Bælius hic ille est cujus dum scripta vigebunt
Lis erit, oblectent, erudiant ne magis.

Jam.^s Smith Sculpsit 1733.

THE
DICTIONARY
Historical and Critical
OF
MR PETER BAYLE.

THE SECOND EDITION,

Carefully collated with the several Editions of the Original; in which many Passages are restored, and the whole greatly augmented, particularly with a Translation of the Quotations from eminent Writers in various Languages.

To which is prefixed,

THE LIFE OF THE AUTHOR,

REVISED, CORRECTED, AND ENLARGED,

BY

M^R DES MAIZEAUX,

Fellow of the Royal Society.

VOLUME THE FIRST.

A——Bi.

LONDON:

Printed for J. J. and P. KNAPTON; D. MIDWINTER; J. BROTHERTON; A. BETTES-
WORTH and C. HITCH; J. HAZARD; J. TONSON; W. INNYS and R. MANBY;
J. OSBORNE and T. LONGMAN; T. WARD and E. WICKSTEED; W. MEADOWS;
T. WOODWARD; B. MOTTE; W. HINCHLIFFE; J. WALTHOE, jun. E. SYMON;
T. COX; A. WARD; D. BROWNE; S. BIRT; W. BICKERTON; T. ASTLEY;
S. AUSTEN; L. GILLIVER; H. LINTOT; H. WHITRIDGE; R. WILLOCK.

MDCCXXXIV.

CT
95
.B3
1734
66371
v.1
A-Bi

The Dictionary Historical And Critical Of Mr. Peter Bayle

MR BAYLE's
Hiftorical and Critical
DICTIONARY.
THE SECOND EDITION.

To which is prefixed,

THE LIFE OF THE AUTHOR,

BY

M^R DES MAIZEAUX,

Fellow of the Royal Society.

VOLUME THE FIRST.

A ——— Bi.

TO

The Right Honourable

SIR ROBERT WALPOLE,

First Commissioner of the Treasury, Chancellor and Under-Treasurer of the Exchequer, One of His Majesty's Most Honourable Privy-Council, and Knight of the Most Noble Order of the Garter.

SIR,

GREAT Writers, who employ themselves for the instruction or entertainment of the World, naturally claim, what they seem naturally to merit, the favour and countenance of Great Men. Whosoever contributes, especially with success, to enlarge the Understandings of Men, and to mend their Hearts, is entitled to the Friendship and Protection of the Governors of Men, I mean of such as would truly answer the noble end of Government; who, if they pursue their duty, and consult the honour and improvement of human nature, will chearfully and generously promote whatever has that good tendency. And they who practise different Politics, by cramping the human Soul, possessing it with false awe, and debasing it through Darkness and Ignorance, do not deserve, but rather disgrace and forfeit, the glorious and endearing title of Magistrates and Protectors.

TRUE and extensive Knowledge never was, never can be, hurtful to the Peace of Society. It is Ignorance, or, which

DEDICATION.

which is worfe than ignorance, falfe Knowledge, that is chiefly terrible to States. They are the furious, the ill taught, the blind and mifguided, that are prone to be feized with groundlefs Fears, and unprovoked Refentment, to be roufed by Incendiaries, and to rufh defperately into Sedition and acts of Rage.

SUBJECTS that are moſt knowing and beſt informed, are ever moſt peaceable and loyal. Whereas the Loyalty and obedience of ſuch, whoſe underſtandings extend not beyond Names and Sounds, will be always precarious, and can never be thoroughly relied upon, whilſt any turbulent or artful men can, by dinn and clamour, and the continual application of thoſe Sounds, intoxicate, and inflame them even to madneſs, can make them believe themſelves undone though nothing hurts them, think they are oppreſſed when they are beſt protected, and can drive them into riots and rebellion, without the excuſe of one real grievance. It will always be eaſy to raiſe a miſt before eyes that are already dark: and it is a true obſervation, " that it is an eaſy work to govern Wiſe Men; but to " govern Fools or Madmen, is a continual ſlavery."

IT is from the blind zeal and ſtupidity cleaving to Superſtition, 'tis from the Ignorance, Raſhneſs, and Rage attending Faction, that ſo many, ſo mad, and ſo ſanguinary evils have afflicted and deſtroyed Men, diſſolved the beſt Governments, and thinned the greateſt Nations. And as a people well inſtructed will certainly eſteem the Bleſſings which they enjoy, and ſtudy public Peace, for their own ſake, there is a great merit in inſtructing the people, and in cultivating their Underſtandings. They are certainly leſs credulous in proportion as they are more knowing, and conſequently leſs liable to be the Dupes of Demagogues, and the property of Ambition. They are not then to be ſurprized with falſe cries, nor animated by imaginary Danger; and wherever the Underſtanding is well principled and informed, the Paſſions will be tame, and the Heart well diſpoſed.

THEY

DEDICATION.

THEY therefore who communicate true Knowledge to their species, are true Friends to the World, Benefactors to Society, and deserve all encouragement from those, who preside over Society, with the applause and good wishes of all men. Such a public friend and benefactor was MR BAYLE. Truth and Knowledge were his mistress, and the pursuit of his life, and he studied to engage all men in that pursuit. A curious searcher of error he was, a constant champion against falshood, imposture, and all dishonest arts; zealous for public tranquillity, and a foe to all who disturbed it; wonderfully qualified for his great undertaking, by an acuteness and penetration never exceeded by any Writer ancient or modern, and with such an accumulation of various, curious, and solid Learning, as perhaps was never equalled by any Writer whatsoever; a great Philosopher, a great Linguist, an universal Historian and Critic, vastly skilled in Divinity and Controversy, and a nice reasoner upon transactions of States, and the arts of Statesmen.

MANY enemies it is true he had; and what other Great Man ever wanted such? their Greatness only is what often produces them. It was therefore no wonder that the outcry and clamour against him was so loud and many-mouthed, even for his most excellent performances. This comfort however attends his memory, and it is likely he foresaw it and enjoyed it in his lifetime; that all that clamour is now dead, and these excellent performances remain, and are likely for ever to remain. What his own admirable talents and many solid defences could not do, time and the infinite merit of his works, and the force of truth have done, silenced his adversaries, and almost made it forgot that he ever had any. This must be a pleasing reflection to all lovers of Truth and of great Merit greatly traduced, and spitefully used, to see such traducers sunk into oblivion, and such merit covered with lustre.

I could, Sir, with your leave and patience, illustrate the fate of MR BAYLE by similar instances; but that

DEDICATION.

that I would no more offend you with the appearance of Flattery, than I would provoke others to charge me with the imputation of defigning, and you of encouraging it. Permit me only to fay, that as this great and applauded Work is like to laft, Pofterity (for Pofterity will judge without anger or envy) will not think it unnatural to fee the name of SIR ROBERT WALPOLE prefixed to the GRAND DICTIONARY of MR BAYLE; and if by this way (this only way) I can purchafe permanence to my own humble name, it is an Ambition which I hope merits pardon. The greateft that I have in the world is to be owned by you, Sir, as what I ftrictly am, with all Devotion and unbounded Refpect,

SIR,

Your moft Dutiful,

and moft Obedient

Humble Servant,

P. DES MAIZEAUX.

ADVERTISEMENT

CONCERNING

This Second Edition.

F the repeated Editions of a voluminous book be a proof of the Approbation of the Public, we may affirm that no book has been more generally esteemed than Mr Bayle's Dictionary. Besides the editions of 1697 and 1702, which he published himself, it was printed at Geneva in 1715, at Rotterdam in 1720, at Amsterdam in 1730, and is just now reprinted in France: so that there have been six impressions of it in six and thirty years; an honour which perhaps was never done to any other book of such a bulk. To these editions may be added the English Translation, published in 1710: for the Translation of a book is in reality a new Edition of it in another dress; and does so much the more credit to the work, as it is the effect of the earnest desires of the curious and inquisitive, who do not understand the original.

That Translation was done from the edition of 1702, the most compleat then extant: but Mr Bayle having left behind him several Articles, which he designed for a Supplement to his Dictionary, they were inserted in the new edition printed at Rotterdam in 1720. But this edition being full of errors of the press, and interpolated in many places, these defects were corrected in the Amsterdam edition of 1730, in which some learned men were employed. They also improved it in several other respects, of which they give us the following account.

I. "We have, say these Editors, collated it with the Editions of 1697 "and 1702, and particularly with Mr Bayle's own Copy of the edition "1702, in which are several additions and corrections written with

VOL. I. [B] " his

Advertisement concerning this second Edition.

" his own hand. By this means several expressions, and whole phrases
" have been restored which had been omitted, changed, or adulterated
" in the preceeding edition.

II. " The Articles of the Supplement, or posthumous Additions, have
" been compared with Mr Bayle's Original Manuscript; by the help of
" which the text has been restored to its purity, and all spurious inser-
" tions struck out.

III. " The several quotations from celebrated Authors, in the Greek,
" Latin, and other languages, have been carefully revised and corrected.

IV. " Some passages, or citations, which were wanting in the
" edition of 1720, and had been only referred to, have been supplied.

V. " The Articles which were misplaced, or put at the end of the
" fourth volume, are placed in their proper order.

VI. " Some Critical Remarks, which had been communicated to the
" Booksellers, and printed at the end of the said fourth volume, have
" been inserted in the Articles they belonged to; but they are distin-
" guished from Mr Bayle's text, being preceeded by a Greek letter for
" a reference and by this mark §, and ending with the words,
" REM. CRIT.

VII. " At the end of the fourth volume is added a piece printed at
" Paris in 1706, intitled *Critical Remarks upon the new edition of Moreri's*
" *Historical Dictionary, published in 1704.* Mr Bayle reprinted this piece
" in Holland, and prefixed to it a long Preface, which contains excel-
" lent instructions towards perfecting Moreri's Dictionary. He likewise
" joined to it several historical and critical Observations, which are to the
" same purpose, and where he shews the errors in fact, and the false
" reasonings of the Author of these remarks. But though he saw that
" this Critic had taken almost all his remarks upon Moreri, from his Hi-
" storical and Critical Dictionary, without citing it, he never reproaches
" him with this piece of Plagiarism, but contents himself with vindica-
" ting some passages which this Censor had misunderstood, or had criti-
" cized without reason. Mr Des Maizeaux has been less indulgent in the
" Observations which he has added to those of Mr Bayle: he has resto-
" red to Mr Bayle all the critical remarks which this Critic had borrowed
" from his Dictionary, and had given as his own. Neither has he
" spared him for his boldness in advancing certain facts without proofs, as
" well as for his loose, equivocal, and sophistical manner of arguing.
" But as the design of that small work is to contribute towards perfecting
" Moreri's Dictionary, Mr Des Maizeaux had taken a particular care to
" point out the corrections that have been made in the late editions, of
" the passages censured by this Author. Future Editors will see at one
" view,

Advertisement concerning this second Edition.

"view, what has been already corrected, and what still remains to be
"rectified with respect to those passages. It does not appear that the
"late Revisors of Moreri were acquainted with these *Critical Remarks*;
"at least it is certain that they have not seen Mr Bayle's Preface and
"Notes. Mr Bayle would not put his name to them, which is the rea-
"son why this piece has been hitherto so little known.

VIII. "To this edition is prefixed the *Life of Mr Bayle*, by Mr Des
"Maizeaux."

In this new English edition of Mr Bayle's Dictionary, we have followed the improved edition of the original, last mentioned; which consequently contains all his posthumous Additions and Corrections. The Readers will also find in the last Volume the *Critical Remarks upon Moreri's Dictionary*, with Mr Bayle's Preface and Notes to it, and Mr Des Maizeaux's Observations: Also, Mr Bayle's *Reflections on a Pamphlet, intitled, the Judgment of the Public concerning Mr Bayle's Critical Dictionary*, (first inserted in the edition of 1720): and an *Historical Discourse concerning the Life of Gustavus Adolphus, King of Sweden*. Mr Bayle designed to write a compleat History of that great Prince; but has left the work unfinished; however, as far as it goes, it is an excellent piece of history, and one may easily see that it comes from a masterly hand. It has been but lately published, and has not been yet inserted in any edition of Mr Bayle's Dictionary. We therefore presume the readers will be glad to see it at the end of the last Volume, where it may, in some measure, supply the want of the Article of the great GUSTAVUS, which is not to be found in the Dictionary.

Besides these Pieces, which were not in the first English edition, this second edition has several other advantages.

I. The Translation is much more exact and correct, and is carefully revised and compared with the original.

II. It has been collated with the original editions of 1697 and 1702, when any doubt has arisen concerning the genuine reading of a word, a date, &c.

III. Several errors of the press which had crept into the edition of 1730, especially in the passages of ancient Authors, have been corrected.

IV. The citations from eminent Writers in various languages, are translated into English, excepting when Mr Bayle himself has fully expressed the sense of them.

V. The

Advertisement concerning this second Edition.

V. The *Life of Mr Bayle* has been revised, corrected, and enlarged by the Author; and some of the Corrections and Additions are very considerable. As soon as this work came out, it was translated into High-Dutch by the learned Dr Kohl, and printed at Hamburgh in 1731, in 8vo: and it has been reprinted at Paris in 1733, in two Volumes in 12mo. But Mr Des Maizeaux was not concerned in these Editions, which however shew that the public entertained a very favourable opinion of that work. Some people may possibly imagine that Mr Des Maizeaux, has insisted too long on Mr Bayle's disputes, and could have wished that he had only given the particulars of his life: but indeed what is the History of the life of a Philosopher, but an account of his works, opinions, and disputes? These are the battles and bright actions of such Heroes. Besides, the knowledge of such books and pamphlets as do not seem to concern the English reader, will be found necessary for the better understanding of numberless passages of Mr Bayle's Dictionary, wherein they are mentioned or referred to; so that this part of his Life is, as it were, a key, or an explanatory introduction, to them.

PREFACE

PREFACE
TO THE
First French Edition.

 I HAVE a thousand things to offer in this Preface; but as I cannot do it without running into an exorbitant length, which would discourage the Readers, I rather chuse to give my self some constraint, than offend their niceness. I shall therefore confine my self to five or six particulars.

I declare first, that this work is not what I promised in the Project I published of a Critical Dictionary in the Year 1692. The objection I had best obviated and answered, is that which was chiefly insisted on, to condemn the plan I designed to pursue; and perhaps it appeared very strong to a great many readers, for no other reason, but because they observed I very much inlarged on it's confutation. But let the cause be what it will, I did not think it prudent to oppose the general taste; and since it has been universally concluded, that the greatest part of the faults I mentioned in the articles of the Project were of little importance to the public, reason required I should give over my undertaking. My design was to compose a Dictionary of errors: the perfection of such a work consists in observing all mistakes, great or small; for doubtless it would be a perfection in a Geographical Dictionary, and in a Map, to specify every town and village. Seeing therefore the best way of executing my project must be the most exposed to the complaints of the public, as it would have multiplied insignificant observations, there was a necessity for me to alter my design; and I could not but believe, that according to the prevailing taste of the age, there was a real imperfection in the very plan of my enterprize, which could never be cured by the execution. If I contest any thing with those who say, that the greatest part of the errors I have censured in my Project are of no consequence, 'tis their supposing that they are not all of that nature; for I maintain, that none of them is important, and that though, generally speaking, they are like those that have been observed by great Critics (1), yet they can contribute nothing to the public good. The fate of mankind does not depend upon them. A narrative abounding with the grossest ignorance is as proper to move the passions, as historical exactness. Let ten thousand ignorant people hear you preach that Coriolanus's mother obtained of him, what " he refused " the sacred College of Cardinals and the Pope himself, who went to meet " him (2)," you will give them the same idea of the power of the Holy Virgin,

I.
WHY this work is not formed upon the plan published in 1692.
[See that Plan at the end of the last Volume.]

(1) If you consider Scaliger's remarks upon Eusebius's Chronicle, you will find that his corrections consist in shewing, that a time, a place, a man's name, &c. have been mistaken.

(2) 'Tis affirmed in the Recueil des bons contes & des bons mots, printed in the year 1693. p. 123. of the Dutch edition, that this was actually preached.

VOL. I.   *   Virgin,

Preface to the first French Edition.

Virgin, as if this was no blunder. Tell them, " 'Tis strange, Christians, " that you should not be moved to see our Saviour JESUS CHRIST " hanging upon the cross, all bruised with blows, when the emperor Pom- " pey was moved with compassion, upon seeing Pyrrhus's elephants pierced " with arrows (3);" you will produce the same effect, as if what you say of Pompey was true. 'Tis therefore certain, that the discovery of errors (4) is not important or useful to the prosperity of the State, or of private persons. Observe now in what manner I have changed my plan, the better to hit the taste of the public. I have divided my composition into two parts: one is purely historical, and gives a succinct account of matters of fact: the other is a large commentary, a miscellany of proofs and discussions, wherein I have inserted a censure of many faults, and even sometimes a train of philosophical reflections; in a word, there is variety enough, to presume that all sorts of readers will find something or other that will please them.

THIS new œconomy has broke all the measures I had taken; most of the materials I had collected were of no use to me, and I was forced to work upon a new foundation. My principal design was to observe the faults of Moreri, and of all other Dictionaries like his. In searching for proofs necessary to expose those faults, and rectify them, I found, that many authors, both ancient and modern had committed the same mistakes. And as Moreri is much more faulty in what concerns Mythology, and the Roman families than in modern history, I had particularly made collections upon the heathen gods and heroes, and the great men of ancient Rome. The work I proposed to publish, would have contained abundance of articles, like those of ACHILLES, BALBUS, and CRASSUS, in my Project. All these vast collections are become useless, because I was informed that these subjects pleased few people, and that a volume in folio, the greatest part of which should run only upon such things, would be left to grow mouldy in the booksellers ware houses. It will appear that I have had a regard to this information: but few articles of this kind will be found in my two Volumes; nor would they perhaps have been there, had they not been wholly composed before I was fully informed of the taste of the readers.

This is one of the reasons that have retarded the publication of this work: many others have contributed to it. I resolved at first to say nothing that has been already said in other Dictionaries, or at least to avoid as much as possible the repetition of facts that are to be found in them; whereby I deprived myself of all the materials that were most easy to be collected, and employed. Nothing can be more easy for the authors of an Historical Dictionary, than to talk of Popes, Emperors, Kings, and Cardinals; or of the Fathers of the church, of Councils, and Heretics; or of great lords, cities, provinces, &c. 'Tis therefore a great disadvantage to lay aside those subjects, as one must do every moment, if he proposes to avoid the articles that are in Moreri's Dictionary. If you design to give the same articles, you must confine yourself to the things that he has omitted: the difficulty of separating them from others in the originals you consult is not small; but that of connecting them together, after the chasms occasioned by this separation, is much greater. Notwithstanding all these Difficulties, I resolved to give an account of most of the persons mentioned in the Bible; but I was informed that a particular Dictionary upon these subjects would quickly come out at Lyons (5). What remained to be done, was to collect what has been said by the Rabbis concerning those persons; but understanding that the late Mr d'Herbelot's Bibliotheque Orientale was printing at Paris, I gave

over

---

(3) *'Tis affirmed in the Furetieriana, pag. 127. of the Brussels edition that Furetiere heard this preached in Flanders.*

(4) *I only mean errors in point of fact, and I except those that concern religion. As to the former, I do not pretend to make any exception.*

II WHY this work could not be composed in a little time.

(5) *'Tis instituled, Le Dictionaire de la bible. 'Tis a Folio book printed, according to the title-page, in 1693. and written by M. Simon, priest, and doctor of divinity.*

Preface to the first French Edition.

over this design (6). Notwithstanding the same difficulties, I would have composed the articles relating to church-history, had I not considered that Mr du Pin furnished the readers of Dictionaries, with all they could desire. His work is adapted both to the learned and unlearned. The Dutch editions have made it very common, and all the curious buy it and read it. I had not, therefore, been excusable, had I mentioned the same things that are to be found there: must one buy the same histories twice? I rather chose to abstain from so fruitful a subject, and easy to come by, than to repeat what may be more conveniently learned elsewhere. (6) *I had already composed the articles of Mr du Pin's Work, &c. ADAM, EVE, CAIN, ABEL, ABRAHAM, &c. which I give in this Work.*

I found myself streightened in other respects. This work was hardly begun, when I heard an English translation of Moreri's Dictionary was printing at London, with abundance of Additions; and that a large supplement to the same work was preparing in Holland. Hereupon I thought myself obliged not to treat of the illustrious men of Great Britain: I concluded, that out of the English edition, they would be inserted in the said supplement, and that the same thing would be bought twice, unless I prevented it by depriving myself of so copious a matter, and so proper to recommend a Dictionary. For the same reason I laid aside my enquiry after the illustrious men who have flourished in the United Provinces (7); and said very little concerning the history or geography of this State. I did not doubt but the supplement, printed in Holland, would give a large and exact account of all these things, and likewise that it would fully treat of all the transactions of Europe in our days. This prevented my touching upon those modern histories. On the other hand, I heard that a new edition of Moreri's Dictionary was going to be published at Paris, with great additions. This made me resolve to suppress a great many things, and put a stop to my enquiry into many subjects, which I could handle but imperfectly, in comparison of those who were engaged in this new edition: they are upon the spot, and at hand to consult libraries, and learned men. I ought therefore to leave them this task entire, and not give them the displeasure of running lightly over a subject, that will be read more eagerly when set off by them in it's full lustre, before others touch upon it. (7) *I have only mentioned some, whose Lives or Funeral Orations I had already by me.*

But besides these new editions, and new supplements of Moreri's Dictionary, other things have much streightened me. Mr Chappuzeau has been a long time about an historical Dictionary in which we shall certainly find, amongst abundance of other subjects, what concerns the situation of nations, their manners, religion, government, and what concerns the royal families, and the genealogies of great men (8); and particularly you will find in it at large, all the electors, princes, and counts of the empire; their alliances, interests, and principal actions. And by that means, you will see the northern countries, and the rest of Protestant Europe. I thought, therefore, that I had better be silent upon those great subjects, than expose the reader to the disagreeable necessity of purchasing the same things twice. Nay, I have found myself confined with respect to the learned men of the XVIth century; for I knew that Mr Teissier was printing, with new additions, the commmentaries he has so curiously compiled upon the Elogies taken from Thuanus (9). I was afraid, in speaking of those learned men, that the facts mentioned by me, would be the same with Mr Teissier's; and that thought has often determined me to suppress my collections. (8) *See the Plan of his Dictionary, which he published in the Year 1694.* (9) *That second edition came out in 1696.*

I do

Preface to the first French Edition.

(4)

I do not enumerate these particulars, in order to enable my friends to make my apology against those who shall despise my Dictionary, and say, "was so much time to be consumed in the composition of such "a Work? the faults of it might be excused, if the author had spent "only a few months in making it: but so poor an effect of so long a "labour deserves no indulgence. Slowness is never tolerable, but when it "produces a master-piece (10)." My friends might answer, that the most diligent writers would be hard put to it, to make their compilations with greater speed, if they abstained from the most copious and easy subjects, and avoided mentioning what some have compiled, and what they foresee will be compiled by others. But I do not desire that these should be alledged in my favour. What I have said, is only designed to resolve such questions as these; "Why so many great men are wanting in my "book? why it contains so many unknown persons, and obscure names? "why it is so barren in some respects, and profuse in others? could the "author be so mistaken, as to pretend to be able to do what Pliny thought "extremely difficult? &c (11)." Let the querist be referred to the account I have given above, and he will find the solution of all these doubts.

I freely own, that laborious and diligent authors will have reason to look upon me as a slow Writer. I have spent above four years in the composition of these two volumes (12). Besides, they are intermixed with long Passages, which cost me no pains; nothing of what I have said of my own, bespeaks an author that revises his work, or corrects his first thoughts, and the first disposition of his words. And therefore, if any one thinks I have been too slow, I shall not wonder at it: I am sensible and ashamed of it, and I should be still more ashamed, were it not that my health frequently interrupted, requires some regard, and does not permit me to perform what strong and laborious men can do. I know, moreover, that the slavery of quoting, which I have submitted to (13), makes me lose much time; and that the prodigious scarcity of books, very necessary to my design, stopped my pen a hundred times a day. Such a work as this requires the most numerous library in the world; whereas I have very few books (14). Shall I dare to own it? The stile is another cause of my slowness: it is very incorrect, and not free from expressions either improper, or which begin to be obsolete, or even from barbarisms. I confess I am, in these respects, without scruple: but, on the contrary, with regard to other things, which give more trouble (15), I am scrupulous, even to superstition. The greatest masters, the most illustrious members of the French Academy, dispense with these scruples, and we have but three or four writers, that are not cured of them. It is, therefore, a great mortification to me, not to be able to get above those niceties, which cost much time, and often spoil the lively and natural agreeableness of the expression, when it is corrected by this Rule. I am so unable to shake off this heavy yoke, that in case this Dictionary be reprinted, it will certainly be my principal care to correct, according to the rigorous rules of our French Grammarians, all the inaccuracies in the language, which still remain in this edition (16). They are not a few; for during the first year I was employed in this Work, I did not so much mind scruples of this sort; so that there are a great many articles which offend the superstitious rules I have now mentioned: they were composed at that time, and I had not the leisure to new-mould them, when I was obliged to send them the press. Such like faults may be found all the work over, occasioned

(10) Diu parturit leæna catulum, 'ed leonem. The slowness goes long with young, but at length brings forth a lion.

(11) Res ardua vetustis novitatem dare, novis auctoritatem, obsoletis nitorem, obscuris lucem, fastidiis gratiam, dubiis fidem. It is a difficult matter to give the grace of novelty to things old, authority to things new, elegancy to things obsolete, light to things obscure, favour to things contemned, and credit to things doubtful. Plin. in Præf. Nat. Hist.

(12) I began this work in July, 1692, and made an end of it in Octob. 1696.

(13) I quote the pages, even when I refer to other places of my Dictionary.

(14) Some persons have very obligingly lent me some books, for which I am very thankful. I would willingly publish here the names and merits of those, who have done me that favour, were I not afraid of offending their modesty.

(15) As to a void equivocal expressions, verses, the use of particles in the same sentence which may refer to different parts of it, &c.

(16) Note, that I found it impossible to perform this promise in the second edition, the printers did not give me the necessary time to revise my first work, and to prepare the new, that is, the additions which have been very numerous.

Preface to the first French Edition.

occasioned either by my being so attentive to other matters, that I have overlooked them in correcting the proofs; or by the printer's not being able to allow me the necessary time to mend what I did not like. The useful advices I have received from Mr DRELINCOURT (17), and his just and elegant corrections, which I have taken care to write in the margin of my copy, will be of infinite use to me in revising that edition.

This is what I had to represent to those who might think it strange that my Dictionary cost me so much time. But I must not neglect those who might believe I have made too much haste. There are many who will be surprized to see two such great volumes in Folio, finished in less than five years. Many authors do not perfect a little book under a year, whether they look upon those thoughts and expressions as mean, which they produce without a long meditation; or whether their business calls them frequently from their studies; or whether a natural laziness, or too scrupulous an obedience to the precept they have learned at school, *interpone tuis interdum gaudia curis*, engage them often to interrupt their labour. Those gentlemen are easily prejudiced against a work that has not cost much time; and they think it has not, unless a hundred printed sheets have taken up three or four Years. They will apply to me, doubtless, the *canis festinans cæcos edit catulos*, and will be confirmed in their prejudice, by reading the particulars above-mentioned. They will abate from the labour spent upon things, all the time I have bestowed upon avoiding verses (18), and to the unity of relatives. They know it is a long and painful task, and that nothing requires more patience than a good series of citations. They will not allow, that under pretence of having inserted a great deal of foreign matter in this work, I may say I have enlarged it in a little time, without making much haste. For, will they say, a just application of vast numbers of passages is a more laborious work, than a long train of reasonings and reflexions (19). These passages must be sought out, they must be read with attention, they must be pertinently placed, and connected with your own thoughts, and with one another. It is impossible to make a quick progress, and do this perfectly well. I grant them this, but I intreat them not to apply to me the *canis festinans*, &c. before they have read my work. Prejudices are deceitful, and if they would have favourable ones, I will tell them that I remember Cato's Distich as well as they, *interpone tuis interdum gaudia curis*, &c. but that I very seldom make use of it. Diversions, collations, journies into the country, visits, and such other recreations, necessary to a great many studious men, as they say, are not my business: I lose no time in them. Nor do I spend it in domestic cares, making interest for preferments, sollicitations, or other affairs. I have been happily delivered from a great many occupations not very suitable to my humour, and I have had the greatest and most charming leisure that a man of letters could desire. By this means an author makes a great progress in a few years; his work may receive considerable additions every day, and that without a negligent performance.

I doubt not but the method I have taken in quoting the passages of authors, will be censured. Many will say, I was resolved to compile a large book with little expence: I have often cited very long passages; sometimes I give the sense of them, and then I set them down in Greek and Latin. Is not this multiplying things without necessity? was it necessary to transcribe a long quotation of a modern book, which is to be had in every bookseller's shop? was it necessary to quote Amyot in his old French?

Preface to the first French Edition.

to give a good answer to those critics, I do not think it necessary to deny that their objections are specious. I confess they are plausible, and they kept me in suspence a long while; but at last more specious reasons determined me to the method I have taken. I considered that such a work as this was to be instead of a library to a great many people. Many, that are lovers of learning, have not wherewithal to purchase books; others have not leisure to consult the fiftieth part of the volumes they buy. Those who have leisure enough, would be very unwilling to rise every moment, to seek out the information they are referred to. They had rather find in the book they have before them, the very words of the authors, that are brought as evidences. If a man wants the edition cited, he loses a great deal of time; for it is not always easy to find in one's edition, the page that an author cites in his own. And therefore out of a regard to the readers who have no books, and to the occupations, or laziness of those that have libraries, I have taken care to shew them at once historical facts, and the proofs of them, with many discussions and circumstances, that their curiosity might be fully satisfied. And because many frauds are committed in the citations of authors, and those who honestly abridge a passage, do not always express the whole force of it, it is incredible how much judicious persons are grown mistrustful. I may justly say, that it is a sort of rashness on a thousand occasions, to believe what is attributed to authors when their own words are not quoted. For which reason I was willing to set the reader's mind at rest; and to prevent his suspecting any fraud in my report, I make every witness speak in his native language; and instead of imitating Castelvetro, who finished his citations with & cætera, even before he had transcribed the necessary passage, I have sometimes lengthened that passage both at the beginning and at the end, that the thing in question might be understood, or something else occasionally learnt. I know this would be absurd in a short moral treatise, in a piece of eloquence, or in an history; but it is not so in such a compilation as this is, in which I propose to relate facts, and then to illustrate them with commentaries. Such a method would be blameable, if instead of one volume it made two; or instead of a pocket-book, it produced a book in Folio or in Quarto. But the question being only, whether a volume in Folio shall be longer or shorter by some sheets, it is not worth the while to constrain one's self. Had it but 250 sheets, it would no more have the advantages of a little book, than if it contained 330 sheets; for it must be well observed, that these large books are not made to be read page by page. They would cost somewhat less, if they contained but 200 sheets, will some say: I answer, that if a bookseller went upon such a rule, he would never print a work consisting of many volumes, though they contained nothing but solid thoughts without a syllable too much; for they would still be too dear for those that are in low circumstances. The trouble of translating Amyot, or Vigenere, into new French, would have been of no service; it suffices that my reader can understand the facts they relate.

WHY Brantome and such like authors are often quoted in this Dictionary.

Men of a grave and severe character will particularly blame the citations out of Brantome or Montaigne, that contain actions and reflexions two free and gallant. I must say a word or two to this. Some persons of merit, who were concerned for the interests of the bookseller, concluded, that so large a book as this, stuffed with Greek and Latin quotations in several places, and full of discussions little diverting, would frighten the readers who are not men of letters, and weary the learned; that therefore it was to be feared the sale would quickly fall, if the curiosity of those who do not

understand

Preface to the first French Edition. (7)

understand Latin was not excited by some other things. I was made sensible, that a work, which is bought only by the learned, seldom pays the printer, and that if any profit is to be made by an impression, 'tis when a book can equally please the learned, and those that have no learning; that it was therefore necessary for the sake of my bookseller, sometimes to relate what authors who take some liberties have published; that the use of such materials is like the liberty a man takes to write his own life; in some persons, 'tis a sign of arrogance (20), in others a just confidence in their virtue (21); and that I might justly place myself in the number of the latter; lastly, that if I was too averse to comply with this advice, I should at least suffer others to furnish the bookseller with such memoirs, and even sometimes with dogmatical reflexions that might excite attention. I promised them to have some regard to those remonstrances, and added, that I had no right to oppose their supplements; that I had left to the bookseller a full authority to insert, even without consulting me, the memoirs his correspondents and friends should send him; and that I could wish they would do with respect to the whole book what they seemed to be willing to do in some places, that is, make such additions, leave out such things, and dispose of my compilations as they should think fit. 'Tis certain I always wished to have no other share in this work, than the care of compiling: I should have been glad if others would have taken the pains to give a form to the materials, and to enlarge and shorten them; and I was well pleased when the persons I speak of assured me they would remember our conversation, which is a thing I desire my readers to take notice of. As for the philosophical reflexions which sometimes have been carried pretty far, I think I need not make an excuse for them; for since they only tend to convince man, that the best use he can make of his reason, is to submit his understanding to the obedience of faith, they seem to deserve the thanks of the faculties of Divinity.

I have but two or three words to say upon a thing which seems very important. I have related the errors of a great many persons somewhat freely. Is not this a rash and presumptuous attempt? The answer to this question would be very long, if I did not refer the readers to what I have said upon it in my project (22). I intreat them to have recourse to it. I only add, that without exceeding the bounds of humility, a man may observe some faults in the books of famous men, and yet have a profound admiration for them. When subaltern officers, or even common soldiers, say freely that their generals have committed some faults in the course of a campaign, they are sometimes in the right; but they do not pretend to be better qualified than they to command an army; they acknowledge themselves infinitely inferiour in capacity as well as in rank (23). That is my case. I further add, that when the question is concerning a thing that is disadvantageous to the memory of a man, I do not warrant the truth of it; I only relate what others say, and I quote my authors. 'Tis therefore to them, and not to me, that a man's relations ought to address their complaints. A modern historian has declared in a preface, " That those who have prescribed the inviolable " laws of history (24), must be applied to, to give an account of those laws, " if any one is dissatisfied with them; and not the historians, who ought " indispensably to obey; all the glory they can hope for consisting in the " execution of their orders." My cause is still more favourable, since I only transcribe the authors already printed. Of the two inviolable laws of history mentioned by that historian, I have religiously observed that which

commands

(20) Plerique suam ipsi vitam narrare fiduciam morum quam arrogantiam arbitrati sunt. Most people have been of opinion, that for a man to write his own life, is rather a mark of a just confidence in his virtue, than of his vanity. Tacit. in vita Agricolæ. cap. 1.

(21) See the remarks of the articles VAYER *and* VIRGIL.

IV. REMARKS on my being so bold as to criticize many authors.

(22) Numero 6.

(23) Consult this verse of Horace. Quum de se loquitur non ut majore reprensi. Sat. 10. lib. 1. v. 55.

(24) Ne quid veri non audeat, ne quid falsi audeat. Cicer. *The words of Cicero, in his second book de Oratore, fol. m. 74. A, are* Quis nescit primam esse historiæ legem, ne quid falsi dicere audeat, deinde ne quid veri non audeat? *Who does not know that the first law of history is, not to dare say any thing that is false, and to dare say every thing that is true.*

Preface to the first French Edition.

commands to say nothing that is false; as for the other, which bids us venture to say all that is true, I cannot boast that I have always observed it. I believe it sometimes inconsistent, not only with prudence but also with reason.

I would not have it thought that I glory to have said nothing but truth. I only can warrant my intention, and not my ignorance. I advance nothing as truth, when I am persuaded that it is a falsity (25); but how many things are there which I have not apprehended, or the ideas whereof have been confounded with one another during the composition? How often does it happen that our pen betrays our thoughts? We intend to put down a figure, or a man's name; and sometimes for want of attention, or even by too much attention to other things, we write another? And therefore I make no doubt, that besides my omissions, which are many, I have committed many faults. I shall think myself obliged to those, who will be so kind as to rectify me: and had I not relied upon the good advices of intelligent and equitable readers, I should have kept this work many years in my closet, according to the advice of the ancients (26), in order to correct it, and render it less unworthy of the public view: but considering I had materials left for two other large volumes, I hastened the publication of it. I easily understood that I should be more usefully and seasonably assisted, when the public should know what I want, and wherein I am wanting. I hope that with those helps the continuation of this work will be more perfect than otherwise it would have been. I shall immediately go about it whilst age will permit me (27). I see nothing wherein I can better and more pleasantly employ the leisure I am bless'd with, a leisure which seems to me preferable to all things (28), and which has always been earnestly wished for by the true lovers of study and learning; for how many men impatiently long for the time, in which they may say,

> Me jam fata meis patiuntur ducere vitam
> Auspiciis, & sponte mea componere curas (29)?

> *At last kind fate has such indulgence shown,*
> *That now my life and labours are my own.*

Besides I think I may reasonably say, that what I am going upon will be more considerable, by the nature itself of the materials, than what I offer at present. Chance and surprize had a greater share in it than a deliberate choice: the thing is this. I put off as long as I could the composition of the articles that seemed the most curious and of the greatest importance. I daily hoped for more materials, and new helps, and in the mean time I was preparing other things; whereby it happened on one hand, that the articles I composed took up a great deal of room; and on the other, that the materials for those I had put off were hugely multiplied. I could not therefore insert them in these two volumes, without prodigiously spoiling the proportion that is to be observed betwixt the letters of the alphabet. This obliged me to keep them till another time; for I cannot prevail with myself to say but little upon a large subject, when I can say a great deal. Therefore I rather chuse to be silent altogether, than to enter upon it. The proportion I have observed betwixt the letters of the alphabet, has been the reason of my referring some articles from one letter to another. The preference was therefore to be given to the articles I had promised; which was the reason why the letter for which they were designed had it's com-

pleat

---

(25) *This ought to be understood of what I advance of my own; and of the great care I have taken faithfully to relate what I think to be the true sense of the authors quoted by me.*

(26) Nonumq; prematur in annum. *Horat. de arte poet.*
Keep it long by you and improve it still. CREECH.

(27) Dum superest Lachesi quod torqueat, & pedibus me porto meis nullo dextram subeunte bacillo, *Juven. sat. 3. ver. 27.*
While I walk upright, and old age is green, And Lachesis has somewhat left to spin. DRYDEN.

(28) Nec otia divitiis Arabum liberrima muto. *Horat. Epist. ~ lib. 1.*
Nor wou'd I sell my freedom and my ease, For rich Arabia or the richer seas. CREECH.

(29) See Virg. Æneid lib 4. ver 340.

Preface to the first French Edition.

pleat extent, before those could be made ready, which were to be very long. I wish my Readers may call this to mind, if at any time they should wonder not to find an account of certain persons in this work.

Here I ought to declare what course I have taken, with respect to Moreri's Dictionary. I. There are many subjects that I have passed over in silence, because they are treated at large in his Dictionary. II. When I have given the same articles, I have been determined to it, either because he was short in his account, or because having by me the lives of some eminent persons, I was able to give a compleat narrative, or because out of many separate and curious things, I could make a pretty large Supplement. In each of these three cases, I have industriously avoided the facts he has mentioned: but it was impossible to do it so absolutely in the second, as in the other two; for in abridging an exact narrative of the life of a great man, it is necessary to give a series of his actions in order, and to make articles well connected, and in some sort all of a-piece. Was it possible to do so, if I had absolutely omitted every thing that has been already said of that person? Therefore in a very few articles of this kind, it will be possible to aver that Moreri's Dictionary had related something, that will be found intermixed with many new facts that I relate. But as this seldom happens, and that in inconsiderable points, I needed not have made this observation; and I only do it through a strong habit of avoiding universal propositions, and having a regard in some cases to the smallest exceptions: besides, there are some occasions in which a man can't be too cautious to prevent cavils. III. If I advance any fact that I have only from Moreri's compilation, I very carefully cite it. I mistrust it very much; and therefore I am resolved to run no risk upon such a security; I abandon it to the critics, it must answer for itself. IV. When I don't cite that writer, and yet I relate any thing that is to be found in his work, 'tis a certain proof I have it from another author. I could swear I have not stollen a word or a syllable from him: I quote him as often as I take the least word from him, which very seldom happens; and I never omit citing him, but when I have discovered the things by as painful searches as if he had never mentioned them. V. I refer the reader to him for facts that are in the least considerable. It would be an absurd thing to make references for the day of a birth, the name of a native place, &c. for such references would take up more room in a page than the things referred to, and would justly disgust the readers. VI. I have not pitched upon this method for fear of being accounted a plagiary. This had been a pannic and a very ridiculous fear; for no one has hitherto carried his extravagance so far, as to accuse of plagiarism such as relate events that another has related, whilst they derive them from the fountain-head, and use neither the turn, nor the order, nor the expressions of another; nor is it likely that it should come into any one's head for the future, to give so absurd a definition of plagiarism; for it would lead us to this utmost point of impertinence, viz. that the most excellent historian, who should undertake to write the life of Charles V, would necessarily be the plagiary of the most wretched chronicler, that collected rhapsodies upon the actions of this great prince. VII. I have put by themselves, in a Remark, the errors I have imputed to Moreri. VIII. I have not touch'd upon those that are found in the articles given by him, and not by me, though they are not less considerable, nor less frequent in these articles than in those I have given. IX. I have followed the edition of Lyons 1688, which is the fifth and last that was printed in France. I am not ignorant that the Dutch editions are much better;

marginal note: V. What course I have taken with respect to Moreri's Dictionary.

but

Preface to the first French Edition.

but I thought it neceffary to proportion my corrections to that, for the fake of a great many people, who only make ufe of the editions printed in France, and who ftill feek and purchafe them preferably to the fixth and feventh (30).

From all this it refults, that my Dictionary is not defigned to leffen the fale of the other; on the contrary it will increafe it, and make the reading of it more ufeful.

For the fake of youth, who want to have their judgment formed, and to be made fenfible of the moft fcrupulous exactnefs, I have taken notice of the leaft faults of Moreri in the fubjects we both handle: as for the miftakes that are in other places, I don't meddle with them, as I have faid before. I don't defire that the contempt this may create for his labour, fhould leffen the acknowledgment that is due to him. I am of Horace's opinion with refpect to thofe who fhew us the way (31): the firft writers of Dictionaries have committed many faults, but they have done great fervices, and deferve a glory, of which they ought not to be deprived by their fucceffors. Moreri took great pains, his performance has been of fome ufe to every body, and afforded fufficient inftructions to a great many. It has brought light into feveral places, where other books would never have done it, and where an exact knowledge of circumftances is not neceffary. It continues to difperfe it into all parts, and with greater purity fince the two Dutch editions. They are infinitely better than thofe of France; for they have been revifed by one of the ableft authors of our age: I mean M. Le Clerc, whofe profound learning, fupported with a juft and penetrating wit, and an exquifite judgment, is admired by all Europe. He has corrected a vaft number of faults and has made excellent additions; and no body could be better qualified to perfect this great work, if nobler and more important occupations would allow him to undertake that task. I can't bear the unjuft caprices of thofe who complain of the frequent editions of Moreri, and look upon the Bookfellers that undertake them as public poifoners.

Thofe, who fhall fee my name in the title-page of this book, and who know that during the time it was printing, I faid on all occafions I would not prefix it, deferve I fhould fay fomething about it in this Preface. I have not only faid this on an hundred occafions, but I have writ the fame to feveral perfons; and many people know that all my friends have ftrongly oppofed my refolution, and that the innumerable arguments, which the fruitfulnefs of their genius, and their generous goodnefs fuggefted to them, could gain nothing upon me. I don't blame thofe who put their names to their works, but I have ever had a fecret antipathy againft it. There is no reafon to be given of antipathies any more than of taftes; and yet I might fay that reflection has confirmed this natural difpofition. That wife indifference, fo much celebrated by the ancient philofophy, has always pleafed me. That illuftrious man, who laboured more to be a good man than to be thought fo (32), who was always concerned how to practife virtue, but never to be praifed for it, feemed to me long ago an excellent model; and never any cenfure appeared more judicious to me, than that which was paffed upon fome Philofophers who put their names to thofe pieces in which they condemned the defire of praife (33). In effect, why do you blame thofe that run after reputation, if you proclaim to the publick that you don't condemn fuch a weaknefs? Purfuant to thefe notions, nothing feemed to me more noble than to fhew in all the fervices that are done to the public, the fame difinterestednefs that the Gofpel prefcribes in works of charity. Thefe were the maxims that moved me to fupprefs my name at the beginning of my Dictionary.

Side notes:

(30) *Thefe are violent Papifts, who have been told that Moreri's zeal has often been check'd in the Dutch editions.*

(31) Hoc erat, experto fruftra Varrone Atacino, Atque quibufdam aliis, melius quod fcribere poffem, Inventore minor: neque ego illi detrahere aufim Hærentem capiti multa cum laude coronam. *Horat. fat. 10. lib. 1. ver. 46. In fatyrs I which Varro try'd in vain. And others too may have a happy ftrain, Yet then Lucilius lefs I freely own, I wou'd not ftrive to blaft his juft renown, He wears and beft deferves to wear the crown.* Creech. VI. *Why the Author has prefixed his name to this work.*

(33) *Cicero relates the thing, but is none of thofe who blame it. Ipfi illi philofophi etiam in illis libellis quos de contemnenda gloria fcribunt, nomen fuum infcribunt; in eo ipfo in quo prædicationem nobilitatemque defpiciunt, prædicari defe ac nominari volunt. Even thefe philofophers have put their names to the books which they wrote concerning the contempt of glory; and defire applaufe and fame by thofe very books wherein they pretend to defpife both.* Cicero *pro Archia poëta fol. m. 164.* D. *See alfo* Cicero. Tufcul. quæft. lib. 1. fol. 247. D. & Valerius Maximus. lib. 8. cap. 14. n. 3. *in ext.*

(32) Vir bonus effe quam videri malebat. *He rather chofe to be good than to be thought fo. See the remark* [H] *in the article* Amphiaraus; *and the remark* [L] *in the article* Cæsar.

But

Preface to the first French Edition.

But I shall not be believed by Detracters; they will think that my scruples were grounded upon the little honour that is to be got by appearing at the head of a large compilation, which they will call *A common shore of Collections, a Rhapsody of a Transcriber*, &c. Of all the employments, will they say, that can be had in the Common-wealth of Learning, there is none so contemptible as that of compilers: they are the drudges of great men. Indeed they are not useless: "Such people, said Scaliger (34), are the drudges of learned men, they bring us all our materials; it is a great help to us, such men are necessary". But are not the vilest professions necessary? and does their usefulness retrieve them from their sordidness? There is therefore more vanity than modesty, in declining the reputation of a drudging author, and endeavouring to get out of the class of those writers, whose productions are not so much the work of their minds, as the work of their bodies, and who carry their brains upon their shoulders. The detracters may believe what they please, there is no reasoning against them; and therefore I shall only say it is not through inconstancy, but in obedience to the supreme authority, that I have done what I have so often said I would not do. It was thought necessary, to compose the difference of some Booksellers, that I should name myself. Without this the Sieur Reinier Leers could not have obtained the licence which he thought he had an indispensible occasion for: I therefore pay a blind obedience; and for that reason should not fear even the rigorous tribunal of Cato the Censor himself (25).

(34) In Scaligeranis, voce *du Maine*, p. m. 148.

I have few words to add concerning my *Errata*, and two or three other small matters.

I comprehend under the word *Errata* my Additions and Corrections. If it was compleat it would contain more pages than it does. I do not lay them all to the Printer's charge, how much soever they exercise our patience, especially when they do not correct all that has been marked in the margin of the proofs. I have had experience of that fatality which attends the trade, and I forget it as much as I am able, *animus meminisse horret*. I however take part of the blame myself, but I beg of those who shall criticize me, to look carefully over my *Errata*. I beg of them also, when they shall find any thing that is wrong, to see whether it be not in the authors quoted by me; for if my translations be not literal, they are at least faithful as to the sense: they must therefore contain an irregularity, when my authors have spoken or thought confusedly.

(25) Ποτέμιον Ἀλζίνον, ἱστορίαν Ἑλληνιστὶ γεγραμμένην καὶ συγγράμμην αἰτιμένον, ἐπιτίμουν, εἰπὼν δεῖσαι εἶναι τὴν συγγράμμην αὐτὸν Ἀμφικτυόνων δεῖσαι καταμέμων ἃ ῥασκαρθεὶς ὑπέμεινε τὸ ἔργον. *Plut. in Catone Majore*. p. 343. B. *He laughed at Posthumius Albinus, who wrote Histories in Greek, and desired his Readers to excuse his inaccuracies; saying, that he ought to be excused if be had been obliged to write in Greek by a decree of the Amphictyons*.

If any think they have been groundlessly criticised in this Dictionary, and if they publish any piece in their justification, wherein they shall use the right of reprisals, I presume they will not take it amiss, that instead of interrupting my work, to answer them, I take the resolution of referring all this to the continuation of this Dictionary. I shall ingenuously confess my errors, and retract them without having recourse to cavilling, as is the common practice. I am sometimes more positive than I should be: but at the bottom I then only propose doubts; and if I speak in another strain, it is that I may the better excite the learned to afford me their instructions, and concur more zealously in the illustration of things.

I have almost every where followed the orthography of the learned; but I have placed the letter *y* in the Articles as if it was *i*. This has not been done in the Index, but I perceived it too late.

The 23d of *October*, 1696.

ADVERTISEMENT

ADVERTISEMENT

CONCERNING THE

Second French Edition.

(1) *In the preface of the first edition.*

THE firſt thing I am to acquaint the Readers with, is, that moſt of the remarks they have ſeen above (1), ſuit with, and ought to be applied to this ſecond edition.

I acquaint them in the ſecond place, that I have been very ſorry that a great many concurring circumſtances, with which it would be to no purpoſe to acquaint them, have put me under a neceſſity of joining to what had already been publiſhed, the new articles I was preparing. I knew that this might offend thoſe who have bought the firſt edition; but at laſt I hoped they would be ſo good as to accept of my excuſes.

They had no reaſon to imagine that the ſecond edition ſhould be no ways preferable to the firſt; for they muſt needs believe that I would correct all the errors which I could obſerve, and that the additions and corrections which were at the end of each volume would be inſerted in their proper places. That alone muſt give the preference to the ſecond edition, and diſpleaſe thoſe who had bought the other. It was therefore impoſſible not to diſoblige them in ſome degree. The queſtion then in that reſpect was only concerning doing ſo more or leſs; but on the other hand we were to give an intire ſatisfaction to thoſe who had not as yet purchaſed the book, but wanted to have it. They would have been very diſcontented if I had divided my work into two alphabets. One might probably preſume that the number of the latter was greater than that of thoſe who had already purchaſed the firſt edition. Long experience has taught us that alphabetic works of this ſort are frequently reprinted, even when they are very defective. We were therefore reduced to this alternative, either not altogether to pleaſe a certain number of people, or to give intire ſatisfaction to a much greater number: reaſon then required that we ſhould chuſe the laſt.

There was a middle way we might have taken: to wit, to print the additions apart, and likewiſe to inſert them in the ſecond edition. They who had not as yet bought it, would by this means have had the whole work under one alphabet; and they who had purchaſed it before, would have only been obliged to procure the additions, and would have found the inconvenience of two alphabets more tolerable than paying twice for the ſame thing. I ſhould have made choice of this expedient, if I had thought the additions would have been ſo large as they have proved; but when this ſecond edition was begun, I fancied they could not amount to more than a

very

Advertisement concerning the &c.

very few sheets, and that it would not be worth the while to print them by themselves. It proved quite otherwise during the course of the impression; but the opportunity of taking that middle way was lost, before we had reason to think that the additions would be sufficient to fill a volume. More care shall be taken of this, if this second edition should be followed by any more; for in that case we shall take our measures, so that every one may have it in his power to buy separately what shall be added.

If this excuse is not sufficient I will give another. The public ought to be so accustomed to frequent editions of Dictionaries, corrected and enlarged in every impression, that it would be unreasonable to take it amiss that I have followed a custom authorized by so many examples. I might produce a great many, but I content my self with alledging Moreri's Dictionary, which has passed thro' nine editions in the space of twenty five years, always with new additions and corrections. The ninth will doubtless be followed by many more, on the same footing, both in France (2) and in Holland. I should not desire to be pardoned if I was guilty of so many relapses; but methinks the public ought to think me sufficiently justified this first time, especially since I have no design of doing so any more.

Let us say something concerning this second edition. It is not twice as large as the first, but it does not want much of it; and if it be not exempt from the faults of the first as much as it should be, and as much as I desired, it is however less faulty. As I was revising the first edition, I have found many mistakes that proceeded from the negligence of the Printers. They have been rectified, as also many others, most of which were occasioned by the authors quoted by me, whom I could not rectify, because I had not by me the books necessary for it. There are some faults which I should not have mended, had I not been informed of them; they will be easily discerned, for I have carefully mentioned the authors of the advices, illustrations, or supplements, that have been communicated to me (3). After all, I am not without great fears that there are more faults remaining than I have removed; 'tis the fate of Dictionaries to arrive slowly and by degree at perfection. Abundance of things are wanting to them when they first come out, which time gives them by slow degrees. Be it how it will, I have been so dissatisfied with my first edition, in bringing it to the test of examination, that I disown and disclaim it (4), and will be answerable only for the things I have caused to be reprinted out of it: I expect from the readers equity, that if they will reprove me, they will take care to observe whether the passage they think faulty is to be found in the second edition. I likewise earnestly desire them to examine whether the passage found fault with, be not corrected in the Errata, or in the Additions placed at the end of these three volumes.

There are some corrections that I have made, as it were *ex officio*, and in consequence of an engagement of which the public was informed (5). I have done it with all imaginable care, and with the strongest intention to satisfy the discontented. To this purpose I have struck out of the article of DAVID every thing that could give offence. This is the greatest suppression that has been necessary: the others are not considerable, either for their number, nor their length. We have been able to amend all the rest at the expence of some few words, or few lines; and chiefly by means of four Explanations which are at the end of this work.

I shall say but little of the Additions, not being willing to prepossess any body: let every one judge of them as they see cause. But I will not dissemble, that the trouble they have given me has not permitted me to correct

(2) *The Literari news from Paris acquaint us that Mr Vautier is employed in a new edition of Moreri; and not only designs to augment and correct it, but also to new mould it. He is very capable of succeeding in it. It was he who gave the edition of Paris 1699.*

(3) *Either in general, or by naming the persons, or placing asterisms or points instead of their names, when I knew or thought they would not be named. There are few exceptions to this.*

(4) *This ought particularly to be understood of the copies that were reprinted, the proofs whereof I did not revise. The Printers have committed great mistakes in those copies.*

(5) *In a Letter concerning what passed in the Consistory of the Walloon church of Rotterdam, in relation to the Critical Dictionary. That Letter is inserted in the Life of Mr Bayle, under the year 1698.*

VOL. I. * * * *

rect the articles of the first edition with all the severity and diligence I designed. It is very difficult for an author, whilst the press goes on without any interruption, to do these three things; to revise two large volumes in folio, to inlarge them above one third part, and to correct the proofs.

Some Additions require that many places should be mended and new moulded, to prevent contradicting one's self, and writing nonsense. To correct a Dictionary well, a man should never enlarge it; for it is with these works, as it is with towns and fruits. A town seldom receives a just symmetry and proportion, whilst greater care is taken to enlarge it, than to repair the old houses. Such an increase serves rather to shew it's disproportions, and irregularities, than to remove them. And as for fruits, it is well known they never ripen, 'till they cease to receive new juices. Such is the common fate of compilations. When they are reprinted, a greater care is taken to add new things, than to put the old ones in a better condition. An author is weary of the old ones he has read so often, and finds in the others the charms of novelty, which take up all his attention. This produces an ill effect; most of the old faults remain, and new ones are added to them.

Having been advised by several people not to suffer the Project or plan which I published in the year 1692, before some essays of this Dictionary, to be lost; I have reprinted it at the end of the dissertations which are in the last volume.

There are certain things of which I have said in sundry places, that I did acquaint my Readers with them once for all. It may happen that they will never light upon these passages, books of this kind not being usually read through, from the beginning to the end: I have therefore been advised to mark here the places where I give any general advertisements. For this purpose I believe it will be sufficient to refer to the following articles: ANAXAGORAS, in the text at the end; ARISTANDER, Remark [B]; BEME; CAMDEN, Remark [D]; CARNEADES, Remark [B]; GOMARUS, Remark [B]; GOURNAI, Remark [D]; HAILLAN; MAHOMET II; PRIOLO.

OBSERVATIONS concerning the Index.

Several people have desired me to place good Indexes at the end of the work. I agree that there are but few books where they are more necessary than in this. I had laid down pretty good plans, and perhaps I might say that there are few people more proper to execute them, than such as have laboured a long while in making vast compilations; for if they have been

(6) Which I have done as often as I could, and always when I had a sufficient number of books.

at the pains to verify the passages (6), they must have been obliged to turn to the indexes every moment; they have been disappointed there a thousand and a thousand times: they have thereby found their defects, and learned what is necessary in order to shun them. Possibly therefore I could have composed a good index; but I neither had the time, nor the patience, which so tedious and tiresome a task requires. Nay, I did not think it proper that the person, who was employed to make one, and who would have been able to have executed very exactly any plan that could have been laid down to him, should engage himself in the detail which some readers desired. They would have a particular index of authors cited, censured, or corrected, and so of an hundred things besides. I considered that such indexes would be so long, that they would disgust many people. I know by my own experience, and by that of many others, that articles of an index, filled with half pages of cyphers, are hardly of service to any body; for where are the people, who in order to find out one passage, will give themselves the trouble to consult twenty? in an index of Salmasius's (7), the article of PLINY contains above three columns of cyphers, that of STRABO two, and that of THEOPHRASTUS near three. Of what use can this be to a reader? will he be stupid enough to employ a whole day to try his chance in this incredible quantity of pages quoted? the way to remedy this, would be to take notice that Pliny is quoted for such and such a thing, but if you do not make a new alphabetical distribution, the sight of two or three pages, filled only with one name, will disgust every body. Now this alphabetical distribution, of what concerns each author that has been quoted, is a task for a gally-slave. Besides, do we not know that there are hardly four readers among an hundred, who mind whether the index is good or not? most people never look into it: we should therefore undertake a most fatiguing task, which would be of use only to very few. It is for these and many other reasons, that I thought it would be sufficient to give the index, which you will find at the end of this work, and to add only another index, which contains nothing but a list of the articles. Be pleased to observe, that the index doth not contain the names of all the authors which I have quoted; and when they are contained in it, all the passages where they are quoted, are not set down. People will therefore deceive themselves if they reason thus, a certain author does not appear in the index, or appears but thrice, therefore he has not been quoted, or he has been quoted only three times.

The chief reason which made me resolve not to execute all the plans of indexes which I had conceived, was, that I thought a word of advice would supply all defects. Let the few readers who make use of that part of a book, only observe what follows.

When they meet with any thing worth remembering, they need only see whether it be in the table; and if it be not, it is but marking it themselves in the margin of the table, under the word which they think most convenient, or on a paper by itself. It is the method that is taken by those who find the tables of books defective, and design to prevent the damage they might receive by them.

Having received too late the memoirs for the article of the town of ETAMPES, and for those of FEVRET, and the house MINUTOLI, which has afforded Cardinals, and many illustrious persons of all ranks, I could not make use of them. I have also received too late an article ready made, and very well drawn up, viz. that of RALPH Archbishop of Bourges, son of Ralph, Count and Lord of Turenne.

It would not have been proper, methinks, to place all these articles in the Addenda, which are at the end of each volume (8). Very few people read these sorts of Addenda, and no body approves that they should fill many pages. I am so much persuaded that they are but little consulted, that I here once more beg of my readers not to condemn me upon any account, before they have examined my Addenda, where many things are corrected. I desire them likewise, particularly to consult there the additions to the articles BRUN (9), and BUDÆUS, in which I mention the ancient nobility of these two families; the addition to the article FONTEVRAUD, and to the article LEO X (10), and the article VERSORIS, which I give entire in the Addenda to the last volume (11).

I have nothing to say to those, who complain that my work does not afford them a sufficient number of things that suit with their taste. It is the unavoidable fate of miscellaneous writings. Each reader finds in them too much of one thing, and too little of another. Those who love genealogies

(7) *Salmasius is the Index of authors quoted in his Exercitationes Plinianæ.*

(8) *These four articles have been inserted in their proper places in this new edition.*

(9) *The Plenipotentiary of Spain at the peace of Munster.*

(10) *I give there two Letters of this Pope, which were never printed, and are very curious.*

(11) *All these Additions have been inserted in their proper places in this edition.*

Advertisement concerning

nealogies do not find enough of them: those who do not love them think there are too many. Those who delight in Philosophical reasonings, would have more of them; and those who do not like them, would not have so many. Some wish I had not given the articles of so many Ministers; others wonder I have omitted so many. I desire them all to call to mind this saying of Pliny, " Let us forgive others their inclinations, that they " may forgive ours (12)." I shall quote upon this, a fine Passage of Scioppius (13).

If I have spoken of one family, rather than of another equally or more considerable, it was without any respect of persons; the only reason of it was, that I had materials for some and not for others.

A particular answer is due to those who have found fault with me for speaking so little of great warriors: two things made me so barren in this respect; one is, as I have sufficiently said (14), that I have avoided falling in with the subjects of other Dictionaries, both as to the present and future editions. Most of the ancient and modern Generals of armies are to be found in Moreri; especially the Constables, Admirals, and Mareschals of France, &c. These articles cost only the pains of transcribing Father Anselme. I was persuaded, that all the famous northern and German warriors, would appear at large in Mr Chappuzeau's Dictionary. I did not therefore think it necessary to turn my thoughts that way. But I had still a stronger reason, which was this: I did not find myself in a capacity to give the articles of great captains, such as I should have desired. Father Anselme's performance is a good and useful work, and required an incredible patience and very labourious enquiries, but it cannot satisfy the reader's curiosity. It is next to nothing to know that in such a year a general took or relieved a town, or won a battel, &c. The reader is besides willing to know what was his character; whether he excelled in courage, as Marcellus, or in prudence as Fabius Cunctator; whether he was better qualified to conquer, than to preserve his conquests; whether his fiery and quick temper dazzled him in a battel, or whether he remained sedate in the greatest danger; by what wise and happy expedient he gained a battle that was almost lost; by what fault he was overcome on such an occasion. The readers are also willing to know, whether in reality he got the victory, as the writers of his party affirm, or whether he lost it, as the Writers of the other side maintain. These disputes are innumerable (15). I should think myself obliged to discuss them, and to compare the relations of both sides, that by establishing as a principle, the facts in which they agree, whether in relation to the battle or to it's consequences, we might there, by way of induction, arrive at some sort of certainty.

For example, if I spoke of the Mareschal de Luxembourg, I would observe the character that distinguished him from other generals, and be particular upon the occasions in which he discovered what he excelled in, and in what his talents was but indifferent. I would avoid the mistakes and omissions which I find about him in Moreri's Dictionary. I would not say that he " defeated the armies of Holland near Bodegrave, in 1672," that he took Bodegrave (16) in 1673, that he raised the Siege of Charleroi in 1674. For the first of these three facts (17) is an inexcusable hyperbole, and the two others are wholly chimerical. I would not say, that in 1673 " he made his way through the enemy's army of seventy thou- " sand men, though he had but twenty thousand:" it is an hyperbole that would not be excused in a poet. I would not say, that in 1678 " he

the second French Edition.

" he beat the Dutch army at St Denys, near Mons; but I would examine the question who won the battle. I would not say, that in 1692 " he took " the enemy's cannon and baggage, &c. at Steinkerke;" it being a fact manifestly confuted by the very relation he gave of this battle, and which was immediately printed in France. I would not omit the rebellion he persisted in from the year 1649, to the Pyrenean treaty. I would not omit his campaign of Philipsburg (18), under pretence that he was mortified upon that account. I would not omit his imprisonment in the Bastille, and would endeavour to dive into the secrecy of the proceedings of the Chamber of the Arsenal against him. This is the more requisite for the honour of his memory, because there went strange and very ridiculous reports concerning his process. I would examine what so many people imagine, though perhaps without much reason, that he would have done greater services to France in his last campaigns, if he had not preferred his particular interest of keeping up the war to the public good, or if his orders had not been too limited. Those men pretend that he headed the army, just as the Pope's legates headed the Council of Trent; that is, he was to wait every post for a new inspiration. Lastly, I would endeavour to find a true medium as to his morals, betwixt his funeral oration, and some pieces that have been printed (19).

(18) *In 1676.*

(19) *I do not mean all; for most of them are so silly and impertinent satires, and so plainly calumnious, that they ought not to be credited.*

Every body will be sensible, that since I am not in a capacity of filling up a plan of this nature, I am very excusable for not touching upon such articles.

I forgot to mention, in the preface of the first edition, one of the reasons why I quote long Latin passages; which is, that many persons who read my book are but little acquainted with French, but they are well skilled in Latin, and so by the help of the citation they can perfectly understand my meaning.

Such as will give themselves the trouble to cast their eyes upon the margins of this Dictionary, are desired to remember, that the quotations I have marked with a figure, are those which I have found in the authors, whose passages I relate. I am not answerable for them.

The 7th of December, 1701.

THE LIFE OF MR BAYLE.

BY
Mr DES MAIZEAUX,
Fellow of the Royal Society.

A Letter from Mr DES MAIZEAUX *to Mr* DE LA MOTTE; *who engaged him to write the Life of Mr* BAYLE, *which was prefixed to the last edition of his Dictionary, printed at Amsterdam in the year* 1730.

SIR,   LONDON, *Dec.* 13, 1729.

I Have at length finished the task you was pleased to prescribe me; but I am very much afraid that the performance will discover the shortness of the time in which I was obliged to compose it, and that my zeal to obey your commands, has thrown me into a precipitation prejudicial to my desire of doing well. Tho' my materials were ready long ago, that was not enough; it was necessary to range and reduce them into order, which was no small matter. I am fully persuaded that you are too much my friend, not to be satisfied with my endeavour, and that you will excuse the defects of this piece, on account of my eagerness to gratify your desire. But tho' a friend regards principally the good intention, the public considers only the performance. It is impossible but being so hurried, I must have sometimes too much contracted what ought to have been enlarged, and too much enlarged what ought to have been contracted. The stile likewise is very incorrect, and I do not even know but I have been guilty of some inconsistencies: for having sent you the sheets as fast as I composed them, I have not as yet seen the work entire, and consequently could not compare the several parts together. I could wish the public were apprized of this, which might incline the reader to excuse my faults: and since you are the occasion of the evil, you are in some sort obliged to apply the remedy. Be so good, therefore, as to join to it a short Advertisement, which may serve as an apology for me. But above all things, do not forget to take notice, that when you engaged me to write these Memoirs, the impression of the Dictionary was finished, and they had actually begun to print the Index.

But after having shown my performance in it's worst light, you may likewise set it off by showing it's fair side. However defective the form may be, you may, Sir, speak with assurance of the matter, since that is none of mine. I had very good materials to go upon. After the death of Mr BAYLE, the Earl of SHAFTSBURY, his friend, desired me to communicate to him all that I could gather concerning his life and writings. I addressed myself immediately to Mr BASNAGE, who furnished me with a great many particulars, which I inserted in the account my Lord SHAFTSBURY had desired of me, a very imperfect English translation of which was published in 1708. Mr BAŸZE acquainted me also with several circumstances relating to Mr BAYLE's youth. He was his relation. I might likewise name Mr DE LA RIVIERE, Mr ABBADIE, Mr HUET, &c. Mr BAYLE's *Letters*, which I have published, were of infinite service to me. Lastly, I had a sure guide to fix the dates of his journies, of his studies, of the composition and impression of his works, and of the different circumstances he was in during the first forty years of his life. This guide is Mr BAYLE himself, who has left us an historical and chronological journal of his life, under the title of *Calendarium Carlananum*. For this journal I am obliged to Mr MARAIS, Advocate in the Parliament of Paris, who was pleased to send along with it such illustrations as I wanted. I am also indebted to him, for the Letters which relate to the Queen of Sweden, and for some other important pieces which you will find in this work.

I have joined to Mr BAYLE's Life three small pieces, which will serve for vouchers, and may be placed at the end by way of appendix. The first is the *Calendarium Carlananum*; the translation of it explains what is either expressed very briefly, or by abbreviations in the original. The second is the *Ordonnance* of Mr DE LA REYNIE, Lieutenant-General of the Police, at Paris, containing a condemnation of the *Critique Generale de l'Histoire du Calvinisme de Mr* MAIMBOURG; there is something very singular in it. The third contains the *Acts of the Consistory of the Walloon Church of Rotterdam, concerning Mr Bayle's Dictionary*; in which is to be found, the whole procedure of that consistory, together with Mr BAYLE's declarations: this piece has not as yet been published.

Out of all this, Sir, you may choose what you think proper for your advertisement. I think you cannot avoid naming the persons who have furnished me with memoirs. This is an acknowledgment which is due to them. But I can safely rely upon you in this matter, my interests cannot be in better hands. It therefore only remains, that I beg the continuance of your friendship, and that I assure you of the great devotion with which I shall always be,

SIR,

Your very humble and most obedient servant,

P. DES MAIZEAUX.

[iii]

THE LIFE

OF

Mr *BAYLE*.

1647. R *(PETER) BAYLE*, was born at Carla, a small town in the county of Foix, betwixt Pamiers and Rieux, on the 18th of November 1647. His Father, descended from a good family, originally of Montauban, was named *JOHN*. He was minister of Carla, and married *Jane de Bruguiere*, whose mother was of the family of Ducasse; so that Messieurs Bayle were related to two families of distinction in the county of Foix, Ducasse, and Chalabre of which that of Bruguiere is a branch. He had two brothers; one elder called *JACOB*, who was colleague to his father, and a younger, named *JOSEPH*, and surnamed *du Peyrat*, from an estate belonging to the family.

Mr Bayle discovered from his infancy, a subtile and lively genius, an easy and quick conception, and a very extraordinary memory; and all these were attended with another talent, absolutely necessary to the improvement of these excellent qualities, a strong desire after knowledge and instruction. He would frequently ask questions of his parents, and wait for their answers with the utmost eagerness and attention, and would not be satisfied with such as they gave him, 'till he fully comprehended them, and what he learned in this domestic school he never forgot. His father cultivated these happy dispositions with the utmost care. After having taught him Latin, he made him study the Greek language at the age of twelve
1660. years and a half (1), and for some years improved his knowledge of both these (1) *June* languages, by the reading of the best authors. But at last the functions of his 29, 1660. ministry taking up a great deal of his Time, and finding his son capable of a greater progress than he could possibly make under him, he took the resolution of sending him to the Academy of Puylaurens. Mr Bayle arrived there in the month of February
1666. 1666 (2). He was then in his nineteenth year; but neither the passions which ordi- (2) *Febr.* narily have the sway at that age, nor his absence from his parents, could in the least 12, 1666. weaken the strong passion he had for letters: he made even the hours that are given to recreation subservient to it; and while the other scholars were engaged in the amusements which are so dear to youth, he used to retire to his chamber, and there devote himself to the pleasures arising from study.

In the month of September following (3), he took the opportunity of the vacation (3) *Sept.* to make a visit to his father. But even this season which is designed for diversion, 9. was to him a time of labour: he applyed himself so closely to his studies, that he fell sick; and hardly was he recovered, when giving himself up a-new to this favourite passion, he sickened again, and in this manner by frequent relapses he was detained
1668. at Carla, above eighteen months. After this he was sent to Saverdun (4), to the (4) *May* house of Mr Bayze, who had married his aunt Paula de Bruguiere. The design of 29, 1668. this journey was for the change of air, and to divert him from study, but unluckily he found books there. Mr Rival, minister of Saverdun, had a large collection of them, which was such a temptation to young Bayle, as almost cost him his Life. His continual study threw him into a dangerous fever, which held him a long time, and of which he with great difficulty recovered. As soon as he was in a condition to go abroad, they removed him to a country house of Mr Bayze's, situate upon the banks of the Auriege, which makes the place very agreeable. The remembrance of (5) *See the* the happy moments he spent near that river, was the occasion of his consecrating an *Article* article to it in his Dictionary (5). Auriege.

When

THE LIFE OF Mʀ BAYLE.

(6) Sept. 28.
(7) Nov. 5.

When he was perfectly recovered, he returned to Carla (6), and soon after to Puylaurens (7), to prosecute his studies. He resumed them with new vigour, and, together with his academical exercises, he read all sorts of books that came in his way, not even excepting books of controversy: but Plutarch and Montaigne were his favourite authors. The long stay he had made at home with his father, before he went to the academy, and his frequent indispositions afterwards, had so much retarded his studies, that he did not begin his Logic, 'till he was one and twenty. So that it is not without reason, that he complains in one of his books (8), that he begun his studies late.

(8) In a pamphlet intituled, *Reflexions sur un imprimé qui a pour titre, Jugement du public sur le Dictionaire Critique,* §. 19. p. 8. That is, *Reflexions on a Pamphlet intituled, The Judgment of the Public, concerning the Critical Dictionary:* which see at the end of the last volume.

1669.

He redoubled his application to make up the time he had lost; and the progress made at Puylaurens, not being in his apprehension sufficiently quick, he resolved to leave that academy in order to go to Toulouse, one of the most celebrated universities in France. He arrived there in the month of February 1669 (9); and taking lodgings in a private house, attended the philosophical lectures, which were read in the Jesuits college. There was nothing very extraordinary in this. The Protestants often sent their children to study under the Jesuits, though this had been forbidden by the synods. Mr Bayle's stay at Toulouse, however, had very melancholy consequences for his family, here he changed his religion. The books of controversy which he had read at Puylaurens, had already shaken him; and his doubts were increased at Toulouse, by some disputes he had with a priest, who lodged in the same house with him. He thought his opinions were false, because he could not answer all the arguments that were objected to him; and, a month after his arrival at Toulouse, he embraced the Roman Catholic religion (10). He was matriculated, and the next day resumed the study of Logic.

The news of his change was in the utmost degree afflicting to all his relations, and particularly to his father, who loved him tenderly. Mr Bertier, bishop of Rieux, rightly judging, that after this step young Bayle had no reason to expect any assistance from his relations, generously took upon himself the charge of his maintenance. Mr Bayle makes a grateful acknowledgment of it in a letter which he wrote in the year 1693, to Mr Pinson, Advocate of the Parliament of Paris [*A*].

(9) Febr. 19.
(10) Mar. 19.
(11) Holding the child Jesus in her arms.

They valued themselves very much at Toulouse upon this acquisition of a young man of so great hopes, and whose merit was heightened by his being son to a minister. When it came to his turn to defend Theses publickly, it was resolved that the solemnity should be performed in a splendid manner. The most distinguished persons, both of the clergy, parliament, and city, assisted there: there had never been seen in that university so august and numerous an audience. The theses were adorned with the picture of the Virgin (11), to whom they were dedicated, and this picture was accompanied with several emblematical figures, representing the conversion of the respondent. The perspicuity, the penetration, and the modesty, with which he answered his opponents, procured him an universal applause.

Mr Ros de Bruguiere, one of his uncles by the mother's side, who was married to a Roman Catholic lady, being at Toulouse when Mr Bayle defended his theses, carried a copy of them to Carla, which Madam Ros de Bruguiere hung up as an ornament in her chamber. Mr Bayle's father being come to visit Mr Ros de Bruguiere, they acquainted him in what manner his son had distinguished himself in the public disputation, the honours which had been done him, and the applause he had received. The good man heard this with pleasure, and seemed for a moment to have forgot the grief with which his son's change of religion had afflicted him. But Madam Ros de Bruguiere having shewed him the theses, as soon as he saw the figure of the Virgin, with these words, *VIRGINI DEIPARÆ* (12), he was seized with such indignation, that he made an effort to get near it; but was stopped least he should

(12) To the Virgin Mother of God.

[*A*] *Mr Bayle makes a gratefull acknowledgment of it in a Letter he wrote to Mr Pinson in 1693.*] What follows had been published in the *MENAGIANA*: Mr Bayle is son to a minister. The bishop of Rieux, who had contributed to his conversion, made him study at Toulouse, at his own charges; but after he had finished his studies, he joined himself again to that sect which he had left. These expressions appeared too general to Mr Bayle. He complained of them to Mr Pinson.

(a) This Letter will never be printed before.

" The manner, says he (a), in which Mr Menage has
" spoke concerning me is a little too loose, and apt
" to give false ideas; every body, from these words,
" will imagine, that I went through all my studies
" under the protection, and by the liberality of the
" bishop of Rieux. the whole of the matter is this.
" After I had finished the studies of Grammar, La-
" tin, and Rhetoric, partly under my father's care,
" partly at the academy of Puylaurens; I began to
" study Philosophy at that academy, and continued
" to do so only about four or five months. After-
" wards I went to Toulouse full of doubts concern-
" ing my religion, occasioned by the reading of books
" of controversy. I chanced to lodge in the same
" house with a priest, who, by his disputes with me,

" increased them, and at last persuaded me that I
" professed a false religion. I separated from it, and
" continued the study of Philosophy in the Jesuits
" college at Toulouse. The bishop of Rieux, in
" whose diocese I was born, hearing of my change
" and the indignation of my family against me, and
" besides, that I was studious, of blameless morals,
" and had some measure of genius, honoured me
" with his protection, and gave me money to pay my
" board, for I received none from home because of
" my father's displeasure. Thus I finished my study
" of Philosophy: that is to say, I staid at Toulouse
" 18 months, after which the impressions of my edu-
" cation having regained the ascendant, I thought
" myself obliged to return to the religion in which I
" was born, and went to Geneva where I prosecuted
" my studies. I do not say this, as if I were asham-
" ed of the favours of that great prelate, I still retain
" the remembrance of them with respect, and with
" the utmost gratitude. But still we are bound, both
" on our own account and that of the public, to pre-
" vent peoples forming false, extravagant, and hyper-
" bolical ideas of things, &c."

have

THE LIFE OF Mr BAYLE.

1670. have tore it to pieces in the transport of his grief. He left the house with precipitation and shed a flood of tears, protesting that he would never return thither, while so ungrateful an object presented itself to his sight.

In the mean time, the catholics, not content with having gained young Bayle, formed a design of bringing over the whole family; and for this purpose they thought it proper to begin with the elder brother. The bishop of Rieux laid his commands on Mr Bayle to write to him, and at the same time assured him, that if he could only persuade him to come to Toulouse his conversion was sure. Mr Bayle believing sincerely that he had embraced the right side, and bearing a great affection to his brother, wrote him the following Letter (1).

(1) *This Letter is dated the 15th of April 1670. I have the original in my hands. The direction is To Mr Bayle, the son, Minister of Carla, at Carla.*

My very dear Brother,

"THE great affection that I have for you, and the passionate desire I have for your happiness, won't permit me to omit any occasion of procuring your welfare. I find myself under a necessity of begging of you, in the most earnest manner, to come and pass a few days in this city, that I may have an opportunity of talking to you of several matters, which are of the utmost importance to you, both with regard to this life, and that which is to come. I persuade myself, that if I had the liberty of discovering to you the state of things as they really are, and the favourable disposition in which they are at present, I should be able to make some impression upon your mind, and make you confess that the supreme wisdom, which governs the world, has laboured in a very particular manner in directing the motion of so many springs; and that as it doth nothing that is not conducive to the advancement of it's own glory and our salvation, it has been pleased, by bringing together so many different things, which all seem to conspire for your advantage, to endeavour the most happy and glorious change, which can possibly be wrought in my father's mind, and in your's.

"You will without doubt say that all these are mysteries which you do not at all understand, that they are riddles to you; but I assure you that if I had but a little conversation with you on this subject, you would easily comprehend my design, and would see as clear as day, what good foundation I had for assuring you, that this disposition which has ordered such a number of things, in which you have a great concern, is so favourable to you, that there is all the reason in the world to hope something supernatural from it.

"I shall not explain myself more clearly upon this subject, because I hope that you will not refuse me the favour I desire of you of coming to see me as soon as possible, and then we shall have an opportunity of talking more at large about it, in the private conversations we shall have together. Come therefore, my dear brother, if it be possible, before the end of this week; come and satisfy the impatience of one who languishes for you, and ardently desires that you would put yourself in a condition of being happy. I assure you that you shall not repent your coming, what I have to say being of such a nature as is proper to satisfy a solid and reasonable mind such as your's.

"And surely I should wrong you, if I believed that you were sick of an incurable distemper, to such a degree too as to approve of nothing but what is agreeable to your own notions. I entertain a better opinion of you, and those who know you make no difficulty of believing, that a person of so good a natural disposition, and of such probity as you profess, may be brought to relish any reasonable opinion, however strange it may appear at first sight, and however strong your prejudices may be to the contrary. Upon this foundation I assure myself, that what I have to say to you will not displease you, nor startle you so far as to make you capable of altogether shutting your ear against whosoever shall desire to talk to you about it.

"If I had addressed myself to a great many people, and begged of them the favour of a hearing which I desire of you, it might indeed happen that they would presently suspect and distrust me, and condemn all I should be able to say to them: but as for you, I believe you are not capable of condemning me without hearing me; and if it was only out of curiosity, methinks you will be desirous to know what this matter may be, and that you will suspend your judgment 'till you know what it is: in which I can observe nothing in your mind but a disposition to do well.

"I should want no more, to give me a foundation for good hopes, than to be assured that you are resolved to form this conclusion, which is founded upon a truth confirmed in the most incontestable manner, by the experience of all ages; to wit, that in matters of religion, all innovations are most pernicious, and that a private person who pretends, by his own authority, to set himself up for a Reformer, can be thought no other than a factious person, a schismatic, a sower of tares, and, in short, a person filled with pride, obstinacy, and envy. And indeed what probability is there, that God should suffer the Christian Church to fall to ruin and desolation, that he should hide his light from it, and deprive it of his illumination; while, in the mean time, he invests a private person, with so extraordinary an abundance of his grace, that he

VOL. I.   b   " shall

THE LIFE OF Mʀ BAYLE.

"shall become the restorer of truth, a light to guide into the right path those who 1670.
"go astray; and, in short, the chanel and vehicle, the base and pillar, of true faith;
"so that one might say of him, as the poet says of a young prince who seemed to
"be born for the glory of that age,

Hunc saltem everso juvenem succurrere sæclo
Ne probibete (1).

(1) Virgil. Georg lib. i. v. 500, 501.

"In truth we must be both rash, imprudent, and blind, to suffer ourselves to be
"persuaded of such chimera's. It is much more agreeable to the order of God's
"providence, and to the care which the Holy Ghost takes of the faithful, in go-
"verning the church, by the communication of his divine assistance, which he be-
"stows upon the vicegerents of the son of God upon earth, that the church should
"instruct, correct, and reform, private persons, and the abuses which they may have
"suffered to creep into their conduct, and cure them of their errors, rather than
"that private persons should reform the church and set it to rights again. For
"as it would be very foolish to maintain, that God, when he intended to preserve
"some persons from the waters of the flood by whom he might restore the human
"race, should drown those who were in the ark of Noah, and at the same time
"should raise up I don't know what person, who had saved himself and his wife
"in some cavern, or who had escaped the fury and inclemency of the waves in
"I don't know what inviolable sanctuaries: so it is as extravagant, and without
"foundation, to pretend that the Holy Spirit, in order to accomplish his design of preser-
"ving always a little of the leaven of faith from the ravages of infidels and heretics,
"has suffered the church, which is his spouse, to fall into idolatry, superstition, and error,
"and has drawn out Luther and Calvin from the obscurity of a cell, or the corner
"of a chapel, to propagate the faith, restore it to it's rights, and raise it up from
"under it's ruins.

"Indeed one might think, tho' without the least appearance of reason or truth,
"that God would preserve these two men to propagate the gospel, during that
"general corruption which they suppose to have spread over the whole face of the
"church, because they had preserved themselves pure and clean from all those dis-
"orders and pretended abominations; as he preserved Lot and Noah, as a reward
"for their not having polluted themselves with the vices of the ages in which they
"lived. But to entertain any such thought, one must be altogether ignorant of things
"the most universally known, since it is notorious, that these two great sticklers for

(2) See Mr Bayle's Critique Generale de l'Histoire du Calvinisme. Lettre xi. § 8; and in the Critic. Diction. the Articles CALVIN and LUTHER, where you will find a defence of these two Reformers.

"Reformation were altogether abandoned and immersed in vice (2); not to observe
"that they set out in an extremely criminal manner, that is to say, that they began
"by violating those vows, of which both piety and justice required the strictest ob-
"servance (3).

(3) See Critique Generale, &c. Lettre ix.

"These, dear brother, are the reflexions with which I would have you fortified,
"when you shall come to this town, for assuredly you will thereby become more apt
"to receive instruction. Besides all this, the precarious and weak condition of your
"whole party, which exists in this kingdom only by toleration, and because the
"King is not in the humour of extirpating you, makes me fear on your account
"every time I think of it. And indeed to subsist only because the fancy of a prince,
"who may do whatever he pleases in this matter, doth not incline him to suspend
"his concourse by which you are preserved, is it not to be exposed to destruction every
"hour of the day, since there is not one in which the humour of a prince may not
"pass from one extremity to another.

"I have therefore great reason to wish, that you would imitate the Pharisees and
"Saducees who came to John's baptism, of whom he asked who had persuaded them
"to fly from the wrath to come? I hope one day we shall be able, through the
"grace of the Holy Ghost and the blessing of God, to ask you a like question, which
"would be both very agreeable and advantageous for you. For this I pray to the
"sovereign Lord of all things, and would willingly bestow the last drop of my
"blood to procure your salvation. This I say not only on your account in parti-
"cular; but likewise on the account of my father, mother, second brother, and all my
"relations: too happy, if, like another Joseph, I could be the instrument of saving
"all my family! Adieu, my dear Brother: reflect on what I have said to you,
"and come as soon as possible, to know what he would say to you who is your
"most humble, most obedient, and most affectionate servant. You will see the ac-

(4) These words are not of St Paul, but of JESUS CHRIST Gospel of St Matb. Chap. vi. ver. 33.

"complishment of that which St Paul says; *he who seeks after the kingdom of God and*
"*his righteousness, all other things shall be added unto it* (4)."

This letter made no great impression upon Mr Bayle's elder brother, with regard to religion. He was equally insensible to the flattering hopes it gave him, and to the common-places of controversy it opposed to him: but he was very much alarmed by some expressions, which made him fear least his brother, together with the Roman Catholic religion, had imbibed that sourness of spirit, with which it inspires it's devotees. His father, more indulgent, attributed them to some busy priest who had

dictated

1670. dictated the letter. He said that he saw nothing of his son in it, and that he hoped to see him very soon return into the good way.

Mr Naudis de Bruguiere, his coufin-german, a young gentleman of a great deal of wit and penetration, was at this time at Touloufe. He lodged in the fame houfe with Mr Bayle. They difputed frequently about religion; and after warmly pufhing the arguments of each fide, they ufed to examine them cooly over again. Mr Naudis was well acquainted with his religion: the ftrict friendfhip that was betwixt them banifhed all bitternefs from their debates, and rendered them more free and more impartial. Thefe familiar difputes, which feemed to be entirely accidental, frequently embarraffed Mr Bayle, and made him fufpect feveral opinions of the church of Rome, infomuch that he fometimes inwardly condemned himfelf for having embraced them without being fufficiently acquainted with them. For he looked upon examination in matters of religion, to be an indifpenfible duty, being the only means to affure one's felf of the truth, and confequently of knowing the will of God, and of putting one's felf in a condition of following it. He was the more confirmed in thefe fentiments by obferving, that whatever fubmiffion the church of Rome exacts, it was notwithftanding by the way of examination, that they thought fit to bring about his converfion.

About the fame time Mr de Pradals de Larbon came to Touloufe. He was one of thofe men, who by their wit, gaiety, and manners, at firft fight gain the affection of all who fee them. Accordingly he was very much careffed by perfons of the greateft diftinction in that province. Mr Bayle, the father, had defired him to vifit his fon as oft as he went to Touloufe: he hoped that Mr Pradals would very foon gain the confidence of the young Bayle; and in fact he fucceeded fo well, that Mr Bayle one day confeffed to him, that he believed he had been a little too hafty in the new party he had chofen, and that now he found feveral doctrines in the Romifh religion, which appeared to him contrary both to reafon and fcripture. Mr de Pradals, charmed with this confeffion, prefently communicated it to Mr Bayle's family, to their inexpreffible fatisfaction. They prefently refolved to fend his elder brother to him, and begged of Mr de Pradals to manage their interview. Mr Bayle's eldeft brother being gone to Touloufe with Mr de Pradals, the latter invited young Bayle to dine with him, as it was his cuftom to do. After fome difcourfe, when the fervants had retired, Mr Bayle the elder, who was in a clofet, came out and fhewed himfelf to his brother. All that joy, grief, and furprize have moft ftrong at once feized the young Bayle, fo that he was not able to utter a word, he threw himfelf at his feet, and burft out into tears. Mr Bayle, the elder, could not refrain his, and raifing him up he fpoke to him in fo tender a manner, that the young Bayle difcovered the bottom of his heart to him, by telling him how impatient he was to leave Touloufe, and renounce the errors which had feduced him. In the mean time, as his efcape would certainly incenfe, the bifhop of Rieux and the Jefuits, they thought it neceffary to take fome precautions, which delayed Mr Bayle's departure for fome days. It was in the month of Auguft 1670, that he put this defign in execution.

He departed fecretly from Touloufe (1), where he had ftaid eighteen months, and retired to Mazeres in the Lauragais, to a country houfe of Mr du Vivié, fix leagues from Touloufe, and three from Carla. His elder brother came there the day after, with certain minifters of the neighbourhood; and the next day (2), Mr Rival, Minifter of Saverdun, received his abjuration in prefence of his elder brother, of Mr Guillemat Minifter of Mazeres, and of Mr Rival Minifter of Calmont and nephew to the minifter of Saverdun. The very fame day they made him fet out for Geneva [B].

(1) Aug. 19.
(2) Aug. 21.

[B] *Mr Bayle has himfelf given us the hiftory of his change of religion, and of his return to the proteftant church.*] " The truth of the matter is (a), that " Mr Bayle, while he ftudied philofophy in the " Academy at Puylaurens, did not confine himfelf fo " clofely to what was dictated by his profeffor, as " not likewife to read fome books of controverfy, " not with the difpofition with which moft people do " fo, I mean to confirm himfelf in his preconceived " notions, but to examine agreeably to the great Pro" teftant principle, whether the doctrine he had been " taught from his infancy was true or falfe: which " requires that we fhould hear both parties. Upon " this account he was curious to fee the arguments " of the Roman Catholics in their own writings. He " found fo fpecious arguments againft the doctrine " which denies that there is any living judge upon " earth, to whofe decifions private perfons are obliged " to fubmit, when there arife difputes about matters " of religion, that not being able to anfwer thefe ob" jections to himfelf, and much lefs to defend his " principles againft fome fubtile controverfifts with " whom he difputed at Touloufe, he thought himfelf " a fchifmatic, and out of the way of falvation, and " bound to join himfelf again to the flock, from " which he looked upon the Proteftant communions " as branches lopped off. Being re-united to it he con" tinued the ftudy of philofophy (b), in the college " of the Jefuits, as do almoft all who ftudy in Ro" man Catholic countries, of whatfoever quality and " condition they be. But the exceffive worfhip he " obferved was paid to creatures, appearing very " doubtful to him, and philofophy having given him " a more perfect knowledge of the impoffibility of " tranfubftantiation, he concluded that there muft " have been fome fophiftry in the objections, which " had overcome him; and upon making a new ex" amination of the two religions, he recovered that " light of which he had loft fight, and followed it " without regarding a thoufand temporal advantages, " of which he deprived himfelf, nor a thoufand in" conveniencies which appeared to him inevitable in " doing fo."

(a) Chimere de la Cabale de Rotterdam demontrée p. 139. & fuiv.

(b) *He had n i tteen ftudied above four or five months in philofophy. See la Chimontrée, p. 151 and the Letter to Mr Pinfon, above, Rem. [A.]*

THE LIFE OF MR BAYLE.

He arrived there the second of September; and resumed the course of his studies. 1670.
He had been taught the peripatetic philosophy by the Jesuits, and as he understood
it well he defended it with a good deal of warmth (1). Yet notwithstanding he
thought himself obliged to examine the Cartesian philosophy, which was taught at
Geneva; and it was not long before he preferred the reasonable principles of the new
philosophy, to the vain subtilties of the followers of Aristotle. A person of Mr
Bayle's merit could not fail of being soon distinguished at Geneva. The reputation
he obtained there, made Mr de Normandie, Syndic of the Republic, desire him to take
the charge of his childrens education (2). Mr Basnage, who studied at that time in
Geneva, lodged with Mr de Normandie, and it was there Mr Bayle became acquainted with him, and formed that union which continued to his death. Mr Bayle likewise
contracted a friendship with Mr Minutoli, which he ever after cultivated by a correspondence, that neither the length of time, nor distance of place, ever made him
neglect. He was likewise intimately acquainted with Messieurs Pictet and Leger, who
have been Professors of Divinity in the Academy of Geneva; and acquired in a very particular manner the esteem and affection of many persons of eminence, both in the State
and in the Church: such as Mr Fabry, the Syndic; Messieurs Turretin, Mestrezat,
Bourlamachi, Sartoris, &c.

Some time after the place of one of the regents of the College becoming
vacant, they cast their eyes upon him to supply it. Upon this he set himself to look
over the ancient Latin and Greek authors; but, after considering the matter maturely,
he could not bring himself to a resolution of teaching a Form, and so he neglected this
sort of establishment.

Mr Bayle had not been two years at Geneva, when the Count de Dhona, Lord 1672.
of Copet, a Barony in the Pays de Vaud, two leagues distant from Geneva, desired
Mr Basnage to find him out a tutor for his sons. Mr Basnage named Mr Bayle to
him as a person extremely fit for that business. At the same time, he spoke of it to
Mr Bayle, who at first had some reluctance to undertake the task proposed to him. He
could not resolve to quit the delights of Geneva, and bury himself in the country.
However at last he went thither (3), and employed himself in the education of the young
Counts de Dhona: Alexander, who was governour and afterwards minister of state to
the King of Prussia; Frederic surnamed Ferrassieres, who was a lieutenant-general in
the Dutch service, governor of Mons, and was killed in the action at Denain (4);
and Christopher, who assisted on the part of the King of Prussia, as elector of Brandenburg, at the coronation of the Emperor Charles VI, and who has distinguished himself
in many other offices both civil and military. He continued two years with this
family, and during that time he endeavoured to divert himself in his solitude, by a
commerce of letters, which he carried on with Mr Minutoli, and with Mr Constant who
afterwards filled the highest stations in the Academy of Lausanne. The letters he
wrote to them turned upon every thing that came to hand, philosophy, literature,
or political news which he loved passionately (5): he owns that he wrote without attaching himself to any regular connexion of thoughts (6). This commerce
however was not capable of hindering his being tired of Copet, so he resolved to
leave that place. He informed Mr Basnage, who had returned to France, of his
design and begged his good offices. Mr Basnage acquainted him, that a relation of
his who was studying at Geneva, was ordered to return to Rouen; he desired Mr Bayle
to accompany him, and flattered him with the hopes of procuring something advantageous for him in that city (7). Mr Bayle received this news with great satisfaction; the only difficulty was to find some pretext for leaving the Count de Dhona.
He made use of the following, which could not fail to prevent the Count's opposing
the loss he was a going to sustain; he told him that his father, who was dangerously
ill, had laid his commands upon him to come to him without delay.

Accordingly he left Copet, the twenty ninth of May 1674, after having provided 1674.
his pupils with another person capable of instructing them (8). He made no longer
stay at Geneva than was necessary to see his friends; and arrived at Rouen with Mr Basnage's relation on the fifteenth of June. Soon after he was appointed tutor to a merchant's
son, and lived in the house with him; this was the post which Mr Basnage had provided
for Mr Bayle. This merchant had a country-house near Rouen, where Mr Bayle was
obliged to go and spend five or six months with his pupil. He found this retirement
as disagreeable as that of Copet had been, and he had recourse to the same remedies;
he wrote letters to his relations and friends, and even composed some small pieces.
When Mr Minutoli pressed him to send them to him, he desired to be excused. "It
" is a sufficient satisfaction to me, (says he in a letter which he wrote to him (9),
" that you are not ignorant how constant a correspondent I was, during my solitude
" in Normandy: and this being a sufficient proof that you are always in my thoughts,
" I won't give you the trouble of reading a confused medley of indigested thoughts, which
" my chagrin has made me put in writing." Being returned to Rouen in the
beginning of the winter, the sole advantage he found there, was the benefit of frequent
conversations with Mr Basnage the father, Mr Bigot, Mr de Larroque, and some
other persons of distinguished learning and merit. He only passed the winter there,
for

THE LIFE OF MR BAYLE.

for finding that his pupil had no disposition to Letters, he acquainted his relations with it, and left him.

1675. His utmost ambition was to be at Paris. The arts and sciences which flourished there, the great number of excellent libraries, the conferences which were weekly held on all sorts of subjects, in the houses of several learned men, where they with pleasure received all who desired to assist at them, were such powerful attractives to Mr Bayle, that he could not resist them. He desired his friends to procure for him some establishment there, to enable him to live in that great city. They proposed that he should take the charge of a young gentleman who was expected there from the country, and Mr Bayle left Rouen, the 1st of March 1675, in order to go to Paris. There he did not indeed find the young gentleman his friends had designed for him, but by the recommendation of the Marquis de Ruvigny, he was chosen tutor to Messieurs de Beringhen, brothers to Mr de Beringhen counsellor in the parliament of Paris, and to the Duchess de la Force. He entered to this charge the 3d of April a month after his arrival at Paris.

While he was still in Normandy his mother had let him know, that she passionately desired to have his picture. He could not refuse her that satisfaction, and employed Ferdinand, a famous painter, whom a President of the Parliament, had at that time invited to Rouen. He sent her this picture after he came to Paris, and along with it a letter so tender, so full of respect, and which shows so well the disposition of his mind, that I think it well deserves a place in these Memoirs. It is as follows (1).

Madam,

" I Had resolved to send you at the same time a portrait of my heart, as well as of
" my face: but not being able to find words strong enough to express the
" greatness of my affection and respect for you, rather than my heart should suffer
" by my not being able to do it justice, I have chosen to send you the work of the
" painter alone. I flattered myself, that it would have been as easy for me to repre-
" sent what passeth in my mind, as it has been to him to give a just representation of
" my features; I already fancied, that a thousand proper and significant words
" strove, which should first present themselves for that purpose. But when I came to
" try it, I found that my imagination was not able to furnish me with any thing
" that I wanted, and so I was obliged, much contrary to my inclination, to abandon
" my enterprize.

" In order to supply this defect, fancy to yourself, my very good Mother, the thing
" on earth which is the most grateful, the most affectionate, and the most respect-
" ful, and you will have an idea of what I am with regard to you, and of what
" I am not able to express in words. It is a great satisfaction to me, that you have
" so much desired to have my picture, and it would be still a greater, if you would
" be persuaded that I am not to blame, that you have waited so long for it. If I
" cannot have yours, at least I shall have you always painted in my heart, on which
" you are impressed as a signet.

" May the good God, who has always displayed his mercies to us, still more
" and more favour our family, and grant to you, my much honoured Mother, a long
" life, free from cares, grief, and sickness; and to me such a share of his protection,
" as may make you taste those joys and pleasures, which usually arise from the
" happiness of persons who are dear to us.

" I am indeed of a disposition neither to fear bad fortune, nor to have very ardent
" desires for good. Yet I lose this steadiness and indifference, when I reflect that
" your love to me makes you feel every thing that befals me. It is therefore from
" the consideration that my misfortunes would be a torment to you, that I wish
" to be happy: and when I think that my happiness would be all your joy, I should
" be sorry my bad fortune should continue to persecute me; tho' as to my own
" particular interest, I dare promise to myself that I shall never be very much
" affected by it. I am with the most ardent affection, Madam my much honoured
" Mother, Your, &c."

Mr Basnage was at this time at Sedan, where he finished the study of Divinity. Mr Bayle communicated to him all the literary news he could meet with, and Mr Basnage used to read his letters to Mr Jurieu, Minister, and Professor of Divinity in the Academy of Sedan. As Mr Jurieu will be mentioned more than once in these Memoirs, I shall begin here to give his character. He had a good deal of sagacity, a fruitful imagination, and wrote both well and with ease. Tho' in many things he departed from the sentiments of the Reformed, he did nevertheless set up for a rigorous defender of Orthodoxy [C]. Being presumptuous he would domineer every where, and his

VOL. I. c pride

(1) *This Letter is dated April 16. 1675. The direction is* To Mademoiselle de Bayle at Carla.

[C] *Tho' in many things, he departed from the sentiments of the Reformed, he did nevertheless, set up for a rigorous defender of Orthodoxy.*] He had published in the year 1670 an Answer to a book concerning the re-union of Christians, written by Mr Dhuisseau, Minister of Saumur: this answer was condemned by the synod of Saintonge, as containing heretical positions. He afterwards composed a dissertation on the necessity of Baptism, wherein he defended one of the errors of the Church of Rome; and it was with much

THE LIFE OF Mr BAYLE.

pride could not bear those, whose merit he looked upon as either capable of equalling 1675. or obscuring that which he thought himself possessed of. His attachment to his friends was measured by the deference they paid to him. To fail in that deference which he exacted, was sufficient to raise his indignation, and make him an implacable enemy. By this imperious and turbulent spirit he brought discord wherever he went, and rendered himself odious to all the world. It was upon this account he had been obliged to quit the churches of Mer and Vitry, and had brought upon himself a great many mortifications at Sedan, where notwithstanding he had a very considerable party.

At this time Mr Basnage having got notice, that the Academy of Sedan designed to appoint a successor to Mr Pithois, one of their Professors of Philosophy aged eighty years, he acquainted Mr Bayle with it, and advised him to take advantage of that opportunity to procure to himself a lasting and honourable establishment. Mr Bayle made him the following answer, the same day on which he took the charge of Messieurs de Beringhen. "I never receive any of your letters, says he (1), without receiving "at the same time, proofs of your friendship, nay of a friendship always watchful "of every thing that can be of advantage to me. The great age of your Pro- "fessor would be a favourable conjuncture, if I was in a condition of making use of "your good offices. But, dear Sir, I must acquaint you, that ever since I left Geneva "I have done nothing else but forget, and want of culture has so blunted my mind, "that I do not know if by a return to study, I should be able to set myself to rights "again. Without doubt that post is a hundred times better than this which I am "going to have, for after all, the character of preceptor is become so contemptible "almost every where, that no personal merit can save a man from that general disc- "steem with which it is attended, therefore it is with the greatest reluctance that I "once more venture into that tiresome road. I do not know but I might have "brought Mr de Beringhen to allow me thirty pistoles if I had higgled with him: "but my natural modesty, my disinterestedness, and the advice of my friends, having "inclined me to leave myself entirely to his discretion, and to assure him that I "would be satisfied with whatever he should please to allow me, I shall only have "two hundred livres. I must be upon the watch, and had it not been for a trou- "blesome delicacy, which obliged me not to depart from the laws of civility, I "might have retracted with considerable advantages towards repairing my bad for- "tune. I am a fool, you will say, for not having done so: I own it, and it is the "shame of appearing fickle, which has been the cause of my folly."

The disagreeable situation that Mr Bayle was in redoubled Mr Basnage's zeal, and made him act with more vigour in his favour. He desired Mr Jurieu to employ his interest for him, and Mr Jurieu promised to serve him to the utmost of his power. He found himself so much the more disposed to do so, that he was afraid least Mr Brazi, who was the other Professor of Philosophy, and whom he hated, should have interest enough to get his son chosen in the place of Mr Pithois. So that it was not so much from the esteem he had for Mr Bayle, as (2) "to flatter his "darling passion, which was the desire of domineering. His party in the Academy "was not so strong as he could have wished, and in case the opposite party had "succeeded in their design of giving the chair of Philosophy to Mr Bayle's compe- "titor, Mr Jurieu foresaw nothing but sorrow and bitterness to himself, so that who- "ever had chanced to have been recommended to him, he would have left no stone "unturned to establish him, in order to exclude a competitor of whom he was "afraid."

Mr Basnage having made sure of Mr Jurieu, represented to Mr Bayle how much what he proposed to him was preferable to his present condition, and pressed him to yield to the desires of his friends. But he continued still to excuse himself, as not being sufficiently qualified, and promised however to look over his Philoso- phy and see what progress he could make in five or six months study. "I admire "you continually, says he (3), and that generous beneficent disposition of yours, "and that indefatigableness to serve those you love. I agree with you, that the "title of preceptor is unworthy of a gentleman, and that I ought to get rid of it "as quickly as possible. I know on the other hand, that the character of Professor "of Philosophy is much more honourable, and not ill suited to my fortune and "situation: your pressing me on that score therefore appears to me perfectly well "judged, and to flow from the most sincere friendship in the world. But, dear Sir, "the misfortune is, you lay your account to find me the same person you knew at "Geneva: then indeed I could dispute indifferently well; I came fresh from a "school, where I had been well instructed in all the scholastic chicanry, and I "may say, without vanity, that I was no bad proficient in it. But the matter is "quite altered now. You know, Sir, that the proposal of teaching a Class, which was

(1) *Letter of April 3, 1675, p. 581, 582, of the fourth Volume of the Miscellaneous Works of Mr Bayle.*

(2) *Letter concerning the small books wrote a-gainst the Cabale Chimerique, pag. 4, 5.*

(3) *Letter of May 5, 1675, in his Works, last cited, p. 592, 593.*

(a) *This hook was published in the year 1674.*

much difficulty, he was persuaded to suppress that piece. They found it no less difficult to make him strike some heretical propositions out of his *Apology for the Morals of the Reformed* (a). Notwithstanding this, he combined with some other divines to perse- cute Mr Pajon, Minister of Orleans, who had a par- ticular system concerning Grace, tho' at bottom it agreed with the doctrine of absolute predestination, and final perseverance, which was taught by the re- formed churches in France (b).

(b) *See Reponse à l'Apologie de Mr Jurieu, by Mr de Beau- val, p. 10.*

1675. "was made me, sent me back once more to study the Classics, and that I began to
"neglect Philosophy, that I laid aside Mr Des Cartes for Homer and Virgil, and
"that by going to Copet I lost two years there, without studying either languages
"or any sort of science, but Philosophy less than any thing. I have continued on
"this footing ever since my return to France, and as I easily lose my ideas, I
"find myself reduced to such a condition at this present time that I write to you,
"that I do not so much as know the first elements of Logic. I know that a year
"employed in the manner I told you of in a former letter, in studying night and
"day, in disputing, defending theses, &c. would bring me in wind again, and give
"me courage to give defiance to all assailants. But here is the point. Where shall I
"find this year, and where shall I find the means to employ it so? in my present
"state, I cannot promise to have it in my power to study a quarter of an hour with-
"out a thousand interruptions. I have not one book of Philosophy, and it is im-
"possible for me to make acquaintances, the few people I know are of so difficult
"access, that I call upon them three or four times without finding them, nay I do
"not so much as know if they have those books which will be necessary for me. In
"fine, dear Sir, my rivals cannot be so far behind in Philosophy, nor in so bad a
"situation to prepare themselves for the engagement, as I find myself in at present.
"I am vexed to the last degree, and am ready to curse my stars, that I am not
"able to answer the advances you made in my favour. I honour and admire Mr
"Jurieu, and should desire earnestly to be near him, that I may improve by his
"great and incomparable talents, and I find myself unable to express my gratitude,
"for his generous inclination to serve me, upon your recommendation. What shall
"I say more to you, dear Sir? I am going to look over my Philosophy, to
"buy or borrow some good system, and study as much as the noise and clamour of
"two foolish ungovernable boys, whom I have upon my hands from morning to
"night, will permit me to do; and according to the progress which I shall be able
"to make, I will resolve upon a journey to Sedan, with great pleasure, five or six
"months hence. If it was only to see Sedan, I would resolve to make this journey, for
"there can be no hurt in it. Dear Sir, I should die with grief, if you had engaged
"yourself for me, and I did not engage myself to disengage you. My friendship to you
"would make me run into any thing, rather than endure that you should not get
"out of this affair, in which you have involved yourself on my account. But once
"more, dear Sir, pray consider that you cannot depend much upon the progress which
"I shall make in Philosophy, by a study so interrupted, and attended with so many
"vexations and so disturbed as mine will be."

This letter surprized Mr Jurieu extremely; he considered Mr Bayle's excuses as mere shifts, and owned that he could not tell what to make of it. The truth was Mr Bayle had a secret reason, which made him averse from going to Sedan. He was afraid least his change of religion, which was a secret to every body in that country but Mr Basnage, should come to be discovered, and that occasion might be taken from the Arret against the Relapse [D], to give him trouble, and to distress the Reformed at Sedan. Mr Jurieu therefore suspecting that there was some other reason than that which Mr Bayle pretended in his letter, would needs know what it really was that kept him back; Mr Basnage could not help letting him into that affair, and Mr Jurieu was of opinion that this ought not to hinder his coming, since they two being the only persons who knew any thing of it, he ran no hazard. Whereupon Mr Basnage removed Mr Bayle's fears, and some time after having wrote to him that the election of a new Professor approached, and that there was no time to be lost, he set out from Paris the 22d of August in order to go to Sedan.

As soon as he arrived there (1), Mr Basnage procured him the acquaintance of several of his friends who were of the party which opposed Mr Jurieu, and particularly of Mr du Rondel, Professor of Eloquence. They promised to do him justice. Mr Bayle soon found the occasion he had for their protection. He had three competitors, and all possible means were used to set him aside, because he was a stranger and his competitors were natives of Sedan. But at last it was left to be determined

(1) *He arrived at Sedan August 31.*

(b) *See the same History Vol. iii. p. 520, 582. and the collection of Edicts, declarations, &c. which is at the end of that vol. p. 109, 112. And vol. iv. p. 18, 3, 4, and the collection of Edicts, &c. of that vol. p. 7, 106.* (c) *See the letters to Mr Minutoli of 1675, pag. 74, and of Feb. 6, 1676. p. 103.*

[D] *The arret against the relapse.*] They called Relapse those of the Reformed, who after having embraced the Roman Catholic religion, abandoned it, and returned to the protestants. From the year 1657 they began to disturb some of the Reformed under pretence, that they were Relapse, but this was without any express order from court (a). The first declaration which appeared against them was given in the month of April 1663, importing that they should be punished according to the rigour of the Ordinances; an expression which properly speaking meant nothing, because no Ordinance had as yet defined the punishment of this new crime. They did not fail, notwithstanding, to take advantage of this declaration to distress the Reformed: they even pretended that it had a retroactive force; which having caused infinite disorders, the King found himself obliged to publish an Arret in the month of September 1664, forbidding the extending of it to any thing which had past before it was registred by the parliaments. In the mean time, that prince not being satisfied with the loose and indefinite terms of his first declaration, published another in the month of June 1665, in which he condemned the relapse to perpetual banishment. Mr Bayle came under this second declaration, which still appearing too moderate, was at last followed by a third in the month of May 1679, whereby it was declared, that the Relapses should be condemned to an amende honourable, be banished for ever out of the kingdom, and have their estates confiscated (b). The fear Mr Bayle was under of being known and punished as a relapse, made him desire his friends to change the spelling of his name in the directions of their letters, and to write *Bele* instead of *Bayle* (c).

(a) *See the History of the Edict of Nantz. Tom. iii. p. 66, 132, 230, 428.*

THE LIFE OF Mʀ BAYLE.

determined by a dispute. The candidates agreed to make their Theses without 1673. books or preparation, betwixt sun rising and sun setting. The subject assigned them was *Time*. They shut themselves up upon the 28th of September, to compose them; and Mr Bayle defended his Theses publickly upon the 23d and 24th of October, in the afternoon. He disputed with such clearness, accuracy and force, that notwithstanding the interest and intrigues of his rivals, the moderators of the Academy adjudged him the victory. These particulars are to be found in the letters which he wrote to Messieurs Constant and Minutoli [*E*].

He was received Professor on the 2d of November: he took the usual oath upon the 4th, and began his public lectures upon the 11th.

Soon after he was informed that the Academy of Geneva had chosen Mr Minutoli Professor of History and Belles Lettres: it was Mr Minutoli himself who informed him of it, not omitting a detail of the examination he had undergone, and of the opposition he had met with. Mr Bayle made his compliments to him upon this new promotion, and thanked him for the particular account he had given him of it. "The cir-
(1) *Letter* "cumstances, says he (1), of your glorious establishment, in the place of Professor,
of April 4, "with which you have acquainted me, have been infinitely agreeable; for tho' I knew
1676, p. "in general that you had given very distinguishing proofs, both of your genius and
104. "learning, and that I had from thence already conceived an incredible satisfaction yet
"the order and detail of it, which you have given me, have redoubled that pleasure: for
"we Philosophers love method in every thing, and without it nothing has charms for
"us. I say this, Sir, to give you hopes of not being henceforth exposed to my ir-
"regularities, and that I shall not any more overwhelm you with a confused heap
"of thoughts and words, as I have done formerly. My new degree inspires me
"with the spirit of method, and you will be sensible of it, or no body will. But
"who could have thought that you should have met with such opposition in your
"own country. No body was surprised here that all sort of means were used to set
"me aside from the Professor's chair, for I was a stranger and my antagonists were
"natives of the place; on the contrary, people were strangely surprised that I found
"any friends at all: but surely there is room for wonder, that all your country men
"did not without hesitation join in your promotion, which will be so advantageous
"and glorious to the Academy."

Whatever opposition Mr Bayle found at his coming to Sedan, his merit soon engaged the love and esteem of every body. The Count de Guiscard, Governour of Sedan, invited him frequently to his house, that he might enjoy his conversation. Mr du Rondel who was afterwards Professor of the Belles Lettres at Maestricht, gave him his friendship, and continued it to his death. Even Mr Jurieu was so touched with Mr Bayle's fine qualities, and was so charmed with the sweetness of his temper, his modesty, and his integrity, that he opened his heart to him, perhaps more than he thought himself capable of to any one. He has acknowledged this publickly in 1691, at a time when he had shamefully broke with him, and was labouring to
(2) *Apolo-* ruin him. "This man, says he (2), was recommended to us, to fill a chair of
gie pour "Philosophy then vacant in the Academy of Sedan, where I had the honour to be
Mr Ju- "Professor of Divinity, and one of the Moderators of the Academy. One of his
rieu, p. 24. "friends gave him the character of a young man of great genius, good learning,
col. 1. "and very capable of making those sciences flourish, which he should be called to
"cultivate. We were not deceived in this. He came and distinguished himself in
"all the public exercises of his examination. But his friend and he not thinking
(3) Mr "it proper to make a secret to me of his revolt and long stay among the Jesuits
Bayle ne- "of Toulouse (3), I was embarassed to the last degree because of the Arret against
ver lived "the Relapses. However as I, upon his protestations, believed that he was
with the "sincere in his return to us, we resolved to keep that matter secret and to proceed.
Jesuits. "He was several years in the Academy, behaving himself decently, and neither
"doing or saying any thing that gave offence. The beauty of his genius and
"his

[*E*] *These particulars are to be found in the letters which he wrote to Messieurs Constant and Minutoli.*]
(1) *Letter of* "It is about four months ago, says he to Mr Con-
December 17 "stant (*a*), since I left Paris, being invited to come
1675, p. 97. "hither, to be a Professor of Philosophy. Upon
98. "my arrival I found matters so embarassed with little
"academical intrigues, that I was obliged to wave
"my Invitation, and submit to the hazard of a Dis-
"pute. I exposed my self to it, and God so assisted
"my ignorance, whether by strengthening my weak-
"ness, or by opposing antagonists to me no stron-
"ger than my self, that at last I gained the victory.
"I take the liberty of sending you the only re-
"maining copy of my Theses, they are these cook-
"ed up in haste, which we agreed to make, with-
"out books or preparation, betwixt sun rising and
"sun setting, to prevent the tricks which auxiliary
"troops might have play'd, if we had been allowed
"to compose them in our own chambers. Unluckily
"for us, the subject was very difficult." See how he speaks of the matter to Mr Minutoli. "Several rea-
"sons, (says he (*b*), having determined me to com- (*b*) *Letter*
"ply with an invitation, which was given me to *of Febr. 6,*
"accept of a Professor of Philosophy's place, I left 16:6, p.
"Paris, about the end of August last, and came hi- 100.
"ther, where I have been obliged in a hurry, to
"rally my scattered ideas of Philosophy, and to
"enter the lists with three rivals, who had kept
"themselves always in wind. I leave it to you to
"judge of my anxiety upon that occasion. At last
"whether by good fortune or the ignorance of my
"competitors I have been received Professor; and
"am obliged to labour like a galley-slave, having a
"course to compose from day to day, besides gi-
"ving five hours a day to my scholars. These
"are drudgeries which have stunned me, and it
"is only because one may be accustomed to any
"thing, that I now begin to breathe."

THE LIFE OF MR BAYLE.

1675. "his honourable principles attached me so to him, that I loved him better than ever I did any person, I confess it."

The composition of his Course of Philosophy employed him during two years: it was an additional labour which filled up all the intervals of his Academical functions, 1677. and left him no time to write to his friends. "I have not been able, says he to "Mr Minutoli (1), to answer your fine letter of the 1st of April, otherwise than by a (1) *Letter* "line or two, because of the fatiguing business which has entirely taken me up these *of the 19th* "two years, I mean the multitude of exercises I was obliged to make for my *of August,* "scholars, and the composition of my Course. I am now, thank God, freed from 130. "that terrible drudgery. I have finished my Course, my Theses for the Master of "Arts degree are defended, and now at last it is Vacation."

But still a long time after this, the vacations were the only time, in which he 1678. could have any relaxation. The revisal of his course, the additions which he made to it, together with his public and private lectures, left him no leisure. This is the account he gives to Mr Minutoli in another letter (2). (2) *Letter*

1679. Mr Ancillon, Minister of Mets, had made him a present of a book of Mr Poiret, *of the 15th* printed at Amsterdam in 1677, intituled *Cogitationes Rationales de Deo, Amma, & malo*; *of Dec* and had desired him to make Remarks upon it. Mr Bayle in the year 1679, sent 1678, *pag*. him a piece in latin, containing the difficulties which had occurred to him, in reading 140. it through. He sent along with it, a Letter of thanks, wherein he excused himself that his affairs had not permitted him to comply with his desire sooner, nor to give that force and regularity to his objections, which he could have wished. Mr Ancillon communicated this piece to Mr Poiret, who wrote an answer to it, which he sent to Mr Ancillon, together with a Letter wherein he thanked him for exciting an adversary against him who showed so much accuracy, judgment, penetration and politeness. Mr Poiret inserted these objections of Mr Bayle's, together with his own answers to them, in a new edition of his book, printed at Amsterdam in 1685, and thereto joined the two letters, which I have now mentioned (3). This small (3) *Mr* piece shows that Mr Bayle was throughly acquainted with the most sublime *Bayle's let-* points of Philosophy. Mr Poiret extricated himself but indifferently from some of *ter is dated* his Objections (4). *April 13,*

Mr Bayle took advantage of the harvest vacation to make a tour to Paris, and from *Poiret's* thence he went to Rouen, to wait upon Mr Basnage (5). *August 14,* 1679.

1680. The affair of the Duke of Luxembourg, at that time made a great noise. He had been accused before the Chamber of Poisons, of impieties, sorcery, and poisonings, (4) *See the* and had surrendered himself a prisoner: but he was declared innocent, and the pro- *letter to* cess against him was suppressed. Mr Bayle who had learnt a great many particulars *Maizeaux* concerning this matter, when he was at Paris, diverted himself in composing an *of July 3,* Harangue, wherein the Mareschal pleads his cause before his Judges, and vindicates 1705. *p.* himself from having made a compact with the Devil, that he might, 1. enjoy all 1027. the women he had a mind to. 2. That he might always be successful in war. 3. (5) *Letter* That he might gain all his law suits. 4. That he might always enjoy the King's *to Mr Mi-* favour. The harangue is divided into these four points: it contains a very smart *nutoli of* satire upon the Mareschal, and several other persons. Mr Bayle afterwards composed *the 1st of* under another name a criticism upon this harangue, still more satirical than the satire *January,* it self. He sent these two pieces to Mr Minutoli, and desired him to give him 153. his opinion of them: and in order to engage him to do it with more freedom, he did not tell him who was the author of them. "I send you (says he) (6), a copy of a (6) *Letter* "Harangue, which some body has composed in the name of the Duke of Luxenbourg, *of the 24,* "to take an opportunity from thence to give us part of his Life. If I have 1680. *v.* "time, I will get copyed for you a sort of criticism upon this harangue. You 162, 163. "will oblige me by giving me your opinion of both these pieces; for a friend of *See likewise* "mine at Paris, who is acquainted with the author of the second of them, *of the 1st of* "and who possibly out of prejudice in favour of his friend, inclines to think that *January* "the harangue is good for nothing, has obliged me to promise to write him my 1681. *p.* "sentiments of both the one and the other. But as I have not leisure, and 169. "besides as you are more capable than I to examine works of this nature, in (7) Senti- "order to show their strong and weak side, I beg, Sir, that you will bestow a mens de "few hours upon them. By this means I shall satisfie my friend's desire, and I am Mr Des "sure he will sooner trust to your judgment, than to mine; for he knows touchant "how to value things, and would much rather that I should pay him out of your l'essence & "pocket that out of my own." les pro-

About this time, Father de Valois, a Jesuit of Caen, concealed under the name of prietez du Louis de la Ville, published a book at Paris, intituled, *The Sentiments of Mr Des* Corps, op-*Cartes concerning the Essence and Properties of Body, repugnant to the doctrine of the* posez à la *Church, and agreeable to the errors of Calvin on the subject of the Eucharist* (7). The author Doctrine not satisfied with opposing the authority of the Council of Trent to the Cartesians, attacks de l'Eglise, them likewise by way of argument, and endeavours to confute the reasons made use mes aux of by Messieurs Clercelier, Rohault, and Father Malebranche, to prove that extention erreurs de is the essence of matter. Mr Bayle read this work and found it very well done. He Calvin sur judged that the author had incontestably proved the point in question, to wit, that rille.

VOL. I. d Mr

THE LIFE OF MR BAYLE.

Mr Des Cartes's principles were contrary to the faith of the Church of Rome, and agreeable to the doctrine of Calvin; which at bottom, says Mr Bayle in a letter to Mr Minutoli, was no hard matter to do (1). As Mr Bayle had a mind to make his scholars defend philosophical Theses, he composed a Dissertation on this subject, wherein he defended Mr Des Cartes's principle, and at the same time restored the arguments of these Philosophers which had been attacked by Father de Valois, to their full force, and destroyed all the exceptions and subtilities of that Father. He endeavours principally to prove that the penetrability of matter is impossible.

In the month of December 1680, there appeared one of the largest Comets that was ever seen. People, that is to say almost every body, were seized with fright and astonishment. They had not as yet got the better of the ancient prejudice, that Comets are presages of some fatal event. Mr Bayle, as he informs us himself (2), was incessantly teized with the questions of a great many people, who were alarmed at this pretended bad omen. He endeavoured to remove their fears as much as possible, but he found that he gained but little upon them by philosophical reasonings; they still made answer that God shows us these great Phænomena's, to give warning to sinners to prevent by their repentance the judgments which hang over their heads. He believed therefore that it would be to no purpose to reason any more with them, except he could find out some argument which would prove that it was inconsistent with God's attributes to appoint Comets for that purpose. Upon examining throughly that matter, he soon bethought himself of the following theological argument, to wit, *That if Comets were presages of evil, God must have performed miracles to confirm idolatry in the world.* He did not remember to have met with this argument, either in books or conversation: so that the novelty of it made him think of writing a Letter on that subject, which might be inserted in the MERCURE GALANT. He began to write it upon the 11th of January 1681, and endeavoured to keep within the bounds of a Letter; but the abundance of matter would not allow him to be so short, he was therefore obliged to consider this letter as a work which must be printed by itself. After this he no longer affected brevity, but enlarged upon every thing as he found occasion; without losing sight however of Mr de Visé, author of the MERCURE GALANT. He resolved to send this letter to him, and to desire him to give it to his printer, and obtain either a licence from Mr de la Reynie, Lieutenant-general of the Police, if that would be sufficient, or the King's Priviledge, if nothing else would do. Accordingly he sent it to him the 27th of May. Mr de Visé kept the manuscript some time without knowing the author's name; and when he wrote to about it, he answered that he was told by a person by whom he had given it to read, that Mr de la Reynie would never take the consequences of printing it upon himself, and that it would be necessary to obtain the approbation of the Doctors, before a Royal Privilege could be applied for, which was a troublesome long and tedious task he had no leisure to engage in. The manuscript was got back, and Mr Bayle gave over all thoughts of printing his letter concerning Comets at Paris. But as he at first composed it with this view, he had assumed the stile of a Roman Catholic, and had imitated Mr de Visé's manner and encomiums upon the administration of affairs. This conduct was then absolutely necessary to those who had a mind to print any thing at Paris, and he thought that to imitate the MERCURE GALANT in some things, would render it more easy to obtain either Mr de la Reynie's licence, or the Royal Privilege. It was upon this account likewise, that he feigns that the letter was wrote to a Doctor of the Sorbonne.

The Reformed in France were at this time in a melancholy situation. The Court had for a long time laboured their destruction. They stript them by little and little of all their privileges, and no year passed without some infringement of the Edict of Nants. At last they resolved to suppress their Academies. There was some reason to hope that they would spare the Academy of Sedan. The principality of Sedan had been a sovereign state until the year 1642. The Duke of Bouillon surrendered it to Lewis XIII, who agreed to leave all things there in the condition he found them. Lewis XIV confirmed this treaty, and it was a-new granted that the Protestant Religion should be maintained there with all the rights and privileges of which it was then possessed. But all these advantages could not save the Academy. Nay Lewis XIV ordered that it should be the first that should be dissolved. The Arret was passed on the 9th of July 1681, and notified the fourteenth of the same month.

There was at this time at Sedan a young gentleman from Rotterdam, named Mr Van Zoelen, a relation of Mr van Zoelen, who was afterwards Burgomaster of that city. This young gentleman (3) had lodged at Sedan with Mr Bayle, and had improved himself in his studies by frequent conversations with him. He had conceived so strong a friendship for his Professor, that upon the same day on which the Arret for the suppression of the Academy came there, he resolved to send a copy of it to Mr Paets, a relation of his, who was one of the Counsellors of the city of Rotterdam, a very learned man, and a patron of men of letters. He acquainted Mr Paets, at the same time that he sent him the Arret, that Mr Bayle was without employment; he gave a very good character of him, and received an answer wherein Mr Paets declared a very great inclination to serve him. Mr Bayle upon this wrote to Mr Paets a letter of thanks,

1680.

(1) *Letter of the 24 of March 1680, p. 165.*

(2) *See the Advertissement concerning the 3d Edition of the Pensées diverses, sur la Comete, &c.*

1681.

(3) *Chimere de la Cabale de Rotterdam démontrée, preface p. clxij. clxiii.*

for

THE LIFE OF Mr BAYLE.

1681. for the favourable sentiments he had of him, and begged the continuance of his favour. Mr Paets, together with a great deal of wit and penetration, had a strong passion for the sciences, particularly for Philosophy. His merit had acquired him a great authority, and would have gained him still more had it not been for the divisions which then prevailed in the Republic. He was considered as the head of the party which opposed the family of Orange (1); and upon this account he found some difficulty to get into the Magistracy again, after his return from being Embassador extraordinary in Spain (2). He notwithstanding triumphed over their jealousy, and the Magistrates of Rotterdam had so great deference for his counsels, that they were guided in all their deliberations by him.

Mr Bayle at the same time endeavoured to procure an establishment at Rotterdam for Mr Jurieu, and engaged Mr van Zoelen to recommend him to Mr Paets. Mr van Zoelen left Sedan in order to sollicit these matters in person at Rotterdam, and insisted so strenuously with Mr Paets, that he was pleased to use his interest likewise for Mr Jurieu (3).

Mr Bayle staid six or seven weeks at Sedan after the suppression of the Academy, waiting for letters from Holland. But at last not receiving any, he grew impatient and left Sedan the 2d of September, and arrived at Paris the 7th of the same month, uncertain as yet whither he should go to Rotterdam or to England, or if he should continue in France (4). Before his departure the Count de Guiscard used all his endeavours to persuade him to embrace the Popish religion. He proposed great advantages to him, but all to no purpose (5). At length when he was ready to set out for Rouen, and from thence to pass over to England, he received an answer from Mr Paets acquainting him that the city of Rotterdam had given him a salary with the right of teaching Philosophy. Mr Paets added that Mr Jurieu's business was in a fair way. Upon this he left Paris the eighth of October, and upon the thirtieth arrived at Rotterdam, where he was very kindly received by Mr van Zoelen's family, and by Mr Paets (6).

Mr Jurieu followed Mr Bayle very soon after; but before he was well settled at Rotterdam, he was guilty of some rash and blunt actions, which very much provoked Mr Paets against him, and which he pardoned only upon Mr Bayle's account (7). The town of Rotterdam erected an ILLUSTRIOUS SCHOOL in their favour; Mr Jurieu was appointed Professor of Divinity; and Mr Bayle Professor of Philosophy and History, with five hundred guilders of yearly appointments. Upon the 5th of December, he delivered his Inaugural Oration with universal applause; and on the 8th he read his first lecture of Philosophy to a great number of scholars.

1682. A little while after he gave his Letter concerning Comets to Mr Leers, a bookseller in Rotterdam, and a man of sense and merit, in order to have it printed. And as he took all manner of precautions not to be thought the author of it, he changed nothing either in the stile of a Roman Catholic which he had assumed, nor in his imitation of the manner and panegyrics of the MERCURE GALANT. He thought that this strain would be very proper to prevent peoples thinking, that this Letter was wrote by one who had left France for his Religion. While they were printing it he added many things that were not in the copy which he had formerly sent to the author of the MERCURE GALANT (8). The impression was finished on the 11th of March 1682, and it appeared under the following title: *A Letter to Mr L. A. D. C. Doctor of the Sorbone. Wherein it is proved by many arguments, both Philosophical and Theological, that Comets are not presages of evil. With several moral and political reflexions and historical observations. Together with a confutation of some vulgar errors. Printed at Cologne by Peter Marteau,* MDCLXXXII (9).

To conceal himself the better, Mr Bayle prefixed to it a Preface or Advice to the Reader under the character of a person publishing this Letter without knowing the author of it. In this preface, after taking notice of several reasons which induced him to make it public, he adds likewise the following: "I have been confirmed in this design " by a yet stronger reason than any of these. I have it from very good authority, " that the Doctor of the Sorbone to whom this Letter was written, is preparing a very " exact and elaborate answer to it, and there would be great reason to fear, con- " sidering his indifference for the character of an author, that he would content him- " self with writing only for his friends use, if we did not by publishing this Letter " which he has received from him, engage him to impart to the public the learned " and fine reflexions he no doubt has made upon several important subjects; such " as the conduct of providence with regard to the ancient Heathens: the question, " *Whether God has wrought miracles among them, tho' he knew that they would thereby* " *become more idolatrous*: the question, *Whether God has sometimes appointed presages* " *among infidels*: the question, *Whether an effect purely natural can be a certain presage* " *of a contingent event*: the question, *Whether Atheism be worse than Idolatry, and if* " *it be necessarily the source of all sort of crimes*: the question, *Whether God would ra-* " *ther choose that men should be without any knowledge of a God, than that they should* " *be engaged in the abominable worship of idols*; and upon many others, concerning " which so great and learned a divine may have very instructive thoughts, and which " well deserve to be made public.

But

xvi THE LIFE OF Mr BAYLE.

But notwithstanding all these disguises, it was very soon known that Mr Bayle 1682.
was the author of the Letter concerning Comets. Mr Leers had shown the manuscript to Mr Paets, and told him from whom he had it; and Mr Paets made no secret of it to his friends (1); nay he thought he did the author a piece of service, by discovering him (2). Mr Jurieu by this means came likewise to know it, either immediately from them, or from others to whom they had told it, and having spoke of it to Mr Bayle, with a kind of reproach that other people knew this secret while he was ignorant of it; Mr Bayle told him how every thing had passed, and satisfy'd him as to some points in the book (3), Mr Jurieu spoke of it with applause (4): but at the bottom he bore with impatience, the honour that Mr Bayle acquired by it; jealous as he was of the honour done his friends.

Madam Paets died at this time, and gave a proof of her esteem for Mr Bayle, by leaving him a legacy of two thousand guilders to buy books. Mr Bayle always preserved a grateful remembrance of this generous gift, as we will afterwards observe.

Mr Maimbourg had just published his *History of Calvinism* (5). This work treated of very important matters: a judgment was to be made concerning the spirit and conduct of the Reformed in France, from the time of their separation from the Church of Rome. Mr Maimbourg had employed all the art he was master of, to draw both the contempt and hatred of the Catholics upon them. Mr Bayle, full of indignation at the disingenuity and pernicious design of this author, resolved to refute his History, and took the opportunity of Easter Vacation to set about it. He wrote his answer by way of Letters, but did not think it necessary to follow its adversary step by step. He was of opinion that in order to undeceive the public, and show how little Mr Maimbourg ought to be regarded, it was sufficient to make some general observations on his History, which even supposing the truth of the facts it relates, might discover his malice, violence, and the cruel and barbarous principles, with which he endeavours to inspire his readers. Mr Bayle diverted himself with several particulars of the life and disputes of this writer, and gave a very just tho' by no means advantageous picture of them (6). "It was not " a sour and morose criticism, but an ingenious sort of raillery, full notwithstanding " of good sense and reason, and more proper to embarass or confound an adver- " sary, than grave and serious arguments."

He began to write these Letters on the 1st of May, and finished them on the 15th of the same month, so that this work tho' pretty bulky (7), was composed in the space of 15 days, as he himself acquaints us in the last Letter. He took all possible precautions to conceal his being the author of them. In the Advertisment prefixed to them, he makes the bookseller say, that this collection of letters having fallen into his hands, he thought himself bound to publish them without delay; and that he was desired to acquaint the reader, that they were really wrote by a country Gentleman of the Province of Maine, and sent to his friend according to their dates. He would not even have them printed at Rotterdam, and having occasion to go to see Amsterdam, he carried his manuscript along with him, and gave it to Abraham Wolfgang, a bookseller there, upon the 30th of May. This book appeared in the beginning of July, with the following title: *A general Criticism on Mr Maimbourg's History of Calvinism. At Ville Franche by Peter le Blanc*. M. DC. LXXXII (8). Mr Bayle received the copies of it, on the 11th of that same month.

This work was approved of, not only by the Reformed, who were so well defended in it from Mr Maimbourg's attacks, but even by the judicious and moderate among the Catholics. A great many copies of it found their way into France, and were eagerly sought after. The Prince of Condé, a prince who was very capable of judging of the merit of books, could never be tired with reading it. It is true indeed he did not love Mr Maimbourg. That historian to please the court, whose pensioner he was, had affected not to take any notice of his Highness, while he made panegyrics upon all his ancestors. Mr Bayle did not fail to expose him upon this account (9), and the Prince took it well. This work touched Mr Maimbourg to the quick: the general approbation with which it was received troubled him extreamly. He applied several times to Mr de la Reynie, to procure a condemnation of it. But that magistrate having read it with pleasure, and not being displeased that Mr Maimbourg had been mortified, put him off from time to time. At last he addressed himself to the King, and obtained an order from his Majesty, directed to Mr de la Reynie, commanding the *General Criticism on Mr Maimbourg's History of Calvinism*, to be burnt by the hand of the hangman; and forbidding all printers and booksellers to print, sell, or publish that book on pain of death. Mr de la Reynie obeyed the order, and put in his Sentence whatever Mr Maimbourg pleased: one may easily discover in it the style of an author, and of an enraged author too (10): but to revenge himself against Mr Maimbourg, he got above 3000 copies of that sentence printed, and posted them up all over Paris, which incited the curiosity of the public to such a degree, that every body would needs have the criticism on Mr Maimbourg.

2   This

(1) Chimere de montrée, preface p. clxxi.
(2) Cabale chimerique, pag. 206.
(3) Preface ubi supra, pag. clxxi.
(4) Chimere demontrée, pag 207.
(5) Histoire du Calvinisme.
(6) Eloge de Mr Bayle by Mr de Bauval.
(7) It was a volume in 12° of 339 pages in a small character.
(8) Critique générale de l'Histoire du Calvinisme de Mr Maimbourg. A Ville Franche chez Pierre le Blanc. 1682.
(9) Letter xix p.268, 269.
(10) This Sentence is to be found at the end of these Memoirs.

1682. This work was sold off in Holland, almost as soon as it appeared; and in the month of August, Mr Bayle prepared a new edition of it. He enlarged it one half, and added a preface to it, wherein he again endeavours to deceive the reader and put him upon a wrong scent. This edition was printed off about the end of November, and he received copies of it, on the 29th of that month.

They sought for a long time in France, among the best pens of the Protestant party for the Author of the Criticism on Mr Maimbourg; and at last fixed upon Mr Claude, who at that time gloriously defended the cause of the Reformed. Even Mr Bayle's friends, who knew that he was the author of the Letter concerning Comets, never dreamt of ascribing this Criticism to him, because of the difference of the stile, and it was a mere accident which discovered it, as he tells us himself, to shew that there is nothing more uncertain than conjectures drawn from the conformity or difference of stile, in order to discover the author of a book. "I know by experience, says he (1), that all the Writings of a man do not resemble one another. The *General Criticism of Father Maimbourg*, was published soon after the *Thoughts concerning Comets*; yet no body seemed to suspect that these two books came from the same hand. The first edition of the Criticism was sold off, before any body so much as suspected the true author. And tho' the second edition possibly might have discovered him better, yet in all probability, if it had not been for a mere accident he had remained still unknown. The accident was this. The author having writ an answer to an Anonymous Letter which his bookseller had sent him, forgot to desire the bookseller not to deliver the original of the answer but a copy. This Anonymous person being a friend of Mr Claude, the son, shewed him my Letter and asked if he knew the hand. Mr Claude having told him whose it was, there wanted no more to put the author under a necessity of making a secret of it no longer. The matter could never have been discovered by the conformity of stile. For although the author did not at all intend it, he wrote the Criticism on Maimbourg in a stile very different from that of the *Thoughts concerning Comets*."

Mr Jurieu likewise wrote an answer to Mr Maimbourg, but more full and circumstantial. It appeared in 1683, under the title of *A Parallel between the History of Calvinism and that of Popery: Or an Apology for the Reformers, the Reformation, and the Reformed: in four parts: In answer to a Libel intituled, The History of Calvinism by Mr Maimbourg* (2). This book was well written; the author refuted Mr Maimbourg with a great deal of force: but one could not find there that easy and natural turn, those lively and poignant reflexions, that manner of exposing the faults of an adversary without bitterness, and of treating matters of controversy without passion; which was the distinguishing character of the *Critique Generale*. Every one was presently sensible of this difference. Even the Catholics, notwithstanding the prejudices of their religion, could not help applauding Mr Bayle's book, while at the same time they affected to despise that of Mr Jurieu. "The Criticism on Father Maimbourg's History of Calvinism is a fine book, said Mr Menage (3) and he himself could not help esteeming it. He confessed to us me, tho' ordinarily he affected to speak of it as a book which he had not read. Excepting what relates to religion, I find every thing Mr Bayle says very lively and very judicious. I had a mind to read what Mr Jurieu has done on the same subject; there is a great difference betwixt them. Mr Bayle writes like a gentleman, and Mr Jurieu like a bigotted old woman, his book is nothing but a wretched repetition of the dullest things alledged by du Moulin, and the rest of them against the Catholic religion." The different esteem shewed to these two books, infinitely displeased Mr Jurieu. He looked upon Mr Bayle as his rival, and could not forgive him for carrying away all the suffrages. This accident sowed the seeds of hatred and jealousy in his mind (4).

Amongst the other men of Letters with whom Mr Bayle contracted a friendship at Sedan, we ought to number Mr Fetizon, a young Minister and a native of that town. He had left Sedan, and was gone to exercise his Ministry in Champagne, in Mr de Bricquemau's family (5). He wrote to Mr Bayle that he had composed by way of dialogue an Apology for the Reformed, with regard to the civil wars of France. Mr Bayle desired to see the book, and Mr Fetizon sent it him, and dedicated it to Philaretus, that is to Mr Bayle himself. Mr Bayle found that it deserved to be published and caused it to be printed (6). It appeared in the beginning of the year 1683, under this title; *An Apology for the Reformed; wherein a just idea is given of the civil wars in France, and of the true foundations of the Edict of Nants. Being a curious dialogue betwixt a Protestant and a Catholic* (7). PATRICIUS, the Roman Catholic, alledges the strongest and most odious things that have been said against the Reformed with regard to the civil wars, and doth not forget the common accusation, that they are animated by a spirit of faction and rebellion; and that they maintain principles opposite to the absolute power of princes. EUSEBIUS, the Protestant, justifies them for taking up arms in defence of their religion, their lives, and the rights of the house of Bourbon; and shews, even by the testimony of Lewis XIII, that they have always been faithful to their lawful princes, and that their principles are so far from being opposite to the sovereign power of princes, that they tend to establish and

xviii   THE LIFE OF Mʀ BAYLE.

confirm it; whereas, on the other hand, the Roman Catholics make that authority 1682.
dependant on the people or on the Pope.

About the end of the year 1682 Mr Bayle was strongly follicited to marry. The
match proposed to him was advantageous. She was a beautiful young lady, of
very good sense, good nature and prudence, was entirely at her own disposal, and
(1) *Letter* had at least fifteen thousand crowns (1). Mademoiselle du Moulin, grandchild of
of Made- the famous Peter du Moulin, sister to Mrs Jurieu, and afterwards wife to Mr Basnage,
moiselle du had set this affair in motion, and had put it in so good a way, that there remained
Moulin to no difficulty except on Mr Bayle's side. He had always appeared very averse to
Mr Bayle, marriage: the cares and troubles of a family did not seem to him to suit a man
of the of letters, a Philosopher who makes all his happiness consist in study and me-
12th of ditation. Besides, as he contented himself with what was necessary, riches appeared
December to him rather an incumbrance than a happiness. Mademoiselle du Moulin spared
1682. In no pains to make him change these sentiments, and to engage him to make use of these
Mr Bayle's advantages, which in a manner offered themselves; but she was unsuccessful.
Letters,
pag. 193.

The Year following Mr Bayle gave a new edition of his Letter concerning Comets, 1683.
fuller and more exact than the first. The impression of it was finished the second
of September 1683, and he received a hundred and twenty copies of it from the (5) Exa-
bookseller to send to his friends. He suppressed the title of the first edition, and men des
substituted the following: *Divers Thoughts written to a Doctor of the Sorbonne, upon* raisons qui
occasion of the Comet which appeared in the month of December, 1680. *At Rotter-* ont doné
(2) Pen- *dam, by Reinier Leers,* MDCLXXXIII (2). He likewise suppressed the long lieu à la
fées diver- preface of the foregoing edition, and instead of it inserted an advertisement in féparation
fes, écrites the bookseller's name, pointing out the advantages of this second edition beyond des Prote-
à un Do- the preceding. ftans, fait
éteur de fans pre-
Sorbonne About this time some of Mr Bayle's Friends sent him some pieces of con- vention
à l'occa- troversy which they had composed, and desired him to get them printed if he thought fur le Con-
fion de la proper. The first which he received was a Confutation of the Memorial drawn up cile de
Comete by the Assembly of the Clergy of France in 1682, wherein they proposed and ap- Trente,
qui parut proved of seventeen Methods, or different manners of disputing against the Re- fur la Con-
au mois formed. This Confutation was wrote by Mr Basnage, at that time minister of feffion de
de De- Rouen. It was accompanied with a Letter to Mr Bayle, in the name of a friend l'oi des
cembre to the author, which contained several curious particulars relating to that Assembly Eglises
1680. A of the Clergy (3). This work came out under the title of *An Examination* Proteftan-
Rotter- *of the Methods proposed by the Assembly of the Clergy of France in the year* 1682 (4). tes, & fur
dam chez Mr Basnage had desired that the manuscript might be communicated to Mr Jurieu, l'Ecriture
Reinier and Mr Jurieu prefixed his approbation to the book. The other pieces which were fainte.
Leers, sent to Mr Bayle, were in answer to a book of Mr Brueys Advocate of Montpel- (6) Le
1683. lier. Mr Brueys had distinguished himself among the Reformed by a confutation Profelyte
(3) *It is* of a book of Mr Bossuet, Bishop of Condom, and afterwards of Meaux, entituled *An* abusé: ou
intituled, *Exposition of the doctrine of the Catholic Church.* But he afterwards changed his Re- luffes
Lettre sur ligion, and according to the common practice of new converts, he wrote against vués de
la derniere the party which he had left. His book appeared in 1683 with the following title, Mr Brueys
Affemblée *The reasons which have given occasion to the separation of the Protestants, examined without* dans l'exa-
du Clergé *prejudice, according to the Council of Trent, the Confessions of Faith of the Protestant* men de la
A. M. B. *Churches, and the holy Scripture* (5). It was wrote in a mild and insinuating manner, and féparation
A. R. *that* had an air of disinterestedness, very proper at first sight to catch weak and superfi- des Protes-
is to say, cial minds: it was thought necessary that it should be answered. Mr Jurieu, who Rotterdam
à Mr Bayle had written a Tract entituled, *Preservatif contre le changement de Religion,* in answer to fur Rei-
à Rotter- the bishop of Meaux's book, published a continuation of it against this piece of nier Leers,
dam. Mr Brueys. Mr de Larroque, son to the Minister of Rouen, who had been received 1684, in
(4) Exa- into the Ministry in one of the last Synods, did likewise enter the lists. He wrote 12°.
men des an answer to Mr Brueys, and sent it to Mr Bayle, who presently put it to the (7) Nou-
Methodes press. The title of it is, *The Proselyte abused: or Mr Brueys's false views in his* velles de
proposées *examination of the separation of Protestants* (6). It has an epistle dedicatory prefixed, *To* Républi-
par Meff. *Mr *** Professor of Philosophy and History at Rotterdam,* wherein Mr Larroque que des
de l'Af- gives an account of the composition, design, and plan of this work. Mr Bayle Lettres,
femblée would not suffer his name to appear before the dedication, though it was easy to *March*
du Clergé those who knew Holland, or had any commerce with men of Letters, to see that 1684, *p.*
de France it was addressed to him. He has spoke very advantageously of Mr Larroque's m. 101.
en l' An- book. " It is (says he (7), the first essay of a young author full of wit, who fol- *See like-*
née 1682. " lows his adversary very close, and shows him that he has made gross blunders. *wise the*
It was " He sometimes makes use of raillery, which is somewhat strong indeed, yet at the *Letter*
printed at " same time delicate; and he acquits himself very well likewise in point of erudition." *to Mr*
Rotterdam Mr Lenfant, who at that time studied Divinity at Geneva, wrote likewise *Lenfant of*
by Pierre against Mr Brueys. But being informed that several learned men were employed *the 26th*
de Graef, on the same subject, he would have suppressed his answer, if Mr Bayle and Mr Ju- *of Novem-*
but the rieu had not pressed him to finish it, and make it public (8). After he had made some *ber 1683,*
title bears stay at Geneva, he went to Heidelberg, from whence he sent Mr Bayle his ma- *pag. 204.*
à Cologne nuscript, and desired him to make what alterations in it he should think proper. (8) *See*
chez Mr Lenfant did not choose to enter into the detail of the dispute, but contented *the Letters*
Pierre himself *to Mr Len-*
Marteau,   *fant of*
in 12°.   *the 8th of*
  September
  and 26th
  of Novem-
  ber 1683,
  pag. 201,
  and the
  following.

THE LIFE OF Mr BAYLE.

1683. himself with reasoning upon general principles. His book appeared about the beginning of the year 1684, with this title, *General considerations on Mr Brueys's book, intituled, An Examination of the reasons which have given occasion to the separation of Protestants, and occasionally upon all those of the same character* (1). There was an advertisement added to it, wherein after shewing how people might be deceived by Mr Brueys's book, and the necessity there was of answering it, they ascribed his change of Religion meerly to worldly motives, and even attacked his Morals. This advertisement was followed by a long *Letter of the Author to a friend, upon sending him his manuscript*, that is to say, to Mr Bayle. Mr Lenfant there gave the character of Mr Brueys's book, and pointed out a great many weak places in it. This answer is written with a great deal of wit, judgment, and moderation, qualities which reign in all Mr Lenfant's writings.

1684. Mr Bayle was always very curious in gathering those sorts of pieces which are called *Fugitives*, because they disappear almost as soon as they come out. The only way to preserve them, is to gather as many of them together as will make a volume. This Mr Bayle did, with regard to several pieces relating to Des Cartes's Philosophy. He published them under the title of *A collection of some curious pieces relating to Mr Des Cartes's Philosophy. At Amsterdam, by H. Desbordes, MDCLXXXIV* (2). He wrote a preface to them, wherein he gave the history of these pieces, and lamented the slavery of the writers in France. "It would be a great misfortune for the whole Republic of Letters, says he, if they were every where as formal and captious with regard to the printing of books, as they have been in France for some time past, where the Inquisition, which they are establishing there apace, prevents the publication of many fine pieces, and discourages the best writers. And who would not be discouraged to see those people, who are appointed to licence books, keep a manuscript for three or four years without looking into it, and then disapprove every thing there that discovers a mind elevated above slavery and vulgar opinions? What mortification for an author, who never thinks the press can go fast enough upon his works, after a delay of three or four years, to find himself commanded to suppress what he thinks is most valuable in his writings, if he would not rather chuse to see them condemned to eternal silence, by being refused the Royal Privilege?" This Collection contains, I. A sort of Concordat, entered into betwixt the Jesuits and the Fathers of the Oratory, by which these last oblige themselves neither to teach Des Cartes Philosophy, nor the doctrine of Jansenius. II. Remarks upon this concordat. III. An Explanation concerning Mr de la Ville, or rather Father de Valois's book (3). This piece was wrote by Mr Bernier, so well known by his Voyages, and his Abridgment of Gassendus's Philosophy. Father de Valois had placed him in the list of the new Philosophers, who destroy the doctrine of Transubstantiation, by maintaining that the essence of matter consists in extension. His book made a great noise in France, and alarmed all the Cartesians. Mr Regis, who held conferences at Paris, was obliged to give them over. Mr Bernier was afraid for himself, and published this explanation, wherein he endeavours to reconcile the principles of his own philosophy, with the decisions of the church. This collection likewise contains, IV. An answer of Father Malebranche to Father de Valois, who had shewed great animosity against him, and particularly endeavoured to raise suspicions of his orthodoxy. This answer was followed by a Memoir, explaining the possibility of Transubstantiation. V. The Theses which Mr Bayle had made his scholars defend, in 1680: *Dissertatio in qua vindicantur à Peripateticorum exceptionibus rationes quibus aliqui Cartesiani probarunt essentiam corporis sitam esse in extentione.* Mr Bayle joined some Philosophical Theses to this Dissertation, where he maintains, among other things, that place, motion, and time, have not as yet been defined in an intelligible manner. VI. A piece which had been printed at Paris, under the title of *Meditations concerning Metaphysics, by William Wander* (4). The Abbé Lanion is the author of it (5). It contains the substance of the Cartesian Metaphysics, and the most valuable things in Des Cartes's Meditations. Nay every thing here seems even better digested, than in Des Cartes's book, and the author appears to have penetrated further than that Philosopher. This is Mr Bayle's judgment of it.

Mr Bernier's Explanation was refuted in a book printed at Paris in 1682, entituled, *The Philosophy of Des Cartes repugnant to the faith of the Catholic church, together with a refutation of the pamphlet lately printed in defence of it* (6). The pamphlet mentioned in this title, is Mr Bernier's performance. The author of this book says, that having seen Mr de la Ville's treatise, he found that the author had very successfully attacked the System of the Cartesians on the subject of the essence of matter, but that their opinion concerning it's accidents and qualities had not been refuted. So that he thought it necessary to handle this last point, and to add to it a new discussion of the first, to make the work compleat. He divides his book into two parts. In the first he shews, "That if the essence of the body consists in actual extension, the body of Jesus Christ cannot be really and actually in the Eucharist, since a thing cannot exist without it's essence, but it must be there only figuratively, that is, purely in imagination and thought, or in imaginary apprehension, which makes us believe it present where

(1) Considérations genérales sur le livre de Mr Brueys, intitulé, Examen des raisons qui ont donné lieu à la separation des Protestans, &c. par occasion sur ceux du meme caractere. At Rotterdam, for Reinier Leers, 1684.

(2) Recueil de quelques pieces curieuses concernant la philosophie de Mr Des cartes. A Amsterdam chez Henry Desborder, 1684.

(3) See above, pag. xiii.

(4) Meditations sur la Metaphysique, par Guillaume Wander.

(5) See Responso aux Questions d'un Provincial, Tom. I. chap. xxvi. pag. 223, 224.

(6) La Philosophie de Mr Des cartes contraire à la Foy Catholique. Avec la Refutation d'un Imprimé fait depuis peu pour sa défense.

it

THE LIFE OF Mr BAYLE.

1684.

"it is not:" and in the second, he proves "That by establishing, as Des Cartes doth, "that there is nothing in the substance but the substance itself, and that the qualities "and accidents which we fancy to exist in it, are only simple appearances that "abuse our senses, and make them believe that there is something really existing "in the substance, which doth not exist there, but only in our thoughts; we destroy "the doctrine of the Church, which teaches us that in the Eucharist, the substance "of the bread and wine being destroyed, and quite changed into the body and "blood of JESUS CHRIST, the accidents, which were in it, remain still, which "necessarily supposeth that the accidents are really distinct from the substance, and "can exist without it." This book is very little known. Mr Bayle doth not mention it, possibly because it never came to his knowledge, and I take notice of it here only because of the relation it has to this Collection which Mr Bayle had published.

The manner of acquainting the public by way of Journal, with what passeth in the Republic of Letters, is one of the finest undertakings of the last age. The honour of it is due to Mr de Sallo, Ecclesiastic Counsellor in the parliament of Paris, who published the *Journal des Sçavans* in the year 1665. This work was received every where with applause, and was imitated in Italy and in Germany. Mr Bayle was surprized to see that in Holland, where there were so many learned men, so many booksellers, and so great a liberty of the press, no body had as yet thought of publishing a Literary Journal. He had been several times tempted to do it, but considering that a work of this kind requires a great deal of time and application, he had laid aside that design. In the mean while there appeared about the end of the month of February 1684, a Journal printed at Amsterdam by Henry Desbordes, with the title of *Mercure Sçavant du mois de Janvier 1684*. This was an attempt of the Sieur de Blegny, a surgeon of Paris, a man fertile in projects, of which take the following instances. Having observed that several people held conferences on Philosophy, and other sciences, he would needs pretend to do the same, and erected an *Academy of new discoveries* in his own house. He read private lectures to the Surgeons apprentices, under the name of a Course of Surgery; and to the Apothecaries apprentices by the name of a Course of Pharmacy: he even undertook to give a Course of Periwigs for the Periwig-makers apprentices. Every body was admitted to them for a certain price. He meddled likewise in physic, and came at last to take the titles of "Counsellor, Physician, "Artist in ordinary to his Majesty and to the Dauphin, and overseer, by his "Majesty's command, of enquiries and examinations of new discoveries in Physic." In 1679 he undertook a sort of Journal, intituled, *New Discoveries in all the parts of Physic* (1). He published it monthly; but his abusive manner of treating several persons of merit, produced an Arret of the Council, which put a stop to it in 1682. The Sieur de Blegny not daring to print his Journal in France, turned his eyes towards Holland, and chose Mr Gautier, a physician of Niort who lived at Amsterdam, for his partner in this project, and furnished him with the materials. This new Journal contained no extracts of Books, but several small pieces generally on subjects relating to physic. It contained likewise songs set to music, poetry, and political news. And he was more abusive in it than he had formerly been in his Journal of Physic.

A work so ill conceived and so ill executed, piqued Mr Bayle and made him re-assume his former design of publishing a Journal. Mr Jurieu pressed him strongly to undertake it. He was glad to have a sure hand to write panegyrics on all the books he should publish (2). Mr Bayle yielded to his sollicitations, and began to set about his Journal the 21st of March 1684. Upon the 4th of April he made an agreement with the Sieur Desbordes for the impression, and resolved to publish it once a month, under the title of *News from the Republic of Letters* (3); and to begin with the month of March. The *Mercure Sçavant* was published only for the months of January and February: whereupon several people fancied that Mr Bayle was the author of it; which obliged him to disown it in express terms (4). The News from the Republic of Letters, for the month of March, did not appear 'till the 27th of May, and those of the month of April 'till the 2d of June: but he laboured so hard, that the Journal of July was published in the beginning of August, and so on, the News of every month appearing in the beginning of the following. In the preface he gives an account of the plan which he had laid down, which did not differ much from that of the other Journalists. He divided every Journal into two parts; the first contained large extracts, and the second a catalogue of new books, accompanied with remarks. This last part of his plan gave him occasion to mention a much greater number of books, and to make a great many Pieces known to the public, of which he did not think it proper to give an extract. He embellished his extracts with a thousand curious and entertaining particulars concerning the history of authors, their works and controversies; and with many ingenious and delicate reflexions. He did not write only for the learned: he intended likewise to please and be of use to the polite world (5). In a word, every thing was lively and animated in his extracts; "he had the art of giving a gay

turn

(1) Nouvelles Decouvertes dans toutes les parties de la medecine.

(2) Chimere demontrée, preface, p. clxxxvii.

(3) Nouvelles de la Republique des Lettres.

(4) In an advertisement which he published at the end of the Nouvelles for the month of May, of the first edition, and which he repeated on the reverse of the title page, in the following editions.

(5) See the Letter to Mr le Clerc of the 18th of June 1684, p. 213, and the following

THE LIFE OF MR BAYLE.

1684. "turn to all sorts of subjects, and of giving the readers a notion of a book in "very few words, without fatiguing them either with a bad choice, or with "dull and tiresome reflexions. He was wise and reserved in judging of the "merit of books, neither desiring to shock authors, nor to expose himself by pro- "stituting his commendations (1)." People were of opinion that at first he praised too much, and this obliged him to be more sparing of his applause (2). He received advice with pleasure, and knew how to profit by it. This work was received with universal applause. Mr Bayle had flattered himself that it would not be prohibited in France, it was forbidden however, but this prohibition could not hinder a great many copies of it from passing there every month. Every body read it with eagerness.

The States of the Province of Friesland, to whom Mr Bayle was known by his *Letter concerning Comets* (3), on the 29th of March, appointed him to be Professor of Philosophy in the University of Franeker, with a salary of nine hundred gilders. This resolution was communicated to him by a letter of the 21st of April, which he received on the 9th of May. He wrote an answer to it next day, desiring to be allowed some time to consider of it; and upon the 9th of June wrote them a letter of thanks, but declined accepting that place, though the salary was near double what he had at Rotterdam.

While Mr Bayle was deliberating about this invitation to Franeker, he had an account (4) of the death of his brother Joseph, a young gentleman of great merit. After he had begun the study of Divinity at Puylaurens, he went to Geneva in 1682 to finish it, where he continued above a year. From thence he went to Paris, where he was invited (5) to be governour to Mr Duffon, son to the Marquis de Bonac (6). He died there the 9th of May 1684, regretted by all who knew him (7). He had a great deal of wit and penetration, together with a great share of piety and modesty. He was learned and laborious, and was likely to make a very considerable Figure in the Republic of Letters. Mr Bayle loved him tenderly, and was no less beloved by him. He was sensibly afflicted with his death. "I am "infinitely obliged to you (says he to Mr Lenfant (8), for the share you have taken "in the loss of my poor brother, every body wrote and spoke of him very ad- "vantageously to me. I loved him dearly, and he loved me, if possible, still more. "Praise be to God, who has been pleased to take him out of this world, and to "deprive me of the comfort I expected from him: you have lost a good friend "who had the utmost esteem for you; so that you have had some interest in la- "menting his Death."

There appeared about this time a third edition of the *General Criticism on the History of Calvinism*. The second edition had been reprinted at Geneva, but notwithstanding this, it was very soon out of print. In the advertisement to this third edition Mr Bayle says, that being convinced that this would be the last time of printing that book, he would very willingly have brought it as near perfection as possible, by making some necessary additions and alterations; but that he durst not venture to do so, least he should disoblige those, who had already bought the two former editions, who frequently complained of new editions revised, corrected, and augmented, because they disgust people at the former editions, and make them regret their having laid out their money upon them. Upon this account he had managed matters so, that this edition did not differ much from the preceding, and he acquainted all those who had the second, that they might be contented with it, and that this edition ought not to tempt them. Not that this (adds he) is not less faulty than the two former, but it is not so to such a degree as to deserve notice. But we must not understand this strictly: this third edition contains many considerable additions and alterations. He likewise made some change in the order of the Letters, but above all he was at particular pains to correct the stile, by striking out all ambiguous expressions and rhymes. He upon this occasion observes how difficult it is in writing French to avoid verses, jingling of words, and phrases wherein one word may relate to different parts of the sentence, and so cause double meanings.

1685. In the beginning of the year 1685, he published a continuation of the *Critique Generale*, under the title of *New Letters of the author of the General Criticism on the History of Calvinism of Mr Maimbourg. Part I. wherein several passages which have been found fault with, as containing contradictions, false reasonings, and other mistakes of that sort are justified, and several curious matters relating to this subject are occasionally bandied. At Ville Franche by Peter le Blanc, MDCLXXXV* (9). To these New Letters a long preface, or advice to the readers, is prefixed, wherein Mr Bayle takes notice that after having, with much difficulty, consented to their being put to the press, he had been frequently tempted to put a stop to the impression, when he considered how rare it was for an author, who ventures to publish a continuation of a book which has been well received, not to miscarry. "These continuations (says he) make people almost always say, that the "author has not held out, that he ought to have rested where he was, that he "ought to have known his strength better, and that he was much in the wrong "to run the hazard of lessening the opinion the public had conceived of him." He

VOL. I.   f   shows

shows that people are sometimes in the right in judging so, but that for the most part they are very much in the wrong, and that when the continuation of a book is less esteemed than what went before it, is not so much the fault of the author as of the readers. But since the misfortune is not the less upon this account, he concludes that excepting a few privileged authors, all others ought to be afraid of the comparison which people will make betwixt their works, if the first has had the good fortune to please. He adds that no body ever had more reason to be apprehensive of this comparison than himself, and takes notice of several circumstances which luckily concurred to procure a good reception to the *General Criticism on the History of Calvinism*, which did not now subsist in favour of these *New Letters*. But that at last he had suffered them to be made public, with a resolution of looking with perfect indifference upon the opinion the public might have concerning them. Mean while he acquaints the reader that he will find in the second Volume several passages which have not all the gravity, which possibly he may expect in that book; nay that he may possibly be of opinion, that some of them are too much a-kin to trifling. For this reason, he declares that he doth not pretend here to write for the learned, but for a great many people who love reading, and not being deep scholars, want, properly speaking, only an innocent amusement whereby they may learn something, but with little trouble. They who would judge of this book, says he, ought to remember that this was the intention of the author. We have only the first part of this work: Mr Bayle intended to publish two parts more, and had even begun to compose them, but did not finish them. "It was originally intended (says he) that this first part "should be followed by two others, the first of which was to have satisfied those "who had said, that several things which deserved great consideration had been too "briefly handled in the *General Criticism*, such as the Conference of Poissy, the "first rising in Arms, the Version of the Psalms, &c. and the second was to have "explained some difficulties in the controversy. But though something has been "prepared a good while ago, for both the one and the other of these parts, yet "in all appearance other business will hinder the author to finish them."

Mr Bayle sent a copy of this book to Mr Lenfant, and assured him that he might let him know the faults in it without fearing to displease him. "I desire (says "he (1), you will accept of a copy of the Continuation of the *Critique Generale*.... "I am not at all pleased with this last book, and you will oblige me if you will "sincerely show me it's faults. Do not be afraid that you will in the least displease "me by doing so. My friends cannot oblige me more than by telling me frankly "the faults they find in my small productions. I have been tried in this matter, "and I can say from experience that their censures do not in the least offend "me."

(1) *Letter of the 2d of April, 1685. pag. 237.*

This Continuation had not the same success with the *Critique Generale*. All that Mr Bayle had said in the Preface, to show the difference betwixt these two pieces, and to give a just idea of this last, was to no purpose. No notice was taken of it. Neither would people understand what he had said in the ninth Letter concerning the rights of an erring Conscience, and concerning innocent Errors; though he had taken all possible precaution to explain himself fully on these heads. He complained of this six months after in the *News from the Republic of Letters*, upon occasion of some reflexions of Father Malebranche's concerning the carelessness of readers. "It "must be confessed (says he (2), that the generality of readers are strange sort of people, "one may take the trouble of acquainting them with a thousand things, one may re"commend this and the other thing to them in the most humble manner, they will ne"vertheless follow their own humour and custom. Good stories have been made con"cerning the useless precautions of mothers and husbands: I am surprised that no body "has given us a history of the useless precautions of authors. I know one whose book "has not been published above six months, who omitted nothing to secure him"self from rash judgments; his preface had given very essential advices, and in those "places where he distrusted his readers, he had expresly warned them that they would "certainly mistake him, if they did not carefully examine the whole series of his "reasoning; he had even carried his precautions so far as to print his real sen"timents in large letters, and to threaten the readers in some sort, that if they "committed any mistakes there, they should be inexcusable. All this signified nothing, "he has been informed, that notwithstanding all his care, even people whose pro"fession it was to know these things, have fallen into those mistakes which he had "been at so much pains to warn them of."

(2) *July 1685. Art. viii. p. m. 780, 781.*

Mr Bayle began the second year of his *News from the Republic of Letters*, that is to say, the month of March 1685, by an addition to the title, which made it no longer an anonymous work; he added these words, *By Mr B ... Professor of Philosophy and History at Rotterdam* (3). He added likewise an Advertisement, wherein he says that he thought himself obliged to let the public know distinctly the place where this Journal was composed, that they might see that the Magistrates of Rotterdam honour the Muses with their protection, and that this work was composed by one of the Professors whom they had settled in their *New Illustrious School*; and declares,

(3) *Par le Sieur B... Professeur en Philosophie & en Histoire à Rotterdam.*

that

1685. that though he doth not dedicate it in the ordinary forms, he doth neverthelefs entirely confecrate it to them. He expreffed himfelf in a ftill ftronger manner, in an article of the month of March, where he is giving the extract from a book, wherein it was obferved, that the town of Rotterdam had always favoured the Belles Lettres. "What this city did three years ago, adds Mr Bayle (1), is a very "evident proof of their love to the Sciences. It is eafy to obferve that I "mean the ILLUSTRIOUS SCHOOL, which the honourable Magiftrates of "Rotterdam generoufly founded in 1681. If the public fhall receive any in- "ftruction, or ufeful amufement from thefe *News from the Republic of Letters*, "they will be obliged for it to thofe gentlemen, fince it is to them that I owe "the fweet tranquillity which enables me to fupport this laborious tafk. It is "under the protection of this glorious Senate that thefe collections are compofed, "*ille nobis bæc otia fecit*, and I am very glad to find here fo natural an occafion, "of teftifying my gratitude, and of declaring, that if the public has any good "opinion of this work, I confecrate it entirely to the glory of this city."

(1) Art. viii. pag. m. 311.

Upon the eighth day of May, 1685, Mr Bayle was informed that his father died upon Saturday the 30th of the preceeding March. This was very afflicting news to him, but his grief was redoubled, when he heard that his elder brother was in prifon upon account of religion. The Bifhop of Rieux did not know what was become of Mr Bayle, 'till the time in which the *General Criticifm on the Hiftory of Calvinifm* made a noife in France, and it was known that he was the author of it.

This Book renewed their vexation for his efcape from Touloufe, and his return to the Reformed Religion. They had endeavoured feveral times to revenge themfelves upon his brother, but that minifter, by his wife and prudent conduct, had ftill efcaped the purfuits of his enemies. At laft they applied to Mr de Louvois, a violent and revengeful man, who at this time was the author of unheard of cruelties againft the Reformed in feveral provinces. Mr de Louvois had given offence at feveral ftrokes in the *General Criticifm* concerning the conduct of the French Court with regard to the Reformed, and fo gave orders that Mr Bayle, the Minifter of Carla fhould be feized. They fent a great number of public officers to his houfe, who dragged him out of his clofet, and carried him to the prifon of Pamiers, upon the 11th of June. From thence he was removed to Bourdeaux, on the 10th of July, to the Chateau Trompette, and confined in a ftinking and infectious dungeon. They ufed all their efforts to make him change his religion, but neither their promifes, their threats, nor their outrages, were capable to fhake him. He fhowed a conftancy and ftedfaftnefs which aftonifhed his perfecutors, and praifed God who had called him to fuffer for the truth. But the delicacy of his conftitution could not bear fuch barbarous ufage: he died the 12th of November, after five months imprifonment. In this manner he "crowned (2) "that piety which he had fhewed during the whole courfe of his life, by an heroic "death, which was admired even by thofe who had done every thing in their "power to make him die a Papift, and over whofe attacks he triumphed glori- "oufly." He was well verfed in facred and prophane hiftory, and in the knowledge both of ancient and modern authors. His zeal for his religion was attended with mildnefs and wifdom. Although he had a very lively fenfe of the many injuries done to the Reformed, yet he ftill preferved an inviolable fidelity to the King's perfon, and a perfect fubmiffion to his commands, being perfuaded that a Chriftian ought to oppofe nothing to his fovereign, but fupplications and tears (3).

(2) Cabale Chimerique, pag. 313.

(3) See his Difcourfe to Mr Da- gueffeau,

Mr Paets was at this time in England, on the affairs of the States, and as the queftion about Toleration was then very much debated there, he wrote a Latin Letter, on the 12th of September, upon that fubject to Mr Bayle, which Mr Bayle got printed at Rotterdam, under the following title: H. V. P. ad B**** (4) *de nuperis Angliæ motibus Epiftola, in qua de diverforum à publica Religione circa divina fentientium differitur Tolerantia*. In this letter, Mr Paets begins with admiring that change, which had been made in the minds and opinions of the Englifh, with regard to James II. He praifed that prince for not diffembling his Religion at his acceffion to the crown; and hoped that he would faithfully obferve the promife he had made to his Proteftant fubjects, of allowing them the peaceable enjoyment of their Religion. The reft of the Letter is employed in confuting thofe who maintain, that Princes ought not to fuffer any Religion but one in their dominions, and that fubjects ought not to fubmit to any Prince but of their own Religion. He fhews that nothing is more oppofite to the fpirit of primitive Chriftianity, than a fpirit of perfecution, and after having examined the reafons adduced by Politicians and Divines againft Toleration, he attacks the infallible authority arrogated by the Church of Rome. In a Poftfcript he clears up and confirms fome things he had faid in the Letter, and fhews that it would be eafy to reduce all the Sects among Proteftants into one fociety. Mr Bayle being of opinion that this Letter was very fit to infpire fentiments of mildnefs and moderation, thought proper to tranflate it into French. This tranflation appeared in the month of August.

Intendant of the Generality of Montauban, and his anfwer to the Comifory of Mazeres, in the Hiftoire de Mr Bayle & de fes Ouvrages, printed at Amfterdam 1716, pag. 98, and the following.

(4) That is, Hadriani Van Paets ad Bælhum.

xxiv THE LIFE OF Mʀ BAYLE.

August. It was likewise tranſlated into Dutch. Mr Bayle gave an abſtract of 1685.
it in his Journal of the Month of October 1685; and Mr Paets being dead after the
impreſſion of that article, he in a new edition added a few words, by way of elogy
upon that great man. "This is not the firſt time, (ſays he (1), that the illuſtrious Mr
"Paets, author of the Letter of which we have been ſpeaking, has reaſoned
"ſtrongly upon the ſubject of Toleration. There are ſome other Letters of his
"upon this ſubject, in the Collection of the *præſtantium ac eruditorum Virorum*
"*Epiſtolæ*, printed firſt in Quarto, and reprinted in Folio at Amſterdam, in the
"year 1684. Theſe are beautiful monuments of his eloquence, and of the ſtrength
"of his judgment. He could have eaſily produced many more conſiderable than thoſe,
"if he had pleaſed to become an author, for he was a great Divine, a great Lawyer,
"a great Politician, and a great Philoſopher, he had a very happy conception
"of things, and a ſurprizing penetration; never did man reaſon more ſtrongly,
"or give a greater air of dignity to what he ſaid: but he was born for greater
"employments than that of an author. The extraordinary embaſſy to Spain, which
"he performed ſo advantageouſly for his country, at that time in a conſternation
"upon account of the great ſucceſs of the French arms, ſhewed what he was ca-
"pable of in affairs of State. What a loſs is it to the public, that ſo great a man
"did not live longer! hardly had he arrived to his 55th year, when he died
"upon the 8th of October of the preſent year 1685; deſerving all manner of
"praiſe as much upon the account of his intrepidity, probity, generoſity, integrity,
"and all the other qualities of a gentleman, as upon the account of his great genius
"and profound erudition. It is in quality of Journaliſt of the Republic of Letters,
"that I am obliged to give this account of him. But what ſhould I not be obliged
"to ſay, if I were to ſpeak agreeably to thoſe ſentiments of gratitude, which fill
"my ſoul for the favours I have received from this illuſtrious perſon?"

Mr Bayle at this time was engaged in a diſpute with Mr Arnauld, upon Father
Malebranche's account. This Doctor in his *Philoſophical and Theological Reflexions on
the New Syſtem of Nature and Grace* of Father Malebranche, had vehemently oppoſed his opinion, viz. "That all pleaſure is a good, and renders the perſon
"who enjoys it actually happy." Mr Bayle, in making an extract of this work
of Mr Arnauld, had declared himſelf for Father Malebranche. "There is no-
"thing, (ſays he (2), more innocent, or more certain, than to ſay that all pleaſure
"renders the perſon happy who enjoys it, for the time in which he enjoys it,
"and that notwithſtanding this, we ought to ſhun thoſe pleaſures which attach us
"to the evil. . . . . But ſome will ſay it is virtue, it is grace, it is the love of
"God, or rather it is God alone who is our happineſs. I agree that he is ſo in
"quality of inſtrument or efficient cauſe, as the Philoſophers ſpeak; but in quality of
"a formal cauſe, it is the pleaſure, it is the ſatisfaction we enjoy, which conſtitutes our
"happineſs." He had obſerved before, that "thoſe who had in any ſort under-
"ſtood Father Malebranche's doctrine concerning the pleaſure of the ſenſes, would no
"doubt be aſtoniſhed that any body ſhould find fault with him on that account;
"and that if they did not remember that Mr Arnauld had made oath of his ſin-
"cerity, in the preface to this laſt book, they would be ready to think that he
"had only cavilled with his adverſary, in order to render his morals ſuſpected."
Mr Arnauld who eaſily took fire, publiſhed a Piece intituled, *An Advice to the Author
of the News from the Republic of Letters* (3), wherein he complained of this reflexion of
Mr Bayle, and maintained that he had not only well underſtood, but likewiſe well
confuted Father Malebranche's opinion. Mr Bayle gave the ſubſtance of this book in
the Journal of December, and promiſed to make uſe of the vacation to examine it
carefully. Accordingly he ſet about it, and the impreſſion of his Anſwer was finiſhed
upon the 25th of February: it was intitled, *An Anſwer of the Author of the News
from the Republic of Letters, to an Advice which has been given him, concerning what he had
ſaid in favour of Father Malebranche about the pleaſure of the ſenſes* (4). Mr Arnaud did
not give up the point, he wrote a Reply under this title, *A Diſſertation concerning
the pretended happineſs ariſing from the pleaſure of the ſenſes, to ſerve for a Reply to an Anſwer which Mr Bayle has made to juſtify what he had ſaid in his News from the Republic
of Letters of September 1685, in favour of Father Malebranche againſt Mr Arnauld* (5).
Mr Bayle would have anſwered this Reply, if he had not been ſick when it appeared,
and he thought it would be too late to refute it when his health allowed him to write.
However he afterwards did deſign to anſwer it, and fully to diſcuſs that ſubject [F].
Notwithſtanding he has only ſaid a word or two about it in one of his works (6).

Mr Bayle

(1) *Art ii. p. 1093, 1394. of the third Edition.*

(2) *Nouvelles of the Month of Auguſt, 1685, Art. iii, pag. m. 876.*

(3) *Avis à l'Auteur des Nouvelles de la Republique des Lettres.*

(4) *Reponſe de l'Auteur des Nou- velles de la Repub- lique des Lettres à l'Avis qui lui a été donné ſur ce qu'il a dit en fa- veur du P. Male- branche touchant le plaiſir des ſens, &c. at Rot- terdam chez Pi- erre de Graef. 1686, in 12mo.*

(5) *Differ- tation ſur le preten- du bon- heur du p'aiſir des ſens, pour ſervir de replique à la Repon- ſe qu'a faite Mr Bayle pour juſtifier ce qu'il a dit dans ſes Nouvelles de la Re- publique de Lettres du mois de Sep- tembre* • *He ought to have ſaid du mois d'Aout.* 1685, en faveur du P. Male- branche contre Mr Arnauld. *Printed at Cologn (Rotter- dam) 1687, in 8vo.*

(6) Criti- cal Dicti- onary, Article Epicu- rus, Rem. [G].

(a) *Nouveau Recueil de pieces fugi- tives d'Hiſ- toire & de Literature, &c.*

(b) *Tom iii. p. 64, & ſeq.*

[F] *Mr Bayle did afterwards deſign to anſwer Mr
Arnauld, and to diſcuſs that ſubject fully.*] This appears by a Letter publiſhed by the Abbé Archimbaut,
in his *New Collection of ſcarce pieces of Hiſtory and Literature, &c (a)*. As this Letter was never printed
except in that Collection (b), which is now pretty
ſcarce, I thought it would not be unacceptable to the
reader to find it here. It was wrote in the year 1694.

"Sir,
"I can aſſure you, that before Mr Abbadie had the
"leaſt thought of writing that book which they have
"reprinted in France (c), I had a diſpute with
"Mr Arnauld, which only lies dormant at preſent,
"concerning our ſenſations. Mr Arnauld has pub-
"liſhed a fine *Diſſertation* againſt me, *On the pre-
"tended happineſs ariſing from the pleaſure of the ſenſes.
"It

(c) *L'Art de ſe connoitre ſoy meme, which they had reprinted at Lyons.*

THE LIFE OF Mʳ BAYLE.

1685. Mr Bayle having observed in the Journal of September 1685 (1), that there were a great many errors in the Treatise concerning anonymous Authors, published by Mr Deckher, Advocate in the Imperial Chamber of Spire; Mr d'Almeloveen, who designed to publish a new edition of this work, desired him to read it, and to point out to him the faults he should find in it. A learned man called Mr Vindingius had before this time wrote a letter to Mr Deckher, which had been printed with the second edition of this book, wherein he corrected some mistakes of the author, and furnished him with some supplements: but neither was this letter free from faults. Mr Bayle corrected both the one and the other, and added a discovery of several anonymous authors, in his answer to Mr d'Almeloveen's letter. He concludes by saying that he could have furnished him with more ample and more curious remarks, if he had time to consult his papers and his friends, and if he had not been afraid of offending authors, who had a mind to be concealed. This letter was written upon the 6th and 7th of March 1686; and Mr d'Almeloveen joined it to a new edition of Mr Deckher's book, printed at Amsterdam with this title: *Johannis Deckherri Doctoris & Imperialis Cameræ Judicii Spirensis Advocati & Procuratoris, de Scriptis adespotis, pseudepigraphis, & suppositiis Conjecturæ. cum Additionibus Variorum. Editio Tertia altera parte auctior.* Mr Bayle mentions it in his new Journal of April 1686 (2), and takes notice of some errors of the press in his letter.

(1) *Art. tit. p. m.* 1013.

(2) *Art. I. Of the Catalogue of new Books, p. m.* 460.

1686. The cruel Persecution of the Reformed in France had very sensibly touched Mr Bayle, but he was quite overcome with grief, when he heard that in the month of October 1685, they had revoked the Edict of Nantes, which was the pledge and security of their rights and liberties; and that they had sent Dragoons into their houses, who lived there at discretion, and committed all sorts of disorders and violence to force them to embrace the Romish Religion. Some among them submitted outwardly, and others fled to foreign countries, that they might serve God there according to the dictates of their conscience. In the mean while the Missionaries and Popish writers, notwithstanding all this, impudently denied that any violence had been used towards them, and there was hardly two or three of them, who confessed the quartering of the troops upon them, which the Protestants called the *Croisade Dragonne*, the Conversions *à la Dragonnade*, or simply the *Dragonnade*. Mr Bayle made several reflexions on this subject in his *News from the Republic of Letters*, with a great deal of wisdom and caution. But at last, the sight of so much injustice, so many cruelties and frauds, put him quite out of patience: being seized with an infinite number of books wherein nothing was talked of but the immortal Glory which Lewis the Great had acquired by destroying Heresy, and rendering *France entirely Catholic*, he published in the month of March 1686, a little book entituled, *A Character of France entirely Catholic under the reign of Lewis le Grand* (3). But that he might not be so much as suspected to be author of it, he feigned in the title that this book was printed at St Omer, and added an advertisement wherein the bookseller said that the manuscript had been given him by a Missionary lately returned from England, who had advised him to print it, being persuaded that it would be a proof of the rage of the Heretics.

(3) *Ce que c'est que la France toute Catholique sous le Regne de Louis le Grand.*

This small piece is composed of three Letters. The second which makes the body of the book, is written to a Canon by a Refugee at London, who had been his friend. It is a very strong and severe censure of the conduct of France with regard to the Reformed. All the Catholics in France are here accused of having been concerned in the persecution: a hideous picture of the Church of Rome is here drawn; treachery and violence (says he) are its distinguishing characters: the pretended Converters are reproached with their ridiculous artifices, and their low and gross cheats: the injustice of the Arrets is complained of, and particularly of that which allowed children of seven years of age to make choice of the Catholic Religion: the falsity of the reasons alledged in the Edict by which that of Nantes was revoked are shown: the dragooning is described in very lively colours: the oaths of Catholics, considered as such, are represented as a meer farce: their pretended zeal is ridiculed: the ruin of the Christian Religion is laid to the charge of the Catholic Clergy:

" It is an Answer to a Defence which I had published of an article of my *News from the Republic of Letters*, wherein I had sided with Father Malebranche, against Mr Arnauld: I had maintained, that the pleasures of the senses are altogether spiritual and incorporeal beings or modifications, and that there is no pleasure, how gross soever or brutish, which in it's own nature may not be a modification of the purest of all created substances. So that if some pleasures are at present criminal, it is only by accident, upon account of the occasions in which they are tasted, that is to say, because they are the consequences of an act of the will, which we know to be forbidden by God. But this doth not relate to the nature itself of the modifications of the mind, but is only an accidental relation, or *ex instituto*, which arises from

VOL. I.

" the laws which God has revealed to man, either by his word, or by reason. From whence it follows, (and I think that I even took notice of this consequence), that the pleasures of taste, of sight, and of touch, may be communicated without the intervention of any corporeal organ, or that the eye may be indifferently the organ of the pleasures either of taste or of hearing, as it is *ex instituto* of those of sight. I was sick when Mr Arnauld answered me, and before I recovered, the subject of our dispute was forgotten, so I have not to this day made any reply to him; but I will set about it when a proper occasion offers, and will show that it is impossible to maintain the spirituality of our souls, without admitting my principle."

g

THE LIFE OF MR BAYLE.

Clergy: the conduct of the Converters is compared with that of the Pagan persecutors: 1686. the Catholics are accused of having rendered Christianity odious to all other Religions; and he maintains that the laws of humanity, and that general benevolence which we owe to all mankind, would oblige an honest man to inform the Emperor of China of what has lately past in France, and acquaint him that the Missionaries, who at first only desire a Toleration, did really intend to become masters, and that he could not rely on the fidelity of their Proselytes; and concludes by saying that Priests and Monks carry discord, sedition, and cruelty, wherever they go. This is a general view of this Letter.

The reader will no doubt be glad to see Mr Bayle's judgment of it in his Journal. "They will possibly find (says he (1), too much fire here, and too great flights of fancy, but the beauty of the thoughts, and their solidity in the main, as to the facts, will very likely make them excuse what is excessive in it. Certainly there is enough said to the Converters in France to cover them with the highest confusion, if people of their trade could blush at any thing. The turn and vivacity which goes through the whole of it, will make few readers think it long, though it were really so."

[(1) Nouvelles of March 1686, Art. III, of New Books, p. m. 346.]

In this manner Mr Bayle speaks of it, pretending not to know the author. The Canon being piqued by this letter, sends it to another Refugee at London, who was a friend of the author's, and desires him to give him his opinion of it. He assures him that he will give thanks to God, for having blest the gentle and charitable methods which had been used against a Religion which had rebelled both against God and the Church, and that he will strive by his prayers to obtain for him the grace of conversion. He afterwards desires him to read St Augustin's Letters, which (says he) shew the injustice of the complaints of the Reformed, and unanswerably justify the means which had been used, in order to reclaim them. This Letter is the first of the three. In the third the Refugee answers to the Canon, with a great deal of mildness and moderation. He condemns the sallies and hyperbolical expressions of his friend, and confesses that there were an infinite number of good people in France, and even Priests and Monks, who had generously sympathized with the miseries of the Reformed, and had done them good offices; and that his friend was to blame in saying, that he had not found one good man in France: but with regard to the Converters, he abandoned them to all the strokes of his friend's pen, and to the utmost extent of his invectives, together with all the Catholic Writers, who had denied that any violence had been used towards the Reformed. He asks some pretty lively questions on this subject, and says that having represented to his friend the great number of honest men they had found among the Catholics in France; in answer to this he had maintained, that these honest men had acted in this matter not as Catholics, but as Frenchmen; and that we ought to depend more upon a person, considered as having been instructed in the laws of civility and honour practised in France, than upon one considered as having been instructed in the Catechism of his Religion by his parish Priest. He adds, that he laughed at this distinction, but that his friend had shewn him some sheets of a manuscript, translated from the English, containing the same thought. "There is here, (says he (2), a learned Presbyterian and good Philosopher, who has wrote a Philosophical Commentary upon these words of the parable, *compel them to come in*, which is not as yet printed. They are at present translating it into our language. They have lent me some sheets of it, which I have read with great pleasure. The English have the most profound genius, and are the most given to meditation, of any people in the world. I do not believe that ever it was more strongly proved, that all constraint in religious matters is criminal and contrary both to reason and scripture. St Augustin, and the two Letters to which we are referred are here quite destroyed, and they shew him that if he had not argued better against the Heretics of his time, than he has done for the Persecutors, the Councils who have condemned Pelagius upon the report and opinion of St Augustin, must have been very easily satisfied or put out of humour. I will hasten the translation and impression of this Book, as much as possible. I am convinced that a great many Catholics will approve of it, notwithstanding the prevailing spirit of those of your cloth."

[(2) Ce que c'est que la France toute Catholique, pag. 125.]

[(3) Commentaire philosophique sur ces paroles de Jesus-Christ, contrain les d'entrer; où l'on prouve par plusieurs raisons démonstratives, qu'il n'y a rien de plus abominable que de faire des Conversions par la contrainte, & où l'on refute tous les Sophismes des Convertisseurs à contrainte, & l'Apologie que St Augustin a faite des persecutions. Traduit de l'Anglois du Sieur Jean Fox de Bruggs. Par M. J. T. A Canterbery, chez Thomas Litwel 1686.]

The book here promised is entitled, *A Philosophical Commentary on these Words of JESUS CHRIST, compel them to come in. Wherein it is proved, by several invincible arguments, that there is nothing more abominable than to make converts by compulsion. With a confutation of all the sophisms of the advocates for constraint, as also of St Augustin's Apology for Persecution. Translated from the English of Mr John Fox of Bruggs. By M. J. T. At Canterbury, by Thomas Letwel, MDCLXXXVI* (3). Mr Bayle inserted this title in his Journal of the Month of August 1686 (4), and added, "In the Journal of last March, *pag.* 345, we spoke of the piece entituled, *Ce que c'est que la France toute Catholique*, which is a small treatise wherein they promise the publication of this Commentary. It will no doubt be a Commentary of a new kind. We had the title of it sent us from beyond sea two days ago, and they promise to send us the work itself very soon. We will then see whether it be so "dreadful

[(4) Art II. of the New Books, p. m. 961.]

1686. "dreadful a ftroke to the whole Tribe of Converters, as they would make us believe
"in the letter of advice we have had about it." But all this was only a feint.
The book was printing at Amfterdam for Wolfgang, who had printed *La France
toute Catholique*. The impreffion was finifhed in the month of October, and
Mr Bayle mentions it in his *Journal* of the month of November (1).

This work is divided into three parts. In the firft, Mr Bayle refutes the literal
fenfe of thefe words *Compel them to come in*; and as this is not a theological or
critical Commentary, but a philofophical one, that is to fay, a work of pure reafon-
ing, he lays it down in the beginning as a principle, "that natural reafon, or the
"general principles of our knowledge, are the fundamental and original rule of
"all interpretation of fcripture, efpecially in what regards to manners;" what
comes to the fame thing, that every particular doctrine, whether advanced as agreeable to Scripture, or propofed in any other manner, is falfe when it can be refuted by the clear and diftinct notions of natural reafon, efpecially if it regards
morality: and he fhews that all Divines, not even excepting the Roman Catholics,
agree to this maxim. After having eftablifhed and proved this principle, he fhews
that the literal fenfe of thefe words is falfe, I. Becaufe it contradicts the moft clear
and diftinct notions of our reafon. II. Becaufe it is contrary to the fpirit of the
Gofpel. III. Becaufe it totally overturns morality, both divine and human; confounds virtue and vice, and by that means opens a door to all imaginable confufion, and tends to the univerfal ruin of focieties. IV. Becaufe it furnifheth Infidels with a very lawful pretence of hindering the preachers of the Gofpel to enter into
their dominions, and of driving them out wherever they are found. V. Becaufe
it contains a general command, the execution of which muft needs be attended
with many crimes. VI. Becaufe it takes away from the Chriftian Religion, a
ftrong proof againft falfe Religions, particularly againft Mahometifm, which was
eftablifhed by perfecution. VII. Becaufe it was unknown to the Fathers of the
Church in the firft three Centuries. VIII. Becaufe it renders the complaints of
the primitive Chriftians, againft the Pagan perfecutions, vain and ridiculous. IX. And
laftly, becaufe it would expofe true Chriftians to continual oppreffion, without leaving
them any thing to alledge, in order to put a ftop to it, but the doctrines themfelves in difpute betwixt the perfecuted and perfecutors, which is only a pitiful begging of the queftion, that would not prevent the world's becoming a continued fcene
of flaughter and cruelty.

In the fecond part, Mr Bayle anfwers the objections which might be raifed againft
him, which he reduces to the following: I. "That force is not ufed in order to
"conftrain the confcience, but to awaken thofe who refufe to examine." He refutes this plea, and examines what it is they call *obftinacy*. II. "That the literal
"fenfe is rendered odious, by our judging of the ways of God by the ways of
"men: and that though men are capable of judging wrong, when they are actuated
"by paffion, yet it doth not follow that God may not make ufe of this means to
"accomplifh his work in the wonderful conduct of his providence." Mr Bayle
fhews how falfe this thought is, and what are the common effects of perfecution.
III. "That things are malicioufly exaggerated, when the conftraint commanded
"by JESUS CHRIST is reprefented under the notion of fcaffolds, wheels, and
"gibbets, whereas we ought only to mention fines, and banifhments, and other fuch
"fmall inconveniencies." He fhews the abfurdity of the excufe, and that fuppo-
fing the literal fenfe, capital punifhments are more reafonable than the chi-
caneries, imprifonments, banifhments, and quartering of Dragoons, which they had
made ufe of in France. IV. "That we cannot condemn the literal fenfe, with-
"out, at the fame time, condemning the laws which God eftablifhed among the
"Jews, and the conduct of the Prophets upon fome occafions." Mr Bayle fhews
that feveral things were permitted, or even commanded by the Old Law, for reafons which were peculiar to the Jewifh Commonwealth, and which have no place
under the Gofpel. V. "That Proteftants cannot find fault with the literal fenfe
"of conftraint, without condemning the moft wife Emperors and Fathers of the
"Church, and without condemning themfelves, fince they in fome countries do
"not fuffer other Religions, and have fometimes punifhed Heretics with death,
"Servetus for example." Mr Bayle blames the conduct of the ancient Chriftian
Emperors, who have been guilty of Perfecution; and cenfures the Non-Toleration
of Proteftant Princes, except when it is an act of policy, neceffary for the good of
the State. On this account, he maintains, that it is lawful to make laws againft Popery,
becaufe it teacheth perfecution, and has always practifed it when it had the power.
"The punifhment of Servetus, (adds he), and of a very few others of that fort,
"who erred in the moft fundamental doctrines, is at prefent looked upon as a
"hideous blemifh on thefe early days of our Reformation, and as fad and deplo-
"rable remains of Popery, and I do not at all doubt, that if the Magiftrates of
"Geneva had at prefent fuch a procefs before them, they would carefully abftain
"from fuch violence."

(1) *Art. iii. of the Catalogue of New Books, p. m. 1347, and the following.*

The

xxviii THE LIFE OF Mr BAYLE.

The sixth objection is, "That the opinion of Toleration cannot fail to throw a 1686.
"State into all sorts of confusion, and to produce a horrible medley of Sects, which
"deform Christianity." Mr Bayle draws a proof of his own opinion from this objection: for if a multiplicity of Religions be hurtful to a State. "It is only, (says he (1),
"because the one will not tolerate the other, but swallow it up by persecution.
"*Hinc prima mali labes*, this is the origin of the evil. If every one of them,
"adds he, enjoyed the Toleration which I plead for, there would be the same con-
"cord in a State, divided into ten Religions, that there is in a City wherein the
"different sorts of mechanics support one another. All the differences it could
"produce, would be an honest emulation which should most signalize itself in
"piety, good morals, and in knowledge; every one would strive to prove itself
"the most beloved of God, by shewing a stronger attachment to the practice of
"good works; nay they would even strive which should show the greatest love
"to their country, if the Sovereign protected them all, and kept an equal ba-
"lance among them by his equity: now it is evident that so beautiful an emula-
"tion would produce infinite advantages, and consequently that Toleration is the
"most proper means in the world to bring back the Golden Age, and to make
"a consort and harmony of many voices and instruments of different tones and
"notes, as agreeable at least as the single harmony of one voice. What is it then
"that prevents this beautiful concert, formed of voices and tones so different from
"one another; it is, that the one of the two Religions wants to exercise a cruel
"tyranny over the minds, and force the others to sacrifice their consciences to it;
"it is that Princes foment this unjust partiality, and lend the secular arm to the
"furious and tumultuous passions of a herd of Monks and Clerks: in a word, these
"disorders proceed not from Toleration, but from Non-Toleration." He afterwards shews in what sense Princes ought to be the *nursing Fathers of the Church*.
The seventh objection is, "That constraint in the literal sense cannot be denied,
"without introducing a general Toleration." Mr Bayle acknowledgeth that this
consequence is just, but denies that it is absurd. He shews that no inconveniencies
would follow from tolerating not only the Jews, but if it were necessary, the
Mahometans and Pagans, and much more the Socinians. He examines the restrictions of those who plead for a partial Toleration; and after making some remarks on what is called *Blasphemy*, he concludes, that Servetus was unjustly punished as a Blasphemer.

The 8th and last Objection is, "That constraint in the literal sense is rendered
"odious by falsly supposing, that it authorises the persecution of the Truth."
Mr Bayle answers that the consequence is just; and that if we admit the literal
sense, Heretics will have the same right to persecute the Orthodox, that the Orthodox pretend to have to persecute the Heretics. In order to prove this, he lays it
down for a principle, that men are always obliged to follow the dictates of their
conscience; that they always sin when they do not follow them, though they may
likewise sometimes sin by following them. That principle is founded on this Maxim,
that whatever is done contrary to the dictates of the conscience is a sin; from whence
it follows, that whoever doth an action which his conscience tells him is bad, or
who omits doing what his conscience tells him he ought to do, offends God and
necessarily commits a sin. So that if God had commanded, by a positive law, that
every man who knows the truth ought to employ fire and sword to defend it; all
those to whom this law should be revealed, would be indispensably obliged to obey
it. But since a Heretic is persuaded that his opinions are true, he is therefore obliged to do that for his errors, which God should have commanded to be done in
defence of the truth; and consequently Heretics would be authorized to persecute
the Orthodox, whom they look upon as maintainers of error, if it was true that
God had commanded to persecute error. He confirms this proof by distinguishing
betwixt absolute truth and seeming truth. He says that as we have no certain mark
whereby to discern whether what seems to be truth to us, be absolutely so; when
it happens that errror is cloathed in the dress of truth, we owe it the same respect
that is due to truth; and that considering the weakness of man, and the state in
which he is placed, the infinite wisdom of God has not permitted that he should
require of us rigorously the knowledge of absolute truth, but that he has laid a
burthen upon us proportioned to our strength, which is to enquire after the truth,
and to stop at that which seems to be such after a sincere enquiry, to love this
seeming truth, and to conform ourselves to it's commands how difficult soever they
may be.

In the Preface intituled *A preliminary Discourse containing several remarks distinct
from those in the Commentary* (2), the author says that he composed this work, at
the desire of a Refugee, who is the author of *France entirely Catholic*; and that having
wrote it in order to it's being translated into French, and upon occasion of the
persecution of the Protestants in France, he had not quoted any English books in
it, but had confined himself to such as were very well known to the French Converters. Here he attacks a-fresh the spirit of persecution, and confutes some Catholic
Controvertists with a great deal of force and vehemence. "The Author (says Mr Bayle,
"speaking

(1) Commentaire Philoso-phique, &c. Part. II, cap 6. pag. 363, 364.

(2) Discours preliminaire qui contient plusieurs remarques distinctes de celles du Commentaire.

THE LIFE OF Mr BAYLE.

1686. "speaking of this work in his Journal (1), has prefixed to his book a long pre- (1) No-
"liminary Discourse, which may be justly called a *Philippic Oration*. The defi- vember,
"nition which he there gives of a Converter is almost as cruel as the thing ubi supra,
"defined; all the rest is very much in the same strain." Before this discourse 1349.
there is an advice to the reader, wherein the bookseller promises to publish speedily
a third part, containing a Refutation of the reasons whereby St Augustin justifies persecution.

The *News from the Republic of Letters* procured Mr Bayle the esteem not only of particular persons, but likewise of several illustrious societies. The French Academy,
to whom he had presented his Journal, thanked him in a Letter wherein he was
assured that they had been unanimous in acknowledging his merit, and the usefulness of the present he had made them (2). The Royal Society in England wrote (2) *Letter*
him a Letter wherein they say (3), *That having observed his particular care in col-* from Mr
lecting every thing curious that happened among men of letters, and the fine genius he of the 18th
discovered in his Journal, they were desirous of holding a fixed and certain correspondence of May
with him, from which *they might reap common advantages*. They add, that *as the first* 1685, p.
mark of their esteem for him, they had sent him *the Natural History of Fishes*, by 242.
Mr Willoughby, revised and augmented by Mr Ray. He received likewise very (3) *Letter*
civil letters from the Society of Dublin (4). It consisted of a number of learned *from Mr*
and curious gentlemen who had formed themselves into a body, in order to *Hoskins*,
contribute to the advancement of arts and sciences: but it continued only a few years. *Secretary*

On the other hand, his Journal engaged him in some disputes; and occasioned *Royal S-*
some complaints which he satisfied either by explaining himself, or by fairly cor- *ciety, of*
recting the mistakes he had made by following some unexact Memoirs which had *the 15th*
been communicated to him. But he was censured in one particular, which gave *of May*
him a great deal of uneasiness, not so much upon account of the manner of the *1686, p.*
complaint, as because it concerned a crowned head. This is one of the most memo- 256.
rable events of Mr Bayle's life, and deserves that I should here publish all the pieces (4) *Letter*
which relate to it. *from Mr*

In the Journal of the Month of April 1686 (5), he took notice of a printed *Smyth, Se-*
paper that was handed about under the name of Queen Christina of Sweden. It *the Society*
was an answer to a letter of the Chevalier de Terlon, wherein that Princess con- *of Dublin,*
demned the persecution in France. "It is very probable (says he) that all the *of the 1st*
"Confessionaries in France would be severe to the Queen of Sweden, if it were *ber, 1686,*
"true that she had answered the Chevelier de Terlon in the manner contained in *pag. 272.*
"the Letter which is handed about, wherein she loudly condemns the conduct of
"France, with regard to the late conversions, and especially when she considers (5) *Art.*
"the behaviour of the Clergy of France, against the head of the Church. There *vi, of the*
"are a great many Protestants who cannot believe that a Princess who professeth *Books, p.*
"the Catholic Religion, has wrote such a Letter." Mr Bayle was desired to *m. 472.*
give this Letter a place in his Journal, and he inserted it in that of the Month
of May (6). It is as follows:
(6) *Art.*
"SINCE you desire to know my sentiments concerning the pretended extirpation *iv, pag.*
"of Heresy in France, it is with great pleasure that I acquaint you with them, 529, *and*
"upon so important a subject. As I pretend neither to fear nor to flatter any *ing.*
"person, I will freely own to you, that I am not well persuaded of the success of
"this great undertaking, and that I cannot rejoice upon that account, as for a
"thing that will be of great advantage to our holy Religion. On the contrary, I
"foresee a great many ill consequences, which will follow upon so strange a pro-
"ceeding."

"Tell me ingenuously, are you well persuaded of the sincerity of those new Con-
"verts? I wish indeed that they may obey God and their Prince sincerely; but
"I fear their obstinacy, and I would not be accountable for all the profanations
"which will be committed by these Catholics, compelled by Missionaries who treat
"our holy mysteries very licentiously. Soldiers are strange Apostles, I imagine they
"are fitter to kill, ravish, and plunder, than to persuade. Accordingly, the accounts
"we have, and of which we cannot possibly doubt, inform us that they acquit
"themselves of their mission very much after their usual manner. I pity people
"who are abandoned to their discretion: I lament the ruin of so many families,
"so many good people reduced to beggary, and I cannot look upon what passeth
"in France at present without being moved with compassion. I am sorry that these
"unhappy people were born in error, but methinks they deserve pity rather than
"hatred; and as I would not for the empire of the world share in their error, so
"neither would I be the cause of their miseries.

"I consider France at present as in the condition of a sick person, from whom
"they cut legs and arms to cure a distemper which a little patience and gentle ma-
"nagement would have entirely removed. But I am much afraid least that distemper
"encrease and at last turn incurable; that this fire concealed under the ashes should
"one day blaze out more fiercely than ever, and least Heresy, under a masque,
"should thereby become more dangerous. Nothing is more commendable than the

VOL. I.   h   " design

"design of converting Heretics and Infidels. But the manner in which they choose
"to go about it is very new. And since our Lord did not make use of that method
"to convert the world, it cannot be the best.

"I admire and cannot comprehend this zeal and these politics, they are out of
"my reach, and I am even glad that I do not comprehend them. Do you be-
"lieve that this is a time to convert Huguenots, to make them good Catholics in
"an age, in which the most notorious attempts are made in France upon the respect
"and submission which is due to the Church of Rome, which is the sole and sure
"foundation of our Religion, since it is to her our Lord has made that glorious pro-
"mise, *that the gates of Hell shall not prevail against her?* Neverthele-s the scanda-
"lous liberty of the Gallican Church was never pushed nearer to rebellion, than it is
"at present. The late propositions, signed and published by the Clergy of France,
"are such as have given too much ground of triumph to Heresy, and I fancy its
"surprise must have been very great, to see itself persecuted by those whose doctrines
"and sentiments are so agreeable to its own upon this fundamental article of our
"Religion.

"These are the strong reasons which hinder me from rejoicing at this
"pretended extirpation of Heresy. The interest of the Church of Rome is without
"doubt as dear to me as my life; but it is upon account of that very interest that
"I see what passeth with grief, and I own to you likewise that my love to France
"is such as makes me lament the desolation of so fine a kingdom. I wish with
"all my heart that I may be mistaken in my conjectures, and that all may ter-
"minate in the greater glory of God, and of the King your master. And I assure
"myself that you will neither doubt of the sincerity of my wishes, nor that I am."

(1) *Art. i. of the new books, pag. m. 522.*

In that same month (1) he said; "We have been assured by very good hands
"that Queen Christina did write the Letter which we have inserted above." And
in that of the month of June (2) he says again: "What we hinted at in our last
"month is confirmed to us from day to day, that Christina is the real Author of
"the Letter concerning the Persecutions in France, which is ascribed to her. It
"is a remainder of Protestantism."

(2) *Art. vi. of the new books, p. m. 726.*

Some time after Mr Bayle received the following letter:

Sir,

"I HOPE you will not take it amiss that I give you a little advice, which
"in process of time may be of some use to you, as you will see. You are
"a man of wit, and people who read your *News from the Republic of Letters*, if
"they have the least taste, confess you have an infinite deal of it: But, Sir, may
"not one be a man of wit without abusing people, and bringing one self into trouble?
"And ought you, who know so many things, to be ignorant of the respect due
"to crowned heads; and that these are sacred things, which are not to be touched
"without danger of the thunderbolt? I say this with relation to the Queen of
"Sweden, of whom you have taken the liberty of talking very licentiously in your
"Journal, upon occasion of a Letter which has been printed under her name. You
"mention it in four different passages, but the last of them surely proceeds from
"a genius which has soared a little higher than became it.

"Although you had added to the illustrious name of *Christina* at least the title
"of *Queen*, you would have done nothing but your duty. Do not tell me that
"great Historians, such as you are, treat the greatest Monarchs in the same man-
"ner, and that they say without ceremony Louis the XIVth, and James the IId,
"in speaking of the Kings of France and of England. The numbers XIVth,
"and IId, carry with them a sort of distinction, and in some sort correct the
"liberty of that expression. But who would say, for example, *Lewis has taken it
"into his head to convert the Protestants, by a mission of Dragoons*; or, *James endea-
"vours by gentle methods to re-establish, if possible, his own Religion in his kingdom*; that
"would be a very ridiculous manner of speaking. It is not less so, Sir, to say as you
"have done in your Journal for the month of June last, page 726, *It is confirmed
"that Christina is the true Author &c.* in speaking of one of the most illustrious
"Queens that has been, or perhaps ever will be, in the universe. You ought sure-
"ly to have accompanied that name with some title, not only because of the respect
"you owe to so great a Princess when you mention her Majesty, but even in con-
"formity to the stile of those who pique themselves upon being good writers."

"But still this is not what is most faulty in that passage of your Journal. The
"worst is two or three words, with which you conclude this Article: *It is a re-
"mainder*, say you, *of Protestantism*. You had done well not to have said this.
"Your great inclination to play the wit has hurried you on; but you have de-
"ceived yourself; there is no wit in it, there is only insolence. No body talks
"at that rate of a Queen who professeth with so much zeal, and in so edifying a man-
"ner, a Religion quite opposite to Protestantism; who has sacrificed every thing
"for it, and who in all her actions contradicts what you have said, that there is
"in her Majesty any remainder of your Religion. To be convinced of this, one need
"only read that very Letter which you mention in your Journal, or a great many
"others

1686. "others which she has wrote on the same subject. She is not indeed a Catholic after the
"manner of France, she is one after the manner of Rome, that is to say, after the
"manner of St Peter and of St Paul. Therefore she doth not approve of these
"persecutions, because in reality this manner of converting Hereticks, had not it's
"original from the Apostles.

"For the rest, all that I say to you here I say from myself, and because my
"duty obligeth me to do so, being one of the Queen's servants. If her Majesty
"happens to read your Journal, I do not know what she will say, or what she
"will do: but believe me, Sir, whatever protection you may boast of from the
"magistrates of the city of Rotterdam, that would not save you from the resent-
"ment of so great a Princess, if she should undertake to do herself justice. And
"the magistrates of Rotterdam are too just and reasonable to undertake to protect
"upon such an occasion.

"Her Majesty doth not disown the Letter which has been printed under her
"name, and which you have inserted in your Journal. There are only the words
"*I am* with which it concludes, which are not her Majesty's. A man of wit, as
"you are, ought to have taken notice of this, and to have corrected it. So great
"a Queen cannot make use of that expression, except to very few persons, and
"Mr de Terlon is not of that number. This single circumstance is sufficient to
"prove that the printing of this Letter was no contrivance of the Queen, as all
"the world knows. If you have a mind to mention it in your Journal, you may;
"but no rallery on this subject, as you have taken the liberty to do in the
"month of April, page 472: make use of this advice, and believe that in this I
"am truly, Sir, your very humble servant.

"P. S. I do not subscribe my name, because is it not necessary, and besides my
"Letter requires no answer. When it shall be proper to make myself known to
"you I will do it: but it is your business to amend, if you think proper."

Mr Bayle justified himself in an Article of the Journal for the month of August (1), intituled, *Reflections of the author of this Journal upon a Letter which has
been sent him concerning what he has said of the Queen of Sweden* (2). His answer
is as follows:

(1) *Art. ix. pag. m. 952, and the following.*

(2) *Reflexions de l'Auteur de ces Nouvelles sur une Lettre qui lui a été écrite touchant ce qu'il a dit de la Reyne de Suede.*

"The writer of this Letter doth not put his name to it, and neither tells us the
"time when, nor the place from whence, he writes. He only acquaints us that
"*all that he has written is only from himself*, and that his duty obliged him to do
"so, being one of the Queen's servants. Let us see what it is he complains
"of, and since it concerns a crowned-head, let us not imagine that the bitterness
"and passion he expresses, shall hinder us from justifying our conduct very cooly."

"He complains first, *That I did not add the title of Queen to the illustrious name
"of Christina in my last month of June, page 726.* But I am very sure that no body
"who judges equitably will be of opinion, that in this I have been wanting in
"the respect due to that great Princess. She has rendered her name so famous,
"that my expression in that passage ought not at all to be thought equivocal. To
"name persons by their names only, without adding some title, is ordinarily in-
"deed either a mark of contempt, or of familiarity; but this is by no means a ge-
"neral rule, for there are some persons whose names alone excite the ideas of
"their great elevation, and in this case it is quite indifferent whether we give them
"their principal titles, or omit them. There is no harm in giving them, it is a
"superfluous addition which at worst can do no hurt. Neither on the contrary is
"there any harm in not giving them, it is an omission of no consequence. Crowned-
"heads are of this number, and hence it is that we say more frequently both in
"conversation and in history, *Francis I. Charles V. Henry IV. Philip II.* than *King
"Francis the Ist, The Emperor Charles V, &c.* It is supposed that the rank to which
"God has raised these Princes makes it impossible for a reader to imagine that their
"titles are omitted out of want of respect, and therefore the shorter expression
"is made use of without scruple. I know very well, as the author of the Letter
"observes, that the number *first*, which is added to the name of *Francis*, carries
"with it a sort of distinction; but this very instance shows, that in case the name
"of *Francis* alone contained a distinction, it would not be necessary to add the
"number *first*. Thus we say every day, that *Alexander* was a disciple of Aristotle,
"that *Soliman* made himself master of Hungary. One has no occasion to say either
"that the first was King of Macedon, or that the second was Grand Signior, or
"to add the ordinal number which belongs to them. Our most exact writers would
"say without scruple *Constantine, Theodosius, Justinian, are the true authors of such
"a law.* Or if we desire an example nearer home, who has not said or wrote, ei-
"ther during the life of Gustavus Adolphus, King of Sweden, or after his death,
"*Gustavus did this or that?* and whence comes it that in speaking of him it is not ne-
"cessary to add the title of King, nor the ordinal number which belongs to him in the
"succession of the Kings of Sweden? It is because he has rendered the name *Gustavus*
"so famous, that he is sufficiently distinguished by it alone. This is the very case in
"question. The Queen of Sweden, his daughter, has given such a lustre to the name

"of

" of *Chriſtina*, that the naming of it alone is ſufficient to awaken all the ideas 1686.
" of her royalty, great qualities, and actions. As therefore it ſhews no want of
" reſpect to the father to call him ſimply *Guſtavus*, ſo it is no want of reſpect
" to the daughter, to name her ſimply *Chriſtina*; but on the contrary, it is giving
" to underſtand that they deſerve theſe names by way of excellence, and that their
" very names contain their panegyric.

" The ſecond complaint turns upon my having ſaid, that this Queen's Letter againſt
" the perſecution in France *is a remainder of Proteſtantiſm*. This is very violently
" complained of. But this proceeds from not having ſufficiently underſtood the force
" of theſe words. They have imagined that I intended to inſinuate that this Princeſs
" had not ſincerely renounced the Proteſtant Religion; which is what never entered
" into my thoughts. It is not neceſſary to a ſincere renunciation of a Religion, that
" we ſhould diveſt ourſelves of every thing we have learned in it, and approve
" every thing that is taught in the communion which we embrace. I ſhould
" think people very unjuſt, who ſhould ſuſpect the ſincerity of a Roman Ca-
" tholic, who after having joined in communion with the Proteſtants, ſhould declare
" that in ſome particulars the Church of Rome ſeemed to him to have the ad-
" vantage of the Proteſtant, ſuch as in the celibacy of the Clergy, in the obſer-
" vation of Lent, and in the faſting on Fridays and Saturdays. One would have
" reaſon to believe that theſe were *remainders of Catholiciſm*; but one might ſay ſo
" and believe at the ſame time, that he had ſincerely abjured his *Catholiciſm*, and
" embraced *Proteſtantiſm*, as the only Religion which leads to ſalvation. It is there-
" fore judging of things without underſtanding them to give my words the ſenſe
" which he gives them. The true ſenſe they ought to have, is the following.

" That if the Queen of Sweden diſapproves of the conduct of thoſe employed
" in the pretended converſions in France, it is owing to the principles of the
" Religion in which ſhe was inſtructed before her journey to Rome, and not to
" the new inſtructions ſhe has received in that country. It is not at Rome that
" one can learn to find fault with perſecution. On the contrary, it is the general
" ſpirit of *Catholiciſm* to extirpate all ſects; for they have not only made public
" rejoicings at Rome for what has been done in France; not only has the Pope
" applauded it in full Conſiſtory, and by his Briefs, but likewiſe all the Catho-
" lics in Europe have ſhown their approbation of it, at leaſt by their ſilence.
" How then could the Queen of Sweden have the principles ſhe has, if ſhe had
" not brought them from her own country? It is (ſays the author of the Letter)
" *becauſe ſhe is not a Catholic after the manner of France, but after the manner of*
" *Rome, that is, of St Peter and St Paul*. But this is what I have called *a re-*
" *mainder of Proteſtantiſm*, and ſo this author and I have really the ſame thought.

" The laſt thing he finds fault with, is that I did not ſtrike out the words *I*
" *am*, out of the copy of the Letter which I inſerted in my Journal. *There is*
" *only this word* (ſays he) *which is not her Majeſty's. So great a Queen cannot make*
" *uſe of that expreſſion except to very few perſons, and Mr de Terlon is not of that*
" *number. This ſingle circumſtance is ſufficient to prove that the printing of this Letter*
" *was no contrivance of the Queen, as all the world knows*. To this I anſwer, that
" I did not think that I could with juſtice ſtrike out this Concluſion, *I am*, be-
" cauſe by doing ſo, I ſhould give people reaſon to ſuſpect that I had ſuppreſſed
" a mark of forgery in that Letter, in order to make it appear more probable to
" the public, that it was written by the Queen of Sweden. Moreover, there has
" lately fallen into my hands a copy of a letter, wherein that Princeſs declares,
" that ſhe is ſurpriſed and diſpleaſed at the publication of the other, though ſhe
" ſtill continues in the ſame ſentiments. The curious will be glad to ſee this ſe-
" cond Letter here at length, but the law of nations doth not allow me to give
" them that ſatisfaction. There is a great difference betwixt theſe two things, the
" inſerting a piece which is in every body's hands, and is already printed; and
" the inſerting a piece which has never been printed. We muſt, with regard to
" manuſcripts, either wait for the conſent of thoſe who have a right to them, or have
" reaſon to believe that they are entirely indifferent what uſe people make of them."

Mr Bayle's unknown correſpondent was not entirely ſatisfied with this anſwer, and wrote him the following Letter:

" Sir,

" THE Queen has ſeen the anſwer you have made to my Letter, and I muſt do
" you juſtice on the one ſide, if you have been to blame on the other. Her Ma-
" jeſty doth not think that it is to be wanting in the reſpect which is due to
" her, to name her ſimply *Chriſtina*. She has indeed rendered that name ſo il-
" luſtrious, that it has now no need of any other diſtinction, and the moſt noble
" and auguſt titles which could be joined to it, could add nothing to the luſtre
" which it has already acquired in the world. I was of opinion that it was not
" a proper expreſſion, with regard to a prince, while he is ſtill living; but I
" have been miſtaken; perſons of ſuch elevated rank, and ſo full of glory, as the
" great

THE LIFE OF MR BAYLE.

1686. "great *Christina*, have rules peculiar to themselves, and their names alone are sufficient to fill the minds of men with that respect and veneration which the titles of others excite. You have got the better in this, Sir, and I submit.

"But the case is quite otherways with regard to the word *Protestantism*, which has escaped you somewhat unseasonably; and which you employ all the subtilty of your wit to justify. You ought to follow my example, and own that you have been to blame. The Queen, who is pretty well satisfied with all the rest of your excuses, is not at all so with regard to this part of your justification. One ought not to seek for evasions before a genius like her's. When one has offended her, the shortest and safest way is to confess it; and after all, a genius such as your's, ought to have suggested something more worthy of her Majesty, than the reasons you have brought in your defence. Not that any thing you can say of her, is capable of giving her the least uneasiness. So great a Queen cannot but equally despise the praises and calumnies of people of a certain kind: but she is born to do justice, and you might have boasted that you are the only person in the world who has offended her with impunity, if you had not taken the course you have done, I mean that of justifying yourself.

"But you must do it effectually, Sir, and retract fully and distinctly what you have said, if you desire to give an entire satisfaction. The Queen at least has a mind that you, together with all the world, should know that she owes nothing to the Protestant Religion; and that if God permitted that she should be born in it, she renounced it as soon as she arrived at the years of discretion, and that without having the least thoughts of returning to it: that ever since that time the Catholic Religion has appeared to her to be the only one, and the true one, and that it was in conformity to it's holy maxims, and not to those of the Protestants, that her Majesty has in her Letter condemned the method used in France in the conversion of the Huguenots, and the Pope has rendered to that Letter the justice it deserved.

"You have no reason to say, as you do, that you are treated with too much *bitterness* and *passion* in the Letter which I wrote to you; on the contrary I am of opinion that you owe me thanks, and that you might possibly have had a great deal more reason to complain, if I had not wrote to you. And I would have you know that I am one of the least of the Queen's servants, and that there are in this Country a great many persons who are proud of being in her Majesty's interest, and who will talk to you in a very different manner than I have done, if you do not take more care for the future.

"I have said nothing to you concerning the word *fameuse*, which you have once more made use of in speaking of the Queen (1), and which has not been agreeable to her Majesty. I know that this word has not altogether the same signification in French, which it has in Latin and in Italian, and that we use it more frequently in a good than in a bad sense. But one ought above all things to avoid these ambiguities in speaking of crowned heads; with regard to whom you know the Proverb says we ought to employ only golden and silken words. And especially with regard to such a Queen as we now speak of; concerning whom we may boldly say, and without fear of offending others, that she has no equal; I say so even in point of rank, for other Queens are properly speaking only the first subjects of their husbands or sons; but the great Christina is a Queen in a manner so noble and elevated, that she knows no superior but God.

"This, Sir, is what I had farther to say to you, and is all the reply I can make to your's. I hope you will continue to make use of my advice, and that time may discover that I am more than you can imagine, Sir, your very humble servant.

"P. S. I had forgot that in your Journal of the Month of August, you speak of a second Letter of the Queen, which has fallen into your hands, and which you make some difficulty of publishing. Her Majesty would be curious to see that Letter, and you will do a thing agreeable to her Majesty, if you send it to her. You might even make use of that opportunity to write to her Majesty. Take this advice; it may be of some service to you: do not neglect it. But I must acquaint you that if you follow it, you must by no means make use of the title *Serenissime* to the Queen. It is a little too common for her, and her Majesty will not have it. You must only direct your Letter; *A sa Majesté la Reyne Christine, à Rome.*

Mr Bayle took the hint that was given him, and on the 14th of November wrote the following Letter to Queen Christina:

(1) Mr Bayle did not make use of this word: He only said that Christina avoit rendu son nom si FAMEUX, (bad rendered her name so famous) &c. the same expression which be afterwards used speaking of Gustavus Adolphus.

"Madam,

"Madam,

"I SHOULD not have taken the liberty of writing this Letter to your Majesty, if a person who has the honour of being in your Majesty's service had not advised me to do so, and to send to your Majesty a copy of a Letter which has fallen into my hands. I hoped, Madam, that an advice of this sort would justify my boldness, and I thought it my duty to make use of this occasion of testifying my most profound respect to the most illustrious Queen in the world. I am ignorant of the name of the person who procures me this great honour. He has not thought fit to make himself known to me by any other title than that of *one of your Majesty's servants*; and I must do him the justice to testify that his zeal for your Majesty's interests is very suitable to the title he assumes.

"It is by him that I have been informed that there are some things in the *News from the Republic of Letters*, which did not seem agreeable to that respect which all the world owes to your Majesty, not only upon account of your Majesty's heroic and extraordinary qualities, but likewise upon account of the sublime rank, in which, from your birth, God has placed your Majesty. As I was sensible of my innocence, I was seized at once with the most inexpressible surprize, and the most unsufferable grief, when I found that my words were interpreted in a manner so contrary to my genuine intention; and to every thing that common sense ought to dictate to every rational creature. For is there any person, Madam, who has the smallest degree of knowledge or reason, who is ignorant of that almost infinite glory which surrounds your Majesty, and of the profound homage which is due to your Majesty from all the world; and if any person has been capable of forgetting this duty, what shame ought not he to feel upon that account? I protest to your Majesty, that ever since I was able to read I have known that your Majesty is the admiration of the universe, and that there is not any one person in the whole Republic of Letters who is more thoroughly sensible of, and more charmed with the just encomiums which have been given to your Majesty by all the learned world. I can with truth affirm that I can still repeat all the passages of *Alaric* (1) which relate to your Majesty, whose august name shines from all quarters. So that I would be the farthest in the world, from either saying or thinking any thing which I apprehended to be contrary to the respect which is due to so great a Queen. My sorrow therefore was exceeding great, when I understood that some persons, who have the honour to serve your Majesty, had judged me guilty. I immediately endeavoured to justify myself, and I am informed that your Majesty has been pleased to declare, that you are satisfied in the main with my defence. This is my greatest consolation; and I am very much persuaded, that it will not be more difficult for me to demonstrate my innocence entirely, when it shall please your Majesty to lay your commands upon me.

"The second Letter which I received upon this subject, acquaints me with a thing which your Majesty desires I should make public. It is, that your Majesty renounced the Religion in which you was born, *as soon as you attained the years of discretion.* If your Majesty command me I will also publish this new explanation; but I was of opinion, that since I have done myself the honour, by the advice of one of your servants, to send to your Majesty the copy of a Letter, and at the same time to pay to your Majesty my most humble homage, it was my duty to wait for your Majesty's commands. I most humbly beg that your Majesty will be pleased to pardon all that may have escaped me, which has given occasion to judge amiss of my intentions; and I protest to your Majesty with the utmost sincerity, that my strongest passion is to testify to all the world the admiration, veneration, and profound submission, with which I am, &c."

(1) *Scudery has composed a pompous Panegyric on Queen Christina, in the XIth Book of his Poem called Alaric ou Rome Vaincuë.*

The Queen upon the 14th of December 1686, wrote to him the following answer:

Mr Bayle. I have received your excuses, and am willing that you should know by this Letter that I am satisfied with them. I am obliged to the zeal of the person, who gave you occasion of writing to me; for I am very glad to know you. You express so much respect and affection for me, that I pardon you sincerely; and I would have you know, that nothing gave me offence but that remainder of Protestantism, of which you accused me. I am very delicate on that head, because no body can suspect me of it, without lessening my Glory, and injuring me in the most sensible manner. You would do well if you should even acquaint the public with the mistake you have made, and with your regret for it. This is all that remains to be done by you, in order to deserve my being entirely satisfied with you.

As

1686. *As to the Letter which you have sent me, it is mine without doubt, and since you tell me that it is printed, you will do me a pleasure if you send me some copies of it. As I fear nothing in France, so neither do I fear any thing at Rome. My fortune, my blood, and even my life are entirely devoted to the service of the Church; but I flatter no body, and will never speak any thing but the truth. I am obliged to those who have been pleased to publish my letter, for I do not at all disguise my sentiments. I thank God they are too noble, and too honourable to be disowned. However, it is not true that this Letter was written to one of my Ministers. As I have every where enemies, and persons who envy me, so I in all places have friends and servants; and I have possibly as many in France, notwithstanding of the court, as any where in the world. This is purely the truth, and you may regulate yourself accordingly.*

But you shall not get off so cheap as you imagine. I will enjoin you a penance; which is, that you will henceforth take the trouble of sending me all curious books that shall be published in Latin, French, Spanish, or Italian, on whatever subject or science, provided they are worthy of being looked into. I do not even except Romances or Satires; and above all if there are any books of Chymistry, I desire you may send them to me as soon as possible. Do not forget likewise to send me your Journal. I shall order that you shall be paid for whatever you lay out, do but send me an accompt of it. This will be the most agreeable and important service that can be done me. May God prosper you.

CHRISTINA ALEXANDRA.

1687. It now only remained that Mr Bayle should acquaint the public with the mistake he had made and with his regret for it, in order to merit that Princess's entire satisfaction. This he did in the beginning of his Journal of the month of January 1687. " We have been informed to our incredible satisfaction, says he, that the
" QUEEN OF SWEDEN having seen the ninth Article of the Journal of August
" 1686, has been pleased to be satisfied with the explanation which we gave there.
" Properly it was only the words *remainder of Protestantism*, which had the misfortune
" to offend her Majesty; for as her Majesty is very delicate on that subject, and de-
" sires that all the world should know, that after having carefully examined the dif-
" ferent Religions, she has found none to be true but the Roman Catholic, and that
" she has heartily embraced it, it was injurious to her glory to give occasion
" for the least suspicion of her sincerity. We are therefore very sorry that we have
" made use of an expression, which has been understood in a sense so very diffe-
" rent from our intention, and we would have been very far from making use of
" it, if we had forseen that it was liable to any ambiguity: for besides the respect
" which we, together with all the world owe to so GREAT A QUEEN, who has
" been the admiration of the universe from her earliest days, we join with the ut-
" most zeal in that particular obligation which all men of letters are under to do
" her homage, because of the honour she has done the sciences by being pleased
" thoroughly to examine their beauties, and to protect them in a distinguishing
" manner."

Thus Mr Bayle extricated himself out of this affair with honour, and had the address not only to appease a provoked Queen, but likewise to procure marks of her favour. She very soon had the unwelcome news of his not being able to perform the *penance* she was pleased to *impose* upon him. He sunk under the weight of an insupportable labour. Besides his public and private lectures, he was employed in composing his Journal, a task which alone required the labour of many persons. The Composition of his *Philosophical Commentary* quite exhausted his strength. On the 16th of February 1687, he was seized with a Fever, which hindered him from finishing the Journal for that month. But as he hoped that this indisposition would be attended with no bad consequences, he gave notice on the back of the title page, " That sore eyes and a slight fever, which had left him several times, and re-
" turned as soon as he attempted to resume his studies, did at last oblige him
" to publish the Journal for this month incompleat, and to acquaint the public
" likewise that the Journal for the month of March should appear very soon."
But his Fever, attended with a head-ach, encreased to such a degree that he was obliged to give over that work. He engaged Mr de Beauval to continue it, and Mr de Beauval began that Continuation, which was printed at Rotterdam by Mr Leers, with the month of September 1687, under the title of *The History of the Works of the Learned* (1). " Ever since the month of April last, says he in the
" preface, the Author of the *Republic of Letters* having being indisposed, and af-
" flicted with pains in his head, which Mr Balzac would call the pangs of his beau-
" tiful productions, proposed to me that I should continue his work, which he was
" by this means forced to give over. I confess that possibly being flattered by my
" vanity upon the account of his having singled me out upon such an occasion,
" I accepted the task without making all the reflexions that such an undertaking
" deserved. I believed that his choice would supply both the place of merit, and
" of excuse with the public, and so resolved to make some attempts at least. Since
" I have entered into this detail, adds he, people would no doubt likewise know
" why

(1) Histoire des Ouvrages des Sçavans.

xxxvi   THE LIFE OF Mʀ BAYLE.

" why I have not continued this work under the same title, that Mr Bayle made   1687.
" use of. I own that this would have been more natural: but my particular at-
" tachments to Rotterdam, the great plenty of the best books which are to be had
" at Mr Leers's, together with some other reasons which it is not necessary to
" mention here, made me think it more proper to change it. After all I thought
" it best to treat the public as we do those who are afflicted with the loss of a person
" very dear to them, whom we must never carry to those places, which may bring
" to mind, or awaken the ideas of the object of their grief. The public would have
" always in the *News from the Republic of Letters*, sought after the illustrious Au-
" thor who gave them birth, and the same title ill supported, would only have served
" to redouble their sorrow for the loss of so inimitable a person."

In the mean time, the Sieur Desbordes, who had printed the *News from the Republic of Letters*, caused them to be continued by Mr Larroque, and some other
persons, until the month of August of the same year 1687, and Mr Barin, a
French Minister, composed them without any assistannce from the month of September to the month of April 1689.

We have seen what pains Mr Bayle was at, that he might not be thought the
author of the *Philosophical Commentary*. He endeavoured even to deceive his friends,
(1) Letter   " These gentlemen at London, says he to Mr Lenfant (1), have a strange itch of
of the 3d   " printing. The public ascribe to them a *Philosophical Commentary* on these words of
February,   " St Luke *compel them to come in*, wherein under pretence of attacking Popish per-
1687. pag.   " secution they aim at establishing a toleration for the Socinians." He feigned that
281, 282.   this *Commentary* came from London, because some Ministers among the Refugees,
who lived there at this time, were thought to be great friends to Toleration, and had
even rendered themselves suspected of Socinianism. Notwithstanding all this he was
still suspected to be the author of it. To put a stop to this suspicion he published on the
(2) There   back of the title-page of the Journal for the month of April 1687 (2), that " certain
are some   " persons, ill-disposed towards the author of the *General Criticism on Mr Maimbourg*,
Copies   " having affected to ascribe to him the *Philosophical Commentary* on the words *compel*
where this   " *them to come in*, he thought himself obliged to complain of this bad office, and
is not to   " to declare that he will look upon all persons as persecutors with regard to him,
be found.   " who shall continue to spread abroad a conjecture so opposite as this is to all the
" rules of Criticism. One might as well, adds he, ascribe Voiture's Letters to Bal-
" zac, or those of Baudius to Blondel."

The Philosophical Commentary did not please Mr Jurieu; and how was it possible for him to relish a book wherein mildness, moderation, or, to say it in one word,
Toleration, was so strongly established. He undertook to refute it, and gave to
his answer the following title, *The rights of the two Sovereigns in matters of Religion,
Conscience, and the Prince*. *In opposition to the indifferency of Religions and universal
Toleration, against a book intituled a Philosophical Commentary on these words of the*
(3) Des   *Parable*, *Compel them to come in* (3). He sets out under the character of a novice in
Droits des   writing, who in obedience to the *commands* of a friend, and out of *vexation* at that
deux Sou-   book, *was a going to be an author in spite of nature and himself*. Afterwards he gives
verains en   his friend his opinion concerning the Commentary, *That it is an original and not a
matiere de   translation*. *That it is of French and not of English extraction*. He adds, *That it is not
Religion,   the work of one single person*. " This appears, says he, to be the work of a cabal,
la Con-   " and a conspiracy against the truth; nothing is more unequal than the stile of it.
science &   " In the first part the expressions are clear and pretty strong, but there are passages
le Prince.   " in the second where one finds a confusion, and obscurities which do not seem to
Pour dé-   " proceed from the same genius that wrote the first. The pretended Translator
truire le   " affects sometimes to make use of old French words, which are not now in use
dogme de   " among good writers; but his fraud is a little too gross, for elsewhere he shows
l'indiffe-   " that he understands French well enough to write more correctly." But in the
rence des   advice to the reader he affirms downright *That the authors of the Philosophical Com-
Religions   mentary are French Divines, and consequently Refugees*. When Mr Jurieu wanted after-
& de la   wards to lay the composition of this book as a crime to Mr Bayle's charge,
tolerance   Mr Bayle always brought him back to this declaration, that it is the work of cer-
univer-   tain French Divines. Observe how he endeavours to soften this false judgment in
selle, con- a satirical piece which he published against a great many French Ministers, and
tre un   particularly against Mr Bayle, in the year 1691. " In the year which followed
Livre in-   " our dispersion, says he (4), there appeared a wicked book intituled, *The Philoso-*
taire Phi-   " *phical Commentary*, &c. wherein the pernicious doctrine of the indifferency of
losophi-   " Religions and Doctrines of the Christian Religion is maintained in so rash and
que sur   " bold a manner, as even goes the length of insolence. I can truly say that this
ces paroles " book wounded and struck me in a very sensible manner. One could easily guess
de la para- " from the third volume of the General Criticism, whence it had it's original. But
bole, Con-   " the stile, and many other circumstances, made us believe that it was the work
trains les   " of a cabal, and published by several persons in concert."
d'entrer.
(4) Apo-   Mr Bayle had finished the third part of his Philosophical Commentary, and given
logie du   it to the Printer before he fell sick. The impression of it was finished before the
Sieur Ju-   end of February, but he did not receive any copies of it 'till the 20th of June.
rieu, p. 4.
col. 2.   2   It

THE LIFE OF Mr BAYLE.

1687. It is intitled, *A Philosophical Commentary on these Words of JESUS CHRIST*, compel them to come in. Part the third. Containing a refutation of the Apology which St Augustin has made for those who use violence in making converts. At Canterbury, by Thomas Litwel, 1687 (1). Here two Letters of St Augustin are refuted, the one wrote to a Donatist Bishop named Vincentius, who had let that Father know how much he was surprized at his inconstancy, having formerly been of opinion that the authority of the secular power ought not to be made use of against Heretics, but only the word of God and persuasion; whereas now he maintained quite the contrary. The other is addressed to Bonifacius, who was a Tribune in Africa, wherein St Augustin pretends that it is lawful to employ the secular arm to destroy Heretics. The Archbishop of Paris had ordered these two Letters to be printed in 1685, with a long Preface intitled, *The Conformity of the conduct of the Church of France in reclaiming the Protestants, with that of the Church of Afric to bring the Donatists into the Catholic Church* (2). This is likewise the title of the whole book. Mr Bayle had refuted some passages of this Preface in his preliminary Discourse. He doth not here confine himself to the two Letters which I have mentioned, but likewise answers what St Augustin has said on this subject in some other Letters.

As soon as he had seen Mr Jurieu's answer, he wrote a letter to his Bookseller, dated from London the 15/25th of May 1687. "If you have (says he) still time "enough, (and it is no matter though you have already sold some copies) I de- "fire you to publish what follows at the beginning of the third part." He says afterwards, that he has just read the treatise *Of the rights of the two sovereigns, &c.* against *a book intitled a Philosophical Commentary, &c.* and that he finds it an unsuccessful and very weak attack on that Commentary. "The author, (adds he) owns in "the beginning, that in spite of himself and of nature, his Chagrin, and the "desire of one of his friends, are going to make him an author. One "must have very little judgment to make such a confession. Chagrin ought to "have no share in the composition of any work. . . . . . . His performance is "faulty in those very places which most essentially require solidity, since it goes "entirely upon a false state of the question, so that he fights against a shadow, "I mean against an opinion which he falsely imputes to me. He is at prodi- "gious pains to prove that men frequently sin and offend God, while they act "according to the light of their conscience. Who denies that? have not I "said so very distinctly in more places than one? he accuses me likewise of intro- "ducing an indifferency of Religions, whereas on the contrary, there never was "any doctrine more opposite to that indifferency, than this which lays it down "as a principle, that we ought always to act according to our consciences. Fal- "lacies of the same sort prevail in the passage where he treats of the legislative "power of Sovereigns in matters of Religion. As for quotations from the scripture, "they are very frequent in his book, but for the most part misunderstood, and "in the manner of St Augustin. To conclude, this author has officiously meddled "with a subject he doth not understand, and has through the whole been guilty "of the fallacy of not proving what was the point in question."

Mr Bayle's indisposition still continuing he resolved to try a change of air, and drink the waters of Aix la Chapelle. He left Rotterdam upon the eighth day of August, and went to Cleves, where he arrived the 13th of that month. Next day he went to lodge at the house of Mr Ferrand, Minister of the Castle of Cleves, and continued there 'till the 15th of September, on which he passed to Bois le Duc, and from thence to Aix la Chapelle, in company with Mr Pielat, Minister of Rotterdam, and Mr Farjon, Minister of Vaals. He returned to Rotterdam upon the 18th of October: but he was obliged to repose himself for some months longer; as he writes to Mr Constant in a Letter of the 22d of March 1688. "It is more "than thirteen months (says he (3), since I fell sick, and all the while have "only lingered and languished, and I now only begin at the return of this spring, "to be able to take a little literary exercise. After my return from Aix la "Chapelle, where I had been to drink the waters, I found your son here. . . . . "but unluckily for me, I was not able to speak much without bringing upon me "a return of my slow Fever, and this has been my continual misfortune during "my illness: if I entered never so little into conversation, I was the worse for "it." He gives Mr Lenfant a more particular account in a Letter of the 20th of July. "You do me a great deal of honour (says he (4), remembering, as "you are pleased to do, a person in a manner dead to the world, and blotted "out of the memory of the living. . . . . I have made a Journey to Cleves, "another to Aix, and upon my return hither, I have, during the whole winter, "immersed myself in the greatest Quietism imaginable, without either reading or "writing. At last, after I thought myself sufficiently reposed, I re-assumed my "Philosophical Lectures, first my public only, and afterwards likewise my pri- "vate ones; but with regard to other matters, I observed and do still keep myself "in a full and absolute inaction. . . . . . . I have not as yet returned to my "books, nay I do not so much as run through the Literary Journals; and

VOL. I.   k   "out

" out of fear of being tempted to break this agreeable charm of indolence, very 1687.
" seldom visit the bookfellers, so that I am quite ignorant what new things they
" have got. I only hear by chance sometimes that this or the other book is
" come out."

All the men of letters were afflicted at Mr Bayle's illness: and they were overjoyed to hear of his recovery. Mr du Tot de Ferrare, a Counsellor in the Parliament of Rouen, a man of great worth, and a great master in the lapidary stile (1), testified his joy upon that occasion, by the following beautiful inscription:

(1) See his Elogy in the Memoires pour l'Histoire des Sciences & des beaux Arts, December 1704, Art. iv. p. 440. and the following of the Dutch Edition.

In
Doctissimi Bælii
Sanitatem restitutam

SOTERIA.

QUÆ TE MORI VETAT GLORIA,
ÆGROTARE PROHIBET.
OMNIBUS CARUS ET UTILIS
SCRIPTORES
CRITICA FACE ELUCIDASTI,
CENSORIA NOTA EMENDASTI.
QUÆSITOR URNAM MOVENS
MAGNUM IN NOMEN ITUROS
ÆTERNITATI
PRONUBA MANU DICASTI.
LABORIBUS TUIS ALIENOS ABSUMIS,
DELICIIS NOSTRIS NUSQUAM ABSUMENDUS.
IN HOC VENERANDUS
QUOD NEMINEM CONTEMPSISTI:
IN HOC VERENDUS
QUOD NEMINEM FORMIDASTI:
DIGNUS QUI VERITATIS ANNOS EXÆQUES.
QUI LABANTEM SUSTENTAS COGNATAM VERITATI
LIBERTATEM.
NON AD UNIUS UTILITATEM REGIONIS NATUS,
ITA EXILIUM TOLERAS
UT VIDEARIS OPTASSE:
ITA CUNCTOS EMINUS COMINUS REFICIS,
UT VIX CREDARIS ULLIBI ABESSE.
THEATRUM ERUDITIONIS CIRCUMDUCTILE
FACTUS EST ORBI.
SUBSELLIA QUÆ DICENDO FATIGARE NON POTES,
TE SILENTEM FERRE
TE QUIESCENTE QUIESCERE
NE SPERA.

VALE, VIVE, SCRIBE.

ENCÆNIA RENOVATÆ FACUNDIÆ
FAUSTIS LITERATORUM ACCLAMATIONIBUS
CELEBRANTUR.

Mr Bayle had once a design to leave Rotterdam. The death of Mr Paets, and 1688. the violent temper of Mr Jurieu, had made him weary of it: accordingly he desired the famous Mr Abbadie, who was then at Berlin, to procure him some establishment in that City. He knew that the Elector of Brandenbourg gave a generous protection to the French Refugees; and besides he had several friends at Berlin. Mr Abbadie upon this addressed himself to the Duchess of Schomberg, who

THE LIFE OF MR BAYLE.

1688. who being well acquainted with Mr Bayle's merit, expressed a great satisfaction at his design of coming to Berlin, and promised to engage the Marechal to speak of it to the Elector. But that great Prince fell sick about this time, and his death (1), a little after, put a stop to the effects of that Lady's good inclinations towards Mr Bayle.

(1) *He died the 9th of May* 1688.

Mr Bayle published the following Advertisement, under the name of the bookseller, on the reverse of the title-page of the News from the Republic of Letters, for the month of October 1687. "We have received a Letter dated from London, by which we are informed that John Fox of Bruggs is the real name annagrammatized of the author of the *Philosophical Commentary*, and that he will very soon give us occasion to speak of the answer, which he has in the press, to the treatise *Of the rights of the two Sovereigns.*" This was in order to prepare the public for a continuation of the *Philosophical Commentary*, which he designed to publish very soon. In effect, it appeared soon after under this title: *A Supplement to the Philosophical Commentary upon these words of JESUS CHRIST*, compel them to come in. *Wherein, among other things, the only refuge that was left to the adversaries is quite destroyed, by demonstrating that Heretics have an equal right with the Orthodox to persecute.* Something is likewise inserted concerning the nature and origin of error. At Hamburg, for *Thomas Litwell* 1686 (2). The author in a long Preface acquaints us, that having heard of a book intituled *The true System of the Church* (3), wherein his opinion concerning Toleration, and the rights of conscience were attacked, and also that the treatise *Of the Rights of the two Sovereigns*, was not the first essay of a young author, but the work of one who had appeared frequently in print, he had resolved to answer them both, and to divide his book into three parts. The first to contain some additions which seemed to him very proper for ever to silence all the advocates for constraint. The second to contain an answer to three chapters of the *true System of the Church*, wherein a doctrine contrary to his is maintained, and an answer to all the objections of the author of *the Rights of the two Sovereigns*, and likewise to every thing that he has advanced directly in favour of his opinion. He adds, that he had laboured so diligently in the execution of this design, that he had finished it before the end of December 1687, and had sent the manuscript to the printer: but having found afterwards that this work would be too bulky, he thought himself obliged to suppress the two last parts, and accordingly "he had ordered the bookseller to put a stop to the impression, of it having happened very luckily that they were not as yet come to what he had said concerning the affairs of England, the Penal Laws, and the taking away of the Test, &c. subjects which were not then seasonable, considering the turn that things were likely to take." He assigns several causes of the encrease of the bulk of his book, and among the others the following: "It has proceeded partly (says he) from this, that the gentlemen who translated my English Original, could not as they pretended, strip it of it's native dress without making use of a diffused stile; they have likewise diverted themselves by mixing a great many different things together, sometimes following one system and at other times another, sometimes imitating the manner of thinking of certain authors, and not their stile, and at other times the stile of others, and not their manner of thinking; designing by this means to make a medley of it, which has caused the Readers, as they pretend, to ascribe my Commentary to a good many different people, without ever guessing at them or me, though my name was only concealed under an Anagram, which deviated but very little from the rules. And they make a diversion of concealing themselves so successfully, and of putting the searchers after the fathers of anonymous and pseudonymous books upon a wrong scent." The rest of the Preface is employed in shewing from a passage of the *true System of the Church*, that the writer of it agrees entirely with Mr Bayle's opinion, and consequently that Mr Bayle is orthodox, and that it is therefore this writer's business to answer himself, and to answer the author of the *Rights of the two Sovereigns*. In this manner Mr Bayle makes Mr Jurieu, who is author of both these books, contradict himself. He adds afterwards some reflexions which serve to confirm what he has said in this Supplement.

(2) *Supplement du Commentaire Philosophique sur ces paroles de Jesus-Christ, contrain-les d'entrer. Où entre autres choses l'on acheve de ruiner la seul échapatoire qui restoit aux adversaires, en démontrant le droit égal des Hérétiques pour persecuter à celui des Orthodoxes. On parle aussi de la nature & origine des erreurs. A Hambourg pour Tho. Litwel, 1688.*

(3) *Le vrai Systeme de l'Eglise. This Book appeared in 1686.*

(4) *Reponse d'un Nouveau Converti à la Lettre d'un Refugié. Pour servir d'addition au livre de Dom Denys de Ste. Marthe, intitulé, Réponse aux Plaintes des Protestants. Suivant l'Imprimé à Paris chez Etienne Noel, à la place de Sorbonne, 1689.*

(5) *Réponse aux plaintes des Protestant touchant la prétendue persecution de France. Où l'on expose le sentiment de Calvin, & de tous les plus celebres Ministres, sur le peines dûes aux Hérétiques.*

At this time Mr Leers was printing Mr Furetiere's *Dictionary*; and the author having died while it was in the press, the Bookseller desired Mr Bayle to write a *Preface* to it. It is an excellent piece.

1689. In the beginning of the year 1689, there appeared a pamphlet entituled, *An Answer of a New Convert to a Letter from a Refugee, by way of supplement to Father de Ste. Marthe's book intituled, An Answer to the complaints of the Protestants.* According to the copy printed at Paris by Stephen Noel in the place de Sorbonne 1689 (4). Father de Ste. Marthe, a Benedictin of the Congregation of St Maur, had published at Paris in 1688, a book intituled *An Answer to the Complaints of the Protestants concerning the pretended persecution in France. Wherein the opinion of Calvin, and of the most famous Ministers concerning the punishment due to Heretics, is shewn* (5). Here he pretended that the Reformed complained without reason of the rigour that had been exercised against them, since they must have been used with much greater severity,

i

xxxix

severity, if they had put the laws of the first Christian Emperors in execution, or 1689. followed the maxims of the Reformers themselves, who teach that Heretics ought to be put to death. He reproached them likewise for taking up arms in defence of their Religion, and accused the Protestants in general of being fond of Independency, and enemies to Monarchy. The *Answer of a new Convert*, which serves for a supplement to this piece, is dated from Paris the 20th of December; and the *Letter of a Refugee* is dated from Amsterdam the 6th of the same month. The Refugee, who had retired to Holland after a tedious imprisonment, puts the new Convert in mind of the disputes they had formerly had, particularly concerning the burning of Servetus, and the rising in arms of the Protestants. He says that his friend always referred him to Father de Sainte Marthe's book; and adds, that instead of engaging himself in discussing all these facts, "he chose rather to employ his time in prayer, "and in meditation on the glorious promises which God has made to the Reformed "in the Apocalypse." But that since his arrival in Holland he has had an opportunity of consulting some of the most learned men of the party, who had furnished him with the four following answers with regard to the affair of Servetus. "I. That at worst it was only a fault of particular persons, the party not having "in the least meddled in that process. II. That if some Doctors have formerly "wrote in justification of such proceedings, they have made no proselytes; and "that it is a long while since they have been cured of these violent sentiments "among the Reformed. III. That the doctrine which some people might have had "on this subject, concerned so small a number of Heretics, that it ought not to "serve for a recrimination to those, whose cruelties are so general. IV. And lastly, "That the practice of the Reformed sufficiently justifies them; for since Ser- "vetus's time we do not find that they have punished the Socinians who have been "among them, or that they have ever extended Calvin's Theory to the Papists." And as to what regards subjects taking up arms upon account of Religion, he says that very learned and very pious men have assured him that it is lawful, when subjects have no other intention by it but to procure themselves the liberty of following the light of their conscience, being ready to shew their fidelity to their Prince in all other matters: and therefore that the Reformed ought not to be ashamed of what their ancestors may have said or done in that respect. He sends him the two last *Pastoral Letters* of Mr Jurieu, and exhorts him to return to the Protestant Church. "You cannot choose a more proper time, says he, to go out from the midst "of spiritual Babylon. You may possibly ruin yourself by continuing in it, in time as "well as to all eternity; and the great success with which God has already favoured the "holy and heroic expedition of the most accomplished Prince who is at present "upon earth, shows us that the time is at last come when the true Church shall "enjoy a flourishing prosperity. You understand me, you know that I do not "only mean that all goes ill for you in England, but likewise that God has struck "your Kings, and above all the Pope, with the most extraordinary stupidity "that ever was known, and the most fruitful in blunders."

The new Convert begins his answer by criticizing one of the Pastoral Letters, and afterwards examines the four answers which the Refugee had been furnished with, concerning Servetus. He reduces them to these four questions. "I. Whether "the punishment of Servetus proceeded from the ill humour of a particular person, or "if it was not generally approved of by the Protestants? II. Whether the Pro- "testants now have different sentiments from those of the last age concerning the "punishment of Heretics? III. Whether the doctrine of the Reformers concerning "the punishment of Heretics, can be justified by saying that it only concerned a small "number of Heretics, in comparison of the great number of erroneous people whom "the Catholic Doctors think punishable? IV. Whether the practice of the Cal- "vinists with regard to the punishment of Heretics can justify the doctrines of their "divines upon that subject." The new Convert answers in the negative to all these questions; and in refuting the second, he refutes at the same time what Mr Bayle in his *General Criticism*, and Mr Jurieu in his *Apology for the Reformation*, had answered to Mr Maimbourg, upon the subject of Servetus; and what Mr Rou, in his *Seduction éludée*, had answered to the Bishop of Meaux upon the same head. Hitherto he preserves a good deal of moderation; but he attacks the Protestants with great violence in the sequel of this pamphlet, intituled, *Reflexions on the Civil-Wars of the Protestants, and the present Invasion of England* (1). He says that the Revolution in England has not at all surprised him, since he knows what that Religion is capable of, which is wont to stir up people to Rebellion. He adds that this event is an apology for the conduct of those Princes who have purged their kingdom from such a sect; and that the quickness of this change, which the Protestants boast of, is a proof that the spring of this affair was not their fear of being oppressed by the Catholics; that King James was dethroned for no other reason than because he would not espouse the passions of the enemies of France, who were envious of her prosperity, but that all the Leagues formed against Lewis XIV served only to increase his glory, and to heighten the idea of his formidable power. He maintains that the Catholic Princes have given greater examples of Toleration than the Protestants;

(1) Reflexions sur les guerres civiles des Protestans, & la presente invasion de l'Angleterre.

1689. testants; and insults the whole body of the Refugees upon the account of the lofty hopes of some among them whom he represents as waiting, like the Jews, for a Messiah who shall conquer all the Popish Kings, and enter Rome in triumph. He taxes the French Protestants with vanity in considering their party in France as the whole Protestant party, and the ruin of their Churches as the ruin of the Protestant Religion. He accuseth them of feeding themselves with visions, dreams, and chimerical interpretations of the Apocalypse, as if the Edict of Nants had been the design and principal object of the inspired Oracles in that sacred book. And lastly he accuseth them of being animated by a *spirit of Rebellion and of Satire*, and of being seized with an *inveterate and incurable disease, of rebelling against their lawful Sovereigns on the one hand, and on the other of filling the whole world with the most infamous calumnies, that ever were imagined*. To this little book is prefixed an Advertisement of the Dutch Bookseller, wherein it is said that the author of this Answer had sent it from Paris in 4to to the author of the Letter: that it was not doubted but Mr Pelisson had a considerable share in it, though the stile of it is different from his, because the Letter which gave occasion to it, was written to one of his intimate friends. It is added, that a very learned author was labouring incessantly at an Answer to it, wherein the public would see the most delicate questions in Morality, especially with regard to these times, treated in the most agreeable and exact manner, and that it was hoped it would be published in a few months.

Mr Bayle mentions this piece in one of his Letters to Mr Rou. " They have cri- " ticised both you and me at Paris lately, says he (1), but not so severely as they " have done Mr Jurieu, in an *Answer of a new Convert, &c.* which they pretend " is wrote by a Disciple or Proselyte of Mr Pelisson. If Mr Pelisson has any " share in it, he must needs have given credit to a very false report, which might " possibly even have reached his ears, that I am the author of a Letter which was " printed at Amsterdam in answer to his *Chimera's of Mr Jurieu* (2), for Mr Pe- " lisson has spoken very civilly of me in his last book; whereas this *New Con-* " *vert* treats me harshly. The piece I am talking of, is short and indifferently " wrote; but very injurious to the party. They have reprinted it in this Country." Mr Bayle gives this account of it from the bookseller's advertisement; but all that was said of it there was a mere feint. This piece was not printed at Paris, and the Answer which the bookseller promised, never appeared.

If we consider this performance as a continuation of the *Philosophical Commentary*, we will be ready to believe that Mr Bayle is the author of it. It is natural to suppose that having seen with grief that his *Commentary*, which was designed to attack the persecutions of the Church of Rome, had been represented by the Ministers as a pernicious book; he may have made use of the way of recrimination in the person of a new Convert, to force them to declare for Toleration, or to give up the cause to the Catholic writers. Besides it is plain, that the author of it strikes particularly at Mr Jurieu, the principal advocate for constraint in religious matters, he laughs at his Interpretations of the Apocalypse, and the chimerical hopes with which he fed the Refugees. He has him likewise in view in a sort of digression, which we find at the end of it, under the title of *Reflections on the Civil-Wars of the Protestants, &c.* as it would be easy to show.

However, in Holland this piece was thought to be Mr Pelisson's (3). They were the more easily persuaded of this, because it was known that he had laboured much in the Conversions, and had published some treatises of Controversy, under the title of *Reflexions sur les differens de la Religion*. Mr Jurieu ascribed this Answer to him without hesitation [G]; and as the Protestants were charged with maintaining

(1) *Letter of the 24th of February 1689, p. 301.*

(2) *It is a piece consisting of 8 pages in 4o, intituled Reponse à l'Auteur des Chimeres de Mr Jurieu.*

(3) *Mr Pelisson disowned it in the Histoire des Ouvrages des Scavans, February 1690, p. 276.*

(d) *Lettre écrite de Suisse en Hollande pour suppléer au defaut de la Réponse que l'on a volt promise de donner, à un certain Ouvrage que Mr Pelisson a publié sous le nom d'un Nouveau Converti, &c.*

(e) *In the month of May 1691.*

(f) *See the Letters to Mr Larsant of the 25th of May, and to Mr Constant of the 2d of July 1690, with the Remarks, pag. 321, 322, 325, 326.*

(g) *Apologie du Sieur Jurieu, pag. 24. al. 11.*

[G] *Mr Jurieu ascribed this Answer to him without hesitation*] In one of his *Pastoral Letters*, which contains some *Reflexions upon the Libels which came* (a) *Pastoral Letter of the 1st of April 1689, pag. 217. cap. 1. of the 4to edition.* *from France on occasion of the affairs of the present time*; after having spoke of the books which were published in France against the Protestants, he adds (a), " We see lately published a Libel under the " title of *An Answer of a new Convert to a Letter* " *from a Refugee, to serve for a Supplement to Dom* " *Denis de St Marthe's book* (b). These gentlemen

(b) *Reponse d'un Nouveau Converti à la Lettre d'un Refugié pour servir d'addition au livre de Dom Denis de Ste Marthe.* " may pretend to hide themselves under feigned " names, they are always found out. We have no " new Convert who can write in that manner, and " with that force upon the subject. One must be " confirmed in a spirit of persecution, and full of " the old leaven to write so. Be not therefore deceived " in this matter, it is not a new Convert (c) but an " old scholar of the Jesuits, who has made great pro- " ficiency in that school." Mr Huet, a Minister and a Refugee, who lived at this time at Dort, and who afterwards went to the Hague, wrote an Answer to

(c) *Mr Pelisson had embraced the Romish Religion in 1670.* this piece which was very much esteemed. It came out under this title: *A Letter written from Switzerland to Holland, to supply the place of an Answer which lies* been promised to a certain book published by Mr Pelisson, under the name of *a new Convert, &c* (d). But as he maintained a political Toleration, and in defending what Mr Bayle had said concerning the punishment of Servetus he had given up Mr Jurieu, the latter was so piqued at it, that he accused him before the Synod of Leyden (e) which was composed of his creatures, and got him suspended from his Ministry. He inveighed afterwards against him in his Libels, and particularly in his *Tableau du Socinianisme*, where he endeavours to establish persecution (f). However it was not Mr Huet he aimed at; Mr Bayle was the person he really had in view. By procuring a condemnation of Mr Huet's opinion concerning Toleration, he wanted to render Mr Bayle odious, whom he looked upon as the author of the *Philosophical Commentary*. He durst not attack him, and so he vented all his spleen upon Mr Huet, and sacrificed him to his rage. He himself has let us into this secret, in recounting his prouess against the Heterodox, with all the ill nature he was master of. " A little while after, says he (g), the *Philosophical* " *Commentary* appeared. And it was the labour of " this book that had almost cracked his brain. I " then

xlii THE LIFE OF MR BAYLE. 1689.

maintaining that it was lawful to make use of the sword to punish Heretics, he says the world would soon see what would be their conduct in that respect. "The first "part of this work, says he, is employed to prove that even according to our "own principles it is lawful to persecute Heretics, and to pursue them even unto "death. God forbid that ever we should go to that extremity. But at least we de- "sire this author to remember this, if we should one day be in a condition of "humbling and depressing his party. If it is lawful to kill Heretics and idola- "trous Christians, with much more reason it must be lawful to mortify them without "forcing their consciences, by all means which may make them reflect upon their "blindness. Time will show which party will henceforth have most occasion for "the moderation of the other."

(1) Bau- val, Ré- ponse à l'Avis de Mr Jurieu, p. 33, 34, 39, 40.

(2) Idem, Lettre sur les diffe- rends de Mr Jurieu & de Mr Bayle, p. 2.

These threatnings were founded upon Mr Jurieu's prophetical System [H]. He had discovered in the Apocalypse, that the persecution of the Reformed in France should cease in 1689, and that the Reformation should be established over all the Kingdom by the King's own authority. The signs and wonders, (says he), that are to be the forerunners of these great events, are already seen in France [I]. If any one doubted of these pretended miracles, he ranked them with the impious and pro- phane [K]. It was upon this score that Mr de Bauval fell under his indignation (1), and that Mr Bayle raised a-fresh all his animosity and resentment (2). But the event showed him that he was mistaken, and then he persuaded himself that the Reformation could not be re-established in France otherwise than by force of arms [L]. This

" then found that the evil was past remedy, but " I could not resolve to break with him entirely, I " satisfied myself with renouncing what they call " openings of the heart, and confidences of friendship. " I believed he was still an honest Pagan (b); In pur- " suing the condemnation of his abominable doc- " trine of the Rights of an erring Conscience in " our synods, a small remain of regard for my for- " mer friendship made me spare his name: especially " seeing there was another name for which I had " less consideration, under which I might carry on " my pursuit."

[H] *These threatnings were founded upon Mr Ju- rieu's prophetical System.*] He had published in 1686 a book intitled, *The Accomplishment of the Prophecies, or the approaching deliverance of the Church. A work wherein it is proved that Popery is the kingdom of Antichrist; that this kingdom is not far from its ruin, and that this ruin is to begin very soon. That the present persecution cannot continue above three years and a half: after which the destruction of Antichrist shall begin, which will be continued 'till the end of this Century, and be finished in the beginning of the next. And at last the reign of Jesus Christ upon earth shall come.* Here he prophesied that the perse- cution of the Reformed in France, could not last above three years and a half. That the Reformation should be established by Royal Authority, and that France should renounce Popery, and the Kingdom should be converted. He added that providence intended to raise that Kingdom very high; that it should arrive to the bright of glory, by building its greatness on the ruins of the Papal Empire; and that the general Refor- mation of France should be brought about without blood (l). Mr Jurieu spoke with so much confidence and so decisive a tone, that he was believed by a great number of the Reformed, both in France and in other Countries. We believe easily what we wish for, and a melancholy and afflicted condition aug- ments our credulity. Several Refugees returned to France to wait there the accomplishment of these great promises. It has been pretended (k) that all this was only an artifice, to engage the Reformed to make an insurrection in France: but Mr Jurieu ima- gined really and sincerely that he had penetrated in- to the profound mysteries of the Apocalypse (l). He looked with admiration upon the prophecies of Dra- bitius, Cotterus, and Christina Poniatovia, and al- most equalled them to the writings of the ancient Prophets.

[I] *The signs and wonders, says he, that are to be the forerunners of these great events are already seen in France.*] He considered as miracles the accounts they had from France at this time, that in Bearn and in the Cevennes, Angels had been heard sing- ing psalms in the air (m); that there was a shep- herdess at Cret in Dauphiné who fell into extasies, during which she spoke many excellent and divine things, and foretold an approaching deliverance (n); that in Dauphiné many hundreds of children had exta-

sies of this kind. "The spirit of God, (said he (o), has "fallen upon the children of that province, in the same "manner in which it has fallen upon the shepherdess "in the neighbourhood of Cret. When that young "girl has seized upon, she declared in the pre- "sence of the judges, that the pains they were at "were to no purpose, that they might put her to "death, but that God would raise up other chil- "dren, who should speak better than she: and this "has come to pass in so wonderful a manner, that "the most blind are obliged to see the finger of "God in it. There are perhaps at this day in one "corner of Dauphiné, without reckoning those in the "other provinces, two or three hundred children who "are seized with extasies, who fall asleep, and during "their sleep declare the wonderful things of God, "pray in an excellent manner, exhort, threaten, pro- "mise, sing the Psalms of David, and even foretel "things to come: and when they awake they re- "turn to their former simplicity. And what is still "more, in the Vivarets the spirit of God has fallen "upon a whole people sleeping and waking, with "signs and wonders, in such sort that since the be- "ginning of the world nothing has been seen like "it, or coming near it. The relation will inform "you of the particulars (p).

[K] *If any one doubted of these pretended miracles, he ranked them with the impious and prophane.*] In the Pastoral Letter which I have just quoted, he treats them as blasphemers, who oppose the spirit of God. "Beware, (says he (q), of that wicked spi- "rit of the world, which opposeth itself to the spirit "of God; and upon this occasion sometimes goes "even to blasphemy. The rashness of those who "who have ridiculed the miracles of the shepherdess, "and of the heavenly voices, which have been heard "by so many faithful witnesses, shall meet with the "just confusion it deserves. I wish that it may be a "saving shame, and that God may not lay this sin "to their charge, but may grant them the favour "of seeing with their eyes, the things foretold by "these preceeding signs. ...... Happy are the wise, "who do not imitate those rash deciders ...... "We do not fear the triumph of those who seeing "the time approaching which is appointed for the "deliverance, insult those who hope for it. The "times and events are in God's hand: they come "to pass when he thinks fitting. We may mistake "in our reckonings, but God is not mistaken in "his." He talked in this manner in the month of March 1689, having seen that nothing of what he had foretold had come to pass.

[L] *But the event showed him that he was mistaken, and then he persuaded himself that the Reformation could not be re-established in France otherwise than by force of arms.*] His *three years and a half,* which commenced at the revocation of the Edict of Nantes, in October 1685, expired in the month of April 1689; and yet no change was seen in France with regard to Religion. This gave people ground to call his

1689. This was his last resource, he turned all his views that way, and in his writings prepared the people for this great revolution [M]. He laboured to prove that the power of princes proceeds from the people, and that there is a mutual contract betwixt the Prince and people (1). He maintains that it is lawful to defend our Religion by force of arms (2). He likewise makes an apology for the Revolution of England, and for King William (3), who was violently attacked in several libels then published in France [N]. There appeared likewise several pieces on this subject composed by Refugees. There were likewise some persons, who abusing the liberty of the press they enjoy in Holland, published romantic and satirical pieces against Lewis XIV, against King James, and against the Queen his consort: but these libels were only relished by the mob, and the greatest part of them were not written by Refugees.

In the heat of this war of political and satirical authors, there appeared towards the end of the month of April 1690, a book entituled, *An important advice to the Refugees, on their approaching return to France. Given for a new year's gift to one of them in 1690. By Mr C. L. A. A. P. D. P. At Amsterdam by James the Censor,* 1690 (4). This book was wrote in form of a Letter to a friend, dated from Paris the first of January 1690. In the beginning the author rallies the Refugees upon the hopes they had conceived of seeing very extraordinary events in 1689. "You " see, (says he), the year 1689 expired without any thing happening very extraordi-" nary. You promised yourselves mighty and wonderful things that year; that it " should be fatal to the Romish Church in general, and more fatal still to France, " that we should see nothing but great crises of affairs, wonderful Revolutions, and " in short every thing most suiting a climacteric year of the world. You have " seen on the contrary every thing go on so naturally, so smoothly, and so alto-" gether of a piece, that it would be hard to find in History a first campaign of " so general a war as this, in the greatest animosity of the parties concerned, " wherein so few remarkable things have fallen out, as in the year 1689. At least " it is certain, that the thing which you looked upon as the most infallible, I mean " your re-establishment, has not happened. I do not say this, (adds he), to insult " you, God forbid; you know my sentiments: you are not ignorant that I always " disapproved the usage you have met with, and I am exceedingly sorry that " France has deprived itself of so many honest people, and so many persons of " merit, who have been obliged to seek shelter in foreign Countries. So that if I " observe with pleasure that the year 1689 has not answered your Predictions, it " is by no means because of the loss you thereby sustain, but because we ought " to be glad for the sake of reason and good sense, that the superstitious confidence " in chimerical calculations, and popular credulity, are belied by such palpable ex-" periences, which may weaken them as much as they would have been confirmed by " events which you expected." After this he congratulates his friend upon the favourable disposition in which the King of France was said to be with regard to the re-establishment of the Reformed, and assures him that in general the most reasonable part of the three estates of the kingdom would approve of allowing them an honest liberty. " But allow me, (continues he), to give one advice to you, and " all your brethren Refugees wherever dispersed, which is to perform a sort of Qua-" rentine before you set a foot into France, in order to purify you from the bad air " you have breathed in the places of your exile, and which has infected you with

"two

(1) *Pastoral Letters of April 15, and May 1, 1689.*

(2) *Letter of Jan. 1, 1689.*

(3) *Letter of May 15, 1689.*

(4) *Avis important aux Refugiez sur leur prochain retour en France. Donné pour Etrennes à l'un d'eux in 1690. Par Monsieur C. L. A. A. P. D. P. A Amsterdam chez Jaques le Censeur, 1690.*

his predictions chimerical, and to laugh at the credulity of those who had given credit to them. He therefore found himself under a necessity of abandoning what he had said concerning the manner in which the Reformation should be established in France. According to his first scheme, that Reformation was to be brought about without violence, without *effusion of blood, by the King's own authority*: but the revolution in England, and the confederacy of so many Princes against France, made him believe that is should triumph there by way of conquest (r); and he declared "that he firmly believed that God " had raised up King William to execute his great " design of abasing and humbling the persecutors in " France (s)." He would needs lend a helping hand himself. "After several nights meditation he con-" trived a sort of pontoons, by means of which they " might land as many troops as they had a mind " in France without much difficulty, and in spite " of the Militia that might be upon the coast (t)."

[M] *In his writings he prepared the people for this great revolution*] He made several reflexions upon the state of affairs in his *Pastoral Letters*, wherein he set forth the wonders of providence, in the present situation of Europe, and particularly of England (u). He exhorted the Reformed in France to be firm and unshaken, and promised them a speedy deliverance. He gave over writing *Pastoral Letters* in the month of July 1689, and in the month following he published a new work, which came out monthly under this title, *Les soupirs de la France Esclave qui aspire après la liberté*. The design of this work was to shew that the ancient liberties of France were lost, and that it was absolutely necessary to reform the government of it, and change it into an Aristocracy.

[N] *The Revolution in England, and King William were violently attacked, in several libels published in France.*] Mr de Vise, besides what he published monthly in his *Mercure Galant*, put out likewise every month a volume concerning the present state of affairs (x). Mr le Noble published also several libels. Father de Ste. Marthe published a book, intituled, *Dialogues concerning the Prince of Orange's enterprize upon England, wherein it is proved that this action fixeth upon the Protestants the character of Antichristianism, with which Mr Jurieu reproacheth the Church of Rome.* Paris, 1689. And no less a man than the famous Mr Arnauld would needs engage in this affair, in a piece intitled, *The true Picture of William Henry of Nassau, a new Absalom, a new Herod, a new Cromwell, a new Nero.* Mr Jurieu refuted this last, in a book printed at the Hague 1689, under the title of *An Apology for their most Serene Britannic Majesties against an infamous Libel, entituled The true Picture of William Henry of Nassau,* &c.

(r) *Chimere demontrée, p. lvi, lvii.*

(s) *Pastoral Letter of July 1, 1689, pag. 173, col. 2.*

(t) *Chimere demontrée, p. lviii, lix.*

(u) *See the Pastoral Letters of the 15th of February, pag. 93, of the 1st of March, pag. 101, and of the 15th of March, pag. 107 of the year 1689.*

(x) *Sur les Affaires du tems.*

"two very dangerous and hateful distempers, the one is a spirit of satire, the other 1689.
"a sort of republican spirit, which tends to nothing less than to introduce Anarchy
"into the world, the greatest plague of civil society. These are two points upon
"which I take the liberty to speak to you as a friend."

Concerning the first point, which regards *satirical writings*, he makes bitter complaints of the many Libels full of calumnies and scandalous stories which were spread abroad every where, and wherein the Refugees seem, says he, to breathe nothing but vengeance. He lays them to the charge of the whole body of the Refugees, because they had not in a public manner disowned them. He even goes back as far as their ancestors, and accuseth them of having first introduced the licence of diffamatory Libels. He maintains that this satirical rage is an infallible mark of Heresy; and shows how much slander is contrary to the spirit of Christianity. He puts the Refugees in mind of the patience of the primitive Christians, and opposeth to the licentiousness of their pens, the moderation of the English Catholics, who were Refugees in France, and of the French writers. He doth not spare the Emperor nor the Pope himself upon the account of their being enemies to France. In the mean while, he represents himself as full of love, charity, and compassion for the Refugees; and protests that he speaks to them in this strong manner for no other reason but to persuade them to reform, and to disavow their satirical Libels in a public manner. In this manner he softens the bitterness of his reproaches and insults. He proceeds to their *seditious writings*, and under this class comprehends all those wherein it is maintained "That princes and their subjects engage themselves to one another
" mutually, and by way of contract to the observation of certain things, so that if
" the Prince fail in the performance of what he has promised, the subjects are there-
" by freed from their oath of allegiance, and may transfer their homage to new
" masters, whether the whole people disapprove the breach of promise of those princes,
" or the most numerous and most considerable part of them agree to it." He pretends that it is on this principle that the Reformed have supported all their civil wars, and founded their seditious maxims. He attacks this doctrine smartly, and makes use of that manner of arguing which they call *reductio ad absurdum*, and maintains the absolute power of Princes with a great deal of warmth. He heaps together all the reproaches which Mr Arnauld in his *Apology for the Catholics*, and other Controvertists have thrown upon the Protestants, on account of the principles of Buchanan, Junius Brutus, and Pareus; and exhorts the Refugees to do something to show that they are not infected with these political Heresies. He chargeth the Presbyterians with the death of King Charles I, and reproacheth the Church of England with abandoning the sound doctrine of submission due to Princes, and embracing the Presbyterian opinion of the lawfulness of bringing Kings to justice; and in a word, he represents the Protestants, and in particular the Refugees, as seditious persons, who bring Rebellion and Anarchy every where; and declares that Princes cannot rely upon their fidelity.

All these invectives are followed by a sort of digression, which he intitles *Reflexions on the irruption of the Vaudois*. He owns that the Vaudois have been unjustly treated, but maintains that they are inexcusable for having entered their own Country in a hostile manner, and made war upon their Prince; and from thence he takes occasion to return to the absolute power of Princes. After this follows the *Conclusion*.
" Now you see, says he, in what consists the *Quarentine* which your best friends
" among the Catholics desire you would perform before your return to France, it
" is to protest in the most public manner, either that you never approved of those
" scandalous and seditious Libels, which your authors have published by heaps, or
" that you sincerely repent your having done so, and are extreamly sorry that
" you were ignorant of their evil tendency, or that you had not the courage to
" declare against them." He once more returns to this subject, and afterwards makes several reflexions on the Campaign of 1689, tending to extol the greatness of France, and the glory of Lewis XIV. From thence he passes to the Revolution in Siam, which was very acceptable to the Hollanders, because of the check it gave to France. He says that the Controversies of the Protestants had grown worse these four or five years past, especially with regard to their civil wars; and he sets in opposition the fidelity of the French Catholics to Henry IV, to that of the English Protestants to James II. He allows his friend to publish this Letter, and make what alterations in it he shall think proper. He concludes with a very devout prayer, and with wishes for the conversion of his friend to the Catholic Religion; but " if the hour, says he, for that happy change is not as
" yet come, may heaven grant that you at least may be endowed with the senti-
" ments which every honest man ought to have for his country."

If one compares this *Advice to the Refugees*, with that part of the *Answer of a new Convert to a Letter from a Refugee*, intituled, *Reflexions concerning the Wars of the Protestants*, he will find a great conformity betwixt them; the same sentiments, the same reproaches, the same insults. The one is only in a manner the prelude or sketch of the other. They both pursue the same design, and follow the same plan, but in a manner different enough to make us doubt, whether these two pieces

come

THE LIFE OF Mr BAYLE.

1690. come from the same hand. In the *Advice* the subject is treated more at length, is more embellished, and more engaging; the stile is more correct, more lively, and more vehement.

To this book is prefixed a Preface, the author of which, a Refugee at London, is as zealous a Protestant, as the writer of the Letter appears to be a zealous Catholic. He says that this piece surprized him extreamly from the very beginning of it: that it was the performance of one of his old friends, an Advocate by profession, but who had employed himself more in reading books of Controversy than at the bar: that he must do him the justice to own that he had loudly condemned the *Dragoonings*; and that he could not imagine why he had made choice of him to be the depositary of a heap of indignities thrown out with the utmost bitterness, both against the whole body of Protestants, and likewise against those who had sought out of France, their cruel step-mother and not properly speaking their country, a sanctuary where they might serve God according to the purity of the faith. " The " ground, says he, of this so severe and so extravagant behaviour, and so con- " trary to the equity and moderation which I have always observed in him, is " first, that the Refugees being in a place where they are at liberty to complain " of the barbarous treatment perfectly worthy of the Religion of Antichrist, as " well as unworthy of all sort of Humanity, which they had suffered in their own " country, had published their complaints against France in a pretty lively manner: " and in the next place, that the Protestants of England and Scotland have not " been so simple, after so long experience as they have had of the treachery and " cruelty of the Church of Rome, to suffer themselves to be led like sheep to the " slaughter, but had rather chosen according to the laws and liberties of their country " to shake off the yoke, and free themselves from slavery, and receive the Deli- " verer whom God had raised up to them, as he did frequently to the people " of Israel in the time of the Judges." He adds that he was resolved to make this old friend of his such an answer as should make him repent his having so highly and maliciously provoked him; but that the public would be better acquainted with the justice of his resentment, if they saw this piece such as he had received it: that he had struck out a great many passages which breathed an unheard of rage, and had only retained certain passages which he designed to examine and to confute exactly in the answer which he was preparing. He gives the plan of this answer, and adds that in the mean while, he had thought it proper to publish this piece that his brethren might know in what light some people considered them, and what envenomed reflexions were made against them; hoping that some body would undertake their Apology, and confine himself to these two general heads, the *satirical writings* and the *seditious writings*, while he would canvass the other articles particularly, and leave nothing without a full and strong answer. He invites the author of the *Letters concerning the present state of affairs* (1) to do this, and says that he is so much the more interested in this matter, that he is one of those writers who are accused as satirical. " It will be, adds he, very easy to vindicate our Refugees, " for I have been assured, by some of my friends in Holland to whom I wrote " on that subject, I. That the pieces wherein they pretend to give an account of " amorous adventures, and wherein persons of the first quality are defamed, were " composed by Papists, before there were any Refugees in that country. II. That " the news writers who have given France the greatest cause of complaint, are not " Refugees, nay some of them are not so much as Frenchmen." He gives an account of the alterations he has made in the performance of his friend, and concludes with a Panegyric on *King William the favourite of God*. " One, says he, may " justly give him that title, and apply to him what the scripture says of David, " that God has found him a man according to his own heart, has led him by the " hand, and placed him upon the throne, with this advantagious difference, that " whereas David was not put in possession of the crown of his father-in-law who " was rejected by God 'till some time after his death, God has anticipated that " favour to King William, having bestowed upon him the crowns of his father- " in-law even while he was still alive." He adds that the Princes who are the greatest enemies of the Protestant Religion, *that the August House of Austria whose zeal for the Catholic Religion is sufficiently known, and all the Catholic Princes in Germany*, had applauded *that happy Revolution*: and that it was visibly a miraculous work of Providence, which had confounded both the counsels of France and of James II, since of a thousand means which they had in their power of giving a powerful check to that enterprize, they had precisely chosen that conduct which rendered it infallible.

The *Advice to the Refugees* was printed secretly at the Hague, and was presently answered by several hands. Mr Tronchin du Breuil vindicated the Refugees in his *Letters concerning the present state of affairs* (2). Mr de Bauval in his Journal (3) showed the injustice and unreasonableness of this author's complaints: and Mr Coulan a Minister and Refugee at London (4), answered him more fully in a treatise intituled: *A Defence of the Refugees against a book intituled An Advice, &c* (5). We may see Mr Bayle's judgment of these Answers, in a Book he published in 1692. Af-

(1) Lettres sur les matieres du tems.

(2) Letter of the 1st and 15th of May; of the 1st of June; and of the 1st of September 1690.

(3) Histoire des Ouvrages des Sçavans, April 1690. Art. x. pag. 364.

(4) Anthony Coulan born at Alais on the 10th of October 1667. He died at London the 23d of September 1694.

(5) La Defense des Refugiez contre un Livre intitulé, Avis, &c. At Deventer in 1691 in 12°. pag. 157.

VOL. I. m ter

xlvi   THE LIFE OF Mr BAYLE.

(1) Projet & Fragmens d'un Dictionaire Critique, pag. 110.

ter having pointed out the *Advice to the Refugees*, he adds (1), "I mean that sort 1690.
"of sermon wherein we are accused of a pretended proneness to libelling and civil-
"wars, with as much vehemence as ever a Minister showed in a fast-day sermon,
"when he lays the breach of the whole Decalogue to the charge of his hearers.
"And since this occasion offers, adds he, it will not be unseasonable to observe
"here, that the violent reproaches of this declaimer have produced a good effect.
"They are not perhaps the cause that those wretched little satirical books do not
"come so thick among us as before; but at least it is certain that they have ob-
"liged the best writers of the party to inform the Public, that it is without reason
"that people pretend to make the whole body of the Refugees accountable for these
"sorry books: so that we shall have cotemporary evidence to latest posterity to
"clear us from the malicious imputations, which some people endeavour to fix upon
"our cause. Let no body alledge, that the excellent writers who have disclaimed
"them, have done it in an anonymous way; for since they have answered for the
"whole body, without any persons entering a complaint against their declaration,
"this proves that the whole body acquiesces in it. Add to this that the name
"of the person who writes every fortnight in so ingenious and judicious a manner
"concerning the present state of affairs, is now known to every body. And as to
"the author of the inimitable History of the Works of the Learned, is there any
"body who doth not know his name?..... And with regard to the person who
"has lately given us the Defence of the Refugees against the *Important Advice*,
"he is no doubt very worthy of credit in what he advances as from his brethren.
"He fully answers all the reproaches which concern this satirical spirit, and sets
"forth his opinion on the other point with a great dexterity of wit. All things
"well considered, it must be owned that though a disavowal which had preceded
"the severe reproaches of the adversary, and had been made by persons appointed
"for this purpose by the Synods, would have been both more honourable and more
"authentic, yet nevertheless none but extravagant cavillers can henceforth renew
"these accusations." Some other Answers were likewise made to this piece [O].

(2) P. 418.

Mr de Bauval in his Journal for the month of May 1690 published an extract of
a Letter from the author of the *Advice to the Refugees* (2). "I confess, says that
"author, that I was surprized to see my performance made public. I did not
"trust my friend with it for that purpose, especially there being several things in
"it which I cannot approve of. I mean the passages wherein I speak of the manner
"in which you have been treated in France. You know very well that though
"I had thought in the manner he makes me speak, I would not have been so im-
"prudent as to say such things in the middle of Paris. I shall perhaps send it to
"you very soon reprinted with the necessary alterations." And in the month of
February 1691 he published an Extract of a Letter from Paris which gave an ac-

(3) Pag. 279, 280.
(4) Jurien, Last Conviction, pag. 19. col. 2. and the Chimera demonstrated, pag. 267, 309.

count that this work was in the press. "They are actually reprinting, says the
"writer of this Letter (3), the *Advice to the Refugees*, with the King's Licence,
"the author who had kept himself concealed upon account of several things which
"could not fail to irritate the Archbishop of Paris and Father de la Chaize, has
"found means of making his peace by adding some things, and taking away what
"might give them offence." In fact, it was reprinting at Paris, with the King's
Licence dated the 20th of October, and the first two sheets of it appeared in
Holland in the month of March following (4). They suppressed the Preface
of the first edition, and substituted the following *Advice to the Reader*: "This piece
"having been sent by the author into foreign parts to one of his friends, it has
"been printed there with several alterations contrary to his intention. This ob-
"liges him to reprint it in France in it's true and natural form. He protests sin-
"cerely that he had no other intention in writing this, but to do his duty by ac-
"quainting those in whom he interests himself, with certain important truths which
"they do not sufficiently reflect upon, and that he has been so far from regarding
"either favour or hopes from the court, that he has even avoided being known
"to it, concealing himself for this good action with as much care as others do for
"bad ones." But this edition was interrupted by the death of the Bookseller: they

(a) Reponse sommaire au Livre intitulé Avis Important aux Refugiés sur leur prochain retour en France. Par Monsieur G. N. A. à M. Musstricht 1690.
(b) Defense de la Nation Britannique; où les Droits de Dieu, de la Nature, & de la Societé sont clairement établis, au sujet de la Revolution d'Angleterre, contre l'auteur de l'Avis aux Refugiez.

set it on foot again a few months after, and the Impression was finished upon the
9th of December 1692, with a new Licence dated the 19th of September, the preamble of which is as follows: "Our well-beloved Mary Magdalen Guellerin, widow
"of Gabriel Martin, late Printer and Bookseller in our good City of Paris, having
"remonstrated

[O] *Some other Answers were likewise made to this piece.*] Mr Nixet, Advocate and Professor of Law at Maestricht, published, in 1690, *A short Answer to the Advice to the Refugees* (a). Mr Abbadie confined himself to what related to the Revolution in England, and printed at London in 1692, *A Defence of the British Nation; Wherein the Rights of God, of Nature, and of Society, are clearly established, with relation to the Revolution in England, against the author of the Advice to the Refugees* (b). Mr de Larrey made a full and large Answer to it under this title: *An Answer to the Advice to the Refugees*, By M. D. L. R. *At Rotterdam for Reinier Leers*, M. DCC. IX (c). This work he was desired to undertake by Mr Leers, who having a mind to publish a new edition of the *Advice to the Refugees*, engaged him to write this Answer to it, to be published along with it. He reprinted the *Advice* from the Paris edition, with the same date, and under the same Printer's name. But he restored the Preface which they had suppressed at Paris. The *Advice* and Mr Larrey's *Answer* make two volumes in 8vo.

(c) Reponse à l'Avis aux Refugiés, par M. D. L. R.

THE LIFE OF MR BAYLE.

1690. "remonstrated to us, that by our Letters of the 20th of October 1690, signed *le Petit*, and sealed, we have given permission to the Author of a book intitled, *An important Advice to the Refugees upon their approaching return to France*, to print, sell, and distribute the said work throughout all our Kingdom for the space and term of ten years, which Author has yielded his right to the said deceased Gabriel Martin, husband to the petitioner; but having affected to continue unknown to the public, he made a difficulty of allowing the said privilege expeded in his name, to be inserted in the Registers of the society of Booksellers of our City of Paris, which together with the sickness and death of the late Gabriel Martin, has interrupted the impression of the said work which was already begun, and will retard it still if we are not pleased, in consequence of the agreement made with the foresaid Author, and with his consent, to allow the said privilege to be registred in the name of the petitioner. For these reasons desiring to show favour to the said petitioner, we have permitted and allowed, and by these presents we do permit and allow the impression of the said book to be continued, &c."

1691. No body in Holland now talked any longer of the *Advice to the Refugees*; this book was quite forgot (1), when Mr Jurieu took it into his head all of a sudden, in the month of January 1691, to send word to Mr Basnage that he looked upon Mr Bayle as the author of that libel, and that he must go out of the seven Provinces. Mr Basnage endeavoured to make him take other sentiments, but he gave no ear to him. Mr Bayle told Mr Basnage that he had formerly intended to answer this book, and that in order to convince Mr Jurieu of his mistake, he was going to set about it again. At the same time he desired Mr Basnage to assure Mr Jurieu that he was ready to confer with him on this subject, and to satisfy all his doubts (2). All this did not appease Mr Jurieu. The hatred which he had of a long time conceived against Mr Bayle was changed into rage: he imagined that he had found a proper occasion of defaming him. Nay if it had been in his power he would have likewise taken away his life. "Since it was not in my power, (says he (3), to get all the punishment which he deserved inflicted upon him, I resolved at least to expose him to public infamy." It was with these dispositions that Mr Jurieu set about an *Examination* of the *Advice to the Refugees*, wherein in the beginning he endeavours to discover the author. After having praised the composition of the book, he undertakes to shew that the author of the book and of the preface, are one and the same person: that this author is a Protestant, and lived in Holland; and that the Preface which he wrote in order to conceal himself had discovered him. In fine, he characterized him in such a manner, that one might easily see that he wanted to point out Mr Bayle, though he did not run the hazard of naming him. But when he comes to give the reasons that could have induced Mr Bayle to write this piece, he found himself extremely embarrassed. "What (says he (4), could be the design of this author? was there ever so whimsical a design? what view could he have? At first I fancied he was one of our Sceptics who designed only to divert himself with truth, and defend both sides of the question; first to make a book against us, and afterwards to destroy it by another for us, to shew that Truth as well in facts as in matters of right lies in the well of Democritus; that one may doubt of every thing, affirm, defend, and attack every thing. And I am still of opinion that a little of this has entered into his views. I believe he would have kept his promise if so much noise had not been made, we should have had a sorry confutation, for in it he would have spoke against his inclinations, and his maxims; whereas here he speaks his real sentiments."

After this Mr Jurieu undertakes to discover the real intention of the Author. He says that this Author, "being extremely fond of the independant and absolute power of Princes, and seeing that for some years past they had wrote against his idol the King of France pretty freely; and being above all full of indignation against the Revolution in England and the dethroning of King James, he had at length lost all patience, and could no longer refrain from writing an apology for the King of France, and for King James (5): and that it was upon this account that he was obliged to screen himself under the mask of a bigotted Papist, and of a violent hater of the Protestant Religion (6)." He confesseth that this mask would have kept him in suspence had it not been for the Preface (7)." However he did not believe that this Author was so animated against the Protestant Religion as he pretended to be. "We do him the justice, (says he), to believe that he is not so malicious against the Protestant Religion as he would make himself appear to be, and that his raving against us is a part of the comedy, that he may under that deep disguise defend both the King of France, King James, and arbitrary power (8)." He did not even believe that any motive of interest had engaged him to write in favour of these Princes. "We must, (says he), do him this justice, that interest could have no share in these appearances of zeal. For he had no design of making a merit of

(1) Caba-le Chime-rique, *pag.* 198, 353.
Last Con-viction.
pag. 35.
col. 1.
Chimera demonstrated, *pag.* 351, 352.

(2) MSS.
Memoirs of Mr Bas-nage. See likewise the Chimera demonstrated, *pag.* 351, 352.

(3) Apology for Mr Jurieu, *p.* 25. *col.* 1.

(4) Examen d'un Libelle &c. *pag.* 36, 37.

(5) Ibid. *pag.* 38.

(6) P. 39, 40, 41.

(7) P. 40.

(8) P. 40, 41.

"this

xlviii THE LIFE OF Mʀ BAYLE.

" this work with thefe powers, fince he has taken all manner of precautions not   1691.
(1) P. 69. " to be known (1)."

But he did this juftice to the author, only to make him appear the more like
Mr Bayle. He did the fame thing in fpeaking of the *Advice*. At firft he faid of
this book all that he thought of Mr Bayle, whom he had in view. He found the
ftile of it flowing, eafy, and lively; that *his figures were natural, his metaphors happy,
his ornaments well chofen and well placed*; that *it engages the reader by a fecret charm*;
that *it was filled with agreeable literature*, and that *his learning was mighty well dif-*
(2) P. 5, *pofed* (2). All this agreed to Mr Bayle in the opinion of the public. Afterwards
6. he fays that this Author ftrikes *blow after blow to overthrow his adverfary, and fets
forth with a great deal of art, and in a very narrow compafs, all the ftrongeft things
that had ever been advanced* againft the Reformed; that *his book was the moft dangerous piece that had been wrote againft them fince the Reformation*; *fhowing the Refor-*
(3) P. 7. *mation in the moft hideous light* (3): becaufe all this was ftill neceffary to his defign,
which was to render Mr Bayle odious. But when he came to anfwer the book, and
was much heated, he forgot all his former defcription of it, it was then a piece fo extravagant at the bottom that it required neither *fyftem*, principles, nor reafon to compofe fuch another. A work which was *all outfide and nothing within*; *a little figure
of wax-work well polifhed and well dreffed, well furnifhed with red and white, but
within had neither flefh, bones, nor nerves*; *there was nothing in it but two very
meagre difficulties which the author had plumped up by the fertility of his imagination, and*
(4) P. 91, *out of the treafure of his common-place books* (4): *two poor difficulties*, all *the reft being
92. mere gilding, embroidery, inveftives, idle ftories, reproaches, trifles, and reflexions no-*
(5) P. 97, *thing to the purpofe*, and which proved *nothing* (5): *a piece wherein there was no
98. fyftem* (6), *a pretty little collection from the Polyanthea and pure pedantry* (7); in fine,
a work *wrote with fo little wifdom and folidity, that the Author muft have confidered*
(6) P. 180. *mankind as brutes, who fuffer themfelves to be led by the nofe or by the ears* (8). His judg-
(7) P. 210. ments were entirely regulated by his paffions. He reprefented the *Advice* as a for-
(8) P. 98. midable work, that he might with the greater probability afcribe it to Mr Bayle;
and he accufed Mr Bayle of having made an apology for the King of France and
for King James, becaufe at that juncture nothing was more proper to incenfe the
public againft him.

About this time there was at Geneva one Goudet, a Merchant, who had but little
bufinefs indeed, but was a great Projector. He took in his head to adjuft the
differences of Princes, and become the pacificator of Europe. He compofed a book
entitled, *Eight Dialogues, wherein Irene and Ariftus lay down meafures for putting an*
(9) Huit *end to the prefent war by a general peace* (9). Thefe Dialogues contained a Project
Entretiens of Peace, wherein Mr Goudet affigned to the Princes and States of Europe the
où Irene Territories they were to poffefs. France for inftance, was to keep Franche-Comté,
& Ariſte
fournif- their conquefts in Flanders, and Luxembourg; but muft reftore all that they had
fent des conquered in Catalonia from the peace of the Pyrenees, and in Germany from
idées pour the peace of Nimeguen, excepting Strafburg. She muft likewife demolifh
terminer Mont-Royal, Fort-Louis, Hunniguen and Fribourg; and in equivalent our
la prefente projector gives her the City of Mons and all Hainault, and fome other ter-
guerre par ritories which lay convenient for her. He gives her likewife Lorrain, and
une Paix
generale. the Duke of Lorrain was to have Servia and Bulgaria, and Belgrade for the
capital of his new Dominions: but afterwards he changed this article, and gave
him Brabant and the reft of the Spanifh Netherlands. France was to reftore to
the Swifs the Town of Fribourg and the fortrefs of Hunninguen, after they were de-
molifhed; and the Emperor was to yield to them the four Foreft Towns, together
with the Brifgau and the Suntgau. He gives up likewife to France the principality of Orange, the County of Avignon, and the Venaiffin; and in exchange he
gives to the Prince of Orange the Baillywic of Gex, and to the Pope an annual
tribute of fifty thoufand Crowns to be paid by the Duke of Savoy, in confideration of which this Duke was to have Cafal and Pignerol. He grants likewife
to the Proteftants in France a perpetual Edict, which fhould fecure to them the fame
liberty of confcience which the Catholics enjoy in Holland: but they were not to
be allowed to write againft the Church of Rome. The Dutch were to have all
the commerce of the Indies, and France was to demolifh certain places in the
Low-Countries, which might give them umbrage. He would have King William
to be acknowledged King of England, and King James made King of Jerufalem
and of all Paleftine. The Chriftian Princes were to unite to deftroy the Ottoman
Empire. The Elector of Bavaria was to be Emperor of Conftantinople, and Count
Tekely was to have Belgrade and the Provinces of Servia, Bulgaria, Bofnia, Rafcia,
Moldavia, and Walachia. Thefe two laft were to be Tributaries of Poland. He
gives alfo to France, Egypt, a part of Syria, and the Ifle of Rhodes, and "the
(10) Se- " advantages that will arife from thence, (faid Mr Goudet (10), is, that by this
cond Dia- " means at the expence of the Infidels, there will be employment found in remote
logue &c. " countries for the unquiet and reftlefs temper of the French, who can hardly
p. 27, 28. " be at eafe themfelves or fuffer other people to be fo, which is not of fmall confe-
" quence to the general intereft." To render this peace perpetual, the Princes of
Europe

THE LIFE OF Mʀ BAYLE.

1691. Europe were to give every year to the Swiss six hundred thousand crowns to maintain 40000 men, who should be always ready to pour in upon any one who should endeavour to disturb it; and these troops in case of need were to be joined by 30000 men whom the Emperor and the Princes of the Empire were to keep on foot.

Mr Goudet admiring the sublimity of his genius in this project of peace which he had formed, communicated it to every body whom he could persuade to read it. He entertained the French Resident with it, who made a jest of it (1). But this did not discourage him. Knowing that Mr Minutoli, to whom he was related, was a friend of Mr Bayle; he desired him to send this scheme of a peace to Mr Bayle, "in order to have his judgment of it, as well as that of many "other illustrious persons in foreign countries (2)." In the month of September 1690, Mr Minutoli sent the first six dialogues to Mr Bayle, without naming the Author, and told him at the same time, "that if they did not design "to take a particular care of the interest of the Protestant Religion, and of his "dear brethren the Refugees in this scheme, he would not have so much as look- "ed into it, but that the person who was concerned in it had assured him that "the sequel would satisfy all the scruples he could have on that head (3)."

The article concerning the Refugees was reserved for the seventh Dialogue, which was not sent to Mr Bayle. Mr Minutoli desired him to communicate the six first to Baron Groeben, Governor to Prince Louis, brother to the Elector of Brandenbourg; to Dr Burnet, Bishop of Salisbury; to Mr Hulst, the State's Resident at Brussels; to Mr Fremont d'Ablancourt, and to Mr de Bauval: and in general he desired him to put it into the hands of as many ingenious men and Ministers of State as possible, and to acquaint him with their opinion of it (4). Mr Bayle caused some transcripts to be made of it, and sent them to the persons named by Mr Minutoli. They did not think very advantageously of it. "Besides that they "did not esteem it well wrote, they found in it chimeras and notions of a Plato- "nic Commonwealth, and of that Christian Republic of which Mr de Sulli has pre- "served the plan (5)." Mr Bayle did not read it, for besides the great aversion he had to the reading of manuscripts, his other affairs, and the indifferent character which was given of it by the persons who had read it, made him neglect it entirely (6). He acquainted Mr Minutoli with their judgment of it, and added, "that the author might lay it down as a thing certain, that any plan of a gene- "ral peace, which did not strip France of all that she had conquered for some years "past, and which did not weaken her to such a degree as to make her neighbours "no longer jealous of her, would be rejected (7)." While they were making copies of this piece, Mr Bayle chanced to go into Mr Acher's shop, a Bookseller in Rotterdam, who "(8) desired him to cast his eyes upon a manuscript "which had been sent him and give him his opinion of it, and tell him whether "it was a piece which would sell. Mr Bayle presently upon looking into "the first page of it knew it, and said aloud, in presence of several Refugees "who were in the shop, that it was a piece which he had given to be copied, and "appeared to be vexed, because he was afraid that the copier had taken it into "his head to give it to the press; for he had only been desired by his friend "at Geneva, to show it in manuscript, and to get the opinion of good judges "concerning it, that the Author might alter it according to the different views "which might be suggested to him. . . . . . . But Mr Acher made him easy on "that head, by telling him that the person from whom he had the copy, would "part with it to no body but to Mr Bayle; and as he believed that Mr Bayle "had the disposal of it, he desired that he would procure him the publication of "it. Mr Bayle answered that he had received no order to get that piece printed, "but that if this should be resolved upon, and the choice of the Printer be left "to him, he would prefer him to any other. He appeared very grateful for "this."

"(9) Some time after Mr Minutoli wrote to Mr Bayle, that the Author was pre- "paring to publish the first six Dialogues at Lausanne, while in the mean time he "was finishing the two others. Mr Bayle told this to Mr Acher, who did not think "fit to alter his design upon that account, since it was not likely that an E- "dition in that country could hinder the sale of one in Holland, which would "be more beautiful and more easily sent every where than that of Switzerland. "He proposed therefore only to oblige Mr Acher, that they should send him "the sheets of the Lausanne edition as they came from the press, there being a "Bookseller at Rotterdam who would reprint them. They agreed to this proposal, "and post after post Mr Minutoli made Mr Bayle hope that they would "send him the sheets with the Author's corrections. He acquainted him that the work "would be considerably enlarged, and that the form of it would be almost wholly "changed for the better; that the author insisted particularly on a Guarrantee, and had "put the article concerning the Refugees on such a footing as had been approved "of by several of them. As the sheets did not come, Mr Minutoli desired Mr Bayle "to keep the Bookseller in hopes, ...

(1) Extract of a Letter from Geneva &c.
(2) Letter from Mr M. nutoli to Mr Jurieu, ibid.
(3) Cabale Chimerique, p. 5, of the second Edition.
(4) Ibid. p. 20. and the following.
(5) P. 13, 14.
(6) P. 7. and the following.
(7) P. 20, 77.
(8) P. 16. and the following.
(9) P. 18, 19.

VOL. I. n "(1) During

THE LIFE OF Mʀ BAYLE.

(1) P 22, 23.   "(1) During this delay of the sheets, Mr Acher told Mr Bayle from time to time, 1691. that he would not print this project until he knew whether it might not give offence. Mr Bayle always told him, that he would do well to give it to read to any body he pleased, and Mr Acher having said that he would be directed by him in that matter, Mr Bayle answered him, that he need not do so, that he had not read it, and would not read it while it continued in manuscript. He even told him plainly the opinion of Messieurs d'Ablancourt and Bauval, and of some others who had read it. This did not discourage him, for Mr Jurieu's prophesies (which he had printed) had taught him by experience, that the most chimerical books, are the very best for

(2) Ibid. p. 24.   the Printer.... At last (2), when Mr Bayle could not tell what to make of this delay of the sheets, he was informed, in the time of the siege of Mons (3), that there

(3) *Mons capitulated on the 9th of April 1691, after 16 days open trenches.*   were copies of the first edition at the Hague. This made him advise the Bookseller to give over the thoughts of printing the Project of Peace, and so much the more because the siege of that place, which ever way it turned, would change the state of affairs: and he found that he had already taken that prudent resolution."

Mr Jurieu's book against the *Advice of the Refugees*, and against Mr Bayle, was actually in the press, when the first six dialogues concerning *the Project of Peace*, printed at Lausanne, came into his hands. He was quite a stranger to this work. (4)

(4) The Chimericalness of the Rotterdam Cabal demonstrated &c. p. 194, 195, in the Note.   "Mr Minutoli, in his letters to Mr Bayle, had never particularly named Mr Jurieu as one of the persons to whom he ought to shew the manuscript. He believed no doubt that it was not necessary to do so, having heard of their intimate acquaintance, and as he desired his friend to shew it to judicious persons in general, he took it for granted that Mr Jurieu would see it among the first. Mr Bayle would not have failed to have shewn it to him at first, tho' his friend had not particularly desired him to do so; but he was afraid least Mr Jurieu should have thought it was with a design to affront him, if he had desired him to read a project of peace, wherein they had departed so far from his system. For Mr Bayle saw plainly from Mr Minutoli's first letter, that according to this project, the religion of the Protestants was not to be the national religion in France. As Mr Bayle had never relished Mr Jurieu's System, and possibly had talked with too much liberty of it before some of his spies, he had already incurred his secret hatred; so that he had reason to fear, that in so delicate an affair, as the glory of having given true or false predictions concerning great events, the smallest matter should pique him, and might be taken, especially coming from such a hand, for an insult."

Mr Jurieu was, in fact, extremely irritated at this *Project of Peace*: but he grew quite outrageous when he understood from Mr Acher, that this work had been long before sent to Mr Bayle, and was told what had passed between Mr Bayle and him concerning the manuscript. Being always full of wild dreams, and become quite furious against Mr Bayle, he built upon this a system a thousand times more chimerical than the chimerical Project of Peace itself. He prefixed to his *Examination of the Ad-*

(5) Examen de l'avis aux Refugiez.   *vice to the Refugees* (5); an *Important Advice to the Public* (6), wherein he declared that all that he had said "concerning the design of the author of the *Advice to the*

(6) Avis important au Public.   *Refugees*, was only the effort of a person groping his way in a dark place. It is true, adds he, that I must have been blind, and at present I can hardly imagine how I could fail of discovering the whole mystery at first sight. (7)...... They

(7) Avis important au Public, p. 3, 4.   who are under suspicion, and are justly so, could find no better means of justifying their friends, than by asking, *cui bono?* and I confess that this difficulty raised a scruple even in me, which did not indeed make me in the least doubt from whence the book came, but which however embarrassed me: when at last God, whose pleasure it is that mysteries of iniquity should be discovered, has permitted that another unexpected discovery should give more light into it. The public must know then, that this is not the work of a private person who designed to defend the authority of Princes. They who have imagined so, have been mistaken

(8) Ibid. p. 5.   (8). This is the work of a Cabal which extends from south to north, and has its center at Paris and at the Court of France (9)." He added, "That there was a

(9) Ibid. p. 7.   French party at Geneva, which was hatched under the wings of the Resident of France; that this party consisted of persons of all ranks and characters; and that this cabal kept a correspondence with another in Holland entirely in the same interests

(10) Ibid. p. 7, 8, 9.   (10). That they both had the same view, which was to relieve France from her present distress, by a peace as advantageous as she could wish for: that their design was to disunite the Allies, to raise a spirit of rebellion in subjects against their Sovereigns, which would force the Allies to receive peace upon any condition: and in fine, that these two parties did nothing but in concert with the Court of France,

(11) Ibid. p. 42, 43.   and by her direction (11)." That in consequence of the views and instructions of the Court of France, Mr Bayle, who was the head of the northern cabal, had wrote the *Advice to the Refugees*; and Mr Goudet, agent for the southern cabal, had composed the *Dialogues concerning a Peace*, which were drawn up by the Resident of France, and corrected at Versailles; that Mr Bayle had undertaken to get them

(12) P. 37, and the following.   printed at Rotterdam, in order to spread them the more easily over all Europe, and particularly in Holland and in England (12). After this he calls Mr Bayle an *Impious*

I

and

THE LIFE OF Mʀ BAYLE.   li

1691. *and prophane perſon, without honour or religion, a traitor, a deceitful man, an enemy to the State ; a perſon to be deteſted and deſerving corporal puniſhment.*
    In the mean while he owned that this accuſation concerning the *Advice to the Refugees,* was founded on ſimple preſumptions only. " It may be, ſays he (1), that "ſome people who would appear to be diſintereſted, will ſay that this is to puſh "people too fiercely, and to expoſe them to the public hatred without having ſuf- "ficiently convicted them ..... but when the public ſecurity is concerned, muſt "we wait for conviction, are not diſaffected perſons diſcovered by ſtrong preſump- "tions, that we may be upon our guard againſt them ? " It is very ſingular, that while he was accuſing Mr Bayle of a deſign to ruin the Proteſtants; ſome confeſ- ſions eſcaped him which deſtroyed this accuſation. "The Author, ſaid he (2), be- "lieved that at laſt this would do them no more hurt than an hundred other libels "which have been wrote againſt them : that this would be forgot like the reſt, "and that for the preſent it would be of uſe to France, and by accident to the "Proteſtants themſelves, becauſe it would contribute to diſſolve the confederacy, "and to bring about a peace." And with regard to the *project of peace,* after having repreſented it as a piece concerted with the court of France, and capable of diſ-uniting the allies, he ſaid *that it was a performance ſo full of chimeras that one muſt be a chimerical man who would ſet about the anſwering of it* (3). But theſe reflexions which were ſufficient to have opened the eyes of a diſintereſted perſon, made no impreſſion on Mr Jurieu : he did not want to vindicate Mr Bayle, he wanted to find him guilty. He likewiſe attacked Mr Bauval. He accuſed him of having forged the Letter which he had inſerted in his Journal, wherein it was ſaid that they were reprinting the *Advice to the Refugees* at Paris (4). But as the firſt ſheets of this new edition had been ſeen in Holland, he pretended that this was an artifice they had contrived to ſcreen themſelves from ſuſpicion ; and that the Royal Licence, printed in the firſt ſheet was forged.
    His book againſt the *Advice to the Refugees* appeared (5) under this title : *An Examination of a Libel againſt Religion, the State, and the Revolution of England, intituled An important Advice to the Refugees upon their approaching return into France* (6). There was prefixed to it *An important Advice to the public,* as we have already obſerved.
    As ſoon as Mr Bayle had read this *Advice to the public,* " he went to the grand "Schout of Rotterdam, and told him that if his accuſer would go to priſon with "him, and undergo the puniſhment which he ſhould deſerve, in caſe Mr Bayle "was found innocent, he was ready to go there (7)." He likewiſe informed two of the chief Magiſtrates of Rotterdam, and two or three other gentlemen at the Hague, diſtinguiſhed by their merit and employments, of Mr Jurieu's accuſations, that theſe accuſations were falſe, and that he deſired nothing of the State but that they would not condemn him without a hearing (8). Poſſibly he would have done well to have gone no further. Mr Jurieu would never have had the confidence to appear before a Magiſtrate with him. He had no legal proof to alledge, they would have ridiculed his preſumptions, and he would have been declared a falſe accuſer. But as he had publickly accuſed Mr Bayle of being the head of a Cabal or conſpiracy againſt the State, Mr Bayle thought himſelf obliged to juſtify himſelf in the ſame manner. He intitled his Anſwer (9), *The chimerical Cabal : or a Refutation of a fabulous Story which has been lately publiſhed with a malicious intention concerning a certain project of peace, in the Examination of a Libel, &c. intituled An important Advice to the Refugees on their approaching return into France* (10).
    In the beginning Mr Bayle gives an account of all he had done with regard to the *project of peace,* agreeably to what we have related above. He takes notice of all the falſhoods in Mr Jurieu's narration, and of all the extravagancies he had been guilty of in this matter. As to the *Advice to the Refugees,* which made the ſecond article of his Accuſation, he ſays he had at firſt deſigned to handle that ſubject in a particular treatiſe ; but conſidering that this work might encreaſe under his hand, and not appear ſoon, he thought it would be beſt in the mean while to give this *prelude of an Anſwer.* He agreed with Mr Jurieu that the *Advice to the Refugees* was the work of a Proteſtant : but he undertook to ſhow by the ſtrongeſt preſumptions that it muſt have been written in France ; and ſo he refuted all the ſuppoſitions which Mr Jurieu had made to prove that it had been compoſed in Holland, and that if the author was at Paris, he would diſcover himſelf. He ſhows the difference betwixt that author's manner of writing and his own. He refuted all the characters by which Mr Jurieu had pretended to point out the author of the *Advice* in order to conclude that it was Mr Bayle. He ſhowed how ridiculous his remarks and chicanery were concerning the new edition of that piece, which they were printing at Paris ; and that Mr Jurieu's preſumptions gave him no right to arraign him publickly as a traitor, an impious perſon, and guilty of high-treaſon both againſt God and man ; and proved that in order to make him appear guilty he had made uſe of deceit, treachery, and the blackeſt malice. He ſhowed that the characters which Mr Jurieu fixed upon the author of the *Advice,* offered preſumptions incomparably more ſtrong that Mr Bayle was not the author of it, than all
that

(1) *Ibid. pag.* 110, 111.
(2) *Ibid. pag.* 57.
(3) *Ibid. pag.* 80.
(4) See above, pag. xlvi, xlvi l.
(5) About the end of the month of April 1691.
(6) Examen d'un Libelle contre la Religion, contre l'Etat, & contre la Revolution d'Angleterre, intitulé Avis important aux Refugiez ſur leur prochain retour en France.
(7) Cabale Chimerique, *pag.* 94 *of the firſt edition.*
(8) *Ibid. pag.* 207, 208.
(9) It was dated the 8th and 13th of May 1691.
(10) La Cabale Chimerique: ou Refutation de l'Hiſtoire fabuleuſe qu'on vient de publier maliciſeuſement touchant un certain Projet de paix, dans l'Examen d'un Libelle, &c. intitulé Avis important aux Refugiez ſur leur prochain retour en France. A Rotterdam chez Reinier Leers, 1691, *in* 12°.

THE LIFE OF MR BAYLE.

that he had alledged to prove that he was. Lastly he re-capitulates Mr Jurieu's 1691. accusations, and reduced them to twenty five Articles, the eighteenth of which was (1), *That Mr Bayle made hardly any secret of his Atheism, that he did not edify the public by any act of Religion; that he was without Religion, and without love to God, so that his supreme deity was called Lewis XIV.* " Here, adds Mr Bayle, are eighteen
" Articles, out of which I am sure my adversary will never extricate himself. The
" last alone is sufficient to employ him for his whole Life, without drawing any thing
" but matter of confusion to himself from it. I wait with a great deal of impa-
" tience 'till he shall come that length. It is so capital a point, that he must either
" conquer or die. He must prove it, either by my writings or by credible wit-
" nesses, or by avouching by unquestionable signs, that God has conferred upon
" him the gift of prophecy to such a degree, that he sees all that passeth in peoples
" hearts. . . . . . Passion has blinded him in such a manner that he could not see,
" that though his cause had been good, he would have ruined it by the great number
" of facts with which he has loaded it. For though he should succeed in all the
" rest of the articles, if he failed in the last could he justly escape hanging? is
" not Atheism punished capitally every where? and ought not an accuser who is
" convicted of false evidence, to suffer the same punishment which the person ac-
" cused would have undergone, if he had been found guilty. . . . . I repeat it once
" more, an accuser who embarasseth himself so stupidly and foolishly excites rather
" our pity than our anger. Who would not laugh to see a Minister undertake to
" prove, that a man who in the sight of the world communicates four times a year,
" and is frequently present at the public prayers, and at the best part of the sermon,
" doth not perform *any religious act*? I will show him that my pretended impiety
" consists only in my not having applauded his false miracles, false prophets, and
" pretended revelations; and I will never be ashamed of having contributed to stop
" my fellow Refugees upon the brink of Fanaticism, and of having indirectly hindered
" Mr Jurieu himself from pushing his chimeras still further (2)." To these eighteen articles he added seven more, and " (3) declared that all that Mr Jurieu could write
" before he had proved these twenty five articles would be lost labour, and that
" his honour would not be at all salved by proving some of them only; for if
" he should fail in others, he would still be convicted as a public calumniator,
" in a matter where life and fame are concerned; and consequently his Ministry
" would be thereby so much dishonoured that he would be a reproach to the Pro-
" testant Church if they did not depose him."

As this was not one of those disputes which arise among men of letters, about points of erudition or science, but an affair wherein honour and even life was concerned, if the treason against the State had been proved; Mr Bayle did not think himself obliged to keep any terms with his accuser, he unmasked him so successfully, that even Mr Jurieu's pride and arrogance were not able to stand so rude a shock. He had recourse to the civil power, and presented to the *Venerable Burgomasters* of Rotterdam a Petition wherein he drew his own picture to the life. It is as follows:

The Sieur Jurieu, who has had the honour for so many years and by so many labours to defend the cause of God, prays for justice from your Lordships, against a horrible Libel composed by the Sieur Bayle, wherein the said Bayle calls him rogue, villain, impostor, calumniator, and wicked man; and calls the Princes who have shaken off the yoke of Popery flagitious men, and assassinators, and says many other infamous things against the Reformation. The Sieur Jurieu implores protection for his innocence, and that the said book may be prohibited, lacerated, and torn to pieces; the author punished as such atrocious injuries deserve; and that the Sieur Jurieu may be permitted to defend himself publickly, he promising to do so with modesty and christian moderation; and that the Sieur Bayle may be forbid to compose any more books against the Sieur Jurieu.

" This is, says Mr Bayle (4), one of the most violent and at the same time the
" most burlesque piece that was ever seen. To desire that an accuser of high-treason
" both against God and man should be allowed to write against the party accused,
" and that the latter should be forbid to write against his accuser; must not one be
" out of his wits to offer such a petition? A Gentleman who should desire his Prince
" to give him leave to fight in single combat with his adversary, after tying him hand
" and foot to a tree, would not be so ridiculous. But his assurance in accusing Mr
" Bayle before these gentlemen, of having in his *Cabale Chimerique* called the *Princes
" who have shaken off the yoke of Popery, flagitious men and assassinators, and of having
" said several infamous things against the Reformation,* is such a furious calumny, that
" tho' he should meet with no other disgrace in this process, but the being convicted of
" having advanced such a falshood in such a petition, he would have good reason to
" repent of his notable accusation."

The Burgomasters of Rotterdam acted a part agreeable to their equity and wisdom.
" They exhorted both Mr Bayle and Mr Jurieu to make up matters as soon as pos-
" sible; and forbad them to write any thing against each other, which should not first
" be examined by Mr Bayer, Pensionary of the city. They prohibited likewise the
" publication of any more anonymous libels, such as had appeared at Rotterdam

" against

THE LIFE OF MR BAYLE.

1691. "against the *Cabale Chimerique* (1)." We shall soon have an occasion of speaking of these libels.

What Mr Jurieu had wrote concerning the pretended Cabal of Geneva, drew upon him both the indignation and contempt of that whole City. One of the Syndics wrote what follows on this subject to a friend of his in Holland (2): *I can assure you, Sir, that people in this Country have been very much offended at Mr Jurieu's manner of writing, and that he has lost his reputation among all men of honour and good sense. One cannot imagine what could make him write in the manner he has done against this City. What he has said is absolutely false, and entirely his own invention. All that is true in the matter is, that one Goudet, a Merchant, has taken upon him to write certain projects of peace &c.*

See likewise what a private Gentleman writes from thence (3): "We cannot but look with indignation upon a man, who, filled with the most deadly poison, bites without distinction every thing that comes in his way, friends and foes, not sparing even Sovereign States. What have the Magistrates of Geneva done to him that he should endeavour to embroil them with their people, and set them at variance with all the Protestants and the Allies? but all that I can say to you on this subject is, that every body here has looked upon his calumnies with the utmost contempt."

Mr Minutoli wrote a letter to Mr Jurieu on the same subject in very strong terms. *I do not know,* (says he (4), *whether our Government, and so many persons of distinction, so unworthily treated in a point which concerns so deeply both their conscience and honour, will not endeavour to give you the most mortifying proofs of their just resentment; but I am very certain that I must have forgot all the rules of justice, if I did not at present appear in favour of Mr Bayle, who by the accident which I will tell you, was brought by me only into that affair, which you are pleased to lay to his charge as a great crime.* He proceeds to give a detail of all that had passed betwixt Mr Bayle and him concerning the project of peace; which agreed in every circumstance with the account Mr Bayle himself had given of it in his *Cabale Chimerique*, and which I have before related. He reproached Mr Jurieu with having upon some frivolous conjectures, placed both Mr Bayle and him in his pretended Cabal. *Tell me upon your conscience,* (says he), *how would you take it, if any body upon such presumptions, which they might have against you, should presently, without farther examination, in a public manner accuse you and your friends as persons without Honour, Faith, or Religion?* He exhorted him to acknowledge his fault, and not to oblige him to make this Letter public for Mr Bayle's justification.

Mr Jurieu received likewise Letters from some friends he had at Geneva, advising him not to give any credit to the story of the Geneva Cabal, and not to consider the project of peace as a serious matter (5). But this did not hinder him to publish without the knowledge, and contrary to the prohibition of the Magistrates, a piece intitled, (6) *New Convictions of the Author of the Advice to the Refugees. Together with the Nullity of his Defences. By a friend of Mr Jurieu.* Part the first. He wrote under the name of a friend, that by this disguise he might not come under the Magistrates prohibition. He maintained in it all that he had before said concerning the Cabal at Geneva, and the project of peace. This first part was soon followed by a second, intitled, *The last Conviction of the Sieur Bayle, Professor of Philosophy at Rotterdam, concerning the Advice to the Refugees, which may serve for a Factum in the complaint laid before the State* (7). In this last piece, he no longer talks of the dangerous Cabal which extended itself from North to South, which had its center at the Court of France, and whose intention was to raise an insurrection in Holland and in England to confound all the Designs of the Allies, and by this means to procure an universal Monarchy to France, and consequently to ruin the Protestant Religion. He saw that he had thereby made himself both contemptible and ridiculous; he therefore changed the state of the question, and only accused Mr Bayle of *having had an intention to publish without the knowledge of the State, A Project of Peace contrary to their intentions and interests* (8). With regard to the Advice to the Refugees he only repeated and amplified the accusations which he had already brought against Mr Bayle: and instead of justifying himself from the falshoods and calumnies which Mr Bayle had reduced to twenty five articles, he gave a loose to abuse and invectives. He had even the boldness to deny that the Magistracy had forbid him to write, as they had done Mr Bayle. " Surely, (said he), one must have a very bad opinion of the Administration both of this City and of the State, to believe that they have put a man accused of treason against the State, upon the same footing with one who through his zeal for the State has brought a complaint against him. It would not be at all just to take the right of defending himself from a man who has been so violently attacked, as Mr Jurieu has been. He is obliged for the edification of the Church to vindicate his name wherever his works have carried it (9)." However as it was very certain that they had been both alike forbidden to publish any thing which had not been examined by Mr Bayer (10): this Magistrate on reading that part of

(1) Chimere demontrée, p. 4.
(2) Ibid. Preface, p xxxv, xxxvi.
(3) Ib'd. p. xxxvi, xxxvii.
(4) Letter from Mr Minutoli to Mr Jurieu of the 14th of May 1691. In the Chimere demontrée &c. p. 189, 190.
(5) Ibid. Preface, p. xi, xii.
(6) Nouvelles Convictions contre l'Auteur de l'Avis aux Refugiez Avec la nullité de ses justifications. Par un Ami de Mr Jurieu. Premiere Partie.
(7) Derniere Conviction contre le sieur Bayle, Professeur en Philosophie à Rotterdam au sujet de l'Avis aux Refugiez, pour servir de Factum sur la plainte portée aux Puissances de l'Etat. Both parts together contain 36 pages in 4°, in two columns small character.
(8) Last Conviction &c. p. 15, col. 1.
(9) Ibid.
(10) Chimere demontrée, p. 215, 216, and Preface, p. lxiv.

VOL. I.   o   the

THE LIFE OF MR BAYLE.

the Factum, was extremely surprized at Mr Jurieu's assurance in maintaining the contrary (1). 1691.

Before the publication of Mr Jurieu's *last Conviction*, there appeared several anonymous libels againſt the *Cabale Chimerique*, wherein his accuſations were repeated and even improved by new calumnies. Of this kind were the *Letter to Mr Bayle, Professor of Philosophy and History in Rotterdam, concerning the Cabale Chimerique* (2). It was a violent declamation wrote by a Miniſter, one of Mr Jurieu's Creatures. *General Remarks on Mr Bayle's Cabale Chimerique, with a first and second Continuation of these Remarks* (3). At firſt theſe *Remarks* were aſcribed to Mr Bazin de Limeville, a Refugee at Rotterdam (4), but he proteſted that he was no ways concerned in them (5), and it was afterwards known that they were written by Mr Robethon. Mr Bayle publiſhed under the name of a friend, a pamphlet of twelve pages, intitled *A Letter concerning the little books published against the Cabale Chimerique* (6), wherein he informed the Public of his reaſons for not anſwering theſe libels. He ſaid that the prohibition of the Magiſtrate had made him ſuppreſs the anſwer which he had promiſed in his *Cabale Chimerique*; and that all the world was convinced that Mr Jurieu had broke the promiſe which he made to the Burgomaſters, by publiſhing his pretended *New Convictions*. He added that he intended to anſwer Mr Jurieu's laſt libel, but that he did not think it proper to ſpend his time in anſwering a great many other pieces which only repeated the ſame things, or commented on ſome miſtaken or mutilated paſſage of the *Cabale Chimerique*, and advanced falſhoods with equal boldneſs and malice. He gives ſome examples of this, taken from the two pieces juſt now mentioned. The Miniſter who was Author of the letter to Mr Bayle thought fit to reply. He publiſhed a pamphlet of twenty one pages, intitled *A short Refutation of a Letter written in favour of the Sieur Bayle in defence of his Cabale Chimerique* (7). He believed that Mr Bauval was author of the letter concerning the little books. I will inſert here one of his accuſations, Mr Bayle's anſwer to it, and the accuſer's reply: this will be ſufficient to give a notion of theſe two pieces, and of the character of their author. The Miniſter after accuſing Mr Bayle of avarice adds (8), " when I ſpeak of " your avarice I do not uſe this word in the ſtrict ſenſe. They ſay you do not " love money with a deſign to hoard it up; I am willing to believe it ſince people " ſay ſo. You love it notwithſtanding for the uſe you are pleaſed to make of " it, with which I do not pretend to meddle........ But, Sir, do you believe " that the world doth not know why you diſcontinued your *News from the Republic of Letters*! we know indeed that the indiſpoſition which ſeized you, fur" niſhed you with a pretence. But we know likewiſe, that you pretended to be " better paid for it than you had been formerly, and that the Bookſeller not be" ing willing to agree to the augmentation you demanded, your agreement was at " an end, and you diſcontinued the work upon that account. That is to ſay, " your appetite increaſed in proportion with your reputation." Who could imagine that a fact could be alledged with ſo much confidence, without taking all the neceſſary precautions to be certain of its truth! However let us hear Mr Bayle. *I do not know*, ſays he (9), *what name to give to a falshood of a certain declaimer, who has lately published as a thing certain, that Mr Bayle discontinued his* News from the Republic of Letters, *only because the Bookseller would not give him all that he demanded for the copy. The Bookseller is still alive: his name is* Henry Desbordes, *he lives at* Amsterdam, *in the* Kalverstraet, *one may be fully informed what truth there is in this, with all the ease in the world; yet here is a man, who without being at the pains of informing himself, which could have retarded the publication of his wonderful Letter only a day or two, dares to entangle himself publickly in an infamous falshood, for which he may be covered with confusion, if he is capable of any shame, by showing Mr* Desbordes's *own handwriting*. But this author was not to be put to the bluſh. He anſwered cooly (10), " We " think ourſelves obliged to conſult Henry Deſbordes about the fact we advanced, " concerning the interruption of the *News from the Republic of Letters*. We have " ſpoke in the manner we have done on the teſtimony a printer, who at that time " worked for the ſaid Deſbordes, becauſe he had no intereſt to diſguiſe matters, and " we believed that he related things as they were. So we leave it as we found it, " becauſe it is a matter of very ſmall importance in itſelf, and neither much helps " or hurts the principal cauſe." This was the common cuſtom of thoſe writers of libels. They publiſhed upon hear-ſay the moſt infamous things they could pick up againſt Mr Bayle, and when they were convicted of falſhood, they ſaid that *they left them as they found them*. And in this they only followed Mr Jurieu's example, who filled his Factums with mere imaginations and falſhoods. It was in this manner that he repeated ſeveral times, that *Mr Bayle had lived with the Jesuits at* Toulouſe *three years;* tho' he had never lived with them, and had ſtaid only eighteen months at Touloufe, as we have already ſeen. He had his ſpies every where, who wrote or told him what paſſed, and for the moſt part very unfaithfully. We may well imagine, that his ſpies were the very ſcum of the Refugees. He had even ſome of them ſo ſcandalous, that his own creatures were aſhamed of it. One of his friends could not forbear writing to him, that he diſparaged himſelf by his correſpondence with a certain Miniſter

(1) *Letter of the 24th of August* 1691. p. 390, 391.

(2) Lettre écrite à M. B. Prof. en Phil. & en Hist. à Rotterdam ſur la Cabale Chimerique.

(3) Remarques Generales ſur la Cabale Chimerique de Mr Bayle: I. & II. Suite *de ces* Remarques.

(4) Bauval *Copy of a Letter from Mr* S.... *concerning the General Remarks on the Cabale Chimerique*, p. 1. *and the following.*

(5) Entretiens ſur le grand ſcandale cauſé par un Livre intitulé la Cabale Chimerique, p. 157.

(6) Lettre ſur les petits Livres publiez contre la Cabale Chimerique.

(7) Courte Refutation de la Lettre écrite en faveur du S B pour la défenſe de ſa Cabale Chimerique.

(8) Lettre écrite à Mr B. ſur ſa Cabale Chimerique, p. 27, 28.

(9) Lettre ſur les petits livres publiez contre la Cabale Chimerique, p. 6, 7.

(10) Courte Refutation de la Lettre écrite en faveur du S. B. pour la défenſe de ſa Cabale Chimerique, p. 15, 16.

THE LIFE OF Mr BAYLE.

1691. nister among the Refugees at London: Mr Jurieu answered him, *He is a knave, it is true; but he is orthodox*: whereupon he was commonly called the *orthodox knave*.

There appeared likewise another piece consisting of twelve pages, against Mr Bayle's Letter, with this title, *A Letter to Mr * * * relating to a Libel intituled, A Letter concerning the little books published against the Cabale Chimerique* (1). The author ascribes this Letter *concerning the little books, &c.* to Mr de Bauval, with more assurance than the author of the *Letter to Mr Bayle* had done. And indeed the same spirit was observable in both. Before these three pieces appeared, Mr de Bauval had published one of eight pages intituled, *A Copy of a Letter written to M. S.... concerning the author of the General Remarks on the Cabale Chimerique* (2). After some fine raillery upon the author of the *General Remarks*, whom he took to be Mr Limeville, he gives us Mr Jurieu's Petition, and shews how ridiculous it is. He made likewise some reflexions upon the unjust distinction that Mr Jurieu pretended should be made betwixt him and Mr Bayle.

The first edition of the *Cabale Chimerique* being very soon sold off, Mr Bayle published another corrected and very much enlarged. On the back of the title-page there is a short advertisement, wherein he desires the reader not to make a judgment of that piece from the first chapters of it, in which he was forced to be dry, and could not avoid a detail of trifling particulars; but that they should find what followed more lively and less tiresome, if they would give themselves the trouble of reading it quite through. This edition did not appear so soon as the impression of it was finished. Mr Bayle put a stop to the sale of it for a considerable time, because the Burgomasters of Rotterdam had forbidden all the Booksellers in that City, to sell any thing that should be printed on this subject (3). But when he saw that Mr Jurieu published his Factums, he thought himself likewise intitled to publish the second edition of his *Cabale Chimerique*. However, he did not mention in the title that it was printed at Rotterdam, or that it was a second edition corrected and enlarged. As this title is somewhat different from the first, I will insert it here: *The Chimerical Cabal: or a Refutation of the fabulous stories and calumnies which Mr Jurieu has lately maliciously published concerning a certain Project of Peace; and concerning a Libel intituled, an important Advice to the Refugees, upon their approaching return into France, in his examination of that Libel* (4).

In this edition Mr Bayle attacked Mr Jurieu very smartly with regard to the accusation of Atheism. He insisted upon this article by all the considerations which could shew the importance of it; he called upon his accuser, in a solemn manner, to prove it, he employed defiances, insults, and, in a word, every thing that is most proper to put an adversary under a necessity of producing his proofs (5). Mr Jurieu seeing himself so pressed, addressed himself to his Consistory, and promised to make good his accusation: but he gave over this design a few days after, and offered only to be their Commissary, if they would furnish him with some Memoirs, which surprized them extreamly (6). He had oftner than once harangued in the Consistory against Mr Bayle with the utmost vehemence, and went even so far as to declare, That *he would no more be reconciled with him than with the Devil* (7). He endeavoured in vain to get the Acts of the Consistory annulled, which amongst other things contained *that Mr Jurieu had desisted from his accusations against Mr Bayle, concerning Religion, and that he should not carry the complaints he might have against him any where but to the Consistory in the first instance* (8). In the mean while he published a piece intituled, *A short review of the maxims of Morality and principles of Religion, of the author of the Thoughts concerning Comets, and of the General Criticism on Maimbourg's History of Calvinism: To serve for an Information to the Ecclesiastical Judges, if they please to take cognizance of it* (9). He here alledges some passages of these two books, and endeavours to shew that they tend to irreligion. The same day that this piece fell into Mr Bayle's hands, he published one under this title: *The Declaration of Mr Bayle, Professor of Philosophy and History at Rotterdam, concerning a Pamphlet lately published under the title of a Short Review of the Maxims of Morality &c* (10). Mr Bayle here shewed that Mr Jurieu changed the state of the question, he calls upon him anew to prove his accusation of Atheism, and engages to justify himself from all Heterodoxy, as soon as this first and principal point is cleared. He adds several propositions extracted from Mr Jurieu's writings, to serve for a supplement to those, a condemnation of which had been desired from the Synod assembled at Leyden in the beginning of May 1691. "The *Short Review* having been distributed among "the members of the Consistory, they resolved to examine a cause of so much "importance: however they did not ground any prejudices against Mr Bayle's opi- "nions, either upon the discourses, or writings of his accuser. They prepared them- "selves to judge the matter in a regular manner; and Mr Bayle declared him- "self always ready to shew his innocence, and it was not owing to him that "they did not come to a final determination (11), but they did not proceed in "the cause."

Some of Mr Bayle's friends sided with him even so far as to write in his favour. Mr de Bauval published *A Letter concerning the differences between Mr Jurieu and Mr Bayle* (12), wherein he demonstrated that Mr Jurieu could never justify his base usage

---

(1) Lettre à Monsieur *** au sujet d'un Libelle qui a pour titre, Lettre sur les petits Livres publiez contre la Cabale Chimerique.
(2) Copie d'un Lettre écrite à M. S.... touchant l'Auteur des Remarques Generales sur la Cabale Chimerique.
(3) Letter to Mr Minutoli of the 27th of August 1691, p. 392.
(4) La Cabale Chimerique: ou Refutation de l'Histoire fabuleuse & des calomnies que Mr J. vient de publier malicieusement touchant un certain Projet de Paix, & touchant le libelle intitulé Avis important aux Refugiez sur leur prochain retour en France, dans son Examen de ce libelle. A Cologne, chez Pierre Marteau, 1691, in 12°.
(5) P. 337.
(6) Chimere demontrée, p. 14.
(7) Ibid. p. 30.
(8) Letter to Mr Lenfant of the 24th of August 1691, p. 389.
(9) Courte Revûe des Maximes de Morale & des principes de Religion de l'Auteur des Pensées diverses sur les Cometes, & de la Critique Generale sur l'Histoire du Calvinisme de Maimbourg: Pour servir de Factum aux Juges Ecclesiastiques, s'ils en veulent connoitre. In 4°. pagg. 8.
(10) Declaration de Mr Bayle, Professeur en Philosophie & en Histoire à Rotterdam touchant un petit Ecrit qui vient de paroitre sous le titre de Courte Revûe des Maximes de Morale, &c. In 12°. pp. 24.
(11) Additions to the Thoughts concerning Comets &c. p. 15, 16.
(12) Lettre sur les differens de Mr Jurieu & de Mr Bayle.

THE LIFE OF Mr BAYLE.

(1) New Convictions, &c. pag. 10. col. 1.

(2) Letter to Mr Minutoli of the 27th of August 1691, pag. 395.

(3) Lettre d'un des Amis de Mr Bayle aux Amis de Mr Jurieu.

(4) Lettre à Messieurs les Ministres & Anciens qui composent le Synode assemblé à Leyden, le 2 de Mai 1691.

(5) Apologie du Sieur Jurieu, Pasteur & Professeur en Theologie, adressée aux Pasteurs & Conducteurs des Eglises Wallones des Pays-Bas.

(6) Apology for the Sieur Jurieu, pag 25 col. 1.

(7) Ibid. pag. 24. col. 2.

usage of Mr Bayle, whether we consider the matter with respect to the conduct becoming a gentleman, or to our common obligations as members of civil society. Afterwards he defends himself from Mr Jurieu's attacks. We have seen that this divine had accused him of forging the Extract of a Letter in his Journal, wherein it was said that they were reprinting the *Advice to the Refugees* at Paris. He repeated this charge in his *Convictions*, and imputed likewise other crimes to him. He accused him of being the publisher of the *Advice to the Refugees*, and of being *a man without Religion*. He maintained that the Extract of the Letter was forged. "We are certain, says he (1), that it is forged. And we defy those Gentlemen "to deposite that Letter, from whence this Extract was taken, in the hands of four "men of honour who shall be chosen on the one side and the other, who may exa-"mine from whence it came, when it was written, and what goes before and after "that passage. We defy them to do this, says he (2), there is none who has wrote any thing "in my favour, except Mr de Bauval, Mr Basnage's brother. Mr Jurieu hates "him, at least as much as he doth me, and brings him into all his Libels with "a perfectly brutal rudeness; and at last joins him with me as author of the *Advice* "*to the Refugees*. Mr de Bauval has therefore wrote a Letter of two sheets and "a half, concerning our differences, which rallies him in a very elegant and dex-"terous manner." Mr Huet likewise published a piece in favour of Mr Bayle, intitled: *A Letter from a friend of Mr Bayle's to Mr Jurieu's friends* (3), wherein he takes to task several passages of the *New Convictions*, and of the *General Remarks*. This pamphlet is wrote with a great deal of good sense and moderation.

Mr Jurieu raised as many complaints by his heterodox opinions, as he did by his violent and persecuting spirit. Some churches petitioned the Synods to examine his books; they made up a list of heresies and profane expressions contained in them [P], and sent it to the Synod then setting at Leyden, under the title of *A Letter to the Ministers and Elders, members of the Synod assembled at Leyden, the second of May 1691* (4). This accusation together with the disputes he had with several Ministers in the Synods, obliged him to publish a piece intituled, *An Apology for the Sieur Jurieu, Minister and Professor of Divinity, addressed to the Ministers and Heads of the Walloon Churches in the Low Countries* (5): but instead of defending his doctrine here, he with a great deal of pride and ostentation sets forth the great services he pretended to have done the Church; and after thus making his own panegyric, breaks out into railing and invectives against the Ministers who had complained of him, and once more inveighs bitterly against Mr Bayle. It is here that he owns that *since it was not in his power to get him punished as he deserved, at least he would expose him to public infamy* (6), and he makes grievous complaints of *the clemency of the State* (7).

As Mr de Bauval's piece had touched him to the quick, he falls violently upon him; and tho' he had refused to abide by the terms of the challenge which he had given; he

---

[P] *The profane expressions contained in the writings of Mr Jurieu*] Mr Jurieu having complained in 1690 that Mr de Bauval had taken all occasions of introducing him in his Journal without the least necessity; Mr de Bauval answered that this was an unjust complaint. "I have done it, says he (a), only "once in treating of Toleration; and I have spared "him on a thousand occasions. He would long ago "have thundered against me, as he has now done, "if I had not shunned him even when he came "naturally in my way. Have I pointed out all the "blunders which Mr de Meaux, and Father de "Sainte Marthe have observed in his writings? His "not the one of them observed with great marks "of astonishment that Mr Jurieu not being able to "fix the time of the fall of Antichrist * has given this "reason for it; *that in matter of prophecies God doth* "*not look so near*? And has not the other reproached "him with a certain chapter † in the *Accomplish-*"*ment of Prophecies*, which has the following fine "title, *Some things put in order which the Holy* "*Ghost has put out of order, with regard to the* "*visions*? Have not others made violent out-cries "against his *Religion of the Jesuits*? After having "recited there a *Motet* wherein the King of France "is introduced saying to King James II, who had "then abandoned his three kingdoms, *Sit thou on* "*my right hand until I make thy enemies thy foot-*"*stool*, Mr Jurieu adds waggishly, *See what an ad-*

(a) Réponse à l'Avis de Mr Jurieu, pag. 26, 27.

* Accomplishment of Proph cies, tom. ii cap. 12. 1st Edit.

† Ibid. tom. ii. cap. 2. 1st Edit.

"mirable metamorphosis here is! *The King is be-*"*come God the Father, the King of England is be-*"*come God the Son; that this Trinity may be com-*"*pleat I think we should make a Holy Ghost of* "*the Prince of Wales*. He had jested pretty much "in the same manner when he found the following "resemblance between Jesus Christ and the Prince "of Wales, *that as Joseph the Virgin's husband,* "*was not the true father of the first Jesus,* "*James II, the Queen's husband, might possibly like-*"*wise not be father of the second*."

These expressions so unedifying and so disrespectful to Religion, were complained of to the Synods. The Author of the *Answer to Mr Jurieu's second Apology* (b) makes a particular article of them under the title of *Profane expressions of Mr Jurieu*, and gives many examples of them, and among others the following: *The Apostles did not imitate these Jugglers, who immediately upon their arrival any where endeavour to perform some master-piece of their art, &c*. The Disciples of Aristotle must needs be much surprized to find that the Eternal Word has turned Cartesian in his old days (c). Mr Saurin in his *Examination of the Theology of Mr Jurieu*, observes that we may add to this railery the following, which very much resembles it: *Can God perform this miracle? possibly they believe he cannot, and that now he is too old to do such great and extraordinary works* (d).

(b) Reponse à un Libelle intitulé, Seconde Apologie du Mr Jurieu.

(c) Réponse à un Libelle &c. pag. 19.

(d) Examen de la Theologie de Mr Jurieu, tom. i. pag. 532.

2

THE LIFE OF MR BAYLE.

1691. he neverthelefs maintained *that he had convicted him of being an accomplice in the Advice to the Refugees*, and of being *the principal actor in the comedy of the Paris edition* (1). Mr de Bauval publifhed an *Anfwer to Mr Jurieu's Apology* (2) wherein he refuted his calumnies, and fhowed how ridiculoufly he had boafted that he was the pillar of the Church, and the champion of Orthodoxy. He called upon him once more to name his arbiters to decide the difference between them with all rigour: but he called upon him in vain. At laft, feeing that he would make him no reparation, nor come to any explanation, he prefented a declaration to the Confiftory of Rotterdam, by which he *protefted that he looked upon Mr Jurieu to be a calumniator and a wicked man* (3).

Mr Bayle publifhed an anfwer to Mr Jurieu's laft pieces under this title: *The Chimera of the Cabal of Rotterdam, demonftrated by the pretended Convictions which the Sieur Jurieu has publifhed againft Mr Bayle* (4). This Anfwer is written under the name of a friend of Mr Bayle, and contains three parts: I. *The Chimera of the Cabal of Rotterdam, demonftrated by the New Convictions publifhed by a friend of Mr Jurieu; or a Letter from a Friend of Mr Bayle to Mr* * * *. It is a Refutation of the Factum or Cafe publifhed by Mr Jurieu, in fupport of his Cabal of the Project of peace. It concludes with the Letter which Mr Minutoli wrote to Mr Jurieu upon that fubject. II. *General Remarks upon Mr Jurieu's Factum againft Mr Bayle concerning the Advice to the Refugees.* He doth not here endeavour to refute particularly every thing that Mr Jurieu advances in his *Laft Conviction*; but lays down a lift of things to be proved by him, without which that piece could be of no force. III. A long *Preface, wherein the way to judge on which fide the victory lies in this procefs, is laid down.* Mr Bayle gives here an account of all the particulars of Mr Jurieu's accufation, and of what had been done in confequence of it. This accufation is reduced to thefe three heads: *the Cabal of Geneva*; *the Advice to the Refugees*; *and the correfpondence with the Court of France*. Mr Bayle joined to it fome *Reflexions on Mr Jurieu's Apology*, wherein he difcovers feveral falfhoods which he had advanced, and amongft others this; that Mr Bayle owed his eftablifhment at Rotterdam to him. Mr Bayle fhows that it was quite the contrary. In the *Advice to the Reader*, he fays that this book was compofed a good while before, except the laft fheets of the Preface; and that it would have appeared a few days after Mr Jurieu's pretended *Convictions*, if the Printers had been as diligent as the Author. He gives an account of the contents of each part, and makes fome reflexions upon Mr Jurieu's fhameful conduct in this whole affair. Mr Bayle treats Mr Jurieu in this work with lefs feverity than he had done in the *Cabale Chimerique*, as he himfelf obferves.

Mr Bayle much about the fame time publifhed, *Dialogues concerning the great fcandal which had been given by a book intitled the Cabale Chimerique* (5). This piece contains five Dialogues. PHILODEMUS and AGATHO, the two dialogifts, confider Mr Jurieu as an eminent fervant of God who has wore out his ftrength in the fervice of the Church; and are very much difpleafed that Mr Bayle has treated him fo harfhly. They acquaint each other with the converfations they have had with fome *Cabalifts*; and repeat the arguments thefe *Cabalifts* had advanced for Mr Bayle, and the manner in which they had anfwered them. It is a perpetual Irony, under which Mr Jurieu's picture is drawn, and Mr Bayle is vindicated on many different fubjects.

The mortifications which Mr Jurieu had received at the laft Synod (6), the neceffity he found himfelf reduced to of preparing his defences for the next Synod, againft the complaints which came from all quarters againft his doctrine, and his grief to fee that, notwithftanding all his oppofition, Mr Bafnage his brother-in-law was received Minifter in ordinary to the Church of Rotterdam; all this together troubled him fo much that he was feized with his ufual vapours in the month of September 1691 (7). He found himfelf unable to write, and there paffed three or four months without any thing appearing in his difpute with Mr Bayle. But at laft his champion, the Author of the *General Remarks*, thought fit to publifh a piece againft the *Chimera of the Cabal, &c.* intituled, *The Philofopher degraded*. Which may ferve for a third part to the General Remarks upon Mr Bayle's Cabale Chimerique (8). Mr Bayle's friends advifed him to neglect this piece: however he thought it neceffary to anfwer it. He gives the following reafons to Mr Sylveftre for doing fo. "If you had read, fays he (9), the Libel which you defire me not to anfwer, I am fure you would approve of my having made that Author fenfible of his infufferable abufes; and I have done this to nip in the bud a thoufand little libels of this fort which he prepares to give us, wherein he would not regard the groffeft falfhoods, if I did not threaten to take him fharply to tafk. And indeed I thought I fhould difoblige Mr Sartre, if I fhould oppofe nothing but filence to his teftimony." To clear up this fact, I muft obferve that Mr Jurieu in his *Short Review* publifhed a Letter from London, wherein it was pofitively affirmed that a perfon *who had ftudied with Mr Bayle at Puylaurens* (that is to fay Mr Sartre a Refugee and Minifter at London) had faid that Mr Bayle *was feduced to fuch a degree that he turned Papift, and even went to ftay at Toulouse with the Jefuits about three years:* that this perfon having wrote to him concerning his change

VOL. I.   p

change of Religion, *had received a sharp answer from him which bespoke him a true* 1691.
Papist and already filled with the spirit of Jesuitism: that he saw him afterwards at
Geneva after he had left Toulouse, and that Mr Bayle *calling to mind this Letter and
the Answer to it, made an apology for it, and begged of him not to mention that
matter*. Mr Bayle denied all these circumstances in his *Chimere demontrée*, except his
change of Religion. He denied that he had ever *lived with the Jesuits*; and called
upon the Author to name the person who pretended that Mr Bayle had wrote a
sharp Answer to him, and afterwards had made *apologies* for it at Geneva: Upon
this Mr Jurieu's emissary, author of the Letter, engaged Mr Sartre to write a Letter
to Mr Bayle, wherein he owned that he had said, that Mr Bayle " being at Puy-
" laurens, had absented himself; and that it was known some days after that he
" had thrown himself into the Jesuits Convent at Toulouse; that he had wrote a
(1) *Letter* " Letter to him on that subject, such as a young man might be supposed to write
from Mr " on such an occasion; and that he had received a very tart answer to it; and that
Sartre to " he had likewise said, that about three years after he had seen Mr Bayle at Ge-
Mr Bayle " neva, and that Mr Bayle signified to him that he would oblige him, by not
of the 6th " speaking of what had passed at Toulouse, because it might do him hurt in the
of October " design he had of making some stay at Geneva (1)." The Author of the *Philo-*
1691, *p.* *sopher degraded* published an Extract of this Letter; but he suppressed the passage
399, 400.
(2) *Advice* wherein Mr Sartre declared, " that he durst not affirm, either that Mr Bayle had
to the lit- " received his Letter, or that he had answered it, and that several persons who saw
tle Author " the Letter which he received in answer to his, were of opinion that Mr Bayle
of the little " was not the Author of it (2)." However the Author of that Libel pro-
books, &c.
p. 29, 30. duced this Letter as a proof of what had been advanced against Mr Bayle, and to
convict him of insincerity. It was this properly that obliged Mr Bayle to answer this
(3) *It is* piece. His answer (3) is intituled, *An Advice to the little Author of the little Books,*
dated the *with relation to his Philosopher degraded* (4). He there produced many instances of
11th of
December the unfairness, stupidity, and vain repetitions of this Author. He likewise discovered
1691. some falshoods which this pretended Athour to prove from this Letter of Mr Sartre, and
acquainted him that he had wrote to that Minister, and waited for his Answer; and
(4) *Avis* that Mr Sartre had already assured him by a common friend, that he would clear
au petit
Auteur up that matter in a manner which should satisfy Mr Bayle.
des petits We have seen that Mr Jurieu being pressed by Mr Bayle to prove the accusa-
Livrets tion of Atheism, which he had brought against him, had promised to his Consisto-
sur son
Philoso- ry to do it; and that afterwards he drew back, and only offered to furnish them
phe dégra- with some Memoirs on that affair; that without waiting for the orders of the Consi-
dé, 1692. story, he published his *Short Review*, which obliged Mr Bayle to publish a *Declaration*, wherein he showed that Mr Jurieu had changed the state of the question; and
(5) *Addi-* at the same time called upon him to prove this principal article. Mr Jurieu an-
tion to the swered nothing to these repeated challenges, and made no further step before the
Thoughts
concern- Consistory that year. But he would needs renew the process as soon as the Con-
ing Co- sistory was changed in the month of January 1692. " At first, says Mr Bayle (5),
mets, &c. " he would not be considered as a party, but a little after he himself agreed that
p. 18, 19.
" he ought to take that character; he excepted against whomsoever he pleased.
(6) *This is* " And as I much about the same time addressed myself to the Consistory to de-
the ordi- " mand justice against the atrocious calumnies he had published against me, all
nary day " things looked as if we should soon have this affair brought to an issue in form; but
wherein
the Con- " the accuser suffered several weeks to pass without appearing, alledging from sunday
sistories " to sunday (6) divers excuses. At length he acquainted the Consistory that he would
meet. " be ready against a certain day. I was informed of it, and did not fail to appear,
" but instead of entering upon the affair, my accuser desired that we should be
(7) *See in* " referred to the Synod. He supported this by all the reasons he could think of.
the Hist.
and Crit. " On the contrary I did all that was in my power to get the Consistory to re-
Dict. the " tain the judgment of the cause in the first instance before themselves, and pro-
Article " posed that they should desire some of the Ministers of the neighbouring Walloon
COME-
NIUS. " churches, and some of the Ministers of the Dutch churches at Rotterdam to join
" with the Consistory, and that they should even desire the Magistrates to ap-
(8) *The* " point some of their body to assist at the discussion of this cause: but all my
Gate of " demands were rejected by the plurality of voices; my adversary obtained that
Heaven
opened to " the affair should be referred to the Synod. He went in person to the Synod
all Reli- " which met a few days after at Ziric-zée, but did not make the least mention of
gions, by " our process, nay would not so much as agree that the proceedings of the Con-
the fa-
mous Mr " sistory should be laid before the Synod, although the Consistory had commissioned
Peter Ju- " their deputies to do so."
rieu Mi-
nister of About this time Mr Bayle, disguised under the name of *Carus Larebonius*, pub-
the Gos- lished a treatise in Latin against Mr Jurieu's book intituled, *The true System of the*
pel and
Professor *Church*: and as there is no title to which the ear is more accustomed than that of
of Divini- the *Janua Linguarum reserata* of Comenius (7). He intiled it, *Janua Cælorum re-*
ty at Rot- *serata cunctis Religionibus; à celebri admodum viro Domino Petro Jurieu, Rotterodami*
terdam. *verbi divini Pastore & Theologiæ Professore. Porta patens esto. Nulli claudatur ho-*
nesto. Amstelodami excudebat Petrus Chayer. M DC XCII, *in* 4to (8). This work
had

I

THE LIFE OF MR BAYLE.

1691. had been composed long before this time; for he makes mention of it in his *Cabale Chimerique* as a piece that was then ready to be sent to the press. "I know a person, says he (1), who has a Latin Dissertation ready for the press, intituled, *Janua Cælorum referata*, wherein he shows that the *System of the Church* of this Author is a spunge to the Reformation, takes away all manner of necessity for it, and saves good people in all Religions." This was to attack Mr Jurieu in the most sensible part: this book was looked upon as the best he had written; and Mr Nicole thought it the only one of all his writings which deserved an answer (2). Mr Bayle shows Mr Jurieu, that as great an enemy as he was to Toleration, he had here opened the gates of heaven, not only to all the sects of Christians, but even to Jews, Mahometans, and Pagans. This book being wrote in a language understood by all the Learned, mortified Mr Jurieu extreamly. He durst not venture to answer it. But at last having published a piece in defence of his doctrine, intituled, *A second Apology for Mr Jurieu: or an Answer to an anonymous Libel presented to the Synods of Leyden, and Naerden under the title of A Letter to the Ministers and Elders members of the Synod assembled at Leyden the 2d of May 1691*; he put at the end of it a kind of Advertisement, wherein he affected to despise that book; and gave extracts of two Letters, written by persons who talked very contemptibly of it, but who confess at the same time that they had not read it. The Authors of the *Letter* addressed to the Synod of Leyden (3), answered this Apology of Mr Jurieu in a piece intitled, *An Examination of Mr Jurieu's Doctrine which may serve for an Answer to a Libel intitled Mr Jurieu's second Apology*. They do not let this pitiful artifice of Mr Jurieu pass unobserved. "There cannot be, say they, a more diverting rodomontade than that of Mr Jurieu concerning the book intituled *Janua Cælorum referata*, wherein people who understand those matters very well, pretend that his *System of the Church* is for ever demolished. He answers it by two extracts of Letters genuine or spurious; the Author of one of which says that he had not read the book, and the other that he had read five or six sections only, which make but ten or twelve pages. This is a very slight way of getting off, and it is taking people for dupes, to believe that the world will be satisfied with the judgment of this unknown person, who possibly is Mr Jurieu himself. As a Latin book is now out of his reach, and as he cannot grapple with it, he makes the judgment of two persons unknown a pretext for despising a work which he is unable to answer." Mr Bayle had advertised in the beginning of the *Janua Cælorum referata*, that it was wrote in the scholastic stile (4). He likewise made use of their dogmatical method, which, together with the harsh stile, disgusted a great many people from reading this book, and made it to be sought after with less eagerness than his other writings; for otherwise one finds there the same clearness and force of reasoning.

The Author of the *General Remarks*, appeared again upon the Stage, by publishing *Letters concerning the differences between Mr Jurieu and Mr Bayle, wherein the contradictions of the latter are discovered, which may serve for New Convictions* (5). These Letters were five in number, they are dated from Copenhagen; but this did not hinder people from soon discovering the Author. He repeats in a new shape what had been wrote against Mr Bayle, and disguiseth or suppresseth what Mr Bayle had answered. Mr Bayle published on this occasion a piece intituled, *New advice to the little Author of the little books. Concerning his Letters on the differences between Mr Jurieu and Bayle* (6). He sets forth the reasons why he doth not answer this Author, and only gives a specimen of the false reasoning, malice, and fraudulent disguises with which his pamphlets are filled. He inserted Mr Sartre's Answer to his Letter, wherein *he owned that by saying that after Mr Bayle's departure from Puylaurens it was known that he was gone to throw himself into the Jesuits Convent at Toulouse; he only meant that this was said at Puylaurens, and believed by every body*; and with regard *to other little circumstances of the time that there might be from Mr Bayle's going to Toulouse to the time when he saw him at Geneva, and concerning the particular place where they first conversed together, that it was about three years or less . . . . . though his memory had failed him in this, it was a thing of very little consequence either to the one or the other*: and with relation to the *Answer* which was wrote to him from Toulouse he said, that *since Mr Bayle did not agree that he had wrote it, he would not pretend to affirm it, being in no ways certain of the matter*; that is to say, he retracted all that he had advanced, and of which Mr. Jurieu and his party had made a matter of triumph. To this piece Mr Bayle joined a *Letter of Mr * * * to the Author of the Advice to the little Author of the little books*. The Author of this Letter praiseth Mr Bayle for having at his desire suppressed the reflexions which he was going to send to the press, concerning the violent assault which Mr Jurieu had made upon the Author of the *Janua Cælorum referata*, in his second Apology. He shows how mortifying that piece was to Mr Jurieu, and makes an ironical Apology for that Minister's anger. He likewise answers to the reproach which had been made to the Author upon account of his Latin. "It is very likely, says he (7), that Mr Larebonius did not expect such a reproach, not only because he declared both at the beginning and end of his book, that he had on purpose made choice of the scholastic stile, but because he did not think his adversary was able to judge

(1) P. 72. See the Article COMENIUS, R. [M].

(2) See the Article CO-MENIUS.

(3) Mr Basnage de Beauvrecueille, Mr de Dieuval, &c.

(4) Non tam odio in Rhetorum scholis quam in Peripateticorum Lyceæo obtinente.

(5) Lettres sur les differens de Mr Jurieu & de Mr Bayle Où l'on découvre les contradictions de ce dernier qui peuvent servir de nouvelles Convictions.

(6) Nouvel Avis au petit Auteur des petits Livrets. Concernant ses Lettres sur les differens de Mr Jurieu & de Mr Bayle. Amsterdam, 1692.

(7) Nouvel Avis, &c p 65. See also the Article COMENIUS, ubi supra.

"of Latin ſtile, otherwiſe than a blind man judges of colours. It is as un- 1691.
"reaſonable to find fault with an Author for making uſe of the ſtile of the
"ſchools in a work of pure reaſoning, as it would be to deſire that one ſhould write
"in elegant French a confutation of a parcel of ſorry Factums in which the Authors
"had only laboured to invent lies and contradictions. How long is it ſince
"people began to pique themſelves in point of ſtile in writings of proceſſes, in Caſes
"and Inventories. Have the accuſer's libels been refuted with that care that is
"taken in the compoſition of a work, which one would make worthy to
"be read upon its own account? It was known that few people would take the
"trouble to read refutations of this ſort; the reading of them was not neceſſary
"to unprejudiced perſons, and the demonſtrations of Euclid would not be
"able to convince thoſe who are prejudiced; this was known, and therefore care
"was taken not to loſe time about ſtile." This friend ſays afterwards that if
Mr Bayle would have taken his advice, he would have abandoned the Author
of little Books to his bad genius, without daigning to give him a word of
anſwer, and that he is ſorry to ſee that he continues ſtill to confute him. You may
as much as you pleaſe, (ſays he), convict him of having reaſoned wretchedly, of
having quoted falſely, and of repeating the ſame things without the leaſt regard to
what has been anſwered to them; all this will not prevent his writing on, and
rekindling the flame in proportion as he obſerves that time begins to extinguiſh
it. He adds, that this Author had advanced many things which Mr Bayle ought
to have expoſed, ſince he had put himſelf on the foot of anſwering him once
more.

(1) *This*   Mr Bayle prefixed an Advertiſement to this piece (1), wherein he owns that the
Advertiſe- greateſt part of his friends had adviſed him not to anſwer the Author of the Re-
ment is da- marks on the Cabale Chimerique; and that if he had followed their opinion he
ted the 2d would not ſeem to know that there were ſuch things in nature as theſe little libels,
of June and that they had been ſorry that he had refuted ſome places of them: however
1692. as this is a matter where ſomething may be ſaid on both ſides, he had not altogether followed their advice, but had choſen a middle way, which was to publiſh
ſomething to acquaint the public why he doth not more particularly anſwer the
writings of this maker of Remarks. "The principal reaſons, ſays he, why I do
"not engage myſelf in anſwers of this ſort are, I. That this Author doth nothing
"but repeat the ſame things without taking any notice of the anſwers, which have
"been made to them. II. That the public is already too much fatigued with
"ſo many trifling diſcuſſions. III. That this Author falſifies ſo groſsly the paſſages
"which he endeavours to refute, that I have reaſon to think that the diſintereſted
"readers themſelves will diſcover the frauds of this kind: but as I ſhould be to
"blame if I expected to be believed in this matter upon my own word, it was
"neceſſary to give ſome proofs of this; and for this purpoſe care has been taken
"both in the firſt and ſecond Advice to the little Author, to ſhow by ſome ex-
"amples what he is capable of in matter of falſe quotation and falſe reaſoning.
"Beſides it has been neceſſary to deſire all the readers who would judge in this
"matter, to confront the writings of both parties throughout: this is the reaſon
"why, on the one hand, I anſwer ſomething to them, and on the other why I
"do not anſwer all." Mr Bayle obſerved that this ſmall piece would have appear-

(2) *Fac-* ed ſooner, if he had not known that Mr Jurieu had a large Factum in the preſs which
tum ſelon was much cried up by his emiſſaries after their uſual manner, and that to prevent
les formes, his being obliged to go twice to the preſs, he had reſolved to delay the publiſhing
ou diſpo- of this ſecond Advice 'till he had by reading this piece ſeen whether it deſerved an
ſition des anſwer, in which caſe he would have refuted it at the ſame time with this other
preuves piece. But as he was now informed that it would not appear for ſome time, he
contre did not think it proper to delay the publiſhing of this New Advice any longer;
l'Auteur and promiſed here beforehand that if it ſhould be worth while he would very
de l'Avis ſoon demoliſh all the new machines of his accuſer.
aux Refu-
giez, ſelon This Factum appeared ſome time after under this title: *A Factum in form, or the proofs*
les regles *againſt the Author of the Advice to the Refugees diſpoſed according to the forms of the Bar:*
du Bar- *which ſhow that upon ſuch proofs criminals are condemned for capital crimes* (2). Mr Ju-
reau: qui rieu ſays in the advertiſement, that a diſtemper which had kept him very weak for
font voir eight months had hindered him from continuing to write againſt the Author of
que ſur de the *Advice to the Refugees*; but that others had ſupplied his place. He adds that
telles this *Factum* was compoſed by an Advocate at Paris, excepting ſome chapters which
preuves, he had added to it. There is nothing new in this piece but the form. Mr Jurieu's
dans les pretended *preſumptions* are here repeated, though a hundred times refuted; they are
crimes ranged under different heads, and accompanied with a commentary drawn from
capitaux, Mr Jurieu's Libels and thoſe of his adherents. Mr Bayle wiſely deſpiſed this piece,
on con- and would not ſo much as read it, as he acquaints Mr Minutoli. "Mr Jurieu,
damne un "(ſays he (3), has anew publiſhed a great *Factum*, or *Caſe*, againſt me, which no
criminel "body adviſeth me to read, (and I have taken this advice), wherein he only re-
accuſé. "peats his old chicanries without ſeeming at all to know that they have been fully
(3) *Letter* "confuted. He has, as I am informed, brought over again the ſtory of the *Cabal*
of the 28th
of Auguſt
1692, p.
445.

l   "of

1691. "of Geneva and the *Project of Peace*, without having the least regard to what he "has wrote to you in acknowledgement of your innocence, nor to the confession "of his most zealous partizans, that he was in the wrong to attack me on that "head, and that he ought to be satisfied with the other accusati n." Mr Jurieu's adherents wished that he had confined himself only to the accusation which related to the *Advice to the Refugees*: but they judged so only after they saw the event, and because they found that all that he had advanced concerning the Cabal of Geneva, and the Project of a Peace was evidently false and chimerical.

This was the last piece which appeared on this subject. Mr Bayle's prudent silence put an end to this dispute. He had refuted all Mr Jurieu's pretended *presumptions*; and the writings of his partizans consisted only, as we have already observed, of heavy and tiresome repetitions, ridiculous reasonings, and false interpretations of what he had written.

In the mean while people did not agree about the true Author of the *Advice to the Refugees*. It was ascribed to Mr Pelisson as soon as it appeared in France. Dr Wellwood, an eminent Physician at London, who published a weekly Paper called the *Observator*, but without setting his name to it, speaks of it as Mr Pelisson's in his Observator of the twenty second of August 1690, six months before Mr Jurieu thought of ascribing it to Mr Bayle. For it was not before the month of January 1691, that he began to say that he believed Mr Bayle was the Author of it, and the book which he published concerning it did not come out 'till near the end of April (1). "There comes very opportunely to my hand, (says Dr Wellwood (2), "a book that makes of late a great noise in the world, called *Avis aux Refugiez*, "Advice to the Refugees; written by a learned pen in France, designedly to throw "dust on the carriage, and actions of the Protestants of Europe in general, with "relation to the late Revolution in England ...... I both know the Author, "and can assure the reader, *that it was written at command of the late King James* "*and the French King, signified to the Author by the Archbishop of Paris.*" Dr Wellwood's *Observator* having been translated into French, and printed in Holland under the title of *A History of the Times* (3). Mr Jurieu declaimed violently against this passage (4). He said *that it was inserted there to serve a turn, and contrived in the same manner as the forged edition, the forged licence, and the extract of the Letter from Paris in the History of the Works of the Learned*. "We were not much puzzled, "(adds he), to guess whence it came: it comes from the same person in England (5) "who is the only man there who denies that Mr Bayle is the Author of the *Advice*; "and who says every where that *the true Author will discover himself at Paris*. And "in the mean time he has thrust this into a Journal in favour of his friends on "this side of the water, and at their desire; nay it is not improbable, that this "has only been foisted into the French translation, for there is no sort of fals- "hood of which those Gentlemen are not capable." And after having treated Dr Wellwood in the most abusive manner, he makes a ridiculous Apology to him (6). He repeats it likewise in the Advertisement before his *Case in form*. "I am obliged to inform the public, (says he), that the harsh expressions which "are in the *Last Conviction* against the Author of the *History of the Times*, ought "to be cancelled. At that time I did not at all know the Author of it. "I have been informed since that he is a very honest, and very learned "man."

Dr Wellwood in 1692, published an Apology for his *Observator*, under the title of an *Appendix*, wherein he justifies some passages of that work, and among others that which relates to the *Advice to the Refugees*. "This book, (says he (7), "had scarce appeared in France, and was not yet seen in England, when from "a worthy and noble person in France, since in chains for his Religion, I had an "account both of the book itself, of its being concerted with the French Court, "and that every body in Paris looked upon Monsieur Pelisson as the Author of "it. In return of a letter of mine in answer to his, my friend told me, *that ac-* "*cording to my desire, he had employed one who was intimately acquainted with Monsieur* "*Pelisson, to inquire of him the truth of that common report*: and that Monsieur Pelisson "*was pleased to allow the person that spoke to him, to think him the author, though he would* "*not positively confess he was so*; adding, that it was not fit for him, or for the King's service, "to acknowledge that book publickly to be his, though he were the author of it. In short, this "worthy Gentleman gave me both his own and the universally received opinion at "Paris, that Monsieur Pelisson was the author of the *Avis aux Refugiez*, and backed "it with a great many probable arguments, needless here to be mentioned. The "book itself appearing here in London a little after, I took occasion to mention "what my friend told me about it, and withal, upon his information said, *I believed* "*I knew the author*, meaning Monsieur Pelisson, with whom I was a little acquainted "at Paris nine years ago.

Mr de la Bastide (8) was likewise of opinion, that Mr Pelisson was the author of the *Advice to the Refugees*. He said so openly, and by that means drew upon himself the hatred of Mr Jurieu (9). Mr de la Bastide's testimony was of great weight. He had lived in a close friendship with Mr Pelisson five and twenty years; he had been toge-

(1) Cabale Chimerique, p. 217, *of the 2d E-dition.*

(2) Mercurius Reformatus, or the New Observator. Vol iii, Numb. 7.

(3) Histoire du Tems.

(4) Last Conviction &c. p. 34, col. 2.

(5) Mr de la Bastide.

(6) P. 36. col. 1.

(7) An Appendix to Mercurius Reformatus, p. 13.

(8) See his Elogy in the History of the Works of the Learned, December 1704, Art. 14, p. 548.

(9) See Revue de l'Histoire de Mr Bayle, in the collection printed at Amsterdam in 1716, intitled, Histoire de Mr Bayle, & de ses Ouvrages, &c. p. 182 and the following.

THE LIFE OF Mʀ BAYLE.

ther with him a Clerk to Mr Fouquet; and after Mr Peliſſon was confined in the 1691.
Baſtille, he kept a regular intercourſe of Letters with him, on matters of controverſy:
for even at that time Mr Peliſſon inclined towards the Catholic Religion. This cloſe
friendſhip had made him acquainted with Mr Peliſſon's turn of wit and favourite expreſſions. Mr de la Baſtide was well acquainted with his works of controverſy, and
had even anſwered ſome of them. When the *Advice to the Refugees* appeared he
found ſo great a conformity betwixt it and Mr Peliſſon's writings, that he made
no doubt of his being the Author of it. However he did not think it proper to
write any thing on this ſubject during Mr Peliſſon's life: but after his death he
compoſed a Diſſertation (1) to prove this conformity. "I propoſed, (ſays he), to
"put in writing ſeveral general and particular obſervations, which all taken to-
"gether evidently ſhew, that the Author of the *Reflexions on the differences about
"Religion*, is likewiſe the Author of the *Advice to the Refugees*, and that this laſt
"piece is properly only a ſupplement, and, as it were, an appendix to the other."
In his general obſervations he takes notice that Mr Peliſſon was very well acquainted with the Belles Lettres, and eccleſiaſtic and prophane Hiſtory: that he had
ſtudied the Scripture, the Fathers, and the writers of Controverſy: that he was very
well ſkilled in the Roman Law, and loved to make uſe of authorities from it on
ſubjects of all ſorts, having frequented the Bar for ſome years: that being appointed to write the Hiſtory of the King, he collected every thing that was publiſhed, and made Memoirs and Obſervations on every thing that paſſed relating to affairs of State or of Religion: and in fine, that in his books of controverſy, we find
apoſtrophes and frequent exhortations to the Proteſtants, elevations and prayers to
God, and panegyrics on the French King: characters which all taken together
agree to the Author of the *Advice*, and appear to agree to him alone. But to
make this conformity more evident, in his particular obſervations he brings a great
number of paſſages of *the Advice*, and compares them with parallel paſſages in the
Reflexions, and particularly in the third volume of the Reflexions publiſhed in 1689,
under the title of the *Chimera's of Mr Jurieu*. He ſhows for example, that near
the end of that piece Mr Peliſſon inſults the Refugees upon account of Mr Jurieu's
Prophecies, which aſſured them of a re-eſtabliſhment in France in the year 1689;
and that the *Advice* begins with this very thing. In the *Reflexions* Mr Peliſſon
had ſaid, that Mr Jurieu *pours out his gall and venom upon our times, againſt the moſt
illuſtrious defenders and protectors of the truth in our days, without reſpect to rank or
merit*: and in the *Advice*, there is nothing, (*ſays the Author*), *ſo auguſt or ſo eminent
which you have thought worthy of your reſpect; crowned heads, which upon all accounts ought to be ſecured from the inſults of your diffamatory libels, have been the objects of the moſt enormous and furious calumny in many of your books*. In the one and
the other, the Roman Law is frequently quoted; the authority of the greater
number is inſiſted upon; the Prophecies of Drabitius, and the little Prophets of
Dauphiné are ridiculed; the preſent ſtate of affairs in Europe is conſidered; and
a great deal of pains is taken to proclaim the glory of Lewis XIV &c. With regard
to the Preface, we may well imagine that Mr de la Baſtide doth not aſcribe it to
the Author of the book itſelf. It did not appear natural to him that an Author ſhould not only anſwer himſelf, but likewiſe ſatirize his own work, and
give a frightful idea of it.

Mr de la Baſtide concludes his Diſſertation, by anſwering a difficulty which naturally offered itſelf. "If one ſhould now aſk, (ſays he), why the Author did not
" name himſelf in this piece as he had done in others, that he might not loſe,
" amongſt thoſe of his own communion at leaſt, the merit of the wit, learning,
" and zeal which he ſeems to diſplay in it? beſides ſecret reaſons which we do
" not always diſcover, it appears pretty plain that it was not his intention to con-
" ceal himſelf entirely or for ever, but only to ſtand behind the curtain for ſome
" time, in order to know the opinion of the public concerning it. For we find that
" towards the end he ſays to the perſon to whom it is addreſſed, that he may *get
" it printed*, and only recommends it to him to be *cautious in uſing his name*; as if
" he would ſay, that it was not proper to name him openly, but he might allow
" people to gueſs at it. Being born a Proteſtant, and being nearly related and
" allied to ſeveral of the Refugees, it was natural that he ſhould have ſome reluctance
" to appear avowedly the Author of a piece which rendered them odious to the ſu-
" preme powers, and ſeemed to ſhut the door againſt their re-eſtabliſhment. But in
" all likelihood his principal reaſon was, that having in ſeveral places of this piece
" dropped ſome pretty free ſentiments, and ſome pretty ſtrong expreſſions againſt the
" manner in which thoſe of our communion had been perſecuted, and this, whether
" by his not ſufficiently reflecting upon the conſequences of them, or that he might
" by this means the more inſinuate himſelf into the favour of the Proteſtants, the
" Archbiſhop of Paris, and the Jeſuits, made a complaint againſt him on that
" account, as was commonly reported. And it actually happened that an edition
" of the *Advice*, begun by Gabriel Martin, Printer or Bookſeller to Mr Peliſſon,
" was ſtopped and interrupted, though it had been undertaken by his order: and
" we have likewiſe ſeen that ſome time before his death, he got a new edition of

" it

(1) *This
Diſſertati-
on was pub-
liſhed in
the collec-
tion intit-
led Hiſ-
toire de
Mr Bayle
&c. p. 297
and the
following.
Mr de la
Baſtide
gave me
a copy of
it which is
more ex-
act than
that which
is printed.*

THE LIFE OF Mr BAYLE.

1691. "it printed under his own direction; but not before he had suppressed or altered "the passages which had offended those of his communion, and had added a short "preface instead of that which was formerly prefixed to it."

It is true however that a short while after the *Advice* was published, Mr Pelisson wrote to Holland to be informed who was the Author of it, and endeavoured to oblige him to discover himself by the hopes of a considerable reward (1). This would suppose that the Author of it was unknown to him, and consequently that it was not he who wrote the *Advice*. But Mr de la Bastide might have answered, that Mr Pelisson did this only to conceal himself the better, and besides that this supposition is destroyed by the licence of the Paris edition, wherein it is set forth that the Author of the Advice *had obtained a licence dated the 20th of October 1690, but he affecting to remain unknown to the public, had made a difficulty of allowing the said privilege to be registered in his name in the registers of the society of Booksellers of Paris*: which proves that the Author's name was known at the Chancellor's Office, and so it was not necessary to write to Holland to be informed of it.

Mr Bayle tells us in one of his Letters written in the month of October 1690, that *the voice of the public* at that time *gave the Advice to the Refugees* to Mr de Larroque (2). Mr de Larroque left France in the month of February 1686, and went to Holland (3), and the year following he published *Critical Remarks* upon the first volume of Varillas's History of Heresy, which were well received. I have already mentioned his answer to Mr Brueys. After having made some stay in England and in Germany, he returned to Holland, and from thence into France in the month of June 1690 (4), that is, about a month or six weeks after the *Advice to the Refugees* was published, and embraced the Romish Religion. When I began to write Mr Bayle's Life in 1707, I desired Mr Basnage to give me some light in this matter, and he wrote to me what follows, concerning the *Advice to the Refugees* (5). "Since you desire me to write to you with full confidence about what "concerns Mr Bayle ; I do not think you ought to awaken the affair of the *Advice to the Refugees*: not that I at all suspect that he was the Author of it. I have "not as yet departed from my first conjecture: which is that being intrusted with the "manuscript, he had got it printed, and added a preface and some strokes of his "own to it. Mr Hartsoeker has confirmed me in my conjecture, for he has as-"sured me that while Mr de Larroque was a prisoner as Paris, he used frequently "to cite this piece as a production of his own : but as this is an odious subject, it "will be better to let it drop, than to set his enemies a clamouring again." He says likewise in a Memoir, which he sent me some time after. " I always believed "(6), and I still believe, that Mr Bayle was Author of the Preface, and that "the manuscript was entrusted with him by Mr de Larroque, who changed his "Religion a short while after, and who always claimed this work as his own. "This, if I am not mistaken, is all the mystery which made Mr Bayle's defences "so weak : he durst not give his opinion of the book and of the Author who had "always been his friend." Mr Basnage observes that Mr Larroque *always claimed this work as his own*; and in fact Mr Larroque always used to say, in speaking of certain things, *I have said*, or *I have proved this in my Advice to the Refugees*; and his friends have often told it as a literary anecdote, that he was the Author of this book. This is a fact attested by persons very worthy of credit.

Here are two opinions, very opposite to one another, which notwithstanding have each of them their followers. However there is still a third, which seems to have most prevailed : many persons ascribe this work to Mr Bayle, though for very different reasons. Some ground this belief upon Mr Jurieu's testimony, but what weight can we lay upon that ? besides he had so interwoven his pretended *Cabal of Geneva* with the affair of the *Advice to the Refugees*, that he could not be allowed afterwards to separate them. The falsity of the one of these accusations being well proved, necessarily destroyed the other. Notwithstanding when he was convinced that the *Cabal* was only a Chimera, he nevertheless persisted in his accusation concerning the *Advice to the Refugees*. But finding afterwards that this separation was not favourable to him, he was not ashamed to have again recourse to the accusation of the *Cabal*.

Others ascribe that piece to Mr Bayle, because they imagine they discover his stile in it. But this is precisely what ought to make people believe that he is not the Author of it : for besides that proofs drawn from the conformity of stile are very uncertain, the stile of it appears to be very different from that of Mr Bayle's other works : it is more pure, more flowing, and more regular. Mr de Larrey, who had well examined the *Advice to the Refugees*, and who was much inclined to ascribe it to Mr Bayle, has not dared to decide. *For my part*, (says he (7), *I am not either sufficiently persuaded myself to undertake to persuade others, nor bold enough to decide in a problematical matter*.

Lastly, this piece is ascribed to Mr Bayle upon the testimony of Adrian Moetjens, who printed it. It is said that Moetjens told several persons that Mr Bayle was the Author of it. For my part, having heard that Mr Louis, who corrected the proofs, confirmed Moetjens's testimony, I desired him to give me some information

(1) Examen de l'Avis aux Refugiez, p. 24, 25. Chimere demontrée, pref. p. cxxi.

(2) Letter to Mr Constant of the 24th of October 1690, p. 339.

(3) Letter to Mr Rou of the 17th of February 1686, p. 251.

(4) Letter to Mr Constant, ubi supra, p. 339, 340

(5) Letter of the 19th of August 1707.

(6) A Memoir MSS. of Mr Basnage.

(7) In the Preface to his answer to the Advice to the Refugees.

THE LIFE OF MR BAYLE.

formation in this matter. He did not think fit to write me any answer: but he said by word of mouth, to a person equally distinguished by his merit and by his works, who did me the favour to deliver my letter to him (1), "That he knew "Mr Bayle's hand writing before he corrected that work, and that since that time "he has had several opportunities of being perfectly acquainted with it: that the "whole manuscript from the one end to the other was wrote with Mr Bayle's own "hand, and that he preserved a piece of it, which he cut from one of the sheets "before he returned it to Moetjens." This is all I have been able to learn of this matter. But though upon this one should no longer doubt that Mr Bayle is the Author of that piece; yet it would still be unjust to accuse him of the pernicious designs and criminal views, which Mr Jurieu attributes to him. The circumstances in which Mr Jurieu revived that book aggravated his accusations. The persecution had forced the Refugees to abandon their estates and the sweets of their native country, and to retire into foreign parts: their wounds were still sore. In this condition we are impatient of reproof, and are provoked by raillery. We take every thing in bad part; we do not consider the intention of the person who speaks, and we make groundless applications of things. And yet it is the intention which ought to guide our judgments. It is by this that we distinguish an innocent raillery from a bitter reproach, and a wholesome advice from a violent invective. Now it is not possible to imagine that Mr Bayle had an intention to blacken the whole body of the Refugees, or designed to make them odious to Princes, and to lay an invincible obstacle in the way of their return. This were to bely his own character, conduct, and all his other books, wherein he has so well defended the Reformed and shewed himself so compassionate to their misfortunes. Besides, the strongest censures in the *Advice* related only to a very small part of the Refugees, a handful of them who retired into Holland. They were the only persons who wrote any thing. The Refugees in Switzerland, Germany, and England, had printed nothing (2). Mr Bayle was not ignorant of this, and therefore could not have them in view, no more than those in Holland who did not write, and who even blamed the conduct of some of their brethren.

So that though Mr Bayle were the Author of the *Advice to the Refugees*, all that one could say concerning the motives that might have induced him to write this book, would only be, That he was vexed to see some people feed the minds of a great many of the Refugees with chimeras and apocalyptic visions, which rendered them the jest of all Europe: That having an extream aversion to satire and calumny, he was full of indignation to see some Refugees write Libels against persons worthy of regard, and even against crowned heads; that they had taken a cruel revenge on his brother upon account of the Criticism on Mr Maimbourg, and that for a much stronger reason there was ground to apprehend that they would revenge themselves for these satirical writings, upon the Reformed who remained in France: That he knew that in that kingdom, Kings look upon themselves as absolute, and that no body there is allowed to say the contrary; and therefore he was willing to intimate that the writings of the Refugees against this absolute power, served only to render them odious and to hinder their return: That having been educated in the doctrine of the independent and absolute power of Princes, a doctrine which was taught in the Reformed churches, we ought not to be surprized to see him attack the contrary opinion with so much vigour: That not being well acquainted with the affairs of England, he did not believe that the Established Religion there was in any danger, and so he considered the Revolution as a political rather than a necessary action: That he had put on the mask of a Roman Catholic, to give the more authority to his remonstrances, to render them more lively, more touching, and more capable of making impression: "That since the Author of the *Advice*, according to Mr Ju- "rieu's own confession, designed *to put the Refugees in a condition of returning to* "*France, which was not the spirit of the French Papists* (3); he must needs, as "Mr Bayle observed (4), have had the interests of the Protestants more at heart "than those of the Papists, so that what he says in the person of a bigotted Papist "must not be thought his own opinion, but the language of one who wanted to "support the character under which he had disguised himself: That this Author, "as Mr Bayle likewise said (5), had only collected the old and new objections of "the most passionate and malicious Catholics, and the reflexions of flatterers upon "the events of the first Campaign, the envenomed reflexions which were thrown "upon the whole body of the Refugees for the faults of a few Authors, &c. and "all this only to give occasion to a disavowal of them which might be very use- "ful, and to an answer which might confound the malice of the persecutors of "the Reformed and the vanity of flatterers, and might free the Refugees from "the ridicule which their prophecies had drawn upon them; a thing which proved "formerly very fatal to the Protestants who had fled out of the Emperor's domi- "nions (6)." To this we might add that Mr Jurieu who infatuated the Refugees with his prophecies, and who had published several pieces which the Author of the *Advice* called Libels; that Mr Jurieu, I say, whom our Author had principally

(1) *Mr de la Chapelle, Minister of the Walloon Church at the Hague.*

(2) *We must, says Mr Jurieu, justify the Refugees who live at London, and those scattered all over England; those who live at Berlin, in Brandebourg, Hesse, Switzerland, all over Germany, and at Geneva; for I do not bear that in all these places there appear any of those little books which they call Libels. The province of Holland is the only place where all these pieces appear.* Examination of the Advice to the Refugees, pag. 67, 68.

(3) *Examination of the Advice, pag. 13.*

(4) *Chimere demontrée, preface, p. cix, cx.*

(5) *Ibid. pag. cxi. cxii.*

(6) *See the Article* COMENIUS, *Rem.* [K].

THE LIFE OF Mr BAYLE.

1692. cipally in view, had acquired a sort of dominion over the Refugees [*Q*], so that it was not possible to obtain a disavowal of those writings of which they complained, otherwise than by interesting the whole body. Even this expedient did not succeed: the Synods, who ought to have disowned them, kept silence, no body daring to speak through fear of being violently persecuted by Mr Jurieu. We might likewise add, that most part of the reproaches which Mr Bayle puts in the mouth of a Catholic, had been refuted a thousand times, and that Mr Bayle himself had answered them very successfully in his Letters against Maimbourg: and lastly that Mr Bayle intended

(*a*) See a-bove, Rem. [G].

(*b*) See a-bove, Rem. [C].

(*c*) La Foi reduite à ses veritables principes, & renfermée, dans ses justes bornes.

(*d*) See the Rem. [C].

(*e*) Letter from Mr Papin to Mr Jurieu, inserted in his Pastoral Letter to the faithful at Paris, Orleans, Blois, &c. p. 6. col. 1.

(*f*) Preface of Mr Papin's book, intitled: les deux voies opposées en matieres de Religion &c. pag. iii, xii. of the Liege edit. 1713.

(*g*) Letter of the 11th of November 1692, pag. 474, 475.

(*h*) Rewoal, Considerations sur deux sermons de Mr Jurieu, &c. pag. 30, 31, and 37.

[*Q*] *Mr Jurieu had acquired a sort of dominion over the Refugees*] Here follow some of his exploits. He assumed the character of Inquisitor of the Faith, and attacked several French Ministers, most part of whom were Refugees in Holland. He accused them of Socinianism, and brought them before the Synods. All their crime was that they were men of moderate principles; for Toleration was, in his way of thinking, the greatest of all Heresies. It was upon this account that he cruelly persecuted Mr Huet (*a*). He likewise accused as Heretics, or favourers of Heretics, Mr de la Conseillere Minister of Hamburg, Mr Jaquelot, Mr Papin, &c. Mr Papin was a nephew of Mr Pajon, and had the same sentiments with relation to Grace (*b*). He defended them against Mr Jurieu in a book intituled *Essays of Theology, &c.* Mr Jurieu resolved to ruin him; and for a pretext chose a little book of Mr Papin, intitled, *Faith reduced to its genuine principles, and confined to its just bounds* (*c*). This work was wrote with the same intention with that of Mr Dhuisseau (*d*), that is to say, to unite Christians by bringing them back to the fundamental principles of Religion, and to inspire them with a spirit of Toleration in controverted points. It was published without Mr Papin's knowledge. The Manuscript was found *in the closet of a gentleman distinguished by his rank and merit* (*e*), and put into Mr Bayle's hands, who added two pages in the beginning, and published it in 1687, with the aforesaid title (*f*). Mr Jurieu got it condemned by a Synod, and persecuted Mr Papin so violently, that he forced him to return to France, and throw himself into the arms of the Bishop of Meaux. Mr Bayle mentions this in one of his Letters to Mr Minutoli. " You know, says he (*g*), that Papin has changed " his Religion: this he would not have done, if " a confutation of a book of our false prophet " which he wrote, had not exposed him to the violent persecution of that Fanatic, who not being " able to deny the contradictions and sophisms of " which Papin had convicted him, revenged himself " by writing every where that they should take " particular care not to employ Mr Papin he being " a dangerous Heretic, &c. Papin in vain fought " bread in Germany, Holland, and England; he " there found every gate shut by the secret practices " of his enemy, so that he was forced by hunger " to return to France, where he put the Letters " which Dr Burnet had wrote to him, in approbation of a little book intitled *Faith reduced to its " due bounds*, into the hands of the Bishop of " Meaux."
When Mr Jurieu found it impossible for him to accuse people of Heresy whom he hated, he endeavoured to make them suspected by the Government, and represented them as ill affected persons. He suspected Mr le Gendre, Minister of Rotterdam, to be author of a piece against the little Prophets of Dauphiné, and upon this account he accused him before his Consistory, *of entertaining correspondence with France, and of being a secret enemy to the State:* but Mr le Gendre demanded satisfaction of him, and declared that he looked upon him to be *a calumniator and a wicked man.* This Declaration was put in writing, signed, and delivered to the Consistory: Mr Jurieu shifted as much as possible, but Mr le Gendre pressed hard upon him without giving any quarter, and he was forced shamefully to yield. His accusation was torn to pieces in his presence, and by his own consent (*h*). His hatred extended even to the relations and friends of those he hated, tho' they themselves had never had any quarrel with him. He used to accuse them to the Ministers of State as traitors and spies of France. Without regard to Confidence, which is the bond of civil society, he published in his Libels whatever was said or wrote to him; and when he came to fall out with his friends, he used to employ against them whatever they had said to him in confidence (*i*).

Here follow some more of Mr Jurieu's features. They are drawn by Mr de Bauval.
" Mr Jurieu, says he (*k*), has brought trouble and " division every where. His hand has been against " all men, and the hands of all men have been against him. Discord entered along with him into " the Academy of Sedan. He divided it into parties " and cabals. They who foretold what we had to " expect from him by the first step he took after " he was settled in the ministry at Rotterdam, have " not been mistaken. He preached upon these " words: *How beautiful are the feet of those who " bring tidings of peace:* and upon coming down " from the pulpit, he brought a process against his " colleague for precedence; he had however the mortification to be worsted in this vain struggle " for preference. For some years past Mr Jurieu " has put all in combustion among us. His vain " and ambitious mind has carried war every where. " *Bella gerimus nullos habitura triumphos.* He has " divided the French nation, which the common " misfortunes of their flight ought to have united; " he endeavours, as it were, to canton his party. The " animosities which he sows and nourisheth with so " much care, are so many barriers to keep them " asunder. He has assumed the character of Inquisitor-General in order to acquire glory at the expence of his brethrens reputation. He acts as " Universal Bishop. He has armed the Churches " against one another, and has debased and vilified " the gravity and dignity of ecclesiastic assemblies, " by the quarrels of which he has been the author. " On the one hand, we have seen members of " the Synods of Amsterdam and Leyden making " complaints to the Hague, that these two Judicatories have at Mr Jurieu's instigation been " guilty of injustice, and, what is worse, of falshood, from which they have not as yet been " able to clear themselves: and on the other hand, " Mr Jurieu dissatisfied with the Synod of Ziric-zee " has addressed a pamphlet to the States full of complaints, wherein he accuseth that Synod *of violence, " oppression, of all sorts of excess, and of endeavouring to violate the fundamental laws of the liberty " both of Church and State.* Nothing renders ecclesiastical assemblies more contemptible than such " mutual complaints, which lessen and dishonour them. " Mr Jurieu is the original cause of all those disorders. He accuseth, he lays about him on both " hands: he declares that the advice of his friends, " who desire him to have some rest, and *he takes " the counsels of flesh and blood* (*l*). He never takes " up the pen but to write defamatory Libels, and " he no sooner has laid down his arms than he takes " them up again upon the first occasion. He is always the aggressor and pursuer. He employs fire " and sword to root out all who do not submit to " his despotic empire; he calls fraud and calumny " to his assistance; and would willingly go under " the standard of Religion to extirpate, after the " manner of the Interdict, all who refuse to bend " the knee before him. Surely Mr Jurieu has made " many Refugees feel a new kind of persecution " possibly more sensible than that which drove them " out of their native Country. He has robbed them " of that repose which they sought after in their " exile: and to compleat their misfortunes and miseries, they have found among their own countrymen an unjust Oppressor, who under other " names makes them feel the iniquity of the furious " zeal against which they had sought a sanctuary."

(*i*) Ibid. pag. 53, 54.

(*k*) Ibid. pag. 7.

(*l*) Apologie du Sieur Jurieu, pag. 25. col. 2.

VOL. I. No XXIX.

lxvi   THE LIFE OF Mʀ BAYLE.

(1) *See* tended to answer the *Advice* (1), and that they ought to have engaged him to set   1692.
the Chi- about it, instead of diverting him from it by outrageous accusations.
mere de-
montrée,   This methinks is the judgment which an equitable and disinterested person might
p. 307. make concerning this piece, and concerning the design of the Author, supposing him
and the to be Mr Bayle. However *Mr Bayle always protested to those who had the greatest*
Answer to *share in his confidence, that he was not the writer of it ; so that it must be struck out*
Mr Ju- *of the catalogue of his works ; at least this is sufficient to prevent its being alledged in*
rieu's A- *proof against him, and since he constantly denied it, equity will not allow that it should be*
pology, by *quoted in evidence to blacken his memory.* These are the very words of Mr de Bau-
Mr de Bau- val (2).
val, p. 8.
               The accusations brought against Mr Bayle had interrupted his literary labours. Study
(2) Eloge requires a perfect tranquillity. Mr de Bauval had in his Journal for the month of Novem.
de Mr 1690 (3), advertised a work intitled : *A Project of a Critical Dictionary, which will*
Bayle. *contain a the correction of a great number of errors to be found both in Dictionaries, and in other*
(3) *P.* 136. " *books* (4). This, (said Mr de Bauval) is the title of a book which a learned man designs
               " to undertake. As he desires to have the advice and opinion of the learned concern-
(4) Projet " ing his design, he is about to print a Preface in which he will give a distinct ac-
d'un Dic- " count of his Project." This Author was Mr Bayle. He proposed to publish
tionaire this *Project* a few months after, and the impression of it was begun in the month
Critique, of December following. The Articles belonging to the three first letters were al-
où l'on most all prepared, and while these were printing Mr Bayle was to finish the others,
verra la together with the Preface. But Mr Jurieu's violent attacks obliged him to lay aside
Correcti- this work after the first sheet of it was printed, so that he laid down that Pro-
on d'une ject very soon after he had formed it. More than a year passed before he took it up
infinité again, and at last when Mr Leers pressed him to set about it, he was obliged to
de fautes
repandues make use of the first subjects which chance presented to him, till he had col-
soit dans lected the books which were necessary to his design (5).
les Dicti-
onaires,   This work appeared in May 1692 (6), under this title : *A Project and Fragment of a*
soit dans *Critical Dictionary* (7). Mr Bayle gives an idea of this Project in a long Preface, addressed
d'autres to Mr du Rondel, Professor of Belles Lettres at Maestricht. He says that he designed
Livres. to compose a *Dictionary*, which should contain all the falshoods and errors of fact which
(5) *See the* are found in other Dictionaries, and a Supplement to their omissions under every Article.
Booksel- He promised likewise to make sallies upon all sorts of Authors as occasion should offer.
ler's Ad- After this he shows how useful such a compilation would be. " Were it not to be wish-
vertise- " ed, (says he), that there was extant a *Critical Dictionary*, to which one might have
ment on   " recourse in order to be sure whether what we find in other Dictionaries, and in all
the reverse " sorts of other books, be true? It would be a touchstone of other books, and you
of the title " know a gentleman who is a little affected in his stile who would not fail to
of the Pro-
ject & Frag- " name such a work, *the Office of Insurance of the Republic of Letters* . . . . . You
ments &c. " see very well that if, for example, I should be able to collect under the word
(6) *The*   " SENECA, all the falshoods that have been advanced concerning this famous Philo-
Booksel- " sopher, one needed only consult that article to know what is to be believed
ler's Ad- " of what one reads concerning him in any book : for if it is a falshood, it would
vertise-   " be taken notice of in this collection, and when one did not find a thing set
ment is   " down here as a falshood, one might depend upon it as true : this instance is suf-
dated May " ficient to show that such a design well executed, would produce a very useful
5, 1692.
(7) *Projet* " work, and very convenient for readers of all sorts." Mr Bayle added that he
& Frag- knew well enough what ought to be done in order to perform such an undertak-
mens d'un ing perfectly, but that he knew still better that he was not able to execute it :
Diction- so that he would confine himself only to give a sketch of it, which should on-
re Criti- ly contain a volume in Folio ; leaving the continuation of it to persons who have
que A
Rotterdam the requisite abilities, in case this Project, rectified in every thing that shall
chez Rei- be necessary, should be thought worthy of the labours of the learned. But as
nier Leers he had foreseen that even this sketch would be extensive enough to engage him
1692. In in a very painful task, and that besides he was very doubtful how he should exe-
8o. cute his project, he had resolved to venture a few fragments of this work abroad,
that he might before-hand know the taste of the public, and be determined
thereby either to pursue or abandon his design. These *Fragments* contained the
Articles of ACHILLES, ANTHONY ARNAULD, JANE OF ARRAGON, COR-
NELIUS BALBUS, of the Author concealed under the name of STEPHANUS
JUNIUS BRUTUS, of CASSIUS in general, and in particular of SPURIUS CAS-
SIUS VISCELLINUS, of L. CASSIUS LONGINUS, of C. CASSIUS LONGINUS,
of T. CASSIUS SEVERUS, which gives him an occasion of making *a digression*
concerning diffamatory libels. He placed there likewise the articles of L. CASSIUS
HEMINA, of C. CASSIUS LONGINUS, of CATIUS, of COMENIUS, of ERAS-
MUS, of the Maréchal de GUEBRIANT, of HIPPOMANES, of the DAY, of
Madam DES LOGES, of the three sisters ANNE, MARGARET, and JANE
(8) *In the* SEYMOUR, of MARY TOUCHET, and of ZEUXIS. All these Articles were
beginning *personal* except those of *Hippomanes* and of the *Day*, which Mr Bayle called *real*,
of the Ar- because they neither related to persons nor places, and consequently did not belong
ticle HIP- to Historical or Geographical Dictionaries (8).
POMANES,
p. 297.

The

1693. The plan of this new Dictionary was not relished, though such a work might have been very useful. Mr Bayle laid it aside, but in the mean while he formed a design of another Dictionary which he forwarded with so much diligence, that the impression of it was begun in the month of September 1693; notwithstanding he had been frequently interrupted in it by the trouble Mr Jurieu gave him. He acquaints Mr Constant with this, in order to excuse himself for not having wrote to him sooner. "I have been, (says he (1), very much embarassed these three or four "months past by the machinations of my accuser, who having interested the Dutch "Consistory in his quarrel with me, has persuaded them to examine my book con- "cerning Comets, and to lay it before the Burgomasters as a book filled with "dangerous and impious propositions, and that therefore it is not consistent with "their duty to give a salary to a Professor who entertains such opinions. This "is the turn he has given it, after being disappointed by the nullity and rash- "ness of his other accusations. I was obliged to make some visits, to undeceive "people concerning the pretended heresies in this book; and here one cannot "do in a fortnight what might be done elsewhere in an afternoon."

(1) *Letter of the 29th of June 1693. pag. 510.*

Mr Bayle attributed the disgrace, which he fell under a short while after, to the sollicitations of these Ministers: see in what manner he speaks of it to Mr Minutoli on the fifth of November. "Our Magistrates, (says he (2), have depri- "ved me of my place of Professor, together with the salary of five hundred "gilders which was annexed to it, they have even revoked the liberty of teach- "ing privately which they had granted me. This resolution was taken by the plu- "rality of voices on the thirtieth of October last; and last monday (3) the Burgo- "masters notified it to me in their chamber. All people of good sense here "cry out against this injustice, and several of our Counsellors of the "longest standing in their Offices, and of the greatest abilities, opposed this "resolution with all their might, but they were outvoted. If they had not last "year turned out seven or eight Burgomasters or Counsellors of this City, in "order to put others in their places, this would not have happened to me. It "gives me comfort to see the general discontent of the City on this account, "the irregularity of their proceedings in this affair, and the unjust ground "of it. This ground is my *Various Thoughts concerning Comets*: the Dutch Mi- "nisters have made the Burgomasters believe that it contains dangerous matters, "and opposite to Christianity. This I offered to refute; and I maintain, and will "prove it as clear as noon-day, that my book concerning Comets advances nothing "contrary either to our Confession of Faith or to the Scripture. But however "this be, they have condemned my doctrine without allowing me a hearing, and "without asking me if I agreed to the justness of the extracts, and to the sense "which they give to my words; neither did the Magistrates give me any oppor- "tunity of answering my accusers. There was nothing said either concerning the *Ad- "vice to the Refugees*; or the *Project of a Peace*, which I intended to publish. This "would have been more odious."

(2) *Letter of the 5th of November 1693, pag. 537, 538.*

(3) *The 2d of November.*

In another Letter to him, he says (4); "You have very probably heard it re- "ported in your country, that I lost my place upon account of the *Advice to the "Refugees*. For the emissaries of you know who, being mortified to the last degree, "at the contempt which our Superiors showed for his pretended information concern- "ing the Cabal of Geneva, and for his repeated calumnious Factums relating to the said "*Advice*, have spread it abroad every where that it was the accusation about "that book which produced this effect. This is a manifest absurdity, for they "would not have satisfied themselves with taking away my liberty of teaching, "if they had founded their proceedings against me upon an accusation of writing "a libel against the State. You may affirm it confidently that the only foun- "dation of it was the complaint of the Dutch Consistory against my book on "Comets; and most people are of opinion that they never read the book, and "some of them were against depriving me of my pension. It was therefore only "upon account of my Treatise concerning Comets. The Dutch Consistory being "almost wholly composed of persons who neither understand French, nor any thing "else, except a few common places of Divinity; who besides were ill affected to- "wards me from my first arrival in this Country, because my Patron who found- "ed the *Illustrious School*, (the late Mr Paets, a great Republican) was very much "hated by them: this Consistory, I say, only consulted a Dutch translation of "some passages out of my book, made by my accuser, with the greatest insincerity "in the world."

(4) *Letter to Mr Minutoli of March 1694, pag. 542.*

Mr Bayle gave the same account, but with some further circumstances, to his cousin Mr de Naudis, on the twenty eighth of December. As this Letter has not been printed, the reader no doubt will be glad to find it here.

"You must know that upon the thirtieth of October last my appointment of "five hundred livres, and the liberty of reading public and private Lectures, "were taken from me by the Council of this City, which is composed of four "and twenty persons, whom they in Dutch call the *Vroedschap*. The Burgomasters "who are four in number, and chosen out of these twenty four, acquainted me with

"with this resolution, without telling me why they now took from me what they 1693.
"granted me in 1681. I have been told that several members of the Council op-
"posed this act of injustice very vigorously, but the plurality of voices carried
"it. Let us distinguish the real cause of this from the pretext.
"The pretext with which they coloured their conduct, when they were spoke
"to in private about it, and which was even alledged by some on giving their
"votes the day on which I was deprived of my place, is, that the book con-
"cerning Comets, which I published here in 1682, contains pernicious doctrines,
"and such as no Christian Magistrate should suffer to be instilled into youth. To
"give more authority to this pretence, the authors of this plot had by a long
"train of intrigues obtained that certain head-strong Dutch Ministers, great ene-
"mies to strangers and to the new Philosophy, and of a violent and seditious
"temper, should take the book concerning Comets into their examination, and
"determine that it contains unsound doctrine. All this was done in a very my-
"sterious manner, and without giving me the least notice of it, and without
"having the least regard to my public declarations, which I have repeated a
"hundred times to the Burgomasters, Ministers &c. in conversation, that I was
"ready to show that my Comets contained nothing contrary either to sound reason, or
"the Confession of Faith of the Reformed Churches. A great number of people
"of merit here are highly offended at this violent procedure, which is not prac-
"tised even in the Church of Rome: for there they hear an Author accused of
"Heterodoxy, and admit him to explain or to retract his errors. This, dear
"Cousin, ought to lessen your regret for not having left France. You will be a
"hundred times the better Protestant, if you only see our Religion where it is
"under persecution: you would be offended if you saw it where it is established,
"but let us come to the cause of my disgrace.
"You must know that a Republican Government has this peculiar to it,
"that every City, nay every little Town is composed of two or more parties.
"In Holland there are two every where: the one is very weak, but composed of
"people of substance and honour; the other governs haughtily, and almost
"constantly makes a bad use of its good fortune. I had upon coming into
"this Country all my patrons, benefactors, and those who received me with ci-
"vility, among the weaker party, which however was not then so weak as
"now: I have always cultivated their friendship, and have never conformed my-
"self to the maxims of Courtiers. I have not endeavoured to make my court
"to those of the other party, which was growing more powerful every day, this ap-
"pearing to me base and mercenary. So that a sudden storm having above a
"year ago happened in this City, which overwhelmed part of our Magistrates, and
"others of this all-powerful party being put in their places, the balance could no
"longer be preserved, and to show their power against those who do not fall
"down before them, and who keep up their correspondence with their old friends,
"they have turned me out of my place. And as doctrines pretended to be dan-
"gerous to the youth was the pretext, they were obliged to take from me the
"liberty of teaching in private as well as in public. By this means they have stopped
"up both the sources of my subsistance. I never received a farthing of my pa-
"trimony, never had a humour of laying up money, and never was in condition
"to save any. I depended upon my salary, which I believed I should have en-
"joyed for life: but now I see there is nothing certain in this world. You may
"judge that I had great reason to be uneasy about the time to come, in a Coun-
"try where living is very expensive. But hitherto by the goodness of God I
"have not felt any uneasiness, but have been perfectly resigned to the will of
"heaven.
"You would be surprized if I should finish my Letter without mentioning that
"French Minister who has published so many libels and calumnies against me.
"I can assure you that all these calumnies have fallen to the ground, and there
"was nothing taken notice of but my book concerning Comets, printed near twelve
"years ago. Besides they were Dutch Ministers who carried on this pursuit a-
"gainst me in a clandestine manner. They have owed me a grudge for a long
"time, because they hated the friends and patrons which I had upon my first ar-
"rival here, and being infatuated with Aristotle, whom yet they do not understand,
"they could not hear Des Cartes named without swelling with rage."
Mr Bayle was ignorant of the true cause of his disgrace: his Judges did not think
it proper to inform him of it. He never suspected that it could proceed from
any circumstance relating to the situation of public affairs, however that was the
occasion of it. France victorious every where, began to be weary of the war.
The efforts which she had made to gain this superiority over her enemies, had drained
her both of men and money. Peace would have been advantageous to her, and
she took all possible steps to obtain it. In the year 1692 she had found means
to propose it to the Emperor, the King of Spain, and the Duke of Savoy, by the
Pope and some neutral Princes; but they did not give the least ear to her proposals. Seeing herself refused on that side, she wanted to try what she could do
in

1693. in the United Provinces, and employed Mr Amelot, her Embaſſador in Switzerland, to make her intentions known to ſeveral conſiderable perſons. She promiſed the States a ſtrong barrier to cover their country, a full and entire liberty of commerce, and all the other advantages they could deſire. Mr Halewyn, Burgomaſter of Dort, ſeduced by theſe great offers, entered into a ſort of negotiation with Mr Amelot, without the knowledge of the States. King William was informed of this, and Mr Halewyn was ſeized, together with his brother who was believed to be his accomplice. Mr Bayle mentions this in one of his Letters to Mr Minutoli. " No
" body knew certainly, ſays he (1), what was the crime of theſe gentlemen until (1) Letter
" their ſentence was publiſhed; for during the proceſs, every thing was managed of the
" with great ſecrecy. They have diſcovered that Mr Halewyn the Counſellor 14th of
" was entirely innocent; but his brother, the Burgomaſter of Dort, has been found September,
" guilty of holding correſpondence with Mr Amelot, the French Embaſſador in 521, 522.
" Switzerland, in order to negotiate a peace in this country. He confeſſed this, 1693, p.
" and pretended that it was the duty of every lover of his country to endeavour to
" put an end to ſo deſtructive a war; that he was not the only man who had given
" ear to the propoſitions of France; and that he had communicated all that he
" knew of this matter to a perſon to whom others had made the ſame propoſitions.
" However he has been condemned to perpetual impriſonment, and confiſcation of
" his eſtate. They have not printed with his ſentence all the anſwers and juſtifications,
" which had been inſerted in the minutes of it; and people are generally of
" opinion that he had no intention of betraying his country, and that he was as
" well affected to the Republic as thoſe who are againſt a Peace; the difference
" between them being only, that the one believes that the continuation of the war
" is advantageous, and the others that it is hurtful. But, unhappily for him, cor-
" reſpondence with the enemy, and meddling in a treaty of peace without a parti-
" cular commiſſion from the Sovereign Powers, is treaſon; and this makes diſin-
" tereſted people ſay that the puniſhment inflicted upon him is too gentle. You
" cannot imagine, adds Mr Bayle, the hopes which our prophet conceived from the
" impriſonment of theſe gentlemen. He hoped that all his pretended *Cabal of Ge-*
" *neva* would be diſcovered, and that you and Mr Goudet, and the Syndics whom
" he aimed at, that Meſſieurs Baſnage and I ſhould be involved in their de-
" poſitions: and he already boaſted that he was the firſt, who had blown up the
" mine of that *wicked plot*, ſaid he, *of the project of peace, which was contriving in*
" *Switzerland*. But all his hopes, as uſual, where chimerical, and it appeared that
" we had thought of nothing leſs than of Mr Amelot and Meſſieurs Halewyn."
Mr Bayle's innocence in this matter did not hinder his feeling the effects of theſe ſecret negotiations: they were the cauſe of his diſgrace. All Mr Jurieu's intrigues among the Magiſtrates were fruitleſs. It is true he perſuaded the Dutch Miniſters to act in his favour againſt Mr Bayle; but their ſollicitations came to nothing. The Regency of Rotterdam had been changed in 1692, by order of King William, who turned out ſeven Magiſtrates who were Mr Bayle's protectors. However they who ſucceeded them had at firſt no bad intentions againſt him: they declared that they would do juſtice, and promiſed to hear his defences, if there ſhould be occaſion for it. But the ſecret practices of France, made King William call to mind the *Project of Peace* of which Mr Jurieu had made ſo much noiſe; and as the peace of Nimeguen had been brought about by ſpreading abroad ſuch pieces at Amſterdam and elſewhere, he thought they had a mind to make uſe of the ſame methods at Rotterdam. That great Prince, not having time to examine this ridiculous Project, was alarmed at the thoughts of a Peace, and imagined that there was, as Mr Jurieu pretended, a cabal to aſſiſt in bringing it about, of which Mr Bayle was the chief perſon who had as yet been diſcovered. He commanded the Magiſtrates of Rotterdam to deprive him of his place of Profeſſor and of the ſalary annexed to it, and this order was put in execution without either citing or hearing him, notwithſtanding the promiſes they had given him to the contrary. It is very certain that the *Advice to the Refugees* had no ſhare in this. King William did not regard the Refugees ſo much, as to trouble himſelf about the complaints they might have againſt that book. But the *Project of Peace* made him uneaſy, he was afraid of the conſequences of it (2). The Magiſtrates of Rotterdam, though better acquainted with (2) *This is* this chimerical project, obeyed the orders of that Prince whoſe creatures they were: *taken from* however they ſeem to have been aſhamed of their conduct, ſince they concealed the *a Memoir* cauſe of it from Mr Bayle. It even appears that they, who were in the ſecret, *of Mr Baſ-* deceived thoſe who were not, and made them believe that the book concerning Co- *nage.* mets was the foundation of their ſentence.

Mr de Bauval bears Mr Bayle witneſs (3) " that he received this diſgrace with (3) Eloge
" a philoſophical conſtancy, and even with too great indifference; eſpecially with- de Mr
" out uneaſineſs with regard to his fortune. He did not mind the gathering of Bayle.
" riches, becauſe really he had no occaſion for them. His temperance and ſobriety
" ſupplied the place of every thing, ſo that having little he wanted nothing. He was
" not however reduced to indigence, very far from it. Neither did he make any ſtep
" to procure a new employment. He found himſelf more free and more at his
" own

THE LIFE OF Mr BAYLE.

"own disposal, now he was released from the tiresome labour of teaching and 1693. reading of lectures." Mr Bayle gives the same account in one of his Letters to Mr Minutoli, who had condoled with him upon his disgrace. "I received it, says (1) *Letter* he (1), as becomes a Christian Philosopher, and I continue, I thank God, *of the 8th* to possess my mind in great tranquillity. The sweetness and repose I find in the *of March* studies in which I have engaged myself, and which are my delight, will make *1694. p.* me stay in this city, if I am allowed to continue in it, at least, 'till the impres- *541.* sion of my Dictionary is finished; for my presence is absolutely necessary in the place where it is printed. Moreover, being neither a lover of riches, nor honours, I shall give myself no trouble to procure an invitation elsewhere; and would not accept of it, though it should be made to me. I am not so fond of the disputes, cabals, and professorial snarlings, which reign in all our Academies. *Canam mihi & Musis.*" And indeed he was so charmed with this quiet and independent situation, that he refused very advantageous offers, and would not so much as make use of the liberty which the Regency were willing to allow him of teaching the sons of some of the Counsellors who desired it earnestly. Mr Basnage sollicited him several times to give them this satisfaction, but in vain. The Count de Guiscard, who was pleased to allow him his friendship at Sedan, desired him to take the charge (2) *See the* of his son's education (2). He offered him a thousand crowns of appointment, and *Article* assured him that he had taken his measures so with the Court, that he should enjoy *Guis-* a full liberty of conscience: but Mr Bayle excused himself upon the necessity he *card.* was under of finishing his *Dictionary*, which was then in the press. *Rem. [C].*

Mr Jurieu's conduct sufficiently shews that he thought it was lawful to hate his 1694. enemies and to persecute them. But he said that *his enemies were the enemies of God*; and declared solemnly that he had taken his duty to *tread under foot all human considerations, and to have no regard to the ties or friendships of this world when the glory of God was concerned.* In this manner he invested himself with the character of Defender of the Cause of God, that he might treat with indignity all those who had the misfortune to fall under his displeasure: and though nothing is more opposite to the maxims of the Gospel than the hatred of our neighbour, he was not ashamed to defend it in two Sermons: the one on these words of David, *shall not* (3) *Psalm I hate those who hate thee? I hate them with a perfect hatred* (3): and the other on *cxxxix,* these of Jesus Christ, *love your enemies, and bless those who curse you* (4). Every *v. 21, 22.* body was offended to hear such scandalous morality taught from the pulpit. Mr Bayle (4) *St* charged him publickly with it, in a loose sheet, intituled: *A new heresy in Morality,* Matt. c. v. *concerning the hatred of our neighbour, preached by Mr Jurieu in the Walloon church of* v. 44. *Rotterdam on sunday the 24th of January, and on sunday the 21st of February 1694. published for the information of all the Reformed Churches, and particularly of the French* (5) *Nou-* *Churches gathered together in the different places of their exile* (5). In the beginning *velle He-* he sets forth the doctrine which Mr Jurieu had preached concerning the love of *resie dans* our neighbour. "I shall not set down particularly, says he, all the pernicious *la Morale,* maxims and propositions which have been extracted from these two last Sermons; *touchant* but shall content myself with acquainting you that his doctrine in general may *la haine* be reduced to that which follows: I. That sentiments of hatred, indignation, and wrath, *du Pro-* are lawful, good, and praise-worthy, against the enemies of God; that is to say, *chain, prê-* as he explained it himself, against the Socinians, and other Hereticks in Holland, *chée par* against the superstitious and idolatrous, &c. II. That we ought to shew these *Mr Jurieu* sentiments of hatred and indignation by breaking all communication with those *dans l'E-* people, by not saluting them, and not eating with them, &c. III. That we ought *glise Wal-* not only to hate these peoples heresies and bad qualities, but that we ought to *lonne de* hate their persons and detest them. One of the objections which he made to *Rotter-* himself, and which he rejected with an air of the utmost disdain, was, that we *dam les* ought to be at enmity with error and vice, but at the same time have charity *Diman-* for the person of the sinner." Mr Bayle next takes notice of the false interpreta- *ches 24 de* tion which this Minister had given of the Scripture in order to draw it to his pur- *Janvier,* pose, the pernicious consequences which may follow upon this doctrine, and how *& 21 de* necessary it was that the Ministers of the Walloon Churches should stigmatize *Fevrier,* this pernicious morality, the tendency of which must be the throwing Holland into *1694. De-* confusion, and putting an end to its commerce. "For what must be the conse- *noncée à* quence, says he, if the Reformed should neither salute those of another Religion, *toutes les* nor eat, nor trade with them? what must be the consequence if they be allowed, *Eglises* and it be thought praise-worthy, to hate the persons of all Papists, of all Arminians, *Refor-* Mennonites, &c. and if we are obliged by the Gospel only to wish them spiri- *mées, &* tual blessings, without being obliged to procure them any temporal good, to draw *nommé-* them out of a ditch if we should see them fall into it, to give them alms if we *ment aux* see them in want? could this country prosper upon such principles? are not *Eglises* they therefore seditious, and tending to overturn the Government, as well as *Françoises* heretical? Is the person, who teaches them, ignorant that this is censuring with *recueillies* an astonishing boldness the supreme powers and the laws of the Government under *dans les* which we live? *différens* *endroits* *de leur* *exil.*

Mr Bayle

THE LIFE OF Mʀ BAYLE. lxxi

1694.   Mr Bayle made too great haste to publish this charge. He was blamed for doing so. Mr Jurieu was actually printing these two Sermons, and they were ready to be published. If he had waited for their publication, they would have furnished visible proofs of his pernicious Morality. As soon as he saw this charge he suppressed them, and published a paper under the title of *Reflexions upon a Libel in a loose sheet, intitled, A new Heresy in Morality, &c* (1), wherein he denied that he had preached the Doctrine he was accused of. Mr de Bauval took occasion from this to set Mr Jurieu's morals in a full light, and to show that this Minister's conduct was agreeable to his morality. This piece is intituled, *Considerations on two Sermons preached by Mr Jurieu, concerning the love of our neighbour: wherein the following curious question is incidentally handled: If we are obliged to hate Mr Jurieu* (2). Mr de Bauval showed very well that Mr Jurieu by suppressing those sermons furnished a proof that he had preached what he was accused of. " If the Morality contained
" in Mr Jurieu's sermons, says he (3), has nothing scandalous in it, it is very
" surprizing that he has put a stop to the impression of them. He might have
" contented himself with a denial of the Libel, without engaging himself further in
" the matter; but we know that they were in the press. The sheets of them have
" been seen, and all of a sudden he changed his resolution. The reason which
" he gives for this interrupting and retarding of them, strengthens the suspicion in-
" stead of weakening it. *We are very well informed (says he) that these Gentlemen
" lie in ambush, and that they have prepared their batteries in order to find heresies
" in these sermons, and we do not think it proper at present to give them the pleasure
" of an engagement, we will wait a little 'till their fire is somewhat spent.* But if
" Mr Jurieu is under no apprehensions with respect to orthodoxy, far from suppres-
" sing his sermons upon account of the menaces of these gentlemen, he ought to laugh
" at their preparations, and make all their batteries useless. These gentlemen whom
" he aims at, are not Knights-errant to go about to fight with phantoms; and after
" all, the public, who is their common judge, would have vindicated Mr Jurieu, if
" they had cavilled him without reason. If they had offended the world by it, hair Mr
" so much the worse for them, it would have been at their own expence and at their Jurieu.
" own peril. As for Mr Jurieu, if his morals are sound, the printing of his sermons
" would have put these gentlemen to silence, and would have stifled all the murmurs
" they have raised on that subject. But it must be confessed that this so sudden inter-
" ruption of a design already begun, is so unlike Mr Jurieu, that he gives ground
" thereby to think that he has stopped the course of the impression for no other reason
" but that his doctrine might not be exposed to the inevitable censure of the publick. It
" is at least a strong presumption, that the *Information* to the public stopped him short,
" and that what ought to have been a further reason for hastening the publication of his
" sermons, has obliged him to put it off to an uncertain time. This prudence of
" waiting *'till these gentlemens fire was a little spent,* seems to be only an artifice to
" let the remembrance of these sermons, which is at present too fresh and recent,
" pass away, that by this means he may afterwards be at liberty with more im-
" punity to give them a quite different form. If Mr Jurieu has taught, as he as-
" sures us he did, *that we ought to forgive our enemies: that we ought not to seek
" to revenge ourselves: that we ought to suffer injuries patiently,* this is without doubt
" the doctrine of the Gospel, he runs no hazard; but his irresolution shows that
" he is embarrassed, and is contriving some trick to save himself: for he promi-
" seth *either the sermons or a treatise.* One would say he doth not know on which
" side to turn himself. A man has not all this uneasiness when he has only preached
" the morality of the Gospel. There has been a clamour raised about these sermons.
" It is therefore these very sermons which ought to appear or nothing. A treatise
" on this subject will not decide the question. Besides, if Mr Jurieu has preached
" no other doctrine than what we have just now mentioned, from whence have those
" rumours and the emotion of his audience proceeded? whence comes it that the Re-
" formed Ministers of Rotterdam have all with once voice disapproved of his mo-
" rality? we defy him to refer himself to their judgment. Whence comes it that
" some of his hearers have been so shocked and offended at him, that they have de-
" clared they will no longer hear him. While he went on in the common road,
" he found no such commotions? But what is still more, from whence ariseth the
" difficulty which the Commissaries of his Consistory make of granting him the
" approbation he desired? How comes it about that they have not as yet found
" sufficient evasions and softenings to make it safe for them to do so? This is a
" strong presumption that his morality startled them. Otherwise they would have
" granted him their approbation without difficulty."
Mr Saurin agrees with Mr de Bauval in his sentiments on this subject. That Divine declares, that " the most favourable thing that we can say of these two ser-
" mons, is that all the good people who heard them were offended, and grieved
" in the highest manner; and that Mr Jurieu's friends were much mortified on ac-
" count of them (4)." He says that Mr de Bauval had very well observed that
it was a poor shift to pretend, as Mr Jurieu did, that he would not publish those
sermons, because his informers *were lying in ambush, and had prepared their batteries*

(1) Reflexions sur un Libelle en feuille volante, intitulé Nouvelle Hérésie dans la Morale, &c.

(2) Considerations sur deux sermons de Mr Jurieu, touchant l'Amour du prochain: où l'on traite incidemment cette question curieuse: S'il faut hair Mr Jurieu.

(3) Considerations on two Sermons of Mr Jurieu, &c. *pag. 2, and the following.*

(4) Examination of Mr Jurieu's Theology, &c. *Tom. ii. pag. 808.*

2   in

THE LIFE OF Mʀ BAYLE.

in order to find heresies in them at any rate. He thinks that pretence very ridiculous. "I admire, (says he (1), Mr Jurieu's bravery who boldly refuseth to "fight, because he sees the enemy ready to offer him battle: if we did not know "from whence he is, we would be ready to think him of another Country than "his own. To speak seriously, Mr Jurieu could not say any thing more poor, or "which gives more matter of triumph to his accusers. Either he was afraid that "those Gentlemen would really find heresies in his sermons, or he was not. If "he was afraid of it, he was conscious of his guilt. If he was not afraid, "he ought to have published his sermons immediately, in order to convict his "accusers of calumny before the whole world." Mr Saurin confirms this argument by several other reflexions, and afterwards speaks of Mr de Bauval's piece. "They "have published, (says he (2), some *Considerations on Mr Jurieu's two Sermons,* "wherein his *Reflections* are answered, and it is proved that he really preached the "hatred of our neighbour, and that he cannot clear himself from it. Mr Jurieu (adds "he) has made a Reply to this piece, in another intitled, *An Apology for the Synod*, "*and for several good people who have been abused in Mr de Bauval's last Satire,* in-"titled, *Considerations on two Sermons &c* (3). One would think, (adds Mr Saurin), that "while he makes an Apology for others, and for himself on some other points, "he ought not to have forgot to have apologized for his doctrine concerning the "hatred of our neighbour. It was this which ought principally to have been done "in his last piece, and it was this which people of sense, who are concerned for the "glory of God, the purity of our morality, and for Mr Jurieu's reputation, wished "and expected to find there. But their hopes have been deceived. Mr Jurieu is "very large on several other matters, but says not one word on this."
It may be thought, perhaps, that I have insisted too long on this subject : but as it is not easy to imagine that rage could carry a Minister of the Gospel so far as to preach the hatred of our neighbour, I thought it necessary to show by good authorities that Mr Jurieu had really preached that detestable doctrine, and that Mr Bayle had good reason to accuse him of it (4).

Mr Bayle published much about the same time a Book intruled, *An Addition to the various thoughts concerning Comets, or an Answer to a libel intitled, A short Review of the Maxims of Morality and Principles of Religion of the Author of the Various Thoughts concerning Comets &c. to serve for information to the Ecclesiastical Judges, who may please to take cognizance of it. At Rotterdam by Reinier Leers.* M.D.C.XCIV. In 12º (5). He here gives the reasons why he did not sooner answer this libel. Mr Jurieu had made no answer to Mr Bayle's summons and defiances concerning his accusation of Atheism, although he had brought it before the Consistory; and had even desisted from it. He had afterwards published his *Short Review*, wherein he arraigns certain propositions out of the *Thoughts concerning Comets*, and out of the *New Letters against Maimbourg*, as dangerous, heretical &c. He had addressed himself to the Consistory to get these Propositions condemned, and when they were ready to examine into that matter, he had desired that it should be referred to the Synod; and yet notwithstanding he had suffered four Synods to pass without mentioning it. This libel contained no objections against the book concerning Comets, which might not be answered by the book itself, and Mr Bayle designed to publish a new edition of it, with additions containing new proofs, new explanations, and new answers to all the objections, which could be made to what he had advanced. It was here that he designed to have answered the *Short Review*. But being informed in the month of February 1694, that Mr Jurieu had got a Committee to be appointed by his Consistory to decide upon the Extracts which he had produced in that libel; so sudden and unexpected a change made him fear some bad design, and obliged him to publish this answer. "Mr Jurieu, (says he (6), has a mind to act a part in "his own Consistory, which hitherto he has not been able to act with regard to me. "He will no longer be my Accuser, he will be my Judge, and manage matters so "that we shall henceforth hear no more of the accusation of Atheism, but they "will only examine whether there be any erroneous and dangerous Propositions in "my writings, which may be punished by Church censures. In all appearance "he designs they should judge without hearing me, and solely upon the credit of "his extracts, and of the consequences which he has drawn from them. Our dis-"pute therefore is now to appear before the Ecclesiastical tribunals, and that too "upon a new foot. But as it may very possibly happen, that every thing shall "pass there without my having the least knowledge of it, it is absolutely necessary "for me to have recourse in this manner to a public Factum, which may serve "for information to the Judges who desire it, and may take away from those who "do not, all room for pleading ignorance. I will confine myself to short ob-"servations, not only because I desire that the long Apology for my Comets, which "will appear in the third Edition, may have the grace of novelty; but likewise "because I will not leave to those who do not care to be informed, their com-"mon pretence in such cases, that the length of the piece discouraged them from "setting about the reading of it."

lxxii

1694.

(1) Ibid. p. 812.
(2) Ibid. p. 827, 828.
(3) Apologie pour les Synodes & pour plusieurs honestes gens, dechirez dans la derniere Satyre du Sieur de Bauval, intitulée, Considerations sur deux Sermons &c.
(4) *In the posthumous editions of the Critical Dictionary, there is a long digression on this accusation, in the article* ZUERIUS BOXHORNIUS.
(5) Addition aux Pensées diverses sur les Cometes, ou Réponse, à un Libelle intitulé, Courte Revuë des Maximes de Morales & des Principes de Religion de l'Auteur des Pensées diverses sur les Cometes &c. Pour servir d'Instruction aux Juges Ecclesiastiques qui en voudront connoitre.
(6) Addition aux Pensées diverses sur les Cometes &c. p. 25, 26. Nouvel Avis au petit Auteur des petits Livrets, in the preface, and pag. 46 and the following.

THE LIFE OF Mʳ BAYLE.

1694. He showed that Mr Jurieu had misrepresented what is said in the Thoughts concerning Comets, and drawn false and absurd consequences from it. For example. This Minister affirms that Mr Bayle in this book pretends that " God never per-" forms prodigies and extraordinary things, in order to be presages of what is to " come, such as earthquakes, extraordinary meteors, signs which are seen in the " heavens and upon earth, apparitions, voices, births of monsters, floods ; and that " he maintains that all these things are brought about by natural and necessary " causes, and that God doth not at all design by things of this sort to foretel " judgments, which he intends to inflict upon men, nor even to manifest his Deity." But this is not at all Mr Bayle's opinion. What he maintains is, that *God never miraculously produces comets, earthquakes, inundations, monsters &c. with a design to threaten Infidels with the judgments which his justice is preparing against them ; for he cannot persuade himself that such a conduct, which appears to him to be proper only to foment the abominable superstition of idolaters, is consistent with our ideas of the goodness, justice, and sincerity of God.* He doth not pretend to deny that God ever performs in any part of the world what we call *prodigies* or *presages*; he says only that things which appear equally and indifferently among heathen nations and among the children of God, are not miraculous productions, appointed to threaten mankind. His doctrine tends to give us such an idea of God, as affords a lively representation of his wisdom, goodness, and truth. It denies certain presages indeed ; but it is because they would be injurious to these divine Perfections.

Mr Bayle likewise entered into a detail of Mr Jurieu's extracts, and discovered both his insincerity, and his want of discernment and penetration. He refuted his objections concerning the Parallel between Pagan Idolatry and Atheism, concerning the morals of Atheists &c ; and proved what he had advanced in his new Letters against Maimbourg, about the Rights of an erring Conscience. He afterwards lays down the true state of the question betwixt him and his adversary, and shews in what manner Ecclesiastical Judges, who shall take cognizance of this dispute, ought to proceed. He subjoins a Petition to the Christian Universities, wherein he desires them to decide upon this representation of his principles which he had made to them : and concludes by impeaching twelve propositions drawn out of the *Short Review*, as false, rash, and impious.

This work broke all Mr Jurieu's measures, and reduced him to silence. This was no easy matter : but Mr Bayle had set his proofs in so evident a light, that it was not possible to make a reply. It was however only the work of a few days. " It cost me so little trouble, (says he (1), that the three or four days which I " bestowed upon it, would have been too much, if I had thought fit to make " a larger answer, but my resolution of being short, made it necessary to employ " more time. I have destroyed that libel so as not leave one stone upon another. " The public will see that my adversary is ignorant of his own Religion, that he " attacks what he has maintained in his other books, and that he denies the most " evident truths : and which is worst of all, his quotations are so unfaithful, that " there is no ground to think that he erred sincerely." [1] Addition to the various Thoughts &c, *in the Advertisement.*

An Officer, a friend of Mr Bayle, having let him know how much he desired to see a reconciliation betwixt him and Mr Jurieu, Mr Bayle showed him that it was impossible. " The nature of this quarrel is such, (says he (2), as can admit of no " reconciliation : there can only be what in your profession is called a *cessation of* " *all acts of hostility*. For the question is, whether I have been in a Cabal which did " conspire both the ruin of Religion and of the Government, or not. He has " accused me of this publickly, and I have shown him that this Cabal is the most " ridiculous chimera, that ever was heard of. He has accused me of being the Au-" thor of a book called *An Advice to the Refugees*, wherein the diffamatory libels which " are printed in this Country against the King of France, and the dethroning of " King James are condemned ; and I have shewn that all the proofs which he has " alledged against me are impertinent. . . . . If he reconcile himself to me, " he must own himself an infamous calumniator ; and if I reconcile myself to him, " I must acknowledge myself guilty. This is what renders our reconciliation im-" possible. For my part, I do not care for any reconciliation. It is sufficient " for me that the Government takes no notice of his accusations : for while there " is no process against me, it is plain they laugh at his pretended proofs. For " as to the place which they have taken from me, that was upon another ac-" count." [2] MSS. Letter to Mʳ *** *of the 20th of November 1694.*

1695. Mr Bayle continued to bestow all his time in the impression of his *Dictionary*. The impression of the first volume was finished in the month of August 1695 (3). The public prepossessed in Mr Bayle's favour, expected it with impatience, but Mr Bayle on the contrary was very much afraid of the reception it should meet with. " If the public, (said he to Mr le Duchat (4), has conceived any hopes or " good opinion of my Dictionary, (of which I have reason to doubt, not knowing " on what it can be founded,) I must expect many complaints ; they will find " themselves disappointed and villainously cheated, for I own ingenuously to you, " that this work is nothing else but a confused compilation of passages tacked to [3] *See the Letter to* Mʳ Constant *of the 22d of August 1695, p. 570.* [4] *Letter of the 9th of January 1696, p. 576.*
" one

VOL. I.   t

"one another, and that nothing can be worse suited to the delicate taste of this age: 1695.
"but there is no remedy, *jacta est alea.*"

However the Booksellers in foreign Countries, in consequence of the taste of the pub- 1696.
lic, demanded so many copies, that the number which was printed of the first volume
was not sufficient to satisfy them; so that Mr Leers was obliged to print a thousand
more copies of the second, and to reprint a like number of the first: this made
(1) *See the* some people imagine that there was a second edition of the whole work published (1).
Letters to Mr Bayle was not concerned in this re-impression; and he complained that there were
Mr Con-
stant of many errors in it (2). He could not correct the proofs of it; the impression of the se-
the 4th of cond volume took him up so entirely that he had not even time to write to his friends.
July
1697, p. "You would excuse my silence (says he to Mr Constant (3), if you knew what a load
654, and "of business I have upon my hands, occasioned by the impression of my Historical and
to Mr Cos- "Critical Dictionary. The Bookseller is resolved at any rate to finish it this year;
15 of the "so that I am obliged to furnish him constantly with new copy, and every day to
said year, "correct the proofs, wherein there are a thousand errors; for my manuscript is so
pag. 660, "full of rasures and references, that neither the Printers nor the Corrector of the
661.
"press can find their way through such a labyrinth: and another thing that re-
(2) *Letter* "tards me very much is, that not having all the books at hand which I have occasion
to Mr le
D E M S. "for, I am obliged to wait till they are procured for me, when any body in this
of the 7th "city has them." He complains likewise that the frequent returns of his head-ach
of July made him lose a great deal of time. "I am very glad, says he (4) that your
1698, p. "megrims have left you; mine would have done me the same favour, if it had
712, and "been in my power to live without study, but obstinate labour nourishes them,
the follow- "and makes them return very frequently. By this means I lose many days in
ing. "every month, which obligeth me afterwards to apply more closely to regain the
(3) *Letter* "time I have lost."

of the 31st They had so advantageous an opinion of Mr Bayle's Dictionary in England, that
of May
1696, p. a person of quality there, no less distinguished by his genius than by his rank and the
588, 589. great posts he enjoyed (5), desired that this work should be dedicated to him. He desir-
(4) *Ibid.* ed Mr Basnage to assure Mr Bayle that he would acknowledge it by a present of two
p. 591. hundred guineas. Mr Bayle's friends, and particularly Mr Basnage, pressed him very
(5) *The* much to give this Nobleman that satisfaction, but in vain. He said that he had
Duke of so frequently made a jest of Dedications, that he would not expose himself by
Shrews-
bury, Se- making one. This however was only a pretence to give a colour to his refusal.
cretary of The real ground of the long and obstinate resistance which he made upon this oc-
State. casion, was, that he would not flatter or praise any person who had any employment
in the Court of a Prince of whom he thought he had reason to complain, and this
(6) *MSS.* Lord was at this time in the ministry (6).
Memoir of The impression of the second volume was finished on the 24th of October, and 1697.
Mr Bas- the work came out under the following title: *An Historical and Critical Dictionary by*
nage. *Mr Bayle. At Rotterdam by Reinier Leers. M.D.C.XCVII* (7). In the beginning
of the Preface Mr Bayle acquaints the Reader, that this work is not what he pro-
(7) *Dicti-* mised in the *Project* published in 1692. His first design was, as we have obser-
onaire
Historique ved, to publish the errors of Dictionaries, and other books, both great and small.
& Criti- But being informed that a mere collection of errors would disgust the readers, and
que, par that they desired something historical, he was obliged to lay aside that undertaking.
Monsieur "See in what manner (says he) I have changed my plan, in order the better to
Bayle. A
Rotterdam "hit the taste of the public. I have divided my composition into two parts: one
chez Rei- "of which is purely historical; a succinct narration of facts; the other is a large
nier Leers "commentary, a medley of proofs and discussions, wherein you find a criticism
1697. "of many errors, and sometimes a long train of philosophical reflexions; in a
"word, such a variety as makes me hope, that in one place or other all sorts of
"readers will find something to their taste." He adds that this change had made
the greatest part of the materials he had prepared useless to him, and that this was
one of the reasons which had retarded the publication of this book. Another reason
was, that he had carefully avoided every thing that is to be found in the Dictionaries already published, or which he foresaw would be contained in those promised
by learned men. He had done the same with regard to Mr Du Pin's Bibliotheque
of Ecclesiastical Authors, and to Mr Teissier's Additions to the Elogies of learned
men, taken from Thuanus's History. He would not put the reader under the
necessity of buying the same thing twice: though in the mean time he had thereby deprived himself of all the materials which are most easily collected and digested.
To these reasons we may add the alteration which he made in the choice of the
articles. At first he intended to give *real* as well as *personal* articles. But he was
told that the former not being historical, would not be relished; which deprived him
once more of a great many materials. However, to prevent the loss of the articles H I P P O M A N E S and of the D A Y, which had appeared in the *Project,* he
placed them at the end of the work under the title of *Dissertations.* He ascribed
likewise the delay of this work to the badness of his health, to the great exactness in his citations, to his want of the necessary books, and to the difficulties arising
from

1697. from the stile, which requires great attention if we would prevent equivocal expressions, verses, and false applications of relatives.

He offered all these considerations, in answer to those who might think it strange that he had spent above four years in composing these two volumes. But as others, on the contrary, might be astonished that he had been able in that time to compose two such large volumes in Folio, and might believe that he had made too much haste; he observes that uninterrupted labour will go a great length in little time, and that he had lost no time in the recreations which are very common among men of letters: "I remember as well as they (says he) the difficulty "of Cato *Interpone tuis interdum gaudia curis &c,* but I very seldom make use of "it. Diversions, games, collations, journies into the country, visits, and such other "recreations necessary to a great many studious men, as they say, are not my business. "I lose no time in them, nor do I spend it in domestic cares, making interest for "preferments, sollicitations, or other affairs. I have been happily delivered from "a great many occupations which were not very suitable to my humour, and I "have had the greatest and the most charming leisure that a man of letters could "desire. By this means an Author makes a great progress in a few Years. His "work will increase daily under his hand, though he be not careless in the com"position of it."

After this he gives his reasons why he has quoted long passages of Greek and Latin Authors, and why instead of translating them himself, he has frequently made use of the versions of Amiot or Vigenere. He adds, that people of grave and severe characters may possibly find fault with him for his quotations from Brantome and Montagne, containing actions and reflexions of too gallant a nature; but that persons of merit, who had the Bookfellers interest at heart, had been of opinion, that, in order to raise a general demand for this Work, it would be necessary that they who do not understand Latin, and do not trouble their heads with Philosophical and Theological discussions, should find some agreeable entertainment in it. He had been told that if he was too averse from taking that advice, he ought at least to allow others, to furnish the Bookseller with such memoirs, and even sometimes with dogmatical reflexions, which might excite some attention. That he had accordingly consented that the Bookseller should insert whatever memoirs should be sent to him: that with relation to the Philosophical reflexions which sometimes had been pushed some length, he did not think it necessary to make any apology for them, for as they only tend to convince man that the best use he can make of his reason, is to subject his understanding to the obedience of Faith; they can't but deserve the thanks of the Divines.

Next follow some remarks upon the liberty he has taken of criticizing the faults of some celebrated Authors, or of pointing out their defects. He declares that he has not the least intention to diminish the reputation they have justly acquired, and that besides for the most part he has only related the observations of others, and only copies from Authors already printed. "Of the two laws of History (says he) I "have religiously observed that which commands to say nothing that is false; as for "the other, which bids us venture to say all that is true, I cannot boast that I have "always observed that; I think it is sometimes inconsistent not only with prudence "but also with reason." In the mean while he was very far from believing that this work was free from faults. "I do not doubt (says he) but besides my omissions, "which are many, I have committed many faults. I shall think myself obliged "to those who will be so kind as to rectify me, and if I had not relied upon "the advice of intelligent and equitable readers, I should have kept this work "many years in my closet, according to the advice of the Ancients in order to "correct it, and render it less unworthy of the public view: but considering that "I had materials left for two other large volumes, I hastened the publication of "it. I easily understood that I should be both more usefully and more seasonably "assisted, when the public should know what I wanted, and wherein I am want"ing. I hope that with those helps the Continuation of this work will be more "perfect than otherwise it would have been. I shall immediately go about it, while "age will permit. I see nothing wherein I can better or more pleasantly employ "the leisure I am blessed with, a leisure which seems to me preferable to all things, "and which has always been earnestly wished for by the true lovers of study and "learning."

He observes likewise how he has behaved with regard to Moreri's Dictionary. That he has passed over several subjects, because they are to be found at sufficient length in that work: that when he has given the same articles which are in Moreri, he has been determined to do so, either because that Author gives a very short account of them, or because having the life of some illustrious person, he found himself able to give a compleat account of him; or because he had as many detached and curious matters, as would make up a tolerable supplement: that he referred the readers to that Dictionary for facts of any importance: that when he gives the same Article with Moreri, he has put the errors he has found in this Author in a remark by themselves; but has not touched those which are to be met with in the

l   articles

articles that are not common to both, though they are neither less considerable nor less frequent in those articles than in the others: from whence he concludes that his Dictionary is not designed to hurt the sale of the other, but on the contrary will encrease it, and make the reading of it more agreeable.

1697.

This is the first and only work to which Mr Bayle has set his name. It was not his intention to do so: he had said upon all occasions during the course of the impression, that he would not let his name appear in it, and he owns at the end of the preface that his friends had endeavoured in vain to make him change his sentiment; but that at last he had been obliged to give his consent that his name should appear. " This doth not proceed from fickleness (says he) but it is in obe-
" dience to authority that I do what I have so often said that I would not. It has
" been thought fit that I should affix my name, in order to terminate some diffe-
" rences among the Booksellers. Without this Mr Leers could not have obtained
" the privilege, which he thought was absolutely necessary to him. I therefore
" pay a blind obedience." The occasion of this difference was, that Mr Leers having applied to the States of Holland for a privilege, the Booksellers who were concerned in the edition of Moreri opposed it, on pretence that Mr Bayle's Dictionary was a work of the same kind with that of Moreri, and that this concurrence had been forbid by the privilege which the States had granted to them, and that this would be a great loss to them. And because they knew that Mr Bayle would not put his name to it, they made use of that circumstance to represent his Dictionary as a work which no body owned. The States notwithstanding this granted a privilege to Mr Leers, but with this condition, that Mr Bayle should affix his name in the title of it (1).

(1) *This condition is expressed in the privilege.*

And indeed Mr Bayle's work has hardly any thing in common with that of Moreri. It is a Dictionary of a new and singular kind. An infinite variety runs through the whole of it. In the Text or body of the articles, he in a very exact and concise manner gives the history of the persons he treats of, but he makes amends for this brevity in the Remarks which are subjoined to the text, and which are a sort of commentary on it. He draws the characters of those persons, he clears up the circumstances of their lives, and the motives of their conduct, he examines the judgment which has been, or may be made concerning them. He treats of the most important points of Religion, Morality, and Philosophy. Nay sometimes the Text seems to have been made for the sake of the Remarks. He takes occasion from the actions or sentiments of an obscure and almost unknown person, to instruct or agreeably to amuse his reader. So that some Articles which seem to promise nothing at all, are frequently accompanied with the most curious matters. He acts throughout the part of an exact, faithful, and disinterested Historian, and of a moderate, penetrating, and judicious Critic. In the articles of the Philosophers, he applies himself to discover their opinions, and to show their strong and weak sides.

Being persuaded that disputes about Religion, which have been the occasion of infinite disorders in the world, proceed only from the too great confidence which the Divines of all parties have in their own understandings; he undertakes to humble them, and to render them more modest and moderate, by showing that even so ridiculous a sect as that of the Manicheans can raise such objections to them concerning the origin of evil and the permission of sin, which it is impossible to answer. He even goes further, and maintains in general that human Reason is more capable of refuting and destroying, than of proving and building up: that there are no points either in Divinity or Philosophy, against which it doth not raise very strong difficulties, so that if we should follow it, with a disposition to dispute, as far as it will go, we should often find ourselves reduced to very great straits: that there are doctrines which are certainly true, to which it opposeth unanswerable objections; that in this case we ought to have no regard to these objections, but acknowledge the narrow limits of human understanding, and oblige it to captivate itself under the obedience of faith, and that in this, Reason doth act inconsistently with itself, since it acts upon very reasonable principles. He at the same time gives several examples of difficulties which Reason finds in the discussion of the most important subjects, and he doth this for the most part without deciding, and meerly as a reporter. He endeavoured to inspire people with the same moderation with regard to historical facts. He showed that several facts which no body has ever called in question are very uncertain, or even evidently false: from whence it is natural to conclude, that we ought not lightly to give credit to Historians, but rather to suspend our judgment 'till by a rigorous examination we are assured of the truth.

The public was agreeably surprized to find that this work surpassed the favourable opinion they had conceived of it. The Booksellers at Paris observing the great demand there was for it, resolved to reprint it, and desired a Licence from Mr Boucherat, Chancellor of France. Mr Boucherat appointed the Abbé Renaudot, Author of the Paris Gazette, to examine it in order to see if it contained any thing against the Government, or against the Catholic Religion. This Abbé instead of confining himself to these two points, drew up a critical Memorial, wherein he says that this

work

THE LIFE OF M.R BAYLE. lxxvii

1697. work is full of *digressions*; that *one can find no system of Religion in it*: that Mr Bayle *never cites the Fathers there but in order to turn them into ridicule*: that he maintains *Pelagianism* and *Pyrrhonism* throughout: that he *had in different places inserted all the harshest things which have been said or written these fifty years past against the Catholic Religion*: that he *every where makes panegyrics upon the Calvinist Ministers, filled with falshoods*: that he *seeks all occasions to render the reign of Lewis XIV odious with regard to the revocation of the Edicts, and the complaints of the Refugees*: that one might *observe every where in it a visible affectation of collecting the most odious and infamous things against the persons of late French Kings*; and that *he had purposely collected several fabulous stories in order to render Henry the Fourth's conversion suspicious*: that in the *article of Francis I, there was a very injurious digression against the King of England, to give ground for establishing the possibility of the supposition of the Prince of Wales*: that it *was full of unsufferable obscenities*: that Mr Bayle *was only acquainted with modern books concerning Religion, and with those wrote by Heretics*: that *he had not the smallest knowledge of History*; that *his knowledge in Antiquity and Literature was all drawn from extracts which he had taken from French Translations*: that *he ridiculously compared the Moderns with the Ancients, and sets up the Abbé de St Real as a rival to Cornelius Nepos, in treating of the merit of Pomponius.* "We may judge, says he, of the abi-
"lities of a person who in an extract of the life of Pomponius Atticus, translates
"*librarii*, Booksellers." This example which the Abbé Renaudot produced of Mr Bayle's ignorance is a very notable proof of his own rashness; for Mr Bayle had observed in the margin that *we ought to understand by that word the Copists and Binders according to the custom of binding books at that time*.

We may see by this what weight this Abbé's judgment ought to have. He had negligently run through Mr Bayle's Dictionary, and saw every thing through the prejudices he had conceived against it. He was besides naturally decisive, rash, violent, and passionate against the Protestants. He piqued himself upon his great reading and profound knowledge of antiquity; but they who have examined his works do not allow that his learning was equal to the opinion which he wanted that the public should have of it. They have found a thousand mistakes in his tract concerning the *Origin of the Sphere*, and showed that he has not so much as understood the Authors whom he has transcribed (1). However, upon his report, they refused the Licence which the Booksellers of Paris desired in order to reprint Mr Bayle's Dictionary, and even prohibited the importing it into France. This was what Mr Bayle wished for (2). "I will tell you as a secret (says he to one of his friends (3),
"that I am exceedingly glad that they have prohibited my Dictionary in France.
"It is not because the prohibition will the more excite peoples curiosity; for *mi-*
"*timur in vetitum*. I have two other reasons. The one is, that if they had allowed
"it to be sold there, the Booksellers at Lyons would have counterfeited it, and com-
"mitted a thousand typographical errors. Their edition would have hindered the
"sale of that of Mr Leers, and would have multiplied the copies of a first edition,
"which is always imperfect when a large work has been composed hastily, and with
"so little assistance of libraries as I have had. This prohibition makes me hope that
"Mr Leers's sole edition will sell, and that he will be obliged to print a second, in the
"correction of which I will employ all my abilities, which are very small I own, but
"which however I will apply to better purpose, and I expect from your knowledge
"and good advice how to direct myself aright in the correction. The other reason,
"which still is of more importance, is, that if my Dictionary had been allowed a
"free admission into France, my enemies in this country, who are a factious kind
"of people, and very artful in giving a bad turn to things, would have inferred
"from hence that my book contains nothing in favour of Protestants, or against
"France: *A proof*, would they say, *of the criminal attachment, of which the Author
"of it is suspected, to the cause of the common enemy of the repose of Europe*. It
"is therefore of advantage to me that my Dictionary has been prohibited; not-
"withstanding, though I wished that this might happen, I have said nothing in
"it which can please our Visionaries. When any thing came in my way relating
"to the affairs of Europe, I have avoided saying any thing either *pro* or *con*: and
"they even complain in England, that I have indirectly condemned the late Re-
"volution, and that I have declared myself too much against the rights of the people,
"in favour of the despotic power of Princes."

Mr Bayle criticized Mr Jurieu in several places of his Dictionary: and in doing so he only followed his plan, which was to take notice of the errors in fact, or of the false reasonings the Authors of whom he had occasion to mention. "I have
"sometimes, says he (4), criticized my enemy with some force; he is enraged at this,
"and searches for all possible means of revenging himself. When I first published
"my Dictionary he set his emissaries a declaiming against it, pretending that it con-
"tained impieties; and after all these snarlings, he has persuaded his Consistory to
"examine it. I have all my defences ready, and I am not at all afraid, provided
"they will, I do not say, exactly follow the rules of equity, but forbear only from
"violating them shamefully and without measure."

(1) *See Mr Des Vignoles's Remarks on this piece of the Abbé Renaudot in the Bibliotheque Germanique, Tom. v. Art. xi, pag. 153, and the following.*

(2) *See Letter to Mr Jexion of the 11th of February 1697, p. 625, 626.*

(3) *Letter to M.* *** *of the 13th of May, 1697, 642, 643.*

(4) *Letter to Mr Constant, July 4, 1697, p. 654.*

VOL. I.   u   Mr Jurieu's

THE LIFE OF Mʀ BAYLE.

Mr Jurieu's party finding themselves superior in the Consistory of Rotterdam, he took that opportunity to have Mr Bayle's Dictionary examined there. In the mean while he published several extracts of anonymous Letters from Paris, London, Geneva, and from some towns in Holland, to decry this work. And indeed the Authors of these Letters said a great deal against it, but most of them had not read it, and spoke of it only by hearsay. Mr Jurieu added the Abbé Renaudot's Memorial, and the extracts which Mr Bayle had given of the books of that Minister in the *News from the Republic of Letters,* " In order, said he, to oppose the high encomiums which " Mr Bayle has given to him and to his works there, to the criticisms in the Dictio- " nary." To all this he added several reflexions, wherein he repeated his ancient calumnies, and made new efforts to disfame Mr Bayle, and disparage his Dictionary. In the mean time he owned that he had not so much as read the title of it (1). He intitled this compilation: *The Judgment of the public and particularly of the Abbé Renaudot, concerning the Sieur Bayle's Critical Dictionary* (2).

Mr Bayle upon this published a piece intitled: *Remarks on a Pamphlet, intitled The Judgment of the Public, &c* (3), wherein he says that his principal design in publishing this piece was to acquaint the public that he was preparing a defence, which would demonstrate to all unprejudiced readers the injustice of his censures: but that this apology not deserving the fate of loose sheets, which for the most part do not outlive the week in which they first appear, he kept it to be placed at the beginning or end of a book in folio. For the same reason, adds he, I refer to it almost every thing considerable that might be said against that piece which is just published, and I confine myself to a few observations made in haste. He takes notice in the beginning that the title of this piece of Mr Jurieu's is deceitful. "This Libel, says he (4), has a " very improper title, it ought only to be intitled: *The Judgment of the Abbé Renaudot,* " *commented upon by the publisher;* for all the other judges are less than phantoms: " they are invisible beings, no body knows whether they are black or white. There- " fore their opinion and a cypher are of the same value...... What manner of " proceeding is this! to make the judgment of the public to consist in such pieces. I " could produce a great many much stronger in my favour, if modesty would permit: " and besides how many Letters could I produce, wherein my adversary is repre- " sented both as a bad writer, and a bad man! but God forbid that I should imi- " tate him in the use he makes of what people write to one another in confidence. " This is a conduct detested even by the Heathens themselves."

He observes that Mr Jurieu out of all his evidences has mentioned only the one who was most exceptionable. "The Author of this pretended Judgment of " the Public (says he (5), has not been very wise in the choice he has made. He " conceals the names of all his witnesses except one whom he ought principally " to have concealed, a name odious and despised in all the countries which are at " war with France. I will not take advantage of the prepossession of the public: " I will not consider him with regard to his Gazette, which discredits him every where " as a man who has got a habit of giving a malicious turn to lies. I will con- " sider him on his fair side.

" The Abbé Renaudot has the character of a very learned man, and of having " a taste so delicate that nothing is able to please him. One can therefore con- " clude nothing from his contempt of any thing: it is an equivocal proof. I have " been likewise told that he is exceedingly devout. We need not therefore be " astonished, that he thinks some things too free, which at bottom do not go beyond " the liberties which an honest man may allow himself, after the example of so many " great authors." He adds, that with regard to the gay passages in his Dictionary, which are complained of as a little too licentious, he does not doubt but every body will be satisfied when they have seen the Apology he is preparing on this head: and he promiseth to revise the article of David in such a manner that it shall not any longer serve for a pretence for the declamations of his detractors. " I have " declared (says he) upon all occasions, and I here declare it publickly, that if " there are any heterodox opinions in my work, I am the first who will detest " them, and that I will throw them out in the second edition. All that I want " is to have them pointed out to me."

He next observes several falshoods which the Authors of the extracts had spread concerning his Dictionary: he refutes Mr Jurieu's calumnies and malicious insinuations; and shows how ridiculously he had boasted that he had reduced him to live upon the pension of a Bookseller: he says that he had criticized him without affectation, and had treated him in the same manner with other authors, whose faults he had taken notice of; that he had done him justice when he had been censured by others without reason, and that it was not his fault that he had not had more frequent occasions of justifying him; that what he had censured in some of his works, was not the same thing which he had formerly commended; that at first he had praised him sincerely, and that afterwards he had criticized him for good reasons, being better instructed.

With regard to Mr Renaudot, Mr Bayle contents himself with observing two or three falshoods in point of fact contained in his Memorial, delaying a thorough examination

---

(1) *I own to you that I have not read this book, nor even the title of it.* Jugement du public, &c. p. 28.

(2) Jugement du public, & particulierement de Mr l'Abbé Renaudot, sur le Dictionaire critique du Sieur Bayle, in 4° pp. 47.

(3) Reflexions sur un Imprimé qui a pour titre, Jugement du public, &c. in 4°, pagg. 16. small character, and in two columns.

(4) Reflexions sur un Imprimé qui a pour titre, Jugement du Public, &c. p. 1.

(5) Ibid. pag. 1, 2.

1697. mination of it 'till that Abbé should declare himself the Author of it. "If I at any time do answer the Abbé Renaudot's Judgment (says he) it will only be after I shall know that he acknowledgeth it to be his, in the manner in which it is printed; for it is so full of mistakes, falshoods, and blunders, that I imagine it not to be agreeable to the original: some false pieces have possibly been added to it in copying. He had prejudiced a great many people, but men of judgment having read my Dictionary, quickly put an end to that prejudice. The Abbé himself is not ignorant of this, for he says in one of his Letters, *That I ought to be satisfied with the approbation of so many people*. And so I am. People were surprized to find so many idle things in his report. The only question was, whether my book contained any thing which could shock either the Church of Rome or France. No body had asked him whether I was acquainted with good Authors, or whether I equal the Moderns with the Ancients. If several of my readers have contradicted him on the head of my ignorance, I disavow them: he has not said enough on this head, I know a great many more circumstances of it, and if he has a mind to draw my picture in this light, I will furnish him with a good many memoirs."

This dispute went no further. Mr de Wit interested himself for the Abbé Renaudot, and made Mr Bayle promise not to write against him. Mr Bayle religiously kept his word; and was even so scrupulous that he was not pleased to see that I designed to insert in Mr de St Evremond's Works, the answer which that celebrated writer had made to the Judgment of that Abbé. "As to what concerns (says he (1), the Apology which Mr de St Evremond did me the honour to write in my favour, as your friendship for me is already publickly declared, I do not know whether the Abbé Renaudot will not think me guilty of an indirect breach of the treaty which Mr de Wit had concluded between us, if any thing should appear in a work reprinted by you concerning the foolish quarrel which that Abbé picked with me. You know that in my *Reflexions* on that Abbé's *Judgment*, I promised to examine and answer it more at large. He is exceedingly techy, and though he is very learned, yet he is afraid of literary disputes. He is very well pleased with the liberty of criticizing by word of mouth, but doth not care to be obliged to come to discussions in writing. The late Mr de Wit, his particular friend, persuaded me very earnestly to peace, and was vexed at the *Reflexions* which I had published. Mr Leers, who is under many obligations to the Abbé, who doth him good offices upon all occasions, received a Letter from him, wherein he signified that it would be against his inclination to enter into a dispute of this nature. In short out of deference to Mr de Wit, and complaisance for Mr Leers, and in consideration of the excuses which the Abbé made for himself, I having a natural aversion to literary disputes of a personal nature, consented that Mr de Wit should make us agree to forget what was passed, and make no more mention of this difference. I have kept my word very scrupulously; for there is not one word in the second edition of my Dictionary which bears the least mark of my remembrance of the Abbé's *Judgment*. I leave it entirely to your discretion, whether by inserting Mr de St Evremond's answer, the Abbé would not have a pretence to say that what I have not done myself I have done by a friend, by thus renewing the memory of that quarrel." Mr de St St Evremond had read Mr Bayle's Dictionary with a great deal of pleasure: and he diverted himself by composing this answer, which contains very fine and delicate raillery (2).

(1) *Letter March 7, 1702, p. 967, and the following.*

(2) *This small piece was inserted in the first edition of Mr de St Evremond's Works, printed at London in 1705, 2 Vols in 4º, and is to be found in all the following editions.*

1698. The first edition of Mr Bayle's Dictionary being almost sold off, they thought of giving a second. It was begun on the 26th of May 1698.

Mr Jurieu had published his pretended *Judgment of the Public*, in order to engage the Ecclesiastical Assemblies to condemn Mr Bayle's Dictionary. He got this libel presented to the Synod, at this time sitting at Delft; but the Synod took no manner of notice of it. The Consistory of Rotterdam itself, acted with great moderation. They granted Mr Bayle a hearing, and communicated to him the remarks which they had made upon his Dictionary; they declared that they were satisfied with his answers, and exhorted him to acquaint the public with every thing that had passed on this subject. This he did in a loose sheet, intituled, *A Letter from the Author of the Historical and Critical Dictionary to Mr D. E. M. S. concerning the proceedings of the Consistory of the Walloon Church of Rotterdam, against this work* (3). It is as follows.

(3) *Lettre de l'Auteur du Dictionaire historique & critique à Monsieur le D. E. M. S. au sujet des procedures du Consistoire de l'Eglise Wallonne de Rotterdam concernant son Ouvrage.*

" Sir,

" I AM informed by your last Letter that a great many contradictory accounts have gone about concerning what passed in the Consistory of the Walloon Church at Rotterdam, when the affair which I had before it concerning the Historical and Critical Dictionary was ended there. All you could gather from so many different reports was, that I had promised to amend that work in a second edition: but this not satisfying you, you desire me to give you a more exact account of that matter, and this I shall now give you.

" Be

"Be pleased therefore to know, Sir, that the Consistory having thought it their 1698.
"duty to take my book into their consideration, on account of the complaints
"which several persons spread abroad concerning it, named a Committee to ex-
"amine it. This Committee read it, took extracts and made remarks, and having
"made their report to the Consistory, and all other preliminaries being regulated,
"so that there remained nothing to be done but to hear me, and then proceed
"to give sentence, I was warned to appear before the Consistory, and accordingly
"I came there upon the day appointed. The state of the case in general being
"laid before me, together with the first article of particular extracts and remarks,
"I was asked what I had to say in my defence. I answered that not knowing
"what should be first considered in this affair, I had prepared only a very
"general discourse. It consisted of these two points. First, that I had a great
"many things to alledge in my justification on every one of the grounds of com-
"plaint; and secondly, that in order to spare the Consistory the trouble of a long
"series of tedious discussions, and to contribute more effectually to peace and edi-
"fication; I chose rather to change the things which had given occasion for complaint
"in a second edition, than to insist upon the reasons which I might advance to
"prove that all the noise which had been made was without foundation; that I
"had already acquainted the public with my dispositions to correct my work, ac-
"cording to the advice which they should be pleased to communicate to me, and
"that in particular I did declare to the Consistory, that I would with the utmost
"docility and respect make use of what information they should be pleased to
"give me; in a word, that if I had advanced any heretical or erroneous opinions
"(which I believed I had not done) I disavowed and retracted them, as I had
(1) *In the* "already declared in a piece printed three or four months ago (1).
Reflecti-
ons on a "This answer being thought too general, I was told that they would commu-
Pamphlet "nicate to me the remarks which the Consistory had made on my Dictionary. Ac-
intitled "cordingly they were communicated to me by the Committee which they had
The Judg- "appointed; they consisted amongst other things of these five heads: I. The ciment of "tations, expressions, and reflexions all over the work, which might offend chaste
the Public "ears. II. The article of David. III. The article of the Manicheans. IV. That
&c, upon "of the Sceptics. V. The praises given to persons who had denied either the
the Criti- "being or providence of God. I answered two things as I had done before: in
cal Dictio- "the first place, that I thought I had a great many reasons to alledge in my
nary, §. iii. "justification on all these heads; and secondly, that notwithstanding this, I was
pag. 2. "ready to strike out of the book all the stumbling blocks which they had found
"there; I added that now that I knew, by the remarks of the Consistory,
"what the things complained of were, I saw more clearly how to correct
"them, that I thought it a very easy matter to remedy every thing, either by
"suppressions, change of expressions, or by additions and explanations. That in
"particular, I would new-mould the article of David in such a manner as no-
"thing should remain there which might give offence to pious souls. That with
"regard to the horrible doctrine of two Principles, that is to say, of Manicheism, I
"had sufficiently declared how much I thought it absurd, monstrous, contrary not only
"to religion and piety, but likewise to the clearest notions of reason and sound
"Philosophy. That I would enlarge more upon this in the second edition; and
"that if in quality of an historian I had thought myself obliged to recite the
"arguments of the Manicheans in their full force, I on the other hand was of opi-
"nion, that this was of no consequence, and that I only enlarged on what the
"most orthodox of our Divines every day tell us in fewer words, viz. that the agree-
"ment of the holiness and goodness of God with the sin and misery of man is
"an incomprehensible mystery, which we ought humbly to adore, being persuaded
"that since it is revealed, it must needs be so, and that we are obliged to silence
"all the difficulties which our weak reason suggests to us. That I had sufficiently
"declared on other subjects, and particularly with regard to the existence of ex-
"tension and motion, that I did not think it a reason to reject a doctrine because
"I could not answer all the objections against it. That I would again examine
"the difficulties of the Manicheans, and that if could find answers, or if the re-
"verend Ministers of the Consistory would furnish me with any, I would put
"them in the best form I was capable of. I made the same answer with relation
"to the article of Pyrrho; and as to the praises bestowed on the good morals of
"some Atheists, I promised an Explanation, which would show how these facts
"which I have found in books, and which I was obliged by the laws of history
"to relate, ought not to give offence, and that in effect they do no hurt to the
"true Religion.
"The Committee having made a report of this Conference to the Consistory, it
"was desired that I should give in writing what I had declared by word of mouth.
"Accordingly I presented a memorial, wherein after having first touched upon the
"two general heads of my verbal answers, I protested that I never had designed
"to advance any proposition as my own opinion, which was contrary to the Confes-
"sion of Faith of the Reformed Church, in which, by God's goodness, I was born,
"and

1698. "and of which I made profession. That if any such propositions were to be found
"in my work (which I did not at all believe) they must have crept in without my
"observation, that I disavowed and retracted them; that if I had in certain respects
"taken a more than ordinary liberty of philosophizing, it was because I thought
"that this would be readily excused in consideration of the nature of my work,
"wherein I sustain both the character of Historian and Commentator, without pre-
"tending to act the Dogmatist; that the pains which I have taken to make my
"Philosophical Reflexions subservient to the confirmation of a fundamental doctrine
"of our Church, and which we constantly oppose to the Socinians, viz. that we
"ought to subject our understanding to the authority of God, and believe what
"he has revealed to us in his word, although the principles of Philosophy should
"not always be conforming to it: this, I say, made me hope that all my Protes-
"tant readers would be rather edified than offended by my Commentaries; that
"I was very sorry that the event had not answered my expectation, and that
"if I had foreseen the consequence of the liberty which I have taken, I would have
"carefully abstained from it; that to remedy what is past I would amend those
"passages in a second edition, and that I would have great regard to the remarks
"which the Consistory had communicated to me. I added to this, the particular de-
"clarations which I had made verbally to the Committee concerning the article of
"David, that of the Manicheans &c.

"Upon this Memorial the Consistory drew up an Act, with such reflexions and
"modifications as they thought proper, and this, Sir, was the amicable conclusion
"of that matter. They signified their desire that without waiting for the publica-
"tion of the second edition, which might be long a finishing, I should publish
"something which might acquaint the public with the sentiments which I had set
"forth in my Memorial. I readily agreed to this, and I now acquit myself of
"that promise; and it has not been owing to me, that I have not done so sooner.
"I am, Sir, yours."

Mr Jurieu being vexed that the Consistory had not gratified his resentment, used all his efforts to engage them to take this affair once more into their consideration. The Consistory had been changed in the beginning of the year 1698, he flattered himself that he should find them more tractable. And indeed they did name a Committee, but did not think it proper to alter any thing in what had been already determined. They confined their examination to the making of some remarks upon the Letter which Mr Bayle had published. The Consistory approved of their report, and declared that this piece had appeared later than they had expected (1); that Mr Bayle had not sent a copy of it to the Consistory; that the number of copies which he had printed was too small; that Mr Bayle had not sufficiently enlarged on what the Consistory had required of him, and had not declared that he submitted to it without reserve: and that upon this account they might justly demand further satisfaction; but that they would be content to represent these things to him verbally, and to exhort him to correct the second edition according to the remarks which they had communicated to him, and to make a good use of the advice which they had given him: that they would draw up a Memorial wherein they might add some new remarks; and that as Mr Jurieu had been very ill used by Mr Bayle in that work, Mr Bayle should be exhorted to behave himself for the future with more moderation, both in the second edition, and in the other books which he should publish. "The Consistory having seen with grief that so little regard had been "shewn to a Minister whose ministry and labours had been and still were of singular "edification to the Church." A Committee was appointed to draw up this Memorial, and they were ordered to communicate it to Mr Bayle. They inserted in it what related to Mr Jurieu. They added likewise some remarks; and amongst other things they desired Mr Bayle "to take care not to refute except upon very "good grounds, what our Divines have reported of certain wicked Popes, since "though he might alledge some conjectures in defence of these Popes, with re-
"gard to certain facts, yet strong reasons might be offered for their condemnation,
"and that it was unjust, without necessity, to side with seducers, who have done
"so much hurt to the Church, and to endeavour to traduce our writers as rash
"accusers." This affair ended here, and Mr Jurieu could not engage the Consistory any farther to gratify the desire of vengeance with which he was animated (2).

1699. In the year 1699 Mr Bayle published a third edition of his *Various Thoughts concerning Comets*. He suppressed the Advertisement prefixed to the second, and substituted another, in the beginning of which he tells us for what reason he had assumed the stile of a Roman Catholic in this work, both in treating of religious and political matters. He next observes upon what occasion this book was composed, and the design which he had of printing it at Paris, together with the other particulars which we related above. He observes likewise that he had promised that this edition should be enlarged with many new proofs and new answers to objections, yet notwithstanding it was entirely the same with the second, without ad-

(1) *The Consistory had been employed in this affair from November 3, 1697, to January 7, 1698. Mr Bayle's piece was not published 'till six months after. It is dated July 6, 1698.*

(2) *The reader will find at the end of this LIFE, the Acts of the Consistory of Rotterdam, with relation to Mr Bayle's Distresses.*

VOL. I.   x   dition

dition or diminution. The reason which engaged him to add nothing to it, is (says he) that this work being already too like those rivers which do nothing but wind about, he could not add new digressions to it without making it very tiresome to the reader: and that on this consideration he had reserved these additions for another volume, which should be published when he had advanced a little further in the composition of his Critical Dictionary, about which he was still employed. "What makes me (says he) refer this to that time, is that having anew examined all "the objections that can be formed against the parallel which I have drawn betwixt "Paganism and Atheism, it seems to me, that they may be all solved by the "principles which I have laid down, and by applying the answers which I have "already made use of. There is therefore no occasion to make haste." This new edition was printed while he was revising and reprinting his Dictionary. When it was finished he had nothing further to divert him from a labour which encreased every day, and which did not allow him the smallest relaxation. "I should be quite inexcusable (says he to Mr Marais (1) for delaying so long to write to you, "if I were not more than ordinarily busy, both in revising my *Dictionary*, of which "they are now printing a second edition, and in correcting the proofs. It is with "much ado that I can perform both these tasks, and it is very happy for me "that my *Thoughts concerning Comets* being finished, I have a little leisure. I have "read over all the sheets of it before they were printed, and though I have ad- "ded nothing, but only made some small alterations in the stile, it has made "me lose a good deal of time." This Edition is in two volumes; and to the second volume was joined a second edition of the *Addition to the Various Thoughts concerning Comets*, which was first published in 1694.

(1) *Letter of September 7, 1699, p. 763, 764.*

About this time Mr le Clerc, concealed under the name of *Theodore Parrhase*, published a book intitled, *Parrhasiana: or Various Thoughts on Critical, Historical, Moral, and Political Subjects*, in which there was an article that concerned Mr Bayle. He had maintained in his Dictionary, that the Manicheans could oppose to Christian Divines difficulties concerning moral and physical evil, which it was not possible to solve by the light of reason. Mr le Clerc on the contrary maintained that Origen's System which has been abandoned by all Christians, was sufficient to take away all these difficulties, and refuted Mr Bayle's Manichean in the person of an Origenist; and concluded "that since a man of that sort can reduce a Mani- "chean to silence, what might not they do who should reason infinitely better than "the disciples of Origen (2)?" But he declared that by answering the Manichean ob- jections, he did not pretend in the least to hurt Mr Bayle, whom he did not at all suspect to be a favourer of them. "I am persuaded (says he (3) that he has "taken the philosophical liberty, of disputing both *pro* and *con* on many occasions, "without concealing the strength of either side, only to exercise those who un- "derstand the subjects of which he treats, and not with an intention of favouring those "whose reasons he explains. One ought to consider the difficulties he proposeth, "as we do the objections which every body is allowed to make in a school of "Divinity or Philosophy; where the further one pusheth a difficulty, the more "honour redounds to those who can solve it. This is a piece of justice which he "has a right to require of his readers, and which ought not to be refused him. "For my own part (says he) I grant it him with all my heart, but I think I have "a right to desire in return, that I may be allowed to answer his objections, with- "out any body's making odious applications to the person, of answers which regard "only the difficulties."

(2) *Parrhasiana, Tom. I, p. 304.*

(3) *Ibid. p. 302, 303.*

In the year following the Princess Sophia, Electress Dowager of Hanover, and her daughter the Electress of Brandenbourg, since Queen of Prussia, had the curio- sity to take a tour through Flanders and Holland. These Princesses, less distin- guished by their elevated rank than by their knowledge and sublime parts, were the admiration of all Europe. They honoured the learned with their particular favour, loved to converse with them, and proposed sometimes very embarassing questions to them. Mr Bayle was perfectly well known to them by his works, their desire of seeing Holland was heightened by the pleasure of being personally acquainted with so celebrated a Philosopher. After having travelled through Flanders, they had no sooner arrived at Rotterdam than they sent to desire Mr Bayle to come to see them. But it being late, and Mr Bayle being in bed tormented with a violent head-ach, he made his compliments, acquainting them how sorry he was not to be in a condition of paying his respects to them. These Princesses next day went to the Hague without having seen Mr Bayle, who was detained at home by his indisposition: but the Count de Dhona, having informed Mr Basnage, who was gone to the Hague, of the desire which their Highnesses had to see Mr Bayle, Mr Bas- nage gave him notice of it. He came, and was received by these two Princesses in a distinguishing manner. The Princess Sophia conversed with him a long time in private, she asked him many questions, and they entered upon very sublime points. In the mean while Mr Basnage entertained the Electress of Brandenbourg, who expressed a great deal of esteem for Mr Bayle and his writings, which she always carried about with her. They staid with the Count de Dhona by their High- nesses

1699.

1700.

THE LIFE OF MR BAYLE.   lxxxiii

1700. nesses order. These Princesses desired their company to Delft, but Mr Bayle not being able to wait upon them, they parted at the Hague (1).

1701. In 1701 there appeared a book intitled, *An Apologetical Dissertation for the blessed Robert d'Arbrissselles, founder of the Order of Font-Evraud, with relation to what Mr Bayle has said of him in his Historical and Critical Dictionary* (2). Mr Bayle, in speaking of Robert d'Arbrisselles, said, that he had been accused of lying with some of his Nuns, that by irritating his passions, he might give the more glorious victory to his virtue. It is certain that Jeffery, Abbot of Vendôme and Cardinal, gave the blessed Robert notice of the reports which went about on that head, and rallied him upon this *new kind of martyrdom* which he had found out. Father de la Mainferme, a Monk of Fontevraud, undertook the defence of the founder of his Order; and Mr Bayle confesseth in his Dictionary, *that the reasons of the Apologist seem very strong,* and that *he doth not pretend to affirm what was reported of Robert.* This confession gave occasion to Father Souri, a Monk of the same Order (3), to examine this subject more accurately, and to place it in a new light. His Dissertation is wrote in form of a Letter addressed to Mr Bayle. He praiseth him for having given to understand that he did not believe what was said concerning the blessed Robert to be true, and at the same time makes great encomiums on his Dictionary. "It is a long time ago (says he (4), since the Republic of Letters
" have been obliged to you, but this last service which you have lately done to
" it, by your admirable Dictionary, has crowned them all. It is not enough to
" say that you have given us a book, you have given us an entire library.
" The novelty of the design, your discernment in historical facts, the exactness of
" your citations, that care and discreet attention which reigns every where in that
" prodigious work of advancing nothing that is false, and of daring to say what
" is true, according to the inviolable laws of a true Historian; all this makes me
" say that it would have been pity, if you had yielded to the temptation of suppres-
" sing so learned a work. As for me, an inconsiderable and private person, I
" received it, with a gratitude which I cannot express to you, and I join
" with the common herd of readers at least, in making the acknowledgments which
" the public owes to you upon account of the great discoveries you have therein
" made, and I shall make a good use of them.

" The difference of party is of no consequence here, every one will be able to
" choose what is proper for him. You do not set a great value upon our Saints,
" but that prejudice doth not at all hinder you from being dissatisfied at people's
" laying evident falshoods to their charge, and we cannot sufficiently acknowledge
" your justice and sincerity in this respect. This love for truth deserves that God
" should one day give you the knowledge of all revealed truths.

" I feel in myself the same equity for your Reformers. I never relished either
" the exaggerations or impostures of zealots; and still less the bold assertions of
" Bolsec, an Author full of resentment; how much soever we may be inclined to
" believe the scandals which are reported concerning your Patriarch, who has de-
" clared himself in so open a manner against the most ancient of Churches. It
" is not by impostures that he ought to be attacked, and the truth of my Reli-
" gion which he endeavoured to destroy, had no occasion for such assistance. I
" do not believe, notwithstanding their Heterodoxy, all that the Catholics say of
" your Doctors, except when they are supported by incontestable proofs, and nei-
" ther doth my Catholicism impose upon me, as to the evil which the Protestants
" say of ours, when their reasons are evident. I do not tell you this, Sir, to
" make you excuse the more easily what I will take the liberty to remonstrate
" to you, nor to set myself up as a model of sincerity to a person who might
" serve for such to others. Although I should not act in this manner, the poor
" example of such an obscure man as I am, would not turn you out of your
" way, and you would still thunder against the forgers of lies. That of which I
" treated here, which has been made concerning the blessed Robert d'Arbrisselles,
" cannot fail *to belong to your Dictionary; for if it is true, your Dictionary may take
" bold of it, as it is historical; and if it is false, may take notice of it, as it is cri-
" tical.*

" But I am very sure you do not believe it to be true. You, Sir, own as
" much yourself. ...... *I do not pretend,* say you, *to affirm what is said of him, for
" the reasons of the Apologist seem very strong.* But will you allow me, Sir,
" to say that possibly you have not sufficiently, in this passage, condemned that
" falshood, nor with so much vivacity as you have done others of that kind, which
" are only founded on HEARSAY."

This is the only thing which Father Souri would have desired of Mr Bayle, for in other respects he is perfectly well satisfied with him. " Once more (says he (5),
" we have only gratefully to acknowledge, upon this occasion, your equity and
" good taste. Shall I dare however (adds he) to tell you that the entertaining
" part of this Article has made you in some measure forget your own maxims,
" and has hindered you from saying any more than the two favourable lines which
" I have just now cited? there never was a story more worthy of your censure than

(1) *A MSS. Memoir of Mr Basnage.*

(2) *Dissertation apologetique pour le bienheureux Robert d'Arbrisselles, Fondateur de l'Ordre de Font-Evraud, sur ce qu'en a dit Mr Bayle dans son Dictionaire Historique & Critique. At Antwerp (Amsterdam) by Henry Desbordes. In* 12°.

(3) *See Reponse aux questions d'un Provincial, Tom. I. chap lxvii, pag.* 684.

(4) *Dissertation apologetique &c. p.* 1, *and the following.*

(5) *Ibid. p.* 8, 9.

"than this. You have indeed a mind to divert your Readers, and you have your 1701.
"reasons for doing so; but it is not your design to divert them at the expence
"of truth, and you have never lost sight of it, in what relates to us."
Mr Bayle gave an account of this piece in an addition to the Article FONT-
EVRAUD. "This Apology (says he) is so well turned and so solid, that every
"reasonable man ought to acquiesce in it; and though I have sufficiently declared
"that I did not give the least credit to the reports concerning the sharing of
"the bed &c, I declare again here, that in all the passages where I have spoke
"of it without repeating this my opinion, I desire it may be understood." Mr Bayle
does Father Souri the justice he deserved. "The civility (says he), the politeness,
"the wit, and erudition of the Author, appear in it in a distinguishing manner,
"and I am very sorry that I do not deserve the praises which so accomplished
"a person has been pleased to bestow by way of compliment upon me."
The second edition of the *Critical Dictionary* was finished on the twenty seventh 1702.
of December 1701, and was published in the beginning of the year 1702. It was
enlarged very near one half. This augmentation was contrary to Mr Bayle's intention. He only designed to make some additions to the Articles already published; and did not think of adding any new ones, he reserved them for a se-
(1) *See the* parate Alphabet, under the title of *A Supplement to the Critical Dictionary* (1). But
Letters to the Bookseller desired that they should be published in this second edition, and
Mr de la Mr Bayle was obliged to consent to it. This change gave him a great deal of
Monnoye, uneasiness as he shows in the Preface. He distinguished the additions in such a
August 19
1697, p. manner that one might discern them at first sight. He very carefully corrected
665; and the faults of the first edition, which he had either discovered himself, or which had
to Mr Ma- been pointed out to him by his friends. He showed his gratitude to those who
rais, Octo-
ber 2, had furnished him with memoirs, and names them when he thought he could do
1698, p. so without offending them. In the mean while he owns that these additions had
727. not allowed him to make the Articles of the first edition so correct as he could
have wished. "I must own (says he) that the trouble which they have cost me,
"has not permitted me to correct the Articles of the first edition, with all the se-
"verity and all the diligence which I would have employed about them. It is
"very hard, while the Printers work without ceasing, for an Author to be able
"to perform these three things, to revise two large volumes in Folio, to enlarge them
"more than one third, and to correct the proofs."
In speaking of the corrections which he had made in the first edition, he doth
not forget those which he had obliged himself to make. "There are (says he) a
"sort of corrections which I have made as it were *ex officio*, and in consequence of
"an obligation of which the public has been informed. I have behaved herein
"with all possible care, and with a very strong intention to give satisfaction to
"those who were offended. For this purpose I have suppressed every thing in the
"article of David, which could give offence. This is the greatest suppression,
"which has been necessary, the rest are neither considerable for their number, or
"their extent. We have been able to amend every thing at the expence of a few
"words, or lines, and principally by means of four Explanations, which are placed
"at the end of this work." Mr Bayle did, in fact, suppress every thing which
the Consistory of Rotterdam had disapproved in the article of David: but even before this edition was compleated, several persons having declared that they would
(2) *See* not buy it, if that article was not published in the same manner as before, the Book-
Letter to seller was obliged to reprint it by itself (2) that they might join it to this new
Mr Pe- edition. Some of Mr Bayle's friends advised him to insert in the *Project* which
cher, Au- he had published in 1692 together with some Essays of his Dictionary, and he
gust 10,
1705, p. accordingly placed it at the end of the Dissertations in the last volume (3).
1041. There is no book which stands more in need of a good Index, than Mr Bayle's
Dictionary. Mr Leers took care to advertise in the beginning of the Project, that
(3) *See* he would not forget this article, and Mr Huet composed a very exact one for the
Letter to first edition: but Mr Leers foreseeing that the printing of it would take up a long
Mr Des time, suppressed the one half of it, which disfigured it in such a manner, that
Maizeaux,
November Mr Bayle thought he was obliged to inform the public of this in a short adver-
1 1701, tisement, which he placed at the end of the Index. The other half was preserved,
p. 839, and given to the Author of the Index to the second edition, who made the best
use of it he could. But this new Index, considering the great number of additions
was very imperfect. Mr Bayle here lays down a method of supplying that defect.
He takes notice at the same time that having learned by experience the qualities
which a good Index ought to have, he could have made such a one, but that he
had neither the time nor the patience which so tedious and toilsome a task required.
He adds, that he had not even thought it proper that the person employed in composing the Index, should engage himself in all the details, which some readers desired, and gives his reasons for it.
He next observes that some persons might complain, that his Dictionary did not
furnish them with a sufficient number of things to their taste. He says that this is
the inevitable fate of all books which contain a medley of many different things,

2   and

1702. and wherein there is a great variety. He declares that if he has made mention of one family rather than of another no lefs, or more confiderable, he has done fo without the leaft refpect of perfons, and only becaufe he had Memoirs concerning the one, and none concerning the other. Laftly, he anfwers thofe who had found fault that he had given fo few articles of great Captains. He fays that this proceeds not only from his having avoided to treat the fame matters which are in other Dictionaries, but chiefly from his not being able to make thefe articles fuch as he could wifh. He gives an example of this, by fhowing upon what plan he would compofe the article of the Maréchal de Luxembourg, if he had the affiftance and knowledge neceffary to draw it up.

He joined four Explanations to this edition, in order to fulfil his engagements with the Confiftory of Rotterdam. He prefixed to them a general obfervation, wherein he gives the reafons why he believed that no body would be offended with the liberty of philofophizing, which he had fometimes take. In the firft Explanation he juftifies himfelf againft thofe who had found fault with him for having faid, that there had been fpeculative Atheifts and Epicureans, who had furpaffed the Idolaters in the foundnefs of their morals ; and fhows that the conduct of thefe Atheifts, could not do any hurt to the true Religion, nor give it the leaft blemifh. But he promifeth to treat of this more at large in the continuation of his book concerning Comets. The fecond Explanation relates to the objections of the Manicheans. He concludes it with the following fix propofitions, which contain the fubftance of his doctrine :

I. That it is the property of the myfteries of the Gofpel to be liable to objections which natural light cannot folve.

II. That Unbelievers cannot juftly draw any advantage from this, that the maxims of Philofophy do not afford folutions to the difficulties which they raife againft the Myfteries of the Gofpel.

III. That the objections of the Manicheans, concerning the Origin of Evil and Predeftination, ought not to be confidered in general as attacking Predeftination, but with this particular regard, that the Origin of Evil, the decrees of God concerning it, and the confequences of it, are the moft inconceivable myfteries of Chriftianity.

IV. That it ought to fatisfy every good, Chriftian that his faith is founded on the teftimony of the word of God.

V. That the fyftem of the Manicheans confidered in itfelf is abfurd, indefenfible, and contrary to the ideas of order ; that it is liable to retorfions, and is not able to remove difficulties.

VI. That in all events, adds he, no body can be offended at my confeffions, unlefs he looks upon the doctrine of the moft orthodox Divines as fcandalous, fince all that I have faid is a natural and neceffary confequence from their fentiments, and that I have only laid down in a more prolix manner, what they teach more compendioufly.

In the third Explanation he fhows, that the objections of the Pyrrhonian Abbé againft fome doctrines of Chriftianity, which he has related in his Dictionary, are of no force againft our Religion. He firft lays it down as a certain and inconteftable principle, *That Chriftianity is of a fupernatural order, and that its analyfis is the fupreme authority of God propofing myfteries to us, not that we may comprehend them, but that we may believe them with all the humility which is due to the infinite Being, who can neither deceive nor be deceived.* From whence evidently follows, adds he, the incompetency of the tribunal of Philofophy to judge of the controverfies among Chriftians, fince they ought only to be carried to the tribunal of Revelation. He draws the character of the Pyrrhonians, and fhows that of all the Philofophers who ought not to be allowed to difpute concerning the myfteries of Chriftianity, before they have admitted Revelation as the rule, there are none fo unworthy of being heard as the followers of Pyrrho. In the fourth Explanation he examines the complaints of thofe who had faid that his Dictionary contained obfcenities. He expreffeth this accufation in the following manner : " That the Author
" relates hiftorical facts which he has found in other authors, whom he carefully quotes,
" which facts are filthy and obfcene, that he adds a commentary upon thefe hifto-
" rical narrations to illuftrate them by teftimonies, by reflexions, and by proofs, &c.
" in which he fometimes alledgeth the words of fome authors, who have wrote
" freely, fome of them as Phyficians or Lawyers, others as Gallants or Poets :
" but that he never fays any thing containing either explicitly, or even implicitly,
" an approbation of impurity ; that, on the contrary, he endeavours upon many oc-
" cafions to expofe it to our abhorrence, and to refute loofe morality." He afterwards proves by reafons, by authorities, and by examples, that thefe forts of obfcenities, are not of the number of thofe which we can reafonably cenfure.

Mr Bayle made an addition to the article of Origen, upon occafion of the *Parrhafiana* of Mr le Clerc. " There are (fays he) in that work fome reflexions con-
" cerning the difpute between the Manicheans and the Orthodox. They are pre-
" ceded by an obfervation as equitable as we could expect from a very honeft man,
" they are preceded, I fay, by a judgment altogether agreeable to equity, truth, and
" reafon, concerning the views which I had in taking the liberty of relating the
" objections

"objections of the Manicheans, and of confessing that natural light doth not furnish 1702. "Christians with any means of solving them, whether we follow the system of "St Augustin, or whether we follow that of Molina, and of the Remonstrants, or "whether we have recourse to that of the Socinians. Theodore Parrhasie main- "tains the contrary, and pretends that an Origenist is able *to stop the mouths of* "*the Manicheans* ...... *If a man of this sort* (says he) *can reduce a Manichean to* "*silence, what might not they do, who would reason infinitely better than the disciples of* "*Origen?* We shall examin what he supposeth *an Origenist might say, after having* "*read all the objections of the Manicheans.*" Mr Bayle reduceth the answer of the Origenist to these propositions: I. God has made us free to make way for virtue and vice, bame and praise, rewards and punishments. II. He damns no man simply for having sinned, but for not having repented of his sins. III. The physical and moral evils of mankind are of so short a duration in comparison of eternity, that we cannot conclude from thence that God is not a beneficent Being and a lover of virtue. It is in this last proposition, says Mr Bayle, that all the strength of the Origenist lies: the reason is because he supposeth that the torments of Hell will not be eternal, and that God after he has judged that creatures, endowed with liberty, have suffered enough, will afterwards make them happy to all eternity. The eternal happiness which will be bestowed on them according to the Origenist, fully answers the idea of the infinite mercy, though it should be preceded by even many ages of suffering; for many ages are nothing in comparison of an infinite duration, and there is infinitely less proportion between the time in which this world shall exist and eternity, than there is between a minute and a hundred millions of years. Therefore we have no reason to wonder that God looks upon the miseries which we suffer as almost nothing; he who alone has an adequate idea of eternity, and who looks upon the beginning and the end of our sufferings, as infinitely more near to one another than the beginning and the end of a minute. We ought to reason in the same manner concerning vice and vicious actions, which with respect to God do not continue a great while, and which in the main do not change any thing in the universe. If an artist should make a clock, which by being once wound up should go exactly during a whole year, excepting two or three seconds, which should not be equal when it is first set a going, could one say that this artist could not pretend to great skill or exactness in his work. In the same manner if God amends in one day for all eternity the disorders which the bad use of liberty has occasioned among men, can any body be surprized that he has not put a stop to them during the moment in which we shall exist upon this Earth.

Mr Bayle observes that a Manichean might answer,

I. That it is not consistent with ideal or infinitely perfect goodness, to bestow a gift of which we foresee the bad effects, without preventing them, though it is in our power: it is the essential and distinguishing property of ideal goodness, that it disposeth the being possessed of it to grant favours, which by the shortest, and most certain means which it can contrive, render the condition of the person who receives them happy. This ideal goodness essentially and necessarily excludes every thing which can agree to a malicious being; and it is certain that such a being would be very ready to bestow favours, the use of which he should know would prove fatal to the persons to whom he should grant them. Now if we consult this idea of goodness, we shall not find that God, an infinitely good principle, can postpone the happiness of his creatures to several ages of misery, nor bestow free will upon them by the use of which he was very certain they would procure their own damnation. But supposing that the infinite goodness of the Creator allowed him to bestow upon his creatures, a liberty of which they might as readily make a bad use as a good one, we must at least allow that it would engage him to watch over their conduct in such a manner, as not to suffer them actually to sin. As to the reason alledged by the Origenist, that it was necessary to bestow liberty upon the creature, in order to make way for virtue and vice, blame and praise, rewards and punishments; we might answer, that this reason instead of being an argument why an infinitely holy and infinitely good Being should give free-will to creatures, is, on the contrary, what ought to have hindered him from doing so. Vice and blame ought to have no place among the works of an infinitely holy cause, every thing there ought to be praise-worthy, virtue alone ought to appear here, and vice be entirely banished. And as every thing ought to be happy under the government of a supream Being infinitely good and infinitely powerful; punishments ought to have no place there. Virtue, praise, and benefits, may very well exist, though vice, blame, and punishments have no other existence than what they call ideal or objective. The Origenist owns that this will be the case when all creatures endowed with freedom of will shall enjoy an eternal happiness, which shall succeed to some ages of suffering. If he answers, that these blessings could not be a reward if creatures had not been endowed with liberty, it might be replied, that there is no proportion between eternal happiness and the good use that man makes of his free-will; and therefore the eternal happiness which God bestows on a good man cannot, properly speaking, be considered as a reward, it is a favour, it is a free gift. It ought

not

1702. not therefore to be pretended, strictly speaking, that it was necessary to confer free-will upon men in order to their deserving the happiness of paradise, and obtaining it by way of reward.

II. Impenitence being nothing else but a bad use of our liberty, it comes all to the same thing, whether we say that God damns men only because they do not repent, or whether we say that he damns them simply because they have sinned. It is true that, generally speaking, it shows a merciful disposition to be willing to remit the punishment to those who are sorry for their faults: but when one promiseth pardon under condition of repentance to such as he very certainly knows will not repent, properly speaking he promiseth nothing, and in this case he is as fully resolved to punish them as if he had offered them no favour at all: if he had a mind in good earnest to exempt them punishment, he would hinder them from being impenitent, which is very easy for God to do who has an absolute power over our hearts.

III. The Origenists would not dare to determine the duration of these torments which preceed this eternal happiness: for not only they are ignorant of it, but likewise they would be afraid of making them too short, least they should be accused of loosing the reins to sinners; or of making them too long, least they should not give a just idea of the mercy of God. They would not dare to make them, for example, either of a hundred or of a million of years. They do not therefore trust to the want of proportion between the duration of a million of ages, and an infinite duration; and we do not see that it solves the difficulty to say that there is infinitely less proportion between the duration of the earth and eternity, than there is between a minute and a hundred millions of years. What can be affirmed of these hundred millions of years, may likewise be affirmed of as many millions of ages, as there are drops of water in the ocean; since there is no proportion between finite and infinite. Yet in the mean while one cannot conceive that the punishment of a creature, which should be continued for a hundred millions of ages, is consistent with the sovereign goodness of the creator. This number of years, which is nothing in comparison of eternity, seems notwithstanding a very long duration considered in itself, and with regard to the person suffering. Now let us diminish this number as much as we will, we shall only thereby make a diminution of rigour, and we shall never arrive at the supreme goodness of God except by suppressing even the last minute of the pains of hell. We commend the skill of a Clockmaker when his clock fails only in two or three seconds in a year; but the exactness of an infinitely perfect artist excludes absolutely all exceptions. His goodness, his holiness, his wisdom, &c. are absolutely simple, and without the least mixture of the contrary qualities, without the least mixture which can be conceived, or which can be in the nature of things.

Mr Bayle observes that "though Origen could answer the objections of the Ma-
"nicheans, it would not follow that therefore they could be much more easily an-
"swered upon better and more orthodox principles: for all the advantage that he
"can find in this dispute, proceeds from falsities which are peculiar to him, he
"giving on the one hand a great deal of power to free-will, and on the other
"hand substituting eternal happiness to eternal misery which he doth not admit." By supposing that eternal happiness will follow the torments which the damned shall endure for some ages, we take away the most embarrassing argument of the Manicheans; for their strongest argument is founded on the hypothesis, that all men, except a few, will be damned to all eternity; which is the doctrine of all the sects of Christians, excepting the Socinians.

In 1701 there was printed at Paris a book intitled *Naudæana & Patiniana. Or Remarkable Particulars, taken from the conversations of Messieurs Naudé and Patin* (1). In works of this kind, they make use of the name of some celebrated author, to introduce a great many historical and literary particulars, which have a relation to the time in which he lived, and which they sometimes even transcribe from his works. These Collections would not be contemptible, if one could depend upon the facts which are related in them; but they ordinarily fill them with an infinite number of things which are either false or uncertain, or which want many essential circumstances. To make them useful they should be attended with a Commentary both to correct them and to supply what is defective. This Mr * * * did with relation to the *Naudæana*. He both made Corrections and Additions of which he gives an account in a short preface. "All the world knows (says he) how greedily the *Ana* are at present
"received. But neither is any body ignorant, that the little exactness which one
"finds in them very much diminisheth the pleasure which the variety of matter
"and liberty of sentiments, inseparable from books of this nature, might give the
"readers. It is therefore to put people in mind of making them henceforth more
"useful, that I have undertaken to add a sort of Commentary to the pretended
"*Naudæana*. The only thing which I propose to do here is to fix the chrono-
"logy of the facts mentioned in it, to add sometimes absolutely necessary circum-
"stances, and lastly not to allow the Author to advance any thing, which is not sup-
"ported by the testimony of some other person worthy of credit." Mr * * * tells us that he had a design of making likewise Additions and Corrections to the *Patiniana*, but that certain reasons had obliged him to confine himself to the *Naudæana*.

Father

(1) Naudæana & Patiniana. Ou singularitez remarquables prises des Conversations de Messieurs Naudé & Patin.

THE LIFE OF Mʀ BAYLE.

(1) By Francis vander Plaats 1703.

Father de Vitry, sent the Additions to the *Naudæana* to Mr Bayle, and he published 1702. them at Amsterdam (1) with the *Naudæana* and *Patiniana*, under the title of *a Second Edition revised, corrected, and enlarged, with Additions to the* Naudæana *which are not in the Paris edition*. Mr Bayle added an Advertisement to it in the name of the Bookseller, wherein he says that this edition is incomparably preferable to that of Paris; that there were a great number of faults corrected in it, which disfigured the proper names so much that they were scarce to be known; that they had brought together all the passages which related to the same person, and which were dispersed all over the book in the Paris edition; and lastly, what was much more considerable, they had given very curious and very necessary supplements, from a manuscript sent them from Paris.

(2) Réponse aux Questions d'un Provincial. A Rotterdam chez Reinier Leers 1704.

The second edition of the Critical Dictionary had fatigued Mr Bayle. To divert himself he composed a book intitled *An Answer to the Questions of a Country Gentleman* (2). He says in the Preface, that in composing it he had proposed to write a book of *a middle kind betwixt those which employ our hours of study, and those which we read only for amusement*. In consequence of this he goes lightly over certain matters which might have been treated in a more compleat manner, he passes quickly from one subject to another, in order to introduce the greater variety, and when it was necessary to enlarge upon some matters, he doth it in such a manner that every chapter shows them in a different light. He observes that he might have employed certain thoughts and facts which have an essential connection with the things which he has treated of, but that he abstained from doing so, to avoid repeating things which are commonly known. He doth not doubt but some readers will think that he has made too many quotations, but he shows that this is a groundless complaint. It is to go against the nature of things (says he) to pretend, that an Author in a work designed to prove and clear up facts, should only make use of his own thoughts, or that at least he ought to quote very seldom. Mr Bayle adds, "That this book "is not written in the taste which has prevailed for some years past, and of "which possibly the public begins already to be tired. It is not a collection of "miscellaneous thoughts, or of maxims or characters, smart repartees or merry "tales. What is it then? It would possibly (answers he) be pretty difficult to define it, and I leave it to every reader to do it for himself; I shall only observe that this work has some resemblance to those books which appeared in so "great number in the XVIth Century under the title of *Diversæ Lectiones*, or some "other title to the same purpose."

This work contains an agreeable and instructive variety of historical, critical, and literary discussions. One finds there likewise some philosophical remarks and some political observations. As soon as this book appeared in Holland, one of my friends informed me that it was written by Mr Bayle. I desired to know of Mr Bayle if this was true, and he made me the following answer. "I do not wonder (said he) that "you have been told that I am the Author of a new book intitled, *An Answer to the "Questions of a Country Gentleman*. Every body here will have it that I have "wrote it, and if I were ambitious I would contradict this report, for this work is "not very proper to give a man a great reputation. It is a heap of little ob-"servations, which can only please those who do not even neglect literary curio-

(3) Letter November 9, 1703, p. 936. See likewise the Letter to Mr Marais, August 4, 1704, p. 1001.

"sities, and do not, after the manner of the generality, look upon them as trifles (3)." Some time after this I desired him to inform me whether this book would have any continuation, and told him the opinion of some people about it. "I will not here "repeat (answered he (4), what I think I told you very plainly, that I renounce "all interest in the *Answer to the Questions of a Country Gentleman*. I know how-"ever that the Bookseller has no intention of publishing any other part to it. I "mean that there is no fixed resolution or plan laid down in this matter, and "there is nothing of that kind in the press. Those people are no doubt in the

(4) Letter February 8, 1704, p. 951.

"right who say that it doth not sufficiently interest the public, but they ought to "consider that an Author cannot interest the public, except he discusses questions "which concern the honour and glory of a whole people, or of a whole Religion, "or at least if he doth not treat of some important doctrine of morality, or poli-"tics. All the other subjects with which men of letters fill their books, are use-"less to the public, and we ought to consider them as only frothy nourishment in them-"selves, but which notwithstanding satisfy the curiosity of many Readers according "to the diversity of their taste. What is there, for example, less interesting to

(5) Nouvelles Additions aux Eloges des Hommes sçavans tirez de l'Histoire de Mr de Thou. Tome troisiéme.

"the public than the *Bibliotheque choisie* of the Sieur Colomiés, which however is "a work that has been looked upon as excellent in its kind, and which almost "charms those who are fond of literary particularities? I could name many other "books to you which are read, though they contain nothing that interests the "public."

In 1704 Mr Teissier published at Berlin, *New Additions to the Elogies of learned* 1704. *Men. Extracted from Thuanus's History. Tom. III.* (5). Mr Bayle had in his Dictionary criticised several passages in the two first volumes: Mr Teissier in this volume agreed that some of Mr Bayle's remarks were well founded, and undertakes to defend the other passages which had been censured. But in the mean time expressed

a great

THE LIFE OF MR BAYLE.   lxxxix

1704. a great esteem and respect for Mr Bayle. " I am obliged to him, (says he (1), for
" taking the trouble of reading this work, and pointing out to me the passages in
" which I have been mistaken ; the other Authors whom he has criticised ought
" with me to express their gratitude, and acknowledge that he has done great
" service to the Republic of Letters, by discovering their errors."

Mr Teissier seemed even to be diffident of the justness of his answers. " I do not
" know (says he) if I have well maintained my cause, for I have to do with a
" formidable adversary, I mean with a Critic of vast erudition, exquisite judgment,
" extreme exactness, and who has signalized himself by several victories which he
" has obtained over the greatest Heroes of the Republic of Letters."

Mr Bayle answered Mr Teissier in a Memoir inserted in the *History of the works of
the Learned* (2). He says that two reasons made him hasten the publication of this
Memoir : the one to show Mr Teissier how sensible he was of his politeness, and the
esteem he had for his work ; and the other to prevent the consequences which might
be drawn from Mr Teissier's answers. " It would (says he) be a very bad preju-
" dice against my whole Dictionary, if among the Critical Observations which relate
" to Mr Teissier's Additions, there were so many of them ill grounded as he pretends.
" I therefore thought myself bound to discuss some of them, in order to put every
" reader in a condition to judge of the dispute." He shows afterwards that Mr Teissier imputes to him things which he had not said ; that he would make him accountable for what is advanced by the Authors he quotes ; that he sometimes has
expressed himself inaccurately, and given occasion to people to mistake his sense ;
and that if he in order to support his opinion has quoted Authors who in effect say
the same thing that he has done, Mr Bayle has cited others to establish his side of
the question, who are of greater weight and authority. He concludes with excusing
the errors which Mr Teissier may have fallen into. " This (says he) is what I
" have to offer in defence of my remarks. I leave it to by my readers to
" judge, whether they are just or not ; but I declare at the same time, that al-
" though they should decide in my favour, they will notwithstanding be obliged
" to think Mr Teissier very excusable, since he has followed Authors who must
" needs have appeared well informed about these matters. No body can be more
" persuaded than I am that my small observations will do no prejudice to his work ;
" and no body is more interested than I am to banish from the Republic of
" Letters, that false and pernicious maxim, that a book cannot be worthy of esteem
" if it is not without errors. Matters do not go ill with some sorts of books, espe-
" cially with Dictionaries, if there are but seven or eight things to be corrected in
" every page taking one with another."

Mr Bayle likewise made use of Mr de Bauval's Journal to defend himself against
the attacks of an anonymous writer (3), who had published a book at Paris intitled,
*The Distinction and Nature, Good and Evil: a Treatise wherein the error of the Mani-
cheans, the sentiments of Montagne, Charron, and of Mr Bayle, &c. are censured* (4). This
piece had been highly commended in some books printed at Paris, and they had
even said that Mr Bayle could not avoid answering it. Mr Bayle sent for it, and
after having examined it found that it required no answer with respect to those
who knew what he had said concerning the Manicheans, and that a short Memoir would be sufficient for those who did not know it. All that he had to do,
was to show that this anonymous Author had entirely mistaken the state of the
question, or at least had pretended to mistake it. In this Memoir (5) Mr Bayle
observed that what this Author had said of his own, or had borrowed from St Augustin
tended only to show. " I. That the system of two principles is false, absurd, and
" evidently contrary to the ideas of the infinitely perfect Being. II. That this system
" is particularly absurd, ridiculous, and abominable in the details, to which the Ma-
" nicheans had descended." But these two propositions were no part of the matter
in debate. Mr Bayle had expressly agreed to them, and consequently there was
no occasion to prove them to him. He had only maintained that the hypothesis
of two principles, how false and impious soever, yet attacks the other hypothesis
with objections which natural light cannot solve. This was the only thing that this
Author ought to have engaged with, and yet it is precisely what he had neglected
to do. He had satisfied himself with acting offensively against the principles of
the Manicheans, instead of standing upon the defensive, and repelling the attacks
which the Manicheans might make against the most orthodox Christians. The business here was not to make thrusts, but to parry those which were made. In this
manner Mr Bayle shows that this Author not having touched the Manichean objections, he did not think himself interested in the dispute, and that it was enough
that he had informed the public why he did not answer him.

This anonymous author had pretended that it was easy to destroy the system of
two principles by maintaining with St Augustin that evil is not a being but a
simple privation : Mr Bayle owns that this being once proved would solidly refute the Manicheans in as far as they affirm that evil is a substance ; but that a
Manichean might easily get out of this difficulty, by showing that this is only a
dispute about words, and a misunderstanding betwixt St Augustin and his adver- saries.

(1) Nou-
velles Ad-
ditions,
&c. in the
Advertise-
ment.

(2) May
1704, p.
200, and
the fol-
lowing.

(3) This
anonymous
writer was
a Carthu-
sian of Pa-
ris, named
Dom A-
lexis Gau-
din. He
was ne-
phew to
Abbé Gau-
din, Canon
of Nôtre
Dame.

(4) La
Distincti-
on & la
Nature du
Bien & du
Mal. Trai-
té où l'on
combat
l'erreur
des Mani-
chéens, les
sentimens
de Mon-
tagne & de
Charron,
& ceux de
Monsieur
Bayle, &c.
Printed at
Paris in
1704, in
12°.

(5) Histo-
ry of the
Works of
the Learn-
ed, August
1704, p.
369, and
the follow-
ing.

VOL. I.   z

faries. He concludes by telling this anonymous Author, that if he thinks it proper to treat this dispute in a regular manner, he must begin anew, since he is not one jot further advanced in it than he was when he first sat down to write: but that if he has nothing to advance but what he finds in St Augustin he had better be silent. "These arguments (adds he) are able without doubt "to set the absurdities of the Manichean sect in a very strong light, but this is "not the affair in hand; the question here is only how to defend, and not at all how "to attack; nay it would not be sufficient to confound the impieties of the Ma- "nicheans by objections; one must enter into a dispute wherein we might get the "better of adversaries who would not give such advantages as they did with whom "St Augustin had to do; we ought to imagine ourselves to be engaged with "Sceptics, who being disgusted with the hypothesis of the two principles, reject it, "and yet will not embrace the other 'till we have freed it from the difficulties "with which it is incumbered. In a word, we must show by the light of na- "ture that there is a close connection betwixt the crimes and miseries of man- "kind, and the ideas of an infinitely holy, infinitely powerful, and infinitely free "being." The anonymous Author having no mind to engage in such a ticklish discussion, chose to be silent.

Mr Bayle at last fulfilled the promise which he had so often made of publishing a defence of his *Thoughts concerning Comets*. He began it in the month of November 1703, and resolved not to give over 'till he had finished it (1). The impression of it was begun in the month following (2), and the book appeared in the month of August 1704, under this title: *A Continuation of the Various Thoughts written to a Doctor of the Sorbonne, on occasion of a Comet which appeared in the month of December 1680. Or, An Answer to several difficulties proposed to the Author by Monsieur* * * * (3). In the Advertisement Mr Bayle, says that though he had promised this work several times for ten years past, he had not made great haste to publish it, for several reasons which he relates: "So that when he all at once "took the resolution of composing it, he had found nothing prepared for that "purpose, and was obliged to awaken, or call very far back, his thoughts on this "subject, so that the materials were brought together and made use of at the same "time. There was only one thing in the Various Thoughts (adds he) which de- "termined me to write an apology, to wit, the parallel betwixt Atheism and Pa- "ganism; but being thus obliged to take up the pen in my own justification, I "thought myself bound to satisfy several difficulties which had been proposed to "me concerning other parts of the work, and I persuaded myself that it was neces- "sary to observe the same order in my answers which they had done in their "objections, in which they had followed the order of my chapters. I have fol- "lowed this method to the end of the first volume, but I was obliged to lay it "aside in the second, to prevent engaging myself in a labour much larger than I "had proposed. I have therefore inserted nothing in the second volume but what "regarded the parallel of Paganism and Atheism, and notwithstanding I have not "been able to go through that subject. There are some objections still left "undiscussed on this subject which I have reserved for a third volume (4)."

Mr Bayle next makes a remark which he thought very essential. "I beg of "the reader (says he) carefully to remember that this long dispute, wherein I have "maintained that Paganism is at least as bad as Atheism, is a question entirely "indifferent to the true Religion. The interests of Christianity are so separated "from those of Pagan Idolatry, that it can neither lose nor gain by Idolatry being "thought either as bad or worse than no Religion. This dispute therefore is of "the nature of those problems, wherein one may indifferently choose which "side he pleaseth, and orthodoxy not be concerned in the matter. It has been "always left to peoples choice to maintain that Arianism is worse than Sabellianism, "or that it is not; that the Nestorian heresy is more or less pernicious than the "Eutychian, and so of several other questions, wherein they who are mistaken "cannot be accused of doing the least hurt to the faith, provided they adhere to "the decisions of the ancient Councils &c." He in the next place obviates some objections, and makes some remarks to clear up this subject. We have seen that he had promised to answer at length in this work a piece of Mr Jurieu called the *Short Review*: he gives us here the reasons why he has not done so. "When I pub- "lished (says he) in 1694 an addition to my Various Thoughts, to answer in a few "words a pamphlet intitled the *Short Review &c.* I promised a full refutation of it, "yet notwithstanding I have taken no notice of it in this work, for I find that my "preliminary answer has been more than sufficient."

The principal objections discussed in the first volume of this *Continuation* of the Thoughts concerning Comets, relate to the following six questions. I. Whether the consent of all nations, in acknowledging a Deity, be a certain and demonstrative proof of the existence of a God. II. Whether there be any certainty in Astrology. III. If the Pagan Religion taught the practice of virtue, or of good morals. IV. If all things were made for man. V. If Historians ought to relate things incredible and superstitious. VI. If the Polytheism of the Pagans has been exaggerated. The

(1) *Letter to Mr Des Maizeaux, November 9, 1703, pag. 936.*

(2) *See Letter to Mr Minutoli December 16, 1703. p. 940.*

(3) *Continuation des Pensées diverses, écrites à un Docteur de Sorbonne à l'occasion de la Comete qui parut au mois de Decembre 1680. Ou Réponse à plusieurs difficultez que Monsieur * * * a proposées à l'Auteur. A Rotterdam chez Reinier Leers, 1705, 2 Vols in 12°.*

(4) *Mr Bayle never wrote this third volume.*

second

1704. second volume is employed in showing that he had reason in his Thoughts concerning Comets to say, *That Atheism is not a greater evil than Idolatry*. Mr Bayle points out the writers whom he had already alledged in that work, and cites several others, among which are Fathers of the Church, and Catholic and Protestant Doctors, who have affirmed that there are things as bad or worse than Atheism, or who have even declared that Idolatry is worse than Atheism, and who have notwithstanding never been exposed to ecclesiastic censures upon that account. From hence he concludes that he was intitled to maintain the same opinion, and that if many writers have been of a contrary sentiment, this only proves that the question in debate is of a problematical nature, and left to every body's discretion, and concerning which every body is at liberty to choose either side without prejudice to orthodoxy.

He likewise here examines the question (1), *Whether a society entirely composed of true Christians, and surrounded by other nations either of Infidels, or of worldly minded Christians, such as all the nations where Christianity prevails are at present, and have been for a long while, would be able to preserve itself*, and declares himself for the negative. Upon this occasion he acquaints us with the notion which a learned man had formed to himself of Christianity. "I was acquainted (says he (2), with a learned man, who fancied that Jesus Christ had not proposed his Religion as a thing which could suit with all sorts of persons, but only with a small number of the wise. He founded his notion upon this, that a whole nation which should practise exactly all the rules of Christianity, would not be able to preserve itself against the invasions of its neighbours. Now it could not be the intention of God, that an entire society should be deprived of all the human means of preserving itself independant of other people. This man would therefore persuade me, that as the Stoic Philosophy which was impracticable for a whole society was designed only for exalted minds, so the Gospel in like manner was only appointed for *Ascetics*, for chosen persons capable of abstracting themselves from the world, and of devoting themselves, in case of necessity, to the solitude of the most frightful deserts. In a word (said he), we ought to consider the Gospel only as a model of the utmost perfection, proposed to those to whom nature strengthened by Grace should give a relish for the most refined spirituality. Thus St Benedict, St Dominic, St Francis of Assise, and other founders of orders, have laid down rules and observances, not for all mankind, but for interior and spiritual Christians the number of which is very small. I answered this learned friend that he was evidently mistaken, since it is plain by reading the Evangelists and Apostles that the law of JESUS CHRIST is proposed to all sorts of people, of what sex and condition soever, not as a choice which they are left at liberty to make or not, but as the only means of avoiding eternal damnation."

This book engaged Mr Bayle in some disputes. He had cursorily criticised the system of Dr Cudworth and Dr Grew concerning *plastic and vital natures*. These Gentlemen suppose that these are immaterial sustances, endowed with a power of forming plants and animals, without knowing what they do. Mr Bayle observed (3), that thereby these Gentlemen, without thinking of it and contrary to their intentions, had weakened the most sensible argument we have for the Being of God taken from the admirable structure of the universe, and gave an opportunity to the Stratonicians to elude it by retortion. For if God could give to a plastic nature the faculty of producing the organization of animals, without its having the idea of what it doth; they will conclude from hence that the formation of the regularity which we observe in the world, is not inconsistent with want of knowledge, and so the world may be the effect of a blind cause.

Mr le Clerc had adopted this hypothesis, and thought himself obliged to defend it (4). He was offended that Mr Bayle had said that it gave ground to elude by way of retortion one of the arguments which most embarasseth the Atheists. He complained that this remark would raise very disadvantageous notions of the Religion and of the abilities of Dr Cudworth and Dr Grew, and that he found himself interested in this matter. He says that if Mr Bayle had sufficiently understood their opinion, he would have seen that it gives no handle to Atheists, because the plastic and vital natures which they maintain, are only instruments in the hand of God, that they have no power but what God has given them, that God governs their actions, that they are instrumental causes, produced and employed by the principal; and that we cannot say that a building was made without art, because not only the hammers, the rules, the squares, the compasses, the axes, the saws, but even the hands of men which made use of these utensils, are things destitute of intelligence: it is sufficient that the mind of the Architect has conducted all these, and employed them to accomplish his designs. It is evident then, adds he, that Atheists, who deny the existence of the intelligent cause which has guided and regulated the formation of all things, cannot retort the argument which these two Philosophers have opposed to them.

Mr Bayle answered (5), that he had not the least intention of doing prejudice either to the orthodoxy or the learning of these Gentlemen, and that he had even taken care

care to prevent any such thought. He adds, that the defect he had found in their 1704. hypothesis, was not peculiar to them: that almost all the Philosophers, both ancient and modern were in the same case. He shows that if these Gentlemen had considered their plastic natures as simple instruments in the hand of God, they would have fallen into all the inconveniences of the Cartesian hypothesis which they designed to avoid; so that it must be supposed that they believed them to be active principles, which do not require being pushed on and directed without interruption, but that it is sufficient, that God set them in their proper places, and watch over their conduct, in order to set them right when it is necessary. Now this being granted, he maintains, that there is room for a retortion. For when we bring the order and symmetry of the world as a proof of the existence of God, we suppose that in order to produce any regular work, the agent must have an idea of it: while according to Dr Cudworth the plastic natures which produce plants and animals have no idea of what they do. If it be answered, that they were created by a Being who knows all things, and that they only execute his idea's, the Stratonician will reply that if they execute them in quality of efficient causes, this is as incomprehensible as the thing objected against, since it is as difficult to execute a plan which we do not know, but which another knows, as it is to follow a plan which is known by no body. Since you allow, will the Stratonician say, that God can give to creatures a faculty of producing excellent works without the least knowledge; you ought likewise to own, that there is no necessary connexion between the faculty of producing excellent works, and the idea of their essence, and of the manner of their production; and consequently you ought not to pretend that these two things cannot be separated in nature, and that nature may not have of itself, what these plastic beings have, according to you, by the gift of God. To abridge this dispute Mr Bayle reduced it to this question of fact: *Have these Gentlemen taught that plastic and vital natures are only passive instruments in the band of God?* Mr le Clerc (says he) seems to affirm it, by his example of an Architect who erects a very regular building, though all the tools of which he makes use be void of understanding. It is evident, added Mr Bayle, that with regard to the Architect, all his tools, and even his hands, are meerly passive instruments, which only move in as far as he pusheth them. If the plastic and vital natures be in the same case, I confess there is no retortion to be feared, but on the other hand God alone in this case will be the next and immediate cause of all generation; which would be to admit the Cartesian doctrine, which they meant to reject.

(1) Bibliotheque choisie. Tom. vi. Art. vii. pag. 422, and the following.

Mr le Clerc replied (1) that Dr Cudworth did not look upon the plastic natures to be passive instruments; that they are under the direction of God, who conducts them, though we do not know in what manner; that though they act regularly, yet it is under the direction of God, who intervenes as he thinks fit, and when he thinks fit; that the sole difference which is between their action and the faculty of beasts, who do several things in a regular manner when men conduct them, tho' they do not know what they do, is, that we do not know how God intervenes, and that we see how men act. But however this be, adds he, the Atheists cannot retort Dr Cudworth's argument against him, because God is Author of the order in which the plastic nature operates; and that according to the Atheists notions, matter moves of itself without any cause which regulates it, or which has given it a power of moving regularly. If any body should say that it has it of itself, that would not be to retort the argument, this would be to make a supposition, which it would be easy to overturn.

(2) History of the Works of the Learned, December 1704. Art. xii. pag. 540, and the following.

Mr Bayle again replied (2), and began with stating the question anew. He said that the retortion was founded on this, that, if we suppose that there are beings which have the faculty of organizing animals without knowing what they do, we cannot refute those who say that the world may have been produced without the operation of an intelligent cause. It would be to no purpose to answer to them, that these beings have received this faculty from an intelligent cause: for by making this answer we would still own the compatibility of the power to organize matter with want of understanding, and consequently would confute ourselves. Mr Bayle next examines Mr le Clerc's Reply. He owns that a creature without understanding may under the direction of God do certain things as regularly as a cause endowed with understanding; but that in that case this creature would be only a passive instrument in the hand of God. And so the plastic natures of Dr Cudworth cannot be the efficient cause of organization, but at most the instrument. They are no more capable of discernment in the first moment of conception, than in all the other moments which follow until the organization is compleated; it is necessary therefore that God apply and direct them without interruption from the beginning to the end: from whence it necessarily follows, that they are only passive instruments in his hands, and so Dr Cudworth cannot avoid the retortion, except by supposing what the Cartesians suppose. The example of beasts, adds he, confirms the difficulty; for if we consider all the services which we draw from them, we shall find that in all things wherein their knowledge doth not serve them for a guide, they must be pushed or directed as if they were pure machines.

Mr le

1704. Mr le Clerc had said, that Madam Masham, Dr Cudworth's daughter, had wrote him a letter, wherein *she complained with reason of Mr Bayle's proceeding with regard to her father*; and that she had allowed him to print it, but that he did not think it proper to do so; because possibly Mr Bayle might change his opinion when he had better understood Dr Cudworth's system. Madam Masham had been prejudiced against Mr Bayle: but he appealed to what he had at first answered to Mr le Clerc, and added that if this Lady, who was very learned, would be pleased to examin the matter, she would find that she had been misinformed. And in fact when she had seen Mr Bayle's explanations, she desired Mr le Clerc to suppress the Letter which she had wrote to him (1).

Mr le Clerc still maintained that Dr Cudworth gave no room for retortion. He said (2), that the conception of a design, such as that of forming animals, is incompatible with a want of knowledge in the first cause; but that it is not so as to the second causes, which act under the direction of this first cause: that it is not necessary that God should direct and push them continually as we do passive instruments, and "(3) that he had proved this by the use which men make of beasts, " whose organs they do not move, which act notwithstanding in a regular manner, " in order to produce a certain effect, which they are entirely ignorant of. They " are not pushed, as Mr Bayle says, in the same manner as if they were pure " machines, since they move their own members. For example, can one say that " a dog, who being placed in a sort of wheel turns it about by going in it, and by " this mean turns a spit and what is tied to it, is employed in the same manner " as a jack? the jack is set a going merely by weights, but we do not give mo-" tion to the limbs of the dog; it is he himself who moves them, and though " we should put in his place any sort of machine it would never produce the same " effect. I own, adds he, that I cannot tell in what manner God applies himself to " matter and directs the immaterial forming natures, without being author of all their " actions; but we cannot reject this opinion as absurd, after the direct proofs which " have been brought of it. Otherwise we must reject every thing of which we have " not compleat or adequate ideas, which would be to fall into a ridiculous Pyr-" rhonism." As to what Mr Bayle had said that he preferred the system of occasional causes to all others, because it seemed to him to be the most proper to establish the being of God; Mr le Clerc declared that he would not engage in any dispute on that subject. "I only thought (said he (4), that after having proposed Dr Cud-" worth's opinion as probable, I was obliged to show that Mr Bayle was in the " wrong to say that it made way for the Atheists to destroy, by a retortion, the " strongest argument which can be produced against them, and which is drawn " from the order of the universe. After having done this, I have no more to add " upon this subject. I will not enter into personal matters, nor penetrate into " designs, which cannot be discovered, without vexing those who might be suspected " of them."

Mr Bayle recapitulated this dispute, and examined it more thoroughly (5). He observed that Dr Cudworth's hypothesis, to wit, that God has the idea of the organization of animals, doth not in the least lessen the incomprehensibility and impossibility of his supposition that the true efficient and immediate cause of organization knows nothing at all; and that the Stratonicians may make use of the second hypothesis in order to contest the other: that they will show him that these two things appear equally impossible, the one that the inventors of a machine know nothing, the other that they should cause it to be executed by persons who have no idea of it. Mr Bayle adds, that the example of a dog who is the cause of a spit's turning about, was out of the case which he had proposed: for he had not said, that we are obliged to *push and direct beasts* in the services which we receive from them, but only that *in all cases in which their knowledge doth not serve them instead of a guide, we must push them or direct them, as if they were pure machines*. " (6) A dog placed in a sort of wheel is not ignorant that he must walk, " and that he will be beaten if he stops; is not he threatened and even beat every " time he interrupts his action? He is not therefore without a certain kind of know-" ledge which serves to direct him, he sees the objects which are round about him, " he is afraid, and he acts by this fear, or by some other passion upon his *loco-" motive* faculty; and in the situation in which he is placed he cannot move him-" self, without at the same time moving the wheel round its center, and by that " means turning the spit. It is not therefore necessary to push him or *make him " move his legs*, it is sufficient to excite some sentiment or passion in him which " may make him move. Let us observe, continued Mr Bayle, that the motion " which he gives to himself is continually under the direction of another cause. It " is not a motion which makes him go from place to place. The dog continues " still in the same place although he never ceaseth to move. From whence proceeds " this? It is because his motion is continually determined by the disposition of the " wheel to be such as it is. Here therefore is an example which proves that " in all cases wherein the knowledge of beasts doth not serve them for a guide, " we must either push or direct them, if we want to make them serve for

VOL. I.   a a   any

(1) See *Letters to M. Coste of the 30th of April, and the 3d of July,* 1705. *p.* 1017. *and the following.*

(2) Bibliotheque choisie, Tom. vii. Art. vii. pag. 281, and the following.

(3) Ibid. pag. 286, 287.

(4) Ibid. pag. 288.

(5) An Answer to the Questions of a Country Gentleman, Tom. iii. chap. clxxxix, and the following.

(6) Ibid. chap. clxxxi p. 1279, 1280.

THE LIFE OF MR BAYLE.

"any purpose. All muleteers and coachmen will confirm this. A coach-
"man may be at rest when his horses know the way, or content himself with taking
"notice when they do not do their duty; but when they are ignorant that they
"must change their road, he is obliged to be active in order to give them the
"necessary direction." Mr Bayle added, that as to the *direct proofs which had been
brought* of the existence of plastic natures, he did not believe them to be so strong
that one must either be a Sceptic, or embrace that opinion; but that he would not
enter upon that enquiry.

(1) *Ibid.*
chap.
clxxxii.
pag. 1286,
1287.

The conclusion of Mr le Clerc's last Reply gave Mr Bayle occasion to say (1),
that Mr le Clerc "had not sufficiently reflected upon a thing which may be
"easily known, to wit, that the same zeal which inclines one man to maintain
"that a reason has a great deal of solidity for the existence of God, may incline
"another man to maintain that it is weak and dangerous. These two men may
"have the same intention, they differ only in their judgment about the quality of
"an argument. They ought both therefore, said Mr Bayle, to abstain from all
"suspicious expressions, to abstain, I say, not by saying that they will abstain from
"them, for this doth not fail to strike home, but by a perfect silence. Equity ought
"immediately to present itself to their mind, and hinder them from saying any
"thing which may be agreeable to the malice of their readers. The warmest de-
"fenders of orthodoxy have always preserved to themselves the liberty of examining
"the arguments for the existence of God, and for any other article of faith, and
"of rejecting such as they thought weak." He shows that in the Church of Rome
they acknowledge a difference betwixt contesting a doctrine, and contesting some of
the reasons brought to prove it; and that this liberty is still greater among Protestants. "But be it as it will, continued he (2), you will easily observe that the
"dispute about Dr Cudworth's plastic natures doth not interest Religion. It is an
"hypothesis lately invented which has very few followers. Whether it doth or doth
"not furnish the Atheists with a pretence to chicane, is of small importance. This
"doth not in the least hurt the many victorious arguments, which this learned Eng-
"lishman has made use of and illustrated in a wonderful manner against Atheism.
"The system of the Peripatetics has been in the same case with these plastic na-
"tures during many ages and is so still: so that the dispute of which I am speaking
"only concerns two private persons, is only a question of Logic, and of Na-
"tural Philosophy. All the question is whether Mr Bayle has reason to say that
"a certain retortion can be made, or if Mr le Clerc has reason to maintain the
"contrary, and has not given occasion to his readers to discover the embarrassing
"consequences and defects of his plastic natures."

(2) *Ibid*
pag. 1290,
1291.

(3) Biblio-
theque
choisie,
Tom. ix.
Art. x.
pag. 361,
362.

Mr le Clerc took this matter very differently. "When Mr Bayle (said he (3),
"accused Dr Cudworth of giving a handle to the Atheists to retort some of the
"arguments which are brought against them; I at first believed that it was be-
"cause he did not sufficiently understand Dr Cudworth's system, for in fact he
"did not understand it . . . . . but as I have seen that he would receive no explana-
"tion upon that subject, after I had explained it to him thrice, I no longer doubted
"that he said this with a design to excuse the Atheists, as he doth in his
"*Thoughts concerning Comets*, and in the *Continuation*. . . . . . Being vexed, as it
"seems, to see Dr Cudworth triumph over the Atheists in a very glorious and ad-
"vantageous manner for Christianity, and not daring to deny this, he thought it
"was necessary at any rate to blacken that great man's manner of philosophizing,
"by accusing him of furnishing arms to those who deny the being of a God."
Mr le Clerc afterwards says that all the difficulty is now reduced to this one proposition: "Whether there can exist an immaterial self-acting nature, which forms
"in miniature, by a faculty which it has received from God, machines such as
"the bodies of plants and animals are, without having an idea of them." He maintained that this is possible, still supposing that the creator of this nature has in himself
perfectly clear ideas of what it doth; without which it would be impossible for a blind nature to act with order. But that it doth not follow from hence, that this nature is a merely passive instrument in the hand of God, because according to the supposition it is a self-
acting nature. He alledged the example of beasts, which men employ as active instruments to draw loaded carriages, and to turn millstones in a certain order; without knowing either what they do, or why they do it, or whether they observe any order or no.
He related likewise the principal actions of birds, and said that how admirable soever
those actions are, yet they were performed without knowledge; since otherwise we should
be obliged to conclude that these animals have a great deal more wit, and reason infinitely better than man, which would be very absurd. He owned that he had not a clear
idea of these plastic natures, that he did not know how God applies them to matter,
nor how he directs them without being author of their actions: but that he had a
very clear idea of an active instrument which is Author of it's own actions, and
yet doth not know what it doth, because he saw that beasts were in many respects
instruments of this nature, and that this was the subject in question. He added, that we
ought not, as Mr Bayle did, to take out one proposition from Dr Cudworth's system,
as if he had advanced only that, and give it up to the Atheists to be retorted:
that

1704.

1704. that Dr Cudworth had not maintained in general, that what has no idea of order can act with order; but that an infinitely powerful Being who has an idea of order may create other Beings which have it not, and who notwithstanding observe it; because he may give them a certain activity which they can only exercise in the manner which he thinks fit, and apply them to matter upon which they act of themselves, although we do not know how. After having thus explained Dr Cudworth's opinion, he says that he will not " stay here to refute particularly all Mr Bayle's " similies, which are not at all just, which make us forget the state of the question, " and which turn only upon confused ideas which he perplexeth with a design to " favour the Atheists. Neither will I take up time (adds he) in exposing his weak " reasonings, to shew that he has not understood me, and has not sufficiently " taken notice with what view I have spoken. This would be to tire the reader, " and one could not avoid troublesome repetitions and fatiguing discussions of " trifles."

Mr Bayle considered his last Answer as the end of this dispute, and contented himself with making some reflexions on Mr le Clerc's reply. " We may hence- " forth (says he (1), look upon the plastic natures of Dr Cudworth as at an end. " Not that Mr le Clerc doth not still make a great noise about it, but he only para- " phraseth what he has already said, and leaves my replies in their full force. It is " not necessary therefore to support them by any new remark; it will be sufficient to " desire the readers to compare them with his last piece." He observes that Mr Leibniz had acknowledged the justness of the retortion of the Stratonicians. " But let " us not talk any more of retortion, adds he; Mr le Clerc obviates this sufficiently " by the necessity which he supposeth there is, that God should intervene in the " work of these plastic natures. It has been proved to him, that an interrup- " ted direction would not be sufficient, from whence it follows that God directs them " without intermission, which shews that they can only be reckoned an instrumental " cause. Now in this case there is no ground for further dispute; for Mr Bayle al- " ways laid down this alternative, that either the retortion of the Stratonician must " take place, or the plastic natures are not the true efficient cause of the organization of " the fœtus. The consequence which ought to be drawn from Mr le Clerc's answer " is, that they are only an instrument in the hand of God, whether he directs them " immediately, or whether he place them like a spring in a machine, the form of " which is the permanent cause of the direction of all the pieces, or whether " he makes use of some other determination equivalent to this. Let no body " object that they are endowed with activity, for this doth not hinder them from being " a mere instrument." He says, that he had shown that Mr le Clerc could receive no advantage from the example of beasts, and that to suppose, as he did, that birds perform many things with a wonderful regularity, tho' they are neither directed by their own knowledge, nor by the laws of mechanism; is to bring back the occult qualities of the Schoolmen. " It would be (adds he (2), a sort of inhumanity to push " Mr le Clerc any farther: he himself owns that he is embarassed, which is a sign " that he is reduced to the last extremity. He is therefore sufficiently punished, " especially if we consider, that being infatuated with his plastic natures, he has ex- " posed himself to the ridicule of all the modern Philosophers. They cannot com- " prehend how a man who has shown a good taste in other things, should chuse ra- " ther to fall into the most absurd galimatias, than to part with his conceit." He says that he was persuaded, that if Dr Cudworth had foreseen the consequences of his System, he would have reformed it; and that if he had been alive when Mr le Clerc's first Answer was published, he would have been very much surprized to see his honour interested where there was so little occasion for it: that Mr Bayle's observation concerned Thomas Aquinas, Scotus, and such superior genius's, as well as Dr Cudworth and Dr Grew: that the last named gentleman gave himself no trouble about it, although Mr le Clerc had in a manner provoked him to it. " Dr " Cudworth (says he (3), would have been no less indifferent about an objection " in which he was no more concerned than almost all mankind, and would have " no doubt suspected that this was only made a pretext to serve for the begin- " ning of a quarrel. He would have imagined that there was a *snake in the grass,* " some old leaven, some abscess which had been forming itself a great while, " and which must needs break at last." Mr Bayle adds that knowing how touchy Mr le Clerc was, he had treated him with the utmost tenderness, and had abstained from reproaching him with not understanding Dr Cudworth's System: that Mr le Clerc to cloak his inability to answer his arguments had treated them as trifling: in a word that the victory obtained over him on the subject of the plastic natures had so confounded him, that he was beside himself whenever he returned to that subject, and that he had loosed the reins to calumny; " like parish Priests " who cry out *Heretic,* if any of their parishioners though agreeing in the main " to the truth of their doctrine, do not agree about the force of the reasons they " make use of to prove it."

Thus ended the controversy which Mr Bayle had with Mr le Clerc concerning the plastic natures of Dr Cudworth.

(1) Answer for Mr Bayle to Mr le Clerc concerning the 3d and 10th Articles of the 9th Tome of the Bibliotheque choisie, pag. 31.

(2) Ibid. pag. 34.

(3) Ibid. p. 35, 36.

About

About the end of the year 1705, Mr Bayle published at the same time the second and third volumes of his *Answer to the Questions of a Country Gentleman*. In the Preface to the second volume he observed that there is this difference betwixt these volumes and the first, that the first contained a great variety of literary and historical particulars, and few matters of reasoning, and these on the contrary contained a great deal of reasoning, and little variety of literary and historical articles. "I have not heard (adds he) that any body complained that there was too much reasoning in the first part, and many have been heard to complain that there was not enough of it there, I have therefore thought it proper to change the proportions, by allowing the greatest share in the continuation of this work to what was only an accessory in the first volume." The plan of this book furnished him with a natural occasion of introducing all sorts of subjects: he took this opportunity of examining some pieces which had been lately published, wherein he found himself interested.

Dr King, Bishop of Londonderry, and afterwards Archbishop of Dublin, had published a treatise concerning the Origin of Evil (1): Mr Bayle examined his principles, but not having the book, and considering that it would have been difficult to find it in Holland, he confined himself to some general observations upon the long extracts which Mr Bernard had given of it in his *News from the Republic of Letters* (2). Dr King had composed this work in order to solve the difficulties which the Manicheans raise in Mr Bayle's Dictionary on the subject of physical and moral evil. Experience teacheth us that man is not only subject to diseases, pains, troubles, and sundry other miseries, but he is likewise liable to commit an infinite number of crimes. The question is how to reconcile these facts with the common notions of the sovereign goodness and sovereign wisdom of the infinitely perfect Being. Dr King had a great deal of penetration, and a very nice judgment. His penetration made him comprehend the whole extent and consequences of the difficulty; he made use of new principles to solve it. He maintains that God's end in creating the universe, was not to procure to himself glory, as the generality of Divines affirm, but to exercise his power, and communicate his goodness: that it is not true that the earth was made for man, that it is the ignorance or pride of man which inspires him with this chimerical imagination; that the quantity of happiness in the world is greater than the misery to be found there, an evident proof of which we have in the horror which all men have at death, and their violent desire for life, even when they are overwhelmed with the miseries, of which they most bitterly complain; that man being created of matter, becomes necessarily subject to diseases, grief &c; but that pain and passions are useful for the preservation of the body, since they warn it of what might destroy it; that the evils are so connected with the good that they are inseparable; that these are inconveniencies which are necessary consequences of the laws of nature; that physical evil is as necessary in the universal System of Beings, as the equality of the diameters is essential to a circle; and that these necessary evils do not at all interest the goodness of God.

But the great difficulty regards moral evil, that is, the bad choices of man, the bad determination of his will, and in a word, all that is called vice. In order to solve it, Dr King has recourse to the ordinary solution, to wit, free-will; but he gives a notion of it very different from that of other Divines. He makes it to consist in the power of choosing, independently of the other faculties of a free agent, and of the quality of objects; so that this power is not determined by the goodness of objects, but the objects are rendered good and agreeable by its choice and determination. This perfect independence is the source of mens happiness, since it makes him master of his determinations, and disposer of his fate. Consequently God would have disturbed the happiness of the first man in its source, if he had not left him at liberty to chuse what he should please. It was necessary therefore that man should be capable of making a bad choice, and falling into sin. God could only hinder the bad use of liberty in the three following manners. I. By not creating any Being endowed with liberty. II. By making use of his almighty power to prevent free agents from abusing their liberty. III. By carrying man to another habitation, where he should find no occasion which could incline him to make a bad choice. But if none of these three be practicable, we must conclude, that the permission of sin is not blameable. Now 1. If God had created no Beings endowed with liberty, the world must have been a pure machine, incapable of any action; for matter is moved, but doth not move itself. Besides, God has created the world to exercise his virtues, and to please himself in his work. Now the more a creature is like to him, and the more self-sufficient it is, the more agreeable it must needs be to him. But we cannot make any doubt that a creature which moves of itself, which is pleased in itself, which is capable of receiving and acknowledging a favour, is more excellent, and must please him who made it, more than one which is not capable of acting, feeling, and of acknowledging a favour. 2. If God should interpose his almighty power, to prevent the bad use of liberty, greater inconveniencies would arise from thence, than from the abuse itself which we can make

(1) De origine mali. Auhore Gulielmo King, S. T. D. Episcopo Derensi. Dublinii, 1702, in 8°. *It was reprinted at London the same year.*

(2) *Months of May and June 1703.*

1705. of this liberty. It requires no less power to hinder the exercise of liberty, than to stop the course of the sun, and besides it would be necessary, that God should entirely change his manner of acting with free agents, which is to keep them in their duty by the motives of rewards and punishments. It would deprive us of what is most agreeable to us in our determinations, which is to be persuaded that we had it in our power not to determine ourselves. It were to deprive God of the exercise of one of his most excellent virtues, to desire that he should interpose his power in order to hinder all the evil determinations of the will, in which his wisdom is exercised in the most excellent manner, and in which it shines with a particular lustre. III. As to the third manner of hindering the bad use of liberty, this were to desire that God should entirely destroy human nature, which was created to dwell upon the earth, and no where else. It is true that good men shall be afterwards carried to another place, where they shall continue to all eternity, but that is only after they have been prepared upon earth, like wild stocks in a nursery before they are transplanted in order to bear fruit elsewhere.

(1) News from the Republic of Letters, February and March 1705.

(2) News &c. February 1705, p. 125.

(3) Conformité de la Foi avec la Raison: ou defense de la Religion, contre les principales difficultez répandues dans le Dictionaire historique & critique de Mr Bayle. At Amsterdam 1705.

Thus Dr King answered the objections founded upon physical and moral evil. As he supposeth that his adversaries do not admit a Revelation, he makes use only of principles drawn from natural reason. Mr Bayle did not think that his system took away the difficulties, and refuted it by several arguments which he lays down with great accuracy and force.

Mr Bernard furnished Mr Bayle with another article of great importance. He gave a critical Extract of the *Continuation of the Thoughts concerning Comets* (1), and attacked Mr Bayle upon the question whether the general consent of nations be a proof of the existence of God, upon the parallel of Atheism and Paganism, and upon the question whether a society entirely composed of true Christians, surrounded with other nations either of Infidels or worldly Christians, could be able to maintain itself. Every body was surprized that Mr Bernard who had always lived upon a footing of friendship with Mr Bayle, should affect to enter into a controversy with him ; and it was thought that being suspected of Arminianism, he wanted by this means to ingratiate himself with the Orthodox. However he used Mr Bayle with great respect. "As I am persuaded (said he (2), that Mr Bayle searcheth after truth sincerely, I "am sure without having consulted him, that he will not be displeased that I propose "some difficulties to him in this Extract, as they shall offer themselves to my mind, not "forgetting in the mean while the rules of good manners, and the esteem, and respect, "which I have for his person and merit." Mr Bayle in the second volume of his *Answer to the Questions of a Country Gentleman*, answered at large Mr Bernard's objections concerning the general consent of nations. In the third volume, he examined what related to himself in a book of Mr Jaquelot's intitled, *The Conformity of Faith with Reason, in answer to the principal difficulties dispersed in Mr Bayle's historical and critical Dictionary* (3). Mr Jaquelot had left the Hague in order to go to Berlin, where he was Chaplain to the King of Prussia. He then declared himself openly for Arminianism ; which he durst not have done in Holland, while under the authority of the Walloon Synods. In 1697 he had published a large volume intitled, *A Dissertation concerning the Existence of God, wherein that truth is demonstrated, by the universal history of the most ancient times ; by a refutation of the System of Epicurus and Spinosa ; by the characters of Divinity which are observable in the Jewish Religion, and in the establishment of Christianity: Containing likewise convincing proofs of the Revelation of the sacred writings* (4). Mr Bayle in quoting this book in his Dictionary (5), made use of an expression which infinitely displeased Mr Jaquelot. "(6) He lost all patience "when he observed that Mr Bayle in quoting his Dissertation concerning the Exis- "tence of God, had only given it the title of a *fine Book*. He made loud com- "plaints of this, and spread them abroad every where. It is true indeed that he "durst not own that they were grounded on Mr Bayle's having made use of the "positive *fine* instead of the superlative *very fine*, or of some sublime epithet. He "pretended that he had used the term *fine* ironically. As soon as Mr Bayle was in- "formed of this he sent a common friend, to protest to him that he had made "use of that epithet in its natural signification, and it is certain that he employed "it in speaking of another book concerning which no body will suspect that he "would pretend to speak ironically (7). Several people from that time foretold that "Mr Jaquelot would write against Mr Bayle with all the animosity of a bitter "enemy, that he would conceal his resentment a little in his first attack, because "he knew that the reply would give him a large field for it." Accordingly Mr Jaquelot *declared* in his Preface, *that he had no intention of attacking either Mr Bayle's person or his morals. I esteem*, said he, *his erudition, his genius, his penetration, and all the fine talents which distinguish a man in the learned world. I say once more*, adds he, *I have no design to dive into his intentions: I leave them to be judged by God and his own conscience. He declares that he proposeth these difficulties with no other view than to obtain an answer to them.*

(4) It is a book in 4° of 705 pages. See Mr Bayle's opinion concerning it in a letter to the Abbé du Bos, December 13, 1696, p. 607, and the following.

(5) In the Article PERGAMUS, a City in Asia. Rem. [C] letter (l).

(6) Entretiens de Maxime & de Themiste, ou Réponse à l'Examen de la Theologie de Mr Bayle par Mr Jaquelot, p. 14, 15.

(7) It was a book of Mr Basnage.

(8) The Dissertation concerning the Messiah appeared in 1699.

The greatest part of this work is only a repetition of what Mr Jaquelot had said in his Dissertations concerning the Existence of God, and concerning the Messiah (8). What relates to Mr Bayle may be reduced to these three heads. I. The liberty of indifference.

VOL. I. N° XXX.   b b

xcviii   THE LIFE OF Mr BAYLE.

difference. II. The Origin of Evil. III. The objections which the Pyrrhonians 1705.
may raife againft fome doctrines of revealed Religion. Mr Bayle obferves upon
this that the title of Mr Jaquelot's book is deceitful, becaufe it makes people
think that it is entirely defigned to refute Mr Bayle, whereas what concerns him makes only the fmalleft part of it. He finds another much more ef-
fential fault in it. " There is no reader (fays he (1), who upon feeing this
" title will not judge that Mr Bayle has attacked Religion, while all that he
" has done is to fhow that the philofophical objections againft what Theology
" teacheth concerning the Origin and Confequences of Sin, are fo ftrong that our
" reafon is too weak to folve them, fo that we ought to behave ourfelves in the
" fame manner with regard to the myftery of predeftination, as with regard to the
" other myfteries of the Gofpel; that is to fay, believe them upon the authority
" of God, though we can neither comprehend them, nor reconcile them to the
" maxims of Philofophers. If he has difperfed fome other difficulties in his Dic-
" tionary, they are all of the fame kind." Mr Bayle adds that if this be to attack
Religion we muft affirm that the moft orthodox Divines do likewife attack it, when
they fay that the Trinity, the Incarnation, Predeftination, and ftill more particularly the Origin of Evil, are myfteries which our reafon cannot comprehend, but
which it ought to believe, fubmitting itfelf to the authority of God who has revealed them. He quotes a great many divines in proof of this, who all with one
voice except againft reafon, and do not afk its affent when the queftion is about revealed articles of faith. He cites particularly Mr Jurieu, who in vain implored the
affiftance of reafon to folve the difficulties which prefented themfelves to his mind.
" When I turn my eyes (fays Mr Jurieu (2), upon the world, upon hiftory, upon
" events, I find abyffes there in which I lofe myfelf, I find difficulties there which
" overwhelm me. It is true that I fee God who created all things good at the
" beginning. Man at coming out of the hands of God was juft, pure, and holy.
" But prefently I find God abandoning this creature whom he had juft placed in
" the world, and fuffering him to fall into fin; fin whofe effects were to be fo
" fatal and terrible . . . . . (3) I find in the conduct of God things which are incom-
" prehenfible to me, I can fcarce reconcile his hatred of fin with his providence . . . .
" (4) Is there any body fo infincere as to fay that he finds no difficulty in this, and
" that he can eafily reconcile this with God's infinite hatred of fin? if God hates fin
" infinitely, why did not he prevent it fince he forefaw it? why has he made crea-
" tures which other creatures may abufe? why, has he created men when he knew
" they would damn themfelves? why doth not he ftop thefe men in their cri-
" minal courfes? why doth not he ftop the moft part of men in thofe courfes
" which lead them to hell? he could have faved a million of perfons, and have fuf-
" fered only one to be loft. On the contrary, he faves but a hundred, and fuffers a
" million to be loft. This poffibly proceeds from his want of power in this matter:
" but who can refift his will, and fince he faves a hundred perfons, why could not
" he, by the fame means, fave millions? . . . . . Could it be faid, that a King had the
" utmoft averfion to the miferies and calamities of his people, who forefeeing that
" three fourths and a half of them were about to deftroy themfelves, and throw
" themfelves down a precipice, fhould open the road to them, make an eafy way for
" them, and fuffer them to run headlong tho' he could prevent it . . . . (5) The
" common fenfe of all men leads them to believe, that he who could have hindered
" the fall of the firft man as eafily as he has permitted it, and who has opened all the
" ways in which men have gone aftray, tho' he could have fhut them fo eafily, may
" be confidered as author of the evil which he ought to have prevented according
" to his principles, and the hatred which he bears to evil, and which he could have
" hindered without the leaft trouble . . . . (6) It is to no purpofe to fay that God,
" before he had decreed any thing concerning the event, forefaw that man, placed in
" thefe circumftances, would fall, and that all his pofterity would be loft: this doth
" not at all leffen the difficulty. For I could ftill anfwer: fince God forefaw that A-
" dam, placed in thofe circumftances, would damn himfelf and an infinite number
" of millions of men, by his free-will, and yet notwithftanding placed him in thofe
" fad circumftances, it is evident that he is the author of all evils . . . . And if we
" would fpeak fincerely, we would confefs that we can anfwer nothing for God,
" which can filence human reafon . . . . (7) To conclude, I maintain that there is
" no fafe medium betwixt the God of St Auguftin, the God of Epicurus who was idle,
" or the God of Ariftotle who meddled with nothing lower than the fphere of the Moon.
" For if we own a general Providence which extends itfelf to all things, in whatever
" manner we conceive it, the difficulty recurrs, and when we think we have fhut one
" gate it comes in at another."

Such were the fentiments of Mr Jurieu in 1686. He fpeaks in no lefs ftrong a
manner in a piece publifhed ten years after. " To what a height of blindnefs,
" fays he (8), muft one be arrived to affirm that we fhould gain our caufe
" before the tribunal of reafon in the matter of the Trinity, the Incarnation, the
" Satisfaction, the fin of the firft man, the eternity of punifhments, and the refurrection
" of the body? they who fay fo, cannot believe it: I fhall never be perfuaded that they
fpeak

1705. "speak sincerely. For all the false lights of reason rebel against these mysteries. And
"these false lights are of such a nature that there is no distinguishing them from
"the true, otherwise than by the light of faith."

This is precisely and in a few words all that Mr Bayle has put in the mouth of the Manicheans in his Dictionary. All his objections concerning the Origin of Evil are contained in these of Mr Jurieu: they all tend to show, that there is no hypothesis which is able to solve the difficulties which our reason offers against the providence of God with regard to evil, and that consequently we ought to hold by revelation alone. Things being so, Mr Bayle asks, why Mr Jaquelot never thought of assisting Mr Jurieu in his difficulties, which oppress him so sorely that he seems to groan under the weight of them; and why he thought himself obliged to take up his pen against Mr Bayle, since he kept silence so long with regard to Mr Jurieu, who however has said the same things?

Mr Bayle next comes to the three principal points which related to him. Mr Jaquelot reproached him with having used all his efforts to destroy free-will, thereby to give the greater force to his objections; and to show that man was unjustly punished for crimes which he was necessarily and inevitably obliged to commit. Mr Bayle answers that he had neither denied nor affirmed any thing expressly concerning free-will: that he took care not to engage himself in a preliminary question which would for ever keep the principal one in suspence. It is a subject so embarrassing and fruitful in distinctions and equivocations, that disputants have endless resources, and that it frequently happens that they fall themselves into contradictions: and that in fine he allowed him to choose whatever hypothesis he should think fit, and to go as far as Pelagianism if he pleased, which is almost the only post wherein we can make use of the liberty of indifference to advantage.

Before he touches upon the question concerning the origin of Evil, Mr Bayle observes that the question between Mr Jaquelot and him doth not concern any article of Faith, and that they are perfectly agreed in the substance of the doctrine. The matter in debate here is only whether our reason can comprehend the real and effectual agreement which is betwixt the Attributes of God, and the system of Predestination, and whether it can solve the difficulties which conceal that agreement from us, and whether reason can not only convince, but likewise enlighten our minds upon this subject. Mr Jaquelot takes the affirmative with the rational Divines, and Mr Bayle takes the negative agreeably to the hypothesis of the first Reformers, and their followers. He then observes what Mr Jaquelot ought to have done in order to succeed in his design: he ought to have proved that the perfect agreement between the theological doctrine concerning sin, and a certain number of philosophical maxims, can be shown to our reason; and he lays down seven theological propositions on the one side, and nineteen philosophical maxims on the other, which must be reconciled together in order to show the agreement betwixt Faith and Reason.

Mr Jaquelot is of opinion, that all the difficulties concerning moral evil may be solved by means of free-will, which according to him consists in "the power which
" man has over his actions, so that he doth what he will, because he will do it,
" so that if he did not will to do it, he would not do it, and would even do the
" contrary." A being, says he, which is possessed of this liberty is the most excellent, and most perfect of all created beings: the power of making a good or bad use of his understanding, and the command over his actions, are surely the things in which man approacheth the nearest to the Deity: God having formed this universe for his glory, that is to say, that he might be known in his works, and that he might receive from his creatures that adoration and obedience which is due to him, it was only a free Being that could contribute to this design; the adoration of a creature not indowed with liberty could not contribute more to the glory of the Creator, than a machine in human shape which should bow down before him by virtue of springs, or a speech in his praise, pronounced by an automaton. God loves holiness. But what virtue could there be in this, if man was as necessarily determined by his nature to follow good, as the fire is determined to burn? Nothing therefore but a free creature could execute God's design. Mr Jaquelot concludes from hence, that although a free creature may abuse its free-will, yet a free agent is something so elevated and so noble, that its excellence and value far exceed the worst consequences which can flow from the abuse which he could make of it.

Mr Bayle answers, that if Mr Jaquelot's principles be true, the love which God necessarily has to virtue would deserve no praise: the holiness of Saints and Angels would be only a mechanical holiness, and the Devils would deserve no blame for their hatred against God, since it is not in their power to do otherwise. He adds, that since it is one of the most sublime perfections of God, that he is so determined to love what is good, that it implies a contradiction to suppose that he may not love it; a creature determined to good, would be more conformable to the nature of God, and consequently more perfect than a creature which has an equal power of loving vice and hating it. Mr Jaquelot said, that the state of the blessed was

a state

THE LIFE OF Mr BAYLE.

a state of recompence, in which their understanding was so purified that it always 1705. inclined their liberty to good, and never tempted them to evil. That is to say, that they should always enjoy free-will, yet notwithstanding they would never turn aside to evil. Now since he declares that this state is a state of recompence, he must consider it as a more excellent and more perfect state than that in which we live. It was therefore in the power of God to have constantly and invariably united in man liberty and the practice of virtue. And in this case, all the value that liberty gives to the worship and obedience which we pay to God, would be found upon earth as it is in Paradice. Consequently the glory and holiness of God have no need of free Beings left to the bad use of their liberty, since they might be confined to a good use of it without being thereby less free. Mr Jaquelot would have more reason to magnify the advantages and prerogatives of liberty, and to make it be esteemed the most extraordinary favour which a creature can receive, if it had served only to render mankind happy. But God having foreseen that this wonderful gift would be the instrument of mens damnation, he could not bestow it upon them out of a principle of goodness. The present was too dangerous, and he would not have raised them so high, except in order to make their fall the greater. He would have done them a greater favour, if he had recalled a gift which has been so fatal to them.

Mr Bayle makes a still stronger answer to Mr Jaquelot. All Divines agree, and Mr Jaquelot with them, that the operation of Grace doth not in the least prejudice free-will, and that God, who is the master of hearts, infallibly directs mens liberty as he pleaseth, without violating the laws of this liberty. From whence it evidently follows, that God by confirming man in a good choice, and by infallibly directing him to good, doth no prejudice to his free-will, and that by finally preserving him from sin, he doth not deprive him of this so precious liberty with which he had invested him. If it be necessary that men should have it in their power to sin, it is not at all so that they should actually sin, and God can prevent their doing so without prejudicing their liberty. Notwithstanding, God far from disposing man constantly to good, constitutes him in such a manner, and places him in such circumstances in which he has foreseen that he will succumb, and has endowed him with a faculty of which he knew very well that he would make a bad use. So that though we allow man even an unlimited liberty the difficulty still recurrs, to wit, whether the permission and foresight of sin, are consistent with the goodness and holiness of God. Mr Bayle makes use of several other arguments to prove that whatever side we embrace, we can never make use of free-will to solve the difficulties concerning the origin and consequences of moral evil; and shows that Mr Jaquelot has been obliged to cover himself with the same intrenchment that the maintainers of Predestination make use of. He shows the terrible consequences of this answer of Mr Jaquelot, to wit, that since the permission of sin was necessary to the manifestation of God's glory, it was just and agreeable to all the divine perfections. He examines Mr Jaquelot's hypothesis concerning physical evil, and the idea which he gives of the eternal pains of hell.

The third point of the dispute between Mr Bayle and Mr Jaquelot relates to the objections which Pyrrhonism may raise against some doctrines of revealed religion. In the *Critical Dictionary* under the article PYRRHO we find the recital of a dispute between a Pyrrhonian Abbé and a Roman Catholic Abbé. The principle in which they both agree is, that the mysteries of the Church of Rome, the Trinity, the Incarnation, Transubstantiation, the fall of Adam, and original Sin, are doctrines undoubtedly true. From this supposition, acknowledged by both disputants, the Pyrrhonian Abbé infers, that evidence is not the certain criterion of truth, since there are several evident propositions which are false if we admit the truth of mysteries. Mr Jaquelot pretends that Mr Bayle by this wanted to prove that the Trinity and the hypostatical union imply a contradiction; and he defends these two mysteries by relating what the Divines say upon these subjects. But Mr Bayle shows him that he has misunderstood the Pyrrhonian Abbé. The design of his objections is only to show that these doctrines are opposite to evident propositions, and that they deprive us of the certainty which we found upon evidence. Mr Jaquelot ought to have proved that this is false, and shewed that this example of the fashood of evident propositions, gives no ground to the Pyrrhonians to distrust propositions which appear the most clear to us. But he mistakes the matter, and raiseth up a phantom in order to fight with it. He takes it to be the same thing, to own that the mysteries of the Gospel ought to be believed though our reason cannot comprehend them, and to endeavour to ruin Religion by pretending that it is always contrary to reason. Mr Bayle wonders that so penetrating a genius has not observed that the question was not to explain the difficulties of our mysteries; the objection supposeth them true, since from hence it is concluded that evidence is not the certain criterion of truth. All that Mr Jaquelot had to do was to destroy this consequence.

I

This

THE LIFE OF Mr BAYLE.

1705. This dispute did not hinder Mr Bayle from doing justice to Mr Jaquelot's merit. He owned that he had a fine genius, a great deal of penetration, and a lively and persuasive stile, that he had joined the study of modern Philosophy to that of Divinity, and had signalized himself in works of reasoning.

Mr Bayle likewise defended the answer which he had made in his Dictionary to Mr le Clerc's Origenist. The latter had given some new explanations in his Reply (1), to shew that the system of the Origenist takes away the difficulties of the Manichean, who maintained that it was impossible to reconcile the permission and consequences of sin with the ideal or sovereignly perfect goodness of God. In order to prove this Mr le Clerc observed,

I. That God, who produced man from nothing, was not obliged to create him so perfect that it should be impossible for him to deviate from his duty; that it is a great proof of his goodness that he gave him the means of being happy by observing the rules prescribed to him, without being under any necessity of violating them.

II. That they exaggerate the damage which liberty has done to men, and which they might have avoided, if he who created them had made them of such a nature that they could not have departed from their duty.

III. That in order to prevent the bad use which man might make of his liberty, and to guide him to happiness, the divine goodness has been pleased to propose to him eternal rewards, and unlimited punishments in the Gospel: and that it is his own fault if he doth not avoid those punishments and obtain these rewards.

IV. God knew what would come to pass; but he was not obliged to make use of his almighty power, in order to prevent the evil which he foresaw would happen by the fault of man, because this evil is of a very short duration in itself, and in all its consequences, and occasions no disorder in the universe which God is not able to redress in a moment, and which he doth not at last redress for all eternity.

V. The inconvenience of passing through evil before the enjoyment of all the effects of the divine bounty, proceeds from the nature of man, which could not exist in the degree of imperfection where it is placed, without being liable to what has happened.

VI. God who foresaw that man would fall, doth not damn him because he falls, but only because having it in his power to rise again, he doth not rise, that is to say, he freely retains his bad habits to the end of his life.

VII. That this is already a very considerable degree of mercy, since no body is damned except for his own fault, and that it is in our power to take advantage of this goodness of God, to amend our faults, and avoid the pains of a future state.

VIII. God has bestowed many other marks of his goodness upon men. He has endowed them with a thousand excellent qualities; and surrounded them with a thousand sensible goods, which they taste with a great deal of pleasure, which make them in love with life; he hath put it in their power to make themselves happy after death, and he gives without delay eternal happiness to those who repent of their faults, and is satisfied by making the impenitent pass through moderate punishments, before he puts them in possession of eternal happiness.

IX. God has considered the miseries of mankind as nothing, in comparison of the happiness which he designs to bestow upon them. The duration of the evils which they suffer here below, and in the other world, are nothing when compared to eternity. If the Manichean should say, that, according to this principle, a certain number of ages, how great soever we suppose it, not having any proportion to infinite duration, torments for many millions of years may be as consistent with the ideas of goodness, and would be as nothing, no less than those which should continue only one day: the Origenist will answer that since there is no proportion betwixt finite and infinite, however long you suppose the torments of a creature, since they are to have an end, neither will there be any proportion betwixt God's severity and his goodness. He will add, that he doth not determine the length of the punishments; they shall be longer or shorter as justice shall require. The duration of punishments shall be shorter when they are more severe; and there shall be as great a variety of punishments, as there hath been of sins. That the arguments against punishments for several ages, do not concern the Origenist; because he is not of opinion that they shall continue so long, though he cannot precisely determine their duration.

X. What has been said above may be equally applied to moral and physical evil, or to the vices and to the sufferings of men.

Mr Bayle answered (2).

I. That the principle which they lay down, to wit, that it is not contrary to the ideas of goodness that one creature should be more perfect than another, is very true; and therefore that men have no reason to complain that they want that perfection which consists in not departing from ones duty. But neither is this the foundation of the objections. They are founded on this, that God has permitted that they should actually depart from their duty; and that they should actually feel the evils of which their nature was created susceptible. This, says he,

(1) Bibliotheque choisie, *Tom. vii. art. viii, p. 330, and the following.*

(2) An Answer to the Questions of a Country Gentleman, *Tom. iii. ch. clxxii, and the following.*

VOL. I.   c c

he, is what doth not appear agreeable to the ideas of goodness, even granting what the Origenist remarks, that if men observed the rules which God has prescribed to them, and which he is under no unsurmountable necessity of violating, he should be happy. We cannot conceive that the goodness of a father is such as it ought to be, when he makes the happiness of his children depend upon a condition which he knows very well that they will not fulfil, and which he permits them not to fulfil, though he could easily procure them sure and infallible means of fulfilling it.

II. The objection is not founded on man's not being immutably determined to good. A creature is essentially mutable, and so it would be absurd to ask why it was not immutable. The question is only, why he was permitted to turn to evil? The consequence from the act to the power is necessary, but from the power to the act is not at all so. The dispute therefore doth not turn upon the possibility of change, but upon the actual change from good to evil. Now God could hinder this without doing any prejudice to free-will. It may be said that God was not obliged to prevent it: but by this the state of the question is changed; for when the Orthodox undertake to satisfy the difficulties of the Manicheans, the question is not always concerning God considered as just; but frequently concerning God considered as good. So that though God considered as just, is not obliged to give his creatures any thing but what he has promised them by way of reward, he is obliged, considered as good, to make them useful presents, that is to say, it is of the essence of goodness to give good gifts. It is not bestowing a good present, to give a thing which one knows will be fatal to the person who shall receive it.

III. God knew that his promises and threats would not hinder men to damn themselves, and that a hundred other assistances, which he doth not bestow upon them, would have conducted them to happiness, without prejudice to their free-will. How can we reconcile such a foresight with the ideas of goodness? Is it not very evident that a real benefactor chooseth the most sure means which he knows, and slights those which he knows to be useless?

IV. Would any body praise the goodness of a Prince who should suffer disorders to reign in his dominions, because at last he could apply a remedy to it? Is it possible not to observe that such a Prince would then apply a remedy not only to the faults of his subjects but to his own, and that he had at least for some time ceased to be good, so that we might find in him a vicissitude of goodness and wickedness?

V. Our nature was made subject to sin, this is certain; but doth it follow from hence that it was necessary that we should sin? Not at all. The goodness of God was therefore at entire liberty not to permit Adam, who was subject to sin, to sin actually; and it is in vain to insinuate that God would have acted contrary to the nature of things, if he had freed men from an inconvenience to which they are subject, that is to say, into which it was possible they might fall. But was it not likewise possible that they should not fall into it?

VI. One doth not less will a thing when he renders the event of it infallible, than when he renders it necessary. Now the causes of the damnation of the reprobate, and consequently their damnation was rendered infallible, since they were placed in conjunctures in which God foresaw that they would sin during their whole lives, and in which he had decreed not to give them any assistance. He therefore created them for sin, and for the pains of hell; and if this objection be strong against the Predestinarians, it must likewise be so against an Origenist.

VII. That it is a considerable degree of mercy, to see a man abuse his free-will for fifty or sixty years, without any assistance from Grace, when it is known that this abuse will damn him, is what the ideas of our reason do not show us. They show us in the most evident manner, that goodness inclines to assist not only those who have not sufficient strength to free themselves from danger, but likewise those who having the necessary strength and skill, do not make use of it.

VIII. The pleasures of this life are mixed with so many miseries, that they cannot come up fully to the character of ideal goodness. As to that innumerable multitude of impenitents, who after a rigorous purgatory pass to the abode of the blessed, we cannot in their lot see the marks of ideal goodness. Here is a representation of the conduct which Origen attributes to God. A Prince designs to make a Gentleman his favourite. He finds him subject to great faults, he has infallible means of correcting them, yet doth not make use of them. He contents himself with making use of promises and threats, which he knows will produce no good effect. The young man is hurried along by his wicked inclinations, notwithstanding the promises and threatnings of his Prince, he is banished, and very severely punished, but at last he is called back to Court, and for the remainder of his life he enjoys the place of favourite. Can such a Prince be said to be eminently good? If we love any person, if we are good to him, we save him, as much as we are able, from the misfortune of committing faults, especially when they are to be followed by punishment; and the only manner of justifying people who expose their friends to any trouble or punishment is, that they cannot by any other means correct their vices. But this is not the present case, since we suppose a King who has effectual means of correcting this Gentleman's

THE LIFE OF MR BAYLE.

1705. man's faults, and yet inſtead of making uſe of them, has recourſe to methods which he knows will be to no purpoſe.

IX. The bounds which are ſet to the duration of the pains of the next life, the degrees and varieties which are ſuppoſed to be in them, are all very proper to prove that the marks of God's goodneſs are infinitely more apparent in the condition of men than the marks of his hatred, and that they have incomparably more reaſon to praiſe the bounty of their Creator, than to complain of his ſeverity. Yet notwithſtanding, infinite goodneſs, which ought to be pure without the leaſt mixture of the contrary quality, ideal goodneſs, in a word, doth not appear in the hypotheſis of Origen: it eſcapes us even tho' we ſoften it after that manner. Would a father who has a moderate love for his children, deſire that the great eſtabliſhments which he deſigns for them, ſhould be preceded by a permiſſion of committing faults, and by a puniſhment of theſe faults, tho' only for ſome days? Would he deſire this, if he could render them equally happy without this preliminary? Few people would deſire to buy the favour of a Prince, at the price of being put to the torture three times a week for ſix months. We ought not to imagine that the torments of hell are ſmall, under pretence that they continue poſſibly only fifty or ſixty years. This term, it is true, is nothing in compariſon of eternity. But it is of a frightful length with regard to human ſenſibility. If one ſhould ſay to a perſon afflicted with the Gout, " the horrible pains which you ſuffer, ſhall only laſt " fifty days together, and after that you ſhall enjoy health for fifty years," he would make him quite deſperate.

X. What the Origeniſt has replied, cannot be equally applied to moral and phyſical evil. Our ideas do not diſcover any equality betwixt theſe two ſorts of evils: they judge a father incomparably more to blame, who doth not hinder his children, when it is in his power, from committing a crime, than a father who allows them to eat what may be prejudicial to their health.

Some perſons of Quality in England had uſed all their efforts to draw Mr Bayle out of his ſolitude and to bring him over to England. They deſired that he would live with them as a friend, that they might have the benefit of his hours of recreation. I ſhall only name the Earl of Huntington, who together with a great deal of learning was poſſeſſed of all the accompliſhments of a gentleman (1). He offered him a yearly penſion of two hundred pounds ſterling for life, with all the liberty and conveniencies which he could wiſh for. He was likewiſe invited to the Hague. The Earl of Albemarle paſſionately deſired that he would come and live with him 1706. (2). Baron Walef went to Rotterdam to propoſe it to him, and redoubled his inſtances in a letter which he wrote to him. " If your friends (ſays he (3), en- " deavour to perſuade you to refuſe the propoſition which I have had the honour to " make to you, their friendſhip muſt needs be intereſted, and they can have no " other motive in doing ſo, but their deſire of poſſeſſing you at Rotterdam. Have " not you ſufficiently honoured that City with your preſence, and has not the Metro- " polis of Holland, with all its advantages, a right to invite you to prefer it to a place " deſigned for commerce? I will not mention here the great eſteem which every body " has for you, nor the regard they will pay to your merit. I know your indifference on " this head. But together with the friendſhip of a noble Lord who has an infinite eſteem " for you, you will find libraries and walks proper to nouriſh, and agreeably to en- " tertain your Philoſophy. Allow me, Sir, to make uſe of your own arms. You " have with your ordinary eloquence ſhown how much a man of Letters ought to pre- " fer an abode in a metropolis to that of inferior towns (4). Either renounce your " own ſentiments, or grant us the favour which we deſire of you. I will not " repeat what my Lord Albemarle has deſired me to ſay to you. You will find " in his family a life more agreeable than I can deſcribe to you. As much as you " excel other men by your profound knowledge, and the ſublimity of your genius, " ſo much he excels by his generous and beneficent mind, by his probity, by that " equality of temper, which is one of the greateſt charms in life, and which is ſo " rarely to be met with among the Great. . . . . . Preſerve, on account of your friends, " a health which you ſpare ſo little with regard to yourſelf, and prevent in a calm and " certain retreat the infirmities inſeparable from an old age ſo worthy of reſpect as " yours is." My Lord Albemarle likewiſe wrote to him, and confirmed all that Baron Walef had told him by his direction. " I wiſh with all my heart (ſaid " he (5), that I could find ſome expreſſion able to perſuade you to grant me the " favour I deſire of you. I will endeavour to live with you in ſuch a manner that " you ſhall not repent the choice which you ſhall make, by leaving you a full " liberty without the leaſt conſtraint, as much as you can poſſibly enjoy at preſent. " This you may depend upon."

Mr Bayle anſwered Baron Walef, that it was very unhappy for him that his preſent ſituation was ſuch as neceſſarily obliged him to continue in it. " Providence (adds " he (6), orders the deſtiny of ſome perſons in ſuch a manner, that when they " would be glad to enjoy a certain happineſs, it doth not preſent itſelf to them, " and when it preſents itſelf, they are no longer in a capacity of enjoying it. This " is my fate. I conſider myſelf as a worn out old man, my conſtitution is ſo weak, " that I cannot eſcape being ſick or very much indiſpoſed, if I depart in the leaſt
" from

(1) This Nobleman died young and unmarried March 2, 1705.

(2) He propoſed to entruſt him with the education of his ſon, when he ſhould be of an age to profit by his inſtructions.

(3) Letter February 9, 1706, p. 1065.

(4) See the Anſwer to the Queſtions of a Country Gentleman, Tom. i, chap. i.

(5) Letter February 11, 1706, p. 1067.

(6) Letter February 12, 1706, p. 1068, 1069.

"from a regularity of life, which a long habit has made necessary to me. I have 1706.
"not advised with any of my friends; for, in examining by myself, the reasons which
"I had the honour to represent to you, and which you opposed with all the wit
"and eloquence imaginable; I have found it too certain, that removing from
"hence will not be at all proper for me . . . . . Good fortune comes to me too late.
"If she had offered herself sooner, she would have made me the most contented man
"in the world: I would with all imaginable satisfaction have complied with the
"reasons which persuade me that living in a metropolis is advantageous to a man of
"Letters. Would to God that about the year 1690, or a little before or after, so
"agreeable and honourable an offer as my Lord Albemarle has been pleased to make
"me, had come in my way! This would have been the height of my wishes, and
"the sure means of obtaining much knowledge, and many degrees of wit, and abi-
"lities which I want, and which I shall never enjoy." Mr Bayle wrote to the Earl
of Albemarle at the same time to thank him for the honour he was pleased to design
for him, but we have not been able to recover this letter.

Mr le Clerc flattered himself that Mr Bayle would acknowledge that his Origenist
had taken away all the difficulties of the Manichean, but seeing him persist in maintaining the contrary, he concluded from thence that Mr Bayle had pleaded his own
cause, and intitled his answer, *A Defence of the Goodness and Holiness of God, against*

(1) Défense de la Bonté & de la Sainteté divine, contre les Objections de Mr Bayle.

the Objections of Mr Bayle (1). " When (says he (2), I read the objections made
"by Mr Bayle in the first edition of his Critical Dictionary, against the goodness
"and holiness of God, and which he maintains no Christian Divine can answer; I
"believed it only a sort of trial of wit, and that he had for his diversion cut
"out a little work for our Divines . . . . I continued in this opinion, until I had
"seen the last two volumes of his *Answer to a Country Gentleman*, wherein he seriously
"maintains the cause of the Manicheans against the goodness of God . . . . (3) But
"since he thinks himself bound in honour to maintain a Thesis opposite to the whole
"Christian world, which he defies methinks in a very odious and very insulting man-
"ner; he will be pleased to excuse us, if, in our turn, we maintain a Thesis, which not
"only honour, but likewise the love of truth and conscience obliges us to defend. I
"flattered myself, that possibly he would of himself acknowledge the goodness and
"holiness of the conduct of God, after the opportunity which I had given him of
"getting out of this ugly affair without hurt to his reputation; by owning that he
"was convinced, and making an end of the dispute by thanking those who had re-
"moved his difficulties, as is the custom in the Divinity and Philosophy schools. But
"as he has done quite the contrary, and pretends that we have not solidly answered
"him; it is necessary to let him see that we are not afraid of his arguments, and that
"we, without sparing him any longer, show how ridiculous they are."

(2) Bibliotheque Choisie, Tom. ix, Art. iii, p.103, and the following.

(3) Ibid. p. 106, 107.

Mr le Clerc having thus assumed the character of Defender of Religion, attacked by
Mr Bayle, begins by recapitulating the whole dispute; and, laying aside the person of
an Origenist, answers Mr Bayle's difficulties in his own name. He declares that
he has no other Confession of Faith but the New Testament, and that this is the only
book which he thinks himself bound to defend. But as the strongest objection of the
Manicheans is founded upon the eternity of punishments, which seems so clearly
revealed in the Gospel; after having rejected the opinion of Origen he lays down
his own. " For my part (says he (4), I would answer that we are not well ac-
"quainted with the nature of the torments of the next life, that we do not know
"whether at first there may not be divers very sensible punishments, differing not-
"withstanding according to the greatness of sins, and whether God putting an
"end to these violent punishments, will not be satisfied to deliver over those who
"have obstinately abused his grace, to the remorse of their own consciences, which
"will reproach them with their faults, and will add to their grief by the reflexion
"that they have lost a happiness which they shall know that others enjoy. This
"possibly will be *the worm which never dieth, and the fire which is never quenched.*
"And in this I do not see that there is any thing but what is most just. Sinners
"might have avoided these punishments by repentance, and yet they have neglected
"to do it. They deserve some punishment on this account." Mr le Clerc determines
nothing concerning the duration or the circumstances of these punishments: he nevertheless says, that probably the condition of the condemned will be tolerable. But
he doth not pretend to advance all these conjectures as certain and evangelical doctrine, he only means to show that we may find a very reasonable sense in the words
of JESUS CHRIST relating to the pains of the next life. He adds that others may
possibly be more happy in their conjectures, yet in the mean while he is persuaded
that there is nothing in the conduct which he attributes to God, inconsistent with
his infinite goodness; but that if there be any thing in what he has advanced
which is unworthy of the justice and goodness of God, he is very certain that God will
not do it. This is (continues he), what I called reasoning infinitely better than Origen,
for Origen assures us of what he knows nothing of, as if he knew it, when he affirms
that the pains of the damned shall not be eternal. However he looks upon Origen's
opinion as tolerable, and infinitely better (says he) than the side Mr Bayle chooses,
by departing from it to accuse God of being neither good nor holy.

(4) Ibid. p. 143.

He

1706.

He endeavours next to shew that Reason cannot deceive us, if we make a right use of it; that it serves to prove the truth of the Christian Religion, and to make us understand the sense of the Holy Scripture: that there are in Divinity, as well as in Philosophy, several things which reason cannot comprehend, but these things are never contrary to reason, and we ought not to reject them because we do not comprehend them: that therefore we ought never to oppose the light of Revelation to the light of Reason, nor suppose that they may contradict one another, unless we reject either the one or the other, and unless we throw ourselves headlong into Pyrrhonism, since truth cannot be contrary to itself: from hence he concludes, that Mr Bayle, who maintains that we ought to renounce our common notions of goodness and holiness, cannot, if he reasons consequentially, believe that God is good and holy; and that he doth not sacrifice his reason to faith, but destroys reason by itself, and involves Revelation in the same fate, while he endeavours to skreen himself by pretending to humble his reason, speaking in the stile of the vulgar Divines, whom he ridicules.

In answer to Mr le Clerc, Mr Bayle published a piece intitled *An Answer for Mr Bayle, to the III and XIII articles of the IX volume of the Bibliotheque choisie* (1). " I easily believed, (says he (2), that Mr le Clerc would be out of humour upon the " defeat of his Origenist, and of the plastic natures, but I did not imagine that he " would be enraged to such a degree, as not to reflect upon the irregularity of the " conduct which he should choose. It is not therefore without surprise that I have " observed the manner of revenging himself, which he has thought fit to take; but " instead of being angry with him, I have had a real compassion for him on this " account. One cannot without pity see a man, who enjoyed a considerable share " of glory in the Republic of Letters, so touched with so trifling a check. He " ought to have comforted himself by reflecting upon his other exploits, in which he " has had better success, or at least not to have abandoned himself to such a chagrin, " as should make him declaim in a manner altogether unworthy of a man of ho- " nour and good sense. He has pretended to dive into Mr Bayle's heart, he has " accused him of horrible designs, he has repeated his accusations a hundred times " over, still in a loose manner, still without the least shadow of proof, still with- " out regard to the clear and distinct declarations, which are to be found in a thou- " sand places of Mr Bayle's writings." He observes, that the Republic of Letters would be a perfect anarchy, if it were allowed to attack our adversaries under pretence that they conceal bad designs in the bottom of their hearts; and he adds, that this conduct doth not at all become Mr le Clerc, who has so well described those who in order to render their adversaries odious, cloak themselves under the pretence of the interest of religion. " Doth it become him, after this, (says he (3), to de- " claim as he has done against Mr Bayle, just when he saw that he could no longer " sustain the shock in the lawful methods of dispute? Doth it become him to give " himself airs of being eaten up with zeal for the house of God? This zeal which has " come so late, would never have appeared, if Mr Bayle had renounced his remark " upon Dr Cudworth, and if he had not refuted the reasons of the Origenist." He opposeth to this conduct of Mr le Clerc, the complaints which he had formerly made against those who accused Grotius of favouring Socinianism, because he gave to some passages of scripture a sense different from that of the common orthodox writers of controversy, and who from thence had concluded that he designed to sap the foundations of Christianity. " No body (said he (4), cried out with more vehemence against " such accusations than Mr le Clerc. With how good a grace therefore doth he now " say, that Mr Bayle writes an apology for Atheists, and intends to destroy religion? " Is this pretended apology any thing else than his having rejected a bad argu- " ment?" He adds, that Mr le Clerc has been obliged several times to defend himself against the accusation of Socinianism, with which he continues still charged.

Mr Bayle afterwards lays down the substance of his doctrine on the subject in question, and reduces it to these three propositions (5):

" I. The light of Nature and Revelation teach us clearly that there is only one " principle of all things, and that this principle is infinitely perfect.

" II. The manner of reconciling the moral and physical evils of man, with all " the attributes of this sole infinitely perfect principle of all things, surpasseth the light " of Philosophy; so that the Manichean objections leave difficulties which human " reason cannot solve.

" III. Notwithstanding of this we ought firmly to believe what the light of Na- " ture and Revelation teach us concerning the unity and infinite perfection of God, " as we believe by faith, and in submission to the divine authority, the Mystery of the " Trinity, the Incarnation, &c.

Mr Bayle adds, that he will without all doubt be thought orthodox in the first and third propositions; and that if he be attacked on the second, Luther and Calvin, and the whole body of the Protestant churches, and even almost the whole Christian world, must be attacked at the same time. He is persuaded that no body will ever be able to prove, that these three propositions are not what he has constantly taught in his writings, or prove that if he has established them in some passages, he has maintained propositions contrary to them in some others.

(1) Réponse pour Mr Bayle au sujet du III & du XIII articles du IX Tome de la Bibliotheque choisie. *This piece is dated April 25, 1706.*

(2) Réponse pour Mr Bayle, *p.* 1.

(3) *Ibid. pag.* 5.

(4) *Ibid. pag.* 7.

(5) *Ibid. pag.* 18.

VOL. I.   dd   He

He next makes some general Remarks on the dogmatical part of Mr le Clerc's piece, not being willing to enter into a more minute criticism which would have led him too far. "I will suppress (says he (1), a great many remarks which would show where Mr le Clerc has misunderstood me, where he disguiseth the state of the question, where he complains, without reason, that I have not understood him, where he discovers chimerical contradictions, where he takes the liberty of distinguishing into two species where there is but one, where he suppresseth what is inconvenient for him, and adds what is convenient, &c." Mr le Clerc charged Mr Bayle with *accusing God of being neither good nor holy*. "What horrible calumny! (cries Mr Bayle (2), what malicious imposture! or at least what want of discernment! but who will be persuaded that so learned a man as Mr le Clerc has erred through stupidity, and by not being able to distinguish here betwixt two things evidently different? the one is to say that God is infinitely good and holy, though our reason doth not know the manner in which this goodness and holiness is reconcilable with the misery and sins of men; Mr Bayle has said no more than this; the other is to accuse God of being neither good nor holy; Mr Bayle has never done any thing like this."

Mr Bayle doth not meddle with Origenism, he pretends that Mr le Clerc hath said nothing new on this subject, and that he has made no reply to the reasons of his adversary; so that they remain in all their force, and it is sufficient to desire the reader to compare the pieces on both sides to be convinced of this. Neither doth he regard what Mr le Clerc had said concerning the excellence and use of Reason. He only observes that the result of the Manichean controversy, which we have recited, was always that we ought from thence to infer the necessity of captivating our understanding under the authority of God, and that this is a principle common to all Christians who admit the mystery of the Trinity, and certain others. "Mr le Clerc (adds he (3), proposeth several difficulties against this, as if the most frightful Pyrrhonism were inevitable, in case revealed truths were not conformable to our common notions. All that I have to say against this is, that the Unitarians have of a long time made these objections, and the Roman Catholics, the Lutherans, and the Reformed have refuted them." He defies Mr le Clerc to dare to say, that he himself has not departed from our common notions, by acknowledging in the Deity three persons really distinct, coëssential, and consubstantial, and consequently that it is his business to answer the difficulties which he proposeth against the common principle of Divines, to the confirmation of which Mr Bayle has made the whole present dispute subservient.

Mr Bayle draws a parallel betwixt his opinion and that of Mr le Clerc, to the end that all the world (says he (4), may judge whether Mr le Clerc had cause to intitle his Reply, *A Defence of the Goodness and Holiness of God, against Mr Bayle's objections*. He makes a supposition that Mr le Clerc and he are disputing with a disciple of Zoroaster about the unity of the principle of all things. Mr Bayle (says he) shall begin the attack, and force the enemy in all his entrenchments. But the difficulty doth not lie there: the question is how to resist the Zoroastrian when he shall attack in his turn, and shall labour to prove that sin and its consequences are not consistent with the idea of one infinitely perfect and holy Being. Mr Bayle will stop him short at once, by declaring that he doth not admit our ideas of goodness and holiness in general, as the rule of the goodness and holiness of God: and by opposing his system to him, which is conformable to the principles of the most orthodox Divines, he will defend with success the following Thesis: "God is infinitely good and holy, though our knowledge is too confined to be able to reconcile his goodness and holiness with the miseries and crimes of mankind in this life, and with the crimes and eternal torments of the greater part of mankind in the life to come". But Mr le Clerc, who will grant to his adversary that the common notions, that is to say, the ideas which we have of goodness and holiness in general, ought to serve us for a rule whereby to judge of the goodness and holiness of God, will be obliged to depart from the opinion of other Christians, at first by denying, with Origen the eternity of hell torments; and not finding even this post tenable, he will be forced to betake himself to conjectures, and reduce the goodness and holiness of God to a problem, the solution of which we shall only learn in the other world. Upon this Mr Bayle observes that Mr le Clerc has fallen precisely into the case on which he founded his accusation. For according to him Mr Bayle's great crime is, that he believes that no Christian system can solve the objections of the Manicheans against the goodness and holiness of God: now Mr le Clerc is persuaded of the same thing, since on the subject of the eternity of punishments, he abandons all the systems of Christians, and even that of Origen, and only intrencheth himself in *may be's* and probabilities. From hence it follows that according to Mr le Clerc there is no Christian system which can solve the objections of Manicheism against the goodness and holiness of God: "This nevertheless (adds he (5), is the sole foundation of his accusation against Mr Bayle: he has therefore wounded himself by the stroke which he aimed at him. He has from this ground of accusation drawn several false consequences, I mean the calumnies which he has raised against "Mr Bayle.

1706. "Mr Bayle. He has said that they who maintain that we cannot answer the Manichean objections, attack the goodness and holiness of God, and accuse him of being neither good nor holy, and that they cannot be admitted to profess that they believe him both good and holy, for having no reason to believe him so, they fall into a manifest contradiction &c. These consequences, and all the rest which I do not particularize here, fall equally upon the accuser and the accused. This can admit of no dispute."

Mr Bayle, to put an end to this debate, offered (1) to Mr le Clerc that he would submit to the decision of the Faculties of Divinity at Leyden, Utrecht, Franeker, Groningen &c. He proposeth to him to draw up a Petition to be presented to these Faculties, in which he should specify the punishment which he desired they would inflict upon the person who should lose his cause. That Mr Bayle should sign that petition jointly with him, and that Mr le Clerc should join to it such propositions as he shall draw out of Mr Bayle's writings, and that he should communicate them to him, and that in case they are to be found in so many words in his works, and without any essential mutilation, he will subscribe them. The Faculties of Theology will know by this petition and those extracts, that what is desired of them is that they may be pleased to determine the following question: *Are the propositions extracted from Mr Bayle's books, good proofs of Mr le Clerc's accusation against him?* Mr le Clerc pretends that they are, *and Mr Bayle denies it*, *and likewise maintains that they contain nothing contrary to the Confessions of Faith of the Reformed Churches in France and the Low-Countries*. But as Mr le Clerc, adds he, declares that before he examined the second and third volumes of the *Answer to a Country Gentleman*, he considered Mr Bayle's objections as a trial of wit only, and that they did not prevent his believing him orthodox; Mr Bayle is of opinion that in order to lessen the trouble of these Professors, it will be sufficient if the Faculties of Divinity shall take the trouble of examining those two volumes. It would likewise (adds he) take away the greatest part of their trouble, if Mr le Clerc would mark the pages from whence he shall extract his propositions, and if Mr Bayle would likewise mark the pages omitted by his accuser, the knowledge of which he shall think necessary to inform his judges more fully of the state of the question.

Mr Bayle's enemies were not content to represent him as a man who endeavoured to destroy Religion, they strove to make him pass for an enemy to the State. This was to imitate Mr Jurieu pretty exactly. But as Mr Bayle's sentiments were too well known in Holland, for such an accusation to make any impression upon reasonable people, his enemies thought it would be better to endeavour to ruin him in England, where they expected to find less difficulty. They left no means unessayed to prejudice the Earl of Shaftsbury against him. But they were disappointed in their attempts upon this noble Lord: he was too well acquainted with Mr Bayle, with whom he had entertained a close friendship, during the stay which he had made at Rotterdam. He perceived the motives of this accusation, and diverted himself with it among his friends. They wrote likewise to the Earl of Sunderland, assuring him that Mr Bayle had conferences with the Marquis d'Allegre, a prisoner of war, when he passed through Holland on his way to England. They added, that Mr Bayle spread every where principles favourable to Monarchy and absolute Power, that he continually extolled the grandeur of France, and talked contemptibly of the power of the Allies, and of the great actions of their Generals &c. My Lord Sunderland being of a warm and impetuous temper, and having as great an aversion to the principles which they attributed to Mr Bayle, as he had a passion for the humbling of France, and the glory of the English General, never spoke of Mr Bayle without transports of indignation and wrath. I endeavoured to undeceive him, but without success, his prejudices were too strong. I own this alarmed me. I was afraid least he should persuade the Court to complain to the States of Holland, who considering the situation of affairs at this time, could refuse nothing to England; and least upon such powerful representations they should order Mr Bayle, a person without great interest, to depart out of the Seventeen Provinces. This in all appearance was what his enemies aimed at. I had recourse to my Lord Shaftsbury, and acquainted him with Mr Bayle's danger. This Lord promised to speak to my Lord Sunderland, but at the same time told me, that it were to be wished that to stop the mouths of his enemies, Mr Bayle should take occasion in some of his works to mention the success of the arms of the Allies, which were principally owing to the activity of the English Ministry, and the conduct of the English General. He added, that this might be done without affectation, and without departing from the character of an historian, and signified to me that I would oblige him by insinuating this to Mr Bayle as from myself.

I thought myself bound to acquaint Mr Bayle with what had passed, and with the conversation which I had had with my Lord Shaftsbury. He answered me (2), that Dr Sylvestre had before informed him that my Lord Sunderland was out of humour with him on account of pretended conferences which he had with the Marquis d'Allegre: but that this was *the most notorious falshood that could be imagined*. As to the other ground of accusation, which was the chief cause of my Lord Sunderland's displeasure,

(1) *Ibid.* pag. 72, *and the following.*

(2) *Letter July 23, 1706. p. 1096, and the following.*

cviii　　　　　　　THE LIFE OF Mʀ BAYLE.

pleasure, Mr Bayle said, "that he defied his most inveterate enemies to find in his works　1706.
" the least shadow of affectation of speaking advantageously of the King of France, his
" Ministers or Generals, or to the prejudice of the Allies: for (adds he) we must not
" reckon here the Thoughts concerning Comets, a book which as I have advertised
" before the third edition, was composed with a design to be printed at Paris, &c.
" It is well known that the Abbé Renaudot alledged this amongst other reasons to
" hinder my Dictionary from passing into France, that it contained things against
" the State." Mr Bayle by no means approved the advice which had been
given him, as the most proper to destroy his enemies calumnies. Being incapable
of flattering on views of interest or even of praising unseasonably, he considered
what was proposed to him in that light, and declared that such a conduct was very
unsuitable to him. "However (says he), the plan which you lay down for me as
" what would disarm my enemies, is the advice of a good friend, and I return you
" most hearty thanks for it, but I find it impossible for me to comply with it. It would
" be very unsuitable for me at the age of fifty nine years, which with regard to the
" weakness of the constitution that nature has given me, is a more infirm old age
" than seventy or seventy five in other men; who besides have struggled more
" than these six months past with a weakness in my lungs, a hereditary distemper
" of which both my Mother and Grandmother died, and which consequently doth
" not permit me to propose to make a long stay in this world: it would be very un-
" suitable for me, I say, to write like a Courtier and flatterer of men in power.
" My enemies would rejoice to have such an inequality of conduct to reproach me
" with."

(1) *Letter July 23, 1706, p. 1100, and the following.*

Mr Bayle wrote likewise to the Lord Shaftsbury (1), wherein he thanked him for
these new marks of his goodness: and protested that it was false that he had had conferences with the Marquis d'Allegre; that he had not so much as known, any other
ways than by the news papers, that the Marquis had been in Holland, and was gone
over to England. He added, that no body knew his principles concerning government better than my Lord Shaftsbury, since he had the honour to converse with his

(2) *Letter October 29, 1706, p. 1123, and the following.*

Lordship more than once on that subject. He prayed that he would undeceive the
Lord Sunderland. My Lord Shaftsbury did it with success. He represented to him
that Mr Bayle being confined to his closet, and entirely taken up with his books and
his works, did not in any sort meddle with affairs of State, that neither his genius nor
his talents lay that way, and that these accusations proceeded only from the animosity of

(3) *Remarques critiques sur la Nouvelle Edition du Dictionaire historique de Morery, donnée en 1704.*

certain authors who had had disputes with him, and endeavoured to render him odious.
My Lord Sunderland at last found that he had been imposed upon, and did Mr Bayle
justice. My Lord Shaftsbury immediately informed him of this, and Mr Bayle in return testified (2) how sensible he was of the generous attention my Lord had shewn
to his interest, and how joyful he was to learn " that the calumnies whereby his ene-
" mies had prejudiced my Lord Sunderland against him, were happily dissipated by
" his Lordship's means."

About this time Mr Bayle received a little book, printed at Paris, intitled, *Critical
Remarks on the new edition of Moreri's Historical Dictionary, published in* 1704 (3). The

(4) *The Abbé Tricauld, now Canon of the Abbey of Ainay at Lyons.*

Author (4) had drawn almost all his remarks from Mr Bayle's Dictionary, and had
given them for his own, yet notwithstanding this he sometimes criticized him. Mr
Bayle thought that this Piece deserved to be known in Holland, and to make it more
useful he thought fit to reprint it (5) with Notes to clear up several facts which the author had either mistaken, or had not related with sufficient exactness. He even pointed
out the faults of his stile, and his ambiguous or equivocal expressions; and lastly,
added a long Preface for the instruction of those who should publish any after editions of Moreri. The relation which this small piece has to Mr Bayle's Dictionary,

(5) *At Rotterdam in* 1706.

engaged one of my friends (6) to desire it of me, that he might add it to the fourth
edition of this Dictionary. I sent it to him, together with some Observations, where-

(6) *Mr de la Motte.*

in I marked the places which the author had borrowed from the Critical Dictionary,
and where I distinguished the errors which he takes notice of in Moreri, and which
are corrected in the later editions, from those which still remain to be corrected in the
edition of 1725.

(7) *At Rotterdam by Reinier Leers, 1707.*

Mr Bayle at the same time published a fourth volume of his *Answer to the Questions
of a Country Gentleman* (7). He says in the Preface, which is dated November 25
1706, that this fourth volume might have appeared much sooner, if the presses of his
Bookseller had not been employed in large works, which had been begun long before,
and which it much concerned him to finish. The five first sheets of it were printed
before the beginning of April. The principal and largest part of this volume relates
to Mr Bernard's Criticism upon the second volume of the *Continuation of the various
Thoughts*, and turns upon the parallel betwixt Atheism and Paganism, and upon the
question " Whether Christianity be proper to maintain Societies?". Mr Bayle flatters himself that his readers will find here such a variety of arguments, authorities, and
histories, as will not allow them to be tired. " They ought not to fear, (says he)
" that because this is an answer to Mr Bernard, they will find nothing interesting in
" it. Every thing here is as dogmatical, and disengaged from personal disputes, as
" if neither Mr Bernard, nor any other particular person had been in view."

2　　　　　　　　　　　　　　　　　　　　　　　　Mr Bernard

1706. Mr Bernard had likewife made critical Extracts of the firft and fecond volume of the Anfwer to a Country Gentleman (1): Mr Bayle fays, that he could have wifhed to have inferted in this fourth volume an Anfwer which he had made to thefe Extracts. "This Anfwer, adds he, has been finifhed a good while ago, and treats of "matters no lefs curious than important. In a word, it is fuch as might render an "Author impatient to have it publifhed. Neverthelefs he had been obliged to reft "content, that the publifhing of it fhould be referred to the volume which is to follow "this." This fifth volume did not appear till after Mr Bayle's death, and he did not live to revife, correct, and enlarge it as he could have done. Notwithftanding he handles feveral important queftions in it, and examines feveral hiftorical facts with a fcrupulous exactnefs. (1) News from the Republic of Letters, January 1706, art. iv p. 49, and February, art. ii. p. 153.

Mr le Clerc did not leave Mr Bayle's laft Anfwer without a Reply. He repeated his accufations with a great deal of vehemence (2); he maintained that Mr Bayle had not anfwered his principal difficulties, and that what he had objected againft him in his laft piece was vain and frivolous. Mr Bayle had offered to fubmit the decifion of their difference to the Univerfities in Holland: Mr le Clerc anfwered, that he had a much eafier and more honourable way, which was, faid he, to defire an approbation of his Dictionary, his Thoughts concerning Comets, and the Anfwers to the Queftions of a Country Gentleman, in which thefe Univerfities fhould declare, that they find nothing in them contrary to their fentiments, particularly in the articles and chapters concerning the Manicheans, and Predeftination. If they grant him fuch an approbation (adds he) I will fay that I was to blame in denying that he is of their opinion. (2) Bibliotheque Choifie, Tom. x. art. viii, p 364, and the following.

Mr Bayle replied in a book intitled *Dialogues betwixt Maximus and Themiftus: or an Anfwer to what Mr le Clerc has wrote in his Xth volume of the Bibliotheque Choifie, againft Mr Bayle* (3). Maximus and Themiftus examine and criticize each in his turn Mr le Clerc's piece. They labour to defend Mr Bayle's principles, and to fhow that Mr le Clerc has drawn falfe confequences from them. They complain that he frequently difguifeth the ftate of the queftion, and takes no notice of the moft ftrong and moft convincing things which have been anfwered to him. We fee that this difpute had degenerated into reproaches of Author againft Author, and had become in a manner perfonal. Thefe reproaches were attended with many harfh and provoking expreffions. The learned and ingenious Lord Falkland (4) faid, that there ought to be no more fharpnefs in a book of controverfy than in a billet-doux. This maxim concerns Philofophers no lefs than the Controvertifts; or rather all the Learned ought to be Philofophers in this refpect: but when an Author fees that his perfon, his honour, and reputation are attacked, it is very hard for him to contain himfelf. He thinks himfelf obliged to repel thefe injuries, and in his turn to wound his enemy in the moft fenfible parts. (3) Entretiens de Maxime & de Themifte: on Réponfe à ce que Mr le Clerc a écrit dans fon x Tome de la Bibliotheque Choifie contre Mr Bayle. At Rotterdam, by Reinier Leers, 1707.

The attacks which were made upon Mr Bayle from all quarters, gave Mr Jurieu frefh courage. He thought the occafion favourable, and that he ought to make ufe of it. He publifhed a little book intitled, *The Philofopher of Rotterdam accufed, attainted, and convicted* (5). He repeats here his old accufations againft Mr Bayle, though they had been refuted in a manner which had reduced him to filence. He beftows great encomiums on Meffieurs Jaquelot and Bernard, whom he had perfecuted on fufpicion of Herefy: he treats Mr le Clerc in the fame manner, whom he mortally hated. But thefe gentlemen had wrote againft Mr Bayle, he brings them in evidence againft him, and he would not difcredit his own witneffes. In the mean while he could not help mixing fome ftrokes of fatire with thefe panegyrics, he malicioufly hints at their former difgraces and heterodox opinions. But he made ufe of a cunning fhift in doing this. He related under the name of Mr Bayle and of his friends, the reafons which might be alledged againft admitting thefe three witneffes, and joins himfelf with them. "He is very diverting (fays he (6), and his friends with him, in the re- "proaches which they throw out againft thefe witneffes. The Rotterdam Divine "is conceited, fond to diftraction of his own productions, vaftly in love with fu- "perlatives, and difcontented with the bad reception of his works. Mr Jaquelot "has been piqued upon hearing that Mr Bayle had fpoke with fmall efteem of "his book concerning the exiftence of God. Befides he is a man more than fufpected, "and has not extricated himfelf with honour out of certain affairs. Another has "been cenfured by the Synods. The third is a Pelagian and Socinian, convicted "of herefy and impiety." Mr Jurieu is at much pains to find fome difference betwixt his principles and thofe of Mr Bayle. We may judge with what fuccefs by the account he gives of his own fyftem, which he reduceth to thefe three points (7): " I. That God could have no other end in his works, in his decrees, in his pro- "vidence, than his own glory; from which it follows that all the difpofitions of "the divine providence are juft, wife, and reafonable, how hard foever they appear "to the flefh and oppofite to the intereft of the creatures. II. That there is nothing "in man, or in human things, like what is in God; the names of *Being, Subftance*, "*Thinking-fubftance, Will, Underftanding, Liberty, Right, Juftice*, and fuch like, are all "equivocal, and do not fignify in God what they fignify in man, fo that it is in "vain to compare the conduct and rights of God with regard to man, with the "rights (4) Killed at the Battle of Newbury September, 20, 1643. (5) Le Philofophe de Rotterdam accufé, atteint, & convaincu. The title bears that it is printed at Amfterdam, but the Printer's name is not mentioned. (6) Le Philofophe de Rotterdam, &c. p. 39, 40. (7) Ibid. pag. 113, and the following.

VOL. I.   e e

"rights of men with regard to one another; and all arguments drawn from thence 1706.
"are sophisms, being founded on comparisons betwixt things not to be compared to-
"gether, to wit, God and the creature, and the rights of God and those of man.
"III. But what *puts an end to all dispute*, is *the sovereign right which God has over
"his creatures*: that power without bounds, ought to silence man, with regard to every
"thing that troubles him, or startles his reason in the conduct of providence; and
"consequently this utterly confounds all the prophane and impious difficulties which
"the Author of the Dictionary furnisheth to the Manicheans and Paulicians, and
"which he displays in so pompous a manner."

Mr Jurieu shows that St Paul had foreseen and mentioned these difficulties in his
(1) *Chap.* Epistle to the Romans (1), and that he answers them by showing that the sovereign
ix *and* xi. right which God has over his creatures ought to silence Reason. Mr Jurieu observes
that St Paul concludes the dispute with this beautiful and sublime exclamation, *O the
depth of the riches both of the wisdom and knowledge of God! how unsearchable are his
judgments, and his ways past finding out! For who hath known the mind of the Lord, or
(2) Le *who hath been his counsellor?* "It is as clear as the sun (adds Mr Jurieu (2), that by
Philoso- "these words the Apostle designs to rebuke the rashness of those pretenders to learn-
phe de "ing, who demand that all difficulties should be solved by the way of human Reason
Roterdam "and of their philosophical axioms, and that we should confess that human reason
&c. *pag.* "is incompatible with Divine Revelation, as if what is above reason must needs al-
128, 129 "ways be against reason." It is plain that Mr Jurieu had Mr Bayle in view here;
but neither doth he forget Mr le Clerc and Mr Jaquelot. "We must confess like-
"wise (adds he), that this pious exclamation of St Paul shows the error of those
"Divines, who would reconcile Reason and Revelation by Pelagian maxims. Surely,
"if it be true, as these Gentlemen pretend, that in order to get out of this labyrinth
"we need only suppose man absolute master of his free-will and of his actions, this
(3) Ibid. "exclamation *O the depth &c*, and *how unsearchable are his judgments &c*, appears
pag. 118, "neither very well grounded, nor very necessary. For there is no difficulty left,
119. "when we say, that God has forsaken man because he made a bad use of his free
(4) Exa- "will." Here he only repeats what he had a little before said in a more strong manner
men de la and more at large. "I would willingly know (says he (3), why so many divines
Théologie "are afraid of this hypothesis, (*of the sovereign right of God over his creatures*); and
de Mr "choose rather to cry up the dignity of a free creature, and the excellence of liberty.
Bayle, ré- "This is good; but it is of no use in this question, and besides it leads to Pela-
panduë "gianism. By shutting one gate, as we imagine, against the impieties of the Mani-
dans son "cheans and Pyrrhonians, we open another, or at least leave another open; for we
Diction- "are under a necessity of owning, that God is the Author of that free-will which he
naire Cri- "has bestowed upon man, and that he is master of it to stop the course of its
tique, dans "disorders when he thinks proper. So that we shall never be able to stop the mouths
ses Pen- "of the prophane by this means."
sée sur les
Cometes, This is precisely what Mr Bayle had said: however he did not think fit to take
& dans ses any advantage from this piece; he did not think it worthy of his notice. He had
Réponses before sufficiently shown the conformity of what he had advanced, with Mr Jurieu's
à un Pro- doctrine.
vincial;
où l'on Mr Jaquelot had not begun his dispute with Mr Bayle to make an end of it so soon,
defend la he returned once more to the charge; but instead of confining himself to the three es-
Confor- sential heads of this controversy, he digressed to other matters which either entered
mité de la only incidentally into it, or which had not indeed the least relation to it. He however
Foi avec by this means pursued his design, which was to represent Mr Bayle as a person who attack-
la Raison, ed Religion. He intitled his Reply, *An Examination of Mr Bayle's Theology, dispersed
contre sa in his Critical Dictionary, in his Thoughts concerning Comets, and in his Answers to a Country
Réponse. Gentleman; wherein the Conformity betwixt Faith and Reason is defended against his An-
(5) *Letter* *swer* (4). Mr Bayle gave the following judgment concerning this performance in a
to Mr la letter to one of his friends (5). "I will tell you in confidence that Mr Jaquelot's
Croze of "book is full of malice, insincerity, and weak reasoning. He departs as well as I
the 25*th* "from the common notions of goodness and holiness, and consequently he is wounded
of October "by all the thrusts Mr le Clerc has made against me. I shall not fail to make this ob-
1706, *p.* "servation which will embarass my accuser; for he is Mr Jaquelot's friend, and even
1121. "revised his manuscript." Mr Bayle answered Mr Jaquelot by way of Dialogue, as he
(6) Entre- had done Mr le Clerc. This Answer is intitled, *Dialogues betwixt Maximus and Themistus:
tiens de or an Answer to Mr Jaquelot's Examination of Mr Bayle's Theology* (6). Mr Bayle in the
Maxime beginning observes, that he might neglect the first three hundred and four pages of
& de The- Mr Jaquelot's Reply which consists of four hundred and seventy two, because they do
miste: ou not concern the main point in the present controversy. The dispute had been reduced
Réponse à to these three points. I. The liberty of indifference. II. The Origin of Evil. III. The
l'Examen objections which Pyrrhonism might found upon some doctrines of Revealed Religion.
de la The- With regard to the first, Mr Bayle observes that it is not necessary to insist upon it.
ologie de "Mr Jaquelot, says he (7), ought to have abandoned it entirely in his Reply, since
Mr Bayle, "Mr Bayle had given him a carte blanche, that is to say, had allowed him to show
par Mr Ja- "himself intirely Pelagian, since he had attacked him concerning the Origin of Evil,
quelot. "without supposing any other principle but the liberty of indifference. Mr Jaquelot
(7) Entre- notwithstanding
tiens de
Maxime
& de The-
miste &c.
p. 4, 5.

THE LIFE OF Mr BAYLE.

1706. "notwithstanding (adds he), has re-handled this question as a matter of great impor-
"tance; Whether man is possessed of this liberty or not. His great itch for rea-
"soning in the Arminian way has occasioned this. He shows the same impatience
"which new converts do, who presently publish the motives of their conver-
"sion."

Mr Bayle reproacheth Mr Jaquelot with five faults. I. That he has attacked Mr Bayle's doctrine, without seeming to know that it is the same with that of the Reformed, and afterwards seems to believe it to be very different from it. II. That he believes that the same doctrine is innocent or blameable according to the different intentions of those who teach it. Mr Bayle had shown that Mr Jurieu had taught, before him, that no system could solve the objections which may be made against the fall of Adam and its consequences, and that he had laid down the same difficulties which Mr Bayle has done. Mr Jaquelot had been asked why he did not sooner attack this doctrine, which as he imagines tends to make God author of sin, and to destroy Religion. To this Mr Jaquelot here answers (1), that he did not (1) Exa-write against Mr Jurieu, *because he believed him sincere in his System*, and that he had men de la *not directly struck at any of the fundamentals of Religion*: but that he thought fit to refute Theolo-Mr Bayle, because he believed him ill persuaded of the System established by the Bayle, p. Synod of Dort, and ill affected towards the principles of Religion. Mr Bayle thinks 66, 67, this a very extraordinary distinction. No body (says he) has ever thought of distinguishing things of this sort. It has been always believed that if two Authors maintain the same doctrine, it was impossible to refute the one without refuting the other. He puts Mr Jaquelot in mind of his declaration in the preface to his first book, *that he had no intention of attacking either Mr Bayle's person or morals, or of diving into his intentions*, which declaration he had repeated in the body of the book in these words: *I do not at all desire to dive into this Author's secret views. . . . . . l:t us forbear rash judgments* (2). But in his second book he continually affirms that Mr (2) Con-Bayle has very bad intentions. Mr Bayle asks him whence he has got this new light, formit de and ascribes this change in his conduct to his being irritated by the bad success of la Raison his attack. He adds that Mr Jaquelot, even when he was writing his Reply, having &c. p. 222. foreseen that the heat of the dispute and the necessity of having pretexts, would oblige him to repeat his rash judgments a thousand times over, had formally disavowed them and made a sort of retractation. *I only wish*, says he: (3), *that the reader* (3) Exa-*may remember that I do not pretend to speak either of Mr Bayle's person or his morals. . . .* men &c. *The title of this chapter*, says he some pages after (4), *sufficiently shows that I do not* p. 60. *desire to speak either of Mr Bayle's intention or of his morals*. (4) Ibid.

The third fault with which he reproacheth Mr Jaquelot, is, that he affirms that p. 78. Mr Bayle deprives man of all sort of liberty. To this it had been already answered, that Mr Bayle had neither affirmed or denied any thing on that subject, and that a discussion of that question was useless, because Mr Bayle had agreed to dispute with him as a Pelagian. He had attacked him all along, even supposing the liberty of indifference, and by showing that this liberty doth not at all weaken the Manichean objections. Mr Bayle therefore was not concerned to refute it, and yet he could have done it without destroying all sort of liberty, since the Contra-Remonstrants who reject the liberty of indifference, nevertheless maintain that man acts freely since he acts voluntarily and deliberately. Now Mr Bayle never undertook to deprive man of this kind of liberty. He next shows what might have deceived Mr Jaquelot, and led him aside from the true state of the question.

The fourth fault of Mr Jaquelot, is, that he attacks Mr Bayle concerning the Conformity of Faith with Reason, and yet says at bottom the same thing that he has done. People believed upon reading the title of his first book, *The Conformity of Faith with Reason, &c.* that he had undertaken to show this conformity according to the plan laid down in the Answer to a Country Gentlemen, which is in substance this " (5) We must show that we not only have philosophical maxims agree- (5) Ré-
" able to our Faith, but likewise that the particular maxims which are objected to ponse aux
" us as not conformable to our Catechism, are really conformable to it in a manner Questions
" which may be distinctly conceived. . . . . (6) This Conformity requires not only vincial,
" that your Thesis be agreeable to several philosophical maxims, but likewise that Tom. iii,
" it be not successfully attacked by any other maxims of reason. Now it will be p. 685.
" successfully attacked by them, if you cannot defend yourself otherwise than by (6) Ibid.
" unintelligible distinctions, or by excusing yourself on account of unfathomable depth p. 687.
" of the subject." It was easy for Mr Jaquelot (adds he) to perceive, even before he read the above plan, that it is this which is wanted when we desire a proof of the Conformity of Faith with Reason. But he has been very far from writing upon this plan. "When I speak of the Conformity of Faith with Reason (says he in his
" first book (7), I mean that we ought not to renounce our Reason, in order to (7) Exa-
" embrace Religion. For though there be Mysteries in Religion which Reason can- men &c.
" not sufficiently comprehend, it doth not follow from this that those mysteries p. 297.
" are contrary to reason. In the same manner it doth not follow that the infinite di-
" visibility of body and motion, are contrary to Reason, though Reason cannot
" answer the difficulties which may be objected against these propositions." It is

observed

observed, that if Mr Jaquelot hath nothing else to advance he has attacked Mr Bayle 1706. very groundlessly, since Mr Bayle never said that we ought to renounce our Reason in order to embrace Religion, and on the contrary has repeated a thousand times, that we cannot act more agreeably to reason, than in preferring the authority of the Scripture to the philosophical maxims which set themselves in opposition to our mysteries. Thus he shows that it is in vain for Mr Jaquelot to pretend to make a difference betwixt his doctrine and that of Mr Bayle, and that it appears by the state of the question laid down by Mr Bayle, that Mr Jaquelot and he do not really differ in their sentiments.

The fifth fault he finds with Mr Jaquelot is, that he has undertaken an accommodation which was not at all necessary. He declares that it is his intention to show that we ought not to renounce our Reason in order to embrace Religion. Now all the world knew that they who admit the Trinity, and the other mysteries of the Gospel, believe themselves very reasonable, and that far from renouncing their reason, they found their belief upon philosophical axioms, which are in the highest degree evident and certain. They found their belief on this, that God can neither deceive nor be deceived, and consequently that what he says ought always be believed; and they employ Reason to find out the true sense of Scripture. Every body likewise knew, that it is not a just cause of rejecting a doctrine, because it is liable to great difficulties; and that the pre-eminence of the divine nature doth not allow us to subject it to the same duties by which men are tied to one another. All these truths are commonly known, and it is not this we expect from those who promise to show the Conformity of Faith with Reason. We expect that they should show that our theological systems are united with Reason by these very maxims, which it furnisheth to the enemy, and on which the objections are founded; and that the solution which they give shall discover the medium by which these philosophical maxims and theological hypotheses are connected together. But this is what Mr Jaquelot hath not done. He has been so frighted at the plan of reconciliation which was pointed out to him, betwixt seven theological propositions and nineteen philosophical propositions, that he has not had the courage to approach them: he has only pretended that these nineteen propositions " are false maxims, which ought not at all to be made use " of in the present question (1)." Mr Bayle had owned that we ought to renounce the common notions of goodness and holiness in judging of the providence of God with regard to evil. This confession had displeased several people. It is upon this that Mr le Clerc grounds his accusation against Mr Bayle of destroying religion. But since Mr Jaquelot likewise refuses our common notions, and affirms that the damned will suffer eternally, he ought to think himself involved in Mr le Clerc's accusation, as an accomplice in the pretended impieties of Mr Bayle. From this he draws another proof, that nothing could be more deceitful than the title of Mr Jaquelot's first piece: *The Conformity of Faith with Reason; or a Defence of Religion, against the principal difficulties dispersed in Mr Bayle's Dictionary.* To rectify this title, we ought to change it as follows: *The imperfect Conformity of Faith, with some maxims of Reason; or a dispute with Mr Bayle, wherein it is acknowledged that the philosophical maxims, which he believed to be irreconcileable with our systems of Divinity, are really so.* After this follows an examination of the five principles which Mr Jaquelot substitutes to the common notions which he has rejected, and it is shown that they are not sufficient to satisfy reason. It is observed, that Mr Jaquelot, not being able to answer the difficulties which Mr Bayle had raised against his first work, had no other resource than to invent a new System, under favour of which he might get rid of these objections which it was not possible for him to evade, if he had continued in his first principles. Mr Bayle shows, that by this new System Mr Jaquelot retracts all that he had said in his first book, in justification of the permission of sin, on pretence that the glory of God is interested in it. He examines this new System, and proves that it is of no use in the solution of the difficulties in question. He maintains, that it evidently follows from Mr Jaquelot's system, that God has willed sin, and is, properly speaking, the cause of it. He proves that this Minister has in vain pretended, that free-will solves all the difficulties touching the origin of evil. He refutes his doctrine concerning the permission of evil, and also what he answered concerning physical evil, and Pyrrhonism, and gives an answer to several remarks which he had made on the third volume of the Answer to a Country Gentleman. Lastly, he gives the reasons why he had not examined the first 303 pages of Mr Jaquelot's reply, and had contented himself with making a few observations, which regard principally the collection of difficulties which he had drawn out of the Critical Dictionary, and to which he had joined some reflexions.

In this work Mr Bayle complains that Mr Jaquelot has made no answer to a great many embarrassing difficulties; that he abounds in shifts and disguises; that he treads sincerity under foot, in order to follow the motions of personal hatred; that he wants only to chicane and conceal difficulties; that he mutilates the passages which he quotes from his adversary, and affects to talk contemptibly of his book: he observes that he is sometimes so confounded that he attacks his own principles; that he abandons himself too much to his presumption; that he is

(1) Pag. 317.

THE LIFE OF Mʀ BAYLE.   cxiii

too proud to acknowledge that he ever has been miftaken, &c. This ftile was not natural to Mr Bayle: he ufed to difpute without departing from the bounds of moderation. On the contrary he ufed to diffemble or excufe the faults of his adverfaries, and foften his criticifms with a thoufand polite and obliging ftrokes. But he was foured and piqued by feeing that his perfon rather than his fentiments was attacked, and that nothing was omitted in order to draw the indignation of the public upon him. This manner of proceeding feemed very unreafonable to difinterefted perfons. Mr de Bauval complained of it. "If Mr Bayle (fays he (1), has " had fecret and dangerous defigns againft Religion, that is Mr Bayle's particular " concern, the public are not interefted in it. They who only feek after truth, will " not be at much pains to examine whether the accufations againft Mr Bayle be " well founded or not. They will mind only the principle caufe. Now it is re- " markable that his antagonifts attack him alone on this head, though it is certain " that almoft all the Roman Catholics, and the greateft part of the Proteftants " loudly maintain the fame thing [R]. Why fhould they fingle him out, and fall
    "fo

(1) Hiftory of the Works of the Learned. December 1706. p. 544.

[R] *The greateft part of the Proteftants loudly maintain the fame thing.*] They who undertook to confute Mr Bayle upon Arminian principles, durft not deny that his doctrine was the fame with that of the Reformed. They faved themfelves only by faying that he had bad intentions. They in the mean while attacked the opinion of the Reformed, and pretended that it was liable to Mr Bayle's objections, Mr Jaquelot feeing that Mr Jurieu had declared, that it was in vain to exalt the free-will of man, and that this hypothefis was not capable of folving difficulties (*a*), made an addition to his laft book, in which he chargeth Mr Jurieu's fyftem with all the confequences of the Manicheans. Thus Mr Bayle's adverfaries refuted one another, and in their turns adjudged him the victory. "I cannot imagine, fays Mr Jaquelot (*b*), how a Divine, who has well underftood Mr Bayle's objections againft the hypothefis of thofe who for all anfwer content themfelves *with impofing filence on reafon*, doth not perceive that it will follow from this method of arguing, that human reafon may be convinced, by good and neceffary confequences, " that God is the caufe of evil, and the author of fin." He declares that " (*c*) all they who will not abandon " the hypothefes on which Mr Bayle has founded his " difficulties, are indifpenfibly obliged to fhew the " falfhood of his confequences, and of his objecti- " ons, in a manner capable of fatisfying the confcience " of a knowing and reafonable man. Otherwife it " is pure obftinacy, and a falfe honour, to refolve to " continue in principles from which fuch horrible " confequences are drawn." Mr le Clerc approved of this judgment. " Mr Jaquelot obferves very well " (fays he (*d*), that if we grant to Mr Bayle, that " Reafon cannot make a good reply to the confe- " quences which he draws againft Religion, from " the doctrine of abfolute Predeftination, this is " to own, that thefe confequences are fairly drawn, " and confequently that the doctrine is falfe. We " muft allow this or renounce all Logic." Mr le Clerc adds, " that the political intereft which fome " people had formerly in maintaining Abfolute Pre- " deftination having ceafed, it was high time to " renounce a doctrine, from which they fee con- " fequences are drawn which they own they cannot " anfwer."

On the other fide, Mr la Placette, not content with Mr le Clerc's and Mr Jaquelot's hypothefes, thought himfelf obliged to anfwer the Manichean objections by the principles of the Calvinifts. But as he was a man of great moderation, he carried his regard for Mr Bayle fo far as not to name him. His book is intitled *An Anfwer to two objections which are oppofed on the part of Reafon to what faith teacheth us concerning the origin of evil, and the myftery of the Trinity &c (e).* "Some diftinguifhed authors, (fays he (*f*), " have undertaken to anfwer thefe objections, efpeci- " ally the firft which is the moft plaufible. But as they " have built upon principles which do not appear to " me to be at all folid, and which are not even uni- " verfally acknowledged; it were to be wifhed " that fome other would undertake this task, and " examine thefe objections by comparing them " with more folid and lefs contefted principles " Mr le Clerc fpeaking of this work of Mr l. Placette, obferved (*g*) " that it was compofed before Mr Bayle's
VOL. I.

" death, but luckily it was not publifhed during his " life. If Mr Bayle had feen it, fays he, I am fure, con- " fidering his humour, that he would have fheltered " himfelf under the reputation of this Divine. He " would have faid, that he was ready to fubfcribe " this book, without changing his opinion, and " would have pretended to be as orthodox as Mr la " Placette, to whom on other accounts no body will " compare him." Was not this to confefs, that Mr Bayle's principles were agreeable to thofe of this learned and judicious Divine?

Mr Naudé in 1708 publifhed a book intitled, *The fovereign perfection of God in his divine attributes, and the perfect integrity of the Scripture taken in the fenfe of the ancient Reformers, defended by right reafon againft all the objections of Manicheifm difperfed in Mr Bayle's writings (h)*. In this work Mr Naudé oppofeth the fyftem of the Supralapfarians to the Manichean objections, being perfuaded that this is the only hypothefis whereby they can be folved. So he is very far from approving of the hypothefis of Dr King, Mr le Clerc, and Mr Jaquelot; nay he even refutes them with a great deal of vivacity, and at length endeavours to fhow that Mr Jaquelot has not folidly anfwered Mr Bayle. He moreover maintains, that Mr Bayle has triumphed over Mr Jaquelot and Mr le Clerc. " Mr Jaquelot, fays he (*i*), fol- " lowing a fyftem merely of human invention, en- " deavours to juftify God from the blame of being " in any fort the author of fin. But he acquits him- " felf very indifferently, fince by drawing confe- " quences which neceffarily follow from his doctrine, " we muft conclude that God is the author of fin, " whatever Mr Jaquelot can fay to the contrary, and " Mr Bayle's laft work (*k*) has proved this in an in- " conteftable manner. Befides, he makes God au- " thor of fin in a much more odious manner. He po- " fitively denies doctrines founded on a hundred paf- " fages of Scripture, he therefore gives it the lie, " which alone is fufficient to pluck up Chriftianity " by the roots. Moreover Mr Jaquelot frequently " contradicts himfelf, and frequently contradicts " right reafon. All Chriftians therefore notwith- " ftanding his anfwer are reduced to the ftraits to " which Mr Bayle pretends to have pufhed them. " Mr le Clerc with his Origenifm, adds Mr Naudé, " is ftill more unfuccefsful than Mr Jaquelot, fince " he more formally contradicts the Scripture, and " falls likewife under the fame inconveniencies. So " both the one and other have been entirely defeated " by this laft book of Mr Bayle. I defire to be " judged in this by thofe who have been fpectators " of the combat.'

The reader will perhaps not be difpleafed to hear Mr Bafnage's judgment of this difpute. " Two " pieces fays, he in a letter to me (*l*), have lately ap- " peared againft Mr Bayle, one by Mr la Placette, " the other by Mr Jaquelot, which I have not feen. " Methinks they may be eafily fet to combat one " againft the other. If a man be a Predeftinarian in " the terms of the Synod of Dort, he will look upon " the anfwers of Meffieurs le Clerc, Bernard, and Ja- " quelot as bad: and the Arminians imagine that he " cannot be well anfwered by the ordinary fyftem. " One cannot fay that he is well anfwered whatever " fyftem they take. For on the contrary, each party
ff   " pretends

(*a*) See above, p. cx.

(*b*) Addition à l'Examen de la Theologie de Mʳ Bayle, &c. p. 475, 476.

(*c*) Ibid. pag. 478.

(*d*) Bibliotheque choifie, Tom. xi. p. 412, 413.

(*e*) Réponfe à deux Objections, qu'on oppofe de la part de la Raifon à ce que la Foi nous apprend fur l'origine du mal, & fur le myftere de la Trinité, &c. primed at Amfterdam in 1707.

(*f*) Réponfe à deux Objections, &c. Preface fol. *3.

(*g*) Biblioth. choifie, Tom. xiii. p. 415, 416.

(*h*) La fouveraine perfection de Dieu dans fes divines attributs, &c. printed at Amfterdam in 2 Vol. in 12mo.

(*i*) La fouveraine perfection de Dieu, Pref pag. xxxiv, xxxv.

(*k*) Entretiens de Maxime & de Themifte, &c.

(*l*) Letter of the 19th of Aug. 1707.

cxiv   THE LIFE OF Mʀ BAYLE.

"so bitterly upon him alone, why do they make no account of the great multitude   1706.
"of Divines who are on his side? This is one of the principal points in the dispute
"betwixt him and his adversaries, on which however they have insisted very little.
"Methinks this is what they ought to have principally laboured: otherwise they
"may be suspected of having designed less to defend Religion, than to revenge
"themselves against Mr Bayle."

Mr Bayle for above six months had been ill of a decay of the lungs, which weakened him sensibly. As this was a hereditary distemper he judged it mortal, and his friends could not persuade him to take any remedy. He saw death approaching without either fearing or desiring it. He laboured constantly, and with the same tranquillity of mind as if death had not been ready to interrupt his work. In a Letter of thanks which he wrote to my Lord Shaftsbury, he gave an account both

(1) *Letter of the 29th of October 1706, p. 1124. See likewise a Letter to Mademoiselle Baricove of the 28th of October 1706, p. 1122, 1123.*

of his occupations and of his illness. "I should have thought (says he (1), that a "dispute with Divines would have put me out of humour, but I find by experience "that it serves for an amusement to me in the solitude to which I have reduced myself. "For as my disease is a disorder in my lungs, nothing pains me more than speaking. "I therefore neither make nor receive visits, but I divert myself with answering "Mr le Clerc and Mr Jaquelot, whom I find constantly guilty of insincerity."

His Answer to Mr le Clerc was already printed, and the larger part of his Reply to Mr Jaquelot: he had answered every thing that was considerable in the last book which the latter had published, and there was nothing left to be done but to make some remarks, which he reserved for the end of it, when death prevented him. Mr Leers wrote what follows to me on that subject. "(2) Mr Bayle died

(2) *Mr Leers's Letter, January 18, 1707.*

"with great tranquillity, and without any body with him. The evening before his "death, after having studied all day, he gave my Corrector some copy of his An-
"swer to Mr Jaquelot, and told him that he was very bad. Next day at nine of the "clock in the morning his landlady entered his chamber, he asked her, but with a "dying voice, if his fire was kindled, and died a moment after, without Mr Baſ-
"nage, or me, or any of his friends with him." He died the twenty eighth of December 1706, aged fifty nine years one month and ten days. He had at first made a Will in favour of Mademoiselle Bayle, his niece, his eldest brother's daughter; but she having died in the month of October, the same year, he made another at Toulouse, whereby he appointed Mr de Bruguiere, his cousin by the mother's side, his heir. He bequeathed to him ten thousand gilders in money, and all his manuscripts, excepting the Articles which he had composed for a Supplement to his Dictionary, which he gave by way of legacy to Mr Leers. He left all his books of Theology and Ecclesiastical History to Mr Baſnage his Executor; and the rest to Mr Paets, Treasurer of the Admiralty of Rotterdam, as a testimony of his gratitude for the favours which he had received from that honourable family. He left likewise to Mademoiselle Paets a golden medal of which

(3) *See Letter to Mr Ancillon August 13, 1702, p. 915.*

the Count de Dhona had made him a present (3). He was buried in the French Church at Rotterdam: he had left a hundred guilders to the poor of that Church.

He was universally lamented. The *Journal de Sçavans* expressed the sentiments of the public by saying, *that the year could not conclude with a more sensible loss to the Republic of Letters* (4). A great many persons of distinction honoured him with

(4) *Journal des Sçavans, January 1707, p. 207, of the Dutch Edition.*

their friendship. His friends in France were, the Duke of Noailles, the Count de Guiscard, the Marquis de Bonrepaux, the Marquis de Bonac, the Marquis de Bougi, Monsieur and Madame de la Sabliere, Mr du Frêne, Counsellor of the Parliament of Mets, Mr Brodeau d'Oiseville, Counsellor of the same Parliament, and afterwards Lieutenant-General at Tours, Mr Thomassin de Mazaugues, Counsellor of the Parliament of Aix, the Abbé Bignon, Father Malebranche, both the Fathers Lamy, the Abbé Nicaise, the Abbé du Bos, Father de Vitry, Father Sagaens, Messieurs Claude, Mr Bayle, Professor at Toulouse, Mr Rainsant and Mr Oudinet, Keepers of the King's Cabinet of Medals, Mr Charles Perrault, Mr de Benserade, Mr Menage, Mr de Longepierre, Mr de la Monnoye, Mr Marais, Advocate in the Parliament of Paris, Mr de Fontenelle, Mr Lancelot, Mr Simon de Valhebert, Mr Naudis de Bruguiere, Mr du Faï, Mr Janiçon, Advocate in the Council at Paris, Mr de Larroque &c. In England: The Earls of Shaftsbury and Huntington, Dr Burnet, Bishop of Salisbury, Mr Justel, Messieurs de la Riviere and Dubourdieu, who had been Ministers at Toulouse and at Montpellier, Mr Abbadie, Mr Cappel, Professor at Saumur, Mr le Vassor, Mr de la Touche, Messieurs Sylvestre, Buissiere, Baÿze, Pujolas, Coste &c. In Germany: The Counts of Dhona and Reckheim, Messieurs
                                                                                                              Leibniz,

---

"pretends that the other mistakes and wanders from "the point, and is not able to sustain the weight "of Mr Bayle's objections. It is not two different "ways which they take to arrive at the same end, "but two opposite roads, of which the one takes "to the right and the other to the left, and each "maintains that his own road is the only true one. "Add to this, that Mr Bayle has obliged Mr Jaque-
"lot to declare himself Arminian, after having eaten "the bread of the Orthodox for eighteen years, and

"after having made solemn protestations in our Sy-
"nods that he was not so. Mr le Clerc has been o-
"bliged to quit the eternity of punishments; he has "abandoned the doctrine both of the Ancients and "Moderns, without being able to justify Providence, "or solve the difficulties which remain still. For "besides moral evil, there are abundance of physical "evils which give ground for the complaints and ob-
"jections of men."

THE LIFE OF Mr BAYLE.

1706. Leibniz, Thomasius, Budæus, Lenfant, la Croze, le Duchat, de Larrey &c. In Italy: Mr Magliabecchi, Library Keeper to the Great Duke of Tuscany. In Switzerland: Mr Constant, Mr Spon &c. At Geneva: Madam Windsor, Messieurs Minutoli, Bourlamachi, Chouet, Turretin, Leger, Pictet &c. In Holland: The Count de Frifen, the Earl of Albemarle, Mr Le-Leu de Wilhem, the Marquis de Bougi, Mr Paets, Mr de Wit, Mr Grævius, Mr d'Almeloveen, Mr le Moine, Professor at Leyden, Mr Fremont d'Ablancourt, Mr Basnage, Mr de Bauval, Mr Basnage de Flottemanville, Mr Huet, Mr du Rondel, Professor at Maestricht, Mr Drelincourt, Professor at Leyden, Mr Regis, a Physician at Amsterdam, Mr Rou &c. In Flanders: The Countess de Tilly, Baron le Roy, Baron de Walef &c.

In his youth he had been at great pains to take extracts from, and make observations on, the books which he read. He had likewise then composed, or sketched out, some books. His collections were of great use to him when he wrote for the public. He then had hardly any thing more to add to them; his memory was sufficient to point out the sources which he had occasion for. The following is a list of the principal Manuscripts which were found among his papers.

Dissertationis super Virgilii & Homeri poëmatis nuper à quodam Gallo compositæ refutatio: incboata 9 Decembris 1671 (1). It is against Father Rapin.

Amico suo charissimo ac plurimum colendo Jacobo Abbadie Epistola super quæstione, an Deus possit sapientiori perfectiorive modo se gerere quam de facto se gessit (2).

Bælius Fetizoni, vel Responsio Bælii ad Observationes Fetizonis super Epistola prædicta (3).

Collectanea quædam ad Chronologiam, Geographiam, & Historiam pertinentia (4).

Lectiones Historicæ (5). These Lectures compose a body of History from the Creation down to the Roman Emperors. The errors in Chronology of Authors are observed here, and the most difficult points in History are explained.

Lectiones Philosophicæ (6). These Philosophical Lectures are mixed with several strokes of erudition. Spinosa is confuted in them in a very lively manner.

Cursus Philosophicus (7). This Course of Philosophy is divided into four parts; Logic, Moral Philosophy, Physics, and Metaphysics. Mr Bayle composed it for the use of his Scholars, and explained it in his public Lectures. He there recites the opinions of the most famous Philosophers both ancient and modern, and points out their strong and weak side.

"An Abridgment of Plutarch's Lives of Illustrious Men, formed on Amiot's "Version, with collections or extracts from the Roman History, which serve to con-"nect the lives of the illustrious Romans." So that by filling up the chasms which are in Plutarch, from the other Historians, Mr Bayle has composed a compleat System of Roman History.

"An Historical Index." This is a collection of every thing either curious or remarkable in History, which Mr Bayle met with in the course of his reading. It begins from the year 1672. The subjects are distinguished by chapters, and ranged in alphabetical order. For example, under the letter A he treats of the Antiquity which the Egyptians and other people boasted of: and of the remarkable things relating to the Empire of Germany (8). Under the letter B he describes some memorable Battles; and the honours paid to Beasts. Under the letter C he describes singular Ceremonies which were used upon different occasions, and particularly those which relate to the keys of cities. He relates in what manner great men have given an account of affairs with which they were charged &c. There are likewise in this volume, some separate collections relating to Chronology and History.

Judgments, or a Journal of Literature (9). "This collection contains critical reflexions on the books which he had read, and those which had been communicated to him by letter or by word of mouth.

"Letters concerning the dispute betwixt Girac and Costar, and some other letters "on various subjects (10)."

"An Harangue by the Duke of Luxembourg to his Judges, and a Letter concern-"ing the said Harangue (11)."

"A Letter concerning Historical Pyrrhonism."

"A Letter in justification of the Reformed, concerning their first rising in "arms."

"An Historical and Critical Letter concerning the Conference at Poissy."

These three Letters were designed as a continuation to the New Letters concerning Maimbourg's History of Calvinism (12).

"An Historical Discourse concerning the Life of Gustavus Adolphus, King of "Sweden." There are only the two first chapters of it, but they are very long. They were composed after the year 1683, for he mentions the last siege of Vienna by the Turks. The first chapter contains Gustavus's actions unto the Treaty concluded with Poland 1629, some time before he entered Germany in order to make war against the Emperor Ferdinand II. The second treats of the origin of the house of Austria, and of the various fates which it hath undergone. It contains the characters of the late Emperors, and shows that Ferdinand brought all his misfortunes upon himself, and destroyed the power of the House of Austria, by giving himself up to the councils

(1) A Confutation of a Dissertation on Virgil and Homer lately wrote by a certain French Author: begun December 9, 1671.

(2) A Letter to Mr Abbadie on the Question, Whether God could act in a more wise and a more perfect manner than he has done.

(3) An Answer to Mr Fetizon's Observations on the foregoing Epistle.

(4) Collections relating to Chronology, Geography, and History.

(5) Historical Lectures.

(6) Philosophical Lectures.

(7) A Course of Philosophy.

(8) Allemagne.

(9) Jugemens ou Journal de Literature.

(10) Lettres sur la querelle de Girac & de Costar.

(11) See above An. 1680, p. xiii.

(12) See above, An. 1685, p. xxii.

2   of

cxvi   THE LIFE OF Mʀ BAYLE.

of Spain, and by cruelly persecuting the Protestants. This chapter contains an account of the transactions in Germany, and in Bohemia, 'till the year 1620. It is pity Mr Bayle did not finish this work: but imperfect as he has left it, and as neglected as the stile is, one may see that it comes from a masterly hand. It is filled with fine and judicious reflexions, and lively and bold strokes both concerning persons and things. It may serve for a model to Historians.   1706.

The new articles which Mr Bayle had prepared for a Supplement to his Dictionary, and which he bequeathed to Mr Leers, are not many. He himself said, that *this Supplement was but little advanced, and that he was disgusted at that sort of labour, since he had for some years been employed in works of reasoning* (1). He had promised that these new articles should not be incorporated with the new edition of his Dictionary, and that they should be printed and sold a-part, that the public might not be obliged to buy the same thing twice (2): but Mr Leers having left off business his stock fell into the hands of two booksellers, who, without regard to Mr Bayle's intentions, caused it to be inserted in their edition of the Dictionary printed in 1720. And what is yet more essential, they disfigured this edition by the alterations they made in it: they have even sometimes pushed their boldness so far as to change Mr Bayle's stile, and to father entire periods upon him. They had maimed and multilated in the same manner the new edition of the *Philosophical Commentary*, printed by the same Booksellers at Rotterdam in 1713; but they have followed Mr Bayle's original edition in the collection of his *Miscellaneous Works*, which contain, in four volumes in folio, all the works which he published (excepting his Dictionary) and some posthumous pieces (3).

They used *Mr Bayle's Letters* no better, which I sent to these Booksellers, and which they printed in 1714. They presumed to make several alterations and castrations in them. They added Notes to them filled with gross blunders in point of Literature, base and malicious insinuations, and calumnious reflexions on several persons of distinction, and did not even spare Mr Bayle himself. I restored these Letters according to the originals, in an edition published at Amsterdam in 1729, and I joined what explanations I thought necessary to them.

Mr Bayle had a lively, shining, and fruitful imagination, a great deal of discernment and penetration; a natural and bold stile, but not very correct. His conversation was lively, chearful, and the more agreeable that it was always useful. His memory was happy and faithful, and seasonably furnished him with every thing he had entrusted to it. He disputed without heat, and without assuming a dictating tone: and we may observe from his writings, that far from giving offence he was on the contrary rather too much inclined to praise. He was faithful and constant in his friendship, and never was any body more ready to do good offices or more disinterested than he. Far from being greedy of presents, it was with difficulty that he accepted of those which he could not handsomely refuse [S]. Having a strong passion for truth he was exceedingly sensible of any assistance which was given him in the discovery of it, and made use of these helps with the utmost gratitude. He abhorred all sort of fraud and insincerity.

Being a true Philosopher he was without ostentation in his manners, without ambition, and gave himself no airs of superiority over any person. He was sober even to frugality, being indifferent about all pleasures but those of the mind, he seemed to know the passions only to talk of them, and not to feel their effects. Modest even to scrupulousness, he would have for ever concealed his name, if it had been in his power to do it, and it was not owing to him that the public ever saw his picture.

---

(1) *Letter to Mr Des Maizeaux September 21, 1706. pag. 1114.*

(2) *See Letter to Mr Minutoli, January 2, 1702, pag. 843, and Letter to Mr Marais, March 6, of the said year, pag. 859.*

(3) *The posthumous pieces are his Course of Philosophy in Latin, together with a French Translation, and the Fragment on the Life of Gustavus Adolphus.*

[S] *Far from being greedy of presents, it was with difficulty that he accepted of those which he could not handsomely refuse.*] What follows is a proof of this, which I thought not unworthy of the curiosity of the public. The late Earl of Shaftsbury having observed that Mr Bayle had no watch, bought one when he went over to England, with an intention of making him a present of it when he should return to Rotterdam. The difficulty was how to make him accept of it. He took it frequently out of his pocket when they were together, as if to see what a clock it was, but Mr Bayle took no notice of it. At last one day he took it in his hand, and after having examined it, could not help saying that he thought it a very fine one. My Lord Shaftsbury laid hold of that opportunity of offering it to him. But Mr Bayle with great confusion, and piqued that my Lord seemed to have taken what he said without design, as an indirect manner of asking his watch of him, excused himself in the most earnest manner and with great emotion. They disputed a long time, And my Lord Shaftsbury could not persuade him to accept of it, 'till he had assured him that he had brought it from England purposely for him, and proved this by shewing him his own watch.

Some years after, that Lord told me that he designed to send Mr Bayle some Greek and Latin books, printed in England, and desired me to draw up a catalogue of those which would be most acceptable to him. I secretly acquainted Mr Bayle with this, that he might let me know what he had most occasion for. But he would not do it. 'It is " not at all necessary, said he (a), to give my Lord " Shaftsbury any list of books I most humbly thank " him for the favour he designs for me: I have a " sufficient token from him of a fine watch which " he was pleased to force me to accept of. At that " time I thought it a very useless piece of furniture, " but at present it is become so necessary to me, " that I could not now be without it, so that I " every moment feel how much I am obliged to " my Lord for so fine a present."

We may by this instance see what judgment ought to be made of those who have affirmed that he was a pensioner of the Court of France, &c.

(a) *Letter of the 3d of April 1705, pag. 1014, 1015.*

1706. Picture [*T*]. He was jealous to excess, and possibly to weakness, of the glory of his Country, and suffered with impatience that it should be attacked, and secretly despised those who had not the same opinion of it which he had.

The fruitfulness of his imagination and the vast extent of his knowledge frequently threw him into digressions, which notwithstanding he had the art to render useful and even necessary to the consequences which he wanted to draw. His penetration made him at first sight perceive all the different sides of the most abstruse subjects; he discovered all their principles, and unfolded all their consequences. The difficulties which he found in them made him very reserved in his judgments, and frequently left him only reasons for doubting. This caution made some people accuse him of Pyrrhonism. But if it is to be a Pyrrhonian to doubt of things doubtful, should not all men be Pyrrhonians?

It has been complained that he has taken a little too much liberty in his Dictionary, and that he has taken great freedoms with regard to the female sex. These however are only quotations from Authors which are in every bodies hands, and which are generally esteemed. Mr Bayle being less touched with strokes of this kind, than probably those who condemn him, was not shocked at the stile of these writers. He considered their coarse and unpolite expressions as the language of undisguised nature, or, if you will, as innocent liberties, and mere sports of wit, because they excited no disorders in his breast. His manners were always so pure and regular, that his most violent enemies never reproached him with any thing on that head. But in this as in all other things he was not scared at the appearance of vice, because he had a solid love for virtue. No body ought to conclude any thing against Mr Bayle's Religion, from his having related in his Dictionary the difficulties which may be raised against some important doctrines. The laws of dispute required that he should make a faithful report on both sides of the question. But it is plain that he had no intention of destroying these doctrines, because the arguments which he has recited in their favour are stronger than those which he opposeth to them. Mr Jaquelot himself owns this in his *Answer* to the *Dialogues of Maximus and Themistus*, which is one continued invective against Mr Bayle. "Libertines (says he (1), who shall read this Philosopher's works, with under- "standing sufficient to comprehend what they read, may easily discover that he "has advanced reasons for the Existence of God, and the spiritual nature of the "Soul, incomparably stronger than those with which he has furnished Pagans and "others to oppose these important truths." He repeats this likewise in the Preface. Mr Bayle (says he (2), reasons with a great deal more force and evidence when *he establisheth the Existence of God, than when he proposeth the difficulties with which he furnisheth Simonides against this truth...... We ought to make the same judgment of the spirituality of the soul, if we read with application what he says of it, pro and con: and consequently to receive the* Existence of God, *and the* Spirituality of the Soul, *the two foundations of Religion, as principles very agreeable to Reason.* But even they who do not approve of Mr Bayle's sentiments, admire the beauty and fertility of his genius, and the extensiveness of his knowledge; and they who do not do him this justice, and who affect, or pretend, to despise him, that they may raise themselves by debasing him, do not so much disparage Mr Bayle as their own discernment,

(1) Réponse aux Entretiens de Mr Bayle &c. p. 256, 257.

(2) Pref. fol. * 5.

[*T*] *It was not owing to Mr Bayle that the public ever saw his Picture.*] It was desired of him in the most earnest manner, in order to be engraved and prefixed to the English Translation of his Dictionary: but he answered that *could not resolve to sit for his picture, nor to allow it to be placed before his book:* that it was not in his power to conquer that reluctance, and *he begged them to pardon that weakness, if they should be pleased to call it so* (a). The picture which he sent to his Mother was designed to remain in the family, and we are obliged for its being made public to Mr Marais, an Advocate in the Parliament of Paris, and to Madam de Merignac a Lady of distinguished merit, and a great admirer of Mr Bayle's memory and writings. They did not know that Mr Bayle had ever been drawn; but the Letter which he sent to his Mother along with his picture (*b*), falling into Mr Marais hands after the death of Mr Bayle, they had notice that this picture was at Montauban, in the house of one of Mr Bayle's relations. Madam de Merignac got a copy of it, which she gave at her death (*c*) to Mr de Francastel under-library-keeper to the Mazarine College, and Mr Marais caused a copy to be made from it. These are the only two copies of it, which are at Paris. The University of Franefort on the Oder, desired a third from Mr Marais, in order to be placed in a Hall where they had already collected eighty two portraits of famous men. Mr Bayle appears in it of a brown complexion, with lively features and very fine eyes. One easily discovers there his wit and vivacity. Some prints have been engraved at Paris from this picture. One of them was engraved by order of Madam de Merignac and Mr Marais. Mr Marais desired Mr de la Monnoye to write some verses to be placed under that print, and he composed the following Latin Distich:

Bælius hic ille est, cujus dum scripta vigebunt
Lis erit obletient, eruditant ne magis.

Such were Bayle's looks, whose writings justly boast
We know not if they please or profit most.

Another was engraved to be placed before the Geneva Edition of his Dictionary printed in 1715, where we find the following French verses of Mr de la Monnoye, which are an imitation of the above Latin ones:

Tel fut l'illustre Bayle, honneur des beaux esprits,
Dont l'élégante plume, en recherches fertile,
Fait douter qui des deux l'emporte en ses Ecrits,
De l'agréable, ou de l'utile.

(a) Letter to Mr Des Maizeaux of the 3d of Apr. 1705, p. 1013; and of the 3d of July, p. 1024.

(b) See above, in the year 1675, pag. ix.

(c) This Lady died November 11, 1712. Her name was Magdalen Faix d'Obrel, she was of a family of distinction in Flanders; and widow to Mr de Merignac.

ment, and discover more presumption than knowledge. It is common to find men of great learning with little genius, of much wit with little erudition, much solidity without any thing agreeable: but it is rare to find one who has so perfectly united all these qualities as Mr Bayle has done. This made Mr de Saint Evremond say (3),

(3) Mr de St Evremond's Works, Letter to Mr Des Maizeaux, Tom. v. p. 377. Edit. of Amsterdam, 1726.

Qu'on admire le grand savoir
L'erudition infinie
Où l'on ne voit sens, ni génie,
Je ne saurois le concevoir:
Mais je trouve BAYLE admirable
Qui profond autant qu'agréable,
Me met en état de choisir
L'instruction, ou le plaisir.

While some the soph profound admire,
Tho' wanting sense, and wit, and fire,
BAYLE stands my favourite confest,
Whose soul, with every talent blest,
Displays in his still various page,
The chearful wit and learned sage.

The end of the Life.

APPENDIX.

APPENDIX.

CALENDARIUM CARLANANUM.
An Historical and Chronological Journal of the Life of Mr Bayle.

ANNI ÆRÆ CHRIST.	EPOCHA NATIVIT. 18. Nov. 1647. ANNI ÆTAT.		YEARS OF THE CHRISTIAN ÆRA	EPOCH OF MY BIRTH. The 18th of November 1647. YEARS OF MY AGE	
1660, 29. Jun.	13. curr.	Initium stud. L. G.	1660, June 29.	13 current	I began to learn Greek.
1661, Fer. 1. sive Domin. die 25. Decemb.	15. iniens.	Iª. Synaxis.	1661, on Sunday Decemb. 25.	15 near the beginning.	I for the first time received the Holy Communion.
1666, Fer. 6. die 12. Febr.	19. curr.	Iª. Profectio ex Lare paterno PdlRm ; ubi ascript. Iª. Class. 3°. Non. Maij, sub Virodunensi Clepoin.	1666, on Saturday February 12.	19 current	I left my father's house and went to Puylaurens where I entered to the first class. Mr Clepoin of Verdun, was my Regent.
1666.	.	Excursio in triduum Castra.	1666,		I made a journey of three days to Castres.
1666 die 9. Sept.	19. curr.	Reditus Carlan.	1666, September 9.	19 current	I returned to Carla.
1668, die 29. Mai.	21. curr.	Profectus Saverd. & mansio usque ad 4. Kal. Oct. proximas.	1668, May. 29.	21 current	I went to Saverdun where I staid 'till the 28th of September following.
1668, die lunæ 5. Novemb.	21. adsectus.	Egressus Carlan. & profectus Pdirm. mansio usque ad d. 19. fer. 3. mensis Febr. 1669. Logicus.	1668, Monday November. 5.	21 near the end.	I left Carla and went to Puylaurens where I continued till Tuesday February 19, 1669. I began the Study of Logic.
1669, die Feb. 19.	22. curr.	Advent. TLSm.	1669, February 19.	22 current	I arrived at Toulouse.
1669, die 19. Mart. fer. 3.	22. curr.	Transit. ad def. sub Ignat ... no cognomine : postera die iterum Logicus, sub Ignat .. no cognomine urbi quæ sedes Imper. (1)	1669, Tuesday March 19.	22 current	I changed my Religion .. : . Next day I resumed the Study of Logic.
1670, die 19. Aug. fer. 3.	23. curr.	Profect. ex TLSm. & advent. ad villam D. dei Vivié ad Mazer.	1670, Tuesday August 19.	23 current	I left Toulouse and came to a Country seat of Mr du Vivié near Mazeres.
1670, die 21. Aug.	23. curr.	Redit. ad patern. Leg. intra privat. par. moderante Rivall. Saverd. Test. Fratre, Guillemat. & Rivall. respectivè Ecclesi... bus Carlan. Mazer. Calmes.	1670, August 21.	23 current	I returned to the Reformed Religion, and made a private abjuration of the Romish Religion in the hands of Mr Rival Minister of Saverdun; in presence of my Brother the Minister of Carla, of Mr Guillemat Minister of Mazeres, and of Mr Rival Minister of Calmont.
1670, die 21. Aug.	23. curr.	Profect. Lemann. advent. die 5. 7br. fer. 3.	1670, August 21.	23 current	I set out for Geneva, where I arrived on Tuesday September 5.
1670, die 21. Nov.	23. adsect.	Ingress. apud Dm. Neustriæ cognom.	1670, November 21.	23 near the end.	I entered to the house of Mr de Normandie.
1672, die 29. Mai.	25. curr.	Transitus Copet .. n' apud Dm. Comit.	1672, November 21.	25 current	I went to Copet to live with the Count de Dhona.
1674, fer. 3. d. 29. Mai.	27. curr.	Profect. ex Copet. & iter in Neustr. apud D. Rip. advent. 15. Jun. proxim.	1674, Tuesday May 29.	27 current	I left Copet and went to Normandie to live with Mr Rip. I arrived there the fifteenth of June following.
1675 Kal. Mart.	28. curr.	Egress. Roth. ad Urbem: inibi ingress. apud Dm. Ber . . gb. 3. apr. prox.	1675, March 1.	28 current	I went from Rouen to Paris, where I entered to Mr de Beringhen's family, the 3d of April following.
1675, fer; 3. die Aug. 27.	28. curr.	Iter Sed. advent. ultima Aug. die proxim.	1675, Tuesday Aug. 27.	28 current	I set out for Sedan where I arrived on the last day of August.
1675, die 28. Sept.	28. curr.	Inclus. cum rival. ad comp. Thes. quæ prop. 22. Oct. & 23. post merid.	1675, September 28.	28 current	I was shut up with my Competitors to compose my Theses which I defended on the 22d and 23d of October in the Afternoon.
1675 die 2. Nov.	28. adsec.	Recept. à curat. & 4. Nov. prox. Sacramenti præst. ad spartam Philosoph. quæ 14 Jul. 1681. interdict. diplom. regio.	1675, November 2.	28 near the end	I was received by the Moderators of the Academy, and on the 4th of November I. took the oath as Professor of Philosophy. The Academy was suppressed by a Royal Edict July 14. 1681.
1675, fer. 2. Nov. 11.	28. adsec.	I. Exercit. in audit.	1675, Monday November 11.	28 near the end	I began my Public Lectures.

(1) We have not been able to discover the meaning of these words: Sub Ignat .. no (Ignatiano) cognomine Urbi quæ sedes Imperii.

CALENDARIUM GARLANANUM.

ANNI ÆRÆ CHRISTI.	ANNI ÆTAT.		YEARS OF THE CHRISTIAN ÆRA.	YEARS OF MY AGE.	
1681, fer. 3. d. 2. Sept.	34. curr.	Profect. Sed. in urbem, advent. die 7. prox.	1681, Tuesday September 2.	34 current	I left Sedan for Paris, where I arrived on the 7th.
1681, fer 4. d. 8. Oct.	34. adf.	Profect. Urbe Rott. vocat. jussu D. Pa..	1681 Wednesday October 8.	34 near the end	I left Paris for Rotterdam where I was invited by Mr Paets.
1681, fer. 5. d. 30. Oct.	34. adf.	Advent. Rott.	1681, Thursday October 30.	34 near the end	I arrived at Rotterdam.
1681, fer. 6. d. 5. Dec.	35. ineunt.	Or. inaug. ob Prof. ppb. & hist. in Sch. ill. recens erect.	1681, Friday December 5.	35 near the beginning.	My inaugural Oration at entering to my charge of Professor of Philosophy and History, in the Illustrious School lately founded.
1681, fer. 2. d. 8. Decem.	35. ineunt.	I. Lect. ppb. 1682,	1681, Monday December 8.	35 near the beginning.	My first Philosophical Lecture.
1682, fer. 4. d. 11. Mart.	35. curr.	Epist. de comet. absol. impress. Jum. compos. 11. Januar. 1681. missa in Urb. 27. Mai. inseq.	1682, Wednesday March 11.	35 current	The Impression of the Letter concerning Comets was finished, it was composed January 11, 1681, and sent to Paris the 27th of May following.
1682, fer. 3. d. 31. Mart.	35. curr.	Nunc. à D. J. Dam. Pa... paulo ante defunctam legasse duo m. Lb. Bibliotb. 9.	1682, Tuesday March 31.	35 current	I was informed by Mr J. that Madam Paets, lately dead, had left me a Legacy of two thousand gilders to buy books.
1682, fer. 6. die 1. Mai.	35. curr.	Inchoata Crit. G. de l'Hist. du C. absol. 15. d. post. tradita 30. Maii Wolfa. accepta ab illo die 11. Jul. dedit libr. in L.	1682, Friday May 1.	35 current	I began the General Criticism of the History of Calvinism; I finished it on the 15th of the same month, and on the 30th I gave it to Wolfgang, from whom I received it printed on the first of July at which time it was published.
1682, mense Aug.	35. curr.	Visa, emend. & aucta. accepta edit. 2ª. die lunæ 29. Nov. dedit libr. in L.	1682, In the month of August.	35 current	I revised, corrected, and enlarged that work, and received a second edition of it, when it was published on Monday November 29.
1682, mens. Oct.	35. exeunt.	Accepta à D. Fetiz. m.s. Apolog. pro bell. civil. quam mihi sub. noe Philar. d. d. & c. impress. Hag. accepta die 21. Feb. 1683.	1682, In the month of October.	35 near the end	I received from Mr Fetizon the M.S. of his Apology for the Civil-Wars, which he dedicated to me under the name of Philaretus, and which was printed at the Hague, from whence it was sent to me February 21, 1683.
1683, fer. 4. die. 2. Sept.	36. curr.	Absol. 2ª. edit. Ep. ad. D. S. contra præ. Com. dedit Typogr. 120. Exempl.	1683, Wednesday September 2.	36 current	The impression of the second edition of the Letter to a Doctor of the Sorbon against the presages of Comets, was finished. The Booksellers gave me 120 Copies of it.
1683, fer. 4. die 24. Nov.	37. ineunt.	Absol. imprimi à Typogr. Graef Examen Method. à D. Bass. Eccl. Rothom. compositum, & mihi dicat.	1683, Wednesday November 24.	37 near the beginning.	Mr Graef finished the impression of the Examination of the Methods by Mr Basnage Minister at Rouen, who dedicated it to me.
1683, mens. Dec.	37. ineunt.	Absol. imp. Profel. ab. in 12. cujus auth. D. La. R. filius mihi dicav.	1683, In the month of December.	37 near the beginning.	The Impression of the Proselyte abused, in 12mo, was finished: it was wrote by Mr de Larroque the son, and dedicated to me.
1684, fer. 6. die 21. Jan.	37. curr.	Accept. Liber Heidelb. in Bruey exarat. à Theol. Cand. Lanf. postea tradit. Leers Typogr.	1684, Friday January 21.	37 current	I received from Heidelberg, a book against Mr Brueys composed by Mr Lenfant a student of Divinity. I gave it to Mr Leers to be printed.
1684, fer. 5. die 16. Mart.	37. curr.	Acceptum exemplar tractat. in quibus dissertat. lat. in L. à Villa denuò excus. Amstel.	1684, Thursday March 16.	37 current	I received a copy of the Collection which contains a Latin dissertation against Louis de la Ville, reprinted at Amsterdam.
1684, fer. 3. die 21. Mart.	37. curr.	Inchoat. Nunc. Reipub. Litterar. & die 4. Apr. inseq. transact. cum Des B. Typ. Amst. & die 27. Maii accepta exempl. mens. 1; die v. 2. Junii accept. exempl. mensis April.	1684, Tuesday March 21.	37 current	I began the News from the Republic of Letters; and on the 4th of April following, I made an agreement with Des Bordes a Bookseller in Amsterdam: on the 27th of May I received copies of the first month (of March) and on the 2d of June I received copies for the month of April.
1684, fer. 3. die 9. Maii	37. curr.	Accept. Littera vocat. data Leoward. 21. April. Sty. vet. ad Philosoph. Profess. Franek. postera die respons. petens: moram: die v. 9. Junii sequente repons. aliud gratias ag.	1684, Tuesday May 9.	37 current	I received Letters from Leewarden of the 21st of April old style, wherein a Professor of Philosophy's chair in the University at Franeker was offered to me. I answered the day after, and desired time to consider of it. And on the 9th of June following I wrote them a letter of thanks.
1684, fer. 3. die 16. Maii.	37. curr.	Accept. Literæ Paris. à D. de Frejeville nunciant. obitum Fratris Jos. qui defunc. Paris. de morb. 9. Maii.	1684, Tuesday May 16.	37 current	I received letters from Paris, by Mr de Frejeville, giving me an account of my brother Joseph's death, who died at Paris May 9.

1685, fer.

CALENDARIUM CARLANANUM.

ANNI ÆRÆ CHRISTI.	ANNI ÆTAT.		YEARS OF THE CHRISTIAN ÆRA.	YEARS OF MY AGE.	
1685. fer. 2. die 5. Mart.	38. curr.	Accept. Exemplar Nouv. Lettres 2. vol. in 12.	1685, Monday March 5.	38 current	I received a copy of the *New Letters concerning the History of Calvinism*, in two Volumes in 12mo.
1685. fer. 2. die 8. Maii.	38. curr.	Accept. nuncius obit. patris qui contigit die Sabb. 31. mensis Martii.	1685. Monday May 8.	38 current	I received the news of my father's death which happened on Sunday March 31.
1685. fer. 4. die 27. Jun.	38. curr.	Acceptæ Amstel. Literæ Saverd. scriptæ nunciant. Fratrem ductum die 10. Jun. in carcer. Appam. inde 10. Jul. transp. Burdig. in arcem quæ vulgò Chat. Tr. ubi obiit die 12. Novembr. in sequent.	1685, Wednesday June 27.	38 current	Letters came from Saverdun to Amsterdam, which gave an account that my brother was carried a prisoner to Pamiers on the 10th of June, and on the 10th of July was removed to Bourdeaux to the Castle commonly called *Château Trompete*, where he died the 12th of November following.
Mense Octobr.	38. exeunt.	Versa Gallicè Epistola A. Paets de nuperis. Vide Novell. p. 1070.	In the month of October.	38 near the end.	I translated into French Mr Paets's Letter *de nuperis* &c. See the News from the Republic of Letters. p. 1070.
1686. men. Feb. die 25. fer. 2.	39. curr.	Absoluta impress. Responsionis ad Monit. Arnal. circa de sens. volupt. opinion. Mallebr.	1686, Monday February 25.	39 current	They finished the Impression of the *Answer to Mr Arnauld's Advice concerning Father Mallebranche's opinion about the pleasure of the senses*.
Die 6. & 7. men. Mart.	39. curr.	Composita Epist. appendix sut. Libri Deckkerri de adesp.	On the sixth and 7th of March.	39 current	I composed a *Letter* to be placed by way of Appendix to Mr Deckher's book concerning *anonymous Authors*.
Die 22. Mart. fer. 6.	39. curr.	* * * * * * * * * * * *	Friday March 22.	39 current	* * * * * * * * * * * *
Die 28. Octob. fer. 4.	39. desin.	* * * * * * * * (2).	Wednesday October 28.	39 near the end	* * * * * * * * * * * *
1687. fer. 1. die 16. Feb.	40. curr.	Incepi morbo laborare quo intermittere coact. Nouv. de la R. non prorsus peract. mens. Febr.	1687, Sunday February 16.	40 current	I was seized with an illness which obliged me to discontinue the *News from the Republic of Letters*, without being able to finish the month of February.
		Abruptum omnino opus transs. in potest. D. de Beauv. qui novum adorn. mens. 7b. Abruptum quoque Colleg.			I entirely laid down that work and resigned it to Mr de Bauval who published a new Journal in the month of September. I also interrupted my lectures.
Die 10. Jun.	40. curr.	Recept. 3. pars Com. ph. quæ ante morb. absoluta fuer. & Typog. trad. & ante fin. Feb. prorsus typis descr.	June 10.	40 current	I received the third part of the *Philosophical Commentary*, which I had finished before my sickness, and given it to the Bookseller, who had finished the impression before the end of February.
Die 8. Aug.	40. curr.	In viam me dedi tend. Cliv. quo perventum die 13. Aug. postero die in hosp. D. Ferrand. pass. in Castello usque ad 15. Septemb. Hinc Sylv. Ducis, inde Aquis gr. cum D. D. Piel & Farjon. Versus 18. Oct.	August 8.	40 current	I made a journey to Cleves, where I arrived August 13. Next day I went to lodge with Mr Ferrand Minister of the Castle, and continued with him till the 15th of September. From thence I went to Bois-le-Duc, and afterwards to Aix-la-Chapelle, with Mr Pielat and Mr Farjon. I returned to Rotterdam on the 18th of October.

(2) These two passages are cut in the original: the one related to the impression of *la France toute Carbosique*; and the other to the first and second parts of the *Commentaire Philosophique*, which appeared at the same time. The third part is mentioned here below, June 10, 1687.

An ORDER of MR DE LA REYNIE, Lieutenant-General of the Police of the City, Provoſtſhip, and Viſcounty of Paris, concerning the GENERAL CRITICISM on Mr Maimbourg's HISTORY OF CALVINISM. By the King, and the Provoſt of Paris, or his Lieutenant-General of the Police.

WHEREAS it has been repreſented to us by the King's Attorney, that certain diſaffected perſons have imported and ſold in this City, ſeveral copies of a book, intitled, *A General Criticiſm on Mr Maimbourg's Hiſtory of Calviniſm*, printed, as the title page bears, at Ville-Franche by Pierre le Blanc in 1682, wherein the Author of the ſaid book, inſtead of a juſt and ſober Criticiſm allowed to men of Letters and erudition, has had the boldneſs, under the ſpecious title of a Criticiſm, to advance ſeveral calumnious and pretended facts, which tend under a falſe zeal for Religion to corrupt the fidelity of ſubjects: and it being for the intereſt of the public that the ſale of ſo pernicious a book ſhould be prevented, and that they who ſhall be found to be the Authors, or Printers, Importers, Sellers, or Venders of the ſame, ſhould be puniſhed according to the rigour of the laws; and the King's Attorney having deſired that we ſhould take cognizance thereof. WE having ſeen the ſaid book, intitled, *A General Criticiſm on Mr Maimbourg's Hiſtory of Calviniſm*, printed at Ville-Franche by Peter le Blanc in 1682, as the title bears, containing 338 Pages, and divided into 22 Letters: WE in purſuance of the ſaid petition have declared the book intitled *A General Criticiſm on Mr Maimbourg's Hiſtory* diffamatory and calumnious, and filled with bold and ſeditious forgeries, and as ſuch we order it to be lacerated and burnt at the Greve, by the hands of the hangman; and that, at the requeſt and by the care of the King's Attorney, informations may be drawn up againſt thoſe who have compoſed, printed, imported, ſold, or vended the ſaid book, and that proceſs may be commenced and proſecuted againſt thoſe who ſhall be found guilty, according to the rigour of the law. EXPRESSLY forbidding all Printers and Bookſellers to print, vend, or ſell, the ſaid book, under the pain of death; and all other perſons, of what quality and condition ſoever, to make any traffic or ſale of the ſame under the pain of exemplary puniſhment: and this preſent Order ſhall be publiſhed and affixed in the uſual and accuſtomed places; and particularly in the Hall of the Bookſellers and Printers of this City, that no body may pretend ignorance of the ſame. Given by Mr GABRIEL NICOLAS DE LA REYNIE Counſellor of State in ordinary, and Lieutenant-General of the Police of the City, Provoſtſhip, and Viſcounty of Paris, the ſixth day of March, one thouſand ſix hundred and eighty three,

Signed

DE LA REYNIE.

DE RIANTZ. SAGOT, Regiſter.

The above Order was read, publiſhed, and affixed with ſound of trumpet, and public proclamation, in the uſual and accuſtomed places, by me Mark Anthony Paſquier, ſworn Cryer in ordinary to his Majeſty, in the ſaid City, Provoſtſhip, and Viſcounty of Paris, living near the Hôtel des Urſins, accompanied with Stephen du Bos, ſworn Trumpeter to his Majeſty, Philip le Sieü and Louis la Coſte, deputy Trumpeters, March 9, 1683.

Signed

PASQUIER.

PRINTED BY DENIS THIERRY, IN THE RUE S. JAQUES.

ACTS OF THE CONSISTORY OF THE WALLOON CHURCH OF ROTTERDAM, CONCERNING THE SIEUR BAYLE'S HISTORICAL AND CRITICAL DICTIONARY.

November 3, 1697.

THE Committee appointed by an Act of the fifteenth of September laſt, having made a report that they had examined the Extracts which Meſſieurs de Superville and le Page, Miniſters, had made of the paſſages of a book of the Sieur Bayle, intitled, *An Hiſtorical and Critical Dictionary*, which relate to obſcenities, and that having compared theſe Extracts with the ſaid book, they had therein found obſcene reflections, indecent expreſſions and queſtions, and a great many obſcene quotations, as is more fully expreſſed in a Memoir which they produced concerning the ſame, wherein theſe paſſages are marked. Whereupon the Conſiſtory have thought fit, that the ſaid Memoir ſhould be kept by their Secretary, to be produced when they ſhall come to a general deliberation with regard to the ſaid book, and mean while the other members of the Conſiſtory, may further examine the ſaid Memoir, and make their remarks upon it betwixt this and a fortnight hence. And it has been thought proper in the mean time that this Act and others of the ſame nature, which ſhall be made on this ſubject, ſhall not be regiſtered in the book of Acts, except by the expreſs order of the Conſiſtory. *November*

ACTS OF THE CONSISTORY &c.
November 17, 1697.

The term of a fortnight appointed by the preceeding Act for making remarks on the Memoir mentioned in the said Act being now elapsed, the other members of the Consistory were asked, if they had made any remarks on the same, and no body having declared that they had made any, the Report contained in the said Memoir was agreed to and held as the opinion of the Consistory.

The same Day.

The Committee above-mentioned having made a Report that they had examined the Extracts which Messieurs de Superville and le Page, Ministers, had made of the passages of the above-mentioned book of the Sieur Bayle, in the Article of DAVID, and that having compared the said Extracts with the said book, they had found that the Sieur Bayle had in general drawn a very frightful picture of the conduct and government of this King and Prophet, and that in particular he treats several of his actions in an unworthy and scandalous manner, as this is more fully expressed in a Memoir which the said Committee produced concerning the same, wherein the passages are marked: whereupon the Consistory have thought fit that this Memoir shall be kept as the foregoing one, and the other members of the Consistory may further examine the said Memoir, and make their remarks upon it betwixt this and a fortnight hence.

December 1, 1697.

The term of a fortnight appointed by the preceeding Act for making remarks on the Memoir which relates to the Article DAVID, mentioned in the said Act, being now elapsed, the other members of the Consistory were asked, if they had any remarks on the same, and no body declaring that they had made any; the Report contained in the same Memoir was agreed to, and held as the opinion of the Consistory.

The same day.

The Committee abovementioned having made a Report that they had examined the Extracts which Messieurs de Superville and Le Page, Ministers, had made concerning the passages in the said book of the Sieur Bayle, in the Articles of the MANICHEANS, MARCIONITES, and PAULICIANS; and having compared these Extracts with the said book, they had found that Mr Bayle had not only advanced the arguments which the Manicheans had made use of anciently, but had likewise formed new arguments in favour of Manicheism, which even tend to oppose the hypotheses of all Protestant Divines, and that he in the conclusion gives the victory to the Manichean hypothesis which had given great offence to the said Committee, as they have expressed it more at large in a Memoir which the said Committee have produced concerning it, wherein the passages complained of are marked: whereupon the Consistory have thought fit that this Memoir shall be kept as the preceeding, and the other members of the Consistory may further examine the said Memoir, and make their remarks upon it betwixt this and a fortnight hence.

December 8, 1697.

The Committee above-mentioned having made a Report that they had examined the Extracts which Messieurs de Superville and le Page, Ministers, had made of the passages of the said book of the Sieur Bayle, in the Article of PYRRHO, and that having compared the said Extracts with the said book, the said Committee had drawn up a Memoir of what they had found there scandalous and blame-worthy, which Memoir they produced to the Consistory; whereupon the Consistory have thought fit that this Memoir shall be kept as the preceeding, and that the other members of the Consistory may further examine the said Memoir, and make their remarks upon it betwixt this and the week following.

December 15, 1697.

The term of a fortnight appointed by the second Act of the first instant, for making remarks with relation to the Article of the MANICHEANS, MARCIONITES ann PAULICIANS, mentioned in the said Act; and likewise the term of eight days, appointed by the Act immediately preceeding this, for making remarks on the Memoir relating to the Article of PYRRHO mentioned in the said Act, being now elapsed; the members of the Consistory were asked if they had made any remarks upon the same, whereupon no body having signified that they had made any, the report contained in the said two Memoirs was agreed to, and held as the opinion of the Consistory.

The same Day.

The Committee abovementioned, having made a report that they had examined the Extracts which Messieurs Superville and le Page, Ministers, had made of the passages of the said book of the Sieur Bayle in diverse Articles with relation to *Atheists* or *Epicureans*; and that having compared the said Extracts with the said book, the said Committee had drawn up a Memoir of such things as they had found scandalous and deserving reproof in it: which Memoir they produced to the Consistory Whereupon the Consistory have thought fit that the said Memoir should be kept as the preceeding, and that the other members of the Consistory may further examine the said Memoir, and make their remarks upon it betwixt this and Sunday next.

The same Day.

Mr le Page, one of our Ministers, informed the Consistory that the Sieur Bayle came to see him on the 10th of this month, to tell him that he had heard that the Consistory were examining his *Critical Dictionary*. That this had surprized him, because he did not think that Dictionaries were subject to examination; that he had been assured that we found fault with the articles of DAVID, the MANICHEANS or PAULICIANS, the PYRRHONIANS, and sundry expressions and citations of too free a nature; that since it was so he designed to soften and rectify these things in a second edition, either by adding or suppressing, and desired that the Consistory might be informed of this his declaration, and that he hoped they would be satisfied with it. Whereupon the Consistory having delibe-

rated,

rated, thought fit to appoint an extraordinary meeting on Thursday next on the affair of the said Sieur Bayle.

Thursday December 19, 1697.

The Consistory being extraordinarily met, according to the abovementioned Act, and having read over the four first Memoirs relating to the affair of the said Sieur Bayle, mentioned in the preceeding Acts, they thought fit to acquaint the Sieur Bayle, by the mouth of their Secretary, to appear before them on Tuesday next in the afternoon, at half an hour after three of the clock, on this affair.

Sunday December 21, 1697.

The time appointed by the second Act of the 15th instant, for making remarks on the Memoir relating to several Articles concerning *Atheists* and *Epicureans*, mentioned in the said Act, being now elapsed, the other members of the Consistory were asked if they had any remarks on the same. Whereupon no body having signified that they had made any, the report contained in the said Memoir was agreed to, and held as the opinion of the Consistory.

Tuesday December 24, 1697.

The Consistory being extraordinarily assembled, according to the Act of the 19th instant, the Sieur Bayle appeared before them: to whom the Consistory having declared, by the mouth of their President, that they had found in his book, intitled *An Historical and Critical Dictionary*, several passages which appeared to the Consistory offensive. And in the first place, that they had found in his said book obscene expressions, quotations, and reflexions; in answer to which the said Sieur Bayle said, " That he was " not prepared to answer, not knowing what the Consistory was to propose to him; and added, " there was a difference betwixt a Philosophical writer or an Historian, and a Divine; that an Hi- " storian ought to be faithful and impartial, and that he is accountable if he gives false relations; " that he might desire of this Consistory twenty audiences, of two hours each, to lay his reasons be- " fore them, but that he would not make use of that method, and that he desired to prevent a long " and tedious process; that he maintained that he had advanced nothing in the said book as his own " opinion, which was contrary to our Confessions of Faith, and that he had defended the principal " points of Religion in it; that they ought not to insist on what was only trifling; that he might cri- " ticize upon the Extracts which the Consistory had made, both with regard to facts, and with re- " gard to right; but that he would not in the least enter into that discussion; that in the preface " to the said book he had declared that he would be ready to correct whatever should be found " in it which deserved correction; and that in the Reflexions which he had published on a " pamphlet intitled, *The Judgment of the Public*, he had made the same declaration; that he de- " clared once more to the Consistory, that he had resolved to change in a second Edition what- " ever the Consistory should find fault with, and that he was already at work in correcting the " said Book."

The Consistory having deliberated on this Answer, and desired the Sieur Bayle to come in, they told him, by the mouth of their President, that they would not at present enter upon an answer to the abovementioned reasons alledged by him, and as to the resolution which he had declared to them, that it appeared to be too general; that he had spoke of correcting in a second Edition, and not of retracting; that the Consistory did not know when that second Edition should be published, and likewise that several accidents might intervene to prevent the execution of it; that the remarks which the Consistory had made upon the said book were of importance. Whereupon the Sieur Bayle had answered " that " he would be ready not only to make alterations in the said book, but likewise to retract what " should be thought deserved to be retracted, and that even now, if there be any propositions " in it which are laid down as his own opinion, which shall be found contrary to our Religion, " that he declared them heretical."

After this the Consistory informed him that they would cause the passages of the said book to be pointed out to him, together with their remarks upon the same, and afterwards appointed Messieurs Pielat, de Superville, and le Page, Ministers; Messieurs de Fanueil, Diodati, and Vermande, Elders; and Messieurs de Tinnebacq and de Peyster, Deacons; to point out to the Sieur Bayle the passages and remarks contained in the five Memoirs which have been made on that subject; and to hear what the said Sieur should say concerning them, and to make a Report of the same to the Consistory.

January 5, 1698.

The Memoirs of the Committee appointed by an Act of the 24th of December last, reported, that having met on the 30th following, they had laid before the Sieur Bayle, the substance of the Remarks contained in the five Memoirs made with relation to his book, mentioned in the said Act, and having heard the explanations and general answers, and likewise the Sieur Bayle's offers on that subject, they had thought it proper that the Sieur Bayle should put what he had said to them in writing, which the said Sieur Bayle having done, they produced a Memoir of the same subscribed by the said Sieur, which being read before the Consistory, after deliberating thereupon, they thought fit to desire the Members of the said Committee to draw up a sketch of an Answer to the said Memoir, and to communicate the same to the Consistory, which shall extraordinarily meet for that purpose on Tuesday next, and ordered that the Sieur Bayle be summoned to appear before them at that time.

A MEMORIAL

OF THE WALLOON CHURCH OF ROTTERDAM.

A MEMORIAL *presented to the Consistory of the Walloon Church of Rotterdam on Sunday January* 5, 1698, *concerning the* HISTORICAL AND CRITICAL DICTIONARY.

"GENTLEMEN,

"WHAT I had the honour to say to you on the twenty fourth of the last month; and to repeat more at large to your Committee on Monday last, when they read their remarks to me, I now give the Consistory in writing with more particular explanations.

"This may be reduced to two points: The first is, that I have a great many things to alledge both by way of reason and of example in my justification, without a discussion of which this matter cannot in equity be determined by way of decision. The second is, that if to prevent a long process, and other inconveniences, the Consistory think proper to terminate this affair by way of agreement, I will do all that is in my power to facilitate it. For that purpose, I in the first place declare in the sincerest manner, that I never intended to insert any thing in my Dictionary which could give just cause of offence to pious souls. I always hoped that the liberty which I took on certain occasions would be favourably interpreted, because people would observe that it is a Layman and a Philosopher who speaks, and that too in a History, a Criticism, and a large Commentary, and that I have been at pains to add, wherever I thought it was necessary, salvo's and explanations which bring back my reader to the most orthodox principle of our Communion, to wit, that the Scripture is the rule of what we ought to believe, whether our reason can comprehend it or not. I likewise hoped that every body would remember that the quality of Historian puts one under a necessity of relating many things concerning the strong and the weak side of every party, which another Author would not say, and that the Fathers of the Church have minutely related impurities and obscenities which create horror.

"I declare in the second place that I am extremely sorry, that, contrary to my intention and hopes, several people have been offended at the liberty which I have taken, and that if I had foreseen this I would have carefully abstained from it. And in order effectually to remedy this I promise to rectify in a second edition which I shall presently set about, all the passages which have been complained of. This appears to me to be very easy to be done either by suppressions, additions, or change of expression. By reading the remarks of your Committee, I know these passages more distinctly than I did before. In my corrections I shall have great regard to these remarks, and the rather that I know that they were made by persons of great abilities, and to the good advice and information, which it shall please the Ministers of the Church to favour me with; and I shall much more consider whether a thing may offend part of my readers, than whether it be at bottom true, and not contrary to our Confession of Faith.

"I promise, in particular, to new model the Article of the Prophet DAVID in such a manner, that no stumbling block shall be left there. As to what relates to the *Manichean* Heresy, I have very distinctly declared that it is horrible, extravagant, contrary to common notions, and that it may be easily overthrown by the Holy Scripture. I have only maintained, that the objections concerning the Origin of Evil cannot be solved by the strength of reason, and I believed that this was saying no more than what all our Divines confess concerning the incomprehensibility of Predestination. Notwithstanding I promise to confider that matter over again, and to seek for philosophical reasons against these objections. And if your Reverend Ministers will be so good as to take the trouble of furnishing me with any, I will make use of them in the best manner I am able, and that with the greater pleasure that Manicheism is an abominable heresy with regard to Morality, and ridiculous and monstrous with regard to Metaphysics. What I promise with relation to this Article ought likewise to be understood in particular with regard to that of PYRRHO.

"In a word, I declare that I will receive with joy, and with an intention to profit by them all the advices that may be communicated to me, in order to render my book more useful to the public, and more edifying to the churches; and especially I will receive with great submission the good advices of the Consistory.

"I have only two things farther, Gentlemen, to declare to you. The first is, that I never designed to advance as my own opinion any doctrine contrary to the Confession of Faith of the Reformed Church, of which I profess myself a member, and in which I beg the grace of God that I may live and die. If therefore there be any such doctrine found in my writings, I disown it, and from this day forth entirely retract it. The second thing is, that I have good ground to hope that the Consistory having nothing in view but the peace and edification of the public, will be fully content with what is above; for methinks it is all that can be required of an Author in such a case. Besides, that by taking the way of a formal process, the Consistory must be sensible that it will be drawn into great length, that I have reasons to offer in my justification on every article; that it may perhaps be necessary to pass from one Court to another, and even come to printed Cases, which will only tend to excite new troubles without any advantage to the Church, and on the contrary will give pleasure to our adversaries.

"If all that I have said above should not be able to bring this matter to an amicable issue, and if notwithstanding thereof this affair should come to be tried by way of process, I desire that nothing that I have said above may prejudice my cause, either as to my pretensions of challenging some persons, if that shall be found necessary, or to the method of appeal, if that be found requisite. I desire likewise that what I have said either to the Consistory, or to the Gentleman of the Committee, may not be taken as part of my Defence."

And it was signed BAYLE.

Tuesday, January 7, 1698.

The Consistory being extraordinarily assembled in consequence of the last Act, and finding that they were not a sufficient number, though all the members were particularly acquainted to meet, that they might come to a resolution on this affair, and considering the shortness of the time, the Consistory

Consistory being to be changed on Sunday next; after having examined the sketch of an Answer drawn by the Committee, mentioned in the preceding Act, they have thought fit only to read the said sketch to the Sieur Bayle, who having desired a copy of it, the Consistory came to no resolution thereupon, but thought proper to meet again on Thursday next.

Thursday, January 9, 1698.

The Consistory being once more extraordinarily assembled, in consequence of the preceding Act, and having read the sketch of an Answer, drawn up by the Committee, and communicated to the Sieur Bayle, as is mentioned in the preceding Act, unanimously approved of the same. The tenour whereof is as follows:

The Consistory continuing to deliberate concerning Mr Bayle's affair, after having heard the said Sieur Bayle's explanations and general answers, both in full Consistory on Thursday the 24th of December last, and on Monday the 30th of this month, in presence of the Committee who communicated to him by word of mouth the substance of the five Memoirs drawn up by the Consistory concerning his Dictionary, and have made a report of the whole on Sunday last, the 5th instant; after having likewise examined the paper presented to the Consistory, on Sunday last above-mentioned, by the said Sieur Bayle, and signed by him, in which he lays down his intentions and designs more distinctly.

The Consistory declare that they are glad to observe,

I. That the said Sieur Bayle protests that he desires to live and die in the profession of the Reformed Religion which it has pleased God to make known to him, and in which he has continued until now, disowning and retracting from this day forth all that he may have advanced in his works contrary to our Confession of Faith, supposing that there be any such thing in them, which he doth not believe, he having always had a contrary intention.

II. That the said Sieur Bayle is extremely sorry that, contrary to his intentions and hopes, many persons have been offended at the liberty which he has taken in his Dictionary, and that if he had foreseen this he would have carefully abstained from it.

III. That he abhors *Manicheism*, as a heresy which is entirely destroyed by the Scripture, and which is abominable, and monstrous with regard to Morality as well as Metaphysics, adding that he will be at all possible pains to refute it, which he also promiseth with regard to *Pyrrhonism*.

IV. That in particular he designs to correct the Article DAVID in such a manner, that no stumbling-block shall remain there.

V. And lastly, that to satisfy the complaints which have been made against his Dictionary, he designs to set about a second edition without delay; in which he will change, correct, rectify, and suppress, every thing that may have given offence, and that in order to render that edition more correct, he will have great regard to the Memoirs which have been communicated to him by the Consistory, and to whatever advice they shall please to give him.

The Consistory is very glad to see Mr Bayle in these dispositions: but they cannot approve of divers other things which the said Sieur Bayle has inserted in his paper, as among other things, that he pretends that he could justify what he has advanced in his Dictionary, if it should come to a discussion, and that he speaks of the reasons which he will then alledge, as reasons which are sufficient to justify him, so that it seems that it is only out of condescendence, and that he may not give offence to pious souls, that he is willing to correct and rectify his work, and not that at bottom he is obliged to do it, or that the work has need of it, because in quality of a Layman, Philosopher, Historian, and Commentator, it was lawful for him to advance many things, which would not be allowed in another Author. The Consistory cannot approve of these exceptions, as the President will represent to Mr Bayle more at large, yet in the mean while being willing to take the most indulgent method to endeavour to put an end to this affair, they are of opinion that in order thereunto it is necessary,

I. That Mr Bayle acquiesce in the remarks which have been made by the Consistory, that he acknowledge the solidity of them, and promise to profit by them, and conform to them in a second edition. These remarks relate 1. to the *Obscenities* dispersed in the work. 2. The Article of *David*. 3. *Manicheism*. 4. *Pyrrhonism*. 5. The excessive praises given to *Atheists*, with the consequences he draws from thence. Concerning which he shall declare his sorrow that he has given ground of complaint.

II. It is necessary that the Sieur Bayle should promise that for the future he will take great care to advance nothing in his writings, which may offend either the purity of Morality, or the truth of Doctrine: but on the contrary that he will dedicate the talents, which God has given him, to the defence of both, and to the edification of the Church.

III. That to repair the scandal already given, and for the edification of the public, Mr Bayle shall be earnestly exhorted, not to wait for a second edition of his Dictionary, which may be a long while hence, but with the first opportunity to print something in which he shall acquaint the public with the sentiments which he has declared to us concerning the points proposed to him.

Afterwards Mr Bayle being come in, the President once more read the before-mentioned sketch to him, which was now held as the opinion of the Consistory, and asked him what he had to answer thereto. Whereupon the said Sieur Bayle declared that he acquiesced in this resolution, and at the same time delivered the following Memoir written and signed by him:

" Gentlemen,

" BEING persuaded that the Consistory have nothing else in view, in terminating this affair, but
" sincerely to promote the edification of the public and the glory of God, and being desirous to
" concur with them to the utmost of my power, in so good a design, I accept of the conditions
" contained in an Act which was read to me on the seventh instant; and I declare in particular
" with regard to the remarks which have been communicated to me by the Consistory, that I acquiesce
" in them as a rule which I will punctually follow in the correction of my Dictionary for a new edition.

" I shall

OF THE WALLOON CHURCH OF ROTTERDAM. cxxvii

" I shall likewise comply with the exhortation of the Consistory to the utmost of my power, concerning
" a piece to be published before the new edition, and I hope that this shall not be long delayed.
" I hope and humbly desire the Consistory that they will be pleased not to allow these remarks and
" other paper srelating to this affair, to fall into the hands of people who may make a bad use of them,
" by publishing pieces which can only do prejudice to the edification of souls, both in themselves
" and by the answers which I may be obliged to make to them. At Rotterdam, January 9, 1698."
And was signed BAYLE.

Thereafter Mr Bayle being withdrawn, the Consistory, after having deliberated on his answer, resolved to rest satisfied with it, because he agreed to every thing which they had desired of him, he acquiesced in the remarks of the Consistory on his Dictionary, and promised to publish, as soon as possible, a piece which should acquaint the public with his good dispositions. They were of opinion, that by putting an end to that affair in this manner, the Church would be more edified than by long debates; besides, that this would be the most effectual means of engaging Mr Bayle to employ his talents for the advancement of our Lord's Kingdom. Being therefore called in again to the Consistory, the President told him, I. That the Consistory was satisfied with his answer. II. That they assured him that the papers which had passed betwixt him and them, should not be given to any body to be published, that this was not the practice of the Consistory, and that they knew very well that after matters were determined, it was not fit to awaken them again by printed papers. III. That neither did the Consistory doubt that he would on his part fulfil his promise of publishing very soon a paper wherein he should inform the public of the good sentiments which he had testified to them, and that the sooner that paper should appear, the better it would be. And this the said Mr Bayle once more promised to do. After which the President represented to him that the more talents God had bestowed on him, the more he was bound to dedicate them to his glory. That he ought to labour to edify the Church, and that they hoped that for the future he would endeavour to do so; that the Consistory earnestly exhorted him to it, and that on that condition they prayed that God would bless his labours. Mr Bayle assured the Consistory that he would answer their expectations, and thanked them for their good wishes.

All the above written Acts down to this day, January 11, 1698, were read and approved of by the Consistory, this 11th of January 1698, and signed LE PAGE, Minister; PIELAT, Minister; DE SUPERVILLE, Minister; BASNAGE, Minister; J. V. KAEREN, Elder; F. VAN SCHONHOVEN, Elder; JOHN FANUEIL, Elder; JACOB VERMANDE, Elder; THEODORE SYSMUS, Deacon and Secretary; D. PRINS, Deacon; GOUERT COOLBRANT; PETER BALDE; ISAAC RERDOES, Deacon; G. ALLART, Deacon; JOHN DE PEYSTER, Deacon.

December 7, 1698.

The Committee appointed by the Act of the 28th of September to consider Mr Bayle's affair, made their Report. Whereupon the Consistory find that

I. The printed Letter of the said Mr Bayle appeared later than they had reason to expect, and that it would have been to be wished that Mr Bayle had published it sooner according to his promise.

II. That the said Mr Bayle did not send a copy of it to the Consistory: notwithstanding he was obliged to show them that he had fulfilled his engagement.

III. That the number of copies of that Letter was too small, and that there have been none to be had at the Booksellers this great while past; so that it seems as if it was intended that the Letter should be suppressed as soon as it was published, and put in the hands of as few persons as possible, which is contrary the intention of the Consistory, which desired that the public should be informed of the declarations which Mr Bayle had made concerning that affair.

IV. And what is more important, that Mr Bayle has passed lightly over the matters which had given offence, and even speaks of them as things that may be defended, pretending that he could defend what he has advanced in his *Dictionary*, because, in quality of Commentator and of Historian, it was allowable in him to speak otherwise than if he had been writing in the dogmatical way: an excuse which he had alledged in his paper of the 5th of January 1698, but which they had told him was by no means to be received, upon which he acquiesced simply in the Remarks of the Consistory, and acknowledged the solidity of them, and promised to submit to the same; which is a circumstance he ought to have taken notice of in his printed Letter, as being necessary to the satisfaction which was required of them.

For these and other reasons, the Consistory being of opinion that Mr Bayle's printed Letter only in part satisfies what he had promised, and so they might justly desire something farther of him, yet notwithstanding that they might not depart from the indulgent method which they had already taken, the Consistory may content themselves with representing these things by word of mouth to Mr Bayle, and earnestly exhorting him to a punctual performance of his promises: and the Consistory will take this method, being persuaded that the Sieur Bayle will, in the second Edition of his Dictionary sincerely correct the things which have been pointed out to him, and will make good use of the advices which they have given him; which is the principal thing that the Consistory proposed to itself in the whole of this affair, because they consider it as of importance to the glory of God, and the edification of the Church.

And farther that Mr Bayle who has promised to make use of the Remarks of the Consistory, may do it the more easily, the Consistory think fit that the Ministers who have already been employed in this affair, should draw up some succinct Memorials concerning the Remarks which the Consistory have made, to which they may add some others on important points, that after the Consistory shall have approved of the said Memorials, they may be put in Mr Bayle's hands, that he may remember and have regard to them.

The Consistory likewise being of opinion that our much honoured brother Mr Jurieu, one of our Ministers, having been very ill treated by Mr Bayle in his work; it is proper to acquaint the latter of the same, and to exhort him for the future to behave with more moderation, both in the

second

ACTS OF THE CONSISTORY &c.

second Edition of his Dictionary, and in the other volumes which he promiseth to the public, the Consistory having observed, not without grief, that so little regard has been had for a Minister whose ministry and labours have been and are of singular edification to the Church.

December 20, 1698.

The Committee, appointed by an Act of the 7th of December, read to the Consistory the succinct Memorials concerning the Remarks of the Consistory on Mr Bayle's paper, and likewise their Remarks on the most important points in the Dictionary of the said Sieur Bayle, which are approved by the Consistory, and it is resolved that the same be communicated to Mr Bayle by Messieurs Pielat, Superville, Le Page, and Fanueil.

A Short MEMORIAL *of the principal things to which Mr Bayle ought to have regard, in order to correct them in the second edition of his* DICTIONARY.

THE Consistory being informed that a second edition of the *Historical and Critical Dictionary*, is actually in the press, think themselves obliged to acquaint Mr Bayle in consequence of what has formerly passed betwixt the Consistory and him. That he ought to remember the following things, in order to have regard to them in the corrections which he promised to make in his book.

1. He shall carefully shun all obscenities, and suppress the impure expressions, citations, questions, and reflexions; remembering that purity of spirit, as well as of body, is one of those things which are most recommended to us in the Scripture, and that all wise men ought to take great care not to favour Libertinism, which is but too common in this age, and to which the youth have but too great propensity.

2. He shall entirely reform the article of DAVID, so that pious souls may no longer be ofended at it, as he has promised: and in order to this he shall conform himself to what the Holy Scripture tells us of that great Prophet. He ought even to write a vindication of him, and observe that during the life of Saul, David was the rightful King; and far from judging of the actions of that Prince by the common and ordinary course of the Kings of the earth, he shall show that he was authorised to extirpate the Canaanites. That the High-Priest, by whose means he consulted God, was a particular rule to him; that we ought to be silent where the Scripture is silent; and that its silence, far from giving a pretence against David, is rather equivalent to an approbation; and, in fine, he shall take care to establish well the prophetical and canonical authority of David's writings.

3. With regard to *Manicheism*, instead of displaying the sophisms of the Manicheans, and lending them reasons and new objections which they never alledged, and endeavouring to free their hypotheses from the difficulties which render it ridiculous, Mr Bayle shall refute them, and shall take care not to give the victory to so detestable and monstrous a heresy. For that purpose he shall correct the articles MANICHEANS, MARCIONITES, PAULICIANS, and likewise divers passages in his book which seem to favour their opinion, or the difficulties which they alledge against the permission of evil.

4. He shall observe the same conduct with regard to the *Pyrrhonians* and *Pyrrhonism*, which extinguisheth all Religion, and reform the article PYRRHO, taking care, both there and every where else, not to injure our mysteries.

5. He shall not give extravagant praises to *Atheists* or *Epicureans*. He shall correct the passages which may contain any affectation in favour of them, and he shall not weaken the necessity of believing a God and a Providence, and even a future life, with regard to the benefit of civil society, and the reformation of manners. He shall rather insert clauses which may serve to inspire his readers with a horror against Atheism; and shall endeavour to show that altho' Atheists have been regular in their manners, that this did not proceed from Atheism, but only from a self-love, which was always irregular. He may even bring examples, which he may know, of many Atheists who have been very vicious and very infamous.

6. Besides these five principal heads, which have been already mentioned to Mr Bayle, and which he has promised to correct, as he has likewise promised to the Consistory to receive all the other informations which they shall give him, and to make use of the same, the Consistory do exhort him to take care, in the sixth place, not to refute, except on very good grounds, what our Divines have advanced concerning certain wicked Popes; since tho' he may alledge some conjectures in defence of these Popes, with regard to certain facts, strong reasons may be opposed to him for their condemnation, and that it is unjust, without necessity, to favour the party of seducers, who have done so much hurt to the Church, and to make our authors pass for rash accusers.

7. He shall likewise revise the Articles of NICOLE and PELISSON, which contain divers things which seem to lead to Pyrrhonism, and are hurtful to the way of Examination, by which Protestants pretend that we can and ought to come to the knowledge of the truth.

8. He shall take care in speaking of Providence, not to exaggerate and magnify the difficulties of the prophane, and not give their objections an air of superiority over our answers, even in refuting those which are agreeable to Scripture: whereupon they particularly point out to him the Article of RUFINUS. He shall likewise revise the Article of XENOPHANES, in which he exaggerates the victories of the Devil.

9. It is likewise to be wished that he would have greater regard to the expressions of the Scripture in the allusions which he sometimes makes.

Mr Bayle shall have regard to all these heads to conform his corrections to them, and shall endeavour to purge his book of every thing that may have given offence to true believers. The Consistory declaring that they have only made these remarks on what appeared to them to be most essential, and that they do not pretend thereby to approve of the rest of the work.

They think themselves obliged to acquaint Mr Bayle, that Mr Jurieu, one of our Ministers, having been very ill used in his book, they desire that he may behave for the future with greater moderation, both in the second edition of his Dictionary, and in the other volumes which he promiseth to the public, and they exhort him to do so, having observed, not without sorrow, that so little regard has been had for a Minister whose ministry and labours have been and are of singular edification to the Church.

Approved and Resolved in Consistory, on the 20th of December 1698.

Mr BAYLE's

Mr BAYLE's
Historical and Critical
DICTIONARY.

A.

AARON, High-Priest of the *Jews*, and Brother of *Moses*. His History is so fully related in the *Pentateuch*, and in the Dictionaries of *Moreri* and Mr *Simon*, that I may be excused from making an Article of it in this place. I shall only observe, That his Weakness in complying with the superstitious Request of the *Israelites*, in the Matter of the Golden Calf, has occasioned a great Variety of fabulous Notions [*A*]. About the Beginning of the XVIIth Century, one *Monceau* or *Moncaius*, published an Apology for *Aaron* (*a*), which was condemned by the Inquisition at *Rome*, as had been foretold to the Author by the Jesuit *Cornelius à Lapide* (*b*). In that Apology it is supposed that *Aaron* designed to represent the very same Form which *Moses* exhibited some time after, namely, a Cherubim; but that the *Hebrews* fell down and worshiped it, contrary to his Intention. An effectual Confutation of this Notion was published in the Year 1609, by one of the Doctors of the *Sorbonne*, who was a Canon of the Church of *Amiens* (*c*). It has been asserted, that this criminal Compliance of *Aaron* was owing to his Apprehensions of being stoned to Death; and that he hoped to have eluded the Desires of the People, by proposing to the Women, on this Occasion, that they should contribute their Ear-Rings;

(*a*) *'Tis intitled,* Aaron purgatus. *It was reprinted at Franckfort in 1675 in 8vo. This differs from the Edition in 12mo at Leipsic, in 1689, mentioned in the 17th Vol. of the Bibliotheque Universelle, in nothing but a new Title which the Booksellers gave it.*

(*b*) Corn. à Lapide Comment. in Exod. cap. xxxii. ver. 4. pag. 605.
(*c*) *His Name was* Vissorius; *and his Book was called,* Destructio Pseudo-Cherubi Moncæi.

[*A*] *Occasioned a great Variety of fabulous Notions.*] I. Rabbi *Solomon* held (1) that the Calf which the *Israelites* worshiped was alive, and that *Aaron* seeing it walk and eat like other Calves, erected an Altar to it. There is something analogous to this in the *Alcoran* (2). II. Several *Rabbies*, in order to excuse *Aaron*, affirm, that he did not make the Golden Calf; that he only contributed so far towards it, as to cast the Gold into the Fire, to free himself from the People's vehement Importunity; but that certain Magicians, who had mingled with the *Israelites* at their coming up out of *Egypt*, communicated to that Gold the Image of a Calf. As the holy Scripture declares it was Cast-work, and fashioned with the Graving-Tool, two Things may be supposed; either, that they prepared a Mould in the Shape of a Calf, into which they poured the molten Gold; or, that, having produced a Mass of Gold, they gave it the Figure of a Calf by the Sculptor's Art. III. Many maintain, that *Aaron* did not make a whole Calf, but only the Head. IV. Some tell us (3), *That the Powder of the Golden Calf burnt by* Moses, *which he mingled with the Water that the* Israelites *drank, stuck in the Beards of those who had worshiped it; by which means their Beards appeared gilt, as a special Mark distinguishing the Idolaters*. This Fable is inserted in the 32d Chapter of *Exodus*, in a *French* Bible, printed at *Paris*, in the Year 1538, by *Anthony Bonnemere*, who says in his Preface, *That this Bible in the* French *Tongue was first printed, at the Desire of his most Christian Majesty* Charles VIII. *in the Year* 1495, *and has since been corrected and reprinted*. And in the same Preface he informs us, That the *French* Translator had inserted nothing but pure Truth, as it is found in the *Latin* Bible; and that nothing was omitted, but what was improper to be translated. So that all which relates to the gilt Beards is to be received as undoubted Fact, as well as another Story of the same kind, which is also inserted in this very Chapter; namely, *That the Children of* Israel *spit so violently in the Face of* Hur, *who had refused to make Gods for them, that they suffocated him*. The Book (4) from which I extract this, was written by a *Walloon* Minister, who fails not to exclaim against the Impudence of adding in some Places, and suppressing in others. But he is guilty of both: in his own Version he has artfully foisted in some things, and drop'd others; besides inserting childish Traditions: And yet he promises in the Preface nothing but pure Truth, and declares, that *this Translation was undertaken not for the Clergy, but for the Laity, Hermits, and the lower Orders of religious Societies, who are not so learned as they should be*. Which is the very Thing that renders the Translator's Unfaithfulness more culpable: for the skillful may escape the Snare; the ignorant cannot. Lastly, The Golden Beard is not the sole Chimera which the *Rabbies* have invented. Another of their Tenets is, that the Water, which *Moses* compell'd them to swallow, impregnated with the Particles of the Gold, whereof their Calf was made, had almost the same Effect as the Waters of Jealousy. It produced Tumours and Ulcers in the guilty, and brought no harm on the innocent (5).

(1) Corn. à Lap. in Exod. pag. 605.

(2) Ascemeli taurum fudit corporeum, emittentem mugitem. i. e. Ascemeli cast a real Bull that bellow'd. Azora xxx. Lat. Cod. xx Arabici ap. Selden. de Diis Syr. Synt. 1. cap. 4. pag. 54.

(3) See Aug. 229. of Jeremiah de Pours's Divine Melody.

(4) *'Tis intitled* La Divine Mélodie du Saint Psalmiste, *printed at Middlebourg in 1644 in 4to. The Author calls himself* Jeremiah de Pours.

(5) See Sàlian, vol. 2. pag. 165. Bocharti Hierozoic. pars 1. lib. 2. cap. 34.

Rings; imagining that they would chuse to renounce the Presence of a Visible Deity, rather than divest themselves of their personal Ornaments: but he found, that nothing is accounted too costly, when the human Mind is intoxicated with Superstition and Idolatry (d). They, who affirm that the Golden Calf was only Wood overlaid with Gold [B], find nothing in the holy Scripture, that can in the least countenance any such Pretence. That GOD suspended the natural Effects of Fire, for the sake of *Aaron*, as he did on behalf of the three Children in the fiery Furnace at *Babylon*, is, I am persuaded, an Assertion not to be maintained; and yet there are some Writers who have held that Opinion [C].

[B] *That the Golden Calf was only Wood overlaid with Gold.*] The holy Scripture tells us expressly (6) that it was a Molten Calf, and, tho it is afterwards said (7) that *Moses* burnt it, and reduced it to Powder, it does not necessarily follow, that the Idol was consisted of combustible Materials: It may only signify, that *Moses* melted down the Gold again, and divided it into very minute Particles, which became imperceptible upon being thrown into the Water; like those with which the Waters of the *Tagus* and *Pactolus* are said to abound. So that *Francis Junius* may be mistaken when he says, (8) *Quamvis non tam existimari possit Vitulus iste totus ex auro fuisse conflatus, quam Auri lamina tantum modo obductus, ut extra ligneus, ut quondam. Littera traducta combustam, atque in Pulveres redactam.* That is, But it is rather to be thought, that this Calf was only covered over with a thin Plate of Gold, the rest of it being nothing but Wood; than that the whole was entirely of cast Gold: since the holy Scripture assures us that it was burnt, and reduced to Ashes. He had more Reason for placing *Aaron* at the Head of his Catalogue of antient Sculptors, Architects, Painters, Statuaries, &c. *Aaron* might have claimed that Distinction by Right of Antiquity, tho the mere Order of the Alphabet had not bestow'd it upon him. This brings into my Mind the Assertion of some who contend that *Moses* was Master of the profoundest Secrets of Chemistry, since he knew how to pulverize Gold. Many are of Opinion, that *Aaron* only ordered the Artificers to cast the Golden Calf, and had no hand in it himself; and that *Moses* did not command the *Israelites* to drink the Powder of that Gold: but, having thrown it into the Stream, the only Place they could possibly drink at, it may justly be said, that he made them swallow the Idol they had worshiped (9).

[C] *There are some Writers who have held that Opinion.*] A *Cordelier*, a Doctor of Divinity, of the Faculty of *Paris*, maintains, that the Miracle of the burning Bush at *Horeb*, which stood unconsumed in the midst of Flames (10), was repeated some time after, when the Fire flew two of *Aaron's* Sons, without damaging their Shirts; and again, when *Aaron* stopt the Plague which had swept away a great Number of *Israelites* (11). *Siquti factum est, quando egressus ignis à Domino Nadab & Abiud ignem alienum & prophanum coram Domino offerentes devoravit, id est, interfecit: vestibus & tunicis eorum linteis intactis remanentibus. Idem judicium est de Aarone summo sacerdote, qui citissimè profectus est ad populum, quem ignis egressus à facie Domini intensficiebat: statitque illaesus inter mortuos ac viventes, licet* effet in medio flammae fulgentissimae & flagrantissimae, *jecundum Josephum*, Lib. 4. Antiq. Cap. 3. (12). That it came to pass when Fire from the LORD devoured *Nadab* and *Abihu*, while they were offering *strange* and profane Fire before the LORD; their Coats and linen Garments remaining untouch'd: The same is remarkable of *Aaron* the High Priest, who ran into the midst of the People, whom Fire, proceeding from the Face of the LORD, was consuming; and stood there unhurt between the Living and the Dead, tho' in the midst of a most bright and intense Flame, according to Josephus, in the 3d Chapter of his 4th Book of Antiquities. To this, among other Examples, he adds that of *Shadrach, Meshach*, and *Abednego*, who escaped untouched out of the fiery Furnace at *Babylon*. Let it be here particularly remark'd, that he quotes not the holy Scripture, but *Josephus*, in relation to *Aaron*. And the Scripture (13) determines not whether the Plague, which *Aaron* stopped, and by which 14700 Persons perished, was a miraculous Fire, or something else. The *Jewish* Historian has entirely suppressed this Miracle: he only mentions the Fire which consumed the 250 Men that offered Incense. The Scripture mentions this likewise (14), but as a Fact preceding the Destruction stay'd by *Aaron*. Observe, *Josephus* contents himself with remarking, that the Supernatural Fire which consumed *Corah*, and the 250 Men that offered Incense, did no hurt to *Aaron*. He does not once touch upon the Circumstances for which *Nodin* cites him. We shall here transcribe his very Words. ὣς δ᾽ ἄντως, ὃι τε διακόσιοι καὶ οἱ πεντήκοντα καὶ Κορῆς, ἕξαντες ἐν᾽ αὐτοῖς, ἐφθάρησαν ὑπὸ τὰ σώματα αὐτῶν ἀφανῆ γεγονότων ὥσπερ οὔτε μένος Ἀαρὼν μηδὲν ὑπὸ τὰ πυρὸς βλαβέντος, τῷ τὸν θεὸν εἶναι τὴν ὃς ἴδεα καλαιν ἀπεχαλύντα (15). That is, *By the Force of which* [Fire] *rushing upon them, the* 250 *Men, together with* Corah, *were so entirely consum'd, that their dead Bodies could not be found*. Aaron *alone remain'd unhurt: because it was* GOD, *who directed the Fire against those only who were guilty.* Here he justly acknowledges the Finger of GOD, but does not particularly inform us, whether the Fire actually touched the Body of *Aaron*, or whether GOD only with-held it from approaching him. Father *Nodin* therefore ought not to have defended from Generals to Particulars; not to have quoted, for that purpose, the *Jewish* Historian. Most of the Faults of this kind, which in Books are infinite, are occasioned, either by Authors not consulting the Originals, or by their having the Confidence to alter them with their Paraphrasts, the better to accommodate them to their own Schemes.

" AARSENS (FRANCIS) Lord of *Somelsdyck*, and *Spyck*, &c. was one of the
" greatest Ministers the United Provinces have produced, for Negotiation [A].
" His Father, who was also a Man of great Abilities, enjoyed such a Post, as enabled

[A] *Was one of the greatest Ministers —— for Negotiation.*] His very Enemies allow him this Character, when they affirm, *That he* (1) *was the most dangerous Genius that ever arose in the United Provinces, and was the more to be dreaded, as he concealed all the Malice and Guile of foreign Courts, under the false and deceitful Appearance of Dutch Candour and Simplicity; that he was zealous and Master of the Art of Persuasion; that he could find Reasons to support the worst of Causes; that he had* (2) *a Genius for Intrigue, and had entered into Leagues and Correspondencies with those Grandees of* France, *whose Conduct was not only suspected, but odious to the King; and that having corrupted the* French *Ambassador's Secretary at the Hague* (3), *he was Master of all the most secret Schemes of the Ministers of that Crown*. I say, when they give him this Character, they describe a Man admirably furnished with all the Talents requisite for the most important Embassies, and the most delicate Negotiations. Farther, Mr *Du Maurier*, who always inveighs most bitterly against *Francis Aarsens*, takes care to prevent the Prejudice his Invectives might raise in his Readers; for he himself tells us, that his Father and this *Dutch* Ambassador *were ever at Enmity* (4); *that there was an irreconcileable Disagreement in their Tempers*; *and that the strong Aversion they had conceived against each other, instead of wearing off, was continually increasing.* He even tells us, That his Father made a Speech against *Francis Aarsens*, on the 13th of November 1613, before the States General (5), wherein *he reproaches him with having presumed to speak disrespectfully of their* Gallic Majesties; *and the Lords of their Council, who were the solid Support of the Liberty of the United Provinces*; and accuses him *of Arrogance and Vanity in his common Discourses, and of Ingratitude, in returning nothing but Insolence for all the kind Offices that* France *had heap'd upon him*. Thus has he furnished us with an effectual Antidote against his Poison; for who does not know, that an Author is not to be understood too rigorously, when he is speaking of his protected Enemy?
" him

AARSENS.

"him to procure an Employ for his Son [B]. *John d' Olden-Barnevelt*, who at that
"Time had the chief Direction of the Affairs of *Holland*, and all the United Pro-
"vinces, sent him into *France*, with the Character of Agent. There he learnt the
"Art of Negotiation, under those great Masters, *Henry* IV. *Villeroy*, *Rôni*, *Silleri*,
"*Jeannin*, &c. and succeeded so well in it, as to gain their Approbation of his Con-
"duct. He had afterwards the Character of Ambassador conferr'd upon him, and
"was the first, whom the Court of *France* considered in that Quality: And it was
"in his Time that *Henry* IV. declared, the Ambassador of the United Provinces,
"should take Place immediately after the Ambassador of *Venice*. He was some
"time after employ'd to that Republic [C], and to several Princes of *Germany* and
"*Italy*, on Account of the Commotions in *Bohemia* [D]. Besides which, he was sent
"upon several extraordinary Embassies into *France* and *England* [E], of which he
"has left very exact and judicious Collections. We may observe from them, that
"all his Instructions, and Credentials, in his later Embassies, were drawn up by
"himself; whence we may judge, that no State ever produced a Minister better
"qualify'd, not only to negotiate, but to instruct an Ambassador in the proper
"Points of his intended Negotiation. And, indeed, in all his Embassies, he did
"Honour to the State, as well as to the Character with which his Masters had in-
"vested him; nor could himself, or his Family, regret the Time [F] he spent
"in the Service of his Country (a)." He died in a good old Age, leaving behind
him one Son, who was esteem'd the richest Man in *Holland* [G], and well known by
the Name of Monsr. de *Sommerdyck* (b).

(a) *Taken from Wicquefor's Ambassador. Tom. 2. p. 435, 43*
(b) *It is thus pronounc'd, tho' the Name is Somelidyck.*

[B] *His Father enjoy'd such a Post, as enabled him to procure an Employ for his Son.*] His Name was *Cornelius Aarsens* (6); and he was Register of the States. He was acquainted with Mr du *Plessis Mornai*, who was transacting Affairs with *William* Prince of *Orange*, whom he intreated to take his Son into his Service. This was comply'd with, and continu'd some Years. In 1598, this young Gentleman, who understood the *French* Tongue, and the Affairs of the Kingdom, succeeded *Levin Calliard*, who died Resident for the United Provinces, at the Court of *Henry* IV. nor was he any thing more than the State's Resident till 1609, when, upon the Conclusion of a twelve Years Truce, in which *Spain* treated with the United Provinces, as with a free People, *Henry* IV. acknowledg'd him for their Ambassador (7). During his Stay in *France*, which was fifteen Years, he received great Favours, and even Honours, from the King; who rais'd him to the Degree of Nobility, and made him a Knight, and a Baron: for which Reason, he was afterwards receiv'd in *Holland*, among the Nobility of the Province. He became at last so odious to that Court, according to Mr du *Maurier*, that they desired he might be recall'd. *See below, the Remark* [D]

[C] *To that Republic.*] To this Juncture of Time must be referr'd what Cardinal *Pallavicini* reproach'd Father *Paul* with *He is in Possession* (he says) *of a Letter* (8) *of the Sieur* de *Zuilichem*, *Secretary to the Prince of* Orange, *in which he relates, that, at an accidental Interview at* Venice *with the Sieur de* Somerdyck, *Ambassador of* Holland, *and* Francis *Paolo, the good Father assur'd that Minister of his extreme Joy in beholding the Representative of a Republic, which held the Pope to be the true Antichrist.* The Author of a Book, entituled *Cancellaria Secreta Anhaltina*, has preserv'd some Fragments of this Letter, by which it appears, that *Francis Aarsens*, when he went to *Venice*, had Authority to negotiate with the Protestant Cantons, and that he receiv'd great Honours from them. This was a Year after the Deputation of the *Swiss* Ministers, to the Synod of *Dort*. *Gratias se imprimis egisse, quod Civitates & oppida non Catholica Prædicantes suos* ANNO PRÆTERLAPSO *ad Synodum Dordracensem dimiserint* (9). He was particularly thankful, that the Protestant States and Towns, had, THE YEAR BEFORE, deputed their Preachers to the Synod of *Dort*.

[D] *On Account of the Commotions in* Bohemia.] This fell out in the Year 1620, and it is remarkable, "that the King of *France* (10) forbad his three Am-
"bassadors, the Duke *d'Angoulême*, the Count de
"*Bethune*, and the Abbot *des Preaux*, to receive the
"Visits of Mr d'*Aarsens*, who was employ'd by the
"United Provinces, to treat with certain Princes of
"*Germany* and *Italy*, concerning the same Affairs of
"*Bohemia*, which were the Purport of the *French*
"Embassy. Their Order imported, that the King
"was not displeased with the States, with whom
"he desired always to live in perfect Harmony, but
"had a particular Dislike to Mr d'*Aarsens*, for ill
"treating the Service and Dignity of his Majesty.
"The Ground of this Displeasure, as any one will
"perceive, who is the least acquainted with the Af-
"fairs of those Times, was this: *Aarsens* had put
"himself at the Head of that Party, which, in 1619,
"oppos'd an Affair, which was negotiated with great
"Earnestness, at the *Hague*, by the King's Ambassa-
"dors *Boissise* and du *Maurier*." Add to these Words
of Mr *Wicquefort*, a Passage of *du Maurier*, which
gives Light into them. "In the Year 1618, *says he*,
"(11) Mr *de Boissise* was order'd by the King to com-
"plain, in his Name, to the States General, of a
"diffamatory Libel, written, sign'd, and publish'd,
"by *Francis Aarsens*, to the great Scandal and Dis-
"honour of the Lords of his Majesty's Council, for
"which, at that Time, he could obtain no Satisfa-
"ction." It is probable, this Complaint was founded upon his having charg'd the Council of *France* with
betraying the King, by favouring those who were plotting in *Holland*, to reduce that Republic once more
under the Yoke of the King of *Spain*: for, if du *Maurier* is to be credited, the grand Common-Place Thesis of Mr *Aarsens*, the constant Theme of all his
Writings, and of the Placards stuck up at the Corners
of the Streets, was, that the Faction of *Barnevelt* was
conspiring with *Spain*, to abolish both the Reform'd
Religion and Liberty, at once, in the United Provinces. We may apply here the Proverb, *Se non e
vero, e ben trovato.*—— *If it is not true, it is well
bit off.* Nothing can be a greater Confirmation of
the profound Abilities of Mr *Aarsens*, than this
Scheme.

[E] *Extraordinary Embassies into* France *and* England.] He was sent Ambassador into *England*, in the
Years 1620, and 1641 (12). The first Time, he was
the Chief of three Ambassadors extraordinary; the Second Time, the Second. In this latter Embassy he
was join'd in Commission with the Lord of *Brëde-
rode*, who took Place of him, and *Heemsohet*, who
was last in the Commission. The Subject of this Embassy, was the Marriage of Prince *William*, Son of
the Prince of *Orange*. The extraordinary Embassy
to *France*, was in the Year 1624 (13). "As Car-
"dinal *Richelieu* was but just come to the Helm of
"Affairs, and was ignorant of the Dislike his Prede-
"cessors had to this Ambassador, he greatly esteem'd
"him, and finding him to be a Man of fine Un-
"derstanding,——made Use of him to compass his
"own Designs." *Aarsens* was appointed Envoy, either
to *France* or *England*, in the Year 1628; but, being
prevented by the Ice from embarking, he return'd
to the *Hague*.——His being accidentally throwm down
by Dogs, was construed by his Enemies to be an
unlucky Omen. *Arsenius à canibus fortè occurranti-
bus in terram dejectus malevolis occasionem præbuit
sinistra ipsi ominandi* (14).

[F] *Regret the Time.*] Du *Maurier* says, that *Francis
Aarsens* died worth an hundred thousand Livres *per
Annum* (15).

[G] *Leaving behind him one Son, who was esteem'd
the richest Man in* Holland.] He was Governor of
Nimeguen,

ABARIS.

Nimiguen, and Colonel of a Regiment of Horse. He left two Sons, the eldest of which nam'd *Francis*, Lord of *la Plaate*, was cast away in his Passage from *England* to *Holland*, after having travell'd eight Years in several Parts of *Europe*. The other, *Cornelius*, bore the Name of *Sommerdyck*. He had been a Colonel in the *Dutch* Army, and afterwards Governor of *Surinam*; where he was kill'd in a Mutiny of the Garrison, in 1688. He married the eldest Daughter of the Marquis *de St André-Mombran*, by whom he had several Children: she died at the *Hague*, in 1695, or thereabout.—Of seven Sisters, which he had, three were married to Persons of Quality: The other four fell into so superstitious a Devotion, that they followed the Sieur *Labbadie*, the Schismatic Preacher, with as much Zeal, as if he had been another Apostle.

ABARIS, a *Scythian* by Nation [*A*], the Son of *Seuthus*. There have been so many fabulous Stories told of him, that *Herodotus* himself made a Scruple of relating them, and of informing himself perfectly concerning them. He only tells us (a) the Story of this *Barbarian*'s carrying an Arrow through the World, and eating nothing. *Herodotus*, it seems, was ignorant of the *marvellous* Part of the Story; for they, who pretend to know it, say, That *Abaris* was carried thro' the Air upon his Arrow [*B*], as

(a) Herod. lib. 4. cap. 36.

[*A*] *A Scythian by Nation.*] It is *Suidas*, who gives him this Character, and who very particularly observes, that he came from *Scythia* into *Greece*; and that, with the Arrow presented him by *Apollo*, he fled back again from *Greece*, to the Country of the Hyperborean *Scythians* (1). Τούτῳ ὁ μυθολογούμενος διῖκε τὸ τοξεύμενον ἀπὸ τῆς Ἑλλάδος μέχρι τῶν ὑπερβορέων Σκυθῶν. Ἐδόθη δὲ αὐτῷ παρὰ τοῦ Ἀπόλλωνος. i. e. *This Person's Arrow is fam'd in Story for carrying him through the Air from Greece (not from Scythia, as is commonly read in the Latin Version) as far as the Hyperborean Scythians. It was given him by Apollo. Eusebius* (2) is likewise of Opinion, that he came from *Scythia* into *Greece*. If the Account of *Abaris*, which is in *Suidas*, were clear and distinct, we might from thence infer, that he therein takes notice of three several Countries; *Scythia*, whence *Abaris* was born; *Greece*, to which he travell'd; and another *Scythia*, called the *Hyperborean*, whither he took another Journey. We might likewise infer, that he made use of his Arrow in flying, only in his second Expedition, and consequently that it was in *Greece Apollo* bestow'd it upon him. All these Conclusions would be reasonable, had we to do with an accurate Writer, or were sure that he related Matters just as they stand at present in his Works; and then we might say, that *Suidas* is very singular in his Opinion, since most other Authors who have mention'd *Abaris*, tell us, that he was an *Hyperborean* (3), and that when he travell'd to *Greece*, he set out from the Country of the *Hyperboreans*; and, whenever they mention his flying Arrow, they constantly observe, that he was possess'd of it before he came to *Greece*.

[*B*] *Was carried through the Air upon his Arrow.*] *Jamblichus* is very express as to this Point, when he says, (1) Οἷος τὸ ἐν Τοιοβορέοις Ἀπόλλωνος δωρηθέντι αὐτῷ ἐνεχόμενος, ποταμούς τε καὶ πελάγη καὶ τὰ ἄβατα διεβαίνων ἀεροβατῶν τρόπον τινά. i. e. *riding upon the Arrow given him by Apollo the Hyperborean, he cross'd Rivers and Seas, and other inaccessible Places, as if he had been an Inhabitant of the Air.* Monsieur *Petit*, (2) in his Account of this Arrow, takes notice of what is commonly reported concerning Witches, riding to their Nocturnal Meetings on a Broomstick. The Journalist, who gives us an Extract of Mr *Petit*'s Book, does not forget the Verse of *Villon*, wherein (3) a Witch is stiled a Broomstick-rider: I will here insert the whole Passage, because it gives us an Opportunity of making a short Remark. Mr *Petit* (4) alledges the Translation of *Elijah*, *the Rapture* of *Habakkuk, that of Pythagoras, and the Arrow which the Hyperborean Apollo gave to Abaris. This* (adds he) *was a miraculous sort of Arrow, and much like the Broomstick, which, they say, Witches make use of to ride thro' the Air, to their Nocturnal Meetings.* Before we make our Remark upon this, it will be requisite to take notice of a Passage in another Journal, which runs thus. (5) Mr *Petit*, from *Jamblichus*, relates the History, or rather Fable, of *Abaris* the *Hyperborean*, *to whom Apollo granted the Power of flying thro' the Air upon an Arrow, just as our Witches go to their Nocturnal Assemblies, astride a Broomstick.* This is the Interpretation the Journalist gives to Mr *Petit*'s Text, which is as follows (6): *Auctor est Jamblichus in vitâ Pythagoræ, cap. 28. id munus Abaridi Hyperboreo ab Apolline concessum fuisse, ut per aërem quocunque vellet cursum magico invehitu jaculo tendere posset.* i. e. Jamblichus, *in his Life of Pythagoras, c. 28. tells us, that Abaris, the Hyperborean, received from Apollo, the Power of directing his Course, as he pleased, thro' the Air, upon a Magic Arrow:* Now here every one may perceive that the Epithet *Hyperboree* may be referr'd either to the Word *Abaridi*, which goes before it, or to *Apolline*, that comes after it: The *Latin* Tongue is full of such Equivocations. But 'tis evident, by the Words of (7) *Jamblichus*, cited by *Petit* (8), that 'tis only *Apollo* that is called the *Hyperborean*. It would be mere trifling to criticise on the Journalist upon this Accoun: ; since, without observing that this Epithet might very well belong to *Abaris*, as may be seen under the first Remark, it is well known that Journalists are not tied up to a rigid Strictness of Translation. We must not forget that this was a Golden Arrow, and so necessary for *Abaris*'s Travels, that he own'd himself (9) obliged to it for directing him the Way he should go. *Pythagoras* artfully extorted this Confession from him, for he robb'd him of his Arrow; and *Abaris*, like a blind Man who has lost his Staff, acknowledg'd his want of it. This puts me in mind of some who pretend, by the help of a certain Wand, to discover the right Road. If all be true that is related on this Subject, I think (all Circumstances considered) their Wand to be as miraculous as the Arrow of *Abaris*: for if, on the one hand, it has not the Power of making them fly, yet, on the other, it not only discovers Treasures, Metals, and the Boundaries of Lands, Thieves and Cut-throats, but likewise the Intrigues of both Sexes. A noted Philosopher (10) who was consulted about this Matter, in the Year 1689, returned for Answer, That *this could never be done, unless by the Assistance of some intelligent Cause, and that this Cause could be no other than the Devil.* Whilst I was writing this, I was inform'd that one of the Principal of those Wand-Conjurers (11) shew'd the last Summer (12) at *Lions*, such surprizing Experiments of his Art, that he was sent for to *Paris*, and on that grand Theatre made such Discoveries (13), as forc'd several to declare, they had now a greater Proof than ever, and that by indisputable Phænomena, of the Power of Dæmons to produce a great variety of Effects, under the Disguise of occasional Causes, such as a Staff, or the like. Upon this footing the Story of *Abaris*'s Arrow may be vindicated; for why might there not have been such an Arrow formerly, since in our Days such wonderful Effects are said to have been wrought by the *Frenchman*'s Staff? It would be worth our Metaphysicians While to enquire how the Wand came into such mighty Request; for the old Proverb, *Virgula Divina*, and the common Saying, *with the Turn of a Stick*, and the Juggler's Phrase, *by Virtue of my little Wand*, seem to be owing to the frequent Use of a Wand in Sorceries, according to the common Tradition. What Virtues did they not anciently ascribe to *Mercury*'s Rod? His Golden Wings, which he fix'd on his Feet, would have been of little Use to him in flying, had not his Rod contributed thereto by it's powerful Energy; and it seems to have serv'd him as an Horse. Thus *Virgil* (14);

Et primùm pedibus talaria nectit
Aurea, quæ sublimem alis, sive æquora supra
Seu terram, rapido pariter cum flamine portant.
Tum virgam capit: Hac animas ille evocat Orco
Pallentes, alias sub tristia tartara mittit,
Dat somnos, adimitque, & lumina morte resignat.
Illa FRETUS agit ventos, & turbida tranat
Nubila.

Hermes obeys, with golden Pinions binds
His flying Feet, and mounts the western Winds:
And

(1) Suidas in Ἀβαρις.

(2) Euseb. Chronic. n. 1454.

(3) Herod. l. 4. c. 36. Diod. Sicul. l. 3. c. 11. Apollonii admir. Hist. Sect. 4. Jamblichi vita Pythag. c. 28. p. 127, &c. Harpocration, in Ἀβαρις. Scholiasta Aristoph. in Equit. Euseb. us, n. 1508, &c.

(1) Jamblich. *in the foremention'd place*, p. 128.

(2) Petitus, de Sibyllis, l. 2. c. 7. P. 200.

(3) *Non oft, le deuston sif 'bruster, comme un Crevaucheur d' escouettes.*

(4) Nouvell. de la Republ. des Lett. Octob. 1686. Art. 1.

(5) Bibl. Universel. Tom. 2. p. 132.

(6) Petit, as above, p. 198.

(7) See *l'Article in Ci. nation* (4).
(8) Petit, p. 199.

(9) Jamblichus p. 131.

(10) Fa'o Malebranche *in the Mercure Gallant for the Month of January*, 1693.
(11) James Aymar, a Peasant of St. Veran in Dauphiné.
(12) *In the Year* 1692.
(13) *See the Note* [G].

(14) Virgil Æn. l. 4. *see likewise* Homer's Iliad. l. 24. *and* Odys. l. 18.
Ovid. Metam. b. 1. *the Story of Argus.*
Horace, Ode 10. *and* 24. *of* b. 1.
Statius, *in his* Thebaid. b. 1.

ABARIS.

as it were upon another *Pegasus*; so that Rivers, Seas, and Places inaccessible to other Men, were no Obstacle to him in his Journey. This Arrow belong'd to *Apollo*, and was apparently the same with which he slew the *Cyclopes*, who forg'd the Thunderbolts, which *Jupiter* made use of against the unfortunate *Æsculapius* (b). *Apollo*, after this Slaughter, hid his Arrow under a Mountain, in the Country of the *Hyperboreans*, and recover'd it after a wonderful Manner, the Winds bringing it back to him, upon a Reconciliation between him (c) and *Jupiter*. It is difficult to determine, when *Abaris* liv'd [C], there being so many different Opinions about it, as to occasion some of the Moderns to fall into Mistakes [D]: But they are more unanimous in assigning

(b) Hygin. Astr. Poet. l. 2. c. 15. p. 386.

(c) Ibid.

> And, whether o'er the Seas or Earth he flies,
> With rapid Force, they bear him down the Skies.
> But first he grasps within his awful Hand,
> The Mark of Sovereign Pow'r, his Magic Wand:
> With this he draws the Ghosts from hollow Graves,
> With this he drives them down the *Stygian* Waves;
> With this he seals in Sleep the wakeful Sight,
> And Eyes, tho' clos'd in Death, restores to Light.
> Thus arm'd, the God begins his airy Race;
> And drives the racking Clouds along the liquid Space.
>   DRYDEN.

(15) De Virgæ Mercurialis potestate & potentia peculiarem Tractationem satis mysteriosam damus in Superstitionum magno Commentario. *Barthius* in Stat. Tom. 2. p. 291.

(16) Hom. Odyss. v, &.

(17) Ibid.

(18) On the Adage *Virgula Divina*, Chil. 1. Cent. 1. n. 97.

(19) Huet. Demonstr. Evang. prop. 4. p. 258.

(20) Exod. vii. and viii.

(21) Philostrat. in Vit. Apollon. l 3.

(22) Apud Harpocrationem.

(23) Eusebii Chron. n. 1568.

(24) Henr. Valesii Notæ in Notas Maussaci in Harpocrat. p. 83.

(25) In the word *ὑπόψιος*.

(26) In Εἰρήνῃ.

If we had the Treatise, which *Barthius* (15) promised on *Mercury's* Rod, we should doubtless have seen a very curious Piece, and probably more instructive than the Tract of *Antisthenes* on *Minerva's* Wand. That Goddess had likewise her Rod, with which she made Persons look either young or old, as the occasion requir'd (16). *Circe* (17), the Sorceress, did more than all this, since with one single Stroke of her Wand, she could transform Men into Beasts, and Beasts into Men. *Erasmus*, who (18) to all those Instances adds the Rod, with which *Moses* wrought so many Miracles, should have taken notice, that the Devil, who mimicks God in all his Works, follow'd him likewise in that in making use of a Rod, as one of his principal Occasional Causes. *Huetius* (19) asserts, That what the Poets feign of *Mercury's* Rod, &c. was all borrow'd from the History of *Moses's* Rod. The Devil was certainly a very ready Mimick for *Pharaoh's* Magicians, by virtue of their Rods, did some Miracles, which resembled those of the true God (20). Nor are we to forget the Brachmans (21), who always carry a Ring and a Staff, to which they ascribe great Virtues. I shall enlarge more on this, under the Article *Rabdomancy*.

[C] *When Abaris liv'd.*] His Embassy to *Athens* is fix'd by some to the 21st *Olympiad*; by *Hippostratus* to the Third, and by *Pindar* to the time of King *Croesus* (22). *Eusebius* is of the last Opinion, having fix'd the Journey of *Abaris*, and the beginning of *Croesus's* Reign, to the second Year of the 54th *Olympiad*; but afterwards he falls into a shameful Blunder, telling us (23), That this Magician flourish'd in the last Year of the 82d *Olympiad*, *Abaris Hyperboraeus Hariolus agnoscitur*. *Abaris is allow'd to be the Hyperborean Augur*. *Valesius* (24) seems to prefer the Opinion of *Porphyry* and *Jamblichus*, according to whom *Abaris* flourish'd in the 2d Year of the 54th *Olympiad*, cotemporary with *Pythagoras*. This is inferr'd from what *Porphyry* and *Jamblichus* say, That *Pythagoras* shew'd his Golden Thigh to *Abaris*, the Priest of *Hyperborean Apollo*. If the Letters ascribed to *Phalaris* were not somewhat romantic, one might conclude that *Abaris* was cotemporary with that Tyrant; but it is not probable, that the Letters in that Collection were ever penn'd by him. However, 'tis an Argument produc'd by some, to prove that *Abaris* and *Phalaris* were cotemporary; for 'tis very likely, that the Sophist, who wrote those Letters, and ascrib'd them to *Phalaris*, kept strict to Chronology, in order to render his Fictions the more probable. *Suidas* places the Reign of *Phalaris* under the 52d *Olympiad*. The Opinion of *Hippostratus* may be back'd by the following Argument: *Suidas* (25) observes, that in the 5th *Olympiad*, the *Athenians* offer'd, in behalf of all the *Greeks*, Sacrifices that were called προηρόσια: They were offer'd before the Land was till'd, in order to obtain the Divine Blessing upon the ensuing Harvest. Now the Scholiast of *Aristophanes* tells us (26), That when the *Athenians* offered the Sacrifices call'd προηρόσια, for the whole Country, there was a great Famine and Pestilence rag'ng over the whole Earth, which forc'd the People to have recourse to the Oracle; and that the Answer of the Oracle was, If the *Athenians* offer a Sacrifice, the Plague shall be stayed. It was therefore at that time so many Ambassadors were sent to *Athens*, and *Abaris*, among the rest, in the Name of the *Hyperboreans*. *Hippostratus*, then, would not have been much mistaken in placing this Expedition of *Abaris* under the third *Olympiad*. If the Conjectures of *Scaliger*, upon a Passage of *Firmicus Maternus*, concerning the *Palladium*, were true, the Time wherein *Abaris* liv'd would be carried up much higher; for, according to some Authors, he must have flourish'd long before the taking of *Troy*. Others bring him down to the Time of *Alexander* the Great; this is indeed the whimsical Notion of an Orator, whose Opinion in this matter is not worth our regard. The Description (27) which the Sophist *Himerus* has left us, of the Equipage, with which *Abaris* made his Appearance before the *Athenians*, is very suitable to a Barbarian: *But*, says he, *he was a Scythian only in his Garb*; *he spoke Greek, and whenever he spoke, you would have thought you had heard an Oration in the midst of the Academy, or the Lyceum*. What an Absurdity! Had *Plato* and *Aristotle* founded these Schools in the Time of *Abaris*? A certain Author (28) endeavours to reconcile these Difficulties, by supposing there were two *Abaris's*; but this Hypothesis is insufficient; five or six are necessary, if he would succeed. Two will not unite these differences.

(27) Apud Photium, p. 1136.

(28) Edw. Simson, Koenig. Bibl. vet. & nova, pag. 1.

[D] *As to occasion some of the Moderns to fall into Mistakes.*] *Vossius* prefers their Opinion, who say, That *Abaris* flourish'd between the 30th and the 38th *Olympiad*. *This Period*, says he, (29) *according to Eusebius, coincides with the Reign of Phalaris*; *Phalaris Tyrannidem exercuit ab Olypiadis xxx* (it should be xxxi) *An. II. usque ad Olympiadis xxxviii. An. II. teste Eusebio*. By this Hypothesis he overthrows the Notion of those, who maintain, that *Abaris* was the Disciple of *Pythagoras*; for he remarks, that *Pythagoras* flourished in the first Year of the 60th *Olympiad*, and died about the latter end of the 70th. He takes notice likewise, that no Disciple of *Pythagoras* could possibly write Letters to *Phalaris*. Lastly, he asserts, That all the Ancients place *Abaris* not only before *Pythagoras*, but even before *Solon*. *Antiqui omnes do* Abari *loquuntur, ut non* Pythagora *modo, sed* Solone *etiam antiquiori* (30). In these Remarks of *Vossius* there is not the least Solidity; since *Eusebius*, upon whose Testimony he builds, has referr'd *Phalaris* to another Period, namely the 3d Year of the 53d *Olympiad*, and the Travels of *Abaris* to the 2d Year of the 54th. *Vossius* should have observ'd this, and have remember'd, that the Passage of *Eusebius*, which he does not cite, was preferr'd by *Scaliger* (31) to that which he quotes. *Scaliger* grounds his Notion upon this, That the beginning of *Phalaris's* Reign was plac'd by *Suidas* under the 52d *Olympiad*. Add to this, that *Orosius* (32) remarks, that *Cyrus* and *Phalaris* were Cotemporaries. It is plain then that the Inferences, which *Vossius* has drawn from *Abaris* and *Phalaris* living at the same time, are not well grounded; for *Abaris* might have written to *Phalaris* after the 52d *Olympiad*, and have seen *Pythagoras* after the 60th *Olympiad* (33). Let this be as it will, it should never have been asserted, That, according to the Testimony of all the Ancients, *Solon* lived after *Abaris*; for we know that he prescribed Laws to the *Athenians* (34) in the 46th *Olympiad*, and that *Eusebius* places his *Abaris* under the 82d (35).

Mr *Moreri* makes a wrong use of the Observations of *Vossius*: He finds a Contradiction between those who say, that *Abaris* liv'd before *Solon*, and those *who place him in the time of* Tullus Hostilius, *or of* Ancus Martius, *Kings of* Rome. But these Sentiments are not contradictory; nor will any Chronologist scruple to assert, that these two Kings preceded *Solon*. Mr *Moreri* was misled by this Passage of

(29) Vossius de Poëtis Græcis, cap. 3. pag. 16.

(30) Ibid.

(31) Scalig. Animad. in Euseb. n. 1452. p. 94.

(32) Id. ib. n. 1390. p. 84.

(33) Note that Abaris, according to Jambl chus, was old when he went in*stru*cted by Pythagoras.

(34) See Scaliger, as above, n. 1422. p. 86.

(35) See the preceding Remark, Citation (23).

Vossius

ABARIS.

assigning the Reason that induc'd him to quit his Country, in order to travel thro' the World. A raging Pestilence (d) (say they) prevailing over the whole Earth, the Oracle of *Apollo* gave no other Answer than this, That the *Athenians* should supplicate the Gods for all other Nations. Hence it was, that several States sent Ambassadors to *Athens*, of whom the *Hyperborean Abaris* was one. He was then very old ; and, since he returned to his Country, to consecrate the Gold (e), which he had gather'd, to *Hyperborean Apollo*, whose Priest he was, it might be said, that a Collection for pious Uses was one of the Motives that induc'd him to travel to *Greece*. During this Expedition, he renew'd the Alliance between the *Hyperboreans*, and the Inhabitants of the Isle of *Delos* (f). He undertook to foretel future Events; and as he spread his Prophecies in all Places thro' which he travelled, he might properly enough be stiled a walking Oracle [E]. Some say it was he who made the *Palladium* [F], That destin'd Pledge of Security to those Cities which possess'd it, and that he sold it to the *Trojans*. He made it of human Bones (g); Materials, which I fancy, the Makers of *Talismans* never employ. They maintain farther, That he could foretel Earthquakes [G], remove Plagues, and lay Storms, and that he offer'd Sacrifices in

---

Vossius (36), *fuerit igitur* (Phalaria) *temporibus Tulli Hostilii & Anci Martii*. And here, by the way, give me leave to say, that he has also suffer'd himself to be impos'd upon, by this Passage of *Cælius Rhodiginus* (37); *Hujus* (Abaridis) *& Gregorius Theologus comeminit in Epitaphio ad magnum Basilium*. *Moreri* is of Opinion (38), that St *Gregory* makes mention of *Abaris* in an Epitaph upon St *Basil* the Great. But I have not met with one Word of *Abaris*, in the Verses which St *Gregory Nazianzen* made on the Death of St *Basil*. I expected to have found among them the five or six Lines, which *Gyraldus* (39) cites, as taken *ex Monodia in Divum Basilium*. The Term *Monodia* seems to refer to a Piece of Poetry ; but here it is a fallacious Direction. I had recourse to the Prose of that great Divine, that is, his Funeral Oration on St *Basil*, and could not meet with one quarter of what *Gyraldus* had cited. There is a particular Mistake, into which *Moreri* has fallen, when he says, that this Epitaph was not compos'd for St *Basil*.

[E] *A walking Oracle.*] *Clemens of Alexandria* has plac'd *Abaris* among those who foretold future Events (40). Προηγόρευσε δὲ καὶ Πυθαγόρας ὁ μέγας προεκίνησεν αἰεὶ, Ἄβαρις τε ὁ Ὑπερβόρεος· Pythagoras the Great always addicted himself to Prognostications; as did also *Abaris* the Hyperborean. A Commentator on this (41) St *Gregory Nazianzen* has related, that *Abaris* visited every part of *Greece*, and there uttered his Oracles. *Apollonius* asserts the same thing, and besides assures us, that these Oracles were still extant. (42) Ἔγραψε δὲ καὶ χρησμοὺς ταῖς χώραις ποσιερχόμενος, οἳ εἶσιν μέχρι τοῦ νῦν ὑπάρχοντες. i. e. *He wrote also Oracles in the Countries through which he passed, which are extant to this day*. The Scholiast of (43) *Aristophanes* says likewise, that there were some extant in his time. *Abaris* was not the only Person who made it his Business to travel thro' the World, and to spread his Predictions wherever he came : it was peculiar to Diviners to do so ; and hence it is, that *Artimedorus* (44) says, when a Man dreams he becomes a Prophet, 'tis generally a sign, that he will undertake a Journey, or some Business: *For*, adds he, *Diviners are accustom'd to be Vagrants*. Φῶμεν δὲ καὶ ἀνοδμιῶσιν πολλάκις καὶ κινεῖσθαι τὸ ἴσασιν τῶν θνείρον, διὰ τὸ τῆς μαντικῆς περινόσιον. *This Dream portends travelling and removing from place to place; for Diviners are generally Ramblers*. They have this in common with Jugglers, and all kind of Strollers. *Abaris* did more than foretel things to come ; 'tis said that he erected Temples ; that the Temple of *Proserpine* in *Lacedemon* (45) was built by him. *Plato* (46) says, That he was a perfect Cheat, or rather an Enchanter, who pretended to cure Diseases by the Charm of a few Words.

[F] *Who made the Palladium.*] This Discovery is owing to the great *Scaliger*, who (47) in two places of a Passage in *Firmicus Maternus* (48) has corrected the Word *Avarus* by substituting *Abaris*. The whole Passage, as it stands thus corrected, is as follows : *Palladii etiam quid sit numen audite. Simulacrum est ex ossibus Pelopis factum. Hoc Abaris Scytha secisse perhibetur. Jam quale sit considerate quod Scytha barbaris consecravit. Estne aliquid apud Scythas humana ratione compositum, & illa offerra genti & crudeli atque inhumanæ semper atrocitate grassata, in constituendis religionibus rectum aliquid potuit invenire? Simulacrum hoc Trojanis Abaris vendidit, stultis hominibus vana promittens.* Hear likewise in what the Divinity of the *Palladium* consists. *It is an Image made of the bones of Pelops. The Scythian Abaris is reported to have been the Artist: but could a barbarous Scythian convey any Sanctity to it? Can the Scythians produce any thing agreeable to human Reason; or can that savage Nation invent any thing fitting and proper in Religious Matters? This Image Abaris sold to the Trojans, making empty Promises to those foolish men.* *Scaliger* has likewise corrected two Mistakes nearly of the same kind, in a Passage of the Scholiast (49) of *Aristophanes*. Instead of θεῖον, he would have us read *Ἄβαριος*; and instead of βαρίδος, *Ἀβάριδος*, which makes the Sense much more intelligible. The Passage, as corrected, is, Ὁ τε δὴ καὶ Ἄβαριν φασὶ τὸν ὑπερβόρειον ἐλθόντα θεωρῶν εἰς τὴν Ἑλλάδα Ἀπόλλωνι θητεύσας, καὶ ὕσω συγγράφαι τὰς χρησμοὺς τῆς νῦν προσαγορευομένης Ἀβάριδος. The Meaning of this is, That *Abaris*, when he travell'd to *Greece* to consult *Apollo*, or to make some Oblation to him, staid in his Service, and wrote the Oracles which still go under the Name of *Abaris*. *Valesius* (50) corrects a Passage of *Proclus* (51), where *Pythagoras* is cited, ἐν τῷ πρὸς Ἄβαριν λόγῳ; he believes it ought to be read *Ἄβαριν*: If so, there must have been some Work of *Pythagoras* (52) address'd to our *Abaris*. All that we know for certain is, that *Pythagoras*, if we will credit *Jamblichus* (53), explain'd to his Treatise concerning Nature, and his other Tract concerning the Gods, to this *Hyperborean*. *Plutarch* (54) makes mention of a Book entituled *Abaris*, and compos'd by *Heraclides*, wherein, I suppose, were contain'd all the Adventures, both real and romantic, of this famous *Hyperborean*. I am surpriz'd, that *Scaliger*, who was in so good a Disposition to discover Mistakes, should refer us to *Gyraldi*, as a Fund of learned Instruction, concerning *Abaris* for, as learned a Man as *Gyraldus* was, yet he was not very accurate in his account of this Matter (55) : He says, That *Valerius Harpocration* has made mention of the Wonders of the Arrow, and that, according to *Herodotus*, it carry'd him through the Air as far as the Country of the *Hyperboreans*: But 'tis certain that *Harpocration* speaks not a Word of the Arrow, and that *Herodotus* says nothing of the Flight of *Abaris*, much less does he determine the particular Place, to which he fled. *Charles Stephens* and *Moreri* fell into this last Mistake; *Legatus Athenas veniens, ad suos Hyperboreos rediit, nihil comedens*, says *Charles Stephens*, i. e. *He return'd from his Athenian Embassy to his Countrymen the Hyperboreans, without eating any thing*. *Moreri* says, that *Returning from Greece into Scythia, he eat nothing during that long Journey*. This however is more excusable than the Rashness of the former, in saying, That we have still extant the Oracles of *Abaris*. This is to copy after another without Judgment, and without considering, that since what was asserted, those Oracles have been lost. We shall elsewhere (56) pass a general Reflexion upon the Blunders that arise from this Principle.

[G] *Foretel Earthquakes.*] *Porphyry* (57) ascribes this Power to *Pythagoras*, as also that of chasing away Pestilences, of stopping Hail, laying Storms, and appeasing of Tempests by Sea, and on Rivers, that his Friends might have a prosperous Passage. He adds, That *Empedocles*, *Epimenides*, and *Abaris*, having learn'd this Secret from *Pythagoras*, put it in practice upon several Occasions: πολλαχῇ ἐνδετελεκέναι τοιαῦτα. A modern Author, having related (58), that *Pherecydes*,

ABARIS.

(b) Jamblich. as above, c. 19. p. 53. & cap. 28. p. 133.
(i) Apollonius also, as above.
(l) Photii Bibl. p.113'.

(n) Strabo, lib. 7. pag. 208.
(o) Casaubon's Notes upon Strabo, lib. 7. p. 113.
(p) Origen l. 3. against Celsus, pag. 129.

in *Lacedemon*, of so great Efficacy (b), that That Country, which was very subject to the Plague, was never troubled with it afterwards. He composed a great many Books (i); such as, *The Arrival of* Apollo *among the* Hyperboreans; *The Marriage of the River* Hebrus; a *Theogony*, wherein he explain'd the Pedigree of the Gods; *A Collection of Oracles*, and another of *Conjurations*, or *Exorcisms*, or, if you please (k), of Expiatory Prayers. All these Pieces were written in Prose, except the first. If we had the whole Speech of *Himerius* the Sophist, of which *Photius* (l) has preserv'd a Part, we could better tell, than by that Fragment, whether the great Encomiums, bestow'd by that Sophist on a certain Person, belong to *Abaris* or not. 'Tis, at least, past all Dispute, that he (m) praises him for his speaking good *Greek*. Others (n) assert, That his affable Behaviour, and plain Dealing, together with his Probity, recommended him to all *Greece*. I do not find, that *Callimachus* and *Lucian*, make any mention of him, though a certain great Critic (o) assures us they did. Had his Arrow been endued with the Virtue attributed to the *Wand* of *James Aymar* [H], he might have been very beneficial to the World, without fearing the Reflexion cast upon him by *Origen* (p), of being useless in his Generation. But we have (q) since been inform'd, that the Credit of this Wonderwor-king *Wand* was but short-liv'd [I], and that it met with it's fatal Doom at the Prince of *Condé*'s Palace.

(i) Suidas on the Word *Abaris*.
(k) The Greek Word in Suidas, καθαρμῶν.

(m) See the Remark [C], towards the End.

(q) This was written in the Year 1693.

ABARIS, a City of *Egypt*. See the Article PITHOM.

(co) He cites Diog. Laert. in Pherecyd. Cicero. I. de Divin.
(60) Concerning Abaris, he cites Apollonius, surnamed Dyscolus, cap. 5. the same token we have quoted above.
(61) See the Remark [B].

Pherecydes, the Master of Pythagoras (59), *and* Anaximander, *and* Abaris (60), foretold Earthquakes, proposes this pleasant Question; *What*, says he, *did they look upon the Earth as a huge Animal, and were they arriv'd at so great a Skill as to know, by feeling her Pulse, when the trembling Fit was coming upon her?* Now whether the Arrow of *Abaris* was the Instrument with which he perform'd so many Miracles, or whether it contributed nothing thereto, it is certain that his Travels might be of great Use to Mankind. See the next Remark.

[H] *Attributed to the Wand of* (61) James Aymar.] Never did any thing make so great Noise, or occasion the writing of so many Books. I have understood since, that those who promis'd themselves so many Advantages, and so great a Victory over the Incredulous, found themselves greatly disappointed in their Expectations. The single History of this whole Matter might well deserve a particular Article; and perhaps I shall give you some Hints of it under the Word *Rhabdomancy*, or upon some other Occasion. But be that as it will, I shall not recant what I advance concerning the Usefulness of this Wand. Being in the Hands of so great a Traveller as *Abaris*, it would reform the Manners of Mankind more effectually, than all the Missionaries and Preachers in the World. For should such a Man return upon the Stage of the World, Jealousy, that Plague of a married Life, would soon be banish'd all human Society: Neither the *Italians*, nor the eastern Nations, would have then occasion to set Guards over their Wives, or watch them with *Argus*'s Eyes themselves; each Man would trust to their Honesty, and they would need no other Test, than this Wand: And the Men would not only be free from an anxious Care (62), which is too often their Ruin, but would find themselves obliged to preserve their Conjugal Fidelity, when the Reputation of it was become so necessary to them. The Appearance of a Court of Justice would strike less Terror into the Souls of Criminals, than the Arrival of an *Abaris*. The greatest Number of Offences, the most dangerous Sins, such I mean as are committed with the Hopes of Secrecy, would be entirely suppress'd, by thinking on the Wand; and then we might with *Horace* truly say:

(63) *Tutus bos etenim rura perambulat,*
Nutrit rura Ceres, almaque faustitas.

(62) *Pareas gravem in Cal be vita, Et gravior canibus custodia cana maritis.* Auf. Idyll. 15. *Painful the Cares, even of a single State.* More racking those which do on Wedlock wait.
(63) Horace, Od. 5. B. 2.

Culpari metuit fides,
Nullis polluitur casta domus stupris.

Laudantur simili prole puerperæ.

Secure in Pastures roams the wanton Steer,
And smiling Plenty crowns the fruitful Year.
Unsully'd Faith in every Bosom reigns,
And the chast Marriage-bed inviolate remains.
Trac'd in the Child, the honest Sire is shown,
And all his Father's Virtues are his own.

I own it is not easy to conceive, that the Devil, the profess'd Enemy of Mankind, should make choice of such Laws of Intercourse with Men, which is not

consider'd by those, who will not allow us either to call in question the Virtues of the Wand, or attempt to explain them mechanically.

[*I*] *The Credit of this wonder-working Wand was but short liv'd.*] It scarce lasted so long at *Paris*, as the Time of composing and printing one single Article of this Dictionary. The Prince of *Condé*, with Discernment, if we consider his Education, must necessarily be fatal to all Impostors, and their credulous Followers, has pull'd down the Trophies set up by the Partizans of *James Aymar*. This poor Wretch was so unsuccessful in the Trials (64) he made of his Art in the Palace of *Condé*, that his Reputation was ruin'd for ever. The Public was made acquainted with the whole Affair, and there was no room to suspect the Truth, since it was by Order of that great Prince, that the World was inform'd of the Cheat. Nor indeed do they pretend any such Thing; they only endeavour to account for the Miscarriages of the Wand, as I shall observe by and by. They who assert, that the Favourers of these Jugglers ill-tim'd the Matter, and that, in such a Philosophical Age as this, such Artists are not to be impos'd upon the World, have, in some Respects, Reason on their Side; but, all Things consider'd, they do not argue right. There are, I allow, many more private Men, at present, than formerly, who are able to oppose the Stream, and combat Error: But then I must answer; that our Age is as easy to be impos'd upon, as any whatsoever; and, after what we have seen concerning an Explication of the *Apocalypse*, we have no Reason to say, *the World is grown wiser now a-days*. It is the same it ever was: Every Delusion, which flatters it's Passions, is pleasing; it is not asham'd of being convinc'd it was impos'd upon; nor has it, upon that Account, the less Respect for the Impostor; and cries out, as much as ever, against the Incredulity of those, who will not suffer themselves to be deceiv'd. Hear what one of our Journalists tells us in Confirmation of this Matter: " The (65) Testimony of a great Prince, and the Letter of one of the principal Magistrates, are such " strong Proofs against *James Aymar*, as none of those " who give credit to the pretended Effects of the " Wand, dare to contradict. But so foolish are those " credulous Creatures, that hardly one of them will " submit to this Evidence. Mr *Vallemont*, who " has lately publish'd a Tract, *concerning the secret " Philosophy of the divining Wand*, goes about to " explain how the Peasant of *Dauphiné* might be mistaken in the Trials of his Skill before that Prince, " though he had really the Power and Gifts, of which " he boasted. This sort of Philosophers, as well as " the Explainers of Prophecies, (for both of them " are of the same Stamp) are a kind of Enthusiasts, " who will never own themselves to have been in " the wrong; and who, though they are convinc'd " of the Falsity of what they have advanc'd, treat, " as Persons of a dull Imagination, those Men of " Sense, who reject their *Chimæras*."

SINCE the Impression of what I have said, three or four Years have elaps'd without the least mention of *James Aymar*: Our Journalists had quite lost sight of him, and gave him over for lost. But at last they brought him again upon their Stage, in the Month of

(64) See the Historical Letters, and the Political Mercury for the Month of May, 1693.

(65) Ibid. p. 565.

April,

April, 1697. and that to make him act a very comical Part, which would be of singular Use, were the Story they tell of it true. "Some time ago, say (66) they (66), the Prior of the Charter-house of *Ville-neuve* in *Avignon,* travell'd through *Orange* with "*James Aymar,* by whose Assistance he pretended "to discover several Boundaries of Land that were "lost: But by chance he was made use of upon ano- "ther Occasion. Three Days before, a Child was "laid at the Gate of the Convent of the *Capuchins*: "The Rector of the Hospital desired *James Ay- "mar* to discover the Person who did it. To this "he readily consented, came to the *Capuchins* Gate, "where the Child had been laid, and in the View "of a great Multitude, took the Way which the Mo- "tion of his Wand directed him to, and went directly "to a Village of the County of *Venaissin,* nam'd *Ca- "meret,* and from thence into a Farm-house, which, "he said positively, was the Place where the Child "was born. I forgot to tell you, that in the Way he "met with a Man on Horseback, and that by the "Motion of his Wand, he discover'd that he was the "Father of the Foundling. The Judge of the Place, "either of his own Accord, or at the Solicitation of "some Persons concern'd, desired *James Aymar,* and "those who set him to work, to make no farther En- "quiry, and that he would cause the Child to be ta- "ken Home again; which was accordingly done." Upon this Narration, give me leave to make three Remarks. In the first Place, we are not certain of the Truth of this Story: for how many Men take plea- sure to invent Romances, and get them inserted in the public Papers? They send them to an Author with- out subscribing their Name: they lay the Scene at some distance; and besides, they know that there are but few, who will give themselves the Trouble of being better in- formed. My second Remark is, that, though all that is related in the *Historical Mercury* were true, yet this will not silence the Incredulous. *James Aymar,* they will say, knew *which Way he was to go; a false Brother, among those who knew the Intrigue of the Lying-in, was impatient to give the Alarm, and to furnish Matter for Conversation.* However, he was a particular Exception to that general Proverb, *A Pro- phet has no Honour in his own Country.* That Dis- grace which he met with in the Metropolis of the Kingdom, that Train, I say, of ill Success, of which Mr *Buissiere* (67) has publish'd an exact Account, was not able to spoil his Credit in his own Province. In the third Place, I observe, That this Property of the Wand would be of vast Advantage to the World: It would ease the Public of the Funds it is forced to establish for the Maintenance of Foundlings; for it would discover those who are their Parents, and force them to maintain them themselves. Besides, it would enhance the Fear of the evil Consequences; which Dread is such a Restraint upon Incontinence, that, without it, there wou'd be more frequent, and more scandalous Acts of Uncleanness committed. The Fe- male Sex, more commonly aw'd with this Fear than Men are, would be more cautious of their Chastity. To chuse out a private Cottage for Lying-in, to send for a Midwife, with her Eyes blinded, and by a round- about Way; to order the Child to be laid in the Streets in the dead of the Night; these and all the other Precautions, would signify nothing, in case the Wand had the Virtue they talk of. It would point out the Way to the very Chamber of the Lying-in-Woman, better than a Hound follows the Scent of the Hare to her Form. It would put an end to all the false Oaths that are taken (68) by those who are not willing to be at the Charge of keeping a Bastard, since the Mo- ther would oblige them to it, by appearing, without Shame, before a Magistrate, for that very Purpose.

As nothing is so proper to undeceive the Credulous, as to shew that *James Aymar* himself confess'd the Cheat, I shall give the most convincing Evidence of it ||. I have a Proof more positive than the Te- stimony of Mr *Robert,* the King's Attorney, at the Chatelet of *Paris.* The Letter (69) which he writ to Father *Chevigny,* Assistant to the Father General of the Oratory, contains only some of the bad Successes of the Wand; and afterwards these Words: "I "have heard say, that this Wand has not been more "succesful in several Experiments made at *Versailles,* "and *Chantilly*; and that he had been convicted of "Falshood, and had confess'd it: But I know this by "common Report only; not thinking myself obliged "to take any Trouble in such a trifling Affair, "which shews how ready men are to believe Things, "which are new, and appear so extraordinary." The following is a clearer and fuller Proof of the Cheat. Mr *Buissiere* did me the Honour to write to me, That Mr *Dodard,* and Mr *Sauveur,* Members of the *Academy of Sciences,* had desired him to print a second Edition of his Letter, and to put his Name to it; which he promis'd to do, *by Order of the Prince of* Condé, *who was desirous to undeceive the Partizans of the Wand*: To which he will add an Account of the Search (70) which *James Aymar* made after those who murder'd a Patroler, in *St Dennis-street*; and that the Favourers of the Wand may be entirely un- deceived, he will add also the Confession which *James Aymar* made to the Prince of *Condé, That he knew nothing of all that had been attributed to him; and that what he had hitherto done, was to gain a Liveli- hood. This sincere Confession procured him a Present of* 30 *Louis-d'ors from his Serene Highness, that he might retire, as soon as possible, to his own Village; because, being no longer under his Protection, the Peo- ple, whom he had falsely accused, would stop him.* Mr *Robert* told me, (these are Mr *Buissiere*'s Words) *That if he had been put into his Hands to be punish'd, he would have caused him to be condemned to the Gal- lies, the Proof being beyond Contradiction.* The same Letter informs me, That a Boy of 14 Years of Age, who had been instructed for that Purpose, had already impos'd upon a great many People; *but as it was too soon after* Aymar's *Tricks, he found People on their Guard. The little Boy fail'd in his Art, to the Confusion of the Gentleman who had produced him.* Mr *Buissiere* was appointed to examine him, and found him very cun- ning for his Age. *They shut him up several Days without any Communication with the Gentleman: A little Money, with some Promises to settle him, and some Threats, made him confess all.* This Letter of Mr *Buissiere*'s is dated from *Paris,* the 25th of *July,* 1698. We will add to this an Extract of a Letter from Mr *Leibnitz,* which the Author, permitted to be publish'd in Mr *Tenzelius*'s Journal, in the Year 1694, with (71) that of Mr *Robert.* He assures us, That he heard the Duchess of *Hanover,* Sister-in-law to the Prince of *Condé,* say, she had dis- cover'd in her House at *Paris,* the Impostures of *James Aymar*; and that she was of the same Opinion with the Prince, That 'twas better publickly to ex- pose the Falshood of these Pretences, than to conceal them, with a view that the Belief of the Divining Wand might fright a great many Rogues, and procure the Restitution of stollen Goods. She declared that *James Aymar* at last confess'd the Fact; that he asked pardon, and excused himself by saying, That his Im- pudence had contributed less to his Success, than the Credulity of others (72). "Is *(Princeps Condæus)* "Aimarum Lugduno accersiverat indaginis causâ: "excussum multis modis homuncionem & deprehen- "sum, tandem ad confessionem fraudis adegit; quam "sibi ignosci petiit supplex, & graviora metuens, cau- "satus non tam propriâ audaciâ, quam aliená credu- "litate hominum falli volentium, & velut obtruden- "tium sibi, quæ alioqui non jactare ausus fuisset, sese "in hæc impulsum eo tandem pervenisse, urde ee- "dem commodè non potuerit referre. Facile con- "donavit homini magnanimus Princeps; sed erant, "qui suaderent dissimulari comperta, & conservari fa- "mam hominis vel artis, utili dolo, quod constaret, "furibus aliisque malis hominibus magnum metum "fuisse injectum, & ob famam adventantis alicubi re- "rum furtivarum pretia fuisse relata. Sed Ducissæ pa- "riter nostræ ac Principis egregii sententia fuit, po- "tiorem habendam rationem veritatis. He (the Prince "of *Condé*) *sent for* Aymar *to Leyden, in order to examine him: at length, after sifting and detect- ing the Fellow several ways, he forc'd him to confess the Cheat; which, thro' Fear of worse Con- sequences, he begg'd pardon for on his Knees; and excus'd himself, by alledging, that it was not so much his own Impudence, as the Credulity of Peo- ple, who were willing to be deceived, and who as it were forc'd that Art upon him, which it otherwise he would not have dared to boast of, that drove him to carry on the Cheat so far that he could not conveniently retreat. The Generous Prince pardon'd the Man: but there were some, who persuaded him to stifle the Discovery, and to keep up the Credit of the Fellow, or his Art, as being of Service to the Publick: it being certain, that Thieves, and other ill-designing Men, stood greatly in Fear of him,* "and

ABBEVILLE.

"and that the Value of stolen Goods had in some Pla-
"ces, been restored, upon the News of his Arrival.
"But our Dutchess, and this excellent Prince, were
"both of Opinion, that Truth was preferably to be
"regarded." Mr Leibnitz has joined to this a Remark worthy of himself: That it had been better to
have examined, how so many Persons of Merit could
he deceived at Lyons, than to endeavour to find out
the Natural Causes of the pretended Virtue of this
(73) Id. ib id. Wand: (73) "Et scripsi nuper Parisios utilius & exa-
"mine dignius mihi videri problema, morale vel lo-
"gicum, quomodo tot viri insignes Lugduni in frau-
"dem ducti fuerint, quam illud pseudophysicum, quod
"tractaverat Vallemontius, meliori materia dignus?
"Quomodo virga corylacea tot miracula operetur?
"Nam moralis illa quæstio, excussa pro dignitate, mul-
"torum errorum popularium origines sæpe speciosas
"aperiret. *I gave my Opinion lately, in a Letter to
"*Paris, that it was a Problem, whether Moral or
"*Logical, of more Use, and more worthy Examina-
"*tion, why so many celebrated Persons at Leyden
"*were impos'd upon, than that false point of Natural
"*Philosophy, which Vallemontius (worthy of a nobler
"*Subject) undertook to discuss, viz. whence it was,
"*that an Hazel Wand could perform such Wonders.
"*For the just and proper Discussion of this Moral Que-
"*stion would unfold the Spring, how specious soever,
"*of many popular Errors.*" I fancy, that if the Magistrates of Lyons, who caused the Murderer to be
hanged, whom *James Aymar* discovered at *Beaucaire*,
had threaten'd to burn the Discoverer alive, as a wicked Magician; and had caused the Executioner to be
present with all the Instruments of the Rack, they
would have made him confess how he had learnt the
Secret of the Assassination, and how he could find at
Beaucaire, in such and such a place, one of the Assassins. 'Tis very probable, that those Persons, who
had a mind to bring him into Reputation, that they
might share the Profit with him, caused him to play
this part. Mr *Buissiere* takes notice in his printed Re-
(74) *Letter* lation (74), That this Man had a *Club of People*, who
concern of the cry'd him up all over *Paris*; and who publish'd in the
real Effects *Mercuré Gallant for February*, 1693. that he had dis-
of the Wand, cover'd such and such a thing: *than which nothing
pag. 13, 14. *was more false.* The Prepossession was so great, that
he would have got vast Sums, if he could but have
maintain'd his Credit. You may judge whether his
Partizans had not very good Reasons to second him.
(75) *Mr Bu-* (75) "There never was an Imposture more credited
issere's Let- "than this; they were so prejudiced in favour of this
ter to me, Ju- "Person, that they made him do things which he
ly 25, 1698. "never thought of, and found out Reasons to ex-
"cuse him when he did not succeed. He impos'd
"on them by the appearance of a simple and rustic
"Air, and speaking only the Gibberish of his Coun-
"try; but he was at the bottom nothing less than
"what he appeared to be: The Motion of his Wand
"was the Cause of the Illusion. They saw the fork'd
"Stick turn so dexterously in his Hand, that they
"did not perceive the insensible Motion of his Wrist,
"which determined it to turn forcibly and quick,
"by the Spring which he gave to his Wand. Besides
"his apparent natural Plainness, he affected to be
"devout, went often to Confession, every Day to
"Mass, and shew'd other external Tokens of a great
"Sense of Religion; and said, That he had very care-
"fully preserved his Virginity, *without which*, as he
"said, *he could not succeed with his Wand*. He
"would not walk in the Streets in the day-time, for
"fear, as he said, of being murder'd by Thieves
"and Pick-pockets. But all this was only because
"the Night serv'd better for his Tricks. However
"ridiculous he was, yet he did not want Admirers,
"and consequently People to cry him up: and if they

"had not taken care to prevent his going out of *Cot-*
"*di-*House, because the Prince, who had sent for him
"to *Paris* to satisfy his Curiosity, would have him
"try some things, which he had thought of, before he
"was publickly set on work, he had been over-run
"by those who came in Crowds to consult him.
"Some wanted to know *whether he could not disco-*
"*ver the Thieves who were guilty of such a Robbery,*
"*at such a time, and such a place, &c.* Others want-
"ed to know, *whether such a Saint was not the true*
"*one, rather than that of another Parish, which pre-*
"*tended to be in possession of him likewise.* Others
"brought Relicks to him, to know whether they
"really belong'd to such a Saint. Nay, I my self
"saw a young *Silk-Weaver*, who was contracted,
"give him two Crowns to know whether the Wo-
"man he was contracted to had her, Maidenhead or
"no. Those, who shared the Profit, took care to
"bring Grist to the Mill; and oblig'd Persons to
"pay the Money before-hand, if they had a mind to
"succeed in their Enquiries."

Such a Man at *Paris* would have been a certain
Source of Gain, and an inexhaustible Mine to those
who were to share in the Profit. Both suspecting,
and suspected, Persons would have strove who should
pay him best. He would have squeez'd Money out
of both Husbands and their Wives, Gallants and their
Mistresses: The Wand would have mov'd, or not
mov'd, according as he was best paid, by one or
t'other. I believe that if we could discover the Mysteries of these sorts of pretended Prodigies, we should
find it to be a Combination of People in order to get
Money: One boasts of an extraordinary Talent; and
others endeavour underhand to establish the Belief of
it. But I believe there are some Cheats, who have no
need of Emissaries; the Credulity of the Publick is a
sufficient Preparation for their acting the Imposture.
'Tis not long, since there went over the Towns of
Holland a sort of *Germans*, who pretended to cure
all Distempers without any Remedies. *The Patients
need only,* said they, *send us their Urine.* Their Success was the subject of the common Talk; every Body
related some wonderful Circumstances; their Lodgings, like the Pool of *Bethesda*, were crowded with
infirm Persons. I don't believe that those who cried
up the Art of those Quacks were Sharers in the Profit: Some pleased themselves in recommending the
thing, because it look'd like a Prodigy; others might (76) *Mr La-*
find something agreeable in it, because the want of *new a very*
Effect of the common Medicines put them out of *ingenious*
Humour with their Physicians. The Cheat did not *Physician of*
last long; a Month or two set all things to rights. *Rotterdam*
This (76) Imposture was detected, and there were *published a*
so many People undeceived, that their Approbation *small Treatise*
was changed into the utmost Contempt. *in Dutch and*
French, to
We must observe that Mr *Leibnitz* takes notice, *shew the Va-*
with a great deal of Reason, (77) That if the Prince *nity and Ri-*
of *Condé* had not discovered the Imposture, no Argu- *diculousness of*
ment could have prevailed to this very Day with those *this Practice.*
credulous People. But it is to be feared, that *James* *See the Hi-*
Aymar's Cheats will be soon forgotten; and that Peo- *story of the*
ple would be pleas'd with the same Farce again, if the *Works of the*
same Motives should revive it seven or eight Years *Learned, by*
hence. "Nisi Princeps Condæus cognoscendæ rei *Mr Banage,*
"tantum studii, imò & sumptus, impendisset, labora- *p. 408, &c.*
"remus adhuc & conflictaremur cum quibusdam in- *And the Pa-*
"geniis, quibus gratius est per mira falli, quam uudæ *ris Journal*
"veritatis simplicitati acquiescere.——Had not the *of Jan. 13.*
"Prince of Condé been at great pains and even ex- *1698. p. 50.*
"pence, in the Enquiry, we might have still contested *of the Dutch*
"the matter with certain Tempers, which are better *Edit.*
"pleas'd to be deceiv'd by something wonderful, than (77) Leib-
"to acquiesce in plain, simple, Truth." nitz ubi supra.

ABBEVILLE, in Latin *Abbatis-villa*, the Capital City of the Dutchy of *Pon-* (b) Sir-
thieu in *Picardy*, on the River *Somme*, five Leagues from the Sea, in the Diocese of mond. Note
Amiens, was formerly, as the Word imports, no more than a Country-Seat belong- in Epist. 36
ing to an Abbot. 'Tis suppos'd, that this Abbot was St *Riquier*, or one of his Suc- *Alexandri*
(a) *Father* cessors, who, perceiving the Situation to be very pleasant and commodious, two *III.*
l'Abbé in Leagues from his Abbey of *Centula*, caus'd first of all an House (a) to be built there, (c) Hariul-
his Métho- and then a Castle, where was a Priory (b) dependant upon the Abbey. *Hugh Capet,* fus a Monk of
dical Ta- willing to make a strong Place of it, in order to stop the Incursions of the *Barba-* *Centula, in*
bles of Royal *rians*, took it away from the Monks (c); and when he had fortified it, gave it to *the Chronicle*
Geography, *Hugh* his Son-in-law, who took upon him the Title of Protector, because the King *of his Mona-*
p. 322. his Father-in-law had committed to him the Protection of the Church of St *Riquier.* *story, l. 4.*
Edit. 12mo. *c. 12. apud*
Hadr Valef.
Notit. Gall.
p. 1.

ABBEVILLE.

His Son *Angelram* was satisfied with this Title, 'till such time as he had killed (d) in Battle the Count of *Boulogne*, and married his Widow; for then he took upon him the Title of Count of *Pontbieu*, which has been continued to his Successors. In process of time *Abbeville* became very considerable. It is at present so large, *that there are scarce ten or twelve Cities in all France which surpass it, or which so much as equal it in Circumference.* (e) *Sanson*, whose Words I just now cited, in his Computation made in the Year 1636, tells us, that *it contained thirty five or forty thousand Souls*. It was his native Country; and 'tis remarkable, that in a short time it produced three skilful Geographers, Himself, *Peter* (f) *Duval*, and Father *Phillip Briet* the Jesuit. The River *Somme* divides itself here into several Branches, which run partly within, and partly without the City. Father *L'Abbé* is not of *Sanson*'s Opinion, who maintains, (g) that *Abbeville* was always the Capital of *Pontbieu* [*A*]; and that the other Cities of that Country were not in comparison near so antient as That [*B*]. Much less will he allow, what *Sanson* pretends, *viz.* That this City was formerly called *Britannia* [*C*]; and that it was one of the most flourishing Cities of all *Gaul*, long before *Jesus Christ*. We shall, in it's due Place, take notice of the whole Contest, which Father *L'Abbé* [*D*] had with him on this Subject. *Abbeville* is endowed with excellent Privileges;

[*A*] *Was always the Capital of Pontbieu.*] Father *L'Abbé* (1) refutes him as to that particular in these Words, "You have not read, Sir, the Titles and Memoirs of the Abbey of *St Riquier*, which inform us, that under *Lewis le Debonnaire*, in the Year 815, there were, within the Walls of *Centula*, Two thousand five hundred Houses, several Artificers, a great many Streets, *&c.* That *Abbeville* is reckon'd among the Towns and Villages which depended upon it." If any Credit may be given to the Verse that is commonly repeated in that Country;

Turribus à centum Centula nomen habet.

The hundred Towers with which the Walls of *Centula* were flank'd, occasioned it's Name (2).

[*B*] *Were not in comparison near so antient as That*] "This is (3) false," say the Inhabitants of S. *Riquier* "What have you in *Abbeville* that carries any Marks of Antiquity? since your Collegiate Church of St *Wulfran* owe it's Foundation to *William* of *Talvas* and *John* his Son, Eleven hundred Years after *Christ*; and the Priory of St *Peter* of the Order of St *Benedict*, was founded but a few Years before: for as to the Parish Church of *Notre-Dame du Chatel*, it only looks like a country Church." As to St *Prodegarius*, whom *Sanson* has cited as his Voucher for the Existence of *Abbeville* in the Time of the Mayor *Ebroinus*; to this 'tis replied (4), That we ought to read in the Ninety sixth Chapter, not, *atque Abecivo villa evadens aufugit*, but *atque à Bacivo villâ evadens aufugit*.

[*C*] *That this City was formerly called Britannia.*] He grounds his Opinion on a Passage of *Strabo*, where he fancies 'tis said (5), "That the Deputies of *Marseilles* appearing before *Scipio*, and being ask'd by him, what they knew of *Britannia*, *Narbo*, and *Corbilo*, not one of them could say any thing in Commendation of them, though they were the best Towns in all *Gaul*." He supposes that it was in the Year of *Rome* 532. that the Deputies of *Marseilles* shew'd themselves so grosly ignorant. His Reason for it, is, that he, who propos'd those Questions, was the same *Scipio*, who lost the first Battle, which *Hannibal* gain'd over the *Romans*. He supposes that *Scipio*, willing to get Intelligence of *Hannibal's* March, sail'd to the Mouth of the *Rhosne*; and that there the Deputies of *Marseilles*, who came to compliment him, could make no Reply to his Questions. This we shall enquire into farther, under the Article of *Pytheas*. Let us at present proceed to the other *Hypotheses* of *Sanson*. He observes, I. That the City of *Narbonne* was one of the most antient, and most flourishing Cities of *Gaul*; and (6) yet it is not nam'd 'till after that of *Britannia*, among the Three, of which *Scipio* desired to be inform'd. II. That the *Belgium*, in the Commentaries of *Julius Cæsar*, was a Region (7) among the *Belgæ*, which comprehended the *Beauvaisis*, the *Amienois*, the *Artois*, and *partly also the Vermendois*, and the *Senlissans*. III. That the Inhabitants of the Coasts of *Great-Britain*, came from (8) *Belgium*, and retain'd the Names of the Cities, from whence they came; as *Cæsar* informs us. IV. That, according to *Pliny's* (9) Calculation, the People, whom he stiles *Britanni*, must have been Inhabitants (10) of *Pontbieu*. V. That of all the Parts of *Belgium*, from whence

People went over into *England*, there is none that ought to come into the Account, so much as that which is situated by the Sea-side; that is, the Country of *Pontbieu*: From all this he infers (11), That the *Britanni* of *Pliny* are the chief Inhabitants of *Belgium*, who went over into *England*; and that at first they retained their antient Name, and at last render'd it universal over the whole Country; and that they would not have called themselves *Britanni*, had not their Capital City been *Britannia*: It follows then, that the Capital of *Pontbieu* was the antient *Britannia* of which *Scipio* desir'd to be inform'd; now *Abbeville* is the Capital of *Pontbieu*: It went therefore under the Name of *Britannia*, the most flourishing City of the *Gauls*, even before the Second *Punick* War.

Doubtless there is Learning and Genius in this long Train of Suppositions and Consequences, considering the Manner wherein the Author was imagin'd it. But, after all, 'tis a meer Romance, an airy Phantom, founded on a Passage not duly understood. The Matter of Fact is this: *Strabo* (12) tells us, that *Polybius* has inserted among the fabulous Stories of *Pytheas*, "That none of the Inhabitants of *Marseilles*, who had an Interview with *Scipio*, could say any thing considerable, when he questioned them about *Britain*, no more than any of the Inhabitants of *Narbonne*, or of *Corbilo*, the two best Cities of the Country." This is the true meaning of the *Greek* Text, as may be collected not only from the Rules of Grammar, but also from the Humour of the Stroller here mentioned; *καὶ ἰς αὐτου Πολύβιος, μηθένος τῶν οὐκ Πυθέα μεθιστορηθέντων ὅτι Μασσαλιωτῶν τῶν συμβαλόντων Σκιπίωνι οὐδεὶς οὐχ λέγειν οὐδεν μνήμης ἄξιον ἔχυστοτίας ὑπὸ τοῦ Σκιπίωνος ὑπὲρ τῆς Βρεττανικῆς; ὡδ᾽ τῶν ἐκ Ναρβῶνος, ὡδ᾽ τῶν ἐκ Κορβιαλῶνος, αἵπερ ἦσαν ἄρισαι πόλεις τῶν ταύτη* (13). This Fellow, to put the better Gloss upon his romantic Stuff and Rhodomontades, used to brag, That he would inform his Readers of a thousand things, of which they never had heard before. No question then but he boldly gave out, that his Relation of *Britain* presented us with the first and earliest Account of that Island; and that, to prove it, he made use of this Argument; *viz.* That *Scipio* could learn nothing about it from the Inhabitants of *Marseilles*, nor from those of *Narbonne*, nor from those of *Corbilo* upon the *Loire*; though these were the most flourishing Cities of *Gaul*. Every one may see how *Sanson* has mistaken the Words of the antient Geographer, to which no question the *Latin* Version has not a little contributed: *Cujus (Corbilonis) mentionem faciens Polybius simul Pytheæ refert commentum, Massiliensium scilicet, qui Scipionem convenerant, nullum quicquam babuisse dignum memoratu quod diceret, interrogatus de Britannia, itemq; Narbonensium & Corbilonensium, cum hæ tres urbes Galliæ omnium essent optimæ.* One might be apt to imagine, at first Sight, that the three chief Cities of *Gaul*, mentioned by the Translator, are call'd *Britannia*, *Narbo*, & *Corbilo*; but upon due Attention, we shall perceive that *Βρεττανικὴ* is here taken for the Island *Britannia*: And thus *Strabo* (14) is us'd to express himself, without the Addition of the Word *Νῆσος*, *Insula*.

[*D*] *The Contest which Father L'Abbé had with him on this Subject.*] He made his Declaration of War,

ABBEVILLE. ABBOT.

Privileges; and as it has never been taken, (b) it is stiled, *The Virgin of the Country*, and has for it's Motto, *semper fidelis, always faithful*. Whoever would be acquainted more at large with what relates to this City, the Privileges of it's Mayors, the famous Men who have been born or died there (i), &c. may consult the genealogical History of the Counts of *Ponthieu*, printed at *Paris*, by Francis Cloufier, 1657. in Folio. The Author only tells us his Name by these initial Letters, F. I. D. J. M. C. D. But 'tis easy to perceive that they mean *Frere Ignace de Jesus-Maria, Carme dechausé*. i. e. Brother Ignatius de *Jesus-Maria, A barefooted Carmelite*. See the Article SANSON (*James*).

(b) Du Val in his Treatise of France p. 70.

(i) 'Tis with great Reason that I have here added an Etcætera, for the Book is full of foreign Matters; Therein is to be found Bayard the Knight, and several other Persons who have no manner of Relation to Ponthieu.

War, and his first Act of Hostility, in these Words: "Brittanniam Abbavillæus Chalcographus interpretatur *Abbeville*, lepidissimo commento, quod non tam ex Pytheæ mendaciis, quam ex ignoratione linguæ Græcæ editum malignam in lucem demonstrabimus alias, cum primum singularem illum de Britannia tra- ctatum nancisci & legere datum fuerit. The *Abba- villæan Chalcographer* (so he stiles *Sanson*) inter- pret: Brittannia *to mean* Abbeville, *upon a plea- sant Hypothesis enough, which we shall shew in an- other place to be unfortunately built, not so much upon* Pytheas's *lying Accounts, as upon an Ignorance of the Greek Tongue, when it shall be in our Powers to procure and read over the remarkable Treatise* De Britannia." Thus he express'd himself in his *Pharus Galliæ antiquæ*, printed at *Moulins* 1644. He had not as yet read the Book, which *Sanson* publish'd on this Subject at *Paris*, 1636. He had only seen the same Appearance of *Brittannia*, not in the large Map of antient *Gaul*, publish'd by *Sanson* in the Year 1627, but in a small Chart publish'd since. Having at last perused the Book, he refuted the Prin- ciples upon which 'tis founded, *Ann.* 1646, in the *Methodical Tables of the Royal Geography*; and did not forget to observe, that, according to the Sense, which the Sieur *Sanson* gives to *Strabo*'s Text, it must be said, that the Inhabitants of *Marseilles* were wholly ignorant with respect to the City of *Nar- bonne, Ann. U. C.* 532. though *Marseilles* had then been built about 400 Years, and *Narbonne* was a very flourishing City. *Sanson* was sensible of the Difficul- ty, and guarded against it as well as he could (15). But who can imagine that the *Marseillians*, because they had frequent Wars with their Neighbours, had not Time to know what *Narbonne* was? The Pas- sage of *Justin* (16), which *Sanson* relates, informs us, that before the Year of *Rome* 362, they had often conquered the *Carthaginians*, and entered into Alli- ance with the *Spaniards*. Father *L'Abbé* was not much the better for his Triumph; for *Sanson* made the same Insults over him in his Turn, which al- most ruin'd the *Pharus Galliæ antiquæ*. Note, That with respect to his Hypothesis concerning *Britannia*, he wrote a Reply (17) which was never printed.

(15) Sanson as before, p. 76, &c.

(16) Justin. L. 43. c. 5, 6.

(17) See the Remark [A] of the Article Pytheas. towards the End.

ABBOT (a) (GEORGE) Archbishop of *Canterbury*, and Author of several Books [*A*], was the Son of a *Cloth-Worker*, and born at *Guilford*, in the County of *Surry*, in 1562. He studied at *Oxford*, and in the Year 1597 was made Master of *University-College*. Two Years after, he was advanced to the Deanery of *Winchester*, which he held 'till the Year 1609, when he succeeded *Thomas Morton* in the Deanery of *Gloucester*. Hitherto his Advancement was not very shining, nor quick; but af- wards it made a very great Progress in a very little Time; for he was made Bishop of *Lichfield*, Dec. 3. 1609, Bishop of *London*, Feb. 1610, and Archbishop of *Canter- bury* in March following (b). His Learning and fine Talent of Preaching contri- buted less to his sudden Advancement, than his Interest with the Earl of *Dunbar*, whose Chaplain he had been. His Conduct was not pleasing to every Body. It was thought strange, that he should have more regard to his Secretary than to his Chap- lains; and that, when he appeared abroad, he should show more Respect to the Laity than to the Clergy. It was supposed, that, having never had any Benefice with the Cure of Souls, that is, having never experienc'd the Difficulties to be met with in the Direction of a Parish, he was thereby become less capable of shewing any In- dulgence to the inferior Clergy. His Severity towards them, and the Countenance he gave to the Nonconformists, were the two principal Reasons of the Clamour that was rais'd against him. The latter of these caused a modern Writer to say, That if *Laud* had succeeded *Bancroft*, and the Project of *Conformity* had not met with an Interruption in the Time of *Abbot*, doubtless the Schism in *England* would have been at an end (c). King *James* was disgusted with *Abbot*, because he oppos'd the Design That King had of marrying the Prince of *Wales* to the *Infanta* of *Spain*. The Ene- mies of the Archbishop, being apprized of this, thought they had a fair Oppportu- nity of crushing him; for they hoped to gain the Ascendant over this superstitious King, by alledging the Sacredness of the antient Canons. For the better under- standing of this, it must be observ'd, that *Abbot* had accidentally kill'd the Keeper of *Bramzel* Park, belonging to the Lord *Zouch*. The Bishop of *Lincoln*, who was then Lord-Keeper of the Broad-Seal, told the Duke of *Buckingham*, That the Arch- bishop was *ipso facto* deprived of his Dignity, upon the Account of the Murther he had committed. For this he appeal'd to the Laws of *England*, and the Seve- rity of the antient Discipline; he added, That it was to be feared the Papists would make an Advantage of it, if they should suffer one to exercise the Office of an Archbishop and Primate of the Realm, whose Hands are defiled with Blood. In short, he gained his Point so far, that a Commission was issued to some Bishops and Peers, to enquire into the Matter of Fact. The Event of this Enquiry was not very agreeable to the Archbishop's Enemies; for it was adjudg'd, That this invo- luntary

(a) Some call him Ab- bat.

(b) Athenæ Oxonienf. Vol. 1.

(c) Fuller's Worthies of England.

[*A*] *And Author of several Books.*] The chief are, *Quæstiones sex Theologicæ totidem prælectionibus dis- putatæ*, printed at *Oxford*, 1598. *Dr Hill*'s *Reasons for Papistry unmask'd* (1) at *Oxford*, 1604. *An Ex- position upon* Jonah, *by way of Sermon*. *The History of the Massacre in the* Valteline. *A Treatise of Geo- graphy*; of which the ninth Edition, which was first the last, is in the Year 1607. And a Treatise con- cerning the *Perpetual Visibility of the Church*, printed at *London*, 1624. to which he has not put his Name.

(1) Dr Hill had embrac'd the Romish Religion.

luntary Murthur had not difqualified him. This happened in the Year 1621. Six Years after, a new Storm was raifed againft him, which quite overthrew him: Nor is there any thing furprifing in it; for the Favourite (d) owed him a Grudge, and could not endure that feveral Perfons, offenfive to him, frequented the Archbifhop's Table, one of the moft fplendid at that time. The Pretence made ufe of, was, That this Prelate refufed to licenfe a Sermon of Dr *Sibthorp*, upon Apoftolical Obedience, though the King had commanded him fo to do: Upon which he was fufpended from all his Archiepifcopal Functions, which were adminiftred by other Prelates; among whom was *William Laud*, who was afterwards his Succeffor (e). *Abbot* retired to the Place of his Nativity, and afterwards to *Croydon* Caftle, where he died on the 4th of *Auguft*, in the Year 1633. His Monument is to be feen, with feveral Ornaments and Infcriptions, in *Guilford* Church. He founded an Hofpital well endowed in that Town. There was another *George ABBOT* [B], who publifh'd, in *Englifh*, a Paraphrafe on *Job*; Short Notes on the *Pfalms*; *Vindiciæ Sabbathi*, &c. (f) He liv'd in the Year 1640.

(d) *The Duke of Buckingham.*

(e) Rufhworth's *Hiftorical Collections,* Tom. 1. *Where is to be feen a large Memorial of George Abbot, upon the Account of his Sufpenfion.*

(f) A hen. Oxon. ib.

[B] *Another George ABBOT*] The Sieur *Henninges Witte* was not aware of this, in his *Diarium Biographicum*; where he attributes to the Archbifhop of *Canterbury* the Works of the other *George*, the Paraphrafes on *Job* and the *Pfalms*, and the *Vindiciæ Sabbathi*. He likewife afcribes to him, *A Treatife againft Bifhops*, and another *againft the Brownifts*. Tho' it feems very odd for a Primate of *England* to write againft Bifhops.

ABBOT (ROBERT) elder Brother to the former, born alfo at *Guilford* (a), and Student of *Oxford* in *Baliol* College: One of his firft Employments was that of Lecturer at *Worcefter*; then he was made Minifter of the Church of *All-Saints* in the fame Place; and a little after Minifter of the Parifh of *Bingham* in *Northamptonfhire*. All this happened between the Years 1581 and 1588. He Commenc'd Doctor of Divinity at *Oxford*, in the Year 1597, and was admitted Chaplain in Ordinary to King *James* I. in the beginning of his Reign. In the Year 1609, he was made Mafter of *Baliol* College; three Years after he was advanced to the Dignity of *Regius* Profeffor in Divinity, in the Univerfity of *Oxford*. In his Lectures he made choice of a Subject fo agreeable to King *James*, and managed it with that Depth of Thought and Learning, as is fuppofed to be the only Reafon of his Advancement to the Bifhoprick of *Sarum*: The Subject he made choice of, was, *The fupreme Power of Kings*; which he maintained againft all the Subtilties and Sophifms of *Bellarmine* and *Suarez*. This is what may be feen in his Treatife, entituled, *De Supremâ Poteftate Regia*, printed at *London*, 1619. He likewife publifh'd, in 1613, a *Latin* Book, no lefs agreeable than his Lectures, viz. An Anfwer to the Apology publifh'd by *Eudæmon Joannes* the Jefuit, in Vindication of his Brother *Henry Garnet*. He did not long enjoy his Bifhoprick, for he was Confecrated Decemb. 3. 1615, and died of the Stone (b) *March* 2. 1618. Within two Years after his firft Wife's Death, he married a fecond, which was highly difpleafing to the Archbifhop his Brother (c). Some have wondered how it came to pafs, that, after he had fhewed his Learning and Merit both by fpeaking and writing; and having been fuccefsful in every thing he undertook, whether preaching, compofing of Books and Lectures, difputing, maintaining of *Thefes*, or folving to a Wonder the moft knotty Queftions, it has been Matter of Surprize, I fay, how he came to be promoted to a Bifhoprick fo late. For this there are three Reafons affigned; Firft, That he was not Ambitious: Secondly, That he was fufpected of being a Puritan: And, Laftly, That his Relations were unwilling to confent, that the Church fhould be Adorn'd with the Spoils of the Univerfity; and that he fhould leave his Profefforfhip to be made a Bifhop (d). This laft Reafon, in my Opinion, is not well grounded. Let this be as it will, thofe, who have made a Comparifon between the two Brothers, prefer *George* as an Eloquent, and *Robert* as a Learned Preacher. They tell us, That *George* was the fitteft for Bufinefs; and that *Robert* was the moft profound Divine: They add, that the Gravity of *George* was attended with an Air of Severity, and that of *Robert* with a fmiling Afpect (e). The latter was reckoned a moderate *Calvinift*; for he explained the Doctrine of Predeftination according to the Hypothefis of the *Sublapfarians*. In the Note we fhall give you the Catalogue of his Works [A]. There has been fince him another *Robert ABBOT*, a Native of *Cambridge*, who has publifh'd feveral Books in *Englifh*. He was a *London* Divine, after he had been a Minifter in *Kent*, and other Places (f). The Catalogue of the *Bodleian* Library makes three *Robert Abbots* out of one, and the Treatifes, which were compofed by one and the fame Perfon, are there divided amongft them.

(a) In 1560.

(b) *The Sieur Witte places his Death March 11. 1817. T at which cov'd in MS. it is. That the Englifh do not fign their Year as other Countries do.*

(c) Athen. Oxonien.

(d) Fuller's *Worthies.*

(e) Id. ib.

(f) Athen. Oxonien.s.

[A] *The Catalogue of his Works.*] Befides thofe I have already mention'd, he compos'd, *A Mirrour of Popifh Subtilties, London*, 1594. *Sermons on the 110th Pfalm*, 1601. *Defence of the Reform'd Catholic of Mr W. Perkins, againft the Baftard Counter-Catholic of Dr Bifhop*, and a Reply to the Anfwer of the fame Doctor; *London*, 1611. *Antichrifti (1) demonftratio contra Pontificios*, Londoni, 1603. *Exercitationes de gratia & perfeverantia Sanctorum*, Ibid. 1618. *Animadverfio in Richardi Thompfoni diatribam de amiffione Juftificationis & Gratiæ*, Ibid. 1618. His Commentary on St *Paul's* Epiftle to the *Romans* was found in his Study; it contains four Volumes, and was given to the *Bodleian* Library by Dr *Edward Corbet*, the Husband of *Margaret Brent*, Daughter of *Martha Abbot*; which *Martha* was the only Daughter and Heir of our *Robert*, Bifhop of *Sarum* (2). That learned Prelate fhow'd his great Skill in *Polemics*, by enlarging on all the Matters of Controverfy, which the Epiftle to the *Romans* affords.

(1) *See the Englifh quoted in this Article.*

ABDAS

ABDAS.

ABDAS, A Bishop in *Persia*, in the time of *Theodosius* the younger, was, thro' his inconsiderate Zeal, the Cause of a very terrible Persecution, which was raised against the Christians, who enjoy'd a full Liberty of Conscience in *Persia*, when this Bishop took the Liberty to pull down one of the Temples, where the *Persians* worshiped the Fire. The *Magi* made their Complaints to the King [*A*], who sent for *Abdas*, and, after a mild Rebuke, ordered him to rebuild the Temple. *Abdas* refused to do it, though that Prince declared to him, that, in case of his Disobedience, he would cause all the Christian Churches to be pulled down. Which Threat he executed (*a*); and all the Christians were delivered up to the Mercy of his Clergy [*B*], who, being angry at the Toleration that had been granted them, fell upon them with great Fury. *Abdas* was the first Martyr, who lost his Life on that Occasion, if we may so call a Man, who by his Rashness [*C*] (*b*) expos'd the Church to so many Misfortunes. The Christians, who had long ago forgot one of the most essential Parts of Christian Patience, had recourse to a Remedy, which occasioned another Deluge of Blood. They implored the Assistance of *Theodosius*, which kindled a long War between the *Romans* and *Persians* (*c*). 'Tis true the latter were worsted: But were there any Certainty that they should not overcome the *Romans*, and that, being flushed with Victory, instead of persecuting only the Christians in *Persia*, they would not exercise a general Persecution against all the other Churches? Thus we see what Mischiefs the inconsiderate Zeal of one Man may occasion. The Fury of the Persecutors could scarce be satisfied in the Space of thirty Years (*d*). They, who (*e*) suppress the Reason of the Rage and Violence of the *Persians*, can't be excused. The Commonwealth of Learning might enter an Action against 'em, as is practised against those Sellers, who (*f*) conceal what they ought to acquaint the Buyers with; and it were to be wished, that the Publick would be more severe against those Historians, who suppress certain Facts: It is so common a Fault amongst those Gentlemen, that it is high time to prevent it for the future, if possible.

(*a*) Ex Theodoret Eccles. Hist. l. 5. c. 39.
(*b*) Vedelius, *a Protestant Divine*, blames that *Bishop*, apud Voet. disp. Theol. Tom. 3. p. 310.
(*c*) Socrates, l. 7. c. 18. Hist. Eccl.
(*d*) Theod. Ibid.
(*e*) See the Remark [C].

(*f*) Cum ea duodecim tua bulis satis est sit ea praestationi quae essent lingua nuncupita, quae qui inficientes esset dupli poenam subiret, à Jureconsultis etiam reticentiae poena est constituta. Quidquid enim esset in praedio visi id statuerunt, si venditor sciret, nisi nonnutim dictum esset, praestari o-portere. Cicero de Officiis l. 3. c. 17. S e l'historie Grotius de Jure belli, l. 2. c. 8. n. 7. and Puffendorf de Jure Nat. l. 5. c. 3.

[*A*] *To the King.*] 'Twas *Isdegerdes*, if we rely upon (1) *Theodoret*; but, according to (2) *Socrates*, the Persecution began under *Vararanes*, Son and Successor of *Isdegerdes*. *Baronius* (3) dares not determine which of the two is in the right.

[*B*] *To the Mercy of his Clergy.*] So I call the *Magi*, who, amongst other things, took care of Religion. It was their business to prevent all manner of Innovation in Religious Matters. *Theodoret* (4) compares them to a Whirlwind, which raises the Waves of the Sea: Τρεάκοντα διεληλυθότων ἐτῶν ἡ ζάλη μεμένηκεν, ὑπὸ τῶν μάγων καθάπερ ὑπὸ τινῶν καταιγίδων ῥιπιζομένη. *The Tempest continu'd more than thirty Years, being rais'd by the Magi, as so many Whirlwinds*; such was their Function in the Storm that tossed so violently the Church of *Persia*. *Socrates* (5) tells us, that they made use of several Impostures to put a Stop to the Progress of the Christian Religion, when they saw that the Love *Isdegerdes* had conceived for the holy Bishop *Maruthas*, gave them Reason to fear, that he would forsake their Religion. They were so bold as to hide a Man under Ground, in the Temple where the King used to worship the Fire; and they order'd him to cry out, when the King came in, "That they ought to turn out That Prince, since "he had been so impious as to believe, that a Chri-"stian Priest was a Friend of God." If what is most falsely said by impious Men were true, *viz.* That Religion is a mere human Invention, set up by the Sovereigns to keep their Subjects within the Bounds of Obedience, may we not assert, that Princes are the first who have been taken in their own Snares? For Religion is so far from making them Masters of their Subjects, that, on the contrary, it gives their Subjects a Power over them, since they are obliged to profess the Religion of their People, and not That, which seems to them to be the best: And if they are resolved to profess a Religion different from that of their Subjects, their Crowns will sit loose upon their Heads. We see how the *Persian Magi* threaten'd their King, though he had only careful'd one Bishop. Has it not been asserted, that the last (6) King of *Siam* was pull'd down from the Throne, for having too much favour'd the Christian Missionaries. The same *Socrates*, who mentions the Artifices made use of by the *Magi*, to put a Stop to the Propagation of the Gospel, tells us likewise, That, after the Death of *Isdegerdes*, they inspired his Son with such a Spirit of Persecution, that the Christians were treated with shocking Cruelty. They had endeavour'd, but in vain, to inspire his Father with the same Spirit; for he was inclined to embrace the Gospel. *Socrates* assures us of this: But he is to blame for not owning

(1) Theod. Hist. Eccles. l. 5. c. 39.
(2) Socrat. Hist. Eccl. l. 7. c. 18.
(3) Baronius ad ann. 420.
(4) Theod. ubi supra.

(5) Socrat. l. 7. c. 8.

(6) This was wrote in 1693.

sincerely, that the rash Action of Bishop *Abdas* afforded the *Magi* a very plausible Pretence. Compare with this the Remark [*B*] of the Article of Junius (Francis) *Professor at Leyden*.

[*C*] *A Man, who by his Rashness.*] All the Church Historians are not guilty of the Insincerity, for which I blame *Socrates*; for *Theodoret* (7) ingenuously confesses, That the Bishop, who pull'd down a Temple, occasion'd the dreadful Persecution of the Christians in *Persia*. He does not deny but that the Zeal of that Bishop; was unfeasonable; but he maintains, that his Refusal to rebuild the Temple is worthy of Admiration, and deserves a Crown: For *it seems to me*, says he, *as great an Impiety to build a Temple to the Fire, as to worship it*. *Nicephorus* (8) does but transcribe *Theodoret*. For my own part, I am of Opinion, That no private Men, whether they be Metropolitans or Patriarchs, can at any time be dispens'd with from obeying this Law of Natural Religion. *The Damage, that has been done to one's Neighbour, ought to be made up by Restitution, or some other Way.* Now *Abdas*, a mere private Man, and a Subject of the King of *Persia*, had destroy'd another's Property, and a Property which ought to have been the more inviolable, as it related to the establish'd Religion of the Country; he was therefore indispensably obliged to obey the Orders of his Sovereign, by restoring what he had destroyed: And it was no good Excuse to say, That the Temple, which he was ordered to rebuild, was design'd for the Use of Idolaters; for he was not to put it to that Use, and he could not be answerable for the Abuse of those, to whom it belong'd. Would it be a good Reason for keeping a Purse, stollen from another, to say that the Man, from whom it was taken, spends his Money extravagantly? Let him do so in you are not answerable to God for the ill Use he makes of his Money: Let him enjoy what is his own; what Right have you to it? Besides, could there be any Comparison between the Destruction of a Temple, without which the *Persians* would have remain'd as great Idolaters as they were before, and the Destruction of many Christian Churches? *Abdas* should have therefore prevented this last Evil by the first, since the Prince put it to his Choice. Lastly, can any thing render the Christian Religion more odious to all the Nations of the World, than to see, that after the Christians had insinuated themselves, as desiring only the Liberty of teaching their Doctrine, they are so bold as to destroy the Temples, consecrated to the Religion of the Country, and to refuse to rebuild them, when the Sovereign commands it? Is it not to give occasion to the Infidels to say; *These Men desire at first a mere Toleration, but in a little Time they will*

(7) Hist. Eccl. lib. 5. c. 39.

(8) Lib. 14. c. 19. *I find apud* Saldenum *Otia theol.* p. 639. *that* Socrates, *vocat exertim rem non opportunam, calls it* an ill tim'd Action, *which was done by the Bishop*. He quotes Hist. Tripart. l. 10. c. 30. but it is certain that That Chapter is taken from Theodoret. Voetius disput. Theol. Tom. 3. p. 310. quotes Eusebius, who could not mention it.

ABDERAME

till pretend to share with us all Employments and Places of Trust, and then become our Masters. At first, they think themselves very happy, if they are not burnt, afterwards very unhappy, if they have fewer Privileges than others: and then again, very unhappy if they are not the only prevailing Party. For some time they resemble Cæsar, who could bear no Master; and then Pompey, who could suffer no Partner?

Nec (9) quenquam jam ferre poteſt Cæſarve priorem,
Pompeiuſve parem.

Superior Power, fierce Faction's dearest Care,
One cou'd not brook, and one disdain'd to share.
ROWE.

The Perſecutors of the *French* Proteſtants maliciouſly inſpired *Charles* IX. with the like Thought. 'Tis ſaid, that that Prince made uſe of theſe Words, ſpeaking to the Admiral *de Coligni* (10), *Per imanzi vi contentavate d'un poco di ſicurza, hora la volete dei pari, fra poco verrette eſſer ſoli, & cacciar noi altri fuori del regno.* i. e. *At first they pretend to be ſatisfy'd with a little Liberty; then they deſire to be upon an Equality; next they aſpire to govern alone; and at laſt, they would drive us out of the Kingdom.* Such are the unavoidable Inconveniences, which They expoſe themſelves to, who maintain ſo warmly, That the Power of the ſecular Arm ought to be made uſe of for the Eſtabliſhment of Orthodoxy. Such were the Principles of *Abdas*. For what would he not have done with force of Arms againſt the Idolaters under a Chriſtian Emperor, ſince, under a Heathen Prince, who tolerated the Chriſtian Religion, he pull'd down a Temple, for which the Heathens had a very particular Veneration. *Compare this with what you will meet with in the Remark* [B], *of the Article* BRAUN (George).

ABDERAME, Governor of *Spain*, for *Iſcham* Caliph of the *Saracens* in the VIIIth Century, endeavoured to extend their Empire over *France*, after they had conquered all *Spain*. They might have been contented [*A*] with the Countries they had already ſubdued; but it was very natural for them not to ſtop in ſo fine a Road of Succeſs. If we had a particular Hiſtory of *Abderame*, written by one of his own Party, it would doubtleſs appear, that he was very well qualified to ſatisfy the exceſſive Ambition of his Maſter; and that he was one of the greateſt Generals in the World. We ſhould meet with nothing but great Actions and Triumphs. I know that ſome Chriſtian Writers ſpeak well of him: And indeed 'tis no ſmall Praiſe to have penetrated, as he did, into the very Heart of *France*: But, after all, there is nothing like a Writer of one's own Party. *Abderame* quickly removed the Obſtacle, which *Eudes*, Duke of *Aquitain*, had raiſed againſt him; having in a little time reduced the (a) Govenor of *Cerdagne*, who had taken up Arms at the Sollicitation of that Duke, to the Neceſſity of killing himſelf. He treated his Widow [B] very civilly, who was Daughter of Duke *Eudes*, and a moſt beautiful Woman. As ſoon as he had ſuppreſt that Inſurrection, he applied himſelf with all imaginable Care to Preparations for War, in order to invade *France*; and (b) the Year following, made an Irruption into that Country with one of the greateſt Armies that had been ſeen for a long time: It ſpread far and wide, and filled every Place with Deſolation and Horror. The Memory whereof is not yet loſt, even amongſt the common People in the Countries, which were ſo cruelly ravaged. 'Tis not known whether the *Gaſcons* [C], whoſe Duke was a Friend to the Duke of *Aquitain*, made any Reſiſtance, or whether they ſubmitted to the *Saracens*: We only know, that *Abderame*, having advanced as far as *Bourdeaux*, took that City, and burnt all the Churches;

[*A*] *Have been contented*] 'Perhaps the World has never ſeen ſuch an Inſtance of a long Series of Victories, and large Conqueſts, as the *Saracen* Hiſtory preſents us with. The Idea which the *Roman* Poet formed of a vaſt Dominion, takes in but part of their Empire.

Latius regnes, avidum domando
Spiritum, quam ſi Lybiam remotis
Gadibus jungas, & uterque Pœnus
ſerviat uni (1).

That Man a wider Empire gains,
Who his own craving Wiſh reſtrains,
Than he, whoſe Sword, and wide Command,
Join diſtant Spain to Lybia's Sand;
Than if they did his Arms obey,
And either Carthage own his Sway.
CREECH.

Reaſon prompted them both to ſtop, and not to ſtop. This ſeems a Contradiction, and yet 'tis very true: If they had ſtopt, they might have been praiſed for it upon ſeveral Accounts; but they had been blam'd likewiſe for ſeveral Reaſons. They might have been charged with Weakneſs and Imprudence. It might have been ſaid, That they neither had the Courage nor the Skill to improve the Opportunities which Providence put into their Hands; and that a little more Boldneſs and Courage would have enabled them to conquer the whole World. They, who do great Actions, are never ſecure from ſuch malicious Reflexions: If it cannot be denied that they have done great Things, it will be ſaid however, that it is nothing in Compariſon of what another would have done in the like Caſe. The Heathens would have called this a Criticiſm on Fortune for the ill Choice of her Favourites.

[*B*] *He treated his Widow, &c.*] I ſhall obſerve in another Place (2), that the Daughter of *Eudes*, who was married to the Governor of *Cerdagne*, was the moſt beautiful Princeſs of her Time; and that, being brought to *Abderame*, he ſent her to the Caliph. A Circumſtance, which a *Saracen* Hiſtorian would not lightly paſs over, as Chriſtian Writers do. He would extol it above all that has been celebrated by the *Greeks*, to the Glory of *Alexander*, and by the *Romans*, to the Glory of *Scipio*. *Alexander* (3) behaved himſelf chaſtly towards *Darius*'s Wife and Daughters, who were his Priſoners. *Scipio* (4) laid a Reſtraint upon his Paſſions, though he had a very beautiful Virgin in his Power, and ſent her back to a Man of Quality, to whom ſhe was contracted. A panegyrical Writer might find in the Circumſtances of *Abderame*'s Conduct ſome Reaſons to give him the Preference. He might have kept for himſelf the Widow of a Rebel-Governor: She was an extraordinary Beauty, and yet he left her untouch'd.

[*C*] *Whether the Gaſcons——made any Reſiſtance.*] The moſt exact (5) Hiſtorians obſerve, That *Abderame* enter'd *France*, through the Country that lies betwixt the *Garonne*, and the Ocean; and they ſay, that Country was at that Time under the Dominion of the Duke of *Gaſcony*, and not under the Duke of *Aquitain*. They make no mention of the Siege of *Arles*, which, *Moreri* ſays, the General of the *Saracens* undertook; before he went into *Aquitain*, and before he made himſelf Maſter of *Languedoc, Querci*, &c. This Account is ſo much the more perplexed and confuſ'd, as it is certain that the *Saracens* were Maſters of *Languedoc*, before *Abderame* paſs'd the *Pyrenees*. The Way he took will furniſh me preſently with a juſtification of the Duke

ABDERAME.

Churches: After which, he was victorious in a bloody Battle [D] over *Eudes*, a little beyond the (c) *Dordogne* [E]. He crossed *Poictou*; he plundered the Church of St *Hilary* at *Poictiers*, and proceeded to *Tours*, in order to plunder the Treasure of St *Martin*'s Church. It was then, that *Charles Martel*, seconded by the Duke of *Aquitain*, stopp'd the Course of that Torrent. The great Army of *Abderame*, the Number of the Towns he plundered, and of the Churches he burnt in his way through *Perigord* and *Saintonge*, made his March so flow, that *Eudes* had time to re-inforce himself with a considerable Army, before he joined *Charles Martel*: After the junction of their Armies, they march'd (d) beyond *Tours* to meet *Abderame*. The two Armies, being in fight of one another, spent near seven Days in skirmishing; but at last, on the seventh Day, which happened to be a *Saturday* of the Month of *October*, in the Year 732 [F], the Battle was fought with a very great Loss to the *Saracens*. Yet we must not imagine the Number of the Dead was so great [G] as some hyperbolical Historians have represented it to be. *Abderame* was kill'd in the Field of Battle; the broken Remains of his Army retired more easily than they could have expected [H] (e). The Duke of *Aquitain*, who has been falsly charged with being the Cause

(c) With respect to the Pyrenees.

(d) With respect to Paris.

(e) See Cordemol's History of France, Tom. 1. p. 43, &c.

---

(6) Histor. Sarracen. l. 2. p. 111, 112.

(7) Isidorus Pacenc. a Chronicle.

(8) Mezerai, Chronol. Abridgment, Tom. 1. p. 293.

(9) Cordemol's History of France, p. 404.

(10) Eudes did not go back, when he heard that Abderame had cross'd the Dordogne; but met, and fought him. Id. ib.

(11) Id. ib.

(12) See Catel's History of Languedoc. p. 525, 520.

(13) Mezerai, ubi supra.

(14) For the History of Languedoc.

of *Aquitain*. The Account of *Augustin Curio* (6) is still more confused: He says, That *Abderame* enter'd *France* before the Death of *Munuza*; that he won a Battle there against *Eudes*; that being returned thither after the Death of *Munuza*, he cross'd the *Rhone*, and made a horrid Slaughter at *Arles*, and afterwards besieged *Toulouse*, without taking it, and then *Bourdeaux*, with very good Success; and at last, that he plundered and burnt St *Martin*'s Church at *Tours*.

[D] *A bloody Battle.*] The loss of the Christians was so great, if we may believe *Isidorus*, Bishop of (7) *Badajox*, that God only knows the Number of the *French* that were slain. According to *Mezerai*, (8) Duke *Eudes* fought with all imaginable Bravery, but at last he was forced to yield, with such a loss of his Men, as is not to be express'd.

[E] *A little beyond the Dordogne.*] I do not apprehend what *Cordemoi* (9) means, when he says, That if *Eudes* had waited for the coming of *Charles Martel*, as he should have done, the *Saracens* had never cross'd the *Dordogne*. Did they not cross it before (10) the Battle was fought, and before *Charles Martel* had pass'd the (11) *Loire*? To what Purpose therefore should he have expected him, in order to prevent the Passage over the *Dordogne*? That Historian should have said, That if *Eudes* had staid for *Charles Martel*, he might have prevented the Irruptions of the *Saracens* into *Saintonge* and *Poictou*; because in that Case he had not lost the Battle; and having all his Troops, he might have kept the Enemy in awe, by the Favour of some advantageous Posts, which he might have secur'd. Thus, preserving his Troops 'till the Arrival of *Charles*, the entire defeat of the *Saracens* would have been more practicable, in whatever Province they had been met with. It is, perhaps, difficult to determine, whether the Eagerness, which prompted *Eudes* to a speedy Engagement, be most worthy of Censure, or the grave and flow March of *Charles* towards the *Loire*. Those two Generals both plaid an artful Part. *Eudes* was desirous to beat the Enemy without the Help of *Charles Martel*; and the latter was not displeased to see *Aquitain* laid waste by the *Saracens*, and the Troops of *Eudes* worsted. By this means he got rid of the Obstacles, which he feared from thence, to his great Design of making himself King; and the Glory of being the Deliverer of *France*, would increase in proportion to the small Share his Rival had in it. Some *Spanish* Writers say (12), That *Eudes* was beaten between the *Garonne* and the *Dordogne*. *Mezerai* made use of better Memoirs, when he said (13), "That *Eudes* durst not stay for " the *Saracens* beyond the Rivers, but retired on this " side the *Dordogne*; and, being there reconcil'd to " *Martel*, he assembled his Troops, expecting that he " should come and join him with the *French* Troops; " but *Abderame* broke his Measures, and marching " forward, cross'd the River to attack him in his " Camp. The Duke staid for him without stirring, " and fought with great Courage." This shews that his Impatience is not so much to be blamed, as *Charles Martel*'s Patience.

[F] *In the Year 732.*] Is it not very strange, that such a Victory as this should not escape Chronological Contradictions? *Catel* places it in the Year 725. pag. 529. of his *Memoirs* (14); but in pag. 531. (to very great Interval) he places it in the Year 728. "The " Year following," says he, which was the Year 728,

" *Eudo* Duke of *Aquitain* died." *Calvisius*, quoting the Annals of *Fulde*, places it in the Year 726; *Petavius* (15) in 725. Formerly most Writers pitch'd upon the Year 725, or 726, but of late they declare for the Year 732. Father *L'Abbé*, *Mezerai*, *Cordemoi*, &c. agree in that, with the Annals of *Metz*, and the most ancient Chronicles.

[G] *The Number of the dead was so great.*] 'Tis commonly computed at 370 or 375 Thousand, and That of the *French* at 1500. This is the Computation of (16) *Anastasius Bibliothecarius*, *Paulus Diaconus*, and several other Historians: But it is now no longer credited. *Mezerai* says, That the whole Army of the *Saracens* consisted but of Fourscore or an Hundred thousand Men. We must remember that they fought till Night (17) without giving ground, and that they were not pursued the next Day, when it was known that they had marched all Night. But it would have been almost impossible to make such a prodigious Slaughter of Men, who stood their Ground. A Slaughter of so many thousand Soldiers can't happen but in pursuit of a flying Army, when no Quarter is given. Since therefore the Night parted the two Armies, what we read in *du Haillan* must needs be a meer romantic Story, *viz. That King* Abderame, *and almost all his chief Officers, were found among the great Heaps of dead Bodies, only suffocated by the Numbers that overwhelm'd them*. If there had been at that time any Weekly News-Writers, we might have better judg'd of the Number of the *Saracens* by the *Gazettes* publish'd before the Battle, than by the Descriptions given afterwards of it. During the March of those Barbarians, the Licens'd News-Writers would have represented their Army as inconsiderable, and weaken'd it every Day by Desertions and Sicknesses: But, after the Victory, they would have corrected themselves, and assur'd us, upon good Authority, that the Army consisted of innumerable Multitudes. One might therefore be impos'd upon both by the former and latter Gazettes; but if I were to chuse, I should rather trust the first Account than the last.

[H] *Retired more easily than they could have expected.*] To rectify the popular Notions of that great Victory, it is requisite to consider what the most accurate Historians have said of it. (18) The *Saracens* " threw their Darts to no purpose; the Shields of the " *French* Soldiers, rais'd one above another, secured " them; and, when the *Saracens* came on Sword in " Hand, all their Efforts being not able to break so great " and so close a Body, did but serve to put themselves " into disorder. The *French*, who knew how to take his " Advantage, immediately attack'd them. A prodi- " gious number of them were killed by the *French*, " who continued to fight very close: *Abderame* himself was kill'd upon the Spot; but the Night coming on put an end to the Fight, before *Charles* " was sensible of all his Advantages. He did not " think it proper to follow the Remains of the *Saracens* Army, to avoid the Ambuscades that are always to be feared, when the Enemy is very numerous. Nay he caus'd his Troops to retire in " good order, and with their Swords in their Hands, " into the Camp, where they staid all Night, and at " break of Day he drew them up again in order of " Battle in Sight of the Enemies Camp. There were " so many Pavillions in it, that, though the Field, " wherein the Battle was fought the Day before, was " cover'd

(15) Petav. temp. Part I. l. 8.

(16) See below, the Remark [K]. (17) See the following Remarks.

(18) Cordemol's History of France, Tom. 1. p. 405.

ABDERAME.

Cause [*I*] of this Invasion, was greatly instrumental in obtainining the Victory [*K*]. It is surprizing, that so important a Victory should not be well described by the Writers of that Time, and yet that the modern Historians should tell us so many Particulars concerning it [*L*].

"cover'd all over with the dead Bodies of the Sara-
"cens, Charles had some Reason to believe ; that they
"had still a great number of Soldiers conceal'd in
"their Tents, and he expected every Minute they
"would sally out ; but at last, after a long Stay, the
"French perceived that the Saracens had abandon'd
"their Camp, and some Spies reported, that they
"had marched all Night towards Septimania. How-
"ever he look'd upon this Flight of an Army, which
"he esteem'd to be more numerous than his own,
"as an Artifice to draw him into some Ambuscade ;
"and was satisfy'd with making sure of the Saracen-
"Camp, where he found all their Baggage, toge-
"ther with the Booty they had gained." This is (19°) Meze- what induc'd Mezerai to say, (19) *That Charles* rai's *Chronol*. *did not well improve the great Advantage he had* *Abregement*. *gain'd*. I am willing to believe he was like many Tom. 1. p. 192. (20) others, better qualified to gain a Victory, than (21°) *See the* to improve it : But perhaps he thought fit to let the *Remark* [*A*], *in the Article* Saracens retire quietly, that they might be the more *of Cæsar*. able to ruin the Duke of Aquitain, whom he looked upon as a dangerous Enemy. With how much Diffi- culty did He and his Son Pepin subdue that Family ? It was the last that submitted to those Usurpers. To conclude ; Notwithstanding the ill Success of Abde- rame, his Successors return'd some Years after into France, and did a great deal of Mischief.

[*I*] *With being the Cause*.] There was never a (21) *See his* more unlikely Accusation than this is. For first, *Art cit*. Eudes (21) had married his Daughter to the Governor of Cerdagne, to engage him thereby in a Civil War, which might prevent the Saracens Irruption into France. His Son-in-law perished in that Enterprize, and his Daughter falling into the Hands of Abderame had been sent to the Caliph of the Saracens. Second- ly, It does not appear that Eudes made any Step to facilitate the Entrance of the Saracens ; he sent them no Passage through his Territories ; they entred into Gaul through the Country of the Duke of Gascony, and so advanced as far as Bourdeaux. Besides, it does not appear that the Saracens had any regard for the Territories of the Duke of Aquitain ; they treated him like an Enemy, from the Beginning to the End ; so far were they from restoring any thing to him of what they had taken from him in their former Expe- ditions ; as they would certainly have done, if they had treated with him concerning Abderame's Invasi- on. Lastly, was there any necessity that Abderame (22) *With* should be sollicited to come into France ? Had not the *respect to Spain*. Saracens entred into France already ? Had they not already taken Narbonne, Carcassonne, and extended their Conquests as far as the Rhone ? Abderame's Expedition was but a Continuation of what his Pre- decessors had so well began ; he was willing to carry on their Conquests (22) beyond the Pyrenees ; and, to give a greater Eclat to his Undertaking, he refus'd to follow a beaten Path. He cross'd the Pyrenees, thro' the Country of Biscay ; which was a ready Way to make new Conquests ; whereas if he had gone thro' Roussillon, he must enter into a Province already con- quered. As for those many Annalists, who throw this Blemish on the Duke of Aquitain, their Testimony cannot counterbalance the Reasons that may be alledg- ed in his Justification ; for they are a sort of Men, who do but transcribe from one another ; and the first took his Account from a Tradition, which ow'd it's Original to the Artifices of the Cabal that favoured Charles Martel. That Cabal had several Reasons to charge the contrary Party with holding Intelligence with the Enemies of the Church and State. We do not find that Isidore of Badajos, Sebastian of Salaman- ca, Roderic of Toledo, and such like Spanish Writers, who are free from the Prejudices of that Cabal, have accused Eudes of having invited the Saracens into France. See what it is to be born under a lucky Pla- net ! I don't believe that Charles Martel invited those Infidels ; and yet he ought to have been sus- pected of it rather than Eudes, since Eudes was the first who was to be oppress'd, and Charles might think, that whilst the Saracens were employ'd in de- livering him from so formidable a Rival, he should have time enough to get his Army ready to fight them, and that a Victory would very much shorten

his Way to the Throne. These are good holds for the malicious Interpreters of the Conduct of Great Men ; and yet Charles has not been suspected of hold- ing Intelligence with Abderame.

[*K*] *Was greatly instrumental in obtaining the Victory*.] There are some Historians, who make no mention of his Engagement with Charles Martel up- (23) Histor. on that Day ; but others expressly assert it. These Longob. lib. are the Words of Paulus Diaconus (23) : "Deinde 6. c. 46. in "post decem annos cum uxoribus & parvulis venien- Catel's Me- "tes, Aquitaniam Galliæ provinciam quasi habitaturi moirs of Lan- "ingressi sunt ; Carolus siquidem cum Eudone Aqui- guedoc, p. "taniæ Principe tunc discordiam habebat, qui tamen 530. "in unum se conjungentes contra eosdem Saracenos "pari consilio dimicarunt, nam irruentes Franci su- "per eos trecenta septuaginta quinque millia Sara- "cenorum interemerunt, ex Francorum vero parte "mille & quingenti tantum ibi ceciderunt ; Eudo "quoque cum suis super eos irruens pari modo mul- "tos interficiens omnia devastavit." *Ten Years after*, (the Saracens) *coming with their Wives and Chil- dren, made an Irruption into* Aquitain, *a Province of* Gaul, *with a Design of settling in it* ; Charles *being at that time at Variance with* Eudo, *Duke of* Aquitain : *but, uniting upon this Occasion, they opposed the* Saracens *with Confederate Forces* ; *for the* Francs, *pouring upon them, slew* 375000 Saracens, *with the Loss of but* 1500 *Men on their own Side* ; Eudo *likewise, setting upon them with his Forces, routed them with a great Slaughter*. Regino like- wise mentions the Reconciliation of Charles and Eudes : He says it was made before the Battle, and that afterwards they jointly attacked the Saracens. Sigebert divides the Glory of the Day between those two Chiefs in such a Manner, that he seems to allow Eudes no other Advantage than that of having for- ced their Camp, and destroyed the Remains of their Army : *Eudo quoque reconciliatus castra Saracenorum irrupit, & reliquias eorum contrivit*. Roderic Arch- (24) Rode- bishop of Toledo will afford us a good Proof ; for he ric's Historia says, (24) that the Forces of Charles Martel consisted Arabum, in chiefly of Germans, Goths, and French, who remain'd Catel's Me- to Eudes after the Victory, which the Saracens ob- moirs, p. 529. tained near the Dordogne. We must not forget the Letter, written by Eudes to Pope Gregory II. where- in he gave him an Account of the Battle. Marianus Scotus, and Otho of Frisingen mention that Letter. (25) Catel's Anastasius the Librarian (25) likewise mentions it ; Memoirs of but 'tis strange that he should ascribe all the Glory Languedoc, of that Day to the Duke of Aquitain, without speaking p. 531. one Word of Charles Martel. As to the Number of the Dead, he makes it 370000 on the side of the Saracens, and 1500 on the side of the French. His Authority is the Letter of Eudes, out of which he extracts a particular Circumstance, which is ridicu- lous enough, namely, That on the Day of the Battel Eudes caused three holy Spunges, sent him by the Pope, *out of those that served for the use of his Table*, to be cut into very small Pieces, and made his Sol- diers eat them : Which had so good Effect, as to se- cure those, who eat of them, from being killed or wounded. The following Words of Martial will explain what is meant by *the use of his Table*,

Hæc tibi sorte datur tergendis spongia mensis (26) Mart. *Utilis* (26). Epig. 144. lib. 14.

This useful Sponge, which Chance has render'd thine, If right apply'd, will make your Table shine.

[*L*] *And yet that the modern Historians should tell us so many Particulars concerning it*.] I shall apply here the judicious Reflexion of the Historian, who has been my chief Guide in this Article. "That (27) Corde- "Day, *says* he (27), can never be too much taken mol's *History* "notice of, and the antient Annalists can never be *of France*, p. "sufficiently blamed, for omitting all the Circum- 506. "stances of so memorable an Action. But on the "other Side, they, who have some love for Truth, "can hardly excuse some modern (28) Authors, tho' (28) *He* "otherwise Writers of great Merit, for being so par- *quotes in the* "ticular in the Description of the Battle. They *Margin* Pan- "speak of it as if they had been present in all the *lus Æmilius* "Councils, *and* Fauchet.

ABDERUS. ABDERA.

" Councils, and had seen all the Motions of both
" Armies: They describe not only the Arms of the
" French and Saracens, but also the manner how
" Charles and Abderame drew up their Troops. They
" give us long Speeches, which are neither real nor
" proper: They mention Abderame's Stratagems, the
" Dexterity wherewith Charles hindered them from
" taking effect, and they conclude with the De-
" scription of the different Postures of the dead Bo-
" dies, that were found in the Field of Battle, not
" omitting even the Groans of the dying, and the
" Praises which Charles and Eudes bestowed upon
" one another."

ABDERUS, the *Favourite* of HERCULES. See the Remark [D] of the following Article.

ABDERA, a Maritime Town of *Thrace*, near (a) the Mouth of the *Nessus*. Some say, That it was (b) built by the Sister of *Diomedes* [A]; and that it took it's Name from her; but that it was rebuilt by the *Clazomenians*; in the 31st *Olympiad*, and that they gave it their Name. According to *Herodotus*, they only laid the Foundations of it under the Conduct (c) of *Timesius*, being driven away [B], and their Designs prevented. The *Teians* only, properly speaking, built *Abdera*, when, being upon the Point of falling into the Hands of *Harpagus*, *Cyrus's* Lieutenant, they chose rather to abandon their Country, than to live under the Dominion of the *Barbarians*. They all, therefore, embarked, and went (d) to finish what had been only begun by *Timesius*. This gave occasion to a (e) Proverb not well understood by *Erasmus* [C]. I pass over the Opinion of those, who ascribe the Foundation of that Town to *Hercules* [D]: I rather chuse to take Notice of some remarkable Particulars, which

(a) Herod. l. 7. c. 109, 226.
(b) Solen. c. 10. See also Mela, l. 2. c. 2.
(c) See his Article.
(d) Herod. l. 1. c. 168.
(e) Strab. l. 14. p. 443.

[A] *The Sister of* Diomedes.] No Reader can believe what *Moreri* says, without being persuaded that *Abdera*, built by the *Teians*, took the Name of *Diomedes*, who reigned in it, and that *Herodotus* gives us this Account of the Matter. But this is only Mistake upon Mistake. For 1st, What concerns *Diomedes*, relates to the poetical Times; the Abandoning of *Toes*, by it's Inhabitants, and their retreat into *Thrace*, where they built *Abdera*, is a Fact of the Historical Times, which falls under the 59th *Olympiad*. 'Tis therefore a strange Oversight to join these two things in such a manner, as to place the Fabulous Times after the Times of True History. If you have a mind to follow *Herodotus's* Account of the building of *Abdera*, by the *Teians*, let us hear no more of *Diomedes*; who, if ever there was such an Hero, must have been dead many Ages before: Or, if you design to speak of That antient King of *Thrace*, give us notice, that you are relating an Opinion different from that, which concerns the *Teians*. 2. When *Herodotus* mentions the building of that Town, he does not speak one Word of *Diomedes*. Lastly, It is not true that *Abdera* was built by the Name of *Diomedes*. *Moreri* should have said, that, according to *Solinus*, The Sister of *Diomedes* built it, and gave it her Name: From whence *Salmasius* (1) was in the right to say, that *Diomedes's* Sister's Name was *Abdera*. There is a Medal in *Goltzius*, which represents the Head of a Woman, with this Legend, (2) ΑΒΔΗΡΑΣ ΚΟΡΑΣ. The most (3) learned Antiquaries understood it of *Diomedes's* Sister, who founded *Abdera*.

(1) Salmasii Exercit. Plinianæ. p. 160.
(2) *The Maid of Abdera.* κόρας Doricè ὑπὲρ κόρης.
(3) Spanheimii Epist. ad Laurent. Begerum.
(4) Herod. l. 1. c. 168.

[B] *Being driven away.*] *Herodotus* (4) says so in express Words, ὑπὸ Ἁρπάγου ἐξελαθέντες, *expell'd by the Thracians.* We shall see in the next Remark a Mistake of *Pinedo*, in relation to this Story. In all appearance the Printers only are the cause of this other Mistake, *Thracibus ejectis*, which is to be found in the learned Letter of Mr *de Spanheim* to Mr *Beger*. They have put it *ejestis*, instead of *ejectus*.

[C] *A Proverb not well understood by* Erasmus.] The Proverb is, Ἀβδηρα καλὴ Τηΐων ἀποικία; Abdera *the fine Colony of the* Teians: the meaning of which, according to (5) *Erasmus*, is, *If you make me uneasy, I know whither to retire. Hoc ænigmate proverbiali significamus, non deesse quo confugiamus, si quis præter modum pergat esse molestus*. *Pinedo*, a *Portugueese*, who was forc'd to fly his Country, to avoid the Pursuits of the Inquisition, understands this (6) Proverb in that Sense; but he adds, that such retreats are not always successful, as he is convinc'd by Experience. " *Quo* (Proverbio) *significabatur non deesse
" quo confugiamus, si nobis contumeliæ inferantur,
" ut fecere Teii, sed hoc non semper feliciter solet
" evenire, & doctus & expertus loquor. The Mean-
" ing of which* (Proverb) *is, That we are never at a
" Loss for a Place of Retreat, when we are reproachful-
" ly us'd; an Instance of which we have in the* Tei-
" ans; *but the Event of it is not always fortunate,
" as I can assure from my own Experience.* Had He

(5) Erasmus, Adag. Chil. 2. Cent. 4. n. 53.
(6) Pinedo in Stephan. de Urbib. p. 5.

no better Reason to complain, than he had to assert, in the same Page, That the *Teians* expell'd *Timesius* the *Clazomenian*, who had begun to build *Abdera*, his Complaints would be very ill grounded. But to return to *Erasmus*. I shall not do much censure him for his Explication of the Proverb, as for what he adds, That perhaps *Cicero* alluded to it in his Epistles to *Atticus*; he quotes two (7) Passages out of them, in which 'tis plain *Cicero* speaks of *Abdera*, only to represent it as a Place, where Affairs were manag'd very foolishly, and, (as we say) without Rhime or Reason. But if *Erasmus*, who made use of a *perhaps*, is, notwithstanding, liable to Censure; what shall we say to *Moreri's* positive Assertion, *without doubt* Cicero *alludes?* What shall we think of it, when we come to know to what he refers that Allusion? It is not to. That Fact, which *Erasmus* conjectured he meant: That would have been, in Comparison, a light Mistake: But he supposes *Cicero* alludes to I know not what Lustre, which (says he) *it is certain the* Clazomenians, *being expell'd from* Asia, *gave to the City of* Abdera, *which made it so famous, as to occasion the Proverb of the* Greeks, ΑΒΔΗΡΑ ΤΗ ΒΕΑUTIFUL. I repeat it again; 'tis plain that *Cicero* mentions *Abdera*, only to ridicule the Government of that Place. 'Tis therefore a great Fault to say, *That without doubt he alludes* to the Lustre, the Glory, and Beauty, of that Town. But besides, it is not true that the *Clazomenians* were the Cause of this pretended Lustre, which occasioned the Proverb. I own, that, according to *Solinus*, they rebuilt *Abdera*, and made it larger than it was before, but this is all that we read of them: And, if we consult *Herodotus*, we shall find that the *Thracians* did not give them time to build it. After all, is it not certain that *Strabo* expresly applies the Proverb to the *Teians*, who, for fear of being exposed to the Insolence of the *Persians*, retir'd to *Abdera*? Is not the Name of the *Teians* included in the Proverb? Besides, let *Moreri* inform us a little, where he has found, that, when the *Clazomenians* came to build that Town in *Thrace*, they had been expell'd from *Asia*. *Herodotus* and *Solinus* spoke not one Word of it. Lastly, I find every body understands this Proverb, rather to the Disadvantage than to the Advantage of *Abdera*. *Erasmus* himself did not reject the Explication of *Vadianus*, though not much to the Reputation of that City: " *Existimat convenire proverbium ubi quis for-
" tunam tenuem, sed cum libertate conjunctam, ante-
" ponit amplis opibus, sed obnoxiis servituti. Cujus
" sententiæ non refragor; nam damnatus est Abderi-
" tarum aër & item pascua. He thinks the Proverb
" is applicable, where any one prefers an humble For-
" tune, with Liberty, to large Possessions, upon the
" hard Terms of Slavery. Which Opinion I have
" no Objection to, for both the Climate and the Lands
" of the* Abderites *are condemn'd."* See *Isaac Vossius*, upon (8) *Pomponius Mela*.

(7) Epist. 16. l. 4. & Epist. 7. l. 7.
(8) Pag. 155.
(9) Salmas. Exercit. Plin. p. 160.

[D] *Who ascribe the Foundation of that Town to* Hercules.] Mr *de Saumaise* proves, only by the Testimony

VOL. I.   E

18 ABDERA.

which have been transmitted to us concerning *Abdera*. The Pasture-Ground about it was of such a Nature, that it (*f*) made Horses mad. There was such a multitude of Frogs and Rats there (*g*) in the Time of *Cassander*, King of *Macedonia*, that the Inhabitants were forced to retire to another Place [*E*]. But either they returned soon after [*F*], or the Town was supply'd with other Inhabitants. The *Abderites* have been very much decried [*G*] for their want of Wit and Judgment; and yet their Town has produced many great Men, such as *Protagoras*, *Democritus*, *Anaxarchus*, the Historian *Hecatæus*, (*h*) the Poet *Nicænetus*, and several others, mentioned in the Catalogues of illustrious Men. Nothing can be more strange than the Distemper,

(*f*) Plinius, l. 25. c. 8.
(*g*) Justin. l. 15. c. 2.
(*h*) Πϊκαιω ᾰ' Ἀβδηρίτας ὑπὸ τῶν ἀναπεμψάντων ἀναγραφῶν. Several of the Abderites are recorded by the Index-Writers. Stephanus Byzant. in verbo Ἀβδηρα.
(10) Apollodori Bibl. l. 2.

Testimony of *Tzetzes*, that the Foundation of *Abdera* was ascribed to *Hercules*. He might have alledged a better Authority: for *Apollodorus* (10) tells us, That *Hercules*, having stollen the Mares of *Diomedes*, had notice given him, that the *Bistones* had taken up Arms; that, thereupon he gave those Mares to the keeping of a young Man called *Abderus*, whom he loved, and march'd against the *Bistones*; that he kill'd part of them, and put the rest to flight; that he slew likewise *Diomedes*; but that, at his return, he found the Mares had torn *Abderus* in pieces: that he built a Town near the Sepulchre of that young Man, and gave those Mares to *Eurystheus*. *Stephen of Byzantium* says only, That the Town of *Abdera* was so called from (11) *Abderus*, *Hercules*'s Favourite: He does not say whether it was built by *Hercules*, or by this favourite Boy. This last Opinion is mentioned by *Marcianus* (12) *Heracleota*; perhaps the seventh Book of *Strabo*, if we had it entire, would determine the Matter. The Extracts we have of it only tell us, that the Name of the City of *Abdera* was taken from a certain Person, who was eaten up by *Diomedes*'s Horses. Observe (13) that *Hyginus* seems clearly to say, That *Abderus* was one of *Diomedes*'s Servants, and that he was kill'd by *Hercules*: " Diomedem regem Thra-
" ciæ & equos quatuor ejus qui carne humana vesce-
" bantur cum Abdero famulo interfecit. He slew
" Diomedes, King of Thrace, *and his four Horses,*
" *who were fed with human Flesh, together with his*
" *Servant* Abderus." *M. de Saumaise* observes upon it, that we must not expect to find a great Uniformity in the antient Fables. His Observation is just: The Writers of the fabulous Times, are full of Contradictions. But perhaps it may be said, that *Hyginus*'s meaning is, that *Hercules*, seconded by *Abderus*, kill'd this cruel King of *Thrace*, who fed his Horses with Man's Flesh. I will not warrant his Construction. *Vigenere* (14) had already observ'd, that *Hyginus* and *Philostratus* contradict one another. He might also have said, that the latter very much differs from *Apollodorus*: for (15) he says, that *Diomedes* gave up *Abderus* to his Mares; and that *Hercules* coming to rescue his Favourite, found him half devoured, and that, to punish *Diomedes*, he caused him to be eaten up by his (16) own Mares. *Philostratus* does not say, as *Apollodorus* does, that *Hercules* built a Town near the Sepulchre of his Friend; as, on the other Side, *Apollodorus* does not agree with *Philostratus*, that *Hercules* appointed certain Games or Exercises, in honour to the Memory of *Abderus*. I believe there is but one (17) Author, who has asserted, that *Patroclus* was *Abderus*'s Brother. Some pretend to prove, (18) by Medals, that the *Abderites* were more willing to ascribe the Name of their Town to *Abdera*, Sister of *Diomedes*, than to the Favourite of *Hercules*.

[*E*] *To retire to another Place.*] *Justin* says, That *Cassander* fearing, least they should invade *Macedonia*, made a Treaty with them, and placed them on the Frontiers. *Cassander*'s Fear (19) has been laughed at: How could a Prince, who kept all *Greece* in awe, be afraid that the Inhabitants of one single Town, who fled from Frogs and Rats, should invade a whole Country against his Will? *Moreri*, who, 'tis likely, never knew that *Justin* was criticiz'd upon that Account, has done all that was requisite to free him from such a Censure; for he declares, *That* Cassander *received very kindly the* Abderites *in* Macedonia. They who depend upon his Dictionary, will not think of criticizing that antient Historian. *Moreri* adds, that this Kindness of *Cassander* is to be referr'd to *the Year*

(11) Ἀπὸ Ἀβδηρου τοῦ Ἑρμοῦ Ἡρακλέους ἐρωμενῶ. *Saumaise* has rightly observ'd, that instead of Ἀβδηρου, it should be Ἀβδηρω; which Name *Apollodorus* (he says *Apollonius*) gave to *Hercules*'s Favourite. *Proclus* and *Berkelius* say, that Passage ought to be thus corrected; but they do not tell us that *Saumaise* had said so before them. The first quotes *Apollonius*, and was not aware that it is a Fault of the Press, or of Memory, in *Saumaise* instead of *Apollodorus*. *Philostratus* might have been quoted.
(12) Apud Salmas. ubi supra.
(13) Hygini Fab. 30.
(14) Vigenere's Annotation on the Sepulchre of Abderus in Philostratus.
(15) Philostrat. in loc. ibid.
(16) Vigenere asserts, falsely, that Tatian in his Discourse against the Gentiles, says, that Hercules found Abderus's Leg entire.
(17) Problem. Phephasti. apud Photium p. 484.
(18) Spanheimii Epist. ad Beger.
(19) See Glareanus, Justin Various orum a' Græviu, p. 333.

of the World 3650. *according to* Eusebius's *Chronology*. Could any one who reads this, believe that *Eusebius* has not one Word of that Action of *Cassander*, and that he does not compute Time according to the *Years of the World*? But, to go to the Bottom of the Matter, I assert, that, according to *Justin*, the *Abderites* were placed by *Cassander* on the Frontiers of the Country, before he destroy'd the Sons of *Alexander*: But according to (20) *Calvisius*, he had entirely got rid of them, in the Year of the World 3641. And therefore *Moreri*'s Chronology is as false, as this Account of *Cassander*'s Kindness is contrary to the only Historian he could follow.

[*F*] *They return'd soon after, or, &c.*] What *Lucian* relates concerning the Distemper of the *Abderites*, happen'd under the Reign of *Lysimachus*, and consequently after they were plagu'd with Frogs; for, according to *Justin* (21), this last Adventure preceeded the Time wherein *Lysimachus* and *Cassander* assumed the Title of Kings. To which I add, that, under the Reign of the late King of *Macedonia*, the City of *Abdera* was in a flourishing Condition. The (22) Prætor *Lucius Hortensius* plundered it, but he was blamed for it by the Senate of *Rome*; and the *Abderites* were restored to their Liberty.

(20) Moreri commonly follows Calvisius's Chronology.
(21) Justin l. 15. c. 2.
(22) Livius l. 43.

[*G*] *The* Abderites *have been very much decried.*] We have already seen how *Cicero* treats them in his Letters to *Atticus*. He is not more complaisant in (23) another Book, wherein, having mentioned an Opinion which he thinks to be ridiculous, he adds, *Quæ quidem omnia sunt patrià Democriti quam Democritis digniora. Which better suits with the Country of* Democritus, *than with* Democritus *himself*. *Juvenal*, who could not deny that *Democritus* was a Man of much Wit, and great Wisdom, pretends 'tis a Proof that great Men may be born in a thick Air, and in a Country of Fools.

Cujus prudentia monstrat
Summos posse viros & magna exempla daturos,
Vervecum in patria crassoque sub aëre nasci. (24)

Learn from so great a Wit, a Land of Bogs,
With Ditches fenc'd, an Heaven fat with Fogs,
May form a Spirit fit to sway the State,
And make the neighbouring Monarchs fear their Fate.
DRYDEN.

Martial did not entertain a much better Opinion of the *Abderites*, when he said,

Si patiens fortisque tibi, durusque videtur,
Abderitana pectora plebis habes. (25)

If Thou believ'st this Wretch a dauntless Wight,
Thy Judgment speaks the A dull *Abderite*.

Vigenere (26) grosly mistakes the meaning of this Passage; he thinks the Words are address'd to a Criminal, who represented on the Stage the Action of *Mutius Scævola*, by putting his Hand into the Fire; but they are apply'd to those, who were so silly, as to mistake it for an Act of Courage, fence that Criminal did it only to keep himself from being burnt alive.

Nam cum dicatur, tunicâ præsente molestâ,
Ure manum, plus est dicere, non facis. (27)

For, were he bid to burn his Hand alone,
The Fire prepar'd, and pitchy Garment on,
Shou'd he refuse — I'd swear 'twere bravely done.

Isaac Vossius, who was often particular in his Way of thinking, has given us an Apology of a new Cast for
the

(23) Cicero de Natur. Deor. l. 1.
(24) Juvenal Sat. 10. v. 49.
(25) Mart. Epigr. 13. l. 10.
(26) Vigenere ubi supra.
(27) Mart. ibid.

ABDERA. 19

per, which raged for some Months [H] in Abdera, in the Time of Lysimachus (i). It was a violent Fever, that came to a Crisis, and so went off, in seven Days; but it so disordered the Imagination of those that were seiz'd with it, that it converted them into Players. They were perpetually reciting Scraps of Tragedy, especially of the *Andromeda* of *Euripides*, as if they were upon the Stage; so that the Streets were full of pale and lean Actors, who were making tragical Exclamations. This continued 'till the next Winter, which proved very cold, and consequently more proper to stop this Raving. *Moreri* gives a very wrong Account of the Matter [I].

Mr Beger

(i) *Lucian's Method of Writing History*, about the Beginning.

---

(28) Isaac Vossius in Pompon. Melam. p. 335.
(29) Hippocrat. l. 3. de morbis vulgar.
(30) Is. Vossius, ibid.

the *Abderites*. He owns (28), that many of them were born, or became mad; but he pretends 'twas not a Sign of Stupidity, since Madness seldom seizes Blockheads and Fools, but frequently attacks the greatest Wits. As to the Passage of *Hippocrates* (29) who mentions many *Abderites*, whose Fever had been attended with Raving, *Vossius* pretends 'twas not that which occasion'd the Proverb relating to that Town, but rather the pleasing Affection of Mind, which (30) succeeded the Fever. *Ex Affectu jucundissimo, qui ipsum febribus succedere solebat, ut testatur Lucianus Scripto de conscribendâ Historia.* They became extreamly fond of Verses and Music, and acted the Part of Comedians in the Streets: Such a polite Phrensy as this, says he, does not fall upon stupid and phlegmatic People: *Tum elegans insania non cadit in crassos & pituitosos; nedum in verrecea capita.* That Author should have remembered *Aristotle's* Maxim, *One Swallow does not make a Summer.* Why does he turn into Custom and Habit the Consequences of a Fever that happened but once? What he quotes out of *Lucian* is a single Fact, on which such Proverbs can't be grounded. I shall observe by the way, that *Erasmus* did not rightly apprehend *Cicero's* (31) Meaning; for it must be inferred from the Words of that *Roman,* not that the Inhabitants of *Abdera* were stupid, but that, through a prodigious Roving of their Imagination, they fell into incredible and groundless Paradoxes. "Abderitanis naturâ peculiarem fuisse mentis stuporem indicat M. Tull. in libris de Natura Deorum. "Cicero, in his Book of the Nature of the Gods, "assure us, that the Abderites were affected with a peculiar Stupidity of Mind," says *Erasmus* (32). Some very learned Men (33) quote them as the very Words of *Cicero:* So true it is, that the Collections of Men of Letters, like *Virgil's* Fame, receive continual Additions by removing from Place to Place.

Mobilitate viget, viresque acquirit eundo (34)

—— Each Moment brings
New Vigour to her Flights, new Pinions to her Wings.
DRYDEN.

They, who pretend that the Word ἀβδηρολόγος, which is proverbially used in *Tatian's* Discourse against the *Grecians,* signifies a Teller of idle Stories, do not, by that, confirm the Charge of Stupidity upon the *Abderites.* People are not imposed upon by Fools and Blockheads. Not to say that *Tatian* applies that Word to the Doctrine of *Democritus,* who certainly was no Fool.

[H] *The Distemper, which raged for some Months.*] *Lucian,* who has described it's Symptoms, pretends to have found out the Cause of it. *Archelaus,* says he, a good Player, having acted *Euripides's Andromeda* before the *Abderites,* in a very hot Summer; many came out of the Theatre in a Fever, and having their Imaginations throughly affected with the Tragedy, the Ravings caused by the Fever represented nothing to them but *Andromeda, Perseus, Medusa,* &c. and so strongly excited in them the Idea of those Objects, and of the Pleasure they had received from the Representation, that they could not forbear reciting and acting in Imitation of *Archelaus.* I make no doubt, but the first, who acted this Farce in the Streets, after their Fever was over, injured several, who were growing well. Every thing contributed then to the spreading of the Contagion. The Mind is subject to epidemical Distempers as well as the Body; and nothing more is wanting, than a lucky Beginning, and due Preparation. Let an Heresiarch, or a Fanatic, start up at such a time, whose contagious Imaginations, and vehement Passions, know how to gain Ground, and they'll infatuate a whole Country in a little time, or at least a great many People.

In other Places, or at other Times, they might not perhaps be able to gain three Proselytes. Recollect the Story of (35) those Virgins of *Miletus,* who were for some time so disgusted at the World, that they could not be cured of the Design of killing themselves, but by threatening to expose those stark naked to public View, who should make away with themselves. The very Remedy shews that their Passion was only a Distemper of the Mind, wherein the Understanding had no Share. Something like this was seen at *Lyons* (36) towards the end of the XVth Century. The Difference between these Distempers and the Plague or Small-pox, is only that the latter are infinitely more frequent. I should be induced to think, the Ravage which the Player *Archelaus,* and the Sun (37), made in the Minds of the *Abderites,* was rather a Sign of Vivacity than of Stupidity: However, It was always a Mark of Weakness; for which I appeal to those, who have observed what sort of Men are most affected with the Representation of a Play (38). "Quos (terrores or errores) auxerunt Poetæ; frequens enim "consessus theatri, in quo sunt mulierculæ & pueri, "movetur audiens tam grande carmen:

Adsum atque advenio Acheronte vix viâ altâ atque ardua
Per speluncas saxis structas asperis, pendentibus,
Maximis, ubi rigida constat crassa caligo inferum.

"The Increase of which (Terrors or Mistakes) is "owing to the Poets: for a full Audience, among "which are Women and Children, are greatly affected with such pompous Numbers, as these.

Behold me here, arriv'd from Hell's Abode,
Thro' gloomy Caverns, and rough, hanging, Rocks,
Where Horror dwells, and everlasting Night,
Forcing my dangerous Way!

[I] *Moreri* (39) *gives a very wrong Account of the Matter.*] 'Tis not true, that the *Abderites* died on the Stage, nor that the Proverb, *Abderitica mens,* was occasioned by the Distemper, they were then affected with. *Moreri* would find it very hard to prove that there was such a Proverb: It is not sufficient to maintain that the *Abderites* were commonly look'd upon as Fools; he should make it appear that these very Words, *Abderitica mens,* were made use of to denote the general Opinion the World entertained of them; but 'tis certain *Erasmus* does not quote any one Author, that used those Words. But I will not insist upon that Incident: nay, I am willing to give up as false the following Reflexion, *viz.* That a Thing of so short a duration, as that Distemper of the *Abderites* was, which has been only mentioned by *Lucian,* who made use of it with no other design, than to form the *Exordium* of a Dissertation; such a Fact, I say, is not sufficient to occasion a Proverb, by which a whole People are for ever render'd infamous. For if it be said, that *the fere sapiunt Phryges* might have proceeded from one single Error of the *Phrygians,* I can't shew a great difference between the two Cases, since It is certain that as soon as the thing became a Proverb, it was not apply'd to the *Phrygians* more than any other Nation: Whereas the Reproach cast upon the *Abderites,* concern'd them literally, and at all times, just as (40) that which is cast upon the *Normans* and *Gascons* concerns them in a most proper Sense. But to consider this as a meer Civil, and to come close to the Point: *Moreri's* Proverb, *Abderitica mens,* was only designed to charge the *Abderites* with great Foolishness; but the Distemper mentioned by *Lucian* was not Folly; it was a disordered Imagination, and a sort of Madness, which falls rather upon Men of great Wit, than upon Fools and Blockheads.

Moreri

(31) *In the 1st Book De Natura Deorum.*

(32) Adagior. Chil. 4. centur. 6. n. 27.

(33) Cicero, *in the Nature of the Gods,* says, Abderitani stupori mentis obnoxii sunt. Laur. Begerus Observ. in Numism. quind. p. 16. *See also* Lloyd *and* Hofman, *in the Word* Abdera.

(34) Virgilii Æn. 4. l. 175.

(35) Plutarch de forti tibus factis mulierum.

(36) Brodæus Miscell. l. 5. c. 27.

(37) *The common Maxim of the Philosoph.r, Sol & homo generant hominem. The Sun and a Man,* was verify'd here in a particular manner.

(38) Cicer. Tuscul. 1. c. 16.

(39) *He is committed many other Faults. See the Remark* [A], [C], *and* [E].

(40) 'Tisterian that the Proverbs which restated upon Normandy and Gascony, are grounded upon ... Faults, which pass from on Ge... to another, ...

ABDERA. ABDIAS.

M. Beger (k), who published his Conjectures on a Medal of the *Abderites* [K], which he fancied was struck in memory of this troublesome Distemper, changed his Opinion, after reading the fine Dissertation written to him (l) on that Subject, which contains several things relating to the City of *Abdera*. I shall mention some of them in the last Remark. There was a kind of Ceremony practised in that Town on certain Days, which might be called, in some Respect, an *Auto de Fe*; for it was without doubt an Act of Religion. I think *Ovid* is the only Author that mentions it: 'Tis one of the Imprecations, with which he loads his Enemy:

Aut te devoveat certis Abdera diebus,
Saxaque devotum grandine plura petant, (m)

A Victim, at *Abdera*, may'st thou bleed,
And all the stony Show'r descend upon thy Head.

The Commentators are silent upon this Passage. I suppose they cannot find the Origin or Circumstances of that Ceremony. I shall take Notice elsewhere of a (n) Temple of *Jason* in *Abdera*, which *Parmenio* destroyed.

Moreri is therefore to blame for saying that his Proverb was grounded on the Phrenzy mentioned by *Lucian*. Tho' I blame *Lucian*, I am not ignorant that *Moreri* has only quoted *Cælius Rhodiginus*, which (41) he has been already censured for. He had that Quotation from *Charles Stephens*. He, and a great many others, have answered, and do answer every day, the Hopes, which that *Italian* Author conceived, when he resolved to quote no body. He hop'd to be quoted himself, which he should not have been, if he had put in the Margins of his Book the Names of the antient Authors, whom he transcribed.

[K] *On a Medal of the Abderites*] It represents a Griffin on the one side, and on the other a Man's Head without a Beard, crowned with Laurel, with these Words, ΕΠΙΔΙΟΣ ΛΑΙΟΤ. Mr *Beger* was of Opinion, that this Medal, consecrated to *Apollo*, under the Title of *Jupiter the Inauspicious, sub Jove sinistro*, (the same as *sub Vejove* at *Rome*) was intended to denote the excessive Influence of the Sun's Heat, which occasioned the Imperfection with which the *Abderites* were reproach'd, and which, notwithstanding, made them good Disciples of *Apollo*. Mr *de Spanheim* understands that Inscription, the (42) Prætor, or Governor, of *Abdera*; and says, That the Griffin having been the Symbol of *Teios*, as appears by many Medals, 'tis no wonder that the Inhabitants of *Abdera*, a Colony of the *Teians*, should have stamp'd the same Symbol on their publick Monuments. It was the constant Practice of the Colonies, with respect to their Mother-Town: The Example of *Syracuse* and *Corfou*, whose Arms were a *Pegasus*, in imitation of *Corinth*, is a Proof of it. As for the Head crowned with Laurel, it represents *Abderus*, *Hercules*'s Favourite, or (43) *Tisamenes*, the *Clazomenian*, who was worship'd as a Hero by the *Teians* settled in *Abdera*. *Isaac Vossius* (44) understands by the Inscription of that Medal, *Jupiter Frumentarius, Jupiter the Harvest-God*, as if Ζεὺς λαῖος was the same thing with Ζεὺς ἰκμαῖος; and he grounds his Explication upon the Fertility of the Soil which surrounded the Town of *Abdera*; whence the *Triballi*, being reduc'd to a great Scarcity, flocked thither, according to (45) *Diodorus Siculus*, it being the most fruitful Spot of Ground they could meet with. Mr *de Spanheim* does not deny; and he mentions another Passage of *Diodorus* (46) *Siculus*, wherein *Abdera* is reckon'd to be one of the most flourishing Towns then in *Thrace*. He mentions likewise another Passage out of a Letter, ascribed to *Hippocrates*, wherein 'tis only said, That *Abdera* is no obscure Town, μία πόλεων ἡ ἀσημος. But, notwithstanding, he refutes *Vossius* concerning the Meaning of the Medal. Before I make an end of this Remark, I must observe, that it would be very wrong to take for an Instance of little Wit, what pass'd (47) between the Inhabitants of *Abdera* and *Hippocrates*, on *Democritus*'s Account. The great Concern they express'd for the Health of *Democritus*, their Fellow-Citizen, is a Sign of their good Judgment. 'Tis true, *Hippocrates* did not confirm the Opinion they had entertain'd of *Democritus*: They took him to be a Fool; but he seem'd to *Hippocrates* to be wiser than his Countrymen. However this proves nothing; for I am sure all the Cities of *Greece* would have judg'd of *Democritus* as his Countrymen did: And we should at present entertain the same Opinion of a Philosopher, who should laugh at every thing; who should say, That the Air is full of Images, who should study the singing of Birds, and shut himself up in Sepulchres, *&c*. And none but Wits of the first Rank, who guard against all Prejudice, would be able to form a right Judgment of him. But that sort of Men are very scarce at all Times, and in all Places. They are as scarce, and perhaps more, than honest Men, who, in *Juvenal*'s Opinion, hardly equal the Number of the Mouths of the *Nile*.

— rari quippe boni: numerus vix est totidem, quot
Thebarum Portæ, aut divitis Ostia Nili. (48)

Good Men are scarce, the Just are thinly sown;
They thrive but ill, nor can they last, when grown.
And shou'd we count them, and our Store compile,
Yet *Thebes* more Gates would shew, more Mouths the *Nile*.

CREECH.

ABDIAS of *Babylon*, an Author who deserves to be ranked amongst the most impudent legendary Writers. He is an Impostor, who pretends to have seen our Saviour, to have been one of the LXXII Disciples, to have been Witness of the Actions and Death of several of the Apostles; to have followed St *Simon* and St *Jude* into *Persia*; and to have been established by them the first Bishop of *Babylon*. The Work, that goes under his Name, is divided into ten Books, and entituled, *Historia Certaminis Apostolici*. *Wolfgang Lazius* (a) found the Manuscript in a Cave at *Carinthia*; and, though he was a learned Man, he suffered himself to be so much imposed upon by that fabulous Writer, that he prepared to publish it, as an important Piece. He gave credit to the Inscription of that Manuscript, importing that *Abdias*, made Bishop of *Babylon* by the Apostles themselves, had writ in *Hebrew* this History of their Lives; and that it was translated into *Greek* (b) by *Eutropius*, and into *Latin* by *Africanus*. He published it at *Basil* (c) in the Year 1551, with some other Lives of

ABDIAS. ABDISSI.

of the Saints. It was since reprinted several times (*A*), in several Places. *Fabricius* remarks, that it is a Mistake to suppose it was inserted in the *Bibliotheca Patrum* (*d*). *Laurence de la Barre* inserted it in his History of the Fathers at *Paris* in 1583 (*e*). 'Tis not Pope *Gelasius*, as *Moreri* would have it, but Pope (*f*) *Paul* IV. who rejected the Work of our *Abdias, as an Apocryphal Piece*. Several Writers, both Catholic and Protestant, have acknowledged that 'tis an Imposture. The latter pretend to have undeceived the others [*B*]: But this is not granted them [*C*]. After all, there is no great Glory in the Discovery; for this Impostor has had the Assurance to quote (*g*) *Hegesippus*, who flourished 130 Years, or thereabouts, after our Saviour's Ascension. He likewise mentions (*h*) a Disciple of the Apostles, called *Crathon*, who, as he says, wrote a *History, in ten Books, of all the Actions and Sufferings of St Jude* in Persia, *for the Space of thirteen Years*; *which History*, pursues he, *was translated into Latin by Africanus the Historiographer*. That *Africanus* can be no other than *Julius Africanus*, who died about the Year 230 (*i*).

[*A*] *Reprinted several times.*] Mr *du Pin*, who mentions the Editions of 1557, 1560, and 1571; and besides, an Edition of *Basil*, in the (1) Year 1532. and one of *Paris*, in 1583. has forgot the first, which I deserv'd most to be mention'd. I have not by me his *Bibliotheque* of the *Paris* Edition; and therefore I dare not affirm, that he takes notice of the pretended Edition of *Basil* in 1532. Now because he mentions but one *Paris* Edition, which is that of 1583; the Reader might very well think, that the others mentioned by him are not of *Paris*: And yet it is certain, that *Abdias* was publish'd there in the Year 1560, in 8vo, with a Preface of a Doctor of the *Sorbonne*, call'd *John Faber*. The Abbreviator of *Gesner*, and *Dr Cave* mention a *Paris* Edition, 1571, in 8vo. 'Tis likely said in *Magirus's Eponymologium*, that this Work was printed the first time at *Paris*, in 1551.

[*B*] *To have undeceived the others.*] Consult *Rivetus* (2) chap 6. of the first Book of his *Criticus Sacer*, where, having observed the Prepossession of *Lazius*, and the Authority which *Harding* and *Bellarmine* ascribe to our *Abdias*, he adds : " Ejus nugas & mendicia non est quod operosius persequamur, quia jam " oculatioribus Pontinicus ita patent EA NOSTRORUM ANIMADVERSIONIBUS, ut eos tam " putidi commenti pudeat. *I may spare my self the " pains of a father Examination of his idle Stories, " and Inventions, since the more judicious Catholics " are so convinced by* MY ANIMADVERSIONS, " *as to be asham'd of so stale a Cheat.*" He quotes *Baronius, Molanus, Possevin,* and even *Bellarmine,* who thought better of it since; he quotes them, I say, as acknowledging the Imposture of that History of the Apostles.

[*C*] *This is not granted them.*] Father *L'Abbé* exclaims in a strange manner against *Rivetus*, on account of the Passage I have just now mention'd. He may be in the right, when he says, the Catholics found out the Imposture, before the Protestants had given them any Insight into the Matter; but he is very much to blame for his sharp and injurious Words; for thus he speaks : " Hasce quisquilias ab otioso fa- " bulatore, qui merito jure Pseudo-Abdias dicitur, " connectis interpolatasve nullius fidei atque auctorita- " tis esse apud eruditos, docuerunt jampridem Catho- " lici Tractatores, Sixtus Senensis, Joannes Hesse- " lius, Joannes Molanus, Cardin, Baronius, Possevi- " nus, Salmero, Miræus, aliique, ut sileam Vossium, " Cocum, Rivetum, similesque Heterodoxos Criticos,

" in alienis ab Ecclesia Catholica castris militantes, " atque ex Catholicorum duntaxat scriptis & observa- " tionibus suffurcinatos. Mentitur enim pro more " Andreas Rivetus, qui libro 1. cap 6. effutire ausus " est, oculatiores Pontificios ex suorum, hoc est, " Hæreticorum hominum, animadversionibus edoctos, " nap.s & mendacia illius operis deprehendisse, ita " ut eos tam putidi commenti pudeat. Sed, amabo, " quis Calvini cærulus hoc commentum subodoratus " est ante Hesselium, Molanum, Sixtum, ipsumque " adeo Paulum IV. Romanum Pontificem, qui inter " scripta ab eo damnata rejicit?—— *Several Catholic Writers, such as* Sixtus Senensis, Johannes Hesselius, Johannes Molanus, Cardin, Baronius, Possevinus, Salmero, Miræus, *and others, not to mention* Vossius, Cocus, Rivetus, *and the like heterodox Critics, who fight under other Banners, than those of the Catholic Church, and are beholden only to the Writings and Observations of the Catholics : All those, I say, have long ago taught, that this Trash, cook'd up by that idle Fabulist, the Impostor* Abdias, *deserv'd to have no Credit or Weight with the learned*. Rivetus, *therefore, would impose upon us, according to Custom, when he has the Assurance, in the sixth Chapter of his first Book, to declare, that his own, that is, the Animadversions of an Heretic, had so undeceived the more judicious Catholics, that they were asham'd of so stale a Device. But, pray, which of* Calvin's *Whelps smelt out this before* Hesselius, Molanus, Sixtus, *and even* Paul IV. *Pope of Rome, who has plac'd this Book in his Expurgatory Index?* " I believe this Book was condemn'd again at *Rome*, since the Death of *Paul* IV. for I don't think that *Claudius Espencæus* means the Condemnation made by that Pope, when he says, " Qualiscunque autor sit Abdias, superiore " certè quam hæc scriberemus anno à Romanis In- " quisitoribus proscriptus est. *Whatever kind of Author* Abdias *may be, it is certain his Book was condemn'd, by the Roman Inquisitors, a Year ago*." These Words are in the 5th Chapter of the 5th Book *ae Continentia*. The Continuator of *M. girus* (4) in the wrong to conclude from thence, that the Year meant in that Passage is 1568; for that Work about Continence was printed (5) in 1569. *Peter Paul Vergerius*, a Protestant Writer, who died in 1564, exclaimed against the Imposture of our *Abdias*, in his *Idolum Lauretanum*.

ABDISSI, [*A*] Patriarch of *Musal* in *Assyria*, beyond the *Euphrates*, came to *Rome* in the Year 1562, and having paid his Homage to *Pius* IV. received the *Pallium* from him. The Council of *Trent* being then met, the Cardinal *de Mula*, Protector

[*A*] ABDISSI.] *Onuphrius Panvinius* (1) calls him *Abdisu*, which, says he, signifies *Servus Jesu*. *Surius* and *Spondanus* give him the same Name. *Ti anus* (2) calls him *Abdisus*, and adds, that he was the Son of *John de Domo Mariæ*, of the Town of *Gezira* upon the *Tigris* I confess I don't well understand what is meant by *domus Mariæ*; and therefore I can give no Translation of those two Words, that can please me; nor approve that of *Moreri*, who renders them *Mar's House*. *Aubert Miræus* (3) calls the Patriarch we speak of *Abdiseho*, and says, That he was a Monk of the Order of St *Pachomius*; that he succeeded the Patriarch *Simon Salleba* (4) a Monk of the same Order, who came to submit to

Pope *Julius* III. that he was a Man of admirable Learning; that he understood many Languages, and was extraordinarily well versed in the Holy Scriptures. *Thomas's* Memoirs imported, that he understood the *Chaldee*, the *Arabic*, and *Syriac*, and gave pertinent Answers to the Questions proposed to him. *Panvinius, Surius,* and *Spondanus*, affirm the same thing with more Circumstances. He says in his Confession of Faith, as it is set down by them, That he had been a Monk of St *Anthony*, in the Monastery of St *Rochas*, and St *John*, two Brothers. He had very much propagated the *Roman* Faith, if we may believe *Aubert Miræus*: but his Successors took no Care to keep it up; to that *Leonard Abel*, Bishop of *Sidon*,

VOL I. P

ABDISSI. ABEL.

Protector of the Eastern Christians, acquainted that Assembly with it. His Letters were read in the XXII Session. They imported that the People under the Jurisdiction of that Patriarch had been instructed in the Christian Faith, by the Apostles St *Thomas* and St *Thaddeus*, and by one of their Disciples, called *Mark*; that their Belief was altogether the same with that of the Church of *Rome*; that they had the same Sacraments and the same Ceremonies; that they had still some Books written from the time of the Apostles; that That Patriarchate reaches into the very Heart of the *Indies*, and comprehends many Nations, some of which are subject to the *Turkish* Emperor, others to the *Sophi* of *Persia*, and others to the King of *Portugal*. The *Portuguese* Ambassador protested immediately, That the Eastern Bishops, subject to the King his Master, acknowledged no Patriarch. Afterwards *Abdissi's* Confession of Faith was read (*a*), bearing date the seventh of *March*, 1562. wherein he promised to observe and teach his Inferiors a perfect and perpetual Conformity of Opinions with the Church of *Rome*. Lastly, they read the Letters he writ to the Council, to excuse himself for not going thither [*B*], and to beseech the Fathers to send him their Decrees, which he promised should be punctually observed. All those things had been read already in a Congregation, without exciting any one's Reflexions; but the Protest of the *Portuguese* Ambassador gave Occasion to take notice of the Absurdities of that Account: Some began to murmur; the *Portuguese* Bishops were ready to speak their Sentiments, when the Proctor, in the Name of the Legates, diverted the Blow. Thus *Fr. Paolo* (*b*) relates the Matter: I shall examine this in another Place (*c*).

the Pope's Nuncio in those Parts, in the Year 1583. found that the Patriarch *Donha Simon*, who was the second since *Abdiesu*, had retired towards the Borders of *Persia*. The Pope's Affairs were not in a better Condition, when *Peter Strozza*, Secretary to *Paul* V. publish'd at *Rome*, and at *Cologne*, in 1617. his Disputation, *De Chaldæorum dogmatibus* (5).

[*B*] *To excuse himself for not going thither.*] This shews that *Moreri* is very much mistaken, when he says, " That *Abdissi* assisted at the Council of *Trent*, " and presented his Confession of Faith in the XXII. " Session." *Aubert Miræus*, committed the same Fault, " qui & Tridentino Concilio interfuit, *who was* " *present likewise at the Council of Trent*," says he (6), speaking of his *Abdiesu*. That which is more surprizing, is, That *Moreri* quotes *Thuanus* and *Spondanus*, though the first says not one Word of that Patriarch's pretended Journey to the Council; and tho' the second expressly says, That they read the Letters, wherein *Abdysu* excused himself for not coming to *Trent*. I shall occasionally observe a Fault, which must needs have crept into *Thuanus's* History: He says (7) That Patriarch came " Ad Apostolorum li- " mina Pontificem salutaturus, ut ab eo confirmatus " partem de corpore Sancti Petri acciperet. i. e. " *He came to the Apostolical See, to salute the Pope,* " *that, being confirm'd by him, he might receive part* " *of the Body of St Peter.*" Any one, who reads these Words, would think that he came to ask an Arm or some other Piece of St *Peter's* Body; for to come to *Rome*, in order to carry away such Presents, is a thing very acceptable to that Court. But I am perswaded that instead of *partem* it should be *pallium*, as we read in *Spondanus*, who uses almost the same Expression with *Thuanus*. We may see this in his Continuation of the Annals of *Baronius*.

ABEL, second Son of *Adam* and *Eve*, was a Shepherd. He brought an Offering to God, of the *Firstlings of his Flock*, at the same Time that his Brother *Cain* offer'd the *Fruits of the Earth*. God accepted the Oblation of *Abel*, but not That of *Cain*: which displeased the latter so much, that *he rose up against the other and slew him*. This is all the Account *Moses* gives us of him (*a*): But we might greatly enlarge this Article, if we would expatiate upon every Thing, which the Curiosity of human Wit has push'd upon the Subject. We shall however avoid entering upon the Detail; nor shall we pretend to guess at the Age of *Abel*, when he was slain. It is impossible to arrive at any Certainty in this Matter; because we know not the Duration of the State of *Innocence* [*A*]; nor how much younger *Abel* was than *Cain* [*B*]; nor

[*A*] *The Duration of the State of Innocence.*] Authors are greatly divided upon this Question: Some assert, that *Adam* fell on the very Day of his Creation; and that he continued in Paradice but six, seven, or ten Hours (1). Others extend the Time to six, eight, or ten Days; others to thirty four Years. Most of them build their Opinions upon a suppos'd Resemblance between *Adam* and *Jesus Christ*: For Instance, if *Adam* be suppos'd to continue in Paradice forty Days, or thirty four Years, the Reason is, because *Jesus Christ* fasted forty Days in the Wilderness, or lived upon Earth thirty Years (2). The Emptiness of these Reasons is obvious to Men of Sense. There are very strong Objections to the Opinion of those, who restrain the State of Innocence to a few Hours; but much stronger against theirs, who continue it to several Weeks or Years: For, with the good Leave of the *Rabbins*, it is certain from *Moses's* Account, that *Adam* did not *know his Wife*, 'till after their Departure from Paradice. Now, why should he defer the Consummation of his Marriage so long? Had he not received the nuptial Benediction from the Mouth of his Creator? Was he not commissioned, in form, to *increase and multiply*, and to *replenish the Earth*? The most substantial Reason for the Delay of this Consummation 'till after the Fall, is that of St *Austin* (3). that " *The Woman was tempted and seduced, almost* " *as soon as formed*. Mox creari mulierē, antequam " conveniret, facti est illa Transgressio " The other Reason he gives, namely, that they were obliged to wait the Command of God, is none at all (4); for I have already observed, that this Command had been authentically notified to them. If it could be once proved, that the Innocence of the *first Man* continued many Days, it would effectually confirm the Opinion of those, who assert, that, had it not been for the *forbidden Fruit*, *Adam* and *Eve* would have preserved their Virginity for ever; and that it was in consequence of God's fore seeing the *Fall*, that they were created of different Sexes. But, be that as it will, we cannot determine certainly at what Age they began to propagate. We shall in another Place (5) refute the Opinion of some, that *Cain* was not conceived 'till a long time after *Adam's* Transgression; either because his Father abstained from the Pleasures of Matrimony, in Mortification for his Offence; or because he had left *Eve* for some other Woman.

[*B*] *How much younger Abel was than Cain.*] The Narration of *Moses* seems clearly to prove, that *Cain* and *Abel*, were not Twin Brothers. Nevertheless, one of the most judicious Interpreters of the Scripture, believed, with some of the *Rabbins*, that they were " Rabbins,

ABEL.

nor in what *Year* of the *World* he he was slain by his Brother [C]. For the same Reason I shall not venture any Conjectures upon the Question, Whether he died a Virgin [D]; nor concerning the Reason of *Cain*'s quarrelling with him. Some say, The Difference between them was a *Religious Dispute* [E]; others, that they quarrell'd about

(6) Corn. à Lap. upon Gen. iv. 2.

"Rabbini, & ex iis Calvinus, putant ex eodem conceptu Evam peperisse gemellos, Cain & Abel (6). The Rabbins, and among them Calvinus, think that Eve brought forth Twins, Cain and Abel." But, tho' we should grant this, the Uncertainty would not wholly vanish; unless we could determine precisely the Year of *Cain*'s Birth. But, farther, it does not appear, that *Abel* was the Twin-Brother of *Cain*; neither is it certain, that he was born after him. However we may conclude it highly probable, that *Cain* was born in the first Year of the World, and *Abel* the Year after. The *Revelation* ascribed to *Methodius*, is an an apocryphal Piece, and meer Invention. It is said to have been revealed to him from Heaven, during his Imprisonment for the Faith (7), that *Adam* and *Eve* left Paradice in a State of Virginity; that they continued in it fifteen successive Years, wholly taken up with lamenting their Fall; that, at the end of this time, they begat a Son and Daughter at once, whose Names were *Cain* and *Calmana*; after which they returned to a State of Continency for fifteen Years more; after which they begat a Son and a Daughter, as before, named *Abel* and *Debora*; and that the Murthur of *Abel* by *Cain* fell out in the one hundred and thirtieth Year of *Adam*; which threw Him and *Eve* into a Fit of Grief, which lasted an hundred Years; after which they begat *Seth*. The Inhabitants of the Island of *Ceylon* pretend, that the salt Lake, found on Mount *Colombo*, is a Collection of Tears, shed by *Eve*, during an hundred Years, for the Death of *Abel* (8). The Rabbins will have it, that *Adam* lamented his Son's Death an hundred Years, in the *Vale of Tears* near *Hebron*, without any carnal Commerce with his Wife (9); which probably would have continued longer, had not an Angel from God commanded him to cohabit with *Eve*, because the *Messiah* was not to descend from the Family of *Cain*. Idle Tales! The State of the World was so far from requiring such a long fit of Sorrow, that, on the contrary, it demanded, that they should comfort themselves by repairing the Loss: So that it is highly probable, that *Adam* and *Eve* presently mollify'd their Grief by the mutual Satisfaction of procuring themselves another Son, in the room of *Abel*, who was slain. Yet one would hardly believe, how industriously this Fable of *Adam* and *Eve*'s long Divorce from the Marriage-bed has been preached up. We shall treat of it under the Article *LAMECH*.

(*) See the Author of Hist. Scholast. in Libr. Hist. Genes. xxv. in Perierius upon Genesis.

(8) See Chevreu i Historie of the World, Tom. 4. p. 255. Dutch Edition, in 1687.
(9) Is Salian, Tom. I. p. 190.

[C] *In what Year of the World he was slain by his Brother.*] Some have thought it probable, that this Murthur was committed the same Year that *Seth* was born; i. e. in the one hundred and thirtieth of *Adam*: It has been thought probable, I say, because *Eve*, in giving the Name of *Seth* to the Child she had brought forth, assigns this as a Reason: *For God hath appointed me another Seed instead of Abel, whom Cain slew* (10). But it must be granted, that this is rather a Proof, that *Seth* was the first Child which *Eve* bore after the Murthur of *Abel*, than that his Death was immediately followed by the Birth of *Seth*. St *Austin* even denies the Right of Eldership to *Seth* over all the Children of *Adam* and *Eve*, born after the Death of *Abel*. He interprets the Words of *Eve* to imply, not *the Appointment of another Son*, but the *restoring of Virtue*; i. e. that *Seth* was considered as Successor to the Piety and Sanctity of *Abel*.
"Potuit Adam (says he) divinitus admonitus dicere, postea quam natus est, suscitavit enim mihi Deus semen aliud pro Abel (11); quando talis erat futurus, qui impleret ejus Sanctuatem (12). Adam, by Divine Inspiration, might well say, at the Birth of Seth, God hath raised me up another Seed instead of Abel; since he was to inherit his Brother's Sanctity." But this can only be Conjecture, and if the Words of *Eve*, cited above, leave us full Liberty of Judgment, we shall carry the Murthur of *Abel* very high; for thus natural Reason will teach us. *Cain* and *Abel* made their Offerings to God, when the one's Crop, and the other's Flock, furnished them with sufficient Means. They immediately perceived how differently their Presents were received by God (13). *Cain*'s Disgust soon after hurried him into the Design of

(10) Gen. iv. 25.

(11) Austin attributes to Adam, *webut, a cording to the Scripture, were the Words of Eve.*

(12) Aug. dt. Civit. Dei. l. 15. c. 15.

(13) *The Scripture speaks that an Oblation of these two Brothers; so that the Supposition of Salian, Tom. I. p. 182. that Cain did not perceive, till after a long Time, and repeated Offerings, that he was rejected, and his Brother in favour with God, is groundless.*

killing his Brother. He murthured him, then, before the Age of sixty; for it was in the fiftieth Year of the World, according to *Eusebius*, that *Adam* allotted to his Sons the Manner of Life he intended they should follow. There was time enough, we are told, for Deliberation in this Affair; since, at that time, the Length of Childhood must have been proportionable to the Length of Life. With all my Heart; I shall not dispute it. I will allow, that *Cain* and *Abel* were not capable before the Age of fifty, the one to till the Earth, the other to keep Sheep; but pray let them be capable at that Age. Now, upon this Supposition, can any thing be more natural, than to believe they made their Offerings at the end of two or three Years at latest; and that in a like interval of time the envious and jealous *Cain* got rid of his Brother? Can any thing be more improbable than the common Opinion, that the two Brothers began to exercise their Occupations in the fiftieth Year of the World; that they made their Offerings in the hundredth, and that *Cain* was slain in the hundred and thirtieth? Neither Reason nor Scripture lead us to imagine, that *Cain* stifled his Resentment for so long a time in his Breast (14). A very judicious Author has fixed the Birth of *Seth* to about an hundred Years after the Death of *Abel* (15). Some Authors place *Abel*'s Death in the Year of the World 102 (16). But the Generality are for the Year 130; which is thought to be the same with the hundred and twentieth ninth of *Abel*. I might, in support of this Opinion, refer to *Cajetan, Torniel, Pererius, Cornelius à Lapide, Salian*, and many other Commentators, whose Works may be compared to Children of the same Family;

(14) *See the Reformer to the Targum of Jerusalem, and the Annals of Eutychius in the Remark* [F].
(15) Cunaeus de Rep. Hebr. l. 3. c. 1.
(16) St Romuald à Camel. Chronol.
(1*) Ovid. Metam. B. 2. v. 13.

——— *Facies non omnibus una,*
Nec diversa tamen, qualem decet esse sororum. (17)

Tho' various Features did the Sisters grace,
A Sister's Likeness was in every Face.
ADDISON.

Thus all Parties, all Bodies, all Societies, have a Variety of Authors, who copy after each other.

[D] *Whether he died a Virgin.*] Some Fathers of the Church have maintained the Affirmative (18); and the Hereticks, taken notice of below, who took their Name from *Abel*, are of the same Opinion: but those who believe, that *Abel* lived an hundred and twenty nine Years, think it improbable he should die a Batchelor. The World stood too much in need of being peopled, for Continency to be a Virtue. Father *Salian* makes no Difficulty to declare, that the Celibacy of *Abel* is absolutely improbable; and shews, that St *Jerom* and St *Austin* did not doubt of his Marriage (19); and that St *Irenaeus* is not to be charged with the Expression imputed to him by *Genebrard* (20), namely, that *Abel* was a *Maid*, *a Priest*, and *a Martyr*: upon the Account of which these Qualifications the Church is said to begin in him. There is another Author, who ascribes these three fine Qualifications to him (21). But if we may depend upon the *Tradition of Eutychius*, produced below, we can no longer question the Virginity of *Abel*, according to that, his Death preceded the Marriage of his two Brothers.

(18) *St Jerom, St Basil, St Ambrose, in Corn à Lapide upon Gen. i. 2. but sewhin, as his Supposition, is a little*

Annals, Tom. I. p. 184. ...
(19) St Jerom ...
not of this Opinion.
(19) Salian's Annals,
(20) Chronolog. B. I.
(21) *The Author of Martha: Sanct. Script. ... Augsb. ...*
Patriis ...
h. lin's ...
Annals ...
(22) Salian's Patriarch.

[E] *Was a religious Dispute.*] The *Targum of Jerusalem* relates, that *Cain* and *Abel* being in the Field, the former asserted that there was no Judgment, nor Judge, nor Life Eternal, nor Rewards for the Good, nor Punishment for the Wicked; and that the World was neither created, nor governed, by the Goodness of God: *For, says he to his Brother, my Oblation was not received, but yours was. Abel* answered him in his own Words, substituting only the Affirmative for the Negative; and, as to his principal Complaint, his Answer was, that *His Works* being better than those of *Cain*, were the Occasion of the Preference given to his Offering. The Dispute growing warm, *Cain* fell upon *Abel*, and slew him (22). This was the impious beginning of Disputes in Religion; and a fatal Presage of the terrible Contentions

24 ABEL.

bout a *Woman* [F]. Nor is there a less Diversity of Opinions concerning the *Manner*, in which this horrid Murther was committed [G]. But it is not so much controverted, in what Manner they discover'd the Preference which God gave to *Abel*'s Offering. The common Opinion is, That Fire from Heaven fell upon *Abel*'s Sacrifice [H]; but that nothing of that kind happen'd to the Offerings of *Cain*. But, as we are very apt to fancy we discover the *Marvellous* in every Story of this Kind, some have said (b), that there appeared the Figure of a *Lion*, in the middle of the Fire, which fell upon *Abel*'s Sacrifice; which, say they, had relation to the *Lion* of the Tribe of *Juda*, whose coming was then already promis'd. I have thrown together in the Remarks a great Variety of Opinions, in relation to *Abel*'s Story. It is indeed a Heap of absurd Notions and Errors; but the Reader, in passing his Judgment upon them, must remember, that such a Collection answers the End and Design of this *Dictionary*: which Caution I here give once for all.

(b) *Salian, Tom. 1. p. 19. and Bidelius's Roman History. Decad. 1.*

Confusions they were to cause in the World. It affords us likewise an Instance of the foolish Vanity of Man; who is never so much led to doubt of a Providence, as when Things do not succeed according to his Wishes. Give him but Prosperity; his Doubts vanish: The Reason is, he thinks he holds too considerable a Rank in the Universe to be overlooked by an equitable and judicious Dispenser of Good and Evil. " Effer to Superi, ait Statius, cum
" contabuisset a periculoso morbo vir eximiæ probi-
" tatis Rutilius Gallicus. At contra, ubi quid con-
" tigerat contra quam æquum esse censerent, Deos
" aut nullos esse, aut crudeles & injustos esse dice-
" bant. —— Itaque in morte Tibulli Ovidius.

Cum rapiant mala fata bonos, ignoscite fallo,
Sollicitat nullos esse putare Deos.

" *I acknowle'ge ye, O ye Gods* cry'd *Statius, when
" Rutilius Gallicus, a Man of distinguish'd Honesty,
" had recovered from a dangerous Disease. On the
" contrary, if any thing fell out, which they did not
" like, they either accus'd the Being of the Gods, or
" charged them with Cruelty and Injustice. Hence
" Ovid, upon the Death of Tibullus,*

*When, just, lost by cruel Fate the Good and Just,
Perish, and sink untimely to the Dust,
(May I the Bad Confession be forgiven)
I almost think there are no Gods in Heaven.*

This is the Language of one of the best Orators of the XVIth Century (23).

[F] *Quarrel'd about a Woman.*] *Eutychius*, Patriarch of *Alexandria*, tells us, in his Annals (24) that *Eve* brought forth, together with *Cain*, a Daughter named *Azrun*, and, together with *Abel*, a Daughter named *Owain*; and that, the time of marrying these two Sons being come, *Adam* allotted *Owain* to *Cain*, and *Azrun* to *Abel*; and treated *Cain* with Severity for desiring his Twin-Sister, who was the most beautiful of the two. *Eutychius* adds, that the two Brothers going to present their Offering upon the top of a Mountain, by the Order of *Adam*, who desired they might perform this religious Act before their Marriage, and that the Success of their Sacrifice might decide their Quarrel; the Devil secretly prompted *Cain* to murther his Brother for the Love of *Azrun*; which, preventing his Offering from being agreeable to God, so enraged *Cain* against his Brother, that they were scarce come down from the Mountain, when *Cain*, with a Stone, dashed out his Brother's Brains. The beautiful *Azrun*, whom *Cain* immediately after, married (25), and carried with him into *Exile*, was indeed the Cause, but the innocent one, of *Cain*'s Crime; and verifies the Assertion of the *Latin* Poet concerning the Antiquity of Wars raised upon the Account of Women;

*Nam fuit ante Helenam Cunnus teterrima belli
Causa (26).*

*E'er Græcian Helen liv'd, the false, the fair,
Beauty has been the fatal Source of War.*

The *Ancients* (27), and the *Cabbalists* (28), agree with this Tradition of *Eutychius* I have read in the Commentary of Father *Merfenne* upon *Genesis*, Page the 1415th, and 1431st, that there are some *Rabbins*, who say, that *Abel* had two Twin-Sisters, and that

Cain desired to marry them both. This, say they, was the ground of their Quarrel. The Inclination then to Polygamy, must be very old. Lastly, it appears by the Citation from the *Targum*, and that from the Patriarch of *Alexandria*, that the Death of *Abel* ensued immediately upon the Sacrifice, wherein God had declared in his Favour. This Chronology is a thousand times more probable, than that which places thirty Years between the Offerings of the two Brothers, and the Murthur of *Cain*.

[G] *The Manner in which this horrid Murthur was committed.*] We have seen, that it was with the Blow of a Stone, according to some Authors. Others say, that *Cain* tore him in Pieces with his Teeth. *Hebræorum nonnulli tradunt eum fuisse morsibus a Cain dilaceratum* (29). Others, that he knocked him down with the Jaw-bone of an Ass: The Painters are directed by this Hypothesis. Some pretend, that he made use of a Pitchfork. St *Chrysostom* puts a Sword into his Hand; St *Irenæus* arms him with a Scythe; *Prudentius* gives him a kind of Hedging-Bill.

*Frater probatæ sanctitatis æmulus
Germana curvo colla frangit farculo* (30).

Envious of his Brother's approved Sanctity, he broke his Neck with a crooked Hedging-Bill.

See *Salian* and *Bosselius*; the one, Page 183 of the first Volume of his *Annals*; the other Page 234 and 254 of the first Tome of his *Illustr. Ruinæ*. " It " is certain, *says an Author* (31), *that Abel was
" neither drowned, nor strangled, for the Scripture
" witnesses, that he died with Effusion of Blood."* Some suppose, that he defended himself bravely; and that at first he had the Advantage; that he threw *Cain* upon the Ground, and gave him his Life; but that *Cain* got up, and slew him. Father *Mersenne* reports this Dream in the 1431th Page of his *Commentary on Genesis*.

[H] *That Fire from Heaven fell upon Abel's Sacrifice.*] St *Jerom* has preserved this Tradition (32), and confirms it from *Theodotion*, who follows him in the Version of the Scripture. " Nisi illa Inter-
" pretatio vera esset, quam Theodotion posuit, & in-
" flammavit Dominus super Abel, & super Sacrifi-
" cium ejus; supra vero Cain & Sacrificium ejus
" non inflammavit (33). —— *Is the Interpretation of
" Theodotion be true, and God sent Fire upon Abel
" and his Sacrifice, but not upon Cain and his Sa-
" crifice."* It is generally approved by the Fathers of the Church, and it is a probable Opinion, because Fire from Heaven has frequently been the Signal of God's Approbation of a Sacrifice. At the Consecration of *Aaron*, God gave this Mark of his Approbation (34). *Gideon, David, Solomon*, (some add *Noæmiah*, were honoured with this extraordinary Favour in some of their Sacrifices (35). *Cornelius a Lapide* says, that *Calvin* and *Luther* laugh'd at this Descent of Fire from Heaven upon *Abel*'s Sacrifice, as a Jewish Fable (36); but Mr *Heidegger* quotes a Passage of *Luther* against him, which plainly proves the contrary. " *Etsi Moses illud signum,
" quo Deus placedit ita Abel numera grata esse, non
" ostendit, tamen verisimile est tale ignem cœlestium,
" denuntiam, quo oblatio hausta & consumpta in odo-
" lis omnium* (37). —— *Though Moses does not record
" on what Sign God declared his Approbation of
" Abel's Offering, yet it is probable that Fire de-
" scended from Heaven, and consumed the Oblation
" in the Sight of all."* The Protestant Divines

ABELARD.

(38) See Sal declare in Crouds for this Hypothesis (38), and some *May be remember thy Offerings, and Services, and*
d... Ora. of them are confirmed in it by the Words of one *reduce thy Sacrifices to Ashes.*
Theol. ❡. P. of the Psalms (39), which *Clement Marot* has thus
317. translated:

(39) Psalm
22.   De tes offertes & services
    Se veuille souvenir,
    Et faire tous les sacrifices
    En cendre devenir.

The Pagans boast of such kind of extraordinary Marks of the Approbation of Heaven in some Places, as we shall show under the Article EGNATIA. We know very well that the Devil mimicks the True God.

ABELARD (*Peter*) in *Latin Abælardus*, was one of the most celebrated Doctors of the XIIth Century. He was born at *Palais* [*A*], a Town four Leagues distant from *Nantes* in *Brittany*: and, as he was of a very subtile Genius, there was nothing in his Course of Studies, to which he apply'd himself with greater Success, than *Logic*. He travell'd to divers Places with no other view, than to exercise himself in that Science; disputing wherever he came, throwing about his Syllogisms, and greedily catching at every Opportunity of distinguishing himself against some Thesis. Never did Knight-Errant more eagerly seek occasion to break a Lance in in Honour of the Ladies. *Abelard* finish'd his Studies at *Paris*, where he met with a celebrated Professor in Philosophy, nam'd *William Champeaux* (a). He became soon his favourite Disciple: but this continu'd not long: the Professor found it so difficult to answer the subtile Objections of his Scholar, that he conceiv'd a Disgust and Hatred towards him. Immediately it became Matter of Party: the older Scholars, envious of *Abelard*, seconded their Master's Dislike. This increased the Assurance of the young Logician so much, that he resolv'd to set up for a Teacher himself. He chose a large Theatre to act this Part on; for he erected a School at *Melun* [*B*], where the Court of *France* resided at that Time. *Champeaux* did all he could to prevent the setting up of this School; but, as he had very powerful Enemies, his Opposition was the principal Cause of his Rival's Success (b). The Reputation of this new Master of *Logic*, made so surprizing a Progress, as to eclipse that of *Champeaux*. *Abelard* was so elevated with this Success, that he remov'd his School to *Corbeil*, in order to press his Enemy close with frequent Disputes; but the great Application, with which he follow'd his Studies, threw him into an Indisposition, which obliged him to retire to his native Air. He stay'd some Years in *Brittany*, and then return'd to *Paris*; where he found that *Champeaux*, who had resign'd his Chair to another, and embrac'd the Religion of the Regular Canons, continued teaching among them. He disputed against him, with such force of Argument, concerning the Nature of *Universals*, that he obliged him to give up his Opinion

(a) Guilielmus Campellensis. He was Archdeacon of Paris.

(b) Quoniam de potentibus terræ nonnullis ibidem habebat æmulos; fretus eorum auxilio voti mei compos extiti, & plurimorum mihi assensum ipsius invidia manifesta conquisivit. *Abelardi Epist. t. p. c.* As he had, there, some Enemies among the great Men, I succeeded by their Assistance; and his manifest Envy procured me the Approbation of many.

[*A*] *He was born at* Palais.] His Father had applied himself a little to his Studies, before he bore Arms; and took great Care of the Education of his Children, particularly the eldest. Whether *Abelard* was this eldest, is uncertain; for he speaks of this Matter so ambiguously, as to give Occasion to two different Opinions. These are his Words: "Primogenitum suum, quanto chariorem habebat, tanto diligentius erudire curavit. Ego vero, quanto amplius in studio literarum profeci, tanto ardentius in iis inhæsi, & in tanto earum amore illectus sum, ut militaris gloriæ pompam cum hæreditate & prærogativa primogenitorum meorum fratribus derelinquens, Martis curiæ penitus abdicarem, ut Minervæ gremio educarer. —— *The more he lov'd his eldest-born, the more Care he took in his Education; For my own Part, the farther Progress I made in my Studies, the greater Desire I had to pursue them; and so fond was I of them, as to leave the Pomp of Military Glory, with the Inheritance and Privileges of Eldership, to my Brothers; and, renouncing the Court of Mars, to be educated in the Bosom of Minerva.*" *Pasquier*, upon the Authority of these Words, makes no doubt of calling him the eldest Son (1): but others positively affirm, that he was a younger Brother. This is the Opinion of *Father Alexander*. "Militaris Gloriæ pompam cum hæreditate primogenitis fratribus derelinquens, says he (2), speaking of *Abelard*, i. e. *leaving the Pomp of Military Glory, with the Inheritance, to his elder Brothers*." Some make him the youngest of the Family (3). If I might chuse, I should not prefer the last Interpretation of the former. Doubtless the Sirname of *Palatinus*, which he bore, was deriv'd from *Palatium*, the Name of the Place of his Nativity. He was so well known by the Name of *Peripateticus Palatinus*, that *Johannes Saresberiensis* never stiles him otherwise (4). Some imagine, that this Epithet was given him on Account of some magnificent Building, where he deliver'd his Lectures (5). But this is without Foundation,

[*B*] *A School at* Melun.] I have not found, in comparing the Relation of *Abelard* with the Abridgment of it, given us by *Pasquier*, that it is abridg'd with great Exactness. The Series of his Adventures, according to the Abridgment, is as follows. *Abelard* went and settled at *Corbeil*, when he first left *Paris*: he returned to *Paris*, when *Champeaux* became a Monk: he was obliged to quit it a second time: and then he retired to *Melun*: he returned to *Paris* again, being informed, that *Champeaux* was gone to reside at his Bishoprick of *Châlons*: *Champeaux*, apprized of his Return, came back to *Paris* to oppose *Abelard*: This latter was at length obliged to quit his Design, and became a Disciple of *Anselm*, Lecturer of Divinity at *Paris*: He became afterwards himself Lecturer of Divinity; and was intreated by a certain Canon to employ one Hour every Day in instructing his Niece. He complied with this Request; and having continued this Occupation for some time, Love made himself of the Party with them. There are many Faults in this Narrative. I. *Abelard* did not settle at *Corbeil* 'till after he had been at *Melun*. II. When he left *Melun* the second time, *Champeaux* was retired to a Village near *Paris*, and not to his Bishoprick of *Châlons*, which was not yet given him; he being then but a Monk. III. And I am surprized that *Pasquier* was not sensible how absurd it was to suppose a Bishop should leave his Episcopal See to dispute with a *Regent of Philosophy* at *Paris*. III. *Abelard* was not conquered in his Dispute; he quitted *Paris* only to pay a Visit to his Mother, who was going into a Convent. IV. *Anselm* read Divinity at *Laon*, and not at *Paris*. V. The *Canon* did not request that his Niece might be instructed; *Abelard* himself entreated to be entertained in the *Canon's* House. VI. *Abelard* desired the Enjoyment of *Eloisa*, before he gave her any Lessons. With what Distrust ought we to read a great Number of Books, when *Pasquier* stumbles so often in so plain a Road?

(1) *Pasquier's* Recherche. de la France. B. 6. ch. 17.

(2) Natal. Alex. Cent. xi. & xii. part 3. p. 2.

(3) Du Pin's Biblioth. T. 9. p. 108.

(4) See his Policraticus, p. 111. and its Metalogicus, p. 745. Edit. Leyden 1639. 8vo.

(5) Jac. Thomasius's Life of Abelard. See below the Cites re (13).

VOL. I.   G   [C] *A*

nion, which at the bottom was a disguis'd *Spinozism* [C]. This brought the Monk into such Contempt, and rais'd the Character of his Antagonist so high, that *Champeaux*'s Logic Lectures were entirely forsaken, and the Professor himself, to whom *Champeaux* had resign'd, thought fit to become the Scholar of *Peter Abelard*. This latter was no sooner in possession of the Chair, than he saw himself expos'd more and more to the darts of Envy. The Regular Canon manag'd it so, that, on pretence of some sinister Management, the Resignation made to *Peter Abelard* was declared void, and a profess'd Enemy appointed to succeed him. Upon this *Abelard* left *Paris*, and retired to *Melun*, to teach Logic there, as before. He continued there not long; for, hearing that *Champeaux* had retired, with his whole Fraternity, to a Village, he came and settled upon Mount St *Genevieve*, and erected his School, as a kind of Battery [D], against the *Parisian* Doctor. *Champeaux*, seeing the Creature of his own raising thus besieged in his School, brought back the Regular Canons to their Convent: but, instead of relieving his Friend, it occasioned all his Scholars to forsake him: This Desertion was follow'd some time after with the Retirement of this poor Philosopher to a Convent. From that time the Contest lay wholly between *Abelard* and *Champeaux*: they alone disputed the ground; but superior Age was not attended with Victory. Whilst this Struggle yet continued, *Abelard* was obliged to pay a Visit to his Mother, who, after the example of her Husband, was preparing to embrace a Religious Life. Returning to *Paris*, he found his Rival made Bishop of *Chalons*: therefore, as he could now give up his School, without the Imputation of flying from the Field of Battle, he determin'd to study Divinity; for which reason he remov'd to *Laon* [E], where his Schoolmaster *Anselm* read Lectures in that Science

[C] *A disguis'd Spinozism.*] I appeal for this to the Judgment of those who understand the following Words. "Erat in eâ sententia de communitate universalium; ut eandem essentialiter non totam simul singulis suis inesse astrueret individuis, quorum quidem nulla esset in essentiâ diversitas, sed solâ multitudine accidentium varietas. He *was of that Opinion, concerning the Sameness of Universals, which asserts, that the same Thing exists essentially and wholly in every one of it's Individuals, among which there is no Difference as to Essence, but only a Variety arising from a Number of Accidents* (6)." The *Scotists*, with their *universale formale à parte rei*, or their *unitas formalis à parte rei*, are not wide of this Notion. Now I say, that *Spinozism* is only carrying this Doctrine farther: for, according to the Followers of *Scotus*, *Universal Natures* are indivisibly the same in every one of their *Individuals*: The Human Nature of *Peter* is indivisibly the same with the Human Nature of *Paul*. Upon what Foundation do they say this? Why, because the same Attribute of *Man*, which is applicable to *Peter*, agrees with *Paul*. This is the very Fallacy of the *Spinozists*. *The Attribute*, say they, *does not differ from the Substance, of which it is predicated: therefore, wherever the same Attribute is found, there is the same Substance; and, consequently, since the same Attribute is found in all Substances, there can possibly be but one Substance*. There is, then, but one Substance in the Universe; and all the Variety we see in the World is but different Modifications of one and the same Substance. *Abelard*'s Antagonist had nothing of Weight to reply to this; and I cannot see what Answer the Cordelier *Frassen* (7), who adheres strictly to the Doctrine of *Scotus*, amidst the Lights of Philosophy, which brighten this Age, could have given to *Spinoza*. But the rest of the Schoolmen had nothing more to do, in order to overthrow this false System, but to distinguish between *Identity* in Number, and *Identity* in Species or Likeness. *Peter* and *Paul* have not the same Nature, nor the same Attribute, if by *same* you mean any thing else than *like*.

(6) *Abelard's* Epist. 1. p. 5.

(7) See the Capucin Cafimir *de Toulouse* in his Atom. Peripatet. T. 5. p. 132.

[D] *As a kind of Battery.*] It will be proper to hear his own Account of this Matter. "Quia locum nostrum ab æmulo nostro fecerat occupari, extra civitatem in monte S. Genovefæ Scholarum nostrarum castra posui, quasi eum obsessurus, qui cum occupaverat nostrum. Quo audito, Magister noster statim ad urbem impudenter rediens, Scholas, quas tunc habere poterat, & Conventiculum Fratrum, ad pristinum reduxit Monasterium, quasi militem suum, quem deseruerat, ab obsidione nostra liberaturus (8). —— *The Place, I enjoyed, being usurped by my Rival, I encamped my School, without the City, upon Mount St* Genevieve, *as it were to besiege my Successor: upon the News of which, my Preceptor, returning confidently to the City,*

(8) *Abelard's* Epist. p. 6.

brought back what Schools he could at that time procure, together with the whole Brotherhood, to their former Monastery, as it were to relieve his own Soldier, whom he had deserted, from my Siege." The Life of *Abelard*, published by M. *Thomasius* (9) in *Germany*, informs me of one Particular, which *Andrew du Chêne*, *Francis d' Amboise*, and perhaps all who have ever spoke of *Abelard*, were ignorant of. It is, that, in the midst of his Troubles and Persecutions, and after he had placed *Eloisa* in the *Paraclet*, he returned to the Reading of his public Lectures on Mount St *Genevieve*. *Johannes Sarisberiensis* confirms this past a Doubt. "Cum primum, *says he* (10), adolescens admodum, studiorum causâ migrassem in Gallias, anno altero postquam illustris " Rex Anglorum Henricus, Leo Justitiæ, rebus excessit humanis, contuli me ad Peripateticum Palatinum, qui tunc in Monte S. Genovefæ clarus Doctor & admirabilis omnibus præsidebat. Ibi ad pedes ejus prima artis hujus rudimenta accepi, & pro modulo ingenioli mei quicquid excidebat ab ore ejus totâ mentis aviditate excipiebam. Deinde, post discessum ejus, qui mihi præproperus visus est, adhæsi Magistro Alberico, qui inter cæteros Dialecticos enitebat, & erat re verâ nominalis sectæ acerrimus impugnator. ——— *When I first travelled into* France, *being very young, in order to prosecute my Studies, a Year after the Death of* Henry *King of* England, *the Lion of Justice, I betook myself to the Peripatetic of* Palatium (11), *who at that time was a celebrated Doctor, and in great Reputation upon Mount* St Genevieve. *There, at his Feet, I was instructed in the first Principles of this Science, and received, to the best of my Abilities, whatever fell from his Lips, with the utmost Eagerness. After his Death, which to me seemed too hasty, I was a constant Follower of the Teacher* Albericus, *who was the most eminent Logician of the Times, and indeed, the most violent Opposer of the* Nominal Sect." This plainly points out the Year 1136. *Abelard* therefore must have been returned to *Paris* long time after the Council of *Soissons*, and have left it a few Years before the Council of *Sens*.

[E] *He removed to* Laon.] *Otho* of *Frisingen* has misplaced Facts, when he says, that *Abelard* studied first under *Rozelin*, then under *Anselm* of *Laon*, and *William des Champeaux*, Bishop, of *Châlons* (12). The Order of Time is not observed: besides this *William* was not a Bishop, at the time when *Abelard* was his Scholar. I have met with a Book (13), in which the Author supposes, that *Abelard* succeeded this *William* in the Divinity-Chair, in the Year 1119: But first, he does not appear, that this pretended Predecessor taught that Science. And it is farther certain, that *Abelard* read Theological Lectures at *Paris*, before the Year 1119: for it is not possible, that all his Adventures, from his first Lectures to the

(9) He is the Son of James Thomasius, Professor at Leipsic, Author of this Life of Abelard, printed at Hall, in 1693. See Citation below (13).

(11) i.e. Abelard, as the Author himself expresses it, p. 814. In hac opinione, ... sayst he, deprehensus est Peripateticus Palatinus Abelardus noster.

(12) Otho of Frif. de Geftis Friderici. lib. 1. cap. 47.

(13) The History of Wisdom and Folly, collected by Christ. Thomafius, Tom. 1. p. 81. *In that we find the Life of Abelard mentioned above, which ..., the rest which lac. Thomasius composed.*

ABELARD.

Science with great Reputation. He was not greatly satisfy'd with this Person's Capacity [F]; and, instead of attending his Lectures, he undertook to read himself to his School-Fellows. He explained to them the Prophecies of *Ezekiel* in so pleasing a manner, that in a short time his new Auditory was crowded. The Jealousy of *Anselm* did not long permit this: he forbid this new Master to continue his Lectures. *Abelard* return'd to *Paris*; explain'd there publickly the Prophet *Ezekiel*; and acquired in a short time as great a Reputation in Divinity, as in Philosophy: besides which he gain'd a great deal of Money. To perfect the Pleasures of Life, he began to think of a Mistress, and cast his Eyes upon *Eloisa*, Niece of a *Canon*, whom he preferr'd to an hundred other Ladies, whom he had it very much in his Power to charm [G]. This Canon, named *Fulbert*, lov'd Money, and was passionately desirous, that his Niece *Eloisa* should be a Scholar. *Abelard* laid hold of these two Foibles to ensnare him. *Admit me to board with you*, says he, and *fix your own Price*. The Good Man, imagining he had found an excellent Tutor for his Niece, who, far from being an Expence to him, would pay him well for his Board, ran headlong into the Snare (c). He intreated Master *Abelard* to instruct the young Girl fully, both Night and Day, and gave him permission to use correction, if she did not perform her Lessons. Our pretended Tutor ill answer'd the Expectation of *Fulbert*: he soon began to talk Love to his fair Scholar; and amus'd himself more in toying and kissing her [H], than in explaining an Author to her. He indulg'd this

---

(14) See Du Chêne's Notes upon Abelard's Narrative, p. 2147.

(15) Dupin's Biblioth. Tom. 9. p. 500. Dutch Edition.

the Council of *Soissons*, could have fallen out in two Years: Now there is good Proof, that this Council was called in the Year 1121. Add to this, that *William des Champeaux* was made Bishop of *Châlons* in the Year 1113 (14); and that this Promotion removing him from the Schools of *Paris*, *Abelard* went to *Laon*, to study Divinity there. I see no Foundation for the Assertion of others, that he engaged in this Study at *Châlons* (15).

[F] *Satisfied with this Person's Capacity*.] He was an old Man, who never had any great Genius; insomuch, that he was easily non-plus'd, when put out of his Road. When he was pushed home, as he frequently was by the acute and subtile *Abelard*, he defended himself with meer empty Words: that his Character will be best known from what I am going to transcribe. "Accessi ad hunc senem, cui
" magis longævus usus, quam ingenium vel memo-
" ria, nomen comparaverat: ad quem si quis de aliquâ
" Questione pulsandum accederet incertus, redibat
" incertior. Mirabilis erat in oculis auscultantium;
" sed nullus in conspectu questionantium. Verborum
" usum habebat mirabilem, sed sensu contemptibi-
" lem, & ratione vacuum. Cum ignem accenderet,
" domum suam fumo implebat, non luce illustrabat.
" Arbor ejus, tota in foliis, aspicientibus à longe con-
" spicua videbatur, sed propinquantibus & diligentius
" intuentibus infructuosa reperiebatur. Ad hanc ita-
" que cum accessisem, ut fructum inde colligerem,
" deprehendi illam esse ficulneam, cui maledixit Do-
" minus, seu illam veterem quercum, cui Pompeium
" Lucanus comparat, dicens,

― Stat magni nominis umbra,
Qualis frugifero quercus sublimis in agro.

" *I applied myself to this old Man, whom long Pra-
" ctice, not Genius or Memory, had made famous;
" who always sent an Enquirer back more uncertain
" than he came. He was the Admiration of his
" Hearers, but the Contempt of his Examiners. He
" had a wonderful Flow of Words; but void of Sense
" and Reason. He was a Fire that filled the House,
" not with Light, but Smoke: A Tree, that appeared
" Fair at a Distance, but, on a nearer View, bore
" nothing but Leaves. When I approached it, in
" hopes of gathering Fruit, I found it to be the Fig-
" Tree which was cursed by our Lord, or that old
" Oak, to which Lucan thus compares Pompey:

Still seem'd he to possess, and fill his Place,
But stood the Shadow of what once he was.
So in the Field, with Ceres's Bounty spread,
Uprears some antient Oak his reverend Head.
ROWE.

This Passage deserves to be copied: It shows *Abelard*'s turn of Wit, and is a true Picture of a great many Persons.

[G] *Whom he had it very much in his Power to charm.*] Vanity was our Hero's distinguishing Foible:

However, being an handsome young Fellow, and in the Flower of his Age; and having a knack at Poetry, a great Reputation, and Money in his Pocket; it is not so strange that he flattered himself with a kind Reception, wherever he should make his Addresses: " Tanti quippe tunc nominis eram,
" & juventutis & formæ gratiâ præeminebam, ut
" quamcumque fœminarum nostro dignarer amore,
" nullam vererer repulsam (16). ― *Such was my*
" *Reputation, my Youth, and Beauty, that I feared*
" *no Repulse from any Woman, whom I should think*
" *worthy of my Affections.*" For a Philosopher, who had lived in great Continence (17), he reasons like a Man of no small Experience in these Matters, when the Conquest of *Eloisa* seems to him more easy, than that of any other Woman; and for this Reason, because *Eloisa*'s Learning gave him the Opportunity of a regular Correspondence with her by Letters, in which he could make more open Declarations, than in Conversation. " Tanto facilius hanc mihi
" puellam consensuram credidi, quanto amplius eam
" litterarum Scientiam & habere & diligere nove-
" ram, nosque etiam absentes scriptis internunciis
" invicem liceret præsentare, & pleraque audacius
" scribere, quam colloqui. ― *The more I found*
" *this Girl improve in Learning, and the fonder she*
" *grew of it, the greater Hopes I had of her Consent:*
" *and it was in our Power to be present, even in Ab-*
" *sence, by the Intercourse of Letters, and to write*
" *more freely, than converse* (18)." Love-Letters, and Amorous Verses, are no weak Instruments in Love; especially when the Lover himself can sing the passionate Songs he has composed. *Abelard* in this Manner touched the Heart of *Eloisa*, and fired her so by his charming Pen, and enchanting Voice, that the poor Lady could never overcome her Passion. " Duo, *says she to him* (19), fateor tibi specia-
" liter inerant, quibus fœminarum quarumlibet ani-
" mos statim allicere poteras, dictandi & cantandi
" gratia. ― *Two Qualifications, I confess, you*
" *was particularly Master of, with which you could*
" *immediately charm the Soul of any Woman, The*
" *pleasing Manner of dictating, and singing, your*
" *Verses.*" See the Remark [F] under her Article, where this Passage, cited more at Length, demonstrates the great Influence of these Things upon that Sex.

[H] *In toying and kissing her.*] The better to disguise his Design from the Uncle, he pretended sometimes to make use of the Liberty given him of correcting *Eloisa*. He tells us, that Love, not the Anger of a Teacher, prompted him from time to time to whip his Pupil; but that the Lashes he gave her, were the softest in the World. He has left us the following Plan of the Lectures he gave this young Lady. " Sub occasione disciplinæ amori penitus vacabamus,
" & secretos recessus, quos amor optabat, studium
" Lectionis offerebat. Apertis itaque libris, plura de
" amore, quam de lectione, verba se ingerebant,
" plura erant oscula, quam sententiæ; Sæpius ad Si-
" nus, quam ad libros, reducebantur manus: crebrius
" oculos amor in se reflectebat, quam lectio in Scrip-
" turam

ABELARD.

this Pleasure the more, as he had never before tasted it. He neglected his public Functions, and employ'd his time in writing nothing but Love-Verses [*I*]. His Scholars soon perceived that his Lectures declined, and they presently guess'd the Cause. The last Person, that heard the Report of *Peter Abelard*'s Amours, was the good Canon *Fulbert*, at whose House the Scene of them was laid. For some time he gave no credit to it; but at length he open'd his Eyes, and dismiss'd his Boarder from his House. Some time after, his Niece found herself with Child, and writ to her Gallant, who thought it proper she should leave her Uncle. He sent her into *Brittany* to a Sister of his, where she was brought to bed of Son (*d*); and, to appease the Canon, he propos'd to him to marry *Eloisa* privately. This Proposal was more pleasing to the Uncle, than to the Niece: for *Eloisa*, through an Excess of Passion not common, chose rather to be the Mistress, than the Wife of *Abelard*, as we shall relate elsewhere (*e*). At length she consented to this private Marriage; but she affirmed, upon occasion, with an Oath, that she was not married. *Fulbert*, who chose rather to cover the Disgrace of his Family, by divulging the Marriage, than to keep his Promise with *Abelard* not to discover it, often express'd his Anger at his Niece, when he perceived her Obstinacy in denying that she was *Abelard*'s Wife. Upon this her Husband sent her to the Monastery of *Argenteuil*, and oblig'd her to take the Habit of a Nun, except the Veil. The Relations of *Eloisa* imagin'd, that he was laying a new Scene of Treachery in that place, and were so enrag'd, that they employ'd certain Persons, who enter'd his Chamber by Night, and dismember'd him of those manly Parts, with which he had dishonour'd the Canon's Family. This Disgrace made him retire, and conceal his Misfortune in a Monastick Life; and therefore it was not Devotion but Shame, which prompted him to take the Habit of a Monk in the Abbey of St *Dennis* (*f*). The Disorders of this Abbey, in which the Abbot was as much superior to the rest of the Monks in all manner of Impurities, as in Dignity, were the Cause of *Abelard*'s leaving it: he cou'd not forbear censuring them; and render'd himself by this means so odious to them, that they were overjoy'd to get rid of him. He chose his Place of Retreat upon the Lands of the Earl of *Champagne* [*K*], and erected there a School, where

(*d*) He was named Astrolabius.

(*e*) In the Article ELOISA.

(*f*) In tam misera me contritione postum confusio, fateor, pudoris potius, quam devotio conversasio ad monasticorum latibula clauStrorum compulit. In this miserable State of Penitence, the Confusion of my Shame, I confess, rather than Devotion, drove me to take Shelter in the Inclosure of a Monastery. *Abelard*'s Epist. p. 18.

" turam dirigebat: Quoque minus suspicionis habere-
" mus, verbera quandoque dabat amor, non furor,
" gratia non ira, quæ omnium unguentorum suavita-
" tem transcenderent. —— *Under the Pretence of In-*
" *struction we gave a loose to Love, and a Lecture pro-*
" *cured us that Privacy, which our Passion desired.*
" *When we open'd our Books, we talk'd more of Love,*
" *than of reading; we repeated Kisses oftener than*
" *Sentences; we Hands were employ'd in her Bo-*
" *som, more than on her Books; and Love oftener*
" *turn'd my Eyes on her, than the Intention of read-*
" *ing directed them to the Scripture: And the more to*
" *prevent Suspicion, Love, not Rage, Favour, not*
" *Anger, gave her Lashes, which were sweeter than*
" *the richest Perfumes* (20)." But it sometimes happen'd, that he had recourse to Punishment in good earnest; either when she was out of humour, or the Solemnity of a Festival inspired him with some Scruple. See the Remark [E], under the Article ELOISA. We must not pass by *Abelard*'s Reflexion on the Simplicity of the Canon. " Quanta ejus simplicitas ef-
" set vehementer admiratus, non minus apud me ob-
" stupui, quam si agnam teneram famelico Lupo com-
" mitteret. Qui cum eam mihi non solum docen-
" dam, verum etiam vehementer constringendam,
" traderet, quid aliud agebat, quam ut votis meis li-
" centiam penitus daret, & occasionem etiamsi nolle-
" mus offerret, ut quam videlicet blanditiis non pos-
" sem, minis & verberibus facilius flecterem? ——
" *I was as much astonish'd at his Folly, as if he had*
" *trusted a tender Lamb to the Care of a ravenous*
" *Wolf. In committing her not only to my Instru-*
" *ction, but even Correction, what was it but to*
" *licence my Wishes, and to give us Opportunities, even*
" *against our Inclination; and to put it in my Power,*
" *if I could not prevail on her by softer Methods, to*
" *force her to Compliance by Threats and Lashes.*" As this Author often cites the antient Poets, I wonder his Thought of the *tender Lamb*, and *ravening Wolf*, did not put him in Mind of these Verses of *Virgil*;

Eheu, quid volui misero mihi? Floribus Austrum
Perditus, & liquidis immisi Fontibus Apros (21).

What have I done? ——
The Boar amidst my Chrystal Streams; I bring,
And southern Winds to blast my flow'ry Spring.
DRYDEN.

(20) *Abelard's Works*, p. 11.

(21) Virg. Ecl. 2. v. 58. See the Nouv. Littér. against the Calvin. of Mainbourg, p. 41.

[*I*] *Nothing but Love-Verses.*] After he had tasted the Pleasures of Enjoyment, he grew weary of reading Lectures, and stay'd in his Auditory as little as possible. The Night was quite lost to his Studies (22): he was otherwise employ'd: he therefore desired to dedicate the Day to Study. This was the Reason why his School was uneasy to him. He repeated only his old Lectures; and if any new Thought came into his Head, it turn'd, not upon any Philosophical Difficulty, but upon amorous Sonnets, which were sung a long time after, in several Provinces. " Ita negligentem
" & tepidum lectio tunc habebat, ut jam nihil ex in-
" genio, sed ex usu cuncta proferrem, nec jam nisi re-
" citator pristinorum essem inventorum; & si qua in-
" venire liceret carmina essent amatoria, non Philo-
" sophiæ secreta. Quorum etiam carminum, sicut &
" ipse nocti, frequentantur & decantantur regionibus,
" ab his maxime quos vita similis oblectat. —— *So*
" *careless was I, and negligent, in reading, at that*
" *Time, that I produc'd nothing new, but was satis-*
" *fy'd with barely reciting my old Compositions; my*
" *Invention was employ'd on Love Songs, not on the*
" *Secrets of Philosophy; many of which Songs are still*
" *Favourites, as you very well know, and sung in the*
" *Provinces, by those especially, who are delighted*
" *with the same kind of Life* (23)." It is certain then, that he had a Genius for Poetry; but I cannot believe, that he was Author of the famous Romance of *the Rose*, nor that he drew the Picture of his *Eloisa*, under the Name of *the Beauty*. Yet this is what I have read in a Book, reprinted in *Holland* (24). I should rather give Credit to him (25), who has taken so much pains to collect, and collate, the Manuscripts of *Abelard*. Now he asserts peremptorily, that the Romance of *the Rose* was wrote by *William de Lorris*, all but the Conclusion, of which *John de Meun* was the Author. Other Writers, who were well informed, declare the same. The History of *Abelard* and *Eloisa* was inserted in this Romance.

[*K*] *Upon the Lands of the Earl of* Champagne.] This appears, by comparing two Passages. The first is, " Ad Cellam quondam recessi, Scholis more solito
" vacaturus. —— *I chose a Place of Retreat, that I*
" *might be at leisure to attend my School as usual* (26)." The other is, " Nocte latenter aufugi, atque ad ter-
" ram Comitis Theobaldi proximam, ubi antea in
" Cella moratus fueram, abcessi. —— *I stole away by*
" *Night, and retreated to the Estate of Earl* Theo-
" bald, *which lay near, and was the Place of my*
" *former*

(22) *Tepidum mihi vehementer erat ad Scholas procedere, vel in iis moram perter & laboriosam, cum nocturnus amori vigiliis, & diurnas studii conservarem. It was both very tedious and tiresome to me, either to go to the Schools, or to stay in them; since my Nights were devoted to Love, and my Days to Study.*

(23) Ibid.

(24) *The History of* Abelard *and* Eloisa, *in* 1693, *in* 12mo.

(25) Francis d'Amboise. See *his Apologetical Preface at the beginning of* Abelard's *Works*, Paris 1616. in 4to.

(26) *Abelard's Works*, p. 19.

ABELARD.

where he gain'd so great a Number of Auditors [L], that the Envy of other Masters, who saw themselves deserted by their Scholars, upon his account, began to raise new Persecutions against him. He had made himself two formidable Enemies at *Laon* (g) who no sooner perceived the Prejudice, which their Schools at *Rheims* receiv'd from his great Reputation, than they fought occasion to ruin him. This was afforded them by a Book, which he wrote upon the Mystery of the *Trinity* [M]: they pretended to discover in it a shocking Heresy; and prevail'd, by the Interest of their Archbishop, to have a Council call'd at *Soissons*, about the Year 1121 [N]. This Council, without giving *Abelard* leave to defend himself, condemn'd

(e) Alberi-cus of Rheims, and Rotul-phus t'e Lombards. The latter is called Lau-taldus Nova-rienss by O-tho of Frisin-gen.*

{27} Abe-lard's Works, p. 26.

" *former Retirement* (27)." *Pasquier* did not understand the former; which he construes thus; " retir-
" ing to the deepest Cell of a Monastery, he read
" Lectures, sometimes in Philosophy, sometimes in Di-
" vinity." *Abelard* by no means erected a School within the Walls of the Abbey of St *Denis*: if he had, he would not have been more favourable to the Monks, whose Irregularities he censur'd, and which was the Reason they were so desirous of getting rid of him, than he had formerly been. Mr *du Cange* explains the Word *Cella* very learnedly, as he does every thing. See the Remark [A], on the Article PARA-CLET, *where I explain the different Situations of* Peter Abelard.

{29} Ibid. p. 20.

[L] *So great a Number of Auditors.*] Concerning the great Number of Scholars, which he had, see the Remark [A] of the Article FOULQUES, Prior of *Deuil*.

{30} Pas-quier's Re-cherch. de la France. B. 6. ch. 17.

[M] *The Mystery of the Trinity*] The occasion, which induc'd *Abelard* to write upon this Subject, was, that his Scholars demanded from him a Philosophical Account of it. " *They were not satisfy'd with Words;
" they desired Ideas; and declar'd loudly, that it
" was impossible for them to believe what they did not
" understand; and that it was an Imposition upon
" Mankind, to preach up a Doctrine equally incompre-
" hensible to the Teachers and the Hearers; which was
" as if the Blind should lead the Blind, according to
" our Saviour himself.* —— Humanas & Philosophicas
" rationes requirebant, & plus quae intelligi, quam
" quae dici possent, effiagitabant; dicentes verborum
" superfluam esse prolationem, quam intelligentia non
" sequeretur, nec credi posse aliquid nisi primitus
" intellectum; & ridiculosum esse aliquem aliis praedi-
" care, quod nec ipse, nec illi quos doceret, intel-
" lectu capere possent, Domino ipso arguente quod
" coeci essent duces coecorum (29)." Upon which he set himself to explain to them the Unity of God, by Comparisons drawn from human Things. *Pasquier* accuses him of maintaining, " That we ought not
" to believe a Thing, of which we can give no Rea-
" son; which, *adds he,* is, in plain Terms, to destroy
" the general Foundation of our Faith (30)." I do not ask this Author, who told him that a Professor approves all the Conceits of his Scholars, when he is so complaisant as to prevent, to the utmost of his Power, the ill Consequences of them. It is indeed probable, that *Abelard* did not disapprove of the Maxims, which he ascribes to his Hearers; but the Passage, quoted by *Pasquier,* is no Proof of this; we ought rather to found it upon these Words of St *Bernard*: " Quid
" magis contra fidem, quam credere nolle quidquid
" non possis Ratione attingere? Denique exponere vo-
" lens (Abaelardus) illud Sapientis, qui credit cito le-
" vis est corde, cito credere est, inquit, adhibere
" fidem ante rationem. —— *Can any thing be more
" contrary to Faith, than to refuse assent to every
" thing, which Reason cannot reach?* Abelard *being
" to explain the Saying of the Wise Man, He, who
" believes hastily is light of Heart; to believe hastily,
" says he, is to give Assent before Reason* (31)." The Treatise, which *Abelard* wrote upon this Subject, was universally approv'd, except by those of the same Profession with himself; I mean the Divinity-Professors. They were so chagrin'd, that another had explain'd and illustrated what they could not, that they cry'd out, he was an Heretic, and alarm'd the People so much, that *Abelard* narrowly escap'd being ston'd. " Duo illi praedicti Aemuli nostri ita me in Clero &
" Populo diffamaverunt, ut pene me populus pau-
" coque qui advenerant ex discipulis nostris, prima
" die nostri adventus, lapidarent, dicentes me tres
" Deos praedicare, & scripsisse, sicut ipsis persuasum
" fuerat —— *My two forementioned Rivals so blacken'd
" me, both to the Clergy and Laity, that, upon the
" first Day of my Arrival, with a few of my Scholars,*

{31} Ber-nard's Epist. 190.

" *the People were near stoning us; crying out, as it
" has been insinuated to them, that I both preach'd
" and writ, that there were three Gods* (32)." Their Cabal were so powerful, as to extort from the Pope's Legate (33), the Condemnation mention'd in the Body of this Article. They made it believ'd, that *Abelard* admitted of three Gods: Nevertheless, it is certain that he was very orthodox in the Mystery of the *Trinity*, and that all the Accusations brought against him in this Affair, were wretched Chicanery, and proceeded either from Malice or Ignorance. The Comparison he fetch'd from *Logic* (for *Logic* was his Strong hold) tended rather to reduce the divine Persons to *One*, than to multiply the Essence of God into *Three*; and yet he was accus'd, not of *Sabellianism* (34), but of *Tritheism*. His Comparison is, that, as the *Three Propositions* of a *Syllogism*, are but *One Truth*; so the *Father,* the *Son,* and the *Holy Ghost*, are but *One Essence*. " Sicut eadem Oratio est Pro-
" positio, Assumptio, & Conclusio; ita eadem es-
" sentia est Pater, Filius, & Spiritus Sanctus (35)." The Inconveniences arising from this Analogy, are not equal to, at least do not exceed, those, which flow from a Comparison of the *Trinity* with the *Three Dimensions* of Matter. Therefore, as no one disputes the Orthodoxy of Mr *Wallis*, the Oxonian Mathematician, who laid great Stress on the Analogy of the *Three Dimensions*, neither ought we to doubt of *Abelard's,* on account of his Comparison of the *Syllogism*. This is certain, that neither the *Syllogism*, nor the *Three Dimensions,* account for the Mystery of the Trinity. Observe, that a certain Protestant Divine made use of the Parallel of the *Three Dimensions,* in the Year 1685. This appears from the *Nouvelles de la Republique des Lettres,* Article the 3d, for *July*; Article the 10th, for *August*; and Article the 12th, for *September*. It was answered by another Protestant Divine, in the Year 1694. See the *Examen* of Mr *Jurieu's* Theology, by Mr *Saurin*, pag. 831.

{32} Abe-lard's Works, p. 20.

{33} Conan, *Bishop of Preneste. He presided at the Council of Soissons.*

{34} Otho of Frisingen, *in his de Gest. Frider. says, re ortels t, that he was accused of the Heresy of Sa-bellius, at the Council of Soissons.*

{35} Abe-lard's Works, p. 20.

[N] *About the Year* 1121.] Father *Alexander* (36) proves this strongly, as well against *John Picard*, a Canon of St *Victor,* who places this Council in the Year 1116, as against *Binius,* who fixes it in 1136. The Chronological Errors of *Binius*, and some others, have been already censured in the Preface to the Works of Peter *Abelard*. We are then told, that *Platina* had plac'd the Synod, which condemn'd *Abelard,* under Pope *Lucius* II; that *Binius* gave into the Mistake of *Platina*; that he is guilty of another, in placing the Council of *Soissons,* and that of *Sens,* in the Year 1140; and that *Genebrard* supposes but one Year to have pass'd between these Councils. To prove these to be Mistakes, it is asserted, that the Pontificat of *Lucius,* which continu'd not a whole Year, is to be referr'd to the Year 1145, and that twenty Years pass'd between the holding of the Councils of *Soissons* and *Sens*; and that the Bishop of *Preneste*, who presided at the Council of *Soissons,* in quality of the Pope's Legate, left *France* about the Year 1120, and never return'd thither. We may observe more Mistakes than one, in these Words of *Platina*, there cited. " Qui (Abaelardus) praesente etiam Lodovico
" Rege, rationibus victus, non modo sententiam mu-
" tavit, sed etiam monasticam vitam & religionem
" induit, ac deinceps una cum discipulis quibusdam
" in loco deserto sanctissime vixit. —— *Who,* (Abe-
" lard) *in the Presence of King* Lewis, *being overcome
" by Arguments, not only renounc'd his Opinion, but
" took upon him the monastic Life, and Religion,
" and afterwards retiring, with some of his Scholars,
" to a desart Place, liv'd a most holy Life.*" First, it is certain, that *Abelard* became a Monk, before any Council was held against him. In the second place, it was at the Council of *Sens,* that *Lewis* VII. assisted, to be Witness of the Transactions in this Heretic's Cause. Now it is false, that *Abelard* submit-

{36} Nat. Alexand. Eccl. Hist. Cent. 11, 12, Part 3. p. 43, &c.

VOL. I.   H

ABELARD.

demn'd him to throw his own Book into the Fire, and to shut himself up in the Cloyster of St *Medard*. He was commanded soon after to return to the Convent of St *Denis*; where the Liberty, he had taken of censuring the corrupt Manners of the Abbot and the *Religious*, had exposed him to the Hatred of them all. He happen'd to say, that he did not believe their St *Denis* to be *Dionysius* the *Areopagite* mention'd in Scripture. This was immediately laid hold of, and carry'd to the Abbot, who was greatly pleas'd at it, as having a Pretence to accuse him, not only of *False Doctrine*, but even of *offending against the State* [O], an Artifice, which these Gentlemen never fail to put in practice, the better to secure their Revenge. The Abbot assembled his Chapter, without loss of time, and declared that he was going to deliver up to the King's Justice one, who had the Assurance to trample upon the Glory and Crown of the Kingdom. *Abelard*, judging that these Menaces were not to be slighted, made his Escape into *Champagne*, and obtained, after the Death of the Abbot, permission to live a monastic Life, wherever he pleased. The Political Reasons, which concurr'd to this, are something curious [P]. In consequence of this Permission,

---

ted to the Reasoning of his Adversaries, and abjur'd his Opinions, in this Council. He appeal'd, from the very first, to the Pope. In the third place, it is no less false, that from that time he liv'd in a desart place, with some of his Disciples: for he pass'd the remainder of his Days amidst the Monks of *Clugni*. It is evident, that *Platina* has confounded what pass'd in the two Councils held against *Abelard*. Most of the Errors, which I have rectify'd, are objected to *Belleforêt*, in the abovementioned Preface; in which he is farther justly censured for having criticiz'd upon the Epitaph of *Abelard*, as if the extravagant Praises, there given him, were a Proof of his Imprudence, and intolerable Vanity. It is certain, that this Epitaph was compos'd by the Abbot of *Clugni*, after the Death of *Abelard*. Many Historians have not rightly distinguish'd between the two Councils, which proceeded against this great Man. *Paulus Æmilius* says, (37) he was examin'd for the first time in that of *Sens* (37): *Du Haillan* confirms this Mistake, and adds several others to it (38); as that *Abelard* was afraid to appear; that all his Works were condemn'd to be burnt; and that, the second time he was summon'd to appear, the Bishops disputed a long time, before they condemn'd him. *Philip* of *Bergamo* maintains, that the Heretic (39) being confuted, in the Presence of King *Lewis*, by the powerful Arguments of the Learned and Catholic Bishops, renounc'd his false Doctrines, became a Monk, and pass'd the remainder of his Life, most Saint-like, in a Desart, with some of his Disciples. We meet with a great many Writers of Chronicles, who have copied the same false Stories. A little Book (40), which I have already quoted, put these Words in the Mouth of *Eloisa*, "What did not those two false Prophets assert, who declaim'd so vehemently against you at the Council "of *Rheims*?" These two false Prophets were St *Bernard*, and St *Norbert*. *Eloisa* never mention'd their declaiming in any Council; and, if she had, it could not be that of *Rheims*.

[O] *Of offending against the State*.] This Artifice has been so often made use of, since the *Jews* employed it against our *Saviour* (41), that it is strange any one should venture at present to put it in practice. Should it not be expected, that so worn out a Contrivance as this should be incapable of Success? No: The World is too unteachable, to profit by the Follies of past Ages. Every Age behaves, as if it were the first; and, as the Spirit of Persecution and Revenge has hitherto endeavoured to engage Princes in it's private Quarrels, so will it endeavour to do to the end of the World: and we may apply to this Purpose the Saying of *Solomon*; *The thing that hath been, it is that which shall be; and that which is done, is that which shall be done; and there is no new thing under the Sun* (42). Our Posterity may say, as well as we,

*Qui méprise Cotin, n'estime point son Roi,
Et n'a, selon Cotin, ni Dieu, ni Foi, ni Loi* (43).

Who slights *Cotin*, affronts his Master too;
No Pardon to such Insolence is due.
All Crimes into that one *Cotin* can draw;
The Wretch, says he, regards nor God, nor Law.

[P] *Something curious*.] *Abelard*, not being able to obtain from the Abbot of St *Denis* permission

to retire, had recourse to the Engines of Policy. He knew, that the more the Monks of St *Denis* plunged themselves into Irregularity, the more Authority the Court exercised over this Abbey, and drew the greater Profit from it. He therefore gave the King to understand, that it was not for his Majesty's Interest, that a Religious as he was, who was perpetually censuring the bad Lives of these Monks, should continue long among them. The Meaning of this was understood at half a Word; and Orders were given to one of the great Men at Court, to demand of the Abbot, and his Brethren, why they would keep by Force a Monk, whose Life was unsuitable to theirs, and who, for that Reason, could be of no Use to them, and might easily bring upon them some Disgrace. The Consequence was, that *Abelard* had leave to retire. * I remember, upon this Occasion, that I one Day asked a Gentleman, who was relating to me numberless Irregularities of the *Venetian* Clergy, how it came to pass, that the Senate suffered a thing so little to the Honour of Religion, and the State. He replied, that the public Good obliged the Sovereign to use this Indulgence; and, to explain this Riddle, he added, that the Senate was well pleased that the Priests and Monks were held in the utmost Contempt by the People, since, for that Reason, they would be less capable of causing an Insurrection among them. *One of the Reasons*, says he, *why the Jesuits there are disagreeable to the Prince, is, because they preserve the Decorum of their Character; and thus, being the more respected by the inferior People, are more capable of raising a Sedition*. I could scarce give Credit to so shocking a Disorder. What would become of us, if the Sovereign Power should have Occasion to support itself by such an Expedient, and if the Clergy should become more formidable by their *good*, than their *bad* Morals? This Confusion would be a thousand times more terrible, than that mentioned by *Tacitus*, when he says, that under a bad Government, a great Reputation is as much exposed to Danger as an ill one. "Intravit animum militaris "gloriæ cupido, ingrata temporibus, quibus sinistra "erga eminentes interpretatio, nec minus periculum "ex magnâ famâ, quam ex malâ. ——— *He was eager "after military Glory, an Ambition odious to the "Times; in which an ill-natured Interpretation was "put upon the Actions of eminent Men, and a great "Character was as much in Danger as an ill one* (44)." But let us hear *Abelard's* own Words: "Intervenientibus amicis quibusdam nostris, Regem & "Concilium ejus super hoc compellavi, & sic quod "volebam impetravi. Stephanus quippe Regis tunc "Dapifer, vocato in partem Abbate & familiaribus "ejus, quæsivit ab iis cur invitum retinere vellent, "ex quo incurrere facile scandalum possent, & nul- "lam utilitatem habere; cum nullatenus vita mea & "ipsorum convenire possent. Sciebam autem in hoc "Regii Consilii sententiam esse, ut quo minus re- "gularis Abbatia illa esset, magis Regi esse sub- "jecta & utilis, quantum videlicet ad lucra tempo- "ralia. Unde me facile Regis & suorum assensum "consequi crediderim, sicque actum est (45). ——— "*By the Interposition of some of my Friends, I ap- "plyed to the King and his Council, and by that "means obtained what I desired. For Stephen, the "King's Cup-bearer, demanded of the Abbot and his "Brethren, why they detained me against my Will;*

ABELARD.

mission, he chose his Retirement in the Diocese of *Troies*, and there built an Oratory, which he named the *Paraclet* (b). A great Number of Scholars follow'd him thither; which again awaken'd that Envy, which had so often pursu'd him. But, in this Encounter, he fell into the most dangerous hands in the World; I mean, he was expos'd to the Attacks of two pretended *Restorers of antient Discipline*, and grand Zealots; who, like new Apostles [Q], had insinuated themselves into the Favour of the People. They spread so many Falshoods concerning him, that they corrupted the Principles of his Friends, and obliged even those, who continu'd to love him, to conceal it from him. They so imbittered his Life, that he was upon the point of abandoning Christendom (i); but his Fate permitted him not to procure to himself this Repose, and engag'd him afresh with Christians, and Monks, worse than *Turks* (k). The Monks of the Abbey of *Ruis*, in the Diocese of *Vannes*, chose him for their Superior [R]. He hop'd he had met with an Asylum in this Place; but he found, that he had only varied his Woe. The incorrigible Behaviour of the Monks, and the Oppression of a certain Lord, who robb'd them of the best part of their Revenues, insomuch that they were obliged to maintain their Concubines and Children, out of their private Incomes (l), expos'd him to a thousand Disquiets, and even to great Dangers [S]. In the mean time, the Abbot of St *Denis* expell'd the Religious from the Monastery of *Argenteuil*. Abelard, struck with compassion for *Eloisa*, their Prioress, made her a Present of the Oratory of the *Paraclet*, where she settled herself with some of her Companions. From that time he made frequent Journies from *Brittany* to *Champagne*, to serve the Interests of *Eloisa*, and to disengage himself a little from the Fatigue of governing his Abbey. Notwithstanding the Mutilation, which the poor Gentleman formerly underwent, he could not escape Scandal [T]. Thus far he has himself carry'd down the Story of his

"since my manner of Life was so different from
"theirs, that it might reflect Disgrace upon them,
"and could not be of any Advantage to them. I
"knew very well, that the King's Council were of
"Opinion, that the more irregular the Abbey was,
"the more subject would it be to the King, in re-
"gard to temporal Profit. I imagined therefore,
"that the King, and his Council, would readily
"consent to my Petition; which fell out according-
"ly." A few Pages after, he says, that a certain *British* Lord had taken Occasion, from the vitious Lives of the Monks of *Ruis*, to seize on their Possessions (46). To take from Men, who by the Sanctity of their Lives have acquired the Veneration of the People: to take from such Men, I say, what the Charity of the Faithful has given them, is no easy Attempt; but there is no great Danger in robbing those, who are a Scandal to the Public.

[Q.] *Like new Apostles.*] Read what follows:
"Quòdam adversum me novos Apostolos quibus
"mundus plurimum credebat excitaverant. Quorum
"alter (S. Norbertus) Regularium Canonicorum vi-
"tam, alter (S. Bernardus) Monachorum se refusci-
"tasse gloriabatur. —— *They raised up against me
"certain new Apostles, who were in great Credit
"with the World. Of whom the one (St Norbert)
"boasted to have revived the Life of the Regular
"Canons, the other (St Bernard) that of the
"Monks* (47)." *Eloisa*, at Page 42. calls them *false Apostles*. See, above, the Remark [N] where I confute the Author of the new *History of Abelard and Eloisa*.

[R] *The Monks of the Abbey of Ruis —— chose him for their Superior.*] The Benedictine, who has taken so much Pains about the Antiquities of *Paris*, was greatly in the wrong in censuring *Belleforêt*, for saying, that Abelard was Superior of an Abbey in *Brittany*. "That he was an Abbot in Brit-
"tany is false; for, when he left the Paraclet, he
"retired to Clugni, and stayed in that Fraternity
"till his Death (48)." This Author was not sufficiently informed. He knew not, that Abelard had an Abbey in *Brittany*, both before and after his leaving the Paraclet. If he had carefully read the Letter (49), from which he quotes some Passages, he would have seen this indisputably proved.

[S] *And even to very great Dangers.*] The Monks frequently endeavoured to poison him, and, not being able to accomplish their Design in his ordinary Food, by Reason of the Precautions he took, they endeavoured to poison him in the Bread and Wine of the Sacrament. One Day, not having eaten of a particular Dish, which was prepared for him, he saw his Companion, who had tasted it, drop down dead. The Excommunications, which he thundered against the most mutinous among the *Religious*, did not remedy the Disorder. At length, he was more in fear of Assassination, than Poison, and compared himself to him, whom the Tyrant of *Syracuse* placed at his Table, under a Sword, which hung only by one Thread (50.)

[T] *Notwithstanding his Mutilation —— he could not escape Scandal.*] So malicious was the World to this unfortunate Man, that tho' they knew he was incapable of gratifying a Woman, they gave it out, that a Reminder of sensual Delight kept him still attach'd to his old Mistress. "Quod me facere fin-
"cera charitas compellabat, solita derogantium pra-
"vitas impudentissime accusabat, dicens me adhuc
"quadam carnalis concupiscentiae oblectatione teneri,
"qui pristinae dilectae sustinere absentiam vix aut
"nunquam paterer. —— *The usual Perverseness of
"Slanderers most impudently misrepresented what
"was the meer effect of Humanity, giving it out,
"that I was yet enslaved to the Desires of Flesh,
"since I was ever impatient at the Absence of my
"old Mistress.*" Thus he complains in the 43d Page of his Narration. He comforted himself with the Example of St *Jerom*, whose Friendship for *Paulus* supported him against Calumny; and he thought that he invincibly refuted the Slander, by remarking, that the most Jealous trust their Wives to the Care of Eunuchs. Father *Theophilus Raynaud* laughs at this Reason, having read many Instances of criminal Conversation between Women, and Men, who were disabled. "Ex quibus omnibus liquet,
"quàm frigida fuerit Petri Abelardi Apologia, cum
"redargutus de nimia familiaritate cum amica qua-
"dam sua, Heloisa, reposuit, Eunuchos, qualis ipse
"factus erat, fore, & absque omni periculo, posse
"versari cum foeminis. —— *From all which it ap-
"pears, how cold an Excuse Abelard made, when,
"being taxed with being too familiar with a cer-
"tain Mistress of his, named Eloisa, he replyed, that
"Eunuchs, such as he was, might safely, and with-
"out Danger, converse with Women* (51)." I shall consider this Matter a little in the Article COMBABUS. *Eloisa* was so passionately fond of Abelard, tho' unmann'd, that his Virtue could not but be in danger in her Company. See my Remarks on the Article of this Lady. The following Words of *Virgil*,

— notumque furens, quid foemina possit,
Triste per augurium Teucrorum pectora ducunt (52).

He knew the stormy Souls of Womankind, &c.
Dire Auguries from hence the Trojans *draw.*
                                    DRYDEN.

ABELARD.

his Misfortunes, in a Letter yet extant. The Remainder of his Life must be trac'd in other Writings; the most material Circumstance of which is, that he was prosecuted a second Time for Heresy before the Archbishop of *Sens*. He demanded leave to vindicate his Doctrine in a public Assembly; which was granted him; and a Council call'd at *Sens*, at which King *Lewis* VII. thought fit to assist in Person. It was in the Year 1140. St *Bernard* was sent thither in the Character of his *Accuser*. They immediately read before the Assembly certain Propositions extracted from the Books of *Peter Abelard*; the reading of which so terrify'd the *Accus'd*, that he interpos'd an Appeal to the Pope. The Council, however, condemn'd the Propositions (*m*); but they pass'd no Sentence against the Person accus'd, and gave an Account of the Matter to Pope *Innocent* II. desiring of him to confirm the Condemnation. The Pope did not fail to do it (*n*): he order'd that the Books of *Abelard* should be burnt, that he should be imprison'd, and forbad him to teach any more. He was appeas'd soon after, at the Sollicitation of *Peter the Venerable*, who had receiv'd, with great Kindness, this Heretic into his Abbey of *Clugni*, and had reconcil'd him with St *Bernard* (*o*), the Promoter of that Injustice [*U*], whose his Innocence had suffer'd in this Council. The Retirement of *Clugni* was the last, which *Abelard* had occasion for. He met with, there, every instance of Charity: he read Lectures to the Monks; he was equally humble and industrious. At length, becoming infirm, and being troubled with the Itch (*p*), and other Disorders, he was sent to the Priory of St *Marcel*, a very agreeable Place upon the *Saône*, near to *Châlon*. He died there the 21st of *April*, 1142 [*X*], aged 63 Years. His Body was sent to *Eloisa* [*Y*], who interred it in the *Paraclet* (*q*). We shall give some Account of his Writings in the Article of *Francis d'*AMBOISE; and as to what regards his Errors, and the Persecutions he met with from Councils, we shall take some Notice of them in the Article of BERENGER of *Poistiers*. It is remarkable, that he made no Secret of his Marriage, tho' he was a Priest, and a Canon (*r*). I am surpriz'd to find that he never mentions his Master (*s*) *Roscelin* [*Z*], who pass'd for a subtile Logician in those times, and is look'd upon as Founder of the Sect of the *Nominals*. He was himself likewise a Favourer of this Sect, which he found agreeable to *that Vivacity of Temper, and that acute and fertile Wit, which he was Master of* (*t*). *By the help of this Science, he so puzzled and confounded People, and made use of such a Variety of Sophistry, and Syllogisms, that he left them not less astonish'd, than incapable of answering him.* I am not of Opinion, that he ever engag'd in explaining the *Civil Law* [*AA*], as

represent in some sort the Conduct of those, who fear'd that the Passion of *Eloisa* might have too great an Influence on the Chastity of her *Abelard*.

[*U*] *The Promoter of the Injustice.*] I have consider'd this in the Article of BERENGER *of Poistiers*.

[*X*] *The* 21st *of April,* 1142.] This shews, that the new Author of the *Life of Abelard* is greatly mistaken, in supposing him alive in the Year 1170. I mean the Author of a little Book, printed at the *Hague*, in 1693, where, beside the *History of* Abelard *and* Eloisa abridg'd, we find three other little Pieces.

[*Y*] *His Body was sent to* Eloisa.] *Pasquier* affirms, that " *Abelard*, by his Will, ordered, that his Body " should be buried in the Monastery of the *Paraclet* " (53)." *Francis d'Amboise* asserts the same (54): but alledges no other Proof, than the Authority of *Pasquier*. What inclines me to disbelieve this, is, that *Peter* the *Venerable* makes no mention of it in his Letter to *Eloisa*, wherein he gives her an account of *Abelard*'s last Moments (55). Farther still, the Absolution of *Abelard* makes it credible, that his Body was sent to the *Paraclet*, only to gratify *Eloisa*. Probably she might petition for the Favour. Besides, what right had the Abbot of *Clugni* to make that a matter of Favour, which was settled by Will? The Calender of the Abbey of the *Paraclet* is a strong Proof of this: for in that we meet with these Words: " VIII of the " Kalends of *January*, died Peter, Abbot of *Clugni*, " by whose GRANT our Church has the Body of " *Peter* our Founder (56)." The Silence of *Andrew* du *Chesne*, in his Notes upon *Abelard*'s *Epistle*, in which he relates his Misfortunes, is a strong Reason with me, against *Pasquier*. Some, without mentioning his Will, say, that the Body of her deceas'd Husband was given to *Eloisa*, because, in his Letters to her, he had often express'd his Desire that it should (57): but they neither cite such Letters, nor any Writer who had cited them. I have met with such a Passage at the 53d Page of his Works. He was, then, at his Abbey of *Ruis*, and was in continual Dread of being assassinated. " Quod si me Dominus in ma-
" nibus inimicorum tradiderit (*writes he to* Eloisa)
" scilicet ut ipsi prævalentes me interficiant, aut quo-
" cunque casu viam universæ carnis absens à vobis in-
" grediar, cadaver obsecro nostrum ubicunque vel

" sepultum vel expositum jacuerit, ad cœmeterium ve-
" strum deferri faciatis, ubi filiæ nostræ, imo in
" Christo sorores, sepulchrum nostrum sæpius viden-
" tes ad preces pro me Domino fundendas amplius in-
" vitenter. —— But, *if Heaven should be pleased to*
" *deliver me into the Hands of my Enemies, and to*
" *suffer them to prevail over me, or by whatever Ac-*
" *cident, in my Absence from you, I may chance to go*
" *the way of all Flesh, I intreat of you, that my Body,*
" *wherever either buried, or expos'd, may be convey'd*
" *to your Church-yard, where my Daughters, rather*
" *my Sisters in Christ, having my Sepulchre frequent-*
" *ly in view, may be the oftener prompted to pour out*
" *their Prayer to God for me.*" The Absolution of *Abelard* is as follows: it was intended to be inscribed upon his Tomb; and it was for that Purpose, that *Eloisa* desired it of *Peter the Venerable* (58). " Ego " Petrus Cluniacensis Abbas, qui Petrum Abælar-
" dum in Monachum Cluniacensem recepi, & corpus
" ejus furtim delatum Heloissæ Abbatissæ & Moniali-
" bus Paracleti concessi, authoritate omnipotentis
" Dei & omnium Sanctorum, absolvo eum, pro
" officio, ab omnibus peccatis suis. —— *I* Peter, *Ab-*
" *bot of* Clugni, *who admitted* Peter Abelard, *a*
" *Monk of* Clugni, *and granted his Body to be pri-*
" *vately convey'd to* Eloisa, *the Abbess, and to the*
" *Nuns, of the* Paraclet, *by the authority of Almighty*
" *God, and all his Saints, do, as is my Duty, ab-*
" *solve him from all his Sins* (59)." *Belleforêt* publish'd a notorious Falshood, when he said, that the Bones of *Abelard* were dug up, and burnt (60). The Apologetical Preface of the *Sieur d'Amboise* proves demonstrably the contrary.

[*Z*] *His Master* Roscelin.] *Salabert*, Priest of *Argen*, in his Dissertation on the Sect of the *Nominalists* (61), leaves it doubtful, whether *Roscelin* was the Preceptor of *Peter Abelard*. We shall examine his Reasons under the Article ROSCELIN.

[*AA*] *That he ever engaged in explaining the Civil Law.*] *Francis d'Amboise* seems to be mistaken, when he fancies, that *Accursius* spoke of our *Abelard*, in his *Gloss* upon the Law *De quinque Pedum præscriptione*. *Accursius*'s Words are, " Sed Petrus Bailar-
" dus, qui se jactavit quod ex qualibet quantumcun-
" que difficili litera traheret sanum intellectum, hic
" dixit,

ABELARD.

as some pretend. The Reader will see in the last Remark a Catalogue of the Mistakes of Mr. *Moreri* [BB]. You will find in a Work of Father *Jacob* (u) a long List of Authors who have spoken of *Abelard*.

"dixit, NESCIO.——— But Peter Bailard *who boasted that he could strike out a good Meaning upon the most difficult Expression, upon this occasion confess'd his Ignorance* (63). *Alciatus* commended the Modesty of this *Peter Bailard*, for so ingenuously acknowledging his Ignorance in this Matter: " *Magnus ille Andreas Alciatus in illo, quem de quinque pedum præscriptione scripsit Tractatu, postquam Petrum Bailardum celeberrem suâ tempestate Professorem laudavit, quod ingenuè fassus esset, eam legem à se non intelligi, &c.——— The great Andrew Alciatus in the Treatise which he wrote concerning the Law De quinque Pedum præscriptione, after he had prais'd Peter Bailard, a celebrated Professor of his Times, for frankly owning, that he did not understand that Law, &c.* These are the Words of *Francis d' Arboise* (63): and he is sufficiently confuted by his own Expressions: for, to make *Alciatus* reason justly, the celebrated Professor, whom he commends, should have been a Professor of Law. Where is the Wonder, that a Professor of Logic should acknowledge, that he does not understand an intricate Passage of the Code? Besides, we find in *Petrus Crinitus*, that this *Bailard* was a Professor of Law: he calls him *Johannes Bajalardus*. We may conclude, that our *Abelard* is out of the Question in that Place; and that *Pasquier*, who fancied he had remarked what ought not to have been passed over, in applying to him *Accursius*'s Words, had better have said nothing about it (64). He ought, at least, to have observed, that, in the Passage of *Accursius*, it is not written *Petrus Abelardus*, as he pretends, but *Petrus Baylardus*. But, if it were true, that this Commentator had our *Abelard* in view, it must be granted, I think, that he was in an Error; for there is no Reason to believe, that *Abelard* ever concerned himself with Law. Consider the Words of *Crinitus*. " Quæsitum est superiori ætate à viris "doctioribus quidnam in Jure nostro Civili præ- "scriptio quinque pedum significaret, qualisque foret " in eâ intellectus. Quam rem Laurentius Valla, " & alii complures, cum non satis perciperent, hâc " unâ ratione se defendebant, quod Johannes Baja- " lardus, inter eos, qui jus CIVILE PROFITENTUR, " consultissimus, ingenuè affirmavit, se illud ignorare. ——— *It was matter of enquiry among the Learned of the last Age, what the Præscriptio quinque pedum, in our Civil Law, meant. Which when Laurentius Valla, and many others were at a loss to understand, they had only this to plead in excuse, that Johannes Bajalardus himself, the most knowing among the* PROFESSORS OF CIVIL LAW, *ingenuously declared his Ignorance of it* (65)." *Thomasius* ought not to have inferred from this Passage, that *Peter Abelard* was sometimes named *Bajalard* (66).

The following Observation was communicated to me by Mr *De la Monnoie*, after he had read my Remark [AA]. As I am certain the Reader will be better able to decide this Dispute, by comparing his Thoughts with mine; he will be pleased to have it in his Power to make the Comparison. *I am* (as Joseph says he, *that Accursius, upon the Law,* Quinque pedum, *means* Abelard. *I agree,* Abelard *did not profess the Civil Law; but he passed for a general Scholar, and one that allowed nothing to be above his Abilities:* qui totum tribule sciebat, *who knew every thing that was to be known, as we are told in his Epitaph.* Accursius, *in the cited Passage, gives us no other Idea than this; and there, who imagine, from the Words of the Commentator, that Petrus Baylardus or Bailardus was a celebrated Professor of Law, are mistaken. There never was one of this Name.* Baylardus *is no other than* Abelard, *and it is one of the ten or twelve Ways, in which this Author's Name is written. The Italians, who are accustomed to this Manner of Contraction, pronounce* Baludus *for* A'elardus, *as* Ragona *for* Arrigona, *Naldo for* Arnaldo, *Berto for* Alberto, *or* Lamberto. *At least, it cannot be denied, that* James Philip *of* Bergamo, *an Augustin Monk, gave our* Abelard *the Name of* Bulardus (67). *This is the Observation of Mr De la Monnoie.* I have one thing to add, which escap'd me in the first Edition. I am

of Opinion, that *Abelard* died before the Study of the *Roman Law* was introduc'd into *France*. It had been reviv'd in *Italy*, some Years before (68), and we must imagine, that the Infancy of it's new Birth continu'd some time. It is therefore improbable, that recourse should be had to our *French Logician*, for the Explication of a particular Law, of great Difficulty as to it's principal Point, and but little in use. Men seldom amuse themselves in unriddling such Matters, 'till they have clear'd up those of the greatest Importance, or when they endeavour to improve upon former Interpreters. If it were allowable to apply Mr *Menage*'s Rules, we might say, that the *Baylardus* of *Accursius* is a Corruption from the Word *Bulgarus*; *Bulgarus, Bailgarus, Bailgardus, Bailardus*. A great Alteration may be introduc'd by Degrees in proper Names, both by transcribing, and by pronouncing them ill.

[BB] *The Mistakes of Mr* Moreri.] First, It is not true that *Abelard* taught Divinity at *Corbeil*, and at *Melun*. 2dly, To alledge, that Authors are unanimous in declaring that *Eloisa* was Niece to the Canon *Fulbert*, is a very weak Argument against *Papirius Masson*, who asserts that she was the *natural Daughter* of a certain *Canon*. *Fulbert* might certainly have a Sister, imprudent in her Conduct : I say a Sister; for he was *Eloisa*'s Uncle by the Mother's Side; her *Avunculus*. I am surpriz'd, that *Andrew du Chêne* (69) could think of confuting *Papirius Masson* by the same Argument, which Mr *Moreri* had made use of. 3div, It does not appear, that *Abelard* introduced himself into the Canon's House, on pretence of teaching *Eloisa* Divinity: Why then is he particular in relating what Authors, whom he ought to follow, deliver only in general? The Words, " Erat cupidus " ille valdè, atque erga nepum suam ut amplius sem- " per in doctrinam proficeret literatoriam plurimum " studiosus.——— *He was very covetous, and at the same Time very desirous, that his Niece should make " a Proficiency in Learning* (70) ; " do not imply Divinity, more than any other Science. 4thly, It does not appear that *Eloisa* had any great Esteem for *Abelard*, before they liv'd together in the same House. 5thly, It is not true, that, upon her leaving her Uncle, he carried her with him into *Brittany*: he sent her indeed into that Province, but continued himself at *Paris*, to guard, in the best Manner he could, against the Attempts of *Fulbert*, 'till he could appease him by offering to marry his Niece Then he went to join her in *Brittany*, as we find in the Relation of his Misfortunes. The *Abridgment of the History of* Eloisa *and* Abelard, *lately publish'd* (71), is not exact in this Point. The Author supposes, that *Abelard* left *Paris*, at the same time that he quitted the Canon's House; that he return'd thither, as soon as he was inform'd that his Pupil was pregnant, and that *he carried her off by Night, in order to marry her privately, 'till her Relations should permit him to espouse her in publick*. He had no Intention of marrying her, when he convey'd her away, nor did he ever pretend, that his Marriage was to be made publick. 6thly, *Eloisa* did not *tell him freely, that she intended not by this Marriage to rob the Church of a Doctor, who, in all likelihood, would soon become one of it's most illustrious Prelates.* Nothing like this occurs in the long Detail, which *Abelard* has left us, of *Eloisa*'s Arguments against their Marriage. See the Article ELOISA, *Remark* [X] 7thly, he does not declare, that he marry'd her *for the quiet of his Conscience*: Why will Mr *Moreri* pretend to know *Abelard*'s Motives to this Marriage, better than himself? 8thly, *The Marriage*, and *the Convent of* Argenteuil, *ought not to have been jumbled together*: there was a Space between these two Circumstances. *Eloisa* was sent to this Convent upon no other account, then the ill Usage of her Uncle, who was angry with her for peremptorily denying her Marriage. 9thly, It is, therefore, a very false account to say, that *this Marriage was not so secret but* Fulbert *had notice of it*: for they receiv'd the nuptial Benediction, at Church, in his Presence. " Post paucos di- " es, nocte secretis orationum vigiliis in quadam Ec- " clesia celebratis, ibidem summo mane, avuncu o " ejus atque quibusdam nostris vel ipsius amicis ob- " silentibus,

ABELIANS. ABELLI.

"*fistentibus, nuptiali benedictione confœderamur — A'ter a few Days, having privately, in the Evening, celebrated Vespers in a certain Church; early in the Morning we were there join'd in Marriage, and receiv'd the nuptial Benediction, in the Presence of her Uncle, and some of our, or his, Friends* [-2) Abelard's Works, p. 1. (72)." 10thly, It is by no Means true, that *Abelard* read Lectures to a great Number of Scholars in *Champagne*, from the Time that the vitious Lives of the Monks of *Ruis*, compell'd him to return thither, and at the Time that the Abbot *Suger* expell'd the Nuns from *Argenteuil*. Father *L'Enfant* has copy'd some of these Errors (73).

ABELIANS, or ABELONIANS, a Sect of Hereticks who rose in *Champagne*, near *Hippon*, and who had been some time extinct in St. *Austin's* Days. They profess'd very odd Principles, and such as were not likely to continue long [*A*]. They ordain'd that each Man should be in possession of his particular Woman; they thought it improper, and would not allow, that a Man should continue single; it was necessary, acccording to the Statutes of the Order, that he should have a Helpmeet like unto himself: but it was not permitted him to lean upon this Prop, that is, to be corporeally join'd to his Wife: She was to be to him the Tree of the Knowledge of Good and Evil, the Fruit of which was forbidden him under severe Penalties. These People were for regulating Matrimony upon the footing of the *Terrestrial Paradise*, in which *Adam* and *Eve* were united only in their Affections; or rather they followed the Example of *Abel*: for they pretended that *Abel* was married, but that he died without ever having any Knowledge of his Wife: and from him this Sect borrow'd it's Name (*a*). When a Man and a Woman enter'd into this Society, they adopted two Children, a Boy and a Girl, who succeeded to their Goods, and who married together upon the same Condition of not getting Children, but of adopting two others of different Sexes. They easily met with poor People in the Neighbourhood, to furnish them with Children. This Account is given us by St *Austin*(*b*); and as he is almost the only Author, who mentions them, we must imagine, that this Sect was known but in a few Places, and of but a short Continuance. It is believed, that it begun in the Reign of *Arcadius*, and ended in that of *Theodosius the younger*. All those, who compos'd it, it being at last reduc'd to one single Village, re-united themselves to the Catholic Church.

[*A*] *Not likely to continue long.*] Such a State of Continency between a Man and his Wife, who had every thing else in common, and whose Union was esteemed a true Marriage, was too great a Violence offered to Nature, to be of long Continuance. *Nullum violentum durabile. Nothing violent is lasting.* The *Abelians* were only a more moderate sort of *Encratites* and *Nicatians*: these latter absolutely condemned Matrimony; the *Abelians* approved of, and retained it. It is true, it was barely the Name: they *preserved it's Appearance, but denied it's Power.* "Hi nomen quidem conjugii & nuptiarum retinuerunt, vim autem & effectum earum prorsus sustulerunt (1)." And they looked upon Marriage to be a Sacrament, their Opinion, in this Point, would have been like that of the *Zuinglians* concerning the *Eucharist*: they would have admitted the Figure, but not the Reality: and this must have contributed towards extinguishing the Sect. You will find in *Furetiere's* Dictionary (2), that

*Boire, & manger, coucher ensemble,
C'est mariage, ce me semble.*

Marriage consists in eating, and drinking, and lying together.

This is the natural Idea of that State: and, in this Description, the last Character passes for the principal, and the specific Distinction. This it is, which is called the *Consummation* of Marriage: without this, the most solemn Contract, the Betrothing, and the nuptial Benediction, pass for meer Preliminaries, which it is easy to be disengaged from. It is this which ties the Knot, and renders it indissoluble. It is the End, the Mark, and the Crown of the Work: It is the *nè plus ultra*. It is therefore very improbable, that such Numbers of People, even after the Notion became common, should chuse to submit both to the Name and the Restraint of Matrimony, and to renounce the most shining Honours of *Celibacy*, without tasting of the Fruits and the Joys of Marriage. When, therefore, I said that the Principles of this Sect were not calculated for a long Duration, it was not necessary, that I should allude to the witty Saying attributed to *Sixtus* the Fifth: "Non si chiava in questa Religione, non durara (3);" as much as to say, they would break thro' such a Precept of Religion as this, in spight of their Teeth. To *adopt* a Child, among them, supplied the Intention of *getting one*; and therefore we cannot apply to the *Abelians* the Remark of *Florus* on the first Inhabitants of *Rome*: "Res erat unius ætatis, Populus Virorum (4). — *It was an Establishment calculated to continue but for one Race, as consisting entirely of Men*;" For, if other Causes had not concurred, this Sect might have continued to the end of the World. "Per sæculorum millia (incredibile dictu) Gens æterna est, in qua nemo nascitur. —— *They are a Race of People, which (incredible to relate !) is never extinct, tho' no one is born among them.*" This *Pliny* says of the *Essenians* (5), and is every Day applied to the Monks.

ABELLI (*Anthony*) Doctor of Divinity, a *Jacobin*, Abbot of *Notre Dame de Livri*, in *Aulnoi*, Confessor to the Queen-Mother, and formerly her Preacher, publish'd *Sermons upon the Lamentations of Jeremiah*, at *Paris*, in the Year 1582. I only copy la *Croix du Maine* and du *Verdier Vau-Privas*, and if I do not correct their Errors, at least I will propose my own Doubts [*A*]. If Mr *Moreri* had done the same, perhaps by this time we might have arrived at the Truth. The Confession of Authors, that they are ignorant of such or such Particulars, is the surest way to excite the curious to communicate their Discoveries to the Public: A Consideration, which will frequently engage me to propose my Doubts. Mr *Moreri* had so many Opportunities, which I have not, of consulting those, who might rectify such things as these, that he ought to have done more upon this Occasion than barely copy *la Croix du Maine*.

[*A*] *I will propose my own Doubts.*] It seems to me a little strange, that a *Jacobin* should be in possession of an Abbey, and receive his Title from it. I know of no Part of *France* called *Aulnoi*. If it should be read *Launoi*, it is another thing: but still I find no Abbey in the Diocese of *Loan* named *Livri* (1) The

ABELLY.

Abbey of this Name is in the Diocese of *Paris*. Lastly, I find, in the Act, by which the University of *Paris* swore Fealty to *Henry* IV. *Apr.* 22. 1594. among those, who subscribed it, one *Francis Abely*, Abbot of *Ivri*, Preacher and Almoner to the King (2). Those, who have Leisure, may consider whether or no what relates to several Persons be not here collected, and applied to one (3).

My Doubts have procured me the following excellent Illustration of this Matter. " *Aunoi*, or *Aulnoi*, " is very right. There is the Abbey of *Nôtre Dame* " *de Livri* in *Aunoi*, in *Alneto* (4), of the Order of " *St Augustin*, in the Deanery of *Chelles*, and Dio- " cese of *Paris*. In order to obtain this Abbey, we " must suppose, that *Antony Abelli* transferred him- " self from the Order of St *Dominic* to that of " St *Augustin*, which is very easily done, and practi- " sed every Day. As to *Francis Abely*, Abbot of " *Ivry*, I suspect it is a Mistake, and that this *Francis*, " who was apparently the Successor of *Anthony*, " ought to be styled Abbot of *Livri*, there being no " Abbey of the Name of *Ivri* in *France*." This Illustration was communicated to me by Mr *De la Monnoie*. The Abbot *Baudrand* has informed me, that the Abbey of *Livri* is three Leagues distant from *Paris*, as you go to *Meaux*, in a little District named *Aulnoy*, in which there are ten or twelve Villages, and that *he knows nothing further concerning it's Boundaries*. These two Accounts sufficiently clear up my Difficulties.

ABELLY (*Lewis*) Bishop, and Earl of *Rhodes*, who died *October* 4. 1691. aged 88 Years (*a*), was a Native of *Paris*, and Rector of St *Josse*, in that City. He wrote several Works, particularly a Treatise of Divinity, entituled *Medulla Theologica* (*b*), upon which Account *Boileau* gives him the Epithet of *Moëlleux*, *Pithy*, or *full of Marrow* [*A*], and which differs widely from the Maxims of the *Jansenists* [*B*]. He was

[*A*] *The Epithet of* Moëlleux, Pithy, *&c.*] In reciting this Passage, I shall make no Scruple to begin it a little higher; for besides, that there is no Danger of any one's being displeased with the Length of the Quotation, it will serve to confirm what I shall advance in the following Remark.

Alain tousse & se leve, Alain (1) ce savant homme,
Qui de Bauni vingt fois a la toute la Somme,
Qui possede Abelli, qui sait tout Raconis,
Et même entend, dit-on, le Latin d'A Kempis.
N'en doutez point, leur dit ce savant Canoniste,
Ce coup part, j'en suis Sûr, d'une main Janseniste,
Mes yeux en font temoins : j'ai vu moi-meme hier
Entrer chez le Prelat le Chapelain Garnier.
Arnaud, cet Heretique ardent à nous de truire,
Par ce ministre adroit tente de le seduire.
Sans doute il aura la dans son Saint Augustin
Q'autrefois Saint Louis erigea ce Lutrin.
Il va nous inonder des torrens de sa plume,
Il faut, pour lui répondre, ouvrir plus d'une volume.
Consultons sur ce point quelque Auteur signale ;
Voions si des Lutrins Bauni n'a point parlé.
Etudions enfin, il en est tems encore,
Et pour ce grand projet, tantôt, dès que l'Aurore
Rallumera le jour dans l'onde enseveli,
Que chacun prenne en main le MOELEUX ABELLI (2).

Then Allen rose, collected and prepar'd,
He regularly hemm'd, then stroak'd his Beard,
And claim'd as Prolocutor to be heard.
The learned Seer Attention might demand,
The only Scholar in the reverend Band.
The learned Seer had oft Abelli *read,*
And fill'd with Raconis *his muddy Head.*
Nay, great A-Kempis *he could construe too ;*
And all his knotty Passages knew.
Then thus he spoke : Believe me, Sirs ! I know
Some Jansenist *must aim this fatal Blow.*
It must be so ; we're in the Prelate's Snare ;
These Eyes saw Chaplain Garnier *enter there.*
Arnaud *endeavours, by this artful Friend,*
The Prelate to his Purposes to bend.
Sirs, be most certainly has somewhere heard,
That this litigious Desk St Louis *rear'd.*
Then, grown polemical, he'll proudly think
To drown us all with Deluges of Ink.
Now 'tis our Duty timely to prepare,
And stand a resolute defensive War,
Consider then ; does Bauni *nothing say*
Of Desks ? None of the Fathers lean that Way ?
I find this Argument will ask much Oil,
Close Reading, indefatigable Toil.
Then, till Aurora *kindles up the Day,*
And lights her Lamp, extinguish'd in the Sea ;
Let each in hand PITHY ABELLI *take,*
And what the learned Doctor dictates, speak.

If these Verses contain'd nothing more than the Agreement between *Bauni* and *Abelli*, they would sufficiently declare the *Anti-Jansenism* of the latter; but there are other Arrows in this Quiver, which are directed to the same Mark, and carry home. The Author has given us, in the Margin, a Note, to explain the Reason of the Epithet, and it was rightly done. When I reflect upon the Conjectures, which the Critics would form, should the *French* Language one Day meet with the Fate of the *Latin*, and the Works of *Boileau* be preserv'd, I represent to myself a thousand Whims. For, suppose that the *Medulla Theologica* of Mr *Abelly* were entirely lost, and scarce any Author extant, who takes notice of it, nor any Note in the Margin of the *Latin*, over against the Word *Moelleux*, what a stir would the Critics make to find out the Reason of this Epithet, and how many Mistakes would they run into (3)? I fancy to myself, that some one of them, ill satisfy'd with the Conjectures of all his Predecessors, would at length pretend to discover, that *Abelly* was distinguish'd by this Epithet, in allusion to the Offerings of *Abel*, which were not dry, like those of *Cain*, but a real Sacrifice of Beasts. Upon this Occasion he would quote the *Sacrum pingue dabo, nec macrum sacrificabo*: he would say, that the Parts of the Victim were not all of equal Efficacy, and that the Fat, under which is comprehended the Marrow, was of singular Use. The more learned he happen'd to be, the farther would he run on from one extravagant Conceit to another, and heap Chimeras on Chimeras. Upon this Occasion, as well as many others, we should see accomplish'd that Expectation in the ninth Satire of Mr *Boileau*,

Et deja vous croiez, dans vos Rimes obscures,
Au Saummaises futurs preparer des tortures.

Thy Rhimes, even now obscure, thro' learned Pains,
Prepare the Rack for future Critics Brains.

It were to be wish'd, says some one, that a good Commentary were wrote upon the Satires of this Author (4). It is certain such Writings soon grow obscure in many Places. The *Catholicon d'Espagne*, and the *Confession Catholique de Sancy*, are a Proof of this. The Publick is very much indebted to the Author, who publish'd Remarks upon the last of these two Satires, in the Year 1693. and upon the first in 1696. He is a curious and discerning Writer, and very fit for this Work.

[*B*] *From the Maxims of the* Jansenists.] One of these Gentlemen complains bitterly, that Mr *De la Berchere*, Archbishop of *Aix*, had ordered the Director of his Seminary, *to follow Abelly*, and no longer teach the *Moral Divinity* of *Grenoble* (5) He asserts, that there are three false Principles in *Abelly's Medulla Theologica*, of which, The first overthrows that most certain Direction of a good Conscience, acknowledged by the Heathens themselves, which forbids the doing of an Action, the Lawfulness, or Unlawfulness, of which is doubtful. The second reduces to nothing the greatest of all the Commandments, namely, that which obliges us to love God above every thing. The third is directly repugnant to that Care, which the Cardinal Grimaldi took to

ABELLY. ABERDEEN. ABGILLUS.

was Author likewise of *The Life of Vincent de Paul*, Founder, and first Superior General, of the Congregation of the *Mission*; a Treatise on the *Principles of Christian Morality*; another on *Heresies*; another on the *Tradition of the Church in relation to the Worship of the Virgin Mary*, &c. This last Work, which was printed a second Time at *Paris*, in the Year 1675, gave great Pleasure to the *Protestants*, as it furnish'd them with good Weapons against the *Converters*, who would make them believe, that whatever there might be extravagant in this kind of Devotion, it was owing wholly either to *Monkish* Opinions, or to Abuses, which the Bishops were every day correcting: The same Book was useful to those of that Persuasion against the Bishop of *Condom*'s Work (c). In truth, Mr *Abelly* became the Patron of the most extravagant Conceits, in relation to the Worship of the *Blessed Virgin*. This was destroying the Attempts of another Prelate, and the Intentions of those, who publish'd, or approv'd, *The wholsome Advice of the Bl ssed Virgin to her indiscreet Votaries*. Mr *Abelly* was a Doctor of Divinity of the Faculty of *Paris*; he resign'd his Bishoprick to another, when his Age would not suffer him to discharge the Duties of his Office, and retir'd to the House of St *Lazarus*. He discover'd a Secret in the *Life of Mr Vincent*, which was pleasing to many [C].

(c) Entitul'd, An Expositi-tion of the Doctrine of the Catholic Church.

secure the Observation of the Rules of St Charles in the Sacrament of Penance, by a forestalling a great Number of Cases, in which the Confessors may either refuse, or defer Absolution. Mr *Abelly* therefore was accused of teaching. First, That one may follow an Opinion less probable and less certain, in doing that which is a Sin according to the contrary Opinion, which seems to be more probable: Secondly, That it is not certain, that the Precept of loving God above all things obliges us always, in virtue of itself, but only by Accident. Thirdly, That one may without Scruple voluntarily dislike those, whose Life is a perpetual Vicissitude of Confessing and Sinning. See the Advertisements to the Reverend Fathers, the Jesuits of Aix, in Provence, concerning a printed Paper, entitul'd, "A Ball, danced at the Reception of the Lord Archbishop of Aix." This Advertisement was published in 1687, in 12mo.

It is easy to see, that Mr *Abelly*'s Book is meant in the following Passage of the *Menagiana*. "As they were talking of the *Marriage* of A—— Mr L'Abbé le Canvs, at present a Cardinal, said, that the Moon was in the Wane, when he wrote it (b)" A new Proof of the Contempt, which the *Jansenists* had for this Work.

[C] A Secret —— which was pleasing to many] He informed the Public, that Mr *Vincent* had drop'd all Correspondence with the Abbot of St *Cyran*, after having heard him declare, that the Council of *Trent* was only a *Cabal*, and an Assembly of *S' kishmen, with the Pope at the Head of them* (n). Whoever is convinced of this, cannot be a *Roman* Catholic

(b) Menagiana, Vol. I. p. 61. Du Pin, Vol. II.

(n) Ant'iv's Life of Vincent de Paul, B 2. c. 12.

ABERDEEN, an Episcopal City of *Scotland*, under the Archbishoprick of *St Andrews*, including an University. It may be considered as separated into two Cities; for there is *Aberdeen* at the Mouth of the *Don*, and *Aberdeen* at the Mouth of the *Dee*. The former is call'd *Old Aberdeen*, the other *New Aberdeen*. They are but a Mile distant from each other. The Bishop's See, and the University, are at *Old Aberdeen*: the other is a richer, and more trading, Place. The University was founded in the Year 1480, the Bishoprick in the Year 1100: it was translated from *Murtlac*, as *Hector Boëthius*, a *Scotch* Historian (a) informs us. This City is call'd indifferently in *Latin Abredonia, Aberdomium*, and *Aberdona*. Mr *Moreri* endeavours to refine upon this Article [A], but without Success.

(a) In Buchanard's Lexic. Geogr. p. 4.

[A] *Mr Moreri endeavours to refine upon this Article*] He quarrels with those, who say, that *Aberdonia*, or *Abredone*, *Abredone*, or *Devana*, is a City. "There is not a City (says h.) in all Scotland of this Name; but there are two Towns, one of which is called *New-Aberdeen*, and the other *Old-Aberdeen*: and if these Names "are jumbled together, it must be in Books or Maps, that are very incorrect." It would be unnecessary to prove, that, not only in common Speech, the Distinction of *Old* and *New Aberdeen* is not made use of, but that, even in Books, it is very little observ'd. For what Author ever said, *The Bishoprick of Old Aberdeen, The University of New Aberdeen*? What Historians are not satisfy'd with bare mentioning *Aberdeen*, when they speak of the Principal City? Mr *Moreri* plainly forgot his own Criticism, when under the Article SCOTLAND, he says, *St Andrews has an University, and Aberdeen another*; for, otherwise, he ought to have said *Old Aberdeen*.

ABGILLUS (*John*), Son of a certain King of the *Frisons*, led so exemplary a Life, that he gain'd the Sirname of *Prêtre*, or the *Priest*. He accompany'd *Charlemagne* in his Expedition to *Palestine*; and, instead of returning to *Europe* with *Charlemagne*, after taking of *Jerusalem*, he advanc'd as far as the *Indies*, made vast Conquests there, and founded the Empire of the *Abyssins*, which from his Name, was called *The Empire of John the Priest*[*]. He compos'd two Histories, one comprehending the Voyage of *Charlemagne* to the *Holy Land*, the other his own Expedition to the *Indies*. This last Work contains a Description of the Country, and of the different People, which inhabit it. If *Suffridus Petri* (a) was capable of imagining these Histories to have been any other than paultry Romances, compos'd in the Ages of Ignorance, and in which *Charlemagne* is introduc'd with such an extraordinary Bravery, as if he had been one of the imaginary Heroës, *Palmerin* of *Oliva*, *Huon* of *Bourdeaux*, or *Geoffrey Great-Tooth*: if, I say, *Suffridus Petri* was capable of conceiving this, he deserves all the hard Words, which *Vossius* has given him (b); for what can be invented more fabulous, than the Conquest of *Jerusalem* by *Charlemagne*?

* We call him in English, *Prester John*.

(a) Historia of his Antiquity, and Frisia, in Well., in Vossius de Scriptor. Frisia.

(b) O Hominem vi le simum!

ABYDUS,

ABYDUS. ABIMELECH.

ABYDUS, a City of *Egypt*. *Stephen* of *Byzantium* calls it a Colony of the *Milesians* [*A*], which receiv'd it's Name from one *Abydus*. *Strabo* speaks of it, as a very ruinous Town; but he says, that it appears to have been very large, and the principal Town of the Country, next to *Thebes* (*a*). The famous King *Memnon* resided in it, and built there a magnificent Palace (*b*). The Temple and Sepulchre of *Osiris* are a great Ornament to this City, and recommend it extreamly. The greatest Lords of *Egypt* affected to be buried there, that they might have their Monuments near that of *Osiris* (*c*). The Oracle of the God *Besa* was no small Ornament to this Place. All the neighbouring People were great Worshippers of this Deity, who gave his Answers in writing to those, who had not the convenience of consulting him in Person. It was sufficient at that time to inform him by Letter of one's Request (*d*). This Oracle was still in being in the Reign of *Constantius*, Son of *Constantin the Great*, and was the Cause of great Disorders [*B*]. *Abydus* was 7500 Paces westward of the *Nile* (*e*) but a Canal was cut, which conducted the Waters of that River to it (*f*). It was above *Diospolis* and *Tentyris* (*g*), and below *Ptolemais* (*h*), which was the largest City of *Thebais*, and as big as *Memphis*. The Inhabitants of *Abydus* had an Aversion to the Sound of Trumpets [*C*]. There has been much talk of certain Thorns, which grew in their Territory [*D*], and which are said to have constantly born Flowers of the Shape of a Crown. The Name of it is thought to be at present *Abutich*. *John Leon* does not say, what Mr *Moreri* ascribes to him, that it stood in the place, where the Patriarch *Joseph* was buried [*E*]. There was a City, called *Abydus*, upon the Side of the *Hellespont*, of which I shall take no Notice at present, tho' *Moreri*'s Dictionary wants to be set right upon this Article.

(*a*) Strabo, L. 17. p. 559. Edit. 1587.
(*b*) Memnonis Regiâ & Osiris Templo inclytum. Fuit is sic the Palace of Memnon, and the Temple of Osiris. Plin. L. 5. c. 9. Strabo, L. 17. p. 559.
(*c*) Plutarch of Isis and Osiris, p. 35.
(*d*) Amm. Marcellinus. L. 19. c. 12. p. 227, 228.
(*e*) Plin. L. 5. c. 9.
(*f*) Strabo, L. 17. p. 573.
(*g*) Plin. L. 5. c. 9.
(*h*) Strabo, L. 17. p. 579.

[*A*] *A Colony of the* Milesians.] This is not clear. I allow that they settled Colonies in *Egypt*; but it was near the Mouth of the *Nile*: Their Power consisted at that time in Naval Force; and their Trade did not require a Situation so distant from the Coast, as *Abydus* was. Besides, They did not settle in *Egypt* 'till the Reign of *Cyaxares*, King of *Media* (1): Whereas *Abydus* was a considerable City before that time; since *Memnon* not only kept his Court, but built likewise a magnificent Palace, there.

[*B*] *Was the Cause of great Disorders.*] The Manner how is as follows: Those, who consulted the Oracle by writing, sometimes left their Letter in the Temple, after they had received their Answer (2). There were People so malicious as to send some of these Letters to *Constantius*; who, being of a mean, suspicious, credulous, and captious Disposition, threw himself into a terrible Passion. " Qui ut erat " angusti pectoris, obsurdescens in aliis etiam ni- " mium serilis, in hoc titulo ima, quod alunt, auri- " cula mollior, & suspicax, & minutus, acri felle " concaluit (3)." Immediately he signed a Commission for prosecuting those who were guilty, on pretence, that many of them had consulted their Deity concerning the Life of the Emperor, and the Name of the Person, who was to succeed him. The Head of the Commission, a violent and avaritious Person, found Means to involve whom he pleased in this Prosecution. This gave Occasion to numberless Acts of Violence, as you may read in *Ammianus Marcellinus*.

[*C*] *Had an Aversion to the Sound of Trumpets.*] This we may learn from *Ælian*, provided we correct him according to the Conjecture of *Berkelius* (4). Σελαινιγγος ηχον βδελυττονται Βυσιρίται, και Ἀβυδος ἡ Αἰγυπτια (it is in the Editions of *Ælian* Ἀβυ ἡ Ἀιγυπτια και Αδυνῦ τελει. ——— *The* Busiritæ, *and the Egyptian* Abydus, *and* Lycopolis, *abhor the Sound of a Trumpet* (5). *Strabo* confirms this Conjecture, when he says, that the Use of Music, both vocal and instrumental, was forbidden in the Preludes to the Sacrifices, which were offered to *Osiris* in the Temple of *Abydus* (6).

[*D*] *Thorns,* which *grew in their Territory.*] *Athenæus* mentions this (7): but we must substitute the Word "Ἀβυδον for "Ἀβυλον in that Place, according to the very probable Conjecture of *Berkelius* (8). The Matter of Fact, according to *Athenæus*, is this. The Thorns, which grew about the Temple of *Tindium*, were thought to be always in Bloom: but the Foundation of this Notion, according to *Hellanicus*'s Remark (9), was that, whenever the People assembled in this Place, the Thorns were covered with Wreaths of Flowers of various kinds. *Demetrius* relates, that such kind of Thorns grew about *Abydus*, and that it was currently reported among the *Egyptians*, that the *Ethiopian* Soldiers, whom *Tithon* sent to King *Priam*, having heard that *Memnon* was slain, threw down their Chaplets of Flowers, before *Abydus*, upon these Thorns, whence it came to pass, that the Flowers, which they produced, resembled Crowns (10).

[*E*] *The Patriarch* Joseph *was buried.*] Mr *Moreri* quotes *John Leon*, p. 8. At first Sight, one would think he meant *Page the eighth*; but we are to look for his Quotation in *Book the eighth*. Now what we meet with there is this: that it is a Mistake to believe, that the City *Mesre Haticbi* was the Residence of the Kings of *Egypt* in the Days of *Joseph* and *Moses*. He confutes this Opinion by alledging, that these antient Kings dwelt on the West Side of the *Nile*; which he proves by two Arguments; the first is, the Situation of that City, which, the Scripture tells us, the *Jews* built for *Pharaoh*: the second is, the Situation of a very antient Building, which is said to be the Sepulchre of *Joseph*. Here marks a few Pages after, that the Town, where this Sepulchre is, stands upon an Arm of the *Nile*, and is at present called *El Filum*. I do not find that he makes any mention of our *Abydus*.

(1) Strabo, L. 16. p. 552.
(2) Amm. Marcellinus. L. 19. c. 12. p. 227, 228.
(3) Amm. Marcell. at the Year 359.
(4) Berkelius upon Steph. de Urbibus, p. 24.
(5) Ælian. de Animal. L. 10. c. 28.
(6) Strabo, L. 17. p. 62.
(7) Athen. L. 15. c. 7.
(8) Berkelius upon Steph. de Urbibus, p. 14.
(9) Upon the Ægyptiaca, in Athen. B. 1. c. 7.
(10) Demetrius upon the Ægyptiaca, in Athen. B. 15. c. 7.

ABIMELECH, King of *Gerar*, in the Land of the *Philistines*, was cotemporary with *Abraham*. This *Patriarch*, being retired with his Family, into the Land of *Gerar*, his Wife *Sara*, tho' Ninety Years of Age (*a*), found herself expos'd to danger: she was taken away by *Abimelech*, who thought her so fair, as to desire to make her his Wife. *Abraham* might have avoided this Accident, by declaring himself to be *Sara*'s Husband: but, fearing to be slain, he pretended, that she was his Sister, and desired her to say, that he was her Brother (*b*). This was the second Time he made use of this Artifice (*c*); which certainly does not deserve the Encomiums, bestowed on it by St *Chrysostom* [*A*]. It is believed, that the *Philistine* King was struck with a Distemper,

(*a*) See the last Remark on the Article SARA.
(*b*) Gen. xx.
(*c*) He made use of it, Gen. xii.

[*A*] *The Encomiums, bestowed on it by* St *Chrysostom*.] We shall point out in another Place (1), what is blameable in this Dissimulation of *Abraham*. Every one may judge, as he pleases, of his second Fall. The Danger which *Sara*'s Honour was expos'd to the first Time, seems, at first sight, to render a Repetition of the Fraud more inexcusable; but, on the other Hand, does it not seem more justifiable to make use of

(1) In the Remarks on the Article SARA.

ABIMELECH.

Distemper, which render'd him *impotent* [B]: but, however that be, it is certain that Divine Providence permitted him not to satisfy the Passion which he had conceiv'd for *Sara*. He was inform'd in a Dream, that she was married to a Prophet, and that he should die, if he did not restore her to her Husband. He fail'd not accordingly to restore her to him, and to reproach him for his Deceit. *Abraham*, in excuse for himself, among other Reasons, alledg'd that he was really the Brother of *Sara*, born of the same Father tho' of a different Mother. Thus the Scripture makes him excuse himself. Mr *Moreri* very improperly supplies the sacred Text with the Words of *Josephus*, who falsly supposes, that *Abraham* pretended, that *Sara* was his Brother's Daughter (d). He follows the same Author, in relation to a Fact, of which the Scripture speaks not a word; I mean, the pretended Alliance contracted between *Abraham* and *Abimelech*, upon the Restitution of *Sara*. The Scripture is content to say, that *Abimelech* made great Presents to this Patriarch, and offered him the Liberty of sojourning in what part of his Country he pleas'd. It is true, there was an Alliance between them; but it was not contracted till some Years after (e): I mean the Treaty of *Beersheba*. *Josephus*, as if he were possess'd of Memoirs

(d) Joseph. Antiq. B. 1. c. 11.

(e) Genes. xxi. 31, 32.

---

of a Remedy, which had succeeded, than at first to make the Experiment of it; and is it not past doubt, that the first Trial had all the Success which *Abraham* could hope for? He not only preserv'd his Life, but was loaded with Presents, and recover'd his Wife untouch'd; a Circumstance, which, perhaps, he did not expect; I say *perhaps*, for I dare not write, what St *Chrysostom* dar'd to preach. "You know, *says* "*he to his Auditors*, that nothing chagrins a Husband "so much, as to suspect that his Wife has been in "the Power of another; and yet this just Man em- "ploy'd all his Efforts, that the Act of Adultery might "be accomplish'd (2)." One would expect, after this, that the Preacher should censure the Patriarch: but, on the contrary, we find him bestowing great Encomiums on his Courage, and his Prudence: On his Courage, which enabled him to conquer the Stings of Jealousy, so far as even to advise an Action of this Nature; on his Prudence, which pointed out to him this Expedient, so certain to extricate him from the Difficulties and Dangers, which surrounded him. St *Chrysostom* does not forget to represent, in lively Colours, the terrible Power of Jealousy, in order to magnify that great Courage, which could surmount this Passion; but, on the other Hand, he derogates from the Prudence of *Abraham*, in saying, that, as he was sensible, that *Sara* was too handsome to be able to escape the Incontinency of the *Egyptian*, whether he called her his Wife, or his Sister, he determin'd to call her his Sister, hoping by that means to save his Life. "Behold, *cries* St *Chrysostom*, with "what Prudence this good Man found out a sure "way to elude all the Snares of the *Egyptians*." After that, he conceives his having consented to the Adultery of his Wife, for this Reason, because Death, which was not as yet dispos'd of his Tyranny, inspir'd at that time great Terror. Ὅτι ἔτι ἦν κατακυ- θεῖσα τῆ ἑαυτοῦ ἃ τυραννὶς διὰ τοῦτο καὶ τῇ μοιχεία τῆς γυναικὸς αἱρεῖται κοινωνῆσαι ὁ δίκαιος, καὶ μονονοὺχὶ ὑπηρετήσασθαι τῷ μοιχῷ εἰς τὴν τῆς γυναικὸς ὕβριν ἵνα τὸν θάνατον διαφύγῃ (3): *Because the Tyranny of Death was not yet dissolved, therefore this just Man consented to the Adultery of his Wife, and was, as it were, subservient to the Adulterer, to his Wife's Disgrace, in order to escape Death.* After this Encomium on the Husband, he goes on to the Praises of the Wife, and says that she freely accepted of the Proposal, and did her utmost to play the Farce well (4). Upon which, he advises Wives to imitate her Example, and cries out, "Who does not admire this "great readiness to obey? Who can ever sufficiently "praise *Sara*, in that, after such Continence, and at "so great an Age, she was willing to expose her- "self to an Adulterer, and give up her Body to "Barbarians, in order to save the Life of her Hus- "band (5)?" I believe no Preacher now a-days would dare to handle so delicate a Subject as this, in such a Manner; he would give too great occasion for Raillery to the prophane; and I very much suspect that the Inhabitants of *Antioch*, naturally given to slander, could not hear such a Sermon, without taking too great a Liberty in making ill-natur'd Reflexions. St *Ambrose* is not less sparing in his Commendations of *Sara's* conjugal Love (6), and we shall see, under the Article ACINDINUS (*Septimius*), that St *Augustin* was under almost the same Illusion. 'Tis strange, that these great Luminaries of the Church, with all

(2) ὁ μὲν τοι δίκαιος σπούδακεν, καὶ πάντα ποιεῖ ὥστε εἰς ἔργον τὴν μοιχείαν ἐμβῆναι. Chrysost. Homil. 32. *in* Genes.

(3) Id. ib.

(4) Πάντα ποιεῖ ὥστε τὸ δρᾶμα καλῶς. She did every thing she cou'd, that the Fiction might be conceal'd. Id. ib.

(5) Τίς κατ' ἀξίαν ταύτην ἐπαινέσειεν, ἥτις μετὰ τοσαύτην ὥραν ἐν ἡλικίᾳ τοιαύτη, ὑπὲρ τοῦ τὸν δίκαιον διασῶσαι, οὐ εἰς τὴν οἰκίαν γυναικὶ καὶ εἰς μοιχείαν ἑαυτὴν ἐξέδωκεν, καὶ εὐνοίας μετέσχετο βαρβαρικῆς. Id. ib.

(6) Ambros. de Abrah. Lib. 1. c. 2.

---

their Virtue, and all their Zeal, should be ignorant that it is unlawful to save either one's own Life, or another's, at the Expence of a Crime.

[B] *Of a Distemper, which render'd him impotent*] To extinguish the Ardour of his Lust, God sent him a Disease, which put all the Physicians Art to a stand. God admonish'd him, in a Dream, to have nothing to do with the Wife of this Stranger. *Abimelech*, finding himself a little better, some time after, declared to his Friends the Cause of his Distemper, and restored *Sara* to *Abraham*. Thus *Josephus* relates the Affair (7); little sollicitous, according to Custom, to adapt his Narration to that of *Moses*; or rather, bold enough to give him the Lie. For does not *Moses* say, that *Abimelech*, after his Dream, rose early in the Morning, and call'd all his Servants, in order to communicate to them, what he had learnt in his Sleep (8)? Could he have done this, had he been given over by his Physicians? *Josephus* was sensible of the Difficulty; but, in order to remove it, he boldly supposes, against the Authority of the Scripture, that this Prince did not communicate his Dream to his Friends, 'till his Distemper was a little abated, some time after his Dream. Some think *Abimelech* was not afflicted in his own Person, but in those of his Women (9): and that, when the Scripture relates that God heal'd him, it only means his taking off the Seal, which he had fixed *to all the Wombs of the House of* Abimelech (10). I could soon be prevail'd upon to approve of this Interpretation; because I see no trace of *Abimelech's* Distemper in the whole 20th Chapter of *Genesis*, except these Words. *God heal'd* Abimelech, *and his Wife, and his Maid-Servants, and they bare Children.* But as the following verse mentions only the Affliction of these Women, it is sufficiently probable, that all the Evil, which God sent upon *Abimelech*, consisted in that. I shall, in another Place (11), answer a Question, which may be put to me: *Why this Prince, if he was in perfect Health, did not gratify that Passion, which had prompted him to take away* Sara. I am not surpriz'd at the fabulous Accounts, which the *Jews* have published, upon this Story; nor should I wonder at their Conduct, if they had invented a thousand Chimeras concerning our *Abimelech*. They say, that all the Channels of the Body were stop'd up, both of Man and Beast, both of Male and Female, so that nothing could either enter, or come out (12). They could no longer eat, nor drink; they could no longer void their Excrements, &c. The Men, besides, were seiz'd with such a Frigidity, that *Abimelech* was incapable of discharging the Duty of a Man, either to *Sara*, or to any other Woman. A celebrated Protestant Divine (13) adopts this Tradition, as far as concerns the latter Part, and rejects the rest, as ridiculous, or superfluous. He says, that, as the Devil sometimes (14), by his Impediments, prevents married People from paying their conjugal Duty, it is not improbable, but that God might send such a kind of Affliction on the Family of *Abimelech*, for a good and holy Purpose; which was to preserve the Chastity of *Sara*, and to make it appear very evident, that she had received no Stain in the House of *Abimelech*. He believes, therefore, that the Domestics of *Abimelech* were struck with the Disease of Barrenness: the Men, by an Impotency like that occasioned by Witchcraft; the Women, by an entire shutting up of the

(7) Joseph. Antiq. B. 1. c. 11.

(8) Genes. xx. 8.

(9) Salian's Annals, T. 1. p. 469.

(10) Genes. xx. 18.

(11) *In the* Remark *of the Article* SARA.

(12) Mercerus. See Rivet in Exercit. in Genes. Op. tom. T. 1. p. 395.

(13) Rivet. Heidegg. Fabius in Sept. Hist. Pat iarch. T. 1. p. 165.

(14) *B n tales rly called* Nouüs l'eguillette.

ABIMELECH.

moirs preferable to those of *Moses* [C], ventures to place this Treaty before the Birth of *Isaac*, whereas the Scripture places it after the Rejection of *Ismaël*, which did not come to pass, till after *Isaac* was weaned. Mr *Moreri* has follow'd the same Guide, when he assures us, that *Abimelech* shew'd great Kindness to *Isaac*, who had retired into the Land of *Gerar*. It is not indeed impossible, but this might be the same *Abimelech*; but it is more probable it was the Successor of him, who took away *Sara* [D]. It is certain that *Isaac*, on account of a Famine, which arose, retired

the Gates of Life, or by a Contraction of the Parts, which rendered them incapable of Conception. That's too much by half, some one may say, *it was sufficient to the Designs of Providence, that the Men were bewitch'd*. But it must be reply'd, that the closing up of the Parts of the Women being a Fact, which *Moses* expresly mentions, it must by no means be drop'd as superfluous. This matter is explain'd two ways: neither of which entirely clears it up. Some say, that *Moses*'s Meaning is, that the Wife and the Maid-Servants of *Abimelech* could not bring forth, when their Time was come: they had violent Pangs, and difficult Labour; but this must be at the time of which the Prophet *Isaiah* speaks: *The Children are come to the Birth, and there is not strength to bring forth* (15). Others say, that his Meaning is, that they did not conceive. The first Interpretation cannot be reconcil'd with *Genesis*, unless we can suppose that all the Women, which belong'd to *Abimelech* were with Child, when *Sara* was taken from her Husband (16): which is not likely. The other supposes *Sara* to have staid longer in this Prince's House, than she really did; for it could not be known in a very short time, whether so great a Number of Women had all lost the Faculty of Conception. This Difficulty oblig'd a very skilful Interpreter to say, that the Punishment, which God sent upon the Family of *Abimelech*, was known in a Manner, of which we have no Notion (17). Lastly, The *Rabins* make but little Difference between the personal Affliction of *Abimelech*, and the personal Affliction of the first Ravisher of *Sara* (18). They say of this latter, that he was seiz'd with the Disease *Ratan*, which is the most troublesome of all Ulcers, and the most destructive of the Joys of Love (19). *Solomon Jarchi* will have it, that the King of *Egypt*'s Plague, was a Disease in his Head, caused by a Worm, bred in his Brain: " *Morbus perturbati cerebri ob innatum ipsi Vermiculum, quo qui laborant, iis gravis fit concubitus, & liberi gignuntur ulcerosi* (20). — *The Disease of a disturbed Brain, caused by a Worm bred in it; which whoever is troubled with, finds it difficult to perform the matrimonial Duty; and his Children are born ulcerous*." Some think, these last Words spoil all; for they imagine, that, for the Honour of *Sara*, the Plague of *Pharaoh* must have render him absolutely impotent. *See the Remark upon the Article of this holy Woman*.

[C] *Memoirs preferable to those of* Moses.] I have a long time conceived an Indignation against *Josephus*, and those who excuse him upon this Head. One, who made an open Profession of *Judaism*, the Belief of which is founded upon the Divinity of the Scripture, has yet the Assurance to relate things otherwise, than he must have read them in *Genesis*: he alters, he adds, he drops Circumstances; in a Word, he sets himself up in Opposition to *Moses*, in such a Manner, that one of the two must be a false Historian. Is this to be born, and ought we not to conclude, either that he did not scruple to scandalize his Nation, or that he thought the particular Opinion he entertained of the Fallibility, and consequently of the Non-Inspiration of *Moses*, was common among the *Jews*? He deserves the following Rebuke of *Theodore Beza* very justly. " Hoc ego " semel pronuncio, quod tu nunquam falsum osten- " des, si verus est multis locis Josephus, mentitum " esse multis locis Mosen & sacros omnes Scriptores. " Sed nos potius ipsos pro veris ipsius Dei inter- " pretibus, illum vero pro sacerdote rerum sacrarum " valdè imperito, atque etiam negligente & pro- " phano Scriptore, habebimus. —— *I pronounce this* " *once for all, which you can never disprove, that* " *if, in many Places, Josephus be in the right*, " Moses *and all the sacred Writers must be in the* " *wrong. But we will rather esteem them the true* " *Interpreters of God himself, but him a very un-* " *skilful Priest of sacred Things, and even a care-*

" *less and prophane Writer* (21)." I am of Opinion, that all the antient Historians have taken the same Liberty with regard to old Memoirs, which they consulted. They have tacked Supplements to them; and, not finding the Facts unfolded and embellished to their Fancy, they have stretched and dressed them up as they pleased; and this is what at present we receive for History.

[D] *It was the Successor of him, who took away* Sara.] I do not build upon the long Life, which we must allow to *Abimelech*, if he was alive at the time when *Isaac* came to *Gerar*. This Journey was later than the Purchase, which *Jacob* made of the Right of Eldership: we may suppose therefore, that *Isaac* was then eighty Years old; for he was sixty when *Esau* and *Jacob* were born: and *Esau* was already a great Hunter, when he sold his Birth-Right. On the other side, *Abimelech*, who took away *Sara*, was a King, and married, before *Isaac* was born: He must then, at least, have been a good hundred Years old, when *Isaac* journied to *Gerar*. But is this much? Did not Men at that time live to above an hundred and fifty Years (22)? One would scarce believe one's own Eyes, that learned Men (23) should be capable of objecting these Words of *The Preacher*, *Omnis potentatus vita brevis* (24): As if, supposing the Canonical Authority of this Book, it was contrary to Revelation, that a Man's Reign should continue an hundred Years. Who does not see, that if this Passage has that Weight, which is attributed to it, we must deny the Truth of all Histories, which inform us, that there have been Reigns which continued upwards of fifty or sixty Years? What then is it which induces me to believe, that *Abimelech*, who took away *Sara*, was not the same who entered into Alliance with *Isaac*? why it is this: This latter *Abimelech* readily believed, upon *Isaac*'s Word, that *Rebecca* was but his Sister; and when he was undeceived, not by the Words, but by the Actions, of *Isaac*, he reproved him mildly for his Deceit, without saying to him, *You follow your Father's Example*: Abraham *heretofore played me the same Trick*. Now is it probable, if he had been already imposed upon by *Abraham*, that he would have again fallen into the same Snare, or if he had, that he would not have passed a severe Rebuke upon *Isaac*, on Account both of his Father's, and his own Hypocrisy? He would hardly have forgot *Abraham*'s, which drew such Misfortunes upon him. St *Chrysostom* thought this so likely, that he boldly declared from the Pulpit, that *Abimelech* actually did reproach *Isaac* with *Abraham*'s Dissimulation. " Rex, adhuc " habens recentem memoriam eorum, quæ tempore " reumque argens dicebat, cur hoc fecisti? — Hanc " deceptionem & olim sustinuimus à patre tuo (25). " —— *The King, having fresh in his Memory what* " *he suffered for the Rape of* Sara *in the Patriarch's* " *Time, reproached him, and charging him with his* " *Guilt, said unto him, What hast thou done?* —— " *Thus was I heretofore deceived by your Father*." But all this has no better Foundation, than Rhetorical Licence, which is sometimes carried as far as that of the Poets and Painters.

—— Pictoribus atque Poëtis

Quidlibet audendi semper fuit æqua potestas (26).

Poets and Painters equally may dare;
In bold Attempts an equal Power they share.
                                                         CREECH.

Two things seem to favour *Moreri*'s Opinion. First, The King of *Gerar*, both in *Abraham*'s and *Isaac*'s Time, had the same Name; and there was a General of his Army, whose Name was *Picol*, at both these Times. Secondly, *Rebecca*, beautiful as she was, was not

ABIMELECH. ABLANCOURT.

tired into the Land of *Gerar*, where one ABIMELECH then reign'd. The Beauty of *Rebecca* occasioned her Husband's making use of the same Policy, which *Abraham* had had recourse to, on account of *Sara*'s Beauty. *Isaac* fearing to be slain, if it should be known that he was the Husband of the beautiful *Rebecca*, made her pass for his Sister. *Abimelech* discover'd the Cheat, by observing, as he look'd through a Window, a certain Sport [E] which passed between them; and having sent for *Isaac*, said to him, *Behold of a surety she is thy Wife, and how saidst thou, she is my Sister?—What is this thou hast done unto us? one of the people might lightly have lien with thy wife* [F], *and thou shouldst have brought guiltiness upon us.* At the same time, he forbad his Subjects, on pain of death, to offer the least Injury to *Isaac*, or *Rebecca*. This Remonstrance, and this Decree, must have been sincere; and we Moderns ought to be careful not to misrepresent these Matters (*f*). The Prosperity of *Isaac* caus'd a change in the Friendship of *Abimelech*. For, perceiving the great Wealth, which *Isaac* acquired, he very freely gave him to understand, that he must depart. He obey'd; and continuing to prosper, notwithstanding the Opposition made to him in several places, on account of the Pits, which he dug, his Alliance was courted by *Abimelech*, whose Offers were favourably receiv'd (*g*).

(f) Tur-ti-lin, *in his* Epist. Hist. p. 10. Edit. in 1692, *is guilty of mistaken interpretation of these Words,* Isaac, *going to* Gerar, *for Corn, by the Providence of God, preserv'd his Wife's Chastity from the Lust of* Abimelech.

(g) Genes. xxvi.

not taken away, as *Sara* had been; the Reason of which might be, that *Abimelech* was grown old, and remembered likewise the ill Consequences of the Rape of *Sara*. I answer, first, that the Kings of certain Countries affected all to take the same Name; as the Kings of *Egypt* did that of *Pharaoh*. Why then might not *Abimelech* be the common Appellation of all the Kings of *Gerar?* Picol might perhaps be the Name of a particular Employ. Perhaps too this Employ might have descended from Father to Son. Secondly, I reply, that *Isaac's Abimelech* might not be a young Man, tho' he was not the same, who took away *Sara*. I frankly own, therefore he was a good old Man; because he formed no Design upon the beautiful *Rebecca*, tho' he did not believe her to be married; and because he does not tell *Isaac*, that she had been in Danger from him, but from his Subjects; and, as these People were so debauched, that every beautiful Stranger, who was thought not to be married, was in great Danger; I can see no Reason more probable for *Abimelech's* Continency towards *Rebecca*, than his old Age. *There is a Time* (say youthful Libertines) *when one is too wise.*

[E] *A certain Sport.*] Some have imagin'd, that the Scripture intended, under the Word *Sport*, to express, modestly, the conjugal Duty, which *Isaac* happen'd to be paying his Wife, at a Time when *Abimelech* was looking out of Window. "Putant qui-
" dem honestè significari eo vocabulo copulam carna-
" lem. Sed non sit verisimile prudentissimum & san-
" ctissimum virum tam incautè rem habuisse cum
" uxore, ut id per fenestram prospicere, ut Scriptura
" inquit, Rex posset Abimelech. Credibilius igitur
" est eo vocabulo significatos esse tales jocos & blan-
" ditias in amplexando & osculando, quales inter con-
" juges agitari turpe non est: extra conjugium vero
" nefas est (27). *—Some think, that carnal Copula-
" tion is modestly hinted at under that Word: but it
" is not likely, that* Isaac, *a prudent and holy Man,
" would have to do with his Wife, in so unguarded
" a Manner, that King* Abimelech, *according to the
" Scripture, could behold it from his Window. It is
" more probable, that that Word implies only such
" kind of sporting and toying, by embraces and kis-
" ses, as is decent between married People, but out of
" Wedlock unlawful.*" Others will not hear of this sort of Explanation; they say, that *Isaac* was too wise, and too prudent, to take his Measures so ill; and that, upon such Occasion, he took care to be in a Place, where the Neighbours could not overlook him from their Windows. " *We must therefore understand,
" say they,* by the Word Sport, *a certain Pass-time,
" which, though it was not the last Act of the
" Play, was yet too familiar between Persons not mar-
" ried, however they might be otherwise a-kin.*" This *Pass-time* must mean something else, than talking familiarly, jesting, and laughing together; for a Brother and Sister may do all this very modestly, and without giving occasion to such a Conclusion as *Abimelech* drew from the sporting of *Isaac* and *Rebecca*. This Explication appears to me incomparably more reasonable, than the former: and, yet, it must be allowed, that Fondness might sometimes hinder *Isaac* from observing that great Precaution, which rigid Moralists would have exacted from the Patriarch: for, in short, it cannot be denied, that *Abimelech*, looking through a Window, surpriz'd him diverting himself with *Rebecca* at a certain Game, whence he could not but certainly conclude they were Man and Wife. Take notice, that they had been marry'd forty Years: *Isaac* was, then, eighty Years old. St *Austin*, in his Book against *Faustus* the *Manichean*, a great Exploder of the Patriarchs, defends *Isaac* in a solid Manner (28); and, indeed, it is too rigorous to expect, that a Patriarch, or a Bishop, if he is married, should not recreate himself a little with his Wife, without closing all his Window-Shutters. For we must have this good Opinion of their Prudence, that if Nature inclines the greatest Men to a little indulgence, they will walk so cautiously upon this slippery Road, as to take care that no Observation shall be made of them from their Neighbour's Window. *Cornelius à Lapide* does not know what it is he is confuting, when he sets himself against the first Explication. " Judæi
" impuri, *says he*, jocum hunc intelligunt copulam
" conjugalem. Sed apage hos Cynicos! Quis crederet
" Isaac publicè, & spectante Rege, tam inverecundum,
" lubricum, & cynicum fuisse (29) ? — *The un-
" chaste Jews understand this Sport of matrimonial Co-
" pulation. But away with these Snarlers! Who can
" believe, that* Isaac *was so immodest, lewd, and bru-
" tish, publickly, and in the King's Sight ?*" This is not the thing: no one pretends, that *Isaac* was, then, in the middle of the Street: he was in his Chamber; and had not sufficiently fasten'd his Window-Shutters: This is the whole Matter; and, if this is too much, you will be obliged to condemn the Patriarch, and to act the *Cato* against him. It is well known that *Cato* expell'd one *Manlius* from the Senate, because at noon Day, and in the Presence of his Daughter, he had given his Wife a Kiss (30). This *Manlius* would have been Consul, probably, the next Election. Some pretend to discover an allegorical Mystery (31) in this Sport of *Isaac* and *Rebecca*, of which certainly neither they, nor the sacred Historian, in the least dreamt. I shall not place these Errors among those which I am compiling. It would be an Attempt like that of drinking the Sea dry. It were to be wish'd, that the greatest part of these mysterious Conceits had been unknown to the World.

[F] *One of the People might lightly have lien with thy Wife.*] The *Philistins* must have been furious Folks in Love-Matters; since *Abimelech*, their King, is surpriz'd, that no one had lain with *Rebecca*, who pass'd only for *Isaac's* Sister. We learn from hence, at the same time, their great regard for Marriage. As for unmarried Women, they seem, in this Country, to have thought they were the first Comer's Right. Witness *Dina*, the Daughter of *Jacob*, who was decoy'd by them, as she was taking a Walk. She was first enjoy'd, and then demanded in Marriage (32).

(28) *Austin against* Faust. B. 22. Ch. 46. *Mr* Thiers *quotes part of this Passage, in the 4th Part of his Treatise of Sports and Diversions.*

(29) Corn. à Lapide *upon* Gen. xxvi.

(30) Plutarch *in his* Cato Major, p. 326.

(31) *See* Pererius *upon* Genesis, *the* xxvi.

(32) Gen. xxxiv.

ABLANCOURT (NICOLAS PERROT, Lord of) *See* PERROT.

ABRABANEL

ABRABANEL.

ABRABANEL (a) (ISAAC) a celebrated *Rabin*, was born at *Lisbon* [*A*], of a Family which pretended to be deriv'd from King *David* [*B*]. He push'd his Interest very far in the Court of *Alphonso* V. King of *Portugal*, and was there honoured with the highest Offices; which he enjoy'd till the Death of that Prince: but he found a great Alteration under the new King. *Abrabanel* was Forty five Years old [*C*], when *John* II. succeeded his Father *Alphonso*. All who were concern'd in the Management of Affairs in the preceeding Reign, were turn'd out; and, if our Rabin is to be credited, there was a secret Design of putting them to death, under pretence, that they had been contriving to betray the Crown of *Portugal* to the King of *Spain*. He was not appriz'd of this, when, in obedience to the Orders he had receiv'd to wait upon the King, he went to *Lisbon* with all haste; but being inform'd upon the Road of the Plot, which was hatching against his Life, he retir'd with expedition into the King of *Castile's* Dominions. All his Estate was confiscated, upon the Return of the Soldiers, who had Orders to bring him dead or alive. He lost, upon that occasion, together with all his Books, the beginning of a *Commentary upon Deuteronomy*, which he was much concern'd at. Some Christian Writers [*D*] do not agree, that the Cause of this Disgrace was so little owing to his Misconduct, as he pretended. They are of the same Opinion, in relation to his other Persecutions [*E*]. Be that as it will, being settled in *Castile*, he apply'd himself to teaching and composing. He wrote, in the Year 1484, his *Commentary on the Books of Joshua, Judges, and Samuel:* after which he was sent for to the Court of *Ferdinand* and *Isabella*, and had Employments conferr'd upon him during eight Years, namely till the *Jews* were driven out of the Territories of the Catholic King, in 1492. He did all he could by his Prayers and his Tears [*F*] to avert this dreadful Storm; but he did not succeed, and was obliged, as well as the rest, to depart with his Wife and Children. He retir'd to *Naples*, and there compos'd, in 1493, his *Commentary on the Books of Kings*. As he was a Courtier, he did not forget to recommend himself, by the Knowledge he had acquir'd in the Courts of *Portugal* and *Arragon*; insomuch that he insinuated himself into the good Graces of *Ferdinand* King of *Naples*, and afterwards of *Alphonso*. He follow'd the Fortune of the latter, when *Charles* VIII. King of *France* drove him from *Naples*; for he pass'd over with him into *Sicily* [*G*]. After the Death of *Alphonso*,

---

[*A*] *Was born at Lisbon.*] His Ancestors were of *Castile*. "E majoribus Castellam Hispaniæ, ex parentibus Olyssiponem Lusitaniæ agnovit patriam.— *He claimed Castile of Spain as the Country of his Ancestors, and Olyssipon Lusitania as the Country of his Parents.*" Thus the Journal of *Leipsic* informs us (1). *Don Nicolas Antonio* will have it, that the Family of *Abrabanel* was settled at *Seville* for many Ages (2). He had it from *Bartolocci*; and he quotes the Rabin *Solomon ben Virga* (3), who has asserted almost the same thing in his *History of the Jews* (4), translated into *Latin* by *Gentius*, and quoted below.

[*B*] *Pretended to be derived from King David.*] *Abrabanel* has in part declared (5), that at the time of the Destruction of the first Temple, two Families of the Race of *David* passed into *Spain*, one of which settled at *Lucene*, and the other at *Seville*, where it left a Posterity. In another Place (6) he gives us the History of this Transmigration. The Rabin *Solomon ben Virga* introduces one *Thomas*, who makes a long Deduction of the same Story to *Alphonso* King of *Spain*, and relates, that the Family of *Abrabanel* descended from the Kings of *Juda*: but *Alphonso* wou'd believe nothing of it, and raised insurmountable Difficulties against these Genealogies (7). The Jews, to get over the Difficulty, suppose, that *Abrabanel* lost his Genealogical Books in the Hurry of his Removal (8). Mr *Huet* relates (9), that *Manassè ben Israël* affirms in his *Conciliator*, that these two Families, sprung from *David*, retired into *Spain*, after the Ruin of the second Temple. This *Rabin* had a very particular Interest in this ridiculous Story; for his Wife was of the Family of *Abrabanel* (10). Farther, it is not easy to know who this *Thomas* is, who conversed so long with this *Thomas*, in the Book of *Solomon ben Virga*. Some call him a King of *Portugal* (11); and as they insist that the *Abrabanel*, whom *Thomas* mentions, is our *Rabin*, we cannot doubt but they take him for King *Alphonso* V. and that this *Alphonso* is the last King of *Castile*, who bore that Name (12). He might speak upon good Grounds thus far; but he is guilty of an Error, when he places near two Centuries between this King and our *Rabin*; for this latter was born in the Year 1437, and that King died in 1350, aged 38 Years.

[*C*] *Forty five Years old*] *Nicolas Antonio* has inserted, at the end of his *Bibliotheque d'Espagne* what Father *Bartolocci* had told him concerning *Isaac Abrabanel*. He has by that corrected some Faults which had been before printed in the Article of this *Rabin*: but he seems to me not to have express'd himself with Exactness, when he says, " *Juvenis* adhuc, sed " benè doctus, in Castellæ regnum transiit, cum Jo- " hanni II. Portugalliæ Regi parum esset gratus. "——*He was yet a Youth, but a good Scholar,* " *when, being disagreeable to* John II. *King of Por-* " *tugal, he went into the Kingdom of* Castile (13)." He talks in that Place of an Age, which generally cannot have afforded time enough to acquire much Learning. This is what cannot be applied to forty five Years of Age. It is certain then, that the Author of the *Bibliotheque d'Espagne* believed that the Rabin was much younger than that, when he fled into *Castile*: he was therefore in an Error.

[*D*] *Some Christian Writers.*] They say that *Abrabanel* deserved the Treatment he met with; and that he would have been punished more severely, upon the Discovery of his ill Designs, if the goodnatured Disposition of King *John* had not been satisfied with banishing him. They add, that Remorse of Conscience made this *Rabin* take the Resolution of quitting *Portugal*, and escaping by Night into *Castile*, with an extraordinary Readiness (14).

[*E*] *They are of the same Opinion, in relation to his other Persecutions.*] They say, that he intruded himself into the Court of *Ferdinand* and *Isabella*, by means of a Bank which he establish'd in the Kingdom of *Castile*; that he amass'd great Treasures, by making use of all the Artifices of his Nation: that he tyrannized over the Poor, that he was very usurious; that he had the Vanity to aspire to the most illustrious Titles, and those which solely belonged to the great Families of *Spain*; and besides that, being a sworn Enemy of the Christian Religion, he contributed more than any one else to the Storm, which overwhelmed him and all his Countrymen (15).

[*F*] *By his Prayers and his Tears.*] He himself relates in one of his Books (16) what he did upon this Occasion. *Solomon ben Virga* gives an Account of it in his History of the *Jews* (17), with a tragical Description of the terrible Miseries, which fell upon three hundred thousand *Jews*, who were obliged, in one Day, to depart out of the Dominions of the Catholic King.

[*G*] *He passed over with him into Sicily.*] *Nicolas Antonio*, correcting his Article of *Abrabanel*, upon the

Alphonso, he retired to *Corfou*, and there began his *Commentary on Isaiah*, in the Year 1495. He had the Satisfaction of recovering, by what Accident I know not, what he had formerly wrote upon the Book of *Deuteronomy*. He came back into *Italy*, the following Year, and went and settled at *Monopoli* in *Puglia* (b), where he wrote many books. He finish'd his *Deuteronomy*, and compos'd his *Sevach Pesach* (c) and his *Nacalath Avoth* (d), in the year 1496. The following year, he compos'd his *Majene Hajeschua* (e); and in 1498, his *Maschmiah Jeschua* (f) and his Commentary on *Isaiah*. Some time after, he went to *Venice*, to make up the difference, which had arisen between the *Venetians* and *Portuguese*, concerning the Spice-Trade, and he shew'd so much Prudence and Ability, that he gain'd the Esteem and Favour of the great Men. At *Venice* he compos'd his *Commentary on Jeremiah*, in the year 1504. Some say, that he compos'd, likewise, at that time, his *Commentary on Ezekiel* and the twelve *lesser Prophets*. In the year 1506, he compos'd his *Commentary on Exodus*; and died at *Venice* in the year 1508, [H], aged 71 years. He left three Sons, *Juda, Joseph*, and *Samuel* [I]. The eldest was a Physician and a great Poet, and compos'd many Verses in Honour of his Father. It is said, that *Samuel* embrac'd Christianity at *Ferrara*, and receiv'd the Name of *Alphonso*, which was That of the Duke. *Abrabanel* wrote many other Books [K] of which we cannot determine the Date, and of which

the Conferences which he had with Father *Bartolocci*, says that this *Rabin* followed King *Ferdinand* into *Sicily*, whom *Francis* had dethroned, and that, after the Death of this Prince, he retired to *Corfou* (18). Here is certainly a Mistake; the Author takes *Ferdinand* for *Alphonso*: it was with *Alphonso* (19) that *Abrabanel* went into *Sicily*, as Father *Bartolocci* remarks (20), and not with *Ferdinand*. He continued at *Messina* 'till the Death of *Alphonso* in the beginning of the Year 1495, and then he went to *Corfou* (21). It was there he began his Commentary on *Isaiah* in 1495. If he had not passed over into this Island till after the Death of *Ferdinand*, we may be sure he could not be there in 1495. Thus the *Appendix* of *Nicolas Antonio* stands in need of another *Appendix* to correct it.

[H] *In the Year* 1508.] Father *Bartolocci* gave D. *Nicolas Antonio* the Hint of this Year, who had already printed, that our *Rabin* was Professor of the *Hebrew* Tongue at *Padua*, about the Year 1510. We have here a Proof of Mr *Moreri's* Negligence. He had by him this Author's *Spanish Dictionary*, and yet did not take the Pains to consult the *Appendixes*, which makes a considerable Part of it, and which clear up, and correct, many Passages of the Work. Thus he has preserved the Mistake relating to this Professorship of *Padua*, without observing that the Author himself had corrected it at the end of his Book, and excused himself, as having been misled by *Buxtorf*. " *Venetiis inde profectus memoratus, ex qua urbe in Germaniam ad in Professorem Patavinam Hebraicae Linguae, quod Buxtorfium & alios secuti nos literis in Bibliothecâ nostra mandarimus, potuit conferre se. Constat autem Venetiis cum Septuaginta* (22) *annos natum superioris seculi anno octavo diem suum obiisse. Quo cum non bene convenit quod circa annum decimum Professorem, ut ibidem diximus, Patavinum egerit* (23). —— *He is said to have gone ſrom thence to Venice; whence he might proceed either to Germany, or to his Hebrew Professorship at Padua, as I have related in my Dictionary, upon the Authority of Buxtorf, and others. But it is certain, that he died at Venice, aged Seventy, in the eightieth Year of the last Century: which does not agree with the Account I have there given of his discharging the Office of Professor at Padua, in the tenth Year* " Thus *Nicolas Antonio* excuses himself. He does not absolutely deny this Professorship at *Padua*; he is satisfied with saying, that he had not exactly marked the Time. Mr *Moreri* therefore ought not to have told us, that, in 1510, Abrabanel taught the Hebrew Tongue at Padua.

[I] *He left three Sons,* Juda, Joseph, *and* Samuel.] At first sight he seems to have left four, if it be true what *N. Antonio* reports (24), that *Leon*, who wrote the Dialogues of Love, was his Son. But we must observe, that the Author of these Dialogues may very well be the same with *Juda*, the eldest Son of *Abrabanel*. This *Juda* was commonly called *Messer Leone* (25). His Book of Love is very well known: *Denis Sauvage*, and *Pontus de Tiard* having translated it into *French*. The Author is generally quoted under the Name of *Leo Hebraeus*. He is called *Mestre Leon Abarbanel Medico Hebraeo*

in a *Spanish* Translation printed at *Venice* in 1568, in 4to.

Juda ABRABANEL left his Father, when the *French* conquered the Kingdom of *Naples*: and retired to *Genoa* to practise Physic there (26). *Samuel* ABRABANEL was alive in the Popedom of *Julius* III. as appears by a Petition, which he presented to Cardinal *Sirlet*, Protector of the *Neophytes*. (27). He left *Naples* in 1540, and carried with him the Value of two hundred thousand Crowns (28). His Father dedicated to him the Commentary on *Pirke Avoth*, which he composed in the Year 1496 (29).

[K] *Abrabanel wrote many other Books*] The following are set down in the *Leipsic-Journal* (30): *Commentaries* on Genesis, Leviticus, *and* Numbers: *Rasch Amana* (31) *Sepher Jeschuoth Meschico*, a Work on the Traditions concerning the *Messiah*: *Zedek Olamim*; this relates to the Rewards and Punishments of another Life: *Sepher Jemoth Olam*; it is an History from *Adam*: *Maamar Muchase Schaddai*; it is a Treatise of the Prophecy and Vision of *Ezekiel*, against the Rabin *Maimonides*: *Sepher Atereth Sekenim*: *Miphaloth Elohim* (32): *Sepher Schamaim Chadaschim*: *Lahakath Nebbiim*. The Sieur *Theophilus Spizelius* remarks, that *John Buxtorf*, the Son, had shown him a great many Dissertations taken from the Words of *Abrabanel*, which he had translated into *Latin* (33). They must be like those of the same Rabin, which the same *Buxtorf* has translated and published with the Book *Cosri*. He shew'd him likewise other Translations, which he had made from some Books of this Rabin. The *Commentary* on Haggai was translated into *Latin* by *Adam Scherzerus*, and inserted in the *Trifolium Orientale*, publish'd at *Leipsic*, in 1663. In the same Town was publish'd, in 1686, the *Commentary* on Joshua, Judges, *and* Samuel. See what is said concerning this Edition, in the *Leipsic-Journal*, whence I have borrowed this Article. In the same Year, 1686, they printed at *Leyden* the *Commentary* on Hosea, with *a Preface on the twelve lesser Prophets*; the whole translated into *Latin*, with Notes, by *Francides Husen*. *M. de Veil*, a converted *Jew*, published at *London*, in 1683, Abrabanel's *Preface to the* Leviticus. See the *Leipsic-Journal*, for the Month of *January*, 1684. *N. Antonio* will furnish you with the Titles of several other Works of this Rabin, sometimes with the Time and Place of the Impression, as far as the *Rabinical Dictionary of Plantavitius* would inform him. Mr *Moreri* ought not to have said, that *Abrabanel* wrote a Commentary on the *Talmud*, but a Piece of the *Talmud*, entituled *Pirke Avoth*. *N. Antonio*, his only Source, might have so well explain'd this to him, as not to suffer him to mistake. Father *Simon*, who tells us many curious Particulars relating to *Abrabanel's* Books, observes that the Book compos'd by this Rabin, under the Name of *Nahalat Avoth*, *Profession of the Fathers*, is a *Commentary on the Treatise* Pirke Avoth, *and that both the one and the other were printed at* Venice, in 4to, *in the Year* 1545: *that there is a very learned Preface of this Author, at the beginning of his Book,* Nahalat Avoth, *in which he explains the Succession of Tradition among the Jews, which is a very obscure point* (34).

ABRABANEL.

which some have not yet been printed. Many of the *Noble Venetians*, and the chief of the *Jews*, solemniz'd his Funeral with great Pomp. His Body was interr'd at *Padua*, in a Burying-Ground without the City. A little while after, the *Rabin*, *Juda Mentz*, Rector of the University, was buried in the same Place. The Siege of 1509 so destroy'd every thing about that Place, that this Burying-Ground was no longer to be distinguish'd. *Abrabanel* was Master of great Talents: he was upon a level with the famous *Maimonides*; and some even rank him above him. The *Jews* pretend, that he entirely overthrew all the Arguments and Objections of the *Christians*. These latter, justly contemning what he wrote in the *Jewish* Controversy, yet greatly esteem his other Interpretations. They find him to be a subtile, clear, learned, and honest, Commentator. He does not canonize the Opinions of his Masters; and censures very freely the Plagiarism, and other Faults, which he found them to be guilty of. His great Weakness was his being too sensible of the Persecutions, which the *Jews* suffer'd, and in which he bore a considerable part. The Memory of this Misfortune animated him with such Fury against the *Christians*, that he treated them with the utmost Indignation. He has scarce wrote one Book, in which his Anger and Thirst of Revenge is not to be trac'd; and the wretched Condition of his Nation is uppermost in every thing he compos'd. He hop'd by this means to revive the expiring *Synagogue* (g); and I suppose he found it a Relief from that Oppression of Choler, which would have choak'd him, had he not discharg'd it upon Paper. Nor is he the only one, who has found Relief from this Remedy. We know some, who have stood in great need of it, tho' they were not ignorant, like him, of the Precepts of the Gospel. I do not meet with his Professorship at *Padua* [L], nor his Journey to the *East* [M]. These are Facts in which Mr *Moreri* is grossly mistaken, as he is in what he relates concerning his Travels into *Germany* [N].

Abrabanel was indefatigable in his Studies: he spent whole Nights in it; and was capable of fasting a long time. He wrote with great Ease: the implacable Hatred, which he shew'd in his Writings against the *Christians* [O], did not hinder his living with them in a civil, chearful, soft, and obliging manner.

(g) From the Acta Eruditt. Lipsf. for the Month of Nov. 1686. p. 528, &c.

[L] *I do not meet with his Professorship at* Padua.] See the Remark [H]. The learned Gentlemen, who have given us an historical Abridgment (35) of the Life of *Abrabanel*, and who have trac'd him almost Year by Year, from his leaving *Spain*, to his Death, would not sure have pass'd over so remarkable a Circumstance: Whence I conclude, that, since they make no mention of it, the Author himself had said nothing of it. Now it is not probable, that, having mentioned so many things not so much to his Honour, as a Professorship at *Padua*, he should say nothing of this Employ, if he had been actually invested with it. And if other Writers had mention'd it upon any good Grounds, I believe the *Leipsic* Gentlemen would not have been ignorant of it, or pass'd it by in Silence. It is therefore a Fact a little apocryphal, to say no worse.

Add to this, that Father *Bartolocci*, who has given us an exact Series of this Rabin's Adventures, takes no notice of it.

[M] *Nor his Journey to the East.*] I look upon it to be false, for the abovementioned Reason; namely, the Silence of these Gentlemen: Nay, though this Journey were real, Mr *Moreri* has still advanc'd a great Falshood. He supposes, first, that *Abarbanel* taught *Hebrew* at *Padua*, in 1510; and, in the second place, that the eager Desire he had to shew his hatred to the *Christians* induc'd him *to go into the East, to live there with those of his own Sect, and that it was there he compos'd that great Number of Books, which are still extant*. We have seen that he died in 1508; which is enough to convince us that all this will fall elsewhere.

[N] *These are Facts in which Mr* Moreri *is grossly mistaken, as he is in what he relates concerning his Travels into* Germany.] I did not dare to treat this as false, whilst I was persuaded, that *D. Nicolas Antonio*, had faithfully cited *Buxtorf*; for, supposing his Quotation just, we must believe, that *Abarbanel* had mention'd in his own Travels into *Germany*, in his Commentary on *Pirke Avoth*. " Profugus ergo is in Germaniam venit, quod ipse ait in Commentariis ad " librum Talmudicum Pirke Avoth, — Buxtorfio " teste, in tractatu de Abbreviaturis Hebræorum, p. " 100 (36). — *In his Exile, he retired to* Germany, " *as he tells us himself, in his Commentaries on the* " *Talmudic Book,* Pirke Avoth, — *according to* Buxtorf, *in his Treatise de Abbrev. Hebr.* p. 100." All I could say, therefore, upon this Supposition, was, that, at least, it was certain, that *Abrabanel* did not visit *Germany*, after his Banishment from the Territories of the Catholic King: because, upon leaving

them, he embark'd for the Kingdom of *Naples*, and arriv'd there soon after. I discover'd likewise *Moreri* to be in an Error; *Abarbinel*, says he, was in the Number of *the Exiles: He retired, first, to* Germany, *and then to* Italy and I had the more Reason to be surpriz'd at this Mistake, as I knew that *D. Nicolas Antonio* had corrected it, upon better Information, from Father *Bartolocci*. But, upon consulting the Book quoted, I found that the Author takes no notice, that *Abrabanel* mention'd his own Travels into *Germany* : See what *Buxtorf* says : " Hic titulus (More- " nu, *i. e. Doctor Noster*) novus est, intra ducentos " annos natus in Germania, inde in Italiam traductus, " quod valde miratus fuit Don Isaac Abarbinel ex Hispania in has terras veniens, ut ipsemet scribit in " Commentario Pirke Abhoth, cap. 6. (37) — *This* " *Title* (Morenu, i. e. *our Doctor) is new, having* " *arose in* Germany, *within these two hundred Years,* " *and from thence transplanted into* Italy ; *which* Don " Isaac Abrabanel *was very much surpriz'd at, as he* " *himself writes in his Commentary on* Pirke Avoth." I could no longer doubt, that *D. Nicolas Antonio* mistook *Buxtorf's* meaning ; and it is an Error, which he does no retract in the Place where he informs us, what Father *Bartolocci* had told him concerning *Abrabanel*. Observe, that this Father proves demonstrably the Falseness of these supposed Travels into *Germany*, which, (says he (38), some mention upon the Authority of *Buxtorf*. I doubt not but this will stop the Course of this erroneous Quotation.

[O] *Which he shew'd in his Writings against the Christians*.] His Commentaries on the Scriptures, but chiefly those he made up on the Prophets, are so full of Venom against *Jesus Christ*, the Church, the Pope, the Cardinals, the Clergy, and all *Christians* in general, particularly the *Roman Catholics*, that Father *Bartolocci* was of Opinion, that the *Jews* ought not to be suffer'd to read them (39) Upon which he remarks, that the reading of the Commentaries on the lesser Prophets had been forbidden them, and that they dared not to keep them, " In his etiam pluri- " bus in locis canino dente Christianam Religionem " mordet & lacerat, adeoque merito illorum lectio & " retentio Judæis interdicta est, nec eos apud se re- " tinere audent, publice saltem & palam, propter me- " tum Christianorum (40). — *For in many Passages* " *of these he tears to pieces the Christian Religion, in* " *so enrag'd a Manner, that the reading and keeping* " *of them is forbidden the Jews, nor dare they be in* " *Possession of them, at least openly, for fear of the* " *Christians.*"

(35) Act. Lips. Nov. 1686, p. 528, &c.

(36) N. Ant. Bibl. Hisp. Tom. 1. p. 823.

(37) Buxtorf de Abbrev. Hebræ. p. 115. Edit. 2.

(38) Bart. Bibl. Rabin. Tom. 3. p. 660.

(39) Bibl. Rab Tom. 3. p. 870.

(40) Id. ib. p. 873.

ABRAHAM,

ABRAHAM.

ABRAHAM, the *Father*, and Source, of the *Faithful*, was the Son of TE- RAH. He defcended from *Noah* by *Shem*, from whom he was diftant nine Gene- rations. The Opinion, which fuppofes him to be born in the 130th Year of *Te- rah* (*a*), feems to me more probable, than that which places his Birth in the 70th Year of the fame *Terah*. There is great probability, that he was born in the fame City, from whence the Holy Scripture tells us his Father retired, in order to go into the Land of *Canaan* (*b*). It was a City of *Chaldæa* named *Ur*. *Abraham* went out of it with his Father, and ftaid with him at *Haran* 'till his Death. After this he re- fum'd his firft Defign, which was a Journey to *Paleftine*. We may read in the Scrip- ture the feveral Stations he made in the Land of *Canaan*; his Journey into *Egypt*, where his Wife was taken from him, who was likewife his Sifter by the Father's fide (*c*); his other Journey to *Gerar*, where fhe was taken from him in the fame man- ner, and reftor'd again, juft as before; the Victory, which he gain'd over four Princes, who had plunder'd *Sodom*; his Complaifance to his Wife, who was willing he fhou'd have Children by their Handmaid *Agar* (*d*); the Covenant, which God made with him, feal'd with the Sign of Circumcifion, his Obedience to the Order which he had receiv'd from God to flay his only Son; the manner in which this Action was ftop'd; his Marriage with *Ketura*; his Death at the Age of 175 Years; and his Burial, by *Sara*, his firft Wife, in the Cave of *Macpelah*. It would be ufelefs to enlarge upon thefe Particulars. The Proteftants have them at their Fingers ends; they fetch them from their Source, from their tendereft Years; and as to the *Ro- man* Catholics, they have no need of any other Dictionary to inftruct them, than *Moreri*'s and *Simon*'s. It would be more agreeable to the Nature of this Collection, to dwell upon the Falfhoods and groundlefs Traditions relating to *Abraham*, but the number of them would be fufficient to tire the Patience of the moft indefatigable Writers. For, what a Variety of Conjectures is there concerning the Motives of his Converfion [*A*]? What Exploits has he not been made to perform againft Idolatry [*B*], both

(*a*) It is, according to the Hebrew, 352 from the Deluge, and 2008 from the Creation.

(*b*) Genef. xi. 31.

(*c*) See the Article SARA.

(*d*) See the Article AGAR.

[*A*] *Concerning the Motives of his Converfion*] It is a common Opinion, that *Abraham* imbibed with his Milk the Poifon of Idolatry; and that *Terah* his Father made Statues, and taught that they were to be adored as Gods (1). The *Jews* fay, that *Abra- ham* for a long time followed the Craft of his Father *Terah* (2): That is, that he made and fold Idols. Others fay, that the Impiety, which reigned in this Country, confifting in the Adoration of the Sun, and Stars, *Abraham* was a long time entangled in this Mire. " Ipfum longo tempore Chaldæorum delirio " de Aftrorum divinitate innutritum fuiffe (3). ——— " He had been educated for a great while in the " Chaldæans fenfelefs Opinion of the Divinity of the " Stars." *Maimonides* lays it down as Matter of Fact, that *Abraham* was educated in the Religion of the *Zabians*, who acknowledged no other God but the Stars (4). He extricated himfelf from it, by the Reflexions he made on the Nature of the Stars. He admired their Motions, Beauty, and Order; but ob- ferved likewife their Imperfections; and concluded from thence, that there was a Being fuperior to the whole Machine of the World, an Author and Di- rector of the Univerfe. *Suidas* does well to cite *Philo*, to prove that *Abraham* arrived at the Know- ledge of God by thefe kind of Reflexions; but, when he reports, upon the Authority of the fame Author, that *Abraham*, from the Age of fourteen Years, was fo highly enlightened, as to have the Courage to fay to his Father *Terah*, *Renounce this pernicious Trade of Idolatry, with which you deceive the World*, this is not a confiftent Account of the long Idolatry of *Abraham*. It is certain, that *Jofe- phus*, without taking Notice that this Patriarch had been a long time infected with Idolatry, maintains, that by his own Genius, and by contemplating the Univerfe, he found out the Unity of God, and a Providence, and that he was the firft, who ventu- red to combat popular Error upon that Head (5). He met with an Oppofition fufficiently formidable to induce him to leave his Country. This is per- haps the firft Inftance of Banifhment for Religion's Sake. Upon this Footing, *Abraham*, under the Law of Nature, fhould be, with regard to this kind of Punifhment, what St *Stephen* was, under the Law of Grace, with regard to his Sufferings. He fhould be the Patriarch of the Refugees, no lefs than the Father of the Faithful. It cannot, I think, be denied, that his Father was an Idolater, fince the facred Scrip- ture, calling him by his Name, affures us of it (6); but all that can be inferred from thence is, that *Abraham*, before the Age of Difcretion, was of the

Religion of his Father. It is the inevitable Fate of Children to follow the Religion of thofe who edu- cate them. At fourteen Years of age, as *Suidas* re- lates, he made ufe of his Reafon: he perceived the Gulph, in which his Father was plunged, and he fled from it, in fuch a Manner, that, upon God's commanding him to leave his Country, *Terah* re- folved to accompany him. St *Epiphanius* relates, that *Abraham* having began in the Time of *Sarug*, Great-Uncle of the Patriarch *Abraham*, the Idols confifted only of flat Painting; and that *Terah* was the firft who made them of Clay (7).

[*B*] *What Exploits has he not been made to per- form againft Idolatry?*] I would not accufe *Philo* of contradicting himfelf; tho' we find him relating in one of his Works, that *Abraham* was a long time infected with the extravagant Opinions of the *Chal- dæans* (8); and in *Suidas*'s Dictionary, that *Abra- ham*, at the Age of fourteen Years, was fenfible of the Abfurdities of Idolatry: for what can be depen- ded upon, or what regard can be had to Numbers and Quotation from an Author, fo mutilated and corrupted, as *Suidas*? Perhaps he might have wrote not *fourteen*, but *fifty* Years. There is an old Tra- dition, which makes *Abraham* of this latter Age, when he left the Bofom of Idolatry. It is related (9), that his Father, having undertaken a Journey, intrufted him with the Sale of his Statues; and that a certain Perfon, pretending to buy, afked him *How old was he? Fifty Years old*, repli'd *Abraham*. *Wretch that thou art*, adds the other, *at the Age of Fifty, to adore a Being of yefterday!* This confounded *Abraham*. Some time after a Woman brought him fome Meal to offer to the Idols; inftead of which he took a Hatchet, and broke them to pieces, pla- cing the Hatchet afterwards in the Hand of the biggeft. *Terah*, upon his Return, demanded the Occafion of this Deftruction. *Abraham* anfwered him, that a Difpute arofe among the Idols, which of them fhould eat firft of an Offering, which a cer- tain Woman brought them; *upon which That God*, (fays he) *which is bigger than the reft, got up, and broke the others to pieces with a Hatchet*. *Terah* anfwered him, that he endeavoured to impofe upon him, and that thefe Idols could not perform fuch a thing. *Abraham* immediately retorted thefe Words of his Father againft the Worfhip of falfe Gods: but *Terah* did not underftand Rallery; he delivered up his Son to the Inquifition. *Nimrod*, the grand Inquifitor, as well as Conqueror, of the Country, exhorted *Abraham* to the Adoration of Fire: At laft, after many Anfwers and Replies on

both

(1) Sudias in Σαρυχ.

(2) *In Ge- nebrard's Chron.*

(3) *Philo in Salian*, Tom. 1. p. 387.

(4) Maim. More Ne- voc. c. 29. p. 3.

(5) Jofeph. Antiq. B. 1. c. 7. *See Ievv fe Re- cognit.* Clem. B. 1.

(6) *Your Fa- thers dwelt on the other Side of the Flood in old Time, even Terah, the Father of A- braham, and Nachor, and th y ferv'd o- ther Gods.* Jof. xxiv. 2.

(7) Epiph. Hæref. B. 14 p. 7, 8.

(8) Καλδαι- ωας μα- νικοι νιν αρχονον Chal. 1. jvng a long time. Philo of A- braham, p. 361.

(9) R.Mofes Hadar- khan in Be- reichet Rab- ba, *in Hei- degger's* Hift. Patr. Tom. 2. p. 36.

ABRAHAM.

both in *Chaldæa*, and the City of *Haran* [C]? How many Sciences [D], and how many Books [E] have not been attributed to him? The *Jews* ascribe to him the Privilege

both Sides, he ordered him to be thrown into the middle of the Flames, saying, *Let your God deliver you*. *Haran*, Brother of *Abraham*, waited impatiently for the Event, resolving in himself to follow the Party which got the better; to be of *Nimrod's* Religion, if *Abraham* was burnt, and of *Abraham's* Religion if he was not. *Abraham* came out whole and untouch'd from the middle of the Flames; and *Nimrod* thereupon having demanded of *Haran, in whom he believed*, and receiving this Answer, *I believe in the God of Abraham*, commanded him to be thrown into a Furnace. *Haran* was so roughly handled there, that he died soon after in the Presence of his Father (10). The Reason, why the Fire had such Power over him, was because his Faith was not so lively as that of *Abraham*, and that he was not predestinated to great Things, as *Abraham* was (11). This is by no means a new Tradition; for St *Jerom* reports it; and he seems even to adopt it, as far as relates to the miraculous Preservation of *Abraham* in the midst of the Fire (12): For, as to the superstitious Cruelty of *Terah*, in acting the Part of an Informer to the Holy Office against his own Son, he says nothing of it. St *Epiphanius*, who is likewise silent as to this Matter, maintains on the contrary, that *Terah* surviv'd *Haran*, as a Punishment for his Blasphemy in making Gods of Clay; and, that before him, no Father had ever seen his Children die a natural Death (13). The Ambiguity of the Word *Ur* (14), may have given Occasion to these Fables. Those, who lay a Stress on the Words of God to *Abraham, I am the Lord, that brought thee out of Ur of the Chaldees* (15), imagine that he saved him from some great Persecution, because he makes use of the same Phrase at the beginning of the *Decalogue*, to signify the Deliverance from *Egypt* (16). But this is to search for Mysteries unnecessarily. We meet with no Footsteps of this Persecution in Scripture; and therefore we may proportionably rank in the same Class of imaginary Notions the Fire, which did no Injury to *Abraham*, and that which *Maimonides* borrows from (17) a certain Treatise of the Agriculture of the *Egyptians*. We find there, that *Abraham*, having maintained in a public Dispute against the Idolaters, that *Fire* was not worthy of Divine Honours, was thrown into Prison, despoil'd of his Effects, and condemned to Banishment. The King was afraid, lest the Authority and Eloquence of so great a Man should convert his People from the Adoration of Fire. *Cedrenus* ascribes the Death of *Haran* to a very unlikely Cause; pretending that it was for endeavouring to snatch the Idols of *Terah* out of the Fire, which *Abraham* had thrown in. This Attempt must be vain, since he himself perished by the Flames.

[C] *And the City of* Haran.] It is pretended, that he became there a Converter; and that, whilst he was labouring to make Proselytes among the Men, *Sara* was doing the same among the Women (18); and that we must understand in this Sense the Words of *Genesis*, where it is said, that *Abraham* went out of *Haran*, with *Sara* his Wife, *Lot*, his Brother's Son, all the Riches they had acquired, and *all the Souls they had gotten* (19). They will not have us understand this of the getting of Children, but of propagating the Faith: And they confirm this Interpretation by a Metaphor, which the Apostle St *Paul* makes use of, at the 19th Verse of the 4th Chapter of his Epistle to the *Galatians*. *My little Children, of whom I am in travail again, until Christ be form'd in you*. It is more probable, that the Souls, which they had gotten, were the Slaves which they had purchas'd, together with the Children, who were born of these Slaves; not but that *Abraham*, without doubt, endeavour'd to instruct the Infidels, as far as his Zeal and his Prudence would permit him; and, if he converted any, they probably follow'd him into the Land of *Canaan*. There are, who think, that his Father did not serve false Gods, till after his arrival at *Haran* (21). But this seems absurd: for, as it is very probable, that (22) this Family abandon'd *Chaldæa*, to avoid a Persecution, which it had reason to fear, on account of it's deserting Idolatry; it would be very strange, if it's Head should not have been tainted with it, till in that very Country, to which they fled for Refuge. But the worship of Idols, of which *Abraham* had cur'd *Terah*, before they left their Country, might possibly revive in the Mind of the good old Gentleman: for, in those times of Ignorance, few Men had Strength enough to master their natural Inclination to Idolatry entirely. It is even believ'd, that *Nachor*, the third Son of *Terah*, was never quite converted, but that, however, he left his Country, in order to join his Father at *Haran* (23). Perhaps it might be he, who reviv'd the Veneration for Idols, in the Mind of the old Man, which *Abraham* had effac'd. It is certain that *Laban*, Grandson of this *Nachor*, was an Idolater. Some of the Fathers of the Church have thought, that *Terah* was neither a Believer in his Life time, nor at the point of Death. See the 31st, and 37th Homilies of St *Chrysostom*. How will they prove this? And how shall the contrary be proved to them? The History of *Abraham* is attended with numberless Difficulties, in which both Sides of the Question do not want for Reasons. But poor Father *Bolduc*, who believ'd that this Patriarch built Monasteries at *Haran*, and carry'd with him into *Palestine* only the youngest of the Monks (24), is not one of those, who can alledge any Reason for his Opinion.

[D] *How many Sciences*.] They say, he understood *Astronomy*. This is what *Berosus* relates of him, without naming him, if we may believe *Josephus* (25). Some will have it, that he taught Arithmetic and Astronomy to the *Egyptians*. *Josephus* affirms this (26); and *Nicolas Damascenus* would have confirm'd it, had he said that *Abraham* taught Geometry and Arithmetic to the *Egyptians*; but he says no such thing. Mr *Heidegger*, at the 144th Page of his second *Tome*, cites the 4th Book of *Nicolas Damascenus's* History, as if this were to be found there; but he mistakes the Words of *Josephus* for those of *Nicolas*, in the 16th Chapter of the 9th Book of *Eusebius's Præparatio Evangelica*. This Patriarch communicated Astronomy to the *Phœnicians*, and *Egyptians*, according to *Eupolemus*, and *Artapan* (27); but, after all, these Things are not Articles of Faith. The Authors, who attribute such sort of Things to him, weaken the Force of their own Testimony, by the Falshoods which they mix with them. One says, that *Abraham* reign'd at *Damas* (28); another, that he sojourn'd twenty Years in *Egypt*, with his whole Family, in the Court of King *Pharethon* (29); a third does him the Injustice to think, that the Motive of his Journey into *Egypt*, was a Desire to be acquainted with the Opinions of the *Egyptians*, concerning the Deity, with a Design of following them, if they were better than his own, or to undeceive that People, if their Belief was erroneous (30). Some Moderns think, that he did not teach Mathematics to the *Egyptians* (31); but, after that, the Reason they give appears to me to be false. They say, that the Detention of *Sara* by the King of *Egypt*, made *Abraham* so uneasy, that he was not capable of reading Lectures on such abstract Sciences as these, which, like Poetry, require ease and freedom of Mind:

Carmina secessum scribentis & otia quærunt.

From Noise and Care the Poet must be free.

But we must carefully observe, that *Josephus* has well distinguish'd the Times; he says that *Abraham's* Conference with the wise Men of *Egypt* was after the Restoration of *Sara*, and when he was contented in his Mind, as well on account of the Favours, which *Pharaoh* heap'd upon him, as because he was justify'd that his Wife had brought back her Honour untouch'd.

[E] *And how many Books*.] There is a Book of the Creation, which was for a long time ascrib'd to him (32). It is mention'd in the *Talmud* (33). The Rabins *Chanina* and *Hoschaia*, were accustom'd to read it on the Eve of the Sabbath. The Author of a Book, entituled *Cosri*, says, that this Work of *Abraham* is very profound, and stands in need of a long Interpretation; that it teaches the Unity of God; that, in one light, it seems to contradict itself, but, in another, that it is very consistent. But the *Jews* do not attribute this Book to this great Patriarch. Some of them declare loudly, that it is a spurious Work, and condemn the boldness of the Rabin *Aki-*

ABRAHAM. ABRAM.

vilege of having been born circumcis'd (e), and to have had the same Soul with *Adam* (f). They believe that this Soul belong'd afterward to *David*, and that it will be That of the *Messiah*, as Bartolocci remarks in his *Rabinical Dictionary*. The *Mahometans* likewise have related several idle Stories concerning this Patriarch, as may be seen in *Al-Koran*, and in one of their principal Authors, named *Kessæus*. They make him take a Journey to *Mecca*, and pretend, that he began there to build a Temple [F]. See the *Bibliotheque Orientale* of Mr d'*Herbelot*, from page the 12th to the 16th; we meet with many curious Particulars there. If we had the Book, which *Hecatæus* compos'd, about *Abraham* (g), we should perhaps see many things, which at present have never been heard of. The Christians resolv'd not to be the only Persons, who have invented no idle Stories concerning *Abraham*; they have made him plant Trees of a singular Virtue [G].

I shall here mention a few more of the Dreams of the Rabins. They say, that the *Egyptian* Bondage was a Punishment for some Faults which *Abraham* had committed; for he had constrained the *Disciples of Wisdom* to take up Arms, and had suffer'd Persons instructed in the Law of God to relapse into Idolatry. Thus they understand those Words of the Scripture, where it is said, *He arm'd his trained servants, which were ere born in his house, three hundred and eighteen* (b); and that he restor'd the Persons (i), which the King of *Sodom* demanded back (k). Father Bartolocci makes a great Bustle about this matter, but does not confute it well [H]. They say likewise, *first*, that the sight of a precious Stone, which hung about *Abraham*'s Neck, cur'd all Diseases; and that God hung this Stone in the Sun, after the Death of *Abraham* (l): *secondly*, That this Patriarch taught his Children Magic, whom he had by his Concubines (m).

ba, whom they look upon to be the real Author of the piece (34). "Quis dedit Potestatem Aquibæ "scribendi librum *Jezira*, nomine Abrahami Patris "nostri (35)? —— *Who gave Aquiba the Liberty of "writing the Book* Jezira, *under the Name of our "Father* Abraham ?" The Supplement to *Moreri* has a very curious Article upon this Subject, taken from the Critical History of Father *Simon*. Consult it, at Page 48, and 536, of the *Rotterdam* Edition. In the first Ages of Christianity, the Hereticks, the *Sethians*, vented an *Apocalypse* of *Abraham*, as St *Epiphanius* remarks (36). *Origen* has quoted a pretended Work of this Patriarch, in which a good and a bad Angel are introduc'd disputing concerning his Salvation, or Damnation (37). The Library of the Monastery of St *Croix*, upon Mount *Amara* in *Ethiopia*, contains, they say (39), the Books, which were compos'd by *Abraham*, in the Valley of *Mamre*, *where he taught Philosophy to those, by whose help he had defeated the five* (40) *Kings, who had taken Lot his Nephew*. The Work of the Creation was printed at *Paris*, in the Year 1552, translated into *Latin* by *Postel*, with Notes. *Rittangel*, a converted *Jew*, and Professor at *Konigsburg*, gave a *Latin* Translation of it, with Notes, in 1642 (41).

[F] *That he began there to build a Temple*.] They contend, that *Adam*, being driven from Paradice, begg'd of the good God, to permit him to build a House on the Plan of that which he had seen in Heaven; a House, I say, which might be a Place for him to direct his Prayers to, and about which he might march in Devotion. Upon which God let fall a Tent, resembling the House, which *Adam* had seen. *Adam* apply'd this Tent to the Uses he desir'd. After his Death, *Seth* built a House of Stone and Mud, upon this Model; the Deluge destroy'd it; but *Abraham* and *Ismael* rebuilt it, by the Order of God. Others successively repair'd it, in proportion as it fell to decay; and, at length, *Hejazus*, in the Year of the Hegira, 74, put it into the Condition it is now in; and it is the Oratory of the Temple of *Mecca* (42). *See the Remark* [I] *of the Article* AGAR.

[G] *Of a singular Virtue*.] Gretser testifies, that he read in a *Greek* Manuscript, in the Library of *Augsbourg*, that *Abraham* planted a *Cyprus*, a *Pine*, and a *Cedar*; which united themselves into one Tree, each, nevertheless, retaining it's proper Root and Branches: That this Tree was cut down, when they were preparing Materials for *Solomon*'s Temple; but that they could not possibly fit it to any Part: That *Solomon*, seeing this, resolved to make a Bench of it: that a *Sybil*, being brought thither, would not sit upon it; and prophecy'd that the Redeemer of Mankind should die triumphantly on this Wood: That *Solomon* encompassed it with thirty Crosses of Silver; and that it continued in this Situation 'till the Death of *Jesus Christ* (43). This puts me in mind of the Oak of *Mamre*, under which *Abraham* is said sometimes to have cooled himself. This Oak, they tell you, was standing in the Reign of *Constantius* (45). "*Drys, i. e.* Quercus Mambre "juxta Hebron, in quâ, usque ad ætatem infantiæ "meæ & Constantii regis imperium, terebynthus "monstrabatur pervetus, & annos magnitudine in- "dicans, sub quâ habitavit Abraham. Miro autem "cultu ab Ethnicis habita est, & velut quodam in- "signi nomine consecrata (46). —— *The Oak of "Mamre, near Hebron, where not many Years ago, "when I was a Child, and in the Reign of* Con- "stantius, *was shewed a Turpentine-Tree very old, "and declaring it's Age by it's Bulk; under which "*Abraham *dwelt. The Heathens have a surprising "Veneration for it, and distinguish it by some ho- "nourable Appellation*." And some have carried the Matter so far, as to say, that it has been seen within these three hundred Years. We must not they say, distinguish it from that *Reed of Seth*, which the Traveller *Mandeville* (a rare Evidence!) saw near the Town of *Hebron* (47).

[H] *But does not confute it well*.] He pretends that these Words of the King of *Sodom*, *Give me the Persons, and take the Goods to thyself* (48), signify in the literal and true Sense, *Suffer those, whom you have instructed in your Belief, to return to the Worship of Idols*; but that *Abraham* protested before the People, that he would not do it. The Author quotes the 22d, and 23d Verses of the 14th Chapter of *Genesis*; and then he accuses the *Talmudists* of Impudence and Blasphemy, in saying that the Patriarch agreed to the Request of the King of *Sodom*. He had reason to condemn them for supposing, that this Prince demanded back Persons converted to the true Religion; for he did not require the Domesticks of the Patriarch, but only those Subjects, whom the four Kings had taken in the Pillage of *Sodom* (49). But Father Bartolocci is greatly mistaken in supposing that *Abraham* did not restore them. What he quotes from Scripture is manifestly against him.

ABRAM (NICHOLAS), a *Lorrain* Jesuit, born in the Diocese of *Toul*, in the Year 1589, enter'd into the Society in 1606; and profess'd the fourth Vow in 1623. He was a polite Scholar; and appear'd to his Superiors so good a Divine, that he was raised to the Professorship of Divinity, in the University of *Pont-a-Mousson*. He exercised this Employ seventeen Years; and died the seventh of *September* 1655. He taught the *Belles Lettres*, before he enter'd upon the
Study

ABRAM. ABSTEMIUS.

Study of Divinity (a). He publish'd several Books [A]. It is something strange, that, being an Author of Distinction, he should be so little known in foreign Countries [B].

(a) Taken from Nathan. Sotuel's Bibl. Script. Societ. Jesu. p. 622.

[A] *He published several Books.*] *Notes on the Paraphrase of the Gospel of St John, compos'd in Greek Verse by Nonnus*: *A Commentary on some of Cicero's Orations*: *A Commentary on Virgil*: A Collection of Theological Tracts, entitled, *Pharus veteris Testamenti, sive sacrarum quæstionum, Libri XV*. *Maxims of a Christian Life* (1) and a *Hebrew Grammar in Latin* Verse. He translated into French, from the Italian of Bartoli, *The Life of* Vincent Caraffa, *The Man of Letters*, and *The Contented Poverty* (1). His Commentary on *Cicero* is a Work of great Labour; his Analysis of Logic is good and exact; the Notes are filled with much Learning; but as he has scattered with great Profusion the Fruits of his Lucubrations, he has fallen into a Prolixity, which is tiresome to the least lazy. This Commentary comprehends only the last Volume of Orations, as far as the *second Philippic* inclusively; and yet it is in two Volumes in Folio. They were printed at *Paris* in 1631. The Commentary on *Virgil* is much shorter; which makes it more useful for Schools. At the end of his *Pharus Veteris Testamenti*, a long Treatise of Truth and Falshood (2); in which he does not give into the Maxims of the rigid Casuists.

Mr *De la Monnoie* has informed me, First, That this Jesuit has supplied, in seventy one *Greek* Verses, after his manner, the *History of the Adulteress*, which was wanting to the eighth Chapter of *Nonnus*'s Paraphrase (3): Secondly, That *Reinesius* speaks of this *Nicolas Abram*, in the 155th Page of his *Letters to Hoffman and Rupert*. I have consulted that Place, and I find there this Elogium : " Si me " cum tot rationibus audire hic notes, vel hujus " (Nic A'brami) auctoritati cede. Est enim sane " quam doctissimus, & maxime idoneus explicando " Tullio.—*If you will not listen to these many Reasons* " *of mine, at least submit to the Authority of this* " *Author* (N. Abram). *For he is indeed a very* " *learned one, and the best qualified to explain Tully*."

(1) From Nathan. Sotuel. Bibl. Script. Soc. Jes. p. 622.

(2) Printed at Paris, in 1643, in Fol.

(3) It is an Error. Fr. Nanstus, who publish'd an Edition of Nonnus, in 1. 589, is the true Author of this Supplement. Mr de la Croze has inform'd me, that F. Simon speaks of it at the 310th Page of his Hist. Crit. of Commentators.

Add to this Testimony that of another learned Person of the same Country. " Ad intelligendas, atque " ad usum transferendas, Orationes Ciceronis sufficit " Commentarius Jo. Thomæ Freigii, nisi quis addere " malit prolixos Commentarios Nic. Abrami Jesuitæ, " multâ rerum varietate instructos (4). —— *The* " *Commentary of Jo. Thomas Freigius is sufficient* " *for the understanding and applying of* Cicero's " *Orations, unless any one chuses to add the long* " *Commentaries of* Nic. Abraham *the Jesuit, which* " *are fraught with a great Variety of Matter*."

[B] *So little known in foreign Countries.*] His Notes upon the Paraphrase of *Nonnus* were printed at *Paris*, for *Stephen Cramoisi*, in 1622; and it does not appear, that *Heinsius* had any Knowledge of them, when, in 1627. he published the same Paraphrase with a large Commentary. It is that, which he calls *Aristarchus sacer*. Neither had Mr *Cave* heard of this Jesuit's Notes, since he takes no Notice of them in that Passage, wherein he reckons up the several Editions of *Nonnus* (5). *Aubert le Mire* and Father *Oudin* are as silent concerning them: the one, in his *Auctarium de Scriptoribus Ecclesiasticis*, printed in 1639; the other, in his *Supplementum de Script. Ecclef.* printed in 1686. The Manner, in which Mr *Simon* often quotes this Work of Father *Abram* (6), shewed that he esteemed it, and that it is a Book, which does not deserve to be unknown. But there is something still more remarkable. *Martin Schoockius*, whose principal Employ was an immense and prodigious Reading, declared in his old Age, that he had never before heard of such an Author, as *Nic. Abram*. " Hanc si tuitus fuisset nescio quis " Nic. Abramus (jam primitus eum nosse incipio) " prolixo examine haud opus fuisset (7). —— *Had* " *one* Nic. Abram *(this is the first time I ever* " *heard of him) seen this, it would not have stood* " *in need of a long Discussion.*"

(4) J. And. Bosius, de Prudentia & Eloquentia comparandâ, p. 400.

(5) Hist. Liter. p. 290. London Edit. in 1688, in Folio.

(6) Hist. Crit. of the New Testament, ch. 23.

(7) Sch. de Fænore unciario, p. 1074, printed in 1668.

ABSTEMIUS (LAURENCE) born at *Macerata*, in the Territory of *Ancona*, apply'd himself to the Study of the *Belles Lettres*, and made a considerable Progress therein. He taught them at *Urbin*, and was Librarian there to the Duke of *Guido Ubalde* (a); to whom he dedicated a little Book, in which he explain'd some difficult Passages of Antient Authors (b). It was in the Pontificat of *Alexander* VI. that he publish'd this Work; and another entitled *Hecatomythium*, dedicated to *Octavianus U-baldini*, Count of *Mercatello*. The reason of this Title was, that the Work was a Collection of an hundred Fables. In the Sequel to it he doubled the Number. They have been frequently printed [A] with those of the Antient Fabulists, *Esop*, *Phædrus*, *Gabrias*, *Avienus*, &c. which *Nevelet* has collected in a body with Notes. Abstemius did not always confine himself to an Imitation of those Antient Originals; he mixes sometimes among his Fables some Droll Tale, and does not always spare the Clergy [B]. We meet with his Conjectures on some Passages of the Antients in the first Volume of *Gruterus*'s *Critical Thesaurus*; we meet with them, I say, under the Title of *Various Annotations*. They are but few in Number, and fill but 15 Pages. There is a Preface of his at the beginning of *Aurelius Victor*, in 1505 (c). I know not whether he surviv'd this Edition long. He is one of those, whom *Laurentius Valla* has censur'd.

Take notice of the Remarks communicated to me [C] since the first Edition.

(a) See Crinter's Thes. Crit. Tom. 1. p. 878.

(b) Opusculum de Nonnullis locis obscuris. See the Ep. to dedicatory of his Hecatomythium.

(c) Epist. Bibl. Gessner ii.

[A] *They have been frequently printed.*] Gesner takes notice of the Edition of *Strasbourgh* in 1522. That, which *Nevelet* made use of, is more modern by eighty eight Years. The Notes, which he has added to it, are but few : and certainly it is not for their sake, that the Impression has been so often repeated. He wrote none upon *Abstemius*'s Fables; as they wanted none.

[B] *And does not always spare the Clergy.*] The following is a Proof of it. The 104th Fable is this: A certain Priest was intrusted by his Bishop with the Care of a Convent, where there were five Nuns, by each of which he had a Boy at the Year's end. The Bishop, hearing this News, was in a great Passion, sent for the Priest, chid him severely, and called him Traytor, and a sacrilegious Wretch, for daring to defile the Temple of the Holy Ghost. *My Lord*, says he, *you intrusted me with five Talents; and lo, I have gained five others*. The Bishop was so well pleased with this facetious Reply, that he gave the Priest full Absolution. The Moral, which the Author has laid down at the end of the Fable, is no better than the Fable itself, in respect of the like Profanation of Scripture. *When we cannot justify an ill Action* (says he) *with good Reasons, we must turn it off with a Jest* (1). It is certain this has often succeeded : but a Bishop, who should excuse such a Profanation as this for it's Pleasantry, would not do his Duty much better, than the Guardian of the five Nuns.

[C] *The Remarks communicated to me.*] " The " Conjectures of *Abstemius*, inserted in the first Vo- " lume of the *Thes. Crit. of Gruter*, are only an " Extract of a Work, entitled *Observorum locorum* " (2), dedicated to the Duke of *Urbins*. Gruter, " who has given us this Extract, has placed at the " beginning a little marginal Note, in which he " says, that *Laurentius Valla* had criticis'd upon " *Abstemius*.

(1) Fabula indicat, peccata, cum ratione nequeant, urbanitate diluenda. *Abstem. Fab. CIV.*

(2) See the Quotation (b) of this Article.

ABUCARAS. ABUDHAHER.

" *Abstemius*. I doubt much of the Truth of this; there not occurring any Footsteps of this pretended Criticism in the Works of *Laurentius Valla*, whom besides *Abstemius* has greatly praised in the Preface to his second *Hecatomythium*, and with whom he could not have much Contention, as he surviv'd him at least forty eight Years. He is the first, I believe, who wrote the Fable of the *Multiply'd Talents*. *Le Bandel*, *Verville*, and others, have related it after him." This is taken from a Letter sent me by Mr *De la Monnoie*.

ABUCARAS (THEODORE) was a Prelate [*A*] very zealous for Orthodoxy, which he shew'd in more than forty Dissertations which he wrote, either against the *Jews* or the *Mahometans*, or the *Hereticks*, or in general on Religious Subjects. *Genebrard* translated into Latin, and publish'd, fifteen of these Dissertations. *Gretser*, adding these to the rest [*B*] which Father *Turrien*, or himself, had translated, publish'd an Edition, which seem'd complete (*a*). But he forgat something; for Mr *Arnold* printed at *Paris*, in 1685, a Treatise by *Abucaras*, which had never yet appeared from the Press. He found it in the *Oxford* Library. He did not accompany it with Notes, not daring to meddle with the grand Mysteries, which the Author examines in that Treatise (*b*): viz. the Incarnation, and the Hypostatical Union. It is uncertain when *Abucaras* liv'd. The Jesuit *Turrien* believes he was the Disciple of *Johannes Damascenus*. This places him in the VIIth Century. *Gretser* places him a little earlier [*C*], not distinguishing him from that *Abucaras*, who was so far engaged in the Troubles of the Church of *Constantinople*, in the Time of the Patriarch *Ignatius* and of *Photius*. This *Abucaras* followed the Party of *Photius*, and undertook to go upon an Embassy for him, with *Zachary*, Bishop of *Chalcedon*, to the Court of the Emperor *Lewis* II. His Business was to present to this Prince the Book, which *Photius* had composed against Pope *Nicolas*, and to exhort him to shake off the Pope's Yoke. But he had scarce began his Journey, when *Basilus* the Macedonian, who had usurp'd the Empire, after having murthur'd the Emperor *Michel*, recalled him, and commanded him to stir no farther in the Affair. Two Years after (*c*) he appeared before the Council of *Constantinople*, and humbly begg'd Pardon for having been in the Interests of *Photius*, and protested that he was drawn in to espouse them by Violence and Artifice. He gained his Ends: the Patriarch reconciled him to the Church, and gave him a Place in the Assembly (*d*). Mr *Arnold* was acquainted with a learned Man in *England*, who believed that *Abucaras* liv'd in the VIIth Century (*e*). The Works of this Author were inserted in the Supplement to the *Paris* Edition of the Collection of the Fathers, in 1624.

(*a*) It is in Greek and Latin, and printed at Ingolstad, in 1606, in 4to.
(*b*) Arnold's Preface.
(*c*) Ibid.
(*d*) Nicet. Paphlag. in the Life of Ignatius, in Cave's Hist. Liter. p. 557.
(*e*) In 869.

(1) Cave's Histor. Liter. p. 557. Oudin's Supplement, p. 250.
(2) Spizelius's Specim. Bibl. Konigius's Bibl. vet. & nov. and Arnold's Preface.
(3) Simler's Epit. Bibl. Gesn.

[*A*] *A Prelate*.] Some stile him *Archbishop of Caria* (1), others *Episcopum Cariæ*, Καρῶν Ἐπίσκοπον, Bishop of *Caria* (2). Mr *Arnold* thinks, that *Abucaras* was Bishop of *Charron* in *Mesopotamia*: this was likewise the Opinion of *Josias Simler* (3). *Photius* had designed him for the Bishoprick of *Laodicea*, as Mr *Cave* observes.

[*B*] *Gretser, adding these to the rest*.] The *Journal des Savans* gives us a wrong Notion of this Jesuit's Edition. *Genebrard* (say they) had translated and published fifteen Dissertations of this Author, and *Gretser* had added them to his Collection of the Works of *Anastasius* the Sinaite, in two Manuscripts in the *Bavarian* Library. Had they understood the Latin of Mr *Arnold*, they would not have been guilty of this Mistake. "Theodori Abucaræ Dissertationes quindecim jam diu Latine vertit & edidit Genebrardus, deinde Theodorum Anastasio Sinaitæ ob argumenti similitudinem conjunxit Jacobus Gretserus, deditque ex duobus codicibus Manuscriptis Ducis Bavariæ Maximiliani.——— Genebrard had, some time before, translated into Latin, and published fifteen Dissertations of Theodorus Abucaras; afterward Jacob Gretser joined Theodorus with Anastasius the Sinaite, on account of the Resemblance between their Subjects, and published them from two Manuscripts of Maximilian Duke of Bavaria (5)." There are three Particulars in this Passage: First, That *Gretser* publish'd the Works of *Abucaras*, after the Publication of fifteen of the Pieces by *Genebrard*; Second, That *Gretser* published them from two Manuscripts of the Duke of *Bavaria*; Third, That he joined them with *Anastasius* the Sinaite. There is nothing of all this in the *Journal de Savans*. We are not there told, that *Gretser* published more Pieces than *Genebrard*, nor that the *Bavarian* Manuscripts were assisting to the Editions of *Abucaras*: it only says, that they were of use to the Edition of *Anastasius*, of which Mr *Arnold* made no mention. Farther, we must not imagine, that all the Works of *Anastasius* the Sinaite were published with *Theodore Abucaras*: there is only the Treatise, entitled Ὁδηγος, *The Guide*, added to the Works of *Abucaras*, in *Gretser's* Edition.

[*C*] *Gretser places him a little earlier*.] In reading Mr *Arnold's* Preface, one is almost convinc'd, that this Jesuit did not dare to advance any thing concerning the Age of *Abucaras*. "Gretserus vero, quis fuerit Abucaras, quo sæculo floruerit, ab Antonio Velfero, S. S. Theol. D. Ecclesiæ Frisingensis Canonico, Præposito Spaltensi, cujus honori librum suum dedicavit, discere volebat (6).——— *But Gretser desired to be inform'd, who Abucaras was, and when he flourish'd, from Antony Velferus, Doctor of Divinity, Canon of the Church of Frisingen, and Provost of Spalta, to whose Honour he dedicates his Book*." Mr *Arnold*, by saying nothing more of *Gretser*, plainly insinuates, that we need look no further in the Preface of this Jesuit. But we find it otherwise: namely, that *Abucaras*, whom he mentions in the Life of St *Ignatius*, Patriarch of *Constantinople*, is the same who compos'd the Dissertations.

(5) Arnold's Preface.
(6) Arnold's Preface.

ABUDHAHER. It is the Name of the Chief of the *Karmatians* [*A*], under whose Conduct they profaned and laid waste *Mecca*, in the Year of the *Hegira*

(1) According to us, the Year 891.

[*A*] *The Karmatians*.] It is the Name of a Sect, which rose in *Arabia*, about the Year of the *Hegira* 278 (1). The first Head of this Sect was a Blasphemer, and an Impostor; who, drawing to his Party those among the Inhabitants of the Fields and Desarts, who had least Religion, gain'd an absolute command over them. We meet with several Etymologies of the Name *Karmatians*, in *Pocock* (2). The Sect was but small at first; but it made an incredible Progress. They possess'd themselves of the greatest Part of the Provinces of *Eraki*, and *Hejazi*; and spread themselves over *Syria*, and as far as the Gates of *Grand Cairo* (3).

(2) Pocock's Notes on Specim. Hist. Arab. p. 371. *This Specimen was printed at Oxford in 1650.*
(3) Ibid.

ABUDHAHER, ABULFEDA.

Hegira [B] 317. They robb'd the Pilgrims, and murther'd 1700 of them, within the very Walls of the *Caaba* (a) whilst these poor superstitious Wretches were marching round this sacred Oratory, as their Form of Prayer directed them. The *Karmatians* were not satisfy'd with this Slaughter; they carry'd away out of the Temple a piece of black Marble, which was had in Veneration there, as a Present from Heaven (b); they pull'd down the Gate of the Temple, and fill'd the Pits *Zamzam*, one of the most sacred parts of the Place, with the dead Bodies. To encrease the Calamity, *Abudbaher* affronted the *Mahometan* Religion many ways; he led his Horse to the Entrance of the *Caaba*, that he might lay his Dung there; and he told the *Mahometans*, they were Fools to call that Building by the Name of God's House; for, added he, *if God had any regard to this Temple, he would have immediately crush'd me with a Thunder-bolt for profaning his House in so outrageous a manner* [C]. The Veneration of the *Mahometans* for this Temple was not lessen'd upon that Account: they continu'd to go in Pilgrimage thither every Year. When the *Karmatians* were inform'd of this, they determin'd to send back the black Marble, which they had kept twenty-two Years. Some time after they rallied the Folly of their Devotions: *This People*, said they, *believe they are in possession of the black Marble: but we sent them another in it's room: the Object therefore of their Veneration is a false and suppositious Being.* They had a more important Design [D] in these Words, than the bare Pleasure of an Insult. They receiv'd for answer, that they need only be witness of the Proof, and that, if the Stone swam upon Water, they might be convinc'd it was genuine. Accordingly it did float in the presence of the *Karmatians*; and by this means all those Doubts and Scruples, which the jesting of these prophane Wretches might raise, were remov'd (c). This is a little Specimen of the Legends of the Eastern People. You will meet with many curious Particulars relating to *Abudbaher*, and the *Karmatians*, in the Oriental Dictionary of Mr *d'Herbelot* (d). He calls them *Carmathians*, and he writes the Name of their Cheif *Abu-Thaher*.

(a) The Name of a Part of the Temple design'd for A-dration and Prayer.
(b) See the Reward [K] of the Attack on the AGAR.
(c) Pocock's Notes upon Spec. Hist. Arab. p. 118, 119. from Abulfeda, and Ebn Yusef.
(d) In the Article CARMATH, p. 256, &c.

[B] *The Year of the* Hegira, 317.] *Abulfeda*, and *Ahmed Ebn Yusef*, point out this Year; and say, that the Stone was not recover'd, till 339: But *Saffioddin* shortens the Time: he places this carrying away of the Stone in the Year 319, and the Restitution of it, in 335 (4).
[C] *In so outrageous a Manner.*] *Ahmed Ebn Yusef* says, that the *Mahometan* Religion never suffered a Calamity comparable to that (5).
[D] *A more important Design.*] They were in Hopes of inviting the Caravans of Pilgrims to them; imagining, that these good People would go where the Stone was kept. This is the Reason, why they would not accept of a Ransom for it: they were deaf to Prayers and Promises. But, finding that *Mecca* was as much frequented as ever, and that no one came to pay their Devotions to the Stone, which they preserv'd, they returned it. To this they did, with a Reserve of some Right in it to themselves; for, when they gave it out that they had returned only a counterfeit Stone, they intended without doubt to raise Scruples in Mens Minds, and to share the Pilgrimages, at least, sooner or later. The People of *Mecca* foresaw the Consequence; and thought proper to give it out, that the Stone had been put to the Proof, and it's Genuineness confirmed.

(4) Pocock's Notes upon Specim. Hist. Arab. p. 119.
(5) Ibid.

ABULFEDA, (ISMAEL) Prince of *Hamah*, a City of *Syria*, succeeded his Brother, in the Year of the *Hegira*, 743 [A], which answers to the Year of *Christ* 1342, and died three Years after, at about the Age of 72 Years (a). He was a Lover of Study, and particularly that of Geography, as may be gathered from a Work entitled, *Chorasmiæ & Mawaralnabræ, hoc est, Regionum extra fluvium Oxum descriptio, ex tabulis Abulfedæ Ismaëlis, Principis Hamah*; i. e. *A Description of Chorasmia, and Mawaralnahre, or the Regions beyond the River Oxus, from the Tables of* Abulfeda Ismaël, *Prince of* Hamah (b). It was printed at *London* in 1650. The Author quotes a great many *Arabian* Writers. It was compos'd long before he ascended the Throne; for it is remark'd at the end of the Book, that it was finish'd in the Year of the *Hegira* 721, which is the 1321 of *Christ*. We are oblig'd to the learned *John Gravius* for the *London* Edition. He added to the Original, which is in *Arabic*, a Latin Translation, and a Preface, in which he informs us, that he consulted five different Manuscripts;

(a) Pocock in his Notes on Specim. Hist. Arab. p. 363. says that he was born in the Year of the Hegira 672.
(b) The Arabic Title signifies Canones, or rather Rectificatio Terrarum, according to Gravius. For which reason Konig was not in the wrong to say that Abulfeda wrote a Geographical Work entitled Directorium Regionum.

[A]-*The Year of the* Hegira 743.] This we are assured of from the *Arabian* Author of a Book entitled *Al Sacerdan* (1). Therefore the Jesuit *Blancanus* was mistaken, when he places *Abulfeda* in the IVth Century of Christianity (2). This Error ought to have led him from another Mistake, in giving this Geographer the Title of *Prince of Syria, Assyria,* and *Persia.* A little Attention might have shewn him, that an *Arabian* Author and a *Mahometan* could not be King of *Persia* 400 Years after *Christ*. *Vossius*, having related the Opinion of *Blancanus*, is content to say, that *Abulfeda* was not so antient by a great deal: but, for the rest, he allows him the Style and Title of Prince of *Syria, Assyria,* and *Persia* (3). He comes pretty near the Truth, as to his Chronology; when he says that it is three hundred Years since *Abulfeda* flourished (4). Instead of this, Mr *Moreri* charges him with believing, as *Blancanus* did, that this Prince of *Syria* liv'd in the IIId or IVth Century: But it is certain, adds Mr *Moreri*, that he lived much later; perhaps in the VIIIth or IXth, or even in the Year 1200. He might have omitted the Word *perhaps*: he might have asserted, that he liv'd in the XIVth Century; since his Work was finished in the 721st Year of the *Hegira*, as is declared at the end of it. There is a false Print in the *Dutch* Edition of *Moreri* in this Place. They make *J. Gravius* say, that our *Abulfeda* lived in the beginning of the XIIIth Century; and yet he has placed the Death of this Prince in 1345. What I am most concerned at is, that the learned *E. Pocock* asserts, that *Abulfeda* took possession of the Government of the Province of *Hamah*, in the 710th Year of the *Hegira* (5). This cannot be reconciled with what *J. Gravius* has ascertained. It is more reasonable to depend upon this latter, than the other, because *Abulfeda* is *Gravius*'s principal Subject; whereas *Pocock* speaks of him only by way of a short Digression. But is't not very hard, that we cannot depend upon Men of such great Abilities in the Eastern Learning, as *Pocock*; and that at the same time that they publish any thing, one of their Colleagues shall shew the Falseness of it?

(1) Gravius's Preface.
(2) He calls him Abilfeda in his Chronol. Mathem.
(3) Vossius de Mathem. Discipl. p. 250.
(4) He calls him Abifeldeas, and Abelfedeas. See the Epitom. Bibl. Gesn.
(5) Pocock's Notes on Specim. Hist. Arab.

VOL. I.   N   [B] *Me*

ABULFEDA. ABULPHARAGE.

nuscripts; the first is *Erpenius*'s Transcript from the Copy in the *Palatine* Library; the second is the same Copy, which is now in the *Vatican*; two others belong'd to *Pocock*; the fifth was bought at *Constantinople*. We learn farther in this Preface, that *Ramusius* is the first, who commended this Work of *Abulfeda*, and pointed out the Use of it; that afterward *Castaldus* made use of it to correct the Longitudes and Latitudes of several Places; that *Ortelius* often mentions it in his *Thesaurus Geographicus*, not as having seen it, but upon the Authority of *Castaldus*; that *Erpenius*, out of concern that no one had given it to the World, resolv'd to publish it, and would have done it, if Death had not taken him off in the middle of his Design; that *Schickard* was the first, who borrow'd from it several Remarks of profound Learning, and 'till then unknown, which he inserted in his *Tarich Persicum*: but as the Copy belonging to the Imperial Library, which was lent him by *Tengnagelius*, was not legible in several Places, he left the greatest part of the Pains and the Honour to *John Gravius* (c). It is surprizing, that Mr *Moreri* cou'd heap together so many Mistakes in one Article [*B*], as he has done in this of *Abulfeda*. *Spizelius* did not know in 1668; nor *Konig* in 1678, that *Abulfeda* had been in *England* (d).

(c) *It follows from hence, that Fabricius, in his Specimen. Ling. Arab. p. 99. was wrong in saying, in Konig, that Schickard had translated into Latin a Work of Abulfeda. Spizelius in his Specim. Bibl. cites the same Fabricius, as saying, that Schickard had translated all that Work.*

(d) *Spizel. Specim. Bibl. Univ.*

[*B*] *Mr Moreri could heap together so many Mistakes in one Article.*] We have already seen some of them. The rest are as follows. First, When he says, that some are of Opinion, that *Abulfeda* was of *Nubia*, he manifestly confounds him with the Author of the *Geographia Nubiensis*, of whom we shall treat in his proper Place. At least, he betrays his Ignorance that these two Authors ought to be distinguished; for, had he known it, he would not have related this Opinion, and let it pass uncensured. Secondly, He confirms this first Observation, by adding that *Abulfeda disposed his Geography into Climates*. This agrees better with the Author of *Geographia Nubiensis* than with *Abulfeda*. This latter has given us only a Description of some Parts of *Asia*, situated beyond the *Oxus*, which he places under the 25th and 26th Climates. The *Nubian* Geography is disposed in a very different Manner. It makes but seven Climates, and adheres to this Division of the Antients; referring all the Description it gives of the known World to That. Let me observe by the way, that *Abulfeda* fixes his *first Climate* in *Arabia*, and not, as the *Nubian* Geography does, on the most western Coast of the *Atlantic* Ocean; and that his *first Meridian* passes thro' Cape St *Vincent*. Thirdly; *We have seen*, says Mr *Moreri*, at present, but the first Climates of Abulfeda; *we are put in Hopes of the remaining ones this Year*: This is a downright Falshood: what is published of *Abulfeda* relates not to the first Climates, but to the 25th and 26th. Fourthly; An Author should not make use of so indeterminate a Phrase as *This Year*; for his Reader, at the end of ten Years, will not know what Year he means; he must have recourse to the Date of the first Impression: this is to be met with but in few Books: and, where it is to be found, it is not always a good Guide, since there often pass many Years between the Composition and the Publication of a Book. This is an Instance of the Difficulty, into which a Reader is led by the Expression *this Year*. Where is the Person, who, in reading *Moreri*, can guess in what Year the other Climates of *Abulfeda* were promised? It is a very long Year; it has reigned to the sixth Edition inclusively. Fifthly, William *Postel was the first who brought this Work into Europe, of which he published an Abridgment in Latin*. Here are two new Errors of *Moreri*. *Simler* is the only Author he quotes, who has any Relation to this. But all that *Simler* says, is, that *Postel*, having brought this Work from the East, left an Abridgment of it, which he had translated at *Venice*, with *Ramusius* (6), who had a Design of publishing the second Tome of his *New World*. There is a great deal of Difference between bringing a Book from the East, and being the first who brought it from thence; between publishing a Book, and leaving the Manuscript for another's Use. It is certain, that *Ramusius* did not publish what *Postel* left with him; and if it be true, that *Abulfeda*, which was in *Arabic* in the *Palatine* Library, as *Moreri* observes, had been brought into *Europe* by *Postel*, and that this was the first Copy we had in the West, this does not acquit Mr *Moreri* of ascribing more to Authors than they really say; and we have reason to complain of such Falsifications. They deserve to be particularly censured.

(6) *Simler calls him Rhamnusius by Mistake; and Spizelius the same.*

ABULPHARAGE (GREGORY) the Son of a Physician named *Aaron*, was himself likewise a Physician, and acquired a great Reputation in this Art; insomuch that they came to consult him from the most distant Countries. He was of *Malatia* [*A*], near the *Euphrates*, and would at this time have been but little known, had he confin'd himself to the Knowledge of Medicine: but he understood History; and there is a Work of this kind, after his manner, still extant, which does honour to his Memory. Not that our Age judges so favourably of it, as the Eastern People do. They are extravagant in their Commendations, either because they have but few truly learned Men among them, or because it is to their Taste. However that be, there are an hundred Historians in the *West*, whose Compositions are not inferior to those of *Abulpharage*, whom no one has yet thought fit to dignify with such Titles, as are given him [*B*]. He liv'd at the end of the XIIIth Century, and profess'd Christianity

[*A*] *He was of Malatia.*] I have in vain looked for this Town in *Pocock*'s Prefaces, in *Ortelius*'s Thesaurus, and Mr *Baudrand*'s Geography. But Chance has been more favourable to me than Enquiry; for in turning over, with other Views, that which is called the *Nubian Geography*, I found; that *Malatia* is a fortified Town, fifty one Miles from *Samosata*, towards the Source of *Euphrates* (1).

Mr *Baudrand* has informed me, that he mentions this Town under the Word *Melitin* and *Meliterie*. It is true: he places it in *lesser Armenia*, upon the *Euphrates*, and says, it is called at present *Malatiah*.

[*B*] *Such Titles, as are given to him.*] Pocock met with this Passage at the beginning of a Copy of *Abulpharage*, wrote in the 900th Year of the *Hegira*:

(1) Geogr. Nub. Clim. 4. p. 5, & 197.

" Dixit Dominus noster, Pater Sanctus, eximius,
" doctrinâ & eruditione insignis, doctorum Rex,
" excellentiam excellentissimus, temporum suorum
" exemplar, fæculi Phœnix, sapientium Gloria, Doctor
" divinâ ope fultus, Mar. Gregorius Abulpharai, fi-
" lius excellenter sapientis Aaronis, Medici Mala-
" tiensis. —— *These are the Words of Mar Gregory*
" *Abulpharai, (Son of the excellently-wise Ahron,*
" *Physician of Malatia) our Lord, and Holy Father,*
" *most excellent of the Excellent, famous for Learn-*
" *ing and Knowledge, King of the Learned, Pattern*
" *of his Times, Phœnix of the Age, Glory of the*
" *Wise, a Teacher favoured by Heaven.*" At the end of another Copy he met with the following: " Pater
" & Dominus noster, Rex doctorum, & corona vi-
" rorum

ABULPHARAGE. ABUMUSLIMUS. 51

Christianity [C]. This did not hinder several Mahometans from studying under him [D]. The current Report of his abjuring his Religion, when he found himself near Death, ought to be rank'd among the numberless Fables of this kind, which are rais'd among all Sects [E]. He has divided the History, which he compos'd in in *Arabic*, into *Dynasties*. It is an Abridgment of *Universal History* from the beginning of the World to his own Time. The Division consists of ten Parts. The Subjects of each may be seen in the Supplement to *Moreri*. *Edward Pocock* (a) publish'd this Book of *Abulpharage*, with a *Latin* Translation, in 1663. He added to it a Supplement, which contains a short Sequel to this History with regard to the Eastern Princes. He had before publish'd, in 1650, a short Extract from the ninth *Dynasty* of this Author, with many learned Notes. The Title of it is, *Specimen Historiæ Arabum, sive Gregorii Abul Farajii, Malatiensis, de Origine & Moribus Arabum succincta Narratio*: i.e. *A Specimen of the Arabic History, or a succinct Relation of the Origin and Manners of the Arabians*, by Abulpharage, of Malatia. *Abulpharage* could not be so exact in the Affairs of the *Greeks* and *Romans*, as those of the *Saracens* and *Tartar-Moguls*. This latter piece is the best of the Work. It relates, in a very instructive and credible manner, the prodigious Conquests of *Zingis-Cham*. All that *Abraham Zacuth* says of them, in his *Juchasin*, is stoln, together with other Matters, from the History of *Abulpharage*. We cannot guess why *Abraham Ecchellensis* (b) gives our Author the Name of *Gregorius Bar Hebræus Syrus* (c) [F].

(a) *Regius Professor of Hebrew at Oxford, and Arabic Lecturer.*

(b) *Pref. Mision. Hauynu'r turc. Paris.*

(c) *Pocock's Præfatio.*

" rorum virtute præstantiam, dubiorum in Theolo-
" gicis occultorum 'Evaoterns, Christianorum Prin-
" ceps primarius, sectæ Jacobiticæ Medulla, Mar.
" Gregorius, dominus, Pater, unicum ævi decus, &
" sæculi Phœnix. ——— *Our Lord and Father, King*
" *of the Learned, and Crown of the Virtuous, Solver*
" *of Doubts in Divinity, Chief Head of the Christians,*
" *Marrow of the Jacobite Sect,* Mar. Gregory, *Lord,*
" *Father, sole Glory of the Age, and Phœnix of the*
" *Times.*" Add to these what he met with at the beginning of a *Syriac* Grammar, composed by this Author: " Pater noster sanctus, Rex Doctorum,
" Mar. Gregorius, Doctor Orientis, qui idem est
" Abul-Pharaj, filius Ahronis, Medici Militiniensis,
" i. e. Malatiensis.

(1) *Pocock's Præf. to Specimen. Hist. Arab.*

[C] *Professed Christianity.*] He was, we see, of the Sect of the *Jacobites*. This is more probable, according to *Pocock*, than what a learned *Jew* has advanced, that *Abulpharage* was of the Sect of the *Melchites*. " Cui potius fidem habemus, quam docto
" cuidam Judæo, qui eum vocat Ebnol Koff, Chri-
" stianum Malatieniem, sectæ Melchitum (2).

(2) *Pocock's Præf. to Compend. Dynast.*

[D] *This did not hinder many Mahometans from studying under him.*] One of *Pocock's* Copies contains these Words of a Mahometan: " Author Libri est
" Abul-Pharaj Ebn Hocima, vir multæ lectionis va-
" riisque Scientiis instructus, & penitus imbutus,
" præcipue autem medicinæ gloriâ sæculo suo clarus,
" adeo ut ad eum de plagis Orientalibus frequentes con-
" tenderent. Christianus erat, à quo tamen didice-
" runt multi è Muslemorum eximiè docti. Ferunt
" ipsum morti propinquum à fide Christianâ desci-
" visse. *The Author of the Book is* Abul-Pharaj
" Ebn Hocima, *a Man of great Reading, and tho-
" roughly vers'd in many Sciences, but particularly
" famous in his Time for his Skill in Physic; inso-
" much that People came in Crouds to him from the
" Eastern Countries. He was a Christian; and yet
" many of the learned Mussulmen were his Disciples.
" He is reported to have renounced the Christian
" Faith, when he was near Death.* Ebn Chalecan, a famous Author, who wrote the Lives of Illustrious Men, was the Writer of these Words, if we may believe the Remark written by another Hand in the same Place of the Copy (3).

[E] *Which are raised among all Sects.*] We have mentioned the Report concerning the last Hours of *Abulpharage*. The *Mahometans* could scarce believe, that so great a Man was inwardly a Christian; they chose rather to think, that he concealed his real Sentiments, 'till the Approach of Death put an end

to his Reasons for dissembling them. This Prejudice universally prevails. Every one imagines, that the Truths of his Religion are so clear, that the Men of Genius of another Party cannot but be convinced of them; and that it is only worldly Motives which prevent their making an open Profession of them. They flatter themselves, that at the fatal Hour, when the eternal Doom affects the Mind most strongly, these Dissemblers will give Truth the Glory, and throw aside the Mask.

Dii longæ noctis, quorum jam numina nobis
Mors instans majora facit (4)!

Ye Deities of everlasting Night,
Whose Forms, in Death, rise larger to the Sight?

For, according to *Lucretius*,

——— Veræ voces tum demum pectore ab imo
Ejiciuntur, & eripitur persona manet Res (5).

Truth then breaks forth, extorted by our Fears,
And all the Man, without Disguise, appears.

It is from this wrong Principle so many idle Stories arise, which are inserted in *Moreri's* Dictionary, relating to *Peter du Moulin, Joseph Scaliger*, &c. It is likewise the Source of I know not how many Discourses, in which certain Persons are made to say, *The Religion I profess is the best for this World, but not in the Article of Death.* See the Remark [DD] of the Article MAHOMET.

(4) *Dido in Sulius Italic. lib. 8. v. 740.*

(5) *Lucret. lib. 3. ver. 57.*

[F] *The Name of* Gregorius Bar Hebræus Syrus.] Upon this Occasion, I shall make this short Remark. *Pocock* repeats two Passages, in which our Author is named *Mar Gregorius*, and one, in which he is called *Mar Gregorius*; he makes no Reflexion upon the first of these Names; he never says, that *Abulpharage* was called *Marc*. Upon which I say, the Supplement to *Moreri* must be mistaken, in saying that the Name of this Author was *Marc Gregory*. The Word *Mar*, which is a Title of Honour as *Mr* in our Language, might be mistaken for the Christian Name *Marc*. I observe the same Fault in the *Perpetuity of the Faith defended* (6); the Patriarch of *Babylon*, who reunited himself to the Church of *Rome*, under Pope *Paul* V. is there styl'd *Marc Elias*; but the Author, cited for it, calls him *Mar Elias* (7).

(6) *B. 5. c. 10.*

(7) *Petrus Strozza, de Dogm. See Assa Mirzaei's Pont. Lexis.*

ABUMUSLIMUS (a) General of the Army under the first Caliphs of the Race of *Abbas*. The Province of *Chorasan* surrender'd to *Abbas* in the Year of the *Hegira* 125 (b). He accepted it, and died the same Year. *Ibrahim*, his Son and Successor, sent *Abumuslimus* into this Country, at the Age of Nineteen. These tender Years did not hinder him from driving out *Nasrus*, who govern'd the Province in the Name of Caliph *Merwan*. After the Death of *Ibrahim*, which came to pass in the Year of the *Hegira* 131, *Saffabus*, his Brother, was raised to the Dignity of Caliph. He left the Government of the Province of *Chorasan* to *Abumuslimus*, and made use of him

(a) *Mr d' Herbelot, who makes a long Article of him, calls him Abou-Moslem.*

(b) *It is an 742.*

52   ABUMUSLIMUS. ACACIA. ACAMAS.

him to get rid of his Counsellor *Abumuſimas*, who became ſuſpected by him. He died in the Year 136, and was ſucceeded by *Almanſor*, his Brother, who, after he had receiv'd the moſt important Services from *Abumuſimus*, treacherouſly cauſ'd him to be murthur'd. *Abdalla* had revolted in *Syria*: *Abumuſimus*, being ſent againſt him at the Head of a gallant Army, entirely routed him. *Almanſor*, more touch'd with the Scandal he pretended *Abumuſimus* had utter'd againſt him, than with the Importance of the Victory, ſent for him, in order to put him to death. *Abumuſimus*, juſtly diſtruſting him, refuſ'd to wait upon his Maſter; but, ſuffering himſelf to be deceiv'd by the Careſſes made to him, he put himſelf into the Power of *Almanſor*, who threw him into the *Tigris*. This was in the 137th Year of the *Hegira*, which anſwers to our 754. It is computed, that *Abumuſimus* cauſ'd the death of 600 Perſons. He paſs'd for one a little verſ'd in Magic, and he was of a Sect, from which That of the unfortunate *Spinoza* was not very different [*A*]. *Erpenius* did not underſtand the Words of *Elmacin* upon this Subject [*B*]. What I have here advanc'd (*e*), and the two Remarks below, are what I will not pretend to warrant. I report them on the Authority of another. Only the Parallel of *Spinoziſme* is my own; and I am not over ſatisfied, that he who criticizes *Erpenius*, knows more of the Point in queſtion, than *Erpenius* himſelf.

(*e*) Taken from Elmacin's Hiſt. Saracen. B. 2. c. 1, &c.

[*A*] *Spinoza was not very different.*] The Sect, which *Abumuſimus* profeſſed, taught a kind of *Metempſychoſis*, but not like that of *Pythagoras* (1). His did not deſtroy the Soul; it only ſent it from one Body to another; but the other *Metempſychoſis* is thus deſcribed by the famous Traveller *Peter de la Valle*, in the Place, where he mentions certain *Mahometan* Heretics, who called themſelves *Ehl Eltabkik*, *Men of Truth and Certainty*. "They believe (ſays he) no other God, but the four Elements —— that there is no Rational Soul, nor another —— Life after this; but that every Man is but a —— Mixture of the four Elements, of which he is —— compoſed during his Life, joined together and animated by that ſtrict Union, which keeps them connected together, and which, upon his Death, is diſſolved and diſperſed among the four ſimple Elements, and conſequently returned to God, out of which it was created; and the ſame, with regard to every thing elſe in the Earth, and in the Heavens: in a Word, that the four Elements are the whole of every Thing, even God and Man; and conſequently the elements are Eternal, and the World, with all it's Viciſſitudes and Changes, is eternal (2)." Whatever Difference there may be between this Opinion, and the Syſtem of *Spinoza*, the Foundation of them both is the ſame: It is maintained on both Sides, that the Univerſe is but one ſingle Subſtance, and that all That, which we call Generation and Corruption, Life and Death, is nothing more than a certain Combination, or Diſſolution of Modes. *Elmacin* calls the *Metempſichoſis* which *Abumuſimus* believed, the *Metempſychoſis* of *Reſolution*.

[*B*] *Erpenius did not underſtand the Words of Elmacin upon this Subject.*] He makes him ſay, that *Abumuſimus* follow'd the Sect of the *Deſcending Succeſſion*, *profitebatur ſectam ſucceſſionis deſcendentis* (3). He ought to have ſaid, that he follow'd the Sect, which taught the *Metempſychoſis of Reſolution*, *profitebatur ſectam eorum qui credunt Metempſychoſim reſolutionis*. It is thus, the Sieur *Beſpier* cenſures and corrects the Tranſlation of *Erpenius* in this Place (4).

(1) *Beſpier's Remarks on Ricaut's Preſent State of the Ottoman Empire.*

(2) *Peter de la Valle*, T. 3. p. 30'. cited by Beſpier *loc.cit.*

(3) *Elmacin Hiſt. Janc.* B. 2. c. 3. p. 100.

(4) *Beſpier's Remarks on Ricaut's State of the Ottoman Empire*, p. 665.

ACACIA *or* ACAKIA (MARTIN). *See* AKAKIA.

ACAMAS, Son of *Theſeus* (*a*), follow'd the reſt of the *Grecian* Princes to the Siege of *Troy*. He was deputed with *Diomede*, on an Embaſſy to the *Trojans*, to demand back *Helen*. This Embaſſy was fruitleſs, as to the principal Deſign of it; but it turn'd to the Advantage of *Acamas*, in what is call'd Good Fortune in Affairs of Gallantry. *Laodicea*, Daughter of *Priam*, fell in Love with him, and having in vain ſummoned to her Aſſiſtance Honour and Modeſty, was obliged to open her Mind to *Philobia*, Wife of *Perſeus*, and to beg her Aſſiſtance in an Affair of the utmoſt Importance (*b*). *Philobia*, touch'd with Compaſſion for her, entreated her Huſband to procure *Laodicea* the Completion of her Deſires. *Perſeus* took pity on the poor Lady; and, being beſides deſirous to oblige his Wife, he made a Friendſhip with *Acamas*, and obtain'd a Viſit, from him in the City, of which he was Governor (*c*). *Laodicea* did not fail to be preſent there, attended by ſome *Trojan* Ladies. There was a magnificent Feaſt; after which *Perſeus* put her to bed with *Acamas*, pretending to him, that ſhe was one of the King's Concubines. *Laodicea* return'd home very well ſatisfy'd; and, at the end of nine Months, was deliver'd of a Boy, which was brought up by *Æthra*, Aunt of *Acamas* by the Mother's Side [*A*]. This Child was call'd *Munitus* [*B*]: we ſhall ſee in the Remarks what became of him (*d*).

Acamas

(*a*) *Pauſan. lib.* 1. p. 5. & *lib.* 10. p. 585. & 543.

(*b*) Παρεκαλεσε τε αυτον μεν μη αδη ερωμενος Λαοδικης *Pauſan. loc. cit.* c. 16.

(*c*) *It was called Dardanus.*

(*d*) Taken from *Hegeſippus de Rebus Mileſ. lib.* 1. *cited by Parthen. in his Erot. c.* 16. *and from Tzetzes upon Lycophon.*

[*A*] *Was brought up by Æthra, Aunt of Acamas by the Mother's ſide.*] You muſt know that *Caſtor* and *Pollux*, making an inroad into *Attica* to recover their Siſter *Helena*, took the City of *Aphidna*, where that fair one was ſent by her Raviſher. *Æthra*, the Mother of *Theſeus*, had been ſent there at the ſame time. They took her Priſoner, and brought her to *Lacedemon*. She was there when *Paris* carried *Helen* away, and was ſent from thence to *Troy*. *Demophoon* and *Acamas* follow'd the (1) other *Greeks*, chiefly to deliver the good old Lady, either by paying her Ranſom, or by taking the City. They met her in the Streets, during the ranſacking (2) of *Troy*; and having underſtood who ſhe was, they mutually embrac'd each other. It was then that *Æthra* (3) made *Munitus* known to his Father *Acamas*. She had educated him; for *Laodicea* had truſted her with the Secret of what had paſs'd in *Perſeus*'s Houſe. *John Cornarius* made a groſs Miſtake in his Tranſlation of *Parthenius*: He render'd thoſe Words, δν ὑπ' αἰθρα τραφέντα μετὰ Τροίας ἁλωσιν διεκόμισεν ἰς' οἰκόν, by theſe, *quem ſub dio enutritum poſt Trojæ captivitatem tranſportavit in domum*. i. e. *whom, having been brought up in the open Air, he carry'd home, after the taking of Troy*. He ought to have ſaid, *having been educated by Æthra*. We ſhall cite *Plutarch* preſently, who ſays, That ſome have called all this a fabulous Story.

[*B*] *This Child was call'd Munitus.*] He follow'd his Father into *Thrace*, where he died by the bite of a Serpent. *Plutarch* calls him *Munychus*, Μοννυχος, in the Life of *Theſeus*; but, ſince *Parthenius*, *Lycophron*, and *Tzetzes* call him conſtantly *Munitus*, *Midnitus*;

(1) *Scholiaſt. Euripid. in Hercul. See Pauſanias, l.* 10. p. 342.

(2) *Quintus Calaber, lib.* 13. v. 406. *See Pauſanias, ib.*

(3) *Tzetzes in Lycoph. cited by Meurſius, on Ovid's Epiſtles*, p. 143.

(4) *Parthen. in Eroticis, c.* 16.

ACAMAS.

Acamas was one of the Heroes, who were hid in the wooden Horse (e). He had, afterwards, an Adventure in *Thrace*, something like the former, but attended with very unfortunate Consequences. *Phillis*, the King's Daughter, fell in love with him: He immediately offer'd her Marriage: the *Fair* was promis'd to him, with the Dowry of a Crown. He demanded permission to return home. *Phillis* oppos'd it with the utmost Intreaties; but obtaining only an Oath from him, that he would return, she presented him with a Box, consecrated, as she said, to *Rhea*, Mother of the Gods. She recommended to him not to open it, till she should have no Hopes of seeing *Thrace* again. *Acamas* landed in the Isle of *Cyprus* [C], and resolv'd to settle there. *Phillis*, upon this, hang'd herself, uttering imprecations against the Traytor. He open'd the Box, and found himself seiz'd with strange Visions. He mounted his Horse, and spurr'd so unluckily, and in so violent a manner, that they were both thrown to the Ground, and *Acamas* accidentally fell upon his own Sword. *Tzetzes* relates this Story (f); but he has confounded *Acamas* with *Demophoon* (g); for, it is with the regard to the latter, that all Authors relate the Fate of the unhappy *Phillis*. See her passionate Letter to *Demophoon*, invented by *Ovid*. It appears by this Epistle, that their Marriage had been consummated:

> Turpiter hospitium lecto cumulasse jugali
> Pœnitet, & lateri conseruisse latus (h).

> But, to admit thee loosely to my Breast
> Is Treason, fatal to my present Rest.   Mr E. LLOYD.

We must not forget, that one of the Tribes of *Athens* was named *Acamantis* [D] from the Name of our *Acamas* (i), and that by the Appointment of the Oracle. *Stephen of Byzantium* makes him the Founder of a City in *Phrygia* the Greater [E], and makes him

---

vitted; it must be believ'd that *Plutarch*'s Text has been alter'd in that Place, or that the Author did not well remember the true Pronounciation of that Word. Does it not happen daily, that when we cite any Author by Memory, we confound sometimes one or more Syllables in his Name? I shall consider this farther in the Article EPHORUS. I do not know whether it ought not to be imputed to forgetfulness that *Plutarch* says, that it was *Demophoon* who lay with *Laodice*. But perhaps he had read it in some Author unknown to us. *Tzetzes* too might have found in some of these Authors, which are lost, that the Adventures of *Phyllis* related to *Acamas*: However it be, neither of the Brothers have been Loosers, at the Foot of the Account; for, if, on one Side, *Plutarch* takes from *Acamas* the delightful Moments he pass'd with *Laodice*, and bestows them on *Demophoon*; *Tzetzes*, on the other Side, deprives the latter of the agreeable Nights he pass'd with *Phyllis*, and gives them to *Acamas*. But, to be serious; if *Meursius* had well weigh'd the Passages, where the Son of *Laodice* is called *Munitus*, he would not have made (5) use of *Plutarch*'s Words, to prove that the Harbour of *Munychia* had not taken it's Name from *Munychus* the Son of *Pantacles*, as is commonly said, but from *Munychus* the Son of *Demophoon* and *Laodice*. *Plutarch*'s Words are (6), Ὅτι δὴ καὶ τοῦτο τὸ ἔτος διαβάλλουσι, καὶ τὴν περὶ Μουνιχιὰν μυθολογίαν, ὃν ἐκ Δημοφῶντος Λαοδίκης ἀφύρα τεκοῦσης ἐν Τροίᾳ συνεκθρέψαι τὴν Αἴθραν λέγουσι. i. e. *some reject this Verse*, ('tis that where *Homer* says that *Helen* brought *Æthra* with her to *Troy*) *as also the Story of Munychus, who, being the spurious Child of Demophoon and Laodice, is said to have been brought up at Troy, under the Care of Æthra.*

[C] *Acamas landed in the Isle of Cyprus.*] There was a Mountain in that Island, which was called *Acamas*, from the Son of *Theseus*. *Hesychius* attests it, and remarks, That the River *Bocarus*, which past by *Salamina*, had it's Source in that Mountain. Geographers (7) speak of Cape *Acamas*, very famous in the same Island; and some observe also (8), that the whole Island was formerly called *Acamas*. But no body that I know of among the Antients said, That Cape *Acamas* borrow'd it's Name from a City, which *Acchamas*, the *Athenian*, *a Friend of the Trojans, that fled from thence*, built on that Cape, and to which he gave his Name. That City, and the *Athenian Acamas*'s Friendship for the *Trojans*, are both alike chimerical. I would fain know where Brother *Stephen* (9) of *Lusignan*, Reader in Divinity to the Dominicans of *Paris*, in the XVIth Century, met with this extraordinary Piece of Learning.

[D] *One of the Tribes of Athens was nam'd Acamantis.*] Mr *Moreri* calls that Tribe *Acamante*; but I meet with no *French* Author, but what says *la Tribe Acamantide*. I shall here take notice of another of this Writer's Mistakes, to save myself the trouble in another Place (10). He says, That *Homer*, in the 2d Book of the *Iliad*, mentions one *Acamas*, a *Thracian* Prince, who came to the Assistance of *Priam*; and of another *Acamas*, *the Son of Antenor*, *whose admirable Modesty caused him to be placed in the Number of the Gods*. It is true, that *Homer*, in the forecited Book, speaks of that *Thracian* Prince; and says (11), elsewhere, that *Ajax* kill'd him. It is true likewise, that he speaks of *Archilocus*, and *Acamas*, Sons of *Antenor*; and describes them as very expert in all kind of Combats, μάχης εὖ εἰδότε πάσης; but he says nothing of the Deification of the chast *Acamas*. Mr *Moreri* wants but little of being the Author of this Story; for, strictly speaking, he would be so, if *Charles Stephens* had not supply'd him with this Foundation to build on: " Fuit & alius ejusdem nominis filius Antenoris, " qui tempore belli Trojani cœlebs erat, & diis similis " habebatur. i. e. *there was also another of the same " Name, the Son of Antenor, who, in the time of the " Trojan War, was a Bachelor, and reverenc'd as a " Godlike Person*." As this Author cites no Writer in proof of this Fact, it was not in my Power to enquire after this pretended Celebacy; and, if I durst freely conjecture, I would say that the Printers have put *cœlebs* for *celebris*, in some Book that *Charles Stephens* copied: Not that I deny, but that *Homer* observ'd sometimes (12) that such and such Heroes were kill'd before they were married. But suppose this *Trojan* was unmarried; and that he is celebrated for being *like the Gods*, must it be concluded from thence, that his Chastity was so extraordinary, as to procure him divine Honours? If all those on whom *Homer* bestows the Epithet θεοείκελος, *God-like*, had been Deified, what would have become of poor *Atlas*'s Shoulders?

— contentaque Sydera paucis
Numinibus miserum urgebant Atlanta minori
Pondere (13).

'*Ere Gods grew numerous, and the heavenly Crowd,
Prest wretched Atlas with a lighter Load.*
                                            CREECH.

[E] *Stephen of Byzantium makes him the Founder of a City in Phrygia the Greater.*] He calls it *Acamantium*. Geographers say nothing at all of it. The Abbreviator of that Writer, or the Copyists, have main'd

---

(e) Tryphiodorus de Excid. Troiæ. See also Pausan. lib. 1. p. 21.

(f) Upon Lycophron.

(g) Who was likewise the Son of Theseus.

(h) Ovid. Phyll. ver. 57.

(i) Pausan. lib. 1. p. 5. & lib. 10. p. 32. See likewise Suidas, and Stephen of Byzant.

(5) Meursius, lib. 1. c. 14. lect. Atticar cited by Meursius who repeats the same Mistake in his Comment. on Ovid's Epistles, p. 144.

(6) Plut. in Theseo, sub fin. p. 16.

(7) Strabo, lib. 14. Ptol. lib. 5. c. 14. Plin. lib. 5. c. 31.

(8) Philonides apud Plin. ibid. Stephanus in the Word Κύπρος.

(9) History of Cyprus, p. 4. & 29.

(10) The 2 ther Faults that were mark'd in the first Edition are suppos'd Less. As true Faults occur in most of the Editions of Moretti, it is thought proper to strike them down in its place. They are as follows: 1st, He cites lest 12 Book of Strabo, in relation to the Promontory Acamas, in the Isle of Cyprus; whereas he ought to have cited the 14th. 2dly, He calls Acamante the Son of Theseus. 3dly, He says, that Suidas mentions an Acamantidae, a Philippine of Eliopolia; whereas Suidas calls him Acamantius.

(11) Iliad. lib. 6. v. 7.

(12) See Iliad. lib. 4. v. 474.

(13) Juvenal. Sat. 13. v. 47.

VOL. I.   O

ACAMAS. ACARNANIA.

him war with the *Solymeans*. I will not pretend to determine, whether *Phædra* or *Ariadne* [F] was the Mother of *Acamas*, upon which point Mr *Moreri* behaves as usual.

maim'd that Passage in such a Manner, that no Sense can be made of it, without supplying something. But supply it as you please, you will be never the better inform'd by it of the War between *Acamas*, and the *Solymeans*.

[F] *Whether Phædra or Ariadne.*] I find two learned Men of a contrary Opinion in this Question. *Meziriac* (14) affirms that *Acamas* was the Son of *Phædra*; but all the Proof he seems to give for it, is, That *Demophoon* the Brother of *Acamas* was the Son of *Phædra*; which he proves by the Letter that *Sabinus* writ to *Phillis* under the Name of *Demophoon*. Mr *de Valois* (15) pretends, That *Ariadne* was the Mother of *Acamas*, and cites the Scholiast (16) of *Homer* for it; he adds, that *Demophoon* was the Brother of *Acamas*, according to that Scholiast; and that *Euripides* (17) confirms it. Neither of those Gentlemen remark'd, That it signifies nothing to the Question, whether *Acamas* and *Demophoon* were Brothers; for they might be so, altho' the one was the Son of *Ariadne*, and the other of *Phædra*.

(14) On O-vid's Epist. p. 137.

(15) Henr. Valesius in Harpocrat. p. 4, & 5.
(16) In O-dyss. O.
(17) In Ioan.

ACARNANIA, a Country situated on the *Ionian* Sea, between *Ætolia* and the Gulph of *Ambracia*. It is said that the *Taphians* and the *Teleboans* were the first Masters of it; and that *Cephalus* conquer'd it, after he was establish'd in the Lordship of the Islands near *Taphos*, by *Amphitryon* (a). They add (b), That *Alcmeon*, the Son of *Amphiaraus*, made himself Master of it, after the second *Theban* War; and that he gave it the Name of his Son *Acarnan*. He had associated himself with *Diomedes*, and they had conquer'd *Ætolia*, which fell to the share of the latter. Some time after, they were summoned to accompany the Expedition to *Troy*: one of them, viz. *Diomedes*, went to join the other *Greeks*, but *Alcmeon* kept himself quiet in *Acarnania* (c). This was of service to the *Acarnanians* several Ages after; for they made a great Merit of it at *Rome* [A], having represented there, that, among all the *Greeks*, their Ancestors alone did not go to the Siege of *Troy*. This notable Reason was alledg'd by the People of *Rome*, when they embrac'd their Party against *Ætolia* [B]. So true it is, that, on certain Occasions, Policy does not refuse to make use of the most ridiculous Pretences. The *Etolians* and the *Arcananians* kept (d) a long time united, either to repulse the *Macedonians* and the other *Greeks*, or to maintain their Liberty against the *Roman* Arms; but at last they were tired, and lost their Courage. The Year consisted of but six Months (e) in *Acarnania*. The Inhabitants of that Country were very lascivious, if we may believe some Dictionaries [C]. It is more

(a) Strabo, lib. 10. p. 317.
(b) Id. ib. p. 318.

(c) Id. ib.

(d) Strabo, lib. 10. p. 317.
(e) Macrobius, Saturn. lib. 1. c. 12. p. 242.

[A] *They made a great Merit of it at Rome.*] The Historian *Ephorus* furnished them undesignedly with an Opportunity of doing this: for, being informed of what he related concerning *Alcmeon*, they ingeniously turn'd it to their own Advantage with the *Romans*, who pretended that the Founder of *Rome* descended from *Æneas*. This is *Strabo's* Conjecture (1): Τίνες δ᾽ ὡς εἰκὸς τοῖς λέγεσιν ἐναπολυθέντες τῶν δι᾽ Αναρνάνες, εὐφνισμένας λέγονται Ρωμαῖως, καὶ τὴν αυτονομίαν παρ᾽ αὐτῶν ἐξαιτήσασθαι, λέγοντες ὡς οἱ μεταχόντες μόνοι τοῖς ἐπὶ τοὺς προγόνους τῶν ἐκείνων στρατείας ὅτε γὰρ ἐν Ἀιτωλικῷ καταλόγῳ φράζοντε, ὅτε ἰδίᾳ ἦθ ὅλοις τὸνωμα τῶν ἐμφέρεται ἐν τοῖς ἔπεσιν.
It is probable the Acarnanians, taking the Hint from this Story, artfully prevailed upon the Romans to allow them the free Use of their Country Laws; pretending, that they alone were not concerned in the War against the Ancestors of the Romans, as not being mentioned either in the Ætolian Catalogue, or separately, or indeed at all in Homer's Verses. But this Pretence was groundless; for *Strabo* (2) shews by the Catalogue (3) in the second Book of the *Iliad*, that the Acarnanians supply'd their Quota for the Expedition to Troy.

[B] *Was alledged by the People of Rome, when they embrac'd their Party against Ætolia.*] After the Death of *Alexander*, the Son of *Pyrrhus*, King of *Epirus*, *Acarnania* had every thing to fear from the *Ætolians*, and did not confide much in that Prince's Widow, who was Guardian of her two Sons; wherefore they implored the Assistance of the *Romans*, which was not refused them. Word was sent to the *Ætolians*, that they should not molest a People, who alone had not assisted the *Greeks* against the *Trojans* (4). "Acarnanes quoque diffisi Epirotis adversus Ætolos auxilium Romanorum implorantes, obtinuerunt à Romano senatu, ut legati mitterentur, qui denunciarent Ætolis, præsidia ab urbibus Acarnaniæ deducerent; paterentur eos liberos, qui soli quondam adversus Trojanos, auctores originis fuæ, auxilia Græcis non miserint. —— The Acarnanians, distrusting the Epirotes, implored the Assistance of the Romans against the Ætolians, and obtained from the Senate an Embassy to be sent to the Ætolians, to demand of them, that they should withdraw their Garrisons from the Cities of Acarnania, and suffer a People to enjoy their Liberty, who alone gave the Greeks no Aid against the Trojans, from whom the Romans were descended." Plutarch reports two as ridiculous Facts as this (5). "Agathocles the Tyrant of Syracuse —— laugh'd at those of Corfu, who ask'd him, for what Reason he ravaged their Island; Because, said he, your Ancestors formerly received Ulysses. And when the Inhabitants of the Island of Ithaca complained to him, that his Soldiers took their Sheep: *And your King*, said he to them, *being arrived in our Country, did not only take our Sheep, but also put out our Shepherd's Eye.*" But the following Account is more ridiculous still (6). "*Mahomet*, the second of that Name, Emperor of the *Turks*, in a Letter to Pope *Pius* the Second, said, I wonder the *Italians* should league against me, seeing we have our common Original from the *Trojans*; and that 'tis my Interest, as well as theirs, to revenge the Blood of *Hector* upon the *Greeks*, whom they favour against me." Thus chimerical Evils, forged by the Poets, have served as an Apology for real Evils.

[C] *Very lascivious, if we may believe some Dictionaries.*] We shall quote Mr *Lloyd* first, "Mollitiei & lasciviæ notati leguntur (*Acarnanes*) teste *Luciano* in Dial. Meretriciis, unde proverbium *Porcellus Acarnanius* in lascivos. i. e. *The Acarnanians, as Lucian witnesses in his Dialogue of Harlots, are branded in History with Effeminacy and Wantonness, whence that proverbial Character of the Lasciviou*, "An Acarnanian Swine." Mr *Hofman* transferred this whole Passage into his Dictionary; and *Moreri's* Account is this: "The *Acarnanians* were accused of being too lascivious and too finical. This was the cause of that reproachful Proverb of the Antients, Porcellus Acarnanius." You may meet with the same Account in *Pinedo's* Notes (7) on *Stephen of Byzantium*. I have consulted the *Dialogue of the Courtezans* of *Lucian*, and do not find there that the Inhabitants of *Acarnania* past for voluptuous and effeminate. It is true, the Courtezan *Musarium*, in answer to her Mother, who reproached her for making no Advantage of the Favours she granted *Chereas*, and who thought it very strange that she should not hearken to a Peasant of *Acarnania*,

(1) Strabo lib. 10. p. 308.

(2) Id. ib.
(3) Homer describes only their Country, and does not mention it by the Name of Acarnania.

(4) Justin. lib 28. c. 1. Sor La Mothe Le Vayer Lettre 95. Tom. 2. p. 325.

(5) Plutarch. de sera Numinis vindicta.

(6) Montagne's Essays, B. 2. c. 36. p. 763.

(7) Tho. de Pinedo in Steph. Byzant. p. 36.

ACARNANIA. ACCARISI.

more certain that Modesty was not to be discovered there in the Womens Garments [D]. It is not true that *Cicero* speaks of a City that was called *Acarnania* [E]. I have observed, that the Inhabitants of this Country, kept themselves a long time united with the *Etolians*; but I must add, that there were frequent Wars between these two People; and that the *Etolians* greatly harass'd the former. *Polybius* tells us this, when he relates, that the *Acarnanians*, upon the first Application made to them by the King of *Macedon*, declar'd War against the *Etolians* (*f*). He commends them for observing a generous Policy, in preferring *the Honourable* to the *Profitable*, and that in the most pressing Dangers (*g*).

nia, said to her, *What! should I quit Chereas to give myself to that Blockhead, who smells as rank as an old He-Goat?* (8) *No! Chereas for my Money: He is smooth, as they say, and a Hog of* Acarnania. *Erasmus* supposes, that by an *Acarnanian* Hog is meant (9) an effeminate Favourite; and that it was an Allusion to the Comedy of *Aristophanes*, where a Hog is the Symbol of the Instruments of venereal Pleasures (10). *Allusum, opinor ad porcellum quem inducit Aristophanes in Ἀχαρνεῦσιν symbolum eorum membrorum quibus obicæna voluptates peraguntur.* I believe the concealed Meaning of *Musarium's* Answer is not understood; for my own Part, I own I do not comprehend it; for which Reason I shall not criticize upon those who assert that the Inhabitants of *Acarnania* were reputed lascivious. If it were true, I wonder Authors should make no mention of it. Lastly, *Erasmus* is not mistaken about the figurative Signification of the Word χοίρινος. The *Latins* had adopted that Figure. *Varro* says (11), "*Nostræ mulieres, maxime nutrices, naturam, qua "feminæ sunt, in virginibus appellant porcum & "Græcè χοῖρον.*—— Our *Women, especially Nurses, "call the Distinction of Sex in Virgins,* Porcus, *in Greek* χοῖρον." See the *Italian* Etymologies of Mr *Menage*, at the Word *Potta*. I am not satisfied with this Conjecture, and propose it only to try if more sagacious Persons than myself cannot account for it better. *Chereas* (12) always paid his Courtezan with Hopes: it was the only Coin he had. *As soon as my Father is dead*, said he, *and I am in possession of my Patrimony, you shall dispose of my Estate, and I will marry you. Musarium*, being allured by these Promises, gave him the Use of herself, and her Purse. Had she not Reason to say to her Mother, *Here is a Gallant that I can neither fleece nor shear! but I feed an Hog of* Acarnania: *the Profit of which will come all at once.* It is indeed the Property of those Animals: nothing is got by feeding them, 'till after all the necessary Expences have been laid out in fattening them; but at last they make amends with Usury. Perhaps *Acarnania* was as *Westphalia* is at this time, a plentiful Country for Hogs: and from thence it was that the Cooks (13) of the great Cities of *Greece* sent for Hogs to fatten them; which may be the Reason why the Courtezan made use of the Epithete ἀκαρνάνιος.

[D] *That Modesty was not to be discovered there in the Womens Garments.*] The Manner in which *Apollonius* censures the *Athenian Ladies*, informs us of this; "From whence have you the Fashion, *says* "*he to them* (14), of those pompous Garments of "Purple, of Carnation, or dried Roses, of Fillemot, "Yellow, Green, and such like, wherewith you "dress yourselves like a Meadow in the Month of "*May?* For it was never seen that the Women of "*Acarnania* ever prankt themselves up in that "Manner." This is according to the *French* Translator*. The *Latin* (15) Translator had said, "Coc"cineæ atque etiam purpureæ croceæque vestes unde "à vobis sumptæ? Cum neque Acarnanides mulie"res ita exornentur." It appears plainly that *Apollonius* would not have argued in this Manner, if the Women of *Acarnania* had not the Repute of dressing themselves in an immodest Manner. This seems to favour the Dictionaries, which assure us that the *Acarnanians* were defam'd as lascivious Persons; nevertheless the Consequence would be somewhat strained. Those Authors want a more precise Authority. *Artus Thomas* quite mistook the meaning of *Apollonius's* Words, which he undertook to comment on. He says (16), "The *Acarnanians* were formerly very expert "in Chariot-Races, according to the Report of *Pau"sanias* in the sixth and last Book of his *Eliacks*, "having formerly been held for wise People, and "very great Politicians, for having so well ordered "their State and Commonwealth, that some (say "*Aristotle* composed an hundred and fifty Books "only on the Subject of the Laws and Govern"ment of that Nation: But the Books are lost with "their Policy. This is the Reason why *Philostra"tus* speaks here of their Wives." Oh!—— the wretched Commentary! the Sense here is quite the Reverse of the Text.

[E] *It is not true that* Cicero *speaks of a City that was called* Acarnania.] Mr *Moreri* however asserts it, and adds, *It is in* Sicily, *and famous for a Temple dedicated to* Jupiter. He cites *Cicero, Orat. in Verrem,* and *Servius in lib 5. Æneid.* Mr *Hofman* goes much farther, for he notes two Circumstances, the one, that that City was near *Syracuse*; the other, that it was burnt by the *Goths*. He had read all this in *Charles Stephens*. The Truth is, *Cicero* does not speak of *Acarnania*, but of *Acradina*, one of the four Parts of *Syracuse* (17). "Ea tanta est urbs ut "ex quatuor urbibus maximis constare dicatur, qua"rum una, *&c.*—— altera autem est urbs Syra"cusis cui nomen Acradina est: In qua forum maxi"mum, pulcherrimæ porticus, ornatissimum pryta"neum, amplissima est curia, templumque egregium "Jovis Olympii.——— *The City is so spacious, that "it is said to consist of four large Towns, one of "which, &c.*—— *Another Part of* Syracuse *is cal"led* Acradina, *in which it a very large Forum, most "beautiful Porticos, a splendid Prytaneum, a mag"nificent Court, and a fine Temple of* Jupiter Olym"pius." *Servius*, cited by *Moreri*, says only (18), that *Acarnania* is a Part of *Epirus*, and not a small Country of *Egypt*, as Mr *Hofman* will have it (19).

(f) Polyb. Hist lib. 4. c. 30.

(g) Id. ib.

• Vigenere.

(15) Alemannus Rhinucinus, p. 167.

(16) Artus Thomas, Lord of Embry, *his Annotations on the Life of* Apollonius, Book iv. ch. 2. p. 800. *of Vol.* 2.

(17) Cicero in Verrem, Orat. 6. fol. 77. verso.

(18) Servius in Æneid. lib. 5. v. 298.

(19) Item Regiuncula Ægypti. Servius in Æneid. lib. *c.* Hofman *on the Word* Acarnania.

(*) Acig μοι Qaeri. λωτομας καί χρωίνονμας ἀνεμώνης. Lucian. Dialog. Meretric. p. 723. Tom. 2.

(9) In molle & amabilem atque in deliciis habitum diceretur. *i.e. It was sophis'd to wear of feminate, de- sirable, and Favourites.* Erasm. chil. 2. cent. 3. n. 69. p. 445.

(10) Id. ib.

(11) Varro de Re rustica, lib. 2. c. 4.

(12) Lucian. Dial. Meretric. p. 723, 724.

(13) Ὅπερ ἐν Ἀκαρνᾶσι τοῖς τὰ Ἀκαρνάνια τρέφουσιν. *As* Cooks *b red up Pigs*. Athen. lib. 14. p. 6; 6.

(14) Philostrat. in vita Apollonii, lib. 4. c. 7.

ACCARISI (FRANCIS) a Civilian, born at *Ancona*, went thro' his Studies at *Sienna*, where *Bargalio* and *Benevolento* gain'd a considerable Reputation in the Science of the Law. He had a great Friendship for them both; but much more for the first, than the other. The Reasons for this difference were natural; *Bargalio's* Closet was always open to him; (*a*) besides, he had praised him very much in a Speech which is printed, and which contains the Elogies of the Family of the *Accarisi*, and on his Death-Bed had intrusted him with the Care of publishing his fine Disputation *de Dolo*. The first Public Employ of our *Accarisi* was to explain the *Institutes* at *Sienna*, which he did during six Years. Afterward they committed the Explication of the *Pandects* to him; and because many *Ultramontanes* went to study at *Sienna*, the Great Duke *Ferdinand* I. determin'd to have a Professor there, who should explain the Civil Law in the same manner as *Cujacius* had explain'd it. *Accarisi* was chosen for that Office, and acquitted himself worthily of it; after which he was promoted to that of Ordinary Professor in Law, vacant by the Death of *Bargalio*, and fill'd that Place honourably for twenty Years. His Reputation was spread abroad: All the Universities of *Italy* desir'd to have him, and offer'd him very advantageous Conditions. He resisted

(*a*) Ab illo fa tus fuerat o.nnium fu- erum studio- rum partu- ceps. i. e. *He praised of All his Studies.* N c. Erythræus, Pinacoth. 2, cap. 25.

ACCARISI. ACCIAIOLI.

sifted these Temptations a long time, in consideration of the Sweetness he enjoy'd at *Sienna*: But the Attack was renew'd so often, that he was at last overcome, and prevailed upon not to persist in the Resolution he had taken to die in his first Post: A Resolution scarce to be parallell'd among Persons of his Character [*A*]. It was *Rainucio Farnese*, Duke of *Parma*, who made him yield to the Temptation, by adding to the Promises he made him, and to the Glory of succeeding *Sforza Oddus*, and *Philip Marini*, the Title of His Counsellor, wherewith he honour'd him. The Great Duke would not suffer *Accarisi* to continue long in the Service of another Prince, but made him soon return [*B*], by giving him the first Professorship in Law in the University of *Pisa*; so that *Accarisi* left the Duke of *Parma*, and went to exercise the Employ which was given him at *Pisa*, in which he continu'd 'till his Death, which happen'd four Years after; he died, at *Sienna*, *Oct.* 4. 1622. The Author (*b*), who furnishes me with this Article, and who is the only Person cited by Mr *Moreri*, does not say that *Accarisi* writ divers Treatises of Law, nor that *Rainucio Farnese* endeavour'd in vain to draw him to him. They are two Mistakes of Mr *Moreri*, who besides did not understand the meaning of IV. *Non. Octobris*, which he interprets to mean the 26th of *September*. We take notice of another Mistake of his in the second Remark.

(*b*) Janus Nicius Erythræus Pinacoth. 2. c. 25.

[*A*] *Scarce to be parallell'd among Persons of his Character.*] One of the most common Faults among Professors is their not fixing in the Universities where they have their first Employ. Instead of looking upon that first Vocation as a kind of Marriage, they consider it only as a transient Engagement, as an *Interim*, and a resting Place: They only stay there in expectation of something better: They have no more Affection for the second Call than for the first, and are not for pitching their Tents for the last time, 'till they have attained the best Professorship. It has been said of some Persons, that they make the Tour of all Religions in a little time; others run through all the Universities as soon as they can. Some of those who do not remove, take care to be well paid for their Constancy. It costs those, who desire to retain them, a considerable Addition of Wages. *Tacitus*, who doubtless comprehended many Defects under the Phrase *Professoria lingua* (1), would not have excluded him, of whom I speak, if he had known him. Churchmen are not exempt from this little Infirmity; we know the Complaints of rigid Moralists against certain Prelates, who, beginning with a Bishoprick of a mean Revenue, rise by Degrees to the most eminent Metropolitan Cities. This is a Spiritual Polygamy, or something worse: For according to the Sense of the antient Canons (2), a spiritual Marriage is contracted between the Pastor and his Flock. The Christian Societies, which belong to the smaller Benefices, are sensible of the Effects of this Humour.

Parcius ista viris tamen objicienda memento (3). See the Remark [*H*] of the Article ALCIATUS (ANDREW).

[*B*] *But made him soon return.*] This was the Success of all that Sollicitation and Bribery, which the Duke of *Parma* made use of to procure *Accarisi*. I confess he gained him at last, but he was soon taken from him again by the same Means he had made use of to take him from others. Yet Mr *Moreri* says, that *Accarisi* did not go to the Duke, and that *he would have done too much Violence to his Inclination, if he had left his Country; where he was detained by the Favours of* Ferdinand, Great Duke *of* Tuscany. A new Fault, which cannot be excused! for we read in *Nicius Erythræus*, that when *Accarisi* went to serve the Duke of *Parma*, it was at least twenty Years since the new Office, which the Great Duke *Ferdinand* had caused to be created in the College of *Sienna*, had been bestowed upon him. We read also in the same Author, that *Accarisi* was Professor but four Years at *Pisa*, whither he was called a little after his Engagement at *Parma*. But he died in 1622. four Years after he had accepted the Professorship of *Pisa*; so that the Duke of *Parma* must have compassed his Design about the Year 1616; at which time there was no Great Duke of the Name of *Ferdinand*. Mr *Moreri* says himself, in his Article MEDICIS, that *Ferdinand* I. died in 1609, and that *Ferdinand* II. succeeded him in 1621.

(1) Annal. lib. 13. cap. 34.

(2) Ne Virginalis pauperculæ Societate contempta dilectioris adulteræ quærat amplexus. Hieron. Ep. ad Oceanum, Tom. 2. p. 744. See the Author of a French Book, entitled, Avis vue to the Jesuits of Aix on an Interlude, p. 37.

(3) Virgil. Ecl. 3. ver. 7.

ACCARISI (JAMES) a Native of *Boulogne*, and Doctor of Divinity. I have but two Particulars to add to Mr *Moreri*'s Account of him. The first is, that the Speeches, which he has published, are Compositions, recited by himself at *Rome*, *Cologne*, *Mantua*, and other Places: The other, that he was four Years Professor of Rhetoric at *Mantua*, in the University founded by Duke *Ferdinand*, *Ann.* 1627 (*a*).

(*a*) Aub. Miræus, Script. Eccl. Sæc. 17. p. 251.

ACCIAIOLI (DONATO) a Person celebrated as well for his Learning, as the great Offices he discharged at *Florence*, the Place of his Nativity. He flourished in the XVth Century. This great Man would have been more eminent for Learning, if the public Affairs had permitted him to dedicate more Time to his Studies, and if the Tenderness of his Constitution had not shortened his Life (*a*). There can be no greater Proof of his Honesty and Disinterestedness than the small Patrimony he left to his Children. His Daughters were portioned for Marriage at the public Expence (*b*), as were formerly those of *Aristides*; which demonstrates, at the same time, how well satisfied the Public was with the Services he had done it. He was sent into *France* to demand Succours against Pope *Sixtus* IV. who extreamly harassed the *Florentines*; but he died, before he had passed the *Alps* (*c*), at *Milan*, in the Month of *August*, 1473, in the 39th Year of his Age (*d*). His Body was carried to *Florence*, and interr'd in the Church of the *Carthusians* (*e*). The Inscription on his Tomb is in the Style and Manner of *Politian*. His Works are principally *A Translation of some of the Lives of* Plutarch [*A*] *into* Latin; *The Life of*

(*a*) Jovius in Elog. ch. 16.
(*b*) Volaterr. B. 21.
(*c*) Jovius in Elog. c. 16.
(*d*) Varillas Anecd. de Florence. p. 269.
(*e*) Jovius in Elog. ch. 16.

(1) Vossius de Hist. Lat. p. 624.
(2) Konig. Bibl. Vet. & Nov. p. 4.

[*A*] *Some of the Lives of* Plutarch.] He should be the Author of Four, if *Vossius* (1) and *Konig* (2) are to be credited; namely, those of *Hannibal*, *Scipio*, *Alcibiades*, and *Demetrius*: but as it does not appear, that *Plutarch* compos'd either the Life of *Scipio*, or that of *Hannibal*; it is more probable, that *Acciaiolus* was originally

ACCIAIOLI.

of Charlemagne; and *Commentaries* on Aristotle's *Ethics* and *Politics*. This *Life of Charlemagne*, being sometimes join'd with those of *Plutarch*, has led *George Wicelius* into a surprizing Blunder. He speaks of this *Life* as if it were the Work of *Plutarch* himself (*f*); so wholly taken up was he in the Learning of the Times. Some have accus'd *Acciaioli* of Plagiarism [*B*] in his *Commentary on* Aristotle's *Ethics*: others, on the contrary, are extravagant in the Praises [*C*] they bestow on him for this Work. He was highly esteem'd by the Cardinal *de Pavia*, as appears by the Letters he receiv'd from him, which are to be found in a printed Collection of the Cardinal's Letters.

The Reader will find below a considerable Supplement to this Article [*D*].

(*f*) Hagiolog. fol. 178. apud Voss. de Hist. Lat. p. 624.

nally the Author of the Lives of these two famous Commanders (3), than that he translated them from the *Greek*. *Vossius* does not seem to be aware of this. He was plainly misled by the Abridger of the *Bibliotheque* of *Gesner*. Father *Ministrier* is positive, that *Acciaioli* impos'd upon the Public, in pretending to have translated the Life of *Hannibal*, from the *Greek* (4).

[*B*] *Some have accus'd* Acciaioli *of Plagiarism*.] It is asserted, that he borrow'd his *Commentary on Aristotle's Ethics*, without acknowledging the Debt. " Scripta, " quæ sub nomine Acciaioli ea de re circumferuntur, " non Acciaioli commentaria, sed Argyropyli Præ- " lectiones Florentiæ habitæ, & ab Acciaiolo descriptæ " editæque, à plerisque existimantur. — *It is generally thought, that the Commentary, which is handed about under the Name of* Acciaiolus, *is not his own, but transcrib'd, and publish'd, from the Lectures of* Argyropylus, *deliver'd at Florence*." After this manner *Simon Simonius* speaks of it in his Dedication to a Book, printed in 1567 (5). *Gabriel Naudé* renew'd this Accusation a long time after in very positive Terms. " Argyropylus Byzantinus, says he (6), cu- " jus Prælectiones, Florentinæ habitas, non absque " manifesto plagii crimine, sibi postea vendicavit Do- " natus Acciaiolus. — Argyropylus, *the Byzantine, whose Lectures, read at Florence, Donatus Acciaiolus claim'd to himself, not without the manifest Guilt of Plagiarism*." Mr *Moreri* has confounded the *Ethics of Aristotle*, with the Commentary upon them. " It has even been thought, says " he, that the Ethics of *Aristotle*, address'd to *Nicho- " machus*, which *Donatus* has publish'd, were in the " Stile and Manner of the same *Argyropylus*; though " *Volaterran* maintains the contrary." Observe this Author's Skill in translating the easiest *Latin*, I mean the *Latin* of *Vossius*. He had read these Words in *Vossius*: " Imo, Commentaria illa in Nicomachia Aristo- " telis multi arbitrantur non ipsius esse Acciaioli, sed " Prælectiones esse Argyropyli, ab Acciaiolo autem " descriptas, inque lucem emissas. Nihil tamen de eo " Volaterranus (7). — *Nay, many are of Opinion, that* Acciaiolus *himself was not the Author of the Commentary on* Aristotle's *Piece to* Nicomachus, *but that he compos'd, and publish'd it from the Lectures of* Argyropylus. *Yet* Volaterran *mentions no such thing*." This is doubly to confound Things: it is to take the Commentary for the Text; and to construe the Silence of an Author into a formal confutation of a Charge. The learned *Conringius* has justify'd *Donatus* against *Naudé*; not by shewing, that *Argyropylus* did not furnish Materials for the Work, but by alledging, that *Acciaiolus* acknowledged to whom he was indebted (8). Can we desire a more authentic Confession, than the following? " Johannes Argyropylus Byzantinus, cum Florentiæ " inter cætera Philosophiæ opera Aristotelis libros, " qui ad Nicomachum de moribus scribuntur, mirifice " esset complexus, eos vno nomine Latinos fecit, pu- " bliceque deinde explicuit, non sine magna audien- " tium approbatione: habent enim libri duo summam " dignitatem, admirabilemque doctrinam, ordinem " vero prope singularem. Itaque si accurata & ex- " quisita quædam explanatio accedat, magnum audi- " toribus afferent fructum; quod ego jam inde ab " initio mecum considerans una cum plerisque aliis, " qui hujus quoque præceptoris disciplinam sequun- " tur, in iis audiendis præcipuam curam diligentiam- " que adhibui. — Postea vero cum viderim hos " libros à te, & ab iis omnibus, qui ingenio vehe- " menter excellunt, libentissime legi, ulterius progre- " diendum ratus, EXPOSITIONEM HUJUS DOCTORIS, " accommodatam præcipue menti Philosophi, literis " mandare constitui, ut ii, qui adesse non potuerunt— " hæc, quæ NOS EX EJUS ORE ACCEPIMUS, perci- " pere & ipsi pro arbitrio possent; quare traductionem

illius ac ordinem explicandi pluribus verbis secuti " sumus, lata interdum & diffusa oratione utentes, ut " explanatio aperta magis magisque omnibus esset " communis (9). — John Argyropylus, *the Byzantine, having, at Florence, among other Philosophical Works, finely introduc'd the moral Writings of* Aristotle, *address'd to* Nicomachus, *translated them, under your patronage, into Latin, and afterwards read public Lectures upon them, not without great Applause from his Hearers; for the Subject of these two Books is very noble, the Instruction admirable, and the Method almost peculiar to them. And therefore the Hearers must receive great Benefit from them, when accurately and judiciously explain'd; which Consideration, from the beginning, induc'd me, and several other Pupils of the same Master, to attend his Lectures, with the utmost Care and Diligence. — But afterwards, when I perceiv'd that those Books became in great Request with you, and all Men of exalted Sense, I determined to publish this great Master's* EXPLANATION, *accommodated chiefly to the taste of Philosophers; that they, who could not attend his Lectures, might, whenever they thought fit, understand what* WE *RECEIV'D FROM HIS OWN MOUTH. I have therefore given his Translation, and method of Explanation at large, making use frequently of a copious and diffuse Style, to render his Interpretation the more intelligible and familiar*." If *Vossius* had ever heard of this Passage, would he have been satisfy'd with opposing the Silence of *Volaterran* to the Accusers of *Acciaioli*? He might have read it in *Gesner's* Works (10). Is it not very strange, that a poor Author, who has so solemnly declared in his Preface, that he publishes only a paraphrastic Translation of the Lectures of *Argyropylus*, should for so long Time be accus'd of Plagiarism?

[*C*] *Extravagant in the Praises*.] This appears by comparing the Text of *Paul Jovius*, with the Paraphrase of Mr *Varillas*. " Erudita & perelegantia " Commentaria magnum lumen attulisse judicantur " Moralibus Aristotelis, explosis scilicet sophistarum " interpretum ineptiis, quum, Bustratii Græci placita " secutus, certiore ubique vestigio niteretur (11). — *He is thought to have given great Light into* Aristotle's *Ethics, by a very learned and elegant Commentary; in which he explodes the foolish Glosses of the Schoolmen, and follows the Opinions of* Eustratius *the* Greek, *as the more certain Foundation*." This is the Text; the Paraphrase is as follows: " He " did not fail to translate the Morals of *Aristotle*, " with much greater exactness, than his Predecessors " in that Work; and to clear them of those ridiculous " Interpretations, which both the antient and modern " Schoolmen had put upon them. This he did in " an excellent Commentary ||, in which he shew'd, " that, whoever engages in this Labyrinth with any " other Guide ‡, than the famous *Eustachius*, can- " not avoid going out of his Way (12)." I need not apprize the Reader, that the Author of the *Anecdotes* goes farther than his Original, as well with respect to *Acciaioli*, as *Eufratius* (13); and that, instead of paying a Compliment to the latter, as was his Intention, he degrades him to the lowest Rank of Interpreters: he should have said, *avec un autre*, not *sans un autre*. Besides, what would Father *Bouhours* say to his *par un admirable Commentaire*? These Words are so ill plac'd, that one would think the Schoolmen had given *their ridiculous Interpretations*, *by an* excellent *Commentary*.

[*D*] *The Reader will find below, a considerable Supplement to this Article*.] I may venture to give it this Character, since it is a Memoir communicated to me by a very able Writer (14). " The Treatise, which " *Matthieu Palmieri*. has left, of the Origin of the " Family of the *Acciaioli*, may be of considerable " Use

---

(3) Poccianti, *de Script. Flor.* p. 57. says expressly, dictavit proprio Marte balia & Scipionis. He had no Assistance in writing the Lives of Hannibal and Scipio.

(4) *See the Journal des Savans, Sept.* 2. 1697. p. 654.

(5) Sim. Simonii Comment. in Aristot. Ethic.

(6) Naud. Bibliogr. polit. p. 16.

(7) Voss. de Hist. Lat. p. 624.

(8) Conring. Introd. in Polit. Arist. p. 649, 659. in Thomasius's Plag. Literar. p. 253.

(9) Don. Acc. Præf. to Cosm. Med. Comment. in Eth. Arist. ad Nichomach.

(10) Gesn. Biblioth. fol. 216.

(11) Jovius Elog. cap. 16.

|| *The Construction of the French is — Interpretations ridicules, que les Schoolmen avoient données, par un admirable Commentaire —*

‡ *The French of* Varillas, *by m/sieur, says, sans un autre guide —*

(12) Varill. Anecd. de Flor. p. 169.

(13) *So it ought to be wrote, and not* Eustachius.

(14) Mr de la Monnoie.

ACCIAIOLI. ACCIUS.

"Use in rectifying and supplying the Article of *Donato Acciaioli*. This Treatise, written in *Latin* by *Matthieu Palmieri*, was translated into *Italian* by *Donato Acciaioli*, Knight of *Rhodes*. The Original has not yet appear'd: the Translation alone was printed at *Florence*, in 4to, in the Year 1588, for *Bartholomi Sermatelli*, as an Appendix to the History of the *Ubaldinis*, and the Life of *Nicolas Acciaioli*, great Seneschal of the Kingdoms of *Sicily* and *Jerusalem*. We are there told that our *Donato* was born in 1428; that he was buried at the public Expence; that *Christopher Laudin* spoke his Funeral Oration*. The other Particulars are too long to be repeated. —— *Sabellicus*, in his Dialogue *de Reparatione Linguæ Latinæ*, (a Dialogue, by the way, commonly cited as the Work of an anonymous Author) and *Vives*, in his 5th Book *de tradendis Disciplinis*, have spoken with Commendation, of the Life of *Charlemagne*, by *Donato Acciaioli*. The *Florentine* History of *Leonard d'Arezzo*, translated from *Latin* into *Italian* by this *Donato*, was printed at *Venice*, in *Folio*, in 1473, according to Father *L'Abbé's* Account, p. 341. of his *Supplem. Nov. Biblioth.* MSS."

* *Porcianthius de Script. Flor.* p. 51.

ACCIAIOLI (ZENOBIUS) a *Florentine*, and Monk of the Order of St *Dominic*, distinguish'd himself by his public Writings. His Office of Librarian of the *Vatican* under Pope *Leo* X. proves him to have been a Man of Letters. He continu'd in this Employ from the Year 1518 to his death, which happen'd in 1520. He liv'd 58 Years. He was skill'd in *Greek* and *Hebrew*, and has translated some Pieces of the antient *Fathers* into *Latin*: viz. Olympiodorus on *Ecclesiastes*; the Treatise of *Eusebius* against *Hierocles*; the twelve Books of *Theodoret de Græcarum Affectionum Curatione*; and *Justin Martyr*. As he was both a Poet and an Orator, he has exercis'd his Talent of Panegyric on every thing, both in Verse and Prose. There are extant his *Poems*, and *Sermons on the Epiphany*, besides *Verses* and *Orations* in Honour of *Leo* X. There are publish'd likewise some *Letters*, which he writ to *Picus of Mirandola*; a Treatise entitled *de Laudibus Urbis Romæ*; *A Panegyric on the City of Naples*, deliver'd in a general Chapter of the Order; and *A Chronicle of the Convent of St Mark at Florence*. He collected likewise in one Volume the *Greek Epigrams of Politian*, and publish'd them in the Year 1495. (a)

(a) *Taken from Ambrosie d'Altamura Biblioth. Ord. Præd.* c. p. 243.

Ambroise d'Altamura, whom I have follow'd Step by Step in this Article, has evidently transgress'd the Laws of Accuracy, as appears from the following account of Mr de la Monnoie. *Of all the Works of Zenobius Acciaioli there are extant only the Translation of Eusebius's Book against Hierocles; and Theodoret's Cure of the false Opinions of the Gentiles. The pieces of Poetry, mention'd by Gyraldus, whether Greek, or Latin, were never printed. Some think he did not dye till the Year 1537, because Jerome Alcander, his Successor in the place of Librarian of the Vatican, did not enter upon his Office till that Year; in like manner as Zenobius began his employ in the Year 1518, after Philip Beroaldus the younger, who died the same Year.*

ACCIUS (LUCIUS) a *Latin* Tragic Poet, Son of a *Freed-Man* [A], was born, according to the Chronology of St *Jerom*, in the Consulship of *Hostilius Mancinus*, and *Atilius Serranus*, in the year of *Rome* 583. But it will appear below, that this Authority is not to be depended upon [B]. He distinguish'd himself before the death

[A] *Son of a Freed-Man.*] The more I consider these Words of *Moreri*, "*Marcinus* and *Serranus*, whom antient *Rome* saw rais'd to the Dignity of "Consuls, were his near Relations," the more difficult I find it to assign any other Reason for his Blunder, than this. He had read in *Charles Stephens* the following Words, "*Natus parentibus libertinis, Marcino & Serano Consulibus,*" and, not sufficiently attending to the Terms *parentibus* and *libertinis*, he thought he might affirm, that the Poet was related to these two Consuls. He ought, however, to have chang'd *Marcinus* into *Mancinus*. See how St *Jerom* expresses himself. "*Lucius Accius, Tragœdiarum* "*Scriptor clarus, natus, Mancino & Serrano Consulibus, parentibus libertinis* (1). —— i. e. *Lucius* "*Accius*, a famous *Tragic Poet, born in the Consulship* "*of Mancinus and Serranus, of free Parents*." Father *Briet* attributes to *A. Gellius* two or three Particulars relating to *Accius*, which St *Jerom* has a right to (2).

[B] *That this Authority is not to be depended upon.*] I say this, without having demonstrative Reasons against this Chronology: I have only Difficulties to alledge on both Sides. *Cicero* often convers'd with *Accius*. This I prove in Remark [H]. Now *Cicero* was born in the Year of *Rome* 647; and it is not likely that he had convers'd much with this Poet before the Age of 20. *Accius*, therefore, must have been alive in the Year of *Rome* 667. He should be at that time 84 Years of Age, according to the Chronicle of *Eusebius*. I confess there is nothing impossible in this; but there is little Appearance of Probability; since *Gyraldus* could not believe, that the Poet, with whom *Cicero* had so often convers'd, was the same *Lucius Accius*, so many of whose Tragedies are quoted. He thinks these were two Poets of the same Name. Add to this, that *Corradus*, who allows not this Distinction, scruples to carry the 20th Year of *Cicero*, higher than the 70th of *Accius*: insomuch, that, on account of a Passage in *Cicero*, he places the Birth of *Accius* 40 Years later, than St *Jerom* has fix'd it (3). But this is not all: *Cicero*, in his First *Philippic*, informs us, that one of *Accius's* Tragedies was perform'd during the Celebration of the Games, which *Brutus* had given, and at which he was not present, having retir'd from *Rome*, upon the Murther of *Julius Cæsar*. This Piece was greatly applauded; but the People's Approbation was more in favour of *Brutus*, than *Accius*. The Applause was too distant in Time, to belong to the Poet; "*Nisi forte Accio* "*tum plaudi & sexagesimo post anno palmam dari* "*putabatis, non Bruto.* —— *Unless you thought, that,* "*after an interval of 60 Years,* Accius, *and not* "Brutus, *received the Applause and the Palm.*" If you reckon these 60 Years from the Death of *Accius* (4), he must have died in the Year of *Rome* 650; and, consequently, we are not to believe *Cicero*, when he pretends to have heard some things from *Accius's* own Mouth. If you count them from the Time, when this Piece first appear'd upon the Stage, you will make the Orator a very weak Reasoner, in supposing that a good Performance on the Stage is never applauded but at the first Representation; which is entirely false. However this Side of the Dilemma is more eligible, than to fix the Death of *Accius* to the 3d Year of *Cicero*. If then the Passage in the First *Philippic* does not prove, that *Accius* died before the Year of *Rome* 667, let us extend the Poet's Life to that Period; but, as we have no sufficient Assurance (5) of St *Jerom's* Accuracy, let us not scruple to affert, that *Accius* might then be between sixty and seventy Years of age; and that, if he liv'd to the

(1) In *Chron. Euseb. the 2d Year of the 166th Olympiad.*

(2) *Brietius de Poët. Lat.* p. 5.

(3) *Corrad. upon Cicero's Brutus.* p. 198.

(4) P. Manucius upon *the first Philipp. counts* it as having forgot what *Cicero says of his Conversations with Accius. Observe by the by, that the Operis recorded in the Supremæ dies Savans, &c. Tom. 2. p. 12. it follows, namely, that Accius died in the Year of Rome 718, in the 61st Olympiad.*

(5) *See the Remark* [O].

A 2

ACCIUS

death of *Pacuvius*; one of his Plays being acted the same year that *Pacuvius* [C] brought a Performance of his own on the Stage. This latter was then eighty years old, the former but thirty. The name of *Accius*'s Play, which was presented that year, is not recorded; but some Authors, who have quoted this Poet (a), have furnish'd us with the Names of Several of his *Tragedies*. He made choice of the noblest Subjects, that ever appear'd on the *Athenian* Stage; such as *Andromache*, *Andromeda*, *Atreus*, *Clytemnestra*, *Medea* [D], *Meleager*, *Philoctetes*, The *Seige of Thebes*, *Tereus*, The *Trojan Matrons*, &c. He did not always borrow the Subject of his Plays from the *Greeks*: He compos'd one, the Story of which is entirely *Roman*: It was call'd *Brutus* [E], and treated of the Dethronement of *Tarquin*. If it be true, that He was Author of a Piece entitled *The Wedding*, and another call'd *the Merchant* (b) we shall have reason to rank him likewise among the *Comic* Writers [F]. His Genius was not confin'd to the Stage. He wrote some other Books, particularly *Annals*, which *Macrobius*, *Priscian*, *Festus*, and *Nonnius Marcellus*, refer to. His Friend and Patron was *Decimus Brutus*, who was Consul in the year of *Rome* 615, and who gain'd several Victories in *Spain*, which procur'd him the honour of a Triumph some time after (c). This *Brutus* was so fond of the Verses, in which *Accius* celebrated him, that

(a) *Nonnius Marcel., Varro, A. Gellius, &c.*

(b) Vossius de Poet Latin cites these two *pocies*, and the latter of them upon the Authority of Varro: but I have not been able to find it in Varro.

(c) In the Year 623. See the Fasti of Sigonius.

Age of *Pacuvius*, there is no reason why we should not apply to him and *Cæsar*, the Story related by *Valerius Maximus*. " Is (Poëta Accius) Julio Cæsari amplissimo & florentissimo viro in Collegium Poëtarum venienti, nunquam assurrexit, non majestatis ejus immemor, sed quod in communium studiorum comparatione aliquanto superiorem se esse consideret. Quapropter insolentiæ crimine caruit, quia ibi voluminum non imaginum certamina exercebantur (6). — *When Julius Cæsar came into the College of Poets, he (the Poet Accius) refus'd to rise from his Seat, though to the most renown'd Hero of the Age: not that he forgot the Respect due to his high Rank, but because he was conscious of some Superiority over him, in their common Attainments. This Behaviour, therefore, was not thought insolent, because in that Place they did not contest the Prize of Birth, but of Learning.*" This last Thought is not unlike that, which the Author (7) of the *Satire against* the French Academy (8) makes use of. I confess, that there is some Difficulty in extending the Life of the Poet *Accius* to the height of *Julius Cæsar*'s Prosperity; and it is this which obliged *Corradus* to suppose, that *Valerius Maximus* meant in this Passage *Sextus Julius Cæsar*. But why may we not suppose him to mean That *Caius Cæsar*, who was kill'd by *Marius*'s Soldiers, and who had so great Credit, though but an *Edile*, that his Disputes with *Sulpitius* the Tribune rais'd a Civil War (9)? He was one of the principal Orators of his Times, and a good Tragic Poet. But, however that be, let it be remember'd, that *Cæsar* had a happy Genius for Poetry. " Feruntur & à puero & ab adolescentulo quædam scripta, ut *Laudes Herculis* & Tragœdia *OEdipus* (10). — *He is said to have been the Author of some Pieces in his younger Days, as* The Praises of Hercules, *and the Tragedy of* OEdipus.

[C] *The same Year that* Pacuvius.] *Cicero* relates it upon the Authority of *Accius* himself. " Ut Accius iisdem Ædilibus ait se & Pacuvium docuisse Fabulam, cum ille octoginta, ipse triginta annos natus esset (11). — *At* Accius *reports, that he and* Pacuvius *taught Dramatic Poetry in the same Edileship, the latter being eighty, himself but thirty Years of Age.*" *Cicero*'s Words are *iisdem Ædilibus*; but, some Manuscripts giving a false Reading, it has been asserted, that these two Poets publish'd their Works *in iisdem Ædibus*, in the same House, *paucis quidem annis interpositis, a few Years the one after the other* (12); which is manifestly a double Mistake. *Corradus* thinks, that *Accius* mentioned this Circumstance of his Life in his *Annals* (13): but *Vossius* is of Opinion, that it was in a Work entitled *Didascalia* (14). The Reason he gives for it is, that *Accius* in this Work expressly treated of Poets and Poetry, as may be gathered from what *Charisius* and *A. Gellius* have cited from it. But this Reason is of no Weight: *Vossius* in proving against *Corradus*, refutes himself. This Writer had recourse to the *Annals* of *Accius*, *because*, says he, *a Poet never speaks of himself in a Dramatic Piece*. But *Terence*'s *Prologues* prove the contrary. How came *Vossius*, who alledges this Reason, not to see, that *Accius* might very naturally acquaint his Audience in a *Prologue*, that a Play of his was brought upon the Stage, at the same time with one of *Pacuvius*'s? Add to this, that, besides his *Annals* and *Didascalia*, *Accius* was the Author of some Books, which had no Relation to the Stage.

[D] Medea] The Conjecture of Father *Lescalopier*, that the Verses, quoted by *Cicero*, in the second Book of *The Nature of the Gods*, are borrowed from the *Medea* of our Poet, is highly probable (15). These Verses describe the Astonishment of a Shepherd, who, having never seen a Ship, discovered, from the top of a Mountain, That which carried the *Argonauts*. The good Father *Crinitus*, in consequence of this Passage, imagined that *Cicero* had quoted a Tragedy of *Accius* entitled *The* Argonauts (16). But, though this Poet had composed such a Tragedy, *Crinitus* is still to be blamed for building upon so uncertain a Foundation. The Author, whose Conjecture I have just mentioned, need not have proved to us, from the Testimony of *Crinitus*, that the Grammarians mention the *Medea* of *Accius*: he might at once have quoted *Nonnius Marcellus* for it. I have found, in the *Fragments* of the Tragic Poets, collected by *Scriverius*, that the Lines relating to the Ship *Argo*, belong to a Tragedy called *Medea*.

[E] *It was called* Brutus] *Manutius* without Reason believes, that it was acted at the Celebration of the Games of *Apollo*, at which the Brother of *Marc Antony* presided in the Room of *Brutus*, who absented himself from *Rome* (17); but it is plain, from *Cicero*'s *Epistles*, that it was the *Tereus* of *Accius*, which was then represented (18). It is surprising, that the greatest Part of the Commentators on *Cicero* should be ignorant of this. *Maturantius* thinks they acted the *Atreus*: *Beroaldus* and *Higenderphin* are for the *Brutus*.

[F] *Among the Comic Writers.*] *Donatus*, the Grammarian, will not suffer us to doubt of it: for he reckons it among the Perfections of *Terence*, that he was content to write *Comedies* without falling under the Temptation of becoming a *Tragic Poet*; *Which, among other things, adds he, was above the Reach of* Plautus, Afranius, Accius, *and almost all the great Comic Writers*. As I have not servilely translated my Author Word for Word, it may be proper to let him speak for himself. " Hæc cum artificiosissima Terentius fecerit, tum illud est admirandum, quod & morem retinuit, ut Comœdiam scriberet, & temperavit affectum, ne in Tragœdiam transiliret, quod, cum aliis rebus minime obtentum esse à Plauto, & ab Afranio, & ab Accio, & multis fere magnis Comicis invenimus (19)." We may gather from hence, that, at first, *Accius* confined himself to *Comedy*: but, his great Reputation arising from his *Tragedies*, *Donatus* seems not to have been so accurate as he should have been, in ranking him among the *Comic Poets*. Mr *Dacier* knew very well that he was a *Tragic Poet*, and has expressly asserted it in his Remark on this Verse of *Horace*:

Nil comis Tragici mutat Lucilius Attî (20)?

Notwithstanding which he translates it after this Manner: *Lucilius ——— ne trouve-t-il rien à changer dans les Comedies d' Attius? — Does* Lucilius *find nothing to alter in the Comedies of* Attius?

[G] Hung

(6) *Valer. Maximus*, lib. 3. c. 7.

(7) St Evremont, according to some, see the Hist. of the Fr. Acad. p. 69. but in the Chevreana this Satire is ascrib'd to the Count d'Etian.

(8) Entitled The Comedy of the Academicians; to which Godeau being said to Colletet, I perceive you to be an excellent Musician; reserv'd this Answer, We are all equal, being the Sons of Apollo.

(9) Ascon. Ped. in his Orat. pro M. Scauro.

(10) Suetonius, in his Life of Cæsar.

(11) Cicero in Bruto.

(12) Crinitus de Poët. Lat. ch. 5. Gl. Adorp. Onomast. p. 3.

(13) Corrad. ap. Cicero's Brutus.

(14) Vossius de Hist. Lat. p. 3.

(15) See Lescalop. Comment. in Cicer. de Nat. Deor. p. 382.

(16) Crinitus de Poet. Lat. lib. 2. ch. 7.

(17) P. Manutius upon Cicero's 1st Philipp.

(18) Cicero Epist. to Atticus, B. 16, Epist. 2, 5.

(19) Don. Ae Trag. & Comœd.

(20) Horat. Sat. 1. lib. 1. ver. 53.

ACCIUS.

that he hung them up at the entrance of the Temples, and Monuments [G], which he built with the spoils of the Enemy. This might, indeed, be owing to a Principle of Vanity rather than of Friendship, and may prove, that, if he was fond of the Poet, he was more so of the Praises he bestow'd upon him: but, in any light, it shews that *Decimus Brutus* thought *Accius*'s Poetry excellent. Besides, he was a Person well qualify'd to judge of this kind of Writing [H]. I do not find, that *Cicero* accuses *Accius* of *Harshness*, and *too much Affectation in his Stile:* this relates to another Poet [I]; as Mr *Moreri* might easily have perceiv'd, had he not servilely copied after others. Not that *Accius*, who, in other respects, was greatly esteem'd as a Poet, (d) was never reproach'd with *Ruggedness* of Stile. *A. Gellius* has a very just Reflexion in answer to this Cavil [K]. The Answer he return'd those, who ask'd him, why he did not plead at the Bar, since he met with such success upon the Stage, carries

(d) See Remark [N].

[G] *Hung them up at the Entrance of the Temples.*] *Cicero* and *Valerius Maximus* relate this. " Decimus " quidem Brutus, *says the former* (21), summus ille vir " & imperator, Accii amicissimi sui carminibus templo- " rum & monumentorum aditus exornavit suorum. — " *That great Commander, Decimus Brutus,* " *adorned the Entrance of his Temples and Monu-* " *ments with the Verses of his dear Friend Accius.*" — *Valerius Maximus* gives this Account: " Simi- " liter honoratus animus erga Poëtam Accium " D. Bruti, suis temporibus clari ducis, extitit, cujus " familiari cultu & prompta laudatione delectatus, " ejus versibus templorum aditus, quæ ex manubiis " consecraverat, adornavit (22). — Decimus Bru- " tus, *a famous General of his Times, shewed great* " *Favour to the Poet Accius, with whose easy Ad-* " *dress, and ready Talent at Panegyric, he was so* " *well pleased, as to adorn the Entrance of the* " *Temples, which he consecrated with the Spoils of* " *War, with this Poet's Verses.*" — *Scriverius* has quoted another Passage in the following Terms: " Amatus etiamnum in tantum Attio, à Decimo " Bruto fuisse dicitur, ut Attianis versibus templo- " rum & monumentorum frontes & aditus exornare " consueverit (23). — Decimus Brutus *was so* " *fond of Attius, that he was wont to hang up his* " *Verses as Ornaments to the Fronts and Entrances* " *of his Temples and Monuments.*" These he gives us for the very Words of *Cicero* in his *Brutus*; but I am sure they are not to be found there. Very likely some modern Author deceived him in this manner. He had quoted *Cicero's Brutus* in relation to the Age of *Pacuvius*, and *Accius*; then he had reported what relates to *D. Brutus*, and had contented himself to express the Sense of *Cicero's* Words, and had cited for it *idem Cicero*. Hereupon *Scriverius*, I suppose, imagined that *Cicero's* own Words were cited; and that they were taken out of the same Book which was quoted before; without taking the trouble of examining into the Truth of the Quotation. Thus you see how the most laborious and the most ingenious Compilers love to find their Work done to their Hands. *Vossius* (24), being doubtless deceived by *Scriverius*, cites *Cicero* pro *Archia* & in *Bruto*, in relation to this Action of *D Brutus*. The Illusion is perhaps still more antient than this *Scriverius* might not have it at first Hand. How careful soever he was to collect all that has ever been related of *Accius*, yet he forgot the Passage of *Columella*, which we shall produce presently (25).

[H] *Qualified to judge of this kind of Writing.*] *Paterculus* (26) has given a great Encomium of this *Brutus* in few Words, in relation to his Military Virtues: But the following is *Cicero's* Elogium on his Learning: " D. Brutus M. filius, ut ex familiari " ejus L. Accio poëta sum audire solitus, & dicere " non inculté solebat, & erat cùm literis Latinis, " tùm etiam Græcis, ut temporibus illis, satis eru- " ditus (27). — Decimus Brutus, *the Son of* Marcus Brutus, *was wont to express himself with great Po-* *liteness, as I have been informed by his intimate* *Acquaintance, the Poet* Accius: *and was well versed* *(considering the time he lived in) both in the Lear-* *ning of* Rome *and of* Greece."

[I] *This relates to another Poet.*] To wit, *Attilius*, whom *Cicero* mentions not only in one of his Letters to *Atticus* (28), Hoc enim Attilius, poëta durissimus, but also in another place. That other Passage deserves to be produced at length, because it shews what Judgment ought to be pass'd upon those who despise their own Tongue, and the Authors of their own Nation (29). " A quibus tantum dissentio, " ut cum Sophocles vel optimè scripserit Electram, " tamen male conversam Attilii mihi legendam pu- " tem, de quo Licinius,

Ferreum scriptorem opinor, verum scriptorem tamen
Ut legendus sit (30).

" Rudem enim esse omninò in nostris poëtis ant in- " ertissimæ segnitiæ est, aut fastidii delicatissimi. Mihi " quidem nulli satis eruditi videntur quibus nostra " ignota sunt. — *With whom I so far differ in Opi-* *nion, that, however beautiful the* Electra *of So-* *phocles may be in the Original, I still think the ill* *Translation of it by* Attilius *deserves to be read;* *whom* Licinius *called An harsh Writer, indeed,* *but a Writer worthy of being read. If our Poets* *are rough and unpolished, it proceeds either from* *the most slothful Neglect, or the most delicate Nice-* *ness. For my own part, I think no Man Scholar* *enough, who is unacquainted with our own Au-* *thors.*" *Suetonius* mentions the *Electra* of *Attilius*, as we shall make appear in that Poet's Article. Doubtless the *Electra* was a Tragedy; yet *Attilius* is only counted in the number of Comic Poets in the Catalogue of (31) *Volcatius Sedigitus*; and, according to *Vossius*'s Remark, the Fragments, which *Cicero*, *Varro*, and *Macrobius* (32) cite of him, relish more of the Sock, than the Buskin. Whoever should pretend to make a difficulty of this, would be greatly deceived. Are not *Corneille* and *Racine* Tragic Poets only and absolutely? yet they have composed Comedies; and if *Moliere* had taken it into his Head to compose a Tragedy, as it is said *Scarron* had a Mind to do at last, would he immediately have ceased to be a Comic Poet? *A majori parte sumitur denominatio.* — *A Thing takes it's Name from that, which particularly distinguishes it.* See the Remark [F]. But to return to the pretended Accusation against *Accius*'s Style: It must be observed, that *Cicero* cited this Poet often; and that in his Oration pro *Sextio* he considered him as a great Poet: Summi Poëtæ ingenium non solum arte sua, sed etiam dolore exprimebat. — *He expressed the Genius of this great Poet not only by his Art, but by his Concern.* The Passage is curious: We learn from it, that the famous Actor *Esop* made use of *Accius*'s Verses which had some Relation to *Cicero*'s Exile: I say he made use of them to make the People sensible of that Injustice. The *Romans* were very apt to apply particular Sentiments of a Play to the present Times. See *Suetonius* (33), and the first and the tenth *Philippic* of *Cicero*: They teach us that while a Tragedy of *Accius* was performing, the People did not cease to testify the Friendship they had for *Brutus* by their Applauses.

[K] *A very just Reflexion, in answer to this Cavil.*] *Accius*, going into *Asia*, pass'd through *Tarentum*, where he saw *Pacuvius*, who was retired thither in his old age. He shew'd him the Tragedy of *Atreus*, which he had in his Pocket, and read it to him. *Pacuvius* found it to be partly very sublime and poetical, and partly very rough and indigested. *Accius* acknowledg'd the friendly Criticism, and promis'd himself from thence Success in his future Productions; the Minds of Men being like Apples, which are never good, if they are not hard and green, before they are ripe. But it is better to weigh the Words of the Original (34). " Tunc Pacuvium dixisse aiunt " sonora quidem esse quæ scripsisset & grandia, sed " videri

(21) Cicero pro Archia Poeta, cap. 11.

(22) Valer. Maxim. lib. 8. cap. 14.

(23) Scriver. in Testim. de Attio.

(24) Vossius de Poët. Lat. p. 7.

(25) In the Remark [N]

(26) Vell. Patercul. lib. 2. cap. 5.

(27) Cic. in Bruto p. 197.

(28) Id. Epist. 20. lib. 14 ad Attic.

(29) Id. de Finib. lib. 1.

(30) Vossius de Poët. Lat. p. 7. places the Words of Licinius in this order.

(31) Apud A. Gell. lib. 15. c. 24.

(32) I believe that Vossius de Poët. Lat. p. 8. is deceived in what relates to Macrobius.

(33) Sueton. in Cæs. c. 84.

(34) A. Gell. lib. 13. cap.

ACCIUS. 61

carries no less good Sense with it [*L*]. Tho' he was short of Stature, he caus'd a very large Statue of himself to be erected in the Temple of the Muses (*e*). The Respect paid to him was so great, that a Player was punish'd [*M*], only for mentioning him by Name upon the Stage. We shall see, in the Remarks, whether *Valerius Maximus*'s Account of one *Accius*, a Poet, who refus'd to rise, and pay his Compliment to *Julius Cæsar*, in an Assembly of the Poets, be applicable to our *Accius*. *Cicero* speaks very contemptibly of one *Accius*, who wrote an History; and, as our Tragic Poet

(*e*) Notatum ab auctoribus & L. Accium Poëtam in Camœnarum æde maximâ formâ Statuam sibi posuisse, quum brevis admodum fuisset. Plin. Hist. Nat. lib. 34. cap. 5. *Charles Stephens is mistaken, in saying that* Dec. Brutus *erected this Statue to him.* Lloyd *and* Hofman *have adopted this Mistake.*

"et videri ea tamen sibi duriora paulum & acerbiora. Ita est, inquit, Accius, uti dicis, neque id sanè me pœnitet, meliora enim fore spero quæ deinceps scribam. Nam quod in pomis est; itidem, inquit, esse aiunt in ingeniis, quæ dura & acerba nascuntur, post fiunt mitia & jucunda: sed quæ gignuntur statim vieta & mollia atque in principio sunt uvida, non matura mox fiunt, sed putria. Relinquendum igitur visum est in ingenio quod diès atque ætas mitificet." This puts me in mind of a piece of Advice *Lipsius* gave to young Men. The extravagant Fondness he had conceiv'd for I know not what conciseness of Style, which disgusts the Readers of that great Man's Letters, or makes them laugh, did not hinder him from condemning those young Men, who affect Brevity. He said it was the direct Road to a meagre, thin Style; and that they ought to have many Superfluities at that Age, which might be pruned, as they advance'd farther in Years (35). "Adeò juventutem ad brevitatem non voco; ut etiam absterream, sive quia tuto assumere vix potest; & brevitatis imitatio facillimè ætatem hanc decipit: sive quia nec utiliter potest, & juvenili illo brevitatis studio aridus plerumque & exsuccus stilus evadit, nec facile ad laudatam illam temperiem venitur, nisi initio ubertas quædam & luxuries sit quam ætas paullatim depascat. ── *I am so far from advising Youth to Brevity, that I deter them from it as much as possible; either because it is unsafe, and apt to deceive tender Years; or because it is useless, and by this juvenile Affectation of Brevity, a Style becomes dry and insipid; nor is it easy to arrive at that happy Temperament in Writing, unless at first there be some redundancy and luxuriancy of Style, which Time, by little and little, may wear off.*" *Balzac* (36) was of the same Opinion. "Amputanda plura sunt efflorescenti illi ætati, quàm inferenda; facileque est remedium ubertatis; sterilia nullo labore superantur. ── *That Age requires more pruning; that cultivating a Redundancy is easily remedied, but Barrenness with great Difficulty.*" But to return to *Accius*, it has been well observ'd in the Dictionary of *Charles Stephens*, and in those that were built on the same Foundation, That *Quintilian* excus'd him, by laying the Blame on the Time in which he liv'd (37). "Tragœdiæ Scriptores Accius atque Pacuvius clarissimi gravitate sententiarum, verborum pondere & autoritate Personarum. Cæterum nitor & summa in excolendis operibus manus magis videri potest temporibus quàm ipsis defuisse. Virium tamen Accio plus tribuitur, Pacuvium videri doctiorem, qui esse docti affectant, volunt. ── *Among the Writers of Tragedy,* Accius *and* Pacuvius *are the most famous, for the Weight of their Sentiments, the Energy of their Expressions, and the Dignity of their Characters. The want of Polishing and Finishing was owing rather to the Times, than to the Poets themselves. The Learned attribute more of Genius to* Accius, *and of Learning to* Pacuvius." One would think that *Quintilian* copies these Verses of *Horace*;

(35) Lips. in Instit. Epist.

(36) Balzac. in Epist. select.

(37) Quintil. Institut. Orat. lib. 10. cap. 1.

Ambigitur quoties uter utro sit prior, aufert
Pacuvius docti famam senis, Accius alti (38).

(38) Horat. Epist. 1. lib. 2. ver. 55.

When Accius *and* Pacuvius *are compar'd*,
Both are esteem'd; both meet with great Reward.
Pacuvius *all the Critics Voices gains*
For Learning, Accius *for his lofty Strains.*

CREECH.

There is a Passage of *Ovid*, which seems to charge I know not what of Savage and Brutal upon *Accius*'s Style; but, every thing considered, I should rather understand by it the cruel Actions describ'd by him in his Tragedies. *Ovid*'s Sentiment is, that if one were to judge of a Man's Manners by his Writings, *Accius* must be accounted Brutal; *Terence* a Lover of good Chear; and

VOL. I.

those who treat of warlike Matters, brave and valiant Men.

Accius esset atrox, conciva Terrentius esset,
Essent pugnaces, qui seri bella canunt (39).

For Cruelty would Accius *censur'd be,*
And Terence *prais'd for Mirth and Jollity.*
Who Wars alarms, and Martial Deeds indite,
Of course must be the Dev'l and all in Fight.

[*L*] *Carries no less good Sense with it*] *Quintilian* has preserv'd this little Circumstance. "Aiunt (40) Accium interrogatum cur causas non ageret; cùm apud eum in Tragœdiis tanta vis esset, hanc reddidisse rationem, quòd illic ea dicerentur quæ ipse vellet, in foro dicturi adversarii essent quæ minimè vellet. ── *In my own Tragedies,* answered he, *I say what I please, but at the Bar, I am oblig'd to hear what I dislike.*" I know a Man of Wit, who made use of a like Reason, to divert his Son from the Study of the Law, and to encourage him to the Study of Divinity. "What is more convenient, *said be to him*, than to speak before Persons who cannot contradict you? This Advantage have Preachers. And what more inconvenient than, when you have done speaking, to hear yourself confuted, and oblig'd, without Mercy, to give an Account of all you have said? This the Condition of an Advocate." This puts me in mind of a Thought of Mr *Montagne*: "As for the Gift of Eloquence (41), *says he*, some have a Facility and Readiness, and which may be called Gift of Utterance, so easy that they are ready upon every Occasion: Others are slow, and speak only what is premeditated and elaborate. ── If I were to give my Opinion in these two different Advantages of Eloquence, of which Preachers and Lawyers now a-days make the chief Profession, the slow speaker seems to me the best qualify'd for a Preacher, the other for a Lawyer; because the Employment of the former gives him as much time as he pleases to prepare himself; and he goes on with the Thread of his Discourse, without any interruption: But the Lawyer is oblig'd to enter every Moment into the Lists, and the unforeseen Answers of his Adversary disconcert his Measures in an Instant (42)." ── The Advocate's Business is more difficult than the Preacher's, and yet we find more tolerable Advocates, in my Opinion, than Preachers, at least in *France*.

[*M*] *A Player was punish'd.*] Being brought before the Judges to give Satisfaction for this Injury, he said in defence of himself, that it was lawful to name a Man who gave his Pieces to be represented on the Stage. *Publius Mutius*, before whom the Cause was try'd, condemn'd him. The satyric Poet *Lucilius*, had not the same Success; for the Comedian, who had offended him, by naming him on the Stage, was acquitted. So true is it, that all Judges are not of the same Humour, or that some Persons are more considered than others. The Author, who reports these two Cases, expresses himself thus (43): "Mimus quidam nominatim Accium poëtam compellavit in scena: cum eo Accius injuriarum agit: hic nihil defendit, nisi licere nominari eum cujus nomine scripta dentur agenda. ── Caius (44) Cœlius judex absolvit eum injuriarum qui Lucilium poëtam in scena nominatim læserat, Publius Mutius eum, qui L. Accium poëtam nominaverat, condemnavit. ── *A certain Player mention'd the Poet* Accius *by Name, upon the Stage:* Accius *sued him for Damages: the other only pleaded in his Defence, that it was lawful to name a Person, who wrote for the Stage.* ── Caius Cælius, *the Judge, acquitted him, who had affronted the Poet* Lucilius, *by naming him on the Stage;* Publius Mutius *condemn'd him, who had offered the same Insult to* Accius." *Glanderpius* did not know where this Story

(39) Ovid. Trist. lib. 2.

(40) Quintil. Instit. Orat. lib. 5. cap. 13.

(41) Montagne's Essays, B. 1. chap. 10. at the beginning, p. 52, 53.

(42) *The same*, p. 54.

(43) Autor Rhetoricor. ad Herenn. lib. 1.

(44) Ibid. lib. 2.

Q Story

ACCIUS.

Poet compos'd *Annals*, some will have it, that *Cicero* abus'd him in this Place. Others deny it [N]. At the same time liv'd an Orator, of no ill Reputation, named *Accius*, against whom *Cicero* defended *Cluentius*. He was of *Pisaurus*; which might make him pass for one of our Poet's Relations [O]. It is not true, that *Cicero speaks likewise of another celebrated Orator of this Name, surnamed* Navius. Mr *Moreri* blunders here. He did not consider, that this *Accius Novius* is no other than a famous *Augur*, whom he takes notice of, a few Pages after, under the Article ACTIUS NÆVIUS (*f*). He is no less deceiv'd, when he distinguishes between the *Tragic Poet*, and the *Annalist*, cited by *Macrobius*. What he adds, that *Aulus-Gellius speaks likewise of Accius the Historian, distinct from the Writer of Tragedies*, ch. 9. Book 3. is doubly false. This Author mentions no *Accius*, in that place; and wherever he speaks of *Accius*, he must be understood to mean the *Tragic Poet*. Some Authors have expos'd themselves to Ridicule for having imitated, or admir'd, the *Latin* of this *Accius* [P], in an Age, when the Language was in much greater Purity.

Story was to be met with, but (45) reports it only on the Credit of a (46) modern Author, whose false Gloss he copies, to wit, that the Defendant was condemn'd, because he had not prefix'd any Titles of Honour or Respect to *Accius*'s Name. *Sine præfationis honori nominaverat*.

[N] *Others deny it.*] I am inclin'd to be of their Opinion; for, besides that *Cicero*, who was so often nam'd, and so often cited our *Accius*, either with Commendation, or, at least, without blaming him, would, with an ill Grace, abuse him in his 1st Book *de Legibus*; I observe, that these Abuses are altogether opposite to the Character of him, who is the Subject of this Article. Elevation, Grandeur, and Force, were the Character of *Accius*; and we have seen (47) the Testimony of *Horace* and *Quintilian*, concerning him; to which we may add two Verses of *Ovid*, and a decisive Decree of *Paterculus*.

Ennius arte carens, ANIMOSIQUE Accius oris
Casurum nullo tempore nomen habet. (48)

Ennius, *the Artless*, Accius *the* SUBLIME,
Shall stand, unmov'd, the rude Attacks of Time.

"Clara (49) etiam par idem ævi spatium fuere inge-
"nia, in togatis Afranii, in Tragœdiis Pacuvii atque
"Attii usque in Græcorum comparationem EVECTI,
"mignumque inter hos ipsos facientis operi suo lo-
"cum; adeo quidem ut in illis limæ, in hoc pene
"plus videatur fuisse SANGUINIS. — *About the
"same time flourish'd*, in Oratory, Afranius, in Tra-
"gedy, Pacuvius, and Accius, *whose Reputation ri-
"vall'd that of the most famous* Greeks; insomuch
"that there seem'd to be more Correctness in the latter,
"but more Life and Spirit in the former.*" If this new Evidence, which I have produc'd, be as strong as the foregoing; this, which follows, goes beyond all I have already reported; for here *Accius* is preferred to the great *Euripides*; "Accius poeta (50) suo
"ingenio præcelluit Euripidem, qui fuit altus & in-
"genio sublimus. — *The Poet* Accius *had a Genius
"superior to That of the lofty and sublime* Euripides." Another (51) celebrates *Accius* and *Virgil* for the two most excellent Poets of *Rome*: "An Latiæ Musæ
"non solos adytis suis Accium & Virgilium recepere,
"sed eorum & proximis & procul à secundis sacras
"concessere sedes? — *Did the* Latin Muses *receive
"not only* Accius *and* Virgil *into their Temple, but
"even Poets of an inferior Class?*" Is it likely that such a Man wrote an History worthy of this Censure of *Cicero* (52): " Nam quid Accium memorem, cu-
"jus loquacitas habet aliquid argutiarum, nec id ta-
"men ex illa erudita Græcorum copia, sed ex librarii-
"olis Latinis? In orationibus autem multus & in-
"eptus, ad summam impudentiam. — *Why should
"I mention* Accius, *in whose wordy Style there is
"indeed some Wit*; but a Wit borrow'd from the
"trifling Productions of the Latins, *not from the
"learned* Græcian *Stores?* Besides, *in his Speeches he
"is tedious and impertinent, even to the highest De-
"gree of Assurance.*" Observe well, that the Annals of the Tragic Poet *Accius* were in Verse; and that *Cicero* speaks here only of those who had writ Histories in *Latin* Prose; for he says nothing of *Ennius*. Our best Critics think that this Passage of *Cicero* is corrupted; and that we must not read *Accium*, but *Macrum*. So that the Censure will fall on the Historian *Licinius Macer*. *Vossius* (53) embraces this Opinion; but when he brings for a Proof the Friend-

ship that was between *Sisenna* and him, whom *Cicero* abus'd, when, I say, he concludes from thence, that *Cicero* did not speak of *Accius*, he is mistaken; for, by his good leave, *Accius* and *Sisenna*, were very near of the same Age. (54) *Sisenna* was old after the Civil War of *Marius* and *Sylla*; that is to say, about the Year 672 of *Rome*, and *Accius* was not dead in 665.

[O] *Pass for one of our Poet's Relations.*] St *Jerome* observes (55), speaking of the Poet *Accius*, That he was carried to *Pisaurum*, when the *Romans* sent a Colony there; and that there was a spot of Ground near the City, called *Fundus Accianus*. It was his Share of the Land, which was divided among the Inhabitants of That new Colony. *Scaliger* observes (56) upon this, That the Colony of *Pisaurum* was not settled 'till four Years after that of *Bologna*; that is, in the Year of *Rome* 568, fifteen Years before *Accius* was born. We may say, therefore, that St *Jerome* was mistaken. *Rome* was a properer place of Residence for a Poet, who was the Glory of the Theatre in those Times, than a Colony: But we must not imagine this Mistake to be without any Foundation. Perhaps the Father of *Accius* follow'd those, who conducted the Colony to *Pisaurum*; and perhaps The Patron to whom he ow'd his Liberty, was one of the chief Commissioners of That new Settlement. Now supposing he follow'd his Patron, he might have had That Land to his share, which was afterwards call'd *Fundus Accianus*, and, among other Children, he might have left the Father of the Orator *Accius*. See how *Cicero* (57) speaks of This Orator. " T. Ac-
"cium Pisaurensem, cujus accusationi respondi pro
"A. Cluentio, qui & accurate dicebat & satis copi-
"ose, eratque præsertim doctus Hermagoræ præcepti-
"quibus etsi ornamenta non satis opima dicendi, ta-
"men ut hastæ velitibus amentatæ, sic apta eque-
"dam & parata singulis causarum generibus argu-
"menta tradantur. — Titus Accius of Pisaurum,
"to whose Accusation I answer'd, in Defence of A. Clu-
"entius; who spoke accurately and fluently enough, and
"was besides vers'd in the Precepts of Hermagoras,
"which, though destitute of the Pomp of Rhetoric, yet,
"like the Darts flung by light-arm'd Soldiers, furnish
"us with apt and ready Arguments, in every kind of
"Cause." *Scaliger* does not censure St *Jerome*, for having confus'd (58) placed the great Reputation and Death of *Pacuvius*, in the third Year of the 156th *Olympiad*, and the great Reputation of *Accius*, in the second Year of the 160th *Olympiad*. This can only serve to confound those, who know that *Pacuvius* was fifty Years older than *Accius*. For if it should be suppos'd, that *Pacuvius* died about 90 Years of Age, in the Year in which St *Jerome* speaks of his Death, it must be said that *Accius* was about 40 Years of Age, in the third Year of the 156th *Olympiad*; and yet, according to St *Jerome*, he was born in the Consulship of *Mancinus* and *Serranus*, which falls under the second Year of the 152d *Olympiad*. So that, as I hinted in the second Remark, we must not depend entirely upon That Chronologist in this Case.

[P] *The Latin of this* Accius.] *Persius* and *Martial* were very severe upon People. (59)

Est nunc (60) Briseï quem venosus liber Acci,
Sunt quos Pacuviusque & verrucosa moretar
Antiopa, ærumnis cor luctificabile fulta.

Some fond are grown of Fustian Accius' *Rage,
Or love* Pacuvius' *antiquated Page.*

So

ACCO. ACCORDS.

So great Antiopa'in Grief appears,
The Tragic Tale dissolves them into Tears.

Here what *Martial* says of them in the 91st Epigram of the 11th Book.

Attonitusque legis Terrai frugiferai,
Accius & quidquid Pacuviusque vomunt.

You are extreamly fond of obsolete Expressions, such as Terrai frugiferai, *and whatever* Accius *and* Pacuvius *pour forth.*

Had they imitated those old Authors, in the manner our finest Wits imitate *Marot* at present, and the other Poets of the XVIth Century, in Fables, Ballads, Pindaric Odes, Stanzas, &c. compos'd designedly in their antiquated Style, I do not see that any Body could reasonably have found Fault with them. But I suppose they made use of that obsolete Style in good earnest, and took it for a Standard of Eloquence, either entirely adopting it, or mixing it with the Language of their own Times. See (61) the good Advice which *Phavorinus* gave a young Man in this Way of thinking. We are not subject at present to this Distemper. More Persons are disgusted even with a common Expression, or run too eagerly after new coin'd Words, than affect to retain obsolete Expressions (62). Whenever the old Language is made use of, it is by way of Pleasantry in Sallies of Wit, and Burlesque Works. It is only in *Latin*, that Authors are yet found, who are fond of the oldest Phrases. Doubtless there was another sort of Men among the antient *Romans*, when *Latin* was come to it's Perfection. These were perpetual Admirers of the old Poets, without using, or intending to make use of, their superannuated Expressions; their Intention was

only to mortify the Writers of their own Time, by extolling those of Antiquity above them. *Horace* apprehended their Design perfectly, when he said,

Sic fautor veterum, ut tabulas peccare vetantes,
Quas bis quinque viri sanxerunt, foedera regum
Vel Gabiis, vel cum rigidis æquata Sabinis,
Pontificum libros, annosa volumina vatum
Dictitet Albano Musas in monte locutas.

Jam Saliare Numæ carmen qui laudat, & illud
Quod mecum ignorat, solus vult scire videri,
Ingenii non ille favet, plauditque sepultris,
Nostra sed impugnat, nos nostraque lividus odit. (63)

So fond of all that's antient are we grown,
Nothing, forsooth, of modern Date will down.
Or'e the Decemvirs Laws devout we pore,
And antient Leagues, with Sabines made, adore.
The Augur's Lawyes transported we admire,
And Bards, grown obsolete, can never tire.
These flow'd not, sure, from any human Skill:
The Muses gave them from th'Aonian Hill.

When Numa's Song above our Verse you raise,
And, what you understand not, dare to praise,
'Tis not, that fond of antient Bards you're grown;
Envy forbids you to applaud our own.

This is a Distemper from which our Age is also exempted. We are contented to place *Grecce* and antient *Rome* above our own Age; but we do not prefer the Speeches and Poems of the XVth and XVIth Centuries, before those which are made at present.

ACCO. *Charles Stephens* reports that she was an Old Woman, who ran mad with Vexation, by seeing in a Looking-glass how homely old Age had made her. He cites the 15th Chapter of the 6th Book of *Cælius Rhodiginus*, but (a) nothing like it is to be found there. The Continuator of *Moreri* adds, That this Woman pleas'd herself with speaking to her Image before a Looking-Glass; and that oftentimes she seem'd to refuse, what she most desired. Plutarch adds, continues he, *that Mothers us'd to frighten little Children, and keep them to their Duty, with her Name*. He cites the 16th Book of *Cælius Rhodiginus*, and Cicero's Second *ad Atticum*. I shall criticise on this Passage [A] below. In the mean time let us hear what *Rhodoginus* says in a Passage, which is not (b) cited. *Acco* doated in such a manner, that when she look'd in her Glass, she entertain'd herself with her Resemblance, as if it had been another Woman; she was seen to make use of Signs, Promises, Threats, Smiles, and of all that is practised in Conversation. Others write, that she endeavoured sometimes to drive a Nail with a Spunge as if she had held a Hammer. Rhodoginus says no more of her. As for Plutarch, he (c) only says, that *Chrysippus* did not approve of frightning us from our Sins by the Divine Justice; For, said he, *we don't want Arguments against what is said about Divine Punishments, which shew that such Discourses resemble those of good Women, who frighten little Children with* Acco *and* Alphito [B], *to hinder them from idling away their time*. Plutarch shews afterwards that *Chrysippus* contradicted himself.

[A] *Criticise on this Passage.*] First, None of the three Authors mentioned have said, That *Acco* ran mad with Vexation, for having seen herself ugly in a Looking-glass; and that she seem'd to refuse what the most desired. This is ascribed to *Plutarch* by Name, and for this Reason, because, after having reported *Acco's* Folly, her being deceiv'd by her own Image, and her Dissimulation, the next Words are, *Plutarch adds*.—But I. This is to assert that *Plutarch* reported these three Facts; and consequently is to deceive the World, since That Author only relates what I have cited of him. II. How careless is it to cite only *Cicero 2d ad Atticum?* Does he mean the 2d Letter or the 2d Book? must the Reader be left to guess which? Must he be at the trouble to examine what Letter, what Book it is? They, who shall have the Patience to look for it, will yet lose their Labour. They will find in the 19th Letter of the 2d Book. *Certi sumus periisse omnia: quid enim ἀναιδίμαθα tam*

diu? My third Censure is, that *Cicero* is falsely cited; He says nothing of *Acco*. The *Greek* Word he made use of, and which many other Authors use to signify what we call wheedling, evading, raising Difficulties about things, which we heartily wish for; that Word, I say, which *Erasmus* (1) plac'd among his Proverbs, gave occasion to suspect that *Acco* was an Hypocrite; but it is only a Conjecture; and it ought not to be permitted an Author to cite *Plutarch*, or *Cicero*, or *Cælius Rhodiginus*, for Conjectures which other Persons have advanc'd.

[B] *Who frighten little Children with* Acco, *and* Alphito.] I do not believe there is any Country in the World where there is not the like Custom. I have heard it condemn'd by very ingenious Doctors. The ancient *Romans* had their *Manducus*, wherewith they threaten'd Children, as I shall observe under that Word.

ACCORDS (STEPHEN TABOUROT, Lord of) Advocate of the Parliament of *Dijon*, and afterwards the King's Advocate of the Bailiwick and Chancery of the same Town, was born in the Year 1549 (a). He was a Man of Wit and Letters, but too fond of Trifles. This appears from a Work of his, entitled *Bigarrures* (The Miscellany),

ACCORDS.

Miscellany), the first Edition of which is of *Paris*, in 1582 [*A*]. I have quoted it upon some occasions (*b*). This was not his first Performance; for he had printed some *Songs* (*c*): which *la Croix du Main*, and *du Verdier Vau-Privas*, were not aware of. His Work, which he calls *Les Touches* (*The Touches*), was printed at *Paris* in the Year

[*A*] *A Work of his, entitled—The Miscellany, the first Edition of which is of* Paris, *in* 1582.] He points out this Year in the Preface to the second Edition, and he ought rather to be believed, than *La Croix du Main*, and *Du Verdier Vau-Privas*, who place the first Edition of the Miscellany, in 1583. The first Book of the Miscellany is divided into twenty two Chapters, which treat, among other Matters, of the *Rebus*'s of *Picardie*, of *Puns*, of *Antistrophes*, of *Allusions*, of *Acrosticks*, of the *Echo*, of *Leonin Verse*, and *other Sorts of Measure, pleasantly and ingeniously contrived*, of *Epitaphs*, &c. All these are full of *Mirth and Gaity*, as *La Croix du Main* assures us (1). The Printer does not dissemble, that he published this Work without the Author's leave, "Who de-
" clared publickly, (*says he*) (2) that Age, Time,
" and his Profession, had altered his Humour and
" Inclination; and that it would ill become him to
" lay claim to what he composed in his early Years,
" and in the Flower and Gaity of his Youth; be-
" ing then scarce eighteen Years old; and that, when
" he shall have given proof of his Abilities, in some
" noble and learned Subject, he would not advise us
" strangle his natural and illegitimate Offspring, got
" out of Marriage; for so he used to call his three
" first Books. Whence I judged that he was only
" looking about for an Excuse; which determined
" me to publish this Copy." Our Author, on his part, does not fail to pretend Ignorance. " I was
" very much surprized, *says he* (3), when I saw the
" first Impression of this Book, the Memory of
" which I thought was extinct. But, upon reading
" it again, as a new Work, not having seen it these
" fourteen Years, I presently discovered my own
" Genius and Style, at a time, when I composed
" it, first, for my own Diversion, and afterwards
" for that of others; in which I observed no Me-
" thod, but threw together my Thoughts, without
" Connexion, as Whim and Fancy directed. The
" Book consists of loose detach'd Pieces, written up-
" on Scraps of Paper, adjusted together at different
" Times, a great part of which I always believed
" was lost. But, as every one is fond of his own
" Work, I had some Thoughts, at that time, of
" sending the Remainder of my Papers, which have
" encreased since that time, together with those,
" which had been omitted." Notwithstanding this He adopts and owns this second Edition. " Upon
" which account, continues he (4), I have read over
" this idle Book from one end to the other, which I
" never did before, in order to re-publish it accor-
" ding to my own true Conception of it. And as
" since that time I have recollected some little
" Pieces of a curious Nature, and others have been
" kindly communicated to me by one of the most
" learned Men in *France*, on the same Subject, I
" have added them to it in the Manner of an Ap-
" pendix by the Author."

Pasquier disapproved of *Tabourot*'s making Additions to his *Miscellany*. It was staying too long, he thought, in places which ought only to be passed by; and which ought to be considered as a Traveller's Inn, not as his Lodging. Such a Work should be looked upon as an Excursion, not as a fix'd Abode. Youth is an excuse for spending a few Hours in such Trifles; but if, some Years after, an Author applies himself to retouch them, and to make Additions, it seems as if he intended *tanquam ad Sirenum scopulos consenescere*, to grow old at the *Sirens* Rocks. After this manner *Pasquier* express'd himself in a Letter to the *Sieur Tabourot*, in the Year 1584. " I have read over your entertaining Mis-
" cellany, and I read it with Pleasure, not only on
" account of that Friendship I bear you, but like-
" wise for that genteel and lively Wit, with which
" it abounds; or rather because it is something
" whimsical, and diversify'd with a great Variety of
" fine Strokes. I could wish there had been no Addi-
" tions made to the first Impression. If I judge
" right, many of the Additions do not relish of your
" Wit; and I should easily be perswaded, that some
" other Hand has bestowed these ill-tim'd Alms up-
" on you. We should consider such Subjects as
" matter of meer Diversion, not as a Duty incum-
" bent on us, and which requires our whole At-
" tention. You will find by this, that I love and
" honour you, since I take the Liberty, for the first
" time, to address myself thus freely to you (5).

I believe *Des Accords* did not regard this Advice, and that he made still farther Additions to his Miscellany, when he reprinted it. I have the *Paris* Edition of 1614, where we find not only *the fourth Book of the Miscellany*; but likewise *the facetious Tales of the Sieur Gaulard, &c. collected by the Sieur Des Accords*. This fourth Book is not preceded either by a second or third; nevertheless the Author gives many Reasons why he calls it the fourth (6), and, among other things, says, that " this whole
" Volume would not have been new and uncom-
" mon enough, if he had followed the Example of
" the generality of Authors." He confesses, that he added the *Tales of the Sieur Gaulard* to promote the Sale. " They, *says he* (7), who have purchased
" only the first Book, in order to laugh and be
" merry, will be induced to buy this likewise for
" the sake of the entertaining Pieces I have mixed
" with it; such as the Apophthegms, or designed
" Blunders, or absurd Reflexions of Mr *Gaulard*;
" which have been imitated by several others in
" *France*; but it is unjust to rob our *Burgundian*
" of the Glory of the Invention. By this means I
" act like the Widow of a certain *Castilian*, who
" would not sell his Horse, without his Cat.

Observe, that the fourth Book of the Miscellany is more serious than the first. It is divided into three Chapters. The first contains *certain Observations useful in the Education of Children*; the second relates to the *Change of the Sir-Name*; the third contains *many particular Remarks on the French Poetry*. The Work ends with a Discourse on *pretended Sorcerers, and their Impostures*. The whole abounds with curious Matters, and may be read with profit. This particular Character of the fourth Book is one of the Reasons, which the Author alledges in justification of his having published it before the second or third. It will be proper to produce his own Words. They will convince us, that he had not given up his ludicrous way of writing, upon *Pasquier*'s Letter to him, since he apologises for continuing it. " I did this (8), *says he* (9), chiefly with a Design
" of shewing by the Stile of this Book, that my
" Mind is disposed to other Subjects, as well as
" of ignorant Detractors, who have maliciously ob-
" jected this to me. And as to those who disapprove,
" that a Man of my Profession should descend to
" such Trifles both in Prose and Verse, I refer them
" to the learned preliminary Letter of the great
" *Pasquier*'s *French* Epistles, who has shewn, as well
" from strong Reasons, as Examples, that we ought
" not to confine our Genius so obstinately to one
" single Profession, as never to allow it to unbend
" itself in more lively and gay Studies. I certainly
" commend those, who, like the *Germans*, can restrain
" themselves from following more than one Profes-
" sion at once; but we must not therefore blame
" others, who, having a Genius for several, are able
" to manage them so well, as in every one to be
" little, if at all, inferior to the particular Professors
" of each. It is well known, that the *French* Genius
" is full of this Vivacity and Variety, and it is against
" our Inclinations when we are tied down to one
" Science. Why then should it be thought wrong
" in me, that I spend That Time (which others trifle
" away) in this honourable Employ, which is not
" empty and fruitless if we examine it nearly?

But he gives another Reason, which particularly shews, that he submitted but a little time to the Attacks of his Critics, and that he had no Intention to suppress the second Book, tho' a little too loose. " In the second, *says he* (10), I treat in the same
" manner of *Periphrases*, *Hyperboles*, *Metonymies*,
" *Metaphors*, *Synechdoches*, &c. and That in the pro-
" perest *French* Terms I could chuse, and with such
" entertaining

ACCORDS.

Year 1585 [B]. It is a Collection of ingenious Pieces of Poetry, it must be confess'd; but for the most part on obscene Subjects, which he handled too freely, according to the vitious Practice of those Times. The same Vein runs thro' his *Miscellany*. He was reproach'd with this, which oblig'd him to justify himself [C]. Some ascribe to him A *Dictionary* of French *Rhimes* [D]. Lastly, *The Lordship of Accords* is an

"entertaining Examples, as must give the Reader Plea-
"sure. At present I shall take no notice of what may
"appear in it too loose and offensive to the Ears of our
"present squeamish Critics, as well as Those former-
"ly; and shall pass on directly to the fourth, in
"order to satisfy Those of a more serious turn of
"Mind, who will have reason to thank me for
"some Discoveries never touched on, I believe, be-
"fore."

[B] *His Work which he calls ———— The Touches, was printed at Paris, in* 1585.] He divided it into three Books and dedicated the first to a Prelate, namely *Pontus* of *Tyard*, Lord of *Bissy*, and Bishop of *Chalon*. He boasts of having composed them (11) *(11) In the Epistle Dedicatory.* in two Months, at *Verdum* upon *Saone*, in the Year 1585 (12); and tells us *they* are a kind of *Epigrams*; *(12) This is a Proof that he did not regard Pasquier's Advice.* to which the Name of *Touches* is properly applied: "For it is a kind of light Fencing, in which we
"my Foil I give only a Touch, which scarce
"scratches the Skin, and cannot wound the Flesh
"(13)." In another place he tells us (14), "That *(13) Epist. Dedicat.* *(14) Advertisement of the Touches, printed with the Miscellany.* "*The Touches* is a Term borrowed from Fencers,
"who call the Thrust given with their Foils a
"*Touch*, the Mark of which appears upon the Cloaths
"of him that was hit, by reason of the Chalk,
"with which the Foil is whiten'd, &c." The *Touches* of *Des Accords*, which are generally printed at the end of the *Miscellany*, are different from those I am here speaking of.

[C] *He was reproached with this, which obliged him to justify himself*] I have quoted his Apology (15) in another place; and shall add here, that *(15) In the Remark [M] of the Article* MAROT. his Printer has thought fit to confirm it. "I have *(16) Andr. Pasquet.* "published, says he (16), the whole Copy, not ca-
"strating any of those Expressions, which may be
"thought too loose and indecent, provided they
"were witty; for, notwithstanding the Author
"would have regard paid to chaste Ears, and would
"designedly have suppress'd several Passages, yet,
"having heard him hint, that it was *ipsum evitare
"Priapum*, and that an infinite Number of fine
"Strokes would lose all their Beauty, without this
"Liberty, I chose rather to follow his Opinion,
"than his Advice. He will pardon me for diving
"so far into his Thoughts; and let the following
"Lines of *Catullus* apologize for me:

Castum esse decet pium Poëtam
Ipsum, versiculos nihil necesse est;
Qui tum denique habent salem & leporem,
Si sunt Molliculi, & parum Pudici * • *Carm.* 16. *ver. 5.*

*Chaste must the Bard in every Action be,
Whilst his gay Muse from this Restraint is free.
Then only Verse can Wit and Humour know,
When wanton and scarce chaste the Numbers flow.*

"And I will venture to affirm, that this ought to
"be so far from offending any Person (some Hy-
"pocrites excepted) that, on the contrary, it will
"serve to put our Youth in mind, not to amuse
"themselves so much in these curious Enquiries,
"since they are to be met with in such Abundance,
"as is enough to create a Disgust towards them; and
"will occasion their applying themselves to the rea-
"ding of good Books, whence they may reap Ad-
"vantage: for I am fully perswaded, that the Mul-
"tiplicity of Books, which we have at present, will
"prevent the mind from examining into, and care-
"fully perusing, the best; even tho' we were sure
"to meet with Authors, who could teach us to find
"out a Hare's Form, or tell us where ready-chaw'd
"Meat was to be had. As to the *Smut*, I cannot
"imagine it will be so offensive, as *Virgil's Pria-
"peia*, the *Epigrams* of *Catullus* and *Martial*, *Ovid's
"Amours*, *Terence's Comedies*, *Petronius Arbiter*, and

"in short, the finest Pieces of Antiquity, which are
"proposed to our Youth as Patterns of Excellency;
"whereas our Author's Immodesty can never be
"considered in such a Light. But farther, every
"thing in this Book is curious, genteel, and inge-
"nious; and the Author need not apologize for
"himself, by alledging the Levity of the Subject." The meaning of all this is, that *Des Accords* did not take this Liberty, in order to favour the Passions of the Heart, but purely to amuse the Imagination, and not to rob his Poetry of that Seasoning, which would render it more agreeable and high-flavoured, according to the Taste, which prevailed for many Ages. He was not ignorant of the Maxim, that *coarse Smut is less dangerous than that which is delicate:* for thus he applys it, in his own Vindication.

"*Des Amadis* (17). *(17) Des Accords in the Touches, printed with the Miscellany, at Paris, for Maucroy, in* 1662. 12mo *pag.* 82.
"Qui voudra voir ces Ecrits,
"Les lise auprès de S'amie,
"Car ils donneront envie
"A tous deux d'être lascifs.

Of The Amadis.

*You who would know the Force these Lines impart,
Read them before the Mistress of your Heart.
The tender Tale the melting maid will move,
And both dissolve in Extacies of Love.*

D'un Lecteur d'Amadis, qui blâmoit les Bigarrures.

Toi, qui permets les lectures
D'Amadis, & ne veux vas
Qu'on lise les Bigarrures,
Cauteleusement çu as
Apperceu que les mot gras
N' entrent vivement dans l' ame,
Pour suborner une dame,
Comme les mignards appas.

On a Reader of the *Amadis*, who found fault with the *Miscellany*.

*Whilst you with wanton Amadis engage,
But shun the Miscellany's sportive Page,
Wisely your nice Discernment you approve,
That soarse Expressions less the Passions move,
Than those soft Touches, which the Fair inspire,
Spight of themselves, with loose and warm Desire.*

This puts me in mind of a Thought of *Sorel*. "The
"Poets, says he (18), who compose Works liable to *(18) Sorel's Remarks on the Extravagant Shepherd, B.* 11. p. 379. *Edit. of Rouen, in* 1646. *in* 2 Vol. 8vo.
"the Censure of the Magistrate, and which are u-
"sually burnt by the Hands of the Executioner,
"are very great Fools, in imagining, that they are
"pleasing to Debauchees: whereas it is impossible to
"read their obscene Collections without desiring to
"quit the Sport, they being so leud and wicked, as
"to create Horror in the Reader." But, not to dissemble any part of his Sentiment, I must observe, that he qualifies this a little. "But, when I give *(19) The same,* p. 379.
"this as my Opinion, *pursues* he (19), I am aware,
"that it may be said, that we ought not then to
"forbid the reading of them, since they inspire Men *(20) Biblioth. Françoise,* p. 136.
"with a hatred to Vice. But generous Minds on-
"ly find the Effect: and we ought not enjoin such
"Penances, as expose Men to Temptation. There *(21) The same,* p. 222. *and observe, that he says, it is Dictionary of French Rhimes was printed at Paris for Guillot du Pre,* 1572.
"are but too many, who take a Pleasure in being
"conversant with Filth."

[D] *Some ascribe to him A Dictionary of French Rhimes.*] *La Croix du Main* had made him Author of a Book, entitled *French Rhimes* (20); but he corrected himself, and acknowledged (21) that it ought to be ascribed to *John le Fevre*, a Native of *Dijon*, Secretary

ACCORDS. ACCURSIUS.

an imaginary Fief, founded upon a Device of his Ancestors [*E*]. Observe that WILLIAM TABOUROT, his Father, who was Advocate of the Parliament of *Dijon*, King's Council, and Master extraordinary of the Chamber of Accounts, is much commended by *Peter* of *St Julian*, in his Work *Of the Origin of the Burgundians* (*d*). He died the 24th of *July* 1561, in the 46th Year of his Age (*e*).

Secretary of the Cardinal *de Givri*, and Canon of *Langres*. This Retractation is just; for *Des Accords* declared, that this Work did not belong to Him. These are his Words, at the end of his Chapter on *French Poetry*: " I shall hereafter, *says he* (22), give " my Opinion more fully, in the Collection I am " preparing of the *French Poetics*; in which I find " the way smooth'd the best, with great Learning " and Labour, by *Pelletier*, divinely and much to " the Purpose by *Ronsard* (as he does every thing), " and with great Address (considering his Time) " by *Quintil* the Critic, and several others: whose " Assistance I shall make use of, mentioning their " Names, and referring to their Text, in compiling " *a Sequel to the Dictionary of French Rhimes*, by my " Uncle, Mr *Le Fevre*, which I shall shortly publish."
What inclines me to believe he kept his Word, is a Passage which I meet with in the *Dictionary of French Rhimes*, printed at *Paris*, in 1596, by the Heir of *Eustace Vignon*, in Octavo. The Author begins thus: " At first, *says he* (23), I collected this " Dictionary, by way of Amusement, almost as it is " at present, as to the Quantity of Words, being " desirous to assist the Defect of a treacherous " Memory. Afterwards meeting with That of " the Sieur *Des Accords*, enriched with several Remarks upon Rhime, I was prompted to review " my own, and to philosophize a little upon this " Subject; which I have not done without Success."
[*E*] *The Lordship of* Accords *is an imaginary Fief, founded upon a Device of his Ancestors.*] Let us hear his own Account: " Since in my Discourse, *says he* (24), on changing the Sir-Name (25), I blame " those who do it; and since, by assuming the Title " of *Lord of Accords*, I declare myself worthy of " the same Censure; I must inform you, that my " Name is composed of the first Letters of the several Chapters of my first Book, by way of *Acrostic*: the 1*st* " *stie* (26); and after the same manner the second " Book informs you of it's Age, and the Place " where it was composed. But to raise the Subject, " I did not put my real Name, but a Lordship " framed upon a Device of my own, which was a " Drum * (27), round which I put these Words " *A tous Accords*, which had been constantly my " Father's, Grand Father's, and Great Grand Father's Motto. In the Chapter of particular Remarks on the *French Poetry*, you will find the Occasion of erecting this Device into a Lordship." It is proper to produce what he relates in the Chapter to which he refers us. He had sent a Song to " a " beautiful and virtuous young Lady, Daughter of " the late learned President of *Bourgogne*, Mr *Begat*, " who, *says he* (28), did me the Honour to be in " Love with me. —— And whereas, *continues he*, " I had subscribed the Sonnnet only with the " Words of my Device *A tous Accords*, she was the " first, who, in her Answer, christen'd me *Seigneur* " *des Accords*, as her Father often afterwards called " me; for which Reason, in all my Writings since " that time, I have made choice of this Sir-Name, " and even in these Books." He gave himself likewise, by way of *Anagram*, the Name of *Tervobatius*, as Mr *Baillet* assures us (29).

ACCURSIUS, Professor of Civil Law in the XIIIth Century, was a *Florentine*. He acquired a very great Reputation by the Comments he composed on the Body of the Law. It is said that he begun but late to study the Law; and that he was 40 Years of Age [*A*] when he first attended the Lectures of the famous *Azo*. He had applied himself before that time to other Studies. The Progress he made in the Civil Law was so great, that he became a famous Professor in that Science, which he taught at *Bologna*; and, afterwards burying himself in Retirement, he compos'd *A Perpetual Comment on the whole Law*, which appeared so convenient and useful to young Students, that the former Glosses were no more spoken of, which doubtless were not so well disposed, nor so compleat. Some think that the Contradictions, which are observ'd in *Accursius*, do not proceed from his Inconstancy, or a Defect of Memory, but from this, *viz.* that in reporting the different Opinions of those, who had preceeded him, he had distinguished them only by the initial Letters of their Names: Which Letters disappearing in several Places, was the Cause of his Readers taking that for His Opinion, which he only produced in Proof of another's Sentiments. His Authority was formerly so great [*B*], that some call'd him the Idol of the

[*A*] *And that he was 40 Years of Age.*] Others say that he was but 28. " Jam quadragenarius, vel, ut " alii scribunt xxviii. annos natus jus civile ab Axone " audivit. —— *At the Age of 40, or as others write* " xxviii, *he learnt Civil Law from Azo.*" These are *Pancirollus*'s Words (1), in the 147th Page of his second Edition, which is That of *Venice*, 1655. Sir *Thomas Pope Blount* (2), citing *Pancirollus*, and *Konig*, puts 37, and not 28 Years. The Citation of *Konig* is good, but that of *Pancirollus* is not, unless my Edition differs from the first. *Forster* would have been more properly cited (3); for he reports, that *Accursius* became a Disciple of *Azo*, at 37 Years of Age. *See the Remark* [*F*].

[*B*] *His Authority was formerly so great.*] I cannot cite any thing more proper or entertaining, in this Place, than a Passage quoted by one of the modern Civilians, with whom the Glossographers were least in Esteem. " Nostis (4) quanta sit sutoritas glossatoris. " Nonne heri dixit Cyn. Glossam timendam propter " præscriptam Idololatriam per Advocatos, significans " quod sicut Antiqui adorabant Idola pro Diis, ita " Advocati adorant Glossatores pro Evangelistis. Volo enim potius pro me Glossatorem quam Textum; " nam si allego Textum, dicunt Advocati diversæ " partis & etiam Judices, *credis tu quod Glossa non* " *ita viderit illum Textum, sicut Tu. & non ita bene* " *intellexerit, sicut tu?* Ego recordor (& sit illud pro " novo) quod dum essem Scholaris, eram satis acutus, & dum semel essemus multi Socii in una collatione, ausus fui unum Textum allegare contra " sententiam Doctoris mei: tantam audaciam habui. " Dixit unus Socius, *Tu loqueris; contra Glossam, quæ* " *dicit sic.* Et ego respondi, *etsi Glossa dicit sic, ego* " *dico sic*; ignarus auctoritatis Glossatorum. Credebam enim quod essent quales sunt in libris Grammaticæ, sicut super Virgilio & Ovidio, sed tamen " non ita est; fuerunt enim Glossatores maximæ scientiæ viri & auctoritatis. Magis ergo standum est " eis qui viderunt totum corpus Juris, quam nobis " qui non vidimus. —— " *You know the great Authority of a Commentator. Was it not said yesterday* " *by Cyn. that a Comment was a terrible thing, on* " *account of That Idolatry always paid to it by the* " *Advocates; intimating, that as the Antients adored* " *Idols for Gods, so the Advocates adored Commentators for Evangelists. I had much rather have* " *the Comment, than the Text, favour my Opinion;* " *for, if I appeal to the Text, the Advocates, on the* " *other side, and even the Judges, cry out, Do you* think

ACCURSIUS.

the Advocates (*a*). Most Interpreters have taken as much (*b*) or more (*c*) Care to explain his Gloss, as to comment on the very Text of the Law. Some Critics, great Lovers of polite Language, have exclaim'd with great vehemence against the barbarous Stile of this Author [*C*], but the general Opinion is, that he was a great Genius; and that his Defects proceeded from the Age wherein he liv'd [*D*]. He liv'd very much at his ease, having both a fine City and Country-House, and two Sons, who were very studious, as we shall see presently. Some Persons say, that he had a very learned Daughter [*E*], and initiated in the Profession of the Civil Law. He died in the Year 1229. at 78 Years of Age [*F*]. His Tomb is to be seen at *Bologna*, in the Church of the *Cordeliers*, with this (*d*) very short and plain Inscription, *Sepulchrum Accursii Glossatoris Legum, & Francisci ejus filii.—The Tomb of Accursius, the Commentator of Law, and his Son Francis.* He said there was no need of Theology [*G*] to teach us Divine Things, since the *Roman* Laws sufficiently instructed

(*a*) Taken out of Pancirollus, lib. 2. cap. 2°. de claris Legum Interpret. p. 147, &c.

(*b*) Arth. Duck of the Use and Authority of the Roman Civil Law, lib. 1. cap. 6. in Pope Blount's Cens. celebr. Autor. pag. 286.

(*c*) Forster's History of the Civil Law, lib. 3. c. 12.

(*d*) Pancirol. ib. p. 149.

"think the Comment did not see the Text, and "understand it, as well as you? *I remember, that,* "*when I was a School-Boy, I was very acute; and* "*that, many of us being together at the same Le-*"*cture, I had the Courage to cite one Text, against* "*the Opinion of my Master.* One of my School-fel-"lows immediately said, *You speak against the Com-*"*ment, which says thus. I reply'd, Though the* "*Comment says so, I say otherwise; so ignorant* "*was I of the Authority of the Commentators. For* "*I consider'd them in the same Light, as the Com-*"*mentators upon Grammatical Books, such as Virgil* "*and Ovid: but the Case is otherwise; for the Com-*"*mentators were Men of the greatest Learning and* "*Authority. It must therefore be safer to rely upon* "*their Authority, who had a full View of the whole* "*Body of the Law, than upon our own Judgment,* "*who have not.*" *Hottomanus* cites some other Passages of the same Author, which confirm the same thing; and informs us, that the Comment, put in Ballance against the Opinion of any Two Doctors, carried it always before the Judges. *Si sententia Glossatoris duobus Doctoribus est contraria, profecto in judiciis praevaleret sententia ipsius Glossae* (5).

(*e*) Raphael Fulgosius, Id. ib. ubi supra.

[*C*]. *Exclaim'd with great Vehemence against the barbarous Style of this Author.*] *Ludovicus Vives* (6) was one of them. See *Bernartius* also in his Treatise of the Profit that reading of History brings. Many Authors have been found among the Civilians of the XVIth Century, who have censur'd This Barbarity of Style. It seems *Alciatus* rous'd them up, and gave them the first taste for uniting Polite Literature with the Civil Law. *Budaeus*, one of the warmest Censurers of *Accursius*, contributed also to it (7). It cannot be denied, but that the Ignorance of good Literature, made the Commentators fall into divers Mistakes. *Albericus Gentilis* declar'd himself much their Partizan; he (8) would not own that *Accursius* put this Maxim in use, *Graecum est, non potest legi*, with which he (9) was reproach'd. He believes that those Words are no where to be found in this Commentator; and makes him more learned in the *Greek* Tongue, than is generally thought. However it be, the Proverb *Graecum est, non potest legi*, passes for having deriv'd it's Original from these Commentators. It is pretended that, when they met with a *Greek* Word, they pass'd it over, and gave for a Reason, that it was *Greek*, and could not be read; and having thus leap'd over this Ditch, they refum'd the Explication of the *Latin*.

(6) Ludov. Vives, de cautis corrupt. artium, lib. 1. p. c2. & lib. 7. p. 206. See also Brevicatus inter Epistol. Eobani Hessi.

(7) See Pasquier's Recherch. de la France, l. 9. c. 39. p. 901. who gives the first Place to *Budaeus*, and the second to *Alciatus*.

(8) Alb. Gentilis de Juris interpretibus, fol. 29.

(9) See Sich. in pref. ad Cod. Theod. & Alcitium, cap. 10. l. 2. Disputat.

[*D*] *That he was a great Genius, and that his Defects proceeded from the Age wherein he liv'd.*] I shall only cite two Authors (10). " Hanc significationem " in animo habuit Fr. Accursius, Glossatorum vete- " rum Coryphaeus, homo ingenii profus stupendi, " qui in tantis disciplinarum tenebris ipsam discipli- " narum disciplinam accuratissime intellexit, cum non " jurisdictionem, sed jurisditionem scribendum censuit. —— *This was the Sense of Francis Accursius, the " Coryphaeus of antient Commentators, a Man of a " prodigious Genius, who, in such a dark Age of " Learning, thoroughly understood all the Principles of " Literature; for he was of Opinion it should be wrote " Jurisditionem, not Jurisdictionem.* This is the Testimony of a *Frenchman*; let us hear a *Frenchman* next (11). " Antiqui (*Interpretes juris*) inter quos Accur- " sius & Bartolus principatum tenent, de sermone non " valdè anxii, rerum quas tractant curam solam habue- " runt: quas cum nossent, quantum in illa barbarie " & codicum depravatione nosse poterant, explicare " nisi incondite & barbarè nequiverunt, quod non

(10) Barthius in Animadv. in Claudiani Rufin. lib. 2. v. 85. pag. 1200, & 1201.

(11) Rolandus Maretius Epist. 40. lib. 1. p. 176, 177. Edit. Lipf. 1687.

" tam eis quam seculo illi tribuendum, quo linguae & " bonae literae prorfus jacebant. —— *The Ancients* " (*the Commentators on Law*) *among whom Accursius* " *and Bartolus claim the Precedence, regardless of the* " *Language, employ'd their whole Concern upon the* " *Matter of their Compositions; which as they under-* " *stood no farther, than That Age of Barbarity, and* " *corrupt Copies of Books, permitted them; it was im-* " *possible they should explain otherwise, than in a* " *rude and barbarous Manner; but this is not so* " *much to be ascribed to them, as to the Age, in* " *which Languages and Learning were at a very low* " *Ebb.*" Note, that *Barthius* gives *Accursius* the Christian Name of *Francis*; and he is not the only (12) Person that does it: I follow'd these Authors in the first Edition, but I reject their Authority in this.

[*E*] *A very learned Daughter.*] *Pancirollus* (13) mentions her only by hear-say. " Filiam quoque habuisse " dicitur, quae jus civile Bononiae publice docuit.—— " *He is reported likewise to have had a Daughter, who* " *taught the Civil Law publickly at Bononia.*" When a Fact of this Nature is doubtful, it is very likely to be false; for such Things are too remarkable to remain in uncertainty, if true. So that I do not give much Credit to what I have just now read in the *Theatrum* of *Paul Freberus* (14), that *Accursius* had Daughters, who for their excellent Erudition, were employ'd to read publick Lectures at *Bologna.* I hope *Freberus* will not take it ill that I should distrust *John Frauenlobius*, of whom he cites a *German* Book.

(12) Arth. Duck, ad Pope Blount de it d sp. See Pope Blount, ubi supra.

(13) Pancir. ubi supra, p. 149.

(14) Paul. Freher. Theatr. Erudit. pag. 784.

[*F*] *He died in the Year* 1229, *at* 78 *Years of Age.*] You see nothing like it in the *Theatrum* (15) of *Paul Freberus*, which was compil'd with so much Labour, and during such a long Time. But you will find, on the contrary, that *Accursius* flourish'd in the Year 1236, that he died in the Year 1279, and that he wrote a Comment on the *Authentics*, in the Year 1236. He is himself cited for this last Particular, by (16) *John Fichardus*, in his Lives of the Civilians. But that Citation is false, as appears from the following Observation communicated to me from good Hands (17). " *Volaterranus* says (18), That *Accursius* be- " gan to study the Law at 40 Years, and that he di- " ed in the Year 1279, in the seventy eighth Year " of his Age; from whence it should follow; that " he was born in the Year 1201. In the mean " time *Accursius* himself informs us, in the *Authen-* " *tic*, *Ut praep. nom. Imper.* at the Word *inditiones*, " that he actually writ in the Year 1229. and on " the last Law but one in the Code *De Accusatio-* " *nibus*, that he writ in the Year 1227. which he " could not have done, if the Calculation of *Vola-* " *terran* were true: Otherwise *Accursius* must have " profess'd the Law a long time before he studied " it. These Epochs of 1220, and 1227, exclude " that of 1236, which is faulty, and cannot be ad- " mitted by those, who place *Accursius*'s Death in " 1229."

(15) Id. ib. à Monnole.

(16) Apud Freher. ib.

(17) Mr de la Monnole.

(18) Volat. Lib. 21. pag. 781.

[*G*] *There was no need of Theology.*] *Conringius* (19) censured him for it, as he ought to do: these are his Words; " Ridicula est Accursii gloriatio in *gl.* " *ad l.* 10. *sect.* 2. *ff. de J. & J.* nihil opus esse " Theologiae studio ad cognoscenda divina, ut quae " ex legum Romanarum libris affatim queat peti. —— *Accursius's Boast* (in *gl.* ad l. 10. sect. 2. ff. " de J. & J.) *that the Study of Theology was of no* " *use towards the Knowledge of Divine Things, they* " *being abundantly contained in the Books of the* " *Roman Laws, is very ridiculous.*

(19) Conrin. de Civili Prudent. c. 3. in Pope Blount, ubi supra.

[*H*] *Mr*

ACCURSIUS.

structed us in them. Mr *Moreri* is very much out in quoting [H] the Sieur *Catel*. *Francis Hotomanus* had no reason to say that *Odofred* taught *Azo* and *Accursius*, for *Odofred* and *Accursius* were both Scholars of *Azo*, and afterwards Professors at the same time at *Bologna*. *Albericus Gentilis* remark'd this Mistake of *Francis Hotomanus* (e).

(e) Alberic. Gentilis in his Dialogue de Juris Interpretibus, fol. 6c.

[H] *Mr Moreri is very much out in quoting.*] Let us compare these two Authors Texts with each other, which will be sufficient to demonstrate the Mistake. *Catel* having said that *Montpellier* was one of the principal Cities of *France* (20), in which the *Roman* Law was read publickly, adds, " For we find that " the greatest and antient Civilian *Placentinus*, who " lived before the Commentator *Accursius*, read the " Law publickly in the City of *Montpellier*, of which " he makes frequent mention in his *Summa*, which " he composed (he tells us in the *Institutes*) during " his abode at *Montpellier*, as those have observed " who wrote his Life. He died at *Montpellier* the " twelfth of *February* 1192, and lies buried in " St *Bartholomew's* Church-yard." Now hear *Moteri*. The Sieur Catel maintains that Accursius died at *Montpellier in* 1192. That which he adds stands in great need of Correction; " Others, *says he*, as " *Fiscardius* and *Tritbemius*, place him in the fol- " lowing Century; nay, the last says, that he pro- " fess'd at *Bologna* in 1240. But they may be mi- " staken, in confounding that Great Man with his " Son *Francis Accursius*, who was a Man of Merit " and Learning; and who was Professor of Law at " *Bologna*, and Counsellor to *Richard* King of *Eng- " land*." The Father ought to have been placed in the XIIIth Century, and then they would not have been in danger of confounding him with the Son: So that Mr *Moreri's* Doubt is very ill grounded. There was no King of *England* at that time, whose Name was *Richard*.

(20) Catel Memoirs of *t* + H. beg of *t. nguedoc, p. 205.

ACCURSIUS (CERVOT) Son of the Foregoing, was more in haste to take his Degree than his Father: For he desired to be *Doctor of Law* before the Age of Seventeen Years, and obtain'd his Request, after it had been a long time discuss'd, whether the Laws (a) permitted it. He apply'd himself to composing Comments, and added them to those of his Father; but they were not much esteem'd. *Deterior Interpres ineptas glossas, & longè à vero distantes, paternis addidit; quæ Cervotianæ vocatæ ut plurimum rejiciuntur*, (b)——Being a worse Interpreter, he added his *own Glosses to those his Father: they were call'd from him Cervotian, and are generally rejected*.

(a) Pancirol. de clar. Leg. Interpr. lib. 2. c. 19.
(b) Id. ibid.

ACCURSIUS (FRANCIS) elder Brother of the Former, was so esteem'd by the *Bolognese*, that when they heard, that he intended to follow the King of *England* into *France*, to teach the Law, they forbad him to absent himself, and threatened to confiscate all his Estate, if he went out of their City. He thought he had out-witted them, by selling all his Estate to a Friend; but his Cunning prov'd ineffectual, for they confiscated it nevertheless. This oblig'd him to return; and he obtain'd the Restitution of his Estate. He had taught at *Toulouse*, and found himself one Day very much puzzl'd on the Subject of Interests. *James* of *Ravanna*, one of the most learned Civilians of his Time, crept in among his Auditors *incognito*, pretending to be one of the Scholars, and urged such Objections to him, as were not easily answered. Some have said that *Accursius*, at his return to *Bologna*, was Professor of Law there with *Bartolus*, and that having had a Dispute with him on the reading of a certain Law, they sent to consult the antient Manuscript of the *Pandects* at *Pisa* about it. But what probability is there, that he lived 'till the Time of *Bartolus's* being Professor [A] (a)?

(a) Ex Pancirol. ibid. pag. 141.

[A] '*Till the Time of* Bartolus's *being Professor.*] *Bartolus* was born in the Year 1313. and was admitted Doctor of Law at the Age of twenty one Years; that is, in the Year 1334 (1). So that *Accursius*, the Son, must have lived at least 120 Years, if he had seen *Bartolus* in his Profession: for he had been (2) emancipated by his Father. Let us suppose, that he was but fifteen Years of Age, when he was emancipated, and that the Year of his Emancipation was the last of his Father, yet we shall find that in 1334, he must have been 120 Years old *Pancirollus's* Conjecture is probable enough; (3) which is, that *Accursius*, who was *Bartolus's* Colleague, was the Son of one *Accursius*, who taught the Law at *Reggio*, his native Country, about the Year 1273, and that he taught likewise at *Padua*. *William Duranti* makes frequent mention of him.

(1) Pancirol. de clar. L.g. Interp. cap. 67.
(2) Id. ib. cap. 23.
(3) Id. Ibid. cap. 42.

Let me add here another Observation of Mr *De la Monnoie*, " *Antonius Augustinus* speaks in several " Places (4) of his *Emendations* on that Dispute of " *Bartolus* in relation to the reading of a certain " Word in the last Paragraph of the Law *Si creditor* " at D. de *Distract. pign.* and is inclined to believe, " that *Bartolus* had that Dispute rather with *Baldus*, " than with *Francis* the Son of *Accursius*. *Alex- " ander* of *Imola*, cited by the same *Antonius Au- " gustinus*, believed also, that the Contest happened " between *Baldus* and *Bartolus*. But *Bartolus* him- " self having positively declared in Writing, that it " was with *Francis* the Son of *Accursius*, the Ex- " pedient, which *Pancirollus* had found out, seems " rather to be admitted :" and I own myself of the same Opinion.

(4) Particularly in the 17th chapter of the 4th Book.

ACCURSIUS (MARIANGELUS) was one of the Critics, who lived in the XVIth Century: He was of *Aquila* [A], in the Kingdom of *Naples*, His ruling Passion

[A] *He was of Aquila.*] Besides the Testimony of *Toppi*, approved by the Silence of *Leonard Nicodemo*; the following Verses confirm this,

Ut volucrum Regina supervolat æthers, & alti
Immotum lumen solis in orbe tenet,
Sic illa genitus Mariangelus Urbe ————
Alite quæ à Jovia nobile nomen habet,
Felici ingenio solers speculatur. ————

As, soaring high in Air, with steady gaze,
The Queen of Birds the Sun's bright Orb surveys,
So Mariangelus,
Sprung from That Town, which bears the Eagle's Name,
On Learning's Wings soars to Immortal Fame.

They are to be met with in a Piece of *Francis Arfillus* (1), printed at the end of a Collection of Verses, entituled

(1) Leonardo Nicodemo mistakes in calling him Aesilius. Addit. alla Bibl. Napolet. p. 170.

ACCURSIUS.

(a) Barth. upon Statius, Tom. 2. p. 399. Tom. 3. p. 1602. upon Claudian. p. 826. *See also the 13th Chap. of the 20th Book of his Adversaria.*

(b) *It was done with regard to Ausonius, in the Edition of Amst. 1671. but not according to the System of the Title, which permits Notæ integræ Accursii; the mere Notes of Accursius.*

Passion was to search for and collate old Manuscripts, in order to correct the Passages of the Ancients. The *Diatribæ*, which he printed at *Rome*, in Folio, in the Year 1524, on *Ausonius, Solinus,* and *Ovid,* shew his Capacity in that kind of Learning. He had taken a great deal of Pains about *Claudian* [B], but That Work was not publish'd, though the Author assures us he had corrected above seven hundred Passages of it from the Ancient Manuscripts. *Barthius* (a) has express'd his Concern, that a Work of this nature was not printed, nor the others (b) reprinted. He does not think *Accursius* contemptible on the score of Wit, and finds him often to be very judicious. This Critic composed *Latin* and *Italian* Verses [C]; he understood likewise both *Music* and *Optics,* and he travell'd to the *North* [D]. They who inform us of this, might add, That he understood the *French, Spanish,* and *German* Languages (c) perfectly: That he collected a great number of *Antiques,* which were reposited in the *Capitol,* and that he spent 33 Years in the Court of *Charles* V. to whom he was very agreeable, and from whom he receiv'd many Favours. It must not be forgot that his Edition of *Marcellinus* (d) is larger [E] by five Books than the preceeding. That Edition is of *Ausburg,* 1533. He pretends to have corrected five thousand Faults in that Historian (e). In the same Year, and in the same City, he publish'd the Letters of *Cassiodorus* in Twelve Books, with the *Treatise of the Soul* added to it; and we are (f) oblig'd to him for the First Edition of That Author. As there were some *Latin* Writers in his time, who affected to make use of the most antiquated Terms, he ridicul'd them very pleasantly in a Dialogue [F], which he published

(c) Nicolo Toppi Biblioth. Napolet. p. 2. 6.

(d) Henry Valesius's *Præface to Ammian. Marcell.*

(e) Toppi, ubi supra.

(f) Leonard Nicodemus's *Additions to the Biblioth. Napolet.* p. 170.

(1) *He was a German, whose Name was Gorits, according to Mr de la Monnoie.*

(2) Lib. 4. Amorum, apud Leon. Nicodem. ubi supra.

(3) Ipse Sallustii civis, Amiterninus nempe, Barth. in Stat. Tom. 2. p. 399.

(4) Mariang. Accurs. In Testudine.

(5) Accursius's Diatr. in Ausonium. *These Words are retrench'd in the Edition of Ausonius of 1671.*

entituled *Coryciana,* which was published at *Rome* in the Year 1524. There is in that Collection, a Protrepticon of our *Accursius ad Coricium* (1), which contains eighty seven Verses. The Title of *Arsilius*'s Piece is, *De Poëtis urbanis ad Paulum Jovium.* Pierius Valerianus, cotemporary with *Accursius,* sirnames him *Aquilanus,* not only in his Commentary on the 11th Book of the *Æneid,* but also in some *Latin* Verses, which he addresses to him (3). We may be certain therefore, that *Barthius* was mistaken in the native Country of *Accursius.* He supposed him to be born at *Amiternum* (4). *Konig,* not being aware of this Mistake, adopts it all along. What led *Barthius* into the Mistake, was the following Sentence of *Accursius:* " Nec placuit reticere, ne quis " (quod Sallustius civis ait meus) modestiam in con- " scientiam duceret (5). ———— *I thought proper not* " *to conceal it, least (as my Fellow-Countryman Sal-* " *lust says) any one should construe my Modesty into* " *Dissimulation.*" The Reason why *Accursius* called *Sallust* his Countryman, *Sallust,* I say, who was born at *Amiternum,* is, because the City of *Aquila* rose upon the Ruins of *Amiternum,* and was in some manner substituted in it's Place. It is but five Miles from the Ruins of *Amiternum.* Consult Mr Baudrand.

[B] *He had taken a great deal of Pains about Claudian.*] Since the Fatigue of his Travels in *Germany* and *Poland* did not hinder him from correcting near seven hundred Faults in That Poet, we may imagine, that he apply'd himself, with great Diligence, to the same Task, at his more leisure Times. " TALIS, " *says he* (6), non ALES, legitur in codicibus (CLAU- " DIANI) etiam novissimè recognitis. Qui tantam " abest ut non etiam nunc versibus sint claudi ac de- " formes, ut eos ex vetustis exemplaribus, dum Ger- " maniam Sarmatiasque nuper peragramus, septin- " gentis fere mendis inter equitandum eluerimus.——— " We read in TALIS, not ALES, in all the Editions *(of* CLAUDIAN) *even the latest revis'd; an Author, so mutilated and deform'd, even at present, in his Versification, that, in my Passage thro' Germany and Sarmatia, I corrected near seven hundred Faults out of the ancient Manuscripts, as I travell'd on Horse-back.*"

[C] *Latin and Italian Verses.*] Hear what *Accursius* himself says of this Matter, in a Fable entituled *Testudo,* which he added to his *Diatribæ.* He relates in it the Persecutions he suffered at *Rome* from his Detractors, who imputed the most innocent Things to him as a Crime. Addressing himself to two young Princes of the House of *Brandenburgh,* to whom he dedicated his Book, he says, " Novitiis ipsi principes, " quàm mihi vestitum prope militarem probro ver- " terint ; tum fidibus scire, musicen callere, philoso- " pho indignum prædictent, quantumque invaserint, " quod & Opticen cum literarum studiis, vernaculos- " que cum Latinis numeris, conjunxerim. ——— *Your* " *Highnesses know, how they even reproach'd me with* " *the Military Garb I wore; then they cry'd, it was*

(6) Accursius's Diatr. in Ausonium. *These Words are retrench'd in the Edition of Ausonius of 1671.*

" *unworthy of a Philosopher to play on the Violin,* " *and understand Music; and how furiously they at-* " *tack'd me for joining Optics to the study of Letters,* " *and the Poetry of our own Language to that of* " *the* Latin." He says likewise, that he was writing the History of the House of *Brandenburgh* from the Memoirs with which he was supply'd.

[D] *And he travell'd to the North.*] We have already heard his own Account of the great Number of Passages, which he corrected on his Saddle, as he cross'd *Germany* and *Poland.* That, which follows, will inform us, that he remarked the most trifling Things, even the Songs with which Children were lulled to sleep; but he drew no very good Consequence from them; as we shall see: " Nuper non in Panno- " nia solum, atque adeo apud septentrionales pleros- " que populos, verum etiam ultra Sauromatas, non " sine admiratione audivimus ad studendum nutricio " more infantibus fomnum dici Li lu, Li lu, tum " & La lu, La lu, & La la, La la; Quod nostrates fere " Nan na, Nan na, & Ni na, Ni na, etiam mora qua- " dam vocem suspendentes, passim dicere consueve- " runt. Movit porro nos majori quadam admira- " tione quod infantes ipsi & horriduli & sordiduli " vix dum fari incipientes mammam atque tatam " Latine balbutiunt, ipsis quoque matribus non " intellecti. Ut videri possint & hæ quoque voces " naturales magis quam arbitrariæ (7). ——— *Lately,* " *says he, not only in* Pannonia, *and among most of* " *the Northern People, but even beyond the* Sauro- " matæ, *I have been surprized to hear* Children " *lulled asleep by their Nurses, with a* Li lu, " Li lu, La lu, La lu, *and* La la, La la; " *which those of our own Country every where call* " Nan na, Nan na, *and* Nin na, Nin na, *with* " *a short Pause of the Voice. But what surprized* " *me more was, that the little dirty Brats, scarce* " *beginning to speak, lisp'd out, in* Latin, Mamma " *and* Tata, *which is not understood even by the* " *Mothers themselves: whence it should follow, that* " *these Words are Innate, and not Arbitrary.*" He was in the wrong to think, that the Mothers did not understand what their little Children would say, for it was they who taught them these Words.

[E] *His Edition of* Marcellinus *is larger.*] *Toppi* had no good Memoirs relating to this Fact: He has omitted what he ought to have said, and advanced what he ought not to say. He has not said that *Accursius* added five new Books to those which were already printed, and mentions only the sixth. But it is not true that the sixth was found; the thirteen first Books of that Historian are yet wanting. *Leonardo Nicodemo* censured *Nicolas Toppi,* as he deserv'd, for it (8).

[F] *In a Dialogue which he published in the Year* 1531.] Because all those who well have my Book may not have that of *Leonardo Nicodemo,* let us copy the Title of that Dialogue at large. " Osco, Volsco, " Romanoque, Eloquentia, interlocutoribus, Dialo- " gus ludis Romanis actus. In quo ostenditur verbis " publica

(7) Id. ib.

(8) Leon. Nicodem. ubi supra.

VOL. I.   S

ACCURSIUS.

publish'd in the Year 1531. He added a small Treatise (g) of *Volusius Metianus*, an ancient Civilian. He wrote also a Book concerning the Invention of Printing [G]. He is accus'd of Plagiarism in his *Ausonius*; for it was said, that he made use of the Labours of *Fabricio Varano*, Bishop of *Camerino*, as his own; but he clear'd himself of it upon Oath, and protested that he had never borrow'd any thing, which he had read in any Book, to adorn his own. The Form of his Oath is remarkable [H]. Several other Works of His wou'd have been printed, if his Son *Casimir*, who was a Man of Learning [I], had liv'd longer (b).

(g) *The Title of it is,* Distributio, item vocabula, ac notæ partium, in rebus pecuniariis, pondere, numero, & mensura.

(b) Toppi Biblioth. Nap. let. p. 2.6.

"publica moneta signatis utendum esse, prisca vero
"nimis & exoleta tanquam scopulos esse fugienda.
"Si quid itaque, lector optime, antiquitatem amas,
"ut sane debes, libellum hunc ingenti quamvis pecu-
"nia à Bibliopola te tibi redemisse non pœnitebit.
"Nam præter quam quod vocibus partim Oscis, par-
"tim Volscis, conscriptus est, Latina quoque istuc
"verba exoletiora nimisque prisca, quibus Aborigines,
"Picus, Evandrus, Carmentaque ipsa loquebantur,
"affatim collata sunt; Quæque omnia apud Ennium,
"Pacuvium, Plautum, aliosve hujus notæ priscos
"Autores abstrusiora leguntur; Itemque recentio-
"rum cacatas Apuleii & Capellæ chartas; hujusmo-
"dive aliorum. Quæ ut certè sunt evitanda, ita
"tamen ab eo qui docti nomen ferat agnoscenda
"sunt, ut cum aliquando in eas offenderit, de illo-
"rum sensu ei turpiter hæsitandum non sit (q). ——
"*A Dialogue held at the Roman Games; The Speakers,
"an Oscian, a Volscian, and Roman. In which is
"shewn, that we ought to make use of Current Phrases,
"and avoid, as Rocks, those which are too old and
"obsolete. If therefore, Courteous Reader, you have
"any Value, as you ought to have, for Antiquity, you
"will not think the Purchase of this little Book too
"dear at any Price. For, besides that it is written
"partly in the Oscian, and partly in the Volscian,
"Language; you will find in it a large Collection of
"the more antient and obsolete Latin Words, made
"use of by the Aborigines, Picus, Evander, and
"Carmenta herself; together with all the abstruse
"Expressions which are read in Ennius, Pacuvius,
"Plautus, and other antient Authors of the same
"Character, likewise the low contemptible Style of
"more modern Authors, such as Apuleius, Capella,
"and the like. Which, tho' we ought certainly to
"avoid imitating them, yet ought they to be so far
"known to him, who pretends to the Name of Scho-
"lar, that, whenever he lights upon them, he may
"not betray his Ignorance of their meaning."* The
following is Andr. Schottus's Opinion of this Work:
"De Apuleio, Metamorphoseos ex Lucio Patrensi,
"seu Luciano, scriptore, audi, amabo, quæ in Dia-
"logo olim ante hos ipsos octoginta annos à Ma-
"riangelo Accursio (homine, ut illis temporibus per-
"erudito, quique Nasonem, Ausonium, ac Solinum
"Diatriba illustravit) Osce ac Volsce conscripto, ut
"sæculi degenerantis nimium à prima eloquentia in-
"saniam veluti aceto asperså satyrâ perstringeret, sæ-
"di inquam, & risum continê si potes, *&c* (10). ——
*Observe, I beseech you, the following Account of
Apuleius, Author of the Metamorphosis from Lucius Patrensis, or Lucian, which was given about
eighty Years ago by Mariangelus Accursius (an
Author very learned for the times, and who criticized upon Ovid, Solinus, and Ausonius) in a
Dialogue written after the Oscian and Volscian
Manner, as a severe Satire upon the Folly of the
Age, which degenerated too much from the ancient
Eloquence; hear, I say, his Account, and forbear
laughing, if you can, &c.*

Observe that this Work of our *Accursius* is in 8vo. but chiefly take Notice of the following Observation, communicated to me by Mr *De la Monnoie*: "The Dialogue of *Mariangelus Accursius* against the Corrupters of the *Latin* Tongue, might have been printed in the Year 1531. but we must believe, that it had already appeared some Years before, seeing *Jeffery Tory* cites it in his *Champ fleuri*, printed by himself in 4to. in the Year 1529. There are besides, says he, a thousand other ways of speaking which *Hieronymus Avancius*, a *Native* of *Verona*, takes notice of in the beginning of his elaborate Annotations on the Works of the ancient Poet *Lucretius*, *which I leave to the Curious, and Lovers of Antiquity, and which may be seen and read at large in a Dialogue, entitled,* Osci & Volsci Dialogus ludis Romanis actus. —— *A Dialogue between an Oscian and a Volscian, held at the Roman Games.* That Piece is hinted at by *Paul Jovius* in the Elogy of *Baptista Pio*, whom it attacked chiefly. The Title of the Dialogue is singular, and of a very modest Length; but I can scarce construe the first Words of it, *Osco Volsco Romanoque eloquentia interlocutoribus*. Perhaps it should be read, *& eloquentia, &c.*"

[G] *A Book concerning the Invention of Printing.*] I do not pretend to have seen it, and only report it on the Credit of *Toppi* (11): but the following I am assured is matter of Fact. It was believed (12) that our *Accursius* had writ with his own Hand in the first Leaf of a Grammar of *Donatus*, printed *en Vellum*; *that this Donatus, with another Book, entitled,* Confessionalia, *were the first Books printed, and that* John Faustus, *Citizen of* Mentz, *Inventor of that Art, had put them to the Press in the Year* 1450. Mr *Chevillier* (13) observes, That That *Accursius* was living in the Year 1500. Yet, for all that, he makes some Difference between his Testimony and That which was given by *Ulric Zel*, Bookseller in *Cologne*, in the Year 1499. I say, he makes some Difference between them, in regard to Time. *Donatus*, says he, had been longer printed, when *Accursius* writ this, than when *Zel* spoke of it (14). Every Man apprehends, that a Year more or less is of no Consequence here. Besides, ought it to be said, that a Man, who passed thirty three Years in the Court of *Charles* V. was living in 1500?

[H] *The Form of his Oath is remarkable.*] It is this: (15) Quod dii hominesque, fas, fidesque audiat, sacramenti religione, ac si quid est jusjurando sanctius, affirmo, idque rite pariter ac sine dolo malo dici, cæterisque accipi volo, me nec ullius unquam scripta perlegisse ac ne conspexisse quidem, unde vel tantillum lucubrationes nostræ redimiri juvaturique datum fuerit. Quin immo laborasse, quoad id fieri licuerit, ut si quippiam alterius, post observationem quoque meam, editum occurrerit, è nostris protinus abolueverimus. Quod si pejerem, tum Pontifex perjurio, malus autem genius Diatribis contingat, usque adeo ut si qua bona aut saltem mediocria in ipsa fuerint, impertiorum tuebæ pessima, doctis leviuscula triciesque viliores censeantur, famæ si qua maneat munera, vento evolent, proque vulgi levitate ferantur. —— *In the Name of Gods and Men, Truth and Sincerity, I solemnly swear, or, if any thing be more binding than an Oath, I affirm upon That, and desire what I say may be received as the Truth, and nothing but the Truth, that I never either read, or so much as saw, the Works of any Author, from whence my own Lucubrations might receive the least Help or Improvement; Nay that I have even laboured, as far as it was possible, whenever any Author has published the same Sentiments with myself, immediately to blot it out of my own Works. And if I am forsworn, may the Pope punish my Perjury, and an evil Fate attend my Criticisms; that, whatever in them is Good or even Indifferent, may appear to the unskilful Many very Bad, to the Learned Trifling and of no Importance; and whatever little Reputation I am still Master of, may it be given to the Wind, and looked upon as the Gift of the ill-judging Vulgar.* How many Reflexions might be made on this Oath!

[I] *His Son Casimir, who was a Man of Learning.*] It is probably He, whom the learned and famous Patron of learned Men, *Vincent Pinelli*, entertained some time in. his House; for although *Gaudo* gives *Accursius*'s Son the Name of *Francis*, he seems to doubt of the Matter. Thus he speaks; "Præter "hos domi habuit Benedictum Octavianum res Phi-"losophicas Theologicasque doctum. —— Marian-"geli Accursii filium Francíscum, ni fallor, insig-"nem Moribus & Doctrina (16). —— *Besides these,* "*he entertained in his House* Benedictus Octavianus, "*learned in Philosophy and Divinity* —— Francis, "*the Son of* Mariangelus Accursius, *if I mistake* "*not, of celebrated Morals and Learning.*"

ACHÆUS,

ACHÆUS.

ACHÆUS, Cousin German of *Seleucus Ceraunus*, and of *Antiochus the Great* [*A*], Kings of *Syria*, became a Powerful Monarch, and held the Dominions, he had seiz'd, a considerable time; but at last his Usurpation was punish'd in a terrible manner. At first he serv'd his Master with wonderful Fidelity; for having accompanied *Seleucus Ceraunus* in his Expedition against *Attalus* (*a*), he caus'd the two Captains, who had kill'd *Seleucus*, to be put to death, and regain'd all the Provinces, which *Attalus* had conquer'd, and refus'd the Title of King, which the Suffrages of his Troops, and Favourable Circumstances, put into his Hands. He resisted those Temptations generously, and would only conquer for the Lawful Successor of the Monarch, whose Death he had revenged; that is, for *Antiochus*, the younger Brother of *Seleucus*. But his Good Fortune blinded him; for, as soon as his Victories had made him Master of all *Attalus*'s Dominions, except only the City of *Pergamus*, he assum'd the Title of King. He maintained this Usurpation with much Prudence and Courage, and no Prince on this side the *Taurus* made himself so much feared, as He (*b*). The Great and Noble Provinces, which he possessed on this side of That Mountain, did not satisfy his Ambition; He projected likewise the Conquest of *Syria*, when he heard that *Antiochus* was gone to make War upon *Artabazanes* (*c*). He was in hopes either that *Antiochus* would perish in That Expedition, or that it would continue so long, that He should have time to take *Syria*, before the return of that Monarch. He relied also much on the Rebellion of some Provinces which had but just revolted. He departed, then, from *Lydia* with a great Army, and in his March he writ to the Subjects of *Antiochus*; but when he drew near *Lycaonia*, he perceived that his Soldiers refused to bear Arms against their Ancient King. This made him declare to them, that he would desist from his Enterprize. He returned back, and, having plundered *Pisidia*, he distributed such a considerable Booty among them, that he entirely regained their Affection (*d*); we may infer from hence by the way, that those, who say, he declared himself King of *Syria*, speak without exactness. *Antiochus*, having gloriously finish'd the War against *Artabazanes*, sent Ambassadors to *Achæus* to complain of his taking the Title of King, and openly favouring the *Ægyptians* (*e*). This Reproach was not altogether ineffectual; for we find, that *Antiochus* (*f*) made a Truce with their Prince, because he knew that *Achæus*, his Ally in appearance, was really in their Interest. This shews, that the Usurper had some regard to the Complaints of *Antiochus*, and that he made a shew of joining with him against *Ptolomy* King of *Ægypt*. This latter endeavoured in vain to include him in the Treaty of Peace; for *Antiochus* always rejected the Proposal, and could not bear, that the King of *Ægypt* should plead in favour of Rebels (*g*). As soon as he was at Liberty, he apply'd himself diligently to recover the Dominions, which *Achæus* had usurped: He gained his point, and obliged the Usurper to take Shelter in *Sardes*, where He blocked him up, and after a long Siege made himself Master of the City (*b*). *Achæus* fell into his Hands by Treachery: Being prevailed upon to sally out of the Citadel of *Sardes*, He was delivered up to *Antiochus*, who caused him to be cruelly and ignominiously put to death. He cut off the Extremities of his Members, and afterwards his Head, which was sewed in an Ass's Skin, and ordered the remainder of his Body to be hung on a Cross (*i*). This happened in the Year of *Rome* 540. It was a fit Example to be made, and doubly useful [*B*]. I shall not remark Mr *Moreri*'s Faults; they may be easily known by only comparing his Narrative with mine; but I shall distinctly point out the Mistakes of *Francis Patricius* [*C*].

[*A*] *Cousin German of* Seleucus Ceraunus, *and of* Antiochus *the Great*.] He was the Son of *Andromachus*, who was the Brother of *Laodice*, Wife of *Seleucus Callinicus* (1), and Mother of those two Princes. Let us observe, that he was a good Son, for knowing that *Andromachus* was imprisoned in *Alexandria*, he forgot nothing to release him out of that Captivity. The *Rhodians*, knowing his Disposition, sent Ambassadors to King *Ptolomy*, to demand *Andromachus* of him. Their Design was to make a Present of him to *Achæus*, to engage him to break the Promise he had made with the *Byzantines* to assist them. There was at that time a strong War between the *Rhodians* and the *Byzantines*. The King of Egypt made some Difficulty to give up *Andromachus*; he knew that such a Prisoner might be useful to him in Time and Place, for he was yet embroil'd with the King of *Syria*, and he was not ignorant of the great Power of *Achæus*. But at last, to oblige the *Rhodians*, he was willing to deliver up his Prisoner to them, that if they judg'd it fit, they might send him to his Son, which they did. And by this, and some other means, they procured *Achæus*'s Friendship, and took from the *Byzantine* the chief Foundation of his Hopes (2). Note that *Achæus* was married (3) to *Laodice*, the Daughter of King *Mithridates*, who had been very well educated by *Logbasi* (4), an Inhabitant of *Selge*, a City of *Pisidia*. This Lady maintained the Siege of *Sardes*, with her Husband, and was constrained to surrender herself, after he was put to Death (5).

[*B*] *It was a fit Example to be made, and doubly useful.*] For it was a Lesson to Men, not to be too credulous, nor to abuse the Favours of Fortune. We will transcribe the Words of *Polybius*, the Author of this Piece of Morality. (6) Κατὰ δύο τρόπους ὡς ἀνωφελεῖς ὑποδείγματα γενόμενος τοῖς ἐπιγινομένοις, καθ᾽ ἕνα μὲν πρὸς τὸ μηδενὶ πιστεύειν ῥᾳδίως, καθ᾽ ἕτερον δὲ, πρὸς τὸ μὴ μεγαλαυχεῖν ἐν ταῖς εὐπραγίαις· πᾶν δὲ προσδοκᾷν ἀνθρώπους ὄντας. —— *An Example of double Use to Posterity; teaching us, first, not to give Credit hastily to any one; and, secondly, that we should not be too much elevated with good Fortune, but expect every thing, as we are Men*.

[*C*] *I shall distinctly point out the Mistakes of* Francis Patricius.] He pretends, that the Subjects of *Achæus*, overburthen'd with Taxes, revolted, and murthered him, with all his Family, and cast his Body into the *Pactolus*, in order to make him drink Golden Waters (7). " Acæus, Lydiæ Mæoniæque
" Rex, gentilitio avaritiæ crimine ardebat: si quidem
" crebra ac gravia populis tributa semper imperabat,
" in quibus exigendis sævus, improbus atque inexo-
" rabilis erat: verum cum tantam injuriam diutius
" populi ferre nequirent, nocturna tessera inter se
" data, subito hominem concursu illum cum omni
" familia trucidaverunt, & regia incensa ejus cadaver
" unco tractum in Pactolum flumen demerserunt,
" ut

ACHÆMENES.

"*ut auriferas aquas semper potaret.* ——— Achæus, "*King of Lydia and Mæonia, was very avaritious,* "*a Vice peculiar to his Family; he imposed frequent* "*and heavy Tributes upon his People; in collecting* "*of which he was cruel, unreasonable, and inex-* "*orable: but his Subjects, unable to bear such inju-* "*rious Usage any longer, conspired together by Night,* "*and the Multitude, surrounding him on a sudden,* "*massacred him and his whole Family, and, setting* "*Fire to the Palace, dragged his dead Body, and* "*threw it into the River Pactolus, that it might* "*drink Golden Waters for ever.*" Observe first that he is mistaken in pretending that our Achæus was a *Lydian* issued from the ancient Kings of the Countrey, and Heir of their Avarice. He had in his Thoughts the Riches of *Crassus*, and the Request of *Midas* (8). He had better have remembered that Achæus was a *Syrian*. But this Fault is small in comparison of the rest; for all the Circumstances of this Narrative are false. Mr *de Boissieu* is persuaded that the bad Interpreters of these Words of *Ovid*,

Morte vel interea capti suspensus Achæi,
Qui miser, aurifera teste, pependit, aqua (9).

Or base *Achæus*'s Sentence mayst thou share,
Suspended on a Gibbet, high in Air,
Whom rich *Pactolus* from his Banks beheld
Aloft exalted o're the *Lydian* Field.

have deceived that Writer. He observes (10) with Reason, that the meaning of them is, that the Body of *Achæus* was hang'd upon the Banks of the *Pactolus*. He adds, that *Zarottus* is the first who div'd into the Poet's Thought, and that *Leopardus* discovered it plainly, and therefore that *Lipsius* ought not to have taken to himself the Reputation of the first Discovery of the true Sense of That Passage (11) " Hanc esse Poëtæ " nostri mentem primus vidit Zarottus, sed quasi per " nebulam ; & omnino Paulus Leopardus, Emendat. " lib. 1. c. 20. ideo non erat, quò Justus Lipsius, l. 1. " de Cruce, cap. 4. principem sibi hujus loci expla- " nationem tribueret. Valeat autem Alciatus cum " sua illa explicatione quam, l. 9. c. 24. Parergon " Juris inseruit. ——— *Zarottus was the first, who* " *discovered this to be the Poet's Meaning, but as it* " *were thro' a Cloud; after him Leopardus thorough-* " *ly saw it, in his Emend. lib. 1. c. 20. Therefore* " *Justus Lipsius had no reason to arrogate to himself* " *the Honour of having first explained it, in his* " *first Book de Cruce, c. 4. But away with Alciatus* " *and his Explanation, which he inserted in the 24th* " *Chapter of his 9th Book of his Parergon Juris.*" However it be, *Francis Patricius* applies his Examples very ill. Achæus was not punished for his Avarice, but for his Ambition. There is nothing in the Punishment of *Aquilius*, whom they (12) associate with him, because *Mithridates* poured melted Gold into his Mouth, which bears any Resemblance to *Antiochus*'s Revenge.

ACHÆMENES was the Father of *Cambyses*, and Grandfather of *Cyrus*, first King of *Persia*, if we may believe *Herodotus* (a). There are other Passages, wherein That Author seems to speak of an *Achæmenes* much ancienter than the other ; for he says that the *Persian* Nation (b) was divided into different Families, whereof the most Illustrious were composed of the *Pasargadæ*, under which were comprehended the *Achæmenidæ*, from whom the Kings of *Persia* descended. In another Place (c) he introduces *Cambyses*, the Son of *Cyrus*, exhorting the Chief Lords of *Persia*, on his Death-bed, and above all the *Achæmenidæ*, not to suffer the *Medes* to recover the Kingdom. This seems to give us the Idea of an *Achæmenes*, the Stock of those *Achæmenidæ*, much ancienter than the Grand-father of *Cyrus*. *Stephen of Byzantium* makes mention of one ACHÆMENES, the Son of *Ægeus*, who, he pretends, gave his Name to a Province of *Persia*, call'd *Achæmenia*. Others say (d) that this *Achæmenes* was the Son of *Perseus* ; others infer it from the Kings of *Persia* being descended from *Perseus* [A]. Almost all the Commentators of *Horace* are unanimous in asserting, that the *Achæmenes*, whom he mentions in the 12th Ode of the 2d Book, as a very wealthy Person, was a King of *Persia* [B] ; but if so, he must have reigned before the *Medes* had subdued the *Persians* ; for from the Foundation of that great Monarchy by the *Medes*, which was the second distinguished by the Name of *Universal*, we do not meet with any King of this Name amongst them. *Cyrus* passes constantly for their first King ; and They, who pretend there were Two before him (e), distinguish them very plainly both from his Father *Cambyses*, and from his Grand-Father *Achæmenes*. However it be, the Epithet of *Achæmenians* is often given the *Persians* in the ancient *Latin* Poets ; and even at this time *Persia* is call'd *Azemia* (f), and the *Persians Agemis* (g).

[A] *The Kings of* Persia *being descended from* Perseus.] Mr *Chevreau* (1) gives it as *Herodotus*'s Opinion, " that the *Persidæ*, that is, those of the House " of *Persis*, or *Persous*, were descended from the " *Achæmenidæ*, Allies of the *Pasargadæ*." He assures us in the same Page, " that, according to the " Testimony of *Herodotus*, the Kings of *Persia* came " from *Perseus* or *Persis*, and that the *Persidæ* were " descended from the *Achæmenidæ*, that is, from the " first who had the Name of *Achæmenes* in that Fa- " mily." This is a very confus'd Account. *Herodotus* does not say in general, that the *Persidæ* descended from the *Achæmenidæ* ; he says (2) it only of the Kings of *Persia*, that is, of (3) *Cyrus*, and of those who reign'd after him. He distinguishes the *Persians* into different Classes, one of which he particularly distinguishes by the Name of *Persian* ; another he calls *Pasargadæ*, under which he places the *Achæmenidæ*. He says in another Place (4) indeed, that the *Persians* acquir'd that Name, from the time that *Perseus*, the Son of *Jupiter* and of *Danaë*, left them his Son *Perseus*, whom he had by *Andromeda* ; but he does not say, as Mr *Chevreau* supposes, That the Kings of *Persia* were descended from *Perseus*. Mr *Chevreau*'s Argument proves thus far, That *Cyrus* was not inferior in Birth to the Kings *Medes*, or to the Kings of *Persia*, seeing these descended from *Achæmenes*, as well

as *Cyrus* : he proves that they descended from him, because the *Persidæ* did. Besides the Mistake I have already remark'd, he supposes farther, That the first, who bore the Name of *Achæmenes*, was antienter than *Perseus* the Son of *Jupiter*. Mr *Dacier* perfectly retain'd what he repeated from his Memory only of this Passage of Mr *Chevreau* (5).

[B] *Was a King of* Persia.] Mr *Moreri* says in plain Terms, That *Achæmenes* was the first King of the *Persians* ; and that all the Princes, who governed that Monarchy to *Darius*, were descended from him. But first of all I would ask him, Why, in speaking of *Cyrus*, he attributes the first Foundation of the *Persian* Monarchy to him, and why in giving us a List of the Kings of *Persia*, he does not place *Achæmenes* before *Cyrus*, but the latter before all the rest ? Besides, I would fain be inform'd, of what *Darius* he speaks ; for there were two or three Kings of that Name in *Persia*. Does he mean him, who was conquered by *Alexander* the Great ? In That Case he would be too decisive ; the Ancients do not agree that That *Darius* was of the Royal Family. If he means *Darius*, the Son of *Hystaspes*, he expresses himself improperly ; the Phrase *all the Princes* is not proper, when we would speak but of two Persons out of more than twelve. I cannot tell why Mr *Dacier* (6) limits the Epithet of *Achæmenidæ* to the

ACHÆMENES. ACHERI. ACHILLES.

the time of *Darius*, the Son of *Hystaspes*; when he says, That the Descendants of *Achæmenes*, King of *Persia*, bore his Name unto That *Darius*. I do not question but they bore it after him. For, besides that his (7) Son *Xerxes* carries up his Lineage in a direct Line to *Achæmenes*, we meet with one *Tigranes*, General of the *Medes* (8), distinguish'd by the Appellation *Achæmenides*: and we find an *Achæmenes*, mention'd above, who was the Brother of *Xerxes*. I say nothing of *Sopor*, called *Achæmenes* in *Ammianus Marcellinus* (9); it is a corrupted Passage. Mr *Chevreau*, wondering, without doubt, to see five Generations between This *Xerxes* and *Cyrus*, believ'd that This Prince counted his paternal Ancestors on the one Side, and his maternal on the other; insomuch that he pretended to descend from *Achæmenes* only by the Mother's Side: but this is not to be found in *Herodotus*; unless we alter the *Greek* Text, according to a very probable Conjecture of Mr *de Saumaise* (10).

(-) Herod. lib. 7. cap. 11.
(8) Ib. cap. 62.
(9) See Valesius upon Amm. lib. 15. cap. 2.
(10) Sal. mas. Excre. Plinian. p. 1183.

ACHÆMENES, the Son of *Darius* I. of that Name (a), King of *Persia*, and Brother of *Xerxes* (b) by Father and Mother, had the Command of *Egypt* (c) after *Xerxes* had again reduc'd it under the Yoak of Obedience, which it had the Boldness to shake off. Some time after he commanded the *Egyptian* Fleet (d), in the famous and fatal Expedition against *Greece*. We do not find what other Employs he had during the Life of the King his Brother; but we find that, *Egypt* being again revolted, after the Death of that Monarch, *Achæmenes* was sent thither to reduce it. This Undertaking was unfortunate; for he was beaten by *Inarus*, Head of the Rebels, assisted by the *Athenians*.

(a) Herodot. lib. 7. cap. 97.
(b) Ib. c. 7.
(c) Ib. c. 97.
(d) Ib. lib. 3. cap. 12. Diod. Sicul. lib. 11.

ACHERI (LUKE de) a Benedictine of the Congregation of St *Maur*, was born at St *Quentin* in *Picardy*, in the Year 1609. He made himself Famous by the Publication of several Books, which lay hid a long time in Manuscript in the Libraries. He began, in 1645, with the Edition of the *Epistle* attributed to St *Barnabas*. Father *Hugh Menard*, Monk of the same Congregation, had a Design to publish This Epistle, and had already illustrated it with several Notes; but, Death preventing him from executing his Resolution, Father *Luke d'Acheri* undertook it. So that, by his Care, the Epistle of St *Barnabas* was printed in *Greek* and in *Latin*, with Father *Menard*'s Notes in the year 1645. At Three Years end Dom. *Luke* publish'd the *Life*, and *Works*, of *Lanfranc*, Archbishop of *Canterbury*, and the Chronicle of the Abbey of *Bec*. In 1651, he publish'd the *Life* and *Works* of *Guibert*, Abbot of *Nogent*, with some other Treatises. Having afterwards collected several rare and curious Pieces, and hoping to get a great many more such, he formed the Design of publishing a most ample Compilation of them that he could, under the modest Title of *Spicilegium*. He publish'd his first Volume in the Year 1655. That Volume was followed by Twelve others; the last whereof was printed in the year 1677 (a). That Collection, in thirteen Volumes *in Quarto*, is very much esteemed by those, who endeavour to clear up Ecclesiastical Matters in every particular: But we meet with no Pieces in it, but such as have been composed since the Decay of the *Roman* Empire in the West. The same Author publish'd the Rule of the *Solitarians*, composed by the Priest *Grimlaic*; and some Ascetic Works [A]. His Prefaces, and small Notes, shew that he had some Learning. He had a hand in the critical Work, which appeared in the first Volume of the *Acts of the Saints of St Benedict's Order*; and it is to him, and to Father *Mabillon*, that the Title of those Acts attributes the Labour of having Collected and Publish'd them. *Luke d'Acheri* died at *Paris* the 29th of *April* 1685, in the Abbey of St *Germain*'s, where he had been Library-Keeper (b).

(a) See in the Journal de Savans of Feb. 28. 1678, why This pecillegium was not continued.
(b) See the Journal des Savans of Nov. 26. 1685. and Mr Baillet, Tom. 3. of his Judgment des a-vans, p. 518.

[A] *And some Ascetic Works*] He did not put his Name to the Collection, which he published of them, and of which I am going to give the Title, as I find it in the *Bibliotheca Bibliothecarum* of Father *L'Abbé*, "Asceticorum, vulgo spiritualium, opusculorum, "quæ inter patrum opera reperiuntur; Indiculus "Christianæ pietatis cultoribus ab Asceta Benedi-"ctino Congregationis sancti Mauri digestus, Parisiis "in 4to. 1648. —— *An Index of the Ascetic, commonly called Spiritual, Tracts, which are found among the Works of the Fathers; digested for pious Christians, by a Benedictine Ascetic of the Congregation of St Maur. Paris, in 4to, 1648.*" Mr *Teissier* says, in his Additions to that Work of Father *L'Abbé*, that *Luke d'Acheri* publish'd the Life of St *Augustin* at *Paris*, in the same Year.

ACHILLES. There have been several of this Name. The first who bore it, had no other Mother than the Earth, and did *Jupiter* a very good Office; for having received the Goddess *Juno* in his Cave, when she fled from the Amorous Pursuits of that God, he entertained her with such persuasive Discourses, that she consented to consummate the Marriage [A]. We are not informed in what manner she testified her Gratitude to her Host, who had inspired her with such Tractableness; but we know that *Jupiter*, in Acknowledgment of this Service, promised *Achilles*, that thenceforth whoever should bear his Name, should be famous. For which Reason, the Son of *Thetis* became an Hero. The Name of the Preceptor of *Chiron* was A C H I L L E S; and from thence it was that *Chiron* gave the Name of A-CHILLES to the Son of *Thetis*, his Pupil. This is sufficient to overthrow all those cold and forced Etymologies of the Word ACHILLES, which depend on the personal Qualities of the Son of *Thetis* [B]. The Inventor of the *Ostracism* among the

(1) Father Schottus translated them wrong by ad Jovem redire.

[A] *That she consented to consummate the Marriage.*] These Words of *Photius*, αυνελθεῖν τῷ Διί, signify so much (1), as appears by what follows; καὶ τοιύτην μίξιν "Ἥρας καὶ Δ.ὸς ταύτην γίνεσθαι φασίν. —— *And it is said, that This was the first time that Jupiter enjoy'd Juno.*

[B] *Etymologies —— which depend on the personal Qualities of the Son of Thetis.*] It is diverting enough

VOL. I. T

ACHILLES.

the *Athenians* was named ACHILLES. A Son of *Jupiter* and of *Lamia* bore that Name. He was so handsome a Man, that, by the Sentence of the God *Pan*, he carried the Prize of Beauty, which was disputed with him. *Venus* being displeased with that Judgment, caused *Pan* to fall in Love with *Eccho*, and metamorphosed him in such manner [C], that he became a frightful Object. Another ACHILLES, the Son of *Galata*, was born with white Hair. There were fifty four others of the Name of *Achilles*, all very famous; two of which were remarkably brutish (*a*). I am going to make a separate Article of the most celebrated Person of this Name.

to read the Inventions of *Greece* on that Subject. It not only deserves the Epithet of *lying* (2), and (3) *fabulous* upon that Account, but also That of *male foriata*, which the *French* Term *oiseuse* does not fully come up to.

Ask the *Greek* Grammarians, why This Hero was called *Achilles*; some will answer you, because he was very troublesome to his Mother, and to his Enemies: Others, because he harass'd the *Trojans* greatly: Others, because, having learned the Secrets of Physic, he quieted Pain: Others, because he had but one Lip: Others, because he was qualified to command: Others, because he had never suck'd; and others, because he went away from his Preceptor *Chiron*, without ever having eat of the Fruits of the Earth. If we were to shew by what *Analysis* of Grammar they found so many Etymologies in the Name of *Achilles*, we should make this place, as it were, stand an end with *Greek*. For which Reason, I refer the Reader, if he pleases, to the great *Etymologicum*, to *Eustathius* (4), to *Tzetzes* (5), &c. Messieurs *Lloyd* and *Hofmen*, who, following the Examples of *Fungerus*, and others, have enrich'd the Article of the Son of *Peleus* with their Etymological Observations, ought at least to have appreh'd us, that much Pains had been taken in vain by those, who will have it, that the Word *Achilles* depends on the personal Qualities of the Hero of the *Iliad*. They might have refuted that Pretension, by shewing that there were *Achilles's* before him, and given us a Reason a thousand times more natural than all the rest, why this Hero was called *Achilles*; I mean That which I have already reported, to wit, that the Preceptor of his Preceptor was called by this Name.

[C] *And metamorphosed him in such manner.*] *Photius* (6), who preserv'd some Fragments of the seven Books, which *Ptolomy*, the Son of *Hephæstion*, has filled with the most curious Trifles of fabulous Antiquity, has maimed what regards *Achilles*, the Son of *Jupiter* and of *Lamia*, in such manner, that a Man must give himself the trouble of guessing that it was with the Goddess *Venus* he contested the Prize of Beauty. This Conjecture is grounded on the Indignation of *Venus* against the Judge, who conferred the Prize on *Achilles*. *Venus*, to punish that Judge, made him in love with *Eccho*, and withal so ugly, that his Figure alone made him the Object of Hatred. Thus *Schottus* understood the Text of *Photius*. But Mr de *Meziriac* (7) divides the Effects of *Venus's* Anger, between *Pan* and *Achilles*; the former became in love, and the latter the ugliest Fellow in the World. It signifies nothing to consult the Original, to know whether the Translation of *Andrew Schottus* is preferable to that of *Meziriac*: For if, on the one side, it may be said, that the Rules of exact Grammar are in favour of *Schottus*; it may be said, on the other side, that the *Greek* Authors do not subject themselves to such Rules; and that it is no uncommon thing, when several Persons are concern'd in the same Period, for the Pronoun *He*, *Him*, to relate indifferently, either to the remotest, or to the nearest Person. The *Latin* Authors are not more scrupulous in this Particular. The Grammar of the *French* Tongue is most wonderfully exact in this Matter; for it requires the same proper Name to be repeated two or three times in a few Lines, rather than to leave the Reader's Mind in suspense. If we consult Reason, either for or against *Meziriac*, and Father *Schottus*, we shall hardly know how to determine the Point. A Person, who has lost his Cause, may, perhaps, revenge himself only on his Judge. Thus *Apollo* was satisfied with punishing *Midas* (8), who had blamed the Sentence of Superiority pronounced in favour of *Apollo*, and in prejudice of *Pan*. Upon this Supposition *Meziriac* would lose his Cause: But a Person may revenge himself sometimes, both on his Judge, and his Rival (9); and upon this footing Father *Andrew Schottus* should be mistaken in his Translation: for, according to him, *Venus* being displeased, takes no Revenge on him, who obtains the Victory. It is true also, that, according to the other Interpreter, she does no great harm to the unjust Judge: she is satisfied with making him in love with a Nymph, who, according to the Tradition of the Ancients (10), had a Daughter by him. When all is done, it seems as if *Meziriac* were in the wrong; and if he were not, *Photius* or his *Ptolomy* would be to blame, for not having declared, that the same *Venus*, who had made *Pan* in Love with *Eccho*, made him unfortunate in his Love. That Circumstance ought particularly to have been mentioned; and there would not have been wanting some, whose Opinion would have confirmed it; for this Nymph's Rigour towards the God *Pan* has been mentioned by some Authors. Of all the Labours of the Pen, That of abridging well, is, perhaps, the most difficult; it requires more than a common Discernment, to judge what are the Circumstances, the Suppression whereof makes an Abridgment obscure or not. *Justin* is not the only Person that wanted This nice Discernment. I have made use of this Thought in some other parts of this Work.

In the former Edition I have perfix'd a kind of Preface to the following Article, which I suppress with Regret. It contained an Elogium of the late Mr DRELINCOURT, *Professor of Physic at Leyden. It was the general Opinion, that I had offended so strangely against Custom, and had introduced this Piece so improperly, that, in order to put a stop to so general a Censure, I am obliged to blot it out. But I declare it my Intention, that this Testimony of my Gratitude and Esteem be considered as given in this Place, in the same manner as if it were repeated Word for Word.*

ACHILLES, the Son of *Peleus* and *Thetis*, was one of the greatest Heroes of Ancient *Greece*. He was born (*a*) at *Phthia* in *Thessaly*; and in his Infancy was dipt in the Waters of *Styx* to make him invulnerable: and he would have been so in every part, if his Mother had had the Precaution to hold him by one Heel, after having held him by the other (*b*), but, as she forgot that, one of her Son's Heels remained capable of being wounded; and it was in that place that Death seized him. Yet we must not imagine, that all Authors agree in this Story; for we meet with some, who mention several Wounds receiv'd by *Achilles*, in different parts of his Body (*c*). I shall mention another Precaution of *Thetis* in the Remarks; which is, that, to make her Son immortal, she anointed him with *Ambrosia* (*d*), and put him under live Coals. He was educated under the Care of the Centaur *Chiron*; it was the best School in the World in those Ages. *Chiron* educated him in a very singular manner; since, instead

ACHILLES.

instead of Milk, or Bread, or such kind of Food, he fed him with Lions Marrow [A].
or

(1) Progym. p. 70. D. p. 97. C. p. 129. A, &c.
(2) In Præexercitat. Rhetor.
(3) Orat. 2. pag. 324. C.
(4) In Iliad. lib. 16.
(5) In 'Αζιλλῶς.
(6) Lib. 3.
(7) Achill. lib. 2.
(8) In Heroic. pag. 701. B. & in Icon. 2. pag. 781. C.
(9) De Pallio: See below Number VIII.
(10) In Iliad. lib. 1. pag. 11.
(11) In χιλή.

[A] *Fed him with Lions Marrow, or with those of some other Beasts.*] Libanius (1) in three Places, and Priscian (2) in one, speak only of Lions Marrow: Gregory Nazianzen (3) adds the Marrow of Stags: the Scholiast of Homer (4) that of Bears: The Author of the great *Etymologicum* (5) mentions only the Marrow of Stags: Apollodorus (6) speaks of that of wild Boars and Bears, and adds the Entrails of Lions to it: Statius (7) joins the Entrails and Marrow of Lions together; or according to the reading of some old Manuscripts, the Entrails of Lions, and the Marrow of She-Wolves. See *Num*. II. below. Philostratus (8) adds to Milk and Honey, the Marrow of Fawns of Hinds, and the Marrow of Roe-Bucks. Tertullian (9) speaks only of the Marrow of wild Beasts in general. Eustathius (10) expresses himself in a more indefinite manner, speaking only of the Marrow of Beasts. Suidas (11) says only Marrow.

I.
Girac should not have demused, that Achilles was fed with the Marrow of Lions.

It is so common a Tradition among the Anciants, that Chiron fed Achilles with the Marrow of Lions, that we cannot enough wonder, that so learned a Man as Mr de Girac should accuse Mr Costar (12) of a gross Ignorance, for having made use of these Words: *You was nourished from your Infancy with the Juice, the Substance, and the Soul of good Books, in like manner as Achilles was with the Marrow of Lions*. Mr de Girac upon this puts a Question unbecoming an exact Critic, seeing it alters the State of the Question, and imputes to Mr Costar more than he really said. *Where did he find*, says he, *that Achilles was nourished only with Lions Marrow?* But what follows is worse still. Having alledged some other Reasons to support his Opinion, that according to *Plutarch*, Achilles *was fed with things which have no Blood*; he adds, *that he does not believe that any Author of Credit ever affirmed, that Achilles was nurs'd with the Marrow of Lions*: And yet, immediately after, he himself cites *St Gregory Nazianzen*, who remarks, that St BASIL had not, like *Achilles*, A Centaur near him, to present him with the Fabulous Marrow of Lions and Stags. *Which shows*, continues Mr de Girac, *that St Gregory look'd upon it as a fictitious and impossible Story.* Be it so: He will still be a credible Witness for all that. For to be so in things of this Quality, it is neither necessary we should be convinc'd of the Truth of the Facts we report, nor that they should really exist, nor even that they should be possible; it is enough that we are not ourselves the Inventors of the Story. Now without doubt this is St Gregory Nazianzen's Case: he does not affirm what he relates of the Centaur *Chiron* and of *Achilles*, without having read of any such thing. I will allow farther, that he does not believe it; but still he did not invent the Story; and this is sufficient to make him worthy of Credit. Neither the Moral nor the Physical Truth is to be inquired into upon this occasion, but only the Truth of the Relation. Mr de Girac, who will have it that the Marrow of Stags was the only Food of Homer's Hero, according to the common Opinion of the Ancients, doubtless esteemed the Authors, who reported it, worthy of Credit, altho' there is no Reason to think either that they firmly believed it, or that the thing is true. He has certainly placed St Gregory Nazianzen upon the same foot, with regard to the *Marrow of Stags*: He cannot therefore reasonably except against him, in relation to that of Lions: And consequently he himself produces a Witness worthy of Credit, immediately after having said, That he did not believe there were any.

II.
Proofs that Achilles was nurs'd with Lions Marrow.

His quoting St Gregory Nazianzen upon this occasion, is not so much to be wonder'd at, as his Ignorance of what two Modern Authors, who are in every body's Hands, have put beyond all Doubt. One is Mr de Meziriac, who has proved, by the Testimony of the Scholiast of *Homer*, on the 16th *Iliad*, by That of *Libanius*, in his two Speeches, the One For, and the Other Against, *Achilles*; and by that of *Statius*, in the 2d Book of his *Achilleid*, that this Hero was fed with the Marrow of Lions. The other is *Barthius*, who, upon this Passage of *Statius*, besides the double Testimony of *Libanius*, cites these Words of *Priscian* (13), as a farther Confirmation of the matter of Fact: "Deinde sequitur victus, ut in "Achille, quod MEDULLIS LEONUM pastus est. This Evidence is as strong, as That, which Mr de Girac produces to prove, that *Achilles* was brought up with another kind of Food.

It must not be dissembled, that *Barthius* deprives us of *Statius*'s Evidence for the Marrow of Lions: For instead of *lubens*, he pretends it must be read *lupæ*, in the Passage, where *Achilles* speaks thus:

Dicor &, in teneris & adhuc crescentibus annis,
Thessalus ut rigido senior me monte recepit,
Non ullas ex more dapes habuisse, nec alnis
Uberibus satiasse famem, sed spissa leonum
Viscera, semianimesque lupæ (14) traxisse medullas.

*Nur'd in a Cave by the Thessalian Sage,
No common Food sustain'd my tender Age;
Nor Mother's Milk did e'er my Thirst assuage:
But the fierce Lion's Entrails, raw in Blood,
And the Wolf's Marrow, were my savage Food.*

What Mr de Girac makes *Plutarch* say, discovers to us, that he did not consult the *Greek*: and as he alledges some of the Remarks, which *Vigenere* made use of in his Notes on *Philostratus*, it is very probable he was misled by these Words of That Author (15): Plutarch *says that* Chiron *nurs'd* Achilles, *form his Birth, with things, which had no Blood* (16). *Meziriac* shewed, many Years ago, that *Amiot* had led *Vigenere* into this Mistake; and that instead of saying with *Amiot* (17), *But this* Philinus, *like a new* Chiron, *feeds his Son, in like manner as* Achilles *was brought up, from his Infancy, with Food, from which no Blood was drawn*; to wit, *with the Fruits of the Earth*, it should be said, *But this new* Chiron *nourishes his Son in a manner quite different from That, in which* Achilles *was brought up* (ἀντιχρύφως τῇ Ἀχιλλέῖ) to wit, *with Meat without Blood*. Xylander may be involv'd in the same Mistake; for his *Latin* Translation imports, Nostrum autem, quo pacto Achillem Chiron nutriens iste statim à natalibus SANGUINE CARENTIBUS. There is an *Hiatus* in the Passage of *Plutarch*: but the Word ἀντιχρύφως must still be understood to mean CONTRARY, a Sense commonly given to it by the *Lexicons*.

What I have urg'd in proof of the Validity of St *Gregory*'s Testimony, shews that Mr de Girac cited *Ælian, Pliny*, and *Aristotle*, to no purpose, to shew that Lions have no Marrow; or that if they have any, it is the least imaginable. He might have appeal'd to *Galen* likewise, in his 11th Book *de Usu Partium*, Cap. 18. And this Fact should seem past Dispute, since the Moderns seldom call the ancient Naturalists to account for it, even when they are accusing them of several Mistakes, in relation to Lions. Consult *Vossius*, in the 52d Chapter of his 3d Book, *de Origine & progressu Idololatriæ*; *Franzius* & *Bochart* in their Treatises, *de Animalibus sacræ Scripturæ*; Father *Harduoin*, in his Commentary on the 27th Chapter of the 11th Book of *Pliny* (18), &c. If *Vossius* were to be credited in this Matter, we might pretend that *Athenæus* found fault with *Aristotle* upon this Subject. But when *Athenæus* (19) himself is consulted, it appears, that he makes no mention of Marrow; and that he only attacks the pretended Hardness of Lions Bones, which *Aristotle* made so great, that Sparks of Fire, he says, fly from them, upon Collision, as from a Flint. This might be denied, without disputing whether they were destitute of Marrow. The Text, then, might be certain; and Mr *Furetiere* should have inserted it among his other Remarks, under the Word LION, if the contrary had not been incontestably prov'd. *Barrichius* (20) mentions two Skeletons of Lions, anatomiz'd at *Copenhagen*, the one sixteen, the other two Years before; and he assures us, that there was a great Quantity of Marrow, *copiosam medullam*, found in the Bones of that Animal; and he quotes *Sevérinus*, who relates, That *Tiberius Cæsar* brought up a Lion, whose Bones were found hollow and full of Marrow, like Those of other Beasts. But though it were certain, that Lions have no Marrow, Mr de Girac should not have had recourse

(13) In Progymn. Rhetoricis ex Hermogene.

(14) Others read lubens.

III.
A Passage of Plutarch ill translated.

(15) Vigenere's Comment. on Philostr. of Achilles's Food, Edit. 1620 pag. 544.

(16) Comment. on the Epistle of Briseis, pag. 249.

(17) Plutarch's Works of Tuble Conversation, ch. 5.

IV.
Property of the Bones of Lions; Whether it be true that they are without Marrow.

(18) Observe, That Hoffman's Continuat. Lexici Universi. Tom. I. p. 1002. attributes this only to the Lions Teeth, as also the producing Sparks of Fire by Collision.

(19) Athen. Deipnosoph. lib. 3. cap. 11.

(20) *In his Treatise, pro Hermetis, Ægyptiorum, & Chimicorum Sapientia, prostat at Copenhagen, 1672.*

ACHILLES.

or with that of some other wild Beasts. The Etymologists, have not neglected their Interests

to that Reason, since Facts, borrow'd from the *Pagan Mythology*, are not to be confuted in that manner, especially when it is affirm'd, that no Author worthy of Credit speaks of them. The Testimony alone of some antient Authors is sufficient to make Him lose his Cause, even though the Naturalists should assure us of the Impossibility of the Thing.

V.
A Remark against Barthius. Decisive Authors find themselves sometimes led into a Scrape.

From whence it appears, That *Barthius* engages himself in a superfluous Refutation, when, in commenting on the Verses of *Statius*, which I have cited below, he cries out very seriously; *It is a strange Fable*, ingens fabula, *since a Child who should take in any such Food, only by sucking, would die*; every thing in Lions, their very Breath, being poisonous, especially to such an Age: in consequence of which he cites a Passage of *Aristotle*, importing that Lions have no Marrow. All this is Labour lost; since the Ancients themselves, who had examin'd things a little, considered these Stories only as Sallies of Wit and Imagination. Would not a Man have little to do, who should spend his time in confuting, from Principles of Philosophy, the Stories of the same *Achilles*'s Heel, and his burnt Lip? It is fabled, that his Mother, having plung'd him in the Waters of *Styx*, to render him invulnerable, could not procure that Advantage to his Heel, because she held her Son by it. *Fulgentius*, in the 7th Chapter of his 3d Book, and the Scholiast of *Horace*, on the 13th Ode of the 5th Book, remark, that he held him by the Heel. Those, who say that he died of a Wound in the Heel, as *Hyginus*, in his 107th Chapter, and *Quintus Calaber*, at the 62d Verse of the 3d Book, agree upon the whole with the other two. *Servius*, on the 57th Verse of the 6th Book of the *Æneid*, says in general, that he was invulnerable, excepta parte quâ à matre, tentus est. *That part excepted by which his Mother held him*. Others have reported, that, to consume all that was mortal in her Son's Body, she laid him every Night under live Coals, and that in the Day she anointed him with *Ambrosia*, and that but one of the Child's Lips was burnt; which was occasioned by his having lick'd that Part.

(21) *Apollodorus*, lib. 3. Scholiast. Homeri Iliad. ɣ. v. 36. Scholiast. Aristoph. p. 184. A.

(22) *See the Commentary of Meziriac, p. 248.*

Many (21) Authors mention This Conduct of *Thetis*; and say farther, that she had destroy'd, by this means, six of her Children; but her Husband, having surpriz'd her in it, was the Cause that *Achilles*, who was the seventh, escap'd. Nevertheless *Tzetzes* (22) condemn'd this Story as false, and says, *that he does not know from whence Lycophron borrow'd this Lie, that Thetis had seven Children by Peleus*. This is another Example, which may be added to that of Mr *de Girac*, to shew the Danger, to which an Author exposes himself by too decisive a Confidence: for Mr *de Meziriac* cites *four very grave Authors, who all agree to what Lycophron writes*. There is good Reason to say, when we hear mention made either of some extraordinary Phrase, or of some uncommon Fact, *that it is a good Bait to draw in Wagerers*, that is, your rash Scholars, who are always ready, on such an Occasion, to lay Wagers that such a thing is not to be found in any Author; and they seldom fail to lose. But what is most astonishing, is, they sometimes deny things the most easy to be met with. I shall give several Examples of this Behaviour in This Dictionary.

(23) Barth. Comment. in lib. 2. Achill. vol. 3. p. 1754.

But we must not take our leave of *Barthius* (23), without observing that he pretends, that thé reading *Lupæ*, instead of *Lubens*, does *Statius* much Honour, who, by this means, does not contradict *Aristotle*, and observes the same Distinctions with *Apollodorus*; the latter having affirm'd that *Chiron* made *Achilles* feed upon the Entrails of Lions, and the Marrow of wild Boars and Bears. But *Barthius*, taking upon himself once more the Air of Confutation, rejects the Marrow of the *She-Wolf*, as a manifest Absurdity; and says he is convinc'd, that if a Child should take that kind of Food but once, he would die before the next Day. *Wherefore*, adds he, Gregory Nazianzen *reconciles it better*, by adding the Marrow of Stags, to that of Lions. *Barthius* here seems to be inconsistent with himself, having said, in the foregoing Page, that the rejecting of the Marrow of Lions was a sign of Judgment in *Statius*, and that the approach of Lions is very dangerous to Children.

VI.
The Fable of Achilles being fed with Lions Marrow was a proper Fiction.

It must be remark'd, That the Reason, why *Apollodorus*, and some others, have rather mentioned the Entrails, than the Marrow, of Lions, as the Food of *Achilles*, seems to be owing to their Opinion, that these Creatures have scarce any Marrow; for otherwise, Marrow was a more suitable Diet, considering the Character, under which the Poets represent him. It is not so much under the Idea of Valour, though they ascribe This to him in an eminent Degree, as under That of an Invincible Anger. *Homer* proposes to himself this Character of him in the Iliad, where, according to the Observation of *Horace*, he takes for his Theme,

—— gravem
Peleidæ stomachum cedere nescii (24).

(24) Horat. Od. 6. lib. 1. ver. 5.

The fierce Pelides' haughty Rage,
Who knew not how to yield.
CREECH.

And begins his Poem thus,

Μῆνιν ἄειδε θεὰ Πηληϊάδεω Ἀχιλῆος,
Οὐλομένην, ἣ μυρί' Ἀχαιοῖς ἄλγε' ἔθηκε.

Achilles' Wrath, to Greece the direful Spring
Of Woes unnumber'd, Heavenly Goddess sing.
POPE.

Now it is certain, that in order to trace this Character to it's Source, in the *marvellous* Fictions of Antiquity, nothing could be better imagin'd, than Lion's Marrow, for the Nourishment of this Hero; since it is the most juicy, and, as is pretended, contains the specific and seminal Parts of the Animal. *Homer* hints to us in the Example of little *Astyanax*, that it was the favorite Morsel of an indulged or spoiled Child:

Ἀστυάναξ, ὃς πρὶν μὲν ἑοῦ ἐπὶ γούνασι πατρὸς
Μυελὸν οἶον ἔδεσκε καὶ οἰῶν πίονα δημόν (25).

(25) Homer. Iliad 22. ver. 500.

Astyanax ——
He, who with tender Delicacy bred,
On Marrow, and the choicest Dainties fed.

And Jesters tell the Mothers sometimes, that it is a *Son-in-law's Bit*. Besides, there is no Beast so angry as the Lion; and it is supposed, that it was from him Prometheus borrow'd the Principle, which subjected the first Man to Anger:

Fertur Prometheus addere principi
Limo coactus particulam undique
Desectam, & insani leonis
Vim stomacho apposuisse nostro (26).

(26) Horat. Od. 16. lib. 1. ver. 13.

When bold Prometheus first began,
As Story goes, to make a Man,
From every thing he snatch'd a Part,
To furnish out his Clay,
And to compleat his rude Essay;
And plac'd the Lion's Fury in his Heart.
CREECH.

Not but that it would have serv'd the Purpose as well, to have given *Achilles* a Lioness for his Nurse. *Virgil* followed This Idea, in some Reproaches of Cruelty;

—— duris genuit te cautibus horrens
Caucasus, Hyrcanæque admorunt ubera Tigres (27).

(27) *Æneid.* lib. 4. See Macrob. Saturn. lib. 5. cap. 11.

False as thou art, and, more than false, forsworn,
Not sprung from noble Blood, nor Goddess-born,
But hewn from hard'ned Entrails of a Rock;
And rough Hyrcanian Tygers gave thee suck.
DRYDEN.

And the Bragadochio in the Comedy of the *Visionaries*, is not far from it in this Rhodomontade:

Le Dieu Mars m'engendra d'une fiere Amazone,
Et je sucai le lait d'une affreuse Lionne.

I was begotten by the God Mars upon a Warlike
Amazon, and suck'd the Milk of a horrid Lioness.

By

ACHILLES.

Interests on this Occasion; they have made their Advantage of this Tradition, for they pretend that the Name of *Achilles* is derived from it [B]. He was not contented to inure his Body to the most laborious Exercises, but he adorn'd his Soul with a great Variety of useful Knowledge. But if we may believe *Homer*, it is to *Phœnix*, and

VII. *Whence the Fiction of the Marrow of a Stag. Swiftness of Foot was formerly an Heroic Quality.*

By this Key we are led to the Reason, why some chose to prefer the Marrow of Stags, before any other, for the Food of *Achilles*: Because they were struck with the Tradition, which ascribes to him great Swiftness in running, and which induced *Homer* to honour him continually either with the Elogy of πόδας ἀκύς, *swift-footed*, or some other Epithet of the same Signification, πυδώκης, ποδώκηης, πόδας ταχὺς, ποσὶ ταχέεσσι, κραιπνοίσι, &c. With us, at present, this is but the Merit of a *Biscaian* Lacquey [*], but anciently (28) it was an heroic Quality: And therefore *Homer*'s only Fault in the use of it, is, His patching up his Verse too frequently with it. It was therefore thought necessary to feign, that an Hero of an extraordinary Swiftness was nourished with the Marrow of Stags; and the Ancients were so fond of this Notion, that they did not take notice, that the Marrow of such a timorous Animal was otherwise very improper for This *Thunderbolt of War*, This *Lion-hearted Hero*.

* *Or Running-Footman. The People of Biscay were fam'd for Swiftness.*

(28) *See the prodigious Swiftness, which Virgil, Æneid. 7. v. 817. gives a young Amazon called Camilla; and Father in Cerda's Observations upon it.*

'Αχιλλῆα ῥηξήνορα θυμολέοντα (29)

who, shewing the utmost Disdain for the General of the Army, among other opprobrious Expressions added;

(29) Homer. Iliad. 7. ver. 228.

Va fac à vin, yeux de chien, cœur de cerf.

So *Vigenere* (30) translates this Verse of the 1st Book of the Iliad.

(30) *Vigenere's Comment on Philostrat. de Notrim. Achill.*

Οἰνοβαρές, κυνὸς ὄμματ' ἔχων, κραδίην δ' ἐλάφοιο

O Monster, mix'd of Insolence and Fear,
Thou Dog in Forehead, but in Heart a Deer!
POPE.

VIII. *Faults of some of Tertullian's Interpreters.*

I do not think that, if the Matter were to be decided by a Majority of Voices, it would be judg'd that *Achilles* was fed with the Marrow of Stags, nor that Mr *de Girac* could support his hasty Assertion, that *Marrow was the only Food of* Homer's *Hero, according to the common Opinion of the Ancients*. But if this should be true, an old (31) *French* Translator of the Treatise *de Pallio* would not be excusable, for having restrained to this Marrow, what *Tertullian* said of That of wild Beasts in general. Translators have no such Right. " Ille ferarum medullis educatus, un-
" de & nominis (32) consilium, quando quidem labiis
" vacuerat ab uberum gustu: ——— *He having been*
" *fed with the Marrow of Stags, from whence he had*
" *his Name, as having never suck'd at the Breast with*
" *his Lips,* &c." *Theodorus* (33) *Marcilius* stumbled likewise at these Words, pretending, that *Tertullian* hints at the Etymology *fine chilo*, ἄνευ χιλῆ, which is visibly false, as *Salmasius* observes. I might have remark'd another Mistake of the same Author, as follows: He says that *Achilles*, according to *Velius Longinus*, cited by *Cassiodorus*, had his Name from the Word χεῖλος, as being one of those Persons who are called *Chilones*; or *Labiones*, that is *Thick-lip'd*. *Lucretius* calls them (34) *Labiosi*, and observes that a Lover, who would excuse the Imperfections of his Mistress, says, *labiosa*, φίλημα, *great Lips are large and spacious Fields for Kisses*. But it is false, that *Achilles* had his Name from χεῖλος, a *Lip*, upon this account; he was rather so called, because he was maim'd in that Part, although *Salmasius* denies it, notwithstanding an express Passage of *Photius*, which I have already mentioned, and what *Agamestor* (35), an old Poet, cited by *Tzetzes*, positively says of it ; *Salmasius*'s Words are (36), " Si chilones dicti à mag-
" nis & improbis labris, Achilles dictus fuerit quasi
" ἄνευ χειλέων, non quod fine labris fuerit, sed quod
" labiorum ministerio non usus fuerit insana. —
" *If the Chilones are so called from their large and*
" *monstrous Lips, Achilles is so called quasi* ἄνευ χει-
" λέων, *not that he had no Lips, but because he made*
" *no use of them in his Infancy*." I do not deny, but that *Apollodorus* says, that the Son of *Thetis*, whose first Name was *Ligyron*, was called *Achilles* by *Chiron*, because he had never apply'd his Lips to the

Breast (37). Ὅτι τὰ χείλη μασοῖς ἐ προσένεγκε, *quod mammis labra minime admovisset*.

(37) *Apollodor. lib. 3. p. 235.*

[B] *That the Name of* Achilles *is derived from it.*] I have taken Notice of the Etymologies of this Name in the Remark [B] of the foregoing Article; but I must speak particularly of That before us at present. It always accompanies the Tradition, which says that *Achilles* was fed with nothing but the *Flesh* and *Marrow* of Animals. The Connexion between these two Things arises from the *Greek* Word χιλὸς, which properly signifies the Nutriment, which the Earth supplies us with. But some Authors build a pleasant Opinion upon this. I shall give it in the proper Terms of Father *Gautruche*, in his Poetical History. I rather chuse This Work, than any other, because it has been printed several Times (38), and in several Languages, and is esteem'd a Book fit for every Body's reading. Now no Faults ought more carefully to be remark'd, than those, which may mislead the greatest Number of Readers. Father *Gautruche* says (39), *Instead of Milk and other common Food*, Chiron *nursed him only with the Marrow of Lions, or of wild Bears, in order to produce in his Pupil the Courage and the Strength of these Animals, Whence, according to the Opinion of some, being nourished without any kind of Meat, he was called* Achilles, *that is to say*, WITH-OUT CHYLE. Though the last Period of this Passage does not appear in the last Edition, yet I shall remark, I. That it is an Error, to say that a Person is nourished without Meat, when he is only fed with the *Marrow of Beasts*: for the Marrow is unquestionably comprehended under the Word *Meat*, and is not comprehended among those Viands, which are permitted in Lent. II. That it is not true, that Marrow is not converted into *Chyle*, or that whoever is fed only with Marrow, must necessarily be without *Chyle*. These Remarks will not seem superfluous to those, who shall consider, that this Doctrine of Father *Gautruche* is in a great many Copies of his Works, and in other Writers (40), and that in the Edition, where his Faults are dropp'd, we are not told, why they were suppress'd.

The Foundation of this Mistake arises from the Term χιλὸς, (which *Euphorion* made use of in some Verses, cited by the Author of the great *Etymologicum*, and by *Eustathius*,) being taken for That soft and whitish Substance, into which the Stomach converts the Aliments, and which the Physicians call *Chyle*, from the *Greek* Word χυλὸς: Whereas by χιλὸς ought to be understood, as Mr *de Mezeriat* (41) took it from *Eustathius*, the *Nourishment we receive from the Produce of the Earth*. *Natalis Comes* (42) has wrong translated *Euphorion*: for he makes him say that *Achilles* had tasted no Milk. *Vigenere* and *Fungerus*, depending upon the Authority of St *Gregory Nazianzen*, have not been more successful. They attribute to St *Gregory* that, which is but in the *Latin* Translation of the Commentaries of *Nicetas Serronius*, Archbishop of *Heraclea*, in the XIth Century, on the Orations of that Father, printed with his Works (43). *Fungerus* concludes, that *Achilles* was nurs'd *sine cibo*, because his only Diet was the Marrow of Stags. The other will have it (44), that χιλὸς signifies *Gravy*, and that *Achilles* was nourished *without Juice*, because he was not fed with the common Food of Men, but with the raw Flesh of Savage Beasts. *Francis Aluanus* adopts one half of this last Error. " Fu nutrito, *says he* (45),
" nel monte Pelio da Chirone Centaurio, ne mai in
" quel tempio mangio cibo cotto, perchè fù nominato
" Achille, perche à in Greco significa senza, & chilos
" CIBO COTTO. — *He was brought up on Mount*
" *Pelion, by* Chiron *the Centaur, and having never*
" *fed upon any thing but raw Flesh, he was called*
" *Achilles, from Alpha, which in Greek signifies*
" *Without, and* Chilos, DRESS'D MEAT." Some, taking the Word χιλὸς simply for *Nourishment*, ground the Etymology of *Achilles* (46) on this, that his Preceptor *Chiron*, after a certain time, neither provided for him the Marrow of wild Beasts, nor any other kind of Food, so that he was oblig'd to support himself by the Fortune of the Chace. But was this to live *without Nourishment*? This is, perhaps, the worst Account of them all.

(38) *An Edition of it was publish'd at Utrecht, in 1690, to which was added the Translation, in Latin and Dutch. The Latin Translation had already appeared by itself. The English publish'd it in their Language in the Year 1671.*

(39) *Poetical History, B. 2. chap. 5. p. 158. Edit. of the Hague, 1681, which is the 4th.*

(40) *Among others, in the Historical Dictionary of Juigné.*

(41) *Comment on the Epistle of Briseis, pag. 248. where the Poet Euphorion is miss-called Nuphorion.*

(42) *Mythol. lib. 6. cap. 12.*

(43) *This Version is printed with the Works of St Gregory.*

(44) *Comment on Philostrat. of the Nurture of Achilles, pag. 543.*

(45) *In sa Fabrica del Mondo, which is a Dictionary on Boccacio, Dante, Petrarch, &c. printed at Venice in 1588. Folio.*

(46) *Comment. on Alciatus's Emblems, p. 624. of the Edition of Thuilius at Padua, 1667. in 4to.*

ACHILLES.

and not to *Chiron* [C], that the Quality of *Achilles*'s Preceptor, and Foster-Father is to

[C] *If we may believe* Homer, *it is to* Phœnix, *and not to* Chiron.] Many Persons are not aware of this. *Decimator* (47) says, that *Achilles*, after having been educated by *Chiron*, who taught him the Military Art, Music, and Morality, was put under the Direction of *Phœnix*, who taught him both to Speak and Live well, as he boasts of it himself. He proves this, as to Music and Morality, from these Verses of *Ovid*, in the 1st Book *de Arte amandi*.

Phyllirides puerum citharæ præfecit Achillem,
Atque animos molli contudit arte feros.

Chiron *his Pupil to the Lyre inclin'd,*
And humaniz'd, by Sounds, his savage Mind.

I set them down without altering any thing, either in the Orthography, or in the *Citharæ præfecit*, which ought to be changed into *Citharâ perfecit*. Every body may see, that there is not a Word of the Study of Morality in those Verses. His Proofs, as to *Phœnix*, are these Words of *Homer*:

Τυνεά με τρέφημε διδασκέμεναι τάδε πάντα,
Μύθων τε ρητῆρ᾿ ἔμεναι, πρηκτῆρά τε ἔργων. (48)

He had me teach thee all the Ways of War,
To shine in Councils, and in Camps to dare.
POPE.

But provided we read with Attention the Book of the *Iliad*, from whence this Authority is borrowed, it will appear, that *Decimator* is mistaken. The Expressions of *Phœnix* testify, that he was the first Preceptor of *Achilles*. *You would eat nothing,* represents he to that Hero, *unless I first took you on my Knees, and carved your Meat. The Wine which you discharged into my Bosom, in your troublesome Infancy, has often fully'd my Cloaths.*

— — — Ἔπει σὺ θαλερὸς ἂν ἄλλῳ
Οὔτ' ἐς δαῖτ᾿ ἴεναι, ἄρ᾿ οὐ παγάμοισι φλοσσέσαι
Πρίν γ᾿ ὅτε δὴ σ᾿ ἐπ᾿ ἐμοῖσιν ἐγὼ γούνεσσι καθίσσας,
Ὄψε τ᾿ ἄσαιμι προταμών, καὶ οἶνον ἐπισχών.
Πολλάκι μοι κατέδευσας ἐπὶ στήθεσι χιτῶνα
Οἴνου ἀποβλύζων ἐν νηπιέῃ ἀλεγεινῇ. (49)

Thy infant Breast a like Affection show'd,
Still in my Arms, (an ever-pleasing load)
Or, at my Knee, by Phœnix *would'st thou stand,*
No food was grateful, but from Phœnix' *Hand.*
POPE.

It was necessary to produce the *Greek*; for it conveys so filthy an Image, that it might else have been thought I had not fairly translated it *. See the 11th Paragraph below. But however it be, this shews, that, if we will make use of the Authority of *Homer*, with respect to *Phœnix*, we must renounce what others report concerning *Chiron*; or that at least we must not give *Chiron* the first Education of *Achilles*, and less still make it continue, until he had taught his Scholar the Military Art, Music, and Morality. When a Person is arriv'd at an Age fit for Instruction in these Sciences, he eats no longer on his Foster Father's Lap, nor throws up his Wine on his Cloaths. Add to this that they, who suppose that *Achilles* was brought up by *Chiron*, say that he was taken away from under his Discipline, to be sent, disguis'd in a Female Dress, to the Court of King *Lycomedes*, where his Disguise soon procured him opportunities of conversing familiarly with the King's Daughter, as appeared by the Child she brought into the World. Now it is not likely that they appointed him a Tutor after he became a Father; and consequently there is no room for placing the Guardianship of *Phœnix* after That of *Chiron*. The Faults of *Decimator* are to be found in the *Thesaurus Scholasticæ Eruditionis* of the last Edition, tho' that Work was often corrected by learned *Humenists* (50). (51) *Dempster* has likewise said, that *Achilles*, having been instructed by *Chiron* in his Infancy, was educated by *Phœnix*, when he was of a more advanced Age. Observe, that I do not intend to deny, that, after *Achilles* became a Father, *Phœnix* was ordered to teach him (52) how to conduct himself in the Trade of Arms, and the Councils of War: But I do not call this appointing him a Tutor.

I cannot tell whether *Malherbe* ever took notice of this; but it is certain that he expressed himself like one, who was well satisfied, that *Achilles* had but one Preceptor. For thus he speaks of that Warrior in the fourth Book of his Poems, *p. 106.*

Ou de Phenix, *ou de* Chiron,
Il est fait son aprentissage.

Whether he serv'd his Apprenticeship with Phœnix *or* Chiron.

We must allow him only *Phœnix*, if we are to be determined by *Homer*, who makes no mention of the Preceptorship of *Chiron*; and only *Chiron*, if we follow the Crowd of Authors. Yet Mr *Menage* has said, in his Notes on this Passage of *Malherbe*, *That* Chiron *was the first Tutor of* Achilles, *and* Phœnix *the second*. I do not rely on the Authority of *Tzetzes*, who, by an Allegorical Explication of what he had read in some Authors, that *Phœnix*, blinded by his own Father, was brought to *Chiron*, who restored him to his Sight, pretends that the meaning of this is, that *Chiron* gave the young *Achilles* to his Care; for, besides that there is nothing more cold, or forced than this Thought; it is certain that *Tzetzes* by no means proves the Fact. By his pretended Allegories he endeavours to reconcile *Homer* with *Lycophron*; but how will he reconcile *Homer*, who says, that *Achilles*, yet a little Child, was under the Conduct of *Phœnix*? I say, how will he reconcile him with those who suppose *Achilles* to have been educated by *Chiron* from six Years of Age (53), to Manhood, 'till he had not only learnt to sit astride on the Back of his (54) Preceptor, but also till he had inured himself to (55) the most violent Exercises; without reckoning many other things, which *Chiron* taught him; as the Military Art, Music, Morality, (as *Decimator* informed us before) and Physick, but particularly Botany and Law, as an ancient Author called *Staphylus* (56), and others inform us? *Statius*, in the second Book of his *Achilleis*; *Claudian*, in his Panegyric on the third Consulship of *Honorius*; and *Sidonius Apollinaris*, in his ninth Poem, specify what *Achilles* learnt of *Chiron*. Note, that on the pretended Testimony of *Homer*, they ascribe to *Chiron*, in the Commentaries on the Emblems of *Alciatus*, what belongs only to *Phœnix*. Nothing is more frequent among Authors than these *quid pro quo*'s.

I said, that *Homer* has taken no notice of *Chiron*'s Preceptorship. You will ask me then, what mean these Words of *Eurypylus* to *Patroclus* in the eleventh Book of the *Iliad*,

— — — ἐν δ᾿ ἄρα φάρμακα πάσσε
Ἐσθλά, τά σε προτί φασιν Ἀχιλλῆος δεδιδάχθαι,
Ὂν Χείρων ἐδίδαξε δικαιότατος Κενταύρων. (57)

With healing Balm; the raging Smart allays;
Such as sage Chiron, *Sire of Pharmacy,*
Once taught Achilles, *and* Achilles *Thee.*
POPE.

I answer, That they do not signify, that *Chiron* was the Preceptor of *Achilles*, but only that he taught him Physic. Every one sees the Difference of these two Things. *Musæus*, in his Travels, names an hundred Persons, who taught him Receipts and Secrets for Cures; yet those People had not been his Schoolmasters, nor had educated him in his Youth. Professors in Physic, who teach their Auditors an hundred good Remedies in public, or communicate some very rare Receipts to distinguish'd Friends in particular, are they therefore what we call Young Master's Tutor or Governor? And, without going farther than this Passage of *Homer*, do we not see that *Achilles* imparted to *Patroclus* Remedies, though he was not his Preceptor? To enter then into *Homer*'s Thought, we must say that *Achilles* was educated by *Phœnix* from three or four Years of Age, 'till he was capable of learning to Discourse well, and perform fine Actions; but yet that, during that time, and afterwards, he did not fail to attend the Lectures of *Chiron*. It

ACHILLES.

to be given. The Uneasiness of *Thetis* did not permit her to leave her Son in *Chiron*'s Cave, so long as she desired; she (*e*) took him from thence when he was but nine Years of Age, and disguising him in a Woman's Habit, hid him among the young Ladies in the Court of *Lycomedes*, King of the Island of *Scyros*, as soon as she was inform'd of the Preparations, which were making against the *Trojans*. The Reason of her Conduct was this; she knew, on the one side, that if her Son went to *Troy*, he would never return from thence; and, on the other, that *Calchas* had foretold that the City of *Troy* should never be taken without *Achilles*. The Device of *Thetis* stood her in no stead; the Seer *Calchas* discover'd to the *Greeks* (*f*) where *Achilles* lay hid, whom they had fought for in divers Places without finding him: Upon this *Ulysses*, being deputed to the Court of *Lycomedes*, easily discover'd *Achilles* [D]; and brought him away

(*e*) Apollodor. lib. 3. p. 235.

(*f*) Statius, Achill. I. b. 2. ver. 493. &c.

is thus a certain Scholiast took *Homer*'s Thought: For he observes, that *Apollonius*, who feigns, that *Chiron* went to the Sea-side to wish the *Argonauts* a good Voyage, and that his Wife attended him, holding *Achilles* in her Arms, and shewing him to *Peleus*, follow'd the Poets, who came after *Homer*, and supposed, with them, that *Chiron* nursed the little *Achilles*; a Thing never mentioned by *Homer*. 'Ηκαλεθημεν Ἀπολλώνιος τοῖς μεθ' Ὅμηρον ποιηταῖς ὑπὸ Χείρωνος λέγων τὸν Ἀχιλλέα τραφῆναι. Ὅμηρος δὲ οὐδὲν τοιοῦτον λέγει (58).

(58) Schol. Apollon. lib. 1. ver. 558.

X.
Authors who have mentioned the Preceptorship of Chiron, and that of Phoenix.

Apollonius is very excusable, since he only followed the Crowd; for who has not spoke of *Chiron*, as having educated *Achilles*? Is it not what *Orpheus* (59), *Pindar* (60), *Euripides* (61), and so many other Poets have sung (62)? *Xenophon* (63), *Plato* (64), *Apollodorus* (65), *Pliny* (66), *Plutarch* (67), *Pausanias* (68), *Clemens Alexandrinus* (69), *Philostratus* (70), *Libanius* (71), St. *Gregory Nazianzen*, (72), and several others less ancient (73), have they not said the same thing? But, on the other side, they (74), who have mentioned the Preceptorship of *Phoenix*, are not fewer in Number. We ought not, then, to be very much surprized, if, according to some ancient Authors, *Phoenix* and *Chiron* are both represented as having been the Preceptors of *Achilles*: We can only say, that these Authors had not examined the thing narrowly enough, or that they had no regard to the Inconsistency, which results from the Circumstances of the Preceptorship of *Phoenix*, and the Circumstances of the Preceptorship of *Chiron*.

(59) Argon. ver. 378.
(60) Nem. Od. 3.
(61) Iphig. in Aul. ver. 209, 709.
(62) Senec. Troad. Act. 3. ver. 233. Stat. Silv. 1. lib. 2. ver. 19. Achill. lib. 1. ver. 196. and in several other places. Valer. Flaccus, lib. 1. ver. 254, & 407. Ausonius Protrept. ver. 20. Claudian. de 3. Consul. Honor. ver. 61.
(63) De Venat. pag. 973. A. & 974. C.
(64) Hipp. Tom. 1. p. 372.
(65) Lib. 3. cap. 13. de Repub. Tom. 2. pag. 391. B.
(66) Lib. 25. cap. 5.
(67) Sympol. lib. 4. cap. 1. pag. 660. F. & de Music. pag. 1146. A.
(68) In Lacon. p. 197.
(69) Stromat. lib. 1. pag. 306. B.
(70) In Heroic. p. 682. A. & 705. A.
(71) Progymn. pag. 71, A; pag. 97, C; pag. 129, A; pag. 142, C; pag. 141, A; & pag. 259, D.
(72) Orat. 2. pag. 324.
(73) Eustath. in Homer. pag. 11. 34. & 340. Scholiast. Homeri in Iliad. lib. 1. ver. 50. & lib. 16. ver. 14. & 36.
(74) *These are the Names of the principal Scholiasts.* Homeri Iliad. 9. ver. 188, & 448. Dictys, lib. 2. Xenophon, Conv. pag. 897, A. Plato 2. de Repub. Tom. 2. pag. 390, E. Cicero 3. de Orat. n. 57. Strabo, lib. 9. pag. 297. Quintil. lib. 2. cap. 3. Stat. Silv. 3. lib. 5. ver. 191. Plutarch. Tom. 2. pag. 4, 26, & 2. Lucian. Dial. Mort. Philoct. Leme. p. 136. Libanius, Progymn. pag. 99.

I had therefore Reason to deny, in my *Plan*, that *Statius*, speaking of *Phoenix* and of *Chiron* as of two Preceptors of *Achilles*, was in the least favourable to *Decimator* and his Party; for besides that *Statius* does not tell us, whether they exercised this Employ both together, or one after the other, or which of the two was the first, he cannot be reconciled with *Homer*, who, in case of Competition, ought to carry it from him with an high hand. Consider these two Passages well:

Non tibi certassent juvenilia fingere corda
Nestor, & indomiti Peleus Moderator alumni,
Quique, rubus acres lituosque audire volentem,
Æaciden alio frangebat carmine Chiron. (75)

(75) Stat. lib. 5. Silva 3. ver. 191.

In forming thee, nor Nestor wou'd employ,
Nor Phoenix, Tutor of th'unconquer'd Boy,
A Guardian's Care; nor He, who cou'd controul,
With softer Notes, Achilles' warlike Soul;
The Martial Music was the Hero's Choice,
And his Heart bounded at the Trumpet's Voice.

This is the first; The other is,

—— tenero sic blandus Achilli

Semifer Æmonium vincebat Pelea Chiron.
Nec senior Peleus natum comitatus in arma
Troica, sed caro Phoenix hærebat alumno. (76)

(76) Id. lib. 2 Silva 2. ver 88.

Thus, for his Pupil, Chiron's flattering Tale
O'er the reluctant Father cou'd prevail.
The Sire refus'd the Grecian Arms to share,
But sent Achilles to the Trojan War,
Trusting the darling Charge to Phoenix' tender Care.

Xenophon (77) and *Lucian* (78), who allot these two Preceptors to *Achilles*, are exposed to the same Battery as *Statius*; and besides they differ from *Homer*, whom *Decimator* alledges: Observe that, tho' *Statius* (79) says, that *Phoenix* accompanied *Achilles* to *Troy*, it does not follow from thence that he supposes he was *Chiron*'s Successor; for he says clearly enough, that *Phoenix* had had the Care of *Achilles* before that Voyage; for he calls the latter the *Alumnus* (the *Pupil*) of *Phoenix* (80). As for *Tzetzes*, who tells us, in his Commentary on *Lycophron*, that *Peleus*, having brought *Phoenix* to *Chiron*'s Cave, where *Achilles* was educated, said to him, *Behold your Son; tutor him as a good Father ought to educate his Child*; he proves nothing against me; nor is he in the least favourable to those who have recourse to the Distinction of *Governor* and *Preceptor*, which is so clear in *Plutarch*, with regard to the Son of *Philip* King of *Macedon*. See the Article LYSIMACHUS. The Poets, I believe, cannot shew us the same Distinction in those remote Ages; and, however it be, it does not appear that *Peleus* joined *Chiron* in the Tutelage of his Son with *Phoenix*. And if *Tzetzes*, expressing himself very ill, meant so, he deserves no Credit. He is too modern an Author to deserve to be followed in a Matter of Fact, which can neither be reconciled with *Homer*, nor with the ancient Authors, who have attributed the Education of young *Achilles* to *Chiron*.

(77) In Conviv.
(78) In Dial. Achill. & Ant.
(79) Ubi supra. & lib. 3. Silv. 2. ver. 96.
(80) Meursius and Canterus understand by the Word παιδαγωγός which Lycophron made use of to denote Phoenix, that the Letter had been Achilles' Fencing Father.

I shall put an end to this Remark, already too long, with a bold Stroke, which I cannot forbear. I dare affirm, that we need only read the Speech of *Phoenix*, in the ninth Book of the *Iliad*, to admire at those, who at present admire That Poem. For is That Speech worthy the Majesty of Epic Poetry? And *Horace*, who, according to Mr *Moreri* (81), boasts in the sixth Satyr of the first Book, that he had learned the *Iliad* by heart, had doubtless forgot that Speech full of a thousand Impertinences; when he gave the Author of the *Iliad* this Elogy, that he always runs directly to the Mark, that he *hastens to the Event*: *semper ad Eventum festinet* (82). If so, would he amuse a Deputy of the *Greek* Army, who had a very important and pressing Commission; I say, would he amuse him with old Wives Stories, and with a Recital of his former Adventures?

XI.
Homer censur'd for the Speech of Phoenix.

(81) In the Article HORACE, but it is a Mistake.

(82) Horat. de Arte Poët. ver. 148.

[D] *Easily discovered Achilles.*] Mr *Moreri* pretends, with little Exactness, that *Ulysses* discovered him, by *causing a Merchant to present him with Toys and Arms*; for if we adhere to what *Ulysses* himself says of it (83), in his Speech to the Generals of the Army, it was He, who not only presented *those Toys and Arms* to *Achilles*, but also to all the young Ladies of the Court. If we refer it to *Hyginus*, and *Philostratus* the younger, it is *Ulysses* again, who presented them, being one of Ambassadors of the *Greeks*, sent to *Lycomedes* to demand *Achilles* of him. If we leave it to *Statius*, it may be said indeed, that it was not *Ulysses* himself, the Chief of the *Greek* Embassy, who presented the Toys, but, nat that he employed a Merchant to do it. Some Moderns (84) say, that he did it himself in the Disguise of a Merchant.

(83) Ovid. Metam. lib. 13. ver. 175.

(84) Textor, Officin. lib. 2. cap. 32. Nat. Comes Mythol. lib. 6. cap. 1. Vincenti in Philostr. in the Summary of Achilles' Nourishment; Pomey in Pantheo Mythico, &c.

ACHILLES.

away without Trouble, tho' he was so much in Favour with the Princess *Deidamia*; the King's Daughter, that she suffer'd herself to be with Child by him [E]. From hence sprung *Neoptolemus*, or *Pyrrhus*, as shall be observ'd in it's proper Place. *Achilles* fought an infinite Number of fine Battles, during the Siege of *Troy*, and before they encamped before the City. The great Quarrel, which arose between Him and *Agamemnon* about their Mistresses, (for (g) *Agamemnon* having restor'd *Chryseis*, who was His, took *Briseis* away, who belong'd to *Achilles*) obliged the latter to keep in his Tent, without troubling himself any more with the War; and nothing was able to make him change his Resolution, but the Death of his dear Friend *Patroclus*, to whom he had lent his Armour (b), of which *Hector* depriv'd him, as well as of his Life. Upon which, *Vulcan*, at the Request of *Thetis* (i), made a new Suit of Armour for *Achilles* [F]. The Death of *Patroclus* was soon after reveng'd [G]; *Achilles* fought

(g) Homer, Il. l. 1. v. 323, &c.

(b) Ib. l. 16. v. 828.

(i) Ib. l. 18. v. 462, &c.

(84) *Upon Cicero de Amicitia*, cap. 20.

chant. I dare not maintain that this is forged; but it very certain, that it is not built upon good Authority. *Langius* pretends (85), that *Lycomedes* did what he could by his Tears and Prayers, to hinder *Achilles* from following *Ulysses*, and accuses *Cicero* for having taken the Son for the Father, in these Words: " Nec enim ——— Trojam Neoptolemus capere potuisset, si Lycomedem apud quem erat educatus cum multis lacrymis iter suum impedientem "audire voluisset. ——— Nor could Neoptolemus have taken Troy, had he suffered himself to have been prevailed upon by the Tears of Lycomedes, who would have prevented his Expedition." *Langius* is mistaken, and not *Cicero*. See the Remark [A] of the Article PYRRHUS, the Son of *Achilles*.

[E] *Suffered herself to be with Child by him*] *Achilles* was so young at that time, that there are but few Examples of such a forward Generative Faculty as his. And yet good Instruction was then more early; nor was there room for the Complaint of *Montagne* in the twenty fifth Chapter of the first Book of his *Essays*, when he says, *They teach us to live when Life is past. An hundred Scholars have had the Venereal Distemper, before having attained to Aristotle's Lessons of Temperance.* But, far from having a mind to moralize on the Poetical History, I should say to *Montagne*, that this Adventure of the Son of *Peleus* is an Admonition, that though Education be implanted never so early, it will sink under the Weight of Nature.

I shall observe by the way, that the Fictions of the Ancients would be more tolerable than they are, had they taken care not contradict each other so much; but it seems they looked on their fabulous History as a Country, wherein every Body did what he pleased, without any Dependance on others. *Apollodorus* says, That *Achilles* was not nine Years of Age (86), when he was carried into the Isle of *Scyros*, and that they had begun already to talk of the Expedition to *Troy*. According to *Statius*, the Preparations of the *Greeks* had already continued a Year, when *Ulysses* was sent to the Island of *Scyros* to fetch *Achilles* from thence. When *Ulysses* came there, *Achilles* was already a Father (87): Judge then whether Nature had been slow in granting him the Abilities of a Man, and whether he long deferred the Exercise of them on young *Deidamia*. *Statius* durst not keep to the Calculation of *Apollodorus*, for he gives *Achilles* (88) at least twelve Years before the taking of him out of *Chiron's* Cave. I cannot tell how *Barthius* could find (89), that, according to the Calculation of *Statius*, the Son of *Achilles* must be above a Year old at the Time of *Ulysses's* Embassy; for though the young Hero had enjoyed the Fair one the very first Day, his Son could have been but three Months old at the Arrival of *Ulysses*. Some have said (90), that he repeated the Dose to his Mistress, after her first Lying-in, and that he had another Son by her. But, seeing he was born (91) before the Voyage of the *Argonauts*, between which, and the Expedition of *Troy*, the Chronologers (92) place at least thirty Years, judge whether the ancient Poets adjusted their Chronology well.

[F] *Made a new Suit of Armour for Achilles.*] No body ought to object that *Charles Stephens* and *Lloyd*, *Hofman*, *Moreri*, &c. speak of the impenetrable Armour, which *Thetis* caused *Vulcan* to make for her Son, for the Expedition of *Troy*. For though she had rendered his Body already invulnerable, by plunging it in the River *Styx*, we know that few Precautions seem superfluous to motherly Fondness. *Malherbe* designed to specify these two Precautions of *Thetis*, when he said:

(85) *Langius* pretends (85), that *Lycomedes* did Langius cites these Words in the 156th and 168th Pages of the 2d Tome of his Commentaries on Statius, and nevertheless he says in the 1584th Page, that Apollodorus does not mention Achilles's Age.

(87) Stat. Achill. ver. 234.

(88) Ibid. 396.

(89) Barth. in Statium, Tom. 3. p. 1684. 1736.

(90) Eustathius in Il. Ιliad. 12. & Ptol. Hephaest. apud Phot.

(91) Apollon. Argon. lib. 1. ver. 558. Valer. Flaccus, Arg. lib. 1. ver. 256.

(92) See Calvisius ad ann. Mundi 2727, & 2767, and F. l'Abbé, Chronol. Franc. Tom. 1. pag. 1270

Bien que sa mere eût à ses armes
Ajoute la force des charmes (93).

*Though to the youthful Hero's Arms
His Mother adds the Force of Charms.*

But yet he did not particularize them, because his Expression rather inclines one to think, that *Thetis* gave her Son enchanted Armour, than that, besides having charmed his Body, she presented him likewise with Armour of Proof. Mr *Menage* (94), who justly censures the Ambiguity of the Expression, acknowledges moreover, that *Thetis* made use of this double Expedient; which in the main does not clash with probability. It is not the Business of a *Distionary Writer* to suppress a Thing under Pretence that it was unnecessary. It is sufficient that he finds it in Authors; being at Liberty, however, if he thinks proper, to arm us with his Philosophical Reflexions. Now it is certain, that an ancient Author called *Philarchus*, or *Phylarchus* has left in Writing, That *Thetis*, finding she could not hinder *Achilles* from going to the Siege of *Troy*, supplicated *Vulcan* to make him a Suit of Armour (95), proof against all human Force. *Vulcan*, having forged the Armour, declared that he would not deliver it, until he had obtained of *Thetis* the greatest Favour she could grant him. She excused herself from it, offering to testify her Acknowledgment by any kind of Service: But, finding he required a Personal Acknowledgment, she promised to pay him with her Person, provided the Armour fitted *Achilles*, which was to be tried upon herself, who was of her Son's Stature. *Vulcan*, satisfied with the Bargain, gave *Thetis* the Armour, who put it on, and run away with it; the poor Cripple, not being able to overtake her, threw his Hammer after her, and hurt her in the Heel.

It may then be said in general, that *Thetis* caused impenetrable Armour to be made for her Son's first Campaign. But since *Homer* is the chief Source, from whence every thing relating to this Article should be drawn, it ought not to have been forgot, that, after the Death of *Patroclus*, from whom *Hector* had taken *Achilles's* Armour, *Thetis* obtained another from *Vulcan*. It is one of the finest Episodes of the *Iliad*, and is served *Virgil* as a Model for one of the best Passages of the *Æneid*. It deserved therefore to be touched upon. Observe, that, according to *Servius* (96), the Armour, which *Patroclus* wore when he was killed, was made at *Peleus* by *Vulcan*.

[G] *The Death of Patroclus was soon after revenged.*] *Moreri* had reason to say, That *Achilles* soon refused the Arms, which the Loss of *Briseis* had made him lay down. In effect, since the *Iliad* comprehends the Actions of but one Year, according to the Sentiment of Father *Mambrun* (97) in his Treatise of Epic Poetry, few Months only must have passed between the Retreat of *Achilles*, and his Return to the Army, after the Death of *Patroclus*. Therefore *Malherbe* fell into a strange Mistake, when he reported as a certain Fact, that *Achilles* had been nine Years before the City of *Troy* without fighting.

Achille à qui la Grece à donné cette marque,
D'avoir en le courage aussi haut que les cieux,
Fut en la même peine, & ne put faire mieux,
Que soupirer neuf ans dans le fond d'une barque (98).

*So Great Achilles, fam'd for warlike Might
Thro' Greece, and equal to the Gods in Fight,*

(93) Malherbe, lib. 3. pg. 75.

(94) Menage's Observations on Malherbe, p. 272.

(95) Apud Natal. Comitem Mythol. lib. 9. cap. 13. Treatise on Lycophron, pag. 36. taken from Notice of it. What I report, and is not proven by Natalis Comes, is in the Scholiast of Pindar. in Nem. Od. 4.

(96) Servius in Æneid. lib. 1. ver. 843.

(97) Mr Menage, in his Observations on Malherbe, p. 443, believes that it comprehends much less.

(98) Malherbe, Poes. L. 5. p. 125.

Nine

ACHILLES.

fought with *Hector* (k), and having kill'd him, fasten'd him to his Chariot, and dragged him round the Walls of *Troy* [H]. *Priam* went in Person (l) to beg the Body of him, and obtain'd it for a great Ransom. There are various Opinions concerning the Death of *Achilles*; some say that *Apollo* killed him (m), or that he (n) assisted *Paris* to kill him, by directing his Dart to the Part, which was not invulnerable; others say that *Paris* (o) killed him treacherously in a Temple, where *Achilles* was gone to treat about his Marriage with *Philoxena*, the Daughter of *Priam*. The *Greeks* made a magnificent Funeral for him, of which *Moreri*'s Dictionary has mentioned some Circumstances, with very little Exactness [I], to say no worse. They

*Nine Years conceal'd within his Vessel lay,
And for his Mistress sigh'd the Hours away.*

Sarrazin, being probably deceived by this Place of *Malherbe*, whom he intended to imitate, has said in a very fine Ode,

*Achille, beau comme le jour,
Et vaillant comme son épée,
Pleura neuf ans pour son amour,
Comme un enfant pour sa poupée.*

Nine Years, Achilles, *fair as Day,
And valiant as his Sword in Battle,
Cry'd for his Mistress, ta'en away,
Like little Master for his Rattle.*

But Mr *Menage* (99) corrected this Fault in the Edition he procured of *Sarrazin*'s Works; he caused *Neuf Mois, Nine Months,* to be put instead of *Neuf Ans, Nine Years.* Finally, the Comparison of *Achilles* to a Child, that *cries for it's Baby,* has it's Foundation in the *Iliad*; where we see that *Achilles*, having lost his Concubine *Briseïs,* runs all in Tears to make his Complaint to his Mother, and that the good Lady comforts him, as if he were a little Boy.

Χειρὶ τέ μιν κατέρεξεν, ἔπος τ' ἔφατ' ἐκ τ' ὀνόμαζε.
Τέκνον, τί κλαίεις; τί δέ σε φρένας ἵκετο πένθος;
Ἔξαυδα, μὴ κεῦθε νόῳ ἵνα εἰδομεν ἄμφω (100).

*She seiz'd his Hand
And thus the Sorrow of his Soul explores.
Why grieves my Son? Thy Anguish let me share,
Reveal the Cause, and trust a Parent's Care.*
Pope.

The Majesty of the *Epic* Poesy suffered these Meannesses in those Times. Therefore let us not regard them. Let us agree that *Homer* was a fine Genius, let us be pleased with the Fruitfulness and Eloquence of his Muse, but let us add,

— Sed illæ,
Si foret hoc nostrum fato delapsus in ævum, &c. (101).

— But He,
Were he to live in these correcter Times, &c.

[H] *Dragged him round the Walls of Troy.*] Perhaps no Poet, before *Virgil*, ever asserted, that the dead Body of *Hector* was dragged three times about the Walls of *Troy*:

Ter circum Iliacos raptaverat Hectora muros (102).

Thrice round the Trojan Walls Achilles *drew
The Corps of* Hector, *whom in Fight he flew.*
Dryden.

The Number of Turns, remarked by *Homer*, relate only to the Sepulchre of *Patroclus*; and it is very probable, that *Virgil* converted the three Circuits about the Sepulchre, of which *Homer* (103) has expressly made mention, into three Compasses round the Walls; I say, that he changed them in that manner, either through a Defect of Memory, or for the sake of the Verse. The Liberty taken in this Alteration has scarce been imitated by any Body; you no more find the three Circuits round the Walls in the Authors who lived after *Virgil*, than in those who preceded him. *Sophocles* (104), *Euripides* (105), *Ovid* (106), *Seneca* (107), *Statius* (108), *Dictys Cretensis*

(109), *Plato* (110), *Cicero* (111), *Hyginus* (112), *Philostratus* (113), *Libanius* (114), *Servius* (115), *Tzetzes* (116), *Eustathius* (117), mention indeed of the dragging of *Hector,* but not the Number of Turns. As much as I can remember, there is only the Author of the *Lesser Iliad,* in *Latin* Verse, who mentions three Courses round the Walls, and thrice round the Tomb. This Author's Name is *Pindarus Thebanus*; he was cited by the old Scholiast of *Statius,* which *Vossius* did not know (118). *Barthius* has mentioned him often in the great Volume of his *Adversaria,* and elsewhere (119). I know that *Ausonius,* in the Summary of the twenty second Book of the *Iliad,* declares that *Hector* was dragged three times round the Walls of *Troy*; but I know also that he was censured for it (120), and that this Error made one of his Commentators believe, that *Ausonius* was not Author of all the Summaries which we have under his Name. Finally, the Treatment of the dead Body, the Discourse which *Achilles* had with *Hector,* ready to expire, the Liberty he granted to every one of insulting and striking the dead Body, that Venal Soul, which suffered itself to be at last perswaded, by rich Presents, to send *Priam* the Body of his Son, are Things so far remote, I will not say from Heroic Virtue, but from the most Common Generosity, that it must necessarily be judg'd, either that *Homer* had no manner of Idea of Heroism, or that he had only a Design to describe the Character of a meer Brute. He represents *Achilles* to us, as wishing himself savage enough to eat *Hector*'s Flesh raw.

Αἲ γάρ πως αὐτόν με μένος καὶ θυμὸς ἀνείη
Ὤμ' ἀποταμνόμενον κρέα ἔδμεναι (121).

*Cou'd I myself the bloody Banquent join!
No!* — *to the Dogs thy Carcase I resign.*
Pope.

The Poet did not so much as comprehend, that, to do more Honour to his Hero, he ought not to have ascribed to him so much Cowardice and Weakness as he does.

[I] *Funeral* — *which* Moreri's *Dictionary has mentioned some Circumstances with very little Exactness.*] This Author has said, that the Gods lamented the Death of *Achilles* seventeen Days; but he ought not to have cited *Homer,* without quoting the Place, where he speaks of it. Now it cannot be in the *Iliad,* for he strictly observed the Rule, which forbids to bury the Hero of an *Epic* Poem, in the Poem itself. *Virgil* observed it also. He ought to have said then, that *Homer* speaks of *Achilles*'s Funeral in the twenty fourth Book of the *Odyssey,* where he introduces that Episode on the Occasion of *Penelope*'s Suitors, killed by *Ulysses.* They have done wrong in the Edition of *Amsterdam,* to put the Continuators in the Place of *Homer* himself. But this is not all: They should not have said *The Gods* in general, without specifying what *Homer* particularly mentions, to wit, That *Thetis,* accompanied by the Sea Goddesses, came to the Camp of the *Greeks,* to solemnize the Funeral Rites of her Son jointly with them, and that the nine Muses assisted with their mournful Elegies. He might have cited *Pindar* for this last Circumstance.

Τὸν μὲν οὐδὲ θανόντ' ἀοιδαὶ
ἔλιπον· ἀλλά οἱ
παρά τε πυρκαὶ τάφον
θ' Ἑλικώνιαι παρθένοι
ἔσαν, ἐπὶ θρῆνόν τε πολύφαμον ἔχευαν. Ἔδοξε ἄρα δ' ἀθανάτοις
ἐσλόν γε φῶτα καὶ φθίμενον ἐ-
μνοις θεᾶν διδόμεν (122).

VOL. I. X

82   ACHILLES.

(n) See the Remark [B] of the Article ACHILLEA.

They buried him in the Promontory *Sigæum* [K]; and after the taking of the City, they sacrificed *Philoxena* on his Tomb, as his *Manes* required. This Warrior, the most violent of all Warriors, and so Brave, that his Name became significant of the Highest Valour [L], was very fond of Music [M] and Poetry (p), and pass'd for the handsomest

> *In Death the Theme of Heavenly Verse,*
> *Each weeping Muse attends his Hearse,*
> *Ordain'd, in never-dying Song,*
> *The Hero's Glory to prolong.*

What the Dictionary adds, on the Authority of *Homer* again, that, after these seventeen Days, *the young Men* of Thessaly *perform'd* Achilles's *Funeral Rites, where they wept, crowned with Flowers of Amaranth,* should, one would think, be found in the same Place of the *Odyssey*, where the seventeen Days Mourning are mentioned. Yet it is not there; and I am much afraid, that Mr *Moreri* made use of some Book, where the Ceremony was ill related, which *Philostratus* takes Notice of in the Picture of *Neopt.lemus*. It is, that the Greeks, having been ordered by the Oracle of *Dudona*, to go every Year and celebrate the Anniversary of *Achilles*, the *Thessalians* were the first, who added Crowns of *Amaranth* to the other Ceremonies.

[K] *They buried him in the Promontory of* Sigæum.] Almost all the Dictionaries observe this. Lloyd rejecting the other Citations of *Pliny*, which he had found much corrupted in *Charles Stephens*, preserves that of the twelfth Chapter of the fourth Book; but not justly; for *Pliny* does not speak there of the Tomb which was at *Sigæum*, but of That, which was said to be in an Island of the *Euxine* Sea. He says, in the thirtieth Chapter of the fifth Book, that there had been a City called *Achilleum*, near the Tomb of *Achilles*, on the Coast of *Sigæum*. It is to be wondered at, that, after the Correction of this Passage, *Isaac* *(123) In Melam. pag. 98.* *Vossius* (123) should yet accuse *Pliny* of placing *Achilles's* Tomb on the Banks of *Rhæteum*, and that of *Ajax* on the Banks of *Sigæum*: *Pliny* has done quite *(124) Polyhist. cap. 4 .* the contrary. *Solinus* (124), by a Mistake common enough to him, transported this Sepulchre to another neighbouring Cape, to wit, That of *Rhæteum*, where the Tomb of *Ajax* was. This Mistake is in the Emblems of *Alciatus*.

(125) Alciat. Embl. 136.

> Æacidæ tumulum Rhœteo in Littore cernis (125)
>
> ------ You see
> Achilles' *Tomb on the* Rhœtean *Shore.*

His Commentators own, that he is mistaken, except *Pignorius*, who maintained the contrary. It is nevertheless certain, by the unanimous Testimony of Authors, that the Tomb of *Achilles* was on the Shore of *Sigæum*. We have already observed, that it was a Custom to go thither every Year, to offer Sacrifices to him; the Tradition was, that his Apparition appeared there in Armour, and in a threatning Po- *(126) Philostr. in vitâ Apollon. lib. 4. cap. 3 & 4.* sture; which did not hinder *Apollonius* from wishing he could converse with it (126). I think it was given out likewise, that Miracles were wrought at his Tomb. See the following Article.

[L] *His Name became significant of the Highest Valour.*] Mr *Moreri* pretends, without citing the Book or the Chapter, that *Aulus Gellius* has said, that when they would speak of a Brave Soldier, they called him an *Achilles*: But it is not true, that *Aulus Gellius* has said any such thing. He says only, in the eleventh Chapter of the second Book, that *Sicinius Dentatus* was called the *Roman Achilles*, for having performed very surprizing Actions in War. Our Author reports some Circumstances concerning them, taken out of that Passage of *Aulus Gellius*, without telling us from whence he borrows them: So that he quotes this Author, not when he ought, but when he ought not; not when he borrows what is really His, but when he gives him what is not his due. *(127) Servius in Virgil. Ecl. 3. ver. 91. & in Ecl. 4. ver. 34.* If he had cited *Servius* (127), he would have alledged a better Proof. Now the Name of *Achilles* was given, not only to denote *Martial Vigour*, but even That shewn in the Wars of *Venus*; witness the *Debauchee*, in *Petronius*, who finding himself already dead in those Parts, which are not to be named, *● Petron. Sat. C. 129.* cries out, *Funerata est illa pars corporis quâ quondam* ACHILLES eram *●*. Perhaps he was more vexed at this, than *Milo* was, when he lost the Strength of his Arms, and *Cicero* would have thought him

more worthy of Censure, than that *Athletè*, for very good Reasons. " Quæ vox potest esse contemp-" tior, quam Milonis Crotoniatæ, qui, cum jam se-" nex esset, athletasque se in curriculo exercentes " videret, adspexisse lacertos suos dicitur, illacrymans-" que dixisse, at hi quidem jam mortui sunt? Non " verò tam isti quam tu ipse nugator, neque enim " ex te unquam es nobilitatus, sed ex lateribus & " lacertis tuis (128). ——— *Can any thing be more ri-* *(128) Cicero de Senect. cap. 9.* " *diculous, than the Complaint of* Milo *the Croto-* " *nian, who, in his old Age, when he saw the Wrast-* " *lers exercising themselves in the Ring, is said to* " *have looked at his own Arms, and to have cried* " *out with Tears, But these, alas! are now dead —!* " *These Men are not such Trifflers, as you are, whose* " *Nobility rose not from any Merit of your own, but* " *from the Robustness of your Sides and Arms.*"

The Dictionary of *Charles Stephens*, in the Edition of Paris 1620. revised and corrected by *Frederic Morel*, Royal Professor, and in that of Geneva 1662. corrected again from a great Number of Faults, as the Title informs us, attributes to *Aulus Gellius*, when rightly quoted, not that *Brave Soldiers*, but that Captains of an extraordinary Valour had the Appellation of *Achilles*; and that *Money*, or *Silver (Argentum)* was called *Achillean*, because it was *insuperable*, or when it was *insuperable*. " Tantæ for- " titudinis fuisse fertur (ACHILLES) ut, teste " *Gell's*, lib. 2. c. 11. insigni fortitudine duces A- " CHILLES appellentur, & Argentum vocetur " ACHILLEUM, quod sit insuperabile & inso- " lubile (129)." The *Latin* Text of *Charles Stephens* *(129) Car. Stephens in Diction. Voc. Achilles.* may be construed both the forementioned ways; and I confess also, that by pleading a Confusion and Inaccuracy in the Period, he may escape the Censure of having imputed to *Aulus Gellius*, what concerns this pretended *Achillean Money*. But neither *Charles Stephens*, nor his Correctors, nor Mr *Lloyd*, nor Mr *Hoffman*, who followed him closely, can justify themselves for having mistaken *argentum* for *argumentum*. For the Epithet, borrowed from *Achilles*, is applied to an *insuperable* Objection. And in the Schools they commonly call the principle Argument of a Sect, it's ACHILLES. Which was not so much because *Achilles* was an invincible Warrior, as in illusion to the intricate Difficulty, which *Zeno* of *Elæa* proposed *(130) See Aristot. lib. 6. Physic. cap. 9. & ib. Simpl'ene, & Themistius. See of Dictionn. Lat. lib. 2. in Zenone.* (130) against the Reality of Motion. He compared a Tortoise to *Achilles*, in order to shew that a flow Motion, which should preceed a quick one never so little, could never be outstript by it. *Calepinus*, who otherwise cites *Aulus Gellius* erroneously, reads *argumentum* and not *argentum*, which teaches us that the Evil proceeds from an ancient Source, which formed as it were two kinds of *Cespitis*. One having, it is probable, lost half of the Word *argumentum*, thro' the Error of the Printer, who substituted *argentum*, were the Cause, that their Descendants preserved this last Word from Hand to Hand; the other have not yet degenerated in this respect; so that those who apply to them, as *Calepinus's* Correctors did, *(131) Lib. 9. ver. 186.* avoid the Blunder of the former.

[M] *Was very fond of Music.*] Mr *Moreri* is not accurate in his Account of this: He says, *That* Homer *has often shewed us, that the Sound of the Lyre* *had a marvellous Power to divert* Achilles's *Anger,* *and calm that furious Passion, which gave the Tro-* *jans so much Trouble.* He adds, *That* Athenæus *observed it also after* Theopompus. But it is certain that we are only told in *Homer*, that the Deputies of the Army found *Achilles* singing the brave Actions of great Men to the Lyre, to divert himself.

> Τὸν δ' εὗρον φρένα τερπόμενον φορμίγγι λιγείῃ
> Τῇ ὅγε θυμὸν ἔτερπεν ἄειδε δ' ἄρα κλέα ἀνδρῶν (132).
>
> *Amus'd at ease, the God-like Man they found,*
> *Pleas'd with the solemn Harp's harmonious Sound*
>
> *With this his Voice he diverts ●, and sings*
> *The martial Deeds of Heroes and of Kings.*
>
> POPE.

(132) Iliad. lib. 9. ver. 186.

● The Reason of the Alteration might be, from what Mr Pope's third Line (which he foaths his angry Soul, &c.) is to a murder of Bayle's Sentiment. Perhaps the Notion might be taken of the Antiquity of the Words. But Mr Pope, with this he foaths his angry Soul, &c., is to answer Bayle's

Achilles,

ACHILLES.

handsomest Man of his Time [N]. If his Beauty made him amiable to the Women, he

Achilles, having been affronted by *Agamemnon*, had at that time abandoned the common Cause out of Spite and Anger. This is all that *Homer* tells us of it. As for Reflexions, he makes none on the Employ, wherein the Deputies found *Achilles*: *Athenæus* (132) indeed concludes from thence that *Homer* intended to signify, that the Lyre was of great help to that Hero, in moderating the violent Heat of his Anger. But it is not true, that *Athenæus* makes this Remark after *Theopompus*, and I am very much mistaken if the Cause of *Moreri's* Error be not a Passage of *Vossius* in his Treatise of Music. This learned Man, having cited *Athenæus* for the Observation, which we have just now seen (133), goes on to say, that the Embassadors of the *Getæ*, who were sent on a Treaty of Peace, or a Truce, to Persons, whose Wrath was to be appeased, presented themselves playing on the Lyre, and alledges *Athenæus* for his Authority, who reports it out of the forty sixth Book of the History of *Theopompus*. Mr *Hofman* is very near in the same Error, as I have observed. They would have found their Account a little better in *Philostratus* (134); for he observes, that *Chiron*, perceiving that *Achilles* could not conquer his Anger, taught him Music.

Some have said, that *Achilles* did not sing the fine Exploits of great Men on the Lyre, but the Evils which Love had made him suffer:

Talis cantata Briseïde venit Achilles
Acrior, & positis erupit in Hectora plectris (135).

Thus to his Lyre his Loss Achilles sung;
(On every Note the fair Briseis hung)
Then rush'd on Hector, doom'd, alas! to prove
The Force of Valour rais'd by injur'd Love.

Ille Pelethronium cecinit miserabile carmen
Ad citharam, citharâ tensior ipse suâ (136).

His Lyre he tun'd to his complaining Song,
Himself more tortur'd, than the Lyre he strung.

These are Slanders on our Hero, which may be refuted by the Answer which *Alexander* the Great made to Him, who offered him the Lyre of *Paris*: *I care but little for This*, said he to him, *but I would willingly see That of Achilles, on which he sung the Actions of the Heroes of former Times.* *Plutarch*, who reports the Thing thus in the Life of This Prince, attributes another Answer to him elsewhere (137), to wit this: *I have nothing to do with it: for I have that of Achilles, to the Sound whereof he repos'd himself, in singing the Praises of valiant Persons; but That of Paris has too soft and effeminate an Harmony, being employed only in Love Songs.* This is not the only Example, which shews that *Plutarch* made himself too a Master of certain Facts, that sometimes he turned and applied them one way, and sometimes another. Surely *Alexander* did not give both these Answers, and it is probable the last is the Invention of the Historian. As for the Words, *for I have that of Achilles*, it is very probable *Alexander* wished to have it, but undoubtedly it is not true, that he was really in Possession of it. *Ælian* (138) relates the Fact conformably to the first Narrative of *Plutarch*. A Commentator on *Ælian* (139) assures us, that *Homer* represents *Achilles*, in divers Places, singing the Exploits of great Captains to the Lyre. But he is mistaken; *Homer* does it but in one Place; and his Error, being that of a Man much superior in Point of Literature, might comfort *Moreri*, if he were yet living. *Kuhnius* (140) does not correct this Mistake. *Statius*, who supposes, against the express Words of *Homer*, that *Achilles* sung his Amours, and his *Brises*, during his Retreat, assures us in other Places, that, from his most tender Youth, he had employed his Musical Instruments in *Chiron's* Cave, to celebrate the great Actions of the Ancients.

----- Nec major in istis
Sudor, Apollineo quam fila sonantia plectro
Cum quaterem, priscosque virûm mirarer honores (141).

No greater Toil, than when the Lyre I strung,
And Heroes were the Subject of my Song.

They were the Combats of *Hercules*, those of *Pollux*, and those of *Theseus*, which he sung before his Mother, who came to visit him in this Cave, to which he added his Father's famous Nuptials.

----- Canit ille libens immania laudum
Semina, qui tumidæ superarit jussa novercæ
Amphytrioniades: crudum quo Bebrycra cæstu
Obruerit Pollux: quanto circumdata nexu
Ruperit Ægides Minoï brachia Tauri.
Maternos in fine thoros, superisque gravacum
Pelion (142).

The Lyre he takes: then, how Amphytrion's Son
Each cruel Labour patiently o'ercome,
Well-pleas'd he sings; and next how Bebryx fell,
(Thy Cæstus, Pollux, sent his Shade to Hell)
The Minotaur and Theseus next employ
His lengthen'd Song; and lost his Mother's Joy,
To grace her Nuptials when the Gods were met,
And Pelion groan'd beneath the Heavenly Weight.

I own *Philostratus* makes him sing several Subjects, under the tuition of *Chiron*, which related infinitely less to War, than to Love; *Hyacinthus, Narcissus, Adonis, Hilas*, &c. (143)

We shall end this Remark with something relating to the Lyre itself of *Achilles*. It is said, that *Cerybas* (144) the Son of *Jasius*, and of *Cybele*, being gone into *Phrygia* with his Uncle *Dardanus*, settled the Worship of *Cybele* there, and gave his Name to the *Corybantes*, who were the Priests of that Goddess, and brought thither the Lyre of *Mercury*. It was kept at *Lyrnessus*, from whence *Achilles* carry'd it away, when he seiz'd on That City. *Homer* is not of this Opinion; for he says (145), that the Lyre of This Hero was found in the City of *Eetion*, that is, in *Thebes* of *Phrygia*, when the *Greeks* plunder'd it. [N] *For the handsomest Man of his Time.*] Instead of this Fact, of which there are such authentic Proofs, Mr *Moreri* observes only, that *Philostratus* says, that *Achilles was of a fine Stature.* *Achilles* boasts Himself, in the twenty first Book of the *Iliad*, that He is both *Tall* and *Beautiful*,

καλὸς τε μέγας τε.

And when *Homer* speaks of *Nireus*, he remarks that, after *Achilles*, he was the handsomest of all the *Greeks*:

Νιρεὺς, ὃς κάλλιστος ἀνὴρ ὑπὸ Ἴλιον ἦλθε
Τῶν ἄλλων Δαναῶν, μετ' ἀμύμονα Πηλείωνα (146).

Nireus, in faultless Shape, and blooming Grace,
The loveliest Youth of all the Grecian Race,
Next to Achilles.

POPE.

See the Scholiast of *Homer* on the 131st Verse of the 1st Book of the *Iliad*, where he says (147), that *Achilles*, the handsomest of all the Heroes, had a Face so like a Woman, that it was easy for him to pass for a Maid at the Court of *Lycomedes*. *Statius* says,

----- Plurimus illi
Invictâ Virtute decor, fallitque tuentes
Ambiguus, tenuique tamen discrimine sexus (148).

A graceful Form cloath'd his Heroic Mind,
Ambiguous, and to either Sex inclin'd.

As for his Stature, I shall pass by what *Philostratus* says, in the Life of *Apollonius* (149), that the Shade of *Achilles*, being conjured up by that Philosopher, appeared at first five Cubits tall, and afterwards twelve, and of a Beauty impossible to be express'd. Neither will I assert with *Lycophron*, that *Achilles* was nine Cubits tall; This is not what we call a fine Stature: It can only be of Service to *Quintus Calaber* (150), who made a Giant of him, and is by no means a Justification of the Sieur *Moreri*. We may say then, that it is very true, that the Author (151) whom he cites,

he lov'd them as well on his side [O]; and it is even said that his Amours extended to Persons of his own Sex [P]. We shall see in the following Article what he did after his Death, and a Miracle he wrought, which *Tertullian* has taken Notice of. I refer you to the *Homericus Achilles* (q) of the late Mr *Drelincourt*, as a Collection of the most compleat Literature that can be met with in Relation to this Hero of *Paganism*.

cites, gives This Hero a fine and tall Stature, and a Face that shot forth Rays, *a Nose neither Aquiline nor hooked, but such as it ought always to continue.* Thus *Vigenere* translates it, apparently from the *Latin* Version: I should choose to render it, *such as it ought to be*, and give This Signification to the Verb μέλλω.

[O] *He loved them as well on his side.*] The Incontinency of *Achilles* was both a forward and a lasting Fruit: We have seen, that he got *Deïdamia* with Child at ten Years of Age: And his future Atchievements of this kind were answerable to this early Beginning. It was not long before *Iphigenia* experienced his Abilities (152), in the same way; and if *Diana* believed that they offered her a Virgin-Sacrifice in the Person of this Daughter of *Agamemnon*, she was deceived. *Achilles* had taken Care, that, if the worst came to the worst, *Iphigenia* should not go out of the World without having tasted both the Joys of Conception, and the Pains of Labour. He saw *Helen* on the Walls of *Troy*, and became so furiously in love with her, that he had no Rest, and was forced to have recourse to his Mother (153), and to beg of her to procure him by some means or other the Enjoyment of this Beauty. A fine Employ for a Mother! *Thetis* accepted of it, and invented a kind of Pimping, which consisted in making her Son believe, that he enjoyed the Fair One: But it was a meer Dream; and yet This imaginary Repast appeased *Achilles*'s Appetite. Though he lost *Briseïs*, he did not lie alone; he was too careful in providing for his Bed. He could find *Relays* at Home in case of Necessity; *Diomedea* (154) supplied the Place of *Briseïs*. He had no sooner seen *Polyxena*, the Daughter of *Priam*, than he desired to make her his Wife; and not being able to satisfy this Desire in his Lifetime, he required that, after his Death, she should be sacrificed to him (155), that he might enjoy her in the *Elysian* Fields. He had so well deserved in this World to be called (156) ἐρωτικός, ἀσελγής, ἀκρατὴς, ἱππομανέστατος (*Amorous, Incontinent*, &c.) (157), that it was thought he would stand in need of Women, even in the other, and therefore they married him there both to *Medea* and *Helen*. He was accused (158) of having fallen in love with the *Amazon* *Penthesilea*, after he had taken her Life away, of having gratified his Passion on her dead Body. We shall take Notice of this in the Article THERSITES. See also the Article TENES.

[P] *Persons of his own Sex.*] Some will have it (159), that *Troilus*, the Son of *Priamus*, died smothered in the Arms of the lascivious *Achilles*, who would have violated him, but found too much Resistance. A very malicious Turn is given to the Choice, which *Ajax* suggested to *Menelaus*, when he advised him to cause the News of the Death of *Patroclus* to be carried to *Achilles* by the handsome *Antilochus*. *Philostratus* (160), who says plainly enough what sort of Acquaintance there might be between the Hero and the Messenger, who was chosen, is mistaken in relation to the Author of this Choice; for it was not *Menelaus*, as he says, who cast his Eyes on *Antilochus*; it was *Ajax* (161), who propos'd it to *Menelaus*. But it is chiefly with respect to *Patroclus*, that they have given a criminal Turn to the Passion of *Achilles*. *Plato* (162) takes his part upon this against *Æschylus*. *Xenophon* (163), is of *Plato*'s Opinion in it. *Sextus Empiricus* (164) handles the Matter like a Man of his Profession, I mean Pyrrhonically. But *Lucian* and *Philostratus* (165) declare him guilty of it: One of them pretends that *Achilles* was not enough upon his Guard in lamenting his Friend's Death, and that he suffered the Truth to escape him in these Words.

Μηρῶν τε τῶν σῶν εὐσεβὴς ὁμιλία
Καλλίων. (166)

Femorum & tuorum sancta conversatio Melior,

What shall we say of this Distich to the 44th Epigram of the 11th Book of *Martial*?

*Bryseïs multum quamvis aversa jaceret,
Æacidæ propior levis amicus erat.*

*What tho' Briseïs lay not by his Side,
His smooth-fac'd Friend her Absence well supply'd.*

ACHILLEA

ACHILLEA, an Island of the *Euxine* Sea, called also the *Island of Heroes*, the Island *Macaron* (a), or the *Island of the Blessed*, *Leuce*, &c. was, according to some, over against the *Borysthenes*, and, according to others, over against the *Danube*. The Name of *Achillea* was given it, because the Tomb of *Achilles* was to be seen there (b), and because it was consecrated to that Hero. *Thetis* (c) or *Neptune* gave it him, and he obtained Divine Honours there, a Temple, an Oracle, an Altar, Sacrifices, and the like. Some speak of this Island (d) as if it were uninhabited, and that it was unsafe to pass the Night in it; which obliged Persons, who went on Shore there, to return on Board toward the Evening, after having seen the Antiquities of the Place, the Temple, and the Gifts, which were consecrated to *Achilles*. This Hero was not there alone; the Souls of many other Heroes had likewise their Abode there [A]; and as for *Achilles*, he must necessarily have been present both in Body and Soul; for he married *Helen* there (e), and had a Son by her, whose Name was *Euphorion*, whom *Jupiter* loved criminally, and without Success, and whom he killed with a Thunderbolt, to punish him for his Refusal. Others say (f), that *Achilles* had *Iphigenia* to Wife in this Island, whom *Diana* had transported thither, after having communicated to her the Gift of Immortal Youth, with a Divine Nature. Lastly, others pretend, that the Wife, whom he married in the other World, was the famous *Medea* (g); but the most common Opinion gives him *Helen* to Wife. It is

[A] *The Souls of many other Heroes had likewise their Abode there* (1)]. This appears from a Passage of *Pausanias* (2), where he relates that *Leonymus*, General of the *Crotoniates*, having been at the Island of *Leuce* to be cured of a Wound, reported, That he had seen there *Achilles*, the two *Ajax*'s, *Patroclus*, *Antilochus*, &c. I wonder *Ammianus Marcellinus* forgot this in the Passage, where he tells us, that this Island was a dangerous Place: " In hac Taurica Insula Leuce sine Habitatoribus ullis Achilli est dedicata; in quam si fuerint quidam forte delati, visis antiquitatis vestigiis temploque & donariis eidem heroï consecratis, vesperi repetunt naves; siunt enim non sine discrimine vitæ illic quemquam pernoctare (3). — *In this Tauric the uninhabited Island of Leuce, is consecrated to Achilles; at which, whoever happen to arrive, after having viewed the Remains of Antiquity, the Temple, and the Gifts consecrated to That Hero, go back to their Ships at Night; for they say, that no one can pass the Night there, without endangering his Life.*"

ACHILLEA.

is the Opinion, which *Philostratus* and *Pausanias* followed (*b*). The first relates (*i*), That if Strangers, who landed upon this Island, could not sail again the same Day, they were obliged to pass the Night in their Ships, where *Achilles* and *Helen* paid them a Visit, and drank with them, and entertain'd them with singing their own Amours, and *Homer's* Verses. He adds, that, at that Time, *Achilles* cultivated the Talent of Poetry, which *Calliope* had bestowed on him [*B*], with so much the more Care, as he was not interrupted by Warlike Occupations. He adds, besides, that those, who sailed near this Shore, heard Music, which fill'd them with an Admiration, mix'd with Horror; and that they heard likewise the neighing of Horses, clashing of Arms, and warlike Shouts. *Maximus Tyrius*, and *Arrian*, tell us things no less surprizing [*C*]. It was here, no doubt, that *Achilles* wrought the Miracle, which *Tertullian* speaks of [*D*]. He wrought many more, among which That, which he perform'd against the Impiety of the *Amazons* [*E*], who endeavoured to plunder his Temple,

(*h*) Pausan. lib. 3. pag. 1c2.
(*i*) In Heroic.

[*B*] *The Talent of Poetry, which* Calliope *had bestowed on him.*] Some will have it, that, when *Plutarch* relates, that *Minerva*, the Goddess of Science, distilled Drops of *Nectar* and *Ambrosia* into the Lips of *Achilles*, who refused all kind of Nourishment, he would intimate to us that This Hero was Master of *Universal Science*. 'Η 'Αθηνᾶ τῷ Ἀχιλλεῖ νέκταρός τι καὶ ἀμβροσίας ἐνεσκαῖε μὴ προεσιαμένη τροφήν (4). *Minerva Achillem, Nutrimentum respuentem, Nectare & Ambrosiâ instillatis alluit.* It is one of the Authorities alledg'd by *Lorenzo Crasso* (5), to prove, that *Achilles* ought to be ranked among the *Greek* Poets. A Punster might call this *infusing Knowledge into him*, or there never was any such thing. But however it be, *Plutarch's* Words are of no use to prove what *Lorenzo Crasso* infers from them: They are to be understood of a real Nourishment of the Body, as appears from the 19th Book of the *Iliad*, from whence they are taken. *Homer* tells us, That *Jupiter*, having perceived that *Achilles* would neither eat nor drink after the Death of *Patroclus*, bid *Minerva* infuse Nectar and Ambrosia into him, to prevent his being starved to Death.

- - - - Οἱ νέκταρ τε καὶ ἀμβροσίην ἐρατεινὴν
Στάξον ἐνὶ στήθεσσ' ἵνα μή μιν λιμὸς ἵκηται. (6)

*E'er Thirst and Want his Forces have opprest,
Haste, and infuse Ambrosia in his Breast.*

Pope.

Recourse must be had to *Philostratus*, to prove this Hero to have been a Poet (7). He is an Evidence, who is very clear in his Testimony.

[*C*] *Maximus Tyrius, and Arrian tell us Things no less surprizing.*] The former tells us, that *Achilles* resided in an Island near the *Euxine* Sea, opposite to the *Danube*, and that he had Temples and Altars there; that it was difficult for any one to land there without first offering Sacrifice; and that Mariners often saw *Achilles* in the Figure of a beautiful Youth, who danced a warlike Dance in golden Armour; some heard him sing, without seeing him; others both saw and heard him. It happened, that a certain Person inadvertently falling asleep in this Island was awaked by *Achilles*, and conducted into a Tent, where he was entertained at Supper. *Patroclus* filled the Wine, and *Achilles* plaid on the Lyre; *Thetis* and the other Deities were present (8). *Arrian* had heard say, and believed it, that those, who were cast a Shore on this Island by a Storm, went to consult the Oracle of *Achilles*, to know whether he would accept of the Victim in Sacrifice, which they themselves should select from the Herd; and that at the same time they deposited on the Altar the Value of it, according to their own Estimation; that, if the Oracle rejected their Propositions, they added something more to the Price, until they found by it's Content, that they had come up to the full Value of it; that, this being done, the Victim presented itself voluntarily in the Temple, without attempting to escape; that *Achilles* appeared in a Dream to those, who came near the Island, and directed them to the most convenient place of Landing; that he shewed himself also sometimes to those, who were awake, &c. (9). *Arrian*, among other Reasons, thought this worthy of Credit, because *Achilles* died *young*, and was remarkably *beautiful*, and so constant in his Love and Friendship, that he would willingly have died for the Objects of his Love. ὥς καὶ ἐκατελευνὸν ἰδέσθαι τοῖς παιδικοῖς. The Ambiguity of

(4) Plutarch. de facie in orbe Lunæ. p. 918. Edit. Paf. 1624.
(5) Istoria de Poeti Greci, p. 6. où if be read ebiolì, and not alluit. Alluit is at least as good.
(6) Homer. Il. 19. ⅴ. 347.
(7) Philostr. Heroic. in Achil. fol. 719. & in Neoptol. fol. 738.
(8) Maximus Tyrius Orat. 27.
(9) Arrian. in Peripl. Ponti Euxini.

the last Word, and the least Reflexion on the Danger, to which he exposed himself, in order to revenge the Death of *Patroclus*, would induce many Persons to rank *Arrian* among those who say, that the Passion of these two Persons exceeded the Bounds of Friendship (10). See the Remark [*P*] of the Article A C H I L L E S, together with one of the strange Stories related below (11) from *Arrian*; I mean the Story of certain Birds, who swept the Temple of *Achilles* every day, in the Island *Achillea*.

[*D*] *The Miracle which* Tertullian *speaks of.*] *Tertullian*, as Mr *Moreri* remarks, informs us, That *Achilles* cured an Athletic in a Dream, whose Name was *Cleonymus* (12): that is, in plain *English*, *Cleonymus* dreamed, that he saw *Achilles*, who directed him to the necessary Remedy. *Tertullian* makes use of this Fact, and many others of the like nature, against the *Epicureans*, who would not acknowledge any thing supernatural in Dreams. This Adventure is but little known, for no traces of it are to be met with in a great Number of Authors, who have amply spoken of *Achilles*. *Pamelius*, in his Commentary on *Tertullian*, only refers us to *Homer*, who, to the best of my remembrance, takes no notice of this Vision. A Passage, cited by *Leo Allatius*, gives some Light into the Matter (13). It imports, that *Leonymus*, General of the *Crotonians*, in the War against the *Locrians*, was wounded by an unknown Hand, in an Attack upon a Party of the Enemies Troops, who took no care to entrench themselves, because they were consecrated to the Heroes, whose Protection was thought to be sufficient; that The General, finding no Cure, consulted the Oracle at *Delphi*, which informed him, that *Achilles*, who had wounded him, would also cure him; upon which he went to the Island of *Leuce*, to offer up his Prayers to That Hero; that he saw certain Heroes in his Sleep; that *Achilles* cured him; that the rest ordered him to discover certain things to Mankind; and that *Helen* in particular charged him to tell *Stesichorus*, who was become blind for having wrote against her, that he must recant, if he would recover his Sight. It is clear that this History, and that which *Pausanias* (14) and *Conon* (15) relate, are the same in the main: But in *Pausanias* it is *Ajax* the Son of *Oïleus*, who wounded *Leonymus*, and afterwards cured him. In *Conon* it is not *Leonymus*, who was wounded and cured by *Ajax*, but *Autoleon*. There are some other Differences, which I omit, contenting myself with conjecturing, that the *Cleonymus* of *Tertullian* came from This *Leonymus*. Lastly, I must not pass over what the Author, cited by *Leo Allatius* (16) says; which is, that *Homer*, keeping some Sheep near *Achilles's* Tomb, obtained, by his Offerings and Supplications, a Sight of That Hero, who appeared to him, surrounded with so much Glory, that *Homer* could not bear the Splendor of it; and that he was not only dazzled, but blinded by the Sight.

[*E*] *That which he performed against the Impiety of the* Amazons.] Give me leave to relate the Fact, according to *Vigenere's* Translation. It has it's Beauties, though the Style be antiquated. After having told us, that the *Amazons* built Ships, in order to go and plunder the Temple of *Achilles*, he goes on as follows. *Estans abordées en l'Isle, la premiere chose qu'elles firent fut de commander à ces estrangers de l' Hellesponte d'aller coupper tous les arbres autour du Temple, &c.* (17) – i. e. Having landed at this Island, the first thing they did was to bid these Strangers of the Hellespont cut down all the Trees round about the Temple: But their Axes, flying back upon them, de-

(10) Some learned Persons leave us to guess that he gives the *Eloy of Adonis* under the Name of *Achilles*, in order to make his Court to the Emperor *Hadrian*. See Causabon in Sparta num, vit. Hadriani, cap. 14, & Tristan. Comment. Hist. Tom. an. in Hadrian.
(11) In the Remark [*F*].
(12) Tertull. lib. de Anima, cap. 46.
(13) Allatius de patriâ Homeri, p. 145.
(14) Pausan. lib. 3. pag. 1c2.
(15) Apud. Photium Cod. 186. Narrat. 18. See Menziac on Ovid's Epistles pag. 322. two centuries some Mistakes made by *Vigenere* on the Passage of *Pausanias*.
(16) His Name is Hermias. The Passage, which Leo Allatius cites, is taken out of a Comment by upon Plato's Phædrus. Pl. loc is not printed.
(17) Philostrat. in the Neoptol. of *Vigenere's Translation, in the 1 tr. Tom. 2. Edit. in 4to.

VOL. I. Y

ACHILLEA.

Temple, was not the least. That which relates to the Flight of Birds [*F*], is misrepresented by Mr *Moreri*, who moreover gives us a separate Article of a Fountain called ACHILLEA [*G*], wherein *Achilles* was wont to bathe himself, and which had a wonderful Quality. *Achilles* was not the only Person, who wrought Miracles in the Island of *Leuce*; his Wife *Helen* shar'd this Reputation with him (*k*), as we shall

(*i*) *See the Remark* [*D*].

stroyed them on the spot, and they fell stone-dead under the Trees. Whereupon the Amazons, crouding about the Temple, fell a spurring their Horses; but Achilles giving them a furious Look, as when he rushed on Scamander before Troy, so terrify'd their Horses, that their Fright proved stronger than their Bridles. So that prancing and curvetting, and imagining that what they carried on their Backs was a new and extraordinary Weight, they threw down the Amazons, and, like wild Beasts, trod them under foot; their Mains standing erect through Fury, and their Ears prick'd up; and thus, like cruel Lions, they tore them to pieces, devoured their Arms and Legs, and made a most horrid Carnage of their Bowels. When they were glutted with this Feast, they fell a prancing and galloping through the Island, full of Rage and Fury, with their Jaws bloody, till they came to the top of a Cape, from whence perceiving the smooth Sea, and taking it for a fine large Plain, they ran headlong into it, and so perish'd. As for the Ships of the Amazons, an impetuous Whirlwind falling upon them (when they were empty and destitute of all their Rigging) caused them to dash one against another, as it were in a Sea Fight; so that they were broke to pieces, especially those whose Sides were attacked by the Beaks and Prows of other Ships, as commonly happens to Vessels which have no Pilots. So that all the Wrecks meeting together near the Temple, where there were many Bodies half dead, and breathing still, and several Limbs horribly scattered up and down, with the Flesh, which the Horses, being not used to such Food, had rejected, That holy Place must needs have been very much prophaned. But Achilles soon purged and expiated it; as it was an easy thing to do, in an Island of such small extent, against which the Sea beat on all Sides. Achilles having therefore let in the Waves, every thing was washed and made clean in a trice.

[*F*] *That which relates to the Flight of Birds.*] What *Moreri* ascribes to *Pliny*, namely, *That no Bird is seen to fly there*, is misrepresented. *Pliny*'s Words are: "*Perdices non transvolant Bœotiæ fines in Attica, nec ulla avis in Ponto, insulâ quâ sepultus est Achilles, sacratam ei ædem* (18). — That is, *Partridges do not fly beyond the Frontiers of Bœotia in Attica; nor any Bird beyond the Temple of Achilles, which is in an Island of the Euxine Sea.*" *Salmasius* pretends, that by these Words must be understood, that no Bird ever soar'd above this Temple; and he proves by a Passage of *Arrian*, that this was anciently believed (19). And, whereas he proves from an express Passage of *Arrian*, that the Birds came into the Temple every Morning to scatter the Water, with which they had wetted their Wings, and to sweep the Temple afterwards with them (20); he insults *Solinus* for having said, *That no Bird comes into the Temple of Achilles; and that if any one happens to come near it, he flies from it again as fast as he can.* *Salmasius* says, That *Solinus* has nothing but what he borrowed from *Pliny*; and that the latter had said the same thing with *Antigonus Carystius*; but it is more likely, that *Pliny* had not the Thought of *Antigonus Carystius* in view, and that *Solinus* had read the Fact elsewhere, adorned with more particular Circumstances, than those of *Pliny*. For what Negligence would it not be in the latter, if, intending to inform us, that Birds did not fly *over* the Temple, he should make use of an Expression which signifies, that they never flew *beyond* it? These two things are so little alike, that there is nothing more easy than never to go over a House, and yet to leave it behind; as it is not more difficult to fly *above* a House, without passing *beyond* it. Besides, the Ancients were so fond of diversifying their Miracles, that it is improbable, after what had been related from the time of *Antigonus Carystius*, that the Story of the Birds flying away at the sight of the Temple of *Achilles*, should not be broached till the time of *Solinus*. However it be, it cannot be proved from *Pliny* against *Solinus*, that the Birds came into it; and after all, Mr *Moreri* will be found to have imputed to *Pliny* more

(18) Plin. lib. 10. cap. 29.

(19) Salmas. Exercit. Plinian. in Solin. cap. 39. pag. 21?.

(20) In *Periplo Ponti Euxini*. *Philostratus* has said almost the same thing. In that Island (says he, according to the Translation of *Vigenere*, Tom. 2. fol. 337.) there is a certain Species of white Birds, which are aquatic, and smell of the Sea, which *Achilles* makes use of to cleanse his sacred Grove, sweeping it with the Wind of their Wings, and sprinkling it with their Feathers, wetted with Sea-water; for which they fly but very little above the Ground.

than he really said, and to have suffered himself to be deceived by these Words of *Charles Stephens*, in the two above-cited Editions (21). *Achilles insulam nulla avis transvolat.* — i. e. *No Bird flies over Achilles's Island.* *Plin.* 10. 29. 10. But he will take his Revenge with Usury on Mr *Hofman*, who attributes the same thing to *Strabo* also. It was owing, no doubt, to his seeing that Mr *Moreri* cited *Strabo* immediately after *Pliny*, and for want of taking notice, that That Citation from *Strabo*, with that of *Pomponius Mela*, which follows it, relate to other Matters contained in the Article. *Nullam hic avem volare*, says he, *Plin. l.* 10. *c.* 19. *habet & Strabo, l.* 13. (22).

(21) *In the Remark* [*E*], *of the Article* ACHILLES, *towards the Middle*.

[*G*] *A separate Article of a Fountain called* ACHILLEA.] This Article appeared to me at first Sight worthy of Criticism; it seemed to me, that this Fountain was not called so *Substantively*; but by way of Epithet, or *Adjectively*, in common with every thing, which belonged to *Achilles*. In a Word, *Fons Achilleus*, and the Fountain of *Achilles*, appeared to me the same thing. Now as it would be ridiculous to make an Article of the Word *Jacobæan*, in giving an Account of That Well of *Jacob*, spoken of in the fourth Chapter of St *John* (23), which a *Latin* Translator might call *Fontem Jacobeum* if he desired; I could not help thinking, that the Epithet *Achilleus*, which *Freinshemius* makes use of, speaking of the Fountain of *Achilles*, ought not to be made a separate Article. But, after having consulted *Athenæus* (24), I found that this Criticism would be precarious, because it appeared to me that it might not appear in it's alphabetical Order, with as much Reason as the Island *Achillea*. It is to be found in the Geographical *Thesaurus* of *Ortelius* (25), under the Word *Achillæum*, and afterwards under the Word *Achilleus fons*; which is however better than the *Achillea, fons* Mileti, of Mr *Hofman*.

(22) *Hofman upon the Word* ACHILLEA.

(23) *Those who transsate it; there was a Well of Jacob there, would do better to render it Jacob's Well; was there, or as the Port-Royal has it, There was a Well there which was called Jacob's.*

(24) 'Εν Μιλήτῳ ἀφανῶς ἴσασι Ἀχίλλειον καλούμενον ἔσωθεν. *Athen.* lib. 2. cap. 6.

I shall not examine, whether *Freinshemius* has well explained the Passage of *Athenæus*, which regards the Singularities of this Fountain (26). I am satisfied with observing, That *Athenæus* ought at least to have been cited, according to *Freinshemius*, that is to say, at his sixth Chapter, and not at the second, of the second Book. Mr *Hofman* follows Mr *Moreri* in quoting, and they were both shewn the Way by *Ortelius*. But this is nothing in Comparison of *Moreri*'s Blunder, who gives us *Aristobulus* the Son of *Cassander*, instead of *Aristobulus* Native of *Cassandria*.

(25) Editn. Hanov. 1611, in 4to.

We cannot complain too much of the Negligence of those who make Supplements to Dictionaries; for very often they tack certain things to them, which contradict those already there, and generally they forget to accommodate the Addition in such manner to the Foundation on which they build it, nor has Dissonance may result from it. It is *Horace*'s Rule,

(26) *Freinsh.* Supplem. in Q. Curt. 4. 7. 24. *ADVICE to those who make Supplements to Dictionaries.*

Primo ne medium, medio ne discrepet imum (27).

The Piece must be consistent with itself.

(27) Horat. de Arte Poët. ver. 154.

For Example, those who enlarged the Dictionary of *Charles Stephens*, made no Difficulty under the Word *Achillea*, to insert these Words of *Ortelius*, crude as they were, and without the least Alteration, "*Video à Nebrissensi Cacæariam, & à Carolo Stephano Cacariam in suis Dictionariis poni, sed pro ponti insula, quam dicunt apud Melam Collisaria dici, ex depravata fortè lectione, &c.* — *I find* Cacæaria *in the Dictionary of Nebrissensis, and* Cacaria *in that of Charles Stephens; but they both appear to be a false reading for an Island of Pontus, which in Mela is said to go by the Name of Collisaria.*" Which is odd enough; for it makes *Charles Stephens* speak of his own Dictionary, in the Dictionary itself, as if he cited another Work; and yet he seems uncertain, in citing himself, of what he had advanced without any Appearance of Doubt in the Passage, which he quotes.

[*H*] *Achil-*

ACHILLEA. ACHMET.

shall observe under the Article STESICHORUS. *Abundance* is here more dangerous than *Scarcity* [H].

[H] *Abundance is here more dangerous than Scarcity.*] If the Reader finds in this Work several Relations of Prodigies, and Miraculous Traditions, he must not imagine, that it is my Intention to put them off for true; I fear no Accusers on this Head. If this were my Design, I would relate but very few of them. I am very sensible that in these Subjects, Credulity is the Source of Abundance (28); but at length it runs into such excess, that it generally cures those who are not incurable. CREDULITY is a Mother, whose own Fruitfulness destroys her sooner or later in the Minds of those, who make use of their Reason. So that it would have been the Interest of the Pagans, who intended to deify their Heroes, to have attributed but few Miracles to them. The Maxim πλέον ἥμισυ παντὸς, *The Half is more than the Whole*, and That other, *ne quid nimis*, *Too much of one thing is good for nothing*, are applicable here. They, who have so multiplied the Sacred Winding-Sheets, the Pictures of the Holy Virgin painted by St. *Luke*, the Hairs of the same Saint, the Head of St *John Baptist*, the Fragments of the true Cross, and an hundred Things of this Nature, ought to reflect on these two Maxims; for, by encreasing the Dose, they have weakened the Force of it, and have administred both the Poison and the Antidote at once; *Ipsa sibi obstat magnitudo* (29). *It's own Bulk is it's Ruin*. *Achilles* had the same Fate in the Island of *Leuce*, as at *Troy*: The same Miracles, which might deceive the Reader, are sufficient to undeceive him; as the same Spear, which wounded *Telephus*, served him as a Balsam to heel the Wound.

Vulnus Achilleo quæ quondam fecerat hosti,
Vulneris auxilium Pelias hasta tulit (30).
Nysus & Æmonia juvenis qua cuspide vulnus
Senserat, hac ipsa cuspide sensit opem (31).

*Ev'n in his Foe a Friend the Trojan found,
And the same Spear both gave and heal'd his Wound.*

But I forget that the Number of those, who are undeceiv'd by the multiplication of Prodigies, is so small, in comparison of those who are not, that it is not worth my while to alter my Course, and to take the two Maxims above for my Polar Star, when I trade in this Merchandise (32). We shall find a Mistake of *Camerarius* in the Remark [Q] of the Article PYRRHUS, King of *Epirus*, concerning a pretended Miracle of our *Achilles*.

ACHMET, the Son of *Seirim*. He wrote a Book of the Interpretation of Dreams, according to the Doctrine of the *Indians*, *Persians*, and *Egyptians*. It was translated from *Greek* into *Latin*, about the Year 1160, by *Leo Tuscus* (a), who dedicated it to *Hugo Echerianus* [A]. It was published in *Latin*, in the Year 1577 (b), from a very mutilated Manuscript, found in the Library of *Sambucus* (c); but it was said to be a Work of *Apomasares* (d). The learned *Leunclavius* inform'd the Public (e) of this Mistake, in his *Annals of the Turks*. Mr *Rigault* is the first who published this Work in *Greek*. He added it to *Artemidorus*, on account of the Similitude of the Subjects, and published them together at *Paris*, in the Year 1603. He alter'd nothing in the *Latin* Translation of *Leunclavius*, and made no Notes on the Text (f). He believes that *Achmet*, the Son of *Seirim*, is the same whom *Gesner* mentions. But the *Achmet* of *Gesner* was the Son of *Habramius* (g), and a Physician, and Author of a Work divided into seven Books, entituled, *Peregrina ntium Viatica*, which was in *Greek*, in the Library of Don *Diego Hurtado de Mendoza*, the Emperor's Ambassador at *Venice*, when *Gesner* composed his Book. *John Anthony Sarrazin* was in possession of the same Work (b), as he assures us, in his Notes on *Dioscorides*. The two *Greek* Copies of the King of *France*'s Library, from which Mr *Rigault* published his Book of Dreams, do not import that the Author called himself *Achmet*, the Son of *Seirim*. It is true, that, as the Beginning is wanting, it may be conjectured, that when they were whole, the Author's Name might appear at the Head. But lastly, these are but Conjectures, which may receive Strength from another Consideration; which is, that the Name of *Achmet* is writ with a fresher Hand on one of the two Copies. That Name did not appear in the Copy, which *Leo Tuscus* made use of in the XIIth Century, in composing his Translation: This is inferred from the *Italian* Translation of that Work, compos'd by *Tricasso* (i). Mr *Rigault* took the Exordium, and gave it in *Latin*; though he supposes that it was not *Achmet* himself, but *Leo Tuscus*, who compos'd it (k). *Barthius* had the Translation of this *Leo*, and believes that his Copy was written in that Translator's Time (l). The Specimen he gives of it makes it appear, that it was not translated literally, and that many Passages of it were omitted. What is most remarkable is, that the Names of *Achmet* and of *Seirim* are in the Title of the Manuscript with those of *Syrnacham*, *Baram*, and *Tarphan*. The first of these three last Persons was Interpreter of Dreams (m), at the Court of the King of the *Indies*; the second at the Court of *Saanisan*, King of *Persia*; and the third, at the Court of *Pharaoh*, King of *Egypt* (n). *Barthius* conjectures from hence, that *Achmet* and *Seirim* were also two Interpreters of Dreams in some *Barbarian* Court. However it be, the Work was compiled by a Christian; for the Author begins it in the Name of the Holy Trinity (o). Mr *Rigault* looks upon the *Greek* Text only as an antient Translation of the Work. The Original was in *Arabic*.

Lambecius makes *Achmet* to flourish in the IXth Century, at the Court of *Mamoum*, Caliph of *Babylon*. Mr *du Cange* is not of that Opinion. See his *Greek* Glossary, at the Word μαμοῦν.

[A] *To Hugo Echerianus.*] *Barthius* calls him *Hugo Eterianus*, and says that he was an Excellent Author, *Scriptorem ævo suo luculentum* (1). There is a false Print in *Barthius*, as well as in these Words of Mr *Rigault*, *Hugoni Echeriano dedicavit*. It ought to have been *Hugo Eterianus*, *Hugoni Eteriano*. *Allatius*, in the eleventh Chapter of the second Book *de perpetuo consensu Ecclesiæ Occidentalis & Orientalis*, is mistaken in citing *Hugo Ætherianus*. *Baronius*, *Bellarmin*, and many others, write *Hugo Etherianus*; but *Eterianus* is more correct. It is the Name of an Ecclesiastical Author of the XIIth Century. This was communicated to me by Mr *de la Monnoie*.

ACIDALIUS

ACIDALIUS.

ACIDALIUS (VALENS) would have been one of the best of the modern Critics, if a longer Life had permitted him to bring the Talents he had received from Nature to Perfection (a). He was born at *Wistoch*, in the Frontiers of *Brandenburgh*, and having visited several Universities of *Germany*, *Italy*, and of other Countries, where he made himself much beloved [*A*], he resided at length at *Breslaw*, the Capital of *Silesia*. He waited a long time for an Employ in this place; but, not succeeding, he went over to the Communion of the Church of *Rome*, where he soon met with the Rectorship of a School [*B*]. It is said, that four Months were hardly expired, when a very strange Accident happened to him. He was following the Procession of the Holy Sacrament, and on a sudden fell into a Phrenzy. He was carried home, and died soon after. Some gave out, that he had killed himself [*C*]. His Death was a great Loss, for he had Wit, and was a very industrious Person. His great Application to Study was the cause of his Death, if we may believe *Thuanus* (*b*), who says, that by sitting up too late, while he was composing his *Divinations on* Plautus [*D*], he contracted a Distemper [*E*], of which he died in three Days, on the 25th of *May*, 1595. He was just entered into his 29th Year [*F*]. We have several Books written by him (*c*). A little Tract, printed in 1595, to shew that *Women were not rational Animals, mulieres non esse homines*, was falsely ascribed to him [*G*].

I have

[*A*] *Where he made himself much beloved.*] The Esteem, which the Illustrious Persons of *Italy* had for him, may be seen by the Literary Correspondence, which he held with *Vincent Pinelli*, *Jerom Mercurialis*, *Antony Riccoloni*, *Asianius Persius*, &c. He resided three Years in that Country (1).

[*B*] *The Rectorship of a School.*] *Barthius* affirms this: *Rector Scholæ Neussanæ factus* (2); says he, *He was made Rector of the School of Neussa*. I believe he ought to have said *Neissanæ*, or *Nissanæ*. *Neisse*, which *Acidalius* always calls *Nyssa* in his Letters, is three or four Leagues from *Breslaw*. The Bishop of this Name resides there (3). He, who was then in That See, had *John Matthew Wacker* for his Chancellor, a Patron of Learning, and the Learned. He invited *Acidalius* to *Neisse*, and lodg'd him at his House. See *Acidalius*'s Letter (4). I have not observed in those, which he writ from that Place, that he ever mentioned the Rectorship of the School.

[*C*] *That he had killed himself* (5).] *Christian Acidalius*, the Brother of *Valens*, durst not speak out plain, when he complained of the Calumnies which were spread abroad concerning his Brother's Death; but it must be no longer questioned, after what *Barthius* writ in one of his Books, that the Subject of his Complaint was the Report which was spread, that *Acidalius* had killed himself; a Theme of great Outcry from the Pulpit. Let us hear how *Christian Acidalius* speaks of it, after having said that his Brother was pompously buried. " Ut mirari satis nequeam " calida multorum in judicando nimium præcipi" tantium & temerariorum ingenia, qui, & ipsius " morbi & loci etiam sæpe ignari, quicquid maledi" cendi libido dictavit, vel fama, quæ

Tam ficti pravique tenax quàm nuncia veri,

" de obitu ipsius sparsit, propagare porro in exteras " etiam regiones & propugnare, imo nescio quas " tragœdias etiam in concionibus ad plebem, ubi reg" nare solent, excitare non erubuerunt. — *So that* " *I cannot sufficiently admire the rash and hasty Judg*" *ments of certain Persons, who were not ashamed to* " *propagate in foreign Countries, the false Reports,* " *which Calumny, and Fame,*

Alike the Voice of Falshood and of Truth,

" *had spread concerning his Death, and to dress up* " *I know not what Tragical Story, in their Ha*" *rangues to the People, whose Passions they command* " (6)." He does not deny that his Brother was disordered in his Brain, which deprived him of his Reason. " Gravissimum illud febrium acutarum " symptoma Paraphrenitidem aliquoties sensit, quod " extremum malorum animam etiam sua sede ejecit " (7). — *He was sometimes taken with a Para*" *phrenitis, that worst Symptom of Acute Fevers, which* " *shakes the very Soul itself from her Seat.*" But he maintains that very able Physicians, and Mr *Wacker*'s Family, at whose House Mr *Valens* lay sick, assisted him 'till he died. Perhaps there is nothing in which Fame oftener deceives us, than in relating the Sickness and Death of illustrious Persons; wherefore Preachers, and all Moralists in general, ought to be very reserved in their Reflections on them. One cannot too much distrust the rash Credulity, or artful Malice of this kind of Newsmongers.

[*D*] *His Divinations on* Plautus.] On the one side he had the Satisfaction to see them promised in the Catalogue of *Francfort* (8); and on the other, the Vexation of being obliged to make an hundred Complaints against the Slowness of his Bookseller. In a Word, they were not published 'till after his Death. *Barthius* set a Value on that Work: " Pauci eum " Comici locum affecuti sunt — solus Acidalius " rectum sensum percepit, ut alia multa in Comico " (9). — *Few* (says he) *have hit the Poet's Sense* " *in that Passage* — Acidalius *alone discovered it,* " *as he did in many others.*" Mr *Teisser* says, That the Commentary of *Acidalius* on *Quintus Curtius* is much esteemed (10). He dedicated it to the Bishop of *Breslaw*, who rewarded him well for it, as it appears from the Author's Thanks in his eighty ninth Letter. He wrote *Notes on* Tacitus, *on the twelve Panegyrics, and on* Velleius Paterculus, *besides Speeches, Letters, and Poems* (11). This last Work inserted in the Delights of the *German* Poets, contains *Epic* Verses, Odes, and Epigrams, which *Barrichius* thought to be of little Value (12). His Dissertation *de constitutione carminis Elegiaci*, pleases *Barthius* (13).

[*E*] *He contracted a Distemper.*] *Thuanus* does not say what that Distemper was; but we learn from another Hand that *Acidalius* heated his Blood in such manner, by sitting up late, whilst he was commenting on *Plautus*, that from that time he became subject to Fevers. This we learn from his Brother. " Uratislaviæ, quæ Silesiorum Metropolis, per sesqui" annum plus minus utrumque se mihi præstitit, " (præceptorem & patrem) donec inde *Nyssam* evo" catus familiari morbo suo, quem ex nimiis vigiliis " in adornandis Plautinis Divinationibus suis, con" traxerat, FEBRI SCILICET ACUTIS" SIMA opprimeretur (14). — *During his A*" *bode, for half a Year, or thereabouts, at* Breslaw, " *the Capital of* Silesia, *I found in him both a Pre*" *ceptor and a Father; 'till being invited to* Nyssa, " *he was there seized with, and died of, that habi*" *tual Distemper, which he had contracted by too* " *great an Application to his Divinations on* Plautus, " *I mean* A MOST ACUTE FEVER." He was more than once dangerously ill in *Italy*, and he informed his Friends in his Letters, that a Fever was his common Disorder in that Country. See Page 97 and 112 of his Letters.

[*F*] *He was just entered into his twenty ninth Year.*] Thus I render *Thuanus*'s Latin Words, *cum vix annum* 28. *excessisset*. Du *Rier* renders them, *having not attained to his twenty eighth Year*. Let the Reader judge which of us has hit the true Sense of *Thuanus*. Mr *Baillet* says that *Acidalius* was but twenty seven Years and some Months old (15). Perhaps he had found out that *Thuanus* had not been exactly informed of this young Author's Age.

[*G*] *A little Tract* — *was falsly ascribed to him.*] *Geisler* cleared him from this false Imputation, as appears from these Words of *Placcius*: " Prioris " auctor quomodo non ex vero sit habitus Valens " Acidalius, vide apud Geislerum decadis 3. n 8. (16).

How

ACIDALIUS. ACINDYNUS.

I have read somewhere, that he was a Physician [H], and that he intended to have wrote Notes upon *Aulus Gellius*, if he had lived longer. *Nisi juveni illi fata quietem miserabiliter properassent.*—Had not Death snatched him away suddenly (d). It appears from his Letters, that he was preparing an Edition of *Apuleius*. Mr *Baillet* places him among his *Famous Children*, and says that *he illustrated* Plautus *at seventeen or eighteen Years of Age*, not to mention several Latin Poems, which are extant, and which he composed at that same Age. One of his first printed Works is *Velleius Paterculus*, publish'd by himself at *Padua*, in the Year 1591. He himself says, That he was ashamed of this early Production of his Pen, and he was surpriz'd when he heard that it had been reprinted in *France* (e). *Lipsius*, who writ some Letters to him (f), wherein he expressed his Love and Esteem for him (g), was of Opinion that he would prove a great Man: *Ipse Valens (non te fallam augur) gemmula erit Germaniæ vestræ, vivat modo.*—Valens *himself (I certainly foresee) if he lives, will become an illustrious Ornament of your Germany.* This he wrote to *Monavius* in 1594. as may be seen in the beginning of *Acidalius*'s Letters.

(d) Sciopp. de Arte Crit. pag. 18.
(e) Val. Acidal. Epist. pag. 70, 78, 132.
(f) Ibid. p. 160, 161, 299, 25.
(g) The Xth and XXVIth of the Centuria ad Ital. & Hisp.

(17) *That it the Dissertation to prove that Women are not rational Animals.*

(18) *Ut id genus hominum lucri cupidum est, cum aviditati ejus e molumentum Editionis non satis respondisset, quæstum persæpe de jacturâ suâ. As they are a Set of Men eager of Gain, because the Profits of the Edition did not answer his Expectation, he often complain'd of his Loss.* Val. Acidal. Epist. Apolog. ad Calcem Epistol.

(19) Ibid.

(20) Ibid.

"—— *How* Valens Acidalius *came to be mistaken for the Author of the former Piece* (17), *See* Geisler, *decad.* 3. *n.* 8. I shall take notice of this Dissertation in the Article of GEDICCUS; but I must here observe how it came to be ascribed to *Acidalius*. Being desirous to indemnify his Bookseller, who had printed his *Quintus Curtius*, and who often complained that he had been a Loser by it (18); he happened to meet with a Copy of the Book I am speaking of, which had been already transcribed by several People: He read it, and, finding it a diverting Piece, he transcribed it, and made a Present of the Copy to the Bookseller, as a Piece which might turn to good Account. However, he did not advise him to print it: He thought, without doubt, that it was sufficient to let him know that it would make Amends for the Loss he had sustained; but he told him, that it was his Business to look to himself, and consider whether the Satirical Strokes of that Piece would not bring him into Trouble. This Discourse did not discourage the Bookseller: he made all the haste he could to get the Dissertation printed. As soon as it came out it was greatly exclaimed against, and the Bookseller prosecuted for it; and because he confessed of whom he had the Copy, there was a terrible outcry against *Valens Acidalius*, who was amazed to see that meer Sallies of Wit should arm People so much. "*Obstupesco ad judicia sæculi* "*nostri, & tam irritabiles animos illorum θεολογουμέ-* "*νων.* Jocos nemo fere jam admittit, & ex levissi- "*ma quisque re gravem calumniandi cussam & an-* "*sam captat* (19). —— *I am astonished at the ill* "*Judgment of the Times, and the captious Temper* "*of the Reverend Gentlemen. At present no Jest* "*will go down, and the lightest Matter gives an* "*Handle to Calumny.*" He desired his good Friend *Monavius* to intercede for the Bookseller with the Magistrates and Professors of *Leipsic*, and to prevent their doing any thing which might bring a Disgrace upon himself. He was afraid that his Enemies would not be contented with those many Aspersions they had cast upon him; nay, he feared that they would raise the Mob upon him; and of all things in the World, he desired to have nothing to do with the Clergy. "*Nomen meum sic traductum jam in vulgus calum-* "*niosis fabulis satis sit, quod est nimio plus satis: ulte-* "*rius ne quid furori populari concedatur.* In primis "à *Theologis & Concionatoribus ne quid noceatur* "*mihi, cum quibus nolo committi, nec quicquam* "*magis opto quam illorum Tribunitiis edictis nun-* "*quam misceri, nec scriptis publicis incessi* (20). "*Let it be sufficient, that my Name is already become* "*the public Object of Reproach: tho' That, I think,* "*is too much: let not popular Resentment be farther* "*let loose against me. But, above all, let me receive* "*no Prejudice from the Ecclesiastics, with whom I* "*desire to have no Quarrel: nor is there any thing I* "*more earnestly wish, than not to be the Object either* "*of their tribunitial Edicts, or their Writings.*" He died some Months after, and because the Scandal occasioned by the publishing of this Book was still fresh in every one's Memory, People were the more disposed to descant upon the Circumstances of his Death. "*Quæ* "*calumniæ inde potissimum natæ sunt, quod recens*

"*adhuc esset fabula illa in Apologetica epistola satis re-* "*futata, quæ multorum animis altè nimis insederat,* "*ut facile esset improbis quidvis in invidiam trahere,* "*&c.* (21) —— *Which Scandal arose from hence, that* "*this Story, which I have sufficiently refuted in my apo-* "*logetical Epistle, was yet fresh, and had taken so deep* "*a root in the Minds of many; insomuch that it gave a* "*handle to unreasonable Men to blacken my Reputa-* "*tion.*" To conclude; I shall observe, that he affirms this Dissertation had been handed about for a considerable time, and that in all likelihood it was written in *Poland*.

Few will wonder, that *Acidalius* was afraid of coming off by the worst, if he brought the Clergy upon his Back; for, as it is very natural, to entertain an ill Opinion of one's Neighbour, these Gentlemen are very often compar'd to *Æolus*;

Æole, namque tibi Divûm Pater atque hominum Rex
Et mulcere dedit fluctus, & tollere ventos (22).

O Æolus! for to thee the King of Heaven
The Power of Tempests and of Wind has given.
Thy Force alone their Fury can restrain,
And smooth the Waves, or swell the troubled Main.
DRYDEN.

But there is this difference in the comparison, that they are more expert at raising, than appeasing a Storm. This latter Effect demands Men of Consequence and Weight:

Tum pietate gravem ac meritis si forte virum quem
Aspexêre, silent——
Ille regit dictis animos, & pectora mulcet (23).

If then some grave and pious Man appear,
They hush their Noise, and lend a lift'ning Ear.
He sooths with sober Words their angry Mood,
And quenches their innate Desire of Blood.
DRYDEN.

The other Effect is more easily produc'd.

[H] *That he was a Physician.*] *Scioppius* calls him so (24). Indeed he took his Doctor's Degree, but it was only *ad honores*; for he never practised Physic, nor ever design'd to do it. "*Medicum τῇ ψυχῇ nec ago,* "*nec agere propositum unquam fuit: certo consilio* "*tamen inter ejus artis candidates nomen dedi, nec* "*pœnitet, &c.* (25) —— *I neither practise Physic, nor* "*was it ever my Intention so to do: though, for cer-* "*tain Reasons, I thought proper to rank my self among* "*the Candidates of that Science.*" He had said a little before, "*Dabam illîc me τοῖς Ἀσκληπιάδαις,* quorum "*sacris & in Italia fuerum initiatus:—It was there I* "*enroll'd my self among the Sons of Æsculapius, into* "*whose Mysteries I was initiated even in Italy.*" What he says in another Place imports something more, "*Inde rediens cum solenni illorum studiorum* "(Medicinæ) *honore* (26). —— *Returning thence with* "*the solemn Honour of that Science* (Physic)."

(21) Christ. Acidal. in Præf. Epist.

(22) Virgil. Æn. lib. 1. ver. 65.

(23) Ibid. ver. 151.

(24) Scioppius de Arte Critica, pag. 18.

(25) Val. Acidal. Ep. pag. 215. See also pag. 194, 209.

(26) Ibid. pag. 249.

ACINDYNUS (GREGORY) a *Greek* Monk of the XIVth Century. He associated himself with *Barlaam*, who, after he had embraced the *Greek* Religion, made it his Business to extirpate the *Hesycastes*, whose Number was very much increased

VOL. I.   Z   among

ACINDYNUS.

(a) *See the Authors quoted by Maimbourg, in his History of the Schism of the Greeks,* lib. 5. pag. 147, &c. *of the Dutch Edition.*

(b) *Orthod. Græc. Tom.* 1. *firſt* pag. 740, & pag. 773.

(c) *In Book* 2. cap. 16. *de Conſenſu in the Appendix to Cave's Hiſtor. Literar. Script. Eccleſiaſt.* Conſult that Appendix about this Article.

among the Monks of Mount *Athos*. The *Heſycaſtes* were contemplative Votaries, whoſe Name is a ſufficient Proof, that, even in thoſe Days, there were *Quietiſts* in the World. In the Rapture of their Devotion they pretended, that they ſaw a Brightneſs, reſembling that which appeared about *Jeſus Chriſt,* when he was transfigured on Mount *Tabor,* and affirmed this Light to be *Uncreated,* tho' altogether diſtinct from the Eſſence of God (a). *Acindynus,* ſeconding the ardent Zeal of *Barlaam,* wrote againſt the Illuſions of theſe Fanatics, and was one of the Sticklers againſt them in the Council of *Conſtantinople.* But he had the Misfortune to meet with Antagoniſts, who had more Credit and Intereſt than either he, or *Barlaam,* and who drew upon them ſeveral Cenſures and Condemnations in ſeveral Councils. The ill Succeſs he met with in That of *Conſtantinople,* about the Year 1337, did not deter him from charging openly with Hereſy the Favourers of *Gregory Palamas,* for which he was cited by the Patriarch of *Conſtantinople* in 1341. He appeared before the Council, and was obliged to hold his Tongue, upon Pain of Excommunication. Six Years after he was yet more vigorouſly purſued, becauſe *John Cantacuzenus,* who was become Emperor, had a Kindneſs for *Palamas.* The Cenſures and Excommunications, which at ſeveral times fell upon *Acindynus,* reduced him at laſt to a more ſedate, and altogether obſcure, Life. *James Gretſer,* a *German* Jeſuit, publiſh'd at *Ingoiſtad* in 1616, *Acindynus's* two Books, *De Eſſentia & Operatione Dei.* *Leo Allatius* has alſo publiſhed a Poem (b), and ſome Fragments of the ſame Author (c), who having had the Fate to paſs for a Heretic [*A*] a conſiderable time, has found at laſt more learned and more equitable Judges [*B*].

[*A*] *To paſs for a Heretic.*] As in the heat of a Diſpute we are only intent upon preſſing our Adverſaries, we are often blinded to ſuch a degree, as not to perceive, that we paſs from one Extream to another; or at leaſt that we ſtretch our Arguments ſo far, that they prove too much. I make no doubt, but this was the reaſon, why *Barlaam* and *Acindynus* laid themſelves open to their Adverſary *Palamas;* and that, being orthodox at the bottom, they often argued like Heretics. *Prateolus* has not fail'd to place them in his Catalogue; but it is impoſſible to make any thing of the Sentence of their Condemnation, in the manner he relates it. What we find leaſt obſcure in his Book concerning *Barlaam* and *Acindynus,* is, That the Council, which was called in order to condemn them, was held in the preſence of the *Bleſſed* and moſt famous Emperor *Michael Andronicus Palæologus,* and *John* his Son, in the Reign of *Henry* VII. Emperor of *Germany,* *John* XXII. being Pope of *Rome,* in the Year of our Lord 1313 (1). This whole Paſſage ſwarms with Errors: For firſt of all, in the Century

(1) *Prateol. in Elench. Hæret.* pag. 86. Edit. Colon. 1605. in 4to.

here in queſtion (2), there was no other Emperor of *Conſtantinople* who could be diſtinguiſhed by the Title of *Bleſſed* by a *Roman Catholic,* but *Michael Palæologus,* who was reconciled to the Holy See, and died in Communion with it. Now he was neither called *Michael Andronicus,* nor had he a Son called *John*; and beſides he died in 1283. Secondly, the Emperor, whoſe Son's Name was *John,* had no other Name but that of *Andronicus Palæologus,* and began to reign in 1328. ſo that neither *John* XXII. nor *Henry* VII. were his Cotemporaries. Laſtly, It is falſe that *Acindynus* was condemned about the Year 1313. Father *Gualtzer,* in his Chronological Tables, does not forget *Barlaam* and *Acindynus,* whom he ranks among the Heretics, upon the Authority of *Prateolus.*

[*B*] *Has found at laſt more—equitable Judges.*] See the Authors quoted by Mr *Moreri*; I mean *Pontanus* upon *Cantacuzenus,* and *Spondanus's* Annals. See likewiſe thoſe of *Bzovius,* Father *Gretzer* (3), Father *Maimbourg* (4), and the Authors cited by him in the Margin.

(2) *The Word Century is taken here in a General Senſe for the Space of 100 Years, beginning with one pleaſes.*

(3) *Gretzeri Notæ in Cant-cu. & in Editione Acindyni.*

(4) *Maimbourg's Hiſt. of the Greek Schiſm,* B. 5.

ACINDYNUS (SEPTIMIUS) was Conſul of *Rome* with *Valerius Proclus,* in the ſame Year that *Conſtantine,* Son to *Conſtantine the Great,* was kill'd, near *Aquilea* (a). He had been Governor of *Antioch,* and during his Government there happened an Event, mentioned by St *Auſtin* (b), which deſerves to be taken notice of. A certain Man, not paying into the Exchequer a Pound of Gold, at which he had been aſſeſs'd, was committed to Priſon by *Acindynus,* who ſwore withal that he would cauſe him to be hang'd, if he did not pay that Sum upon a certain Day, which he appointed. The limited Time was near expiring, and the poor Fellow ſtill unable to ſatisfy the Governor: He had indeed a beautiful Wife, but who was bare of Money as well as himſelf; and yet it was from her alone he began firſt to be in Hopes of Liberty. A very rich Man being deſperately in love with this Woman, offer'd her the Pound of Gold, on which her Huſband's Life depended, and aſked no other Recompence for it but a Night's Lodging (c). She, being inſtructed by the Scripture, that *She had no Power over her own Body, but her Huſband,* communicated the Offer of this Gallant, telling him withal, that ſhe was ready to accept of it, if he would give his Conſent, he who was the true and lawful Maſter of his Wife's Body; and if he thought his Life worth redeeming at the Expence of a Chaſtity, whereof he had the ſole Diſpoſal. He thank'd her for it, and gave her leave to lie with her Lover. She obey'd; giving her Huſband the Uſe of her Body, not in the common way of gratifying the Appetite of the Fleſh, but to indulge the Deſire he had to live (d). The Spark gave her a Purſe with the promiſed Sum of Money, but ſtole it afterwards cunningly from her, and impoſed upon her another Purſe filled with Earth. The Good Woman, returning home, (for ſhe had met her Gallant at his Country-Houſe) no ſooner found out the Cheat, but ſhe complained of it publickly, and demanded Juſtice of the Governor, to whom the very ingenuouſly related the Fact. *Acindynus* began with accuſing himſelf, as having by his Severity and Menaces drove theſe innocent People to ſuch deſperate Remedies, and firſt of all condemned himſelf to pay the Pound of Gold into the Exchequer; afterwards he adjudged to the obedient Wife That Piece of Ground, out of which the Earth had been taken, which was

(a) *In* 340. *according to Calviſius.*

(b) *Auguſtin on our Lord's Sermon on the Mount,* B. 1. c. 16.

(c) *Pollicens pro una Nocte, ſi ei miſeri velet, ſe auri libram daturum. Id. ib.*

(d) *Illa Corpus non niſi marito dedit, non concumbere, ut ſolet, ſed vivere cupienti. Id. ib.*

found

found in the sham Purse. St *Augustin* dares not decide [*A*] whether this Woman's Conduct be right or wrong, and inclines rather to approve than to condemn it [*B*]; which is somewhat surprizing [*C*]. We have observed before (*e*), the same loose Principle of Morality in St *Chrysostom*, in relation to *Abraham* and *Sarah's* Conduct.

(*e*) *In the Remark* [*A*] *of* ABIMELECH.

[*A*] *Dares not decide.*] This is plain from these Words " *Nihil hic in alteram partem disputo: liceat cuique æstimare quod velit* (1). — *I do not decide upon this Question, let every one judge as he pleases.*" In another place he questions whether a Woman's Chastity would be violated, in case, to save her Husband's Life, and by his own Order, she should lie with another Man; " *Scrupulosius disputari potest utrum illius mulieris pudicitia violaretur, etiam si quisquam carni ejus commixtus foret, cum id in se fieri pro mariti vita, nec illo nesciente sed jubente, permitteret, nequaquam fidem deserens conjugalem, & potestatem non abnuens maritalem* (2). — *It is a nice point to be determined, Whether that Woman's Chastity would be violated, even tho' she should be carnally known by another, who should submit to this for the sake of her Husband's Life, and that by his own Consent; in which she neither deserts her conjugal Faith, nor denies the Authority of her Husband.*" *Rivetus*, having quoted these Words, adds (3), That St *Augustine* relates, that the same Case happened under the Emperor *Constantine* (4), when *Acindynus*, &c.

[*B*] *Rather to approve than to condemn it.*] This evidently appears by these Words: " *Non ita existimandum ut hoc etiam femina, viro permittente, facere posse videatur;* — *Quamquam nonnullæ causæ possint existere ubi & uxor mariti consensu pro ipso marito hoc facere deberet videatur* — *Nihil hic in alteram partem disputo* — *Sed tamen narrato hoc facto, non ita respuit hoc sensus humanus, quod in illa muliere viro jubente commissum est, quemadmodum antea, cum fine ullo exemplo res ipsa poneretur, horruimus* (5). — *We are not to imagine in general that it is lawful for the Wife to do this, even with her Husband's Permission* — *tho' there may happen Cases, in which such a Liberty may be allowed* — *I pronounce nothing in this point* — *However, now I have mentioned this Fact* (to wit, the Case of the Wife, whose Husband was imprisoned by *Acindynus*) *this Woman's Behaviour, in Obedience to her Husband, is not so contrary to the general Sense, nor shocks us so much, as at first sight it may do, when the Question is proposed without any Instance.*" I know not what Grounds the *Protestant* Divine, whom I have quoted in the foregoing Remark, has for his Assertion, when he assures us, that St *Augustin* rather inclines to condemn than to justify the Woman. " *Quo facto Acindyni explicato, liberum unicuique permittit Augustinus æstimare quod velit, quamvis in eam partem propensior videatur, quod id fieri non liceat* (6). — *After laying down this Story of Acindynus, St Austin gives every one leave to judge as he thinks fit; tho' he seems more inclined to condemn the Lawfulness of the Action.*"

(1) St *Austin, contra Faust, Manich. lib.* 22. *cap. 1.*

(2) *Id. contra Faust. Manich. lib.* 22. *cap.* 47.

(3) *Rivetus Exercitat.* 71. *in Genes. Oper. Tom.* 1. *pag.* 281.

(4) *It is Constantius, in the book of St Austin, which I have quoted.*

(5) *St Austin, Ubi supra.*

(6) *Rivet. Ubi supra.*

[*C*] *Which is somewhat surprizing.*] So great a Divine as he was, ought surely to have known, that our Life, which is but a temporal and a perishing Good, ought not to be so dear to us, as to be thought worthy of being redeemed by our Disobedience to the Law of God. For as Disobedience is a Sin, which makes us liable to eternal Punishment, and a Moral Evil, which offends an Infinite Being, it is no less against common Prudence, than the Dictates of sound Reason, to chuse to commit a Sin, rather than lose one's Life. I say nothing of those wide Abysses of Corruption, which are opened every where under our Feet, by asserting, that an Action, which would be criminal, if done without a design to save one's Life, becomes innocent, when done to prevent Death. *Acindynus*'s Prisoner would have acted the shameful Part of a Pander, no doubt, and consented to the Act of Adultery, properly so called, if he had suffered his Wife to lie with the Spark merely to gain a Pound of Gold: but because he consented, only to save his Life, it ceases to be a Consent to Adultery; nay, it becomes a lawful thing. Who does not see, that if this Morality took place, there is not one Precept in the Decalogue, to which the Fear of Death might not dispense with our Obedience? Where are the Exceptions in favour of Adultery? If a Woman may be dispensed with for violating the Command of *not defiling her Body*, when by that means she may rescue her Husband from Capital Punishment, she will likewise be free to transgress it, when her own Life comes in question; for God no where exacts from us, that we should love another more than ourselves. Therefore we may with Impunity, it seems, violate the Law of Chastity, in order to avoid Death. And why will not the same Reason make Murther, Theft, Perjury, the abjuring of one's Religion, &c. lawful? The greatest Men are apt to mistake and lose their Way, even in the smoothest and most beaten Roads. Is it so difficult to find, that St *Paul* did not pretend, that a Husband had Power to dispose of his Wife's Body to whom he pleased; when he said, That *the Wife has no power over her own Body, but her Husband?* Nevertheless you see that St *Austin* puzzles himself with these Words of the Apostle, and that he lays great Stress upon the Distinction, *marito jubente, potestatem non abnuens maritalem.* We shall take notice elsewhere (7) that he has made use of this Doctrine of St *Paul* to justify *Abraham* and *Sarah* in relation to *Agar*'s Concubinage. Let us now hear a Divine, who tho' he lived several Ages after This Father of the Church, yet proves a better Casuist in this Point. " *Qua in re (that is, concerning the Adventure of the Wife whose Husband was Acindynus's Prisoner) mirum est talem ac tantum virum potuisse dubitare, cum ex sacra Scriptura constet apertissime malum aliquod pœnæ nunquam esse redimendum maio culpæ, & vitam potius esse deponendam, quam ut eam nobis aut aliis servemus id facientes ex quo Deus offenderetur. Nullo modo itaque censendum est licitum esse adulterii remedium vel marito, vel uxori, vitandæ alterius necis causa; quin potius mortem expectare convenit, imo vero ultro expetere, quam alterutrius castitatem prodere, ob cujus conservationem multæ pudicissimæ fœminæ non solum ab aliis occidi sustinuerunt, sed etiam (quod tamen probare nolim) sibi ipsis vim intulerunt, non solum inter Ethnicas, sed etiam inter Christianas* (8). — *It is strange, that so great a Man should hesitate in this Matter, when it is plain from the sacred Scriptures, that no Evil of Punishment is ever to be bought off at the Expence of the Evil of Sin, and that we should rather part with Life, than preserve it for ourselves or others, by doing what will offend God. And therefore we must by no means think, that either the Husband or the Wife is at liberty to have recourse to the Remedy of Adultery, in order to save either's Life: they ought rather to await Death, nay even voluntarily to seek it, than betray each other's Chastity; for the sake of preserving which many the most chast Women, not only among the Heathens, but even Christians, have not only submitted to die by the Hands of others, but have violently destroy'd themselves; which latter Action, however, I by no means approve.*". He quotes the Example of *Sophronia,* of whom in it's Place. Consult the *Amœnitates Juris* of Mr *Menage* in the Chapter, entituled, *De mariti lenocinis: Adulterarum viros ordinare non potuisse.* 'Tis the 10th Chapter of this Work; See the 52d Page of it, in the *Leipsic* Edition of 1680, in 4to.

(7) *In the Remark* [*I*], *of the Article of* SARA.

(8) *Rivet. Ubi supra.*

ACONTIUS, (JAMES) a Philosopher, Civilian, and Divine, born at *Trent*, in the XVIth Century (*a*). He embraced the Reform'd Religion, and going over into *England* in the Reign of Queen *Elizabeth*, he received many Instances of That Princess's Bounty, as he acknowledges himself in the Frontispiece of the Book [*A*], which he

(*a*) Moreri *falsly places him in the* XVth *Century.*

[*A*] *In the Frontispiece of the Book, which he dedicated to her.*] Instead of an Epistle Dedicatory, he contented himself with a Canonizing Inscription, which begins with, DIVÆ ELIZABETHÆ ANGLIÆ, FRANCIÆ, HIBERNIÆ REGINÆ. He declares, that he inscribes his Book

ACONTIUS.

he dedicated to her. I mean the famous Collection of the *Stratagems of the Devil*, which has so often been translated, and reprinted. The first Edition of it is That of *Basil*, in 1565. soon after which the Author died in *England* (*b*). *James Grasserus* procured a second Edition of it in 1610. wherein we find indeed *Acontius*'s Letter, *de Ratione Edendorum Librorum*, containing very wholsome Cautions to those, who design to set up for Authors; but the Editor has omitted his *Treatise of Method* (*c*); which is a good Piece [*B*], tho' the Author only published it as an Essay (*d*). He had composed in *Italian* a Book of Fortification, which he himself turn'd into *Latin* during his Stay in *England* (*e*); but I think it was never printed. He was also writing a System of Logic (*f*), which I suppose Death hindered him from finishing. 'Twas great Pity, for he was a Man of a just way of Thinking, and great Discernment and Penetration. He had framed to himself the most rational Idea of such a Work, and thought himself obliged to bestow the more Pains and Care upon it, because he foresaw, that an Age more refined, than that he lived in, was advancing [*C*]. His Conjecture was well grounded [*D*]. His Principles in Religion were not the same with those of *Calvin*; he had a great Inclination to Toleration, and held in general certain Tenets, which have render'd him very odious to some Protestant Divines [*E*]. I have met with but few Particulars of his Life. He says of himself, by the

to her, as a Testimony of his Gratitude: "In sig-
"num memoriamque grati animi ob partum ejus li-
"beralitate, quum in Angliam propter Evangelicæ
"veritatis professionem extorris appulisset, humanis-
"simeque exceptus esset, literarum otium. — *As
"the Sign and Memorial of a Mind full of grate-
"ful Sentiments for That Tranquility, which her
"Bounty afforded his Studies, when, exiled for pro-
"fessing the Protestant Religion, he took Shelter in
"England, and was received with the greatest Hu-
"manity.*" In his Letter to *Wolfius*, he says, That his Pension relieved in some measure his Indigence, and afforded him leisure to Study. "Ut autem
"quicquid est operæ id istam in artem (*muniendo-
"rum oppidorum*) conferrem, ex parte privatis sum
"rationibus adductus, etenim in hoc voluntario
"meo exilio inopiam UTCUNQUE sublevat,
"& otii ad alia studia suppeditat NONNIHIL,
"impetrato mihi ab hujus sapientissimæ atque op-
"timæ Reginæ liberalitate honestâ stipendio (1). —
"*I am induced, partly by private Reasons, to culti-
"vate this Science* (Fortification) *as far as I am
"able; since, in this my voluntary Exile, it procures
"me a* KIND OF MAINTENANCE, *and affords
"me* SOME *Leisure for other Studies, by obtaining
"for me an honourable Pension from the Liberality
"of this Wise and Good Queen.*" What Restrictions are here! And how well they shew the Difficulty of satisfying the Expectations of Refugees? Observe, that he obtained this Pension, not as a *Divine*, but as an *Engineer*, which appears by the Reason he himself alledges, why he spent his time principally in the Study of Fortification.

[*B*] *Which is a good Piece.*] This is the Judgment which a learned *Cartesian* gave of it (2), in a Letter which he wrote to Father *Mersennus*, soon after the Publication of *Des Cartes*'s Meditations. "He said,
"he relished above all things the Method which
"Mr *Des Cartes* had made use of in handling his
"Subject; he admired it's Usefulness, and extolled
"it's Excellencies above That of the Schools: More
"particularly he esteemed his Judgment, and the
"Reasons he had to prefer the *Analytical* or *Resolu-
"tive Method*, to the *Synthetical* or *Compound*, as
"well in teaching, as demonstrating. He had not
"'till then met with any thing like it, except the
"little Book *De Methodo*, composed by *James Acon-
"tius*, who, besides that excellent Treatise, has also
"given a fine Specimen of the *Analytical* Method,
"in his Book of the *Stratagems of the Devil*, which
"he recommends to the Perusal of all those, who love
"the Peace of the Church; though *Acontius* plain-
"ly discovers in it the Prepossession of his Sect, and
"intended by it to Favour those of his own Party (3)".
That little Piece of *Acontius*, under the Title of, *Methodus sive recta investigandarum tradendarumque artium ac scientiarum ratio*. — (*The Method, or right Rule, of investigating and delivering Arts and Sciences*), was inserted in a Collection of Dissertations *de Studiis bene instituendis*, printed at *Utrectht*, in 1658.

[*C*] *That an Age more refined — was advancing.*] We must hear what he says himself, after having mentioned the other Reasons which rendered his Design very difficult in the Performance: "Intelligo etiam

"me in seculum incidisse cultum præter modum,
"nec tam certe vereor eorum qui regnare nunc vi-
"dentur judicia, quam exorientem quandam seculi
"adhuc paulo cultioris lucem pertimesco. Etsi enim
"multos habuit habetque ætas nostra viros præstan-
"tes; adhuc tamen videre videor nescio quid magis
"futurum (4). — *I am sensible too, that I am
"fallen into an extreamly polite Age; and yet I am
"not so apprehensive of the reigning Geniuses, as the
"approaching Brightness of still politer Times: for
"though the present Age has produced, and continues
"to produce, many Great Men, yet I fancy I foresee
"an Æra of superior Politeness arising upon us.*"

[*D*] *His Conjecture was well grounded.*] I am of opinion, that the XVIth Century produced a greater Number of Learned Men, than the XVIIth, and yet the former was not so enlightned as the latter. Whilst the Reign of *Criticism* and *Philology* continued, every Part of *Europe* produced Prodigies of Erudition. The Study of the new Philosophy, and of modern Languages, having introduced another Taste, That Universal and Profound Literature has disappeared; but in recompence, a certain Genius more refined, and accompanied with a more exquisite Discernment, has spread itself over the Commonwealth of Learning. People are now-a-days less learned, and more subtle. Therefore *Acontius* had Reason to foresee, at a Distance, an Age, which would be a more formidable Judge of the *Logic*, he intended to write, than That wherein he lived. However, I would not be thought to presuming, as by my own Authority to adjudge the Superiority to our Age: for in this I do but conform myself to the Opinion of the most acute and refined Critics. "We live
"in an Age, says one of them (5), wherein People
"attend more to good Sense and Reason, than any-
"thing else; and it may be said in our Commenda-
"tion, that we are already better acquainted with
"the Character of ancient Authors, and more inti-
"mately familiar with their Genius, than those,
"who went before us. The Difference between
"them and us, is, That, in the last Age, People
"were more ambitious of Erudition than they are
"at present. — 'Twas the Genius of those times,
"wherein nothing was more in Vogue than a vast
"Capacity, a great Memory, and profound Litera-
"ture. They studied Languages to the bottom;
"applied themselves to reform or restore the Text of
"ancient Authors by far-fetched Interpretations;
"cavilled about an equivocal Word; laid stress up-
"on a Conjecture, in order to establish a Correction;
"in short, they stuck to the literal Sense of an Au-
"thor, because they had not Force enough to raise
"themselves up to his Spirit, and to be thoroughly
"acquainted with him, as we have at present, be-
"cause we are more Reasonable, and less Learned;
"and set a greater Value upon plain good Sense,
"than an extensive, but perverse, Capacity."

[*E*] *Odious to some Protestant Divines.*] That I may not be arraigned for advancing this without any Ground or Proof, I shall quote the Words of a Minister of the *Hague* (6): "Jacobus Acontius (de
"quo jure quod de Origine dici solet, *ubi bene nemo
"melius, ubi male nemo pejus*) — fuit — vir
"verè doctus, sed ingenii, ut acris quidem, ita &
"elatioris,

ACONTIUS. ACOSTA.

the by, that he had bestowed a great part of his Life in the Study of *Bartolus*, *Baldus*, and such like barbarous Writers, and many Years at Court (g). *Acontius's* Letter, which was published in 1696 (h), shews a clear and exact Genius, and which was acquainted with sound Logic. It is dated from *London* the 5th of *June* 1565. and serves to illustrate a thing which he had advanced concerning *Sabellius*, and which had been censured. Note, That tho' most Protestant Divines look upon this Man with Horror, yet some amongst them have very much commended him [F].

(g) Id. ib.
(h) By *Mr.* Crenius, p. 131, &c. if the'ad part of his Animadversiones Philologicæ & Historicæ.

"*elatioris*, & justo liberalioris: quin à nescio quali "scepticismo & indifferentissimo in ipsam *Theolo*- "*giam* introducendo haudquaquam alieni, quod tracta- "tu suo de *Stratagematis Satanæ* testatum satis fecit, "*libello*, (Simone Goulartio judice) *omnium malo-* "*rum pessimo* *. Voetius ei adscribit † *quod* "*vel imperitè vel subdolè communem confessionis* "*conceptum molitus sit, sub cujus vexillo militari* "*possunt & ipsi Ariani.* —— James Acontius (*to* "*whom may be applied what is generally said of* "*Origen, that where he did well, no one did* "*better, where he did ill, no one worse*) *was a* "*truly learned Man, but of a Genius too Elate and* "*Free, and too Sceptical in Matters of Religion, as* "*appears by his Treatise* de Stratagematis Satanæ: A "Book (*according to* Simon Goulartius) *of all bad* "Books *the worst*. Voetius charges *him with cun-* "*ningly, or unskilfully, drawing up a Confession* "*of Faith, under whose Banner the Arians them-* "*selves might fight.*" What is here mentioned of *Simon Goulart* is not to be found (as far as I know) in any of his Books; I believe it is taken from *Uytenbogardus*, who says in one of his Works, that, when he studied at *Geneva*, he was censured by *Simon Goulart* for reading *Acontius*, who told him, that his Book of the *Stratagems of the Devil*, was the worst Book in the World, *esse librum omnium malorum pessimum* (7). I have met with another Passage of *Voetius* concerning this Matter, wherein that Doctor places *Acontius* among the Hereticks, who came out of *Italy*, under Pretence of Reformation (8), and assures us, that if the Venom which lies hid in some Places of his Book ‖, had been taken notice of, he had either been Excommunicated, or constrained to sign a Confession of Orthodoxy. "Judicetur quis anguis "in herba latuerit, quod hic vir in fundamentalibus "assertionibus nunquam τὸ ὁμοούσιον trium personarum "statuerit, nec adversarios, Samosatenum, Photinum, "Arrium, Eunomium, Pneumatomachos, at eorum "errores rejecerit, conversos folos illos rejectos, qui "negarent filium non esse alium à patre (9). —— "*Judge what a Snake is concealed in the Grass, when* "*this Author, in his Fundamental Assertions, never* "*lays down the* SAMENESS OF ESSENCE *of the Three* "*Persons, nor rejects the Errors of* Samosatenus, Pho- "tinus, Arrius, Eunomius, *and the* Pneumatomachi*, "*being contented with disclaiming only those, who de-* "*nied, that the Son is not distinct from the Father.*"

[F] *Some amongst them have very much commended him.*] Mr Crenius furnishes us with Proofs for both these Assertions. He observes (10), That *Conradus Bergius* declares, that *Acontius* argued prudently and piously. This *Bergius* was Minister and Professor of Divinity at *Bremen*. The Book, wherein he speaks to this Purpose, is entituled, *Praxis Catholica divini Canonis contra quosvis hæreses & schismata, &c.* and printed at *Bremen*, in 1639. in 8vo. Rivetus,

* Triglind. Hist. Eccles. pag. 232.
† Voet. Polit. Eccles. part. III. in Indice, & pag. 31. & 398.

(7) Uytenbogardus in his History written in Belgic, cap. 1. pag. 7. Edit. in 4to.

(8) Voetius's Theological Disputations, Tom. 1. p. 495.

‖ Pag. 114, 123, 141. Edit. Basil. 1610.

(9) Voetius, ubi supra, pag. 501.

* Opposers of the Divinity of the Holy Ghost.

(10) Thom. Crenius's Philological and Historical Animadversions, part. 2. pag. 32.

being in Possession of one of these Books, *ex dono autoris*, wrote in it some Remarks, of which I shall mention That, which relates to *Acontius*. "Miror "cur, p. 524. tanti faciat vir doctus judicium Aconti, hominis ambiguæ fidei & Socinianorum vel "prodromi, vel commilitonis, cujus rei gratia ab "Arminianis toties recusus est & commendatus, etiam "in varias linguas vulgares translatus. Huic homini "scopus fuit, ut ex toto libro appareat, ad tam pauca "necessaria doctrinam Christianam arctare, ut om- "nibus sectis in Christianismo pateret aditus ad "mutuam communionem. Vellem doctiss. & pium "virum à talibus laudandis & imitandis abstinuisse "(11). —— *I wonder this Learned Author, at* "*his 524th Page, should so highly extol the Judg-* "*ment of* Acontius, *a Man of ambiguous Principles,* "*and either the Fore runner or Fellow-Soldier of the* "Socinians; *upon which account he was so great a Fa-* "*vourite with the* Arminians, *that they reprinted his* "*Work many Times, translating it into several Vul-* "*gar Languages.* This *Gentleman's Aim, as appears* "*from his whole Book, was to reduce the* Christian "*Doctrine to so few Fundamentals, as to open the* "*Door to a general Communion of all the Sects in* "Christendom. *I wish this learned and pious Au-* "*thor had abstained from commending and imitating* "*such Writers.*" The Book, whence I had this Passage, informs me farther, that *Isaac Junius* (12), Minister at *Delft*, plac'd *Acontius*, the *Remonstrants*, and *Socinus*, in the same Class, and look'd upon the first as a Man, who had a mind to reduce all Sects into one, and enclose them in the same Ark, as *Noah* did all sorts of Animals in his, wherein they were preserved, though sustain'd by different Food. We see in the same Book, the Account which *Peltius* gave of *Acontius*, which is, that by reducing to a small Number the Points necessary to Salvation, and requiring a Toleration for the particular Opinions, which were against the other Articles, he opened a wide Door to all manner of Heresies (13). Lastly, we find in the same Book, that not only *Arminius* and *Grevinchovius* have given great Commendations to our *Acontius*, but also that *Amesius* and *George Pauli* (14), two Reformed Divines, have very much applauded him. "Jacobo Arminio tamen in Respons. ad Excerpta Theol. "Leidens. p. 65. Acontius est *divinum prudentiæ ac* "*moderationis lumen*, —— (Acontius *is a* divine Luminary of Prudence and Moderation). Amesio præfat. ad Puritan. Anglicanos & Grevinchovio in Abstertione calumn. Simoutii, p. 125. apud B. Hulsemannum in Dedicat. Supplementi Breviarii Theologici, p. 6. idem Acontius est *σπάρμα τῶν* τοῖς "*σπέρμασι, qui sementem Ecclesiæ Anglicanæ caliore* "*& rore cælesti fovit sedulo.* —— (The same Acontius "was very mightly in the Scriptures † and one, who "diligently cherished the Growth of the *English* "Church, with Warmth and Heavenly Dew (15)."

(11) Rivetum, ibi. pag. 3.

(12) Isaac Junius in Examine Apologiæ Remonstrantium, pag. 4. apud Crenium, ibid.

(13) Peltius in Dedicatione Harmoniæ, apud Crenium, ib. pag. 31.

(14) In Refermato Augustano, seu Apologia pro dictatis Iuis de Aug. Confess. See Crenius, ibid. p. 32.

(15) Cren. ibid. p. 36.

ACOSTA (URIEL), a *Portuguese* Gentleman, was born at *Porto* about the end of the XVIth Century. He was educated in the *Romish* Religion, which his Father sincerely profest (a), though descended from one of those *Jewish* Families, which were constrain'd to receive Baptism. He was educated like a Person of Quality, and, after several Studies, apply'd himself at last to Civil-Law. Nature had endow'd him with good Inclinations [A], and Religion had made so deep an impression upon him, that he ardently desir'd to fulfil all the Precepts of the Church, in order to avoid Eternal Death, which he very much dreaded. Therefore he diligently apply'd himself to the reading of the Gospel, and other spiritual and godly Books; and

(a) Pater meus verè erat Christianus. —— My Father was truly a Christian. Uriel Acosta in his Exemplar Vitæ Humanæ, inserted by Mr Limborch, at the end of his Friendly Conference with a *Jew*, concerning the Truth of the Christian Religion.

[A] *Nature had endow'd him with good Inclinations.*] He was so tender-hearted and compassionate, that he could not forbear shedding Tears at the recital of any Misfortune, that had befallen his Neighbour; and Modesty had taken so deep Root in his Soul, that he feared nothing more than what might offend it, and put him to the Blush. He was courageous,

and susceptible of Anger on a lawful Occasion, and check'd the Insolence of those rude Men, who take delight in insulting others, still chusing to side with the weaker. This is the Character he gives of himself. *Infirmorum Partes adjuvare cupiens*, says he (1), *& illis potius me socium adjungens.*

(1) Uriel Acosta *in his Exemplar Vitæ Humanæ*, p. 140.

VOL. I.   A 2   [B] *When*

ACOSTA.

and often consulted the Decisions of Casuists about the Heads of Confession; but the more Enquires he made, the more he found his Scruples and Difficulties increase, till, at last, they entangled him to such a Degree, that, being unable to get out of the Labyrinth; he fell into most terrible Agonies of Mind. He did not think it possible for him punctually to discharge the Duty and Conditions, which Absolution requires, according to sound Casuists, and thus he despair'd of Salvation, in case it could not be obtain'd any other Way. But, because it was difficult for him to abandon a Religion, to which he had been accustom'd from his Infancy, and which had taken deep Root in his Mind, thro' the Force of Persuasion, all he could do in his Condition was to examine, whether All the Notions he had imbibed of a Future State were not meer Fiction, and whether They were agreeable to Reason. He fancy'd that Reason incessantly suggested to him Arguments against Them. He was then 22 Years of Age, and This was the Course he took: He first turn'd *Sceptic*, and afterwards concluded, that the Road, into which Education had led him, would never carry him to Salvation. In the mean time, he studied the Law, and obtain'd a Preferment *(b)*, at 25 Years of Age. Now, being unwilling to be without Religion, and the Profession of the *Roman Catholic* Religion affording him no Rest, he apply'd himself to the Reading of *Moses* and the *Prophets*, and, having found them more satisfactory than the *Gospel*, he was at last persuaded, that *Judaism* was the true Religion; but, not being permitted to profess it in *Portugal*, he resolv'd to leave his Native Country. Accordingly he resign'd his Place, and embark'd for *Amsterdam* with his Mother and Brothers, whom he had the Courage to catechise [*B*], and whom he had effectually brought over to his Opinions. As soon as they arriv'd there, they were admitted into the Synagogue, and were circumcis'd according to Custom: upon which he chang'd his Name of *Gabriel* into that of URIEL. It was not many days, before he found that the Manners and Customs of the *Jews* were not conformable to the Laws of *Moses*: He cou'd not forbear censuring this *Nonconformity*; but the Chief of the Synagogue gave him to understand, that he must follow their Tenets and Customs in all Points, and that if he receded from them never so little, they would excommunicate him. These Threats did not discourage him; He thought it would not become a Man, who had abandon'd the Conveniences of his Native Land for Liberty of Conscience, to yield to Rabbies who had no Authority [*C*]; and that it would argue want of Spirit and Piety, if he
should

(b) The Dignity of a Treasurer of a Collegiate Church.

[*B*] *Whom he had the Courage to catechise.*] He does not forget the Circumstances, which were proper to heighten the Sacrifice he made to his Religion. He observes that he relinquished a profitable and honourable Post, and a fine House, which his Father had built in the best Part of the City (2). He adds the Dangers of embarking: for the Descendants of the *Jews* cannot go out of the Kingdom, without the King's particular Leave. *Navem adscendimus non sine magno periculo: non licet illis qui ab Hebræis originem ducant à regno discedere sine speciali Regis facultate* (3). Lastly, he says, That if it had been known, that he entertained his Mother and Brothers with his Thoughts about the *Jewish* Religion, it would have been his utter Ruin; but his Charity made him overlook the Danger. *Quibus ego fraterno amore motus ea communicaveram, quæ mihi super religione visa fuerant magis consentanea, licet super aliquibus dubitarem: quod quidem in magnum malum meum poterat recidere, tantum est in eo regno periculum de talibus loqui* (4). We may here observe by the Way, that the *Spaniards* and *Portuguese* have omitted nothing, that the subtilest and severest Politics can invent, to maintain a Party. They have made use of every Method, for the Support of *Christianity*, and the Destruction of *Judaism*; and they cannot be accused, without Injustice, of having committed the Church to the Protection of Heaven, with a temper of Mind, dispos'd patiently to expect every thing from the Efficacy of their Prayers. On the contrary, one would think they followed the Advice which the Heathen Poet has given in an Affair relating to Agriculture,

Non tamen ulla magis præsens fortuna laborum est,
Quam si quis ferro potuit rescindere summum
Ulceris os: alitur vitium, vivitque tegendo;
Dum medicas adhibere manus ad vulnera pastor
Abnegat, aut meliora deos sedet omina poscens (5).

*Receipts abound; but, searching all thy Store,
The best is still at hand, to launce the Sore,
And cut the Head; for, till the Core be found,
The secret Vice is fed, and gathers Ground:
Whilst, making fruitless Moan, the Shepherd stands,
And, when the launcing Knife requires his Hands,
Vain Help, with idle Prayers, from Heav'n demands.*
DRYDEN.

Or else one would be apt to say, that they have squared their Conduct by the Reproaches which *Cato* made to the *Romans*, when he blamed them for confiding solely in the Assistance of the Gods, who, added he, never hear the Prayers of the Slothful, for Sloth is a Sign of the Anger of Heaven. "Vos — " inertia & mollitia animi alius alium expectantes cun- " ctamini, videlicet diis immortalibus confisi, qui " hanc rempubl. in maximis sæpe periculis servavere. " Non votis, neque supplicus muliebribus auxilia " deorum parantur; vigilando, agendo, bene consu- " lendo, prospere omnia cedunt. Ubi socordiæ " tete, atque ignaviæ tradideris: nequicquam De- " os implores: irati infestique sunt (6). ———— Un- " active and Effeminate in Mind, you stand idly ga- " zing on each other, relying on the Assistance of the " Immortal Gods, who have often preserv'd this Re- " public in the greatest Danger. But be assured, that " the Assistance of Heaven is not to be obtained by " Wishes, and womanish Supplication: Success attends " alone on Vigilance, Action, and wise Councils. If " you give yourself up to Sloth and Idleness, it is in " vain to implore the Gods; they are angry and un- " propitious." Lastly, one may say, that the Lesson which they are most apt to practise, is the latter part of the Axiom, which a Modern has set down in these Words: *We must, as it were, so wholly abandon ourselves to Providence, as if all human Prudence were useless; and we must so govern ourselves by the Dictates of human Prudence, as if there were no Providence* (7). Without doubt they would laugh at an Author, who should blame them for using *Christianity* like an old Palace, so much decay'd, that it wants Props on every Side; and *Judaism*, like a strong Fortress, which one must cannonade and bombard continually, in order to weaken it. We may justly condemn certain Methods of supporting the *Good Cause*; but after all, as good as it is, it stands in need of Support; and *Distrust is the Mother of Safety*. See the Remark [*E*], of the Article LUBIENI-ETSKI, and the Remark [*B*], of the Article DRABICIUS.

[*C*] *To Rabbies who had no Authority.*] There is certainly a great Difference between the Tribunal, which our *Acosta* stood in fear of in his own Country, and the Tribunal of the Synagogue of *Amsterdam*.
This

(2) Ibid. pag. 347.
(3) Ibid.
(4) Ibid.
(5) Virgil. Georgic. lib. 3. v.r.452.
(6) Sallust. in Bello Catilin. pag. 160,
(n) Cerin, Oeuvres Galantes, Tom. 1. in his Discourse on t'e Truth of Dreams, p. 260.

ACOSTA.

should betray his Sentiments upon this Occasion; wherefore he persisted in his former Course. Accordingly he was excommunicated, which had such an effect, that his very Brothers, I mean those, whom he had instructed in the *Jewish* Religion, durst neither speak to him, nor so much as salute him, when they met him in the Streets. Under these Circumstances he compos'd a Book in Justification of himself; wherein he shewed that the Rites and Traditions of the *Pharisees* were contrary to *Moses*'s Writings. He had scarce begun this Book, when he embrac'd the Opinion of the *Sadducees*; for he was fully persuaded, that the Punishments and Rewards of the Old Law respected this Life only; grounding His Opinion principally upon this, that *Moses* makes no mention either of the Joys of Heaven, or of the Torments of Hell. When his Adversaries were inform'd, that he had embrac'd this Opinion, they were extreamly pleas'd, because they foresaw it wou'd be a good Plea in justifying to the Christians the Proceedings of the Synagogue against him. This was the Reason, why, even before his Book went to the Press, they publish'd a Treatise concerning the Immortality of the Soul, compos'd by a Physician (*c*), who forgot nothing, that might contribute to brand *Acosta* for an Atheist: Nay They even encourag'd Children to abuse him in the Streets, and to throw Stones at his House. Nevertheless he publish'd a Book against the Physician, wherein he strenuously oppos'd the Immortality of the Soul (*d*). The *Jews* had recourse to the Tribunals of *Amsterdam*, and impeach'd him, as a Person who overthrew the Principles both of *Judaism* and *Christianity*. He was imprison'd, and admitted to Bail in 8 or 10 days. The Impression of his Book was confiscated, and the Author fin'd 300 *Gilders*. All this did not stop him: Time and Experience push'd him on much farther. He examin'd whether the Law of *Moses* came from God, and fancied he had found sufficient Reasons to be convinc'd, that it was a meer Contrivance of Human Wit; but instead of concluding from thence, *Therefore I ought not to return to the* Jewish *Communion*, he drew this Consequence, *Why should I obstinately remain separated from it all my Life-time, expos'd to so many Inconveniencies, and a Stranger as I am, in a Country, the Language whereof I cannot speak?* Having consider'd all these things he return'd to the Pale of *Judaism* 15 Years after his Excommunication, recanted what he had said, and subscrib'd whatever they pleas'd. Some days after, a Nephew of his, who lodg'd in his House, inform'd against him. This was a Youth, who had taken notice, that his Uncle did not observe the Laws of the Synagogue, either in point of Diet, or otherwise. This Accusation was attended with strange Consequences: For one of *Acosta*'s Relations, who had reconcil'd him to the *Jews*, thought himself obliged,

(*c*) *In the Year* 1623.

(*d*) *Entitled*, Examen Traditionum Philosophicarum ad Legem Scriptam. — *The Philosophical Traditions compared with the written Law.* [*Perhaps* Philosophicarum *is a Mistake for* Pharisaicarum.]

---

(8) Uriel Acosta, ubi supra.

This latter can only inflict Canonical Punishments, whereas the *Christian Inquisition* can put a Man to Death, for it delivers over to the Secular Sword all those it condemns. Therefore I do not wonder, that *Acosta* was less afraid of the *Jewish* Inquisition, than of that of *Portugal*: He knew that the Synagogue had no Tribunals, which intermeddled with any Process, Civil or Criminal, and therefore look'd upon their Excommunications as a meer *brutum Fulmen*; he did not find this Canonical Sentence attended either with Death, Whipping, Prison, or a pecuniary Mulct. Wherefore he thought, that since he had Courage enough not to betray his Religion in *Portugal*, he ought, with much more Reason, have the boldness to speak, according to his Conscience, among the *Jews*, even at the Peril of Excommunication from them; which was all he had to fear from Men, who have no Magistrates of their own. "Quia " minimè decebat, ut propter talem metum terga " verteret, ille qui pro libertate natale solum, & uti- " litates alias contemperat; & succumbere hominibus, " præsertim JURISDICTIONEM non habentibus, in " tali causa nec pium nec virile erat; decrevi potius " omnia perferre & in sententia perdurare (8). ── " *As it was unbecoming a Person to turn his Back* " *thro' such a Fear; one who had forsaken his na-* " *tive Land, with all it's Conveniencies, for the sake* " *of Liberty; and as, in such a Case, it was neither* " *pious nor manly to submit to Men, especially such* " *as had no* JURISDICTION, *I determine rather to* " *hold it out to the last, and to persist in my Opinion*." But it fared with him as with most People, who judge of complicated Evils. They imagine 'tis in the Union of two or three Punishments that a Misfortune consists; and that a Man would deserve but little Pity, should he suffer but one of them; but They Experience the contrary, when Providence exposes them to but one of these two or three Disgraces. They feel it much heavier than they imagined it would prove. The Inquisition of *Portugal* seem'd dreadful to the *Jew* Acosta: Why so? Because he beheld it join'd with the Power, either mediately or immediately, of imprisoning, torturing, and burning, Criminals: If he had considered it only with relation to it's Excommunication, he would not have been much afraid of it. This was the Reason of his contemning the Menaces of the Synagogue of *Amsterdam*. But he was sensible, by Experience, that the bare Power of Excommunication is very terrible, tho' altogether unaided by the Secular Sword. Every body look'd upon him as a Monster after his Excommunication: His very Brothers avoided meeting him, and durst not take notice of him. *Ipsi Fratres mei, quibus ego Præceptor fueram, me transibant, nec in plateâ salutabant, propter metum illorum* (9). The Boys hooted at him in the Streets, and loaded him with Curses; they gathered in Crowds about his House, and threw Stones at his Windows; *jamque faces & saxa volant*, He could not be quiet either at home or abroad. *Pueri istorum, à Rabinis & parentibus edocti, turmatim per plateas conveniebant, & elatis vocibus mihi maledicebant, & omnigenis contumeliis irritabant, hæreticum & defectorem inclamantes. Aliquando etiam ante fores meas congregabantur, lapides jaciebant, & nihil intentatum relinquebant ut me turbarent, ne tranquillus etiam in domo propria agere possem* (10). The Evils, to which his Excommunication subjected him, were so violent, that at last he found himself unable to support them; for as great an Aversion as he had to the Synagogue, he chose rather to return to it by a seeming Reconciliation, than to be openly separated from it. For this Reason, he said to certain *Christians*, who had a mind to turn *Jews*, that they did not know what Yoke they were going to submit their Necks to. *Nesciebant quale jugum suis verticibus imponerent* (11). But how great was his Perplexity, when, having refus'd to undergo the ignominious Penance impos'd on him by the Synagogue, he saw himself still detained by the Bonds of Excommunication? Those, who met him in the Streets, spit at him, and Children were taught to do the same. *Multi eorum transeunte me in plateâ spuebant, quod etiam & pueri eorum faciebant ab illis edocti; tantum non lapidabar, quia deerat facultas* (12). His Relations persecuted him, and no body would attend him, when he lay sick. To be short,

(9) Acosta. Exempl. Vitæ Humanæ. pag. 347.

(10) Ibid.

(11) Ibid. pag. 348.

(12) Ibid. pag. 349.

ACOSTA

obliged, in Honour, to prosecute him with the utmost Severity [D]. The Rabbies, and all the People under them, were acted by the same Spirit, especially when they heard that our *Acosta* had dissuaded two Christians, who were come from *London* to *Amsterdam*, from turning *Jews*. He was summon'd before the grand Council of the Synagogue, who declar'd to him they would excommunicate him a second time, if he did not give them the Satisfaction which they shou'd require of him. He found the Terms of it so very hard, that he answer'd, he cou'd not submit to them. Whereupon they resolv'd to drive him from their Communion; and 'tis impossible to relate the many Insults offer'd him from that time, and how much he was persecuted by his Relations. Having past seven Years in this sad Condition, he resolv'd to declare, that he was ready to submit to the Sentence of the Synagogue; for they had given him to understand, that, by means of this Declaration, he would easily come off, because the Judges, being satisfy'd with his Submission, would mitigate the Severity of the Discipline. But he was deceiv'd, and made to undergo with the utmost Rigour the Penance, which they had at first impos'd upon him [E]. This is what I have extracted, without any Disguise or Alteration, (and without pretending to warrant the Truth of the matters of Fact) out of a small Piece compos'd by *Acosta* (*e*) and publish'd and confuted by Mr *Limborch* (*f*). 'Tis thought he writ it some few days before his Death, having first resolv'd to lay violent hands upon himself. He executed this strange Resolution a little after he had fail'd in his attempt of shooting his principal Antagonist as he passed by his Door (*g*); for, his Pistol missing Fire, he lock'd himself up, and with another Pistol shot himself (*h*). This happen'd at *Amsterdam*, though in what Year is not certainly known [F]. This Instance favours those, who condemn the Liberty of philosophizing in Matters of Religion; for the principal stress of their Arguments lies in this, that such a Method leads a Man insensibly either to *Atheism* or *Deism* [G]. I shall just mention the Reflexion, which

(*e*) Ext. i. d, Exemplar Humanæ Vitæ.
(*f*) See the Citation (*a*).
(*g*) It was either his Brother or his Cousin. Limborch in Præf. ad Exemplar Vitæ.
(*b*) Limborch, ibid.

---

short, they tormented him to such a Degree, that at last they extorted from him the Submission they desired. *Duravit pugna ista per annos septem, intra quod tempus incredibilia passus sum* (13).——This Struggle continued for *seven Years, during which I suffered incredible Persecutions.* We shall see in the Remark [*E*], what kind of Punishment they impos'd upon him, He was then more than ever sensible, how terrible even those People are, who, without any legal Jurisdiction, inflict the Laws of Discipline.

I am cautious of declaring my Approbation of the Reasons of the *Independants*; who think it so unjust, that the Church should arrogate to herself the Power of Excommunication, that is, of inflicting Punishments, which are sometimes more ignominious and defaming than a Branding-Iron; and which exposes a Man to more temporal Misfortunes, than the afflictive Pains which the Civil Magistrate imposes. The Sentence of the Judge does not set aside the Acts and Offices of Humanity, much less the Duties of Consanguinity. But Excommunication often arms Fathers against their Children, and Children against their Fathers; it stifles all the Sentiments of Nature; it breaks the Bonds of Friendship and Hospitality; and reduces People to the Condition of such as are infected with the Plague, nay sometimes to a worse and more abandon'd State.

[*D*] *One of his Relations —— thought himself obliged, in Honour, to prosecute him with the utmost Severity*] These are the ill Offices he did him: *Acosta* was upon the point of marrying a second Wife; he had a great many Effects in the Hands of one of his Brothers, and it concerned him very much to continue his Partnership with him. Now this Relation cross'd him in all these Particulars; for he broke off the March, and engaged *Acosta*'s Brother to detain all his Effects, and to have no more Dealings with him. This Procedure ought to be considered as one of the Reasons, which confirmed *Acosta* in his Impiety; for without doubt he persuaded himself, that this Violence and Injustice was authorized by some Passages of the Old Testament, wherein the Law commands Brothers, Fathers, and Husbands, not to spare the Lives of their Brothers, Children, and Wives, in case of Apostacy (14). And we must take notice, that he made use of this as a Proof against the Law of *Moses*; for he pretended that a Law, which overthrew Natural Religion, could not proceed from God the Author of Natural Religion (15). For, argued he, Natural Religion establishes a Bond of Amity among *Relations*, &c. See how Mr *Limborch* has answered this Sophism (16).

[*E*] *With the utmost Rigour the Penance, which they had at first imposed upon him*] His own Account of

it is as follows. A great Crowd of Men and Women being assembled in the Synagogue, to see this Spectacle, he entered the Place, and, at the time appointed, went up into the Pulpit, and read with a loud Voice a Paper, wherein he acknowledged that he had deserved Death a thousand Times, for not keeping either the Sabbath-day, or his promis'd Faith, and for having dissuaded the Conversion of certain *Christians*, who were inclined to embrace *Judaism*: That, in Atonement for these Crimes, he was ready to suffer whatever they should decree, and that he promis'd never to relapse into the same Faults. Being come down from the Pulpit, he was ordered to retire to one of the Corners of the Synagogue, where he stripped himself naked, from the Waste upwards, and pulled off his Shoes; then the Door-keeper tied his Hands to one of the Pillars; after which the Master-Chanter gave him thirty nine Stripes with a Whip, neither more nor less; for in these Ceremonies they take care not to exceed the Number, which the Law prescribes. Next came the Preacher, who ordered him to sit on the Ground, and declared him absolved from his Excommunication, and that *the Doors of Paradise were not shut against him as before. Et ita jam porta cœli mihi erat aperta, quæ antea fortissimis seris clausa me à limine & ingressu excludebant* (17). *Acosta* put on his Cloaths again, and went and laid himself down flat on his Belly, at the Door of the Synagogue, and all that went out trod over him. I thought the Reader would be pleased to find here this small Specimen of *Jewish* Ceremonies (18).

[*F*] *Though in what Year is not certainly known.*] 'Tis very probable that he kill'd himself soon after the Ceremony of his Absolution, enraged at the Treatment he had received, contrary to the Hopes he had entertained of a mitigated Punishment. But this will not precisely determine the time of his Death, because it is not known in what Year he performed this Penance. If it were known how long he had been under Excommunication, when the Physician's Book was published, in 1623, it would not be difficult to make an exact Computation, since he observes, that his first Excommunication lasted fifteen Years; that the second continued seven, and soon followed the other. It is supposed, in the *Bibliotheque Universelle*, that he killed himself in the Year 1647 (19), but others say it was in 1640 (20).

[*G*] *That such a Method leads a Man insensibly either to Atheism or Deism.*] *Acosta* serves them for an Example. He would not acquiesce in the Decisions of the Catholic Church, because he did not find them conformable to his Reason; and he embraced *Judaism*, because he found it more agreeable to his Natural Notions. Afterwards he rejected an infinite Number

(13) Acosta, ubi supra, pag. 343.

(14) See Deuteronomy, xiii.
(15) Uriel Acosta, ubi supra, pag. 352.
(16) Philip a Limborch in his Confutation of Uriel Acosta pag. 361, &c.

(17) Acosta, ubi supra, pag. 350.
(18) Take from the Exemplar Humanæ Vitæ of Uriel Acosta, pag. 349, 350.
(19) Bibliotch. Universelle Tom. 7. pag. 327.
(20) Joh. Helvicus Willemerus in his Philosophical Dissertation concerning the Sabbatarians, He quotes Mullerus's Judism, Proleg. pag. 71.

which *Acosta* made on the *Jews* endeavouring to render him the more odious, by affecting to say, That he was neither *Jew*, *Christian*, nor *Mahometan* [H].

Number of *Judaical* Traditions, because he thought they were not contained in the Scripture; nay, he rejected the Immortality of the Soul, upon pretence that the Law of God makes no mention of it: And lastly, he denied the Books of *Moses* to be divinely inspired, because he thought that natural Religion did not agree with the Ordinances of That Legislator. Had he lived six or seven Years longer, he would, perhaps, have denied Natural Religion itself, because his wretched scanty Reason would have puzzled him with Difficulties about the Hypothesis of Providence, and of the Free Will of the Eternal and Self-existent Being. It is certain, that Mankind, even in making use of their Reason, stand in need of Divine Assistance; without which it will prove a blind and erroneous Guide: And we may compare Philosophy to certain Powders so very corrosive, that, having consumed the proud and spongy Flesh of a Wound, they would corrode even the quick and sound Flesh, rot the Bones, and penetrate to the very Marrow. Philosophy is proper at first to confute Errors, but if she be not stopped there, she attacks Truth itself; and when she has her full Scope, she generally goes so far, that she loses herself, and knows not where to stop. This must be imputed either to the Weakness of Man's Understanding, or to the ill use he makes of it's pretended Force. By Good Fortune, or rather through a wise Dispensation of Providence, there are few Men, who are capable of thus abusing their Reason.

[H] *Affected to say, that he was neither Jew, Christian, nor Mahometan.*] This Accusation, answered he, carries both Malice and Ignorance with it; for, had he been a *Christian*, they would have looked upon him as an abominable Idolater, who, together with the Founder of Christianity, deserved to be punished by the true God, as an Apostate. If he had followed the Religion of *Mahomet*, they would not have made him less odious: Therefore he had no way of escaping the Lash of their Tongues, but by devoutly addicting himself to the *Pharisaical* Traditions. Let us consider his own Words: " Scio adversarios istos, ut nomen meum coram indocta plebe " dilanient, solitos esse dicere, iste nullam habet re- " ligionem, Judæus non est, non Christianus, non " Mahometanus. Vide prius, Pharisæe, quid dicas, " cæcus enim es, & licet malitiâ abundes, tamen sicut " cæcus impingis. Quæso, dic mihi, si ego Christianus essem, quid tuisses dicturus? Planum est, " dicturum te, fœdissimum me esse idololatram, & " cum Jesu Nazareno Christianorum doctore pœnas " vero Deo soluturum, à quo defeceram. Si Mahometanus essem, norunt etiam omnes quibus me ho- " noribus fuisses cumulaturus: & ita nunquam linguam tuam possem evadere: unicum hoc effugium " habens, nempe ad genua tua procumbere, fœ- " dissimos pedes tuos, tuas inquam nefarias & pudendas " institutiones, osculari (21).—— *I know that* " *my Adversaries, in order to blacken my Name in* " *the Sight of the ill-judging Vulgar, were wont to* " *say, This Man has no Religion; He is neither Jew,* " *Christian, nor Mahometan. Consider first, thou* " *Pharisee, what thou sayest; for thou art blind, and,* " *in spight of thy abundant Malice, thou stumblest like* " *a blind Man. Pray tell me, if I were a Christian,* " *what would you say? It is certain you would call* " *me a vile Idolater, and condemn me, together with* " *Jesus of Nazareth, the Teacher of the Christians,* " *to expiate by Punishment my Apostacy from the* " *True God. Were I a Mahometan, every one knows* " *with what kind of Honours you would load me. Thus* " *I could never escape your Censure: One way indeed* " *there is; namely, to fall down at your Knees, and kiss* " *your filthy Feet, I mean your wicked and shameful* " *Institutions.*" He makes use of another Answer: For he asks his Adversaries, whether, besides the three Religions they have mentioned, (and of which the two last were, in their Opinion, not so much Religion, as an Apostacy from God) they acknowledge any other? He supposes that they acknowledge Natural Religion as true, and as a Means of rendering

(21) Acosta, ibid. pag. 351.

us acceptable to God, and sufficient to save all Nations, the *Jews* excepted. 'Tis That, he tells them, which is contained in the *seven Precepts*, which *Noah*, and his Descendants down to *Abraham*, observed. *Thus*, said he, *according to yourselves, there is a Religion, on which I may depend, although I descend from the Jews; and if my Prayers cannot engage you to give me leave to mingle with the Crowd of other Nations, yet I shall not fail to assert this Liberty to myself.* Upon which he launches out in the Praises of *Natural Religion*.

By the first of his Answers we may plainly see, that the Objection of the *Jews* was more specious than strong; more glittering than solid; more proper to serve their own Ends, than agreeable to the exact Rules of Argumentation; and at the bottom somewhat fallacious. What makes it look plausible and specious is This: The Mind of Man is so contrived, that, at the first Impression, a *Neutrality* in the Worship of God is more shocking to him than a False Worship; and therefore, when he hears of any one's abandoning the Religion of his Fathers, without embracing another, he is seized with more Horror, than if he were told that such an one had quitted a better Religion for a worse. This first Impression dazzles and affects him to such a Degree, that he makes it his Standard to judge of such Persons by; and his Resentment is thereby proportionably raised. He does not allow himself time maturely to examine, whether in reality it is better to lift one's self under the Devil's Banner, in some of those False Religions, which That Enemy of God and Man has introduced, than to observe a *Neutrality*. Therefore we may imagine, that the *Pharisees*, who persecuted *Acosta*, laid so much stress upon their Objection, only because they found it proper to startle and confound the People, and to engage the *Christians* in their Quarrel. I confess they would not have made so much Bustle, had he embraced Christianity at *Amsterdam* or Mahometanism at *Constantinople*; but, in effect, they would not have accounted him less abandoned, less damned, or less an Apostate: Their Temper would have been owing to their Policy, and the effect of their just Fear of the Resentment of the *Religion Established*. If we judge from the first Impressions of Things upon us, there are but few Protestants who, upon the News that *Titius* had left the Profession of the Reformed Religion, without embracing any other Persuasion, would not assert that he was more criminal than if he had turned Papist: But I would fain ask these Protestants, *Have you good Ground for This? Have you well examined what you would say, in case he were become a great Bigot to Popery; if you should see him loaded with Relicks; running mad after Processions; and, in short, practising all the Extravagancies of Idolatrous and Superstitious Monks? Could you answer, that you would still say the same, if you should be informed that he was turned Jew or Mahometan, or a Worshipper of the Pagods of China?* To repeat it once more, the Mind of Man is thus contrived at the first thing, that strikes it, is the Rule of it's Passions: We lay hold of the present Circumstance, and do not consider what we should say in another Conjuncture. This private Person has left us, and has embraced no other Sect: we must attack him on this side.—— His Indifference is now his greatest Crime; but if he were turned Heathen, we should attack him on that side too, and we should say, at least we should think, *if he had but stood Neuter, and attach'd himself in general to the Religion of Nature, it were something; but, as it is, &c.*

By the second Answer, *Acosta* deprived his Adversaries of a great Advantage; for he sheltered himself against this strong Battery, *It is better to be of a false Religion than of none.* However, upon the whole, we must conclude,, that he was of a detestable Character, and a Genius so ill turned, that he miserably lost himself in the Labyrinths of his mistaken Philosophy.

How much the Notion of Neutrality in Matters of Religion, offends and provokes the Minds of Men.

ACRONIUS (JOHN), taught *Mathematics* and *Physic* at *Basil*, with a great deal of Reputation, and compos'd some Books, *De Tetræ motu*; *de Sphæra*; *de Astrolabii & Annuli Astronomici confectione*. He was of *Friesland*, and died at *Basil* in the

the Flower of his Age, in the Year 1563. This Author has escap'd the Diligence of *Vossius* (a) though *Swertius*, and *Valerius Andreas* had given him a Place in their *Bibliotheque* of the *Netherlands*; wherein however they have forgot to insert another JOHN ACRONIUS, who was a Minister, and perhaps a Native of the same Province with the former. This Minister was of a Restless, Seditious, Spirit; he abandon'd the Congregation of *Wesel*, at a time when she was threatened with an imminent Danger; They found, at *Deventer*, that they could not chuse him Pastor of their Church, without admitting at the same time a very disagreeable Member into their Society; He left the Church of *Groningen* with disgrace; and at *Franeker* he discover'd his want of Abilities to discharge the Trust of Professor of Divinity, into which he had intruded. Lastly, he was Minister at *Haerlem*, where he behav'd himself as usual; that is, he contradicted, oppos'd, and censur'd every one, without distinction. The Historiographer of That City does not deny him the Character of a very Learned Man, but gives him at the same time That of a Turbulent Spirit (b). Some have compared him to *Heshusius*, against whom the following Distich was handed about.

(a) *He makes no mention of him in his Book De Scientia Mathematica.*

(b) *Theodorus Screvelius.*

    Quæritur, Heshusi, quarta cur pulsus ab urbe?
    In promptu causa est, seditiosus eras.

    The Cause, Heshusius, of thy Exile's known;
    Thou wert a Mover of Sedition grown.

Acronius wrote in *Flemish* a Book *de Jure Patronatus*, wherein he inserted several Quotations from the Canon-Law (c). I am inclin'd to ascribe to him the *Elenchus Orthodoxus pseudo-religionis Romano-Catholicæ*, printed at *Deventer* in 1615. He may very well be the Author of the Treatise, *De studio Theologico*, which Mr *Konig* attributes to Him, who wrote about the *Sphere*. The same *Konig* speaks of one RUARDUS ACRONIUS, who publish'd some *Catechetical Expositions* in 1606. He might have added, that, in the beginning of the Troubles of *Arminianism*, he wrote something against the *Arminian* Hypothesis, concerning the Power of Magistrates in Matters of Religion; and that 'twas He, who publish'd a Sermon, which *Uytembogard* had preach'd at the *Hague* before the Troubles, much different from the Doctrine, which he afterwards maintain'd, in relation to the same Question (d). *Ruardus Acronius* was one of the six Advocates for the *Reform'd* against the *Arminians*, in the Famous Conference held at the *Hague* in 1611.

(c) *See Martin Schookius. Exercitat. sacr. pag. 255. Edit. in 4to.*

(d) *Ex Vocell Polit. Eccles. Tom. 1. pag. 126.*

ACTOR [*A*] is the Name of several Persons mention'd in *Fabulous History*. I. It is the Name of one of *Hercules*'s Companions in the *Amazonian* War, who having receiv'd a Wound, resolv'd to return home, and died by the way (a). II. It is also the Name of *Patroclus*'s Grandfather; for *Menetius*, *Patroclus*'s Father, was Son of ACTOR and *Ægina*. This *Actor* was a *Locrian*, according to some (b), but he settled himself in the Island of OE*none*, after having married *Ægina*, Daughter to the River *Asopus*; by whom he had *Menetius*. Others say, that he was a *Thessalian*, Son of *Myrmidon*, who was Son of *Jupiter* (c), and that the Nymph *Ægina* having already had a Son by *Jupiter*, call'd *Æacus*, went into *Thessaly*, where *Actor* made no scruple to marry her, notwithstanding the Apprenticeship she had serv'd in Matters of Love (d). He had by her several Children, who conspir'd against him, which oblig'd him to send them into Exile, and bestow his Kingdom upon *Peleus*, with his Daughter *Polymele*. *Peleus* was Son to *Æacus*, and consequently *Ægina*'s Grandson, and had fled for Sanctuary to *Phthia*, where *Actor* reigned ; thither, I say, he fled, after he had kill'd his Brother *Phocus*. III. There was likewise one ACTOR, Son of *Hippasus*, who sail'd with the *Argonauts* (f). IV. Another, who was Son of *Neptune* and *Agamede* [*B*], Daughter of *Augeus* (g). V. Another, who was Son of *Axeus* [*C*], and Father

(a) *Charles Stephens in his Historical Dictionary.*

(b) *Scholiast on Homer. in Il. 18.*

(c) *Eustath. in Iliad. 1. Schol. Apollon. in lib. 4.*

(d) *Scholiast on Pind. in Olymp. 9.*

(e) *Eustath. in Iliad. 2.*

(f) *Hygin. cap. 14.*

(g) *b. cap. 157.*

[*A*] ACTOR] Mr *Moreri* has, without any reason, changed this Word into *Astorius*; but this is a small Fault in comparison of that, into which he falls some few Lines after, when, by these Words, *Quæ fuit Astoride cum magno semper Achille*, he pretends to prove, that *Ovid*, from whom he quotes them, has made mention of one *Astorius*. How came he not to see, that there is no mention made in that Passage of any Person called either *Astorius* or *Astoride*, but only of *Patroclus*, whom the Poets, for the sake of Versification, are used to denote by the Patronymic ACTORIDES, i. e. *descended from* ACTOR?

[*B*] *Son of Neptune and Agamede.*] *Muncerus* in his Commentary upon the 157th Fable of *Hyginus*, pretends that *Homer*'s Scholiast makes this *Actor* Son of *Neptune* and *Mollone*; but the Scholiast says no such thing. *Homer*, in the 749th Verse of the 11th Iliad, mentions two Brothers whom he calls *Ἀκτορίωνε Μολίονε, Actoriones Moliones*. Whereupon his Scholiast says, that by these Words we must understand *Cteatus* and *Eurytus*, Sons of *Actor* and *Molione*; or, according to some, of *Moliones* and *Neptune*. *Homer* thought them Sons of That God, for he adds, That they would have been slain, had not *Neptune*, their Father, succoured them in the Engagement, by covering them with a thick Mist.

    Ἐι μὴ ἄφαρ πατὴρ εὐρυκρείων Ἐννοσίγαιον
    Ἐκ πολέμου ἐσάωσε, καλύψας ἠέρι πολλῇ (1).

*Neptune, their Sire, to save his Offspring, shrouds;
The youthful Heroes in a Veil of Clouds.*

[*C*] *Who was Son of Axeus.*] *Homer* calls him *Azeus*.

    Οὓς τέκεν Ἀστυόχη δῖα Ἀκτορος Ἀζείδαο (2).

Meziriac remarks a Fault (3) of the Author of the Great *Etymologicum*, who thought that the same *Actor*,

(1) *Homer. Iliad. lib. 11. ver. 750.*

(2) *Id. Ibid. lib. 2.*

(3) *Upon Ovid's Epistles pag. 44.*

ACTOR. ACTUARIUS. ACUNA.

(1) Homer. Iliad. 2. Pausan. in Bœot.

(2) Pausan. lib. 9. p. 248.

Father of *Astyoch*, (*b*), by whom the God *Mars* had two Sons, who at the Siege of *Troy* commanded the Forces of *Aspledon*, and *Orchomenus*, two Towns of *Bœotia*. VI. Another ACTOR, Son of *Phorbas*, built a Town in *Elis*, his Native Countrey, which he call'd *Hyrmine*, after his Mother's Name (*i*). *Augias* King of *Elis*, who according to some, was his Brother (*k*), and whose Stables, clean'd by *Hercules*, have made so much noise, associated both him and his two Sons in his Kingdom (*l*). His two Sons were call'd *Eurytus* and *Cteatus*, and poetically *Molionides*, because their Mother's Name was *Molione*; see the Article MOLIONIDES. VII. Lastly, there was one ACTOR, describ'd as an Hero of the first Rate among the *Aurunci* [D].

(i) Apollodor. Bibl. lib. 2. pag. 158. Edit. Salmur.

(k) Pausan. ubi supra.

(4) Pausan. lib. 9. pag. 311.

Actor, mentioned here by *Homer*, was the Father of *Patroclus*. 'Tis what *Homer* never meant. He speaks of one *Actor* a *Bœotian*, Grandson to *Erginus*, and Great-Grandson to *Clymenus*. *Meziriac* quotes for this Pedigree *Eustathius* upon the second *Iliad*, and *Pausanias* in his *Bœoticis*: but *Pausanias* makes *Clymenus* Grandfather to *Actor*, but not Great-Grandfather (4).

[D] *One Actor, describ'd as an Hero of the first Rate among the Aurunci.*] He is thus describ'd by *Virgil*, in the twelfth Book of the *Æneid*:

—— *Validam vi corripit hastam,
Actoris Aurunci spolium, quassatque trementem,*

*Vociferans: Nunc O numquam frustrata vocatis
Hasta meos, nunc tempus adest: te maximus Actor,
Te Turni nunc dextra gerit* —— (5).

He seiz'd *the Launce Aruncan Actor wore;
Which with such Force he brandish'd in his Hand,
The tough Ash trembled like an Osier Wand.
Then cry'd, O pond'rous Spoil of Actor slain,
And never yet by Turnus toss'd in vain,
Fail not this Day thy wonted Force.* ——

DRYDEN.

(5) Virgil. Æneid. lib. 12. pag. 93. &c.

ACTUARIUS [A], a *Greek* Physician, of whom there are extant several Works [B]. *Ambrosius Leo* of *Nola*, who has translated some of them, and gives him great Commendations, owns that he could not discover who he was, nor of what Country (*a*). *Peter Castellan*, in his *Lives of Illustrious Physicians*, and *Wolfgang Justus* in his *Chronology of Physicians*, confess the same thing (*b*). Mr *Moreau*, in his Treatise of *Bleeding in the Pleurisy*, believes that he liv'd about the Year 1100 [C].

(a) Apud Gesner. Bibl. fol. 3. verso.

(b) See Merckl. in his Lindenius Renovatus, pag. 6.

[A] *Actuarius.*] Some call him *John*, Son of *Zacharias* (1); others chose rather to make him Son of *John Zacharias* (2). *Vossius*, who approves the latter, in the thirteenth Chapter of his Book, *De Philosophis*, mentions a little after one *John Actuarius*, who lived in the Time of *Constantine Ducas* (3), as is inferred from his having a Sister, upon whom *Michael Psellius* composed a Monody. If it should happen, that This *John Actuarius* did not differ from the Physician here in question, *Vossius* will have been in the wrong to distinguish them, and not to give the Physician the Name of *John*: But by the Remark [C] it will appear, that there's little likelihood of their being the same Person. Mr *Du Cange* shews, that the Title of *Actuarius* denotes a particular Dignity belonging only to the Physicians at the Court of *Constantinople*; and he confesses he is ignorant of the Reason of it, notwithstanding the Enquiries of Father *Possinet*. He owns also, that he does not know, whether our *Actuarius*, whom he calls *John*, Son of *Zacharias*, was in possession of that Dignity (4).

[B] *Of whom there are extant several Works.*] They were printed at *Paris*, in 1 Volume in Folio, by *Henry Stephens* in the Year 1567. having been printed before in another Place in three Volumes in 8vo. They have likewise been printed singly more than once. The chief of them are, *De actionibus & affectibus spiritus animalis, ejusque nutritione*. Libri II. *De Urinis*, Libri VII. first translated into *Latin* by *Ambrosius Leo*, and printed at *Venice* in 1519. and afterwards revised and illustrated with Notes, by *James Goupil*. *De Medicamentorum Compositione: Raul* has translated this Treatise. *Methodi Medendi Libri* VI. translated by *Henry Mathisius* of *Bruges*, and printed at *Venice* in 1554 (5).

[C] *That he lived about the Year 1100.*] Mr *du Cange* durst not place him in the Reign of *Alexis* (6), although his Book, *De affectibus Spiritus Animalis*, is dedicated to *Joseph Rastenphites*; and though *Nicetas*, in the third Book of the History of *Alexis*, n. 5. speaks of one *Rastendytes*. He approves what *Lambecius* decided concerning this Physician's Time (7); which is, that he lived in the Reign of *Andronicus* the Elder; because in the Manuscript of one of his Books, which is in the Emperor's Library, there is a Title, which shews that it is dedicated to *Apocauchus*. But we know that *Apocauchus* lived under That *Andronicus*. Mr *du Cange* observes, that *Actuarius* relates in the beginning of his *Method of Cures*, that the Emperor his Master sent him to the *Hyperborean Scythians*. Mr *Moreau* is therefore a little out in his Reckoning; for *Andronicus* the Elder did not begin his Reign before the Year 1333.

(1) Hyde's Catal. Bibl. Oxon. & Mercklinus in Linden. renovato.

(2) Gesner. Bibl. and his Abridgers.

(3) He began to reign in 1059.

(4) Glossar. Græc. pag. 46.

(5) See Mercklinus in Lindenio renovato, pag. 6, 7.

(6) He meant, but be had done better to have experienc'd it, *Alexis Angelus* who began to reign in the Year 1195.

(7) De Bibl. Cæsar. lib. 6. pag. 113.

ACUNA (*a*) (CHRISTOPHER) a *Spanish* Jesuit, born at *Burgos*, enter'd into the Society in the Year 1612, at 15 Years of Age. After having spent some Years in Study, he went into *America*, and labour'd to convert the Natives of the Kingdoms of *Chili*, and *Peru*, and was Professor of Moral Divinity. He return'd to *Spain* in the Year 1640, and gave the King his Master an Account of the Commission he had receiv'd to examine the River of the *Amazons*. The following Year he publish'd a Relation of that River at *Madrid*. He was sent to *Rome* in the Quality of Procurator of his Province; and having pass'd into *Spain*, honour'd with the Title of *Qualificator* of the Inquisition, he return'd to the *West Indies*. He was at *Lima*, when Father *Sotuel*, from whom I have extracted this Account, publish'd the *Bibliotheca* of the *Jesuit Authors* at *Rome* in the Year 1675. The Relation of our d'Acuna is entituled, *Nuevo descubrimiento del gran rio de las Amazonas. A New Description of the great River of the Amazons*. The Author was ten Months successively on that River, and had Orders to inform himself exactly of the State of It, that the King might be enabled to make the Navigation of it easy and commodious. For this purpose, he embark'd at *Quito* (*b*) with *Peter Texeira*, who had advanc'd thus far up the River, and whom they thought proper to send back again thither. They embark'd in the Month of *February* 1639 [A]; and did not arrive at *Para*, till the Month

(a) It is renumbred *Acugna*, but the *Spaniards* never accent it.

(b) It is a City of *Peru*.

[A] *In the Month of* February 1639.] I own freely, that I have not by me the Relation of Father *Christopher de Acuña**; and therefore I take this Date from Mr *Chevreau*, and prefer it to the Month of *January*,

the Spaniards do not put an Apostrophe between the Article &c. and a proper Name which begins with a Vowel.

* *I J. not still heard* Acuña's *for I have observ'd in* D. Nic. Antonio*, that*

ACUNA. ADA.

Month of *December* following. It is believ'd that the Revolutions of *Portugal*, which made the *Spaniards* lose all *Brazil*, and the Colony of *Para* at the Mouth of the River of the *Amazons*, were the cause that the Relation of this Jesuit was suppress'd (*c*), for fear that, being useless to the *Spaniards*, it might become serviceable to the *Portuguese*. The Copies of it became very scarce, insomuch that the Publishers of the *French* Translation at *Paris* (*d*) declar'd that there remain'd no more of them, except that which the Translator had made use of, which is perhaps That of the *Vatican*. Mr *de Gomberville* is the Author of this *French* Version, but it was not publish'd till after his Death; and a long Dissertation is added to it, which deserves the perusal. The Relation itself likewise is well worth reading. Those who have it not, may meet with a Specimen of it in the Journal of *Paris* (*e*), in that of *Leipsic* (*f*), and in Mr *Chevreau*'s History (*g*).

January, noted in the Journal of *Leipsic*; because the Faults, which the Printers of that Journal have committed in the foregoing Page, give me some Reason to distrust them. I find at Page 324. of That Journal, that the Governor of *Brasil* caused *Peter Texeira* to go up the River of the *Amazons* in the Year 1639. and that *Texeira* could not arrive at *Quito* in less than a Year's time (1). He did not therefore embark again at *Quito* in the Month of *January* 1639. as is asserted at Page 325. Mr *Chevreau* is more to be credited, when he declares, that *Peter Texeira* departed in the Month of *October* 1637. and gave an Account of his Voyage to the Viceroy of *Peru* (2). in *September* of the Year 1638. Mr *Chevreau* (3) does not name the Author of the *Relation* right, for he calls him *Christopher d' Alcuna*.

ADA, Daughter of *Hecatomnus* (*a*), and Sister of *Artemisia*, Queen of *Caria*, married her own Brother *Idrieus*, and reign'd with him in *Caria*, after the Death of *Artemisia*, who surviv'd her Husband *Mausolus* but two Years (*b*). *Idrieus* reign'd seven Years [*A*], and died of a Distemper, without leaving any Posterity. His Widow, having reign'd about four Years, was dethron'd, by *Pexodares* her younger Brother (*c*), who, to maintain his Usurpation, allied himself to a *Persian* Lord, whose Name was *Orontobates*, to whom he gave his Daughter in Marriage [*B*]. Her Name was *Ada*, as was That of the dethron'd Queen; and her Mother's Name was *Aphneis*, Daughter of *Synnesis*, King of *Cappadocia*. *Orontobates* succeeded his Father-in-Law in the Kingdom, at the end of six Years, and defended *Halicarnassus* against *Alexander* (*d*). The Revolutions of those Times were favourable to *Ada*. She implor'd that Conqueror's Protection against the Usurper, deliver'd the City of *Alinda* to him, which continu'd faithful to her, and promis'd to endeavour to make him Master of many others (*e*). *Alexander* gave her a very kind Reception, and re-establish'd her in her former Authority over all *Caria*, after having subdued the City of *Halicarnassus*. Out of Gratitude for his Favours, she sent him all kind of Refreshments, Comfits, Pastry, and delicate Meats, with the best Cooks she could find: But he return'd her for answer, that he had no occasion for such Things, and that his Governor *Leonidas* had already provided him with more excellent Cooks, in teaching him, *that to dine with Appetite, he must rise early and walk; and that to make a good Supper, he must eat but a slender Dinner* (*f*).

[*A*] *Idrieus reigned seven Years.*] *Diodorus Siculus* tells us this (1). Mr *Chevreau*, who has converted the Years into Months (2), would perhaps have had more Reason to lengthen the time, than he had to shorten it; for *Idrieus* was yet living, when *Isocrates* wrote his *Philippic*. Now if we believe *Hermippus* (3), he composed a little before his own Death, and That of *Philip*: So that *Philip* must have lived 'till the tenth *Olympiad*, seeing *Isocrates* died a few Days after the Battel of *Chæronea*, which was fought in the second Year of the tenth *Olympiad*, about two Years after the Death of *Philip*. Because therefore the Reign of *Idrieus* did not begin 'till about the third Year of the hundred and seventh *Olympiad*, (for I have shewn in the Remarks on the Article ARTEMISIA, that her Husband *Mausolus*, whom she survived two Years, did not die 'till the end of the hundred and sixth: the seven Years which *Diodorus* gives him, are not sufficient. Yet I believe his Chronology is more to be depended upon than that of *Hermippus*. Where would *Hermippus* place the Reign of *Ada*, and that of *Pexodares*, whereof the one continued four Years, and the other six, and both of which preceded the Expedition of *Alexander*?

[*B*] *He gave his Daughter in Marriage.*] *Valesius* thought that *Philip* King of *Macedon* demanded this Daughter of *Pexodares* for his Brother *Arideus*, and cites *Plutarch* for it (4). But that Historian does not tell us, whether the Daughter of *Pexodares*, of whom he makes mention, was called *Ada*; but it may very well be inferred from his saying, that she was the Eldest (5), for we know besides, that *Orontobates*, having married a Daughter of *Pexodares*, thought himself lawful Possessor of the Kingdom of *Caria*. So far then *Valesius* seems to me to be in the right; but he had no reason to say, that *Philip* desired that Alliance for his Brother *Arideus*; *Pexodares* first offered it, and sent Ambassadors to *Philip* for that Purpose. On the other side, *Arideus* was not the Brother, but the Son of *Philip*. *Plutarch* says it expressly. He adds a Circumstance, which affords us a remarkable Instance of the Intrigues of Courts. *Alexander*'s Friends alarmed him on the Proposals of *Pexodares*'s Ambassador: They suggested to him, that *Philip*'s Aim in this Alliance was to put *Arideus* in a better Capacity of succeeding to the Kingdom. *Alexander*, to ward against this Blow, dispatched a Person to *Pexodares*, to represent to him, that he ought rather to cast his Eyes on *Alexander*, than on *Arideus*, who was a Bastard, and almost a Fool. *Pexodares* did not hesitate in his Choice; but *Philip*, discovering what was carrying on, reproved *Alexander* sharply, telling him he would shew himself unworthy of being his Successor, if he was satisfied with the Daughter of a *Carian*, and Vassal of a *Barbarian* Prince. At the same time he exil'd all his Son's Confidents, and writ to the *Corinthians* to send him the Messenger, bound Hand and Foot, whom *Alexander* had sent to *Caria*. He was a Comedian, whose Name was *Thessalus*.

ADAM,

ADAM.

ADAM, the Stock and Father of all Mankind, was produc'd immediately by God on the Sixth Day of the Creation. His Body having been form'd of the Dust of the Earth [*A*], God breath'd into his Nostrils the Breath of Life; that is to say, he animated him, and made him that Compound Creature, which we call *Man*, comprehending an Organized Body, and a Rational Soul. The same Divine Being, which produc'd *Adam*, plac'd him a fine Garden (*a*), and, to give him an opportunity of imposing Names on the Brute Creation, he caus'd them all to appear before him. Afterwards he caus'd a Deep Sleep to fall on *Adam*, and took out of him a Rib [*B*], of which he form'd Woman. *Adam* knew that This Woman was *Bone of his Bone, and Flesh of his Flesh*; and liv'd with her, without any Shame on account of their being naked. There was a Tree in the Garden, of which God had forbid them to eat, on pain of Death. Yet the Woman, seduced by a Serpent (*b*), did not abstain from eating of it, and persuaded *Adam* to eat of it likewise. From that time they perceived that they were naked [*C*], and made themselves Aprons with Fig-leaves sewed together. God came and pronounced on them the Punishment, which he resolv'd to inflict upon them, drove them out of the Garden, and made them *Cloaths of Skins*. *Adam* called his Wife *Eve*, and consummated his Marriage. He became the Father of *Cain*, and of *Abel*, and afterwards of *Seth*, and of many other Sons and Daughters, the Names whereof are not known, and died at the Age of 930 Years (*c*). This is all that is certain in this matter. A great number of other things, which have been related of him, are either very false, or very uncertain; it is true, we may judge of some, that they are not contrary to the Analogy of Faith, nor to Probability. I place in this rank what is said of his prodigious Knowledge [*D*]: We read indeed nothing in *Genesis*, but what is less proper to

(*a*) *It is commonly called the Terrestrial Paradise, and the Garden of Eden.*

(*b*) *See the Remarks on the Article* EVE, *concerning this Serpent.*

(*c*) *See the first Five Chapters of Genesis.*

[*A*] *Of the Dust of the Earth.*] If we may believe Father *Garasse* (1), *Photius* reports, the Egyptian Tradition, *That Wisdom laid an Egg in the Terrestrial Paradise, out of which came our first Parents like a couple of Chickens.* I believe *Photius* has said no such thing, and I am much mistaken, if it be not a licentious Paraphrase of that Jesuit, forged on what *Photius* relates concerning a certain Mariner, whose Name was *Oé*, whom some made to issue ἐκ τῶ ὠρογόνω ᾠᾠ (2), that is, according to Father *Garasse* in another Book (3), *of the Race of the first Man, whose Name was* Oon (Egg): Or, according to Father *Schottus*, *à primo parente* Ωu. Many Enquiries might be made about this Egg, which served, according to the Doctrine of the Ancients, for the Generation of Things, when the *Chaos* was reduced into order. We shall touch upon some Particulars of it under the Word ARIMANIUS.

[*B*] *And took out of him a Rib.*] A modern Author (4), designing to shew, that the *Roman* Catholics are in the wrong to think themselves more learned than the Protestants, reproaches them, among other Mistakes, with that of a Preacher (5), who said that *Adam* was form'd of one of *Eve*'s Ribs. He reported, that a Philosopher having proposed these three Questions to *Theodorus*, a Disciple of St *Pacomus*: *What Man is he, who was not born, yet is dead? What Man is he, who was born, yet did not die? And, What Man is he, who was both born and died, yet is not rotten?* Had for Answer, that the three Persons in Question were *Adam*, *Enoch*, and *Lot*'s Wife. *Adam was not born*, added the Preacher, *for he was form'd of one of* Eve's *Ribs*. His Sermon was printed at *Vienna*, in *Austria*, in the Year 1654, with the Approbation of the Sub-Dean of the Professors in Divinity, who was at that time Father *Leonard Bachin*, a Jesuit. That Approver declares, that he read the Book, and he found nothing in it contrary to our Faith, or Manners: A Proof of the little Attention wherewith Censors of Books examine certain Manuscripts.

[*C*] *They perceived that they were naked.*] The Scripture says, that *their Eyes were opened*. This Expression made some People believe that *Adam* and *Eve* were *blind*, till they had transgress'd the Commandment of God. "Neque enim cœci creati erant, "ut imperitum vulgus opinatur (6).——*For they were "not created blind, as the ill-judging Vulgar think.*" St *Austin* refutes this Mistake very strongly, in several Parts of his Writings (7), and tells us, that this opening of our first Parents Eyes consisted in their being sensible of certain corporeal Motions, which they were ignorant of before; and that it was this, which inspired them with Shame. "Extitit in motu corporis quædam "impudens novitas, unde esset indecens nuditas, & fe- "cit attentos, reddiditque confusos (8). ——— *There "was a certain impudent Novelty in the Motion of* "*their Bodies; whence Nakedness became indecent; "and which excited their Attention, and put them to "the blush.*"

[*D*] *What is said of his prodigious Knowledge.*] Mr *Moreri* is not contented with affirming in general, that *Adam* had a perfect *Knowledge of Sciences, and chiefly of Astrology, of which he taught his Children several curious Secrets*; he adds also, That *Josephus* says, that *Adam ingraved some Observations he had made on the Course of the Stars on two different Tables.* I have search'd for this in *Josephus*, but find only, that the Descendants of *Seth*, the Son of *Adam*, invented Astronomy, and caused their Inventions to be engraven on a Pillar of Brick, and a Pillar of Stone, to preserve them from the general Destructions, which, according to the Predictions of *Adam*, were to happen, once by Fire, and once by a Deluge (9). When a Person is capable of falsifying in this Manner an Author, whom he cites, he seldom regards the Evidence so closely, as to make them say nothing, but what they really depose; so that I do not wonder, that Mr *Moreri* attributes to our first Father the Imposition of Names on Plants; I say I do not wonder at it, though the Scripture makes him only Author of the Names of Beasts. They, who infer from this Imposition of Names, that *Adam* was a great Philosopher, do not deserve to be refuted. To return to the prodigious Knowledge attributed to *Adam*; I say, that, according to the common Opinion (10), he knew more the very first Day of his Life, than any Man besides can learn by long Experience. Scarce any thing, besides future Events, escaped his Knowledge. *Cajetanus*, who ventures to rob him of the perfect Knowledge of the Stars, and of the Elements, was much censured for it. Some, having made it a Question, whether *Solomon* ought not to be excepted out of the general *Position*, which gives the Preference to *Adam*'s Knowledge, above That of all other Mortals, have been reduced to acknowledge, That *Adam* was more knowing than *Solomon*. It is true, *Pinedo* excepts *Politics*; but no Regard is paid to his particular Opinion; and it is determined, that the *speculative Understanding* of the first Man was endow'd with all the Philosophical and Mathematical Knowledge, which human Nature is naturally capable of; and that his *practical Understanding* possess'd a consummate Prudence, with respect to every thing which Men ought to do, either in a private or public Capacity; and, besides, contain'd all moral Sciences, and all the liberal Arts, Rhetoric, Poetry, Painting, Sculpture, Agriculture, Writing, &c. Every one knows, with what Emulation Mankind have strove to heap Praises upon *Aristotle*. Every Idea, and every Comparison had been exhausted, when a good *Carthusian*, being willing to outdo the most extravagant of all his Panegyrists, maintained, That

(1) *Garasse's Curious Doctrine,* pag. 232.

(2) Phot. ex Helladio, Biblioth. pag. 1583. fl. 279.

(3) *Theological Summary,* pag. 26. *where he reports this with many Alterations.*

(4) Daniel Francus, de indicib. Libror. prohibit. Epist. Dedicat.

(5) *His Name is Florentine Schilling, Regular Clerk of St Paul, and a Barnabite.*

(6) August. de Civit. Dei. lib. 14. cap. 17.

(7) Ibid. & lib. 11. de Genesi ad liter. cap. 31. & lib. 1. de Nupt. & Concupisc. cap. 5. & lib. 1. Locutionum in Genes. n. 9. & lib. 2. de Peccat. Merit. & Remiss. cap. 21.

(8) Ibid. de Civit. Dei, lib. 14. cap. 1.

(9) Josephi Antiquitat. lib. 1. cap. 2.

(10) *See* Salian's Annals Tom. 1. pag. 107, 113.

VOL. I. C c *Aristotle's*

ADAM.

(d) So God created Man in his own Image, in the beginning of God created be him, Male and Female created be them. Gen. i. 27.

to give us this Notion, than the contrary; and yet it is very probable, that *Adam* came out of the hands of his Creator endued with innate Science, and that he did not lose it by Sin; as the bad Angels are not become less knowing since their Fall, and as the Crimes of Learned Persons do not deprive them of that Knowledge they enjoy'd before. What some affirm concerning the Beauty of *Adam* [E], may be also plac'd in the rank of probable things; but it is altogether false that he was created of both Sexes [F]. It is a gross mistake of the words of Scripture (d) to imagine any such thing. The Revelations of *Antoinette Bourignon* [G], would be improperly

(11) Henry de Hassia. He Lived in the beginning of the XVIth Century.

(12) See Rivinus's Serpent. seduct. pag. 5.

(13) Idem, pag. 49, 56, 57.

(14) Ibid. pag. 56.

Aristotle's Learning was as extensive as That of *Adam* (11). Some Rabins have been satisfy'd with equalling the first Man to *Moses* and *Solomon*, in point of Learning (12); but others have maintained, that he excelled the Angels themselves, and have alledged the Testimony of God himself, in proof of it (13). They say, that the Angels having spoke of Man with some Disdain, when God consulted them on his Creation, God answered them, That Man was more knowing than they; and, to convince them of it, he presented all kinds of Beasts to them, and ask'd them their Names. They could not tell what to answer; and then he ask'd the same Question of Man, who named them all after each other; and being interrogated, what should be his own Name, and what was God's Name; he answered right, and gave to God the Name of *Jehovah*. According to the same Rabins, the meaning of this Aphorism of their Doctors, that *Adam's Stature extended from one end of the World to the other*, is, *that he knew all things* (14).

[E] *Concerning the Beauty of* Adam.] If some Authors had been contented to say, that he was a fine Person, and well made, they would have said nothing but what was probable: but instead of this, they have fallen into the Galleties of Rhetoric, and Poetry, and even into visionary Notions of this Matter. It has been fabled, that God, intending to create Man, assumed a perfect, and beautiful, human Body: and that he formed the Body of *Adam* on that Model, whence God might say, in relation to this Body, that *he made Man after his own Image*. They add, That this Apparition of God, under an human Form, was the first prelude to the Incarnation; that is, that the second Person of the Trinity cloathed himself with the Appearance of the same Nature he was one Day to assume in the Flesh, and that, under the likeness of the finest Man that ever was, he laboured in the Production of *Adam*, whom he made a Copy of that great and divine Original of Beauty, which he had assumed. "Hanc speciem divinamque pulchritudinem " clementissimus formosissimusque assumens, quam " erat post multa tempora usque ad carnem & ossa as- " sumpturus, creabat hominem, largiens ei speciem " hanc tantam, ipse primus Archetypus, speciosissimus " ipse speciosissimæ prolis creator (15). *The*

(15) Eupibin. in Cosmopora apud Salian. Annal. Tom. i. pag. 106.

(16) Id. ib.

(17) Id. ib.

(18) Salian. Tom. i. p. 16.

" *most Clement and Fair, assuming this divine Form* " *and Beauty, which he was in process of time to* " *cloath himself withal, even to Flesh and Bones, crea-* " *ted Man, bestowing on him this noble Form, himself* " *the Original Archetype, the most beautiful Creator* " *of a most beautiful Creature.*" It can be no wonder, after this, that these Exclamations should be made: "Quantum qualemve credas fuisse primi hominis illius " venustatem! quantum in ore decus, quas gratias " insedisse (16)? ——— *What, and how great, must be* " *the Beauty of the first Man? And what Charms must* " *dwell in his Countenance?*" For in short, the Form, which the WORD assum'd, was like That, which was seen by St *Peter* on Mount *Tabor*, and by *Moses* on Mount *Sinai*, and like That, which *Moses* and *Elias* appeared in on the Day of the Transfiguration. But what is still more wonderful is, That *Adam* himself saw his own Maker, and the manner how his Body was formed by the fair Hands of it's Author. "Cum fingeretur homo, manus illas divinas aspexit, " ambrosioique vultus illos, pulcherrima brachia cor- " pus suum fingentis, singuloisque artus ducentia (17). " ——— *When Man was created, he beheld those di-* " *vine Hands, that ambrosial Countenance, and those* " *beautiful Arms, which form'd his Body, and fashion-* " *ed every Member of it.*" A very learned Man published these airy Notions (18); and there are People enough, who approve, at least, one part of them.

[F] *That he was created of both Sexes.*] Many of the Rabins believed that *Adam's* Body was created double, Male on one Side, and Female on the other; and that both these Bodies were joined together by the Shoulders; the Heads looking towards places directly opposite, like the Heads of *Janus* (19). Now they pretend that, when God made *Eve*, he only divided This Body into two: That, which was of the Male Sex became *Adam*, and That, which was of the Female, became *Eve*. *Manasseh Ben Israel*, the most learned Rabbi of the XVIIth Century, maintained this fantastical Opinion, if we believe *Heidegger* (20). The learned *Maimonides*, the Honour and Glory of the *Jewish* Nation, had (21) already maintained it, if we may believe the same Witness. *Eugubinus* varied from it, only as to the Situation of the two Bodies; for he pretends that they adhered together by the Sides, and that they resembled each other in all things, except the Sex. The Male Body was on the right, and embraced the other by the Neck with his left Hand, while the other did the like to him with the right Hand. Both were animated; both fell into a deep Sleep, when God intended to form *Eve*, that is, separate her from the Male Body. We need only be able to read the Scripture, to confute all those chimerical Notions. Before I pass on to other Matters, I shall just take notice of those *Androgynes*, of which *Plato* has spoke so largely (22). They were Hermaphrodites, with four Arms and four Legs, and two Faces turned towards each other on one Neck. This duplicity of Members gave them much Force, and made them very insolent upon that account; so that they thought on nothing less than making War with the Gods. A Consultation was held in Heaven on the manner of reducing them to Reason; and *Jupiter's* Opinion was followed, which was to divide them asunder. Each of the Parts preserved a strong Inclination to a Re-union; and this is the Origin of Love, according to this Philosopher. But some Alterations were necessary to be made in the Situation of certain Members, in order to make their Re-union fruitful. I shall observe by the way, that they, who speak of these *Androgynes* of *Plato*, seldom report the Matter as it really is. They make him say, that Men, in general, were of this kind at first; but his Account relates only to certain of them: He acknowledges that there were also Males and Females, of the same kind with those at present. See the Remark of the Article SALMACIS. The Author of a Book entituled, *The New Visionary of Rotterdam* (23) assures us, that, according to the Rabins, *Adam* and *Eve* were both Hermaphrodites before their Fall (24). He is the only Author I know of, who ascribes this Opinion to the Rabins.

(19) See Heidegger's Histor. Patriarch. Tom. i. pag. 128.

(20) Conciliat. in Genesim apud Hoornbeeck who refutes him in the first Chapter of the fourth Book concerning Judaism.

(21) In More Nevoch. pag. 2. cap. 30. apud Heidegg. Tom. i. pag. 128. But observe, as Mr Van Dale has informed me, that Heidegger does not give a faithful Account of the Opinion, which Manasseh ben Israel and Maimonides have most approv'd.

(22) Plato in Convivio, pag. 1185. Edit. Francof. 1602.

(23) It was printed in the Year 1686.

(24) P. 76.

[G] *The Revelations of Antoinette Bourignon.*] This Lady's Works prove, that she had very particular Opinions; but perhaps she advanc'd nothing more strange, than what concerns the first Man. She pretends, that, before the Fall, *Adam* had the Principles of both Sexes in himself, and the Power of producing his Likeness, without the help of a Woman: And that the Necessity, which both Sexes are under, at present, of uniting for the sake of Propagation, is a Consequence of the Alteration Sin made in the human Body. "Men, *says she* (25), think they were " created by God as they are at present, though it " is not true; seeing Sin has disfigured the Work of " God in them, and instead of Men, as they ought " to be, they are become Monsters in Nature, divi- " ded into two imperfect Sexes, unable to produce " their like alone, as Trees and Plants do, which " in that Point have more Perfection than Men or " Women, incapable to produce by themselves, but " in Conjunction with each other, and accompany'd " with Pain and Misery." The Particulars of this Mystery are explain'd in another Work, as it was revealed from God to Mrs *Bourignon* (26). She believed that she had seen, in an Extacy, how *Adam* was made before Sin, and in what manner he was able alone to produce other Men. Nay, she believ'd she had learn'd, that he had put this rare Fecundity in practice,

(25) Pref. of the Bit entitled, The New Heaven and the New Earth, Amst. 1679.

(26) Continuation of Midam Bourignon, pag. 315.

ADAM.

perly alledg'd in confirmation of this false Gloss. The romantic Narrations of *James Sadeur* [H] might as well be employ'd for that Purpose. Neither is it more true that *Adam* was produc'd with Circumcision (e), and that, being displeas'd at it, he committed the Fault of those, whom St *Paul* mentions in one of his Epistles (f). We may place likewise in the rank of *Fable*, what has been said of his gigantic Stature [I],

his

practice, by the Production of the human Nature of *Jesus Christ*. Though the Passage is somewhat long, yet I shall beg leave to transcribe it, as it will shew us to what Extravagancies the human Mind is liable.

"God represented to her in a Vision, without the Assistance of corporeal Eyes, which could not have endured such Brightness, the Beauty of the first World, and the manner how he form'd it out of the original *Chaos*: All was bright, transparent, and radiant, with an ineffable Light and Glory. In the same spiritual manner he made the first Man *Adam* appear to her, whose Body was more pure and transparent than Crystal, all light and flying, in appearance; In and through which were seen Vessels and Streams of Light, penetrating from the inside to the outside, through all his Pores; Vessels, which contained most lively and diaphanous Liquors of all Sorts and Colours, not only of Water and Milk, but also of Fire, Air, &c. His Motions were wonderfully harmonious; every thing obey'd him; nothing resisted nor could annoy him. He was of a larger Stature than Men are at present; his Hair short and curl'd, inclining to black; his upper Lip covered with small Hair: And, instead of the bestial Parts not to be named, he was made like as our Bodies shall be restored in eternal Life, after a manner which I know not whether I dare reveal. In this Region of his Body, was situated the Structure and Resemblance of a Face; which was a Source of admirable Odors and Perfumes: From thence likewise Men were to spring, whose Principles he had all within himself: for there was a Vessel in his Belly, which bred small Eggs, and another Vessel full of Liquor, which impregnated the Eggs. And when Man grew enflamed with the Love of his God, the Desire he had that there should be other Creatures, besides himself, to praise, love, and adore the divine Majesty, made that Liquor, by the Fire of God's Love, to spread itself on one or more of these Eggs with unconceiveable Delight; which, being impregnated, came out some time after from the Man, by the forementioned Canal, in the form of an Egg, and a little after hatch'd a perfect Man. After this manner there will be an holy and endless Generation in the Life eternal, quite different from that which Sin produc'd by the means of the Woman, whom God form'd of the Man, by taking that Vessel out of *Adam* which contained the Eggs, which the Woman now possesses, and from which Men proceed at present, according to the new Discoveries in Anatomy. The first Man, whom *Adam* produc'd by himself in this glorify'd State, was chosen by God to be the Throne of the Divinity, the Organ and Instrument by which God would communicate himself eternally with Mankind; that is, *Jesus Christ*, the First-Born, united to the human Nature, both God and Man (27)."

I wish the Author of The *New Visionary* of Rotterdam had not insulted, in so gay a manner, the Visions of this Maid, and those of the Minister, whom he attacks. He might have turn'd the latter into Ridicule, for his Notions concerning *Adam* and *Eve's* Marriage, without playing the Buffoon so much upon the Subject. I only add two short Remarks. The first is, that *Antoinette Bourignon* ought not to have expected her own Resurrection: for, according to her Principles, the gross Matter, which was added to Man's Body after the Fall, and which rots in the Grave, will not rise again (28); and the Resurrection is nothing else but the re-establishing of Man in his State of Innocency: A State wherein, according to the fine Revelations of *Antoinette*, there were no Women. An Heretic, whose Name was *Amaury*, was formerly condemn'd at *Paris* (29), among other Errors, That at the end of the World both Sexes shall be re-united together in one Person, and that this re-union began in Jesus Christ; and that if Man had continued in the State, wherein God produc'd him, there would not have been any distinction of Sexes (30). *Faber Stapulensis* believ'd, that, in the State of Innocency, *Adam* might have begotten a Man like himself, without the help of a Woman (31). So that Mrs *Bourignon* was not the first who broach'd this Opinion, though she has added much of her own to it; for instance, That perpetual Propagation, which, she says, will be in Paradise, in the same manner that Man would have multiply'd, if he had preserv'd his Innocency. What shall we say to *Paracelsus*, who believ'd that our first Parents had not the necessary Parts of Generation before they sinned, but that, after the Fall, they came out of them, like Excrescences, or Tumours in the Throat? *Negabat primos parentes ante lapsum habuisse partes generationi hominis necessarias, postea accessisse ut strumam gutturi* (32). My second Remark is, that This Lady attributes to *Jesus Christ*, born of *Adam*, all the Apparitions of God, spoken of in the Old Testament: and that she believes, that when he *resign'd to cloath himself with the Corruption of our Flesh and Blood*, in the Womb of the Holy Virgin, *he enclos'd his Body there, either by reducing it to the smallness it had at its first Conception or Birth, or some other way inconceivable to our gross Reason* (33).

These two Reflexions, which were sufficient in the first Edition of this Work, are not so in this; for there are Persons so captious, as to object, that my Article of ADAM contains intolerable Obscenities. I answer, that They are too nice and scrupulous; and that they are ignorant of the Privileges of History. They, who write the Life of a wicked Man, may and ought to represent, in general, the excesses of his Debauchery; and what choice soever they make of Words, they must necessarily relate impure things, and such as fully the Imagination. This is inevitable. All they can do is to avoid Particulars, and too gross Expressions; and this I have done. They likewise, who write the History of Sects, whose Doctrines or Actions have been impure, find themselves under the same Necessity. The most cautious Style can never hinder them from presenting filthy and obscene Images to their Readers. That which justifies me in particular, is, that I relate Absurdities contain'd in a Book, which is publickly sold. Besides, I have the Example of the ancient Fathers on my side, who have inserted the most shocking Impurities of Heretics in their Works.

[H] *The romantic Narrations of* James Sadeur*]* It is a pretended relation of certain Hermaphrodite Nations of *Terra Australis*. See the Article SADEUR.

[I] *His gigantic Stature.*] *Philo* believed that *Adam* exceeded the size of all other Men both in Body and Soul (34); but the *Talmudists* go much farther; they affirm, that *Adam* was extended from one end of the World to the other, when God first form'd him; that after he had transgress'd, the Hand of the Lord was heavy upon him, and reduc'd his Stature to the Measure of an hundred Ells (35). Some say that God did it at the Request of the Angels, who were afraid of so gigantic a Creature; but they suppose that God left to the first Man the height of nine hundred Cubits. See the first Volume of the *Rabinical Dictionary* of Father *Bartolocci*, pag. 65, 66. *Barcepha* takes notice of certain Authors, who say, that the Terrestrial Paradise was separated from our World by the Ocean, and that *Adam*, being driven out of this Paradise, cross'd the Sea on foot, to come into our World, and that he found it every where fordable; his Stature was so enormous (36). This is just the *Orion* or the *Polyphemus* of the Poets;

— *quam magnus Orion*
Cum pedes incedit medii per maxima Nerei
Stagna viam scindens, humero supereminet undas (37).

— *He stood,*
Like tall Orion, *stalking o'er the flood:*
When with his brawny Breast he cuts the Waves,
His Shoulders scarce the topmost Billow laves.
DRYDEN.

summo

ADAM.

his Books [K], his Sepulchre [L], and of a Tree planted on that Sepulchre [M], &c. But we must be careful not to doubt of his Salvation, as the Abbot *Ruperius* did (g), and least of all to believe him condemn'd to Infernal Flames, as the *Tatianites* did (h). Nor are we oblig'd to adopt the Opinion of *Origen*, St *Augustin*, St *Athanasius*, and others, that *Adam* was one of the first of those, who rose from the dead with JESUS CHRIST (i); and we are yet less oblig'd to believe, that his Repentance would have kill'd him with Grief, if God had not sent the Angel *Raziel* to comfort him (k). But Reason requires us to believe, that his Faith and his Prayers obtain'd Mercy for him, and that he made a very good End; without imagining at the same time, that he made a Speech to his Children before his Death, and recommended to them particularly to honour their Mother, and to bury her near him. It is

(g) *Rupertii Comment. in Genes. cap. xxxii.*
(h) *Epiphan. Hæres. 46. Eusebii Hist. lib. 4. cap. 27.*
(i) *Apud Cornel. à Lapide in Genes. cap. v. vers 5.*

――― summo cum monte videmus
Ipsum inter pecudes vasta se mole moventem,
Pastorem Polyphemum, & littora nota petentem (38).

――― When, on the Mountain's Brow,
We saw the Giant-Shepherd stalk before
His following Flock, and leading to the Shore.

――― graditurque per æquor
Jam medium, necdum fluctus latera ardua tinxit (39).

――― Thro' Seas he strides,
And scarce the topmost Billows touch'd his Sides.
DRYDEN.

(38) *Virgil. Æneid. lib. 3. ver. 655.*
(39) *Id. ib. ver. 664.*

The *Arabians* have no less an Idea of the Stature of our first Parents, than *Moses Barcephas's* Authors. The following is a Narrative of Mr *Monconys*. " My " *Arabian* told me how the Caravan of *Cairo* arriv'd " first at *Mecca*, and how, after having offer'd their " Prayers, they went to the Foot of the Mountain, " which is a League distant from thence, to wait " for the other Caravans of *Damascus* and *Bagdat*, " which came the following Days to *Mecca*; and " that being all arriv'd on the ninth of the twelfth " Moon, which is *Diel Hegbe*, at the end, I say, of " the ninth Day, which is *Affor*, all the three Ca- " ravans ascended to the top of the Mountain, on the " Summit whereof (which is very low, like those " Hillocks, which stand alone in the midst of Plains) " they believe that *Eve* laid her Head, when *Adam* " knew her the first Time; and that her two Knees " were two Muskets shot distant from each other, " on two other Hillocks in the bottom of the Plain ; " on each of which places they have erected a round " Pillar, between which (to be a good *Agi*, that is, " Pilgrim) you must pass, both ascending and de- " scending the Mountain, on the top of which is " a Mosque, made like a Niche, into which but se- " ven or eight Persons can enter (40)." I find that one *John Lucidus* is cited, who believed that *Adam* was one of the greatest of all Giants (41), and who us'd to prove it by these Words of Scripture, according to the Vulgar Translation, *Nomen Hebron ante vocabatur Cariatharbe: Adam maximus ibi inter Enacim situs est* (42). Upon the Authority of this Passage, St *Jerom* fancies that *Adam* was buried at *Hebron* (43). But it was proved to him, that neither the *Hebrew* Text, nor the Translation of the LXX, make mention of *Adam*, or of any Sepulchre (44). The *Geneva* Translation renders it, *the Name of Hebron before was Kariath-Arbah, which Arbah had been a very great Man among the Hanakims*. The *English* Version renders it after the same manner. There is a Mountain in the Island of *Ceylon*, called the Peak of *Adam*, because, according to the Tradition of the Country, it was the place of his Residence (45). The prints of his Feet are yet to be found there, above two Palms in length. *Pythagoras* would not infer such a gigantic Stature from thence, as that which others attribute to *Adam*; I say, *Pythagoras*, who judg'd of *Hercules*'s Stature by the length of that Hero's Foot (46). It is also said that there are some Remains on that Mountain, of the Tears which were shed for the Death of *Abel*; but others say, that *Adam* and *Eve* lamented his Death in a Cave in *Judæa*, where their Beds of Stone are to be seen of thirty Foot length (47).

[K] *His Books.*] The *Jews* pretend that *Adam* wrote a Book concerning the Creation of the World; and another on the Deity (48). *Mosius* mentions the former (49). A *Mahometan* Author, whose Name is *Kis-*

(40) *Moncon. Travels, part 1. pag. 172. 3°. Edition of Lyons.*
(41) *Joh. Lucidus, lib. 1. de Emendat. Temp. cap. 4. apud Pererium in Genes. lib. 4. quæst. 3.*
(42) *Jothua, cap. xiv. ver. ult.*
(43) *Hieron. in Matth. cap. xxvii.*
(44) *Pererius ubi supra.*
(45) *Ludev. Romanus Patricius in sua Navigat. apud Bissilium illustr. Ruinar. Decad. 1.*
(46) *A. Gellius Noct. Att. lib. 1. cap. 1.*
(47) *Apud Salden. Otia Theol. pag. 346.*
(48) *Heideg. Hist. Patr. Tom. 1. pag. 481.*
(49) *See Salian. Tom. 1. pag. 230.*

saus, reports, that *Abraham* being gone into the Country of the *Sabæi*, open'd *Adam*'s strong Box, wherein he found his Books with those of *Seth*, and *Edris* (50). This last Name is that which the *Arabians* give to *Enoch*. They say that *Adam* received twenty Books fallen from Heaven, which contain'd divers Laws and Promises, and Threatnings, from God, and Predictions of many Events (51). Some Rabbies attribute the 92d Psalm to *Adam*, and there are some Manuscripts, where the *Chaldait* Title of that *Psalm* imports that it is a Song of Praise, recited by the first Man on the Sabbath-day (52). The good *Eusebius Nierembergius*, who was Credulity itself, reports two Canticles, which he faithfully copied out of the Revelations of the ever blessed *Amadeus*, in the Library of the *Escurial* (53). It is said, that *Adam* was the Author of these two Pieces; he made the one the first time he saw *Eve*; the other is the penitential Psalm, which he and his Wife sung after their Fall.

[L] *His Sepulchre.*] We have already seen, that St *Jerom* imagined, without any ground, that *Adam* was buried at *Hebron*; but we have as much Reason to be of his Opinion in that, as to think with many others, that *Adam* was buried upon Mount *Calvary* (54). I confess the latter Opinion is preferable *per la predica, for the Preacher's Use*; for it is much more fertile of Allusions, Antitheses, moral Application, and all kind of Rhetorical Figures: But such a Reason is fit for little else, than to serve as an Answer to those, who may ask, why St *Jerom*'s Opinion had fewer Followers than the other. But, Comparisons aside, it is enough for us to be informed, that the Fathers generally believed, that the first Man died in the Place, where *Jerusalem* was built afterwards, and that he was buried on a neighbouring Hill, which was called *Golgotha*, or *Calvary*; which is that where *Jesus Christ* was crucified. If you ask me how *Adam*'s Grave could resist the Waters of the Deluge, and how his Bones could maintain their place, in order to receive the sprinkling of the Blood of our Lord; for there lies the Mystery;

Hic hominem primum suscepimus esse sepultum,
Hic patitur Christus: pia sanguine terra madescit,
Pulvis Adæ ut possit, veteris cum sanguine Christi
Commixtus, stillantis aquæ virtute lavari (55);

Here Tradition says the first Man was buried; Here Christ suffered: The pious Earth is wet with Blood, that the Dust of Adam, *mixt with the Blood of Christ, might be wash'd with the Virtue of the distilling Water*.

If, I say, you put this Question; *Barcepha* will quote a Doctor upon you, very much esteem'd in *Syria* (56), who said that *Noah* dwelt in *Judæa*; that he planted the Cedars, wherewith he built the Ark, in the Plains of *Sodom*, that he took *Adam*'s Bones with him into the Ark; that, after he was come out of the Ark, he divided them among his three Sons; that he gave the Skull to *Shem*; and that the Offspring of *Shem*, having taken possession of *Judæa*, buried this Skull in the same Place where *Adam*'s Grave had been.

[M] *A Tree planted on that Sepulchre.*] *Cornelius à Lapide* says, that the *Hebrews* have a Tradition, that by the Command of an Angel *Seth* put some of the Seed of the forbidden Tree into *Adam*'s Mouth, who was already buried; and that it produc'd a Tree, of which the Cross of *Jesus Christ* was made; and that it was but just that the same Wood, which had caus'd *Adam* to sin, should be That, on which *Jesus Christ* should expiate *Adam*'s Sin (57). That Jesuit refers us to *Pineda*, who

(50) *See Stanley's Eastern Philosophy, B. 3. cap. 3.*
(51) *Hotting. Hist. Orient. pag. 22. cited by Lyserus in Polygamiâ Triumphatâ, pag. 145.*
(52) *Gaspar Schottus Technic. Curios. pag. 556.*
(53) *Lib. 2. cap. 17. de Orig. Sacræ Script. cap. 13. apud Schottum, ibid.*
(54) *See Salian. Ann. Tom. 1. pag. 225. where he proves that St Jerom himself, at times, seemed Opposite to some places.*
(55) *Tertullian. Carm. contra Marcion. lib. 2. c.p. 4.*
(56) *Dom. Jacobus Orobaitis (sive Edesseus) St Ephrem who liv'd in the IVth Century was his Disciple. See Salian, Corn. à Lapide, p. 15.*
(57) *In Genesim. cap. ii. ver. 9. pag. 74.*

ADAM.

is giving one's self too much Liberty, to forge such direct Speeches [*N*]. We have related elsewhere (*l*) the Opinions concerning the *Duration* of his *State of Innocence.*

(*l*) *In the Remark [A] of the Article* ABEL.

(58) *See concerning this Rabbin, and his Works, the Nouv. Liter. for July* 1686. *Art.* 3. *pag.* 770. *taken from* Morhius *of the Brazen Serpent.*

who related this Fable at length. But what does he mean by the *Hebrews*? Doubtless he means the *Jews*. Now, do the *Jews* own that *Jesus Christ* expiated *Adam*'s Sin by the Punishment of the Cross, to which their Nation condemn'd him under *Pontius Pilate*? When an Author is full of a thing, he thinks others are so too, and does not always perceive the Absurdity of attributing his own Thoughts to them. Lastly, this Fable has been variously reported: for we find in a Rabbi, who liv'd long before *Jesus Christ*, and whose Work is entituled, *Gale Rasejab* (58), that the Angels brought to *Adam*, in the Desert, a Branch of the Tree of Life, which *Seth* planted, and that it became a Tree, whereof *Moses* made good Use; for, after having made out of it the Rod, with which he wrought so many Miracles, he sweetned the bitter Waters with it, and erected likewise the Brazen Serpent on part of it. Some say that *Adam* sent *Seth* to the Gate of the Garden of *Eden*, to desire the Angel's who defended the Entrance, to grant him a Branch of the Tree of Life, which they comply'd with (59).

[*N*] *To forge such direct Speeches.*] I have *Salian* in view, in this Censure. Not contented with the Speech, he made a long Epitaph for *Adam*, wherein he denotes his own Name by these three Letters, *J. S. P.* (60). He made Epitaphs also for *Abel, Abraham*, and *Sarah*, &c. In truth this is scarce pardonable, except in Authors, who are just come from teaching Rhetoric; and I am fully persuaded that the *Sirmonds*, the *Petavius*'s, the *Hardouins*, and the rest of the great Authors of the Society of the Jesuits, will judge of it, as I do.

(59) *See Salden's Otia Theolog. pag.* 608.

(60) *They signify, Jac. Sallianus Pontius Salian Potifu.*

ADAM, Archdeacon of the Patriarchal Chamber, and Superior of the Monks of *Chaldæa*, was sent to *Rome* at the beginning of the XVIIth Century, by *Elias, Nestorian* Patriarch of *Babylon*. This Patriarch, having caus'd the Profession of Faith, which *Paul* V. had sent him, to be examin'd by his Bishops, commission'd *Adam* to present it to That Pope, with the Alterations he had made in it; but order'd him at the same time to correct what the Pope should find amiss in it. This Embassy of our *Adam* was an Embassy of Obedience. This Monk, being come to *Rome*, acquitted himself of his Commission with all imaginable Care. He had brought a Writing with him, wherein he pretended to reconcile the Faith of the *Eastern* Churches with That of the Church of *Rome*, and to make it appear that their Differences were but a *Verbal Dispute* [*A*]. He had first shewed this Writing to his Patriarch, and afterwards, by his order, to all the Bishops of the Party, and he had employ'd a whole Year in going from City to City to procure the Approbation of those Bishops. *Peter Strozza*, Secretary to *Paul* V. was order'd to answer this Writing. The Answer favour'd more of Inflexibility than Condescension; for he explain'd every thing with the utmost Rigour; and the Legate of the Patriarch was not only oblig'd to submit to the Doctrines, but to the very Expressions of the Church of *Rome*. He sign'd whatever the Pope propos'd to him, and, not satisfy'd with abjuring all the Errors of his Nation, he wrote several Books, and address'd them to his Countrymen, to communicate to them the new Lights he had acquir'd at *Rome*. He departed from thence after an abode of Three Years; and carry'd with him a Brief from *Paul* the V. to his Patriarch *Elias*, rejecting all the Terms of Accomodation, which *Patriarch* had propos'd, and obliging him to condemn every Expression, which might cover any Error (*a*). *Adam* was accompanied by two Jesuits (*b*), who had Orders to labour at the entire Re-union of that Sect.

(*a*) *Taken from the* 10*th Chapter of the* 5*th Book of the Perpetuity of the Faith defended. Mr Arnaud cites this Treatise of* Peter Strozza, *de Dogmatibus Chaldæorum.*

(*b*) Nic. Godign. s. lib. 1. de Rebus Abassinorum apud Aub. Miræum, de Stat. Relig. Christ. pag. 226.

(1) Moni's Critical History of the Belief and Customs of the Nations of the Levant, pag. 93.

[*A*] *Their Differences were but a verbal Dispute.*] The *Sieur de Moni*, in his *Critical History of the Levant*, seems fully persuaded, that the Patriarch *Elias* had reason to maintain, that there is but a mere verbal Difference between the *Nestorians* of the present Time, and the *Catholics*. The *Nestorianism of the present Time*, says he (1), *is but an imaginary Heresy; the Difference of their Opinion consists only in Equivocation;* the Nestorians *understanding the Word* Person *in another Sense, than the* Latins. Why then did they not acquiesce in the Explanation, which the Patriarch of *Babylon* gave of their Notions? The Reason was, because, in order to keep up a *Decorum*, and out of a false Punctilio of Honour, it was necessary to maintain that *Nestorianism* was a dangerous Heresy; otherwise they would have prostituted the Honour of the *Oecuménical* Councils. This is what the Sieur *de Moni* would have said in a free Country; but in *France* he was obliged to qualify his Expressions: *The Councils*, says he (2), *having condemn'd the Heresy of* Nestorius, *it seemed necessary to make it appear at* Rome, *that* Nestorianism *was a true Heresy, since it had been condemn'd by the Church in a general Council.* He adds, with the same caution, *That some might infer, from the very Acts of the ancient Councils, that* Nestorianism *is but a nominal Heresy; and that if* Nestorius *and St* Cyril *had understood each other, they might have reconcil'd their Opinions* (3).

(2) Id. ib.

(3) Id. ib.

ADAM, (JOHN) a *French* Jesuit, was a famous Preacher of the XVIIth Century [*A*]. He was of *Limousin*, and enter'd among the Jesuits in the Year 1622, at 14 Years of Age (*a*). His Superiors, finding him qualify'd to succeed in the Pulpit, apply'd him to it, after he had taught Humanity, and Philosophy. He exercis'd the Trade of Preaching Forty Years, and was follow'd in the chief Cities of *France*, and in the *Louvre* itself (*b*). He began, as it was reasonable he should, in the Provinces; but when he had sufficiently signaliz'd himself in them, he was sent to Display his Talents on the grand Theatre of the Kingdom. The Circumstances of the Times favour'd him, the Disputes of *Jansenism* having already heated the People; and never was Man more fit than Father *Adam*, being a rash Adventurer, to be let loose against That Party. He was hot and undaunted, and had all the Qualifications of a great Declaimer. The Sermons, which he preach'd in *Lent* at *Paris* in St *Paul*'s Church in the Year 1650, made a great Noise. The Preacher push'd Matters so far, that,

(*a*) Sotuel, Biblioth. societatis Jesu, pag. 397.

(*b*) Id. ib.

(1) *It is the title of the* 13*th part of the Letters of the Latter*.

[*A*] *Was a famous Preacher of the XVIIth Century.*] See the Letter which Mr *de Balzac* writ to him | on the 15th of *January* 1643, after having read the fifteen Sermons, which that Jesuit had sent him (1).

[*B*] *They*

VOL. I. D d

ADAM.

that, had it not been for powerful Patrons, they would have forbad him the Pulpit [*B*]. He had Honesty enough to acknowledge [*C*], that St *Austin* was no ways favourable to *Molinism*; and was very angry with that Ancient Doctor. The *Jansenists* did not pass by this Affront [*D*]. They publish'd an Answer to his Sermon, and were not satisfy'd with apologizing for St *Austin*; but refuted some other Propositions of that Jesuit, and particularly That, which related to the Inspiration of the *Canonical Writers* [*E*]. Father *Adam* had no regard to the Complaints, which were made

---

(a) Patin's Letter 7.
p. y. t. 2.
of the 1st
part, Edit.
of Geneva,
1691.

(3) *Defence of St Austin against Father Adam.*

(4) *The same.*

* Third Part, cap. 7. pag. 622.

[*B*] *They would have forbad him the Pulpit*] This we learn from a Letter of *Guy Patin*, written the twelfth of *April*, 1650: Our *Archbishop*, says he, *has forbid the Pulpit to Mr* Broussel, *a Doctor of* Navarre, *and Canon of St* Honore, *who is a great* Jansenist, *for having preached within these three Days a little too boldly*. Father *Adam*, *a Jesuit, would have felt the same rigour, for having preached against* St Austin *in* St Paul's *Church, and for having called him the hot African and the petulant Doctor, if the Credit of the Jesuits and of the Capuchins had not diverted the Archbishop from it* (2).

[*C*] *He had Honesty enough to acknowledge.*] This must be understood, *cum grano salis*, with some Restriction; and we should be deceived, if we imagined, that this Jesuit retained nothing of the Artifices of those, who pretended that St *Austin* is neither favourable to the *Calvinists*, nor to the *Jansenists*: For in the same Sermon, which raised such an outcry, and which he divided into two Parts, he designed by the second *to shew from the Doctrine of That Father, that* Jesus Christ *died for all Men, without Exception*; and he had already published a Book, entitled, Calvin *defeated by himself, and by* St Austin's *Weapons, which he has unjustly usurped in his Doctrines of Grace, Free-will, and Predestination* (3). Now he made no Difficulty to say, that *Jansenius* and *Calvin* taught the same thing in the Doctrine of Grace; and a few Days after his Sermon, he replied to one, who reproached him for it, *I fear nothing; no one can attack my Sermon, nor my Book about Grace, without undertaking at the same time to support* Calvin (4). Why are we to understand then by the *Honesty* which I ascribe to him? Why, that the Liberty he took in giving his Opinion of St *Austin's* Errors, plainly intimated, that he did not esteem him a proper Model of Faith in those Matters.

[*D*] *The* Jansenists *did not pass by this Affront.*] A few Days after, they published a Pamphlet of sixty Pages in *Quarto*, entitled, *A Defence of St* Austin, *against the Errors, the Calumnies, and the scandalous Invectives which Father* Adam, *the Jesuit, preached in* St Paul's *Church on the second* Thursday *in* Lent, *on this Text of the Gospel*, " I am not sent but to the " lost Sheep of the House of *Israel*." They accused him of having said, " I. That St *Austin* was intricate " and obscure in his Writings; that, being an *African*, " violent and full of Heat, he was often too pas- " sionate, that he ran into Extreams, and had ex- " ceeded the Bounds of Truth in opposing the Ene- " mies of Grace; as it happens sometimes, that a " Man, who designs to strike his Enemy, does it " with such Violence, that he dashes him against a " Tree, and gives him a Counter-Blow contrary " to his Intention. II. That St *Austin* himself, in " establishing *Original Sin*, against the *Pelagians*, " was carried away to an excess of Error, in saying " *that Original Sin was punished in Children, who* " *died without Baptism*, with the Torments of Fire, " and with Damnation. III. That St *Austin* was not " steady in his Notions, since, according to the Ob- " servation of Mr *Gamache*, he changed his Opinion " three times about the Doctrine of Grace." These Reproaches, and some others of the same kind, had already appeared in a Book of Father *Adam*. Those, who have not that Book, may find them in a Work, which is easy to be consulted; I mean the *Vindictæ Augustinianæ*, wherein Father *Adam* is the first of St *Austin's* modern Adversaries, whom Father *Norris* refuted.

[*E*] *Which related to the Inspiration of the Canonical Writers*.] " It is not surprizing, that Father *Adam* " should assert in his Sermon, That St *Austin* was " carried too far by the Ardor of his Zeal, since, in " a naughty Book, full of Falsities and Errors, he " has laid it down *, *That this Weakness is not so* " *criminal, but that God suffers it in those Authors,*

" *whom he inspires, and whom we call Canonical* " ———— *and that the Natural Fire of St* Paul *was* " *likewise apt to incline him to Expressions of this* " *nature* ———— To prove that there are some Frail- " ties in *Canonical Authors*, and that they *follow* " *their own Imaginations in expressing the things* " *which God has revealed to them*, he says, *That* " *when the Prophet* Elias *complained of the Impiety* " *of the Age, he said to God, that Faith was ex-* " *tinguished in the Hearts of all Men, and that he* " *alone remained of all who adored him on the Earth.* " ——— David *affirms, that there was never more* " *Corruption and Disorder seen, than in his Time,* " *that there was not one Man to be found who would* " *perform a good Action*." This is the Doctrine which Father *Adam's* Censurers reproached him with. The result of it is, that the inspired Doctrine, and the Expressions of those who are inspired, are two different things; that God is the Author only of the first, but that he left the other to the Imagination of the Person inspired, and that this did not hinder his Imagination from exceeding the Dictates of the Holy Spirit. Without doubt this was Father *Adam's* Sentiment; for the Examples of *Elias* and *David*, which he alledges, would not serve the Purpose of one, who believes, that it was revealed by God, that *Elias* was the only Worshipper of the True God, and that in *David's* Time there was not one good Man on the Earth. Whoever therefore makes use of such Examples must be convinced, that God only revealed, that the Number of good Men was small. Thus the Imagination of an inspired Author may make that *universal* which is given him with Restriction; and thus he may fall into the Sophism, *à dicto secundum quid ad dictum simpliciter*: In a Word, This is to adulterate Revelation, to deceive the Church, to lie. The *Jansenists* did not fail to exclaim against this Doctrine, as being impious, and opening a Door to a thousand Attempts against the Authority of the Scripture (5). " For, said they (6), " if God suffers any Frailty in the Canonical Au- " thors, whom he inspires, if there is a Natural Fire " in St *Paul*, which is not from God; every thing, " which the Libertine or Heretic finds in Holy Writ " contrary to his Sentiments, he will say proceeds " from the Frailty or Natural Fire of the Writer, " and not from the Spirit of God. ———— To allow " of any Infirmity, or any Influence of meer Na- " tural Disposition in the sacred Writers, is to give " every one the Liberty of judging of This, and of " throwing out of the Scripture what he pleases, " as proceeding rather from the Weakness of Man, " than the Spirit of God. ———— The Libertine will " deny the Eternity of Hell Torments, and when " St *Matthew* says, Go ye cursed into everlasting " Fire, he will say it was an extravagant Expres- " sion denote the long Continuance, and Greatness of the " Torments prepared for the Wicked, proceeding from " to the Imagination of the Evangelist (7)." Those Gentlemen pretended that Father *Adam* only made use of this Doctrine, *that he might shift off the Force of St* Paul's *Expressions, which seemed hard to him, and contrary to his Sentiment, and to teach us the Art of playing with the Words of the Apostle of the Gentiles about Grace and Divine Predestination, as well as with those of St* Austin If he finds himself pressed by the Ninth Chapter of the Epistle to the Romans, *where* St Paul *says*, that God will have Mercy, on whom he will have Mercy, and whom he will he hardens; he may answer, that St Paul's Natural Fire carried him into Expressions of this Nature; that it is a Frailty which God suffers in Canonical Authors; that it is the Expression of a thing revealed after the Imagination, Disposition, and Temper of St Paul (8).

I omit their Answer to the Instances of *Elias* and *David*; and shall only observe, that they found a great Mistake in matter of Fact in the first of those Citations; for the Canonical Author, who relates

(5) Ibid. pag. 11.

(6) *The same.*

(7) Pag. 16.

(8) *Compare this with what is said pag. 5. 4. in the Advice to the Refugees.*

ADAM. 107

made against his Sermon, and against a Book, wherein he had thrown out several Expressions concerning St *Austin*, which gave great Offence. He retracted nothing, and continued writing in the same Strain. The *Jansenists* renew'd their Complaints; and their Writings; and a particular Conflict arose between them and Father *Adam*. They criticiz'd the Books, which he publish'd, some of which he compos'd for the use of pious Minds, in Opposition to those Gentlemen. To this end, he publish'd the *Psalms* of *David*, the Hymns and Prayers of the Church in *Latin*, and in *French*. Every body knows that the *Jansenists* endeavour'd to recommend themselves by their *French* Translations of those Books. They attack'd likewise the Poetry of Father *Adam* ; I mean the Translation, which he had made, of the Hymns in *French* Verse [F]. But this Paper War continued but a very little time between them. His Writings began in 1650. and ended in 1651 [G]. It is plain, they found that he did the Church and the Society more Service by his other Talents, than by his Pen. He was therefore sent to *Sedan* to settle a College of Jesuits there. He would have found it very difficult to succeed in this Design, had the Marshal *de Fabert* liv'd, who was of all Men the least a Bigot, and most firmly settled in the Principles of Honesty. The Protestants were very easy under his Government; but the Scene was chang'd after his Death (c). They met with great Molestation from This Jesuit, and were oblig'd to pay large Sums of Money, and to establish Funds, which put him in a Capacity of founding the College he had projected. He publish'd a Scheme to which Mr *de St Maurice*, Professor in Divinity at *Sedan* (d), return'd an Answer which remain'd without Reply. He liv'd some Years at *Sedan*, where he promoted the Interests of his Order, and the business of making Proselytes, to the utmost of his Power.

(c) *Which happened in the Month of May 1662.*

(d) *He liv'd at Maestricht, upon his leaving France after the Revocation of the Edict of Nantes, till his Death, which fell out in the Year 1700, Aug. 20. Father Adam laid many Snares in his way, but he found an Adversary, who avoided them ingenuously.*

---

relates *Elias*'s Complaint, does not mention it as the Expression of a Man inspired, but as the Expression of a Man who was deceived, and to whom God revealed that he was in an Error. Therefore that Author did not deviate from the utmost Historical Exactness in reporting this False Complaint of *Elias*. These Gentlemen put the Public in mind, " That among the Propositions extracted from the Public " Lectures of the Jesuits of *Lowain*, acknowledged " by them, and censured by the Faculties of *Lowain* " and of *Douay*, in the Year 1588. are the two following: 1. *To constitute Holy-Scripture, it is not* " *necessary that the Words should be inspired by the* " *Holy Ghost.* II. *It is not necessary that the sacred* " *Authors should be immediately inspired by the Holy* " *Ghost, with every Truth and every Sentiment, con-* " *tained in their Writings.*" But, whatever Appellation these two Propositions deserve, yet they are very different from the Doctrine of Father *Adam*, and much less dangerous (9).

I have enlarged upon this, because I observed that it was an unknown Fact to those who, on Occasion of the *Sentiments of some Divines of* Holland, have lately wrote so much concerning the Inspiration of the sacred Books. All Communions have their Father *Adam*; there are Writers to be found every where to whom the same Lecture ought to be read, which was read to that Jesuit. The following are the Words of Mr *Saurin*, Minister of *Utrecht*, to Mr *Jurieu*, Minister of *Rotterdam* (10). " The " Comparison which *M. J.* made between the Imagination of the Prophets, which received Impressions from above, and a Wheel, which, being set " a-going, continues in Motion, though the Hand, " which impelled it, be removed (11), is another " Prophanation. For though he did not apply it to " the greater Prophets, it will necessarily lead to " them; unless he can shew that their Imagina- " tions, when wrought upon, did not run beyond " the Impression, by their own Impetuosity, like the " Wheel, which is put in Motion, as he says hap- " pened to other *inspired Persons*, in *whom God* " *produced these extraordinary Motions for Signs and* " *Prodigies, and who often went farther, than they* " *ought to do.* By what Mark would he have us " distinguish those Prophets, whom God sends for " Signs, if their Imagination, being once stirred, con- " founds what comes from God with their own Folly, " and if they report Truth and Falshood together, un- " der the external Appearance of Persons *out of their* " *Senses, and disordered in their Imaginations?* This " Mixture of Divine Inspiration, and Extravagancy " concealed under the exterior Resemblance of *Mad-* " *ness*, is inconsistent with the Idea which we have " of the Wisdom of God (12)." Some Persons are of so warm an Imagination, that they never report any thing that is told them without improving upon it: They only retain the thing, and never remember the Expressions of him, who related it to them: They substitute others in their room, cloathed with all their Fire, and consequently an unfaithful Representation of what was told them. These Persons easily believe that the Prophets and Apostles treated in the same manner the Idea's which the Holy Ghost communicated to them.

[F] *The Translation, which he had made, of the Hymns in French Verse* (13).] What is to found in relation to this in the *ninth* Part of the Difficulties proposed to Mr *Steyaert*, deserves to be reported. " No Liturgy, for these many Years, has been " more esteemed than that whereof the Title is: " *The Office of the Church, and of the Virgin,* " in Latin and French, with the Hymns translated " *into Verse*; otherwise called *les Heures de Port-* " *Royal*; or, the Port-Royal Primer. Four Editions were published of it in one Year; which " gave so much Jealousy to the Jesuits, that they left " nothing undone to cry it down. They made silly " Objections against it, which were immediately answered. They opposed to it Father *Adam*'s Prayer- " Book, under the Name of *Les Heures Catholiques*, " *the Catholic Primer*, as if the other was Heretical. The Hymns in it were also translated into " Verse, but so ridiculously, that it only served to " falsе the Credit of those of the *Port-Royal*. Lastly, " they informed against them to the Inquisition of " *Rome*, and made use of all their Credit to have " them condemned there (14)." Cardinal *Spada* intimated to Mr *de St Amour*, that if that Work of Father *Adam* was presented to the Tribunal of the Inquisition, they would condemn it. Mr *de St Amour* answered, That *if the Primer, which be defended, was to be decried. - - - - they might as well condemn it without that of Father* Adam: *And that he did not think it proper to accustom those Fathers to compose a silly Book, whenever they saw a good one appear, which did not please them, in hopes of having them both condemned, under pretence of holding the Balance even, and of keeping both Parties in Peace* (15).

[G] *Begun in* 1650. *and ended in* 1651.] Father *Sotuel* mentions but five of Father *Adam*'s Works. The last is his Answer to a Letter of Mr *Daillé*, which came out in 1660. These are the Titles of his other Books: *Calvinus à seipso & à S. Augustino profligatus*, (Calvin *defeated by himself and St* Austin) Parisiis 1650. in 8vo. *Psalmi Davidis Latinè & Gallicè cum Canticis undecim quibus utitur Ecclesia*, (*The Psalms of* David *in Latin and French, with eleven Hymns used by the Church*) Parisiis 1651. in 12mo. *Fidelium regula ex Sacra Scriptura & sanctis Patribus deprompta*, (*A Guide to the Faithful, extracted from the Sacred Scriptures, and the Holy Fathers;*) Parisiis 1651. in 12mo. *Preces Catholicæ Latinè & Gallicè*. (*Catholic Prayers in Latin and French*.) Parisiis 1651. in 8vo. and 12mo.

(9) *See Mr Simon's Answer to the Opinions of some Divines of Holland, cap. 12. and his Critical History of the New Testament, cap. 23. the Bibliotheque Universelle, Tom. 10. pag. 132. Tom. 11. p. 80. and Tom. 19. pag. 499.*

(10) *In* 1692.

(11) *See the 20th Pastoral Letter of* 1689.

(12) *Saurin. Examination of Mr* Jurieu's *Doctrine, designed as an Answer to a Libel entitl'd, Mr* Jurieu's *Second Apology, pag. 21.*

(13) *See M. Daillé's Reply, Part 2. pag. 19. and Part 3. pag. 234, & 424.*

(14) *Difficultes proposed to Mr Steyaert, part 9. pag. 42.*

(15) *Ibid. pag. 45.*

[H] *An*

ADAM.

Power. At length, the Government itself was disgusted at him; and, whether it was that they dreaded his bold and intriguing Spirit, or that they perceiv'd, that his Manner of Preaching had not all the Gravity requisite in a Place, where there was a *Protestant* University, they were pleas'd that his Superiors recall'd him: I have been told, that some Instances were made for it. He had been sent to preach at *Loudun*, while the *Protestants* held a National Synod there, about the end of the Year 1659. It is likely, this engag'd him in the composing of a Work, which made him known to the *Protestants* of *France*, more than any thing else, and more than many Authors of the First Rank are known to them. A Minister of *Poictiers* (e) having chang'd his Religion, a little after the breaking up of that Synod, wrote a Letter, wherein he maliciously censur'd the Fact, which That Assembly had enjoyn'd all the Reform'd Churches of the Kingdom to keep (f). Mr *Daillé*, who had been Moderator of the Assembly, answer'd his Letter. The other reply'd; Father *Adam* would engage in the Controversy, and publish'd an Answer to Mr *Daillé*'s Writing in the Year 1660 [H]. Mr *Daillé* reply'd to them both in one Book. Perhaps he never succeeded better than upon this Occasion, nor was any Piece so much read by all sorts of Persons among the *Protestants*; which is the Reason, why Father *Adam*, who appears almost in every Period in it, and often under such a Character as makes an Impression, is more known to them than an hundred Authors, who surpass him. This Work of Mr *Daillé* remain'd without Reply [I], and it is not to be wonder'd at: They, who ought to have answered it, were inferior to such an Adversary, who could have triumphed over them even in a bad Cause. I do not know in what Year Father *Adam* was Procurator of the Province of *Champagne* at *Rome*; the *Bibliotheque* of the Jesuits does not remark it (g); but it informs me, that in 1674. he was Superior of the *Maison Professe* at *Bourdeaux*. I think he died in that Employ about the Year 1680. He publish'd some Controversial Sermons on the *Eucharist*, which was the *Gospel of the Day* all over *France*, during the Quarrel between Mr *Arnaud* and Mr *Claude*; I say, he publish'd them since the Impression of Father *Sotuel*'s Work, and I think he preach'd them in the height of the Contest. They are not ill turn'd, but they are a little too Dramatic, Mr *Claude* being sometimes introduc'd as speaking in them. I say this only upon hear-say. Father *Adam* pass'd through the hands of Father *Jarrige*, but met with a milder Treatment, than from many others, and came off at a small Expence [K]. He was not the first who spoke

(e) *His Name was Mr* Cottibi.

(f) *See Mr* Daillé's *Life pag.* 33, &c.

(g) Rexit Collegium Sedanense in Provincia Campaniæ, à qua electus est Procurator ad Urbem. ---- He govern'd the College of Sedan in the Province of Campania, from whence he was elected Procurator for the City. Sotuel Biblioth. Soc. Jesu, pag. 397.

[H] *An Answer to Mr* Daillé's *Writing in the Year* 1660.] Father *Sotuel* entitled that Work, *Responsum ad Epistolam D. Allii Ministri Charentonensis Haeretici*. This is to latinize Mr *Daillé*'s Name after a wretched manner, and is a Sign that Father *Sotuel* read but few Books of Controversy. For is there any Controvertist, to whom Mr *Daillé*'s Latin Works are unknown, and who consequently does not know that That Minister's Name in *Latin* is *Dallæus*? They, who have a confused Notion, that there was a Minister of *Charenton*, whose Name was Mr *Allix*, would believe without Hesitation, that Father *Adam* wrote a Book against him, if they had no other Light than what the Article of that Jesuit affords in the Continuator of *Alegambus*; and thus the least Mistake in Proper Names is enough to lead the Reader into an Error. Any one, who should once mistake Mr *Allix* for the *Allius* of that Continuator, might very well give him a place in the Catalogue of the *Famous Children*, and send him to Mr *Baillet* (16) as an Additional Article; for he would imagine that That Book was printed in the Year 1660. and refuted by a famous Jesuit.

[I] *This Work of Mr* Daillé *remained without Reply.*] The Curious will be glad to see here what the Son of that Learned Minister observed concerning This Book. He says, "It is in every body's hands, "and was so well received, that two Editions have "already been made of it. Those of our Communion, "for whom it was chiefly composed, find, with Sa"tisfaction, most of our Controversies treated in it "after a manner very proper to instruct them, and "our Religion cleared from every thing which it's "Enemies commonly charge it with. And if we "may draw any advantage from the Silence of our "Adversaries, it seems as if they had condemn'd "themselves, seeing hitherto neither of them have "oppos'd any thing against it; tho' they often pro"mis'd the contrary, and have been reproach'd for "it several times (17)". Mr *Daillé*, the Son, has mention'd one thing, which clearly insinuates, that Father *Adam* was the Converter of the Minister *Cottibi*. It ought, therefore, to be taken Notice of, as one of the great Actions of the Hero of this Article. Let us hear then Mr *Daillé*'s Historian once more. "Not only the new converted *Roman*, who was the

(16) *He published a Book intituled,* Of the Children which became famous by their Studies or their Writings.

(17) *Abridgment of Mr* Daillé's *Life, printed in* 1670.

"Party concerned, defended himself by publishing a "large Answer; but as if his Cause had not been se"cure enough in his own Hands, a famous Jesuit "came to his Assistance, of whom some of his Com"munion said, that he was the first Man of the "World only by his Name. The Reader will easily "see, that Father *Adam* is meant by this, who, to de"fend his PROSELYTE, published a second An"swer at the same time, of the same Size, and Force "with his.

The Phrase, *First Man*, made use of in the above Passage, supply'd me in the first Edition of this Dictionary, with a Marginal Note, which shall make, at present, part of the body of this Column. It is as follows: "I have heard say, that the Queen-Mother "having asked a great Lord, who attended her to "one of Father *Adam*'s Sermons, what he thought of "it; he thanked her for his having been so well "convinced by it of the Hypothesis of the *Pra-Ada*"*mites*. Being desired to explain this Riddle, he "answered, *This Sermon convinces me that Adam is* "*not the first Man of the World*." You will find this Story in the Continuation of the *Menagiana* (18); and you will farther be informed, that the great Lord, who gave the Queen this Answer, was the Prince de *Guemené*, and that the Sermon which gave occasion to the Jest, *was very ill received both by the City and the Court* (19). Father *Adam* made *a very odious Compa*"*rison in it between the Parisians and the Jews, who cru*"*cified our Lord*. He compared the *Queen* to the *Virgin*; and Cardinal *Mazarine* to *St* John *the Evangelist*. Note that others ascribe this Witticism to *Benserade*. Read his *Life* before the last Edition of his Works (20).

[K] *Came off at a small Expence.*] I find three Passages relating to this, in the Works of the Ex-Jesuit *Jarrige*. The first is as follows: *Father* John Adam, *one of the best Preachers they have, interpre*"*ted the Treatise of Generation to one Ursuline of the* "*Convent of St* Macaire, *and gave as exact a Descrip*"*tion of the Parts, which contribute to the Procreation* "*of Children, as the Sieur* du Laurens *in his Anatomy* (21). The second contains these Words; *All those* "*who were of the College of Poictiers in the Year* 1646. *know the Quarrel between* John Adam *and* James Biroat. *They attacked each other in such an hostile man*"*ner,*

(18) *Page* 30. *of the Edition of* Holland.

(19) *It was a Sermon on the Passion, preached by Father A. dam at St* Germain de l'Auxerrois.

(20) *That of the Year* 1697.

(21) Jarrige, *the Jesuit placed on the Scaffold, cap.* 1.

ADAM.

spoke disrespectfully of St *Austin* [L], and who endeavour'd to persuade, that St *Paul* often carry'd his Subject farther than it wou'd bear [M], thro' too lively an Imagination.

(22) Ibid.

(23) Jarrige, *Answer to James Beaulieu*, cap. 14.

A Doubt proposed to the Casuists on an Anatomical Curiosity.

(24) See Sarrau's Letter, pag. 196.

(25) *Defence of St Austin against Father Adam*, pag. 24.

ner, that, by the Providence of God, all their Impurities came to Light, and James Biroat remained convicted, &c. (22) The third informs us (23), that *John Adam, the most excellent of their Preachers, was the Son of a Taylor.* Of these three Passages, the first alone can hurt the Memory of Father *Adam*: for the second makes the Impurities, which were discovered in consequence of their Quarrel, fall on *Biroat*'s Head alone. Thus all, that the scandalous Chronicle, and private Memoirs, had revealed to Father *Jarrige,* concerning Father *Adam*, is reduced to some Lectures of Anatomy read to a Nun, on the Generation of Children. Once again, this is to come off cheaply out of the Hands of *Jarrige*. This will be allowed me by any one, who reflects but the least on the Character of that Author's Works. If he had told us the Nun's Age, we might form a better Judgment of the Nature of the Offence. To discourse on such Points before a young Nun is doubtless a great Sin, because it is morally impossible that such a Conversation might excite in her impure Thoughts; but I would willingly have a Casuist of good Sense, who is neither of too loose, nor too rigid Morals, examine this Question : *Would a Nun of such an advanced Age, that she could bear a Lecture of Anatomy on the Organs of Generation, with the same Indifference as an Explication of the Parts of the Ear, commit a Sin by her Curiosity in hearing such a Lecture ?* I believe it will be granted me, that it is very lawful for a Woman, of what Condition soever, to be acquainted with all that is said concerning the *Circulation of the Blood* : It is no Sin for her to know that the most subtle Parts of the *Chyle* pass from the *Intestines* into the *Lacteal Veins,* and from thence successively into the *Reservoir of the Chyle,* into the *Ductus Thoracicus,* into the *subclavian Vein,* into the *hollow Vein,* into the right *Ventricle* of the *Heart,* into the *Artery* of the *Lungs,* into the *Vein* of the Lungs, into the left *Ventricle* of the *Heart,* and into the *great Artery.* There is no harm in her understanding the opening and shutting of the *Valves*, which are at the Extremities of the Veins and of the Arteries, the *Anastomoses,* the Secretion of the *Urine,* &c. Why then would it be criminal in her to finish her *Course of Anatomy,* and to acquaint herself minutely with the Structure both of the Internal and external Parts, designed for the Procreation of Children? The Crime cannot consist in the bare Knowledge of these things; it must consist then in the impure Thoughts which might accompany, precede, and follow such a Study: But I suppose, in the present Case, the Person to be as calm, as if she was studying the Anatomy of the *Ear*. This is the point, on which the Argument must turn. I do not set up here for a Casuist, but leave the Question to be decided by those, to whom it properly belongs; and shall only remark, that, for the greater Security of their Virtue, it is better, that Persons, who are not of a Profession, which obliges them to know these things, and chiefly those, who have made a Vow of Chastity, should never have such a Curiosity, or ever satisfy it : so that Father *A. dam* could not have owned the Fact, without acknowledging that he had committed a Fault. The most charitable Construction is, that his Pupil had a mind to apply this Maxim : *Amare licet, si potiri non licet. Dum caremus veris, gaudia falsa juvent.— We may love, tho' we can't enjoy; and, whilst we are deprived of real Pleasures, let us divert our selves with imaginary ones.*

[L] *He was not the first, who spoke disrespectfully of St* Austin.] Mr *Sarrau* in a Letter to Mr *de Saumaise* in 1646, tells him that the Jesuits affirmed every day from the Pulpit, that St *Austin* was not a Rule of Faith, and that he had advanced many things indiscreetly, to clear himself from the Objections, which were made to him. *Non est hic Pater regula fidei. Ut se expediret ab argumentis haereticorum sui temporis multa liberius & inconsideratius dixit quibus non tenemur* (24). Father *Adam,* four Days after his Sermon, confessed to a Person, who represented to him the Prejudice his Sermon might cause, *That* Gabriel à Porta, *a* Jesuit, *said often, that it were to be wished that St* Austin *had never wrote concerning Grace* (25). Some Divines had very freely declared, long before the Birth of *Jansenism,* that St *Austin* had pushed

things too far, and that when he determined to oppose certain Errors, he receded so far from them, that he generally ran into the opposite Extream : For Example, when he opposed the Error of the *Pelagians*, he seemed to incline too much towards that of the *Manichees*; and, in opposing the *Manichees,* he seemed to adopt the Heresy of *Pelagius.* An *Irishman*, whose Name is *Paul Leonard,* cites *Genebrard, Cornelius Mussus,* Bishop of *Bitonto, Cajetanus,* and *Sixtus Sinensis,* for this (26). But Father *Annat* cites many others in the same Book; wherein he endeavours to prove that St *Austin* is not of *Jansenius*'s Opinion (27). See what Father *Norris* answered to that great Cloud of Witnesses, produced against the great Bishop of *Hippo.* Some Protestants are not far from the same Thought, that St *Austin* over-strained things. I do not speak of the *Philosophical Commentary* (28), wherein Father *Adam*'s Judgment is approved in some measure; nor of the *Bibliotheque Universelle* (29), wherein St *Austin* is represented just as Father *Adam* could have desired it : I speak of Mr *Daillé*, who not only involves St *Austin* in the general Accusation he raises against the Fathers, of seeming to fall down one Precipice, when they would shun another (30), but charges him likewise with having treated his Subjects too much after the fluctuating manner of the *Academic Philosophers* (31). A little Book was published some time ago, entituled, *An important Advice to Mr* Arnaud, *on a Project of a new Bibliotheque of* Jansenist *Authors*; which speaks of a third Party then forming, which was to be neither *Jansenist,* nor *Molinist,* and which would place St *Austin* between Heaven and Earth, neither too high, nor too low. Such a Medium would reconcile Animosities, if People would but be reasonable. Upon this Scheme, every one would be at liberty to be *Jansenist* or *Molinist,* as he pleased. Ought it not to suffice the Jesuits that St *Austin* is not a Rule of Faith? Or do they require more in the Books, out of which the Deputies of the *Jansenists* extracted above an hundred Propositions levelled against the Authority of this Father? (32)

[M] *To persuade, that St* Paul *often carried his Subject farther than it would bear.*] There is a Passage of Father *Cauffin* in the Censure of Father *Adam*'s Sermon (33) where St *Paul* and St *Austin* are compared to "two great Seas, which pour so violently over one "Shore, by the impetuosity of the Wind, that they "seem as if they would leave the other dry for a "while ; but as the Ocean after having spread itself "largely on one side, returns within the Bounds pre- "scribed to it by God ; so these, after having launch'd "out against the rebellious Spirits, which rise against "the Truth, return to a peaceable Equality, to edify "the House of God *." This is that Wheel which takes more Turns than it is commanded, to which we have seen that Minister compare the prophetic Spirit (34). St *Paul* and St *Austin* overflow their Banks sometimes, but, like the Tide, they return afterwards to the Bounds which God has set them. A fine way of answering all the Passages of St *Paul* which displease ! It is but saying he had then overflowed all the Country, and that his Return must be expected into the Channel, which God had allotted him. Sir *Edwin Sandis* informs me of a thing, which is too much to the Purpose to be omitted here. He says (35), *I have it from very good Hands, that in Italy they have such a lively Jealousy against some Parts of the Scripture, and chiefly against the Epistles of St* Paul, *that not long ago some* Jesuits, *exalting St* Peter *as an excellent Man, in their public Sermons, and among their Favourers in private Conversation, censured St* Paul *as a Person of a petulant and hot Brain, who in most of his Disputes had suffered himself to be carried away so immoderately by the Sallies of his Zeal, and the Acrimony of his Spirit, that no great account was to be made of his Assertions; and that the reading of him is very dangerous, favouring of Heresy in divers Places; and perhaps it had been better that he had never writ. In conformity to which I have heard Roman Catholics say many times, that they have already often consulted among themselves about censuring and reforming St* Paul's *Epistles. Though, to speak my Sentiments, I cannot give credit to it; the*

(26) *Paul Leonard's Answer to the Expositulat. contra Scientiam mediam,* pag. 117, 118.

(27) *Annati Augustinus vindicatus à Bajanis.*

(28) *Part* 3. pag. 4. *See also the Supplement*, p. 2.

(29) *Tom.* 14. pag. 287.

(30) Daillé *of the Use of the Fathers,* pag. 153.

(31) Ibid. pag. 391.

(32) *In* 1653. *See the Historical Memorial concerning the five Propositions,* p. 82.

(33) Pag. 17.

* *In his Holy Court, Tom.* 3. Maxim 6. *of Praedestin.* §.

(34) *Above, how it is the end of the Remark* [E].

(35) *Account of Religion,* chap. 26. pag. 245.

VOL. I.   E e   *Undertaking*

Undertaking in itself being so blasphemous and abominable, and the Scandal so desperate in these Times. But, however, it is certain, that they esteem St Paul below all the sacred Writers: And I can affirm from my own Knowledge and Hearing, that some of them teach in their Pulpits, that that holy Apostle had no other Assurance of his Doctrine, than the Conferences he had with St Peter; and that he durst not publish his Epistles before St Peter had approved them. Behold the Absurdity of these Men! If the Epistles of St Paul were approv'd by St Peter, they are as authentic as can be desired.

ADAM (MELCHIOR) liv'd in the XVIIth Century. The indefatigable Care he took to collect, frame, and publish the Lives of a great number of learned Persons, deserves, that somebody should do him the like Office; and yet I think no body has yet done it. Mr *Moreri* undertook to record him, but he forgot his Promise when the Time of performing it presented itself (*a*). The Promise and the Non-performance have subsisted hitherto in all the Editions of his Dictionary (*b*). One would think it difficult to forget a Writer, to whom we are oblig'd for so many Articles. As for me, who find my self very much indebted to his Labours, I would testify my Gratitude to him by giving the Particulars of his Life at large, but I can no where find the necessary Materials for it. All that I have met with is as follows: MELCHIOR ADAM was born in the Territory of *Grotkaw* in *Silesia*, and perform'd his Studies in the College of *Brieg*, where the Dukes of that Name took great Care to encourage Literature, and chiefly the Reform'd Religion (*c*), I mean that, which a *Roman*-Catholic would call *Calvinism*. The young Man learn'd to be a good Protestant in that School. To continue his Studies, he had his Share in the Bounty, which a great Lord (*d*) bestow'd for the Maintenance of a certain number of Scholars. He became Rector of a College at *Heidelberg* (*e*), and it was in that City that he publish'd the first Volume of his *Illustrious Men* in the Year 1615. The first Volume, which contain'd the *Philosophers*, and, under that Name, the Poets, the Humanists, the Historians, &c. was follow'd by three others: That, which contain'd the *Divines*, was printed in the Year 1619. That of the *Civilians* follow'd it; and lastly, That of the *Physicians*. These two last were printed in 1620. All the Learned, whose Lives we see in these Four Volumes in 8vo. liv'd in the XVIth. Century, or in the beginning of the XVIIth. and are *Germans* or *Dutchmen*; but there is a Series of twenty Divines of other Countries, whose Lives our Author publish'd separately in the Year 1618. All his Divines are *Protestants*. Although he compos'd but few Lives, yet he bestow'd much time on that Work, and took great pains with it, because he abridg'd the Writings, which furnish'd him with the Materials; whether they were Lives properly so call'd, or Funeral Orations, Programmas, Elogies, Prefaces, or Family Memoirs. I say nothing of the Summaries, which he plac'd in very great numbers in the Margin. He omitted some Persons, who were no less considerable, than many of those he has taken notice of [*A*]. The *Lutherans* are not pleas'd with him (*f*): they find him too partial, and will not allow his Collection to serve as a Rule to judge of the *German Literati* by (*g*). He died in the Year 1622. He compos'd other Works [*B*]. Consult Mr *Baillet*, in the 177th and 178th pages of the 2d Tome of his *Judgment of the Learned*.

[*A*] *He omitted some Persons, who were no less considerable, than many of those he has taken notice of.*] He acknowledges this himself; but he declares that there was no Affectation in it, and that a want of Memoirs was the only Cause of it. He proposed to himself to supply this Defect in some other Volumes. These are his Words; " Quædam mihi monendus aut rogandus " es, mi lector. Primum ne præteritos aut omissos " non paucos queraris, haud Indignos, qui hoc in " theatro apparerent. In eo mea, mi lector, culpa " nulla est: sed penuria fecit historiæ; quam nancisci " nullam uspiam potui. Malui itaque prorsus tacere " de multis præstantibus viris; quam, ut ille de Car- " thagine, pauca dicere, & trita illa *Natus est; obiit; " scribere*. Suppleri tamen poterit hic defectus, vo- " lente Deo, & mutuas operas tradentibus bonis pa- " trisque amantibus; si hujus Voluminis tomus se- " cundus fuerit adornatus. Quod idem dictum volo, " de reliquis vitis *Jurisconsultorum & Politicorum, " Medicorum, ac Philosophorum* (1).——*I have some " things, Reader, to inform you of, and some things " to request of you. First, that you would not com- " plain of the Omission of many Persons, not unwor- " thy to appear upon this Stage. The Fault, Reader,* " is not my own, but is owing to the want of Materials, " which I could by no means procure. I chose therefore " to say nothing of many excellent Persons, rather, " than like him of Carthage, to say but little, and to " write down the thread-bare Account. He was born; " he died. However, this Defect may be supplied, " God willing, by the Assistance of good Men, " and Lovers of their Country; when the second " Tome of this Work shall be prepared. Which No- " tice I desire may be understood to regard the other " Lives of Civilians, Politicians, Physicians, and Phi- " losophers."

[*B*] *He compos'd other Works.*] To wit, *Apographum monumentorum Heidelbergensium. Notæ in Orationem Julii Cæsaris Scaligeri pro M. T. Cicerone contra Ciceronianum Erasmi. Parodiæ & Metaphrases Horatianæ* (2). It is not true, as is asserted in the Catalogue of *Oxford*, that he was the Author of an *Historia Ecclesiastica Ecclesiæ Hamburgensis & Bremensis*. It is the Work of a Canon of *Bremen*, whose Name is *Adam*, who lived in the XIth Century. *Cenringius* and *Possevinus*, who placed him in the Xth, are mistaken. See *Molleris*, at the 65th Page of the first part of the *Isagoge ad Historiam Chersonesi Cimbricæ*.

ADAM, a Joyner of *Nevers*, and a *French* Poet. Look for BILLAUT.

ADAMITES (*a*), a ridiculous Sect, a Branch of the *Carpocratians* and *Valentinians* (*b*). *Theodoret* assigns one *Prodicus* as it's Founder [*A*]. St *Epiphanius* pretends, that they deriv'd their Name of *Adamites* from

[*A*] *Theodoret assigns one Prodicus as it's Founder* (1).] *Baronius* places him in the Year 120, and makes him more antient than *Valentinus;* which induces him in another place (2) to censure those, who reckon him among the Disciples of *Valentinus*. If this be true, *Lambertus Danæus*, whom I have cited, deserves no Credit: I shall speak of this *Prodicus* in a separate Article.

ADAMITES.

from one *Adam*, who liv'd at the time, when they were so call'd (c). It is more likely, that *Adam*, the Stock of all Human kind was the Original, whence this Name was borrowed, as St *Austin* informs us (d); for these Wretches imitated the Nakedness, in which our first Parents liv'd, during the State of Innocency, and condemn'd Marriage, because *Adam* did not know *Eve* till after his Fall, and Expulsion from Paradise. They believ'd, then, that if Man had persevered in his Innocency, there would have been no Marriage. Therefore they made Profession of Continency, and a Monastic Life (e). As for their Nakedness, they only observ'd it, when they were assembled for the Exercise of their Religion (f) [B]. Their Place of meeting was in a Stove, where they expell'd the Cold by means of a Fire kindled under the Chamber; they put off their Cloaths upon going into it; and Men and Women sat together, the Ecclesiastics as well as the Laity, in the same condition as when they came out of their Mothers Womb. They seated themselves without Order upon Benches, rais'd one above the other; then they perform'd their Devotions; after which they put on their Cloaths again, and went home. Whoever committed an offence, was no more receiv'd into their Assembly [C]. They said, that such an One, having, like *Adam*, eat of the forbidden Fruit, was to be driven, like him, out of Paradise; so these People call'd their Church. This is St *Epiphanius*'s Account of this Sect [D], not founded on the Authority of Books, or the Report of any one among them; but on the Relation of some other Persons. He does not know, whether this Sect was entirely abolish'd in his time, or whether it was yet subsisting

(c) Epiphan. in Synopsi Tomi 2. lib. 2. p. 397.
(d) August. de Hæres. cap. 31.
(e) See the Remark [C].
(f) Epiph. Hæres. 52.

[B] *They only observ'd it; when they were assembled for the Exercise of their Religion.*] *Danæus* is in the wrong, then, when he places among their Errors, that Christians of both Sexes ought to go naked in the Streets. *Oportere Christianos homines versari in* PUBLICO, *in cœtu Ecclesiæ, in precibus, nudos, sive mares sint sive fæminæ* (3).

[C] *Was no more receiv'd into their Assembly.*] St *Epiphanius* testifies, that these Persons profess Continency, and the monastic Life, and that they condemn'd Marriage. Μοναζοντες τε και εγκρατευομενοι εισιν, και γαμον μη δεχομενοι (4). — *Monachorum ac continentium instituta sectantur, nuptiasque condemnant.* So that we cannot doubt, but that their Discipline condemn'd Fornication and Adultery, and that they excommunicated those from their Assemblies, who were guilty of these Crimes. And it is observable, that though this ancient Father will not allow of what the *Adamites* pretended, namely, that they stripp'd themselves naked, because they were no more ashamed of their Nakedness, than *Adam* was; I say, it is remarkable, that though St *Epiphanius* rather attributes their Conduct to an insatiable Lust, which required Incitements in view (5); yet he does not say, that any impure Actions were committed in their Assemblies. So that *Baronius* falsly charges him with calling their Assemblies Brothels, *lupanaria*. He made use of the Terms φωλεος *latibulum*, and σπηλυγγα, *caverna* (6), implying a Den, Cave, or Cavern; as appears by his remarking, that it is the Name he would give to Hæretical Conventicles; where he plainly alludes to what is said in the Gospel, that They (*the Buyers and Sellers in the Temple*) had made the House of God *a Den of Thieves* (7). The Notion of corporeal Impurity, or carnal Commerce between the Sexes, has no room here. Father *Gaultier* is much in the wrong then, to say, in citing St *Epiphanius*, That the *Adamites*, leaving their Cloaths at the Door of their Assemblies, mix'd indifferently with the Women, which fell in their Way, *mulieribus promiscuè utentes* (8). As for the Citation of *Alphonsus de Castro*, which we see after That of St *Epiphanius*, in the Margin of Father *Gaultier*, it only multiplies the Number of False Accusers. *Lambertus Danæus*, who accuses the *Adamites* of the same Impurity, does not cite St *Epiphanius*, but *Clemens Alexandrinus*, quoted by *Theodoret*. " Extinctis " in suo cœtu lucernis, promiscuè coëunt, quemad- " modum ex Clemente Strom. notat Theodoretus (9). " — *Putting out the Lights in their Assemblies,* " *they mix promiscuously, as* Theodoret *remarks from* " Clement. Strom." It will soon appear that this Passage was not produc'd to the purpose. It is something strange, that neither St *Epiphanius*, nor St *Austin*, heard of any such thing; for Fame seldom lets such Transactions die, when once it has them in her Power, unless they are found to be notoriously false. Yet it does not always happen that Fame loses it's hold even in this Case. See, in the following Remark, the means of reconciling these two Fathers with *Clemens Alexandrinus*.

(3) Danæus, in August. de Hær. cap. 31. fol. 83.
(4) Epiphan. in Synopsi Tom. 1. lib. 2. pag. 397.
(5) Εχουσι ασφαλιας ἀ-ξονσιν αφορμας αφθαρ-σιαν, εμπα-θωνος την θελειν. Id initiatos, libidini tribuunt quæ ejusmodi o-culis illece-bras objicit. Epiphan. Hær. 52. pag. 460.
(6) Ibid. pag. 459.
(7) Matth. xxi. 12.
(8) Gaulter. Tab. Chronogr. Seculo 2. cap. 33.
(9) Danæus, ubi supra.

[D] *This is St* Epiphanius's *account of this Sect.*] He does not say, that every Man seiz'd his Woman in their Assemblies: This has been touch'd upon in the preceeding Remark. Neither does he impute to them the Heresies of *Prodicus* which Father *Gaultier* gives a List of (10), and which *Moreri* imputes to them in general. But *Moreri* is not so much to blame in this, as in asserting, That St *Epiphanius* calls their Temples *infamous Places on account of the abominable Crimes, which they committed in those Caves of Horror and Prostitution*. This Author adds, That they rejected Prayer. *Danæus* says the same, on the Credit of *Clemens Alexandrinus*. " Deum " à nobis precandum esse orandum esse negant, quia " scit ipse per se quibus egeamus. Clemens hoc de " illis tradit. Lib. 7. Strom. (11) — *They deny,* " *that we ought to pray to God, because of himself* " *he knows our Wants*. Clemens *reports this of* " *them in his* Strom. Book 7." Yet St *Epiphanius* and St *Austin* say the contrary; Γυμνοι γαρ δε ἐν μητροπι --- συνάγονται, και ἐπως τας ἀναγνωσεις και ευχας και τας ὁσας ἐντελπων. *They assemble, as naked as they came out of their Mothers Wombs, and in this Condition they read and say their* PRAYERS, *and perform their other Exercises of Religion.* Thus speaks St *Epiphanius*, in the Summary of the 2d Book of the 1st Tome: And St *Augustin*'s Words are, " Nudi itaque " mares fœminæque conveniunt, nudi lectiones au- " diunt, nudi ORANT, nudi celebrant sacramenta " (12). — *The Men and Women meet together na-* " *ked; they bear Sermons naked; they say their* " *Prayers naked; and administer the Sacraments* " *naked.*" The means of reconciling these two last Fathers with *Clemens Alexandrinus* would be, to suppose that the *Adamites*, to whom the latter gives *Prodicus* for Founder, did not follow all the Errors of *Prodicus*. This Supposition has nothing extraordinary in it. Generally thirty or forty Years are sufficient to render the Principles of a Sect very unlike those of it's Founder. Therefore it betrays want of exactness to attribute all the Extravagancies of *Prodicus* to the *Adamites*, under pretence that he was their Founder. In truth it is certain, from the Testimony of St *Epiphanius* and St *Austin*, that they stript themselves quite naked in their Assemblies; but *Clemens Alexandrinus* (so far is he from saying any such thing of the Followers of *Prodicus*) observes, that before they came to an Engagement, they caus'd the Candles to be taken away, which might have put them to the blush. Τα κατασχουσιν αὐτων την πορνειαν ταυτην δικαιοσυνην ἐποδιδον τοιπαμενος φησι της τε λυχνε παρεπχυη μιγνυσθαι (13). *Lumine amoto, quod eorum fornicatorium hanc justitiam pudore afficiebat, eversa lucerna coire.* So that *Danæus* had no Reason to apply to the *Adamites*, what that Father reported of the Followers of *Prodicus*. In a Word, when I consider the Calumnies of the Pagans against the Primitive Christians, and those of the Catholics against the Protestants, as to their Nocturnal Assemblies, I do not readily believe all the Imputations of the prevailing Party.

(10) Ubi sup.
(11) Ibid.
(12) Augustin. de Hæres. cap. 31.
(13) Clem. Alex. Strom. lib 3. pag. 431.

[E] *In*

ADAMITES.

subsisting. *Evagrius* makes mention of some Monks of *Palestine*, who, thro' an excess of Devotion, and to mortify their Bodies, went, Men as well as Women, into solitary Places, quite naked, excepting those Parts, which Modesty forbids to name; where they expos'd themselves in a very strange manner [*E*] to the Extremities both of Heat and Cold (g). We shall speak of the *Modern* ADAMITES, under the Article PICARDS. I find, that both Catholics and Protestants reproach each other [*F*] with having *Adamites* among them: but perhaps neither Party has more reason than the other for this Charge. If I had no other Authority, than that of *Lindanus* (b), I shou'd scarce believe, that, in the year 1535, *Adamites* were seen in *Amsterdam*, among the richest and most noble Families, who ran about stark naked; some of whom were fanatical enough to climb up on Trees, where they waited in vain for Bread to fall from Heaven to them, till they fell themselves half dead to the ground. I shall quote an Author (i) in another place (k) who attests part of these Facts.

(g) Evagr. Hist. Eccl. lib. 1. cap. 21.

(h) Lindan. Dubitantii Dial. 2. pag. 171.

(i) Lambert. Hortens. in Hist. Tumult. Anabaptist.

(k) In the Remarks of the Article PICARDS.

[*E*] *In a very strange manner.*] They outdid the other Monks, whom the same *Evagrius* mentions; who, having no Garment of their own, (since the same, which one Monk wore one Day, serv'd another the next Day) had, at least, the use of some Garment (14). The Solitaries, of whom I speak, were satisfied with wearing only a Girdle, and as for the rest, they renounc'd Humanity as much as they could; they would not eat of the Food which serv'd other Men; but fed like Beasts, and eat but just as much as would keep them alive: At last they became like Beasts; their Figure alter'd, and their Sentiments also. When they saw other Persons, they ran away, and if they found themselves pursued, they fled, as fast as they could, to some inaccessible Hole. Some of them appeared in publick again, and pretended to be Fools, to shew the greater contempt of Glory. They went to eat in public Houses; they entered into the public Baths; they convers'd, and wash'd, with the other Sex; but with so much Insensibility, that neither the Sight, nor Touch, nor even the embraces of a Woman, caus'd any Emotion in them. They were Men with the Men, and Women with the Women; they would be of both Sexes. Μετὰ ἀνδρῶν δὲ ἄνδρες εἶναι, μετὰ γυναικῶν τὸ αὖ γυναῖκας, ἱκατέρας τε μετέχειν θέλειν φύσεως, καὶ μὴ μιᾶς εἶναι (15) — *Cum viris quidem viri sunt, fœminæ vero cum fœminis; non enim unius, sed utriusque simul sexûs, esse cupiunt*. It is likely they had not much trouble in counterfeiting the Fool, and that they were so in reality; we may, at least, apply to them what *Rutilius Numatianus* said, though unjustly, of all kinds of Solitaries :

Quænam perversi rabies tam stulta cerebri
Dum mala formides, nec bona posse pati (16) ?

What Madness 'tis, whilst Evil you avoid,
To fly the Good, and leave it unenjoy'd ?

Lastly, Their Nakedness was very contrary to the Principles of those *Religious*, of whom I shall speak in the following Remark, neither would it agree well with the Doctrine of Father *Sanchez*.

[*F*] *Reproach each other*] Mr *Moreri* assures us, that there are *Adamites* in England, *who hold their Assemblies by Night, and teach only these Words*, Swear, Forswear, *and do not discover the Secret*. It was proper to inform him, in the Edition of *Amsterdam*, that there were no such People in *England*, that the Civil Government there is too good to *suffer an Infamy of that nature, which could not be concealed, and that it is likewise very improbable, that there are any in* Poland; for he had said, that there are *still remaining some of these mistaken Pe.ple in that Country.* He could not defend himself, by saying that he does not pretend, that these People shew themselves naked in public, but only that they undress themselves in their Nocturnal Meetings, which the best Government may be ignorant of; I say, he could not alledge this in his Justification, since he just before mentioned the *Adamites of Bohemia*, who went always naked, as is pretended. So that, if Mr *Moreri* understood what he said, he must assert, that there are yet People in *England*, both Men and Women, who go always naked, out of a Principle of Religion. Now this is what the Government would not suffer, and cannot be ignorant of. Behold there are *Adamites* in *Protestant* Countries. I say nothing of those idle and ridiculous Stories concerning *Holland*, which are to be seen in the *Sorberiana*, pag. 17. Let us produce, on the other side, a Minister who says there are Monks in *Italy* call'd *Adamites*, who go naked, in consequence of the Vow they make, and in compliance with the most sacred Rules of their Order. " Ac ne nunc quidem, *says* " he (17), nomen ejus (hæresis Adamianorum) ex- " taret, nisi Monachi quidam, qui se falsò pietatis & " vitæ austeritatis prætextu commendant, horum hæ- " reticorum impudentes prorsùs mores retinuissent, " & inter sanctissima ordinis & regulæ suæ præcepta " posuissent, quales ii qui etiam nunc hodie Adamitæ " dicuntur, vigentque plurimum in Italia — Vivunt, " enim nudi, non necessitate quidem adacti vel inopia " vestimentorum, sed ex voti professione. —— *The very Name of this Heresy* (of the *Adamites*) *would be extinct, did not certain Monks, who recommend themselves under the false Pretence of Piety and Austerity of Life, retain the very impudent Manners of these Heretics, and place them among the most sacred Precepts of their Order and Institution ; such as are Those, who even at this time are called Adamites, and flourish chiefly in Italy. —— For they live naked, not compelled by Necessity, or for want of Garments, but in compliance with their Vow.* I wish he had been more eager to prove this Fact, than to make a Comparison between the Conduct of these People, and that of the ancient Monks, who never saw themselves naked (18), and who said, that a Man of their Profession could not contemplate his own Nudity, without behaving unworthy of himself (19). A modern Casuist, who is none of the most rigid (20), counts it nevertheless a venial Sin, *propriâ verenda aspicere ex quadam curiositate absque alia mala intentione* ; and a mortal Sin, *aspicere verenda alterius sexus, operta vestibus ita subtilibus, ut parum espectui obstent* (21). To see a Person, of a different Sex, swim naked, is, according to him, a mortal Sin. Two Men of a grave Character, as two Bishops, who should look upon each other naked, commit, says he (22), a mortal Sin. De Bernia tells us of a Man, who never handled his *Pudenda* without his Gloves (23). Why might not a Casuist require, that a Man should abstain from touching them naked, as well as from contemplating them naked ? An ancient Philosopher, thro' an Affectation of Chastity, never touched them with, or without a Glove ; he receded in that respect very far from the Principle of *Anacharsis* (24). This ancient Philosopher was the severe *Xenocrates*. *Aristoteles, irridens Chalcedonium Xenocratem, quod mejendo virilibus non admoverct manum, inquit,* " purâ quidem manus at inquinatâ " *mens* (25)."

We shall prove in the Remark [*N*] of the Article HADRIAN VI, that *la Mothe, le Vayer* ought not to have taken the Passage of *Bernia* in a literal Sense.

(14) Evagr. Hist. Eccl. lib. 1. c. 21.

(15) Ibid.

(16) Rutil. Itiner. lib. 1. ver. 445.

(17) Lamb. Danæus in Aug. Hær. cap. 31.

(18) Apud Socrat. Hist. Eccl. lib 4. cap. 23. & Sozomen. lib. 1. c. 13.

(19) See in the Historia Ladicrs of Balthasar Bonifacius, pag. 181. how St Jerome maintain'd, that a Virgin ought to blush at seeing certain naked, and some Examples of this quoted by Theodoret.

(20) Sanchez de Matrimon. lib. 9. Disputat. 46. n. 27, 28.

(21) Ibid. n. 25, 26.

(22) Ib. n. 27, 28.

(23) Apud la Mothe le Vayer, Hexam. Rust. pag. 79.

(24) Plutarch de Garrulitate, pag. 105, & Clemens Alexand. lib. 5. Stromat. pag. 568.

(25) Athen. lib. 12. p. 530.

ADONIS,

ADONIS.

(a) See the Article MYRRHA.
(b) Ovid. Metam. lib. 10. v. 337.
(c) Hygin. cap. 164.

ADONIS, Minion of the Goddess *Venus*, was the Son of *Cinyras* King of *Cyprus* [*A*]. The Poets have pretended, that *Myrrha* (*a*), that King's Daughter (*b*), became so desperately in Love with her Father, that she caus'd her self to be introduc'd into his Bed, without his knowing who she was. Some say she made use of the Artifice of *Lot*'s Daughters (*c*). *Adonis* was the Fruit of this Incest. He was perfectly beautiful, and appeared so lovely in the Eyes of *Venus*, that she stole him away [*B*], and devoted herself wholly to his Company. Heaven itself seem'd an unpleasant abode to her in Comparison of the Hills and Woods, where she follow'd *Adonis*, who was a great Hunter [*C*]. Judge whether the Poets did not exert all the Figures of their Art (*d*), to represent the inexpressible Grief, which seized the Heart of that Goddess, when a wild Boar had kill'd her dear *Adonis* [*D*]. Never was a Mourning

(d) Ovid's Metam. lib. 10. Bion εἰδύλλ. ἄδερ also εἰδύλλ. Μέ. Theocritus, εἰδύλλ. Μέ. and among the Moderns Mr Menage in his Greek Poems, pag. 167.

---

(1) See Meursius of the Island of Cyprus, lib. 2. cap. 9.
(2) Apollod. lib. 3. pag. 258.
(3) Metam. lib. 10. vers. 480, & 513.

[*A*] *The Son of* Cinyras *King of* Cyprus.] Almost all Authors agree that *Cinyras* reigned in that Island (1), though some have said, that he first reigned in *Assyria* (2). See the Article BYBLUS. *Ovid* makes him to be born in the Island of *Cyprus*; but he says, That *Myrrha*, flying from her Father who would have killed her, after he had discovered her Incest, travelled through *Arabia*, and was delivered of *Adonis*, in the Country of the *Sabæi* (3). He would have done well to have remarked in few Words, that *Cinyras* had past from the Island of *Cyprus* to *Arabia*, or that *Myrrha* had embarked in that Island. When *Adonis* was born, his Mother had been already metamorphosed into the Tree, from whence *Myrrh* distills. We understand from *Ptolomy*, the Son of *Hephæstion*, That *Venus*, seeking *Adonis*, of whose Death she had heard, found him at *Argos*, a City of *Cyprus*, in the Temple of *Erithian Apollo*. Whence some have affirmed, that he was killed in that Island. *Propertius* is of this Number, when he says in the thirteenth Elegy of the second Book,

Testis, qui niveum quondam percussit Adonim
Venantem Idalio vertice, durus aper.

Witness the cruel Boar, fated to kill
Adonis, hunting on th' Idalian *Hill.*

(4) Pausan. in Bœoticis.
(5) Strabo, lib. 16. pag. 520.
(6) Antonin. Liberalis, cap. 34.
(7) See Muncker's Notes on Hygin. cap. 58.

There was a Temple of *Adonis* and *Venus* at *Amathus*, in the Island of *Cyprus* (4). *Strabo* says, that *Byblus* was the Residence of King *Cinyras*, and that there were some Temples of *Adonis* to be seen there (5). Note, That *Antoninus Liberalis* relates, that *Myrrha*, whom he calls *Smyrna*, was born on Mount *Libanus*, and that her Father's Name was *Theias* (6). *Panyasis* plainly gave him the same Name, and not that of *Thoas*, as we read at present in *Apollodorus* (7). We read the same likewise in *Probus*, on the tenth Eclogue of *Virgil*, with this additional Circumstance, that the said *Thoas* was King of *Syria* and *Arabia*: *Probus* borrowed this from *Antimachus*.

[*B*] *She stole him away.*] This Fact was but little remarked by the ancient Writers: I wonder at it; for it was universally known. The Painters made it the Subject of their Pictures, as they did the Rape of *Ganymede*. This *Plautus* informs us of.

ME. Dic mihi; numquà vidisti tabulam pictam in
pariete,
Ubi aquila catamitum raperet, aut ubi Venus
Adoneum?

(8) Plaut. in Menæchmis Act. 1. Sc. 2. v. 34.

PE. Sæpe (8).

ME. *Tell me; did you never see a Picture on a Wall, where the Eagle carries away the Catamite, or Venus Adonis?*

PE. *Often.*

[*C*] *An unpleasant Abode to her in comparison of the —— Woods, where she followed Adonis, who was a great Hunter.*] Read this Passage of *Ovid*:

Abstinet & cœlo: cœlo præfertur Adonis:
Hunc tenet: huic comes est: assuetaque semper in
umbra
Indulgere sibi, formamque augere colendo,
Per juga, per silvas dumosaque saxa vagatur (9).

(9) Ovid. Metam. lib. 10. ver. 532.

Ev'n Heav'n itself with all it's Sweets unsought,
Adonis far a sweeter Heav'n is thought.
On him she hangs, and fonds with every Art;
And never, never knows from him to part.

She, whose soft Limbs had only been display'd
On rosie Beds beneath the Myrtle Shade,
Whose pleasing Care was to improve each Grace,
And add more Charms to an unrivall'd Face,
Now, buskin'd, like the Virgin Huntress, goes
Thro' Woods, and pathless Wilds, and Mountain
Snows.
EUSDEN.

Virgil represents *Adonis* under another Idea than that of a Hunter,

Nec te pœniteat pecoris, divine poeta,
Et formosus oves ad flumina pavit Adonis (10).

(10) Virgil. Ecl. 10. ver. 18.

The Sheep surround their Shepherd, as he lies:
Blush not, sweet Poet, nor the Name despise;
Along the Streams his Flock Adonis fed,
And yet the Queen of Beauty blest his Bed.
DRYDEN.

Few Authors, I think, have represented this Favourite of *Venus* under the Character of a Shepherd. *Servius*, upon this Passage, relates some Particulars no less different from the common Tradition, than This. Some have said, that he was inspired by the Muses with this Inclination for Hunting (11). It seems they bore a Grudge to *Venus*, for causing some of them to fall in Love with Mortals. To be revenged of her, they sung several Airs before *Adonis*, which gave him a violent Passion for Hunting. Perhaps he became odious to *Diana* upon this Account; for two of a Trade seldom agree. Whence some have said, that *Diana*'s Anger was the Occasion of a wild Boar's killing this Boy (12).

(11) Tzetzes on Lycophron.
(12) Apollod. lib. 3. pag. 258.

[*D*] *When a wild Boar had killed her dear Adonis.*] *Theocritus* feigns, that *Venus*, having caused the wild Boar to be brought before her, chid him roughly; but that he alledged in his Excuse the violent Passion, which had seized him at the Sight of so fine a Thigh: that he was eager to kiss it; but did it in too passionate a manner; that he was so displeased with himself for what he had done, that he thought his Tusks deserved to be cut off, and that he burnt them himself (13). Thus a learned and polite Writer (14) explained the last Verse of that Idyll of *Theocritus*. The Editions have it ἴσας τῆς ἴμερας, *exussit amores*; but he believes it should be read ἰδόντας, *dentes*, instead of ἴμερας. This cruel Kiss puts me in mind of a Thought of the Chevalier *Marini*: He introduces the God *Pan*, who boasts that the Spots which are seen in the Moon, are Impressions of the Kisses he gave it. Surely he attacked her very forcibly. What *Caresses!* by adding a little more to them, they would be like those of Apes, who, it is said, smother their young ones sometimes with embracing them. What would *Horace* have said to this, since upon a much slighter Occasion, he expresses himself thus,

(13) Theocrit εἰδύλλ. 31, or 30. according to other Editions.
(14) Mr de Longepierre: See his Translation of Bion, pag. 47. Edit. of Paris 1686.

sive puer furens
Impressit memorem dente labris notam.
Non si me satis audias
Speres perpetuum dulcia barbare
Lædentem oscula, quæ Venus
Quinta parte sui nectaris imbuit (15).

(15) Horat. Od. 13. lib. 1.

Or, when the ruffling amorous Youth
Hath press'd thy Lips with eager Tooth,
And left a Mark behind:

ADONIS.

(e) Servius in Eclog. 10.
Firm. Maternum. pag. 22.
Nonnus. Dionyf. l. 41.
Cyrillus in Eſai. n.

(f) Ptolem. Hephæſt. apud Phot. pag. 4 2.

(g) Διότι Βοι λομιδόνων Ἄφρο-δίτην ἀντὶ τῆς Ἄδονιδος μιδύως. Quod poſt congreſſum cum Adoni-de lavit am Venerem vidiſs et. Ibid.

Mourning more famous, and more immortaliz'd than this; Almoſt all the People in the World perpetuated the memory of it by a long Train of Anniverſary Ceremonies [E]. Some Authors ſay, that it was not a wild Boar, but a God under the Form of that Beaſt, who kill'd *Adonis*. According to ſome it was *Mars* (e); according to others *Apollo* (f). The former ſay, that *Mars* did it to ſatisfy his Jealouſy, and to be reveng'd of *Venus*, who preferr'd this Rival before him. The latter ſay, That *Apollo* was hurry'd to this Exceſs of Violence, to revenge his Son *Erymanthus*, who was ſtruck blind, for having ſeen *Venus*, while ſhe was bathing, being newly come from the Arms of her *Adonis* (g). The place of the Wound ſeems to indicate ſome principle of Jealouſy.

> Trux aper inſequitur, totoſque ſub inguine dentes
> Abdidit (b).
>
> *And now too late to fly the Boar he ſtrove,*
> *Who in his Groin his Tuſks impetuous drove.* EUSDEN.

(b) Ovid. Metam. lib. 10. ver. 715.

But the ſecond Tradition does not agree with their Account, who reported that *Adonis* was an Hermaphrodite, who enjoy'd *Venus* as a Male, and, as a Female, gave himſelf to *Apollo* (i). Others, without aſcribing to him both Sexes, have not ſcrupled to ſay that he was the Minion of *Venus* and *Bacchus* [F]. There is a Scholiaſt, who aſſures

(i) Prolem. Hephæſt. ubi ſupra, pag. 483.

Coy Lydia, all thy Hopes are vain,
Still to endure the pleaſing Pain
 Of a ſurprizing Kiſs;
Which Venus doth in Nectar ſteep,
And hang upon the balmy Lip,
 To draw us on to Bliſs.
                    CREECH.

Perhaps we may ſpeak of theſe amorous Bites under the Article FLORA.

(16) Venus in Idyl. 3.
Theocr. calls him Εὔμαρ τὸν ἄνδρα·
Tuum meum virum perculiſti Biconem b:
Illud oſ the Death of Adonis repreſents Venus.
Βοννζα τὸν ἀνέρι·
upon he Husband & Cicero de Nat. Deor. l. 3.
pag. 302. speaks of a Venus of Syria, married to Adonis.
So the 15th Idyll of Theocritus, & Firm. Maternus, de Err. Prof. Relig. pag. 21.

Note, That a very good Critic has informed me that the Correction ἐδόντας for Ἰρωτας is not neceſſary. He ſays, *the true Explication of that Verſe is, That the Boar τὸ πυρὶ πρωελθὼν, caſting himſelf into the Fire, ignes τὰς Ἰρωτας, burnt at the ſame time his Love. There is not only Reaſon, but alſo ſome Wit in ſaying, that this Boar, being firſt burnt by his Love, had in his turn found the means to burn it.* Politian made uſe of this Thought in the Epigram, which he made on Picus Mirandula who caſt his Love Verſes into the Fire. *Add to all this, that it is very difficult to imagine how the amorous Boar could have put his Teeth into the Fire, and burnt them, without burning himſelf likewiſe.*

(1-) Amm.
Marcell. lib. 19. cap. 1.

(18) Athen. lib. 7. pag. 292.

(19) Theocr. Idyl. 15.

(20) Cicer. de Nat. Deorum. lib. 1. cap. 15.

(21) Auguſt. de Civitat. Dei, lib. 6. cap. 7. See alſo Firm. Matern. ubi ſupra.

[E] *Long Train of Anniverſary Ceremonies.*] *Ariſtophanes*, in his Comedy of *Peace*, reckons the Feaſt of *Adonis* among the chief Feſtivals of the *Athenians*. Almoſt all the People of *Greece* celebrated it: The Women acted the chief Part in it, in lamenting the Death of this Gallant, or Husband, of *Venus* (16). "Fœminæ miſerabili planctu in primævo flore ſuc-"ciſum ſpem gentis ſolitis fletibus conclamabant, ut "lacrymare cultrices Veneris ſæpe ſpectantur in ſol-"lemnibus Adonidis ſacris (17). ——— *The Women, "with mournful Cries, bewailed the Hopes of "the People cut off in the Flower of his Age; "in like manner as the Votaries of Venus are "often ſeen to do, upon the ſolemn Feſtivals of "Adonis."* They repreſented Funerals in Picture, as *Plutarch* tells us in the Life of *Alcibiades*, and in that of *Nicias*. The Courteſans were not the leaſt forward to celebrate this great Solemnity, as may be gathered from a Paſſage of the Poet *Diphilus*, reported by *Athenæus* (18). They did not forget to make two Beds, on one of which they laid the Figure of *Venus*, and on the other that of *Adonis*. This is what we learn from *Theocritus* (19). The Wits laugh'd at a religious Worſhip, which conſiſted in weeping. " Quid abſurdius, quam ——— homines " jam morte deletos reponere in Deos, quorum om-" nis cultus eſſet futurus in luctu (20). ——— *What "more abſurd, than to deify Perſons already dead, "while worſhip was to conſiſt wholly of Grief?"* St *Auſtin* approves this Raillery; " Sacra ſunt Vene-" ris, *ſays he* (21), ubi amatus ejus Adonis, aprino " dente extinctus, juvenis formoſiſſimus, plangitur. " ——— *There are Rites of Venus; wherein her Fa-" vourite Adonis, a moſt beautiful Youth, killed by " the Tuſks of a Boar, is commemorated with La-*

" mentations." The People of *Syria* were yet greater Fools in this reſpect, than the *Greeks*: for, not contented with Sighing and Weeping, they diſciplined themſelves likewiſe; and, after having whipped themſelves, and wept ſufficiently, they performed the Sacrifice of the Dead to *Adonis*, and ſhaved their Heads. The Women, who refuſed to be ſhaved, were obliged to proſtitute themſelves a whole Day to Strangers, and the Money which they got by it, was employed in a Sacrifice, which was offered to *Venus*. The Mourning ended with Joy; for they feigned that *Adonis* was reſtored to Life. *Lucian*, who tells us thoſe Circumſtances, ſays farther, that the *Syrians* pretended that *Adonis* was killed by a Boar in their Country (22). See the Remark [*f*] where we ſhall obſerve, among other things, that this Feaſt was ſtill celebrated at *Alexandria* in St *Cyril's* Time. The Proceſſion was pompous; for the Queen herſelf carried the Image of *Adonis* in it. *Arſinoë*, the Wife of *Ptolemy Philadelphus*, received the Incenſe of Praiſe from *Theocritus* for this (23). The Women, who accompanied the Queen, carried Flowers and Fruits, and a hundred other things. 'Tis ſaid, that all theſe, and the Image itſelf of *Adonis*, were to be caſt into the Sea, or into Fountains. See *Heſychius, Zenobius, Suidas*, the Scholiaſt of *Theocritus*, cited by *Fuſidus* at the ſeventy fifth and ſeventy ſixth Pages of his *Hierology* of the ancient *Greeks*. The Gardens of *Adonis* became proverbial to ſignify any thing of no long Continuance. It is plainly in this Senſe, that *Plato, Plutarch*, and the Emperor *Julian* made uſe of that Proverb; the Original whereof came from thoſe Pots and Baſkets of Flowers, which were carried in Proceſſion at the Feaſt of *Adonis*. See *Eraſmus* at the twenty third Page of his *Adagies*. Laſtly, it is probable that the Celebration of this Feſtival continued as long at *Antioch* as at *Alexandria*. *Julian*, the Apoſtate, made his Entry into the firſt of thoſe Towns in the Year 362. when they celebrated the Feaſt of *Adonis* there, which was taken for a bad Omen. " Evenerat autem iiſdem " diebus annuo curſu completo Adonia ritu veteri " celebrari, amato Veneris, ut fabulæ fingunt, apri " dente ferali deleto. Et viſum eſt triſte, quod am-" plam urbem Principumque domicilium introeunte " Imperatore, nunc primum ululabiles undique plan-" ctus & lugubris ſonus audiebantur (24). ——— *It " happened at the ſame time, that the annual Rites " of Adonis were celebrated, the Favourite of Venus, " as Story tells, who was killed by the Tooth of a " wild Boar. And it ſeemed ominous, that, upon the " Emperor's making his public Entry into a large " City, the Reſidence of Princes, there ſhould be heard " on all Sides Howlings and mournful Cries."* A like Accident appeared a bad Omen to the *Athenians* upon two Occaſions (25).

(22) Theocr. Eidyl. 15.
See the Summary of that Idyll.

(24) Amm. Marcell. lib. 22. cap. 9.

(25) Plut. in Alcib. pag. 200. in Nicia, pag. 532.

[F] *Minion of Venus and Bacchus.*] In the Place, where *Athenæus* mentions ſome Examples of Ænigmatic Expreſſions (26), he does not forget the Oracle, which was given to *Cinyras*; it is as follows:

(26) Athen. lib. 10. cap. 22. pag. 456.

'Ω Κενύρα

ADONIS. 115

assures us, that *Adonis* was beloved by *Jupiter* (k); and that *Proserpine* fell in Love with him in Hell [G]. Yet she had some Compassion for her disconsolate Rival, who earnestly desir'd the Restitution of her Lover (l): She consented to his Absence for six Months, in favour of *Venus*. It was reported, then, that *Adonis* pass'd six Months with *Venus*, and six Months with *Proserpine*. The Scholiast, whom I have cited, contradicts himself hereupon [H]; and some do not speak so advantageously of *Proserpine*'s Complaisance (m). This division of the Year has been allegoris'd; as if we were to understand by it either the successive Stages of the Seed, which at first lies under ground, and afterwards rises above the Surface of the Earth (n), or the Period of the Sun's alternate Revolution thro' the Southern and Northern Signs of the Zodiac (o). These Explications seem not so solid to me, as the Sentiment of those, who reduce the Fable of *Adonis* to the History of *Osiris* (p). The Ancients do not agree about the Country, where the Scene of *Adonis* was laid; some placing it in *Syria*, others in the Island of *Cyprus*, or in *Egypt*, as will appear in the Remarks. Two things are related of *Hercules*, very opposite to each other, in relation to our *Adonis*; one is, that he was in love with him, and that Jealousy made *Venus* direct the Centaur *Nessus* how he might lay an Ambush for *Hercules* (q): The other, That this Hero, seeing many People come out of a Temple, in a City of *Macedonia*, had a mind to enter and perform his Devotions there; but, hearing that *Adonis* was the Divinity of the Place, he ridicul'd the Worship paid to him (r). Some report, that *Adonis* was born of *Jupiter*, without the concurrence of a Woman (s). St *Jerome* believ'd, that the Prophet *Ezekiel* spoke of the Festival of *Adonis* [I]. Lastly, It is difficult

'Ω Κινύρα βασιλεῦ Κυπρίων ἀνδρῶν ἐκπρεπεστάτων,
Παῖς σοι κάλλιςος μὲν ἴςω θαυμαςότατός τε
Πάντων ἀνθρώπων, δύο δ' αὐτὸν δαίμον' ἔχησετον
Ἡ μὲν ἐλαυνομένη λαθρίοις ἐρετμοῖς, ὁ δ' ἐλαύνων·

*A Son, O Cynyra, is given to thee,
Who fairest of the Human Race shall be:
Two Deities his Favours shall contest;
One he shall press, by t'other shall be prest.*

Athenæus adds, that *Venus* and *Bacchus* are meant in these Lines; for both of them were in love with *Adonis*. *Plato*, the Comic Poet, had reported this Oracle (27). He is not the only Poet, who has taken notice of this Amour of *Bacchus*. We find two Verses in *Plutarch*, which tells us, that *Bacchus*, having seen the Fair *Adonis*, in the Island of *Cyprus*, fell in love with him, and carried him away (28). What *Plutarch* adds, is curious, and may serve upon occasion for a Lesson to those, who give us so many Oriental Genealogies of the Pagan Religion, and Mythology. One of the Personages of *Plutarch*'s Dialogue maintains very seriously and gravely, That *Adonis* and *Bacchus* are the same Divinity, and that the *Jews* abstained from Swine's Flesh because *Adonis* was killed by a wild Boar. Now he pretends, that their Religion, their Feasts, their Ceremonies were much the same with those practised in *Greece* to *Bacchus*; and he says likewise, that their *Levites* were so called from Λύσιος, Εὔιος, *Lysius, Evius*, two Names of that Deity. *Ausonius* declares, that *Bacchus, Osiris, Adonis*, &c. were one and the same God (29). *Macrobius* goes yet farther (30).

[G] *Proserpine fell in love with him in Hell*.] If we may believe *Apollodorus* (31), she did not stay so long before she fell in love with him; she was enamoured of him in his very Cradle. *Venus*, being charmed with the Beauty of this Child, put him in a strong Box, and shewed him only to *Proserpine*; who protested that she would keep him. *Jupiter* was obliged to decide the Quarrel; and this was his Sentence: That *Adonis* should be at his Liberty the first four Months of the Year, and that he should stay the next four Months with *Proserpine*, and the last four with *Venus*. It had been better to have placed *Adonis*'s Portion in the middle of the Year; and perhaps it was so before the Abbreviators or Copiers of *Apollodorus* had put his Book into the Condition we now find it in. However it be, *Adonis* refused the Vacation which *Jupiter* allotted him, and renounced it in favour of *Venus*; for he presented her with his own four Months. Others say (32), I. That the Muse *Calliope* being charged with the Decision of the Dispute by *Jupiter*, ordained that *Adonis* should belong six Months to *Venus*, and six Months to *Proserpine*. II. That *Venus*, angry that she was not allowed to engross his whole Time, inspired all the Women of *Thrace* with so violent a Passion for *Orpheus*, the Son of *Calliope*, that each endeavouring to take him from the other, tore him in Pieces. One of the Complaints, which *Venus* makes of her Son, in the Dialogues of *Lucian*, is, That he sends her sometimes to Mount *Ida* in favour of *Anchises*, and sometimes to Mount *Libanus* for the fair *Assyrian*, half of whom he had robbed her of, by the Care he had taken to make *Proserpine* in love with him (33). *Arnobius* (34), and *Clemens Alexandrinus* (35), mention this Goddess's Passion for *Adonis*; and it is without Reason that *Sylburgius* would place in the *Greek* Father 'Αιδωνεῖ instead of 'Αδώνιδι; for if we should read 'Αιδωνεῖ we should make *Clemens Alexandrinus* affirm a Fasthood, to wit, that *Proserpine*'s Love for *Adonis* was an *Adultery*. *Meziriac* is the Author of this last Remark. See the 403d Page of his Commentary on *Ovid*'s Epistles. *Calliope*'s Judgment puts me in Mind of these two Verses:

*Et vitula tu dignus & hic, & quisquis amores
Aut metuet dulces, aut experietur amaros* (36).

*So nice a Difference in your singing lies,
That both have won, or both deserve the Prize.
Rest equal happy both, and all who prove
The bitter Sweets and pleasing Pains of Love.*
DRYDEN.

[H] *Contradicts himself hereupon*.] He tells us, on the one side, and with little Probability, That *Adonis* abode six Months with *Proserpine*, and six Months with *Venus*, without touching them, they having separate Beds. Ἄνευ τῆς συγκαθευδήσεως καὶ προσερπύσεως (37); and, on the other side, that he pass'd six Months in the Arms of *Venus*, and as many in the Arms of *Proserpine*. Ἕξ μῆνας ἐκοίμησιν ἐν ταῖς ἀγκάλαις τῆς Ἀφροδίτης, ὥσπερ καὶ ἐν ταῖς ἀγκάλαις τῆς Περσεφόνης (38). Observe, that the like was related concerning the Agreement between *Ceres* and *Pluto*; namely, that *Proserpine* should remain six Months with Him, and that she should go and finish the Year with *Ceres*. The Ancients had not variety enough of Invention: they apply'd the unravelling of their Fables to too many Subjects. Besides, *Egypt, Phœnicia*, and the Island of *Cyprus*, which were the Scenes of *Adonis*, are not distant enough from the Sun, from the Month of *September*, to the Month of *March*, to induce one to say, That *Adonis* is then in the Grave, or in the Shades below: And I wonder what Mr *Moreri* meant by his *six Months, in which the Days are so short, and the Nights so long*. For in the Countries, which I speak of, the Difference of the longest and shortest Day of the Year, gives no room for this Expression. Many more things might be corrected in the *Adonis* of that Author.

[I] *That the Prophet* Ezekiel *spoke of the Festival of* Adonis.] St *Jerome* thought that the *Tammuz* in these Words of *Ezekiel, Then he brought me to the Door of the Gate of the Lord's House, which was towards the North, and behold there sat Women weeping for*

difficult to comprehend why the Ancients feign'd that *Venus* hid, or buried her Favourite under Lettuces [K], since they obſerv'd, that that Plant cauſes Impotency. Perhaps their Allegory may be explain'd, by ſuppoſing they meant, by it, that *Venus* had exhauſted her Favourite, and paſs'd him ſo often thro' the Alembic, that he was only fit to be compar'd to the *Terra Damnata*, and the *Caput Mortuum* of the Chymiſts: But they do not hint at any ſuch Meaning. They do not all agree, that he died of his Wound [L]. There was a River near *Byblus* call'd *Adonis*, which deſcended from Mount *Libanus*; it became red once a Year, becauſe the Winds drove a large quantity of Duſt into it of the Colour of Vermillion. They thought this a proper time to lament *Adonis*; it being the ſeaſon, when they ſuppoſ'd he was wounded on Mount *Libanus*, and his Blood ran down into the River (*t*).

for Tammuz (39), is *Adonis*. He did not forget to remark the two Faces, under which this Feſtival appeared: Firſt of all they bewail'd *Adonis* as dead; and afterwards they ſung, and celebrated him as reſtored to Life. *Plangitur à mulieribus quaſi mortuus, & poſtea reviviſcens canitur atque laudatur* (40). St *Cyril* relates ſeveral Particulars of This Feaſt: He ſays, That it was ſtill celebrated in *Alexandria* (41); and, when he explains theſe Words, *Wo to the Land —— that ſendeth Ambaſſadors by the Sea, even in Veſſels of Bulruſhes upon the Waters* (42); he will have it to be underſtood of the Letters, which were ſent to make known the Arrival of *Adonis*. "They took, *ſays he* (43), an earthen Veſſel, and "writing a Letter to the Women of *Byblus*, as if "*Adonis* were really found again, and putting it "into the Veſſel, they ſeal'd it up, and caſt it in-"to the Sea, after having uſed ſome Ceremonies. "This Veſſel, as they aſſerted, came of itſelf to *By*-"*blus*, on certain Days of the Year, and certain Wo-"men, favour'd by *Venus*, having received it there, "ceaſ'd from weeping, after having open'd the Let-"ter; as if *Venus* had found her *Adonis* again." *Lucian* ſays, That he ſaw the Paſt-board Head at *Byblus*, which the *Egyptians* ſent thither every Year, without any other Ceremony, than caſting it into the Sea. The Winds carry'd it directly to *Byblus*, in ſeven Days, which was the uſual time ſpent in going from *Egypt* to that City. *Procopius Gazæus* relates this as well as St *Cyril* (44) According to the latter, the *Greeks* believed, that *Venus* deſcended from Hell to recover *Adonis*; and, it being known, ſaid they, at her return, that ſhe had found him (45), it was proper that the mournful Beginnings of the Feaſt ſhould terminate in great Rejoicings.

[K] *Under Lettuces*.] It is *Callimachus* who tells us, That *Venus* hid *Adonis* under Lettuces (46). According to *Cratinus* ſhe did the ſame by *Phaon*, of whom ſhe was greatly enamour'd. What had *Athenæus* done with his Wits, when he advanc'd, that the Poets intended to ſignify by this Allegory, that Lettuces cauſe a kind of Impotence in thoſe, who commonly eat of them? Would *Venus* have made choice of them to cover her Favourites with, had they had ſuch an Efficacy? Would ſhe not have abhorr'd the very Name and Sight of them? Would ſhe not have fear'd, that the very touch of them would have been attended with ill Conſequences? Obſerve a Difference between *Callimachus* and *Eubulus*; the latter ſaid, That, when *Adonis* was dead, *Venus* buried him under Lettuces; from whence he infers, that That Plant is of no uſe but for the Dead (47). The Original of all theſe Stories might very well proceed from the Report, That *Adonis*, having eaten of a certain Lettuce, which grew in the Iſland of *Cyprus*, was kill'd by a wild Boar. They, who conſider in what part the Boar wounded him, will eaſily find the unravelling of all this. *Adonis* was become impotent, from having eaten too many of thoſe Lettuces: This is the Reaſon why it is feign'd, That afterwards he receiv'd a mortal Wound in the Groin. So that the Word κατεφαγυὰν ought not to be ſubſtituted in the room of κατεφαγυν (48); and it is much more reaſonable to think that *Nicander* ſpoke of this Lettuce, as having been the Food of *Adonis*, than to think, that he ſpoke of it as of an *Aſylum*, which *Adonis* ſought, to eſcape the Boar.

I muſt acquaint my Reader, that Mr *de la Monnoie* is not of this Opinion. He was pleaſed to communicate to me the following Remark upon this Subject. "The κατεφαγυν of the Manuſcripts is much to be "prefer'd before the κατεφαγυν of the printed Co-"pies. *Nicander*, in the Place, which *Athenæus* "cites, ſpeaks of a kind of Lettuce, under which, he "ſays, *Adonis* took Shelter, when the Boar kill'd

"him. This makes very good Senſe; whereas there "would be little Senſe in ſaying, That *Adonis* had "eat too much of that Lettuce, when the Boar kill'd "him; the Expreſſion would not be clear, nor co-"herent, and it would only be a confuſ'd Mixture "of Allegory and Fable. Moreover it muſt be con-"ſidered, that θρίδαξ being of the Feminine Gender, "there ſhould be ἧς or ἣν καταφαγών, becauſe ϑ is "then adverbially taken for *quâ.*" It is certain, that *Caſaubon* prefer'd καταφαγών to καταφαγων (49). He confirm'd his Opinion by the Words, which are found in the ſame Page of *Athenæus*, ἐν καλαῖς θριδακίναις ἀποκρύψαι (50), *in pulchris lactucis abdidiſſe*: But he ſhould have obſerved that *Athenæus* does not report them, 'till after having quoted a long Paſſage of a Poet, who ſaid, That if any one eats of theſe Lettuces, he can do nothing with a Woman (51). Obſerve well, that this Poet's Words follow immediately upon what *Nicander* ſaid. Now it is a ſign that *Athenæus* did not write ϑ καταφαγών, but ἣν, or ἧς καταφαγών. And it is a more evident ſign of it, becauſe we ſee, that That Author, having cited *Callimachus*, who ſaid, That *Venus* hid *Adonis* under Lettuces, obſerves that it is an Allegory, deſign'd to ſhew that thoſe who commonly eat of that Herb, become weak and impotent with regard to *Venus*. Ἀλληγορούντων τῶν ποιητῶν ὅτι ἀςθενεῖς εἰσι πρὸς ἀφροδίσια διʼ συνεχῶς χρώμενοι θρίδαξι. *Ea quidem allegoria Poëtis innuentibus qui aſſiduè lactuca veſcuntur ad venerem eſſe invalidos*. It is of no Importance, that *Nicander* has confounded Allegory with Fable: The Poets are full of ſuch Mixtures. Beſides it is obſervable, that he miſunderſtood the Word he would explain. Ἔνδυον λέγεσθαι φησὶ παρὰ Κυπρίοις θρίδακα (52). *Lactucam à Cypriis dicit vocari Brenthin*. He miſtook a Firr-Tree for a Lettuce (53). This Miſtake induc'd him to alter the Tradition; for he was ſenſible, that it would be ridiculous, to ſuppoſe, that *Adonis* hid himſelf under a Lettuce; and therefore he ſays, that he fed upon it.

[L] *They do not all agree, that he died of his Wound.*] Conſult the third Volume of the *Bibliothèque Univerſelle* (54). We may add to the Remarks we find there, a Paſſage of *Ptolemy*, the Son of *Hephæſtion* (55); it is That, where he ſays, that this Verſe of the *Hyacinthus* of *Euphorion*,

Κωκυτὸς μοῦνος τὸν ἀφάρμακα νίψεν Ἄδωνιν,

Coeytus only waſh'd Adonis' Wounds;

was not underſtood. It ſignifies quite another thing, from what it is generally thought to imply; for it informs us, that one *Cocytus*, a Diſciple of *Chiron*, had cur'd *Adonis* of his Wound, receiv'd by the wild Boar. The Ceremonies of the Feſtival, may convince us, that *Adonis* did not die of it. His Votaries mourn'd at firſt, as if he were really dead, and afterwards rejoic'd, as if he were return'd into the World again. "It is obvious to conjecture, that this Fable "was built upon ſome ſtrong Expreſſions of the *Egyp*-"*tians*, or the *Phœnicians*, who uſed to ſay, that "They, who recover'd from a great Fit of Sickneſs, "or eſcap'd any imminent Danger, were raiſ'd again "out of the Grave. Many Examples of it are found "in the *Pſalms* (56)." Add to this, "That it was the "Cuſtom of the *Oriental* Nations, to conſecrate "Golden Figures of the Parts of the Body, in which "they had ſuffer'd any Inconvenience. We find an "Inſtance of this in 1 *Sam.* vi. 4. *Adonis* having been "wounded in the Groin, and being cur'd of his "Wound, conſecrated a Golden *Phallus* —— They "had a very great reſpect for that Figure in the My-"ſteries of *Oſiris* (57)." We find here a Confirmation of the foregoing Remark; The Clouds vaniſh, and

ADRASTUS.

and the Day begins to appear. *Venus* thought she had lost for ever, not the Life, but the Sex of her Husband; whether it was that a wild Boar had actually injured him in That; or that Witchcraft, or some other Principle, unknown to us, had brought a fatal Mortification upon those Parts. *Hinc illæ lacrimæ*; This was the Cause of her Tears. But the Wound, being heal'd, or the Charm remov'd, *Venus* was persuaded, that her Husband reviv'd again, and that he return'd to her from the lowest depths of *Erebus*; and this was the Occasion of her Joy: And, in order to preserve the Memory of all this more mysteriously, and more honourably, the Festival of *Adonis* was ordered to be celebrated every Year, in such and such a manner. It would be easy to adapt the Explications of *Macrobius* to this Hypothesis; his Sun descending to the inferior Parts of the Zodiac, and remounting afterwards to the superior Parts; his wild Boar, the Image of Cold, and consequently of those, who are included in the *Canon-Law* under the Title *De frigidis & maleficiatis*; his *Venus* despairing, because she was the Widow of her Sun; and afterwards rejoicing at the return of that beautiful Luminary, which rendered her fruitful. Every body sees, that it would not be difficult to make a proper use of the Agreement between *Venus* and *Proserpine*; I mean those Seeds concentered in the Bosom of the Earth for some Months, out of which they spring afterwards for the Propagation of the Species.

ADRASTUS, King of *Argos*, the Son of *Talaüs* and *Lysianassa* (*a*), the Daughter of *Polybius*, King of *Sicyon*, acquir'd a great Reputation in the Famous War of *Thebes*, wherein he engag'd to maintain the Rights of his Son-in-Law *Polynices* [*A*], who was excluded from the Crown of *Thebes* by his Brother *Eteocles* (*b*), notwithstanding the Agreement pass'd between them. *Adrastus*, being followed by *Polynices*, and *Tydeus* his other Son-in-Law, by *Capaneus*, and *Hippomedon*, his Sister's Sons, by *Amphiaraus*, his Brother-in-Law, and *Parthenopeus* (*c*), march'd against the City of *Thebes*; and this was the Expedition of the seven *Worthies*, so much sung by the Poets: They all perish'd in it, except *Adrastus*, whom his Horse sav'd. It was a Horse of consequence, whose Name was *Arion*; we shall speak of him in his place. This first War was follow'd by some others; for *Adrastus*, not having been able to obtain the Bodies of the *Argians*, who were kill'd before *Thebes*, had recourse to the *Athenians* (*d*), who, under the Conduct of *Theseus*, constrain'd the new King of *Thebes* (*e*) to comply with *Adrastus*'s Request. This Satisfaction did not put an end to the War; for the Sons of those, who had succeeded so ill in the first Expedition, wag'd a second War, ten Years after, which was call'd the War of the *Epigones* [*B*], and ended with the taking and plundering of *Thebes*. None of the Chiefs perish'd in it (*f*), except *Ægialeus*, the Son of *Adrastus*. It was a kind of Compensation, some times practis'd by Fortune (*g*). This Loss touched *Adrastus* so sensibly, being moreover weakened by old Age, that he died with Grief [*C*] at *Megara* (*h*), as he was leading the victorious Army back, which had taken the City of *Thebes*. It is a Proof, that he was personally present in the second Expedition [*D*], which, nevertheless, but few Writers have taken notice of. Those of *Megara* greatly honour'd his Memory; but it was nothing in comparison of what those of *Sicyon* did [*E*]. These built him a Tomb in the most conspicuous part of their City, and instituted Feasts and Sacrifices to him, which they celebrated every Year with great Shew and Magnificence. We may see in *Herodotus* in what manner *Callisthenes*, Tyrant of *Sicyon*, abolish'd

(*a*) Pausan. lib. 2. pag. 50.

(*b*) Ibid. lib. 9. pag. 286.

(*c*) Hygin. cap. 7. Apollod. lib. 3. Diodor. Sicul. lib. 5. cap. 6.

(*d*) Pausan. lib. 1. pag. 37.

(*e*) Eteocles nd Polynices bath kill'd each otier.

(*f*) Hygin. cap 71.

(*g*) See the Remark [H].

(*h*) Pausan. lib. 2. p. 41.

[*A*] *The Rights of his Son-in-law Polynices.*] *Pausanias* says, that *Adrastus* had married his Daughter to *Polynices*, before the Dispute about the Succession of *Thebes* (1); but others pretend, that this Marriage was not made, till *Polynices*, excluded by his Brother, had retir'd to *Adrastus*. They relate, that *Tydeus* fled for Refuge thither at the same time, and that the latter of these two Refugees was cover'd with the Hide of a Boar, and the former with the Hide of a Lion; which was the reason of *Adrastus*'s giving them his Daughters in Marriage; for he recollected the Oracle (2), which had commanded him to marry them to a Boar, and a a Lion (3). The Supplement of *Moreri* says falsely that *Tydeus*, being ask'd why he wore the Hide of a wild Boar, answer'd, that it was because his Father *Oeneus* was the Conqueror of the *wild Boar of Calydonia*. He did not give this Answer; and it was not *Oeneus*, but *Meleager* who kill'd that furious Boar. The Oracle, which was given to *Adrastus*, is likewise mis-reported in that Supplement.

[*B*] *The War of the* Epigones.] Had they been aware, in the composing of the third Volume of *Moreri*, that this War was only ten Years later than the First, they would not have translated the Word *Epigones* by, *they, who were born after the Siege of Thebes*: they would only have said, *they, who surviv'd their Fathers*: or, in general, *the Descendants of the first Chiefs*.

[*C*] *That he died with Grief.*] The Supplement pretends *that he cast himself into his Son's Funeral Pile*, and cites *Hyginus*, Fab. 242. and *Herodotus*, Lib. 5. Now it is observable, that *Herodotus* says nothing of *Adrastus*, which has been taken notice of in that Article of the Supplement. The only thing, which may be suspected to have been borrow'd from *Herodotus*, is at the Beginning of the Article in these Terms: *Adrastus was obliged to retire to King Polybius, in the City of Sicyon, who gave him a good Reception, and*

(1) Pausan. lib. 9. pag. 286.

(2) *It is in the Scholiast of* Euripides, ad Phœniss. ver. 41. See Stat. in als, Theb. lib. 1. ver. 395.

(3) Hygin. cap. 69. Apollodorus, lib. 3. says, *That one of them bere the Head of a Boar on his Shield.*

his Daughter Amphitea *in Marriage*; but this does not agree with the Account of *Herodotus*, who says that *Polybius* left his Kingdom by his Will to *Adrastus* his Daughter's Son. See the following Remark. The Citation of *Hyginus* is yet worse; for *Hyginus* does not speak of our *Adrastus* there, but of another, who was the Father of *Hippoïnoüs*, and who cast himself into the Fire to obey an Order of *Apollo*. *Hipponoüs* did as much, upon the same Principle. The Author of the *Index* of *Hyginus*, in the Edition of *Amsterdam* in 1681. gives to *Hercules* for Sons the *Adrastus*, and *Hipponoüs*, we are here speaking of; and yet he pretends, that the same *Adrastus* is the Father of *Ægialeus*, of whom *Hyginus* speaks in the 71st Chapter, and who is manifestly the Father-in-law of *Polynices*, and the Son of *Talaüs*. He mistook the Sense of these Words: " Hercules Jovis fi-
" lius ipse sese in ignem misit. Adrastus & Hipponoüs
" ejus filius ipsi se in ignem jecerunt ex responso
" Apollinis (4). ——— Hercules, *the Son of* Jupiter,
" *threw himself into the Fire*. Adrastus, *and* Hip-
" ponous *his Son, threw themselves into the Fire, in
" Obedience to the Oracle of* Apollo."

[*D*] *That he was personally present in the second Expedition*.] I can add a second Evidence to *Pausanias*: I mean *Pindar*, who asserts positively, that *Adrastus*, having collected, and taken away his Son's Bones, brought back his Army safe to *Argos* (5.) He does not, then, suppose he died by the way at *Megara*, as *Pausanias* does; but still these are two consistent Authorities to ground the present Fact on, namely, that *Adrastus* was at the second War of *Thebes*.

[*E*] *In comparison of what those of* Sicyon *did*.] The Scholiast of *Pindar* (6) reports, that *Dieutychides* maintains, that they had only the *Cenotaph* of *Adrastus* at *Sicyon*, and that his real Tomb was at *Megara* (7).

(4) Hygin. Fabul. cap. 242.

(5) Pindar. Pyth. Od. 8.

(6) Schol. Pindari in Od. 9. Nem.

(7) Dieutychides, lib. 5. Hist. Megarica.

[*F*] *Being*

ADRASTUS. ADRIANI.

lish'd these Ceremonies, out of Hatred to the *Argians* (i). You must understand, that *Adrastus* was King of *Sicyon* (k), in virtue of the Will of *Polybius*, his Grandfather by the Mother's side, to whom he once fled for Refuge, being constrain'd to depart out of *Argos* [F]; and that, during his Reign, he made the City of *Sicyon* very famous (l), by the *Pythian* Games, which he establish'd there (m). Some Writers remark, that his Hereditary Kingdom was that of *Sicyon*, and that he obtain'd that of *Argos* by Election; the Mildness of his Nature occasioning the *Argians* to invite him [G], to come and civilize their barbarous Manners. *Homer* does not say so much; but only, that he reign'd first at *Sicyon* (n). *Servius*, on Æneid. Lib. 6, gives the same account; and we read the same thing in *Pindar* (o), and in his old Scholiast. They give him commonly but two Daughters, *Argia*, the Wife of *Polynices*, and *Deipila* the Wife of *Tydeus* (p), but he had besides two Sons, *Ægialeus* and *Cyanippus*: and a Daughter, whose Name was *Ægialea*, who married *Diomedes*, the Son of *Tydeus*, and gave him great uneasiness by her immodest Behaviour. Some say, that he was the first, who built a Temple to the Goddess *Nemesis*, and that upon that account she had the Name of *Adrastea* [H]. But I am certain they confound him with another *Adrastus*. He, who built the first Altar to that Goddess, erected it on the River *Æsepus* in *Phrygia* (q). We do not find that our *Adrastus* was ever in *Asia*; and yet we meet with a King of that Name in *Phrygia*, at the time of the Siege of *Troy* (r). There is more reason, therefore, to attribute the Establishment of the Worship of *Nemesis* to an *Asiatic* Prince, whose Name was *Adrastus*, than to a King of *Argos* of that Name. *Herodotus* speaks of an ADRASTUS, who fled to the Court of *Cræsus* King of *Lydia*, and who kill'd that King's Son by an Accident (s). The Article of that *Adrastus* in *Moreri*'s Dictionary is tolerably good [I].

[F] *Being constrained to depart out of* Argos.] It is said, in the Supplement to *Moreri*, that *Adrastus was driven out of the Kingdom of* Argos *by his Brother-in-law* Amphiaraus, *and obliged to retire to the City of* Sicyon; but, by an inexcusable neglect, they have not cited any Authority for this. The Reader must traverse a great deal of Ground to meet with Evidences. I have searched so long, that at last I have discovered the Source in *Pindar*, where I find that *Adrastus* left *Argos*, and retired to *Sicyon*, by reason of *Amphiaraus*'s Attempts, and the overthrow of the Family of *Talaüs*, which were no longer in possession of the Sovereign Power (8). That Poet adds, that *Adastrus* stopped the Course of this Evil; and that the Marriage of *Eriphyle* with *Amphiaraus* was the Bond which re-united the contending Parties, and quieted the Troubles. *Amphiaraus* was not therefore the Brother-in-law of *Adrastus*, when the latter was obliged to retire to *Sicyon*. *Pindar* does not say, that this Fugitive Prince married King *Polybius*'s Daughter, nor that *Talaüs* was killed by *Amphiaraus*; but both these Facts, the former of which is so contradictory to *Herodotus*, are in the Scholiast of *Pindar*. *Diodorus Siculus* says, That the Marriage of *Amphiaraus* with *Eriphyle* the Sister of *Adrastus*, did not appease the Differences, since a little before the Wars of *Thebes*, the two Brothers-in-law were yet contending for the Crown (9). They were divided on another Point; *Amphiaraus* was unwilling to be of the Expedition, and *Adrastus* passionately desired that he might. *Eriphyle* was chosen Arbitress of their Dispute, and gave the Cause for her Brother. *Apollodorus* says partly the same Thing, though confusedly enough (10). *Barthius* has misrepresented what *Diodorus Siculus* says; for he supposes, that *Eriphyle* was the Daughter of *Adrastus* (11). The *Latin* Translation of that Historian, printed at *Basil* in 1548. says falsly, That *Eriphyle* adjudged the Crown to her Husband.

[G] *The* Argians *to invite him*.] If Mr *Moreri* had known this Particular, he would have taken care not to have affirmed, That *Adrastus quitted the City of* Sicyon *after four Years Reign, without any body knowing the Reason of it, and came to reign at Argos, where he had two Daughters*, &c (12). However, be it here it be, here is a Subject for Historical Pyrrhonism; namely the Disagreement of the Ancients about the two Kingdoms of *Adrastus*; I mean in relation to the Title, and the Order of Succession. See the Article TALAUS.

[H] *And that upon that Account she had the Name of* Adrastea.] The Scholiast of *Pindar* says, That this Name was given to the Goddess *Nemesis*, on account of the Compensation I have taken notice of. *Adrastus* was the only Chief, who survived at the first Siege of *Thebes*, and his Son was the only Chief, who was killed at the second. The Balance is much more just, according to the Hypothesis of those, who ascribe the whole Conduct of the second War to the *Epigones*; but they who pretend that *Adrastus* was present, and who give him the Glory of leading back the Victorious Army, necessarily suppose that he commanded there. He should have perished, therefore, in this second Expedition, to make the Balance even between Him and the six Colleagues who accompanied him in the first.

[I] *The Article of That* Adrastus *in* Moreri's *Dictionary is tolerably good*.] I only find these small Faults in it. I. He makes *Adrastus* to be the Son of *Gordias*, instead of making him the Son of *Midas*, and Grandson of *Gordius*, conformably to the *Latin* Translation of *Herodotus*. I know very well that the *Greek* Text imports that he was the Son of *Gordius*, and Grandson of *Midas* (13); but I am certain likewise on the one side, that *Moreri* had not Abilities to rectify Translations of the *Greek* Originals; and on the other side, that there is a *Greek* Reading agreeable to that Translation. II. He should not have omitted, that *Cræsus* used such Expiatory Ceremonies in favour of *Adrastus*, as were used for the Purification of involuntary Homicides. III. It ought not to have been said, That *Adrastus* killed himself on the Body of the Son of *Cræsus*, but on his Tomb; for *Herodotus* notes, That *Cræsus*, having excused and comforted the Murtherer, caused his Son to be buried. IV. Lastly, he ought not to have cited *Clio*, or *Li*. The Names of the Muses, given to the Books of *Herodotus*, are of no use in Quotations, especially when a *French* Book is composed for such Popular Use as *Moreri*'s Dictionary; however he ought to have settled the distinct Estimate of *Clio*, by adding, *or, the first Book*.

ADRIANI (JOHN BAPTIST) born at *Florence*, in the Year 1511, of a Patrician Family, wrote the History of *his own Times* in *Italian*. His Work is a Continuation of *Guicciardin*, and begins at the Year 1536 [A]. Judgment and Sincerity, Diligence

[A] *And begins at the Year* 1336.] Not having it by me, I must be contented with the Testimony of *Thuanus*; but I apprize my Reader, That, according to *Spondanus* (1), our *Adriani* begun his History at the Year 1537. and finished it at the Year 1574. It comprehends twenty two Books, and was printed at *Florence* by the *Giunti*, in the Year 1583. in Folio, and at *Venice*, in two Volumes in 4to. in the Year 1527. *Marcello Adriani*, the Author's Son, published this History, and dedicated it to *Francis de Medicis*, Great Duke of *Tuscany*. It contains the Space of forty four Years, if we may believe *Bocchi* (2).

[B] Had

ADRIAN. — ADRICHOM.

Diligence and Exactness reign through out it; and it appears that *Cosmo*, Great Duke of *Tuscany*, a Prince of a prodigious Genius, and consummate Prudence, had communicated his Memoirs to the Author [B]. *Thuanus*, from whom I borrow this, acknowledges ingenuously, that he was oblig'd to this History for many things, and that none supply'd him with more Materials (a). He thinks it strange that the *Italians* do not consider *Adriani* according to his Merit. Besides this History, there are extant six *Orations* of this Author's Composition, to wit, the Funeral Oration of *Charles* the Vth; that of the Emperor *Ferdinand*; that of *Eleonora* of *Toledo*, Wife of *Cosmo*, Duke of *Florence*; that of *Isabella*, Queen of *Spain*; that of *Cosmo*, Great Duke of *Tuscany*; and that of *Jane* of *Austria*, the Wife of *Francis de Medicis* (b). He died at *Florence* in the Year 1579. I believe him likewise to be the Author of *A* long Letter concerning the Ancient Painters and Sculptors, which we meet with at the beginning of the 3d Volume of *Vasari*. He was the Son of the Learned MARCELLO VIRGILIO (c), Secretary of State to the Republic of *Florence*, and Professor of Literature in that University. He succeeded him in the Place of Professor (d), and left a Son nam'd MARCELLO ADRIANI, who was very learned, and who exercis'd the same Function (e), and took the Title of, *Il Torbido*, (*The Troubled*) in the Academy *de Gli Alterati* (f). There are some Authors, who find our *John Baptist* a little partial against Pope *Paul* III (g).

[B] *Had communicated his Memoirs to the Author.*] *Thuanus* had already declared his Opinion of this in the thirty seventh Book, on Occasion of the private Conferences, which *Catherine de Medici* had with the Duke of *Alba*, at the Interview of *Baionne*. The Protestants, says he, *who are a very suspicious People* (3), *gave out, That the Extirpation of their Sect was contrived in these Conferences. What happened afterwards will plainly shew Posterity whether it was false, or not.* He adds, *That John Baptist Adriani,* a very sincere and judicious Historian, and whom, it is likely, the Memoirs of the Duke of *Florence* had supplied with many Particulars (4), has reported, that according to the Advice of the King of *Spain*, explained by the Duke of *Alba*, it was concluded at the Interview, That the Heads of the principal Protestants should be cut off, and that afterwards they should fall upon them all, after the manner of the *Sicilian Vespers.* I wish *d'Aubigné* had not exceeded the Author, whom he copied. Almost all *Historians,* says he (5), *and amongst them* John Baptist Adrian, *who had the Cyphers and the Secrets of the Duke of* Florence, *unanimously agree, that the Wars of the* Netherlands, *and the Massacres, which followed afterwards, were projected there.* It is not to be questioned but that *Thuanus* is the Original which *d'Aubigné* copied; but does not the Copier give himself too much Liberty? Does he not lay that down as matter of Fact, which *Thuanus* only advanced as a Probability? Does he not speak of the Great Duke's Cyphers and Secrets, of which *Thuanus* has not said a Word? For *Commentarii* does not signify *Cyphers and Secrets.* The more heinous an Accusation is, the more we ought to attend to the Terms of the Deposition, even when Appearances are favourable, as in this Case. If *Zeidler* had cast his Eyes on this Passage of *Thuanus*, he would not have ventured to say, that *Adrian's* History ended with the Death of *Charles* V. (6)

ADRIANUS, or *Adrian*, Emperor, Pope, &c. Look for HADRIAN.

ADRICHOMIA (CORNELIA), a Nun of the Order of St *Augustin*, in the XVIth Century, the Daughter of a *Dutch* Gentleman, acquir'd much Reputation by the Knowledge of Poetry, which she made use of conformably to her Profession; for she translated *David's* Psalms into Verse, and compos'd several other *Sacred Poems*. *James Faber Stapulensis* admir'd this Lady's Wit and Learning. *Cornelius Musius* kept a strict, but very honourable, Correspondence with her. This is what *Francis Swertius* relates of her (a). I wonder, that *Valerius Andreas*, whose Collection of the Writers of the *Netherlands* is much more copious, than that of *Francis Swertius*, takes no notice of this Illustrious *Dutch* Maid. He could not be ignorant of what the other had said of her.

ADRICHOMIUS (CHRISTIAN) was born at *Delft* in *Holland*, in the Year 1533. He was a Priest zealous for his Religion, and apply'd himself to Study. He was a considerable time Director of the Nuns of St *Barbara*, the Place of his Birth; but the Religious Civil Wars obliging him to go into Exile, he retir'd first into *Brabant* [*A*], and afterwards to *Cologne*, where he undertook a considerable Work, which was printed after his Death [*B*]. The Subject of it was a Description of the *Holy-Land* in general, and of the City of *Jerusalem* in particular; as we find by his *Theatrum Terræ Sanctæ*, printed with Geographical Maps at *Cologne* in 1593 in Folio. It is pretty well esteem'd, and would have been yet more, if the Author had not trusted too much to the *Manethon*, and *Berosus*, and such other Chimerical Writings, of the Monk *Annius* of *Viterbo*. He sometimes assum'd the Appellation of *Christianus Crucius*; under which Name he publish'd the Life of *Jesus Christ* at *Antwerp* (a), with an Oration *de Christiana Beatitudine*, which was deliver'd in a General Chapter (b). He died at *Cologne* in the Month of *June* 1585, being the thirteenth Year of his Exile, and was bury'd in the Monastery of the Canonesses of *Nazareth*, of which he had been Director for some time (c).

[*A*] *Into* Brabant.] The Author, quoted by Mr *Moreri* and my self, expresses himself thus; *Inde à primis Geusio-Calvinistis pulsus, Machliniæ, Trajecti & Coloniæ vixit* (1). I do not question in the least, but that *Moreri* is mistaken in taking *Trajectum* for *Utrecht*; he had better have translated it *Maestricht*.

[*B*] *Which was printed after his Death.*] What Mr *Moreri* asserts, That *Adrichomius* himself published this Work, and that his *Theatrum Terræ sanctæ* is distinct from the Description of the *Holy Land*, &c. is false.

ÆGIALEA. ÆRODIUS. AFER.

ÆGIALEA, Daughter of *Adrastus* King of *Argos*. See EGIALÉA.

ÆRODIUS, a Learned Civilian of the XVIth Century. Look for AYRAULT.

AFER (DOMITIUS) a famous Orator under *Tiberius*, and under the three following Emperors, was of *Nismes* (a). After his Prætorship, not finding himself greatly rais'd, and being ambitious of exalting himself by any Method, he turn'd Accuser against *Claudia Pulchra*, Cousin to *Agrippina* (b). He gain'd his Cause, and by this Success he found himself in the Number of the First Orators, and in the Favour of *Tiberius*, who bore an implacable Hatred to *Agrippina* [A]. The Commendations his Eloquence receiv'd from this Emperor made him relish the Trade; insomuch that he was seldom without some *Accusation*, or some *Defence*, upon his Hands; which gain'd greater Reputation to his Tongue, than his Honesty; till at length he lost much of his Fame, even as an Orator, when old Age, having wore out his Mind (c), could not prevail with him to leave off Pleading [B]. The Accusation of *Claudia Pulchra* fell out in the Year of *Rome* 779. The Year after her Son *Quintilius Varus* was accused by the same Orator, and by *Publius Dolabella* (d). No body wonder'd, that *Afer*, who had been a long time poor, and who had not well manag'd the Gains of the former Accusation, shou'd return to the Charge; but it was thought strange, that a Relation of *Varus*, and of so great a Family, as *Publius Dolabella* was, shou'd join with this Informer. *Afer* died in the Reign of *Nero*, in the Year of *Rome* 812 (e). It was reported that he died at Table of excessive Eating (f). *Quintilian*, who, in his youth, was greatly attach'd to this Person [C], makes frequent Mention of him

(a) Euseb. Chron. n. 2060.
(b) Tacit. Annal. lib. 4. cap. 52.
(c) Nisi quod ætas extrema multum etiam Eloquentiæ dempsit, dum fessa mente retinet silentii impatientiam. Id. ib. See in the Remark [B] a Passage of ch. 11th Chapter of the 12th Book of Quintilian.
(d) Tacit. Annal. 66.
(e) Id. Ann. lib. 14. cap. 19.
(f) Euseb. Chron. n. 2060.

[A] *Tiberius, who bore an implacable Hatred to Agrippina.*] This Princess was so well satisfied, that it was the Emperor, who occasioned the Process against her, that she shewed no Resentment for it to *Domitius*. The latter meeting her one day in the Streets, turned from her: She imagined this Behaviour proceeded from Shame, and having caused him to be called, she bid him fear nothing, and told him, That it was not he, but *Agamemnon*, who was the Cause of all this: Θάρσει Δομίτιε ὐ γάρ σύ μοι τούτων αίτιος αλλ' Αγαμέμνων Bono sis animo, Domiti; non enim tu horum causa es, sed Agamemnon (1). It is a sign that she had read the *Iliad*.

(1) Dion. Cass. lib. 59. ad an. 792. pag. 752.

[B] *Old Age, having wore out his Mind, could not prevail upon him to leave off pleading.*] This is too common an Infirmity. Few Persons know how to retreat in time, or can say with *Horace*;

Est mihi purgatam crebro qui personet aurem;
Solve senescentem maturè sanus equum, ne
Peccet ad extremos ridendus & ilia ducat (2).

(2) Hor. Epist. 1. lib. 1.

*There sounds, methinks, still thro' my well-purg'd Ear
A little Voice, fond Horace have a care,
And whilst 'tis well releast thy aged Horse,
Least, when he runs but with unequal Force,
And stretches hard to win, he breaks his Wind,
And, laugh'd at, distanc'd, basely lags behind.*
CREECH.

Poets and Orators ought to be most careful of withdrawing from their Business at a proper time; because they stand most in need of the Warmth of Imagination: yet it too frequently happens that they persist in their Career till the lowest Decline of Age. They think the Public is obliged to drink the very Dregs of their pretended *Nectar*. But, if formerly the Legislators limited the Time, wherein People might marry, (for they prohibited it to Women of 50 and Men of 60 Years of Age) (3) and, if they supposed that, after a certain Age, it was time to leave off thinking of Procreation, either because of the Extinction, or the Weakness, of the Faculties; every Author ought, for the same Reason, to set Bounds to himself in the Production of Books, which is a kind of Generation, for which every Age is by no means proper. The Comparison, which *Horace* makes use of, puts me in mind of a Precept, which *Virgil* has left us; and which old Poets ought to apply to themselves.

(3) Quid est quare apud poetas salacissimus Jupiter desierit liberos tollere? trum sexagenarius factus est, & illi lex Papia sibu'am irrogauit? Lucbart. lib. 1. cap. 16. Capit. Papiæ Popperæ lesa a Tiberio Cæsare, quasi sexagenarii generare non possent, addito alrogavit. Suet m. in Claud. c. p. 23. & ibi Commentatores.

Hunc quoque, ubi, aut morbo gravis aut jam senior annis,
Deficit, abde domo, nec turpi ignosce senectæ.
Frigidus in Venerem senior, frustraque laborem

Ingratum trahit, &, si quando ad prælia ventum est,
Ut quondam in stipulis magnus sine viribus Ignis,
Incassum furit (4).

But, worn with Years, when dire Diseases come,
Then hide his not ignoble Age, at home.
For, when his Blood no youthful Spirits move,
He languishes, and labours in his Love.
In vain he burns, like hasty stubble Fires,
And in himself his former self requires.
DRYDEN.

(4) Virgil. Georg. lib. 3. ver. 95.

I say, old Poets ought to profit by this Lesson, and not think to climb *Parnassus*, when they are become like that Horse which *Pliny* spoke of, after *Aristotle* (5): " Generat mas ad annos triginta tres.——Opun- " te & ad quadraginta duraste tradunt adjutum modo " in attollenda priore parte corporis.——*The Male ge- " nerates till thirty Years of Age.—At Opus they say " he holds out till forty, with the Assistance however " of lifting up the fore part of his Body.*" They obscure their first Glory by it, in Imitation of our *Domitius Afer*. See the Article JOHN DAURAT. Some dedicate their Muses to *divine Poetry* in their old Age; these are commonly insipid Productions (6): I say commonly, for there are very excellent Works compos'd by old Men on all Subjects.

(5) Plin. lib. 8. cap. 42.
(6) See Baillet's Judgment of the Poets, Tom. 3. pag. 246.

[C] *Was greatly attach'd to this Person.*] *Charles Stephens*, *Lloyd*, and *Hofman*, in their Dictionaries, *Glandorpius*, at the 306th Page of his *Onomasticon*, and others, remark, that *Quintilian* informs us of this Particular in his 5th Book: *Confitetur senem Domitium sibi adolescentulo cultum*: But they all agree, that the Authority, which *Domitius* had acquir'd, was much diminished, *sed priore autoritate multum imminuta*. I have not found this in that Passage of *Quintilian*; he says (7), " Sufficiebant alioqui " libri duo à Domitio Afro in hanc rem compositi, " quem adolescentulus senem colui, ut non lecta " mihi tantum ea, sed pleraque ex ipso fint cognita.— " *The two Books of Domitius Afer upon this Subject " were otherwise sufficient; for I was a Follower of " the old Orator in my Youth; so that I receiv'd In- " struction as well from the Author, as his Writings.*" He should have quoted the 11th Chapter of the 12th Book of *Quintilian*. It is there we meet with the Decline of *Domitius*'s Authority; which affords us a Confirmation of the Precept, which the Author had before given, concerning the Retreat, which Orators ought to make, when their Age will not suffer them to maintain their former Character. " Non quia pro- " desse unquam satis sit, & illa mente, atque illa facul- " tate prædito nonc conveniat operis pulcherrimi quam " longissimum tempus; sed quia decet hoc quoque " prospicere, ne quid pejus quam fecerit, faciat. Ne- " que enim scientia modo constat Orator, quæ augetur " annis,

(-) See also when he says of his Judgment in old Age, Tom. 1. of his Judgment of the Learned, pag. 389.
(7) Quintil. lib. 5. cap. 7.

AFER. 121

him (g). He tells us, that there were many agreeable Narrations in his Pleadings; and that there were public Collections of his Jests, some of which he relates. He mentions likewise two Books which this Orator publish'd concerning Evidences. It was well for him, on a certain occasion, that he had a ready, as well as a flattering, Wit, or else he had been undone. It was when *Caligula* became his Accuser (b), and pleaded in Person against him (i). *Domitius*, instead of defending himself, repeated that Prince's Plea [D], with signs of Admiration, and then kneeled down, and begg'd Pardon, declaring that he dreaded *Caligula*'s Eloquence, more than his Imperial Quality. He was not only pardon'd, but rais'd to the Consulship, by the Deprivation of those, who were then in Office. His Crime was very slight; he had erected a Statue to *Caligula*, and remark'd in the Inscription, That that Prince was in his second Consulship, at the Age of 27 Years. He thought to make his Court by it; but the Emperor brought an Action against him for it, pretending that he reproach'd him for his Youth, and his infringing the Laws (k). *Afer* had some adopted Children: *Pliny* the Younger will inform you so, and tell you besides some curious Circumstances concerning them [E]. The Abbot *Faydit*, in his Remarks on *Virgil*, pag. 5. makes him of the Royal Family of the *Domitians*.

Marginal notes:
(g) Quintil. lib. 5. cap. 7. & lib. 6. cap. 3. See also Pliny's Epist. 14. lib. 2. & ibi Catanæum, pag. 1214.
(b) Dion Cass. lib. 59. ad Ann. 792.
(i) He read his Plea.
(k) Dion. lib. 59.

" annis, sed voce, laterum firmitate; quibus fractis
" aut imminutis, ætate, seu valetudine, cavendum
" est, ne quid in Oratore summo desideretur, ne in-
" terstistat fatigarus, ne quæ dicet parum audiri sentiat,
" ne se queratur priorem. Vidi ego longe omnium
" quos mihi cognoscere contigit, summum oratorem,
" Domitium Afrum valde senem, quotidiè aliquid ex
" ea quam meruerat autoritate perdentem, cùm, agente
" illo, quem Principem fuisse quondam Fori non erat
" dubium, alii (quod indignum videbatur) riderent,
" alii erubescerent, quæ occasio fuère illis dicendi,
" malle eum deficere quam desinere. Neque erant
" illa qualiacunque mala, sed nimiora. Quare ante-
" quam in has ætatis veniat insidias, receptui canet,
" & in portum integra nave perveniet (8). ——— *Not
" that it is sufficient once to have been useful, or that
" the longest possible Continuance of so fine a Profes-
" sion is improper for a Person endu'd with these
" Abilities; but because he ought to provide against
" this likewise, that he does not degenerate from his
" former Excellency. For Science (which indeed in-
" creases with Years) will not alone make an Orator;
" he must have Lungs, and Strength of Sides; and if
" these are broken or impair'd by Age or Sickness, he
" must take care that the great Orator is not found
" deficient, that he does not stop short for want of
" Breath, that he is not sensible he is not heard, and
" that he is not the first to complain of himself. I
" myself saw the greatest Orator, of all I ever knew,
" Domitius Afer, in his very old Age, continually
" losing part of that Authority, which he had meri-
" ted; insomuch that, when he pleaded, (he, who un-
" doubtedly was once the first at the Bar) some, which
" appear'd very indecent, laugh'd, others blush'd for
" him; which occasioned them to say, they had rather
" he would faulter, than conclude. Nor was this a
" slight Inconvenience, but a Matter of great Conse-
" quence. Wherefore an Orator, where he falls into
" these Snares of Age, should sound a Retreat, and
" sail into Port with a sound Vessel."* I omit *Moreri*'s great and capital Omissions; they may be well enough known only by comparing. I shall only remark, that his Citation of *Suetonius*, and of *Dion*, in *Caligula*, is nothing to the purpose. For besides that it is not customary to cite *Dion* without refering to such or such a Book, and that it is only his Abbreviator *Xiphilinus*, who is cited with reference to such or such an Emperor, it is not true that *Suetonius* speaks of *Domitius Afer*, either in the Life of *Caligula*, or in any Work, which we have remaining of his. So that, when *Scaliger* advances, in his Notes on the Chronicle of *Eusebius*, that what has been said of that Orator by St *Jerome*, was taken out of *Suetonius*, he must necessarily have regard to Books that are lost since the Death of That Father. Mr *Hoffman* gives us two *Domitius Afers* instead of one, and makes use of the bad Citation, for which we have censur'd Mr *Moreri*.

[D] *That Prince's Plea*.] *Caligula* was so charm'd with that Piece of his own, that when one of his freed Men, who had contributed much to pacify him, ventur'd to reproach him for the Process enter'd against *Domitius*, he answered, *I ought not to have suppress'd a Discourse of such Importance*. As much as to say, *What, should I have taken so much Pains about this Plea for nothing? should I rather have renounc'd the Praises which my Rhetoric deserv'd, than expose

the Life of Domitius?* There are but too many great Men of *Caligula*'s way of thinking: They believe every thing ought to be sacrificed to their Passions. They, who said, that the Cardinal *de Lorrain* chose to expose the Catholic Religion to all the Dangers of the Conference of *Poissy*, rather than deprive himself of the Honour of displaying his Learning and Eloquence upon that Occasion (9), argued him pretty well.

[E] *Curious Circumstances concerning them*.] *Domitius* adopted two Brothers, whose Names were *Domitius Tullus*, and *Domitius Lucanus*. He caus'd afterwards their Father's Estate to be confiscated, and left them his own in some manner against his Intention; for it is very probable that he was prevented by Death from revoking the Will, which he had made in their Favour. *Domitius Lucanus*, Son-in-law of *Curtius Mantia*, render'd himself odious to his Father-in-law. He had a Daughter, in whose Favour *Mantia* would not make his Will, but on condition, that *Lucanus* should set her at Liberty; but, when she was made free, *Domitius Tullus* adopted her. This was a Collusion of the two Brothers: They enjoy'd their Fortunes in common; wherefore, by the Daughter's being again in her Father's Power, by means of this Adoption, *Domitius Lucanus* came in for a share of *Mantia*'s Inheritance, though the latter had used many Precautions to hinder him from it (10). *Domitius Tullus* was his Brother's Heir, preferable to the Daughter, who was common to them. He fed many with Hopes of being his Heirs; by which means he procured all the Caresses, all the Presents, and all the officious Assiduities, to himself, which are used to rich old Men, whose Inheritances are courted; but he deceived them all. The Young Lady, whom he had adopted, was his Heiress, and all his Legacies were given to his Relations. He particularly remembered his Wife, for he left her a good Estate. She undervalued herself in marrying him, considering the wretched Condition, to which Age and Diseases had reduced him. He might have disgusted a Woman, in his Condition, though she had been his Wife in his Youth and Vigour. How much more Reason was there for his being disagreeable to a Wife, who began her Correspondence with him when he was so infirm. Nevertheless this Lady bore the distastfulness of her Condition so patiently, and supported her Husband's infirm and decay'd Life with so much Charity, that she regain'd the good Opinion of the Public. This poor Wretch was so impotent in all his Limbs, that his Servants were obliged to wash and clean his Teeth, which caus'd him to complain of being every Day obliged to lick his Slaves Fingers. Yet he had no mind to die (11). *Pliny*'s Words, which give us this Account, and which contain so many *Characteristics of Manners*, deserve to be produc'd at length. " Accepit (*uxor*) amœnissimas villas, ac-
" cepit magnam pecuniam uxor optima & patientis-
" sima, ac tanto melius de viro merita, quanto magis
" est reprehensa, quod nupsit. Nam mulier, matalibus
" clara, moribus proba, ætate declivis, diu vidua,
" mater olim, parùm decorè sequuta matrimonium
" videbatur divitis senis, ita perditi morbo, ut esse
" tædio posset uxori, quàm juvenia, sanúsque duxisset.
" Quippe omnibus membris extortus & fractus, tan-
" tas opes solis oculis obibat; ac ne in lectulo qui-
" dem, nisi ab aliis, movebatur. Quinetiam, fœdum
" miserandumque

Marginal notes:
(8) Quintill. lib. 12. cap. 11 pag. 590.
(9) See the Remark [D] of the Article LORRAIN (Charles of).
(10) Fuit fratribus illis quasi fato datum, ut divites fierent invitissimis à quibus facti essent. —— It was the Fate of these Brothers, to become rich even in spight of those, by whom they were made so. Plin. Epist. 18. lib. 8.
(11) Ibid. pag. 493.

VOL I. H h

AFRANIUS. AGAR.

"miferandumque dictu, dentes lavandos fricandof-
"que præbebat. Auditum eſt frequenter ab ipſo,
"quum quæreretur de contumeliis debilitatis ſuæ, ſe
"digitos ſervorum ſuorum quotidie lingere. Vivebat
"tamen, & vivere volebat, ſuſtentante maximè uxore,
"quæ culpam inchoati matrimonii in gloriam perſe-
"verantia verterat (12). ——— *She* (his Wife) *came
"into Poſſeſſion of the fineſt Villas, and a large Eſtate;
"a Wife, the beſt and moſt patient, that ever was,
"and who deſerv'd ſo much the more from her Huſ-
"band, as the Cenſure ſhe underwent in marrying was
"the greater. For it was thought ſcarce decent, that
"a Lady, of great Birth, of Reputation, advanc'd in
"Years, who had been long a Widow, and formerly a
"Mother, ſhould be fond of marrying a rich old Man,
"ſo worn with Diſeaſes, that he might have diſguſted
"a Wife, whom ſhe had married in his Youth, and in
"Health. For he was ſo diſtorted and broken in all
"his Limbs, that he could only enjoy his great Wealth
"in Sight; nor even ſo, without being turn'd in his
"Bed by others. Nay, which is filthy and wretched
"to relate, he was oblig'd to have his Teeth waſh'd and
"clean'd by others. He was frequently heard, in com-
"plaining of his Infirmities, to ſay, that he every
"Day lick'd his Servants Fingers. Yet he liv'd, and
"deſired to live, being ſupported chiefly by his Wife,
"who turn'd the falſe Step of beginning ſuch a Mar-
"riage to her own Honour by perſevering in it.*"
This Lady's Virtue would certainly have been more
worthy Admiration, had ſhe foreſeen the long Continuance of her Huſband's Infirmities. But, after all,
ſhe deſerves to be praiſed; for tho' the hopes of
purchaſing a large Jointure, at the price of ſome very
vexatious, but ſhort, Diſguſts deceiv'd her, yet her
Condition never appear'd to fit uneaſy upon her; but
ſhe did her Duty always with a good Grace. What
fine Deſcriptions are there in that Letter of *Pliny*!
how ſtrongly does that miſerable, impotent Wretch,
in his Fears of Death, repreſent human Weakneſs! An
Infirmity, of which we ſhall ſpeak elſewhere (13), and
which was in thoſe Times much more ſcandalous than
at preſent; for it was taken for a courageous and re-
ſolute Action to put an end to too tedious a Sickneſs.
How perpoſterous is it, on the other ſide, to ſee a
Man, who had a Daughter, and Grand-children,
give out that he expects an Heir out of another Family; and that they need only lay a formal Siege to
his Inheritance to take the Place! What ſordid Traffic! What Cunning! It was ſuch like Perſons as this,
who found their Account in thoſe, who courted their
Inheritance.

——— *Dominus tamen & Domini Rex
Si vis tu fieri, nullus tibi parvulus Aula
Luſerit Æneas, nec filia dulcior illo.
Jamdudum & carum ſterilis facit uxor amicum* (14).

*Wou'dſt thou become his Patron and his Lord,
Wou'dſt thou be in thy turn by him ador'd?
No young Æneas in thy Hall muſt play,
No ſweeter Daughter lead thy Heart aſtray.
O! how a barren Wife does recommend!
How dear, how pleaſant is a childleſs Friend,*
Rev. Mr BOWLES.

But if this Avarice was baſe, That of the Perſons,
whom it cheated, was no leſs ſordid. They would
have been leſs blamable, if they had courted the Favour of one, who had no Children, and if they had
not exclaimed againſt *Domitius Tullus*, after his Death.
Their Complaints were laugh'd at, as they diſcovered
their Shame; the deceaſed was praiſed, and his Conduct was thought uſeful to ſuch a corrupt Age as
That. Let us once more employ *Pliny's* Pencil. "Va-
"rii tota civitate ſermones: alii fictum, ingratum, im-
"memorem loquuntur, ſeque ipſos, dum inſectantur
"illum, turpiſſimis confeſſionibus produnt, qui de illo,
"uti de patre, avo, proavo, quaſi orbi quærantur: alii
"contra hic ipſum laudibus ferunt, quod ſit fruſtratus
"improbas ſpes hominum, quos ſic decipere pro mori-
"bus temporum prudentia eſt (15).——— *The whole City
"was divided; ſome call'd him falſe, ungrateful, and
"forgetful; and, whilſt they reproached his Memory,
"betray'd themſelves by ſcandalous Confeſſions, com-
"plaining of him, as if they had been diſinherited by
"a Father, Grand-Father, or Great-Grand-Father;
"others extol him for this very thing, in that he diſ-
"appointed the unreaſonable Hopes of ſome Men, whom,
"conſidering the Morals of the Times, it was Wiſdom ſo
"to deceive.*"

AFRANIUS *Quintianus*, a *Roman* Senator of a bad Reputation by reaſon of
his infamous Lewdneſs, enter'd into the grand Conſpiracy againſt *Nero*, which coſt *Seneca* his Life, in the Year of *Rome* 818. He had a perſonal Reaſon to hate that Prince,
who had compos'd a ſevere Satire in Verſe againſt him. He denied, a long time, that
he was an Accomplice in that Conſpiracy, but confeſt it at laſt, in hopes of his Pardon. He ſhewed more Courage in his Death, than his manner of Life promis'd (*a*).

AGAR *, the Handmaid, and afterwards the Concubine of the Patriarch
Abraham, was an *Egyptian* (*a*). There is ſome probability, that he took her into his
Service, when he was return'd from *Egypt*, and had recover'd his Wife, whom King
Pharaoh had taken from him. But it is falſe to ſay, as the *Jews* do [A], That *A-
gar* was That King's Daughter. Every one knows, that *Sarah*, finding herſelf bar-
ren a long time [B], deſired her Huſband to try whether he could have Children by
this Servant; and that *Abraham*, overcome by her Sollicitations, and doing alſo an
Act

[A] *As the Jews do.*] It is thought that the *Chaldee Paraphraſt* was the firſt, who publiſhed this falſe
Tradition. He pretends, that *Pharaoh*, having taken
away *Sarah*, gave her his own Daughter *Agar* for an
Handmaid; and that *Sarah* brought her with her into the Land of *Canaan*. Rabbi *Joſua* is of the ſame
Opinion (1). Another Rabbi gives this turn to the
Story; that *Pharaoh*, ſtruck with the Prodigies,
which were wrought upon his own Perſon, ſince
he had taken away *Sarah*, ſaid to *Agar*, *My Daughter, it is better for you to be a Servant in this Family, than Miſtreſs in another* (2). But *Abraham
Zacuth* will not allow her to be of ſuch illuſtrious
Extraction; he ſays, that ſhe was a Servant of *Churia*, the Wife of *Pharaoh*, and that *Churia* gave her
to *Sarah*, after the Death of her Huſband (3). St
Chryſoſtom ſays, that *Pharaoh* himſelf gave this Handmaid to *Abraham* (4). The Scripture obſerves, indeed, that, among other Preſents, which he made
him, he gave him *Women Servants* (5). If he gave
him this Damoſel, we need not queſtion, but that
he choſe her from among thoſe of a ſervile Rank.
I could willingly believe, what *Philo* ſays, that ſhe
embraced *Abraham's* Religion (6); but as to what
he adds, that That Patriarch abſtained from enjoying.
her, as ſoon as he perceived that ſhe was with Child,
I am not concerned either to deny or affirm it. Theſe
are Myſteries, which we ought not to pry into; it
muſt be ſuppoſed that they paſt under the Veil of
Night, or behind the Curtain, and we muſt leave
them to the Covert of their natural Darkneſs. The
Jews, always ſoaring up to the *Marvellous*, attribute
Agar's Converſion to the Miracles, which were performed in *Pharaoh's* Houſe on Account of *Sarah's*
Rape (7).

[B] *A long Time.*] It is ſaid, in *Geneſis*, that *Abraham* had dwelt ten Years in the Land of *Canaan*,
when he firſt lay with *Agar*; from whence the
Jews have inferred, that an Huſband ought not to
cohabit with a Woman after he has found her barren for the Space of ten Years (8). An abſurd Conſequence; as well becauſe *Abraham* had been married above ten Years to *Sarah*, when ſhe propoſed
her Handmaid to him (9), as becauſe he had not

the

AGAR.

Act of Obedience, according to the Translation of some Interpreters [*C*], went in unto *Agar* with all the Success that his Wife could have desired; I say, his Wife; for it was upon her own Account, that she desir'd her Servant might bear Children, and, being incapable of giving her Husband any Herself, she was willing to oblige him by Proxy (*b*). They, who shall think it little agreeable to the Practice of our Age, that so much Sollicitation was requisite to prevail with *Abraham* to comply with such a Request, and are chiefly surpriz'd that this Request came from his own Wife, ought to remember, that all Times, and all Nations of the World, are not alike. However it be, *Agar*, finding herself with Child, became as proud, as if she had done a very great Exploit; but her Insolence was soon abated. *Sarah*, who could not brook her haughty Behaviour, treated her with such Severity, as oblig'd her to leave the House [*D*]. *Agar* did not return, till she had humbled herself, according to the order she had receiv'd from an Angel, who told her that she should be delivered of a Son, who should quarrel with every body [*E*]; soon after which she was deliver'd of *Ishmael*, who was educated with his Father till he was at least 15 or 16 Years of Age [*F*]. It is not known, whether these two Women agreed very well all that time; but we find that *Agar* was at last oblig'd to depart with her Son. *Sarah* would absolutely have it so, because she had seen *Ishmael mocking* at something [*G*]. *Abraham* sent the Mother and the Child away with a very small *Viaticum*. The Bottle of Water, which he gave them, being emptied, poor *Agar* saw the Hour that her Son must die of Thirst [*H*]. To avoid this Sight, she went and sat down at a distance from the

(*b*) Ecce conclusit me Dominus ne parerem, ingredere ad ancillam meam, si forte saltem ex illa suscipiam filios: Behold now the Lord hath restrained me from bearing; I pray thee go in unto my maid, it may be that I may obtain children by her. Genes. xvi. 1.

the least Intention of forsaking her, after he had lived ten Years with her in the Land of *Canaan* without Issue.

[*C*] *Doing also an Act of Obedience, according to the Translation of some Interpreters.*] The Vulgar Translation says, *Cumque ille acquiesceret deprecanti*; and the Version of *Geneva*, *And Abraham obeyed the Word* of Sarah (10). St *Austin* gives this latter Sense to the Words of Scripture; for, after having observed, that *Abraham* was so complaisant, as to cohabit with, or to leave, *Agar*, just as it was agreeable to *Sarah's* Inclinations, he makes this Exclamation, "O virum viriliter utentem fœminis, conjuge
"temperanter, ancilla OBTEMPERANTER, nulla in-
"temperanter (11)! — *O illustrious Man, in the*
"*Use of Women a Man indeed; yet conversing with*
"*his Wife temperately, with his Handmaid* OBE-
"DIENTLY, *and with no Woman intemperately!*" He had already made use of this Expression, "Usus est
"ea (*concubina*) non ad explendam libidinem, nec
"insultans, sed potius OBEDIENS conjugi (12).
"—— *He conversed with her* (his Concubine) *not*
"*to gratify his Lust, or to insult her, but rather in*
"OBEDIENCE *to his Wife*.

[*D*] *Treated her with such Severity, as obliged her to leave the House.*] Who would ever have thought that this would have one day served as an Apology for Persecution? Yet the copious and inventive Mind of St *Austin* found this Secret in it. He maintained, from *Sarah's* Conduct towards *Agar*, that the True Church may inflict Chastisements on the False, exile it, torment it, and so on. He was severely reprimanded for this Assertion in the *Philosophical Commentary* on the famous Words, *Compel them to come in* (13).

[*E*] *Who should quarrel with every body.*] The Angel said to her, *He will be a wild Man; his Hand will be against every Man, and every Man's Hand against him* (14). If it were permitted to look for Types here, as St *Austin* did, one would think, that *Ishmael* was an Emblem of certain snarling Polemical Writers, who are for snapping at every body, and who, to declare War the better against human kind, run every Moment out of their Sphere, scribbling on every Subject, right or wrong, and always in a defamatory and libellous Style. All Ages and Countries produce these Copies of *Ishmael*. Some of them indeed differ from their Original in this, that, tho' they cast Stones at every body, few Persons take the trouble to return them; but let them quietly enjoy a wretched Impunity, which increases their Insolence, and their Frenzy.

[*F*] *Till he was at least fifteen or sixteen Years of Age.*] It is proved thus: *Ishmael* was fourteen Years old, when *Isaac* was born; for he was born when *Abraham* was eighty six Years of Age (15), and *Abraham* was an hundred Years old, when *Sarah* was delivered of *Isaac* (16). Now the latter was weaned before *Ishmael* was sent away; therefore, *&c.* I shall not amuse you with the Opinion of those *Jews*, who believe, that *Isaac* sucked twelve or fifteen

(10) Genes. xvi. 2. The English Version in like manner gives it, And Abraham hearkened unto the voice of Sarah.

(11) August. de Civit. Dei, lib. 16. cap. 25.

(12) Id. ib.

(13) Comment. Philos. part. 3. pag. 62.

(14) Genes. xvi. 12.

(15) Ibid. xvi. 16.

(16) Ibid. xxi. 5.

Years (17); for if there were any Foundation for this Opinion, I should have allowed a longer time for *Ishmael's* abode with *Abraham*, than what I have here advanced. See the Remark [*H*].

[*G*] *Had seen Ishmael mocking at something.*] The Translation of the LXX imports, that *Sarah's* ill Humour proceeded from her having seen *Ishmael* play with *Isaac*. The Vulgar Translation followed them in it; *Cum vidisset Sara filium Hagar Ægyptiæ ludentem cum filio suo*. The Hebrew Text particularizes nothing; it leaves us to guess, whether the Son of *Agar* laught at *Sarah* or *Isaac*, or at the Feast that was made when *Isaac* was weaned, or at something else; or whether he made himself too familiar with, or superior to, *Isaac*; or lastly, whether he attempted to beat him. Some Interpreters have advanced many idle Notions hereupon; for they believe, that either *Sarah* saw *Ishmael* perform some Acts of Idolatry, or that he played some lewd Tricks, or that he endeavoured to kill *Isaac*. " Hebræi nonnulli acci-
"piunt de lusu idololatriæ, quasi videlicet idola fin-
"gentem & colentem Ismaëlem vidisset Sara —
"Alii venereum hunc fuisse lusum statuunt — &
"detectionem turpitudinis. Neque desunt qui Is-
"maëlem fratri necem molitum esse existimant (18). Some pretend, that he shot an Arrow at him with a Design of killing him (19). It is said, that the *Hebrew* Word for *Mocking* (20) has four Significations, in Scripture, *viz*. Pastime, Idolatry, an amorous Game, and a desperate Fight. To prove the third Signification, they alledge the twenty sixth Chapter of *Genesis*, where it is said, *That Abimelech looking out at a Window, saw Isaac sporting with Rebecca his Wife*. But it is to extend the Signification of the Word beyond it's due Limits, to pretend, that it implies, in that Passage, *the Work of the Flesh*. It is sufficient to understand by it a certain Familiarity, which shewed that they were not Brother and Sister, but Husband and Wife: for that was the Conclusion *Abimelech* drew from it. The most probable Account of the Matter seems to me to be this: *Ishmael* gave himself some Airs of Contempt, which made *Sarah* fear, that he would one day dispute the Birthright, if it was not prevented in time.

[*H*] *That her Son must die of Thirst.*] Supposing, that the mocking, which *Sarah* was offended at, was on occasion of the Feast that was made when *Isaac* was weaned, *Ishmael* must have been sent away at about sixteen Years of Age. If it be supposed, that this Mockery was much later in time, than that Feast, his Age will be so much the more increased at his leaving his Father. But make him as young as you can (which will be to allow him at least sixteen Years of Age) will it not appear very strange, that his Mother was obliged to carry him on her Shoulders at that Age, to lay him under a little Tree, to take him up again, to carry him in her Arms, and to give him drink? Read that Passage of Scripture concerning *Ishmael*; it represents to us a Child in swaddling Cloaths, or very near it. We cannot get out of this Plunge by supposing that this Fact

(17) Apud Hieronymi cap. 21. in tract. Hebraicis. See also Tom. 1. Corn. à Lapide in Genes. p. 199. takes it for granted, that Isaac was not weaned till five Years of Age; Salian p. 474. cites St Jerome, Del Rio, and Per. rius for the same Opinion, which is his own.

(18) Heidegg. ibid. pag. 205.

(19) R. Eliezer Pirk. cap. 30. ap. Heidegg. ib. who cites also Baal Hathurim.

(20) Lyranus apud Pererium in Gen. xxi.

AGAR.

the place, where she had laid *Ishmael*. An Angel came to her Relief, and discover'd a Well to her, where she fill'd her Bottle; and by this means she sav'd her Son's Life. She married him afterwards to an *Egyptian* Woman. Thus far the Scripture carries the History. Many of the *Rabbins*, pretend, without any Reason, that *Agar* is the same with *Ketura*, who was *Abraham's* Wife after the Death of *Sarah* (*c*). But this Error is much more tolerable than the ridiculous Superstition of the *Saracens*, who honoured the Stone, on which *Agar* [*I*], as they said, granted *Abraham* the last Favour, as an holy Relick. Their Writers do not mention the Reason; and acknowledge but a very remote Relation between *Agar*, and the Stone [*K*]. An Author, cited by *Eusebius*, certainly meant this *Agar*, when he said that *Abraham* married an *Egyptian* Servant-Maid, by whom he had twelve Children, who seiz'd on *Arabia*, and divided it among themselves (*d*). The *Rabbins* have advanced another Fable, to wit, that *Ishmael* came to Life again, before he was born; for, say they, his Mother lost her Fruit for a Punishment of her Vanity, and by the Fatigue of her Journey; but her deference for the Angel who advised her to humble herself to her Mistress, obliged God to re-animate her Child. *Cornelius à Lapide* assure us in the 171st Page of his Commentary on the *Pentateuch*, that *Tostatus* believ'd this Story.

Calvin is falsly accused of inveighing bitterly against *Abraham* and *Sarah*, on account of the Concubinage of *Agar*. But there is more Reason to say that St *Austin's* Apology for the Patriarch's Conduct is very weak. See the Remarks [*I*] and [*K*] of the Article SARAH.

(*c*) Targum Jonathanis, Pamphrasis Hierosolym. Jarchius, R. Eliezer apud Heidegg. Hist. Patriarch. Tom. 2. pag. 136.

(*d*) Meloa apud Alexand. Polyhist. cited by Euseb. Præp. Evang. lib. 9. cap. 19.

Fact was misplaced; for it is expresly declared, that *Sarah* sent *Ishmael* away because she would not have him share the Inheritance with *Isaac*. And therefore *Ishmael* was not sent away 'till after *Isaac* was born; and consequently he was as able to seek for Water, as his Mother; he was no longer ἐπι τῶν ὤμων αὐτῆς, an Infant to be carried upon her Shoulders, &c. (21) I foresee that I shall be told, that neither the Translation of the LXX. nor the Vulgate import, That *Ishmael* was carried on his Mother's Back; and that it ought therefore to be concluded, that the *Hebrew* Text does not clearly favour my Supposition. With all my Heart; the rest of the Narrative is sufficient for me, and I submit it to the Judgment of every Reader, who considers the thing without Prejudice. Perhaps the best Solution would be to say, that, as they lived longer in those Ages, they did not come out of Childhood so soon as we: This would do very well, if it were not attended with the Consequence of making *Ishmael* twenty Years old when he was thrust out of doors; for, according to this Answer *Isaac* must have sucked longer, than they sucked him in the Time of the *Maccabees*. Now in that Age Children sucked three Years (22); we ought therefore to acquiesce, with St *Jerome*, and many of the Moderns, in the old *Hebrew* Tradition, which I took notice of, to wit, that *Isaac* was not weaned 'till five Years of Age. Tho' I cannot but express my wonder, that they, who follow it (23), should not perceive the difficulty attending it; which does not cease to be very great, even supposing, as I do, that *Isaac* did not such suck at the Breast so long as was usual in the time of the *Maccabees*.

[*I*] *The Stone on which Agar, &c.*] What idle Stories! as if *Abraham*, who was a great Lord, and whose Retinue amounted to above three hundred Domesticks, able to bear Arms, could not provide a Bed for a Concubine of this kind. He did not take her, but at the Sollicitation of his Wife; *Sarah* performed in some manner the Functions of the *Paranymph*; it was more like a Wedding, than any thing else; and yet they tell us, that a Marriage of this sort was consummated on a Stone. This Story might be probable enough, if it were related of a Master of a Family, who was afraid of his Wife, and whom a thousand reasons might induce to do the Feat by Stealth, and wherever Occasion offered; being persuaded, that if he missed his Opportunity, in hopes of a better, he might be disappointed for Life. However it be, we understand by *Euthymius Zigabenus*, that the *Saracens* honoured and kissed a Stone, which they called *Brachtan*, and when they were asked the Reason of it, some answered, it was, because *Abraham* knew *Agar* on that Stone; others, that it was, because he tied his Camel to it, when he prepared to offer up his Son *Isaac* (24). The same Author says, That this Stone was the Head of the Statue of *Venus*, the Deity, which the ancient *Ishmaelites* worshipped. The form of the *Anathemas* which a *Saracen* is obliged to recite who embraces Christianity, confirms this Author's Account; for it imports, that That Stone was the Image of *Venus* (25), and that the *Saracens* spoke of it as of a thing, which had served *Abraham* for the abovementioned Purposes. On this Occasion, I shall observe, that the Stone, which was worshipped by the *Arabians*, and which they took for the God *Mars*, was black and unhewn. Τὸ δὲ ἄγαλμα λίθος ἦν μέλας, τετράγωνος, ἀνώνυτος. —— Simulacrum autem est lapis niger, quadratus, nullam figuram incisam habens (26). Ridetis temporibus priscis Persæ fluvium coluisse —— INFORMEM Arabas lapidem (27). *You think it ridiculous, that in ancient Times the Persians worshipped a River — the Arabians an UNHEWN Stone.* *Maximus Tyrius*, who had seen it, says only, that it was square (28). The Mother of the Gods, whom the *Phrygians* adored with a very extraordinary Zeal, was nothing more than a plain Stone; and they gave only a Stone to the *Roman* Ambassadors, who desired to establish the Worship of that Divinity at *Rome*: "Is legato "comiter acceptos Pessinuntem in Phrygiam deduxit, "sacrumque iis lapidem, quem matrem Deûm incolæ "esse dicebant tradidit, ac deportare Romam jus- "sit (29)." How absurd soever the Idolatry of those was, who worshipped the Stone which *Jacob* set up for a Pillar, and anointed and consecrated to God (30); it was yet more tolerable, than That of the *Saracens*; for *Jacob's* Stone served him for a Pillow, in a Night, which he past, as no one may say, with God, the Dreams and Visions, with which he was entertained, representing heavenly Things in so lively a manner to him. The *Saracens* durst not have said so much, in relation to their pretended Stone of *Agar*. *Scaliger* has collected a great deal of curious Learning concerning this Stone of *Jacob* (31); but what the learned *Pocock* has said concerning That, which the *Saracens* honoured, is no less considerable. I am going to take some Notice of it.

[*K*] *But a very remote Relation between Agar and that Stone.*] You must consult *Pocock*, if you would be exactly inform'd of their Religion hereupon (32). The black Stone, which they adore, is in the Temple of *Mecca*, in a Corner, two Cubits and one third from the Ground. They suppose that it was one of the precious Stones of Paradise, and that it descended from thence with *Adam*: that it was carried thither again at the Time of the Deluge; that it was sent into the World again, when *Abraham* built the Temple; and that the Angel *Gabriel* put it into the Hands of that Architect (33). It was, at first, whiter than Snow, and brighter than the Sun; but it become black, by being touched by a Woman who had her *Menses*. Others say, That the Sins of Men made it lose it's Whiteness and Lustre; others affirm, that it was fully'd by being much kissed and handled. It would be very difficult to prove from the *Arabian* Authors, what St *John Damascenus* and *Euthymius* assert, That there was a *Venus's* Head engraven upon it. There is another Stone, which they esteem sacred, and on which they pretend a Figure is to be seen; but it is a Figure of Feet, and not of a Head; it is the Print of *Abraham's* Feet, when he rested on that Stone, either, building the Temple (34), or while his Daughter-in-law (35) washed his Head, when he made

(21) *That is to say*, As Men go now, such Men as live in these degenerate days.

(22) *The Mother of the Maccabees told her Son*, that she suckled him three Years, 2 Maccab. vii. 37.

(23) Moreri is of this Number.

(24) Euthym. Zigab. in Panoplia, apud Vossium de Orig. Idol. lib. 2. cap. 71. & lib. 6. cap. 39.

(25) Ἑνοδιώσασθαι τῆς Ἀφροδίτης ἐκείνης εἰκόνα Veneris habere. See Vossius ibid. lib. 2. cap. 31. pag. 467. Edit. Francofurt.

(26) Suidas in voce ΧΑΒΑΡ. pag.

(27) Arnobius, lib. 6. pag. 196.

(28) Maxim. Tyrius Dissert. 38. pag. 384.

(29) Livius lib. 39. cap. 11.

(30) Genes. xxviii. 18.

(31) Scalig. Animadv. in Euseb. n. 2150.

(32) Pockii Notæ in Specim. Histor. Arab. pag. 113, &c.

(33) *See the Remark* [*P*] *of the Article* ABRAHAM.

(34) Ex Abulfeda.

(35) *The Wife of Ishmael.*

AGATHON.

made *Ishmael* a Visit (36). This last Stone is shut up in an Iron Chest. *Ahmed Ebn Yusef* pretends to have seen and kiss'd it, and to have drank Water there out of the Well *Zamzam*, and to have taken notice, that the Print of the Right Foot is deeper than that of the Left, and that the Toes are as long as the Fingers of the Hand (37). They hid this Stone in one of the Hills of *Mecca*, when the *Karmatians* committed a thousand Prophanations in the Temple, and carried the *black Stone* away (38). Now since *Euthymius*, and the Catechism for the Use of the converted *Saracens*, remark, That the Stone, on which it was pretended that *Abraham* had to do with *Agar*, or to which he tied his Camel, was in the middle of the Oratory, *in medio æræ τῆς εὐχῆς*, this must not be understood of the Black Stone (for that is fix'd in a Corner of the Temple); but of the Stone, in which *Abraham's* Footsteps are to be seen. Besides, though no *Arabian* Writer says, That the Reason why they venerate that Stone, is, because it serv'd the Patriarch for the Purposes mentioned by *Euthymius*, we must believe, that the Tradition, which *Euthymius* speaks of, relates rather to the Stone, in which *Abraham's* Footsteps are imprinted, than to the *Black Stone*; from whence two Things are to be concluded. I. That *Euthymius*, and the Catechist of the *Saracens*, had not a distinct Knowledge of these People's Errors, as to the Worship of Stones. II. That the *Arabian* Writers did not acknowledge any neat and direct Relation between *Agar* and the venerable Stones of *Mecca*. *Agar* is no farther concern'd in it, than inasmuch as *Abraham* set his Feet on it; while her Son *Ishmael's* Wife wash'd his Head. There is a third remarkable Stone at *Mecca*; it is white, and passes for *Ishmael's* Sepulchre; it is in a kind of Inclosure, near the Foundations of the Temple. From all these Particulars we may infer, That it is very easy to deceive a Man in Matters of Religion, and very difficult to undeceive him in them. He is fond of his Prejudices, and finds Leaders, who indulge him in them, and who say within themselves, "*quandoquidem populus vult decipi, decipiatur.* ——— Since "*the People will be impos'd upon, let them be impos'd* "*upon.*" They find their Account in this, both in point of Authority and Profit: When the Disease is become inveterate, the most disinterested fear, that the Remedy may prove worse than the Disease. These dare not cure the Wound, and it is the Interest of others, that it should not be cur'd. Thus an Abuse is perpetuated: Dishonest Men protect it; and honest Men tolerate it.

AGATHON, a Tragic and Comic Poet [*A*] Disciple of *Prodicus* (a), and *Socrates* (b), is greatly celebrated for his Beauty in *Plato's* Dialogue (c), in which he is farther commended for his Good Nature (d). Some Authors report, that he was a very Good Man, and that his Table was magnificent (e). Perhaps they found this on the splendid Entertainments he gave, after his first Tragedy had obtained the Prize (f), and he had been crowned in the Presence of above 30000 Men (g), in the 4th Year of the XCth *Olympiad* (b). *Plato* supposes, that the *Discourses*, which he recites, on the *Nature of Love*, in one of his Books (i), were held the day after that Solemnity, at the second Entertainment, which *Agathon* gave. The Pieces of This Poet were so full of *Antitheses*, that he replyed one day to a Person, who was for expunging them, *You are not aware, that you rob Agathon of himself* (k). He was the Darling of *Pausanias* the *Ceramian*, and follow'd him to the Court of *Archelaus*, King of *Macedon* (l). He often quarrelled with him; but it was with a view of affording him a more sensible Pleasure by their Reconciliation. Thus he explained himself to that Prince, who asked him the Cause of their frequent Quarrels, as *Ælian* informs us in the XXI *Chapter* of the *Second Book* of his *Various History*. I have taken notice, in another place (m), of what is related concerning *Euripides's* Passion for *Agathon*. The Answer of the former is misrepresented in the Historical Dictionaries [*B*]. The Scholiast of *Aristophanes* seems to assure us, that *Agathon*

[*A*] *A Tragic and Comic Poet.*] No body questions his writing Tragedies; it will be sufficient therefore to prove, that he was a Writer of Comedies. For this I may appeal to the Scholiast of *Aristophanes*, on the second Scene of the first Act of the *Frogs*. Οὗτος ὁ Ἀγάθων κωμῳδοποιὸς τὲ Σωκράτους διδασκάλου. *This A-* *gathon, a Writer of Comedies, whom Socrates taught.* Observe, that he speaks of the same Poet, who is one of *Plato's* Interlocutors in the *Feast*, and who most certainly compos'd Tragedies. I appeal likewise to these Words of *Philostratus*, Καὶ Ἀγάθων δὲ ὁ τῆς τραγῳδίας ποιητὴς ὃν ἡ κωμῳδία σοφόντε καὶ καλλιεπῆ οἶδε, πολλαχοῦ τῶν ἰαμβείων γοργιάζει (1). *Agathon*, the Tragic Poet, whom the Comic Muse acknowledged skillful and elegant, frequently imitates the Style of *Gorgias in his Iambics.* I am aware, that these Words may signify, that he was praised in Comedies; but they may be taken in this Sense, That he shewed both his Capacity and Elegancy in the Comedies, which he composed. A learned Critic conjectures. That *Socrates* hinted at our *Agathon*, when he said, that it was the business of the same Poet to compose both Tragedies and Comedies; and that whoever has a Genius for Tragedy, is equally capable of excelling in Comedy (2). Τοῦ αὐτοῦ ἀνδρὸς εἶναι κωμῳδίαν καὶ τραγῳδίαν ἐπίστασθαι ποιεῖν, καὶ τὸν τέχνῃ τραγῳδοποιὸν ὄντα καὶ κωμῳδοποιὸν εἶναι (3). *Ejusdem viri officium esse tragœdiam comœdiamque componere, eumque qui arte tragicus est esse quoque comicus.* It is, I think, to multiply Beings unnecessarily, to give us a Comic Poet *Agathon*, different from ours. It is what *Vossius* (4), *Moreri*, *Hofman*, &c. have done.

[*B*] *The Answer of the former is misrepresented in the Historical Dictionaries.*] I have set it in it's true Light, in another Place (5): the following is a very confused Account of it: "Agatho Philosophus Pythagoricus, frequens antithesis, adhibitus quondam convivio Archelao rege, cujus erat familiarissimus, interrogatusque ab eo, cum jam esset annorum 80, "si robur adhuc illum servaret? Sane, inquit, non "solùm ver, sed autumnus solet bona & prosperitatem adferre (6). ——— Agatho, the Pythagorean Philosopher, a great Lover of Antitheses, being once invited to a Banquet by King Archelaus, with whom he was very intimate, and being asked by him whether, at the Age of fourscore, he yet retained any Vigour; reply'd, surely not only the Spring, but the Autumn, is wont to produce good things and Prosperity." Let us reckon up the Mistakes of this Account. I. The *Agathon*, who was fond of Antitheses, and was in the Court of *Archelaus*, was not a Pythagorean. II. He was but about forty Years of Age, when *Archelaus* gave occasion for the abovementioned Reply (7). III. It was not *Agathon*, but *Euripides*, who gave this Answer. IV. The Question did not turn upon personal Strength, but upon Beauty; and the Answer had no regard to the Goods of Fortune. V. It would be an Absurdity to use the Age of eighty Years for the Autumn of Life. VI. I believe no Philosopher, of the Sect of *Pythagoras*, was called *A- gathon*. All these Faults of *Charles Stephens* are to be found in the second Edition of *Lloyd*; nay we see the pretended Testimony of *Ælian* more exactly remark'd in it (8). This Exactness is prejudicial to the Author; for, since he was not ignorant in what Chapter the Fact was to be found, he is more inexcusable in copying all the Mistakes of the Dictionary which he undertook to correct. Mr *Moreri* followed him Letter by Letter, and distinguish'd between this *Agathon* and Him, who was at the Court of *Archelaus*. Mr *Moreri* speaks also of a *Pythagorean* Philosopher, named *Agathon*, who, at the Age of eighty Years, answered

VOL. I.   I i

AGATHON.

Agathon died at the Court of *Archelaus* (C); and we may conclude from the Words of *Aristophanes*, that he was not living, when the Comedy of the Frogs was acted [D], that is in the second Year of the XCIIId Olympiad (*n*). There remains nothing of *Agathon* but what we find in *Aristotle*, in *Athenæus*, &c. who cited him. They are beautiful Sentences enough, and confirm what has been said of his Passion for Antitheses [E]. I shall give an Instance of them, wherein we meet with a very judicious Maxim relating to the Deceitfulness of Appearances [F]. *Aristophanes* satirizes

(n) See Sam. Petit's Miscellany, lib. 1. cap. 14. pag. 50.

answered that Monarch, That *the Autumn produced Flowers and Fruits, as well as the Spring*. He mentions afterwards *Agathon*, a Tragic Poet; and *Agathon* a Comic Poet.

[C] *That Agathon died at the Court of Archelaus.*] Ἀρχέλαον τῷ Βασιλεῖ μέχρι τελευτῆς μετὰ ἄλλων πολλῶν συνῆν ἐν Μακεδονίᾳ (9). That is, *He lived with many others in Macedonia at the Court of King Archelaus until his Death.* This may either signify, 'till the Death of *Archelaus*, or 'till the Death of *Agathon*. For which Reason I do not give these Words as a certain Proof.

[D] *That he was not living, when the Comedy of the Frogs was acted.*] We find these four Verses there,

HP. Ἀγάθων δὲ ποῦ ἐστιν; ΔΙ. ἀπολιπών μ' ἀποίχεται, Ἀγαθὸς ποιητής, καὶ ποθεινὸς τοῖς φίλοις.
HP. Ποῖ γῆς ὁ τλήμων; ΔΙ. ἐς μακάρων εὐωχίαν (10).

HE. *But where is Agatho?*
BA. *He has left me, and is gone.* —— *A good Poet, and dear to his Friends.*
HE. *Unhappy Man! to what Country is he gone?*
BA. *To the Banquet of the Gods.*

[E] *What has been said of his Passion for Antitheses.*] *Kubmius* has given us three *Sentences* of *Agathon*, as a Specimen of his Taste (11). The two first were cited by *Aristotle*, and the other by *Athenæus*. The Sense of the latter is, *If I tell you the Truth, I shall not please you; and if I please you, I shall not tell you the Truth* (12). Those cited by *Aristotle* signify, the one, that the only impossible thing with God is, to cause, That what has been created, should not have been created (13); the other, That Fortune loves Art, and Art loves Fortune (14). *Vossius* imagin'd, that this last Sentence belong'd to *Agathon* the Comic Poet (15) ; but he had better have ascrib'd it to the Tragedian, and have observ'd, that the Spirit of *Antitheses* adjudges it to him. I say this without pretending, that it is certain that *Agathon*, the Tragic Poet, differs from *Agathon* the Comic Poet. Mr *Moreri* copied *Vossius*, according to Custom. I wonder *Kubmius* did not produce this;

Τὸ μὲν πάρεργον ἔργον ὡς ποιούμεθα,
Τὸ δ' ἔργον ὡς πάρεργον ἐκπονούμεθα (16).

Operis loco ducimus accessorium,
Et in opere satagimus ut accessorio.

[F] *A very judicious Maxim on the Deceitfulness of Appearances.*] *Agathon* observes, That it is likely several Things may happen, which are not likely. Εἰκὸς γίνεσθαι πολλὰ καὶ παρὰ τὸ εἰκός. *Verisimile est & multa fieri præter verisimile*. Thus *Vossius* reports this Sentence; and he observes, that *Aristotle* alledg'd it in more than one Place (17). That great Philosopher cited it in the following manner, in the 24th Chapter of the 2d Book of his Rhetoric.

Τάχ' ἄν τις εἰκὸς αὐτὸ τοῦτ' εἶναι λέγοι,
Βροτοῖσι πολλὰ τυγχάνειν οὐκ εἰκότα (18).

*Fortasse aliquis verisimile id ipsum esse dixerit,
Mortalibus multa evenire non verisimilia.*

We may compare, with this Maxim, that of St *Bernard: Ordinatissimum est, minus interdum ordinate fieri* (19); that is, *It is very consistent with Order, that sometimes things should be done out of Order*. Mr *de Balzac* reports this Thought so ill, that of a very fine Maxim he makes frightful Untruth. *That the Affairs of the World*, says he (20), *sometimes alter their Course, and go into an unusual Channel*; *and though this is only likely, as Agathon said, That many things happen against Likelihood, nevertheless, generally speaking, like Enterprizes produce like Events*. The Adverb *only* produces a Monster here, and if it was an Error of the Press (21), I wonder the Corrector was not startled at it. For what is more monstrous, than to maintain, that it is never probable that a thing should happen agreeable to probability? This is the fine Axiom ascribed to our *Agathon*, in the *Prince* of *Balzac*: but the Sequel of the Discourse shews, that if the Poet's Thought was marr'd on the Paper, it was not so in the Mind of the Writer: It is certain that Mr *de Balzac* meant to say, with *Agathon*, that this very Thing is likely, that many Things happen against likelihood. *Euripides* was so fond of this Maxim, that he has repeated it five Times; for, as Mr *Coftar* says (22), he ended his *Medea*, his *Alcestes*, his *Andromache*, his *Bacchæ*, and his *Helena*, with the following Sentence;

Πολλὰ δ' ἀέλπτως κραίνουσι θεοί,
Καὶ τὰ δοκηθέντ' οὐκ ἐτελέσθη,
Τῶν δ' ἀδοκήτων πόρον εὗρε θεός.

The meaning is, *The Gods sport with human Foresight, and equally deceive our Hopes and our Fears. Sometimes they divert Events which all Men expected, and, opening Passages and Ways unknown, make Designs to succeed, which were in Appearance impossible.* *Seneca* made a very good use of this Thought, to encourage those who are terrify'd at the likely and probable Approaches of ill Fortune. *How many things*, says he, *have happened, which no body expected? How many others have never appear'd, tho' every body expected them? Nothing is so sure among those things, which we fear, but it is yet more certain, that our Fears and our Hopes prove sometimes groundless.* *Seneca*'s Words are more strong: It will be better to transcribe them. "Venisimile est aliquid futurum mali? Non statim verum est. Quàm multa non expectata venerunt, quàm multa expectata nunquam comparuerunt?—— multa interveniunt, quibus vicinum periculum vel prope adreptum, aut substitit, aut destinat, aut in alienum caput transiit —— habet etiam mala fortuna levitatem: Fortasse erit, fortasse non erit. Interim dum non est, meliora propone —— nihil tam certum est ex his quæ timentur, ut non certius sit & formidata subsidere, & sperata decipere (23). —— *Is any Misfortune likely to befal you? It does not therefore immediately become certain. How many unexpected things have come to pass? How many look'd for Events have never happen'd? —— Many things intervene, by which an approaching Danger may stop short, or cease to be a Danger, or fall upon another Head. —— Even ill Fortune has her Fickleness: Perhaps it will be; perhaps it will not be. In the mean time, whilst it is not, hope the best. —— Nothing, in all the Ills we dread, is so certain, but it is still more so, that what we fear sometimes vanishes, and what we hope for sometimes disappoint us.*" Cardinal *Palavicin* is very angry with *Fra-Paolo*, who took the Reception of the Doctrine of *Zuinglius* by the Evangelical Cantons, as a manifest Proof, that an higher Cause, than *Zuinglius*, was the influencing Motive. I omit *Palavicin*'s Reflexions, but shall copy what he borrows from *Aristotle*, namely, That it happens sometimes, that the most probable things are false; for if they were always separated from Falsehood, they would be certain and not probable. I am going to shew, that he builds upon this Maxim, when he accuses those of Rashness and Presumption, who pretend to judge of the Providence of God. Such a Person is a devout Christian, therefore he is predestinated to Salvation: Such a Person is a *Mahometan*, and wicked, therefore he is predestinated to Damnation. Rash Consequences; and which are often groundless! This is Cardinal *Palavicin*'s Remark: The whole Passage is as follows. " Per tanto chi ascrive le prosperità della miglior causa ad una volontà che doi habbia di farla stabilimente prevalere alla rea, discorre con pietà probabile à leggia: quantunque talora s'ingannà, secondo l'insegnamento

AGATHON. AGESILAUS.

rizes him severely on account of his Morals, in one of his Comedies (o). I believe we ought to distinguish him from that *Agathon*, whom the Philosopher *Plato* lov'd so tenderly [G]. The Mistake of *Budæus* was doubtless voluntary, when he said in the 27th Chapter of the *Institution of a Prince*, that *Euripides* kiss'd a Lady, at *Archelaus*'s Table, who was called the Fair *Agatha*.

(o) *In Thesmophoriazusis.*

" segnamento del Filosofo: Che talvolta il più pro-
" babile è falso; perciòche se da falsità fosse esente,
" non saria probabil, mà certo. E se basta il potersi
" ingannare acciòche ogni giudicio, quantunque
" dubitativo della Providenza divina chiamisi pre-
" sontuoso; chiamerassi presontuoso chiun que dall'
" haverlo Dio fatto nascere fra Christiani e viver
" divotamente, prende conghiettura che l'habbia de-
" stinato alla vita eterna; e'l contrario s'avvisa di chi
" nacque Saraceno e vive sceleratò: Essendo manifesto poter succedere che il primo si danni, e'l secondo si salvi (24). ———— Thus he, who *ascribes the Success of the better Cause to the immediate Influence of Heaven, reasons probably and justly; tho' he may sometimes be deceived; according the Sentiment of the Philosopher, that the most probable Thing sometimes proves false, because, if it were exempt from Falsity, it would not be probable, but certain. Now, if the bare Possibility of being mistaken renders all Judgment concerning divine Providence, though express'd with Doubt, presumptuous, certainly it is great Presumption in any one to imagine, that because he is born a Christian, and lives devoutly, therefore he is predestin'd by God to eternal Life, and to judge the contrary of one; who is born a Saracen, and lives wickedly; it being evidently possible, that the former may be damn'd, and the latter sav'd.*"

Not only the Physicians, but the News-Writers, likewise, ought to profit by the Sentence of *Agathon*. A Professor of *Leipsic* exhorts Physicians not to speak without much Precaution, if they would do Honour to Physic. He would not have them promise too much, nor terrify their Patients so greatly, but speak always conditionally, and with a perhaps (25). All this, in virtue of *Seneca*'s Maxim produc'd above. The like Advice may be given to your great Coffee-House Politicians: I mean those among them, who have a good deal of Sagacity and Judgment. Their Conjectures are generally right; nor have they often occasion to repent of their decisive Air, with which they deride the Hopes or Threats of the Gazetteers. This gives them a still greater Boldness to reject magisterially every piece of News, which shocks Probability; but they are sometimes mistaken; for the Event confirms, upon some Occasions, the most impertinent and the most extravagant News that can be reported, and which they had condemn'd as Chimera's, or as Things inconsistent with the Wisdom, which had 'till then appear'd in the Councils of the State. This Rule is not always safe, and sometimes ensnares those Reasoners upon public Affairs, who trust too much to it. It is therefore Prudence to act considerately, and not to pronounce definitive Decrees, under pretence of having the most plausible Appearances on our side. But if in this Case it is not reasonable to play the Dictator, what Blame do not they deserve, who promise the greatest Successes, against all Appearances, and publish these Promises as grounded on St *John*'s Revelation?

[G] *From that Agathon, whom the Philosopher Plato lov'd so tenderly.*] That Philosopher compos'd a very tender Distich, and so full of Sense, that a *Latin* Poet found Matter in it for seventeen Verses. Let us transcribe a whole Chapter of *Aulus Gellius* here (26). " Celebrantur duo isti Græci versiculi, multorumque doctorum hominum memoriâ dignantur, " quod sunt lepidissimi & venustissimæ brevitatis. Neque adeo pauci sunt veteres scriptores, qui eos *Platonis* esse Philosophi affirmant; quibus ille adole-

(24) Palavicin. Istor. del. Concilio, lib. 3. cap. 8. in fine. p. 303.

(25) Bibl. Universelle, Tom. 4. p. 80, 81: in the Extrait of the Miscellanea Curiosa Medica of Christianus Langius.

(26) Aulus Gellius, lib. 19. cap. 11.

" scens luserit, quum tragœdiis quoque eodem tempore faciendis præluderet.

Τὴν ψυχὴν, Ἀγάθωνα φιλῶν, ἐπὶ χείλεσιν ἔσχον.
Ἦλθε γὰρ ἡ τλήμων ὡς διαβησομένη (27).

" Hoc distichon amicus meus, οὐκ ἄμουσος adolescens, " in pluris versiculos licentius liberiusque vertit: " qui quoniam mihi quidem visi sunt non esse mèmoratu indigni, subdidi.

Dum semihulco savio
Meum puellum savior;
Dulcemque florem spiritus
Duco ex aperto tramite:
Animula ægra & saucia
Cucurrit ad labias mihi,
Rictumque in oris pervium,
Et labra pueri mollia,
Rimata itineri transitus,
Ut transiliret nititur.
Tum si moræ quid plusculæ
Fuisset in cœtu osculi;
Amoris igni percita
Transisset, & me linqueret;
Et mira prorsum res foret,
Ut ad me fierem mortuus,
Ad puerum at intus viverem.

(27) *Notat Diogenes Laërtius, lib. 3. n. 32. sæpius, mentioning that two Greek Verses, that they were made y Plato for Agathon; They are thus translated in the Greek, and Latin Editions of Diogenes Laertus. Suavia dans Agathoni, animam ipse In labra tenebram? Ægra etenim properans tanquam abitura fuit.*

" That Greek Distich is much celebrated, and though " worthy of being recorded by many learned Men, as " being most witty and most beautifully concise. Nor " are there a few among the antient Writers, who " affirm it was compos'd by Plato the Philosopher; " with which he diverted himself in his Youth, and " at a time when he was making Essays towards " Tragedy."

Τὴν ψυχὴν, Ἀγάθωνα φιλῶν &c.
*My Soul (in kissing Agathon)
Flys to my Lips, and wou'd be gone.*

" *A young Gentleman, a Friend of mine (no Enemy* " *to the Muses), has paraphras'd this Distich in several* " *Verses; which, as they seem to me not unworthy of* " *being produc'd, I have here subjoin'd.*"

Dum semihulco savio, &c.

*Whilst on thy Lips, to taste the Bliss,
I print the burning, amorous, Kiss,
And drink thy balmy Breath; my Soul,
Thro' Love impatient of controul,
Mounts to my Lips in extasy,
And fain would pass, to dwell in Thee.
If, then, Dear Youth, we should delay,
And on the Kiss prolong our stay,
The wanton Thing would take her Flight,
Struck with Love's Fire, and leave me quite;
And strange would my Condition be,
Dead in myself, but yet alive in Thee.*

Observe that *Plato* was but fourteen Years of Age, when our Poet *Agathon* obtain'd the Prize of Tragedy, so that it is not very likely, that he sigh'd for him, but for an *Agathon* much younger (28).

(28) Athen. lib. 5. s. p. 18. p. 217.

AGESILAUS, the first of the Name, King of *Sparta*, succeeded his Father *Doryssus*, who was the fifth King from *Eurysthenes*. The Reign of this *Agesilaus* was very long [*A*], and yet it affords an Historian scarce any materials. The Histories
of

[*A*] *Was very long.*] In saying this, I rely more on the Authority of *Eusebius* than on that of *Pausanias*. The latter assures us, that *Doryssus*, and his Son *Agesilaus*, did but just shew themselves on the

Throne: Ἄι ὀλίγον ἐδεῖ τὰ χρεὼν ἰσολαβὸν ἀμφοτέροι.
———— *Death soon seized them both* (1). But *Eusebius* makes them reign seventy three Years: he gives twenty nine Years to the Father's Reign, and forty four

(1) Pausan. lib. 3. p. 82.

AGESILAUS

(a) The Reign of A G E S I‑ L A U S 1. bet in the Year of the World 2992. according to Helvicus, 34 Years after the Death of Solomon.

of those Remote Times *(a)* have not been preserved. *Pausanias* ought not to have said, that *Lycurgus* gave Laws to *Lacedemon* [B] in this Reign *(b)*. *Charles Stephens*, *Lloyd* and *Hofman* confound this *Agesilaus* with *Agesilaus* II. for they say of the latter, that he was the Sixth King of *Lacedemon*.

(b) Pausan. lib. 3. pag. 82.

to the Son's. *Calvisius* quotes *Pausanias* for this Duration: This is to make a judicious Choice of one's Witness.

[B] *That Lycurgus gave Laws to* Lacedemon.]

Meursius proves, in his Antiquities of *Lacedemon*, that *Lycurgus* published his Laws in the thirtieth Year of *Archelaus*, the Son and Successor of *Agesilaus*.

AGESILAUS, the second of the Name, King of the *Lacedemonians*, was the Son of *Archidamus*. He had perhaps Ambition enough to desire the Kingdom in exclusion of his elder Brother *Agis*; but, however that be, it was not perceived, till after the Death of *Agis*, that he was desirous the Order of Succession should be broke in upon for his sake. This Desire had all the Success he could expect; for they did *Leotychides*, Son of *Agis*, the Injustice [A] to exclude him from the Crown in Favour of *Agesilaus* (a). The latter repaired by a great number of fine Actions what was irregular in this first step, and tho' he was of a diminutive Stature, an unpromising Aspect, and lame [B], he justly acquired the Reputation of a great Captain. He was brave, vigilant, and ready; he improved every Advantage to the utmost, and knew how to make the best use of Occurrences; he understood all the Stratagems of War, and he had the Art of deceiving his Enemies, at the same time that he let them know his

(a) This happened according to Calvisius, in the 3d Year of the 95th Olympiad.

[A] *They did Leotychides —— the Injustice.*] We cannot give their Treatment of him any other Name, if we examine well the Reasons of it. *Agesilaus* did not deny, but that, according to the Laws of the Country, the Crown belonged to his Brother's Son; but he maintained that *Leotychides* was not the Son of *Agis*; and made use of these two Methods of Proof. He said in the first Place, that *Timea*, the Mother of *Leotychides*, was so fond of *Alcibiades*, who had fled to *Lacedemon* for Refuge, that her Husband suspected, that the Child, which she had some time after, had no other Father, than that Gallant. This concerned *Leotychides*. It was of Him that *Timea* was delivered about that Time: It was He, whom *Agesilaus* did not acknowledge for his Son but on his Death-bed. *Agesilaus* alledged in the second Place the Testimony of *Neptune*. He said, That *Agis* was driven from his Wife's Bed by an Earthquake, and that *Timea* was brought to Bed of *Leotychides* above ten Months after (1). These two Reasons stand for nothing; the Maxim, *Pater est quem nuptiae demonstrant*, —— *Wedlock makes the Father*, ruins them entirely. If, whenever a Husband takes Umbrage at seeing his Wife pleased with the Visits, or private Conversations, of a Stranger, he should exclude from the Inheritance the Children born about that Time, What a Confusion would it introduce? Therefore, though it should be true what an Historian says, That *Timea* made no Scruple of calling her Son by the Name of *Alcibiades*, before her Women, instead of *Leotychides* (2), nothing could be legally concluded from this Fact in favour of *Agesilaus*. *Timea* herself ought to have declared what she meant by this Language (3), and whether she used it in earnest, or by way of insult, or meerly in jest. Much less could they have alledged the Indiscretion of *Alcibiades*, if it had been true that he boasted of his Familiarity with *Timea*, not thro' a Principle of Gallantry, but out of an Ambition of giving Kings to *Lacedemon* (4). An hundred Reasons of this kind ought not to have balanced the Act, by which *Agis* acknowledged *Leotychides* for his Son, in the Presence of good Witnesses, on his Death-bed. The second Reason of *Agesilaus* was an idle Story; for let *Neptune* be never so much the cause of Earthquakes, how could it be proved, that *Agis* durst not lie with *Timea* after the Earthquake in question? A Lying-in ten Months after the last Caresses of an Husband (5), is no Proof in Law. The Maxim, *Pater est quam nuptiae demonstrant*, and the Decisions of Physicians, remove all Suspicions. So that it may be said that the *Lacedemonians*, a People who piqued themselves upon a very rigid Morality, took away a Crown for Reasons, which, in a well regulated Court, would have been insufficient to have excluded a Man from the Inheritance of an Acre of Land. But the Misfortune of *Leotychides* was, that *Lysander* the most intriguing, the most deceitful, and the most factious of all Men, who had gained a Reputation in the City proportionable to his Abilities, and the Victories which he had

obtained over the Enemies, took it in his Head to cause *Agesilaus* to be crowned (6). No fundamental Law can hold against such Persons: If you alledge the Divine Law to them, they explain it their own way. This *Lysander* did, when he heard that a Prophet of *Lacedemon* would have pleaded, in favour of *Leotychides*, an Oracle, which forbad the *Lacedemonians* to suffer a lame Person to reign. *This*, says *Lysander*, *does not relate to the Defects of the Feet, but the Defects of the Blood; and it is* Leotychides, *who would make your Kingdom halt, not being of the Race of your Kings*.

[B] *Tho' he was of a diminutive Stature, an unpromising Aspect, and lame*] He was always the first to rally his own Lameness (7), as is commonly practised by Men of Wit in the like case; by which means they disconcert the Schemes of the Laughers. " Materia petulantibus, & per contumeliam urbanis " detrahitur, si ultro illam & prior occupes. Nemo alias " risum praebuit, qui ex se cepit. Vatinium hominem natum & ad risum, & ad odium, scutram fuisse venustam ac dicacem, memoriae proditum est. " In pedes suos ipse plurima dicebat, & in fauces " concisas: Sic inimicorum, quos plures habebat " quam morbos, & in primis Ciceronis urbanitatem, " effugit (8). —— *The Invectives of the ill-natured, " and the Raillery of the Witty, are disappointed by " being beforehand with them. No one is liable to " be laughed at by others, who first laughs at himself*. *Vatinius, a Man designed by Nature the " common Object of Ridicule and Contempt, is reported to have been an ingenious and talkative Droll. " He was always jesting upon his own Feet, and his " little Mouth: Thus he escaped the Ridicule of his Enemies, of whom he had more in Number than Diseases, " and particular of Cicero*." The Pleasantry of *Agesilaus*, and the Strength wherewith he endured the most painful Exercises, made amends for all his bodily Defects (9), for without these his despicable Outside would have been very prejudicial to him. Λέγεται τε γενέσθαι καὶ ὄψιν εὐκαταφρόνητος. *He is said to have been small of Stature and of a contemptible Aspect* (10). The *Ephori* had fined his Father for having married a little Woman (11), from whence they concluded would spring but a diminutive Race of Kings. *Cornelius Nepos* speaks more expresly of *Agesilaus's* ill Mein than *Plutarch*. " Atque hic tantus vir, " says he (12), ut naturam fautricem habuerat in " tribuendis animi virtutibus, sic maleficam nactus est " in corpore, exiguus & claudus altero pede, quae res " etiam nonnullam afferebat deformitatem, atque ig- " noti faciem ejus cùm intuerentur, contemnebant. " —— *This great Man, as the experienced Nature's " favourable in bestowing on him the Virtues of the " Mind, so he found her unpropitious in regard to his " Body, being little and lame of one Foot, which rendered him in some manner deformed; insomuch " that those who were unacquainted with him, at " first Sight were apt to despise him*." Never was the *minuit praesentia famam* more true than with respect

(1) Ex Plut. in Agesil. p. 597. & Xenoph. de Rebus Graecis. lib. 3. pag. 214.

(2) Duris, apud Plut. ubi supra.

(3) According to the Maxims of the Law, the Evidence which a Person gives against himself is not received.

(4) Plut. in Agesil. pag. 214.

(5) Note, that the Ancients allow'd ten Months for the Term of Childbearing; Matri longa decem tulerunt fastidia menses. Virg. Ecl. 4. ver. 61. & La Cerda upon that Passage.

(6) Plut. & Xenoph. ubi supra.

(7) Plut. ib. pag. 569. Ea

(8) Seneca de Constantia Sapientis, cap. 17. pag. 292.

(9) Plut. in Agesil. pag. 596.

(10) Id. Ib.

(11) Id. Ib.

(12) Corn. Nepos in ejus Vita, cap 8.

AGESILAUS.

his True Intentions [*C*]. He was desirous they shou'd understand the Trade of Arms; otherwise it wou'd have been difficult for him to have drawn them into his Snares (*b*). He had the Art likewise of deceiving his own Soldiers, by giving them, instead of the bad News he received, a fictitious Relation of some great Triumph (*c*). This deserves to be remarked, to undeceive those, who believe, that it is only since the Invention of the *Gazette*, that the Public has been imposed upon in this way. As soon as *Agesilaus* was on the Throne, he advised the *Lacedemonians* to prevent the King of *Persia*, who was making great Preparations for War, and to attack him in his own Dominions (*d*). He was chosen for this Expedition, and gained so many Advantages over the Enemy, that if the League, which the *Athenians* and *Thebans* had formed against *Lacedemon*, had not crossed his Enterprizes, he would have carried his victorious Arms into the Center of the *Persian* Monarchy. He quitted all these Triumphs with a good Grace, to come to the Assistance of his Country, and freed it very fortunately, by the Battel which he gained over the Allies in *Bæotia* [*D*]. He gained another Battel near *Corinth* (*e*); but he afterwards had the Vexation to see the *Thebans* obtain signal Victories over the *Lacedemonians*. These Misfortunes raised many Malecontents against him; but, after all, they did not obscure his Glory. He had been sick during the first Advantages, which the Enemy gain'd (*f*); and when he was fit for Action, he prevented, by his Valour and Prudence, the Consequences of the last Victories of the *Thebans*; insomuch that it was the general Opinion, that, had he been in Health at the beginning of the War, the *Lacedemonians* would not have been worsted, and that they would have been entirely subdued in the end without him (*g*). It cannot be denied that he loved War, more than the Interests of his Subjects required (*h*); for if he could have lived in Peace, he would have saved his Country many Losses, and would not have engaged it in Undertakings, which ended only in a very great Diminution of the Power of the *Lacedemonians*. This insatiable Thirst for War and Slaughter, push'd him, in his old Age, on an Enterprize, which was generally disapproved (*i*). He was above eighty Years of Age, when he undertook to lead Troops into *Egypt*, to support *Tachus*, who had revolted against the *Persians*. But, being disgusted at *Tachus*, he forsook him to take the part of *Nectanabus*, a Relation of *Tachus*, whom he powerfully assisted; after which he designed to return to *Lacedemon*; but he died of a Fit of Sickness by the Way, in the third Year of the CIVth *Olympiad* [*E*]. He was Eighty four Years of Age, whereof he had reigned Forty one (*k*). Mr *Moreri* has committed

(*b*) Plut. in Agesilao, pag. 617. E.

(*c*) Ibid. pag. 605. Xenophon. de Rebus Græcis, lib. 4. pag. 214.

(*d*) Cornel. Nepos in Agesil. vita, cap. 2.

(*e*) Ex Cornel. Nepote, ibid.

(*f*) Plut. in Agesil. pag. 611. B.

(*g*) Talem se imperatorem præbuit, ut eo tempore omnibus apparuerit, nisi ille fuisset, Spartam futuram non fuisse. Corn. Nep. ibid. cap. 6.

(*h*) Plut. in Agesil. pag. 616. B.

(*i*) Id. ib. C.

(*k*) Plut. p. 611, 618. Corn. Nepot in Agesil.

---

respect to him. Fame went before him into *Egypt*, and represented him there under the most pompous Ideas. As soon as they heard of his landing, they ran in Crowds to see him: Judge then how they were surprized, to see a little Man lie on the Grass in a mean and slovenly Garment. They could not forbear laughing, and applying to him the Fable of the Mountain, which brought forth a Mouse (13). Their Contempt was not lessened, when they saw the Choice he made of the Refreshments sent him by the King (14). See below the Remark [*G*].

[*C*] *He deceived his Enemies, at the same time that he let them know his true Intentions.*] The Reason was, They did not believe him, and a General would discover his Designs. " Vidit, si quo esset iter " facturus palam pronunciasset, hostes non credituros, " aliasque regiones occupaturos, nec dubitaturos aliud " esse facturum ac pronunciasset. Itaque cum ille " Sardis se iturum dixisset, Tissaphernes eandem Cariam defendendam putavit (15). *He knew that if* " *he publickly declared the Rout he was about to take,* " *the Enemy would not believe him, and would post* " *themselves in a quite different Place, nor would* " *doubt of his acting contrary to his Declaration. Accordingly, when he gave out, that he would march* " *to Sardes, Tissaphernes thought proper to stay and* " *defend Caria.*" We should improperly apply here the Thought of Mr *Wicquefort*: Sir George Downing, Ambassador of England, *had not Probity nor Prudence enough to be perswaded, that no Minister deceives more securely nor more pleasingly, than be who never deceives; because in keeping the High-road, those, who look for By-ways and Evasions, can never meet him*(16). The Comparison between such a Minister, and our *Agesilaus*, would be a very lame one; for this King of *Lacedemon*, in publishing his Intentions, deceived his Enemies, only because on other Occasions he had concealed his Intentions. A General, who pursues this Scheme, can seldom make use of a more successful Stratagem, than that of spreading a true Report of his Marches. The Contrivance will be good, because it is new, and the Enemy has not yet been deceived by it. Read this Passage of *Xenophon*; it is *Cambyses* who speaks to his Son *Cyrus*, and who

compares new Stratagems in War to new Airs of Musick. Καὶ ἐφέδρα μὲν καὶ ἐν τοῖς μουσικοῖς τὰ νέα διδασκεῖ, πολὺ δὲ καὶ ἐν τοῖς πολεμικοῖς μᾶλλον τὰ καινὰ μηχανήματα εὐδοκιμεῖ, ταῦτα γὰρ μᾶλλον καὶ ἐξαπατᾶν δύνανται τοὺς πολεμίους (17). *And as in Music what is new is most esteemed, so in War the newest Stratagems are the best; for they are most likely to deceive the Enemy.* We shall observe in another Place (18), that some Men, by dint of Folly, avoid being imposed on.

[*D*] *Which be gained over the Allies in* Bæotia.] The Battle was fought at Coronea. *Xenophon*, who served under *Agesilaus* in it, gives the same Account (19); as does *Plutarch* (20). Lambinus, in his Commentary on these Words of *Cornelius Nepos*, *apud Coroneam quos omnes gravi prælio vicit*, would, without necessity, correct the Word Χαιρώνειαν of *Plutarch*, by that of Κορωνείαν. *Plutarch* mentioned these two Places, without pretending, that the Battle was fought in the first. But, says Lambinus, could *Agesilaus*, *going from Phocis*, *advance into Bœotia*, *as far as Chæronea*, *if Chæronea is in Phocis?* No, doubtless; but this IF is false, and Lambinus shews by it, that he was but little versed in Geography. See the Commentary of *Kirchmaierus* on *Cornelius Nepos*, at pag. 722. *Charles Stephens* erred yet more grosly, when he placed *Chæronea* in *Peloponnesus*. *Lloyd* and *Hofman* followed him in this Error.

[*E*] *He died of a Fit of Sickness by the Way, in the third Year of the hundred and fourth Olympiad.*] A Storm having obliged him to put into Harbour, he was carried into a Desart Place, called the Port of *Menelaus*, where he died (21). *Hic cum ex Ægypto reverteretur* — *venissetque in portum qui Menelai vocatur, jacens inter Cyrenas & Ægyptum, in morbum implicitus decessit* (22). It was in the third Year of the hundred and fourth *Olympiad*, according to *Calvisius*: But we see by this, that his Calculation is false; for from the third Year of the Ninety fifth *Olympiad*, the beginning, as he says, of the Reign of *Agesilaus*, to the third Year of the hundred and fourth *Olympiad*, there are but thirty six Years: And yet he allows forty one Years to that Reign.

(13) Plut. Ibid. p. 626. See the Artic. *TACHUS*.

(14) Corn. Nepos, ubi supra.

(15) Ibid. cap. 3. See also Plutarch in Agesilao, pag. 600. F.

(16) Wicquefort's Ambassador, pag. 170.

(17) Xenoph. Cyropæd. circa fin. pag. 21.

(18) In one of the Remarks of the Article S I-M O N I-D E S.

(19) Xenophon. de Rebus Græc. lib. 4. pag. 225.

(20) Plut. in Agesil. pag. 605.

(21) Plut. pag. 618.

(22) Corn. Nepos. in Vit. Agesil. sub fin.

AGESILAUS.

mitted some Mistakes here [F]. We shall see in the Article CONON, whether *Cornelius Nepos* and *Justin* have done their part in the History of *Agesilaus*. This Prince would never suffer his Effigies to be made either in *Relievo*, or in Flat-Painting (*l*); nay he forbad it by his Last Will. Some have been of Opinion, that he did this, because he was sensible he was not an handsome Man, *diffidens formæ suæ* (*m*). Never any Person lived in greater Simplicity than he [G]. But he knew very well how to couch the Spirit, the Heart, and the Religion of a Sovereign [H], under this outside

Reign. Let us then place the beginning of it, with *Helvicus*, in the second Year of the Ninety third *Olympiad*, and the end in the third Year of the hundred and fourth.

[F] *Mr Moreri has committed some Mistakes here.*] It is false; I. That *Leotychides* was the Natural Son of King *Agis*. II. That *Lysander* zealously maintained *Leotychides*'s Pretensions (23). III. That *Agesilaus* ever encamped near the City of *Hermees*, in *Bæotia* (24). IV. That he had a noble Presence, and full of Majesty (25). V. That he said, That the Oracle which excluded the Lame from the Crown, ought to be understood of the Imperfections of the Mind, or of Birth. These two last Faults belong to the Supplement of *Moreri*. I pass over his giving the *Egyptians* a wrong Name, to whom *Agesilaus* did Service: His Name was not *Nastenebon*.

[G] *In greater Simplicity than he.*] He was the worst cloath'd of any Person in his whole Army (26). After his *Asiatic* Expedition, wherein he had acquir'd such an high Reputation, which had received an additional Lustre from the Battle of *Coronea*, he liv'd in *Sparta*, as a good *Lacedemonian* of the old Times would have done. He alter'd nothing in his Garments, in his Bathings, or in his Meals; and, what was perhaps more difficult, he would not suffer his Wife to be better dress'd than before, nor permit her to distinguish her Daughter, in Processions, by finer Cloaths than those of other young Ladies. He would not repair the Gates of his House, though they were so old and ruinous, that they seem'd to be the same, which *Aristodemus* had built in that place (27). Observe, That *Aristodemus* was one of the *Heraclidæ*, to whose Share the City of *Sparta* fell, and from whom descended the Kings of *Lacedemon*, divided into two Families on account of the two Sons which he left. " In hoc (*Agesilao*) " illud in primis fuit admirabile, cum maxima mune- " ra ei ab regibus & dynastis civitatibusque conferren- " tur, nihil unquam in domum suam contulit, nihil " de victu, nihil de vestitu Laconum mutavit. Do- " mo eadem fuit contentus, quâ Eurysthenes proge- " nitor majorum suorum (28) fuerat usus, quam qui " intrarat nullum signum libidinis, nullum luxuriæ " videre poterat; contra plurima patientiæ atque ab- " stinentiæ. Sic enim erat instructa, ut nulla in re " differret à cujusvis inopia atque privati (29).— " What was the most worthy of Admiration in him, " (Agesilaus) was, that, though he receiv'd the most " magnificent Presents from Kings, Dynasts, and Re- " publics, he apply'd no Part of them to his own Fa- " mily, made no Alteration in his manner of living, " nor any change in his Lacedemonian Dress. He was " content with the same House, in which Eurysthenes, " the Progenitor of his Ancestors, liv'd; which who- " ever enter'd, could perceive no Signs of Luxury or " Excess, but many of Content and Frugality. For it " was furnish'd in all respects like the House of an in- " digent and private Person." When it was known that *Agesilaus* was arrived in *Egypt*, they sent him all sorts of Provisions: He chose only the most common; and left the Perfumes, Comfits, and Delicacies (30) to his Servants. The *Egyptians*, instead of admiring his Behaviour, derided the Prince, and took him for a silly Fellow, who did not know what was good. " Ille præter vitulina, & hujusmodi genera " obsonii, quæ præsens tempus desiderabat, nihil ac- " cepit, unguenta, coronas, secundamque mensam " servis dispersit, cætera referri jussit. Quo facto " eum barbari magis etiam contempserunt, quod eum " ignorantia bonarum rerum illa potissimum sump- " sisse arbitrabantur (31)." You will find in *Plutarch*, I. That this Prince behav'd in the same manner, when the *Thracians* sent him Presents. II. That he derided them, when they offer'd him divine Honours (32).

[H] *The Spirit, the Heart, and the Religion of a Sovereign.*] *Plutarch* testifies, that those, who govern'd in *Lacedemon*, acknowledg'd no other Justice, than that which tended to the Advantage and aggrandizing of the State (33). It was among them the Rule and the Measure of Law and Honesty; if a thing was useful to the Public, it immediately pass'd for lawful. I believe *Plutarch* says the Truth; but he ought not to have confin'd his Observation to the City of *Sparta* alone. Those of *Athens* (34), and *Thebes*, had no better Principles; and, generally speaking, they are the Maxims of all States: The only Difference is in Degrees; some save Appearances better than others. However, *Agesilaus* was quite abandon'd to this iniquitous Morality. Being suspected to have induc'd *Phœbidas* to surprize the Citadel of *Thebes*, in full Peace, and by a Fraud, which made all *Greece* exclaim, he represented, That they ought first to examine, whether the Action was of Advantage to the State; and that every Person ought, in his private Capacity, to do what tended to the Advantage of the State (35). He obtain'd, that *Phœbidas* should be acquitted, and that a Garrison should be sent into the Citadel. In his *Egyptian* Expedition, did he not abandon *Tachus*, who had hired his Assistance, and embrace the Interests of *Nectanabus*, for this Reason alone, because it was more for the Interest of the *Lacedemonians* to support the latter than the former? An Action, which under the Mask of public Good, was downright Treachery, as *Plutarch* himself observ'd. Ἀντοῦ μὲν ἀλλοῖον ποιήσαντος παρανομωτάτην τὸ συμφέρον τῆς πατρίδος χρησάμενος ἐπεὶ τούτον γε τῆς πατρίδος ἀφαιρέσεως ἡ δικαιοτάτου ἄνομα τῆς πράξεως ἦν πρόφασις (36). *Absurdo & indigno facinori commodum prætexens patria: quando hoc quidem velamento detracto nomen istius facti verissimum erat proditio.* In Conversation *Agesilaus* talk'd of nothing but Justice; his Discourses upon this Subject were the finest in the World (37). Hearing that a certain thing was pleasing to the great King (38), he demanded, *How is he greater than I, if he is not more Just?* Fine Theory! but his Practice did not answer it, when his Kingdom was in question. I am apt to believe, that, for private Views, he could not easily have acted against Conviction; and this is the Reason why I pretend, he had the *Religion of a Sovereign*. How many Kings and Princes are zealous for their Religion, Just and Honest in themselves; but if it be thought for the public Good to annoy their Enemies, most of them, if not all, follow the Maxims of *Lacedemon?* I believe a Book, entituled, *The Religion of a Sovereign*, would sell well; it would cause the *Religio Medici* to be forgotten.

Two Days ago I heard a Person of Merit say, that an *Italian* Prince, demanding too advantageous Conditions, in negotiating a Treaty of Peace with a powerful Monarch, who had taken most of his Dominions from him, the Envoy of that Monarch answered him, *But what Security will you give the King my Master, if he complies with all your Demands?* Answer him, reply'd the Prince, that *I engage my Word to him, not in quality of a Sovereign, for, as such, I must sacrifice every thing to aggrandize myself, and lay hold of every Opportunity of contributing to the Glory and Advantage of my Dominions; tell him, then, that I engage my Word to him, not in this Quality (which would be to promise nothing) but as a Gentleman, and an honest Man.* Though this Language does not answer the Ideas of those, who have introduc'd, in the Style of the *Chancery*, the set Form, *We promise upon the Faith and Word of a King*, yet it is very Sincere, and very Just.

Let us make two Remarks more. First, I distinguish between the Belief of *Urban* VIII, and that of *Maphœus Barbarini*. The Religion of a Sovereign, as such, and Religion, personally speaking, are two things.

My other Remark is this. *Agesilaus* had a very great respect for his Gods; he would not suffer their Temple to be plundered nor prophan'd, neither in *Greece*, nor in the Country of the *Barbarians*; and he reckon'd those as sacrilegious, who treated an

Enemy

outside of Regularity, and philosophical Frugality. He had such a great Tenderness for his Children, that he would amuse himself with them in the most childish Exercises [*I*], such as riding on a Hobby-horse.

It will not be useless to remark the small Account he made of those, who greatly prided themselves in feeding and dressing Horses for the Races of the *Olympic* Games. He wou'd persuade them it was a trifling Ambition; and that it was an Affair of Expence, not a Proof of Merit or of Virtue; and for this purpose he persuaded his Sister to dispute this Prize (*n*). This Lady having prepared her Horse for the Exercise, came into the Lists and gained the Victory. She was the first Woman who obtained this Honour (*o*). Her Name was *Cynisca*. I cannot think *Dicæarchus* was ignorant of this, tho' he complains that he could not find what the Name of *Agesilaus*'s Daughter [*K*] was. He might have known it, if he had done what *Plutarch* did [*L*].

(39) Corn. Nepos, in Vit. Agesil. cap. 4.

Enemy ill that had taken Refuge in a Temple (39). During the March of his Troops, he lodg'd always in the most sacred Temples, that the Gods might be Witnesses of his most private, domestic, Actions. Ἐκεῖνο μὲν γὰρ ἀποδημῶν καθ᾿ αὑτὸν ἐν τοῖς ἁγιωτάτοις ἱεροῖς ἃ μὴ πολλοὶ καθορῶσιν ἀνθρώποι πράττοντας ὁρᾷς, τούτων θεοὺς ποιούμενος ἐπόπτας καὶ μάρτυρας. *Tendebat enim, cum iter faceret, solus in sanctissimis delubris, ac quibus rebus paucos adhibemus arbitros, earum Deos*

(40) Plut. in Agesil. pag. 603.

faciebat inspectores (40). This was his *Personal* Religion; but when he considered himself in the Character of a *King*, the Good and Advantage of his Kingdom were his principal Divinity, to which he sacrificed Virtue and Justice, divine and human Laws. I cannot tell, whether all, who quote this Sentence of *Euripides*,

(41) Cic. de Offic. lib. 3. cap. 21.

Nam si violandum est jus, regnandi gratia
Violandum est: aliis rebus pietatem colas (41).

for if *Justice* be ever to be violated, it is to be violated for the Sake of a Kingdom: in other Cases follow Virtue; whether every one, I say, who cites this, comprehends the full Force of it. It represents the Sentiments of those, who acquire Kingdoms, and of those who govern States; they fall sometimes into Superstition. Consider *Agesilaus*'s private Conduct; it was very regular, *aliis rebus pietatem colas*; he does not swerve from Equity; but in the Capacity of a King, *regnandi gratiâ violandum est*. As a Man, he will deal with you sincerely, *amicus usque ad aras*; but, as a Prince, if he speaks his real Sentiments, he will tell you, *I will observe the Treaty of Peace, so long as the Good of my Kingdom requires it; I will despise my Oath, when Maxims of State will have it so*. If he would rather have the *Persians* break the Truce, than begin to violate it himself, it is because he expected to find his Account in this Conduct of the *Persians*. " Multum in eo consequi se dicebat, quod

(42) Corn. Nepos, ubi supra, c. 2.

" lienaret, & Deos sibi iratos redderet (42)."
" *This*, he said, *would be much for his Advantage; since* Tissaphernes, *by his Perjury, would lose the Favour of Men, and incur the Anger of the Gods*." Our good *Agesilaus*, who would have thought it an Offence against good Morality, to be well clothed, and to live luxuriously, made no Scruple to usurp a Kingdom. Thus certain Casuists damn every Woman without Remission, who dresses too delicately: They cannot bear their Ribbons, or their Jewels; but at the same time they not only permit Men to revolt, and to engage in Civil Wars, but even exhort them to it.

(43) Plut. in Agesil. pag. 610. See Dionysius Æmilian. Var. Hist. lib. 12. cap. 5.

[*I*] *In the most childish Exercises*.] Being surprised one Day riding, among his Children, on a Hobby-Horse, he only said to him, who saw him in that Posture, *forbear to speak of it, 'till you are a Father* (43). We must not, upon this Occasion, apply these Verses of *Horace*.

Ædificare casas, plostello adjungere mures,
Ludere par impar, EQUITARE IN ARUNDINE
LONGA

(44) Horat. Sat. 3. lib. 2. ver. 247.

Si quem delectet barbatum, amentia verset (44).

If any, grown a Man, delights to raise
Dirt-Pies, and, like a Child, at Push-pin plays,

Yokes Rats and Mice unto a little Plough,
And RIDES UPON AN HOBBY-HORSE, or so
Sure he is Mad.   CREECH.

For the Poet is not describing those, who, in Compliance to their own Children, amuse themselves at home in this Manner. La Mothe le Vayer is not exact, when he says, that King *Agesilaus*, as well as Alcibiades, *was surpris'd in* playing boyish Tricks among Children, and that the Philosopher *Socrates* gloried in it (45). He cites *Seneca* in the last Chapter, of the first Book *de Tranquillitate*. Here are many Errors: I. He ought to have specified, that *Agesilaus* play'd the Boy only with his own Children. II. The Treatise *de Tranquillitate* contains but one Book. III. Nothing is said either of *Alcibiades*, or of *Agesilaus*, in the Chapter cited. IV. It is not said there, that *Socrates* gloried in playing with Children; it is only said that he was not ashamed of it. *Cum pueris Socrates ludens non erubescebat*. V. *Valerius Maximus*, and *Ælian*, who mention this Sport of *Socrates*, say that *Alcibiades* surpris'd him at it. " Non erubuit tunc, cum inter-
" positâ arundine cruribus suis cum parvulis filiolis lu-
" dens ab Alcibiade risus est (46). — He did not
" blush, *when, riding upon an Hobby-horse among his
" little Sons, he was laugh'd at by* Alcibiades. Ἐωρακέναι δὲ κατειληφότα ποτὲ αὐτὸν Ἀλκιβιάδης παίζων μετὰ τῶν Λαμπροκλέους ἔτι νηπίου (47). Socrates *was once surpris'd by* Alcibiades, *playing with* Lamprocles, *yet a Child*." But I do not remember to have read, that others surpris'd *Alcibiades* at it. VI. These two Authors observe that *Socrates* plaid with his own Children.

[*K*] *I cannot think that* Dicæarchus *was ignorant of —— the Name of* Agesilaus's *Daughter*.] *Cynisca* was not only the first Woman who obtain'd the Prize in the Chariot-Races of the *Olympic* Games, but the most Illustrious of all those Ladies, who obtain'd the like Victory afterwards (48). The Poet *Simonides* honour'd her with an Epigram (49). She consecrated Horses of Brass as a Monument of her Victory, which were placed at the Entrance of the Temple of *Jupiter Olympius* (50). Her Statue, made by *Apelles*, and adorn'd with divers Inscriptions, was to be seen in the Temple of *Juno* at *Elis* (51). The *Lacedemonians* erected a Monument like that of a Hero, ἥρῳον, to her (52). So that it is not likely that the Name of *Agesilaus*'s Sister was unknown to any *Greek* Historian.

[*L*] *He might have known it, if he had done what* Plutarch *did*.] This latter Historian informs us, that *Dicæarchus* was very angry, that neither the Name of *Agesilaus*'s Daughter, nor of *Epaminondas*'s Mother, was known. Ὁ Δικαίαρχος ἐσχετλίακεν ὅτι Stomachabatur Dicæarchus, &c. *As for myself*, continues he, *I have found in the Registers of the* Lacedemonians, *that* Agesilaus's *Wife's Name was* Cleora, *and that the Name of one of his two Daughters was* Apola, *and the Name of the other* Prolyta. I am not surpris'd, that *Dicæarchus* was vex'd at the Negligence of the Historians; for we are naturally desirous of knowing the Families of great Men. It was a little strange, that the Names of *Agesilaus*'s Wife and Daughters were only to be met with in the Archives of *Lacedemon*.

AGESIPOLIS, the first of the Name, King of *Lacedemon*, succeeded his Father *Pausanias*, who had taken Refuge in a Temple, (*a*), when he found, that his Conduct, in concluding a Peace with the *Thebans*, was disapprov'd. They permitted him

AGESIPOLIS.

him to continue in that Asylum, and placed his Son *Agesipolis* on the Throne, under the Guardianship of *Aristodemus* (b). This happened in the 3d Year of the XCVIth Olympiad (c). He was of Age, when the *Lacedemonians* resolved to attack the *Athenians* and *Thebans* at the same time: but as they judged it imprudent, in such a War, not to be secure of the *Argians*, they began with them (d). *Agesipolis*, who was to command against them, made a scruple of it, because they demanded a Truce of him. He desir'd to satisfy his Doubts, by consulting with *Jupiter* upon this case of Conscience; which he did in Person, in the famous *Olympian* Temple. He demanded, whether he might reject the Proposals, which the *Argians* made, of a Truce; and whether he might not pretend, that they had mis-timed their Proposition, by delaying to talk of Peace, till the *Lacedemonian* Troops were upon the Point of attacking them? The Oracle answered, that the Demands of the *Argians* were unjust, and that they might honourably be refused (e). *Agesipolis*, as a still farther Precaution, immediately had recourse to the Oracle of *Delphi*, that he might inform himself, whether the Opinion of the Son (f) was agreeable to That of the Father (g) [*A*]. The Answer of *Apollo* was the same with That of *Jupiter*; upon which *Agesipolis* hesitated no longer, but caus'd his Army to march towards *Argos*. The *Argians* sent two Heralds to him, to desire Peace: He answered, that the Gods thought proper he shou'd reject their Offers, and continued his March. There happened an Earthquake the first Day of his encamping in their Country; and as Part of his Troops looked upon it as an Admonition to them to return, he dissipated their Superstition, by remarking that this Prodigy had come to pass after their Entry into the Enemy's Country. Upon this he marched farther, approached the City of *Argos*, and pressed the Siege of it closely. He wou'd, perhaps, have taken it, had not the Loss of some of his Soldiers by a Thunder-clap, and other Omens, obliged him to retire (b). We must not forget his Emulation: When he had entered the Country of the *Argians*, he informed himself how far *Agesilaus* had formerly ravaged it; and this Curiosity was only that he might surpass the Exploits of that Commander, as if he had rivalled him in the Athletic Games (i). The general Peace which the *Lacedemonians* procured to *Greece* (k) by the Negotiations of *Antalcides*, their Ambassador, at the Court of *Persia*, in the Second Year of the XCVIIIth Olympiad, was soon followed by a particular War, which they declared against the Inhabitants of *Mantinea*. *Agesilaus* declining the Command of the Troops, *Agesipolis* marched against the Enemy. He ravaged the Territory of *Mantinea*, and at length took the City. The Stratagem he

---

[*A*] *If the Opinion of* Apollo *was agreeable to that of* Jupiter.] We may collect from hence a Truth, which is otherwise evident enough; namely, that the Pagan Religion was founded upon Notions of the Deity as false as Atheism. I do not speak of the Sentiments of the common People only, or the Abuse of particular Persons: I speak of the public Worship, performed by the most eminent Persons, and supported by the Authority of the State. We have here an Instance of a King of *Lacedemon*, who, after having offered solemn Sacrifices, as Preparative to an Expedition (1), and even after a favourable Answer from the greatest of the Gods, goes and consults another Deity, being uncertain whether he will contradict, or confirm this Answer. He was, therefore, of Opinion, that the Decisions of *Jupiter* could not always be followed with a safe Conscience, and he supposed, that the Sentiments *Apollo* were not always conformable to those of *Jupiter*. Was not for this to believe, that all the Gods, without excepting the greatest, were limited in their Knowledge, and that between Them and Men there was only the Difference of *more* or *less*? At this rate, the *tot capita, tot sensus,* —— *so many Men, so many Minds,* was applicable to Inhabitants of Heaven, as well as Earth. They consulted *Jupiter*, as we consult the most famous Advocate of Parliament, when we intend to commence a Law-Suit. This Advocate's Answer does not satisfy a cautious Client; but he desires to have the Advice of other Counsel; and there are, who consult the most able Doctors in every Court of the Kingdom. The *Pagans* did so with respect to their Oracles: They consulted several of them upon the same Point, to see whether the Gods would contradict each other, and to take their Measures the better, by comparing their respective Answers. Thus their Gods were as chimerical, as the Deity of *Spinoza*; for it is as impossible that a limited Nature should be God, as it is impossible that the World should be the Supream Being which governs all things by a wise Providence. To confirm what is here advanced concerning the false Ideas, which the *Pagans* entertained of God: They were not scandalized at the different Fate of their Victims.

Those which were offered to one Divinity encouraged their Hopes, while those offered to another alarmed their Fears. *Apollo* and *Diana*, Twins of *Jupiter*, often contradicted each other; the Brother rejecting an Offering, the Sister accepting it. *Paganism* found nothing scandalous in this. The Heathens would willingly have found a greater Harmony in the Promises of good things; but in short they did not believe, that the Divine Nature was free from Ignorance, Caprice, and Disagreement: So that they acquiesced in this, as an unavoidable Effect of the Nature of Things. We must not imagine, that *Cicero's* Objections opened the Eyes of many among them. " Quid quum pluribus Diis immolatur, qui " tandem evenit ut litetur aliis, aliis non litetur ? " Quæ autem inconstantia Deorum est, ut primis mi- " nentur extis, bene promittant secundis? Aut tanta " inter eos dissensio, sæpe etiam inter proximos, " ut Apollinis exta bona sint, Dianæ non bona " (2) ? —— *Whence is it, that in consulting seve- " ral Gods at a time, we sacrifice to some and not " to others ? And what Inconstancy of the Gods is it, " to threaten in the first Entrails, but to appear " propitious in the second ? Or is there such a Dis- " agreement among them, even those who are nearest re- " lated, that Apollo's Victims shall promise Success, " but Diana's not ?*

A modern Author has made use of this Conduct of *Agesipolis*, to shew that, in relation to the Oracles, the greatest of the Gods of *Paganism* did not preserve his Advantage, or his Superiority. He says, (3), *The Oracles of Jupiter, such as those of Trophonius, Dodona, and Hammon, had not so much Credit as That of Delphi —— For they never equalled the latter either in Esteem, or in Duration. And this is proved, besides the Consent of most Authors who have spoke of it, by what Xenophon reports of Agesipolis*, who, after having consulted Jupiter Olympias, and received his Answer, had recourse to Apollo at Delphi, as a Judge without Appeal, whether he was of the same Opinion with his Father.* Aristotle imputes this kind of Religious Ridicule to one *Hegesippus in the second Book of his Rhetorics.* This Passage furnishes Matter for two Observations. The

AGESIPOLIS.

he put in practice upon this occasion is too curious to be omitted [B]. There is some Probability, that it was in this War, that *Pelopidas* and *Epaminondas* extricated themselves from a Danger [C], to which their Valour and Friendship exposed them. He was sent some years after [D] with a fine Army against the *Olynthians* (*l*). *Amintas*, King of *Macedon*, and *Desdas*, Prince of *Elymea* (*m*), gave him a powerful Assistance. He marched towards *Olynthus*, and, finding no Army to oppose him, he ravaged the Country, and made himself Master of *Torona*. But, as he fatigued himself extreamly, notwithstanding the violent Summer-Heats, he was seized with a Continual Fever, which carried him off in seven days (*n*) in the fourteenth year of his Reign (*o*). See my Critical Remarks on Mr *Moreri* [E]. *Agesilaus* was not pleased with this Loss, as

it

The first is, that the Notions of the Gallican Church concerning the Council, and the Pope, tho' speaking ex cathedra, may be compared to those of Paganism concerning the Oracles of Jupiter, and of Delphi. The Olympian Jupiter, when he answered a Question, met with great Esteem in the Minds of the People; much Deference was paid to his Authority; but in short, his Opinion, tho' delivered ex cathedra or rather ex tripode, did not pass for Infallible. Behold the Pope of the Gallican Church! The Apollo of Delphi was the Judge without Appeal: Behold the Council! My second Observation is, That Agesipolis was in earnest in what he did; there was no Religious Banter in the Case. As for what concerns Hegesippus, I answer nothing for him. He was perhaps malicious enough to attempt ensnaring the Oracles, that he might insult them if they did not agree. He might have said, It is a shame for you to answer Yes, and No. Ἡγήσιππος ἐν Δελφοῖς ἐπηρώτα τὸν θεόν, μεχημένος προτερον Ὀλυμπίασιν, εἰ αὐτῷ ταὐ τὰ δοκεῖ ἄπερ τῷ πατρί, ὡς αἰσχρὸν ὂν τἀναντία εἰπεῖν (4). *Hegesippus, having received an Answer from the God at Olympia, interrogated him at Delphi, whether he was of the same Opinion with his Father, as if it were scandalous for the Gods to disagree in their Answers. If our Agesipolis had had any ill Design against Apollo, in Imitation of that malicious Person, whose Story Esop relates* (5), *he would have been bit: for the Answer of Delphi was the same with that of Olympia.*

[B] *The Stratagem he put in practice upon this Occasion is too curious to be omitted*] He stopped the Current of the River, which ran through the middle of the City: This caused an Inundation, which weakened the Foundations of the Houses and Walls in such a manner, that the Inhabitants feared they would fall; and, as they foresaw, that if any part of the Wall should fall, their City would be taken by Assault, they capitulated. They obtained but very hard Conditions; for they were forced to go and live in the Country, being divided into four Cantons, and their City was dismantled: Their Magistrates would have been punished with Death, had not *Agesipolis*'s Father not interceded for them (6). *Xenophon* who relates these Particulars, omits a particular Circumstance, which *Pausanias* takes Notice of. *Agesipolis* turned the Course of the River towards the Walls of the City. Now the Brick, of which the Wall was made, not being burnt, melted in the Water, as Wax melts by the Heat of the Sun. The Reason, why the *Mantineans* preferred crude to burnt Brick, was, because it was not so apt to break, when the Walls are battered. *Agesipolis* did not invent this Stratagem, but put it in Practice, upon hearing that *Cimon* had made use of it, to take the City of *Eione* on the River *Strymon* (7).

[C] *Pelopidas and Epominondas extricated themselves from a Danger.*] *Plutarch* relates, that the *Thebans* sent Succours to the *Lacedemonians*, in the Expedition of *Mantinea*, and that the Wing, where these two celebrated Warriors fought, giving way, they did not retire. *Pelopidas* received seven Wounds, and fell on a heap of dead Men. *Epaminondas* ran to him, and opposed himself alone against many, fully resolved to die, rather than forsake his Friend. He was wounded in two Places; yet he defended himself vigorously, when *Agesilaus* came at the Head of some Troops of the other Wing of the Army, and rescued them both (8). You will tell me, that *Xenophon* does not mention any Battel, when he relates what past in this War of *Mantinea*: but I answer, that *Pausanias* observes, that *Agesipolis* had gained a Battel, before he laid Siege to the City; Ὡς δε ἐπεκράτησεν ὁ Ἀγεσιπολις τῇ μάχῃ, καὶ ἐς τὸ τεῖχος κατέκλεισεν τοὺς Μαντινέας (9). *After that Agesipolis had subdued the Mantineans in Fight, had drove them*

within the Walls of the City. And I add, that *Xenophon* himself remarks, that there were some Auxiliary Troops in the Army of *Lacedemon* (10). Note, that the Event mentioned by *Plutarch*, preceded the Stratagem, by which *Phæbidas* made himself Master of the Fortress of the *Thebans* (11). This Chronological Character agrees with the Expedition of *Agesipolis* against *Mantinea*.

[D] *He was sent some Years after.*] I only make this Remark, to censure *Pausanias*, who reports that *Agesipolis*, abandoning with regret the *Argian* War, turned his whole Resentment against the *Olynthians*. Οὕτω μὲν δὴ ἐκ τῆς Ἀργολίδος ἀνέζευξεν ἄκων, ἐπὶ δὲ Ὀλυνθίους ἐποιεῖτο αὐθις στρατιάν (12). *Invitissimus itaque ille ex Argivorum finibus castra movit, & contra Olynthios belli impetum convertit.* Who would not believe, in reading this, that the Expedition of *Olynthus* succeeded immediately that of *Argos*? Who would not imagine, that *Agesipolis*, when he left the Territories of *Argos*, took the way of *Macedonia*: yet it is false. Some Years past between these two Expeditions. The War of *Mantinea*, of which the same *Pausanias* has taken some Notice, followed That of *Argos*, and preceded that of *Olynthus* six Years. Let us, upon this Occasion, remark a Fault of *Calvisius*. He has placed the War of *Argos* in the fourth Year of the Ninety sixth Olympiad, a little after the Death of *Pausanias* King of *Macedonia* (13). Now *Agesipolis* came to the Throne the same Year, in which this *Pausanias* died (14), and, being a Minor, was put under the Tuition of *Aristodemus* (15). So that if *Calvisius* was exact, the War of *Argos* must concur nearly with the first Year of the Reign of *Agesipolis*, and must have been conducted by *Aristodemus*; for it is certain, that, under the Minority of *Agesipolis*, his Tutor was placed at the Head of the Army, when this King was obliged to take the Field (16). *Calvisius* does not fail to observe, that *Aristodemus* went thither in the third Year of the Ninety sixth Olympiad, because *Agesipolis* was under Age (17). He is mistaken in placing the first Year of his Reign in the second Year of the Ninety sixth Olympiad, and the War of *Argos* too soon after the Death *Pausanias* King of *Macedonia*.

[E] *See my Critical Remarks on Mr Moreri.*] "*Agesipolis* was surprized with a burning Fever, and "returned continually to the Coolness of the Wa-"ters of a certain Temple of *Bacchus*, which was "at *Aphitis*, whither he caused himself to be carried, "and died on the seventh Day of his Fever, after "he was gone out of the Temple, that he might "not defile it by his Death." These are Mr *Moreri*'s Words. It would be unjust to criticise on this Expression, *returned continually to the Coolness*, (*revint toujours à la fraicheur*) for it is easy to see that the Printers have have put *revint* (returned) instead of *rêvant* (thinking of, or raving after) (18). But two Observations may be made: One is, that he ought to have expressed himself thus; *Remembring the Temple of Bacchus, which he had seen at Aphitis, he desired to enjoy it's Shade, and the Coolness of the clear Waters, which were there.* He was carried thither alive, but died out of the Temple the seventh Day of his Fever (19). In the second Place, it is a chimerical Gloss to tell us, That out of a religious Respect for the Sanctity of the Temple, he would not die in it. Has *Xenophon*, or any other Author worthy of Credit, said so? To save myself the Trouble in another Place, I shall here remark an Error, which Mr *Moreri* has committed in his Article of AGESIPOLIS II. He assures us that That Prince, having been a Hostage in his Youth, answered those, who reproached him with it, *that it was because Kings suffer for the Faults of their Kingdom.* This Answer is as false, as it is contrary to the satirical Sentence,

Quidquid

AGESIPOLIS. AGIS.

it was expected he wou'd have been [F]; but bewailed and regretted it a long time, as *Xenophon* informs us (p). Observe, that *Agesipolis* left no Posterity (q); and that *Cleombrotus* his Brother and Successor was the Father of AGESIPOLIS II. (r), who reigned but one Year (s), and whose Apophthegms were more memorable than his Actions: For we meet with no Account of the former, whereas *Plutarch* has preserved a small Collection of the latter (t).

(p) *See the Remark* [F].
(q) *Paufan. lib. 2. p. 86.*
(r) *Id. ibid.*
(s) *Diod. Sicul. lib .15. cap. 60.*
(t) *Plut. in Apophthegm. Lacon. pag. 215.*

Quidquid delirant Reges, plectuntur Achivi (20).

The People suffer, when the Prince offends.
CREECH.

The Matter of Fact is this. It was said to him one Day, *As great a King as you are, you have been an Hostage, with the chief of the Youths of Lacedemon; but your Wives and your Children were not. Because*, replied he, *it was just, that we should bear the Punishment of our own Faults ourselves* (21).

[F] *Agesilaus was not pleased with this Loss, as it was expected he would have been.*] *Xenophon* inclines us to believe, that an Emulation reigned between those two Princes, very fit to produce Enmity. But *Plutarch* represents them to us as strictly united in Friendship. He observes that *Agesipolis* was mild and modest, and interested himself but little in public Affairs, and that he suffered himself to be gained by his Colleague *Agesilaus* (22), who knowing him to be of an amorous Complexion, was always talking to him of handsome Boys, and not only flattered his Passion for them, but even assisted him in the Gratification of it. Εἰδὼς ἔχοντα τοῖς ἐρωτικοῖς τὸν Ἀγησίπολιν, ὥσπερ ἦν αὐτὸς, ἀεί τινος ὑπῆρχε λόγω περὶ τῶν ἐν ὥρᾳ· καὶ προῆγε τὸν νεανίσκον εἰς ταυτὶ, καὶ συνήρα καὶ συνέπραττε (23). *Qui autem teneri sciret Agesipolim, sicut se, amoribus, sermonem assiduus de formosis adolescentibus inserebat, eodem illum impellebat, sociusque erat ei in amore & adjutor.* He adds, that these kind of Amours were not looked upon as criminal in *Lacedemon*. The following Passage informs us, that *Agesilaus* regretted the Loss of this Colleague. Ἀγησίλαος δὲ τοῦτο ἀκούσας, ἤχθη τις ἂν οἴεται, ἐφήσθη ὡς ἀντιπάλῳ, ἀλλὰ καὶ ἐδάκρυσε καὶ ἐπόθησε τὴν συνουσίαν (24). *Agesilaus*, upon this News, did not rejoice, as was expected, at the Loss of a Rival, but shed Tears, and lamented the Death of a Friend.

(20) *Horat. Epist. 2. l. 1. ver. 14.*
(21) *Plut. in Apophth. Laconic. pag. 215.*
(22) *Plut in Agesil. pag. 607. A.*
(23) *Id. Ibid.*
(24) *Xenophon. de Reb. gestis Græc. lib. 5. pag. 330.*

AGIS, King of *Lacedemon*, descended from *Agesilaus* II. in a direct Line (a), met with a very unfortunate End. He intended to reform his Kingdom, by the re-establishing of *Lycurgus*'s Laws; but he sunk under the weight of an Undertaking, which could not but be displeasing to those, who possessed great Estates, and who had so much accustomed themselves to the Sweets of a voluptuous Life, that they were no longer capable of relishing the ancient Discipline of *Lacedemon*. *Agis*, in the Flower of his Age, conceived the Design of this Reformation, out of a refined Desire of Glory [A], and practised it first of all in his own Person: His Cloaths, and his Table, were according to the manner of the old times; which deserved so much the more Admiration, because his Mother *Agesistrata*, and his Grand-mother *Archidamia*, had brought him up effeminately (b). Upon sounding the Disposition of his Subjects, he found the younger sort less averse to his Project, than those, who had enjoyed the Relaxation of Discipline for many Years. The greatest difficulty, he feared, was from the Women [B]. They were in more Credit at that time than ever; for they never reign more absolutely, than when Luxury is in Fashion. The Mother of *Agesilaus* did by no means find her account in this Reformation; she would have lost her great Wealth by it, which enabled her to be concerned in a thousand Intrigues: and therefore she immediately opposed the Design of *Agis*, and called it a chimerical Project. But her Brother *Agesilaus*, whom *Agis* had engaged in his Interests, knew how to manage her in such a manner, that she promised to second the Enterprize. She endeavoured to gain the Women; but, instead of suffering themselves to be persuaded, they addressed themselves to *Leonidas*, the other King of *Lacedemon*, and most humbly intreated him to frustrate the Designs of his Colleague. *Leonidas* durst not openly oppose it, for fear of exasperating the People, to whom the Reformation was pleasing, because it would be useful to them. He only crossed it by Intrigues, and spreading Suspicions, as if *Agis* aspired to the Tyranny by depressing the Rich, and raising the Poor. Nevertheless *Agis* propos'd his new Laws to the Senate, which contained the Abolishment of Debts, and a new Division of Lands. *Leonidas*, supported by

(a) *He was five Degrees remov'd from him. Plut. in Agide, pag. 796.*
(b) Ἐντεθραμμένος πλούτοις καὶ τρυφαῖς γυναικῶν τῆς τε μητρὸς Ἀγησιστράτας καὶ τῆς μάμμης Ἀρχιδαμίας, αἳ πλεῖστα χρήματα Λακεδαιμονίων ἔκέκτηντο. *Enutritus essent in opibus & deliciis mulieribus matris Agesistratæ & aviæ Archidamiæ, quæ in Lacedæmoniis erant pecuniosissimæ. Id. p. 797.*

[A] *Out of a refined desire of Glory.*] *Plutarch*'s Narrative (1) insinuates plainly to us, that *Agesistrata* shewed her Son the Prejudice he would do himself by his Plan of Reformation, considering the great Estate she possest; but he desired her to be willing to sacrifice her Riches to her Son's Glory. *For*, said he to her, *I can never equal other Monarchs on the Score of Riches: The Servants of the Satrapæ, the Servants of the Financiers of Seleucus, and Ptolemy, are richer than all the Kings of Lacedemon; but if, by my Temperance, and the Greatness of my Soul, I can raise myself above the Luxury of those Princes, and if I can introduce an Equality of Goods in my Kingdom, I shall attain to true Grandeur; I shall pass for a great Prince. This is to refine upon Self-love: You will be surpassed, what Progress soever you make in a certain Road; take quite the contrary, wherein you shall have no Rivals: They, who make a Comparison between you and others, will maintain, that, in it's kind, your Merit is by no means inferior to that of others. But could this be said, if the Dispute turned on Qualities of the same kind, some manifestly Inferior, and others* manifestly Superior, as the Opulency of *Agis*, and That of the King of *Syria*, would have been?

[B] *From the Women.*] The *Lacedemonians* were the best Husbands in the World; they communicated the Affairs of the Common-wealth to their Wives, much more than their Wives communicated their Domestic Affairs to them (2). At the time we are speaking of, almost all the Riches of *Lacedemon* were fallen to the Distaff; they were at the disposal of the Female Sex, which frustrated the Designs of this Prince. The Ladies fear'd they should lose their Riches, their Pleasures, and their Credit, all at once; and perhaps they were not mistaken. But let us hear *Plutarch* himself. *Now it must be observed, that most of the Riches of Lacedemon were at that time in the Hands of the Women, which made the Undertaking more difficult: For the Women not only were against it, because it would deprive them of their Pleasures, in which they plac'd their Happiness, for want of knowing the true Good, but also because they saw that the Honour, which was paid them, and the Power and Authority which they had, on account of their Riches, would be taken from them* (3).

[C] *Alledged*

(1) *Plut. in Agide, pag. 798.*
(2) *Plut. ibid.*
(3) *Plut. ibid.*

AGIS.

by the Rich, opposed this Project so powerfully, that there was one Voice more for throwing it out, than for carrying it. He paid dear for the Success of his Affair. *Lysander*, one of the *Ephori*, who had been the great Promoter of the Reformation, brought an Action against him, alledged the Celestial Signs [C], and persuaded a Prince of the Blood Royal, whose Name was *Cleombrotus*, and who was Son-in-Law to *Leonidas*, to secure the Kingdom to himself. *Leonidas*, seized with Fear, took Refuge in a Temple, where his Daughter, the Wife of *Cleombrotus*, came to him. He was cited, and because he did not appear, he was declared degraded from his Dignity, which was conferred on *Cleombrotus*. He obtained leave to retire to *Tegea*. The New *Ephori* entered a Process of Innovation against *Lysander* and *Mandroclidas*: These latter persuaded the two Kings to unite, and to make void the Election of these *Ephori*. Which being done, but not without raising great Commotions in the City. *Agesilaus*, one of the *Ephori*, who succeeded those, who were turned out, would have caused *Leonidas* to have been killed on the Road to *Tegea*, if *Agis* had not escorted him with a sufficient Guard. The Reformation might have been established at that time, if *Agesilaus* had not found Means to elude the good Intention of the Two Kings. During these Transactions, the *Achæans* desired assistance; it was granted them, and *Agis* had the command of the Troops. He acquired a great Reputation in That Campaign [D]. At his Return he found Affairs so embroiled by the ill Conduct of *Agesilaus*, that it was impossible for him to support himself. *Leonidas* was recalled to *Lacedemon*; *Agis* retired into one Temple, and *Cleombrotus* into another. The Wife of the latter behaved in such a manner, as to gain an universal Applause (*c*). *Leonidas* was satisfied with the Exile of his Son-in-Law; after which he applied himself wholly to the Ruin of *Agis*. One of the *Ephori*, who was unwilling to restore what *Agesistrata* had lent him, was the chief Instrument of the Misfortunes of that Family. *Agis* did not come out of his Place of Refuge, but only to bathe himself: As he was returning one Day from the Bath to the Temple, this *Ephorus* seized him, and dragged him to Prison. He was tried, condemned to Death, and delivered to the Executioner. His Mother and Grandmother earnestly sollicited, that at least a King of *Lacedemon* might have leave to plead his Cause before the People. But it was feared his Words would make too great an Impression; and that very Hour they strangled *Agis*. The Ephorus, who was Debtor to *Agesistrata*, suffered that Princess to enter into the Prison; he permitted the Grandmother to do the like; and then caused both of them to be strangled one after the other. *Agesistrata* died gloriously (*d*). The wife of *Agis* (*e*), a very rich Princess, and very wise, and one of the finest Women of *Greece*, was forced out of her House by King *Leonidas*, and constrained to marry that Prince's Son. He was a Youth as yet incapable of Marriage. He succeeded his Father; his Death was at least as tragical as that of *Agis*, whose Designs he had endeavoured to execute. His Name was *Cleomenes* (*f*). Mr *Moreri* misrepresents what *Agis* said [E] to those, who pitied his Fate. Other Dictionaries are very faulty on this Article [F]. *Meursius* ought not to have said that this *Agis* reigned Nine Years (*g*); for the Passage of *Diodorus Siculus*, which he appeals to, relates to another *Agis*. The AGIS of this Article lost his Life in the CXXXVth *Olympiad*. *Plutarch*'s Considerations on this King's Punishment may be seen under the Article AMPHARES.

(*c*) Her Name was CHELONIS. See her Article.

(*d*) See the Article AMPHARES.

(*e*) Her Name was Agiatis.

(*f*) Taken out of Plutarch, in Vita Agidis & Cleomenis.

(*g*) Meursius de Regno Lacedæmon. pag. 87.

[C] *Alledged the Celestial Signs.*] The Affair was this (4). Once in every nine Years the *Ephori* contemplated Heaven in a serene Night, and without a Moon; and if they saw a Star fall, they judg'd that the Kings had sinned against God; upon which they were suspended from their Dignity, 'till an Oracle from *Delphi*, or *Olympia*, re-establish'd them. *Lysander*, pretending to have seen this *Phænomenon*, entered an Action against the King, and produc'd Witnesses, who declared that *Leonidas* had had two Children by an *Asiatic* Woman. Now there was an ancient Law, which forbad the *Heraclidæ* (5) to have Children by a foreign Woman. Is it not very odd, that such a Government as this, wherein the Fortune of Kings depended on the good Pleasure of an *Ephorus*, who had seen a Star fall, should subsist so long?

[D] *Acquired a great Reputation in that Campaign.*] Having join'd *Aratus*, General of the *Achæans*, near *Corinth*, his Advice was to give the Enemy Battle on the other side of the *Isthmus*; but he submitted his Judgment to that General's Opinion, who thought it better not to come to an Engagement. *Aratus* own'd this himself in his Book. Yet one *Baton* of *Sinope* pretended, that *Agis* dissuaded the Fight, which *Aratus* had resolved upon (6). Is it not very strange, that an Historian should relate things concerning a General, which are contrary to the Relations of that General himself? Is it credible, that his Account should be false, to the prejudice of it's Author? This Boldness may be suffer'd for some Months, and for certain Reasons; but, when Events have pass'd that Term, the Actions of great Men ought no longer to be contradicted.

[E] *Mr Moreri misrepresents what Agis said.*] *Agis* seeing one of the Serjeants weep, said (7), *Weep not, for since they put me to Death by such a crying Act of Injustice, my Merit is greater than that of the Authors of my Death*. Instead of this, Mr *Moreri* makes him say, *Weep not, for those who weep, are much more to be pitied than I am.* This is not the only Fault of that Article. Mr *Moreri* says falsly, I. *That in the beginning of* Agis'*s Reign, an* Ephorus, *whose Name was* Epitadeus, *caus'd an Order to be made, That Fathers might disinherit their Children*. II. *That* Agis *rectified the Words of that Order, which re-peopled the City in a little time.* III. That the most Considerable lent a helping hand to the Design of *Agis*. Read *Plutarch*, and you will see, First, That *Epitadeus* had caus'd his Decree to be pass'd a long time before. Secondly, That *Agis* had not the good Fortune to procure the least Alteration. Thirdly, That the richer People oppos'd his Design. Is this to consult Originals ? Is this to understand them ?

[F] *Very faulty on this Article.*] Charles *Stephens* confounds this *Agis* with another more ancient, and distinguishes him from him, whom the *Lacedæmonians* hang'd. Mr *Hofman* is guilty only of the former of these two Mistakes; *Lloyd* corrects neither of them.

(4) Plut. in Agide, pag. 800.

(5) *That is, the Descendants of Hercules, of which Number were the Kings of Lacedæmon.*

(6) Plut. in Agide, pag. 801.

(7) Ibid. pag. 808.

AGREDA

AGREDA

AGREDA (a) (MARY de) a *Religious Visionary*, and famous for a Work, which the *Sorbonne* censured, lived in the XVIIth Century. *Francis Coronel*, her Father, and *Catherine d'Arena*, her Mother, who lived at *Agreda*, a Town of *Spain*, founded a Convent in their House on the 19th of *January*, 1619. A Particular Revelation induced them to it. This *Mary* took the Nun's Habit in it, at the same time with her Mother and Sister; she professed, with her Mother, on the Second of *February*, 1620 (b). She was elected Superior, in the Year 1627. and during the first Ten Years of her Superiority, she received several Commands from God, and the Virgin *Mary*, to write the Life of the Holy Virgin. She resisted these Orders *till the Year 1637: when she began to write it*. Having finished it, she burnt it with several Writings, which she had composed on other *Subjects*: She followed in this *the Counsel of a Confessor*, who *directed her in the absence of her Ordinary Confessor*. Her Superiors, and the first Confessor, reprimanded her severely for it, and commanded her to write the Life of the Holy Virgin a *second time*. God and the Holy Virgin repeated the same Command to her. She began to obey on the 8th of *December*, 1655 (c). She divided the Work *into three Parts, contained in eight Books*, which have been printed at Lisbon, at Madrid, at Perpignan, and at Antwerp. *The first was translated out of* Spanish *into* French, *from the Edition of* Perpignan, *by Father* Crofet, *a Recollect*. This Translation was printed at *Marseilles* in the Year 1696 (d). There are so many Absurdities in the Work [*A*], and yet so capable of pleasing the passionate Votaries of the Holy Virgin, that the Faculty of Divinity of *Paris* judged it proper to censure it [*B*]. They attained their End, in

(a) She is commonly call'd so for brevity sake, but it is not her Family Name; it is only the name of the Town, where the Monastery was, of which she was Superior.

(b) The Profession of her Sister was defer'd because she was not of age; Journal of the Learned of the 16th of Jan.1696. pag. 53, 54. Edit. Holl.

(c) It is the Day of the Conception of the Virgin in the Kalender.

(d) Taken from the Journal of the Learned, ubi supra.

[*A*] *There are so many Absurdities in the Work.*] We find there, "That, as soon as the Virgin was "born, the Almighty order'd the Angels to carry the "lovely Child into the Empyreal Heaven, which "they did several times; that God appointed an "hundred out of each of the nine Choirs of Angels, "that is to say nine hundred, to serve her: And that "he appointed twelve others to serve her in a visible "and corporeal Form, and eighteen more of the "highest Rank of those, who descended on *Jacob's* "Ladder, to carry Embassies from the Queen to "the great King; That, to regulate this invincible "Squadron the better, *Michael*, Captain of the "heavenly Militia, was plac'd at the Head of it: "That the first Conception of the Body of the most "Holy Virgin was on a *Sunday*, correspondent to "that of the Creation of Angels: That if the Virgin "did not speak as soon as she was born, it was not "because she could not, but because she would not: "That before she was three Years of Age, she swept "the House, and the Angels assisted her, &c. There "are I know not how many such like Extravagancies "in it." This is the Extract, which a *Protestant* Journalist gave of it (1). Another Journalist, who is a good Catholic, assures us (2), that *nothing is to be found in the six first Chapters, but Visions, by which Sister Mary of Jesus says, That God discover'd the Mysteries of the Holy Virgin to her, and the Decree he had made of creating all things*.—That, in the twentieth Chapter (3), *She gives an Account of what happen'd to the Holy Virgin in the Womb of St Anne; that she comes afterwards to the Birth of the Holy Virgin, to the Name which was given her, to the Angels, who were commission'd to guard her, to the Employments of the first eighteen Months of her Childhood, to the Conversation she had with God at the end of those eighteen Months, to her Conversations with St Joachim, and St Anne, and to the holy Exercise, wherein she employ'd herself, 'till she was carried to the Temple of* Jerusalem. If any one imagines, that, among so many Visions, there is nothing relating to St *John's Revelations*, he will be greatly mistaken; for our Visionary, not satisfy'd with explaining the twelfth Chapter of the *Revelations*, has enlarg'd very much on the twentieth first, which she expounds *of the Conception of the Holy Virgin* (4). It would be very surprizing indeed, if, in failing so long upon such a Sea, she should never dash upon this Rock. If you desire to know the Title of her Work, in the Translation of *Thomas* Crofet, read what follows. *The mystical City of God, Miracle of the Almighty, Abyss of Grace, divine History of the Life of the most holy Virgin* Mary, *Mother of God, our Queen and Mistress, manifested, in these last Ages, by the Holy Virgin to Sister Mary of Jesus, Abbess of the Convent of the Immaculate Conception of the City of Agreda, of the Order of St Francis, and written by the same Sister, by Order of her Superiors, and Confessors*.

[*B*] *The Faculty of Divinity at* Paris, *judg'd it proper to censure it.*] I have met with the Censure, which they published, only in the *Journal of the Learned*, wherein I find. I. That the sixth Proposition imports, *That God gave the Holy Virgin all that he would, and would give her all that he could, and could give her all that was not of the Essence of God* (5). II. That the seventh Proposition, is conceived in these Terms. "I declare, by the Force of Truth, "and of the Light, in which I see all these ineffable Mysteries, that all the Privileges, the Graces, "the Prerogatives, the Favours, and the Gifts of the "most pure *Mary*, comprehending the Dignity of "the Mother of God in it, depend and take their "Original from her having been Immaculate, and "full of Grace, in her Conception, insomuch that, "without that Privilege, all the rest would appear "faulty, or like a stately Building without a solid and "proportionable Foundation (6). *That* the ninth Proposition applys literally to the Holy Virgin, the Words of the eighth Chapter of *Proverbs*, and insinuates, that her Kings are raised and supported on the Throne, Princes command, and the Rulers of the Earth administer Justice (7). IV. *That* the thirteenth Proposition is, that if Mens Eyes were penetrating enough to see the Light of the Holy Virgin, it would suffice to conduct them to a blessed Eternity. V. *That*, besides these Propositions, several others are compriz'd under the fourteenth Article, and which are respectively condemned as rash, contrary to the Wisdom of the Rules, which the Church prescribes; to which is added, that most of them are like the Fables and Ravings of apocryphal Authors, and expose the Catholic Religion to the Contempt of impious Men and of Heretics (9). VI. *That* finally the Faculty declares, "that it does not pretend to approve several other "things contain'd in the Book, and chiefly the Passages, where the Author wrests the Text of Scripture, in applying it to her own Sense, and those "wherein she affirms, that some Opinions, which "are meerly Scholastic, were reveal'd to her." Let us make a few Reflexions upon this.

In the first Place, the School-men unanimously teach, that the distinct Character of God, and of his Creatures is, that God has nothing which comes from without, and that the Creatures have nothing, but what proceeds from without. This is what they express by the barbarous Words *aseitas*, and *abalietas*; from whence they conclude, that all the Attributes of God are communicable to the Creature, except the *Aseitas*; and, consequently, that it is possible for a Creature to be eternal, *à parte ante*, & *à parte post* (10), and infinite as to Knowledge, Power, local Presence, Goodness, Justice, &c. They commonly teach, that, by Power *Obediential*, Creatures are susceptible of the Faculty of working all sorts of Miracles, and also of creative Power. So that, if God did effectually confer on the Holy Virgin all that he could confer upon her, it follows, according to the Doctrines of the School, which Sister *Mary of Jesus* esteemed much, that the Holy Virgin existed from Eternity, that she can do all things, that she knows all things, that she fills all Places, and that she is infinite

(1) History of the Works of the Learned, Nov. 1696. pag. 140, 141.

(2) Journal of the Learned, of Jan. 16th 1696. pag. 52.

(3) Ibid. pag. 53.

(4) Ibid.

(5) Ibid. of Nov. 26. 1696. pag. 727.

(6) Ibid.

(7) Ibid. pag. 728.

(8) Ibid. pag. 729.

(9) Ibid. pag. 730.

(10) That is, That it may neither have Beginning nor End.

AGREDA.

in spite of the Opposition, and terrible Outcry of some of the Doctors of that Society [C]. How just soever the Censure was, it gave Offence to a great Number of Persons. It is thought that the Apprehensions of the Scandal it might cause obliged the Company

finite in every respect. I need not suppose, that our Abbess of *Agreda* followed the Doctrine of the *Spanish* Schoolmen; for I am not concern'd whether she knew, or was ignorant of it. She teaches plainly, that God gave the Holy Virgin all that he could give her, and that he could give her all his Attributes, except the divine Essence itself. This justifies the Conclusion, which I have drawn : Upon which, we may very well wonder, that the *Sorbonne* should only say, That *this Proposition is false, rash, and contrary to the Doctrine of the Gospel* (11). Is such a Censure severe enough? Ought they to have been contented with such weak Appellations? Is it enough to affirm, that it was a rash Mistake, to apply to the Virgin *Mary*, in a literal Sense, these Words of *Solomon*, *By me Kings reign, and Princes decree Justice* (12).

My second Reflexion is this. They who have carefully examin'd all that has been said of the Power of the Holy Virgin, and the Share which is given her in the Government of the Universe, have observed, that the last Comers, desirous to surpass those, who have gone before them, have been the Cause, that at last the utmost Bounds of Flattery have been found out. But, as the Reasons for continuing to proceed farther have never ceas'd (for when the Devotion of the People is to be a Maintenance for many Persons, who desire to live at their Ease, it must be quicken'd and reviv'd from time to time with new invented Incitements) I say, considering this, there is reason to wonder that the Barriers have not been broke, and that, among so many Monks and Nuns, who have been such great Refiners, no one has yet said, that the Holy Virgin governs the World alone. How comes it to pass, that *Spain* has not yet produc'd Writers, who have pretended to discover by Revelation, that a long Experience having convinc'd God the Father of the infinite Capacity of the Holy Virgin, and the good Use she has made of the Power, wherewith he had invested her, had resolv'd to abdicate the Empire of the World; and that God the Son, believing he could not follow a better Example, had embrac'd the same Resolution, and that the Holy Ghost, always obedient to the Will of the two Persons, from whom he proceeds, approving this fine Design, the whole Trinity had committed the Government of the World to the Hands of the Holy Virgin ; and that the Ceremony of the Abdication, and That of the Translation of the Empire had been solemnly perform'd in the Presence of all the Angels ; that an Act of it had been drawn up in the most authentic Form; that, since that Day, God concerns himself with nothing, and relies altogether on the Vigilancy of *Mary*; that Orders were given to several Angels, to notify this Alteration of Government upon Earth, that Men might know to whom, and in what Manner, they ought to have recourse for the future, in their Prayers; that it was no longer to God, since he had declar'd himself *emeritus, & rude donatus*, nor to the Holy Virgin, as to a Mediatress, or a subordinate Queen, but as the Sovereign and absolute Empress of all things? Once more ; how comes it to pass, that such an Extravagancy is yet to be brought forth ? I was ask'd once, if I had never heard of such a Conceit ? No, reply'd I, but *I would not swear, that this Thought has never appear'd, and yet less, that it will never be hatch'd in a Brain, sick with Devotion* : and, perhaps, if *Mary d'Agreda had liv'd ten Years longer, she would have brought forth this Monster* (13), *and, given us a Copy of the Act of Abdication; wherein we should have seen, that the Trinity, willing to live henceforth a quiet Life, and acknowledge their Obligations to the Holy Virgin, who for many Ages has so wisely born a considerable Share of the Fatigues of the Regency of the World, thought they could do nothing more proper, nor pitch upon a Reward more suitable to her, than to divest themselves, in her Favour, of their absolute Authority over all things*. Yet it must be confess'd, that the Idea of the *unalienable Action* of God is so clearly understood in all the Christian Communions, that there is no Reason to apprehend that this Monster of *Abdication* could live any time, supposing it could be produc'd. We ought not to fear it in our Days : Let this satisfy us ; nor let us trouble ourselves with

what may come to pass an hundred Years hence ; *nostros maneat ea cura nepotes.* Let Posterity look to that.

I observe, in the third Place, that there is nothing more true, than the Remarks of the *Sorbonne*, that the Book of the Abbess of *Agreda* contains several things, which expose the Church of *Rome* to the Contempt of Impious Men, and of Heretics. It was well for the Christian Religion, that the *Celsus*'s and *Porphyry*'s of those times had it not in their Power to attack it with such Weapons, as these Books, infinite in Number, can furnish at present. What would not a *Pagan* Author have objected to the Church in those Times, who should have had the Heat and the Character of *Arnobius* ? If *Henry Stephens*, and *Philip de Marnix*, were to return into the World, what Supplements would they not make, by the help of the *Mystical City* of our *Mary of Agreda*, the one to his *Apology* for Herodotus, and the other to his *Description of the Differences in Matters of Religion* ?

IV. Lastly, I remark, that our pretended inspired Authors endeavour to impose upon Mankind. They give us for Revelation, what they have learn'd by reading. For does not the Abbess of *Agreda* affirm, *That some Opinions, which are meerly Scholastic*, were taught her by Inspiration (14) ?

[C] *In spite of the Opposition — of some of the Doctors of that Society.*] The following are Extracts from a Printed Book, entituled, *The Case of Mary d'Agreda, and the Manner how her Condemnation was plotted in the Sorbonne* (15). It is a Letter from an anonymous Author, to an anonymous Person. " The Odour of Sanctity, in which this good Religious died, and the Canonization which is sollicited at the Court of *Rome*, gave me such an high Idea of her Person, that I was surpriz'd to hear that the Faculty of Divinity, at *Paris*, had met to condemn her Works." These are the Authors Words (16). Afterwards he supposes, " That they were " some mercenary Souls, who at the Sollicitation " of three Prelates, to whom they were devoted, " pursued the Condemnation of them (17). The " whole Intrigue, *continued he* (18), is as follows. My " Lord Bishop, being more addicted to the Opini- " ons of St *Thomas*, than a young *Jacobin*, who " ought only to swear *in verba magistri*, could not " bear that the Faculty should, with so much Preci- " pitation, give into the immaculate Conception of " the Virgin. The hatred he bore to Brother *Thomas* " *Crojset*, a *Recollect*, and Translator of that Book, " occasion'd by the Report which was spread of what " the Translator had said against him, upon his re- " fusing him a Benefice in his Diocess, and the De- " sire of indemnifying *A*—— the King's Printer, for " the considerable Loss he had sustain'd by his Works, " and who had made use of the Impression of this " Book, printed by *H*——, at *Marseilles*, were the " Foundation of the Commotions among the Facul- " ty ; for the ready way to make a Book sell well " is to get it condemn'd. Every body runs to it, as " to a House on fire, and the Book, which was worth " but twenty Pence, *A*—— sells for ten Livres, be- " sides what is sold under hand of a pirated Impres- " sion. This Prelate, to succeed the better in his " Design, prepossess'd my Lord *** one of the most " moderate Prelates in the Kingdom : both join'd " with my Lord ✝✝✝✝✝✝ a Man of a very mean Ge- " nius, who may be easily prejudic'd, and who is " fond of Ceremonies and Trifles; you must know " that these Lords go hand in hand. This Trumvi- " rate influenc'd their Creatures, and gain'd Mr *le* " *Fevre*, Syndic of the *Sorbonne*, who presented " the Book of *Mary d'Agreda* to the Faculty, on " the 20th of *May*. Deputies were appointed to " examine it. They reported sixty eight Proposi- " tions (19), which they call'd heretical, rash, scan- " dalous, and offensive to chaste Ears. They were " printed, as qualified by the Deputies, and distribu- " ted among the Doctors (20), that they might give " their Opinions of them, in the next Assembly (21). " Father *Meron*, a Cordelier, of whom we have some " fine Performances, both in Philosophy and Chro- " nology, desired the Faculty not to be too hasty in " condemning

Vol. I. M m

Company to infert a Declaration in their Act [*D*], which otherwife would have been very fuperfluous; fince the Queftion did not relate to the Things fpecified in the Declaration. We muft not forget that the Father of *Mary d'Agreda* became a Monk in a Monaftery of the Order of St *Francis, wherein two of his Sons had already entered themfelves Fryars, and that he lived there a very exemplary Life, and died a Saint* (*e*). Much lefs ought we to forget, that great Intereft has been made at *Rome* to procure the Canonization of *Mary d'Agreda*. See the beginning of the Remark [*C*].

(*e*) *Journal of the Learned,* Feb. 16. 1696. p. 51.

"condemning a Book, which the fovereign Pontiff "had referv'd the Cognifance of to himfelf, and "had deputed Cardinals, who were at that time "examining it (22). —— The Cabal were enrag'd "at him, and he was obliged to declare, that, if they "proceeded, without regarding his Remonftrance, "he appeal'd from all that was done againft the "Book to the Pope. He declares, however, That "if this Appeal injur'd the Rights of the *Gallican* "Church in any manner, he would defift from it "(23). From that Day, 'till the meeting of the Affembly, there was nothing but caballing. The "Day of the Affembly being come, Meff. *du Sauffoy* "and *Gabillon* condemn'd the Book (24). —— "But "Monf. *le Caron* pretended there was nothing in it, "which deferv'd to be cenfured; which he fupported with good Reafons. Each of them had his Partizans, who appear'd in twenty nine fucceffive Affemblies. The *Syndic* gave thofe of Monf. *le Caron*'s Party the Name of *Agredians*, a Name which "they ftill retain. The Affair was terminated the "feventeenth of *September*. "There was fuch a Noife "in the Hall of the Affembly, that it feem'd like a "Market (25). —— The next Day Meff. *du Flos* "and *du Mas*, formerly Counfellors in the Parliament of *Paris*, protefted againft the Validity of the "Cenfure, and caufed their Proteft to be notify'd to "the Dean and Syndic of the Faculty, which is ftill "in Force, they not having retracted it by any Act "(26). Some time after, the Syndic and the Deputies affembled again, and procur'd another Cenfure "—— which was read the firft of *October*; but, before the reading, the Syndic declar'd to the Faculty the Oppofition which was fignify'd to him by "thofe two Gentlemen. He faid moreover, that "my Lord of *Paris* having caus'd them to come "to his Palace, had convinc'd them by fuch good "Reafons, that the Abbot *du Mas* yielded to them, "and that he was fure that when Monf. *du Flos* fhould "hear the reading of the Cenfure, as it was drawn "up, he would affent to it. The Work of the Syndic was read, and they were furpriz'd that there "were new and cenfur'd Propofitions in it, which "they had not heard of in the Faculty, and that they "had retrench'd feveral of the condemned ones (27)." My Readers may judge as they pleafe of thefe Extracts.

[*D*] *That the Apprehenfions of the Scandal it might caufe obliged the Company to infert a Declaration in their Act.*] They protefted in the moft folemn manner, "That by this Cenfure they had no Defign "to diminifh any thing of the lawful Worfhip, which "the Catholic Church pays to the Holy Virgin; "that they honour'd her as the Mother of God; that "they had a particular Confidence in her Interceffion; that they held the Sentiments of their Fathers, concerning the immaculate Conception, and "that they believed her Affumption into Heaven, "both in Body and in Soul (28)." The Author of the Letter, of which we have produc'd fome Extracts in the foregoing Remark, fays, That the Cenfure, wherein they acknowlege the Conception and the *Affumption of the Virgin*, was made by the Syndic and the Deputies, after the Body of the Faculty had finifh'd the Judgment (29). This fhews that they had not the Courage to publifh the Cenfure of the Faculty, without qualifying it; and we may judge from thence, to what Dangers they expofe themfelves, who difapprove the moft palpable Errors, which magnify the Honours of the Holy Virgin. They not only expofe themfelves to the Indignation of the People, but alfo to that of the Monks, and of many other Ecclefiaftics: Whence they endeavour to ward off the Blow by ftudied Prefaces (30). What Servitude! and what a Proof that the Difeafe is incurable! What *Livy* faid of the Republic of *Rome*, agrees at prefent with the Church of that Name. "Labente "deinde paulatim difciplinâ, velut defidentes primo "mores fequatur animo; deinde ut magis magifque

(22) Ibid. pag. 30.

(23) Cafe of Mary d'Agreda, p. 31.

(24) Ibid. pag. 35, 36.

(25) Ibid. pag. 37.

(26) Ibid. pag. 38.

(27) Ibid. pag. 39.

(28) *Journal of the Learned,* Nov. 1696. pag. 716, 717.

(29) Cafe of Mary d'Agreda, pag. 30.

(30) *Note, that, in relation to the Vot vets, thefe two Verfes of Boileau have been apply'd.*
Un Auteur à genoux dans une humble Preface, au Lecteur qu'il ennuie a beau demander grace,
An Author on his Knees, in an humble Preface, does evil to beg pardon of the Reader, whom he is going to torture.

"lapfi fint, tum ire cæperint præcipites, donec ad "hæc tempora, quibus nec vitia noftra nec remedia "pati poffumus, perventum eft (31). —— *We may "trace the Decay of their Morals, from the firft Relaxation of Difcipline, through the feveral Stages "of Degeneracy, to the prefent times, in which we can "neither bear our Vices, nor their Remedies.*" The Work of *Mary d'Agreda*, is evidently full of Fables, and abfurd Doctrines; yet, becaufe it favours the falfe Ideas which People will entertain of the high Dignity, and unlimited Power of the Holy Virgin, all kind of Machines muft be fet at work to get it cenfur'd at *Paris*. The Author of the Letter (32) does more harm to his Church and Nation than he apprehends, when he recounts the Cabals, which were made ufe of by thofe, who wanted to have the *Myftical City* of the *Spanifh* Abbefs cenfured. There would have been no need of caballing, if the Minds of the People had not been ftrangely obftinate; Nor need they have had recourfe to Softenings. The Cenfure would have pafs'd, and no one would have murmur'd at it. All the Courts of the Inquifition would have prevented the Faculty of Divinity of *Paris*(where they have all remain'd filent hitherto, if I am not miftaken; though they are fo ready to condemn all Works, which oppofe ever fo little the moft doubtful Traditions, if they favour the Worfhip of the Saints (33).

Note, That there is a particular Reafon, which may oblige the *Sorbonne* to be cautious, and expofe themto the Oppofitions of many Doctors: Which is, that fo many Confequences have been drawn from the Epithet *Mother of God*, that there is fcarce any extravagant Opinion concerning the Excellence and Power of the Virgin, but what may be maintained in fome Meafure by Arguments *ad hominem*, which thofe Confequences afford. Your Adverfaries lead you by Degrees where they pleafe; you are undone by the Subtilties of the Schoolmen: If you retreat, you ftand convicted of denying Confequences; from whence it happens, that thofe, who pretend to argue confequentially, and to favour the popular Devotion at the fame time, chufe rather to advance ftill farther, than to retreat. And yet their Syftem is not regular. The Divinity of *Mary*, in the literal Senfe, is wanting to it: fince the Mother of God ought to be a Goddefs of courfe, and of the felf-fame Nature with her Son. And fhe would be fo, if they would adopt the Imagination of the Cavalier *Berri* (34), but it has been condemned. Perhaps a time will come when they will find the Neceffity of it, and by that means fquare this irregular Figure. It is thought that many wifh for it.

—— O fi Angulus ille
Proximus accedat, qui nunc deformat Agellum (35).

—— *Oh! that the Gods would yield That Nook, which fpoils the Figure of my Field.*
Creech.

Such a thing might be done in certain Circumftances, if there was a Combination of temporal and fpiritual Interefts. Every thing paffes, when Princes concur with the Heads of an Ecclefiaftical Party, during certain Difpofitions of general Affairs.

Let us conclude with obferving, that, if the Faculty of Divinity of *Paris* were in hopes that their Cenfure would remove a Stumbling-Block out of the way of thofe, who are called the *New Re-united*, they were deceived; for the Oppofition they were forced to encounter with its own Body, and the Difcontent which broke out after the Publication of the Cenfure, have much more fcandalized the *Re-united*, than the Cenfure could have Edified them. Befides that, what gives them the greateft Offence remains entire in the Preface to the Cenfure; a Preface, which is a Signal of the Continuation of a Capital

(31) Liviue, lib. 1. init.

(32) *The Title of it is as the beginning of the Remark* [*C*].

(33) *The Acta Sanctorum of the Jefuits of Antwerp have been condemn'd by the Inquifition of Toledo.*

(34) *See the Article* BORRI.

(35) Horat. Sat. 6. lib. 2. ver. 8.

AGRICOLA.

Capital Controversy, I mean, in relation to a Worship, whose Excesses have excited some curious Persons to philosophize, in order to discover the Original of it (36).

(36) *See the Remark [N] of the Article NESTORIUS.*

AGRICOLA almost an infinite number of Authors bear this Name, but as there are but three or four of considerable note, I shall only take Notice of them.

AGRICOLA (GEORGE) a *German* Physician, excelled in the Knowledge of Metals. He was born at *Glaucha*, in *Misnia*, on the Twenty fourth of *March*, 1494. The Discoveries he made in the Mountains of *Bohemia*, after his Travels in *Italy*, so strongly inclined him to go to the Bottom of the Metallic Science, that when, by the advice of his Friends, he had engaged himself in the Practice of Physic at *Joachimstal* (*a*), he employed as much time as he could in the Study of Fossils. To satisfy this Passion the better, he retired to *Chemnits*, where he gave himself up wholly to this Study. He spent there not only the Pension, which was obtained for him from *Maurice* Duke of *Saxony*, but also part of his own Estate; insomuch that he got much more Glory by his Labours, than Profit. He composed many Works on the Subject he had most at Heart, and some others on Miscellaneous Subjects [*A*]. He examined what *Budæus*, *Leonard Portius*, and *Alciatus*, had observed concerning Weights and Measures, and found them greatly mistaken. *Alciatus* undertook to defend himself, but he was foiled in the Argument. *Bodin* maintains, that, in Comparison of *Agricola*, *Aristotle* and *Pliny* saw very little into the Metallic Science (*b*). It must not be forgot, that, when Duke *Maurice*, and Duke *Augustus* marched to join the Army of *Charles* the Vth in *Bohemia*, *Agricola* followed them, to shew his Fidelity, though he was obliged to abandon the Care of his Estate, his Children, and his Wife, who was with Child (*c*). He died a very good Papist at *Chemnits* on the Twenty first of *November*, 1555. The Zeal, with which he opposed the Protestant Doctrine in his latter Days, to which he seemed not much averse to at first [*B*], rendered him so odious to the *Lutherans*, that they let him lie five days unburied [*C*]. They

(*a*) *That is, The Valley of* Joachim. *It is a City of* Misnia.

(*b*) Bodin, in Method. Histor. *See* in Sir Tho. Pope Blount *his* Censura celebr. Authorum, *pag.* 413. *a great number of very honourable Elogies of* Agricola.

(*c*) Uxore prægnante cum dulcissimis liberis domi relicta, fortunis etiam omnibus posthabitis, cum dumo, quo eis erat devinctus, nullo modo negligendum putaret, in exercitu eorum pene sepex militavit. *Melch. Adam. Vit. Medic. pag.* 79.

[*A*] *Many Works on the Subject he had most at Heart, and some others on miscellaneous Subjects.*] The Titles of some of them are as follows. *De ortu & causis subterraneorum* (Of the Origin and Causes of Subterraneous Things). *De natura eorum quæ effluunt ex terra* (Of the Nature of those things, which flow out of the Earth). *De natura fossilium* (Of the Nature of Fossils). *De medicatis fontibus* (Of medicinal Springs). *De subterraneis animantibus* (Of Subterraneous Animals). *De veteribus & novis metallis* (Of old and new Metals). *De Re metallica* (Of the Metallic Science). I look upon his Speech *De bello Turcis inferendo* (1) (Of making War upon the *Turks*), to be a Political Work; his Treatise *De traditionibus Apostolicis* (Of Apostolical Traditions), a Controversial Piece; and his Treatise *De Peste* (Of the Plague), a Physical Dissertation. *Melchior Adam* does not know whether these two last Works were ever printed; I am also ignorant of it, as to the Treatise of Controversy, but I know that the other appeared at *Basil* in the Year 1554. and that it was since twice printed before *Melchior Adam* published his Book. *See Marklinus* in his *Lindenius renovatus*.

[*B*] *Seemed not much averse to it at first.*] He not only disapproved the sordid Traffic of Indulgences, but many other Practices likewise. The following four Verses of his making were affixed in the Year 1519. in the Streets of *Zwickaw* (2). They concern the Indulgences of *Rome*.

(1) *Printed at* Basil *in* 1538.

(2) *He taught Greek there.*

Si nos injecto salvabit cistula nummo,
Heu nimium infelix tu mihi pauper eris!
Si nos, Christe, tua servatos morte beasti,
Jam nihil infelix tu mihi pauper eris.

*If without Gold Salvation can't be bought,
How curs'd the Wretch who is not worth a Groat?
But if Christ's Death has purchas'd for us Peace,
Rejoice, ye Poor, and bid your Miseries cease.*

Melchior Adam was of Opinion, that four things hindered the Conversion of *Agricola*. 1. The rash Writings of some Divines. 2. The scandalous Lives of some Reformed Sectaries. 3. The breaking of the Images, and revolt of the Country People. 4. The Inclination he had for Pomp and Ceremony (3). The three first of these gave *Erasmus* an entire Dislike to the Protestant Party. A great Number of other Persons, who wished for a Reformation of the Church, fell into the same Snare with *Erasmus*.

(3) Melch. Adam in Vit. Medic. *pag.* 80.

Whence it was, that *Theodore Beza* encountered so many Persons, who had at first tasted of the good Seed, and afterwards returned to their wallowing in the Mire (4). When we talk thus to Men of Sense and Reason, they tell us, that, considering the State of things at that time, it was impossible to support or propagate one's Cause by downright Meekness and Patience; and that therefore the Providence of God, whose ways are always Wise, permitted, that Men should appear, such as they are, in the great Work of Reformation, to attain more naturally to his Design, which was, as Experience teaches us, to hinder either of the two Religions from quite ruining each other. This is a good Plea. There are certain means, which, for this very Reason, that they are proper to bring about half the Work, are insufficient for the perfecting of it.

(4) *See his History of the Churches.*

[*C*] *They let him lie five Days unburied.*] *Scaliger* condemned this Conduct with Reason; he says "Agricolam, quo nihil doctius, Lutherani mortuum sepelire noluerunt, quia manserat Pontificius. Italus quidam scripsit & hortatus est ut sepelirent hominem Christianum; barbaries magna. (5). ——— The *Lutherans* refused to bury the very learned *Agricola*, *because he died a Papist. A certain Italian wrote to, and exhorted them, to bury a Man, who was a Christian: this was an Instance of Great Barbarity.*" I dare not maintain, that it is false, that an *Italian* exhorted the *Lutherans* to this Office of Humanity by Letter, but I see no probability of it; and it may be imputed to Forgetfulness in *Scaliger*, or His Boarders. There is a Letter of *Matthiolus*, wherein he complains, that such a venerable old Man, as *George Agricola*, could not find Earth enough in his own Country to cover his Body. *Id. Matthiolus ad Caspar. Næuium Med. (lib. 2. Epist.) queritur, hunc præclarum probumque jenem in patria tantum terræ non invenisse quo suum operiretur cadaver* (6). From hence they might pretend, that an *Italian* exhorted by Letter those, who had the Body, to bury it. Let it not be thought strange, that I lay but small Stress upon what the great *Scaliger* says here; for how can I depend upon him in relation to *Agricola*, when he has told us, upon another Occasion, that he was a very impious Man, who scarce deserved to be buried? " Non minus eruditus & in censenda metallorum natura curiosus fuit quam vere impius, nulli addictus religioni, ut post mortem vix sepeliri meruerit (7). ——— *He was as Learned and Curious in examining the Nature of Metals, as he was truly impious, and addicted to no Religion; insomuch that he scarce deserved funeral Rites after his Death.*"

(5) *In* Scaligerana, *pag.* 5.

(6) Melch. Adam. ubi *supra.*

(7) Scaligerana prima, *pag.* 80.

AGRICOLA.

They brought his Corps from *Chemnits* to *Zeits*, where he was interred in the principal Church (d). Such are the Fruits of a blind Zeal [D].

(d) Id. ibid. pag. 77, &c.

[D] *Such are the Fruits of a blind Zeal.*] There is no Protestant at present, who does not condemn this Treatment of his Corps; and I do not question, but that, at that time, most of the *Lutherans* condemned it. *Melchior Adam* seems to lay all the Blame of it on the Minister of the Place. It is more easy, at present, to see the Mischiefs of this false Zeal; Time has calmed those Passions, which like impetuous Storms rob us of the Sight of Heaven:

Eripiunt subito nubes cœlumque diemque
Teucrorum ex oculis: ponto nox incubat atra (8).

(8) Virgil. Æneid. lib. 1. ver. 88.

———— *sable Night involves the Skies,*
And Heaven itself is ravish'd from their Eyes.
DRYDEN.

What will not Men do to make Reprisals, and when there is Reason to speak thus?

Res dura & regni novitas me talia cogunt
Moliri (9).

———— *my Cruel Fate,*
And Doubts attending an unsettled State,
Force me to guard my Coasts.
DRYDEN.

(9) Dido apud Virgil. Æn. lib. 1. ver. 563.

Freberus remarks, that *Agricola* fell into so great a Passion in a Theological Dispute, that he contracted a violent Fever, of which he died (10). He cites only *Melchior Adam*, who says nothing of it. It is very likely, that *Agricola* had enraged the *Lutherans* by the Appearance of an excessive Aversion. *Peter Albinus* represents him (11) as an obstinate Roman Catholic. I desire you to compare this with the first *Scaligerana*.

(10) Paul. Freher. in Theatr. Viror. illustr. pag. 1238.

(11) In the Chronicle of Misnia.

AGRICOLA (JOHN) a *Saxon* Divine, born at *Islebe* (a) on the Twentieth of April 1492 (b), was the Cause of great Troubles to the Protestant Religion, which he embraced. It has been said, that he followed the Elector of *Saxony*, in Quality of his Minister, to the Diet of *Spire*, in the Year 1526. and to that of *Augsburg* in the Year 1530. But it is certain, that he made those two Journeys, only in Quality of Minister of the Count of *Mansfeld*. It is true this Count accompanied the Elector of *Saxony*, and, during that time, his Minister preached sometimes before the Elector; and this is the Original of the Mistake. *Agricola* had tolerable Success in preaching, which made him fancy himself a great Man, and set himself up in competition with *Melancthon*. For this Reason he wrote against him in 1527 (c). His restless and ambitious Temper prompted him, in 1536, to ask leave to quit his Country, where he exercised the Ministry, and was Principal of the College. His Request was accompanied with Complaints; and seemed so unreasonable to the Count of *Mansfeld*, that he did not obtain his Dismission without Reproaches of Ingratitude, Avarice, and Drunkenness; besides being charged with exercising his Function carelesly, and with having disputed more against the Protestants, than against the Catholics. He went to *Wittemberg*, where he obtained the Chair of Professor and Minister. He taught no very instructive Doctrine in relation to the use of the *Law* under the *Gospel*; in a word, he became the Founder of the *Antinomian* Sect (d). *Luther*, who had been his good Friend [A], attacked him very roughly, and obliged him to promise that he would recant his Errors; but while they were employed in drawing up the Formulary, which he was to sign, *Luther* published some new Writings, at which *Agricola* was so piqued, that he presented (e) a very abusive Petition to the Elector against his Antagonist, wherein he complained, among other things, that they imputed Opinions to him, which were not his. *Luther* answered him with all his Fire, and, to clear himself from the Character of a Public Libeller, he sent for Attestations from *Islebe*, in relation to some particular Instances of *Argricola*'s Behaviour. The Divines of *Wittemberg* ran to the Assistance of *Luther*, and said, That his Accusations were well-grounded. The Elector of *Saxony*, much embarrassed with the Affair, appointed Arbitrators between the Parties, and recommended to them to find out some means of an Accommodation; after which he made *Agricola* promise, that he would not retire, before the Process was ended. This Promise was broke: *Agricola* retired privately to *Berlin* (f), without waiting for an Answer to the Demand he had made for Leave to depart. The Elector of *Brandenburg* endeavoured to reconcile him with *Luther*; but there was nothing to be done in it, except upon one of these two Conditions, either that *Agricola* should return, and wait the decision of the Process, or that he should retract his Errors, and the abusive Language he had given *Luther* in writing. He chose the latter [B], and published a Book at *Berlin*, wherein

(a) A Town in the County of Mansfeld. He was as well known by the Name of Islebius as by that of Agricola.

(b) Melch. Adam. In Vitis Theol. pag. 409.

(c) It was in relation to the Formulary of Ecclesiastical Visitation, drawn up by Melancthon.

(d) See the Article IS-LEBIANS.

(e) The 30th of March, 1540, during the Assembly at Smalcalde.

(f) In 1540.

[A] *Luther, who had been his good Friend.*] They were of the same City. We find that *Agricola* served *Luther* as Secretary in the Conference at *Leipsic*, in 1519 (1), and that he was sent to *Francfort* in 1525 (2), with a Recommendatory Letter from *Luther* to the Magistrates, to be one of the Ministers of the Gospel there. The Author, whom I cite (3), censures Mr *Varillas*, who said, that *Luther* undertook nothing considerable without *Agricola*. This is to push things too far, and he cannot produce any Proof of it.

[B] *He chose the latter.*] There are probably two Reasons for this Piece of Condescension. First, He had no Hopes of finding his Account in the Decision of the Controversy; for he could not gain his Point without *Luther*'s being declared a Slanderer of his Brethren. Now he must have been the most credulous of Men to entertain any Hopes of Success, at this Expence, in *Saxony*. The People would have stoned the Judges, who should have sullied the Reputation of a Reformer in this manner. They would have pretended, that the Church stood in need of the good Fame of *Luther*, and that the Papists would draw too great an Advantage from his Disgrace. Have we not seen some, who were but Pigmies in comparison of *Luther*, escape, by this means, the Canonical Punishments which they have deserved? *Agricola*'s second Reason, probably, was, that by not submitting, he was in danger of losing the Quarter's Salary which was due to him. Read what follows: " Neque tamen hoc scripto sta- " tim

(1) Seckendorf, Hist. Luther. lib. 1. pag. 92. liter. r.

(2) Ibid. p. 243. lit. a.

(3) Seckendorf, ubi supra, lib. 3. pag. 126. n. 1.

AGRICOLA.

wherein he asked Pardon of those, whom he might have offended by his Errors, and of *Luther* by Name, and professed that he would Live and Die in the Faith, which he had opposed. *Luther* did not depend upon these fine Protestations; *Agricola* complained of this to the Elector of *Saxony*, and assured him, that nothing had ever given him greater uneasiness, than this Contest with the Man of God (g); and that, since his Offer of giving his Oath wou'd not avail him, he referred his Cause to the Judge of the World; humbly entreating the Elector, at the same time, to order him the Payment of his Salary, which was due for Three Months, and which he stood in need of for the Maintenance of his Wife and Nine Children (b). I believe he never wou'd have regained the Favour either of the Elector, or *Martin Luther*. No doubt he comforted himself with the Reputation, which his Office of Preacher at the Court of *Berlin* gave him, and with the Choice, which they made of him for composing a Work, which made a great Noise. I mean the *Interim*, which he drew up with *Julius Phlug*, and *Michael Heldingus* (i), in the Year 1548. It is pretended, that the Emperor rewarded *Agricola* largely for the Pains he had taken on this Occasion. The War, which arose some time after, in *Germany*, between the Protestant Divines (k), made it appear that this Minister was a Man of a dangerous Spirit, and a great Intermeddler. He was officious in composing Animosities, and did not spare the Gift of Elocution, which he was Master of, in the Conferences, which were held about these Matters; but he heal'd no Differences. He died at *Berlin* in 1566. He had been Superintendant (l) of the *March* of *Brandenburg* (m). It is said that he would have reviv'd the use of Holy Oyl for the Sick, and that he did not question, but that miraculous Cures would have attended, it as in former times (n). He wrote but few Books [C]. They carry Things too far, who say that he relapsed to Popery [D].

(g) See Remark [B].

(b) Taken out of Seckendorf's Ansewer to the Lutheranism of Father Maimbourg, lib. 3. from pag. 306. to pag. 310.

(i) He is commonly called Michael Sidonius, because he was titular Bishop of Sidon.

(k) It was on the Question about things indifferent in Religion.

(l) So the Lutherans call the Ministers, who have the Inspection of several Churches.

(m) Michel. Hist. Eccles. pag. 733. Edit. 1679.

(n) Melch. Adam. in Vitis Theol. pag. 411.

" tim, ut speraverat, Luthero de vera conversione
" sua fidem fecit; id quod ipse *Agricola* literis d. 19.
" Decemb. apud Electorem Saxoniæ queritur, nihil-
" que tota vita sibi gravius accidisse, quam simulta-
" tem illam cum viro Dei, quem ipse patris loco ve-
" neratus sit, & in cujus obsequio mori vellet, apud
" quem tamen nihil proficiat ne juramenti quidem ob-
" latione, ideo se Deo causam committere. Petit tamen
" ut sibi ad alendam uxorem novemque liberos trime-
" stre, quod restare sibi dicit, salarium non denegetur,
" se enim id diligenti lectione promeritum (4).
" Nor did he by this Writing presently convince Lu-
" ther of his Conversion, as he pretended; which *Agri-
" cola* himself complained of in his Letters of the
" nineteenth of December to the Elector of Saxony;
" in which he declares, that nothing had happened
" so afflicting to him in his whole Life, as his
" Quarrel with the Man of God, whom he reve-
" renced as a Father, and in whose Favour he de-
" sired to dye; with whom as his Offer of an Oath
" could not prevail, he committed his Cause to
" God. However he petitioned, that they would
" not deny him his Quarter's Salary, for the Mainte-
" nance of his Wife and nine Children, *which he said
" was due to him*, and which he had merited by his
" constant Attendance on Preaching."

[C] *He wrote but few Books.*] The Explication of three hundred *German* Proverbs was one of the first. He abused *Ulric* Duke of *Wirtemberg* much in it (5). Complaints were made of it, which obliged the Author to acknowledge his Fault in a very submissive Letter. This did not hinder Duke *Ulric* from alledging, among other Grievances, at the Diet of *Franckfort*, in the Year 1536, that they protested *John Agricola* in the County of *Mansfeld*, by whom he had been publickly affronted (6). The Author increased his Work with above four hundred Proverbs more in the second Edition. He wrote a Commentary on St *Luke*; he refuted the Explication of the nineteenth Psalm, published in *German*, by *Thomas Muncerus*, &c. (7).

[D] *That he relapsed to Popery.*] It is certain, that, leaving *Saxony*, he retired to the Court of *Brandenburg*, and that the Elector *Joachim* II. who had established the Reformation in his Dominions, in the Year 1539, (8) received him honourably, and made him his Preacher. It is as certain that he enjoyed that Prince's Favour all his Life-time; so that it is false to say, as *Melchior Adam*, and *Paul Freherus* do, that *Agricola* was a Papist, *tunc Pontificiis sese adjunxerat*, when *Charles* V. employed him in drawing up the *Interim*. I own he made great Concessions in that Piece; but did not *Phlug*, and the Bishop of *Sidon*, do the same? Were they therefore *Lutherans*? The Project of these three Persons was neither satisfactory to the Protestants, nor the Catholics; this is very certain: But there is a manifest Distinction to be made between those, who, for the sake of Peace, give up part of the Reformation, and those who actually forsake the Protestant Communion, to embrace the Communion of *Rome*. *Agricola* was doubtless one of the first Class, but, having never been of the second, he ought not to pass for a Papist. Censure therefore these Words of *Micrælius*; " Joh. Agricola - - - - noster primo,
" deinde suus, tandem Pontificiorum (9). ——— John
" Agricola - - - - *who was first of our Sect, then
" of no Party, and lastly a Convert to Popery.*" I cannot tell, whether, when he says three Lines after, " Homini Epicuræo similior quam pio Theologo, ut
" scribit *Osiander* ad annum 1566. quo obiit *Agri-
" cola*. ——— *More of an Epicurean, than a pious
" Divine, as* Osiander *writes, at the Year* 1566, *in
" which* Agricola *died* ——— He means a Voluptary, or one indifferent to all Religions.

(4) Id. ibid. pag. 310. n. 16.

(5) Id. lib. 2. pag. 135.

(6) Ib. pag. 412. lit. b.

(7) Melch. Adam. in Vitis Theol. pag. 411.

(8) Seckendorf, lib. 3. pag. 234, & seq.

(9) Micrel. Syntagm. Histor. Ecclef. p. 733.

AGRICOLA (MICHAEL) a *Lutheran* Minister at *Abo* in *Finland*, was the first who translated the New Testament into the Language of the Country, which contributed much to the Propagation of *Lutheranism* (a).

(a) Ex Micrælio, Hist. Eccles. pag. 733.

AGRICOLA (RODOLPHUS) was one of the most Learned Men of the XVth Century. *Italy*, which in those times called all beyond the *Alps* barbarous, produced nothing, to which *Friesland* could not compare her *Agricola*, without fearing to be overcome. This great Man was of mean Birth [A]; he was born about the Year

[A] *Was of mean Birth.*] I am aware, that, in the Life of *Agricola*, among those of the Professors of *Groningen*, it is affirmed, that he was of one of the most considerable Families of *Friesland*; *Ex Agricolarum familia, apud Frisios inter honora-tiores semper habita, vir hic incomparabilis oriundus*: ——— *This incomparable Person sprung from the* Agricolæ, *a Family in* Friesland, *esteemed amongst the most honourable*. But as this Life is the same with that, which we find in *Melchior Adam*, it cannot balance

VOL. I. N n

AGRICOLA

Year 1442. in the Village of *Baflon*, two Miles from *Groningen*. He gave early proofs of his future Reputation; and he had scarce received the Degree of Master of Arts at *Louvain*, but he might have been advanced to a Professor's Chair, if he had desired it: but his Inclination was rather to travel. He went from *Louvain* to *Paris*, after having lived in the former of these Two Cities the Life of an Athletic, I mean with great Sobriety, Chastity, and Application to Labour [B]. From *Paris* he went to *Italy*, and staid Two Years at *Ferrara* [C], where the Duke conferred many Favours on him. *Theodore Gaza* explained *Aristotle* in that City. *Agricola*, who was one of his Auditors, was heard in his Turn, and admired no less for his Style, than his Elocution. The *Italians* regretted, that so great a Man was not born in their Country. It was his own fault, when he returned home, that he did not possess considerable Employs; but his love of Books hindered him from thinking of any Settlement of this kind, or at least made him soon quit it. He at last accepted a Post, in *Groningen*, and followed the Court of *Maximilian* the First Six Months, to take care of the Affairs of That City. He acquitted himself happily of this Commission, and had no great Reason to boast of the Gratitude of his Masters; therefore he left them, and went to travel again. He was such a Lover of Liberty, that he refused to accept the Headship of a College, which the Inhabitants of *Antwerp* offered him; and I know not how he could with Honour have accepted it, since he had refused to enter, under very advantageous Conditions, into the Service of the Emperor *Maximilian*? He preferred Quiet and Independency to every thing. After having led a very roving Life, he settled in the *Palatinate*, where the Bishop of *Worms*, whom he had instructed in the *Greek* Tongue, found means to engage his Stay. It was in the Year 1482, that he came into the *Palatinate*; where he spent the remainder of his Life [D], sometimes at *Heidelberg*, and sometimes at *Worms*. The Elector *Palatine* took

---

(1) Ubbo Emmius, lib. 30. Histor. Frisiæ ann. 1490. pag. 437.

(2) By Mr de la Monnoie.

lance the Testimony of *Ubbo Emmius*, who was best acquainted with *Friesland*, his own Country, of any Man: " Obscuris natalibus apud Bastoot ortus (*Rodolphus Agricola*) tantum sibi in literis nomen paravit per " omnem Europam, ut, &c. (1) —— RODOLPHUS " AGRICOLA born at Basston, of obscure Parents, " gained such a Reputation for Learning over all " Europe, that, &c."
I have been shewed (2) two Proofs of *Emmius's* Opinion in *Agricola's* Letters. The one is, that his Twin-Sister was sent to *Groningen* to learn the Skinners Trade, pelliceam operam & texturam pulvinariam; the other is, that the Father of this Girl was Receiver of the Church of his Village. He was much grieved with one of his Sons robbed him of an hundred *Florins*, of that sacred Money, which, you know, he has the care of. Our *Rodolphus*, being at *Groningen*, wrote this to *John* his Twin-Brother. " Venit ad me pater tuus turbatus & gemens, & prope " cum lacrimis questus est mihi, Henricum fratrem " nostrum pridie ejus diei clam sibi abstulisse centum " florenos nostræ monetæ ex pecunia sacra cujus " curam, ut scis, ille gerit. —— Your Father came " to me greatly discomposed, and sighing, and complained to me almost with Tears, that Henry, our Brother, had, the Day before, stolen from him an hundred Florins, of that sacred Money, which, you know, he has the care of."

[B] *The Life of an Athletic, I mean with great Sobriety, Chastity, and Application to Labour.*] The Ancients remark, that the Athletics enured themselves to Labour, and abstained from Wine and Women.

(3) Horat. de Arte Poët. ver. 412, &c.

Qui studet optatam, cursu contingere metam,
Multa tulit fecitque puer; sudavit, & alsit:
ABSTINUIT VENERE ET VINO (3).

He, who, ambitious of the Victor's Place,
Courts the first Honours of the dusty Race,
Enures himself to Toil from childish Years,
And Cold, and Heat's Extreams alternate bears;
Flies the strong Grape's entoxicating Joys,
And Venery, which manly Strength destroys.

This Abstinence was remarkable in *Agricola*, and very uncommon in the Country where he lived, with regard to the first Particular. " Lovanii vixit honestissime ab omni compotatione ac commessatione " contra gentis suæ morem alienissimus. Tantus erat " in eo bonarum literarum amor, tam indefessum " studium, ut turpis Veneris fornices & lustra ne " noverit quidem (4). —— He lived an exemplary " Life at Louvain, not complying with his Country's " Manners in revelling and feasting. So fond was " he of good Literatures, that he was wholly unacquainted with the scandalous Seats of Debauchery."

(4) Melch. Adam in Vitis Philos. pag. 15.

It was uncommon likewise every where, and is so still, with respect to the other Particular. For, to the shame of Christianity and of Learning be it said, there appears almost nothing in Scholars but shocking Inclinations to Debauchery. They were perhaps no better in ancient Times; for which reason I wonder why this did not become a Proverb, *Sine Venere & Baccho friget Musa*, as well as this, *Sine Cerere & Baccho friget Venus*. For this long time, the Youth, who study, have behaved as if the Birth of these Maxims was true.

[C] *And staid two Years* (5) *at Ferrara.*] He learned *Greek*, and taught *Latin* there: He contended with *Guarin* which had the best Talent at writing in Prose, and disputed with the *Strozza's* the Praise of Poetry; as for Philosophy, he treated of it with *Theodore Gaza* (6).

(5) In 1476. & 1477.

(6) Ex Valerio Andr. Bibl. Belg. pag. 798.

[D] *It was in the Year* 1482, *that he came into the Palatinate, where he spent the Remainder of his Life.*] *Melchior Adam* asserts this. " Cum hoc (*Joanne Camerario Dalburgio*) ab anno 1482, partim *Heidelbergæ* partim *Wormatiæ* ad ultimum vitæ actum " usque vixit conjunctissime (7). —— He lived in " strict Friendship with this Person John Camerarius Dalburgius), partly at Heidelberg, and partly " at Worms, from the Year 1482. to his Death." But Mr *de la Monnoie* found fault with this Account; for this is his Remark: " *Rodolphus Agricola*, in a " Letter, which he wrote to *James Barbirianus*, dated, by Mistake, XCII. instead of XXCII. in " another of the same date to his Brother *John*, " says, that, upon taking a Journey the same Year " to *Heidelberg*, he gave his Word to *John* of *Alburg*, Chancellor of the Count *Palatine*, and Bishop of *Worms*, that he would return to him again " the following Year. Yet we find, by his other " Letters, that he did not return thither before the " middle of the Year, 1484. So, that the Calculation of *Vossius*, pag. 566. *De Histor. Lat.* " concerning the three Years of the Regency of *Rodolphus* at *Heidelberg* (8), is not right. *Sigismond* " of *Foligni*, otherwise *Sigismundus Fulginas*, is also " mistaken, when he says, that *Rodolphus*, died by " the way in his return from *Rome* to his own Country. *Rodolphus* departed from *Rome* in 1480. and " died five Years after at *Heidelberg*. It does not appear by the reading of his Works, that he exercised the Function of Professor at *Worms*." There is a Letter from *Peter Schottus*, dated the eighteenth of *February*, 1484, in which he says, That he was well pleased with *Agricola's* having begun to read Lectures to the Youth at *Heidelberg*. " Argentinam reversus cum intellexissem --- te Heidelbergæ " cœpisse purgare, & linguas Juvenum & aures, ut " illa nil scelerosum balbutiant, hæc vero, tuja tam " peritis

(7) Melch. Adam. in Vitis Philos. pag. 16.

(8) Note, that Melch. Adam does not say that Agricola ever taught Philosophy at Heidelberg. Vossius supposes that he taught it there three Years.

AGRICOLA

took a pleasure in hearing him discourse on Antiquity, and desired him to compose *An Abridgment of ancient History*, which *Agricola* performed with great Learning. He read public Lectures at *Worms*, but his Auditors, having a greater Taste for the Chicanery of Logic, than for polite Literature, were not in the way of Thinking he desired. He began to study Divinity at Forty Years of Age; but despairing to succeed in it without the Knowledge of *Hebrew*, he apply'd himself to the Study of that Language, and, by the assistance of a *Jew*, he had made a considerable Progress in it [*E*]. Death, which seized him at *Heidelberg*, on the Twenty eighth of *October* 1485 (*a*), did not permit him to proceed. He submitted, with a Christian Resignation, to the Orders from above, and was buried, in a *Cordelier's* Habit, in the Church of the *Minor Friars* of that City. The Description, which is given, of his Character, may easily satisfy us, that he was a very good Man, plain, without Malice, moderate, and of a good Disposition. He was never married, tho' he had been in Love, or seemed to have been so. He had resolv'd to marry in his Youth; but, after having seriously examined what he was going to do, he laid aside his Design, not so much for fear of domestic Inconveniences, as out of a certain natural Indolence of Temper [*F*], which made him sink under the least Cares. One would scarce imagine, that a Person, who had div'd so far into the Study of Antiquity, as he had, should be capable of singing to Instruments Songs of his own Composition ; yet in this manner he sometimes entertained the Ladies [*G*]. It is pretended, that, in the Affair of Religion, he had a Fore-taste of that Light [*H*], which appeared in the following Age. He left his Books to *Adolphus Occo*, a Native of *Friesland*, and Physician at *Augsburg* (*b*). Mr *Moreri* had no foundation for saying, that *Erasmus* and *Agricola* became acquainted at *Ferrara* [*I*]. *Paul Freherus* did not understand all that

(*a*) *Erasmus therefore was mistaken when he laid that Agricola died before the Age of 40 Years.* Also. Chif. F. cent. 4. n. 39.

(*b*) *Taken out of Melchior Adam's Vit. Philos.* pag. 25, & seq.

---

(9) Centur. Epist. Philolog. à Goldasto Edit. rum, pag. 55, 56.

"peritia & dulcibus elegantiis delibatae, omnes illas "sciolorum insulsas & verbosas ineptias quasi magicas "incantationes declinaret : num ego vehementer sum "gravisus (9). ———Returning to *Argentina*, when I understood, that you had began at *Heidelberg* to purge the Tongues and Ears of the Youth, that the former might not utter any thing *futilely* or wicked, and that the latter, by the Infusion of your skilful and pleasing Elegancies, might avoid all the insipid and wordy Follies of Pretenders to Learning, as so many magical Incantations ; when I understood this, I was greatly pleased."

(10) Melch. Adam. ibid. pag. 18.

[*E*] *Had made a considerable Progress in it.*] We learn from himself that at first this Study seemed very difficult to him ; "Studia Hebraea ——— primum "ei plurimum negotii, uti scribit ipse, exhibuerunt, "ut sibi videretur cum Antaeo luctari (10)." *The Study of the Hebrew Tongue, according to his own Account, gave him at first a great deal of Trouble, insomuch that it seemed to him, as if he was wrestling with Antaeus.* Meeting afterwards with a *Jew* who understood that Language indifferently well, he made such a Progress in a few Months, that he could translate some of *David's* Psalms without Faults. *Nactus Judaeum ejus linguae utcunque peritum paucis mensibus tantum profecit, ut aliquot Psalmos Davidicos in Latinam linguam citra culpam transtulerit* (11). This will not authorise us

(11) Id. ibid. pag. 19.

(12) De Historia. Lat. pag. 566.

to say, with *Vossius*, that *Agricola* was very skilful in the *Hebrew* Tongue, *Hebraicè doctissimus* (12) ; we may degrade this *Superlative*, without any Injustice, and treat it like a Trooper, who is dismounted, to be incorporated with the Infantry. *Geisner* distinguished better than *Vossius* ; the latter has bestowed a Superlative on *Agricola's Latin, Greek,* and *Hebrew*, indifferently. But *Geisner* expresses himself thus : *Graeci & Latini sermonis peritus, & Hebraicae linguae non ignarus* (13). ——— Skilled in the Latin and Greek Tongues, and not ignorant of the Hebrew. He borrows these Words from *Trithemius*. *Konig* outdoes *Vossius* ; for he makes use of the Superlative *callentissimus*, must knowing. See *Varillas's* third Mistake below. We may observe likewise, that *Trithemius* does not speak with Exactness, when he assures us, that *Agricola* had translated the Psalter from the original *Hebrew* (14) ; for we do not reckon the Exercises of an Author in learning a Language among his Works ; but it is plain, that the Translation, which *Agricola* made of some of *David's* Psalms, was an Exercise, which his *Jew* corrected for him. This *Jew* was converted to the Christian Religion. *John Dalburg*, Bishop of *Worms* (15), kept him in his House only for the sake of *Agricola*, if we may believe *Valerius Andreas*, "Primus esse- "lantes è Germanis Graecas restituit litteras, quibus "aetate provectior etiam Hebraicas adjecit, praeceptore usus Judaeo quodam ad fidem converso, quem

(13) Gesn. in Biblioth. fol. 585.

(14) Apud Valer. Andr. Bibl. Belg. pag. 708. Gesner asserts it likewise.

(15) *And not Heidelberg, as Bullart says in his Academ. of Sciences,* Tom. 1. pag. 276.

"Wormatiensis Episcopus *Johannes Dalburgius*, solius "*Rodolphi* causâ, domi suae alebat (16). ——— He "was the first who restored the exiled Greek Learning in Germany ; to which, in his riper Years, he added the Hebrew, by the Instruction of a certain converted Jew, whom the Bishop of Worms, John Dalburg, entertained in his House, solely upon Rodolphus's Account."

(16) Valer. Andreas, Bibl. Belg. 708.

[*F*] *As out of a certain natural Indolence of Temper.*] Because I cannot pretend to reach the Force of his Expressions. I shall set down the Greek Words, which he made use of. "Uxorem nunquam duxit : "quanquam in priori aetate dusturum destinarat. Sed "postquam incepit diligentius se ipsi introspicere, "aversus est ab eo consilio non incommodis rei oeconomicae, sed deterruit ipsum genus vitae suae, & "animus levissimis etiam curis impar, καὶ ἀφαγχώς "γε τῆς φύσεως (verba sunt ipsius epistolâ quâdam ad "Capnionem) ὅτε μάλαν Δυσηγυμονός καὶ ἀκωμωσὰ "τοῖς παντὸς τε βοῇ (17). ——— *He never married : "though formerly he had resolved to marry. But, "after that he began to look more carefully into himself, he gave up that Resolution, not in Consideration of the Inconveniences of a married State ; but his own manner of Life, and his natural Disposition, unequal to the lightest Cares, deterred him from it.*"

(17) Melch. Adam. Vit. Philos. p. 19. *See also the Life of Agricola among those of the Professors of Groningen.*

[*G*] *Sometimes entertained the Ladies.*] See what his Historian says : "Puellas amare se nonnunquam "simulabat, verum numquam deperibat. In earum "gratiam vernacula lingua quaedam carmina (scripsit "elegantissimè : quae virginibus primariisque amicis "praesentibus voce & testudine modulatissimè canebat (18). ——— *He sometimes pretended to be an Admirer of the Ladies ; but was never desperately in love with any of them. For their Sakes he wrote some very elegant Latin Verses in his mother Tongue.*" He understood all kinds of Music : "Canebat voce, flatu, pulsu (19). ——— *He performed "with his Voice, his Breath, and his Fingers.*"

(18) Melch. Adam. Vit. Philosoph. pag. 18.

(19) Id. ibi.

[*H*] *A Foretaste of that Light.*] Some one, who heard *Agricola* and *Wesselus* discourse together, testifies, that they deplored the Darkness of the Church ; and that they blamed the Mass, Celibacy, and the Doctrine of the Monks concerning Justification by Works (20).

(20) Id. ibid. In Vita Professorum Groningens.

[*J*] *Mr Moreri had no Foundation for saying, that Erasmus and Agricola became acquainted at Ferrara.*] This is easily proved. *Erasmus* was born in the Year 1467. He studied at *Deventer* at twelve or thirteen Years of Age. *Agricola* was at *Ferrara* in the Year 1476, and 1477. How could he then have consulted an eternal Friendship with *Erasmus* in that City ? If Mr *Moreri* had read *Agricola's* Prognostic concerning *Erasmus*, he would not have said that they became acquainted at *Ferrara*. *Agricola* was returned from *Italy*, when, having

AGRICOLA

that he transcribed out of *Erasmus* [K] in praise of *Agricola*. We understand from the same *Erasmus*, that *Agricola* died for want of timely Assistance from the Physicians [L]. *Reuchlinus* has taken notice of the Funeral Oration of this Learned Man (c). *Varillas* will supply us with many Faults here [M], and give us an occasion to relate what concerns the publication of one of *Agricola*'s Books, entitled *De Inventione Dialectica* [N].

(c) Valer. Andr. Bibl. Belg. pag. 798.

ving read the Themes of *Hegius*'s Scholars at *Deventer*, he found I know not what in that of *Erasmus*, which made him desire to see the Child, and, having well observed him, he pronounced, that he would be a great Man. *Erasmus* was not twenty Years of Age, when *Agricola* died, and had not yet emerged from the Darkness, wherein impertinent Tutors had detained him: so that there could not be that Friendship between him and *Agricola*, which Mr *Moreri* speaks of. Here are some other Mistakes of that Author. *Agricola*, says he, *was learned in all kind of Literature, and even in the Greek Language*. This is, as if one should say, *Such a one is learned in all Parts of Divinity, and even in the Questions about Grace*. Is not the *Greek* Tongue one of the noblest Parts of Literature? I do not know where Mr *Moreri* has read, that *Agricola* was two Years Syndic of the City of *Groningen*.

[K] *All that he transcribed out of* Erasmus (21)] He applies That to our *Agricola*, which *Erasmus* said of another. You must know, that *Erasmus*, having highly prais'd *Agricola*, confesses, that one of the Reasons, which made him so inclin'd to praise him, was, that he (*Erasmus*) had been instructed by one (22), who had been a Scholar of *Agricola* (23). Upon which he displays his Master's Merit; and says, among other Things, That Envy itself could not cavil at him, but for having too much despis'd Fame, for having had too little regard for Posterity, and for having wrote nothing but by way of Amusement. *Freberus* reports this Remark, as if it related to *Agricola*, wherein he attributes a Falshood to *Erasmus*; for *Agricola*'s Works, collected in a Body (24), and printed at *Cologne*, in the Year 1539, prove, that he wrote many Things with Care, and with all his Industry.

[L] *He died for want of timely Assistance from the Physicians.*] Let us see *Erasmus*'s Account of this Matter: It will not be disagreeable to read it in his own Words. " Veluti si quis in morbo capitali Medicum opperiatur insignem aut procul accersendum; quæ res Hominem illum vere divinum extinxit Rodolphum *Agricolam*; etenim, dum cunctatur Medicus, Mors antevertit (25). ——— *At if any one, in a mortal Distemper, should wait for an eminent Physician, or one a great way off; which was the Occasion of the Death of the great Rodolphus Agricola; for Death was before-hand with the tardy Physician.*

[M] *Mr Varillas will supply us with many Faults here.*] I. He says (26), That *Agricola had such a prodigious Memory, that he never forgot any thing that he had learned.* This is an Hyperbole, for which I find no ground in that great Man's History, though they have very much enlarg'd on his Talents. Would they have forgot this, which is the most extraordinary that can be met with? II. *He became learned to a Prodigy, by Books, which were borrowed, and without a Master.* The Hyperbole here is accompany'd with a palpable Falshood; for we read in his Life, that he was sent very early to the College (27), and that after he had studied *Grammar*, he went to *Louvain*, where he lodg'd in the College of the *Faulton*, and perform'd all the Exercises of a Student in Philosophy, and became acquainted with several, who had a taste for good *Latin*. He was also a diligent Auditor of *Theodore Geza* at *Ferrara*. ——— *Ibi Theodorum Gazam, Aristotelis Scripta enarrantem, diligenter audivit* (28). It is very true, that he carried but few Books with him, in his Travels, and that, leaving the rest of his Library with his Friends, he made use of borrow'd Books, according as he wanted them: But, besides that there is no learned Man, who does not do the like in travelling; can it be said that *Agricola* gain'd all his Learning in his Travels? III. *He began his Studies, where others use to end them*; that is, with the Hebrew *Tongue*. *He was not only desirous of understanding it in it's Purity, but with all the Alterations, likewise, which Time, and the refining of the Rabbies, have produc'd in it. He was equally industrious in acquainting himself with*

the Greek *Tongue*. ——— *Lastly, he apply'd himself to* Latin, *without any regard to the Remonstrances of those, who pretended to dissuade him from it, because the Habit of writing and pronouncing the* Hebrew *seem'd to have introduc'd into his Mind an Incompatibility with the* Roman *Phrases and Expressions.* Who can read this without Astonishment, when he is inform'd that our *Rodolphus* 'did not learn *Hebrew* 'till a few Years before his Death, and that the Progress he made in it was but small (29): I fancy Mr *Varillas* was deceiv'd by this Passage in *Latin*: it is an Apostrophe to *Agricola*, " Transiisti enim Hebraicas, Græ-" casque literas, usque adeo fluperida celeritate, ut " nequaquam Groningiæ in ultima Frisia, sed Hiero-" solymis Athenique natus ac educatus à doctissimis " crederere. Latinas porro tanta felicitate didicisti, do-" cuissique ut, &c. (30) ——— *You went through the* Hebrew *and* Greek *Learning with such a surprizing Celerity, that you seem'd to have been born and educated, not at* Groningen *in farthest* Friesland, *but at* Jerusalem *and* Athens. *You attain'd likewise to the* Latin, *and taught it so successfully, that, &c.*" This seems to me to be the Reason, why Mr *Varillas* imagin'd, that *Agricola* first learnt the *Hebrew*, then the *Greek*, and last of all the *Latin* Tongues, and that he often compos'd, and spoke in *Hebrew*. IV. *He made such a surprizing Progress in the* Latin, *that* Erasmus, *so little accustom'd to praise in others the Riches which himself possess'd, was never weary of commending him, especially after he had publish'd his Commentaries, so polite, and so worthy of the Age of* Augustus, *an* Aristotle's Rhetoric *and* Logic. *Erasmus* was so inconsiderable a Man, when *Agricola* died, that the Progress of his Admiration must not be look'd for in the Years, which preceeded the Death of *Agricola*. Besides, it is an Anachronism to say, that this illustrious *Frieslander* liv'd 'till the Time when his own Possession of polite Literature hinder'd *Erasmus* from *praising* it *in others*. I have yet two Observations; The Commentaries on *Aristotle's* Logic did not appear 'till after the Death of the Author. *Erasmus* informs us of this, and says also, that they were mutilated. " Latitabant apud nescio quos commentarii " Dialecticis, nuper in publicum prodierunt, sed mu-" tili (31). ——— *The logical Commentaries lay conceal-" ed in the Possession of I know not who; lately indeed " they have come abroad, but imperfect.*" Certainly it is not in this Work, that *Agricola's* Latin, or the polite Manners of the Age of *Augustus*, are to be admired. V. *The Elector Palatine* ——— *caus'd* Agricola *to come to* Heidelberg ——— *gave him the first Professorship of Eloquence in the University* ——— *and made him his Counsellor of State*. Neither the Life of *Agricola* among those of the Professors of *Groningen*, nor that in *Melchior Adam*, say any thing like this. The Bishop of *Worms* is said to have invited *Agricola* into the *Palatinate*.

[N] *Entituled*, De Inventione Dialectica.] The following Remark was communicated to me since the first Edition. " *Rodolphus Agricola* compos'd no re-" gular Commentaries on *Aristotle's* Logic or *Rhe-" toric*. We have only his three Books *de Inventione " Dialectica*, which were first printed at *Louvain*, " in the Year 1516, by the Care of *Alard of Am-" sterdam*, who published them confusedly, just as " he could meet with them. Some time after, one " *James le Febvre*, at *Deventer*, gave out that he " had a Manuscript of the *de Inventione Dialectica*, " more ample, by three Books, than the Edition of " *Louvain*; but this was false. *Alard*, who went on " purpose to this *le Febvre* at *Deventer*, having seen " his Manuscript, found it neither more ample, nor " more correct than that, from whence the Edition " of *Louvain* was publish'd. He reproach'd *le Febvre* " for it, who excused himself as well as he could, " though badly enough. Since the Year 1528, *Pom-" py Occo*, having obtain'd *Agricola's* own Manu-" script by the Inheritance of his Uncle *Adolphus*, " gave it to *Alard*, who, finding it very compleat, " and well preserv'd, caus'd it to be printed at *Co-
" logne,*

AGRIPPA.

" *logue*; in 4to, with long Commentaries, in the
" Year 1539. Some Years before, *John Matthew*
" *Prissemius*, to whom *Alard* had communicated his
" Manuscript, had caused it to be printed in the same
" City, with his own Comments." This Work, which
" is *Rodolphus's* Master-piece; was always universally
" esteem'd for the Exactness of the Style (32), and
" of the Arguments." This comes from the same
hand with the Observation, contain'd in the Remark [D] (33).

of the Augustan Age, and less eloquent than some other Pieces of Agricola. (33) *Mr de la Monnoie.*

AGRIPPA (HENRY CORNELIUS), a great Magician, according to some [*A*], was a very Learned Man of the XVIth Century. He was born at *Cologne*, on the fourteenth of *September*, 1486 (*a*), of a Noble and Ancient Family [*B*]. Desiring to walk in the Steps of his Ancestors (*b*), who for many Generations had been employed by the Princes of the House of *Austria*, he entered early into the Service of the Emperor *Maximilian*. He had at first the Employ of Secretary; but as he was equally qualified for the Sword, as the Pen, he afterwards turned Soldier, and served the Emperor seven Years in his *Italian* Army [*C*]. He signalized himself on several Occasions, and, as a reward of his Brave Actions, obtained the Title of *Knight*. He had a mind to add the Academical Honours to the Military [*D*]; He therefore commenced Doctor of Law, and Physic. It cannot be denied, that he was a very great Genius, and had a very extensive Knowledge of Languages [*E*] and Things; but his too great Curiosity, his too free Pen, and his inconstant Temper, rendered him unhappy. He changed his Situation perpetually; he brought himself continually into Trouble; and, to compleat his Misfortunes, he drew upon himself the Hatred of the Clergy by his Writings. We find by his Letters, that he had been in *France* before the Year 1507 (*c*), that he travelled into *Spain* in the Year 1508 (*d*), and that he was at *Dole* in 1509 (*e*). He read Public Lectures there [*F*], which engaged him in a Contest with the *Cordelier Catilinet*. The Monks in those Times suspected, whatever they did not understand, of Error or Heresy; How then cou'd they suffer *Agrippa* to explain the mysterious Works of *Reuchlinus de Verbo mirifico* with Impunity? It was the Subject of the Lectures, which he read at *Dole* in the Year 1509, with great Reputation. The Counsellors of the Parliament themselves were his Auditors (*f*). To insinuate himself the better into the Favour of *Margaret* of *Austria*, Governess of the

[*A*] *A great Magician, according to some.*] *Paul Jovius*, *Thevet*, and *Martin Del Rio* are his principal Accusers. We shall see, in the Remark [*P*], the Mistakes, into which they fall; they are palpable; and yet a great number of Persons are still perswaded, on the Authority of these Writers, that *Agrippa* was perfect in the Art Magic.

[*B*] *Of a noble and ancient Family.*] It's Name was *de Nettesbeym.* Mr *Teissier* assures us, in the 99th Page of the second Volume of his Additions to the Elogies taken out of *Thuanus*, that *Agrippa was born at* Nettesheym, *in the Country of* Cologne. *Melchior Adam*, whom he quotes, does not say so; he makes him to be born at *Cologne* itself (1), and refers us to a Letter of *Agrippa*, wherein we read these very Words, address'd to the Magistrates of *Cologne*; " Possem vobis horum verissima exempla referre, nisi
" civium vestrorum pudori parcendum, & patriæ meæ
" rationem habendam ducerem. Sum enim & ego,
" si forte nescitis, civitate vestra oriundus, & prima
" pueritia apud vos enutritus (2). ———— *I could give you undoubted Examples of these things, had I not a regard for your Citizans, and for the Place of my Birth. For I must tell you, if you are ignorant of it, that I was born in your City, and brought up from my Infancy in it.*" *Thevet* is still more mistaken in saying, *That* Agrippa *was born in the City of* Neustra (3). I know nothing of our *Agrippa's* Father, but that he serv'd the House of (4) *Austria*, and that he died about the Beginning of the Year 1518 (5).

[*C*] *Serv'd the Emperor seven Years in his Italian Army.*] *Freherus*, who ventures but seldom to go beyond the Bounds of those, whom he transcribes, had a Mind here to play the Master, and to shew that he could tell us something, omitted by *Melchior Adam*. But he has been very unlucky in it; for he makes these seven Years commence in 1508, and end in 1515. If he had been well acquainted with the History of *Agrippa*, he would have known, that this Author was in *Spain* in the Year 1508, at *Dole* in the Year 1509, and in *England* in the Year 1510. This *Week of Years* must have begun in 1511, and *Agrippa* must necessarily have pretended that he serv'd under the Emperor, all the time he liv'd in *Italy*. But his own Letters would have betray'd him. We do not find, that he had any Employment in the Army, after he was made Professor at *Pavia*, in 1515. *Freherus*, in the rest of his Extract from *Melchior Adam*, contents himself with the Faults of That Author, and adds no other to them. See his *Theatrum*, pag. 1221.

[*D*] *Add the Academical Honours to the Military.*] It is proper to produce here his own Words. " Utriusque Juris & Medicinarum Doctor evasi, antea etiam
" Auratus Eques; quam ordinem non precario mihi
" redemi, non à transmarina peregrinatione mutuavi,
" non in Regum inthronisatione impudenti insolentia
" surripui, sed in publicis præliis, media acie, bellica
" virtute commerui (6). ———— *I went out Doctor of Laws and Physic, having before receiv'd the Honour of Knighthood; the conferring of which Order upon me was not the Effect of Sollicitation, not borrowed from my Travels beyond Sea, nor impudently and insolently extorted from the Inauguration of Kings; but gloriously earn'd by Martial Bravery, and in the Field of Battle.*"

[*E*] *Extensive Knowledge of Languages.*] He understood eight, and there were but two, out of this great Number, which he did not understand to Perfection. He will give us this Account himself, without too much Modesty: We need not be afraid of injuring him, by esteeming him, according to the value he sets upon himself. " Octo linguarum mediocriter doctus, sed illarum sex adeò peritus, ut
" singulis non loqui modo & intelligere, sed & eleganter orare, dictare, & transferre noverim; stum
" præter multimodam etiam abstrusarum rerum cognitionem, utriusque Juris & Medicinarum Doctor
" evasi (7). ———— *I was moderately vers'd in eight Languages; of which six were so familiar to me, that I not only understood and spoke them, but was able to play the Orator in them, dictate in them, and translate from them: then, besides an extensive Knowledge of the most abstruse things, I commenc'd Doctor of Laws and Physic.*" He was betimes in search of the Philosopher's Stone, and it appears that he had been recommended to some Princes, as very fit for the grand Projection, which made him run the Hazard of his Liberty sometimes (8). It is certain, that a Person thought capable of making Gold, might well be afraid, that some Prince would imprison him, in order to employ him for himself, exclusive of other Princes.

[*F*] *He read public Lectures there.*] He seems to contradict himself on this Subject; for sometimes he says that he did it without Reward, and sometimes that he was rewarded for it. " Publicis prælectionibus quas ad honorem Illustrissimæ Principis Mar-
" garetæ Dolani feci GRATIS.—*In the public Lectures, which I read* GRATIS *at* DOLE, *in honour of the most illustrious Princess* Margareta. Thus he speaks

VOL. I. O o

AGRIPPA.

the *Netherlands*, he composed at that Time a Treatise of the *Excellency of Women* (*g*); but the Persecution he suffered from the Monks hindered him from publishing it. He gave up the Cause, and went into *England* (*b*), where he wrote on the Epistles of St *Paul* (*i*), though he had another very private Affair in hand. Being returned to *Cologne*, he read Public Lectures there on the Questions of Divinity, which are called *Quodlibetales*; after which he went to the Emperor *Maximilian*'s Army in *Italy*, and continued there, till Cardinal *de Sainte Croix* sent for him to *Pisa*. *Agrippa* would have displayed his Abilities there in quality of Theologist of the Council, if That Assembly had continued. This would not have been the way to please the Court of *Rome*, nor to deserve the obliging Letter he received from *Leo* X. [*G*], and from whence we may conclude that he altered his Opinion. From that Time he taught Divinity publickly at *Pavia*, and at *Turin* (*k*). He read Lectures on *Mercurius Trismegistus*, at *Pavia*, in the Year 1515 (*l*). His leaving That City, the same, or the following Year, looked more like running away, than retiring. This appears by the 49th Letter of his first Book, compared with the 520th. He had a Wife and Children at That Time [*H*]. It appears by the Second Book of his Letters, that his Friends in his Complaint against the *Cordelier Catilinet* (*q*). But he says elsewhere, That he was admitted into the Society of the Professors of Divinity, and gratify'd with a Pension (10). " In *Dola Burgundiæ* publ. lectura " sacras literas professus sum, ob quam ab hujus studii " Doctoribus in Collegium receptus, insuper regen- " tia & STIPENDIIS donatus sum. ――― At *Dole*, " in *Burgundy*, *I read public Lectures in Divinity*; *upon which Account I was admitted by the Doctors of that Faculty into the College, and was besides rewarded with the Place of Regent, and a PENSION.*" The way to reconcile these two things, is to say, That at first he read *gratis*, and afterwards for Money.

[*G*] *The obliging Letter he receiv'd from Leo X.* (11) It is dated from *Rome*, the twelfth of *July*, 1513, and sign'd *Petrus Bembus*. He is there commended for his Zeal for the holy Apostolical See, on the good Character which the Nuncio had given of him. " Ex literis venerabilis fratris Eanii Episcopi Verulani " nuncii nostri, aliorumque sermonibus, de tua in " sanctam sedem Apostolicam devotione, deque tua " in ejus libertate incolumitateque tuenda studio di- " ligentisque intellectimus: quod quidem nobis gratissimum fuit. Quapropter te in Domino magnopere " commendamus, laudamusque istam animum atque " virtutem (12). ――― *We have been inform'd, by the Letters of our venerable Brother Eanius, Bishop of Verulam, our Nuncio, and from the Report of others, of your Devotion to the holy See, and your Care and Diligence in defending it's Privileges and Safety; which gave us great Satisfaction. Wherefore we greatly commend you in the Lord, and praise this virtuous Disposition.*" Let me remark, that This Brief is of no use towards clearing *Agrippa* from the Imputation of Necromancy (13), for it proceeded his ill Reputation several Years.

[*H*] *He had a Wife and Children at that Time.*] Though I make use of the Plural Number, yet I know he had but one Son. " Quorsum, quæso, in " tam suspecta tempestate, una cum uxore filioque ac " familia confugissem, relicta Domo ac supellectile, " rebusque omnibus? ――― *How could I leave my House, Furniture, and all my Effects; and whither, in such suspicious Times, could I fly with my Wife, my Son, and my Family?*" Thus he speaks in the forty ninth Letter of the second Book. He was very happy in his Wife, whom he thus describes in another Place; " Ego quidem Deo omnipotenti innumerum " habeo gratiam, qui uxorem mihi conjuratis secundum cor meum, virginem nobilem, bene moratam, " adolescentulam, formosam, quæ ita ad meum vivit " consuetudinem, ut ne contumeliosum verbum in- " ter nos intercidat, atque, quo fœlicissimum me " dixero, quorsum se res vertant, in prosperis & ad- " versis, semper æquè mihi benigna, affabilis, con- " stans, integerrimi animi, sani consilii, semper apud " se manens (14). ――― *I give abundant Thanks to Almighty God, who bestow'd on me a Wife after my own Heart, a young Lady of a good Family, well bred, young, and handsome, who lives with me in so complaisant a manner, that we never exchang'd an angry Word; and, to compleat my Happiness, the same both in Prosperity and Adversity; alike affectionate, affable, and constant; bone, prudent, and ever employ'd in the Care of her Family.*" One thing he forgot to tell us, I mean, whether she was rich or not; for otherwise he represents her as endow'd with all he could desire, handsome, young, virtuous, of a noble Family, and of a perpetual Complaisance. He lost her in the Year 1521, and, for what Reason I know not, he would have her buried at *Mentz*, where he no longer resided (15). He took Care to order, that all the Anniversaries should be performed, which he had founded for the Soul of the deceas'd (16). He married again at *Geneva*, in the Year 1522 (17). He praises this second Wife as much as the first, for he says, " Ante biennium hoc secun- " dam uxorem duxi virginem nobilem pulcherrimam- " que, quæ adeo ad meam vivit consuetudinem ut " nescias istane priorem, anne hæc illæ, usæ alteram, " in amando obsequendoque æquet, an superet (18). ――― *Two Years ago, I married a second Wife, a young Lady of a good Family, and very beautiful; who behaves with so much Complaisance towards me, that you would be at a loss to determine which of the two equals, or exceeds, the other in Duty and Affection.*" The latter was more fruitful than the former; he had but one Son by the first; the second lay in three times in two Years, and a fourth time the Year following; " Duos ista mihi filios peperit, ambo " superstites, filiamque unam quæ vita excessit (19). ――― Uxor mea jam partui proxima est (20). ――― *She has already brought me two Sons, both alive, and one Daughter, who is dead. ――― My Wife is at this time near her Delivery.*" He does not say whether she was rich; but one of his Friends assures us, that she was. " Te nunc probâ, nobili, for- " mosâ, ac locupletæ ductâ uxore, &c. (21) ――― *Having now married a virtuous, noble, handsome, and rich Wife, &c.*" But this does not convince me; for *Agrippa*'s Letters, after his second Marriage, breath as much Poverty, as before. The Cardinal of *Lorrain* was Godfather to his third Son, by his second Wife (22). When he set out from *Paris* for *Antwerp*, in the Month of *July*, 1528, he left his Wife big with Child at *Paris* (23). She was brought to Bed of her fifth Son, at *Antwerp*, the thirteenth of *March*, 1529 (24), and died in *August*, 1529, at *Antwerp*, extreamly lamented by her Husband, as appears by the eighty first Letter of the fifth Book; she was near twenty six Years of Age. I do not find that he makes mention of his third Marriage in his Letters; but we find that he divorc'd his Wife in the Year 1535. *Ubi conjugem Mechliniensem Bonæ repudiasset anno tricesimo quinto supra sesquimillesimum.* This was what *John Wierus* (25) informs us of, who had been his domestic Servant. If *Thevet* had known these Particulars, he would not have been satisfied with telling us that *Agrippa married Mrs Louyse Tyssie, of a very noble Family, at twenty three Years of Age, and in the Year of our Lord 1509* (26); he would at least have mention'd the other two Marriages in general. *Melchior Adam* knew more of them than *Thevet*; for he was not ignorant that *Agrippa* had been twice married: *Duxum uxorum maritus nobilium, & liberorum aliquot parens*: but, besides that he seems to know nothing of the third Marriage, he is guilty of several Chronological Errors, in speaking of the first. These are his Words, " Mortuo *Maximiliano*, sub diversis & principibus & " civitatum magistratibus, per *Italiam*; *Hispaniam*; " *Angliam*, *Galliam*-egit, multaque egregia facinora " designavit. Tandem, laborum terræ marisque ex- " antlatorum satur, ac quietis & otii cupidus, desera

" uxore

AGRIPPA.

Friends endeavoured in several Places to procure him some Honourable Settlement, either at *Grenoble*, *Geneva*, *Avignon*, or *Metz*. He preferred the Post, which was offered him in this last City, and I find that, in the Year 1518 (*m*), he exercised there the Employment of Syndic, Advocate, and Orator of the Town (*n*). The Persecutions, which the Monks raised against him, as well upon the account of his having refuted the common Opinion concerning the three Husbands of St *Anne*, as because he had protected a Country-Woman, who was accused of Witchcraft [*I*], made him leave the City of *Metz*. What induced him to treat of the Monogamy of St *Anne*, was his seeing, that *James Faber Stapulensis*, his Friend, was pull'd to pieces by the Preachers of *Metz*, for having maintained That Opinion (*o*). *Agrippa* retired to Cologne, his native City, in the Year 1520. willingly forsaking a City, which the Seditious Inquisitors had made an Enemy to Learning, and true Merit (*p*). It is indeed the Fate of all Countries, where such Persons grow powerful, of whatsoever Religion they are. He left his own City in the Year 1521, and went to *Geneva* (*q*); but his Fortunes did not much improve there; for he complained, that he was not rich enough to make a Journey to *Chamberi* (*r*), to sollicit the Pension, which he was made to hope for from the Duke of *Savoy*. This Expectation came to nothing; upon which *Agrippa* went from *Geneva* to *Friburg* in *Swisserland* (*s*), in the Year 1523 (*t*), to practise Physic there, as he had done at *Geneva*. The Year following he went to *Lyons*, and obtained a Pension from *Francis I*. He was in the Service of That Prince's Mother, in Quality of her Physician, but made no great improvement of his Fortune there; neither did he follow That Princess (*u*), when she departed from *Lyons*, in the Month of *August*, 1525, to conduct her Daughter to the Frontiers of *Spain*. He was suffered to dance attendance at *Lyons*, and imploy the Interest of his Friends in vain, to obtain the payment of his Pension: and, before he received it, he had the Vexation to be informed that he was struck out of the List (*x*). The Cause of his Disgrace was, that, having received Orders from his Mistress to inquire, by the Rules of Astrology, what Turn the Affairs of *France* would take, he expressed his Disapprobation too freely, that the Princess shou'd employ him in so vain a Curiosity, instead of making use of him in more important Matters. The Lady took this Lesson very ill (*y*); but she was yet more angry, when she heared, that *Agrippa*'s Astrology promised the Constable of *Bourbon* new Triumphs [*K*]. *Agrippa*, finding himself discarded,

" uxore, virgine nobili, sedem in Allobrogibus fixit,
" ut procul negotiis sibi ac musis viveret. Invitatus
" autem ab inclyta *Mediomatricum* repub. munus syndici, advocati & oratoris obivit (27). ——— *After the Death of Maximilian, he liv'd successively under several Governments, in Italy, Spain, England, and France, and distinguish'd himself by many famous Actions. At length, tir'd with the Fatigues he had undergone both by Sea and Land, and desirous of Ease and Retirement, he married a Wife, a young Lady of Birth; and settled in the Country of the Allobroges, in order to retire from Business, and enjoy himself, and the Muses. But, upon the Invitation of the illustrious Republic of Metz, he discharg'd the Offices of Syndic, Advocate, and Orator.*" Observe, that the Emperor *Maximilian* died the 12th of *January*, 1519, and that *Agrippa* travell'd into *Spain* in 1508, and into *England*, in 1510. Here is already one Anachronism. After his return from *England*, he staid some time at *Cologne*, and afterwards went into *Italy*, where he still resided in the Year 1517 (28). He was at *Metz* in the Year 1518 (29). He did not return into *Italy* after his Departure from thence for *Metz*: here is, then, another Anachronism. Remark farther, that he was already married, in the Year 1515 (30). Where are then those great Fatigues, which he underwent both by Sea and Land, after the Death of the Emperor *Maximilian*, which Matrimony was to free him from? How could he settle with his Wife in the Country of the *Allobroges*; he, who liv'd a roving Life with her in *Italy*? Add to this, that he did not settle in the Country of the *Allobroges*, before his Journey to *Metz*: and that he was Syndic of *Metz* before *Maximilian* died. *Melchior Adam* is full of the like Mistakes. Part of those, which I have observed, are so much the more excusable, as they are committed on the Authority of *Agrippa* himself, who, through Forgetfulness, or otherwise, told *Margaret*, Queen of *Hungary*, That he had travell'd to such and such Places, after the Death of *Maximilian*, &c. See the twenty first Letter of the seventh Book. I should be glad to see some one undertake to reconcile *Melchior Adam* with *Thevet*. According to the latter, *Agrippa* married at twenty three Years of Age; according to the former, not 'till after an infinite Number of Travels, and a world of Affairs; when, being fatigu'd and worn out, he desir'd at last a retir'd Life.

[*J*] *A Country-Woman, who was accused of Witchcraft.*] The *Dominican*, *Nicholas Savini*, Inquisitor of the Faith at *Metz*, propos'd to put this Woman to the Torture, upon a meer Prejudice; grounded on her being the Daughter of a Witch, who had been burnt (31). *Agrippa* did what he could to prevent so irregular a Proceeding; but could not hinder the Woman from being put to the Question; however he was instrumental in proving her Innocence. Her Accusers were condemn'd in a Fine (32). The Penalty was too mild, and far from Retaliation. [This Country-Woman was of *Vapey* *, a Town situated near the Gates of *Metz*, and belonging to the Chapter of the Cathedral. There appear'd in *Messin*, the principal Accuser of this Woman, such sordid Passions, and such a total Ignorance of Literature, and Philosophy, that *Agrippa*; who, in his Letter of the second of *June*, 1519; treats the Town of *Metz*, as, " Omnium bonarum literarum virtutumque Novercam. ——— *The Stepmother of Learning and Virtue* ——— *Agrippa*, I say, might, by this satirical Reflexion, give rise to the Proverb, " *Metis avara, scientiarum noverca* ——— " *Metz the Covetous, and Stepmother of Arts and Sciences.*" Rem. Crit.]

[*K*] *Promis'd the Constable of Bourbon new Triumphs.*] His Complaint of being employ'd in the Follies of Astrology might well give Offence. " Scripsi Seneschallo, ut admoneat istam, ne ad tam indignum artificium ingenio meo diutius abutatur, nec in his nugas ulterius impingere cogar, qui multo fortioribus studiis illi inservire queam (33). ——— *I wrote to the Seneschal, desiring him to advise her not to misapply my Abilities any longer in so unworthy an Art; and that I might for the future avoid these Follies; since I had it in my Power to be of Service to her by much happier Studies.*" But the Misfortune was, these Follies predicted Success to the opposite Party. " Rediit in mentem scripsisse me Seneschallo; comperisse me in *Borbonii* natalitiis revolutionibus; illum prostratis vestris exercitibus etiam in bane omnium victorem fore ——— dixique intra me, ô infelix prophetia! hoc vaticinio jam omnem Principis tuae gratiam concacasti: Hoc est ulcus, hic anthrax, hic carbo, hic cancer iste, quem noli me tangere dicunt, quem tu imprudenter retigisti etiam cauterio (34). ——— I remember I told the *Seneschal*, in a Letter, that in casting the Constable of *Bourbon*'s Nativity,

* Villa Vapeys.

148 AGRIPPA.

discarded, murmured, stormed, threatened [L], wrote, and did, all that his Impatient Humour suggested to him; but, in short, he was obliged to look out for another Settlement. He cast his Eyes on the *Netherlands*, and, having after long waiting obtained the necessary Passes, he arrived at *Antwerp* in the Month of *July*, 1528 (z). One of the Causes of these Delays was the rough Proceeding of the Duke of *Vendôme*, who, instead of signing the Pass, tore it, saying, He would not sign it for a Conjurer (aa). In the Year 1529, *Agrippa* found himself invited at once by the King of *England*, by the Emperor's Chancellor, by an *Italian* Marquis, and by *Margaret* of *Austria*, Governess of the *Netherlands* (bb). He accepted the Offers of the latter, and was made Historiographer to the Emperor, a Post procured him by That Princess. He published, by way of Prelude, *The History of the Government of* Charles V, and soon after he was obliged to compose That Princess's Funeral Oration, whose Death was in some manner the Life of our *Agrippa*; for She had been strangely prejudiced against him [M]. The same ill Office was done him with his Imperial Majesty (cc).

" I had discovered that he would this Year likewise
" gain the Victory over your Armies; upon which
" I exclaim'd within myself, *O unhappy Prophet!*
" *By this Prediction, you have forfeited all the Favour*
" *of your Mistress: This is the Ulcer, the Quicksilver*
" *Earth, the Coal, the Concert, which we must not*
" *touch; which yet, imprudent as thou art, thou hast*
" *ventur'd to touch even with a Burning iron.*" They, who are acquainted with the History of those Times, see plainly, that our Astrologer could not make his Court worse than to the Mother of *Francis* I. than by promising good Success to the Constable. From that time *Agrippa* was look'd upon as a *Bourbonist* (35). To silence this Reproach, he represented the Service he had done to *France*, by dissuading four thousand foot Soldiers from following the Emperor's Party, and by engaging them in the Service of *Francis* I. He alledged his refusal of the great Advantages, which were promis'd him, when he left *Fribourg*, if he would enter into the Constable's Service. It appears by the *fourth* and *sixth* Letter of the *fifth* Book, that he held a strict Correspondence with that Prince, in the Beginning of the Year 1527. He advis'd, and counsell'd him, yet refusing to go, and join him, and promis'd him Victory. He assur'd him, that the Walls of *Rome* would fall down, upon the first Attack; he only forgot the chief Point, which is, that the Constable would be kill'd there. " Jam sata illis propinquam
" stragem suamque perniciem denunciant: Mox illa
" superba moenia vix oppugnata corruere videbis. Eja
" ergo nunc, strenuissime Princeps, quem tantae victoriae ducem fata constituunt, rumpe moras, perge
" intrepidè quò coepisti prosperè, aggredere fortiter,
" pugna constanter; habes electissimorum militum
" armatas acies: Adest coelorum favor, aderit & justi
" belli vindex Deus; nihil formidaveris, ingens siquidem te manet gloriae triumphus (36)." *The Fates*
" *already denounce their approaching Ruin: You will*
" *soon see those proud Walls demolish'd, upon the slightest*
" *Attack. Go on, then, most valiant Prince, whom*
" *the Fates have plac'd at the Head of so signal a Victory; make no delay; go on, and prosper, as you*
" *have begun; attack vigorously; fight undauntedly;*
" *you have an arm'd Force of chosen Soldiers: Heaven*
" *assists you, and God himself will fight for righteous a*
" *Battle; fear nothing, for a glorious Triumph awaits*
" *you.*" The Death of the Constable, which happened before *Agrippa* went out of *Lyons*, puts me in mind of three Errors of *Melchior Adam*. He says, that *Agrippa*, being invited first by the Constable, and afterwards by the Chancellor, went to the Court of *Burgundy*, and a little while after was very unfortunate in the loss of these two Patrons. This is to fall into three Anachronisms. I. The Constable was dead, before *Agrippa* left *France*, and he never had any Design of inviting him to the Court of the Princess *Margaret* (37). II. The Chancellor *Gattinara* did indeed invite him, but it was to the Court of *Charles* V. and it was an Invitation which *Agrippa* distinguished very plainly from That, which was offer'd to him, in relation to the Court of *Margaret* (38). III. He was already in the *Netherlands*, when the Chancellor made Proposals to him.

[*L*] *Agrippa*, finding himself discarded, murmur'd, storm'd, threatned.] He had used Menaces, before his Pensions was taken from him. Enrag'd at his Salary's being stopp'd, and seeing himself despis'd, he declar'd he was tempted to perpetrate some base Act. " Crede mihi
" *(says be in a Letter to a Friend)* (39) eò se incli-
" nant res meæ, atque animus, ni tuis precibus celeri-
" que adjuver auxilio, malo aliquo utar consilio, si-
" quidem & malis artibus nonnunquam bona fortuna
" parata est. ——— *Believe me, my Affairs, and my*
" *Mind, are in such a Posture, that, unless I am prevented by your Intreaties, and speedy Advice, I shall*
" *attempt something vile; since good Fortune is sometimes procur'd by base Arts.*" When he knew that he was cashired, he wrote several thundering Letters, and threatned to publish a Discovery of all the Intrigues of those Courtiers, who had ruin'd him (40). He was so brutish as to say, That for the future he should look upon the Princess, whose Counsellor and Physician he had been, as a cruel and perfidious *Jezabel*: *Nec ultra illam ego pro principe mea (jam enim esse desiit) sed pro atrocissima & perfida quadam Jesabele mihi habendam decrevi* (41). What would he not have done in such a Rage, and in such a thirst of Revenge, if he had had so much Credit with the Devil, as they pretend he had? No Author, I believe, has asserted, That this Indignation of *Agrippa* was fatal to any Person of the Court of *France*. This unfortunate Man was not better pleased with the Court of *Charles* V. He presented a Petition to That Prince's Privy Council, wherein he represented what Harm and Good he could do: His Menaces were the most intelligible in the World; but no ill Consequence attended the Council's disregard of them. " Cogeretis me accep-
" tam ea repulsâ injuriam ad novarum rerum licen-
" tiam transferre, & malo aliquo consilio (ceu quale
" Hermocles dedit Pausaniae) uti oportere ——— Quin
" & malis artibus saepissimè bona fortuna parta est ———
" Sed interea memineritis inter Æsopi Apologos esse,
" murem aliquando, subvenisse leoni, & scarabaeum
" expugnasse Aquilam (42). ——— *You would drive*
" *me, by this unjust Repulse, to new Plots, and wicked*
" *Designs; such as Hermocles advis'd Pausanias to.*
" *Nay very often Success attends upon base Arts.*
" *——— but remember, in the mean time, that, in Æsop's Fables, a Mouse once assisted a Lion, and a*
" *Beetle got the better of an Eagle.*

[*M*] *For she had been strangely prejudiced against him.*] He gives us the following Account of the Matter, after having complained that they suffered him to perish with Hunger. " Quod ad te scribam non habeo aliud
" nisi quod ego hic egregie esurio, ab istis aulicis diis to-
" tus praeteritus. Quid magnus ille Jupiter, suspicari
" nequeo. Ego quanto fuerim in periculo, jam primum
" rescivi; tantum enim dictum est mihi; praevaluerant
" culliones illi apud Dominam, sed muliebriter
" religiosam principem, ut nisi illa mox periisset,
" jam ego, quod maximum crimen est, monachalis
" majestatis sacraeque cuculiae reus, tanquam in reli-
" gionem Christianam impius, periturus fuissem (43). *I have only to inform you, that I am here*
" *perishing with Hunger, being wholly neglected by*
" *yon Deities of the Court. What the great* Jupiter
" *himself* (44) *intends, I cannot guess. I have just*
" *learned what great Danger I was in; for it has*
" *been hinted to me; that the Brethren of the Cowl*
" *had so influenced this bigotted Princess, that, had*
" *not her Death intervened, I should have been convicted of Treason against the Majesty of Monkery,*
" *and the sacred Cowl, (a Crime of the most heinous*
" *Nature) and have suffered as a Blasphemer of the*
" *Christian Religion.*" Generally speaking, a Mistress is more to be feared than a Master, when any Person is accused of Irreligion.

[V] P

AGRIPPA. 149

jesty *(cc)*. His Treatise of *the Vanity of Sciences*, which he caused to be printed in 1530, terribly exasperated his Enemies *(dd)*. That which he published soon after at *Antwerp (ee)*, of the *Occult Philosophy (ff)*, afforded them a still farther pretence to defame him. It was well for him that Cardinal *Campegio*, the Pope's Legate, and Cardinal *de la Mark*, Bishop of *Liege*, were his Advocates *(gg)*. But their good Offices could not procure him one Penny of his Pension, as Historiographer, nor prevent his being imprisoned at *Brussels*, in the Year 1531 *(hh)*. But He was soon released. The following Year he made a Visit to the Archbishop of *Cologne* (*ii*), to whom he had dedicated his *Occult Philosophy*, and from whom he had received a very obliging Letter *(kk)*. The fear of his Creditors made him stay longer in the Countrey of *Cologne*, than he desired *(ll)*. He strenuously opposed the Inquisitors, who had put a stop to the printing of his *Occult Philosophy*, when he was publishing a new Edition of it, corrected, and augmented, at *Cologne*. See the XXVIth and the following Letters of his Seventh Book. In spite of them, the Impression was finished, which is That of the Year 1533. He continued at *Bonn* till the Year 1535, and was then desirous of returning to *Lyons*. He was imprisoned in *France* for something, which he had wrote against the Mother of *Francis* I, but was released, at the Request of certain Persons, and went to *Grenoble*, where he died the same Year, 1535 *(mm)*. Some say, That he died in the Hospital; but, according to *Gabriel Naudé*, it was at the House of the Receiver General of the Province of Dauphiné, whose Son was first President of Grenoble *(nn)*. Mr *Allard*, at p. 4. of the *Bibliotheque of Dauphiné*, says that *Agrippa* died at *Grenoble*, in the *House*, which belonged to the Family of Ferrand, in Clerks-street, and was then in the possession of the President Vachon, and that he was buried in the Convent of the Dominicans. He lived always in the *Roman* Communion; therefore it ought not to have been said that he was a *Lutheran* [*N*]. I do not believe that

[*N*] *It ought not to have been said that he was a Lutheran.*] I confess, I have not observed in his Letters, that, when he speaks of *Luther*, or his Followers, he makes use of opprobrious Language, or injurious Reflexions. I own farther, that he inquired particularly into the Tenets of *Luther*, and his Followers, in controversial Points; but this does not shew, that he approved of that Reformer's Doctrine. May not the most rigid Protestants of the Confession of *Geneva* give orders to purchase for them all the Books, which the Sectaries of *Transilvania* cause to be printed; and would it not be very ridiculous to pretend, that therefore they agree in Opinion with those Heretics? They, who embraced the Reformation of *Luther*, did not treat That Doctor with That Indifferency, which we meet with in *Agrippa*'s Letters, I mean, without praising, or blaming him. If *Agrippa* was the Author of the eighty second Letter of the third Book, it could be no longer doubted, that he was a stanch *Lutheran*; but tho' That Letter is inscribed, *Agrippa ad amicum*, it is certain that it was not written by *Agrippa*: which I thus demonstrate. The Author of That Letter tells that his Wife was brought to bed of a Son, in the Month of *November* 1525. Now *Agrippa*'s Wife was brought to bed of a Son in the foregoing Month of *July*; this is plain by the seventy sixth Letter of the third Book, wherein it appears likewise that the Cardinal of *Lorrain* was God-father to the Child. It is incontestable, then, that *Agrippa* did not write the Letter in question. I omit the he was not at *Strasbourg*, but at *Lyons*, at the time, when That Letter was written from *Strasburg*. So that they, who would produce this as a Proof in favour of *Sixtus Sienensis*, who said that *Agrippa* was a *Lutheran* (45), would supply him with an insufficient Evidence. [The Truth is, *Agrippa*, in the nineteenth Chapter of his Apology, speaks in such lofty Terms of *Luther*, and with such Contempt of the principal Adversaries of that Reformer, that it is plain *Sixtus Sienensis* was induced from thence to affirm, that *Agrippa* was a *Lutheran*. As this was a proper Place for producing this Piece, rather than certain of *Agrippa*'s Letters, there is reason to believe Mr BAYLE had not read it so carefully, as he had done the Letters. REM. CRIT.] *Quenstedt* confuted *Sixtus Sienensis* by the sixth Chapter of the Treatise of the *Vanity of Sciences*, wherein *Agrippa* calls *Luther* an Arch-Heretic. This Confutation is infinitely more solid, than That which a Divine of *Utrecht* made use of, by alledging the Professorship of Divinity, to which *Agrippa* was preferred at *Dole* and at *Pavia*, and the Post he enjoyed under the Cardinal *de Sainte Croix*, for the Council of *Pisa* (46). This proves nothing at all; because all those Honours of *Agrippa* preceded *Luther*'s first preaching against the Pope. If any one asks me, why *Agrippa* speaks in harsher Terms of *Luther*, in his Books of the *Vanity of Sciences*, than in his Letters, I shall not answer, that it is a Work, wherein he proposed to censure the whole World: I chuse to offer another Reason. When he composed this Treatise, it is likely he had given up the Hopes he at first conceived of *Luther*. I believe, that, at first, he, as well as *Erasmus*, looked upon this Reformer as an Hero, who would put a stop to the Tyranny, which the mendicant Friars, and the rest of the Clergy, exercised over the Minds and Consciences of Men. Being ignorant and voluptuous, they encouraged a thousand paultry Superstitions, and would not suffer, that any one should study polite Literature; they would neither emerge from their Barbarity, nor suffer others to do it: Insomuch that to be Witty, Learned, and Polite, was sufficient to expose a Man to their Hate and Indignation. *Agrippa*, *Erasmus*, and some other great Geniuses, were pleased, that *Luther* had broke the Ice; they expected the critical Hour of honest Mens Deliverance from Oppression; but when they saw that things did not take the Turn they expected, they were the first to cast a Stone at *Luther*. Let us observe, however, that *Agrippa* was very fluctuating in his Sentiments. He protested to *Erasmus*, when he sent him his Declamation on the *Vanity of Sciences*, that he held no other Opinions, than those of the Catholic Church. *Illud te admonitum volo, me de his quæ ad Religionem attinent nequaquam secus sentire quam sentit Ecclesia Catholica* (47). He withed, in his Dedication of the Apology for this Declamation to the Pope's Legate, that God would purge his Church from the Impiety of Heretics (48); and a little after he wrote to *Melancthon* in a most obliging manner (49), and defired him to compliment, in his Name, the invincible Heretic *Martin Luther*. "*Salutabis mihi invictum illum hæreticum* "*Martinum Lutherum, qui, ut in Actibus ait Paulus,* "*fervit Deo secundum sectam quam hæresim vocant* "——*Pay my Compliments to the Invincible Heretic,* "*Martin Luther, who, as St Paul says in the Acts,* "*worships God after the way, which they call Heresy*;" and expresses at the same time his earnest Desire to come out of *Babylon*. For, speaking of *Charles* V. he says, " *Utinam hic Nabuchodonosor aliquando ex* " *bestia redirit in hominem, aut ego relinquere pos-* " *sem istud Ur Chaldæorum* (50). —— *I wish this* " *Nabuchodonosor would return from the Beast to* " *the Man, or that I could depart out of this Ur* " *of the Chaldees.*" There was a time when the Brethren were recommended to him (51); into, what we have seen that he wrote to *Melancthon*, was a return of certain former Emotions, which his Disgraces, and the unjust Proceedings of the Catholic Divines, had inspired him with. However, it is ve-

VOL. I.   P p

AGRIPPA.

that he wrote in favour of the Divorce of *Henry* VIII [O]. As to Magic Art, of which he is accused, every one may judge as he pleases. One thing I assert; which is, that the Letters, which he wrote to his intimate Friends, without any apparent design of printing them, carry all the Marks of a Man used to religious Reflexions, and the Language of Christianity. His Accusers were not well informed of his Adventures [P]; which weakens their Testimony. We shall have Reason to be surprized at

ry certain, that he lived, and died, in the *Romish* Communion. We shall touch upon some of his Opinions in the Remark [*T*].

[O] *That he wrote in favour of the Divorce of* Henry VIII.] I have read, in the Work of a very learned Man (52), "That *Cranmer*, going into *Germany*, where he became acquainted with the famous *Cornelius Agrippa*, discoursed with him concerning the Divorce, and so strongly represented to him the Necessity of it, that this great Man, warmly defending King *Henry*'s Pursuits, was treated with great Rigour by the Emperor, and at last died in Prison." He, who criticised on this Work, answered among other things; I. *That* R. Wakefield, *who wrote at that time for* Henry VIII. said positively, that he answered the Book of the *Bishop of Rochester, and another, which was believed to be wrote by* Vives, *or* Agrippa. II. *That* Agrippa died in France, and was never Prisoner in Germany (53). I find some things in *Agrippa*'s Letters, which convince me that he was not of *Cranmer*'s Opinion. His Imperial Majesty's Ambassador at *London* (54) wrote to *Agrippa* on the twenty sixth of *June*, 1531. to exhort him to maintain the Queen's Interest (55); and put him in mind of a Passage of *the Vanity of Sciences*, wherein *Henry* VIII. is censured. " Hodie adhuc nescio cui regi persuasum audio, ut liceat sibi jam plus viginti annorum uxorem dimittere, & nubere pellici (56). — *I am informed, there is a certain King, at this time t' Day, who is persuaded, that it is lawful for him to divorce a Wife, to whom he has been married those twenty Years, and espouse an Harlot.*" *Agrippa* answered, that he would willingly engage in this Undertaking, provided the Emperor would send him his Orders, or his Permission. He shewed very strongly, that he detested those cowardly Divines, who approved of the Divorce. The following Passage relates to the *Sorbonne*. " Non est mihi incognitum queis artibus res hæc apud Parisiorum Sorbonam tractata est, quæ cæteris tanti sceleris ausum temerario porrexit exemplo. Vix me continere queo quin imitatus poetam illum exclamem, *Dicite Sorbonici in Theologia quid valet aurum?* Quantum pietatis & fidei illorum pectore clausum putabimus, quorum venalis magis quam sincera conscientia est, qui extimescendas universo orbi Christiano determinationes auro venales fecerunt, ac servatam tot annis fidei & sinceritatis opinionem nunc tandem extrema avaritiæ infamia corruperunt (57). — *I am not to learn how artfully this Affair has been managed by the* Sorbonne *at* Paris, *which set the rest a rash Example of so vile an Attempt. I can scarce forbear exclaiming, in the Language of the Poet,* Tell me, ye Sorbonists, *the mighty Power of Gold in Divinity. What share of Piety and Fidelity can we think dwells in their Breasts, whose Conscience is rather mercenary than sincere; who have exposed to sale Decisions shocking to the whole Christian World; and have corrupted the Reputation of Fidelity and Sincerity, maintained by them for so many Years, by the utmost Infamy of Avarice?*" Nevertheless he represents the Danger, to which he should expose himself, by writing against a Divorce, which so many Divines had approved, *who*, says he, *bear me a Grudge on account of my Vanity of Sciences.* The Ambassador returned to the Charge, and put him in Hopes, that the Queen of *England* would write to the Emperor, or to the Queen of *Hungary*, concerning the Method of writing on That Subject; and explained to him the reason, why *Erasmus*, *Vives*, and other good Pens of the times ought not to be preferred to him (58). *Agrippa* looked upon himself as engaged in the Work; for, in the Letter, which he wrote to the Queen of *Hungary*, after he retired to *Bonn*, he represented, how he had applied himself altogether to his Office of Historiographer, though he had not yet reaped any Profit by it. *I collect Memoirs,* says he, *for the History of the War of* Italy *and* Hungary; *and I have still a greater Design in my Head, which is to write in favour of your Aunt,* Queen Catherine. " Sed longe majus his negotium pro vestri sanguinis decore, pro tua, inquam, matertera, Angliæ celebratissima Regina, meis humeris impositum suscepi, in quo licet multi hactenus operam suam collocarunt, nullus adhuc nodum rei difficult (59). — *But I have undertaken a much greater Task than this, for the Honour of your Family, I mean, in favour of your Aunt, the most illustrious Queen of* England; *in which though many have employed their Pens, no one has hitherto solved the Difficulty.*" I believe this Design was never executed; for the Author, being in Disgrace at the Imperial Court, doubtless thought it not proper to expose himself to the Indignation of the King of *England*. If *Cranmer* gained him over, he must have made a Convert of him at soonest in the Year 1532; and if *Robert Wakefield* published his Book before the Year 1532 (60) it is certain, that the Treatise, which he confutes, and which was ascribed to *Vives* or to *Agrippa*, by no means belongs to *Agrippa*. Note, that *Sanders*, who mentions the Names of several Authors, who wrote against the Divorce (61), takes no notice of the latter. [*Agrippa* was not yet gained over, in the Year 1533, the time, in which, if I mistake not, he published his *Apology* against the Doctors of *Louvain*; and he could not do it afterwards, without the same scandalous Prevarications, which he charges the *Sorbonne* with. Eadem, says he, speaking of *that famous Body*, his recentibus annis determinavit, Papam non posse dispensare, ut frater uxorem ducat fratris mortui fine liberis, atque propterea matrimonium inter Angliæ Regem & Cæsaris amitam, velut contra jus naturale & divinum, indispensabile, pro incestuoso, abominabili, & sacrilego adulterio damnarunt, magna Sorbonæ infamia: cum non multis annis ante pro Augustino Furnario Civi ac Patricio Genuensi determinavisset oppositum *. — *The same Society determined lately, that the Pope could not dispense with a Brother's marrying the Wife of his Brother, dying without Children; for which Reason they condemned, for an incestuous, abominable, and sacrilegious Adultery, the Marriage between the King of* England *and* Cæsar's *Aunt, as being contrary to Laws Divine and Human, and not to be dispensed with, to the great Scandal of the* Sorbonne; *which not many Years before, had decreed the very reverse, in favour of* Augustinus Furnarius, *Citizen and Senator of* Genoa." It is not only in the Edition of 1536, that I find this Passage, which *Crenius* tells us was omitted in the Treatise of *the Vanity of Sciences* in the Edition of *Lyons*. This Passage appeared again in the Edition of 1539; and it is to be met with in all the preceeding Editions of that Treatise. REM. CRIT.

[*P*] *His Accusers were not well informed of his Adventures.*] I said in the first Remark, that *Paul Jovius*, *Thevet* and *Martin del Rio* are his chief Accusers, and I promised to shew their Faults; I will now be as good as my Word.

I. *Paul Jovius* makes him at *Lyons* in a Hedge Tavern, and charges him with the infamous Suspition of Magic, for a Reason, which I am going to produce. *Agrippa*, says he (62), *had always a Devil with him, in the Shape of a black Dog; as they profit'd him to repent at the Approach of Death, he took off a Collar from the Dog's Neck adorned with Studs, which formed some Necromantic Inscriptions, and said to him,* Go unhappy Beast, who art the Cause of my everlasting Ruin. *The Dog ran immediately to the Saone, and, casting himself into the River, never came out again.* This Author has greatly commended *Agrippa* for his Wit, and Learning, so far as to say that his Learning had procured him the Dignity of a Knight, which the Emperor had bestowed upon him. *Vir educatus in literis,*

AGRIPPA

at their Overfights, and the Effects they have produced, notwithstanding the Negligence, wherewith they enquired into those Facts. After all, if he was a Magician, he

(63) Id. ib.

(64) See above the Remark [D.]

(65) Jo. Wierus de Magis, cap. 5. pag. 111.

& à Cæsare eruditionis ergò Equestris ordinis dignitate cohonestatus (63). Let us begin our Criticism with this.

It is certain, from the Testimony of *Agrippa*, that his Order of Knighthood was the Reward of his Military Exploits (64). Besides, he did not die at *Lyons*; and lastly, *John Wierus*, his Domestic, testifies, that the black Dog was a true Dog, and that he often led him with a hair String. "*Silentio involvi,*" says he (65), *diutius ob veritatis prærogativam non patiar quod in diversis aliquot scriptoribus legerim, Diabolum forma canis ad extremum Agrippæ halitum comitem ipsi fuisse, & postea nescio quibus modis evanuisse. Satis equidem mirari hic nequeo tantæ existimationis viros tam insulsè aliquando loqui, sentire, & scribere, ex inanissimo vulgi rumore. Canem hunc nigrum mediocris staturæ, gallico nomine Monsieur* (quod Dominum sonat) *nuncupatum novi ego si quis alius familiarissime, quem nimirum non raro, ubi Agrippam sectarer, loro ex pilis concinnato alligatum duxi; at verè naturalis erat canis masculus, cui alias fœmellam fere colore & reliqua corporis constitutione similem, quam Gallicè Madamoisselle (Dominam) appellabat, me præsente, adjunxit.* —— *In justice to Truth, I shall not conceal the Matter of Fact of what I have read in several Authors, that a Devil, in the Shape of a Dog, attended Agrippa to his last Breath, and afterwards disappeared I know not how. I cannot sufficiently express my wonder, that Men of such Reputation speak, think, and write so sillily, upon no other Foundation than Common Fame. I was perfectly acquainted with this black Dog; who was of a middle Size, and called by the French Name of Monsieur; whom I have often lead after Agricola by a String of twisted Hair. He was a real Dog; and his Master, in my Presence, gave him for 'n Companion a Bitch of the same Colour, Size, and kind; which he called Madamoiselle.*" This Author adds, that *Agrippa* was very fond of this Dog; that he kissed him often; that he made him eat sometimes at his Table; that he took him to bed with him; and that, when *Wierus* and *Agrippa* studied at the same Table, the Dog always lay between them among a heap of Papers. Now, because *Agrippa* continued whole Weeks without going out of his Stove, and yet was acquainted with almost every Transaction in several Countries of the World, some silly People gave out that his Dog was a Devil, from whom he had all his Information. It is not long, since a Soldier, who is a *French* Refugee, told me very seriously, that when Mr *de Melac* (66) had his Mastiff with him, he always returned victorious. He assured me, that, in the general Opinion of the Soldiers, that Dog was a familiar Spirit, who revealed all the Enemies Posts, their Numbers, Designs, &c. to his Master. Perhaps Mr *de Melac* was not displeased, that It was so believed. Such a Notion might make his Soldiers fear nothing under his Conduct (67). Thus you see, on what sort of Reports *Paul Jovius* founded his Opinion.

(66) Lieutenant General of the Armies of France: He served in the Armies of Germany, during the War, which was ended in the Year 1697. See the Remark [B] of the Article LANDAU, towards the End.

(67) See what Plutarch relates of Sertorius's Hind, in the Life of that General.

(68) Thevet's History of Illustrious Men, Tom. 7. pag. 221. Edit. of Paris, 1671. in 8 Vol in 12°

(69) Id. ib. pag. 223.

II. Let us go on to *Thevet*. "It cannot be denied, says he (68), "but that *Agrippa* was miserably enchanted to the most cunning and execrable Magic, that can be imagined, and of which he made such evident Profession, in the Sight, and to the Knowledge of every one (as the following Discourse shall justify), that it is impossible to deny it by Palliations or Disguises." Let us see what the Proofs, which this *present Discourse* brings, are reduced to. In the first Place, "*Antony de Leve* was so fond of this Man, that, by his Counsel, Advice, and Prudence, he compassed his high Designs, and ambitious Undertakings; which made some Persons, who were jealous of That *Spaniard's* Victories, say, That, by Magic Art, he gripped his Enemies with his crooked and gouty Hands, in such a Manner, that many valiant Captains could not do the like, with the clashing of their Arms, and a furious Fight (69)." In the second Place, that *Agrippa*'s Instructions are so unreasonable, that Dr *John Wierus*, though he praises and exalts him greatly in several Places of his Works, as his

" good Master, yet is sometimes obliged to give him
" a kick o' the Breech, and disown him (70)." He refers us to the forty fourth Chapter of the second Book of the Illusions and Apparitions of Spirits (71); as a Proof that *John Wierus* laughed (with *Cardan* in the eighteenth Book of *Subtility*) at *Agrippa's wild Imaginations, which invented more than ridiculous Apparitions*. In the third Place, "His Book "of Occult Philosophy was condemned and censu-
" red by the Christians ——— and for that Reason
" *Agrippa* was forced to leave *Flanders*, where he
" was not suffered to profess Magic; so that he went
" to *Italy*, where he lived about three Years, and
" poured out his Poison in such abundance, that se-
" veral good Persons, perceiving that he had infected
" the Air of *Italy* with it in so little a time, pur-
" sued him so close, that he retired to *Dole*, where he
" publickly read upon the Book *de verbo mirifico* (72)."
In the fourth Place, "He darken'd *Burgundy* in such
" a manner with the Smoak and Mist of his Black
" Art, that if he had not fled for it, it is to be
" feared, they would have enlightened him with
" Fire nearer than he would have desired." In the fifth Place, "He went to *Lyons* in a wretched Con-
" dition, and destitute of Money; where he tried
" all the means he could to subsist; and got so little,
" that he died in a pitiful Tavern, abhorred by every
" body, who detested him as a cursed and execrable
" Magician, because he always carried with him a
" Devil in the Shape of a Dog." *Thevet* adds to this the remaining part of the Story, which *Paul Jovius* inserted in his Elogies.

It would be easy to shew the Insufficiency of these five Proofs. It is not necessary to refute the first, since *Thevet* acknowledges that *Antony de Leve* did not apply to *Agrippa* for any *necromantic and wicked Charm* (73), *but rather on account of his surprizing and uncommon Genius* (74); and, that the Emperor did not take him into his Service at the Interception of *Antony de Leve*, but upon the Assurance which was given him, that, by his mature and settled Judgment, he was capable of putting an end to the weighty Affairs he had then in hand. So that the accused Person is cleared by the very Confession of the Accuser himself: It will be much more difficult to clear the latter from the Imputation of very gross Ignorance. I have not observed any Traces in *Agrippa*'s Letters of his Correspondence with *Antony de Leve*; and I wonder that so many learned Persons have reported, on the Credit of such an Author as *Thevet*, that *Agrippa was a Favourite of* Antony de Leve, *and a Captain in his Troop* (75). He was never in the *Spanish* Service; but served only in the Troops of the Emperor *Maximilian*; and I believe he never bore Arms, after the Speech he made at *Pavia* in the Year 1515. Part of That Harangue is as follows: "Neque mireris, Marchio Illustris, Joannes
" Gonzaga strenuiss. militum dux, quod cum me
" proximis his annis fœlicissimis Cæsareis castris Præ-
" fectum cognosceres, nunc me sacrarum literarum
" præpositam pulpito cernas (76). —— Nor wonder,
" Illustrious Marquis, and most valiant Commander,
" John Gonzaga, that you now see me in the Rostrum,
" at the Head of sacred Literature, whom not long
" since you beheld a Leader in Cæsar's victorious
" Army." He continued likewise some time in *Italy*; his Patron there was *William Paleologus* Marquis of *Monferrat*, to whom he dedicated his Treatise *De triplici Ratione cognoscendi Deum — of the three ways of knowing God, in the Year* 1516 (77): He taught at *Turin*, and repassed the *Alps* about the beginning of the Year 1518 (78). Let any one shew me that *Antony de Leve* served the Emperor *Maximilian*. But he is guilty of a still more inexcusable Ignorance. *Agrippa* did not obtain the Title of Counsellor and Historiographer to *Charles* V, but by the Interest of certain Friends, whom he met with at the Court of the Princess *Margaret*, Governess of the *Netherlands*. *Charles* V. was not at that time in the *Low Countries*, but came thither some time after, so prejudiced against *Agrippa*, that if it had not been for the good Offices of Cardinal *Campegius*, and Cardinal *de la Mark*, he would have caus'd him to have been imprison'd. The Sieur *Clavigni* of St *Honorine*, says, that

(70) Id. ib. pag. 225.

(71) I have not met with any Book with this Title, or such a Division, in the Works of John Wierus, printed at Amsterdam, 1660. in 4to.

(72) Thevet. ubi supra; p. 226.

(73) Id. ib. pag. 223.

(74) Id. ib. pag. 225.

(75) Naudé's Apology for Great Men, pag. 405. See also Teissier, Eloges taken out of Thuanus, Tom. 1. pag. 99. See, besides, Citation (79).

(76) Agrip. Oper. Tom. 2. p. 1075.

(77) Ibid. p. 480. & 718.

(78) See his Letters, pag. 728, 730.

AGRIPPA.

he is a strong Proof of the Impotency of Magic; for never any Man miscarried more frequently than he, nor was oftner in fear of wanting Bread. We shall have reason to think the Financiers of *Francis* I. and those of *Charles* V. were very well satisfied of his Innocency in this respect; if we consider how they diverted themselves with him, when he apply'd for his Pension. There are some Errors of Fact in the manner of some

that *Agrippa*'s End would have been as tragical as that of *Lucilius Vaninius*, if Cardinal *Campegius*, and *Anthony de Leve*, his Protectors, had not prevail'd upon *Charles* V. not to punish him (79). He did not see *Agrippa*; neither did he order him his Salary; so far was he from making use of his Counsels to extricate himself *from the great Affairs he had in hand*. It is a pleasant Proof of *Agrippa*'s great Abilities in the Civil Law, to alledge, that *Charles* V. *admitted him into the Number of his Counsellors*. *He had attain'd*, says Thevet (80), *to so great a Knowledge in the Civil Law, that (as I have observed above)* Charles V. *admitted him into the Number of his Counsellors*. He had said in the foregoing Page, *that* Agrippa *was so well receiv'd at the Emperor's Court, that he was one of his Counsellors*. Is it not well known, that the Title of King's Counsellor is given to many Persons, to Physicians, Historiographers, and Authors, who have as little share in the Councils of their Prince, as the meanest Citizen? Thevet's second Reason proves nothing. *Agrippa* had spoke of some Apparitions so ridiculous, that one of his best Friends laugh'd at them; therefore he was a Magician. What would become of *Bodinus*, *Martin del Rio*, *le Loyer*, and most of the *Demonographers*, if such a way of arguing was admitted? His third Reason swarms with Falshoods. If *Agrippa* had profess'd Magic, they would not have been satisfy'd with banishing him from *Flanders*. Such a Profession is not so mildly punish'd. He was never in *Italy* after the Censure of his Occult Philosophy. This Work did not appear 'till the Year 1531. If *Agrippa had pour'd out* the Poison of his Magic, in such abundance, in *Italy*, would Cardinal *de Sainte Croix* have chosen him for one of the Divines of the Council of *Pisa*? Would the Pope have address'd so complaisant a Brief to him in the Year 1515 (81)? So far is it from being true, that *Agrippa*, upon his being expell'd *Italy*, retir'd to *Dole*, that he did not go into *Italy*, 'till after he had left *Dole*. The fourth Reason takes for granted what is false. *Agrippa* brought himself into a Scrape at *Dole*, by favouring the Hypothesis of *Capnio*, whose Book *De verbo mirifico* he explained. The long Quarrel between the Monks and *Capnio* is well known. The *Cordelier Catilinet*, choosing rather to preach against *Agrippa* before the Princess *Margaret*, than to enter the Lists with him at *Dole*, took occasion to vent his Spleen against him at *Ghent*, in the Pulpit of Truth. But he does not accuse him of Magic; he charges him only with addicting himself to the *Jewish Cabala*, and preverting the Scripture by cabalistical Explications (82). The ill-tim'd Declamations of that *Cordelier*, who, instead of prejudicing the Court and the People against an absent Professor, ought to have accus'd him in Form before the Academical Judges, did not hinder the famous *John Collet* from lodging *Agrippa* in his House at *London*, nor the Emperor *Maximilian*, Grandfather of the Princess *Margaret*, from employing him in *Italy* (83). The fifth Reason of *Thevet* has already been refuted; he has only copied *Paul Jovius*, and both of them have been so imprudent as to take notice of *Agrippa*'s Poverty. A fine means of convincing a judicious Reader that he was a great a Magician! A rare Way to persuade the People of it, when they know, on the contrary, that *whenever Fortune smiles on a Prince or Lord, it is presently cast in his Dish, that he courts* Agrippa (84).

III. As for *Martin del Rio*, he relates these three or four Particulars: I. When *Agrippa* travell'd, he paid his Reckonings in Money, seemingly *good and lawful*; but, after some Days, it was discover'd, that he had paid his Host with pieces of Horn, or Shells (85). II *Charles* V. expell'd him from his Court and Dominions, and with him two other Persons of Quality, who had promis'd him great Treasures by the means of Magic (86). III. The same Emperor did not remit the Sentence of Death against *Agrippa*, but condemn'd him to Banishment, after he had heard that he was fled (87). IV. *Agrippa* had a Boarder in *Louvain*, who was very inquisitive. One Day, as he was going out of Town, he order'd his Wife not to let

any body go into his Closet: Nevertheless this Boarder obtain'd the Key of it; he went in and read a Book of Conjurations: upon which there was a great knocking at his Door; which he heard two or three times, without leaving off his reading. It was the Devil who knock'd at the Closet-Door, and demanded, who it was that call'd him, and what he wanted; but, receiving no Answer, he strangled him. *Agrippa*, returning home, sees the Spirits dancing on the top of his House; he calls them, and they inform him of what had happen'd; he order'd the Homicide to enter into the Body, and to walk some Turns, in the Place, which the Scholars frequented most, and then quit it. This was done. The Boarder, having walk'd three or four turns, fell down dead; and it was believ'd a long while, that he died suddenly; but certain marks of Suffocation appearing, began to make the thing suspected. At length Time discover'd all, and *Agrippa*, being obliged to fly into *Lorrain*, begun to give vent to the Heresies, which he had conceiv'd in his Heart (88).

Agrippa's Poverty, and the frequent Fear he discovers, in his Epistles, of being starv'd for want of common Necessaries, are a sufficient Confutation of the first of these Stories. When a Man has so compendious a Method of discharging his Debts, he need not fear wanting Bread. It is not true that *Charles* V. ever expell'd *Agrippa* out of his Dominions; he was too great a Politician, to punish, in such a manner, a Magician, who was a distributer of Treasures; he would have fear'd, that other Princes might make use of the Secrets of such a considerable Exile to his detriment. *Del Rio* refutes the second Story by the third; for he pretends in the third, that his Imperial Majesty would have put *Agrippa* to Death, had it been in his Power, and that the Decree of Banishment came out after the Magician's Flight. These are mere Stories. *Agrippa* presented Petition upon Petition to the Emperor's Council, either for the payment of his Salary, or for his Dismission (89); and when he was tir'd with his ill Success, he went to *Cologne*, where he exclaim'd with great Freedom, before the Magistrates, against the Monks, who stopt the printing of his Works (90). He liv'd quietly at *Bonn*, 'till he went from thence to *France*. Would *Charles* V. have permitted this in a Man whom he had banish'd his Dominions? Would he have suffer'd this in a Magician, who had avoided Death only by Flight? As to the fourth little Tale, I refer him to *Gabriel Naudé*, whose Words are these; *We have more Reason to deny it, as* Ludwigius * *did, than* Del Rio *has to affirm it, since he has translated it Word for Word out of a Book, entituled*, The Theatre of Nature, *published in* Italian *and in* Latin, *under the Name of* Stroza Cicogna, *and in* French *and* Spanish, *under the Name of* Valderama (91). We may refute it another Way: as thus, *Del Rio* observes, that the Wife, who lent the Key to the Boarder, was afterwards divorced by *Agrippa*. It must be, then, the third Wife of this Magician. Now the second did not die 'till the Year 1529. So that the Adventure of the Boarder must have happen'd after the Year 1529. *Agrippa*, must therefore, have fled towards *Lorrain* after the Year 1530, or thereabouts; he must have taken a House at *Louvain*, after he was install'd in the Office of Historiographer of *Charles* V, for Boarders: but nothing is more false than this. For, first, he did not go into *Lorrain* as a Fugitive; he went thither to exercise a noble Office at *Metz*, which was offered to him with all possible Advantages, at the same time that he was press'd to accept of honourable Employments elsewhere (92). II. He did not go into *Lorrain* 'till 1518, and at that time his first Wife was alive. III. The Doctrines he maintain'd in that Country, for which he was expos'd to the Persecution of the Monks, were neither Magical nor Heretical; they turn'd on this Question, Whether *St. Anne*, the Mother of the Holy Virgin, had three Husbands, and a Child by each; or whether she had but one Husband, and one Daughter. *Agrippa* maintain'd the latter Opinion (93), which did infinitely more Honour to *St. Anne*'s Memory. IV. It does not

appear

AGRIPPA.

some Persons apologizing for him [*Q*]. *Moreri* declared strongly in his favour; which
was

appear that he liv'd any where else, than at *Antwerp*, and at *Mechlen*, from the time of his being made the Emperor's Historiographer, 'till he retir'd to the Elector of *Cologne*; and I do not believe that ever he had any Boarders at *Louvain*: So that we might have been dispens'd with from answering *Martin del Rio*, and his Partizans, 'till they had rang'd their Circumstances of Time and Place in better order.

I wonder that the famous *Naudè* had not the precaution to object to the Accusers of *Agrippa* the great Number of Historical Falshoods, of which I have convicted them.

[*Q*] *There are some Errors of Fact in the manner of some Persons apologizing for him.*] I have Gabriel *Naudè* in view. He endeavours to justify *Agrippa*, among other Reasons, from *the Favour of two Emperors, and as many Kings* (94); which is to suppose, that *Charles* V. had a Kindness for *Agrippa*; but we need only read the Complaints of that Author, to discover the contrary (95). Farther, *Naudè* supposes, that they did not think of crying down the *Occult Philosophy*, 'till a long time after it was publish'd; he pretends that they exclaim'd against that Work, only in Revenge for the Injuries, they believ'd they had receiv'd in That of the *Vanity of Sciences*. It is true, this latter Book gave great Offence to many. The Monks, the Members of the Universities, the Preachers, and the Divines, saw themselves drawn to the Life in it: *Agrippa* was of too warm a Complexion. " Ex ejus " Libri (*de Vanitate Scientiarum*) qualicunque gustu " deprehendi hominem esse ardentis ingenii, variæ " lectionis, & multæ memoriæ, alicubi tamen majore " copia, quam delectu, ac dictione tumultuosâ verius " quam compositâ. In omni genere rerum vituperat mala, laudat bona. Sed sunt, qui nihil aliud " sustinent, quam laudari (96).—— *The least taste of* " *his Book* (of the Vanity of Sciences) *convinc'd me,* " *that he was an Author of a fiery Genius, extensive* " *Reading, and great Memory; but sometimes more* " *copious, than choice, in his Subject, and writing in* " *a disturb'd, rather than a compos'd, Style. He lashes* " *Vice, and commends Virtue, every where, and in* " *every person; but there are some, with whom no-* " *thing but Panegyric will go down.*" His Paintings were too strong; his Shades too dark, and his Touches too lively. This gave them uneasiness, I confess; but it is not true that this Resentment spent itself on a Work, which had lain in Obscurity for many Years. *Naudè* would have done better to have reserv'd this Thought for another Application; he might have met with an Opportunity sooner or later, though he had not been a Man of such great Reading, as he was. To explain myself: It is no rare thing for Zealots to take no notice of a Book, or the Author of it, for a long time, whatever it be, provided it does not personally attack them. But, if after ten, fifteen, or twenty Years, they happen to quarrel with the Author; if some new Work comes out, containing Discoveries of what they carefully endeavour to conceal from the People; the former Work immediately becomes heretical, impious, and fit to be burnt. They begin then to be *eaten up with the Zeal of God's House*; and thereby impose upon honest People. But They, who are no Dupes, perceive plainly what shameful Passions they cover under the fair Mask of the Interest of Piety. Let us do Justice to the Divines of *Louvain*: they do not deserve the Reproach, which the Apologist of *Agrippa* throws on them, upon this Account. The *Occult Philosophy* was not printed, 'till after the Declamation of *The Vanity of Sciences*; and it is sufficient to charge them with having made use of a thousand Cavils, to discover some damnable Propositions in That Declamation. See the solid Answer, which was given them: It is in the second Volume of *Agrippa*, and begins at *pag*. 252.

HISTORY of the Occult Philosophy.

Let us, in a few Words, describe the History of the *Occult Philosophy*. *Agrippa* compos'd this Work in his younger Days (97), and shewed it to the Abbot *Tritbemius*, from whom he had learnt many things (98). *Tritbemius* was charm'd with it, as appears by the Letter which he wrote to him on the 8th of *April*, 1510 (99); but he advises him to communicate it only to those, whom he could confide in. I know not whether the Author communicated it to too many Persons, or whether the first, who had a Copy of it, was indiscreet. The Truth is, several Manuscript Co-

pies of it were dispers'd almost all over *Europe*. It is not necessary to observe, that most of them were faulty; which never fails to happen in the like Cases. They were preparing to print it from one of these bad Copies; which made the Author resolve to publish it himself, with the Additions and Alterations, with which he had embellish'd it, after having shew'd it to the Abbot *Tritbemius*. Melchior *Adam* was mistaken in saying, that *Agrippa*, in his more advanc'd Years, having corrected, and enlarg'd, this Work, shew'd it to the Abbot *Tritbemius*. He had refuted his *Occult Philosophy*, in his Book of the *Vanity of Sciences*, and yet he publish'd it, to hinder others from printing a faulty and mutilated Edition of it (100). He obtain'd the Approbation of some Doctors of Divinity, and some Persons, whom the Emperor's Council appointed to examine it. " Liber ille jam nuper per aliquos " Ecclesiæ Prælatos & doctores sacrarum humanarum- " que literarum eruditissimos, & ex Cæsaris consilio " ad hoc specialiter deputatos commissarios, examinatus & probatus fuerit, deinde etiam totius Cæsarci " consilii assensu admissus, & ejusdem Cæsareæ Majestatis authentico diplomate, & appensâ in rubrâ ce- " râ Cæsaris aquilâ privilegiatus, insuper Antverpiæ, " & posteà etiam Parisiis, sine contradictione impressus " & publicè venditus sit (101). — *This Book has " been lately examin'd, and approv'd, by certain Prelates of the Church, and Doctors, thoroughly vers'd " both in sacred and prophane Literature, and by Commissaries, particularly deputed for that Purpose, by " Cæsar's Council; after which it was admitted by the " assent of the whole Council, and licensed by the authentic Diploma of his Imperial Majesty, and the " Stamp of the Cæsarean Eagle in red Wax; and was " afterwards publickly printed and sold at Antwerp, " and then at Paris, without any Opposition.* Upon this Approbation he obtain'd a Licence from his Imperial Majesty; and caus'd his Book to be printed at *Antwerp*, and dedicated it to the Elector of *Cologne*. His Epistle Dedicatory is dated at *Malines*, in the Month of *January*, 1531; and it is the thirteenth of the sixth Book of his Letters. This Book was publish'd in the Year 1531. It was presently reprinted at *Paris*. These two Editions were sold without any Opposition. The Author set about a third at *Cologne*. Father *Conrad* of *Ulm*, Inquisitor of the Faith, had notice of it, and caus'd the Impression to be stopp'd; but the vigorous Instances of *Agrippa* to the Magistrates had doubtless their Effect; since there is an Edition, of *Cologne*, of the *Occult Philosophy*, in 1533. It contains three Books; whereas the former Editions contain'd only the first (102). After the Death of *Agrippa*, a fourth was added to it by another Hand. " Optimo jure hic (*libris magicis*) annumeretur abo- " minabilis libellus nuper in lucem sb impio homine " emissus, tributuque Henr. Corn. Agrippæ, meo " olim hospiti & præceptori honorando, ultrà annos " quadraginta jam mortuo, ut hinc falso ejus manibus " jam inscribi sperem, sub titulo quarti libri de Oc- " culta Philosophia, seu de Ceremoniis magicis: qui " insuper clavis librorum trium de Occultâ Philoso- " phia omniumque magicarum operationum jactatur " (103). — *To these* (Books of Magic) *may very justly be " added an abominable Work, lately publish'd by an " impious Wretch, and ascrib'd to my late honoured " Host and Preceptor*, Henry Cornelius Agrippa, *who " has been dead more than forty Years; whence I conclude, that It is unjustly inscribed to his Manes, " under the Title of* The fourth Book of the Occult " Philosophy, *or of* Magical Ceremonies; *which pretends, likewise, to be a* Key *to the three former " Books of the* Occult Philosophy, *and all kinds of " Magical Operations.*" Thus *John Wierus* expresses himself. " I have seen an Edition in Folio of the *Occult Philosophy*, in 1533, without the Place, where it was printed. The Privilege of *Charles* V. is prefix'd to it, dated, if I mistake not, from *Mechlen*, the 12th of *January*, 1529.

Let us now examine the Falshoods contain'd in these Words of *Naudè*; " The Divines of *Louvain* " censur'd his Declamation against the Sciences with " great Severity: *John Catilinet*, a *Cordelier*, de- " clam'd publickly against his Explication of the *de " Verbo Mirifico*, at *Dole*: The *Dominican* of the " City of *Metz* wrote against the Propositions, which " he had advanc'd, in support of the Opinion of

Fa-

was not to be expected from his Pen. His Faults are not many in this Article [R]. I have already mentioned the chief Works of *Agrippa*, and shall speak more particularly of them in the Remarks. It will be sufficient to add, that he wrote *A Commentary on the Art of Raimundus Lullius*, and *A Dissertation on the Original of Sin*, wherein he teaches, that the Fall of our First Parents proceeded from their unchaste Love. He promised a Work against the *Dominicans* [S], which would have pleased many Persons, both within, and without, the Pale of the Church of *Rome*. He held some uncommon

" *Faber Stapulensis*, concerning the Monogamy of St *Anne*; and yet not one of these Censurers could find any thing offensive in the two first Books of his *Occult Philosophy*, which were printed LONG BEFORE all those Pieces, as well at *Paris*, as at *Antwerp*, and elsewhere (104)." —— Observe, that he repeats these Words LONG BEFORE, in the 416th Page. To understand the whole Mistake, we must remember, that *Catilinet* declaim'd, in the Year 1509; that the *Jacobins* of *Metz* wrote concerning St *Anne*, in the Year 1519; and that the Declamation on the *Vanity of Sciences* appear'd in 1530, a Year before the *Occult Philosophy*. " The Avarice of the " Booksellers, and the Vanity of certain Persons, —— " adds *Naudé* (105) —— injure this Author's Memory, " by attributing a fourth Book to him, full of magi-" cal, vain, superstitious, and abominable Ceremo-" nies, and by publishing it with the three Books of " the *Occult Philosophy*. —— *Wierus**, in defence of " *Agrippa*, says, that this Book was not publish'd " 'till twenty seven Years after his Death, and that " it is very certain he was not the Author of it (106)."

These Words of *Naude*, *twenty seven Years after his Death*, compar'd with the *Latin* Passage cited above (107), may embarrass the Matter; but to clear it, it is sufficient to take notice of the several Editions of *John Wierus*. He revis'd, and enlarged his Work six times. *Naudé* had doubtless an Edition, which the Author prepar'd in the Year 1526. There were at that Time twenty seven Years past, since the Death of *Agrippa*. My Edition was prepared thirteen or fourteen Years after; this is the Reason why the Author makes use of this Phrase in it, " ultra annos " quadraginta jam mortuo —— *more than forty Years* " *dead*." —— He always retain'd his *nuper*, and is to blame for it; since by this means he deceives his Readers. He makes them believe, that the fourth Book *Philosophiæ Occultæ* was not printed 'till twenty seven, or forty Years after the Death of *Agrippa*; which is false. Authors, who enlarge their Books several times, seldom take proper Care to alter the Dates.

In favour of those, who have not *Agrippa's* Works, I shall in this place inform them, how it is proved, that the Declamation against the Sciences was printed in the Year 1530, and the *Occult Philosophy*, in the Year 1531. By a Letter, printed with those of *Agrippa*, and dated the 10th of *January*, 1531 (108), we understand, that the Elector of *Cologne* had receiv'd a Copy of the *Vanity of Sciences*, and seen some Sheets of the *Occult Philosophy*, which was printing at *Antwerp*. The Author of the *Bibliotheque of Dauphiné*, has taken a very unnecessary Trouble in his *Errata*: He has changed 1467, into 1567. His Book says, that the Treatise of the *Vanity of Sciences* was compos'd at *Grenoble*, in the Year 1467. If you correct it according to the *Errata*, you must suppose that the Book was compos'd thirty two Years after the Death of its Author. He had better have made no Correction at all. I think it would be a Mistake, whatever Year should be inserted; for I believe the Author had not resided long at *Grenoble*, when he died there.

[R] *His Faults are not many in this Article.*] I. He says *Cubert* instead of *Gobori*; *Gattinaria* instead of *Gattinara*; *Rauchin* instead of *Reuchlin*; *Carniletus* instead of *Catilinetus*. II. He tells us, That *Agrippa* obtained a *Professorship* at *Padua*; which is false, he ought to have said *Pavia*. Mr *Teissier* was also deceived by the Resemblance of the Words; he put *Paris* for *Pavia*: Perhaps it is an Error of the Press; however the Reader ought to be advertised, that he must not believe what he finds in Mr *Teissier*, to wit, that *Agrippa* was *Professor of Holy Writ* at *Dole*, and at *Paris* (109). It is to be feared, that some Compiler, who shall collect all that he finds dispersed in several Authors, will tells us, some time or other, that *Agrippa* professed Divinity at *Dole, Paris, Pavia, Turin, Padua, Cologne*, &c. By this Means no doubt it often happens that a Man's

Employments are multiplied without Reason; which occasions many advantageous Reflexions on the extent of his Merit. III. The following Passage is confused. *The Cardinal de Sainte Croix would have engaged him to follow him to the Council, which was to be assembled at Pisa; and at the same time the King of England, Margaret of Austria, and Gatinaria, Chancellor of the same Charles V. invited him into their Service*. The Rules of Grammar lead us to refer all this to one and the same time; and at this rate *Moreri* will have told a downright Falshood; for it was in 1529, a long time after the Affair of *Pisa*, that *Agrippa* was invited by *Henry* VIII. by *Margaret of Austria*, and by the Chancellor of *Charles* the Vth. IV. There is no Chicanery to be found out in vindication of what follows: *But* Agrippa, *who loved Liberty extreamly, preferred the Pleasure of Travelling before these Advantages; and, after having spent some time at* Friburg, *at* Geneva, *and elsewhere, he retired to* Lyons. A pitiful Anachronism, and which involves other Mistakes. *Moreri* pretends, then, that none of these Offers were accepted; yet That of the Princess *Margaret* was, and, when it was offered, *Agrippa* thought no more of travelling; he had satisfied his Curiosity; he had been at *Geneva*, at *Friburg*, and at *Lyons*. V. It is not true, that *Paul Jovius, Del Rio, Thevet*, and others, maintain, that *Agrippa* kept two Spirits *in the form of two little Dogs, and that he called one of them* Monsieur, *and the other* Mademoiselle. *Paul Jovius* and *Thevet*, &c. speak only of one Dog, without mentioning his Name. VI. He ought not to have distinguished between the Book of the Vanity of Sciences, and the other Works of *Agrippa*, which compose two Volumes; for that Work is at the beginning of the second Volume. I say nothing of the Confusion, which runs through *Moreri's* Narrative, with respect to Chronology.

[S] *He promised a Work against the* Dominicans.] They were the chief Directors of the Inquisition, it is no wonder, that he was more incensed against them, than against others. His Patience was lost, when he saw them so indulgent to the Errors of their Brethren, and so severe against the equivocal Propositions of other Persons. This Indulgence would have been less scandalous, had they alone been guilty of it; but the Misfortune is, People are such Fools, that whilst they commend the Zeal of an Inquisitor, who discovers Heresy wherever he thinks fit, they will not suffer any Recrimination to be used against him, and that his own pernicious Doctrines should be laid open to the Public. *Agrippa* intended to be very free with the *Dominicans* on this Head, and upon several others. " Neque tamen putetis, *says he to the Magistrates of* " Cologne, hunc solum articulum apud illum reperiri " hæreticum: sed alii multi, quos, cum hic nimis " longum vobisque tædiosum foret referre, enume-" rabo alibi, in eo scilicet libro quem de Fratrum " Prædicatorum sceleribus & hæresibus inscripsi, ubi " infecta sæpius veneno sacramenta, ementita sæpis-" sime miracula, interemptos veneno Reges & prin-" cipes, proditas urbes & respublicas, seductos po-" pulos, assertasque hæreses, & cætera ejusmodi he-" roum illorum facinora flagitiaque in varias transfusa " linguas, omnique populo exposita, dilucidè narra-" bo (110). —— *Nor would I have you think, that* " *this Article of His is the only Heretical one; there* " *are many others of the same Stamp, which, as it* " *would be tedious to lay them before you at present,* " *I shall enumerate in another Place; namely, in the* " *Treatise I am composing of the Vices, and erro-* " *neous Opinions, of the* Dominicans, *in which I shall* " *expose to the whole World their vicious Practices,* " *such as the Sacraments often infested with Poison,* " *numberless pretended Miracles, Kings and Princes* " *taken off by Poison, Cities and States betrayed,* " *the Populace seduced, Heresies avowed, and the rest* " *of the Deeds of those Heroes, and their enormous* " *Crimes*."

AGRIPPA. 155

uncommon Opinions [*T*], and never any Protestant spake more forcibly against the Impudence of the Legendaries than he did (*oo*).

We must not forget the Key of his *Occult Philosophy*. He kept it only for his Friends of the first Rank, and explained it in a manner, which differs but little from the Speculations of our Quietists [*U*]. Let me observe likewise, that the Edition of his

(*oo*) *See the Preface to his Treatise of the Monogamy of St Anne,* Oper. Tom. 2. p. 1053.

[*T*] *Some uncommon Opinions.*] I have already mentioned That, which concerns the Fall of *Adam*. The rest were not of so dangerous a Nature, and their only Crime was their being agreeable to the Doctrines of the Reformers. His Dissertation concerning Marriage, dedicated to *Louisa* of *Savoy*, Mother of *Francis* I. strikes at the Law of Celibacy, and shews plainly, that Adultery breaks the Conjugal Engagement. One of his Friends (111) gave him notice, that this Dissertation had displeased the Court, and that at first they were afraid to present it to the Princess. I refer you to his Answer. He did not approve of the use of Images, and with all his Heart would have consented to a Reformation, which would not have occasioned the raising of Altar against Altar (112).

[*U*] *Which differs but little from the Speculations of our Quietists.*] I shall produce another Observation of *Naudé*, designed to shew, that, under pretence of this Key, it cannot be maintained, that *Agrippa* was the true Author of the fourth Book of the *Occult Philosophy*. " Nor must it be objected, *says he* (113), " that the same *Agrippa* says in some Passages of his " Epistles *, that he reserved the Key of the three " Books, which he had published (114), to himself: " For, besides that it may be answered with great " shew of probability, that he amused the World " with this Key, in order to make himself courted " by the Curious; as *James Gohory* † and *Vigenere* ‖ " say, that he pretended, with the same View, to " be master of the Practice of the Mirrour of *Pythagoras*, and the Secret of extracting the Spirit " Gold from it's Body, in order to convert Silver " and Copper into fine Gold, from which it had been " separated: I say, besides this Reason, he explains " sufficiently what he meant by such a Key, when " he says in the nineteenth Epistle of the fifth Book. " Hæc est illa vera & mirabilium operum occultissima Philosophia, Clavis ejus intellectus est, quanto " enim altiora intelligimus, tanto sublimiores induimus virtutes, tantoque & majora, & facilius & efficatius operamur. —— *This is that true and Occult Philosophy of the Wonders of Nature's it's Key is the Understanding; for the higher we carry our Knowledge, the more sublime are our Attainments in Virtue, and we perform the most extraordinary things with greater Ease, and more effectually.*" *Naudé* stopt here, but Mr *de la Monnoie* went farther. He did me the favour to acquaint me, that *Agrippa's* Sentiments agree perfectly well with those of the Quietists. You will be convinced of this, if you examine what I am going to say. *Agrippa* makes mention of this Key in two Letters, which he wrote to a Religious (115), who addicted himself very much to the Occult Sciences. He represents to him, that, whatever is to be found in Books concerning the Virtue of Magic, Astrology, and Alchimy, is false and deceitful, when literally understood; that a Mystical Sense is to be looked for in them; a Sense, which none of the Masters had yet found out, and that it was almost impossible to discover it, without the Assistance of a good Interpreter, unless by Divine Inspiration, which happens to very few Persons (116). " O quanta leguntur scripta de inexpugnabili magicæ artis " potentia, de prodigiosis astrologorum imaginibus, " de monstrificis alchimistarum metamorphosi, deque " lapide illo benedicto, quo, Midæ instar, contacta " æra mox omnia in aurum argentumve permutantur. Quæ omnis comperiuntur vana, ficta & falsa, " quoties ad literam practicantur (117). What surprizing Accounts do we meet with in Authors of " the invincible Power of Magic, of the wonderful " Schemes of Astrologers, of the amazing Metamorphoses of the Alchymists, and of that blessed Stone, " by which, as by the Touch of Midas, all Metals " are transmuted into Gold: All which are experienced " to be empty, fictitious, and false, when put in " practice literally. We must not, adds he, look for " the Principle of these great Operations without " ourselves: It is an internal Spirit, which can very " innocently perform all that the Mathematicians, " Magicians, Alcymists, aud Necromancers promise;

(111) Capellanus, *Physician to* Francis I. *See Agrippa's Letters,* pag. 832, 833, 836.

(112) *See* Gesner *in* Biblioth. fol. 509. verso.

(113) Naudé, *ubi supra,* p. 414, 415.

* Epist. 56. lib. 4. & Ibid. 14. lib. 5.

(114) *Naudé is mistaken, they were not then printed.*

† Lib. de Myst. Not. Comment. in Paracels. de Vita longa, fol. 61.

‖ *In his* Cyphers, fol. 26, & 27.

(115) Aurelius ab Aquapendente Augustinianus.

(116) Nisi fuerit divino numine illustratus, quod datur paucissimis. *Agrippa* Epist. 14. lib. 5. pag. 904.

(117) Id. ib.

" I shall not explain this to you in Writing; for it " is a Thing not to be committed to Paper. It is " communicated from one Spirit to another in a " few mystical Words. This wonderful Operator " comes not from Heaven or Hell, but is the Inhabitant of our own Breasts." " Atque hoc est, " quod te nunc scire volo, quia nobis ipsis est omnium mirabilium effectuum operator: Qui, quicquid portentosi Mathematici, quicquid prodigiosi " Magi, quicquid invidentes Naturæ persecutores Alchimistæ, quicquid dæmonibus deteriores malefici " Necromantates promittere audent, ipse novit discernere & efficere, idque sine omni crimine, sine " Dei offensa, sine religionis injuria. In nobis, inquam, est ille mirandorum operator,

Nos habitat, non tartara; sed nec sydera cœli.
Spiritus in nobis qui viger, illa facit.

" Verum de his nobis quam latissime tecum conserendum esset, & coram. Non enim committuntur hæc literis, nec scribuntur calamo, sed spiritu " spiritui paucis sacrisque verbis infunduntur, idque, " si quando nos ad te venire contigerit (118)." *This* is taken from a Letter, dated from *Lyons* the twenty fourth of *September*, 1527. The other Letter was written in the same City the nineteenth of *November* following: *Agrippa* unfolds his Mystery in it: He says, That true and solid Philosophy consists in being united with God by an Essential and Immediate Contact, which may transform us into God. He adds, " The Understanding is the Key of this " Philosophy; but, to be united to God, it must " be freed from Matter, and dead to the World; to " the Flesh, to all the Senses, and to the whole natural Man." His Latin will express this Fustian better: " Quod ad postulatam philosophiam attinet, " ite scire volo, quod omnium rerum cognoscere " opificem ipsum Deum, & in illum tota similitudinis imagine, ceu essentiali quodam contactu sive " vinculo transire, quo ipse transformeris, efficiareque Deus, ea demum vera solidaque philosophia " sit: Quemadmodum de Moyse ait Dominus, inquiens: *Ecce ego constitui te Deum Pharaonis.* Hæc est illa vera & summa mirabilium operum occultissima Philosophia. Clavis ejus Intellectus est. " Quanto enim altiora intelligimus, tanto sublimiores " induimus virtutes, tantoque majora & facilius & " efficacius operamur. Verum intellectus noster carni inclusus corruptibili, nisi, viam carnis superaverit, fueritque propriam naturam sortitus, divinis " illis virtutibus non poterit uniri (non enim nisi " sibi quam similibus congrediuntur) ac pervidendis " illis occultissimis Dei & Naturæ secretis omnino " inefficax est: Atque

Hoc opus, hic labor est, superas evadere ad auras.

" ——— Mori enim oportet, mori, inquam, mundo " & carni, ac sensibus omnibus, ac toto homini animali, qui velit ad hæc secretorum spenetralia ingredi: Non, quod corpus separetur ab animo: " Sed, quod anima relinquat corpus. De qua morte " Paulus scribit Colossensibus, *Mortui estis, & vita vestra abscondita est cum Christo:* & alibi clarius " de seipso ait, *Ÿsio hominem, in corpore, vel extra corpus, nescio; (Deus scit) raptum usque ad tertium " cælum:* Et quæ reliqua sequuntur (119). —— *As to the Philosophy you enquire into, you must " know, that the only true and solid Philosophy consists in knowing God the Creator of all things, " and being transformed into the perfect Resemblance " of Him, by an essential Contact or Union, and becoming God: as the Lord said to Moses,* See I have " made thee a God to Pharaoh. *This is that True " and Occult Philosophy of wonderful Things. It's " Key is the Understanding. For the higher we carry " our Knowledge, the more sublime are our Attainments in Virtue, and we perform the most extraordinary things with greater Ease, and more effectually. But our Understanding, inclosed in corruptible Flesh, unless it soar above the Ways of the " Flesh, and exert it's own proper Nature, cannot be " united*

(118) Id. Ib. 13. l. b. 5. pag. 909.

(119) Ibid.

his Works published at *Lyons* in two Volumes in 8vo. is castrated in a place, which might have displeased the Gentlemen of the Church [*X*].

" united to those divine Virtues (for they have no
" Communication but with what is most like them-
" selves) and is unqualified to look into those most
" abstruse Secrets of God and Nature.

To soar above, and view the chearful Skies,
In this the Task and mighty Labour lies.
                                                DRYDEN.

" ···· He must die; He must die, I say, to the
" World, the Flesh, all the Senses, and the whole
" Animal Man, who would enter into these secret Re-
" cesses: I do not mean, that the Body must be sepa-
" rated from the Soul; but that the Soul must re-
" linquish the Body: of which kind of Death St Paul
" writes to the Colossians, Ye are dead, and your
" Life is hid in Christ; and in another Place he
" says more plainly of himself, I know a Man, whe-
" ther in the Body, or out of the Body, I cannot
" tell (God knows) such an one caught up to the
" third Heaven; and so on. This precious Death,
" continues he, is granted but to a small number of
" People, beloved by God, or favoured with a
" propitious Influence of the Stars, or supported by
" their own Merits, and the Secret of the Art.

To few great *Jupiter* imparts this Grace,
And those of shining Worth, and heavenly Race.
                                                DRYDEN.

" Hæc, inquam, preciosa in conspectu Domini morte
" mori oportet, quod contingit paucissimis, & fortè
" non semper. Nam id

         ····· Pauci, quos æquus amavit
Jupiter, aut ardens evexit ad æthera virtus,
Diis geniti, potuere.

" Primùm qui non ex carne & sanguine, sed ex Deo
" nati sunt: Proximè qui Naturæ beneficio ac cœlo-
" rum genethliaco dono ad id dignificati sunt:
" cæteri meritis nituntur & arte, de quibus viva vox
(12.) Id. ib.   " te certiorem reddat (120)." He acknowledges in-
            genuously that he is not one of these Favourites of
            Heaven, and that he has no Hopes of attaining to this
(121) Com- high Degree of Happiness; for he had always found
pare this himself hurried away by the Vortices of Matter, a sen-
with les   sual Man, attach'd to a Wife, to the Flesh, to the
Suisses de la World, and to domestic Cares, &c. he desires only
Foi, whereof to be considered as a Door-keeper, to introduce others
the Sieur Pa- (121). " Verùm hoc te admonitum volo, ne circa
visot, speaks " me decipiaris, ac si ego aliquando divina passus tibi
in his Book " ista prædicem, ut tale quid mihi arrogare velim,
La Foi de- " vel concedi posse sperem, qui hactenus humano san-
voillée par " guine sacratus miles, semper ferè aulicus, tum car-
la Raison. " nis vinculo charissimæ uxori alligatus, omnibusque
There are " instabilis fortunæ flatibus expositus, totusque à carne,
some Extracts " & domesticis curis transversùm actus, tam sublimia
of it in the " immortalium deorum dona non sum adsecutus: Sed
Nouvelles " accipi me volo velut indicem, qui ipse semper præ
de la Rep.
Lit. Octob.
1685. pag.
1140, &c.

" foribus manens, aliis, quod iter ingrediendum sit,
" ostendo (122)."   (122) A-
                                                           grippæ, Ep.
[X] *Castrated in a Place, which might have dis-*   19. p. 909.
pleased the Gentlemen of the Church.] The Author, in
that part of the Work, exclaims against the Law of
Celibacy; and insinuates, that those who were the
Defenders of it, connived at Fornication, rather than
allow'd of Marriage, in Priests, because they drew a
great Revenue from permitting them to keep Concubines. He adds, That he had read of a certain Prelate
who boasted at Table, that he had eleven Thousand
Concubinary Priests in his Diocese, who paid him
each a Crown a Year. This Passage is not in the
Edition of *Lyons*. *Crenius*, who made the Discovery,
complain'd much of the Imposition: These are his
Words. " Mala fide, per Beringos fratres Lugduni
" anno M.DC. in 8vo. edita sunt Henrici Cornelii A-
" grippæ ——— Opera; utpote in qua multa omissa
" sunt Editione, quæ in prioribus erant. Atque ut
" hoc gratis dixisse videar, capias exemplum è tractatu
" de Incertitudine & Vanitate Scientiarum atque Arti-
" um, in cujus C. LXIIII. p. 189. de Lenonia, se-
" quentia hæc, quæ ex optima, recognita, plena, &
" scholiis *marginariis* (retineo vocem in titulo libri po-
" sitam) illustrata editione, fine loci adjectione, anno
" M. D. XXXVI. in 8vo. excusa, admodùm rara, datu-
" rus sum, in Lugdunensi planè dempta sunt: *Jam*
" *verò etiam Leuocinitis militant Leges atque canones,*
" *cùm in potentum favorem pro iniquis nuptiis pug-*
" *nant, & justa matrimonia dirimunt; Sacerdotesque,*
" *sublati honestis nuptiis, turpiter scortari compellunt:*
" *Maluerantque illi legislatores sacerdotes suos cum in-*
" *famia habere concubinas, quàm cum honesta fama*
" *uxores, forte quia ex concubinis proventus illis est*
" *amplior. De quo legimus gloriatum in convivio quen-*
" *dam Episcopum, habere se undecim millia sacerdotum*
" *concubinariorum, qui in singulos annos illi aureum*
" *pendant.* Hæc omnia, & alia forte plura, neque
" enim integrum hactenus contuli, pro more eraserunt
" Adversarii, clarum relinquentes documentum, illo-
" rum quid editionibus tribuendum sit (123). ——— *The* (123) Tho-
Works of Henry Cornelius Agrippa *were unfaith-*   mas Crenius,
fully publish'd, at Lyons, *by the Brothers* Beringi, Animadv.
in the Year M. DC. *in* 8vo. *: there being many things* Philolog.
omitted in this Edition, which were in the former.   Histor. part.
To confirm this, I instance, in his Treatise of The   secunda.
Uncertainty and Vanity of Arts and Sciences, in   p. 13, 14.
the 64th Chapter of which, pag. 189, De Lenonia,
the following Passage, which I am going to produce
from the best Edition of his Works, revis'd, entire,
and illustrated with Marginal Scholia (I retain in
the Phrase, as it stands in the Title Page) printed in
8vo. *in the Year* M.D. XXXVI. *and now very*
scarce; the following Passage, I say, is omitted in
the Lyons *Edition.* Jam verò etiam Lenociniis
militant Leges, &c. This, and, perhaps, many more
Passages, (for I have not collated the whole) have
been eras'd, according to Custom, by the Enemies of
this Author: whence we may judge how far we are
to depend upon their Editions.

AGUIRRE. The *Bibliotheque* of the *Spanish* Writers furnishes Five or Six Authors of this Name. The most eminent among them, is, I think, MICHAEL de AGUIRRE, born at *Aspeitia*, in the Diocese of *Pampelune*, in the Province of *Guipuscoa*. He was a Civilian, who, whilst he was Member of St *Clement*'s College at *Bologne*, wrote in favour of the Pretensions of *Philip* II. King of *Spain* [*A*] to the Crown of *Portugal*. He exercised the Office of a Judge in several Courts of the Kingdom of *Naples*, and afterwards he had the dignity of Counsellor in the Council of *Granada* in *Spain*. He
(a) N. An- died in 1588 (a). They, who shall continue the Work of Don *Nicolas Antonio*, will
ton. Bibli- have an AGUIRRE, infinitely more famous, to insert in it. I mean JOSEPH SAENZ
oth. Script. de AGUIRRE, a *Benedictin*, one of the Learned Men of the XVIIth Century. He
Hispan.   was Censor, and Secretary of the Supream Council of the Inquisition of *Spain*, First
Tom. 2.   Interpreter of the Scripture in the University of *Salamanca*, and had been more than
pag. 102.
(b) *An Edi-* once Abbot of the College of St *Vincent*, when, in 1686, he was honoured with a
tion of all Cardinal's Hat by Pope *Innocent* XI. He had undertaken a very great Work (b),
the Councils
held in Spain.

[*A*] *Wrote in favour of the Pretensions of* Philip II.
King of Spain.] His Book was printed at *Venice*, in
the Year 1581, with this Title, *Responsum pro succes-*
sione regni Portugalliæ pro Philippo Hispaniarum rege

adversus Bononiensium, Patavinorum, & Perusinorum
collegia. Besoldus inserted it in his Collection of Councils.

[*B*] *The*

which he continued with the same diligence after his Promotion to the Purple. They, who would form a just Idea of it, should read the *Prodromus*, which he published at *Salamanca* [B], in the Year 1686, or, if they have it not, the Abstracts, which the Journalists gave of it [C]. He was thought, for some time, to be the Author of a very Learned Work against the Decisions of the Clergy of *France*, in the Year 1682 [D]. But at last the contrary appeared (c). The Conjecture was not improbable, considering this Cardinal's Attachment to the Doctrines of the *Ultramontanes*, and the pains he took to prevent the Agreement between the Courts of *Rome* and *France*, which was, nevertheless, concluded in the Month of *October* 1693. The Expence he was at in printing two Volumes of his old Friend Don *Nicolas Antonio*, is very commendable. I shall take notice of it in the Article ANTONIO.

(c) *See the Remark* [D].

[B] *The Prodromus which he publish'd at* Salamanca.] The Title of it is; *Notitia Conciliorum Hispaniæ atque novi Orbis, Epistolarum decretalium & aliorum monumentorum sacræ antiquitatis ad ipsam spectantium, magna ex parte hactenus ineditorum, quorum editio paratur Salmanticæ cum notis & dissertationibus, sub auspiciis Catholici Monarchæ Caroli II. Studio & vigiliis M. Fr. Josephi Saenz de Aguirre. Salmanticæ apud Lucam Perez, Universitatis Typographum, 1686, in 8vo.* —— Memoirs of the Councils of *Spain*, &c. Note, that this Cardinal did not entirely execute the Plan of his Work, according to his first Ideas of it. They, who have not the four Volumes in Folio, which he publish'd at *Rome*, under the Title of *Collectio maxima Conciliorum omnium Hispaniæ & Novi Orbis*, &c. need only read the Abstracts, which the Journalists of *Leipsic* gave of them in their *Acta Eruditorum*, for the Year 1696.

[C] *The Abstracts, which the Journalists gave of it.*] The Gentlemen of *Leipsic* took notice of it in their *Acta*, of the Month of *February*, 1688. The Abbot *de la Roque* gave an Abstract of it in his Journal of the 13th of *January*, 1687. I wonder That Journal did not appear in the Editions of *Holland*. The Article relating to the Work before us is very curious; it gives Advice, in an artful manner, to Cardinal *d'Aguirre*, on his declaring that he would not warrant divers *Decretals* for genuine, which all the Learned judge to be spurious.

[D] *He was thought —— to be the Author of a very learned Work* (1) *against the Decisions of the Clergy of* France, *in* 1682.] The Title of it is : " Tractatus " de libertatibus Ecclesiæ Gallicanæ, continens amplam " discussionem Declarationis factæ ab Illustrissimis Ar- " chiepiscopis & Episcopis Parisiis mandato regio con- " gretatis anno 1682, Auctore M. C. S. Theolog. " Doctore Leodii apud Matthiam Hovium 1684 su- " periorum permissu." I have read a Preface of the Abbot *Faydit* (2), wherein, among other things, he promises " a Confutation of the principal Maxims of " the Treatise, *de Libertatibus Ecclesiæ Gallicanæ* " *adversus quatuor propositiones Cleri*, printed at " *Liege*, and attributed to Cardinal *d'Aguirre*, and " and to Monsr *Cozzoni*;" and thus he expresses himself at the 148th Page. " The Author of the " Treatise *de Libertatibus Ecclesiæ Gallicanæ*, or " rather the Authors, for I understand that several " Persons have had a hand in that Work, and that " all the *Roman* Doctors have exhausted their whole " Stock of Learning in it, though it is but a mean " Performance, these Authors, I say, maintain, &c." But let us consider a little what the Author of *the Letter of an Abbot to a Prelate of the Court of* Rome, *on the Decree of the Inquisition of the 7th of* December, 1690, against thirty one Propositions, advanc'd. " We ourselves (3), in our Assemblies, have not even " the Liberty of proposing what we may judge of Ad- " vantage to our Cause. You know whose fault it is."

(1) *See what was said of it in the* Nouvelles de la Rep. Lit. *for the Month of* July 1685, *Artic*. 3.

(2) *See the Abstract of a Sermon preach'd on St* Polycarpus's *Day at St* John's *in Grieve at* Paris, *printed at* Liege 1689.

(3) *It is a Bishop who is supposed to speak*, p. 59.

" Which is the Reason, why one of the Books, " which ought to have been most rigorously oppos'd " by our Divines, and even render'd infamous by an " Episcopal Censure, is spread all over *France* with " Impunity, and that the Abettors of the Opinions " contain'd in it, disperse, and commend it every " where, boasting that we dare not answer it. He " presently nam'd to me the Book *de Libertatibus Ec- " clesiæ Gallicanæ*, which is a thick Volume in Quarto, " the Author of which is better known than he ima- " gines. It is a shameful thing, *continues he*, that the " Clergy of *France* should tamely permit the Author, " who is a *French* Monk, to teach a Doctrine which " we all hold to be heretical; for he maintains openly, " that our Episcopal Jurisdiction is not of Divine " Right." The Anatomy of the Sentence against Father *Quesnel*, informs me (4), that the Book *de Libertatibus Ecclesiæ Gallicanæ* was compos'd at *Rome*, at the Instance of the Ministers of the Holy See, and printed by their Order, under the Inspection of the Nuncio of *Brussels*, at *Brussels* itself. But if Cardinal *d'Aguirre* be not the Author of that Treatise, it is however certain, that he wrote against the Decisions of the Assembly of 1682. The Letter I have quoted informs me of This, in a manner, which deserves the Reader's notice, as it will inform him how this Cardinal's Book is receiv'd in *France*. " Our four Ar- " ticles were scarce come out, *adds the Author* (5), but " a Crowd of Writers appear'd in opposition to them; " though scarce any one in *France* undertook their " Vindication. I do not say, that the Writings of " our Adversaries are formidable; most of them excite " our Pity; yet they do mischief in Countries, " where the People are already dispos'd in favour of " the Doctrines, which they defend. —— Lastly, " The noble Rewards, wherewith the Court of *Rome* " knows how to pay the Zeal of those, who declare " for her, give a Lustre to the least considerable, and " the most obscure Works. Is it not by this means " alone that Cardinal *d'Aguirre*, from a *Spanish* " Monk, rose to his present Dignity? Was not the " Abbot of St *Gall* nominated to a Bishoprick, with a " Design of raising him to the Purple (6), as a Reward " for his writing against the four Articles, as well as " Cardinal *d'Aguirre*?" Lastly, public Complaints (7) were made three Years before the printing of the Letter, out of which this Passage is taken, that the Pensioners among the Clergy left the Tract *de Libertatibus Ecclesiæ Gallicanæ* unanswered *The History of the Works of the Learned* has inform'd us (8), that the Author of that Tract is a *French* Priest, whose Name is *Antony Charlas*, who fled to *Rome* on account of the *Regale* *. Perhaps he ought to be called *Charlas*, for he is probably of the same Family with the Monk of that Name, Native of *l'Isle en Jourdain* (9), who died in Exile, after having suffer'd many Disgraces in the Service of the Bishop of *Pamiers* (10).

(4) *Pag*. 76, 77.

( ) *Letter of an Abbot*, &c. *a Prelate*, *pag*. 55, 56.

(6) *He was made a Cardinal in the Year* 1516. *His Name was Monsr. drais, and le died some time after*.

(7) *In the Sentiments of* Fra[...], *publish'd at* Cologne, *in* 1685, *pag*. 155.

(8) *Of the Month of* May 1691, *pag*. 426.

* *A Right belonging to the Kings of* France, *of disposing of benefices during the Vacancy of an Episcopal See*.

(9) *In the Diocese of* Toulouse.

(10) *Francis de Caulet*.

AJAX, the Son of *Oïleus*, was one of the Chief Lords, who went to the Siege of *Troy*. As he was the Son of a Prince, whose Dominions were of great Extent in the Country of the *Locrians*, it was easy for him to fit out Forty Ships for This Famous Expedition (a). He signalized himself on many Occasions; and it is pretended that there are Three Verses in the 2d Book of the *Iliad*, which are not *Homer*'s, because they give a remarkable Superiority to *Ajax*, the Son of *Telamon*, over the *Ajax* of this Article (b), which by no means agrees with *Homer*'s Account of these Heroes in another (c) Place. It is certain that our *Ajax* may be compared with any other Prince in the *Grecian* Army (d) for Courage, Boldness, and Activity [A]. As for

(a) Homer. Iliad. lib. 2. v. r. 41.

(b) *See the Scholiast of* Homer *on* Iliad lib. 2. ver. 35.

(c) Homer. Iliad. lib. 13. ver. 01.

(d) Plutarch. in Heroic.

[A] *And Activity*] *Homer* generally gives him the Epithet ταχὺς, *swift* (1). The three Hands, given him by others, signify only the Rapidity of his Action in Fight. " A multis historicis Græcis tertium ma-

(1) *See particularly the last Verses of the 14th Book of the* Iliad.

AJAX.

for Judgment and Conduct, they are out of the question; they are not part of his Character. The Poets have described him as so undaunted, that they even tell us, that the Gods, with all their Thunder and their Storms, could not subdue his Insolence; insomuch that they found it easier to destroy than to humble him [*B*]. The Action, which exposed him to the Anger of the Gods, was infamous, and brutish to the last degree. He had violated *Cassandra*, the Daughter of *Priam*, in the Temple of *Minerva*, whither she fled for Refuge. The *Greeks* themselves were offended at such a prophane Violence, and *Ulysses* advised to stone him (*e*). It appears, from some Passages of Ancient Authors, that *Ajax* denied the Fact, and offered to clear himself of it upon Oath (*f*). He confessed indeed, that he took the Maid in the Temple of *Minerva*, and that he pulled her away from the Image of the Goddess, which she had embraced (*g*); but he protested that he did not violate her; and pretended, that *Agamemnon* had spread this malicious Report, that he might keep *Cassandra*, whom he had seized, and whom *Ajax* claimed, as the first Possessor. We shall see, in the Remarks, how *Minerva* revenged herself on him for this Injury [*C*]. The Body of *Ajax* was thrown ashore by the Waves of the Sea on the Island *Delos*, where *Thetis* buried

(*e*) Pausan. lib. 10. pag. 347.
(*f*) Id. ib. pag. 343.
(*g*) Philost. in Heroic.

"num dicitur post tergum habuisse, quod ideo est
"fictum, quia sic celeriter utebatur in prælio mani-
"bus, ut tertiam habere putaretur (2). —— Many
"*Greek Historians relate, that he had a third Hand;
"the Ground of which Fiction is, that he was so
"quick in the use of his Hands, that he seem'd to
"have a third.*" Several interpreters apply these Words of *Horace* to him.

—— & celerem sequi
Ajacem (3).

Ajax, swift in pursuit.

Mr *Hofman* adopts their Explication, and confirms it by *Homer*'s Description of him.

----- Οἰλῆος ταχὺς υἱός

The swift-footed Son of Oileus.

At first I could not guess what he meant by confirming what the Compiler of his Dictionary had said concerning the Swiftness of *Ajax*'s Feet, from the Authority of *Homer*. *Quod autem supra, Ajacem pedibus velocem fuisse scribit hujusce Dictionarii compilator, Homerum habet authorem*; I thought it strange, and incomprehensible, that Mr *Hofman* should speak of the Compiler of his Dictionary, as of an Author distinct from himself; but at last I met with a Solution of this Enigma. Mr *Hofman* had taken Word for Word, what I have just now cited, out of *Lloyd*'s Dictionary. The thing has no Difficulty in *Lloyd*; because that Author publish'd his Dictionary only as an Addition to, and Correction of That of another. There are a great many Obscurities in Books, which proceed from the same Principle, as That of this Passage of Mr *Hofman*. The Authors forget to make the proper Alterations, when they abridge or transcribe the Passages of another Author (4).

[*B*] *Easier to destroy, than to humble him.*] *Minerva* was, in some measure, put to her last Shifts to punish him; she rais'd a furious Storm; he saw his Ship sink; and yet he escap'd upon a Rock.

Καὶ νύ κεν ἔκφυγε κῆρα, καὶ ἐχθόμενός περ Ἀθήνῃ,
Εἰ μὴ ὑπερφίαλον ἔπος ἔκβαλε, καὶ μέγ' ἀάσθη (5).

By *Neptune* rescu'd from *Minerva*'s Hate,
On *Gyræ*, safe *Oilean Ajax* sat,
His Ship it's o'erwhelm'd; but, frowning on the Floods,
Impious he rear'd Defiance to the Gods.
Pope's *Odyss.*

His Triumph at his Escape was horridly blasphemous.
In spite of the Gods, said he, *I am safe*.

Ὅττι ῥ' ἀέκητι θεῶν φυγέειν μέγα λαῖτμα θαλάσσης (6).

*To his own Prowess all the Glory gave,
The Pow'r defrauding, who vouchsaf'd to save.*
Id. ibid.

Neptune, being angry at this Insolence, split the Rock in two with his Trident, and the Part, on which *Ajax* sat, fell into the Sea. Thus *Homer* relates it,

in the 4th Book of the *Odyssey*. *Quintus Calaber* is much more particular on this Subject, and so prolix, that this single Passage shews he was not a great Master of Writing. However, he informs us, that *Minerva*, not being satisfy'd with the Thunderbolts, which *Jupiter* had given her, desired *Neptune* likewise to lend her all his Storms. It was the most dreadful Tempest imaginable; *Minerva* darted Thunder every Minute, and burnt and split *Ajax*'s Ship; yet this *Furioso* sav'd himself amidst the wildest Tumult of the Waves, and brav'd the Gods from the Rock which he gained.

Ὡς δ', καὶ οἱ μάλα πάντος ἐλάσσωσιν εἰς ἐν ἑαυτὰς
Χυέμενοι, καὶ πᾶσαν ἀνασχόμενοι θάλασσαν,
Ἐκφυγέειν (7).

The Gods ——
*Shou'd dart united Vengeance on his Head,
And tempest Ocean from it's deepest Bed,
Still to escape he fear'd not ——*

In order to destroy him, they were obliged to crush him by the fall of a Mountain, as they formerly did *Enceladus*. *Seneca*, in the Tragedy of *Agamemnon*, confirms this; read the first Scene of the third Act; you will there see a Description of Resistance and Fierceness carried to the highest Degree. The *Festin de Pierre*[*] is nothing to it. Poets would not be allowed at present to carry their Fictions so far on the Stage. Thus we have one *Latin*, and two *Greek* Poets, who ascribe the Death of *Ajax* to *Neptune*; but *Virgil* and *Hyginus* (8) ascribe the whole Honour of it to *Minerva*.

[*] *A Comedy of Moliere's from whence our Shadwell borrowed his Don Johan.*

—— Pallasne exurere classem
Argivûm, atque ipsos potuit submergere ponto,
Unius ob noxam & furias Ajacis Oilei?
Ipsa, Jovis rapidum jaculata è nubibus ignem,
Disjecitque rates, evertitque æquora ventis.
Illum expirantem transfixo pectore flammas
Turbine corripuit, scopuloque infixit acuto (9).

*Could angry Pallas, with revengful Spleen,
The Grecian Navy burn, and drown the Men?
She, for the Fault of one offending Foe,
The Bolts of Jove himself presum'd to throw;
With Whirlwinds, from beneath, she toss'd the Ship,
And bare expos'd the bosom of the Deep;
Then, as an Eagle gripes the trembling game,
The Wretch, yet hissing with her Father's Flame,
She strongly seiz'd, and, with a burning Wound
Transfix'd and naked, on a Rock she bound.*
Dryden.

[*C*] *How Minerva reveng'd herself on him for this Injury.*] See the foregoing Remark. I shall only add here, that the Storm, she rais'd, cast a great many Ships away near the Rocks of *Capharæum*, in the Neighbourhood of the Island of *Eubœa*, called at present *Negrepont*. We cannot, without extreem Imprudence, and without imputing to them, a false Principle, condemn the *Greek* Poets for representing a whole People as punish'd by that Goddess, for the Crime of a particular Person.

(2) Servius in Æneid. lib. 1. ver. 41.
(3) Horat. Od. 15. lib. 2. ver. 19.
(4) See the Remark [*G*] of the Article ACHILLEA, towards the end.
(5) Homer. Odyss. lib. 4. ver. 502.
(6) Id. ib. ver. 504.
(7) Quint. Calaber. lib. 14. pag. 564.
(8) Hygin. cap. 116.
(9) Virgil. Æneid. lib. 1. ver. 39.

Unius

AJAX.

buried it [D]. Some Authors say, that he escaped from the Storm, and arrived safely at home [E]. The Locrians had a singular Veneration for his Memory (h). We shall relate, in the Article CASSANDRA, in what manner they were obliged to expiate his Crime. He tamed a Serpent fifteen Foot long, in such a manner, that it followed him like a Dog, and eat at his Table (i).

> Unius ob noxam & furias peccantia Oilei.
>
> *She, for the Fault of one offending Foe,*
> *The Bolts of Jove himself profan'd so threw.*

Or, as another Poet says,

> Quidquid Oïlides commiserat, omnibus unus
> Peccavit Danais, omnibus ira nocens (10).
>
> *What mighty Ills upon the Greeks were brought,*
> *By rash Oilides' bold and single Fault?*
> Mr SALISBURY.

The Objection would prove too much, and might be retorted against the History of David. It is not only true in Prophane, but likewise in Sacred Writers, that

> Quidquid delirant reges plectuntur Achivi (11).
>
> *The People suffer, when the Prince offends.*
> CREECH.

[D] *The Island Delos, where Thetis buried it.*] Lycophron informs us of this Particular (12), since the Interpreters have found it out among his Enigmas. See what Canterus and Meursius have said upon it; but do not believe all they say; for they are mistaken in relation to the Passage of Pausanias, which they make use of to confirm their Conjectures. Pausanias does not speak of the Tomb of the Son of Oileus (13), but of That of Ajax, the Son of Telamon. Meursius's Criticism on the Greek of Pausanias is not right; instead of reading τὴν Ἰσοδον πρὸς τὸ μνῆμα ἢ χαλεπὴν ποιῆσαι, he reads τὴν Ἰσοδον πρὸς τὸ μνῆμα οὐ χαλεπὴν ποιῆσαι. According to this Correction, the Mysian, who spoke to Pausanias, told him, That the Sea had render'd all Access to That Tomb difficult to him; whereas, on the contrary, he related to Pausanias, That the Sea, had been the occasion of discovering the largeness of one of Ajax's Bones. Wherefore the meaning of it is, That the Sea having wash'd part of the Land away, had made the Place more accessible, less steep, &c.

[E] *Some Authors say, that he escap'd from the Storm, and arriv'd safely at home.*] Mr Lloyd has cited these Words of Timaeus Locrus, Hist. lib. 2. Μετὰ τῆς Τροίας ἅλωσιν πολλοὶ τῶν Λοκρῶν περὶ τὰς Γυρείας ναυαγήσαντες διεφθάρησαν· οἱ δὲ λοιποὶ σὺν Αἴαντι μόλις εἰς Λοκρίδα διεσώθησαν. That is, *After the taking of Troy, many Locrians were shipwreck'd, and perish'd near the Gerean Rocks* (14); *the rest hardly escap'd, with Ajax, and return'd home to Locris.* There is some Probability, that, instead of Timaeus Locrus, he ought to have cited Timaeus Tauromenita.

AJAX, the Son of *Telamon* (a), was, next to Achilles, the most valiant of the Grecian Captains [A] at the Siege of Troy; where he commanded the Troops of Salamis (b), and performed many Heroic Actions, which are described in the Iliad, in Dictys Cretensis, in Quintus Calaber, and in the XIIIth Book of the Metamorphoses, in the Speech, which he made upon the Dispute concerning the Arms of Achilles. He lost his Cause; for they were awarded to his Competitor Ulysses. He was so enraged at it, that he ran mad (c). He attacked the Cattle, and made a great Slaughter among them, fancying he was destroying his Rivals for the Arms of Achilles, or his Judges, who gave them to another: But, finding that he destroyed only Cattle, he became yet more furious, and killed himself. It is said, That his Madness was of great Service to the Besiegers [B]. According to some, he was condemned, not by

[A] *Was, next to Achilles, the most valiant of the Grecian Captains.*] It is on the Authority of several Poets, that I make this Restriction:

Ἀνδρῶν δ' αὖ μέγ' ἄριστος ἔην Τελαμώνιος Αἴας,
Ὄφρ' Ἀχιλλεὺς μήνιεν. (ὃ γὰρ πολὺ φέρτατος ἔεν) (1).

Ajax in Arms the first Renown acquir'd,
While stern Achilles in his Wrath retir'd.
POPE.

Pindar calls Ajax κράτιστον, Ἀχιλλέος ἄνευ, μάχᾳ (2) *strenuissimum, excepto Achille, in pugna.* Sophocles says as much of him (3). And Horace no less,

———— *Ajax, Heros ab Achille secundus* (4).

Plutarch reports, as a Tradition, which admits of no Difficulty, That *Ajax* was the Handsomest, the Greatest, and the most Valiant of all the *Greeks*, next to *Achilles* (5). This is built on these Words of Homer:

Αἴαντ', ὅς περὶ μὲν εἶδος περὶ δ' ἔργα τέτυκτο
Τῶν ἄλλων Δαναῶν μετ' ἀμύμονα Πηλείωνα (6).

With Tow'ring Ajax, an illustrious Shade:
War was his Joy, and pleased with loud Alarms;
None but Pelides brighter shon in Arms.
POPE's Odyss.

Plutarch builds upon this the Objection, which he makes to Plato, who feigned, that the Soul of *Ajax* was but the twentieth, that was enrolled. Τί ἂν (εἴποι) οἱ δευτερᾶται μὲν ὁ Αἴας κάλλει καὶ μεγέθει καὶ ἀνδρείας ἀεὶ φέρεται μετ' ἀμύμονα Πηλείωνα; *What!* (says he) *was not Ajax always esteemed second to Achilles in Beauty, Stature, and Courage?* Mereri misrepresents this Passage entirely; his Words are; Plutarch *remarks, in his Table-Talk, the reason, why* Plato *gives but the twenty second Place, after* Achilles, *to the Soul of* Ajax, *who was esteemed the first in Beauty, Strength, and Courage: and he makes it appear, that That Philosopher played upon the different Signification of Names.*

[B] *His Madness was of great Service to the Besiegers.*] We must not, however, conclude from hence, that true Courage stands in need of such Assistance. The Benefits, which sometimes arise from Vice, do not justify the being in it's own Nature evil. I appeal to this fine Passage of Cicero: "Non desiderat fortitudo advocatam iracundiam; satis est instructa, parata, armata per se. Nam isto modo quidem licet dicere utilem vinolentiam ad fortitudinem, utilem etiam dementiam, quod & insani & ebrii multa faciunt saepe vehementius.

Semper Ajax fortis, fortissimus tamen in furore.
Nam facinus fecit maximum, quum, Danais inclinantibus,
Summam rem perfecit manu, praelium quum restituit insaniens.
Dicamus igitur utilem insaniam (7).

"———— *True Bravery stands in no need of being assisted by Rage and Fury; it is sufficiently equipped, prepared, and armed by itself. By the same Argument, otherwise, we might prove Drunkenness and Madness to be useful to Bravery, because Madmen and Drunkards often perform great Feats.*

Ajax, for Valour constantly renown'd,
Was most an Hero, in his Madness found;
When he restor'd the Fight, the Grecians giving
Thus Madness has it's Use."
(Ground.

AJAX

by the Votes of the *Grecian* Princes, but by the Decision of the *Trojans*, of whom it was demanded, which had done them most mischief, *Ajax* or *Ulysses* (d). This Opinion is founded upon an express Passage in the Eleventh Book of the *Odyssey*. *Ajax* resembled *Achilles* in many things; he was equally passionate and impatient (e); and every where invulnerable, excepting one part of his Body [C]. It would betray a very little acquaintance with Fabulous History, should we believe that there have not been various and even contradictory Accounts of the Causes and Circumstances of his Death [D]. One part of *Ajax*'s Character was Impiety [E]; it consisted, not in believing, that the Gods were not endued with great Power, but in imagining, that there was no great Glory in conquering by their assistance, since the arrantest Cowards might do so. He would only be indebted for Victory to his own Courage. It is feigned, that his Soul, having the Liberty of chusing a Body (f) to return into the World with, preferred That of a Lion to That of a Man: such was his Detestation of Mankind, when he remembered the Injustice, which was done him, in relation to the Arms of *Achilles*. We shall, in another place (g), take notice of his Posterity, from whence proceeded the Family of *Miltiades*. The Poets have given *Ajax* the same Elogy, which the Holy Scriptures give King *Saul*, as to his Stature (h). He was the subject of several Dramatic Pieces, both in *Greek* and *Latin* (i). The famous Comedian *Æsop* refused to act them (k). The *Greeks* highly honoured this valiant Captain after his Death (l). They erected a stately Monument to him on the Promontory

(d) Eustathius and the Sch. h. ff. on Odyss. lib. 11. Schol. Aristophan. in Equit.

(e) Plutarch. Symposiac. lib. 1. sub fin. p. 629. See it. Cicero de Officiis, lib. 1. cap. 31.

(f) Plato de Republ. lib. 10. pag. 76;.

(g) In the Article TECMESSA.

(h) See Remark [G].

(i) Augustus had begun one of them. See Suetonius, in his Li. i, c. 85.

(k) Cicero de Offic. lib. 1. cap. 31.

(l) See Remark [E]. Quintus Calaber, lib. 5. Dictys Cret. lib. 5.

[C] *Every where invulnerable, excepting one Part of his Body*] The Origin of this particular Circumstance is as follows. *Hercules*, seeing *Telamon* uneasy, because he had no Children, begged of *Jupiter* to give him a Son, who should have a Skin as tough as that of the *Nemean* Lion, and be as courageous as the Lion itself (8). He saw an Eagle, after he had finished his Petition, and, taking it for a good Omen, he promised *Telamon* such a Son, as he had just been praying for, and ordered, that the Child should be named *Ajax*, from the Eagle (9), which had given the Presage. He returned to visit *Telamon*, after the Birth of *Ajax*, and, causing the Child to be brought to him naked, he wrapped him in the Skin of his *Nemean* Lion, which rendered the whole Body of *Ajax* invulnerable, excepting that Part, which happened to be under the Hole in the Skin, at the Part where *Hercules* carried his Quiver (10). Authors are not agreed, which this Part was; some place it under the Arm-pit (11), others in the Neck (12), others in the Side (13), others in the Breast. *Tzetzes* upon *Lycophron* is of the last Opinion. Which seems likewise to be *Ovid*'s in the thirteenth Book of the *Metamorphoses*, v. 391.

Dixit, & in pectus, tum denique vulnera passum,
Qua patuit, ferro letalem condidit ensem.

*He said, and, with so good a Will to die,
Did to his Breast the fatal Point apply.
It found his Heart, a way 'till then unknown,
Where never weapon enter'd, but his own.*
DRYDEN.

[D] *Various and even contradictory Accounts of the Causes and Circumstances of his Death*.] For some Authors say, that he killed himself in the transport of Passion, which seized him, upon the loss of *Achilles*'s Arms; others, that his Dispute with *Ulysses* was not in relation to those Arms, but to the *Palladium*, which was carried away from *Troy*, when the City was plundered. These two Accounts are incompatible; for the Arms of *Achilles* were awarded to *Ulysses*, before the taking of *Troy*, and *Ajax*'s Madness immediately followed this Decision. However it be, *Dictys Cretensis* relates, that *Ulysses* carried the *Palladium* against *Ajax*, by the Judgment of the Chiefs, and that *Ajax*, transported with Anger, threatened to kill those, who had done him this Injustice; but that, the next Day, he was found dead in his Tent, transfixed with a Sword (14). *Ulysses*, being suspected of the Murder, and perceiving the Murmurs of the Army, embarqued, and sailed away, as fast as he could. *Suidas* (15) and *Cedrenus* confess indeed, that *Ajax* and *Ulysses* disputed the *Palladium*, but not that the Judges pronounced in favour of either of them. They say, that they separated without coming to any Determination; and that *Ajax* was found dead the Night following. Some will have it, that his Combat with *Paris* was as fatal to himself as his Adversary; that he received a Wound in

(8) Pindar. Isthm. Od. 6. See also Apollodorus lib. 3.

(9) The Greeks call an Eagle αἰετός.

(10) See Suidas in Ἀσφάδικτω. The Scholiast of Sophocles in Ajacem, That of Homer in Il. l. 23. & Tzetzes in Lycophr.

(11) Suidas in ἀσφάδικτω.

(12) Apud Tzetzen; item Scholiastes Homeri in Il. l. 23.

(13) Scholiast. Sophoc. in Ajacem.

(14) Dict. Cret. lib. 5.

(15) Suidas in voce Παλλάδιον.

it, of which he died (16), at the same time that he killed *Paris* (17). Others say, that the *Trojans*, being told by an Oracle, that Iron could not hurt his Body, and that, if they would kill him, they must overwhelm him with Dirt, actually put him to Death in that manner (18).

[E] *One part of Ajax's Character was Impiety*.] When he went to the Army, his Father recommended to him to add always the Assistance of God to his own Courage. *Ajax* answered him, That Cowards are often Victorious, with such Help; as for himself, he stood in no need of it; and that he was sure to conquer without it.

Τέκνον, δορὶ
Βώλει κρατεῖν μὲν, σὺν θεῷ δ' ἀεὶ κρατεῖν.
Ὁ δ' ὑψικόμπως ἀφρόνως ἠμείψατο,
Πάτερ, θεοῖς μὲν κἂν ὁ μηδὲν ὢν ὁμοῦ
Κράτος κατακτήσαιτ' Ἐγὼ δὲ καὶ δίχα
Κείνων, πέποιθα τοῦτ' ἐπισπάσειν κλέος (19).

Mi fili, inquit, virtute
Vellis vincere, sed auxiliante Deo semper velis
vincere.
Ipse vero superbe ac stulte respondebat:
Adjuvante Deo, inquit, etiam ignavi
Vincere solent. Ego vero, vel absque
Auxilio divino, confido me istam attracturum esse
gloriam.

There is a Passage of the like Import in the same Author.

- - - - - Εἰ δε τις ὕμων
Βλάπτει φυγὼν ἂν χώ κακὸς τὸν κρείσσονα (20).

*If Jove refuse, from Heaven's ætherial Height,
To aid the Warrior in the Day of Fight,
In vain the Bravest in the Battle go:
Edgeless their Swords against the Dastard Foe.*

Minerva offered one day to give him Advice; but he answered haughtily; *Trouble not yourself about my Post: I shall give a good Account of it; you may keep your good Offices for the other Greeks* (21). Another time, she offered to drive *Ajax*'s Car in the Battle; but he would not suffer it (22): Nay he even effaced the Owl, which was painted on his Shield (23). He was afraid, no doubt, that this Picture should be taken for an Act of Devotion to *Minerva*, and a distrust of his own Strength. It would be unjust not to inform the Reader here, that *Homer* does not represent him quite so irreligious; for, if he does not himself pray to *Jupiter*, in preparing for his Combat with the valiant *Hector*, he desires, at least, that others should supplicate That God; but *in secret*,

- - - - - *Least the Foe should hear,
And deem their Prayers the mean Effect of Fear.*
POPE.

(16) Dares Phrygius, and the Scholiast of Sophocles on the Argument of Ajax.

(17) Dares Phrygius.

(18) Apud Schol. Sophocl. in

(19) Sophocl. in Ajace in, pag. 80, 81.

(20) Ibid. pg. 52.

(21) Ibid. pag. 81.

(22) Scholiast. Sophoclis.

(23) Idem.

Or

AJAX.

montory *Rhœteum* [F]. Some miraculous Adventures have been related concerning this Tomb [G]. The Mistake, which *Ronsard* believed he had committed in relation to *Ajax* [H], was corrected in a new Edition.

(24) Hom. Iliad. lib. 7. ver. 194.

Or rather *Aloud*; for, adds he, *I stand in Fear of no Man* (24);
From warlike Salamis I drew my Birth,
And, born to Combats, fear no Force on Earth.
                                                Ibid.

(25) Comm. in Emblem. 127. Alciati pag. 54;-

This is not sufficient to set him up for a Model of Devotion, as is done in the Commentary on the Emblems of *Alciatus*. "Recte Ajax apud Homerum, " qui Deos invocat sese ad arma componens; neque " enim putat sibi felicius rei bene gerendæ auspicium " capere posse, quam ab invocatione numinis (25). " ——— Ajax, in Homer, *does right to invoke the* " *Gods, when he prepares himself for the Fight;* " *he thought an Invocation of the Deity the happiest* " *Prelude to Success.*" This is to misrepresent the Fact: the Passage of the seventeenth *Iliad,* v. 645. is of no use here. He would not have the *Trojans* know, that the *Greeks* prayed to Heaven for the Success of his Arms; This may admit of two Explications: He feared, perhaps, that the *Trojans* would take this Invocation of the Deity for a Sign that he distrusted his own Courage; or else He feared, that the *Trojans,* apprized of the Vows, which the *Greeks* were offering up for him, would do the same, and even more fervently, for *Hector.* The first of these two Explications makes him guilty of a Vanity very injurious to God; the second represents him fully persuaded of the Divine Power. But what is this to the Purpose, since he consents they should pray aloud; I say, consents to it, in confidence of his own Strength and Dexterity; in a word, for this Reason, because he fears nothing, and is unconcerned, whether the *Trojans* offer up counter Prayers or not? Is this an Example of Piety, which the Commentator of *Alciatus* ought to have proposed? A certain Person was saying the other Day, that the Catholic Princes were in the wrong to suffer the Pilgrimages of *Loretto,* the Offerings, the Vows, the Prayers of forty four Hours, which they appoint, in order to obtain a glorious Campaign, to be put in the *Gazettes*; for, as soon as their Enemies are informed of this, they practise the same thing, and make yet larger Vows to the Saints of both Sexes. It was replied, that this shewed the plain dealing of those Princes: They will not surprize the Decrees of Heaven; they will not, like *Ajax,* hide the Knowledge of their Requests from their Enemies, and the means of providing against them. This would be to desire that Judgment might be given, before both Parties were heard.

[F] *They erected a stately Monument to him on the Promontory* Rhœteum.] It was one of those, which *Alexander* desired to see and honour (26). I have observed, in another Place (27), that *Pliny* is unjustly accused of being ignorant of the true Situation of this Sepulchre. But if it be true, that the *Greeks* erected this Monument, what does *Horace* mean by censuring *Agamemnon* for having left *Ajax* unburied?

(26) Diod. Sicul. L 17.

(27) *Is the Remark* [K] *of the Article* ACHILLES.

Cur Ajax, heros ab Achille secundus,
Putrescit, toties servatis clarus Achivis.
Gaudeat ut Populus Priami, Priamusque inhumato,
Per quem tot juvenes patrio caruere sepulchro (28).

(28) Horat. Sat. 3. lib. 2. ver. 193.

Say, why does Ajax, born the Greeks to save,
Rot on the Earth, unhonour'd with a Grave;
Whilst Priam's Sons with hostile Joy deride
HIS cold Remains, their Funeral Rites denied;
Whose Hand had hurl'd to Pluto's gloomy Reign
So many Trojan Chiefs, untimely slain;
Whose Limbs, unburied on their native Shore,
Devouring Dogs, and hungry Vultures tore?

I answer, that The Poet makes use only of one of the Incidents of the Tragedy of *Ajax;* it is That, wherein *Sophocles* feigns, that *Agamemnon* would not consent, that *Ajax* should be honoured with Funeral Rites. He yielded at last to the pressing Instances of *Teucer.* Observe, that some Authors say, that the Body of *Ajax* was not burnt, and others that it was. *Dictys Cretensis* and *Quintus Calaber* are of the latter Opinion; *Philostratus* of the former. He tells us, that *Calchas* declared it contrary to the Precepts of Religion to permit those to be burnt, who had killed themselves (29). See in the same *Philostratus,* how the *Athenians* distinguished themselves in honouring this Hero. *Pausanias* informs us, that one of the Tribes bore the Name of *Ajax* (30); and that the Honours they decreed to him and his Son *Eurysaces,* were yet subsisting (31). Those of *Salamis* had a Temple to *Ajax* (32). The whole *Greek* Nation invoked him some time before the Battle of *Salamis* (33), and afterwards consecrated to him one of the Ships, which they had taken from the *Persians,* in that memorable Day, as being part of the first Fruits dedicated to the Gods (34).

(29) Philostr. in Heroic.

(30) Pausan. lib. 1. pag. 4. See Plut. Sympos. lib. 1. Quæst. 10. p. 628.
Herodot. lib. 5. c. 66.

(31) Pausan. ibid. pag. 33.

[G] *Some miraculous Adventures* ——— *relating to this Tomb.*] *Ulysses,* having suffered Shipwreck on the Coasts of *Sicily,* lost, among other things, the Armour of *Achilles.* The Shield was afterwards thrown a shore by the Waves near the Sepulchre of *Ajax,* where it hung; but the next Day it was struck with Thunder. This is what *Ptolemy* the Son of *Hephæstion* reports (35). *Pausanias* says, in general, that the Storm threw the Arms of *Achilles* on *Ajax's* Tomb, after the Shipwreck of *Ulysses* (36). The Story was curious, and afforded too many moral Reflexions, to be omitted by the Poets. See in the *Anthologia* what the *Greeks* have sung on this Subject (37). *Alciatus* borrowed one of his Emblems from thence (38). As for the Prodigies, or Miracles, for which *Ajax* was famed after his Death, see *Pausanias,* at the thirty fourth Page of the first Book. Before I end this Remark, I shall add, that the Waves having half opened the Tomb of *Ajax,* People were curious to look into it, and observed that one of his Knee-Bones was as big as one of the *Discus's* or Quoits, which were made use of in the Games (39). The Person, who related it to *Pausanias,* would have him judge from thence of *Ajax's* Stature (40). *Homer* says that he was remarkably tall.

(32) Id. ib.

(33) Herodot. lib. 8. cap. 64.

(34) Id. ib. cap. 121.

(35) Apud Photium, pag. 484.

(36) Pausan. lib. 1. p. 34.

(37) Anthol. lib. 1. c. 22. initio.

(38) *It is the* 28th.

(39) Pausan. ubi supra.

'Ανὴρ ἠΰς, τε μέγας τε,
"Εξοχος Ἀργείων κεφαλήν ἠδ' ἔυρέας ὤμους (41).

----- *With Giant Strength endu'd,*
Whose brawny Shoulders, and whose swelling Chest,
And lofty Stature, far exceed the rest.
                                                POPE.

(40) *See some Mistakes in relation to this Passage of Pausanias, in Rem ark* [D] *of the foregoing Article.*

(41) Hom. Iliad. 3. ver. 226.

[H] *The Mistake, which* Ronsard *believed he had committed.*] He had ranked *Ajax* among the Heroes who took *Troy*; but he left him out in the second Edition of his *Franciad,* having been told by *Florens Christianus,* that *Ajax* killed himself before the taking of the Town (42). He was plainly ignorant, that, according to some Authors, this great Captain did not die, 'till after the sacking of *Troy*; for, if he had known it, he would have told *Florens Christianus,* that he was not ignorant of what *Homer, Sophocles, Ovid,* and others have related; but that he knew likewise the Opinion of others; and that he chose rather to follow *Dictys Cretensis,* than *Homer*; and thus he might have avoided the Acknowledgment of a Mistake: A Confession very ungrateful to a Poet, and even to other Authors.

(42) *See* Florens Christianus's *Notes on the* Philoctetes *of* Sophocles.

AJAX, the Son of *Teucer,* caused a Temple to be built to *Jupiter* in *Olbus,* a City of *Cilicia.* The Priest of That Temple was Lord of the Country called *Tracheotis.* Several Tyrants endeavoured to invade this Country, and to support themselves in it, so that it became a true Theatre of Robberies. After these Tyrants were extirpated, it was called the Country of *Teucer,* and the Priesthood. These are the Names it had in *Strabo's* time, who adds, that most of it's Pontiffs had born the Name of *Teucer,* or That of *Ajax*; and that *Aba,* the Daughter of *Zenophanes,* one of the Tyrants, being

AJAX. AIGUILLON.

being allied to that Family by Marriage, became Mistress of the Country, after her Father had governed it in quality of her Guardian. She was confirmed in the Possession of it by *Marc Antony* and *Cleopatra*, to whom she had made her Court with great Address. After her Death, the Country returned into the Power of the lawful Possessors (*a*). We may infer from hence, that the Supplement to *Moreri's* Dictionary is very erroneous in this Article [*A*].

(*a*) See Strabo, lib. 14. pag. 462.

[*A*] *The Supplement to Moreri — is very erroneous in this Article.*] After having thoroughly considered the Matter, I find the shortest way is to set down the whole Article of the Supplement: Here it is. Ajax, *the Son of* Teucer, *King of* Salamis, *in the Island of* Cyprus, *having succeeded his Father, consecrated a Temple to* Jupiter, *in the City of* Olbus. *He maintained himself in the Possession of this Kingdom, against several Princes, who endeavour'd to make themselves Masters of it, and left it to his Posterity, who most of them bore the Name of* Ajax, *or of* Teucer. Strabo, *lib.* 14. I observe, in confutation of this Account, I. That it deceives the Reader, by inducing him to believe, in virtue of this Narrative, that the Town of *Olbus* was in the Island of *Cyprus*. II. That it is not true, that *Strabo* says, *Ajax* succeeded his Father in the Kingdom of *Salamis*. The indefatigable *Meursius*, who took so much pains to discover the Names of all those, who reign'd in the Island of *Cyprus*, did not meet with a single *Ajax* (1). III. That it is not true, that several Princes endeavour'd to wrest the Kingdom of *Salamis* from *Ajax*. Their Attempts were aim'd against *Tracheotis*, the Patrimony, or Demesn of the Church of *Olbian Jupiter*, in *Cilicia*; and *Strabo* does not say, that they endeavour'd to dispossess *Ajax* of it, nor that *Ajax* was in Possession of it. A Man may build a Temple without being the Priest of it, and without possessing the Revenues, with which it is endow'd. IV. That, supposing *Ajax* had been both Prince and Priest of *Tracheotis*, it would be false, that he kept the Possession of it, and that he left it to his Descendants; it is plain, from the Relation of *Strabo*, that the Series of lawful Successors was sometimes interrupted.

(1) See his *Treatise* de Cypro, lib. 2. cap. 7. & seq.

AJAX, an Ecclesiastic, famous for his Piety, and Exemplary Life, in the Reign of *Theodosius*. He had a Brother, whose Name was *Zeno*, who was equally virtuous. They distinguished themselves for the practice of Virtue, at first, not in a Solitude, but in the City of *Gaza*; afterwards they addicted themselves to a Monastic Life. They were often very ill treated, for courageously maintaining the Orthodox Faith against the *Pagans*. *Ajax* had married a very handsome Woman; but it is said he knew her but Three times, from whence proceeded Three Sons; after which, he separated himself from her, as to Conjugal Commerce, and wisely governed the Church of *Botolium*. He brought up Two of his Sons to the Study of Divinity, and to Celibacy, and married the Third (*a*).

(*a*) Sozem. lib. 7. c. 28.

AIGUILLON, a small Town of *Guienne*, on the Confluence of the Rivers *Lot* and *Garonne*, four Leagues below *Agen* [*A*], was erected into a Duchy, with the Dignity of Peerage annexed to it, in favour of the Duke of *Maienne*, in the Year 1599. The Letters Patents for it were confirmed in Parliament the Year following (*a*); but, the family of that Duke being extinct, the Erection of it was renewed in the Reign of *Lewis* XIII, in the Year 1638, by Letters-Patents, which were confirmed the same Year (*b*). Cardinal *Richelieu* caused this to be done, in Favour of his Niece, the Lady *de Combalet*, who was afterwards so well known by the Name of the DUCHESS OF AIGUILLON. We shall speak of her in her proper place (*c*). She left this Dutchy by Will to her Niece *Mary Magdalen Teresa de Vignerod*, Sister to the Duke of *Richelieu* (*d*). Nothing is more remarkable in History, than the Resistance made by the Town of *Aiguillon* [*B*] in 1346, against the Duke of *Normandy*, who was afterwards King *John*. We are ashamed to read the account of it at present; and our Military Men cannot sufficiently express their Wonder, that the Art of War was at that time so inconsiderable in respect to what it is now. If the Duke of *Normandy*, eldest Son to the King of *France*, had taken *Aiguillon* after fourteen Months Siege, he would have deserved the greatest Triumph; and yet, at present, such a Town, as This was at that time, would hardly do honour to a Colonel,

(*a*) The 2d of March.
(*b*) The 19th of May.
(*c*) In the Article (VIGNEROD Mary de).
(*d*) See the State of France, Tom. 2. p. 88, 80. Edit. 1680.

[*A*] *Below* Agen.] If I had thought proper to observe, in the middle of what Towns *Aiguillon* is situated, I should not have pitch'd upon *Agen* and *Nerac*, as Mr *Moreri* did; for these three Places form a Triangle; but I should have chosen *Agen* and *Tonnains*, the one above, the other below *Aiguillon*, on the *Garonne*. This Fault is so much the more considerable, as there is no Reader but will conclude from it, that *Nerac* is situated on the same River.

[*B*] *Is more remarkable — than the Resistance made by the Town of* AIGUILLON.] *Papyrius Masson* says, that the Siege continued fourteen Months. "*Acilionem* (1) urbem irrita Joannis, postea Regis Francorum, & tunc Ducis Normanniæ, quatuordecim mensium obsidione memorabilem (2). — The City Acilio (AIGUILLON) *famous for the fourteen Months fruitless Siege of* John, *afterwards King of* France, *and then Duke of* Normandy." The numerous Army of the Duke of *Normandy* is no less to be considered, than the length of the Siege. "This Duke came to *Toulouse*, in the beginning of "*January*, with an hundred thousand Men bearing "Arms. All this dreadful Multitude did nothing in "three Months, but take some paltry Towns in *A-* "*genois*, and afterwards the City of *Angouleme*, from "whence they attack'd *Tonneins*, and then besieg'd "*Aiguillon* ——— very well stor'd, and fortify'd, for "those times (3)." The manner of the Attack is a third remarkable Particular. "This whole Century (4) "has not produc'd a more memorable Siege, if we "consider either the Attack or the Defence. It was "attack'd three times a Day for a whole Week to-"gether; afterwards they plied it with Artillery and "Engines, both by Land and by Water." The following Citation takes in the two Passages of *Mezerai*. I fetch it from *Catel* (5). "*Froissard*, in the 121st Chap-"ter of his first Volume, says, That when the Duke "of *Normandy* besieg'd, with a hundred thousand "*French*, the City of *Aiguillon*, in possession of the "*English*, he sent to *Toulouse* for eight of the greatest "Engines that were in that City, and when the In-"habitants of *Aiguillon* were upon the point of being "attack'd, it was agreed by the *French* Lords; that "those of *Toulouse*, *Carcassonne* and *Beaucaire* should "attack them from Morning 'till Noon, and those, of, "*Rouergue*, *Cahors*, and *Agenois*, from Noon 'till "Night (6)." *Mezerai* makes the three Assaults in a Day continue, but a Week, which does not answer the Expectation,

(1) Baudrand calls it Aguillionum.
(2) Papyr. Masson's *Description of the Rivers of* Gaul.
(3) Mezerai, Abreg. Chron. ad ann. 1346. Tom. 3. pag. 14. Holl. Edit. 1673.
(4) It was the XIVth Century.
(5) Id. Ibid.
(6) Catel's *Memoirs for the History of* Languedoc, pag. 563.

AIGUILLON. AILLI. 163

Colonel, who should take it at the first Onset. The *Romans* made almost the same Reflexion, when they compared the first Conquests of their City [C] with the Victories they gained afterwards. *Mezerai* strangely puzzles the Affair I am speaking of (*e*). *Aiguillon* had not altogether the same Success against the *English*, as against the Duke of *Normandy*; for, when they besieged it in 1430, they did not take the Castle; they took only the Town, and plundered it (*f*).

(e) See Mezerai [B].

(f) Darna[ii] Antiquii of Aquit. pag. 100.

Expectation he had raised in his Readers; for what is a Week in fourteen Months? The Idea he gives us of the Attack is certainly too narrow and confin'd. Besides, he is guilty of a Chronological Error. According to his Account, the Duke of *Normandy* came to *Toulouse* in the Month of *January*, 1346, and spent three Months in taking some paltry Towns; afterwards he took *Angouleme*, and then return'd towards the *Garonne*, took *Tonneins*, besieg'd *Aiguillon*, and rais'd the Siege of it by reason of the Battle of Creci. This Battle was fought on the 26th of *August*, 1346. According to this Narrative of *Mezerai*, it is not only impossible, that the Siege of *Aiguillon* should have lasted fourteen Months, but even, considering the Custom of those times, that the Siege should have been very long: And it is to speak improperly, to say, that the Duke of *Normandy* push'd it vigorously (7). We must place the Arrival of this Prince at *Toulouse* in the Year 1345.

(-) Mezerai. ibid.

[C] *When they compar'd the first Conquests of their City.*] See *Florus* and his exclamatory Style. " Sora " (quis credat?) & Algidum terrori fuerant: Satricum " atque Corniculum provinciæ. De Verulla & Bo- " villis pudet, sed triumphavimus. Tibur, nunc sub- " urbanum, & æstivæ Præneste deliciæ, nuncupatia " in Capitolio votis, petebantur. Idem tunc Fæsulæ, " quod Carræ nuper; idem nemus Aricinum, quod " Hercynius saltus: Fregellæ, quod Gefericum: Ti- " beris, quod Euphrates. Coriolus quoque (pro pu- " dor!) victus adeò gloriæ fuit, ut captum oppidum " Caius Marcius Coriolanus, quasi Numantiam aut " Africam, nomen induerit (8).—— *Even Sora (who would think it?) and Algidum struck Terror: Satricum and Corniculum were Provinces.* *We blush'd and Bovillæ, (though now we are asham'd of it) were matter of Triumph. We made solemn Vows in the Capitol for the Conquest of Tibur, now Rome's Suburbs, and Præneste's Summer Pleasures. Fæsulæ was, then, what Carræ was lately; the Aricinian Grove, what the Hyrcinian Wood; Fregellæ, what Geforicum; Tiber, what Euphrates. The Victory gain'd over Coriolus (I am asham'd to say it) was thought so glorious, that Caius Marcius Coriolanus assum'd the Captive City's Name, as it had been another Numantia, or Africa.* " But what shame soever it was to the *French*, not to be able to take *Aiguillon*, with so many Men, commanded by their King's eldest Son, it was a great Honour to the *English*, that they defended the Post so long.

(8) Florus. cap. 11.

AILLI (*a*) (PETER de) Bishop of *Cambray* (*b*) and Cardinal, was born at *Compiegne* in *Picardy* [*A*], in the Year 1350. His Family was very obscure; some say He was (*c*) Under-Porter of the College of *Navarre*; but they are mistaken. He was not entered in That College till about the Year 1372. He was admitted a Pensioner there, among the Students in Divinity. He was at that time Sollicitor for the *French* Nation in the University of *Paris*, and capable of setting up for a good Author, as he made it appear by his *Treatises of Logic* [*B*] according to the Hypotheses of the *Nominals*, and his *Treatises concerning the Nature of the Soul*, *and that of Meteors*. He shewed such great Penetration and Elegance in his Works, that he laid thereby the Foundation of That high Reputation, to which he raised himself. He had as good Success in his Explication of *Peter Lombard*, in the Year 1375. This happy Application to Scholastic Learning did not hinder him from being a good Preacher. He took his Doctor's Degree in 1380, and had a Canonship given him at Noion. He was recalled to *Paris* Four Years after, to exercise the Office of *Great Master of the College of Navarre*. He had a great Number of Scholars there, and among others *John Gerson*, and *Nicolas de Clemangis*. He pleaded with so much Force in 1387, before the Pope (*d*), against a *Jacobin* (*e*) who had appealed from the Judgment, which the Faculty of Divinity of *Paris* had pronounced against him, that he obtained a Confirmation of the Sentence. He wrote likewise a Treatise against the same *Jacobin*. This gained him so great a Reputation, that, in 1389, he was made Confessor and Almoner

(*a*) In Latin Petrus de Alliaco, or ab Alliaco, or ab Alyaco, or Alliacensis, or Alliacus, or Alliacus, &c.

(*b*) The et, & Vossius de Hist. Lat. pag. 45 & de Cient. Mathem. p. 182, 228, & de hist: p of that City.

(*c*) See Remark [*A*].

(*d*) It was the Antipope Clem. VII. who resided at Avignon.

[*A*] *Born at Compiegne in Picardy.*] This appears by the public Registers of the Church of *Cambray* (1); so that we may place in the List of *Thevet's* Untruths what he says concerning *Peter d'Ailli's* native Country. " He was born, *says* he (2), in a very obscure " Village of Germany, called *Ailly*, from which, to " hide the meanness of his Extraction, he took his " Name. He was so poor, that he was obliged to " serve as Under-porter to the College of *Navarre*, " to support himself in his Application to the Study " of Literature." *Volaterran* had already publish'd, " that Peter d'Ailli was a German (3).

[*B*] *By his Treatises of Logic*] He understood it perfectly, and was indebted to it for that Strength and Skill, wherewith he supported his own Opinions, and overthrew those of others. The famous *Wesselus* of *Groningen* speaks of him in this manner. " Quis " unquam ad illum apicem Theologiæ, quo Petrus " de Alliaco conscendit, absque definitionibus, divi- " sionibus, argumentationibus, instantiis logicalibus " perveniret? In disputationibus dico, ubi discussione " diserta opus est. Quomodo Petrus Joannem de " Monteson in Rota de errore quatuordecim illarum " conclusionum concussisse, nisi distinctione multi- " plici, aut elenchi ignorantia antecedente vel conse- " quente delusam docuisset? Opus igitur Theologicis " Logicam inferre. Et *GERSON* iste quo tandem " tantus ipse Theologus, nisi per accuratissimam il- " lam suam Magistri Petri Logicam, evasit (4)?—— " *Who can ever arrive at that Heights of Divinity*, " *to which Peter d'Ailli attain'd, without Definitions*, " *Divisions, Syllogisms, and Logical Instances? I* " *mean, in Controversies, which require a rational* " *Disquisition. How could he have convinc'd John* " *de Monteson of Error in his fourteen Conclusions*, " *before the Pope, had he not shew'd in what manner* " *he was led into them, either by heaping Distinction* " *upon Distinction, or by an Ignorance of the Argument in the Antecedent, or Consequent? Divinity* " *therefore stands in need of Logical Conclusions. And* " *how could the famous GERSON ever have been* " *the great Divine he was, without this accurate Logic of Peter d'Ailli?*" We must remark, that Mr *de Launoi* is of Opinion, the Words *Rota de errore*, &c. in the foregoing Passage, were the Title of a Book written by *Peter d'Ailli*; but I chuse to understand by *Rota*, the Place, where the Pope heard the Disputants. Without doubt Logic contributed much to the following Elogy of *Peter d'Ailli*: " A- " quila Franciæ, atque aberrantium à veritate malleus " indefessus (5).—— *The Eagle of France, and the* " *indefatigable Combatant of Heretics*."

[*C*] *Almoner*

(1) Apud Launoium Hist. Coll. Navari, pag. 137.

(2) Thevet's Illustrious Men, Tom. 7. pag. 80. 12mo.

(3) See Gesner. Bibl. fol. 543. verso.

(4) Wesselus de file Auth ty of the Pope, &c. apud Launoium Hist. Navar. pag. 469.

(5) Launoi, ibi supra, pag. 136, 476.

164 AILLI.

Almoner to *Charles* VI [C], and Chancellor of the University. Five Years after, the first Dignity of the Holy Chapel of *Paris* was conferred upon him; to wit that of Treasurer. So many different Employments did not hinder him from applying himself earnestly to find out the most effectual means of putting a stop to the Schism, which divided the Church of *Rome*. He went from the King to the Anti-Pope *Benedict* XIII. in 1394, and gave such an advantageous Character of him at his return, that it was resolved, in the King's Council, to acknowledge him for lawful Pope. He obtained the Bishoprick of *Puy* in *Vellai* (*f*), at the end of the Year 1395, and That of *Cambray*, in the beginning of the Year following. He was much esteemed by *Boniface* IX. and he made use of his interest with him in procuring a Doctor of Divinity to be established in all the Episcopal Churches of the Kingdom. He preached at *Genoa*, in the Year 1405, on the Mystery of the Trinity, before *Benedict* XIII. and persuaded That Pope to enjoin all the Churches to celebrate the Feast of the Trinity. He was admired for his Learning and Prudence in the Council of *Pisa*, in the Year 1409. He maintained, in all the Assemblies of *Paris*, which debated concerning a Remedy for the Schism, that the only way to put a stop to it was to call a General Council. Two Years after, he was promoted to the Purple (*g*). He went into *Germany*, in the Year 1414, in Quality of the Pope's Legate. He presided at the third Session of the Council of *Constance*; he composed Three Pieces during the sitting of the Council: One, *De emendanda Ecclesia*; another, *De duodecim honoribus beati Josephi*; another, *De modo & forma eligendi Papæ*: And no Person had a greater share, than He, in the Affairs of That memorable Assembly, which lasted Three Years. He died in the Year 1425 [D], and was buried in his Cathedral of *Cambray*. He was a great Benefactor to the College of *Navarre* [E], and left great Sums, by his Will, for Services to be performed in several Churches for the Repose of his Soul (*h*). Mr *de Launoi*, who supplied me with this Account, does not forget to look upon *Peter d' Ailli*'s Doctrine concerning the Ecclesiastical Power, as a Blemish in a beautiful Body. He imputes it to the Misfortunes of the Times (*i*); but I wonder he forgot another Blemish of This Doctor, I mean his Fondness for Judicial Astrology [F]. Lastly;

our

[C] *Almoner to Charles VI.*] See *du Peyrat*, pag. 345, of the Antiquities of the King's Chapel. He observes there, that "*Peter d'Ailli* never had the "Quality of great Almoner of *France*, nor of the "King's great Almoner: They were Titles unknown "at that Time, and did not come in Fashion, 'till "the Reign of *Charles* VIII. and of *Francis* I. whatever the Author of the *Gallia Christiana* may say, "in which the Continuator of the Annals of *Baronius* is likewise mistaken."

[D] *He died in the Year 1425.*] It is strange, that a Person of this Rank and Distinction should die, without our knowing certainly where, or in what Year. Some say that he died in *Germany*, in the Year 1416. Others, that he died at *Avignon*, on the 8th of *August*, 1425, when he was the Pope's Legate in *France* (6). Others allow, that he died at *Avignon*, but place his Death in the Year 1426 (7). Mr *de Launoi* is contented with placing it in the Year 1425, in the 479th Page of his Book; but he had said, (Page 129) that *Peter d'Ailli* died, when he was Legate of the Holy See in *Germany*, in the Year 1423 (8). "Anno postquam vastatum est à "Burgundionibus quinto. — *Five Years after it "was laid waste by the Burgundians*." Now, in the 126th Page of the same Work, he has placed this Ravage in the Year 1418. The Register of the Church of *Cambray* says, that he died on the 9th of *October*, 1425, being Legate of the Holy See in the Lower *Germany*, and that, on the 9th of *July* following, his Body was carried to *Cambray*, where it was buried behind the great Altar. The difference of 1416, and 1426, proceeds from an Error of the Press; the Figure 1 being, by mistake, plac'd instead of the Figure 2, occasion'd two different Opinions.

[E] *He was a great Benefactor to the College of Navarre.*] He was called it's second Founder (9). He built the House of the Divines, but not the Library. *Spondanus*, who affirms it, is mistaken; it was the Work of *Charles* VIII. "Spondanus in annalibus "Ecclesiasticis prodidit ab eo extructam esse bibliothe- "cam. Sed aberrat; id est opus Caroli octavi Re- "gis, cujus & nomen μονόγραμμον in Bibliotheca "vitro centies depingitur, & statua in occidentali tur- "binati parietis cono erecta conspicitur (10)." It is true, indeed, *Peter d'Ailli* would have part of his Benefactions to the College laid out in purchasing Books; and that he often presented them with Books (11). I cannot tell, whether he gave them his own Library, as *Aubert Miræus* assures us he did: "Alliacus, says he (12), anno 1425, Avenione mo- "riens, bibliothecam suam legavit Navarræo Pa- "risiis Collegio, quam ibi magna cum voluptate ali- "quando vidimus. — D'Ailli, *dying at Avignon "in the Year* 1425, *left his Library to the College "of Navarre at Paris, which I have formerly seen "there with great Pleasure.*" I don't find, that Mr *Launoi* says so; his Silence alone is sufficient to refute this *Flemish* Writer.

[F] *His fondness for Judicial Astrology* (13).] *Bellarmin* has not overlooked this Blemish: "Unum "est, says he (14), in quo reprehenditur hic auctor, "quod videlicet sensifle videatur Christi nativitatem "prænosci potuisse ex genethliacis observationibus, "atque ad hoc adduxerit apparitionem stellæ, quæ "apparuit Magia. — *There is one thing, for which "This Author deserves Censure; I mean, his Opinion, "that the Nativity of Christ might have been cal- "culated Astrologically, and his appearing, in proof "of this, to the Phænomenon of the Star, which ap- "peared to the Wise Men.*" Others observe, that *Peter d'Ailli* maintained, in his Book *de Concordia Historiæ & Astrologiæ Divinatricis*, that *Noah's* Flood, the Birth of JESUS CHRIST, and such other Miracles, and all the Prodigies, might have been foretold by Astrology (15); and that he referred the Origins, Revolutions, and Destructions of Commonwealths, and Religions, to the Conjunctions of the Higher Planets (16). *Bodin* adds, That *Johannes Picus, Prince of Mirandola*, takes the Hypothesis of *Peter d' Arliac* (17) *for certain, without enquiring any farther after the Truth*; *though, out of thirty six great Conjunctions, which That Cardinal observed, from 115 Years after the Creation of the World, 'till the Year of our Lord 1385, not six of them proved true* (18). [*De Alliaco* is the vulgar *Latin* Name of *Peter d' Ailli* (*Alliacus)*: from whence *Bodin* formed his *Arliac*, by changing the first of the two *ll* into an *r*, as in *Varlet, Merlin, Merlusine*, from *Vallet, Melin, Melusine*. Rem, Crit.] This Passage of *Bodin* was thus drawn up in the *Latin* Edition, *Mirum mihi visum est quamobrem J. Picus Mirandulæ princeps illius hominis errores sane pudendos in cœlestium orbium doctrina pro certis & compertis demonstrationibus habuerit; cum enim post orbem conditum anno centesimo decimo quinto usque ad annum Christi 1385, triginta sex Jovis & Saturni concursus tradiderit, vix tamen sex illos es quo docuit loco ac tempore descripserit*. The same *Bodin* attacks the very Foundation of these Hypotheses: "Cardinal *d' Arliac*, says he "(19), begins with the great Conjunctions at the "Time of the Creation of the World, supposing,

"according

our *Peter d'Ailli*, who submitted Scepters and Crowns to the Ecclesiastical Power; who endeavoured to multiply Festivals; who founded such a great number of Masses for the Repose of his Soul; and who condemned *John Hus* to Death [G]; appears nevertheless in the *Catalogue of the Witnesses of the Truth* [H], as a Forerunner of *Luther* and of *Calvin*. The *Cartesians* likewise rank him in the Number of their Forerunners, in

"according to his Account, that there are 7158 Years, following the Error of *Alphonsus*, which was rejected by all the *Hebrews*, and at present with common Consent by all Churches.——And therefore it is an intolerable Error to suppose the great Conjunction of the three higher Planets to have fallen out in the Year of the Creation 320, and to lay it down, that there are at present 7118 Years elapsed, which is carrying it up to twelve hundred Years before the Creation of the World." This manner of opposing *Peter d'Ailli* cannot be decisive at present, when we consider, that several learned Men prefer the Calculation of the *Greek* Bible, concerning the Duration of the World, before the Calculation of the *Hebrew* Text. *Vossius* had more reason to insult him, on the rise of the Arian Heresy, than on the Duration of the World. These are *Vossius*'s Words; and we find by them, that our Astrologer placed the beginning of That Heresy seven hundred Years after *JESUS CHRIST*, which betrays a very gross Ignorance. "Valde etiam futile est fundamentum quod arti isti ponit. Ait ab initio mundi usque ad diluvium fluxisse annos 2042. à diluvio ad natalem Christi 3102. His ita constitutis, totus est in eo ut ostendat, quandocunque mirandum aliquid contigit in terris, etiam illustrem aliquam stellarum conjunctionem apparuisse in cœlis. Atqui falsissimum est quod sibi sumit de anno vel diluvii vel natalis Domini: Nec levis est error, sed spississimus; in priori quidem numero, annorum pene sexcentorum, in altero autem, paulo pauciorum. Quid mirum? omnino Cameracensis fuit Chronologiæ imperitissimus, ut vel arguit quod Arrianam Hæresim cœpisse dicat anno Christi septingentesimo, quam verisimilius tum pene extinctam dixisset. Ortam vero constat sere initio seculi quarti.—— The Foundation, which he lays of This Science, is very weak. He tells us, that from the Creation to the Deluge were 2042 Years [20]; from the Deluge to the Birth of Christ 3102. If this were admitted, it would yet rest upon him to shew, that, upon every wonderful Event, there appeared in the Heavens some remarkable Conjunction of the Stars. But his Hypothesis concerning the Year of the Deluge, and the Birth of Christ, is most false. Nor is it a trivial Error, but a very considerable one; being no less, than a Mistake of near six hundred Years in the former, and something less in the latter [21]. Nor are we to wonder at it; since the Bishop of Cambray's utter Ignorance of Chronology appears in his placing the Rise of the Arian Heresy in the 700th Year of Christ, which he might, with more appearance of Truth, have said was extinct at that Time. For it is certain it commenced at the beginning of the fourth Century [22]." If *Thevet* had wrote with Judgment, would he have spoke of *Peter d'Ailli* in the following Terms? "I could wish that all, who set up for Astrologers, would carefully peruse his Books; it would not be Labour lost. For besides the extraordinary Observations I have related [23], they would find there a Sentence drawn up against those, who, under the Name of true Astrology, take a Pleasure in being imposed upon by the false Mask of Astrology, introducing an *Astral Idolatry*, altogether abominable [24]." This pretended Idolatry was no more to be feared in *Thevet's* Time, than the religious Worship of the Earth: So that if *Peter d'Ailli's* Books were only fit to convert this kind of Idolaters, they were almost useless. But, as, on the other side, they were calculated to keep up the Credit of Astrology, by reason of the Influences, which the Author attributes to the Conjunctions of the Planets, things of which *Thevet* says never a Word, the reading of them was much more prejudicial, than useful.

[G] *Who condemned* John Hus *to Death*.] It was not without exhorting him to submit, and assuring him it was the best way he could take. "Examinatis dictis testium, & recitatis articulis erroneis, in Patrum confessu, Cardinalis Cameracensis, judex causæ deputatus à Concilio, dixit ad Joannam Huss:

En viæ duæ propositæ sunt tibi; ut ex his eligas unam; aut te offeras omnino totum in potestatem & gratiam Concilii, ejúsque decretis super hac re acquiescas; ita namque fiet ut Concilium ob honorem domini nostri Regis Romanorum nunc præsentis, ac fratris ejus Bohemiæ Regis, clementer acturum sit tecum; aut si ex dictis articulis quosdam tenere ac defendere intendas, & desideras aliam audientiam, concedetur tibi quidem; sed tunc scias hic esse magnos & illuminatos viros, qui fortissima habent adversus articulos tuos fundamenta, & verendum est ne inde gravioribus involvaris erroribus. Id consulendo dixerim tibi, non ut judex [25]. —— *The Witnesses having been examined, and the erroneous Articles recited, in the Assembly of the Fathers, the Cardinal Bishop of* Cambray, *having been deputed Judge of the Cause by the Council, addressed himself to* John Hus, *in the following Manner. You have your Choice of two Ways; either to throw yourself wholly upon the Power and Favour of the Council, and acquiesce in their Sentence; which will induce the Council, in respect to our Lord the King of the Romans now present, and his Brother the King of Bohemia, to deal mildly with you; or, if you have thoughts of maintaining and defending any of the aforesaid Articles, and desire another hearing, it shall be granted you; but be assured, here are great and enlightened Men, who can produce strong and fundamental Arguments against your Articles; and you must take care you do not involve yourself in still greater Errors. I give you this Advice, as your Friend, not as your Judge.*" Mr de *Launoi*, having related this, adds, that This Heretic chose rather to maintain his Opinions obstinately, and to be burnt, than to follow the wholsome Advice of Cardinal *d'Ailli*. Verum litigiosus homo dogmata sua nimis pertinaciter propugnare maluit & comburi, quam usque adeo salubre Cardinalis Alliaci consilium sequi.

[H] *Appeared nevertheless in the Catalogue of the Witnesses of the Truth*.] "He was delegated, by the Determination of the Council of the *French* Church, to require the two Popes, who contested the Papacy, to resign the Papal See. He was answered, that the Popes of *Rome* are never guilty of Schism; but that the *French* Prelates were purposely Schismatics. He was afterwards sent back again, according to the Advice of the Council, held at *Paris*, with the Sieur *John Mangre*, Marshal de *Boucicaud*, who afterwards spoke his Mind very freely to the Anti-Pope at *Avignon*; nor was Cardinal *d'Ailli* behind hand in severely reproving him [26]. And this seems to be the Reason, why *Henry Pantaleon* ranked him among those, who, at that time, exclaimed, and wrote against the Ambition of the Popes, the Corruption of the Church, and the Schisms and Divisions, which sprang up daily; telling us, That he wrote a Book, entituled, *Of the Reformation of the Church*; which however is not to be met with in the Catalogue of his Books, which is very large, both in Diviinity and in Mathematics [27]." Nothing is more true, than what *Pantaleon* affirms concerning this Book of *Peter d'Ailli*. As to the Catalogue of *the Witnesses of the Truth*, published by *Francis Illyricus*, we find *Peter d'Ailli* in it condemning the Doctrine of Transubstantiation, and laying before the Council of *Constance* a Project of Reformation; according to which, the Court of *Rome* was to be deprived of the numberless ways and means of heaping up Money; the Prelates were to be compelled to live an exemplary Life, and to discharge their Duties; the Pomp of Ceremonies, the unnecessary Holydays, the Abuse of Fasts, and the Canonization of Saints, were to be abolished; and the Number of Monks, Images, and Churches to be diminished [29]. We may be sure that all the Writings of *Peter d'Ailli* are not calculated to please the Court of *Rome*, since three or four of them have been inserted in the Appendix of the *Fasciculus rerum expetendarum & fugiendarum* [30]. Orthuinus Gratius

in the Question relating to Accidents [*I*]. He had been turned out of his Episcopal Church, if we may believe *Erasmus*; who adds, That his Exile procured him a Cardinal's Hat (*k*). He wrote many Books [*K*], some of which were never printed [*L*]. He composed likewise Verses, such as they were, in the Vulgar Language [*M*]. Consult the Authors cited by *Moreri*, and, instead of *Frissart*, to whom he refers us; read *Froissard*.

Gratius had already inserted in That *Fasciculus* this Cardinal's Treatise *de Emendatione Ecclesiæ*. What I have said concerning the Diminution of the Number of Monks, does not agree with what *Thevet* had been informed of; to wit, That *Peter d'Ailli* had composed a Book entituled, *The Buckler of Poverty*, wherein he apologised for the Mendicant Fryars (31).

[*I*] *The Carthusians likewise ranked him in the Number of their Forerunners, in the Question relating to Accidents.*] A Professor of *Louvain*, one of the most strenuous Opposers of Mr *Descartes*, became "one of his most zealous Followers, after he had found "in some Authors, very much approved of by the "Church, his Opinion concerning Transubstantia- "tion, which was almost the only Point, which "stuck with him. Some time after, he inferred, "in his Theological Theses, an Abstract of a Book, "which Cardinal *d'Ailli*, Bishop of *Cambray* com- "posed on the Master of the Sentences, to shew, "that the Cardinal proposes Mr *Descartes's* Opinions, "concerning the Accidents of the Eucharist*, and re- "conciles it with the Definition of the Oecumeni- "cal Council of *Constance* (32).

[*K*] *He wrote many Books.*] His *Commentaries on the Master of the Sentences*, and the *four Treatises* inserted in the Appendix to the *Fasciculus rerum expetendarum*, were printed at *Strasburg* in 1490. A Volume of his *Treatises* and *Sermons* was printed in the same Place, at the same time. Part of his Treatises was reprinted at *Douay*, in the Year 1634. under the Care of *Leander de St Martin*, Hebrew Professor at *Douay*. *Thevet* assures us, "That he had "a Work of *Peter d'Ailli*, which was printed in "the Year 1410, on the twelfth of *August*, when "the Art of Printing began to be in use in *France*, "in which there is a great Number of Mathema- "tical Figures (33)." This cannot be; for the Art of Printing was not discovered 'till about the Year 1440. He might have said, that the *Sacramentale* of this Author was printed at *Louvain* in 1487, and his *Quæstiones in sphæram mundi Joannis de Sacrobosco cum Commentariis Petri Cirveli Darocensis Hispani*, at *Paris* in 1488 (34). His *Meteors* was printed at *Strasburg*, in the Year 1504. and at *Vienna*, in *Austria*, in 1509. His Life of Pope *Celestin* V, was printed at *Paris* in the Year 1539 (35). and is to be met with in the Lives of the Saints compiled by *Surius*. There is a Difficulty in the Title of this Book, as it ascribes to *Peter d'Ailli* the Dignity of Confessor to *Charles* V. but we had better suppose, that *Charles* V. is mistaken for *Charles* VI. than to say, there was another *Peter d'Ailli*. *Possevin*, who believed it, is much mistaken. The Cardinal appears to have nothing so much at Heart as Astrology; for, besides that he presented to the Council of *Constance* a Plan for the Reformation of the Calendar, he composed the following Books: *Tractatus de vero cyclo lunari. Vigintilogium de concordantia Astronomicæ veritatis cum Theologia. Tractatus de concordia Astronomicæ veritatis & narrationis Historicæ* (36). *Tractatus elucidarius Astronomicæ concordiæ cum Theologia & cum Historica Narratione. Apologetica defensio Astronomicæ veritatis* (37). *Alia secunda Apologetica defensio ejusdem* (38). *Tractatus de concordia discordantium Astronomorum*.

Du Peyrat assures us (39), That *Bodin, in his Preface to the Dæmonomania of Sorcerers*, mentions a Book, composed by Cardinal d'Ailli, *wherein he maintained, that there is not one necessary Demonstration in Aristotle, except That, whereby he has demonstrated the Unity of God*. There are two Particulars, which deserve Censure, in this; for *Bodin* does not say, as *du Peyrat* intimates, That *Peter d'Ailli* wrote a distinct Treatise on this Subject; and he declares, that the Author had remarked some other Demonstrations in *Aristotle*, though but few in Number (40).

[*L*] *Some of which were never printed*.] They are in the Library of the College of *Navarre* (41); Mr *de Launoi* gives us a List of them. Some of them contain an Answer to certain very curious Questions, as, *Utrum esse tria supposita unius naturæ sit perfectio* (Whether three *Substrata* of one and the same Nature be the Perfection of that Nature): *Utrum libertas creaturæ rationalis ante & post lapsum intrinsece sit æqualis* (Whether the Free-Agency of a rational Creature before and after it's Fall be intrinsically equal): *Utrum Creaturæ rationalis conscientia erronea ejus actum excusare possit* (Whether the erroneous Conscience of a rational Creature can excuse it's Act). This latter Question puts me in mind of certain Papers, which appeared some time ago in *Holland*, concerning the Privileges of an erroneous Conscience; in which it was so demonstratively proved, that every Action, committed against the Light of Conscience, is essentially evil, and that it must necessarily and indispensibly be avoided; that the Opposers of this Doctrine fell into this shocking Opinion, *That a Man must not always act according to the Light of his Conscience*: From whence it follows, that it is sometimes justifiable to act contrary to the Dictates of Conscience. A monstrous Doctrine! destructive of all Morality; and in comparison of which the most extravagant *Probabilism* is an innocent Opinion. What makes this the more strange is, that they were Fanatics, who ran into this Extream; tho' They, of all Men, are most concerned to assert the Rights of Conscience.

[*M*] *He compos'd likewise Verses, such as they were, in the Vulgar Language.*] I quote my Authority in the Margin, who says, "That *Peter d'Ailli* wrote "many French Verses in Rhime, such as was pra- "ctis'd in his Time, which were translated into "Latin by *Nicolas de Clemangis*. I have seen "some of them, *says he* (42), which were printed a- "bove an hundred Years ago. He adds, That the "same Author wrote a Book in *French*, entituled, "*The seven Steps of the Ladder of Penitence, figured "and set forth under the seven penitential Psalms*; "printed at *Paris*." I am afraid *la Croix du Maine* imposes upon us in relation to this last Work; for Mr *de Launoi* positively asserts, That *Antony Belard* made a French Translation of the *Latin* Treatise of *Peter d'Ailli*, on the seven Penitential *Psalms*, and that *Denys de Harsi* printed this Translation at *Lyons*, in the Year 1544, in 16° (43).

Add the following Observation: "The *French* "Verses of *Peter d'Ailli*, which *la Croix du Maine* "spoke of, are only thirty two in Number, and con- "tain a short Description of a Tyrant's Life. *Nicolas "de Clemangis* paraphras'd them in *Latin* Hexame- "ters, printed with the *French* Verses of *Peter d'Ailli*, "at the end of a Book, entituled, *The Contempt of "the Court*, translated from the *Spanish* of *Guevara*, "into French, Italian, and High Dutch, at *Geneva*, "in 16°, by *John de Tournes*, 1605. The Para- "phrase of *Clemangis* is to be met with at the end "of his Epistles, page 355, of the Edition of *Leyden*. "As for the Translation of *Antony Belard*, *Antony "du Verdier* says, page 51 of his *Bibliotheque*, that "it was printed in 1542, by *Denys de Harsi*, in 16°, "at *Lyons* (44).

AIMON, Prince of the *Ardennes*, was, were are told (*a*), the Father of those Four Worthies, so celebrated in our Old Romances. They are commonly called *The Four Sons of* Aimon. They had but one Horse in common to them all, whose Name was *Bayard*. I should not have taken notice of so Idle a Tale, had it not been for the sake of observing, that these romantic Extravagancies have even crept into the Sanctuary. Popular Superstition has introduced them into Religion; and if any one had objected to these Impertinent Writers, *Hæ nugæ seria ducent in mala* (*b*),

he

AIMON. AYRAULT.

he would not have been a False Prophet. The History of *Luxemburgh*, composed by *John Bertels*, Abbot of *Epternach*, informs us, that *Renauld*, the Eldest of these Four Brothers, died a Martyr to the Name of JESUS CHRIST; that he was canonized; that the Church celebrates his Festival; that Temples were consecrated to him, and, among others, the Church of St *Renauld*, in the Country of *Cologne*, to which is annexed a Convent of Nuns. There is also a Church dedicated to the same Saint at *Cologne*, near That of St *Maurice*; and the representation of the Four Brothers is painted on the Walls of the Church. They are all four on one Horse, and *Renauld*, the Eldest, has a Diadem round his Head, as a Mark of his Saintship. It is pretended, that, after having been a great Warrior under *Charlemagne*, he turned Monk at *Cologne* (c); that he died a Martyr, and that, because he wrought Miracles after his Death, a Church was built to him (d).

(c) Ferrarius in Catalog. Sanctorum ad 7. Januar.

(d) See Voetii Disput. Theolog. Tom. 3. pag. 508.

AYRAULT (PETER), in Latin *Ærodius*, Lieutenant Criminal in the *Presidial* Court of *Angers*, his native Country, was born in the Year 1536. He studied *Humanity* and *Philosophy* at *Paris*; afterwards he applied himself to the Civil Law at *Toulouse*; from thence he went to *Bourges*, to improve himself by the Lectures of *Duarenus*, *Cujacius*, and *Doneau*, three of the most Excellent Civilians of That Time. After taking his Bachelor's Degree at *Bourges*, he returned to his own Country, where for some time he read Public Lectures in Civil Law, and pleaded at the Bar. He was then 22 Years of Age. Some time after he returned to *Paris*, where he became one of the most famous Advocates of the Parliament [A]. In the Year 1563, he published, there, the *Declamations* of *Quintilian*, which he corrected in several Places, and accompanied them with Notes. The Year following, he published a Treatise *of the Power of Redemption*, composed by *Francis Grimaudet*, the King's Advocate at *Angers*, to which he prefixed a Preface, *concerning the Nature, Variety, and Alteration of the Laws*. In the Year 1567, he published a Book entituled *Decretorum rerumve apud diversos populos ab omni Antiquitate Judicatarum Libri duo—Accedit tractatus de origine & auctoritate rerum Judicatarum*. He enlarged it considerably in the following Editions [B]. He left *Paris*, the Year following, to exercise the Office of *Lieutenant Criminal* in his own Country: Which he executed with so much Justice, that, like another *Cassius*, he was called *the Rock of the Accused*. During the Confusions of the *League*, he exercised, in the Interim [C], the Office of President in the same Court, of which he acquitted himself with the same Integrity. The City of *Angers* expressed their Esteem for him several ways; especially by conferring upon him the Office of Perpetual *Echevin* *. He had a great Quarrel with *Philip Gourreau* Master of the Requests, his Countryman, and published an *Apological* Letter against him in 1577 (a). He was heartily attached to the honest Party against the *League*; and he was obliged to be so, not only on account of his Office in the *Presidial* Court, but because he was Master of the Requests to the Duke of *Anjou*, a Place

* *A kind of Magistrate somewhat like an English Sheriff.*

(a) *He published two Editions of it, in one Tome, at Angers, the second more ample than the first. This Piece is in Latin.*

[A] *One of the most famous Advocates of the Parliament.*] *Antony Loisel*, in his Dialogue of the Advocates of the Parliament of *Paris*, places our *Ayrault* in the List of the most famous, and gives him the Pre-eminence over *Bodin*. It is true he remarks, that *Bodin* had no Success at the Bar. These are *Loisel's* Words: "Master *Peter* *Ayrault* was likewise promoted to the Post of *Lieutenant Criminal* at *Angers*, where he was born, and retir'd thither about the latter end of the extraordinary Sessions of *Poitiers*, in the Year 1567, though he was a skilful and learned Pleader, and succeeded much better than *John Bodin* of *Angers*; for, notwithstanding the latter was a compleat Scholar, his Pleadings at the Bar had never any Success (1)." Some of *Peter Ayrault's* Pleadings were printed at *Paris*, in the Year 1568 (2). They were reprinted at *Rouen*, in 1614, with the Notes and Additions of a young Civilian. Mr *Menage*, who tells us this (3), might have added, that they were printed at *Paris*, in 1598, in 8vo. with some other small Pieces of *Peter Ayrault*. The Secular Priests of *Paris* chose him, in 1564, to plead their Cause against the Jesuits; yet he did not plead it; perhaps, because it was not thought proper, that the Interest of the Clergy should be distinct from That of the Bishop of *Paris*. This is the Conjecture of *du Boulai* (4). However it be, his Pleading was published, as I just now observ'd in the marginal Note (2).

[B] *He enlarg'd it considerably in the following Editions.*] The second Edition is of *Paris*, 1573, in 8vo. and contains six Books. The Third is in Folio, and the Title of it is, *Rerum ab omni antiquitate judicatarum Pandecta*. There is a *Paris* Edition of it likewise, in 1588. After the Death of the Author, the same *Pandects* were printed at *Paris*, in the Year 1615, with the small Treatise *de Patrio Jure*. He had re-

(1) *Loisel, apud Menag. in Testim. de P. Ærod. prefix'd to his Life, p. 26.*

(2) *There are 22 of them; of which the 20th is That, which he had prepared for the Secular Priests of Paris against the Jesuits, in 1564.*

(3) *In his Life of Peter Ayrault, pag. 26.*

(4) *In the History of the University of Paris, Tom. 6. p. 266. apud Menag. in Testim. de P. Ærod. pag. 77.*

vised and corrected them. Mr *Menage* had promis'd (5) a new Edition of them, with short Marginal Notes, wherein he designed to shew, from whence *Ayrault* borrowed his Examples. This is a very learned Work. "Continet enim res ab omni antiquitate apud Indos, Judæos, Græcos, Romanos, Francos, aliosque, judicatas (6). —— For it contains *Cases adjudg'd from all Antiquity among the Indians, Jews, Greeks, Romans, French, and others.*" That, which he wrote in *French*, *Of the Judiciary Forms, which the ancient Greeks and Romans made use of in public Trials, compared with the Practice of our French*, is useful and curious. It was printed, the first time, at *Paris*, in 1575, in 8vo. The second Edition, which is of *Paris*, in 1588, in 4to, was enlarg'd by two Books: The third was enlarged by one Book, at *Paris*, in the Year 1598, in 4to (7). So that this Work contains four Books. The fourth Book, which treats *of the Proceedings against dead Bodies, Ashes, the Memory of a Person, Brute Beasts, things inanimate, and Criminals who refuse to appear before the Judge*; was printed at *Paris*, in 1591. I forgot to observe, that his Treatise *de decretis rebusque apud diversos populos ab omni antiquitate judicatis*, was printed at *Francfort*, in the Year 1580, from the first Edition. The Abbreviators of *Gesner* had no other Knowledge of our *Peter Ayrault*, but what the Edition of *Germany* afforded them. They were mistaken, in supposing his Name was *Paul*.

[C] *In the Interim.*] Mr *Menage* makes this *Interim* to continue two Years; *Eo Præturæ munere per biennium functus Ærodius est* (8); and yet he says, That *Ayrault* was not nominated to this Office, 'till the 11th of *May*, 1589, and that *Henry* the Great presented another Person to it, in the beginning of the Year 1590, *ineunte Anno* 1590.

(5) *Ubi supra, pag. 28.*

(6) *Menage in the Life of Peter Ayrault, p. 27.*

(7) *It is thus we must translate the Words of Mr Menage, Quarto posthac anno 1588, duobus libris, & anno 1598, tribus auctiorem in eadem urbe publicavit.*

(8) *Id. ib. pag. 24.*

(9) *Ib. pag. 23.*

[D] *Was*

Place which he had jointly with the Civilian *Baudouin*, before That Prince came to the Throne. The *Speech*, which he made before That Duke, upon his Entry into *Angers*, on the 7th of *January*, 1570, was printed with the *Discourse*, which he addressed to him [D] in praise of his Victories, and of the Restoration of the University of *Angers*. This Discourse turns chiefly on *Baudouin*'s having dedicated two Ancient Panegyrics to That Prince; viz. That, which *Eumenius* made upon *Constantius*; and That, which *Pacatus* made upon *Theodosius*. The *Discourse*, which *Ayrault* published, in the Year 1589, *on the Death of Henry* III. *and the Prejudice which the Church received by it*, testifies his Adherence to that Monarch's Party. He neither put his own, nor the Printer's Name to it. *Thuanus* speaks of it with Commendation (*b*). A *Latin* Translation of it by the Author himself was found among his Papers. He wrote a Discourse at that time, in which he exhorted *Henry* IV. to become a Catholic: But, of all his Works, That which made him most known in Foreign Countries, and chiefly among the *Protestants*, is his Treatise of Paternal Power [E]. He composed it during a Law-Suit, which he had with the Jesuits, on account of his Eldest Son, who had taken the Habit of their Order (*c*). He had sent him to their College at *Paris*, to render him the more capable of succeeding him; and, some time after, had the Vexation to hear, that they had persuaded him to enter himself among their Order. He complained of This Proceeding to the Parliament of *Paris* (*d*); and, being informed, that they had secreted him, he presented a Petition to the Pope, and obtained Letters from *Henry* III. to Cardinal *d'Est*, Protector of the Affairs of *France*, and to the Marquis *de Pisani*, Ambassador of that Crown (*e*); by which Letters the King pressed them to obtain an Order from the Pope for the Release of the Young Man. But all was in vain. The Treatise of Paternal Power, which he addressed three Years after to this Disobedient Son, did not prove more effectual. Although *Ayrault* had other Sons, yet he was exceedingly concerned at the loss of This. He had married *Anne des-Jardins*, at *Paris*, in the Year 1564. She was Daughter of *John des-Jardins*, Physician to *Francis* I, by whom he had 15 Children [F], of which Ten were living, when he died at *Angers*, the 21st of *July*, 1601, aged 65 Years (*f*). I borrow this Article from Mr *Menage* (*g*).

[D] *Was printed with the Discourse, which he addressed to him*] Mr *Menage* has not rightly adjusted the Date of the Impression of these two Pieces; he says they were printed in 1577, and that the Prince, who is celebrated in them, was then King of *Poland*, and Duke of *Anjou*. This is plainly to tell us, that he was not King of *France*; and yet the Duke of *Anjou* was Inaugurated at *Rheims*, in the Month of *February*, 1575, and he was look'd upon as King of *France*, the very Day that *Charles* IX. died (10). You may take it for granted, that the Speech and Discourse, in question, came out in 1570, and consequently that the Subject of them was no longer King of *Poland*.

[E] *His Treatise of Paternal Power*.] The Author wrote it in *French* and *Latin*; one of his Countrymen, whose Name was *Jacob Frubert*, translated it into *Italian* (11). Let us see what Mr *Menage* says of it; " Egit cum fugitivo filio tanquam cum absente reo, " hoc est annotatione & programmate.

Qualis populea mœrens philomela sub umbra
Amissos queritur fœtus (12);

" Et quæ sequuntur; notum enim tibi carmen est;
" Talis Petrus Ærodius amissum filium insolabiliter in
" scriptis suis queritur. Vide quæso —— quo ipse
" questus fundat in libro tertio Ordinis judiciarii, mo-
" do fratrem Johannem Ærodium, modo Renatum fi-
" lium compellans. Quis vere tam ferus ac ferreus
" est, qui cum querelas ejus legat in libello illo aureo,
" & tot laudibus à Stephano Pascasio (13) celebrato,
" quem de patrio jure ad fugitivum filium contra Jesu-
" itas scripsit, à gemitu & lacrimis temperare possit?
" At non solus Ærodius facum suum gemuit;
" ingemuere & alii; lege Stephani Pascasii & Johan-
" nis Bodini (14) ea de re ad Petrum Ærodium Epi-
" stolas. Lege Antonii Arnaldi Advocati Parisiensis
" —— Orationem pulcherrimam habitam in Senatu
" Parisiensi contra Jesuitas anno M. D. LXXXXIV (15).
" ——— *He considered his Fugitive Son as a Defen-*
" *dant, who refuses to appear at the Suit of the Plan-*
" *tiff, and treated him in the usual Forms*.

*As, close, in Poplar Shades, her Children gone,
The Mother Nightingal laments alone;*

" *and so on; you know* Virgil's *Simile; just so the dis-*
" *consolate Ærodius laments, in his Writings, the Loss*

" *of his Son*. —— *Do but read his Complaints in the*
" *third Book of his Judiciary Forms, one while calling*
" *upon* John Ærodius *his Brother, then on his Son*
" Renatus. *But who is so steel'd to all Sense of Pity,*
" *as to refrain from Sighs and Tears, when he reads*
" *his Complaints in that Golden Work* Of Paternal
" Power, *so much commended by* Stephen Pascasius,
" *which he wrote against the Jesuits, and address'd*
" *to his Fugitive Son?* —— *But* Ærodius *did not la-*
" *ment his Fate alone; others sympathiz'd with him;*
" *read* Stephen Pascasius' *and* John Bodin's *Letters to*
" Peter Ærodius *upon this Subject. Read those of*
" Antony Arnauld, *Advocate of* Paris; *and the beau-*
" *tiful Oration, delivered in the Senate of* Paris, *a-*
" *gainst the Jesuits, in the Year* M. D LXXXXIV."
Mr *Menage* relates, in his Remarks, what *Antony Arnauld* said upon this Subject, and the Answer return'd him by *Peter Barai*, Attorney to the Jesuits of the College of *Clermont*. The Answer runs thus, That the *Jesuits* would never receive *Renatus Ayrault* in *France*, though he was at least eighteen Years of Age; but that, *without discovering to them his Design, he went into Germany, where he was receiv'd* (16). See the Remark [A], of the following Article.

[F] *By whom he had fifteen Children*.] We set apart a particular Article for his eldest Son: His second Son *Peter AYRAULT* succeeded his Father in his Virtues and Office, and was President in the Seneschal's Court of *Angers*, Counsellor of the City, and Mayor. He obtained, in the Year 1603, a Professorship of Civil Law, in the University of *Angers*, for *William Barclay*. The Speech he made before *Mary de Medicis*, the Mother of *Lewis* XIII, at *Angers*, on the 16th of *October*, 1619, may be seen in the 6th Tome of the *French Mercury*. He was deputed to the Assembly, which call'd themselves *Les Notables*, *The Eminent or Remarkable Men*, who met at *Rouen*, in 1617. He left a Family. His Brother, *John AYRAULT*, was Advocate in the Parliament of *Paris*. Their Brother, *William AYRAULT*, a *Benedictin* Monk, Doctor of the *Sorbonne*, was in favour with *Lewis Servin*, Advocate General in the Parliament of *Paris*. *Guyonne AYRAULT*, one of their Sisters, married *William Menage*, the King's Advocate in the *Presidial* of *Angers*. From that Marriage sprang the late Mr *Menage* (17), one of the most learned Men of *France*.

AYRAULT. AITZEMA.

AYRAULT (RENATUS) Eldeſt Son of the foregoing, was the Cauſe of great Uneaſineſs to his Father. He was born at *Paris*, on the eleventh of *November*, 1567, and was put to School to the *Jeſuits* (a). *Peter Ayrault* had a good opinion of them at that time (b); and was ſo fond of them, that he would hardly have undertaken the *Pariſian* Clergy's Cauſe againſt them, at that time, as he actually did afterwards in the Year 1564. Perceiving in this his Eldeſt Son a lively Wit, great Memory, and many other good Qualities, he earneſtly intreated the Provincial of the Jeſuits, and the Rector of the College of *Clermont*, when he committed his Son to their Care, not to ſollicit him, in any manner, to enter into their Order; and aſſured them he had other Children, whom he intended to dedicate to the Church; but that he deſigned this Son ſhould ſucceed him in his Poſt, and intended him for the Support of his Family. They promiſed to grant his Requeſt. However the Young Gentleman's great Abilities made the Jeſuits deſirous of having a Subject of this Importance in their Society; at length, after he had ſtudied *Rhetoric* Two Years under Father *James Sirmond*, they gave him the Habit of their Order in 1586. His Father, without whoſe Conſent or Privacy this was done, made a great ſtir about it. He accuſed them of Plagiariſm, and ſummoned them to deliver up his Son. They anſwered, That they knew not what was become of him. *Ayrault* obtained a Decree of Parliament, whereby the Jeſuits of the College of *Clermont* were ordered not to receive *Renatus Ayrault* into their Order, and to notify this Prohibition to the other Colleges. This Decree was not obeyed; the Young Man was removed from Place to Place, his Name was changed, and he was ſent into *Lorain*, *Germany*, and *Italy* [*A*]; Henry III. cauſed his Ambaſſador, and the Protector of his Affairs, to ſollicit the Pope; *Ayrault* wrote to his Holineſs about it; the Pope cauſed the Liſt of all the Jeſuits in the World to be ſhewed him; *Renatus Ayrault*, going under another Name, did not appear in this Liſt (c). Three Years of Trouble and Enquiry being employed to no Purpoſe, the Father had recourſe to his Pen, and wrote a Book concerning the Paternal Power, and addreſſed it to his Son *Renatus* (d). *Renatus* anſwered it; but his Superiors did not think fit to publiſh his Anſwer. They employed *Richeome*, Provincial of the Jeſuits of *Paris*, to refute *Peter Ayrault's* Book [*B*]. *Renatus*'s Adventures are as follows. He entered into the Order, at *Triers*, on the 12th of *June*, 1586. He went afterwards to *Fulde*, where he renewed his Study of *Rhetoric*. He paſſed through *Germany*, and was taken there by the *Proteſtants*; He went to *Rome*, where he ſtudied Philoſophy a Year, under *Mutius Vitelleſchi* (e). He continued this Study, the Year following, at *Milan*, and finiſhed it at *Dijon* (f). Having taught the Claſſes, in the ſame City, during four Years, with great Succeſs, he left it, when the Jeſuits were baniſhed from ſeveral Cities of the Kingdom, in the Year 1594, and went into *Piedmont*, where he taught for two Years. He came afterwards to *Avignon*, where he ſtudied Divinity four Years. After which he returned to *Rome*; from whence he was ſent to *Milan* to teach Rhetoric. This he did for ſome Years; and returned afterwards into *France*; where he paſſed through the moſt illuſtrious Employments of his Order; He taught Philoſophy; he Preached; He was Superior of a College. He was Rector at *Rheims*, *Dijon*, *Sens*, *Dole*, and *Bezançon*; He was the Provincial's Aſſiſtant, and Procurator of the Province of *Champagne*, and afterwards of That of *Lyons*, at *Rome*. Laſtly, he died at *la Fleche* on the 18th of *December*, 1644 (g). His Father, by a Deed executed before a Notary and Witneſſes, deprived him of his Bleſſing in the Year 1593. but he did not keep his Reſentment till his Death; for a Writing was found among his Papers, in which he gave him his Bleſſing [*C*].

[*A*] *Into* Lorain, Germany, *and* Italy.] *Antony Arnauld* ſet forth, in his Plea of the Year 1594, that the Jeſuits *had enticed away* Renatus Ayrault, *when he was but fourteen Years of Age, and that they kept him in* Italy *and* Spain. It does not appear, that they ever ſent him into *Spain* (1), and he wanted but little of his 19th Year, when he took the Jeſuits Habit.

(*B*) *They pitch'd upon* Richeome——*to refute* Peter Ayrault's *Book.*] His Anſwer, as well as *Renatus Ayrault's*, was never printed. " Quia indecorum viſum " eſt adverſus parentes ſcribere filios, prohibitus eſt à " Rectoribus ſuis reſponſionem vulgare. Igitur id " aggreſſus eſt Ludovicus Richeomus—quod me " docuit privata ipſius Renati Ærodii ad ipſum Ri- " cheomum epiſtola, cujus exemplar, quæ ſua eſt " humanitas, miſit ad me Româ Petrus Poſſinus, " Preſbyter Societatis Jeſu doctiſſimus, idemque Je- " ſuiticæ Hiſtoriæ Scriptor celeberrimus. Sed ne- " que reſponſionem ſuam vulgavit Richeomus: qua " de cauſâ neſcio (2).——*He was forbid by his Supe-* " *riors to publiſh his Anſwer, becauſe it was thought* " *indecent for Children to write againſt their Parents.* " *For which reaſon* Lewis Richeome *undertook it*—— " *as I am inform'd by a private Letter of* Renatus Ay- " rault's *to the ſame* Richeome; *a Copy of which* Pe- " ter Poſſin, *a learned Preſbyter of the Society of Je-* " *ſus, and the celebrated Author of the Hiſtory of Je-* " *ſuitiſm, was ſo good-natur'd as to tranſmit to me at* " Rome."

[*C*] *A Writing—in which he gave him his Bleſſing.*] It was ſign'd with his own hand, and contain'd as follows; " God give his Peace, his Love, and his " Grace, to my Son *Renatus Ayrault*. I give him " my Bleſſing, in the Name of the Father, and of the " Son, and of the Holy Ghoſt. And I forgive him " every thing wherein he may have offended me. " And I pray God to aſſiſt him with his holy Spirit, " whatever State, or Calling, he may undertake (3).

AITZEMA (LEO *de*) a Gentleman of *Frieſland*, born at *Doccum*, in the Year 1600, was Counſellor of the *Hans-Towns*, and their Reſident at the *Hague*. He compiled an *Hiſtory of the United Provinces*, which ſold very well, and is of great uſe to thoſe, who ſtudy Politics; for it contains, Word for Word, the Treaties of Peace, Inſtructions

AITZEMA. AKAKIA.

Instructions and Memoirs of Ambassadors, Letters and Answers of Sovereigns, Capitulations of Towns, and other Public Acts, each in its Original Language, and then translated into *Dutch*, in which Language the History is written. There are two Editions of it [*A*]. Although it is chiefly considerable, for the Authentic Pieces, which the Author collected with much Patience and Application, I would not judge of the rest, as Mr *de Wicquefort* did [*B*]. I have been told that this Historian speaks in an impartial Manner of whatever relates to Religious Disputes. Mr *Arnaud* cited him for a Particular not very advantageous to the Protestants (*a*). *Valerius Andreas* mentions one *Leo Aetsma*, a *Frieslander*, who printed his Juvenile *Latin* Verses at *Franeker*, in the Year 1617 (*b*). Some think this Poet is the same with the Historian, who is the Subject of this Article (*c*). LEO de AITZEMA died at the *Hague*, on the 23d of *February* 1669. after having been employed there, about forty Years, in quality of Resident for the *Hans-Towns*, which was procured him by FOPPIUS de AITZEMA his Uncle, Resident of *Holland* [*C*], at *Hamburgh*. Our *Leo* was a very good Man, Serviceable to his Friends, Affable, Liberal to the Poor, and well versed in Politics. He spoke several Languages, *German*, *French*, *Italian*, and *English*. His Father was Secretary of the *Admiralty* of *Friesland* (*d*). It will not be improper to observe that there are already published Three Volumes, in *Folio*, of the Continuation of *Aitzema*; the first reaches from 1669 to 1679. the Second from 1679 to 1687. the Third from 1687 to 1692 (*e*). A Minister, whose Name was AITZEMA, wrote a *Dutch* Book concerning the *Sibyls*.

(*a*) *See the Apology for the Catholicks, part 2. pag. 267.*

(*b*) *Valer. Andr. Bibl. Belg. p. 623.*

(*c*) *Konig. Bibl. p. 19.*

(*d*) *It resid'd at that time, at Doccum; at present it resides at Harlingen.*

(*e*) *The first was printed at Amsterdam in 1685. the second in 1688; and the third in 1698.*

[*A*] *There are two Editions of it.*] The first contains fifteen Volumes, in *4to.* which were printed separately; the first in 1657, and the last in 1671: the first begins at the Cessation of the Truce, which was concluded, by the Interposition of *Henry* the Great, between *Spain* and the *United Provinces*, and reaches from the Year 1621 to the Year 1625. The last contains the History of the Year 1668. The second Edition is in seven Volumes in *Folio*, which were printed in 1669, and in 1671. The last of these Volumes contains a general Table of the other six, with an Account of the Peace of *Munster*, and a Treatise intitled, *The Lion rester'd*; and which is a Narrative of the Transactions in the *United Provinces* in 1650, and 1651, in relation to the filling up of some considerable Posts. This Treatise had already appear'd in *4to* in the Year 1652. The Account of the Peace of *Munster* had been printed in *Latin* in the Year 1654.

[*B*] *As Mr de Wicquefort did.*] He speaks of *Aitzema* in the following Words. "The History, or the Account of the Affairs of State and of War, which was written in *Holland*, in fourteen or fifteen Volumes, contains a great Variety of Treaties, Resolutions, and other authentic Pieces; that may serve as an Inventory to those, who have no Access to the Archives of the State: but what the Author has added of his own, is beneath the Gazette, in whatever Light it be considered. He is Master of no Style: His Language is altogether barbarous, and the whole Texture of the Work is a meer Chaos. This is common to our Author with most of those, who, in that Country, attempt to write History, without express Order and Permission; and, generally speaking, they do it without Judgment and without Sincerity (1)." It must be confessed, This Censure is very disadvantageous to our Author's Character; and indeed gives offence to many Persons.

[*C*] *Foppius d'AITZEMA his Uncle, Resident of Holland.*] I have met with a Passage relating to him in one of *Puffendorf's* Volumes. I find there, that, in 1636, this *Foppius*, Envoy of the *United Provinces* to the Emperor, affirmed at *Ratisbon*, that *Salvius* had inform'd him by Letter, that the *Swedes* intended to negotiate a Peace at the Court of *Vienna*; but that *Salvius* denied it (2). Nevertheless *Foppius* was very busy in negotiating the Peace; but *Sweden* did not think him qualified for such a Work; and it was thought ridiculous in him to intermeddle in such a Design, especially considering that, since he had gone over to the *Roman* Communion, he had employ'd every Art to insinuate himself into the Emperor's Favour. *Nec Aitzema idoneus tantæ rei autor habebatur, omnibus qui hominem norant irridentibus, quod iste heic se ingerere non dubitaret, quem præsertim post susceptæ sacra Romana gratia Cæsaris omnibus modis adrepere constabat* (3).

(1) *Wicquefort's Ambassador, Tom. 1. p. 172. See also p. 448.*

(2) *Puffendorf de Rebus Suecicis, lib. 9. pag. 296. n. 53. ad ann. 1637.*

(3) *Id. Ib.*

AKAKIA (MARTIN) Professor of Physic, in the University of *Paris*, in the XVIth Century, was of *Chalons* in *Champagne* [*A*]. His Name was *Sans-malice*, (*without Malice*) [*B*]; but, according to the Custom of those times, he changed it to *Akakia*, which signifies the same in *Greek*, as *Sans-malice* does in *French* [*B*]. He transmitted it to his Posterity, who have always bore it to this present time. He made a considerable Progress at *Paris*, under the Professor *Peter Brissot* (*a*), and acquired from

(*a*) *Moreau, in vita Brissoti.*

[*A*] *Was of Chalons in Champagne.*] *Moreri*, not knowing what *Catalaunensis* meant, thought, in good earnest, that *Akakia* was a *Catalan*. He was of Catalonia, says he; and he refers us for it to *Quenstedt*, who has positively declared, that This Physician was of *Chalons*; a City, the Bishop whereof assumes the Title of Count and Peer of *France* (1).

[*B*] *His Name was Sans-Malice, but——he changed it to Akakia, which signifies the same in Greek, as* Sans malice *does in French*] We learn this from *Renatus Moreau*, in his Life of *Sylvius*, and *Gabriel Naudé*, in his *Judgment on Augustin Niphus* (2). See likewise *le Mothe le Vaier*, at the 277th Page of the 12th Tome of his Works; and Mr *Menage*, in his *Origin of the French Language* (3). Father *L'Abbé* believes, that all this is but an ex post facto, or pretty Allusion, made afterwards, or perhaps a Nickname, which was given him, and which grew afterwards into a Family Name (4). He assigns two Reasons for this Opinion; the first is that 'Ακακία does not signify a MAN *free from Malice*, but, simply, a *Freedom from* Malice. The second is, that This Physician of *Francis* I. would have wrote himself *Acacia* or *Akakia*, if he had borrow'd a Name from the *Greek* Tongue. To confirm the first he adds, that This Physician, *if it be true that his Name was, at first, Sans-malice, would have done better to quit the Feminine Name* 'Ακακία, *and assume one more Masculine, and which should have some relation to* 'Ακακιθ, Acacius, *Words in use among the Greeks and Latins. Who would not laugh at the Simplicity or Ignorance of him, who, having the Family Name of Bald or Virtuous, should turn his Name into Greek, and call himself* 'Ακακιλια *or* 'Αρετῆ? These Reasons are very weak. As for the second, we may allow, that he ought to have wrote himself *Acacia* or *Akakia*; and I think That learned Physician did actually subscribe himself after the latter. As for the other Reason, it is easy to see, that Father *L'Abbé* advances nothing material; for the Masculine 'Ακακιθ does not so fully come up to the *French* Word *Sans-malice*, as the Feminine 'Ακακία does. The Comparison of *Bald* or *Virtuous* is improper; since it is certain,

(1) *Quenst. de Patriis Vicor. Eruditor. p. 51.*

(2) *Fol. o, iii.*

(3) *At the 4th Page of the Paris Edition in 1694.*

(4) *L'Abbé's Etymologies of French Words, pag. 10.*

AKAKIA.

from him most of what he published afterwards on *Galen* [C]. He was created Doctor of the Faculty of Physic of *Paris*, in the Year 1526. *Francis* I, one of whose Physicians in Ordinary he was, had a great esteem for him. I cannot determine in what Year he became Professor of Physic; but he was so, when *Gesner* published his *Bibliotheque*, that is, in the Year 1545. He died in the Year 1551. His Coat of Arms was, *Gules and a Cross d'Or, with four Cubes d'Or*, with this Motto, *Quæcunque ferat fortuna, ferenda est*. He married *Mary Chauveau*, Widow of *Silvan de Montbelon*, by whom he had a Son, who was Professor of Physic, as we shall see. Most of his Descendants have followed the same Profession; though one among them had other Affairs upon his hands besides Physic [D]. They, who place the Death of our *Martin Akakia* in the Year 1605, are strangely mistaken [E]. *Marot* spoke of him with Commendation: Mr *Menage* has cited his *Elogium* of him (*b*).

(*b*) Menage's *Origin of the French Tongue*, pag. 4.

tain, that *Sans-malice* has not the Nature of an Adjective Noun; and that, if a Person, whose Name happens to be *Avec-peleure*, should have a mind to *Grecise* it, he ought rather to take the Name of *Synalopecia*, than That of *Synalopecius*.

(5) Gesner, Biblioth. fol. 500.

[C] *What he publish'd —— on Galen*.] In 1538, he publish'd a *Latin* Translation of *Galen's* two Books, *De ratione curandi*, and accompanied it with a Commentary (5). Afterwards he translated the *Ars Medica, quæ & Ars parva*, of the same *Galen*. This Work was printed at *Lyons*, in 1548. He is likewise Author of a Book, printed at *Paris*, in the Year 1555, with the Title of "Synopsis eorum, quæ quinque "prioribus libris Galeni de facultatibus simplicium "medicamentorum continentur. —— *A Synopsis of "the Contents of the five first Books* of Galen, *Of "the Qualities of Simple Medicines.*"

(6) It came out in Sept. 1693.

[D] *Tho' one among them had other Affairs upon his Hands besides Physic.*] A Letter of *Guy Patin*, dated the twenty second of *July*, 1664, contains these Words: "The King has caused the Brother "of M. *Akakia*, our Colleague, to be confined in "the *Bastile*, for having wrote something, which "displeased his Highness the Prince. It is not long, "since he was employed about the Marriage of the "Duke of *Enguien*, and had been Secretary of the "Embassy to *Poland*." Every one has heard of the Complaints, which a Friend to the House of *Austria*, disguised under the Name of *Stanislaus Lysimachus*, *A Polish Knight*, published in 1683, against the Correspondence, which *France* carried on with Count *Tekeli*, by the means of *Akakia* and *du Vernai-Boucauld*. I have just read, in the *Journal* of *Amsterdam* (6), that the same *Akakia* had a great share in the Intrigues, which were formed, to place the Crown of *Poland* on the Head of the Duke of *Longueville*, by deposing King *Michael*. It is affirmed, in this Journal, that the Emperor complained of this to the King of *France*, and that, among others, he named Mr *Acakia as one of the chief Conductors of That Affair*; that Mr *Acakia was committed to the Bastile*; *but that he pursued the Scheme, which he had begun, rather with more Application, and had more leisure to keep up the Correspondence he had settled* ; *and that his Letters and Negotiations continued their Train, notwithstanding his Imprisonment* ; and that

the Business was so far advanced, that nothing but the Death (7) of the Duke of *Longueville* hindered the Execution of it. The Medals were already prepared. This second Imprisonment of Mr *Akakia* lasted but five or six Months, if I can depend upon one, whom I have consulted, since the reading of That Journal. This Person told me farther, that Mr *Akakia* was so overjoyed to find himself pitched upon, as a proper Person to foment the Troubles of *Hungary*, that, though he was then very sick, he soon recovered Health enough to set out on the Expedition. Not daring to take the way of *Germany*, he went into *England*, where he embarqued for *Sweden*, from whence he went by Sea to *Riga*, and from thence to *Poland*; where he died. He was a Man of Intrigue; and acted vigorously for the Conclusion of the Peace of *Oliva*.

(7) He was kill'd as the *Passage of the Rhine*, June 12, 1672.

[E] *They, who place the Death —— in the Year* 1605, *are strangely mistaken.*] This the Author of the *Diarium Biographicum* did (8) : Thus he expresses himself, under that Year: "Martinus Akakia, Gallus, "CATALAUNENSIS, Medicinæ Doctor & "Professor Lutetiæ Paris. —— Martin Akakia, *a "French Man, of* CHALONS, *Doctor of Physic, "and Professor at Paris*." After which he gives us the Titles of some Books, of which *Akakia, of Châlons*, is the true Author. If he had known, that *Brissot*, whose Disciple our *Akakia* was, was no longer in *France*, in the Year 1519, he would not have prolonged the Life of this Disciple of his to the Year 1605; or he would have taken some Notice of so remarkable an old Age, as his would have been. His Mistake might arise from hence, that a Physician died in the Year 1605, whose Name was *Akakia*. He was a Grand-Child of *Brissot*'s Disciple. *Guy Patin* speaks of him in this manner, with his Cynical Liberty: "Two Doctors of our Society conspired "in writing the Apology for *Theodorus Mayerne "Turquet* : to wit, *Seguin*, who always supported "the Quacks, and his Brother-in-law *Acakia*, who "died in the Year 1605, of the Pox, which he "brought with him from *Italy*, whither he went "with M. *de Bethune* Ambassador at *Rome* (9)." If our *Martin Akakia* was capable of getting such a Disease at the time of this Embassy, he must, without all Contradiction, have been the oldest Whoremaster in *Europe*.

(8) Henningus Witte, Professor at Riga, in Livonia.

(9) Patin, Letter VIII. *of the first Edition.*

AKAKIA (MARTIN) a *Parisian*, Son of the preceeding, was created Doctor of Physic of the Faculty of *Paris*, in the Year 1572. *Tristan de Rostaing*, Knight of the Order, and *Amiot* Bishop of *Auxerre*, became his Patrons [*A*]; and, at their Sollicitation, *Charles* IX. gave him the Office of first Reader and *Regius Professor* of Chirurgery in the Year 1574. Four Years after, he was made Second Physician to *Henry* III (*a*). As he was ambitious of producing the most elaborate Lectures in the Royal Schools, which took up a great deal of his time, he feared, that the visiting of his Patients, and the Function he was obliged to discharge at Court, would be too heavy a Burthen for him. So that, to preserve himself from sinking under so many Labours, he resigned his Professorship, with the King's leave, to *John Martin*, a Person

(*a*) See Remark k [*A*].

[*A*] *Tristan and Amiot became his Patrons.*] An apter Proof cannot be given of this than the Words, which I am going to cite out of a Panegyrick of *Henry* III. It is *Martin Akakia* who speaks: "Vix dum "injtur in publica professione, qua nos Carolus Rex "Christianissimus, Tristando Rostagnio Equite Tor-"quato fortissimo, & Jacobo Amyoto Altissiodoren-"sium Episcopo de nobis referentibus, cohonestave-"rat, quadriennium compleveramus, cum Tu nos "inter tuos Medicos allegisti & conscripsisti. —— "*I had scarce compleated four Years in the Exercise* "*of That public Profession, with which the most Chri-*"*stian King* Charles, *at the Request of the brave* "Tristan de Rostaing, *Knight of the Order, and* "James Amiot, *Bishop of* Auxerre, *had honoured* "*me, when you gave me a Rank among your own* "Physicians." This Panegyric was printed at *Paris* in the Year 1578, with this Title: *Martini Akakiæ Regii & Medici & Professoris ab suam in ordinem Regiorum Medicorum co-optationem Panegyricus*, *Henrico Valesio Regi Christianissimo dictus*.

[B] *At*

AKAKIA. AKIBA.

son very capable of That Office, as his Writings testify [B]. But *John Martin*, rightly judging that it would be incompatible with his other Employs, if he would discharge it conscientiously, restored it to *Martin Akakia*; who disposed of This Employment in favour of his Son-in-Law *Peter Seguin*, and died very soon after, in the Year 1588, being about Forty nine Years of Age. He left Two Sons, of whom I am going to speak, and a Daughter, who was married to *Peter Seguin*, one of the most learned Physicians of the Faculty of *Paris*, and who exercised his Father in-Law's Profession in the Royal College from the Year 1588, to the Year 1599. The Treatise *de Morbis muliebribus*, and the *Consilia Medica*, of our *Martin*, are scarce known to any one, but under the false Supposition, that they come from the same hand, as the Treatises of *Martin Akakia* of *Chalons*. I have not met with any Bibliographer, who distinguishes the Father's Writings from Those of the Son; both are ascribed to *Martin Akakia Catalaunensis*. I should have been deceived in this point as well as *Moreri*, had I not consulted some Friends [C] about it. The Two Books *de Morbis muliebribus* were inserted in the Collection, which a Physician, whose Name is *Israel Spachius*, published at *Strasburg*, in 1597, of several Treatises concerning the Diseases of Women; and, as for the *Consilia Medica*, they are to be found in a Collection of the like Works published by *Scholzius* at *Franckfort*, in 1598. It is highly probable, that *Israel Spachius* believed the Two Books *de Morbis muliebribus* to be a Work of the Disciple of *Brissot*. It was, doubtless, He, who inserted in the Title, *Martini Akakiæ Medici Regii & in Universitate Parisiensi Professoris Medicinæ doctissimi, &c.* This Work had never been printed, but had been handed about in Manuscript. *Spachius* knew, in general, that *Martin Akakia* wrote it; and he innocently believed, that This *Akakia* was the same Author, who had published some Works already; thus he gave him the Titles of the *Akakia* of *Chalons*, and not That of *Regius Professor*, which the Author would have assumed, if he had published his Book himself.

[B] *As his Writings testify.*] *Renatus Moreau* took care to publish two Pieces of this Author: to wit, *Prælectiones in librum Hippocratis Coi de morbis internis, Parif.* 1637. *Prælectiones in librum Hippocratis Coi de aëre, aquis, & locis, Parif.* 1646. He prefixed the Author's Elogy to the first. There are likewise some *Latin* Verses of *Antony Mornac* prefixed to the second, in praise of the same *Martin*, who was one of the Commissioners at the famous Conference of *du Perron*, and *du Plessis*.

[C] *Had I not consulted some Friends.*] The Professor *Dreslincourt* was pleased to inform me, that *Martin Akakia*, Author of the Treatise *de Morbis muliebribus*, not only cites *Fernel* and *Amatus Lusitanus*, but also *Scaliger's* Work against *Cardan*, and the *Cosmocritice* of *Cornelius Gemma*. *Fernel* dedicated his Books to *Henry* II. who did not begin his Reign till the Year 1547. *Amatus Lusitanus* composed his *Second Century* at *Rome* (1) in the Year 1551 (2): I say at *Rome*; whither Pope *Julius* III. had invited him. *Scaliger's* Book against *Cardan* was not printed till 1557. That of *Cornelius Gemma* was written on occasion of the *Star*, which appeared in the Year 1572. and was not printed till 1575. This *Martin Akakia*, therefore, must have been living in the Year 1575. Mr *Dreslincourt's* Remarks prove this plainly. Now, as I had read (3), that *Martin Akakia* was Royal Professor of Physic, in the Year 1577, and that *Peter Seguin* succeeded him, on the twentieth of *September*, 1594; I was desirous of knowing what *William du Val* had said upon this Subject, in his Catalogue of the Professors of the Royal College. This I accomplished by the Assistance of Mr *Pinsson de Riollet* (4), who took the Pains, in a most obliging manner, to send me several Particulars concerning the *Akakia's*. He informed me among other things, I. That the *Martin Akakia* of *Chalons*, Physician to *Francis* I, died in the Year 1551. From this Fact, and the Remarks of Mr *Dreslincourt*, it necessarily results, that the Author of the Book *de Morbis muliebribus*, is not *Martin Akakia Catalaunensis*. II. That it is true indeed, that *Peter Seguin* had a Grant, in the Year 1588, of the Office of Royal Lecturers of Chirurgery, upon the Resignation of *Martin Akakia*, his Father-in-law, but that he was obliged to take out new Letters, in the Year 1594. And the Reason was this: During the Civil Wars, the Number of Royal Lectures increased much more than the Foundation could support; several Persons having surreptitiously obtained Grants of that Place. *Henry* IV. chastised Part of those Lecturers, in 1594, and gave out new Letters to those, whom he retained. *Peter Seguin* was one of the latter. And for this Reason his Promotion was dated in the Year 1594. by the Author of *the Antiquities of Paris*; but, if That Author had been exact, he would not have been contented to say, that *Peter Seguin* succeed *Martin Akakia* on the twentieth of *September*, 1594. He would have been afraid of making his Readers imagin, that *Martin Akakia* died the same Year, and that *Peter Seguin* commenced from that Time Royal Professor. Now whoever should say this, would be guilty of two great Mistakes.

(1) *'Tis that, which Akakia quotes without naming it; but what he quotes is in Centur. 2. Curat. 39. pag. 289.*

(2) *He says so himself, pag. 136.*

(3) *In the Antiquities of Paris, by Father Du Breul, pag. 568.*

(4) *Advocate in the Parliament of Paris.*

AKAKIA (MARTIN) Son of the Preceeding, was created Doctor of Physic, at *Paris*, in 1598. He was made Royal Professor of Chirurgery, the Year after, by the Resignation of *Peter Seguin*, his Brother-in-Law (*a*). He took a Journey to *Rome*, and died of a Distemper, at *Paris*, in the Year 1605, without leaving any Posterity. He lies buried with his Father at St *Germain de l'Auxerrois*. His Brother JOHN AKAKIA, created Doctor of Physic, in the Year 1612, was Physician to *Lewis* XIII; and died in *Savoy* in the Year 1630. He left many Children [A].

(*a*) *He resigned his Place on being made Royal Reader in Physick, on the tomb of Sept. 1609. by the Resignation of John Duret.*

[A] *He left many Children.*] I. MARTIN AKAKIA, Royal Professor of Chirurgery (1), who resigned his Place in favour of *Mathurin Denyau*, and died some Years after, in 1677, leaving a Son, who was Clerk to the Comptroller General of the Finances, and a Daughter married to Mr *le Vayer de Boutigni*, Counsellor in the Parliament of *Paris*. II. ROGER AKAKIA. He is the Man of Intrigue, taken Notice of in the Remark [D] of the first *Akakia*. III. CHARLES AKAKIA: a very pious Clergyman, attached to the *Port-Royal*. IV. SIMON AKAKIA *de Plessis*, Agent for the *Port-Royal* Ladies. V. N. AKAKIA, known by the Name of Mr *da Lac*. He has the Care of the Edition of the late Mr de *Saci's* Books on the Scripture. There were other Children of *John Akakia*, besides these five.

(1) *He had the Post, when Wissliam du Val publish'd his Catalogue in 1644.*

AKIBA

AKIBA.

AKIBA, a famous Rabbin, flourished, a little after *Titus* had destroyed the City of *Jerusalem*. He was a *Jew* only by the Mother's side; and it is pretended, that his Father was a Descendant of *Sisera*, General of the Army of *Jabin*, King of *Tyre*. *Akiba* lived in the Country, till he was forty Years of Age; where he had no very Honourable Employ; for he kept the Flocks of *Calba Schwa*, a rich Citizen of *Jerusalem*. At length he applied himself to Study, at the Instigation of his Master's Daughter, who promised to marry him, if he made a great Progress in the Sciences. He applied himself so earnestly to Study, for twenty four Years, in the Academies, that, afterwards, he found himself surrounded with a crowd of Disciples, as one of the greatest Masters, that had been in *Israel*. He had twenty four Thousand Scholars. He declared for the Impostor *Barcochebas* (a), and maintained, that the Words of *Balaam*, *A Star shall come out of Jacob*, were to be understood of him, and that he was the true *Messiah* (b). He was not satisfy'd with anointing him (c), as *Samuel* did the two first Kings of the *Jews*; He even submitted to become his Equerry (d). The Forces, which the Emperor *Hadrian* sent against the *Jews*, who, under the Conduct of this false *Messiah*, had committed horrible Massacres, extinguished this Faction. *Akiba* was taken, and punished with a cruel Death (e): His Flesh was torn with Iron Combs; but in such a manner, that they lengthened out the Torture, and put him to Death, as it were with a slow Fire (f). He lived one Hundred and twenty Years, and was buried, with his Wife, in a Cave, on a Mountain not far from *Tiberias*. His twenty four Thousand Disciples were buried below him in the same Mountain (g). I mention these particulars, without pretending, that they all deserve Credit. It is thought, that he wrote a spurious Book, under the Name of the Patriarch *Abraham* [A]. Some say, he was guilty of a more unpardonable Offence than this; namely, that he altered the *Hebrew* Text of the Bible [B], in order to answer an Objection of the *Christians* [C]. The *Jews* give him great Commendations [D]; and look upon him as a Man, who taught them all the unwritten Law [E]. The Remark, which we shall make upon this, will contain some Particulars

(a) *The word signifies in Hebrew, Son of the Star.*
(b) *See Joh. à Lent. Schediasma Historico Philologicum de Judæorum Pseudo-Messiis, pag.* 9.
(c) *Ibid. p.* 14.
(d) *Ibid. p.* 9, & 15.
(e) *Ibid. p.* 14. ex Tractatu Talmudico E-ruf, fol. 21.
(f) *Ibid. p.* 15. ex Tractatu Talmudico Berachos, fol. 61.
(g) *Ibid. p.* 15. ex Autore libelli de Cippis ab Hottingero editi, & Latine translati.

[A] *That he wrote a spurious Book, under the Name of the Patriarch* Abraham.] It is entitled, *Sepher Jezirah*; that is, *The Book of the Creation*. See the Remark [E] of the Article A B R A H A M, and add there this Supplement. *Lambecius* ought not to have said that this Book of the Creation was printed the first time at *Mantua* (1); for the Edition of *Mantua* in 4to, with the Commentary of *Abraham Ben-Doir*, and several other Rabbies, whose Names you may find in the 536th Page of the *Critical History of the Old Testament*, had been preceded by the *Paris* Edition, in 8vo, 1552. The same Book was printed at *Basil* in *Folio*, in the Year 1587, with several others of the same Stamp. It is of great Weight with the Cabalists; they say, they work Miracles by it (2).

[B] *He altered the* Hebrew *Text of the Bible*.] This Alteration relates to the Age of the Patriarchs, when they began to have Children. Every one knows, they were older at that Time, according to the Bible of the LXX, than according to the *Hebrew* Bible. For Example: *Adam*, according to the *Hebrew* Text, was one hundred and thirty Years old, when his Wife brought forth *Seth*; but, according to the Translation of the LXX, he was, at that time, in his two hundred and thirtieth Year. Most Divines prefer the *Hebrew* Text to the *Greek*. They, who contend for the *Greek*, are but few in Number, but, in Recompence for this, they are commonly Men of singular Learning. Father *Paul Pezron*, a Monk of the strictest Order of *Cistertians*, and Doctor of Divinity of the Faculty of *Paris*, is one of this Minority. He pretends, among other things, that the *Jews* altered the *Hebrew* Text in relation to the Times which past between the Destruction of *Jerusalem*, under *Titus*, and the twelfth Year of the Emperor *Hadrian* (3). He proves this by the Translation of *Aquila*, published in the twelfth Year of That Emperor, which agrees very well with the *Hebrew* Text at this present time. Now as *Aquila*, going over from the Christian to the Jewish Religion, put himself under the Tuition of *Akiba*; it seems very probable to Father *Pezron*, that This Alteration of the Scripture ought to be imputed to That Rabbi. It is certain that *Akiba* was "at that time in great Esteem "among the *Jews*, and chiefly among those of *Pa-*"*lestine*; for he was about forty Years Master of a "College, which they had at *Jabne*, or at *Tiberias*, "near the Lake of *Genezareth* (4). ―――― He had "many Disciples; he passed for the most learned "Man among the *Jews*; and had so much Credit "with them, that it was he, who declared that *Bar-*"*cochebas* was the *Messiah* (5)."

[C] *In order to answer an Objection of the Christians.*] "The *Christians* never disputed more strong-"ly against the *Jews*, than in those Times, says "the *same Author* (6), and never opposed them more "effectually. For they had nothing more to do, "than to shew them the *Gospel* on the one side, and, "on the other, the Ruins of *Jerusalem*, which were "before their Eyes, to convince them that *JESUS* "*CHRIST*, who had so plainly foretold it's Destru-"ction, was the Prophet whom *Moses* had promi-"sed. ―――― But they pressed them very close with "their own Traditions, which imported, That "*CHRIST* should manifest himself at the end of "about six thousand Years, by shewing them, that "this Number of Years was actually accomplished. "This greatly embarrassed them, and is doubtless the "Reason, why it is said, in the *Talmud*, that *Akiba* "and *Samsai* computed the Years (7) out of which "such powerful Arguments were drawn against "them." It is certain, that the *Jews* might have answered the Objection drawn from the six thousand Years, had the Bible been such, as we have it at present; for it wants much of that Number of Years, from *Adam* to *JESUS CHRIST*.

[D] *The Jews give him great Commendations*] They called him *Sethumtaah* (8), that is, *The Authentic*. One of them (9) says, it would fill a whole Volume to speak of him according to his Worth. His Name, says another, ran all over the Universe, and we have received all the Oral Law from His Mouth; *Hujus nomen (inquit autor libri Zemach David) exiit ab uno extremo mundi usque ad aliud, atque totam legem Oralem ex ejus ore accepimus* (10).

[E] *Look upon him as a Man, who taught them all the unwritten Law.*] See the Passage just now quoted, and the Book, which Father *Paul Pezron* published at *Paris* in the Year 1691 (11). We find there (12), that Rabbi *Akiba*, the Son of *Joseph*, was the first Compiler of the *Deuteroses*, or *Jewish* Traditions, and the chief of the *Traditionaries*: that he collected the Traditions, which *Hillel*, *Simeon*, and other antient Doctors had invented; that he added others of his own Invention to them; that they were in vogue together 'till the end of the Vth Century, at which time others were added to them, of which the *Talmud* was composed; that *Akiba* (13) imployed the Rabbi *Meir*, the most famous of all his Disciples, *to commit part of these Traditions to Writing, out of which the Misna was afterwards com-*
posed

(1) Lambecii Histor. Literar. Prodrom. p. 53. apud Placcium de Pseudonymis, pag. 134.
(2) Placcius, Ibid.
(3) Pezron, *of the Antiquity of Times*, cap. 16. pag. 289. Edit. of *Paris* 1687, in 4to.
(4) Ibid. p. 290.
(5) Ibid. p. 291.
(6) Id. ib.
(7) Talmud in Tractatu de Synedrio.
(8) See Joh. à Lent de Pseudo-Messiis, pag. 9.
(9) Zacutus in Juchasin, pag. 66. apud Lent, pag. 19.
(10) Kœnig. Biblioth. pag. 19.
(11) Entitled, A Defence of the Antiquity of Times.
(12) Page 61.
(13) Page 63. ex Talmach Divid, p. 95.

AKIBA. ALABASTER.

culars of his Life. If we were to judge of his Lectures by his Precepts relating to the Close-Stool [F], we should have reason to treat them as ridiculous.

posed (14), that he was the Patriarch's Assistant (15), and the Master of *Aquila*, and of Rabbi *Jose*, who was the Author of the *Grand Council* of the *Jews* (16); that he became the Head of the *Jewish* Schools, in the same Year that *Josephus* finished his Antiquities; that he continued in this Place forty Years; that he is often cited in the *Pirke-Eliezer*, and that he wished eternal Damnation to all those, who should read the Works of the *Christians*.

[F] *By his Precepts relating to the Close-Stool.*] The *Jewish* Nation was devoted to a Spirit of such childish and chimerical Observances, that their gravest Doctors have extended their Ritual, even to the most Mechanical Actions, such as That of going to the Necessary-House. Unhappy for him who could not find out the East; for the four Cardinal Points of the Horizon are not equally favourable. I shall give the rest of their ridiculous Superstitions in this Matter in the following Words. "Dixit R. Akiba, ii. gressus sum "aliquando post Rabbi Josuam in sedis secretæ locum, "& tria ab eo didici. Didici I. quod non versus "Orientem & Occidentem sed versus Septentrionem "& Austrum converterem nos debeamus. Didici II. "quod non in pedes erectum, sed jam confidentem "se retegere liceat. Didici III. quod podex non "dextra sed sinistra manu abstergendus sit. Ad hæc "objecit ibi Ben Hasas; usque adeo vere perspicuisti "frontem erga magistrum tuum ut cacantem observares? Respondet ille, Legis hæc arcana sunt ad "quæ discenda id necessario mihi agendum fuit (17). "— R. Akiba *said, I once follow'd Rabbi* Josua "*into the* — *and learned three Things from him*; "I. *That we must turn ourselves, not Eastward and "Westward, but Northward and Southward, when "we* — II. *That we must* — *not standing, but "sitting.* III. *That we must wipe* — *not with our "right Hand, but with our left.* Upon this Ben "Hasas objected; *Are you so burden'd in Impudence, "as to watch your Master, when he is at* — ? *He* "reply'd, *These are Secrets of our Law, to learn which "I was obliged so to do.*" Behold a wonderful Doctor, who explain'd the Mysteries of the Law, on his Close-Stool, without speaking a Word!

ALABASTER (WILLIAM) an *English Divine*, was born at *Hadley* in *Suffolk*. He was one of the Doctors of *Trinity* College at *Cambridge*, and accompanied the Earl of *Essex*, as his Chaplain, in his Expedition to *Cadiz*, in the Reign of Queen *Elizabeth*. It is said, that his first inducement to change his Religion was the Pomp and Splendor of the *Romish* Churches, and the great Respect paid to their Priests; and that, as he became wavering, some of that Communion worked upon these Dispositions, and so dextrously took advantage of the Complaint he made of being neglected in *England*, that he immediately turned *Papist*, being satisfied, that he had no reason to expect better Preferment, at home. However that be, he embraced the Communion of the Church of *Rome*; but did not find his Expectations answered. He was soon disgusted with it; he did not like a Discipline, which would not admit any of the Degrees, to which he had been already promoted; and it is probable he was not better pleased with their Creature-Worship, which the Protestants are used to look upon with Horror; therefore he returned into *England* to resume his former Religion. He obtained a Canonship in St *Paul*'s Church, and afterwards the Living of *Tharfield* in *Hertfordshire*. He understood the *Hebrew* Tongue very well, but spoiled himself by the Study of the *Cabala*, of which he was very fond. He gave Proofs of it in the Sermon, which he preached, when he was created Doctor of Divinity at *Cambridge*. He took for his Text the beginning of the First Book of the *Chronicles*, *Adam, Seth, Enoch*, and, after having touched upon the Literal Sense, he fell into the Mystical, and maintained, that *Adam* signified, *Unhappiness* and *Misery*; and so of the rest (*a*). His Method of explaining the Scripture did not please the *Roman* Catholics [*A*]. I shall give their Sense of it in the Remarks, and shew, how he got clear

[*A*] *His Method of explaining* — *did not please the Roman Catholics.*] Francis Garasse, a Jesuit, having mentioned a very whimsical Opinion of *Isidorus Pelusiota* (1), goes on thus. "*Alabaster's* Exposition is "yet farther from common Sense; for he tacks together certain *Rabbinical* Conceits, which are pleasant enough, if they were but as solidly founded, "as they are subtilly invented. He tells us, in his *Apparatus*, chap. 9. That *Jonas* and our Saviour "remain'd punctually three Days and three Nights, "the one in the Bowels of the Earth, and the other "in the Whale's Belly, in the following Manner. "*Jonas*, says he, *was carried to the very Center of "the World, as he himself acknowledges*: Ad extrema "montium descendi, terræ vectes circumdederunt me. "— *I went down to the bottom of the Mountains; "the Earth with her Bars was about me for ever.* "*Jonah* ii. 6. *Now, being thus situated, he had both "Day and Night at one time; for, looking towards "our Hemisphere, he had the Day before, and the "Night behind him, and, the next Day, quite the "contrary; so that, remaining but one Day and a "half, he continued there in reality three whole Days; "forasmuch as the Space of Time must be doubled, because he enjoy'd at once, what we have successively. "Thus our Lord being in the Womb of the Earth, "had, like Jonas, Day and Night both at one time; "forasmuch as his Soul went down to the Center of "the Earth, in order to have the Day on one Side, "and the Night on the other, and thereby to shorten "the Term of his abode, without wresting Truth; so "unwilling was he to leave his Disciples in a disconsolate Condition.* This Hypothesis, I say, is injurious to the holy Scripture; as it is too much "strain'd, and sophisticated, and is just like the Fancies "of the Rabbins; and therefore it was not without "Reason, that *Alabaster's* Book was condemn'd at *Rome*: But he was so excessively fond of his own "Conceits, that he behav'd worse, than *Heliodorus*; "for he chose to forsake his Religion, rather than "quit his dangerous and idle Notions concerning the "holy Scriptures (2).'' I shall add the Judgment of a *Flemish* Jesuit to That of the *Frenchman*. *Bonfrerius*, having condemn'd those, who, by the help of the *Cabala*, find any thing in every Passage of the holy Scripture, goes on thus: "Quod nuper fecit "insulse nimis & irreligiose Gulielmus Alabaster, qui "in illo suo Apparatu ex inanibus ejusmodi fundamentis, ne dicam quisquiliis, conatus est nobis suam "Mysticam Theologiam, & (ita ipse vocat) interiorem "Scripturæ sensum ac medullam (re ipsa aliud nihil "quam deliramenta & somnia) exprimere. Qua ex "re male audit, & Romæ censorium Ecclesiæ virgulam merito expertus est. Quis enim ferat quempiam "in re tam seria, Scripturæ inquam interpretatione, "pro probatis mercibus vendere quæ ipse parum sano "cerebro deliravit (3) ? — *Which was lately practised, with too much Folly and Irreligion, by "William* Alabaster, *who, in That Apparatus of his, "endeavour'd, upon this idle Foundation, not to call it "a Founda-

ALABASTER. 175

clear of the Objection made in relation to the Three Days and Three Nights, which JESUS CHRIST was to pass in the Bowels of the Earth, as *Jonas* did in the Whale's Belly (*b*). I must not omit, that his Poetry was very much esteemed. He wrote a Latin Tragedy, called *Roxana*, at the Representation of which, in a College at *Cambridge*, there happened a very remarkable Accident (*c*). A Lady was so frighted with the Last Word of the Tragedy, *Sequar, Sequar*, which was pronounced with a very furious Air, that she was distracted all her Life-time after. *Alabaster* was yet living in 1630. His *Apparatus in Revelationem Jesu Christi* was printed at *Antwerp* in the Year 1607. As for the *Spiraculum tubarum, seu fons spiritualium expositionum ex æquivocis Pentaglotti* (*d*) *significationibus*, and his *Ecce sponsus venit, seu tuba pulcritudinis, hoc est demonstratio quod non sit illicitum nec impossibile computare durationem mundi & tempus secundi adventus Christi*; they were printed at *London* (*e*). From these Titles we may judge of the Author's Taste; but we shall form a better Notion of it from the Words of *Andrew Rivet* [*B*], which I shall produce. We must not forget his *Lexicon Hebraicum, in Folio*. I have taken no Notice of his *Motives of his Conversion*, which he published, after having embraced the Catholic Religion; we know well enough that this is the Practice of those, who change their Religion; A Custom more in vogue at that Time, than at present. The Public had not, then, leisure to be disgusted at this sort of Books. That of *Alabaster* was refuted by *Roger Fenton* (*f*).

(a) See Remark [A].

(c) Fuller's Worthies.

(d) So says the Catalogue of the Bodleian Library: But it should be Pentateuch.

(e) See the Catalogue of the Bodleian Library.

(f) His Reply is entitled, An Answer to W. Alabaster's Motives. Lond. 1599. in 4to

---

"a Foundation of Weeds and Refuse, to explain to us
"his *Mystical Theology*, and (as he himself calls it)
"the internal Sense and Marrow of the Scripture;
"though in reality, nothing else but a Madman's
"Dreams. Upon which account it was (of ill repute,
"and deservedly felt the Church's censorial Rod, at
"Rome. For who can bear, that, in so serious a
"Matter, I mean in explaining the Scripture, any
"one should vend for approved Wares, what are but
"the delirious Productions of his own distemper'd
"Brain?" He gives afterwards some Examples of this Author's Explications.

I shall quote presently a *Protestant*, who reproaches the *Roman Catholics* for tolerating the idle Fancies of *Alabaster*.

I have been informed by a learned Person, that most Readers do not love to be told, in general, that such or such an Author has advanc'd a chimerical Opinion. This excites their Curiosity, and they want to have it immediately satisfy'd, and even without being obliged to have recourse to some other Book, which they have in their Library. This learned Person therefore, would have thought I ought to have said nothing of *Isidorus Pelusiota*, or that, having observ'd, in general, that his Opinion is grotesque, I ought to have produc'd it; especially considering that Father *Garasse's* Book is seldom found in the Library of private Persons. I profit by this Advice, and find by experience it is well founded; for which Reason I have chosen, upon many Occasions, to add to my Commentaries, rather than excite the Curiosity of my Readers in vain: *Isidorus Pelusiota*, then, in order to compleat the Number of Days, suppos'd, That the Darkness, at the time of the Passion, ought to be taken for one Night, and that the return of the Light 'till Sun-set ought to be consider'd as a Day. Read what follows: "I answer, That it is true, there is

(A) It is That of the 12th Chapter of St Matthew, where it is said, that the Son of Man shall be three days and three nights in the heart of the earth.

"some Difficulty in reconciling this Passage (4) with
"the Truth of History; and that it was one of the
"chief Arguments, by which *Julian*, the Apostate,
"endeavour'd to overthrow the Truth of the Gos-
"pel; however it is not so desperate, but that a
"true and natural Exposition may be given of it,
"without having recourse to Fancies; which some
"have done, though without any ill Design; as we
"have seen above, concerning the Hour of the Re-
"surrection. *Isidorus Pelusiota*, in the 114th Epistle
"of the first Book of his Epistles, gives us a new
"Explication of it in these Words: —— Sic habeto;
"sextâ horâ Parasceves in crucem actus est Dominus,
"ab hac horâ usque ad nonam tenebræ extiterunt;
"hæc tu noctem intellige: Rursus horâ nonâ lux;
"hæc tu pro die habe: Nox rursum Parasceves:
"Tum dies Sabbathi: Tum nox Sabbathi Dominici
"Diei. —— Take it thus; Our Lord was crucified
"at the sixth Hour, on Good Friday; from this
"Hour to the ninth, there was Darkness; call this
"one Night; again, at the ninth Hour there was
"Light; let this stand for one Day; Then follow'd
"the Night of Good Friday: Then the Day of the
"Jewish Sabbath: Then the Night of the Christian
"Sabbath, or Lord's Day. —— It is true, indeed, ac-
"cording to this Exposition, that JESUS CHRIST re-
"mained three Days and three Nights, in the Bowels

"of the Earth; but they are Days and Nights redu-
"ced to a very narrow Compass (5).

[B] *A better Notion of it, from the Words of* Andrew Rivet.] "Anno, 160-, says he (6), qui-
"dam Pontificius Anglus *Gulielmus Alabastrus*, edi-
"dit Antverpiæ librum, cui titulum fecit, *Appara-*
"*tus in revelationem Christi*, in quo profitetur se no-
"vam & admirabilem rationem afferre investigandi
"Prophetiarum mysteria ex Scriptura se ipsam inter-
"pretante. Ibi novam Cabbalam instituit, ex qua
"quidlibet ex quolibet educit, & mutatis, vel inver-
"sis, aut separatis, & disjunctis, Ebræorum vocabu-
"lorum literis, aut syllabis, novis etiam significationi-
"bus contra grammaticæ rationem assignatis, diversis
"nominibus aut verbis, omnia pervertit, & ipsi adeo
"commentum placet, ut, quamvis sæpe excipiat se
"nolle præjudicare Latinæ versioni, cum tamen vi-
"deat ex ea nullis fiduciis sensum, quem sibi propo-
"nit, posse erui, non veretur dicere, pag. 61, *De-*
"*um Christi & Religionis Christianæ mysteria per*
"*illam verborum formam in Ebrææ legis codice ex-*
"*pressisse, quæ sensum carnalem, & à divina mente*
"*alienum, lectori prima fronte offerret, atque ita*
"*voluisse ut in Ecclesia Christiana nulla passim lege-*
"*retur versio, quam quæ secundum Ebræorum ver-*
"*borum corticem conciperetur, ut loc mode sapientia*
"*divina non esset cuivis profano obvia*. Sed postea
"idem, per totum illud opus, ita sapientiam illam
"divinam ex Scripturæ, si Deo placet, penetralibus
"haurit, ut ne ulli quidem hactenus ex Patribus san-
"ctissimis vel unius loci talis interpretatio in men-
"tem unquam venerit, ne ipsis quidem omniscuis
"Pontificibus. *In the Year* 1607, *a certain*
"*English Roman Catholic, named* William Alabaster,
"*published, at* Antwerp, *a Book, entituled* Apparatus
"in Revelationem Christi, *in which he professes to
"give us a new and admirable Method of investiga-
"ting the mysterious Sense of the Prophecies, by
"making the Scripture it's own Interpreter. In
"this Work, he drew up a new Cabala, by the help
"of which he extracts any thing from any thing;
"and perverts the whole Scripture, by changing, or
"inverting, or separating, and disjoining, the Let-
"ters of the Hebrew Words, or Syllables; sometimes
"by assigning new Significations to them, contrary
"to the Rules of Grammar, or by substituting new
"Nouns or Verbs: Nay he is so fond of his own
"Comment, that, tho' he frequently assures us he in-
"tends no Prejudice to the Latin Version, yet, when
"he cannot, with all the torturing imaginable, wrest
"That to the Sense, he would extract from it, he
"is not asham'd to declare, pag. 61, That God ex-
"press'd the Mysteries of CHRIST, and the Christian
"Religion, under That Form of Words, which is
"in the Hebrew Code of the Law, which, at first
"sight, presents to the Reader a carnal Sense, and
"wide of the Divine Intentions, and that it is his
"Will, that no Version should be publickly read in
"the Christian Church, but what is conceiv'd accor-
"ding to the Bark, or external meaning of the He-
"brew Words; that by this means the Divine Wis-
"dom might not be obvious to the Prophane. Yet
"this very Author afterwards, through his whole
"Work, so exposes his divine Wisdom, by drawing

(5) Garasse's Curtius Doctrine, pag. 592, 593.

(6) Rivet. Isagoge ad Scripturam sacram, cap. 15. Oper. Tom. 2. pag. 937.

ALAINS.

" it out of it's Recesses, that none of the Holy Fa-
" thers, not even the Popes themselves, with all their
" Infallibility, ever dream'd of one single Interpreta-
" tion, such as our Author gives us." Rivet, having
produc'd two Examples of the visionary Notions of
this Author (7), continues his Discourse thus; " A-
" lia hujus farinæ multa, pag, 57. & seqq. afferuntur
" à nugatore blasphemo, quibus syllabas unius nomi-
" nis & verbi seorsim accipiens, & à sua radice di-
" vellens, omnia sursum deorsum vertit: Et tamen
" in regno Pontificio toleratur hæc novitas, ubi sim-
" plex Scripturæ ex ipsâ Scripturâ interpretatio hæ-
" reseos insimulatur. Sed de his hactenus. Videant
" Pontificii, an suo Alabastro non debeant nigrum
" præfigere theta: Nos hominis insolentissimam au-
" daciam detestamur, etsi eum Jesuita Possevinus suis
" Catholicis Scriptoribus inseruerit, Appar. Sacri
" Tomo primo. ——— This blasphemous Trifler has
" given us more of the same Stamp, Page 57, &c.
" in which, by taking the Syllables of a single Noun
" or Verb apart, he overturns the whole Sense. And
" yet this novel Practice is tolerated in a Roman Ca-
" tholick Country, where the simple Interpretation of
" Scripture by itself is charged with Heresy. But
" so much for this Subject. I leave it to the Roman
" Catholics to judge, whether their Alabaster ought
" not to undergo the Sentence of Condemnation: For
" my own part, I detest the shameless Impudence of
" the Man, notwithstanding the Jesuit Possevin has
" inserted him among his Catholic Writers." Observe
I. That the Work, out of which this is taken, was
publish'd the first time in 1626, and that the Edition in
Folio, printed in the Year 1652, which I make use
of, had been revised, corrected, and enlarged by the
Author. II. That Alabaster's Book had been condemn'd at Rome, the 30th of January, 1610, and
that the Author was return'd to the Bosom of the
Church of England, a considerable time before the
first Edition of Rivet's Book. The Congregation of
the Index express themselves in the following Terms;
I set them down, because they seem to infer that the
Apparatus of Alabaster was reprinted at Rome, with
some Alterations and Corrections. Apparatus in Revelationem Jesu Christi Auctore Gulielmo Alabastro
Anglo, Antverpiæ 1607. Et Antithesis, Benedicti à Benedictis Veneti, contra Gulielmum Witackerum, nisi
fuerint ex CORRECTIS AB AUCTORIBUS ET
ROMÆ IMPRESSIS, cum approbatione P. Mag.
Sacri Palatii. But perhaps they meant only, that,
in case those Authors should correct their Works,
and suffer them to be printed at Rome, with the
Approbation of the Master of the Sacred Palace, they
would then license the new Edition. I believe this
to be the true Sense. Samuel Andreas, a German
Divine, wrote a Book (8) against the Cabala of Dr
Henry Moor (9), wherein he produces some Instances
of Alabaster's Chimeras (10).

ALAINS, in Latin ALANI, a barbarous People, who greatly contributed to
the Ruin of the Roman Empire. Pliny places them in Europe, beyond the Mouths
of the Danube (a); but Josephus points out their Situation more exactly; for he places
them near the Palus Mæotis, and the Tanais (b). He describes a furious Eruption,
which they made into Media, and Armenia, in the Reign of Vespasian. It was at that
time, that Vologeses, King of the Parthians, desired That Emperor to send him
Assistance against the Alani, under the Command of one of his Sons; upon which
Domitian used his Endeavours to obtain this Commission (c). This might induce
Moreri to tell us, though a little confusedly as to Chronology, that these Barbarians
had already made themselves known from the Time of Domitian. But this want of Chronological Exactness is nothing in comparison of the rest. He tells us, that the Alani
joined with the Vandals, with the Suevi, and afterwards with the Goths, in the beginning of the Fifth Century; that they fought against the French in the Year 505; that
they ravaged Gaul; that Gunderic, the Son of Aodegigilus, was their Chief; that,
about the Year 509, they passed into Spain, where they settled; and that they were
defeated there by Vallia, King of the Goths, in 418. Such gross Mistakes, surely,
must fly in the Reader's Face; for in short, a People, conquered in 418, in a Country, into which they came about the Year 509, is a Story, sufficient to awaken the
most languishing Attention. The Truth is, Moreri is guilty of an Anachronism of no
less than an Hundred Years. The Alani advanced, in 406, from the Banks of the
Danube to the Rhine, without meeting any Resistance; and being joined by the
Vandals, who had escaped from a Battel lost against the Franks, they entered Gaul.
Their King's Name was Respendial: the King of the Vandals's Name was Gunderic, the
Son of Godisigil, who had been killed in the late Battel. Several other Nations of
Barbarians joined them, and caused a prodigious Desolation in all the Gauls. Part
of the Alani, under the Conduct of Utacus, who had succeeded Respendial, passed
into Spain, in the Year 409, and settled in the Province of Carthagena, and in Lusitania; the other Part kept their Ground in Gaul, under the Conduct of Two Kings.
The Alani in Spain, defeated by Vallia, King of the Goths, near Merida, in 418,
were forced to submit to Honorius. Their King Vatacus lost his Life in the Battel
(d). We meet with certain of the Alani, in the Year 464, who threw off the Yoke
of the Huns, after the Death of Attila, and entered Italy in order to settle there;
but Ricimer, marching against them with the Forces of the Empire, defeated them in
such a manner near Bergamo, that not very few of them escaped, and their King
Beorgor was killed in the Battel. The Huns, having committed great Ravage and
Slaughter in the Country of the Alani, had a long time before associated themselves
with those, who escaped their Fury. This we read in Ammianus Marcellinus (e).
He gives us a long Description of the Manners of the Alani (f) and says, they were
the same People, to which Antiquity gave the Name of Massagetæ [A]; he pretends
they

[A] The People to whom Antiquity gave the Name of Massagetæ.] There are two Passages in relation to this in Ammianus Marcellinus (1); the first is in the fifth Chapter of the twenty third Book, and will admit of no Difficulty; " Lucullus, per Albanos & " Massagetas, quos Alanos nunc appellamus, hac " quoque natione perruptâ, vidit Caspios lacus. ——— " Lucullus, by the Albani and Massagetæ, now cal- " led Alani, forcing his Way thro' this People, came " in sight of the Caspian Sea." The other is in the second Chapter of the thirty first Book, in a Place where the Manuscripts are so confused, that we must have Recourse to Critical Conjectures, to find in it what I attribute here to Marcellinus. It is, therefore, only upon the Conjecture of the learned Va-lesius, that This Historian is made to say adæque

ALAINS. ALAIS.

they inhabited the vast Solitudes of *Scythia*, and gave their Name to the Neighbouring Nations, as fast as they subdued them, and spread this Name as far as the River *Ganges*. Though he represents them Cruel and Savage [*B*], yet he does not make them equal the *Huns* in Brutality; and he remarks that they pillaged and plundered as far as the *Palus Mæotis*, and as far as *Media* and *Armenia*.

Alanos pervenit, veteres Massagetas. —— *He penetrated as far as the Alani, formerly the Massagetæ.* Now, as the first Passage plainly proves, that *Marcellinus* placed the *Alani* in *Asia*, we may, I think, contest, with this learned Commentator, the Explication he gives of these Words of the Text: " *Hister* " *Sauromatas prætermeat ad usque amnem Tanaim* " *pertinentes, qui Asiam terminat ab Europa.* Hoc " *transito in immensum extentas Scythiæ solitudines* " *Alani inhabitant* (2). —— *The River Ister (or the* " *Danube*) *flows by the Country of the Sauromatæ,* " *which reaches as far the River Tanais, the Boun-* " *dary of Asia and Europe, beyond which, the Alani* " *inhabit the immense Deserts of Scythia.*" *Valesius* will have *hoc transito* (*beyond which*) to relate to the *Danube*, and not to the *Tanais*; and, in proof, he alledges *Pliny, Dionysius Characenus, Orosius,* and *Tzetzes*, who place the *Alani* in *Sarmatia*, and beyond the *Danube*; but the Question is not what others have said of it, but only what *Marcellinus's* Opinion was; and, upon this Foot, it seems to me, that *hoc transito* must be referred to the *Tanais*; for, besides that the *Massagetæ* did not inhabit between the *Tanais* and the *Danube*, we find a little after, that this Historian places the *Alani* in the Neighbourhood of the *Amazons*, and makes them rob and plunder, on the one side, as far as *Media* and *Armenia*, and, on the other, as far as the *Palus Mæotis*, and the *Bosporus Cimmerius*. " *Parte alia prope Amazonum* " *sedes Alani sunt Orienti adclines, diffusi per populo-* " *sas gentes & amplas, Asiaticos vergentes in tractus,* " *quos dilatari ad usque Gangen accepi fluvium* (3). " —— *latrocinando & venando ad usque Mæotica* " *stagna & Cimmerium Bosporum, itidemque Arme-* " *nios discurrentes & Mediam* (4)." All this shews, that he has not followed the Opinion of those Authors, who placed the *Alani* in the *European Sarmatia*; for where would be the wonder, if Robbers, thus situated, should ravage not only *Media* and *Armenia*, but likewise the *Palus Mæotis*? *Marcellinus* would not be the only Author, who places these *Barbarians* in *Asia*; Does not *Valesius* cite *Procopius* (5), who places them between *Caucasus* and *Caspiæ Portæ*? Lastly, What does *Moreri* mean by these Words: *Pliny places them in the European Sarmatia, where Lithuania is at present*? Doubtless he means, that the *Sarmatia* of the Ancients is the present *Lithuania*: But this is false; for *Lithuania* is but

(a) Amm. Marcell. lib. 31. c. 2.

(3) Id. ib.

(4) Id. ib.

(5) Henr. Valesius in Marcell. lib. 31. c. 2.

a small Part of the ancient *European Sarmatia*. Observe, that *Ptolemy* acknowledges two Nations of *Alani*, one in *Europe*, the other in *Asia*.

[*B*] *He represents them Cruel and Savage.*] They had no other Houses than their Waggons; in them they begot, and brought up, their Children, and abode no longer in a Place, than till they had consumed their Provisions. Flesh and Milk were their only Food; and they did not manure their Ground. " *Nec enim ulla sunt illis tuguria aut versandi vome-* " *ris cura: Sed carne & copia victitant lactis, plau-* " *stris superstidentes.* —— *absumptisque pabulis ve-* " *lut carpentis civitates impositas vehunt, maresque* " *supra cum feminis coëunt, & nascuntur in his &* " *educantur infantes* (6)." They accustomed themselves early to ride on Horseback, and looked upon it as mean to travel on Foot. They were so fond of War, that they esteemed those happy, who died in it, and loaded those with Injuries, and Reproaches of Cowardise, who died of Age and of Sickness. They took a pride in nothing more than in having killed a Man; they cut off the Heads of those, whom they killed; they flayed them, and made use of their Skins as Ornaments for their Horses; they had no Temples, nor worshipped any thing but a naked Sword stuck in the Ground. It was their God *Mars*, the Patron of the Countries, which they inhabited. They foretold future Events by the help of certain Rods, selected with magical Incantations. " *Judi-* " *catur ibi beatus, qui in prælio profuderit animam:* " *Senescentes enim & fortuitis mortibus mundo di-* " *gressos ut degeneres & ignavos conviciis atrocibus* " *insectantur: Nec quidquam est quod elatius jactent,* " *quam homine quolibet occiso: Proque exuviis glo-* " *riosis, interfectorum avulsis capitibus detractas pelles* " *pro phaleris jumentis accommodant bellatoriis. Nec* " *templum apud eos visitur, aut delubrum, &c.* (7)." This is the Picture, which *Ammianus Marcellinus* draws of these *Barbarians*; and it is not improper to represent to those, who are acquainted only with civilized Nations, that there are others so savage, as more nearly to resemble Brute Beasts, than the Human Species. This may afford many Reflexions both Physical and Moral, and make us wonder at the infinite variety of Customs and Dispositions of which our Nature is susceptible, and, among which, for one that is good, we may count above an Hundred thousand bad.

(6) Amm. Marcell. lib. 31. c. 2.

(7) Id. ib.

ALAIS, a City of *France*, in the *Sevennes*, in the Diocese of *Nîmes*, five Leagues from *Usès* (*a*), is the Capital of an Ancient Lordship, which was erected into an Earldom, and possessed by *Charles de Valois*, Duke of *Angôuleme*, a Natural Son of *Charles IX*. *Lewis Emanuel de Valois* was long known by the Name of Count *d' Alais* (*b*); he was Colonel General of the Light Horse of *France*, Governor of *Provence*, and Son of This Duke of *Angôuleme*, and Father of *Frances Mary de Valois*, Wife of *Lewis* of *Lorrain*, Duke of *Joyeuse*. By this Marriage the Earldom of *Alais* fell to the House of *Lorrain*, settled in *France*; for, from the Marriage of the Duke of *Joyeuse* with *Frances Mary de Valois*, sprung *Lewis-Joseph* of *Lorrain*, Duke of *Guise*, who died at *Paris* of the Small-Pox, the 30th of *July* 1671, aged twenty one Years (*c*). The City of *Alais* became Episcopal after the Revocation of the Edict of *Nantes* [*A*]. Some will have it to be the *Alesia* described by *Julius Cæsar*, in the seventh Book of his Commentaries. Mr *de Mandajors*, who is Mayor of it, wrote a Dissertation on this Subject. See *the Journal of the Learned*, of the 9th of *May*, 1695, at the 321st Page of the Edition of Holland.

(a) *From Baudrand's Lexic. Geograph.*

(b) *It is he, of whom Gassendus speaks so often, and to whom he wrote so many Letters, Ludovico Valesio.*

(c) *Father Anselm's General 33 of the House of France, pag. 175, 17...*

[*A*] *The City of Alais became Episcopal after the Revocation of the Edict of Nantes* (1).] It is not without reason that I mark this Period of Time; for it is certain, that the Suppression of That Edict occasioned the Erection of This new Bishoprick. This Country was full of Protestants, who were forced, by a Mission of Dragoons, to sign a Popish Formulary. It was, therefore, thought expedient not to let them be so far distant from their Prelate, as they would have been, if they had been subjected to the Diocese of *Nîmes*. This new Episcopal Church " is compo- " sed of two Collegiate Churches, That of *Psal-*

(1) In 1685.

" *modi*, and That of the City of *Alex*, and has twen- " ty three Canons, and twelve Prebendaries: It's " first Bishop *Francis*, Knight of *Saulx*, Abbot of " *Psalmodi*, and Doctor of the *Sorbonne*, was consecrated, by Cardinal *de Bonzi*, Archbishop of *Narbonne*, in the Church of the Nuns of the Visitation of *Montpelier*, the twenty ninth of *August*, " 1694. He is descended from one of the most an- " cient and noblest Families of *Poittou* (2)." See the Letter which Mr *Pontier* wrote to him, and which he published at *Paris* in 1695. The *Journal of the Learned* takes notice of it (3).

(2) *Journal of the Learned, May 9th, 1695. p. 322. Edit. of Holland.*

(3) *Id. pag. 321.*

VOL. I.   Y y   ALALCOMENIUM.

ALALCOMENIUM. ALAMANDUS.

ALALCOMENIUM, a small Town of *Bœotia*: It was so called from *Alalcomeneus*, the Foster-Father of *Minerva*, according to some (*a*); or from *Alalcomenia*, one of the Daughters of *Ogyges*, who nursed *Minerva* [*A*], according to others (*b*). The Goddess was born in this Place (*c*), and had there a Temple, and a Statue of Ivory, held in great Veneration by the People (*d*). This Veneration was the Cause, as *Strabo* tells us, that *Alalcomenium*, though easy to be taken, was never plundered, and that every body abstained from using Violence towards This Place (*e*). But *Pausanias* assures us, That the Statue of *Minerva* was taken from thence by *Sylla*, and that the Temple began afterwards to be neglected. He adds, that, in his Time, the Walls of it were split, a great Trunk of Ivy having shot forth it's Branches between the Stones. Among the Epithets of *Minerva*, That of *Alalcomenian*, Ἀλαλκομενηίς, which *Homer* gives her, is not the least worthy of Consideration (*f*). *Plutarch* reports, That *Ulysses*, having been born in *Alalcomenium*, gave this Name to a City of *Ithaca*, the better to preserve the Memory of the Place, where his Mother lay in of him (*g*). *Stephen of Byzantium* says nothing of this, when he speaks of *Alalcomenium*, and calls a City of the Island *Ithaca*, *Alalcomenium*. What *Moreri* says, That *Alalcomenium* was remarkable for the Tomb of *Tiresias*; and, that, according to *Plutarch*, it was afterwards called *Ithaca*, is false (*h*). *Hofman* is still more faulty than *Moreri* [*B*].

(*g*) Plut. Quæst. Gr. pag. 301.   (*h*) See the Article *TIRESIAS*.

[*A*] *Alalcomenia* —— *nursed Minerva.*] *Scaliger* pretends, I. That *Pausanias* owns, that some have ascribed the Education of *Minerva* to *Alalcomenia*, the Daughter of *Ogyges*: But this is rather to guess what one believes, that *Pausanias* should, or would, have said, than to keep close to his Text, as every one must acknowledge, who examines the Original. II That *Stephen of Byzantium* mentions This Daughter of *Ogyges* (1). This is not to be found in the Place where that Author speaks of the City of *Alalcomenium*.

[*B*] *Mr Hofman is still more faulty than Moreri.*] He says, I. That *Alalcomenium* was a City of *Bœotia*, denominata à *Bœotorum Alalcomenæo*. It is most certain, that he took this last Word for the Name of a Man, but for That of a Town, as *Lloyd* did (2). *Lloyd* is in the right: these are his Words; "Alalcomenæ urbs Ithacæ denominata à Bœotorum *Alalcomenæo*, ut Plut. in Hellen. refert pag. 537. Edit.

" Steph. afferens simul causam nominis." All this is true; but *Hofman*, by putting *Urbs Bœotiæ* instead of *Lloyd's Urbs Ithacæ*, and preserving the rest without any Alteration, is fallen into a double Mistake: On the one side, he says, That a Town of *Bœotia* took it's Name from itself; and, on the other, that *Plutarch* says it. II. He charges *Plutarch* falsly with advancing, Page 537, That the Sepulchre of *Tiresias*, and the Temple of *Minerva*, made this Town of *Bœotia* famous; whence the Poet said Ἀλαλκομενηίς Ἀθήνη. *Lloyd* ascribes the same thing to *Plutarch*, except what relates to the Tomb of *Tiresias*. III. *Hofman* gives us, as another Town, That which he calls *Alalcomenium*, op. *Bœotia ad locum Copaïdem inter Haliartum & Coronæam*, *Templo Minervæ clarum*; this is to multiply Beings unnecessarily. I believe none of the Authors, quoted by *Moreri*, say, that Prince *Alalcomeneus* set up the Statue of *Venus* in the Town of *Alalcomenium*.

ALAMANDUS (LEWIS), Archbishop of *Arles*, and Cardinal with the Title of *St Cecilia*, was one of the greatest Men of the XVth Century. They who speak of the Affairs, in which he was concerned, usually call him the Cardinal of *Arles*. He was of a *Burgundian*, as some Authors have said, but wanted little of being so; for the Country of *Bugei* gave him Birth. This is what *Guichenon* has shewn in his History of *Bresse*, as *Moreri* observes. Not to repeat what he says of him, I shall confine my self to other Particulars. The Cardinal of *Arles* presided in the Council of *Basil*, which deposed *Eugenius* IV, and elected the Anti-Pope *Felix* V (*a*). He was much commended by *Æneas Silvius*, as a Man perfectly qualified to preside in such Assemblies, resolute and active, famed for his Virtue, learned, and of an Admirable Memory to recapitulate what the Orators and Disputants had urged (*b*). As he was one Day haranguing against the Pope's Superiority over the Council, he was so much admired, that many saluted him, and others crowded to kiss his Robe. They extolled his Abilities to the Heavens; Abilities, which, though he was a *Frenchman*, enabled him to surpass the *Italians*, with all their Subtilities (*c*). He knew very well how to employ the Artifices of Devotion; for, upon a Session-Day, he caused all the Relicks, which were to be found in *Basil*, to be brought into the Assembly by the Priests, and to be placed in the room of the absent Bishops. This produced such an Effect, that when, according to Custom, they came to invoke the Holy Ghost, every one shed Tears. He drew Tears, likewise, from the Assistants, when he officiated on the Day of another Session, and when, with his bare and bald Head, he distributed the Communion to all those, who presented themselves, giving them the Kiss of Charity; and exhorting them to communicate worthily (*d*). He was inflexible, during the Plague, which arose in the City; neither the Death of part of his Domesticks, nor any Intreaties, could prevail upon him to leave the Place; he chose rather to lose the Council, at the peril of his own Life, by his Presence, than to save his Life, at the peril of the Council, by his Absence (*e*). He was very laborious, and of such Sobriety, that some of the Conclavists could not bear, when their Expences were retrenched, to be put in mind of the Cardinal's Example. The Answer of a *Polander*, upon that Occasion, deserves to be read [*A*]. We need not ask,

[*A*] *The Answer of a Polander, upon that Occasion deserves to be read.*] "What a Comparison you " make, (said he when they proposed the Example of " *Lewis Alamandus* to him)? You tell me of a sober " *Frenchman*, who has no Gut, or rather, who is " no Man; I can see all his Actions through the " Curtain, which is between us; I never yet saw " him eat or drink; he neither sleeps in the Night,
" nor

ALAMANDUS.

ask, whether Pope *Eugenius* thundered his Anathemas against the President of a Council, in which he had been deposed. He deprived him of all his Dignities, and called him the Son of Iniquity [B]. Yet, notwithstanding This, *Lewis Alamandus* died in the Odour of Sanctity [C], and wrought so many Miracles, after his Death, that, at the Request of the Canons, and the Celestins of *Avignon*, and at the Sollicitation of Cardinal *de Clermont*, Legate *à latere* of *Clement* VII, he was canonized by that Pope in the Year 1527 (*f*). *Odoricus Raynaldus* pretends, that he repented of all that he had done in the Council of *Basil*; but no Proof can be given of This Repentance (*g*) nor can we contradict this Matter of Fact, that, a Year before his Death (*h*), he was one of Those, who, in the Council of *Lausanne*, represented the Council of *Basil*, as a Holy and Sacred Assembly (*i*). He died at sixty Years of Age (*k*), on the 16th of *September* 1450 (*l*). Some say he died in *Savoy*, at the Abbey of *Hautecombe*, where the Monks built a Chapel to him, and invoked him in the Celebration of the Mass (*m*); others say, that he died at *Salon* (*n*). His Body lies at *Arles*: The Bull of *Clement* VII permits the Removal of it from the damp Vaults under Ground to any other more convenient place in the same Church. Some affirm, after *James Philip de Bergamo* (*o*), that *Lewis Alamandus* published several small Works, not unworthy of his Pen; but I meet with no mention of their Titles, or the Libraries, where they are.

The *Jansenists*, who censured *Odoricus Raynaldus* for the Pretended Repentance of our *Lewis Alamandus*, are themselves liable to Censure [D].

(*f*) See the Bull for it in Launoi, Epist. 11. part. 1. pag. 79, 80. Edit. Cantab. 1689. Folio.

(*g*) Launoi, ibid. p. 81.

(*h*) Anno 1449.

(*i*) Sacri Basileensis Concilii, Diploma Concilii Lausanensi apud Raynaldum ad ann. 1449.

(*k*) See the Bull of Clement VII. in Launoi, ubi supra, pag. 79, 80.

(*l*) 'Tis apparent from his Epitaph.

(*m*) Petrus Monodus in Amedeo Pacifico, cap. 6. in Launoi, ubi supra, p. 81.

(*n*) Moreri.

(*o*) Jacob. in Philippus Bergom. lib. 15. Chronicor.

" nor in the Day; he is ever reading or negotiating; " he thinks on nothing less than his Belly; he is " not a Man for my Money. There is not the least " Resemblance between us." " *Quos inter (they are the Words of Æneas Silvius, concerning the Diet of the Canalovisi.)* *Cracoviensis Archidiaconus denunciationem (cibariorum) tulit. Cui cum aves & arietinæ carnes afferrentur, substractæ aviculæ sunt, orante in portâ famulo, ut, quod plus esset, id Domino dimitteretur; sperabat namque ex arietæ partem, ex avibus autem non sperabat : Dominus tamen aviculam præoptasset. Ideoque, cum spolium sensit, utique conquestus est publicoque testatus, nunquam se dictâ, postquam Sacerdos fuit, tussse pejorem. Ac cum rogaretur ne admiraretur sibi hoc, quoniam id obligisset Cardinali (Arelatensi), Proh, inquit, Cardinalem mihi æquiperas, hominem Gallicum, parcum, ventrem, aut ut verius loquar non hominem. Ego apud eum meo infortunio sum locatus, unam quam facis per lustra mihi certina indicat, nec adhuc bibere cum, aut comedere vidi : & quod mihi molestius est, insomnes noctes insomnesque dies ducit (quamquam nulla est apud nos dies) aut ligis semper, aut negotiatur. Nulla ei minor quam ventris est cura ; mihi nihil cum eo commune est* (1).

" ——— Among whom the Archdeacon of Cracow was " abridg'd in his Diet. For, when they were bringing " him a Dish of Wild Fowl, and another of *Venison*, " the Wild Fowl was taken away; his Servant at the " Door intreating, that they would allow his Master " the largest Dish; for he was in hopes part of the *Venison* might fall to his Share, which he could not have " expected from the Wild Fowl; whereas his Master " would have preferr'd the Latter. When the Archdeacon found himself robb'd of half his Dinner, he " complain'd of it, and publickly declared, that it was " the most unfortunate Day he had met with, since " he first went into Orders. And, when he was desir'd " not to be surpriz'd at it, since the same thing " had happen'd to the Cardinal of *Arles*, he exclaim'd, What a Comparison you make! you tell me of a " sober Frenchman, &c." Such is the bodily Constitution of those, who, in the greatest Affairs, are able to surmount the strongest Obstacles. This requires Men of Labour, detach'd from sensual Pleasures, and intrepid. The following is the *Latin* Description of *Lewis Alamandus*'s Resolution of Mind, against the Fear of the Plague. " Neque illum pestes, neque domesticorum funera, flectere potuerunt, volentem " potius cum vitæ periculo salvare Concilium; quam " cum periculo Concilii salvare vitam ; sciebat enim, " quoniam se recedente pauci remansissent, facileque " committi fraus in ejus absentia potuisset (2)."

(1) Id. ib.

(2) See Launoi Epist. 11. part. 1. p. 45. p. 80.

[B] *And call'd him the Son of Iniquity.*] In a Bull dated at *Florence*, in the Year 1442, he calls him *Iniquitatis filium, rebellionum & factionum multorum reum* ; and he says that the Council of *Ferrara*, and *Florence*, had condemn'd him to be stript of all his Dignities ; *à Ferrariensi & Florentino Conciliis damnatum & universis dignitatibus privatum fuisse* (3).

[C] *Yet, notwithstanding this, Lewis Alamandus died in the Odour of Sanctity.*] This Instance, and the Beatification of *Peter* of *Luxemburgh*, by the same Bull of *Clement* VII (4), are a little puzzling to the Controvertists of the *Roman* Party ; for, in short, if, as they pretend, every one, who is not united to the Pope, is out of the Pale of the Church, how came these two Persons to merit the Rank of Saints ? The best answer to this, is, that the Distinction between the true and the false Pope being above the Capacity of private Persons, and a mere Question of Fact, the Error was invincible, and consequently ought not to prejudice those, who acted with sincerity; as to the Question of Right. But this is a case of the Reply, and the Consequences, which result from hence in favour of other Errors.

[D] *The Jansenists are censur'd — are themselves liable to Censure.*] They alledge, first of all, the Continuator of *Baronius*'s injurious Treatment of the Cardinal of *Arles*, and they observe afterwards, " that he " was forc'd to confess, in two several Places, to " wit, in the Year 1446, *n*. 26, and in the Year " 1450, *n*. 20, that God confirm'd the Holiness of " this Cardinal, by such visible and well attested Miracles, that *Clement* VII placed him in the Number of the Blessed (5). — The manner in which " this Author endeavours to clear himself, continue " they, is most shocking, and cannot be founded but " on a most pernicious Maxim; which is, that Persons, guilty of publick Crimes, may become Saints, " and be acknowledged as such by the Church, " without giving any Proof of their having repented " of their Crimes, and though there is the greatest " Reason, on the contrary, to believe, that they " persevered in them. For if the Cardinal of *Arles* " was guilty of certain Crimes, and ought to be " esteemed as a very wicked Man for his Behaviour " in the Council of *Basil*, never was Man more constant in his Offence; since, when the Fathers of " the Council of *Basil*, in which he presided, recon- " ciled themselves to *Nicolas* V, it was not by ac- " knowledging in any manner, that they had done " amiss, either in opposing *Eugenius*, or in deposing " him, or in electing *Amedeus* ; but, on the con- " trary, they protested, that they had done nothing; " but with a view to the good of the Church, and " that they did not declare for *Nicolas* V otherwise, " than by re-electing him, after the voluntary Resignation of *Felix* ; and this Union was made, without " obliging them to recant any thing they had done ; " on the contrary, *Nicolas* V, confirm'd all the Proceedings of the Council of *Basil*. Therefore if all " that the Cardinal of *Arles* did in That Council was " criminal, never any Man shew'd greater Obstinacy " in his Crimes. Whence it follows, that if this did " not hinder him from becoming a Saint, the Consequence will be, that Perseverance in the greatest " Crimes is no Bar to any one's Beatification ; which " is shocking. And yet this necessarily follows from " the Words of *Raynaldus*, in the Year 1450, *n*. 20. " ——— Hoc Anno Ludovicum Alamandum Archi- " episcopam Arelatensem — vitâ cessisse tradunt; " atque miraculis post mortem coruscasse affirmant ; " eaque Clemens VII, veluti Sanctus, coli permisit " exarato

(3) See Launoi Epist. 11. part. 1. p. 45, p. 80.

(4) See Mr Claude's Defence of the Reformation. part 3ᵈ, towards the end.

(5) Remarks on the 18th Tome of the Ecclesiastical Canons, pag. 213. Those Remarks are printed with a Collection of several Pieces in Defence of the Censures of the Faculty of Divinity at Paris, against a Brief and a Bull of Alexander VII. I make use of the Edition of Geneva; they have put the Title at Munster by Bernard Raesfeldi, in 1667, in 8vo.

" exarato diplomate Pontificio 9 Apr. an. 1527. Ita-
" que adoranda est divina misericordia, quæ exiguo
" temporis fluxu Ludovicum ipsum, nefandi & perni-
" ciosissimi schismatis auctorem, propagatorem hære-
" seos, qui ex erronea conscientia innumera in Dei
" Ecclesiam mala invexerat, ac tot annorum cursu in
" pertinacia obfirmatus profanaverat Sacramenta, pœ-
" nitentem ac reversum in gremium Ecclesiæ ad san-
" ctitatis culmen brevi evexit. —— *This Year, they*
" *say, died Lewis Alamandus, Archbishop of Arles,*
" *who became famous for Miracles after his Death,*
" *and was permitted to be adored as a Saint, by a*
" *Pontifical Bull of* Clement VII, *dated April* 9,
" *Anno* 1527. *We ought therefore to adore the Di-*
" *vine Compassion, which, in so short a time, rais'd*
" *to the highest Pitch of Sanctity, this* Lewis, *Author*
" *of a wicked and most pernicious Schism, a Propagator*
" *of Heresy; and who, out of an erroneous Con-*
" *science, was the occasion of numberless Evils to the*
" *Church of God, and who, confirm'd in Perseverance,*
" *prophan'd the Sacraments for so many Years; but*
" *at last repented, and return'd to the Bosom of the*
" *Church.* —— If this Author had only said, that
" the great Zeal of this Holy Man, for the Refor-
" mation of the Church, had carried him too far,
" though he acted upon good Motives, it would
" have been tolerable, and not so contrary to the
" Testimony which God gave of his Sanctity. But
" to represent him as a wicked Man, and as an ob-
" stinate Heretic and Schismatic, who had sacrile-
" giously prophaned the Sacraments; and to tell us,
" that, in a Year or two afterwards, he became a
" Saint, fit to be canoniz'd, without giving any
" Proof of his Repentance of so many Crimes, as
" as are imputed to him, is to have a strange Idea of
" Holiness, or rather it is to join Wickedness and
" Sanctity together, to avoid confessing, that a Pope
" was mistaken, in declaring a Man a Sinner, whom
" God himself had declared a Saint. But the Bull
" of *Clement* VII, relating to the Beatification of this
" holy Man, reported by *Ciaconius*, is sufficient to
" confute this Writer; since it appears from thence,
" that the Pope does not alledge his sincere Repentance
" of the Crimes he had committed; but that he
" yielded up his most pure Soul to God, after having
" liv'd sixty Years." These Gentlemen censure *Rey-*
naldus very justly for his bold Assertion of *Alaman-*
dus's Repentance; and they demonstratively confute
what he advances; but they are in the wrong to accuse him of That shocking Doctrine, which they so
pompously display: It is not true, that he joins Sanctity and Impenitence together; for he supposes, on
the contrary, that the Cardinal actually did repent;
and in That he acknowledges the adorable Mercy
of God. If I assert here, that Mr *Claude* has reproach'd the *Jansenists* with Inconsistencies in relation
to *Odoricus Reynaldus* (6), it is only to shew, that the
Remarks, which I attribute to them, have been ascribed to them by others.

(6) Claude's Preface to the Answer to the Perpetuity of the Faith defended, pag. 28, 29.

ALAMOS (BALTHAZAR) was born at *Medina-del-Campo* in *Castile*. Having studied the Civil-Law at *Salamanca*, he entered into the Service of *Antony Perez*, Secretary of State to King *Philip* II, and had a great share in his Master's Esteem and Confidence; which was the reason, why they secured his Person, after That Minister's Disgrace. He was kept in Prison eleven Years. *Philip* III, upon his Accession to the Throne, set him at liberty, in compliance with the Orders which his Father left him in his Will. *Alamos* led a private Life, till Duke *d'Olivarez*, Favourite of *Philip* IV, called him to the discharge of public Employments. He was promoted to the Post of Attorney-General in the Court of Criminal Causes, and in the Council of War; afterwards he was Counsellor in the Council of the *Indies*; and lastly in the Council of the *Royal Patrimony*. He was Knight of St *James*, a Man of Wit and Judgment, and had a better Pen than Tongue. He lived Eighty eight Years, and left only Daughters. He acquired a great Reputation by his *Spanish* Translation of *Tacitus*, and by the Political Aphorisms, which he inserted in the Margin; but there are different Opinions of this Work [*A*]. It was published at *Madrid* in the Year 1614.

[*A*] *There are different Opinions of this Work.*] This Difference of Opinions relates much more to the Aphorisms, than the Translation, as will appear by the following Citations. " As for the Aphorisms of
" *Alamos*, they are not such, as they are thought to
" be; for you will scare meet with any thing in them
" like an Aphorism, or that comes near the force of
" what is express'd in the Text of the Translation.
" And whereas Aphorisms ought to be more sen-
" tentious than the Text; the Words of the Text are
" always more sententious, than his Aphorisms. Last-
" ly, to be short, his Aphorisms are generally mere
" paraphras'd Translations of the Translation itself;
" an insipid and tedious thing to a Reader of Under-
" standing and Taste. This being suppos'd, I shall
" not scruple to say, That *Alamos*'s Translation is
" much better than his Aphorisms. And it is a Judg-
" ment, which the Author of the Historical and Po-
" litical Bibliography has made before me, in the
" Article of the *Latin* Historians. *Tacitus illustra-*
" *ted,* says he, (it is the Title of *Alamos*'s Translation)
" *is much esteemed by our Travellers*; but, to judge
" *rationally of it, the Notes are no better than the*
" *impertinent* New Thoughts of Lewis d'Orleans *on*
" *this Author, or than the* Aulic and Political Re-
" marks of Count Hanibal Scot of Piacenza, *which*
" Lipsius *rightly calls* Leaden Notes. — Yet a certain
" *Spanish* Secretary, whose Name is *Juan Oñate*, took
" the Pains to rank these Aphorisms under particular
" Titles, in an Alphabetical Order, and made no Dif-
" ficulty to entitle them, *Alma de Cornelio Tacito*.
" Nay farther, one *Jerome Canini* translated them in-
" to *Italian*, and inserted them in the *Italian* Version
" of *Adriano Politi*, as something very excellent:
" witness the Title, —— Operi di Corn. Tacito illu-
" strate con NOTABILLISSIMI AFORISMI del Signor
" D. Baldassar Alamo (1). —— *The Works of* Corne-
" lius Tacitus, *illustrated with the* CELEBRATED
" APHORISMS *of Signor D.* Belthassar Alamos."

Here are already two Authors, who speak with Contempt of these Aphorisms, and two, who set a great Value on them. This difference of Opinion will be less surprizing, if we reflect, that, in the Year 1683, Mr *Amelot* had not the same Notion of them, as he had in 1686, and in 1690. Let us consult the Preface to his *Tiberius* (2). " It is very true,
" *says he,* that *Alamos* not only translated *Tacitus,*
" but wrote likewise a great number of Remarks up-
" on him; which he calls Aphorisms, and which
" *Antony de Covarruvias*, who approved his Book,
" represents as the principal Part of the Work *———
" I confess that it is excellent, both in respect of the
" Translation, which is as perspicuous as the Original
" is obscure, as likewise of the Aphorisms, which are
" in every Margin; most of which are properly Pa-
" raphrases and Versions of the Sentences of *Tacitus*,
" and the rest moral or political Conclusions, drawn
" from the Events, which he relates; but, notwith-
" standing the great Reputation of this Author, I hope
" my Work will be very well received by those, who
" are proper Judges in this Matter; and the more, be-
" cause my Undertaking was much more difficult than
" that of *Alamos*. For all his Aphorisms—are so many
" detach'd Pieces and Scraps, and, as the Proverb
" says, *Sand without Lime or Cement*; whereas, in my
" Chapters, I throw into a continued Discourse all
" the *Latin* Citations, which are in the Margins,
" and collect into an uniform Body all these distinct
" Pieces. Upon this Occasion *Justus Lipsius* says,
" a Man must undertake such a Work, to know how
" difficult it is." The Words of *Lipsius*, as they are cited by *Amelot*, are as follows. " Nec vero nudas
" & sparsas sententias dedimus, ne diffluerent, & effet,
" quod dicitur, Arena sine Calce: Sed eas aut inter

* The Soul of Cornelius Tacitus.

(1) Amelot de la Houssaye's Critical Discourse before his Translation of Tacitus's *Annals*, printed in 1690. This Discourse had already appeared before his Morals of Tacitus, in 108. It is a little enlarg'd in the Edition of the Annals.

(2) Printed at Amsterd. in 1683.

* Aun es la principal parte y documento de su Obra.

ALAMOS. ALBERTUS.

1614, and was to have been followed by a *Commentary* [B] which was never printed, that I know of. The Author composed these Two Works, during his Confinement, and endeavoured, in that Condition, to obtain a Licence for the Impression [C]. He left some other Works, which were not printed: *Advertimientos al govierno*, addressed to the Duke of *Lerma*, about the beginning of the Reign of *Philip* III: *El Conquistador*; it contained Advices in relation to the Conquests to be made in the New World: *Puntos politicos o de Estado*. *Dom Garsias Tellode de Sandoval*, Knight of *Calatrava*, Son-in-Law to *Alamos*, gave notice of these Manuscripts to *Dom Nicolas Antonio* (*a*), from whom I have borrowed the greatest part of this Article.

" se haud indecenter vinximus, aut interdum velut
" cœmento quodam commisimus nostrorum verborum,
" è mille aliquot particulis uniforme hoc & cohærens
" corpus formantes. Hoc totum quam arduum mihi
" fuerit, frustra dixerim apud non expertum ——
" eo major mihi molestia, quod per hæc aliena vesti-
" gia sic iverim, tanquam in libérrimo ingenii cur-
" su †.

[*B*] *Was to have been followed by a Commentary.*] The King's Licence expresly mentions this Commentary. *Antony Covarruvias* speaks of it as of a Book, which he had read, and tells us also the Disposition, and principal Parts of the Work, in his Approbation, prefix'd to the Translation, Another Approbator speaks of this Commentary by Name. *Alamos* mentions it several times in his Prefaces, and promises to clear up the Obscurities of *Tacitus* in it: Yet *Nicolas Antonio* is silent in this Matter; and, what is more strange, does not so much as mention the Translation; he only tells us, That *Alamos* wrote Aphorisms on *Tacitus*.

[*C*] *Endeavoured, in that Condition, to obtain a Licence for the Impression.*] I make this Observation, not to lengthen out the Article, as some Readers of precipitate Judgments may imagine. I propose a Breviate of a Case, in relation to a small Process entered against *Don Nicolas Antonio*, with great Appearance of Reason. He pretends that *Emanuel Sueiro* translated *Tacitus*'s Works into *Spanish*, after *Antony de Herrera* had translated part of them, and after *Balthasar de Alamos* and *Carlos Coloma* had translated them entire. " Post Antonii de Herrera aliqualem, Balthasaris de

" Alamos & Caroli Coloma illustrium virorum in-
" tegram operam, in hujusmet autoris interpretatione
" positam (3)." Now, he acknowledges, that *Sueiro*'s Translation was printed at *Antwerp* in 1613; and it is certain, That That of *Alamos* was printed at *Madrid* in 1614. It is the Date, which *Don Nicolas Antonio* gave to the Aphorisms of *Alamos* (4). Farther, *Alamos* sets down in his Preface the Reasons why he continued his Design of publishing his *Tacitus*, after *Sueiro*'s Translation appeared. It is therefore, I think, impossible to vindicate *Don Nicolas Antonio* against the Objection of Mr *Amelot de la Houssaie*; *which shews*, says he, citing what I have just now produced, *that Don Nicolas Antonio mistook, when he supposed the Translation of Emanuel Sueiro to be later than That of Alamos* (5). There is but one thing to be pleaded in his Excuse, which is to say, that perhaps *Sueiro* was not ignorant, when he undertook his Work, that *Alamos* had already obtained a Licence for publishing one of the same kind, which had been read and approved by *Antony Covarruvias*. The News of it might reach him at *Antwerp*; for in the Year 1594, King *Philip* II. ordered *Covarruvias* to examine the whole Work of *Alamos*; and, in the Year 1603, *Philip* II. granted a Permission to print it. *Alamos* relates all this in his Advertisment to the Reader, which by the by, overthrows the Conjecture of those, who fancy that he filled the Margins of his Translation with Aphorisms, *only to excel That of Sueiro* (6). The Aphorisms were a principal Part of his Work, from the time, that it was approved by *Antony Covarruvias*.

ALBERTUS MAGNUS, a *Dominican*, Bishop of *Ratisbon*, and one of the most famous Doctors of the XIIIth Century, was born at *Lawingen*, on the *Danube*, in *Suabia*, in the Year 1193, or 1205 [*A*]. *Moreri*'s Dictionary gives us an Account of the several Employs, which were conferred upon him, and the Success of his Lectures in several Towns (*a*). I shall confine my self to some Fabulous Reports concerning him. It has been said, that he practised the Art of Midwifery; and it was thought improper for a Person of his Profession to set up for a Man-Midwife (*b*). The Foundation of this Story is, That there went a Book under the Name of *Albertus Magnus*, containing several Instructions for Midwives, and so much Knowledge of their Art, that it was thought he could not have been so well skilled in the Trade, if he had not exercised it. But the *Apologists* for *Albertus Magnus* maintain, that he was not the Author of that Book [*B*], nor of another *De Secretis Mulierum* [*C*], wherein

[*A*] *In the Year* 1193, *or* 1205.] *Vossius* justly censures *Nicolas Reusnerus*, who placed the Birth of *Albertus* in the Year 1293, and his Death in the Year 1382; thus setting out with a Mistake: " Quæ mag-
" na est *διςφωνία* peccantis in ipso operis ingressu,
" velut cantherius in porta, ut dici solet, nam ab
" hoc Alberto decem & elogia sua auspicatur (1)." Thus *Vossius* expresses himself, without remembering that, through as great a Mistake as this, he had (*page* 62) placed *Albertus*'s flourishing Condition in the Year 1160, and his Death, at Eighty seven Years of Age, in the Year 1208; and that he had made him cotemporary with *Urban* IV. and the Emperor *Rodolphus*.

[*B*] *That he was not the Author of that Book.*] It is entitled, *De Natura rerum*, and treats at large, and minutely, of the Practice of Midwifery. The Author maintains, that this Subject is not unworthy the Pen of a Monk, since the Ignorance of Midwives destroys many Children, and deprives them for ever of heavenly Bliss. *Peter of Prussia*, a Monk of the Order of St *Dominic*, maintains that This Book, *De Natura rerum*, was composed by *Thomas Cantipratanus*, a Disciple of *Albertus*; and he does not deny, that several Precepts are to be met with in it, for procuring a happy Delivery, which cannot be expressed without obscene Words; But it is not Nature, he says,

but human Sensuality, which sullies these Ideas (2). " Admodum succenset in blaterones illos, qui Alberto
" imposuerunt quod egisset obstetricem: Fassus tamen
" Cantipratanum ad instructionem obstetricum, in
" Opere perperam supposito præcepto ejus Alberto,
" tradidisse modos & vias fœlicis obstetricationis, cu-
" jus præcepta chartis commisti, nec voce tradi pos-
" sunt, absque expressione Multorum quæ libido non
" natura fordavit (3)." It would be curious enough, to have seen *Albertus Magnus* undertake to deliver a Woman, and set his Hand to the Work. See the Remark [*A*] of the Article HIEROPHILUS.

[*C*] *Nor of another* De Secretis mulierum.] *Naudé* makes use of these two Proofs: I. *Albertus*'s Name is not prefixed to the Work; if he who commented upon it would deceive us, when he maintains the contrary. II. *Albertus*'s Authority is often made use of in this very Book; and therefore the Author *lived some time after him* (4). These two Proofs are inconclusive; and the Consequence drawn from the second is of no weight. Many Reasons may oblige a Man not to put his Name to a Book; and no Authors cite themselves more willingly than those, who suppress their Names; nor is any thing more common, than to quote cotemporary Authors. See the Remark [*K*].

[*D*] *Some*

in are many Things, which could not be expressed but in obscene and filthy Terms; which raised a great Clamour against the pretended Author of it. His *Apologists* cannot always have recourse to a positive Denial of Matter of Fact; They acknowledge there are some Questions in his *Commentary on the Master of the Sentences* relating to the Practice of the Conjugal Duty [D], in which he was obliged to make use of Terms, which gave Offence to chaste Ears (*c*); but they alledge, what he observes himself in his own Justification, that so many monstrous Things are revealed in Confession, that it is impossible not to touch upon such Questions. It is certain, that *Albertus* was the most inquisitive of Men. He exposed himself, upon that account, to other Accusations. It has been said, that he was in search of the Philosophers Stone [E]; and even that he was a notorious Magician [F], and that he had formed a Machine,

(*e*) Theoph. Rayn. ubi supra.

[D] *Some Questions — relating to the Practice of Conjugal Duty.*] *Peter of Prussia,* when he could not deny the Fact, endeavoured to justify the Lawfulness of it; and shews, in the eighteenth Chapter of his Book (5), That it is useful, and even necessary, for us to be acquainted with natural Things, not excepting the most obscene; and that, therefore, *Albertus* and other Casuists were in the right to treat of Subjects full of Obscenity; for, without it, Confessors would not be qualified to remedy the Complaints of their Penitents. "Qualia item "multa ab Alberto de usu conjugii in 4. S. d. 31. "*sub finem,* scripto comprehensa fatetur, illud ex ipso "Alberto ibidem præfatus [dicendum primo, quod "hujusmodi turpes quæstiones nunquam tractari de- "berent, nisi illa cogerent monstra quæ his tempo- "ribus in confessione audiuntur] ne ergo Confessa- "rii rudes sint medicinæ, quam facere debent adeo "frequentibus morbis, justum censuit Albertus in illud "oletum stylum demittere (6)." We are told, that it were to be wished, that none but Confessors would concern themselves with such Obscenities; but that there must be Books, to which we may have Recourse in Cases of Conscience, which relate to That filthy Subject. "Necessarium est enodationem soli- "dam atque legitimam dubiorum circa fœditates "illas emergentium prostare alicubi apud probatos "Doctores cujusmodi fuit Albertus, qui proinde re- "prehensione vacat, etiamsi illum veluti scriptionis "putorem suis commentariis immiserit (7)." But it would be yet more necessary to abolish that which makes this sort of Writings necessary, for, how good soever an Author's Intention may be, it is to Books of this Nature, rather than to numberless others, we ought to apply *Horace*'s

- - - - Peccare docentes
- - - - - - - Historias - - - - (8).
- - - - *Tales, the Bawds to Vice.*

CREECH.

(*c*) *The Title of the Chapter is, Quod scire naturalia etiam impudica utile sit & necessarium.*

(6) Theoph. Raynaud. ubi supra.

(7) Id. ibid.

(8) Horat. Od. 7. lib 3. ver. 19.

[E] *That he was in search of the Philophers Stone.*] *Naudé* informs us, that *Moyer*, the great Patron of the Alchymists, was not ashamed to affirm in his *Symbols of the Golden Table of the twelve Nations **, that *St Dominic* was the first who had the Knowledge of the Philosophers Stone; *and that those, to whom he left it, communicated it to* Albertus Magnus, *who by that means cleared all the Debts of his Bishoprick of* Ratisbon *in less than three Years* (9). *Moyer* builds his Opinion upon three Books of Chymistry, which he ascribes to *Albertus Magnus. Naudé* answers, that he is in the wrong to attribute them to him (10), and for this reason, because *not one of them has been inserted among his Works, or specified by* Trithemius; and because That of the *Quintessence* was falsly ascribed to him by *Francis Picus* †. To prove this last Fact, he does not imitate *Velcurion* ∥ and *Guilbertus* **, who maintained, that *Albertus* laughed at Alchymists, *and their pretended Transmutations, in his third Book of Minerals* ‡. He does not alledge this Proof, since *Albertus in That* maintains a quite contrary Opinion; but he shews, that the Author of the *Quintessence* styles himself *Monk of the Order of* St Francis, and says, that *he composed it, when he was in Prison.* These two Circumstances *must undoubtedly relate to* John de Rupescissa.

* Lib. 6.

(9) Nawdé, ubi supra, pag. 515.

(10) Ibid. pag. 520.

† Lib. 2. de Auro.

∥ Lib. 3. Physic. cap. 13.

** Alchym. Impugnatæ, lib. 2. c. 7.

‡ Tractatu 1. cap. 9.

[F] *That he was a notorious Magician.*] *Trithemius* endeavoured long ago to justify him from this Accusation. This appears from these Words: "Non "surrexit post eum vir similis ei, qui in omnibus "literis, scientiis, & rebus tam doctus, eruditus, & "expertus fuerit. Quod autem de Necromantia ac- "cusatur, injuriam patitur vir Deo dilectus (11). ——— "There arose no one after him, who deserved to be compa- "red to Him, for universal Knowledge and Experience. "As to the Accusation of Necromancy brought against "him, it is an Injury to this Favourite of Heaven." *Naudé* pretends, that this Accusation can only arise from two Works, which went under the Name of *Albertus Magnus*, and on the *Androïs*. So that here are two Proofs: Let us see then what he says of each.

I. The first of these two Books is entituled, *de Mirabilibus*; the other is *the Mirrour of Astrology, which treats of the licensed and prohibited Authors, who have wrote on this Science* (12). *Francis Picus **, and *Martin Del Rio* ‡‡ agree, that they do *Albertus Magnus* a great Injury, who believe him to be the Author of the Book *de Mirabilibus*, and therefore the latter clears him in these very Terms: "Alberto "Magno tributus liber de Mirabilibus, vanitate & "superstitione refertus est, sed magno Doctori partus "suppositius. ——— *The idle and superstitious Book* "de Mirabilibus, *ascribed to the famous Dr* Albertus "Magnus, *is a spurious Work.*" The Mirrour of Astrology "was condemned by *Gerson* ∥∥ and *Agrippa* ‡‡, as superstitious to the highest Degree; and "by *Francis Picus* **, and many others, because the "Author of it asserts a very erroneous Opinion, in "favour of Books of Magic; which, he maintains, "ought carefully to be preserved, because the Time "approaches, in which, for certain Reasons, which "he does not specify, Men will be obliged to peruse "and consult them on some Occasions (13)." It seems, then, that if our *Albertus* had composed such a Book, he must have been considered as a Magician; but *Naudé* does not allow this Consequence, since the Jesuit *Vasquez* expresly declares ††, "that Books of "Magic are necessary, and that Magicians are tole- "rated by God, that Libertines may in some Mea- "sure be reclaimed from Atheism (14)." Besides, *Naudé* takes it for granted, that *Roger Bacon* is the Author of That Work, as *Francis Picus* maintains, in his first Book against Astrologers (15). So much for the first Proof of the Accusation. Let us see how the second is answered.

(11) Trithem. de Scriptor. Ecclef p. 195.

(12) Naudé, ubi supra, p. 523, 524.

* Lib. 6. de Prænot. cap 7.

†‡ Disquisit. Mag. lib. 1. cap. 3.

∥∥ Libro de libris Apocryph. non tolerandis, Propost. 3.

‡‡ In Epistolis.

** Lib. 6. de Prænot. cap. 2.

(13) Naudé, ubi supra, pag. 525.

†† Part. 1. Q. 8. 1. Art. 3. Disput. 2. cap. 4. *at the beginning.*

(14) Naudé, ubi supra, pag. 527.

II. Some Persons have believed, that *brazen Heads* might be made *under certain Constellations*, which would give Answers, and direct a Man in all his Affairs. One *Tepes* relates ***, that *Henry de Villeine* had made one at *Madrid*, which was broke to pieces by the Command of *John* II. King of *Castile. Virgil, Pope Silvester, Robert of Lincoln*, and *Roger Bacon*, had the like Heads, if we may believe certain Writers (16). *Albertus Magnus* was judged to be more ingenious; for it is pretended that he "had formed "an entire Man of this sort, having worked thirty "Years without interruption, in forging him under "divers Aspects and Constellations; as for Example, "the Eyes, --- when the Sun was in a Sign of "the Zodiac correspondent to such a part; which he "cast of mixed Metals, and marked with the Cha- "racters of the same Signs and Planets, and of their "divers and necessary Aspects; and thus the Head, "Neck, Shoulders, Thighs and Legs, fashioned at dif- "ferent Times, and connected together in the Form of "a Man, had the Ingenuity to reveal to the said *Al- "bertus* the Solution of all his principal Difficul- "ties (17)." This is what is called the *Androïs* of *Albertus Magnus*. It was broke, they say, by *Thomas Aquinas*, who could not bear it's everlasting Tittle tattle with Patience. *Henry de Assia* and *Bartholomew Sibylla* assure us, that it was "composed "of Flesh and Bones; but by Art, not Nature: "Which

(1) Idem, pag. 526.

*** Apud Emanuel de Moura, §. 2. cap. 15. art. 6.

(16) Naudé, ubi supra, pag. 528.

(17) Idem, pag. 529, 530.

ALBERTUS. 183

a Machine, in the shape of a Man, which served him for an Oracle, and explained all the Difficulties, which he proposed to it. I could easily be induced to believe, that, as he understood the Mathematics, he had made a Head, which, by the help of Springs, might form certain articulate Sounds; but what Folly is it to ground an Accusation of Magic upon this? Some pretend that he was justify'd from this Imputation by an extraordinary Miracle [G]. Though he was as well qualified, as any Person, to be the Inventor of Artillery, there is Reason to believe that they, who ascribe the Invention of it to Him, are mistaken [H]. It is said (d), that he had naturally a very dull Wit, and that he was upon the point of leaving the Cloister, because he despaired of attaining to what his Fryar's Habit required of him; but that the Holy Virgin appeared to him, and asked him, in which he would chuse to excel; in Philosophy,

(d) See Vol. I. of Bzovius's Annals.

(18) Idem, pag. 531. He cites Peregr. Quæst. 3. Decad. cap. 2. Qu. 3.

" Which being, however, judged impossible by mo-
" dern Authors, and the Virtue of Images, and pla-
" netary Rings and Seals, being then in great Vogue,
" it has been always believed since ---- that such
" Figures were made of Brass, or of some other Metal,
" which was fashioned under the Influence of Hea-
" ven, and of the Planets (18). Upon this foot
Naudé refutes Albertus's Accusers; namely, by supposing, that the pretended Androïs was composed of
Metal. He shews, by very strong Reasons, that it
could neither hear, nor speak, nor serve the Devil as an Instrument for Speech; and that, if the
Devil had spoke through this Machine, he would
have done it without the help of the metallic Organs, of which it was composed. So that it would
not have been necessary to employ so much Time,
and so many Ceremonies, in forging such a Machine;
A Bottle or a Trumpet would have been as proper
to resolve all the Difficulties of Albertus. Lastly,
Naudé remarks, that They, who mention This Androïs, bring no Proof of the Fact. Tostatus, notwithstanding all his Wit and Learning, was very credulous; therefore his Authority proves nothing. If any
one will maintain, that such a Tradition must have
some Foundation, Naudé assigns a very plausible
one (19), which is, that Albertus might perhaps have
in his Closet a Head, or Statue of a Man, like those
Machines of Boëthius, of which Cassiodorus speaks
††† : " Metalla mugiunt, Diomedis in ære grues
" bucciniant, æneus anguis insibilat, aves simulatæ
" fritinniunt, & quæ propriam vocem nesciunt ab
" ære dulcedinem probantur emittere cantilenæ. ——
" Metals bellow; Diomedes's Cranes chatter in Brass;
" A brazen Serpent hisses; Imitated Birds chirp;
" and Things, which have no Voice of their own,
" are found, in Brass, to counterfeit the Sweetness of
" singing."
[G] He was justified from this Imputation by an extraordinary Miracle.] According to Father Theophilus Raynaud, the Accusers of Albertus say, that, on Twelfth-day, he treated William Earl of Holland, and King of the Romans, who past by the City of Cologne; and that, to make his Entertainment the more remarkable, he changed the Winter into a Summer full of Flowers and Fruits. " Horridam hye-
" mem in florigeram fructiferamque æstatem vertit,
" ut scribit Trithemius in Chron. Spanh. anno 1254
" (20)." Trithemius in effect relates this. They add to this the speaking Head, the Book de Mirabilibus, and That de secretis mulierum. Father Theophilus does not refute these Accusations by the Elogies, which several Historians bestow upon the Virtues of the Accused. He has recourse to the Testimony, which God himself gave of the Sanctity of Albertus by several miraculous Operations, and by preserving his Body from Corruption to this Day: Testimonium quod ejus sanctitati Deus perhibuit patratis in ejus gratiam miris plerisque operibus, & ipsius Alberti corpore ad hunc usque diem à tabe & putrefactione exempto. This Apologist adds, that the Metamorphosis of Winter into Summer, and the speaking Head, are two great Falsities; and that the two Books in Question are falsly attributed to Albertus Magnus; and that St Thomas does not say *, that he himself formerly broke the speaking Head, in his Master's House. " Hyems in veris amœnitatem versa, & caput æne-
" um articulate loquens, ad Deum Fabulorum sunt
" ablegenda tanquam confiſta & falso jactata de tanto
" viro ---- libri autem Magici, qui Alberto affin-
" gebantur, sunt suppositiii (21)." See what this Jesuit relates of certain Machines, which utter very harmonious Sounds. He will allow, that Albertus might have a Head so ingeniously contrived, that

the Air, which was blown into it, might receive the Modifications requisite to form a human Voice. As to the Exemption from Putrefaction, read the following Extract from Thevet; " Our Albertus, ha-
" ving lived Eighty seven Years, died in the Year
" of our Redemption 1280, at Cologne, whither he
" had retired to Study; and there his Body is bu-
" ried, in the middle of the Quire of the Convent
" of the Dominicans, and his Entrails were carried
" to Ratisbon; his Body was yet entire in the Time
" of the Emperor Charles V. and was taken up by
" his Command, and afterwards replaced in it's first
" Monument (22)". The Jesuit Raderus wrote some Latin Verses on the Preservation of his Body from Putrefaction (23). They end thus;

Illius doctas mirentur sæcula chartas,
Miror ego salvas post tria sæcla manus

Let the famed Writings of the wond'rous Sage (24)
The Admiration prove of every Age;
Thy learned Hands, Albertus, I admire,
After Three Centuries preserved entire.

Moreri says but Two hundred Years, instead of Three hundred. Neither his usual Practice, nor his Disposition, incline him to lessen Things of this Nature.
[H] *They, who ascribe the Invention of it to him, are mistaken.*] " *John Matthew de Luna* *, who liv'd
" above an Hundred and twenty Years ago (25),
" maintains, though against the constant Opinion of
" Polydorus, Mazius, Meyer, Pancirolus, Florentius,
" Rivault, and Bezoldus, that *Albertus Magnus* found
" out the Use of great Guns, Fusils, and Pistols; but
" I cannot find, in all those Authors, any thing which
" comes near this Opinion, except that the Experi-
" ment was made of these Engines in his Time, by
" a *German* Monk, whom they call *Bertbold Schu-
" wartz*, or by a Chymist, who, in the Judgment
" of *Carnazanus*, an ancient Author, liv'd in the
" City of *Cologne*, in which it is certain that *Alber-
" tus* continu'd to reside, after he took the Habit of a
" *Dominican* (26)." Thus *Naudé* refutes *John Matthew de Luna*. The last thing he affirms is false; for the Historians of *Albertus* tell us, That he enter'd into the Order of St *Dominic*, in the Year 1222; That, after his Superiors had sent him to *Cologne*, to teach Divinity and Philosophy, and he had acquitted himself of that Employment to the astonishment of his Auditors, he distinguish'd himself at *Hildesheim*, at *Friburg*, at *Ratisbon*, and at *Strasburg*; that he return'd to *Cologne*, in the Year 1240; that, among other Disciples, he had *Thomas Aquinas* there, to whom he resign'd his Chair, when he went to profess in the City of *Paris*; that, having taught three Years at *Paris*, he return'd to *Cologne*; that he was made Provincial of his Order, in the Year 1254; that he perform'd the Visitation of the Provinces on Foot; that he went to *Rome*, by order of *Alexander* IV, where he was made Master of the Sacred Palace, and read Divinity Lectures; that he returned into *Germany* in the Year 1260; that he was elected Bishop of *Ratisbon* there; that, at three Years end, he obtained leave to resign his Bishoprick; that he return'd to his Cell at *Cologne*; that the Pope commanded him, a little while after, to preach the Crusade all over *Germany* and *Bohemia*; that, in 1274, he assisted at the Council of *Lyons*; that he had the Character of the Emperor's Ambassador there; and that, at last, he returned to *Cologne* (27). How could *Naudé*, who was so deeply read, be ignorant of these several Stations of *Albertus Magnus*?

[I] Our

(19) Naudé, ubi supra, p. 539, 540.
††† Lib. 1. Variar. Ep. 45.

(20) Theophil. Rayn. Hoploth. §. 2. Serm. 1. cap. 14. pag. 149.

* III. contra Gent. cap. 104.

(21) Theophil. Raynaud. p. 150.

(22) Thevet's Hommes Illustres, Tom. 2. pag. 87.

(23) Bullart, Academy of Sciences, Tom. 2. pag. 143. mentions them.

(24) l. e. Aristotle.

* Libro de Rerum invent cap. 12. fol. 10.

(25) These are Naudé's Words, pag. 618. of his Apology for Great Men, Paris 1625.

(26) Moreri, in'e'id f th s, eaks only of Gunpowder, f ou. ch Naudé ays nothing.

(27) See Bullart's Academy, Tom. 2. p. g. 140, &c.

ALBERTUS. ALBRET.

losophy, or Divinity; that he made choice of Philosophy; that the Holy Virgin assured him he should surpass all Men in that Science; but that, as a Punishment for his not chusing Divinity, he should, before his Death, relapse into his former Stupidity. They add farther, That, after this Apparition, he shewed a prodigious deal of Wit, and improved in all Sciences, with a Quickness, which astonished all his Masters; but that, Three Years before his Death, he forgot, in an instant, all that he knew; and that, being at a stand, in a Lecture of Divinity at *Cologne*, and endeavouring in vain to recal his Ideas, he was sensible that it was the Accomplishment of the Prediction. Whence it was said, the he was miraculously converted from an Ass into a Philosopher, and afterwards from a Philosopher into an Ass. It is needless to observe that this is a meer Story; they who will believe me in this, stand in no need of my Opinion, and would form this Judgment without expecting it; and as for those, who judge otherwise of it, they will not change their own Opinion, by finding here, that I am of a different. Our *Albertus* was a very little Man [*I*]. He died at *Cologne*, the 15th of *November* 1280, being Eighty seven or Seventy five Years old. He wrote such a prodigious number of Books, that they amount to twenty one Volumes in Folio, in the Edition of *Lions*, 1651. A *Dominican* of *Grenoble*, called *Peter Jammy*, procured it.

(*e*) *By Mr de la Monnoie.*

Two or three Particulars, which have been communicated to me (*e*), shall be produced below [*K*].

(28) Id. ib. pag. 148.

[*I*] *Our* Albertus *was a very little Man.*] " Some " write, That, kissing his Holiness's Feet, upon his " Arrival at *Rome*, the Pope commanded him to rise, " thinking he was yet on his Knees; though he was " really standing (28)." The same Story is told of some other Persons. See the Remark [H], of the Article ANDRE (JOHN): and remember the Logicians Distinction between *quantitas molis*, and *quantitas virtutis*. Little Albett *the Great* puts me in mind of it (29).

(29) The non eſt in tanto corpore mica salis, carried the same Distinction.

(30) Simler Epitome Bibl'oth. Geln. pag. 332.

[*K*] *Particulars, which*——*shall be produc'd below.*] " The Book *De Secretis Mulierum*, falsely ascribed to " *Albertus*, is the Work of one of his Disciples, " named *Henry of Saxony*; under whose Name it has " been printed several times. These are *Simler's* " Words: ——— Henrici de Saxonia Alberti Magni " discipuli liber de secretis mulierum, impressus Au- " gustæ anno D. 1498, per Antonium Sorg (30).——— " Henry of Saxony, *the Disciple of* Albertus Mag-

" nus, *his Book* De Secretis Mulierum, *printed at* " Ausbourg, *in* 1498, *by* A. Sorg. — And in *Thua- " nus's* Catalogue you meet with — Henrici de Saxo- " nia de secretis mullerum, de virtutibus herbarum, " lapidum, quorundam animalium, aliorumque in 12°. " Francof. 1615 (31). ——— Henry of Saxony, *of the* " *Secrets of Women, of the Virtues of Herbs, Stones,* " *of some Animals, and other Things, in* 12°, Franc- " fort, 1615. ——— *Albertus's* Name being more fa- " mous than That of *Henry*, plainly gave occasion " to this Supposition.——— *John* Picus de Mirandula, " says, That *Albertus*, in his riper Years, condemn'd " the Books of Magic, which he had compos'd in " his Youth.——— *Androïs* is not the Term made use " of, when they speak of *Albertus Magnus's* Artificial " Man. It is a Word absolutely unknown, and in- " vented by *Naudè*, who boldly applies it, as if it " had been generally received."

(31) *In the* 136th Page *of the second* Part.

ALBRET, a Family. It was, for some Ages, one of the most Illustrious of *France*, for the great Men it produced, whose Merit was distinguished by the most Eminent Dignities of the Kingdom. Every one knows that this Family was in possession of *Navarre* and *Bearn*. *Moreri* speaks of it at large; I refer my Readers to him, without examining into the Truth of every thing he has advanced in relation to it. I shall only take Notice of one Omission; Namely that this illustrious House was extinct, by the Death of the Marquis *d'Albret* (*a*) who was killed in *Picardy*, in the House of the Marquis *de Buffi-Lamet*. He married the only Daughter of his Uncle, the Mareschal *d'Albret*, in the Year 1662; but this Marriage produced no Children. It is probable the Mareschal consulted the Interests of his Family, more than the Inclinations of the two Cousins; for it is said, there was but little Harmony between the Husband and the Wife. She married again with the Count *de Marsan*, one of the Sons of the Count *d'Harcourt*. Her first Husband, the Marquis *d'Albret*, was in a fair way of being advanced to the Chief Military Offices: He was already Field-Mareschal, and would have ended the Campaign, of 1678, under Mareschal *Schomberg*, who was sent to the Frontiers of *Champagne*, in the beginning of the Month of *August*. Whilst his Flying Camp drew near *Charleville*, the Marquis *d'Albret* demanded of him a Furlough for a few Days. It was not questioned, but it was upon an Affair of Gallantry. However it be, he was slain at the above mentioned Gentleman's House, who cleared himself by proving, that he was then in another place (*b*). This was the Bed of Honour, in which the only remaining Branch of such a line of Heroes ended his Life. His Family deserved to end on a more glorious Occasion. The Marshal *d'Albret* died Governor of *Guienne*, two Years before. He had obtained the Staff of Mareschal of *France* in 1653. They, who pretend that he earned it by securing the Prince of *Condé*, are ignorant of the Matter of Fact. It was not he, (but Mr *de Guitaud*) who arrested him(*c*): He only conducted the Prince to *Bois de Vincennes*. He commanded, at that Time, the *Gendarmes* of the Guard. He learned the Trade of War in *Holland*, and was called the Count *de Miossens*. It is under this Name that he is so greatly celebrated by Mr *de St Evremont* (*d*). He was Knighted the first of *January*, 1662, and made Governor of *Guienne* in the Month of *November*, 1670. In 1645, he married *Magdalen de Guenegaud*, youngest Daughter of *Gabriel de Guenegaud*, the King's Treasurer (*e*). He was one of *Scarron's* Heroes, as appears evidently from that Writer's Works.

(*a*) *His Name was Charles Amanieu d'Albret.*

(*b*) *See the 120th Letter of Bussi-Rabutin, part 1. p. g. 202. Edit. Holl.*

(*c*) *See Beniaminus Priolus de Rebus Gallicis, lib. 5. c. 5.*

(*d*) *See St Evremont's Miscellaneous Works, Tom. 2. pag. 71, 77, &c. Edit. Holl. 1693.*

(*e*) *See Father Anselme, Tom. 2 pag. 285.*

ALBUNEA,

ALBUNEA. ALBUTIUS.

ALBUNEA, a Famous Place (*a*), near *Tibur* in *Italy*. See the laſt Remark of the Article TIBUR.

(*a*) *At preſent Tivoli.*

ALBUTIUS SILUS (CAIUS) a Famous Orator in the Reign of *Auguſtus*, was born at *Novara*, and had raiſed himſelf there to the Office of *Ædile*; but quitted his Poſt on occaſion of an Inſult offered him by ſome Perſons, who had loſt their Cauſe. He was their Judge, and gave Sentence againſt them; upon which they dragged him by his Feet from the Tribunal. This Affront induced him to leave his Country immediately, and repair to *Rome*; where he became acquainted with the Orator *Munacius Plancus*. Emulation breeding ill blood between them, he ſet up a ſeparate Auditory; and at laſt ventured to plead Cauſes. He met with ſome Diſgraces at the Bar [*A*], which obliged him to quit it. Being old, and troubled with an Impoſthume, he returned to *Novara*, where, aſſembling the People, he repreſented to them, in a long Speech, the Reaſons, which gave him a diſreliſh of Life, and then ſtarved himſelf to death (*a*). *Seneca* the Father, who had often heard him plead, gives an ample Account of him, and recites ſeveral Abſtracts from his Speeches (*b*). He commends him as one, who would neither ſuffer, nor do an Injury; and this he calls the higheſt degree of Probity; *Homo ſummæ probitatis, qui nec facere injuriam, nec pati ſciret*. *Seneca*, the Philoſopher, would have defined the Nature of *Probity* better. *Albutius* compoſed a Treatiſe of Rhetoric, as may eaſily be inferred from a Paſſage of *Quintilian* (*c*).

(*a*) Sueton. de Clar. Rhetor. c. 6.

(*b*) Seneca, Prætat. lib. 3. Controverſ. & alibi paſſim.

(*c*) *Albutius non obſcurus Proſeſſor ate que autor, Scientis bene dicendi eſſe contentus (Rhetoricam, Albutius, in ſeptem Partes diviſerat, Auctor, alibi vocat Rhetor's to be the Science of ſpeaking well. Quint. Inſtit. lib. 2. cap. 5.*

[*A*] *He met with ſome Diſgraces at the Bar.*] It happened, once, that he addreſs'd himſelf to his Adverſary in theſe Words, intending nothing more by them, than a fine Rhetorical Figure, *Swear by the Aſhes, and by the Memory of your Father, and you ſhall gain your Cauſe*. After he had illuſtrated and ſet off the Thought to the beſt Advantage, the Advocate on the other ſide reply'd, *We accept the Condition*. *Albutius* anſwered, that he intended to offer no ſuch Terms; that it was only a rhetorical Figure, and that all figurative Expreſſions muſt be excluded, if Things were thus taken literally. The other Advocate reply'd, That Men could live without theſe Figures, and that they might be baniſh'd, with all his Heart. The Judges gave it for the Oath, and *Allutius* loſt his Cauſe, for a rhetorical Flouriſh. He was ſo vex'd at it, that he renounc'd the Profeſſion (1). The ſame Account is given of it by *Suetonius*; " Cum, in lite qua-" dam centum virali ab adverſario, quem ut impium " erga parentes inceſſebat, jusjurandum quaſi per fi-" guram ſic obtuliſſet; Jura per patris matriſque ci-" neres, qui inconditi jacent, & alia in hunc modum : " arripiente eo conditionem, nec judicibus aſpernanti-" bus, non ſine magna ſui invidia negotium afflixit " (2)." From that Time, Maſters have recommended to their Diſciples not to apply theſe Figures unſeaſonably (3).

(1) Seneca, Præf. lib 3. Controv.

(2) Sueton. de Claris Rhetor. c. 6.

(3) Quintil. lib. 9. c. 2.

ALBUTIUS (TITUS) a Philoſopher of the *Epicurean* Sect, went, in his Youth, from *Rome* to *Athens*, and gained ſuch a Taſte for the Manners of the *Greeks*, that he was fonder of paſſing for a *Greek*, than a *Roman* (*a*); which occaſioned a Jeſt of *Scævola* [*A*], to which *Lucilius* gave a very malicious turn in one of his Satires, as we learn from *Cicero* (*b*). The ſame Author informs us, I. That *Albutius* was a zealous *Epicurean*(*c*), and that he would have been a better Orator, had he been leſs attached to the Sect of *Epicurus*(*d*). II. That he was well verſed in the *Greek* Learning (*e*), and that he publiſhed ſome Harangues (*f*). III. That he had ſerved in ſome of the Offices of the Republic; that he governed *Sardinia* in the Quality of *Pro-Prætor* (*g*); and that he could

(*a*) Cicero in Bruto, cap. 26, 35.

(*b*) Id. l. 1. de Finib. cap. 3.

(*c*) Id. lib. 1. de Nat. Deorum, cap.33.

(*d*) Id. in Bruto, cap. 26, 35.

(*e*) Ibid.

(*f*) Ibid.

(*g*) Ibid. de Provinc. Conſular. cap 7. & in Piſonem, cap. 38.

[*A*] *A Jeſt of Scævola*.] It conſiſted in this; when he received a Viſit from *Albutius* at *Athens*, he ſaluted him in *Greek*, and made all his Attendants ſalute him in the ſame Language. The Ridicule cannot be conceived without thinking on the Action itſelf. *Cicero*, upon this Occaſion, expreſſes himſelf thus. " Res vero bonâ verbis electâ graviter ornate-" que dictatas quis non legat niſi qui ſe planè Græcum " dici velit, ut à Scævola eſt Prætor ſalutatus Athenis " Albutius, quem quidem locum cum multa venu-" ſtate & omni ſale idem Lucilius, apud quem præ-" clare Scævola,

Græcum te, Albuti, quam Romanum atque Sabinum
Municipem Ponti, Titii, Anni, Centurionum,
Præclarorum hominum ac primorum ſigniferumque,
Maluiſti dici. Græce ergo Prætor Athenis
Id quod maluiſti, te, cum ad me acceſſi' ſaluto :
Χαῖρε, inquam, Tite: Lictores, turma omni', cohorſq;
Χαῖρε. Hinc hoſtis Muti Albutius, hinc inimicus (1).

(1) Cicero de Finib. lib. 1. c. 3.

" —— *Who would refuſe to read a good Subject treated
" of with Weight and Beauty, and in choice Phraſes,
" but one, who plainly affects the Manners of Greece;
" ſuch as Albutius; who, when he was Prætor at
" Athens, was ſaluted in Greek by Scævola; a Cir-
" cumſtance repreſented with great Elegance and Wit
" by the Poet Lucilius, who introduces Scævola ad-
" dreſſing himſelf thus to Albutius;

*So fond of Grecian Cuſtoms was you grown,
That you abjur'd the Citizen of Rome.*

Hence, when at Athens, once ('tis known to Fame)
To viſit me, a Prætor there, you came,
Χαῖρε, O Titus! was my Compliment,
And Χαῖρε, Titus! thro' the Circle went.
—— *The Jeſt too keen Albutius could not bear,
And Wit divided the once friendly Pair.*

In this Paſſage *Cicero* expreſsly declares, That *Albutius* was, at that Time, Prætor at *Athens*, and yet the Verſes of *Lucilius* teſtify, that *Albutius*, upon viſiting *Scævola*, was ſaluted in *Greek*, and in a bantering manner; which offended him, and made him *Scævola*'s Enemy. Is it not very evident, that, according to *Lucilius*, it was *Scævola*, and not *Albutius*, who was then Prætor? Had *Albutius* been Prætor, he would have received, not made Viſits; or if he had made any, he would not have met with ſo ſatirical a Reception. It is therefore ſurpriſing, take it which way you will, either that *Cicero* ſhould ſay, that *Albutius* was Prætor; or, if he ſaid that *Scævola* was, as it is very likely he did, that the Error, which has crept into the Editions, has never been corrected. It ought to be read, *ut à Scævola eſt Prætore ſalutatus Athenis Albutius* (2); and not, *ut à Scævola eſt Prætor ſalutatus Athenis Albutius*. Mr Dacier cites theſe Verſes of *Lucilius*, and tranſlates them in ſuch a manner, as to declare, that *Scævola* was Prætor at *Athens*, when he derided *Albutius*, who was come to pay his court to him (3). *Corradus* thinks, that *Albutius* ſtudied at *Athens*, and that *Scævola* paſs'd through it, in his Way to *Rhodes*, as mentioned in the firſt Book de Oratore (4).

(2) Corradus, in Brutum Ciceronis, pag. 189. *would have corrected thus. Other Critics are of the ſame Opinion. See the Cicero of Mr Gronovius.*

(3) Dacier in Horace, Sat. 2. l. b. 2. burg. 121. Edit. Holl.

(4) Corradus ubi ſupra.

[*B*] *That*

ALBUTIUS.

could not obtain from the Senate the Proceffion [B] which he defired, to thank the Gods for his Exploits; that he was accufed of Bribery and Corruption [C], and banifhed [D]; and that he went to philofophize at *Athens* (b). *Scævola*'s Jeft fowed the Seeds of Difcord between

(b) Cicero Tufcul 5. cap. 3.

[B] *That he could not obtain from the Senate the Proceffion, &c.*] Cicero relates this, in order to deprive the Friends of *Gabinius* and *Pifo* of the Confolation they drew from it. He fhews them that the Cafes were not parallel : " Hac confolatione utuntur, " etiam T. Albutio fupplicationem hunc ordinem de- " negaffe, quod eft primum diffimile : Res in Sar- " dinia cum maftrucatis latrunculis à Proprætore " una cohorte auxiliaria gefta, & bellum cum maxi- " mis Syriæ gentibus ac tyrannis confulari exercitu " imperioque confectum. Deinde Albutius, quod à " Senatu petebat, ipfe fibi in Sardinia ante decreve- " rat : Conftabat enim, Græcum hominem ac levem " in ipfa provincia quafi triumphaffe. Itaque hanc " ejus temeritatem Senatus fupplicatione denegata no- " tavit (5). —— *They comfort themfelves with this " Reflexion, that Titus Albutius was denied a public " Thankfgiving by the Senate ; but there is a manifeft " Difparity between the two Cafes ; firft, between the " Tranfactions of a Pro-Prætor in Sardinia, with but " one auxiliary Cohort, and a War with the greateft " Nations and Kings of Syria, carried on and finifh'd " with a confular Force. In the next place, Albutius " had decreed himfelf, in Sardinia, the very Thing " he petition'd the Senate for : For it is well " known, that this Mimic of Greece, this Trifler, " celebrated a kind of Triumph in That Province. The " Senate therefore branded this his Prefumption with " the refufal of a public Thankfgiving."* It is thought, that *Albutius* commanded in *Sardinia*, in the Year of *Rome*, 639 (6).

(5) Cicero de Provinc. Confular.

(6) Father Prouft in his Commentary in ufum Delphini, on Cicero de Caris Oratoribus.

[C] *That he was accufed of Bribery and Corruption*] The following Paffage puts this paft difpute ; " Mu- " tius autem Augur, quod pro fe opus erat, ipfe dice- " bat, ut de pecuniis repetundis contra T. Albutium. " Is oratorum in numero non fuit ; juris civilis intel- " ligentis, atque omni prudentiæ genere præftitit (7). —— *The Augur Mutius* (Scævola) *fpoke, in perfon, " to what regarded himfelf ; as in the Accufation of " Bribery and Corruption againft T. Albutius. He " was not an Orator ; but excell'd in a thorough Know- " ledge of the Civil Law"* It is not very certain, that *Mutius Scævola* was the Accufer : I fhould chufe to fay, that he was only concern'd in the Caufe, and obliged to clear up, or maintain, fome Point, which related to it, and was part of the Accufation againft the Defendant. He had Eloquence enough for a thing of this nature ; but otherwife he was no Orator ; as plainly appears from the Words I have quoted. Some Critics prefer this reading ; *Mutius autem Augur, quod opus erat, per fe ipfe dicebat* (8) ; with all my Heart ; this reading will ftill leave room to conjecture, that *Scævola* was only accidentally engaged in the Caufe, and fpoke but to fome particular Circumftance of it. This Conjecture, which I fhall mention again in the Remark [F], is ftrongly confirmed by a Reafon, which *Cicero* alledg'd againft the Perfon, who contefted with him the Right of accufing *Verres*. He fays, That *Caius Julius*, having a like Difpute with *Cnæus Pompeius*, in the Affair of *Albutius*, made ufe of two Arguments ; the one was, that *Pompey* had been Quæftor to *Albutius* ; the other, that the Inhabitants of *Sardinia* had defired him to accufe *Albutius* (9). It was adjudg'd, that *Pompey* fhould not be the Accufer. This Office, therefore, remained with *Caius Julius*. The Reader, if he knew it not before, may learn from hence, by the way, that the *Romans* did not approve, that a fuperior Magiftrate fhould be accufed by his Subaltern. " Neque here unquam venit " in contentionem de accufando qui Quæftor fuiffet, " quin repudiaretur. Itaque neque L. Philoni " C. Servilius nominis deferendi poteftas eft data, " neque M. Aurelio Scauro in L. Flaccum, neque " Cn. Pompejo in T. Albutium : Quorum nemo prop- " ter indignitatem repudiatus eft, fed ne libido vio- " landæ neceffitudinis autoritate judicum comproba- " retur (10). —— *No Quæftor ever demanded the Right " of Accufation, but he was rejected.* Thus L. *Philo " was denied the Liberty of accufing* C. Servilius, *M. " Aurelius Scaurus of accufing* L. Flaccus, *and* Cn. *Pompeius of accufing* T. Albutius : *None of which " were fet afide as unworthy ; but, left the Authority " of the Judges fhould feem to countenance an Inclina-*

(7) Cicero in Bruto.

(8) Corradus in Brutum Ciceronis, pag. 189. Douza in Lucilium, pag. 99.

(9) Cicero, Divinat. in Verrem.

(10) Id. ib.

" tion to violate the Laws of Relation or Friendfhip." *Apuleius* feems to confute what I have endeavoured to prove ; for he fays, in his fecond Apology, That *C. Mutius* accus'd *A. Albutius*. But it is eafy to anfwer this Objection ; for, on the one fide, the Perfons of whom *Apuleius* fpeaks, have different Names from thofe whom I am here fpeaking of ; and, on the other, what *Apuleius* fays of his *C. Mutius* cannot be applied to our *Scævola*. It is certain that our *Albutius*'s Name was *Titus*, and not *Aulus*, and that our *Scævola* was called *Quintus Mucius* ; and, as he was Augur, he was often denoted by that Office ; *Quintus Mucius Scævola Augur*. The Accufer, whom *Apuleius* fpeaks of, was a young Man, who then made his firft Appearance at the Bar. " Neque autem gloriæ causâ me " accufat, ut M. Antonius Cn. Carbonem, C. Mutius " A. Albutium —— quippe homines eruditiffimi ju- " venes laudis gratiâ primum hoc rudimentum foren- " fis operæ fubibant, ut aliquo infigni judicio civibus " fuis nofcerentur, qui mos incipientibus adolefcenti- " bus ad illuftrandum ingenii florem apud antiquos " conceffus, diu exolevit (11). —— *He does not accufe " me, with a view of eftablifhing a Reputation, as " M. Antonius did, when he accufed* Cn. Carbo, *and " C. Mutius, in his Accufation of A. Albutius. —— " Thefe were young Gentlemen of promifing Geniufes, " who, ambitious of Fame, made thefe firft Effays at the " Bar, in order to diftinguifh themfelves by fome no- " table Caufe to their Fellow Citizens : A Practice, " which the Antients allowed in Youth, at their firft " fetting out, to difplay their opening Talents ; but is " now difufed."* This does not agree with our *Mutius Scævola*: He was Conful in the Year of *Rome* 636 (12) ; he was old, when *Cicero* was but eighteen Years of Age, that is to fay, in the Year of *Rome* 665 ; and *Albutius* was not accus'd, till after his return from *Sardinia*, where he was Pro-Prætor, in the Year 649. See the following Remark. Perhaps the Tranfcribers of *Apuleius* have by degrees chang'd *C. Julius* into *C. Mutius.* It is certain, that *C. Julius* was the Accufer of *Albutius*, and, if *Apuleius* had nam'd him, he would have been exact in this refpect ; but he cannot be juftified in what he advances, that all the Accufers, he names, were young Adventurers, who endeavour'd to fignalize their fetting out in the World, by fome famous Caufe. He borrows all thefe Examples from *Cicero*, as the famous *Grævius* has judicioufly obferved (13) ; why then does he reduce them all to one Species, fince *Cicero* ranks them under different Claffes (14) ? Is it not, becaufe they would not have ferv'd his purpofe, if they had been divided ? This is a fruitful Source of Falfifications in matters of Facts. If they do not fuit an Author's Purpofe, as they ftand, it is but turning and wrefting them as he pleafes, and they anfwer his Intention.

(11) Apul. Apolog. 2.

(12) Cicero in the beginning.

(13) Grævius, Notæ in Ciceron. de Offic. lib. 2. cap. 14.

(14) He alledges his *Accufation* as a *ginff Verres* as one Example : *Therefore he did not pretend to cite on'y there, who had it up for Accufers in their Youth.*

[D] *And banifh'd.*] We do not meet with this in the fame Paffages of *Cicero*, where *Albutius*'s Trial is mentioned, and it muft not be wondred at ; for, when an Author does not write the Life of a Man, he fays no more of him, than what relates to the Subject in hand. When *Cicero* took fome notice of *Albutius*'s Trial, he had only in view the Perfons who had fpoken, or intended to fpeak, againft the Accufed ; it was not, therefore, neceffary, that he fhould mention the Iffue of the Caufe. When he fpoke of *Albutius*'s Banifhment, his only aim was to fhew the good Ufe a Man may make of his Exile ; and therefore it was not neceffary to remark the Caufe of *Albutius*'s Banifhment. It is our Bufinefs to weave thefe different Paffages into one Contexture ; by which means we fhall find, that *Albutius*, having been accufed of Corruption, upon the Petition of the Inhabitants of *Sardinia*, was condemn'd, and banifh'd. " Albutius, cum in Sardinia triumphaffet, Romæ " damnatus eft (15). —— *Albutius, after he had triumph- " ed in Sardinia, was condemn'd at Rome.* —— Quid " T. Albutius, nonne animo æquiffimo Athenis exul " philofophabatur ? Cui tamen illud ipfum non acci- " diffet, fi in republica quiefcens Epicuri legibus pa- " ruiffet (16). —— *Did not Titus Albutius philofo- " phize, with great calmnefs of Mind, at Athens ; " which he could not have done, had he ftaid at home, " and obey'd the Laws of Epicurus."* *Gaffendus* cited this

(15) Cicero in Pifone.

(16) Id. lib. 5. Tufculan. cap. 37.

ALBUTIUS.

between them [E]. The Dictionaries are not free from Faults upon this Subject [F]. I do

this Passage very ill; for, instead of *si in republica——paruisset*, he gave it, *nisi in republica ——paruisset* (17). They, who require a Proof of my Assertion, that *Albutius* was accused, at the Petition of the Inhabitants of *Sardinia*, may find one in the following Words. " Julius hoc secum authoritatis ad accusandum asserebat, quod, ut hoc tempore nos ab Siculis, " sic tum ille ab Sardis rogatus ad causam accesserat " (18). —— Julius *claim'd the Right of Accusation*, *upon this Authority, that he undertook the Cause*, *at the Request of the Sardinians, as we do now at* *the Request of the People of Sicily*." To which may be added these Words of the 14th Chapter of the 2d Book *de Officiis*: *Aut patrociniis, ut nos pro Siculis, pro Sardis Julius*. So we must read it with *Lambinus*; or *pro Sardis contra Albutium Julius*, with *Manutius*. Consult *Suetonius* (19).

[E] *Scævola's Jest sow'd the Seeds of Discord between them.*] This is what *Lucilius* particularly took notice of in his Satires,

Hinc hosti Muti Albutius, hinc inimicus.

A Jest divided the once friendly Pair.

A learned Man believes, that they were frequently engaged on contrary Sides, particularly in the Cause of *Granius*, accused by *Albutius*, and defended by *Mutius*. He says, that at least, *Mutius* was much pleased, that *Granius* was acquitted. He proves this by a Passage of *Cicero*, to which he confesses that others give a different Explication; to wit, That *Albutius* accused *Mutius* of Corruption. " Sæpe inter se dissentirent " & contenderent; ut, quum Albutius Granium oppugnabat, & Mutius eum defendebat, certe illo absoluto gaudebat, ut libro secundo de Oratore scriptum videbis, quamvis aliter alii verba illa sint interpretati, & putarint ipsum Scævolam ab Albutio de pecuniis repetundis accusatum fuisse, quod ut nos de viro tali credamus adduci non possumus (20)." I can neither reconcile myself to the Sense, which this Critic rejects, nor to that which he approves. I should rather think *Cicero* meant, that *Scævola* was concern'd in the Process of Corruption, entered against *Albutius*; and so far concern'd, that the Justification of *Albutius* was to result from *His* Condemnation. I suppose, in consequence of this Conjecture, that *Scævola's* Cause depended upon that of *Albutius*, and that from hence it was that he pass'd for *Albutius's* Accuser. He was acquitted, I suppose, honourably; which occasioned the Conviction of *Albutius*. I suppose farther, that the latter appeal'd to the Crier *Granius's* Registers, in order to convict *Scævola*, and that his Proof was judg'd insufficient. *Granius* was pleas'd at *Scævola's* Acquitment, and was rallied as if he had rejoic'd, that the Judges had no regard to his Books, or his verbal Processes. This I take to be the Import of *Cicero's* Words, " Bella etiam est familiaris reprehensio quasi errantis, ut quum objurgavit Albius Granium, quod quum ejus tabulis quiddam Albutio probatum videretur, & valde absoluto Scævola gauderet, neque intelligeret contra suas tabulas esse judicatum (21)." If any other Proof is required of the Enmity between *Albutius* and *Scævola*, I can add, that *Lucilius* introduced *Scævola* jesting upon *Albutius's* Style (22). I should be glad to know whence Father *Prouft* had it, that *Lucilius's* Anger against our *Scævola* proceeded from the Affection he had for *Albutius*, against whom *Scævola* had pleaded (23). If *Lucilius* was *Albutius's* Friend, he verify'd the Maxim, *That a Jester prefers his Jest to his Friend*;

—— dummodo risum
Excutiat sibi, non hic cuiquam parcit amico (24);

for we have seen how this Satirist diverted himself at the Expence of *Albutius*.

[F] *The Dictionaries are not free from Faults upon this Subject.*] I. *Charles Stephens* pretends, that *Varro* spoke of our *Titus Albutius*, as of a Poet, who had wrote Satires after *Lucilius's* Manner, *Luciliano Stylo*. But, when we consult *Varro*, we find that he speaks of one *Lucius Albutius*. " Nonne item Lucius Albutius, homo (ut scitis) apprimè doctus, cujus Lucilia- " no charactere sunt libelli, dicebat, in Albano fundum " suum pastiunibus semper vinci à villa, agrum enim " minus dena millia reddere, villam plus vicena (25)? " *—— Did not Lucius Albutius, a very learned Man* " *(as you know) and whose Writings are in the Style* " *and Manner of Lucilius, say, that the Revenue of* " *his Farm at Alba was scarce half that of his Vil-* " *la?* " II. It is not true, that *Lucilius* laugh'd at *Albutius* as one, who intermix'd *Greek* with *Latin* Words; *Charles Stephens* did not take the Poet's Meaning; he fancied that the χαῖρε belongs to *Albutius*; whereas it must be referr'd to *Scævola*, and his Attendants. *Lloyd* and *Hofman* have not corrected these two Faults. Observe, that I do not pretend to deny, that *Albutius* intermix'd *Greek* Phrases with *Latin*. III. What *Charles Stephens*, *Lloyd*, and *Hofman* suppose, is very precarious; to wit, That the Father of the Witch *Canidia* was the same *Albutius*, spoken of in the second Satire of the Second Book of *Horace*. Mr *Dacier* believes they are two *Albutius's* (26). IV. These three Dictionary-Writers are mistaken, when they take the *Albutius* of the second Satire of the second Book of *Horace* for a downright Miser. We shall soon see the contrary. V. *Moreri* is mistaken, when he fancies, that the *Albutius*, whom *Cicero* speaks of, in the beginning of the first Book *de Finibus*, is not the same with him, whom he mentions in the first Book *de Naturâ Deorum*, and in the fifth Book of the *Tusculan* Questions. VI. It is not true that *Horace* says, That there was an *Albutius*, *the most covetous of all Men, who was wont to correct his Servants before they executed his Commands, for fear, as he said, he should forget to do it, if they did not exactly obey his Orders*. *Moreri*, who ascribes all this Discourse to *Horace*, was deceived by *Charles Stephens*; though the latter does not expresly ascribe this little Fable to *Horace*. All that *Horace* says of the Matter is this.

Mundus erit, qui non offendet sordidus, atque
In neutram partem cultus miser: hic neque servis,
Albuti senis exemplo, dum munia didit,
Sævus erit: neque, sic ut simplex Nævius, unctam
Conviviis præbebit aquam (27).

—— *He lives well, who keeps the middle State*,
And neither leans too much to this, nor that:
Such, when he bid his Slaves do this and this,
Will not be rigid, as Albutius is;
Nor yet, like Nævius, when he makes a Feast,
With costly Ointment will he wash his Guest.
                                                                    CREECH.

The meaning is, that true Cleanliness lies in the middle between Nastiness, and *a too scrupulous, and over nice Exactness* (28). If he had seen the excessive and servile Care that is taken by the People in keeping their Houses clean in some Parts of *Holland*, he would have call'd it a *false Neatness*. *Albutius* and *Nævius* are produced as two Examples of vicious Extreams: the former as an Instance of too much Formality; the latter of too little. Some Interpreters have changed the Characters; and mistaken *Nævius* for a Prodigal, and *Albutius* for a covetous Man (29). But, perhaps, the Words of *Horace* do not relate to Covetousness and Prodigality; but only rather to Neatness and it's contrary. This latter Defect is sometimes attended with superfluous Expences. Some Persons are extravagant in Dress, in Furniture, and in Eating; and yet have not the Reputation of being well dress'd, of disposing the Ornaments of their Appartments to Advantage, or of keeping a good Table. However it be, *Albutius* here is not an Example of Covetousness. I shall conclude, by observing, that *Albutius's* Severity towards his Slaves is not a Circumstance forg'd by *Moreri*; he had read it in his Patron (30); but did not know that the Original of it is in an ancient Scholiast. " Asper in exigenda à singulis im- " pensi ratione castigandoque, adeo ut servos nonnum- " quam castigaret prius, & cæderet; quum peccassent, " dicens vereri se ne cum peccassent cædere tunc ei " non vaceret (31). —— *Rigid in exacting an Account* " *from every one of their Tasks; to such a Degree, that* " *he sometimes corrected, and beat his Servants, be-* " *fore they offended, pretending, that he fear'd he* " *should not, then, have an Opportunity of doing it*."

(17) Cassiend. de Vita Epic. lib. 2. cap. 6. pag. 188. *in Folio. where the Citations in the Margin are very erroneous.*
(18) Cicero, Divin. in Verrem.
(19) Sueton. in Jul-o, cap. 55.
(20) Corradus in Brutum Ciceronis, p. 285.
(21) Cicero, lib. 2. de Orat. c. 70.
(22) *See below the Remark* [G].
(23) Prouft Comment. in Ciceron. de Orat. lib. 3. n. 72. In usum Delphini.
(24) Horat. Sat. 4. lib. 1. ver. 34.
(25) Varro de Re rustica, lib. 3. cap. 2.
(26) Dacier's Remarks on Sat. 1. lib. 2. pag. 40.
(27) Horat. Sat. 2. lib. 2. ver. 65.
(28) *See Mr* Dacier *on this Passage*.
(29) *The old Commentators*, Lambinus, Cruquius, &c. *&c.*
(30) Charles Stephens.
(31) Vetus Commentator in Horat. d. l.

[G] I

188   ALBUTIUS. ALCASAR. ALCÆUS.

I do not believe, that our *Titus Albutius* is the same, whom *Horace* speaks of [G] in the second Satire of the second Book. We meet with nothing concerning the Physician ALBUTIUS, whom *Pliny* ranks among the most Famous (*i*).

[G] *I do not believe, that our* Albutius *is the same, whom* Horace *speaks of.*] We have seen, that *Horace*'s *Albutius* was a Man of too great Exactness; that he never forgave his Domesticks an Offence; that he would have one do precisely this, and another that; and that he descended to Particulars, in a pedantic manner. He, whom *Lucilius* describes, as one *who affected so much the Greek Politeness and Elegancy, that he desired to pass for a Greek* (32), was cut out to furnish *Horace* with the Example he wanted; since every Person, who affects the Manners of foreign Countries, mixes with them I know not what of forced and extravagant, which turns the thing into Ridicule. See the Behaviour of the Country 'Squires so often ridiculed by *Moliere*, with regard to Fashions in which they never observe a Medium. I can scarce believe, that *Horace* brought upon the Stage the Person of the *Albutius* of *Lucilius*; nor do I think it strange, that *Torrentius* believed he did. Mr *Dacier* chuses to say, That the *Albutius*, mentioned by *Horace*, was the Son of him, whom *Lucilius* satirized. I believe, that *Albutius*'s Affectation of what was *Greek*, related chiefly to the Language. We find, besides, from a Jest of *Lucilius*, that he was too nice in the disposition of his Words. "Collocationis est componere & struere verba, sic ut "nerve aspere eorum concursus neque hiulcus sit, sed "quodammodo coagmentatus & levis. In quo lepide "soceri persona lusit is, qui elegantissime id facere "potuit, Lucilius.

Quam lepide lexeis compostæ, ut tesserulæ omnes Arte, pavimento, atque emblemate vermiculato.

"Quæ cum dixisset in Albutium illudens, &c. (33) "—— The Collocatio (or Disposition) *consists in* "*ranging the Words in such a manner, that the Period shall neither be harsh, nor discontinuous, but* "*as it were cemented and polish'd.* Lucilius rallied "*this careful Style very elegantly, as he was very* "*capable of doing, in the Person of* Mutius *the Augur* "(34), *comparing it to* small Tyles, wrought artificially, upon a Pavement, into variety of emblematical "Figures. *Applying this in a bantering way to Al*- "*butius,* &c." The Verses of *Lucilius* represent a sort of Style in Writing, which may be called *Inlaid*, or *Mosaic*, Work.

ALCASAR (LEWIS de) a *Spanish* Jesuit (*a*), was born at *Seville*, in the Year 1554. He entered among the Jesuits in the Year 1569, in spite of the Opposition of his Family, which had great Possessions. After teaching Philosophy, he taught Divinity above Twenty Years at *Corduba*, and at *Seville*. He applyed himself chiefly to discover the Mysteries contained in St *John*'s *Revelations*, and employed near Twenty Years in this Work (*b*). The Book he composed upon this Subject is one of the best, which the *Roman* Catholics have produced on the *Apocalypse* [*A*]. It is entituled, *Vestigatio Arcani Sensus in Apocalypsi*, and has been printed several times [*B*]. It is pretended that *Grotius* borrowed many of his Notions from it (*c*). The Author maintains, that the *Apocalypse* is fully accomplished as far as the twentieth Chapter, and finds the Two Witnesses in it, besides *Elias* and *Enoch* (*d*). He makes no Scruple of rejecting the Ancient Fathers; and, as his Principal Studies tended only to the Explication of this Book, the other Work, which we have of his, is but a Commentary on the Passages of the Old Testament, which have some relation to St *John*'s *Revelation*. It was printed, after his Death, with this Title, *In eas Veteris Testamenti partes quas respicit Apocalypsis, nempe Cantica Canticorum, Psalmos complures, multa Danielis, aliorumque librorum capita, libri V.* So that here are Two Volumes in Folio, which are, properly speaking, but a Commentary on the *Revelations*; but there is an *Appendix* to each: That of the First Volume is a Treatise *de Sacris ponderibus & mensuris*; and That of the Second a Treatise *de malis Medicis*. *Alcasar* died at *Seville*, the 16th of *June*, 1613. aged sixty Years (*e*). You will find an *Examen* of some of his Apocalyptic Hypotheses, in a Work, which Mr *Heidegger* published at *Leyden*, in the Year 1687, entituled, *Mysterium Babylonis magnæ*.

[*A*] *The Book —— is one of the best, which the* Roman *Catholics have produc'd on the* Apocalypse.] This is *Nicolas Antonio*'s Account of it. "Insignem "posuit operam in adornando atque illustrando *Apo-* "*calypsis* libro obscurissimo. Edidit namque lucubrationes suas ad ipsam ingeniosas quidem, eruditas, "elaboratasque, ut censet Cornelius à Lapide. Sed "quisnam sponsor erit, telo eum quamvis acuto & "forti scopum tetigisse (1). —— *He took remarkable* "*Pains in explaining and illustrating that obscure* "*Book,* The Apocalypse. *For he published his own* "*Lucubrations on it, ingenious indeed, and elaborate,* "*in the Opinion of* Cornelius à Lapide. *But, as* "*sharp and strong as his Arrow may be, who will an-* "*swer for him, that he has hit the Mark?*" I am certain there is no Bankrupt, or impriso'n'd Debtor, but could find Security much easier, than your Interpretors of the *Apocalypse*, were there a Tribunal on Earth to assess those at a large Fine, who should warrant false Interpretations. When a Man flatters his Passions, where no Danger attends his Opinions, he is apt to be credulous; but it would be in vain to demand such Securities, as *Don Nicolas Antonio* would require.

[*B*] *Printed several times.*] Father *Alegambus* mentions only the Edition of *Antwerp*, by *John Keerberge*, in 1614, and immediately after says, that the other Volume was posthumous. If the first had been printed but in 1614, it would have been Posthumous, and so there would have been no Reason to distinguish the one from the other. We must believe then, as *Don Nicolas Antonio* observes, that the first was printed at *Antwerp*, by *Keerberge*, in the Year 1604. Besides this Edition, *Nicolas Antonio* speaks of that of 1619: *Antverpiæ apud Nutios*, and that of *Lyons*, 1616. *Draudius* quotes these two last Editions, and besides them one of *Antwerp*, by *Keerberge*, in 1611 (2). Father *Sotuel*, besides the Edition of 1614, mentions only the two last of *Nicolas Antonio*, and says also, that the other Volume is posthumous. So that his Revision of *Alegambus* is not so exact as it ought to be.

ALCÆUS, a Native of *Mitylene* in the Island of *Lesbos*, was one of the greatest Lyric Poets of Antiquity. Some say, That he was the Inventor of this Species of Poetry.

—— Age, dic Latinum,
Barbite, carmen,
Lesbio primum modulate civi (*a*):

Begin,

ALCÆUS.

Begin, sweet Harp, a Roman Strain
Those Measures and those Airs maintain,
First struck by great Alcæus' noble Hand. CREECH.

He flourished in the forty fourth *Olympiad* (b) at the same time with *Sappho*, who was likewise of *Mitylene*. The Scandalous Chronicle [A] says, that *Alcæus*, one day, requested I know not what Favour of *Sappho*, but that *Sappho*, who was not, at that time, in so good a Humour as she used to be, refused him what perhaps she offered him the next day (c). However it be, he had other business upon his Hands besides making Verses: he wanted to give a Proof of his Courage in War, but was not very successful in it; for he ran away, and left his Arms behind him, when the *Athenians* gained a Battel against the *Lesbians* (d). But it was some Comfort to him in his Disgrace, that the Conquerors caused his Arms to be hung up in the Temple of *Minerva* at *Sigeum*; which they would not have done, with such a Mark of Distinction, had they not thought it a glorious Monument of their Victory (e). *Alcæus* did not forget this Circumstance in the Verses he wrote on this unlucky Adventure [B]. His Muse, whom he employed in the midst of War, either in Catches, or Love Songs, or in celebrating his Mistress (f), who was such another trusty Support as himself [C]: His Muse, I say, was not silent on the Defeat of the *Lesbians*. It is well known, that she was not always ludicrous, and that she could treat the gravest Subjects with a suitable Dignity

(b) Euseb. in Chronic.
(c) Le Fevre's Lives of the Greek Poets, pag. 27.
(d) Herod. lib. 5. cap. 95.
(e) Id. ibid.
(f) Horace. See his words below in the Remark [C].

[A] *The scandalous Chronicle.*] I have set down Mr *le Fevre*'s own Words, and am very much mistaken, if he fetch'd this little Fable any where else than from *Aristotle*'s Rhetoric. *Aristotle* cites these Words of *Alcæus* ;

Θέλω τὶ τ' εἰπῶν, ἀλλά με κωλύει
Αἰδώς.

And this Answer of *Sappho*,

Αἰ δ' ἦχες ἐσλῶν ἵμερ⊕, ἢ καλῶν,
Καὶ μὴ τι εἰπῶν γλῶσσ' ἐκύκα κακόν,
Αἰδώς κε τυ σ' οὐχ ἄχεν ὄμματ'·
Ἀλλ' ἔλεγες περὶ δικαίω (1).

(1) Aristot. Rhetor. lib. 2. cap. 6. Note, that I read, and accent these Greek Words, as Scaliger did in Euseb. p. 85. Edit. 1658.

The Import of the Verses is This. *Alcæus* declares he has something to say, but that Modesty forbids him: *Sappho* replies, that if his Request were honourable, and his Tongue were not prepared to utter something immodest, Shame would not have appear'd in his Face, and he would not be at a loss to make a reasonable Proposition.

ALCÆUS.
Fain wou'd I speak, but must, thro' Shame, conceal
The Thought my eager Tongue wou'd strait reveal.

SAPPHO.
Were your Request, O Bard, on Honour built,
Your Cheeks wou'd not have worn these Marks of Guilt;
But in prompt Words the ready Thought had flown,
And your Heart's honest Meaning quickly shown.

They, who are qualified to judge of Mr *le Fevre*'s Books, Mrs, as he says in his first *Journal*, whose Souls are capable of different Forms, and who understand, at half a Word, wherein the Beauty of Thoughts and Expressions consists, are sensible, that these Words of *Alcæus* are one of those Declarations of Love, which require the critical Minute, and that *Sappho* apprehended perfectly what he meant. Her Answer is wise, but it is perhaps too serious upon this Supposition.

[B] *The Verses he wrote on this unlucky Adventure.*] HE, among all the *Latin* Poets, who most resembles *Alcæus*, confesses, as well as He, in his Poems, that he fled from the Battle, and threw down his Arms, as being useless in Flight.

Tecum Philippos & celerem fugam
Sensi, relictâ non bene parmulâ,
Quum fracta virtus, & minaces
Turpe solum tetigere mento (3).

(3) Horat. Od. 7. lib. 2. ver 9.

The bloody Wars, Philippi's *Field,*
Ignobly having lost my Shield,
With thee I saw, secure from Wound;
I saw the Flight, when Pompey *proud*
To Cæsar's *stronger Virtue bow'd,*
And basely bit the bloody Ground.
CREECH.

The same Adventure happen'd to *Archilochus* before *Alcæus*, and he confess'd it publickly (4). Perhaps *Horace* would not have been so ingenuous, if he had not had these great Examples before his Eyes. *Chabot* is mistaken, when he maintains, that *Plutarch* refutes *Herodotus* in relation to *Alcæus*'s Flight (5). *Plutarch* says only, that *Herodotus* suppress'd a fine Action of *Pittacus*, but not the cowardly Behaviour of *Alcæus* (6).

[C] *His Mistress, who was such another trusty Support as himself.*] *Horace* informs us, that *Alcæus*'s Mistress was a Boy, whose Name was *Lycus*, and who had black Eyes and black Hair.

Qui ferox bello ; tamen inter arma,
Sive jactatam religarat udo
    Littore navim,
Liberum & Musas, Veneremque, & illi
Semper hærentem puerum canebat,
Et Lycum nigris oculis, nigroque
    Crine decorum (7).

He fierce in Arms ; yet, midst his Cares,
When Dangers press'd, and naisy Wars,
And stain'd his charming Harp with Blood ;
Or, when he stemm'd the angry Seas,
Or when, arriv'd, he sat at ease,
And laugh'd at all the Fury of the Flood ;
The Muses he in sounding Verse,
Wou'd sing, and Venus' *Praise rehearse,*
With her th'attending wanton Boy ;
Or Lyco's *Face, surprizing fair,*
With coal-black Eyes, and auburn Hair,
By Nature fitted to entice to Joy.
CREECH.

It is apparently He, who had a Mole upon his Finger, which, in the Poet's Eye, was a beautiful Ornament. *Nævus in articulo pueri delectat Alcæum, at est corporis macula naevus, illi tamen hoc lumen videbatur* (8). *Cicero* says, in another place, that, though *Alcæus* had shewed a great deal of Courage, he had filled his Verses with an excessive Pederasty ; *Fortis vir in sua republica cognitus, quæ de juvenum amore scripsit Alcæus* (9) ? He was so amorous, that he compares himself to a Hog, who, whilst he eats one Acron, devours another with his Eyes ; *Just so,* says he, *when I am enjoying one Girl, I am wishing for another.* Ἀ υε τὰν βάλανον τὰν μ̔ ἔχω, τὰν δ' ἐράσμαι λαβεῖν. Κάτω παῖδα καλὴν τὰν μ̔ ἔχω, τὰν δ' ἐράμαι λαβεῖν. *Scipio Gentilis* relates this in his Notes on *Apuleius*'s Apology, pag. 65.

(4) See Remark [H] of Lit. article.
(5) Chabot, in Horat. Od. 13. lib. 2.
(6) Plut. de Malign. Herodoti, pag. 858.
(7) Horat. Od. 32. lib. 1. ver. 6.
(8) Cicero de Natur. Deor. lib. 1.
(9) Id. Tuscul. Quæst. 4. cap. 33.

ALCÆUS.

Dignity [D]; particularly the fine Common-place Topic against Tyrants. *Alcæus*, in That, followed an Inclination, which was confirmed by his own Adventures, and his personal Interests; for he had vigorously opposed the Invaders of the Liberty of his Country, and particularly *Pittacus* [E], who became an Usurper, though he was one of the Seven *Sages* of *Greece*. He set *Alcæus* at Liberty, whom he had taken Prisoner, saying, that it was better to forgive, than to punish, an Offence (g). Some say, that *Alcæus* was *expelled with many others; but that at length he put himself at the head of the Exiled, made War against the Tyrants, and drove them out* (b). I find in *Dionysius Halicarnasseus* nothing more, than that the Inhabitants of *Mitylene* elected *Pittacus* for their General, against the Poet *Alcæus*, and his Adherents, whom they had banished (i). Others say, that, having abused *Pittacus*'s Clemency, and continuing to cabal, and inveigh against him, he had no longer Favour shewn him (k); which *Ovid* expressed in these Words;

> Utque lyræ vates fertur periisse severæ,
> Causa sit exitii dextera læsa tui.

> Or may thy Satire too severe be found,
> And Thine, like poor Alcæus' Muse, be crown'd
> With Vengeance from the Hand it dares to wound.

This is the more probable, as *Alcæus* pass'd for one, who did not oppose Innovations, as such, but because others had introduced them (l). It is a very common Infirmity. There are only some small Fragments of his Poems remaining.

[D] *His Muse —— could treat the gravest Subjects with a suitable Dignity.*] This made *Horace* say,

> Et te sonantem plenius aureo,
>   Alcæe, plectro, dura navis,
>   Dura fugæ mala, dura belli.
> Utrumque sacro digna silentio
> Mirantur umbræ dicere: sed magis
>   Pugnas & exactos tyrannos
>   Densum humeris bibit aure vulgus (10).

> Alcæus too, whose golden Strings
> With manly Strokes sound loftier things;
> He sings the Dangers, and the Fears,
> Of Flights, of sailing, and of Wars.
> With silent Awe the Shades admire
> The tuneful Numbers of his Lyre:
> The vulgar Ghosts throng most to hear
> Of Kings depos'd; of Feats of War
> And drink them with a greedy Ear.
>   CREECH.

Mr *Dacier* remarks on these Words, I. That *Alcæus's Style was noble and strong, and that he treated of more lofty Subjects, than Sappho, who says of him in Ovid*,

> Nec plus Alcæus consors patriæque Lyræque
> Laudis habet, quamvis grandius ille sonet.

> --- *The wide World resounds with Sappho's Praise.*
> *Tho' great Alcæus more sublimely sings,*
> *And strikes with bolder Rage the sounding Strings,*
> *No less Renown attends the moving Lyre,*
> *Which Cupid tunes, and Venus does inspire.*
>   POPE.

II. That *Horace gives him a Golden Plectrum, because he is speaking of that Part of his Works, wherein he describes the Civil Wars, which happened at Mitylene, and the different Factions of the Tyrants* Pittacus, Myrsilus, Megalagyrus, *the* Cleanactides, *and others* (11), *and that those Poems were called Στρασιωτικὰ ποιήματα, Poems on Seditions.* He cites this Passage of *Quintilian*: " Alcæus in parte operis aureo
" plectro merito donatur, qua tyrannos infectatur.
" Multum etiam moribus confert, in eloquendo bre-
" vis & magnificus, & diligens, plerumque Homero
" similis, sed in lusus & amores descendit, majoribus
" tamen aptior (12). —— *Alcæus deserves the Golden Plectrum, which is given him, in that Part of his Poems, in which he lashes Tyrants. In this he is greatly useful to the Manners of Mankind, being concise and majestic in his Language, and much like Homer; However he sometimes descends to Mirth and Love; tho' naturally qualified for loftier Subjects.*"
Add to this the Epithet of *Threatning*, given to his Muse:

> ----- Alcæi MINACES
> Stesichorique graves Camænæ (13).

[E] *Had vigorously opposed —— Pittacus.*] He inveighed against him in very vulgar Terms. He called him *Splay-Foot, Fat-Guts, &c.* as we learn from *Suidas* under the Word σαράπους, and from *Diogenes Laertius* in the Life of *Pittacus*. The Moderation of the latter was very praise worthy, and appeared so to *Valerius Maximus*: " Pittaci quoque modera-
" tione pectus instructum, qui Alcæum poetam &
" amaritudine odii & viribus ingenii adversus se pertina-
" cissimè usum, tyrannidem à civibus delatam adep-
" tus, tantummodo quid in opprimendo posset admo-
" nuit (14). —— *Pittacus likewise was a Person of great Moderation, who, having seized on the kingly Power, abolished by the People, only shewed the Poet Alcæus, who employed all the Bitterness of Hatred, and the Force of Wit, in abusing him, what he could have done in the way of Oppression.*"

ALCÆUS, an *Athenian* (a), and a Tragic Poet, was the first, according to some, who composed Tragedies. If we may believe *Suidas*, he is not the same with the Comic Poet ALCÆUS, the Fifth of the Ancient Comedy, and the Son of *Miccus*. It seems, he renounced his Country, which was the City of *Mitylene*, and passed for an *Athenian* (b). He left ten *Pieces*, whereof one was entituled *Pasiphaë*: It was that which he produced, when he disputed with *Aristophanes* in the Fourth Year of the Ninety seventh *Olympiad* (c). *Athenæus* cites some others: It is not certainly known, whether the *Endymion*, cited by *Pollux*, belongs to *Alcæus* the Tragic, or *Alcæus* the Comic Poet: But it is probable, that the Piece entituled *Cælum*, was written by the former, since *Macrobius* cites it as a Tragedy (d). I find, in *Plutarch*, a Poet ALCÆUS, different from all the preceeding (e), and who is perhaps the same, whom *Porphyry* mentioned as a Writer of Satirical *Iambic* Verses, and Epigrams,

ALCÆUS. ALCHABITIUS. ALCHINDUS.

grams, and who wrote a Poem concerning the Plagiarism of the Historian *Ephorus* (*f*). The *Alcæus* of *Plutarch* lived in the Hundred and forty fifth *Olympiad*, in the Year of *Rome* 555, as appears by the *Ode* he composed on the Battle, which *Philip*, King of *Macedon* lost in *Thessaly*. This *Ode* represented *Philip* as running away faster than a Stag, and magnified the Number of the Slain, in order to chagrin him the more. Nevertheless *Plutarch* tells us, that *Titus Flaminius*, who gained the Battel, was more offended at *Alcæus*'s Verses, than *Philip*; because the *Ode* mentioned the *Ætolians* before the *Romans*, and seemed thereby to give the *Ætolians* the chief Honour of the Victory. *Philip* defended himself against *Alcæus*'s Song by another [*A*]. It must be confess'd, that *Plutarch* makes the *Roman* Consul too apt to take Offence. We are told likewise of one A L C Æ U S, a *Messenian*, who lived in the Reign of *Vespasian*, and in That of *Titus* (*g*). Some of his Epigrams are in the *Anthologia*. I know not which of these *Alcæus*'s suffered a very remarkable kind of Death [*B*] for his Lewdness. *Vossius*, at the forty second Page of his Notes on *Catullus*, believes it was He, who satirized *Philip* King of *Macedon*. He takes him for the Comedian by mistake; for the Comic Poet was cotemporary with *Aristophanes*.

(*f*) Porphyr. apud Euseb. Præp. Evangel. lib. 10. cap. 3. pag. 467.

(*g*) Tzetzes in Lycophr. apud Gyrald. de Po. t. Dialog 10. pag. 511. Edit. 1696.

[*A*] *Philip defended himself against Alcæus's Song by another.*] *Plutarch* gives us the Substance of it in these two Lines:

"Αφλοιθ· ἠ ἀφυλλθ·, ἰδ'υσίρε, τῷ ἰπὶ νότῳ
Ἀλκαίῳ ταυσθι πάςτω θ ηλίκθι (1).

This leafless, barkless Trunk, O Passenger, is erected as a Gibbet for Alcæus.

[*B*] *Suffered a very remarkable kind of Death.*] *Isaac Vossius* gives us (2) this Epitaph, taken out of an *Anthologia*, which was never printed:

Αλκαῖυ τάφθ· ἵτ θ·, ὃν ἰκπαπν ἡ ̔ λαϊδίφυλλθ·
Τιμωρὸς μοιχῶν γᾶς θυξάτης ἰφοριθ·.

This is Alcæus's Tomb, who died by a Radish, the Daughter of the Earth, and Punisher of Adulterers.

The meaning of this is, that *Alcæus* suffered the Punishment of Adulterers, which consisted in a certain manner of impaling. They thrust one of the largest Radishes they could find up the Adulterer's Fundament, or, for want of Radishes, they made use of a Fish, with a very large Head; as the Scholiast of *Juvenal* informs us, on these Words of the tenth Satyr:

 ---- Quosdam Mœchos & * Mugilis intrat.

This helps us to understand this Menace of Catullus:

Ah tum te miserum, maliq; fati,
Quem, attractis pedibus patente porta,
Percurrent raphaniq; mugilesq; (3).

(1) Plutarch. in Flamin. pag. 373.

(2) Isaac Vossius in Catullum, pag. 42.

* *The Mugilis is a Sea-Fish with a large Head.*

(3) Catull. Epigr. 11. See Parthenius, Muretus, and Achilles Statius on this Passage.

Ah! wretched Thou, and born to luckless Fate,
Who art discovered by the un-shut Gate!
If once, alas! the jealous Husband come,
The Radish, or the Sea-Fish, is thy doom.

Lucian speaks of this sort of Punishment, but does not say whether the Criminal died of it, and differs but little from his Scholiast. They both tell us, that the Adulterer was usually well beat; but the Scholiast says, that the Radish was not thrust up his Fundament, till he was ready to expire under the Blows he had received. *Lucian* insinuates the quite contrary; for the Letcher, of whom he speaks, having been foundly beat, leaped down from the Tiling, and ran away with the Radish sticking in his Posteriors. Καὶ τῦ τέλυς ἀληφθὼ θρύφυ βαφανῖδι & σύγχῳ βυ-Cυυρθυ (4). *De tecto desiliens aufugit natibus raphanos oppletis. Vossius* ought not to have concluded from this Passage of *Lucian*, that this Punishment was not Mortal; for it is very probable, that if the Patient had not run away, it would have cost him his Life sooner or later. The two Verses, which *Vossius* cites, and which he takes for the Discourse of an Adulteress, who said to her Godmother, that if the Punishment of the Cross was inflicted upon their Gallants, instead of the Radish, no one would have any thing more to say to them, are a better Proof, than the Words of *Lucian* (5). The Commentators on *Diogenes Laertius* rightly apprehended what *Menedemus* aimed at, when he said to an insolent Adulterer, that the Juice of Radishes was useful: Πεφὶ ἢ τὸν Δεριοινοίδωον μοιχὸν, ἀγεοιῶς, έφη, ὅτι ὁ μέσος κοιμᾶΣα χυλὸν ἔχει χρνσὸν, ἀλλὰ ἡ βαφα-νίδας (6). *Audacter exultanti adultero, ignoras, inquit, non modo brassicæ succum inesse utilem, sed & raphano.*

(4) Lucian. de morte Peregrini.

(5) Ex Hesychio in μεραινιβω-θῆναι. See also the Scholiast of Aristophanes in Nubibus.

(6) Diogenes Laert. lib. 2. n. 128. See Aldobrandinus & Menage.

A L C H A B I T I U S, an *Arabian* Astrologer, composed an Introduction to the Knowledge of the Celestial Influences [*A*]. He wrote likewise concerning *The Conjunction of the Planets*, and a Treatise of *Optics*, which was found in a Convent of *Germany*, and brought to the Author of the Book *de Lumine Animæ*. His Astrological Works, translated by *John of Seville* (*a*), were printed at *Venice* in 1491, with the Exposition of *John of Saxony*, and, in 1521, with the Corrections of *Antony de Fantis*, a Physician of *Treviso* in *Italy* (*b*). It is not well known at what time *Alchabitius* lived.

(*a*) Gesner *in Miscellan*.

(*b*) Gesner in Bibl. & ex eo Vossius de Scient. Mathem. pag. 3. 4. & 319.

[*A*] *Composed an Introduction to the Knowledge of the Celestial Influences.*] The Title of the Book in *Gesner* and in *Simler*, is, *Isagoge ad magisterium judiciorum astrorum, vel ad scrutanda stellarum magisteria. Vossius* gives it in another manner, but which comes to the same Sense: *Isagoge ad scrutanda astrorum indicia* (1). But *Moreri*, mistaking one Word for another in *Vossius*, *initia* for *indicia*, gives us an incomprehensible Title: *An Introduction to the Knowledge of the beginning of the Stars.* It appears that *Vossius* thought it ought to be *indiciorum*, where *Gesner* and *Simler* have put *judiciorum*.

Note, That *Alchabitius*'s Treatise of the Conjunction of the Planets was translated into *French* by *Orontius Finæus* (2), and that Mr *de la Mare*, in his Preface to the Works of the four Brothers *Guimes*, quotes the Manuscript Notes of *Peter Almatius*, Counsellor in the Parliament of *Dijon*, on *Alchabitius de inimicitiis Planetarum*. I have this from Mr *de la Monnoie*.

(1) Vossius de Scient. Mathem. pag. 399.

(2) See du Verdier, pag. 20. of his Bibliotheque.

A L C H I N D U S, a Physician and Astrologer among the *Arabians*. *Cardan* reckoned him among the Twelve Sublime Geniuses, whom he looked upon as the chief of those, who excelled in the Sciences (*a*). This is to exceed *Albobazen Haly*, and *Haly Rodoan*, who call him the great Astrologer, and even *Rasis* and *Mesue*, who style him the most Learned and most Experienced Physician, and even *Averroes* and *Wimpina*, who call him the Subtile Philosopher. One may judge of his Parts and Learning by his Two printed Books, *De Temporum Mutationibus*, and *De Gradibus Medicinarum*

(*a*) Card. de Subtilit. lib. 16.

Naudé in his Apology for Great Men, pag. 324. *Simpliciss.* Cardan's Tyranny too much.

Medicinarum compoſitarum inveſtigandis. We meet with many others, which are very often cited by Authors, under the Titles, *De ratione ſex quantitatum: De quinque eſſentiis: De motu diurno: De vegetabilibus,* and *De Theoricâ magicarum artium.* This laſt Work induced all the Demonographers to repreſent *Alchindus* as a dangerous Magician. *Francis Picus,* and *Conrad Wimpina,* have amply diſcourſed of the Hereſies, Blaſphemies, and Abſurdities, which are to be met with in this Book. The famous *John Picus* does not ſeem to have judged ſo diſadvantageouſly of him, ſince he ſays, that he knew but Three Men, who had ſo much as touched upon the natural and lawful Magic, to wit, *Alchindus, Roger Bacon,* and *William* Biſhop of *Paris.* What is moſt to be depended upon, according to *Gabriel Naudé,* from whom I borrow this Article, is I. That this Work is full of Superſtition, and Doctrines quite contrary to our Faith, and ſuch as are to be expected from a *Mahometan,* who writes his Thoughts with great Freedom. II. That he cannot be accuſed of Magic, ſince he was ſo far from amuſing himſelf with the *Theurgic* or *Goetic* Magic, that his ſole View was to account in a natural Way for all that is attributed to good or bad Angels; which *Petrus de Apono* and *Pomponatius* have done after him *(b).* Theſe Philoſophers, in ſupport of their Opinion, maintain that Sublunary things depend wholly on the Heavenly, and that they mutually receive their Properties from each other, and that each receives them from the whole, by means of certain material *Effluvia,* which, paſſing from the leaſt to the greateſt, are the Cauſe, they tell us, of all the *Phænomena* in Nature. We cannot certainly ſay when *Alchindus* lived; but we muſt not place him in the XII Century, ſince *Averroes* makes mention of him. There is a JAMES ALCHINDUS, whom ſome confound with the ALCHINDUS of this Article *[A].*

(b) Naudé, Ibid. *and the following Page.*

[A] *Whom ſome confound with the* Alchindus *of this Article.*] *Wolfgang Juſtus* ſays, that *James Alkindus* lived under Pope *Eugenius* III. in the Year 1145, cotemporary with *Averroes* and *Avicenna*: He ſays, that he was an *Arabian* Phyſician and Philoſopher (1). The Bibliographers attribute the ſame Books to *Alchindus,* and to *James Alkindus. Voſſius* ſeems to diſtinguiſh between them; for, when he ſpeaks of *Alchindus,* he aſcribes to him only the Treatiſe *de ſex quantitatibus,* and does not mention his Age; but he places *James Alkindus* in 1235, and aſcribes to him, among other Books, a Treatiſe *de radiis ſtellarum* (2). It is, doubtleſs, the ſame Book, which *Geſner* alledges under the Title *de radiis ſtellicis,* and which he believes to be a Work of *James Alkindus,* though the Name of *James* is not joined there with that of *Alkindus.* One would imagine by the Title alone, that it belongs to Him, who was ſuſpected of Magic.

(1) Apud Merklinum in Lindenio renovato.

(2) Voſſius de Scientiis Mathem. pag. 61. & 179.

ALCIATUS (ANDREW) a great Civilian, flouriſhed in the XVI. Century. He was the Son of a rich Merchant of *Milan [A],* and was born in the Month of *May,* 1492 *(a).* It is pretended, that his Mother in bringing him forth, felt ſcarce any of the uſual Pains of Labour *(b).* Having ſtudied Humanity under *Janus Parrhaſius,* who taught at *Milan (c),* he applied himſelf to the Civil-Law at *Pavia* and at *Bologna (d),* and attended chiefly the Lectures of *Jaſon* in the former of theſe Univerſities, and thoſe of *Charles Ruinus* in the latter *(e).* After he was created Doctor, he betook himſelf to the Bar in the City of *Milan (f),* till he was called to the Profeſſorſhip of Civil-Law by the Univerſity of *Avignon [B].* He filled the Chair

(a) See Remark *[E].*

(b) Panzirol. de Claris Legum Interpret. lib. 2. cap. 169.

(c) Minos in Vita Alciati.

(d) Mr. Teiſſier in his *Eloges taken from* Thuanus, Tom. 1. pag. 35. *quoting Minos, ſays, that* Alciatus *ſtudied at* Verona: *but I have not found this.*

(e) Panzirol. ib. d.

(f) Minos in Vita Alciati.

[A] *He was the Son of a rich Merchant of* Milan] I have followed *Panzirolus,* the only Author, whom I have conſulted, who makes him the Son of a Perſon of that Profeſſion: "Ex Joanne pecunioſo negotiatore Mediolani ferè nullo parentis dolore natus "& educatus fuit (1)." Others make him rather the Son of a Gentleman of an ancient Family; "Andreas Alciatus in pago Alciato ſeu Alzato Mediolanenſi natus è nobili Alciatorum familia." This is the Opinion of *Claudius Minos* (2). It cannot be objected to me, that in ſome Countries the quality of Merchant, and That of Gentleman, are not incompatible: for, where they are united, an Hiſtorian ſeldom takes notice of the leaſt, without ſpeaking of the moſt conſiderable. Wherefore, ſince *Panzirolus* has only mentioned the Occupation of *Alciatus's* Father, he ſeems not to have been of *Claudius Minos's* Opinion.

[B] *He applied himſelf to the Bar in the City of* Milan, 'till he was called ——— *by the Univerſity of* Avignon] I ſhall be cautious of adopting the Narrative of *Panzirolus.* I have thought fit to aſſert, that *Alciatus,* having been created Doctor of the Civil and Canon Law, in the Year 1517, being a little above twenty two Years of Age, taught firſt at *Pavia,* and afterwards at *Avignon; Primum itaque Ticini profeſſus, poſtea Avenioni docuit* (3). But this would be giving the Lie to *Alciatus* himſelf, who declares in a Speech, which he made at *Pavia,* that, when he obtained ſix hundred Crowns Salary, at *Avignon,* he had never appeared in any Chair. "Avenioni cum nunquam ad eam diem cathedram "aſcendiſſem ſtipendium ſexcentorum mererer (4)." *Panzirolus's* Account is, moreover, ſuſpected of Falſhood: he betrays an extream Negligence; we find there, that *Alciatus* was not quite Twenty three Years of Age in 1517, and yet his Epitaph, related by *Panzirolus,* three Pages after, declares, that he was near Fifty nine Years of Age in the Month of *January* 1550: he was therefore Twenty five in 1517. What *Panzirolus* affirms, that *Alciatus* publiſhed his *Paradoxes* and his *Diſpunctiones* about the Year 1517, cannot be cleared up by *Claudius Minos;* for there never was a Chaos of a Book more abſurd, than the Paſſage where this laſt Writer ſpeaks of the Edition of *Alciatus's* Paradoxes. "Duodecim poſt "annos, ſays he (5), cum civilis & pontificii juris profeſſoriis inſignibus donatus eſſet, Paradoxa "& Diſpunctiones in publicum emiſit, opus, ut ipſe "dicit, elaboratum horis ſucciſſivis, & à candidato adhuc & tirone.— *Twelve Years after, whenbe was inveſted with the Profeſſorſhip of Civil and Canon Law,* "*he publiſhed his* Paradoxa *and* Diſpunctiones, *a* "*Work, according to his own Account, compoſed at his* "*leiſure Hours, and when be was as yet but a Candidate and a Student.*" It is not eaſily ſeen, to what the Word *duodecim* relates: for all that goes before is an Account of *Alciatus's* different Stations, and of his manner of teaching the Civil Law. If theſe Words of *Minos* imported, that *Alciatus* publiſhed his Paradoxes twelve Years after his Promotion to the Doctorate, all this Chaos would be reduced into order; but, then, what would become of *Panzirolus,* who places the Edition of That Book about the time of his taking the Degree of Doctor; that is, about the Year 1517? What would become of *Tiraquellus,*

(1) Panzir. de Claris Legum Interpret. lib. 2. cap. 169. pag. 353.

(2) Minos, in Vita Andreæ Alciati, Ghilini, Lorenzo Craſſo, Paul Freher, Bullart, &c. *ſay he deſcended from a noble and ancient Family.*

(3) Panzir. ubi ſupra.

(4) *See the* Commentari*us that is his* Apologia Prima, *Tomi 4.* Oper*um* 1582.

(5) Minos in Vit. Alciati.

ALCIATUS.

Chair with such great Abilities, that *Francis* I. thought him a proper person to promote the Study of the Civil-Law in the University of *Bourges*. He invited him thither in 1529 [C], and, the Year following, he doubled his Pension, which was at first Six hundred Crowns. *Alciatus* professed the Civil-Law Five Years at *Bourges*, and acquired a great Reputation there. But he made use of an Artifice to obtain an Increase of his Salary [D]. He mixed a great deal of Literature with the Explication of

---

(6) Tiraq. de Jur. Primigen. pag. 158. apud Baillet, Enfans celebres, p. 126. *where you will find the following Authors quoted, viz.* Ghilin. Theatr. Literat. pag. 1. & Picinel. Athen. Milan. pag. 26, 28.

(7) Baillet Enfans Celebres, pag. 126.

(8) Pasquier's Recherches, lib. 9. cap. 39. pag. 901.

(9) See the Preface to the Paradoxes, prefix'd to the Edition of 1529.

(10) Beginning the Year in January.

(11) Epist. Godii, &c. pag. 76.

(12) Ibid. pag. 78.

(13) Ibid. pag. 96.

(14) Ibid.

(15) Ibid. pag. 106.

(16) He says, *in the first Page of his History of Calvinism in Berri, that Alciatus read his first Lecture at Bourges, on Monday, Apr. 19. 1529.*

(17) Panzir. de claris Legum Interpr. lib. 2. cap. 169.

Tiraquellus, who says, that *Alciatus* wrote a considerable Work before he was twenty Years of Age (6)? "It is That, which is extant under the Title of *Paradoxes of the Civil Law*, which he divided into "six Books, and dedicated to the Chancellor *du Prat*, "when he was at *Bourges* in 1529, twelve Years after having published it in his own Country, when "he assumed the Doctor's Cap: but seventeen or "eighteen Years after the Composition of it (7)." The Work, which I cite, informs me, that *Alciatus's* first Essay was an Explication and Correction of the *Greek* Terms, which we meet with in the *Digests*; that this Book was published first in *Italy*, and some time after at *Strasburg*, in 1515. I have read, in a certain Author (8), that *the first Dedication Alciatus* made of his Works, is dated in 1513, and that it is That of the three last Books of the *Code*. What is very certain, is, that he published his *Paradoxes*, dedicated to the Chancellor *Antony du Prat*, about the Year 1517 (9). He published his *Dispunctiones* about the same time, dedicated to *John Selve*, President of the Senate of *Milan*, and his *Prætermissa*, dedicated to *James de Minut*, Counsellor in the same Senate, and ancient Professor of the Civil Law at *Orleans*. He was Professor at *Avignon* in the Year 1521; for he says, in the Epistle Dedicatory of his Treatise *de Verborum significatione*, dated at *Bourges* the first of *May*, 1529, that he had dedicated it to his Scholars eight Years before.

I have been informed, that *Budæus*, in a Letter written to *Christopher Longueil*, in the Month of *February* 1520 (10), mentions a Visit, which *Alciatus* made him some time before at *Avignon*. Mr *de la Monnoie* communicated to me this Particular. I add, that some Letters of our *Alciatus* were published at *Utrecht*, which shew, that he was Professor of the Civil Law at *Avignon* in the Year 1518 (11); that his Salary amounted to Five hundred Crowns, and that he had Seven hundred Auditors. Two Years after he wrote, that they allowed him Six hundred Crowns, besides other Gratuities; and that his Auditory was composed of above Eight hundred Persons, among whom there were some Prelates, Abbots, and Counts (12). He left That Professorship, and returned to *Milan*, about the end of *October* 1522. Among other things, which induced him to this Retreat, the principal was, that his Salary was not punctually paid him, the City of *Avignon* being in debt by Reason of the Contagious Distemper. Besides, they gave him to understand, that if the Plague returned, he must consent to a Diminution of his Salary. But he rejected the Condition (13). He applied himself to the Bar in his own Country, and found this Employment more advantageous than he expected (14). He stayed in *Italy*, 'till he accepted the Professorship which was offered him in the University of *Bourges* (15).

[C] *He invited him thither in* 1529.] I choose to follow *Minos* and Mr *Catherinot* (16), rather than *Panzirolus*. The latter anticipates this Invitation by an whole Year. "Deinde anno 1528, Biturages, "quo magna studiosorum multitudo ad ejus famam "confluxit, amplo 1200 aureorum stipendio à Rege "Francisco est conductus (17). —— *At length, in* "*the Year* 1528, *he was retained at Bourges by* "*King Francis, with a Salary of Twelve thousand* "*Crowns; whither the Fame of his Abilities drew* "*from all Parts a great Number of Students*." I do not object to *Panzirolus*, that his Pension was at first but Eighteen hundred *Livres*, and that, being doubled, the next Year, it amounted to the Sum which he has laid down: I have greater Instances of Inaccuracy to charge him with. He says, I. That *Alciatus* lived but few Years in *France*; because *Francis Maria*, Duke of *Milan*, ordered him to return, and threatned him with the Confiscation of all his Effects in case of Disobedience. II. That *Alciatus*, being returned home, taught for some Years at *Pavia*; 'till he retired to *Bologna* in 1532, on account

of the Wars, It is certain, that *Alciatus* lived five Years at *Bourges*: This appears by the Verses, he wrote on his leaving it.

Urbs Biturix, invitus amans te defero amantem,
Quinque per æstates terra habitata mihi (18).

And therefore, since, according to *Panzirolus*, he was invited thither in the Year 1528, he could not have left it till 1533. How could he then have taught for some Years at *Pavia*, after his Removal from *Bourges*, and retire afterwards to *Bologna*, in the Year 1532? His *Dissertation concerning Duels*, dedicated to *Francis* I, is dated from *Avignon* the first of *March*, 1529. The Preface to his *Paradoxes* is dated from *Bourges* the Twenty fourth of *August* 1529. This is decisive against *Panzirolus*. There remain yet two Errors to be censured, one of *Moreri*, the other of *Paul Freherus*. The former says, that *the Liberality of Francis I. drew Alciatus into France, where he taught at Avignon*; according to the latter, *Alciatus* went to teach in That City, immediately upon his leaving *Parrhasius*'s School (19). It is an absurd Mistake to say, that the Liberality of a King of *France* invited a Professor into another Prince's Country; and who does not know, that when *Alciatus* left *Parrhasius*'s School, he went to study at *Pavia* and at *Bologna*, and that he took his Doctor's Degree in 1517, and that he published some Books before he was Professor at *Avignon*?

[D] *He made use of an Artifice to obtain an Increase of his Salary.*] He contrived the matter so by his Intrigues, that a Professorship was offered him by the University of *Padua*. *Vossius*, who informs me of this, was afraid, lest by deferring to return an Answer to the Offer, which was made him of a Professorship in the University of *Cambridge*, he should be suspected of the same Artifice; for, adds he, it is a piece of Cunning generally put in Practice: "Quis, rerum mearum ignarus, aliud sibi persuadere "possit, quam diutinam hanc in respondendo cessa-"tionem inde duntaxat, aut potissimum saltem, pro-"manare, ut Vocatione Anglicana aliquid mihi apud "Batavos lucelli acquiram? Scimus id plerisque me-"ris esse. Nec notam hanc effugit summus Juris-"consultus, Andreas Alciatus, cùm Biturigibus Pa-"tavium vocaretur. Et ille quidem callide hoc ege-"rat ipse, ut vocaretur. Mihi, ut scis, ne per som-"nium tale quid cogitanti sponte apud vos professio "oblata est. Ille item, immane quantum aucto sti-"pendio, apud Biturigas remansit. Ego, uti hoc "nunquam egi, ita nec quicquam accessionis (quam "quidem scio mihi minimè invideres) consequar re-"manendo, nisi simul accessio fiat forte novi la-"boris (20). —— *Who, that is unacquainted* "*with the State of my Affairs, would put any other* "*Construction on my long Neglect in returning an* "*Answer, than that I hoped this Invitation from* "*England might be improved to my Advantage in* "*Holland? Nor was the great Civilian, Andrew* "*Alciatus, clear from this Suspicion, when he was* "*invited from Bourges to Pavia. He indeed art-*"*fully contrived this Invitation. As for myself,* "*you know, that I never so much as dreamt of the* "*Professorship in your University, 'till it was offered* "*me. He, likewise, continued at Bourges, upon his* "*Stipend being greatly augmented. I, as I never* "*asked in this manner, so I shall receive no addi-*"*tional Advantage (which I am sure you would not* "*envy me) by continuing here; unless at the same* "*time an additional Service be required of me.*" I should feel some Remorse of Conscience, did I not acknowledge, that Mr *de la Monnoie* acquainted me with this Passage of *Vossius*. Besides which, He has imparted to me the following Particulars. "It appears, by the twelfth Letter of the second Book "of *Sadolet's* Letters, that *Alciatus*, from the first "Year of his Abode at *Bourges*, had, or pretended "to have, a Design to profess the Law at *Bologna*.

---

(18) *S. r Minos, ubi supra.*

(19) Freher. in Theatr. Viror. illust. pag. 826.

(20) Vossius Epist. 43. pag. 91, 92. *It is dated from Leyden,* June 1. 1625.

"Two

ALCIATUS.

of the Laws, and happily banished That barbarous Language, which had prevailed, till then, in the Lectures and Writings of the Civilians. *Thuanus* extols him highly for This: I say, *Thuanus*, who, otherwise, was but little acquainted with his History [E]. This Professor's Extemporary Harangue to *Francis* I, who came into his Auditory [F], pleased that Monarch much. *Francis Sforza*, Duke of *Milan*, thought himself obliged to recal into his Country so eminent a Man, and compass'd his Design by giving him the Dignity of a Senator, besides a great Salary. *Alciatus*, therefore, went to teach the Civil-Law at *Pavia*; but a little after he came to the University of *Bologne* (*g*), where he resided Four Years. Afterwards he returned to *Pavia*, from whence he went to *Ferrara* (*b*), being invited thither by Duke *Hercules d'Est*, who endeavoured to make that University famous. It recovered it's Splendor under a Professor, who was so much followed; but, at the end of Four Years, *Alciatus* left it, to return to *Pavia*, where at last he met with the true Remedy for his inconstant

(*g*) *He made his Inaugural Speech there on the 3d of Nov.* 1537.

(*h*) *He made his Inaugural Speech there in* 1542.

---

(21) *These Letters of Bembus, are in the 645th and 646th Pages of the Collection, entitled,* Letters di XIII. Huomini illustri, *printed at Venice,* 1560. *in* 8vo. *See likewise the 29th and 30th Letter of the 16th Book of Bembus.*

(22) *Cum tu nummos aureos solares petieris, illa tibi tantum aureos est pollicita.* Pet. Bembus Epist. 20. lib. 6. pag. 634.

(23) Idem, Epist. 30. lib. 6. pag. 635.

(24) Coll'd Franciscus Calvus.

" Two *Italian* Letters of *Bembus*, one of the seventh
" of *July*, 1533, and the other of the Twenty third
" of *February*, 1533, contain many Particulars con-
" cerning the Design, which the Republic of *Venice*
" had of inviting *Alciatus* to *Padua* (21). The Pro-
" fessors of That University were in terrible Appre-
" hensions about it; and among others, *Franceschin*
" *da Corte*, in *Latin*, *Franciscus Curtius*; who, to
" prevent the coming of such a Colleague, spread a
" Report, That the Duke of *Milan*, *Francis Sforza*,
" erroneously called *Francis Maria* by *Panzirolus*,
" had forbad him, on very severe Penalties, to leave
" the Professorship of *Pavia*, *Sotto pena di confisca-
" tione, Upon pain of Confiscation of his Goods.*" To
clear this Account from all Intricacy, we must, I
think, suppose, that the Twenty third of *February*,
1533, in the Letter of *Peter Bembus*, is of the Year
1534; beginning the Year in the Month of *January*: for, without, it we cannot be persuaded, that
Alciatus was at *Pavia*, when that Letter was dated;
He, who had professed five Years at *Bourges*, and
who did not begin to profess there 'till 1529. In
consulting the *Latin* Letters of the same *Bembus*, I
find, that he writ to our *Alciatus* on the fifteenth
of *July*, 1532, to exhort him to come and take Possession of the Professorship, which was offered him
in the University of *Padua*. He removes the
Objection which kept him in suspence, which was,
that the Republic of *Venice* would not promise
him the same Species of Crowns, which he demanded (22). *Bembus* tells him, that he ought not
to disengage himself from his Promise on so trivial an Account, and *if you come*, says he, *I will undertake, that you shall have in a very little time all
the Money, which you desire, and other Advantages
too.* He wrote to him again on the Tweaty first of
April, 1534. *Alciatus* was then at *Pavia*, but ill-
contented. *Bembus* declares, that, as for his Part, he
was very well satisfy'd with his Excuses; but that
the Curators of the University of *Padua* were not;
and that they were persuaded, that the Request which
he had made of the Professorship of Civil Law a-
mong them, was grounded on a Motive of Interest;
that is to say, That *Alciatus* would not have desired the Professorship in the University of *Padua*,
but in order to make use of the Offer of this Post
to procure a larger Salary from the Duke of *Milan*.
" *Utinam tam æqui in te Judices præfecti ludi Pa-
" tavini essent, neque sibi persuasissimum haberent,
" te propterea profitendi Jus Civile hac in urbe locum
" postulavisse, ut eo tradito apud Ducem istum tuum
" uterere, ad largius atque uberius ab eo stipendium
" promerendum* (23)."

Alciatus had before made use of the same Artifice,
at *Avignon*. He employed one of his Friends (24) to
contrive the Matter so, that he might be invited to
Bologne or *Padua*. He had no Intention of accepting these Offers; but he hoped to procure a better
Salary by this Means. This appears from some Letters he wrote at that Time, and which were printed
at *Utrecht* in the Year 1697. " Si mille mihi aurei
" *Ferrariæ constituerentur, eo non irem: Et satis
" non possum mirari, qui tibi in mentem venerit,
" hanc conventionem cum eo tractare; cum de Pa-
" tavino, aut Bononiensi Gymnasio solum tibi mea-
" data dederim: Quamvis nec mihi displiceant tua
" ista consilia: Non quod in has Academias ven-
" turus sim, sed quod Avenionenses, si sciverint ab
" aliis quoque me sollicitari, ne eos deseram time-
" bunt, & augebunt stipendia. Quare cum eis po-
" tissimum velim hæc dissemines, quos conjectabis ido-*

" neos esse; ut in Avenionensem Academiam literas
" harum rerum indices dent (25). —— *If they would
" settle upon me a thousand Crowns a Year at* Ferrara,
" *I would not go thither; and I cannot enough won-
" der how you could think of entring into such a No-
" gotiation, since I commissioned you to treat only con-
" cerning the Bolognian and Pavian Schools: however
" I am not displeased with your Designs; not that I
" have any Thoughts of ever coming into those Uni-
" versities, but because the People of* Avignon, *when
" they find I am courted by others, will fear I
" should desert them; to prevent which they will aug-
" ment my Stipend. Wherefore I desire you would
" impart this Design to those, whom you shall judge
" proper for it, that they may send Letters to the
" University of* Avignon, *in Confirmation of these
" Matters.*" His Friend caballed at *Padua*, to induce
the *German* Scholars to desire the Republic of *Venice* to send for *Alciatus* (26). The latter desired
him not to trouble himself about it, since he was engaged for two Years in the City of *Avignon*. His
Letter is dated the Twenty sixth of *September*, 1520.
What Meanness! What sordid Love of Gain!

[E] *Thuanus* —— *who, otherwise, was but little
acquainted with his History.*] He supposes, I. That
Alciatus, after having taught a long time at *Bourges*,
was Professor at *Avignon*; but the contrary is true.
II. That *Alciatus* left *France*, in the decline of his
Age; whereas he was but forty Years of Age, or thereabouts. III. That *Alciatus*, being return'd into *Italy*,
read first at *Bologna*, and afterwards at *Ferrara*. He
read at *Pavia*, before he went to *Bologne*. IV. That
Alciatus died in the Year 1551; but his Epitaph says
it was on the 12th of *January*, 1550. It is true, some
Authors report, That *Alciatus*'s Epitaph mentions Fifty eight Years, eight Months, and four Days, which
would prove that he died the 12th of *January*, 1551;
but others report, that it gives him but Fifty seven
Years, eight Months, and four Days (27). *Thuanus*'s
Mistake is not so considerable, as that of *Forster*, adopted by Mr *Doujat* (28), and that of *Imperialis*. The
latter places the Death of *Alciatus* in the Year 1559
(29). *Forster* places it in the Year 1548 (30). But
let us particularly remark the Error of the Astrologer, who, having said that *Alciatus* died at *Ferrara*, in the Year 1546, adds, that it was of a
Wound from *Saturn* and the *Sun*. " Andreas Alcia-
" tus didicit literas Græcas à Pomponio Gaurico Pa-
" tavii —— obiit Ferrariæ anno 1546, ex Saturno
" in oppositione horoscopi, & Sole Martis tetragono
" sauciato. In conversione annua non solum directi-
" ones Aphetarum, sed annuæ conversiones penitus
" commaculatæ interimunt (31)." This is what *Luke
Gauric* notes, under the Figure of the Nativity of our
Civilian. He supposes him to be born, the eighth of
May, 1492, at one Hour, and thirty Minutes, after
Sun-rising. Is not this a pretty Art? It has Rules,
according to which a Man ought to die several Years
before his Death. I have seen one of *Alciatus*'s Letters,
dated the third of *September*, 1530, wherein he says,
that he is just entered upon his Thirty seventh Year,
or that he is but little more than Thirty seven Years of
Age. *Vix trigesimum & septimum annum attingenti*
(32). This would prove that he was born in 1494,
or 1493.

[F] *This Professor's extemporary Harangue to* Francis I. *who came into his Auditory.*] *Minos* reports
this Fact: *Panzirolus* says nothing of it; but, instead of it, tells us, That the *Dauphin*, having assisted at one of *Alciatus*'s Lectures, presented him with
a Medal, to the value of Four hundred Crowns. It
was

(25) Epist. Godii, &c. pag. 79.

(26) Ibid. pag. 78.

(27) Ghillini Teatro al Litterati, parte 1. pag. 11.

(28) Doujat Præsat. Canon. p. 619.

(29) Imper. in Musæo Histor. pag. 52.

(30) Forster. Histor. Juris Civil. lib. 2. cap. 41. pag. 542.

(31) Lucas Gauricus in Schemat. fol. 73.

(32) Epist. Godii, &c. pag. 106.

ALCIATUS. 195

stant Humour [G], I mean Death, on the 12th Day of *January*, 1550 (i). He was not full Fifty eight Years of Age. *Paul* III. gave him an honourable Reception, in his Passage through *Ferrara*, and offered to advance him to Ecclesiastical Dignities. *Alciatus* was contented with that of Prothonotary, and would not renounce the Profession of the Civil-Law [H]. The Emperor created him a Count Palatine, and a Senator. *Philip*, King of *Spain* (§*), passing through *Pavia*, presented him with a Gold Chain. It is thought that *Alciatus* died of a Surfeit, which he got by over eating himself (k); for he was not only very covetous, but likewise a greater Eater [I].

He

(l) Panz'r. de Claris Leg. Interp. lib. 2. cap. 16c. *See concerning the Time of his Death, the Remark* [E] *towards the End.*

(33) Tom. 4. pag. 870. Edit. of Francfort 1617.

(34) Teisser, Eloges des Hommes Illustres, Tom. 2. pag. 335. Edit. Geneva, 1683.

(3) *See the Speech he pronounced at Ferrara, in* 1543. Oper. Tom. 4. pag. 852. *and Claud. Minos in his Life.*

(35) *See Remark* [A] *of the Article* FOULQUES.

(k) Ex cibo, quem largioram fumere confueverat, morbum contraxit. Id. ib.

(37) Plot. in Apophth. Lacon. init. pag. 208.

A REFLEXION on the Rambling Humour of some Professors.

(38) *In the Remark* [A], *of the Article* AC-CARISI.

(39) Alciat. Epist. ad Paulum Jovium. It is *prefix'd to the first Volume of* Jovius's *Histories, and dated from Pavia, the Seventh of October,* 1549.

(40) Teissier. Elog. Tom. 2. pag. 304. Edit. 1683. & Tom. 1. Edit. 1696.

---

was the same, which the Inhabitants had given the Dauphin. I have already said, on other Occasions, That, when a Fact of this nature is variously reported by Authors, or does not appear in most of those, who write a Person's Elogy, it cannot be depended upon. Yet this Fact ought to be excepted out of this Rule: for we find among *Alciatus*'s Works (33) the Discourse, which he made when *Francis* I. assisted at one of his Lectures.

[G] *The true Remedy for his inconstant Humour.*] If I had taken Advantage of all that I have met with in Authors, concerning the several Stations of *Alciatus*, I should have represented him as more inconstant, than he really was. It is sufficient, that he went from *Avignon* to *Bourges*, from *Bourges* to *Pavia*, from *Pavia* to *Bologne*, from *Bologne* to *Pavia*, from *Pavia* to *Ferrara*, from *Ferrara* to *Pavia*, and all this before sixty Years of Age. *Thevet* so ill disposes his Account of this learned Civilian, that any Reader would infer from it, that *Alciatus* returned into *France*, after the Duke of *Milan* had recall'd him from *Bourges*. We have seen that *Panzirolus* makes him go from *Pavia* to *Avignon*. *Moreri* sends him from *Bourges* to *Orleans*, and from *Orleans* to *Padua*. Mr *Teissier* makes him Professor at *Milan* (34). He cites *Pasquier*, in the Twenty ninth Chapter of the ninth Book of his *Recherches*: He should have cited the Thirty ninth Chapter; but *Milan* is not to be found there. These are *Pasquier*'s Words: " I heard " three or four of *Alciatus*'s Lectures in the City of " *Pavia*. Coming from thence to *Bologne*, where " *Marianus Socinus*, the Nephew of *Bartholomew*, " read Lectures, I found that the *Italian* Scholars, " in general, had a greater Esteem for him, than for " the other. Nay, those, who had any Suit in Law, " chose rather to make use of *Socinus*, because, *said* " *they*, he never lost any time in the study of hu" man Learning, as *Alciatus* did." Mr *Teissier*, citing this Passage, says, *That Bartholomew Socinus taught the Civil Law at* Bologne, *when* Alciatus *was Professor at* Milan. These two Facts are not to be found in *Pasquier*. If I would have made a general Collection of all the Circumstances, which a Weathercock should I have made of our sickle Professor? but I should have been a thousand times more to blame, than the Authors of these Falshoods, if I had made use of them to his prejudice. He was not ignorant, that he was censured for his frequent Changes of Universities, and, among other Reasons, he endeavour'd to justify himself by this, that no one finds fault with the Sun, for running round the Earth, to animate all things by it's Heat, and it's Beams: He added, That when any one praises the fixed Stars, he does not design to condemn the Planets (35). There was an insufferable Vanity in these Comparisons; it was to consider himself as a Source of Light, which was to run successively through all the Republic of Letters, that the Darkness of Ignorance might be expell'd from every Place by his Presence. But let us allow him his Comparison, and tell him, that he ought to have resembled *Copernicus*'s Sun, have kept his Center, and illuminated from thence all who approach'd him. It is much more honourable for a Philosopher to be visited by a great Number of Scholars, in the place of his Residence, as *Abelard* was (36), than to travel up and down in search of Scholars. And, doubtless, if the love of Glory alone possesses a Man's Soul, without being mix'd with the love of Gain, or a fantastical Humour of being soon disgusted with the same Things, we should not see so many Persons struck with *Alciatus*'s Distemper. The Idea of true Glory would inspire a Man with a Resolution not to wander in search of great Theatres of Action, but to convert the Place of his own Residence into such a Theatre, how small soever it be: He would remember *Agesilaus*'s Answer. He happened to be placed, on a Day of Ceremony, beneath his Rank; Εὔγε,

says he, δείξω γὰρ ὅτι ἐκ οἱ τόποι τὰς ἀνδρας δοξαζοῦσι, ἀλλ' οἱ ἄνδρες τὰς τόπους ἐπιδυκνύουσι — *I am satisfy'd; for I will shew that a Man does not receive Honour from his Place, but his Place from him* (37). He would see that it is much more glorious to do a thing *gratis*, than for Reward, and that the nearer a Man comes to a free Gift, that is, to a Profession without a Salary, the nearer he approaches to what is great and noble; whereas he recedes from it, and becomes a Man of a mean and mercenary Spirit, in proportion as he increases the Wages, which he extorts. This is to reduce the Profession of Learning to the Nature of the most Mechanic Arts. A Shoemaker, or a Hatter, who will be better paid for his Work than another, gains the Reputation of an excellent Workman by it. To pretend, that an Encrease of your Salary is a Proof that you are esteem'd the greater Preacher, or more learned Professor; is it not to judge of your Trade, as we judge of that of a Shoemaker, or a Hatter? This is the direct way to cry down Learning, and to draw Contempt upon those, who profess it; for a false Taste of Glory, join'd with Covetousness, generally occasions the Fault, for which *Alciatus* was blamed; I mean the violent Desire of making the Tour of all the Universities; which I have already taken notice of in another Place (38). Surely this is to set up one's Learning to public Sale, and to proclaim, That he who bids most shall have it.

[H] *And would not renounce the Profession of the Civil Law.*] He congratulates himself upon it, in a Letter which he wrote to *Paul Jovius*, whom Pope *Paul* III. had amus'd a long time with deceitful Promises. *I am very glad*, says he, *that I did not suffer myself to be deceived by that Pontiff, who invited me to go to* Rome, *upon the Promise of great Rewards*. Upon this he set forth the solid Advantages of his Profession, in opposition to the imaginary Hopes of a Cardinalship. " *Mihi gratulor, quod ab eo (inveterati* " *astus, sed Principe) me decipi non sim passus, quum* " *me, uti scis, magnis propositis præmiis Ticino,* " *Ferraria, atque Bononia, in Urbem accerseret.* " *Tum enim ex jure meo magis cautus fui, quam tu* " *ex sapientia praeceptis prudens Philosophus. Cur* " *enim pro inani aut incerta spe purpuræ, hos tantos* " *primi suggestus honores relinquerem, opimis præ-* " *sertim firmatus stipendiis? Cur has tantas contem-* " *nerem circumfusæ juventutis salutationes? & hanc* " *denique tot consultoribus januam pulsantibus existi-* " *mationem magno lucro, & non obscura cum laude* " *quæsitam, ineptæ stulteque desererem* (39)? — " *Per why should I quit these first-rate Honours, at-* " *tended too with great Advantages, for the vain and* " *uncertain Hopes of the Purple? Why should I de-* " *spise that awful Respect, which is paid me by the* " *surrounding Croud of Students? and why should I* " *foolishly forsake the great Reputation I acquire, not* " *without considerable Gain, from such a Number of* " *Persons, who are continually knocking at my Door to* " *consult me?"* Note, by the by, that this confutes those who say, that he refus'd a Cardinal's Hat, which the Pope offer'd him (40). This Story is the fruit of an Hyperbole, the darling Figure of many People. The whole Truth of the Matter is this, That the Pope, the better to persuade *Andrew Alciatus* to come to *Rome*, gave him to understand that it would be a means to open his Way to the Sacred College. Such a Discourse is very far from the Offer of a Cardinal's Cap.

(§*) [*Alciatus*, to whom it is said that *Philip* made a Present of a Gold Chain, died in 1550. Now this Prince came to the Crown but upon the Abdication of the Emperor his Brother. If Mr *BAYLE* had recollected this, he would have said the *Prince of* Spain, and not the *King of* Spain. This little Piece of Inadvertency is properly *Panzirolus*'s, whom Mr *BAYLE* only copies here. Rem. Crit.]

[I] *For he was not only very covetous, but likewise a great Eater*.] *Panzirolus* expresses himself thus; *Avarior*

ALCIATUS.

(l) Vir fuit corpulentus, procera statura. *Pamur. de Claris Leg. Interpr. lb. 2. cap. 169. Mr Teissier, Tom. 2. p. 304. of his Eloges, says he was a Man of a middle Stature.*

(m) *It is not therefore true that there was at Naples, in 1688, a Grandson of the Great Alciatus. See Dr Bonnet's Travels into Italy. If there was, he must have been very old.*

He was a corpulent and tall Man (l). After the Death of his Mother, who was much advanced in Years, he had a mind to lay out his Estate in founding a College; but, having received an Affront from some insolent Scholars, he gave over that Design, and made choice of *Francis* ALCIATUS for his Heir, a Young Man of great Hopes, whom he had educated (m), though he was not nearly related to him (n). This *Francis Alciatus* succeeded to *Andrew*'s Estate and Professorship, and made himself famous at *Pavia* by his Lectures in Civil-Law. Cardinal *Borromeo*, who had been his Disciple, invited him to *Rome*, and was so good a Patron to him, that he obtained for him, from Pope *Pius* V, a Bishopric, the Office of a Datary, and a Cardinal's Hat (o). There are some Treatises of Civil-Law wrote by this Cardinal *Alciatus*, who died at *Rome* in the Month of *April*, 1580, being a little above fifty Years of Age. See *Nicius Erythræus*, in the Forty seventh Chapter of the second *Pinacotheca*. Those, who say that our *Alciatus* lived always a single Life, are mistaken [K]. He set up for an Author betimes, as I have observed in the Remark [B]. He published many Law Books, and some *Notes on Tacitus*, whose Latinity appeared to him very harsh [L]. *Muretus*, in one of his Speeches, very much inveighs against this Delicacy (p). *Alciatus* was not sensible of this; for he was already dead; but other Critics, particularly *Floridus Sabinus*, who attacked him in his Life-time, made him feel their Teeth and Nails (q). His *Emblems* were very much esteemed, and some Learned Persons have adorned them with Commentaries [M]. His Poems were

(n) *Moreri 1735, &c. in his Nephews.*

(o) *Panzir. ubi supra.*

(p) *'Tis the 11th of the 2d Tome. See all Bodin, Meth. Histor. cap. 4. pag. 25.*

(q) Cl. Minos in Vita Alciati.

Avarior habitus est, & cibi avidior. He adds, That *Alciatus*, having once received Three hundred Crowns for his Advice, and hearing, that *Marianus Socinus* had received a larger Fee upon the same Occasion, said, they had found a better Merchant, but not a better Lawyer. Take this by the way, for a Confirmation of what has been quoted out of *Pasquier* (41). " Here are more Tidings of *Alciatus*'s Co-
" vetousness. He is taxed with two Things. The
" one is, That his Method favours of I know not
" what Ostentation of the Doctor. —— The other
" is, that Covetousness had so far got the Ascendant
" over him, that his Tongue, his Pen, and his Do-
" ctrine, seemed to be at the Service of that Lord,
" who paid him best. Nay, I remember, that speak-
" ing of *Jason*, in his *Parerga*, he seems to preach
" in favour of Money: for he praises him, because
" his Salary had been augmented; which *Alciatus*
" knew very well how to make his Advantage of,
" having drawn Twelve hundred Crowns from the
" University of *Bourges*, besides his Licences and
" Degrees; the Prices of which he caused to be
" trippled, following the Steps of Dr *Jason*, who was
" the first that took fifty, and an hundred, Crowns,
" for the Degrees and Honours he confer'd on the
" Civilians : whereas before his Time they were
" wont to pay but three or four Crowns. And,
" therefore, he says, it is lawful for himself, *Decius*,
" *Ruinus*, and the other Doctors, to enrich them-
" selves by these Gratuities paid by the Scholars.
" From whence it is easy to gather, that he did
" not fail to alledge the Example of *Jason* against
" those, who censured him for being so fond of Mo-
" ney, that they, who had a Mind to take a Doctor's,
" Bachelor's, or Licentiate's, Degree from him, were
" obliged to pay down their Crowns in abundance.
" That which makes me persist in this Opinion, is,
" that, in the last Chapter of the fifth Book of his
" *Parerga*, renewing his Discourse concerning *Ja-
" son*, he complains of Princes, and Lords, who set
" such a mean Value on learned and knowing Men;
" whereas in former Times, and even in *Vespasian*'s
" Time (according to the Report of *Suetonius*) That
" Emperor caused Fifteen hundred Crowns of the pub-
" lic Money to be given to the *Greek* and *Latin* Ora-
" tors, and Rhetoricians : He also adds the Authority
" of the Rhetorician *Eumenius*, who exercised his
" Profession at *Autun*, to whom Fifteen thousand
" Crowns of the public Money were given yearly,
" by Order of the Emperors *Dioclesian*, and *Maxi-
" milian*." These are *Thever*'s Words, in the 279th Page, of the seventh Tome, of his History of Illustrious Men.

[K] *Those, who say that our Alciatus liv'd always a single Life, are mistaken.*] Let us see what he says in a Letter, which he wrote to his Friend *Francis Calvus*, after he came from *Milan* to *Avignon*. " Vice
" versâ & ego te rerum mearum admoneo: multis
" affectum me ærumnis patria excessisse, Uxorem
" vivam & sospitem ibi reliquisse; cæteros sato lu-
" ctos; fortunis plerisque amissis, virtuti soli inni-
" xum non omnino concidisse. Libros & Bibliothe-

" cam omnem conservasse. In præsentia Jus Civile
" Avenione profiteo (42). —— *I will now, in my
" turn, give you an Account how my Affairs stand :
" I have left my Country in great Affliction of Mind :
" I have left behind me my Wife, alive, and in
" Health : the rest of my Relations are dead* (43)
" *my Virtue alone supports me from entirely sinking
" under the Loss of the greatest part of my Fortunes :
" I have preserved my Books, and my whole Library,
" and, at present, I profess the Civil Law at Avig-
" non.*" Let us then correct these Words of Mr *Teissier, he liv'd always a single Life* (44).

[L] *Whose Latinity appeared to him very harsh.*] This Complaint escap'd him in a Letter to *Paul Jovius*: " Alciatus non dubitat affirmare dictionem ejus
" præ illa Pauli Jovii esse senticeta (45) —— Alciatus
" *does not scruple to affirm, that his Style, in Compa-
" rison of Paul Jovius's, is like a Place covered with
" Thorns and Briars.*" On another Occasion, he expresses himself in a very different manner: " Certat
" in Tacito sermonis gravitas cum elegantia (46). ——
" *In Tacitus, Dignity of Style contends with Ele-
" gance.*" I refer the Examination of this to the Article TACITUS.

[M] *His Emblems were very much esteemed, and —— adorn'd with Commentaries.*] Scaliger the Father, who was not lavish of his Praises, as every one knows, gives this Account of That Work : " Alciati præter
" emblemata nihil mihi videre contigit. Ea vero
" talia sunt, ut cum quovis ingenio certare possint.
" Dulcia sunt, pura sunt, elegantia sunt, sed non
" fine nervis; sententiæ verò tales, ut etiam ad usus
" civilis vitæ conferant (47). —— *I have not met
" with any Work of Alciatus, except his Emblems.
" But they are, I think, equal to any Work of Ge-
" nius. They are entertaining, chaste, and elegant,
" and not without Strength : the Sentences likewise
" are such, as may even be of Service to the Purposes
" of Civil Life.*" These *Emblems* were translated into *French, Italian*, and *Spanish* (48). There are at least three *French* Translations; That of *Bartholomew Aneau*, That of *John le Fevre*, and That of *Claudius Mines* (49) The latter not only translated, but commented upon them : One of the most learned Humanists of *Spain* (50) thought them worthy of a Commentary of his own composing. *Pignorius*, a learned *Italian*, formed the same Judgment of them; and after them, a Professor of *Friburg* (51), published them with their's and his own Notes, and added those of *Frederic Morel* at the end. This Edition is a very good one : 'Tis pity we cannot distinguish in it what belongs to each Commentator : It came out at *Padua*, in the Year 1661, in 4to. I do not mention *Sebastian Stockhamerus*, whose Labours are not much esteemed. " Sebastianum Stockhamerum vix Com-
" mentatoris nomine dignor, quia in sola epigram-
" matis resolutione occupatur, paucissimis, iiique sa-
" tis vulgatis, sententiis & fabulis additis; ad hæc
" vix mediam emblematum partem hoc suo more ex-
" plicat (52). —— Sebastian Stockhamerus *scarce de-
" serves the Name of a Commentator; for he is
" wholly taken up in the Analysis of an Epigram,
" adding*

ALCIATUS.

were much commended, as Mr *Baillet* ingeniously observes in the Third Volume of his *Jugemens sur les Poëtes*, n. 1286. He is not one of those, who have persisted in their first Sentiments; for we find, in his *Parerga*, a Work, which he published in his old Age, a Retractation of several things, which the fire of Youth had occasioned him to advance with too great Precipitation; and, when his *Disputationes* were printed in 1529, he gave the Public to understand (*r*) that, in revising this Work, he did not pretend to give his Approbation to every thing he had inserted in it in his Younger Days, nor to deprive himself of the liberty of altering his Opinions. This Remark was made by an Apologist of the Emperor *Justinian* (*s*).

A Letter was printed at *Leyden* (*t*), in 1695, wrote by *Andrew Alciatus*, which he did not intend to make public; for it contains a lively Description of the Abuses of a Monastic Life. He wrote this Letter to *Bernard Mattius*, who had been his Colleague, and who turned a Fryar of the Order of St *Francis* on a sudden, and without consulting his Friends. He represented to him his Imprudence with great Learning and Eloquence. This Piece of *Alciatus* was composed in four Days; and was found in *Scriverius*'s Closet (*u*). It is dated the 7th of *June* 1553 [N].

" adding a few, and those the most trite and common
" Sentences; besides, he does not explain half the Em-
" blems, after this his Manner." I omit likewise the Jesuit, who explained the same Emblems publickly at *Paris* (53); but I believe the Reader will not be displeased to see the Title, which *Bartholomew Aneau* (*Bartholomæus Anulus*) prefixed to His Translation. It is This. Andrew Alciatus's *Emblems translated Verse for Verse, according to the Latin, and digested into Common Places, with Summaries, Inscriptions, Schemes, and brief epimythic Expositions, according to the Natural, Moral, or Historical Allegory.* The Editions of this Work of *Alciatus* are numberless; there are Two hundred and twelve Emblems in That of *Thuilius*, which I make use of; I am therefore surprized, that *Paul Freherus* should say, That this Book contains but One hundred Emblems (54).

[N] It is dated the 7th of June, 1553.] If this Date be right, we must reject all the Authors, who place *Alciatus*'s Death on the twelfth of *January*, 1550, or 1551, and who alledge his Epitaph as a Proof (55). But there is a Mistake in the Date of this Work, and I believe it was composed before the Year 1520, and that it is the same Piece, which *Alciatus* feared *Erasmus* would cause to be printed. " Quod ut fa-
" cias te quoque ipso oro: Nec minus ut de ungui-
" bus Erasmi reglutines orationem illam meam ad
" Matthiam Minoritam, cum id quæso, ne, si in ci-
" nerariorum istorum manus inciderit, parata sint
" mihi cum eis æterna bella (56). ——— *This I in-
" treat you to perform; as also, that you would get
" out of* Erasmus's *Clutches That Oration of mine to
" Matthias* Minorita; *lest, if it falls into the Hands of
" those Blowers of the Coals, I should be drawn in to
" wage eternal War with them.*" This is what he wrote to his Friend *Francis Calvus*, the Twenty sixth of *September*, 1520. Some of this Civilian's Letters were published at *Utrecht* in 1697, which inform us of many Particulars, and chiefly of the Encomiums he bestowed upon himself with all a Boaster's Vanity.

ALCIATUS (JOHN PAUL) a Gentleman of *Milan*, was one of those *Italians*, who left their Country in the XVIth Century, to embrace the *Protestant* Religion, and who afterwards refined so much upon the Mystery of the Trinity, that they formed a New Party, equally odious to the *Protestants* and *Catholics*. *Alciatus* had bore Arms; he began his Innovations at *Geneva*, together with a Physician, whose Name was *Blandrata*, and an Advocate, whose Name was *Gribaud*, to whom *Valentinus Gentilis* associated himself (*a*). The Precautions, which were taken against them, and the severe Proceedings carried on against the latter, made the rest more timorous, and induced them to look out for another Stage (*b*). They made choice of *Poland*, where *Blandrata* and *Alciatus* sowed their Heresies with good Success. They invited *Gentilis* thither [A], who did not fail to join them (*c*). He had obligations

[A] *They invited* Gentilis *thither.*] I have followed *Aretius* and *Theodorus Beza*, who agree in this, That *Gentilis* did not go into *Poland*, 'till after *Blandrata* and *Alciatus* had published their Opinions there (1); and I give up the Author of the *Bibliotheca Antitrinitariorum*, who affirms that *Alciatus* and *Gentilis* went into *Poland* together about the Year 1562 (2). *Stanislaus Lubieniezky* says almost the same thing. " *Valentinus* iste & *Paulus Alciatus* Pedemontanus,
" cum Genevæ ob odia Calvini acerrima subsistere
" non possent, anno 1563 in Poloniam venerant (3).
" ——*This* Valentinus *and* Paulus Alciatus *of* Piedmont,
" *when they could no longer continue at* Geneva, *on
" Account of the inveterate Prejudices against* Calvin,
" *in the Year* 1563, *came into* Poland." But these Authors are not exact enough to deserve the Preference. *Hornius* deserves it still less, who says, That *George Blandrata*, and *Paul Alciatus*, both Physicians, (he is mistaken in regard to *Alciatus*) fled from *Switzerland* into *Poland*, being terrified at the Punishment of *Servetus* and *Gentilis*. In the same Page of his Ecclesiastical History, he affirms, that they followed the Tritheism of *Valentinus Gentilis* (4). But it is certain that *Alciatus*'s Heresy was meer *Socinianism*. *Hornius*'s Chronology cannot be better confuted, than by a Letter of *Peter Martyr*, written at *Zurich*, the eleventh of *July*, 1558. He informs *Calvin*, in this Letter, that he had seen *Gregory* the Physician, and *John Paul* the *Piemontois*; that they

were exhorted not to disturb the Union of the Church, and to conform themselves to the Formulary of the *Italian* Church of *Geneva*; that they could not prevail with them, and that, upon *Bullingerus*'s Opinion, they were advised to leave the City; that they did so; that the Physician said, he was going into *Transylvania*; and that *John Paul* went to *Chiovenne*. We must not read *Gregorum Medicum*, in *Peter Martyr*, but *Georgium Medicum*; who is no other than *George Blandrata*, as *Johannes Paulus Pedemontanus* is no other than our *Alciatus*. It *Calvin* had not expressly said, that all these Heterodox *Italians*, and by Name *John Paul Alciatus*, signed the Formulary, I should be much tempted to think, that those, whom *Peter Martyr* speaks of, refused to subscribe to it. However it be, they were not at *Geneva* a little after their Subscription; for they subscribed on the eighteenth of *May*, 1558, and were at *Zurich* the eleventh of *July* following. *Gentilis* was not executed 'till 1566. He left *Geneva* some Months after the Subscription, and went into the Country of *Gex*, where he conferred with *Alciatus*; which shews, either that *Alciatus* did not go to *Chiovenne*, when he left *Zurich*, or that he did not long continue there. See the Article BLANDRATA, where I endeavour to clear up the Chronology in relation to these Persons.

tions to *Alciatus*, at whose Request the Bailiff of *Gex* had released him out of Prison [B]. It is pretended, that they went from *Poland* into *Moravia*. We shall relate in it's proper Place what *Gentilis*'s Fate was. As for *Alciatus*, he went to *Dantzic*, where he died in the Opinions of *Socinus* [C]; for it is not true that he turned *Mahometan* [D]. He had wrote Two Letters to *Gregorius Paulus*, the one in 1564, and the other

[B] *At whose Request the Bailiff of Gex had released him out of Prison.*] 'Tis not certain whether his Request alone effected this: *Sandius* intimates, that there was a Brite in the Case: " In oppido no- " mine Gajum in carcerem conjiciatur (*Gentilis*), un- " de, cum evadere non posset, quod esset pauper, à so- " cio suo Paulo Alciato redimitur. Quem utpote locu- " pletem, præterea vero nobili genere ortum, immo " & militem, simili modo non audebant aggredi (6). " ——— *In the Town of* Gex, *Gentilis was thrown* " *into Prison: out of which, when he could not escape* " *by reason of his Poverty, he was redeemed by his* " *Associate* John Paulus. *They dared not proceed against* " *the latter in the same manner, on Account of his* " *Wealth, the Nobility of his Extraction, and his* " *Profession, which was That of a Soldier.*"
[C] *Where he died in the Opinions of* Socinus.] This cannot reasonably be questioned, after the Proofs which *Martin Ruarus* (7) has given of it. He says, That this Person, having lived some Years at *Dantzic*, as a good Christian, when he was dying, recommended his Soul to *JESUS CHRIST* his Saviour; and then adds (8) " *Catherine Wemera*, " my Wife's Grandmother, who was intimately ac- " quainted with him, and who assisted at his Death, " told it often to her Husband, *David Werner Buttel*, " who is yet living; and she died but three Years " ago. My Mother-in-law told me but yesterday, " that she had often seen *Alciatus*'s Widow in this " City, who survived her Husband some Years." He adds occasionally, that he heard *Andrew Wolda-vius* say, That *Alciatus*, being in danger of his Life from the Scholars of *Cracow*, who took him for an *Arian*, eluded their ill Designs, by telling them, that he was not an *Arian*, but a *Marian*; for that he believed in *JESUS CHRIST* the Son of the Living God, and of *Mary*; the Name of *Mary* saved him: " Ridiculo schemate evasisse, cum se non Arianum " sed Marianum esse diceret, quod cum illi quid sibi " vellet quærerent respondisse, credere se Jesum " Christum Dei vivi & Mariæ filium. Illi, non mi- " nore stupore quam malitia obsessi, audito veneran- " do Mariæ nomine incolumem dimiserunt." This is a Case, in which the Maxim of the extravagant Votaries of the Holy Virgin was verified, *That one is sometimes more speedily saved by invoking the Name of Mary, than That of Jesus* (9).
[D] *It is not true that he turned Mahometan.*] We have just now seen the Proofs of it; and who can forbear saying, upon this Occasion, that it were to be wished, that those, who maintain the good Cause, were not subject to certain Faults, which prevail among the Persecutors of Orthodoxy? An Excess of Credulity, a mistaken Hate, I mean an Hate, which comprehends the Person of the Heretic, as well as his Heresy, makes us swallow all the Stories, which are reported to the Disadvantage of an Heresiarch. If it be reported, that he has killed himself, that the Devil has carried him away, or that he died raving and blaspheming, it is believed, without waiting 'till the Report be confirmed. Accounts of it are dispersed up and down by Letters; nay, what is worse, it gets into Print; and thus a Falshood is sown, the Seed whereof is never lost, so fruitful is the Soil it falls upon. The first is not long the only Publisher of it. Care is taken to convey it from Book to Book, as a great Motive of Zeal, or a Subject for Reflexions. The *Protestants* have been as much mistaken as the Catholics, as to the pretended *Mahometism* of *John Paul Alciatus*. Both have been careful enough to report it:

Iliacos intrà muros peccatur & extra (10).

Spondanus inserted it in his Ecclesiastical Annals; and no doubt Father *Maimbourg* copied it from him (11), though he did not cite the Author, as *Moreri* does. The famous *Calovius* published it; *Ruarus* wrote to him as above: His Letter had been printed two Years, when a new Edition was published of *Micrælius*'s Ecclesiastical History; yet he, who took so much Pains to add many Things to it, did not throw out the Falshood, for which *Calovius* was censured. I cannot tell, whether *Ruarus* made a true Discovery of the Original of this Fable. He believes, that a Letter from *Theodorus Beza* (12) was the Foundation of it. This Letter relates, that *Valentinus Gentilis*, being interrogated concerning his Friend *Alciatus*, answered, *He is turned Mahometan, and I have had no Correspondence with him a long Time.* The two Conjectures of *Ruarus* are not amiss: I. *Gentilis* thought this would please the Judges, by whom he was tryed. We meet with, every day (13), something like this in our Gazettes; to wit, That Deserters relate a thousand things, which they think will tickle the Ears of those who question them. II. *Gentilis*, who acknowledged a very singular Generation or Filiation in our Lord, was inclined enough to place the *Samosatenians* and *Mahometans* in the same Category. Two Sectaries, which quarrel, hate each other more at first, than they hate the Stem, from whence they are separated: So that *Gentilis* was an improper Evidence concerning *Alciatus*, after the violent Disputes, which disunited them in *Poland*. *Vottius* (14) and *Lætus* (15) cited only this Letter of *Theodorus Beza*, when they said that *Alciatus* turned *Mahometan*. *Hornius* quotes no Author, though he reports the thing with the utmost Confidence: " Alciatus, *says he* (16), transiit ad Tur- " cas, ac Muhammedismum amplexus, inter eos vitam " finiit. ——— *Alciatus went over to the Turks,* " *and, having embraced* Mahometanism, *ended his* " *Life among them.*" *Hornbeck* likewise cites no Authority in the *Apparatus* to his Disputes against the *Socinians*, where he says, two or three times, that *Alciatus* embraced *Mahometism*. " Dignam er- " nam dedit, quando eum Deus ad Muhammedanos pro- " labi sivit; nempe ne alibi quam inter Infideles istos " nomen ultra suum profiteretur (17). ——— *God deserved-* " *ly punished him, by suffering him to desert to the Ma-* " *hometans; that his Name might be no longer heard* " *of, but among those Infidels.*" It may be suspected, that this Story was not moerly grounded on *Beza*'s Letter, if we do but lightly examine the History of the *Polish* Reformation; for, when we find there, that the Author, having mentioned one *Adam Neusserat* (18) who was at last obliged to fly to *Constantinople*, adds, that *Alciatus* had a like Fate, we can scarce doubt of the Truth of it, since such an Historian reports it. But if this Author's Words be closely examined, it will be found that his Testimony amounts to nothing. Thus he expresses himself, Page 200. " Exacto trimestri necesse habebat (*Adamus Neusserus*) " periculo sibi ad exploratoribus Cæsareis imminente " solum vertere, & Constantinopolim (quam Al- " ciati fortunam fuisse supra vidimus, adeo Turcæ " ante Christianos æquitate & humanitate longe " sunt!) confugere. ——— *After three Months* Adam " Neufferus *found it necessary to change his Resi-* " *dence, to avoid the Danger, which threatened him* " *from* Cæsar*'s Spies, and to fly to* Constantinople; " *which was the very Fate of* Alciatus, *as we have* " *seen above; so far do the* Turks *extel the Christians* " *in Equity and Humanity.*" These Words refer us to a foregoing Passage; I think it is to Page 109. Now if, on the one side, we find there, that some Authors have charged *Alciatus* with turning *Mahometan*; we find, on the other, that they were his Enemies, who forged this Imposture. This is, doubtless, what the Sieur *Stanislaus Lubieniezky* meant. The Reader must perceive it, notwithstanding the Typographical Errors, which wretchedly maim That Work. " De *Alciato*, *says he* (19), scriptum accepi " eum, epistolis ad Gregorium Pauli anno 1564, & " 1565, Husterlirxii datis, dissiuasisse sententiam quod " Christus extiterit antequam ex Maria nasceretur, & " acerrimè dogmati vulgari de Trinitate restitisse, " ita ut Mahometismum consilii in primordio refor- " mationis sat ancipiti & arduo ignarus ei prætulisse " scribatur, sed à Calvino & inventorum ejus æmu- " lis odio interneeino iri eum & alios veritatis aman- " tes flagrantibus (20). ——— *I have been informed,* " *that*

other in 1565, dated from *Husterlitz*, in which he maintained that JESUS CHRIST did not exist before he was born of the Holy Virgin (d). There was Reason, then, to blame *Moreri*, who made him an *Arian*, and afterwards a *Mahometan* (e). Perhaps, before he went to *Dantzic*, he made the Tour of *Turkey*, without any design of turning a Renegado, but only to secure himself from Persecution [E]; which perhaps occasioned the Report of his pretended *Mahometanism*. *Calvin* and *Beza* represented him as a Madman [F].

(d) Bibl. Antitrinit. p.g. 28.

(e) See his *Dictionary* in the Article ALCIATUS, where he is censured.

" that Alciatus, *in his Letters to Gregorius Paulus,*
" *dated at* Husterlitz, *in the Year* 1564 *and* 1565, *dis-*
" *suaded him from the Opinion, that Christ existed be-*
" *fore he was born of Mary and strenuously opposed the*
" *Vulgar Notion of the Trinity; insomuch that he is*
" *said inadvertently to have recommended to him a*
" *kind of Mahometanism, even in the doubtful and*
" *hazardous beginnings of a Reformation; but that*
" *it was found out by Calvin and his Followers,*
" *who were inflamed with the most deadly Hate to-*
" *wards him, and all Lovers of Truth.*"

[E] *Perhaps* —— *he made the Tour of Turkey*
—— *to secure himself from Persecution.*] This puts me in mind of *Peter Abelard*, who was on the Point of seeking an Asylum among the Infidels, against the Agents or Promoters of Orthodoxy. He had been very ill treated, and was more alarmed than any other; for, whenever he was told that there would be speedily an Assembly of Ecclesiastics, he immediately believed it was designed to condemn HIM. Besides he found, by Experience, the great Credit of those Agents; and it was not easy to escape them under Princes of their own Party. They send circular Letters; and, before their Enemy arrives at any Town, the Description of his Errors has already alarmed the Inhabitants of it, and exasperated them against him. There was a Time, when they, who had the Pope's Ear, could make the best part of *Europe* an uninhabitable Country to a Person, whom they were resolved to decry as an Heretic; and the poor Wretch might, in some Sense, apply to himself the Psalmist's Exclamation, *Whither shall I go then from thy Spirit; or whither shall I go then from thy Presence? —— If I take the Wings of the Morning, and remain in the utmost Part of the Sea;* —— *even there also thy right Hand shall hold me.* Psal. cxxxix. —— Therefore, it is no wonder, that *Peter Abelard* was induced to retire among the *Mahometans* or *Pagans*. He was in hopes, that, in paying Tribute, he might have the Liberty to profess Christianity, out of the Sphere of Activity of the *Odium Theologicum*, and he fear'd, that, unless he did so, he should always find himself within the Influence of That Sphere. These are his Words. " *Deus ipse mihi testis est,*
" *quoties aliquam Ecclesiasticarum personarum con-*
" *ventum adunari noveram, hoc in damnationem*
" *meam agi credebam.* Stupefactus illico, quasi fu-

" pervenientis istum fulguris expectabam, ut quasi hæ-
" reticus aut profanus in consiliis traherer aut Synago-
" gis —— Sæpe autem (Deus scit) in tantum lap-
" sus sum desperationem, ut, Christianorum finibus
" excessis, ad Gentes transire disponerem, atque ibi
" quietè sub quacumque tributi pactione inter inimi-
" cos Christi christianè vivere (21). —— *God himself*
" *is my Witness, that, as often as I heard, that an*
" *Assembly of Ecclesiastics was to meet, I fancied it*
" *was called for my Condemnation. In the utmost*
" *Consternation thereupon, I immediately expected,*
" *as some Thunder-Clap, to be dragg'd before Coun-*
" *cils and Synagogues, and to be accused as an He-*
" *retic, or profane Person. —— Often likewise (God*
" *knows) I fell into such Despair, that I purposed to*
" *quit Christendom, and to take Refuge among the Pa-*
" *gans; there, at the Expence of a Tribute, to live*
" *as a Christian, among the Enemies of Christ.*" Now, as *Alciatus* had yet more to fear from Popery, than *Abelard*, and that he found but little Safety in Countries, where other Christians were Masters,

- - - - Tenent Danai, quâ deficit Ignis (22);

Where'er the raging Fire had left a Space,
The Grecians enter, and poss[s]s the Place.
DRYDEN.

his capricious Humour might well create in him a Desire of trying the Toleration of the *Turks*, and then might induce him to change his Mind, and resolve upon going to *Dantzic*. Let us learn from hence to distrust certain Accounts, though adopted by considerable Authors.

[F] *Calvin and Beza represented him as a Madman.*] The former says, that, on the Day, when the *Italians*, suspected of Heterodoxy, were required to sign a Formulary, *Alciatus* flew into a violent Passion.
" Inter quos Princeps fuit Joannes quidam Paulus Al-
" ciatus, homo non stolidi tantum & vesani ingenii
" sed plane phreneticus ad rabiem usque (23). ——
" *Among them the Chief was one* John Paulus Al-
" ciatus, *a Man, not only Foolish and Ignorant, but*
" *Frantic even to Rage.*" —— The latter says, that he was a giddy-headed, and frantic Fellow; " Paulus
" quidem Alciatus, Mediolanensis, homo jam antea
" planè phreneticus & vertiginofus (24)."

(21) Abælardi Oper. pag. 32.

(22) Virgil Æn. lib. 2. ver. 505.

(23) Calvin. adversi. Valent. Gentil. pag. 6,9. Tractat. Theolog.

(24) Beza Ep st. 81.

ALCIATUS (TERENCE) an *Italian* Jesuit, descended from the same Family as *Alciatus* the Civilian, was born at *Rome* in the Year 1570. He studied the Civil-Law five Years before he turned Jesuit, and entered into That Society in the Month of *March*, 1591. The Employments he had in it testify, that they looked upon him as a considerable Man. He was thirteen Years Præfect of the College of *Rome*; he taught Philosophy five Years, and Divinity seventeen in That City. Afterwards he was Director of the Penitentiary of the *Vatican*, and Sub-Superior of the *Maison Professe*. He assisted at the Ninth General Congregation of the Jesuits, as Deputy of the Province of *Rome*, and, when he died of an *Apoplexy* on the 12th of *November*, 1651, he was Sub-Provincial. He was not less esteemed out of the Society; for, besides that he was a long time *Qualificator* of the Congregation of the Holy Office, and *Consultor* of the Congregation of Rites, he was chosen by Pope *Urban* VIII to refute Father *Paul*. He prepared an Edition of the *Acts* of the *Council of Trent*, which he intended as an Apology for that Assembly against all kind of Adversaries, and particularly against This Formidable *Venetian*. He had already collected a great number of Materials for this Important and Laborious Work, when Death took him out of the World (a); but, though he had spent several Years upon this Undertaking, he had scarce began to digest it into Form. Father *Sforza Palavicini*, who was engaged in the same Design, informs us why Father *Alciatus* was so backward in his Performance [A]. If *Moreri* had but cast his Eye on the Preface of Cardinal *Pallavicini*,

[A] *Father* Alciatus *was so backward in his Performance.*] He laid it down as a Rule, never to deny a thing, without bringing Proofs of the Negative; insomuch that he spent many Years in search of Memoirs, which might furnish him with Proofs. Cardinal *Palavicini* pretends, that this was a Work of Supererogation; because no Law obliges a Man to prove what he denies: It lies upon the Accuser to pr[ove]

ALCIATUS. ALCINOE. ALCINOUS.

Palavicini, he would not have put *the Acts of the Council of* Trent among Father *Alciatus*'s Works. We muſt only inſert among them one *Sermon on the Paſſion*, preached before Pope *Clement* VIII in 1602, and the Life of *Peter Fabri*, a Companion of St *Ignatius Loyola*. Father *Alciatus*, diſguiſed under the Name of *Eminius Tacitus* (b), tranſlated it into *Italian* from the *Latin* of *Nicolas Orlandino* (c). This Tranſlation was printed at *Rome* in 1629. The *Latin* was printed at *Lyons* in 1617. *Moreri* obſerves, that Pope *Urban* VIII declared, that Father *Alciatus* deſerved a Cardinal's Hat. *Nicius Erythæus* reports the ſame (d). If it be aſked, what prevented this Jeſuit from obtaining what he deſerved; I anſwer, had not *Urban* the VIIIth the diſpoſal of theſe Hats? The Reply is very obvious; This Dignity is to be conferred on ſuch a number of Perſons for Political Reaſons, that, they, who are thought worthy of it, cannot always be admitted to it.

prove his Charge; and if he does not do it, he deſerves the Puniſhment of Retaliation. But the accuſed Perſon may content himſelf with a bare *I deny it*: This is ſufficient to acquit him, whilſt nothing is proved againſt him: "Là dove queſti s'era fatto lecito, "d' accuſare ſenza provare, il che dalle leggi è punito "colla pena del talione; quegli non volle negare ſenza "haver la prova della falſità; dal che ogni legge il di "obligava. Quindi fu che ſpece moltiſſimi anni in "cercar memorie certe di que' ſucceſſi (1)." By this Cardinal's good leave, I do not think, that, upon this occaſion, it was ſufficient to deny what Father *Paul* affirmed. When the Laugh is againſt us, we cannot bring too many Proofs in ſupport of our Cauſe. The Cardinal adds, that Father *Alciatus* compoſed very ſlowly, as being ſcrupulouſly exact in whatever he wrote; beſides which, Old Age, and the Affairs of the Society, were new Obſtacles. "Dapoi la fred "dezza dell' età decrepita, la natura perpleſſa, la pen- "na altrettanto lenta, quanto eſquiſita, le occupazioni "de' noſtri governi domeſtici hanno cagionato ch' egli "ſia morto con laſciar ſolo qualche veſtigio dell' opera "conceputa in idea (2)." We may learn from hence, that ſome Perſons, through too much care of becoming good Authors, never become Authors at all.

ALCINOE, Daughter of *Polybius*, the *Corinthian*, and Wife of *Amphilocus*, ran mad for Love of one *Xanthus*, of the Iſland of *Samos*, who lodged at her Houſe. This was not the ſtrangeſt part of her Adventure; the great Matter of Surprize is, that it was *Minerva* who inſpired her with this Diſeaſe of Love, to puniſh her for not having diſcharged her Promiſe to a Woman, who had worked for her. This Woman prayed to *Minerva* to revenge her; and thus her Prayers were heard. *Alcinoe*, influenced by this Goddeſs, fell ſo deſperately in Love with her Gueſt, that ſhe forſook her Houſe and her young Children, and embarked with him. But, at Sea, ſhe reflected on her Conduct, ſhe bewailed it, ſhe remembered, with Tears and Cries, her young Huſband, and her Children; laſtly, all the good Words of *Xanthus*, who promiſed to marry her, being too feeble a Conſolation, ſhe caſt herſelf into the Sea (a). A great Exploit, and highly worthy of the Goddeſs *Minerva*! See the Remark [C] of the Article E G I A L E A, and the Remark [D] of the Article M Y R R H A.

ALCINOUS, King of the *Phæacians*, in an Iſland, which is, at preſent, called *Corfu*, was the Son of *Nauſithoüs* (a), and Grandſon of *Neptune* and *Periboëa* [A]. He married his Niece *Arete*, the only Daughter of *Rexenor*, the Son of *Nauſithoüs*, and had five Sons by her, and a Daughter whoſe Name was *Nauſicaa*, whom *Homer* greatly celebrates (b). He praiſes the Mother much more, and makes a Heroine of her. He gives us likewiſe very long Deſcriptions of *Alcinous*'s Palace and Gardens. According to his Account, theſe Gardens produced the moſt excellent Fruits in the World, without any viciſſitude of Winter and Summer, and in every Month of the Year. It was, doubtleſs, by his Gardens that *Alcinous* chiefly immortalized his Memory [B]. He received *Ulyſſes* with great Civility [C], whom a Storm had caſt a-ſhore

[A] *Grandſon of Neptune and Periboëa*,] *Britannicus* aſſures us, that *Alcinous* was the Son of *Phæax*, and that *Phæax* was the Son of *Neptune*, and of *Corcyra* (1). I find indeed the latter of theſe two Circumſtances in *Stephen of Byzantium*, but not that this Son of *Neptune* and *Corcyra* was the Father of *Alcinous*.

[B] *It was doubtleſs, by his Gardens, that* Alcinous *chiefly immortaliz'd his Memory*.] The Poets, in general, ſtrive to out-do each other in ſpeaking of his Gardens. *Lloyd* uſes many Paſſages from them; let us content ourſelves with this of *Juvenal*:

———— Illa jubebit
Poma dari, quorum ſolo paſcaris odore,
Qualia perpetuus Phæacum autumnus habebat (2).

To him are ordered, and thoſe happy few,
Whom Fate has rais'd above Contempt and you,
Moſt fragrant Fruit; ſuch in Phæacian Gardens grew;
Where an eternal Autumn over ſmil'd,
And golden Apples loaded Branches fill'd.
Rev^d. Mr WILLIAM BOWLES.

And let us add to this the Teſtimony of an Author in Proſe. " Antiquitas nihil prius mirata eſt quam " Heſperidum hortos, ac regum Adonis & Alcinoi " (3) ———— Antiquity admired nothing beyond the " Gardens of the Heſperides, and thoſe of the Kings " Adonis (4) and Alcinous." *Lloyd* cites *Theophilus*, Patriarch of *Antioch*, who mentions theſe Gardens in his third Book *ad Autolicum*, but he ſays that we muſt correct the Reading *Antinous*, and ſubſtitute *Alcinous*. He cites likewiſe theſe Words of St *Gregory Nazianzen*;

Ἡ ᵹ τϱαπεζα κ᾽ ἁλσος Ἀλκινοοιο
Τεϱπνοτεϱη (5).

Thy Table is pleaſanter than the Gardens of Alcinous.

I have not obſerved, that the Poets feign, that this Prince was the *Orchard-Keeper*, as *Moreri* will have it. *Charles Stephens* led him into this Error; for in his Dictionary we find an *Alcinous* different from the King of the *Phæacians*, and diſtinguiſh'd by the Office of *Hortorum cuſtos*; which the Author proves by the ſecond Book of *Virgil*'s Georgics, and by ſome Verſes of *Ovid* and *Statius*; which relate, not to this, but only to *Alcinous*'s Gardens. Probably this Miſtake might ariſe from a Blunder of ſome Tranſcriber, or Printer, who put *cuſtos*, inſtead of *cultor*.

[C] *He receiv'd Ulyſſes with great Civility*.] Several Authors, as *Raviſius Textor* (6), and *Decimator* (7), attribute

ALCINOUS. ALCYONIUS.

a-shore on the Coast of the *Phæacians*; he offered him his Daughter, and caused him to be conducted to *Ithaca* loaded with Presents. Now, as *Ulysses* told the Company an hundred old Women's Stories, during the Feast, to which he was admitted, it is thought that this occasioned certain Proverbs, which were in use among the Ancients [D]. However it be, *Alcinous*'s Kingdom was a jovial Country; the People there loved good Cheer, and the Conveniencies of Life [E], which however did not hinder them from being active, and very good Seamen (c), and *Alcinous* from being a very just Prince, as appears from these words:

Ἀλκίνοος ———— δικαιότατος βασιλήων (d).

Alcinous ———— *the justest of Kings*.

(c) Homer. Odyss. lib. 6. ver. 270. lib. 7. ver. 35, 107. lib. 8. ver. 247, 253, &c.

(d) Orpheus.

attribute this Reception to *Nausicaa*, the Daughter of *Alcinous*, without allowing the Father any share in it. But they forget, that she only gave *Ulysses* Cloaths, and Advice, without the City; and that she had a Father and Mother, who perform'd all the Honours of Reception, and Hospitality. See the Article NAUSICAA.

[D] *Certain Proverbs, which were in use among the Ancients.*] *Moreri* says, that "*Ulysses* related the Fable "of the *Cyclopes*, of the *Læstrigones*, and others, "leaning, as they say, with his Elbow on the Table; which gave occasion for that Proverb of the "Ancients, which *Erasmus* did not forget, "*Alcinous*'s Table*?* or, as *Plato* expresses it, Must I relate the Story of *Alcinous* to you?" This is nothing to the Purpose. I. The Phrase *and others* is obscure, and quite careless. II. The Proverb of *Alcinous*'s Table did not arise from *Ulysses*'s Story-telling, but from the good Cheer, which *Alcinous* usually provided. See the following Remark. Besides, it is not true, that *Plato* expresses himself by way of Question: He declares only that he will not repeat the Fable of *Alcinous* (8). It is yet more false, that what he says is, in other Terms, the same thing with *the Table of Alcinous*. It is certain that we find, in the Index of *Erasmus*'s *Adagia*, *Alcinoi Mensa*, and *Alcinoi Apologus*, as two different Proverbs. The first is not an Article in the Body of the Book; it is only added, by way of Supplement to the Proverb, *Sybaritica Mensa* (9); and is taken from these Words of *Gregory Nazianzen*, Οὐκ ὡς Λωτοφάγοι θυσίαι, ἀλλ' ὡς Ἀλκίνου τράπεζα; *non ad Lotophagorum inopiam, sed Alcinoi mensam*. *Hadrian Junius*, who made a Collection of Proverbs after *Erasmus*, wherein he places *Alcinoi Horti* as a capital Proverb, cites, in the Explication of it, this other Passage of the same Father, concerning the Table of *Alcinous*;

(8) Plato de Rep. lib. 10.

(9) It is in the 65th of the 2d Cent. in the 2d Chiliad.

Καὶ δόμον αἰγλήεντα ᾗ Ἀλκινόοιο τράπεζαν.

The Dome magnificent could'st thou afford,
And rich Alcinous *hospitable Board.*

Lloyd cites another Passage, in which this holy Doctor makes use of the same Phrase. As for the *Alcinoi Apologus*, *Erasmus* repeats it twice. First he understands it of old Wives Tales, *de longis & anilibus fabulamentis*, and justifies it by the Stories, which *Ulysses* told at the Table of *Alcinous*. "Prodigiosas "ac deridiculas fabulas & protentuosa mendacia de "Lotophagis, Læstrygonibus, Circe, Cyclopibus attigit genus aliis plurimis miraculis, fretus videlicet Phæacum insicitia barbarieque (10). — *His monstrous and absurd Tales, and portentous Lies, concerning the* Lotophagi, *the* Læstrigons, Circe,

(10) Erasm. Adag. n. 72. cent. 4. chil. 2. p. 469.

"the Cyclopes, *and the like wonderful Events, which* "*he told, relying upon the Ignorance and Barbarity of* "*the* Phæacians." But, in another Place (11), he tells us that he had met with another Signification of the same Proverb, in the fourth Book of *Aristotle*'s Rhetoric (12), but that he would suspend his Decision, till he saw more clearly into the Matter, either by the Commentaries of St *Gregory Nazianzen* on those Books of *Aristotle* (13), or by some other means. I scarce meet with any one, who pays the least Regard to this latter Passage of *Erasmus*. They stop at the first; as if the true Sense were to be found there: But it is far from being to be met with in that place; for if we consider never so little what *Erasmus* says on *Aristotle*'s Words, we shall wholly distrust the Explication he has given in another Place. I own this Passage of *Aristotle* is obscure, that it is differently read, and that perhaps there is an Hiatus in it; but there is no probability, that by the Apologue of Alcinous, we ought to understand *a Tale of a Tub*. Yet *Gilbert Cousin*, who made a Collection of Proverbs after *Erasmus*, fancies so; though he considers the thing only according to *Aristotle*'s Citation (14). There is a Passage in *Ælian*, where Alcinoi apologi, Ἀλκίνου ἀπόλογοι, can only be taken for the Discourses of *Ulysses* to that Prince in the *Odyssey* (15).

[E] *The People there liv'd good Cheer, and the Conveniencies of Life.*] *Alcinous* made no Secret of his to *Ulysses*: *We love*, said he to him, *Feasts, Music, Dancing, change of Apparel, Bathing, and the Bed*.

(11) Id. n. 82. cent. 1. chil. 5. pag. 1057.

(13) *I never heard of the 3d Book in the Edition of Geneva, 1605.*

(14) Cognat. in Proverb. n. 210. *He quotes, as* Erasmus does, *the fourth Book of the Rhetorics*.

(15) Ælian. var. Hist. lib. 13. c. 13.

Αἰεὶ δ' ἡμῖν δαίς τε φίλη, κίθαρίς τε, χοροί τε,
Εἵματά τ' ἐξημοιβά, λοετρά τε θερμά, ᾗ εὐναί.

To dance, to dress, to sing, our sole Delight,
The Feast, or Bath, by Day, and Love by Night.

POPE'S Odyss.

(16) Homer. Odyss. lib. 8. ver. 248.

Horace expresses it in this Manner;

———————— Alcinoique
In cute curanda plus æquo operata juventus,
Cui pulcrum fuit in medios dormire dies, &
Ad strepitum citharæ cessatum ducere curam (17).

Alcinous' *idle Youth, whose sole Design*
Aim'd at soft Blandishments, and being fine,
Indulg'd at ease, who slept out half the Day,
And lull'd their Cares with Dancing, Songs, and Play.

I need not observe, that by *Alcinoi juventus*, must be understood the young Lords of *Alcinous*'s Court. *Athenæus* somewhere remarks the voluptuous Life of the *Phæacians*.

(17) Horat. Epist. 2. lib. 1. ver. 28.

ALCYONIUS (PETER) was one of those learned *Italians*, who cultivated useful Literature in the XVIth Century. He acquired a considerable Knowledge of the *Greek* and *Latin* Tongues, and wrote some Rhetorical Pieces, which deserved the Approbation of good Judges. He was a long time Corrector of the Press at *Venice*, in the House of *Aldus Manutius* [A], and ought consequently to have a share in the Praises,

[A] *A long time Corrector of the Press at Venice, in the House of* Aldus Manutius.] *Paul Jovius*'s Account falls short of this. He only says, "Cum "diu in Chalcographorum Officinis, corrigendis er"roribus menstrua mercede operam navasset, multa "observatione ad præcellentem scribendi facultatem "pervenit (1). — *Having been employ'd a long time* "*in Printing-Offices, in correcting Errors of the*

(1) Paul. Jovius, in Elog. c. 125. pag. 265.

"Press, for a monthly Stipend, by long Observation he "arriv'd at an excellent Faculty of Writing." What relates to Aldus Manutius, is borrowed from *Varillas*, and I confess that I do it trembling, considering the great Number of Faults, which that Writer committed, about the learned Men, whom he has mentioned in his *Anecdotes* of *Florence*. "The Public, says "he (2), is obliged to him for that Exactness of Aldus "Manutius,

(2) Varillas Anecdot. pag. 105.

VOL. I. Eee

ALCYONIUS.

Praises, which are given to the Editions of that Learned Printer. He translated several Treatises of *Aristotle* into *Latin* (a), but without Success. *Sepulveda* wrote against these Translations, and observed so many Faults in them, that *Alcyonius* found no better Remedy for his Disgrace, than to buy up as many Copies of *Sepulveda*'s Works as he could find, in order to burn them [B]. *Paul Jovius* accuses him of a second Fault, which is more disgraceful than the first; namely of having been an impudent Parasite [C], who made no scruple of eating two or three times a day out of his own House. I cannot tell whether we ought to give entire Credit to *Paul Jovius* in this Matter; for he quarrelled with *Alcyonius* (b) upon hearing, that he was his Rival in the Commission of writing History [D]. The Treatise, which *Alcyonius* published *concerning Exile*, contained so many fine Passages among other very mean ones, that it was thought he had tacked several Parts of a Treatise of *Cicero de Gloria* to his own Thoughts, and afterwards, to prevent being convicted of the Theft, had thrown into the Fire that Manuscript of *Cicero* [E], which was the only one in the World (c). The Two Orations, which he made, after the taking of *Rome*, in which he

(a) *See the List of them in the Bibliotheque of Gesner.*

(b) *Epistles of Princes, fol. 92. verso.*

(c) *Jovius, Elog. c. 123.*

" *Manutius*, in printing the best *Greek* and *Latin* Au-
" thors, which we admire at present; for he was all
" his Life-time Corrector of that famous Printing-
" Office." This last Particular is false, for *Manutius*
was Professor at *Florence*, under the Pontificate of
Hadrian VI.

[B] *Sepulveda* ———— *observ'd so many Faults in
them, that* Alcyonius *found no better Remedy, &c.*]
Paul Jovius remarks this. " Quum aliqua ex Ari-
" stotele perperam insolenterque vertisset, in eum Se-
" pulveda vir Hispanus, egregiæ de literis meritus,
" edito volumine peracuta jacula contorsit ————
" tanto quidem eruditorum applausu, ut Alcyonius
" ignominiæ dolore misere consternatus, Hispani ho-
" stis libros in tabernis, ut concremaret, gravi pretio
" coemere cogeretur (3). ———— *Having translated
" some Pieces of* Aristotle, *after a wretched and igno-
" rant Manner,* Sepulveda, *a Spaniard, well deser-
" ving of the learned World, attack'd him very severe-
" ly upon it* ———— *with such Applause from the learn-
" ed, that* Alcyonius, *greatly afflicted with Grief,
" at the Ignominy thrown upon him, was forced to
" buy up, at a great Price, the Books of his Spanish
" Enemy, that he might burn them.*" See the *Epistles of Princes*, collected by *Ruscelli*, and translated
by *Belleforet*, Fol. 93. See also the Twenty seventh,
and the last Letter of the third Book of *Longolius*.
" Si bene te novi, ipse tu denuncabis, ut hominis,
" ad tantæ contumeliæ nuncium, vultum videas:
" quod unum sanè spectaculum tibi magnopere invi-
" deo (4). ———— *If I know you well, you will your-
" self carry the News* (namely, that *Sepulveda's*
" *Work was printed*), *that you may observe the
" Man's Looks, when he hears of such a Slur upon
" his Character; a Sight, which I greatly envy you the
" Pleasure of.*"

[C] *Paul Jovius* accuses him ———— *of having
been an impudent Parasite.*] Let us set down his own
Words : " Cùm nulla ex parte ingenuis, sed planè
" plebeiis ac sordidis moribus sœdaretur; erat enim
" impudens gulæ mancipium, ita ut eodem sæpe die
" bis & ter, aliena tamen quadra, cœnitaret ; nec in ea
" fœditate malus omnino modicus, quod domi de-
" mum in lecti lumine per vomitum ipso crapulæ o-
" nere levaretur (5) ———— *He was a Man, not of
" ingenuous, but downright plebeian and sordid, Man-
" ners ; he was a shameless Slave to his Appetite ;
" insomuch, that, in one and the same Day, he would
" dine three or four times, but always at another's
" Expence ; nor was he altogether a bad Physician
" in this beastly Practice ; since, afterwards, before he
" went into Bed, he discharged the intemperate Load
" of his Stomach.*" *Varillas* mentions only *Alcyonius's* Drunkenness : he accuses him *of getting drunk
as often as he had an Opportunity for it*. *Lætomus*,
whose Verses *Paul Jovius* alledges, mentions two of
this Person's Excesses; that of Drinking, and that of
Eating too much.

[D] *His Rival in the Commission of writing History.*] He, who informs us of this, adds, That it was
not true, that *Alcyonius* was to compose an History,
and that *Paul Jovius* was told so, only to make them
quarrel (6). Cardinal *de Medicis* diverted himself
with the Feuds of the Learned; he took delight
in disquieting *Alcyonius*, by protecting *Sepulveda*.
Note, that *Alcyonius* extolled to the Skies the first
Decad of *Paulus Jovius*'s History, in the second Part
of his Treatise *de Exilio* [7].

[E] *Had thrown into the Fire That Manuscript
of Cicero.*] *Paul Jovius* is not the only Person, who
mentions this unlucky Trick. *Paul Manutius* in his
Commentary on these Words of *Cicero* ; *librum tibi
celeriter mittam de gloria* (8), ———— (*I will speedily
send you my Book de Gloria*), speaks of it thus : " Li-
" bros duos significat, quos de gloria scripsit : qui ul-
" que ad patrum nostrorum ætatem pervenerunt.
" Nam Bernardus Justinianus in indice librorum suo-
" rum nominat Ciceronem de Gloria. Is liber postea,
" cum universam bibliothecam Bernardus monacha-
" rum monasterio legasset, magna conquisitus cura,
" neutiquam est inventus. Nemini dubium fuit, quin
" Petrus Alcyonius, cui monachæ medico suo ejus
" tractandæ bibliothecæ potestatem fecerant, homo
" improbus furto averterit. Et sane, in ejus opusculo,
" de Exsulio, adspersa nonnulla deprehenduntur,
" quæ non olere Alcyonium auctorem, sed aliquanto
" præstantiorem artificem, videantur. ———— *He means
" the two Books, which he wrote de Gloria; which
" were handed down to the Age of our Fathers. For
" Bernardus Justinianus, in the Catalogue of his Books,
" mentions* Cicero *de Gloria. This Book, purchased
" not without great Pains, when Bernardus bequeathed
" his Library to a Monastery of Nuns, was after-
" wards not to be found. It was generally believed,
" that Peter Alcyonius, Physician to the Monastery,
" to whom the Nuns entrusted the Management of this
" Library, privately made away with it. And, to
" say the Truth, there are some scattered Passages in
" his Work* de Exsulio, *which do not favour of Alcyo-
" nius's Pen, but of a more excellent Artist.*" We
understand, by this Passage, that *Alcyonius* was a Physician by Profession. See the Remark [F]. Now
since he was Physician to a Convent of Nuns, it cannot, I think, be true, that he spent all his Life in
Manutius's Printing-Office. This is a new Proof of
Varillas's Error.

I have two things to remark against this Historian. The first is, that, in the Fragment of his *Lewis*
XI, he imputed the Plagiarism, and the Destruction
of the Treatise *de Gloria* to *Philelphus*, and cited the
lesser Elogies of *Paul Jovius*. He was informed (9),
that there was no such thing there. No doubt he
profited by this Advice, in publishing his *Lewis* XII ;
for, after having observed the same thing concerning
Philelphus, he adds : " Nevertheless it is not certain
" that he was guilty of this Crime, which passes
" for one of the greatest that can be committed in the
" Affair of Literature : and some Authors impute it
" to a learned Person of the same time, whose Name
" is *Alcyonius*, and maintain that he appropriated
" this Work of *Cicero* to himself, after having chang-
" ed the Title of it, which was *de Gloria*, into that
" of *de Exsulio*. (10)." To this latter Fact he applies
the Citation of *Paul Jovius*. Had he entirely suppressed what concerns *Philelphus*, he would have come
off better; for where could he find that *Philelphus*
was accused of this Fraud? Besides *Alcyonius* is not
charged with publishing *Cicero*'s Book, and changing
only the Title of it; his Vanity might easily have
been forgiven, if he had only been guilty of this ; the
Pleasure of having that Work of *Cicero* would make
one forget the Trick; but he is accused of having
taken a rich Embroidery out of it, and tacking it to
his own Rags, and afterwards of burning that whole
Work of *Cicero*. " Ex libro de Gloria Ciceronis,
" quam nefaria malignitate aboleverat, multorum ju-
" dicio

(3) *P. Jovius ubi supra.*

(4) *Longolius Epist. ultim. lib. 3. Epist. 25. verso.*

(5) *P. Jovius Elog c. 123. pag. 265.*

(6) *Letters of Princes, fol. 93.*

(7) *Ibid.*

(8) *Cicero, Epist. 27. lib. 15. ad Atticum.*

Remarks upon *VA-RILLAS*.

(9) *Nouvelles de la Rep. de Lettres, June 1685. Article 1/5, towards the End.*

(10) *Varillas, Hist. of Lewis XI. Book 1 pag. 30. of the Dutch Edit.*

ALCYONIUS.

he very eloquently reprefented the Injuftice of *Charles* V, and the Barbarity of his Soldiers, removed in fome meafure the Sufpicions, which were entertained againft him (d). They are Two very good Pieces. There is mention of a Speech which he compofed upon the Knights, who died at the Siege of *Rhodes* (e). He was Profeffor at *Florence* in the Pontificate of *Hadrian* VI; and, befides his Penfion, had Ten Ducats *per* Month from Cardinal *de Medicis*, for Tranflating a Work of *Galen* (f). Having heard that this Cardinal was elected Pope, he defired Letters of Difmiffion from the *Florentines*; but, not obtaining them, he went neverthelefs to *Rome*, full of the hopes of raifing himfelf there (g). He loft all his Eftate, in the Troubles, which the *Colonnas* excited in *Rome*; and, fome time after, when the Emperor's Forces took the City, in the Year 1527, he received a Wound, as he was making his Retreat to the Caftle of St *Angelo*; into which he forced his way, notwithftanding the Soldiers, who purfued him, and joined *Clement* VIIth. He was afterwards guilty of bafe Ingratitude towards That Pope; for, upon the raifing of the Siege, he went over to Cardinal *Pompey Colonna*, at whofe Houfe he fell fick, and died in a few Months.

(d) Jovius, ibid.
(e) Letters of Princes, fol. 93.
(f) Pius. De partibus Animalium.
(g) Letters of Princes, fol. 95.

(11) Jovius, Elog. cap. 125. p. 266.
" dicio confectum crederetur. In eo enim tanquam
" vario centone præclara excellentis purpuræ fila, lan-
" guentibus cæteris coloribus, intertexta notabantur
" (11). —— *It is thought he compofed it out of*
" *Cicero's Book* de Gloria, *which he wickedly and*
" *malicioufly deftroyed. For in this Patch-work Com-*
" *pofition there appear interfperfed feveral beautiful*
" *Threads of the fineft Purple, whilft the reft of the*
" *Colours are faint and languid* (12)." My fecond Remark is, that when *Varillas* mentions *Francis Philelphus*, in his *Secret Hiftory of Florence*, he imputes nothing to him in relation to the Book *de Gloria*; he accufes *Alcyonius* alone of That fcandalous Action. He fays (13), that " this wretched Plagiary was o-
" bliged to comfort the Proveditor *Cornaro* in the
" Exile, to which he was condemned, for having
" been defeated in the War againft the *Turks*, tho'
" it was not his own Fault. *Algienus* (14) fent him
" the Book, entitled *De fortiter toleranda exilii for-*
" tuna. And as this Treatife was only compofed out
" of Sentences, though very ill thrown together, of
" *Cicero's* Book *de Gloria*, it was much efteemed;
" notwithftanding the more judicious obferved that
" there was no Coherence in it. *Algienus*, ravifhed
" with the Succefs of his Work, altered his Defign
" of publifhing This Piece of *Cicero*. And, know-
" ing very well that no one, befides himfelf, had a
" Copy of it, he threw it into the Fire, for fear it
" fhould be found fome time or other among his Pa-
" pers, and his Theft fhould be difcovered by that
" means." If we compare this Relation with That, which is in the Life of *Lewis* XI, we fhall have reafon to wonder, how one and the fame Man could relate the fame Fact with fo many inconfiftent Varieties. Having not this Treatife of *Alcyonius*, I cannot determine, whether *Varillas* has juftly remarked the Subject and Occafion of it. I can only fay, that the Title he gives it does not agree with That which *Gefner* fet down, *Medices Legatus, five de Exilio liber*; and that a Paffage of this Book (15) difcovers to me, that *John de Medicis*, who was Pope *Leo* X, is introduced fpeaking in it. But what I cannot determine by myfelf, I can affirm on the Word of a Friend of mine, whofe Exactnefs and Capacity I am thoroughly acquainted with (16). His Obfervation, communicated to me, is as follows: " The *Legatus Medices, feu de Exilio, of Petrus Alcyonius* is fo far
" from being wrote for the Confolation of the pre-
" tended Proveditor *Cornaro*, that it is dedicated by
" the Author *ad Nicolaum Shomberg*um *Pontificem*
" *Campanum* (17), and there is not one Word in the
" whole Book that can either directly or indirectly
" relate to *Cornaro*. This Work, printed at *Bafil* in
" 1546, is divided into two Books, the Title of which
" runs thus: *Petri Alcionii Medices Legatus, feu de*
" *Exilio, ad Nicolaum Shombergum Pontificem Cam-*
" *panum*. It is written by way of Dialogue; and
" *John de Medicis*, who was afterward Pope *Leo* X,
" *Julius de Medicis*, and *Lawrence de Medicis*, are the
" Interlocutors. This is the Reafon, why *Medices*
" is put in the Title; and, becaufe the Author fup-
" pofes that thefe Interlocutors difcourfed together a
" little while after Pope *Julius* II. had fent *John*
" *de Medicis* as his Legate, at the Head of the Ar-
" my, which was to retake *Bologna*, the Word *Le-*
" *gatus* was added to that of *Medices*." What follows is certainly a great Miftake. Neverthelefs he repented of it before his Death (to wit, *Alcyonius*) and made a kind of Honourable Amends *, prefixed to the two Speeches, which he compofed at* Venice *on the Defolation caufed by the Lutherans at* Rome (18). Doubtlefs *Varillas* intended to tranflate thefe Words of *Paul Jovius*: " Verum non multo poft confirmatæ fufpi-
" cionis invidiam duabus fplendidiffimis orationibus
" peregregiè mitigavit, quum in clade urbis vehe-
" mentiffimè invectus in Cæfarem, populi Romani
" injurias & barbarorum immanitatem fumma per-
" fecti Oratoris eloquentia deplorafiet. —— *Not long*
" *after he wonderfully took off from the Odium of a*
" *confirmed Sufpicion by two moft elegant Orations,*
" *when, upon the City's Defolation, he inveighed moft*
" *vehemently againft Cæfar, and lamented the Inju-*
" *ries of the Roman People, and the Cruelty of their*
" *inhuman Foes, with all the Eloquence of a perfect*
" *Orator.*" Is there the leaft Shadow of any thing relating to the *Lutherans* in this Paffage? Is there any Traces of Repentance in it? any Footfteps of an Honourable Amends on Account of the Book *de Gloria*? Has *Jovius* any other Defign than to fhew that *Alcyonius's* Speeches were fo much admired, that People were the more inclined to believe, that he might be the Author of the fine Paffages in the Book, entitled, *de Exilio*? I don't believe thefe Speeches were compofed at *Venice*.

I am furpized, that *Pierius Valerianus*, who regretted the Suppreffion of a Work, with which he charged *Alcyonius*, took no notice of the Suppreffion of the Treatife *de Gloria*. Having related that *Peter Marcellus* could not put the laft Hand to fome Works by Reafon of his Sicknefs; he adds: " Quatuor tamen
" libros exactiffimæ interpretationis in Mathematicas
" difciplinas Braccius ejus filius ab interitu vindicavit,
" vel ipfius auctoris de fe teftimonio abfolutos: at-
" que il Barbarorum manus effugerant, Braccii ip-
" fius diligentia in Arcem Æliam afportati. Sed
" enim in Petri Alcyonii manus cum incidiffent,
" ita fuppreffi funt, ut aufquam amplius apparu-
" rint (19). —— *However, his Son Braccius preferv-*
" *ed from Deftruction four Books of moft exact*
" *Lectures upon Mathematical Learning, which were*
" *perfectly finifhed, as appears from the Author's own*
" *Teftimony. Thofe efcaped the Hands of the Barba-*
" *rians* (20), *being conveyed by the Care of* Braccius
" *to the* Ælian *Tower. But when they fell into*
" Peter Alcyonius's *Hands, they were fo fuppreffed,*
" *as never afterwards to appear.*" Since the firft Edition of this Dictionary, Dr *Bourdelot*, Phyfician to the King, and to the Duchefs of *Burgundy*, did me the Favour to fend me his Copy of the Treatife of *Alcyonius*. It is a fmall Book in 4to, printed at *Venice* in the Year 1522; it contains two Parts (21), which are both dedicated *ad Nicolaum Schonbergium Pontificem Campanum*. I found the Information, which Mr *de Larroque* had fent me concerning this Work, to be true. It does not contain any thing which relates to the Exile of the *Venetian* Proveditor. The three Interlocutors confider only their own Condition. They were all of the Houfe of *Medicis*, and continued ftill under the Misfortune of Banifhment. *John de Medicis* comforts himfelf, and them too: He is the chief Actor in this Piece, and alledges the Reafons and Examples; in a Word, the Author beftows upon him his Erudition, and his elegant Style. Note, that this Book of *Alcyo-*

* Amende Honorable.

(18) Varillas, Anecdot. pag. 168.

(19) Pierius Valerian. de Litterat. Infellicit. p. 76.

(20) He means the Army of Charles V. which plundered Rome in 1527.

(21) The firft Title of the firft is, Medices Legatus prior; and the fecond Title of the fecond is, Medices Legatus pofterior.

ALCYONIUS.

Months (b). His Vanity hindered him from becoming more learned [F], and his Practice of Detraction raised him many Enemies [G]. The Supplement to *Moreri's* Dictionary is nothing to the purpose in this Article [H]. For it is only a faithful Copy of *Varillas's* enormous Faults. Some learned Men have very much commended *Alcyonius*, and his Translations [I].

We find something concerning him in the Letters of *Longolius*, which is not much to his Advantage [K].

nius was printed at *Geneva*, in the Year 1624, in 8vo, with two Treatises of *Cardan* (22).

[F] *His Vanity hindered him from becoming more learned.*] This is the Opinion of *Pierius Valerianus*: "Non displicuisset mihi Alcyonius, si, quantum stylo "profecerat, amicorum consilium de rebus adhibere "voluisset, qui, nisi ipsimet sibi tantum arrogasset, "futurus omnino fuerat è primoribus; multam enim "Græcis, Latinisque literis operam impenderat, & "disciplinis variis oblectatus erat (23). —— Alcyonius "*would not have displeased me, if, as he was Master* "*of a good Style, he had but consulted his Friends* "*in relation to the Subject-matter of his Compositions;* "*for, had he not depended so much upon his own Judg-* "*ment, he would have been one of the first Class of* "*Authors; for he had bestowed great Pains in the* "*Greek and Roman Learning, and was Master of* "*many Sciences.*"

[G] *His Practice of Detraction raised him many Enemies.*] Let us hear the same Evidence again: "Is eo primum infelicitatis incommodo flagellatus est, "quod dum de literatis omnibus male sentit, dica- "cissima omnes obtrectatione lacerabat, unde om- "nium tam doctorum quam imperitorum in se odium "concitarat. —— *He was particularly unhappy in* "*this Respect, that, having an ill Opinion of the Learn-* "*ed in general, he was perpetually detracting from* "*their Merits; by which means he drew upon him-* "*self the Hatred both of the Learned and the Igno-* "*rant.*" See below the Remark [*K*].

[H] *The Supplement to Moreri's Dictionary is nothing to the Purpose in this Article.*] I. They have not taken notice, that the *Algionus* of *Varillas's* Anecdotes is a Chimera of the Transcribers. No doubt the Author gave it *Alcionius* in the Original of those Memoirs; and consequently they should not have distinguished the pretended *Algionus* from *Peter Alcyonius*, whom *Moreri* had justly placed in the XVIth Century. This put me in mind, that *Claude du Verdier*, in his *Censura in omnes penes autores* (p. 73.), says, that *Peter Avionius* had remarked many Errors in *Apuleius*'s Book *de Mundo*. The Errata corrects *Avionius* by *Alcionius*. Notwithstanding which, *Avionius* is cited in the fifty sixth Page of the *Plagiariorum Syllabus*, printed at *Amsterdam*, in 1694, with the *Amœnitates Theologico-Philologicæ* of Mr *Almeloveen*. II. They should have considered, that, according to *Varillas*, this pretended *Algionus*, having deplored the Ravages, which *Charles* the Fifth's Army committed at *Rome* in the Pontificate of *Clement* VII. should have been placed in the XVIth Century. III. That which was taken out of the *Anecdotes* is not purged from any Errors.

[I] *Some learned Men have very much commended* Alcyonius, *and his Translations.*] I shall only mention what was wrote to *Erasmus* by *Ambrosius Leo Nolanus*, in the Year 1518. This Friend, who was an able Physician, informed him, that the Senate of *Venice* had caused it to be proclaimed by Sound of Trumpet, that all those, who aspired to the Professorship of the *Greek* Tongue, vacant by the Death of *Mark Musurus*, should present themselves; and that two Months should be appointed for taking their Names; and examining their Abilities and Knowledge of the *Greek* Authors. "Statutum est tempus duo- "rum mensium quo competitores & nomina dent, "& legendo & aperiendo Græcos autores ostendant "qui viri sint, & quantum lingua & ingenio polle- "ant (24)." *Leo* adds, that several of *Musurus's* Disciples prepared themselves to dispute his Succession, and that *Alcyonius*, one of the most polite among them, distinguished himself by many admirable Translations. It is better to express this according to the Original; "Inter eorum elegantiores unus *Petrus* "*Alcyonius* multa è *Græco* in *Romanum* sermonem "elegantissimè vertit. Nam Orationes plerasque *Iso-* "*cratis* ac *Demosthenis* tanta *Arpinitate* expressit, ut "*Ciceronem* ipsum nihilominus legere videris. *Ari-* "*stotelisque* multa vertit tam candidè ut *Latium* glo-

"riabundum dicere possit; en *Aristotelem* nostrum ha- "bemus. Idem ipse juvenis, ut est literarum opti- "marum utrarumque maximus alumnus, ita tui quo- "que amantissimus, ac studiorum tuorum laudator "summus (25). —— *Among the more polite of these,* "*Peter* Alcyonius *rendered many things from the* "*Greek into the Roman Tongue, with the greatest* "*Elegance. For he express'd several of the Orations* "*of* Isocrates *and* Demosthenes, *so nearly in the Ci-* "*ceronian Style, that you would imagine you was* "*reading* Cicero *himself. And so fairly did he trans-* "*late many of* Aristotle's *Pieces, that* Latium *might* "*boast an* Aristotle *of it's own. This young Author,* "*as he is the greatest Follower of the best, and of* "*both kinds of Learning, so is he very much your* "*Friend, and extreamly fond of your Works.*" *Erasmus*, answering this Letter, the fifteenth of *October*, the Year following, caus'd *Peter Alcyonius* to be complimented in his Name, and confess'd, that he had never heard of him. It were to be wish'd, since there are different Opinions about *Alcyonius's* Translations, that the learned Mr *Huet* had done him the Honour to take notice of him, when he compos'd his Dialogues *de Interpretatione*.

I shall add at this time another Testimony to that of *Leo Nolanus*. I find that *Gabriel Naudé* very much commends *Alcyonius's* Translations, in his Treatise *de Fato & Vitæ Termino*. He tells us, that this Translator, having examin'd three Objections, which may be made to those, who say that the Treatise *de Mundo* is a Piece of *Aristotle's*, has recourse, afterwards, to every thing, which may prevent his being obliged to confess, that it is a spurious Piece, concluding with these Words: *But let us leave these disagreeable Questions to the Grammarians.* "Difficultates "ejusmodi amoliri tentet: atque ne suppositionem "hunc fœtum, quem una cum legitimis aliis ELE- "GANTISSIMÈ de Græco Latinum fecerat, agnoscere "cogeretur, vertit se in omnes partes, tandemque his "verbis concludit: *Sed morositatem ejus generis quæ-* "*stionum Grammaticis relinquamus* (26)."

[K] *We find something concerning him in the Letters of* Longolius, *which is not much to his Advantage.*] We have already seen (27), that, in the Opinion of *Longolius*, *Alcyonius's* Looks, upon the News of the publication of *Sepulveda's* Book, would be an entertaining Sight. Here is something worse. *Alcyonius*, having passionately desired to carry one of *Longolius's* Letters to *Mark Antony Flaminius*, went away without taking it with him, upon which *Longolius* makes this Reflexion: "Nosti hominis ingenium: Ille enim "& cornæ quam ei opiparam hic dederamus, & lau- "dum quibus à nobis ornatissimus discesserat, & lite- "rarum quas summa contentione ut festinanter scri- "berem pervicerat, oblitus, profectus esse dicitur. "Quod vos idcirco scire volui, ut meis verbis hac de "inhumanitate cum eo expostuletis (28). —— *You* "*know the Nature of the Man: After an handsome* "*Entertainment, which I prepared for him, and the* "*many Praises I bestowed upon him, he forgot it all,* "*and went away, without taking with him the Let-* "*ters, which, at his own earnest Sollicitation, I had* "*written in haste. This I thought fit to inform you* "*of, that you may expostulate with him in my Name,* "*concerning this uncourteous Treatment.*" *Longolius* adds, That it was fortunate enough; since he had said some things in his Letters, which he desired *Alcyonius*, as well as others, should never be acquainted with. Is not this to insinuate that he was thought capable of breaking open a Letter? "Quanquam id ipsum de "quo queror non omnino incommodè nobis cecidit- "se videri possit, ea enim iis literis incautè commise- "ram quæ illum in primis celatum esse cupiebam. "Perfecerat scilicet pristinæ nostræ consuetudinis usus, "ut magis quibuscum agerem in mentem mihi veni- "ret, quam cui literas daturus essem satis meminis- "sem (29)." If he be the Person mentioned in another Letter of *Longolius* (30), as a learned Man conjectures (31), what a Picture is drawn of him? What unpolite

ALCMAN.

unpolite Behaviour, what outrageous Detraction is imputed to him; and what Contempt is shewn for his Person! What makes it doubtful whether our *Alcyonius* is intended in that Letter, is, that a little after *Longolius* mentions him without any seeming dislike to him; but this Reason for doubting is no convincing Proof; since the Picture given of him agrees with that, which another Author, of the same Age, has drawn of the same *Alcyonius*. *Gyraldus*, having said (32), That *Pierius Valerianus* was a sincere Man, adds immediately after; " diversæ naturæ est " Petrus Alcyonius Venetus, mordax & maledicus, " nec pudens magis quam prudens ------ mitte de " hoc nebulone plura, qui bellum bonis omnibus in-" dixit, flagris & fuste coërcendus - - - - 3. . . Peter " *Alcyonius, the Venetian, was of a different Dispo-" sition; a Back-biter, and a Detractor, nor more " modest than prudent. -------- But no more of " this paultry Fellow, who was at open War with " all good Men; and who deserves the Correction of " the Whipping-post, or a good Caneing."* Note, that the same Author owns, that he composed very good Lyric and Iambic Verses, and that he boasted to have wrote an excellent Tragedy on the Death of *JESUS CHRIST* (33).

ALCMAN, a *Lyric* Poet, flourished in the Twenty seventh Olympiad (*a*). Some say he was a *Lacedemonian*, and others, that he was born at *Sardes*, the chief City of *Lydia*. What is certain, is, that he was a Freeman of *Sparta* [*A*], and that the *Lacedemonians* thought it much to their Honour, that they had supply'd *Greece* with such a Genius [*B*]. He wrote many Verses, of which there are but few extant, which are cited by *Athenæus*, or some other Ancient Author. He was a Man of a very Amorous Disposition, and is looked upon as the Father of *Genteel Poetry* [*C*]. Nay, it has been said, I think, that he was the first, who introduced the Custom of singing Love-Songs in Company (*b*). The Name of one of his Mistresses is preserved (*c*): She was *Megalostrata*, a Poetess. If he had stopped here, there would not have been so much Reason to complain of him; but it is said, that he was likewise in love with one *Chæron* (*d*). *Alcman* was one of the greatest Gluttons of his time (*e*); this Quality would have been attended with great Inconveniences, if Poetry had been in those Times upon the same Foot it has often been; I mean, very unfit to maintain it's Master. He died of a very singular Disease; for he was eaten up with Lice (*f*). He must not be distinguished from the Poet *Alcmæon* [*D*], and I see no necessity for acknowledging Two *Alcmans*, one of *Lacedemon*, and the other of *Messena* [*E*].

[*A*] *A Freeman of Sparta.*] This appears from an Epigram, which *Plutarch* inserts in his Treatise of *Exile* (1). The Author of that Epigram makes *Alcman* say, That if he had been educated in *Sardes*, the Country of his Ancestors, he had been only a poor Priest of the Goddess *Cybele*, deprived of his Manly Parts; but that he is at present a Citizen of *Lacedemon*, well instructed in the *Greek* Learning, which makes him superior to the Kings of *Lydia*. The *Latin* Interpreter has ill translated the first Verse of that Epigram,

----- Σάρδεις ἀρχαῖος πατέρων νόμος.

----- *O mea majorumque meorum Patria Sardes!*

for we must conclude from this Translation, that *Alcman* was born at *Sardes* (2), which the *Greek* Words do not import: Thus it happens, that a Translator is sometimes a sower of Dissension, when he least thinks of it. The Translator of the *Greek* Epigram into *Latin* was not aware, but that, by adding the Word *mea*, he should induce many Authors obstinately to maintain, that *Alcman* was not born at *Lacedemon*. How many Writers are there, who consult only the Versions, and who make use of all the Proofs, which the Version supplies them with, whether the *Greek* Original will allow it or not? *Salmasius* has learnedly corrected this Epigram (3); but I do not well apprehend what they mean, who refer us to him, as to a Judge, who has put an end to the Dispute about *Alcman*'s Country. The Question is, whether this Poet was born at *Lacedemon*, or at *Sardes* in *Lydia*. *Suidas* maintains the former Opinion (4), *Crates* the second (5). *Velleius Paterculus* (6), and *Ælian* (7), deny what *Suidas* affirms. Of what use is the Epigram in putting an end to this Dispute, if it does not inform us, where *Alcman* was born, but only that he was not educated in *Sardes*, the Country of his Ancestors; that he was educated after the *Greek* Manner, and that he enjoy'd the Freedom of *Lacedemon*? This may equally signify these two things: either that *Alcman* was carried into *Greece*, being a Child, or that his Father went and settled there, before this Son was born. In this latter Case, *Alcman* might have been born in the City of *Lacedemon*. *Scaliger* was of this Opinion, but he founded it upon a bad Reason. "Ego "Laconem fuisse arbitror, quum Laconica dialecto "usus fit (8).——*I am of Opinion that he was a La-"cedemonian, since he writes in the Doric Dialect.*" If he had thought of the Epigram, mentioned by *Plutarch*, he would have seen the insufficiency of this Reason. *Alcman*, not having been educated in *Lydia*, but in *Greece*, and living at *Lacedemon*, must needs have made use of the *Doric* Dialect, which was that of *Sparta*. How harsh soever it was, yet he wrote his Poems in it. Ὦ ποισάκις ἀσμυλι, ἰδὼν ἐς ἀδο-ντὴν αὐλῶν ἐλυμήνατο τ̂ Λακαίνων ἢ γλῶσσα, ἐκί-σα παρέρχονθιν τὸ εὔφωνον (9). *Cui in canticis pangenĳs nihil omnino Laconica lingua obfuit, etsi nihil eo in vocibus appellandis habet suavitatis.*

[*B*] *The Lacedemonians thought it much to their Honour, that they had supply'd Greece with such a Genius.*] The Passage of *Paterculus*, which I have cited, proves this; these Words of *Statius*

---- & *tetricis Alcman cantatus Amyclis* (10).

Alcman the Theme of rough Amyclæ's Song;

is a farther Proof. Add to this the Monument erected to *Alcman*, near the Temple of *Helen* (11).

[*C*] *It looked upon as the Father of* Genteel *Poetry.*] This is evident from this Passage of *Athenæus* (12). Ἀρχύτας δ' ὁ Ἁρμονικός, ὥς φησι Χαμαιλέων, Ἀλκμᾶνα γεγονέναι τ̂ ἐρωτικῶν μελῶν ἡγεμόνα, ἢ ἐκδοῦναι πρῶτον μέλος, ἀκόλαστον ὄντα ᾖ τὰς γυναῖκας ᾖ τ̂ τοιαύτην μῦσαν εἰς τὰς διαξείξας. Archytas Harmoniacus *writes, as* Chamæleon *tells us, that* Alcman *was the first Inventor of Love Verses, that he had a great Passion for Women, and was the first, who introduced that kind of Poetry, which is sung in Meetings and Assemblies.*

[*D*] *He must not be distinguished from the Poet* Alcmæon.] St *Jerome*, in the Chronicle of *Eusebius*, having spoke of *Alcmæon*, under the thirtieth *Olympiad*, mentions *Alcman* under the Forty second, and makes use of this Citation, *ut qu:busdam videtur*. *Scaliger* reads *Alcman* in the first Passage, instead of *Alcmæon*. It is plain, by the Reign of *Ardys*, King of *Lydia*, in whose Reign *Crates* plac'd *Alcman*, that this Poet flourished about the thirtieth *Olympiad*, which is the Time, wherein *Alcmæon* is placed in the Chronicle of *Eusebius*. If this Reason is not sufficient to shew, that those two Names belong to one and the same Person, it will undeniably prove, that *Alcman*, Ἀλκμαίων, and *Alcman*, Ἀλκμάν, differ only in the Dialect; and that the first ought to be changed into the second, by the Rules of the *Doric* Dialect. See the Commentary of *Salmasius* on *Solinus*, pag. 885. The *Alcman* of the Forty second *Olympiad*, is a Chimerical one. *Eusebius* placed him there, because he had read some Authors, who were mistaken, in relation to *Alcman*'s Age.

[*E*] *I see no necessity for acknowledging two* Alcmans, *one of* Lacedemon, *and the other of* Messena.] *Suidas*

ALCMENA.

Suidas is the only Author, who makes this Distinction. But his Authority is not very great, when he quotes no Author, and mentions no Circumstances. This is the Case of his *Alcman* of *Messena*; he says nothing of him. Let us remember that he said, That the true *Alcman* was born at *Messoe*, τὰς Μεσσόας. This Place being not famous, some Transcribers thought it should be τὰς Μεσσήνης, in the Authors who had reported the same thing with *Suidas*. Their pretended Correction produced a new *Alcman*, who was tack'd to *Suidas*'s Patch-work. This Conjecture appears to me more probable, than That of *Lilius Gyraldus*. He acknowledges but one *Alcman*; but he will have him to be born at *Messena*, and changes τὰς Μεσσόας in *Suidas* into τὰς Μεσσήνης. *Scaliger* justly rejects this Conjecture (13).

(13) Scalig. Animadv. in Euseb. n. 1360.

ALCMENA, the Daughter of *Electryon*, King of *Mycena* [A], was the Wife of *Amphitryon*, and the Mother of *Hercules*. She was delivered of this Son, whilst her Husband was living; and yet *Hercules* was not the Son of *Amphitryon*, but of *Jupiter*, who, assuming the Form of *Alcmena*'s Husband [B], was admitted without any scruple to the Matrimonial Functions. He was so well pleased with the sport, that he continued the Night to three times it's usual Length [C]. Behold the Origin of *Hercules!* most Modern Authors say, that *Alcmena* was already with Child, by *Amphitryon*; but *Apollodorus* insinuates plainly enough, that she was yet a Maid [D]; which is more for the Honour of *Jupiter*. However it be, *Amphitryon* returned home the same Day, which

[A] *The Daughter of Electryon, King of Mycena*.] The Poet *Asius* says she was born of *Amphiaraus*, and *Eriphyle* (1). Others say indeed, That *Electryon* was her Father, but, according to them, her Mother was *Anaxo*, the Daughter of *Alcæus*, the Son of *Perseus* (2), and not *Lysidice*, the Daughter of *Pelops* and *Hippodamia*, as *Charles Stephens*, *Lloyd*, *Hofman*, &c. say she was (3). The Scholiast on *Pindar* is for *Lysidice* (4).

(1) Pausan. l. 5. p. 165.
(2) Apollodor. Bibl. lib. 2. p. 96. Scholiast. Homeri in Iliad. ξ. ver. 323.
(3) *See their Dictionaries*.
(4) In Olymp. Od. 7.

[B] *Assuming the Form of* Alcmena's *Husband*.] *Diodorus Siculus* observes, that *Jupiter* took this Method, because he would not use any Violence, and because, in the way of Persuasion, he had no Hope of prevailing upon so chaste a Lady as *Alcmena* was (5). The same Historian observes, that, on this Occasion, *Jupiter* was not moved by that lascivious Passion, which he had felt so often for other Women, and that his only Inclination was to get an Hero. For which Reason he did it not in haste; he employ'd much time in the Work, three successive Nights. Our Physicians would laugh at such a Reason. I cannot tell why *Plautus* makes *Jupiter* speak thus to *Amphitryon*.

(5) Diodor. Sicul. l. 5. cap. 2.

Tu cum Alcmena uxore antiquam in gratiam
Redi: haud promeruit quamobrem vitio verteres,
Mea vi subacta est facere (6).

(6) Plaut. in Amphitr. sub finem.

— *Be reconciled, as before, to your Wife* Alcmena; *she has not deserved your Reproaches; my Power compelled her to this Action.*

For, since *Jupiter* had put on the Form of the Husband, it was not necessary to use any Violence; and we have just now seen that he assumed this Shape, only because he would not employ any violent Methods. A modern Author alledges this Example of *Alcmena*, to prove that a sincere Ignorance is a good Excuse, and quotes some fine Lines of *Moliere* (7). A thousand things might be said upon this Subject; it affords Matter for a great variety of Reflexions.

(7) *See the new Letters against Maimbourg's History of Calvinism*, pag. 280, &c.

Note, that some Persons will have *Plautus*'s Thought to be this. *Alcmena was constrained to let me enjoy her, since I had the Power of assuming your Resemblance.* If it be so, it must be said, that the Intention of the Poet was much better than his Expression.

[C] *He continued the Night to three times it's usual Length.*] *Jupiter was so well pleased with the Lady, that he made the Night last all that Day, and the Night following*; which moved *Lycophron* to call *Hercules* τριέσπερον λέων, *the Lion of three Nights*, as *Lucian* did likewise (8). Perhaps *Vigenere* alluded to these Words of *Hyginus*: *Qui unus libens cum ea concubuit, ut unum diem usurparet, duas noctes congeminaret* (9). The Dialogue of *Lucian*, which takes notice of the long Night, which *Jupiter* spent with *Alcmena*, informs us, that *Mercury* went with Orders to the Sun, to stand still three Days, that *Jupiter* might have time enough for the Production of *Hercules*; one Night not being sufficient for the Generation of so great a Warrior. It seems *Jupiter* did his best; for the Weight of the Child had like to have burst his Mother. Τέρον ἔρ᾽ ἐν μιᾷ νυκτὶ δύνασθαι οὐδ᾽ ἐξ θεὰς ἀνδείλιδος (10). *Hoc una nocte absolvi non potest*.

(8) Vigenere upon Philostrat. Tom. 2. fol. 17. Edit. 4to.
(9) Hygin. c. p. 29.
(10) Lucian. Dial. Merc. & Solis. *Ser*. Diod. Sicul. lib. 5. c. 2.

Tendebat gravitas uterum mihi, quodque ferebam
Tantum erat, ut posses auctorem dicere tecti
Ponderis esse Jovem (11).

(11) Ovid. Metam. lib. 9. ver. 283.

*My Womb extends with such a mighty Load,
As Jove the Parent of the Burthen shew'd.*

Mr GAY.

Many Authors are of opinion, that this Night was not trippled, but only doubled (12). Others say, that it lasted nine times longer than usual. St *Jerome*, who might have read this in the Writings of two Fathers of the Church (13), made no use of it, and kept to the Tradition of the double Night: *In Alcmenæ adulterio duas miscet Jupiter copulavit*. From that Time *Jupiter* took his leave of Women; *Alcmena* was the last Mortal whom he lay with. *Niobe* was the first; sixteen Generations pass'd between the one and the other (14). Such was the Duration of *Jupiter*'s Intrigues on Earth. Now, as his Diversion with *Alcmena* was the last of the kind he was to take in this World, was it not reasonable that it should last longer than usual? *Alcmena* wondered at the length of the Night (15): It seem'd therefore long to her; this makes for her Honour. And indeed she was a very virtuous Woman (16), and would not have merited, though she had lost her Sight, the Satire of the following Distich.

(12) Amor. lib. 1. Eleg. 13. Propert. lib. 2. Eleg. 22. Capella, lib. 2. c. 39.
(13) Clem. Alexandr. in Protrept. pag. 20. Arnobius, lib. 4. pag. 145. *vide Verba are these*, Quis illum in Alcmena novem noctibus fecit pervigilem continuit?
(14) Diodor. Sicul. lib. 5. cap. 2.
(15) Hygin. cap. 29.
(16) *See Remark [A]*.

Cum longas noctes Moreta ab amore rogaret,
Favit amor votis, perpetuasque dedit.

Long Nights Moreta (17) *ask'd, in love to burn;
Love heard her Wish, and gave her Night eterne.*

Sosia, Amphitryon's Valet, made an Observation worthy of him, when he perceived that the Night was longer than it used to be; he wish'd those Gallants Joy, who had paid dear for their Bargains.

(17) *The Camera de* Moret, Henry the Great's Mistress.

Ubi sunt isti scortatores qui soli inviti cubant?
Hæc nox scita'st exercendo scorto conducto male (18).

Where are those intriguing Sparks, who, against their Will, lie alone? This Night is calculated for the full Enjoyment of a dear-bought Womb.

(18) Amphitr. Act. 1. scen. 1. ver. 130.

[D] *That she was yet a Maid*.] *Apollodorus* relates, That *Electryon*, going to revenge the Death of his Sons, put his Kingdom, and his Daughter *Alcmena* into the Hands of *Amphitryon*, after having made him swear, that he would abstain from *Alcmena*, till his Return (19). *Amphitryon*, having inadvertently killed him, a little while after, was obliged to seek a Retreat. He went with *Alcmena* into *Bæotia*, and as she declared that she would marry Him, who should revenge the Death of her Brothers, he engaged in pursuit of this Revenge, and, associating himself with others, made War with the *Teleboes*, who had killed *Alcmena*'s Brothers (20). Being returned to *Thebes* victorious, and triumphant, he understood that ANOTHER HIMSELF had enjoy'd the Lady. It is plain that he had not the first Favour; doubtless *Alcmena* had put off the Ceremony of the Wedding, or at least the Consummation of her Marriage, till *Amphitryon*

(19) Apollodor. Biblioth. lib. 2. pag. 99.
(20) Id. ib. pag. 102.

ALCMENA. 207

which succeeded the Long Night, which That God had passed with *Alcmena*. He was not so well received by his Wife, as he might have expected, after Absence; and he soon discovered the Reason of it, by the account, which She gave him of the Transactions of the preceeding Night. They, who shall put themselves in his Place, may tell us what he thought of the Matter. He immediately had recourse to the Soothsayer, and learnt from *Tiresias*, that *Jupiter*, in the Form of *Amphitryon*, had enjoyed *Alcmena*. He must bear it, as well as he could; and it does not appear, that his Chagrin continued very long; for, the Night following, he got his Wife with Child, who was already so by a God (a). *Juno*, out of her usual Jealousy, prevented the Delivery of this Lady, as long as she could; it was only the Dexterity of a Servant Maid, which eluded the Ill Intentions of *Lucina* [E], who hindered *Alcmena* from being

(a) Hygin. c. 29. says, That he lay no more with her, and speaks only of Hercules. See Apollod. Biblioth. lib. 2. pag. 97.

---

phitryon had conquered the *Teleboes*. *Jupiter*, knowing that *Amphitryon* was upon his Return, and that there was no other time to crop this Flower of Virginity, but whilst *Amphitryon* was on his Journey, prevented him, and did his Business before the Husband's Arrival. *Apollodorus* adds, That *Amphitryon*, having enjoy'd *Alcmena*, got her with Child; this Child was a Night younger than *Hercules*. Ἀλκμήνη ᾗ δύο ἐγήνατο παῖδας. Διὶ μὲν Ἡρακλέα μιᾷ νυκτὶ πρεσβύτερον, Ἀμφιτρύωνι Ἰφικλέα (21). *Alcmena vero duos peperit filios: Jovi quidem Herculem una nocte grandiorem, atque Amphitryoni Iphiclem.* This is a farther Confirmation of what I am to prove. The Scholiast upon *Homer* is more precise than *Apollodorus*: He says plainly, That the Marriage was not consummated 'till after the return of *Amphitryon* (22). In *Plautus's* Comedy Matters go otherwise. *Amphitryon* leaves his Wife with Child, when he goes to the War (23). A great Temptation indeed to *Jupiter*! It would be much worse, if *Plautus* had observed the Unity of Time, as Mademoiselle *le Fevre* will have it. In that Case, it must be said, That *Jupiter* interrupted the whole course of Nature, by stopping the Sun, to divert himself the longer with a Woman big with two Children, and so near her time, that, if he had stay'd a little longer, the Midwife would have been obliged to say to him, *give me your Place*. This is an unlucky Alternative for *Plautus*. For either the Time of his Comedy must be several Months; or he must suppose a Woman, ready to be delivered of Twins, a very tempting Morsel to the greatest of all Monarchs; and this, with supposing at the same time, that the King of Gods and Men had already begot one of these Twins. Take notice that the Poet does not feign, that *Jupiter* disguised himself in the Shape of *Amphitryon*, to come like a good Husband to the Assistance of *Alcmena*, in her Labour; it was the Visit of a very amorous Spark. See how *Mercury* expresses himself in the Prologue,

Et meus Pater nunc intus hic cum illa cubat,
Et hæc ob eam rem nox est facta longior,
Dum ille qua cum volt voluptatem capit.

My Father, within there, is now in Bed with her; and it is upon this Account that the Night is longer than usual, to give him an Opportunity of satisfying his Appetite.

As for these Words of *Sosia*,

Hæc nox scita est exercendo scorto malè conductâ.

This Night is calculated for the full Enjoyment of a dear-bought Wench.

He illustrates them thus:

Meus Pater nunc pro hujus verbis rectè & sapienter facit
Qui complexus cum Alcumena cubat amans animo obsequens (24).

—— *My Father in this Business acts a very wise Part; as he loves the Sport, he has pitched upon Alcmena for a Bedfellow.*

He congratulates himself for having removed all Interruptions to *Jupiter's* Joy, and prepares to continue his good Offices, 'till the Gallant be satisfied.

Bene & prosperè hoc hodie operis procesfit mihi;
Amovi à foribus maximam molestiam.

(21) Id. Ib. pag. 103.

(22) Schol. Homeri in Iliad. ξ. ver. 323.

(23)

(24) Gravidam ego illam hic reliqui cum abeo. Act. 2. Scen. 2. ver. 34.
Et cum te gravidam, cum te pulcrè plenam adspicio, gaudeo. Ibid. ver. 52.
Mercury affirms the same thing in the Prologue.

(24) Plauti Amphytr. Act. 1. Sc. 1. ver. 133.

Patri ut liceret tuto illam amplexarier.

Erroris ambo ego illos & dementiæ
Complebo, atque omnem Amphitruonis familiam
Adeo, usque satietatem dum capiet Pater
Illius quam amat (25).

Thus far Success attends upon my Counsels: I have removed the greatest Obstacle from the Door, that my Father may take his swing of Pleasure in full Security.
—— *I will perplex them both with Mistakes, and fill them with Madness; and not only the Master and Man, but Amphitryon's whole Family's 'till my Father is cloy'd with the Enjoyment of his Mistress.*

[E] *The Dexterity of a Servant Maid, which eluded the ill Intentions of* Lucina (26).] I follow *Ovid's* Narrative. *Alcmena* had been seven Days in Labour, with horrible Pains. *Galanthis*, one of her Women, came in, and went out, and, being apprehensive of some Charm, upon seeing a Woman setting at the Door, and muttering to herself, with her Hands joined on her Knees, she told her that *Alcmena* was delivered. *Lucina* (for it was she, who was fitting in that Posture) no sooner heard these Words, but she disjoined her Hands, and rose up, which caused *Alcmena* to be delivered.

—— subsedit in illâ
Ante fores arâ, dextroque à poplite lævum
Pressa genu, digitis inter se pectine junctis,
Sustinuit partus, tacitâ quoque carmina voce
Dixit, & inceptos tenuerunt carmina partus.

Una ministrarum, media de plebe, Galanthis
Flava comas, aderat, faciendis strenua jussis,
Officiis dilecta suis. Ea sensit iniqua
Nescio quid Junone geri, dumque exit & intrat
Sæpe fores, Divam residentem vidit in arâ,
Brachiaque in genibus digitis connexa tenentem;
Et, quæcunque es, ait, dominæ gratare; levata est
Argolis Alcmene, potiturque puerpera voto.
Exsiluit, junctasque manus patefacta remisit
Diva potens uteri: vinclis levor ipsa remissis (27).

*She hears the groaning Anguish of my Fits,
And on the Altar at my Door she sits.
O'er her left Knee her crossing Leg she cast,
Then knits her Fingers close, and wrings them fast.
This stay'd the Birth; in muttering Verse she pray'd.
The muttering Verse th' unfinish'd Birth delay'd.
— — — — — — — — — — — — — —
Among the Theban Dames Galanthis stands,
Strong limb'd, red hair'd, and just to my Commands.
She first perceiv'd, that all thefe racking Woes
From the persisting Hate of Juno rose.
As here and there she pass'd, by chance she sees
The seated Goddess; on her close-press'd Knees
Her fast-knit Hands she leans; with chearful Voice
Galanthis cries, whoe'er thou art, rejoice,
Congratulate the Dame, she lies at Rest,
At length the Gods Alcmena's Womb have blest.
Swift from her Seat the startled Goddess springs,
No more conceal'd, her Hands abroad she flings;
The Charm unloos'd, the Birth my Pangs reliev'd;
Galanthis' Laughter vex'd the Pow'r deceiv'd.*

GAY.

(25) Ibid. Act. 1. Sc. 2. v. 1, 2, 3, 5, &c.

(26) She was the Goddess of Childbirth.

(27) Ovid. Metamorph. lib. 9. ver. 298, &c.

Pausanias,

being delivered. She was brought to bed of Two Boys; He, of whom *Jupiter* was Father, was called *Hercules*; and He, who was the Son of *Amphitryon*, was named *Iphiclus* (*b*). It is said, That she married *Rhadamantbus*, after the Death of *Amphitryon*, and that her Tomb was to be seen adjoining to That of *Rhadamantbus*, near *Haliartus*, in *Bæotia* (*c*). Others say, That she was buried at *Megara*, and that the Oracle ordered it so, when *Hercules*'s Children consulted it, on a Dispute between them, some being willing that she should be carried to *Argos*, and others maintaining that she ought to be brought to *Thebes* (*d*). She died on the Frontiers of *Megara*, as she was returning from *Argos* to *Thebes* (*e*). *Hercules* was already dead; she survived him for her great Grief; but on the other hand she had the Satisfaction of holding in her hands the Head of *Hercules*'s Persecutor, and of tearing out his Eyes [*F*]. It is related, that her Corps disappeared in the Ceremony of the Funeral, and that a Stone was found in her Bed (*f*). Which made *Pausanias* say, That she was metamorphosed into a Stone (*g*). *Antoninus Liberalis* tells us, that, whilst the *Heraclidæ* were preparing the Funeral Rites of *Alcmena*, *Jupiter* ordered *Mercury* to steal her away, and to transport her to the *Fortunate Islands*, in order to marry her to *Rhadamantbus*. This Order was obey'd; and a Stone was placed in her Coffin. They who carried it, finding it very heavy, opened it, and, instead of a dead Body, found a Stone, which they deposited in the sacred Grove, where was afterwards a Chapel of *Alcmena*, at *Thebes* (*h*). *Diodorus Siculus* remarks only, That she disappear'd, and that the *Thebans* paid her Divine Honours (*i*). They continued to shew her Chamber in *Pausanias*'s Time (*k*). Her Altar was seen at *Athens* at the same time (*l*). The Present, which she received from *Jupiter*, for the long Night's Lodging he had with her, was shewed many Ages after at *Lacedemon*, as a singular Curiosity (*m*). Very surprizing things have been related concerning her Tomb [*G*]. Consult the Article AMPHITRYON.

Pausanias does not relate the Story with the same Circumstances. He says, That the Figures of certain Women (28) were seen at *Thebes*, whom *Juno* had sent to prevent *Alcmena*'s Delivery. The Daughter of *Tiresias* (29) deceived them, by crying out that *Alcmena* was delivered (30). In *Pliny*'s Time they looked upon the Posture I have mentioned as a kind of Witchcraft. "Assidere gravidis, vel cum remedium alicui adhibetur, digitis pectinatim inter se implexis, veneficium est: idque compertum tradunt *Alcmena Herculem pariente*. Pejus, si circa unum ambove genua: item poplites alternis genibus imponi (31). — *To sit by Women with Child, or when a Medicine is administred to any one, with one's Fingers joined together in the Fashion of a Comb, is Witchcraft; and this was experienced, when Alcmena was in Labour of Hercules. The Charm is stronger, if this be done upon one or both Knees; as also if the Posture be cross-legged.*" We shall see in another Place the Licence, which *Plautus* took, in supposing that *Alcmena* was delivered without Pain (32). [*Rabelais*, B. 3. *cap*. 48. has very properly rendered the Text of *Ov.d* and *Pliny*. If Mr *BAYLE* had known this, he would doubtless have produced it here. REM. CRIT.]

[*F*] *The Satisfaction of holding in her Hands the Head of Hercules's Persecutor, and of tearing out his Eyes*] *Apollodorus* informs us, that the Sons of this Hero found a good Asylum in *Athens* against *Eurystheus*; and that *Hyllus*, one of them, having killed him, cut off his Head, and gave it to *Alcmena*, who dug out the Eyes with a Weaver's Shuttle: Καὶ ἢ μὲν κεφαλὴν Ἀλκμήνῃ δίδωσιν, ἣ ἡ κερκίσι τοὺς ὀφθαλμοὺς ἐξώρυξεν αὐτῷ (33). Ejusque caput amputatum Alcmenæ dedit. Hæc autem illi textoriis radiis oculos effodit.

[*G*] *Very surprizing things — concerning her Tomb.*] *Agesilaus*, King of *Sparta*, intending to remove the Relicks of *Alcmena* to *Lacedemon*, sent some People to *Haliartus*, who opened her Monument. They found in it two earthen Vessels, a Bracelet of Brass, and a copper Table, on which certain Letters were engraven, which no one understood. As they resembled the *Egyptian* manner of Writing, *Agesilaus* caused them to be transcribed, and sent the Copy to the King of *Egypt*, desiring him to enquire of his Priests the Purport of them (34). *Plutarch* adds, that *Agetoridas*, who was deputed for this Purpose by *Agesilaus*, went to *Memphis*, where the Prophet *Chonuphis* decyphered the Inscription. It contained a Precept addressed to the *Greeks*, to live in Peace, to honour the Muses, and to compose their Differences according to the Rules of Equity. The Letters of the Inscription were like the writing, which *Hercules* learnt in the Reign of King *Proteus*. The most remarkable Particular is, that the Inhabitants of *Haliartus*, having had a very bad Harvest, and great Inundations, believed that the e Evils proceeded from having permitted the Removal of *Alcmena*'s Tomb. We read the same Reflexions in divers Legends, concerning the dismembring or translating of the Bodies of Saints.

ALCMÆON. Many Persons have been called by this Name. The last Perpetual *Archon* of *Athens* was called ALCMÆON. After him other *Archons* were created, whose Office continued but ten Years. This Alteration happen'd in the VIth Olympiad, a little before *Romulus* built the City of *Rome* (*a*). *Herodotus* speaks of an ALCMÆON, who lived at *Athens* in *Cræsus*'s Time, and who performed many good Offices to the Ambassadors, whom That King sent to *Delphi* (*b*). *Cræsus*, having heard of it, invited him to his Court, and gave him leave to take as much Gold out of his Treasury as he could carry. We read, in *Herodotus*, the Expedient, which ALCMÆON made use of to carry a great Weight of it. *Cræsus* made him many other Presents, insomuch that he put him in a Condition of adding a very great Lustre to his Family at *Athens*, where it became one of the most considerable. The ALCMÆONIDÆ (so they called ALCMÆON's Posterity) distinguish'd themselves on several Occasions, and chiefly by strenuously opposing the Tyranny, which *Pisistratus* and his Sons endeavoured in vain to perpetuate there. I believe this ALCMÆON was the same, who was General of the *Athenians*, in the War, which was undertaken for the Protection of the Temple of *Delphi*, at the Sollicitation of *Solon* (*c*). I find an ALCMÆON in *Plutarch*, who was a great Enemy of *Themistocles* (*d*). There are many Faults in *Moreri*'s Dictionary relating to the Word

ALCMÆON.

ALCMÆON [*A*]. I am going to give separate Articles of two Persons who bore this Name.

[*A*] *There are many Faults in Moreri's Dictionary relating to the Word Alcmæon.*] I. It is not true, that *Alcmæon*, the last perpetual *Archon*, lived about the Year 301, or 300, of *Rome*. *Eusebius*, who is cited for it, places the end of the perpetual *Archons* before the Foundation of *Rome*. II. Besides, the Year. 301 of *Rome* does not answer to the Year of the World 3300, but to the Year 3530, or thereabouts, according to *Petavius*; or the Year 3498, according to *Sethus Calvisius*. III. *Alcmæon*, the perpetual *Archon*, is not the same *Alcmæon*, who received so many Presents from *Crœsus* (1). He preceded the beginning of That King's Reign about One hundred and ninety Years. IV. The last Year of That Reign answers to the 206th Year of *Rome*. V. *Herodotus*, who is cited, does not say, that *Alcmæon* succeeded his Father *Megacles* in the Office of Annual *Archon*; nor that the Ambassadors of *Crœsus* asked *Alcmæon*, whether he would accompany their Master to *Delphi*; nor that, after he had promised them to do it, That King presented him with as much Gold as he could carry; nor that, perceiving that *Alcmæon* had loaded himself with Gold beyond his Strength, he caused him to be carried with the Burthen to his House, because he could not walk under it. I cannot imagine for what Reason *Herodotus* is quoted, when his Narrative is so strangely falsified. VI. *Alcmæon*, the Son of *Amphiaraus*, did not marry *Callirhoe*, after the Death of *Alphesibœa* his first Wife; the latter was yet living at the time of the second Marriage.

Amphilochi frater ne Phegida semper amaret,
Callirhoe fecit parte recepta tori (2).

Lest *Phegeus'* Daughter shou'd engross his Heart,
Callirhoë in his Bed obtained a Part.

VII. *Plutarch* does not say, that the Fable of *Alcmæon* signifies that he killed his Mother, that is to say, his Part, in order to go and live in the Country, which is expressed by the River his Father-in-law. One would think, that *Moreri* read in *Plutarch*, that *Alcmæon* castrated himself; which seems to be the Natural Sense of these Words, *he killed his Mother, that is to say, his Part.* I am willing to believe, that instead of *Partie* (Part), the Author gave it *Patrie* (Native Country); but this does not justify him: for *Plutarch* does not say that *Alcmæon* killed his Native Country, or that he abused it: On the contrary he tells us, that *Alcmæon*, shunning Magistracies, Seditions, Factions, and Calumnies, made choice of a small Retreat, in order to live quietly, and that thus he fled from the Furies (3). VIII. The Chronicle of *Eusebius* is cited still more improperly, to explain what the Fable says of *Alcmæon*; for of what use is it towards explaining this Fable, to say,

That the City of *Thebes* was plundered, that *Tiresias* was taken Prisoner, and that his Daughter *Manto* was consecrated to the Service of *Apollo*? IX. It is not true, that *Eusebius* relates these Things, as falling out in the One hundred and eighty seventh Year of *Abraham*. He says nothing of the sacking of *Thebes*; he speaks in general of the Seven Captains, who attacked this City, and of their Posterity, which renewed the War; I say, he speaks of the first of these two Expeditions under the Year 784, and of the last under the Year 823. X. Neither *Eusebius*, nor any other Historian, observe that *Alcmæon's* Expedition against *Thebes* was unsuccessful (4); for it was at that Time that the *Epigones* plundered the City, &c. XI. They did not carry away the poor Blind *Tiresias*: He had fled, with the other *Thebans*, before the Enemy entered the City. XII. They did not collect a great Booty, to revenge the Disgrace of their Fathers. It ought to have been said, that, to revenge the Disgrace of their Fathers, they undertook a second Expedition. XIII. It is not true, that the Philosopher *Alcmæon* made it appear, that the Moon has a peculiar Property, which never ends: he supposed the Eternity of this Planet: It can only be a Supposition; and it is a more unpardonable Negligence in a Priest, than any other Author, to say, That it has been made appear, that the Moon is eternal, and that the Immortal Soul turns continually as the Sun. XIV. *Eusebius* does not speak of *Alcmæon* the Philosopher; doubtless he meant the Poet, when he said; *Alcmæon, clarus habetur, & Lesches Lesbius, qui parvam fecit Iliadem. ——— Alcmæon is reckoned famous, as is Lesches of Lesbos, who wrote the lesser Iliad.* XV. These Words of his are in the Thirty first *Olympiad*, and not in the Sixty ninth. XVI. It is equally false, that *Plutarch*, in the *Life of Solon*, cites an Historian, whose Name is *Alcmæon*. These are *Plutarch's* Words; they will serve to shew how hasty Transcribers fall into the greatest Mistakes. Ὀυ μέντοι σφόδρα ὁμολογοῦσι τοῦτο ἀπαδείξειν ὁ πόλεμον, ὡς λέγουσιν ἐνιοι, Ἑρμιππος ἐυάγθη τοῦ Σαμίου. Ὀυδ' ὁ Αισχίνης ὁ ῥητωρ τῶτ' εἰρηκεν, ὡς ἐν τοῖς τοῦ Δελφῶν ὑπομνήμασιν Αλκμαίων, ὁ Σόλων, Ἀθηναίων στρατηγὸς ἀναγορευθεις (5). He was not appointed General for this War, as *Hermippus* says *Euanthes* of *Samos* delivered. For the Orator *Aeschines* says no such thing, and, in the *Commentaries* of *Delphi*, *Alcmæon*, not *Solon*, is the *Athenian* General. *Lloyd* and *Hofman* found the pretended Historian *Alcmæon* in this Passage of *Plutarch*: *In Delphorum Commentariis*, say they; *citatur à Plutarcho in Solone*. It is plain that these *Commentaries of Delphi* are the Work, which they ascribe to *Alcmæon*, and which they pretend to have been cited by *Plutarch*. I wonder that *Vossius* fell into this Mistake: *Alcmæon*, says he (6), *in Delphorum commentariis*, Αλκμαίων ἐν τοῖς τ Δελφῶν ὑπομνήμασι, *citatur à Plutarcho in Solone*.

(1) *Tet it is so affirmed in the Dutch Edition of Moreri's Dictionary. The Supplement to the Dictionary says only, that this Alcmæon had been an annual Archon of Athens.*

(2) *Ovid. de Remed. Amor. vers. 455.*

(3) *Plut. de Exilio. pag. 602.*

(4) *Moreri, both in the Lyons Edition, 1688, and in that of Holland, expresses himself thus, After his unfortunate Expedition to Thebes.*

(5) *Plut. in Solone. pag. 84. A.*

(6) *Vossius de Histor. Græc. pag. 501.*

ALCMÆON, the Son of *Amphiaraus* and *Eriphyle*, the Sister of *Adrastus*, kill'd his Mother in obedience to his Father's Command. I am going to tell you the Reason of so strange a Command. *Amphiaraus* looked upon *Eriphyle* as the Cause of his Death. He had resolv'd not to go to the *Theban* War; for, being a great Soothsayer, he foresaw, that, if he went, he should die there. Moreover, he had promised with an Oath, That, if he should have any Dispute with *Adrastus*, he would refer the whole Matter to the Decision of his Wife. They differ'd about the Expedition to *Thebes*. *Adrastus* would have *Amphiaraus* engage in it; but *Amphiaraus* refused, and dissuaded others from it. *Eriphyle* decided the Affair, as *Adrastus* desir'd, being bribed by a fine Necklace (a), which *Polynices* offered her (b), and which she accepted, contrary to her Husband's Command not to take any thing of *Polynices*. Hence she has furnished many Topics and moral Thoughts to the Censors of the Fair Sex. It is well known, that *Amphiaraus*, flying, when the Army was routed, was swallowed up in an Abyss, which a Clap of Thunder opened under his Feet. He had ordered his Sons, before he march'd against *Thebes*, to kill *Eriphyle*, as soon as their Age would permit. All the Generals, except *Adrastus*, perished in this War. Ten Years after, their Sons resolv'd to revenge this Affront, and made choice of *Alcmæon* for their Generalissimo. *Eriphyle*, bribed again by Presents, sollicited them to this War. *Thersander*, the Son of *Polynices*, presented her with a Necklace (c), and a Robe (d). *Alcmæon*, tho' greatly inclin'd to kill his Mother before he accepted the Command of the Forces, yet marched against *Thebes*, without executing *Amphiaraus's* Order. This Expedition proved very fortunate: the *Thebans*, by the Advice

(a) *See concerning this Necklace the Remarks on the Article CALLIRHOE.*

(b) *Hyginus says, c. 73. That Adrastus gave her the Necklace, and that Eriphyle discover'd the Place where Amphiaraus hid himself.*

(c) *Diod. Sic. cautious is rather to be credited, who says, That Thersander gave his eye to the Poison, as Robe's, his could not give the Necklace, since Eriphyle had it already.*

(d) *Called in Greek πέπλος.*

of *Tiresias*, abandoned their City; it was plundered, and destroyed. *Alcmæon*, transported with new Rage, upon hearing, that *Eriphyle* had suffered herself to be corrupted by Presents against him also, no longer scrupled to kill her, after consulting the Oracle about it. Some maintain, that his Brother *Amphilochus* assisted him in this Parricide; but most Authors deny it. *Alcmæon*, haunted by the Furies for this Action, retired to *Psophis* in *Arcadia*, where he expiated his Crime, with the usual Forms, under the Protection of *Phegeus*, and married *Arsinoe* (*e*), the Daughter of the same *Phegeus*, to whom he made a Present of the Necklace and the Robe, which were given to *Eriphyle*. A great Famine arising, recourse was had to the Oracle, which ordered *Alcmæon* to fly to *Achelous*. He arrived there, after much rambling up and down, where he renewed the Ceremonies of the Expiation, and married *Callirhoë*, the Daughter of *Achelous*; and settled on a Corner of Land, which that River had form'd by throwing up a quantity of Sand [*A*]. *Callirhoë* declared she would not lie with him, if he did not make her a Present of *Eriphyle*'s Necklace and Robe. This obliged him to return to *Phegeus*, from whom he obtained the Necklace, having made him believe that the Oracle had declared to him, that the Furies would not cease to persecute him, 'till he had offered the Necklace to *Apollo*. *Phegeus* was afterwards informed, that *Alcmæon* designed this Present for *Callirhoë*; upon which he ordered his two Sons to pursue and kill him, which they did: And, because *Arsinoe* was offended at it, they carried her in a Box to *Tegea*, and charged her with the Murther. Some say that *Alcmæon*, during his Madness, diverted himself with the Prophetess *Manto*, the Daughter of *Tiresias*; and that he had two Children by her (*f*). See the Sequel to this in the Article of CALLIRHOE. *Alcmæon*'s Furies made a great Noise on the Stage of Ancient *Greece* (*g*), but we have none of those Tragedies left [*B*]. What has been said of his Tomb, deserves to be considered [*C*]. The *Oropians*, who were beforehand with all other Nations in placing *Amphiaraus* among the Gods, excluded *Alcmæon* from Divine Honours, which they conferred on his Father and his Brother (*h*), on account of his Parricide (*i*). It is observed, that a *Persian*, called *Orontes*, resembled him perfectly (*k*).

Some Historians say, that, after the second War of *Thebes*, *Alcmæon* went into *Ætolia*, being invited thither by *Diomedes*, and that he assisted him in conquering That Country, and *Acarnania*; and that being both summoned to accompany the Expedition of *Troy*, *Diomedes* went, but *Alcmæon* staid in *Acarnania*, and built a City there, which he called *Argos* of *Amphilochus*, in Honour of his Brother (*l*). Note, that he practised the Trade of Divination in *Acarnania* (*m*).

[*A*] *He settled on a Corner of Land, which that River had formed by throwing up a Quantity of Sand.*] It will not be amiss to illustrate *Apollodorus* by a Passage of *Pausanias*, which imports, that, after *Alcmæon* had killed his Mother, he fled from *Argos* to *Psophis*, where he married *Alphesibœa* the Daughter of *Phegeus* (1). His Marriage did not cure him of his Phrensy; so that he had recourse to the Oracle, which ordered him to retire to a new Land, which was made since the Murther of *Eriphyle*. He was assured that the Furies would not pursue him thither. Meeting, then, with a Piece of Land, thrown up by the Waters, at the Entrance of the River *Achelous*, he settled there, and married *Callirhoe*.

[*B*] *We have none of those Tragedies left.*] I question not but the two Verses, mentioned by *Plutarch*, in one of his Books, are taken out of some of those Pieces. The common-place Topic, which *Plutarch* there touches upon, is of greater Importance than is generally believed to be. It relates to a general Fault, to wit, of those who reproach their Neighbours with a Vice, which they themselves are guilty of; of which is less than their own. *Alcmæon* reproaches *Adrastus* for being the Brother of a Woman, who had killed her Husband: *Adrastus* answers, *And you* have killed your own Mother. He, who is very guilty himself, must not set up for a Cato, and a Censor.

Οὐκοῦν μηδὲ μοιχὸν λοιδοροῦμεν, αὐτὸς ὢν παράδαμενις. Μηδ' ἀσωτον αὐτὸς ὢν ἀνειλάθερος,
Ἀνδροκτόνῳ γυναικὸς ὀνειδισας ἔρως;
Τὸν Ἀδρηστον ὁ Ἀλκμαίων. Τί δ' ἐκεῖνο; ὁ σὸν
ἀλλότριον ἀλλὰ ἰδιον ἐαυτοῦ στιγιῶ ὄνειδος.
Σὺ δ' αὐτόχειρ γε μητρὸς ἢ σ' ἐγείνατο (2).

Non itaque adulterium objice altari, ipse insano puerorum amore flagrans, neque prodigalitatem sordidus ipse. Alcmæon Adrastum hoc maledicto incessit,

Tibi quæ maritum ferro interfecit est soror.

Quid Adrastus? Non alienum sed proprium ei reponit opprobrium,

Matrem necasti tu manu tua tuam.

[*C*] *What has been said of his Tomb, deserves to be considered.*] This Tomb was at *Psophis* in *Arcadia*; it was but indifferently adorned; but it was surrounded with such high Cypresses, that they covered with their Shade the Hill, which commanded the City. They were never cut, because it was thought they were consecrated to *Alcmæon*: and they were called *the Virgins* (3).

ALCMÆON, born at *Crotona*, was a Disciple of *Pythagoras*. It is thought he was the first who wrote upon *Physics* (*a*). He held very heterodox Opinions; as, that the Moon was eternal, and that the Soul always turned round like the Sun. This is what *Laertius* says of him. *Cicero* represents this Philosopher's System better; for how careless it is, among all the Planets, to which *Alcmæon* attributed an eternal Nature, to pitch upon That, whose Alterations are the most sensible, I mean the Moon! *Laertius* should therefore have said, as *Cicero* did (*b*), that This Philosopher ascribed a Divine Nature to all the Celestial Bodies, and even to our Souls. But, as it is the Fate of false Systems to be incoherent, we find that our *Alcmæon* argued very inconsequentially, when he made so great a Distinction between the Knowledge of the Gods, and that of Men. He saith that the Gods knew things evidently, and Men only conjecturally. This may be said by those who acknowledge One only True God; but they who take the Planets, and human Souls, for so many Gods, become ridiculous

ALCMÆON. ALDRINGER.

culous when they pretend, that Human and Divine Knowledge do essentially differ. It is not true that *Alcmæon* died of a pedicular Distemper [*A*].

[*A*] *It is not true that he died of a pedicular Distemper.*] *Antigonus Caryſtius* mistook the one for the other, when he said (1) that *Alcmæon* the Philosopher, had this Disease; he took *Alcmæon*, the Disciple of *Pythagoras*, for *Alcmæon* the Poet. *Charles Stephens* does not only say, that the Philosopher *Alcmæon* died of a pedicular Disease, but also that he was the first, who died of it; for which he alledges *Ælian*. Both these Assertions are false; *Ælian* is not speaking of our *Alcmæon*; but observes several things concerning *Alcman* the Poet: Having said, that the Philosopher *Pherecydes* died of the Distemper here in Question (2), he would doubtless have given him the Precedence over *Alcmæon*, if he had mentioned the latter in relation to this kind of Disease. *Charles Stephens*'s Errors are likewise to be met with in Father *Lescaloplier* (3).

ALDRINGER, a famous General, in the Reign of the Emperor *Ferdinand* the Second, raised himself solely by his Merit. He was of the Country of *Luxenburgh*, and of very obscure Birth [*A*]. In his younger Days he engaged in the Service of some Gentlemen, who went into *France*; he apply'd himself with them to Study, and made a great Progress in it. Being come into *Italy*, he was made Chancellor to Count *Madrucci*. He went afterwards to *Trent*, where he had an honourable Employment in the Chancery; but the Jealousy of his Colleagues, and their Conduct, so greatly disgusted him, that he left his Post, and, enrag'd at Fortune, determined to follow the Profession of the first Man he should meet with in his Way. He took the Way of *Inspruck*, and, meeting a Soldier near the Bridge, who was returning into *Italy*, he entered himself a private Soldier. He became a Sergeant soon after; and, as he was Master of his Pen, he was employ'd to draw up all the Accounts of the Company, and to write the Answers, which the Captain was to give. He gave his Captain such an Insight into Affairs, as opened to him the Way to an higher Employment. This Promotion occasioned the Lieutenant of the Company to be made Captain, and *Aldringer* to be advanced to the Lieutenant's Place. He defended himself so well, with but fifty Men, in a disadvantageous Post, that he maintained it, notwithstanding all the Attacks of the Enemy. From that time the Reputation of his Courage spread as far as that of his Capacity: Several Colonels offered him a Company; the Nephew of the Archbishop of *Saltzburg* was one of them. On account of his Youth, he had occasion for such a Man in his Regiment; he gained him, and acquired so much Honour, by *Aldringer*'s good Counsels, that, to testify his Acknowledgment, he made him his Sergeant-Major. *Aldringer* was afterwards Lieutenant-Colonel, and then Colonel; and made it so fully appear, that he understood his Profession thoroughly, that he was thought worthy to command in Chief, in the Expedition to *Mantua* (*a*). He joined the broken Remains of the Battle of *Leipsic* (*b*), very opportunely, with the Troops which he brought from *Italy*; and perhaps, if Count *Tilly* had delay'd giving Battle till the Arrival of these Troops, as he was advised to do, the Enemy would not have been so fatal to the Imperialists. *Aldringer* left *Tilly*, some time after, to retire into *Bohemia*, on account of the Jealousies, which the ill State of Affairs sowed between the *Imperialists* and the *Bavarians* (*c*); but this Disunion did not continue long. He was, in the Month of *March* 1632, with *Tilly* on the Banks of the *Leck*, to dispute the Passage of that River with the King of *Sweden*. He was at that time Great Master of the Artillery (*d*). The Wound, he received in his Head, contributed much to the Advantage the Enemy had in passing the River; but did not hinder him from serving the same Campaign; he joined Count *Wallestein* in *Bohemia*, notwithstanding the Efforts of the Enemy to hinder this Junction: he was obliged to return in haste into *Bavaria*, to oppose General *Horn*'s Troops. The Success was various, on both sides, in those Parts, all the Remainder of that Year, and the beginning of the following. The most glorious Exploit of *Aldringer*, during that time, was his contributing, in 1633, to the raising the Siege of the City of *Constance*. He march'd afterwards to join the Duke of *Feria*, who had brought some *Spanish* Troops from *Italy*. It has been thought, that *Wallestein* had given *Aldringer* private Orders to frustrate the Duke's Designs [*B*]; and

[*A*] *Of very obscure Birth.*] *Puffendorf* says, Hamilt *apud Luxemburgicos loco ortus*; and adds (1), that he was, at first, Footman to certain *French* Barons, and afterwards a Secretary. According to another Historian, his Condition was not so mean; he makes him first study, then go to the War, then serve as a Secretary, and afterwards take up Arms again. "Lauemburgi tenui sed honesto loco ortus, primam ætatem literis dedit (2). —— Born at *Luxemburg*, "of private, but reputable, Parents; he spent the first part of his Life in Study." He makes him naturally abstemious, *ingenio promptus æque acri, & adversus vini oblectamenta* (3). which was a very bad, and very prejudicial, Quality, in a Soldier, in *Germany*.

[*B*] *It has been thought, that Wallestein had given Aldringer private Orders to frustrate the Duke's Designs.*] The *Historian of Bavaria*, whom I have cited, says (4), "That the *Swedes* desired only to come to a general Engagement, though they were not so advantageously posted, as the Catholics. The Duke of *Feria*, continues he, seeing a fair Opportunity, endeavoured in vain to oblige *Aldringer* to engage with the Enemy, and could never obtain any thing from a Man, who was under the Correction of *Wallestein*: and the *Swedes* retiring as it were in Triumph, about the end of *October*, the ill Conduct of *Aldringer*, which cost the Catholic Union dear, displeas'd the Duke of *Feria* so much, that he died soon after of Grief." This Historian had said, in the foregoing Page, that "*Aldringer*, being in the Secret of *Wallestein*, seldom acted without his Orders; and that a Piece was published, at that time, which imported, that, whilst *Wallestein* wrote to the Emperor, that he was about to send *Aldringer* to the Duke of *Bavaria*, to get rid of him entirely, he gave him private Orders to serve him only

ALDRINGER. ALDROVANDUS.

and that this was the true Reason, and the secret Motive, why *Aldringer* would never consent to give Battle. However we must not imagine, that he was privy to all the Plots of *Wallestein*; he had only a certain Complaisance for him, which, without ruining the Affairs of their common Master, very much advanced the private Interests of That General. The like Intelligences are practised in most Armies. He was kill'd in the Year 1634, at *Landshut* a Town of *Bavaria*, and it was never known, whether it was by his own Soldiers, or by the *Swedes*. He had been created a Count (*e*). He was a Man of excellent Qualities [C]; 'tis pity they were attended with an excessive Avarice and Cruelty [D]. Such is commonly the Fate of Man; He resembles those Lands, which promiscuously produce both good and bad Herbs.

" only by acting upon the defensive with the little
" Reinforcement, which he commanded: Which *Al-*
" *dringer* not having punctually performed, *Galas*
" let him know from *Wallestein*, that he would never
" pardon him this Disobedience."

[C.] *He was a Man of excellent Qualities.*] He had a very quick and penetrating Wit, great Skill, a refined Understanding, and great Courage; he distinguished himself in Councils of War by the Force of his Reasons, and by the Probability of his Conjectures; he was besides a good Writer; he spoke several Languages, and had extracted the Quintessence of the Maxims of several Countries. The Politics of an Italianiz'd Spaniard did not out-do his; " Le da
" lui praticate varie nationi, l' osservate diverse mas-
" sime, è gli investigati genii è inclinationi di molti
" popoli lo resero cosi accorto nelle attioni, che alcuno
" Spagnuolo Italianato non lo avanzava (5)"

[D.] *Attended with an excessive Avarice and Cruelty.*] He was void of Compassion, and exacted Contributions with the utmost Rigour; he had no regard to the necessities of the Soldiers, so that he was neither belov'd by the People, nor by the Army. He made a good hand of it at the sacking of *Mantua*; and no Officer in the Imperial Army gained so large a share of Plunder as he (6). It was believed that his own Soldiers slew him on the Bridge of *Landshut*, the Opportunity of doing it without discovery being favourable. " Fu colpito è fatto cader morto, non senza sus-
" petto cio divenisse dalla parte de' suoi per vendetta
" d' alcune ingiurie fatte loro, essendo egli per la sua
" severita piu temuto che amato della militia (7)."

ALDROVANDUS (*a*) (ULYSSES) Professor of Philosophy, and Physic, at *Bologne*, his Native Country, was one of the most inquisitive Men in the World with respect to Natural History. His Cares, his Labours, and his Expences, on that account, are incredible. He travelled into the remotest Countries, without any other Motive, than that of enquiring into the Productions of Nature there. Minerals, Metals, Plants, and Animals, were the Objects of his Enquiries, and of his Curiosity: But he applied himself chiefly to the Knowledge of Birds; and, in order to have very exact and lively Representations of them, he employed the most excellent Artists of *Europe* [A], for above thirty Years, at his own Expence. These Expences ruin'd him; he found himself at last reduced to the utmost Necessity; and it is said that he died in the Hospital of *Bologne*, loaded with Years (*b*), and blind, in the Year 1605 (*c*). A remarkable Example both of Publick Ingratitude [B], and Private Curiosity. A thousand Reflexions might be made on this Adventure; but I leave them to others, and shall only content myself with this single Observation, That Antiquity does not afford any Example of so extensive and difficult an Undertaking, as This of our *Ulysses*, with regard to Natural History. *Pliny*, I confess, treats of a greater Variety of Subjects, but he only glances upon them, and says but little of each; whereas *Aldrovandus* collected every thing he could meet with. His Compilation comprehends several large Volumes in Folio (*d*); but the whole Honour of it must not be ascribed to him [C]; for there came out a Work, after his Death, in which it is thought

[A] *He employ'd the most excellent Artists of Europe.*] Let us see what *Aubertus Miræus* has collected on this Subject: " Pictori cuidam ea in arte
" unico triginta & amplius annos annuum aureorum
" ducentorum stipendium persolvit. Delineatores ce-
" leberrimos, *Laurentium Benninum* Florentinum,
" & *Cornelium Suintum* Francofurtensem ære suo con-
" duxit, nec non *Jacobi Ligotti*, Serenissimi *Etruriæ*
" ducis Pictoris eximii, opera in hac eadem provincia
" Florentiæ quandoque usus est, ut quo maximo fieri
" posset artificio aves eæ designarentur. Tandem Sculp-
" torem habuit insignem *Christophorum Coriolenum*
" Norimbergensem, atque ejus nepotem, qui eas
" adeo venustè adoeque eleganter exsculpserat, ut
" non in ligno sed in ære factæ videantur (1).
" ———— *He paid an annual Stipend of Two hundred*
" *Crowns, for more than thirty Years, to a Painter,*
" *the first of his Profession. He hired the most cele-*
" *brated Drawers, Laurentius Benninus the Floren-*
" *tine, and Cornelius Suintus of Francfort; besides*
" *which he employ'd, at Florence, the most serene*
" *Duke of Tuscany's famous Painter,* James Ligotius,
" *to delineate his Birds, in the most exquisite manner*
" *possible. At last he engag'd, as his Sculptors,* Chri-
" stopher Coriolanus, *of Nuremberg, and his Ne-*
" *phew, who carved them so beautifully, and elegant-*
" *ly, that they seemed not express'd in Wood, but in*
" *Brass.*"

[B] *A remarkable Example of publick Ingratitude.*] We must not imagine that no one helped this Naturalist in the Expences he was at. " The Senate of
" *Bologne,* Cardinal *Montalto, Francis Maria*, Duke
" of *Urbino,* and others of the chief Persons of *Italy,*
" contributed willingly to it, by supplying the Pain-
" ters, and Sculptors, which *Aldrovandus* had under
" him, with Money for their Maintenance ————
" After having dedicated twelve Books of his *Orni-*
" *thologia,* or History of Birds, to Pope *Clement* VIII,
" and some others to those, who had favour'd his
" Labours with their Benefactions, he bequeathed the
" the rest by Will to the magnificent Senate of *Bo-*
" *logne* ———— who assigned a considerable Sum of
" Money to *John Cornelius Uterverius,* born at *Delft,*
" in *Holland,* Professor in that University, and since
" to *Thomas Dempster,* a *Scotch* Gentleman, Professor
" likewise in the same Place, to collect, and cause
" these Books to be printed, which so highly deser-
" ved Publication (2)."

[C] *The whole Honour of it must not be ascribed to him.*] It appears, by the Catalogue of Books of Physic, that most of the Volumes of *Aldrovandus*'s Natural History, were printed after his Death (3). The *Ornithology* (4), in three Volumes in Folio, and the Seven Books of *Insects,* in one Volume of the same Size, are the only Works, which he published. The Volume of Serpents, the three Volumes of Fourfooted Beasts, the Volume of Fishes, that of Bloodless Animals. The History of Monsters, with the Supplement to that of Animals, in twelve Volumes, the Treatise of Metals, and the *Dendrology* (5), came out at different Times, under the Care of different Persons, after the Death of *Aldrovandus.* The Volume

ALDROVANDUS. ALEANDER.

thought he had no other share, than that of furnishing the Plan [D], or at most some imperfect Memoirs. I explain this in the Remarks. It is impossible, I think, that he could write such a prodigious Number of Books, as *Imperialis* gives us a Catalogue of (*e*); and it is not to be wondered at, that, being imploy'd in such different Researches, which require the greatest Attention, he often gave for Verse, what was most contrary to the Rules of Poetry (*f*); and that he was not much skilled in *Greek* (*g*). A Poet, who was once Pope, has given us a pretty Elogium of him [E].

[D] *There came out a Work after his Death, in which he had no other share, than that of furnishing the Plan.*] The Abbot *Gallois* has so well represented the Judgment, which ought to be formed of this great Work, that I believe I shall oblige the Reader more by producing the Passage at length, than by abridging it. His own Words, then, are as follows. "*Aldrovandus* is not the Author of this Book (8), nor of many others, which nevertheless were published in his Name. But it happened to the Collection of Natural History, of which these Books make a part, as to those great Rivers, which, during their whole Course, preserve the Name they had at their Spring, though, at last, the greatest part of the Waters they disembogue into the Sea, does not belong to them, but to other Rivers, which mix with them. As the six first Volumes of this great Work were *Aldrovandus*'s, though the others were composed by different Authors, after his Death, they are yet ascribed to him, either because they are a Continuation of his Design, or compiled out of his Memoirs, or wrote upon his Plan, or, perhaps, with a View of recommending the latter Volumes by so famous a Name (9)." They, who would be acquainted with the Plan of this Compilation, need only cast their Eyes on the following Words; the Abbot *Gallois* goes on thus: "There is scarce any thing written about these Trees but what has been collected in this Volume. For this Author is not satisfy'd with mentioning all that he had read in Naturalists concerning them; but he observes also, according to the Method of *Aldrovandus*, what the

"Historians have wrote, what the Legislators have "ordained, and what the Poets have feigned, about "them. Moreover he explains the different uses "these Trees are put to in Oeconomics, in Physic, "in Architecture, and in other Arts. Lastly, he "takes Notice of the moral Sayings, Proverbs, De-"vices, Enigmas, Hieroglyphics, and many other "things, which relate to his Subject (10)." He did not forget to consult Medals, and to borrow from them what might be useful to his Design (11).

[E] *A Poet, who was once a Pope, has given us a pretty Elogium of him.*] I mean *Maphæo Barberini*, or *Urban* VIII. He wrote the following Epigram, in Praise of *Aldrovandus*.

Multiplices rerum formas, quas pontus & æthet
Exhibet; & quidquid promit & abdit humus,
Mens haurit, spectant oculi, dum cuncta sagaci,
Aldrobande, tuus digerit arte liber.
Miratur proprios solers industria fœtus,
Quamque tulit moli se negat esse parem.
Obstupet ipsa simul rerum fœcunda creatrix,
Et cupit esse suum quod videt Artis opus (12).

*Curious retiring Nature to pursue,
And dress'd in all her Shapes the Pow'r to view ;
Whether in Earth's dark Womb conceal'd they lie,
Or on her Surface catch th' admiring Eye ;
Whether in Seas they swim, or cut the yielding Skies ;
Thro' ev'ry Form thy tow'ring Genius soars,
And all the vast Variety explores.
Great Nature's Comment, hence, these Volumes rose ;
Here Art, sagacious, all her Beauties shews.
See Industry, unconscious of her Worth,
Start at her Offspring, and deny the Birth ;
While Nature fain would claim the better Part,
And call that Her's, which is the Work of Art.*

Lorenzo Crasso has given us another Epigram with this.

ALEANDER (JEROM) Archbishop of *Brindisi*, and Cardinal, in the XVIth Century. *Alexander* VI. desired to have him in his Service [A], and intended him for Secretary to his Son. He changed his Mind soon after, and sent him to negotiate in *Hungary*; but *Aleander* happened to be sick at that time, and could not go from *Venice*, where he resided. *Lewis* XII. sent for him into *France*, in the Year 1508 [B], to be Professor of Philology in the University of *Paris*. *Aleander* was then Twenty eight

[A] *Alexander* VI. *desired to have him in his Service.*] I make use of this Expression, because the Author, whom I follow, reduces the thing to a meer Design, which was never put in Execution. According to his manner of Expression, *Aleander* was never in the Service of this wicked Pope. If so, all those Reflexions, which were made to the Disadvantage of *Aleander*, occasioned by the pernicious School of *Alexander* VI, and *Cæsar Borgia*, wherein it is pretended that he was educated, stand for nothing. I shall not pretend to decide the Matter, and leave the Reader the trouble of examining into the Affair. "*Aleandrum* (qui paulo ante *Cancellarius Leodiensis*, "& olim famosissimi *Cæsaris* illius *Borgia* seu *Ducis* "*Valentini Secretarius* fuerat, famulus hero dignus, "& pars aulæ *Romanæ* sub *Alexandro* VI.) pessime "describit *Lutherus* (1). —— *Luther* gives a very bad "Character of *Aleander, who a little before was "Chancellor of *Leige, and lately Secretary to the "most infamous Cæsar Borgia, or Duke Valentine; "a Servant worthy of his Master, and part of the "Roman Court, in the Pontificat of Alexander VI.*"

[B] *Lewis* XII. *sent for him into* France, *in the Year* 1508.] *Pallavicini* does not mention this Year;

but, because he says that *Aleander* was sent for to *Paris* at Twenty eight Years of Age, I did not think myself mistaken in setting it down; since, as a farther Confirmation, *Aleander*'s Epitaph imports, that he died in the Year 1542, aged Sixty two Years within thirteen Days (2). He was therefore born the thirteenth of *February*, 1480. For those, who remark the Day of his Death, place it on the first Day of *February* (3). I am surprized at the Negligence of the Authors of his Epitaph. They say that he was born in *Carniola*, in the Year 1479, and that he died at *Rome* in the Year 1542, being within thirteen days of Sixty two Years. This cannot be true, except by supposing, that the Year 1479 did not begin in *January*, and that the Year 1542 begun with it: Now it is ridiculous to suppose, in an Epitaph, a manner of reckoning time so destitute of Uniformity. I wonder that the Author of the *Nomenclator* did not perceive this false Supposition. He says one thing, which is inconsistent with Father *Pallavicini's*; to wit, That *Aleander* was but twenty Years of Age; when he taught in the University of *Paris*.

[C] *He*

214 ALEANDER

eight Years of Age. He gained a great Reputation in this Post. He entered into the Service of *Everard de la Mark* Bishop of *Liege*, who sent him to *Rome*, to facilitate his Promotion to the Purple, against the Opposition of *France*. *Leo* X. found him a Person of such good Parts, that he desired to retain him, to which the Bishop of *Liege* consented. *Aleander* was at first placed with the Cardinal *de Medicis* (*a*), whom he served as his Secretary: After the Death of *Accialoli*, he was made Library-Keeper of the *Vatican*. But the great Stage, on which he began to appear with considerable Lustre, was *Germany*, at the beginning of the Troubles, which the Reformation raised there. He was sent thither as the Pope's Nuncio, in the Year 1519. He acted the Part of an Ambassador, and a Doctor, as occasion required. He spoke three Hours successively in the Diet of *Worms*, against the Doctrine of *Luther* (*b*), but it is said, that he did not represent it faithfully (*c*). He could not prevent *Luther*'s being heard in that Diet, and refused to dispute with him; but he obtained, that his Books should be burnt, and his Person proscribed; and drew up the Edict which proscribed him (*d*). He was the Pope's Nuncio to *Francis* I, before *Pavia*, in the Year 1525, and fell into the Hands of certain Soldiers, who used him ill [C]. He was sent a second time into *Germany*, in the Year 1531, where he found a considerable Alteration of Affairs, if we may believe what we are told he wrote concerning them. The People, in the Protestant Towns, had in some measure laid aside their Animosity against the Pope; but, in the Catholic Towns, they shewed an extream Desire to shake off the Yoke of *Rome*, and to enrich themselves with the Treasures of the Church, as the Protestants had done. The Occasion of this Change in the latter was, that, having expected great Liberty, provided they could shake off the Pope's Yoke, they found, that the Yoke of the Secular Power, under which they lived, was not easier. *Aleander* did what he could to hinder *Charles* the Fifth from making a Truce with the Protestants of *Germany*, but without Success. He was created Cardinal by *Paul* III, and designed to preside in the Council with two other Legates (*e*). In the mean time he went into *Germany* as the Pope's Legate, in the Year 1538. This Commission continued a Year. His Death happening on the first Day of *February* 1542, hindered him from presiding in the Council. Some say that he died by the Ignorance of his Physician [D]. I have not mentioned all his Nunciatures. *Moreri* will supply what I have omitted. *Aleander* published some Books [E]. He understood *Hebrew* and *Greek* very well: and they attribute a surprizing Memory

[C] *He fell into the Hands of certain Soldiers, who used him ill.*] We meet with the following Account of this Matter in a Letter of *Jerom Negro* to *Mark Antony Michiels*, dated from *Rome* the twentieth of *March*, 1525 (4). "The Archbishop of "*Capua* has related to us a strange Adventure of "*Aleander*, Bishop Elect of *Brindisi*, and *Nuncio* of "his Holiness to the Most Christian King: namely "that, in the greatest Fury of the Fight, and "in such a Confusion as you may imagine, the "poor Gentleman running away, drest in a manner "becoming his Episcopal Dignity, fell into the Hands "of three *Spaniards*, who, not knowing him, forced "him with Threats and Bravadoes to set himself at "Three thousand Ducats Ransom, and led him in "this Equipage through the Camp, turning sometimes back, and commanding him sharply to fol- "low them. The frighted Bishop ran after them like "a Footman, without daring to discover that he "was an Apostolical *Nuncio*. But, being come to "*Pavia*, he was known by the Viceroy of *Naples*, "and by the Marquis of *Pescara*, who delivered "him with great Trouble and Difficulty from this "Prison and Servitude: Nevertheless, to acquit himself of his Oath, he was obliged to give each of "the aforesaid Soldiers Two hundred Ducats, to "satisfy them. I understand he is going to *Venice*; "he will tell you the Story of his Misfortunes himself.

[D] *Some say that he died by the Ignorance of his Physician* (5)] This does not well agree with his Epitaph, which testifies, that a languishing Disease contracted by the Toils of his Embassies, killed him; *Max diversis legationibus pro summis Pontificibus ad omnes fere Christianos Principes fideliter & diligenter perfunctis, & IDEO IN TABEM DELAPSO.* Perhaps a Passage of *Paul Jovius*, ill understood at first, and afterwards metamorphos'd, from hand to hand, into different Senses, occasioned what has been said of the Ignorance of *Aleander*'s Physician. However it be, we learn from *Paul Jovius*, that *Aleander* ruined his Health by taking too much care of it, and that he was a very bad Physician to himself, in making use of too many unnecessary Remedies. *Lætatus est ea purpura per annos quinque tres, perva-* *surus haud dubie ad exactam ætatem, nisi nimia tuendæ valetudinis solicitudine intempestivis medicamentis, sibi hercle insanus & infelix medicus, viscera corrupisset* (7).

[E] *Aleander published some Books.*] Mr *de la Roche-pozai* (8) gives me new Reason to complain of his Carelessness. He says, that *Aleander*, though very capable of treating on the most sublime Subjects, condescended to write on Human Learning, and to publish some small Pieces, the Subject whereof was very inconsiderable: *De re - - - literaria licet inferiori bene mereri non dedignatus est, exilis argumenti opusculis editis, quæ tamen autoris nomen & famam nec elevant neque imminutum eunt* (9). Every one, who reads this, will expect to find nothing but *Opuscula* in the Catalogue of *Aleander*'s Works, which follows these Words of the *Nomenclator*. Yet the next Sentence runs thus. "Scripsit vastum opus adversus sin- "gulos disciplinarum professores, in quos censuram "acerbius & felicem exercuit calamum: Tabulas in "Grammaticam Græcam, seu potius Grammaticam "ad literas Græcas; Dialogos duos festivissimos, "quorum alter Cicero relegatus inscribitur, alter ve- "ro Cicero revocatus; Carmina quædam illustrium "poetarum Italorum carminibus indita: Epistolas "multas, quarum quatuor habes inter epistolas Fede- "rici Nauseæ, & alias in quibus de rebus Ecclesiasti- "cis agit; Annotationes item quasdam in Bibliothe- "ca Cardinalis Sirleti. ——— *He wrote a very large* "*Work against Professors of all kinds: whom he cen-* "*sured with great Bitterness, and upon whom he ex-* "*ercised his happy Talent of Writing.* He wrote like- "wise *Tables of the Greek Grammar, or rather a* "*Grammar itself of the Greek Tongue: Two very di-* "*verting Dialogues, one intitled* Cicero banish'd, "*the other* Cicero recall'd (10): *The Works of some* "*famous Italian Poets inserted among his own Poetical* "*Compositions: Several Epistles; four of which you* "*have among the Epistles of* Frederic Nauseas; *and* "*others, in which he treats of Ecclesiastical Matters:* "*Lastly, Some Annotations on the Bibliotheca of Car-* "*dinal Sirlet.* If the Reader is offended at finding a large and immense Work, where he expected but a small Dissertation; his Disgust encreases, when he finds in a Catalogue of an Author's Works no Mark of Distinction between what is printed,

and

ALEANDER.

Memory to him [F]. I do not believe there was any reason to say, that the *Hebrew* was his Mother-Tongue, or, to express myself more plainly, that he was born a *Jew* [G]. There was more reason to accuse him of being passionate (f). He wrote his own

and what is not. This Defect reigns throughout the *Nomenclator*, the *Athenæum* of Oldoini, and several other Bibliographers. *Aleander*'s great Work, wherein he censured all sorts of Professors, was never printed. It is said, that he was finishing it, when he died. *Mentre andava componendo una vastissima Opera contra i Professori di tutte le Scienzes, fu assalito in Roma dalla morte* (11). This is what *Moreri* meant by these Words, *He died the first of February* 1542, *when he was about publishing a considerable Work*. Most Writers have copied *Paul Jovius* in this Point. "*Quum vastum opus vasta illa memoria adversus* "*singulos disciplinarum professores agitaret, Romæ* "*interiit* (12). — *He was preparing a prodigious* "*Work, by the help of that prodigious Memory of* "*His, against Professors of all kinds, when Death* "*seized him at Rome*." The Continuators of *Gesner* and *Konig* were acquainted only with the Tables of the Greek Grammar, among *Aleander*'s Works. *Draudius* did not know so much. The Catalogue of *Oxford* contains but a small Poem of this Author's.

[F] *Attribute a surprizing Memory to him.*] I look upon *Paul Jovius*'s Account of this Matter as a most Poetical Flight, tho' he gave it in Prose; which is, that *Aleander* remembered every thing that he read, and could repeat it a long time after, without mistaking Things, or Words. "*Detur hoc incomparabili* "*inusitatæ memoriæ felicitati, quæ in Hieronymo* "*Aleandro supra cujusque vel antiqui sæculi captum* "*admiranter excelluit, ut ejus ex vero depicta facies* "*vel in pudenda ingenii sterilitate inter fœcunditi,* "*mas imagines conspiciatur, quando nihil eum cun-* "*cta volumina cupide perlegentem vel rerum vel* "*verborum omnino subterfugerit, quin singula me-* "*moriter vel à multis annis longo sepulta silentio* "*recitaret* (13). *We must ascribe this to that un-* *common Happiness of Memory, which was remark-* *able in* Jerom Aleander, *beyond the Comprehension* *even of ancient Times*; *insomuch that a true Picture* *of this Author, tho' of a shameful barrenness of* *Genius, might claim a Place among the Represen-* *tations of the most fertile Wits*; *since, notwithstand-* *ing his universal Knowledge of Books, which he* *read over with great Eagerness, nothing, either as* *to the Matter or the Expression, escaped his Me-* *mory*; *but he could repeat every Particular by Heart,* *though many Years after he first read them.*" It is hard to believe this without Experience: but, as a Memory does not cease to be very good, though it does not come up to the Degree, which *Paul Jovius* mentions, I do not question the perfect Knowledge of divers Languages, which *Aleander*'s Epitaph attributes to him: *Hebraicæ, Græcæ, Latinæ, aliquotque aliarum linguarum exoticarum ita exacte docto, ut eas recte & apte loqueretur & scriberet.* — *So perfectly skilled in the Hebrew, Greek, Latin, and other foreign Tongues, that he could both speak and write them justly and properly.*

[G] *I do not believe there was any Reason to say* ———— *That he was born a Jew.*] *Luther* and his Disciples gave it out as a certain Truth, during *Aleander*'s first Nunciature in *Germany*; and we find the following Account of it in *Luther*'s Works (14). "Ve- "nit his diebus Hieronymus Aleander, vir sua opi- "nione longe maximus, non solum propter linguas "quas eximie callet, siquidem Ebræa illi vernacula "est, Græca à puero illi coaluit, Latinam autem "didicit diutina professione, sed etiam mirabilis suis "videtur ob antiquitatem generis. Nam Judæus na- "tus est, quæ gens immodice gloriatur de Abrahamo "vetustissimo se originem ducere. An vero baptisatus "sit nescitur. Certum est eum non esse Pharisæum, "quia non credit resurrectionem mortuorum, quoniam "vivit perinde atque cum corpore sit totus periturus, "adeo nullum à se pravum affectum abstinens. Ut- "que ad insaniam iracundus est, quavis occasione "furens. Impotentis arrogantiæ, avaritiæ inexple- "bilis, nefandæ libidinis & immodicæ, summum "gloriæ mancipium, quamquam mollior quam qui "possit elaborato stylo gloriam parare, & pejor quam "qui vel conetur in argumento honesto. At ne ne- "sciamus, cessit felicissimæ simulata defectio ad Chri- "stianos. — *Here is just arrived* Jerom Aleander,

"*in his own Opinion the most famous of Men, not* "*only on account of the Languages he perfectly under-* "*stands; for* Hebrew *is his Mother-Tongue,* Greek "*grew familiar to him from his Youth, and* Latin "*he attained by long exercise*; *but admired likewise* "*by his own Country-men for the Antiquity of his* "*Race. For he was a* Jew *by birth*; *a People which* "*boasts extravagantly of their Descent from* Abraham "*who lived so many Ages ago. Whether he was* "*ever baptized, is unknown. But it is certain that* "*he is not a* Pharisee, *because he does not believe the* "*Resurrection of the dead*; *since he lives, as if he* "*were to perish entirely with the Body, and denies* "*himself no Gratification of his depraved Affections.* "*He is choleric even to Madness, falling into a* "*Passion upon every Occasion*; *of outrageous Arro-* "*gance, unsatiable Avarice, shameful and immoderate* "*Lust*; *an abandoned Slave to Fame, though too in-* "*dolent to acquire it by an elaborate Style* (15), "*and too dishonest even to attempt it by just and* "*proper Reasoning. As for his pretended Conversi-* "*on to Christianity, it has turned out greatly to his* "*Advantage.*" This Picture represents *Aleander* to us not only as a Jew, who pretended to become a Convert to Christianity, and whole Baptism was doubtful, but also as one, who did not believe the Immortality of the Soul, and who plunged himself into the most infamous Pleasures; as a Man furiously passionate, covetous, and proud to the highest Degree. He answered the Accusation of being born a *Jew*, and declared before the Diet of *Worms*, that his Ancestors had the Dignity of Marquis in *Istria*, and that he had given good Proofs of his Noble and Illustrious Extraction, when he was made Canon of *Liege*. He appealed to several Persons, who heard him, and knew his Family. Mr Seckendorf informs us of this Particular. He found it in the Archives of the Duke of *Weimar*, where the Acts of the Diet of *Worms* are kept, among other Manuscripts of that time. *Aleander*'s long Speech is abbreviated in those Acts, and it is from thence that this illustrious *Lutheran* furnished us with the above-mentioned Account of *Aleander*'s Family, which he translated from his own Words into Latin (16). "*Tandem* "*questus est à* Luthero *spargi quasi* Aleander *gente* "Judæus *esset: Deum immortalem! dixit, multi hic* "*sunt boni viri quibus notus sum ego & familia mea,* "*& asserere ego vere possum, majores meos Marchio-* "*nes in* Istria *fuisse* (17); *quod vero parentes mei* "*ad inopiam redacti sunt, fato tribui debet. Natales* "*meos ita legitimavi, ut in Canonicum* Leodiensem "*receptus sim, quod factum non foret, nisi ortus* "*essem ex* familia *illustri vel spectabili.*" What induces me to believe, that this Reproach of being born a *Jew* was unjust, is no trifling Reason. *Hutrus* Hutten published an Invective against *Aleander*, wherein he was so angry, that he threatened to kill him: "*Omnem adversam diligentiam, omne adhi-* "*bebo studium, omnia tentabo conaborque, ut qui* "*furore, amentia, & iniquitate gravis accessisti, vita* "*inanis hinc efferaris. Neque enim exspectandum* "*adhuc tibi est, ut filios hic doctorum virorum sen-* "*tias, sed futurum crede, ut fortium gladiis conso-* "*diare* (18). — *I will watch every Opportunity,* "*I will make it my whole Business, I will try every* "*Art and Means, that one so full of Rage, Mad-* "*ness, and Iniquity, may not depart with his Life.* "*For you must not expect, that the Learned here will* "*express their Resentments against you with their* "*Pens*; *depend upon it, the Swords of the Brave* "*will revenge their Quarrel on you.*" He was not ignorant that our *Nuncio* had refuted the Reproach of *Judaism* before the Diet, and had boasted that he descended from a most illustrious Family; but he is so far from engaging to maintain this Charge, that he denies it was ever brought against him. I am not concerned, whether he had reason to deny it, or not; the Proof I draw from his Silence is the same; for if he had believed there was any Ground for this Accusation, he would, at least, have maintained, that *Aleander* denied his *Jewish* Extraction falsly. But, on the contrary, does he not affirm, that the Counts, to whom he said he was related, did not acknowledge

own Epitaph, which shews that he was not dissatisfied with his Condition, as some have charged him with being [H]. *Erasmus* mentions him frequently in his Letters, and almost always to his Disadvantage [I]. He complains, among other things, of the

acknowledge him for their Kinsman? "Nihil intellexisti proxima auditione, cùm multis quidem excusares Judaicam originem, nemo objiceret. Nam esse malum, quacunque etiam gente editum, sciebant omnes. Itaque nemo magnopere putabat generis pravitatem tibi objiciendam : adversùm mores fremebant insensè multi. Et poterat sentiri jam manifestè quæ esset animorum commotio: tu tamen, quasi illic potissimum expurgationem opus esset, multis tractatus locum eum ad fastidium usque audientium: sed tanta cum fiducia, ut planè certus tibi esse videreris neminem intelligere, quam impudenter ibi mentireris omnia. Illo enim post multa erupisti, ut ad nobilissi. Comitum, qui te penitùs ignorant, & quos tu haud satis nosti, genus, originem tuam referres (19). ——— *At the next Hearing, you behaved quite like a Fool, when you took so much Pains to refute, what no one objected to you, the Charge of having been born of Jewish Parents. Every one knew you to be a Rascal, whatever was your Extraction. Therefore no one thought it of much Importance to object to you the Vileness of your Origin; whereas many inveighed strongly against your Morals. The Disposition of the Audience towards you was very evident; yet, as if the Refutation of this Charge was of the highest Consequence, you dwelt upon it with such tiresome Prolixity, that the Hearers were quite sick of the Subject; and That, with such an Air of Assurance, as if you were convinced, that no one understood, how impudently false every thing you said was. For, at last, you had the Confidence to refer your Birth and Origin to a Noble Family of Counts, who knew nothing of you, and whom you yourself know very little of.* " Now, at the least Story, which is handed about, becomes at last considerable; I would not deny, that the Slander, which was spread against this *Nuncio*, was grounded upon what *Paul Jovius* says, that the *Jews* admired *Aleander*'s Skill in the *Hebrew* Tongue, and that they were much inclined to believe that he was of their Nation: " Latinæ Græcæque literæ quum sæpe alacriter jactabundo pro vernaculis haberentur, Hebraicas admirantibus Judæis & suæ stirpis eum facile credentibus, solertissimè didicit (20)." They, who shall have a mind to criticize upon me, are desired to observe, that I do not pretend, that *Paul Jovius*'s Book occasioned this Calumny; the Notion, I think, might have been broached long before *Paul Jovius* took any Notice of it.

"What *Luther* says, that *Aleander* was very choleric, is very true: We may believe *Josse Gentin*, this Cardinal's Secretary, in a Letter to *Nausea* Bishop of *Vienna**. He tells him, with the greatest Simplicity, after having informed him of the Death of *Aleander*, that he knows not where to go, after the Death of his Master, for fear of finding one more passionate still. Haslenus, says he, alium Mecenatem Romæ non quæsivi, eo quod immodestia & furor hujus mei defuncti inculcat mihi timorem ne faciam Glauci cum Diomede permutationem. ——— *Hitherto I have not looked out for another Mecenas at Rome; for the intemperate Disposition of my deceased Patron makes me afraid of making* Glaucus's *Exchange with* Diomedes." See the Margin (21).

[H] *He wrote his own Epitaph, which shews that he was not dissatisfied with his Condition, as some have charged him with being.*] It consists of two *Greek* Verses, importing, that he died willingly; since he should thereby avoid being a Witness of many things, the Sight of which was more insufferable than Death.

Κάτθανον ἐκ δικῶν, ὅτι παύσομαι ὢν ὑπομάρτυς
Πολλῶν, ὧντεπ ἰδεῖν ἀλίων ἢν θανάτε.

This would be the Disposition of all Men, if Reflexion, Reason, and Sense were capable of surmounting those Mechanical Impressions, which make us in love with Life. Setting aside this profound Morality, I say it is very strange, that *Paul Jovius* should produce such an express Evidence against himself, as this Epitaph. He had said, that *Aleander*,

angry with his Fate, which took him off one Year before his Climacteric, died complaining of this Anticipation: *Interiit fato suo vehementer indignatus, quum se præreptum anno uno ante climactericum inter anxia supremaque suspiria quereretur* (22): and, immediately after, he adds, that *Aleander* ordered, by his Will, that a *Greek* Distich of his own Composition, should be inserted in his Epitaph, containing this Thought:

Excessi è vitæ ærumnis facilisque lubensque,
Ne pejora ipsa morte dehinc videam.

*Tranquil of Heart, and with a willing Mind,
The World, and all it's Miseries, I resign'd;
Pleas'd to awake from Life's uneasy Dream,
Nor longer see what worse than Death I deem.*

Lorenzo Crasso gives nearly the same Account of *Aleander*'s Indignation at his Fate: " Fu assalito in " Roma dalla Morte, contro la quale mostrossi anche " negli ultimi sospiri sdegnato (23). ——— *He was seized with Death at Rome, at which he expressed great Indignation, even with his last Breath.*" He foretels, says *Paul Jovius*, new Misfortunes ready to fall on our Heads, *novas clades imminere nobis ominatur*; but nothing is more false than this: *Aleander* considered the time to come only accidentally; all his Thoughts were employ'd on the past; he only declared his Belief, that the World would not mend. So that here is a second Error of *Paul Jovius*. As to the first, he cannot be justified, without being moreover charged with monstrous Calumny, in representing *Aleander* as a Cheat upon his Death-bed, who ordered, by his Will, that Posterity should be made to believe a notorious Falshood; to wit, that he died in great Discontent of Mind. *Lorenzo Crasso* says, that *Scraderus* inserted the Sepulchral Inscription of *Aleander* in his Monuments of *Italy*, with the *Latin* Translation of the two *Greek* Verses (24); This Translation is the same which *Paul Jovius* mentions; and is about as good as this: " Non in- " vitus obii, quia quiesco; testis multorum quæ " videre pejus ait mors (25). ——— *I did not die unwillingly, because I am at Rest; having been Witness of many things, which to see is worse than Death.*" This is the Consequence of making use of a Language but little known; all the Force and Grace of the *Greek* Distich have escaped the Translators.

Let me insert in this Place a Remark, which was communicated to me by a learned Person: Josse Gentin *says, in his Letter to* Nausea, *that* Aleander, *having disposed his Affairs three Days before he died, servitoribus & aliis præsentibus pronunciavit suum quod fieri cupiebat epitaphium,* ——— *declared to his Servants and others what kind of Epitaph he desired to have,* quod hoc distico clausit: κάτθανον, &c. *which he concluded with this Distich,* κάτθανον, &c. *This shews*, adds he, *that the Epitaph did not consist altogether of two Verses, but that they were only the Conclusion of the Epitaph.* I am not of this Opinion. I believe Gentin meant that his Master comprehended in this Distich all the Inscription he intended for his Tomb.

[*I*] Erasmus *mentions him frequently in his Letters, and almost always to his Disadvantage.*] *Aleander*, being naturally of a warm Temper, and being moreover interested in the Ruin of Lutheranism, by his Quality of *Nuncio*, sent into *Germany* to stifle that Party in it's Birth, could not suffer the Moderation of *Erasmus*. This was not all; *Erasmus*'s Enemies did not cease to defame him, as a Favourer of Lutheranism: Thus the reciprocal Friendship and Esteem, which was between him and the *Nuncio*, suffered a great Diminution upon *Aleander*'s first coming into *Germany*. " Hieronymum Aleandrum Nun- " cium apostolicum, hominem apprimè doctum, mi- " hique vetere ac jucundissimâ necessitudine conjun- " ctum, miris mendaciis in me conati sunt irritare " ——— Quid multis? persuaserant homini, ut acri " ingenio prædito, itâ credulo, me parùm amice de " ipso & sentire & loqui. Nec defuerunt qui coalef- " centem

ALEANDER.

the ill Offices he had done him with the Bishop of *Liege*, with whom *Aleander* had

"centrem amicitiam novis subinde delationibus discinderent (26). —— *They endeavoured by surprizing Fal-* "*stood to exasperate against me* Jerom Aleander, *a very* "*learned Person, and my old and intimate Friend.* —— "*In short, he was so credulous, though a Man of acute* "*Parts, as to be persuaded by them, that I thought and* "*spoke of him not like a Friend. Nor were there want-* "*ing some, who contrived, by new Calumnies, to pre-* "*vent the Renewal of our Friendship.*" This is to speak but slightly of *Aleander*'s ill Dispositions, if it be true, as it is highly probable, that it is He, who is denoted elsewhere (27), by the Title of *Bull-Carrier*, δυπλωματοφόρος; for That *Bull-Carrier* did his utmost Endeavours to ruin *Erasmus*; and it was well for the latter, that the Emperor did not comply with every thing he desired of him: "Me quo minus oppresserit, per illum non stetit: perierat Erasmus, si pronas aures Principum reperisset. —— *If I* "*was not ruined, no Thanks to him*: Erasmus *had* "*been lost, if the Great had lent a favourable Ear* "*to him.*" A Letter, which *Erasmus* had written to *Luther*, and which the Friends of the latter had made public, exasperated *Aleander* to that Degree, that he endeavoured to ruin his ancient Friend, both with the Pope, and with the Bishop of *Liege*. "Hæc "(Epistola) dedit ansam Aleandro, jampridem ini-"quo in me animo, ut me perditum iret, conatus "Leonis animum irritare in me, simul Leodiensis "Episcopi, qui prius pene deperibat, ut ita loquar, "Erasmum. Nam ipse Leodiensis ostendit mihi li-"teras, quas ad eum à Roma scripserat Aleander, "satis odiosè me attingentes (28). —— His Letter "induced *Aleander*, already prepossessed against me, to "contrive my Ruin, which he endeavoured to do, "by exasperating Pope Leo against me; as also the "Bishop of Liege, who before was dotingly fond, "if I may use the Expression, of Erasmus. For the "Bishop himself shewed me the Letters, which Aleander wrote to him from Rome, in which he suf-"ficiently discovered his Spleen against me." He affected to say that *Erasmus*'s Works were the Source of all the Heretical Doctrines, then maintained. "Jam "audio multis persuasum ex meis scriptis extitisse "totam hanc Ecclesiæ procellam. Cujus vanissimi "rumoris præcipuus autor fuit *Hieronymus Aleander*, homo, ut nihil aliud dicam, non superstitiose "verax (29). —— *I am now informed, that it is a* "*general Persuasion, that all this Storm, which has* "*fallen upon the Church, was raised by my Writings.* "*The chief Author of this groundless Report was* Je-"rome Aleander, *a Person, to say no more of him,* "*not over scrupulous with regard to Truth.*" He not only found fault with *Erasmus*'s Religion, but reflected also upon that great Man's Learning, and his Works. This appears by a Letter, which *Erasmus* wrote to him in the Year 1524 (30), in which he opens his Heart to him. He looked upon him as so enraged an Enemy, that he took him for one of the chief Promoters of the Censures, which the *Sorbonne* had published against his Books, and for the true Author of the Invective, which passed under the Name of *Julius Cæsar Scaliger*. "Non tamen "erant proditoræ Censuræ, nisi quidam oleum camino "addidissent. Lutetiæ fuit Eccius, &c, ut suspicor, "Aleander; quem suspicor has de causâ præcipue "venisse, ut Erasmo moliatur exitium. *Julii* Sca-"ligeri libellum tam scio illius esse, quam scio me "vivere. Id tamen dissimulandum est, ne magis in-"saniat prodito fuco (31). —— *However these Cen-* "*sures would never have appeared, had not a certain* "*Person thrown Oil upon the Fire. It is well known,* "*that* Eccius *was at Paris, and, as I suspect,* Ale-"ander; *whose principal Design in coming thither, I* "*suspect to have been, a Plot against* Erasmus. *I am* "*as sure, that the Book of* Julius Scaliger *is His,* "*as that I am now alive. But this must be dissembled,* "*least he should grow more furious, upon pulling off the* "*Mask.*" I have shewn elsewhere (32), that *Erasmus* was mistaken in relation to this last Fact; *Scaliger*'s Oration was the Work of Him, whose Name it bears; and, to say, that, in the Year 1531, *Aleander* went to *Paris*, chiefly to contrive *Erasmus*'s Ruin, is to think one's self too considerable a Man, and to be ignorant of the Nature of the Charge, which the Pope gave his Nuncio. We shall see in another

Place (33). whether *Erasmus* had reason to attribute a Book, which bore the Name of *Dolet*, to *Aleander*. He meant this Nuncio in the twenty fourth Letter of the twenty fifth Book. *Aleander*'s Passion must therefore have been extream; for he, whom *Erasmus* complains of, had handed about a Paper (34) at the Court of *Rome*, wherein he told the Pope, that he wondered that, so many thousands of Men having perished in *Germany*, in the War of the Peasants, *Erasmus*, the Author of this furious Tumult, was yet living. We cannot be ignorant, who the Author is, whom *Erasmus* denotes, since we find these Words in another Letter: "In me impudentissimis "argumentis causam agit (*Albertus Pius*) & agit "hostiliter, docens laboram, me fuisse occasionem, "causam, autorem & principem, totius hujus negotii. "Quod idem agit *Aleander* in suo *Racha*, demirans "me adhuc spirare, quum in *Germania* tot hominum "millia sint trucidata (35). —— Albertus Pius car-"*ries on the Cause against me with most impudent* "*Argument, and declares open War against me*: "*taking a great deal of Pains to shew, that I was* "*the Occasion, the Cause, the Author, and Ring-* "*leader of this whole Affair.* Aleander *does the* "*same, in his* Racha, *in which he expresses his Won-* "*der, that I am yet alive, after the Slaughter of* "*so many thousand Men in* Germany." In another Place (36) he denotes him by the Name of VERPUS, which shews that he believed still, that *Aleander* was born a *Jew*. If *Aleander* wrote this Book, he held a very strict Correspondence with *Erasmus*, and had the same Table, the same Chamber, and the same Bed with him; and had received besides good Offices from him; for thus *Erasmus* expresses himself: "Cum altero fuit mihi olim non tectum "modo ac mensa, verum etiam cubiculum & lectus "communis: adeoque à me nulla læsus est injuria, "ut, quam illi res essent angustiores, commendatri-"cibus literis meis nonnihil etiam adjutus sit, nec "usquam illius in scriptis meis nisi honorifica men-"tio (37). —— *The other shared not only my House* "*and my Table, but even my Bed* (38); *and so far* "*was He from receiving an Injury from me, that,* "*when his Circumstances were a little embarassed, I* "*assisted him in some measure by Letters of Recommen-* "*dation*; *nor did I ever mention him in my Writings* "*but with Respect.*" We must necessarily understand this of *Aleander*, when we remember another Letter (39), wherein we find these Words: "Ut "video, tibi propemodum persuasit (*Aleander*); at "ego, qui è domestico convictu ac lectuli quoque "contubernio totum intus & in cute nôvi, tam scio "esse ovum illius, quàm scio me vivere. —— *I find,* "*Aleander* has persuaded you of the contrary; *but* "*I, who, from my Intimacy with him, see into his* "*very Thoughts, am as certain* This *Work* (40) *is* "*His, as that I am alive.*" Let us end this disadvantageous Relation with a Passage, which concerns *Aleander*'s Morals. If we may believe *Erasmus*, he lived at *Venice* the Life of an Epicurean in the Year 1533. Nunc Venetiis plane vivit Epicureum, non sine dignitate tamen (41). —— *Not without Dignity.* Doubtless he means, by this Dignity, the double Mitre, which he had mentioned in the sixtieth Letter. *Aleander* gemina mitra insignitus, nam Brundusinus & Oretinus est; apud Cæsarem agit legatum Anglicum (42). This latter Term is equivocal, and perhaps *Erasmus* did not write *Anglicum*, but *Angelicum*, to denote the Office of Apostolical Nuncio, which *Aleander* had at that time in *Germany*. However, it had not been amiss to have hinted, in a marginal Note, that he was not the King of *England*'s Ambassador to the Emperor *Charles* V; for the Reader will naturally understand it so. Monsieur *de la Monnoie* happily conjectures, that *Anglicum* was owing to *Erasmus*'s having written, by way of Abbreviation, *Aplicum* for *apostolicum*.

The Reader should, at least, see one Passage of *Erasmus*, to the Advantage of *Aleander*: "Etiamsi "nominasses istum, qui *Aliundrum* Erasmo præfert "in omnibus, nihil erat periculi. Nam & ipse plu-"rimum tribuere soleo *Aleandro*, præsertim in lite-"ris, nihiloque magis me lædi puto, si doctior est, "quam quod ditior est aut formosior (43). —— *You* "*might safely have named him, who prefers* Aleander "*to* Erasmus *in every thing. For I alway; pay a* "*great*

VOL. I.   I i i

ALEANDER. ALEGAMBUS.

had a Brother, who was a much greater Master, than he, of the Art of Dissimulation [K].

"*great Deference to Aleander, especially in Matters of Learning; nor is it more injurious to me, if he is a better Scholar, than if he is richer, or handsomer.*" The Letter, wherein Erasmus speaks thus, is dated the Thirty first of *August*, 1524.

[K] *He had a Brother ------ a much greater Master, than he, of the Art of Dissimulation.*] Erasmus, who informs us of this Particular, adds, that this Brother was, upon this Account, more dangerous than *Aleander*, who knew not so well to conceal his Designs. I will give you his own Words: " Habet " Fratrem apud Leodiensem hoc perniciosiorem, quod " omnia potest dissimulare, id quod non potest Aleander (44)."

(44) Ep. cr. lib. 2:. pag. 1011.

(a) *They are distinguished by the Appellations of Aleander the elder, and Aleander the younger.*

ALEANDER (JEROM) of the same Family with the Preceding (a), and Grandson of *Jerom Amaltheus*, by the Mother's side, was one of the learned Men of the XVIIth Century. Upon his quitting *Frioul*, his Native Country, to go to *Rome*, he was made Secretary to Cardinal *Octavio Bandini*, which Employ he discharged with Honour near twenty Years. He ventured early to appear in Print; for he had scarce taken his Degree of Civilian, before he published a *Commentary on the Institutes of Caius*. He did not suffer his Pen to be idle at *Rome*; for being one of the first who was admitted into the rising Academy of the *Humourists*, he had always some Composition ready to produce before them, and wrote likewise a very learned Treatise, in *Italian*, on the Device of that Assembly. The Fertility of his Genius, and his Studies, appeared in several Works on different Subjects. He explained some Pieces of Antiquity [A]; he wrote on the Question concerning *Suburbian Churches*, and published a Book against That, which an anonymous Author (b) had composed on this Subject, in Favour of the Protestants. A Volume of his *Verses* was published, and was followed by an Apology for the *Adonis* of the Cavalier *Marini*, against the rude Attacks of the Cavalier *Stiliani*. Urban VIII. expressed his Esteem for him advantageously; for he laboured to draw him from the Service of Cardinal *Bandini*, in order to place him in That of the *Barberinis*: so that *Aleander* became Secretary to Cardinal *Francis Barberini*, the Pope's Nephew. He went with this Cardinal into *France*, when he was sent thither with the Character of Legate *à Latere*. He did not sink under the Fatigues of this long Journey, but bore them with Resolution, notwithstanding the Weakness of his Constitution, and his want of Health. He was not so much Master of himself, with regard to good Cheer. He had agreed, with some of his intimate Friends, to treat one another every three Days by turns. Amidst such a Variety of Delicacies, he could not forbear eating more than was proper, considering his weak Stomach; so that he fell sick, and could not recover of his Illness (c). The Cardinal his Master, made a magnificent Funeral for him in the Academy of the *Humourists*, and his Brethren, the Academics, carried his Body to the Grave (d). *Gaspar de Simeonibus* spoke his Funeral Oration on the 31st of *December* 1631. It was printed at *Paris* in the Year 1636. *Aleander* had such an elegant and genteel way of writing, that the Compliment, which one of his Friends made him upon it, deserves our Notice [B].

(b) Salmasius.

(c) *Mr Baillet, in his Judgment on the Poets, n. 1431. and Witte in his Diarum Biograph. part. 2. pag. 40. place his Death in the Year 1631. Witte calls him Aleander.*

(d) *Taken from Nicius Erythræus, Pinacoth 1. See also Alathus in Apibus Urbanis, pag. 123, 124, 125.*

[A] *He explained some pieces of Antiquity.*] They were two Marbles, a Table, and a Statue. The Table contained the Figure, and the Symbols, of the Sun; the Statue was surrounded with a Girdle full of carved Work. The Title of this Work of *Aleander* is as follows: Explicatio antiquæ tabulæ marmoreæ solis effigie symbolisque exculptæ: explicatio sigillorum zonæ veterem statuam marmoream cingentis. It is in Quarto, printed at *Rome*, in the Year 1616, and at *Paris*, in the Year 1617. I do not question but his Acquaintance with Father *Morin* was owing to this Work. It appears, by the Book, entituled, *Ecclesiæ Orientalis antiquitates* (1), that they corresponded by Letters.

[B] *Such an elegant and genteel way of Writing, that the Compliment ------ deserves our notice.*] Nicius Erythræus told him often, *When I read your Works, I find myself a learned Man*; *but when I read those of other Writers, who pretend to Eloquence, I find myself very Ignorant*; *for I understand nothing in them.* How few *Latin* Authors are there, at present, who deserve this Compliment? I do not speak of those, who write in the Chancery, or Scholastic, Style, but of those, who write as Orators, and who labour their Phrases. They are generally fit only to mortify the Presumption of their Readers, who find themselves every Moment stopt by some Allusion, or some Metaphor, so confusedly exprest, that they are altogether in the Dark. The Misfortune is, that the Reader is seldom mortify'd by this means, since Self-love prompts him to impute the Cause of these Obscurities, not to his own Ignorance, but to the Nonsense of the Author. However, I fancy the Reader will be pleased to read Nicius Erythræus's genteel Compliment in the Original. " Scribendi ejusdem ratio tum in soluta " oratione tum in versibus adeo erat pura, adeo perspi- " cua, ut sæpe ex me audiret tum demum me mihi- " met doctum eruditumque videri, cum sua legerem; " cum autem in aliorum scripta, qui se eloquentes fa- " ci vellent, incurrerem, tum plane me indoctum om- " niumque rerum rudem agnoscere, eò quod verbum " prorsus in illis nullum intelligerem (2)." This ought to have been a strong Inducement to him, not to leave any Obscurities in his Elogies; and yet they are not altogether free from it. Some think he has not exprefs'd clearly, whether it was at *Rome* or *Paris*, that good Cheer was so fatal to *Aleander*; they believe it was at *Paris* (3). As for myself, I do not question the contrary; the Agreement of treating one another two or three times a Week, by turns, favours more of Persons, at ease, and at Home, than of Travellers. Besides, the Journey, which the Legate *Francis Barberini* took into *France*, in the Year 1625, lasted but few Months; and *Aleander* did not die 'till the Year 1631.

(1) *It was printed at London in 1682. and at Francfort in 1683. 12mo.*

(2) Nicius Ervthr. Pinacoth. 1. pag. 46.

(3) *See the Judgment of the Learned on the Poets, Tom. 4. n. 1430. pag. 54.*

ALEGAMBUS (PHILIP) a *Flemish* Jesuit, was born at *Brussels*, the Twenty second of *January* 1592. He studied Classical Learning in his own Country; after which he went into *Spain*, and entered into the Duke of *Ossuna*'s Service; whom he followed into *Sicily*, when he went to take upon him the Office of Viceroy there. Finding within himself a Call to a Religious Life, he took the Jesuit's Habit at *Palermo*,

ALEGAMBUS.

lermo, on the seventh Day of *September*, 1613. He performed his Noviciate, and his Course of Philosophy, in the same City, and his Divinity Studies at *Rome*; from whence he was sent into *Stiria*, to teach Philosophy in the University of *Gratz*. Having discharged the Duties of this Function to the Satisfaction of his Masters, he was made Professor of School-Divinity, and solemnly promoted to the Doctorate in the Year 1629. During these Transactions, the Prince of *Eggemberg*, Favourite of the Emperor *Ferdinand* II, had a mind to send his Son to travel, and to appoint a prudent and learned Jesuit to be his Confessor in his Travels. Father *Alegambus* was thought fit for this Employ, and was taken out of the Schools to travel with this young Lord. He was five Years with him, and saw *Germany*, *France*, *Spain*, *Portugal*, and *Italy*. Being returned to *Gratz*, he taught Moral Divinity there, and was the Spiritual Father of the Youth. In the Year 1638, the young Prince, whom he had accompanied in his Travels, was nominated by the Emperor *Ferdinand* III, for the Embassy of Obedience to Pope *Urban* VIII. He desired Father *Alegambus* to accompany him; upon which this Jesuit travelled to *Rome*, in Quality of the Ambassador's Confessor. When this Function was over, the General of the Jesuits retained him to be his Secretary for the *Latin* Dispatches, which related to *Germany*. *Alegambus*, having discharged the Duties of this laborious Function for four Years successively, was obliged to leave it; a continual Application to Writing having greatly impaired his Sight. Upon this they gave him the *Prefecture of Spirituals* in the *Maison Professe*, and the Office of confessing in the Church; of which it is said he acquitted himself with great Applause. He died at *Rome* of a Dropsy, on the sixth Day of *September* 1652 (a). He wrote but few Books [*A*]; and yet he deserves the Elogy of a very good Author; for the *Bibliotheque of the Writers of his Order* is a good Book in it's kind, and excels by much all the Works of this Nature, which were wrote before That time. He must necessarily have taken a great deal of Pains in collecting the Materials; a Work, which requires two Talents, seldom found together, great Patience, and great Eagerness. He was obliged afterwards to put these Materials in order; and this was the most laborious part of his Work; because a Man is no longer supported by the strong Inclination, which prompted him to search for the Materials, which he wanted. It was at *Rome* that *Alegambus* composed his *Bibliotheque*; for which he had collected so many Memoirs (b); and it was printed at *Antwerp* in 1643. He so greatly enlarged the Work, which the Jesuit *Ribadeneira* had begun on this Subject [*B*], that, whereas the Work of the latter is but a very small *Octavo*, his is a pretty large *Folio*. I shall mention, in the Remarks, what has been said for or against it [*C*]. He intended a new Edition, and, during the nine Years he survived the former,

(a) *Taken from Sotuel's Bibl. Scriptor Societ. Jesu. Rome 1675. pag. 706, 707.*

(b) *Sotuel, Ibid.*

[*A*] *He wrote but few Books.*] The Catalogue of his Works, according to Father *Sotuel*, is as follows: *Bibliotheca Scriptorum Societatis Jesu, Antverpiæ*, 1643, in Folio. *Vita P. Johannis Cardin Lustani ex Societate Jesu, Romæ*, 1649, in 12°. *Heroes & Victimæ charitatis Societatis Jesu, Romæ*, 1658, in 4to. *Mortes illustres & gesta eorum de Societate Jesu, qui in odium fidei ab Hæreticis vel aliis occisi sunt, Romæ*, 1557. in Folio.

[*B*] *The Work, which the Jesuit* Ribadeneira *had begun on this Subject.*] That the Reader, who desires to know the History of the *Bibliotheque*, of which we speak, may not have the trouble of turning to another Volume, I shall observe here, that *Peter Ribadeneira* began, in the Year 1602, the Catalogue of the Jesuit Authors. This Catalogue consisted of but few Sheets; he enlarged it afterwards, and published it at *Antwerp*, in the Year 1608. It was printed at *Lyons*, the Year following, with some Additions, and Corrections, in relation to some Particulars concerning the *French* Jesuits, with which the Author was unacquainted. Father *Julius Nigroni* perceived, that this Work stood in need of Correction in many other Places, particularly with respect to the *Italian* Jesuits: upon which a new Edition was published, in the Year 1613, at *Antwerp*. Father *Andrew Schott* had the Care of it; and it was considerably enlarged (1); but was still a very defective Work; which was the Reason why *Alegambus* undertook to put it into a better Condition, and to make it fitter to give an advantageous Idea of the Erudition of the Society. He published it in the Year 1643. It was still farther enlarged by the Jesuit *Sotuel*, whose Edition was published at *Rome*, in the Year 1675, and no doubt it will require still farther Additions, both because the Society of the Jesuits continually affords new Authors, and because many things escaped the last Continuator, which might make the *Bibliotheque* of the Order more perfect. The second Tome of the *Bibliotheque Romaine* (2), informs us, that the Jesuit *Bonanni* is preparing a Catalogue of the Writers of his Society, who have published any thing since the Year 1675. The

(1) *See Alegambus's Preface.*

(2) *Printed at Rome in 1692. The Author's Name is Professor Mandosio.*

Exactness of *Alegambus* is doubtless wonderful; but yet there are some Faults, both of Omission and Commission, in his Book. He does not always mention the first Edition of Books, which is a considerable Fault, to be found in all the Compilations, which have hitherto appeared. No one has yet undertaken to publish an exact Collection of all the Editions, and carefully to observe the first. *Gesner*, and his Continuators, have been very negligent in this respect. Father *Sotuel*, willing to avoid the minute Particulars, on which *Alegambus* sometimes enlarges a little too much, is too concise and barren. He was not so well qualify'd for this Work, as *Alegambus*. The Curious, and even those, who excuse him on account of the Orders, which he might have received from his Superiors, in relation to the anonymous, and pseudonymous Writers, look upon his Work, in this respect, as much inferior to that of the former, in which so many obscure Authors are brought to light.

[*C*] *What has been said for or against it.*] Mr *Baillet* will supply us with a Comment on the Text of this Remark. Let us begin with the fair side.

He says (3), that "the *Bibliotheque* of the Writers of the Society ———— is a grand Collection, which surpasses all those of the same Nature, and that it ought to be considered as one of the most perfect of the kind:" That, according to *Nicolas Antonio* (4), "the Jesuits have shewn, by this Work, how curious and industrious they are in the things which concern them, and that, having built on the Foundation of *Ribadeneira*, they raised this great Edifice; the Beauty whereof consists particularly in the Exactness and Proportion of it's Parts, and of which the whole Credit is due to *Alegambus*, a Writer so careful and exact, that there is no Danger of being deceived by him; because he is not only free from Confusion, and never takes one Author for another, but also because he does not attribute any Book to the Jesuits, which they did not write, and because he is exact and faithful, in his Representation of those, which really come from the Society." Mr *Baillet* adds, "that it is no small Praise

(3) *Baillet's Judgment of the Learned, Tom. 2. n. 112. p. 130.*

(4) *Pref. Biblioth. Scriptor. Hispan.*

to

ALEGAMBUS.

mer, he collected many Particulars, which might serve for Corrections, or Additions. Father *Sotuel* made use of them, when he published a new Edition of this *Bibliotheque* at *Rome*, in 1675 (c).

(c) Id. Ibid.

It cannot be denied that there are many inconsiderable Authors taken Notice of in this Book, and many Authors of the first Rank. But some pretend, that should it be continued, there would be a very sensible Disproportion in it; that is to say, the great Men would be incomparably fewer in the Continuation, than in what has hitherto appeared. This gives me an Opportunity of communicating to the Public what passed in a Conversation between some learned Persons in the Year 1697 [D].

" .... to have avoided a Fault with so much Care, into which most of the other Regulars have fallen, who have given an account of the illustrious Men of their Order; who, thinking to do Honour to their Communities, by increasing the Number of their learned Men and Saints, indifferently, and without Choice, have plac'd a great many Authors among their Brethren, who did not belong to them; whereas there is scarce one to be seen in the *Bibliotheque* of the Society, who had not been a Jesuit. Nay, that the Writers, who left their Society, as *Papyrius Maffo, Gaspar Scioppius, Mark Antony de Dominis, Christian Francken*, &c. do not appear in it." Or that if they are seen there, it is only in relation to their Works, which preceded their Departure; that, in this View, we find there *Francis de Macedo*, a *Portuguese*, who from a Jesuit became a Cordelier, and *Claudius Dausquey*, a *Fleming*, who left the Society for a Canonship at *Tournay*. Lastly, Mr *Baillet* observes, that, according to the Taste of the *News from the Republic of Letters* (5), *Alegambus*, "suited himself to the Taste of our Age, that is, of all Persons of good Sense; that this Taste consists in observing a Chronological Exactness in every thing relating to History; that it is this, which occasioned the Approbation of the Applauses bestowed upon *Alegambus*, who takes notice every where of the Time, and Place, of the Birth of Authors, the Age when they became Jesuits, their Employments, and their chief Actions, according to the Series of Time, and that there is something extreamly pleasing in this Exactness.. Lastly, continues Mr Baillet (6), as the Society of the Jesuits has been hitherto the most Learned of all regular Societies, that is to say, at least, the most abundant in all sorts of Writers (except in Physic) .... one may judge from thence of the Advantage, which may be drawn from this copious *Bibliotheque*, which is well enough written, without any affectation of a particular Style, and without too far-fetch'd Ornaments .... dispos'd in a very fine Method, and embellish'd with a great Number of laborious and useful Tables." This is the fair Side of it's Character. Let us now proceed to the Imperfections of this *Bibliotheque*.

Mr Baillet says (7), that "as the most perfect Bodies are not always free from Spots and Defects, when their Beauty consists only in the Size and Proportion of their Parts, it will be no surprize to hear, that this fine *Bibliotheque* has met with it's Censors as well as others; that some think they discover in it something of that Affection for one's own Society, which inclines a Man to represent the Writers of it always to their Advantage; that they add, that, in effect, there is nothing to be met with in this huge Volume, but Elogiums; and that, among such a great Number of Authors and Books, it does not appear that *Alegambus* and *Sotuel* acknowledge one that is bad, except, perhaps, those, who have been put into the Inquisition, or been in the *Index*; that others have observed, that there is scarce one Writer in all this *Bibliotheque*, who is not represented to us as a Saint. It is true, that reasonable Persons ought to be satisfied with seeing a solemn Protestation at the beginning, and end of the Book, that he does not pretend to warrant what is said of the Holiness and Virtues attributed to his Brethren, no more than the other Encomiums, which are bestowed upon them." It is more difficult, according to Mr Baillet (8), "to answer two other Accusations; the first is, that *Alegambus*, being deceived by some false Memoirs, which ill affected Persons sent him, calls Mr *Marion*, Mr *Servin*, and some other illustrious Magistrates, and good Catholics, Heretics. The second is, that he was so indiscreet as to reveal certain things, which it was of the utmost Importance to the Society, to keep private and suppress; as for Example, when he affirms, that the *Amphitheatre of Honour* [* §], written against the Royal Authority, by one *Bonarsius*, is the Work of a famous Jesuit, though Father *Coton* had assured King *Henry the Great* of the contrary; and that some other Books, written against Episcopacy and Hierarchy in general, and against the Clergy of *France*, and the *Sorbonne* in particular, were composed by some Fathers of the Society; though the chief among the Jesuits of *France*, who governed the Houses of *Paris*, having been called upon to answer this Charge, had protested, even under their own Hands, that the Jesuits were not the Authors of these Libels." Mr *Baillet* adds, that " *Sotuel*, was more discreet in this Point than *Alegambus*; for in his Edition we do not find the Writings of the false *Smith*, and of the false *Of-Jesu*, which gave so much Offence; nor the Books of *Guimenius*, of *Vernant*, and of the *Apologist for the Casuists*; nay, he took care to tell us beforehand, that his Silence, in relation to these Books, ought to pass for a disowning, and a private Condemnation, which the Society makes of them. But it cannot be denied, on the other side, that he has preserved *Alegambus*'s Faults in many other Places, and that his Edition is not so exact and fine, as that of *Alegambus*." See the foregoing Remark. I shall take notice of a small Defect of this *Bibliotheque*, at the End of the Remark [C], of the Article ANNAT.

[* §] [This Book is ascribed to the Jesuit *Carolus Scrivonius*, in the Catalogue of *Rhodeneira*: at *Lyons*, in 8vo. for *Pillehotte*; and, at *Antwerp*, *ex officina Plantiniana*, 1613, 8vo. REM. CRIT.]

[D] *What pass'd in a Conversation of some learned Persons in the Year 1697.*] Some Gentlemen, who came to *Delft*, with the Plenipotentiaries of *France*, being one Day in Company with some *French* Refugees, and some Persons of the Country, the Conversation, according to the Custom of Men of Letters, turned upon Books and learned Men. Most of them acknowledged the Decay of Learning; and they observed, more than once, with great Joy, that the Society of Jesuits scarce produces any learned Men at present. *The Bellarmins, the Sirmonds, and the Petaviuses*, add they, *have left no Successors; their Places, and those of many other left famous Men, are still vacant.* Mr *,*,*, was almost the only Person, who did not approve of this Censure, and who desired the Company to consider, that those, who take Delight in such Discourses, are guilty of two Faults; for in the first place, *said he*, they lightly touch upon what concerns other Orders, and Communities, but insist much on That of the Jesuits. This respect of Persons is very unjust. Have the Universities of *France* any Professors of Physic, which make so great a Noise as *Fernel*, and *Sylvius*? Or any Professors of the Civil Law, who come near *Deneau, Duaren, Hotman*, and *Cujacius*? Shew us, if you can, a *Casaubon*, a *Scaliger*, or a *Salmasius*, in the Protestant Party. Shew us a *Grotius*, an *Heinsius*, or a *Vossius*, in *Holland*. Did not these Men die without leaving any Successors? Have they left Places, which are filled up? Let us confess then, that the Decline, which you affect to appropriate to the Jesuits, is common to all the Parties and Communities of *Europe*: it is a Defect of the Times, and not of their Society. Do not imagine, *says he, (which was his second Reflexion)* that I pretend, that this part of the XVIIth Century, in which we live, is inferior to the former Part, or to the foregoing Age. I believe, on the contrary, that, upon the whole, it ought to have the Preference, and that it is the Alteration of our Taste, which is the only Reason of what you call the Decay of Literature. The Study of Critical Learning is fallen; Men apply themselves to the reason-

ALESIUS.

"ing Part (9); they improve their Minds much "he was their Countryman. Can a more extensive
"more than their Memory; they are desirous to think "share of Literature be seen, than That of Father
"delicately, and to express themselves politely. This "*Hardouin*? Is not Father *Commire* one of the best
"Application does not indeed produce those great "*Latin* Poets at present in the World? Is there any
"Volumes, which impose on the Publick, and which "Writer, who exceeds Father *Bouhours* in the Pu-
"raise a Man to a great Reputation; but in truth it "rity of the *French* Language, and in the Beauty of
"strikes out more Light, and forms a Genius more "his Compositions, or Father *Jouvency*, in point of
"valuable than the great Learning of the Gram- "Philology, or Father *de la Brunne* in a fine *Latin*
"marians, and Philologers. The *Jesuits* have fol- "Style, by whose Care Father *Sirmond*'s Works have
"lowed this new Taste; and this is the Reason, why "been lately published? Are there better Pens in *France*
"their learned Men are not of the same Stamp with "than Father *le Tellier*, Father *Daniel*, Father *Dou-
"those, who lived formerly. Have you observed, "*cin*, &c.? I name you some of them, but without
"as I have done, *continued he*, the considerable Num- "pretending to wrong many others, whom I do not
"ber of illustrious Men, at present in their College "name." This was the Discourse of Mr *⁎⁎⁎*, if
"at *Paris*? Father *Bexier* is so consummate in Lan- "the Person, who informed me of this Conversation,
"guages, that all the Strangers of *Europe* and *Asia* "related it faithfully. My Readers may judge of it as
"desire his Company, and converse with him, as if "they think fit.

ALESIUS (ALEXANDER) a famous Divine of the Confession of *Augsburg*, and Author of several Books (*a*), was born at *Edinburgh* in *Scotland*, the Twenty third of *April* 1500. He made a wonderful Progress in School-Divinity; and entered early the Lists against *Luther*. It was at that time the Controversy in fashion, and the great Field of Battle, wherein young and old Authors endeavoured to give Proofs of their Merit. He had his Share, a little while after, in the Verbal Dispute, which *Patrick Hamilton* maintained against the Ecclesiastics [*A*], concerning certain new Opinions, which he had gained a Relish of at *Marpurg*. He endeavoured to bring him back to the Catholic Religion, but could not prevail upon him; and began himself to entertain Doubts concerning his own Religion, from this Gentleman's Discourse, but much more from the Constancy he shewed on the Wood-Pile, on which *David Beton*, Archbishop of *St Andrews*, caused him to be burnt. The Doubts of our *Alesius* would perhaps have been attended with no Consequence, if they had let him quietly enjoy the Canonship, which he possessed in the Metropolitan Church of *St Andrews*; but he was persecuted with so much Violence, that he was forced to retire into *Germany* [*B*], where at length all his Doubts vanished. At first indeed he wavered a little between the two Religions, as may be seen in his Answers to *Cochleus*: But at last he embraced *Lutheranism*, and persevered in it to his Death. It is true, that, between several Parties, which arose in that Sect, he sometimes inclined to the side of the less Orthodox. Thus, in 1560, he maintained the Doctrine of *George Major* concerning the Necessity of Good Works [*C*]. I forgot to observe, that the Alteration, which happened in *England*, with respect to Religion, after the Marriage of *Henry* VIII with *Anne Bullen*, occasioned *Alesius* to repair to *London* in 1535. He was greatly

countenanced

[*A*] *He had his Share, a little while after, in the Verbal Dispute, which* Patrick Hamilton *maintained against the Ecclesiastics.*] *Beza* has, in few Words, given us the Elogy of this Protestant Martyr, who was of a Family related to the Kings of *Scotland*. He places his Martyrdom in the Year 1530 (1). *Buchanan* places it in the Year 1528 (2), and says, the Earl of *Arran*'s Brother was his Father, and the Duke of *Albigni*'s Sister, was his Mother. He observes, that, a little after his Execution, the Death of a Dominican, who had been his Accuser, occasioned a great Consternation in the Minds of the People. This Dominican's Name was *Alexander Campbell*; he was a young Man of great Genius, and Learning: He had often discoursed with *Hamilton*, about the Interpretation of Scripture, and had confessed to him, that he acknowledged most of the Doctrines for true, which pass'd at that time for Paradoxes. *Hamilton*, remembering this Confession, treated him as a vile Wretch, when he found that he was his Accuser, and cited him before the Throne of God. These Words affected him in such a Manner, that he lost his Senses, and died mad some time after (3). *Alesius* relates many Particulars concerning the Execution of *Patrick Hamilton* (4), which *Rabus* inserted in his German History of Martyrs.

[*B*] *He was persecuted with so much Violence, that he was forced to retire into* Germany.] This Persecution was raised against him, for preaching warmly before a Provincial Synod, in 1529, against fornicating Priests. The Provost of *St Andrews*, whose lewd Intercourses were known to every body, apply'd the Sermon to himself, and fancied it was preach'd on purpose to turn the Eyes of the whole Congregation upon him. He resolved to be revenged the first Opportunity; and, as he was of a Temper a thousand times more fit for a Soldier than a Canon, he made choice only of violent means. Hearing that the whole Chapter was assembled to send Complaints against him to King *James* V, he came to the Assembly with an armed Retinue, and ordered *Alesius* to be seized; who exhorted him to moderate his Anger; nay, he drew a Sword upon him, in answer to his just Remonstrance. The poor Canon was so terrified, that he threw himself at the Provost's Feet, and humbly begged his Life of him. He came off with a kick on the Stomach, which made him fall into a Swoon: After which he was carried to Prison: All the rest of the Canons were likewise imprisoned; but the King, being informed of the Matter, ordered them to be set at Liberty. *Alesius* alone was not released; on the contrary, he was clapped into a dreadful Dungeon, where he remained One and twenty Days. His Liberty was of no long Continuance; he thought he ought to acquaint the Magistrates with the ill Treatment he had suffered: Whereupon the Provost, who had forbid him to acquaint them with it, caused him to be imprisoned again, and represented to the Archbishop, that he had published heretical Opinions in his Synodal Sermon, and that he deserved to be punished. He was so vexed at *Alesius*'s being let out of Prison, while he was on a Journey, that he wanted by all means to send him thither again, without suffering him to finish a Mass, which he had began. But at last the Intreaties of the Canons softened him; he waited 'till the end of the Mass, to remand him back to Prison. Now, as they knew he would be confined again in the Dungeon the next Day, they advised the Prisoner to make his escape in the Night, and to leave *Scotland*. He followed this Advice, and went into *Germany*, in the Year 1532 (5).

[*C*] *He maintained the Doctrine of* George Major, *concerning the Necessity of good Works.*] The Title of his Book is, *De necessitate & merito bonorum operum disputatio proposita in celebri Academia Lipsica, ad xxix diem Novemb.* 1560. This Dispute is the fifth *inter Anti-Tapperianas*; and thus we have an *Anti* to add to Mr *Baillet*'s Collection. Upon this Occasion, I shall set down the Titles of his principal Works. *Commentarii in Evangelium Joannis, & in utramque*

Epistolam

ALESIUS.

countenanced there by *Cranmer*, Archbishop of *Canterbury*, by *Latimer*, and by *Thomas Cromwell*, who was at time in great Credit with the King; and he taught publickly. The Fall of these Favourites obliged him to return into *Germany*, where the Elector of *Brandenburgh* made him Professor of Divinity, at *Francfort* on the *Oder*, in the Year 1540. *Alesius* had a Dispute, there, two Years after, upon the Question, *Whether the Magistrate may and ought to punish Fornication* [D]. He held the Affirmative,

Epistolam ad Timotheum. Expositio in Psalmos Davidis. De justificatione, contra Osiandrum. De sancta Trinitate, cum confutatione erroris Valentini Gentilis. Responsio ad 32 articulos Theologorum Lovaniensium, &c.

[D] *He had a Dispute —— upon the question, whether the Magistrate may and ought to punish Fornication*] This Dispute did not turn upon Adultery, but on simple Fornication: for though the Punishment of Adultery is as rare, as the Crime is frequent, yet it is accounted lawful among Christian Doctors. So that *Alesius* had only an Antagonist to oppose, who maintained against him, that the Magistrate neither can, nor ought, to punish Fornication. The final Decision of this Dispute was put off; and it is very probable, that *Alesius*, being angry at this Delay, would live no longer among People, who appeared such Favourers of the Impunity of Fornication. "Cum A. 1542, *says* Thomasius (6), inter ipsam & alium quendam "exorta esset controversia de quæstione, possit ne ac "debeat Magistratus Politicus scortationem punire? "veramque sententiam, hoc est affirmantem, ac Philippi quoque Melanchthonis calculo approbatam *, defenderet Alesio, nihilominùs hujus disputationis "decisio juberetur differri: offensus, ut apparet, hâc "bonæ causæ procastinatione Alesius, non expectato "Principis adventu, discessit †." Such an indignation did not ill become a Professor of Divinity, who had seen the rise of the Reformation, and who would naturally wish that he might not live to see Morality return to it's former Relaxation. Nothing could reflect greater Honour upon the Protestant Religion, than the Severity of it's Maxims, in relation to Chastity; for the Observation of these Maxims is the most difficult Victory we can obtain over Nature, and that which best shews our Dependance upon God, by the reciprocal Ties of his Protection and Love. It was, therefore, matter of great Scandal, that, in the Year 1542, a Protestant Divine, who maintained, that Magistrates may, and ought to, punish Fornication, should meet with Opposition, and, in some measure, sink under it. At present, as we are accustomed to a Toleration of this Crime, scarce any one is offended at it. A very honest Man assured me, lately, that the Magistrates of *Strasburg* have such an Indulgence for a Girl, who suffers herself to be got with Child, that, provided she pays the Fine, at which this kind of Fault is taxed, they restore her to her former Character, and inflict Penalties on those, who dare, in the least, to reproach her for the future. This is, doubtless, a more singular Privilege, than that of restoring, by Patent, such Families as have derogated from their Nobility; and if I may be allowed to laugh upon so serious an Occasion, I would say, that the Magistrates of *Strasburg* ought to have stipulated the Preservation of this Privilege, when they capitulated with *France*, and when, after the Peace of *Ryswick*, they demanded a Renewal of their Capitulation (7). I am aware, that they do not pretend, by this Prerogative, to overthrow the Truth of that ancient and undeniable Axiom.

---- Nulla reparabilis arte
Læsa Pudicitia est, deperit illa semel.

*No Art can Modesty, when lost, restore,
Once forfeited, 'tis ne'er recover'd more.*

They do not pretend, physically speaking, to restore a lost Maiden-head; this would be to oppose the true Sense of the Axiom: but, morally speaking, they pretend to restore it; since they patronize the Reputation of a lewd Girl, and secure her from Reproach; in omuch that she may carry her Head as lofty as an honest Woman. Nay, 'tis said, that the Efficacy of their Sentence is such, that Women, who have had Children, and who, by paying their Fine, have renewed their Reputation, meet with Husbands as easily, and almost as advantageously, as if they had not committed the Fault. But I would rather ascribe this to the weakness of the Men, who marry them, than to their Persuasion of the Efficacy of the Sentence (8). However, we may apply to those, who suppose that the Payment of a Fine makes amends for Crimes of this Nature, what was said to those, who fancied that a little fair Water could wash away the Stain of Murder.

Ah! nimium faciles, qui tristia crimina cædis
Fluminea tolli posse putatis aqua (9).

*Fools! on external Sprinklings Stress to lay,
And think that they can wash the Stains of Guilt away.*

The same honest Man assured me, that what he knew for certain of the Customs of *Strasburg*; he had been informed was practised in some other Parts of *Germany*. Such Laws would have made the Divine, whose Article I am writing, very angry; for this is so far from punishing Fornication, that it is in some degree to reward it, since the Advantage of appearing every where without fear of Reproach, is a Benefit, which greatly exceeds the Damage sustained by the Payment of the Fine, which sometimes is not one half of the Money, which is got by Prostitution.

I have heard some very judicious Persons say, that the Practice of a great many Countries is rather a Reward, than a Punishment, of Fornication. This Practice requires, that whoever owns himself to be the Father of a Bastard, shall be condemned to keep it, and to give the Mother a Sum of Money. An Order for the Maintenance of the Child cannot pass for a Punishment; since the Law of Nature plainly lays this Obligation on every Man. Nothing therefore but the Money, which is paid to the Girl, can be called a Punishment; but, besides that it is a very light Punishment to the Father, it is, properly speaking, a Reward to the Mother. "Now it is very "strange, *say those Gentlemen*, that Christian Tribunals should decree Rewards to Women for losing their Honour, and scandalizing the Public." Some one replied, that the Loss they suffered, and which rendered it more difficult for them to get a Husband, required some Amends, as an Act of Justice. "No, *answered they*, it is not an Act of "Justice, but meer Favour and Grace: Justice does "not require, that those who suffer by a voluntary "Transgression of the Laws of God, and of Human "Honour, should be indemnified. And, if the Sovereign will bestow Favours, he ought to make "choice of more worthy Objects. Would a Man "be obliged to reward a Girl, who, in committing "a Robbery for his Sake, or through his Instigation, should lose an Arm or a Leg? The Judge "would be so far from decreeing her any Reparation for the Loss she sustained, that he would condemn her to a corporal Punishment. The same "would happen in all punishable Cases, wherein "she should lose a Limb, in executing her Lover's "Counsels. Fornication alone is excepted out of this "Rule: Let us call it then *the common Offence, and* "*the privileged Case*. Words separately appropriated to other things (10), and about which a Book "was published at *Paris*, in the Year 1611 (11)." Upon this some one alledged, that the Magistrates of *Amsterdam*, being tired with the Complaints of so many Servant Maids, who accused their young Masters of having got them with Child, made a Law, that, for the future, these sort of Creatures should be paid but twenty five *Florins*; for which they should be obliged to keep the Child; that they thought by this means to lay a restraint upon Lewdness: for they were sensible that the Profit, which accrued to these Girls from their ill Conduct, induced them either to make Advances, or to yield to the first Sollicitation; and that, in a Word, their Lewdness ought to be deprived of all Hope of Gain, and not encouraged by the Expectation of what the Courts

ALESIUS.

tive, with *Melancthon*. I cannot tell, whether he took it ill, that the Decision of this Dispute was delay'd; and whether this Discontent was the occasion of his leaving *Francfort* with so much Precipitation; but it is certain, that the Court of *Brandenburgh* complained of him, and that they wrote to the University of *Wittemburgh* to have him punished. The Affection he had for *Melancthon* made People believe, that he was retired to *Wittemburgh* [*E*]; but he chose rather to go to *Leipsic*, where he refused, in 1543, a Professorship in the University, which *Albert*, Duke of *Prussia*, designed to erect at *Konigsberg*, and which was erected there the following Year. It is not certain, whether he had a Professorship in the University of *Leipsic* at that time; or whether they only gave him Hopes of the Divinity-Chair, which he afterwards enjoy'd till his Death, which happened on the seventeenth of *March* 1565 [*F*]. He was miraculously preserved from Death in his Youth [*G*]. The Esteem and Authority he possessed appear from the great Number of Conferences, at which he assisted [*H*]. He married an *English* Woman, by whom he had two Daughters, and a Son.

Courts should think proper to adjudge them. To this it was answered, that it is not certain, that such Laws have been made at *Amsterdam*, tho' the Fame of them was spread over other Towns of that Country. Whether it be true or false, it is very certain, that this proves, that People are not ignorant, that the common Conduct of the Courts of Judicature is too favourable to Fornication, and that it encourages young Women to Debauchery, rather than lays a Restraint upon their Modesty. And this is plain from hence, that Sovereigns, in punishing Transgressors of the Decalogue, are not directed by the Sinfulness of the Action, but by the temporal Prejudice, which the State receives from it. Hence it is that they punish Robbers and Murderers; but, because Fornication seems more useful than prejudicial to the temporal Good of the State, they connive at it, and behave in such a manner, as to make People think, that they are not displeased with having their Towns peopled *per fas & nefas*. If they laid the Law of God to Heart in this Point, they would increase the Fear of Infamy, instead of removing it; they would impose large Fines, to be paid, not to the Girls, who transgress, but to Hospitals; they would brand with Disgrace both the Tempter, and her, who could not resist the Temptation: and, because Infamy is not sufficient among Persons of mean Birth to stop a certain Coquetry, which animates the Tempter, which prevents him, and assures him of Victory with the utmost ease, they would inflict a more sensible Punishment, for which they could not fail of finding the proper Methods.

Ecclesiastical Discipline is very near fallen into the same Relaxation. It is but few Years (12) since a young Gentleman's Tutor made his Addresses, in a Town of - - - - to a young Coquet; and soon obtained what he desired of her. As soon as her Relations perceived that she was with Child, they endeavoured to marry her to our Spark. He refused it; for, besides that the easiness of his Conquest was no great Inducement to him to think of marrying her, he did not believe himself to be the only Person, who had a Finger in the Pye, or that the Child was more his own Manufacture than another's. The only Method of obliging him to take her to Wife, was to threaten him, that, if he did not marry her, he should lose the Benefice he had in *England*. He married her, and thereby preserved his Benefice. Such was the Reward of Coquetry; a Coquetry, which had been carried to the most scandalous Excess. What would the ancient Fathers say, if they were to return into the World? they might well cry out, casting their Eyes on the Face of the Church, *O domus antiqua, quam dispari dominaris domino!* It is the Fate of all Religions, as well as all Politic Bodies, to be the worse for Age. Men, indeed, are more corrupt in their Youth, than in an advanced Age. But it is quite otherwise with Republics. There is nothing like new Laws (13). Laws are like Bread and Eggs, *pan d'un di, ovo d'un' hora*. ——— Bread for a Day, an Egg for an Hour. The flourishing State of a Code, (I mean the Practice and Observation of the Laws) is That of Infancy. See the Complaint of a Poet, who had described some Abuses of *Augustus*'s Age. It resembles That of *Jesus Christ*, from the beginning it was not so (14).

- - - - - Non ita Romuli
Præscriptum, & intonsi Catonis
Auspiciis, veterumque norma (15).

Not so, at first, great Romulus prescribed;
Severe the Laws, when Cato was our Guide.
With better Principles our Fathers liv'd,
And juster Maxims were, of old, receiv'd.

In this respect, Sects and Communities, &c. resemble MAN, who is innocent only in the Cradle, and a Year or two after. Let us observe, that there are some Protestant Countries (16), where they still use some Severity against Fornication, both with respect to Women and Men. But I am sure that our *Alexander Alesius* would require something farther still. What would he say of other Countries?

I must farther observe, that the Courts, which adjudge a Pecuniary Profit to loose Women, or which condemn them to marry those, who debauched them, do it to avoid many Inconveniencies: but they increase thereby the Disorders of Impurity; for every Sentence they pronounce of this kind is a real Advantage to one naughty Woman, and a Motive of Hope to twenty more. Every Girl, who gets a Husband this way, is an Encouragement to others to attempt the same Methods. This abuse has been perceived in *France*: The new Laws are not so favourable there, as the old ones were, to those Ladies, who make too great an Advantage of the Privileges of Marriage. It is a Sacrament, which has a retroactive Virtue, and which, like that of Penance, is a Plank after Shipwreck. It makes one enter again into the Port of Honour; it repairs old Breaches; it legitimates Children unlawfully begotten (17); To say nothing of the thick Veil, with which it covers new Breaches, current Frailties, and daily Offences.

[*E*] *The Affection, which he had for* Melancthon, *made People believe he was retired to* Wittemburgh.] *Melancthon*, in his Two hundred and ninetieth Letter, expresses some uncertainty, whether *Alesius* did not doubt of his Friendship. In his Two hundred eighty eighth Letter, he declares, that he observed in him certain Whims and Starts of Temper, τραχυτέλους κ τραχυλόγους θυμούς.

[*F*] *His Death happened on the seventeenth of* March 1565.] The Calendar of *Peter Eberus* notes, that *Alesius* died on the eighteenth of *March*, 1565, being Seventy five Years of Age: the first Fault is very small, since it is but of one Day; but the second is of ten Years, and therefore more considerable. *Alesius* himself wrote, in the Register of the University of *Leipsic*, that he was born in the Year 1500. *Bucholcerus* (18), and *Reusnerus* (19), give him as long a Life as *Paul Eberus*. This whole Remark is taken out of *Thomasius*. *Bucholcerus* might have been reprimanded for another thing, viz. for saying that *Alesius* lived and taught in *Germany*, after his coming to *Wittemburgh*; that is to say, after the Year 1533.

[*G*] *He was miraculously preserved from Death in his Youth.*] He says, in one of his Books (20), that he often recollects (but that the Thought chills his very Blood), that as he was tumbling towards a Precipice, on the Top of a very high Mountain, he felt himself transported to another Place, without knowing how, or by whom; which he attributes to the Faith of his Relations, and not to the small Papers, which he carried about him, containing some Verses of St *John*'s Gospel, according to the Custom of Children in those Times.

[*H*] *The great Number of Conferences, at which he assisted.*] In the Year 1555, when those of *Norimberg* desired *Melancthon* to come and compose the Dissensions

a Son. He had but one Daughter living, when he died. I have extracted this from a Speech of *James Thomasius*, Professor at *Leipsic*, in the Year 1683, in 8vo. His whole Account is accompanied with Citations. I did not think my self obliged to copy them: They, who would apply to the Originals, will easily meet with the Speech, which points them out.

Diſſentions, which the Diſciples of *Andrew Oſiander* cauſed in their City (21), he brought *Aleſius* with him, who performed his Part very well in the Diſputes they engaged in (22). *Melanchthon* knew him to be very capable of this; he had had him for his Aſſiſtant in 1554, in the Conference of *Naumburg*, which was held to appeaſe the Theological Troubles of *Pruſſia*. *Camerarius* praiſes *Aleſius* very much on this Account. "Alexander Aleſius, patria Scotus, "valde carus Philippo Melancthoni, rei Theologicæ "intelligentiſſimus, & artifex excellens congruentium "diſputationum, & vir dignitate atque doctrina ex-"quiſita præſtans (23). —— Alexander Aleſius, a "Scotch Man, greatly in Favour with Philip Melanchthon, thoroughly verſed in Divinity, *who had an excel-* "lent Talent at Diſputation, and famous for his extra-"ordinary Merit and Learning." He had obſerved in another Place, that *Graunvelt*, who preſided in the Conference of *Worms*, in the Name of *Charles* V, in 1541, would not let *Aleſius* ſpeak, whom the Elector of *Brandenburg* had ſent thither. "Qui qui-"dem & paratus erat & cupidus conflictus, ſed huic "obſtitit juſſum præſidis, qui & Aleſium ad pugnam "inſtructum ſciret, & talem adminiſtrationem rei vi-"cioſam eſſe animadverteret. —— *Who was both* "*ready and eager to engage; but was prevented by* "*Order of the Preſident, who knew that Aleſius was* "*come prepared for the Combat, and obſerved, that* "*ſuch a Management of the Affair would be wrong.*"

ALEXANDER AB ALEXANDRO [*A*], a *Neapolitan* Civilian of great Learning, flouriſhed about the end of the XVth Century, and beginning of the XVIth [*B*]. He applied himſelf to the Profeſſion of the Law with ardor, firſt at *Naples*, and afterwards at *Rome* (*a*); but he ſpent all the Time he could ſteal from the Fatigues of Pleading, in the Study of polite Literature, and at laſt entirely quitted the Bar, to lead a more calm and agreeable Life with the Muſes. The Reaſon he alledges for abandoning the Profeſſion of an Advocate [*C*], was the Ignorance or Corruption of thoſe who adminiſtred Juſtice; which inclined him rather to live a retired Life, than to take much Pains in ſtudying the Civil Law, ſince his Labours would avail nothing againſt the Raſhneſs of a corrupt Judge (*b*). He had ſeen many Examples of this Diſorder at *Rome*, which he mentioned to *Raphael Volaterranus*, who aſked him the Reaſon of his Retreat. It is ſomewhat ſtrange, that, among ſo many Men of Learning, who were his Cotemporaries, or who wrote Elogies of the learned Men of thoſe

[*A*] Alexander ab Alexandro.] I give him his *Latin* Name according to the Grammarians. They who tranſlate it *Alexander of Alexandria* are miſtaken (1). Our Author was of a *Neapolitan* Family of the Name of *Alexander*. It is pretended, that it had before produced ſome Illuſtrious Perſons, as *Moreri* relates after *Lorenzo Craſſo*. Every one knows *Balzac*'s pleaſant Reflexion. "Was there not, *ſays he* (2), "a Grammatico-Civilian in the Kingdom of *Naples*, "who aſſumed the Name of ALEXANDER AB "ALEXANDRO? Can any thing be more mag-"nificent and more glorious than to be twice an "*Alexander*, an *Alexander* by one's Name, and an "*Alexander* by one's Lordſhip (3)?"

[*B*] *Flouriſhed about the End of the* XV*th* *Century and beginning of the* XVI*th*] My reaſon for ſaying this, is, that our Author, ſpeaking of the Calamities of the Kingdom of *Naples*, carries them down to the Death of *Frederic*, the Son of *Ferdinand* I (4), that is, to the Year 1504. beſides, he ſpeaks of *Jovianus Pontanus*, as of a Perſon no longer in being (5). Now *Jovianus Pontanus* did not die before the Year 1505. This is what eſcaped thoſe, who placed the Death of our *Alexander* in the Year 1494, in which *Moreri* gives them a much ſtronger Proof of his Approbation than of his Uncertainty.

[*C*] *The Reaſon he alledges for abandoning the Profeſſion of an Advocate*] To give the Author's Reaſon in it's full Force, I muſt ſet it down in his own Words "Quæ cum viderem, *ſays he* (6), patro-"niſque contra vim potentiorum aut gratiam nihil "præſidii eſſe, nihil opis, fruſtra nos in legum con-"troverſiis & ediſcendis tot caſuum varietatibus tam "penſiculate editis tantum laboris & vigiliarum ſuſ-"cipere, tantoque nos ſtudio fatigari dicebam, cum "ad ignaviſſimi impuriſſimique cujuſque temeritatem, "qui juri dicendo præſideret, quem leges virum bo-"num eſſe volunt, non æquo jure ſed ad gratiam "& libidinem judicia ferri, decretaque legum tanto "conſilio edita convelli & labefactari viderem. —— "*When I ſaw theſe things, and that it was impoſ-*"*ſible for the Advocates to ſupport their Clients a-*"*gainſt the Power and Favour of the Great, I ſaid,* "*it was to no Purpoſe to take ſo much Pains, and* "*undergo ſo great a Fatigue, in ſtudying the Law,* "*and thoroughly conſidering all it's Variety of Caſes;* "*ſince I could not but obſerve, that the Iſſue of Suits* "depended not on the *Juſtice of the Cauſe, but on* "*the Favour and Affection of a lazy and corrupt* "*Judge, whom the Laws ſuppoſe to be a good and* "*upright Man; and that the judicial Decrees, ſo* "*equitably contrived, were every Day broke in upon,* "*and weakened.*" It was much better to quit the Bar, than to imitate the Practice of ſome Advocates, who, having loſt many good Caſes, undertake to defend the worſt. I have read not long ago, "That "one of the moſt famous Advocates of this Age, "whom his Brethren aſked, why he took upon him "to plead bad Cauſes, anſwer'd them ſmiling, that "He did it, becauſe he had loſt a great many good "ones. This is a bad excuſe, *continues the Author*; "an Advocate, who, having examined a Cauſe, "finds it unjuſtifiable, ought to leave it (7). I have met with another Paſſage in the Book of *Alexander ab Alexandro*, which ſhews the Integrity of his Heart (8). One of his Friends, ſeeing, that he did not puſh his Fortune, adviſed him to make uſe of the Expedients, which had ſucceeded ſo well with ſuch and ſuch Perſons, whom he named to him; who had been raiſed by Favour to Honours and Mitres, in ſpite of the Merit of their Competitors, and who had attained to Favour by unlawful Methods. Our Author was not ignorant of theſe Examples, and knew ſome that were worſe; he had ſeen in his Youth a very honeſt Man, well verſed in *Latin* and *Greek*, who, having ſtruggled with an extream Poverty, while he relied only on his Virtue and Learning, reſolved to try another way: He engaged in ſuch villanous Arts, as are improper to be mentioned, and in a little while he became Rich and Powerful, and was poſſeſſed of good Preferments. "Eo veſaniæ proceſſit, ut, coactus "inopia, obſcœnis & libero homine indignis artibus "vacaret (quibus vero artibus non libet dicere, ita "fœdæ & pudendæ ſunt) conſectaque fuit ſibi res "ex ſententia; namque haud multo poſt & ſacerdotio "ex opibus auctus, affluens & beatus, tranquilliſſime "vitam egit (9)." But theſe Examples did not ſtagger our Advocate; he choſe rather to be contented with a mean Fortune, than to hazard his Conſcience. "Longe igitur multumque præſtat, ſatiuſque fuit "uti ingenio meo, vacuumque his moleſtiis modico "civiliuſque cultu contentum eſſe, neque in ambitio-"nem non neceſſariam incurrere, quam bona animi, ſi "quæ ſibi homo ſtudio & labore paravit, ea turpi quæſtu "peſſimo

ALEXANDER ab ALEXANDRO.

those times, scarce any one mentions him [D]. We should know but few Particulars of his Life, if he himself had not touched upon some of them in his Work (c). We find there, that he lodged in a House, at *Rome*, which was haunted with Spirits (d) so that here is an Evidence to be produced against the Incredulous; an Evidence, I say, who pretends to have seen, and who relates the surprizing Pranks of the Apparition, which disturbed the House. He tells us farther, that, when he was very young, he went to *Philelphus*'s Lectures, who explained *Cicero's Tusculan Questions* at *Rome* (e). We may gather from the Twenty first Chapter of the fourth Book, that he was at *Rome*, when *Nicolas Perottus*, and *Domitius Calderinus*, read public Lectures there on *Martial* [E]. I do not find, that he speaks of the Office of Prothonotary of the Kingdom of *Naples*, which it is said he exercised with great Reputation (f). I cannot tell when he died, but I know that he was buried in the Monastery of the *Olivetans* (g). Every one blamed him for the Affectation he shewed, in not quoting the Authors, who furnished him with his Materials (h). *Tiraquellus* remedied this Omission by a learned Commentary, which was printed at *Lyons* in 1587 (i). It was reprinted at *Leyden* in two Volumes in 8vo, in the Year 1673, with the Notes of *Dionysius Gothofredus, Christopher Colerus*, and *Nicolas Mercerus*, on the same Text. I find by *Gesner*'s *Bibliotheque*, that the Edition, published at *Paris*, of this Work of *Alexander ab Alexandro*, in the Year 1532, was more exact than the rest, and that *Gerard Morrhius*, who corrected it, had collated with the Originals the Passages, which the Author had taken from others. He must, then, have collated a great many; for the six Books of the *Dies Geniales* are scarce any thing but a large Collection, relating to the History and Customs of the ancient *Greeks* and *Romans*; besides several Grammatical Questions. Exactness is not in it's Perfection in this Work [F]. I do not believe, that the *French* Translation of this Work, by *Bernard de la Roche* (k), was ever printed. The Author of the *Neapolitan Bibliotheque* had no Success in the Article of our *Alexander* [G]; but the Additions of *Leonardo Nicodemo* are very curious on this Subject [H].

Alciatus

"pessimo Exemplo foedare (10)." The Advice, which was given him, is much like this.

Aude aliquid brevibus Gyaris & carcere dignum,
Si vis esse aliquis. Probitas laudatur & alget (11).

Would'st thou to Honours and Preferments climb?
Be bold in Mischief, dare some mighty Crime;
Which Dungeons, Death, or Banishment deserves,
For Virtue is but dryly prais'd, and starves.

DRYDEN.

He dedicated his Book to the Duke of *Atri*. This Duke was very learned, as we shall observe under AQUAVIVA.

[D] *Scarce any one mentions him.*] Yet, if we may believe *Moreri*, all the great Men of That Age, as *Georgius Trapezuntius, Theodorus Gaza, Domitius Calderinus, Pontanus*, &c. *were his Friends and his Admirers*. All that can be gathered from the Book itself of *Alexander ab Alexandro*, is, that, in his Youth, he heard the Lectures, which *Philelphus* read at *Rome*, who was then very old (12), and that he was entertained sometimes, together with some very learned Men, at the Houses of *Jovian Pontanus* (13), *Hermolaus Barbarus* (14), *Sannazarius* (15), *Gabriel Altilius* (16), &c. This is not a sufficient Warrant to affirm, that certain Persons admire certain Persons. See the following Remark.

[E] *Was at Rome, when Nicolas Perottus, and Domitius Calderinus, read public Lectures there on Martial.*] This is all that can be gathered from what he relates concerning *Nicolas Perottus*, and *Domitius Calderinus*: As for that great Intimacy, which *Panzirolus* pretends there was between them (17), it must be looked for elsewhere, and I cannot tell whether it be possible to find any Proofs of it. I question not, but *Panzirolus* trusted to his Memory for this Particular, without considering, that the Memory is a Mould, in which Objects change their Form very easily.

[F] *Exactness is not in it's Perfection in this Work.*] I chuse rather to alledge the Testimony of one of the Commentators, than to pass this Censure on my own Authority. Let us hear then what *Nicolas Mercerus* says. "Est profecto, mi Linoceri (18), verum quod aiant. "Fuit Alexander vir eruditus & multae lectionis: mul- "ta ad utilitatem publicam scripsit eleganter, mul- "ta tamen, ut hominum est infirmitas, minus accu- "rate, vel memoriae vitio, vel imprudentia lapsus. "Quae lectoribus indicari magni interfuit. —— *The*

common Opinion, Friend Linocerius, *is very true. Alexander was a Man of Learning and great reading. He wrote many Things for public Use with Elegance; but in many things, such is human Infirmity, he was deficient, for want either of Memory or Skill. It was highly proper to inform the Reader of this.*" I am not the only Person, who complains, that Editors of Books, *cum notis Variorum*, leave out the Epistles Dedicatory, and the Prefaces (19). They should do, as was done in the last Edition of *Diogenes Laertius* (20). If the same had been practised in that of *Alexander ab Alexandro*, I might have given a better account of this Author and his Book.

[G] *The Author of the* Neapolitan Bibliotheque *had no Success in the Article of our* Alexander.] He only refers his Readers to three or four other Books (21), and was ignorant, that *Alexander Jurisconsultus Neapolitanus*, Author of the four Dissertations, of which he gives the Title (22), is the same with *Alexander ab Alexandro*; insomuch that he speaks twice of the same Man, without knowing that they are different Authors. The Title of the four Dissertations is as follows. "Alexandri Jurisconsulti Neapolitani Dissertationes quatuor de rebus admirandis, quae in Italia nuper contigere, id est, de somniis quae à viris spectatae fidei prodita sunt, inibique de laudibus Juniani Maii somniorum conjectoris: de umbrarum figuris & falsis imaginibus: de illusionibus malorum dæmonum, qui diversis imaginibus homines delusere: de quibusdam ædibus, quæ Romæ infames sunt ob frequentissimos lemures, & terrificas imagines, quas author ipse singulis fere noctibus in Urbe experte est: Romæ, in 4to. Absque anno nec apud quem. —— Alexander, *the* Neapolitan *Civilian, his four Dissertations concerning the wonderful Things, which have lately happened in* Italy, *viz. of Dreams, related by Men of unquestionable Veracity, herein this of the Praises of* Junianus Maius, *Interpreter of Dreams; of the Shapes and deceitful Appearances of Spectres; of the Illusions of Evil Spirits, who deceive Men by various Appearances; of certain Houses at* Rome, *which are infamous on account of frequent Apparitions, and frightful Sights, which the Author himself was very Night a Witness of at* Rome, *in 4to.*" They have neither set down the Printer's Name, nor the Year of the Impression. We shall see, in the following Remark, that these Pieces have been incorporated with the *Dies Genialis*.

[H] *The Additions of* Leonardo Nicodemo *are very curious on this Subject.*] He proves, that *Alexander*

VOL. I. Nº. VIII.

ab

Alciatus believed, that ALEXANDER *ab Alexandro* was yet living, in the Year 1521. I shall give his own Words, because they contain his Opinion of this Writer [*I*].

ab Alexandro is the Author of the four Dissertations, because most of the Particulars they contain are to be met with in the *Dies Geniales*: For Example, that which relates to the Praises of *Junianus Maius*, and the Interpretation of Dreams (23), is to be found in the eleventh Chapter of the first Book, where this *Junianus* is represented as one, who had daily a crowd of Dreamers attending him, whose Dreams he interpreted in a very intelligible manner, whereby many Persons avoided Death, or great Troubles. Read the Twenty third Chapter of the fifth Book (24), where you will find what concerns the Apparitions and Hobgobblings, which haunted the Author's own House. We find the Title of an Edition in Folio, of the *Dies Geniales* in *Nicodemo*'s Additions: I should take it for the first, if a Passage of *Alciatus* did not hinder me (25). The Title is this. " Alexandri de Alexandro " *Dies Geniales*. Ne quis opus excudat denuo infra " septennium, sub diris imprecationibus Apostolica " autoritate interdictum est. —— Alexander ab Alex- " andro, his *Dies Geniales*. *It is ordered by Apostolical Authority, and upon pain of dreadful Anathemas, that no one reprint this Work, 'till seven Years are expired*." There is at the end, " Romæ, in ædi- " bus Jacobi Mazochii, Rom. Academiæ Bibliopolæ. " Anno Virginei partus 1522, Kalend. April. Pontif. " S. D. N. de cujus nomine pontificali adhuc non " constat, anno primo. —— *At* Rome, *sur* James Ma- " zochius, *Bookseller to the Academy of* Rome, *in* " *the Year of Christ* 1522, *the Kalends of* April, *in* " *the first Year of the Pontificate of* S. D. N. *whose* " *pontifical Name is not yet known*." *Nicodemo* mentions a Fragment of a Letter of *Jerome Niger* (26), which is not very complaisant to the *Neapolitans* in general, or our *Alexander* in particular. " Quel libro " d' Alessandro de gli Alessandri è intitolato *Dies Ge-* " *niales*, à similitudine delle notti Attiche d' Aulo Gel- " lio, è de' Saturnali di Macrobio, cose cavate di quà " è di là. Ed in vero ha molto del Napoletano, con " sopportazion del Sannazaro parlando. Vendesi sel " carlini, al parer mio troppo caro. —— *This Book* " *of Alexander ab Alexandro is entituled*, Dies Ge- " niales, *in imitation of the* Noctes Atticæ *of* Aulus " Gellius, *and the* Saturnalia *of* Macrobius, *which* " *are Collections from different Authors. In truth it* " *savours much of the* Neapolitan, *in speaking of* San- " nazarius *with Patience. It is sold for fix* Carlins, " *a Price, in my Opinion, much too great*." I shall give an Article concerning *Junianus Maius*, the *Artemidorus* of his Age.

[*I*] *I shall give his own Words, because they contain his Opinion of this Writer.*] I take them out of a Letter, which he wrote from *Milan*, the sixth of *May*, 1521, and which was printed in the Year 1697 (27). " Alexandri Jurisconsulti Neapolitani librum, " quem ad nos misisti, diligenter legi. Vir est do- " ctus & diligens, & non parum studiosos adjuvabit: " suspicor tamen eum quandoque falli. —— Si is " aliqua tecum familiaritate junctus est, velim ab eo " exquiras, ut Alpheni Jurisconsulti vetustissima scrip- " ta, commentariosque Senatus consultorum, quæ vi- " disse se, emiseque Romæ, ait, commodato det. " Eorum autem mentionem facit capite quarto & sep- " timo primi libri: suspicor enim nescio quid Parrha- " sianum, quem scis eos authores plerumque adducere " solitum, quos nunquam viderat. —— *I have carefully perused the Book of Alexander the Neapolitan Civilian, which you sent me. He is a learned and industrious Writer, and not a little useful to the Studious; but I suspect he is sometimes mistaken.* —— *If you have any acquaintance with him, pray beg the favour of him to lend you the ancient Works of* Alphenus *the Civilian, and the Commentaries on the* Senatus Consulta, *which he says he saw, and purchased, at* Rome; *he mentions them in the fourth and seventh Chapters of his first Book: For I suspect him of imitating* Parrhasius, *who, you know, was wont to alledge Authors, whom he never saw*."

ALEXANDER THE GREAT, King of *Macedonia*. Look for MACEDONIA.

ALEXANDER VII. Pope. Look for CHIGI.

ALEXANDER VIII. Pope. Look for OTTOBONI.

ALEXIS, a *Piemontois*. There is a Book of SECRETS under the Name of this *Alexis*. It was printed at *Basil* in 8vo, in the Year 1563, being translated from the *Italian* into *Latin* by *Wecker* (*a*). It was likewise translated into *French*, and printed several times with Additions. There is a Preface to it, wherein Signor *Alexis* informs the Public, that he was born of a Noble Family; that he applied himself to study from his Childhood; that he learned *Latin*, *Greek*, *Hebrew*, *Chaldee*, *Arabic*, and several other Languages; that, being particularly fond of the Secrets of Nature, he had collected as many of them as he could in his Fifty seven Years Travels; that he had piqued himself upon not communicating them to any one, but that, at the Age of Eighty two Years and seven Months, seeing a poor Man dead at *Milan*, whom he could have cured, if he had communicated one of his *Nostrums* to the Chirurgeon, he was touched with so great a Remorse of Conscience, that he nearly turned Hermit, and in this Solitude disposed his *Recipes* for Publication. The Hawkers carry them to Country-Fairs, with their other little Books, covered with blue Paper. It is true they have only the choice Remedies of Signor *Alexis*; the whole Collection would be too great a Volume for them.

ALFENUS VARUS (PUBLIUS) born at *Cremona*, first a Shoemaker, and afterwards a Disciple of the famous Civilian, *Servius Sulpitius* (*a*), and at last Consul, was a very learned Man in the Civil Law [*A*]. He was buried at the Public Expence. This is all that is said of him by one of the old Scholiasts upon *Horace*, in his

[*A*] *A very learned Man in the Civil Law.*] This Passage of *Ammianus Marcellinus* against the Advocates of his Time: " Hi, ut altius videantur jura " callere, Trebatium loquuntur, & Cascellium, & " Alfenum, & Auruncorum Sicanorumque jamdiu le- " ges ignotas (1). —— *These Men, that they may be* " *thought more deeply versed in the Science of the Law,* " *are ever talking of* Trebatius, Cascellius, *and* Alfenus, " *and the obsolete Laws of the* Aurunci *and* Sicani." This Passage, I say, is sufficient to convince us of the great Authority of the Name of *Alfenus*, in matters of Law. Add to this the Testimonies alledged by *Bertrand*, in the first Book of his Civilians (2).

[*B*] On

ALFENUS. 227

his Notes on a Passage, which relates to our *Alfenus* [B], whose Consulship, they say, fell out in the Year of *Rome* 754 (b). I will not warrant this. *Alfenus* wrote Forty Books of *Digests*, which are mentioned in the Index of the *Pandects*, and some Books of Collections, *Collectaneorum*. *Aulus Gellius* cites both these Works; and, tho' he refutes what he quotes out of them, yet he represents the Author as a Man, who was a great Enquirer into Antiquities [C]. The Civilian *Paulus* wrote an Abridgment of *Alfenus*'s Books (c). If it were true, that there was an *Alfenus* among the Counsellors of the Emperor *Alexander Severus* [D], who was a Disciple of *Papinian*, as some affirm from a very intricate Passage of *Lampridius*, he might be descended from the other; tho' it must be confessed that there were some *Alfenus*'s different from the Disciple of *Sulpitius*. There was an *Alfenus* mentioned by *Cicero* in his Oration for *Quinctius*, and an *Alfenus*, General of the Army under *Vitellius*, and Prefect of the *Prætorium*, who did not behave like a Man of Courage, when his Party was overcome by That of *Vespasian* (d). *Donatus*, in the Life of *Virgil*, speaks of an *Alfenus* [E], who, with some others, exempted the Lands of that Poet from the Fate, to which those of the Neighbourhood were exposed, when, after the Defeat of *Brutus*, they were assigned to the Soldiers. Very learned Persons believe, that He, who did *Virgil* that kind Office, was the same *Alfenus*, who had been formerly a Shoemaker, and the same *Alfenus*, whom *Catullus* speaks of (e). This is attended with some Difficulty [F]. See my Remarks, in which *Moreri* is sometimes shewn to be guilty of unpardonable Mistakes.

(b) See Cruquius in Hor. Sat. 3. lib. 1.

(c) Guil. Grot. Vitæ Jurisconf. pag. 86.

(d) Tacit. Histor. lib. 2. cap. 29, 43. & lib. 3. cap. 36, 55, 61. & lib. 4. cap. 11.

(e) Ducier upon Horace Sat. 3. lib. 1.

[B] *On a Passage, which relates to our* Alfenus.] The Words of *Horace* deserve to be produc'd.

——— *Alfenus vafer, omni*
Abjecto instrumento artis, clausaque taberna,
Sutor erat, sapiens operis sic optimus omnes
Est opifex, sic rex solus (3).

Skilful Alfenus, though he lost his Awl,
And threw away his Last, and shut his Stall,
And broke his Threads, yet was a Cobler still;
Thus each Mechanic, if he has but skill,
Is wise, and only King. CREECH.

(3) Horat. Sat. 3. l. 1. ver. 130.

[C] *Aulus Gellius* ——— *though he refutes what he quotes out of them, yet represents him as a great Enquirer into Antiquities.*] This relates to the Signification of these Words, *argentum purum putum*, which were in the Treaty of Peace, concluded between the Republic of *Rome*, and that of *Carthage*. The *Romans* were to receive every Year a certain Tribute of Money, *purum putum*, that is of good Alloy. *Moreri* imagined, that the proper name of that Tribute was *purum putum*, which is a pleasant Conceit enough. *Aulus Gellius* rejects, not without reason, the Sense, which *Alfenus* gave to these Words (4); and, if we were to judge of this Civilian's Capacity from hence, he would soon lose his great Reputation. He believed that *purum putum* was formed from *purus*, as *novicius* and *propicius* are form'd from *novus* and *propius*, in order to give more Force to the Signification of the primitive Word. *Aulus Gellius* refutes him solidly, and shews that *putum* signifies That, from which all Superfluities are retrench'd. He does not cite the Book, which *Moreri* quotes, to wit, the fourth and thirtieth of the *Digests*, nor That, which *Bertrand* alledges, to wit, the thirtieth of the same *Digests*; but he cites the Thirty fourth. As for the other Work, which he cites, it is entituled, *Conjectaneorum*, in the Edition of *Henry Stephens*; but I find that *Bertrand*, and *William Grotius*, read it *Collectaneorum*. This last Title seems to agree better with the Passages of the *Pandects*, where *Servius* is cited upon the Testimony of *Alfenus*, *Servius apud Alfenum notat, putat*; but it would be wrong to prefer, upon this Account, the latter Title to That, which *Henry Stephens* preferred. *Bertrand* makes *Aulus Gellius* say what he does not, to wit, that the Work, entituled *Collectanea*, consisted of four Books. These are *Aulus Gellius*'s Words: *In libro digestorum trigesimo & quarto, conjectaneorum autem secundo, in sordere, inquit,* &c (5). I do not question, but that, since *Bertrand* said, that *Aulus Gellius* quoted the thirtieth Book of the *Digests*, he believed that *& quarto* related to the following Words, and that, without taking notice of what follows, he concluded, that the fourth Book of the *Collectanea* had been cited; from whence, nevertheless, he had no reason to infer, that the Work contained but four Books, and that *Aulus Gellius* said so. Neither the critical Remarks on the Work of *Bertrand*, inserted in the Edition of *Leyden*, nor *William Grotius*, have taken notice of these small Mistakes. *Aulus Gel-*

(4) Aulus Gell. lib. 6. cap. 5.

(5) Id. Ib.

lius speaks to the Advantage of *Alfenus*: "*Alfenus* "Jurisconsultus, Servii Sulpitii Discipulus, Rerum- "que antiquarum non incuriosus (6). ——— *Alfenus,* "*the Civilian, Disciple of* Servius Sulpitius, *and a* "*curious Enquirer into Antiquity*."

(6) Lib. 6. cap. 5.

[D] *That there was an* ALFENUS *among the Counsellors of the Emperor* Alexander Severus.] The Passage of *Lampridius*, as it is printed, is so erroneous in some respects, that nothing can be concluded from it, for the Existence of an *Alfenus*, in the Reign of *Alexander Severus*. See *Casaubon* on that Passage. However *Moreri* should not have cited *Horace*, nor *Aulus Gellius*, for his *Alfenius*, *surnamed the younger,* who lived, says he, *in the Reign of* Alexander Severus.

[E] Donatus ——— *speaks of an* ALFENUS.] *Moreri*, giving an Article of this Person, pag. 170, calls him *Alphenius Varus*, *a Roman Knight*, and cites *Donatus in vita Virgilii*. But *Donatus* does not stile him a *Roman Knight*; and, besides, in the best Editions (7), it is *Alphenus, Varius*, as two different Persons, and not *Alphenius Varus*, as one Person. It must, nevertheless, be confess'd, that these Verses of the ninth Eclogue of *Virgil*, ver. 26.

(7) That of Hackius at Leyden 1680.

Immo hæc, quæ Varo necdum perfecta canebat,
Vare, tuum nomen (superet modò Mantua nobis,
Mantua væ miseræ nimium vicina Cremonæ)
Cantantes sublime ferent ad sidera cygni;

Or what unfinish'd be to Varus *read;*
Thy Name, O Varus *(if the kinder Powers*
Preserve our Plains, and shield the Mantuan *Towers,*
Obnoxious by Cremona's *neighbouring Crime)*
The Wings of Swans, and stronger-pinion'd Rhyme,
Shall raise aloft, and soaring beat above,
Th' immortal Gift of Gratitude to Jove.
  DRYDEN.

are applied, by the Grammarian *Servius*, to an *Alfenus Varus*, who was sent by *Augustus* to command beyond the *Po*, after *Pollio* had lost that Government. The same Grammarian observes, that some Persons have applied these other Verses of *Virgil* to the Civilian *Alfenus Varus*, Successor of *Servius Sulpitius*;

Nam neque adhuc Varo videor, nec dicere Cinna
Digna, sed argutos inter strepere anser olores (8).

I nor to Cinna's *Ears, nor* Varus *dare aspire,*
But gabble, like a Goose, amidst the Swan-like Quire.
  DRYDEN.

(8) Virgil. Eclog. 9. ver. 35.

The reason was, because *Alphus Varus* the Civilian was something of a Poet. *Servius* confutes them, by shewing, that this Elogy ought to be understood of the Poet *Varius*, whom *Horace* praised so much.

[F] *This is attended with some Difficulty.*] A Person, who applies himself with such Ardour to the Civil Law, that, by his great Progress, he not only wipes off the Disgrace, arising from the Mechanic Trade, which he

ALFONSUS. ALYPIUS.

he had exercised in his Native Country, but succeeds likewise the greatest Civilian at that time in the Republic of *Rome*, must probably be too sedate, to join with *Catullus*, and other Sparks of the same Stamp, in their Debauchery. But the *Alfenus*, of whom *Catullus* speaks, was of this Knot of Rakes.

(9) Catull. Epig. 31. Mr Dacier upon Horace, Sat. 3. lib. 1. cites the 27th Epigram of Catullus.

Alphene immemor, & unanimis false sodalibus (9)!

Forgetful Alphenus, *and false to your unanimous Companions!*

He introduced *Catullus* to his own Whore;

(10) Catull. Epig. 10.

Varus me meus ad suos Amores
Visum duxerat è fore otiosum,
Scortillum, ut mihi tum repente visum est,
Non illepidum, nec invenustum (10).

Varus *carried me Home from the Forum, being disengaged, to see his Mistress; who appeared to me, upon a sudden View, a smart, pretty, Wench.*

And therefore it is not very likely, that he was the Disciple of *Sulpitius*. *Muretus* was censured for saying, that *Varus*, who carried *Catullus* to his Mistress, was *Quintilius Varus*; and the Censure was grounded on this, that there were at least Fifty seven Years between the Defeat of the three Legions of *Varus*, and and the Visit, which *Catullus* speaks of. I make use of this Reason (11). There must be fifty Years, more or less, between this Visit, and the Consulship of *Alfenus* (12), and therefore it is very unlikely, that the Shoemaker of *Cremona*, if he was Consul in the Year of *Rome* 754, had such an intimate Acquaintance with *Catullus* fifty Years before: For a Country Shoemaker, who leaves his Trade; in order to study in the Capital City, can be no Boy; when he is intimate with Persons of Distinction. Add to this, that he, who did *Virgil* that good Office, commanded beyond the *Po* forty Years before the Consulship in Question (13). So that there is reason to doubt, whether *Alfenus*, who was Consul in the Year of *Rome* 754, be the same with *Virgil's* Benefactor: For it is seldom that a Man attains to great Dignities, when the usual time of arriving at them has been long over. This was the Case of those, who, after a Government of a Province, were forty Years without obtaining the Consular Dignity.

(11) Scilig. in Catull. Epigr. 10.

(12) It is placed in the 754th Year of Rome.

(13) Servius in Ecl. 9. ver. 29.

ALFONSUS. See the Kings of this Name under That of their respective Kingdoms.

ALYPIUS, of *Antioch*, lived in the Reign of *Julian* the Apostate. He had already commanded in *England*, when That Prince took it into his Head to rebuild the Temple of *Jerusalem*, and appointed him Overseer of the Work. *Alypius* promoted the Design with great Application, and was assisted in it by the Governor of the Province (a). Yet he was obliged to desist from the Undertaking; the Flames, which issued out of the Earth, rendring the Place inaccessible. Eight Years after, he found himself involved in a terrible Persecution, which destroyed a great number of People, and which was first raised against those, who had made use of Magic to discover the Successor of *Valens*. When the Commissioners for informing against the Guilty had set the Affair a-going, nothing was to be seen but accused Persons, who were immediately Condemned and Punished. *Alypius*, who had betaken himself to a private Life, in order to enjoy the Pleasures of Quiet, was attacked by the Informers, and accused of being a Poisoner (b). He was banished, and all his Estate confiscated. His Son *Hierocles*, being condemned to Death on the same Accusation, was happily saved, as he was led to the Place of Execution (c). The News of this fortunate Event mitigated *Alypius's* Affliction in his Exile. It is very probable, that the Author of the *Geographical Piece*, which pleased *Julian* the Apostate very much, is the same with our *Alypius* [A]; but I do not believe, that this Work is a Description of the Old World, which *James Godfrey* translated out of *Greek* into *Latin* [B]. I know nothing of one ALYPIUS, who wrote a Treatise of Music, entitled Εισαγωγη μουσικη, *Introductio Musica*, mentioned by *Cassiodorus*; *Meursius* was

(a) See Remark [A].

(b) See Remark [A].

(c) See the manner below, in the Article HIEROCLES.

[A] *The Author of the Geographical Piece, which pleased* Julian *the Apostate, is the same with our Alypius.*] This Author lived in the Reign of *Julian* the Apostate. We have two Letters, which that Prince wrote to him, which testify, that *Alypius* was the Brother of *Cæsarius*, and that he exercised a considerable Employ (1). This last Character agrees admirably well with *Alypius* of *Antioch*, who, after having been Deputy-Governor in *England*, was sent to *Judæa* to superintend the Building of the Temple. *Ammianus Marcellinus* informs us of these Particulars. "Ambitiosum quondam apud Hierosolymam templum. —— instaurare sumptibus cogitabat immodicis: Negotiumque maturandum Alypio dederat Antiochensi, qui olim Brittannias curaverat pro præfectis. Cum itaque rei idem fortiter instaret Alypius, juvaretque provinciæ rector, metuendi globi flammarum prope fundamenta crebris assultibus erumpentes fecere locum, exustis aliquoties operantibus, inaccessum (2).—— He resolved to rebuild the magnificent Temple, which was formerly at Jerusalem, at an immense Expence, and committed the Dispatch of the Work to Alypius of Antioch, who had formerly commanded in Brittain under the Præfects. But, as Alypius was carrying on the Work with great Expedition, and was assisted in it by the Governor of the Province, there issued forth dreadful Balls of Fire, with frequent Eruptions, near the Foundations; which sometimes burnt the Workmen, and rendered the Place inaccessible."
Thus he speaks in the Twenty ninth Book: " Ecce autem Alypius quoque, ex Vicario Britanniarum, placiditatis homo jocundæ, post otiosam & repositam vitam (quoniam huc usque injustitia tetenderat manus) in squalore maximo volutatus, ut veneficii reus, citatus est cum Hierocle filio (3).—— Alypius too, formerly Deputy-Governor of Brittain, a Man of a pleasant and easy Temper, after a Life of Ease and Retirement (for the Hand of Injustice reached even thither) was treated as the greatest Criminal, and arraigned for poisoning, with his Son Hierocles."
[B] *I do not believe, that this Work is the Description of the old World, which* James Godfrey *translated out of* Greek *into* Latin.] This Description is an anonymous Work, composed in the Reign of the Emperors *Constantius* and *Constans*. There was an ancient and very barbarous *Latin* Translation of it, which *Salmasius* communicated to the learned *James Godfrey*, who caused it to be printed, with the *Greek* Text, and with a new Translation, accompanied with Notes (4). *Vossius* seems to believe, that the Author of this Description is the same *Alypius*, who sent a Geographical Treatise to *Julian* the Apostate: but *if so*, continues he, *it must be said, according to the Remark of* James Godfrey, *that A-lypius composed it before he commanded in England, for there is nothing said of that Island in it, but on the Credit of others:* "Britannia Provincia, sicut qui fuerunt narrant, valde maxima." As for me, I should readily conclude from this Passage, that *Alypius* did not write this Description; and this is my Reason. It was long, since his having been Lieutenant in *England*, when *Julian*

(1) See Remark [B].

(2) Ammian. Marcell. lib. 23. cap. 1. pag. 350. ad ann. 363.

(3) Id. lib. 2. cap. 2. pag. 556. ad ann. 371.

(4) Vossius de Scient. Math. pag. 243.

ALYPIUS.

was the first who published it in *Greek* (d). have omitted this Article entirely [C].

Mr *Hofman* would have done better to

Julian gave him a Commission to rebuild the Temple of *Jerusalem*. "Negotiumque maturandum Alypio "dederat Antiochensi, qui OLIM Brittannias cura- "verat pro Præfectis (5). —— He committed the "*Dispatch of the Work to Alypius of Antioch, who* "*had* FORMERLY *commanded in* Britain *under the* "*Præfects*." He sent his Geography to the Emperor, while he commanded under him in some Province. He was therefore able to speak of *England*, as an Eye-witness. He is not, then, the Author of the Description of the old World, in which there is nothing said of that Island, but on the Credit of others, who had travelled thither. Let no one object to me, that he wrote two Books, the one before he went into *England*, the other under *Julian* the Apostate, and that the first is the Description, published by *Godfrey*; for it is very probable, that, if he was Author of that Description, he would have inserted it in the Work, which he sent to *Julian*, and thus the first Work would have been disregarded. It would have been lost, then, and the Book, which *Godfrey* translated and adorned with Notes, would not be extant at this present time. We understand from *Julian*, that *Alypius* was a Poet: "Ἔχει γὰρ, says he (6), καὶ τὰ διαγεράμματα τ̂ περιόδου βιβλίον, ἡ καλλιμμώσας αὐτὸ ᾖσαντος τὸν ἰαμβον. —— It contains likewise much better Descriptions than the former; besides which you have given it a Poetical Turn by the Iambics, which you have added to it. Afterwards he approves of the manner, in which *Alypius* treated the People, and praises him for using sometimes Mildness, and sometimes great Resolution. Πῆδε ᾗ ᾗ διοίκησις τ̂ πεαγμάτων, ὅτι πρέποντος ἅμα ᾖ πρᾴως ἀνατάξῃ πεποίησαι, γεγθυμῶς, σωφρόθμεθα, μίξας ᾗ ἀρδρείᾳ ᾗ εὐμεριάων ἀνδρεία. ᾗ πρᾷον, ᾗ τῇ μὲ χρηςὸς πρὸς τοὺς ὑπακούοντας, τᾷ ᾗ ὅτι τ̂ πονηρὸν ἀναφιλέτως πρὸς ὑπερβολὴν, ᾗ μικρὸς τῶν φύσεως, ἰδ᾽ ἀρέτης ἰσῶν. —— *As to your Conduct in Affairs of Government, I am pleased to find, that you study to transact every thing with Assiduity and Humanity; for it requires no small Ability and Virtue so to temper Lenity and Moderation with Vigor and Resolution, as to use the former towards good Men, and exert the latter for the Punishment of the bad.* V. That *Ammianus Marcellinus* asserts This. This is all Mr *Hofman's* Account; in which there are many Faults of Omission; but the worst is, the little he has said is quite full of Faults of Commission.

[C] *Mr Hofman would have done better to have omitted this Article entirely*] I. In the first Place, he writes *Alypius*. II. He says, that *Alypius* of *Antioch* is Author of the Description of the old World. III. That this Description was published in *Latin*, in the Reign of *Constantius* and *Constans*. IV. That there was another *Alypius* of *Antioch*, who wrote a Treatise of Geography.

ALYPIUS, a Philosopher of *Alexandria*, cotemporary with *Jamblicus*, and one of the subtilest Logicians of his Time, was as little as a Dwarf; but his Wit made up for this Imperfection. He had many Disciples, to whom he gave only verbal Instructions, without dictating any Thing to them. Which was the reason why they left him, to follow *Jamblicus*, under whom they might improve both by Lectures and Writings. *Jamblicus*, having had some Conversation with our *Alypius*, admired his Judgment, and his Genius; and even composed his Life, wherein he praised his Virtue, and the firmness of his Soul. *Alypius* died, very old, in the City of *Alexandria* (a).

ALYPIUS, Bishop of *Tagasta*, where he was born (a), was one of St *Austin's* good Friends. He was baptized, with him, at *Milan*, in the Year 388. Five Years after, he travelled into *Palestine*; and if, on the one hand, the great Character he gave St *Jerom* of St *Austin*, served to cement the Friendship of those Fathers, it seems, on the other hand that, at his return into *Africa*, he cooled St *Austin's* Affection. This is ascribed to his relating the scandalous things, which St *Jerom's* Adversaries spoke of him at *Jerusalem*. *Alypius* was not promoted to the Bishoprick of *Tagasta*, till the Year 394, a Year after his Travels into *Palestine*. He assisted at the Council of *Carthage*, in the Year 403, in which an Attempt was made to bring over the *Donatists* to the Unity of the Church. The Benefactions, which *Pinianus* bestowed on the Church of *Tagasta*, when he went thither in the Year 409, with the two *Melania's*, and *Albina* his Mother-in-law, exposed *Alypius* to Calumny, as if, by his fine Discourse and Dexterity, he had extorted too much from these good and charitable Persons. The Inhabitants of *Hippo* murmured furiously against him, because they looked upon him as the cause of their loosing the Prey, which they thought they had in their Hands. They had obliged *Pinianus*, even against his Will, to promise them that he wou'd embrace the Priesthood in their City; His great Estate induced them to this Violence; but, the next Day, he left *Hippo*, and returned to *Tagasta*, and did not think himself obliged by such a forced Promise as his was. *Alypius* was one of the seven Catholic Prelates, who disputed, in 411, with seven *Donatist* Bishops, in the famous Conference of *Carthage*. In 419, he was deputed to *Honorius*, by the Church of *Africa*. Pope *Boniface* received him with many Marks of Friendship, and employed him to transmit to St *Austin* some artful Letters, which the *Pelagians* dispersed in the Churches. St *Austin*, the best Writer of his Time, was desired to refute them. He undertook it, and exerted all his Skill in it (b); but *Alypius* confuted this Heresy more strongly, by the severe Decrees, which he obtained at the Court of *Honorius*, against the *Pelagians* [A]. We should be better acquainted with his Actions and

[A] *The severe Decrees, —— against the Pelagians.*] *Baronius* does not affirm, that the *African* Churches sent *Alypius* to the Emperor, to desire leave to make use of the secular Arm against the Followers of *Pelagius*; he only conjectures it; and grounds his Conjecture on the Orders, which were dispatched, in the same Year, by the Emperor *Honorius*, against the *Pelagians* of *Africa*. But Mr *Maimbourg* does not speak of this as a doubtful Matter; for, having made an odious Comparison between the Conduct of the Protestant Ministers and that of the *Pelagians*, he adds (1), "That which has filled

ALYPIUS.

and his Merit, if we had the Work, which St *Auſtin* promiſed, in a Letter, which he wrote to St *Paulinus* [B]. To conclude, *Alypius* was very near being married. See the Remark [B] of the Article St AUGUSTIN.

"filled all *France* with Joy, is, that ſo juſt a Decree was ſoon followed by That famous Edict of *October*, which gave the fatal Blow to this Hereſy, by forbidding the public Exerciſe of the pretended Reformation, deſtroying all their Temples, and baniſhing thoſe Miniſters, who refuſed to renounce their Errors. And this is exactly what the Emperor *Honorius* did againſt the *Pelagians*, at the Requeſt of the Clergy of *Africa*, preſented by *Alypius*. For, by the Edict which that Prince granted him for the Good of the whole Church, that Hereſy was exterminated out of the Empire; they, who might yet be ſuſpected of it, were forbidden to meet, and thoſe falſe Biſhops, who would not ſubſcribe to it's Condemnation, were expelled from their Sees."

(a) It is the 32d. [B] *The Work, which St Auſtin promiſed in a Letter ——— to St Paulinus.*] Becauſe what he ſays in that Letter (1) may give a general Notion of *Alypius*'s Merit, it will not be improper to produce it here, "Eſt etiam aliud quo iſtum fratrem amplius diligas, nam eſt cognatus venerabilis & verè beati Epiſcopi Alypii, quem toto pectore amplecteris & merito: nam quiſquis de illo viro benigne cogitat, de magna Dei miſericordia & de mirabilibus Dei muneribus cogitat. Itaque, cum legiſſet petitionem tuam, quâ deſiderare te indicaſti, ut hiſtoriam ſuam tibi ſcriberet, & volebat facere propter benevolentiam tuam, & nolebat propter verecundiam ſuam, quem cum viderim inter amorem pudoremque fluctuantem, onus ab illo in humeros meos tranſtuli: nam hoc mihi etiam per epiſtolam juſſit. Cito ergo, ſi Dominus adjuverit, totum Alypium inſeram præcordiis tuis: nam hoc ſum ego maximè veritus, ne ille vereretur aperire omnia, quæ in eum Dominus contulit, ne alicubi minus intelligenti (non enim abs te ſolo illa legerentur) non divina munera conceſſa hominibus, ſed ſeipſum prædicare videretur, & tu, qui noſti quomodo hæc legas, propter aliorum cavendam infirmitatem, fraternæ notitiæ debito fraudareris. ——— *This Brother has ſtill a farther claim to your Affection; for he is related to the venerable, and truly bleſſed Biſhop* Alypius, *whom you embrace with your whole Heart, an deſervedly: for whoever thinks favourably of him, reflects upon the great Mercy, and the wonderful Gifts, of God. Therefore, when he had read your Petition, in which you expreſſed your Deſire, that he would write to you his own Hiſtory, he was inclined to do it out of good Will to you, but deterred from it by his own Modeſty; whom when I ſaw fluctuating between Love and Modeſty, I transferred the Burthen from his Shoulders to my own; as he had deſired me by Letter to do. Speedily therefore, with God's Aſſiſtance, I ſhall infuſe all* Alypius *into your Breaſt; for my greateſt Fear was, leaſt he ſhould conceal Part of the Favours beſtowed on him by God, out of a dread of appearing to the Ignorant (for you would not have been his only Reader) rather to preach up himſelf, than the Divine Gifts beſtowed on Men; and that, out of Regard to the Weakneſs of others; yea, who would have rightly underſtood him, would be defrauded of the Debt of Brotherly Information.*"

ALYPIUS (FALTONIUS PROBUS) Brother of *Q. Clodius Hermogenianus Olybrius* (a), was Prefect of *Rome* in the Reign of the Emperor *Theodoſius*. *Baronius* proves it by ſome Inſcriptions (b). He adds, that there are ſeveral Letters from *Symmachus* to this *Alypius* [A]; he cites the *Roman* Martyrology, which ſays, that St *Almachius* was killed by the *Gladiators* [B] in the Prefecture of *Alypius*. Laſtly, he conjectures, I. That *Alypius*, Governor of *Egypt*, with whom *John* the Hermit had a Conference [C], is the ſame with Him, who is the Subject of this Article. II. That this Converſation with the Hermit converted *Alypius*. A learned *Engliſhman* conjectures, that the Martyr St *Almachius* is an imaginary Saint, and that the Title of the *Almanack* produced this wonderful Canonization [D].

(a) Demetrias, his Daughter, is very much praiſed by the Fathers.

(b) Baronius ad Ann. 395. n. 2. & 3.

[A] *There are ſeveral Letters from* Symmachus *to this* Alypius.] His Words are theſe: "Ad eundem quoque Alypium complures extant Epiſtolæ Symmachi, deque eo, meminit in Epiſtola ad Flavianum (1)." He cites the Eighty ſecond Letter of the ſecond Book of *Symmachus*. In my Edition, I find, at the Eighty ſecond, theſe Words; "Jampridem Domino & fratri meo Alipio comitatum ſacrum viſere atque adire cupienti. ——— *My Maſter and Brother* Alypius, *deſirous of going to ſee and attend the ſacred Proceſſion.*"

[B] St Almachius *was killed by the Gladiators.*] He endeavoured to ſuppreſs the Worſhip of falſe Gods, on the Day of the Octave of *Chriſtmas*, (which is the firſt Day of the Year) and it coſt him his Life. Theſe are the Words of the Martyrology, on the firſt of *January*, "Romæ S. Almachii martyris, qui, jubente Alypio Urbis præfecto, cum diceret, hodie Octavæ Dominici diei ſunt, ceſſate à ſuperſtitionibus idolorum, & à ſacrificiis pollutis, à gladiatoribus occiſus eſt (2). ——— *St* Almachius, *Martyr at* Rome; *who, at the Command of* Alypius, *Prefect of the City, having ſaid,* To Day is the Octave of Chriſtmas; *lay aſide your idolatrous Superſtitions, and polluted Sacrifices; was thereupon ſlain by the Gladiators.*" *Theodoret*, in the Twenty ſixth Chapter of the fifth Book of his Eccleſiaſtical Hiſtory, ſpeaks of a Monk, whoſe Name was *Telemachus*, who came from the utmoſt Parts of the Eaſt to *Rome*, to endeavour at the aboliſhing the Shews of the *Gladiators*. He had the Courage to catechiſe theſe People; but the Spectators were ſo offended at it, that they ſtoned him to Death. *Honorius*, hearing of it, cauſed him to be ranked among the Martyrs, and commanded theſe ſort of Games to be aboliſhed. *Baronius* (3) would reduce what you have juſt now read, and what I have cited out of the Martyrology, to one and the ſame Fact, and would willingly make us believe, that *Theodoret* called Him *Telemachus*, whom he ought to have called *Almachius*; that he placed in the Reign of *Honorius* what was done in that of *Theodoſius*, and that he imputed the Action of the *Gladiators* to the Spectators. At this rate *Theodoret* muſt be guilty of three Miſtakes.

(1) Baronius ad Ann. 395. n. 12.

(2) Ibid. n. 19.

(3) Baron. ad ann. 395. n. 20.

[C] Alypius ——— *with whom* John *the Hermit had a Conference.*] *Baronius* cites hereupon a long Paſſage (4), by which we are given to underſtand, that Good *Palladius* took it very ill, that the Hermit ſhould leave him, to go and converſe with *Alypius*, Governor of the Province. His Reſentment hereupon inſpired him with ſome Contempt for the Hermit, and with a Reſolution to retire. He would have done ſo, if the Hermit had not ſent him Word to defer his Intentions a little while. *Palladius* perceived from hence, that the *Man* had a great Fund of Spirituality in him, and a very particular Talent of gueſſing at a Man's Thoughts. He ſtaid 'till the Governor was gone, and then the Hermit made his Excuſes.

(4) Palladius Lauſiac. cap. 22. apud Lipom. tom. 3.

[D] *The Title of the Almanack produced this wonderful Canonization.*] They, who cannot procure the *Engliſh* Book, printed at *London* in 1688, entitled, *The Enthuſiaſm of the Church of Rome*, may conſult the eleventh Volume of the *Bibliotheque Univerſelle*, at the One hundred thirty ninth Page. They will ſee there, that, according, to the Conjecture of the *Engliſh* Author, "Some ignorant Monk, of the VIIth or VIIIth Century, ſeeing at the beginning of the Calender, S. *Almanachum*, written, by way of abbreviation, according to the Cuſtom of thoſe Times, S. *Almáchum*, took the Word, ſeldom uſed in thoſe Times, for the Name of a Saint, "gave

ALKINDUS. ALLATIUS.

" gave it a Termination in *us*, and placed it *on the*
" *first Day of the Year*. Ignorance and Chance had
" no sooner brought this new Saint into World, but he
" found Martyrologists, who affirmed that he was kil-
" led in the Amphitheatre of *Rome* in the Prefecture of
" *Alypius*, by the Gladiators, whom he endeavoured
" to hinder from fighting. No ancient Author men-
" tions this holy Courage (5). *Alcuinus* * is the first, who
" speaks of it, but with some Doubt."

(5) *Yet Theodoret describes it to the Monk Telemachus*. See Remark [*B*].

* De Divin. Offic. cap 4.

ALKINDUS. Look for ALCHINDUS.

ALLATIUS (LEO) Librarian of the *Vatican*, born in the Island of *Chios*, was one of the most famous Writers of the XVIIth Century. He was laborious, and indefatigable, greedy after Manuscripts, endowed with a great Memory, very fit to collect Materials, and consequently deserving of the Place which he enjoyed; though he had no very great Penetration, nor a manner of arguing, which favoured of the good Logician. I omit the Employments which he had, before he was made the Pope's Librarian, nor have I examined, whether *Moreri*, who speaks of him at large, is very exact. If I have any thing to say upon this Head, it shall be in the Remarks [*A*]. So that, omitting here what may be found in his Dictionary, I shall only touch upon some Particulars, which he has omitted. *Allatius* was very serviceable to the Gentlemen of *Port-Royal*, in the Dispute they had with Mr *Claude*, about the Belief of the *Greeks* in regard to the Eucharist. Mr *Claude* often calls him *the great Author of Mr* Arnaud, and gives him but an indifferent Character [*B*]. Mr *Simon* represents him as a Man of no Sincerity [*C*]. Never was a *Latin* by Birth more zealous against the schismatical *Greeks*, than *Allatius*, nor more devoted to the See of *Rome*. He never was married, nor in Ecclesiastical Orders; the Reason he gives for it deserves to be known [*D*]. It would be difficult to find in the History of Authors, a more remarkable Particular, than That, which relates to a Pen, which he used [*E*]. He published several Manuscripts, several Translations of *Greek* Authors and several Books of his own composing. The List of them in *Moreri*'s Dictionary does not

distinguish

[*A*] *If I have any thing to say upon this Head, it shall be in the Remarks.*] I find in *Lorenzo Crasso* (1), that *Leone Allacci* (so he calls him) was but nine Years of Age, when he was carried from the Island of *Chios* into *Calabria*, where he met with the Protection of a powerful Family (2). After some time, he was sent to *Rome*, where he studied classical Learning, Philosophy, and Divinity, in the *Grecian* College. He was elected at *Naples* great Vicar to *Bernard Justiniani*, Bishop of *Anglona*. He returned to his Native Country; but, finding nothing there agreeable to his Inclinations, he returned to *Rome*, where he studied Physic under *Julius Cæsar Lagalla*, and was admitted Doctor in That Science. Afterwards he applied himself to Polite Literature, and taught *Greek* in the College of his Nation. The death of *Gregory* XV. deprived him of the Reward of the Commission, which he had received, to transport the Library of the Elector *Palatine* to *Rome* (3). Some time after, he went into the Service of Cardinal *Bichi*, afterwards of Cardinal *Francis Barberini*, and at last had the Care of the Library of the Vatican from Pope *Alexander* VII. *Lorenzo Crasso* says nothing more in the Book, which I have quoted. I add, that *Allatius* had been a long time Librarian to Cardinal *Barberini*.

[*B*] Mr *Claude* ——— *gives him but an indifferent Character*.] " *Allatius* was a *Greek*, who had left his
" Religion to embrace the *Romish*; a *Greek*, whom
" the Pope had made his Library-keeper, a Man the
" most attached to the Interest of the Court of *Rome*,
" a Man the most malicious, and most outrageous
" against Persons; a Man the most zealous against
" the *Greeks*, who are called Schismatics, particu-
" larly against *Cyril*, and, after all, a true Dealer in
" Smoak (4). ——— His Zeal for the Court of
" *Rome* appears in the very beginning of his Book,
" *De perpetua Consensione*: for thus he speaks in fa-
" vour of the Pope * : *The Roman Pontiff holds of*
" *no one* ; *he judges every one, and is judged of none* ;
" *Obedience is to be paid to him, though he governs*
" *unjustly* ; *he gives Laws without receiving any* ; *he*
" *alters them as he pleases, he creates Magistrates,*
" *he determines Matters of Faith, he orders the great*
" *Affairs of the Church, as he pleases*. *He cannot*
" *err, if he wou'd ; for no Infidelity or Error can*
" *come near him* ; *and if an Angel should say other-*
" *wise, being invested as he is with the Authority*
" *of* Jesus Christ, *he cannot change*. The ill Nature,
" with which he treats those, against whom he dis-
" putes, as *Chytræus*, *Creygthon*, the Archbishop of
" *Corfu*, and others, whom he attacks out of Wan-
" tonness, appears from the meer reading of his
" Works; each Period honours them with some of
" these fine Appellations: *Fools, Lyars, Blockheads,*
" *Rotten Mushrooms, Infernal Mouths, Wicked, Im-*
" *pudent*, and such like Terms †, which are not
" the Marks of a Temper extreamly moderate. To
" prove to us the Conformity of the *Greek* Church
" with the *Romish* in Essentials, he lays it down as
" a Principle, that we must acknowledge, as the true
" *Greek* Church, no other Party, but that which
" obeys the See of *Rome*; as for the other *Greeks*,
" whom he calls *Hereticks* and *Schismaticks*, he fairly
" maintains, that it would be right to reduce them
" to obedience by Fire and Sword. *That Hereticks*
" *ought to be proscribed, exterminated, and punished,*
" *and, if they are obstinate, put to death and burnt* ‖.
" They are his own Words." Had *Moreri* reason then to call him *good Man* ? Is this contemptuous Elogy due to those, who talk of nothing but penal Laws, Extirpation, and Fire and Sword, when the Question is, How Hereticks are to be dealt with?

[*C*] Mr *Simon represents him as a Man of no Sincerity.*] The Design of the whole first Chapter of the *Critical History of the Levant*, is to shew, that *Leo Allatius* had no Reason to be in a Passion with *Caucas*, Archbishop of *Corfu* : that *Caucas* has not imputed any Opinions and Practices to the *Greeks*, which they disown; and that *Allatius*, *to please Pope Urban* VIII, *who had at that Time formed the Design of re-uniting the Greeks to the Church of Rome by softning Methods*, had abated of the Rigour of several of the *Greek* Opinions. This is plainly to insinuate, that he wanted Sincerity; for if *Caucas* was in the right, he could not be contradicted, out of Complaisance to the Pope, without sacrificing Candour to Maxims of State.

[*D*] *The Reason he gives for it deserves to be known.*] Pope *Alexander* VII. asked him one Day, why he did not take Orders. *It is*, answered he, *because I would be always ready to marry*. *Why then*, replied the Pope, *don't you marry* ? *It is*, replied *Allatius*, *because I would always be at liberty to take Orders* (5). Thus he spent his whole Life in deliberating between a Parish and a Wife: Perhaps, at his Death, he repented, that he had not chosen one or other of them; but he might have repeated thirty or forty Years successively, if he had actually made his Choice.

[*E*] *A remarkable Particular relating to a Pen, which he used.*] This Particularity comes from the same Hand with the foregoing, to wit, *John Pastricius*, *Allatius*'s good Friend, Heir of his Books,

and

(1) Lorenzo Crasso Istoria de' Poeti Greci, pag. 306. See also his Elogii d'Huom ni Letterati, Tom. 1. pag. 197. &c.

(2) *That of the* Spinelli.

(3) Moreri *places this in the Year* 1621. *but* Heidelberg *was not taken till* 1622.

(4) Claude's Answer to Mr Arnaud, Book 3. ch. 17. Tom.1. pag. 452. Edit. 8vo.

* Allat. de Perpet.Cons. lib. 1. c. 2.

† Ibid. lib. 3. cap. 16, 26, 27, 18. & adverf. Creygth. paffim.

‖ Allat. de Perpet.Conf. lib. 2. c. 13. Ibid. lib. 3. cap. 11.

(5) Mabillon Muscum Ital. Tom. 1. pag. 61.

ALLATIUS. ALMAIN.

distinguish these Three sorts of Works, nor does it comprehend all that *Allatius* published. There is more of Reading and Learning in his Productions, than of Wit and Judgment. He knew how to discover the Faults of those, against whom he wrote, but he did it with too much Sharpness, and after an insulting manner. This is chiefly to be seen in the Dissertations, which he published against Mr *Creyghton* (*a*), concerning the Council of *Florence*. His Genius and his Memory appear in the Digressions he made from one Subject to another in the same Volume. Mr *Sallo* was far from being his Admirer upon this Account [*F*]. *Allatius* died at *Rome*, in the Month of *January*, 1669 (*b*), being Eighty three Years old. He often wrote *Greek* Verses. He composed a Poem in *Greek* on the Birth of *Lewis* XIV, wherein *Greece* is introduced Speaking. This Poem was printed before his Book, *de Perpetua Consensione*, which he dedicated to that King. I forgot to observe, that the Gentlemen of *Port-Royal* did not fail to reply to Mr *Claude*, in Favour of *Allatius* [*G*].

(*a*) *See the Journal des Scavans of No. 15. 1666.*
(*b*) *Henn. Witte, Diarium Biograph. Morteri places his Death in 1670.*

and Principal of the College *de propaganda fide*. He told *Mabillon* (6), that *Allatius*, having made use of the same Pen (7) for forty Years in writing *Greek*, and loosing it at last, was ready to cry for Grief. He wrote very fast; for he transcribed in one Night the *Diarium Romanorum Pontificum*, which *Hilarion Rancatus*, a *Cistertian* Monk had lent him (8). *Allatius* was not permitted to publish it.

[*F*] *Mr Sallo was far from being his Admirer on this Account.*] Having observed, that the chief Piece of one of *Allatius*'s Works was a Complaint of the Virgin, he goes on thus: " This Complaint " was composed by *Metaphrastes*, from which *Leo* " *Allatius* - - - - takes occasion to give us an Elo- " gium of *Metaphrastes*, written by *Psellus*. And, " because *Metaphrastes*'s Name was *Simeon*, he takes " occasion likewise from hence to make a very long " Dissertation on the Lives and Works of great " Men, of the Name of *Simeon*. From the *Simeons* " he proceeds to the *Simons*, from those to the *Si-* " *monides*; and lastly to the *Simonasides*. This way " of writing is the Taste of *Leo Allatius*. For he " had before composed Dissertations on the Lives " and Works of some Authors, who had *equivocal* " Names, as That of *George, Methodius, Nicetas,* " *Philo*, and *Psellus*. This is a new invented Pro- " ject; at least we have nothing like it in the Works " of the Ancients (9)." *Diogenes Laertius* seldom forgets to mention, at the end of each Philosopher's Life, those who bore the same Name; and he cites *Demetrius Magnes*, who had wrote a Book, περὶ ὁμωνύμων ποιητῶν τε καὶ συγγραφέων (10). *Of Poets, and Authors, of the same Name.* See the Remark [*H*] of the Article APOLLONIUS TYANEUS. Nor is *Allatius* the Restorer of this Project: *Meursius* had published several Treatises of this Nature before him. See Mr *Teissier*, in his *Catalogus Authorum Bibliothecarum*, where he gives us a List of the Authors, who exercised their Pens on this Subject (11). He calls them *Scriptores de Homonymis*. According to Mr *Sallo*, *Homonymi* ought to be translated *those who have Equivocal Names*; but, by his Leave, This would be a wrong Translation. It was never said, that Princes of the same Name, as the *Charles*'s, the *Lewis*'s, the *Henry*'s, had *equivocal* Names. Names of this Sort are such as may be taken in different Senses; such is their Species and their Use, both in Logic, and in common Speech. But,

(6) Ibid.
(7) See the Article of LANCELOT an Olivetan Monk.
(8) Id. Mabillon, pag. 77.

(9) Journal des Scavans, of Jan. 19. 1665.
(10) Dieg. Laert. in Epimenide, lib. 1. n. 112.
(11) Teissier, Catalog. pag. 355.

to return to *Leo Allatius*, I must observe, that he was very fit to draw up Lists or Catalogues. He made this appear when he published his *Apes Urbanae*: it is a Book, which grows scarce, and is already very dear in *Holland* (12). It contains a List of all the learned Men, who flourished in *Rome*, from the Year 1630 to 1632, with a Catalogue of their Works. The Reason of the Title is taken from the Bees, which Pope *Urban* VIII bore in his Coat of Arms. There is another List of *Allatius*, which is less known than this, the Title whereof is *Dramaturgia*. It relates to Dramatical Works, and their Authors. The Book, which he published at *Rome*, in the Year 1636, *De Erroribus magnorum virorum in dicendo*, contains several Remarks stollen from *Claudius Du Verdier*. Mr *Morhof* charges him with It (13).

(12) *It is not to be met with in Rick'el's Stores, but sometimes at Auctions.*

(13) *Morhof. de Paten. ad Polyhist. pag. 179.*

[*G*] *The Gentlemen of Port Royal did not fail to reply to Mr Claude in Favour of* Allatius.] First, they mention part of what Mr *Claude* says of him; and then they go on thus. " But, besides, that these empty " Reproaches carry an ill Face; that *Allatius*'s " Writings give quite another Idea of him, and that " his Brethren * speak of him in a very different " manner, and cite him with Commendation; they " are likewise contrary to good Sense: for a Man " may be zealous or bitter against an Author, whom " he refutes, without being a Cheat, and a Forger " of false Passages, and false Stories; and there is no " Consequence from the one to the other. It is not " with the Vices, as it is with the Virtues of Men; " there is no Affinity between them; nay, they are " often contrary the one to the other; and Persons " may be Passionate, Violent, Flatterers, Interested, " without giving any occasion to believe, that the " Passages, which they cite, are supposititious. There " is yet less Reason to believe it of *Allatius*, than of " another, because some Books, which he cited, when " they were but in Manuscript, having been after- " wards printed, have justified his Faithfulness; and " because it appears, farther, that he always pretend- " ed to the Reputation of a learned Critic; and it is " well known, that such Persons are very far from " falsifying Authors." It is certain, that Mr *Drelincourt* cites him with Commendation, and makes use of his Doctrine concerning the Witch of *Endor*, who conjured up the Ghost of *Samuel*. He cites his Treatise *De Engastrimytho*, published in the Year 1630.

* *Drelincourt, de la defcente aux enfers, pag. 200, &c. Note, That is too juvenal, too much in pompe &*c. *and ve*·· *to*··

ALMAIN (JAMES) Professor of Divinity at *Paris*, in the College of *Navarre*, flourished in the beginning of the XVIth Century. He was born at *Sens*, and acquired the Reputation of one of the most subtle Logicians, and best Schoolmen of the Times. The great Inclination he had for the Doctrine of *Scotus*, and that of *Occam*, and *Gabriel Biel*, shews the Character of his Genius. He taught Logic and Physics, before he was admitted into the *House of Navarre*, in the Year 1508, and published some Treatises on these two branches of Philosophy, in 1505, and 1508. He took his Doctor of Divinity's Degree in the Year 1511, and the Year following he explained the three Books of *Sentences* in the College of *Navarre*. He was employed at the same time to write for King *Lewis* XII against Pope *Julius* II, and to vindicate the Authority of the Councils against a Piece of Cardinal *Cajetan*. The Council of *Pisa* had sent that Cardinal's Book to the Faculty of Divinity of *Paris* to be confuted by them; they made choice of *Almain* for this Drudgery, and had no reason to repent of their choice. This Doctor died very young in the Year 1515. An Edition of all his Works was published [*A*] at

[*A*] *An Edition of all his Works was published.*] *Oliver Lugdunens* took this pains, and added a Pre- | face to it, wherein *Almain* is amply praised. The best of his Works are four moral Treatises. Exposi-

ALPAIDE. ALSTEDIUS.

at *Paris* two Years after (*a*). They who pretend, that he was a Monk, are mistaken [*B*].

(*a*) Launoius Histor. Gymn. Navarr p. 614.

fitio circa decisiones quæstionum Magistri Gulielmi Occam de potestate summi Pontificis. De auctoritate Ecclesiæ & Conciliorum. Dictata super sententias Magistri Roberti Holcot (1).

[*B*] *They who pretend that he was a Monk, are mistaken.*] Father *Labbé* (2) accuses *Gesner*, and his Abbreviator *Simler*, of having falsly advanced this Fact; *Moreri* did not fail, in this point, to copy after Father *Labbé*. Mr *de Launoy* is more particular in his Accusation against *Gesner*; he blames him for saying, in his Bibliotheque, that *Almain* was of the Order of the *Franciscans*: He adds, that *Possevin*, in his *Apparatus*, makes him only a Monk (3). Father *Labbé* did not make use of this Distinction; he says that *Almain* was a Monk, according to *Gesner*; but that, according to others, he was of the Order of St *Francis*. I do not believe, that *Gesner* has said what is imputed to him; for I have not been able to find any Passage in his *Bibliotheque*, which mentions *Almain*. I find indeed a Benedictin, whose Name was *Almannus*; but he makes him live in the Year 890. As for *Simler*, it is true he says, that *James Almain*, a Monk, wrote a Book against Cardinal *Cajetan*. *Moreri* was not acquainted with this Writer's Age; he flourish'd still, says he, *in the beginning of the XVIIth Century*. Say rather, that he did not begin to flourish 'till that time.

(1) Lonnoius Hist. Gymn. Navarr. pag. 611.
(2) De Scrip. Eccles. Tom. 1. pag. 438.
(3) Ibid. pag. 614.

ALPAIDE, a Concubine of *Pepin*, and Mother of *Charles Martel*. Some Authors say, without good Grounds, that *Pepin* married her, after he had divorced *Plectrude* [*A*]. It is a general Opinion, that *Lambert*, Bishop of *Liege*, was never so much a Courtier, as to approve of *Pepin*'s Amours with this Lady; and that *Alpaide*, enraged at the Liberty he took in censuring them, made *Pepin* consent to the Design she had formed against that Prelate's Life [*B*]. They add, that *Dodon*, *Alpaide*'s Brother, executed this villanous Design, and that, having committed the Murder, he fell into a Distemper, which bred a prodigious Number of Worms in his Body, and obliged him to throw himself into the *Maese* (*a*). *Lambert* has been canonized: He was the only Prelate, they say, who durst tell *Pepin* the Truth [*C*], for which he met with the Fate of *St John* the Baptist. His Morality was so refined, that he refused the Benediction, which was desired of him at Table, for *Alpaide*'s Glass [*D*]. This Lady retired at last into a Monastery (*b*), where she died. A Cloister is commonly to this kind of Persons, what *Leghorn* was formerly to Bankrupts.

(*a*) Mezerai, Abregé Chron. Tom. 1. pag. 171. ad ann. 707. Cordemoi, Hist. de Fr. Tom. 1. pag. 382.

(*b*) Moreri says, that this Monastery had born her name, and is by Alpaide at Orp-le-grand in Brabant.

[*A*] *Some Authors say, without good Grounds, that Pepin married her, after he had divorced Plectrude.*] Mr *de Cordemoi* (1) observes, that they built only on the Authority of the second Continuator of *Fredegarius*, who says that *Pepin* married *Alpaide*. " But " besides that this Author, who wrote (as every one " knows) by the Order of *Charles Martel*'s Brother " and Nephew, took care not to represent the Amours " of *Pepin* and *Alpaide*, otherwise than as a Marriage; " he does not say, that *Plectrude* was divorced: Nay, " there are several Acts remaining, which shew that " *Plectrude* was never separated from *Pepin*; so that, " according to Ecclesiastical or Civil Laws, *Alpaide* " could not be look'd upon as his lawful Wife, and " if he married her, he had two Wives at once."

[*B*] *Enrag'd at the Liberty he took in censuring them ------ she form'd a Design against that Prelate's Life.*] We need not wonder, that the second Continuator of *Fredegarius* should say nothing of *Lambert*'s Conduct, nor of the fatal Consequences it was attended with. He could not touch upon it, without incurring the Displeasure of *Charles Martel*'s Relations, who made use of his Pen; and therefore his Silence is no Weight: But the Author of the *Gesta* likewise says nothing of it (2). An Author, who liv'd in those Times, says only, " That St *Lambert* " was killed by a Lord, whose Name was *Dodon*, " in revenge for the Death of two of his Relations, " whom the Servants of that holy Bishop had slain, " without his Knowledge (3)." If we knew of what Party this Author was, whether he was for *Charles Martel*, or for *Plectrude*, and what he had any thing to hope for, or to fear, we might know how to judge of his Silence. Mr *de Cordemoi* adds, that it does not appear " by any Memoirs of that Time, either " that *Dodon* was the Brother of *Alpaide*, or that she " induced him to kill St *Lambert*; that there are in- " deed some Expressions in the Martyrologies expos'd about that time, which shew, that this Vio- " lence had been done by Order from the Court, " and that, as *Pepin* was Master of it, those, who " wrote afterwards, thought they ought to explain, " to the Disadvantage of that Prince, and of *Alpaide*, " the conceal'd meaning of the Martyrologies (4)." The safest way, I think, is to place this in the Number of doubtful Facts. They, who tell us, that *Lambert*, Bishop of *Liege*, was the only Person, who durst reprimand *Pepin*, and speak openly of his Bigamy *as of a public Adultery*, without suffering himself to be influenced either by the Promises, or the Threats, of *Dodon*, *Alpaide*'s Brother (5), *did not write 'till a long time after* (6); which makes their Testimony less to be depended upon: Besides, the Son of *Alpaide* was so formidable a Person, that nothing can be inferred from the Silence of cotemporary Writers.

[*C*] *The only Prelate, who durst tell* Pepin *the Truth.*] An Author of an Historical Dictionary will have a thousand Opportunities of observing, that there are no greater Flatterers of Princes than Churchmen. Their Sermons, their Prayers, their Speeches, their Epistles Dedicatory, are so full of extravagant Elogies, that the Condition they put an honest Hearer or Reader into, cannot be better represented, than by the Proverb, *Date mihi pelvim* *. ----- *Give me the Bason.* If it be said that *Pepin* was no King; I answer, that he had the Key of Tongues and Pens, Rewards and Punishments in his Hands; he only wanted the Title of Sovereign; he had the Reality, and performed the Functions of it. Flatterers do not regard a meer Title: They adore him more devoutly, who has the Power without the Title, than him who has the Title without the Power.

[*D*] *He refused the Benediction, which was desired of him at Table, for* Alpaide's *Glass.*] Let us see how a modern Historian relates the Matter. " Ad epulas " invitatur (*B. Landebertus*) à principe. Pippinus, " cæterique illustres viri qui aderant, scyphum quis- " que suum ab Antistite benedici, aut, ut alii dicunt, " de manu ejus poculum accipere, pia ambitione cu- " piebant. Cum Alpais (nam & ipsa pleno convivio " intererat) scyphum suum à Landeberto signari op- " taret, indignabundus Episcopus palatio excessit, con- " vivarum hilaritate confusa (7). ------ Lambert *was* " *invited by the Prince to an Entertainment.* Pepin, " *and the rest of his illustrious Guests, were piously* " *ambitious, that their Glasses might be bless'd by the* " *Prelate, or, as others say, to receive the Glass from* " *his Hand. But when* Alpais *(who was present at* " *this grand Feast) desired, that her Glass likewise* " *might receive* Lambert's *Benediction, the Bishop* " *left the Palace with Indignation, to the Interrup-* " *tion of the Company's Mirth.*" Compare with this the Stories related in the new Letters against Maimburg's History of *Calvinism* (8).

(1) Cordemoi's Hist. of France, Vol. I. pag. 381.

(2) Ibid.

(3) Godescalc. in Vita S. Lamberti, cap. 7. apud Cordemoi, ibid.

(4) Cordemoi, ibid. pag. 382.

(5) Anselm. Licdicenf. Canonicus Sigibert. Monachus Gemblacenf. Nicolaus Lacodic. Canon. Ecclef. Vener. *and others cited by* Cordemoi, pag. 381.

(6) Cordemoi, p. 381.

* *A Proverbial saying of Those, who, when any thing becomes so very troublesome, as not to be any longer born, (for instance, a Bason full; no longer) call for a Bason, or Pot, as if they were sick, and wearied to discharge. See* Sub: as, *and* Erasmus Adag.

(7) Heinan. Valesius Rerum Franci- carum, lib. 33.

(8) Pag. 614 &c.

ALSTEDIUS (JOHN HENRY) a *German* Divine of the Reformed Religion, was one of the most voluminous Writers of the XVIIth Century. He was an indefatigable

ALSTEDIUS. ALTAEMPS.

tigable Author, and one who answered his Anagram perfectly well (a). He was a long time Professor of Philosophy and Divinity at *Herborn*, in the County of *Nassau*, from whence he went into *Transylvania*, to be Professor at *Alba-Julia* (b), where he died in the Year 1638, being fifty Years of Age. He was one of the Fathers at the Synod of *Dort*. His chief Employment was to compose *Methods*, and to reduce the several Branches of Arts and Sciences into certain *Systems*. His *Encyclopædia* (c) found Favour with the *Roman* Catholics [*A*]; for it was reprinted at *Lyons*, and sold very well in *France*. Some are of Opinion, that one of his best Works is his *Thesaurus Chronologicus*, of which there are several Editions; others speak with Contempt of it. *Vossius* says nothing of it; he only mentions the *Encyclopædia* in general, and in particular the Treatise of Arithmetic (d). He acknowledges, that the Author had read much, and that his Learning was very extensive. They, who judge of him with the least Flattery, own that there are some good things in his *Methods* and *Systems* [*B*]. He did not persuade many People of what he endeavoured to prove in his *Triumphus Biblicus*, that the Materials and Principles of all Arts and Sciences may be fetched from the Scripture. It was impossible for him to publish so many Books, without making use of the Labours of others; but he borrowed too much from other Authors, whom he transcribed without any Scruple [*C*]. *John Himmelius*, a Divine of the Confession of *Augsburg*, and Divinity-Professor at *Jena*, is one of those who wrote against him [*D*]. *Moreri* was not acquainted with the Year of *Alstedius*'s Death [*E*], and he had better have said nothing about it.

I must not omit, that he was a *Millenarian*. He published, in 1627, a Treatise *De Mille Annis*. He taught, that the Faithful shall reign, with JESUS CHRIST, upon Earth, a Thousand Years; after which will be the General Resurrection, and the last Judgment. He pretended, that This Reign would commence in the Year 1694. We are fully assured he was mistaken. His Son-in-law *Bisterfeldius* was of the same Opinion (e).

[*A*] *His Encyclopædia found favour with the Roman Catholics.*] *Lorenzo Crasso* places *Alstedius* among the great Men, whose Elogies he has published. It is very probable, that *Moreri* borrowed from thence the Incense, which he bestows upon *Alstedius*. I find the Reader is referred to a Work of *Sorel* (1), to be informed concerning this learned *German*. He must have been better known, and more esteemed than many others among the *Roman* Catholics. Father *Lami*, of the Oratory, is of Opinion, that *Alstedius is almost the only one among all the Writers of Encyclopedias, and Systems of Sciences, who deserves to be read, and to keep his Rank in a choice Library* (2). See the following Remark.

[*B*] *There are some good things in his Methods and Systems.*] The following Quotation from Mr *Baillet* is borrowed by him from the anonymous *German*, who wrote the *Bibliographia curiosa Historico-philologica*. " *Alstedius* has indeed many good things; but " he is not exact enough in many Places: Never- " theless, upon his first Appearance, he was received by " the Public with great Applause, and he is of some " use to those, who, being destitute of other helps, " and not having the Authors, would acquire some " Knowledge of the Terms of each Profession or " Science. One cannot sufficiently praise his Patience " and Labour, and his Judgment and Choice of good " Authors, out of whom he made his Abridgments, " for they are not mere Scraps and unconnected Rhap- " sodies; but he lays down the Principles of Scien- " ces and Arts with great Order, and endeavours to " be uniform every where, though some Pieces are " better than others, and some of them are of no " value, as his History, Chronology, &c. ...... " It must be confess'd, that he is often confus'd, by " endeavouring to be too concise; that he is too full " of Divisions and Subdivisions, and that he affects " a Method too much constrain'd (3)." *Lorenzo Crasso* says, that though there is much more of Labour, than Genius, in *Alstedius*'s Works, yet they are esteemed, and that People admire his Industry, which gives him admittance into the Temple of Fame. " Con gloria del suo nome s'e ammirata la fatica fatta " nelle Storie, e nella Cronologia de' Tempi: le qua- " li cose, quantunque in libri diversi di Scrittori illu- " stri sacri e profani truovansi, è vi concorra in tale " raccoglimento piu sudore che ingegno, tuttavia l'or- " dine dato da Giovanni Errico alle sudette fatiche " storiche è stato da gli huomini amatori delle anti- " chita, è dell' eruditioni assai commendata (4). ------ " *The great Pains he has taken in History and Chro- " nology, is much to the Reputation of his Name: " which Sciences, though they are to be met in seve- " ral Works of illustrious Authors, sacred and pro- " phane, and though more of Labour than Genius is " requisite in such Collections, nevertheless the Order " bestowed by* John Henry, *on the aforesaid Historical " Labours, has been sufficiently admired by the Lovers " of Antiquity and Learning*."

[*C*] *Whom he transcribed without any Scruple.*] Read this Passage of *Thomasius* (5). Hunc in Paratitlis Theologicis quicquid de silentio sacrorum effert *, observo prope de verbo descripsisse è Casaubono †, quem nominari tamen etiam lectoris interest, ut sciret unde plura sibi haurienda forent. ------ vereor autem ne quercum eandem alibi quoque excusserit, cum in ipso ad lectorem principio reperiam periodum unam alteramque dedicationis Casauboni- ane. ------ *Whatever this Author advances, in his " Theological Titles, concerning the Silence of the sa- " cred Writers, he has copied, I find, Word for Word " from* Casaubon; *whom it was the Reader's Interest " he should have nam'd, that he might know where to " have farther recourse. But I am afraid, he has " shaken the same Oak elsewhere; for, in the very be- " ginning of his Address to the Reader, I find a " Period or two* Casaubon's *Dedication.*

[*D*] Himmelius ------ *is one of those, who wrote against him.*] His Work is entituled *Anti-Alstedius, sive examen Theologiæ Polemicæ Johannis Henrici Alstedii*. Though this Remark should serve only to give the Title of one of *Alstedius*'s best Works, it would not be altogether useless.

[*E*] *Moreri was not acquainted with the Year of* Alstedius's *Death.*] *Alstedius*, says he, *died about the Year* 1645, *or* 46; *others say in the Year* 1640, *being the Fifty second Year of his Age*. Two of the three Authors, whom he cites (6), say nothing of it. *Lorenzo Crasso*, who is the third, says only, that *Alstedius* published the four *Tomes* of his *Encyclopædia*, at the Age of *Fifty two Years* (7).

ALTAEMPS (MARK) Son of a Sister of *Pius IV*, was one of the Cardinals, who presided in the Council of *Trent*. *Wolfgang Altaemps*, his Father, was a Count of the Empire in the Diocese of *Constance*. How splendid soever the Dignity of the Pope's Legate was in That Council, this Cardinal obtained it only by the Artifices of some ill affected Persons. The *Borromeo*'s, related to the Pope in the same Degree

with

ALTENSTAIG. ALTHAMERUS.

with him, desiring to remove him from Court, caused him to be sent to *Trent* (a), where he remained from the Month of *January* 1562, till about the Beginning of Spring 1563 [*A*]. The Pope recalled him, to raise Troops; for, hearing that the Dukes of *Saxony* and *Wirtemberg*, and the Landgrave of *Hesse*, were raising Forces, and that the *Germans* had a mind to plunder *Rome*, where they had found so great a Booty in the Year 1527; he was not willing to be surprized (b). This Cardinal was very much displeased with *Pibrac*'s Speech. His Opinion was, that it ought to be strongly answered; and said *that the Insolence of this Civilian ought to be restrained, who was accustomed to treat only with Persons of the meanest Rank* (c). He was promoted to the Purple in the Year 1561, and, a little before his Legation, the Canons of *Constance* had chosen him for their Bishop. He had neither the Learning, nor Experience, requisite for presiding in a Council; but his Uncle, *Pius IV*, was not ignorant that the other Presidents would supply what was wanting in him (d), and would teach him the Intrigues of Oecumenical Councils. When That Pope sent him Nuncio to the Emperor *Ferdinand* in the Year 1560, he sent with him the famous *Cornelius Musso*, Bishop of *Bitonto*, as his Instructor (e). *Altaemps* was then Bishop of *Cassano*. That Family rose in Dignity afterwards; for we find a Duke of *ALTAEMPS*, who died in the Year 1620 (f). He was a Man of Learning; and, if I am not mistaken, it was He, who collected the Library, which was so long famous at *Rome*, under that Name, and which was not quite sold, when Father *Mabillon* travelled into *Italy* (g). This Duke of *Altaemps*'s Name was *John Angeli*, and he published the Life of Pope *Anicetus*. Another Duke of *ALTAEMPS*, whose Name was *Gaudentius*, and who died in the Year 1677, was no less curious in Books, nor less learned. He published the Life of St *Chrysostom*, and the *Persecuted Sanctity triumphant* (h).

[*A*] *Where he remained from the Month of* January, 1562, *'till about the beginning of the Spring* 1563.] *Pallavicini* reproved Father *Paul* for having said, that Cardinal *Simonetta*, and Cardinal *Altaemps*, were named the Pope's Legates both at one time, to be added to the Legates that were already named. He knew not, that *Simonetta* was honoured with the Legation of the Council, at the same time with *Osius* and *Seripandus*, several Months before Cardinal *Altaemps* was made their Colleague (1). He censures him for another thing; which is, his mentioning *Osius* and *Seripandus*, only when he is speaking of what happened a considerable time after their Legation. Such Faults are not very material; yet it cannot be thought wrong in a Censor, to take notice of them; since it is the Duty of an Historian to avoid them.

ALTENSTAIG (JOHN) Doctor of Divinity, lived in the XVIth Century. He was of *Mindleheim*, in *Germany*, and composed a *Lexicon Theologicum*, which is tolerably good [*A*].

[*A*] *He composed a* Lexicon Theologicum, *which is tolerably good.*] He dedicated it to the Bishop of *Augsbourg*, the first of *October*, 1517. *Konig* places the first Edition of it in 1519 (1). I never saw it; but I have met with the second, which is of *Antwerp*, for Peter Bellerus, in 1576, in Folio; with this Title: " Lexicon Theologicum continens Vocabulorum Descriptiones, Definitiones, & Interpretationes perutiles, Theologiae Studiosis concinnatum. —— *A Theological Lexicon, containing very useful Descriptions, Definitions, and Interpretations of Words, compiled for the Use of Students in Divinity.*"

ALTHAMERUS (ANDREW) a *Lutheran* Minister at *Nuremberg*, about the middle of the XVIth Century (a), published, not only some Works in Divinity [*A*], but likewise Notes on the Treatise of *Tacitus*, *De Situ, Moribus, & Populis Germaniae*——*Of the Situation, Manners, and People of* Germany. They were printed at *Nuremberg* in the Year 1529, in 4to (b), and at *Amberg* in the Year 1609, in 8vo (c); and they were inserted by *Simon Schardius* in the first Volume of the *German Authors*. He was so eager to reject the Doctrine of the *Merit of Works*, that he attacked the Apostle St *James* with the utmost Brutality (d). This gives us an Opportunity of examining a Passage of the Controversy between *Grotius* and *Rivetus* [*B*]. We shall see in this Disquisition, that our *Althamerus* assisted, in 1528, at the Conferences of *Bern*, which were the Forerunners of the Ecclesiastical Reformation in this Canton.

[*A*] *Not only some Works in Divinity.*] The Titles of them are; *Conciliationes Locorum Scripturae, quae Specie tenus inter se pugnare videntur. Annotationes in D. Jacobi Epistolam. De Peccato Originis. De Sacramento Altaris.* He composed likewise a Dictionary of the proper Names, which are to be met with in the Bible, *Sylva Biblicorum Nominum*, &c. This Work was printed at *Basil*, in 1535. The *Conciliationes Locorum Scripturae*, was printed at *Nuremberg*, the same Year, and at *Wittemberg*, in the Year 1582. The Abridgment of *Gesner* takes notice of but these two Editions; but it is certain they were preceded by another, which appeared before the Year 1528 (1).

[*B*] *An Opportunity of examining a Passage of the Controversy between* Grotius *and* Rivetus.] The first Piece of this Part of their Dispute contains these Words (2): " Gaudeo D. Rivetum non accedere is, " qui Jacobi Epistolam rejecerunt, quorum quidam " hoc amplius dixere, *Mentiris Jacobe in caput " tuum*; that is, *I am pleased, that* Rivetus *does not " follow those, who reject the Epistles of St* James, *" among whom some go still farther, and in plain " Terms give St* James *the Lye.*" The second Piece is This: *Rivetus* demanded (3), *Who are They, who talk in this manner? How many are They?* and added, that, having searched among the Writings of the Jesuits, and other Controvertists, who eagerly collect Facts of this kind, whether the Protestants were ever reproached with a Blasphemy of this Nature, he had met with no such thing. The third Piece shews us, that *Grotius* mentioned no Author by Name, in his Reply to his Adversary (4), who had called upon him so expressly and warmly. This Silence made *Rivetus* conclude, that *Grotius* had no *Author* to alledge. *Quod nunc Autores non nisset harum contumeliarum, ostendit se nullos habere* (5). We find, by the fourth Piece, that *Grotius*, in rejoyning, cited the Words of *Andrew Althamerus*: " Is, qui Jacobum accusavit Mendacii, fuit Andreas " Althamerus

ALTHUSIUS.

"Althamerus (6). Liber editus est Argentorati, Anno CIƆIƆXXVII. Verba ejus inter cætera sunt: *Vult nunc probare suam sententiam, sed directè contra scripturam agit. Non possumus hic defendere Jacobum. Citat enim scripturas falsò, & solus spiritui sancto, Legi, Prophetis, Christo, Apostolicis omnibus, contradicit. Testimonium ipsius vanum est. Uni ipsi testi non esse credendum, supra annotavimus, præsertim cum quo ipse Spiritus sanctus & tot testes veritatis dissentiant. Credendum Multitudini. Paulus multo dignius sanctiusque rem tractat. Si Abraham ex operibus justificatus, habet quod glorietur, sed non apud Deum; quid enim dicit scriptura? Abraham credidit Deo, videlicet promissioni divinæ de semine; & reputatum, scilicet quia credidit, illi ad justitiam. Nonne quod ex filii immolatione justificatem dicit, rectè mentitus est in caput suum? Quindecim enim annos ante immolatum Isaachum justificatus fuit Abraham, etiam nondum nato Isaaco; non ex circumcisione, neque filii immolatione, sed ex sola Fide. Dicit enim scriptura, Credidit, &c. ut nihil habet Jacobus ad quod refugiat. Nos Fidei magistrum constituimus, & jam sui ipsissimis verbis scimus, nescivisse quid sit Fides. Et in fine Libri; Ne igitur succenseas nobis, Lector, si durius & vehementius calamo quandoque in Autorem invecti sumus. Meretur enim hoc Odium & hunc Spiritus vehementiam, dum aliam à nobis perfectionem atque Justitiam contendit, quam Fidei.* — He, who gave St James the Lye, was Andrew Althamerus. His Book was published at Strasbourg, in the Year 1527. His Words, among others, are These. He then endeavours to confirm his Doctrine; but his Proof is directly contrary to Scripture. We cannot here vindicate St James. For he cites Scripture falsly, and opposes his single Authority to That of the Holy Ghost, the Law, the Prophets, Jesus Christ, and all the Apostles. His Testimony is nothing. I have shewn above, that his single Evidence is not to be believed, especially when it clashes with That of the Holy Ghost, and so many Witnesses of the Truth. We must be governed by Numbers. St Paul treats the Subject with greater Dignity and Sanctity. For, if Abraham were justified by Works, he hath whereof to Glory, but not before God. For what saith the Scripture? Abraham believed God (to wit, the Divine Promise in relation to his Seed) and it was counted to him (namely, his Faith) for Righteousness *. Does not St James truly lie against his own Head, in saying that he was justified by the offering up of his Son? For Abraham was justified fifteen Years before the intended Sacrifice of his Son Isaac; even before Isaac was born; not by Circumcision, nor by the Sacrifice of his Son, but by Faith alone. For the Scripture faith, *He believed*, &c. So that St James is left without Excuse. I formerly looked upon this Apostle as a Rule of Faith; but am now convinced, from his own Words, that he did not himself know what Faith was. *And at the end of his Book*, Be not angry with me, Reader, if I sometimes inveigh too roughly and vehemently against this Author. For he deserves these Reproaches, and this Indignation of Mind, for requiring of us another kind of Perfection and Justification than that of Faith." The last Piece shall be, that *Rivetus*, finding at last an express Citation, answered (7), that it was insufficient; that *Grotius* had used the Plural Number; and that one is not *many*; *unus non sunt multi*. He condemns the Words of *Althamerus*; but he complains, that *Grotius* had not declared, that he was not a Calvinist. He proves, that He was a Lutheran; and charges him with having undertaken the Popish Cause, at the Conferences of *Bern*, and with having maintained the Doctrine of the *Real Presence*. " Qui cum in disputatione Bernensi (8), quam secuta est Reformatio Anni 1528, libera ei facta est disputandi copia, volens passus est se à parte Pontificia deligi, ut Oratoris munere in suggestu fungeretur, & carnalem Christi præsentiam in cœna defenderet. —— *At the Conference of Bern, which was followed by the Reformation of the Year 1528, tho' he had free Liberty of Disputation, yet he suffered himself to be chosen by the Pope's Party, to play the Orator in the Rostrum, and to defend the corporeal Presence of Christ in the Eucharist.*" His injurious Treatment of St *James*, concludes *Rivetus*, does not in the least affect us. The whole Disgrace of it recoils upon the Papists, and the Lutherans, whose Cause he pleaded."

From what we have here produced, it is easy to judge; I. That *Rivetus* ingaged unnecessarily in an incidental Dispute. He might have passed by this Remark of *Grotius*, without any Prejudice to his Cause; and he might have been satisfied with demanding the Names of Those, who had the Boldness to treat an Apostle with such Indignity. II. That he was mistaken, in believing, that his Adversary could not name any such. III. That, by dint of importunity, he occasioned a Discovery of his own Ignorance in a Matter of Fact; the Knowledge of which might have been to the Credit of his Reading and his Library. IV. That he flies for Refuge to little Evasions, which only serve to prolong Disputes, and to multiply unnecessary Additions. It is certain, that, in common Speech, when we know that an Author has published any thing, it is very allowable to say, that Authors have advanced it. Nor are we obliged to produce more than one Witness; unless when we expresly say, that *several* Persons have cast such a Reproach. But this is not *Grotius*'s manner of speaking; his Expression is indeterminate; *quidam dixere, there are, who have said*; or, *some have said*. He would have fully acquitted himself, tho' the Author, whom he cited, were not a Calvinist, but a Lutheran; and it is idle in *Rivetus* to alledge what passed in the Conferences of *Bern*. That is no Proof of *Althamerus*'s being a Papist. We can only conclude from thence, that he was so opposite in Opinion to the *Zuinglians*, on the Doctrine of the *Real Presence*, that he made no Scruple of maintaing it, even in favour of Popery. If *Rivetus* was Self-content in this part of his Dispute, it is a Proof, that Controvertists know not how to distinguish between what is to the Purpose, and what is meer caviling.

ALTHUSIUS (JOHN) a *German* Civilian, flourished near the End of the XVIth Century. He wrote a Book of Politics. Some Civilians of his Country are strangely angry with him, for maintaining, that the Sovereignty of States belongs to the People [*A*]. He wrote a Treatise *De Jurisprudentia Romana*, another *De Civili Conversatione*, another intituled *Dicæologia*, &c. I forgot to observe, in the former Editions,

[*A*] *Some Civilians — are strangely angry with him for maintaining, that the Sovereignty of States belongs to the People.*] *Boeclerus* maintains, that *Althusius*'s Principle is only fit to break all the Bonds of Civil Society, and that his Work is so far from deserving to be recommended to Students, as is done by several Persons, that it rather deserves to be burnt. " Omnes reges nihil aliud esse quam Magistratus — *Althusio* inter solennia carmina placet, cujus *Politica* non tradit sane, qui civitatis finis & felicitas & tranquillitas obtineri debeat, sed quibus modis omne vinculum societatis ac salutis civilis dissolvi ac everti possit. *Demagogica* appelles meritò; & tamen, quia Jurisconsulti nomen præfert, & quædam subinde in ostentationem ejus scientiæ jacit, " commendari juventuti Academicæ audimus librum, " orco, damnandum, judicio eorum qui venena à " cibis distinguere didicerunt (1). —— *That all* " *Kings are nothing but Officers of the People* —— " *is Althusius's darling Principle; whose Book of Po-* " *litics is not designed to shew, how the End, the* " *Happiness, and Tranquility of a State is best to be* " *obtained, but in what manner every Tye of Society* " *and Civil Security may be dissolved, and overturned.* " *It may properly be called* Democratical Politics; " *and yet, because the Name of a Civilian is prefixed* " *to it, and there is here and there a purpose Display of that Science in it; the Book is, we hear,* " *recommended to the University Youth; though in the* " *Opinion of those, who have learned to distinguish*

ALTIERI. ALTILIUS.

Editions, that he was of the *Protestant* Religion; that, after having been Professor of Law at *Herborn*, he had the Dignity of *Syndic* conferred upon him at *Breme*, and that the Jesuits, in answering the *Anti-Coton*, placed him in the List of those *Protestants*, who have spoken disrespectfully of the Regal Power [*B*].

" *Poison from wholesome Food, it deserves the severest* " *Censure.*" The learned *Conringius*'s Opinion of it is as follows: " Fundamentum doctrinæ suæ politicæ " collocat in eo, quod summa Reip. cujusvis jure " sit penes solum populum: qui error pestilens est, " & turbando orbi aptus (2). —— *He lays the Foun-* " *dation of his Political Doctrine in this; that the* " *Sovereignty of every Republic is in the Hands of* " *the People; which is a contagious Error, and cal-* " *culated to disturb the Repose of the World.*" Another *German* Writer expresses himself with more Force: " In classem istam, *says* he (3), referendi sunt " illi politicorum qui majestatis πρῶτον δεικτικόν " populum faciunt, inde *politici populares*; &, quia " jugulum omnium principum ac Regum petunt, " *Monarchomachi* dicti. Horum hominum nefanda " dogmata refertim habet Althusius in sua politica, " Vulcano publico edicto consecranda. —— *In this* " *Class we must rank those Politicians, who make the* " *People the Source of all Majesty; hence they are* " *called Popular Politicians; and, because they would* " *cut the Throats all Princes and Kings, they are* " *called Anti-Royalists.* Althusius *has made great* " *use of those Gentlemens wicked Doctrines in his* " *Politics; a Work, which deserves to be publickly con-* " *demned to the Flames.*"

[*B*] *The Jesuits* - - - - *placed him in the List of those Protestants, who have spoken disrespectfully of the Regal Power.*] I will give you the Words of Him, who presented to the Queen-Mother an Apologetical Answer to the Anti-Coton: " After *Hotto-* " *man*, *says* he (4), let us add the Doctrines and ex- " presss Words of *John Arthusius* (5), Doctor of " Law, in his Politics, methodically digested, and " printed at *Herborn*, in the Year 1603, in his Chap- " ter of the *Ephori*; in which, to look no farther, " he asserts, among other things, that *it is lawful* " *to dethrone a Tyrant, to take from him the Ad-* " *ministration of Affairs, with which he was in-* " *trusted*; *and even to put him to death, if no other* " *Remedy can be found, and to substitute another in* " *his Place.*" Althusius's Words are these (6). " E- " jusmodi Tyrannum ab officio removere, admini- " strationem demandata privare, imo etiam, si aliter " contra vim se defendere non possunt, interficere, " & alium in ejus locum substituere, possunt."

(2) Conring. de Civ. Prudent. c. 14.

(3) Meyer. in Analys. libri 3. Polit. Aristot.

(4) Réponse. Apolog. à l'Anti coton p. 185, 180.

(5) *It should be* Althusius.

(6) Althusii Politica methodicè digesta, cap. 14.

ALTIERI. The Dictionary of *Moreri* mentions two Cardinals of this Name. The One died in the Year 1654; the Other was Pope *Clement* X. We may add to these two the Cardinal *Altieri*, who died at *Rome*, the 29th of *June*, 1698.

ALTILIUS (GABRIEL) born in the Kingdom of *Naples*, flourished about the End of the XVth Century (*a*). He was chiefly esteemed for his *Latin Verses*, which shewed, that he cultivated polite Literature, and that he read the Ancients to great Advantage. This contributed to his Advancement in the Court of *Ferdinand*, King of *Naples*, which still retained some thing of the good Taste it had acquired in the Reign of King *Alphonsus*. He was chosen Preceptor to the young Prince *Ferdinand* [*A*]. It appears also, that he was employed in State-Affairs, and that he accompanied *Jovian Pontanus* to *Rome*, upon a Negotiation of Peace between King *Ferdinand* and Pope *Innocent* VIII (*b*). He had a great Share in the Friendship and Esteem of *Pontanus*, as appears from the Writings of the latter (*c*). *Sannazarius* gave him likewise several Marks of his Esteem in his Poems (*d*): These two Authors are not the only Persons, who have commended him [*B*]. One of *Gabriel Altilius*'s finest Poems, is That, which he composed on the Marriage of *Isabella* of *Arragon* [*C*]. One would scarce believe, that *Latin* Poetry raised him to the Prelature; but it is certain, that it greatly contributed to his obtaining the Bishoprick of *Policastro*. Some find fault with him for neglecting the Muses, after his Advancement, which had

(a) *And not of the* XIVth, *as* Moreri *says*.

(b) Pontanus Præf. Tractatus de Magnificentia.

(c) *He wrote an Epitaph for* Altilius, *and dedicated to him his Treatise de Magnificentia. See likewise his Dialogue* Ægidius, *pag.* 14, 1.

(d) Eleg. 12. ver. 27. & Epigr. 7.

[*A*] *He was chosen Preceptor to the young Prince* Ferdinand] This is what *Paul Jovius* meant, when he used this Expression, *junioris Ferdinandi regis* (1). *Ughelli* makes use of it likewise (2). *Toppi* is of another Opinion: " Fu maestro, *says* he, di Re Ferdinando I. " d' Aragona, è Vescovo di Policastro nel 1471 (3). I believe he is mistaken. *Ferdinand* I. died in the Year 1494, being above seventy Years old: So that he must have been born about the Year 1424; and *Altilius* must have been his Preceptor about the Year 1440. The Preceptor of a King's Son is seldom very young; he must have had time to gain the Reputation of a Man of Learning: And doubtless King *Alphonsus*, who was himself learned, and surrounded with learned Men, would not have chosen *Altilius*, without full Proof of his Abilities. Upon this Supposition *Altilius* must have been thirty Years of Age, in 1440; but, at that time, he was scarce born. He lived but a little more than sixty Years (4); and died in the Year 1501 (5).

[*B*] *These two Authors are not the only Persons, who have commended him.*] *Gyraldus* mentions him greatly to his Advantage. *Basil Zanchius* wrote several Verses in praise of *Altilius*, which are to be found in the *Delights* of the *Italian Poets*. *John Matthæus Toscanus* speaks well of him both in Verse and Prose (6). But if any one is desirous to see an Encomium upon his Wit and Disposition of Mind, let him read *Alexander ab Alexandro*, who describes at large the manner how he and some others were entertained by *Altilius*, when they went to wish him Joy of his Bishoprick (7). He gave them a Supper more becoming his first Condition, that the Dignity of a Bishop, with which he was then invested; he had not yet dismist the Muses, his first Mistresses (supposing he ever dismissed them); thus the Conversation turned upon some Verses of *Martial*, which were sung by a young Musician.

[*C*] *One of* Gabriel Altilius's *finest Poems is That, which he composed on the Marriage of* Isabella *of* Arragon.] It was by This, and by his Elegies, that he acquired his Reputation. " Usque adeo molliter ac " admirande in Elegis & Heroico carmine excelluit, " sicuti ex Epithalamio Isabellæ Arragoniæ perspici " potest, ut Pontani atque Actii testimonio antiquis " vatibus æquaretur (8). —— *He was so great a* " *Master of Elegiac and Heroic Poetry (as may be* " *seen by his Epithalamium of* Isabella *of* Arragon) " *that, in the Opinion of* Pontanus *and* Actius, *he* " *was equal to the antient Poets.*" *Julius Scaliger* found too great a Profusion of Thought and Expression in his *Epithalamium*. His Opinion of it is this: " Gabriel Altilius Epithalamium cecinit longe opti- " mum, excellentissimum vero futurum, si sibi ille " temperasset. Dum enim vult omnia dicere, affi- " cit auditorem aliquando fastidio tanto, quanta in " aliis voluptate. Est enim nimius, quod vitium " illi genti est proprium. Est enim totis illis Italiæ " tractibus perpetua loquendi fames (9). —— Gabriel " Altilius *composed an excellent Epithalamium*; *which* " *however*

(1) Jovius Elog. cap. 225.

(2) Ughelli Italia sacra, Tom. 3. pag. 790.

(3) Toppi Bibliotheca Napoletana, pag. 101.

(4) Jovius in Elog. cap. 225.

(5) *See below* Citat. (17).

(6) In Peplo Italiæ.

(7) Genial. dierum, lib. 3. cap. 1.

(8) Jovius, ubi supra.

(9) Jul. Cæsar Scalig. Poetic. l. 6. pag. 736.

ALTILIUS. ALTINGIUS.

had been so serviceable to him [D]. They discover Ingratitude and Shamelessness (e) in the precipitate manner of his leaving them; and his Fault would seem unpardonable to them, had they not some Regard to the Excuses he might make, that Episcopacy required he should apply himself earnestly to the Study of Holy Writ. I shall endeavour to rectify what is said concerning the time of his Death (f). We find only the *Epithalamium* of *Isabella* of *Arragon* in the Collection of *Gruterus*, and in That of *John Matthæus Tuscanus* [E]. It is very probable that most of *Altilius's* other Verses are lost.

"however would have been much better, had he re-
"strained his Genius. For, by endeavouring to say
"every thing upon this Subject, he becomes as tedious
"to the Reader, as he is entertaining upon others.
"He is too diffuse; a Vice peculiar to his Nation;
"for in all that Tract of *Italy* they are never tired
"with talking." This is not very complaisant to the *Neapolitans* (10).

[D] Some find Fault with him for neglecting the *Muses*, —— which had been *so serviceable to him*.] 'Tis hard of Digestion, that a Bishop should be the Author of this Reproach, and that he should express it in such harsh Terms: "Is virtutis merito Policastri (ea "arbs olim Buxentum fuit) antistes factus, à Musis, "per quas profecerat, celeriter IMPUDENTERQUE "discessit, MAGNO HERCLE INGRATI animi PIACULO, "nisi ad spem non injustæ veniæ ob id culpa tege-"retur, quod ad sacras literas nequaquam ordinis ob-"litus tempestivè configgisset (11). —— Being raised, "on Account of his Virtues, to the Bishoprick of Po-"licastro (formerly Buxentum), he quickly and "SHAMEFULLY deserted the *Muses*, his *Benefactresses*; "Guilty, in this, of the HEINOUS CRIME of IN-"GRATITUDE; unless he thought to screen himself "from reproach, by pleading that, in consideration "of his Order, he had opportunely applied himself to "the Study of the Scriptures." See Mr *Baillet's* judicious Reflexions upon this (12). These four Verses of *Latomus* are not amiss.

Audiit Altilius desertis transfuga Musis,
In quarum tabulis nobile nomen erat.
Sed quid peccavit, si demereatur, ut olim
Carminibus Phœbum, nunc pietate Deum?

*Censures the Bard Altilius they accuse
Of base Desertion from his friendly Muse;
But where's the Crime,
If He, who in Apollo's Temple trod,
His Priest --- now serves in pious Prose his God?*

Altilius would have been more to blame, if, after having obtained a Mitre by preaching, he had behaved like many others, who preach no more, after they are made Bishops. The reason is, because, to preserve this kind of Power, it is not necessary to continue the same Expedients, which had made use of to procure it (13). *Paul Jovius* is as unfortunate in Point of Fact. He pretends, that *Altilius* left off writing Verses, after his Promotion to a Bishoprick: and that the finest of his Poems is his *Epithalamium* of *Isabella* of *Arragon* (14). I make no doubt but this *Isabella* is she, who was contracted, the first of *November* 1472, to *John Galeas Sforza*, Duke of *Milan*. I cannot therefore persuade myself, that *Altilius* is guilty of the Desertion, with which he is charged. He was made a Bishop in 1471: now the best of his Poems was composed after this time: ought we therefore to complain that the Mitre made him abandon *Parnassus*? Observe, that He wrote this *Epithalamium*, not at the time of the Contract, but upon the Nuptials of *Isabella* of *Arragon*; that is, in the Year 1489 (15). This is proved by the first Lines of it.

Purpureos jam læta sinus Tithonia Conjux
Extulerat, roseoque diem patefecerat Ortu,
Cæruleum tremulo percurrens lumine pontum,
Qui cupido sua vota viro DESPONSAQUE DUDUM
Connubia, OPTATOSQUE locos & gaudia ferret.

*Aurora now, from Tithon rising gay,
Blush'd in the Rosy East, and gave the Day;
Whilst trembling Beams upon the Ocean play;
The Day, which is the Happy Bridegroom's Arms
Consigns the PROMIS'D Fair, with all her Charms.*

By this we may convict the Abbot *Ughelli* of a gross Mistake: who says, that *Altilius* died in his Bishoprick of *Policastro*, in the Year 1484 (16). It may be proved, that he did not die 'till about the Year 1501; for *Jovian Pontanus* observes, in mentioning the News of his Death, that *Sanazarius* was upon the point of going into *France* with King *Frederic* (17).

[E] *We find only the* Epithalamium *in the Collection of* Gruterus, *and That of* J. M. Tuscanus.] I understand by this Collection the Work, entituled *Deliciæ CC. Italorum Poëtarum, collectore Ranutio Ghero*. The Collection of *John Matthæus Tuscanus* is entituled, *Carmina illustrium poëtarum Italorum*. This Author says, in his *Peplum*, that he had only read the *Epithalamium*, and some few Epigrams of *Altilius*. He, who procured a new Edition of *Sanazarius's* [*] *Latin* Poems, in 1689, and illustrated them with Notes, observes, that he does not remember to have seen any printed Pieces of *Altilius*, but the *Epithalamium*, and an Epigram; from whence he infers, that many of them are lost, since *Paul Jovius* mentions this Poet's Elogies, and *Sanazarius* ascribes some Odes to him (18). To repair this Loss in some measure, he has given us, in the Notes on *Sanazarius*, three or four Pieces of *Altilius*, which he had in Manuscript. *Toppi* mentions three Pieces of *Altilius* inserted " ne' fiori delle Rime de' Poëti "illustri raccolti & ordinati da Girolamo Ruscelli, "stampati in Venetia, nel 1558. in 8vo. —— *In* "*the Poetical Flowers of the celebrated Poets collected and disposed by* William Ruscelli, *and printed* "*at* Venice, *in* 1558, *in* 8vo." These three Pieces are, *Gabrielis Altilii lamentatio, Ejusdem Epithalamium, Ejusdem Elegia*.

[*] [It was the late Mr *Bruckhusius*. REM. CRIT.]

ALTINGIUS (HENRY) Professor of Divinity at *Heidelberg*, and at *Groningen*, was born at *Embden*, the 17th of *February* 1583. His Family had been a long time very considerable in *Friesland*. He was designed, from the Cradle, for an Office, wherein his Father had signalized himself [A], I mean the sacred Ministry. For this end

[A] *An Office wherein his Father had signalized himself.*] His Name was *Menso Altingius*; and he was the Grandson of another *Menso*, who was given in Hostage to the Duke of *Guelderland* by the States of *Drent* in the Year 1523. Another *Menso Altingius*, Great Grandfather to Him, who was given in Hostage, had been Counsellor to *Reinold the Fat*, Duke of *Guelderland*, and retired into the Country of *Drent*, in the Year 1361 (1). *Menso Altingius*, the Minister, was the first, who, with two others, preached the Reformation in the Territory of *Groningen*, about the Year 1566, during the Tyranny of the Duke of *Alba*, Sub ipsâ Albani ducis grassante *Tyrannide* (2). He was also the first Minister, who preached in the great Church of *Groningen*, after the Reduction of That Place to the Power of the States-General, in the Year 1594. He served the Church of *Embden* thirty eight Years faithfully, and opposed, with great Courage, the Fury of the *Anabaptists*, and the Plots of the *Ubiquitarians*. He died, the seventh of *October* 1612, the same Day that his Son and *Abraham Scultetus* were in danger of being cast away on the Lake of *Harlem*. "Subita ac pro-"cellosâ coortâ tempestate, naufragio ac submersioni "proximi (Scultetus & Altingius) ægrè tandem, "toto corpore madentes, salve tamen, divinâ cle-"mentia

ALTINGIUS. 239

end he was sent very early to the Schools, and, after he had acquired Classical Learning, and gone thro' a Course of Philosophy at *Groningen*, he was sent into *Germany* in the Year 1602. He was three Years at *Herborn*, where he made so great a Progress under the famous *Piscator*, and under *Matthias Martinius*, and *William Zepperus*, that he obtained leave to teach Philosophy and Divinity. He was preparing to travel into *Switzerland* and *France*, when he was made Preceptor to three young Counts (a) who studied at *Sedan*, with the Electoral Prince Palatine. He entered upon this Employ, the beginning of *September* 1605. The Storm, which threatened the Duke of *Bouillon* from *Henry* IV, and which was attended with no Consequence, induced the Electoral Prince to leave *Sedan*, with these young Lords, in the Year 1606. *Altingius* followed them to *Heidelberg*, where he continued to instruct the three young Counts. He was also admitted to read some Geographical and Historical Lectures to the Electoral Prince, and became his sole Preceptor in the Year 1608. We may meet with Proofs of this in the *Vatican* Library [B]. He accompanied him to *Sedan* in this Quality, and instructed him in so accomplished a manner, that the young Prince, upon his Return to *Heidelberg*, in 1610, being interrogated on all Points of Religion before the Duke of *Deux Ponts*, Administrator of the Electorate, and several other Persons of Note, answered very pertinently, and in *Latin*. He was one of those, who was chosen to accompany the young Elector into *England*, in the Year 1612, where he became acquainted with *George Abbot*, Archbishop of *Canterbury*; Dr *King*, Bishop of *London*; and Dr *Hakwell*, Preceptor of the Prince of *Wales*. He had likewise the Honour to converse with King *James*. The Marriage of the Elector with the Princess of *England* being celebrated in *London* in the Month of *February* 1613 (b), *Altingius* went before with his former Pupils, and arrived at *Heidelberg*, the First of *April*. In the Month of *August* following, he was made Professor of Divinity Common Places; and, because he could not preside in the Disputes, without being Doctor of Divinity, he took that Degree in the Month of *November*, with the usual Ceremonies. In 1616, he had a laborious Office conferred upon him, which was the Direction of the Seminary, if I may be permitted so to call the *College of Wisdom* at *Heidelberg*. He was offered the Professorship, vacant by the Death of *Coppenius*, in the Year 1618, which was the second Professorship in the Faculty of Divinity; but he refused it, and procured it for *Sculetus*. He gave great Proofs of his Learning in the Synod of *Dort*, whither he was sent with two other Deputies of the *Palatinate* (c). It was at that time that the Degree of Doctor, which the University of *Leyden* had suffered to be extinct, was revived. *Altingius* solemnly created the Professor, *John Polyander*, Licentiate in Divinity, who afterwards received his Doctor's Degree from *Sculetus*, by which means he became invested with the Authority requisite for conferring the Degree of Doctor on his Colleagues. *Altingius*, no doubt, entertained great Expectations a little after his Return to *Heidelberg*. The Troubles of *Bohemia* gave a Crown to the Elector Palatine; but these happy Beginnings were soon attended with a dreadful Ruin. *Tilly* took *Heidelberg* by Assault, in the Month of *September*, 1622, and suffered all imaginable Disorders to be committed in it [C]. *Altingius*, having escaped the Fury of the Soldiers, as it were by Miracle [D], followed his Family, which he had sent some time

---

(1) Vit. Hen. Altingii.

(a) The Counts of Nassau, Solms, and Ilenberg.

(4) Vit Jacobi Alting.

(b) König dates not allow him a proper time, when he says visit anno 1613. His most flourishing State was not then arrived.

(c) Vita Hen. Altingii.

(c) Abraham Sculetus, and Paul Toffanus. The latter was deputed by the Ecclesiastical Senate, and the other two by the University.

(6) Ex Vita Henr. Alting.

" mentia in proximam ripam evaserunt (3). —— *A sudden and stormy Tempest arising, They* (Scultetus *and* Altingius) *were in danger of being cast away and drowned; but, at last, they providentially escaped, drenched and wet to the Skin, on the next Shore*." His Life, written at large by *Ubbo Emmius*, is among the Papers of his Heirs (4).

[B] *We may meet with Proofs of This in the Vatican Library.*] The Exercises of the King of *Bohemia*, corrected by *Altingius*, are preserved there, and shewn to Travellers, as the Author of That Professor's Life informs us. He adds, that these Monuments deserve as much to be shewn to the Curious, as most Relicks which they see. "*Hujus magisterii ejus ne unquam apud posteros intestata queat esse industria, vel Roma, quod miremur, faciet, quæ in Bibliotheca Vaticana inter Heidelbergensia cimelia, dicam an spolia, ostentat themata & exercitia styli Regis Bohemiæ Altingii manu emendata, eruditis peregrinatoribus minimeque superstitiosis visenda, atque non minus credo, quàm pleræque ipsorum reliquiæ* ἀξιοθεατα, *digna spectatu* (5).

[C] *Suffered all imaginable Disorders to be committed.*] They plunder'd, they ravish'd, they kill'd, they tortur'd; in a Word, they committed every Outrage, which the Fury of Soldiers, animated by a false Zeal for Religion, is capable of. "*Urbs —— impetu & vi capta, omniaque dira exempla passa direptionis, lanienæ, libidinis, quæ militaris licentia, victoris insolentia, odium religionis, barbarorum Croatarum feritas comminisci potuere, aut patrare —— Ea nocte insomni & moesta, inter lamenta & ejulatus, quibus omnia undique perstrepebant, aut sequioris sexus vim patientis, aut virorum equuleis subditorum, ac per varia tormenta ac vulnere lenta citave morte affectorum*, &c. (6) —— *The Town was taken by Assault; and every dreadful Instance was permitted, of Plunder, Butchery, and Lust, which the Licentiousness of an Army, the Insolence of a Conqueror, religious Hatred, and the Brutality of barbarous Croatians, could contrive or perpetrate. —— In that sleepless and calamitous Night, amidst the Cries and Groans, which were heard on all Sides, either of violated Women, or Men suffering variety of Tortures, some dying a quick, some a lingring Death,* &c." These are the usual Fruits of War; enough to make those tremble, who undertake to advise it, to prevent Evils, which, perhaps, may never happen, and which, at the worst, would often be less than those, which necessarily follow a Rupture. I shall have occasion, more than once, to remark the Anguish of Mind, to which great Commanders have been reduced, when their Consciences have reproached them with the Ravages they have occasioned.

[D] *Having escaped the Fury of the Soldiers, as it were by Miracle.*] The Circumstances of his Escape deserve to be related. He was in his Closet, when he heard that the Enemy, being Masters of the City, began to plunder it. He bolted his Door, and betook himself to Prayer. One of his Friends, accompanied by two Soldiers, came to him, and advised him to retire, by the Back-door, to the Chancellor's House, which was put under a strong Guard; Count *Tilly* intending to secure all the Papers, which were there. The

ALTINGIUS.

time before to *Heilbron*. He met it at *Schorndorf*; where with much Difficulty he abode a few Months: for the *Lutheran* Ministers put in practice the Doctrine of Non-Toleration against him [*E*]. In the Year 1623, he retired with his Family to *Embden*, and went from thence to wait upon the King of *Bohemia* at the *Hague*. This Prince retained him as Preceptor to his eldest Son (*d*), and would not permit him to serve the Church of *Embden*, which desired him for their Minister, nor the University of *Franeker*, which offered him, in the Year 1625, the Professorship of Divinity, vacant by the Death of *Sibrandus Lubbertus*. This Prince was prevailed upon, with great Difficulty, to give him leave, the next Year, to accept of a Professorship of Divinty at *Groningen*. *Altingius* took Possession of it, the sixteenth of *June* 1627, and kept it 'till he died. It is true, that, in 1633, he was fully resolved to leave *Groningen* for *Leyden* ; but it was upon this Condition, that the States of *Groningen* should consent to it, which they refused to do. It is true likewise, that he listened to the Proposals, which Prince *Lewis Philip* (*e*) made him in 1634, to come and re-establish the University of *Heidelberg*, and the Churches of the Palatinate; and that he was already arrived at *Francfort*, through many Dangers; but this Design proved abortive by reason of the Battel of *Norlingen*, which the Imperialists won. He was obliged to return to *Groningen* through By-ways. It does not appear, that he had any Thoughts afterwards of removing to any other Place. The last Years of his Life were full of Trouble ; Grief and Diseases gave him great Uneasiness. He was so afflicted at the Death of his eldest Daughter in 1639, that he fell into an obstinate Melancholy, which brought him into a Quartan-Ague, of which he was with great Difficulty cured, though not perfectly ; for the Remains of it turned to a Lethargy in 1641. Scarce had the Physicians, by repeated Applications, removed this Distemper, when a domestic Affliction came upon him, which occasioned his bodily Infirmities to return upon him stronger than ever. *Altingius* lost his Wife in the Year 1643, and grieved so much for her, that he was no longer able to overcome his Melancholy. From this time to the Day of his Death his Infirmities continued

(*d*) *He was cut away in the Sea of Palm, an. 1629.*

(*e*) *He was at Ad intra of the Palatinate, and in 1633, forced to make Altingius Professor of Divinity, and Ecclesiastical Senator.*

The Lieutenant Colonel of the Regiment of *Hohenzollern* guarded this House : With this Battle-axe, said he, *I have killed ten Men this Day* ; *Doctor Altingius should soon be the eleventh, if I knew where he lies hid: Who are you?* continued he, directing his Discourse to the Doctor. *Altingius* was not so confounded, but he readily replied ; *I was Teacher in the College of Wisdom* ; an Answer not the farthest from Truth. The Author of his Elogium compares this Answer to that, which St *Athanasius* made, " Sanè " ille Vultus, ille Habitus, ille Sermo, is rerum ar- " ticulus, quemvis alium percellere poterat: at noster " imperterritus, solerti tamen usus responso, nec " aperte se negavit Altingium, nec tamen intempestive " se prodidit, eadem fere qua olim in casu simili S. A- " thanasius dexteritate usus, Ego, (inquit) Ludimagi- " ster fui in Collegio Sapientiæ. ——— *In truth, such* " *a Look, such a Mein, and such Language, might* " *have confounded any one else : But our Hero, undis-* " *may'd, returned, however, an artful Answer; nei-* " *ther positively denying that he was Altingius, nor* " *unseasonably betraying himself* ; *in which he had re-* " *course to the same Artifice, which was put in practice,* " *in a like Case, by St Athanasius.* I *was a School-* " *master,* says he, *in the College of Wisdom."* The Lieutenant Colonel promised to save him. The next Day the Jesuits took Possession of the House, and sent away this Officer so suddenly, that he had not time to enquire after his *Teacher of the College of Wisdom*. Thus *Altingius* found himself in the Hands of the Jesuits ; but he hid himself in a Garret ; and, by good Fortune, a Cook of the Electoral Court was employed by Count *Tilly*, whose Kitchen was in the Chancellor's House. This Man privately convey'd Victuals to *Altingius* in the Garret, and even gave him an Opportunity of going to see what past at his own House, attended by three Soldiers of the *Bavarian* Army for his Guard. *Altingius* found his House in great Disorder, and his Closet in the Power of a Captain ; who told him, either in a bantering way, or out of Civility, that he gave him leave to carry away what Book he pleased. He declined the Offer, and only answered, that, if those things belonged to him, he desired God would give him a longer Possession of them, than their first Master had. *Altingius* ran many Dangers in his return ; and, after three Days, *Tilly* gave him leave to retire. I have read, somewhere, that, had not *Altingius* been afraid of being thought a Plagiary, he might have saved many Books of the Electoral Library : and that he had removed many of them to the College of *Wisdom* ; but I confess I do not understand this ; I find a Contradiction in it. If he convey'd no Books out of the Electoral Library in- to his own Closet, for fear of being accounted a *Plagiary*; why do you say, that he carried away several of them to the College of *Wisdom*, and that he might have saved many ? Besides, according to the Author of his Life, he was permitted only to carry away one Volume. Read the following Passage. " Hunc (*Quin-* " *tilianum*) & alios illius Bibliothecæ libros sua manu " in Collegio Sapientiæ exceperat Henricus Altingius, " atque ex communi illo incendio Bavarico eripuisset, " nisi suis reculis timuisset, & ne plagiarius haberetur, " si antiquus liber in ejus supellectile reperiretur, ve- " ritus fulsset (7). ——— Henry Altingius *had picked* " *out this* (Quintilian) *and other Books of that Library,* " *with his own Hands,* in *the College of* Wisdom ; " *and might have saved them from that general Bava-* " *rian Conflagration, had he not been afraid of pos-* " *sing for a* Plagiary, *if the ancient Copy was found* " *in his Possession.*"

[*E*] *The* Lutheran *Ministers put in practice the Doctrine of* Non-Toleration *against him.*] At the Request of the Elect'ress, he obtained leave of the Duke of *Wirtemberg* to reside at *Schorndorf*. He continued there 'till the Month of *February*, which followed the Desolation of the Palatinate. The *Lutheran* Ministers murmured at his living there, and at the Permission, which the Duke had given him ; the Reason of their Discontent was, that *Altingius* was a Professor of *Heidelberg.* " Ibi ad Februarium usque hæsit, fa- " cultate hac per serenissimam Electricem impetrata " à Duce Wirtembergico, cujus alias Ministri Lu- " therani, quasi Ponti Axeni accolæ, aut aves Dio- " medeæ, quæ solos socios gratanter accipiunt, id re- " rebant ægerrime, non alia de causa quàm quod Al- " tingius Professor esset Heidelbergensis (8). ------ " *He continued there 'till* February, *having obtained* " *leave from the Duke of* Wirtemberg, *by means of* " *the Serene Elect'ress* ; *which was taken ill by the* " Lutheran *Ministers, for no other Reason, but because* " Altingius *was Professor at* Heidelberg, *resembling* " *in this the People bordering on the* Euxine *Sea, or* " Diomedes's Birds, *who receive joyfully only their* " *Fellows.*" I believe they would have more strictly observed the Laws of Hospitality towards a Merchant of the Palatinate, or towards a *Calvinist* Professor of a very remote Country, than towards a Professor of *Heidelberg*. The Palatinate was near the Dutchy of *Wirtemberg* ; the Professors of *Tubingen*, and those of *Heidelberg*, frequently attack'd each other in Disputations, and Polemical Writings. Behold the Source of Theological and Professorial Enmity ! But after all, we cannot excuse their ill Treatment of *Altingius*. He had escaped from the Popish Flames ; the Injuries he had received from the com-

(7) Lomeier de Biblioth. pag. 278. *I vow not whether a Man may be called a Plagiary, who Steals, not the Thoughts of an Author, but a Book or a Volume in kind, without publishing it in his own Name.*

(8) Vita Altingii.

mon

ALTINGIUS. 241

continued to increase. He died christianly, and devoutly, on the Twenty fifth of *August*, 1644. He was a Man of great Merit. The Books he composed [*F*] are a Proof of his Learning, and his Application to the Discharge of the Academical Duties; and it is well known, that he employed his Abilities other ways, in serving his Neighbours. He went to see the King of *Bohemia* every Year, and reviewed the Studies of the Royal Family. He took a great deal of Pains in the Collections, which were made every where in the Protestant Countries for the Churches of *Germany*, and particularly for those of the Palatinate. He was one of the three Commissioners for the Collections from *England*, and disposed of the Alms of *Lewis de Geer*. I omit the two considerable Commissions he was charged with; one relating to the Revisal, which was made at *Leyden*, of the new *Dutch* Translation of the Scripture, and the other relating to the Visitation of the County of *Steinfurt*. He had Colleagues in the first; but he was sole Inspector-General in the second; the Count of *Bentheim* having sent for him to make Inquisition against *Socinianism*, which threatened his Country, and to regulate the Churches. *Altingius's* Elogy says, that he was not a quarrelsome Divine [*G*]; he did not spend his Time in trifling, insignificant, Scruples; he was not fond of Novelty; he was zealous for the antient Doctrine; an Enemy to the Subtilties of the Schools; and relied only on the Scripture [*H*]. All Persons of his Profession ought to imitate his Conduct in the Management of their domestic Affairs [*I*]. They were spoken of no otherwise, than as being, in general, right. They afforded no other Topic for Conversation. He married at *Heidelberg* in the Year 1614, and had seven Children, of which one Daughter and two Sons survived him. The eldest was Professor of the Civil Law at *Deventer* (*f*). The following Article treats of the other.

(e) *Juvenal. Sat.* xv. ver. 33.

mon Enemy, should have served as a powerful Recommendation of him; his Belief did not differ from that of *Wirtemberg*, but in things not essential. If Men must hate and persecute each other for Religion, they should wait, at least, 'till they are like the People of *Egypt*, some in the Service of one God, and some in the Service of quite a different God.

Inter finitimos vetus atque antiqua simultas,
Immortale odium, & nunquam sanabile Vulnus,
Ardet adhuc Ombos, & Tentyra, summus utrinque
Inde furor vulgo, quod numina vicinorum
Odit uterque locus, quum solos credit habendos
Esse deos, quos ipse colit (9).

Ombus and *Tentyr*, neighb'ring Towns, of late
Broke into Outrage of deep-fester'd Hate.
A Grudge in both, time out of mind, begun,
And mutually bequeath'd from Sire to Son.
Religious Spite, and pious Spleen, bred first
This Quarrel, which so long the Bigots nurst.
Each calls the other's God a senseless Stock,
His own Divine: tho' from the self-same Block
One Carver fram'd them. TATE.

Thus we see, that the Promoters of Ecclesiastical Wars always suppose, that their religious Disputes are of the greatest Consequence. *It is a Gangrene*, say they, *it is undermining the Foundations of Religion.*

[*F*] *The Books he compos'd.*] Those, which have been published, are as follows. *Notæ in Decadem problematum Johannes Behm, de gloriosi Dei & beatorum cœlo*, Heidelbergæ, 1618. *Loci communes cum didactici tum elencthici: Problemata tam theoretica quàm practica: Explicatio Catecheseos Palatinæ cum vindiciis ab Arminianis & Socinianis*, Amstelodami, 1646, in 3 Volumes. *Exegesis Augustanæ Confessionis una cum syllabo controversiarum Lutheranarum*, Amstelodami, 1647. *Methodus Theologiæ Didacticæ & Catecheticæ*, Amstelodami, 1650. Those, which are not published, are more in Number, and some of them are imperfect: The List of them is to be seen at the end of the Author's Life. I find there, that the *Medulla Historiæ Prophanæ*, published by *Daniel Pareus*, is a Work of our *Altingius*. It is a *Plagiarism*, which has not been observed by *Thomasius*, nor Mr *Almeloveen* (10) The Ecclesiastical History of the Palatinate, from the Reformation down to the Administrator *John Casimir*, is one of the most considerable among the Manuscript Works of *Altingius*.

[*G*] *He was not a quarrelsome Divine.*] I shall set down the very Words of his Historian. "Alienus à jurgiis & vitilitigiis cuminisectorum, ab iis distinctiunculis & ineptiis Sophistarum, quibus mysteria salutis potius implicantur quàm explicantur; à scrupulositatibus præcisistarum, qui nodum quærunt in

(10) *H. has published a Catalogue of the Progress of the End of the Armenians Theologico-Philologica, Amst.* 1694.

scirpo, colant culicem, camelum deglutientes (11). ----- *He avoided all Quarrels and Disputes about Trifles, together with the idle Distinctions of the Sophists, in which the Mysteries of Salvation are rather taken for granted, than explained; likewise the scrupulous Behaviour of the Fanatics, who carry Religion to Superstition, strain out a Gnat, and swallow a Camel*". The Sect of the Fanatics made a noise in *Holland*, about forty Years ago (12). It is very well characterised by these Words; they strain out a Gnat, and swallow a Camel*; they open a Door to Disputes, which serve only to furnish the Prophane and Libertine with Arms. To go on; "Ab omni denique καινοφωνία & novatione in Theologicis, quasi illud semper Tertulliani tenens, *primum quodque verissimum*. ----- *Lastly, he avoided all Innovations in Divinity*, adhering always to that Maxim of Tertullian, The first is the truest". There is no doubt, but that the love of Novelty is a Plague, which, having thrown Universities and Synods into a Flame, shakes and disorders a State, and sometimes overthrows it: So that we cannot too much commend those Professors, who recommend to their Pupils to avoid this Spirit of Innovation. I confess, the Care, which is taken to recommend the Observation of the ancient and commonly received Doctrine, seems to imply a Principle of Authority in the Church, which is constantly rejected by the Protestants, when they have occasion to dispute with the *Roman* Catholics. But this ought not to discourage any one from preventing Innovations; for if a Reason were never to be made use of, 'till it were free from all Difficulties, every thing would be at a stand.

[Give me leave to remark here, an Error in our *English* Version of this proverbial Saying. We render it *strain* AT *a Gnat, and swallow a Camel*; whereas both the *Greek* Term διυλιζω, and the *Latin Colo*, signifie to STRAIN OUT any thing, out of a Cup, or drinking Vessel, for instance, into which a *Gnat* or other Insect may have fallen. REM. CRIT.]

[*H*] *An Enemy to the Subtilties of the Schools, and relied only on the Scripture.*] See what follows: "Theologiam probabat ac tuebatur solidam ac masculam, non ex lacunis Scholasticorum, etsi illarum inexpertus non esset, sed ex fontibus Siloë & Scripturarum derivatam; ut gloriæ sibi duceret, se ab imperitis nonnullis ac nasutis Palæmonibus traduci, tanquam Theologum Scripturarum & Biblicum (13). ----- *He approved of, and maintained, a sound and manly Divinity, not derived from the standing Pools of the Schoolmen, though he was not unacquainted with them, but from the running Brooks of* Siloë, *and the Scriptures*; *insomuch that he thought it an Honour to be traduced by ignorant and scoffing Grammarians, as a Scriptural Bible-Divine.*"

[*I*] *Persons of his Profession ought to imitate his Conduct, in the management of their domestic Affairs.*] It was only known, that no one knew the Transactions

(f) *Taken from James Altingius's Life, among those of the Professors of Groningen, from the Life, in* 1654.

(11) Vit. Jacobi Alting.

(12) *I wrote this in* 1698.
* See REM. CRIT. below.

(13) Vita Altingii.

VOL. I. Ppp

ALTINGIUS.

ons of his Family, farther than that all things were done decently, and according to the fear of God. " Hinc in familia ejus omnia semper pacata, omnia " ordinata, de qua hoc solum sciretur, quod à nemi- " ne sciretur quid in illa fieret, nisi quod piè, com- " posite, decenter omnia fieri neminem lateret (14)." This is much better than that whatever is said or done in a Minister's House should be the Subject of pub- lic Conversation. *Such a Piece of News was talk'd of there this Morning*, says one (15); *last Night such a Re- flexion of a News-Writer was controverted there*, will another say; *he may excuse himself as Adam did*, says a third, and say, *The Wife whom thou gavest me, made me do it*. What I says a fourth, *you only heard this Circumstance at that Place; I mistrust it; it is an ill Office of Intelligence: The Nympha loquax, who prejudes there, adds what she pleases to Relations:*

Give me none of her Glosses, or her Commentaries; I appeal to the Text, how uncertain soever it may be. It can be no wonder, that *Altingius* was so incon- solable after the Death of his Spouse, if it be true, as his Historian Relates, that he lived near thirty Years with her, without any Complaint or Quarrel. *Cum ea per annos prope* 30 *fine rixa fine querela conjunctis- sime vixit* (16). Few Persons can make this boast, and complain, that they are ignorant, whether the Effects of Reconciliation are as sweet in Marriage, as in Gallantry.

Amantium iræ amoris redintegratio est (17).

Quarrels of Lovers only prove New Fewel to the Fire of Love.

ALTINGIUS (JAMES) Son of the preceding, was Professor of Divinity at *Groningen*. He was born at *Heidelberg* on the Twenty seventh of *September* 1618, du- ring his Father's Deputation to the Synod of *Dort*. His Childhood was a perpetual change of Place [*A*]. He went thro' his Studies at *Groningen* with great Success; and, having a great Inclination to the Oriental Languages, he went to *Embden*, in the Year 1638, to study under Rabbi *Gumprecht Ben-Abrabam*. He went into *England*, in the Year 1640; where he made himself known to the greatest Men: he preached there, and was admitted a Priest of the Church of *England* by the learned *John Prideaux* Bishop of *Worcester*. He had once resolved to pass his Life there; but he accepted the *Hebrew* Professorship, vacant by the Death of *Gomarus*, at *Gro- ningen*. He was installed there, the thirteenth of *January* 1643, the same Day that *Samuel Des Marets* was installed in the Professorship of Divinity, which the same *Goma- rus* had exercised. *Altingius*'s Titles and Offices increased with Time; He was ad- mitted Doctor of Philosophy, the Twenty first of *October* 1645; Academical Preacher in the Year 1647; and Doctor and Professor of Divinity in 1667. He tra- velled twice to *Heidelberg*; once in the Year 1651, and afterward in the Year 1662, and had received a thousand Marks of Esteem from the Elector Palatine *Charles Lewis*; who sollicited him several times to accept a Professorship of Divinity there; but he civilly declined it. He soon quarrelled with *Samuel Des Marets*, his Colleague, and it was almost impossible it should be otherwise; since their Method of teaching was quite different, nor did they agree in Principles on several Points. *Altingius* ap- plied himself to the Scripture, without any Mixture of Scholastic Divinity; He was in the full Career of Glory; he still pressed forward, and wanted neither Wit nor Learning to support his Opinions. The first Lectures, which he read, at his own House, on the *Catechism*, drew so many Auditors, that, for want of Room in his Chamber, he was obliged to make use of the University Auditory. He had most of the Foreign Students on his side. His Colleague accustomed himself to the Di- stinctions and Method of the Schoolmen; he had been a long time famous; he published many Books, had a ready Wit, and great Learning; and the Students in Divinity of that Country applied themselves to him, as the surest way to obtain a Church; for all the Parishes were served by Ministers, who had studied according to his Method. This was more than sufficient to raise, and keep up a Division, tho' Temper were not concerned in it. *Altingius* had very great Obstacles to sur- mount. The Majority of Voices, and Authority of Age, were on his Adversary's side: Besides, *Des Marets* had an Advantage in his Favour, sufficient to arm all the World against his Antagonist, and to awaken the most venerable Prejudices; which was to represent *Altingius* as an Innovator; one who removed the sacred Boundaries, which our Fathers had so wisely placed on the Confines of Truth and Falshood. He set up for a publick Accuser; and imputed Thirty one Erroneous Propositions to *James Altingius*. The Curators of the University sent the Accuser's Writing, and the Answer of the Accused Person, to the Divines of *Leyden*, without giving the Parties notice of it, and desired them to give their Opinion upon it. The Judgment they gave deserves to be taken notice of [*B*]. *Altingius* was declared innocent

of

[*A*] *His Childhood was a perpetual Change of Place*] For, at two Years of Age, he was sent to *Christian Chytræus*, Minister of *Bretten*. The Year following, his Mother was obliged, on account of the impending Siege of *Heidelberg*, to retire to *Heilborn*, notwithstanding her being with Child, and she carried him with her; from whence, at the end of the Year, they were obliged to retire to *Schorndorf*. " Se- " quente mox anno, propter imminentem Heidelbergæ " obsidionem, matre etiam comite, eaque tum gravidà, " Hulbronnam, indeque exacto anno Schorndorfium " missus est (1)." His Father, *Henry Altingius*, after- wards brought his whole Family to *Embden*, through By-ways. From *Embden* he removed to *Leyden*, where he was Preceptor to the King of *Bohemia*. The

Plague obliged him to go from *Leyden* to *Honslaerdijk*; lastly, he went from *Honslaerdijk* to *Groningen*, being invited thither to be Professor of Divinity, in the Year 1627. *James Altingius* was then nine Years of Age.

[*B*] *The Judgment they gave deserves to be taken notice of*.] I pretend not to take any part in the parti- cular Affair here in question; and shall content my- self with remarking, that, in general, one cannot for- bear, on occasion of the like Disputes, to judge, as the Divines of *Leyden* did. They, who advance new Hypotheses, pique themselves too much upon maintaining them, to the prejudice of Peace, and of the Ecclesiastical and Academical Tranquillity. They may be as Orthodox as they please; but they have not

Prudence

ALTINGIUS.

of Heresy; they only blamed his Imprudence in framing new Hypotheses; on the other hand, *Des Marets* was declared to want Modesty and Charity (a). The latter refused to acquiesce in this Judgment, and would not accept the Offer of Silence. He insisted upon having the Cause examined by the Consistories, the Classes, and the Synods; but the Superiors would not consent to it, and prohibited writing either for or against the Judgment of the Divines of *Leyden*: Thus *Des Marets*'s Book, *Audi & alteram partem*, was suppressed. This Contest made a great Noise, and might have been attended with bad Consequences, by the calling of *Des Marets* to the University of *Leyden* (b); but he died at *Groningen* (c) before he took Possession of that Employ. He made a kind of Reconciliation on his Death-Bed [C]; I shall speak of it in the Remarks. *Altingius* thought he had reason to complain, that he was play'd upon [D]; and was not easy after he was delivered from so formidable an Adversary. The Clergy murmured continually against what they called Innovations [E]; but the Secular Power calm'd by it's Prudence these Synodal or Consistorial Storms, and threatened to interdict those, who should revive the Quarrel of these two Champions in any Ecclesiastical Assembly. *Altingius* enjoyed but little Health during the three last Years of his Life; at length a continual Fever, which lasted but nine Days, took him out of the World on the Twentieth of *August*, 1679. He died piously, resigning himself to the Will of God; and recommended the Edition of all his Works several times to his Cousin *Menso Altingius*, Burgo-Master of *Groningen*.

(a) *Cum Altingium ab omni Hæreseos notâ absolverent, in ipso autem prudentiam in procuendis novis inventis, in Maresio modestiam & charitatem requirerent. Vit. Jac. Altingii.*

(b) *Et res mixtam habituræ catastrophen, Maresio quamquam sene ad Theologicam Professionem Lugdunum id Batavis vocato. Ibid.*

(c) *In May 1673.*

Prudence enough: They are guilty of Rashness; for it is rash Conduct to disturb the public Peace, without great and urgent Necessity. They, who oppose a new Method of Teaching, betray too much Passion: I am apt to believe, that, sometimes, they are not guided by any personal Considerations in their Proceedings; but they carry matters too far, they alarm the whole Church for trifles; they spread Apprehensions among the People of a total Depravation of the Confession of Faith, when there is yet no Attempt made against it. They are zealous, but neither moderate, nor charitable, nor equitable. Nay, they are as impudent, as their Adversaries: They do not consider, that a new Method, of which no notice appears to be taken, falls of itself; whereas, if it be zealously opposed, it degenerates into a Party. The new Methodist shall have some Relations in the Government, who will support him with all their Interest; and thus you will soon see a Combination of the Civil and Canon Law, and the Factions of the Church and State, matched together. What may not one apprehend from such a Conflict? How many Evils would Religion and the State avoid, if People were only contented to oppose Fundamental Innovations?

[C] *A kind of Reconciliation on his Death-Bed.*] A Minister of *Groningen*, seeing *Des Marets* past recovery, proposed to him a Reconciliation between him and his Colleague; and, having his Consent, went and proposed the same thing to *Altingius*; who answered, that the Silence he had observed, notwithstanding the Clamours, and the Writings of his Adversary, was a Proof of his peaceable Disposition; that he was always ready to accept of Peace on reasonable Terms; but that he desired Satisfaction for the Injuries, which had been published against his Honour; and that he did not see, how any one could desire any Friendship with him, while he thought him to be such a Person, as he had represented him. The Mediator went away, without proposing any thing farther. A little while after, a Report was spread all over the Town, that Mr *Altingius* was so hard-hearted, as to refuse to be reconciled to his dying Colleague: So true it is, that Town Reports are little consistent with Truth. The Mediator returned with another Minister to Mr *Altingius*, and got a Formulary of Satisfaction from him. This Formulary did not please the sick Person; and That, which the sick Person dictated, did not please *Altingius*; more Goings and Comings were employed, than in the Capitulation of a Fortress. At last, the Alteration, which *Altingius* inserted in the Formulary of *Des Marets*, being accepted, on condition, that *Altingius* should accept what *Des Marets* should add to it, that the Conditions might be equal on both Sides, they signed it; and this was all the Reconciliation. Note, that the Parties retracted only personal Injuries; as for doctrinal Accusations, the Accuser left them to the Judgment of the Church (2).

[D] *Altingius thought he had reason to complain that he was play'd upon.*] He founded his Complaint on the last Edition of *Des Marets*'s System, in which he was very ill treated. He pretended, that his Adversary was bound to suppress all Monuments of their Disagreement; and that, since he had not suppress'd so outrageous a Libel, his Reconciliation was not sincere. " Posteaquam autem ad plures abiit (*Maresius*) - - - - monitus fui ego (3) de Systematis novi perpetuis " annotationibus, quæ irrisandis maledictis cum in alios, " tum in me, constarent. Liber ille paucis ante mor- " tem ipsius diebus vendi quidem cœperat, sed non- " dum in meas ædes fuerat illatus. - - - - - - Curavi " ergo asserri, atque inde didici quantopere D. Mare- " sius mihi illustiset, quando in speciem concordiæ " redintegrari expetiit. Etenim quotiescunque verum " illud est ac sincerum votum, non tantum verbis " pax initur, sed etiam abolentur omnia monumenta " prioris inimicitiæ. Tenera namque conscientia ad " suam ipsius infamiam spectare retur, si, quod ipsa- " met damnavit, atque ex sua memoriis abolitum vo- " luit, universorum notitiæ ac Memoriæ infixum de- " derit, editis contumeliosis chartis per universum " orbem disseminatis. - - - - - - *After the Decease of* " *Des Marets, I was informed of the perpetual Com-* " *mentary of the New System, which was fraught with* " *unjust Aspersions, both on others, and myself. The* " *Book indeed begun to be sold a few Days before his* " *Death, but had not, as yet, come to my Hands. I* " *took Care to procure it, and was convinced by it,* " *how greatly Des Marets imposed upon me, when he* " *appeared to sollicit a Reconciliation. For, when such* " *a Desire is real and sincere, a verbal Reconciliation* " *is not thought sufficient, but all Remains of former* " *Enmity are abolished. A tender Conscience will* " *scruple to perpetuate and spread over the World,* " *by libellous Writings, what itself has condemned,* " *and would willingly forget.*" If I may be allowed to speak my Opinion freely, it seems to me unreasonable to expect that *Des Marets* should suppress a whole large Volume; if he had, the Bookseller ought certainly to have been indemnified; and thus the Expence of the Reconciliation would not have been a meer *unsaying*, a *nollem factum*; it would have been a pecuniary Loss to the Family. The Question was not concerning three or four Leaves only, but the whole Work, as *Altingius* himself acknowledged. " Cum in ipsius " effet potestate totum opus suppressisse, quæ unica " supererat in opere usque quaque sibi conformi emen- " datio (4). - - - - - - *When it was in his own Power* " *to have suppress'd the whole Work; which was the* " *only Emendation left in a Work so uniform from Be-* " *ginning to End.*" It was enough, that he declared in a Writing under his Hand, that he retracted whatever he might have said or published against his Adversary's Reputation. " Ita ut indicta velit Cl. D. " Maresius, si quæ in dictis & scriptis ipsius in famam " Cl. D. Altingii incurrere videantur (5)." With that alone he might die in form; *è morte canonicamente**, as they say beyond the Alps.

[E] *The Clergy murmur'd continually against what they called Innovations.*] The following Words will inform us of the Matter. " Qualis fuerit utriusque ante " mortem mutua reconciliatio, ipsiusmet Autoris *Epi- " stola*, initio *Mantissæ* tomi quinti posita, testatur. " Quiescente

(2) *Taken from a Letter of James Altingius, in the 5th Volume of his Works.*

(3) *Alting. Tom. 5. Mantissæ, pag. 425.*

(4) *Id. ibid.*

(5) *Id. ibid.*

* *He died canonically.*

Groningen. His Requeſt was complied with ſome Years after his Death, by the Publication of Five Volumes in *Folio* [*F*]. He lived a ſingle Life, 'till he was almoſt Thirty Years of Age; at which time he grew weary of that State, and married [*G*]. He purpoſed, if he had lived longer, to have compoſed two Books, one in *Latin*, and the other in *Dutch*; the firſt was to have been *An Apology for his Doctrine*, and the other *An Hiſtory of his Life*, from the time of his Profeſſorſhip; by which means we ſhould have ſeen the Injuſtice which was done him (*d*), in creating him ſo many Troubles [*H*]. This is what I have extracted from his Life, prefixed to the Firſt Volume of his Works. If any one finds Miſtakes in this Article, I deſire him not to impute them to me, who have only faithfully reported what I find in the Book, which I have cited. I advertiſe once for all, that I will not warrant the Truth of ſuch Accounts. I conclude with this Remark; that *Altingius* was a Divine much attached to the Text of the Scripture, and to *Cocceianiſm* and *Rabbiniſm*. This latter Application expoſed him to a terrible Injury [*I*]. He preached well in three Languages, in *German*, *Dutch*, and *Engliſh*.

(*d*) Ex Vita Jacobi Altingii, in limine Operum, Edit. Amſt. 1687.

"Quieſcente *Mareſio*, non ſic tamen quieſcendum ſibi duxerunt, qui ipſius partium fuerant. Nihil autem adeo dediſſe operam videntur, quam ut via quaſi eccleſiaſtica per Synodos, Claſſes, & quas dicimus Correſpondentias, *Altingii* opinionibus obſiſterent. Ita variis quidem fluctibus poſtea jactatus vir optimus, ſuæ autem ſententiæ tenaciſſimus, tandem fere enatavit; ſiquidem quotieſcunque aliquid proponeret Eccleſiaſticorum ordo, illud mox procerum edicto vel conſulto rejectum eſt. Imo exauctorationis etiam pœna in eos conſtituta, qui de controverſiis *Mareſio-Altingianis* in cœtu aliquo Paſtorum quidquam moverent. Ita factum ſæpius eſt, ut generalibus etiam verbis concepta gravamina *de periculoſis novitatibus* in ſpongiam incubuerint (6)."

(*) In Vita Jac. Alting.

[*H*] *The Injuſtice which was done him, in creating him ſo many Troubles.*] They, who chooſe the Words of the Original, rather than my Abridgment, may here be ſatisfy'd. "Dixit inter alia (*Altingius*) ſi Deus ſibi vitam vireſque concederet, ſtare ſibi animum duos libellos in lucem mittendi, alterum quidem, quem orſus etiam eſt, quo ſe purgaret coram Eccleſiâ ab heterodoxias & hæreſeos crimine ſibi intentato, alterum verò quo hiſtoriam vitæ ſuæ publicæ panderet, ab eo tempore quando in Academiâ docere cœpiſſet; unde cuivis judicandum relinqueret, quo jure qua injuria tantum ipſi moleſtiarum creatum fuiſſet. ----- Præ cæteris autem conquerebatur à malevolorum inſidiis atque inimicitiis ſtetiſſe, quo minus ut vellet publico inſervire potuiſſet (10). ----- Altingius declared, among other things, that, if God granted him Life and Strength, he had determined to publiſh two Books; one of them (which he had even begun) in Vindication of himſelf, before the Church, from the Charge of Heterodoxy and Hereſy, which had been brought againſt him; the other, the Hiſtory of his public Life, from the time of his commencing Teacher in the Univerſity; from whence every one might judge, how juſtly, or unjuſtly, he had been involved in ſo many Troubles. ------ But he particularly complained, that the Treachery and Enmity of ill deſigning Men, had prevented his being as ſerviceable to the Public, as he could have wiſh'd." It is certainly a very melancholy Conſideration, that Civil Diſcord ſhould prevent ſo many excellent Operators from exerting their Abilities in the Service of their Community, and againſt foreign Enemies; againſt whom all the Forces of a Party ought conſtantly to be kept united. I do not ſpeak of the Scandal it occaſions; for, on the contrary, we ought to be ſcandaliz'd at the little Scandal it gives. Is it, becauſe to be properly diſguſted requires a Degree of Wit, to which few Perſons attain? Is it becauſe Cuſtom readers Men at length leſs ſenſible; *ab aſſuetis non fit paſſio*? Whatever the Cauſe of it may be, it is certain that People have an exceſſive Indulgence for thoſe, who keep up Diſcord, by violent, injurious, and cavilling Writings, under the falſe Pretence of Zeal. Nothing would more effectually correct the prevailing Itch in ſome People of libelling their Brethren by Book after Book, than for the World to ſhew they are offended in earneſt at ſuch a Conduct, and publickly to expreſs their Contempt and Indignation. But while we ſee them follow the Party, which knows how to make the moſt Noiſe and Buſtle, the Diſeaſe muſt be look'd upon as incurable.

(10) Ibid.

In what the Scandal of Controverſy at preſent conſiſts.

"What kind of mutual *Reconciliation was between them before his Death, we learn from the Author's own Epiſtle*, at the beginning of the fifth Tome of the Mantiſſa. Though Des Marets ſaid *aſide his Reſentment, thoſe of his Party did not ſo eaſily quit theirs. But they had no other Aim, than to oppoſe* Altingius's *Opinions, in an Eccleſiaſtical Way, by Synods, Claſſes, and what we call Correſpondencies. Thus this beſt of Men, but tenacious to the laſt of his Opinions, after being toſſed with various Storms, with much Difficulty at length ſwam a-ſhore; for, whenever the Order of Eccleſiaſtics propoſed any thing againſt him, it was immediately rejected by the Authority of the Civil Power. Nay, the Penalty of Deprivation was decreed againſt thoſe, who ſhould, in any Aſſembly of Paſtors, revive the* Mareſio-Altingian *Controverſy. Thus Complaints of dangerous Novelties, though touched in general Terms, often undergo the Spunge.* Hence it appears, that *James Altingius* would have been in great Danger from the Divines, if he had not been protected by the Magiſtrate. It is certain that the Secular and Eccleſiaſtical Power ſtand in need of each other: The Latter ſerves ſometimes as a Spur to the former, and the former as a Bridle to the latter.

—————— alterius ſic
Altera poſcit opem res, & conjurat amicè (7).

Thus mutually they need each others Aid.
ROSCOMMON.

(7) Horſt. de Arte Po t. ver. 410.

[*F*] *By the Publication of five Volumes in Folio.*] The late Mr *Bekker*, then Miniſter at *Amſterdam*, who had been a Diſciple, and good Friend of the Author's, took a particular Care of this Edition. It was publiſhed at *Amſterdam*, in the Year 1687, and contains ſeveral kinds of Treatiſes, *Analytical*, *Exegetical*, *Practical*, *Problematical*, and *Philoſophical*, which witneſſes not only the laborious Life of *James Altingius*, but likewiſe his great Knowledge. His Diligence may be diſcovered in another Inſtance. Moſt learned Men become at length tired of writing Letters; but he never knew this Fault: He wrote Five thouſand Letters; but they publiſhed but few of them. "Loquuntur Epiſtolæ, quarum tam paucas "ex 5000 publicari potuiſſe, id equidem dolendum. "Erat autem ad ſcribendas literas impiger (8). The bare Names of the Divines, with whom he correſponded, ſhew that he was no *Voëtian*.

S. Vita Jacobi Al. t g.

[*G*] *He lived a ſingle Life 'till he was almoſt thirty Years of Age ----- and then married.*] Vitam cælibem ad annum ætatis trigeſimum fere perduxit, cujus tandem pertæſus junxit ſibi tori ſociam (9). Of eight Children, which God had given him, but three were

(8) Ibid.

living when he died; one whereof was a Phyſician, another an Advocate, and the third bore Arms. The firſt and the laſt died ſoon after their Father.

[*I*] *This latter Application expoſed him to a terrible Injury.*] He was called a half *Jew*: one who differed from a *Jew* only in the Foreſkin; in ſhort, one, who complained ſometimes of not being Circumciſed, and whoſe Foreſkin was troubleſome to him. The Occaſion of theſe Abuſes was, his having maintained, that the Points of the *Tetragramma* are not proper to That Name, and that therefore the true Pronunciation of it is not known, and that we ought not to accuſe thoſe of Jewiſh Superſtition, who read it *Adonaï*. The Judgment paſſed upon this Opinion was as follows: "Impudentia eſt Grammaticorum "nonnullorum & filiorum Bicri negare ex ſuperſti- "tione Judaica oriri, quod id nomen aliter pronun- "cietur quam legitur ---- Sed per nos homines ſemi- "Judæi doctrina, ſtudio, affectu, commercio, & qui ſola "fere

AMABLE. AMAMA.

" fere pondere præputii, & quò interdùm se gravari do-
" lent, distant à recutitis, infantant ut libuerit — Vestræ
" est impudentiæ, petulantiæ, & superbiæ in primo gra-
" du, quod ausitis dicam scribere imperitiæ & ignoran-
" tiæ tot illustribus Ecclesiæ viris vobis etiam longe
" doctioribus, quod id nominis enuncient & pro-
" nuncient uti scribitur (11). —— *It is downright
" Impudence in certain Grammarians, and Sons of* Bicri,
" *to deny, that the Pronunciation of this Word dif-
" ferently from what it is read is owning to Jewish
" Superstition* ——— *But let these Men, who are Half-
" Jews in Doctrine, Study, Affection, and Commerce,
" and who differ from the Circumcised almost only in the
" Weight of the Prepuce, with which they sometimes
" complain of being burthened; let these Men, I say,
" be as mad as they please* ——— *Your Impudence,
" Sauciness, and Pride, is of the highest Degree, in
" daring to charge with Unskilfulness and Ignorance
" so many Ornaments of the Church, whose Learning
" far exceeds your own, for uttering and pronouncing
" this Name as it wrote.*" Was this a sufficient Reason for being so very angry? and have we not here
an Example of what an Heathen Philosopher judiciously remarked? " Crede mihi, levia sunt, propter
" quæ non leviter excandescimus, qualia quæ pueros
" in rixam & jurgium concitant. Nihil ea his, quæ
" tam tristes agimus, serium est, nihil magnum. Inde,
" inquam, vobis ira & insania est, quod exigua
" magno æstimatis (12). —— *Believe me, we fall
" into a violent Passion for meer Trifles; such as set
" Children a fighting. None of those things, which
" give us so much Uneasiness, are serious; none of
" them of Importance. From hence, I say, arises this
" childish Anger of your's, that you set a great Value
" upon things of little Moment.*" Could there be a se-
verer Censure, than this, of one who should set his Apostacy to sale, and should only wait for the Solution of
three or four small Difficulties in order to turn Jew?

AMABLE, a Priest of *Riom* in *Auvergne*, in the Vth Century, is praised by
Gregory of *Tours*, as a Man admirable for his Holiness, and who wrought many Miracles (*a*). It is said he had *Power over Serpents*: Thus that Historian expresses himself; but he speaks of another Particular, as an Eye-Witness. *I have seen at his Sepulchre,* says he, *a Dæmoniac dispossessed*; *I have seen a perjured Person there become as stiff
as an Iron Bar, and, after confessing his Crime, become as free as before.* When such a Man
as *Gregory* of *Tours* makes use of an *it is said*, 'tis a sign, that the thing is not very certain; nevertheless this Empire over Serpents has passed for the most unquestionable
Fact among all that are attributed to St *Amable*. One would think it was his Lot,
or, to speak like a *Mallebranchist* (*b*), that God had established him the occasional
Cause of the Cure of those, who were bit by Serpents. A modern Author, tho' a
Canon in the City, of which St *Amable* is Patron (*c*), confesses *that he does not believe
all the Miracles, which are reported of him in the Lives of the Saints of* Auvergne, *and
in several other Legends* (*d*); *but declares on the other side, that he firmly believes That
Saint had a Sovereign Power over Serpents, because the wonderful Effects of it had been uni-
versally attested for the Space of* 1300 Years [A], *and because he had had the Happiness of
seeing some of them himself* (*e*). He questions much the Truth of a certain Tradition, *which prevailed at* Riom *concerning this Saint*; *to wit, that, when he went to* Rome *on foot, the
Sun attended upon him as his Valet, and carried his Gloves and Cloak in the Air, like an
Umbrello, during the great Heat, and kept off the Rain from him in bad Weather* (*f*). *This
Tradition passeth for so certain in that Country, that they seldom draw St* Amable's *Picture,
without his Gloves and his Cloak being supported in the Air by a Sun-Beam.* Credat Judæus
Appelles (*g*), says he, *non ego*. This is sufficient, without any Reflexion of my own, to
give to this Article the Form, which this Dictionary seems to require. A mere Relation of such things is an Heap of Errors.

[*A*] *The wonderful Effects of it were universally
attested for the Space of* 1300 *Years*.] This Calculation does not agree exactly with what is said in the
following Page; that *Gregory of Tours lived but about
fifty or sixty Years after St* Amable. It is not necessary to prove, that the Words do not signify, that
he was born fifty or sixty Years after that Saint; it
is plain enough that they import, that he was arrived
to Manhood, when St *Amable* had been dead fifty
or sixty Years. According to this, the Death of this
Saint should fall about the beginning of the VIth
Century; for *Gregory of Tours* lived but about Fifty two Years, and died in the Year 594 (1). Now if
the Miracles of this Saint of *Riom* had been seen for
the Space of 1300 Years, about the end of the XVIIth
Century, he must have flourished about the end of
the IVth Century; and, upon this Supposition, it
cannot be said that a Man of twenty Years of Age in
562 lived fifty or sixty Years after him.

AMAMA (SIXTINUS) Professor of the *Hebrew* Tongue, in the University of
Franeker, was a very learned Man. He was of *Friesland*, and had been a Disciple of
Drusius [*A*]. The University of *Leyden*, which endeavours to procure the most famous Professors of the neighbouring Universities, by offering them more considerable
Advantages, endeavoured to draw him from the University of *Franeker* (*a*). It was
to succeed *Erpenius*, who had been one of the most learned Men of his Age in the
Oriental Languages. *Amama* did not absolutely refuse this Invitation, neither did
he absolutely accept of it; he consented, upon condition of obtaining his Dismission
from his Superiors of *Friesland*. But they did not grant it (*b*), and no doubt they
gave him such additional Advantages, that he had no reason to repent his not being
Professor at *Leyden*. The first Book he published was a Specimen of a noble Design
he had conceived. He had undertaken to censure the Vulgar Translation, which the
Council of *Trent* had declared authentic; and, before his whole Design was executed,
he published a Criticism on the Version of the Pentateuch (*c*); Thus he commenced
Author (*d*). He was preparing the Continuation of this Criticism, when he was called off

[*A*] *And had been a Disciple of* Drusius.] This is
evident from several Passages of the *Antibarbarus
Biblicus*. As for *Sinesius*, whose Disciple they make
him in the Supplement to *Morreri's* Dictionary, I
confess he is absolutely unknown to me; and I question much whether they ever heard of him in the
United Provinces.

246 AMAMA.

off to other Matters; I mean to collate the *Dutch* Verfion of the Scripture with the Originals, and the exacteft Tranflations. This *Dutch* Tranflation had been made from *Luther's German* Verfion. He gave the Public an Account of his Labours, in a Work, which he publifhed (*e*) at *Amfterdam* in the Vulgar Language, intituled *Bybelfche Conferentié*. This Work is taken notice of in the Supplement to *Moreri's* Dictionary [*B*]. This Care of collating was full Employment for *Amama*; infomuch that the Publication of this Book, and of fome *Grammatical Pieces*, prevented him a confiderable time from applying himfelf to his Cenfure of the Vulgate (*f*). He refumed this Work, upon hearing that Father *Merfennus* had undertaken to refute him, as to the Six firft Chapters of *Genefis* [*C*]. Leaving, then, every other Work, he applied himfelf to juftify his Criticifms againft that Author. His Anfwer is one of the Pieces, of which the *Anti-Barbarus Biblicus*, which he publifhed in 1628, is compofed. The other Pieces are a Criticifm on the Vulgate in relation to the Hiftorical Books of the Old Teftament, on *Job*, the *Pfalms*, and the Books of *Solomon*; with fome particular Differtations. One of them is on the famous Paffage of the *Proverbs*, *The Lord poffeffed me in the beginning of his Way*, wherein *Amama* fhews, that they, who accufed *Drufius* of favouring *Arianifm*, were downright Calumniators. The *Anti-Barbarus Biblicus* was intended to confift of Two Parts, each containing three Books. The Author publifhed only the firft. It was reprinted after his Death [*D*]; and the fourth Book was added to it, which contains the Cenfure of the Vulgar Tranflation, on *Ifaiah* and *Jeremiah*. It is impoffible to ward the Blows he gives to the Vulgate, and to anfwer the Reafons, by which he fhews the Neceffity of confulting the Originals. And indeed few learned Men of the *Romifh* Communion will deny it; they only maintain (to fave the Honour of the laft Council) that they did not pretend to fubmit the Originals to the Authority of the Vulgar Tranflation. It is not the Queftion here to examine, whether this can be faid in earneft. Our *Sixtinus* fo ftrongly perfuaded to the Study of the Original Languages of the Bible, that fome Synods, influenced by his Reafons, ordered, that thenceforth no one fhould be admitted a Minifter, without at leaft a moderate Skill in the *Greek* and *Hebrew* of the Bible [*E*]. I muft not forget the Zeal he fhewed in putting

[*B*] *This Work is taken Notice of in the Supplement to Moreri's Dictionary.*] The Supplement fays, that, according to Mr *Simon*, *The defign of Sixtinus Amama, in his Book, is to fhew*, that the Dutch *Bible*, *which was read among the Proteftants of the Low Countries*, *and had been tranflated from the German of Luther*, *was full of Faults*; *this he fhews very plainly*, *and they*. To give the Reader fuller Information in this Matter, I fhall fet down the very Words of the Author, who is here cited. *The Proteftants of the Low Countries*, fays Mr *Simon*, in his Letter to Mr *P.* concerning the Infpiration of the facred Books, Page 10. *built their Reformation only on a Dutch Verfion, which was made from that of Luther*; *but at laft* —— *they refolved to fet about a new Tranflation*. *For this Purpofe Sixtinus Amama compofed a Book in Dutch, entituled* Bybelfche Conferentié, *wherein he fhews at large, that it was neceffary to publifh a new Bible for the Dutch Churches. He fays*, that the Dutch *Tranflation, which they read in their Churches, and which had been taken from that of* Luther, *contained in certain Places more Faults than Verfes*; *and gives a great many Examples of it in that Work*. At Page 11. Mr *Simon* has thefe Words —— *It is true that the Calvinifts of the* Netherlands *rejected their ancient Tranflation, and compofed a new one. But if they followed, in their new Tranflation, the Method, which Sixtinus Amama propofes in his* Bybelfche Conferentié, *it cannot be exact*; *for, to make his Reformation, he only follows* Pagninus, Junius, *and* Tremellius, *the Bible of* Zurich, *the French of* Geneva, *the German of* Pifcator, *the Spanifh of* Cyprian de Valera, *the Italian of* Diodati, *the Englifh of* Geneva, *and other new Tranflations* —— *which are all faulty*.

[*C*] *Father Merfennus had undertaken to refute him, as to the fix firft Chapters of Genefis.*] *Rivetus* informed him of it; otherwife he had run the Rifque of being unacquainted with it a long time; for he had never before heard of fuch a Man as Father *Merfennus*. Thefe are his Words, in his Epiftle Dedicatory (1). " Abfque te fuiffet, Cl. *Rivete*, nomen Merfenni, qui VI. " priorum Genefeos capitum adverfus meas ftricturas " fufcepit patrocinium, etiamnum juxta cum ignaffi- " fimis ignoraffem. Tu primus mihi indicium, tu vo- " luminis copiam fecifti, tu ad modeftam & manfue- " tam replicationem hortamentis tuis me animafti. " —— *Had it not been for you*, Rivetus, *I had known*

" *no more*, *than the moft ignorant*, *of the Name of* " Merfennus, *who has patronized the fix firft Chap-* " *ters of* Genefis *againft my Strictures*. *You gave me* " *the firft Notice of*, *you procured me a Sight of*, *the* " *Work*, *and you animated me by your Advice to a* " *moderate and good-natured Reply*." I wonder he did not infert in his *Antibarbarus* the Prelude to his Anfwer, which he had publifhed in the Year 1627, with this Title *Epiftola παράινεσις ad Marinum Merfennum* (2). *Crevius* has inferted it in the third Part of his *Animadverfiones* (3).

[*D*] *It was reprinted after his Death.*] At *Franeker*, in 4to, in the Year 1656. Mr *Baillet* mentioned this Edition in his *Anti's*, at the Three hundred and fifteenth Page of the Second Tome. " I muft not forget, fays he, the *Anti-Barbarus*, which a Profef- " for of *Hebrew* of the Univerfity of *Franeker*, in " *Friefland*, whofe Name is Sixtinus Amama, pub- " lifhed on the Text of the Holy Scripture, in the " Year 1656, in 4to, in the Town where he taught. " —— The Work is intermixed with feveral fmall " Differtations and Difcourfes, which fpoil it's Oeco- " nomy." Note, that they have inferted in the new Edition of the *Great Critics* (4), his Criticifm on the Vulgate of the *Pentateuch*, and his Notes on the *Hiftorical Books*, on the Pfalms, Proverbs, and Ecclefiaftes, which had never been printed.

[*E*] *Some Synods*, *influenced by his Reafons*, *ordered*, *that thenceforth no one fhould be admitted a Minifter without a moderate skill in the* Greek *and* Hebrew *of the Bible*.] Thefe are the Words of the Act, which was paffed upon this Account by the Synod of *Friefland*, held at *Harlingen* in the Year 1624. " Decretum eft, ut in pofterum Theologiæ " Candidati quotquot ad examen Minifterii Ecclef. " admitti defiderabunt, præter teftimonia Senatus Aca- " demici & Theologiæ Profefforum, exhibeant etiam " teftimonia Profefforum Ebreæ & Græcæ linguæ, " quibus doceant fe in prædictis linguis eos faltem " progreffus feciffe, ut originalem Veteris Novique " Teftamenti textum mediocriter poffint intelligere, " utque in Claffe ifta, cujus examini fe offerunt, e- " jus quoque rei fpecimen edere teneantur. —— *It* " *is decreed*, *that*, *for the future*, *whatever Candi-* " *dates in Divinity fhall defire to be admitted to the* " *Examination of the Miniftry of the Church*, *be-* " *fides the Teftimonials of the Univerfity Senate*, *and* " *the Profeffors of Divinity*, *fhall produce likewife* " *Thofe*

AMAMA. AMASÆUS.

putting a Stop to a Vice, which prevailed as much in the University of *Franeker*, as in those of *Germany*, I mean Drunkenness [*F*]. He made a warm Speech on this Subject in 1621. They were so well satisfied with him in *Friesland*, that, after his Death, which happened in the Month of *December* 1629 (*g*), they were very liberal to his Children, as *Nicholas Amama*, one of them, testifies with great Acknowledgment, in the Epistle Dedicatory of a certain Book [*G*].

(*g*) Konig, *who says he was living in 1630, and Father Ma-rin, who supposes*, Exercit. Bible. part. 1. pag. 61, *that he taught at Franeker, in* 1633, *are therefore mistaken.*

(5) *It is a part of the Anti-barbaros Biblicus, and had been already printed twice.*

"Those of the *Hebrew* and *Greek* Professors, testi-"fying, that they have made such a Progress at least "in the aforesaid Tongues, as to have acquired a mo-"derate Skill in the Original Text of the Old and "New Testament; and that they shall be obliged to "give a Specimen of their Abilities, in that Class, "to whose Examination they offer themselves." It appears, by the same Act, that it was the *Supplex Paraenesis* of *Amama* (5), some Copies of which had been distributed among the Assembly, which occasioned the taking of this good Resolution.

[*F*] *The Zeal he shewed in putting a Stop to Drunkenness.*] We must not ascribe the vigorous Resolutions, which were taken against this Irregularity, principally to *Sixtinus Amama*; it is enough if we say that he contributed to it; and had he only harangued, and publickly congratulated those, who reformed the University in this respect, he would merit great Praise. He acknowledges, that *Amesius*, Professor of Divinity, and *Hachting*, Professor of Logic, having been admitted into the Academical Senate, and finding themselves supported by the Rector of the University, undertook the Reformation of this Disorder courageously, and with happy Success. He congratulates them upon it, and dedicates his Speech *de barbarie morum* to them upon that account. The Reader will be pleased to see how he expresses himself, and the Difficulties which those Reformers met with. " Ad " primam occasionem ———— intrepidis & commac-" ulatis animis horrendas illas & feroces belluas " Ebrietatem & Licentiam, quæ hic stabulabantur, " ex Academia ejecitis, ac Christianam disciplinam, " jam desperatam, Deo supra quam à quoquam spe-" rari potuisset benedicente, Academiæ redonastis. " Cujus præclari & æterna gratitudine dignissimi fa-" cinoris, sicuti invidiam apud dissolutam & barba-" ram juventutem sustinuistis, & quasi præpilatis hastis " objecti fulstis soli, ita & æquissimam censeo, ut

" vobis quoque præ aliis tam egregii operis gloria " transcribatur (6). ———— Upon the first Opportunity " ———— with great Courage and Resolution, you drove " out of the University those horrible and fierce Mon-" sters, Drunkenness and Licentiousness, which had " here stabled, and, by an extraordinary Assistance " from Heaven, restored to the University That Chri-" stian Discipline, which it despaired to recover. And " as this glorious Exploit, so worthy of eternal Gra-" titude, exposed you to the Envy and rude Attacks " of a dissolute and barbarous Youth, so I think it " but just, that the Honour of so excellent a Work should " be principally ascribed to you." He gives a shocking Account of the Debauchery, which reigned in some Universities. All the new Comers listed themselves in the Service of *Bacchus* with certain Solemnities, and were obliged to swear by a St *Stephen* of Wood, that they would spend all their Money. If any one had more regard to the Oath, which he had taken to the Rector of the University, than to this pretended Bacchanalian Oath, he was so persecuted by the debauched Scholars, that he was obliged either to leave the University, or to comply with the rest. He added to his Speech some Fragments of *Alstedius*'s Complaints on the same Subject. *Bellarmin* deplores, with great Vehemence, in his twentieth Sermon, the Drunkenness, which prevailed in the University of *Lovovain* (7).

[*G*] NICOLAS AMAMA ———— *testifies, with great Acknowledgment, in the Epistle Dedicatory of a certain Book.*] It was printed in the Year 1651. It is an Octavo of Six hundred Pages, entituled, *Dissertationum marinarum decas*, wherein there is much Reading; and the Author departs in many things from *Aristotle*'s Opinions, without addicting himself to the new Philosophy. He has innovated in the very Orthography.

(6) Sixt. A-mama, in Præliminar. Anti-barbari Bibl.

(7) Amama *observes this in the Epistle Dedicatory of his Speech de Ebrietate.*

AMASÆUS (ROMULUS) Professor of *Greek* and *Latin* at *Bologne*, in the XVIth Century [*A*], and Secretary to the Senate (*a*), distinguished himself by his Learning, and his Employments. He was originally of *Bologne*, and born at *Udine*, in *Frioul*. Pope *Paul* III appointed him Preceptor to his Grandson, *Alexander Farnese* (*b*). He was afterwards employed in more important Affairs; he was deputed to the Emperor and to the Princes of the Empire, and to the Court of *Poland*. No Man of Learning appeared with greater Lustre at the Court of *Rome*, under the Pontificate of *Julius* III. He was that Pope's Secretary. He gave Proofs of his Knowledge in the *Greek* Language by a *Translation* of *Pausanias*, and another of a Work of *Xenophon* (*c*). He composed likewise a Volume of Speeches, and a Work intituled *Scholae duae de ratione instituendi*. As for the two Pieces he had written, in which he made it appear, that the *Latin Language is more beautiful than the Italian*, they were never printed (*d*). Some say that he died in the Year 1558, being 69 Years old [*B*]. He left a Son, whose Name was *Pompilius*, and who did not degenerate; for he understood, and translated, *Greek*. He was likewise Professor of That Tongue at *Bologne* (*e*). I believe he translated only

(*a*) *See Remark* [*B*].

(*b*) *And not his Nephew, as Du Rier renders the word* Nepos *of* Thuanus.

(*c*) *His Expedition of Cyrus the younger.*

(*d*) Thuan. lib. 21 pag. 412. *and the Additions of Mr* Teissier.

(*e*) Bumaldus *cited by Baillet*, Jugem. des Savans, Tom. 4. pag. 400.

[*A*] AMASÆUS (ROMULUS) *Professor of Greek and Latin ———— in the XVIth Century.*] Moreri was not mistaken in his Chronology: It should not therefore have been altered, as it is, in the *Dutch* Edition, where, instead of the XVIth Century, they have put the XIVth. Three things wanted Correction in this Article, which ought not to have been passed over. I. It was too dry, and lean. II. It should have been under AMASÆUS, not RO-MULUS. III. It should not have been said, that *Amasaeus* translated the Works of *Xenophon*, but that he translated the seven Books, which *Xenophon* composed of the *Expedition of Cyrus the Younger*.

[*B*] *Some say, that he died in the Year* 1558, *being Sixty nine Years old.*] *Thuanus* is mistaken in placing the Death of *Romulus Amasaeus* in the Year 1558. For this *Romulus* was dead from the Year 1552. We have a Proof of this in a Letter of *Giovanni Antonio Serone*, an intimate Friend of *Romu-*

lus, dated the twentieth of *October of That Year*, and inserted in the Collection of *Turchi*, pag. 257. This is what M. de la Monnoie did me the Favour to write to me. Besides, if *Amasaeus* died in the Year 1558, there would be reason to say, that he lived Sixty nine Years; for the Day of his Birth is marked, in the Figures of *Luke Gauric*, on the Twenty fourth of *June* 1489 (1). I have met with three or four Particulars in This Work of *Gauric*, which I shall insert here. *Amasaeus* was lean, very tall, bald, and had a small Head. He was Secretary to the Senate of *Bologne*, and taught Eloquence in the same City, having a Salary of Three hundred Crowns *per Annum*. He taught afterwards at *Rome* in the Time of *Paul* III, having a Pension of Six hundred Crowns, *nuta Pauli III. ex lectura in urbe habebat 600 aureos*. *Thuanus* was ignorant of this.

(1) *Figures of* Gauric, folio 72. Edit. Venet. 1552.

[*C*] *Translated*

only two Fragments of the sixth Book of *Polybius* [C]; in which he discovered a greater Capacity, than *Perottus* and *Musculus* did in translating That Author (*f*). Yet a learned Man accused him of omitting all the difficult Passages, and contenting himself with referring the Reader elsewhere, for the Interpretation of them (*g*). As for his Father, it is agreed, that he was a great Lover of Elegancy, and Perspicuity; he enlarged what was too concise, and contracted what was too diffuse; and cleared up obscure Passages (*h*). His Translation of *Pausanias* stood in need of *Sylburgius*'s Revisal.

[C] *Translated only two Fragments of the sixth Book of Polybius.*] *Pompilius Amasæus,* having translated those Fragments, which treat of the Military Discipline of the *Romans,* explained them in a Commentary, which is among the Manuscripts of *Thuanus*'s Library (2). This Manuscript is in *Italian.* The Author translated those Fragments both into *Latin,* and his Mother Tongue.

AMASTRIS, Niece of the last *Darius,* and Wife of *Dionysius* Tyrant of *Heraclea.* Look for her History in the Article of That *Dionysius.* You will likewise find there the Town of AMASTRIS, built by this Princess.

AMBOISE (FRANCIS d') a *Parisian,* deserves to be ranked among those, whom the Profession of Letters raised to worldly Honours. He was the Son of a Chirurgeon to *Charles* the Ninth, and was maintained, by the Liberality of That Prince, in the College of *Navarre,* whilst he pursued his Rhetorical and Philosophical Studies. He taught afterwards in That College; for we find, that, in 1572, he had already taught the second Class four Years. He was then made Procurator of the *French* Nation. He applied himself afterwards to the Civil Law, and became a very good Advocate in the Parliament of *Paris*; after which he had the Post of Chancellor in the Parliament of *Brittany*; lastly, he was Master of the Requests (*a*), and Counsellor of State (*b*). He travelled into several remote Countries [*A*]. He published several pieces of *French* Poetry in his Youth, and some *Latin* Verses; which doubtless he did not think much to his Reputation, when he was advanced to Dignities; for they represent to us a Poet, who sent his Muse backwards and forwards, sometimes with Compliments of Condolance, at other times with Compliments of Congratulation; in a word, they gave us the Idea of a Compliment-Bearer of *Parnassus* to the great Lords. You will see below the Titles of some Books of our *Francis d'Amboise.* They seem to me less fit to immortalize his Name, than the Pains he took in collecting the Manuscripts of *Peter Abelard* [C], and in adding an *Apologetical Preface,*

[*A*] *He travelled into several remote Countries* (1).] *Du Verdier Vau-Privas* remarks, that *Francis d'Amboise made a Description of the Kingdom of Poland at Warsaw, when the Duke of Anjou, at present King of France, was elected King of Poland* (2). This was one of his Expeditions. It cannot be determined by the Words, which I have cited, whether he went into *Poland* in the Retinue of the new King, or whether he was there, when the Duke of *Anjou* was elected. This latter Sense would be the only one, which ought to be given to these Words, if *du Verdier Vau-Privas* were an exact Writer. See *Francis d'Amboise*'s *Treatise of Devises,* where we find (3), that, at the Time of that Election, he was in That, Country at the House of the Bishop of *Valence.* This *Treatise of Devises* is a Posthumous Work. It was printed at *Paris,* for ADRIAN d'AMBOISE, the Author's Son. This Son published, the following Year, at *Paris,* a little Treatise of his own, entitled *Moral Devises.*

[*B*] *The Titles of some Books of our Francis d'Amboise.*] Viz *An Elegy on the Death of* Anne de Montmorency, *Peer and Constable of France, with a Latin Panegyric, and a French Ode on the Disaster of France, in 1568* (4). *A Panegyric on the Marriage of* Henry *of* Lorrain, *Duke of* Guise, *and* Catherine *of* Cleves, *Countess of* Eu, *in 1570* (5). *The Tomb of Messire* Giles Bourdin, *the King's Attorney-General in the Parliament at* Paris, *being three Sonnets, an Elegy translated from the Latin of* Antony Valet, *and some Latin Hendeca-syllabic Verses, in 1570* (6). *The Loves of* Clio; *in which there is a Poem intituled,* The Desperadoes, *or* Amorous Eclogues, *in 1572* (7). *Comical Amours, containing several facetious Histories, and,* among others, That, which he calls the *Neapolitan Ladies, in 1584.* The *Neapolitan Ladies* is a Translation of an *Italian* Comedy. He calls himself at the beginning of this Translation *Thierry de Timophile G. Picard,* and he takes the same Disguise in the Title of the *Funeral Lamentations of certain Animals,* which he translated from the *Italian* in 1576, and in the Title of the *Familiar Dialogue of Young Ladies,* which he published in 1583. *La Croix du Maine,* who informed me of this, says that this Author understood many Languages, and that he had published several Works in *Latin.* His Collection of *Devices* was published after his Death, in the Year 1620.

[C] *The Pains he took in collecting the Manuscripts of* Peter Abelard] His Diligence in this deserved a publick Acknowledgment. We are indebted to him for a very good Edition of the Writings of that famous Logician. It contains I. The Letters, which passed between *Abelard* and *Heloisa,* to which is prefixed his own Account of his Misfortunes. II. The Letters which he wrote to other Persons; with those of *St Bernard*; the Abbot of *Clugni,* &c. concerning his Errors, his Condemnation, or his Death; and some Treatises, which one of his Disciples published for him. III. Some Dogmatical Treatises of *Abelard*; as his Exposition of the Lord's Prayer, That of the Apostle's Creed; That of St *Athanasius*'s Creed; His Answer to some of *Heloisa*'s Questions; a Commentary on St *Paul*'s Epistle to the *Romans.* IV. Several Sermons on the principal Holidays. V. An Introduction to Theology, containing his Book of the Trinity. VI. The learned Notes of *Andrew du Chesne* on the History of *Abelard*'s Calamities. There are besides some other Works of this Author, which are not printed. You may find the Titles of them in the Supplement of Father *Oudin* (8), with the Libraries where they are to be found. *Francis d'Amboise* procured a *French* Translation of the Rules, which *Abelard* prescribed to the Nuns of the *Paraclet.* His Apologetical Preface displeased several People, and it was the Opinion of some, that it occasioned the Proceedings of the Court of *Rome* against the Work, which he published. "And if, not long ago, the printed Works "of *ABAYELARD* were put in the expurgatory "Index of *Rome,* I believe the Fault is not so much "to be imputed to the Author, as to the Preface-"Writer, who, instead of cautioning the Reader a-"gainst such and such Passages of *ABAYELARD,* "undertook to defend them." They are the Words of the Author of the Antiquities of *Melun,* Advocate in the Parliament of *Paris* (9). It cannot be said, that he wrote the Life of *Peter Abelard* (10); he only

AMBOISE 249

Preface, which is prefixed to the Edition of the Year 1616 [D]. This Preface informs me of a Particular, which I have not met with in the History of the College of *Navarre*; to wit, that he published a small Treatise of the Council, and a Preface to the History of *Gregory* of *Tours* [E]; in which he vindicates that Historian from the Accusations of *Flacius Illyricus*; but gives him up in relation to the two *Dionysius's*, the *Areopagite*, and him of *Corinth*. He holds his Rank, under the fictitious Name of *Thierry de Timophile*, in the List of *Disguised Authors*, published by Mr *Baillet*. I have something to add concerning the Edition of *Peter Abelard's* Works commonly ascribed to our *Francis d'Amboise* [F].

CHARACTER of Abelard's Works.

(11) Hist. of Melun. pag. 342.

(12) Launous, Hist. Gymn. Navarr. p. 801.

(13) *Father Oudin.* Supplem. de Script. Eccl. pag. 413.

(14) Spizelius Specim. Biblioth. Universal. Konig. Bibl. vet. & nov. Christoph. Hendreich. Pandectae Brandenburgicae, initio.

(15) *Prefacs,* to *Gregor. Turonensis.*

(16) *It is not to be found in Allard's* Bibliotheque de Dauphiné.

(17) *A Manuscript Memoir communicated by Mr* Lancelot *one of the Under-Librarians of the Mazarine Library at Paris.*

only gave a short Account of his principal Adventures. There are many Errors in that Account; this is not a proper Place to take notice of them: But, without departing from the true Subject of this Remark, I may very well say, that *Francis d'Amboise* did not procure to *Peter Abelard* all the Glory he intended him by the Edition of his Works. The Public did not find, in the Writings of That Author, that great Subtilty, and Force, which rendered him so Famous during his Life. Let us hear *Sebastian Rouillard* once more: "As to *ABAELARD's* Writings, they "do not seem to me to answer the great Praises "and Encomiums bestowed upon him by so many "eminent Authors. And therefore I am persuaded, "that the Excellency of That Author consisted in "a ready Wit, an eloquent and copious Discourse, "and a Philosophical Genius, which rendered him "formidable and invincible in all kinds of Disputa- "tion. As, in our time, we have seen two or three "Persons, who acquired a great Esteem by some "of these Perfections; and yet what they have print- "ed has fallen very short of what every one would "have expected from them (11)."

[D] *An Apologetical Preface, which is prefixed to the Edition of the Year 1616.*] The Conveniency of Arithmetical Figures has likewise it's Inconveniencies. Printers commit a thousand Faults in them, which Correctors overlook; this multiplies Beings extravagantly, and without any Necessity. We have an Example of it here. Some place this Edition of *Abelard* in the Year 1606 (12), others in the Year 1626 (13). No doubt This will induce some Authors to say, that *Abelard's* Works were printed three times in the Space of twenty Years; and, as some tell us they were printed in *Folio* in the Year 1616 (14), this is another way of multiplying the Editions without Necessity.

[E] *A Preface on the History of Gregory of Tours.*] I question not but it is that, of which the Abbot *de Marolles* speaks thus (15): " His History of the *French* " (speaking of *Gregory* of *Tours*) which is the finest of " all his Works, was formerly translated by *Clau-* " *dius Bonnet*, a Gentleman of *Dauphiné* (16), who " stiled himself Doctor of the Civil and Canon Law; " on which Mr *Henry d'Amboise*, Master of the Re- " quests, made a pretty long Preface, address'd to " Madame *Henrietta de Balzac*, Marchioness of *Ver-* " *neuil*, which was printed at *Paris*, in 8vo, for " *Claudius de la Tour*, in 1610."

[F] *I have something to add concerning the Edition of* Peter Abelard's *Works, commonly ascribed to our* Francis d'Amboise.] This Remark is not my own; I give it in the express Terms of it's Author (17). " There are Copies of *Abelard's* Works, which carry " in their Title-page the Name of Mr *d'Amboise*; " but there are others, to which the Name of *Andrew* " *du Chesne* is prefixed, with this Title; " *Petri* " *Abaelardi, Sancti Gildasii in Brittannia Abbatis, &* " *Heloissae conjugis ejus, quae postmodum prima coe-* " *nobii Parachletensis Abbatissa fuit, Opera, nunc pri-* " *mum eruta ex M.SS. Codicibus, & in lucem edita,* " *studio ac diligentia Andreae Quercetani, Turonensis,* " *Parisiis, Nic. Buon, 1616, in 4to.* ——— *The* " *Works of Peter Abelard, Abbot of St Gildas, in* " *Brittany, and Eloisa his Wife, afterwards first Ab-* " *bess of the Covent of the Paraclet, now first publish-* " *ed from the Manuscripts, by* Andrew du Chesne *of* " *Tours,* Paris, N. Buon, 1616, *in* 4to." It is highly probable, that we are indebted to this famous Native of *Tours* for this Edition. In the Abstract of the Privilege, prefixed to the Copy, which bears the Name of *du Chesne*, we are expresly told, " that these Works were printed under the Care of " *Andrew du Chesne, edita Studio Andreae Querce-* " *tani*; whereas in the Copy, which bears the Name " of *Amboise*, the Privilege says not a Word of the " Person, who had the Care of collecting these " Works. Whence, if a Conjecture may be allowed, we may infer, that, through some secret Motive, " which it was not thought proper to transmit to " Posterity, *du Chesne* made over the Credit of " this Work to Mr *d'Amboise*, who, at that time, " was in a Condition of being obliged to him for " such a Sacrifice. However this be, the two Copies " of *du Chesne* and *d'Amboise*, which I have seen, " are not in all respects alike; for instance, that of " *du Chesne* begins with an Epistle Dedicatory, ad- " dress'd to Monsr. *Benjamin Brichanteau*, Bishop of " *Laon*, and Abbot of *St Genevieve*. This Dedica- " tion is wanting in the pretended Edition of *d'Am-* " *boise*, as well as the Preface, which *du Chesne* ad- " ded; in which, after telling us, in general, who " *Abelard* and *Eloisa* were, he gives an Account of " what he had done, to render this Edition of that " famous Logician as perfect as he could: He speaks " respectfully of all those, who had assisted him with " their Manuscripts; and acknowledges himself obli- " ged to Mr *d'Amboise* for the Letters, and other " small Pieces. After this Preface follow the *Test-* " *monia Veterum de Abaelardo & Heloissa*, which are " wanting likewise in the Copy of Mr *d'Amboise*. " The Edition of this Counsellor of State, on it's " Part, has an Apological Preface for *Abelard*, " which is wanting in *du Chesne's* Edition. In every " thing else they are alike; and the two Copies answer " Page for Page. It will not, perhaps, be unneces- " sary to inform the Public of this double Title, for " fear it should occasion hereafter another increase of " the Editions of *Abelard*, as has been already re- " marked."

AMBOISE (ADRIAN d') younger Brother of the preceding, advanced himself no less than *Francis*; for he was made a Bishop. He had his share likewise in the Liberality of *Charles* IX; who maintained him a considerable time in the College of *Navarre*; and he met with the same Favour from *Henry* III. He was of the House of *Navarre* (a), when, in 1579, he was chosen Rector of the University of *Paris*. During his Rectorship, the University petitioned the King for a Confirmation of their Privileges; and he was their Speaker, attended by a great number of Doctors. He took his Licentiate's Degree in Divinity, in the Year 1582, and was preconiced * on that occasion by *Michael Thiriot*, who, among other Encomiums, said, that he was descended from a very noble Family [A]. He was the King's Preacher and Almoner, and

(a) Socius Navarricus, Fellow of the College of Navarre; Launoius, Hist. Gymn. Nav. p. 360.

* Preconiser le French signifies to make a Report in the Pope's Consistory, that the Party presented to a Benefice is qualified for the same.

[A] *Said he was descended from a very noble Family.*] Nevertheless this Author mentions the Ocupation of the Father, who was a Chirurgeon, in his Elogy of the Son. I borrow this *Nevertheless* from Monsr. *de Launoi*, for thus he expresses himself. "*At-* " *tamen Thiriotus ait,* Hadrianum fundatissima & no- " bilissima satum esse familia. *His enim verbis utitur:* " *Franciscus primum in duorum inferiorum Navarrae* " *sodalitiorum disciplinam receptus est, & Caroli IX.* " *liberalitate ac Rhetoricas ac Philosophicas institutio-* " *nes eruditus. Deinde humaniores literas ibidem* " *docuit, &c.* (1) ——— Nevertheless Thiriot says, " that

(1) Launoius Hist. Gymn. Navarr. pag. 799, 800.

AMBOISE.

(b) Id. pag. 371, 372.

and Great Master of the College of *Navarre* (b), when, in 1594, the University of *Paris* took an Oath of Allegiance to *Henry the Great*. About this time he obtained the Rectory of St *Andrew* at *Paris*; and, lastly, in the Year 1604, he was made Bishop of *Treguier*. He died the Twenty eighth of *July* 1616, and was buried in his Cathedral,

"that Adrian *was descended from a substantial and honourable Family*. For these are his Words. Francis "was first initiated in the Studies of the two inferior "Classes of the College of *Navarre*; and brought up, "by the Liberality of Charles IX. to Rhetoric and "Philosophy. Afterwards he taught Classical Learning in the same Place." A very good Way to reconcile these two Authors, would be to say, that *Nobilissima Familia* does not signify what the *French* call a *very noble Family, a Gentleman's Family*; for if *Thiriot* understood his *Latin* so, he would not have expressed himself with Accuracy. Chirurgery is not the Profession of a Gentleman in *France*. If Monf. *de Launoi* had understood it in the same Sense, he would have produced Proofs unnecessarily; nor would his Proofs have been of any Force. It is superfluous to prove that the Quality of Gentleman has been ascribed to any one, when it has been said in express Terms, that he was descended from a very noble Family, in the Sense in which the *French* understand this Phrase; and if, in proof of a Fact of this Evidence, any one should alledge the Quality of Fellow of a College, and that of Teacher of the second Class, which such an one had possessed in the College of *Navarre*, it is certain he would speak very inconsiderately. Such Proofs of Nobility were never admitted. Perhaps, then, not only *Michael Thiriot*, but also Monf. *de Launoi*, took *Nobilissima Familia* for a considerable Family, and which had made a good Figure, and not for a noble Family. This must be carefully remembered in reading the *Latin* Elogies of Men of Letters; we should be mistaken, if we should take all those to be nobly descended, of whom it is said, *nobili loco, nobili genere, nobili prosapia oriundi*. I am not ignorant, that *Francis d'Amboise* styles himself *Esquire*, in the Edition of *Abelard*; but the most this proves, is, that his Father or himself were ennobled, but not at all that his Father was both a Chirurgeon, and a Gentleman. A Conjecture is just come into my Mind, which is at the Reader's Service; and that is, that perhaps, the Predecessors of *Francis d'Amboise* having been degraded, he obtained the Restoration of his Family. Nay, how do we know but he might descend from a Bastard of the illustrious Family of *Amboise*? This seems to be the most probable Conjecture; for he tells us, that he went to the Convent of the *Paraclet*, to collect what he could of the Works of *Peter Abelard*; and that he was very well received by the Abbess *de la Rochefoucaut, whose Grandmother, by the Father's side*, says he, Antoinette d'Amboise, *Wife of the Lord* de Barbesieux, *Knight of the Order, was the only Daughter of* Guy d'Amboise, *and Grand-daughter and Heiress of* Charles, *Lord of* Chaumont, *Marshal of* France: So that the whole Succession of that most ancient Family devolved upon her; and she transferred the Estate of the eldest Branch into the Family of la *Rochefoucaut. Totam vetustissimam familiam crevit, & primogenita* NOSTRA *ad Rupisfocaldos transfulit* (2). It is very extraordinary, that the Son of a Chirurgeon of *Charles* IX should speak thus. Note, that we must not absolutely deny, that a Branch of the illustrious Family of *Amboise* remained in, or fell into, Obscurity. The Chirurgeon of *Charles* IX was, perhaps, of this Branch.

(2) Franc. Amboefius, Præfat. Apologet. in Oper. Abelardi.

[This Person's Family takes it for granted, at present, (but falsly) from a sameness of Name, that it is a Branch of the illustrious Family of *d'Amboise*; but we can positively affirm,

I. That *JOHN d'AMBOISE*, Father of *Francis d'Amboise*, was a Native of the Town of *Douay*, in *Flanders*; that he was successively Chirurgeon to *Francis* I, *Charles* II, and *Henry* III; that he was naturalized by Letters of the Twenty ninth of *January*, in the Year 1566, being at that Time in quality of *Valet de Chambre* and Chirurgeon to *Charles* IX; that he died on the thirteenth of *December*, 1584; and that he was buried in the Church of St *Jervase*, at *Paris*, with *Mary Fromager*, his Wife, Daughter of *John Fromager*, sworn Chirurgeon to the *Chatelet de Paris*, and Chirurgeon to the King.

II. That *FRANCIS d'AMBOISE*, son of *John*, was Baron of *Chartre* on the *Loire*, and Lord of *Hemeri* and *Vezeul*, in *Touraine*, &c. Counsellor, then President of the Parliament of *Bretagne*; Advocate General to the Grand Council, in the Year 1586; Master of the Requests, in 1597; and Counsellor to the Privy Council; afterwards Counsellor of State, in 1604; that he married, on the 15th of *January*, 1594, *Margaret Cousinet*, Daughter of a Notary of the Town of *Meaux*, who was still alive in the Year 1634; that, in the Month of *July*, of the Year 1589, King *Henry* III. created him a Knight, in Consideration of his Father's Services done to four of this Prince's Predecessors. A Copy of this Letter of Knight-hood is as follows.

Letters of Knight-hood; granted by King Henry III, *in the Month of* July, 1589, *to* FRANCIS d'AMBOISE, *President of the Parliament of* Bretagne.

"HENRY, by the Grace of God, King of "*France* and *Poland*, to all present, and to "come, greeting. Whereas it is just and reasonable, "that Persons of eminent Virtue should be distinguish- "ed by a Title and Degree of Honour suitable to their "Merit, that others may be encouraged thereby to "rise by their Virtue to the same, or greater Digni- "ty and Exaltation; we give you to understand, that, "being fully satisfied of the noble, commendable, "and virtuous Deeds, Actions and Conduct, of our "dear and well beloved Monf. *Francis d'Amboise*, "Lord of *Vezeul*, our Counsellor, and Advocate "General in our Grand Council, and President of "our Parliament of *Bretagne*; in remembrance of "the Services, which his late Father shewed to four "Kings, our Predecessors, and to ourselves; and in "Consideration of the great, acceptable, and faithful "Services, which the said *d'Amboise* has done to us, "as well in the several Charges and Commissions, "which he has had in this our Realm, and the "Journey which he took into *Poland*, at the time "of our Election, as in the Exercise of his two "Functions, in two of our supreme Courts; and "which Services the said *d'Amboise* continues ordi- "narily to perform near and about our Person, in se- "veral and various Ways; and in Expectation of his "farther and still greater Services; WE, being wil- "ling to reward him in some measure, and to raise "him to the Title and Degree of Honour, which his "said Virtues and Actions deserve, that his own De- "scendants, and other Persons of Honour and Vir- "tue may be induced, by his Example, to be equally "serviceable to us and our Crown; these and other "Reasons moving us thereto, we have made and cre- "ated him A KNIGHT; and have honoured, and do "honour him with this Title, in the Presence of se- "veral Lords and Princes of our Blood, and other great "and noble Personages of our Court, and have permit- "ted him to enjoy, and for the future to assume, the "said Title of Knight, with all the Rights of Nobi- "lity, Honours, Authorities, Privileges, Exemp- "tions, Prerogatives, and Precedencies, in all ho- "nourable Assemblies, as well in Courts of Justice, "as elsewhere, where it shall be needful; in like "manner as is enjoy'd by other Knights, created "as well by Our Hand, as by that of our Royal "Predecessors. In Consequence of which, we have "directed our trusty and well-beloved, the Bailiffs, "Seneschals, Judges, or their Deputies, belonging to "our Courts of Parliaments, and our well-beloved "Justices, Officers, and Subjects, in their respective "Capacities, to cause, suffer, and permit, the said "*d'Amboise* to enjoy fully and peaceably the said "Rights of Knight-hood, Honours, Prerogatives, "Privileges, Franchises, and Liberties, thereto be- "longing, as is above declared, and as is customary "upon the like Occasion. For such is our Pleasure; "and to the Intent that this our present Gift and "Grant may be, and remain for ever, in Force, to "the Honour of the said *d'Amboise*, and his Succes- "sors, and that there may be a perpetual Memo-

AMBOISE. 251

thedral, where his Epitaph bestows great Commendations on him [B]. I know not whether he wrote any thing beside a *French* Tragedy, entituled, *Holophernes*, which was printed in the Year 1580 (c).

(c) Launoius Hist. Gymn. Navarr. pag. 800.

" rial thereof, we have affixed our Seal to these Pre-
" sents."

Given at Pontoise; *in the Month of* July, *Anno Dom.* 1589, *in the sixteenth Year of our Reign.*

Signed HENRY, *and on the Fold by the King,* POTIER; *and on the Side is written* VISA CON-TENTOR; *signed* COMBAND; *and seal'd with the Great Seal of green Wax, with Strings of green and red Silk.*

III. That ANTONY d'AMBOISE, his Son, Baron of *Hémeri,* &c. espoused, on the twentieth of *October,* in the Year 1632, *Anne de la Hilière,* Daughter of *John Gabriel de la Hilière,* Governor of *Amboise,* and of *Louisa de Gast* ; and that, after having been Lieutenant of the Artillery, in 1634, then Camp-Master of the Regiment of *Touraine,* and Governor of the Town and Citadel of *Trin* in *Piedmont,* he died Lieutenant-General of the King's Armies.

IV. That CHARLES *JULIUS d'AMBOISE*, his Son, Camp-Master likewise of the Regiment of *Touraine,* espoused, on the Twenty second of *September,* 1672, *Charlotte du Gast,* his Cousin. And

V. That from this Marriage sprang GILES-AN-TONY *d'AMBOISE,* now living, and dwelling in the City of *Amboise,* in *Touraine,* where he espoused, on the seventeenth of *January,* 1700, *Paula Guichard,* Daughter of the Mayor of the said Town, by whom he has had one Son and two Daughters, all alive in 1716.

It is supposed, in a small Book, entituled, *Index Funereus Chirurgorum Parisiensium ab Anno* 1315 *ad Annum* 1714, printed at *Trevoux,* for *Stephen Ganeau,* in 1714, in 12mo, that *Francis, Adrian,* and *James d'Amboise* *, Sons of *John,* sprang from the illustrious House of *Amboise* †; and it is upon this false Suppo-

* JAMES, AVTOIS; Brother of Francis, espoused Mary Longis Daughter of Joseph Longis, Procurator of the Parliament; he died the 5th of Aug. 1605; and was buried in the Church-Yard of St Nicolas in the Fields at Paris. He was the Father of Anne d'Amboise, his only Daughter, married to David de Mondestir, Governor of Fère in Picardy, afterwards Depty.-Governor of Verdun.   † JOHANNES d'AMBOISE, Pater, Cassaleti Chirurgia Regius, ex nobilissima Amboisanorum gente oriundus, tres habuit filios, in suo quisque statu percelebres.----FRANCISCUS, scilicet, ADRIANUS, & JACOBUS. *Index funereus Chirurgorum Parisiensium,* pag. 22, 30, 32, &c.

sition, that the only one at present remaining of the Posterity of *Francis d'Amboise* assumes the Arms entire of this powerful House.

Had the late Mr BAYLE, when he set about his Historical Dictionary, consulted me, he might have treated with more exactness and certainty, than he has done, several Genealogical Facts, which he has advanced in his Work; which have never yet been set right, and which continue, in Opposition to Truth, in all the Editions, as yet published, of this excellent Work ‖. REM. CRIT.]

‖ Taken from a Memorandum, communicated by Mr d'Hozier in 1716.

[B] *His Epitaph bestows great Commendations on him.*] I believe the Reader will be pleas'd to find it here. I take it from Monsr. *de Launoi.*

Amboesi, pater eruditionum,
Argiva & Latia madens Minerva,
Paulina in Cathedra diserte præco,
Idemque hæresios severe censor,
Priscorum nova norma Episcoporum,
Antistes pie, pauperum patrone,
Custos virginitatis atque amator,
Tu quocumque ieris, sequeris agnum.

Capacious Soul, with Learning fraught,
From Stores of Greece *and* Latium *brought,*
Persuasive from the Preacher's Chair,
Censor of Heresy severe;
By whose Example taught, we see,
What Bishops were, and ought to be;
Prelate, with ev'ry Virtue crown'd,
Still to the Poor a Patron found;
Adorn'd with Christian Piety;
Guardian and Friend of Chastity;
Where'er thou go'st, the Lamb shall be
A Guide, divine Amboise, *to Thee.*

AMBOISE (JAMES *de*) younger Brother of the foregoing, followed his Father's Profession, and became very skillful in it; but, after he had sufficiently distinguished his Capacity in Chirurgery, he advanced some degrees higher, and became Doctor of Physic [*A*]. This Promotion fell out between the Year 1582, and 1597; for *Pinæus* declares, in the Book, which he wrote, in 1597, concerning the Tokens of Virginity, that at that time *James d'Amboise* was Doctor of Physic; but that he was only Master of Arts and Batchelor of Chirurgery, when, with great Dexterity, and in the Presence of many great Masters, he dissected a Woman, who was hanged in the Year 1579 for destroying her Child (a). We know, farther, that he was nothing more than Chirurgeon in the Year 1582 (b), and that he was Licentiate in Physic, and the King's Physician in the Year 1594, when he was chosen Rector of the University of *Paris* (c). The Oath, which that University took to *Henry the Great,* and the Process which they entered against the Jesuits, fell out under his Rectorship. There are two *Latin* Speeches, which *James d'Amboise* made to the Parliament, in quality of Rector, on the 12th of *May,* and the 13th of *July* 1594; they are very severe against the Jesuits. He had been a Member of the College of *Navarre,* before he was Rector (d).

(a) See Remark [A].
(b) Mich. Thriot. Laud. Hadr. Amboesii, 1584, apud Launoium, Hist. Gymn. Nav. pag. 799.
(c) Launoius, Hist. Gymn. Nav. pag. 358. See likewise the Apology for John Chauvet, p. 194.
(d) Launoius, ibid.

(1) Apud Launoium, Hist. Gymn. Nav. pag. 799.
(2) Pinæus, de Virginit. Not. 1. lib. 2. cap. 8.

[A] *He advanc'd some Degrees higher, and became Doctor of Physic.*] This appears from two Passages; one is of *Thriot* (1) ; " Natu minimus paternam, " hoc est ulceribus medendi artem, amplexatus, mul- " tis salutarem manum felicissime præbet. —— *The* " *youngest Son, embracing his Father's Profession of* " *Chirurgery, has great Success in the Cure of his Pa-* " *tients.*" The other of *Pinæus* (2) ; " Jacobus Am-

" boësianus, in Artibus Magister, & in Chirurgia Bac- " calaureus, nunc autem in utraque Medicina Do- " ctor, & Medicus Regius. —— James Amboise, *Ma-* " *ster of Arts, and Batchelor of Chirurgery; now* " *Doctor of both Faculties, and Physician to the King.*" Monsr. *de Launoi* understands by this the Chirurgeon of *Charles* IX; but he is mistaken.

AMBOISE (MICHAEL *de*) Esquire, and Lord of *Chevillon,* lived in the XVIth Century. He gave himself in his Works a Nick-Name, or rather a Poetical one (a), which was no great Ornament to them, and did not prevent his falling, with his Numberless Poems, into the Obscurity of Oblivion. He does not appear, any more than *Francis d'Amboise,* in the vast Collection of Mr *Baillet:* Yet he seems to have expected, that the Title of his Works would continue to excite the Curiosity of Readers a long time. One of his Books entituled, *Amorous Epistles, Fancies, Com-plaints,*

(a) L'Es-clave fortuné, The happy Slave.

AMBROSIUS. AMELIA. AMELIUS.

plaints, Epitaphs, Thirty Four Roundo's, and Three Ballads, was printed at Paris in 1556. Another is entitled, *The Encomium of the Tooth* (b). The *Counter Epistles of Ovid* (c), that is, Letters composed in answer to those, which the Heroines of *Ovid* wrote to their Husbands or Gallants, seemed to promise great Entertainment; and yet they underwent the Fate of his other Poems; They are quite unknown. He undertook some Translations; he turned four Satires of *Juvenal* (d) into *French* Verse, the 10th Book of *Ovid's Metamorphosis*, the Eclogues of *Baptista Mantano* (e), and the *Italian* Treatise of *Antonio Phileremo Fregoso*, entituled, *Ris de Democrite, & pleur d' Heraclite* (*Democritus*'s Laughter, and *Heraclitus*'s Tears) (f). He wrote in Heroics *A Lamentation for the Death of* Messire William du Bellai, Lord of Langey (g), and the *Standard of the Soldiery* (h) in Prose. See the *Bibliotheque of du Verdier-Vau-Privas*.

(e) *Printed at Lyons, in 1537.*
(c) *Printed at Paris, in 1541.*
(d) *Printed at Paris, in 1543.*
(e) *Printed at Paris, in 1530.*
(f) *Printed at Paris, in 1547.*
(g) *Printed at Paris, la Croix du Maine, Bibl. Franc. pag. 322.*
(h) *Printed at Paris, in 1543.*

AMBROSIUS, General of the Order of CAMALDOLI. Look for CAMALDOLI.

AMELIA, a City of *Italy*. It was anciently called AMERIA. It is situated between the *Tiber* and the *Nera*. *Cato* says it was founded 964 Years before the War of *Perseus* (a): So that, as this War began in the Year 581 of *Rome*, it should follow, that *Ameria* was 383 Years older than *Rome*. *Festus* calls the Founder of this City *Amirus*. It appears from Inscriptions, that it became one of those Cities, which the *Romans* called *Municipia*. *Cicero* confirms this in his fine Oration in defence of *Roscius Amerinus*. It acquired the Privileges of a *Roman* Colony under *Augustus* (b). It stands in a fruitful Soil; and the Hills, which surround it, are covered with fine Vineyards (c). It is not certain that the Vines of *Ameria* were formerly in great Esteem. My View in this Article is only to rectify That of *Moreri* [A], and therefore I forbear enlarging upon it. *Leander Albertus* wants likewise to be set right [B].

(a) *Apud Plinium, lib. 3. cap. 14.*
(b) *See Cluverius, Ital. Antiq. lib. 2. cap. 7.*
(c) *Leandri Alberti Descript. Ital. pag. 144.*

[A] *My View in this Article, is only to rectify that of* Moreri.] I. No Author *says, that* Ameria *was built at the time of the War of* Perseus. II. Pliny *does not maintain, that it was built in* 964, *before the War*. He only tells us, that *Cato* had said so. III. *Cicero* did not plead for a Comedian, born in that Town; *Roscius Amerinus*, for whom he pleaded, was different from *Roscius* the Player, whose Cause he likewise undertook. IV. These Words of *Virgil*,

Atque Amerina parant lentæ retinacula viti (1).

—————— and *twine*
AMERIAN *Twigs, to tie the straggling Vine*.
   DRYDEN.

(1) Virgil. Georg. lib. 1. ver. 265. *This Verse is a very ill cited by* Moreri. *Atque* Amerina parent lentæ retinacula vitæ.
(2) Servius in Virgil. ibid.

do not prove, that *the Vines of* Ameria *were esteemed* in his time. This Verse only implies, that in the Territory of that City there was found a great quantity of Boughs, as pliant as Ozier, which they make use of in dressing their Vineyards. "Virgas de quibus vites relligantur: quæ virgæ abundant circa Amerinum "oppidum ——— alii genus salicis dicunt, dispari colo- "re à cætera salice: nam est rubra & ad connectendum "aptior, quia præter morem lenta est (2). ——— *Twigs,* "*with which Vines are tied*; *they are found in great* "*plenty about* Ameria. ——— *Others say, it is a* "*kind of Willow, of a different Colour from other* "*Willows*; *for it is red, and fitter for tying, as* "*being uncommonly pliant*."

[B] Leander Albertus *wants likewise to be set right*.] He makes *Cato* say, that *Ameria* was rebuilt above Nine hundred Years before the War of *Perseus*, and that it was first built by the *Vejentes*, a People of *Tuscany*, under the Conduct of *Amerus*, Daughter of the *Italian Atlas*, and of *Pleione*. He supposes, that *Pliny* said it was built Nine hundred sixty four Years before the War of *Perseus*, and represents *Cato* and *Pliny* as being of two different Opinions. Afterwards he endeavours to reconcile them; which he does in the following manner. "The Chronology of the "one, *says he*, agrees well enough with the Chrono- "logy of the other: *Cato* mentions above Nine hun- "dred Years before the War of *Perseus*, and *Pliny* "speaks of Nine hundred sixty four Years before that "War: So that it is easy to reconcile them. Tho' "one of them uses the Term *Rebuilding*, and the "other the Term *Building*, it must not be inferred "from thence, that they affirm contrary things; for "the Word *condere*, which *Pliny* makes use of, is "indifferently taken both for *Founding* and *Repair- "ing*." These vain and chimerical Disputes fall to the Ground, to the shame of their Author, as soon as *Pliny* is consulted; for it appears, that he gives no Opinion of his own; and is contented to say, "Ame- "riam ——— Cato ante Persei bellum conditam annis "964 prodidit (3). ——— *Cato gave out, that* Ameria "*was built* Nine hundred sixty four Years *before the* "*War of* Perseus."

(3) Plin. lib. 3. cap. 14. in fine.

AMELIUS, a Platonic Philosopher, of the IIId Century, was of *Tuscany*. His true Name was *Gentilianus*; and he preferred the Sirname of *Amerius* to That of *Amelius*. He was 24 Years a Disciple of *Plotinus* at *Rome*, after which he retired to *Apamea*, a City of *Syria*, where he resided, when *Plotinus* died. He adopted one *Justin Hesychius*, born in the same City (a). This doubtless occasioned the Mistake of *Suidas*, who said that *Amelius* was of *Apamea*. He is not less mistaken, when he affirms, that *Porphyry* was a Disciple of *Amelius* [A]. What is certain is, that *Amelius* was

(a) *Porphyrius in Vita Plotini.*

[A] Suidas ——— *is mistaken, when he affirms, that* Porphyry *was a Disciple of* Amelius.] *Porphyry* himself tells us (1), that, when he began to be a Disciple of *Plotinus*, *Amelius* had studied eighteen Years under that Philosopher. He adds, that he was *Amelius*'s Fellow-Pupil six Years; after which they both departed from *Rome*, himself for *Sicily*, and *Amelius* for *Apamea*. They continued in the Places, to which they had retired, at least 'till the Death of *Plotinus*. Now as *Porphyry* was then about Thirty eight Years of Age, and was in greater Reputation at *Rome*, than *Amelius*, it is improbable he should be a Disciple of the latter. Add to this, that *Amelius*, in dedicating

(1) Porphyr. in Vita Plotini.

to him his Apology for *Plotinus*, desires him to excuse and correct the Faults of it (2). Lastly, the Silence of *Porphyry* is a very strong Argument against *Suidas*. *Porphyry* mentions *Amelius* every Moment, in the Life of *Plotinus*; and would he not have said something of his having been the Scholar of such a Master? *Suidas* might have been deceived by *Theodoret*, who *calls* Amelius *the Head of* Porphyry's *School* (3), *that is*, according to the Interpretation of Monsr. *de Tillemont*, *of* Plotinus's *School, in which* Porphyry *studied* (4). *And indeed* Suidas *says be was* Porphyry's *Master*: (They are Monsr. *de Tillemont*'s Words.) We may reckon likewise among his Disciples Castricius Firmus,

(2) Ibid.
(3) Theodor. Græcor. Affect. pag. 500.
(4) Tillem. Hist. des Emper. Tom. 3. pag. 1084. printed at Brussels.

AMELIUS. AMESIUS.

was very much esteemed by his Master, and that he returned This Esteem by a singular Veneration for *Plotinus*. When he began to study under This famous Philosopher, all he knew was what he had learned from one *Lysimachus* (b); but by his great Application, he soon surpassed all his Fellow Pupils. He retained Part of *Numenius*'s Lectures by heart, having collected and transcribed most of 'em. He made likewise ample Collections of all that he had heard in the Philosophical Conferences; and out of these Collections he drew up an hundred Treatises, which he gave to his adopted Son. He had not yet ventured to produce any thing else, when *Porphyry* came to *Rome* (c); that is to say, after having profited by *Plotinus*'s Instructions for the space of 18 Years. Afterwards he composed 40 Books against *Zostrianus*, one of those ancient Heretics, both in Philosophy, and Religion, who made such an horrible jumble of the Doctrines of the Gospel, and of the Philosophers. There arose a great number of these Heretics in *Plotinus*'s time, which obliged him to declare War against them. He undertook the Defeat of the *Gnostics*, whilst *Amelius* opposed *Zostrianus*, and *Porphyry* attacked the pretended Revelations of *Zoroaster*. *Amelius*, having heard afterwards, that *Plotinus* was accused of adorning himself with the Spoils of *Numenius*, took Pen in Hand to justify his Master, and, in three days, wrote a Book, which he dedicated to *Porphyry*, and which the latter entituled, *Of the difference between the Doctrine of* Numenius *and That of* Plotinus. What I am going to say is sufficient to shew the Esteem, which *Plotinus* had for *Amelius*. *Plotinus* took no great pains to exert himself; upon which Account he generally left some doubts upon the Minds of his Hearers, and stood in need in some manner of being forced to shew the best side of his Doctrine. This made *Porphyry* propose several Objections to him in Writing, to prove that our Ideas are distinct from our Understanding (d). This Doctrine Father *Mallebranche* has revived in our days. *Plotinus*, having read these Objections, gave them *Amelius* to refute 'em. The Opponent replyed; *Amelius* rejoined; and at last *Porphyry*, apprehending *Plotinus* Doctrine, approved of it, and read his Retractation in a full Auditory. *Longinus*, whose Taste was so just, and whose Censures were so formidable, found indeed *Amelius*'s Writings to be too verbose; but ranked him nevertheless among the few Philosophers, whose Works seemed to him worthy of Consideration [B]. He wrote a long Letter in answer to That, which he had received from *Amelius*, concerning *Plotinus*'s Philosophy. *Amelius* was a Votary of Paganism, and a great Observer of new Moons and Feasts (e) [C]. In one of his Books he cites the beginning of St *John*'s Gospel, in confirmation of *Plato*'s Doctrine. *Eusebius* alledges this Passage (f), but not so fully as *Theodoret* (g) and St *Cyril* (h).

Firmus, *a Man* ——— *who was very serviceable to* Amelius. So that here is a modern Author, who falls into the Error of *Suidas*, and goes still farther; for it is plain from the Life of *Plotinus*, to which he refers us concerning *Castricius*, that it was in *Plotinus*'s Lifetime that *Castricius* had so great an Inclination for *Amelius* at *Rome*. Now it is undeniable, that, whilst the latter was at *Rome*, he had no Disciples. He was *Plotinus*'s Disciple, and did not set up Altar against Altar.

[B] Longinus ——— *ranked him among the few Philosophers, whose Works seemed to him worthy of Consideration.*] The Number of them was so small, that it comprehended but two Authors, *Plotinus* and *Amelius*. The Reputation of the latter was upon this Account the greater; yet this did not prevent his Writings from losing, in a little time, their first Reputation. *Eunapius* places them in the same Category with those of two other Fellow-Students of *Porphyry*, and passes this Censure upon them all: Συγγράμματά γε αὐτῶν περισεύζεται, λόγῳ δὲ αὐτῶν οὐδέν εἰς (5). *Their Works indeed are extant, but their Reputation is nothing.* He gives this as a Reason for it, that they were destitute of the Ornaments of Language, and meerly dogmatical.

[C] *A great Observer of New Moons and Feasts.*] I am aware, that, instead *of New Moons*, it would be better to say, *the first Days of the Month*, as *Marsilius Ficinus* did (6), but I thought my Expression would be more easily understood. These are *Porphyry*'s Words: Φιλοθύτης δὲ γέγονεν ὁ Ἀμέλιος, καὶ τὰ ἱερὰ κατὰ νουμηνίαν, καὶ τὰς ἑορτὰς ἐκπεριιών (7). Amelius *being fond of Sacrifices, and a religious Observer of new Moons and Feasts.* After this let any one say, that Philosophers are impious Men? If they had been so, they would not have wrote so much in favour of Paganism; they would not have been the only Writers, whom the Christians had to oppose; for, as for the Priests and Sacrificators, they did not concern themselves with it; their Ignorance excused them from it.

AMESIUS (WILLIAM) an *Englishman*, and Professor of Divinity at *Franeker*, flourished in the XVIIth Century. He was concerned in the *Arminian* Controversy; and wrote several learned Books against That Sect [A]. He is one of the reformed Divines, who have treated Cases of Conscience most exactly and methodically. It is almost needless to observe, that he wrote against *Bellarmin* (a); for no one is ignorant, that in those times the Works of that Jesuit were refuted by the greatest part of the Protestant Controvertists. *Amesius* wrote a Book entituled, *Medulla Theologiæ*. He wrote likewise against the *Socinians*, and against Metaphysics, and in favour

[A] *He wrote several learned Books against that Sect.*] He begun the Controversy *viva voce* with *Grevinchovius*, Minister of *Rotterdam*; but, being prevented by frequent Interruptions from speaking his whole Mind, carried on the Dispute by Letters, and published what he had objected, and his Adversary's Replies. The Points in question were, The Redemption of Man by the Death of *JESUS CHRIST*, and Election grounded on the *Fore-sight* of Faith. *Grevinchovius* published another Edition of their Dispute at *Rotterdam*, in the Year 1615, in 4to. *Amesius* replied, in a Piece entitled, *Rescriptio Scholastica & brevis*, &c. He wrote a Book likewise under the Title of *Coronis ad Collationem Hagiensem*, in which he replied to the Answers, which the *Arminians* had made to the Objections of the Ministers of *Holland*.

favour of Puritanism, of which he was a strict Follower [B]. He published this last Work in *England* in 1610. I say nothing of his Lectures on the *Psalms*, nor of his Explication of the Epistles of St *Peter*. He did not die in the Year 1639, as *Henningus Witte* affirms in his *Diarium Biographicum*. The Epistle Dedicatory of his *Lectures on the Psalms*, in 1635, are a proof that he was then dead. We find in the same Epistle, that, after having been twelve years Professor at *Franeker*, he had obtained his Dismission, in order to be Professor at *Rotterdam*.

His Work, entituled, *Anti Synodalia*, contains some Remarks on the *Scripta Synodalia* of the Remonstrants. It was printed at *Franeker* in the Year 1629.

[B] *He wrote —— in Favour of Puritanism, of which he was a strict Follower.*] You will find in the Preface, which I cite (1), some Extracts of the Book, which he published against Episcopacy, in the Year 1610, where you will see, that, in his Opinion, there were no good Men in *England*, but the Puritans. They distinguished themselves by their Aversion for Stage-Plays, Oaths, Dancing, Gaming, and Treats: The rest were only Gamesters, Drinkers, Swearers, and Children of Belial. There was no *Medium* between these two Extreams, either to suppress Episcopacy, or to bring back the Church of *Rome* from Hell. "Hi scil. soli inter Anglos *vivi* " boni, simplices, quadrati: quos *ex scelerifugio* fit " cognoscere, quibus ex repudio spectaculorum, ju- " ramentorum, chorearum, alearum & commessatio- " num, inditum sit nomen *Puritanorum*: reliqui ve- " ro insignes aleatores, potatores strenui, religionis " officia susque deque habentes, versati institores pa- " pistarum, ambitionibus pravis corrupti, juratores " impii, homines denique vani, injusti, turpes, & " omnes filii Belial. —— Adeoque vel è medio tol- " lendum *cruentatum hunc Episcoporum ordinem, vel* " *denuo Papam revocandum ab orco* (2).

(1) Grevinchovii Præf. Dissertat. Theolog. de duabus Quæstionibus.

(2) Grev. Ib. fol. **** iii.

AMESTRIS, Wife of XERXES King of *Persia*. See the first Remark of the Article MASISTES.

AMYOT (JAMES) Bishop of *Auxerre*, and Great Almoner of *France*, was one of the most illustrious learned Men of the XVIth Century. He was born at *Melun* the Thirtieth of *October* 1514. His Father and Mother, who were good honest Folks, but of a very mean Condition [A], used all their Industry to maintain him at *Paris*, where he went thro' his School-Learning, and a Course of Philosophy, in the College of Cardinal *le Moine*. He had naturally a heavy Genius; but Labour and Application supplied this Defect. Having taken his Master of Arts Degree at 19 Years of Age, he continued to study under the Royal Professors, whom *Francis* I. had established. He heard *James Tusanus*, who explained the *Greek* Poets, *Peter Danæus*, who was Professor of Eloquence, and *Orontius Finæus*, who taught Mathematics. He left *Paris* at Twenty three Years of Age, to go to *Bourges* with the Sieur

[A] *His Father and Mother —— were but of a very mean Condition.*] Some say that *Amyot*'s Father, was a *Currier* of *Melun* (1); according to others *he made and sold Purses, and tagged Points* (2); lastly, others say that he was a Butcher. I find there good Authorities for this latter Opinion, *Thuanus* (3), *Papyrius Masso* (4), and *Brantome*. I believe the Reader will not be displeased to see the Words of this last mentioned Author a little at length, for they contain another Particular, which deserves to be known, though it should be false. *Brantome*, having said, that *Charles* IX. in a Speech to the Parliament, said, *with a couragous and threatning Boldness*, "It is " your Business to obey my Ordinances, without dis- " puting or contesting them; for I know better, than " you, what is fit and expedient for the Good of my " Kingdom", Adds: "Being as yet beardless, he spoke " these Words before those old and wise Men, who " all wondered at such a bold and grave Speech; " which savoured much of a generous Courage, than " of the Lessons of his Preceptor, Mr *Amyot*; who " had nevertheless instructed him well, and whom " he greatly loved, and had given him very good " Benefices, and made him Bishop of *Lizieux* (5), " and called him always his Master; and sometimes, " in jest, reproached him with his Avarice, telling " him, that he lived only on Neats-Tongues; and " indeed he was a Butcher's Son of *Melun*, and might " well be fond of the Meat, which he had seen his " Father prepare. Setting aside his Avarice, he " was a Great and Learned Man, both in *Greek* " and *Latin*; witness the beautiful and elegant Tran- " slation he made of *Plutarch*; though some envious " Persons gave out, that he was not the sole Author " of it; but that he was assisted by a certain great " Man, well skilled in the *Greek* Tongue, who hap- " pened, luckily for him, to be confined in the Pri- " son of the Palace of *Paris*, and in Necessity; whom " he released and took into his Service;" and that " they two privately composed this Translation, " which *Amyot* afterwards published in his own " Name. But this is entirely false, for He alone " wrote it; and they, who were acquainted, and " conversed with him, can truly say, that he wanted " no Assistance in such a Work. To conclude, he " educated That brave King very well, and chiefly " in the Catholic Religion." Were I to call in question the three mean Professions, which are ascribed to our *Amyot*'s Father, my reason would not be, because his Son has mentioned none of them in the Manuscript of his Life; He was contented to say, that he was born of Parents more virtuous than rich, *parentibus honestis magis quam copiosis* (6). This Reason has no Weight with me; for there are few great Men, of mean Extraction, who are not very willing to pass lightly over the Obscurity of their Birth: Particulars on that Subject are disagreeable to them. They will own in general, that they were not Men of Quality; but you must not expect that they should give you any Memoirs, in which you may read, that their Fathers were Butchers, Coblers, Sellers of tagged Points, or Matches; that they lived upon Alms in their Childhood, &c. They, who make such Confessions, and are willing they should be inserted in their Elogies, are so few, that, though it were true, that *Amyot* had begged for some time in the Streets of *Paris*, I should not be surprized, that he did not mention such a Particular in his Memoirs of his Life. I shall not therefore refute by his Silence what is related of his Beggary, and of his having been a Foot-Boy, and of his Abode in the Hospital of *Orleans* (7). It is true, I cannot reconcile his Silence with That part of his Will, wherein he leaves Twelve hundred Crowns to That Hospital, *as an acknowledgement for the Charity, which he had met with there* (8). It has been observed, that in his *Works* he *never adds his Country's Name to his own*, and that, during his prosperous Condition, he had *very little Correspondence* with the Place of his Birth (9). No doubt he was weak enough to be mortified at That City, and to fancy that his Correspondence with *Melun* would make People talk of the Meanness of his Birth. Yet I have read, that he advanced some Persons of his Family. "He died " invested with great Dignities, and worth above Two " hundred thousand Crowns, besides a great many " other means which he had of advancing his Re- " lations, some of which shared in his Liberality (10)."

(1) St Real, Of the Use of History, p. 74.

(2) Roulliard's Antiquities of Melun, pag. 605.

(3) Thuan. Histor. lib. 100. ad ann. 1591. pag. 405.

(4) Lanlii filius erat, Meloduno oppido ortus, vir excellenti ingenio, Latinæque & Græcæ doctissimus. Carolus Magistrum eum appellabat, inter jocos avaritiam obiciens & sordes, quod linguis uterentur. *Papyr. Masso in Historia Vit. Caroli IX.*

(5) *This is a Mistake; he should have said Aux re; and not Lisieux.*

(6) Rouilliard, ubi supra.

(7) St Real, ubi supra, pag. 76.

(8) Id. p. 75.

(9) Rouilliard, ubi supra.

(10) *They are la Popeliniere's Words, pag. 250. of his Idea of History.*

[B] He

AMYOT. 257

Sieur *Colin* (a), who was possess'd of the Abbey of St *Ambrose* in that City [B]. At the Recommendation of this Abbot, a Secretary of State there (b) took *Amyot* into his House to be Tutor to his Children. The Progress they made under him induced their Father to recommend him to the Princess *Margaret*, Duchess of *Berry*, only Sister of *Francis* I. Upon this Recommendation *Amyot* was made public Lecturer in *Greek* and *Latin*, in the University of *Bourges*. He read two Lectures every day for ten Years, a *Latin* Lecture in the Morning, and a *Greek* one in the Afternoon. It was during that time that he translated into *French*, *The Loves of Theagenes* and *Chariclea* (c). This Translation pleased *Francis* the First so well, that he soon provided the Author with a Benefice. He gave him the Abbey of *Bellosane*, which became vacant by the Death of *Francis Vetablus* [C]. That Prince died soon after; upon which *Amyot* thought it more for his Interest to go into *Italy*, in hopes of Preferment there, than to expect any thing from the Court of *France*. He went to *Venice* with *Morvillier*, whom *Henry* II. sent on an Embassy thither. *Morvillier* employed him in some Affairs, and sent him to carry the King's Letters to the Council of *Trent*, in 1551 [D]. Being recalled from his Embassy, *Amyot* refused to repass the Alps with him, and chose rather to go to *Rome*, where he met with a very kind reception from the Bishop of *Mirepoix*. He lodged about Two Years at his House. It was then, that, examining the Manuscripts of the *Vatican*, to which *Romulus Amasæus*, who was the Keeper of That famous Library, gave him free Access, he discovered, that *Heliodorus*, Bishop of *Trica*, was the Author of *the Loves of Theagenes*. He met with a more correct and more perfect Manuscript of This Work, than That which he had translated, and was not wanting in taking proper Care to publish a better Edition. His learned Occupations did not take off his Thoughts from the Interest of his Fortune. He made his Court very dexterously to Cardinal *de Tournon*, and insinuated himself so far into his Favour, that the Cardinal nominated him to the King, when That Prince, having recalled him to *France*, desired him to recommend to him a good Preceptor for his Two Younger Sons (d). This was about the Year 1558. Thus *Amyot* became Preceptor to Two of *Henry* the Second's Sons. Whilst he was in this Post, he finished his Translation of *Plutarch's* Lives, and dedicated it to That Prince (e): Afterwards he undertook a Translation of *Plutarch's* Morals, and finished it in the Reign of *Charles* IX, to whom he dedicated it. *Charles* IX. was his great Benefactor; He gave him the Abbey of St *Cornelius* of *Compiegne*, and made him Great Almoner of *France*, and Bishop of *Auxerre* [E]; and, as the Dignity of Great Almoner,

(a) He was Reader of Lectures to Francis I.

(b) William Bouchetel, Sieur de Sassy.

(c) 'Tis Book is usually called Heliodorus's Ethiopic History.

(d) They reigned successively, under the Names of Charles IX. and Henry III.

(e) He began it in the Reign of Francis I. to whom he presented some of Those Lives written in a fair hand by Adam Charles, a Writing-Master of Paris, Knulliar's Antiquities of Melun, pag. 605.

[B] *He left Paris —— to go to Bourges with the Sieur Colin, who was possess'd of the Abbey of St Ambrose in That City.*] *Bullart*, who generally follows the Antiquities of *Melun*, goes out of his way here, to inform us of a Particular very little known (11), which is, that *Amyot* turned Monk in the Abbey of *St Ambrose* in the Town of *Bourges*. But that the Abbot, judging him worthy of a more conspicuous Life, than that of a *Cloyster*, brought him acquainted with the Sieur de Sacy Bouchetel. 'Tis pity he quotes no written Authority for a Particular so little known.

[C] *He gave him the Abbey of Bellosane, which became vacant by the Death of Francis Vetablus.*] This is altogether inconsistent with the Narrative of the Abbot *de St Real*. The Author will have it, that, in the Reign of *Henry* II, *Amyot* was still in the Obscurity of a small Tutorship, in the House of a Gentleman, *who was a Friend of his*, and that M. de *l'Hospital*, *who did not know him*, recommended him only on Account of a *Greek* Epigram, which was presented to That Monarch (12). This must necessarily be false, if it be true, as the Manuscript of *Amyot's* Life says, that this learned Man had been several Years Professor at *Bourges*, before the Death of *Francis* I; and that his Works, which were presented to That King, procured him a very good Abbey. Can any one believe, that M. de *l'Hospital* was unacquainted with a *Frenchman*, who had published, in 1549, at farthest (13), a Translation of *Heliodorus's Historia Æthiopica?* How are we sure, that *Henry* II. took a Journey to *Bourges* before the first Edition of That Translation? Add, that the Manuscript Life of *Amyot* makes him go into *Italy* soon after the Death of *Francis* I. Reconcile this if you can with the Abbot *de St Real*, who makes him a Tutor at *Bourges* at the Time of *Henry* the Second's Journey to That Town.

[D] *Morvillier —— sent him to carry the King's Letters to the Council of Trent, in 1551.*] It will be necessary to correct the Author, who supplies me with this Article (14), though he tells us, that he made use of a Life of *Amyot*, begun by himself, and finished by his Secretary. We have a Letter of *Amyot*, which contains the Relation of his Journey to *Trent*.

A few Days after this Journey, he wrote to Mr *de Morvillier*, Master of the Requests. Now he is so far from saying, that Mr *de Morvillier*, Ambassador of *France* at *Venice*, had sent him to carry the King's Letters to the Council, that he declares in express Terms, that he was chosen for That Business by Cardinal *de Tournon*, and by the Ambassador *de Selve*. This is a convincing Proof, that *Morvillier* was not Ambassador at *Venice*, at that time: and this appears still plainer by *Amyot's* Letter: for it is directed to M. *de Morvillier* at Court. Observe well these Words of *Amyot*: *Cardinal* de Tournon, *and the Ambassador* de Selve, *were pleased to pitch upon the Man to execute this Commission, when such a thing was the farthest from my Thoughts* (15). —— *It is observable, that not only I was not so much as mentioned in That Letter* (16), *but the worst is, They had not so much as sent a Copy of it, by which one might know the Contents of it. So that I never saw any Thing so ill managed* (17). It was not then the King, who sent him to protest in his Name against the Council; but it was Cardinal *de Tournon*, and the *French* Ambassador at *Venice*, who made choice of him to carry the King's Letter, and to read his Majesty's Protestation Word for Word before the Assembly. He acquitted himself very well of this Commission. You see what I aim at. The Abbot *de St Real* takes it for granted, that *Amyot* was Preceptor of the Children of *France*, before the Negotiation, which I have just now mentioned; and he supposes that *Henry* II. employed Him in that Business, because he had experienced the Reality of the good Character which M. *de l'Hospital* had given of him, when he told the King, that *Amyot deserved to be Preceptor of the Children of* France. All this is irrefragably confuted by *Amyot's* Letter to *Morvillier*. Correct, therefore, without Fear, this Falshood, in *de Saussai*. "Cæterum Amyotus, adhuc Abbas, ad Concilium Tridentinum ab Henrico II. missus fuit, negotiorum "magni momenti causâ (18). —— *But Amyot, yet "an Abbot, was dispatched by* Henry II. *to the Council of* Trent *upon Affairs of great Moment.*" *Henry* II. had no Part in This Transaction.

[E] *Made him Great Almoner of France, and Bishop of Auxerre.*] The first of these two Dignities was conferred

(11) Acad. des Sciences, Tom. 1. p. 166.

(12) S. Real, ubi supra, pg. 80.

(13) I express myself thus, because du Verdier Vau-Privas mentions an Edition of 1549. But this does not prove that it was the first.

(14) Sebast. Roulliard's Antiquities of Melun.

(15) Instructions and Letters of the Most Christian King, and other Papers relating to the Council of Trent.

(16) It is that, which the King wrote to the Fathers of the Council of Trent.

(17) Instructions and Letters, &c. pag. 23.

(18) Andr. Suassaius, da Scriptor. Eccles. n. 52.

AMYOT.

Almoner, and the Office of Curator of the University of *Paris*, were vacant at the same time, he presented him to them both. *Thuanus* complains very much of this Plurality *(f)*. *Henry* III. had perhaps yielded to the importunate Sollicitations of the Bishop of *St Flour*, who had followed him into *Poland*, and earnestly desired the Dignity of Great Almoner; but the Duchess of *Savoy*, the King's Aunt, so strongly recommended *Amyot* to him, when he passed through *Turin*, in his Return from *Poland*, that not only His Office was continued to him; but a new Lustre was added to it, in his Favour: for when *Henry* III. made *Amyot* Commander of the Order of the Holy Ghost *(g)*, he ordained that, in Consideration of his Merits, all the Great Almoners of *France* should, for the future, be, in virtue of their Office, Commanders of That Order. *Amyot*, in the midst of his Dignities did not neglect his Studies; he carefully revised all his Translations, and compared them with the *Greek* Text, and made many Alterations in them: in a word, he designed to publish a more perfect Edition, with the various Readings of the Manuscripts; but he did not live to finish this Work. The Civil Wars and the rebellious Spirit of the People of his Diocese gave him a thousand Disquiets *[G]*: He was robbed, in his Return from the States of *Blois*, in 1589. He died the 6th of *February* 1593, in his 79th Year *[H]*. He had preached sometimes on solemn Festival days. He made use of the *Latin* Tongue in composing his Sermons, though he spoke them in *French*. He had a very particular Custom in Preaching; He turned the Door of the Pulpit towards the People, and sat in the middle of it, on a great Chair. He attempted Poetry, but without Success *[I]*. This is what I have extracted out

---

ferred on *Amyot*, the sixth of *December*, 1560, by *Charles* IX. at *Orleans*. Du *Peyrat*, who had perused the Registers of the Great Almaners of *France*, mentions this Date as extracted out of the Registers of *Amyot* (19). It is therefore matter of Fact. Now by this means above one half of the History, which the Abbot *de St Real* relates concerning This Prelate's Fortune, comes to nothing. He says, that *Amyot*, in the Reign of his Pupils, *Francis* II. and *Charles* IX. had only the Abbey of *Bellosane*, with the Honour of having spoke the *judicious* and *bold* Protestation of *Henry* II. *before the whole Council*, and that his *Fortune would probably have stopped there, had it not been for a lucky Chance, which raised him higher than ever he had hoped for, and which wonderfully shews the Spirit of the Court*. This lucky Hit was This: It happened one Day, that, at That *Prince's* Table, *Charles* V. *was praised for several things, but chiefly for having made his Preceptor a Pope. — — This made such an Impression on Charles the Ninth's Mind, that he said, that upon Occasion he would do as much for his own. And, in fact, soon after the Place of Almoner of France became vacant, the King gave it to Amyot.* All this falls to the Ground, when we consult the Registers of this Great Office, in which we find the Post of Great Almoner conferred on *Amyot*, the second Day of the Reign of *Charles* IX. Besides, *Francis* II. was not a Disciple of *Amyot*, but of *Peter Dancs*. But to proceed; M. *de St Real* supposes, that the Queen-Mother, upon hearing what *Charles* IX. had done for his Preceptor, *sent for the latter into her Closet, where she received him with these dreadful Words*: " I have made the *Guises* and " the *Chatillons*, the Constables and the Chancellors, " the Kings of *Navarre*, and the Princes of *Condé*, " buckle to, and shall an insignificant little Priest " pretend to oppose me." *Notwithstanding the Submission of Amyot, the Conclusion was, That if he had the Office, he was not to live Twenty four Hours*. The Abbot says afterwards, that *Amyot* absconded, and that *Charles* IX. *immediately guessing at the Occasion of it, — — fell into such a Passion — — that the Queen, who had much ado to govern him, and who feared him, as much as she loved him, gave immediately Orders to look for Amyot*. This is to suppose, that *Charles* IX. had been King, long before he gave the Office to his Preceptor. But nothing can be more false; He gave it to him the next Day after his Accession to the Crown, before *Catherine de Medicis* had tasted of the Regency, and had exerted her Power over so many Persons. Every one knows how little Influence she had in the Reign of *Francis* II. After all, I allow the Reflexions of M. *de St Real*, on this Occasion, considered in themselves, to be fine and solid. As for the Bishoprick of *Auxerre*, it was not given to *Amyot* in the Year 1568, as *du Peyrat* affirms (20), but in the Year 1570 (21), after the Death of Cardinal *Pelisbert Babou*, who was possessed of it.

[F] All the Great Almoners of France were, for the future, to be, in Virtue of their Office, Commanders of That Order.] Another Author (22) gives this Account of it. " *Henry* III. in the Year 1578, instituting the Order of the Holy Ghost, ordained, " in * Favour of *Amyot*, that the Great Almoner, " and his Successors, should be associated in the same " Order with the Title of Commanders; who nevertheless *(say he)* shall not be obliged to prove " their Nobility; which he added, to gratify the " said *Amyot*, who was not of a noble Extraction, " but entered into the Temple of Honour through " that of Virtue." See in *du Saussay* (23), King *Henry* the Second's Answer to the Courtiers, who murmured at the Promotion of a Man of such mean Birth. The same Author says, that *Amyot* drew up, with Skill and Learning, the Statutes and Litanies, or rather the Office of the Order; *Hujus statuta & horarias preces scite & scienter composuit*.

[G] The rebellious Spirit of the People of his Diocese gave him a Thousand Disquiets.] Thuanus makes a Remark, very disadvantageous to the Memory of our *Amyot*; for he accuses him of having forgot the Favours, which the two Princes, his Pupils, had heaped upon him, and of having too much indulged the Seditious and Factious Rage of the Inhabitants of *Auxerre*. The Love of Study, together with old Age, induced him to reside upon his Diocese; and he had not the Courage to oppose the Torrent of Rebellion (24). *Sebastian Roulliard* does not speak of him in this manner; but insinuates that he was ill used for his Fidelity. " Afflictions, *say he* (25), overtook him, " when he left the States of *Blois*, in the Year 1589 " for, through the Fury of the Troubles, which grew " hot at that time, he was robbed and plundered " half-way in his return to *Auxerre*; and, being arrived there, he met with great Vexation from the " Inhabitants, and even his Clergy. At last, things " were pacified by Degrees; so that he continued " his Residence, but daily complained, that the Loss " of his Estate, and of the Conveniencies he enjoyed " before, deprived him of the Pleasure of Study." *Sammarthius* owns indeed, that some ill Reports had been spread, but does not believe them to be true (26).

[H] He died the sixth of February 1593, in his Seventy ninth Year.] Thuanus applied himself to Persons, very ill informed concerning *Amyot*, since they could neither tell him, when he died, nor at what Age. He says, in general, that *Amyot*, whose Death he places in the Month of *July*, 1591, was above sixty Years of Age. *Sammarthius* places it in the Year 1592. " *Triennio post Henricum tertium detestabili parricidarum coitione sublatum è vivis excessit* (27). — *He died three Years after the detestable Assassination of Henry III.*"

[I] He attempted Poetry, but without Success.] Sebastian Roulliard, his Countryman, would doubtless have spared him on this Head, if it had been possible. These are his Words: " As for the *Latin* " Poem,

AMYOT.

out of a Life of *Amyot*, begun by himself, and finished by his Secretary (*b*). His Translations are the best of his Compositions [*K*], though the Critics are not all favourable to him [*L*] upon this Account; some of whom tax him with Plagiarism [*M*]. Others have imputed Avarice to him [*N*]. The Abbot *de St Real* was acquainted with many curious Particulars, which are not in the Life of *Amyot* (*i*). They are to be seen in *Moreri's* Dictionary: Which is the Reason why I omit them, though I have no reason to question the Truth of them. If I have any Supplement, or Explication, to add to what I have said, I shall give them in the Remarks.

What *Varillas* relates concerning *Amyot* is full of Falshoods [*O*]. It stands in need of a Critical Examination; which may serve to disembroil the Chaos.

(b) It is in Latin, and has not been printed; but Seba'tian Roulliard Advocate in the Parliament of Paris, who resided it, published an Abstract of it in his Antiquitez de Melun, pag. 605. I have taken this Article from that Abstract.

(28) Roulliard's Antiquities of Melun, pag. 614.

(29) Id. ib.

(30) It is thus we must render the Poimenica of Thuanus, and not with du Ryer, The Poimenics of Longus.

(31) Baillet's Academy of Sciences, p. 368.

(32) Du Verdier Vau-Privas, Prosopograph. Tom. 3. p. 2572.

(33) Jugemdes Sçavans, Tom. 4. p. 421. See also Sir Thomas Pope Blount, Censura celebr. Aut. pag. 521.

(34) Thuan. Hist. L. 100. pag. 405.

(35) Girac's Reply to Costar, § 52. pag. 438. Dutch Edit.

* *Amiotus hic Poemenicos Longi, Heliodori Æthiopica, Diodori Siculi Historias, ac postremo Plutarchum in linguam nostram Gallicam de Græcis verterat, sed hunc majores elegantia quam fide, dum maribus nostris placere, quam de sensus veritate laborare, potius existimat. Thuan. de Vita sua, Lib. 5.*

† *L'Oiseau, de l'action hypotheque (Of Mortgaging) book 3. Τοῖς τε προϋπηρεγμενοις τῆς ὄψεις δυελὰς πελλαχᾶ ποσπηρότας. Quod sustulit signa oppignoratis Terris passim affixa.*

‖ *Marks or Signals to distinguish mortgaged Lands.*

"Poem, which he wrote on the Coronation of King
"*Charles* IX, it appears from thence that he had
"read *Horace* very much; but he would have proved
"a very indifferent Poet (28)." The Translation of
Greek Verses into *French*, to which *Amyot* confined
himself in his *Plutarch*, is frightful. *Charles* IX thought
it very coarse, *in which his Opinion was followed by
many others* (29). Roulliard alledges a pitiful excuse:
"It is, *says he*, a Collection out of several Authors,
"and of different Styles." His Opinion of *Amyot's*
Prose is This. "In short, *says he*, in my Opinion
"he was more happy in Translation, than in
"Composition, either in *French* or *Latin*: for what
"I have seen of the latter appears to me strangely
"heavy and dull."

[*K*] *His Translations are the best of his Compositions.*] The first was That of *The Loves of Theagenes* and *Chariclea*; but That of *Plutarch* procured him his chief Reputation. He translated likewise the Pastorals of *Longus* (30), several Books of *Diodorus Siculus*, and some *Greek* Tragedies. The Duchess of *Savoy*, not finding in *Plutarch* the Life of *Epaminondas*, nor that of *Scipio*, desired him to compose them. He did so; but they were not published. The Preface was ready. *Peter Matthieu* saw it (31), and therefore we may believe that *Amyot* had put the last hand to That Work. It is said (32), that he was afraid to undertake a Translation of *Philostratus*, though King *Henry* III. had often desired him to set about it; but he excused himself, on the Impossibility; and, when that Prince, having been the Version of *Vigenere*, said to *Amyot*, *Well, Sir! you told me that Philostratus could not be translated*; *Amyot* answered, that 'till then he had thought so.

[*L*] *The Critics are not all favourable to him.*] Mr *Baillet* has happily collected the Praises bestowed upon *Amyot's* Translation of *Plutarch* (33). These are fine and greatly to his Credit. I add to them what I heard Mr *Conrart* say in the Year 1675, upon being told, that most of the Copies of *Plutarch*, translated by the Abbot *Tallemant*, had been lost in the burning of a Bookseller's Warehouse; *The Loss*, said he, *will be easily born, whilst we have the Translation of Amyot, which contains the finest Turns of our Language, and the best Oeconomy of our Periods*. Mr *Baillet* has not been less careful in collecting the Censures of That Work: He did not forget, that *Thuanus* commends This Translator's Elegancy in his Versions of *Diodorus* and *Plutarch*, more than his Faithfulness. *Diodoro ac præcipue Plutarcho, licet majore plerumque elegantia quam fide, Gallice reddi tis* (34). But he forgot another Passage of *Thuanus*, mentioned by Mr *de Girac*. This last Author shall be the only one, whose Words I shall alledge, as a kind of Supplement to Mr *Baillet's* fine Collection; "As for *Epitimius*, *says he* (35), who is killed in
"*Amyot*, whereas in the *Greek* Text it is only his
"Horse; I should rather think, that this famous In
"terpreter made use of Copies, different from those
"at present, than say, as *Thuanus* does *, that *his
"Versions are much polite, than Faithful, and
"that he was not so curious after Truth, as studious,
"even to Affectation, of pleasing delicate Ears. I
"know that a learned † and wise Civilian charges
"him with not comprehending a fine Piece of An
"tiquity in relation to a Law of *Solon*; for, instead
"of saying, that this Lawgiver had boasted some
"where in his Poems, that he had delivered the
"*Athenians* from all the Debts they had contracted,
"and taken away the Wisps of lighted Straw, or
"Pennons ‖, which were fixed in many Places on
"Mortgaged Lands; he had rendered it *Removing the*
"*Boundaries* ‡, *which before separated the Inheri
"tances of the whole Territory of Attica*. I could
"add several Remarks on many Passages, in which
"good *Amyot* was mistaken; but I cannot commend
"Mr *de Meziriac*, who ** in a Discourse concerning
"Translations, *after having praised the Wit, Labour,
"and Style of this Eloquent Translator in his Version
"of Plutarch*, pretends to shew that he has grosly mi
"staken the Sense of Plutarch in *Two thousand Places*."

[*M*] *Some of whom tax him with Plagiarism*.] We have seen (36), what *Brantome* says on this Subject. Let us now see what others have said concerning it. "I have heard M. *Patin* say, *says* Mr *Colomies* (37), that he had it from the good Man *Lawrence Bochel* (who caused the Decrees of the *Gallican* Church, &c. to be printed) that *Amyot* had translated *Plutarch's* Lives from an old *Italian* Version in the King's Library, and that this was the Cause of the Faults he had committed. I cannot tell whether this Version be That, which *Baptist Alexander Jaconel* of *Rieti* made from the *Latin*, in the Year 1428, which is in the same Library." *La Popeliniere* censures *Amyot* for denying *Turnebus* the Honour which was due to him, in not informing the Public of the Assistance he had from him in understanding the difficult Passages (38). He pretends, that *Turnebus* sent him *whole Passages turned into French*, where *Amyot* was at a loss, and that several other learned Men assisted him with their good Advice (39).

[*N*] *Others have imputed Avarice to him.*] I have cited a long Passage of *Brantome* in the Remark [*A*], wherein *Charles* IX. taxes his Preceptor with this Fault. Another Book informs me, that *Amyot*, asking one Day a Benefice of a great Revenue, That Prince said to him, *How now Master? you told me, that if you had a thousand Crowns a Year, you would be satisfied; I believe you have that and more. Sir*, answered he, *Appetite comes by eating; and yet be obtained what be desired* (40). You may if you please look upon the Two hundred thousand Crowns, which he amassed, as an ambiguous Proof of his Avarice (41).

[*O*] *What Varillas relates — is full of Falshoods*.] He says, that, the Court of *Francis* I. stopping some Hours at the Castle of a Gentleman of *Berry*, *Amyot*, who was Preceptor in the Gentleman's House, "took
"Occasion to present to his Majesty an Epigram
"of four *Greek* Verses, which he had just composed.
"The learned Persons, who followed his Majesty,
"were so well pleased with the Epigram, that it
"was thought improper to leave the Author of it
"any longer in a Province so remote from *Paris*.
"The King took him into his Service, and gave
"him a considerable Pension (42). This whole Account is full of Transpositions of Circumstances; for we have seen (43), that the good Effect which some of *Amyot's Greek* Verses, presented to *Henry* II, produced, is attributed to *Michael de l' Hospital*. *Varillas* relates in another Book (44), that *Amyot*, Professor of the *Greek* Tongue at *Bourges*, made himself known to the Court *by his Politeness in writing French*, and that *Bouchetel* and *Morvillier*, Secretaries of State, recalled him at that time to *Paris*, and, having brought him back to *the Communion of the Catholick Church*, recommended him to Cardinal de *Tournon*, *who procured him the Abbey of Bellosane, and the Commission of Secretary to the Ambassador at Venice, from whence he set out to execute the King's Orders at Trent, in the Year* 1551. Thus this Historian refutes in one Book what he advances in another. He adds, that *Amyot* made a Speech before the Fathers of the Council: He gives the Substance of it, and quotes *Amyot's* Speech. But this Speech is a Chimera; *Amyot* only read the King's Protest. What Assurance is it to cite Manuscripts, which ne-

(i) See his Treatise of the Use of History. Mr Tessier has borrow'd from it whatever relates to Amyot, (always citing his Author) in his Additions to the Eloges taken from Thuanus, Tom. 2. pag. 152.

‡ The Word ὅρος signifies indifferently a Boundary, and a Mark of a Mortgage.

*** Pellisson's History of the Academy, p. 232.*

(36) Above, in Remark [A].

(37) Colomes, Opusc. pag. 124. Edit. of Utrecht.

(38) Popelin's Compleat Idea of History, lib. 3. pag. 259.

(39) History of Histories, pag. 359.

(40) Du Verdier's Prosopography, Tom. 3. pag. 2573.

(41) See Remark [A] at the end.

(42) Varillas's History of Hereſy, lib. 10. pag. 320. Dutch Edit.

(43) In Remark [C].

(44) Varillas's History of Henry II. lib. 2. pag. 204.

ver were in Being? *Varillas* affirms, that, at the Age of ten Years, *Amyot* was found fick on the Road to *Paris* lying near a Ditch, and that "a Gen- "tleman going by - - - - - - fet him upon his Horfe, "and carried him to a Houfe, which was near; where "he recovered, and was charitably furnifhed with "fixteen Pence for the Expences of his Journey "home; which he afterwards repaid with Ufury, "by leaving to the Heirs of his Benefactor Sixteen "hundred Crowns a Year (45)." 'Tis faid in *Amyot's* Life, that he left Twelve hundred Crowns to the Hofpital of *Orleans* (46). It was there that the Gen- tleman carried him; there he was cured; and there he received fixteen Pence: It was to That Hofpital that he *left afterwards a Legacy of Twelve hundred Crowns,* according to the Relation of Mr *de St Real* (47). Why does *Varillas* alter thefe Circumftances, and ex- aggerate *Amyot's* Gratitude? Why does he by his Hy- perboles convert a meer Legacy of Three thoufand fix hundred Livres into a yearly Rent of Six thou- fand two hundred Livres (48). He tells us, that "*Amyot,* being a Student, changed his Religion, "and was inftrumental in feducing his School-Fel- "lows; 'till, being difcovered, he fled to *Bourges*: "where the fame *Volmar,* who had inftructed *Cal- "vin* and *Beza,* procured him a Tutor's Place in "the Houfe of the Abbot of *St Ambrofe,* whofe

(45) Varil- las, ibid. p. 203.
(46) See Re- mark [*A*].
(47) St Real, of the Ufe of Hiftory, pag. 75.
(48) Varil- las, ibid. pag. 204.

"Nephews were committed to his Care; and "chofe him aftwards for his Succeffor in teaching "*Greek. Amyot* was foon weary of teaching pub- "lickly." This Account cannot be reconciled with the Memoirs of *Amyot's* Life, publifhed by *Sebaftian Roulliard.* We find there, that he was about Twen- ty three Years of Age, when he went to *Bourges* with the Abbot of *St Ambrofe,* who perfuaded him to undertake That Journey (49), and therefore he went thither in the Year 1537. Now *Volmar* left *Bourges* in the Year 1535 (50), and confequently it was not He, who introduced him to the Acquaintance of that Abbot. We find in the fame Memoirs, that *Amyot* filled the Profeffor's Place *ten Years,* and that *he was often heard to fay among his Friends, that he had a fufficient Maintenance; that he had never en- joyed better Times than thofe; and that he took great Delight in performing That Function, becaufe he was perfectly at his Eafe* (51). And therefore 'tis not true, that he was foon weary of teaching publickly. *Varillas* obferves, that *Bouchetel* and *Morvillier* re- prefented to him *the Obftacles, which his Herefy threw in the Way of his Salvation, and of his Fortune, and that he profited by their Advice. Bouchetel* knew him, then, to be a *Calvinift*; but would he, in fuch a Cafe, have made him Tutor to his Children, as he actually did (52)?

(49) Roul- liard.'s An- tiq. of Me- lun. p. 607.
(50) Melch. Adam. in Vitis Philo- foph. p. 253.
(51) Roul- liard, ubi fupra.
(52) Roffil- ard. ibid.

AMYRAUT (in *Latin* AMYRALDUS) (MOSES) Minifter, and Profeffor of Divinity, at *Saumur,* was one of the moft illuftrious Divines of *France,* in the XVIIth Century. He was of a good and ancient Family, which came originally from *Orleans* [*A*]; and he was born at *Bourgueil,* a fmall Town of *Touraine,* in the Month of *September,* 1596. Having performed his Courfe of Philofophy, he was fent to *Poitiers,* to ftudy the Civil Law; and applied himfelf to it with fo much diligence, that he fpent 14 Hours every day in Study. He became a Licentiate at the end of one Year (a), but proceeded no farther. Mr *Bouchereau* his Countryman, and Mini- fter of *Saumur,* advifed him to ftudy Divinity. The reading of *Calvin's Inftitutions* gave him an high Relifh for this Advice; fo that, having told his Father, who had his views in defigning him for the Bar [*B*], that he paffionately defired to be a Mini- fter, he obtained, though with much difficulty, the Confent, which he defired. He went to ftudy at *Saumur,* under *Cameron,* who loved and efteemed him in a particu- lar manner; and he was for a confiderable time a Student in Divinity. When he was admitted a Minifter, he was prefented to the Church of St *Aignan,* in the Country of *Maine,* where having lived eighteen Months, he was invited to *Saumur,* to fucceed Mr *Daillé,* who quitted his Poft, to be Minifter of *Charenton* (b). At the fame time, that the Church of *Saumur* defired to have him for their Minifter, the Acade- mical Council caft their Eyes upon him for the Profefforfhip of Divinity. By this means the Church of *Rouen* and *Tours,* who at the fame time requefted him of the Synod, were difappointed in their Hopes; for the National Synods had made a Re- gulation, that the Intereft of the Univerfities fhould be preferred to That of the Churches. His Admiffion to the Profefforfhip in 1633, his Examination, which preceded it, and his Inaugural *Thefis, de Sacerdotio Chrifti,* procured him great Ap- plaufe. Two other excellent Profeffors were admitted with him, to wit, *Lewis Cap- pel,* and *Jofhua de la Place*: Thus the Univerfity of *Saumur* obtained, at one and the fame time, Three Perfons who were extremely well qualified to make it flourifh; for, befides

(a) In 1616.

(b) *We find in* Mr Daillé's *Life, that he was invited to* Paris *in* 1626.

---

* A kind of Sheriff.

† The Ger- man Horfe, which came Into France, during the Regency of Catherine de Medicis.

(1) In his Notes upon fome Ex- tracts of Ed- ward De- ring's Speeches. That was printed at London, in 1649, with a Piece inti- tuled, Nun- cius à mor- tuis, (News from the Dead) which it is a Dialogue between the Ghofts of Henry VIII. and Charles I.

[*A*] *Of a good and ancient Family, which came ori- ginally from* Orleans.] His Great-Grand-father, *Ste- phen L'Amyrault,* was *Echevin** of *Orleans,* when the Common Law was reformed there in 1509. The Verbal Procefs of the Common Law proves this. It is pretended, that the firft of the Family was one *L'Amyrault,* on whofe Tomb is infcribed the Year 1370; which is to be feen in the Church of *St Pierre en Pont.* His Epitaph fays, that he came from *Ha- guenaw,* a Town of *Alface,* being Captain of a Com- pany of *Reifters* †. This Family were Benefactors to the Convent and Church of the *Minimes* at *Orleans*; and, as fuch, their Coat of Arms is to be feen upon the Glafs Windows of the Church. Let me obferve, by the way, that an *Englifhman* of the *Romifh* Com- munion has very ill latiniz'd the Name of *Amyraut*; for, inftead of *Amyraldus,* he calls him *Amurath.* This would be but a fmall Fault; if, by a cold and mean Allufion, he had not added to it a very ridicu- lous Doubt. "*Mofes* quidam *Amurath, fays he* (1), Mi- "nifter Salmurienfis, homo faltem nomine (nefcio an "& progenie) Judaeo-Turca - - - - - One Mofes Amu- "rath, Minifter of Saumur, *a Man, in Name at leaft* "(*if not by Birth*) *a Jew-Turk.*" In the following Pages he calls him *Amyrath.* The following Words of Father *Bartolocci* are very furprifing. "Mofes "Amyraldus, *fays he* (2), videtur *Judaeus Converfus* "*ad fidem,* fcriptifque eruditiffimam & Catholicum "differtationem de Myfterio Trinitatis, deque voci- "bus, & phrafibus, quibus tam in fcriptura, quam "apud Patres explicatur. *Pars IV. quae eft de Pri- "mordiis Revelationis Myfterii Trinitatis in veteri* "*Teftamento, habetur in libro Wagenfeilii infcripto,* "*Tela Ignea Satanae,* pag. 140. ——— Mofes Amyraut "*feems to have been a Jew,* converted to the Faith; "*he wrote a moft Learned and Catholic Differtation* "*on the Myftery of the Trinity, and on the Words and* "*Phrafes, by which it is explained, both in Scrip- "tures, and in the Writings of the Fathers. The* "*fourth Part, which treats of the Beginning of the Re- "velation of the Myftery of the Trinity, in the Old* "*Teftament, is to be found in a Book of* Wagenfeilius, "*entitled,* The Fiery Darts of Satan." Thus the moft famous Authors are fometimes unknown to one ano- ther. Father *Bartolocci,* not knowing Mr *Amyraut,* otherwife than by a Piece adopted by Mr *Wagen- feil,* took him in earneft for a converted *Jew.*

[*B*] *His Father, who had his Views in defigning him for the Bar.*] He intended him for the Office of Se- nefchal, poffeffed by his Uncle, who had no Children. [*C*] He

(2) Bartol. Biblioth. Rabin. Tome 4. pag. 66.

AMYRAUT. 261

besides their great Learning, there was a wonderful Sympathy between them; which produced a very useful and happy Agreement; a Circumstance, which deserves the greater Commendation, as it is rarely to be met with in Academic Land. Mr *Amyraut* was deputed to the National Synod of *Charenton* in the Year 1631. This Assembly chose him to make a Speech to the King, and to represent to his Majesty their Complaints concerning the Infractions of the Edicts. He was particularly charged to order it so, as not to deliver his Speech upon his Knees [C], as the Deputies of the last National Synod had done; and he managed the Affair with so much Dexterity and Resolution, that he was at last admitted to his Audience according to the ancient Usage, and according to the Desire of the Assembly (c). This Deputation brought him acquainted with Cardinal *de Richelieu*, who was surprized to find so many Qualities in him, which did not favour of the Man of Study. Some time after he published a Piece, wherein he explained the Mystery of Predestination and Grace, according to the Hypothesis of *Cameron* [D]. This Piece raised a kind of Civil War among the Protestant Divines of France [E]. They, who disliked this Hypothesis, decried it as a Novelty, especially when they saw the great *du Moulin* join them; who incessantly accused Mr *Amyraut* of opposing the Synod of *Dort*, and of favouring *Arminianism*. The Authority of this famous Divine, who had gained the Veneration

(c) *The Speech, which he made to the King, is inserted in the Mercure François for 1631.*

[C] *He was particularly charged to order it so, as not to deliver his Speech on his Knees.*] Mr *Amyraut* was the Person, who represented the State of the Question to the Synod; and who promised, at the same time, to make all possible Instances, if the Assembly gave him their Instructions about it. They charged him, then, to demand the Restoration of the Privilege, which the Ministers had enjoy'd, of speaking to his Majesty standing, as the Clergy of the Kingdom do. He went, accompanied by two Elders, to *Monceaux*, where the Court was; and, having applied to Monsr *de la Vrilliere*, Secretary of State, he understood from him, that the King expected, that the Deputies of the Synod should not address him in any other Manner, than those of the preceding Synod had done. There being always a Commissary on the part of the King in our Synods, he, who assisted at that Time in the National Synod of *Charenton*, had notified to the King, what they had commissioned the Deputies to ask; and, the Court not thinking fit to grant their Request, Monsr. *de la Vrilliere* was ordered to declare this Resolution immediately to the Deputies. Mr *Amyraut* represented to him very dextrously, and, at the same time, very respectfully, the Reasons of the Synod; and above a Fortnight passed without any Concessions on either Side. Cardinal *de Richelieu*, being informed of this Minister's Resolution, desired to confer with him on that Subject, and endeavoured to persuade him not to insist any longer upon it. He answered, and replied to all the most plausible Reasons alledged by the Cardinal; at last an Audience was granted, in the manner Mr *Amyraut* desired. The Cardinal discoursed several times with him concerning the Complaints of the Protestants, and was mightily pleased with this Minister's Wit and Behaviour.

[D] *He published a Piece, wherein he explained the Mystery of Predestination, according the Hypothesis of Cameron.*] A *Roman* Catholic of Quality occasioned this Piece. He had dined, with Mr *Amyraut*, at *Bourgueil*, at the Bishop of *Chartres*', to whom this Minister was very well known (3). After Dinner, he turned the Conversation upon a Matter of Controversy, and charged the Protestants with teaching very harsh Doctrines concerning Predestination. Mr *Amyraut* took up the Dispute; and there ensued a kind of Controversy, in a very civil way, between him and the Bishop of *Chartres*, on this difficult Question. The Evening being come, the Company parted: the next Day Mr *Amyraut*, in his return to *Saumur*, called upon the Person of Quality (4), as he had promised, and found him well affected to the Protestant Religion, but very unsatisfied with the Doctrine of Predestination, as *Calvin* had explained it. He removed his Scruples, as well as he could; and, in compliance with the Gentleman's Request, who desired him to write a Treatise, in which the Subject might be more fully discussed, than it could be in Conversation, he wrote and published (5) the Book, which I am speaking of. This is what I find in my Manuscript Memoirs. Mr *Amyraut* does not give this Reason for composing this Piece; he assigns another, which is very different (6).

[E] *A kind of Civil War among the Protestant Divines of France.*] This Dispute was considerable enough to furnish out a large Article in the Ecclesiastical Annals of the Protestants. The *English* Author of a very curious History of our Synods of France (7), can inform us of the Quarrels, which the Doctrine of Universal Grace raised there. I think it would be a cruel Reflexion, to say, that the first Movers of this Question would have done it, though they had foreseen all the Evils, which were to result from it: For where is the Use, the *Cui bono* of such Disputes? Will no Difficulty remain, provided the Hypothesis of *Cameron* be admitted? Is it not true, on the contrary, that there never was a Remedy more palliative than that? Something farther is wanting to satisfy Reason; and if you stop here, you might as well have staid where you was, and have stuck to *Particularism*. But granting, that *Universalism* has in some respects the Advantage, and furnishes the best Answers to some Objections; is that sufficient to counter-balance so many spiritual Crimes, which Factions draw after them, so many wicked Surmises, so many sinister Interpretations, so many false Imputations, so much Animosity, so many injurious Words, so many Libels, and so many other Confusions, which attend upon such a Theological War? If you believe, that *Particularism* damns People, you do well to refute it at any rate. I say the same to those, who may take *Universalism* to be a damnable Heresy. But, since, on either side, you do not pretend to relate a pernicious Opinion, dispute no farther than is consistent with the Public Peace; and be silent, when the Event shews you, that you divide Families, or that two Parties are forming. Continue not to rouze a thousand Passions, which ought to be chained up, like so many wild Beasts; and Wo be to you, if you are the Occasion of their breaking their Chains. Thank Heaven, the Civil War of universal Grace, and some others, have not deserved the Application, which was made, in my hearing, of some Verses to schismatical Disputes. The Preparations, and the auxiliary Troops of the two Leaders, were compared to these Decorations of the Stage.

(3) *He was of the House of Estampes Valençai, and was afterwards Archbishop of Rheims.*

(4) *At Plessis-Rideau.*

(5) *In 1634.*

(6) *Præfat. Speciminis Animadvers. de Gratia Universal.*

(7) *John Quick, a London Minister; His Book, intituled, Synodicon in Gallia reformata, was printed in Fol. 1692.*

A Reflexion on the Mischiefs occasioned by Theological Disputes.

Aigles, Vautours, Serpens, Griffons,
Hippocentaures, & Typhons,
Des taureaux furieux, dont la gueule beante
Eût transi de frayeur le grand cheval d' Atlante,
Un char que des dragons étincelans d' éclairs
Promenoient en fifflant par le vuide des airs,
Demogorgon encor à la triste figure,
Et l' Horreur & la Mort s'y voyoient en peinture (8).

*Theatric Horrors strike upon the Sight;
Eagles and Vultures on the Scene arise;
With hissing Serpents, winged Griffins join,
Typhons with Hippocentaurs: furious Bulls,
Whose gaping Mouths affright Atlanta's Horse;
A Car, by fiery Dragons drawn through Air,
With Demogorgon, dreadful to behold;
And Death and Horror close the pictur'd Scene.*

(8) *See Æschylus's Life, written by Tanaquil Faber.*

Mr *Amyraut* had the Satisfaction to be reconciled to his most violent Opposers; and, tho' it be not necessary, that the Great should always interpose in pacifying Quarrels;

ration of the People by many Books of Controversy, made such an Impression upon several Ministers, that, though Mr *Amyraut* had published a piece (*d*), in which he maintained, that *Calvin* had taught the Doctrine of Universal Grace, there appeared, in the National Synod of *Alençon* (*e*) several Deputies, charged with Instructions against Him; some of whom were so hot, that they talked of nothing but deposing him [*F*]. The Deputies of the Provinces beyond the *Loire* were the most violent against him. Nevertheless the Assembly, having heard Mr *Amyraut*, who explained his Opinion in several Sessions, and who solved the Difficulties, which were proposed to him, honourably acquitted him, and enjoyned a Silence in respect to these Questions, which was not too well observed. Complaints were made against Mr *Amyraut*, in the National Synod of *Charenton*, in 1645, *for having acted contrary to the Regulation*, which imposed this Silence; and He, in his turn, complained *of some Violations of the same Regulations* (*f*). The Assembly, *by an holy Amnesty*, suppressed these reciprocal Complaints, renewed the Injunctions of Silence, dismiss Mr *Amyraut* with Honour, and permitted him to oppose Foreigners, who should write against him, in what manner the Synod of *Anjou* should think proper. This Synod permitted him to publish an Answer to the three Volumes of *Spanhemius* concerning *Universal Grace* [*G*], which occasioned many other Books (*g*). During the National Synod of the Year 1645, Mr *Amyraut* was desired by the Assembly to enter into Conference with Mr *de la Milletiere*, in order to bring him over to His Opinion. The Conference continued several Days; but they did not come to a better Agreement in this oral Disputation, than they had done in the Books, which they had already published against each other. The Doctrine of Mr *de la Place* concerning Original Sin was attacked in That Synod. Mr *Amyraut*, hearing of it, appeared before the Assembly, to plead the Cause of his Colleague, and shewed, in a long Discourse, that the Doctrine complained of was not at all dangerous. This Action was not only extolled on account of the great Skill, with which the Doctrine of Mr *de la Place* was defended, but also because Mr *Amyraut's* only aim was the Interest of his Colleague; for his own Opinion in that point was not That of Mr *de la Place*. If I add, that Mr *Cappel* dissented from the common Opinion of the Protestants concerning the Antiquity of the Points of the *Hebrew* Text, I shall have mentioned all the Complaints, which were made against the Academy of *Saumur*. But, notwithstanding these Complaints, a great Number of Students in Divinity reforted thither; which visibly decreased, after the death of these three illustrious Professors (*h*). Mr *Amyraut* survived his two Colleagues, and had time to publish a very great

(*d*) *Intituled A Specimen of Calvin's Doctrine.*

(*e, In* 1637.

(*f*) Blondel, *A les authent. p.* 36.

(*g*) Blondel, *ibid. pag.* 40, 41.

(*h*) *They are the Authors of what is called Theses Salmurienses; a Work very much esteemed.*

Quarrels; yet the Prince of *Tarentum* imploy'd his good Offices in this Reconciliation, in the Year 1649. I know not whether the contending Parties gave him more trouble, than the Marshals of *France* meet with from the Differences, which fall under their Cognisance; however he succeeded in his Undertaking (9), and perhaps better than a Synod would have done. As to his Reconciliation with Mr *du Moulin*, it was brought about by Mr *de Langle*, Minister of *Rouen*. Upon the first Proposal, Mr *Amyraut* joyfully consented, and offered to make all the Advances. He wrote a Letter first; which Mr *du Moulin* answered very civilly. These letters were published for the Edification of the Church. They are dated in the Year 1655. Mr *Daillé* has inserted Mr *du Moulin's* Answer in one of his Books (10). Reason and Charity allow us to believe, that they, who made so much Noise, and raised so many Storms against a Doctrine, which they afterwards acknowledged to be harmless, and the Asserter of which seem'd at last, in their Opinion, a faithful Servant of God, did not die without being covered with Shame and Confusion, at least before the Throne of the Divine Majesty, when they reflected on that mortifying Prepossession, which had represented to them an innocent, inoffensive, Hypothesis, as a dangerous and shocking Doctrine. See what follows.

[*F*] *Some of whom were so hot, that they talked of nothing but deposing him.*] Had they lived thirty or forty Years longer, they must have been greatly mortified; for, at last, that Doctrine, which they judged worthy of the most thundering Anathema's, was found to be that of the greatest Men, who served the reformed Churches of *France*. It was the Doctrine of Mr *Mestrezat*, Mr *le Faucheur*, Mr *Blondel*, Mr *Daillé*, Mr *Claude*, Mr *du Bosc*. The *Particularists* were soon obliged to acknowledge the Favourers of *Universal Grace* for their Brethren, and faithful Ministers of *JESUS CHRIST*; and we have seen, that the *French* Ministers, who fled into *Holland*, and who sign'd a Formulary in the Synod of *Rotterdam*, in the Year 1686, were not obliged to make any Declaration, which reflected in the least upon the System of Mr *Amyraut* (11). From whence, then, came the Clamour, which was raised at first against

(9) He reconciled (in the Castle of Thouars, October 16, 1649) Mr Amyraut with Mr de Champvernou, Minister of Taillebourg, and with Mr Vincent, Minister of Rochelle. See the Actes Authentiques, by David Blondel, pag. 85. This Champvernou was called William Rivetus, and was the Brother of Andrew Rivetus, Professor of Divinity at Leyden.

(10) Vindiciæ Apologiæ, &c. pag. 418.

(11) See Remark [M] of the Article Doillé.

that System? Whence was it, that the same Doctrine was accounted at first a Monster, and afterwards an innocent Thing? Must we not in this acknowledge the Finger of Original Sin, and the Influence of a thousand dark Passions, which ought at last to produce in us, if we are of the Number of the Elect, a salutary and mortifying Humiliation? The worst is, Men do not profit by what is past; every Generation betrays the same Symptoms, sometimes in a greater, sometimes in a less Degree. For we shall often have occasion to say, when we see Cases, Denunciations, Apologies, and Disputations, take the Field, and whole Vollies of Books fly about;

Jamque faces & saxa volant—— (12).

Now Stones and Brands in rattling Vollies fly,
And all the Arms, which Fury can supply.
DRYDEN.

but let them alone; they will soon agree;

Hi motus animorum, atque hæc certamina tanta
Pulveris exigui jactu compressa quiescunt (13).

Yet all these dreadful Deeds, this deadly Fray,
A cast of scatter'd Dust will soon allay,
And undecided leave the Fortune of the Day.
DRYDEN.

But this cannot always be said. Things are sometimes carried to extremities: *Res in nervum erumpit*.

[*G*] *This Synod permitted him to publish an Answer to* Spanhemius's *three Volumes concerning* Universal Grace.] It is entituled, *Specimen Animadversionum in Exercitationes de Gratia Universali*; and was printed at *Saumur*, in 1648, in 4to. It is not true, as is inserted in the *Melange Critique*, Tom. I. pag. 129, that Mr *Amyraut* attack'd *Spanhemius* first, nor that his Work is against the Thesis of *Spanhemius*. It is against a Work of the latter, in three Volumes; who was likewise the Aggressor.

(12) Virgil. Æneid. lib. 1. ver. 154.

(13) Virgil. Georg. lib. 4. ver. 86.

[*H*] *He*

AMYRAUT. 263

great number of Books [*H*]. He wrote as readily as he spoke; and this is to say a great deal; for he had a surprizing Fluency of Tongue both in *Latin* and *French*, and as well in his Divinity Lectures, as in his Sermons. He knew the World; and could furnish a great Variety of Matter for Conversation, in Points, which did not belong to his Profession: And, doubtless, it was This, which contributed, as much, or more, than the Reputation of his Learning, to the Happiness he enjoyed, all his Life, of being considered and respected by the great Men of the Contrary Religion. I have already observed, that Cardinal *de Richelieu* had a great Esteem for him: I shall not add, that he communicated to him his Grand Design of re-uniting the two Churches [*I*]; for this would not be a sufficient Proof of his great Regard for him; since the Cardinal had founded several Ministers upon this Head, who were much inferior to *Amyraut*. The Marshal *de Breze* [*K*], and the Marshal *de la Meilleraie* [*L*], ought to be reckoned among the great Lords, who had a particular Esteem for our *Amyraut*. Mr *le Goux de la Berchere*, first President in the Parliament of *Burgundy* [*M*], and

---

[*H*] *He published a great Number of Books.*] He published his *Treatise of Religions* in 1631. Five Years after he published *six Sermons on the Nature, Extent, &c, of the Gospel*. He published several other Sermons at different Times. His Book concerning the *Elevation of Faith, and Abasement of Reason* appeared in 1641. The *Defence of Calvin in relation to the Doctrine of Absolute Reprobation* appeared in *Latin* the same Year, and in *French* in the Year 1644. He begun his *Paraphrases on the Scripture* in 1644. The *Epistle to the Romans* was paraphrased first; he then proceeded to the other *Epistles*, and concluded with the *Gospels*; but he had the Prudence, as well as *Calvin*, not to meddle with *St John's Revelation*. For fear his Name should hinder the *Roman* Catholics from reading his Paraphrases, he did not prefix it. In 1647, he published *an Apology for the Protestants*, a *Treatise of Free Will*, and another *De Secessione ab Ecclesia Romana, deque pace inter Evangelicos in negotio religionis constituenda*. He treated more amply afterwards of the Re-union of the *Calvinists* and *Lutherans*, in his *Irenicum*, printed in the Year 1662. His Book, *Of the Calling of Pastors*, was published in 1649. He preached on that Subject before the Prince of *Tarentum*, during the holding of a Provincial Synod, of which he was Moderator. This Prince desired that the Sermon might be printed, and that the Matter might be more amply treated; for it was a great Common-Place Topick among the Missionaries. For which Reason Mr *Amyraut* not only printed his Sermon, but published also a compleat Treatise on that important Controversy, and dedicated the whole to the Prince of *Tarentum*. His *Christian Morality*, in six Volumes in Octavo, the first of which was printed in the Year 1652, was the Product of the Conversation he had often had with Mr *de Villarnoul*, a Lord of extraordinary Merit, and one of the most learned Gentlemen of *Europe*, who was Heir, in this respect likewise, to Mr *du Plessis Mornai*, his Grandfather, by the Mother's Side. There are but few Subjects, on which Mr *Amyraut* did not write. He published a *Treatise of Dreams*; two Volumes concerning the *Millenium*, in which he refutes an Advocate of *Paris*, whose Name is Mr *de Launai*, who was a great *Chiliast* * (14); the Life of the brave *la Noue*, surnamed *Bras de fer*, i. e. *Iron-Arm*: and several other Works which I omit, or mention in the Sequel of this Article. He mounted likewise on *Parnassus*; for he wrote a Poem, entituled, *St Stephen's Apology to his Judges*. This Work was attack'd from a Quarter, which was the less to be dreaded for certain Reasons: for the Attack was not made by the Poets, but by the Missionaries. They pretended, that the Author had spoken *of the holy Sacrament of the Altar*, with the utmost Irreverence; but he published a Piece in his Vindication, of which I can say nothing more to the purpose, that what Mr *Daillé* has said of it. Let us hear him then. "As for *St Stephen's Apology to his Judges*, which you (15) make use of to "convict us of having abused your Sacrament; if you "and they, who are so much offended at it, had vouchsaf- "ed to read the Letter, which the Author has published "in Vindication of himself, you, and they, would "not have consented to ill an Opinion of it; nay, "you would perhaps have wondered at the Illusion, "which your Prejudices had produced in your Mind, "in pretending, that what he has written against the "Extravagancy of Pagan Idolatry, was meant of you "and your Transubstantiation (16)."

* Millenarian.

(14) *See pag. 129, 130. of Tom. 1. of M. Ancillon's Melange Critique de Literature.*

(15) *He addressed himself to Father Adam.*

(16) *Daillé, Reply to two Books of Adam and de Cottiby, part 2. chap. 17. p. 108.*

[*I*] *Cardinal* de Richelieu -------- *communicated to him his grand Design of re-uniting the two Churches.*] The Jesuit, who discoursed with Mr *Amyraut* upon this Subject, was Father *Audebert*. Mr *de Villeneuve*, who was, at that time, the King's Lieutenant at *Saumur*, having engaged them to dine together, and with so much Complaisance for the Minister, that he gave him the upper Hand of the Jesuit, and that no Grace was said at his Table for that Time, contrived it so, after Dinner, that they had a private Conference. It is true, Mr *Amyraut* declared he must necessarily communicate to his Collegues the whole Subject of their Conference. The Jesuit told him, that the King, and his Eminence, had sent him to make Proposals of Agreement in Matters of Religion; and then gave him to understand, that they would sacrifice to Peace the Invocation of Creatures, Purgatory, and the Merit of Works; that the Pope's Power should be limited, and that, if the Court of *Rome* should refuse to consent to it, they would take occasion from thence to create a Patriarch; that the Cup should be given to the Laity; and that, perhaps, they might give up some other Points, if they found a sincere Inclination in the Protestants to Peace and Re-union. But he declared, when Mr *Amyraut* mentioned the Doctrine of the Eucharist, that they were determined to make no Alteration in that; upon which the other replied, that, if so, there was an end of the Affair. Their Conversation lasted about four Hours; the Jesuit would have exacted Secrecy. But Mr *Amyraut* protested to him, that, according to the Declaration he had made at first to Mr *de Villeneuve*, he must communicate their Conference to his Collegues; but that he would answer for their Discretion. That very Evening he gave them an Account of the Conference, and made no scruple to speak of it, upon Occasion, after the Death of Cardinal *de Richelieu*, and Father *Audebert*.

[*K*] *The Marshal de Breze* ——— *had a particular Esteem for him.*] He was Governor of *Saumur*, and never went thither, without sending to desire Mr *Amyraut* to come and visit him. He often invited him to his Castle of *Milly*, where he commonly resided; and, when he received the News of the Death of his Son, the Duke of *Fronsac*, Admiral of *France*, he would always have Mr *Amyraut* near him. He received several Visits from him in his last Sickness, and even recommended himself to his Prayers, and desired to be prayed for in the Protestant Church of *Saumur*. He died in the Castle of *Milly*, in 1650.

[*L*] *The Marshal de la Meilleraie* ——— *had a particular Esteem for him.*] When he was a Protestant, he studied with Mr *Amyraut* at *Saumur*. He always remembered his old Acquaintance, and, the Day after his coming to *Saumur*, when the Court was there, in 1652, he sent to compliment this Minister; who did not fail to go and pay his Respects to him immediately; and he was received by him, as usual, with a thousand Marks of Esteem. This Marshal hearing of Mr *Amyraut's* last Sickness, sent a Gentleman to see him, and to tell him, that if his Gout would have permitted him to bear the Motion of a Coach, he would have paid him a Visit. He was at that time at his Castle of *Montreuil-Bellai*, four Leagues from *Saumur*.

[*M*] *Mr le Goux de la Berchere* ——— *first President in the Parliament of Burgundy, &c.*] He was exiled to *Saumur*, in the Year 1637, where he lived 'till the Year 1644. Being himself a Man of great Merit and Learning, he was fond of learned Men of

VOL. I.   U u   all

and the Intendants of the Province of *Anjou* [N], are of this Number; and we may add to them some Bishops and Archbishops [O], and, above all, Cardinal *Mazarine* [P], whose Civilities to this Professor were extraordinary. It is very probable he found Favour with this Cardinal, among other Reasons, because he declared openly for the Doctrine of the Obedience of Subjects to their Princes. His Declaration was of Use to the Court of *France*, during the Commotions, in which the Fortune of Cardinal *Mazarine* was so much tossed; and, on several other occasions, he shewed that it was his favourite Doctrine [Q], so far as to quarrel about it with a Minister of *Rochelle*

all Religions. He soon desired to be acquainted with Mr *Amyraut*, and found him so worthy of his Friendship, that they became very intimate. They saw each other commonly twice a Week; so that it is no wonder, if this Minister could supply some Memoirs for the Life of this President. It is not necessary to observe, that Mr *de la Berchere* died first President of the Parliament of *Grenoble*, and that his Brother succeeded him; but it may be proper to remark, that the latter, desiring to have his Brother's Life written, requested Mr *Amyraut* to communicate his Memoirs of the Particulars, which passed between them. Mr *Amyraut* sent him, among other things, the Account of the Conference, which he had with Father *Audebert*; for, as soon as the Report was spread in *Saumur*, that he had a private Conference with that Jesuit, Mr *de la Berchere* desired an Account of it from his own Mouth. Mr *Amyraut* recited a great part of it, and desired him not to mention it. That part of his Memoirs was not made use of in the Life of Mr *de la Berchere*, which was published. In 1648 he dedicated his Book, *Of the Rights of Marriage*, to that illustrious Magistrate, who was at that time first President of *Grenoble*.

[N] *The Intendants of the Province of* Anjou.] He never failed to wait upon them, and they all returned him his Visit, and shewed a great Respect for him. When he went, in 1658, to drink the Waters of *Bourbon*, he received many Civilities at *Bourges*, from Mr *Mandat*, Intendant of the Province. He might have lodged at that Intendant's House, who desired it. He dined, there, with the Archdeacon of *Bourges*, and some other Clergymen.

(1⁰) *In Remark* [D].

[O] *Bishops and Archbishops*] See what is said above (17), concerning the Bishop of *Chartres*. I add here, that, in the Year 1662, the Archbishop of *Paris*, *Hardouin de Perefixe*, being gone to *Saumur*, on a Vow, which the Queen-Mother had made to *Our Lady des Ardilliers* (18), sent Word to Mr *Amyraut*, that he should be very glad to see him. Mr *Amyraut* was very ready to pay him a Visit, but he let him know that he would not style him *My Lord*. The Archbishop, agreeing to this, received two Visits from this Minister, discoursed two Hours with him every time, and treated him very civilly. They talked, among other things, of Mr *Daillé's* Books, which the Prelate gave a good Character of, as to the Learning in them.

(18) *In the Church of the Fathers of the Oratory, at the End of a Suburb of Saumur.*

[P] *And above all Cardinal* Mazarine.] He came to *Saumur* in 1642, some Days after the King and the Queen-Mother; and, hearing, that a Sermon of Mr *Amyraut* had been much talked of at the Queen's Table, he desired the Count *de Comminges* to tell that Minister, that he should be very glad to be acquainted with him. This Count was Governor of *Saumur*, and had a great Affection for Mr *Amyraut*: He promised him, that the Protestants should meet on *Sundays* as usual, though the King was in the City; just he told him, at the same time, that they must omit their Assemblies the three first Days after the King's Arrival. This Promise was performed. Mr *Amyraut* preached on the *Sunday*, upon these Words, *Fear God, Honour the King*, and was heard by many Persons of the Court, who were very well satisfied with him, and spoke of his Sermon with Commendation, not only to the King, as soon as they came from Church, but likewise in the Evening, during the Queen's Supper. It was then, that Cardinal *Mazarine* heard of this Sermon, and was informed by Mr *de Comminges* of the Zeal, which Mr *Amyraut*, and all the Protestants of those Parts, had expressed for the King's Service in the last Troubles. The Cardinal was so desirous to see this Minister, that he sent him word of it the very next Morning, by the Judge of the Provostship: So that Mr *de Comminges*, finding that he was not the first Messenger, said to Mr *Amyraut*, smiling: *I see, Sir, that we shall soon stand in need of your Intercession with his Eminence; which*

will convince you of the Usefulness of the Invocation of Saints. The first Visit was very short; but Mr *Amyraut* was desired to come again the next Morning at eight o'Clock. The Cardinal shewed him all manner of Respect, made him sit near the Fire, talked with him about State-Affairs, gave him a particular Account of all the Efforts, which were used in *Xaintonge*, to bring over the Protestants to the Prince's Party, and desired him to endeavour to make all those Attempts useless. Mr *Amyraut* assured him, that there was nothing to fear from the Protestants of *France*, and that he would write to several Ministers of *Xaintonge*, to the end that the Synod, which they were speedily to hold, should authentically testify their Fidelity. The thing was performed. Two Days after this Audience, the Cardinal, under pretence of seeing the Protestant College, and the Library of Mr *du Plessis Mornay*, had another Conference with Mr *Amyraut*, in that Minister's Closet. They conversed about the Edict of *Nantes*, and, upon Mr *Amyraut's* being asked, whether *Henry* IV. was under an Obligation of making it, and answering yes, but that, if it were a meer Favour at first, the Observation of it would be indispensable at present; the Cardinal told him, he was in the right, and cited this Maxim of Law, *quod initio fuit voluntatis, ex post facto fit necessitatis*. i. e. *What at first is Voluntary, becomes afterwards Necessary*. The Reader will be pleased to find here, what Mr *de Guitaut* (19) said to Madam *de la Trimouille*, in the Queen's Presence. "His Eminence is with "the Minister *Amyraut*; they are both Ecclesiastics; "but I am sure they will not talk of Religion; his "Eminence will not find his Account in it." During the five Weeks that the King was at *Saumur*, Mr *Amyraut* paid the Cardinal several Visits, and was always kindly received by him; and, when he took his leave, his Eminence told him, that he might write to him directly, whenever he had any Request to make, either for the Party in general, or for his own private Interests. He made no use of this Permission, 'till after the Journey he took to *Paris*, about the end of the Year 1658. He saw his Eminence three or four times, who used him with great Civility. He spoke to him about the National Synod, the calling of which had been desired so many Years. The Cardinal answered, that the Reasons, which had prevented the granting of it, still subsisted, and desired Mr *Amyraut* to write to him about it. He did himself the Honour to write twice to him upon this Affair. The Cardinal answered him with his own Hand; and afterwards, whenever he returned him an Answer, he made use of his Secretary's Pen, but signed *Proprio pugno*, with his own Hand.

(19) *He was Captain of the Queen's Guard, and was Uncle to M. de Comminges.*

[Q] *And, on several other Occasions, he shewed, that it was his favourite Doctrine.*] In the Apology, which he published for the Protestants, in the Year 1647, he excuses their Civil Wars in *France*, as well as he can; but he declares, nevertheless, "That he will "not in any wise pretend to justify the taking up Arms "against one's Prince, upon any Occasion whatever, "—— and that he always believed it much more a"greeable to the Nature of the Gospel, and the "Practice of the Ancient Church, to have recourse "to no other Arms, than Patience, Tears, and "Prayers (20). —— And every time, *says he* (21), "that I reflect upon the History of our Fathers, I "cannot help sensibly regretting, that they did not "crown so many other fine Virtues, of which they "have left us Examples, with an Imitation of the "first Christians, in that invincible Patience, which "they shewed under the Persecutions of the Empe"rors." A *Latin* Piece (22) which he published two Years after, shews how he maintained his Cause against the Complaints of a Minister of *Rochelle*, who would have done better not to have taken notice of Mr *Amyraut's* Book, than to have taken Offence at it. The Book entituled, *Of the Sovereignty of Kings*, published

(20) *Apology for the Protestants, pag. 75.*

(21) *Ibid. pag. 76.*

(22) *Latinè, sive Epistolae Historicae Criminationes Mosis Amyraldi Defensio.*

AMYRAUT. 265

Rochelle (i): but this did not hinder him, at the same time, from declaring, that, in *Cases of Conscience*, a King is not to be obeyed [R]. I need not say, that he was much respected by the great Protestant Lords. This is sufficiently evident of itself. He quarrelled with a Minister of *Saumur*, whose Name was Mr *d'Huisseau*, and did not meet with all the Satisfaction, which he expected, in the National Synod of *Loudon* (k). It is thought, that his great Reputation was prejudicial to him on this occasion; like a great Tree, which shades the little ones, and whose Branches must therefore be lopped. Besides, the Relations of those, who had declared against the Doctrine of Universal Grace, favoured his Enemy as much as possible. He would, 'tis probable, have been one of those, who sat at the Table in This Synod [S]; to which he was deputed by his Province, if he had not been thought to be personally concerned in the Affairs of Mr *d'Huisseau* with the Church of *Saumur*. He died very christianly on the Eighth of *January* 1664 (l), and was interred with all the Academical Ceremonies. He had a great Command of Mind in his last Sickness, which gave him an Opportunity of making several very edifying Discourses, and of giving strong Proofs of his Faith, in the Presence of many Persons of both Religions. Among his other Virtues, his Charity to the Poor ought to be observed. He gave them the Salary of his Ministry during the Ten last Years of his Life. He gave Alms without distinction of Catholics and Reformed: the Mendicant Friars, who applied to him, never went away with empty hands; and he recommended to Mr *Hervart* (m) the Recollects of *Saumur*, when they had recourse to the King's Treasury for rebuilding their Cloyster, which was burnt: They thanked him for the good Effect of his Recommendation. He left but one Son, who was a very learned Advocate in the Parliament of *Paris*, and who fled to the *Hague*, after the Revocation of the Edict of *Nantes*. He had a Daughter, who died in 1645, Eighteen Months after her Marriage with *Bernard de Harmont*, who was afterwards the King's Advocate at *Saumur*. The Grief, which this Loss threw his Wife into, induced him to write a Treatise *of the State of the Faithful after Death*; which he dedicated to her. It was printed the Year after. The Reader will be pleased to see here the Distich which Mr *du Bosc* wrote with his own hand under a *Print* of Mr *Amyraut*. It is an Allusion to what the *Jews* have said in praise of the famous Rabbi *Moses Maimonides*.

(i) *Philip Vincent.*

(k) *In* 1659.

(l) *König in his Bibliothe. and Witte in his Diarium, places his Death (wrong) in 1665.*

(m) *Hervart Comptroller of the Finances.*

A Mose ad Mosem par Mosi non fuit ullus:
More, ore, & calamo, mirus uterque fuit.

From Moses down to Moses, none,
Among the Sons of Men,
With equal Lustre ever shone,
In Manners, Tongue, and Pen.

It published in 1650, on occasion of the Tragical Death of *Charles* I. King of *England*, is a yet stronger Proof of Mr *Amyraut's* Opinion in relation to Subjects taking up Arms against their Prince. There was no room to be silent; for the Catholics incessantly imputed this Tragedy to the Presbyterian Party, and drew a thousand odious Consequences from it against the Protestants of *France*. Mr *Amyraut* thought proper not to leave the Injustice of these Reproaches unanswered. During the Troubles of the last Minority, This Minister constantly exhorted the People, in his Sermons, to Obedience; and, being consulted in what manner to behave, he answered, *That the only way was to adhere to the Royal Party*. It is probable that the Persons, who consulted him, were sincere, and did not dive into the Artifice, which prevails in these kinds of Confusions. Rebels ever pretend, that their Aim is only to remedy Abuses, and drive away evil Counsellors from about their Master's Person. One must be very weak to be catched in this Trap, and to want the Opinion of a Casuist. The Distinction of the Pope and the Holy See is not so gross a Sophism. Lastly, Mr *Amyraut* spoke his Thoughts fully in the Epistle Dedicatory of his *Latin* Paraphrase on the *Psalms*. It is there that he maintains and lays down, that, according to the true Principles of Christianity, Subjects ought not to take up Arms against their Sovereigns. He declares openly for that which is called *Passive Obedience*. That Work was dedicated to *Charles* II. King of *England*, soon after That Prince's Restauration. The Author had made himself acquainted at *Paris* with one of that Prince's Chaplains, in the Year 1658. Two Years after, he expressed to him his Joy for the King's Restauration, and congratulated him on the Bishoprick of *Durham*. He was answered, that the King thanked him. This encouraged Mr *Amyraut* to dedicate to him his Paraphrase on the *Psalms*, but not 'till he knew from the Bishop of *Durham*, whether That Monarch would be pleased with it.

[R] *That, in Cases of Conscience, a King is not to be obeyed.*] This appeared, when the *Seneschal* of *Saumur* notified to him an *Arrêt* of the Council of State, which ordered all the Protestants to put out Hangings before their Houses on *Corpus Christi* Day. He communicated it to him, on the Eve of that Feast, and desired him to order the Protestants to conform to it, for fear their Disobedience should excite the People against them. Mr *Amyraut* answered, that, on the contrary, he was going to exhort his Flock, to put out no Hangings, and that he would be the first, who should refuse it; That he had always preached up Obedience to the Superior Powers; but that he never meant it in such things as concern the Conscience. Leaving the *Seneschal*, he went from House to House to exhort his Parishioners rather to suffer any thing, than to obey that *Arrêt*. The *Seneschal* caused it to be published with Sound of Trumpet; the Consistory met, thanked Mr *Amyraut* for his Conduct, and charged the Elders to take care that there should be no Hangings put out. The King's Lieutenant refused to assist the *Seneschal*, and prevented the Tumult, which began to be raised. The *Arrêt* was revoked some time after.

[S] *He would, 'tis probable, have been one of those, who sat at the Table, in this Synod.*] If all my Readers were *French* Protestants, this Remark would be unnecessary, but it will not be so to other Readers. In our Synods of *France* there were commonly four Persons, who formed what was called *the Table*. One of these four Persons was the President of the Company, and was called the *Moderator*, the other three were the Moderator's Assistant, the Secretary, and the Collector of the Acts.

[T] I

AMYRAUT. AMYRUTZES.

It was some Years after the Death of this Professor, that his Picture was engraved by his Son's Care (*n*).

Some Particulars concerning Mr *Amyraut* are to be found in a Work entituled *Melange Critique de Literature recueilli des Conversations de feu Mr* Ancillon (*o*).——— *A Critical Miscellany of Literature, collected from the Conversation of the late Mr* Ancillon; by which it appears, among other things, that a Passage in a Letter of Mr *Balzac* (*p*), wherein the Author of an Apology is much praised, is to be understood of him. We find also there, that *Patin* esteemed him very much: But take notice, that what is disobliging in *Patin*'s Letter does not relate to the Minister of *Saumur*. I shall take notice of this in a Remark, as also of some other trifling Mistakes [*T*].

[*T*] *I shall take Notice of it in a Remark, as also of some other trifling Mistakes.*] *Patin* says, in his Hundred and thirteenth Letter of the first Edition (23), " That there was a Physician of *Nyort*, in 1663, " whose Name was Mr *Lassaud*, who proposed to " publish an Apology for the Physicians, against those, " who accused them of trusting too much to Nature : " he says, that This Physician had principally in view " Mr *Amyraut*, a Minister of *Saumur*, who cast this " Reflexion upon them in the last Volume of his *Christian Morality*." ---- He seems (24) not to be very well satisfied with Mr *Amyraut* on this Account; for he adds, " If Mr *Amyraut* will be pleased to give " himself the trouble to answer that Book, he is " one who can say fine Things upon the Occasion, " which *Lassaud* is unacquainted with, and which " are not in his Book. I have suggested some " of them to him, *says he*, and among others, " fine Passages, and good Authorities; but he pays " no Regard to them" This plainly disgusted him; for he afterwards expresses himself thus : " And in- " deed he is in a Province, which is not far from " *Gascony*, where they are generally more vain than " learned, &c." I omit the rest of the Passage as it stands in Mr *Ancillon*, which is very disobliging; but I must inform my Readers, that the Person, so much abused by *Patin*, is the Physician of *Nyort*, and not the Divine, who makes the Subject of this Article. I must also acquaint them, that the *Treatise of Religion against those who think them indifferent*, is not Mr *Amyraut*'s only Book, of which there have been two Editions (25). I am very certain, that the Apology for the Protestants was printed more than once; that the Treatise of Predestination, printed in 1634, was reprinted at *Saumur* in the Year 1658, with the Specimen of *Calvin*'s Doctrine, and the Reply to Mr *de la Milletiere*, concerning his offer of a Friendly Conference to examine his Method for procuring a Reunion (*o*): that these two last Treatises had been published in the Year 1638, and that the Bookseller, who reprinted them in 1658, with the Treatise of Predestination, declares (26), that he republishes these three Books, because they were not to be met with. I am assured likewise, that eleven of *Amyraut*'s Sermons on several Texts of Scripture were reprinted in the Year 1653; that the Life of *la Noüe* was reprinted at *Leyden*: that the *Theses* of This Professor, and those of his Colleagues, were reprinted at *Geneva*; and that his Treatise of the State of the Faithful after Death, was printed at *Lindun* in *English*, and at *Utrecht* in *Dutch*.

AMYRUTZES (*a*), a Peripatetic Philosopher, born at *Trebizond*, was greatly esteemed in the Court of the Emperor *David*, his Master, and wrote in Favour of the *Greeks* against the Decisions of the Council of *Florence* (*b*); but he lost all his Reputation by his Apostasy. He was one of those, who accompanied the Emperor *David* to *Constantinople*, when *Mahomet* II. caused him to be brought thither, after the taking of *Trebizond*, in the Year 1461. This Philosopher, being gained over by the Promises of the *Sultan*, renounced Christianity, and turned *Turk*, with his Children ; one of whom, under the Name of *Mehemet-beg*, translated several Books of the Christians into *Arabic*, by order of *Mahomet* II. This Prince gave *Amyrutzes* considerable Employments in the Seraglio, and conversed sometimes about Learning and Matters of Religion with Him, or with *Mehemet-beg* (*c*). According to *Allatius*'s manner of Expression, one would be apt to take this Philosopher for *Groom of the Stole* to the Emperor of *Trebizond* [*A*]. I must not forget to observe, that *Amyrutzes* did not *then* begin to be in Esteem with Princes, when the Emperor of *Trebizond* honoured him with his Affection; for he had been a long time greatly respected in the Court of *Constantinople*. He was one of the chief learned Persons, whom the Emperor *John Paleologus* consulted about his Journey into *Italy* (*d*), and he accompanied that Emperor in his Expedition (*e*), as he himself relates (*f*) in his Account of what had passed in the Council of *Florence*, and which he inscribed to *Demetrius* Governor of *Napoli di Romania*. He affirms, among other things, that the Patriarch of *Constantinople* was strangled during the Session of that Council, and that the Physicians attested the Fact (*g*).

[*A*] *According to* Allatius' *manner of Expression, one would be apt to take him for Groom of the Stole to the Emperor.*] *Allatius*, in the Nine hundred and thirty sixth Page of his *Perpetuus consensus*, speaks only by Conjecture of the Book, which this *Amyrutzes* composed against the Council of *Florence* ; but, in the Additions, he tells us, that the Work itself was sent him from the Isle of *Chio* : Afterwards he says, that *Dorotheus*, Archbishop of *Monembasa*, * discovers the Condition of this Person *, cujusnam conditionis vir iste fuerit.* He inserts the Passage of *Dorotheus* in *Greek* and *Latin*. The *Greek* imports, that *Mahomet* caused the Emperor *David*, and some other Persons to embark for *Constantinople*, and among others τὸν φιλόσοφον Ἀμυρύτζην τὸν πρωτοβεστιάριον, *Philosophum Amyrutzium Protovestiarium*. Thus *Allatius* translates and Points. And therefore doubtless he believed, that *Amyrutzes*, and the *Protovestiarius*, were one and the same Person, and that he understands of him the Sequel of the Passage of *Dorotheus*, which informs us, that this Person was first Cousin of *Mahomet Bassa*, and that he had betrayed the Emperor *David*, and that, after the taking of *Trebizond*, he received great Honours from his Cousin, and from *Sultan Mahomet*; that he was Cunning, Tall, Well-shaped, a good Archer, and qualified for every thing. His Relation to *Mahomet* arose from his Mother's being *Mahomet*'s Mother's Sister ; these two Sisters were Daughters of *Jagrus*. I give no great Credit to this Account ; for I find that Mr *Guillet*, citing the *Turco-Græcia* of *Crusius*, says, that the Name of the *Protovestiarius* (*Groom of the Stole*) of the Emperor of *Trebizond* was *George*; that he was of a graceful Mien, and had such great Skill in Archery, that he surpassed therein all the *Greeks* and *Turks*; that he was the Son of a Daughter of a Christian Prince, called *Jagrus*, who had married his other Daughter in *Servia*, where she had a Son, who was the Renegado

AMMONIUS.

negado *Machmut* (1). I would willingly therefore place a *Comma*, in the Paſſage of *Dorotheus*, Ἀμυρῆσιν, in order to make This Philoſopher, and the *Protoveſtiari-us*, whom *Allatius* confounds together, Two Perſons.

AMMONIUS. Many Writers have been called by this Name. *Athenæus* cites two Works of a very different Nature, compoſed by an Author, whom he calls AMMONIUS. One of them treats of *Altars and Sacrifices* (a); the other of the *Courtezans of Athens* [A]. He does not poſitively ſay, that theſe two Books were wrote by the ſame *Ammonius*; neither does he ſay any thing, which intimates the contrary; beſides he makes no mention of the Author's Country, nor of the Age, in which he lived. We are informed by another Author, that he, who wrote the Book concerning *Altars and Sacrifices*, was a Native of *Lampria* (b) [B]. *Suidas*, ſuch as we have him at preſent, ſpeaks only of *Ammonius Saccas*: but, without doubt, he mentioned an *Ammonius* different from this; for what we find in his Dictionary cannot be applied to one and the ſame Perſon. It is impoſſible, that the ſame *Ammonius* ſhould have abjured the Chriſtian Faith, and have ſucceeded *Ariſtarchus* in the School of *Alexandria*, before the Reign of *Auguſtus*. Theſe are the two Particulars we find in *Suidas* concerning *Ammonius*. Was he ſo ignorant as to believe they were not inconſiſtent? I ſee no probability of it. One Author (c) conjectures, that there is an *Hiatus* in this Paſſage (d), and that *Suidas* might have ſpoken in this *Hiatus* of the *Ammonius* mentioned by *Athenæus*. If this were true, we muſt ſay, that the Treatiſe of Sacrifices and Altars, or that of the Courtezans of *Athens*, or both, were written by a Grammarian, who was *Ariſtarchus*'s Succeſſor. The ſecond AMMONIUS, I propoſe to ſpeak of, is a Philoſopher of *Egypt* (e). *Plutarch*, whoſe Preceptor he was, makes frequent mention of him. See particularly the 70th and 385th Pages of his *Moral Works* in the Edition of *Francfort* 1620. But it is falſely pretended in *Moreri*'s Dictionary, that he ſpeaks of him *with Praiſe, particularly towards the end of the Life of* Ariſtotle [C]. *Moreri* is not more ſucceſsful in his Account of AMMONIUS the Son of *Hermeas* [D]; to whom he attributes, among other Works, a Book compoſed in the Reign of *Valentinian*. That *Ammonius* was Son and Brother of a Philoſopher (f). The Learned believe, that he flouriſhed in the Reign of *Anaſtaſius*, in the beginning of the VIth Century; and that it is He who compoſed the Commentaries we have, under the Name of *Ammonius*, on ſome Treatiſes of *Ariſtotle*, and particularly on his Book *de Interpretatione* (g). The Author of this laſt Commentary ſays, at the beginning, that he was a Diſciple of *Proclus*. It is to him that ſome aſcribe the Life of *Ariſtotle*, which goes under the Name of *Ammonius* (h). He is the ſame, no doubt, who was refuted by *Zacharias Mitylenenſis*: See the Remark [H] of the following Article. He is likewiſe the ſame, of whom *Jonſius* (i) underſtands a Paſſage of *Photius*, in which he mentions One *Ammonius*, who took great Delight in explaining the old Poets, and making Critical Remarks on the *Greek* Language (k). This induces ſome to believe, that the Treatiſe *Of the Difference of* Greek *Words* ought to be aſcribed to him (l). But Mr *Menage* ſays, that *Herennius Philo* was the Author of it (m). The ſame *Ammonius*, to whom the abovementioned Paſſage of *Photius* relates, had an Aſs of a wonderful

[A] *Of the Courtezans of Athens* (1).] They, who, in theſe latter times, have wrote Books entituled *The Harlotry of* Rome, or of ſome other great City, were not original Authors. Antiquity ſaw many Works of this Nature, which are happily loſt. Not one of them is come down to us.

[B] *We are informed by another Author, that he who wrote the Book — was a Native of* Lampria.] We are not indebted to *Harpocration* for this Information, as Mr *Lloyd* affirms, but to the Author of the Book *De differentiis vocum*. *Voſſius*, and ſeveral others, call him *Ammonius*. If Mr *Lloyd* had tranſlated *Voſſius* right, he would not have ſaid, *Ammonius hiſtoricus ἐν τῷ περὶ βωμῶν καὶ θυσιῶν citatur ab Harpocratione in* Ἀμαζόνιον, uti & in voce Ἐσχάρα, *Ex quo etiam diſcimus Lampriensem fuiſſe, ut Gesnerus falſò Alexandrinum vocet*. — *Ammonius the Hiſtorian, in his Treatiſe of Altars and Sacrifices, is cited by* Harpocration *under the Words* Ἀμαζόνιον *and* Ἐσχάρα, *who informs us likewiſe, that he was of* Lampria; *for* Gesner *is miſtaken in ſaying that he was of* Alexandria. This is one of the Faults of the Abbreviators, which I have ſo often mentioned. *Voſſius*, having ſaid, as far as the Word Ἐσχάρα, what I have juſt now quoted from *Lloyd*, adds *ἐν πρώτῳ περὶ θυσιῶν ab Ammonio lib. de differ. voc. in* βωμός. *Ubi & Λαμπριενὺς fuiſſe dicitur, ut Gesnerus falſò Alexandrinum vocet* (2). *Lloyd*, being unwilling to transcribe the whole Paſſage of *Voſſius*, and having ſkipt a Line of it, fell into a great Miſtake; for it is not true, that *Harpocration* informs us, that *Ammonius*, whom he cites, was a Native of *Lampria*. If he had a mind to have omitted any part of it, he ſhould have left out the laſt Line, in which *Voſſius* tells an Untruth.

Gesner does not ſay, that *Ammonius*, the Author of the Book concerning Sacrifices, was an *Alexandrian*. There is a third Paſſage of *Harpocration* (3), in which our *Ammonius* is cited: Ἀμμώνιος δ' ἐν τετάρτῃ περὶ βωμῶν γράφει ταυτὶ: *Ammonius in the fourth Book of* Altars *writes theſe things*. The learned *Mauſſac* has thus corrected the Text of *Harpocration*; he puts βωμῶν (*Altars*) inſtead of κωμῶν (*Towns* or *Villages*), becauſe no one ever ſaid that this Author wrote a Book, *De oppidis vel pagis*. *Valeſius* approves of this Correction (4). One might conjecture, that, ſince *Ammonius* wrote a Book concerning the Courtezans of *Athens*, he likewiſe compoſed one of *Feaſts* or *Revellings*, περὶ κώμων: upon which Suppoſition, there will be no occaſion to pretend, that, according to the common reading of *Harpocration*, the Book of *Ammonius* related to the Towns, or the People, of *Attica*: Yet *Mauſſac*'s Correction appears to me highly probable. It appeared ſo to *Voſſius*, who mentions it as his own. *Valeſius* cites a Paſſage of the Scholiaſt upon *Hermogenes*, in which the Author of the Book concerning *Altars* is called *Ammonius of* Lampria (5).

[C] *It is falſly pretended in* Moreri's *Dictionary, that* Plutarch *ſpeaks of him with Praiſe, particularly towards the end of the Life of* Ariſtotle.] This Life of *Ariſtotle* is a Chimera. *Moreri* ſhould have ſaid *Themiſtocles*, and not *Ariſtotle*. Now it is true, indeed, that *Plutarch* mentions *Ammonius* at the end of the Life of *Themiſtocles*; but it is not true, that he praiſes him. He ſpeaks neither well nor ill of him.

[D] Moreri *is not more ſucceſsful in his Account* of Ammonius *the Son of* Hermeas.] He has committed at leaſt three or four groſs Faults. I. He is ignorant, that *Proclus* flouriſhed in the Reign of *Theodoſius the Younger*, and a long time after; for, if

AMMONIUS.

wonderful Taste for Poetry; for he would abstain from eating his Provender and suffer hunger, rather than interrupt his Attention, upon the reading of a Poem (*n*). The third AMMONIUS, of whom I intend to speak, was a Poet, who lived in the Vth Century. He composed a Poem on the War with *Gainas* King of the *Goths*, and, upon his repeating it before the Emperor *Theodosius* the younger, was greatly applauded (*o*). I propose to speak, in separate Articles, not only of some Moderns, who have born the Name of *Ammonius*, but likewise of an ancient Philosopher, who has given greater Lustre to it than all the rest.

(n) Phot. Biblioth. n. 241. ex Damascio, in Vita Isidori Philosophi.

(o) Socrates, Hist. Eccl. lib. 6. c. 6. & ex e. Niceph. lib. 13. cap. 6.

(6) Proclus *in the Reign of Julian; the second Ammonius, his Disciple, who wrote so well on Aristotle's Book of Interpretation, in the Reign of Valentinian. Rapin Compar. de Platon. & d'Aristote, pag. 391.*

he had known it, would he have said that *Ammonius*, Disciple of *Proclus*, wrote a Book *in the Reign of* Valentinian? Would he have been such a faithful Transcriber of Father *Rapin*'s Errors (6)? II. What a strange way is this of denoting Emperors? There were three of this Name; and the first must be understood to be meant, when we talk of *Valentinian* without any Addition. The first *Valentinian* died in the Year 375; judge then whether the Disciple of *Proclus* could write in That Emperor's Reign. III. If *Moreri* had understood the Author, whom he followed, I mean Father *Labbé*, he would have learned, that *Ammonius*, the Disciple of *Proclus*, and Son of *Hermeas*, flourished in the Reign of the Emperor *Anastasius*; who did not begin to reign 'till above thirty five Years after the Death of *Valentinian* III. IV. Father *Labbé* observes, that frequent mention is made of One *Ammonius* in the *Catenæ of the Greek Fathers* on St *John*'s Gospel, and other Books of the Scripture; and he believes, that *Ammonius*, the Son of *Hermeas*, is different from Him. Instead of this, Mr *Moreri* tells us, that some Authors ascribe the Explication of the *Greek* Fathers on the Gospel of St *John* to *Ammonius*, the Son of *Hermeas*.

AMMONIUS, firnamed *Saccas* [*A*], was one of the most famous Philosophers of his Time. He flourished about the beginning of the IIId Century. He was of *Alexandria*, and, as he was bred up in the Christian Faith from his Infancy, he persevered in it to the last, as his Works testify. *Eusebius*, who says this, accuses *Porphyry* of a manifest Falshood (*a*), in saying, that *Ammonius* renounced Christianity, in which he had been educated, and embraced the public Religion, when he was of Age to philosophize [*B*]. This great Philosopher gave a wonderful Lustre to the School of *Alexandria*, and put the Science, which he professed, upon an honourable Foot. He found it miserably depraved by the vain Subtilties of the Disputants. We have seen, in *Christendom*, what they are able to do; I say, we have seen it in the Controversies of the *Thomists* and *Scotists*, and of the *Realists* and *Nominalists*. They all professed to follow *Aristotle*, and yet they multiplied Disputes *in infinitum*. What can we think, then, of the Disputes, which prevailed in ancient times, when, the Philosophers, being divided into several Sects, under different Heads, some condemned *Plato*, and others *Aristotle*, &c.? It was a Chaos of mere Chicanery, which dishonoured the Profession. The right way to restore the Science to it's former Credit was to banish all useless Disputes, and to adhere to the Doctrines, in which *Plato* and his Disciples were agreed. No doubt they were the most certain, and consequently, the most important, Doctrines. This was the Reason, why *Ammonius* thought himself particularly obliged to reconcile these two Heads of Sects [*C*], and to clear up the Misunderstanding, on which their pretended Oppositions were built; and it is difficult to express the great Reputation he acquired by this manner of philosophizing. He was extoll'd as a Person inspired, as one taught by God [*D*]; and

(a) Euseb. Hist. Eccl. lib. 6. cap. 19.

[*A*] AMMONIUS, *firnamed Saccas*] *Ammianus Marcellinus* (1) and *Suidas* (2) witness, that he had this Sirname. It is generally believed, that, by his first Trade, he was a Carrier of Sacks, and *Suidas* is alledged in proof of it. These are the Words of the learned *Henry Valesius*: " *Saccas videtur ex eo* " *dictus Ammonius, quod mercibus ex portu Alex-* " *andrino comportandis victum sibi quæsivisset, cu-* " *jusmodi homines Saccarios antiqui vocabant; ut* " *videre est in Codice Th. tit. de Saccariis portus ur-* " *bis Romæ.* Suidas, πλοΐζων, inquit, μαΐνθής " Ἀμμώνιν τῷ πρώην γενομένω σακκοφόρῳ (3). —— " *Ammonius seems to have been firnamed Saccas*, " *because he gained his Living by carrying Goods from* " *the Port of* Alexandria; *which kind of Men were* " *called by the Ancients* Saccarii; *as may be seen in* " Cod. Th. tit. *Of the Saccarii of the Port of* Rome." Suidas says, *Plotinus*, a Disciple of *Ammonius*, who " was originally a Sack-Bearer."

(1) Amm. Marcell. lib. 22. circa fin.

(2) Suidas in Ἀμμώνιος.

(3) Henr. Valesius in Amm. Marcell. lib. 22.

[*B*] *A manifest Falshood, in saying that* Ammonius *renounced Christianity, - - - when he was of Age to philosophize*] Let us see the Original. "Ὅτε τῆ φρονήσει καὶ τῆς φιλοσοφίας ἥψατο, εὐθὺς πρὸς τὴν κατὰ νόμους πολιτείαν μετεβάλετο (4). —— *As soon as he was capable of thinking for himself, and had begun to taste Philosophy, he exchanged his manner of Life for That which was agreeable to the Laws.* Porphyry, *in saying this, was animated by the Spirit, which I have mentioned in the Remark [E] of the Article* ABULPHARAGIUS.

(4) Porphyr. lib. 3. adv. Christianos, apud Euseb. Hist. Eccl. lib. 6. c. 19.

[*C*] *Thought himself particularly obliged to reconcile these two Heads of Sects.*] We learn this from *Hierocles*, Author of a Book concerning Providence, of which we have some Extracts in the *Bibliotheque de Photius*. According to this Author, none but Men, governed by a Spirit of Contradiction, and an itching Desire of Disputation, or by their Prejudices, and the Darkness of their Minds, found any Disagreement between the Doctrines of *Plato* and *Aristotle*. Τὰς μὲν ἐκόντας ἑκυτοὶ καὶ ἀπονοία σφᾶς αὐτοὺς περικαταθέντας, τοὺς δὲ καὶ περιλίψει καὶ ἀμαθίᾳ δεδωκυμένες (5). —— *Some voluntarily giving themselves up to Strife and Malice, others enslaved to Prejudice and Ignorance.* The first of these kind of Disputants were very numerous, before the Light of *Ammonius* came to enlighten the World. " Donec Ammonii aliquando sapientia orbi illuxit, " quem etiam *divinitus eruditum* appellari prædicat. " Hunc enim veterum philosophorum opinionibus " perpurgatis, & refectis quæ utrimque excreverant " nugis, in præcipuis quibusque & maxime necessa- " riis dogmatibus concordem esse Platonis & Aristote- " lis sententiam demonstrasse (6). —— *Till at length the Philosophy of* Ammonius *shone upon the World, who, he tells us, was called the* Inspired. *For, having thoroughly purged the Doctrines of the old Philosophers, and pared off every useless Excrescence, he demonstrated, that* Plato *and* Aristotle *agreed in the principal and most important Points.*"

(5) Photii Biblioth. n. 214. p. 543.

[*D*] *He was extolled as a Person Inspired, as One taught by God.*] I have set down a Passage of *Hierocles*, wherein these Words are to be found "Ὃν καὶ θεοδίδακτον ἐπικαλεῖσθαί φαμεν, *who, he tells us, was called the* INSPIRED. I shall add another, in which the same Author relates, that the Followers of *Plato* and *Aristotle* were so fond of perpetuating their Quarrels, that they corrupted the Text of these two great Philosophers, to demonstrate more easily the Opposition between them. This Disorder, adds He, continued 'till the Time of *Ammonius*,

(6) Hierocl. apud Phot. ibid.

AMMONIUS.

and whom a Divine Inſtinct had guided into this Path. *Moreri* and many others were ignorant of the true Foundation of this Elogy [*E*]. Others are no leſs miſtaken, when they ſay, that *Ammonius* taught his Diſciples the Myſteries of the Goſpel, under the Seal of Secrecy [*F*]. Some have confounded his Theological Works with thoſe of other Writers [*G*]; but at laſt they have been diſtinguiſhed. He had, among other Scholars, *Plotinus* and *Origen*. He died about the Year 230 (*b*). I believe we ought to

(b) According to Cave, Hiſtor. Liter. pag. 72.

---

nius, the Diſciple of the great God; for, being carried away by an Enthuſiaſm in ſearch of Philoſophical Truth, he dived into the bottom of both Sects, and reconciled them together, and gave his Hearers, particularly his learned Equals, *Plotinus, Origen,* and their Succeſſors, a Syſtem of Philoſophy free from Strife and Contention. Ἕως Ἀμμωνίω τῶ θεοδιδάκτω· ἐπ᾽ αὐτῷ γὰρ πρῶτῳ ἐνθυσιάσας πρὸς τὸ τῆς φιλοσοφίας ἀληθινὸν, καὶ τὰς τῶν πολλῶν δόξας ὑπεριδὼν, τὰς πλεῖςον ὄνειδῷ φιλοσοφίᾳ περιεποιομένας, εἶδέ καλῶς τὰ ἑκατέρω, καὶ συνήγαγεν εἰς ἕνα καὶ τὸν αὐτὸν νῦν καὶ ἀπάσιασιν τὴν φιλοσοφίαν παραδέδωκε πᾶσι τοῖς αὐτῷ γνωρίμοις, μάλιςα δὲ τοῖς ἀρίςοις τῶν αὐτῷ συγγεγονότων Πλωτίνῳ καὶ Ὠριγένει καὶ τοῖς ἑξῆς ἀπὸ τούτων (7). *Uſque ad divinitus edoctum Ammonium. Hic enim primus æſtu quodam raptus ad Philoſophiæ veritatem, multorumque opiniones, qui magnum dedecus Philoſophiæ attulerunt, contemnens, utramque ſectam probe calluit, & in concordiam adduxit, & à contentionibus liberam Philoſophiam tradidit omnibus ſuis auditoribus, & maxime doctiſſimis æqualibus ſuis Plotino & Origeni & ſucceſſoribus.*

(*) Hierocl. apud. Phot. n. 251. pag. 1381.

[*E*] *Moreri and many others were ignorant of the true Foundation of this Elogy.*] According to Mr *Moreri, Ammonius* " applied himſelf more particularly " to the Divine Philoſophy of JESUS CHRIST. " He acquired ſuch an Eſteem by it, that he was " looked upon as a Man, who had been particularly " inſtructed by God, and for that Reaſon he had " the Name of *THEODIDACTUS* given him." He is miſtaken: I ſhall not not conteſt with *Ammonius* his Theological Learning; but certainly, it was not upon that Account, that he was called *Theodidactus*. He was honoured with this Title on Account of his Philoſophical Lectures, which ſpoke only of *Plato* and *Ariſtotle*, but made no mention of JESUS CHRIST and the Goſpel. His Auditors were divided; ſome profeſſed Paganiſm, and others Chriſtianity; and therefore it was neceſſary he ſhould ſet aſide Matters of Religion, and chiefly thoſe, which related to Piety. Would *Hierocles*, who was a Pagan Philoſopher, have expreſſed himſelf in the manner he has done, if the Knowledge of the Goſpel had procured *Ammonius* the Elogy we are ſpeaking of? I can eaſily believe, that *Ammonius* was not accounted a Chriſtian among the Pagans, and that it is This, which moved *Porphyry* to ſay, that *Ammonius* renounced Chriſtianity, as ſoon as he was capable of philoſophizing. He was known to be a Chriſtian among his Brethren, and gave Proofs of his Faith in certain Writings, which were, in all likelyhood, little known to the Pagans. Would *Plotinus* have followed *Ammonius* ſo long, if he had believed him to be an Enemy to the Eſtabliſhed Religion? The Chriſtians were not yet ſo conſiderable.

[*F*] *Others are no leſs miſtaken, when they ſay, that* Ammonius *taught his Diſciples the Myſteries of the Goſpel, under the Seal of Secrecy.*] I was ſurprized to find Father *Labbé* ſo greatly miſtaken in theſe Words. " *Idem Porphyrius, ſays he (8) in vita Plotini Platonicæ ſectæ Philoſophi, narrat Ammonium Religionis Chriſtianæ arcana diſcipulis ſuis ſub ſilentii religione communicaſſe, & Herennium, Origenem atque Plotinum obſtrinxiſſe, eumque Herennius primus eam fregiſſet, nec Originem nec Plotinum promiſſis ſtetiſſe.* —— *The ſame Porphyry, in the Life of Plotinus, a Philoſopher of the Platonic Sect, relates, that Ammonius communicated the Myſteries of the Chriſtian Religion, to his Diſciples, upon an Oath of Secrecy; which when Herennius had firſt broken, neither Origen nor Plotinus ſtood to their Promiſe.*" Here are two notorious Miſtakes: Firſt, it is not true, that *Ammonius* made his Diſciples ſwear not to impart to any one what they had learned of him. In the ſecond place, it is falſe, that *Porphyry* ſpeaks of any other Doctrines, but Thoſe of Philoſophy. All that he ſays may be reduced to this. *Erennius, Origen,* and *Plotinus,* had

(8) Labbé de Script. Eccl. Tom. 1. pag. 58.

agreed not to make public the Leſſons they had been taught by *Ammonius*, and which appeared to them to be greatly laboured, and very refined. *Plotinus* kept his Word; but *Erennius,* having broke his, was ſoon imitated by *Origen*. This is not a proper place to ſhew, that this *Origen* is not He, who wrote ſo many Books, and who ſo greatly allegorized the Scripture; but, as great part of my Readers may not have a *Plotinus* at hand, I ſhall ſet down his own Words. Ἐρεννίῳ δὲ καὶ Ὠριγένει καὶ Πλωτίνῳ συνθηκῶν γεγονυιῶν μηδὲν ἐκκαλύπτειν τῶν Ἀμμωνίῳ δογμάτων ἃ δὴ ἐν ταῖς ἀκροάσεσιν αὐτοῖς ἀνεκεκάθαρτο, ἔμενε καὶ ὁ Πλωτῖνῳ, συνὼν μέν τισι τῶν προσιόντων, τηρῶν δὲ ἀνέκπυστα τὰ παρὰ τῶ Ἀμμωνίω δόγματα. Ἐρεννίω δὲ πρῶτε τὰς συνθήκας παραβάντῷ, Ὠριγένης μὲν ἠκολούθει τῷ φθάσαντι Ἐρεννίῳ (9). *Cum vero Erennius & Origenes & Plotinus olim inter ſe conſtituiſſent, ne Ammonii dogmata ederent, quæ audita ab eo tanquam in primis purgata præcipue comprobaverant; Plotinus quidem ſtetit promiſſis, familiariter quidem nonnullos excipiens ſalutantes, inſtituta verò Ammonii ſecreta integraque conſervans. Erennius autem primus pacta diſſolvit, & Origenes anticipantem Erennum eſt deinde ſequutus.*" Another Cauſe of wonder is, that theſe two Faults of Father *Labbé* are to be found likewiſe in *Lucas Holſtenius* (10).

(9) Porphyr. in Vita Plotini.

[*G*] *Some have confounded his Theological Works with thoſe of other Writers.*] St *Jerom* places *Ammonius* among the Eccleſiaſtical Writers, and aſcribes to him, among other Works, the Invention of the Goſpel-Canons (11), and adds, that *Euſebius* copied after this Model upon a like Deſign. If this were true, *Euſebius* would be a great Impoſtor, ſince he affirms in a Letter (12), wherein he explains the Nature and Uſe of his ten Canons on the Harmony of the Goſpels, that he invented them, on occaſion of a Book of *Ammonius*. This Book is entituled, *Monoteſſaron*, or *Diateſſaron*. It's Difference from the Goſpel-Canons conſiſts in this. "Theſe Canons are only Indexes of the Paſſages of the Goſpels, which are " continued in one, two, three, or four Evangeliſts; " whereas *Ammonius*'s Harmony (*the ſame with the* " *Diateſſaron or Monoteſſaron*) contained the entire " Text of the four Evangeliſts, which *Euſebius* had " made uſe of in compiling his Canons; which related to this Harmony, and were in the Nature " of an Index to it (13)." 'Tis therefore a Miſtake to ſay, as *Moreri* does, that the *Goſpel Canons,* and the *Harmony of the Goſpel,* are the ſame thing. *Victor,* Biſhop of *Capua*; *Zacharias,* Biſhop of *Chryſopolis, Trithemius,* and ſeveral modern Authors, relying upon St *Jerom*'s Authority, and not attending to the abovementioned Letter of *Euſebius,* ſay, that *Ammonius* invented the Goſpel-Canons. Here is another Confuſion. There are in the *Bibliotheca Patrum* two Harmonies of the four Goſpels. One of them was aſcribed to *Tatian* by *Victor*, Biſhop of *Capua*, who tranſlated it into Latin (14) about the Year 545, and added a Preface to it (15). Hence it came to paſs, that the other Harmony was aſcribed to *Tatian* by the Biſhop of *Capua*, cannot be That Author's, ſince it contains all the Genealogies of JESUS CHRIST mentioned by the Evangeliſts; whereas *Tatian* left out of his Harmony all the Paſſages of the Goſpels, which ſhew that JESUS CHRIST ſprung from *David* (16). On the other hand, the Harmony, aſcribed to *Ammonius,* wants theſe Paſſages (17). *Sixtus Sieneſis, George Ederus,* and ſeveral others have followed *Victor*'s Error. But *Zacharias,* Biſhop of *Chryſopolis,* made it appear, above Five hundred Years ago, that *Ammonius* is the Author of That Harmony (18), which is *Baronius*'s Opinion. We ought to take particular notice of a Circumſtance, which we learn from Father *Oudin, viz.* that the Harmony, to which *Ammonius*'s Name is prefixed, which is in the *Bibliotheca Patrum,* printed in the Year 1575, and which has been tranſlated into Latin by *Ottomarus Luſtinius,* is neither *Ammonius*'s, nor *Tatian*'s

(10) Lucas Holſten. de Vita & Script. Porphyr. p. 28.

(11) Hieron. de Script. Eccl. c. 55.

(12) Ad Cardinalem; it is prefixed, with the ten Canons de Conſonantia quatuor Evangeliorum, to the Greek Teſtament of Rob. Stephens, Paris 1550. See Father Labbé de Script. Eccl. Tom. 1. p. 308. item pag. 58.

(13) Du Pin. Biblioth. Tom. 1. p. 130. Edit. Amſt.

(14) Oudin, Supplem. de Script. Eccl. pag. 216.

(15) Labbé, de Script. Eccleſ. Tom. 1. pag. 57.

(16) Euſebius and Theodoret affirm this. Labbé, ubi ſupra, p. 57.

(17) Cave, Hiſtor. Literar. p. 72.

(18) Comm. in eam Harmoniam, apud Labbé, ibid.

to distinguish him from the Peripatetic AMMONIUS [H], who was, according to *Philostratus*, the most learned, and the best read Man of his Age.

I find a very gross Mistake in one of the Commentators upon *Boëthius*. He says, Our *Ammonius* corrupted *Plato*'s Doctrine about the Eternity of the World more than any one else: but nothing can be more false, than this Accusation [I].

(19) *Oudin*, *ubi supra*. *Tatian*'s (19). We have lost *Ammonius*'s Book, *de consensu M.sis & Jesu*. If we may believe *Henry Valesius*, all his other Books are also lost: *Hujus Ammonii, quod sciam, hodie nihil extat*, says he, in his Commentary upon the last Chapter of the Twenty second Book of *Ammianus Marcellinus*. Had he forgot the *Harmony of the Gospels*, which is to be found in the *Bibliotheca Patrum*, or did he believe that *Ammonius* was not the Author of it? *Hadrian Valesius*, having made no Observation upon this in the second Edition, plainly shews, that he is of his Brother's Opinion.

[H] *I believe we ought to distinguish him from the Peripatetic* Ammonius.] A very learned Man seems not inclined to make this Distinction. " Hic esse vi- (20) *Hadr. Valesius in Amm. Marcell. lib. 22. pag. 344. Edit. Folio.* " detur, says he (20), Ammonius Peripateticus Phi- " losophus, quem πολυγραμματώτατον fuisse sae- " culi sui testatur Philostratus in Sophistae Hippo- " dromi vita, quo qui plura legisset neminem se " vidisse. —— *This seems to be the Peripatetic Phi- " losopher* Ammonius, *who, according to* Philostra- " tus, *in his Life of the Sophist* Hippodromus, *was " a Man of the most extensive Reading he had ever " met with*." But if he had attended to the Words of *Longinus*, inserted in *Plotinus*'s Life, he would have made no scruple to distinguish between these two Philosophers. *Longinus* observes, that some Philosophers composed Books, and others taught only *viva voce*. He mentions some of each of these two Classes; some are Platonists, others are Stoics or Peripatetics. He reckons *Ammonius* and *Origen* among those of the second Class, and says they followed *Plato*'s Philosophy. He adds that he was acquainted with them, and that they surpassed all the Philosophers of their Time. Οἷς ἡμεῖς τὸ πλεῖστον τοῦ χρόνου προσφοιτήσαμεν, ἀνδράσιν ἐκ ὀλίγω τῶν καθ᾽ ἑαυτοὺς εἰς σύνεσιν διενεγκόντες (21). *Quibuscum nos* (21) *Longinus, apud Porphyr. in Vita Plotini.* " *diu versati sumus, viris profecto intervallo non parvo " in sui saeculi Philosophos intelligentia superantibus*. Afterwards he names some Stoics, who belonged to the second Class of Philosophers, *viz.* of Those, who wrote nothing, or but very little. Lastly, he mentions two Peripatetics of the same Class, *viz.* *Ammonius* and *Ptolemy*, who exceeded all the learned Men of their Age in Philology: This he says particularly of *Ammonius*. Ἀμμώνιος καὶ Πτολεμαῖος φιλολογώτατοι μὲν τῶν καθ᾽ αὑτοὺς ἁπάντων γεγόνασι, καὶ μάλιστα ὁ Ἀμμώνιος· οὐ γὰρ ἐστιν ὅτις ἐκείνῳ γέγονεν εἰς πολυμαθείαν παραπλήσιος (22) *Id. ib.* (22). *Ammonius atque Ptolemaeus, disciplinarum am- " bo professi maxime omnium suo tempore pleni, prae- " sertim Ammonius: nullus enim ad disciplinarum illum " copiam prope accessisse videtur*. Here we have the Philosopher *Ammonius* mentioned by *Philostratus*; he is therefore a very different Person from Him, who taught Philosophy at *Alexandria*, and who was the Master of *Plotinus* and *Origen*. It appears from *Longinus*'s Letter, that these learned Peripatetics wrote only some Poems and Orations. This great Critic supposes they did not intend those Pieces for Posterity; for, says he, if they had, they would have been more exact in their Compositions.

[I] *Nothing can be more false than this Accusation.*] I shall set down the Words of the Commentator at large, that the Reader may the better understand his Error. " Nulla autem Platonis sententia est, " quam foedius corrupierint, & obstinatius defenderint, " veteres Platonis interpretes; seu quia eorum alii " ita sentirent, seu ut Christianam fidem impugna- " rent. Eorum signifer Ammonius fuit, fidus alio- " quin ac illustris doctrinae Platonicae assertor; quem " Zacharias dialogo, cui Ammonius titulus est, con- " futavit. Mox ejus discipuli, Plotinus passim libr. " suis; & quod mirum est, ne a magistro dissentiret, " fax illa fidei Origenes; cujus errorem S. Metho- " dius lib. περὶ τῶν γενητῶν, ut est apud Photium, " redarguit (23). —— *There is no Doctrine of* (23) *Ravattos Vallicus, Not. ad lib. 5. Boëtii de Consolat. Philosoph. pag. 96.* " Plato, *which has been more basely corrupted, and " more obstinately defended, by the ancient Interpre- " ters of* Plato, *than This: either because some of " them really thought so, or with a view of opposing " the Christian Faith. At the Head of these is* Am- " monius, *in other Respects a Faithful and Illustrious " Assertor of* Platonism; *whom* Zacharias *confuted " in his Dialogue entituled* Ammonius. *Next to " Him were His Disciples,* Plotinus *in several Parts " of his Works, and, what is wonderful, That Lumi- " nary of Faith,* Origen, *who would not differ from " his Master; whose Error* S. Methodius *refutes in " his Book* περὶ τῶν γενητῶν, *as it is in* Photius." You see plainly, that he speaks of *Ammonius*, who was *Origen*'s Master. Would he have been guilty of such an Oversight, if he had consulted the Originals, and if he had not cited the Treatise of *Zacharias* upon the Authority of Others? For we read at the very beginning of That Treatise, that *Ammonius*, against whom it was written, was still living, and taught at *Alexandria* with great Ostentation, after he had been *Proclus*'s Disciple at *Athens*. The Author, I mean *Zacharias* Bishop of *Mitylene*, lived in the VIth Century; for he assisted at the Council of *Constantinople*, in the Year 536; and therefore 'tis not true, that he confuted *Origen*'s Master. But it is true, that the Philosopher *Ammonius*, whom he refuted, taught, that God and the World were, and would always be, Co-eternal. This Book of *Zacharias* was translated out of *Greek* into *Latin* by *Genebrard*, and inserted in the *Bibliotheca Patrum* (24). (24) *It is in Vol. 4. of the Biblioth. Patrum, p. 33, &c. de Paris Ed. dictus 1644.* *Possevin* observes, that *Canisius* censures *Gesner*, for saying, that *Zacharias*'s Book *de Mundi Aeternitate* was different from That, which is entituled *Ammonius* (25). (25) *Possevin. Appar. Tom. 2. p. 352.* This Censure would be very well grounded with respect to *Simler*, who abridged *Gesner*: but it is unjust with respect to *Gesner* himself, who says, in express Words, that the Dialogue, entituled *Ammonius*, seems to him to be the Same with the Treatise *de Rerum Aeternitate*. I must observe, that I was surprized to find that a Heathen Philosopher was permitted to be a Professor at *Alexandria*, in the VIth Century, and to teach openly the *Eternity of the World*, in opposition to the Doctrine of the Christians. He was so far from concealing his Opinion, that he publickly maintained it in his Lectures, and no one could be ignorant that many of his Scholars imbibed This Doctrine. One of them (26), who was afterwards the chief Professor of Physic in That City, warmly maintained the Same Opinion. This appears from the Treatise of *Zacharias Mitylenensis*. (26) *His Name was Gessius. See the Biblioth. Patrum, Tom. 11. pag. 339.*

AMMONIUS (ANDREW) born at *Lucca*, went to seek his Fortune in *England*, towards the beginning of the XVIth Century, and would probably have advanced himself there, if he had lived longer [A]. He applied himself to polite Literature, and

[A] *Would probably have advanced himself there if he had lived longer.*] This is not my own Conjecture; it is the Sentiment of *Erasmus*. " Periit, (1) *Erasm. Epist. 24. lib. 2. pag. 332. scripta anno 1518.* " says he (1), & apud *Gallos* Faustus, & apud Bri- " tannos Andreas Ammonius, quorum alter diu reg- " navit Lutetiae, alter ad summam dignitatem emer- " surus erat, si vita diuturnior contigisset. —— *In " France died* Faustus, *in England Andrew* Ammo- " nius; *the former of whom flourished long at* Paris; " *the latter would have risen to the highest Honours,* " *had he enjoyed a longer Life*." He gave this Judgment of him, not only whilst the Wound was fresh, that is, when, a little after the Death of *Ammonius*, Affliction prompted him to celebrate his Praise, but even when a considerable number of Years had effaced the first Impressions of Regret and Sorrow. " Quam " multos, *says he in a Letter, which he wrote in " the Year* 1524 (2), hic ex vetere sodalitio desidero. " Primum Andream Ammonium Lucensem. Deum " immortalem quanta ingenii dexteritate, quam fideli " memoria (2) *Id. Ep. 5. lib. 23. p. 1210.*

AMMONIUS.

and *Latin* Poetry: His Merit, as an Author, arises chiefly from his *Latin* Verses [B]. *Erasmus* and He were intimate Friends, and maintained a constant Epistolary Correspondence. *Ammonius* lodged some time with Sir *Thomas More* (a), and afterwards in St *Thomas*'s Hospital (b), for he had not Money enough to hire, and keep, a House. He declared to *Erasmus*, that he repented of having left *Rome*, and that he was not very well pleased with his Condition in *England* (c). The Advice *Erasmus* gave him was very conformable to the fraudulent Ways, which are necessary to be used in advancing ones self in the World [C]; but we must suppose that *Erasmus* gave it only in jest. He wrote very fine Iambic Verses in his Praise, which shew, that *Ammonius* had a great many Perfections both of Body and Mind (d). But we must not rely much on Poëtical Elogies; *Erasmus*'s Prose (which we shall produce in our Remarks) will be a greater Confirmation of the Worth of his Friend. Fortune becoming more favourable to *Ammonius*, He was made Secretary to King *Henry* VIII (e), and had likewise a public Character in the Court of That Monarch, conferred upon him by Pope *Leo* X (f). Had he not died before the Age of Forty Years, he might have been advanced higher. He was in the Army in the Year 1513 (g), when the *English* gained the Battel of the *Spurs*, and took *Terouenne* and *Tournay*; he wrote Verses on these Victories, as also on that which they obtained over *James* IV, King of *Scotland*. He died of the Sweating Sickness in *England* [D], in the Year 1517 [E]. One of the greatest pieces

(a) Erasm. Epist. 2. lib. 8. pag. 408.
(b) Id. Epist. 23. pag. 422.
(c) Id. Epist. 25. pag. 426. Item Epist. 11. pag. 413.
(d) Id. Epist. 22. pag. 422.
(e) Balæus, apud Simlerum Epist. Gesneri.
(f) Andreæ Ammonius tuæ Sanctitatis apud Anglos Nuncius Iiteris significabit. — — Ammonius, your Holiness's Nuncio in England, will inform you by Letter. Erasm. Ep. 6. lib. 2. pag. 104.
(g) Id. Epist. 40. lib. 6. pag. 434.

" memoria præditum! Tum animus quàm erat ex-
" celsus, quàm alienus à livore, quàm alienus à sor-
" dibus! Hunc & suis dotibus & omni principum
" applausu florentem, maximis rebus destinatum, su-
" bita mors intercepit, natu minorem annis quadra-
" ginta. Cujus equidem decessum non possum non
" dolere, quoties in mentem venit quàm mihi fuerit
" jucunda ejus familiaritas. —— *How many of my
" old Acquaintance do I lament the Loss of in this
" Place? First, Andrew Ammonius of Lucca; a Man,
" blest with the Happiest Genius, and most Faithful
" Memory. Then his Mind, how free was it from
" Envy, how remote from every thing Low and Sordid!
" This Illustrious Man, flourishing by his own Abi-
" lities, and the general Applause of the Great, and
" destined to the highest Honours, was taken off by
" a sudden Death, before he was forty Years old. Whose
" Decease I cannot but lament, when I recollect how
" happy I was in his Acquaintance and Conversation.*"

[B] *His Merit, as an Author, arises chiefly from his Latin Verses.*] The Abridgment of *Gesner*'s *Bibliotheque* gives us this Catalogue of *Ammonius*'s Poems. *Scotici conflictus Historia* lib. 1. *Bucolica, seu Eclogæ* lib. 1. *De rebus nihili* lib. 1. *Panegyricus quidam* lib. 1. *Epigrammata* lib. 1. *Poëmata diversa* lib. 1. *Balæus* is quoted for it. What is called here *Panegyricus quidam* is a Poem on the Victories, which the *English* obtained, in the Year 1513, at the Battel of the *Spurs*, at the taking of *Terouenne*, *Tournay*, &c. *Erasmus* gives his Opinion of this Poem in a Letter (3) which is dated on St *Thomas*'s Day, 1510. This is an undeniable Proof, that sometimes they have added the date of his Letters without any care; besides they are misplaced. The Answer precedes, sometimes by several Pages, the Letter, which is the Subject of the Answer (4).

[C] *The Advice Erasmus gave him was very conformable to the fraudulent ways, which are necessary to be used in advancing ones self in the World.*] " Be
" ashamed of nothing, said he to him, interfere in
" every one's Business;

Coudoyez un chacun, point du tout de quartier (5).

Elbow each one; no Quarter ever give.

" make your Interest the Rule of your Love and
" Hatred; give nothing but to those, who will re-
" turn it with Usury; be complaisant to every one
" in every thing; have two Strings to your Bow;
" suborn some to invite you away; pretend you are
" going, and seem to prepare for your Departure;
" produce Letters, in which you are promised a thou-
" sand Advantages." " Principio perfrica frontem,
" ne quid usquam pudeat. Deinde omnibus omnium
" negociis te misce, protrude quemcunque potes cubi-
" to. Neminem nec ames nec oderis ex animo, sed
" omnia tuo compendio metiare. Ad hunc scopum
" omnia vitæ ratio spectet. Ne quid des, nisi unde
" speres fœnus: assentare omnibus omnia. At ista
" vulgaria sunt, inquis. Age quando ita vis, accipe
" peculiare consilium, sed heus in surem. Nosti τὴν
" Βερταυνικὴν ζηλοτυπίαν, hac in tuum bonum a-

" butere. Duabus sedeto sellis. Suborna diversos
" procos qui te ambiant. Minare & appara discessum.
" Ostende literas quibus magnis polliciris avocaris.
" Subducito te nonnunquam, ut subtracta copia de-
" siderium acuat (6)." *Alciatus* made use of the last mentioned Artifice (7).

[D] *He died of the Sweating-Sickness in England.*] Consult the History of the Divorce of *Henry* VIII. composed by Mr *le Grand*, and you will find there what kind of Sickness This was. It was called the *Sweat*, because People died Sweating. This kind of Plague began to be felt the first time in 1486, and was not known before. All the Remedies, which were used against it, were in vain, and it carried off a great Number of People, before the Physicians knew how to treat it. It was a Scourge, with which God was pleased at first to punish the *English* alone. In what place soever they were, they were attacked with it, without it's having any Effect upon Strangers, with whom they conversed (8)." Among the Proofs which Mr *le Grand* has produced (9), there are some Letters from the Bishop of *Bayonne*, the *French* Ambassador in *England*, which speak of this Disease. *Anne Bullen* was infected with it, as also that Ambassador. This Distemper had already infected, for some time, others besides the *English*; for our *Italian Ammonius* died of it in the Year 1517, notwithstanding the Hopes he had conceived of preserving himself from it by his great Sobriety. Sir *Thomas More* wrote to *Erasmus* about it in these Terms. " In his, (quod
" tibi quoque dolori esse doleo) Andrea nostro Am-
" monio, in quo & literæ & omnes boni magnam
" fecere jacturam. Is valdè sibi videbatur adversus
" contagionem victus moderatione munitus: qua fa-
" ctum putavit ut quum in nullum pene incideret
" cujus non tota familia laboraverat, neutiquam dubio
" è suis id malum attigerit; id quod mihi & multis
" præteres jactavit non admodum multis horis ante-
" quam extinctus est, nam hoc sudore nemo nisi pri-
" mo die perit. Ego uxoremque ac liberi adhuc intacti,
" reliqua familia tota revalvit. Hoc tibi affirmo, mi-
" nus periculi in acie quàm in urbe esse (10). *Among
" Those, who have died, is our Friend* Andrew
" Ammonius, *in whose Death Learning and all good
" Men have suffered a Loss. He thought he had suf-
" ficiently guarded against the Contagion by Sobriety
" and Moderation in his Diet; which was the Reason,
" as he thought, why none of his Domesticks had been
" visited with the Distemper, at the same time that
" he scarce met with any one, whose whole Family
" was not afflicted with it. This he boasted of to me
" and several others not many Hours before he died;
" for This Sweat is not mortal after the first Day.
" I and my Wife and Children have hitherto escaped;
" and the rest of my Family has recovered from it.
" This I affirm to you, that there is less danger in
" a Field of Battel, than in this City.*"

[E] *He died in the Year 1517.*] Sir *Thomas More*'s Letter, from whence I have just now cited a long Passage, is dated the nineteenth of *August*, 1520. It seems, then, as if *Ammonius* did not die in the Year 1517; for how unlikely is it that Sir *Thomas More* should

(3) The 20th of the 8th Book.
(4) See the Article CARMILIANUS.
(5) Moliere, in his Remerciment au Roi. The whole Passage is as follows: Jettez vous dans la foule, & tranchez du notable; Coudoyez un chacun, point du tout de Quartier; Poussez, Pressez, Fendez le Diable, Pour vous mettre le Premier.

(6) Erasm. Ep. 13 lib. 8. pag. 414.
(7) See the Remark [D] of the Article ALCIATUS.
(8) Le Grand's History of the Divorce of Henry VIII. He cites Goodwin.
(9) Ibid. Tom. 3. pag. 137, 152, &c.
(10) Mori Epist. 4. lib. 7. among those of Erasmus.

AMMONIUS. AMPHARES.

pieces of Service he did *Erasmus*, was his supplying him constantly with the best Wines at *Cambridge* [F]. He uses an hyperbolical Expression in one of his Letters, in which he says, that so many Heretics were daily burnt, that it raised the Price of Wood [G].

(11) *Ammonii mortem acerbissime fero.— I am greatly afflicted at the Death of Ammonius.* pag. 198.

(12) *Apud Simlerum Epit. Gesneri.*

(13) *The 23d of the 2d Book.*

should let three Years pass without taking any notice of it to *Erasmus?* I answer, that this Objection can be of no Force against the Letters, in which *Erasmus* himself mentions the Death of *Ammonius*. He observes in the Twenty fourth Letter of the second Book, and in the twentieth of the third Book, both dated in the Year 1518, that That Year was fatal to learned Men, as *Musurus, Paleottus, Pauftus, Andrelius*, and *Ammonius*. In the Thirty first Letter of the third Book, dated the ninth of *September*, 1517, he mentions *Ammonius's* Death (11). This Letter is dated right; for *Erasmus* mentions the Departure of the King of *Spain* as a Piece of News. Now it is well known, that the King set sail in the beginning of *September*, 1517. Let us say, then, that *Baleus* is mistaken one whole Year, when he places the Death of *Ammonius* in the Year 1518 (12). *Erasmus* might well say, in the Year 1518, that several great Men had died that Year. One of his Letters, in which he says so, is dated in *March*; when he said *this Year*, he meant the ten or twelve preceding Months. This is confirmed by a Letter of *Bombasius* (13), justly dated the sixth of *December*, 1517, in which we find, that *Musurus* died at *Rome* the last Autumn, and that *Paleottus* died eight Months before.

[F] *His supplying him constantly with the best Wines at* Cambridge.] The Letters of these Friends frequently mention the sending of Wine; but the following Passage proves, that *Erasmus* was not quite averse to this Liquor, and that he rather chose to stay in a Country infected with the Plague, than drink Water. "Simul atque Anglicum solum tetigi, ubi loco- "rum esses rogare cœpi, siquidem Cantabrigiensem "pestem fugere te scripsisti. Unus tamen Sixtinus "mihi dixit, te quidem Cantabrigiam ob pestem re- "liquisse, & concessisse nescio quo, ubi cum vini "penuria laborares, & eo carere gravius peste duceres, "Cantabrigiam repetiisse, atque inibi te nunc esse.

"O fortem Bassrei commilitonem, qui in summo "periculo ducem deserere nolueris (14). —— Upon "my first Arrival in England, I immediately enquired "the Place of your Abode; for you had informed me "by Letter, that you had left Cambridge for fear of "the Plague. Sixtinus at last told me, that you had "indeed left Cambridge for fear of the Plague, and "had retired I know not whither; but that, not meet- "ing with plenty of Wine, the want of which you e- "steemed worse than the Plague itself, you were re- "turned to Cambridge; and that you continue to re- "side there. O valiant Fellow-Soldier of Bassareus, "who in the greatest Danger didst refuse to desert "your Leader!" Thus *Ammonius* writes to *Erasmus*.

(14) [*Ammonius*, Epist. ad Erasm. inter Erasmi.] Epist. 40. lib. 2.

[G] *He uses an hyperbolical Expression in one of his Letters, in which he says, that so many Heretics were daily burnt, that it raised the Price of Wood.*] They were neither those Papists, nor Protestants, who ran equal Hazard of being punished in *England*, under King *Henry* VIII, after he had renounced the Pope's Supremacy, but another Set of Men; since the Letter, which mentions these Executions, is dated in the Month of *November*, 1511. The Flames could not extirpate their Opinions. Read this. "Lignorum "precium auctum esse non miror: multi quotidie "Hæretici holocaustum nobis præbent, plures ta- "men succrescunt. Quin & Frater Germanus mei "Thomæ, stipes verius quam homo, sectam (si diis "placet) & ipse instituit, & discipulos habet (15). —— "I do not wonder, that the Price of Wood is enhanced; "for though every Day afford us Holocausts of Here- "tics, yet more daily spring up. Even the Brother "of my Friend Sir Thomas More, a Stock rather "than a Man, is, forsooth, Author of a Sect, and "has his Followers."

(15) *Ammonius*, Epist. 8. lib. 8. inter Erasmi Lib.] pag. 410.

[* They were the Remains of the *Wicklissites*. See Burnet's *History of the Reformation*. Rem. Crit.]

(a) *Erasmus calls him so. Valerius Andreas says Levinus.*

(b) *Livinus Ammonius, vir eruditione juxta ac pietate insignis. Erasm. Epist. 23. lib. 28. pag. 2704.*

AMMONIUS (Livinus) (a) distinguished himself among the *Carthusians* in *Flanders*, not only by the Character of Procurator, with which he was honoured at *Ghent*, the Place of his Birth, but also by his Learning and Piety (b). *Erasmus* had a great Esteem for him; and it appears, by two Letters (c), which he wrote to him, that he thought he was free from the Prejudices and Passions of Persons of his Rank [A]. *Ammonius* discovered to him the Uneasiness of his Situation, and the Resolution he had taken to submit to the Hardship of his Condition. We may easily conjecture, that he could have wished for more leisure to improve his Mind and Studies. But his Superiors were not pleased that he should; they rather desired that he might be ignorant, and attend only to the external Observances of their Order. However, he had the Credit of being an Author: The Titles of his Works are to be seen in *Moreri*; but there is no depending upon the Citation of *Vander-Linden* [B].

(c) *The ninety fourth of the twentieth Book, and the twentieth of the Seventy fifth.*

[A] *Erasmus—thought he was free from the Prejudices and Passions of Persons of his Rank.*] If he had not, he would not have taken the Liberty of telling him, that, when he recollected what kind of Persons the Monks were, he could not help thinking, that the Enemy of Mankind had a share in the Institution of Monasteries; he added, that to these Places the Ignorant acquire the greatest Esteem by placing their Merit in the exact Observation of outward Ceremonies. "Quum interdum mecum reputo, Ammoni "charissime, cujusmodi ingenia premantur ac sepeli-

"antur in istis ceremoniis, interdum subit animum "cogitatio fortassis humana, istiusmodi vitæ erga- "stula non sine instinctu satanæ fuisse instituta. —— "Ac fere sit ut quo quisque indoctior stupidiorque "est, hoc in isto vitæ instituto pluris habeatur, tu- "midus fiducia ceremoniarum, & alieni spiritus ini- "quus æstimator (1)."

[B] *Upon the Citation of* Vander Linden.] This Author did not write the *Bibliotheca Belgica*; he is there put for *Valerius Andreas*. It was the *Bibliotheca Medicorum*, which he composed.

(1) *Erasm. Epist. 20. lib. 25. pag. 1361.*

(a) *In the Article* AGIS.

AMPHARES, one of the *Lacedemonian* Ephori, was the chief Instrument in the Tragical Death of King *Agis*. We have observed in another Place (a), that, after the Re-establishment of his Colleague *Leonidas*, This Prince took Sanctuary in a Temple. *Amphares* was one of those, who familiarly visited him there, and accompanied him, when he went from thence to the Bath, and back again to the Temple. As he was returning one day in this manner from the Bath, *Amphares* seized on him, and obliged him to appear before the *Ephori*, and give an account of his Conduct: He carried him by force to a Prison; The *Ephori*, and their Assistants, immediately repaired thither to set in Judgment upon the King. He assured them, that he had no other Intention than to settle Affairs on the same foot as *Lycurgus* had left them, and that he should never repent of so good a Design. Whereupon he was condemned to Death, and the Officers were commanded to conduct him to the

Place

AMPHARES. AMPHIARAUS.

Place of Execution *(b)*. The Officers thought it so strange and unheard of a thing to lay violent Hands on the Person of a King, that they expressed an Abhorrence of their Orders *(c)*, and *Demochares*, a Friend of *Amphares*, was obliged in Person to perform the Office. *Agesistrata*, the Mother of *Agis*, and her Mother *Archidamia*, came immediately to the Prison Doors, and requested, that This Prince might be permitted to plead his Cause before the People; which occasioned the Execution to be hastened. As soon as *Agis* was strangled, *Amphares* came out, and assured *Agesistrata* that no Injury should be offered to her Son, and that, if she pleased, she might go in and see him; the same Permission was granted to the Grand-mother; and both went into the Prison. *Amphares* caused *Archidamia* immediately to be hanged; and then ordered *Agesistrata* to be brought to the Place, where the Execution was performed. The first thing, which presented itself to the View of this Lady, was the dead Corps of her Son, extended on the Ground, and next that of her Mother yet hanging. She assisted the Executioners in taking her down, and laid her near the Body of *Agis*; then, kissing her Son, she cried out, *That he had undone himself, and drawn them into these Misfortunes, by his too great Lenity*. *Amphares*, hearing these Words, told her, *That since she approved the Conduct of Agis, she should be treated like him*. *Agesistrata*, without showing any Surprize, held out her Neck to the Executioner to be hanged, saying only, *That she wished all Things might turn to the Good and Welfare of her Country (d)*. The People were incens'd at such an extraordinary Piece of Cruelty, and murmured at it; but it was attended with no farther Consequences. Then was verified the Truth of a Maxim, which may by applied on several Occasions, *People clamour, and then are quiet*. The strongest Inducement to *Amphares* to perpetrate this Crime, was the Desire of not returning what *Agesistrata* had lent him. *Plutarch*, from whom I have borrow'd this Article, tells us what was said of the Execution of King *Agis* [A], which I set down according to my Promise *(e)*.

[A] *What was said of the Execution of King* Agis.] These three Executions did not put the People into such a Consternation, as prevented them from discovering that they were extremely afflicted at them, and that they detested *Leonidas* and *Amphares*. It was thought, that nothing more cruel or abominable had ever been perpetrated at *Lacedaemon*, since the Dorians came and peopled *Peloponnesus*. For their very Enemies shewed always, in Battel, a great regard for the Persons of the Kings of *Sparta*: and, when they saw them approach, they turned aside from them, out of Veneration for their Majesty: And hence it was that, in so many Battels, which the *Spartans* fought with the other People of *Greece*, before the Reign of *Philip*, the Father of *Alexander the Great*, there was but one King of Sparta killed (1). The *Messenians* were not allowed to say, that *Aristodemus* had killed *Theopompus*, but only that he had wounded him. *Agis* is the first King of *Lacedaemon*, who was put to death in the City; A Prince, who had entertained a very noble Design, and most worthy of his Country, and at an Age, in which those who commit Errors are generally excused. His Friends blamed him with more Justice, than his Enemies; his Friends, I say, who upbraided him for being too good Natur'd, and for having saved *Leonidas*, and trusted too much to others. His Mother's Words are remarkable, Ἡ πολλὴ ὅς, ὦ παῖ, εὐλάβεια καὶ τὸ πρᾷον καὶ φιλάνθρωπον ἀπώλεσέ μεθ᾽ ἡμῶν. *Your too great Moderation, Lenity, and good Nature, have ruined you, together with us*. This is what *Plutarch* informs us of, in the Life of *Agis*. I have relate it without adding or omitting any thing. Let me subjoin this Observation, That, upon a careful reading of History, it will appear, that more Princes have been dethroned for being too Good, or too Weak, than for being too Wicked. The latter find more Strength in their own Wickedness against the Plots of their Enemies, than the former do in the Justice of their Cause, and the Fidelity of their People. See the Remark [F], of the Article of EDWARD IV.

AMPHIARAUS, one of the greatest Prophets of *Paganism*, was the Son of *Oicles*, and Great-Grand-Son of *Melampus* [A], who had received part of the Kingdom of *Argos* as a Reward for a considerable piece of Service, which he did to the Women of that Country *(a)*. This Division of the Kingdom was a Source of Discord; the fatal Effects of which appeared in the Time of *Adrastus*, King of *Argos*, who found himself obliged to leave his Dominions, not being able to support himself against the Faction of *Amphiaraus* [B]. The latter had caused *Talaus*, the Father of *Adrastus*, to be put to Death, and had seized on the Crown *(c)*. This Quarrel was made up by the Marriage of *Amphiaraus* with *Eriphyle*, the Sister of *Adrastus*; upon which the latter was restored. I mention this in another place *(d)*; not forgetting the new Contests, in which *Eriphyle*, being appointed Judge, declared in Favour of *Adrastus*, to the Prejudice of her Husband. The Trick, which she put upon

[A] *And Great-Grand-Son of* Melampus.] This is the Genealogy of *Amphiaraus*. His Father *Oicles* was the Son of *Antiphates*, Son of *Melampus*, Son of *Amythaon*, Son of *Cretheus* and *Tyro*, who was the Daughter of *Salmoneus*, whose Great-Grand-father, by his Father's side, was *Deucalion* (1). This you will find in *Diodorus Siculus*. If you consult Homer (2), he will carry you no farther than to *Melampus*, Father of *Antiphates*, Father of *Oicles*, Father of *Amphiaraus*. Each of these two Authors makes *Melampus* to be the Great-Grand-father of *Amphiaraus*; but he is only his Grand-father, in the Scholiast upon *Æschylus*; who reckons the Descent thus. *Amphiaraus*, the Son of *Oicles*, Son of *Melampus*, Son of *Amythaon*, Son of *Cretheus*, Son of *Æolus*, Son of *Hellen*, Son of *Jupiter* (3). Let us remember, that *Hypermnestra* (4), Daughter of *Thestius* (5), was the Mother of *Amphiaraus*, and that some Authors say he was the Son of *Apollo* (6). Note, That we read in *Apollodorus*, as also in the Scholiast upon *Æschylus*, that *Cretheus* was the Son of *Æolus* (7), and therefore he was the Brother of *Salmoneus*, and of *Sisyphus*, &c. Before he married his Niece *Tyro*, he had had Twins, *Pelias* and *Neleus*, by *Neptune* (8). He had three Sons by her, *Æton*, *Amythaon*, and *Pheres* (9). The eldest was the Father of *Jason*. Consult *Apollodorus*, who will inform you, that *Amphiaraus* was related to most of the illustrious Persons of *Greece*.

[B] *He*

AMPHIARAUS.

upon her Husband, at the Time of the Preparation for the *Theban* Expedition, was a villanous Action. *Amphiaraus*, discovering by his prophetic Spirit, that he should perish in this War, concealed himself, and refused to go; but his Wife, being bribed by a Present, discovered where he was (*e*). He was obliged, therefore, against his Will, to accompany the other Princes to the Expedition of *Thebes*; which proved unfortunate; and he perished in it after a very extraordinary Manner; for, the Earth being opened by a Thunder-bolt, he was swallowed up in the Abyss, with his Chariot [*B*]. They (*f*) who pretend, that this Misfortune happend to him the same Day

(*e*) See the Article ALCMÆON, Son of AMPHIARAUS.

(*f*) Charles Stephens, and Lloyd, in their *Dictionaries*. Oliveri et Cruserius, Vit. Max. lib. I. sub. finem, and many others.

[*B*] *He was swallowed up in the Abyss, with his Chariot.*] *Pindar* and *Apollodorus*, are among those who say that a Thunder-bolt opened the Earth, and that it was a Stroke of Favour from *Jupiter*; for otherwise *Amphiaraus* would have had the Disgrace of being killed by *Periclymenus*, who pursued him.

---- ὁ δ᾽ Ἀμφιαρηῒ
σχίσεν κεραυνῷ παμϐίᾳ
Ζεὺς τὰν βαθύστερνον χθόνα,
κρύψεν δ᾽ ἅμ᾽ ἵπποις,
Περὶ Περικλυμένῳ πρὶν
νῶτα τυπέντα μαχατὰν
θυμὸν αἰσχυνθῆμεν (10).

(10) Pindar, Nemeor. Od. 9. pag. 611, 612. See Apollodorus, lib. 3. pag. 193.

Jove *saw* Amphiarus' *threatned Shame,*
And *darted from on high the missive Flame.*
The *Womb of Earth, disclosing at the Blow,*
Absorpt *the Hero to the Shades below,*
Quick *with his Car descending; 'ere the Spear*
Of *Periclymenus, approaching near,*
Had *in his Back infix'd the Coward Wound,*
And *an inglorious Death the warlike Chief had found.*

You find in this, and another Passage of the same Poet (11), that *Amphiaraus* and his Chariot fell both together into the Precipice. This is the most general Tradition (12): But others pretend, that he fell from his Chariot during the Battle, and that the Chariot was afterwards transported empty to another Place (13). Their Reason is, because the Temple of *Amphiaraus* was but a little distant from a certain Village, which was called *Harma* [*], and which borrowed it's Name from his Chariot. They pretended, that the Temple was built where the Prophet died, and that the Village *Harma* was built where the Chariot was transported (14). *Pausanias* calls it a Town, and says expresly, that it was built, where it is pretended that the Earth had swallowed up *Amphiaraus* and his Chariot (15). This was the Pretension of the *Tanagrians*; for those of *Thebes* shewed another Place, situate on the great Road from *Potniæ* to *Thebes*, and encompassed with Columns, concerning which they related two pleasant Miracles. One was, that the Birds never perched on those Columnes; the other, that no Beast touched the Grass, which grew in that Place (16). *Stephen* of *Byzantium*, in mentioning the Town of *Harma*, entirely contradicts the Tradition, and the very Author, whom he cites (17); for he asserts, that this Town was so called, because it was said, that *Amphiaraus* retreated thither in his Chariot, and that the Inhabitants would not deliver him up to those, who pursued him (18). Is not this to pretend, that he saved his Life, and to give the Lye to a great number of Authors, who tell us, that he was swallowed up in the Bowels of the Earth? The great *Salmasius* imagined, that there are wanting two or three Words in this Article of *Stephens*; namely, that, after mentioning the Chariot of *Amphiaraus*, he turned the Discourse to that of *Adrastus*; so that what relates to the Refusal of the Inhabitants, must be referred to the latter (19). This Conjecture is ingenious, and may be confirmed by a Passage of *Strabo*, where it is said, that the Inhabitants of *Harma*, in *Bœotia*, saved the Life of *Adrastus*, after his Chariot had been broke in that Place (20). The like Conjecture cannot be made in Favour of *Eustathius*. It must be affirmed, without any Hesitation, that, according to his Account (21), the Chief, whom the Inhabitants of *Harma* saved, was *Amphiaraus*, and not *Adrastus*.

Note, That *Strabo* has committed a Mistake, which *Salmasius* has not failed to censure. Ἐνταῦθα δὲ σὺ καὶ τὸ Ἀμφιαράειόν ἐστι τετιμημένον ποτὲ μαν-

(11) Id. Pind. Od. 6. Olymp. pag. 98.

(12) See Diodorus Siculus, lib. 4. cap. 68.

(13) Strabo, lib. 9. pag. 2, 8.

[*] *Ἅρμα*, in Greek, signifies a Chariot.

(14) Id. ib.

(15) Pausan. lib. 9. pag. 296.

(16) Id. ib. pag. 288.

(17) *He quotes the 9th Book of Pausanias.*

(18) Steph. Byzantin. in voce Ἅρμα.

(19) *See* Berkelius's *Notes upon this Passage of* Steph. Byzant.

(20) Strabo, lib. 9. pag. 278.

(21) Eustathius, in Il. Lib. 2. pag. 266.

τεῖον, ὅτε φυγιόντα τὸν, Ἀμφιάρεων, ὡς φησὶ Σοφοκλῆς,

Ἐδέξατο ῥαγεῖσα Θηϐαία κόνις,
Αὐτοῖσιν ὅπλοις, καὶ τετραρύμῳ δίφρῳ (22).

Near *which Place was the Oracle of Amphiaraus, formerly had in Veneration, where, according to Sophocles,*

*The Theban Earth, wide opening, swallowed down
The sinking Chief, his Chariot, and his Arms.*

Strabo would prove, that the Oracle of *Amphiaraus*, in the Territory of *Oropus*, was situated in the same Place, where this Prophet was swallowed up by the Earth; and, as a Proof of this, he cites two Verses of *Sophocles*, which testify, that the Earth opened itself in the Territory of *Thebes*, to swallow up *Amphiaraus* and his Chariot. *Salmasius* censures this with a great deal of Reason (23). *Isaac Vossius* has taken *Strabo*'s part; but, on this Occasion, he has made it appear, that too eager a Desire of finding Faults in the Writings of an Adversary is a dangerous guide. "Desinat quoque mirari, *says he* (24), quod multi "Oropum urbem in regione sive agro Thebano col- "locarint. Recte enim hoc ab illis factum, cum "Oropus non sui juris, sed propria fuerit Thebano- "rum. Hoc manifestè Dicæarchus docet, ἃ δέ φή- "λεῖς τῶν Ὀρωπίων οἰκεῖα Θηϐῶν ἐςι. ---- *Let him cease to wonder, that many place the City of* Oropus *in the Region or Territory of* Thebes. *For this is rightly done by them, since* Oropus *is not an independant Town, but under the Jurisdiction of* Thebes. *This* Dicæarchus *plainly teaches*; 'The "City of *Oropus*, says he, belongs to *Thebes*." In the first place, what is advanced by *Dicæarchus*, being taken in general Terms, and so as to suit to all Times, is not true. *Oropus* was a long time a Matter of Dispute between the *Athenians* and the *Thebans*. At last the former obtained a full Possession of it, after *Philip* of *Macedon* had taken the City of *Thebes* (25). In the second place, because *Oropus* belonged to the *Thebans*, it does not follow, that it was in the Territory of *Thebes*, in *agro Thebano*. An Author, quoted by *Plutarch*, affirms that the Town of *Harma* was built, where the Battel was fought between the *Argives* and *Thebans*, and where *Amphiaraus* was swallowed up (26). It is a Geographical Error; but much less ridiculous, than what the same Author relates, that, on the Day, which preceded the Battel, an Eagle carried away the Lance of *Amphiaraus*, while the Generals were at Dinner together, and, having carried it aloft, let it fall again: It took root in the Earth, and became a Tree. Τὸ παχὺ ἐν γῇ πάγην ἐγίνετο (27). *Being fixed in the Earth, it became a Laurel.* The following Words of the Scholiast upon *Statius* have been censured. "Civitas "in illo loco post est condita, in quo hiatus terræ "Amphiaraum recepit, quæ Amphiarma vocatur, ut "Homerus ait, quod illic curru, quem Græci ἅρμα "vocant, deciderit, in quo etiam Oraculum est, "quod Græcè Amphiaraon vocatur. ------ *A City was afterwards built in the Place, where the open- ing Earth swallowed up* Amphiaraus, *which, according to Homer, is called* Amphiarma, *because there he fell from his Chariot, called by the Greeks* ἅρμα; *where likewise is an Oracle, called in Greek* "Amphiaraon." *Barthius* (28) pretends, that this Scholiast alledges, improperly, the Testimony of *Homer*, since nothing like it is to be found in the Book of the *Odyssey*, where mention is made of *Amphiaraus* (29). He adds, that, perhaps, the Name of *Homer* crept in by the Error of the Copyists; and that, without this Supposition, we must say, that the Scholiast's Memory failed him; a Misfortune to which he is frequently subject, as well as others. "Vel alium "ergo autorem nominavit intrusò nunc Homeri ti-

(22) Strabo, Ibid pag. 275.

(23) Salmas. Exercit. Plin. pag. 267.

(24) Is. Vossius, in Pomp. Melam. pag. 152.

(25) Paus. lib. 9. pag. 357. See In Pindar's Nemea tom Stephano Byzantino, voce Ὀρωπός, sine Passage, how that this Town belonged to the Athenians γῆν Λάφνην ἐγίνετο.

(26) Trismachus, lib. 3. de conditis urbibus, apud Plut. In Parallelis, pag. 30".

(27) Id. ib.

(28) Barthius, in Statii Theb. lib. 8. ver. 207. pag. 352. Tom. 2.

(29) Odyss. Θ. ver. 243.

2

AMPHIARAUS.

Day the Army drew near *Thebes*, are mistaken; for he did not die till the Day of the Retreat; and the Siege had continued for some time. This Tragical Adventure has been the Theme of many Writers; whence it has happened, that the Circumstances have not been uniformly related. Several weak Reflexions have been made on this kind of Death [C]. It was believed, that *Amphiaraus* returned from Hell

"Ὅτι τ' ἀμφ' Ἀρμ' ἐνέμοντο (31)

Or *Harma, where Apollo's Prophet fell.* POPE.

In the third place, that the Oracle of that Prophet was not at *Harma.*

I shall conclude this Remark with a Passage of *Barthius*, who informs us, that some have thought, that the Pagans alluded here to the Story of *Korah* and *Abiram.* "Placet non plane absurdam conjecturam veteris adnotatoris proponere; per hunc casum alludi à paganis scriptoribus ad vindictam divinam in Sacerdotes Hebræi populi, *Datamum* nimirum, & *Abiramum,* quos, non rite rebus sacris ministrantes, Deus Omnipotens coram omni illa gente vivos ad inferos per hiatum terræ subitum dejecerit. Ei rei respondere nonnihil etiam posterius dicti vocabulum; facile enim ex *Abiramo* gentilium deliria *Amphiaraum* fecisse, quem, *Israëlitæ* gente jam eo loco remota, quo loco ista absorptio accidierit, consecrasse postmodum, Satana instituente oraculum. Et inde cultum impii hominis aliorsum longe lateque propagatum (32). ------- *I shall set before you the plausible Conjecture of an old Annotator; namely, that the Pagan Writers, in this Event, alluded to the Divine Vengeance on the Hebrew Priests,* Dathan *and* Abiram, *whom, at the Command of God, the Earth opening swallowed up alive, in the sight of all the People, as a Punishment for their prophane Ministration of the Sacred Rites. And indeed the Name of the last mentioned in some manner confirms this Conjecture; it being easy for the wild Imaginations of the Gentiles, to convert* Abiramus *into* Amphiaraus; *and, as the People of* Israël *were removed from that Place, where this swallowing-up happened, they afterwards deify'd this Person; the Devil at the same time instituting an Oracle to him. Thus the Worship of an otherwise impious Man was spread far and near.*"

[C] *Several weak Reflexions have been made on this kind of Death.*] Some have thought, that the Order of Nature was overturned by it; That Order, I mean, according to which the Parts of a Compound, when dissolved, ought to return each to it's proper Place: For Example, when a Man dies, his Soul ought to fly up to Heaven, from whence it came; and his Body, taken from the Earth, should return thither. *Amphiaraus* did not enjoy this Privilege; for the Earth swallowed him up, Body and Soul: She was not satisfied with resuming what belonged to her; she must needs detain likewise what she had no right to. The Soothsayer *Theodamas* seems to complain of this.

- - - - - - liceat, precor, ordine belli
Pugnaces efflare animas, & reddere cœlo.
Ne rape tam subitis spirantia corpora bustis,
Ne propera: veniemus enim quo limite cuncti
Qua licet ire via (33).

Let us the common Fate of Battel share;
O! let us breath our warlike Souls in Air;
Permit the Hero's Spirit, when he dies,
Ascending to regain it's native Skies;
Nor bid our Chiefs thus immaturely go,
Alive and breathing, to the Shades below.
Forbear to hasten Life's approaching Date,
Nor thus anticipate the Hero's Fate.
Death, suited to their Lives, awaits the Brave,
And soon we all shall reach th' appointed Grave.

A Commentator says hereupon, "Iniquitas manifesta Telluri hic exprobratur, qua animam Amphiarai cum corpore egerit deorsum (34) ------ *The Earth is here charged with a manifest Act of Injustice, in carrying downwards the Soul of* Amphiaraus, *together with his Body.*" He had just before mentioned an excellent Doctrine of *Epicharmus.* *Man was made by an Union of two Parts: they separate; and each returns from whence it came; the Earth to the Earth, and the Spirit on high: There is nothing amiss in this.* Καλῶς οὖν Ἐπίχαρμ⸗, συνεκρίθη, φησί, καὶ διεκρίθη, καὶ ἀπῆλθεν ὅθεν ἦλθε πάλιν, γᾶ μὲν εἰς γᾶν, πνεῦμα δ' ἄνω. τᾶν δὲ καλετὸν ὑδ' ἐν. *Præclarè igitur Epicharmus, concretum, inquit, fuit, & discretum est, rediitque unde venerat, terra deorsum, Spiritus sursum. Quid ex his omnibus iniquum est? nihil* (35). This Thought is to be met with in the Writings of several Pagan Authors (36), and even in the Verses of *Lucretius,* as I have observed in another Place (37). This was at least to have a general Notion of the Truth: But they, who imagined that the Soul of *Amphiaraus* did not enjoy the Liberty of re-uniting itself to it's Principle, were grosly mistaken. Although it had not been immaterial, but of the Nature of the Stars, it would easily have found the Means of remounting. The Poets, who said, that he was yet alive, when he came into Hell, made the return of his Soul to the Celestial Regions more difficult; for it seems to be more easy to mount upwards, if the tendency that way begins but a little below the Surface of the Earth, than if we sink to the Center of it, before we begin our Flight towards Heaven. But these Poetical Fancies are not serious enough to be regarded, and I fear my Readers will scarce excuse me, if I insert the following Lines.

------ vecte alte præceps humus, ore profundo;
Dissilit, inque vicem timuerunt sidera, & umbræ.
Illum ingens haurit specus, & transire parantes
Mergit equos: non arma manu, non frena remisit;
Sicut erat, reflos defert in Tartara currus (38).

- - - - - - *when lo! the Ground,*
Parting, disclos'd it's opening Mouth profound.
Stars trembled at the Sight; Ghosts fled dismay'd,
And mutual Fear both Heav'n and Hell betray'd.
As o'er the Plain the rattling Car he drove,
And to o're-leap th' Abyss his Horses strove,
Deep in Earth's Womb engulph'd the Hero fell,
And, arm'd, descended to the Shades of Hell.
Even in his Fall, he govern'd still the Car,
And, sinking, brandish'd still the threat'ning Spear.

He was yet alive, when he first saw the *Destinies;* they did not cut the Thread of his Life, 'till after their surprize at seeing the Prophet in his Chariot, in the infernal Regions.

- - - - - - quin cominus ipsa
Fatorum deprensa colus; visoque paventes
Augure, tum demum rumpebant stamina Parcæ (39).

His Thread of Life not yet it's Length had run;
The Wheel revolv'd, and still the Parcæ spun.
When Pluto's *Courts they saw the Augur tread,*
Then first th' astonish'd Sisters cut the Thread.

It will be thought less strange, that I observe the Contradiction, into which this Poet is fallen. He supposes, that *Amphiaraus,* a little before he was swallowed up, restored to *Phœbus* the Prophetic Ensigns, as things, which ought not to be carried down to *Pluto's* Kingdom.

Accipe commissum capiti decus, accipe laurus,
Quas Erebo deferre nefas (40).

AMPHIARAUS.

Hell [D], and the Scene of his Resurrection has been described: he was placed among the Gods: Temples were consecrated to him: His Oracle was very famous [E]. The Games, which were instituted in Honour of him (b), made a great Noise.

'Tis

(b) See Benedictus upon Pindar. Od. 7. Olymp. pag. 243.

> — — — — — — and now,
> Receive these Laurels, Phœbus, from my Brow.
> To Death, thus crown'd, your Prophet must not go,
> Nor bear these Honours to the Shades below.

In another place, he supposes, that Phœbus confessed, that his Prophet descended into Hell, with all the Ensigns of his Office:

> — — — — utinam indulgere precanti
> Fata darent! en ipse mei (pudet) irritus arma
> Cultoris, frondesque sacras, ad inania vidi
> Tartara, & in meimet versos descendere vultus (41).

(41) Id. ib. lib. 9. ver. 652.

> O! that Apollo might have lent an Ear,
> Propitious, to his dying Prophet's Prayer!
> But Fate withstood: Unable to assist,
> I saw descend to Hell my fav'rite Priest.
> MY Laurels grac'd him, in that fatal Hour,
> And all the sacred Ensigns of my Power.
> In vain with supplicating Looks he pray'd;
> In vain Apollo's Priest implor'd Apollo's Aid.

Barthius, who has taken notice of this Mistake, observes, that there are several of the same Nature in the Thebaid of this Poet. " Hoc genus plurima con- " nivet magnanimus hic Vates; & duodecim tamen " annorum limam referre vult suam Thebaidem (42). " — — This lofty Poet has inadvertently let slip se- " veral Errors of this kind, and yet he pretends, " that his Thebaid carries the Polish of twelve " Years."

(42) Barth. in Stat. Tom. 3. pag. 773.

[D] *It was believed that Amphiaraus returned from Hell.*] Some Authors affect to say, that he *disappeared*: Ἀμφιάρεω δὲ χανοῦσα τῆς γῆς ἐμπεσεῖν εἰς τὸ χάσμα μετὰ τοῦ ἅρματος ἅπαντα ἐγένετο (43). *Amphiaraus vero dehiscente terra cadens in hiatum cum curru inconspicuus evasit.* Apollodorus adds this Reason, because *Jupiter* had immortalized him. Ὁ δὲ σὺν τῷ ἅρματι — — ἐκρύφθη, καὶ Ζεὺς ἀθάνατον αὐτὸν ἐποίησεν. *Is vero cum curru absorptus est, & postea nunquam visus: illum enim Jupiter immortalitate donavit* (44). This was sufficient to induce the Hebraizers to say, that the Plague alluded in him to the History of Enoch. Some other Authors are positive in the matter: They suppose that *Amphiaraus* died, and that he actually descended into *Pluto's* Kingdom; but that, afterwards, he re-ascended to the upper Regions; nay they marked the very place, where he ascended; which was a Fountain near the Temple, which the Inhabitants of Oropus (45) built in Honour of him. The Devotion paid to this Fountain was remarkable: No Sacrifices were offered there; the Water of it was not used, either in Purifications, or in washing of Hands; only those, who were healed of any Disease, by means of the Oracle, cast a piece of Gold or Silver into it. Ἔστι δὲ Ὠρωπίοις πηγὴ πλησίον τοῦ ναοῦ, ἣν Ἀμφιαράου καλοῦσιν, ὅτε θύοντες οὐδὲν ἐς αὐτήν, οὐδ' ἐπὶ καθαρσίοις ἢ χερνιβι χρῆσθαι νομίζουσιν. Νόσου δὲ ἀκεσθείσης ἀνδρὶ μαντεύματι· γίνομένου, καθέστηκεν ἄργυρον ἀφεῖναι καὶ χρυσὸν ἐπίσημον ἐς τὴν πηγήν, ταύτῃ γὰρ ἀνελθεῖν τὸν Ἀμφιάραον λέγουσιν ἤδη θεόν (46). *Est etiam apud Oropios fons templo proximus, quem Amphiarai nuncupant: ad quem neque divinam rem faciunt, neque aut ad lustrandum, aut ad manus lavandas, aqua ea uti fas putant: Solum, qui morbo oraculi monitu levati fuerint, signatum aurum argentumve more majorum in fontem abjiciunt. Hinc enim jam deum Amphiaraum ascendisse tradunt.* Note, that the Resurrection of *Amphiaraus* was not universally believed, and that there were some, who ventured to deny it upon the Stage: Witness this Verse, quoted by *Cicero*.

(43) Diodor. Sicul. lib. 4.

(44) Apollodor. lib. 3. pag. 193.

(45) A Town situated between Attica and Bœotia.

(46) Pausan. lib. 1. p. 33.

> Audisne hæc, Amphiarae sub terram abdite (47)?
> From Earth's dark Womb, O Prophet, do'st thou hear?

(47) Cicero Tuscul. Quæst. l. 2. sub fin.

[E] *Temples were consecrated to him: His Oracle was very famous.*] The Inhabitants of Oropus were the first, who deified *Amphiaraus*. They built a Temple to him, twelve Stadia from their Town, in the place where the Earth opened and swallowed up him, and his Chariot (48). We have already seen (49), that there were divers Opinions about the true Situation of the Place, where he was swallowed up. However it be, all *Greece* joined with the *Oropians* (50), in the Apotheosis of this Prophet. They agreed, that the Oracle of this new God was to be consulted in the Temple, which they had built to him. *Pausanias* informs us, that a Collection of Oracles in *Hexameter* Verse contributed greatly to give the People an high Opinion of *Amphiaraus*; because the Author of this Collection inserted the Answer, which this Diviner had given, concerning the War of *Thebes*. This was much to his Reputation; for People were prejudiced with an Opinion, that, in former times, only Persons inspired by *Apollo* gave Answers *viva voce*; I mean, after the manner of an Oracle. Other Soothsayers were employed only in explaining the Presages of Birds, and Victims, or Dreams. But, whatever Advantage this gave our *Amphiaraus* over his Fellows, yet People were not persuaded, that his true Function was the same with that of the Divinity of *Delphi*; for they consulted him only to receive Answers from him by Dreams; which is a Proof, that, during his Life, he chiefly applied himself to the Interpretation of Dreams. This seems to me to be the Substance of *Pausanias's* Narrative (51). I do not find that *Romulus Amasæus* has rightly translated it; and I chuse to depend upon the Version of *Vigenere*, though not very exact. It is this. " Jophon Cnosfien, l'un des interpretes des Oracles, publia ceux " d'Amphiaraus, en vers hexametres, &c. i. e. *Jophon* " of *Cnossos*, one of the Interpreters of Oracles, pub- " lished those of *Amphiaraus* in *Hexameter* Verse; " which had such an Influence upon the People, " that they flocked to them on a sudden from " all Parts. For none of the Soothsayers, except " those, who formerly were inspired by the Enthu- " siasm of *Apollo*, pronounced any Oracles, but " were all Interpreters of Dreams, or foretold things " to come by the Flight of Birds, or by the En- " trails of sacrificed Beasts. Whence it appears, that " *Amphiaraus* addicted himself chiefly to the Interpre- " tation of Dreams; which we infer from hence, " that, after his Deification, he instituted this man- " ner of Divination. And, in the first place, those, " who go to his Oracle, must be well and duly puri- " fied: Which Purgation or Cleansing consists in or- " derly sacrificing to this God, and performing the " requisite Ceremonies as well towards him, as to- " wards all the rest, whose Names are written there. " After this, having offered a Sheep, they stretch the " Skin on the Ground, and sleep upon it, expecting " the Answer to their Request, which they are to re- " ceive in a Dream (52)." *Philostratus* informs us of some other Ceremonies, which were observed in that Place. " The Gods, *says he* (53), are wont to " grant Oracles to those, who are sober; for there " was once a Prophet in *Greece*, whose Name was " *Amphiaraus*. I believe, interrupted the *King*, you " mean him, who was the Son of *Iocles*, who, in " his return from *Thebes*, was swallowed up by the " Earth. Him, and none else, answered *Apollonius*, " who, to this Day, pronounces Oracles in the *Athe- " nian* Territory, and sends to those, who require it " of him, an Answer to their Demands by Dreams. " But the Priests of the Place enjoin those, who come " thither to consult him, to abstain a whole Day from " all manner of Flesh, and three Days from Wine, to " the end that they may the better conceive and retain " in their pure Thoughts the Reasons of the Things, " which shall be declared to them in Dreams. If Wine " were a proper means to cause Sleep, the sage *Amphia- " raus* would, without doubt, have preferred it to " the Dreamers; and would have enjoined them to " eat and drink to excess, before they descended into " the most private Recesses of the Temple, where " such Oracles were given." Observe, that *Philostratus* assures us, that, in the Time of *Apollonius*, the Oracle of *Amphiaraus* was still in Repute; and yet *Plutarch* confesses, that all the Oracles of *Bœotia* (54), among

(48) Pausan. ubi supra.

(49) In Remark [B].

(50) Pausan. ibid.

(51) Id. ib.

(52) Vigenere upon the Amphiaraus of Philostratus, p. 400. Tom. 1.

(53) Philostrati Vita Apollon. lib. 2. cap. 12. pag. 476. agreeable to the Translation of Vigenere.

(54) Plutarch. de Oraculorum defectu, pag. 411.

AMPHIARAUS.

'Tis thought that he chiefly excelled in Divination by Dreams; but this was not all; for he was the Inventor likewise of Divination by Fire [F]. He conceived such an inveterate Hatred against his Wife, that he commanded the Children, whom he had by her, to kill her (*i*), as soon as their Age would permit. Great Praises have been bestowed upon him; and among others This, That he endeavoured to be an honest Man,

(*) He ex-
cepts that of
Leb. dii.

among which he reckons this, were ceased (55). Let us lay no Stress upon *Apollonius*'s placing this Oracle in *Attica*, and not, as *Plutarch* does, in *Bœotia*. They both mean the same Place; for the Country of *Oropus* being contested between the *Athenians* and the *Thebans*, the former pretending it belonged to *Attica* (56), and the latter, that it was part of *Bœotia*; hence it was, that some Authors tell us, that the Temple of *Amphiaraus* was in *Bœotia*, and others, that it was in *Attica*. *Clemens Alexandrinus*, objecting to the Pagans the Cessation of their Oracles, mentions That of *Amphiaraus* by Name (57); thus here is a second Evidence against the Hero of *Philostratus*. Let us remark by the Way, that he takes notice of it in another Place, which his Translator has perverted. It is this: "Η τὸν Ἀμφιάρεον τὸν σὺν τοῖς ἐπὶ Θήβας ςρατεύσασι μίαν γενεὰν τῆς Ἰλίου ἁλώσεως προτέρω γενόμενον" The Translator says *Aut Amphiaraum, qui, cum septem qui adversus Thebas bellum gesserunt, fertur Troja capta una generatione fuisse posterior.* He should have said prior (58). The Sense is; Or *Amphiaraus*, who, with the seven, who warred against *Thebes*, is said to have lived one Generation before the taking of *Troy*.

Herodotus can inform us, how much this Oracle was esteemed; for he says, that of all those, which *Crœsus*, King of *Lydia*, sent to consult, this alone, and That of *Delphi*, returned proper Answers, and received noble Gifts from that Monarch (59). I am surprized at what he observes, that the Presents, sent by *Crœsus* to the Oracle of *Amphiaraus*, were deposited in the Temple of *Apollo Ismenius*, in the City of *Thebes* (60). Why were they not consecrated in *Amphiaraus*'s own Temple? Or why, in default of this, were they not rather carried to any other City, than *Thebes*, whose Inhabitants had incurred a Mark of Ignominy, with respect to this Oracle; for they were forbidden to sleep in the Temple of *Amphiaraus*; which was the only way to be informed of future Events in that Place? The Reason of this Prohibition was, that, *Amphiaraus* having offered the *Thebans* to be their Soothsayer, or their Fellow-Soldier, they made choice of the latter. You will find these Particulars in *Herodotus* (61), with so clear a Distinction between the Temple of *Apollo Ismenius*, and that of *Amphiaraus*, that I wonder how *Barthius* (62) could say, there was no Difference between them. *Herodotus* relates this, (speaking of an *European*, who was sent by *Mardonius*, to consult the Oracles of *Greece*. He could not tell by what Dream *Amphiaraus* discovered to this General of the King of *Persia* the ill Fortune which attended him. *Plutarch* was better informed of it; for he relates the Dream (63). Some Authors say, that *Amphiaraus* appeared to those who consulted him. Ἀμφιάρεως μὲν γὰρ καὶ Τροφώνιος ἐν Βοιωτίᾳ καὶ Ἀμφίλοχος ἐν Αἰτωλίᾳ χρησμῳδοῦσί τε καὶ φαίνονται. Ἔτοι δὲ παντάχη τῆς γῆς διαλάττουσιν ὥσπερ ἀσὴρ περίπολοι (64). I believe they mean, that he appeared to them in a Dream. However it be, his Oracle was no less esteemed, than that of *Delphi*, or that of *Dodona*, or that of *Jupiter Hammon*. *Valerius Maximus* tells us this. "Eadem gens "summo consensu ad Amphiaraum decorandum in-"cubuit, locum, in quo humatus est, in formam con-"ditionemque templi redigendo, atque inde oracula "capi instituendo. Cujus cineres idem honoris pof-"sident, quod Pythicæ Cortinæ, quod aheno Do-"donæ, quod Hammonis fonti datur (65)."------ "*The same People were unanimous in honouring Am-"phiaraus, by building a Temple over the Place, where "he was buried, and ordering that he should be en-"quired of, as an Oracle. The same Honour was paid "to his Ashes, as to the Pythian Tripod, the Cauldron "of Dodona, and the Fountain of Jupiter Hammon.*" *Cicero* does not say so much; yet he speaks with Commendation of it. "Amphiaraum sic honoravit "fama Græciæ, deus ut haberetur, atque ut ab ejus "solo, in quo est humatus, oracula peterentur (66). ------ *Amphiaraus was so honoured by Greece, that "he was deified, and the Place, where he was buried, "became oracular.*"

Note, That there was at *Corinth* a Temple of *Amphiaraus* (67); but give no credit to *Pomponius Mela* (68), nor to *Solinus* (69), who say there was one at *Rhamnus*; for they are mistaken: it was not there, but near *Oropus*, as I have already observed, and as may be proved from *Dicæarchus*, *Strabo*, and *Pausanias*, &c. See *Isaac Vossius*, pag. 151 of his Commentary on *Pomponius Mela*.

[F] *He chiefly excelled in Divination by Dreams ------ for he was the Inventor likewise of Divination by Fire.*] As to this Invention, I can only cite these Words of *Pliny*: "Aruspicium Delphus (in-"venit) ignispicia Amphiaraus, auspicia avium Tire-"sias Thebanus, interpretationem ostentorum & som-"niorum Amphictyon (70).------ *Delphus was the "Inventor of Divination by the Entrails of Beasts, "Amphiaraus of that by Fire, Tiresias the Theban of "that of Birds, and Amphictyon of the Interpreta-"tion of Prodigies and Dreams.*" *Statius* makes no mention of this Particular; though he is pleased frequently to take notice of the Ability of *Amphiaraus*, in prophesying by several Methods. His Words are;

Quis mihi sidereos lapsus, mentemque sinistri
Fulguris, aut cæsis saliat quod numen in extis,
Quando iter, unde moræ, quæ sævis utilis armis,
Quæ pacem magis hora velit, quis jam omne futurum
Proferet? aut cum quo volucres mea fata loquentur (71)?

*Who now shall read the Omens of the Skies,
Or tell the Thunder's meaning, as it flies?
Who in the panting Entrails shall explore
What Heaven decrees, and read each lucky Hour;
For journeying which or best or worst is found;
When War or Peace shall with Success be crown'd?
Who, after him, Futurity shall scan,
And from the Birds enquire the Fate of Man?*

Thus he expresses the Grief of the whole Army for the Death of this Prophet. He says, in another place:

----- quantum subito diversus ab illo,
Qui tripodas laurusque sequi, qui doctus in omni
Nube salutato volucrem cognoscere Phœbo (72).

*How on a sudden chang'd from him, who late
Learn'd from the Tripod the Decrees of Fate;
Skilful (due Honours first to Phœbus paid)
The winged Oracles of Air to read!*

I omit several other Passages of the same Nature; chusing rather to observe, that this Poet would insist on the chief Character of this Prophet, which was to foretel by Dreams, as I have already observed (73). He was the first who abstained from Beans, as being prejudicial to this Science (74). Πρῶτος δ' ἀπέσχετο κυάμων Ἀμφιάρεως διὰ τὴν δι' ὀνείρων μαντείαν· *Amphiaraus primus abstinuit à fabis ad divinationem per somnia* (75). It will not be improper to take notice, in this place, how he became a Prophet. "He went into a certain House, "as ignorant of Futurity as any one else; but the "next Day he came out of it perfectly qualified to be "a Prophet. The House was shut up from that "time, and was called *Fatidica*, *The House of Pre-"diction*." It had, with respect to Divination, the same Virtue, which the Poets ascribed to *Parnassus*, with respect to Poetry.

Nec in bicipiti somniasse Parnasso
Memini, ut sic derepente Poeta prodirem (76).

*Nor on Parnassus (well I know it)
Slept I myself into a Poet.*

It made a Man a Prophet in one Night; and it might then be said, that Good comes by sleeping. We learn this from a Passage of *Pausanias*; and that this
Metamorphosis

278 AMPHIARAUS.

Man, and not to appear so [G]. A noble Subject for Reflexions [H]. If I am not mistaken,

(77) *A Town of Peloponnesus.*

Metamorphosis of *Amphiaraus* came to pass at *Phthia* (77). "Ὅπισθεν δὲ τῆς ἀγορᾶς, ἐστὶν οἶκ@· ὀνομαζόμεν@· ὑπὸ Φλιασίων μαντικὸς. ἐς τέτον Ἀμφιάρεως ἐλθὼν, καὶ τὴν νύκ]α ἐγκαθακοιμηθεὶς, μαντ]ούεσθαι τίτε πρῶτον, ὡς οἱ Φλιάσιοι φασὶν, ἄρξατο. τέως δὲ ἦν Ἀμφιάρε@· τῷ ἐκείνων λόγῳ, ἰδ ιώτης τὲ καὶ ὁ μάντις. καὶ τὸ οἴκημα ἀπὸ τέτε συγκέκλειται τὸν πάν]α ἤδη χρόνον. In postica fori parte domus est, quam *Phliasii* Fatidicam nuncupant: in eam enim ingressus Amphiaraus (quemadmodum ipsi narrant *Phliasii*) cum noctem unam obdormisset, statim divinare cæpit, cum antè induclus planè fuisset. Id cum ita evenisset, in reliquum omne tempus *inclusæ illæ ædes fuerunt.*

[G] *Great Praises have been bestowed upon him* ...... *that he endeavoured to be a Virtuous Man, and not to appear so.*] *Adrastus*, in his Complaint for the Death of *Amphiaraus*, declares, that he had lost the Eye of his Army, both a Prophet, and a good Soldier.

Ποθέων ἐρετίας
Ὀφθαλμὸν ἐμᾶς, ἀμφότερον,
Μάντιν τ' ἀγαθὸν
Καὶ δυρὶ μάρνεσθαι (78).

(78) Pindar. Od. t. Olymp. p. 99.

Desidero exercitus oculum mei
Utrumque vatem bonum & ad pugnandum hasta.

Indeed he was a Diviner, not active in Mind alone; His Arm of Flesh was formidable, and he excelled in bodily Exercises. It is said that he made a terrible Slaughter of the Enemy the Day in which he died.

Ardet inexpleto sævi mavortis amore,
Et fruitur dextra, atque anima flagrante superbit.
Hic hominum casus lenire & demere satis
Jura frequens, quantum subito diversus ab illo, (80).
Innumeram ferro plebem, ceu letifer annus,
Aut jubar adversi grave sideris, immolat umbris
Ipse suis (81).

(80) *Why at its meaning, be e, but b en cited in the foregoing Remark.*

(81) Statius, Thebaid. lib. 7. ver. 703.

Insatiate Love of Battle fires his Breast,
And his Soul's cruel Transport stands confest.
He triumphs in his own unconquer'd Might,
Exults in Slaughter, and enjoys the Fight.
He, who was wont to mitigate, of late,
The Woes of Mortals, and controul their Fate,
How on a sudden chang'd, &c.
By his dire Sword, with Blood of thousands red,
(So baleful Stars their murd'rous Influence shed,)
To his own Ghost, e'er yet it sunk to Hell,
Whole Hecatombs of human Victims fell.

In a Word, he was an Hero, as well as a Prophet; a Quality proper for one, who to Royalty joined the Knowledge of Futurity. *Statius* calls him the Royal Prophet.

Jamque erit ille dies, quo te quoque conscia fati
Templa colant, reddatque tuus responsa sacerdos,
Talia FATIDICO *peragunt solennia* REGI (82).

(82) Id. Ib. l. 8. v. 206.

Altars and Temples soon shall rise to Thee,
And Priests, thy own, reveal the Fates Decree;
Such Rites be thine, as at his Votaries Heads
Even now the sage PROPHETIC KING *demands.*

As for what concerns his Dexterity in the Exercises, in which the *Greeks* strove so much to obtain the Victory, I need only observe, that our *Amphiaraus* obtained the Prize of the *Race*, and That of the *Discus*, in the *Nemean* Games, which the Generals celebrated in their March against the City of *Thebes* (83). Take notice of these Words of *Stesichorus*:

(83) Apollodor. lib. 3. pag. 189.

Θρώσκων μὲν γὰρ Ἀμφιάρα@·
Ἄκον]ι δὲ νίκασεν Μελέαγρ@· (84).

(84) Athen. lib. 4. c. 21. pag. 172.

Amphiaraus bore away the Prize in Vaulting, Meleager in throwing the Launce.

As to the rare Qualities of his Soul, see the eighth Book of the *Thebaid*, and the Tragedy of *Æschylus*, entituled ἑπτὰ ἐπὶ Θήβας, *septem contra Thebas*, out of which I shall produce a Passage in the Remark [*I*], and three fine Verses in the following Remark. See likewise the Commendations bestowed on his Modesty, in a Fragment of the Emperor *Julian* (85).

(85) *Pag.* 307, *Of Julian's Works, Edit. Lips. 1696.*

[*H*] *A noble Subject for Reflexions*] The Matter of Fact, according to *Plutarch*, is this. "*Aristides* " was never puffed up with any Honour which was " paid him, nor dejected and troubled at any Re- " pulse or Refusal; being always of Opinion that a " good Citizen ought to offer himself Body and Soul " for the Service of his Country without hoping or " expecting the mercenary Hire either of Riches or " Glory. For which Reason it was, that, at the re- " cital of these Verses of *Æschylus*, on the Stage, in " Commendation of the old Augur *Amphiaraus*,

Οὐ γὰρ δοκεῖν ἄριστος, ἀλλ' εἶναι θέλει,
Βαθεῖαν ἄλοκα διὰ φρενὸς καρπέμενος,
Ἐξ ἧς τὰ κεδνὰ βλαςάνει βελεύματα *.

* Æschyl. Ἕπτα ἐπὶ Θήβας, vs. 598.

He aims at being just, not seeming so;
The Fruit of Virtue grows up in his Mind,
Whence sage Advice and prudent Counsels spring;

" The Eyes of all the Spectators were immediately " turned on *Aristides*, as if the Elogium of this Vir- " tue was particularly applicable to him. For he was " a most strenuous Champion for Justice, nor was " ever induced to violate it, either by Favour and " Friendship, or by Hate and Resentment (86)." This is the finest Encomium in the World. *Amphiaraus* was worthy of Admiration, if he deserved it: *Aristides*, who seemed to deserve it, is an incomparable Man.

(86) Plutarch. in Vit. Aristid. pag. 320. & in medio. Post. p. 72.

Let us make a few Reflexions on a Subject, which will afford an infinite Number, and observe, I. That if the Pagans did not practise true Virtue, at least they perfectly understood it; for they praised those, who, in doing a good Action, did not propose to themselves either a pecuniary Interest, or public Applause; and they despised those, whose End, in the Exercise of Virtue, was Reputation, Glory, or the Applause of their Neighbour. Be as disinterested as you please with respect to Riches and Employments; if you are not so, with respect to Praise, you still act meanly; you are not recovered from the Disease of Self-love; you are only disengaged from the grossest Snares; you only wear finer Chains: In a word, you will find your Picture drawn in the Treatise of Mr *Esprit*, concerning the Deceitfulness of human Virtues. Apply to all Virtues the excellent Rule, which *Seneca* has prescribed concerning Liberality, and then they will be *True;* but, without That They will not be so. The Philosopher answers this Objection, *May not he, to whom I have done good, know of whom he has received it?* "Quid ergo? ille nesciet à quo accepit? " Primum nesciat, si hoc ipsum beneficii pars " est: deinde multa alia faciam, multa tribuam, per " quæ intelligat & illius auctorem. Denique ille " nesciat accepisse se: ego sciam me dedisse. Parum " est inquis; parum, si foenerare cogitas; sed si dare " quo genere accipienti maxime profuturum erit, da- " bis, contentus eris te teste. Alioquin non benefa- " cere delectat, sed videri benefecisse. Volo, inquis, " sciat: debitorem quæris. Volo utique sciat: quid, si " illi utilius est nescire? si honestius? si gratius? non in " aliam partem abibis? Volo sciat: ita tu hominem " non servabis in tenebris? Non nego, quoties pa- " titur res, percipiendum gaudium ex accipientis " voluntate: sin adjuvari illum & oportet, & pudet; " si quod præstamus, offendit, nisi absconditur: be- " neficium in acta non mitto. Quidni? ego illi " non sum indicaturus me dedisse; cum inter prima " præcepta sic maxime necessaria sit, ne unquam ex- " probrem, imo ne admoneam quidem? Hæc enim " beneficii inter duos lex est, alter statim oblivisci " debet dati, alter accepti numquam (87). — *What*

(87) Seneca de Benefic. lib. 2. c. 10.

" *Shall he not know to whom he is obliged? I answer,* " *first, not if this very Ignorance be Part of the Be-* " *nefit. I will continue to be his Benefactor, I will* " *oblige him farther, 'till by repeated Services he* " *discovers the Author of them. Nay, let him not* " *even know, that he has received a Favour, so long*

AMPHIARAUS.

mistaken, *Apollodorus* is the only Author, who has inserted him in the Catalogue of the *Argonauts* (k); for neither *Apollonius*, nor *Hyginius*, nor *Valerius Flaccus*, have done so. He is ranked among the wise Men, who have had the misfortune to be engaged in Undertakings directed by hot-head Men [*I*]. This is without doubt a very deplorable

(k) Apollod. lib. 1. pag. 52.

" *as I am conscious of having conferred one on him. This*
" *is too little, you say. Too little indeed, if you propose th*
" *lend out your Favours to Usury; but, if you will bestow*
" *them in the manner most advantageous to the Receiver,*
" *you will freely give them; you will be satisfied with*
" *your own Consciousness. Otherwise you are not pleased*
" *with being serviceable, but with appearing to be*
" *so. Still you insist upon his knowing it. But,*
" *What if it is more to his Advantage not to know*
" *it, if it is more honourable, if it is more acceptable?*
" *Will you not alter your Opinion? Still you persist.*
" *Will you not even upon these Accounts; keep him in*
" *the Dark? I do not deny you the Pleasure, which*
" *arises from the Disposition of the Receiver, when-*
" *ever it is proper: but, if your Assistance be required,*
" *where it is inconsistent with Decency to let it be*
" *known; if the Service you do offends, unless it be con-*
" *cealed; the Benefit must not be made public. Why*
" *not? Shall I not let him know, that I am his Be-*
" *nefactor, because it is one of the principal and most*
" *necessary Precepts, that I must never reproach ano-*
" *ther with, nor even hint at, the Favours I have*
" *once conferred upon him? For This is a Law be-*
" *tween the Giver and Receiver, that the former*
" *ought immediately to forget, that he has bestowed,*
" *the latter never, that he has received, a Benefit.*"
My second Reflexion is, That it seldom happens, that the Desire of Applause is the only End of those, who are not satisfied with the Testimony of their own Consciences. Observe the Persons, who aspire to these two Things; the one to *be* virtuous, and the other to *appear* so; and you will find, that the Ambition of the former is not contented with the Reality, nor That of the latter with the Appearance, of Virtue. The meer Steam of Incense does not satisfy their Desires; they wish for something more solid to attend it. Reputation alone seems to them a Reward too spiritual; they endeavour to incorporate it with the Conveniencies of Life: They soon make a Merit of the Praise and Approbations of the World to those, who have the Distribution of Honours and Employments, and from thence make use of this Credit, to enrich themselves, or to gratify all their Passions. The surest Way therefore to preserve the Purity of the Soul, is to follow the Example of *Amphiaraus* and *Aristides*. Endeavour to *be* a virtuous Man; let That be your chief End; seek not to *appear* so, for such an Endeavour is attended with more dangerous Consequences, than you are aware of.

III. *Socrates* is reported to have said, " That the
" shortest way of attaining to Virtue, was to endea-
" vour to be such as one would desire to be thought."
" *Semper id agisti, ut qualis haberi velles talis esses:*
" *quam viam ad gloriam proximam & quasi com-*
" *pendiariam Socrates esse dicebat* (88)." *Socrates*'s own Words are: Συντομωτάτη τε καὶ ἀσφαλεσά-τη καὶ καλλίςη ὁδὸς, ὦ λεϊςόκλε, ἔτι ἂν βέλη δοκεῖν ἀγαθὸς εἶναι, τᾶτο καὶ γενέσθαι ἀγα-θὸν πειρᾶσαι (89). " Velim, O Critobule, scias
" hanc esse brevissimam, securissimam, optimamque
" ad hæc omnia viam, in quocunque volueris bonus
" apparere, in eodem effici quoque bonus conari." So likewise *Horace*

Tu recte vivis, si curas esse quod audis *.

This Advice is very judicious; for the Desire of appearing with Lustre, and of obtaining public Applause, is so strong and common, even among those, who have no great Inclination to be internally virtuous, that we may expect great Advancements in Virtue from him, who will endeavour to produce a perfect Conformity between the real State of his Soul, and the Opinion he would have others entertain of Him. But it must be confessed, that there is less disinterestedness in This way, than in That of *Amphiaraus.* " Seem to be an honest Man, and be so: enjoy
" a fair Reputation, but deserve it; do not usurp
" the Esteem of your Neighbour:" This is the Counsel of *Socrates:* He would not deprive any one of the Incense of Praise. *Amphiaraus* would have said, " Be an honest Man, and do not trouble yourself

(88) Petrus Alcyonius, in Medico legato priore, circa finem.

(89) Xenophon. Memorab. l. 2. pag. 474. See also Plato, Epist. 4. pag. 1274. and Cicero, de Officiis, lib. 2. c. 12.

* Lib. 1. Epist. 16. See Postel on this Passage, in the Epistle Dedicat. to his Oriental History.

" whether it be known to others, or whether you are
" praised for it.
IV. You will say, perhaps, that these two things generally go together, and that, if a good Reputation may be acquired by false Virtues, that is to say, by the Art of concealing a bad Heart under the Appearance of Honesty, it may be more certainly obtained by real Virtues. You will conclude from hence, that *Amphiaraus*, and others like him, valued themselves upon despising a thing, which they very well knew they could not want. I answer, that oftentimes it is easier to be an honest Man, than to be accounted so; and that there is no necessary Consequence from one of these things to the other, wherever you begin. To become a virtuous Man, you have nothing to do but to conquer your own Passions; but to appear so, you must conquer those of others, and triumph over them. You have cunning and violent Enemies, who spread many ill Reports of you: Those who hear them give Credit to them, and become new Spreaders of Calumny: If they are incredulous, they form Difficulties, by which they teach your Enemies how to propose their Calumnies after a more plausible manner. Sometimes you are ignorant of these Machinations; and, if you knew them, either wholly, or in part, can you go from place to place to justify yourself? If you are an honest Man, as I suppose you to be, are you able to discover the Contrivances of your Enemies, and the oblique ways of working upon the Minds of the Vulgar? Had you not rather leave the Vulgar in an Error, than spend all your Leisure in disputing the ground with Calumniators? Will your Vigilance be sufficient to remove the Impressions, which their Malignity has made upon credulous Men, who are infinitely more susceptible of Calumny, than of the best Reasons you can alledge in your Vindication?
You may see in the Remark [*L*] of the Article CÆSAR, that the same Commendation, which *Æschylus* bestows upon our *Amphiaraus*, was bestowed by *Sallust* upon CATO of Utica.

[*I*] *He is ranked among the wise Men, who have had the Misfortune to be engaged in Undertakings directed by hot-headed Men*] It is of little Consequence, whether I myself, or another, furnish a Commentary on this Text. We are not here to consider Style, but Facts, and Sentiments. I shall therefore boldly produce the Old *French* of the Commentator on *Philostratus* (90). " Icy pouvons nous remarquer,
" & appercevoir des eschantillons de nostre pouvrete
" & misere, &c. i. e. Here we have an Instance of
" our Wretchedness and Misery; since prudent and
" good Men are obliged to suffer for the Folly of
" those, who are inconsiderate and wicked. Is it
" not strange, that *Tideus*, a hot-headed, peevish,
" quarrelsome, and brainless Fool, a disturber of the
" public Quiet, though a Stranger, and notwith-
" standing all the Remonstrances, Predictions, and
" Admonitions of the wisest Man of *Greece*, who was
" also accounted a Prophet, should have a Voice in
" the Council, and be so far credited, as to cause a
" War to be undertaken, which was no way neces-
" sary, and would turn to the Ruin and Destruction
" of them all? Nay, those who oppose the same with
" the most probable and best Reasons, must be Par-
" takers of, and even have a great share in, the Danger
" of these giddy-headed Men. So true it is, that bad
" and pernicious Counsels have always prevailed over
" good and wholsome ones! Wherefore, not without
" Reason, or at Random, the Poet *Æschylus*, in the
" Tragedy, entituled *Septem contra Thebas*, laments,
" in the Person of *Eteocles*, the good and wise *Am-*
" *phiaraus*, in this manner:

Φεῦ τῦ ξυναλλάσσοντος ὄρνιθος βροτοῖς
Δίκαιον ἄνδρα τοῖσι δυσσεβεςέροις.
Ἐν παντὶ πράγει δ᾽ ἐσθ᾽ ὁμιλίας κακῆς
Κάκιον, ὀδὲν καρπὸς ὁ κομιςέος.

" *What an unhappy thing it is,* says he, *that a*
" *good Man should be associated with impious and*
" *wicked People! Certainly there is nothing worse*
" *than bad Company; from whence no Good can*

(90) Vigenere upon the *Amphiaraus* of Philostratus, p. 403, 404. of the first Vol. Edit. in 4to.

AMPHIARAUS.

deplorable Case, and is but too common. The manner, in which he comforted a Woman, who bewailed the Death of her Son, deserves a Remark [K]. I would willingly see the Particulars of the Action, which the Farmers of the Taxes * brought against his Priests [L]. I have shewn, in another place (*l*), the Invalidity of an Argument,

(?) In Remark [F] of the Article MELAMPUS.

* In French Les Partisans.

"come ------ This Soothsayer (I mean the Son "of Oicleus) a prudent, just, sincere, and devout "Man, a Foreteller of things to come, by keeping "Company with Men, wicked and presumptuous, "and deprived of all Sense and Reason, who endea- "vour to come against us with a great Army, (*Ju- "piter* permitting it to be so) shall be drawn in "with them to his final Perdition and Ruin." This is what *Vigenere* says. We must not imagine that *Amphiaraus* was in hopes, that the Errors of the Managers would be repaired by the Justice of the Cause (91). He was too understanding a Man to believe This: he knew that a just War stands as much in need of human Assistance, as an unjust one (92), and that, without being at least very near as powerful as the Defenders of Injustice, we shall generally come off by the worst. He is therefore justly alledged as an Example of the Sacrifice, which upon some Occasions we ought to make of our Lives or our Prudence to other Considerations. Read these Words of *Cicero* (93). "Valuit apud me plus pudor meus, "quam timor. Veritus sum deesse Pompeii saluti, "cum ille aliquando non desuisset meæ. Itaque, vel "officio, vel famæ bonorum, vel pudore, victus, ut in "fabulis Amphiaraus, sic ego prudens & sciens ad "pestem ante oculos positam sum profectus. —— "Upon this Occasion, Shame had a greater Influence "on me than Fear. I was afraid of being wanting "to Pompey's Health, who once was not wanting to "mine. Therefore, being prevailed upon by Duty, or "Reputation, or Shame, like Amphiaraus in the Fable, "I ran prudently and knowingly into the midst of "a Plague, which was before my Eyes." To conclude; there is some Reason to upbraid this Prophet with the Imperfection of his Knowledge, and to rally him upon this Account. He foresaw, that, if he went to the War, he should be killed; but he did not foresee, that he should go, and that, notwithstanding his Precautions, he should be forced to engage in the Undertaking (94).

[K] *The manner in which he comforted a Woman* ----- *deserves a Remark.*] *Plutarch*, having mentioned the Reasons, which ought to be employed in comforting those, who are afflicted at the untimely Death of their Children, adds (95): "And *Amphia- "raus*, in a Poem, seems to me to offer no imper- "tinent Consolation to the Mother of *Archemorus*, "who was uncommonly afflicted for the Loss of his "Son, who died unexpectedly: For he says to her: "*No Man was ever happy all his Life; he produces "Children upon the Earth; then buries them; at "last he dies himself; and Men always lament those, "whom they carry in their Coffins to their Grave, "in like manner as Ears of Corn grow out of the "Earth, and are afterwards cut down. Thus it must "be, that some, newly born, come into Being, and "others go out of it. Why then should Men grieve "for all this, which, according to the Course of Na- "ture, ought always to be so? It is never grievous "to suffer, or do, what cannot be avoided by Man. "In general, every one, whether in meditating by "himself, or in discoursing with others, should take "this for a Rule, that not the longest Life is the best, "but That, which is the most virtuous.*" *Plutarch* seems to me to have alledged this Passage improperly; for it doth not relate more to the Death of young People, than of others. I might observe likewise, that the Comparison drawn from *Ears of Corn* would be absurd, if the Design was to moderate an Affliction, grounded on the Youth of the Person, who is bewailed; for, according to the usual course of things, the Harvest of Corn is not 'till the Ears are ripe. It would be more proper to make the afflicted Person consider the State of Fruit-Trees. Count the Apples, when they are in the Bud; and count them every Week afterwards, and you will find that the Number of them is always decreasing. It is extraordinary if one half of them remains 'till the time of gathering. As for the other Reasons of *Amphiaraus*, they are good enough; but there is nothing in them but what is common; nay, he concludes with a Maxim, which in one Sense is more apt to encrease

(91) The Thebans were wholly to blame in this War, and yet they came off victorious in the Battle.

(92) See Remark [C] of the Article BRUTUS (MARCUS).

(93) Cicero, Epist. 6. lib. 6. ad Familiar. p. 319.

(94) See the Commentary on the Life of Apollonius, translated into French by Vigenere, Book 2. chap. 11. p. 488.

(95) Plutarch. de Consolatione ad Apollonium, p. 110, 111. Mr Bayle cites the French Version of Amyot; which therefore we follow.

Grief, than to cure it (96). We shall see presently how the Philosopher *Carneades* censured this Reasoning.

Amyot has not justly rendered the *Greek* of *Plutarch*, ὁ παρὰ τῷ ποιητῇ Ἀμφιάραος, by *Amphiaraus, in a Poem* *. This Version manifestly insinuates, that *Amphiaraus* wrote a Poem; but *Plutarch* means, that there was a Poet, who introduced *Amphiaraus* making use of those Reasons. It was *Euripides*. "Dicuntur "nonnulli in mœrore, quum de hac communi om- "nium conditione audivissent, eâ lege nos esse na- "tos, ut nemo in perpetuum esse possit expers mali, "graviùs etiam tulisse. Quo circa Carneades, ut vi- "deo nostrum scribere Antiochum, reprehendere "Chrysippum solebat laudantem Euripideum carmen "illud:

Nemo mortalis est, quem non attingat dolor, Morbusque: multi sunt humandi liberi, Rursus creandi: multi sunt humandi omnibus. Quæ generi humano angorem nequicquam afferunt.

Reddenda est terræ terra (97). Tum vita omnibus Metenda ut fruges, sic jubet necessitas.

"Negabat genus hoc orationis quicquam omnino ad "levandam ægritudinem pertinere. Id enim ipsum "dolendum esse dicebat, quod in tam crudelem ne- "cessitatem incidissemus. Nam illam quidem oratio- "nem ex commemoratione alienorum malorum ad "malevolos consolandos esse accommodatam (98). — "It is said, that some Persons in Affliction, when "they have been put in mind of the common Fate of "all Men, that the Condition of our Birth is such, "that no Man can be perpetually exempt from Mi- "sery, instead of receiving Consolation, have thought "This an Aggravation of their Misfortunes. For which "reason Carneades, as Antiochum informs us, was "went to reprove Chrysippum for commending those "Verses of Euripides:

No mortal lives, whom Grief does ne'er attack, Or whom Diseases spare; our Children die; Others are born; and Death attends us all. No Anguish hence the human Breast should feel; Earth must to Earth, and Dust to Dust, return; And Life be gathered like maturest Fruit: Such is th' inevitable Law of Fate.

"He denied that this way of speaking tended in the "least to mitigate Sorrow. For this very thing, he "said, was matter of Affliction, that we are obnoxi- "ous to so cruel a Necessity: For such a Consolation, "as arises from the Recollection of other Men's Mis- "fortunes, can administer Relief only to the Ill-na- "tured." Let us now produce the Answer to this Criticism of Carneades: "Mihi vero longè videtur "secus. Nam & necessitas ferendæ conditionis hu- "manæ quasi cum deo pugnare cohibet, admonet- "que esse hominem, quæ cogitatio magnopere luctum "sevat: & enumeratio exemplorum, non ut animum "malevolum oblectet, assertur, sed ut ille, qui mœret, "ferendum sibi esse sentiat, quod videat multos mo- "derate & tranquille tulisse (99). — *I am of a very "different Opinion. For the Necessity of submitting "to the Condition of Humanity both restrains us from "fighting, as it were, against God, and admonishes "us, that we are Men; a Consideration which con- "tributes greatly to mitigate Affliction: Besides which, "the setting Examples before our Eyes is not intended "to gratify a malevolent Ill-natured Disposition, but "to convince the afflicted Person, that his Grief is "to be born, by shewing him that many have endured "the like with Patience, and Composure of Mind.*"

[L] *The Action which the Farmers of the Taxes brought against his Priests.*] Give me leave to apply this Application to those, who levy'd the Tribute of the *Roman* Republick in the Provinces. There was a Law, which exempted the Lands consecrated to the immortal Gods from all Taxes; upon which *Amphiaraus*'s Priests pretended to this Exemption,

(96) See Remark [E] of the Article FOULQUES.

* Amphiaraus, en un Poeme Ancien.

(a) The Greek Verse mentioned by Plutarch, which answers this, is, εἰς γῆν φέροντας γῆν ἀναγκαίως ἔχει. Barthius in Statium, Tom. 3. p. 37. conjectures that it should be read, εἰς γῆν φέροντας γῆν, ὦ' ἀναγκαίως ἔχει.

(98) Cicero Tuscul. Quæst. l. 3. cap. 25.

(99) Id. Ib.

AMPHIARAUS. AMPHILOCHUS.

gument, by which they pretended to prove the Certainty of his Prophecies. He left several Children [M], one of which was the Founder of *Tibur* in *Italy*. *Pliny* makes this Remark in a Paffage, wherein he relates several curious Particulars concerning the long Life of Trees.

and maintained, that the Lands, which belonged to that Deity, were not subject to any Taxes; and without doubt they pretended, that *the Text of the Law was clear and express in their Favour*. The Farmers replied, that these Lands did not come within the Intent of the Law; since they were consecrated to a dead Man, and that it was plain, that a Person, who is dead, is not one of the immortal Gods. This Argument, though suggested to them by Covetousness, and not by a Zeal for Religion, which such Men seldom regard, where their Interest is concerned, yet it was so demonstrative, that they ought to have carried the Cause: But I believe they lost it. It is pity all the Records of this Trial are not extant: All we know of it is this: " An Amphiaraus Deus erit " & Trophonius? Nostri quidem publicani, cum ef- " fent agri in Bæotia deorum immortalitas excepti " lege censoria, negabant immortales esse ullos, qui " aliquando homines fuissent (100)—— *The Queftion* " *was, whether Amphiaraus and Trophonius should* " *be esteemed as Gods. Our Publicans, allowing the* " *Censorial Law, by which the Lands in Bæotia, con-* " *secrated to the immortal Gods, were exempt from* " *Taxation, denied those to be Immortals, who had once* " *been Men.*" If they had been suffered to go on, they might have affess'd most of the Gods, and have subjected much consecrated Ground to Taxes; for what Titles to Divinity or Immortality would have been Proof against their Exceptions? If Farmers of the public Revenues were ordered to make an Enquiry into false Worships, the Number of them would quickly decrease. But where would such Inquisitors be safe? We shall see in another place (101), how false this Argument appeared to many Heathens; *He is dead, therefore he ought not to be worshipped as a God.*

[M] *He left several Children.*] I have composed the Articles of *ALCMÆON* and *AMPHILO-CHUS*, who were his Sons. I do not find that any *Greek* Author, now extant, mentions *Tiburtus*, who was likewise his Son; but they mention *Eurydice*, *Demonassa*, and *Alcmena*, Daughters of *Amphiaraus* and *Eriphyle* (102). *Pliny* speaks of *Tiburtus* in this Manner: " Tiburtes originem multo ante urbem Romam " habent. Apud eos exstant ilices tres, etiam Ti- " burto conditore eorum vetustiores, apud quos inau- " guratus traditur. Fuisse autem eum tradunt filium " Amphiarai, qui apud Thebas obierit una ætate ante " Iliacum bellum (103). —— *The Tiburtes are more* " *ancient than the building of Rome. They shew* " *three Oaks, older than Tiburtus their Founder,* " *where Tradition says he was inaugurated. They tell* " *us he was the Son of Amphiaraus, who died in the* " *Expedition to Thebes, about an hundred Years be-* " *fore the Trojan War.*" I fancy *Pliny's* Account of this Matter is not true: how could the three Oaks, under which *Tiburtus*, Founder of *Tibur*, and Son of *Amphiaraus*, was inaugurated, have remained 'till the Time of *Vespasian?* Note, that *Solinus* says, that *Tiburtus* was Grand-Son, and not Son of *Amphiaraus*. I shall set down his Words in the Article TIBUR.

AMPHILOCHUS, the Son of *Amphiaraus* and *Eriphyle* (a), was a famous Soothsayer. He accompanied his Brother *Alcmæon* to the second War of *Thebes* (b), and some say he assisted him in the Murther of *Eriphyle* (c); but most Authors are of a different Opinion. The Altar, which was consecrated, to him at *Athens* (d) contributed much less to the Glory of his Name, than the Oracle which he had at *Mallus* in *Cilicia* [A]. He and *Mopsus* founded That City after the *Trojan War* (e); afterwards they quarrelled, and kill'd each other in a Duel, as I have observed elsewhere (f). Some affirm, that *Amphilochus* was kill'd by *Apollo* (g). He was both a King and a Prophet (h), for he reigned at *Argos*. It is true he could not support himself in That Kingdom, but left it in discontent, and built a City upon the Gulph of

[A] *The Oracle which he had at Mallus in Cilicia.*] *Pausanias* affirms, that, in his Time, there was no Oracle so much to be depended upon as this: From whence we may infer, that all the *Pagan* Oracles did not cease upon the planting of Christianity. Τῷ μὲν 'Αμφιλόχῳ καὶ πᾶς 'Αθηναίοις ἐςὶν ἐν τῇ ἀρ- χαίᾳ βωμός, καὶ Κιλικίας ἐν Μαλλῷ μαντεῖον ἀ- ψευδέςατον τῶν ἐπ' ἐμοῦ (1). *Amphilocho in ipsa urbe apud Athenienses ara sua est: in Cilicia vero urbe Mallo ejusdem oraculum quod omnium ego ætate mea extant minime fallax.* The Answers of this Oracle were given by Dreams. Ἔςιν ἐν Μαλλῷ πόλει τῆς Κιλικίας 'Αμφιλόχου χρηςήριον, καὶ χρᾷ δι' ὀνειράτων (2). *Est Malli, quod est oppidum Ciliciæ Oraculum Amphilochi, quod per somnia consulentibus respondet.* They, who consulted it, passed the Night in the Temple, and what they dreamed was the Resolution of their Question. *Dion Cassius* mentions a Picture, wherein *Sextus Condianus* caused the Answer, which he had received from this Oracle, in the Reign of *Commodus*, to be represented (3). The following Passage of *Lucian*, induces me to believe, that *Amphilochus* was accounted a great Prophet at that time. Ὅπότε γὰρ ἐξ Αἰγύπτου ἐπανήειν οἴκαδε, ἀκέων τὸ ἐν Μαλλῷ τοῦτο μαντεῖον ἐπιφανέςατόν τε καὶ ἀληθέςατον εἶναι, καὶ χρᾷν ἐναργῶς πρὸς ἔπος ἀποκρινόμενον, οἷς ἂν ἐγγράψας τις εἰς τὸ γραμματεῖον παραδῷ τῷ προφήτῃ, καλῶς ἔχειν ἡγησάμην ἐν παράπλῳ πειραθῆναι τοῦ χρηςηρίου, καί τι περὶ μελλόντων συμβουλεύσασθαι τῷ Θεῷ (4). —— *When I returned from Egypt, and was informed that the Oracle at Mallus was the plainest, and at the same time the truest, and that it's Answers were so clear, as to give a particular and distinct Solution of all Questions, which were proposed to the Pro-* phet, *written on a scroll of Paper; I thought it would be right, as I sailed by, to try the Oracle, and propose some Questions to this Divinity, concerning future Events.* Take notice of the Circumstance mentioned by *Lucian*, which is, that the Questions, to which an Answer was demanded of *Amphilochus*, were proposed in Writing. Let no one say, that *Lucian* forged the Stories, which he relates in this Work; for this does not weaken our Proof; since it is certain he would not have said, that this Oracle was famous, if it had never been consulted for the space of an hundred Years. Thus Mr *Van Dale* solves this Objection (5). He cites another Passage, taken out of the History of the false Prophet *Alexander*, wherein *Lucian* testifies, that the Oracle at *Mallus* was famous. He might have quoted a third Passage, which I find so favourable to this Observation, that I will give it at length. Τὸν Ποδαρείον, ὦ Ζεῦ, καὶ ὃ μάλιςά με ἀποπνί- γει, τὸν 'Αμφίλοχον. ὃς ἐναγοῦς ἀνθρώπου, καὶ μητραλοίου υἱὸς ὤν, θεοπροπεῖ ὁ γενναῖος ἐν Κι- λικίᾳ, ψευδόμενος τὰ πολλά, καὶ γοητεύων τοῖν δυοῖν ὀβολοῖν ἕνεκα (6). — *I am more angry, O Jupiter, with Amphilochus, than with Trophonius: for the former, though the Son of a Villain and a Parricide, yet is famous for prophecying in Cilicia, lying much, and playing the Wizzard for two Oboli.* I shall examine hereafter what *Lucian* says, that *Amphilochus* was not the Son, but the Grand-Son of *Amphiaraus*. In the mean time I shall observe, that the Oracle of *Amphilochus* was still famous in *Plutarch's* Time. Ἔτι κομιδῇ ἐν ἡμῖν περιηνέςι, καὶ τὸ Μόψου καὶ τὸ 'Αμφιλόχου μαντεῖον (7). *Cum autem etiam in Patria, floreant adhuc Mopsi & Amphilochi Oracula.*

[B] *He*

AMPHILOCHUS.

of *Ambracia* [B]. *Livy* has mistaken him for another, in a Passage which I shall quote [C]. *Moreri* too is liable to Censure [D]. We must not confound our Soothsayer with one *Amphilochus*, whom a Goose fell in Love with [E]. In the Remark below I shall give *Pliny's*, and other Authors, Account of this Matter.

[B] *He left Argos in discontent, and built a City upon the Gulph of Ambracia.*] We have this from a grave Historian. Ἄργ⟨ος⟩ τὸ Ἀμφιλοχικὸν καὶ Ἀμφιλοχίαν τὴν ἄλλην δεξίως μετὰ τὰ Τρωικὰ οἰκασθῆ ἀναχωρήσας, καὶ οὐκ ἀρεσκόμενος τῇ ἐν Ἄργει καταστάσει Ἀμφίλοχος ὁ Ἀμφιάρεω, ἐν τῷ Ἀμπρακικῷ κόλπῳ, ὁμώνυμον τῇ ἑαυτοῦ πατρίδι Ἄργος ὠνόμασε. Καὶ ἦν ἡ πόλις αὕτη μεγίστη τῆς Ἀμφιλοχίας, καὶ τοὺς δυνατωτάτους εἶχεν οἰκήτορας (8). *Amphilochus, the Son of Amphiaraus, returning home, after the Trojan War, and being dissatisfied with the State of Affairs at Argos, founded Amphilochian Argos, and all the Region of Amphilochia, upon the Gulph of Ambracia, calling the City, after the Name of his native Town,* Argos *: which City was the largest and most powerful of the whole Amphilochian Territory. Strabo* alledges this Testimony of *Thucydides*: but adds a Circumstance to it; to wit, that *Amphilochus*, being dissatisfied with the Government established in *Argos*, went into *Acarnania*, where he took possession of his Brother's Estate (9). *Thucydides* does not say this; and consequently *Strabo* is in the wrong to ascribe it to him. They, who pretend, that he follows the Opinion of *Thucydides* (10), are mistaken; for he seems to prefer the Historian *Ephorus*, who said, that the City of *Amphilochian Argos* was built by *Alcmæon*, and that it's Founder gave it the Name of his Brother. Μετὰ δὲ τὴν Ἀμφιλοχίαν τὸ Ἄργος ἔτι τὸ Ἀμφιλοχικὸν κτίσμα Ἀλκμαίωνος καὶ τῶν παίδων (11). *After Ambracia follows* Amphilochian Argos, *a City built by* Alcmæon *and his Sons*. It cannot be said, that *Apollodorus* has neither followed *Thucydides*, nor any other Writer, when he says that *Amphilochus* was the Son of *Alcmæon* (12); for he reports this only on the Credit of *Euripides* (13). *Note*, He observes, that this *Amphilochus* went, by the Advice of *Apollo*, to live at *Amphilochian Argos*.

I must take notice of a great Difference between *Thucydides* and *Strabo*. The one says, that *Amphilochus*, being returned to *Argos*, after the taking of *Troy*, and not finding Affairs in such a Condition as he could have wished, retired towards the Gulph of *Ambracia*, where he built a Town (14). The other tells us, that *Amphilochus*, having built *Mallus* in *Cilicia*, after the taking of *Troy*, returned to *Argos*, and being displeased with the posture of Affairs there, went back into *Cilicia*, where he was killed, and buried (15). But there are other Difficulties still. *Euripides* says, that *Alcmæon*, being mad, lay with *Manto*, the Daughter of *Tiresias*, by whom he had a Son and a Daughter; the Son was called *Amphilochus*, and the Daughter *Tisiphone* (16). This *Amphilochus*, in Obedience to an Oracle, settled in *Amphilochian Argos*. We have seen (17), that *Lucian* says, that *Amphilochus*, whose Oracle was so famous at *Mallus*, was the Son of *Alcmæon*: others say that he was the Son of *Amphiaraus*. Amidst all this Confusion there are two ways to choose. One is, to say, that there was but one *Amphilochus*, whose History has only been related by Piece-meal, that is, by Authors who have omitted part of his Adventures. The other is to assert, that there were two *Amphilochus's*, one the Son of *Amphiaraus*, and the other the Son of *Alcmæon*; and that Authors have sometimes ascribed to one what belonged to the other. I could easily believe that *Amphilochus*, whose Oracle was in *Cilicia*, was the Son of *Amphiaraus*; and that he, who settled in *Acarnania*, was the Son of *Alcmæon*. The City of *Argos*, in that Country, was built by *Alcmæon*, in that Country, was built by *Alcmæon*. Τὸ Ἄργος τὸ Ἀμφιλοχικὸν κτίσμα Ἀλκμαίωνος καὶ τῶν παίδων (18). *Argos Amphilochicum Urbs ab Alcmæone ejusque liberis condita.* This is my first Argument. *Amphilochus*, the Son of *Alcmæon*, was admonished by the Oracle to go and reside in this City of *Argos* (19). This is my second Argument. *Pausanias* observes, that the Posterity of *Melampus* reigned in *Argos*, 'till *Amphilochus*, after the taking of *Troy*, retired into the Country, which was called, from his Name, *Amphilochia* (20). This is the *Amphilochian Argos*, and the adjacent Country. Now there are six Generations from *Melampus* to this *Amphilochus*: Ἀπὸ δὲ Μελάμποδος γενεαί τε ἓξ καὶ ἄνδρες ἴσοι μέχρις Ἀμφιλόχου τε Ἀμφιαρέω (21). *A Melampode sex per totidem ætates usque ad Amphilochum Amphiarai filium*: and therefore the latter cannot be the Son of *Amphiaraus*, as *Pausanias* affirms, but of *Alcmæon*. And indeed *Melampus* was the Father of *Antiphates*, who was the Father of *Oicles*, who was the Father of *Amphiaraus*, who was the Father of *Alcmæon*, who was the Father of *Amphilochus*. If you end with *Amphilochus*, the second Son of *Amphiaraus*, you will not find the six Descents which *Pausanias* mentions. This is my third Argument.

[C] *Livy has mistaken him for another*, &c.] He has mistaken the Son for the Father, in these Words of the Forty fifth Book: "Oropum Atticæ, ubi pro "Deo vates Amphilochus colitur, templumque vetu"stum est fontibus rivisque circa amœnum (22). —— "Oropus *of Attica; where the Prophet* Amphilochus "*is worshipped as a God, whose Temple is pleasantly "situated amidst Fountains and Rivulets.*" It is certain that the chief Deity of the Temple, which this Historian mentions, was *Amphiaraus*: he should therefore have said, *ubi pro Deo vates Amphiaraus* (not *Amphilochus*) *colitur*. *Pausanias*, who made these things his particular Study, and had a Genius capable of Success therein, is much more to be credited than *Livy*. Now he not only affirms, that the Inhabitants of *Oropus* built a Temple to the Soothsayer *Amphiaraus*; but seems likewise to say, that *Amphilochus* had no share in the Altar, which was divided into five Portions, each of which belonged to some Hero or God (23). Indeed we find in this Partition the Children of *Amphilochus*, but not *Amphilochus* himself. I confess, the Sequel of the Reasoning might induce one to believe, that *Pausanias* has not omitted him. I could willingly make a Correction in the Greek Text of this Author: I would read, καὶ τῶν παίδων Ἀμφιλόχῳ, & filio Amphilocho, and not καὶ τῶν παίδων Ἀμφιλόχων, & filiis Amphilochi; see the Margin (24). But, after all, this is no Proof, that *Amphilochus* was the God of the Temple of *Oropus*.

[D] *Moreri too is liable to Censure*] I. *Amphilochus* is not a certain Greek Captain, whom Homer mentions in his Odyssey: for Homer only says, that *Alcmæon* and *Amphilochus* were the Sons of *Amphiaraus* (25). II. This being so, *Moreri* should not have expressed himself in this manner, *It is said that he was the Son of Amphiaraus and of Eriphyle.* He should have had more Regard to the Authority of Homer; and no Author, ever so little acquainted with the Ancients, would have made use of an, *It is said*, upon this Occasion. III. *Amphilochus*, mentioned by *Plutarch*, is not different from the *Amphilochus* of *Homer*: It was the same, whose Oracle was consulted at *Mallus* in *Cilicia*. IV. He ought not to have said, that *he carried the Oracle to one* Thespesius *of* Solos (26). This is to metamorphose a God into a Messenger. V. He has omitted a Circumstance, which should have been expressed, *viz.* That this *Thespesius* led a good Life after his Resurrection. See *Plutarch* (27).

[E] *Our* AMPHILOCHUS, *whom a Goose fell in Love with*] *Pliny's* Account is this: "Quin "& fama amoris (anseri) Ægii dilecta forma pueri "Olenii (28). —— *It is reported that a Goose fell in "Love with an Olenian Youth at Ægium.*" Thus Father *Harduin* has corrected this Passage. In the other Editions it runs thus, *Argis dilecta forma pueri nomine Olenii.* Thus two Errors had crept into the Text of *Pliny*: one concerning the Place, where the Goose was in Love, and the other concerning the Name of the beloved Youth. This Adventure did not happen at *Argos*, but in the Town of *Ægium* (29). The Goose's Favourite was called *Amphilochus*, and not *Olenus*; but, because he was born at *Olenus*, he had the Appellation of *Olenius*. A Passage of *Ælian* enabled Father *Harduin* to correct the Passage of *Pliny*. Ἐν Αἰγαίῳ τῆς Ἀχαίας παιδὸς Ὀλενίου χὴν ἠράσθη, ὄνομα Ἀμφίλοχον ἡράσθη χήν. Θεόφρα<ς>ός λέγει τοῦτο (30). *At* Ægium, *a Town of* Achaia, *a Goose fell in love with a Youth of* Olenus, *named* Amphilochus.

AMPHITRYON.

ehus. Theophraſtus *relates this*. *Athenæus* relates the ſame Story, and quotes *Clearchus* and *Theophraſtus*; but correct a Fault, which has crept into his Book. Read ἐν Ἀργείῳ, and not ἐν Ἀργείῳ. Were it not for this, it might be ſaid, that Father *Hardouin* is too bold in theſe Words, "Neque enim Argis ſed Ægii " prope Sicyonem res geſta narratur (31). —— *The* " *Affair did not happen at Argos, but at Ægium* " *near Sicyon.*" Do we not find in the Tranſlation of *Athenæus*, apud *Argivos puerum amavit anſer*, and in the *Greek*, ἐν Ἀργείῳ δὲ παιδός τις μνάςτην χῆν (32)? *At Argos, a Gooſe fell in love with a Boy:*

(31) Hardouin. ibid.

(32) Athen. lib. 13. c. 8. pag. 6. 6.

AMPHITRYON, the Son of *Alcæus* [*A*], Son of *Perſeus*, is leſs known by his Exploits, than by the Adventure of his Wife *Alcmena*, who afforded a Subject to the Comic Poets [*B*]. She was the Daughter of *Electryon*, King of *Mycenæ*. The Sons of *Pterelaus* had made an Incurſion into the Territories of This Prince, which proved fatal to them; for they all periſhed in it (a); but they had before deſtroyed all the Sons of *Electryon* (b). The latter, making the neceſſary Preparations to revenge the Death of his Sons, left his Kingdom and his Daughter *Alcmena* in the hands of *Amphitryon*, and made him promiſe, with an Oath, not to lie with his Daughter. They, who accompanied the Sons of *Pterelaus*, had brought the Flocks of *Electryon* into the Country of *Elis*. The Flocks were recovered by *Amphitryon*; but, in delivering them up to their Maſter, he had the Misfortune to be the innocent Cauſe of the Death of That unhappy Prince [*C*]. Upon this, being obliged to leave the Country of the *Argians* (c), he retired with *Alcmena* to *Creon* King of *Thebes*, and received from him the Ceremonies of Expiation. After this he made Preparations for a War againſt the *Teleboës* [*D*], in Revenge for the Death of *Alcmena*'s Brothers; a Condition, which ſhe required of the Perſon, who deſired to marry her [*E*]. In order to engage *Creon* to follow him, he reſolved to free him from a Fox, which did him a great deal of Miſchief: This he did by the Aſſiſtance of *Cephalus*, who lent him the Dog, which *Procris* had brought from the Iſle of *Crete*. *Amphitryon*, aſſiſted by ſeveral Nations, entred the Territories of *Pterelaus*, and ravaged them; but the great Succeſs of this War was owing to the Treachery of *Cometho*, the Daughter of *Pterelaus*. This Lady fell in Love with *Amphitryon*, for whoſe ſake ſhe plucked off the golden Lock of Hair from her Father's Head, on which his Life depended. The unhappy Father died immediately; and *Amphitryon* took poſſeſſion of all his Dominions. He cauſed *Cometho* to be put to death, and returned to *Thebes*, loaded with Booty. The firſt News, with which he was greeted, was, that He had ſpent the laſt Night with *Alcmena*, tho' he had good reaſon to be aſſured, that it was falſe. At laſt it was diſcovered, that *Jupiter* had play'd this Trick, by aſſuming the Shape of *Amphitryon*. The latter, without any Concern for the matter, lay with *Alcmena*, and made her an inſtance of *Superfœtation*, which has been quoted a thouſand times. She had already conceived *Hercules*, and became pregnant with another Son. But, to diſtinguiſh which was his own Son, and which was *Jupiter*'s, he threw two Snakes on their Beds. *Hercules* was not afraid of them; but the other fled. There wanted no other Proof, to ſhew, that *Hercules* was not the Son of *Amphitryon*. It is ſaid, that *Alcmena* put an Ornament on her Head, which informed the World, that *Jupiter* had tripled

(a) Except one, who fled, but made his way toward the Shore. Apollodor. lib. 2. pag. 97.

(b) Except the Son of Lyſidice, the Daughter of Pelops; and others ſay, that Laonome, the Daughter of Guneus, was his Mother.

(c) Iſ this were not true, as is ſaid in the Supplement to Moreri's Dictionary, that Amphitryon ſuccorded Electryon.

(4) Except Licymnius, a Baſtard. Id. pag. 95.

[*A*] *The Son of* Alcæus.] *Apollodorus* ſays, that *Hipponome*, the Daughter of *Menœceus*, was the Mother of *Amphitryon* (1). Others make him the Son of *Lyſidice*, the Daughter of *Pelops*; and others ſay, that *Laonome*, the Daughter of *Guneus*, was his Mother (2). Note, that he was Uncle to his Wife; for his Siſter *Anaxo* was the Mother of *Alcmena* (3).

[*B*] *Who afforded a Subject to the Comic Poets.*] *Amphitryon* is one of the beſt of *Plautus*'s Comedies, in the Opinion of Madam *Dacier*, who tranſlated it into *French* with excellent Notes. See the laſt Remarks of the Article TELEBOES. *Moliere* wrote a Comedy with the ſame Title; which is one of his beſt Pieces. He has borrowed many things from *Plautus*, but gives them a different turn: And, were a Compariſon between theſe two Pieces to decide the Controverſy, which has been raiſed of late Years, about the Superiority or Inferiority of the Ancients, I believe Mr *Perrault* would ſoon carry his Cauſe. There are many fine Turns in the *Amphitryon* of *Moliere*, which greatly exceed the Pleaſantry of the *Latin* *Amphitryon*. How many things in the Comedy of *Plautus* were neceſſary to be omitted, which would not have ſucceeded on the *French* Stage? How many Ornaments and Touches of a new Invention has *Moliere* been obliged to inſert in his Work, to procure it the Applauſe, which it has received? The bare Compariſon of the Prologue is ſufficient to adjudge the Advantage to the modern Author. *Lucian* has furniſhed the Subject, on which the Prologue of *Moliere* turns, but not the Thoughts. A good Judge will never ſay upon this Occaſion, that of a good Original he has made a bad Copy, applying the Words of *Terence* Qui bene vertendo, & eas deſcribendo male, ex Græcis bonis Latinas fecit non bonas (4).

I beſeech the Reader not to take me wrong: I grant, not only that the *Amphitryon* of *Plautus* is one of his beſt Pieces, but alſo that it is moſt excellent in ſome Reſpects. It ſeems it was ſtill acted in the Time of *Arnobius*. "Ponit animos Jupiter, ſi Amphitryo " fuerit actus pronuntiatuſque Plautinus (5). —— " *Jupiter lays by haughty Carriage, in the Repreſenta-* " *tion of the* Amphitryon *of* Plautus." I wiſh we had the *Amphitryon* of *Euripides*, and the two *Amphitryons* of *Archippus*.

[*C*] *In delivering up the Flocks to their Maſter, he had the Misfortune to be the innocent Cauſe of the Death of that unhappy Prince.*] The thing fell out thus: "Cum bos una aufugeret, in ipſam Amphi- " tryo tum quam manibus forte clavam geſtabat im- " miſit, quæ de bovis cornibus repulſa in Electryonis " caput reſiliens ipſum vita privavit (6). ------ " *One of the Cows endeavouring to run away,* Am- " phitryon *threw a Club after it, which by hap-* " *pened to bove on his Hand; which rebounding from* " *the Horns of the Cow daſhed againſt* Electryon's " *Head, and killed him.*" In the Supplement to *Moreri*'s Dictionary inſtead of a *Club* it is a *Stone*.

[*D*] *He made Preparations for a War againſt the* Teleboës.] I obſerve in another Place (7), who the *Teleboës* were, and wherein *Apollodorus*, whom I follow, differs from the Scholiaſt on *Apollonius*.

[*E*] *A Condition, which ſhe required of the Perſon, who deſired to marry her.*] We ſhall ſee in the Article, to which I refer the Reader in the foregoing Remark, that *Alcmena* chiefly required, that the Death of her Father ſhould be revenged.

(1) Apollod. lib. 2. p. 97.
(2) Pauſan. lib. 8. pag. 248.
(3) Id. ib.

(4) Terent. Prol. Eunuch.

(5) Arnob. lib. 7. pag. 238.

(6) Apollod. lib. 2. p. 99.

(7) In the Article TELEBOES.

[*F*] *Put*

tripled the length of the Night, in order to caress her the longer [F]. It is not true, that *Amphitryon* taught Men to mix Water with their Wine [G]. *Alcmena* survived her Husband (d). The Ruins of their House were still to be seen at *Thebes*, in the Time of *Pausanias* (e). We must remember, that *Amphitryon* was born at *Argos* (f). Some Authors call him King of *Thebes* (g).

(d) Pausan. lib. 1. p. 39.
(e) Id. lib. 5. pag. 29c.
(f) Plaut. Amphitr. in Prolog.
(r) Servius in Æneid. lib. 8. ver. 103.

[F] *Put an Ornament on her Head, which informed the World, that Jupiter had tripled the Length of the Night, in order to caress her the longer* [8].] This is very singular. She might have been satisfied with seeing the Head of her Husband loaded with Horn-work and half Moons, which might have vied with the Towers of the Goddess *Cybele*.

(8) Apollod. lib. 2. p. 97.

— — — — qualis Berecynthia mater
Invehitur curru Phrygias turrita per urbes (9).

(9) Virgil. Æneid. l. 6. ver. 785.

High as the Mother of the Gods — — — —
Then, when in Pomp she makes the Phrygian round,
With Golden Turrets on her Temples crown'd.
DRYDEN.

Why did she wear three entire Moons on her Forehead?

— — — — parvoque Alcmena superbit
Hercule, tergemina crinem circumdata Luna (10).

(10) Statius, Theb. lib. 6. ver. 288.

Proud of her Son, behold Alcmena wear
Three Moons, an Ornament to grace her Hair.

Most Interpreters understand these three Moons to be a Symbol of the three Nights, which *Jupiter* passed with her. A fine Trophy for poor *Amphitryon*! A noble Monument of the Safety of his Honour! Would she have every one, who looked on her Head-dress, remember the triple Night, which her Charms had produced. Her Husband could not be well pleased with such a Dress. I appeal to *Moliere*, who makes him approve the Reflexions of his Servant. *Amphitryon's* Friends being informed, that *Jupiter* was willing to make amends for the Injury, began to express their Joy: But *Sofia* interrupted them.

Messieurs, voulez-vous bien suivre mon sentiment?
Ne vous embarquez nullement,
Dans ces douceurs congratulantes:
C'est un mauvais embarquement,
Et d'une & d'autre part, pour un tel compliment,
Les phrases sont embarrassantes.
Le grand Dieu Jupiter nous fait beaucoup d'honneur,
Et sa bonté sans doute est pour nous sans seconde,
Il nous promet l'infaillible bonheur,
D'une fortune en mille biens feconde,
Et chez nous il doit naitre un fils d'un très-grand cœur;
Tout cela va le mieux du monde.

Mais enfin coupons aux discours,
Et que chacun chez soi doucement se retire.
Sur telles affaires toûjours
Le meilleur est de ne rien dire.

Gentlemen, will you please to follow my Advice?
— *By no means embark in these Congratulations:*
'tis a scurvy Venture: and both one side and t'other is at a loss to find Expressions for such a Compliment. The great God Jupiter does us abundance of Honour, and his Goodness towards us is, undoubtedly, not to be equalled; he promises us the certain Felicity of a Fortune, abounding with a thousand Blessings; and in our House shall be born a mighty stout-hearted Son.
— *All this goes on the best that can be. But, in short, let's cut the Discourse off here, and let every Body go Home in Peace. In these kind of Affairs, 'tis always best to say nothing.*

MOLIERE *translated by several Hands.*

Amphitryon found this so reasonable, that by his Silence, he gave entire consent to it.

[G] *It is not true, that Amphitryon taught Men to mix Water with their Wine.* If *Athenæus* may be believed, this Invention is another's (11). But this other's Name being *Amphitryon*, a learned Critic has confounded him with the Husband of *Alcmena*. I make no doubt, that the like Mistakes often occasion the various Opinions, which are to be found among Authors. Read *Athenæus*, and you will say that *Amphitryon*, King of *Athens*, invented the mixing of Water with Wine. Read *Casaubon* and you will ascribe this Secret to *Amphictyon*, King of *Thebes*. Whence it will happen, that some pretty good Compilers will form two Opinions: *Some*, will they say, *ascribe this Invention to* Amphitryon, *and others to* Amphictyon. *Casaubon's* Words are: " Quod mox de Amphitryonis (*I make no Alteration in the Orthography of the Words*) invento temperandi vinum sequitur quo pertinet subobscurum est. Spectat autem eo, ne quis miretur, quod postea dicit Homerum varia temperamenta vini habuisse nota, cum τᾶς τῦ οἴνυ κεράσιος inventor sit Amphitryo, quem ante Iliaca Tempora Thebis regnasse nemo dubitat. (12). — *The Design of mentioning* Amphitryon's *Invention of tempering Wine is to prevent any one's being surprized, to find, that Homer was acquainted with the various ways of mixing Wine, since no one doubts, that* Amphitryon, *the Inventor, reigned at Thebes before the Trojan War."*

(11) Athen. lib. 4. cap. I 27. p. 179.
(12) Casaub. in Athen. p. 323, 324.

ANABAPTISTS, a Sect, which sprung up soon after the Rise of *Lutheranism*. *Nicolas Storch*, *Mark Stubner*, and *Thomas Munzer*, gave birth to it, in the Year 1521. It was founded upon the Abuse of a Doctrine, which they had read in a Book, published by *Luther*, in the Year 1520, *De Libertate Christianâ*. This Proposition, which they met with in it, *A Christian Man is Master of every thing, and is subject to no one*, and which *Luther* intended in a very good Sense [A], seemed to them

[A] *It was founded upon the Abuse of a Proposition* — — — *which Luther intended in a very good Sense.*] Namely That, which he affixed to it, in explaining his meaning, when he perceived in what manner these People perverted his Expressions. " Quæ verba sano sensu à Luthero — Scripta & " prolixè ἐξηγητῆς declaratis, oppositoque apho" rismo, eundem omnium servum esse, & omnibus " subjectum, exposita, detorta fuere in sensum sequio" rem ab hominibus suæ pariter & alienæ quietis " impatientibus (1). — *Which Words, written and interpreted by* Luther *in a good Sense, and explained by the opposite Aphorism, The same is a Servant of All, and Subject to All, were perverted by a worse meaning by Men, impatient of their Own, and the Peace of Others."* His most zealous Adversaries confessed, that he disapproved of a seditious

(1) Frider. Spanhemius, de Origine, Progressu, Sectis, & Nominibus, Anabaptistarum, p. 196. *I make use of the Edition inserted in the Gangræna Theologia Anabaptistica of Cloppenbourg.*

Behaviour, which seemed to be accidentally owing to his Doctrine. Father *Maimbourg* relates, that the Rebels, having sent their public Declaration to *Martin Luther*, were disappointed in their Expectation of it's receiving his Approbation (2); " For, adds " he, *Luther* perceiving that many accused him of " giving Occasion to this Rebellion, by the Books, " which he had written in the Vulgar Tongue, in " Defence of Evangelical Liberty, against the Ty" ranny of those, who overlaid it by human Tradi" tions, answered this Accusation in a long Dif" course, in which he shews them, that the Scrip" ture enjoins Obedience to Princes and Magistrates, " even though they should abuse the Power, " which God has intrusted them with; that they " ought to address themselves to God, and in " the mean time suffer with Patience, in Expecta" tion

(2) Maimbourg's History of Lutheranism, Book I. pag. 114. *Dutch Edit.*

ANABAPTISTS. 285

them calculated to influence the Vulgar. This they employ'd all their Industry in doing, each according to his Abilities. *Storch*, being wholly illiterate, boasted of Divine Inspiration. *Stubner*, who had Wit and Knowledge, looked out for crafty Explications of the Word of God. *Munzer*, who was bold and vehement, trusted to Assurance, and gave the Reins to the most restless and disorderly Passions. They were not satisfied with decrying the Ecclesiastical Tyranny of the Court of *Rome*, and the Authority of Consistories; they taught likewise, that the Power of Princes was meer Usurpation, and that, under the Gospel, Men ought to enjoy full and absolute Liberty. They *re-baptized* their Followers; and, the better to encourage this Practice, they taught that *Infant-Baptism* was invalid. As to the rest of their Tenets, they insisted much on strict Morality; they recommended Mortifications, Fasts, and a Simplicity of Dress; by which means they gained a prodigious number of Followers. After these successful Beginnings, *Munzer* became so rash, as loudly to exhort the People to resist Magistrates, and constrain Princes to divest themselves of their Authority. A Gospel of this kind was so pleasing to the Peasants of *Germany*, who were weary of their Masters Yoke, that they rose in several Places, and committed infinite Disorders. They were soon reduced, and great numbers put to death. *Munzer*, who had seduced them by his Pretences to Inspiration (*a*), was taken, and beheaded, in the Year 1525 (*b*). His Disciples, whom he had left in *Switzerland*, increased the Sect in that Country, and were the occasion of great Troubles; insomuch that the Magistrates were obliged to have recourse to the most severe penal Laws, to stop the Progress of *Anabaptism*. The same was necessary in several Towns of *Germany*, and other Places. The Protestant Clergy, it is true, were very diligent in refuting these Sectaries; but as this was found not effectual, the Magistrates interposed, and supplied this Defect by their Authority [*B*]. The *Anabaptists*

"tion of his good Pleasure; and that the Way of "Arms, which they had taken up, would be the "Occasion of their Damnation, if they refused to "lay them down." We shall see in the Article MUNZER, that he rejected the Propositions of this Fanatic.

[*B*] *The Protestant Clergy were very diligent in refuting these Sectaries; but —— the Magistrates interposed —— with their Authority.*] It would have been difficult for the most violent Opposers of Lutheranism to conceive a more effectual way of stifling it in the Birth, than this Schism of *Munzer* and his Adherents. They preached up a Doctrine destructive of all Society, and they put it in practice with inconceivable Havock and Devastation. They had been united to *Luther*, and agreed with him in this, that Christianity ought to be reformed according to the pure Word of God (3). Thus the Resentment, conceived against *Them*, recoiled upon *Him*, and his Followers; and, when Men beheld the fatal Consequences, which the Enterprize of the Reformation had so soon produced, they were tempted to believe, that it was not the Work of God. This, no doubt greatly retarded the Progress of *The Reform.* We are not to wonder, that the Protestant Divines called it the Depths of *Satan*; and said, that the Enemy of our Salvation had made use of this Artifice to support his Kingdom against the new Apostles, which God had raised up against him (4). This Language is the natural Result of Theological Hypotheses. The Disputants of the Romish Party took Advantage of this Conjuncture with extraordinary Address, to cry down the Reformation, and to animate all the Powers against it. But the Reformers were not less vigilant to guard against the *Odium*, which their Enemies attempted to throw upon them. They exclaimed with all their Force against the *Anabaptists*; they refuted them by Writing; they engaged them in Disputation as much as possible. " Ut " labem istam sibi neque ac doctrinæ Evangelicæ ad- " spersam abstersum irent, Heroes illi Dei causam " publicis scriptis sibi agendam censuêre. Quod inter a- " lios alacriter præstitere *Lutherus, Melanchthon, Zwing- " lius, Bullingerus, Menius, Regius*, alii, & in seditiones " & seditiosos graviter invecti, subditos perduelles, de " suo erga potestates superiores officio ex Dei verbo " monendo, tribunitios istos concionatores perstrin- " gendo, & omnes ad quietam & debitam Principibus " suis reverentiam hortando, nihil reliqui fecere, ut im- " petum hominum ad scelera & cruces furibundis ani- " mis ruentium sufflaminarent. *Lutherus* vel impri- " mis concitatior non *παρεινετικα* tantum scripta " contra seditiosos, verum etiam *ελληκτικα* emisit, " & peculiari libello *contrà Latrones & Homicidas* " *Rusticos* vulgato ipse classicum in illos cecinit, Prin- " cipes hortatus, ut vi & armis latrociniorum isto- " rum impetum sisterent, & eos ad quietem coge- " rent, qui persuaderi nollent (5). —— *To wipe off* " *these Aspersions from themselves and the Doctrine* " *of the Gospel, these Heroes determined publickly to* " *write in Defence of the Cause of God. This was* " *readily undertaken, among others, by* Luther, " Melanchthon, Zwinglius, Bullinger, Menius, Re- " gius, &c. *who inveighed strongly against Sedition* " *and the Seditious, admonishing rebellious Subjects,* " *from the Word of God, of their Duty towards* " *the higher Powers; reproving those turbulent Ha- " ranguers of the Mob; and exhorting all to a peace- " able and due Reverence for their Princes: in short* " *they omitted nothing, which might restrain the Fury* " *of Persons, rushing on to Acts of Villany and Out- " rage.* Luther *in particular, more zealous than the* " *rest, published not only Exhortatory Writings, but* " *even* Invectives *against the Seditious; and, in a* " *singular Work against the rustic Robbers and Mur- " derers, founded the Alarm against them, exhorting* " *Princes to repress by Force of Arms their violent* " *Proceedings, and oblige those to be quiet by Com- " pulsion, who refused to be so by Persuasion.*" The Minister, whose *Latin* I cite, mentions certain Towns, in which these Sectaries were confounded in Disputation; but the Burden of the Song is always, that at the last the Magistrates exerted their Authority. He tells us, that, at *Zurich*, the Heads of the *Anabaptists*, having disputed three times, to their Confusion, with *Zwinglius* (6), were condemned to Silence by a solemn Decree. " Senatus Tigurinus solenni " Edicto Pædobaptismum sancit, & Anabaptismi Do- " ctoribus silentium & quietem imperat (7). —— *The* " *Senate of* Zurich *confirms Infant-Baptism by a* " *solemn Edict, and enjoins the Teachers of* Anabap- " *tism to be silent."* *Balthasar Hubmeyer*, one of them, having promised to make a public Recantation, yet continuing to preach up his Errors, was compelled to abjure them, and then expelled the City (8). And, because this Sect encreased daily, in spight of all Obstacles, it was thought necessary to have recourse to the most violent Remedies. The Senate published an Edict, condemning to death the Anabaptist Teachers, and laying a severe Fine upon those, who gave them Reception. " Capitis pœna in Ana- " baptistarum Doctores decreta, & gravibus in eo- " rum receptatores mulctis (9)." This Decree was made in the Year 1530. *Oecolampadius* disputed at *Basil* with these Hereticks, in the Years 1525, 1527, and 1529. He maintained his Cause with great Force of Reason, but could not surmount the Obstinacy of these People. For which Reason the Magistrates laid such Restraints upon them, that the Church recovered it's Peace. " Causæ quidem abundè satisfa- " cit;

ANABAPTISTS.

Anabaptists made a considerable Progress in *Moravia*, and would have done so more, in spight of the Severity, with which they were opposed by the Secular Arm, had they not been divided into two Factions (c). No Town was more infested with these People, than That of *Munster* [C]. Every one knows, that they became Masters of it; and that *John* of *Leyden*, King of this New Jerusalem, defended himself as long as he could; but that at length, the Town being taken, he was put to death in the Year 1536. The *Anabaptists* of *Friesland* and *Holland* disapproved, in many things, of the Conduct of their Brothers of *Munster*; and yet they were the occasion of great Troubles (d). One of their principal Chiefs was named *Mennon*. The most effectual Means that could be thought of were put in practice for the Extirpation of this Sect; but in vain (e). It still subsists in the *United Provinces*. It is true, the principal Follies of the Sect have by degrees been worn off [D]: It no longer pretends to Enthusiasm;

(c) *That of the Hutterians, and that of the Gabrielists.*

(d) *See Remark* [D] *of the Art. the* PICARDS.

(e) *T. len from a D'l. sertat on of Frider. Spihem. the Father, De Origine, Progressu, Sectis & Nominibus Anabaptisarum; printed at Leyden. John Ciopinbourg Las in'erted t in his Conguine Theologiæ Anabaptisticæ, printed t Francfort 1 1556, in 4to.*

" cit; actoribus vero pervicacibus non item; ita in " prudentissimi senatus, & strenui Gloriæ divinæ " vindicis, in Anabaptistarum sectariis coërcendis au- " thoritate, Ecclesiæ Basiliensis tranquillitati simul & " puritati consulendum ibidem fuerit (10)." They were refuted at *Bern*, in a public Disputation, in the Year 1527; yet they privately declared, that their own Reasons still appeared to them to be good. In order therefore to confirm the Triumph of Truth, another Disputation was appointed; which lasted nine Days. The Acts of it were published. This had great Effect; but the rigorous Edicts of the Senate of *Bern* were incomparably more useful (11). These seditious Persons would have established their safe Retreat at *St Gal*, had not the Magistrates banished them from thence (12). It was there, that *Thomas Schucker* cut off his Brother's Head, in the Year 1527. He called together a numerous Assembly, and declared to the Company, that he perceived himself under the Influence of the Spirit of God. Upon which, he commanded his Brother to kneel down, and took a Sword. His Father, and Mother, and some others, demanded what he was about to do. *Be satisfied*, replied he, *I will do nothing but what is revealed to me by our heavenly Father*. The Company waited impatiently for the Event; when they saw him draw the Sword, and cut off his Brother's Head. He was punished by the Magistrates as his Crime deserved; but he shewed no Signs of Repentance, and declared upon the Scaffold, that he had only executed the Orders of God. You may imagine, that the Decrees of Banishment were repeated with greater Severity, upon such an Instance of Fanaticism (13). At *Strasbourg*, there were both Disputations, and rigorous Edicts, against this Sect (14). *Melchior Hofman*, one of it's Ringleaders, was condemned there, and died in Prison (15). The Sect spread itself over *Moravia, Bohemia, Poland, Hungary, Austria*, and *Silesia*. Some of it's Heads were delivered over to the Executioner. *Balthasar Hubmeyer*, being conducted to *Vienna*, was burnt there. This Execution passed with the Sect for a Martyrdom, and inflamed their Zeal.

Add to this, that, upon their first Arrival in *England*, in the Year 1560, Queen *Elizabeth*, by a Proclamation, commanded them instantly to leave the Kingdom (17). The Elector *Palatine* drove them out of his Dominions, in the Year 1594. The Diets of *Spire*, in the Years 1529, and 1544, and That of *Ausbourg*, in the Year 1551, put out cruel and bloody Decrees against them (18). *Philip* II. ordered the Governess of the *Netherlands* to be very severe in punishing the *Anabaptists* (19). Consult the Annals of *Spain*, composed by *Henry Ottius*; you will there find an ample Recital of all the Edicts published against them in several Parts of *Europe*. That which is sometimes said of Artillery, that it is *the last Argument of Kings, Ratio ultima Regum*, is applicable to penal Laws: they are the *Ratio ultima* of Divines, their most convincing Argument, their *Achilles* *, &c.

(10) *Spanhemius, ubi supra, pag. 203.*

(11) *Id. Ib. p. 203, 204.*

(12) *Turboneus urbe ejecti fuere. Id. ib. pag. 204.*

(13) *Id. ib.*

(14) *Id. Ib. pag. 205.*

(15) *Id. Ib. pag. 212.*

(17) *Hornbeeck summa Contraversi. pag. 381.*

(18) *Id. Ib.*

(19) *Id. Ib. citing Strada's Hist. Belg. lib. 4.*

* *An invincible Argument is properly called Argumentum Achilleum. See the Article ACHILLES. Remark* [L]. REM. CRIT.

(20) *He was Governor of the Sons of the Duke of Cleves, and afterwards Counsellor to the Duke, and was at the Siege of Munster.*

[C] *No Town was more infested with these People, than that of* Munster.] What passed in this Town, from the time that *Anabaptism* got footing in it, to the Death of *John* of *Leyden*, is one of the most memorable Events of the XVIth Century. We meet with an Account of it in several Books. See particularly the Letter, which was written to *Erasmus* by *Conrad Heresbachius* (20), in the Year 1536, and which was printed at *Amsterdam*, in the Year 1637, *cum Hypomnematis ac notis Theologicis, Historicis, ac Politicis, Theodori Strackii, Pastoris Pudericensis*. See likewise *Lambert Hortensius's* Book, *De Tumultibus Anabap-* *tistarum*, That of *John Wigand, De Anabaptismo Publicato*, and the Relation of *Henry Dorpius*, a Citizen of *Munster*, published in the Year 1536.

[§ Mr BAYLE has omitted, through inadvertence I believe, a *Latin* Heroic Poem in two Books, composed by *Herman Kersenbroeck*, recited by the Author in a full Assembly of the University of *Cologne*, and printed at *Cologne* in the Year 1445, in 8vo. This Piece is dedicated to the Bishop of *Munster* and *Osnabrug, Francis*, Count of *Waldeck*; and the Title is, *Belli Munstercensis contra Anabaptistica Monstra Gesti brevis atque succincta descriptio*. REM. CRIT]

[D] *The principal Follies of this Sect have by Degrees been worn off.*] It is upon this Account, that the *Anabaptists* of these times complain, that they are refuted in the same manner their Ancestors were. An illustrious Divine of the *Dutch* Academy found himself exposed to this Censure, in a Letter, which an *Anabaptist* published in *Dutch*: but he replied to the Author, that he did not pretend to impute all the Errors he had taken notice of to the Sect in general. "His (*Sectas*) ut minime confundimus in " controversiis *singulis*, ita nec notatos errores *omnes* " *omnibus* imputamus - - - - - minus voluimus imputa- " tos illis qui intra *Waterlandorum* dictas confessiones, " bona fide, procul fallaciis Mennoniticis, hærere sese " profitentur. Absit ut cuiquam invito & deprecanti " Hæresim impingamus! Sed nec isti aliorum apolo- " giam suscipiant, aut alios esse ac fuisse agent, " quoa hic Elenchus sub generali *Enthusiastarum* & " *Anabaptistarum* nomine, ne nesciat Juventus nostra, " coarguit. Factum tamen novissime, ut diximus " modo, à *Rypensi* scriptore *Epistolæ* in modum Bel- " gico sermone mihi opponendæ. Qui errores hic " complures notatos dum à suis Waterlandis amolittur, " si modo verè & sincerè, hoc ipso non se aut suos " in talibus controversiis peti, sed familias alias ex " dicto grege, intellexisse debuit. Frustra ergo est " omnis ipsius expostulatio, quasi ignorem quid Ry- " penses Anabaptistæ sentiant, aut quasi Lectoribus " meis imponam (21). —— *As I do not confound* " *these several Sects in particular Controversies, so* " *neither do I impute all the Errors, which I remark,* " *to all without Distinction - - - - - much less would* " *I impute them to those, who profess to adhere to* " *the aforesaid Confessions of the Waterlandians, in* " *Sincerity, and free from the Fallacies of Mennon.* " *Far be it from me to fix Heresy upon any Man a-* " *gainst his Will, and against his express Declara-* " *tion to the contrary. But let not such Men under-* " *take the Defence of others, and deny that there are,* " *or ever were, such others, as this Table, for the* " *Information of our Youth, reprehends under the ge-* " *neral Name of Enthusiasts and Anabaptists. Yet this* " *was lately done, as I observed before, by the Ry-* " *pensian Author of an Epistle against me in the* " *Dutch Language. Who, whilst he endeavours to* " *vindicate his own Waterlandians from many Errors* " *here taken notice of, if indeed he does it with Truth* " *and Sincerity, might in this very Attempt have seen,* " *that neither himself nor his Friends were aimed at* " *in such kind of Controversies which were levelled* " *against other Folds of the abovesaid Flock. All his* " *Expostulation therefore, insinuating that I am unac-* " *quainted with the Opinions of the Anabaptists of* " *Rypen, and that I impose upon my Readers, is no-* " *thing to the Purpose.*" *Hornbeeck* has been so just, as not to impute the Heresies of particular Persons to the Sect in general. "Hic quidem imprimis à " *communibus* illorum & *singularibus* cœtuum dogma- " tis secernenda sunt *propria* aliqua doctorum ipso- " rum (22). —— *We must here distinguish between* " *the*

(21) *Frider. Spanhem. F. filius, in Elencho Controversiarum pag. 87. Edit. Amst. 1694.*

(22) *Hornbeeck summa Controversiarum. pag. 189.*

ANABAPTISTS.   287

Enthusiasm; it does not oppose Magistrates; nor does it at present preach up an entire Freedom from all Subjection, a Community of Goods, and the like. It has been split into a great Variety of Subdivisions [E]; as must always happen to every Sect, which is not supported by Authority. It boasts of a great number of Martyrs [F]: It's Martyrology is a large Volume in Folio. I believe no Author has represented this Sect with so much Justice, as *George Cassander* [G]. The Protestant Divines

" *the particular Opinions of some learned Men among them, and the common and singular Tenets of the Sect.*" He mentions two by Name, the Opinion of *James Outreman*, and That of *Woke Walles*. The former admits three Essences in the Deity, and pretends, that the Essence of the Father is confined to Heaven, and does not pass this Boundary. The other teaches, that *Judas* was a good Man, and that he was saved; that he committed no Crime in betraying *JESUS CHRIST*; that the Priests and Scribes were no more guilty, in persecuting our Lord even to Death; and that both the Thieves were saved. *Outreman* taught at *Harlem* in 1605. *Walles* taught in the Territory of *Groningen*, in 1673. He was banished from the Province; and, as he retired into *Friesland*, the Protestant Synod, which was held at *Franeker*, in the Year 1644, caused him to be expelled that Country.

[E] *It has been split into a great Variety of Subdivisions.*] I should be afraid of tiring my Readers, were I to produce here the Catalogue of the several *Anabaptist* Sects: I shall content myself therefore with pointing out a Book, where the Curiosity of those, who desire to see this List, may be satisfied. Consult, then, the *Preface to* John Henry Ottius*'s Annals of* Anabaptism.

[F] *It boasts of a great Number of Martyrs.*] Could it only produce those, who were put to Death for Attempts against the Government, it's bulky Martyrology would make but a ridiculous Figure; but it is certain, that several *Anabaptists*, who suffered Death courageously for their Opinions, had never any Intention of rebelling. Give me leave to cite an Evidence, which cannot be suspected. It is that of a Writer, who has exerted his whole Force in refuting this Sect (23). He observes, that it's great Progress was owing to three Things. The first was, that it's Teachers deafened their Hearers with numberless Passages of Scripture: The second, that they affected a great Appearance of Sanctity: The third, that their Followers discovered great *Constancy in their Sufferings* and *Deaths*. He shews, that not one of their three Particulars is a Mark of Orthodoxy. Concerning the last, he expresses himself thus. " The third Distinction, by which the *Anabaptists* seduce the Simple and Wavering, is their Constancy in Sufferings and Death. But this can never make their Anti-Christian Doctrine good and wholesome; since, according to St *Cyprian*, it is not the Punishment that makes the Martyr, but the Cause, for which he suffers. The Scripture (24) assures us, that those only are truly Martyrs and Saints, who suffer for Righteousness, for Truth, and for the Name of *CHRIST*. But the *Anabaptists*, which is to be lamented, do not suffer for this Truth, but for a Doctrine of Anti-Christ. And surely Princes and Kings do not take the proper Method to extirpate this Sect, when they put to death these ignorant Wretches, the greatest part of whom have been seduced. They should rather imitate the good Kings *Ezechias* and *Josias*, who extirpated all kinds of Idolatry out of their Kingdom, and, as far as they could, reformed the true Religion. Thus they should cause the true Apostolical Doctrine to be publickly preached; and, when this done, I am of Opinion, there would be no Occasion for so much Fire, to put to death these poor, ignorant, seduced, People (25)." Afterwards he alledges Examples of Persons, who have suffered courageously, though not in the Cause of Justice. He instances in the impenitent Thief, the *Essenians*, the Popish Martyrs, *Arians*, *Mahometans*, and the Philosophers *Zeno*, and *Socrates*. But he gives not the least Hint, that the *Anabaptist* Martyrs suffered Death for taking up Arms against the State, or stirring up the People to Rebellion. He represents their Martyrs, as weak, ignorant, People. See what is cited below, in relation to *George Cassander*.

Observe, by the Way, that this Author refutes his Adversaries, just as the Catholics refute the Protestants.

" The first Mark, *says he* (26), by which they impose upon so many People, is, when, without Sense, Judgment, or Reason, they quote numberless Texts of Scripture at random, as if they fed upon the Bible; whereas, generally speaking, they know not an Hawk from an Handsaw, according to the Proverb. However, the poor Wretches are at a stand, and amazed at such a Profusion of Scripture; and believe they have met with most learned Instructors. But I beseech these poor Wretches to consider, that there never was an Heresy, which did not make use of Scripture, by corrupting and perverting it, to support it's Blasphemies. The Knowledge of Scripture is not the Occasion of Error and Heresy, but the contrary, according to Christ. *Do ye not therefore err, because ye know not the Scripture* * As to the second Mark, by which the *Anabaptists* seduce and subvert the Minds of the Simple, namely, the Appearance of Sanctity," he proves by Examples, that it is often the Character of false Teachers. It is certain, that the Catholics had to reply to these three Difficulties, I. That the Protestants talk of nothing but the Bible, and are for ever citing it; II. That they condemn Dancing, Finery, frequenting Taverns, &c. III. That many among them die courageously for their Religion. They refute these Difficulties, just as the Protestant Author above-mentioned has refuted them. This is a farther Proof, how greatly prejudicial the Sect of the *Anabaptists* has been to the Protestants; who were obliged to refute it by Arguments, which were turned against themselves by the Papists.

There are some *Anabaptists*, likewise, in the Martyrology of *Geneva*. Take notice, that they have published two Martyrologies, one at *Haerlem*, in the Year 1615, the other at *Horn*, in 1617. These two Works discovered the Disagreement between the *Anabaptists*; for those of *Horn* censured (27) the Martyrology of *Haerlem*, as an unfair Work. In answer to this Censure (28), they had recourse to Recrimination; they charged the Compilers of the Martyrology of *Haerlem* with inserting Persons, who had subscribed the Confession of the Reformed, in relation to the Article of the Incarnation of *JESUS CHRIST* (29). The principal Compiler of the Martyrology of *Horn*, was one *James Outerman*. The Preface to this Work is as injurious to the *Lutherans* and *Calvinists*, as to the Papists: It accuses them all of Tyranny (30).

[G] *No Author has represented this Sect with so much Justice as* George Cassander.] He says, that the *Mennonites* discovered an honest Mind, a pious Mind; and that they erred from the Faith through a mistaken Zeal, rather than an evil Disposition; that they condemned the outrageous Behaviour of their Brethren of *Munster*; that they taught, that the Kingdom of *JESUS CHRIST* was to be established only by the Cross: *They deserve therefore,* adds he, *to be pitied and instructed, rather than to be persecuted;* and he applies to them a fine Passage of St *Austin*. " Hujus, " quem dixi, Mennonis, cui nunc hic Theodoricus " successit, Sectatores ferè sunt omnes, qui per hæc " Belgicæ & Germaniæ inferioris loca huic Anabap- " tisticæ Hæresi affines deprehenduntur: in quibus " magna ex parte pii cujusdam animi Argumenta cer- " nas, qui, imperito quodam zelo incitati, errore " potius quam animi malitia à vero divinarum litera- " rum sensu, & concordi totius Ecclesiæ consensu, " desciverunt; quod ex eo perspici potest, quod Mo- " nasteriensibus & Batenburgicis furoribus, novam " quandam restitutionem regni Christi, quod in de- " letione impiorum per vim externam positum sit, " meditantibus, acerrimè semper restiterunt, & in " sola Cruce regni Christi instaurationem & propaga- " tionem consistere docuerunt; quo fit, ut qui hujus- " modi sunt, commiseratione potius & emendatione " quam infectatione & perditione digni videantur. " His enim multo magis convenire videtur, quod de " Manichæis disputans inquit Augustinus †. Quan- " quam

(23) Guy de Bres, *Epistle Dedicatory to his Racine, Source & Fondement des Anabaptistes. This Book was printed in 1565.*

(24) Matth. v. 11. 2 Pet. iv. 20. 2 Joh. iv. 3.

(25) Guy de Bres, ubi supra, p. 9.

(26) Ibid. pag. 5.

* Mark xii. 24.

(27) *In the Preface to the Edition of* 1626.

(28) *They answered it in a Dutch Piece printed at* Haerlem *in* 1630, *and compiled by* Haris Alenson.

(29) Ottius's *Annals*, ad ann. 1615. num. 6. pag. 233.

(30) Id. ib. ann. 1626. num. 2. pag. 251.

† Contra Epistolam Fundamenti.

ANABAPTISTS.

Divines have zealously opposed It in the *United Provinces*, and have obtained at different Times several Edicts to restrain it [*H*]. Yet it continues to be tolerated there. They say that Mr *van Beuning* reasoned one Day upon this Affair with Mr *de Turenne* [*I*] in a very strong and lively manner. The Books, which have been wrote concerning

‖ "quam Dominus per servos suos regna subvertat Er- "roris, ipsos tamen homines, in quantum homines "sunt, emendandos esse potius quam perdendos ju- "bet. —— Atque Utinam, qui atrociore in hosce mi- "seros sunt animo, mansuetudinem & prudentiam "hujus sancti viri imitentur, qui in disputatione ad- "versus Manichæos —— his verbis est usus ‖. Illi, "inquit, in vos sæviant, qui nesciunt cum quo labo- "re verum inveniatur, & quam difficile caveantur "Errores. Illi in vos sæviant, qui nesciunt cum "quanta difficultate sanetur oculus interioris Hominis, "ut possit intueri solem suum. Illi in vos sæviant, "qui nesciunt quibus suspiriis & gemitibus fiat, ut ex "quantulacunque parte possit intelligi Deus (31).——— "*Almost all those of Lower Germany, who lean to* "*the Anabaptist Heresy, are followers of* Mennon, "*who is now succeeded by* Theodoric; *in which Peo-* "*ple you may, in general, discover Marks of a certain* "*pious Disposition of Mind; who, carried away by a* "*Zeal, not according to Knowledge, have, erroneously,* "*not maliciously, departed from the true Sense of the* "*Inspired Writings, and the general Consent of the* "*whole Church; which is evident from hence, in that* "*they always strenuously opposed the rash Attempts of* "*those of* Munster, *who were contriving a new sort of* "*Establishment of the Kingdom of* CHRIST, *which* "*consisted in destroying the Impious, by external Force;* "*and have always taught, that the Establishment and* "*Propagation of* CHRIST's *Kingdom depended* "*solely upon the Cross; whence it is, that such Per-* "*sons as these seem rather to merit Pity and Instru-* "*ction, than Persecution and Extirpation. And indeed* "St Austin's *Words, in his Controversy with the Ma-* "*nichæans, is more applicable to these People. Though* "*the Lord,* says he, *overthrows the Kingdom of Error* "*by his Servants, yet be commands that Men, con-* "*sidered as Men, should be instructed and set right,* "*not destroyed. —— And I heartily wish, that they,* "*who are so very angry with these poor Creatures,* "*would imitate the Temper and Prudence of this holy* "*Man, who, in his Controversy with the Manichæ-* "*ans, expressed himself thus. Let those,* says he, *be* "*angry with you, who know not the Difficulty of com-* "*ing at Truth, and avoiding Error. Let those be* "*angry with you, who know not the Difficulty of cu-* "*ring the Mind's Eye, and enabling it to bear the* "*Light of it's proper Sun. Let those, I say, be angry* "*with you, who know not with what Groaning and* "*Pains the least Knowledge of the Deity is acqui-* "*red.*" Thus our Author expresses himself in a Book, which he dedicated to the Duke of *Cleves*, in which he proves, that Infant Baptism was always allowed by the Primitive Church. He looked upon the universal Consent of all Christians for many Centuries, as so strong, a Proof that a Doctrine is Apostolical, that he thought the *Anabaptist* could not be better refuted, than by the force of this Argument. He had experienced it's Virtue; for he tells us, that an *Anabaptist* Teacher, who was Prisoner in the Castle of *Cleves*, together with several of his Adherents, were converted, upon seeing this Collection of Testimonies, in proof of the Antiquity of Tradition in this Point. It was this, which induced *Cassander* to publish his Work. Let me observe, that he had two Conferences with the *Anabaptists*, the first at *Cologne*, with one *Matthias*, in the Year 1556; the other with *John Kremer*, who was Prisoner in the County of *Mark*, in the Year 1558. I transcribe the Method of the Writer I borrowed this from; for his *Iterum* is a Contradiction. "Georgius Cassander, *says he* (32), bis "cum illis coram disputavit, de quo inter ejus Opera fol. "1227: semel cum Johanne Kremer, a. CIƆ IƆ LVIII "captivo in comitatu Marciæ, iterum, a. CIƆ IƆ LVI, "cum Matthia aliquo, Coloniæ."

[*H*] *The Protestant Divines have zealously opposed this Sect in the* United Provinces, *and have obtained several Edicts to restrain it.*] They have often challenged the *Anabaptists* to Disputation. The Synod of *Horn* passed an Act hereupon, and even had recourse to the Authority of the Governor. "Ecclesiæ nostræ "semper bonum ac utile censuerunt, Adversarios ad "Disputationem & Colloquia provocare. Synodus "Hornana, a. CIƆ IƆ LXXX, & a. CIƆ IƆ LXXVI, "imploratâ etiam in finem Gubernatoris Theod. Son- "noyi auctoritate—decernit provocandum, *&c* (33)." Three or four Synods passed like Acts before the End of the XVIth Century (34). The Churches thought proper, in the Year 1599, to compose a Work, comprehending a Body of *Anabaptist* Controversies. *Arminius*, Minister of *Amsterdam*, undertook it, and began it; but laid it aside, when he was made Professor of Divinity at *Leyden*; and alledged the Reasons, in the Synod of *Alcmaer* in 1605, why he could not go on with such a Work. The Synod of *Enchuyse*, in the Year 1624, employed two Ministers to examine the Confessions of the *Mennonites*, and discuss the Points in question. One of them being left alone, in the Year 1626, demanded a new Partner; the Synod of *Amsterdam*, in 1628, appointed *Doreslaar* to be his Assistant. They applied themselves diligently to their Commission, and published a very good Book, in *Dutch*, in the Year 1637. It is a Body of *Anabaptist* Controversies; in which the Variations of this Sect are exactly distinguished (35). The Author, who tells us these Particulars, observes, that the Churches, in Conjunction with the Secular Arm, took care, that this Sect should not encrease; they stand Centinel, *says* he, to check it, if it produces new Branches, or attempts to exceed it's Bounds. *Pro coërcendis aut noviter pullulantibus aut sua pomæria extendentibus juxta cum Politicis Ecclesiæ vigilant* (36). He adds, that the Synod of *Friesland* is perpetually sollicitting the States of that Province, to revive the Edict, which was published against the *Anabaptists*, in the Year 1598; and that they press the Execution of it, with regard to the new Assemblies, and new Places of Worship, which this Sect has ventured to set up. He adds farther, that it being discovered, that the Synod of the *Anabaptists*, held at *Haerlem*, in the Month of *July*, 1649, had set up several new Congregations, it behoved the Orthodox Pastors to restrain, by some Means or other, these Innovations; and the rather, as they were authorized so to do, by an Edict of the Year 1651, by which their High Mightinesses decree, that the Sects should be restrained, and not suffered to spread. *Sectas cohibendas & in ordinem redigendas, neque permittendum ut in plura loca quam hodie sunt diffundantur* (37). After the same manner, the Protestants, in *France*, were forbid all Places of religious Worship, which they could not prove they were in possession of at the time of the Edicts. See *Voëtius*'s *Politica Ecclesiastica* (38), in which he examines, whether this Sect ought to be tolerated; he distinguishes upon it; but, generally speaking, he inclines most to the Negative.

[*I*] Mr van Beuning *reasoned one Day upon this Affair, with Mr* de Turenne.] Mr *de Turenne*, being in a Coach with this Ambassador, expressed to him his dislike of the Toleration, which the *States General* granted to all sorts of Religions. I omit Mr *van Beuning*'s Answer, with regard to the other Sects; and confine myself to that Part of it, which respects the *Mennonites*: "Why are you, *says* he, averse to a Toleration of this Sect? They are very honest People, "and the most easy in the World; they never aspire "to Employments; they thwart no Man's Ambition; "they traverse no Man's Views, by Competition or "Intrigues. It were to be wished, that in every "Country half the People would make a Conscience "of aiming at Dignities; the other half would arrive "at them with less Difficulty, and without employ- "ing so many mean Arts, and unlawful Methods. "We have no reason to apprehend the Rebellion of a "Sect, one of whose Articles of Faith is, that it is "unlawful to bear Arms. How great a Security "is it to a Sovereign, to know that his Subjects "are restrained from mutinying by such a Bridle, "whatever Imposts or Tallage are laid upon them? "The *Mennonites* contribute their Share to the "Charges of the Government. This is sufficient; "with this we levy Troops, which are more useful to us, than these People would be, were they "to enlist themselves. They edify us by the Simplicity,

ANABAPTISTS. 289

concerning this Sect, and against it's Tenets, are innumerable [K]. I must not omit, that they have not been able as yet to extinguish it in Switzerland, notwithstanding the rigorous Methods made use of at different times (f). I shall produce some of the Reasons alledged in Justification of their Severity [L]. The Dutch Edition

(f) See Stumpf. Reign. of Holl. Lett. 4. pag. 100, &c. But, principally, See Ottius's Annals of Anabaptism, printed at Basil, 16; 8.

"city of their Manners; they apply themselves to
"Arts and Business, without squandering away their
"own Patrimony, or the Wealth they acquire, in
"Luxury and Vice. Other Communions behave
"differently: Voluptuousness, and the Expences of
"Vanity, are in them a constant Source of Scandal,
"and a weakening of the State. But they refuse to
"swear; a mighty matter indeed. The Authority
"of the Tribunals receive no Prejudice thereby.
"These People think themselves as much obliged by
"an Affirmation of the Truth, as they could be by
"an Oath. All the use of administering an Oath
"consists in this, that the Person, who violates it,
"is in fear of being the more severely punished by
"God, and exposes himself to Infamy, and even cor-
"poral Punishment from Men. The Mennonites fear
"the same Consequences, if they violate their Af-
"firmation; they are therefore bound by the same
"Obligation with other Men."

[K] *The Books, which have been wrote concerning this Sect, and against it's Doctrines, are innumerable.*] I have pointed out some in the Remark [C]. Others are as follows. *Herman Modæus* wrote a Book *de initiis Sectæ Anabaptisticæ.* *Andrew Meshovius* wrote, in Latin, *An History of the Anabaptists.* An anonymous Author published, in Dutch, *The Anabaptistic Succession,* printed at Cologne, in the Year 1603. There is likewise a Book in Dutch, *De Origine & Progressu Sectarum inter Anabaptistas.* Mr *Ottius,* Protestor at *Zurich,* compiled the Annals of this Sect, down to the Year 1671. All these Works are taken notice of, either by *Hornbeeck* (39), or by *Micraelius* (40), or by *Spanheim* (41). I do not find, that they mention a Book, which *Cassander* describes after this manner. "De Origine vero hujus Anabaptisticæ
"Sectæ, ejusque Progressu, & quæ ex hoc capite
"monstra quam varia & absurda atque inter se pug-
"nantia prodierunt, luculente, copiose, summáque
"cum fide scripsit Nicolaus Blesdick, qui, quod alli-
"quando hujusmodi errore per imperitism ætatis de-
"ceptus fuerit, eo nunc instructior & vehementior
"est in iis erroribus refellendis, id quod el cum B. Au-
"gullino commune est (42). —— *As to the Origin
"and Progress of this Sect, with the various, absurd,
"and discordant Monsters, which it has produced,
"they have been clearly, fully, and faithfully described,
"by* Nicolas Blesdick, *who, having been formerly de-
"ceived by this Error, through the unskilfulness of
"Youth, was the better qualified, and the more eager
"to oppose it; a Circumstance common to him with
"St Austin."* *Hornbeeck* mentions only an *History of* David George, composed by *Nicolas Blesdick,* Son-in-law of this *David,* and published by *Revius* (43). *An History of the Anabaptists,* in French, was published at *Amsterdam,* in 1695, and one more ample in 1700. The Authors, who have wrote against them, are *Zwinglius, Luther, Calvin, Melanchthon, Oecolampadus, Urbain Regius, Justus Menius, Bullinger, John Lascus, Guy de Bres, Taffinus, Huninus, Ofiander, Cloppenbourg, Spanheim,* and several others, whom it would be tedious to recount (44). But I must not forget a Book called *Babel,* published in the Year 1621, by *Herman Faukelius,* Minister of *Middelbourg,* and one of the Fathers of the Synod of *Dort.* He shews, in this Work, the prodigious Variety of Opinions, which prevail among the *Anabaptists.* The latter appealed from him to a Confession of Faith, which they published in the Year 1624, at *Amsterdam.* They made Reprisals; for they published *a Babel of Pædobaptists* (45). The Author of it was *Antony Jacob* (46). Observe, that, at first, they wrote but few Books; at length they produced several Authors, and published many Books, some Didactic or Historical, others Polemical. They printed, at *Horn,* in 1624, *A Confession of Faith,* which they confirmed by Passages of Scripture, and other Authorities. At the end of twelve Years, they published another (47), to shew the Agreement of their Sentiments. There have appeared *Apologies for their Confessions;* likewise *Catechisms,* and *Manuals of Religion.* They refute the Declaration of Zurich, in 1644. *Abraham de David* (48), one of them, published a

Book, the same Year, against a Minister of *Haerlem,* named *Bontemps,* entituled, "Smegma Holandicum
"contra maculas quas P. Bontemps Mennonitiis ad-
"spersit. —— *The* Dutch Soap against the Aspersions,
"which* Peter Bontemps *has thrown upon the Menno-
"nites."* The same Minister was attacked in other Works; in the *Abstersio Accusationum gravium Petri Bontemps, facta per P. V. K.* 1643; the *Confutatio argumentorum quibus P. Bontemps probare conatur, Anabaptistas injuriosos esse in Deum & Homines,* 1643; the *Spongia ad abluendas Maculas Petri Bontemps contra certam Anabaptistarum Sectam;* the *Judici Henrici Lixivium contra ejusdem maculas;* and the *Probatio Lixivii D. Bontemps ubi per G. V. V. fidei potissimum Authoris & Methodus agendi solicitatur* (49).

[L] *Some of the Reasons alledged in justification of their Severity.*] Let me produce here the Substance of a Letter, written the Twenty first of August, 1642, to Mr *Hotten,* Minister of the *Walloon* Church at *Amsterdam,* by Mr *Bretinger,* Dean of the Ministers of the Church of *Zurich.* A War being kindled almost all over *Europe,* in 1622, the Magistrates of *Zurich* gave orders, that, conformably to the usual Practice of all times, in the like Cases, the People of that Canton should be exercised to the Trade of Arms by Reviews. The *Anabaptists* refused to obey, and represented to those, who were preparing to comply, that a War ought to be considered as a divine Chastisement, and that the State was to be defended by a good Life, and not by taking up Arms. They intimated, that they should chuse to abandon their Country, their Wives, their Children, and all their Possessions, rather than repulse the common Enemy by Arms. The good Subjects conceived such Indignation at this, that they were for extirpating the whole Sect; but the Magistrates tried Expedients of a milder Nature. They employed the wisest Heads of the Senate, to regulate with the most moderate Divines, what was to be done in this Conjuncture. This Committee began with recommending themselves to the Prayers of the whole Church; after which they came to these Resolutions; that nothing should be omitted, which might seem proper to remove the ill-grounded Scruples of the *Anabaptists;* that none of them should be condemned either to Death, or to the Gallies; and that nothing should be done, which favoured of Cruelty, Precipitation, or Passion. After this, it was thought proper to confer with them; and they had their choice of three Places to assemble at, where they might hear what was to be proposed to them. They met at an appointed Place; where the principal Points of the Christian Faith were proposed to them, both by Word of Mouth, and in Writing; all of which they admitted, except one, which related to Magistracy. The Senate, being informed of what passed in these Assemblies, sent for some of their Heads. They appeared; they gave in their Reasons, which were answered with Calmness; but nothing could influence them: yet they were dismissed with a great deal of Clemency. They retired, however, as if they were afraid of some Design upon their Persons; which they confessed the next Day, when they were asked why they shewed a Distrust of the safe Conduct, which the Magistracy had granted them. This Mildness of the Government was displeasing to many Persons; however, it was resolved to try moderate Methods still farther. The principal Heads of the *Anabaptists* were called together; they were assured, that the usual Oath upon these Occasions should be dispensed with, and that the Government would be satisfied with their Affirmation, or Negation: that they should be excused from bearing Arms, provided they would contribute, by their Prayers, and other pious Means, to the public Good; and that, in requiring of them to be present at the Sermons of the Ministers, they did not pretend to abridge them of the Liberty of disapproving what they should judge contrary to the Word of God; that they only desired they would not pass their Censures, 'till they had conferred either with their Pastors, or with some other Ecclesiastical Person. They concluded with Promises of Protection, and pathetic Exhortations. But when

ANABAPTISTS.

dition of *Moreri* distinguishes the Tenets, which are at present peculiar to the *Anabaptists*; for which reason I shall not give a particular Account of them. It is certain, that the Description, which the Sieur *Moreri* gives of this Sect, does not agree with the Time, in which he wrote; and I doubt a little, whether ever there was reason to charge them with two Doctrines, which he imputes to them [*M*]: one is, that they held, that *a Woman was obliged to consent to the Passion of those, who desired to obtain her*; the other is, that *they condemned the Marriage of Persons, who did not adhere to their Sentiments*. We must consider as a Legendary Tale what is reported by some Authors, that there have been *Roman* Catholics, who, upon becoming *Anabaptists*, have immediately been able to read, and discourse on Matters of Religion; but who, upon returning to Popery, have forgot every thing, and become as ignorant as before (*g*).

(*f*) Lindanus, Dial. 3. Dubitanti, & Thyreus de Dæmoniacis, cap. 21. apud Thenaud. Theologiæ Natur. Dist. 4. n. 310. p. 404.

when they found, that these People persisted in their Opinion, they civilly entreated them to retire somewhere else; they gave them permission to carry away as much of their Effects, as was necessary for their Subsistance; they promised Restitution to those, who, being cured of their Errors, should return; and they declared, that the Children and Wives, who should renounce the Sect, and continue in the Country, should enjoy a suitable Portion of the Goods of their Fathers and Husbands. The *Anabaptists* replied, that the Earth is the Lord's, and not the Magistrate's, and rejected the Conditions. Then they had recourse to Mulcts and Fines; and, upon their refusal to pay them, and protesting against the Tyranny of these Proceedings, they confiscated their Estates. They now murmured more; they assembled by Night; they petitioned Heaven to repress the Madness of the Government by Plague, Famine, and such other Calamities. It was now absolutely necessary to have recourse to more effectual Remedies; several were imprisoned; most of whom made their escape (50) thro' a Breach, which they made in the Wall, and appeared no less turbulent than before: They were remanded to Prison; they were exhorted from time to time to submit, or willingly to quit the Country; they persisted to demand unconditional Liberty. They offered to give an account of their Doctrine before the whole People; this was denied them; but it was thought proper to offer them a Disputation in Writing, and even to propose to them the Points of Controversy: Their constant Answer was, that they could not defend themselves, whilst they were in Prison. Note, that those of them, who escaped, spread grievous Complaints every where, of the barbarous Treatment they pretended to have met with, during their Imprisonment.

(50) *The Day after Rogation Sunday.*

This Apology, you see, is founded upon that long Patience, which preceded so rigorous a Treatment; but there are other more particular Reasons, resulting from the Nature and Constitution of the Government of this Country. The *Swiss* do not repulse the Enemy with auxiliary or hired Troops, but by fighting every Man in Person; and one way of their Subsistance is the Permission they give, of levying Troops among them, for the Service of Strangers. It is therefore for the Interest of their Governors, that all their Subjects should be trained to Arms, and be fond of War. This is the Reason, why the *Anabaptists* were disagreeable to them; People who would neither wound nor kill any one, and who endeavoured to intimidate the most Warlike, by inspiring them with Scruples of Conscience, in relation to the effusion of human Blood, and the Passions inseparable from the Trade of Arms.

[*M*] *I believe there never was reason to charge them with the two Doctrines, which* Moreri *imputes to them.*] He learned from *Prateolus*, that, according to the *Anabaptists*, the Women were obliged to lend the Use of their Bodies to every Man, who demands it of them; and that the Men, in their turns, are obliged to satisfy the Desires of every Woman, who requires it. *Dicunt postremo quamlibet mulierem obligatam esse ad coëundum cum quolibet viro eam petente, & contrà eodem vinculo adstringunt omnem virum ad tantundem reddendum cuilibet mulieri hoc ab illo petenti* (52). Upon this Principle, there would be a natural Marriage between all Men, and all Women; I mean, that the Sexes would be mutually obliged, in point of Duty, to gratify each other upon Demand. The Duties, which St *Paul* lays down (53), which teach, that *the Husband has not Power over his own Body*, and that he ought to consider it as transferred to his Wife; and that she, in like manner, ought to consider *the Power over her Body*, as transferred to her Husband; those Duties, I say, so just and reasonable in the Marriage of one with one, would have no Bounds; they would extend to the Power of every Man over every Woman, and of every Woman over every Man; a Doctrine so extravagant, so villanous, so abominable, that it is difficult to conceive, that any Sect of the *Anabaptists* really taught it. The Laws of Nature would, upon this Foundation, be much more difficult to be fulfilled, than the Laws of the Gospel; and we might justly, upon this Account, renew the Complaint, *It is a Yoke, which neither we, nor our Fathers, were able to bear.* In a Word, it cannot be a Law of Nature; for Nature obliges us to nothing impossible (54). Beauty, and a tender Conscience, united under such a Law, would be a Weight, under which the most Vigorous and Robust would sink. The Handsome, and the Conscientious would have the most reason to complain. And observe, that the Doctrine of a Community of Wives, is much less shocking than this. That does not deprive us of the Liberty of refusing; it does not tie down the Conscience to an indispensible Compliance.

(52) Prateolus in Elencho Hæreseōn.

(53) 1 Cor. vii. 4.

(54) Impossibilia nemo tenetur.

Perhaps I shall not be mistaken, in conjecturing, that the Writers of *Heretical Catalogues*, *Prateolus*'s Originals, have forged this Chimæra, by giving a bad turn, through Ignorance or Malice, to one of the Consequences of the Doctrine of *Equality of Condition.* It is certain, that the *Anabaptists*, at first, taught this Equality; the Consequence of which was, that a young Lady, of a good Family, ought not to refuse Propositions of Marriage from the Son of a Peasant, and that a Gentleman ought not to decline the Courtship of a Country Girl. If our Catalogue-Writers built the absurd Doctrine, which they impute to the *Anabaptists*, upon this Foundation, are they less impertinent, than the Doctrine itself?

I am as little satisfied, that these Sectaries looked upon the Marriage of other Christians as unlawful; and that they confounded Bastards with the Children of married Persons; that they thought, for instance, that the Birth of *Calvin* was not less sullied, than that of *Erasmus*. But Mr *Moreri* did not look so nearly into the Matter; and, provided he could diffame Heretics, he was satisfied.

ANACREON, a *Greek* Poet, born at *Teos*, a Town of *Ionia* [*A*], flourished, when *Polycrates* reigned in *Samos* [*B*], and when *Hipparchus* enjoyed at *Athens* the Dominion

(1) Calvisius makes him say, that Anacreon flourished in the 24th Olympiad, I don't find this in Eusebius's Chronicon, published by Scaliger.

[*A*] *Teos a Town of* Ionia.] In the Article TEOS I confute those, who say, that *Anacreon* was a Native of *Teium*, on the *Euxine* Sea.

[*B*] *Flourished when* Polycrates *reigned in* Samos.] I have not set down the Olympiad; for I think we need not be so very exact, in regard to a Person who lived Eighty five Years; and indeed those, who pretend to it, differ very much. *Eusebius* (1), who pitched upon the LXIId Olympiad, could not hinder *Suidas* from chusing the XXXIId, and *Tanaquil Faber* (2) from pitching upon the LXXIId. But I shall decide nothing as to *Suidas*; for his Text is certainly corrupted, and his Translators are unpardonable, for having suffered the horrid Blunder, which is

(2) Life of the Greek Poets.

ANACREON. 291

minion, which his Father *Pisistratus* had usurped. This cannot be doubted of, if we read *Plato* and *Herodotus*; for we find in *Plato*, that *Hipparchus* invited *Anacreon* to come to *Athens* (a) [C]; and *Herodotus* says, that *Anacreon* was in the Chamber of *Polycrates*, when Audience was given to an Envoy of *Oretes*, Governor of *Sardes* (b) [D]. *Cambyses* was then King of *Persia*: This I observe, that my Readers may more readily apprehend the Time, in which *Anacreon* lived. This Poet had a delicate Genius; and there are inexpressible Graces, and Charms, in his Poetry: but he was too fond of Pleasures; and of such an amorous Complexion, that he must have Boys, as well as Girls [E]; and, besides, he was addicted to drinking. Doubtless this last Fault made him very remarkable at *Athens*; since his Statue, which was erected there, represented him as a drunken Man singing (c). If we had all his Poems, we should find in them many Strokes of his voluptuous Humour [F]; but the few Remains we have of them sufficiently prove it. There we

(a) Plato in Hipparcho. Ælian. Var. Hist. lib. 8. cap. 2.

(b) Herodot. lib. 3. cap. 121. See also Pausanias, lib. 1. p. 2.

(c) Pausan. ibid. p. 23.

is found in his Book, to pass uncorrected. It is said there, that *Anacreon* lived in the Time of *Polycrates*, Tyrant of *Samos*, in the LIId Olympiad; or, according to others, in the time of *Cyrus* and *Cambyses*, in the XXVth Olympiad. It appears from *Herodotus*, that *Polycrates* and *Cambyses* died much about the same time (3). *Eusebius* makes them Cotemporaries under the LXIIId Olympiad; and he is in the right: Therefore it is not true, that we ought to reckon Twenty seven Olympiads between these two, and bring back *Cyrus* from the LVth Olympiad, in which the Epoch of the *Persian* Monarchy is generally fixed, to the XXVth. *Vossius* makes *Suidas* say, that *Anacreon* lived in the LXIst or LXIId Olympiad (4), which is not to be found in the printed *Suidas*. As for *Tanaquil Faber*, who pitched upon the LXIId Olympiad for the exact time of the Life of *Anacreon*, it is easier to confute his Arguments, than to shew that our Poet did not live at that time. This Critic argues thus: *Anacreon* came to *Athens* in the time of *Hipparchus*: The latter had a Brother, whose Name was *Hippias*, *who solicited Darius, the Son of Hystaspes, to undertake the Expedition, which he made against the Athenians*. This being so, says he, *see exactly the Year 489, before JESUS CHRIST, and the LXXIId Olympiad*. I confess, that the Expedition of the *Persians* against the *Athenians*, spoken of here, in which *Darius* was not in Person, though the Expression of *Tanaquil Faber* implies that he was, belongs to the LXXIId Olympiad, and the Year 489 before JESUS CHRIST (5). But we must remember, that this pretended Expedition of *Darius* was not 'till twenty Years after that *Hippias* was expelled from *Athens* (6), and that his Expulsion was in the fourth Year after the Death of *Hipparchus*, and the eighteenth after the Death of *Pisistratus*; from whence it must be concluded, that *Hipparchus* had reigned fourteen or fifteen Years. It is therefore very possible, I. That he might have invited *Anacreon* to come to *Athens* thirty Years before *Darius* the Son of *Hystaspes* complied with the Instigations of *Hippias* against the *Athenians*. II. That the Death of *Anacreon* might have fallen out some Years before the LXXIId, and the Four hundred and eighty ninth Year before JESUS CHRIST, which is so precisely set down by *Tanaquil Faber*, as the time, in which *Anacreon* lived. I have another Remark to make. He wrote his *Lives of the Greek Poets* in 1659 (7). Now in his *Anacreon*, printed in 1660, he makes this Poet flourish Five hundred and fifty five Years, or thereabouts, before JESUS CHRIST; and he agrees with *Suidas*, that *Anacreon* might have lived in the LIId Olympiad, *Since*, says he, *he lived very familiarly with Polycrates, who flourished at the same time that Amasis reigned in Egypt*. This Critic has been therefore a little too inconsistent in his Chronology as to *Anacreon*. It can never be said, without a Mistake, of one, who might have flourished in the LIId Olympiad, that he lived precisely in the LXXIId Olympiad. Besides, it is a wrong way of proving, that a Man might live in the LIId Olympiad, to alledge his Intimacy with *Polycrates*, who was Cotemporary with *Amasis*: For the latter died at the end of the LXIVth Olympiad; and the former two Years after (8).

[C] *Hipparchus invited* Anacreon *to come to* Athens.] I pretend not to censure *Tanaquil Faber* for saying, that " *Hipparchus*, the Son of *Pisistratus* (9), " sent a Ship of fifty Oars to *Teos*, with very civil " and obliging Letters, in which he invited *Ana-*

(3) Herod. lib. 3. cap. 120. & seq.

REMARKS on *Tanaquil Faber*.

(4) Vossius, de Poët. Gr. pag. 22. Hofmann says the same after him; but Moreri, who transcribes him likewise, says 60 instead of 61.

(5) See Calvisius.

(6) Petav. Ration. Temporum, lib. 5. cap. 8. & part. 2. lib. 3. c. 9.

(7) See the End of the Preface.

(8) See Calvisius.

(9) Moreri and Hofmann say Philostratus.

creon to cross the Ægean Sea, and make a Voyage " to *Athens*; assuring him that he would find there " some Admirers of his Virtue, who were good " Judges of the value of noble Compositions, and of " the Merit of excellent Persons." I shall not censure these Words, on pretence that I find nothing in *Plato* but this; 'Επ' Ἀνακρέοντα τὸν Τήιον πεντηκόντορον στέλλει ἐκόμισεν εἰς τὴν πόλιν (10). *He caused* Anacreon, *born at* Teos, *to come to our City, by sending a Vessel of fifty Oars for him*; nor on pretence that Ælian uses the same general Expression (11). For, besides that *Faber* might have read, in Books unknown to me, the Particulars, which he relates; the Rules of Probability will allow, that *Hipparchus* wrote, or caused obliging Letters to be written, to *Anacreon*: and then we may adopt the Supposition of this Critic; I say, we may adopt it with the less scruple, because a Narrative would generally be jejune and ungrateful, if the Originals were literally translated. But I confess I cannot forbear censuring him, when he alledges *Plato* as his Author.

[D] *He was in the Chamber of* Polycrates, *when Audience was given to an Envoy of* Oretes, *Governor of* Sardes.] This is all the Account *Herodotus* gives us of it; nevertheless I am very sure, that *Tanaquil Faber* might say, as he did, *That* Polycrates, *Tyrant of* Samos, *generally kept* Anacreon *near his Person, and would have him hear a share both in his Business and Pleasures*. For, it being certain on the one hand, that *Anacreon* (12) was in great Favour with *Polycrates*, and on the other, that the chief Employment of this Tyrant (13) was his Diversions, we run no great Risque in believing *Faber's* Account. *You know it* (adds he); *for 'tis not two Years ago since* Herodotus *was read at your Father's Table*. This to me does not seem exact; since there is nothing in *Herodotus*, from whence we may reasonably infer, that *Anacreon* had any concern in the Affairs of *Polycrates*. I am sorry, that some Men of good Parts, and great Learning, should believe, without examining the Matter, that *Plato* and *Herodotus* have said all that this learned Critic has fathered upon them. They should have distinguished the Text from the Flourishes and Glosses of the Author, who quotes it.

[E] *Of such an amorous Complexion, that he must have Boys, as well as Girls*.] Besides *Bathyllus*, and *Smerdias*, of whom more hereafter (14), he was in love with the fair *Cleobulus*. He had like to have killed him in the Arms of his Nurse, by rudely jostling her, as he reeled one Day through the Streets, when he was in his Cups; and, not content with this, he abused the Child with railing Language (15). The Nurse wished, that he might one Day commend him more, than he had then abused him. Her Wishes were fulfilled; for *Cleobulus* grew to be a beautiful Youth: *Anacreon* fell in love with him, and wrote several Verses in his Commendation (16). Behold a pretty kind of Punishment, and a Nurse finely revenged!

[F] *Many Strokes of his voluptuous Humour*.] The following Passages, among others, mention the general Theme of his Poetry. Ἀποτῷ ὁ Ἀνακρέων, ὁ πᾶσαν αὐτοῦ τὴν ποίησιν ἐξαρτήσας μέθης (17). *Foolish* Anacreon, *whose Poetry turns upon nothing but Drinking*. Ἀνακρέων ὁ Τήϊος φαντὶ μετὰ Σαπφῶ τὴν Λεσβίαν τὰ πολλὰ ἐν τῷ γράφειν ἐρωτικὰ ποιήματα (18). Anacreon *of* Teos, *who first, after* Lesbian Sappho, *spent the greatest Part of his Poems in Love Matters*. Let us hear what *Horace* says of the Amours of *Anacreon*;

(10) Plato in Hipparcho.

(11) Ælian. lib. 8. c. 2.

(12) Pausan. Ælian. ubi supra, l. 9. cap. 4. Strabo, l. 14.

(13) Athen. lib. 11. cap. 9, 10.

(14) *In Remark* [G].

(15) Maximus Tyr. Orat. 11. circa init.

(16) Dion Chrysostom mentions some of them.

(17) Athen. lib. 10. c. 7.

(18) Prusanias, lib. 1. pag. 23.

VOL. I. N°. X.   D d d d   Non

we meet with his violent Paſſion for *Bathyllus* [G]; and if, as this ſort of Love was not then branded with Infamy, as it is among Chriſtians, he does not merit ſuch Deteſtation, as a Chriſtian Poet would in the like Caſe, the hardened Age he lived in ought to ſuffer for him: I mean, That the Reader ought to vent his Indignation againſt the Times, when it cannot diſcharge itſelf againſt particular Perſons. *Anacreon*, notwithſtanding his Debaucheries, lived Eighty five Years, if we may believe *Lucian*, who places him among the long-lived. It is ſaid, that he ſupported himſelf, at this great Age, by eating dry Grapes; and that a Grape-Stone, happening to ſtick in his Throat, choaked him. *Valerius Maximus* aſcribes ſo eaſy a Death to a particular Favour of the Gods [H]. No Author that I know of has remarked either the Time or Place of his Death [I], or decided what was his Father's Name [K].

There

(19) Horſt. Epod. 14. ver. 9.

Non aliter Samio dicunt arſiſſe Bathyllo
Anacreonta Teium,
Qui perſæpe cava teſtudine flevit amorem (19).

Thus ſoft Anacreon *for* Bachyllus *burn'd,
And oft his Love he ſadly mourn'd;
He to his Harp did various Grief rehearſe,
And wept in an unpoliſh'd Verſe.*

CREECH.

See alſo *Cicero* in the fourth Book of his *Tuſculan Queſtions*, and *Suidas*.

(20) Ælian. Var. Hiſt. lib. 9. cap. 4.

(21) Id. ib.

[G] *His violent Paſſion for* Bathyllus.] This Inſtance refutes the exceſſive Charity of *Ælian*, who will not allow us to entertain any ill Suſpicion of our Poet's Love for *Smerdias*, one of *Polycrates*'s Minions (20). What is moſt to be wondered at is, that *Ælian* goes upon this general Reaſon, that we ought not to accuſe *Anacreon* of Incontinency, and Intemperance. Μὴ γὰρ τις ἡμῖν διαβαλλέτω πρὸς Θεῶν τὸν Ποιητὴν τὸν Τήϊον, μὴ δ' ἀκόλαςον εἶναι λεγέτω (21). *I intreat that no one would ſlander the* Teian *Bard, or call him intemperate.* *Polycrates* became furiouſly jealous, when he perceived, that our Poet had inſinuated himſelf very far into the good Graces of *Smerdias*, by the flattering Verſes he made on him; and his Jealouſy roſe ſo high, that he cauſed the Youth to be ſhaved (22). The Rival, apprehending very well the meaning of this, very complaiſantly wrote a Poem upon the Occaſion, in which he took care not to diſpleaſe *Polycrates*. They, who remember theſe four Verſes of *Petronius*,

(22) M. ib. See alſo Athenæus, lib. 12. cap. 9.

Quod ſolum formæ decus eſt, cecidere capilli,
Vernanteſque comas triſtis abegit hyems.
Nunc umbra nudata ſua jam tempora mœrent,
Areaque * attrita ridet aduſta pilis.

* Area, Ulceris genus eſt in capite. *Cell. A Sore in the Head, which makes the Hair fall.* REM. CAIT.

*His Form's ſole Ornament, his Locks are ſhed;
Cropt are the ſpringing Honours of his Head,
And his vex'd Temples mourn their raviſh'd Shade.
Whilſt the gall'd Wound rejoices to be bare,
Free from the fretting Load of cumbrous Hair.*

(23) Strabo, lib. 14.

will conclude, from the Action of *Polycrates*, that he had rather his Minion ſhould loſe his Beauty, than find him unfaithful. *Strabo* obſerves, that *Anacreon* perpetually mentions this Tyrant of *Samos* in his Verſes; τούτῳ συνεξίωσεν Ἀνακρέων ὁ μελοποιός, καὶ δὴ καὶ πᾶσα ἡ ποίησις πλήρης ἐςὶ τῆς περὶ αὐτοῦ μνήμης (23). *Cum hoc vixit* Anacreon *Lyricus, & mentione ejus oppleuit ſua carmina*; from whence *Voſſius* had Reaſon to conclude, that it was no wonder he was beloved by him. " Polycrati, *ſays he* (24), carus " fuit. Quod mirum? cum verſibus ſuis cum cele- " braret? *It ſhould be quid mirum?* cum verſibus ſuis " eum celebraret? —— *He was dear to* Polycrates *, and no wonder, ſince he be celebrated him in his Verſes.* We ſhall ſee, in the Article BATHYLLUS, how *Tanaquil Faber* has juſtified the Amours of *Anacreon*.

(24) Voſſ. de Poët. Græc. pag. 22.

[H] *A Grape-Stone* —— *choaked him.* *Valerius Maximus* aſcribes ſo eaſy a Death to a particular *Favour of the Gods.*] His Words are theſe: " Cui " quidem (Pindaro) crediderim eadem benignitate " Deorum & tantum poëticæ facundiæ, & tam pla- " cidum vitæ finem attributum; ſicut Anacreonti " quoque, quamvis ſtatum humanæ vitæ modum ſu- " pergreſſo; quem uvæ paſſæ ſucco tenues & exiles " virium reliquias foventem unius grani pertinacior " in aridis faucibus humor abſumpſit (25). —— *This*

(25) Valer. Max. lib. 9. cap. 12. See alſo Plin. l. 7. cap. 7.

" *Poet* (Pindar), *in my Opinion, owed his great Genius " for Poetry, and the eaſineſs of his Death, to the " ſame Kindneſs and Favour of the Gods; as was like- " wiſe the Caſe of* Anacreon, *though he had exceeded " the uſual Bounds of human Life; for, as he che- " riſhed his little Remains of Strength with dried " Grapes, the Stone of one, which he endeavoured in " vain to ſwallow, was the cauſe of his Death.*"

[I] *No Author that I know of has remarked the Time or Place of his Death.*] It is true, *Suidas* ſays, that *Anacreon*, being driven from *Teos*, on account of the Revolt of *Hiſtiæus*, retired to *Abdera*, in *Thrace*: But this does not imply, that he died there; we can only conjecture from it, with ſome Probability, that he did. And, indeed, *Anacreon* muſt have been very old at that time, ſince the Victories, which the *Perſians* obtained over the Favourers of the Revolt of *Hiſtiæus*, are much later than the Death of *Hipparchus*, and fall under the LXXIſt Olympiad. It may be conjectured from this Paſſage of *Suidas*, that, after *Anacreon* had left *Athens*, whither *Hipparchus* had invited him, he retired to *Teos*; which makes it probable, that he retired alſo to *Teos*, after the Ruin of *Polycrates*; and that *Hipparchus* ſent him thither the Fifty-Oar'd Veſſel, as *Tanaquil Faber* aſſerts. We need not wonder, that *Anacreon* made choice of *Abdera* for his Retirement; it being a Town, which thoſe of *Teos* had built, after they had left their Habitations, when *Harpagus*, the Lieutenant of *Cyrus*, made himſelf Maſter of *Ionia* (26). *Strabo* does not ſpeak of their Tranſmigration in this manner; He only ſays, that the *Teians*, in the time of *Anacreon*, being unable to bear the Inſults of the *Perſians*, retired to *Abdera* (27). This may be the ſame Event, mentioned by *Herodotus*; for *Harpagus* invaded *Ionia* in the LIXth Olympiad, at which time *Anacreon* made ſome Figure in the World.

(26) Herod. lib. 1. cap. 168.

(27) Strabo, lib. 14.

[K] *No Author has* —— *decided what was his Father's Name.*] *Suidas* mentions four Perſons, who have paſſed for the Father of *Anacreon*. If it be a Compliment to *Homer*, that ſeveral Towns contended for his Birth; it muſt be confeſſed, that this is a very poor one to *Anacreon*; for, in ſhort, it is a Proof of the Obſcurity of his Family, rather than any thing elſe. For had his Father been a noted Man in *Teos*, Authors would not ſo eaſily have loſt ſight of him, or have confounded him with others. Nevertheleſs I find, that Madam *Dacier* cites *Plato* to prove, *That* Anacreon *was a Man of great Birth, and related to* Solon, *whoſe Father was of the ancient Family of King* Codrus, *and his Mother Couſin German to the Mother of* Piſiſtratus (28). She pretends to prove this from a Paſſage in the Dialogue of *Temperance*, where ſhe finds, that the Father of *Charmides* deſcended from the ancient Family of Dropidas, and of Anacreon, and Solon, *which had been always diſtinguiſhed from others by their Beauty, Virtue, and Riches*. Perſuaded as I am of the Learning of this Lady, I find myſelf reduced to believe one of theſe three things; either that *her Plato* is very different from *mine*; or that ſhe has not taken this Paſſage from the Original; or that ſhe has too cloſely followed the ill Tranſlation of *Serranus*. I find in *my Plato* nothing more, than that the paternal Family of *Charmidas* had been celebrated by *Solon, Anacreon*, and ſeveral other Poets, as being remarkably endowed with the Advantages of Beauty, Virtue, &c. Ἥ τε γὰρ πατρῴα ὑμῖν οἰκία ἡ Κριτίου τοῦ Δρωπίδου καὶ ὑπὸ Ἀνακρέοντος καὶ ὑπὸ Σόλωνος καὶ ὑπ' ἄλλων πολλῶν Ποιητῶν ἐγκεκωμιασμένη παραδέδοται ἡμῖν ὡς διαφέρουσα κάλλει τε καὶ ἀρετῇ καὶ τῇ ἄλλῃ λεγομένῃ εὐδαιμονίᾳ. This is the Paſſage, as it ſtands in the Edition of *Frankfurt* in 1602. That of *Serranus* diſ-

(28) *Life of* Anacreon.

Whether A-NA CRE-ON was a Man of great Birth.

fers

ANACREON.

(d) Tanaquill. Faber, Notis in Anacreon. Madam Dacier *&c*, does not always agree with him in this. See her Preface to Anacreon.

There are several Translations of his Poems [L]: But some Criticks will not allow, that all the Verses, which are at this day extant under his Name, are His (d). They, who have mentioned his Love for *Sappho*, have not regarded Chronology, as I shall prove in the Article of That Lady. It is said that a Present of Money, which *Polycrates* sent him, gave him so much disturbance, that he could not sleep for several Nights; and that he returned it to That Prince. This is not very probable, tho' *Stobæus* gives us *Aristotle* for his Voucher. *Gyraldus* cites only the *Greek* Collections of *Arsenius* in proof of it (e).

(e) Gyrald. Hist. Poet. Dial. 9. pag. 471.

fers only in the Word ἐγκεκραμένη, which, by a Mistake of the Printers of *Frankfort*, has been put instead of the ἐγκεκραμμένη of the Edition of *Serranus*; but *Ficinus*'s Version is much better, though perhaps not so good as the following. "Nam, "quæ paternum vobis genus est, domus Critiæ filii "Dropidæ, tum ab Anacreonte, tum à Solone, mul- "tisque aliis Poetis laudata nobis tradita fuit, ut "præcellens formâ, virtute, cæterisque quæ felicitatis "nomine veniunt.——*For we find, that the House of* "*Critias, the Son of Dropidas, from which you are* "*descended by the Father's side, was celebrated by* "*Anacreon, Solon, and many other Poets, as being* "*remarkable for Beauty, Virtue, and other Perfe-* "*ctions, which Happiness includes*." *Serranus*'s Version is as follows. "Nam Paternum quidem Genus, "quod cum isto Critia commune habes, à Dropida, "Anacreonte, Solone, & aliis multis celeberrimis "Poetis, deducitur, & vobis traditur, veluti robore "& virtute & alio omni genere felicitatis instructis- "simum. — *For your paternal Descent, which is* "*common to you with Critias, is derived from Dro-* "*pidas, Solon, and many famous Poets; and descends* "*to you adorned with Strength, Virtue, and every* "*kind of Happiness*." I omit observing, that one might be descended, by the Father's Side, from *Solon* and *Anacreon*, without *Solon* and *Anacreon* being related to each other. Every Person has two sorts of paternal Relations, the Family of his Father's Father, and That of his Father's Mother.

[L] *There are several Translations of his Poems*.] Those, which Madam *Dacier* has mentioned, are as follows. The Reader will be pleased to see her Opinion of them. "It is a long time, *says she*, since "*Anacreon* was translated into *French* by *Remi Bel-* "*leau*; but, besides that his Translation is in Verse, "and consequently very unfaithful, it is in such an "antiquated Style, that it is impossible to find any "Pleasure in reading it. It was translated into *Ita-* "*lian* some Years since; but the Translator has no "more kept to the *Greek*, than *Remi Belleau*; ne- "vertheless his Translation is pleasing enough, tho' "it be sometimes very different from the Sense of "*Anacreon*, and though he takes every Moment so "great a Liberty, that it ought rather to be account- "ed a Paraphrase, than a Translation. The *Latin* "Version, part whereof was done by *Henry Stephens*, "and the other by *Elias Andreas*, which is gene- "rally used, seems to me to be the best; yet it is "not without Faults, and, being also in Verse, it "is often very obscure, and, in several Places, at- "tributes to *Anacreon* what he never thought of." This is what Madam *Dacier* says, in the Preface to her *Anacreon*, published at *Paris*, in the Year 1681, with the *Greek* Text on one side, and the Translation in *French* Prose on the other, and some Remarks on each Piece of *Anacreon*. Give me leave to add, that the Translation of *Remi Belleau* appeared in the Year 1556. It has been said, that *Daurat* was the true Author of the Translation, which *Henry Stephens* ascribed to himself. *Colomies* assures us, that *Isaac Vossius* told him, *That he had an Anacreon in* *his Possession, in which Scaliger has remarked with* *his own Hand, that Henry Stephens was not the* *Author of the Latin Version of the Odes of That Poet,* *but John Dorat* (29). The *Italian* Translation, which Madam *Dacier* speaks of, is That of *Bartholomeo Corsini*, which Mr *Regnier des Marais* caused to be printed, at *Paris*, in the Year 1672 (30). I do not wonder, that Madam *Dacier* takes no Notice of the Translation of *Anacreon* done by a Youth, who is since become very famous under the Name of the Abbot *de la TRAPPE*; for I believe That Translation was never printed. Mr *Baillet* informs us of many things relating to it. "He knew so well, "(*says he* (31)) *speaking of* Armand Bouthillier de "Rance) how to improve under his Masters, by his "Assiduity and Application to his Studies, that at

(29) Colomies, Opusc. pag. 108.

(30) See the Acta Erudit. 1693. pag. 236.

(31) Baillet, Enfans celebres, p. 359.

"ten Years of Age, he understood the *Greek* Poets "very well, especially *Homer*; and he had scarce at- "tained to the Age of twelve or thirteen Years, "when he published a new Edition of the Works "of *Anacreon*, with *Greek* Remarks, which were "admired by the Learned. This Edition appeared "in 8vo, at *Paris*, in the Year 1639; and Time "has not in the least diminished the Astonishments, "which these Remarks still gave to those, who com- "pare them with the tender Age of the Author. "I say nothing of a *French* Translation, which he "then composed of the same Poet; tho' it pleased "very much those, who, at that time, were per- "feeling our Language, and shewed, that he could "write as politely in *French*, as he understood *Greek* "and *Latin*. Mr *Baillet* mentions neither the Place, nor the Year of the Impression, and does not so much as say, in general, that the Work had been published; which makes me believe, that It had only appeared in Manuscript. I am the more confirmed in this Thought, by finding, that Mr *de Longe-Pierre* says not a Word of this Translation; though he takes notice, that *Henry Stephens* rendered the same same *Odes* of Anacreon into *French Verse*, which he afterwards turned into Latin. He observes likewise, that *Ronsard* translated many of them; he says this in the Preface to his Version. His Work was published in the Year 1684. The *Greek* (2) is on one side, and the *French* Translation in Verse on the other: And there are critical Remarks at the end of each Piece. Mr *Regnier des Marais*, perpetual Secretary to the *French* Academy, gave, in the Year 1693, a Version of *Anacreon* in *Italian* Verse, with Remarks.

(32) See the Nouvelles de la Republiq. des Lettres, for Novem. 1683. Art. 8.

The following curious Supplement is taken Word for Word out of a Letter, which I have received from Mr *de la Monnoie*. "No care has been "taken, hitherto, to collect, and examine several "curious Particulars, concerning the Poems, which "are extant, of *Anacreon*. It has been said, that "*Henry Stephens* first brought them to light; but, "Where or How, few Persons know. He met with "the Ode Λέγουσιν αἱ γυναῖκες, on the Cover of "an old Book, as we read in *Victorius*, who inserted "it in the seventeenth Chapter of the twentieth "Book of his *Variæ Lectiones*. Till then, nothing "had been seen of *Anacreon*, but what *Aulus Gellius* "and the *Anthologia* had preferred. By chance two "Manuscripts, containing several Pieces of this Poet, "fell into the Hands of the same *Henry Stephens*. "He was obliged for the first to *John Clement*, an "*Englishman*, Servant to Sir *Thomas More*; and he "brought the second, after a long Journey, from "*Italy* into *France*. And, having carefully compared "the one with the other, he formed the Edition, "which he published, the first time, at *Paris*, in "the Year 1554. This Book met with a Reception "attended with different Opinions. Most of the "Learned looked upon it as an happy Discovery: "some distrusted it. *Robortel*, in his Dissertation "concerning the Art of correcting Books, did not "acknowledge it to be genuine. *Fulvius Ursinus* "inserted no other Poems of *Anacreon* in his Edi- "tion of the *Greek* Lyricks, but those, which he "found mentioned by the ancient Authors, as sus- "specting the rest. It were to be wished, that the "two Manuscripts, before mentioned, and which "are the only ones, which have been seen, had "been preferred. But *Henry Stephens*, unhappily "falling into a kind of Distraction towards the latter "end of his Days, suffered them to perish with se- "veral others, which he communicated to no one, not "so much as to his Son-in-law *Casaubon*. He trans- "flated into *French* Verse the same *Odes* of *Anacreon*, "which he rendered into *Latin* Verse. *Eas Ana-* "*creontis Odas*, says he, in the Preface to his An- "notations upon the *Paris* Edition of *Anacreon*, in "4to, 1554, *quas jam ante Gallicas fecerant, in e-* "*liquet*

" liquet, amicorum gratiam Latinè quoque aggressus " Richard Renvoisy, Master of the singing Boys of
" suam vertere. What has been reported of Isaac Vos- " the Holy Chapel at Dijon, made, according to
" sius, who said, that he had an Anacreon in his " the Testimony of Antony du Verdier, page 34 of
" Possession, wherein Scaliger had noted with his " his Bibliotheque, another French Version of the
" own Hand, that John Dorat was the Author of the " Odes of Anacreon. In This probably du Verdier is
" Latin Translation of this Poet, ascribed to Henry " mistaken. I take it to be the Version of Belleau,
" Stephens, ought not to be regarded. Either Vos- " which Renvoisy set to Musick in the Year 1558,
" sius was mistaken, or Scaliger was misinformed. " or 1559; which du Verdier himself gives us suf-
" Henry Stephens, who was no Plagiary, was very " ficiently to understand, when, at Page 1222, he
" capable of making such a Version as That; and, " quotes this Renvoisy only as a Musician. As for
" if it had been Dorat's, he would not have failed " the French Version of the same Poet, composed by
" to have laid claim to it. It was from this that " Mr Beuthillier de Rance, at the Age of twelve
" Remi Belleau made his in French Verse, which " or thirteen Years, it was never printed; and it
" perhaps appeared so fine to Henry Stephens, that, " is very likely, that, if there was such an one,
" after he had read it, he durst not publish That, " it was in Prose, though the Authors, who have
" which he had composed in the same Language. " mentioned it, do not positively say so."

(a) In Latin Tabernæ. Hence it is called Tabernas.

ANANIA (JOHN LAURENCE d') a Native of *Taverna* (a) in *Calabria*, lived about the End of the XVIth Century. He is Author of a Geographical Book in *Italian*, and a *Latin* Work, intituled, De Natura Dæmonum, which was printed at *Venice*, in the Year 1582, in 8vo. The other Work is intituled Cosmographia, overo l'universale Fabrica del Mondo———Cosmography, or the Universal Fabric of the World, and was printed at *Venice*, in the Year 1576, in 4to (b). *Vossius* has omitted this Author in his Catalogue of Geographers.

(b) Baudrand Tom. 1. pag. 441. mentions only the Edition of Venice in 1584.

ANAXAGORAS, one of the most illustrious Philosophers of Antiquity, was born at *Clazomenæ*, in *Ionia*, about the LXXth Olympiad, and was a Disciple of *Anaximenes*. His noble Extraction, his Riches, and the Generosity, which induced him to resign his whole Patrimony to his Relations [*A*], made him very famous. He applied

[*A*] *To resign all his Patrimony to his Relations.*] Before the Gospel had taught Men to renounce the World and it's Riches, in order to make a swift Progress towards Perfection, some Philosophers were sensible of this, and parted with their worldly Goods, to attend more freely to the Study of Wisdom, and the Search of Truth. They believed, that the Cares of a Family, and an Inheritance, were Clogs, which hindered our Advancement towards the End most worthy of our Esteem. *Anaxagoras* and *Democritus* (1), were of this Opinion. " Quid ergo, *(says* Cicero) (2), " aut Homero ad delectationem animi ac voluptatem, " aut cuiquam docto desuisse unquam arbitramur? " An ni ita se res haberet, Anaxagoras, aut hic ipse " Democritus, agros & Patrimonia sua relinquissent, " huic discendi quærendique divinæ delectationi toto " se animo dedissent ? ——— *What then can we think* " *wanting to compleat the Satisfaction and Pleasure* " *of* Homer, *or any other learned Man? Without* " *this perfect Happiness, would* Anaxagoras, *or this* " Democritus, *have resigned their Possessions and Patrimonies, and given themselves up entirely to the* " *divine Pleasure of acquiring Knowledge?* " It was to such a Renouncing of the World, that *Anaxagoras* thought himself indebted for his Learning, or, to use his own Expression, for his Safety. " Quali porro " studio Anaxagoram flagrasse credimus? Qui, cum " è diuturna peregrinatione patriam repetiisset, posses- " sionesque desertas vidisset, " non essem," inquit " " ego salvus," nisi ista perissem (3). ——— *How* " *eager after Knowledge must we suppose* Anaxagoras " *to have been; who, upon returning home, after a* " *long Absence from his native Country, and seeing* " *his Possessions lying desolate and in ruins, made use of* " *this Expression,* " *Had not these perished, I myself* " *should not have been safe.*" Socrates, with his usual Irony, shews, that " the Sophists of his Time were " wiser than *Anaxagoras*; for, instead of quitting " their Patrimonies, as he had done, they took a " great deal of pains to enrich themselves, being " convinced of the Folly of the old Times, and per- " suaded, that the principal Wisdom consisted in pro- " moting one's own Interest: that is to say, in the Art " of heaping up great Riches." Τέταρτον γὰρ Ἀναξαγόρᾳ φασὶ συμβῆναι ἢ ὑμῖν. καταλειφ- θῆναι γὰρ αὐτῷ πολλὰ χρημάτων καταμελῆ- σαι, καὶ ἀπολέσαι πάντα. οὕτως αὐτὸν ἀνοήτα σοφίζεσθαι. λέγουσι δὲ καὶ περὶ ἄλλων τῶν πα- λαιῶν ὑπέρ τοιαῦτα. τοῦτο μὲν οὖν μοι δοκεῖς καλὸν τεκμηριον ἀποφαίνειν περὶ σοφίας τῶν νῦν πρὸς τῆς πρότερον, καὶ πολλοῖς συνδοκεῖ, ὅτι τὸν σοφὸν αὐτῷ αὐτῷ μάλιστα δεῖ σοφὸν εἶναι. τοῦτο δ' ἐστὶν ὅρος ὃς ἂν πλεῖστον ἀργύριον εἰργάσηται (4). *Cum Anaxagoras, contra ac vobis* contigit, amplum patrimonium cum accepisset, neglexisse dissipasseque dicatur, adeo stulte philosophatus est: deoque cæteris illorum temporum sapientibus alia quædam hujusmodi tradunt. Quapropter optimam hanc attulisse conjecturam videris, quod sapientes nostri superioribus præstant, multique in hoc consentiunt, sapientem in primis sibi ipsi sapere oportere. Hujus autem hæc est summa, ut argentum plurimum acquiratur. This puts me in mind of a Distinction which I have read in *Aristotle.* " We find, *says* he (5), that *Anaxagoras*, " and *Thales*, and such like Philosophers, were wise, " but not prudent Men, because they were ignorant " of what was useful to them (6): They were ac- " quainted with abstruse, lofty, wonderful, and di- " vine Things; but they turned to no account: for " they disregarded the good things, and Advantages " of this Life." This is the Sense of a great many Men; they condemn all Employments, which do not tend to raise a Fortune. Whatever does not treat *de pane lucrando*, or is of no use, πρὸς τὰ ἀληθῆα, that is, in the vulgar Phrase, *to make the Pot boil* (7), seems to them vain and superfluous. *Anaxagoras* had quite another Notion. He abandoned his Lands to the Mercy of the Sheep, that he might apply himself wholly to Astronomy and Physic. *Philo* (8), *Plutarch* (9), *Philostratus* (10), *Himerius* (11), and *Suidas*, speak of it. *Democritus* and *Crates* are seldom forgot upon this Occasion. The Fathers of the Church likewise mention it (12): But St *Chrysostom* (13) declares, that the Conduct of these Philosophers was mere Folly, and not a Contempt of Riches. The Devil, says he, *has always been studious to depreciate and defame God's Creatures, because of the Incapacity of some Men to make a right use of their Money.* This is paying the Heathens in their own Coin, who accounted all the Christians, who parted with their Possessions, and retired into Solitudes, Fools and Madmen (14). Thus things are praised or blamed, according to the different Prejudices of Men. Observe, that *Apollonius Tyanæus* censured the Conduct of *Anaxagoras*, as the Action of a Philosopher, *who had more regard to the Advantage of the Beasts, than that of Men* (15). *Vigenere* has miserably rendered the Passage of *Apollonius*: he makes him say, that *Anaxagoras, giving himself up to the feeding of Camels, and white Cattle, employed his Philosophy rather in the Service of the Brute Creation, than of Men*. The Latin Version of *Rhincuccinus* is equally bad. *Aiebat Clazomenium Anaxagoram* & *camelorum armenti nutriendis intentum pecorum gratia magis quam hominum philosophatum esse.*

(1) See Remark [B] of the Article DEMOCRITUS.
(2) Cicero, Tusculan. lib. 1. circa finem.
(3) Valer. Maxim. l. 3. cap. 7. n. 6. in extern.
(4) Plato, in Hipp. a majore, (and not in Phædro, as Menage quotes it, in Diog. Laërt. lib. 2. n. 6.) pag. 1246.

3. cap. 22. Origen. contra Celsum, lib. 2. (13) See lib 7th Homily upon the Acts of the Apostles, pag. 67. Edit. Parif. 1636. (14) See Rusinus Nomafianus, in his Itinerarium. (15) Philostr. in Vita Apollo. li. l. 1. cap. 1.

(5) Arist. Endemii 1. lib. 6. cap. 7. pag. 134.
(6) ἐσ τις δὲ σοφίας ὀνομάζουσι τοὺς ἄκρως οἶκε ἐν ἄκρως ἐξαίρετος.
(7) Poor pow'd dirt-eating houfelire to nourish.
(8) Philo de Vita contempl.
(9) I quote his Words in the Remark [A] of the Article DEMOCRITUS.
(10) Philostr. la Vit. Apollon. lib. 1. c. 8.
(11) Himer. apud Phot. pag. 1088.
(12) Lact. l. 3.

This

ANAXAGORAS.

applied himself wholly to the Study of Nature, without intermeddling in any public Affairs; which occasioned some One to ask him, whether he had no Concern at all for his Country. His Answer was admirable; nor could a Christian Philosopher have given a better; *Yes*, said he, stretching his Hands towards Heaven, *I have an extraordinary Concern for my Country* (a). He was asked, another time, *To what End are you born?* he replied, *To contemplate the Sun, the Moon, and the Heavens* (b). Accordingly he placed the supreme Good, or the End of Human Life, in Contemplation, and that Freedom of Condition, which it produces (c). He was but Twenty Years of Age, when he began to philosophize at *Athens* (d). Some Authors say, He was the First, who removed the School of Philosophy thither, which had flourished in *Ionia* from the Time of it's Founder *Thales*; which I shall examine in the Article of the Philosopher ARCHELAUS. It is certain he had several Famous Disciples at *Athens*, and particularly *Pericles*, and *Euripides*; and some add *Themistocles* and *Socrates*. But Chronology is against them as to *Themistocles* (e). There is scarce any thing, which gives us a greater Idea of his Ability, than the Nature of the Progress, which *Pericles* made under him; for he inspired him with those grave and majestic Manners, which enabled him to govern the Republic (f); he qualified him for that sublime and victorious Eloquence, which made him so powerful (g); and he taught him to fear the Gods (h) without Superstition. Add to this, that his Counsels assisted him greatly in supporting the Weight of Government (i). He distinguished himself by the Novelty and Singularity of his Doctrines. He taught, that there were Hills, Vallies, and Inhabitants in

(a) Diogen. Laert. l. 2. c. 6, 7.

(b) Id. ib. n. 10.

(c) Clem. Alexandrin. Strom. st. lib. 2. pag. 416.

(d) Diogen. Laërt. ibid. n. 7.

(e) Plutarch. in Themist. pag. 112.

(f) Id. in Pericle, pag. 154.

(g) See Remark [B] of the Article PERICLES, at the end.

(h) See Remarks [A] and [B] of the same Article.

(i) See Citation (19).

This Censure looks like a Cavil; for, to say nothing of the Profit, which public Pasturage bring to Men, is it not plain, that *Anaxagoras* had reason to believe, that those Lands, which he forsook, would be cultivated by his Relations? The four Verses in the Life of *Virgil*, which begin with *Sic vos non vobis*, contain a great Truth, which is, that the Care, which is taken of Sheep, Oxen, &c. redounds to the good of Men. *Eusebius* has been more just to *Anaxagoras*, than *Apollonius Tyanæus*: for he represents the abandoning of his Lands, as a greater Proof of his Attachment to Philosophy, than all the other Philosophers had ever given. Φασὶ γοῦν ὡς ἄρα τῷ μάλισα παρὰ τὰς περὶ αὑτὸν ἐθαυμασε φυσιολογίαν μηλοβότον γῆ τοι τὴν ἑαυτῷ χώραν δι᾽ αὐτὴν εἴασε (16). *Et vero superiores omnes quantum is Physiologiæ studio superarit, vel ex eo intelligi, quod agros ipse suos magnitudine passionis uberrimos ejus amore reliquerit*. I make use of the Vulgar Version, which is that of *Francis Vigerus*; but I observe, that It is faulty as to μηλόβοτον χώρας, which ought to be rendred *agros ovibus deposcendos*, and not *agros magnitudine passionis uberrimos*.

There remain still some Remarks to be made on the Disinterestedness of *Anaxagoras*. He was one, who would have very well discharged the Duties of public Offices; for his Counsels were not only very serviceable to Him, who governed the *Athenians*, but even necessary (17); yet he always avoided interfering with the Government. He would never make use of the Authority and Credit of *Pericles*, to raise himself to Employs; but confined his Desires to Philosophical Speculations, being altogether free from all Ambition, which many other learned Men are incapable of subduing, even when they have not, as he had, an insight into Affairs of State, or the Protection and Favour of those in Authority. I question not but *Cicero* had our Philosopher particularly in view, when, speaking of several great Men, he says, That it was a Misfortune to the Commonwealth, that they wholly applied themselves to the Study of Nature. His Words are, " *Eadem autem alii prudentia, sed consilio ad vitæ studia dispari, quietem atque otium secuti, ut Pythagoras, Democritus, Anaxagoras, à regendis civitatibus totos se ad cognitionem rerum transtulerunt; quæ vita propter tranquillitatem, & propter ipsius scientiæ suavitatem, quâ nihil est hominibus jucundius, plures quàm utile fuit rebus publicis delectavit* (18). —— *With the same Prudence, but with a view to different Studies, others, seeking for Retirement and Ease, as Pythagoras, Democritus, and Anaxagoras, have quitted the Government of States, to give themselves wholly up to the Study of Nature; a Life, which, on account of it's Tranquillity, and the Sweetness of Knowledge itself, has engaged more Persons to embrace it, than the public Good can spare.*" He not only slighted all Honours, but was careless, even with regard to the Necessaries of Life. He considered not, how easy it was for him to heap up Riches, by the Credit and Friendship of *Pericles*; nor did he provide against the Wants of old Age. His Enquiries into the Secrets of Nature swallowed up all his other Passions. He found, at last, that his Contempt of Riches ought not to have been so great; for, in his old Age, he was reduced to Want, and, in this Necessity, he took up a calm Resolution to starve himself to death; but *Pericles*, having notice of it, prevented it. Let us hear Plutarch; " *Pericles*, says he (19), assisted several poor " People with his Riches, and, among others, *Anaxa-* " *goras*; of whom it is related, that, *Pericles* being " so busy, that he had no leisure to think of him, " he found himself forsaken by every one in his old " Age, and, having muffled up his Head, laid him- " self down with a Resolution to die of Hunger. " *Pericles*, being informed thereof, went immedi- " ately to him in great Concern, and earnestly en- " treated him to alter his Resolution, and live, bewail- " ing, not *Anaxagoras*, but himself, that he should " lose such a faithful and wise Counsellor in the Oc- " currences of public Affairs. *Anaxagoras*, upon this, " uncovered his Face, and said to him; " They, " *Pericles*, who desire the Light of a Lamp, put " Oil into it to keep it alive." Would you see another Proof of the little Ambition of this Philosopher? They offered to pay to his Memory all the Honours he could desire; but he rejected the Favour, and only desired, that the Day of his Death might be a Play-day for School-Boys. Τὰς δεδομένας αρεὶς τιμὰς, ητήσατο τὴν ἡμέραν ἐκείνην καθ᾽ ἢν ἂν τελευτήσῃ τοῖς παισὶ ἀφεῖσαι παίζειν σχολάζειν ἀπὸ τῶν μαθημάτων (20): *Honoribus qui offerebantur recusatis, postulavit ut ea qua decessisset è vivis die pueris scholarum vacatio & discendi concederetur*. Was not this to wish, that his Death might be a Subject of Pleasure to many, and not of Affliction; and that he had an extraordinary contempt for every thing, which flatters most the Vanity of Mortals?

I shall make two short Reflexions on this Passage of the Life of *Pericles*. It informs us, that *Anaxagoras* was very well skilled in Politics, though he only made Profession of speculative Philosophy. Why then should we not believe, that he composed the Treatise *de Regno*, out of which *Ælian* alledges a Sentence (21)? Granting it to be the Work of another *Anaxagoras*, as *Meursius* and *Menage* suppose (22), yet the Reason, which *Menage* gives for it, is not a good one (23): He himself would have been sensible of it, if he had recollected this Passage of *Plutarch*. This is my first Reflexion. The other is, that the old Age, ascribed to our Philosopher, does not agree with the Account of those, who say, that he came to *Athens* at twenty Years of Age, and that he lived there thirty Years. He must then have received *Pericles*'s Visit, mentioned by *Plutarch*, at about fifty Years of Age. I shall conclude with a Passage of *Ovid*, which tells us, that the first Astronomers must needs have been free from Sensuality, and from the Care

(16) Euseb. Præpar. Evang. lib. 14. cap. 14. pag. 730.

(17) See below, Plutarch's Words, Citation (19).

(18) Cicero de Oratore, lib. 3. c. 15. (and not l. 2. 2. Menage quotes it in Diog. Laërt. n. 7. fol. 91. B.

(19) Plutarch. in Vit. Pericle, pag. 162.

(20) Id. in Præcept. Resp. gerendæ, p. 820. D. Diog. Laërtius, as appears by the Text of this Article, relates the Circumstances somewhat differently.

(21) Ælian. Var. Hist. lib. 4. c. 14.

(22) See Kuhnius's Notes upon this Passage of Ælian.

(23) Alius igitur fuerit ab Anaxagora nostro, &c. Menag. in Laërt. l. 2. n. 7. ibi de oros it's Consequence from Anaxagoras's never applying himself to Affairs of Government.

VOL. I. Eeee

ANAXAGORAS.

in the Moon; and that the Sun was a fiery Mass of Matter [B], and bigger than Peloponnesus (k). He said, that Snow was black (l), for which he assigned a very poor reason; for he built his Notion, on the one Side, upon this, that Snow is condensed Water; and he supposed, on the other side, that black is the true Colour of Water (m). He believed, in general, that our Eyes are incapable of discerning the true Colour of Objects, and that our Senses deceive us; and that therefore it is the business of Reason, not of our Eyes, to judge of things (n). He held that the Heavens were made of Stone (o), and that it was the Swiftness of their Motion, which hindered them from falling (p). Others assure us, that he believed the Heavens to be *of the Nature of Fire as to their Essence*; and that the Stones of the Earth being snatched upwards, and set on fire, by the Rapidity of it's Revolution, became Stars (q); and that, at the beginning, Animals were formed out of the Earth, and a warm Moisture (r), and that afterwards they produced each other, the Males on the right side, and the Females on the left (s). He admitted as many sorts of Principles, as compound Bodies; for he supposed, that each kind of Body was made up of many similar Particles, which he called *Homœomeriæ*, by reason of this Conformity. But this led him to grant a thing, which perplexed his System; namely, that the Seeds, or Principles, of all Species, are to be found in each Individual. Moreri has misrepresented this Opinion [C]. Lucretius has well explained, and solidly refuted

(k) Diogen. Laërt. lib. 2. n. 8.
(l) Cicero, Acad. Quæst. lib. 2. cap 23, & 31. Lactant. lib. 5. cap. 3.
(m) Sextus Empiricus, Pyrrhon. Hypotypos. lib. 1. c. 13.
(n) Id. adv. Mathem. l. 7. p. 133.
(o) See the beginning of the Remark [I].
(p) Diogen. Laërt: n. lib. n. 12.
(q) Plutarch. de Placitis Philosoph. lib. 2. c. 13.
(r) Diogen. Laërt. ibid. n. 12.
(s) Id. ibn. 9.

Care of attaining to Honours and Riches: Anaxagoras is a pregnant Instance of it.

Felices animos, quibus hæc cognoscere primis,
Inque domos superas scandere cura fuit!
Credibile est illos pariter vitiisque locisque
Altius humanis exseruisse caput.
Non Venus & vinum sublimia pectora fregit;
Officiumque fori, militiæve labor.
Nec levis ambitio, perfusaque gloria fuco;
Magnarumve fames sollicitavit opum.
Admovêre oculis distantia sidera nostris;
Æthereaque ingenio supposuere suo.
Sic petitur cœlum : non ut ferat Ossan Olympus;
Summaque Peliacus sidera tangat apex.
Nos quoque sub ducibus cœlum metabimur illis,
Ponemusque suos ad stata signa dies (24).

(24) Ovid. Fast. lib. 1. ver. 297.

Thrice happy they, who first, with Souls refin'd,
To these Pursuits their generous Care confined;
Who, nobly spurning Earth's impure Abodes,
Assay'd to climb the Mansions of the Gods.
Such Breasts, sublime, Intemp'rance never broke;
Such ne'er submitted to Love's shameful Yoke.
Such fled the wrangling of the noisy Bar,
The hideous Din of Arms, and painful Toils of War;
Foes to Ambition, and her idle Lure,
From Thirst of Fame, from Thirst of Gold, secure.
Such Souls, examining the distant Skies,
Unveil'd it's hidden Lights to mortal Eyes.
Let huge Olympus lofty Ossa bear;
Let Pelion tow'r on Ossa high in Air;
Mountains on Mountains short of Heav'n must rise;
This only Ladder reaches to the Skies.
Led by these Guides, to measure Heav'n we try,
And to each Sign it's stated Days apply.

[B] *He taught —— that the Sun was a fiery Mass of Matter*] I make use of this general Expression, because the Interpreters do not agree about the true Sense of these Words of *Diogenes Laërtius*: Τὸν ἥλιον μύδρον εἶναι διάπυρον (25). Some will have them to signify a Mass of burning Iron; others rather understand by them a flaming Stone; and others, a fiery Globe, neither of Iron nor Stone. *Videtur mihi Anaxagoras*, (thus speaks *Casaubon*) *per μύδρον διάπυρον non tam lapidem aut ferrum, quàm globum quendam igneum, λιθώδη & βαρὺν, ut ait Plutarchus, intelligere voluisse* (26). Most of those, who have mentioned this Doctrine of *Anaxagoras*, have adhered to the second Explication; which agrees perfectly with the Hypothesis of this Philosopher, as will appear hereafter (27). I begin with *Xenophon's* Words. Φάσκων δὲ τὸν ἥλιον λίθον διάπυρον εἶναι, καὶ τοῦτο ἠγνόει ὅτι λίθ. μὲν ἐν πυρὶ ὢν ἔτε λάμπει, ἔτε πολὺν χρόνον ἀντέχει. ὁ δὲ ἥλι⊕· τὸν ἀεὶ/α χρόνον πάντων λαμπρότερ⊕· ὢν διαμένει (28).

(25) Diogen. Laërt. lib. 2. n. 8.
(26) If. Casaub. in hunc locum Diog. Laërtii.
(27) In Remark [I].
(28) Xenophon. Memorabil. l. 4.

This is, according to Mr *Charpentier's* Translation, Saying also, *That the Sun was only a fiery Stone, he did not consider, that a Stone does not shine in the Fire, neither can it continue long there, without being consumed; whereas the Sun continues always, and is an inexhaustible Source of Light.* *Plato* shall be my second Evidence. He introduces *Socrates*, who, finding himself charged with saying, that the Sun was a Stone, and the Moon an Earth, answers, *They take me for Anaxagoras, whose Books are full of such Discourses; and they fancy that I am so foolish as to teach young People these absurdities: They would laugh at me, if I should ascribe to myself a Doctrine, contained in the Works of another Man, which are sold very cheap* (29). I have only given a general Notion of the Words of *Plato*; and therefore I shall set down the very Words of that Philosopher, for the Satisfaction of those, who are not contented with the Substance of an Evidence. Ἀναξαγόρου οἴει καθηγορεῖν ὦ φίλε Μέλιτε· καὶ ὕτω καταφρονεῖς τῶνδε, καὶ ἀπείρους ἀτέχνως γραμμάτων εἶναι, ὅτε ἐκ εἰδέναι ὅτι τ' Ἀναξαγόρου βιβλία τοῦ Κλαζομενίου γέμει τούτων τῶν λόγων. καὶ δὴ καὶ οἱ νέοι ταῦτα παρ' ἐμοῦ μανθάνουσιν ἃ ἔξεςιν ἐνίοτε, εἰ πάνυ πολλᾶ, δραχμῆς ἐκ τῆς ὀρχήστρας πριαμένοις, Σωκράτους καταγελᾷν, ἐὰν προσποιῆται ἑαυτοῦ εἶναι, ἄλλως τε καὶ ὕτως ἄτοπα ὄντα (30). *Anaxagoram tu quidem, ô amice Melite, accusare tibi videris, atque ita hos parvi facis, existimasne eos literarum ignaros esse, quasi nesciant libros Anaxagoræ Clazomenii ejusmodi opinionibus esse plenos. Juvenes vero hæc à me discunt? quibus liceret interdum, etiam si multa sint, unius drachmæ pretio ementibus ex orchestra Socratem deridere, si sua esse fingeret, præsertim quum tam absurda sint.* You will find in *Plutarch*, that *Anaxagoras* was condemned as an impious Man, for having said, that the Sun was a Stone (31). *St Cyril of Alexandria* (32), and *St Austin* (33), are to be reckoned among those, who have said, that, according to *Anaxagoras*, the Sun was a fiery Stone. *Suidas* renders μύδρον διάπυρον, in *Diogenes Laërtius*, by πυρινοῦ λίθου. And therefore I wonder, that Mr *Charpentier* chose rather to say, that *Anaxagoras* maintained, that *the Sun was only a fiery Mass of Iron* (34).

(29) Plato in Apologia Socratis. pag. m. 484. A.
(30) Id. ibid.
(31) Plutarch. de Superstitione, pag. 169. E.
(32) Cyrillus lib 6. contra Julian.
(33) August. de Civ.tat. Dei, lib. 18. cap. 41.
(34) Charpentier's Life of Socrates, p. 7.

[C] *Moreri has misrepresented this Opinion.* Lucretius *has well explained, and solidly confuted it.*] I shall sum up, in this Remark, all the Mistakes of *Moreri*.

I. He supposes, that *Anaxagoras* taught, *That the first Causes of Things had in them the Characters of the Parts*; for, *as Gold is composed of small Particles united together, so likewise this great World is composed of similar Particles, which make up the whole, and are the Primum Mobile of all things*. What Nonsense! What Darkness! Did ever *Heraclitus* express himself so obscurely? To what purpose is the Example of *Gold composed of small Particles united together?* Does this belong to Gold, more than to any other compound Body? He should have added, that those little Particles, of which Gold is compounded, are also Gold themselves. This *Anaxagoras* taught: He believed, that a visible Bone was composed

ANAXAGORAS.

refuted it. This will give us an Opportunity of making some Reflexions on this Doctrine. What was most excellent in his System, was, that, whereas, till then, they had reasoned about the Formation of the World, by admitting only, on one side, *unformed Matter*, and, on the other, *mere Chance*, or a *blind Fatality*, which put it

posed of several invisible Bones, and that the Blood, which we see, was composed of divers small Drops, each whereof was Blood ; and therefore he called his Principles ὁμοιομερείας (35), *similaritates*. Read these Verses of *Lucretius*.

(35) Plutarch. de Placit. Philosoph. l. 1. c. 3. p. 876. Diog. Laërt. lib. 2. n. 8.

Nunc & Anaxagoræ scrutemur Homœomerian,
Quam Græci memorant, nec nostrâ dicere linguâ
Concedit nobis patrii sermonis egestas.
Sed tamen ipsam rem facile est exponere verbis,
Principum rerum quam dicit Homœomerian.
Ossa videlicet è pauxillis atque minutis
Ossibus ; sic & de pauxillis atque minutis
Visceribus victus gigni ; sanguenque creari
Sanguinis inter se multis coëuntibu' guttis ;
Ex aurique putat micis consistere posse
Aurum ; & de terris terram concrescere parvis ;
Ignibus ex ignem ; humorem ex humoribus esse.
Cætera consimili fingit ratione, putatque (36).

(36) Lucret. l. 1. v. 830.

Now let's examine with a curious Eye
Sage Anaxagoras' Philosophy,
By copious Greece term'd Homœomery.
For which our Latin Language, poor in Words,
Not one expressive single Voice affords.
Yet by an easy short Periphrasis
We plainly can discover what it is.
For this it means: That Bones of minute Bones,
That Flesh of Flesh, and Stones of little Stones,
That Nerves take other little Nerves for Food,
And Blood is made of little drops of Blood.
That Gold from parts of the same Nature rose,
That Earths do Earth, Fires Fire, Airs Air compose ;
And so in all things else alike to those.
CREECH.

I will not repeat all the Arguments alledged by *Lucretius* against this Doctrine ; I shall only insist on the first. He shews, that, upon his Hypothesis, the first Principles of things would be as corruptible as the most Compound Bodies themselves. This Consequence draws two great Inconveniencies after it ; one is, that the Difference, which ought to be between Principles and Compounds, is not to be found in *Anaxagoras*'s Hypothesis. The Difference I speak of is, that the first Principles (37) ought always so continue the same, how often soever Compound Bodies be destroyed. Compound Bodies alone are born, and die, and pass through a thousand Vicissitudes of Generation and Corruption ; but Principles retain their Nature unchangeably under all the Forms, which are successively produced. *Anaxagoras* could not say this of HIS Principles ; for (to give an Instance) if those of Flesh had the Nature of Flesh, they would be no less subject to Destruction, than a great Mass of Flesh ; and so of the rest, for he admitted no indivisible Parts in Matter.

(37) I understand by This Word the Matter, or Subjectum ex quo.

Nec tamen esse ulla parte idem in rebus inane,
Concedit, neque corporibus finem esse secandis (38).

(38) Lucret. lib. 1. v. 843.

But he admits no void, he grants no least,
And therefore errs in that, with all the rest.
CREECH.

We shall see hereafter (39), whether he could have supposed, that Principles, being eternal and unerested, ought to be Incorruptible. The other inconvenience is, that the Destruction of first Principles is the same with what is called *Annihilation* ; for when they cease to be, they do not resolve themselves into other things, of which they are composed, since the Simplicity, which is peculiar to them, will not admit of any Composition. They perish therefore entirely, and are annihilated. Now the Light of Nature cannot conceive the Possibility of such a Change.

(39) In Remark [G].

At neque recidere ad nihilum res posse, neque autem
Crescere ex nihilo, testor res ante probatas (40).

But former Arguments have clearly taught,
That things nor perish to, nor rise from, nought.
CREECH.

(40) Lucret. ib. ver. 857.

The Destruction of Compound Bodies is not liable to this Difficulty ; they subsist always in their Principles ; for instance, Wood, when destroyed by Fire, ceases not to exist as Matter, or extended Substance. Thus there is a great Defect in the System of *Anaxagoras* : His Principles are composed of Matter and Form, and have not consequently the Simplicity and Immutability, which Order requires. This Defect could not be remedied, by supposing, that the Intelligence, which presides over Generations, never suffers them to be destroyed. Was it not a sufficient Inconveniency, that of their own Nature they were subject to Corruption, and could not be preserved from it but by a Privilege, or, rather, by a Miracle ? I say nothing of their great Number, which is likewise a remarkable Defect ; for it is essential to a good System, that an infinite number of Effects should flow from a very few Causes.

Lucretius was not aware of an Objection, which would have destroyed the very Foundation of *Anaxagoras*'s Hypothesis. This Philosopher's Motive, in his Supposition of the *Homœomeries*, or *Homogeneities*, was, that no Being can be made out of Nothing, or reduced to nothing (41). Now if the Earth, for Example, was formed of Things, which were not Earth, it would be made of nothing ; and if, having been Earth, it should cease to be Earth, it would be annihilated : It must then be formed of what is Earth, and, in that which is called Destruction, or Corruption, it must needs be reduced to, or resolve itself into, Parts, which are Earth. According to this, there is no Generation, or Corruption, properly so called ; no Birth, or Death. The production of an Herb is nothing else but the Assemblage of several small Herbs : The Destruction of a Tree is nothing but the Separation and Dispersion of several Trees. " We see, added " be (42), that the simplest Food, as Bread and Wa- " ter, is converted into Hair, Veins, Arteries, " Nerves, Bones, &c. there must be therefore little " Hairs, Veins, and Arteries, &c. which indeed our " Senses do not discover ; but they are not invisible " to our Reason or Understanding." It is evident, that he went upon this false Supposition, to wit, that something would be made out of nothing, if the parts of Bread, which supply the Bones with Nourishment, had not the Nature of Bones, in the Bread itself. It is surprizing, that so great a Genius should reason in this manner. Could he not perceive, that a House is not made out of nothing, though it be built with Materials, which are not an House ? Do not four Lines, none of which are squares, make a Square ? Is it not enough, that they are placed in a certain manner ? Is not a Doublet made of several Pieces of Cloth, none of which is a Doublet ? Is there any Creation in this ? Since, then, in artificial Things, the bare change of Figure, and situation of Parts, is sufficient to form a whole, which, as to it's Species and Properties, differs from each of it's Parts ; could he not apprehend, that Nature, which infinitely exceeds human Art, can form Bones and Veins, without putting together Parts, which are already Bones and Veins ; and that it need only work upon such Particles, as are capable of receiving such or such a Situation or Figure ? By this means, without any Creation, properly so called, That, which was not Flesh, will become Flesh, &c. This is what *Lucretius* might have objected to our *Anaxagoras* ; and by this he would have entirely destroyed his Hypothesis of the *Homœomeriæ*. I proceed to other Faults of *Morire* (43).

(41) Plutarch. ubi supra. See also Aristot. Physicor. lib. 1. c. 4. pag. 256.

(42) Plut. ibid.

(43) I shall not take notice of his wrong Quotations. He quotes Plutarch, only in Vita Niciæ, sit it sould be Nicliæ) besides he mentions reciting of what Plut. r h. says there ; and there are other Tracts of Plut reli, which might have been more properly quoted.

II. *Anaxagoras*, says he, was sirnamed Νῦς, or the *Mind*, *on account of the Subtilty of his Doctrine*. *Diogenes Laërtius* says nothing of this Reason ; he only tells us, that he had this Sirname given him, because he taught, that an intelligent Being had cleared up the Chaos

2

ANAXAGORAS.

it in order; he was the First, who supposed, that an Intelligence produced Motion in Matter,

Chaos (44). *Timon* (45), and *Harpocration* (46), say the same. I do not deny, that *Plutarch* mentions the Reason alledged by *Moreri*; but, since he alledges also That, which we find in *Diogenes Laërtius* (47), and which is the more probable one, *Moreri* should not have suppress'd it.

III. He falsely charges our *Anaxagoras* with having admitted of Atoms (48). This Error is so much the grosser, because he had before said, that *Anaxagoras* admitted *of infinite Parts in all Bodies*. These two Opinions destroy each other; for, though, generally speaking, the *Atomic* System may admit of an Infinity of Corpuscles; yet it requires, that their Number should be determinate in each Body; since one of the Reasons of the Atomists, in their System, is, that they avoid the Absurdities of a *Divisibility in infinitum*, which necessarily follows from the Supposition, that each Body is composed of an infinite Number of Parts.

IV. It is not true, that *Lucian* feigns, that *Jupiter* struck *Anaxagoras* dead with a Thunder-bolt. We shall see, below, the Words of *Lucian*.

V. I know not upon what Foundation *Moreri* says, that *Anaxagoras* travelled into Egypt, *where he learned the Secrets and Mysteries of the learned Men of that Country*: I do not remember to have read this in any ancient Author. For I desire I may be allowed to place *Theodoret* among the Moderns, in this respect; *Theodoret*, I say, who mentions this Journey of *Anaxagoras* (50), but who is otherwise mistaken, in supposing this Philosopher to be cotemporary with *Pythagoras*. However, I shall have still reason to censure *Moreri*, since he has not quoted *Theodoret*, nor any Author, who mentions this Journey.

VI. He believed, that the Stars (they are *Moreri*'s Words) *had at first a confused Motion, which was afterwards regulated*. This was not at all the Opinion of *Anaxagoras*. According to *Diogenes Laërtius*, he believed, that, at first, the Stars moved in such a manner, that the Heavens, being in the Form of a Vault, the Pole, which never sets, was vertical to the Earth, but that it inclined itself afterwards (51). By his leave, this was to have a very imperfect Knowledge of the Sphere. He was ignorant, that the North Pole, inclining to the Horizon of *Ionia*, and several other Countries, is no less vertical to the Earth, with respect to a certain Place, than it could be at the beginning. If *Anaxagoras* meant, that this Pole, being formerly in the Zenith of *Ionia*, afterwards declined towards the Horizon, he expressed himself very ill, and must have believed, that *Ionia* was formerly a very miserable and unhappy Country. *Plutarch* relates this somewhat differently. He says, that *Anaxagoras* believed, that, after the World was created, and the Earth had produced living Creatures, the Earth of itself (ἐκ τῦ αὐτομάτυ) inclined towards the South; perhaps providentially (ἵσως ὑπὸ προνοίας) that there might be habitable and uninhabitable Parts, through excessive Cold, scorching Heat, and Temperature (52).

VII. It is not true, that *Diogenes Laërtius* mentions an Orator, whose Name was *Anaxagoras*, and who was Disciple of *Socrates*. He makes him a Disciple of *Isocrates* (53).

VIII. It is still falser, that our *Anaxagoras* taught, that the *similar Parts* were *the Primum Mobile of all Things*. We shall see, in the following Remark, that, according to his Opinion, the *first Mover* was a Spirit, distinct from the *Homœomeriæ*. If *Moreri* had understood the Author of the Life of this Philosopher, he would not have fallen into this Mistake. ʼΕκ τῶν ὁμοιομερῶν μικρῶν σωμάτων τὸ πᾶν συγκεκρίσθαι, καὶ τῶν μὲν ἀρχὴν κινήσεως (54). *Ex parvis similium partium corporibus hoc totum esse compositum*, MENTEMQUE INITIUM ESSE MOTUS.

IX. *Moreri* has misrepresented the Sense of the first part of this Greek of *Diogenes Laërtius*. *All this great World*, says he, *is made up of similar Parts, which constitute the whole*. I have already complained of the Nonsense of these Words; but I shall here consider them more fully, in order to shew, in what manner a Modern Writer ought to guard against Ambiguities, to which he is liable, when he forgets, that an Expression, which was clear to the *Greeks*, may be very obscure at present, unless expressed by a Periphrasis.

I say this, without intending to justify good *Diogenes Laërtius*, who generally did not know what he said, when he abridged the Opinions of the Philosophers. I wish *Moreri* had expressed himself thus; *The World is the Effect or Result of the Choice of small similar Parts*. According to his own Expression, one would take the World to be an Whole, each of whose Parts has the same Name and Quality with all the rest (55). This is so false, that it is but opening one's Eyes, to be convinced of it. The very Blind may know it, and cannot be ignorant of it; for they know, that they are composed of Flesh and Bones; and that their Hair is not like their Nails. They, who have the least Tincture of School-Philosophy, know, that an *Homogeneous* Compound is That, whose Parts have the same Nature and Qualities with the Whole; and that an *Heterogeneous* Compound is That, whose Parts are not named as their whole is, and have not each the same common Properties. Water, Milk, Wine, Flesh, and Bones, are *Homogeneous* Compounds; for Instance, each drop of the Liquid, which composes a River, is called Water, and has the Essence of it. But it is quite otherwise with an *Heterogeneous* Compound; it's Parts have not it's Name, nor it's Nature; neither have they the Names and Qualities of each other. Such, for Example, is the Body of an Ox; it is composed of Blood, Flesh, and Bones, and of several other Parts, which have each their distinct Names and Qualities. This being so, no one can say, that the Universe is an *Homogeneous* Compound. Some of it's Parts are opake, and others transparent; some liquid, and others hard: Here is Earth; there Air and Water; here a Meadow, and there a Wood. *Anaxagoras* would have been more extravagant, than the most absurd Visionary that ever was put into a Mad-House, had he entertained any Doubts about it; and yet *Moreri*'s Expressions plainly intimate, that he taught, that the Universe was *Homogeneous*; and therefore he falsely charges him with a shocking Absurdity. He should have made use of another Phrase to describe his Opinion, and pitched upon such Terms, as would have explained the *collective Sense* of the Word *Whole*, with the *distributive* (56). I will explain myself by an Example. Let us suppose, that all the Citizens of a great City are divided into ten Classes; and that those, who have Twenty thousand Livres are placed in the first, those, who have Fifteen thousand, in the next, and the rest accordingly. Now whoever should say, *This Town is composed of Inhabitants equally Rich*, must intend it only in a *distributive* Sense. His meaning must be, that the ten Parts, which constitute this People, are each of them composed of Men equally Rich; But his Thought would be involved in improper, obscure, and intricate Words; and, to make himself understood, he ought to add, *That this equality of Riches is only to be found, in comparing the People of the same Class with each other; for if th se of the tenth Class be compared with those of the first, there will be a great Inequality*. This is the ill Office, which those do our *Anaxagoras*, who maintain, that he said, that the Universe was altogether composed of similar Parts: They make their Readers suspect, that he advanced a ridiculous Enigma; and, if the Writer does not explain himself by a *that is to say*, they are at a Loss to understand him, and grow very angry with such an Author. To free them from such a Perplexity, I will endeavour to explain the Sentiment of this Philosopher.

His meaning seems to me to be, that the Intelligence, which formed the World, had, in infinite Matter, found infinite Kinds of minute Corpuscles, which resembled each other; but which by a confused Mixture were surrounded with other Corpuscles, or small Bodies, not of the same Nature. The Intelligence united the several Corpuscles of the same Species; and, by this means, formed here a Planet, there a Stone, in other places Water, Air, Wood, &c. This Action divided the Universe into several Masses of similar Parts; but in such a manner, that the Particles of one Mass did not resemble those of another. And, therefore, the Word *All* or *Whole*, must not be taken in a *Collective*, but in a *Distributive* Sense; otherwise you will have as much Reason to say, that the World is made of Dissimilar, as of Similar, Parts. *Ludovicus Vives*, having observed, that this Passage of *St Austin*,

Anaxagoras

ANAXAGORAS.

Matter, and reduced the Chaos into Form [D]. This was, without doubt, the true Reason,

Anaxagoras ——— dixit ex infinita materia quæ constaret dissimilibus inter se particulis, &c. ——— Anaxagoras ——— said, *that of infinite Matter, consisting of dissimilar Particles, &c.* ——— was read in the old Manuscripts, *Similibus inter se particulis* ——— *of similar Particles* ——— adds, *utrumque recte* ——— *both Readings are right.*

As to the Objections, which *Anaxagoras* had to fear, I shall take some notice of them in the Remark [G].

[D] *He was the first, who supposed that an Intelligence produced motion in Matter, and reduced the Chaos into Form.*] These are Facts well attested. Πρῶτος τε τῆς ὕλης τῶν ἑτέρων, ἀψάμενος ὅτι τῆς συγγράμματος, ὃ ἐςιν ἡδίως καὶ μεγαλοφρόνως ὑπομενούμενον. πάντα χρήματα ἢν ὁμοῦ, εἶτα νοῦς ἐλθὼν αὐτὰ διεκόσμησε (57). *He was the first, who superadded a* MIND *to Matter, expressing himself at the beginning of his Work, in this pleasing and sublime manner ;* "all Things were confused ; afterwards an Intelligence, interposing, reduced them into Form and Order." I thought it proper to begin with this Passage of *Diogenes Laërtius*, because it contains *Anaxagoras*'s own Words (58).

Let us take a view of *Aristotle*'s Remarks on this Subject. He condemns the Philosophers, who, treating of the Principles of Things, stopped at the material, without searching for the efficient, Cause of Generation and Corruption. *The material Cause*, says he, *never changes ; Brass does not convert itself into a Statue, nor Wood into a Bedstead ; there is another Principle of this Change. To search after this Principle, is to ascend to the first Mover.* His Words are so remarkable, that it is proper to repeat them. Εἰ γάρ ὅτι μάλιστα πᾶσα φθορὰ καὶ γένεσις ἐκ τινὸς, ὡς ἐνὸς ἢ καὶ πλειόνων ἐστὶ, διὰ τί τοῦτο συμβαίνει, καὶ τί τὸ αἴτιον ; ὁ γὰρ δὴ τὸ γε ὑποκείμενον αὐτὸ ποιεῖ μεταβάλλειν ἑαυτό. λέγω δ' οἷον, ὅτε τὸ ξύλον ὅτε ὁ χαλκὸς αἴτιος τοῦ μεταβάλλειν ἑκάτερον αὐτῶν. ἐδὲ ποιεῖ τὸ μὲν ξύλον κλίνην, ὁ δὲ χαλκὸς ἀνδριάντα, ἀλλ' ἕτερον τι τῆς μεταβολῆς τὸ αἴτιον. τὸ δὲ τοῦτο ζητεῖν, ἐστι τὸ τὴν ἑτέραν ἀρχὴν ζητεῖν, ὡς ἂν ἡμεῖς φαῖημεν, ὅθεν ἡ ἀρχὴ τῆς κινήσεως (59). *Nam etsi quàm maxime omnis corruptio, & generatio ex aliquo ut ex uno aut ex pluribus fit, cur hoc accidit, & quæ causa est ? Non enim ipsum subjectum sese mutari facit, utputa, dico quod neque lignum, neque æs causa est, ut utrumque eorum mutetur. Neque lignum quidem lectum, æs vero statuam facit, sed aliud quippiam mutationis causa est. Hoc autem quærere, aliud principium quærere est, perinde atque id, quod nos unde principium motus dicimus.* He adds, I. That, when the Insufficiency of the Elements came to be known, the Force of Truth obliged the Philosophers to look for another Mover. II. That it is not probable, that Fire and Earth, &c. are the Causes of the beautiful State of certain Beings, and of the Generation of others ; nor that those ancient Philosophers believed it. III. That it would be unreasonable to attribute so grand an Effect to Chance and Fortune. Οὐδ' αὐτῷ αὐτομάτῳ καὶ τύχη τοσοῦτον ἐπιτρέψαι πρᾶγμα καλῶς ἔχει. *Nec rursus Casui & Fortunæ tantam attribuere rem probè se habet* (60). IV. That, for this Reason, *Anaxagoras*, who said that there is a Spirit in Nature, as well as in Animals, which is the Author of the World, and of Order, seemed to be a Person of good Sense, in comparison of the Philosophers his Predecessors, who were great Talkers about nothing. There is more Force in the Original, than in the Idea which I give of it. Those, who are able to understand the *Greek*, which I am going to produce, will find my Confession sincere. Νοῦν δέ τις εἰπὼν εἶναι, καθάπερ ἐν τοῖς ζώοις καὶ ἐν τῇ φύσει τὸν αἴτιον καὶ τοῦ κόσμου, καὶ τῆς τάξεως ἁπάσης, οἷον νήφων ἐφάνη παρ' εἰκῆ λέγοντας τοὺς πρότερον. φανερῶς μὲν ὁ Ἀναξαγόρας ἴσμεν ἀψάμενον τοῦτων τῶν λόγων (61). *Wherefore he, who said, that an Intelligence, in Nature, as well as in Animals, produced the World, and the Order of Things, appeared a sober Reasoner, in comparison of the vain Discourses of the more ancient Philosophers.* We know, that Anaxagoras was the Person, who openly taught this Doctrine. If these Testimonies are express, That of *Plutarch* is, perhaps, still

more so. Let us produce the Words of That Author. Ὅτι (Ἀναξαγόρας) δὲ τῷ' ἄνθρωπος τῶν προγεγονότων, εἶτε τῶν σύνεστιν ἀνδρῶν μεγάλην τὶς φυσιολογίαν καὶ περιττὴν διαπαρεῖσαν θαυμασταῖς, εἰδ' ἔτι τοῖς ὅλοις πρῶτος ὁ τύχων ἐδ' ἀλόγων, διακοσμήσεως ἀρχήν, ἀλλὰ τὸν ἐπιστῆμον καθαρὸν καὶ ἄκρατον, ἐμμεμιγμένον πᾶσι τοῖς ἄλλοις, ἀποκρίνοντα τὰς ὁμοιομερείας (62). *Who* (Anaxagoram) *was by his Cotemporaries stiled* The Mind, *either because they admired his singular and excellent Penetration in Natural Philosophy ; or, because he was the first, who did not ascribe the Formation of the Universe to Chance or Fate, but to a simple and uncompounded Intelligence, which separated the similar Particles of Matter from all others, with which they were confused.* This Passage is quoted by some Authors, as if it ought to be read ἐμμεμιγμένον, instead of ἐμμεμιγμένος ; but I choose to reject both these readings, and substitute ἐμμεμιγμένος. So the Author of the *Latin* Translation supposes it ought to be read, *Quem* (Anaxagoram) *illius temporis æquales* Mentem *appellavere, vel quod perspicaciam ejus singularem excellentemque in Naturâ perscrutandâ admirarentur ; vel quòd universitatis, non Fortunam neque Fatum ordinatæ descriptionis Principium, sed mentem puram ac sinceram præstiterit, cum omnibus aliis confusa*m *inveniretur particulas similes*. Though *Vossius* quotes this Passage in *Greek*, with the Word ἐμμεμιγμένον, yet he renders it as if it was ἐμμεμιγμένος : This is his Translation (63) ; *Non fortunam neque fatum ordinatæ descriptionis Principium, sed mentem puram ac sinceram præstiterit, ad aliis omnibus* A D M I X T I S *similes particulas inveniretam*. Within a few Pages after, he makes use of the same Passage, to prove, that *Anaxagoras* taught, that God is entirely blended with Matter. *Quare ex ejus sententia ipse mundi Deus est, ut in Plutarcho antea monitum, nec καθαρὸς καὶ ἄκρατος ἐμμεμιγμένῳ πᾶσι, Mens pura ac sincera omnibus permixta* (64). I do not believe, that *Plutarch* intended any Mixture of the Divine Nature with the parts of Matter : this would be inconsistent with the Epithets καθαρὸς & ἄκρατος, which he had just before made use of, and by which he clearly shews, that *Anaxagoras* believed, that God is a pure and unmixed Spirit, distinct and separate from Matter. His meaning, in my Opinion, is, That this Immaterial Spirit separated the *Homœomeriæ*, or similar Parts, which lay confused with all other Bodies. Thus we see how difficult it is for the most learned Men, such as *Vossius* was, to write much, and to be always upon their Guard : Their Attention frequently fails them, and they forget, in one Place, what they have said in another : Nay, sometimes what they say in the beginning of a Period does not perfectly agree with the Conclusion of it.

I have farther Reason to believe, that *Plutarch* meant what I attribute to him ; for, besides what I shall alledge out of *Tertullian* (65), I find in *Aristotle*, that *Anaxagoras* said, that the Spirit, which had put Matter into Motion, was free from all Mixture. Πλὴν ἀρχή γε τὸν νῦν τίθεται μάλισα πάντων. Μόνον γὰρ φησὶν αὐτὸν τῶν ὄντων ἁπλοῦν εἶναι, καὶ ἀμιγῆ τε καὶ καθαρόν. ἀποδίδωσι δ' ἄμφω τῇ αὐτῇ ἀρχῇ, τό, τε γινώσκειν καὶ τὸ κινεῖν, λέγων τὸν κινῆσαι τὸ πᾶν (66). *He says* down an Intelligent Mind as the Principle of all Things ; and says, that That alone, of all Things, is simple and unmixed, pure and uncompounded. And to this Principle he ascribes two Properties, to wit, Knowledge and Motion ; saying that the Mind put the Universe into Motion. This is more clearly expressed in the following Words. Φησὶ ('Ἀναξαγόρας) δ' εἶναι μεμιγμένα πάντα, πλὴν τὸ νοῦ· τοῦτον δ' ἀμιγῆ μόνον καὶ καθαρόν (67). Anaxagoras taught, that all things were compounded, except the Mind, but that This was unmixed and pure. The next is the Testimony of *Plutarch* ; from which it manifestly appears, That *Anaxagoras* ascribed to God the first Production of Motion and Order. Ὁ δ' Ἀναξαγόρας φησὶν ὡς εἰκηκεὶ καθ' ἀρχὰς τὰ σώματα, νοῦς δ' αὐτὰ διεκόσμησε θεοῦ, καὶ τὰς γενέσεις τῶν ὅλων ἐποίησεν. ὁ δὲ Πλάτων ἔχει ἐκεῖνα ὑποδιδὲ τὰ πρῶτα σώματα, ἀτάκτως δὲ κινεῖμενα. διὸ καὶ ὅ σὲ (φησὶν) ἐπεσήσαιεν ὡς τάξεις ἀτάξιας ἐσι βελτίων, διακόσμησε ταῦ-

VOL. I.   F f f f

ANAXAGORAS.

Reason, why this great Philosopher was firnamed Νᾶς, that is to say, *The Mind, or Understanding* (u). But his Orthodoxy was not sufficiently refin'd [E]; there remained still

τα. (68). Anaxagoras *taught, that, in the beginning, Matter was without Motion, and that the Mind of God put it in order, and gave rise to every thing.* Plato laid it down, that the *first Bodies were not motionless, but that they moved irregularly. But God,* says he, *perceiving that Order was preferable to Confusion, adjusted them.* You see here a remarkable Difference between *Anaxagoras* and *Plato.* The firſt ſuppoſes, that God found Matter at Reſt. The ſecond, on the contrary, that God found it in Motion. I am amazed at the Reflexion, which *Plutarch* makes upon theſe two Doctrines; it not only contains an horrible Impiety, but likewiſe a very groſs Contradiction. He had blamed the Philoſophers, who acknowledged but one Principle. He had ſaid (69), that "it is impoſſible, that Matter ſhould be the "ſole Principle of all things, and that an efficient "Cauſe muſt be added to it; for Silver alone is not "ſufficient to produce a Veſſel, unleſs there be a "Workman to make the Veſſel. The ſame may be "ſaid of Braſs, Wood, and of all other Materials." In the ſame Page he had commended *Anaxagoras* for admitting an Intelligence, which had united the ſimilar Particles; Τὰς μὲν ὁμοιομερείας ὕλην, τὸ δὲ ποιοῦν αἴτιον τὸν νοῦν τὰ πάντα διαλεξάμενον (70). *Homœomerias ſtatuit materiam, cauſam vero efficientem mentem quæ diſponeret univerſa*: that is, for adding the efficient Cauſe to the paſſive Subject, and the Artificer to the Materials. Ἀποδεκτέος ἔςος ἐςὶν ὅτι τῇ ὕλῃ τὸν τεχνίτην προσεζεύξεν (71). *Hic Approbandus eſt, quod materiæ Artificem adjunxerit.* What does he mean then, when, five Pages after, he cenſures *Anaxagoras* and *Plato*; the firſt for having attributed to God the Motion and Diſpoſition of Bodies, and the latter for having attributed to Him the ranging of them? *Their common Error,* ſays he, *is in thinking, that God takes care of human Things, and that he has framed a World to that end.* Κοινὸς ἐν ἀμφοτέροις ἀμφότεροις, ὅτι τὸν θεὸν ἐποίησαν ἐπιςρεφόμενον τῶν ἀνθρωπίνων, ἢ καὶ τότε χάριν τὸν κόσμον καταςκευάζοντα (72). *Communis ambobus hic eſt error, quod deum facium res humanas curantem, at ea de cauſa mundum adornantem.* After which, he lays down the moſt ſpecious Reaſons, which an Atheiſt can alledge, againſt thoſe, who attribute to God the Creation and Government of the World. How then? Does he approve of *Anaxagoras* for admitting an Intelligence, which was the firſt Mover of Matter, and the efficient Cauſe of the World; and does he blame him for taking this firſt Mover to be God? Can any one reaſon in a more pitiful and incoherent manner than he does? And, ſhould we ſuppoſe, that there is no Contradiction in this, muſt we not confeſs at leaſt, that he has confuted, in this Place, a great many other Paſſages in his Books, in which he ſuppoſes a Providence?

I ſhould be tedious, were I to ſet down all the Teſtimonies, which prove one or both of theſe Truths. I. That *Anaxagoras* admitted an Intelligence, which put Matter in Motion, and formed the World, by the choice of the *Homogeneities*. II. That he was the firſt Philoſopher, who advanced This Syſtem. Let it ſuffice, then, to point out *Plato* (73), *Tertullian* (74), *Clemens Alexandrinus* (75), *Euſebius* (76), *Themiſtius* (77), St *Auſtin* (78), *Theodoret* (79), *Proclus* (80), and *Simplicius* (81). I ſhall not do the ſame with reſpect to *Cicero*; but I ſhall produce his Words; becauſe they furniſh a Particular, which ought to be examined. "Inde Anaxagoras, ſays "he (82), qui acceptit ab Anaximene diſciplinam, "PRIMUS omnium rerum deſcriptionem & mo"dum mentis infinitæ vi ac ratione deſignari ac "confici voluit. In quo non vidit, neque motum "ſenſui junctum & continentem in infinito ullum "eſſe poſſe, neque ſenſum omnino, quo non ipſa na"tura pulſa ſentiret. Deinde ſi mentem iſtam qua"ſi animal aliquod eſſe voluit, erit aliquid interius "ex quo illud animal nominetur. Quid autem in"terius mente? Cingitur igitur corpore externo. "Quod quoniam non placet, aperta ſimplexque mens "nulla re adjuncta quæ ſentire poſſit, fugere intelli"gentiæ noſtræ vim & notionem videtur. ————— *Anaxagoras next, who was brought up at the Feet*

"of Anaximenes, *was the* FIRST, *who held, that* "*the Diſpoſition and Order of all Things was planned* "*and effected by the Power and Underſtanding of an* "*infinite Mind. In which he is not aware, firſt,* "*that there can be no Motion joined with Senſe in* "*what is infinite, nor any Senſe at all, which can*— "*not affect it's Nature. In the next place, if he* "*would have this Mind to be a kind of Animal, there* "*will be ſomething more internal, from whence to de*— "*nominate this Animal. But what is there more in*— "*ternal than a Mind? It is therefore ſurrounded with* "*an external Body. Though you will not allow this,* I "*am of Opinion, that an unbodied, ſimple, Mind, unaſſi*— "*ſted by any thing, which may have Senſe, is beyond the* "*Force and Comprehenſion of our Underſtanding.*" It is ſomewhat ſurprizing, that *Cicero* ſhould ſay, that *A*naxagoras was the firſt Philoſopher, who acknowledged ſuch a Doctrine, ſince he had before told us, that *Thales* (83) had acknowledged a Mind, or a God, who had formed all things out of Water. "Thales Mileſius, qui "primus de talibus rebus quæſivit, aquam dixit eſſe "initium rerum: deum autem, eam mentem, quæ "ex aqua cuncta fingeret (84). How could *Cicero* ſo ſoon forget his own Words? Can it be imagined, that he meant, that *Thales* only aſcribed to God the Power of converting Water into other Bodies; but that *Anaxagoras* made God the Author of the Order and noble Symmetry of the Parts of the World? This does not ſeem to me to be probable, and I ſhould rather ſuſpect that this Paſſage is corrupted. The Confuſion and Obſcurity, which is to be found in the following Words, may confirm this Conjecture. However it be, I would not have this Teſtimony of *Cicero* be oppoſed to thoſe of ſo many ancient and celebrated Writers, who unanimouſly affirm, that *Anaxagoras* was the *firſt*, who ſuperadded the efficient Cauſe to the material, that is to ſay, who acknowledged an Intelligence to be the Author of the Oeconomy, or Architecture, of the Univerſe. St *Auſtin* paid ſo little regard to this Teſtimony of *Cicero*, that, in the very Place, where he mentions the Opinion of the Philoſophers of the *Ionian* Sect, agreeably to that of *Cicero* in other Reſpects, he expreſſly contradicts him as to what concerns *Thales*. "Iſte autem Thales, ————— rerum naturam ſcru"tatus, ſuiſque diſputationes literis mandans, eminuit "————— aquam ————— putavit rerum eſſe princi"pium, & hinc omnia elementa mundi ipſumque "mundum, & quæ in eo gignuntur, exiſtere. NI"HIL autem huic operi, quod, mundo conſiderato, "tam admirabile aſpicimus, EX DIVINA MEN"TE præpoſuit (85) ———— *This* Thales, *examining* "*into the Nature of Things, and committing his Diſ*— "*putations to Writing, taught that Water was the* "*Principle of all Things; and that to This the ſeve*— "*ral Elements of the World, the World itſelf, and* "*all things in it, owed their Exiſtence. He ſuppoſed* "NO DIVINE MIND *to preſide over the won*— "*derful Works of the Creation*." Obſerve, that *Cicero* himſelf, in another Book, denies, that *Thales* was the firſt, who taught the Doctrine we are ſpeaking of, and that he aſcribes it ſolely and abſolutely to the Philoſopher *Anaxagoras*. I ſhall ſet down his Words in the Remark [F].

The Jeſuit *Leſcalopier* (86) endeavours to reconcile this Contradiction, by ſuppoſing, that *Anaxagoras* was the firſt, who *publiſhed* this Doctrine; the Philoſophers, who lived before him, having only taught it in their Auditories. This is no very good Solution; for, ſince the Doctrines of the Predeceſſors of *Anaxagoras* were known, and wherein they differed from each other; I ſay, ſince this was known, tho' *Anaxagoras* was the firſt, who publiſhed Books, it might as well have been known what they taught concerning the efficient Cauſe of the World. As to the Objections againſt the Doctrine of this Philoſopher, contained in the above-cited Paſſage of *Cicero*, I refer you to St *Auſtin*, who confutes them ſolidly (87).

[E] *His Orthodoxy was not ſufficiently refin'd.*] *Tertullian* blames him for being inconſiſtent with himſelf; for, on the one hand, he ſaid, that God was a pure and ſimple Intelligence, and, on the other, he mixed and confounded him with the Soul. "Quam "Anaxagoras turbata ſententia eſt! initium enim om"nium commentatus animum, univerſitatis oſcillum "de

ANAXAGORAS.

still many Imperfections in it; which is less to be wondered at, than to find, that the Philosophers, who lived before him, were ignorant of the great Truth, which he discovered; a Truth so very plain, and so often sung by the Poets [F]. It will be proper

"de illius axe suspendens, purumque eum adfirmans, & simplicem & incommiscibilem, hoc vel maxime titulo segregat ab animæ commissione, & tamen eundem alibi animæ addicit (88)." *Aristotle* had made this Remark before *Tertullian*. 'Αναξαγόρας δέ έοικε διαφορεῖ περὶ αὐτῶν. πολλαχῇ μὲν γὰρ τὸ αἴτιον τοῦ καλῶς καὶ ὀρθῶς τὸν νοῦν λέγει ἑτέρωθι δε, τὸν νοῦν εἶναι τὸν αὐτὸν τῇ ψυχῇ. ἐν ἅπασι γὰρ ὑπάρχειν αὐτὸν τοῖς ζώοις, καὶ μεγάλοις, καὶ μικροῖς, καὶ τιμίοις καὶ ἀτιμιωτέροις. οὐ φαίνεται δὲ ὅ γε κατὰ φρόνησιν λεγόμενος νοῦς, πᾶσιν ὁμοίως ὑπάρχειν τοῖς ζώοις, ἀλλ᾽ οὐδὲ τοῖς ἀνθρώποις πᾶσιν (89). But *Anaxagoras is less explicit in this Matter*; for, in many Places, he ascribes the Origin of Good and Right to a Mind; but, in other Places, he asserts the Soul itself to be a Mind; for he tells us, that there is a Mind in all Animals, both great and small, excellent and less excellent. But This Mind and Understanding, to which he ascribes Prudence, does not seem to be contained in all Animals alike, nor even in all Men. This Passage of *Aristotle* informs us, that *Anaxagoras* admitted of a Soul in Brutes, to which he gave the same Name of a *Mind* or *Intelligence*, which he had given to the first Mover of Matter, and the Director of the Fabric of the World. The same *Aristotle* observes, that "*Anaxagoras admitted an Intelligence for the Production of Things, only as a Θεὸς ἀπὸ μηχάνης; that is, he never had recourse to it, but in Cases of necessity, and when all other Reasons failed him.*" 'Αναξαγόρας τε γὰρ μηχανῇ χρῆται τῷ νῷ πρὸς τὴν κοσμοποιΐαν, καὶ ὅταν ἀπορήσῃ διὰ τίν᾽ αἰτίαν ἐξ ἀνάγκης ἐστὶ τότε ἕλκει αὐτόν. ἐν δὲ τοῖς ἄλλοις πάντα μᾶλλον αἰτιᾶται τῶν γινομένων ἢ νοῦν (90). Nam & *Anaxagoras tanquam machina utitur Intellectu ad mundi generationem. Et cum dubitat propter quam causam necessario est, tunc eum attrahit. In cæteris vero, magis cætera omnia, quam intellectum, causam eorum, quæ fiunt, ponit.* This is, without doubt, the Foundation of an Observation, made by *Clemens Alexandrinus*, that *Anaxagoras* has not supported the Rights and Dignity of the Efficient Cause, whose Functions he attributed to a Mind; for he mentioned several Revolutions, which were made without the Knowledge or Co-operation of This Spirit. This, if I am not mistaken, is the true Sense of the *Greek* Words of that Father of the Church. 'Αναξαγόρας πρῶτος, φησὶ δὲ, ἐπέστησε τὸν νοῦν τοῖς πράγμασιν᾽ ἀλλ᾽ οὐδὲ οὗτος ἐτήρησε τὴν ἀξίαν τὴν ποιητικὴν, δίνας τινὰς ἀνοήτους ἀναζωγραφῶν, σὺν τῇ τοῦ νοῦ ἀπραξίᾳ τε καὶ ἀνοίᾳ (91). *Primus Anaxagoras mentem rebus adhibuit. Sed nec ille dignitatem servavit efficientem, nescio quas amentes describens revolutiones cum mentis ab agendo cessatione & amentia.* Without doubt *Eusebius* copied this Passage, when, giving it another turn, he said, that *Anaxagoras* did not preserve safe and found his Doctrine, which teaches, that all things were produced by an Intelligence. Λέγεται δὲ μηδὲ οὗτος σῶον φυλάξαι τὸ δόγμα. ἐπείσεται μὲν γὰρ τὸν Νοῦν τοῖς πᾶσιν, ἐκεῖνο δὲ κατὰ τὸν καὶ λογισμὸν τὴν περὶ τῶν ὄντων ἀποδύναι τὴν φυσιολογίαν (92). *But even he himself did not preserve his own Doctrine safe and sound: For he professes a Mind to All Things, in such a Manner, as to dispute concerning the Nature of Things inconsistently with the Rule of a Mind and Reason.* Which he proves by this Argument, that *Anaxagoras* philosophized upon Nature, and explained it's *Phænomena*, without supposing such an Intelligence. I know it may be said, that *Eusebius* does not mean so; and that he only declares, that *Anaxagoras* assigned physical Reasons, which were contrary to good Sense. But three things convince me, that my Interpretation of *Clemens Alexandrinus*'s and *Eusebius*'s Words, is truer than This. In the first Place, it is no good Proof, that a Philosopher deserts or weakens the Hypothesis of a Providence, and of the universal Activity of God, to say, that he argues sometimes impertinently, foolishly, or irregularly. All the Sects of Philosophy among the Christians reproach each other after the same manner; and yet they do not accuse each other

of Heterodoxy, with respect to the universal Interposition of God, the first Cause of all Beings. Therefore, if no other Complaint could be brought against *Anaxagoras*, but that, in explaining several Effects of Nature, he reasoned ill, and without Sense; it would have been unjust to reproach him with abandoning or spoiling the Hypothesis, in which he admitted of an Intelligence, which presided over the Production of the World. This Reproach therefore must have been grounded, not upon the impertinent Explications, which he gave, but upon what he advanced to the Prejudice and Exclusion of that Intelligence. In the second place, *Eusebius* alledges, as his Authority, a long Passage of *Plato*, which contains a Complaint, that *Anaxagoras* explained Things, without having Recourse to an Intelligence, or to the Causes of the Beauty and Order of the Universe; but that he stopped at the Air, the Æther, the Water, &c. as the Causes of Beings (93). Who does not perceive from hence, that 'tis very probable *Eusebius* meant the same Defect? In the third place, I observe, that *Anaxagoras*, as *Plutarch* informs us, taught, that certain things come to pass by Necessity, others by Destiny, others by Deliberation, others by Fortune, and others by Chance. "Α μὲν γὰρ εἶναι κατ᾽ ἀνάγκην, ἃ δὲ κατὰ εἱμαρμένην, ἃ δὲ κατὰ προαίρεσιν, ἃ δὲ κατὰ τύχην, ἃ δὲ κατὰ τὸ αὐτόματον (94). *Fieri enim alia necessario, alia fato, alia instituto animi, alia forte fortuna, alia casu.* There is no question, but that, in the detail of these inexplicable Distinctions, he robbed the Divine Intelligence of several Events; and that this was the Reason of the Complaint of *Clemens Alexandrinus*, copied by *Eusebius*.

I know not whether what *Anaxagoras* said of our Hands ought to be placed among his Errors. He asserted, that they have been the Cause of the Wisdom and Industry of Man. *Plutarch* takes him to task for this. "The contrary is true, *says* he (95), for "Man is not the wisest of Animals because he has "Hands; but, because he is naturally rational and "ingenious, he has obtained such Tools from Na- "ture." The Books of *Anaxagoras* are not extant; and therefore it cannot be decided, whether he gave occasion for this Censure; but I am apt to think he did not deserve it. His System engaged him to think quite otherwise in this Matter, than those Philosophers did, who attributed to Chance all the Beings, of which the World is composed. This impious Tenet induced them to maintain, that Organs were not given to Man for his Use, but that, finding them fit for certain Purposes, he employed them to such Uses. See the fourth Book of *Lucretius* (96).

Observe these Words of a Father of the Church: "Anaxagoras autem, qui *Atheus* cognominatus "eft, dogmatizavit facta animalia decidentibus è cœlo "in terram seminibus, quod & hi ipsi in matris suæ "transtulerunt semina, & esse hoc semen seipsos sta- "tim consistentes apud eos qui sensum habent, & ip- "sos esse quæ sunt Anaxagoræ *IRRELIGIOSI* lc- "mina (97). *But Anaxagoras, sirnamed the* ATHEIST, "taught, that Animals were formed of Seeds, which "fell from Heaven; which these Persons have trans- "ferred to the Seeds of their Mother, and for the ac- "knowledging to Men of Sense, that this Seed is "Themselves, and that Themselves are *IMPIOUS* "*Anaxagoras's Seeds.*" You see here, that *Anaxagoras* was sirnamed the ATHEIST; and that St *Irenæus* treats him as an IMPIOUS Man. *Vossius* does not complain of this; he only says, That *Justin Martyr*, in his Exhortation to the *Greeks*, calls this Philosopher an Atheist; and he makes some Reflexions upon it (98). I meet with nothing like it in this Work of *Justin Martyr*; and I think *Vossius* had better have reserved his Excuses for St *Irenæus*. If *Justin Martyr* stands in need of them, it is only for having misrepresented the Doctrine of *Anaxagoras*. He supposes the beautiful Part of it; and says nothing of the Intelligence, the first Mover, but only speaks of his *Homœomeria* (99).

[F] *The Philosophers, who lived before him, were ignorant of the great Truth - - - - - so often sung by the Poets.*] We might bring a Cloud of Witnesses in proof of this Fact, that *Anaxagoras* is the first Philosopher, who

ANAXAGORAS.

per to examine, whether the Doctrine of the *Homœomeriæ* does not imply many Contradictions

[100] *See the Remark* [D].

who ascribed the Arrangement of Matter to the Wisdom of a first Mover (100). *Thales*, *Anaximander*, and *Anaximenes*, who preceeded him in the School of *Ionia*, endeavoured to explain every thing without it. "Princeps Thales, unus è septem, cui sex reli-
"quos concessisse primas ferunt, ex aqua dixit con-
"stare omnia. At hoc Anaximandro populari &
"sodali suo non persuasit. Is enim infinitatem na-
"turæ dixit esse è qua omnia gignerentur. Post ejus
"auditor Anaximenes infinitum aëra, sed ea quæ ex
"eo orirentur definita; ignis autem terram, aquam,
"& ignem, tum ex his omnia. Anaxagoras mate-
"riam infinitam, sed ex ea particulas similes inter
"se minutas, eas primum confusas, postea in ordi-
"nem adductas mente divina (101). —— Thales,

[101] Cicero, Academ. Quæst. lib. 4. cap. 37.

"one of the seven, whom they say the remaining six
"acknowledged as their Master, was the first, who
"taught, that all Things were formed of Water. But
"he could not convince his Countryman and Compa-
"nion Anaximander of this. For the latter held, that
"all things sprung from an infinite Nature. After
"him, his Scholar Anaximenes taught, that Air was
"infinite, but that those things, which were produced
"from it, were finite; that Earth, Air, and Fire,
"were first produced; then all things out of these;
"Anaxagoras held the Infinity of Matter; but that
"it's minute similar Parts, which were at first con-
"fused and blended together, were afterwards reduced
"into Order by a divine Mind." Who can forbear
wondering, that such great Men should be guilty of
such gross Ignorance? This Reflexion has not been
neglected by the Jesuit *Pererius*. "Ferunt primos

[102] Pererius, de communibus omnibus rerum naturalium principiis, lib. 4. cap. 4. pag. 206.

"Philosophorum, *says he* (102), Pherecydem Syrum
"& Anaxagoram, illum quidem, immortalitatem
"animi nostri, hunc autem, Deum, quem ipse Men-
"tem vel Intellectum vocabat, esse mundi cunctarum-
"que rerum opificem, Græcos docuisse: ut permi-
"rum sit, priores Philosophos, qui hæc ignorarunt,
"sapientum nomen, & honorem habuisse; & duas has
"res, quarum cognitio cunctis mortalibus optatissima
"est, & ad bene pieque vivendum maxime necessaria,
"tam serò ad Græcorum notitiam pervenisse. ——
"The Chief of the Philosophers, Pherecydes and A-
"naxagoras, are said to have taught the Greeks,
"the one, that our Souls are immortal; the other,
"that God, whom he calls the Mind or Intelligence,
"created the World, and all things in it; whence
"it is very strange, that the preceeding Philoso-
"phers, who were ignorant of these things, were
"honoured with the Name of wise Men; and that
"these two Principles, the Knowledge of which is so
"highly beneficial to all Mankind, and so necessary
"to a good and pious Life, should so late come to the
"Knowledge of the Greeks." Father *Thomassin* has

[103] Thomassin's Method of studying and teaching Philosophy, Book 1. chap. 14. pag. 162, 163. See also sag. 165.

a remarkable Sentiment upon this Occasion. "All
"the Poets, *says he* (103), who were the most ancient
"Philosophers, and all the Sages of the fabulous
"Times, as they are called, not having mentioned,
"or celebrated, in their Writings, any other Cause,
"than the first and supreme Deity; how came it
"to pass, that, presently after, *Thales*, and his im-
"mediate Successor, were ignorant of, or passed
"over in Silence, that which had employed all the
"Sages, and every Age 'till then? It is therefore
"probable, that these first *Ionian* Philosophers, pre-
"supposing what was incontestable, and, 'till then
"uncontested, concerning the first efficient Cause of
"all Things, treated only of second Causes, which
"were 'till then unknown, and had not been so much
"as enquired after. They were afraid, that, if they
"should refer all particular Effects to God, Men
"would fall again into the old Custom of neglecting
"to enquire into second Causes, and resting con-
"tented with the first. The same may be said of
"Angels. *Homer*, and the other ancient Poets or
"Philosophers, made them the sole Authors of all
"Things, under God. The Disciples of *Thales*, to
"establish the Power of corporeal or immediate
"Causes, omitted the mention of Angels. ·······
"But, at last, *Anaxagoras* judged, that, in his time,
"the World was able to apprehend the Subordi-
"nation of corporeal Causes to angelical Substances,
"and of both to the Wisdom and Power of God.
"······ It was purely on a Supposition of the
"Truth of these Parts of Philosophy, in which the
"World had been sufficiently instructed, that *Thales*

"and his Disciples made no mention of Ethics, or
"Metaphysics; and with a View of engaging Mens
"Attention wholly in cultivating that Branch, which
"'till then was unknown. But, when it was per-
"ceived, that the Knowledge of second Causes was
"very uncertain, and that it was to be feared it would
"make Men forget the Knowledge of God, of An-
"gels, and Morality, which was more constant, use-
"ful, and necessary, *Anaxagoras*, *Socrates*, and *Plato*,
"restored Theology and Morality to their ancient
"Lustre and Credit."

This is a fine Sentiment; an ingenious Notion: But perhaps it has more of Brilliant than Solid; for we see, that *Anaximenes*, the Master of *Anaxagoras*, did not treat of Philosophy, as one, who supposed, that the Existence of God, in quality of the first Cause, was so well known, that there was no occasion to mention it. He spoke of the Gods; but he was so far from considering them as Principles, that he maintained, that they themselves owed their Existence to the Principle, which he established. "Qui
"(*Anaximenes*) omnes rerum causas infinito aëri de-
"dit: nec deos negavit aut tacuit: non tamen ab
"ipsis aërem factum, sed ipsos ex aëre ortos cre-
"didit (104). —— *Who* (Anaximenes) *ascribed the*

[104] August. de Civit. Dei, lib. 8. cap. 2. See also Cicero, lib. 1. de Nat. Deorum pag. 38. *where he says*, Anaximenes Deum statuit, cumque signi.

"*Causes of all Things, to the infinite Air; nor did*
"*he deny the Gods, or was silent concerning them;*
"*yet he did not believe, that the Air was created*
"*by them, but that They were formed of the Air.*"
Cicero attributes a like Opinion to *Anaximander*, Master of *Anaximenes*. "Anaximandri opinio est
"nativos esse deos, longis intervallis orientes, occi-
"dentesque, eosque innumerabiles esse mundos. ——
"*Anaximander was of Opinion, that the Gods were*
"*born and died; that they rose and set at very di-*
"*stant Intervals; and that they were innumerable*
"*Worlds.*" Note, that the two Disciples of *Anaximenes* (105) corrected the Hypothesis of their Master;

[105] *Viz.* Anaxagoras, & Diogenes Apolloniata.

either by admitting an Intelligence distinct from Matter, and the Cause of the World; or by supposing, that the Air, the Principle of all Things, was a Principle, only as it was endowed with a Divine Spirit. The first of these two Suppositions is That of *Anaxagoras*; the other That of *Diogenes Apollonius*. "Diogenes quoque, Anaximenis alter auditor,
"aërem quidem dixit rerum esse materiam de qua
"omnia fierent, sed eum esse compotem divinæ ra-
"tionis, sine qua nihil ex eo fieri posset. (106). ——

[106] August. ubi supra. *See also* Cicero, ubi supra. *where he says*, Quid enim, quo Diogenes Apolloniates utitur Deo?

"Diogenes likewise, the other Disciple of Anaxi-
"menes, held, indeed, that the Air was the Prin-
"ciple of all Things; but that it was endowed with
"a divine Mind; without which it was incapable of
"producing any thing." All this contradicts Father *Thomassin*. The Question is not concerning the Philosophers, who only passed over in silence the Doctrine of the Existence of God; the Question relates to those, who spoke of it; but in a manner quite contrary to That of the Poets, and of *Anaxagoras*. I add, that their Silence is a strong Proof; for, in those Times, the Philosophers went back as far as the Chaos, and the first Origin of all Things (107).

[107] *See* Cicero Tuscul 5. *circa* init.

Namque canebat, uti magnum per inane coacta
Semina terrarumque, animæque, marisque, fuissent,
Et liquidi simul ignis; ut his exordia primis
Omnia, & ipse tener mundi concreverit orbis *.

* Virgil. Ecl. 6. vers. 31.

He sung the secret Seeds of Nature's Frame;
How Seas, and Earth, and Air, and active Flame
Fell thro' the mighty Void, and in their Fall
Were blindly gather'd in this goodly Ball.

DRYDEN.

It was therefore necessary that they should explain themselves about the Nature of God, and exhaust the whole Doctrine of first Principles; after which they might be permitted to account for the particular and constant Effects of Nature, without going back to the first Cause. At present the Philosophers consider only second Causes, Matter, and Form, &c. But it is not, because they suppose, that the Knowledge of God, as the first Cause, is sufficiently established. It is, because they treat of it at large, in a part of their Course of Philosophy, distinct from Physics

ANAXAGORAS. 303

Contradictions [G]. It seems to me to be full of them; and, in general, the Ideas of

(108) In their Metaphysics.

(109) As in Hesiod's Theogony; in which are so many absurd things concerning the Gods; and even, as Lactantius complains, lib. 1. cap. 5. the Chaos is there represented as being more ancient than the Gods.

(110) Arist. Metaphyl. lib. 3. c. 4. pag. 662. B.

(111) Plato in Apologia Socratis, p. 27. F.

(112) Lact. lib. 1. c. 5.

(113) Diog. Laert. in Proœm. n. 4.

(114) Arist. de Anima, lib. 1. c. 2. pag. 479.

(115) Theodor. de Gr. Affect. Serm. 2. p. 489.

(116) See the 7th Chapter of the 1st Book of his Metaphysics, and the 4th Chapter of the 1st Book of his Physics.

(117) In Remark [C].

Physics (108). However, we may be sure, that these ancient Philosophers were not ignorant of what the Poets had said of God. Why then did they not imitate them? Was it, because they laid no great stress on Poems, in which they found so many Trifles, and so many popular Opinions, which were not proof against a philosophical Enquiry (109)? *Aristotle* insinuates this Reason (110). Did they judge of the Poets, as *Socrates* did, when he said, that they resembled Fanaticks, and that, like them, they understood not what they advanced? Ἔσμεν ὧν αὖ καὶ περὶ τῶν ποιητῶν ἐν ὀλίγῳ τοῦτο, ὅτι ἦ σοφία ποιοῖεν, ἀλλὰ φύσει τινί, καὶ ἐνθυσιάζοντες, ὥσπερ οἱ θεομάντεις καὶ οἱ χρησμῳδοί. καὶ γὰρ οὗτοι λέγουσι μὲν πολλὰ καὶ καλὰ, ἴσασι δὲ οὐδὲν ὧν λέγουσι. τοιοῦτόν τί μοι ἐφάνησαν πάθος καὶ οἱ ποιηταὶ πεπονθότες (111). I soon discovered this in the Poets; namely that they were not directed by Wisdom, but by a kind of natural Enthusiasm; not unlike those, who prophesy by Inspiration. For these indeed utter many excellent Things; but they understand nothing of what they say. After the same manner the Poets appear to me to be affected. It is certain, that the most Orthodox Poets have greatly erred concerning the Nature of Gods; for *Orpheus*, who sung, that God made Heaven, calls him only the Firstborn of all Creatures, and says, that the Air was his Father,

Πρωτόγονος Φαέτων περιμήκεος ἠέρος υἱὸς (112).

Primo-genitus Phaeton, Alti Aëris filius.

Diogenes Laërtius pretends, that *Anaxagoras* borrowed one of his Tenets from the Poet *Linus* (113), but it was not with respect to the Intelligence, the first Mover. Note, that *Aristotle*, in this Particular, makes a great Difference between *Anaxagoras* and *Thales* (114). I shall conclude with a fine Passage of *Theodoret*, from whence it appears, that the Philosophers, who lived before *Anaxagoras*, were altogether ignorant of the first Cause. Ἀναξαγόρας — τῶν πρὸ αὐτοῦ γεγενημένων φιλοσόφων οὐδὲν περαιτέρω τῶν ὁρωμένων νενοηκότων, πρῶτος ὑφ᾽ ἑαυτοῦ ἐφαίνετο τῷ κόσμῳ, καὶ τοῦτον εἰς τάξιν ἐκ τῆς ἀταξίας ἀγαγεῖν τὰ στοιχεῖα (115). Anaxagoras — whereas the Philosophers before him carried their Thoughts no higher than the Visible Creation, was the FIRST, who taught, that an Intelligence presided over the World, and reduced the Elements from Confusion into Order.

[G] *Whether the Doctrine of the Homœomeria does not imply many Contradictions.*] I shall not make use of *Aristotle*'s Arguments (116), however solid and refined they may be; and, if it appears that my Reflexions agree with his, it will be meerly accidental.

I. We have seen (117), why *Anaxagoras* taught, that every thing was composed of similar Particles: This he asserted, to shew, that Bodies were not made out of nothing. Now, as the simplest Food may administer Nourishment to all the Parts of an Animal, he was necessarily obliged to acknowledge, that the Grass of a Meadow contains Bones, Nails, Horns, Blood, Flesh, Skin, Hair, &c. It is not therefore composed of similar Particles; it is rather a Collection of all kinds of *Heterogeneities*: To what purpose then was the Doctrine of the *Homœomeria*? Was he not obliged to depart from it in all particular Cases, after having supposed it in general? What I have said of Grass, may be applied likewise to Milk, Wine, Water, Bread, and many other things. Is there any Body, which does not serve as Nourishment to several others, in the Changes, which are called Generation and Corruption? Therefore these first Principles both are, and are not, *Homogeneous*. They are Homogeneous, according to the Supposition of *Anaxagoras*; but in reality they are not so; for since compound Bodies, according to his Opinion, ought to be of the same Nature with their Principles, and are only a Mixture of dissimilar Parts, it follows, that the Principles are of *Heterogeneous*. I shall retouch this Argument in the Vth Paragraph.

II. Besides, it will be found, that, upon this Supposition, Names have been wrong imposed; for (to give an Instance of it) if the Blood of Animals was contained in the Herbage they have fed upon, it would better deserve the Name of Blood, than that

of Hay. *Anaxagoras* answered, that certain Particles being more numerous in a compound Body, or placed on the Surface, make it appear uniform, and procured it a specific Name (118). *Lucretius* has refuted this Answer by the false Consequences which arise from it. *It would result from hence*, says he, *that, when Corn is bruised, some Particles of Blood may be drawn from it, or of some other Organs, of which our Body is composed. But this is contrary to Experience.*

Linquitur hîc tenuis latitandi copia quædam;
Id quod Anaxagoras sibi sumit, ut omnibus omnes
Res putet immixtas rebus latitare: sed illud
Apparere unum, cujus sint plura mixta,
Et magis in promtu, primæque in fronte locata.
Quod tamen à verâ longe ratione repulsum est.
Conveniebat enim fruges quoque sæpe minutas,
Robore cùm saxi franguntur, mittere signum
Sanguinis, aut alium, nostro quæ corpore aluntur.
Consimili ratione herbas quoque sæpe decebat,
Et laticis dulces guttas, simílique sapore,
Mittere, lanigeræ quali sunt ubera lactis:
Scilicet & glebis terrarum sæpe friatis
Herbarum genera, & fruges, frondesque videri,
Dispertita, ac in terris latitare minutè:
Postremo in lignis cinerem fumumque videri,
Cum præfractæ forent, igneisque latere minutas.
Quorum nil fieri quoniam manifesta docet res,
Scire licet non esse in rebus rea ita mixtas (119).

(118) See Aristotle's Physics, lib. 1. cap. 4. pag. 456.

(119) Lucret. lib. 1. ver. 874.

But there's a little Shift, a slight Excuse,
Which Anaxagoras's Scholars use.
Tho' such lie mix'd in All, That Part alone
Appears, That only to the Sense is shown.
Which, in the Composition, does comprize
The greatest Part, and on the Surface lies.
But this is false; or, through the weighty Mill,
From broken Corn wou'd bloody drops distil,
Or some such Parts, as in our Bodies grow,
From Herbs and Flow'rs a milky juice would flow;
Some lurking, scatter'd, Herb, or Leaf, or Tree;
And in cleft Wood, and broken Sticks, admire
Smoak, Ashes, Flame, and little Sparks of Fire.
But, since, on strictest Search, no Parts appear,
We must not fondly fancy they are there.

CREECH.

This Confutation is not amiss; for, in short, mix several Sorts of Grain together as you please; take an hundred times more Wheat, than Barley; put as many Grains of Barley as you can in an Inclosure of Wheat; what will you get by it? Will you make People believe, that there is nothing but Wheat there? Will any one continue in this Error, even after your Heap is scattered? Will no Grain of Barley appear? Nothing can be more foolish, than such an Assertion. *Anaxagoras* could not have solved this Objection, but by supposing, that each sensible Part of a Grain of Corn is so qualified, that the *Heterogeneities* are there in a less Number, and wrapt up in the Particles of Corn; and that this is the Reason why, when Corn is bruised between two Mill-Stones, we never discover the *Heterogeneous* Parts; but that, if we could proceed in the Division as far as the insensible Particles, then the Blood, the Flesh, the Bones, &c. would appear to Eyes finer than ours. In a word, he could not get clear of this Difficulty, but by the divisibility of Matter *in Infinitum*; which is to imitate a Man, who, to avoid the thrust of a Sword, throws himself headlong down a Precipice of an inconceivable Height. But I will insist only on the Difficulties, which imply some kind of Contradiction.

III. I say, in third the place, that *Anaxagoras* ought to have supposed, that the similar Particles are found, both in *greater* and *lesser* Numbers, in Bread: In greater Numbers, because the Compound is called Bread; in lesser Numbers, because a few Hours after the Bread is

VOL. I.   Gggg

ANAXAGORAS.

of the Ancients, who have mentioned the Chaos, were no less confused than the Chaos itself.

is eat, it becomes *Chyle*, and discovers nothing in all it's sensible Particles, but the Qualities of *Chyle*. This Objection will be more easily apprehended, if Dough be compared with Corn, or Bread with Dough. It will appear, that this Philosopher must have owned, that the *Homogeneities* are both more and less numerous in the same mixed Body; In Dough, for Instance; for, while it is Dough, it contains more Corpuscles of Dough, than of any other Species of Body: But, when it is converted into Bread, it contains fewer Corpuscles of Dough, than of Bread; and yet the Corpuscles of Bread are only derived from Dough.

IV. Here follows another Contradiction. It is contradicting one's self, to lay down an Hypothesis, which involves on one side the same Inconvenience it removes on the other. This is the Misfortune of *Anaxagoras*'s System. This Philosopher, having supposed, that the Parts of Matter had eternally been in a State of Confusion; that is to say, that the smallest *Homogeneous* Particles had been every where surrounded with *Heterogeneous* ones, supposed, that, at last, an intelligent Being put an end to This Disorder, by separating the similar Particles from those, which were dissimilar. But He himself overthrew his own Supposition; being obliged to confess, that all the kinds of *Homoeomeriae* were blended together in all kinds of Bodies; and This even with respect to the insensible Particles. According to His Opinion, there is an Infinity of small Bones, and little Drops of Blood, &c. in each Blade of Grass, and in each Morsel of Bread: Every thing was mixed with every thing, since every thing was made of every thing. Διὸ πᾶσί πᾶν ἐν παντί μεμίχθαι, διότι πᾶν ἐκ παντὸς ἑώρων γινόμενον (120). *Qua propter inquiunt quodque in quolibet esse mistum, quia quodlibet ex quovis oriri videbant.* Ἀναξαγόρας μεμίχθαι πᾶν ἐν παντί φησι (121). *Anaxagoras omne in omni misceri ait.* Can there be a greater State of Confusion? It was *Plato*'s Opinion of it; for more than once he alledges the Doctrine of *Anaxagoras* as a Symbol of the Chaos. Κἂν εἰ συγκρίνοιτο μὲν πάντα, διακρίνοιτο δὲ μὴ, ταχὺ ἂν τὸ τοῦ Ἀναξαγόρου γεγονὸς εἴη, ὁμοῦ πάντα χρήματα (122). *Moreover, if all things were confused, and never separated,* Anaxagoras's *Doctrine would presently be verified, that all Things were together.* He says, in another place, Τὸ τοῦ Ἀναξαγόρου ἂν πολὺ ἦν, ὦ φίλε Πῶλε ---- ὁμοῦ ἂν πάντα χρήματα ἐφύρετο ἐν τῷ αὐτῷ, ἀκρίτων τ' ὄντων τῶν τε ὑγιεινῶν καὶ ἰατρικῶν καὶ ὀψοποιητικῶν (123). *That of* Anaxagoras *would come to pass, Friend Polus.---- All things would be blended together, Those which relate to Medicine, and Health, and Those which relate to Cookery.* Menage tells us, that Luther called those Divines *Anaxagorists*, who find every thing in every Text of Scripture. "Atque inde est, quod "Luthero *Theologicus Anaxagoricus* dicitur is, qui "quodlibet in quolibet loco scripturae sacrae inveniri "possit (124)."

V. His first Principles were, and were not, such: they were first Principles, according to his Supposition; and were not in reality so; since they were as much compounded and corruptible, as any other Body. He admitted of a Divisibility *in Infinitum*; and therefore must have believed, that there is an Infinity of Corpuscles in the least Drop of Water; and consequently that it contains as many of them, as the whole Earth. Besides, this infinite number of Corpuscles was an Heap of all kinds of *Heterogeneities*. It was not, then, more simple than a Tree; and, in this respect alone, it differed from mixed Bodies, that human Eyes could not discover the *dissimilar* Parts, as they discover them in a Tree. Lastly, the Intelligence, which moved Matter, could as easily have divided these pretended first Principles, as Fire divides Wood: They were, then, as perishable as Wood; from whence it follows, that, if they existed in the Nature of things, it was not in quality of first Principles. Besides, can any thing be more absurd, than to lay down for Principles what has no Existence at all? Now, according to the Hypothesis of *Anaxagoras*, it is certain there were no *Homoeomeriae* in the Universe.

Let us examine an Answer, which he might have made: He might have supposed, that the Essence of the *Homoeomeriae* does not consist in the Resemblance of all their Parts, but in the Conformity, which is found, between the Contexture of the *Heterogeneities* of a small Bone, for instance, and the Contexture of the *Heterogeneities* of any other Bone. He might have said; "I do not pretend, that a Bone "of ten Inches, divided into an Hundred thousand "Parts, or, which is the same thing in my Hypo-"thesis, into an Hundred thousand Bones, does not "absolutely contain any Particle, but what is simi-"lar to all the rest. I own, that each of these small "Bones is a Mixture of all kinds of Principles; it "contains Flesh, it contains Blood and Membranes, "&c. But, because these different Materials are "ranged according to the same Symmetry in each "of these small Bones, I have reason to maintain, "that the Collection of an Hundred thousand of these "small Bones is an *Homogeneous* Compound, or an "Heap of *Homoeomeriae*; and, whereas I suppose, that "the Intelligence, which made the Choice of them, "found them ready made; I may very well assert, that "each of them, taken separately, is incapable of De-"struction; for they always existed of themselves."

This Answer consists of two Heads: one is the Explication of the Hypothesis with respect to the Sense of the Word *Homoeomeriae*; the other concerns the Incorruptibility of these *Homoeomeriae*. I am going to illustrate the first by an Example. Put all the Copies of the same Book, bound after the same manner, into a Library: it will be a Collection of Books, which are all alike; an *Homogeneous* Collection: not because each of these Volumes is composed of Parts, which are perfectly alike; but because the White and the Black, the Spaces, Letters, Accents, Points, Comma's, and the other *Heterogeneous* Parts, have the same Symmetry in one, as in all the rest. Setting aside this Explication of *Anaxagoras*, I shall only argue against the second Part of his Answer.

VI. I ask him not, why the Intelligence, which he acknowledged, left the *Homoeomeriae* in Confusion, from all Eternity; nor how It came to think so late of moving and uniting them; nor why he denies, that something may be formed out of nothing; he, who confesses, that Motion had a beginning? These three Objections, and some others, strangely puzzle those, who admit of a Matter, eternal, uncreated, and distinct from the divine Being; but, because these Difficulties may be urged against other Philosophers, as well as against *Anaxagoras*, it will not be proper to insist upon them. I will only illustrate the last. It is certain, that the Production of a Quality, distinct from it's Subject, does not differ from a true Creation. This the modern Philosophers (125), prove demonstratively against the *Aristotelians*; who admit an Infinity of substantial and accidental Forms, distinct from Matter; for, since they are not composed of any pre-existent Subject, it follows, that they are formed out of nothing. The best Answer, that the Followers of *Aristotle* can make, is to retort this Objection, and to say, that the *Cartesians* are obliged to acknowledge, that Motion cannot be produced, but by Creation. The *Cartesians* own this Consequence; and attribute the Production of Motion only to God; and they say, that to put Matter in Motion, is to create it at every Moment, in different Places. Let us conclude from hence, that *Anaxagoras*, and several others, contradicted themselves, when, on the one side, they would not acknowledge, that something might be made out of nothing, and owned, on the other side, that Motion, or some other Modification, had a beginning in the eternal Chaos (126). But, waving this, I shall only insist on the Difficulties, which relate particularly to *Anaxagoras*.

VII. I alledge this Maxim against him: All things, which are distinct between themselves, may be separated or divided from each other; and from hence I conclude, that each *Homoeomery* may be divided *in infinitum*; for it is composed of all Kinds of Principles jumbled together. And, therefore, since Motion is a necessary Principle of Division, and God has produced Motion in Matter, it follows, that, by this moving Force, he might disunite each part of the Universe, and break in pieces any *Homoeomery* whatever, which you would take for an Unit. If it was an *Epicurean* Atom, a Body perfectly simple, single, and free

ANAXAGORAS.

itself. I may venture to say, without an Hyperbole, that they are not just, and that these Philosophers

free from all Composition, I own, that nothing could divide it: but *Anaxagoras* does not acknowledge any such Bodies, nor any *Homœomery*, be it ever so little, but what contains an Infinity of distinct Corpuscles, and even different from each other in their Qualities. It is therefore true, that what he calls first Principles are as subject to Destruction, as the most compounded Bodies; for instance, an Ox; this, I say, is very true, even though it be supposed, that the *Homœomeriæ* exist eternally of themselves; for it is sufficient, that an external Cause can make them pass from Motion to Rest; though it has not the Power of giving them Being, or of annihilating them. To recur to a Progress *in infinitum*, would be unnecessary upon this Occasion. It cannot be said, in answer to this Objection, that, the *Homœomeriæ* being composed of an Infinity of Corpuscles, those, which compose a small Bone, may be divided *in infinitum*, without ceasing to be a small Bone, and that they only become a smaller Bone, after each Division. This is no good Reply; for there are two things to be considered in each *Homœomery*: I. That it contains an Infinity of Particles; this is common to it with others. II. That the Particles are ranged after a certain Manner; this is peculiar to it; this is it's specific Form; it's Essence; by this it is either a little Bone, or a drop of Blood, rather than any other Species of the first Principles. And, therefore, in order to take from the *Homœomery* of a Bone it's Essence, and it's Species, it is sufficient to range the Particles, which compose the same, after another manner. Now, if it be admitted, that the Intelligence, which was the first Mover, could divide Bodies, and disentangle them from each other, it might also have divided the Corpuscles of each particular *Homœomery*, and given them another Combination; it would therefore change their Species, as Flower changes it's Species, when it is kneaded; that is, when it's Particles are jumbled and combined in a different manner.

I do not object to this Philosopher, That he acknowledged a Difference between the Parts of Matter, before they were put in Motion. This Objection always appeared to me very weak. I conceive very clearly, that a Division supposes a Distinction, and that an Iron Pin, fixed into a piece of Wood, and perfectly at Rest, is as different from the Wood, as if it moved together with the Wood.

VIII. I proceed to the last Objection. What would be the Consequence, if we should grant this Philosopher, That the same necessity, which causes Bodies to exist, causes them to exist distinct, in an infinite Number of *Homœomeriæ*; each of which must necessarily continue for ever entire; the Nature of things being such, that there must be fixed Bounds in each Species; as we usually say, there is a *minimum quod sit* (127), in each Species of living Bodies? Would not such a Concession be of great Service to the Hypothesis of *Anaxagoras*? Would it not allow him the Incorruptibility, and internal Immutability, of his first Principles? Would they not be so small a Bone, that, becoming less by the actual Division of their Parts, they would cease to be a Bone; and so with regard to other Species? And would it not signify, that natural Necessity made them Indivisible? I allow all this; but it is only avoiding one Inconvenience by another: I should still find this Fault with the System; that the Νῦς, or Intelligence, would come in, against all Rules, to undertake the easiest Task, after the most difficult was performed by a blind Necessity. It is incontestably true, that every Philosopher, who will give a good Account of the Order, which appears in the several parts of the Universe, must suppose an Intelligence as the Author of this beautiful Regularity. He need not fear, that reasonable Persons will reproach him with imitating certain Poets, who introduce a God, a *Deus ex machina*, upon the Stage, to unravel Difficulties, which are not worth his Trouble. But if, after having supposed, that the *Homœomeriæ* were formed without the Direction of an intelligent Cause, he pretends, that such a Cause disentangled, and put them in order, he may be told, that he imitates such Poets, contrary to all Rules,

Nec Deus intersit, nisi dignus vindice nodus Inciderit (128).

(128) Horat. de Art. Poet. ver. 191.

Never presume to make a God appear,
But for a Business worthy of God. ROSCOMMON.

To be sensible of the Force of this Objection, we need only observe, that it is much more difficult to make good Watches, than to separate them from a parcel of Medals and Shells, with which they are intermixed, and then to range and mix them after a better manner. A young Apprentice, a Child, could make this Choice, and produce this new Regulation. Every one will grant me, that the Formation of Men (129) is a Work, which requires more Direction and Ability, than the Art of ranging them according to Military Evolutions. The greatest part of modern Philosophers suppose, that the general Laws of Nature are sufficient to make a Fœtus grow, provided it has been well formed, and well organized, in the Seed; but they suppose, that the *Animalcula*, which are organized in the Seed, are the Work of a most wise and powerful Creator. They believe, therefore, that the principal Difficulty, which stands in need of the Direction of an Intelligence, consists in the first formation of an organized Machine; that is to say, in the forming those *Animalcula*, which they suppose to be in the Seed. To speak properly, each of these *Animalcula* is an *Homœomeria* of *Anaxagoras*. It is, therefore, more difficult to form *Homœomeriæ*, than to cause Animals to grow by the help of Nourishment. It is, therefore, in order to explain the Formation of the *Homœomeriæ*, that the Direction of an intelligent Being is chiefly requisite; for every *Homœomeria* is a certain Collection of infinite kinds of Bodies: And this Collection must be made according to certain Proportions and Situations: The Collection, necessary for the *Homœomeria* of a Bone, is different from that, which is necessary for the *Homœomeria* of Flesh; and, if you were not exactly to follow this Symmetry, you would not have the first Principles of Blood or Marrow, but those of some other Mixture. Now *Anaxagoras* did not suppose the Necessity of an Intelligence, towards the Formation of infinite Species of *Homœomeriæ*: each of which is a certain Conjunction of all kinds of Bodies, mixed together in such a manner, that those of one Species must prevail in Number, and be placed in one certain manner, rather than in any other, and that, in general, one Proportion and Symmetry must prevail more than another. He has therefore assigned a blind Necessity as the Cause of what was most difficult. And therefore he did not reason consequentially, when he believed an Intelligence to be necessary for what was less difficult. According to his Doctrine, the whole Function of the Intelligence consists in ranging what was confused, in moving what was at Rest, in separating such things as were mixed, and adorning those, which were destitute of Ornament. Ἀναξαγόρας ––– ταῦτα παιδεύει, ἀρχὴ πάντων ὁ νῦς, καὶ ἔτι ἀπ᾽ ἀυτοῦ καὶ κίνησις τῶν ὅλων, καὶ περίχυσις τάξιν τοῖς ἀτάκτοις, καὶ κίνησιν τοῖς ἀκινήτοις, καὶ διάκρισιν τοῖς μεμιγμένοις, καὶ κόσμον τοῖς ἀκόσμοις (130). *Anaxagoras hæc docet. Mens omnium est initium, eaque causa & omnium dominà est, & ordinem confusis præbet, & motionem immobilibus, & discrimen commixtis, & ornatum inornatis.* He might have been attacked both in Front and Rear. He might have been told, *You say both too much, and too little. If you believe, that Nature, without any Direction or Knowledge, formed all the* Homœomeriæ, *you must believe, that she could have moved, separated, and distributed them:* And therefore your Intelligence is superfluous. But if you believe it necessary for the Separation and Distribution of these Homœomeriæ, *you ought likewise to ascribe to it their Formation; you do not extend it's Influence wherever it is wanted.* Thus one part of your System destroys the other: It is not made up of well sorted and well connected Pieces (131). If this Philosopher's Works were extant, or all those of *Theophrastus* (132), we might perhaps find, that he answered some of the Difficulties, which I have just now started; that he owned he was not satisfied with his own Hypothesis; and that he sunk under the weight of the Mysteries of Nature. He said, that every thing was surrounded with Darkness. *Anaxagoras pronuntiat circumfusa esse tenebris Omnia* (133). Several other Philosophers make the same Complaint;

(129) *I do not mean what Parents contribute towards it; I do not mean the Material, but the Efficient Cause, which organizes the Fœtus, and forms this admirable Machine.*

(130) Hermias in Philosoph. Irrisione. This Work of Hermias is to be found in the Bibliotheca Patrum, and at the end of Justin Martyr's Works, Paris, 1636, and Cologne, 1686.

(131) See a Passage of Aristotle in Remark [R].

(132) He wrote a Book περὶ τῶν Ἀναξαγόρου, de Anaxagoræ decretis. See Laert. in Theophr. lib. 5. n. 42.

(133) Lact. lib. 3. c. 2. pag. 217.

ANAXAGORAS.

Philosophers could not pretend, with any shew of Reason, that this state of Confusion subsisted no longer [*H*]. It is related, that *Anaxagoras* foretold, that the Stone, which fell from Heaven into the River *Ægos*, and was preserved and honoured as a holy Relick, would fall from the Body of the Sun [*I*]. Some other Predictions are likewise ascribed to him (*x*). He applied himself very much to Geometry (*y*); and it was found, that, in Prison, he wrote concerning the Quadrature of the Circle (*z*). His vast Genius was equal to every thing; the most difficult *Phænomena* of Nature, Comets, the Milky-way, Earthquakes, Winds, Thunder, Lightening (*aa*), the overflowing of the *Nile* (*bb*), Eclipses, and such like things, which he accounted for. All These, together with his Astronomical and Geometrical Speculations, did not prevent his reading the Poems of *Homer*, with the attention of a Man, who was desirous of making Discoveries, and improving Litterature. He was the first, who supposed them to be Moral Works, in which Virtue and Justice are explained by Allegorical Narrations (*cc*). The Circumstances and Issue of the Action, which was brought against him at *Athens* for Impiety, are variously reported; some say, that he was condemned; others,

(x) See Remark [*I*].

(y) Proclus Diadochus, lib. 2. in I. librum Euclidis.

(z) Plutarch. de Exilio, pag. 607.

(aa) Diog. Laërt. lib. 2. n. 9.

(bb) Diod. Sicul. lib. 1. cap. 38.

(cc) Diogen. Laërt. lib. 2. n. 12.

Complaint; so far as to imagine, that the removal of the Darkness mentioned by *Moses*, which was upon the Deep, before God created the Light (134), was only with respect to the corporeal Eye; for, say they, *the Darkness of the Mind still covers the Face of the Deep. The Light of Truth, concentrated in this Abyss, never emerges from it; it only sends out a few Rays, which reach our Minds, after so many Reflexions and Refractions, and after having mixed their Brightness with so many obscure Corpuscles, in the dark Spaces, through which they pass, that they are only proper to form false Images.*

[*H*] *They could not pretend, with any shew of Reason, that this State of Confusion subsisted no longer.*] I had resolved to make some Reflexions on this Subject; but since the foregoing Remarks, and those which remain to be made, will sufficiently, if not too much, enlarge this Article, I have altered my Resolution, to avoid Prolixity. I shall not want an Opportunity of giving, in another Article, what I suppress here.

[*I*] *Anaxagoras foretold, that the Stone ——— would fall from the Body of the Sun.*] This is related by Diogenes Laërtius (135); and *Plutarch* mentions this Prodigy in these Words: " Others fancied, that a " Stone, which seemed to fall from Heaven, was an " Omen of this great Overthrow (136). It was of " a vast bigness; and fell by the River *Ægos*. The " *Peloponnesians* esteem it very much; and shew it " among their Curiosities to this Day. And it is said, " that the Philosopher *Anaxagoras* foretold, that one " of those Bodies, which are fixed to the Vault of " Heaven, should one day be loosened by a violent " Shock or Convulsion of the whole Machine, and fall " to the Earth. For he said, that the Stars were not " in the very places, in which they were first formed; " seeing they were heavy Bodies, and of the Nature of " Stones; and that they shone by the Reflection of the " elementary Fire, and had been drawn up by force " and were kept there by the Impetuosity and Violence of the circular Motion of the Heavens; " having been placed there at the beginning of the " World, and hindered from falling upon the Earth, " when cold and heavy bodies were separated from " the other substances of the Universe (137)." I have set down the whole Passage, that the Tradition of this Prodigy, and the Singularity of the Doctrine of *Anaxagoras*, may be seen at the same time. The Words of *Pliny* deserve no less to be quoted. " Celebrant Græci, *says he* (138), Anaxagoram Clazomenium, Olympiadis septuagesimæ octavæ secundo " anno, prædixisse cœlestium literarum scientia, quibus diebus lapis casurum esset è Sole. Idque factum interdiu in Thraciæ parte ad Ægos flumen. " Qui lapis etiam nunc ostenditur, magnitudine vectis, colore adusto, comete quoque illis noctibus flagrante. Quod siquis prædictum credat, simul fateatur necesse est, majoris miraculi divinitatem Anaxagoræ fuisse : solvique rerum naturæ intellectum, " & confundi omnia, si aut ipse Sol lapis esse, aut " unquam lapidem in eo fuisse credatur: decidere " tamen crebro, non erit dubium. In Abydi gymnasio ex ea causa colitur hodieque, modicus quidem, " sed quem in medio terrarum casurum idem Anaxagoras prædixisse narratur. Colitur & Cassandriæ, " quæ Potidæa vocitata est. ——— *The Greeks have a Tradition, that, in the second Year of the Seventy eighth Olympiad*, Anaxagoras *of* Clazomenæ *fore-*

" *told, by his Knowledge of the Heavens, at what time* " *a Stone would fall from the Sun*; *which came to pass* " *in the Day-time, in a part of* Thrace, *by the River* " *Ægos. This Stone is still shewn, of the bigness of* " *a Bar, and of a burnt Colour, and as having been* " *attended with the Appearance of a Comet. But if* " *any one really believeth, that this Prodigy was foretold, he must own, at the same time, that the divine Knowledge of* Anaxagoras, *is the greater Miracle of the Two*; *and that the Knowledge of natural Causes is destroyed, and all things confused,* " *if it be believed, either that the Sun is a Stone,* " *or that there ever were Stones in it*; *though there* " *would be no room to doubt of their frequent falls.* " *Upon this Account a Stone is at present had in reverence by the School of* Abydus; *it's Size is but* " *small*; *but it is that, whose fall to the Earth was* " *foretold by* Anaxagoras. *It is reverenced likewise* " *at* Cassandria, *now called* Potidæa." By this you see, that *Anaxagoras* had more than once foretold the falling of these Stones, and that the Worship of them increased proportionably. Note, that *Ammianus Marcellinus,* and *Tzetzes,* make use of the Plural Number, in relation to the Prodigy of the River *Ægos*. They pretend, that *Anaxagoras* foretold, that Stones would fall from Heaven (139). *Philostratus* has expressed himself after the same manner. I shall set down his Words at length, because they will afford Matter for Criticism. " *Apollonius*, then, would have " been unjustly charged with Impiety and Error, for " having foreseen several things, and foretold others, " after the same manner as *Socrates* was fully informed of them by Spirits, before they came to pass. " And *Anaxagoras* also: for who knows not, that, " once upon a time, being gone to the *Olympic* " Games, covered with a Cloak, as a Prediction that " it would Rain (140), though the Day was so clear " and serene, that there was no probability of it; yet " a little while after it rained violently? Having, another time, foretold that a House would fall in a few " Days, it fell accordingly. Again, having foretold, " that the Day at Noon would be in an Instant become " as dark as Night; and, another time, that great " Stones would fall from Heaven into the River " *Ægos*, it came so to pass. Now, if it be acknowledged, that these Things, and others of the like " Nature, foreseen by *Anaxagoras*, were only a Proof " of his very great Skill, how can they be imputed " to *Apollonius* as Art Magic (141)." Upon this a Commentator has made a very ridiculous Observation. " There are no Astrologers at present, tho' " ever so mean, who cannot do as much as *Philostratus* says *Anaxagoras* did, in foretelling Rain, " and the fall of a Stone from Heaven, and the " like (142)." What an Absurdity is this! As great Fools as the Astrologers of our Days may be, they have not the Rashness to foretel, that Stones will fall from Heaven. Our Almanack-makers, and our most renowned Calculators of Horoscopes, are careful not to hazard their Reputation so shamefully. They know too well, that to foresee such Falls surpasses all their Skill. *Pliny* had reason to say, that the Prediction of *Anaxagoras* would have been a greater Miracle, than to see the Stone fall from the Body of the Sun (143). Observe, that there is an Interval of about sixty Years between the Time of this Prediction, according to *Pliny,* and it's Accomplishment, according to *Plutarch.* I have another Observation to make.

(134) See Genesis I.

(135) Diog. Laërt. lib. 2. n. 10.

(136) Namely, The Destruction of the Athenian Fleet by Lysander.

(137) Plutarch. in Lysandro, pag. 439.

(138) Plin. lib. 2. c. 58.

(139) Amm. Marcellin. lib. 22. c 8. pag. 308. Tzetzes chil. 2. ver. 892.

(140) Diog. Laërt. lib. 2. n. 10. Ælian. de Animal. l. 7. cap. 8. and Suidas, mention it likewise.

(141) Philostr. in Vita Apollonii, lib. 1. cap. 2.

(142) Artus Thomas, Sr. d'Embri, *Annotations on the Life of Apollonius,* Tom. I. p. 9.

(143) See his Words above, Citat. (138).

Photius,

ANAXAGORAS.

others, that he was acquitted [K]. *Pericles*, who protected him on this occasion, was suspected of Atheism, for having been instructed by such a Master. I have taken notice of this in another place (*dd*). *Diogenes Laërtius*, in reporting a witty Saying of Anaxagoras,

(*dd*) *In the Remarks* [C] *and* [D] *of the Article* PERICLES.

Photius, in his Abstract of the Life of *Apollonius*, pretends, that *Anaxagoras* was accounted a great Prophet, for having foretold, by Magic, that it would rain (144). I cannot believe, that *Photius* so little understood *Philostratus*'s Meaning; I ascribe this egregious Mistake to the ill State his Work has been put into by Transcribers. And I cannot sufficiently wonder, how the Translator (145) could resolve to let this Passage be printed. His Translation is a Series of such gross Impertinence, and monstrous Reasoning, and withal so expressly contrary to the Original of *Philostratus*, that we can comprehend nothing of his Conduct. Did he believe, that the Text of *Photius* was correct? He must, then, have dream't of something else. Did he believe his Readers would be so stupid as to think his Performance a good one? He was, then, strangely secure. I desire those, who are qualified for it, to examine this Passage of *Photius*; they will find such Wounds in it, as require the Dexterity of the ablest Hand; and perhaps they may heal them, by the Assistance of the Manuscripts, compared with the Text, of *Philostratus*.

[*K*] *Some say that he was condemned, others that he was acquitted*.] He was accused of Impiety, by *Cleon*, for having said, that the Sun was a Mass of inflamed Matter; and, notwithstanding *Pericles*'s Protection, he was condemned to Banishment, and fined five Talents, as *Sotion* relates (146). But others say, that *Thucydides* informed against him, and accused him not only of Impiety, but of Treason likewise; and that the Accused was condemned to Death for Contumacy (147). Others relate, that he was in Prison, when Sentence of Death was pronounced against him. They add, that *Pericles*, addressing himself to the Judges, said, *Do you find that he has committed any Crime?* And, perceiving that none was imputed to him, he said, *I am his Disciple; destroy him not, therefore, through Prejudice: believe me rather; and give him his Liberty*. He obtained his Request; but the Accused took his Trial so much to heart, that he resolved to die (148). Others report, that he was brought before the Judges by *Pericles*; and that his Melancholy had reduced him so low, that he could scarce walk; insomuch that he was discharged; not on account of his Innocence, but because of the Compassion, which he excited (149). I have observed elsewhere (150), that *Pericles* found no better means of saving this Philosopher, than by causing him to leave *Athens*.

Take notice of four Things. I The Accusers of *Anaxagoras* (151) were Men of a Faction contrary to *Pericles*. It was not, therefore, out of Zeal for Religion, that they persecuted this Philosopher; but with a Design of supporting their Cabal, and weakening the Authority of *Pericles*, by maliciously causing the Suspicion of Irreligion to fall upon him. The most probable means of succeeding in this Design was to accuse *Anaxagoras* of Impiety. This is generally the first Inducement to this kind of Accusations; we went to be revenged of some one, or to remove an Obstacle to our Authority, and Fortune; we call the Passions of the People to our Assistance, and pretend, that the Honour of God is concerned in our Cause. II. It is not true, that the Accusers of *Anaxagoras* grounded their Accusation on his acknowledging, that the divine Intelligence created the World; they proceeded upon this, that, in saying the Sun was a Stone, he robbed it of it's Divinity; which was likewise the Foundation of his Sentence of Condemnation (152) And therefore *Vossius* is guilty of an Error in these Words. " *Laërtii* industria nobis ipsa " *Anaxagoræ* verba conservavit. Sunt autem hujus- " modi: Πάντα χρήματα ἦν ὁμοῦ. εἶτα τὰς ἐλ- " θὼν αὐτὰ διεκόσμησε. *Omnia simul erant: de- " inde accessit Mens, eaque composuit*. Quàm apertè " hic opificem ab opificio distinguit! Hoc ferre non " potuere Athenienses, ac ἀθεότητα vel ἀσέβειαν " vocarunt (153). ——— *We are obliged to the Care of Diogenes Laertius, for preserving the very Words of* Anaxagoras; *they are these*: All things were confused; afterwards an Intelligence, interposing, reduced them into Order. How plainly does he distinguish here between the Workmanship and the Ar-

" *tificer!* The Athenians could not bear this; and " charged him with Atheism or Impiety." *Anaxagoras* was not condemned merely for distinguishing between God, and his Works; but for not teaching, as the Poets did, that the Sun was both the Work of God, and itself a God: For, according to the Belief of the People, grounded upon the Writings of the Poets, the Sun was *Apollo*, the Son of *Jupiter*, and one of the great Deities. *Vossius*'s Error is, as if one should say, That the Inquisition has condemned a Person to death, for teaching, that God alone, the Author, Preserver, and sovereign Lord of all things, deserves the supreme Worship, Λατρεία, and that no Creature in Paradice merits our Invocation, or the Worship Δελεία. This Doctrine comprehends two Points; and a Man would be punished in *Salamanca* only for the second. Would not a Protestant be in the wrong to say, that such a Man was punished for maintaining the first Point? However, *Eusebius* had reason to think it strange, that *Anaxagoras* was in danger of being stoned, as an Atheist, notwithstanding his Orthodoxy as to the Existence of a God, the Author of this World; a Doctrine, which he was the first who taught, among the *Greeks*. Θαυμάσαι δ᾽ ἐςὶν ὡς ἐτῷ πρῶτῳ πᾶς᾽ Ἕλλησι τούτου θεολογήσας τὸν πρῶτον, δέξας Ἀθηναίοις ἄθεος εἶναι, ὅτι μὴ τὸν Ἥλιον ἐθεολόγει, τὸν δὲ Ἥλιον ποιητὴν, μιχρῆ δεῖν καταλευσθεὶς ἔθανε (154). *In quo sanè permirum illud est, qui princeps apud Græcos eam Theologiæ rationem intulerat, eum Atheniensibus, quod non tam Solem, at Solis ipsius effectorem Deum statueret, athewm esse visum, ac propterea parum abfuisse, quin ab iis lapidibus necaretur*. This, I say, is astonishing; for, in short, (which is my third Remark) it is scarce conceivable, that, in so learned a City as *Athens*, a Philosopher could not explain the Properties of the Stars by Physical Reasons, without running the risque of his Life. Is it not a deplorable thing for a Man to be more knowing than a superstitious Mob, conducted by senseless Men? To what purpose serves this Superiority of Genius and Knowledge among such a People? Is it not rather a Crime? Does it not expose a Man to a thousand Infamies and Dangers? And might we not enjoy the Conveniencies of Life much better, by following the Current of Ignorance and Superstition? Οἱ προεςραμμένοι τὸ χρεὼν κατὰ τὸ ἀνθρώπινον ἐπερχθῆναι τὰ πράγματα διωθεαι καὶ ἀλέξαι, ὡς ἀσεβεῖς καὶ περιττοὶ εἰς δικαστήρια ἤγοντο (155). *The Philosophers before* CHRIST *were dragged before Tribunals, as impious and officious Persons, for endeavouring to speculate upon, and explain, things, to the Understanding of Men*. I observe, in the fourth Place, that we cannot but wonder, that so remarkable a Trial as That of *Anaxagoras*, in which *Pericles*, the chief Man of *Athens*, was so far concerned, was not better known to Historians. They mention it with a Thousand Variations; nay, some of them, in the principal Points, assert what others deny; which is not for the Honour of Antiquity.

I must not omit a fine Passage of *Lucian*, in which he supposes, that the greatest of the Gods endeavoured to crush *Anaxagoras* to pieces, but that he missed him; and that the Thunder-bolt, being averted by *Pericles*, burnt a Temple, and was almost broken to pieces against a Rock. Δίκην δ᾽ ὥσπερ ἐπαυδὰν τὸν κεραυνὸν ἐπισκευάσω καθωπλισμένα γὰρ αὐτῷ, καὶ ἀποςομωμένα εἰσὶ δύο ἀκτίνες αἱ μάλιςαι, ὑπότε φιλοτιμότερον ἠκόντισα πρῴην ἐπὶ τὸν σοφιστὴν Ἀναξαγόραν, ὃς ἐπειθε τὲς ὁμιλητὰς μηδὲ ὅλως εἶναι τινας ἡμᾶς τὲς θεές. ἀλλ᾽ ἐκείνου μὲν διήμαρτον. ὑπερέσχε γὰρ αὐτῷ τὴν χεῖρα Περικλῆς. ὁ δὲ κεραυνὸς, εἰς τὸ Ἀνάκειον παρασκήψας, ἐκείνο τε κατέφλεξε, καὶ αὐτὸς ὀλίγου δεῖν συνετρίβη παρὰ τὴν πέτραν (156). *They shall smart for it, as soon as my* Thunder *is in Order. For two of it's largest Forks were bent and broken; when, not long ago, I darted it too eagerly at the Sophist* Anaxagoras; *who endeavoured to persuade his Acquaintance, that there were no such Folks, as we Gods. I missed my aim, it is true; for* Pericles *interposed with his Hand, and protected him; and the averted Bolt, falling on the Temple of* Castor *and* Pollux, *burnt it

(144) Phot. Biblioth. cod. 241. pag. 1017.

(145) Andr. Schottus.

(146) Sotion, in Successionibus Philosophorum, apud Diogen. Laërt. lib. 2. n. 12.

(147) Satyrus, in Vitis apud Diogen. Laërt. ubi supra.

(148) Hermippus, in Vitis apud Diog. Laërt. ubi supra, n. 13.

(149) Hieronymus, in secundo libro Commentor. Varior. apud Diog. Laërt. ubi supra.

(150) *In Remark* [M] *of the Article* PERICLES.

(151) Cleon, or Thucydides. See Plutarch *in the Life of Pericles, p.* 170, & 155.

(152) See Josephus, l. 2. contra App. p. 1079. F. S. Cyril. lib. 2. contra Julian.

(153) Vossius de Orig. & Progr. Idolol. lib. 1. cap. 1. p. 5.

(154) Euseb. Præpar. Evang. l. 14. cap. 14. pag. 750. C.

(155) Just. Martyr. Apol. 1. p. 48.

(156) Lucian. in Timon. p. 65. Tom. 1. Operum.

VOL. I.   H h h h   *down*,

ANAXAGORAS.

Anaxagoras, has committed a Blunder in Chronology [L], which I wonder has been so long unobserved. The Constancy of this Philosopher on the News of his own Condemnation, and at That of the Death of his Sons, was wonderful [M]. He was very little concerned, whether he lived and died out of his own Country (*ee*); and he had a true Discernment of human Happiness [N]. Some Authors pretend, that he was never seen to laugh, or even to smile (*ff*). Cicero ascribes a remarkable Gravity to him; *Maxima fuit & gravitatis & ingenii gloria* (*gg*). He died at *Lampsacus*, where he had an honourable Burial, and a very glorious Epitaph; nay, they went so far as to build

(ee) See Remark [M].
(ff) Ælian. Var. Hist. lib. 8. c. 13. Plutarch *in the Life of Pericles.*
(gg) Cicero, Quæst. Academ. lib. 2. cap 13.

down, and was itself almost broke in pieces against a Rock. *Vossius*, who says only, that *Jupiter* darted his Thunder-bolt against this Philosopher (157), occasioned *Moreri* to say, that *Anaxagoras* was crushed to pieces by it. It was very natural to believe so; for we cannot easily conceive, that a Thunder-bolt, designed for the Death of any Person, should not kill him. But this should teach us to have recourse to the Originals, and not to stop at modern Authors, who mention only such Circumstances of a Fact, as they have present Occasion for. *Vossius*, for Example, who had no occasion, in this Place, to tell us, whether *Jupiter* succeeded or not, suppressed *Lucian*'s Raillery. This Omission led *Moreri* into a Snare, which he might have avoided, if he had but translated the *Latin* of *Vossius*. Why did he act the part of a Paraphrast? *Lambert Bartenus*, commenting on this Passage of *Lucian*, asserts, that *Anaxagoras* was accused of Atheism, on account of his Doctrine concerning the divine Intelligence, The first Mover, &c (158). This is an Untruth, which he borrowed from *Vossius*, and which I have already confuted. He says, further, that a Talent was promised as a Reward to any one, who should kill this Philosopher (159). This seems to me to confound *Anaxagoras* with the Atheist *Diagoras*. Lastly, in point of Orthodoxy, he compares *Anaxagoras* with *Lucian*, and complains, that *Justin Martyr* ranks *Lucian* among the Atheists. " Anaxa" goræ non absimilis fuit Lucianus noster, quem " immerito ἄθεον vocat Justinus Martyr, in oratione " contra Græcos (160). — Our Lucian *was not " unlike Anaxagoras, whom Justin Martyr, in his O" ration against the Greeks, unjustly styles* The " Atheist." But his Comparison is as false, as his Complaint; the Occasion of his Error was as follows. He had read in *Vossius*, " Lucianus, in Timone, ait " Jovem in Anaxagoræ caput - - - - fed Lucianum " quid dico? Ecce Justinus Martyr, oratione ad Græ" cos, *cum ἄθεον* vocat (161) - - - - Lucian, *in his " Timon, says, that Jupiter darted on the Head of " Anaxagoras* — *but why do I mention* Lucian? " Justin Martyr, *in his Oration against the Greeks, " calls him an* Atheist?" And he did not apprehend, that *eum (him)* relates to the Philosopher *Anaxagoras*, and not to *Lucian*.

(157) Vossius de Philos. Sectis, p. 27.
(158) Lambert. Bartesius in Luciani Timon. pag. 62.
(159) Id. Ib.
(160) Id. Ib. pag. 63.
(161) Vossius de Orig. & Progr. Idol. lib. 1. cap. 1. p. 5.

[L] *Diogenes Laërtius, in reporting a witty Saying of* Anaxagoras, *has committed a Blunder in Chronology.*] He says, that *Anaxagoras*, seeing the Tomb of *Mausolus*, cried out, *It is a Monument of the Conversion of Gold into Stone*. I do not confine myself to a literal Translation; but these are the *Greek* Terms: Τάφο₰ πολυτελὴς λελιθωμένης ἐστὶν οὐσίας εἴδωλον (162). *Monumentum pretiosum in lapides conversarum divitiarum imago est.* We may suppose, that he really expressed himself thus, at the Sight of a sumptuous Sepulchre; but it was not upon seeing That of *Mausolus*; for his Death preceded the building of that Monument by several *Olympiads*. " Anaxagoras " Olymp. LXXXVIII. mortuus est. Mausoli autem " sepulchrum ante Olymp. CVII. conditum non est. " Aut igitur hæc verba Philosophus ille non dixit: " aut alia certè occasione dixit : Mausoleum enim " nunquam vidit : quod ab Illustratoribus Laërtii non" dum opinor observatum est. Verba sunt Joannis " Pearsonii viri undecunque doctissimi, in libro de " epistolis Sancti Ignatii, pag. 9. secundæ partis ; " quibus ego assentior. Id ipsum observatum à Gis" berto Cupero in antiquis numismatibus explicatis " viro elegantissimi ingenii (163). — Anaxagoras " *died in the* LXXXVIII*th Olympiad. But the Se" pulchre of* Mausolus *was not built 'till the* CVII*th " Olympiad. Either, therefore, our Philosopher did " not speak these Words, or he spoke them on some other " Occasion; for he never saw the Mausoleum; which " I think has never been observed by the Commentators " on* Laërtius. *They are the Words of* John Pearson, *a " Man of great Learning, in his Book concerning the E" pistles of* St Ignatius, p. 9. Part II. *with which I agree. " The same Observation was made by That great Genius " * Gisbert Cuperus, *in his ancient Coins explained.*"

(162) Diog. Laërt. lib. 2. n. 10.
(163) Menage, in Diogen. Laërt. p. 77. col. 2.

[M] *The Constancy of this Philosopher on the News of his own Condemnation, and at That of the Death of his Sons, was wonderful.*] On the first News, he said, *Nature has long ago pronounced her Sentence as well against them* (164), *as against me*; and on the second, *I knew very well, that I begot them mortal* (165). *Diogenes Laërtius* intimates, that he lost them all; and adds, that, according to *Demetrius Phalereus*, his Sons buried him with their own Hands (166); which would be a Contradiction among Authors. But it may be cleared up, by supposing, that, after he had shewed this Constancy, he had other Children; or that he gave this Answer, only upon hearing of the Death of one of his Sons. *Cicero* employs the singular Number. " Quem (*Anaxagoram*) ferunt " nunciata morte filii, dixisse, sciebam me genuisse " mortalem (167). —— *Who* (Anaxagoras) *is report" ed, upon hearing of the Death of his Son, to have " said, I knew that I begot him mortal.*" *Valerius Maximus* (168), *Plutarch* (169), and *Simplicius* (170), use the same Number ; but *Ælian* observes, that *Anaxagoras* had only two Sons, and that he spoke these Words, upon hearing of the Death of both (171). Note, that he received this News, whilst he was reading a Lecture in Philosophy (172).

I shall insert here his Answer to his Friends, who asked him, at *Lampsacus*, whether he desired, after his Death, to be carried to *Clazomenæ*, where he was born. *That is unnecessary*, said he, *the Infernal Road is as short from one Place, as from another. Præclarè Anaxagoras, qui quum Lampsaci meriretur, quærentibus amicis, velletne Clazomenas in patriam, si quid ei accidisset afferri, nihil necesse est*, inquit, *undique enim ad inferos tantundem viæ est* (173). *Diogenes Laërtius* supposes, that he said this to a Person, who was unwilling to die out of his own Country (174). I have often wondered, that the fine Sayings of the Ancients are so variously reported : I have enquired into the Reason of it ; and the most probable seems to be this. Readers retain the Substance of a Fact better than the Circumstances ; and therefore, when they have a mind to relate it, they supply what they have forgotten in the best manner they can ; and, as their Tastes are different, it happens, that some supply one thing, and some another. I say nothing of the Supplements, which are designedly made to accommodate things better to the Subject in hand. They are artificial Variations, and proceed from Insincerity : I say nothing of them. What I have said of Readers, may be universally applied. We are still more apt to falsify what we hear, than what we read.

(164) There it, against his Judges.
(165) Diog. Laërt. l. b. 2. n. 13.
(166) Id. Ib.
(167) Cicero, Tuscul. Quæst. l. 3. fol. 261.
(168) Valer. Max. lib. 5. in fine.
(169) Plutarch Consol. ad Apollon. p. 118. de cohibenda irá, p. 463. & de tranquill. Animi pag. 474. Mr Menage in Laërt. lib. n. 13. qu. net, as two Treatises of Plutarch, the Treatise de cohibendâ irá, and quæl dapper ælog.
(170) Simplic in Epictet. Enchirid. c. 22.
(171) Ælian. Var. Hist. lib. 3. cap. 2.
(172) Plutarch. de Consol. ad Apollon. p. 118.
(173) Cicero Tusculan. Quæst. l. 1. fol. 252. D.
(174) Diog. Laërt. lib. 2. n. 11.

[N] *He had a true Discernment of human Happiness.*] He believed those to be most happy, who seem least to be so; and that we must not look, among the Rich and Great, for Persons, who taste true Happiness : but among those, who, till a small Parcel of Ground, or apply themselves to the Sciences, without Ambition. *Valerius Maximus* will express it better than I can. " Nec parum prudenter Anaxago" ras interrogari cuidam, quisnam esset beatus: " Nemo, inquit, ex his quos tu felices existi" mas : sed eum in illo numero reperies, qui à te " ex miseris constare creditur. Non erit ille divi" tiis & honoribus abundans : sed aut exigui ruris, " aut non ambitiosæ doctrinæ fidelis ac pertinax " cultor, in secessu quam in fronte beatior (175). " —— Anaxagoras, *being asked, who was happy, re" plied, with great Prudence, none of those, whom " you esteem to be so, but He, whom you think to be " miserable, will not be one, who abounds with Riches and Ho" nours ; but either one, who cultivates a small Farm, or " is a true and constant Follower of unambitious Sciences, " happier in his Retirement, than he appears to be.*"

(175) Valer. Max. lib. 7. cap. 2. & 9. in extern. pag. 604.

[O] He

ANAXAGORAS. 309

build an Altar to Him [*O*]. A little before his Death, the Chief Persons of the City paid him a Visit; and asked him whether he had any Commands for them; to which he answered, That he only desired, that Children might be permitted to play, every Year, in the Month of his Death (*bb*). This was performed; and the Custom still continued in the Time of *Diogenes Laërtius*. It is said, that he lived Seventy two Years (*ii*). It is not certain, that he maintained the Doctrine of Predestination [*P*]. He is the first Philosopher *, who published Books [*Q*]. *Socrates*, who expected to be informed of certain Particulars by them, was dissatisfied with the Perusal of them: This was plainly his own Fault [*R*], as I shall shew in the Reflexions

(bb) Diogen. Laërt. lib. 2. n. 14. See R mark [*A*] towards the end.
(ii) Id. ib. n. 7.
* Id. ibid. n. 11.

I have

[*O*] *He had —— a very glorious Epitaph: Nay, they went so far as to build an Altar to him.*] *Ælian* and *Diogenes Laërtius* have preserved this Epitaph; which consists of these two Verses.

(176) Diog. Laërt. l. 2. n. 15.

'Ενθάδε πλεῖστον ἀληθείας ἐπὶ τέρμα περήσας
'Ουρανίε κόσμε κεῖται Ἀναξαγόρας (176).

Entomb'd here Anaxagoras *lies,
Who taught the Secret of the Skies.*

There is as much Energy in this Distich as in these seven *French* Verses, which contain a like Encomium.

*Descartes, dont tu vois icy la sepulture,
A desfillé les yeux des aveugles mortels,
Et gardant le respect que l'on doit aux Autels,
Leur à du monde entier demontré la structure.*

*Son nom par mille ecrits se rendit glorieux,
Son esprit mesurant & la terre & les cieux
En penetra l' abime, & perca les nuages* (177).

(177) Baillet's Life of Descartes, t. 2. p. 443.

*Descartes, whose Ashes here are laid,
Dispell'd the Mists from mortal Eyes;
And, due respect to Altars paid,
The Structure shew'd of Earth and Skies.*

*A thousand Works his Name shall spread;
Who, measuring Nature's wond'rous Frame,
Div'd to Earth's deepest, central Bed,
And, soaring, reach'd the Ætherial Flame.*

(178) Ælian. Var. Hist. lib. 8. cap. 19.
(179) Kahnius upon this Passage of Ælian.
(180) Arist. Rhetoricor. lib. 2. c. 23. pag. 445.

Diogenes Laërtius says nothing of *Anaxagoras*'s Altar. But *Ælian* mentions it in (178), and seems to say, that two were consecrated to him, one under the Name of *The Intelligence*, the other under That of *Truth*. But a very learned Critic (179), does not understand the Passage so; he says, it signifies, that, according to some, the Altar was dedicated to the *Intelligence*, and according to others, to *Truth*. *Aristotle* observes, that the Inhabitants of *Lampsacus* continued to honour *Anaxagoras* (180). We may observe, that, in St *Austin*'s Time, the Authority of this Philosopher was still very considerable. " Quam (veritatem) si sensit " *Anaxagoras, eamque Deum esse vidit, mentemque* " *appellavit, non solum nomen* Anaxagoræ, *quod* " *propter literatam vetustatem, omnes, ut militariter* " *loquar, literatores libenter sufflant, nos doctos &* " *sapientes non facit, sed ne ipsa quidem ejus cog-* " *nitio, qua id verum esse cognovit* (181). —— *If* " Anaxagoras *was sensible of Truth, and saw that* " *it was God, and called it The Mind or Intelli-* " *gence; the Name of* Anaxagoras, *which the Learn-* " *ed, on account of it's literary Antiquity, willingly* " *blow up, to express myself in a military Phrase;* " *the Name of* Anaxagoras, *I say, does not only not* " *make us learned and wise; but even his Judgment, by* " *which he discovered it to be true, contributes no-* " *thing towards making us so.*"

(181) August. Ep. 56. pag. 272.

(182) Communi hominum opinioni de Fato quantum potuit reluctatus est. Naud. de Fato et Vit. termino, pag. 20.

[*P*] *It is not certain, that he maintained the Doctrine of Predestination.*] It is said, that he strenuously opposed this Doctrine (182), and confuted it in his Works; but *Alexander Aphrodisiensis* is the only Author, who asserts this; and he does it in such a manner, as to keep us in suspence; for he observes, that *Anaxagoras* confuted this Doctrine, by engaging in Controversy, and not out of a premeditated and previous Choice. It was necessary for him to oppose it, in order to maintain another Doctrine; that is, being sensible, that, without opposing it, he should be unable to answer those, who should attack That Doctrine, he wrote against *Fate*.

Alexander Aphrodisiensis judiciously observes, that such a Circumstance renders the true Opinion of *Anaxagoras* doubtful. And, indeed, an Author will do any thing, in the Heat of a Dispute, to deprive his Adversaries of the Advantages, which they might draw from his Silence, or Confession. He will rather contradict himself, and affirm what he does not believe, than suffer his own Weapons to be turned against himself. However, read this Passage of *Gabriel Naudé*. " *Obtulit se tandem Alexander ex Aphrodisiade **;* " *facemque in his tenebris versanti prætulit, quam-* " *quam eo scrupulo injecto, quod fide dignus Anaxa-* " *goras, dum istud assereret, minime fuerit, non* " *quod propositio ejusmodi vera non esset, verum* " *quia in alterius opinionis suæ defensionem, quam* " *suscipere cogebatur, non autem ex sola determina-* " *taque voluntate adversus fatum scribendi, illam* " *protulisset* (183). —— *At length* Alexander A- " phrodisiensis *appeared, and in some Measure cleared* " *up this Obscurity: tho' with this Difficulty in the* " *way, that* Anaxagoras, *in this Assertion, by no means* " *deserved Credit; not because the Proposition, which* " *he laid down, was not true; but because he produced* " *it in Defence of another Opinion, which he was* " *obliged to support, and not through a fixed Intention* " *of writing against Fate.*" This Author had just said, that the Moderns, who assert, that *Anaxagoras* opposed Predestination, quote no ancient Author, who takes any notice of it. He had said likewise, that *Diogenes Laërtius, Cicero, Galen, Plutarch,* and *Origen,* are silent in this Matter.

** Lib. de Fato, cap 1. & lib. de Animâ, cap. ult.

(183) Id. ib.

[*Q*] *He is the first Philosopher, who published Books.*] *Diogenes Laërtius* expressly asserts this. Πρῶτος δὲ 'Αναξαγόρας καὶ βιβλίον ἐξέδωκε συγγραφῆς (184). *Anaxagoras was the first, who published a Book of his own Writing.* But, as he seems to declare, in another Place, for *Phavorinus,* who said, that *Alcmæon,* the Disciple of *Pythagoras,* was the first, who wrote upon Physics (185), he renders his own Testimony very doubtful. *Clemens Alexandrinus* leaves the Matter undecided; he only says, that some ascribe to *Alcmæon* the first Work, which was published concerning Nature; and that others pretend, that *Anaxagoras* was the first, who gave the Public a Book (186). Both these Opinions would be false, if *Thales* had wrote Books, as St *Austin* asserts (187), and if the *Greek* Tradition, mentioned by *Suidas* (188), were true, *viz.* that the Philosopher *Pherecydes* was the first, who wrote Books. Note, that *Aristotle* observes, that the Writings of *Anaxagoras* were later than those of *Empedocles,* tho' the latter was younger than *Anaxagoras* (189).

(184) Diog. Laërt. lib. 2. n. 11.
(185) Id. lib. 8. n. 83.
(186) Clem. Stromat. lll. 2. pag. 308.
(187) See above. Citat. (85).

[*R*] Socrates —— *was not satisfied with the perusal of them: This was plainly his own Fault.*] I propose two things; an Abridgment of *Socrates*'s Complaint, and afterwards some Reflexions upon it.

" Being informed, *says he* (190), that *Anaxagoras* " had laid down, in one of his Books, that an In- " telligence produces and governs all things (191), " I was well pleased with this kind of Cause; and " imagined, that the Consequence must be, that each " Being was circumstanced, and situated, after the " most excellent manner. I expected therefore, with " great Joy, to find, at last, in this Book of *Anaxa-* " *goras,* a Master, who should instruct me in the " Causes of every thing, and inform me, whether " the Earth be round or flat; and then give me the " Reason of his Determination; and, as I believed, " that this Reason would be grounded on the Idea " of the highest Perfection, I was in hopes he would " shew me, that the State, in which the Earth is, " is the best it could have; and that, if he placed " it in the Center, he would tell us, why This Si- " tuation is the best of all. I resolved to look for " no other Cause, provided he made This clear to " me;

(188) Suidas in Ἐχαται—ος.
(189) Arist. Metaphys. lib. 1. c 3. See heretupon Fonseca's Commentary, pag. 218.
(190) Plato in Phædone, pag. 72, & seq.
(191) Τὰς ἀρα νῶς ἐςὶν ὁ διακοσμῶν τε καὶ πάντων αἴτιος. Mentem omnium exornantem, omnium- que causarum esse. Id. ib.

ANAXAGORAS.

I have to make on his Discourse. One of the Reasons, why he neglected Astronomy, was, because *Anaxagoras*, who had extreamly applied himself to it, was very much mistaken

"me; and only to enquire, with respect to the Proportions of Swiftness and Revolution, &c. which are found between the Sun, Moon, and other Planets, what is the best Reason that can be assigned, why these Bodies, in Quality of Agents and Patients, are what they are; for I could never have imagined, that a Philosopher, who says, that an Intelligence governs all these Things, would alledge any other Cause; but prove, that the State, in which they are, is the best that can be. I believed likewise, that, having in this manner explained the particular Nature of each Body by such a Cause, he would, in general, explain their common Good. Full of this Hope, I applied myself with the greatest Eagerness to the reading of his Writings, that I might speedily know what is most excellent, and what is wrong; but I found that this Philosopher does not employ an Intelligence, nor any Cause of Arrangement; but refers all Things to the Air, the Æther, the Water, and such other impertinent Subjects, as to their Original (192). This is just as if any one, after having said, that whatever I do, I do by my Understanding, should afterwards account for all my particular Actions after this manner. *Socrates* sits, because his Body is composed of Bones and Nerves, which, by the Rules of Mechanism, are the Cause, that he can bend his Limbs. He speaks, because the Motion of his Tongue impels the Air, and conveys it's Impression to the Ear, &c. Such an one would forget the true Cause, to wit, that the *Athenians* having judged it best to condemn me, I thought it better for me to sit down here; and that it was more just, that I should suffer the Punishment, which they have ordained. Now, if any one objects, that, without my Bones and Nerves, &c. I cannot perform what I would, he judges right; but if he pretends, that I perform it, because of my Bones and Nerves, &c. and not thro' a Choice of what is best, since he supposes that I act by my Understanding, his Discourse is very absurd (193).

You see plainly the Taste of *Socrates*. He had forsaken the Study of Natural Philosophy, and applied himself wholly to Moral; wherefore he required, that all Natural Things should be explained by moral Reasons, and by the Ideas of Order and Perfection. I dare assert, that he censured *Anaxagoras* improperly. Every Philosopher, who has once supposed, that an Intelligence has moved Matter, and ranged the Parts of the Universe in order, is no longer obliged to have recourse to This Cause, when he is to give a Reason for each Effect of Nature; his Business is to explain, by the Action and Re-action of Bodies, by the Qualities of the Elements, by the Configuration of the Parts of Matter, &c. the Vegetation of Plants, Meteors, Light, Gravity, Opacity, Fluidity, &c. Such is the Method of the Christian Philosophers, whatever Sect they are of. The Schoolmen have an Axiom, That a Philosopher ought not to have recourse to God, *Non est Philosophi recurrere ad Deum*: They call this Recourse the Sanctuary of Ignorance. And indeed what could you say more absurd, in a Piece of Physics than this; Stones are hard, Fire is hot, and Cold freezes Rivers; because God has ordered it so? The *Cartesians* themselves, who make God not only the first Mover, but also the only, continual, and perpetual Mover of Matter, make no use of his Will and Actions in explaining the Effects of Fire, the Properties of the Loadstone, Colours, Smells, &c. they only consider the second Causes, the Motion, Figure, and Situation of the Corpuscles. So that if the Remark of *Clement Alexandrinus*, mentioned above (194), was grounded only on this Discourse of *Socrates*, it would be very unjust. To approve of it, we should know, not that *Anaxagoras* explained many Things without mentioning the Divine Intelligence; but that he expresly excluded it, in explaining part of the *Phænomena* of Nature. Perhaps, he had said in some Parts of his Writings, what his Disciple *Euripides* afterwards said, *viz.* that God concerns himself only with great Things, and leaves the lesser to Chance: Τῶν ἄγαν γὰρ ἀπτεῖαι Θεὸς, τὰ μικρὰ δ' εἰς τύχην

ἀνεὶς ἐᾷ, κατὰ τὸν Εὐριπίδην (195). *Summa procurat modo Deus, inque fortunam minora rejicit, ut ait Euripides*. As if the World was like the Tribunal of the Prætors; *de minimis non curat Prætor*. We have observed above (196), that this Philosopher attributed some Effects to Chance, and others to Necessity, &c. and that he only called the supreme Intelligence to his Assistance, when he could not make it appear, that Necessity had produced a Thing (197). It may be supposed, in general, that he had not fully explained his System, and that he had left many Parts of it ill connected. *Aristotle* intimates as much, when he speaks of the first Philosophers, who acknowledged two Causes, the Material, and the Efficient. He compared them to Men, who have not learned the Art of Fighting, and yet often wound their Enemies; which they do, without observing the Rules of That Art. In like manner these Philosophers were not Masters of their Subjects. Οὗτοι μὲν ἐν - - - - - δυεῖν αἰτίαιν ἐφήψαντο - - - - - - τῆς τε ὕλης, καὶ τῆς ὅθεν ἡ κίνησις. ἀμυδρῶς μὲν τοι καὶ ἰδὲν σαφῶς, ἀλλ' οἷον ἐν ταῖς μάχαις οἱ ἀγύμναστοι ποιῦσι. καὶ γὰρ ἐκεῖνοι περιφερόμενοι τύπτυσι πολλάκις καλὰς πληγάς. ἀλλ' ὅτε ἐκεῖνοι ἀπ' ἐπιστήμης, ὅτε οὗτοι τοικασιν εἰδότες λέγειν ἃ λέγυσι (198). *Atque hi quidem - - - - duas causas - - - - - - attigerunt, materiam, & unde motus obscure tamen, & non clare: sed quemadmodum incxercitati in prælio faciunt. Etenim illi circumeuntes, egregias plerumque plagas infligunt. Sed nec illi ex scientia, nec isti videntur scire quid dicant*. You will see in another Place (199), that there are some Things, which *Anaxagoras* did not explain, and which he would infallibly have admitted, if any one had made the Discovery to him; and, lastly, that many fine Doctrines would result from his Principles, if they were cleared up and explained.

I should not condemn *Socrates* for desiring such an Explication of the Universe, as he mentions; for what could be more excellent, or curious, than to know distinctly and particularly, why the Perfection of the Machine of the World required, that each Planet should have the Figure, Magnitude, Situation, and Swiftness, which it has, and so of all the rest? But this Science was not designed for Man; and it was very unjust to expect it from *Anaxagoras*. And unless we had the Idea, which God followed in creating the World, it will be impossible to give the Explications, which *Socrates* desired. All that the greatest Philosophers can say, upon this Occasion, amounts to this: That, since the Earth is round, and situated at such a Distance from the Sun; This Figure and Situation were necessary to the Beauty and Symmetry of the Universe; the Author of this vast Machine having an infinite Intelligence, and Wisdom. From hence we know, in general, that every thing is right in this Machine, and that there is no Defect in it: But, if we should undertake to make it appear, Piece by Piece, that every thing is in the best State it could possibly be in, we should infallibly assign very wrong Reasons. We should ask like a Peasant, who, having no Notion of a Clock, should undertake to prove, that, the Wheel, which he sees through a Chink, must necessarily be of such a Thickness, and Bigness, and precisely placed in such a Place, great Inconveniences would follow. He would judge of this Machine, as a blind Man doth of Colours, and without doubt he would be a wretched Reasoner. The Philosophers are not much better qualified to judge of the Machine of the World, than this Peasant of a Clock. They know but a small part of it, and are ignorant of the Model of the Artist, his Design, his Ends, and the reciprocal Relation of all the Parts. If you say, that the Earth must be round, that it may turn the easier on it's Axis, you may be answered, that it would be better if it were square, that it might turn more slowly, and afford us longer Days. What could you reasonably reply, if you were obliged to specify the Inconveniencies the World would suffer, if *Mercury* were greater, or nearer the Earth? Would Sir *Isaac Newton*, who has discovered so many Mathematical and Mechanical Beauties in the Heavens, pretend to warrant,

ANAXAGORAS. 311

mistaken in it [S]. What is observed concerning the *Treatise*, in which he reasoned about Eclipses, is very curious. You will find it at the End of the Remark [B] of the Article PERICLES. I must not forget, that Mount *Mimas*, near *Clazomenæ*, was the Place, from whence he viewed the Stars (*kk*). Much less should we forget, that the Strength and Sublimity of his Genius, his Labour, his Application, and his many Discoveries, led him only to Uncertainties; for he complained, that every thing was full of Darkness (*ll*). This was, perhaps, what obliged him to say, that all things consist in Opinion, and that Objects are such as we would have them, that is, such or such, according as they appear to us (*mm*). Tho' he taught, that the Soul of Man was an aërial Being (*nn*), yet he believed it to be immortal (*oo*). He honoured It more than the World; for he was one of those, who judged, that Heaven and Earth would perish (*pp*); and being asked, If the Mountains of Lampsacus *should one day be part of the Sea*, he answered, *Yes*, provided Time does not fail them (*qq*). I have observed, elsewhere (*rr*), what his Opinion was concerning the Souls of Beasts. 'Tis pity He was not a Friend of *Democritus*, and that these two great Men did not concert together their Hypotheses; the Defects of the one might have been supplied by the Perfections of the other; but there was no Intimacy between them. *Anaxagoras* bore *Democritus* a Grudge; because the Visit, which he offered to make him, was refused (*ss*). *Servius*, and *Sidonius Apollinaris*, were ignorant of his Opinions [T]. To avoid being too tedious in this Article, I have referred such Chronological Enquiries, as I have to propose, to another place (*tt*).

---

warrant, that, if Things were not such, as he supposes them, as to Magnitude, Distances, and Velocities, the World would be an irregular Work, ill built, or ill contrived? Is not the Divine Understanding infinite? God has therefore the Ideas of an Infinity of Worlds, different from each other, all of them Beautiful, Regular, and Mathematical, to the last Degree. Do you think he could not, from an Earth of a square Figure, and nearer *Saturn*, draw such Uses, as would be equivalent to those of our Earth. Let us conclude, then, that *Socrates* ought not to have expected, that *Anaxagoras* should prove to him, by a Particular Deduction, that the present State of every thing is the best it can be. God only can prove it after this manner.

How should we perform what *Socrates* required, with regard to the Machine of the World; since we are at a loss to do it, with respect to the Machine of an Animal, after so many Dissections, and so many Lectures of Anatomy, which have taught us the Number, Situation, and Use, &c. of it's principal Organs? By what particular Reasons can it be proved, that the Perfection of Man, and That of the Universe, require, that our two Eyes be situated as they are, and that six Eyes, placed round the Head, would occasion a Disorder in our Body, and in the Universe? It may be reasonably pretended, that, in order to give a Man six Eyes round his Head, without departing from the general Laws of Mechanism, the other Organs must have been so altered, that Man's Body would have been framed after another Model, and would have been another kind of Machine: but no particular Reasons can be given for this; for all that you could say would be opposed with Objections as probable as your Proofs. We must stick to this general Reason: The Wisdom of the Artificer is infinite; therefore the Work is such as it ought to be; the Particulars are out of our reach; and they, who pretend to engage in a Detail of them, generally expose themselves to ridicule (200).

We can prove, by this Discourse of *Socrates*, that he was not the Disciple of *Anaxagoras*; for, if he were, would he have stood in need of being informed, by one, who had read the Books of *Anaxagoras*, that, according to That Philosopher, a Divine Intelligence was the Cause of all things (201).

[S] *Socrates neglected Astronomy ------ because Anaxagoras, who had extremely applied himself to it, was very much mistaken in it.*] That *Socrates's* Thoughts upon this Subject may more clearly appear, I shall set down at length the Words of his Historian. "He "was of Opinion, that some time should be spent "in Astronomy, in order to know what o' Clock "it is by the Stars; and in what Day of the Month, "and what Season of the Year, we are; to know "when a Centinel is to be relieved in the Night; "when it is proper to travel by Sea, and when "by Land; and this, he said, would easily be learned "by conversing with Seamen, or Night-Hunters. "But, to endeavour to drive farther, so far as to "know, what Planets are not in the same De- "clination; to aim at explaining all the different Motions of the Planets; and to know their "Distances from the Earth; in what time they per- "form their Revolutions; and what their Influences "are; was what he very much dissuaded others "from; for these Sciences appeared to him quite "useless, not because he was ignorant of them, but "because they required the whole Man, and diverted "him from several other useful Occupations. In a "Word, he advised, not to search too curiously into the admirable Art, with which the Gods have "disposed the Universe; because it is a Secret, which "the Mind of Man cannot comprehend. And the "Gods are displeased, that any one should endeavour "to discover, what they intend to conceal from us. "He believed, moreover, that there was Danger "of falling into Error in these high Speculations; "as *Anaxagoras* did, who boasted of being greatly "skilled in them. For, teaching, that the Sun "is the same thing with Fire, he did not consider, that Fire does not dazzle the Eyes; but "that it is impossible to bear the Brightness of "the Sun (202)." I omit two other Reasons, alledged by the Historian, against this Doctrine of *Anaxagoras*. They are no better than the first, and deserve not so much Attention, as the Idea, which *Socrates* entertained of the Gods: He believed them to be very jealous of their Secrets, and much inclined to be displeased with those Men, whose Curiosity led them to enquire into them. *Xenophon's* Words are; "Ὅλως δὲ τῶν οὐρανίων ᾗ ἕκαστα ὁ Θεὸς μηχανᾶται, φροντιστὴν γίνεσθαι ἀπέτρεπεν· οὔτε γὰρ εὑρετὰ ἀνθρώποις αὐτὰ ἐνόμιζεν εἶναι, οὔτε χαρίζεσθαι Θεοῖς ἂν ἡγεῖτο τὸν ζητοῦντα ἃ ἐκεῖνοι σαφηνίσαι οὐκ ἐβουλήθησαν (203). *Ut una omnia complectar, cœlestium unumquodque quomodo Dii machinentur scrutari dehortabatur, neque enim hominibus facile esse adinvenire; neque Diis eos sacere grata arbitrabatur, qui ea quærant, quæ ipsi Dii in promptu & manifesta esse noluerunt.*

Note, that *Aristotle* entertained a more Advantageous Opinion of the Deity; He does not deny, that, if God were capable of Jealousy, he would chiefly envy Man the Knowledge of the sublimest Sciences: but he denies what the Poets affirmed of the pretended Envy of the Gods. His Words are very remarkable. Εἰ δὲ λέγουσί τι οἱ ποιηταὶ, καὶ πέφυκε φθονεῖν τὸ θεῖον, ἐπὶ τούτου συμβαίνειν μάλιστα εἰκὸς, καὶ δυστυχεῖς εἶναι πάντας τοὺς περιττούς. ἀλλ᾽ οὔτε τὸ θεῖον φθονερὸν ἐνδέχεται εἶναι, ἀλλὰ κατὰ τὴν παροιμίαν πολλὰ ψεύδονται ἀοιδοί (204). *But if, according to the Poets, the Divine Nature be capable of Jealousy, it is most probable it would be so in this Instance, and that all those would be unhappy, who aspired after Knowledge, which is above them* (205). *But neither is the Deity capable of Envy, and the Poets are Lyars to a Proverb.*

[T] *Servius and Sidonius Apollinaris were ignorant of the Opinion of* Anaxagoras.] The first affirms that he assigned Fire as the Principle of all things (206): This is to confound him with *Heraclitus*. The other pretends, that, like *Thales*, he asserted, that Water was the Principle of all Bodies, and that he superadded an Intelligence to this Principle. This

ANAXANDRIDES.

This is to rob him of his Doctrine of the *Homœomeriæ*. It was not unknown to *Sidonius Apollinaris*; but he ascribed it, without Reason, to the Philosopher *Anaximander*. He attributed likewise to him the παντοσπερμία, that is, that the Seeds of all things were every where; a Doctrine, which belonged to the Philosopher *Anaxagoras*. It was likewise *Democritus's* Doctrine, as *Aristotle* has observed, in the fourth Chapter of the third Book of his Physicks.

.... sed rebus inutile ponit
Principium, dum credit aquis subsistere mundum.
Hujus discipuli versâ est sententia, dicens,
Principiis propriis semper res quasque creari,
Singula qui quosdam fontes decrevit habere
Æternum irriguos, ac rerum semine plenos.
Hunc etiam sequitur, qui gignere cuncta putabat
Hunc aërem, pariterque Deos sic autumat ortos.
Quartus Anaxagoras Thaletica dogmata servat:

Sed divinum animum sentit, qui fecerit orbem (207).

An useless Principle to Things He (208) *gives,
Who Water makes the World's Original.
A different Sentiment his Scholar held;
That all Things had their proper Principles;
Each Principle it's everlasting Spring,
From whence the Seeds of all things ever flow'd.
Him follow'd That Philosopher, who taught,
That this surrounding Air gave Nature birth,
And peopled Heaven itself with all it's Gods.
The fourth in order,* Anaxagoras,
*Subscrib'd to Thales' Doctrine; yet acknowledg'd
A Mind Divine, Creatress of the World.*

(207) Sidon. Apoll. Carm. 15. ver. 81. p. 152, 257.

(208) L. e. Thales.

The learned *Severus* has taken no Notice of these Mistakes in his Remarks on this Poem of *Sidonius Apollinaris*.

ANAXANDRIDES, King of *Lacedemon*, the Son of *Leo*, was the only Man of his Country, who had two Wives at once (a). It was not so much his own Fault, as That of the *Ephori*, who would have obliged him to divorce his Wife, because she was barren, and to marry another, who might bring him Children: As he was very fond of his Wife (b), he protested, that he would never divorce her. The *Ephori*, finding him resolute, proposed to him to marry another Wife, without divorcing the first; and gave him to understand, that, if he refused, it would be the worse for him. He accepted the second Proposal; but would not lodge his two Wives under the same Roof, but in separate Houses. His new Spouse was soon delivered of *Cleomenes*: This good Fortune of *Anaxandrides* extended likewise to his first Wife: she also proved with Child. The Domesticks of the other Queen, being displeased at this, spread many scandalous Reports, and pretended it was but a Feint to deceive the World by a supposititious Child. These Slanders had such an Influence on the *Ephori*, that, when the time of her Delivery drew near, they placed Guards about the Queen (c), to prevent being deceived. It proved no Feint; for the Lady was delivered of a Boy, who was named *Dorieüs*. Some time after she was delivered of Twins, one of which was the brave King *Leonidas*, who died so gloriously at the Streights of *Thermopylæ*; the other's Name was *Cleombrotus* (d). The Son of the second Wife had scarce common Sense; on the contrary *Dorieüs* surpassed his Equals in every thing. Nevertheless his Pretensions, which were, that they should pay more regard to Merit than Birthright, were rejected; and *Cleomenes*, notwithstanding his Unworthiness, succeeded to the Crown (e): the Laws of the Country required it, and were observed. *Anaxandrides* was more favoured by Fortune, than the Kings his Predecessors, with respect to the *Tegeates*; for the *Lacedemonians* began to conquer them in his Reign (f); I mean about the LXth Olympiad [A]. *Plutarch* has left us a Collection of the Apophthegms of *Anaxandrides* among those of the *Lacedemonians*. The Supplement to *Moreri's* Dictionary is full of Mistakes on this Head [B.]

(a) Pausan. lib. 3. p. 84.

(b) She was the Daughter of Anaxandrides's Sister.

(c) The words of Herodotus may be render'd so as to import, That They themselves were the Queen's Inspectors, or Guards.

(d) Some say, that Leonidas and Cleombrotus were born at different Times.

(e) Herodot. lib. t. c. 39. & seq. See also Pausan. lib. 3. p. 84.

(f) Pausan. ibid. Herod. lib. 1. cap. 67.

[A] *The Lacedemonians began to conquer the Tegeates about the LXth Olympiad.*] Historians observe, that the *Tegeates* were not overcome by the *Lacedemonians*, 'till the latter had transported to their City the Bones of *Orestes*, who was buried at *Tegea*. This Translation was made in the LVIIIth Olympiad. " Priscorum autem testantur molem etiam " Orestis supremâ, cujus ossa Olympiade quinquage- " sima & octavâ Tegeæ inventa à Spartanis Oraculo " monitis discimus implesse longitudinem cubitorum " septem (1).—*The Ancients inform us likewise of the* " *Stature of* Orestes: *whose Bones, which the* Spartans, " *by the Advice of the Oracle, found at* Tegea, *in the* " *LVIIIth Olympiad, were seven Cubits long."* We know farther, that *Cleomenes*, the Son and Successor of *Anaxandrides*, was exhorted to wage War against *Polycrates*, Tyrant of *Samos* (2), who died a miserable Death, in the second Year of the LXIVth Olympiad (3). I omit, that *Cleomenes* had reigned a considerable time, when the Successors of *Pisistratus* were obliged to leave *Athens*, which happened about the LXVIIth Olympiad (4). *Moreri* ought not to have said, That *the Time, when* Anaxandrides *lived, is unknown,* nor that *the Ephori obliged him to divorce his first Wife,* nor that the eldest Son of his first Wife was called *Dorceus*. He should have called him *Dorieus*. I say nothing of his Omissions, tho' they are not inconsiderable. I must not pass over in Silence, that it is not difficult to reconcile *Solinus* and *Herodotus*, with respect to Chronology. *Solinus* places the Translation of *Orestes's* Bones in the LVIIIth Olympiad. But, according to *Herodotus* (5), the *Lacedemonians* had already obtained several Advantages over the *Tegeates*, after this Translation, when *Crœsus* courted their Alliance; which he did, before he made War with *Cyrus*; and his Expedition against *Cyrus* fell out at the end of the fifty sixth Olympiad (6); how then can the Chronology of *Solinus* be reconciled with That of *Herodotus*? However it be, *Moreri* ought not to have said, that the time, when *Anaxandrides* reigned, is unknown; for do we not find in *Herodotus*, that he reigned in the Days of *Crœsus* (7)?

[B] *The Supplement to* Moreri's *Dictionary is full of Mistakes on this Head.*] To the Three Faults of *Moreri*, which I have mention'd, I add those of his Continuator. I. It is not true, that *Anaxandrides* was the Son of *Eurycrates* the Second: He was his Grandson, (8) and the Son of *Leo*. II. It is not true, that *Anaxandrides* took the City of *Tegea*, before the Bones of *Orestes* were carried away from thence. It was not till after this Translation, that Fortune ceas'd to favour the *Tegeates*. How then could their Capital City have been taken before the Removal of these Bones? Is not the taking of the Principal City the entire Ruin of such little Republics? III. It is not true, that *Glycas* (9) made his Entry into *Tegea* in the Retinue of the Victorious *Anaxandrides*: He enter'd it, as People, in peaceable Times, do the Cities of their Neighbours. IV. It was not He, who found the Tomb of *Orestes*, and carried his Bones away; He only reported, at his Return to *Lacedemon*, that he believ'd

(1) Solinus, cap. 1. p. 9.

(2) Plut. in Apoph. pag. 233. C.

(3) Calvisius, ad Ann. mundi 3448.

(4) Id. ib. ad Ann. mundi 3440.

(5) Lib. 1. cap. 68, 69.

(6) Ser Calvisius, ad Annum mundi 3359.

(7) Herodot. lib. 1. c. 67.

(8) Pausan. lib. 3. p. 83.

(9) It should be Lychas, as before.

ANAXANDRIDES.

believ'd, that the Sepulchre of *Orestes* was at a Blacksmith's in *Tegea*. For this Blacksmith had inform'd him, that, as he was digging a Well in the Court of his House, he met with a Tomb of seven Cubits, and that it appeared, by the Bones, that the Person, for whom it was made, was of That Stature. *Lychas* concluded from hence, that it was the Tomb of *Orestes*, because the Oracle had said, that it should be found at *Tegea*, in a Place, where two Winds were driven with Violence, and where a Representation of a Fight, and Wounds upon Wounds, were to be seen. He applied all this to the Smith's Bellows, Hammer, and Anvil. He only conjectur'd this; and communicated it to his Superiors, who thereupon banished a Criminal. This Man retired to *Tegea*, and hired of the Blacksmith the Place, where the Tomb of seven Cubits had been discover'd; and took away the Bones of *Orestes*, and brought them to *Lacedemon.* V. It is not true, that the Oracle had said, *That, in order to this Translation, the Winds, the Striker, and the Strick*-*ers, were to be removed, with the Plague and Ruin of Men. Herodotus,* who is quoted in the Supplement, says no such Thing. VI. There was no occasion to remove *all these things,* in order to find the Tomb of *Orestes*; for it was not under the Forge; but in a Court, where the Smith set himself to dig a Well. VII. *The War did not cease* as soon as the Bones of this Prince *were buried at Lacedemon. Herodotus* says only, that from That time the *Lacedemonians* had the Advantage in all their Wars with the Inhabitants of *Tegea*. Ἀπὸ τότε τὸ χρόνο ὅσον ἐπειρῶντο ἀλλήλων πολλῶ κατυπέρτεροι τῶ πολέμῳ ἐγίνοντο οἱ Λακεδαιμόνιοι (10). *Quo ex tempore Lacedæmonii, quoties cum Tegeatibus congressi sunt, superiores extitere.* VIII. And therefore it is not true, that the latter were *wholly subdued by the Lacedemonians,* as soon as the Bones of *Orestes* were buried in *Lacedemon.* IX. There was no occasion to quote *Plutarch*; for he says nothing of what the Article imports.

ANAXANDRIDES, a Comic Poet, a Native of *Camirum* [*A*], in the Isle of *Rhodes*, flourished about the ClSt Olympiad [*B*]. According to *Suidas*, he was the first, who brought upon the Stage Love-Adventures, and the Disgrace, which attends young Ladies, who forfeit their Virginity (*a*). I can easily believe, that it was not till the Cth Olympiad, that they began to introduce upon the Stage a Character so difficult to support as is That of such young Ladies; but I cannot believe they deferred till that time intermixing Love in their Comedies. *Anaxandrides* was tall, and of a graceful Mien; he was very careful of his Hair, and dressed magnificently; he wore a purple Gown fringed with Gold (*b*). This Equipage did not suit with a Poet. He affected Pomp to such a degree, that, on a day, when he was to read a Poem at *Athens*, he rode to the appointed Place, and recited part of the Piece on Horseback. This Behaviour makes what is farther said of him probable; viz. That he was extremely disgusted, whenever his Pieces did not obtain the Prize (*c*). He did not, like Others of his Profession, revise and correct his Comedies, that they might enter the Lists again with more Advantage. This capricious and morose Behaviour towards his Audiences occasioned the Loss of several fine Comedies of his Composition. But his Disgust must have often given way to paternal Affection; for he carried the Prize but ten times (*e*), and we find above twenty of his Plays quoted (see, in the Remark [*C*], the Reflexion of *Athenæus*); he composed Sixty five (*f*). The *Athenians* condemned him to be starved to Death, for censuring their Government [*D*]. Perhaps the Comic Poet *Alexandrides* is only a Fault of the Transcriber; if so, we may substitute our *Anaxandrides* wherever we meet with the other [*E*].

[*A*] *A Native of* Camirum (1).] *Suidas* says so as well as *Chamæleon*; but he observes, that it was not the Opinion of all Authors. They were divided in their Sentiments concerning it; some of them would have *Anaxandrides* to be a *Colophonian*; others a *Rhodian*.

[*B*] *He flourish'd about the ClSt Olympiad.*] The anonymous Author of the Olympiads agrees, in this, with *Suidas*; and, as the latter observes, that *Anaxandrides* assisted at the Games of King *Philip* of *Macedon*, he gives us a Matter of Fact, which fixes this Age of *Anaxandrides.* Besides, it is well known, that this Poet abused *Plato* (2), and that some of his Comedies were cited by *Aristotle* (3). He must, therefore, have lived at the time mention'd by *Suidas.*

[*C*] *See in the Remark the Reflexion of Athenæus.*] Having quoted (4) a Verse out of the *Tereus* of *Anaxandrides*, a Piece of no great Value, he takes an opportunity of mentioning what I have quoted from *Chamæleon*: after which, he asks, with an Air of Astonishment, how it came to pass, that the *Tereus*, and such other Pieces of the same Author, which had not come off with Victory, were preserv'd? He might have found the Solution of this Difficulty in the very Words of *Chamæleon*; for they clearly intimate, that *Anaxandrides* did not vent the Spleen, he had conceived from the Judgment of the Spectators, against his own Pieces, till he was an old Man. He, therefore, spared several of his vanquish'd Comedies, before Old Age had soar'd his Temper. Πολλὰ ἔχοντα κομψῶς τῶν δραμάτων ἰαυτοῖς, δυσκολαίνων τοῖς θεαταῖς διὰ τὸ γῆρας (5). *He destroy'd many excellent Performances, being exasperated, through the peevishness of old Age, against the Spectators.*

[*D*] *The Athenians condemn'd him to be starv'd to Death, for censuring their Government.*] In one of his Comedies he has this Verse,

Ἡ πόλις ἐβούλεθ' ἃ νόμων οὐδὲν μέλει,

that is,

The State will have it so; *the State, which pays no regard to the Laws.*

He only alter'd a single Word in this Verse of *Euripides.*

Ἡ φύσις ἐβούλεθ' ἃ νόμων οὐδὲν μέλει (6).

that is

Nature, which observes no Laws, will have it so.

See *Eustratius*, on the Tenth Chapter of the Sixth and Seventh Books of *Aristotle's* Morals. It is thought, that *Ovid* intended this Punishment of *Anaxandrides*, when he said in his Poem, in *Ibin.* ver. 523.

Utque parum stabili qui carmine læsit Athenas,
  Invisus pereas deficiente cibo.

Depriv'd of Food, may starving be thy Fate,
Like His, whose Satire lash'd the Athenian State.

[*E*] *We may substitute our* Anaxandrides *wherever we meet with the other.*] This is the Opinion of *Casaubon* (7). His Reason is, because *Suidas* makes no mention of *Alexandrides*; and because the same Piece (8), which he ascrib'd to *Alexandrides*, in the Eleventh Book of *Athenæus* (9), is cited under the Name of *Anaxandrides*, in the Fourteenth Book (10). *Casaubon* adds a Third Reason. *Pollux*, in the Sixth Chapter of the Ninth Book, quotes the *Anchises* of *Alexandrides*: Now it is certain, that *Anaxandrides* compos'd a Piece with this Name; *Athenæus* cites it in the 18th Chapter of his 6th Book (11). *Meursius* is altogether of *Casaubon's* Opinion. He will have the two or three Dramatic Pieces, which are ascrib'd to *Alexandrides*.

ANCHISES.

(12) Suidas in 'Αβέλτερ pag.
(13) Id. in Αποσταγής.
(14) Vossius de Poët. Gr. pag. 49.
(15) Diogen. Laert. l. 3. n. 26.
(16) In Alcestid. Init.
(17) Plut. in Lysandro, pag. 443.
(18) Id in Quæst. Romanis, pag. 232.

Alexandrides, in the Editions of *Athenæus*, to belong to *Anaxandrides*. And he ascribes the *Helena* (12) and the *Pisander* (13), mention'd by *Suidas*, under the Name of *Alexandrides*, to *Anaxandrides*. See page 87. of his Treatise of the Isle of *Rhodes*. *Vossius* is of the same Opinion (14). So that, according to this Account, which is probable enough, there are Thirty Pieces of *Anaxandrides* quoted. His *Theseus*, mention'd by *Diogenes Laertius* (15), was unknown to *Meursius*. There is the like Confusion with respect to one ANAXANDRIDES of *Delphos*. The Scholiast upon *Euripides* cites him, (16) Αναξανδρίδης ὁ Δελφὸς, in relation to the Penalty, impos'd on *Apollo*, of serving *Admetus* for Wages, as a punishment for having kill'd the Serpent *Python*. *Plutarch* cites him, (17) Αλεξανδρίδης ὁ Δελφὸς, in relation to the Money, which *Lysander* deposited in the Temple of *Delphos*. He mentions elsewhere (18) an *Anaxandrides*, in speaking of the Times, when the Priestess of *Delphos* delivered her Oracles. At first she delivered them but once a Year. A long time after, she delivered them once a Month. It is very probable, that, in these two Places, *Plutarch* quotes the same Author, and that this Author is the same with Him, who is mention'd by the Scholiast upon *Euripides*. The Question is, whether his Name be *Alexandrides* or *Anaxandrides*. *Vossius* cannot tell what to think of it (19). Without doubt, The Work, mention'd in the Collection of Proverbs, publish'd by *Andreas Schottus*, from a Manuscript of the *Vatican*, must be ascrib'd to the same *Anaxandrides*. The Subject of the Work, mention'd in That Collection, relates to the Sacrileges committed in the Temple of *Delphos*, Περὶ τῶν συληθέντων ἐν Δελφοῖς ἀναθημάτων, *de anathematis quæ sacrilegio Delphis fuere sublata*; and was written by one, whose Name was *Anaxandrides*. He relates a Story, which occasion'd the Greek Proverb, ἄκρῳ λαβὲ, καὶ μέσον ἕξεις, *Take the upper Part, and you'll be sure of the Middle*. See *Vossius*, pag. 320. *de Historicis Grædis*.

(19) Voss. de Hist. Græc. pag. 502.

ANCHISES, a *Trojan* Prince, descended from *Dardanus*, and the Son of *Capys* (a), pleased *Venus* so much, that she appeared to him in the Shape of a Nymph, in order to declare her Passion to him. She told him, that her Destiny obliged her to offer herself to him in Marriage; assuring him, that he should find her a Virgin (b), and intreating him to present her to his Relations, that the Contract of Marriage might be speedily drawn up. *Anchises* replied, like a brisk Man, that, since she was no Goddess, nothing should hinder him from enjoying her upon the Spot (c). She took him at his Word, and to Bed they went, &c. Towards Evening, *Anchises* fell asleep, and, when he awaked, he perceived, that he had lain with a Goddess. He feared he should not long survive such an Adventure [A]; but *Venus* revived his Spirits, and told him, she should have a Son by him, whose Name should be *Æneas*; that she would employ the Wood-Nymphs to nurse the Child, 'till he was five Years of Age; and that, then, he should be put into His Hands. She desired him to beware of boasting, that he had lain with *Venus*; and assured him, that if ever he should be so indiscreet, he would be Thunder-struck by *Jupiter* (d). It is said, that *Anchises* could

(a) Homer. Il. lib. 20. v. 239.

(b) Ἀτρυγέτην Θαλάτταρος, imperitam venerei congressús à Hom. in Hymno Veneris.

(c) Πρὶν ἐς φιλότητι μιγῆναι ἀυτίκα νῦν, Quæ minus tibi in amore miscear statim nunc. Id ib.

(d) Il. 2.

[A] *He fear'd he should not long survive such an Adventure.*] It was a Tradition, in those Times, that Mortals, who lay with Goddesses, were not long liv'd. Wherefore *Anchises*, discovering his Adventure, supplicated *Venus* to have Compassion on him.

Ἀλλά σε πρὸς Ζηνὸς γουνάζομαι αἰγιόχοιο
Μή με ζῶντ' ἀμενηνὸν ἐν ἀνθρώποισιν ἐάσῃς
Ναίειν ἀλλ' ἐλέαιρ', ἐπεὶ ὁ βιοθάλμιος ἀνὴρ
Γίγνεται, ὅς τε θεαῖς εὐνάζεται ἀθανάτῃσι (1).

(1) Homer. in hymno Veneris pag. 843.

*By Jove I beg, the Pow'r who gave thee Birth,
Let me not drag a wretched Life on Earth;
But, O! some pity show; since short the Date
(Such is th' irrevocable Will of Fate)
Of Him, who takes a Goddess to his Arms,
And boasts th' Enjoyment of immortal Charms.*

This Sentiment of the Antients appears, at first View, to be ill-grounded; for this intimate Union of Mortal with Immortal Beings, this Mixture, this Confusion of Principles, ought to have been look'd upon as productive of Immortality, not as tending to shorten Life. Hence it is, that the most refined *Cabala* teaches, that the Elementary Inhabitants repair the Misfortune of their Destiny, which subjects them to Annihilation, *by the Alliance, which they contract with Mankind—Thus a Nymph, or Sylphid, becomes immortal, and capable of the Beatitude, to which we aspire, when she is so happy as to be married to a Philosopher: And a Gnome, or Sylphe, ceases to be mortal, as soon as he marries one of our Females* (2). But if we consider the Matter in all it's Lights, we shall find, that *Anchises*'s Fear, and the Maxim he alledged, were founded upon a specious Reason. According to the Notions of the *Pagans*, The Gods were jealous of their Superiority, and took great Care, that Men should not forget their Inferiority: It was therefore their Business to exclude them from the Enjoyment of Goddesses, to make them understand, that such dainty Morsels were not for Them. It was proper to threaten an exemplary Punishment, such as a speedy Death, if they presumed to taste a Pleasure of this Nature, which the Gods reserv'd for themselves. It was requisite to deter Mortals, not only from being so bold as to tempt a Goddess, but even from yielding to Declarations of Love made them by Goddesses, tho' under the Appearance and Disguise of Women. Don't we see, that Human Laws punish with Death Servants, who debauch their Masters Wives, or Daughters? 'Tis in vain for them to alledge in their Excuse, that they have resisted repeated Sollicitations; and that so many Advances have been made them, and so many Threatnings denounc'd against them, that it was impossible for them to avoid the Snare; the Judge delivers them up to the Executioner, even upon a Supposition that their Excuses are real and undeniable. The Gazettes have lately (3) inform'd us, that a Footman was hang'd at *Paris* for such an Act. And, as, in some Cases, the Publick Interest requires, that the Rigour of the Law should go beyond Justice, because an Injury done to a private Person (4) is less an Evil, politically speaking, than the Publick Advantage, which accrues from it, is a Good; I do not believe, that Judges, animated with a rigorous Zeal for the Preservation of Chastity in Families, would regard the Apology of a Servant, who should alledge, that his Master's Daughter, or Wife, came to him in the Disguise of a Servant-Maid, &c. It is necessary, that Lacqueys should have no Pardon to hope for, even when they can plead Ignorance; because such Severity will keep them more upon their Guard, and make them look with Horror upon the pretended Advantage of being belov'd. It will serve them as a Precaution against Promises, Threats, and cunning Disguises. If they could promise themselves Impunity, in case they debauch'd a Lady in Disguise, they would expect it in the Case of Simple Seduction; and, might they hope to go unpunished, by pleading Sollicitation, they would quickly venture to turn Sollicitors themselves, wherever they had the least Hopes of Success. It is necessary, therefore, to keep them in awe as much as possible; for a Master, who has no reason to believe, that his Servant will be so honest as to resist all Sollicitation, can never be entirely free from Suspicion. Now, as the Pagans look'd upon Men of the highest Rank to be more inferior to the Gods, than a Lacquey is to a Great Lord, we cannot wonder, that the Courts above expos'd *Anchises* to a severe Punishment, tho' he enjoy'd *Venus* under the Disguise of a Woman.

(2) *See the Comte de Gabalis*, p. 54.

(3) *I write this in 1698.*

(4) *See Tacitus, Annal. l. 14. c. 44.*

[B] *It*

ANCHISES.

could not keep the Secret of his good Fortune [B]; and that it escaped him, as he was one day drinking with his Friends. *Venus*'s Menace had it's Effect; he was struck with a Thunder-Bolt; but was not killed by it [C]. Some say he only lost his Sight by it [D]; others pretend, that the Wound could never be closed [E]. It is

[B] *It is said, that Anchises cou'd not keep the Secret of his good Fortune.*] Yet *Venus*'s Menace was very terrible.

Εἰ δέ κεν ἐξείπῃς καὶ ἐπεύξεαι ἄφρονι θυμῷ
Ἐν φιλότητι μιγῆναι ἐυστεφάνῳ Κυθερείῃ,
Ζεύς σε χολωσάμενος βαλέει ψολόεντι κεραυνῷ. (5)

(5) Homer. in Hymni. Vener. sub finem.

But, indiscreet, should'st thou reveal my Love,
Thunder shall blast Thee from the Hand of Jove.

This Adventure is a Picture, which is often copied. Ladies of the highest Quality, who fall in Love with their Inferiors, are obliged to make all the Advances. They exact Secrecy, and threaten Indiscretion with terrible Punishment: And yet The Favourite, when he is a little heated with Wine, will be blabbing. Sometimes Vanity prompts him to say too much, even when he is sober. I shall quote some Authorities in relation to this Indiscretion of *Anchises*. " Fulminatus est Anchises, quia se cum Venere concubuisse jactabat." ——— *Anchises was thunder-struck for boasting, that he had lain with Venus.* They are *Servius*'s Words (6). *Hyginus* says, " Venus Anchisem Assaraci filium amasse, & cum eo concubuisse dicitur: Procreavit Æneam, eique præcepit ne id apud homines enunciaret. Quod Anchises inter sodales per vinum est elocutus. Ob id à Jove fulmine est ictus (7). ——— " *Venus is said to have fallen in Love with Anchises, the Son of Assaracus* (8), *and to have lain with him. She conceiv'd Æneas by him, and enjoyn'd him not to reveal it to Men. But Anchises in his Cups disclos'd the Secret to his Companions; for which Reason he was thunder-struck by Jupiter*".

(6) Servius in Æneid. lib. 2. ver. 649.

(7) Hyg. cap. 94.

(8) Hyginus *should have said that Cassius was his Father, and not Assaracus, who was Capys's Father.*

[C] *He was struck with a Thunder-bolt, but was not kill'd by it.*] *Venus*, discovering that *Anchises* had boasted of the Favours she had bestowed upon him, made her complaints to *Jupiter*, and obtain'd that he should be Thunder-struck: But, not being willing to destroy him, and knowing he could not recover from the Stroke of a Thunder-bolt, she took care to turn it aside. " Cum inter æquales exultaret Anchises, gloriatus traditur de concubitu Veneris, quod cum Jovi Venus questa esset, emeruit ut in Anchisem fulmina mitterentur. Sed Venus eum cum fulmine posse vidisset interimi, miserata juvenem in aliam partem detorsit. Anchises tamen afflatus igne coelesti semper debilis vixit (9)." This is another Original, of which Copies have been taken in all Ages. The Fair are angry with an indiscreet Gallant, and are fond of making him sensible of his Fault; but They do not carry it too far; there is room left for Repentance.

(9) Servius in Æneid. lib. 2. ver. 649.

[D] *He only lost his Sight by it.*] *Servius* informs us, that *Anchises*'s Sight was blasted by Lightning for boasting of the Favours he had received from *Venus*; *Quod cum jactaret Anchises afflatus est fulmine, oculoque privatus est* (10). The Singular *Oculo* must not make us think, that he lost but one Eye; for, in another Place (11), *Servius* makes use of the Authority of *Theocritus* to inform us, that it was a real Blindness.

(10) Servius upon these two Lines of the first Book of the Æneid; Tunc ille Æneas, quem Dardanio Anchisæ Alma Venus Phrygii genuit Simoentis ad undas?

(11) In Æneid lib. 2. ver. 687.

[E] *Others pretend, that the Wound could never be closed.*] In *Virgil*, he complains only of a great Weakness, which the Thunder had occasioned in him.

(12) Virgil. Æn. lib. 2. ver. 647.

Jampridem invisus divis & inutilis annos
Demoror, ex quo me divum pater atque hominum Rex
Fulminis adflavit ventis, & contigit igni (12).

'Tis long, since I, for my cœlestial Wife,
Loath'd by the Gods, have dragged a lingring Life;
Since ev'ry Hour and Moment I expire,
Blasted from Heav'n by Jove's avenging Fire.

DRYDEN.

I wonder, that *Scarron*, whose Burlesque Paraphrase of this Passage of *Virgil*, shews that he was not ignorant of the Cause of this Misfortune, has not given it a more humorous Turn; the Subject, I think, was capable of being set in a very ludicrous Light, especially in the Hands of such a Poet. However, this is his Translation.

Vieil, cassé, mal propre à la guerre,
Je ne sers de rien sur la terre;
Spectre qui n'ai plus que la voix,
J'y suis un inutile poids.
Depuis le tems que de son foudre
Jupin me voulut mettre en poudre,
Depuis le tems qu'il m'effraya
Ce grand Dieu qui me giboya,
Par une vengeance secrette;
Mais je suis personne discrete,
Je n'en dirai point le sujet;
Suffit que j'aurois eu mon fait
Sans Venus qui sauva ma vie.
J'ay depuis eu cent fois envie
De m' aller pendre un beau matin,
Et finir mon chien de destin.

Crazy, and old, I curse my Birth,
An useless Load to Mother Earth;
Since Jove, to crush Anchises dead,
Darted his Thunder at my Head.
A secret Vengeance on me fell;
The Reason why ----- I must not tell ---
A Vengeance, which had been my end,
Had not Dame Venus stood my Friend.
An hundred times I have intended
This wretched Corps should be suspended;
And, hanging on some fatal Tree,
To end That Bitch, my Destiny.

If we compare together a Passage of *Plutarch*, and another of *Dionysius Halicarnasseus*, we shall prove, that the Thunderbolt inflicted a Wound, which never closed up. *Plutarch* says (13), that if Musk gives a good Scent to the most ragged Cloaths (14); on the other hand, an Ulcer makes the richest Garments stink. This is his Thought; but, whereas I make him speak in general, he instances particularly in *Anchises*. The Greek runs thus;

(13) Plutarch de Virtute Vitio & Virtute, Opera moral. pag. 100.

(14) *I keep to the Sense, not the Words, of Plutarch.*

Τῷ δ᾽ Ἀγχίσου τὸ ῥάκος ἡχώρα πονηρὸν ἐξεδίδε,
Μυρῷ καταστάζοντα βύσσινον φάρος.

Now, since, according to the common Acceptation, the Word ῥάκος signifies Rags and Tatters; it is not probable, that it is the true reading of the *Greek* Text: Wherefore a learned Critic reads ἕλκος, *a Wound*, or *an Ulcer*, instead of ῥάκος (15). The Sense, then, is This; Anchises's Wound, oozing thro' the dressing, distained his Linnen Garment. It it not sufficient to know, that *Plutarch* quotes the Words of a Poet; we should know who he is (16). *Meziriac* will inform us of this; He found them in *Dionysius Halicarnasseus* (17), who quotes some Lines of *Sophocles*, the third whereof is the same which *Plutarch* quotes.

(15) Meziriac, Ovid's Epistles, p. 671.

(16) Ibid. pag. 670.

(17) Dion. Halicarn. lib. 1. c. 48.

Νῦν δ᾽ ἐν πυλαισιν Αἰνείας ὁ τῆς θεοῦ
Πάρεστ᾽ ἐπ᾽ ὤμων πατέρ᾽ ἔχων, κεραυνίῳ
Μυρῷ καταστάζοντα βύσσινον φάρος (18).

(18) *The Verses of Sophocles are taken from his Laocoon.*

Next the Son of Venus appeared at the Gates; carrying his Father on his Shoulders, whose Wound, caused by Thunder, still continued to stain his Linnen Garment.

Meziriac has corrected a Fault in the beginning of the third Verse of *Sophocles:* instead of νότῳ, as we read in all the Editions *Dionysius Halicarnasseus*, he has put μυρῷ. To which there is nothing contrary to the Rules of Criticism. The comparing of Authors, who

VOL. I. Kkkk

ANCHISES. ANCILLON.

is said he lived to the Age of Eighty Years, and was buried on Mount *Ida* [*F*], where his Tomb was honoured by the Shepherds. This Opinion differs very much from That of *Virgil*; for, according to That Poet, the same Night that *Troy* was taken, *Æneas* took his Father upon his Shoulders [*G*], and carried him to a Place of Safety; nor did the old Man die, before the *Trojans*, who joined *Æneas*, arrived in *Sicily*, after innumerable Fatigues. This Affection of *Æneas* for his Father, and the Care he took to save the *Penates*, are the Foundation of the Character, which distinguishes him from other Heroes: This Character consists in Piety (*e*). Some say, that *Anchises* lived 'till his Son's Arrival in *Italy*, That Land of Promise, which the Destinies commanded him to go in search of, amidst a thousand Dangers (*f*). *Cato*, *Dionysius Halicarnasseus*, and *Strabo*, are of this Opinion. See the end of the Remark [*F*]. Lastly, the Love of *Venus* for *Anchises* was not a transient Passion; her first Lying-in did not satisfy her; she bore a second Son to *Anchises*, as *Apollodorus* tells us in the third Book of his *Bibliotheca*.

(*e*) Virgil often calls him Pius Æneas.

(*f*) See among other Passages the first Book of the Æneids, ver. 205, & 258.

who have, at different times, quoted the same Passage, often discovers the true Reading. *Sylburgius*, who revised the *Latin* Translation of *Dionysius Halicarnasseus*, done by *Sigismund Gelenius*, has not corrected the third Verse of *Sophocles*. *Gelenius*'s Version of the three Lines is This;

Nunc in porta est Æneas Deæ filius,
Humeris bajulans Patrem fulminata
Terga amicium fluxa veste byssina.

Here is nothing of the suppurating Wound; besides, *Anchises* is represented as wounded in the Back; that is, the Translator has omitted what *Sophocles* said, and added what he did not say. If the ancient Writers were to return into the World, they would be amazed to find so many things in their Books, which they never dreamt of.

[*F*] *He was buried on Mount* Ida.] *Eustathius* relates this (19), but *Pausanias* is of a different Opinion. He says, that *Æneas*, going to *Sicily*, put into *Laconia*, and built there two Cities; and that *Anchises*, dying at the Foot of a Mountain in *Arcadia*, was buried there; for which Reason the Mountain was called *Anchisia* (20). *Pausanias* adds, That the Ruins of a Temple of *Venus* were seen near this Sepulchre of *Anchises*; and that the Inhabitants of *Troy* could no where shew the Tomb of This old Man. *Stephen* of *Byzantium* says, that *Anchises* was buried in a City of *Thrace*, built by *Æneas* (21): or rather, he quotes an old Scholiast, whose Name was *Thom*, who said so. *Tzetzes* is of the same Opinion; only he says, that This City was in *Macedonia* (22). *Virgil* carries the good Man as far as *Sicily*, where he makes him die; with this he concludes the long Story, which his Hero related to Queen *Dido*.

Hinc Drepani me portus & illætabilis ora
Accipit. Hinc pelagi tot tempestatibus actus,
Heu genitorem, omnis curæ casusque levamen,
Amitto Anchisen. Hic me, pater optime, fessum
Deseris, heu tantis nequicquam erepte periclis (23).

(19) Eustathius, in Iliad. l. 12.

(20) Pausan. lib. 8. pag. 247.

(21) Steph. Byzant. in Αινεια.

(22) In Lycophr.

(23) Virgil. Æn. lib. 3. ver. 707.

At length on Shore the weary Fleet arriv'd;
Which Drepanum's unhappy Port receiv'd.
Here, after endless Labours, often tost
By raging Storms, and driven on ev'ry Coast,
My dear, dear Father, spent with Age, I lost;

Ease of my Care, and Solace of my Pain,
Sav'd thro' a thousand Toils, but sav'd in vain.
DRYDEN.

Servius tells us, that *Anchises*'s Tomb was on Mount *Eryce* near *Drepanum* (24). I have named three Writers, who say, that *Anchises* died in *Italy*. *Cato* (25), *Dionysius Halicarnasseus* (26), *Strabo* (27), are my Authorities.

[*G*] *Took his Father upon his Shoulders.*] The Words of *Virgil* are so excellent, that they deserve to be inserted in this place.

Ergo age, chare pater, cervici imponere nostræ,
Ipse subibo humeris, nec me labor iste gravabit (28).

Hæc fatus, latos humeros subjectæque colla
Veste super, fulvique insternor pelle leonis,
Succedoque oneri. Dextræ se parvus Iülus
Implicuit, sequiturque patrem non passibus æquis (29).

Nunc omnes terrent auræ: sonus excitat omnis
Suspensum, & pariter comitique onerique timentem (30).

Haste, my dear Father, ('tis no time to wait)
And lead my Shoulders with a willing Freight.

Thus, ordering all that Prudence could provide,
I cloath my Shoulders with a Lion's Hide,
And yellow Spoils; then on my bending Back
The welcome Load of my dear Father take:
While on my better Hand Anchises hung,
And with unequal Paces tript along.

At ev'ry Shadow I am seiz'd with Fear,
Not for myself, but for the Charge I bear.
DRYDEN.

The Poets have highly extolled this Action; and it deserved it. They say, that the Flames had a regard for *Æneas*, and that, for fear of hurting a Son, who shewed so great an Affection for his Father, they divided, and left a free Passage for him (31).

(24) Serv. in Æn. lib. 1. ver. 570.

(25) Apud Servium ib.

(26) Antiq. lib. 1. c. 64.

(27) Lib. 5. pag. 158.

(28) Virgil. Æn. lib. 2. ver. 707.

(29) Ibid. ver. 721.

(30) Ibid. ver. 728.

(31) See several Authorities for this in La Cerda's Commentary upon this Passage of Virgil.

ANCILLON (DAVID), Minister of the Reformed Church at *Metz*, was born in that Town (*a*), the Seventeenth of *March*, 1617. At Nine or Ten Years of Age, he studied in the College of the Jesuits, which was then *the only One at Metz, where good Literature was taught* (*b*); and from the very first he proved so hopeful a Youth, that the chief Persons of the Society neglected nothing to give him a Relish of their Religion, and make him one of their Order; but he vigorously opposed them; and from that time took up a Resolution to study Divinity (*c*). He was so indefatigable in his Studies (*d*), that it was often necessary to employ the paternal Authority to interrupt them; for *he was excessively, and, if I may so say, intemperately studious* (*e*). He took a Journey to *Geneva*, in the Year 1633 (*f*), where he went through a Course of Philosophy under Mr *du Pan* (*g*), and studied Divinity under the Professors *Spanheim*, *Deodati*, and *Tronchin*, who had a particular Love and Esteem for him (*h*). He left *Geneva*, in the Month of *April* 1641, and presented himself to the Synod of *Charenton*, to be admitted into the Ministry (*i*). His Examiners admired his Capacity, and the Ministers of *Paris* his Modesty (*k*); and the whole Assembly

(*a*) Discourse on the Life of Mr Ancillon, p. 6.

(*b*) Ib. p. 8.

(*c*) Ib. p. 9.

(*d*) Ib p. 13.

(*e*) Ibid. p. 13, 14.

(*f*) Ibid. pag 14.

(*g*) Ibid. pag. 18.

(*h*) Ibid. pag. 20, 21.

(*i*) Ibid. pag. 32.

(*k*) Ibid. pag. 35.

ANCILLON. 317

sembly was so well pleased with him, that they gave him the most considerable vacant Benefice (*l*); which was That of *Meaux*. He exercised his Ministry there, with all imaginable Satisfaction, 'till the Year 1653. He was tenderly beloved by his Flock; and He married very advantageously [*A*]. He acquired a great Reputation by his Learning, Eloquence, and Virtue; and the *Roman* Catholics themselves had a particular Esteem for him. He display'd his fine Talents, with greater Lustre and Success, at *Metz*, where he was Minister from the Year 1653, 'till the Revocation of the Edict of *Nantz* in 1685. After this fatal Blow, he retired to *Francfort* (*m*), and, having preached in the *French* Church at *Hanaw*, *the whole Congregation were so edified, that they immediately desired a meeting of the Heads of each Family, to request him to afford them his Ministry* (*n*). — He agreed to the Proposal, which was made to him by some Deputies, who *obtained all that they desired*. He began to exercise *his Ministry in That Church, at the end of the Year* 1685 (*o*). We shall see, why he soon returned to *Francfort* [*B*]; where he would have taken up his Residence, had not the Condition of his Family, which was numerous, obliged him *to go where he might settle them* (*p*). He made choice of *Berlin*, and met with a very favourable Reception from his Electoral Highness of *Brandenburg* (*q*). He was made Minister of *Berlin*, and had the Satisfaction to see his eldest Son appointed Judge and Director of the French, *who were in that City* (*r*); and his other Son gratified with a Pension, and maintained in the University of *Francfort* on the *Oder*, and at last Minister in Ordinary of the Capital (*s*). He had likewise the Satisfaction of seeing his Brother *made Judge of the French*.

(*l*) Ibid. pag. 36.

(*m*) Ibid. pag. 352.

(*n*) Ibid. pag. 353.

(*o*) Ibid. pag. 354.

(*p*) Ibid. pag. 366.

(*q*) Ibid. pag. 372, &seq.

(*r*) Ibid. pag. 375.

(*s*) Ibid. pag. 397.

[*A*] *He married very advantageously.*] The manner how this Affair was managed is very curious. "The chief Heads of the Families at *Meaux*, being "sensible of the great Worth of their Minister, and "and hearing him often give out, that he would "return to *Metz*, to visit his Father, and his Re- "lations, whom he had not seen for several Years, "were afraid of losing him. They sought a thou- "sand Expedients to engage his longer Continuance "among them. The surest way, they thought, "was to marry him to a rich Person, worthy of "him, and whose Estate lay in that Country, or in "the Neighbourhood. Some one recollected, that "he had heard say, that Mr *Ancillon*, having "preached one Sunday Morning at *Cherentou*, met "with a general Applause; but that, above all others, "Mr *Macaire*, a venerable old Man, of an exem- "plary Virtue and Piety, and who had a great Estate "in *Paris*, and about *Meaux*, bestowed on him "a thousand Benedictions, and Praises, and said in "the hearing of many, who sat near him at Church, "*That he but one Daughter, his only Child, whom "he tenderly loved, but that, if That Gentleman,* "meaning Mr *Ancillon*, *should come and demand her "of him in Marriage, I would give her to him "with all his Heart.* They went to him, and asked "him, whether he continued in the same Mind. "He answered, that he did; and added new Testi- "monies of Esteem and Affection for Mr *Ancillon*; "insomuch, that the Marriage was concluded in the "Year 1649, and consummated a little while after. "D. *Mary Macaire*, his Spouse, was very young, "being but fourteen Years of Age. But, having, at "these tender Years, every growing Virtue, it will "appear, by the Sequel of this Discourse, that she "proved not only an Help to him in Piety, and "an agreeable Companion; but that he relied upon "her entirely in the Management of his domestic "Concerns (1).

(1) Discourse on the Life of Mr Ancillon, pag. 75. &seq.

[*B*] *He soon returned to* Francfort.] His Sermons were soon the Subject of Conversation at *Hanaw* (2). "Several Persons, who had left the *French* Congre- "gation out of Discontent, returned to it again. "The Professors of Divinity, the *German* and *Dutch* "Ministers, were often his Hearers. The Count of "*Hanaw* himself, who had never been seen in that "Church, was pleased to come and hear Mr *An- "cillon*: They came thither from the neighbouring "Places, and even from *Francfort.* ----- People, "who did not understand *French*, came thither in "Crouds, saying, *it was a Pleasure to them to see "him speak. Inde iræ & lachrymæ.* This Distinction "gave Jealousy to the other two Ministers: Nature, "disordered by this Passion, forgot her Duty (3). "They took Umbrage at the Marks of Esteem and "and Affection, which were shewn to this new Col- "league; they were chagrin'd at it; and created him a "thousand Disquiets, to oblige him voluntarily to quit "a Post, from which they could not drive him. "The Virtue of Mr *Ancillon* was exposed to a second

(2) Ibid. pag. 354.

(3) Ibid. pag. 356.

"Trial. For his two Relations (4), who had shewn "a great Readiness to oblige him, and seemed to "wish they could turn Stones into Bread, for his "Comfort, all the Time he was in their City, as "a Stranger, began to shun him, when he had the "Direction of their Flock: They created him a thou- "sand Mortifications; and, if it had been in their "Power, they would willingly have turned Bread in- "to Stones, to expel him; so burthensome was he "grown to them. ------ This Conduct pro- "duced two considerable Effects (5): One was, That "the *Roman* Catholics, and the Prophane, made it "a Subject of Raillery. The other, that it exaspera- "ted the People (6). Mr *Ancillon* was their Favo- "rite, and, if he would have made use of it, might, "perhaps, have surmounted the Malice of his Ene- "mies; but, as he was of Opinion, that a faithful "Pastor ought not to establish himself at the expence "of a Division between the Flock, and their Mini- "sters, and as he had ever been an Enemy to Parties, "and exclaimed against Cabals and Factions, he would "take no Advantage of the Disposition of the People "towards him, nor suffer them to stir in the Affair. "------ Having, therefore, tried whatever Charity "and Honesty suggested to him, in Order to bring "these two Men to their Duty, he resolv'd to leave "*Hanaw*; a Town, which he had looked upon as a "Place of Refuge, or a secure Harbour, after a "Storm; but which was now become a Field of "Battel, in which he must continually fight, and "where his Patience, which had already undergone "several great Trials, might at last be overcome; he "therefore determined to abandon it (7). ------ He "left *Hanaw*, without Noise, when it was least ex- "pected; or rather, he suffered himself to be rescu- "ed out of the Hands of his Enemies, and of his "Friends (8). The former, holding him, as it were, "by one Hand, treated him ill; the latter, holding "him by the other, endeavoured to rescue him from "Oppression; and both were ready to come to an "Engagement, and try their Strength. To avoid "this Scandal, he sacrificed his Interest to the Pub- "lic Peace; he went away privately, least his Friends, "by endeavouring to stop him, should kindle a Fire, "lurking under the Ashes, which he was willing to "extinguish."

(4) One of them had been married to Mr Ancillon's Sister, and the other was actually married to his Niece. Ibid. pag. 353.

(5) Ibid. pag. 357.

(6) Ibid. pag. 359.

(7) Ibid. pag. 360.

(8) Ibid. pag. 361.

I have observed, I think, elsewhere (9), that the Jealousy of Eloquence is of all the most violent; the scandalous Divisions it produces are but too frequently seen. The Reflexions, which may be made upon it, are only fit to be suppressed. The Subject is too nice, and too invidious. I shall only remark, without al- luding to any particular Case, that, in this Affair, the People do not behave with due Prudence and Charity. They should chuse Pastors of nearly equal Abilities; or, if one among them is remarkably supe- rior to his Colleagues, they should not distinguish him in so particular a manner. They have no regard to human Weakness; they run in Crowds to the Ser- mons of one Preacher, and leave the Auditory of the rest

A Remark upon the Jealousy of Eloquence.

(9) *In the Remark* [*H*] *of the Article* ATTICUS.

ANCILLON.

French, in the *States of* Brandenburg [C]; and Mr *Cayart*, his Son-in-law, Engineer to his Electoral Highness (*t*). He enjoyed these Comforts, and several others, 'till his Death, which he underwent with all the Sentiments of Piety of a true Minister of JESUS CHRIST, at *Berlin*, on the 3d of *September* 1692, being Seventy five Years of Age (*u*). I could have made this Article much longer than I have done; for the Book, out of which I have taken it, contains many Particulars: But it being a Work, which it will be more easy to consult, than to procure this Dictionary, I thought it more adviseable to refer the Reader to it, than to make too many Extracts from it (*x*). I should take another Method, if I had only Manuscript Memoirs. I shall insist but upon two Particulars; one of which relates to the Library of the late Mr *Ancillon*, and his manner of studying [D]; the other relates to the Books, which

rest almost empty. They take so little Care to conceal their Preference, that their Imprudence may be accounted the chief Cause of the Discord. It is a Seed of Dissension: wise Men are not so indiscreet: All Auditors should follow this Model; but, because it can scarce be expected that the People will be so prudent, perhaps the best way would be, that those, who proceed to Elections, should avoid too great an Inequality of Talents, and consider, that, in some Professions, many Persons approve of this Law of the *Ephesians*, *Let no one among us excel; and, if any one be this Advantage, let him be rather any where else, than in our City* (10). This Law was condemned by *Heraclitus* (11); but he was a Philosopher. The following Remark was made by the Author of the Book, which I have often quoted. "Mr *Ancillon*, says he (12), having none of the Faults, which have been observed to be the usual Cause of the Divisions, which happen among Ministers of the same Church, *viz.* I. A fond Conceit of one's own Opinions, and a Desire of spreading them; II. A love of Esteem and worldly Glory; III. A love of Power; IV. A love of Interest; and having besides a respect for Mr *Ferry*'s old Age (13), and his Merit, which was Proof against a great Number of Years, forced, as it were, that great Man to remain constantly united to him."

[C] *He had the Satisfaction of seeing his Brother made Judge of the French, in the States of Brandenburg.*] An Office, which he still actually exercises with Honour; but, as laborious as it is, it does not so wholly engross his Time, as to prevent him from publishing several solid and judicious Pieces, in the Journals of *Berlin*, which shews the Solidity, and vast Extent, of his Knowledge and Learning (15)."

[D] *The Library of the late Mr Ancillon, and his manner of Studying.*] The Estate, which he gained by his Marriage, having put him in a Condition of gratifying his favourite Passion (16), he bought all the capital Books, which may be called *the Pillars of a great Library*; such as the most curious Bibles, either for the Editions or Notes; several Dictionaries; the most excellent Commentaries on the Scripture; the Works of the Fathers; Collections of Councils; Ecclesiastical Histories; and several others of the like Nature; all of the best Editions (17). He observed this Maxim ever after, and gave good Reasons for it. An Account of which would be too tedious: however, the Substance of them, in few Words, is this. He said, "that the less the Eye is fatigued in reading a Book, the more at liberty the Mind is to judge of it. That, as the Beauties and Faults of it are more easily perceived, when it is printed, than in Manuscript: so the same Beauties and Faults are more clearly seen, when it is printed in a fair Character, and upon good Paper, than when it is printed on bad Paper, or with a bad Letter. Having thus laid a good Foundation for a Library, he increased it with all the good Books, which came out afterwards. He had the Pleasure of reading all the new Books; for his Friends in *Paris*, *Holland*, *England*, *Germany*, *Switzerland*, and *Geneva*, with whom he kept a strict Correspondence, sent them to him, as soon as they were exposed to Sale. The Opinion of those, who say, that the first Editions are the least valuable, because they are of no use, but to make the Works of an Author appear in a fairer Character, did not abate his Curiosity. He was not ignorant, that the famous Mr *Menage*, Dean of St *Peter*'s, at *Angers*, in his Epistle Dedicatory to his Etymologies of the *French* Tongue, speaking to Mr *Du Puy*, tells him, That he had formerly learnt from him, that Mr *Loysel*, a famous Advocate in the Parliament of *Paris*, used to say of first Editions, That they only serve to make the Works of an Author appear in a fairer Character; that it was very probable this Judicious Gentleman said this of all sorts of Books, but that it was more true of Dictionaries, than of any other kind of Books. He knew very well, that others were of Opinion, that the first Editions of Books were only to be looked upon as imperfect Essays, which Authors propose to the Learned, to have their Opinion of them. But this was no restraint to his Eagerness; and, the Event teaching him afterwards, that he ran no great risque (18), he did not discontinue it. And, indeed, we have seen, hitherto, but few Authors, in this respect, like Cardinal *du Perron*, who spared neither Pains nor Expence in his Works, and who had them twice printed; the first time, to distribute only a few Copies to particular Friends, on which they might make their Observations; and the second time, to give them to the Public, such as he at last determined to publish them; and who, to prevent their being published against his Will, after the first Manner, caused them to be printed in his own House, where he set up a Printing-Press for that purpose."

Mr *Ancillon*'s Library was "very curious and large; he increased it, daily, with all that appeared new and valuable in the Republic of Letters; insomuch, that, at last, it became one of the finest of any private Man in the Kingdom. Foreigners of Curiosity did not fail to see it, as they went through the City of *Metz*; it being the greatest Rarity of that Town (19)." As soon as he saw the Catalogue *of the pretended Heretical Books*, drawn up by the Archbishop of *Paris*, in the Year 1685, he selected all the Books, "which were ordered to be suppressed, which made up his Library in foreign Countries (20); his own having been, as it were, given up to be plundered, after the Revocation of the Edict of *Nantes*. None would have remained, if those, which he concealed, had not escaped the Greediness, with which the rest were carried away. —— The Monks, and the Clergy of *Metz*, and the adjacent Towns, had long coveted Mr *Ancillon*'s Library (21); his forced and hasty Departure supplied them with a fair Pretence to appropriate it to themselves. Some proposed to buy it in the Gross; others would have it sold by Retail; but neither of them intended to pay for it; they only desired to get it into their Possession. The last Expedient was followed, as being more proper to favour this unjust Design: A Crowd of Ecclesiastics of all Orders came in, from all Parts, to this noble and rich Library; which had been Forty four Years in collecting, with Pleasure and Choice; and which consisted only of rare Books, and worthy of the Curiosity of the most learned Men: They made several Parcels of them, and, going away, they gave Money to a young Girl, of about twelve or thirteen Years of Age, who was looking upon them, that they might say they had paid the Price of them. In this manner Mr *Ancillon* saw his precious Collection dispersed, which he had made, and on which he had set his Affections, and, as we may say, his very Heart." Note, That the loss of this Library was attended with the loss of a vast Number of Letters, which were designed for the Press (22), and which Mr *Ancillon*

ANCILLON

which he published [E]. As to the rest, I shall observe, in general, that the *Discourse*, which

cillon had received from many learned Men. He designed chiefly to print those, which Mr *Daillé*, his intimate Friend (24), had wrote to him. What a Loss was this!

This may afford copious Matter for Reflexion: For is it not a deplorable Consideration, to think, that a single Day may undo, what has been compleated with a thousand Cares, and, at a vast Expence, during many Years? Is it not a melancholy Fate, to be exposed to lose, in a Moment, what has been a long time purchasing, by innocent Means, and been treasured up, as a perpetual Source of very lawful Pleasure, and honest Instruction? To be deprived, in a Moment, of a vast Number of Volumes, which have been so carefully collected, and so much one's Delight, is it not an hard and cruel Destiny? If the Flames had devoured them, one could more easily bear the Loss; but, without a special Grace of God, one cannot support, that they should become the Prey of an unjust Possessor, who is at no other Trouble, than that of transporting them to his own House. The *Triumvirate*, which dispossest of their Lands, those, who had cultivated them, during their whole Life, and gave them to others, who had contributed nothing towards their Improvement, did not occasion so sensible a Grief, as that of the Learned, who have seen their Libraries plundred, and fallen into the Hands of a Persecutor, worthy of hatred, if he acted against his Conscience, and deserving of Pity, if his false Devotion persuaded him, that it was a thing acceptable to God.

Impius hæc tam culta novalia miles habebit,
Barbarus has segetes (25)?
Did we for these Barbarians plant, and sow?
On these, on these, our happy Fields bestow?
DRYDEN.

This was the Complaint of those good People of *Italy*, who found themselves obliged to surrender their Patrimony to the Soldier of the *Triumvirate*.

— — — en! queis consevimus agros!
Insere nunc, Meliboee pyros, pone ordine vites (26).

Now let me graft my Pears, and prune my Vine;
The Fruit is theirs, the Labour only mine.
DRYDEN.

— — — vivi pervenimus advena nostri,
Quod nunquam veriti sumus, ut possessor agelli
Diceret, hæc mea sunt, veteres migrate coloni (27).

The Time is come, I never thought to see,
(Strange Revolution for my Farm and me)
When the grim Captain, in a surly tone,
Cries out, pack up, ye Rascals, and be gone.
DRYDEN.

Mr *Ancillon*, and many others, might have adapted most of these Expressions to their Fortune. Perhaps, it were better to have no Affections, than to let them on a Library; since, perhaps we may be reduced to address it in this manner:

Nuper sollicitum quæ mihi tædium,
Nunc desiderium, curaque non levis (28).

O! lately, thou, my anxious Fear,
Now my sad Loss, and heavy Care!

But, if possible, let us forget the unhappy and fatal Revocation of the Edict of *Nantz*, which was attended with so many Acts of Injustice. Let us rather cast our Eyes on Objects, which do not raise the Passions into a Ferment. Let us praise, the good Taste of this able Divine. He was for, having the first Editions of Books, though it was very *probable* they would be reprinted, with Additions and Corrections (29). This was to understand things; this we may call Love of Books, and Eagerness after Instruction: But they, who can rest satisfied without a Book, 'till it be reprinted, make it appear, that they are satisfied

with their Ignorance, and that they had rather save a few Pistoles, than acquire Instruction. I speak of those, (and the Number of them is very great) who are persuaded, on the one side, that a new Book will afford them much Information; and who, though they are able to purchase it, defer the buying of it, because they are told, that there will be published better, or cheaper, Editions. This Delay cannot be sufficiently blamed: It is a shameful Neglect of Learning. Mr *Bigot* told me, one Day, that a Man of *Rouen*, who applied himself to the Study of Genealogies, would willingly have improved by the Works of Father *Anselm*; and yet he did not purchase them; but waited for the second Edition, which never came out; thus he died, without satisfying his Curiosity. Mr *Bigot* represented to him, several times, that it was better to have two Editions of a Book, than to deprive one's self of the Advantage, which might accrue by reading the first; and that a Man judges wrong of the value of things, who prefers three or four Crowns to such a Profit. They, who can afford it, ought to provide themselves with the first Editions. I confess the foreign Editions of Books are not so expensive: But are they faithful? Is there nothing altered in, or added to, them? Did not the Abbot *de la Roque* publickly complain (30), that the Printers of *Holland* had corrupted his Book? I have been assured, but a few Days ago, that the History of *Davila*, and That of *Strada*, printed in the *Netherlands*, are not exactly the same with the *Italian* Editions; the Booksellers of *Flanders* having suppressed, or altered, some things, out of Complaisance to some illustrious Families. I may be told, that the Author often corrects his Faults in the second Edition: I own it: But they are not always real Faults; they are Alterations, which he sacrifices to prudential Reasons, to his Repose, and to the Injustice of his too powerful Censurers. The second Edition, which *Mezerai* publish'd, of his Chronological Abridgment, is the most correct; for he left out some Mistakes; but he omitted likewise some Truths, which were ungrateful; and, for this Reason, the Curious endeavour to get the Edition in Quarto, which is the first; and pay a great Price for it. I say nothing of the Advantage of comparing Editions. It is so great, when an able Writer has carefully revised his Work, that his first Essay deserves to be kept. All this will make you sensible, that Mr *Ancillon* knew very well what belonged to a Library.

I proceed to his Method of Studying. "He spent "no time in vain and useless Studies. He read, "indeed, all sorts of Books, even the ancient and "modern Romances. He believed, that there was "no Book, but what might be useful; and used to "repeat these Words, ascribed to *Virgil, Aurum ex* "*stercore Ennii colligo* (31). —— I collect Gold out "of Ennius's Dung. We find, said he sometimes, "even in neglected Authors, very curious Particulars, "which are not to be met with elsewhere; and, if "it were only the Style, there is always something "to be got by the reading of them. But he did not "apply his Mind to them; he made only important Books, and serious Things, the principal Subject of his Studies. —— He made a very great Difference between the reading of Books, which, as "he himself said, he only looked into, that he might "not be ignorant of any thing, and the reading of "those, which were useful to his Profession. He "read the first but once, and curiously, *perfunctoriè*, "and, as the *Latin* Proverb says, *sicut canis ad Nilum bibens & fugiens*; but he read other Books "several times over, with Care and Application. "The first time, he said, served only to give him a "general Notion of the Subject, and the second enabled him to observe the Beauties of it. Indexes, "which other great Men have called *The Soul of* "*Books*, were entirely useless to him, because he "read them with Application, and often more than once. "Besides, he had a very happy Memory, and, particularly, a local one, of great use to Men of Letters. He read them exactly, without omitting the "very Title, the Name of the Printer, or the Place, "and Year, of the Impression. In his Opinion, "every thing was of some use. He marked his Books "with his Pen, as he read them, and placed in the Margin References to other Authors, who had treated

Marginal notes:
(24) *Estand of the usual Talk Monsieurs, they called each other My Dear Atticus.* Ibid.
REFLECTION on the Fate of some Libraries, and the Indolence of those, who wait for second Editions.
(25) Virgil. Ecl. 1. ver. 71.
(26) Id. Ib.
(27) Idem, Ecl. 9. v. 2.
(28) Horat. Od. 14. lib. 1. ver. 17.
(29) *He often found that this probable week without any Effect. See, above, Cicer. (18).*
(30) *In a Preface to his Journal des Sçavans. See also the Remark [F] of the Article PELISSON, towards the end.*
(31) *Discourse on the Life of Mr Ancillon, p. 107.*

ANCILLON.

which has been published, *on his Life*, represents him as a Person of extraordinary Merit. It is, properly speaking, the Idea of an accomplish'd Pastor. He appears in it Learned, Eloquent, Wise, Pious, Modest, and Charitable; dispensing his Censures meekly, or rigorously, according to the Exigency of the Case; practising what he

"the same Subject, or had made use of Expres-"sions a-kin to what he read (32). ———— Sometimes he "changed his Reading, which served him instead of "Rest †. He did not read every Book through; "sometimes he studied the Subject thoroughly, and "then consulted Authors, who had treated of it; he "often met with the same thing in different Books, "at which he was not disgusted; on the contrary, "he said, they were so many new Strokes, which "compleated the Idea he had conceived, and brought "it to an entire Perfection. He had a great Table "in the midle of his Chamber, which was common-"ly full of Books, most of them open (33). The "famous Fra-Paolo, whom I have mentioned, studied "also in the same manner; and, as the exact and "faithful Author of his Life inform us, he never "left off, 'till he had seen all; that is to say, 'till he "had confronted Authors, Places, Times, and Opi-"nions. He persisted in this Practice, that he might "have no more Occasion to doubt, or think again "on the same Subject; and that he might know what "to depend upon. Thus Mr *Ancillon* studied some-"times, and he has often been heard to give the "same Reasons for it. As he read much, he found "many things worth taking notice of; and, though "he had an admirable Memory, he had Books, in "which he collected what he thought most consider-"able. He was not ignorant, that *Govean*, for Ex-"ample, who would not have so much as an Ink-"horn in his Study, *Salmasius*, *Menage*, and several "other great Men, have condemned Collections, "and that, so far from thinking, that they facilita-"ted the Acquisition of Learning, on the contrary, "they looked upon them as an Obstacle, which in-"terrupts the Course of Reading and Meditation, "and destroys the Effect of them. But he was of "Opinion, that, since, thro' the Unhappiness of the "present Age, it is not sufficient to be Master of a "Subject, and all the Reasons, on which it is built, "but it is necessary likewise to produce Authorities, "and express Texts; there was occasion for a Book, "which, like a Vein, or Stream of Water, may di-"rect one to the Fountain Head, and the rather, be-"cause, being to speak in public before certain Peo-"ple, who were rather his Spies, than his Hearers, "and who often diminished of him Authorities and "Proofs for what he advanced; it was in some "sort necessary to have a Repertory, to assist his Me-"mory, and to prevent his looking a long time for "what he wanted, according to the different Con-"junctures he was in." These Particulars may, I think, be of use to many Readers. I shall speak be-low (34), of his confused Application to Study.

[E] *The Books he publish'd.*] In the Year 1657, he publish'd a Relation in Quarto at *Sedan*, *wherein the whole Controversy concerning Traditions is fully and jointly examined* (35). 'Tis a faithful Relation of what passed in the Conference, which he had with Mr *de Bedacier*, *Doctor of the Sorbonne*, *Bishop of Augusta*, *and Suffragan of the Bishop of Metz* (36). He disputed with him; First, in his own House (37), in the Presence of many Persons, and afterwards at the Bishop's Palace (38), before a Crowd of People. All the Articles were committed to writing, and sign'd. "He maintain'd this Disputation with Ho-"nour, and finish'd it with Success. Having answer'd; "methodically, all the Objections, which were made "to him, he represented, that He was likewise to "propose his Arguments, in his Turn; but, as "he had given several Mortal Blows to Error, in "his Answer, it was fear'd he would utterly destroy "it, if he was allowed to establish what he preten-"ded to be the Truth. Mr *de Bedacier* resolv'd to "break up the Conference, and, in order to conceal "the real Motives of his Conduct, he pretended, that, "for the future, it would be better to carry on the "Dispute in Writing, than by Word of Mouth: "Nevertheless it was agreed, on both Sides, that "neither Party should cause the Acts of This Con-"ference to be printed (39)". But there was a Monk, who publish'd spurious Acts of it, (40). And whose Impudence was so great, that, though Mr *Ancil*-lon had obtain'd very great Honour in This Conference, he endeavour'd to persuade the Publick, that it had prov'd fatal both to him and his Party, and that he had been entirely vanquish'd (41). This oblig'd Mr *Ancillon* to publish the Work I have mention'd. *Hottinger* commends it very much, in the 6th Chapter of the 3d Book of his *Bibliothecarius Quadripartitus* (42). Father *Clivier*, a *Minime*, and Provincial of his Order, *undertook to confute this Work*; *in order to which*, *he compos'd a Book*, *intituled*, Le Fort des Traditions abbatu par les Maximes de Mr *David Ancillon*. ———— *The Fort* (or *strong Hold*) *of Traditions demolish'd by the Maxims of Mr* David Ancillon. Others wrote Satires against it; but all these Libels were unsuccessful (43). The *Roman* Catholics themselves advised Mr *Ancillon* not to answer them, as he had undertaken to do; they assur'd him, that He, and his Book, *were so far superior to these Hackney Writers*, *that it was beneath him to enter the Lists with them* (44). As soon as the *Method* of Cardinal *Richelieu* came out, "He wrote a large and excellent Answer "to it. But he was inform'd, that Mr *Martel*, Pro-"fessor at *Montauban*, had wrote one, which was "just upon the Point of being publish'd; and that "Mr *Claude*, who had the same Design, had laid it "aside for the like Reason, as it now appears by the "Sixth Letter, in the Collection of his Letters, in "the Fifth Volume of his Posthumous Works. He, "therefore, suppress'd what he had wrote; and no-"thing of it was made Publick, but a few Sheets, "which contain'd an Answer to the 6th Chapter of "That *Method*, or, to speak more properly, an "Apology for *Luther*, *Zuinglius*, *Calvin*, and *Be-*"*za*, which is the Title of it in the Edition of "*Hanow*, 1666. Mr *Ancillon* wrote the Life of "*William Farel*; or, *The Idea of a Faithful Mini-*"*ster of Christ*. The famous Mr *Conrart*, who was "one of his intimate Friends, read, and approv'd "of it, and with his own Hand wrote some Notes "in the Margins of the Manuscript. It was a "Work, which deserved to be publish'd; but he "could not be persuaded by any means to give his "Consent to it; and his Refusal occasion'd a Copy, "full of Errors, to be taken from it, which fell into "the Hands of a Bookseller in *Holland*, who put it "to the Press, on the Reputation of the Author. "Every one was surpriz'd to see such a wretched "Edition, as That was; and, if ever the same Book "should be printed from the Copy, revised by Mr "*Conrart*, This Piece will appear so mangled, that "it will not easily be known again. Tho' Mr *Ancillon* "had expounded some entire Books of the Holy "Scripture, and committed all his Sermons to Writ-"ing, he could never be persuaded to print them --- "(45) All of this kind, which was printed, is a Ser-"mon, which he preach'd at *Metz*, on a Fast-day: "His Consistory exerted some Authority over him, "to force it out of his Hands, and caus'd it to be "printed at *Paris* in the Year 1676. This Ser-"mon, was compos'd on the 18th and 19th Verses "of the third Chapter of St *Paul's* Epistle to the "*Philippians*, and is intitled, *The Tears of St* Paul. "Lastly, he wrote an excellent Answer to the *Pa-*"*storal Advice*, the *Circular Letters*, and the *Me-*"*thods*, which the Clergy address'd to the Re-"formed of *France*, in the Year 1682; but he kept "it close in his Study, till, some considerable Persons "having oblig'd him to publish it, he sent it to his "old Friend Mr *Turretin*, Professor of Divinity at "*Geneva*, giving him full Liberty to dispose of it, "as he should think fit; but it is probable, that the "Copy miscarried, for it has been never heard of "since. Mr *Ancillon* had so little concern for his "own Works, that he never enquir'd after it; and "yet this was the Answer, which the Public ex-"pected, and of which mention is made in the "Preface to a solid and judicious Book, intituled, "*Examen des Methodes*, &c. In the Place, where it "is said, *There will be publish'd an Answer by an* "*able Hand at* Metz (46).

[F] He

ANCILLON.

he preached (7); wholly employ'd in the Discharge of his Ministry [F], without interfering, as many others do, with what belongs only to Laymen; or keeping his Doors open to Informers, and Newsmongers [G]. How learned his Conversation was [H],

[F] *He was wholly employ'd in the discharge of his Ministry.*] They, who devote themselves to the Pastoral Office, "Stand in need of all their time, to "study, labour, and to perform worthily the Duties "of their Calling; and, without doubt, this is the "reason, why the Sixth Canon, among those which "are call'd Apostolical, imports, that no Bishop, "Priest, or Deacon, shall meddle with Secular Matters, or engage in any Public Office; and that the "Sixth Canon, among those of *Africa*, forbids Persons of This Character to take upon themselves the "Management of the Affairs, or Law-Suits, of other "People. The Loss of time, which is spent in these "Worldly Occupations, is not the least Motive of "these excellent Constitutions; but I believe they "are not the only Considerations, which occasion'd "them. Experience has made it appear, that the "Intrigues of the World, the Hurry of Business, "and the Ambition of making their Court to great "Persons, are three Rocks, which have always been, "and ever will be, fatal to them. They depart insensibly from That Apostolical Simplicity, which "ought to be one of their chief Ornaments; they "learn the Maxims of the World; they accustom "themselves to it's Subtilties, and Artifices, and are "led insensibly to practise them (47)." The Minister, I am speaking of, shunn'd all these Rocks; he "lov'd Study, Repose, and Retirement; and never "embarrass'd himself with Worldly Affairs (48). "He "was appointed, by the Laws of his Country, and "against his Will, Guardian to his Brother and Sister: But he left the Administration of the Estate, "and the Management of Affairs, to his Brother, "who, though under Age, was already, a very able "Man ——— So that, the Pupillage being ended by "the Majority of the Orphans, the Minor gave an "Account to his Guardian, and the Guardian, for "Form sake, did the like to his Minors; quite "contrary to the usual, natural, and common Custom. He absolutely renounced all Worldly Affairs, "and, like a true Anchoret, banish'd himself from "the Conversation of Men, and employ'd his whole "Thoughts on God, and his Church (49). He had "a very curious and large Library ——— He was always to be found in it. ——— (50). He never went "out of his House, but in order to go to Church, or "to perform, elsewhere, some other Function of his "Office. He never left his Books, but upon this "Account; and, as if the Day were not long enough, "he spent part of the Night in Meditation, or Study. Though he had several Country Houses, and "One had been purchas'd for him very near the City, "the more easily to engage him to spend a few Days, "or at least Hours, at it; yet he was never "seen there above three or four times, in two, and "thirty Years, that he exercis'd his Ministry at *Metz.* "He was constantly in his Chamber, being a "Stranger to Jealousy, which makes other Men "pass so many uneasy Moments: In this manner he "liv'd peaceably at home, regardless of the Credit "which is got by frequent Visits, troublesome Cares, "and great Measures, which are exactly to be observ'd."

This is the Model, by which all Ministers of the Gospel should regulate their Lives. They have all, like *Mary*, chosen the good part (51); but some of them imitate *Martha*, who was careful and troubled about many things (52). They meddle with State Affairs; They enter into the Intrigues of the Town; They are inquisitive after all kinds of News; They traffick in them, and make use of them in making their court to their Superiors. Nay, They sometimes venture to suggest Advice, in regard to War, or Negotiations; and are not discouraged at the Contempt, which is artfully shewn for their idle Projects. They are often seen in the Anti-Chambers of Princes; and wait impatiently for an Opportunity of being introduced; not upon Matters of Conscience, but to ask a thousand Favours, to recommend their Children, their Relations, and their Friends, with respect to honourable and profitable Places. They have the first Intelligence of a Vacancy, and endeavour to get it fill'd up upon their Recommendation. They would deserve Commendation, if they employ'd their Credit only in procuring Bread to those, who want it; but they employ it chiefly in favour of those, who are already rich, and who wou'd not dare to have recourse to their Sollicitations, if they believ'd them to be true Ministers of JESUS CHRIST; for then they would expect a Censure; they would be afraid of being put in Mind of St *Paul's* Precept, that, provided we have Food and Raiment, we shou'd be therewith content (53). It is not the Duty of a Pastor to procure to his Flock a stronger Attachment to worldly Things; he should rather endeavour to draw them off from it, and combat their Covetousness and Ambition; and no doubt he would do so, were he himself free from the gnawing Cares of Vain-glory. But, because, in order to gratify his Passions, he wants to have the Offices of a Town in the Hands of Men, who may be obliged to him for them, and who, by way of Acknowledgment, or in hopes of new Favours, will always be ready to serve him, he uses his utmost endeavours to raise them; he commends their ambitious Views; and, to support himself in the Management of Affairs, he is obliged to be a Man of Intrigue, and to have his Emissaries every where. Such a Man stands in need of being threatned, as Bishops are sometimes, when they set against the Canons, which oblige them to Residence; and little thinks, that his Office is of such a Nature, that the utmost Human Ability is scarce sufficient for it. They, who consider this, will imitate Mr *Ancillon*, and not throw away so much time in Visits of Interest.

Forumque vitat, & superba civium
Potentiorum limina (54).

The Clamours of contentious Law,
And Court and State he wisely shuns,
Nor, brib'd with Hopes, nor dar'd with Aws,
To servile Salutations runs.
DRYDEN.

Note, that they, who do not imitate his Conduct, sometimes employ their Interest for Persons, who are distress'd in their Circumstances: but if you observe, you will find, that these Persons are serviceable Men, fit for any thing, and inclin'd to consecrate all their Leisure to the Passions of Him, whose Protection has procur'd it for them. He is their Deity;

—— Deus nobis hæc otia fecit;
Namque erit Ille mihi semper Deus; illius aram
Sæpe tener nostris ab ovilibus imbuet agnus (55).

These Blessings, Friend, a Deity bestow'd;
For never can I deem him less than God.
The tender Firstlings of my woolly Breed
Shall on his Holy Altar often bleed.
DRYDEN.

They acknowledge themselves his Creatures, and perform all the Duties, which This Character requires.

[G] *His Doors were not open to Informers and Newsmongers.*] "He neither loved Tales, nor "Tale-bearers; and laid it down as a Maxim, that "little Credit was to be given to them; saying, that "a Report is never so pure, but it relishes of the "Passions of him, who makes it; and that It is like "Water, which always retains the Quality of the "Veins of Earth, or Minerals, through which it "runs. He had, particularly, a vast Aversion to "those, who go into Houses to learn what passes "there, and to set People a talking, and then report "what they have, as it were, extorted from their "Mouths by Cunning and Artifice —— (56). He "said, that it was very dangerous lightly to believe "what is said of others. He was upon his Guard "in this Respect (57). The House of such a Pastor "was far from being a Place of Resort for News-"Writers. I have consider'd this matter above, in "the Remark [H] of the Article ALTING (HENRY)

322   ANCILLON. ANCRE. ANDLO.

(z) *In Remark [F] of the Article FERRI.*

was [H], cannot be better known, than from the Book mentioned in the Remark [G]. I shall, in another Place (z), examine some Particulars concerning a Print of Him. But I must not pass over in silence, That he was the Son of a Learned Civilian; that one of his Ancestors *was formerly President au Mortier in one of the chief Sovereign Courts of France*; and that *Georgin* ANCILLON, *one of the Principal Members of the Church of* Metz, *was also one of the first Founders and Governors of it* (aa).

(aa) *Discours, &c. pag. 7.*

"(HENRY) and I shall farther consider it in the " Remark [N] of the Article GRUTERUS " (JANUS).

(58) *See the Acta Eruditorum for June 1698. pag. 287.*

[H] *How Learned his Conversation was.*] The Work, from whence we have our Information, is intituled, *Melange critique de Litterature*, and was collected out of Mr *Ancillon's* Conversations (58). It was printed at *Basil*, in the Year 1698, in Two Volumes in Twelves, by the Care of Mr *Ancillon* the Advocate, eldest Son to This Minister, who had already distinguish'd himself in the Common-Wealth of Learning (59). I shall have frequent occasion to speak of this Miscellany; and if, sometimes, I do not find every thing in it so exact as it should be, I do not intend to prejudice, thereby, the Author or Publisher of these Pieces. It is much more surprizing, that the late Mr *Ancillon*, in speaking off-hand, should be so exact in many things, than strange, that his Memory fail'd him in some particulars. As to his Son, it was his Duty to deliver things as he had them from Mr *Ancillon's* Mouth. See what I have observed concerning the *Menagiana* (60); the Case here is the same. You may see, in the Preface to This Miscellany, why it was intituled *Ancilloniana.*

(59) *He publish'd several Books; word of them anonymous.*

(60) *In Remark [A] of the Article MENAGE.*

ANCRE (The *Mareschal d'*). Look for CONCINI.

ANDLO (PETRUS AB), a fictitious Name, under which a *Cartesian* disguised himself, in order to write against the Dissertation *De Abusu Philosophiæ Cartesianæ surrepente, & vitando in rebus Theologicis & Fidei.* Mr *Des Marets*, Professor of Divinity at *Groningen*, the Author of this Dissertation, published it in the Year 1670, to represent to the Protestant Churches the great Evils, which were to be feared, if the Opinions of *Des Cartes* were suffered to pass from the Schools of Philosophy to those of Divinity. Some Months after, there came out a Piece intituled, *Petri ab Andlo Batavi Specimen Confutationis Dissertationis de Abusu Philosophiæ Cartesianæ*, &c. Never was any Confutation written in a more vehement Style. *Des Marets* was treated in it after the most disobliging manner. He quickly published an Apology, intituled, *Vindiciæ posteriores Dissertationis de Abusu Philosophiæ Cartesianæ*, in which he loaded his Adversary with all kinds of Abuse. He treated him as a most impudent *Socinian*, a *Spinozist*, an impious and unchristian Man, and an Atheist. *Petrus ab Andlo* speedily published a Reply, intituled *Animadversiones ad Vindicias Dissertationis, quam Samuel Maresius edidit, de Abusu Philosophiæ Cartesianæ*: If he was passionate in his first Dissertation, he was still more so in his second; intermixing, nevertheless, as he had done at first, several Strokes of Raillery with his Anger. He positively denied, that he had any Acquaintance with *Spinoza*, that he had ever seen him, or that he approved his Opinions (a). *Des Marets* received this second Piece of *Petrus ab Andlo*, the Nineteenth of *December* 1670, and confuted it so speedily, that his Rejoinder was finished the Third of *January* following (b). It was intituled, *Samuelis Maresii Clypeus Orthodoxiæ, sive Vindiciarum suarum priorum pro sua Dissertatione de Abusu Philosophiæ Cartesianæ*, &c. The Author declared, that he would write no more against so obscure an Author [A], but should be always ready to enter the Lists, in Defence of Truth, with a Learned, and Honest Adversary, who was not ashamed of his Name. He kept his Word; for he left the third Piece of *Petrus ab Andlo* unanswered; It was intituled, *Specimina Bombomiachiæ Samuelis Maresii se defendentis Clypeo Orthodoxiæ, seu vindiciis vindiciarum Dissertationis de Abusu Philosophiæ Cartesianæ.* Thus ended this Controversy, which verified the Proverb, *Nullum violentum durabile,——— Nothing violent is of long Continuance*; tho' it frequently proves false in a Paper-War [B]. *Des Marets* could never discover the true Name of his Adversary [C]. There appeared, in 1673, a small Book in 4to, intituled DANIELIS AB ANDLO, *Petri filii,* Καγαζοεσε αδελφοδν ελεξχομενο, *sive ad Clarissimi Theologi Samuelis Maresii Tractatum brevem de Studio Theologico Nota breves.*

(a) *Spinozam nec novit Petrus, nec vidit, nec audivit, nec absurda ejus dogmata probat. Animadv. ad Vindicias, pag. 7.*

(b) *Vindic. Vindiciarum Dissertat. sub fin.*

(c) *Petrus de Andlo.*

Note, That there is a true ANDLO among Authors (c). He was a Native of *Alsace*, Doctor of the Canon Law, and Canon of *Colmar* (d). The two Books, which he wrote, *De Imperio Romano, Regis & Augusti Inauguratione*, &c. *deque Officio & Potestate Electorum*, &c. were published at *Strasburg*, with Notes, in the Year 1603, by *Marquardus Freberus.*

(d) *Mich. Hertzius, Biblioth. German. n. 224.*

[A] *Declar'd he would write no more against so obscure an Author.*] The Term he makes use of, is the same, which the Scripture uses against the Gods of the Gentiles, calling them Gods of Dung. " Animo non ulterius hanc ferram cum hoc sterco- " reo homine reciprocandi (1) ——— *Having resolv'd* " *to dispute no longer with this dirty Fellow*". " In " antecessum me protestari nihil amplius mihi futurum " negotii cum hoc hominis sterquilinio & infami ne- " bulone quem pudet sui ipsius (2). ——— *I pro-* " *tested before-hand, that I wou'd have nothing more* " *to do with this Dunghil of a Man; this in-* " *famous Rascal, who is asham'd of being known.*

(1) *Maresf. Vindic. Vindiciarum Dissert. sub fin.*

(2) *Id. in Judicio de Theolog. Pacifica Wittichii sub fin.*

[B] *The Proverb* nullum violentum durabile *frequently proves false in a Paper-War.*] I need not go far to find an Instance of what I say. The Quarrels between *Des Marets* and *Voëtius* were extremely violent, and continued near thirty Years, as long as the *German* War, which ended at the Peace of *Munster*.

[C] *Des Marets could never discover the true Name of his Adversary.*] All his Conjectures, and the Enquiries of his Friends, were to no purpose: So that, being weary of such an unsuccessful Chace, he resolved to leave his Adversary masked. *Quis sit ille larvatus* Petrus ab Andlo, Batavus ——— *ut nec hactenus conjectura assequi, nec amicorum diligentia rescire potui,*

ANDRADA.

patui, ita nolo amplius inquirere. —— *Who this disguised Petrus ab Andlo Batavus is —— as I could never yet guess, nor discover by the Diligence of my Friends, I resolve to make no farther Enquiry after him.* This is what he says, at the beginning of his *Clypeus Orthodoxiæ.* He had Friends every where, who, being more zealous than discreet, which is the usual Character of those, who are accounted the Flail of Innovators, made him believe, that there was a Minister in *Zealand,* whose Name was *Petrus ab Andlo,* married to the Daughter of *Cocceius.* He published this News; but, being informed, that the Son-in-law of *Cocceius* was called *Anselaer,* he caused his Excuses to be made to him. "Apud R. D. An- "selaer curavi me honestè excusari, quod id mihi "exidisset ex relatione honesti cujusdam R. viri, "etiam in Cartesianismum ---- pronioris, cui non "erat cur ultro asserenti fidem detractarem (3). —— "I took care to excuse myself honourably to Anselaer "for spreading a Report, the Truth of which I could not "question, as it came from a Reverend and Honourable "Person, and one who was even inclined to Carte- "sianism." He says somewhere (4), that there was a Report, that three Persons had been concerned in the Defence of *Wittichius,* and that they had published their Work under the feigned Name of *Petrus ab Andlo.* We shall see, whether Mr *Placcius,* or Mr *Baillet,* will be more lucky, than I have been, in unmasking this Pseudonymous Writer, whom I take to be *Regnier Mansvelt,* Professor of Philosophy at *Utrecht.*

ANDRADA (Diego de Payva d'), in *Latin Andradius,* a learned Portuguese, born at *Coimbra,* signalized himself in the Council of *Trent,* whither King *Sebastian* sent him, as one of his Divines (a). He preached before the Assembly, the second *Sunday* after *Easter,* 1562. He was not contented with the Service he did, in explaining the Matters, about which he was consulted; he employed his Pen likewise in Defence of the Canons of That Council. This he did in a Book, intituled, *Orthodoxarum Explicationum Libri X* (b). In which he particularly answers a Piece published by *Chemnitius* against the Doctrine of the Jesuits [A], before the breaking up of the Council of *Trent*; and, as *Chemnitius* took this Opportunity to write a very large Book, which he intituled, *Examen Concilii Tridentini; Andrada* thought himself obliged to vindicate his first Piece against this learned Adversary [B]. He, therefore, composed a Book, which his two Brothers published after his Death at *Lisbon,* in the Year 1578. It is intituled, *Defensio Tridentinæ Fidei Catholicæ, quinque Libris comprehensa, adversus Hæreticorum calumnias, & præsertim Martini Kemnitii.* These Works of *Andrada* have been printed several times (c), and yet they are so scarce at *Paris,* that Mr *Pellisson* could not meet with them in the *Rue de St Jaques* * [C]. There is scarce any Catholic Author, who has been more quoted by the Protestants,

[A] *A Piece published by Chemnitius against the Doctrine of the Jesuits.*] A Lutheran Minister, who wrote an Encomium upon *Chemnitius,* expresses himself thus: "Breve quidem, sed nervosum scriptum, "durante adhuc Concilio Tridentino, Jesuitarum "Theologiæ opposuit, cujus opusculi cum Andra- "dius Lusitanus in se suscepisset refutationem, Chem- "nitio occasionem subministravit conscribendi insigne "illud ------ opus, quod Tridentini Concilii exa- "men nuncupavit (1). ----- *During the Session "of the Council of Trent, he wrote a short, but ner- "vous, Piece against the Doctrine of the Jesuits; "which when Andradius the Portuguese undertook "to refute,* Chemnitius *laid hold of the Opportu- "nity of writing That famous Work, which he called, "An Enquiry into the Council of Trent.*" To which I add a Passage of *Eisengreinius,* because it will give occasion to a small Remark. This Author pretends, that *Andrada* did Wonders against the Hereticks, in his Orthodox Explications, and chiefly against *Chemnitius*: "Præsertim contra Martini Kemnitii "petulantem audaciam, qui Coloniensem censuram "quam à viris societatis Jesu compositam esse ait, "una cum ejusdem sanctissimæ Societatis vitæ ra- "tione temere calumniandam suscepit (2). —— *Par- "ticularly against the insolent Boldness of* Martin "Chemnitius, *who took upon him to abuse the Cen- "sure of* Cologn, *which he says was drawn up by the "Jesuits, together with the manner of Life of the "Gentlemen of That venerable Society.*" *Nicolas Antonio,* having quoted this Passage, censures *Eisengreinius,* for believing that *Andrada* was a Jesuit. *Hæc ille,* says he, *falsus, saltem in eo quod Andradam nostrum unum ex Jesuitico sodalitio credidit.* If this Censure be only grounded upon the Words, quoted by *Don Antonio,* I believe it to be false.

[B] *Thought himself obliged to vindicate his first Piece against this learned Adversary.*] This Epithet is due to *Chemnitius*; and, at the Bottom I lay no more in his Favour, than *Don Nicolas Antonius* does. At first Sight, indeed, these Words of the *Spanish* Author, "Cui cum reposuisset profligatissimus hæreticus "librum, in quo gravissimas adversus universalem "Ecclesiam contumelias intorquebat, descendere de- "nuo in campum sibi opus esse Paiva vidit, ut im- "manem hostem totis viribus profligaret. —— *This "abandoned Heretic having published a Reply, in "which he most scandalously abused the whole Church,*" "Payva *thought himself obliged to enter the Lists "once more, and exert his whole Strength in demo- "lishing this Gigantic Adversary.*" These Words, I say, at first Sight, appear not very much to the Credit of *Chemnitius*; but, if they be well considered, they will be found to redound greatly to his Honour; for must it not be very pleasing to a Man, to find himself represented as the *Goliath,* or the *Polyphemus,* of his Party, by those of the contrary Side; when, besides, he believes himself engaged in a good Cause?

[C] *That Mr Pellisson could not meet with them in the* Rue de St Jaques.] An Account of this Matter will not displease the Curious. Mr *Leibnitz,* in his Remarks on the *Reflexions on the Disputes in Religion* (3), alledged, among other things, that *Andrada* had composed a Work entitled, *Explicationes Orthodoxæ de controversiis Religionis capitibus;* in which he teaches in express Terms, "That the Philosophers, "who used all their Industry to come at the Know- "ledge of the true God, and to honour him reli- "giously, had That Faith, by which the Just live. "------ That it would be the greatest Cruelty in "the World *(neque immanitas deterior ulla esse potest)* "to condemn Men to eternal Torments, for wanting "a Faith, which they could not attain to (4)." Mr *Pellisson* immediately replied, "That he had "never met with This Author, and that, to satisfy "his Curiosity, he would enquire after his Book, "when he came to *Paris* (5)." Some time after he acquainted the Public, that he had *carefully enquired after the Book of the* Portuguese *Doctor,* Payva Andradius; but he added, "It is no easy thing to "find it in *Paris*: It is unknown in the *Rue de "St Jaques*; nor is it to be met with in the most "voluminous Libraries; no, not In That of the Je- "suits; which is very remarkable, because he wrote "in their Favour. At last, It has been found in "the Library of the *Sorbonne.* The Abbot *Pirot,* "a Person of Merit, if there be one this Day in "*France,* or elsewhere, and one of the most emi- "nent and illustrious Members of that House, who "knew as little of the Author, as myself, has given "himself the Trouble to peruse it at my Request. "------ This Writer has Merit, and is no dry or "jejune Scholastic, as so many others are; he dif- "covers a more than ordinary Elegance, and Viva- "city; in a Word, he answers the Reputation, "which he bore in the Council of *Trent* (6)." It is surprizing,

ANDRADA. ANDREAS.

Protestants, than He, because he maintained some Opinions a little too extravagant, concerning the Salvation of the Pagan Philosophers. He was a Preacher; His Sermons have been published in three Parts; the second of which was translated out of *Portuguese* into *Spanish*, by *Benedict de Alarcon* (d). The *Bibliotheque* of the *Spanish* Writers does not mention all his Works [D]. Many Encomiums have been bestow'd upon *Andrada* [E], which may be seen in the Remarks.

(d) Id. ib.

prizing, that a Book, so little known to the greatest Booksellers, and scarce to be found in the largest Libraries, should be quoted by an hundred Authors, whose Collections are very small. This, I say, is surprizing to those, who are ignorant, that the *Enquiry into the Council of Trent*, by *Chemnitius*, is a very common Book, and that Dr *Andradius* is frequently quoted in it. An hundred other Authors have expressed them as positively as he has done on this Subject, as *la Mothe la Vayer* shews in one of his Books (7). How comes it, then, that they have not been quoted so often as *Andradius*, when the Question was to excuse *Zuinglius*, by way of Recrimination, or to object to the Papists, that they have leaned towards the *Pelagian Heresy*? What, I say, can be the Reason of this, if I have not hinted at the true Cause of the frequent Quotations of *Andradius*?

[D] *The Bibliotheque of the Spanish Writers does not mention all his Works.*] The Book he wrote concerning the Pope's Authority, during the Council, in the Year 1562, is not to be found in it (8). The Pope's Legates, being very well pleased with This Work, sent it to Cardinal *Borromeo*. The Court of *Rome* liked it extreamly, and the Pope very obligingly returned the Author Thanks. I believe this Work is the same with That, which is entituled, *De Conciliorum Autoritate*, the first Book of which has been quoted by *Palavicini* (9).

[E] *Many Encomiums have been bestowed upon Andrada.*] You have already seen Mr *Pelliffon*'s Opinion of him. *Osorius*, in his Preface to the Orthodox Explications of *Andradius*, ascribes to him a great Wit, an eager Application, a Knowledge of Languages, and the Zeal and Eloquence of a good Preacher. *Reymede* speaks of him thus: " Ad Concilium Tridentinum & profundissimi Theologi mentem, & linguam eloquentissimi Oratoris, attulit (10). — He carried with him to the Council of *Trent* the Understanding of a most profound Divine, and the Eloquence of a consummate Orator."

ANDREAS (JOHN), a famous Canonist of the XIVth Century, was the Son of a Priest [A], and was born at *Mugello*, near *Florence*. He was yet very young, when he went to study at *Bologne* (a); where he would have scarce been able to maintain himself, had he not met with a Tutor's Place; but, by the help of this Employment, he was in a Condition to apply himself, at his Ease, to the Study of the Canon Law, in which he made a great Progress, under the Professor *Gui de Baif* (b). He had always a particular Respect for the Person, and Glosses, of this Professor; He paid as great a Deference to his Glosses, as to the Text itself. He was beholden to him in a Particular, which we are, generally, more thankful for, than for Instruction. *Gui de Baif*, perceiving, that, for want of Money, he durst not petition for his Doctor's Degree, put him upon demanding it, and obtained it for him *gratis*. *Andreas* himself confesses this (c). The same *Gui* encouraged him likewise to stand for a Professorship; which was attended with all the Success he could wish. Our *Andreas*, we find, was Professor at *Padua*, about the Year 1330, and also at *Pisa*; but he was recalled to *Bologne* (d), where he acquired a greater Reputation, than any where else. We are told wonderful things concerning his austere Life [B]. He mortified

[A] *Was the Son of a Priest.*] All Authors agree, that the Father of *John Andreas* was a Priest, but not that he was so, when he begot this Child. " Patrem constat Presbyterum fuisse; an filium ante, an post Sacerdotium genuerit, incertum. — — It is certain, that his Father was a Priest, but uncertain whether he begot his Son before, or after, his Priesthood" Thus Mr *Dupat* speaks of him (1), after having read *Panzirolus*, who positively asserts, that *John Andreas* was born, before his Father was a Priest. " Is ex Andrea Presbytero, antequam Sacerdos fieret, & matre nomine Novella, genitus (2)." It is a Sign Mr *Dupat* laid no great Stress on *Panzirolus*'s Decision of the Matter; and for what Reason, I desire to know, should the latter be credited in it, rather than *Volaterran*, who has affirmed the quite contrary? " Joannes Andreas patre Andrea Presbytero & matre concubina natus, apud Mugellum agri Florentini Oppidum, juris scientia virtutibusque aliis natalium pudorem contexit (3). — — John Andreas, Son of John Andreas, a Priest, and his Concubine born at Mugello, near Florence, covered the meanness of his Birth by his Knowledge of the Law, and his other Vertues." He has expresly said, that *John Andreas* was the Son of a Concubinary Priest; and no one will venture to affirm, that *Novella* was ever married to the Father of *John Andreas*. It is, therefore, past doubt, that our celebrated Canonist was, at least, born, like *Erasmus*, out of lawful Marriage, of a Father, who was a Priest. We must not imagine, that *Forster* says he was not ordained a Priest, 'till after he had begot this Child. He only means, that the Father of *John Andreas* was a Priest, in the Place, where he was born. " Patre Joanne Andrea, cive initio, deinde Presbytero Mugellano, natus est (4). — — — — Son of John Andreas, first a Citizen, afterwards a Priest, of Mugello."

[B] *We are told wonderful Things concerning his austere Life.*] The following Commentary has been communicated to me (5): I make no Alteration in it. " What you observe concerning the austere Life of *John Andreas*, is attested by good Authors. But if the Story, which *Poggius* tells of him, in his *Facetiae* be true, there is Reason to believe, that afterwards this Doctor degenerated very much from his former Continence. Joannem Andream, ajys Poggius, Doctorem Bononiensem, cujus fama admodum vulgata est, subaqitantem ancillam domesticam uxor deprehendit. Re infueta stupefacta mulier in virum versa: ubi nunc, ait, Joannes, est sapientia vestra? Ille nil amplius locutus, in vulva istius, respondit: lotu admodum sapientiae accommodato." Perhaps the Translation of these Words into *French* Verse will not be unacceptable to the Reader.

Jean dit André, fameux docteur és loix,
Fut pris un jour au peché d'amourette:
Il accolloit une jeune soubrette.
Sa femme vint, fit un signe de croix.
Ho ho, dit-elle, est ce-vous? non je pense;
Vous, dont par tout on vante la prudence.
Qu'est devenu cet esprit si subtil?
Le bon André, poursuivant son negoce,
Honteux pourtant: ma foi, repondit-il,
Prudence, esprit, tout gist dans cette fosse.

In *English*, thus,

A learned

ANDREAS. 325

tified his Body with Fasting and Prayers, and slept every Night, for twenty Years together, on the hard Ground, wrapped in a Bear's Skin (*e*). He pretended, that he had obtained several things by his Prayers (*f*). He married a Woman called *Milantia*, whom he mentions sometimes in his Writings; and confesses, that he had learned several things of her; and, among others, that, if Names were to be sold, Fathers and Mothers ought to buy fine ones for their Children (*g*). I forgot to tell you, that his Mother's Name was *Novella*, and that he had a Daughter of the same Name, who was so learned, that she read Lectures for him [C], when he had no leisure to mount the Chair. It was out of Love to his Mother and Daughter, that he intituled his Commentary on the Decretals of *Gregory* IX, *Novellæ* (*h*). He had a Natural Son, whose Name was *Banicontius*, who published some Books [D]; and it is said, that, having lost him, he adopted *John Calderini*, a learned Canonist, and married him to his Daughter *Novella* [E]. He had another Daughter, whom he married to a celebrated Professor of the Canon Law at *Bologne*. Her Name was *Betina*; and she died at *Padua*, in the Year 1355 (*i*), whither her Husband had been invited, to accept of the like Professorship. *Andreas* died of the Plague at *Bologne*, in the Year 1348, after he had been Forty five Years Professor, and was buried in the Church

(*e*) Volaterr. lib. 21. pag. 782.
(*f*) Apud Panzirol. ubi supra.
(*g*) In cap. cum secundum, Extravag. de præbend.
(*h*) Panzirol. de claris Legum Interpret. lib. 3. cap. 19.
(*i*) His Epitaph is to be seen in Panzirolus, ubi supra.

> A learned Canonist, of Fame,
> (John Andreas *was the Doctor's Name*)
> Once on a time in bed was laid,
> Solacing it with Madam's Maid.
> When Chance, That Sower of all Strife,
> Brought in, curst Luck! the Doctor's Wife.
> And is it you, the Lady cries?
> Bless me, I scarce can trust my Eyes.
> Inconstant Wretch, of shameless Brow!
> Where is your boasted Wisdom now?
> 'Tis here, the Doctor, blushing, cries,
> 'Tis here, dear Wife! my Wisdom lies:
> A proper Place (the Place he shows)
> For wearied Wisdom to repose.

Since it is agreed, on all Hands, that *John Andreas* had a Bastard, this Story might be true at the bottom, and perhaps his Wife surprized him with the Mother of *Banicontius*: If it be so, we may place him in the List of the *Menagiana* (6).

(6) *See the Remark* [E] *on the Article* BRISEIS.

[C] *His Daughter read Lectures for him.*] I have met with this Particular, not in *Forster*, or *Panzirolus*, or Mr *Doujat*; but in the *Cité des Dames*, written by *Christina de Pise*. This Book was printed at *Paris*, in the Year 1536, and composed in the Reign of *Charles* VI. The following Passage is taken from it. "To speak of the late times, without quoting Ancient Histories, about sixty Years ago *John Andreas*, a noted Civilian at *Bologne*, did not think there was any harm in a Woman's having some Learning. For he took care, that his handsome Daughter *Novella*, whom he was very fond of, should be bred a Scholar; and so well versed was she in the Knowledge of the Law, that, when he had not leisure to read Lectures to his Scholars, he sent his Daughter *Novella*, to supply his Place in the Schools; and, to prevent her Beauty from diverting the Thoughts of the Auditors, a little Curtain was drawn before her. Thus she sometimes assisted her Father, who loved her so well, that, to preserve the Memory of her, he wrote a famous Book of Law, which he intituled *Novella*, it being the Name of his Daughter (7)." It is strange, that a Particular of this Nature, so singular and rare, should not be found in all the Authors, who mention *John Andreas*, or at least in most of them; and I confess this inclines me to doubt of the Truth of it. But, be that as it will, it may occasion a diverting Problem, *viz.* Whether this Lady promoted, or retarded, the Improvement of her Hearers. An hundred things may be said *pro* and *con.* I am apt to think the Scholars would have amused themselves so much with her Beauty, as to be little attentive to her Lectures; but, on the other hand, what proceeds from a fine Mouth, is much more taking, and persuasive; and some Women, though charmed with the good Air and Mein of a Preacher, remember, nevertheless, what he says. What an ancient Poet says of Virtue, that it is more pleasing in a beautiful Body, *Gratior & pulchro venens in corpore virtus* (8); may be applied to Learning. However it be, if the Daughter of the Professor, *John Andreas*, drew a Curtain between her and

(7) Cite de Dames de Christine de Pise, part 2. cap. 38.

(8) Virgil, Æn. lib. 5. ver. 344.

her Hearers, least the Darts of her Beauty should wound their Hearts, and interrupt their Attention, she made them a considerable Sacrifice, which they would willingly have dispensed with. They would, probably, have been very well pleased to see her; and she, on her part, would not have been displeased to be seen, had she not preferred *their* Improvement to her *own* Satisfaction. This is a probable and natural Account; since she was not one of those learned Women, who have reason to say, with *Sappho*,

> *Si mihi difficilis formam natura negavit,*
> *Ingenio formæ damna rependo meæ* (9).

(9) Ovidius Epist. Sapph. ver. 31.

> *To me what Nature has in Charms deny'd,*
> *Is well by* Wit's *more lasting Charms supply'd.*
> POPE.

[D] *Banicontius, who published some Books.*] It was the Name of his Grandfather. The Books he published are, *De privilegiis & immunitate Clericorum: De accusationibus & inquisitionibus: De appellationibus.* This I find in *Panzirolus.*

[E] *And married him to his Daughter* Novella.] The ancient practice of Adoption would not have permitted such a Marriage (10): And perhaps the Adoption of *Calderini* is only to be understood in this Sense, that *John Andreas* made him his Son in-law. It is said, that *Calderini* frequently consulted his Wife. *Is conjugem velut eruditis parentibus (Milentia,* the Wife of *John Andreas,* was a learned Woman*) ortam prudentem nactus sæpe ob sapientiam consulere consueverat* (11). But, if we may judge of other Points, in which he had recourse to this domestic Oracle, by that which *Calderini* has mentioned, we shall find nothing, which comes up to the Character *Christina de Pise* gives us of *Novella*: and most Women may be said to be as knowing, as she was. The Fact is this. "*Calderini* asked his Wife, one Day, whether he, who gives an Invitation, ought to send to the Persons invited, when the Hour of Eating is come: She answered, that this ought to be done to Ladies and Strangers, but not to others, unless they happen to be Persons of Importance." *Francis Hotomanus* tells us this Story in his ludicrous Way. *Verum enimvero medius fidius,* says he (12), *nequaquam inficiandum aut dubitandum est quin mulieres concilium dare possint, quando quidem (& dignam historiam & digito lignadam) refert* Joh. Calderinus Canonist. famossissimus, *quod semel consuluit suam uxorem, an convivator teneatur hora prandii mittere ad convivas, ut veniant; quæ sapienter & tanquam altera Sybilla respondit, ad fœminas & extraneos esse mittendum, qui se facile non ingerunt, sed non ad alios nisi essent graves personæ.* Johan. Calderin. in c. ult. de renunt. & post eum Ægid. Bell. in c. quidam col. 3. verf. tertio quæro. eo. ti. & Panormit. in c. cum inter universa' in fin de elect. & de hoc etiam per Collect. in cap. à crapula, Ext. de vit. & hon. cleric. & Bal. in proœm. Gregor col. 5. verf. quære, quidam scholaris. What most inclines me to believe, that *Calderini* was married to a Daughter of *John Andreas*, is, that one *John Calderini*, who caused the Tomb of *John Andreas* to be repaired, in the Year 1501, calls him his fourth Grand-Father, his *Atavus*; and says, that one *John Calderini* was his

(10) Octavium Claudius, antequam Neroni traderet, ne sororem is suam ducere videretur, Claudii & ipse filius adoptivus, in illam familiam adoptandum dedit.----- Claudius, before he gave Octavia in marriage to Nero, lest it should seem as if he married his Sister, being himself the adopted Son of Claudius, caused him to be first of all passed into another Family. Torrentius in Sueton. Claudii, cap. 3. ex Xiphili. & Zonara.

(11) Panzirol lib. 3. cap. 21.

(12) Adversus Italo-gallium Matharelli, pag. 214.

ANDREAS.

Church of the *Dominicans*. He wrote many Books [F]. Extravagant Commendations have been bestowed upon him [G]; but he is said to have been an egregious Plagiary [H]. We are told, that the excessive Smallness of his Stature made the Cardinals laugh heartily [I], at the Audience, which *Boniface* VIII. gave him in a full Consistory. It is said, that he foretold his Death a Year before it happened (k).

his third Grand-Father, his *Abavus* (13). I question whether the Adoption of these latter Ages has laid down such Degrees of Kindred, to the fifth Generation. And I scarce think, that, if *Mademoiselle de Gournai* had left a Family, her Descendants would, at this Day, simply and absolutely stile themselves, in a public Inscription, the Grand-Children, or Great-Grand-Children, of *Michael de Montagne*.

[F] *He wrote many Books.*] His first Work was a Gloss on the sixth Book of the Decretals. He was very young, when he composed it; afterwards he revised, and enlarged it. He wrote also some Glosses on the *Clementines*, and afterwards a Commentary on the *Decretals*, which he entituled *Novellæ*, for the Reason above-mentioned. He published a Commentary, *In regulas Sexti*, which he entituled *Mercuriales*; either because he wrote it on *Wednesdays*, or because he inserted his *Wednesdays* Disputations in it. He enlarged the *Speculum of Durandus*, in the Year 1347. I omit some other Treatises, which he published. It is pity he followed so closely the Method of the *Pyrrhonists*; for he very strongly confirmed his own Opinion, when he thought proper; but this he very seldom did; he chose rather to report the Sentiments of others, and to leave his Readers in the middle of a Controversy (14).

[G] *Extravagant Commendations have been bestowed upon him.*] In the Epitaph of his Daughter *Betina*, he is called *Archidoctor Decretorum* ――― *Arch-doctor of the Decretals*; in his own Epitaph, he is stiled *Rabbi Doctorum, lux, censor, normaque morum.* ――― *The Rabbi of the Doctors, the Light, Censor, and Rule of Manners.* It is reported, that Pope *Boniface* VIII. called him *Lumen Mundi* ------ *the Light of the World* (15).

[H] *He is said to have been an egregious Plagiary.*] Most of his Additions to the *Speculum of Durandus* were taken, Word for Word, out of a Work of *Oldradus* (16); insomuch, that *Baldus*, who discovered it, could not forbear calling him *a notorious Pilferer of other Men's Works, insignis alienorum fur* (17). This was the more inexcusable, because, in these very Additions, he proves *Durandus* to have been a great Plagiary (18). He is accused likewise of having stolen the Treatise *De Sponsalibus ac Matrimoniis*, composed by *John Anguisola* of *Cesena* (19).

[I] *The excessive Smallness of his Stature made the Cardinals laugh heartily.*] Some Decretals, they say, being suspected of Falsity, the University of *Bologne* deputed *James de Castello*, a little ugly Man, to *Boniface* VIII. He came into the Consistory, attended by a great many Persons. The Pope received him very graciously; and, thinking that he was still upon his Knees, ordered him, three times successively, to rise (20). The Deputy was so ashamed, that he had not a Word to say. A Cardinal said, That he was another *Zaccheus*; which raised a general Laugh. Many Writers affirm, that it was not *Castello*, but our *Andreas*, a Man of small Stature, and very ugly, who met with this Adventure (21).

ANDREAS (JOHN), Author of a Book, intituled *The Sect of Mahomet demolished*, was born a *Mahometan*, at *Xativa*, in the Kingdom of *Valencia*, and succeeded his Father in the Dignity of *Alfaqui*, in the same Town. He was converted to the Christian Faith, by a Sermon, which he heard in the Great Church of *Valencia*, on the Day of the Assumption of the Blessed Virgin, in 1488 (a). He demanded Baptism, and, remembering the Call of St *John* and St *Andrew*, he obtained the Name of *John-Andrew*, or *Andreas*. " Having received Holy Orders *(says he)* (b), " and, from an *Alfaqui*, and Slave of *Lucifer*, become a Priest and Minister of " CHRIST, I began, like St *Paul*, to preach and publish the contrary to what I " had falsly believed and affirmed; and, by the Assistance of the most high Lord, " first converted, and led to Salvation, several Souls, among the unbelieving Moors, " who would otherwise have lost them in Hell, under the Power of *Lucifer*. After " which I was invited by the most Catholic Princes, King *Ferdinand* and Queen " *Isabella*, to come and preach to the Moors of the Kingdom of *Granada*, which " they had conquered. By my preaching, and the Will of GOD (who would have " it so) a prodigious Number of Moors renounced *Mahomet*, and were converted " to CHRIST. A little after I was created a Canon by their Bounty, and was " again invited by the most Christian Queen *Isabella*, to come into *Arragon*, and " endeavour the Conversion of the Moors of that Kingdom; who, to the great Con- " tempt and Dishonour of our crucified Saviour, and the Peril of the Christian " Princes, persevere to this day in their Error; but this most pious Intention of Her " Highness was prevented, by her Death, from taking Effect." He adds, that, *to employ his leisure Hours, he translated, out of Arabic into the Language of* Arragon, *the whole Law of the Moors*, to wit, *The Koran*, and it's Glosses, and the Five Books of *Suna*. He did This at the Command of *Martin Garcia*, Bishop of *Barcelona*, and Inquisitor of *Arragon* (c). After he had finished this Undertaking, he wrote the Work, which I mentioned at the beginning [A]; and which has been thought tolerably good [B].

[A] *The Work, which I mentioned at the Beginning.*] I mean the Book, entituled, *The Sect of* Mahomet *demolished*. It contains twelve Chapters; in which the Author has collected *The fabulous Inventions, Impostures, Follies, Absurdities, Inconsistencies, Impossibilities, Lies, and Contradictions, which the Impostor* Mahomet, *to deceive the ignorant People, scattered up and down in the Books of the Sect; particularly in* The Koran; *which, he tells us, was revealed to him, in one Night, by an Angel, in the City of* Mecca; *though, upon the other Occasions, he affirmed, in Contradiction to himself, that he was twenty Years in composing it; which aforesaid Work I have intituled,* The Sect of Mahomet demolished. He informs us (2), that he composed this Work, *to the end, that Christians, not only the Wise and Under-* *standing, but the Simple and Ignorant likewise, may, on the one side, laugh at such Follies and Absurdities, and, on the other side, express their Concern for the Blindness and Perdition of this People.*

This Work, which was first published in *Spanish*, has been translated into several Languages; particularly into *French*, by *Guy de la Boderi*, from the *Italian*; and was published at *Paris*, for *Martin le Jeune*, in the Year 1574. in 8vo.

[B] *This Work* ――― *has been thought tolerably good.*] All the Writers against *Mahometanism* cite it frequently. Among others, see *Hornbeeck* in his *Disputatio de Muhammedismo* (3); *Hottinger*, in his *Historia Orientalis*, and *Samuel Schultetus*, in his *Ecclesia Mahummedana breviter delineata*.

[A] *Where*

ANDREAS.

ANDREAS (TOBIAS) Professor of History, and the *Greek* Tongue, at *Groningen*, was born at *Braunfels*, in the County of *Solms*, the Nineteenth of *August* 1604. His Father was Minister of the Count of *Solms-Braunfels*, and Overseer of the Churches dependant on That Count. His Mother was the Daughter of *John Piscator*, a famous Professor of Divinity at *Herborn*, in the County of *Nassau*. He went through his School-Learning at *Herborn*; and, then, studied Philosophy, in the same Place, under the Direction of *Alstedius*, and his Uncle *Piscator* (a); after which, he went to *Bremen*, where he lived seven Years [A]. He was one of the most constant Attendants on the Lectures of *Gerard de Neuville*, a Physician, and a Philosopher; and, as he aspired to the Office of Teaching publickly, he prepared himself for it, by reading private Lectures in Philosophy. He returned to his own Country in the Year 1628; and, after a short Stay, he went to *Groningen*, being invited thither by his good Patron *Henry Altingius*. He read there, for some time, private Lectures in all Parts of Philosophy: After which *Altingius* gave him his Children to instruct; and, when they had no longer occasion for a Tutor, he procured him the same Employment with a Prince *Palatine*; this continued three Years, which he spent partly at *Leyden*, and partly at the *Hague*, in the Court of the Prince of *Orange*. In the Year 1634, he was invited to *Groningen*, to succeed *James Gebhardus*, who had been Professor of History, and the *Greek* Tongue (b). He discharged the Duties of this Employ with an extraordinary Application, till his Death, which happened the Seventeenth of *October* 1676 (c). He had been Library-Keeper to the University, and a great Friend of *Des Cartes* [B]; which he testified, both during the Life [C], and after the Death, of that Illustrious Philosopher [D]. He wrote some Books in his Vindication, as will appear in the Remarks. He married the Daughter of a *Swede* (d), who, among other things, was famous for her Charity towards those, who suffered for the sake of the Gospel.

(a) *Son of the Professor of Divinity.*

(b) *See the Lives of the Professors of Groningen*, pag. 124.

(c) Witte, *Diar. Biograph.*

(d) Lewis de Geer.

[A] *Where he lived seven Years.*] My Reader ought not to have believed this, if the Author of the Lives of the Professors of *Groningen* had not been more exact in this Calculation, than he is, as to the time, when *Tobias Andreas* was at *Herborn*. It is strange, that a Corrector of the Press should overlook such Errors in the Space of five or six Lines, though the Avocations of the Author hindered him from perceiving them. You will find, in the Life of our *Andreas*, that he went to *Herborn*, in the Year cɪɔ ɪɔ cxvɪɪ; that he studied five Years, there, in the Schools, and one Year in Philosophy, and that he pursued the same Studies at *Bremen*, for seven Years; and that, afterwards, having taken a turn home, he came to *Groningen*, in the Year cɪɔ ɪɔ cxxvɪɪɪ. There is nothing written in Cyphers; the Errrors, probably, were in the Copy. *Paul Freberus* has very innocently transcribed it (1), without perceiving any Error in the Calculation.

[B] *A great Friend of Des Cartes.*] He heartily served him in his Law Suit with *Martin Schoockius*, Professor of Philosophy at *Groningen*. This Professor was prosecuted by *Des Cartes* for Scandal, in having publickly accused him of Atheism. Though *Des Cartes* had not seen our *Andreas* more than once in his Life, he recommended his Cause to him, perceiving, that he was very much in his Interest. The *French* Ambassador, Monf. *de la Thuillerie*, and *Des Cartes's* Friends acted on one Hand (2); the Enemies of *Voëtius*, at *Groningen*, acted on the other; and by this means *Des Cartes* had Justice done him. His Accuser acknowledged his Innocence (3), and was thereupon acquitted; which was a scandalous Indulgence, and a bad Example: For, if they had made him suffer the Punishment of Retaliation, as he very well deserved, it would have restrained, in some measure, the boldness of those seditious Writers, who so readily, and so rashly, accuse so many honest Men of Atheism. "*Des Cartes* wrote, the Twenty sixth "of *May*, 1645, to Mr *Andreas*, to thank him for "his good Offices, and to desire him to return his "most humble thanks to the Judges. Seeing how "mildly his Adversary had been treated, though he "deserved to be punished as a Calumniator; "he nevertheless acknowledged, that the Judges had "given him all the Satisfaction he desired, or could "lawfully pretend to. For, *said he* (4), *to the Ma- "gistrates of Utrecht*, private Persons have no right "to demand either the Death of their Enemies, or "that they should suffer in their Honour or Estates. "It is sufficient they are indemnified by the Judges. "Any thing farther does not concern them, but the "Public alone." The Text of my Remark necessarily obliging me to mention the good Offices done by *Andreas* to *Des Cartes*; I believed the Reader would be pleased to know, in general, the Issue of this Affair, without turning to another Page.

[C] *Which he testified during the Life, &c.*] We have just seen a Proof of this. I add, that he favoured *Des Cartes's* Disciples, and procured him as many Followers as he could. It was by his Advice, that *Claubergius* became a *Cartesian* (5); which was a glorious and useful Victory for the whole Party.

[D] *And after the Death of that illustrious Philosopher.*] He wrote in his Defence, against a Professor of *Leyden*, whose Name was *Revius*, and published a vigorous Reply, in the Year 1653, entituled, *Methodi Cartesianæ assertio opposita Jacobii Revii - - - - Præf. Methodi Cartesianæ considerationi Theologicæ.* The second Part of this Answer came out the following Year. He wrote also, in the Year 1653, against Mr *Regius*, in Vindication of the Remarks, which *Des Cartes* had made on a *Programma*, containing an Explication of the human Mind (6). He taught, in his own House, the *Cartesian* Philosophy, though his Profession did not require it of him, and even when Age had very much impaired his Strength. Mr *Des Marets* informed me of these Particulars, on account of a *Swiss* Student in Divinity, who durst not attend the Philosophical Lectures of *Andreas*, for fear it should be known in his own Country, and should prove an Obstacle to his Promotion to the Ministry. " Nec defuit unus ex illis, cujus nomini "parco, bene alias doctus, & in Philosophiam Car- "tesianam valde propensus, qui, dum hic esset, pro- "fessus est, non audere se frequentare Collegia Car- "tesiana Cl. Tobiæ Andreæ (qui, Clinicus licet, "quod summopere doleo, Deumque veneror ut illi "suas vires restituat, ea solet habere in superpondium "suæ professionis, nec enim ad philosophiam, sed "ad linguam Græcam & Historias est vocatus) ne "hoc in sua patria resciretur, & suæ promotioni obes- "set (7). — Nor was there wanting one, *among "them, whose Name I forbear to mention*; *a Man, "otherwise, of good Learning*; *who, during his abode "here, declared, that he durst not frequent the Car- "tesian School of Tobias Andreas, lest it should be "known in his own Country, and hinder his Pro- "motion*: *I mean the Cartesian School of That An- "dreas*; *who, tho' almost Bed-rid (which I am very "much concerned for, and beg of God to restore him "to his Strength) yet continues to teach a Science, "over and above his Profession*; *which requires of him "a Knowledge of History, and the Greek Tongue, not "of Philosophy."*

(1) *Theatr. Vivorum Illustr.* pag. 2558.

Tu ex offensive Indelgence towards him, who accused him of Atheism.

(2) *The Condemnation of Schoockius fell indirectly upon Voëtius.*

(3) *See the Life of Des Cartes by M. Baillet*, Tom. 2. p. 212. & seq. ad annum 1645.

(4) Tom. 3. *of his Letters* pag. 17. ap. Baillet, ubi supra, pag. 257.

(5) Claubergius Epist. Dedicat. Logicæ.

(6) *This Piece is intituled, Brevis Replicatio brevi Explicationi Mentis Humanæ Dn. Henrici Regii reposita.*

(7) Marestius, in Judicio de Theologia pacificæ Wittichii, *printed in* 1671.

ANDREINI.

ANDREINI (ISABELLA) born at *Padua*, was, towards the end of the XVIth and beginning of the XVIIth Century, one of the best Actresses of *Italy*. This was not the only Qualification, for which she was admired; she was likewise a compleat Poetess. This we learn, not only from the Praises, which many learned Men, and great Wits, have bestowed upon her, (tho' this would be but a doubtful Proof) but also by the Works, which she published. The *Intenti* (a) of *Pavia* thought it an Honour to them to admit her into their Society; and, to testify her Acknowledgment, she never forgot, among her Titles, That of *Academica Intenta*; but, without doubt, she looked upon it as an Honour done to her. Her Titles were, *Isabella Andreini, Comica Gelosa, Academica Intenta, detta l'Accesa*. In one thing she excelled the most excellent Actresses; for she was a beautiful Woman; so that, on the Stage, she charmed, at once, the Eyes and Ears of the Audience [*A*]. Cardinal *Cinthio Aldobrandini*, Nephew to *Clement* VIII, had a great Esteem for her, as appears by many Poems, which she composed for him, and by the Epistle Dedicatory of her Works. She came into *France*, and was graciously received by their Majesties, and Persons of the first Quality at Court (b). She composed many Sonnets in their Praise, which are to be seen in the second Part of her Poems. She died, at *Lyons*, the Tenth of *June* 1604, of a Miscarriage, in the Forty second Year of her Age. Her Husband, *Francis ANDREINI*, buried her in the same City; and honoured her with an Epitaph [*B*], which imports that she was very pious and chaste. Since That, he discovered, how greatly he regretted [*C*], and esteemed her. The Death of this excellent Actress set all *Parnassus* in Tears. Nothing but Funeral Elegies appeared, in *Latin* and *Italian*. Many of them were prefixed to her Poems, in the Edition of *Milan*, 1605. Nor did they forget the ingenious Inscription, made in her Praise, whilst she was still alive, by *Erycius Puteanus*, at that Time Professor at *Milan* (c). Besides her *Sonnets, Madrigals, Songs*, and *Eclogues*, there is a Pastoral of her Composition, intituled *Myrtilla*. There are extant likewise some of her Letters, which were printed at *Venice*, in the Year 1610. She sung well, and play'd admirably on several Instruments; she was not ignorant of Philosophy (d), and understood *French* and *Spanish*.

(a) So the Academicians of Pavia are called.

(b) See the Epistle Dedicatory of the second Part of her Poems.

(c) See Remark [A].

(d) See the Verses wrote in her Praise, prefixed to her Poems.

[*A*] *She charmed, at once, the Eyes and Ears of the Audience.*] This supplied Flatterers with many Thoughts. These Words were wrote under her Picture, " Hoc Histricæ eloquentiæ caput, lector admi- " raris? quid si auditor fies? —— *Do you admire*, " *Reader, this Head of Theatric Eloquence? What* " *would you have done, had you been her Hearer?* " The *Antitheses* and Witticisms of *Erycius Puteanus* turn chiefly upon this.

Hanc vides, & hanc audis;
Tu disputa, Argus esse malis, ut videas,
An Midas, ut audias.
Tantum enim sermonem vultus,
Quantum sermo vultum commendat.
Quorum alterutro æterna esse potuisset,
Cum vultum omnibus simulacris emendatiorem,
Et sermonem omni Suada venustiorem possideat.

You see her; and you hear her;
Consider now, whether you would be an Argus, *to see,*
Or a Midas, *to hear.*
For her Looks as much recommend her Voice,
As her Voice her Looks.
Either of which might have rendered her Immortal;
Since no Painting can equal the Charms of her
Face;
No Music the Harmony of her Voice.

[*B*] *Her Husband —— honoured her with an Epitaph.*] If it be but to undeceive those, who talk so much of the Rigour of the Church, in regard to the Burial of Players in Holy Ground, I shall copy the Epitaph of *Isabella Andreini*, in which her Profession, as an Actress, is mentioned next to her Hopes of the Resurrection

D. O. M.

Isabella Andreina, Patavina, mulier magna virtute prædita, honestatis ornamentum, maritalique pudicitiæ decus, ore facunda, mente fecunda, religiosa, pia, Musis amica, & artis Scenicæ caput, hic resurrectionem expectat.

Ob abortum obiit 4. Idus Junii 1604. annum
agens 42.
Franciscus Andreinus mœstissimus posuit.

Isabella Andreini, *of* Pavia, *a Lady remarkable for Virtue, Honour, and Conjugal Fidelity, Eloquent, and Ingenious; Religious, and Devout; A Friend to the Muses, and Head of the Theatric Art; lies Here, in expectation of the Resurrection.*

She died of a Miscarriage, June 10, 1604.
Ætat. 42.

This Monument was erected by Francis Andreini, *her afflicted Husband.*

You will see, in the next Remark, how tenderly she was beloved by her Husband *Francis Andreini*.

[*C*] *Since That, he discover'd, how much he regretted her.*] The Preface to his *Bravure del Capitano Spavento*, informs us, that he was born at *Pistoia*, and that, whilst he was among the Company of Comedians *Gelosi*, he took great delight in acting the Part of a Braggadocio, He took upon him the Title of *Capitan Spavento da Vall' Inferna, Captain Bluff of the Infernal Vale*; and left off personating the part of a Lover, in which he had chiefly signaliz'd himself: *io lasciai di recitare la parte mia principale, laquelle era quella dell' innamorato*. This Company of Players acquir'd a surprizing Reputation; which began to decay after the Death of *Isabella Andreini*. Her Husband thought it best from a Player to turn Author; and, for the Subject of his Works, he made choice of That, in which he had distinguish'd himself on the Stage, I mean the Rhodomontades of a *Captain Bluff*. He publish'd some Dialogues, or *Ragionamenti*, in Prose, with the Title above-mentioned. The 4th Edition, which I make use of, is of *Venice*, 1625, in Quarto; but, the Licence being dated in the Year 1607, the first Edition ought to be placed in That Year. The Complaints of the Shepherd *Corinto alla defunta sua Fillide* (he calls her his Wife) *& alla sua Bosccareccia Sampogna*, are prefixed to the Book. Never did Lover utter more tender Expressions, or complain more strongly of the inexorable Rigor of Destiny. They are *Andreini*'s Lamentation for the Death of his *Isabella*; the following Words put it past doubt:
" Finito che fu quel termine, e venuto meno il vi-
" vere d' Isabella mia dilettissima consorte (la quale
" fu lume e splendore di quella virtuosa e honorata
" compagnia) fui da molti amici miei consigliato à
" scrivere alcuna cosa e donarla alla stampa per lasciar
" qualche memoria di me, e per seguitare l'honorato
" grido della moglie mia, la quale haveva lasciato al
" mondo

ANDRELINUS.

"mondo cantanta sua gloria e con tanto suo honore il suo bellizzimo Canzoniero, la sua bellissima Mirtilla Favola Boscareccia, e il compendio delle sue bellissime lettere (1). —— *After the Death of my dearest Consort Isabella (who was the Light and Ornament of this ingenious and honourable Company), I was advised by many of my Friends to write, or publish something, to perpetuate my Memory, and to emulate the Reputation of my Wife, who left behind her, so much to her Glory, and so much to her Honour, her beautiful Collection of Sonnets, her Pastoral of Myrtilla, and the Abridgement of her beautiful Letters.*" There is one *John Baptist* ANDREINI, who wrote a Tragedy, entituled *La Florinda*; printed at *Milan*, in the Year 1606.

ANDRELINUS (P. FAUSTUS) born at *Forli*, in *Italy*, was a long time Professor of Poetry in the University of *Paris*. *Lewis* XII. made him Poet Laureat (*a*). I know not, whether Queen *Anne* of *Bretagne*, or some other Queen, honoured him with her special Protection; but I am not ignorant, that *Erasmus*, who was intimately acquainted with him, says, that he was not only Laureat to the King, but to the Queen likewise [*A*]. He was not contented with Poetry; He wrote likewise some *Moral, and Proverbial, Letters* in Prose, which have been printed several times. They were printed at *Strasburg*, in the Year 1517, and again, from the second Revisal of the Author, in the Year 1519 (*b*). *Beatus Rhenanus* prefixed a Preface to them, in which he greatly commends them [*B*]. *John Arboreus*, a Divine of *Paris*, wrote a Commentary upon them. Most of his Poetry consists of Distichs; they have been printed, with a Commentary of *Jodocus Badius Ascensius*, being translated, Verse for Verse, into *French* by a Poet of *Paris*, whose Name was *Stephen Privé* (*c*). This Translation came out in 1604, and is only fit to bring the Original into Contempt. *John Paradin* had before turned (*d*) into *French Tetrastics* about an hundred Distichs, which *Andrelinus* inscribed to John Ruzé, Treasurer-General of the Finances of King *Charles* VIII, to return him Thanks for a large and honourable Pension, which that Prince caused to be paid him with extraordinary Care; and which did not deserve the Contempt this pleasant Poet designed to throw upon it, by leaving us room to think he was paid for his Verses by the Quarter, or the Hundred (*e*) [*C*]. The Poems of *Andrelinus* have been inserted in the first Volume of the *Delights of the Italian Poets*; tho' good Judges set

[*A*] *Erasmus, who knew him very intimately, says, that he was not only Laureat to the King, but to the Queen likewise.*] These are his Words. "Faustus "Andrelinus Foroliviensis, poëta non solum laureatus, "verum etiam regius, atque etiam, si diis placet, re-"gineus, vetus congerro meus, qui plus quam triginta "jam annos in celeberrima Parisiorum Academia poëti-"cen docet, in carmine quod de Pavimento Parisiensi "inscripsit, adagionem (*Syracusana Mensa*) in Angloe "derivavit, Mensa, inquiens, Britanna placet (1). "—— *My old Friend,* Faustus Andrelinus, *of* Forli, "*Poet-Laureat both to the King and Queen, who has* "*taught Poetry more than thirty Years in the famous* "*University of* Paris, *in his Poem de* Parisiensi Pavi-"mento, *applies the Adage* Syracusana Mensa *to* "*the* English, *saying,* Give me a British Table". There are, among *Erasmus's* Letters (2), two or three Billets, which *Andrelinus* wrote to him, in such a Laconick Style, that *Brutus's* Letters, if compared with them, would pass for long ones. *Erasmus*, who answer'd him in the same Style, is somewhat more diffuse, when he desires him to promote the Sale of his *Adagies* (3); and when he describes the Pleasures of *England*, to induce him to take a Journey into that Country (4). I shall, by the way, take notice of an ill Custom, which prevails among Authors, of denoting the time, when they write, by such general Words only as, *Nunc, jam, &c.* whereas they ought precisely to mark the Year; for, besides that some Books take up an Author several Years, or are not publish'd till a long time after they are finish'd, are there not many printed several times? How, then, can a Reader know, at what time a Book was written, when he meets only with these Words, *hoc anno, nunc*, and the like? *Erasmus* speaks of *Andrelinus* as one, who was then alive, and had taught Poetry at *Paris*, for the space of 30 Years. This he says, in a Book printed in 1546; there is no Date to the Preface; but the Epistle Dedicatory is dated the 13th of *August* 1528. Wou'd not this induce one to believe, that *Andrelinus* was alive in the Year 1528? and must we not infer from hence, that the greatest Men, when they revise their Works for a new Edition, leave a great many things in them, which cease to be true? I have observed this Fault in the last Edition of the large History of *Mezerai*.

[*B*] *Beatus Rhenanus* —— *greatly commends them.*] These are *Gesner's* Words. "Beatus Rhenanus, in "præfatione, commendat has epistolas tanquam eru-"ditas, lepidas, & utiles; etsi enim hic Author "(inquit) in nonnullis opusculis genuino poëtarum "more lasciviusculus sit, hic tamen integrum ac mo-"destum oratorem agit (5). —— Beatus Rhenanus, in "his Preface, commends these Epistles, as being learn-"ed, entertaining, and useful. For" "Tho' this Au-"thor (says he) like other Poets, is a little too obscene, "in some of his Works; yet here he assumes the per-"fect and modest Orator.

[*C*] *By leaving us room to think, he was paid for his Verses by the Quarter or the Hundred.*] M. Baillet proves it by these four Verses, translated from the Latin of *Andrelinus*, by Paradin (6).

Croissez mes vers, soyez en plus grand nombre,
Car c'est aux frais & salaries du Roi.
Seure richesse, empeschant tout encombre,
Exige vers en copieux arroi.

A fresh Recruit, my Muse, of Numbers bring;
'Tis at a Monarch's sole Expence you sing.
The sure Reward, which bids each Care retire,
With copious Fewel feeds the Poet's Fire.

We meet with a remarkable Instance in the Tenth Eclogue of *Andrelinus*; I mean of a Poet, who, far from complaining of the Ingratitude of the Age, or finding fault with the Muses for not taking care to maintain those, who engage in their Service, acknowledges that he had a large Pension, and that, when he recited his Poem on the Conquest of *Naples*, before *Charles* VIII, that Prince presented him with a Bag of Money, which he had much a-do to carry upon his Shoulders.

Dum stupeo totus visu defixus in isto,
Jupiter ecce venit magno stipatus honore,
Ipse olim vultus inter nutritus agrestes.
Admiror primo aspectu; mox poplite flexo
Ante ipsum quæsita Jovem modulamina fundo;
Scilicet ut bello claram expugnavit aperto
Parthenopem, patrios victorque rediit in agros,
Quamvis Hesperio vetitus foret orbe regressus.
Nescio qua nostri captus dulcedine cantus
Ipse fuit, fulvi saccum donavit & æris;
Vix istis delatum humeris, cunctosque per annos
Pensio larga datur, qualem non lentus habebat
Tityrus umbrosis resonans sua gaudia sylvis.

Whilst on this Sight, with fixt Regard, I gaze,
See Jupiter in splendid Pomp appear;

Himself

ANDRELINUS.

no great Value on them [D]. His Death is placed in the Year 1518 [E]. The Letters, which he wrote, by way of Proverbs, were thought worthy of a new Impression at *Helmstadt*, in the Year 1662, after the Edition of *Cologne* of the Year 1509 (f). The Morals of this Author, tho' none of the best, were not taken notice of, because he was an Ornament to the University of *Paris*. He was so happy, that the Liberty he took of offending the Divines brought him into no Trouble. *Erasmus* informs us of these Particulars [F].

Note, That I have left this whole Article, in this Edition, just as it stood in the first, tho' I have been informed, that it stood in need of Correction in several Places. I thought it would be more modest to give the Corrections, which have been since imparted to me, by themselves [G]. You'll find them in the Remark [G].

(f) Morhof. Polyhist. pag. 258.

Himself once conversant with Rustic Looks;
At first, in Admiration lost, I stand;
Then, on my Knee, present the Verse, required;
The Verse, which paints Parthenope destroy'd,*
And from Hesperia † Charles's blest Return,
In vain forbidden, to his native Land.
Pleas'd with the Numbers, which his Conquests sung,
A Load of Gold the generous Prince bestow'd,
Too weighty for the sinking Bard to bear;
A Pension too, larger than what of old,
Reclin'd at Ease, gay Tityrus ‖ enjoy'd,
Courting his Muse beneath the Beechen Shade.

* *Naples.*
† *Italy.*
‖ VIRGIL, under the Character of TITYRUS.

[In this Poem, *Andrelinus* says, that the Brand (the *Stigmata*) of *Charles* VIIIth's Victories, appeared still imprinted on the Brows of the Italians. *Brantome*, who, instead of *vera Stigmata*, read *vera Stemmata*, makes this Poet say, that the Victories and warlike Actions of *Charles* VIII appeared on the Brows of the *Italians*, as so many Crowns or Laurels. See *Brantome's Illustrious Frenchmen*, Tom. 4. pag. 25. REM. CRIT.]

[D] *Good Judges set no great Value on them.*] *Vossius* mentions three Authors, who abounded in Words without Meaning (7); the first is the Orator *Anaximenes*; the second is *Longolius*, who was likewise an Orator, and the third is the Poet *Andrelinus*. As to the first he says, that *Theocritus of Chios*, seeing him about to make a Speech, cried out, *A River of Words begins to flow with but a Drop of Sense.* Ἀρχέται λέξεων μὲν πόταμος, νοῦ δὲ σταλαγμός. He says, upon the Authority of *Francis Lusinus*, that *Constantin Lascaris* passed the same Judgment upon *Longolius*; and that *Andrelinus* was still more liable to Censure, in whose Poems there was wanting but one Syllable, as *Erasmus* very ingeniously observed. This Syllable was νοῦς, which signifies *Sense, Understanding, Wit*. If I knew where this Passage of *Erasmus*, so little agreeable to the great Compliments and Praises he bestows upon *Andrelinus* (8), is to be found, I would inform the Reader. I make no doubt, that the Judgment, which *Julius Scaliger* passed on the Poet *Faustus*, relates to our *Andrelinus*, rather than *Gerhardus Faustus*. " *Fausti facilitas, says he* (9), " *viventis in scribendo secundo plausu excepta est;* " *scholas tamen sapit illa juniorum, à qua nihil aliud* " *quam hoc ipsum expectes.* ----- *The Knack of* " *Writing, which Faustus, when alive, was Master of,* " *was received with Favour and Applause; yet it sa-* " *vours of the Schools of Youth; from which you can* " *expect nothing farther.*"

[E] *His Death is placed in the Year 1518*] I shall not cite *Konig's Bibliotheque*, nor the Letters of the learned *Reinesius* to *Dauminus* (10). I can produce a cotemporary Writer, who, in a Letter, dated the sixth of *March*, 1518, takes notice, that That Year had carried off several learned Men. " *Hic annus* " *multos eximios viros tui similes absumpsit, Marcum* " *Musurum Romæ, jam Archiepiscopum designatum,* " *& ante hunc Paleotum Camillum, Lutetiæ Fau-* " *stum immortalitate dignum* (11). ——*Several great* " *Men, like yourself, have died this Year; particu-* " *larly, Marcus Musurus, Archbishop Elect, at Rome,* " *and, before him, Paleotus Camillus; at Paris, Fau-* " *stus, worthy of Immortality.*" It cannot be concluded, from these Words, that *Andrelinus* died in the Year 1518; for it is certain, that *Musurus* died in the Year 1517 (12).

[F] *Erasmus informs us of these Particulars.*] The Reader will not be displeased to see the Original. " *Parisiensis Academiæ candorem ac civilitatem jam* " *olim sum admiratus, quæ tot annos Faustum tulerit,*

(7) Voss. Instit. Poet. pag. 2.

(8) See the 21st Letter of the 7th Book of *Erasmus*.

(9) Jul. Cæs. Scalig. de Poetic. l. 6. pag. 716. See Baillet, ubi supra.

(10) Pag. 15.

(11) Erasm. Epist. 20. l. 3. ad Petrum Barbirium. See also Epist. 24. lib. 2.

(12) See the Rem. (1) in his Art.

" *nec tulerit solum, verum etiam aluerit evexeritque.* " *Cum Faustum dico, multa tibi succurrunt quæ no-* " *lim literis committere. Quæ petulantia solitus est* " *ille in Theologorum ordinem debacchari? Quàm* " *non casta erat istius professio? Neque cuiquam ob-* " *scurum erat qualis esset vita. Tantum malorum* " *Galli doctrinæ hominis condonabant, quæ tamen* " *ultra mediocritatem non admodum erat progressa* " (13). ——*I have long wondered at the Good nature* " *and Courtesy of the University of* Paris, *which bore,* " *so many Years, with* Faustus; *and not only bore* " *with, but supported, and advanced, him. When* " *I mention* Faustus, *many things occur to you* (14), " *which I avoid committing to Writing. How viru-* " *lently was he wont to inveigh against the sacred* " *Order? How far from Chast was his Profession?* " *Nor was his manner of Life a Secret to any one.* " *The French, however, pardoned his bad Qualities,* " *in respect to his Learning, which yet did not very* " *far exceed the Bounds of Mediocrity.*" You may observe, that *Erasmus's* Letters to *Andrelinus*, and those he wrote to others concerning him, are written in a very different Strain. However, it cannot be denied, that he sometimes commends him in his Letters to other Persons (15).

(13) Erasm. Epist. 20. lib. 21. pag. 1090.

(14) He writes to Lodovicus Vives.

(15) See Remark [A].

[G] *Give the Corrections, which have been imparted to me, by themselves.*] The following Remarks were communicated to me by Monsieur *de la Monnoie*. I. Instead of *P. Faustus*, it should be *Publius Faustus*; at length; least any one should think that *P.* signifies *Petrus, Paulus*, or some such other Christian Name. It is probable, that *Faustus* assumed the Name of *Publius* at *Rome*, in imitation of those Academicians, great Lovers of Antiquity, of whom *Pomponius Lætus* was the head. II. It ought not to be said, in a Dictionary, that *Faustus* was only Professor of Poetry in the University of *Paris*. He taught, there, not only Poetry, but Rhetoric, and the Doctrine of the Sphere, and even explained the *Psalms of David*. III. It was at *Rome*, long before the Reign of *Lewis* XII, that *Faustus*, who was not then Twenty two Years of Age, carried the Laurel (16). His Love Verses divided into four Books, entituled, *Livia*, which was his Mistress's Name, appeared so fine to the *Roman Academy*, that they adjudged him the Prize of the *Latin Elegy*; which was the Reason why, when he printed his *Livia* in 8vo, at *Paris*, in the Year 1490, and his three Books of Elegies, four Years after, in the same City, he filled himself *Poëta Laureatus*, and afterwards *Regius*, and *Reginæus*, with respect to *Charles* VIII, *Lewis* XII, and Queen *Anne*. IV. To find the thirty Years that *Faustus* was Professor at *Paris*, we must suppose, that *Erasmus* made this Computation in the Year 1517. By this means we go back as far as 1487, at which Time, or thereabout, *Faustus* settled at *Paris*. This Chronology is so much the more certain, because there was an Edition of *Erasmus's Adagies* (17), in 1517, which he mentions in the *Chronici* as *insideas*. V. *Faustus* did not compose above two hundred Disticks, and consequently they were but a very small part of his Poems; for, besides the four Books of his Love Verses, and the three Books of Miscellaneous Elegies, which I have mentioned, there are twelve Eclogues of his writing, printed in 8vo, in the Year 1546, in the Collection of Thirty eight Bucolic Poets, published by *Oporinus*. *Faustus* promised several other Pieces in Prose and in Verse; *Ten moral Satires; an hundred Epistles;* and *the Christian Advent;* (which, perhaps, is the same with what he calls, in another place, *a Treatise of the true Religion;*) *a Dialogue on the Sphere;* and *Observations on the Latin Tongue.*

(16) The ceremony was performed by Alexander Albertus, whom I have quoted.

(17) Erasmus's Fault, as I have observed in the Remark [A] of this, that he did not shew the Chronology in the last Editions.

I shall

ANDRINOPLE. ANDROMACHE.

I should certainly have supplied the Defects of my Article of ANDRELINUS, if I had had the Works of this Author; but, not being able to procure them, I was obliged to follow those, who have mentioned him, without consulting them; and thus *the Blind lead the Blind*. It is a great Misfortune, not to have all the necessary Books, in the Composition of such a Dictionary, as this; but it is a Misfortune, I cannot avoid, in the Situation I am at present in.

ANDRINOPLE, or ADRIANOPLE, a City of *Thrace*. It owes it's Name to the Madness of the Emperor *Hadrian*. *Moreri* mentions this; but very confusedly [*A*]. It has been said, that this Town was built by *Orestes*, and bore his Name [*B*]. It was also called *Uscudama* (a). The two *Latin* Verses, quoted by *Moreri*, serve only to shew, that he was a careless Writer [*C*]. I omit what he further says of *Andrinople*: The Reader may have Recourse to his Dictionary.

(a) *See the Roman* *h* [C].

[*A*] *Moreri mentions this; but very confusedly.*] These are his Words. "Some Pagan Authors say, "that this Prince, having been cured there of a Drop- "sy, by invoking the mad *Orestes*, took delight in "beautifying this City." These Pagan Authors are not *Spartian*, and *Ammianus Marcellinus*, the two cited by *Moreri*; and I am very much mistaken, if we must not reduce them to *Ælius Lampridius* alone. Let us see then how the latter expresses himself. "Et "Orestam quidem urbem Adrianus suo nomini vin- "dicari jussit, eo tempore quo furore coeperat labo- "rare, ut ex responso quum id dictum esset ut in "furiosi alicujus domum vel nomen irreperet. Nam "ex eo emollitam insaniam ferunt, per quam multos "senatores occidi jusserat (1)." If we compare these Words with Those of *Moreri*; we shall find him guilty of three, or four, gross Mistakes. I. It is not true, that *Hadrian* was cured in the City of *Adrianople*. II. It is not true, that his Distemper was a Dropsy. III. It is not true, that he recovered his Health, by invoking *Orestes*. IV. It is not true, that he took delight in beautifying This City, after his Recovery. *Lampridius* only says, "That *Hadrian*, being fallen "into a Phrenzy, commanded the City *Oresta* to "be called by his Name, in Obedience to an Oracle, "which advised him to seize on the House, or Name, "of some Mad-Man;" and we are told, that by this Means his Fitts of Madness went off.

[*B*] *That it was founded by Orestes, and bore his Name.*] I shall cite only *Lampridius* for this. "Et "Orestem quidem ferunt, says he (2), non unum "simulachrum Dianæ, nec uno in loco posuisse, sed "multa in multis. Posteaquam se apud tria flumina "circa Hebrum ex responso purificavit, etiam Orestam "condidit civitatem, quam sæpe cruentari hominum "sanguine necesse est. Et Orestam quidem urbem "Adrianus suo nomini vindicari jussit, &c. —— "They say likewise, that Orestes erected, not one "Statue alone of *Diana*, or in one Place only, but "many in several. And after that, in Obedience "to the Oracle, he had purified himself at three "Streams, near Hebrus, he built, likewise, the Ci- "ty Oresta, which must frequently be polluted with "human Blood. This City, Oresta, Hadrian ordered "to be called by his own Name, &c." I have set down this Passage at length, to shew what City of *Adrianople* is here meant. The Emperor *Hadrian* gave his Name to several Towns at a great Distance from each other (3): But it is plain, that *Lampridius* meant That of *Thrace*; and that *Orestes* built it, where the *Hebrus* receives two other Rivers. Note, that *Pinedo* makes *Lampridius* say, that *Heliogabalus* built a Town near the *Hebrus*, which he called *Oresta*; and that, afterwards, *Hadrian* gave it his own Name (4). This is an Instance of the usual Distraction of Mind, from which the most learned Writers are not free.

[*C*] *The two Latin Verses, quoted by Moreri —— shew, that he was a careless Writer.*] These are his Words. " It is said to have been built, first of all, by "*Orestes*, who called it *Oresta*; which Name was af- "terwards changed into That of *Uscada* or *Uscudama*.

Tandemque Uscudamæ mutato nomine prisco
Matricida suo de nomine dixit Orestam.

At length the Parricide Orestes, changing it's ancient Name Uscudama, called it Oresta, after his own Name.

These two Verses prove quite the contrary to what *Moreri* produces there for. They evidently prove, that *Orestes* found This Town with the Name *Uscudama*; and that he afterwards changed it to his own. *Ammianus Marcellinus*, cited by *Moreri*, at Lib. 4. (5), informs us, in the fourth Chapter of the Twenty seventh Book, that *Adrianople* had been called *Uscudama*. *Post banc Æmimuntus Hadrianopolim habet, quæ dicebatur Uscudama.*

(1) Lamprid. in Antonino Heliogabalo, pag. 809.

(2) Id. Ib.

(3) Quum titulos in operibus non amaret, multas civitates Adrianopolis appellavit, ut ipsam Carthaginem & Athenarum partem. Spartianus in Adriano cap. 20. *See Ibrum's* Ortelius's Thesaurus Geographicus.

(4) Pinedo, in Steph. Byzant. pag. 211. n. 45.

(5) The thirteen first Books of this History are lost.

ANDROMACHE, Wife of the Valiant *Hector*, was the Daughter of *Ætion*, King of *Thebes* in *Cilicia* (a). She was advantageously married on all accounts; for, besides that her Husband was accounted the Bulwark of his Country, and the greatest Support of the Throne, he proved very kind to her; and they say, that she was free from the Disquiets, which commonly attend the Wives of Great Heroes; I mean, that he ever preserved his Conjugal Fidelity towards her [*A*]. *Euripides* denies this; but, at the same Time, he informs us, that it did not in the least disturb the Happiness of this Lady; her Disposition being very easy and complaisant in this respect

(a) Homer. Il. lib. 6. This Cilicia was not far from Troy.

[*A*] *Hector —— ever preserved his conjugal Fidelity towards her.*] *Andromache*, in some Verses of *Euripides*, declares, that she loves the very Mistresses of her Husband, to please him, and that she gave suck to his Bastards (1). The Scholiast upon this says, that *Anaxicrates* gave out, that *Hector* left behind him two legitimate Sons (2), who escaped from the Hands of the *Grecians*, and a Bastard (3), who was taken at *Troy* (4), but he pretends, that *Euripides* and *Anaxicrates* advance a Falshood; and maintains against them, that *Hector* never had a Bastard, and that it must be very inconsiderate to advance the contrary. *Ovid* represents *Hector* as a good Husband; who overlooked every thing, that was disagreeable, in his Wife.

Felix Andromache, certo bene nupta marito!
Utor ad exemplum fratris habenda sui (5).

Happy Andromache, *who justly art
Possessed of a firm and loyal Heart.*

*A Faith like Hers Thou hast beheld in me,
And Hector's Virtue should have shined in Thee.*

Mr J. COOPER.

Thus he makes OEnone, the Wife of *Paris*, express herself. In another Place he says, that every one thought *Andromache* too tall; but that she seemed to her Husband to be of a middle Stature.

Omnibus Andromache visa est spatiosior æquo.
Unus, qui modicam diceret, Hector erat.

Colomies has rightly observed (7), that *Marcerus*, in his Notes on the fourth Book of *Dictys Cretensis*, should not have said, *That Antiquity knew nothing of Hector's loving any Woman beside his Wife, or that he had Children besides those she brought him.* *Marcerus* had forgot the Historian *Anaxicrates*, and the Poet *Euripides*. But *Colomies*, who farther observes, that this Historian was unknown to *Vossius*, should have told us, that he had from *Mezeriac* the

(1) Eurip. in Androm.

(2) Amphineus, and Scamandrius.

(3) Called Palæmorus.

(4) Anaxicrat. Argolicor. lib. 2.

(5) Ovidius, in Epist. Oenon. ad Paridem, vers. 107.

(6) Id. lib. 2. de Arte Amandi.

(7) Bibl. choisi. pag. 109.

VOL. I. O o o o Passages

ANDROMACHE.

spect [B]. The Death of *Hector* proved, therefore, a terrible Blow to *Andromache*; yet she survived it, as well as the Grief she conceived, some time after, upon the taking of *Troy*, upon the Loss of her dear Son *Astyanax*, who was thrown headlong from the Top of a Tower, and her own Slavery. She fell to the Lot of a Master, who, tho' of a fierce and bloody Disposition, used her very kindly. *Pyrrhus*, the cruel Son of the cruel *Achilles*, proved gentle and tractable towards *Andromache*; shared his Bed with her [C], and made her Condition so happy, that the beautiful *Hermione*, whom he married some time after, grew very jealous at it (*b*). After the Death of This Prince, or even in his Life-time, *Andromache* married *Helenus* [D], the Son of *Priam*, her Fellow-Captive; and reigned with him in part of *Epirus*. She had Children by *Pyrrhus* [E], and one likewise by *Helenus*. Some Authors are of Opinion, that the Kings of *Epirus* down to That *Pyrrhus*, who made War with the *Romans* (*c*), descended from a Son of *Pyrrhus* and *Andromache*. This Princess had seven Brothers, who were slain by *Achilles*, together with their Father, in one and the same Day (*d*). An Author tells us, that she accompanied *Priam*, when he went to beg of *Achilles*, that he would sell him the dead Body of *Hector* (*e*); and that, to excite the greater Compassion, she carried with her her two Sons, who were but Infants (*f*). She has been the Subject of many fine Tragedies both Ancient and Modern

(*a*) Euripid. in Andromache.

(*c*) See the Rem. k [E].

(*d*) Il. lib. 6. ver. 414, & seq.

(*e*) Dic'ys Cretensis, lib. 3.

(*f*) Astyanacla quem nonnulli Scamandrum appellabant, & Laodamanta parvulos admodum filiosque habuisse dicunt. — — Carrying with her Astyanax, whom some call Scamander, and Laodamas, as yet but Infants. Id. ibid.

(8) Passages alledged by him, and that *Maillincrot* (8) mentions *Anaxicrates*, without saying any thing of the Work quoted by the Scholiast upon *Euripides*: He only says, that *Strabo* alledges the Authority of *Anaxicrates*, in speaking of *Arabia*, in the fourteenth Book.

[B] *Her Disposition was very easy and complaisant in this Respect.*] See the foregoing Remark. It does not appear from hence, that *Andromache* carried her Complaisance so far, as *Livia* and *Cromwell*'s Wife did. The latter, out of Ambition, favoured the amorous Intrigues of her Husband (9). *Livia* occasionally acted the Part of a Bawd to *Augustus*, to keep up her Credit. " Circa libidines hæsit (*Augustus*) " postea quoque ut ferunt, ad vitiandas Virgines " promptior, quæ sibi undique etiam ab uxore con " quirerentur (10). - - - - - *Augustus* continued afterwards *his Debaucheries*, being fond of violating " young Women, whom even his Wife procured for " him from all Parts." *Andromache* proposed only domestic Peace, by giving her Husband no Disquiet.

[C] *Pyrrhus - - - - shared his Bed with her.*] *Virgil*, in order to sooth a *Decorum*, introduces *Andromache* grieving chiefly at This; for *Æneas* no sooner asked her, whether *Hector*'s Widow was married, but she cast down her Eyes, and told him, blushing, that she was so against her Will; and that she envied the Fate of *Polyxena*, whom Death had freed from the like Necessity. We are not obliged to understand this altogether in a literal Sense.

Hectoris, Andromache, Pyrrhin' connubia servas?
Dejecit vultum, & demissa voce locuta est,
O felix una ante alias Priameïa Virgo,
Hostilem ad tumulum Trojæ sub mœnibus altis
Jussa mori, quæ sortitus non pertulit ullos,
Nec victoris heri tetigit captiva cubile!
Nos, patria incensa, diversa per æquora vectæ
Stirpis Achilleæ fastus, juvenemque superbum,
Servitio enixæ tulimus, qui deinde secutus
Ledæam Hermionem Lacedæmoniosque Hymenæos,
Me famulam famuloque Heleno transmisit habendam (11).

Still are you Hector*'s, or is* Hector *fled,
And his Remembrance lost in* Pyrrhus *Bed?
With Eyes dejected, in a lowly Tone,
After a modest Pause she thus begun.
Oh only happy Maid of* Priam*'s Race,
Whom Death deliver'd from the Foe's Embrace!
Commanded on* Achilles *Tomb to die;
Not forced, like us, to hard Captivity,
Or in a haughty Master's Arms to lie.
In Grecian Ships unhappy we were born;
Endur'd the Victor's Lust, sustain'd the Scorn.
Thus I submitted to the lawless Pride
Of* Pyrrhus, *more a Handmaid, than a Bride.
Cloy'd with Possession, he forsook my Bed,
And* Helen*'s lovely Daughter sought to wed.*

*Then Me to Trojan Helenus resign'd,
And his two Slaves in equal Marriage joyn'd.*

DRYDEN.

But we must do her Justice; she is not represented as a Woman of an amorous Complexion. Tho' she was a Mother, *Ovid* could scarce believe, that she had lain with her Husband.

Nunquam ego te, Andromache, nec te, Tecmessa,
  rogarem,
Ut mea de vobis altera amica foret.
Credere vix videor, cum cogar credere partu,
Vos ego cum vestris concubuisse viris (12).

*When youthful Heat, inspir'd by female Charms,
Prompts me to take a Mistress to my Arms;
Nor you,* Andromache, *should gain my Voice,
Nor you,* Tecmessa, *be the Poet's Choice.
Scarce can I think such cold and lifeless Dames
(But that the Fruit the sure Embrace proclaims)
'Ere blest the Nuptial Bed, or burnt in* Hymen*'s
  [Flames.*

[D] *Or even in his Life time.*] I thought this Alternative necessary, because Authors are not agreed about the Time, when *Andromache* married *Helenus*. We have just now seen, that, according to *Virgil*, this Marriage preceeded the Death of *Pyrrhus*. *Justin* is of the same Opinion (13). But, according to *Servius*, the only Reason for her becoming *Helenus*'s Wife, was, that *Pyrrhus* ordered it so upon his Death bed (14). *Pausanias* likewise places their Nuptials after the Death of This Prince. Τέλος γάς Ἀνδρομάχη αὐτοίκασιν ἀπισδυθέντος ἐν Δελφοῖς Πύῤῥου (15). *Huic enim Andromache nupsit, mortuo Delphis Pyrrho.*

[E] *She had Children by* Pyrrhus.] Some compute, that she had three Sons by him, *viz. Molossus, Pielus,* and *Pergamus* (16); or *Pyrrhus, Molossus,* and *Æacides* (17). Others mention only *Molossus* (18), from whom, according to *Euripides* (19), the Kings of *Molossia* descended. *Pausanias* says, they sprung from *Pielus*. As for *Pergamus*, the same *Pausanias* informs us, that he went into *Asia*; that his Mother *Andromache* followed him thither; and that he killed *Atreus*, Prince of *Teuthrania*, having fought with him in single Combat for the Sovereignty; that he called the Town by his Name; and that his Tomb, and That of his Mother, were to be seen there. *Servius*, upon the Seventy second Verse of the sixth Eclogue of *Virgil*, gives a very different Account of the whole Matter. As for the Son of *Helenus*, by *Andromache*, his Name was *Cestrinus*; and he went and settled, with a Company of *Epirots*, who willingly followed him, in a Province situated above the River *Thyatis*: This he did after his Father's Death, and when the Kingdom had been restored to *Molossus*, Son of *Pyrrhus* (20).

[F] *She*

(8) Paralipom. de Histor. Græcis, pag. 5.

(9) Letts Life of Cromwell, in Monsi. de Beauval's Journal, 1692, pag. 499.

(10) Sueton. in Aug. cap. 71.

(11) Virg. Æneid. lib. 3. ver. 320.

(12) Ovid. de Arte Amandi, lib. 3. ver. 519.

(13) Justin lib. 17. cap. 3.

(14) Servius in lib. 3. Æneid. ver. 519.

(15) Pausan. lib. 1. p. 20.

(16) Id. ib.

(17) Schol. Euripid. in Andromach.

(18) Servius in Æneid. lib. 3. ver. 319.

(19) In Andromach.

(20) Pausan. lib. 1. p. 20.

ANDROMACHE

Modern [F]. Her lofty Stature was known to all Posterity [G]. Her Dialogue with *Hector*, in the sixth Book of the *Iliad*, is one of the best Passages of That Poem [H].

She was so careful of *Hector*'s Horses, that she fed and watered them, before she served Him (g). Some have alledged this Example, to shew, that Women ought to condescend to the most servile Offices of a Family [I]. *(g) Homer. Iliad. lib. 8. ver. 188.*

[F] *She has been the Subject of many fine Tragedies both ancient and modern.*] That of *Euripides* is still extant; and, if the Reader desires to know what was the Success of That, which was acted upon the *French* Stage at *Paris*, he need only read what *Montfleury*, a famous Player, says, in the *Parnassus Reformed*; to which he may add a Passage of a modern Poet. "If any one desires to know what I died "of, (they are *Montfleury*'s Words) he must not "ask, whether it was of a Fever, a Dropsy, or the "Gout: No, it was of *Andromache* --- I wish all "those Writers of Tragedies, who invent these mur- "th'rous Passions, had to do, like *Corneille*, with "such a Man as the Abbot *d'Aubignac*; they would "abate of their Fury. But what vexes me most, "is, that *Andromache* will grow more famous by "the Circumstance of my Death; and that, for the "future, every Poet will want to have the Honour "of killing a Player once in his Life (21)." Add to this these few Verses.

(21) Gueret's Parnassus Reformed, pag. 108, 109.

— — — — — Un Marquis
Enflé de son savoir chez les Dames aquis,
Ennemi du bon sens qu'à grand bruit il attaque,
Va pleurer au Tartuffe & rire à l'Andromaque.

— — — — — A Marquis
Vain of Experience, gain'd among the Fair,
And Foe to Sense, which rudely he attacks,
Shall, by inverted Rule, make Tartuff weep,
And paint Andromache a laughing Dame.

[G] *Her lofty Stature was known to all Posterity.*] I have already produced two Verses of *Ovid* upon this Subject, in the Remark [*A*]. Here are two more of the same Author.

Parva vehebatur equo: quod erat LONGISSIMA, *nunquam*
Thebais Hectoreo nupta resedit equo (22).

(22) Ovid. de Arte Amandi, lib. 3. ver. 777.

The Dapper only shou'd the Steed bestride;
The Wife of Hector *walk'd, too tall to ride.*

Martial refutes *Ovid*, as well in this Particular, as in what has been already cited. These are his Words,

Masturbabantur Phrygii post ostia servi,
Hectoreo quoties sederat uxor equo (23).

(23) Mart. Epigr. 105. lib. 11. ver. 23.

Behind the Doors the Phrygian *Slaves were fired,*
Oft as on Hector's *Horse his Consort rode.*

Juvenal was not ignorant of *Andromache*'s Stature; for, speaking of those Ladies, who raised several Stories of Ornaments and Hair upon their Heads, he says, they resembled so many *Andromache*'s before, but appeared very little behind.

Tot premit ordinibus, tot adhuc compagibus altum
Ædificat caput. Andromachen à fronte videbis,
Post minor est (24).

(24) Juv. Sat. 6. ver. 500.

With Curls on Curls they build her Head before,
And mount it with a formidable Tow'r.
A Giantess * *she seems; but look behind,*
And there she dwindles to the Pigmy kind.

An Andromache.

DRYDEN.

Thus the old *Roman* Ladies wore something like our *Top-Knots*. Another Poet expresses himself in the following Manner,

(25) Stat. Silv. 2. lib. 1. ver. 113.

Celsæ procul aspice frontis honores
Suggestumque comæ (25).

— — — — *behold the tow'ring Honours of her Head,*
The rising Mount of Hair.

(26) Quatro Berecynthia mater Invehitur curru Phrygias turrita Virg. Æn. lib. 6. ver. 785.

The Mother of the Gods, with her Towers upon her Head (26), would be nothing to our Ladies, if once they should enlarge the Mode of their *Top-Knots*. See M' *Almeloveen*'s *Amœnitates Theologico-Philolo-*

gicæ, where you will find (27) a Collection of curious Learning about the Antiquity of *Top-Knots*. See also the Article *Candle*, and this Passage of *Xenophon*, Μέλλει γὰρ (28), speaking of a Bride, καὶ εἰς τὴν ὑστεραίαν ἐσίδυμιν ταινιωσεσθαί τε καὶ πυρφόρος καδαντο ἢ Κυβέλη πυρσιαλίσεσθαι. *She will be adorn'd with this Head-dress, these seven Days, and walk about, like* Cybele, *with Turrets on her Head.* But, to return to *Andromache*, I must observe, that *Dares Phrygius* says, she was endowed with many fine Qualities; and he does not forget her tall Stature, "*Andromacham oculis claris, candidam,* LON-"GAM, *formosam, modestam, sapientem, pudicam,* "*blandam.* — *Andromache, Fine-Eyed, Fair,* "TALL, *Handsome, Modest, Wise, Chaste, and* "*Good-natur'd.*"

(27) Pag. 106, &c.
(28) Synes. Epist. 3.

[H] *Her Dialogue with* Hector --- *is one of the best Passages of That Poem.*] This is the Judgment M' *Perrault* passes upon it. He translated This Dialogue into *French* Verse, and read his Version to the *French* Academy, when the Abbot *Fenelon* was admitted into it (29). He first made a short and ingenious Discourse, in which he declared, that he believed *Homer* to be the most Excellent, the most Copious, and the finest Genius, Poetry ever knew; and that, in order to convince the Incredulous, that he honoured him according to his Merit, he had translated This Part of the *Iliad* into *French*. He owns, that he has left out some Digressions, which seemed to him too languid. This is *Homer*'s Fault; he is too talkative, and too downright; though otherwise a Writer of great Genius, and so full of noble Thoughts, that were he now alive, he would write an Epic Poem, free from all Defects. He would not introduce *Andromache*, among other Complaints for the Death of her Husband, lamenting, that young *Astyanax* must now no longer eat, upon his Father's Knees, the Fat and Marrow of Sheep. This is to paint after Nature, it must be confessed; but such Simplicity is not allowable, at present, in Epic Poetry; it appears to us too Citizen-like; and only fit for Comedy. I believe our Countesses and Marchionesses would think they expressed themselves too much like City Dames, should they say, as the Queen of *Carthage* does in *Virgil*,

A REFLECTION on the Epic Poetry of the Ancients.

(29) On the Thirty first of March, 1693. This Version was printed in the first part of the Recueil de Pieces curieuses, at the Hague, for Moetjens, 1694.

— — — — *si quis mihi parvulus Aula*
Luderet Æneas.

This Fault is not to be ascribed to the ancient Poets, but to the time they lived in. Properly speaking, the Question is not, whether Men have better Parts now, than they had in former times; but whether we have better Notions of Perfection, and may apply to *Homer* what *Horace* says of another Poet.

— — — — *sed ille,*
Si foret hoc nostrum fato dilapsus in ævum,
Detereret sibi multa, recideret omne, quod ultra
Perfectum traheretur (30).

(30) Horat. Sat. 10. lib. 1. ver. 67.

Yet did he now again new Life commence,
He wou'd correct; he wou'd retrench his Sense,
And pare off all that was not Excellence.

CREECH.

[I] *Some have alledged this Example, to shew, that Women ought to condescend to the most servile Offices of a Family.*] Read these Words of *Tiraquellus* (31). "*Qua loca Franciscus Barbarus in suo libello de re* "*uxoria quem apud Gallos imprimendum primi om-* "*nium dedimus, solerter sciteque annotavit, monens* "*his exemplis uxores ne rea hujusmodi contemnant* "*quas Andromache, &c.* — *& hoc quoque è no-* "*stris commemoravit Jo. Lupus in rep. rubr. de don.* "*inter vir. & uxor. &. Bo. Curtil. in tract. nobilitatis,* "*in 38. privilegio.* — *Which Passages* Franciscus "Barbarus, *in his Treatise de re* Uxoria, *first publish-* "*ed by me in* France, *wisely distinguished, putting Wives* "*in mind, from these Examples, not to overlook such* "*things, which* Andromache, *&c.* — *The same* "*Remark has been made by our Countryman* Jo. Lupus, "*in his Rep. Rubr. &c. and by Bo. Curtil. in his* "*Treatise*

(31) Andr. Tiraquell. de Nobilit. cap. 20. n. 101. pag. 78.

"*Treatise* de Nobilitat. &c." *Tiraquellus* made no Reflexion upon this Circumstance, *viz.* that *Andromache's* Husband was not first served. Doubtless he thought this Example would prove too much; and that the Reader ought not to be entertained with such a Notion.

ANDROMACHUS. I shall mention but six Persons of this Name. The First ANDROMACHUS, born in *Sicily*, was the Father of the Historian *Timæus*, and the Founder of *Tauromenium*, now called *Taormina*. He was a Man of Courage, and very rich. He gathered together (*a*) upon a rising Ground, called *Taurus*, near *Naxus*, the Inhabitants of That Town, who had fled away, when the Tyrant *Dionysius* destroyed it. He supported himself a long time in this Post; which was the Reason why he called it *Tauromenium*. The Fugitives of *Naxus* were very prosperous in this new Habitation; so that in a little time it became a very considerable Town (*b*). *Andromachus* received *Timoleon* into it, and permitted him to make it a Place of Arms. This *Corinthian* General came only to deliver *Sicily* from the Tyrants, who oppressed it. *Andromachus* was a professed Enemy to Tyrants, and had a long time sollicited the *Corinthians* to undertake the Deliverance of *Sicily*. He, therefore, and *Timoleon*, quickly resolved to act in Concert, in order to restore the Public Liberty (*c*). The Second ANDROMACHUS served under *Alexander* the Great, and was Governour of *Cælo-Syria*. The *Samaritans* burnt him alive; but *Alexander* punished the Authors of this cruel Action according to their Deserts (*d*). I find no other *Andromachus* in *Quintus Curtius*, tho' *Moreri* pretends there are many Persons of this Name mentioned by That Historian. The Third ANDROMACHUS was Brother-in-law to *Seleucus Callinicus* King of *Syria*, and had a Son (*e*), who invaded the Provinces, situated on this side of Mount *Taurus*, and caused him to be proclaimed King, in the time of *Antiochus* the Great. This *Andromachus* was kept Prisoner a considerable time in *Egypt*. The *Rhodians* obtained his Liberty, not from *Ptolemy Evergetes*, as is said in the Supplement to *Moreri*'s Dictionary, but from *Ptolemy Philopator* [*A*]. The Fourth ANDROMACHUS was a Traytor, who discovered to the *Parthians* all the Designs of *Crassus*, and, being chosen as a Guide, led the *Roman* Army into a Place, where they could not avoid being cut to pieces. See *Plutarch*, pag. 562, of the Life of *Crassus*. The Fifth ANDROMACHUS was *Nero*'s Physician, who makes the Subject of the following Article. The Sixth ANDROMACHUS was a Sophist, who taught in *Nicomedia* under the Reign of *Dioclesian*; as we read in *Suidas*.

[*A*] *The Rhodians obtained his Liberty, not from* Ptolemy Evergetes —— *but from* Ptolemy Philopator.] The Fault of the Supplement to *Moreri*'s Dictionary will be manifest to any one, who considers, that, when the *Rhodians* obtained *Andromachus*'s Liberty, his Son had been gone, two Years, over Mount *Taurus*, with *Seleucus Cerasnus*, King of *Syria*, to make War upon *Attalus*, King of *Pergamus*. Now this Expedition was undertaken the same Year, that *Ptolemy Evergetes* died, and was succeeded by *Ptolemy Philopator* (1). It was therefore *Ptolemy Philopator*, who set *Andromachus* at Liberty, to please the *Rhodians*, who wanted to deprive the City of *Byzantium* of the Favour of *Achæus*, and who thought, that the most effectual way to make a Friend of that Prince, was to procure the Liberty of his Father. See the Remark [*A*], of the Article ACHÆUS.

ANDROMACHUS, a Native of the Isle of *Crete*, and Physician to the Emperor *Nero* (*a*), is chiefly known by the Antidote, which he invented, by mixing the Flesh of Vipers with *Mithridate* (*b*). This Antidote was called *Theriace*, on Account of this Mixture. We call it *Treacle*. Θηρίον signifies a Beast; but Physicians understand by Θηρία particularly venomous Beasts (*c*). This Antidote banished the use of *Mithridate*, which 'till then had been in great Esteem (*d*). *Andromachus* wrote a Description of his Antidote in Elegiac Verse, and dedicated it to *Nero* (*e*). His Son, whose Name was ANDROMACHUS, wrote the like Description in Prose (*f*). *Democrates* did it in Iambic Verse, in a Poem which he wrote concerning Antidotes (*g*). We read, in *Galen*, that *Andromachus*, the Father, wrote a Treatise *De Medicamentis compositis ad adfectus externos* (*h*), and that he was a Learned and an Eloquent Man (*i*). *Erotian* dedicated his *Lexicon* to him. I wonder how *Meursius* could forget so famous a Physician, in his List of the Illustrious Men of the Isle of *Crete*, in the fourth Book of his Treatise of That Island. Some will have it, that this Physician was a good Astrologer [*A*].

[*A*] *That this Physician was a good Astrologer.*] I begin with *Vossius*'s Words. "Circa Olympiadem "CXI, (*the Printer has left out a* C; *it should be* "CCXI) ac deinceps, nempe extremis Neronis temporibus, & sub Vespasiano, magnum sibi decus "hac scientia peperit Andromachus, Cretensis, qui "primus dicitur edidisse theoricas Planetarum. —— *About the* CCXIth *Olympiad, and afterwards, namely, about the end of the Reign of* Nero, *and in that of* Vespasian, Andromachus, *of* Crete, *acquired great Reputation in this Science, who is said to be the first, who published Theories of the Planets.*" This is *Vossius*'s Text in the Hundred sixty first Page of his Book, *de Scientiis Mathematicis*, to which he adds the following Commentary, according to his usual Method. "Consentiunt de eo Lucas Gauricus, "& Christophorus Clavius, nisi quod Gauricus perperam Andronicum vocat, qui Clavio rectius Andromachus. Illum vide in Calendario Ecclesiastico*, "hunc Commentario † in Sphæram Juan. de Sacrobosco. —— Luke Gauric, *and* Christopher Clavius, *agree in relation to this Person; except that* Gauric, *by mistake, called Him* Andronicus, *whom* Clavius *rightly calls* Andromachus. *See the former in his Ecclesiastical Calander, the latter in his Commentary on the Sphere of* John de Sacrobosco." I wonder *Vossius* did not tell us, whether, or no, he believed this *Andromachus*, the Astrologer, to be the same, with him, who invented Treacle. The Time, wherein he places him, and the Country, he says he was born in, would induce one to think he means one and the same *Andromachus*. I am apt to believe, that

that *Voſſius*'s Silence in this matter was the Effect of Prudence: He wanted farther Information; and therefore would not venture to decide peremptorily. *Moreri*, a much bolder Author, affirms, that *Andromachus*, *Nero*'s Physician, and *Andromachus* the Astrologer, the first who wrote concerning the Theory of the Planets, are one and the same Person. *Andromachus*, the Astrologer, seems to me to be a Chimera; for Mr *Drelincourt*, whom I never consulted, without admiring his vast and accurate Learning, was pleased to acquaint me, among many other things, which I make use of in this Article, that the Words *Inventor Theoriacarum*, in *Clavius*, ought to be read *Inventor Theriacarum*. This Correction utterly destroys the two Authorities alledged by *Voſſius*, as to what concerns the Theory of the Planets; one speaks only of *Andromachus*, and the other ascribes the Invention of Treacle alone to *Andromachus*. We have here a plain Instance of the Mistakes of learned Men, occasioned by the Errors of Printers and Transcribers. *Blancanus* places *Andromachus* among the Mathematicians: "Andromachus Cretensis, quem Theoriacarum inventorem facit Clavius (1)."——Androma-

(1) Blancan. in Mathem. Chronol. pag. 30.

"chus *of Crete*, *whom* Clavius *makes the Inventor of* "*Theories*." The same may be said of *Voſſius*. So that they, who pretend, that *Andromachus* was the first, who wrote concerning the Theory of the Planets, have no Ground for it, but a False-Print, by which the Word *Theriacarum* has been changed into *Theoricarum*. Mr *Drelincourt* alledged this Reason, among others, for his Conjecture, *viz.* that the Epithet *Inventor* has nothing to do with the Theory of the Planets; which, besides, was known before *Nero*'s Reign; whereas *Inventor*, added to *Theriacarum*, is very properly applied to *Andromachus*. Perhaps the same kind of Mistake of the Printers, or Transcribers, occasioned our *Andromachus* to be taken for an Astrologer, by *Clavius*, or by the Author, whom *Clavius*, mediately, or immediately, followed. The Word *Andromachus* was, perhaps, printed instead of *Andronicus*, or some such Name. Whence it was, that they, who knew, that one *Andromachus*, of *Crete*, was *Nero*'s Physician, and the Inventor of Treacle, added these Titles and Encomiums to the Word *Andromachus*, in their Lists of Astrologers.

ANDRONICUS, a *Peripatetic* Philosopher, born in the Island of *Rhodes*, came to *Rome*, in the time of *Pompey* and *Cicero* [*A*]; where he laboured powerfully to raise the Credit of *Aristotle*, whose Works he brought into request [*B*], after having regulated, and disposed them after a better Method [*C*]. There was something very singular in the Fate of these Writings, as I shall shew in another place (*a*). One cannot sufficiently express, what great Service *Andronicus* did to the Sect of the *Peripatetics*. Perhaps, It had never been so famous, if he had not taken a particular Care of the Works of it's Founder. *Andronicus* acquired a great Reputation by it (*b*). Some learned Men do not ascribe to him the *Paraphrase* upon Aristotle's

(*a*) In the Remarks on the Article TYRANNION.

(*b*) Quem cum acutum diligentemque Aristotelicorum laborum & judicem & reparatorem inolcuaverit antiquitas. Boetius Proœm. Libri de interpretat.

[*A*] *Came to Rome in the Time of* Pompey *and* Cicero.] This may be inferred from two Passages of *Plutarch*; one in the Life of *Sylla* (1), and the other in the Life of *Lucullus* (2). The first informs us of three things; I. That *Sylla* sent, from *Athens* to *Rome*, *Apellicon*'s Library, in which most of *Aristotle*'s Works were to be found. II. That the Grammarian *Tyrannion* took many Books out of *Sylla*'s Library. III. That *Andronicus*, the *Rhodian*, had *Aristotle*'s Works from *Tyrannion*. We learn, from the second Passage of *Plutarch*, that *Tyrannion* was taken by *Lucullus*, when *Mithridates* was defeated, and that *Murena*, having asked him of *Lucullus*, gave him his Freedom. We know, besides, that this Grammarian enriched himself at *Rome*, and collected a large Library. *Andronicus* must, therefore, have been at *Rome*, at the time I have mentioned, since he had *Aristotle*'s Works from *Tyrannion*. We shall see, in the Remark [*C*], whether Father *Rapin* is in the right, to say, that *Andronicus* did not come to *Rome*, 'till after the Death of *Tyrannion*.

[*B*] *Whose Works he brought into request.*] This supposes they were before unknown at *Rome*; and I have reason to affirm it, since *Cicero* does; nay, *Plutarch* tells us, that they were little known to the *Athenians*, when *Sylla* seized on *Apellicon*'s Books (3). Father *Rapin* has before observed, what I here suppose. "It was That *Andronicus*, says he (4), who brought "*Aristotle* into request at the time, when *Cicero* was "raising himself, by his great Reputation, to the "most considerable Dignities of the Republic. — "*Cicero* had heard of *Aristotle* in *Greece*. He was ac- "quainted with part of his Merit, which was not "very well known at *Rome*; as appears from the "Surprize of *Trebatius*, who paid a Visit to *Cicero*, "at his Country Seat of *Tusculum*, and, going into "his Library with him, happened to light upon *Ari*- "*stotle*'s Topics, of which *Cicero* had a Copy. *Tre*- "*batius* asked him, what Book it was, and what "it treated of; for, though he was no ignorant "Man, he had never heard of *Aristotle*. *Cicero* told "him, That it was no wonder, *since that Philosopher* "*was known to very few* (5)." I cannot forbear saying, that this agreeable Writer is not exact, in reporting this Passage of *Cicero*. This, I think, ought not to be ascribed to Inadvertency; but to a Desire of Brevity. It is an Inconvenience inseparable from exact Writers; they cannot avoid a Prolixity, which tires the Reader; who is better pleased with an easy and short Account of a thing, though not perfectly exact, than with a long one, however ever so

VOL. I.

accurate. Father *Rapin*, in order to give the Substance of *Cicero*'s Passage, should have said, that *Trebatius*, turning over several Books in *Cicero*'s Library, met with *Aristotle*'s Topics; that, being surprized at the Title, he immediately asked *Cicero* what Book it was, and, being informed, desired him to explain it to him; that *Cicero* advised him to read it himself, or to get it explained to him by an able Rhetorician; that *Trebatius* tried both these Methods without any Success, being himself discouraged by the Obscurity of the Book, and being told by the Rhetorician, that *Aristotle* was an Author unknown to him; that *Cicero* was not surprized at it, though such an Ignorance appeared to him inexcusable; and that, at the Request of *Trebatius*, who was a learned Civilian, he wrote upon *Aristotle*'s Topics (6). "Utrumque, ut à te audie- "bam, es expertus. Sed à libris te obscuritas reje- "cit. Rhetor autem ille, magnus ut opinor, Ari- "stotelica se ignorare respondit. Quod quidem mi- "nime sum admiratus, cum Philosophum rhetori "non esse cognitum, qui ab ipsis Philosophis præter "admodum paucos ignoretur. Quibus eo minus ig- "noscendum est, quod non modo rebus iis quæ ab "illo dictæ & inventæ sunt allici debuerunt; sed di- "cendi quoque incredibili quandam cum copia, tum "etiam suavitate (7). —— *You have, as you yourself* "*informed me, try'd both these Methods. But* "*the Obscurity of the Books deterred you. Besides* "*which, your Rhetorician, of great Fame, I think,* "*replied, that he knew nothing of* Aristotle *Which* "*I was not at all surprized at; namely, that* "*a Rhetorician was unacquainted with this Philoso-* "*pher, who is unknown to the Philosophers themselves,* "*a very few excepted. This they are the less to be forgi-* "*ven since not only the Subject of his Writings, but even* "*the wonderful Copiousness and Elegance of his Style,* "*ought to have engaged them to read him.*" To conceal nothing from the Reader, I must acquaint him, that *Strabo* informs us (8), that the Library-Keeper of *Sylla* permitted the Booksellers to get *Aristotle*'s Works transcribed; but that they made use of ignorant Transcribers, who, besides, did not compare the Copies with the Originals; which occasioned these Works to be published with abundance of Faults. This cannot be alledged in confutation of what I have said; for I may answer, that *Andronicus*'s Edition, being more correct, raised the Curiosity of the Learned, who made no account of the faulty Editions. See the Marginal Note (6).

[*C*] *Disposed them after a better Method*.] *Plutarch* says, that *Andronicus*, having received *Aristotle*'s and

Pppp *Theophraſtus*'s

ANDRONICUS.

Aristotle's *Ethics* [D]; others pretend he is the Author of it, and likewise of a small Treatise *on the Passions*, published by David Hoeschelius, in 1593. It is certain, that Andronicus was an Author; for *Aulus Gellius*, in a Chapter (c), wherein he mentions the two kinds of Lessons, which *Aristotle* gave his Scholars, sets down word for word a Letter of *Alexander* to *Aristotle*, and *Aristotle*'s Answer; and informs us, that he met with these two Letters in a Work of the Philosopher *Andronicus*. No one can say, whether this Work was the Paraphrase upon the Categories, or That on The Physics. It is well known, that *Andronicus* paraphrased those two Treatises of *Aristotle* [E]. I am not of Opinion, that he was *Strabo*'s Master [F].

(c) *It is the fifth of the twentieth Book.*

Theophrastus's Books from *Tyrannion*, published them with Indexes. Παρ' αὐτῷ τὸν Ῥόδιον Ἀνδρόνικον ευπορήσαντα τῶν ανλιγράφων εις μέσον θεῖναι, και αναγράψαι τοὺς νῦν φερομένους πίνακας (9). The following Passage of *Porphyry* may be added to this of *Plutarch*. Μιμησάμενος δ' Ἀπολλόδωρον τὸν Αθηναῖον, καὶ Ἀνδρόνικον τὸν Περιπατητικὸν, ὧν ὁ μὲν Ἐπίχαρμον τὸν κωμωδιογράφον εἰς δέκα τόμους φέρων συνέταξε, ὁ δ' Ἀριστοτέλους καὶ Θεοφράστου βιβλία εἰς πραγματείας διείλας, τὰς οἰκείας ὑποθέσεις εἰς ταὐτὸ συναγαγών, οὕτω δὴ καὶ ἐγώ (10). *Imitatus Apollodorum Athenienſem & Andronicum Peripateticum, quorum ille Epicharmum Comicum in decem collegit tomos, iste vero Aristotelis & Theophrasti libros in tractatus distribuit, proprias suppositiones in idem conducens; sic & ego.* I confess I do not very well understand the *Greek* Words, τὰς οἰκείας ὑποθέσεις εἰς ταὐτὸ συναγαγών. Much less do I understand the Translation, *proprias suppositiones in idem conducens*; but I think either of the two following Senses may be allowed. *Porphyry* means, either that *Andronicus* collected into one Body all the Tracts, which belonged to the same Subject, or that he added a proper Summary to each Tract. The first Sense seems to me the best, and agrees better with *Plutarch*, and the Comparison, which *Porphyry* makes between *Andronicus* and himself; for *Porphyry* only prefixed Titles to the Writings of his Master *Plotinus*, and digested them into several Classes. I have not met with any Author, who says what I have read in Father *Rapin*; and, as he quotes only *Plotinus*, I know not, whether he had it from a Work, which I have not consulted, or whether he paraphrases *Plotinus* and *Plutarch*. However it be, these are his Words, which have been faithfully transcribed by *Moreri*. "After *Tyrannion*'s Death, *Andronicus*, "the *Rhodian*, came to *Rome*, and, being sensible "of *Aristotle*'s Worth, having been bred up in the "*Lyceum*, he bought those Writings of *Tyrannion*'s "Heirs, and examined them so carefully, that he "was, in a manner, the first Restorer of them, as "*Porphyry* affirms in *Plotinus*'s Life. For he not "only restored what had been injured by length of "Time, and the Carelessness of those, who were in "possession of these Works, but took them out of "that strange Confusion they were in, and got them "transcribed (11)." The beginning of this Passage contradicts *Plutarch*, who affirms, that *Andronicus* had *Aristotle*'s Works from *Tyrannion* himself. I confess, *Plutarch* is not so exact, but we may give up his Authority in Circumstances; but, since we have no Author, who says, that *Tyrannion*'s Heirs, and not *Tyrannion* himself, sold to *Andronicus* the Writings of *Aristotle*; I think we had better adhere to *Plutarch*, since Chronology is not against him. See the Remarks on the Article TYRANNION. Some say, that *Andronicus* was the tenth Successor of *Aristotle*, and that he flourished in the CLXXXth Olympiad (12).

[D] *Some learned Men do not ascribe to him the Paraphrase upon* Aristotle's Ethics.] Daniel *Heinsius*, who translated this Paraphrase into *Latin*, plainly enough intimates, that he takes it to be the Work of this famous Peripatetic. He published it, in *Greek* and *Latin*, at *Leyden*, in the Year 1607, in 4to. It had never been printed before, either in *Greek*, or *Latin*. Many Errors crept into this Edition, which were corrected, at least in part, in That of the Year 1617, in 8vo. *Heinsius* prefixed the Name of *Andronicus Rhodius* to the second Edition. He was contented, in the first, to ascribe this Work to an ancient Philosopher, who was a famous Peripatetic. There is a Parenthesis in a Passage of *Naudé*, which may serve to vindicate him against *Placcius*. " Cui se Danielis Heinsii ..... diligentiâ socium "non ita pridem adjunxit Andronicus Rhodius (aut "potius Olympiodorus.) talem enim appellationem in "posteriori editione consulto sortitus est, cum in priori "ab eodem Heinsio facta Lugduni Batavorum sub "anonymi nomine latens ..... fuisset. ..... avide "à cunctis receptus. ..... *To whom* Andronicus "*Rhodius joined himself, by the Care of* Daniel "*Heinsius ; (or rather* Olympiodorus:) *for this Ap-*"*pellation was purposely assumed in the latter Edi-*"*tion since, in the former, published by the same* Hein-"*sius at* Leyden, *though without a Name, He was* "*eagerly received by the Public*." They are *Naudé*'s Words, in his *Bibliographia politica*; upon which *Placcius* makes this Remark: " Ubi lapsu memoriæ "fit oportet, quod de *Olympiodoro* memorat, cum "ejus nullam unquam in alterutra editione mentio-"nem Heinsius fecerit (13). ..... *Where his Me-*"*mory certainly fails him, as to what he says of* "Olympiodorus ; *since* Heinsius *makes no mention* "*of him in either Edition*." It appears from *Naudé*'s Parenthesis, that the Words *Andronicus Rhodius* only, and not *Olympiodorus*, are to be referred to *Heinsius*. *Meursius* does not doubt, that *Andronicus* is the Author of this Paraphrase, and of the Treatise περὶ παθῶν, published by *Hoeschelius*, from two Manuscripts; one of which he received from *Margunius*; the other was sent to *Sylburgius*, from *Spain*, by *Andrew Schottus* (14). *Vossius* ascribes this last Work to one *Andronicus*, not so ancient, as He who makes the Subject of this Article (15). *Reinesius* is of *Meursius*'s Opinion (16); but *Salmasius* asserts, that *Andronicus Rhodius* was not the Author of the Paraphrase, translated by Daniel *Heinsius* (17). *They*, says he, *who first published this Para-*"*phrase, injudiciously ascribed it to* Andronicus ; and he laughs at them for boasting, that they had met with very good Proofs of it, in the ancient Interpreters of *Aristotle* (18). He shews, that the true *Andronicus*, in *Aulus Gellius*, explains *Aristotle*'s ἐξωτερικὰ and ἀκροατικὰ differently from the Paraphrast. *Salmasius* enlarges very much upon this: "This Paraphrast does not agree with *Aristotle* in many things (19). " In tam multis abit "à mente Aristotelis, ut Andronici esse genuinum "opus soli possint credere, qui nihil in literis his "vident. ..... *He departs in so many things from* "Aristotle's *meaning, that They alone, who are whol-*"*ly unacquainted with these Studies, can possibly mi-*"*stake it for the Genuine Work of* Andronicus." He cannot believe, that so great a Philosopher as *Andronicus* would have mispent his time so far as to paraphrase a Book the most intelligible in the World. *Quis credat tanti nominis Peripateticum otium suum occupasse in Studiis Aristotelis paraphrasi elucidandis, quo libro nihil lucidius?* This last Proof seems to me to be very weak.

[E] *Andronicus paraphrased those two Treatises of* Aristotle.] *Simplicius* witnesses this in several Passages of his Commentaries. See *Franciscus Patricius* (20).

[F] *I am not of Opinion, that he was* Strabo's *Master.*] I know not, whether the Printers have omitted some Words, or Lines, in *Reinesius*'s Copy, or whether *Reinesius* be the true Author of these Words, pag. 312 (21). *Amasiæ Magister* (Andronicus *Rhodius*;) Strabonis: *his lib.* XIV. They mean, that *Strabo* says, in his fourteenth Book, that he was *Andronicus Rhodius*'s Scholar at *Amasia*. But it appears, that he was the Disciple of the Grammarian *Aristodemus* at *Nysa* (22), and of *Xenarchus*, the Peripatetic Philosopher, in another Place (23). And, if I am not very much mistaken, all that he says of *Andronicus*, in his 14th Book, is, That he was one of the illustrious Men of the Island of *Rhodes* (24); and I dare affirm, that he no where says, in his Writings, either that he was *Andronicus*'s Scholar, or that *Andronicus* taught at *Amasia*.

ANDRONICUS

ANDRONICUS.

ANDRONICUS (MARCUS POMPILIUS) a *Syrian*, taught Grammar at *Rome*. His too great Application to the Study of Philosophy [*A*] disqualified him for performing the Part of a Grammarian as diligently, as he ought to have done; which occasioned his School to be neglected. When he saw, that *Antonius Gniphon*, and even some Grammarians, inferior to himself, were yet preferred to him, he quitted his School, and retired to *Cumæ*, where he spent his time in writing Books. This Employment was no Relief to him in his wretched Condition. His great Poverty obliged him to sell the Best of his Works at a very low Price [*B*]. This Work was suppressed; but *Orbilius* repurchased it, and published it under the Author's Name; at least he pretended so to do. *Andronicus* followed the Sect of *Epicurus*, and lived in *Cicero's* time (*a*). *Moreri* has been guilty of many Errors in relation to this Person [*C*].

(*a*) Ex Suetonio de Illustrib. Grammaticis, cap. 8.

[*A*] *His too great Application to the study of Philosophy.*] *Suetonius* makes use of very proper Terms. "Studio Epicureæ sectæ desidiosior in professione Grammaticæ habebatur, minusque idoneus ad tuendam scholam. — — — His Attachment to the Sect of *Epicurus* was thought to have rendered him too indolent for the *Profession of Grammar*, and unfit for the Care of a School." This ought to serve as a Lesson to those, who desire to have a great many Scholars. They ought to apply themselves entirely to their Profession, or take care, at least, that no one knows they follow other Studies. A Philologist, who sets up for a Philosopher, who is curious after Physical Experiments, and carefully examines, whether *Des Cartes* has been more successful, than *Gassendus*, runs a great hazard of seeing his Class deserted. A Physician, fond of Medals, Mathematics, and Genealogies, must not expect to have a great many Patients. And this was the Reason, why Dr *Spon* thought fit to acquaint the Public, that they would be very much mistaken, if they thought, that he made the Study of Antiquity his principal Employ (1). He found, by Experience, that this Opinion was very prejudicial to him, in respect to his Practice, as a Physician. Besides, it is certain, that a Professor, who is known to write many Books, is not looked upon as a Man fit to improve his Scholars; and therefore they, who desire to grow rich by teaching Youth, will not succeed in it, if they set up for Authors.

[*B*] *Obliged him to sell the best of his Works at a very low Price.*] *Suetonius* calls it a *small Tract. Opusculum*, says he (2), *Annalium Elenchorum*. The Title, therefore, of this Work must have been *Elenchi Annalium*. Some Manuscripts of *Suetonius* have the following Reading, *Opusculum suum Annelium Ennii elenchorum* (3). *Achilles Statius* (4), and *Vossius* (5), declare for this Reading; and I think they are in the right. Whatever Reading we follow, it appears, that *Andronicus* had censured an Annalist.

[*C*] *Moreri has been guilty of many Errors, in relation to this Person.*] I. He calls him *Pompinius*, instead of *Pompilius*. II. He falsly says, that *Andronicus had been Preceptor to* Julius Cæsar, *and that* Cicero, *though a Prætor, was very well pleased to be one of his Hearers*. III. He renders *Annalium Elenchi*, Annals *digested into Tables*. IV. He says, that *some have ascribed these Tables to* Ennius. Thus he understands these Words of *Vossius*, *in quibusdam tamen libris est* annalium Ennii Elenchorum. V. He weakens *Suetonius's* Argument. That Historian mentions two Circumstances, which plainly discover *Andronicus's* Poverty: One of them is taken from the Importance of what was sold; *viz,* the best of the Author's Works; the other from the small Price, at which it was sold. *Moreri* thought he expressed the whole Sense of *Suetonius* in these Words: *He was so poor, that he was obliged, in order to support himself, to sell a small Tract, which he had composed*. How came he not to perceive, that he enervated, in a great Measure, the Proof of This Historian? The Reader will not be displeased to see what was the Occasion of his second Mistake, which contains two or three notorious Falshoods. He did not apprehend *Vossius's* Argument. That Author was to prove, that *Andronicus* lived in the time of *Sisenna*, and *Quadrigarius*, and some others. He proves it by this Reason: because *Antonius Gniphon*, and *Andronicus*, lived at the same time; and, because *Gniphon*, as *Suetonius* relates, taught in the House of *Julius Cæsar*, and had *Cicero* among his Hearers. He taught in *Cæsar's* House, when *Cæsar* was but a Child. *Cicero*, who was Prætor, went to hear him: Here are two Circumstances of Time, which *Vossius* alledges out of *Suetonius* to fix the Age of *Pompilius Andronicus*; to which he adds another Particular, attested by *Suetonius, viz.* that *Andronicus* and *Gniphon* kept School at the same time. *Moreri* understands of *Andronicus* what *Vossius* says of *Gniphon*. Besides, he thought that the keeping of a School in a Person's House meant only being Tutor to his Son.

Advice to those who excite any particular Protection.

(1) See the Letter, *ou il se be nourir to the Author of the* Nouvelles de la Republique des Lettres, *for* January, 1685, Art. 5.

(2) Suetonius de Illustr. Gramm. cap. 8.

(3) See Casaubon, upon this Passage of Suetonius.

(4) In Sueton. ibid.

(5) De Hist. Latin. pag. 47.

ANDRONICUS, of *Thessalonica*, was one of the Fugitive *Greeks*, who restored Learning in the West, in the XVth Century. He passed for the best Professor, next to *Theodorus Gaza*; and perhaps he exceeded him in the Knowledge of the *Greek* Tongue; for he had read all the Authors, who had wrote in that Language, and was a perfect Master of *Aristotle's* Philosophy. He taught at *Rome*, and lodged in Cardinal *Bessarion's* House. His Salary was so inconsiderable, that Poverty obliged him to leave *Rome*. He went to *Florence*, where he was Professor a considerable time, and had a great many Hearers; but, hoping to meet with better Fortune in *France*, he removed into That Country, and died there soon after, being very far advanced in Years. He had a bad Pronunciation; and regarded nothing but his Studies (*a*). *Platina* gives him the Character of being perfectly skilled in the *Greek* and *Latin* Tongues (*b*). I shall take notice, in the Remarks, of a Mistake of *Gabriel Naudé* [*A*]. There

(*b*) Greek & Latin linguæ apprime eruditus Platina in Panegyr. Bessarionis.

(*a*) Taken from Volaterran lib. 21. pag. 775.

[*A*] *A Mistake of* Gabriel Naudé.] Having said, that one *Hermonymus* of *Sparta* taught at *Paris*, he adds: *Afterwards there arrived another, called* Tranquillus Andronicus Dalmata, *who was the last of those, who came thither in the Reign of* Lewis XI. (1). It is plain, that he confounds *Andronicus* of *Thessalonica* with him, who is the Subject of the following Article. *Moreri* has committed the same Fault; and, by endeavouring to distinguish, he is become more embroiled. He will have it, that *Tranquillus Andronicus*, Professor of the *Greek* Tongue at *Paris*, was not the same, who *had a great Share in Cardinal Bessarion's Friendship*; and yet 'tis certain, that the Client of That Cardinal is the same with him, who was Professor at *Paris*. *Moreri* should not have called him *Calixtus Andronicus*, but *Andronicus Calistus*. Consider these Words; which inform us, that he was related to the famous *Theodorus Gaza*. "Gaudeo equidem plurimum, *they are* Philelphus's *Words*, *in a Letter, which he wrote, from* Milan *to* Gaza, *the Twenty first of* January *1469*, Eruditissimum virum mihique amicissimum Andronicum Kallistum, necessarium tuum, apud vos agere, id est in Musarum & sapientiæ domicilio, quem ut verbis meis salvere jubeas abs te peto, meque τοῖς περὶ Ἐνοῦοντα φιλοσοφεῖν τὸν φιλοσώτην commenda (2) — — — *I am*

(1) Naudé's Addition to the History of Lewis XI. pag. 187.

(2) Philelph. Epistol. lib. 29. See also a Passage of the sixteenth Book, and another of the seventeenth. These Passages were printed out to me, by Monsr. de la Monnoie.

ANGIOLELLO. ANGLUS.

There was, at the same time, another ANDRONICUS, a Native of *Constantinople*, who taught at *Bologne* [B].

"*am overjoyed, that my dear Friend, and your Relation, the learned Andronicus Callistus, is with you, that is in the Residence of Philosophy and the Muses: whom I desire you to compliment in my Name; and commend me to Bessarion's Family.*" This *Andronicus Callistus* was a Peripatetic, and wrote a Book *de Physica scientia & fortuna*, another *de misera Constantinopoli*, and some other Tracts mentioned by Father *Labbé* (3). Once more; *Moreri* should not have distinguished between him and the other, who taught at *Paris*; nor should he have said, that the latter was Professor at *Basil*. The Author of the *Athenes ancienne & nouvelle* places *Antonicus* among the learned *Greeks*, who came into *Italy*, about the middle of the fourteenth Century (4). He meant, doubtless, *Andronicus*, and put *fourteenth* instead of *fifteenth*.

[B] *There was, at the same time, another* ANDRONICUS, *a Native of* Constantinople, *who taught at* Bologne.] *Philelphus* commends him in several of his Letters. I shall transcribe but one Passage out of the first Letter of the Twenty fourth Book, dated the last of *October*, 1464. " Quare "non possum vos omnes, qui Bononiæ agitis, non "mirari plurimum, quod cum vobis viri doctissimi "eruditi copia data fit ad Græcam disciplinam pe- "nitus consequendam, malitis indocti esse quam "docti. Nunquam equidem discendi gratia trajecis- "sem in Græciam Constantinopolim, qua in urbe "septennium egi, si istiusmodi mihi Andronicus By- "zantius esset oblatus. - - - - - *Wherefore I cannot* "*sufficiently wonder at all you, who live at* Bologne, "*who chuse to continue in Ignorance, when the Pre-* "*sence of one of the most learned Men puts it in your* "*Power to acquire a perfect Knowledge of the Greek* "*Tongue. For my own Part, I should never have* "*passed into Greece, as far as* Constantinople, *where* "*I resided seven Years, for the sake of learning it,* "*if it had been in my Power to have had Recourse,* "*at Home, to such a Byzantian Andronicus.*"

ANDRONICUS (TRANQUILLUS) born in *Dalmatia*, towards the end of the XVth Century, was about a Work, which he promised to publish [A]. He taught in the University of *Leipsic*, at the same time with *Mosellan* [B]. It will appear by my Remarks, that he was an Author (a). *Erasmus* wrote a Letter to him: It is the Tenth of the fourth Book.

[A] *Was about a Work, which he promised to publish.*] *Paul Jovius* having said, that the sad Condition *Dalmatia* had been reduced to, by the *Turks*, was an Obstacle to the Study of Literature; and that, therefore, he would not mention any learned Men of That Country, adds, *unless* Tranquillus *Andronicus acquaints us with the Merit of his Countrymen*. Let us produce the very Words of *Paul Jovius*. " Sic ut nemo dignus eloglo compare- "at, nisi in Lucem studiosè producat cives suos "Tranquillus Andronicus, præclarus Ciceronis æmu- "lator, dum gravissimarum actionum ac Othomanicæ "legationis obscurorumque nobis itinerum Commen- "taria perscribit (1). —— *Insomuch that there seems* "*to be no one worthy of an Elogy, unless* Tranquillus "Andronicus, *the famous modern* Cicero, *shall dis-* "*play the Merits of his Country-men, in his Commen-* "*taries on the important Transactions of the dark Em-* "*bassy to* Turkey." This Passage intimates, that *Andronicus* took a Journey to *Constantinople*, either as Envoy, or in the Retinue of an Ambassador. *Konig* is not so reserved; he says positively, that *Andronicus* was deputed to *Turkey*, and wrote a Book concerning his Negotiation: *Legationem ad Turcam obiit, eamque suis commentariis illustravit.* Authors, who amplify what they quote, cannot be sufficiently censured for it. *Jovius* speaks only of a Work, which *Andronicus* was about; *Konig* converts it into a Book actually publish'd.

[B] *He taught in the University of* Leipsic, *at the same time with* Mosellan.] This I find in *Simler*: " Hic, says he (2), *literas docuit Lipsiæ Pet. Mosellani tempore*. He calls him *Tranquillus Parthenius Andronicus, Dalmata*, and makes him the Author of a Speech, printed at *Ausburg*, in 1518, and at *Vienna*, in 1541. The Subject of this Speech is to exhort all the Princes of *Germany* to make War against the *Turks*. There is another Speech of his *de Laudibus Eloquentiæ*, and some *Latin* Verses (3). *Du Verdier's* Supplements mention a Dialogue of the same Author, entituled *Sylla* (4): The Interlocutors are *Cæsar*, *Sylla*, *Pompey*, and *Minos*. It was printed at *Leipsic* in 8vo. The Year of the Impression is not set down in *Du Verdier's* Supplements.

ANGIOLELLO (JOHN MARIA), a Native of *Vicenza*, wrote an History of *Mahomet* II, in the *Italian* and *Turkish* Languages; which he dedicated to him. It was very well received by that haughty *Sultan*, who not only greatly caressed *Angiolello*, but gratified him likewise with a Reward. The Author had been an Eye-witness of what he related; for, being one of the Slaves of the young *Sultan Mustapha*, he followed him in the Expedition to *Persia*, in the Year 1573. I speak of the dreadful War, which *Mahomet* made, in Person, with near Two hundred thousand Men, in the States of *Ussun-Cassan*. We may well wonder, that *Angiolello*, who doubtless knew the Haughtiness of this *Turkish* Emperor, ventured to insert, in his History, the injurious Words, spoken by *Ussun-Cassan* against *Mahomet*; when, discovering his Army from a rising Ground, near the *Euphrates*, he reproached him with Illegitimacy. Perhaps *Mahomet* never knew, that these Reproaches were perpetuated in this History; for Princes are not acquainted with every thing, which is contained in Books dedicated to them. However it be, *Angiolello's* Work was kindly received, and well rewarded (a). They, who say, that he flourished in 1524 (b), are not exact; but what they add, that he wrote the Life of *Ussun-Cassan*, is more accurate. A Work of *Giov. Mario Angiolello, della vita è de' fatti di Re di Persia,* —— J. M. Angiolello, *of the Life and Actions of the King of* Persia, was printed at *Venice*, in 1553 (c). And I find in the Catalogue of *Thuanus's* Library (d), *Relatione della vita è de' fatti del Signor Usuncassan,* —— A Relation of the Life and Actions of Usuncasson, by our *Angiolello*. The Year, and the Place of the Impression, are omitted.

ANGLUS (THOMAS) an *English* Priest, distinguished himself no less by the Singularity of his Opinions, than by a Multitude of small Books, which he published in the XVIIth Century. He was of a very good Family; which he took Care often to acquaint the World with, in the Title-Pages of his Books [A]. He went by several Names [B]; and made some stay in most parts of Europe. He was Principal of a College at *Lisbon*, and Sub-Principal at *Douay* (a). *Rome* and *Paris* afforded him long Stations. He was a considerable time a Domestic of Sir *Kenelm Digby*'s, for whose Opinions he had a very particular Value [C]. He resolved to continue a Peripatetic, and to oppose the Lights, which Mr *Des Cartes* would have afforded him [D]. Nay, he undertook to clear up the most impenetrable Mysteries of Religion by *Aristotle*'s Principles; and, in order to it, he discussed the Doctrines of Liberty and Grace; in which he entangled himself; and, because He gave free Scope to his private Opinions, he pleased neither the *Molinists*, nor the *Jansenists*. He was a Man of a penetrating and vast Genius; but he had not the Talent of distinguishing those Ideas, which are proper to serve as a Rule and Foundation, or of clearing up Difficulties (b). There was something Irregular in his Philosophy and Theology. Some of his Works were censured at *Rome* by the Congregation of the *Index*, and by some Universities [E], elsewhere. He

(a) *See the Book, entituled, 'tatera appends, pag. 5.*

(b) *See the Remark [D] in regard to his Objections.*

[A] *Which he often took care to acquaint the World with, in the Title-Pages of his Books.*] For Instance, his three Dialogues *De Mundo*, printed at *Paris* in 1642, have these Words in the Title-Page, *Authore Thoma Anglo, è generosa Albiorum in Oriente Trinobantum prosapia oriunda*.

[B] *He went by several Names.*] Mr *Baillet*'s Remark (1) on this Subject is This, "Sir *Kenelm Digby* entertained the famous *Thomas Anglus*, an "*English* Gentleman, and a Catholic Priest, of one of "the most ancient Families in *England*. He had "an *Irish* Outside, and lived in great, but voluntary, Poverty. His true Sirname was *White*; "which he disguised sometimes under That of *Candidus*, sometimes That of *Albius* *; sometimes "he called himself *Bianchi*, and sometimes *Richworth*: but he is scarce known in *France* by any "other Name, than That of *Thomas Anglus*. — — "*Des Cartes* generally called him Mr *Vitus*." *Thomas Anglus* subscribes himself, at the end of several Epistles Dedicatory, *Thomas ex Albiis*.

(1) *Baillet's Life of Des Cartes, Tom. 2. p. 245. ad ann. 1644.*

* *Albius was an equivocal Word, as alluding to Albion, or Albius.*

[C] *For whose Opinions he had a very particular Value.*] This is the Title of one of his Books, printed at *Lyons*, in 1646. *Institutionum Peripateticorum ad mentem summi viri clarissimique Philosophi KENELMI EQUITIS DIGBÆI. — Peripatetick Institutions, according to the Opinions of the Great and Famous Philosopher Sir Kenelm Digby*. The Reason of this Title is to be seen in the Preface: "Quòd ad mentem summi viri & clarissimi Philosophi "Kenelmi Equitis Digbæi scriptas pronunciem, inde "est quod cum invidendo illo de animæ immortalitate libro totam naturæ compositionem à prima corporis ratione usque ad invisibiles animæ spiritualis "articulos defecuerit, & in omnium oculos intulerit, "alia quam ipse præcesserat incedere neque volui neque potui. Quicquid itaque de illo subjecto vides, "inde translatum est. ——— *The Reason, why I "say, they are according to the Opinions of the "Great and Famous Philosopher Sir Kenelm Digby, "is, because, in that admirable Book, of the Immortality of the Soul, This Great Man having dissected, "and explain'd, the whole Human Composition, from "the first OEconomy of the Body, to the invisible "Construction of the Spiritual Soul, I neither would, "nor could, tread in a different Path from him. "Whatever, therefore, you meet with, in relation to "this Subject, is borrowed from That Work*." He acknowledged himself indebted to him, not only for his Philosophical Knowledge, but likewise for his great Skill in Divinity, with respect to the greatest Mysteries; as appears from his Book, intituled, "*Quæstio Theologica, quomodo secundum principia "Peripateticæ Digbæanæ, five secundum rationem, "& abstrahendo quantum materia patitur, authoritate, humani arbitrii libertas sit componenda, & "cum gratia efficaci concilianda* (2). ——— *A Theological Enquiry; How, according to the Principles of the Digbæan Peripateticism, or according "to Reason, and by abstracting from the Passiveness of "Matter, Free-will is to be explain'd, and reconcil'd "with Effectual Grace*." He publish'd, in 1652, his *Institutiones Theologicæ, super fundamentis in Peripatetica Digbæana jactis, extructæ*.

(2) *It is a Book in 12mo, without the Place, or the Year, of the Impression. It appears, from the Preface, that the Author was, at that time, an old Man.*

[D] *And to oppose the Lights, which Mr Des Cartes wou'd have afforded him.*] *Thomas Anglus* (to have recourse once more to M. *Baillet*.) (3) "was a Peripatetick, more extraordinary still, than Sir *Kenelm Digby*; and certainly he exceeded him in the Ob-

(3) *Baillet, ubi supra.*

"scurity of his Notions, and the Incomprehensibility "of his Thoughts. He was, otherwise, one of "the most subtle Philosophers of his time, and had "shaken off the Yoke of the Schools, which most "Peripateticks submit to. *Des Cartes* — conceiv'd "an high Esteem for him, from the advantageous "Character given of him by Sir *Kenelm Digby*. He "willingly suffer'd *Thomas Anglus* to propose his Objections. The Nature of these Objections, and the "high Idea Sir *Kenelm* had given him of his Genius, made *Des Cartes* hope, that he would soon be "one of the Followers of his Philosophy; but it "appear'd, by the Event, that he depended too "much on the Tractableness of *Thomas Anglus*. *Anglus* puzzled his Brains with the knotty Questions concerning Predestination, Liberty, and "Grace, which began to make a noise in the Universities of *Louvain* and *Paris*. Being persuaded, "that *Des Cartes* was not a Man appointed by God to "give him the Solution of these Supernatural Difficulties; he chose rather to have recourse to the "Lights of *Aristotle*, in order dispel this mysterious "Darkness. What he wrote concerning these Matters, by the help of *Aristotle*, is not unlike the Obscurity of Oracles; which, perhaps, made him unintelligible to the *Roman* Congregation of the *Index* (4), and was the Reason, why the Jesuits consider'd him as a savage Divine (5)". It will not be improper to take notice, in this Place, of his Answer to those, who charg'd him with being an obscure Writer: It will farther discover to us the Character of his Genius. "I value, myself, said he, (6), upon "a Brevity, which becomes the Masters and Dispensers of Sciences. If my Writings are obscure, "it is the fault of the Divines, who give me no "Opportunity of explaining myself. In short, either "the Learned understand, or do not understand, me : "If they understand me, and find me in an Error, "they may easily confute me: If they do not understand me, they have no reason to exclaim against my "Doctrine". This favours of one, who is extremely desirous of being talk'd of; and concern'd, that he has not a sufficient number of Adversaries to excite the Attention of the Publick. *Riferunt aliqui hominem quod evidentiam jactet, cum tamen probscure ipsum scribere, quotquot eum legant, queritentur. Respondet ille, se brevitati scientiarum traditoribus aptæ studere: Theologos in causa esse quod obscura maneant ipsius scripta, dum sese explicandi ansam præbere resugiunt. Addit vel doctos cum intelligere posse, unde &, si errores scribat, ipsum confutare in proclivis est : vel non intelligere, & sic neque debere ipsi exclamitare: cum pessimus sit animi morbus calumniari quod nescis*. This Dilemma is somewhat sophistical.

(4) *Decret. sacr. congr. collect.*

(5) *Labbæo dishus Theologæ.*

(6) *Prefat. Stat. ræ appennæ.*

(-) *He publish'd, in 1643, Sonus buccinæ sive Thomas Anglus had publish'd, in 1653, Sonus buccinæ, cum append ice adversùs mentem divinitus innocente X.*

[E] *Some of his Works were censur'd at Rome, by the Congregation of the Index, and by some Universities.*] This Congregation, by a Decree of the 10th of *June* 1658, condemn'd these Four Treatises of *Thomas Anglus*: *Institutiones Peripateticæ*; *Appendix Theologica de origine mundi*; *Tabula suffragialis de terminandis fidei litibus ab Ecclesia Catholica fixa*; *Tesseræ Romanæ evulgatio*. The two last Pieces were publish'd against the famous Father *Macedo*, who, in a Paper War, was a perfect Knight-Errant; always ready to enter the Lists. He attack'd *Thomas Anglus* (7), but, instead of replying to the *Tabula suffragialis*, and to the *Tesseræ Romanæ evulgatis*, he made use of Intrigues, by which he caused these Pieces to be condemn'd by the Congregation of the *Index* (8). The

(8) *See the Preface to the Book, entituled, Statera spoensiis, quoad similia ad equi. nsue frequentem, printed at London, 1652, in 12mo.*

ANGLUS. ANICIUS.

He held a very particular Opinion, in relation to the State of departed Souls, and the Easiness of obtaining Salvation. I know not in what Year he died: He was still living, when *Charles* the Second was restored to the Throne of *England*. I have seen some Works of His, written after the Marriage of That Prince with the *Infanta* of *Portugal*. He was no Friend to the Jesuits; and he would willingly have been thought worthy of their Resentment [*F*]. I have been told, that, in the beginning of the War between *Charles* the First, and the Parliament, he wrote an *English* Book, in Defence of *Passive Obedience*, according to the Doctrine of the Church of *England*.

The Divines of *Douay* censured Twenty two Propositions, extracted out of *Thomas Anglus's Institutiones Sacræ*.

He publish'd a *Supplicatio postulativa Justitiæ*, in Opposition to their Censure; wherein he complain'd, that they had been contented with an indeterminate Censure, attended with a *respective*, without particularizing each Proposition (9). He shews them, that they acted like prevaricating Divines. And, in truth, all simple People are by this means in danger of being mistaken, or of slandering their Neighbours. If you pronounce, in general, on Thirty Propositions, that they are *respectively* rash, dangerous, and heretical, may not any one take That to be heretical, which is only rash, and That, which is downright Heresy, to be only a rash Assertion? This Reflexion will appear more strong in the Words of an anonymous Writer, who seems to be a Man of Parts and Judgment. He speaks in the following manner *concerning the Decree of the Inquisition, of the 7th of* December 1690, *against Thirty one Propositions*. "I know not, Sir, "says the Prelate, addressing himself to the Doctor, "whether you have observ'd all the Address and "Art of the Censure. You are not ignorant how "these Gentlemen usually style Propositions; they "do not say, that Each of them, in particular, is "scandalous, or erroneous, &c. but they set them "all down, one after another, though there were Five "hundred, and then qualify these Propositions, thus "placed in a heap, as they think fit; adding a "*respective* at the end. So that private Divines are "left to guess which of these Propositions have been "condemn'd only as Scandalous, and which as Heretical, or in another Sense (10)". In the next Page a Counsellor of the Parliament is introduc'd expressing himself thus: "We should think it a Contempt "of Justice, and a just Cause of being laugh'd at, "and exposed to the Indignation of the Publick, "should we, when we give Judgment in a Cause, "set down, on one side, all the Heads of it, and all "the Claims of the Parties; and, on the other, the "different Decisions confusedly, and in a heap, with "a *respective*; by which means the Judgment, being "unintelligible, would occasion a thousand endless "Suits". See the Reflexions, made on the same Decree of *Alexander* VIII, by the Author of the Difficulties proposed to M. *Steyaert* (11). To return to *Thomas Anglus*; he had raised several Doubts in relation to each Censure of the Divines of *Douay*; pretending, that, if they were not vindicated, it would redound to Their shame, and his own Glory (12). When Intrigue has a greater share in the Censure of a Book, than Reason, the censured Person seldom fails to get the better of his Censors. We need only remember the Letter written by M. *Arnauld*, in 1683, to the University of *Douay*.

I have something more to add, concerning the Censures past upon *Thomas Anglus's* Books. His *Statera morum* no sooner appear'd, but the Archbishop of *Mechlen*, and the Bishop of *Antwerp*, complained of it to the Internuncio at *Brussels*. A pragmatical Fellow went into *England*, to extort Subscriptions against the Doctrine of This Author (13), and it appears, that the Bishop of *Chalcedon* disapproved of the Treatise *de medio animarum statu*; and that a Report was spread, that he had publickly censured it (14). Father *Baron* observes, that the *Sonitus buccinæ* was censur'd, and that the Author maintains in it, that the Church has not the Power of determining, but only of giving her Testimony, concerning Tradition (15).

[*F*] *He would willingly have been thought worthy of their Resentment*] This appears from the Preface, I have so often quoted (16). The Author of the Preface, and of the Book printed with it, is, perhaps, The same with *Thomas Anglus*. Perhaps he himself wrote against his *Statera morum*, as well to clear up some Difficulties, as to make the Publick take notice of a Book, which was in danger of being confounded with the Multitude of new Books. However it be, the Author of That Preface seems to be well acquainted with *Anglus's* Opinions, and well affected towards him. He expresses himself thus concerning the Jesuits. "Increbuerunt sæpiuscule "rumores comminatam esse doctam illam Societatem "se contra D. Albii Opera structuram calamum. "Hoc idem ab iis maxime expectabant omnes, ut "quos præcipue ac pene unice scriptis suis lacessi- "verat. Attamen, sive ex motivis prudentialibus "suppressi sint libri illi jam scripti, sive nulli omnino "scripti fuerint, nihil dum editum est. Hic triumphat maxime D. Albius, & causam suam hoc dis- "cursu tueri solet; Minas illas, quas intendebant, "clamores, quibus ipsi passim obstrepebant, manifesta "esse indicia non defuisse *voluntatem* illum confu- "tandi: Neque eo genio esse PP. Societatis ut "quicquam fama sua charius habeant; unde eviden- "ter constare solam eis defuisse *potentiam*, postquam "ad tam insignem ignominiam propellendam adeo "tardi extiterint. —— *It was frequently given "out, that This Learned Society had threatned to "draw their Pens against the Works of* D. Albius. "*This was generally expected from them, and for "this Reason in particular, because This Author had "principally, and almost solely, exerted himself against "the Jesuits in his Writings. But, whether the "Books, already written, were suppress'd for pruden- "tial Reasons, or whether none were ever written, "nothing as yet has been publish'd against him. In "this* Albius *chiefly triumphs; to this he appeals in "Defence of his Cause; that the Threatnings, which "they gave out, and the Clamour, which they every "where rais'd against him, were plain Proofs, that "they did not want the Will to confuse him; that "their Reputation was the dearest Thing to the Society; "consequently, that they wanted only the Power; "since they enter'd the Lists so late in Defence of "themselves, against so strong an Attack upon their "Reputation*." This Man, you see, who could not procure himself the Honour of being attack'd by the Jesuits, takes Advantage of their Silence, by imputing it to their Inability, not to their Insensibility.

ANICIUS, a *Roman* Family. It was more Illustrious under the Christian Emperors, than in the time of the Republic, though it produced some Consuls before the Birth of *Julius Cæsar*. We read, in *Pliny*, of one Q. ANICIUS *Prænestinus*, who was made *Curule Ædile* in the Vth Century of *Rome* (a). L. ANICIUS *Gallus* was Prætor in the following Century; *viz.* in the Year 585, and was so successful in *Illyricum*, that, in a Month's Time, he conquered it, and took King *Gentius* Prisoner [*A*]. He obtained the Honour of a Triumph the Year following (b).

[*A*] *In a Month's time he conquered* Illyricum, &c.] This was the first time, that the End of a War was sooner heard of at *Rome*, than the beginning of it; and yet *Anicius* was obliged, in carrying it on, to take *Scodra*, a very strong Place. His Victory was so compleat, that the King of this Country fell into

ANICIUS. ANNA.

One of the Consuls of the Year 593 was called *L. ANICIUS Gallus*. I find, under the first Emperors, but one *ANICIUS Cerealis*, who was nominated to the Consulship in the Year of *Rome* 818 (*c*). He was engaged in a Plot against *Nero*; and killed himself in the Year of *Rome* 819. His Death was the less lamented, because it was remember'd, that he had discovered to *Caligula* a Conspiracy carried on against his Life (*d*). Many Persons of this Family were raised to the Consulship, after *Dioclesian*'s Reign; and it had never been seen, that two Brothers were Consuls at the same time, before the Year of *CHRIST* 395, when *Probinus* and *Olybrius* discharged this Office. They were the Sons of *Probus*, of whom I shall speak in his proper Place, and descended from *ANICIUS*, the first Great Man of *Rome*, who turned Christian [*B*]. The great Riches of this Family exposed it to many Slanders, as I shall shew, in speaking of *Probus*. The *Benedictine* Monks pretend, that the Founder of their Order was of the Family of the *Anicii*, and have published some Books, wherein they endeavour to prove, that the August House of *Austria* likewise derives it's Pedigree from it. This Fable was confuted by *Streinius*, in a Book intituled *Anti-Anicianus*, which was never printed: the Manuscript Copy is in the Emperor's Library (*e*). I shall take notice of a curious Particular in relation to the Subject of this Work [*C*].

(*c*) Tacit. Ann. lib. 15. cap. 74.

(*d*) Id. lib. 16. cap. 17.

(*e*) Lambecius, Commentar. Biblioth. Vindobon. Tom. I. n 50.

his hands, together with his Mother, his Wife, his Children, his Brother, and all the chief Persons of his Dominions; and he obtain'd a considerable Booty. This is *Livy*'s Account of the matter: *Anicius bello Illyrico intra triginta dies perfecto nuncium victoriæ Perpennam Romam misit, & post dies paucos Gentium regem ipsum cum parente, conjuge, ac liberis, ac fratre, aliisque principibus Illyricorum. Hoc unum bellum prius perpetratum, quam cæptum Romæ auditum est* (1). "*Hoc Bellum* (says Florus) (2) *ante finitum est, quam geri Romæ nuntiaretur.* —— *This War was at an end, before it was known at Rome, that it was begun*." These Prisoners of Quality were only part of the Ornaments of the Triumph: The Wealth, and Spoils brought from *Illyricum*, and the Liberalities bestowed upon the Soldiers, made it very considerable. The General was more applauded by his Army, than *Paulus Æmilius*, who had triumphed not long before, was by his. *Lætior hunc triumphum est secutus miles, multisque dux ipse carminibus celebratus* (3). *Lloyd* observes, that the Consul of the Year 593 is the Son of Him, who conquered *Gentius*; but he quotes no Authority for it.

(1) Livius, lib. 44. cap. 32.

(2) Florus, lib. 2. cap. 13.

(3) Livius, lib. 45. cap. 43.

[*B*] ANICIUS, *The first Great Man of Rome, who turned Christian.*] These Words of *Prudentius* are the only Proof I can alledge for it:

Fertur enim ante alios generosus Anicius urbis Illustrasse caput (4).

(4) Prudent. in Symm. lib. 1. ver. 553.

The Noble Anicius *is reported to be the First Ornament of the City.*

Baronius conjectures, that this Poet meant *Anicius Julianus*, who was Consul in the Year 322. *Lloyd*, being more positive, affirms, without quoting any Authority for it, that *Anicius Julianus* was the first *Roman* Senator, who embrac'd the Gospel; and that this was the Reason why most of the Emperors, from that time, took the Sirname of *Flavius*, and most of the Senators That of *Anicius*. I should be glad to see some Proofs of this. If *Baronius*'s Conjecture be well grounded, *Anicius Julianus* may be compared to That *French* Lord, who procured himself to be the first baptiz'd in Imitation of *Clovis*, and took this Motto, *God preserve the first Christian*. 'Tis said, that the Lords *de Montmorency* are descended from Him; for which Reason they stiled themselves *the first Christian Barons*.

[*C*] *I shall take notice of a curious Particular, in relation to the Subject of this Work.*] Mr *Baillet* is of Opinion, that *Streinius*'s Manuscript will never be printed, for two Reasons: One is That mentioned by *Lambecius, viz.* that it is an imperfect Work; the Second, more important than the First, and of which he took care to say nothing, is, that the " *Anti-Anicianus* does " not favour the Prejudices of the Vulgar, in the " hereditary Countries, nor the Notions of those, " who, to make their Court to the Emperor, have " derived the Pedigree of the House of *Austria* " from the *Anicii* of ancient *Rome*. —— The Author " undertook this Work, in Opposition to the *Benedictine* Monks, who seem to be infatuated with " their being related to the House of *Austria*, and " particularly to confute the Book of a *Flemish* Benedictine, called *Arnold Wion*, who, by a Concatenation of extravagant Conceits, produced the two " Branches of the *Roman* Family *Anicia*, one, as the " Origin of the Princes of the House of *Austria*, the " other of his Patriarch St *Benedict* (5)." Mr *Baillet* adds, that *Streinius* said nothing of the *Anicii*, in his Book concerning the *Roman* Families, *because it was not one of the Families of the old Stock*. He informs us, that " *Lambecius* designed to answer " *Streinius*'s *Anti-Anicianus*, in his *Prolegomena* to the " Annals of *Austria*, which he promised." —— And that it seems, he " had chosen for the Ground and " Model of his Answer (6), the Book, which a *Benedictine* Abbot, but of the Order of the *Cistertians*, " whose Name was *John Seyfrid*, published twelve " Years after *Streinius*'s Death, under the Title of " *Arbor Aniciana*; but that, though *Seyfrid* had intended to write against the *Anti-Anicianus*, it may " be said, that *Streinius* would have been sufficiently " revenged by *Scioppius*, who published, in the Year " 1651, a small Dissertation, to ridicule this *Seyfrid*, " and those of the same Stamp; at the very same " Time, that another Monk, called *Bucelin*, to increase the Number of the Ridiculous, published his " *Aquila Imperii Benedicta*. *Scioppius*, (Mr *Baillet* " goes on) was not, upon this Occasion, the slanderous and satirical Writer he usually is; he appears " a faithful and zealous Servant of the House of " *Austria*; a Counsellor to the Emperor, and the " King of *Spain*; engaged in the Interest of the " Princes of their Name, upon several Accounts; infinitely more learned, than these idle Dreamers; " and who had made himself formidable, in point of " false Genealogy, above forty Years before, by his " *Scaliger Hypobolimæus*. If, therefore, *Scioppius*, " though otherwise devoted to the House of *Austria*, thought himself obliged to oppose the Vanity and idle Fancies of these Monks, concerning " the *Anician* Genealogy; we may very well infer " from hence, that their Inventions are not for the " Honour of the Princes of the House of *Austria*, or " of St *Benedict*'s Disciples; and that *Streinius*'s *Anti-Anicianus*, must needs be a considerable Work. —— " Though *Seyfrid* gave out, that St *Thomas* was descended from the illustrious Family of the *Anicii*; " it is not to be expected, that a *French Dominican* " will ever publish an *Aquila Imperii Thomistica*. " This is reserved, perhaps, for some *German*, or " *Spanish Dominican*, a zealous Friend to the House " of *Austria*." I desire the Reader to consider me, in this whole Matter, as a bare Transcriber.

(5) Tom. 2. of the Antiq. n. 114. pag. 228, & seq.

(6) Tom. 2. Comment. Biblioth. Vind. pag. 418, & seq.

ANNA, the Name of some Persons, mentioned in the Scripture. The Mother of the Prophet *Samuel* was called ANNA or HANNAH. She was a very pious Woman, and very much beloved by her Husband *Elkanah*. She was barren; and this Misfortune afflicted her the more sensibly, as it exposed her to the Raillery and Insults

Infults of the other Wife of *Elkanah*. She fo importunately petitioned Heaven for a Son, that her Prayers were at length heard (a); for God gave her *Samuel*, and afterwards three Sons, and two Daughters (b). The Book of *Tobit*, an Apocryphal Book among the Proteftants, mentions one ANNA, the Wife of *Tobit*, and Mother of *Tobias*. In St *Luke*'s Gofpel, we read of ANNA the Prophetefs, Daughter of *Phanuel* (c). She was a very devout Woman, about Eighty four Years of Age, and had lived but Seven Years with her Hufband. *Baronius*, who makes her a Cloyfter'd Religious, is miftaken [*A*]. The Gofpel mentions, likewife, a Man named ANNAS, who was High-Prieft, among the *Jews*, in our Saviour's Time. His Son-in-law, *Caïphas*, had the fame Dignity, when CHRIST was put to Death. As for SAINT ANNE, Mother of the Holy Virgin, and the moft celebrated Lady of this Name, among the *Roman* Catholics, fhe is no where fpoken of in the Scriptures, nor in the Writings of the Three firft Centuries. St *Epiphanius* is the firft, who mentions her; and yet the following Ages trumped up a long Legend concerning St *Anne*, as may be feen in the Article of S. JOACHIM, her Hufband. I am furprized, that *Erafmus* met with but three Women of the Name of ANNA in ancient Books [*B*].

[*A*] *Baronius, who makes her a Cloyfter'd Religious, is miftaken.*] Thefe are his Words: "Quomodo autem Anna nunquam è templo difceffiffe dicatur, ut merito eamdem S. Cyrillus * Hierofoly mitanus religiofiffimam monialem appellet, confule quæ fuperius dicta funt de præfentatione Dei genitricis in templo (1). ----- *How Anna is faid never to have departed from the Temple, upon which account St Cyril of Jerufalem juftly calls her a moft devout Nun, confult what has been faid, above, concerning the Prefentation of the Mother of God in the Temple.*" Here are two things: I *Baronius* takes in a literal Senfe St *Luke*'s Phrafe, *She departed not from the Temple* (2). II. He thinks S. *Cyril* very much in the right in calling *Anna* a moft religious Nun. But it is plain, that St *Luke*'s Words ought not to be ftretched beyond the Senfe, which is commonly put upon fuch Expreffions, when, to fignify that a Man goes frequently to any Particular Houfe, we fay, *That he never ftirs from it, that he is there Night and Day*. This is particularly faid of your devout Ladies, who go to Church feveral times in a Day; we ufually fay, that *they never ftir from Church, that they are continually praying at Church*. As to what concerns St *Cyril*, it is not true, that he calls the Prophetefs *Anna* a Nun. The *Latin* Tranflator of That Father fhould have confidered, that the Words ἀσκήσης, ἀσκήσεια, were ufed, not only to denote Monks and Nuns, but all thofe, likewife, who exactly practifed religious Exercifes. This is what the learned *Cafaubon* clearly fhewed againft *Baronius* (3).

[*B*] *I am furprized, that* Erafmus *met with but three Women of the Name of* Anna *in ancient Books*.] The firft is *Dido*'s Sifter; and he fays, *fhe was placed among the Gods, on account of the extraordinary Affection fhe fhew'd for her Sifter.* The Adventures of this *Anna* are fo fully related in other Dictionaries, that I think it unneceffary to mention them. The fecond is *Elkanah*'s Wife: *It is fufficient Commendation of her,* fays he, *to fay, that, by the particular Favour of God, fhe brought forth, in her old Age,* Samuel, *who was a very pious Prieft, and a moft uncorrupt Judge.* "Cujus ad laudem abunde fatis eft, quod & anus, & aufpice Deo, Samuelem pepererit, non utique fibi fed Deo quidem facerdotem religiofiffimum, populo vero judicem incorruptiffimum (4)." The third is the Mother of the Holy Virgin. He fays, that this laft *Anna* was greatly celebrated by *Rhodolphus Agricola*, and *Baptifta Mantuanus*. Thus *Erafmus* is guilty of Errors both of Omiffion and Commiffion. How came he to forget *Phanuel*'s Daughter, and *Tobias*'s Mother? Where did he find, that *Samuel*'s Mother was an old Woman? The facred Writer fays no fuch thing; but rather gives us to underftand, that fhe was ftill young enough. Had fhe not five Children, after fhe had weaned *Samuel*? The fame Hiftorian makes her reply to the High Prieft *Eli*, who charged her with Drunkennefs, that fhe had drank neither Wine, nor Beer. *Jofephus*, not thinking this Anfwer extraordinary enough, furnifhes her with another, to wit, that fhe never drank any thing but Water. Mr *Morreri* chofe to follow the Jewifh Hiftorian, rather than the Scripture. By the way, the Lady, to whom *Erafmus* wrote the Letter, which mentions thefe three *Anna*'s, might very well deferve an Article: He calls her *Anna Berfala Princeps Veriana*. If I can difcover her Family and Adventures, I here engage myfelf to take Notice of her.

Since the firft Edition of this Work, I have made fome Difcoveries in relation to this Lady. See the Article BERSALA.

ANNAT (FRANCIS), Confeffor to *Lewis* XIV, was a Native of *Rovergue* (a). He was born the fifth of *February*, 1590, admitted Jefuit in *February* 1607, and profeffed the fourth Vow, in the Year 1624. He taught Philofophy at *Toulouse*, for the fpace of fix Years, and Divinity for the fpace of feven; and, having honourably difcharged the Duties of thofe Places, he was invited to *Rome*, to exercife the Function of Cenfor-General of the Books publifhed by the Society, and That of Theologift to the General of the Order. Being returned into his own Country, he was made Rector of the College of *Montpellier*, and afterwards of That of *Toulouse*. He affifted, as Deputy of his Province, at the eighth General Affembly of the Jefuits, held at *Rome*, in 1645, and gave fo many Proofs of his Merit, that Father *Vincent Carafa*, General of the Jefuits, found no better qualified to fill the Place of Affiftant of *France*, which became vacant fixteen Months after. The ninth General Affembly gave him again the fame Employment, under *Francis Picolomini*, General of the Society; after whofe Death he was made Provincial of the Province of *France*. Whilft he was invefted with this Dignity, he was chofen Confeffor to *Lewis* XIV; and, after he had been fixteen Years in this Poft, he was obliged to demand his Difmiffion, his great Age having very much impaired his Hearing. As the King was very well pleafed with him, it was with Reluctance He granted his Requeft. Father *Annat* lived but four Months, after his leaving the Court, and died in the *Maifon Profeffé* of *Paris*, the fourteenth of *June*, 1670. Father *Sotuel*, who fupplies me with thefe Particulars, reprefents him as a Man endowed with great Virtues; as perfectly difinterefted, modeft, and humble; and exact in practifing the

Obfervances

Observances and Discipline of his Order; as never employing his Interest for his own Advantage, or in order to raise his Family; and as expressing a great Zeal for Religion (b). He was the Flail of Heretics, (says Sotuel) (c), and particularly attacked with incredible Zeal, the new Heresy of the Jansenists; he left nothing unattempted to get their Heresy condemned by the Pope, and restrained by the Authority of the Most Christian King; besides, he wrote with such Force of Reason against it, that his Adversaries have not been able to make any solid Reply. Some will not grant Father Sotuel this last Point; but as to what concerns the Disinterestedness of Father Annat, it will easily meet with Credit; for they, who would be informed, may know, that this Father Confessor never raised his Family. It is reported, that the King had been heard to say, that he did not know, whether Father Annat had any Relations (d). Some he had, who did not forget themselves, and who paid him a Visit at the Louvre; but they did not return with any Preferment. There are times, when the Greater and Lesser Nepotism, are both in vogue; sometimes the Lesser Nepotism prevails, whilst the Greater is suppress'd. In Father Annat's Time, the greater Nepotism was at it's Height (e); but the Lesser, with regard to the Father Confessor's, was, in Paris, at it's lowest Ebb. I make use of this Restriction, because there are many other dignified Clergymen, who heap upon their Relations all the Preferments they can procure. Many, no doubt, followed the usual Course, whilst Father Annat gave no Encouragement to his greedy Relations of Roüergue. We may read, in the Amours du Palais Royal, that he desired to lay down his Place [A], when Madam de la Valiere was taken into Favour. Were this true, it would be the finest Circumstance of his Life, and the noblest Subject for Encomium, that the Life of a King's Confessor can afford. The Author of this Satire, who, according to the Nature of this kind of Works, made it his Business to give a malicious Turn to every Thing, was very sensible of this; and, therefore, took care, that the Reader should find nothing commendable in it. A Satire of a much later Date has been handed about, which, besides Father Annat's desiring his Dismission, whether true or not, contains so many notorious Falshoods [B], that it is hard to conceive how any Man can tell publick Lyes

(b) Biblioth. Scriptor. Societ. Jesu, pag. 211.

(c) Hæresum malleus, & nominatim Jansenistarum hæreseos oppugnator acerrimus. Ibid.

(d) Adeo ut dixisse aliquando perhibeatur sua Majestas nescire se an P. Annatus haberet aliquos sanguine sibi conjunctos. Ib.

(e) That of the Court of Rome.

[A] *We may read, in the Amours du Palais Royal (1), that he desired to lay down his Place.*] Here is the Passage. "Poor Father Annat went also to him, by "the Suggestion of the Queens, and pretended a "Desire of quitting the Court, artfully insinuating, "that it was on account of his Amours. The King "fell a laughing, and immediately granted him his "Dismission. The Father, finding himself taken at "his Word, would fain have accommodated the "Matter; but the King, laughing on, told him, "that, for the future, he would have no other Confessor than the Rector of the Parish. It is difficult "to express, how vexed the whole Society was at "his Indiscretion." Upon this, I may be asked three Questions. I. Whether it be true, that Father Annat desired to lay down his Place. II. Whether it was a mere Feint, and out of Complaisance to the Queens. III. Whether he actually left the Court; or whether the Jesuits made up the Matter. All I can say, in Answer to the first Question, is, that I know nothing of the Matter, and that the Authority of a Satirist is of no Weight. I believe him, no farther than he proves what he advances. Writers of History are dispensed from taking an Oath, and producing their Witnesses (2); their Word is sufficient to procure Credit to what they say; but as to Writers of Libels, it is a Favour, a piece of Civility, to believe them, even upon their Oath, confirmed by Witnesses. I am still more ignorant, as to the second Question: I do not pretend to dive into the Hearts of Men. And, as to the third, I only know what is publickly known, viz. that Father Annat was the French King's Confessor, without Interruption, 'till the Spring of the Year 1670.

[B] *A Satire of a much later Date (3), ———— contains so many notorious Falshoods, &c.*] The Author of this Satire supposes, that Father La Chaize was very instrumental in moving the Pope to grant what the King desired of him, and that Cardinal Mazarin, as an Acknowledgment for this Service, was very kind to him, recommended him to the King, and even got him admitted into the Council of Conscience, which was properly to make him the Confessor's Coadjutor (4). The Year 1663 is set down in the Margin, for the Date of the Cardinal's first Marks of Favour, and the Year 1665, for the Admission into the Council of Conscience. What an Ignorance of modern History is here! Who does not know, that Cardinal Mazarin died, in 1661? The Author adds, that Father La Chaize supplanted Father Annat, by excusing the King's Love for Madam de la Valiere, from the Infirmity of Human Nature, whilst the Confessor teazed the King every Day on that Account, and would never suffer him to rest (5). He farther adds, that Madam de la Valiere, being informed of Father la Chaize's Maxims, desired to have him for her Confessor, and proposed it to him, by Mr de Montauzier (6); but, having afterwards discoursed with this Jesuit, she chose rather to procure him Father Annat's Place; and, having spoke to the King about it, the Affair was concluded in a few Days; Father Annat, who denounced the dreadful Judgments of God, and desired leave to retire, being taken at his Word (7). The Year 1667 is set down in the Margin. This is an unaccountable piece of Assurance; for it is notorious, that Father Annat did not take leave of the Court, 'till the Year 1670; and that a Jesuit of Roüergue, called Father Ferrier, succeeded him in his Place of Confessor to the King; and that Father la Chaize had not this Employ, 'till after the Death of Father Ferrier, who died the Twenty ninth of October 1674 (8). What do these Writers mean, when they publish such gross Falshoods? Do they not perceive, that they act contrary to their main Design? For do they not prejudice the Reader against their Books, when they appear so ignorant of Things, which are publickly known, or so void of Shame, as boldly to publish evident Untruths? Do they approve the Maxims of those, who preach up pious Frauds to a numerous Congregation, reasoning with themselves in this manner? Far-one Hearer, who will know that I am mistaken, a thousand will not discover it; a thousand, therefore, will be edified by my Fraud; one only will be offended at it; the Mischief, therefore, will be trifling, in comparison of the Advantage, which will accrue from it: It is therefore a Point of Charity and Prudence to maintain such a Falshood before this numerous Assembly. I know not whether our Libellers argue in the same manner; but I am sure they would succeed better in their Design, if they took more care to observe Chronology, and the Rules of Fiction. *Est ars etiam maledicendi*, says Scaliger (9); there is an Art of Slandering; they, who are ignorant of it, do not so much defame their Enemies, as shew how desirous they are of defaming them. To conclude, I make this Remark, rather for the Advantage of the Public, than for the Interest of any private Person. It is fit, that, in our Age, we should be able to judge of the Satires, which have been published within these thousand Years; and that Posterity should know how to judge of those, which appear in

(1) Intrigues of the Court. The Rock made it's first Appearance about the Year 1665.

(2) Quia unquam ab Historico juratores exegit? Seneca de morte Claudii imp.

(3) Entituled, History of Father La Chaize, a Jesuit, and Confessor to Lewis XIV. Cologne, for Peter Marteau, 1693, in 12mo. The second Part was pri'ted two Years after.

(4) Pag. 106.

(5) Pag. 107.

(6) Pag. 108.

(7) Pag. 115.

(8) Ex Nathan. Sotuelli Bibloth. Societ. pag. 449.

SOME Thoughts concerning Satire.

(9) Scaligerana 2 pag. 10.

ANNAT. ANNIUS. ANSELM.

Lyes with so little Caution. Father *Annat* wrote many Books [C], both in *French* and *Latin*. The *Latin* are much more in Esteem, than the *French*; because he was more capable of handling a Point of Divinity, according to the Dogmatical Method of the Schools, than of turning it according to the Genius of the Age he lived in. Nevertheless his *French* Works are very much commended in an Answer to the *Lettres Provinciales* (f). What I have said in general of the Nephews of this Father Confessor, ought not to prejudice any one against them; for One of them, who is General of the Fathers of the Christian Doctrine, is accounted a very learned Man, and has published a *Latin* Book of Divinity, which is very much esteemed. It is *A Methodical Apparatus to Positive Divinity* (g). You will meet with an Abstract of it in the *Journal des Sçavans*, of the Thirteenth of *September*, 1700.

(f) See the end of the Remark [C].

(g) Nouvelles de la Republique des Lettres, for April, 1700. pag. 477.

our Days. In order to judge rightly of them, we must pay no regard to this Principle, *It is not probable, that, if this thing were evidently false, any one would dare to publish it.*

This will, no doubt, be the principal Use of this Remark; for, in short, the best grounded Reflexions or Censures will never be able to stop the Pens of this Species of Writers. Notwithstanding the Indignation of honest Men against the fabulous and satirical History of Father *la Chaize*, another Piece, much worse than this, appeared five Years after. It is, from beginning to end, an Heap of Falshoods and chimerical Adventures, related with the utmost Impudence, and in a Style stuffed with Obscenities. The Title of this fine Performance is as follows. *Histoire des Intrigues amoureuses du P. Peters, &c.* — *The History of the amorous Intrigues of Father Peters, a Jesuit, Confessor to* James II, *late King of* England, *containing his most private Adventures, and his true Character, and likewise the Counsels he gave to that Prince, concerning his Government.* Cologne, *for Peter Marteau, junior,* 1698. As long as there are Persons, who take a Pleasure in purchasing this kind of Books, there will be Booksellers, who will be at the Charge of the Composition and Impression of them, and, consequently, base and mercenary Writers will never be wanting for such a Work. It is therefore an incurable Disease.

[C] *Father Annat wrote many Books.*] His *Latin* Treatises, published at several Times, were collected into three Volumes, in 4to, and printed at *Paris*, for *Cramoisy*, in 1666. The first contains a Work entituled *De Scientia media contra novos Jesu impugnatores, una cum exercitatione scholastica sub nomine Eugenii Philadelphi, & appendice ad Guilhelmum Camerarium.* — *Of the middle Science, against it's new Opposers; together with a Scholastic Discourse, under the Name of* Eugenius Philadelphus, *and an Appendix to* William Camerarius. The second contains a Piece entituled *Augustinus à Bajanis, hoc est Jansenianis, vindicatus.* — *St Austin vindicated against the Jansenists.* The following Treatises are in the third. *Catholica disputatio de Ecclesia praesentis temporis.* — *De inconcessa libertate contra novum Augustinum Iprensis Episcopi, Vincentium Lenem, Apologistam Jansenii & Commentatorem quinque propositionum.* — *Informatio de quinque propositionibus ex Theologia Jansenii collectis, quas Episcopi Galliae Romano Pontifici ad censuram obtulerunt.* — *Jansenius à Thomistis gratiae per se ipsam efficacis defensoribus condemnatus.* — *Cavilli Jansenianorum contra latam in ipso à sede Apostolica sententiam, seu confutatio libelli trium Columnarum* (10). i. e. *A Catholic Disputation concerning the present Church.* — *Of unrestrained Liberty, against the new* Augustin *of the Bishop of* Ypres, Vincentius Lenes, *Apologist for* Jansenius, *and Commentator on the five Propositions.* — *An Information concerning five Propositions collected from the Divinity of* Jansenius, *presented by the French Bishops to the Pope, for his Censure.* — Jansenius *condemned by the Thomists, Defenders of the Notion of Grace efficacious of itself.* — *The Cavils of the Jansenists against the*

(10) *It is in Father Sotuel Calumniarum.*

Sentence pronounced against them by the Apostolical See; or a Confutation of the Book of three Columns. Thus there are five Treatises in the three Volumes; to which are prefixed some Advertisements to the Readers, and some Notes on the *Journal de Santi-amour.* The following are the Titles of some of his *French* Works. *An Answer to a Book entituled,* la Theologie morale des Jesuites. — *An Answer to some Queries about Mr* Arnauld's *first Letter.* — *The Fairness of the Jansenists in quoting their Authors.* — *A Collection of several Libels, and Impostures, contained in the Journal of what passed in* France, *on Account of the Morality and Apology of the Casuists* (11). *Remedies against the Scruples, which hinder the subscribing the Formulary.* — *Remarks on the Conduct of the Jansenists in printing and publishing the New Testament, printed at* Mons. — Jansenius's *Doctrine contrary to the Holy Apostolic See, and to St* Augustin. I omit the Titles of some other Books, which may be seen in Father *Sotuel*. But, let me observe, by the way, that He, and *Alegambus* his Predecessor, have forgot one thing, which should not have been omitted. They should have set down the Titles of Books in the Language the Author made use of, and then have translated them into *Latin*. It is a common thing to be disappointed, when we enquire after a Book, not by it's true Title, but by the Sense of it, when, perhaps, it is really in the Bookseller's Shop or Warehouse. To conclude, though Father *Annat* was a very old Man, at the time of the Dispute with the *Jansenists* about subscribing the Formulary, and the Version of *Mons*, he published several small Works, in 4to. He was not contented to use his Interest with the Prince, in order to serve the Cause, but defended it, likewise, with his Pen, to the last Drop of his Ink.

I must not forget the Praises, bestowed upon him, in an Answer to the *Lettres Provinciales* of Mr *Pascal*, which was reprinted in *Holland*, in the Year 1696 (12). "As for the Jesuits, who ventured to "write against *Pascal*, what do you think of Father *Annat*, who is the Author of the Book, en-"tituled, *La bonne foy des Jansenistes*; and to whom "the seventeenth and eighteenth *Provincial Letters* "are inscribed? Father *Annat*, answered *Cleander*, "was, in my Opinion, a Man of very good Parts: "The Jesuits published nothing better, than what "he wrote on the Points controverted at that Time, "This good Man (for I knew him to be such; and "indeed he was Modesty itself) would have been "qualified for a Writer, even in *French*, if he had "but applied himself a little more to the Study "of our Language. He has some Strokes as ele-"gant, as lively, and as agreeable, as any I ever met "with in other Authors. I am of your Opinion, "replied *Eudoxus*; And, not to mention his Virtue, "for which I have heard him commended even by "some of the contrary Party, I have besides ob-"served in him an accurate Judgment, and some-"times such a Delicacy of Expression and Raillery, "as is seldom to be met with, in a Scholastic Di-"vine."

(11) *The Clergy of* Paris *made an Apology for this Journal, in the seventeenth and ninth Writings.*

(12) *Entretiens de* Cleandre *&* Endoxe, pag. 70, 80. *Dutch Edition.*

ANNIUS of *Viterbo*, a famous Impostor. See NANNIUS.

ANSELM, Archbishop of *Canterbury*, one of the most illustrious Prelates of his Times, died the Twenty first of *April*, 1109, in the Seventy sixth Year of his Age (a). He wished to have lived a little longer, to finish a *Treatise on the Origin of*

(a) Cave's Historia Literaris Scriptorum Ecclesiast. pag. 627.

ANSELM. ANTESIGNANUS.

the Soul [*A*]. His Article is very long in *Moreri*'s Dictionary, to which I refer the Reader. The Monks of *Lerins*, who placed this great Prelate in the Chronology of their Saints and famous Monks, are confuted by the Author (*b*) of a Book, intituled, *The Monks travestied* (*c*). We shall see, below, that he made use of an Argument for the Existence of a God, which Mr *Des Cartes* very much improved [*B*].

(*b*) He calls himself Monf. Peter Joseph. His Work was printed in 1698, in 12mo.

(*c*) Moines Travestis, Tom. 1. pag. 49.

[*A*] *He wished — — — to have finished a Treatise on the Origin of the Soul.*] This Wish of his made a Doctor of *Louvain* say, That the Doctrine of the Propagation of Souls subsisted to the end of the eleventh Century. These are his Words. "Imo usque ad tempora S. Anselmi, hoc est Annum Christi M. C. in Occidente durasse videtur hæc de animarum traductione dubitatio. Nam cum paulo post moriturus S. Petrus decumberet, dixisse scribit familiaris & convictor ejus Edinerus, *Si Deus mallet me adhuc inter vos saltem tam diu manere, donec questionem, quam de animæ origine mente revolvo, absolvere possem, gratiosus acciperem: eo quid nescio, utrum aliquis eorum, me defuncto, sit absoluturus* (1). ———— *This doubtful Opinion concerning the Propagation of Souls; ex' traduce, seems to have continued to the Time of St Anselm*; i. e. *to the end of the eleventh Century*. For Edinerus *, his Acquaintance, and Companion, informs us, that the Holy Father, on his Death-bed, said; I should be thankful, if God would grant me a longer Life; at least till I have finished the Question, which imploys my Thoughts, concerning the Origin of the Soul*; since I know not, whether, after my Decease, any one will undertake to finish it." I have elsewhere (2) cited *Thomas Bartholin*, who has made a Reflexion on this Thought of *Anselm*.

[*B*] *He made use of an Argument for the Existence of a God, which Mr Des Cartes very much improved.*] The Catalogue, which Mr *Baillet* has given of the Authors, whom they say Mr *Des Cartes* pirated, contains these Words. "St *Anselm* likewise is placed "in the Number of the Ancients, to whom Mr *Des* "*Cartes* † was obliged for his Argument, in proof "of the Existence of a God, drawn from hence, "That a most perfect Being, or at least the most "perfect that we are able to conceive, implies Existence. The Argument is to be found in a Book, "which this Saint wrote against *The Fool*, in Answer to an anonymous Author, who had wrote "in Defence of *The Fool*, against an Argument, "which St *Anselm* had advanced in his Book, entituled, *Proslogion* (3)." Observe, that *Huetius* remarks, that *Thomas Aquinas* refuted this Argument. "Celebris illa argumentatio — — — tota est Anselmi, & in Proslogio, & in Apologetico contra Gaunilonem; eandemque exposuit Thomas Aquinas, & refellit (4). — — — *This famous Argument — — — belongs solely to Anselm, both in his Proslogion, and his Apologetic against Gaunilo: it has been explained and refuted by Thomas Aquinas.*"

(*r*) Elbertus Flemouthuanus Philosoph. Christ. de Anima, lib. 4t cap. 1. pag. 8122.

* Ediner. in the Life of S. Anselm apud Surium, April 21.

(2) *Is the Remark [E] of the Article* AVERROES.

† Tom. 2. of his Letters, pag. 276, &c.

‖ Wilh. Leibnitz. Epist. MS. Anselm. Edit. Colonien.

(3) Baillet's Life of Des Cartes, Tom. 2. pag. 336.

(4) Huetii Cens. Philos. Cartes. pag. 204.

ANSELM, a bare-footed *Augustin*, born at *Paris*, will be too often quoted in this Dictionary, and has supplied Mr *Moreri* with too many Materials, not to deserve a Place here. He died at *Paris*, the seventeenth of *January*, 1694, in his Sixty ninth Year. He passed fifty Years of this Time, free from all Monastical Offices, and applying himself wholly to the Duties of a religious Life, and the Writing of Books. He was preparing a second Edition of his *Genealogical History of the House of France* [*A*], and *the great Officers of the Crown*, with Corrections and Additions, which had employed him a long time. He had also undertaken a Work, which treats of the *Royal Houses, and other most illustrious Families*, of *Europe*, and had already put the finishing Hand to it (*a*). I know not what will become of his Manuscripts; but I wish they may be published.

(*e*) Mercure Galant, for the Month of January, 1694. See also the Journal des Savants, of the eighth of February, 1694. pag. 157.

[*A*] *He was preparing a second Edition of his Genealogical History of the House of France, &c.*] He published it, together with That of the great Officers of the Crown, in the Year 1694. in two Volumes in 4to. A large Work of his, had already appeared, entituled, *The Palace of Honour, or the Historical Genealogies of the Illustrious House of France, and of several noble Families of Europe*. This Work was printed at *Paris* in the Year 1663. It contains an Abstract of several Particulars, relating to the Heraldry, the Coronation of Kings, solemn Entries, Baptisms of the Children of *France*, Royal Funerals, Military Orders, &c. This large Volume was not so correct, as the two which followed: it is, though they all stand in need of a new Edition, Revised, Corrected, and Augmented. They have certainly been of great Use: and it is difficult to conceive the Pains this good Monk must needs have taken, to collect so many Names, so many Marriages, so many Births, and so many Dates. It is in vain to resist; where Nature strongly inclines to any one. Thing, the Monk's Habit never cures a Man of it. Father *Anselm* was born with a Talent for tracing Genealogies. The little Relation such Matters have to That kind of Life, which he had vowed, did not alter the Bent of his Inclination. One of his Brethren, though not of the Barefooted Order, was perpetually running after Geographical Discoveries (1). This was his natural Inclination; the Habit of an *Augustin* did not change it.

(1) *Father Lublin. He died at Paris, the seventh of May, 1695. See his Elegy in the Journal des Savants, March 28, 1695.*

ANTESIGNANUS (PETER), born, if I mistake not, at *Rabasteins* [*A*], a small Town of *Languedoc*, in the Diocese of *Alby*, was one of the best Grammarians of the XVIth Century. He had his Employ so much at Heart, that he chose to render himself serviceable to Youth, by applying himself to the Explanation of those Things, which render the first Entry upon Study difficult, rather than aim at Honour by the Explication of greater Difficulties [*B*]. He acquired Reputation enough to provoke

[*A*] *Born, if I mistake not, at Rabasteins.*] What induces me to believe so, is his writing himself *Rapistagnensis*, at the beginning of his Works. I know no Town, which can better give this Appellation, than That of *Rabasteins*: which is called in *Latin Rapistanum*, or *Rapistagnum* (1). I take it for granted, that the Printers have committed an Error in the Place, where *Papyrius Masson* speaks of this Town. They have put *Rupistagni incolis*, instead of *Rapistagni incolis* (2). The three Radishes, which are the Arms of *Rabasteins* (3), persuade me, that *Papyrius Masson*, or the Printers, have put the Letter *u* for the Letter *a*.

[*B*] *He chose to render himself serviceable to Youth — — — rather than aim at Honour by the Explication of greater Difficulties.*] Let him inform us of this Himself; and let us cite his own Words at length: They are Indications of a good Heart, and may perhaps be an useful Lesson to those ambitious Minds, who aim only at gaining the Applause of Those like themselves, but never study the Advantage of those, who stand most in need of Instruction. He had observed just before, that several learned Commentators had written on *Terence*; "and

(1) Catel affirms this in the 306th Page of his Memoirs of the History of *Languedoc*, Mr Bertrand mentions this Town under Rapistanum.

(2) *At the Four hundred ninetieth Page of the* Descriptio Fluminum Galliæ, Edition of Paris, 1685. (3) Catel, ubi supra.

provoke the Lash of Envy [C]. What he published on *Terence* may convince us, that he was the most indefatigable Man in the World [D]. I believe he taught a considerable time at *Lyons*. The Epistle Dedicatory of his *Terence* is dated from thence, in *August* 1556 (a). He inscribes it to three Brothers, whom he taught. His *Greek* Grammar has been reprinted several times. He understood *Hebrew* well enough to deserve a Place in the *Gallia Orientalis of Colomies* (b); and yet he is forgotten in it.

(a) *Idibus Augusti.*

(b) *He wrote a Letter in this Language to Peter Costus, which has been printed. See Gesner's Epitomy.*

—and then adds, " *Verum pueri novitii, ad quos maxi-*
" *me hujus laboris fructus pertinebat, vix ullum ex*
" *accuratis & meditatis istorum commentationibus*
" *emolumentum percipere potuerunt. Videntur enim*
" *viri illi graves incubuisse in eam curam & cogita-*
" *tionem, quæ sibi summam dignitatem & gloriam*
" *esset allatura. Itaque ardua tantum & obscuriora*
" *interpretando explanasse contenti, minutiora cætera,*
" *quorum doctrina & tractatio præcedere, vel certe*
" *conjungi debuerat, leviter attigerunt: Ut Adoles-*
" *centuli, qui his studiis initiantur, se ad cognitio-*
" *nem hujus rei, quam ex communi quadam homi-*
" *num opinione reconditissimam arbitrantur, despe-*
" *rent posse pervenire. Ut igitur eos ab hujus-*
" *modi desperatione ad spem revocarem, ad minima*
" *ista me demittere non recusavi. Neque hic dif-*
" *ficilia tantum enodavimus, sed ne unam quidem*
" *totius Terentii syllabam reliquimus intactam, quam*
" *ad unguem non excusserimus, idque absque ulla*
" *verborum pompa aut magnificentia, sed nudis li-*
" *terarum notis, & methodo quam potuimus bre-*
" *vissima & facilima. Doctrinæ opinionem affectent*
" *alii: Ego pro mea virili parte me puerorum &*
" *formandis & promovendis studiis omnem meam*
" *operam addixisse aperte & ingenue fateor* (4). - - - -
" *But School Boys, who have the best claim to the*
" *Fruit of these Labours; reaped scarce any Advan-*
" *tage from such accurate and laboured Commentaries.*
" *For these great Men seemed to have studied only*
" *their own Honour and Reputation. Upon which ac-*
" *count, they were contented to explain the more dif-*
" *ficult and abstruse Points, but passed lightly over*
" *those of less Importance; the explaining and hand-*
" *ling of which ought to precede, or, at least, ac-*
" *company That of the others: insomuch, that Boys,*
" *when they are initiated in these Studies, despair*
" *of acquiring the Knowledge of what, from the ge-*
" *neral Opinion, they are taught to look upon as very*
" *difficult and abstruse. In order, therefore, to re-*
" *move this Despair, I have condescended to explain*
" *the most trifling Passages. I have, here, not only*
" *cleared up what was difficult; but have left not*
" *a Syllable of Terence untouched, or not fully ex-*
" *amined; and That without a pompous Shew of Words;*
" *but by simple literal Marks, and as briefly as possible.*
" *Let others affect the Reputation of Learning; I free-*
" *ly own, My whole Care has been to form and promote*
" *the Studies of Youth.*" Compare with this the following excellent Passage of *Erasmus*. They relate to the Pains he had taken in enlarging a Dictionary: " *Scimus*
" *hoc laboris genus esse minime gloriosum, præsertim*
" *quum pauci reputant quot autores sint excutiendi;*
" *ut voces aliquot ab aliis præteritas seligas. Verum*
" *hoc plus debetur illis gratiæ qui publicæ utilitatis*

(4) *Petrus Antesignanus,* Epist. Dedicator. Terentii init.

" *gratia non detrectant ingloriam ac molestiæ plenam*
" *industriam* (5). - - - - *I know very well that there*
" *is little Reputation to be gained by this kind of*
" *Labour; especially since so few consider, how many*
" *Authors are to be turned over, in order to select*
" *certain Words omitted by others. But, for this very*
" *Reason, They deserve the greater Thanks, who, for*
" *the sake of publick Utility, do not decline an in-*
" *glorious and troublesome Task.*"

[C] *He acquired Reputation enough to provoke the Lash of Envy.*] This he insinuates by a Common-Place Topic, which is seldom omitted in Epistles Dedicatory He says, that They, to whom he dedicated his *Terence*, seemed to him the properest Persons to screen him from the Attacks of his Enemies. " *Digni maxime atque idonei videbamini, qui nostra*
" *a morsu malevolorum fortiter & industrie tutari*
" *possetis* (6)." There are few Compliments falser than this. Critics have no regard to the Dignity or Capacity of the Person, to whom a Book is dedicated. The *Sieur des Accords* ridicules, wittily enough, the Hopes grounded on the supposed Protection of those, to whom Books are dedicated (7). *D'Aubigny* found the Reflexions of this Author so just, that, after giving them a new Turn, he adopted them for his own (8).

[D] *What he published on* Terence *may convince us, that he was the most indefatigable Man in the World.*] He published the Comedies of this Poet three several Ways: First, he published them with short Notes, and Contents at the Head of each Scene, marking the Accents of all the Words of above two Syllables; and setting down the Measure, and way of scanning each Verse, by it's Side. In the second Place, he published them with the Annotations of almost all the Authors, who have written on *Terence*. Lastly, he published them with new marginal Notes, and with a *French* Translation, and Paraphrase, on the three Comedies. He included every thing in the Translation, which was not in express Terms in the Original, between Crotchets; he marked all the References from the Translation to the Paraphrase with Letters. The *variæ lectiones* have each their Parentheses, and Notes of Reference. This is sufficient to shew, that our Author was extremely laborious. Note, that, in the two last Impressions of his *Terence*, he inserted all that was contained in the first. *Matthieu Bonhomme*, a Bookseller of *Lyons*, was the Person he employed in this tripple Edition. The King's Licence is dated in 1556. The indefatigable Pains of the Author appears no less in his Treatise intituled, *Thematis verborum investigandi ratio*, and in his *Praxis Præceptorum Linguæ Græcæ*. They are to be found in divers *Greek* Grammars.

(5) *Erasmi præfationes in Lexicon. It is the 23d Letter of the 28th Book,* pag. 1702. *See, likewise, the end of the first Chapter of the 18th Book of Pliny's Natural History.*

(6) *Antesign. Epist. Dedicat. Terentii.*

(7) *See the Preface to the Bigarrures de des Accords.*

(8) *See the Epistle Dedicatory to the Confession of Sancy.*

ANTHERMUS, a Sculptor, and Native of the Isle of *Chios*, was the Son of *Miciades*, and Grandson of *Malas*, who had both been Sculptors. He left two Sons, who were of the same Profession; the Name of the one was *Bupalus*, and That of the other *Athenis* [A]. It was against Them that *Hipponax* wrote some very satirical Verses, in revenge for the ridiculous Representation they had made of his Deformity (a). I speak of this, more at large, in the Article of That Poet. See likewise the Article BUPALUS.

(a) Plin. lib. 36. cap. 5.

[A] *The name of the one was* Bupalus, *and that of the other was* Athenis.] So *Suidas* calls him (1): In the Editions of *Pliny*, he was call'd *Anthermus*: But Father *Hardouin* has struck out this Word, and put *Athenis* in the room of it. See the Remarks [C] and [B] of the Article HIPPONAX. The Dictionaries of *Charles Stephens*, *Lloyd*, *Moreri*, and *Hoffman*, call him *Anthermus*, in spite of *Suidas*.

(1) In *Ἰππῶναξ.*

ANTINOE, or ANTINOPOLIS [A], a Town in *Egypt*, on the *Nile*

[A] ANTINOPOLIS.] Mr *Baudrand* says, twice in the same Page, that *Stephen of Byzantium* calls it so. I have not found it so, either in the Edition of *Pineda*, or in that of *Berkelius*: I find in both of them, nothing more, than that the City 'Aντίνοια, *Antinoia*, was likewise call'd *Adrianopolis*. Mr *Moreri* was not aware, that the latter Name, and *Adrianople*, are not different; he gives them as if they were.

ANTINOE. ANTINOUS.

Nile [B], and built, or repaired, by the Emperor *Hadrian*, in Honour of *Antinous*. If we may believe an Author of the IVth Century (a), it was once the Metropolis of *Thebais*. The same Author adds, that it was so populous, that, in his Time, it contained twelve Monasteries of Women (b). *Ammianus Marcellinus* mentions it as one of the three most celebrated Towns of all *Thebais* (c). It is not true, that *Leo Africanus* said it was called *Antbios* [C]. See the Remark [D] of the Article ANTINOUS; you will meet with some Particulars there concerning this City.

[B] *A Town in Egypt, on the Nile.*] *Dion Cassius* positively asserts, that *Adrian* caus'd it to be built in the same Place, where *Antinous* died. Ὅς καὶ πόλιν ἐν τῷ χωρίῳ ἐν ᾧ τοῦτ᾽ ἔπαθε, συνοικίσας καὶ ὀνομάσας ἀπ᾽ αὐτῷ. *Ut urbem in eo loco, in quo ille obiisset, restitutam ex eo nominari voluerit* (1). He had said, that, according to *Adrian's* Relation, this unhappy Youth fell into the *Nile*. Since *Adrian*, then, would have the World believe, that *Antinous* was drown'd in this River; we must conclude, that the Town, which be dedicated to this Favourite, was built on the Banks of the *Nile*, and near the Place, where he said the young Man was lost. *Pausanias* expresly remarks, that This Town stood on the *Nile*: Ἔπι τῷ Νείλῳ πόλις Ἀντινόου ἐστὶν ἐπώνυμῷ· Ἀντίνου (2). *In Ægypto apud Nilum urbs de Antinoi nomine ab appellata*. From hence we may conclude, that the Ruins, which are seen Ten Leagues from the *Nile*, as *Moreri* says, are not Those of *Antinopolis*. At the same time, likewise, this concludes more strongly against the Ruins of the Town, which Mr *Baudrand* has situated Forty Nine Leagues from the *Nile*.

[C] *It is not true, that Leo Africanus said, It was call'd Anthios*.] This is another of Mr *Baudrand's* Mistakes. I believe I shall not judge amiss, if I ascribe his Mistake to the Liberty some take of paraphrasing Authors, whom they make use of. Consider well these words of *Ortelius*; " Anthios hodie dici ex Joannis Leonis Africæ descriptione " deprehenditur: ——— *It appears from* John Leo's *Description of Africa, that it is at present call'd* " Anthio". Compare them with these of Mr *Baudrand*, " Nunc in ruinis jacet, Anthios dicta teste " Leone Africano: ——— *It now lies in Ruins, having been call'd* Anthios, *according to* Leo A- " fricanus." You will perceive, that if this latter Writer had scrupulously confin'd himself to the Terms of the former, he had not made such a Slip. *Ortelius* might have disputed the Point, by wresting *Leo Africanus's* Words to his own Purpose; but Mr *Baudrand* cannot have recourse to Applications or Conjectures; it is incumbent upon him to shew, that *Leo* has positively said, that the Ancient City of *Antinoe* is called at present *Anthios*. Now this can never be made out; for *Leo Africanus* says only, that *Anthios* was built by the *Romans* on the River *Nile*, on the side of *Asia*; and that several *Latin* Inscriptions in Marble are yet to be seen there (3). He speaks of it as a very beautiful City, rendered considerable by the Industry, and good Disposition, of the Inhabitants; so far is he from being able to quote him as a Proof, that it is now quite ruin'd. Mr *Baudrand* adds, that it lies Forty Nine Leagues Eastward from the *Nile*. It is not, then, the *Anthios* of *Leo Africanus*. For Mr *Moreri* deducts Thirty Nine of these Leagues; *It's Ruins*, he says, *are to be seen Ten Leagues from the* Nile. We have prov'd, in the preceding Remark, that *Antinopolis* stood upon This River.

ANTINOUS, Minion of the Emperor *Adrian*, was a Native of *Bythyne*, in *Bythinia* (a). We meet with nothing concerning his Family. His Beauty inflamed the Heart of *Adrian* in such a manner, that a more unbridled or extravagant Passion, than That of the Emperor for this young Man, has scarce been known. It never broke out so furiously, as after the Death of *Antinous*; for there were no Divine Honours, which *Adrian* thought too sublime for this Object of his Love [A]. Some say, that *Antinous* had given him the highest Instance of Affection, that is, had died for him [B]. Others affirm, that he drowned himself in the *Nile*, during the Stay which *Adrian* made in *Egypt*, about the CXXIId Year of the Christian Æra. However it be, the Emperor mourned for him with the most effeminate Grief (b), and ordered Temples and Altars to be erected to him; which was performed with all the

[A] *There were no Divine Honours, which* Adrian *thought too sublime for this Object of his Love*.] I insist not on the great Number of Statues, or Representations, which he caus'd to be made of him, almost in every Part of the World (1). I appeal to the Temples, which he order'd to be built to him; to the Priests, which he appointed him, and to the Sacred Games (2), and Mysteries, consecrated in Honour of him (3). *Pausanias* observes, that, by the particular Care of this Emperor, the Worship of *Antinous* was settled at *Mantinea*, because *Antinous's* Country was a Colony of it (4). Games were celebrated there every five Years, in honour of this Favourite; but the Mysteries consecrated to him were celebrated every Year. They, who publish upon this, that there were Priests of *Antinous*, who assum'd the Title of Prophets; they, I say, who build upon this, and thence conclude that he had an Oracle, seek for Mysteries where there are none (5). These Prophets were only the Priests of *Antinous*, in That particular Town, which bore his Name in *Egypt*, and which was the Mother Church, and Center of this New Religion (7). Now, in the Colleges of the *Egyptian* Priests, They were call'd Prophets, who were in the Nature of Deans, or Superiors. See the Proofs of this, which the Learned *Henricus Valesius* furnishes, in his Annotations on *Eusebius* (8). There is an Inscription preserv'd, in which *Antinous* is placed on the same Throne with the *Egyptian* Gods, σύνθρονος τῶν ἐν Αἰγύπτῳ θεῶν (9). The Dignity of an *Assessor to the Gods* was much inferior to This. I shall not dissemble, what the Philosopher *Celsus* insists on, that the *Egyptians* would never suffer *Antinous* to be compar'd with *Jupiter* and *Apollo* (10). *Origen* maintains the contrary; but I confess he advances it without any Proof; or I do not understand his Reasoning.

[B] *Some say* ——— *that* Antinous ——— *died for him.*] *Adrian* did not say so much: But *Dion* has no regard to the History of That Emperor, where he had read, that *Antinous* fell into the River *Nile*, and was drown'd. He delivers it as a constant Truth, that a certain Magic Operation, on which *Adrian* was employ'd, requir'd, that some one should voluntarily lay down his Life, and that *Antinous* accepted the Condition. The Abbreviator *Xiphilin*, probably, has robb'd us of some Circumstances, which might clear up this Mystery a little; for it is not to be imagin'd, that *Dion Cassius* should report a Circumstance of this Nature in so concise, or rather so maim'd, a Manner. However it be, we cannot infer from the Narration of *Xiphilin*, that *Antinous* laid down his Life, to save, or prolong, That of *Adrian*. We should rather conclude, that he submitted to Death, that the Augurs, by inspecting his Entrails, might be enabled to discover That Point of Futurity, which the Emperor searched for. Nor let it be alledged, after one of our Antiquaries (11), " That, had the Emperor been only curious to consult the Entrails of some Youth, in a Point of Divination, there had been no Necessity of making the Experiment on Him, whom he loved of " all Men living: There were Youths enough, besides him, of exquisite Beauty, in That great Em-

the Diligence, which might be expected from a Nation accustomed of old to the grossest Flatteries [C]. He would fain have persuaded the People, that *Antinous* delivered Oracles; and some were published in his Name; but it was generally believed, that *Adrian* had forged them (c). He caused the Town, in which his Favourite died, to be rebuilt, and called it after his Name [D]. He was overjoy'd, when they told him, that a new Star had appeared in the Heavens, supposed to be the Soul of *Antinous* [E]; and he himself was wont to say, that he had seen the Star of
Antinous

(c) *See the Remark* [D]. *it was at the end.*

(12) *He ought not to have expressed himself doubtfully in this Point. See Apuleius, Apolog. pag.* 301.

(13) *Lampridius in vita Heliogab. cap.* 8.

(14) *Justin. in Apologia, pag.* 65. *See Salmasius on Spartian, in Adriano, pag.* 136. *and Apuleius in Apologia, pag.* 301.

(15) *Aurel. Victor. in Cæsaribus.*

(16) *Spart. pag.* 135.

(1*) *Casaub. in Spart. Vit. Adr. pag.* 137.

(1'3) *Athen. lib.* 1 *c. cap.* 6. *pag.* 677.

" pire (had Beauty been material (12)) who might
" have serv'd for this Infamous Mystery." Let not
this, I say, be alledged; for this Writer was himself
apprized of the Invalidity of this reason, when he added these Words immediately after; But, perhaps, " The
" Secret of the Necromantic Art required, that He
" alone, as being his best beloved, should be sacrificed, to make the Ceremony more efficacious."
He should have added the Words of *Dion*, that it
was necessary the Victim should be a voluntary one.
Now, Other Youths, whom the Emperor might have
design'd for this Sacrifice, would not voluntarily have
submitted to it. Do you not think it was necessary to
use extreme Violence towards those beautiful Youths,
whom *Heliogabalus* delivered to his Magicians?
" Cædit & humanas hostias, lectis ad hoc pueris nobilibus & decoris per omnem Italiam patrimis &
" matrimis, credo ut major esset utrique parenti dolor. Omne denique magorum genus aderat illi,
" operabaturque quotidie hortante illo, & gratias diis
" agente quod amicos eorum invenisset, quum inspiceret exta puerilia, & excuteret hostias ad ritum gentilem suum (13). —— *He sacrificed, likewise, human Victims, selecting for this purpose noble and
" beautiful Youths, whose Fathers and Mothers were still
" living*; I suppose, that both Parents might feel the
" *greater Affliction*. *Lastly, he was attended by all
" sorts of Magicians, whom he daily employ'd, returning the Gods Thanks, that he had met with
" their Friends, when he inspected the Entrails of
" the Children, and examin'd the Victims after his
" own Pagan Rites*". The Magic of those Ages
requir'd Victims of this kind; and St *Justin* observes,
that it made choice of Youths of unspotted Chastity.
Νεκυομαν]εἶαι μὲν γὰρ καὶ αἱ ἀδιαφθόρων παιδῶν ἐπεοπ]ἠσεις· Necyomantiæ ipsæ & incorruptorum puerorum speculariæ inspectiones (14). *Antinous*
would, in this respect, have been very unfit. To return to *Adrian*, I think we must suppose, 1. That
the Necessity was extremely pressing, which made
him consent to the sacrificing of his Favourite.
II. That the Desire of avoiding Death was to him a
stronger Motive, than the Curiosity of diving into
Futurity: I chuse therefore to follow *Aurelius Victor*,
rather than *Xiphilin*. *Aurelius Victor* expresses himself thus, " Quæ quidem alii pia volunt religiosaque,
" quippe Hadriano cupiente fatum producere, cum
" voluntarium ad vicem magi proposuissent, cunctis
" retractantibus Antinoum objecisse se referunt (15)".
—— " *Others look upon it as a pious and religious
" Act*; *for*, *Hadrian being desirous of seeing into Futurity*, *and the Magicians requiring a voluntary Sacrifice for this Purpose*, *when all others declin'd it*,
" *Antinous*, *they say*, *offer'd himself*." Add, if
you please, these Words of *Spartian*. " De quo (*Antinoo*) varia fama est, aliis eum devotum pro Hadriano asserentibus (16). —— *Concerning whom*
" (*Antinous*) *there are various Reports*, *some affirming*
" *that he devoted himself for* Hadrian".

[G] *Accustom'd to the grossest Flatteries*.] Among the
Instances of base Complaisance for the Passions of *Adrian*, *Casaubon* reckons what the Poet *Pancrates* did
(17). He shewed *Adrian*, as a Miracle, the *Lotos* Flower,
which is not unlike a Rose, telling him it ought to
be named the *Antinoian*, and that it grew on the
very Spot, which had been sprinkled with the Blood
of a Lyon, which He, the Emperor, had kill'd in
Hunting. The Emperor was so pleased with this
Discourse, that he ordered *Pancrates* a Pension in the
Musæum of Alexandria (18). *Athenæus* does not explain the Reason, why the Poet would have this
Flower called after *Antinous*; but we may easily conjecture, that *Pancrates's* Design in it was to do honour to the Name of This Favourite. I imagined for
some time, that this Passage of *Athenæus* had been
the Occasion of a Mistake of Mr *Moreri's*, which I
have mention'd at the End of this Article: But I alter'd my Opinion, upon Reading these Words of a
Modern Author. *Adrian* —— *gave the Name of
this wretch* (*Antinous*) *to a City of* Egypt —— *as
he had also given it to a Planet*, *to a Flower*, *to
Temples*, *to Sacrifices*, *to Oracles*, *to Solemn Games*;
in short, *he made a God of him* (19). They, who
compare this Passage with the *Antinous* of *Moreri*,
will be able to judge whether That Writer knew
how to make use of the Books he consulted.

[D] *He caus'd the Town*, *in which his Favourite
died*, *to be rebuilt*, *&c.*] I have followed the Translator
of *Xiphilin*, who speaks only of a City repaired;
though *Xiphilin* makes use of the Word συνοίκισας.
Others, not examining the Text so closely, say, that
Adrian built a Town, which bore the Name of *Antinous*. Πόλιν ἔκτισεν ἐπώνυμον Ἀντίνου (20). Urbem condidit *Antinoo* cognomine. It was situated
in *Thebais*, and was anciently called *Besa*, which was
also the Name of the particular Deity adored there.
Casaubon affirms this (21), and observes, that the
Egyptians, leaving the new Name to the *Greeks*, continued to call it *Beza*; but some, joining together the
old and new Name, call'd it *Besantinous*. *Helladius*,
who was born there, did so (22). Let us not forget,
that *Antinous's* Tomb was to be seen there. St *Epiphanius* informs us of it in these Words: Ὡς ὁ Ἀντίνοος ὁ ἐν Ἀντίνου κεκηδευμένος ὑπὸ Ἀδριανοῦ
κατετάγη (23). *After this manner* Antinous, *being
buried by* Hadrian *in the City of his Name*, *was
rank'd among the Gods*. We learn from *Origen*,
that Miracles were said to be wrought in This Temple of *Antinous* (24). It is there *Salmasius* places
the pretended Oracle of This false and ridiculous
Divinity. " Licet in multis Græciæ urbibus templa & sacerdotes habuerit Antinous, præcipue tamen eum coluisse videntur Ægyptii, in ea urbe,
" quæ ab ipso nomen accepit; nam ibi sepultus est,
" ibi Oracula per eum reddi credebantur, ibi & prophetas habuit (25). —— *Tho'* Antinous *had Temples
" and Priests in many Cities of* Greece, *yet the
" Ægyptians seem to have been the principal Worshippers of Him*, *in that City*, *which had it's Name
" from Him*; *for There he was buried*; *There Oracles
" were thought to be deliver'd by Him*; *and There
" he had his Prophets*." What relates to the Oracle is attested by *Origen* (26), if the Passage be read
as *Salmasius* has quoted it; Πνεῦν Θεϊλεγον ἀπὸ
τῦ Ἀντίνου αὐτοῦ (27). See also *Scaliger* on *Eusebius*,
n. 2135, where his Quotation differs from That of
Salmasius; tho' *Spencer* vindicates the latter Reading,
in the Forty fourth Page of his Annotations on *Origen* against *Celsus*. What induc'd me to call it a pretended Oracle, was this: I recollected these Words
of *Spartian*: " Et Græci quidem, volente Adriano,
" eum consecraverunt, oracula per eum dari asserentes, quæ Adrianus ipse composuisse jactatur (28).
" —— *The* Greeks, *to please* Adrian, *deified Him*, *affirming that he gave Oracles*; *which* Adrian *himself is
" said to have composed*.

[E] *A New Star*, —— *supposed to be the Soul of* Antinous.] The like Flattery had been practised before,
in Favour of *Julius Cæsar*. " Ludis quos primo
" consecratos ei hæres Augustus edebat, stella crinita
" per septem dies continuos fulsit, exoriens circa undecimam horam, creditumque est animam esse Cæsaris in Cœlum recepti, & hac de caussa simulacro
" ejus in vertice additur Stella (29). —— *At the first
" Celebration of the Games*, *consecrated to him by* Augustus, *a Comet appeared for seven Days successively*, *rising about the eleventh Hour*; *and it was
" thought to be the Soul of* Cæsar *receiv'd into the
" Heavens*; *for which Reason a Star is plac'd on the
" Head of his Statue*". *Ovid* concludes his Metamorphoses by That of *Cæsar's* Soul into a Star.

Vix ea fatus erat, media cum sede Senatus
Constitit alma Venus nulli cernenda, suique
Cæsaris eripuit membris, nec in aëra solvi

(19) Trist Comment. Histor. Tom. 1. pag. 541.

(20) Hegesippus apud Euseb. Hist. Ecclef. lib. 4. cap. 8. *See also* Amm. Marcellin. lib. 22. cap. 16.

(21) *Casaub. in Spart.* V.t. Adriani. 138.

(22) Apud Photium, Biblioth. pag. 1596.

(23) Epiph. in Ancorato, n. 108.

(24) Origen adversus Celsum, lib. 3. pag. 132.

(25) Salmas. in Spart. vit. Adriani, pag. 143.

(26) Origen. *ibi supra.*

(27) Salmas. *ubi supra.*

(28) Spart. in Adriano, pag. 137.

(29) Sueton. in Cæsare, cap. 88. *See the* Penses Diverses sur les Cometes, pag. 219.

Passa

ANTINOUS. ANTIPATER. 349

Antinous (d). What is most surprizing in all this, is, not the prophane Complaisance for this Prince's Weakness, which in private was a Jest (e); but that the Worship of this new Deity should subsist a long time after his Death, and be still in vogue in the Reign of *Valentinian* (f), when there was no longer occasion to flatter this Prince, or to fear the special Edict, ordaining this Worship (g). So that the Adoration of *Antinous* subsisted entirely on a ridiculous Fondness in People for every thing, which they find established. The Fathers of the Church made the Advantage of this foolish Superstition, to expose the Vanity of the Pagan Religion. It was easy to trace this new Divinity to the Source, and thence bring the Original of all the rest into suspicion. People talked very differently of *Antinous*, according to the Differences of the Times; when they addressed themselves to *Antoninus Pius*, the adopted Son and Heir of *Adrian*, or to *Marcus Aurelius*, adopted by *Antoninus Pius*, according to the Intention of *Adrian*, they were not so imprudent, as to hint at the infamous Cause of his Deification. They touched upon that String with the gentlest Hand (h). But *Tertullian*, who lived at a greater Distance from those Times, and under Emperors, who had not the same Interest in the Affair, observed no Measures. *Prudentius* has pleasantly observed, that *Adrian's* Minion was raised to an higher Station than *Jupiter's* [F]; for *Antinous* sat down to Table, while *Ganymede* fill'd the Liquor. The former might have said,

——— mediis videor discumbere in astris
Cum Jove, & Iliaca porrectum sumere dextra
Immortale merum (i).

Methinks amidst the Stars reclin'd I lye
With *Jove*, th' Imperial Master of the Sky;
There from the Hand of the fair *Trojan* Boy
The Cup receive, and quaff immortal Joy.

The Children of this World have, in all Ages, made their Court more exactly to the Gods of the Earth, than to those of Heaven. I cannot imagine, why Mr *Moreri* says, that Adrian believed, that Antinous *was changed into a Flower*, and into a *Temple* (k), and even ordered an Altar to be raised to him. Is not this supposing, that he built no Temples in Honour of him? And is this any truer, than the metamorphosing him into a Flower?

Passa recentem animam, cœlestibus intulit astris.
Dumque tulit, lumen capere atque ignescere sensit,
Emisitque sinu. Luna volat altius illa,
Flammiferumque trahens spatioso limite crinem
Stella micat *.

* Ovid. Metam lib. 15. ver. 843.

*This spoke; the Goddess to the Senate flew;
Where, her fair Form conceal'd from mortal View,
Her Cæsar's Heavenly Part she made her Care,
Nor left the recent Soul to waste to Air;
But bore it upwards to it's native Skies:
Glowing with new-born Fires she saw it rise;
Forth-springing from her Bosom up it flew,
And, kindling, as it soar'd, a Comet grew:
Above the Lunar Sphere it took it's Flight,
And shot behind it a long Trail of Light.*
WELSTED.

The Greek Poets had long before employed the same Thought in Favour of *Berenice's* Hair: The Emperor *Adrian* was too learned to be ignorant of it. Yet he relished the Flattery, though destitute of the Charms of Novelty. What could they be thinking of, who placed this Darling in the lowest Region of the Heavens? Some there were, who raised him no higher than the Orb of the Moon. Πῶς ὁ τεθνεὼς Ἀντίνοος μειράκιον ἐν τῇ σελήνῃ οὐρανὸν καθίδρυται

(30). ——— *How came the young Antinous, when he died, to be placed near the Moon?*

[F] *Prudentius has pleasantly observed, that Adrian's Minion was raised to an higher Station, than Jupiter's*.] His Verses deserve to be more correctly cited, than the Sieurs *Tristan*, in his *Historical Commentaries on the Medals of the Roman Emperors* (31), and *Moreri*, in his *Historical Dictionary*, have given them. I transcribe them from the Edition of *Nicolas Heinsius*.

Quid loquar Antinoum cœlesti in sede locatum?
Illum deliciæ nunc Divi Principis; illum
Purpureo in gremio spoliatum sorte virili,
Hadrianique Dei Ganymedem; non cyathos dis
Porgere, sed medio recubantem cum Jove fulcro
Nectaris ambrosii sacrum potare lyæum,
Cumque suo in templis vota exaudire marito (32)?

Why shou'd I mention Fair Antinous,
*The Royal Lover's Minion, and Delight;
Rank'd, with His Master, now, amidst the Gods,
His other Ganymede; yet not, like Him,
The Cup to fill; but, near great Jove reclin'd,
To quaff Ambrosial Nectar with the Gods,
And, jointly with his Master, hear the Vows,
Which Mortals at their Altars humbly pay?*

ANTIPATER, an Idumean by Nation [A], illustrious for his Birth

[A] *An Idumean by Nation*.] *Eusebius* makes him an *Ascalonite* (1). "A Band of Robbers, *says he*, who had plundered a Temple near *Ascalon*, carried *Antipater* with the rest of the Booty into *Idumea*, where he lived a long time; his Father not having wherewithal to redeem him." What I shall observe in the following Remark confutes this Story. *Photius* seems to me to deserve Censure upon this Occasion. In giving the Extract of *Josephus*, he affirms, that *Herod* was the Son of *Antipater*, who had served in the Temple of *Ascalon*, Ὁ τῷ Ἀντιπάτρῳ τῷ Ἀσκαλωνίτῃ τῷ ἱεροδούλῳ (2). He did not find this in *Josephus*; and yet what Reader questions, whether every thing cited by *Photius* be in the Books he refers to? He, elsewhere, says (3), that *Antipater* was an *Idumean*, of the City of *Ascalon*, and a great Enemy to *Hircanus*, on account of the Love he bore to *Aristobulus*. This last Fault ought not to be imputed to *Photius*; for all his following Discourse shews, that he makes *Antipater* and *Hircanus* good Friends.

ANTIPATER. ANTONY.

Birth [B], his Riches, and his good Sense, artfully made his Advantage of the Confusions, into which the Differences betwixt *Hircanus* and *Aristobulus* had thrown *Judea*. These were two Brothers, who disputed the High-Priesthood. *Antipater* warmly espoused *Hircanus*'s Interest, and engaged *Aretas*, King of the *Arabians*, in it, and, afterwards, *Pompey*, the *Roman* General; in such a manner, that *Hircanus* got the better (*a*). *Antipater* had the sole Management of Affairs under his Government, and always turned them to the Advantage of the *Romans*, whenever an Opportunity offered. This made the *Roman* Generals, *Scaurus*, *Gabinus*, and *Cassius*, honour him with several important Commissions, and pay a great deference to his Councils (*b*). He did *Julius Cæsar* a singular Piece of Service, in the War of *Alexandria*, by supplying him with Provisions and Troops, and assisting him couragiously in Person. Insomuch, that, besides great Commendations, he obtained from *Julius Cæsar* the Freedom of a Citizen of *Rome*, and the Administration of *Judea* (*c*). The Complaints of *Antigonus* (*d*) prevailed nothing against him; his Application to Business, and his great Abilities, gained him such an high Esteem, that he was little less honoured, than if he had been formally invested with the Royal Authority (*e*). The manner, in which he seemed to guard against any Reverse of Fortune, by giving one of his Sons the Government of *Jerusalem*, and another That of *Galilee*, with the Command of Troops, created a just Suspicion of his designing to have no Superior, either in Name, or Effect. A *Jew*, named *Malchus*, suspecting this, resolved to prevent the Evil, and, finding no better way, than That of sending *Antipater* out of the World, he poisoned him (*f*). By this Act he became guilty of the blackest Ingratitude; for the Person, whom he destroyed, had loaded him with Benefits, and had, besides, saved his Life (*g*). Among other Children, *Antipater* left the famous *Herod*, who was afterwards King of *Judea* (*h*).

(*a*) Joseph. Antiq. lib. 14. cap. 2. & seq.
(*b*) Ibid. cap. 9. & seq.
(*c*) Ibid. cap. 14, 15.
(*d*) He was the Son of Aristobulus.
(*e*) Ibid. cap. 17.
(*b*) His Wife, called Cypris, was of a great Family in Arabia. Joseph. de Bell. Jud. lib. 1. cap. 6.
(*f*) Ib. cap. 19.
(*g*) Ibid. cap. 18.

Friends. They, who published this Author, must share in the Blame as to this Point; but he alone is answerable for the other Fault. *Ascalon* was not a Town of *Idumea*; and, after all, *Josephus* does not say, that *Antipater* was of *Ascalon*. Now *Photius* gives it as an Extract from *Josephus*.

[B] *Illustrious for his Birth*] His Father, whose Name was likewise *Antipater*, was Governor of *Idumea* under *Alexander Jannæus*, King of *Judea*. *Eusebius* calls him *Herod*, and makes him a Servant in a Temple; and so poor, that he was not able to redeem his Son, who was fallen into the Hands of Robbers. Τῦτον δὲ Ἡρῴδη τινὸς Ἀσκαλωνίτη τῶν περὶ τὸν νεὼ τῦ Ἀπόλλων Θ' ἱεροδύλων καλυμένων γεγονέναι (4). *Huic vero Herodem quemdam Ascalonitam unum ex numero servorum templi Apollonis quod Ascalone est patrem fuisse.* But the Learned make no doubt, that both *Eusebius* and *Africanus*

(4) Euseb. l. 1. cap. 6. Vide ibi Valesium.

whom he copies, have followed false Memoirs in this Point; and that more Credit ought to be given to *Josephus*, who affirms, that King *Alexander*, and his Queen, gave the Government of *Idumea* to *Antipater*, who, by many Presents, obtained the Friendship of the *Arabs*, and That of the Inhabitants of *Gaza* and *Ascalon* (5). *Josephus*, speaking in another Place of *Antipater*, the Son, observes, that he was the most considerable Person of *Idumea*, as well for the Antiquity of his Family, as for his Riches (6). *Hegesippus* says of the same *Antipater*, that he was famous in his own Country for his Ancestors (7). It has ever been common to debase the Birth of those, whom Fortune raises to the highest Dignities (8). By the way, the Ambiguity of a Passage in *Josephus* has made some imagine, that *Herod*'s Grandfather's Name was not *Antipater*, but *Antipas*.

(5) Joseph. Antiquit. lib. 14. cap. 2.
(6) Id. de bello Judaico, lib. 1. cap. 5.
(7) De Excid. lib. 2. cap. 14.
(8) See the Remark [A] of the Article TOUCHET.

ANTONY, a *Roman* Family, in *Latin*, *Antonia*, descended, according to an old Tradition, from *Anton*, the Son of *Hercules* (*a*), produced two Branches: The one a *Patrician*, with the Sirname of *Merenda*; the other a *Plebeian*, without almost any kind of Sirname. It does not appear, that the *Patrician* Branch lasted long, or produced any other Persons, mentioned in History, except *T. ANTONIUS MERENDA*, and *Q. ANTONIUS MERENDA*. The first was one of the *Decemvirate*, abrogated on account of the tyrannical Cruelty of *Appius Claudius*, in the Year of *Rome* 304; and one of those, who went into a voluntary Exile, and whose Goods were confiscated, after the Trial of *Appius Claudius*, and *Sp. Oppius* (*b*). The latter was a Military Tribune in the Year of *Rome* 333 (*c*). But the *Plebeian* Branch continued a long time, and made a great Figure in *Rome* [*A*]; for, besides that it could boast of having twice enjoyed the Post of Captain-General of the Cavalry, Six times the Consulship, Once the Censorship, and Thrice the Honour of a Triumph (*d*); It saw itself, in the Person of *Marc Antony*, the *Triumvir*, Mistress of Half the Empire. We shall proceed to particular Articles of the chief Men of this Ancient Family [*B*].

(*a*) Plutarch. in Marc. Antonio, pag. 917.
(*b*) Livius, lib. 3. pag. 88.
(*c*) Id. lib. 4. pag. 128.
(*d*) See Glandorp Onomast. pag. 66.

[*A*] *The Plebeian Branch continued a long Time, and made a considerable Figure in Rome.*] We must not forget, that *Marc Antony* the Orator, who died in the Year 667, was the first, who brought the Honours of the Consulate, the Triumph, and Censureship into This Family.

[*B*] *Of This ancient Family.*] They, who have most Reading, most Collections, and most Materials for a Library, fall, sometimes, into strange Oversights. Father *Vavassor* is an Instance of this, in his excellent Treatise of the Burlesque Stile, when he censures *Photius*, for having believed, that *Antonius Diogenes*, Author of a Romance, flourished not long after the Death of *Alexander*. Οὐ λίαν πόῤῥω τῶν χρόνων τῦ βασιλέως Ἀλεξάνδρου (1). *Non ita diu post Alexandri Magni tempora floruisse.* He alledges several Reasons against this; among which he thinks this the strongest, That the Family *Antonia* was not, then, in being; and that the Name was not so much as known. *Neque, quod gravissimum est, tum nata gens Antonia, aut facta vox, aut audita temporibus illis* (2). Than which nothing is more false. We have produced, on the Credit of *Livy*, one *Titus Antonius*, a *Decemvir*, in the Year of *Rome* 304; and, about thirty Years after, one *Quintus Antonius*, who was a Military Tribune. We find, in the same *Livy*, one *Marcus Antonius*, appointed Master of the Horse by the Dictator *Cornelius Rufinus*, in the Year 421. Now it is certain, that *Alexander* died in the Year 430. I do not alledge the Tradition, recorded by *Plutarch*; I might justly be answered, that *Anton*, Son of *Hercules*, was no more the Stem of the *Antony*'s in *Italy*, than *Cocceius Nerva* was the Stem of the House of *Cossé* in *France*.

(1) Photius, n. 67. pag. 364.
(2) Vavassor, de ludicra Dictione, 148.

ANTONY.

ANTONY (MARC) the Orator, was the greatest Ornament of his Family. At his Entrance on Public Business, he distinguished himself in a manner, which deserves to be related. He had obtained the Quæstorship of the Province of *Asia*, and was already arrived at *Brundusium*, to take shipping there, in order to go and take Possession of his Office, when his Friends informed him, that he was accused of Incest before the Prætor *Cassius*, the most rigid Judge in the World; whose Tribunal was termed the *Rock of the accused*. *Marc Antony* might have pleaded a Privilege, which forbad the receiving Accusations against those, who were absent in the Service of the Republic; but he chose to justify himself in Form, and returned to *Rome*, stood his Trial, and was acquitted with Honour (*a*). *Sicily* fell to him during his Prætorship; and he gave chace to the Pirates, who infested those Coasts. He was made Consul, with *A. Posthumius Albinus*, in the Year of *Rome* 653, and courageously and happily suppressed the turbulent Attempts of *Sextus Titus*, Tribune of the People. Some time after, he was made Proconsul of *Cilicia*, and performed so many great Actions in this Post, that he obtained the Honour of a Triumph. We must not forget, that, to improve his wonderful Talent of Eloquence, he would in some manner become the Disciple of the most noted Orators of *Athens* and *Rhodes*, in his Passage to *Cilicia*, and his Return to *Rome*. He afterwards exercised the Office of Censor, with great Glory; having gained his Cause before the People, against *Marcus Duronius*, who had entered an Accusation of Bribery against him, in Revenge for his expelling him out of the Senate; which this wise Censor thought he deserved; because, while Tribune of the People, he repealed a Law, restraining the immoderate Expences of Feasts (*b*). He was one of the best Orators That ever pleaded in *Rome*; and, as *Cicero*, a proper Judge in these Matters, says, he was an Instance, that *Italy* could boast of equalling *Greece* in the Art of Speaking well. Among other Persons, he defended *Marcus Aquilius*, and so moved the Judges by the Tears he shed (*c*), and the Scars he shewed on his Client's Breast, that he gained his Cause. The Character of his Eloquence, and his Actions, may be seen at large in the Books I quote (*d*). He never published any of his Pleadings [*A*]; least he should be convicted of speaking in one Cause, contrary to what he might have alledged in another. The Morality of the Bar thought it no Scandal, in those Days, for a Pleader to contradict himself in Favour of his Client. The Precaution of this Advocate is necessary to Persons of his Profession [*B*]; and yet is not always sufficient

(*a*) Valer. Maxim. lib. 3. cap. 7. n. 6. *ubi mentions* lib. 6. cap. 8.) *the Constancy of this Marc Antony, in denying that his Master was guilty.*

(*b*) Glandorpius, ubi supra, pag. 68. ex Epit. Liv. Cicer. &c.

(*c*) Cicero de Orat. lib. 2. cap. 47. & in Verr. 5.

(*d*) Id. in Bruto, & de Orat. c. 37.

[*A*] *He never published any of his Pleadings.*] This Fact, and the Reason of it, deserve to be confirmed by Proofs. *Cicero* and *Valerius Maximus* shall be my Vouchers. Let us hear *Cicero* first: "Hominem ingeniosum M. Antonium aiunt solitum esse dicere, idcirco se nullam unquam orationem scripsisse, ut si quid aliquando non opus esset ab se esse dictum, posset se negare dixisse (1). ----- *The ingenious Orator*, Marc Antony, *they tell us, was wont to say, that his Reason for never publishing any of his Orations, was, that, whenever it was proper he should not have said a Thing, he might deny that he had said it.*" *Valerius Maximus*'s Words are: "Jam M. Antonio remittendum convitium est, qui idcirco se aiebat nullam orationem scripsisse, ut si quid superiore judicio actum ei, quem postea defensurus esset, nociturum foret, non dictum à se affirmare posset: qui facti vix pudentis tolerabilem caussam habuit, pro periclitantium enim capite non solum eloquentia sua uti, sed etiam verecundia abuti, erat peratus (2). — Marc Antony *is to be excused from Censure; who said, that he, therefore, published no Orations, that, if what he had pleaded in a foregoing Cause should appear to be prejudicial to a subsequent Client, he might deny his own Words. Thus he assigned a tolerable Reason for an Action, otherwise scarce honourable; for he was ready, not only to employ his Eloquence, but even to sacrifice his Modesty, in Defence of the Distrest.*" No Critic, I think, can be so unreasonable, as to maintain, that I translate the Word *scribere* wrong. Every Reader of common Sense will perceive, that *Marc Antony* never meant to say, that he pleaded *Extempore*; that he never drew up his Pleadings in Writing; for, if this had been his Meaning, he would have assigned an impertinent Reason for his Conduct; since his only Intention was to prevent any one's turning his own Weapons against him. Now this he might equally have done, whether he wrote down his Pleadings, or not, provided he did not publish them. A Manuscript, which is locked up, can never convict an Orator, at the Bar, of having formerly maintained an Opinion quite contrary to what he advances at present. He may deny it, with the same Assurance, as if he had pleaded *Extempore*; without any Fear of being condemned to produce the Original of his Pleas; there are many ways of guarding against This.

(1) Cicero in Oratione pro Cluentio. cap. 50.

(2) Valer. Maxim. lib. 7. cap. 13. n. 5.

We may conclude, then, that the present Question is not, whether he wrote, or did not write down, his Pleadings, but whether he published them, or not. Were it necessary to offer Proofs in so clear a Case, I could foon produce two very strong ones. The first should be taken from a Passage in *Cicero*, where *Brutus* complains, that *Marc Antony*, the Orator, had published but one very small Book. "Vellem aliquid Antonio præter illum de ratione dicendi sane exilem libellum ------ libuisset scribere (3). ---- *I could wish, that* Antony *had thought fit to publish something more, than That very small Treatise of the Art of Speaking.*" Here, you see, he makes use of the Word *scribere*. The second might be taken from That Oration of *Cicero*, in which the Fact in Question is mentioned; for *Cicero*, intending to shew, that *Marc Antony*'s Precaution was not so effectual as he imagined, represents, not that an Advocate is obliged to produce the Original of his Pleas; but, that there are Auditors, who remember, a long time after, what they have heard a Lawyer advance. "Perinde quasi quid à nobis dictum aut actum sit id nisi literis mandaverimus hominum memoria non comprehendatur (4). ---- *As though the not committing to Writing, what we have formerly advanced in our Pleadings, would prevent it's being retained in the Memory of others.*"

[*B*] *The Precaution of this Advocate is necessary to Persons of his Profession*] I remember, in a Letter, which was published in the Year 1685, an Enquiry into the Causes of the Contradictions of Authors (5). The Lawyers are there brought upon the Stage; and what is said, on their Article, is as follows. "It is sometimes diverting enough to hear the same Lawyer plead, in one and the same Week, for a Husband against his Wife, and for a Wife against her Husband. If he has a fruitful Imagination, he dwells altogether, in his first Plea, upon the Power of Husbands; he grounds his Arguments on Nature, on Reason, on the Word of God, and on Custom. He quotes the Scriptures; he quotes the Fathers; the Civilians, and the Writers of Travels. He declaims against Women, and dwells only on general Propositions. Two Days after, the Scene changes; he entertains other Thoughts, quite contrary to the former. He calls the Husband's Authority, Usurpation; he runs over the Holy Scriptures,

(3) Cicero in Bruto, cap. 44.

(4) Cicero, in Orat. pro Cluentio.

(5) *The second of the new Letters against* Maimbourg's *History of Calvinism*.

A REFLEXION *on the Contradictions to be found in Authors.*

VOL. I. Tttt

sufficient to save their Honour [C]. He ever affected not to pass for a learned Man

"tures, the Code, Physic, History, and the Moral Law, in favour of Women, still haranguing on general Principles; for a vehement Spirit thinks it proves nothing, unless it affirms and denies, without Exception; and consequently, if obliged to maintain opposite Interests, must necessarily contradict itself." It must be owned, that a Lawyer, who has publickly pleaded with all the Fire of Imagination, for the Privileges of Women, may be confuted with all imaginable Ease, the next time he pleads for the Privileges of Men. It is but referring him to his own Minutes. Our Orator, Marc Antony, would fain have avoided this great Inconveniency, and have enjoyed the Privilege of contradicting himself, by maintaining one thing to Day, and another to Morrow, according as the Interest of his Clients required. It would be easy to shew, that Lawyers are not the only Persons, who make use of this Practice; Polemic Divines do the same, according to the different Tenets of those they have to deal with (6). *Bellarmin*, in disputing against the Enthusiasts, maintains, that the Scripture abounds with Characters of it's being Divine; but insists, against the Protestants, that it is obscure, and stands in need of the Authority of the Church (7). A certain Minister, whom I forbear to name, maintains, against those of the *Romish* Church, that the Scriptures every where shine with Characters of Divinity; but, writing against Mr *Pajon*, he speaks another Language (8). This Privilege ought to be left wholly to Poets and Orators. "*In different Places, they say very different Things, as it best suits their Purpose.* Non Poetarum more, uti se res dederit, ita vel populi, vel eruditorum hominum sententiam nostro quodam jure sequimur, atque allas, si sit opus, aliter de eadem dicimus, says the excellent *Monsignor* della Casa, *Archbishop* of Benevento, in one of his *Letters* to Victorius. But *Eustathius* has observed, on the eighteenth Verse of the second Book of the *Odyssey*, and on the Two hundred and forty third of the twelfth of the *Iliad*, that *Homer* has said things in these Places, concerning Auguries, quite contrary to what he said elsewhere; which he calls ἀμοιβηρὸν λόγον. Thus, in the first Parts of my Poems, which I have just now quoted, I have said, that an old Poet is a wretched thing, because it suited no my purpose; but this does not hinder me from saying the quite contrary elsewhere, if occasion requires (9)." How do I love this Sincerity! and how should I be overjoyed to find it in *Bellarmin*, or the Minister! but it is not to be expected. We shall hear *Cicero* presently on the Right of Lawyers, with regard to the Privilege of contradicting themselves: See the Remarks [H] and [I] of the Article BALDUS.

[C] *This Precaution — is not always sufficient to save their Honour.*] We have seen (10), how *Cicero* has observed, that the good Memory of their Hearers is to be dreaded by Lawyers, who contradict themselves (11). If he had given Examples of this, he might better have made it appear, that the Precautions of *Marc Antony* were insignificant. But it must be own'd, that what he adds is sufficient to justify the Conduct of That Orator. It is this: *Marcus Brutus*, pleading against *L Plancius*, who was defended by *L. Crassus*, got two of his Friends to stand up in Court, and read certain Passages in an audible Voice, which he had selected out of two Speeches of *L. Crassus*; some raising the Authority of the Senate very high, the others depressing it. This disconcerted the Orator a little, and put him upon excusing himself, from the Difference of Times, and Causes, which had extorted from him these contradictory Maxims (12). "Ego vero, says *Cicero* (13), in isto genere libentius cum multorum tum hominis eloquentissimi & sapientissimi L. Crassi autoritatem sequor, qui quum L Plancium defenderet accusante M. Bruto, homine in dicendo vehementi & callido, quum Brutus duobus recitatoribus constitutis ex duabus ejus orationibus capita alterna inter se contraria recitanda curasset, quod in dissuasione rogationis ejus, quæ contra Coloniam Narbonensem ferebatur, quantum potest de autoritate Senatus detraxit; in suasione legis Serviliæ summis ornat Senatum laudibus, & multa in Equites Romanos quum ex ea oratione asperius dicta recitasset, quo animi illorum Judicum in Crassum

incenderentur; aliquantum esse commotus dicitur. Itaque in respondendo primum exposuit utriusque rationem temporis, ut oratio ex re & causa habita videretur. — — *For my own Part, I willingly follow, in This, the Authority of many Others, as also of the most eloquent and wise* L. Crassus *; who, having undertaken the Defence of* L. Plancius, *against the Accusation of* M. Brutus, *a vehement and artful Speaker; and Brutus having procured two Persons to repeat alternately Passages out of two of his Orations, which were contradictory to each other; for, in the one side, in his Oration against the Law, which was proposed against the Colony of* Narbo, *he detracts as much as possible from the Authority of the Senate: whereas, in That for the Servilian Law, he highly extolls the Senate; and* Brutus *having recited out of That Oration some Reflexions on the Roman Knights, in order to exasperate the Minds of the Judges against* L. Crassus; *he is said, upon this Occasion, to have been a little at a Loss. In his Reply, they say, he sets forth the different Junctures of Time; that what he had said might appear to result from the particular Circumstances of each Cause.*" *Cicero* disapproved of the Conduct of L. *Crassus* on this Occasion; *Cicero*, I say, who was once in the same Circumstances; his Adversaries having repeated a Passage, in one of his Orations, quite contrary to an Argument he was then upon. He answered, That what they had repeated did not contain his true Sentiments; and that what a Man offers, as an Advocate, ought not to be considered, as if spoken by him in quality of a Witness; that it is the Language of the Cause, and not of the Orator. This is plain enough; they must speak according to the Interest of their Cause, and the Conjuncture of Time, and not according to their private Opinions. "Ego si quid ejusmodi dixi, neque cognitum commemoravi, neque pro testimonio dixi: & illa oratio potius temporis mei quam judicii & autoritatis fuit. — — — Errat vehementer si quis in orationibus nostris quas in judiciis habuimus autoritates nostras consignatas se habere arbitratur. Omnes enim illæ orationes causarum & temporum sunt, non hominum ipsorum aut patronorum. Nam si causæ ipsæ pro se loqui possent, nemo adhiberet oratorem: nunc adhibemur ut ea dicamus, non quæ nostra autoritate constituantur, sed quæ ex re ipsa causaque dicantur (14). *If I, indeed, said any thing of this kind, I neither offered it as of my own Knowledge, nor in quality of an Evidence; it was rather the Language of the Juncture of Time, than of my own Judgment and Authority. It is a great Mistake in any one, to look upon the Orations, which I have spoken in several Causes, as so many written Opinions under my own Hand. They are all the Language of the particular Cause and Time, not of the Orator himself. For could Causes speak for themselves, no one would have recourse to an Orator; and it is our Business to speak, not our own Determination of the matter, but what the particular Cause, we are engaged in, requires.*" Add to this the Words, which *Cicero* puts in the Mouth of the Orator *Marc Antony*. "Oratoris omnis actio opinionibus non scientia continetur, nam & apud eos dicimus qui nesciunt, & ea dicimus quæ nescimus ipsi: ita & illi alias aliud iisdem de rebus & sentiunt & judicant, & nos contrarias sæpe causas dicimus, non modo ut Crassus contra me dicat aliquando: aut ego contra Crassum, quum alterutri necesse sit falsum dicere, sed etiam ut uterque nostrum eadem de re alias aliud defendat, quum plus uno verum esse non possit. Ut igitur in ejusmodi re quæ mendacio nixa sit, quæ ad scientiam non sæpe perveniat, quæ opiniones hominum & sæpe errores aucupetur, ita dicam (15). — — — *The whole Business of Oratory consists in Opinion, not in Knowledge; for we speak, not only before the Ignorant, but in Causes, where we ourselves are ignorant. Therefore both our Hearers think and judge of the same things differently at different Times; and we ourselves often patronize opposite Causes; insomuch that not only* Crassus *sometimes speaks against me, and I against* Crassus, *in Causes, where we are both obliged to speak against our Opinions; but even that we both take different Sides of the Question, in relation*

(6) See Remark [M] of the Article ADAM (JOHN).

(7) See the Efforts, which the Jesuit Mulliusieu made in the Auditorium Primum Speculi Miserarum Paresi, to reconcile their Contradictions. See the Remark [D] of the Article BELLARMIN.

(8) See the Supplement to t'e Philosophical Commentary, and pag. 207 and 216 of Mr Saurin's Answer to This Commentary.

(9) It is Mr Menage, who says so, in the Anti-Baillet, Tom. 2. p. 174, 175.

(10) Above Citation (4).

(11) It is not less to be feared by Preachers, who, far from extravagating themselves, repeat from time to time, and almost word for word, the same Sermon.

(12) See Cicero Orat. pro Cluentio, cap. 50, &c. and de Oratore, c. 55. how he was revenged on Brutus, by bringing three Readers into Court.

(13) Cicero Orat. pro Cluentio, cap. 51.

(14) Idem, ibid. c. 50.

(15) Idem, de Oratore, lib. 2. cap. 7.

ANTONY. 353

Man [D]. His Modesty, and other good Qualities, made him no less beloved by a great Number of Illustrious Persons, than his Eloquence gained him the Admiration of the whole World. He perished unfortunately in the bloody Confusions occasioned by *Marius* and *Cinna*. He was discovered in the Place, where he had concealed himself, and Soldiers were immediately sent to kill him. His Address mollified them; nor had any of them Brutality enough to kill him, except their Commander, who had not heard his Discourse, but entered his Chamber in great Anger, that his Men had not executed their Orders (*e*). His Head was exposed on the Chair of the Orators, *pro rostris* (*f*); a Place he had formerly adorned with Triumphal Spoils. This happened in the Year of *Rome* 667. He left two Sons, of whom I am going to speak.

(*e*) Plutarch. in Mario, pag. 431. Valer. Max. lib. 9. c. 9.
(*f*) Cicero, de Oratore, lib. 3. c. 3.

" *to the same Cause, upon different Occasions; when*
" *but one side can possibly be right. In this Matter,*
" *therefore, which depends upon Falshood, which seldom*
" *comes up to Science, and which catches at the Opi-*
" *nions, and often the Errors, of Men*, &c." I assure myself, that the greatest Part of my Readers will be so pleased to find, that these two great Orators held such Principles, and so well knew the Foible of their Profession, that they will pardon whatever may favour too much of Digression in this Remark. Note, that these Principles subsist still.

Compare the Pleadings of Mr *Erard* against Madam *Mazarin* with the Answer to the *Factum* of This Lady. In particular read these Words of the Answer. *Mr* Erard *represented to Madam* Mazarin *the Occurrences of the then Times, in such a manner as she herself must have considered them. It is true, Time and different Events make us think and speak differently.*

[D] *He ever affected not to pass for a learned Man.*] If I am not mistaken, this was more through Policy than Modesty. He saw himself already established in the Reputation of a great Orator. And might he not imagine, that he should be still more admired, if it was believed, that he ow'd his Eloquence to his Genius alone, and not to a long Application to the Study of *Greek* Authors? He had a farther meaning in it; he believed his Rhetoric would have more Influence on the People, if they took it for the meer Production of Nature, than if they looked upon it as the Result of Art. For People are apt to distrust Those, who are practised in all the Tricks of their Profession. As for the Judges, *Marc Antony* believed, that nothing would influence them more in his favour, than to make them believe, that he spoke unprepared, and carefully to conceal from them those fine Touches of Rhetoric, which are generally employed to set off a Cause. And yet, at the bottom, he was a learned Man, and acquainted with all the best Authors among the *Greeks*. Let us prove this by some Passages of *Cicero*. " Magna nobis pueris, Quinte
" frater, si memoria tenes, opinio fuit, L. Crassum
" non plus attigisse doctrinæ quam quantum prima
" illa puerili institutione potuisset, M. autem Antonium omnino omnis eruditionis expertem atque
" ignarum fuisse ---- Quum nos ---- ea discere-
" mus quæ Crasso placerent, & ab his doctoribus
" quibus ille uteretur erudiremur, etiam illud sæpe
" intelleximus ---- illum & Græce sic loqui, nul-
" lam ut nosse aliam linguam videretur, & doctoribus
" nostris ea ponere in percontando, eaque ipsum omni
" in sermone tractare, ut nihil esse ei novum nihil
" inauditum videretur. De Antonio vero quanquam
" sæpe ex humanissimo viro patruo nostro accepera-
" mus, quemadmodum ille vel Athenis vel Rhodi
" se doctissimorum hominum sermonibus dedidisset,
" tamen ipse adolescentulus, quantum illius ineuntis
" ætatis meæ patiebatur pudor, multa ex eo sæpe
" quæsivi. Non erit profecto tibi quod scribo hoc
" novum (nam jam tum ex me audiebas) mihi illum
" ex multis variisque sermonibus nullius rei, quidem esset in his artibus de quibus aliquid existi-
" mare possem, rudem aut ignarum esse visum. Sed
" fuit hoc in utroque eorum, ut Crassus non tam
" existimari vellet non didicisse quam illa despicere,
" & nostrorum hominum in omni genere pruden-
" tiam Græcis anteferre. Antonius autem probabi-
" liorem hoc populo orationem fore censebat suam,
" si omnino didicisse nunquam putaretur. Atque ita
" uterque se graviorem fore, si alter contemnere, alter ne nosse quidem Græcos, videretur. ---- *If*
" *you remember, Brother* Quintus, *it was a prevail-*

" ing Opinion, when we were Boys, that Lucius Cras-
" sus had attained to no greater Degree of Learning,
" than what he had gained at School; but that Marc
" Antony was entirely ignorant, and void of all Eru-
" dition. But, when we applied our selves to Cras-
" sus's favourite Studies, and were instructed by such
" Preceptors, as he had made use of, we had frequent
" Opportunities of being convinced, that he spoke the
" Greek Language as well, as if he had never known
" any other; that he had put such Questions to our
" Preceptors, and handled such Points in every thing
" he said, that he seemed to be familiarly acquainted
" with the whole Circle of Science. As for Antony;
" though I had often learned from That Best-natured
" of Men, my Uncle, his attachment to the Conver-
" sation of the learnedest Men at Athens, or Rhodes,
" yet, as far as the Modesty of Youth would permit,
" I often applied myself to him for Instruction. And
" what I now assure you of, is no new thing to you
" (for I then declared to you the same) that, in the
" many and various Conversations I had with him,
" he appeared to me to be perfectly skilled in every
" Science, of which I could then form any Judg-
" ment. But this was peculiar to them both; that
" Crassus desired not so much to decline the Reputation
" of Learning, as to appear to despise it, and to
" prefer our own native Skill to That of the Greeks;
" and that Antony thought his Words would have
" the more Weight with the People, if they believed he
" had never been instructed; both of them thus aiming
" at Success, the one by appearing to despise, the
" other to be quite ignorant of, the Greek Learning.*"
Thus the second Book *de Oratore* begins. Add to this what he there says of himself (16), that he read the *Greek* Writers only by way of Amusement; and that the Books of the Philosophers were quite unintelligible to him. " Verbum prorsus nullum intel-
" ligo, ita sunt angustis & concisis disputationibus
" illigati;" that, in this Respect he had nothing to say to the Poets, whose Language was not human; and that he confined himself to the Historians, or Orators, who condescended to the Understandings of the half-learned; *Videantur voluisse esse nobis, qui non sumus eruditissimi, familiares.* In what follows, it is not *Cicero*, who speaks, but *Marc Antony*, who, among other things, expresses himself thus: " Ego
" ista studia non improbo, moderata modo sint: opi-
" nionem istorum studiorum & suspicionem artificii
" apud eos qui res judicent oratori adversariam esse
" arbitror; imminuit enim & oratoris autoritatem,
" & orationis fidem (17). ------ *I do not disapprove of*
" *these Studies, provided they are followed with Mode-*
" *ration; but I am of Opinion, that to be famed for them,*
" *and to be suspected of Artifice in the Judges, is pre-*
" *judicial to an Orator, for it lessens his own Autho-*
" *rity, and the Weight of what he says.*" Here he gives the Reason of That Conduct, which *Cicero* ascribes to him; " Erat memoria summa, nulla medita-
" tionis suspicio, imparatus semper aggredi ad dicen-
" dum videbatur, sed ita erat paratus, ut judices illo
" dicente nonnunquam viderentur non satis parati ad
" cavendum fuisse (18). ------ *He had a happy Me-*
" *mory; was never suspected of Premeditation, and*
" *seemed, whenever he began to speak, to be unpre-*
" *pared; yet was he in reality so much so, that the*
" *Judges always seemed sufficiently prepared by what*
" *he was saying to give their Opinions.*" I remember, on this Occasion, a Remark of Mr *Daillé*, on the Difference between *acting the Orator, and being one* (19). This Remark is very just.

(16) Id. cap. 14. See likewise cap. 19.

(17) Id. de Oratore, lib. 2. cap. 37.

(18) Id in Bruto, c. 37.

(19) Daillé, Reponse au P Adam, 3. part. p. 156.

ANTONY (MARC), Eldest Son of the foregoing, had the Sirname of *Creticus* (*a*). He never rose higher than the Prætorship; but he exercised this Office with a more

(*a*) Plut. in Antonio, init. p. 915.

ANTONY.

a more extensive Power than usual; his Commission to convoy Corn to *Rome* giving him a Command over the Seas (b). This Prerogative he obtained by the Favour of the Consul *Cotta* (c), and by the Faction of *Cethegus* (d); nor did any Party murmur at it, as they certainly would have done, if he had been a Person of more Merit [A]. It is said, that he suffered himself to be instigated by evil Counsels, to commit Extortions in the Provinces; and, indeed, he was guilty of many (e). Those of *Sicily* have been represented in a few Words by *Cicero* (f). The War of *Crete*, the good Success of which he thought so certain, that he had provided fewer Arms on board his Fleet, than Chains to bind the conquered (g), having miscarry'd, he fell sick, and died of Grief. He was unable to support the cutting Reflexions, which arose in his Mind, when he remember'd, that the Enemy, having taken several of his Ships, had hung up the *Roman* Soldiers at the Yard-Arm, and had failed up and down with this Spectacle, triumphing insolently over the Republic in a thousand Places. He had three Sons by *Julia*, his second Wife [B], to wit, *Marcus Antonius*, *Caius Antonius*, and *Lucius Antonius* (h), of whom we shall speak hereafter.

I shall have some Errors to correct [C], and perhaps the Encomium *Plutarch* bestows on *Antony* will be one [D].

(b) Paterculus, lib. 2. cap. 31.

(c) *I shall examine, under the Article CETHEGUS*, *whether Cotta was Consul when M. Antony retrieved this Commission.*

(d) Asconius Pedianus in Orat. Cicer. contra Verrem, pag. 113.

(e) Asconius Ped. ubi supra.

(f) Cicero, Orat. 2. in Verrem, cap. 03. See *libram's* Oratio. 2. c. 3.

(g) Florus, lib. 3. cap. 7.

(h) Glandorp. Onomast. p. 73.

[A] *If he had been a Person of more Merit*] *Velleius Paterculus* supplies me with this Thought, in that Part of his History, where he relates, that *Pompey*, about two Years after, obtained a Commission, which rendered him Master of almost all the World. This Commission was not granted him without Opposition; whereas nothing had been said against the Decrees, which had trusted the like Power in the Hands of *Marc Antony*. The Reason was, that they did not judge the latter capable of rendring himself formidable; but *Pompey's* Merit was looked upon as dangerous to the Public Liberty. "Idem hoc
" ante biennium in M. Antonii praetura decretum
" erat; sed interdum personae, ut exemplo nocet, ita
" invidiam auget aut levat. In Antonio homines
" aequo animo passi erant; raro enim invideretur eo-
" rum honoribus, quorum vis non timetur. Contra
" in iis homines extraordinaria reformidant, qui ea
" suo arbitrio aut deposituri aut retenturi videntur,
" & modum in voluntate habent (1). ----- *The
" same thing was decreed two Years before in the
" Praetorship of Marc Antony; but there is some-
" thing in the different Characters of Men, which
" increases or diminishes the Odium of a Thing. In
" the Case of Antony, the People were very well
" satisfied; for we seldom envy those Men Honours,
" whose Power we are not afraid of; whereas any
" extraordinary Degree of Authority alarms us in
" Those, who, we think, can resign, or keep, their Au-
" thority just as they please, and whose only Restraint
" is their Will.*" This is a fair Text for the Compilers of Political Commentaries: I leave it to them almost entire, and content myself with this small Observation. It is thought a just ground of Complaint, that the same Qualities, which should recommend a Man to great Offices, prevent his obtaining them. *George de Monte Mayor* used to say, *Estamos á tiempo, que mererer la cosa es principal parte para no alcanzarla*. That is, (and they are the very Words of the President du Vair,) *Nothing, in these times, hinders good Men from rising to Riches and Honours, so much, as their deserving them* (2). This Complaint is often too well grounded; but there are certain Cases, in which it is not quite so just; for, in order to deserve an Office, it is not sufficient to have the necessary Qualifications for the honourable discharge of it; but it is farther requisite, that those Qualities be not mixed with certain Vices, which prompt a Man to make an ill Use of the Glory, which redounds from the Discharge of this Office, with Capacity and Success. To speak properly, a Mixture of these Vices may render those unworthy of an Office, who, considered with regard to their great Accomplishments, might be the most deserving of any. It is not, therefore, always an Act of Injustice to refuse an Office to one, who is most capable of discharging it; it may be a reasonable Precaution, a Point of necessary Prudence; especially in Republics. Eminent Qualities inspire Men with Ambition. Give those who possess them Opportunities of doing their Country considerable Service; and you kindle the Fire of this Ambition more and more; the Glory they acquire, by worthily discharging an important Trust, inspires them with Thoughts of making an ill use of their Reputation, and shews them, that it is not impossible to climb a Step higher. They try their Fortune, aspire sometimes to the Sovereignty, and, whether they succeed or no, occasion a thousand Disorders, which might have been avoided, by bestowing such Offices upon Persons of moderate Merit.

[B] *Julia, his second Wife*] She was the Daughter of *Julius Caesar*, who was Consul in the Year of *Rome* 664; and Sister of another *Julius Caesar*, who was Consul in the Year 690. Her Virtue and Merit equalled her to the most illustrious Ladies of her Time. Ταῖς ἀρίςαις τότε καὶ σωφρονεστάταις ἐναμίλ λον. *Cum praestantissimis & pudicissimis illius me- matriae matronis comparanda* (3). She was not the happiest in Husbands; for, after the Death of *Marcus Antonius Creticus*, she married *Publius Cornelius Lentulus*, who was an Accomplice in *Catiline's* Conspiracy, and one of those, who was put to Death for it. What She did to save her Brother *Lucius Caesar*, deserves Admiration (4). He was proscribed in the Time of the *Triumvirat*, and hid himself in her House. The Soldiers went thither to search for him, to put him to death; but She placed herself at the Door, and declared they should never pass, 'till they had killed her; She, who had brought that *Marc Antony* into the World, whose Orders they were now to execute. This made them retire (5). The Name of our *Antony's* first Wife was *Numitoria*: She was the Daughter of *Quintus Numitorius Pullus*. She is called the Daughter of a Traytor, in *Cicero's Philippics* (6).

[C] *Some Errors to correct*] *Thysius*, Professor of Oratory in the Academy of *Leyden*, has made a Remark, which might give us an ill Opinion of his Learning. It relates to these Words of *Lactantius*. " De Neptuni forte manifestum est, cujus regnum
" tale fuisse dicimus quale M. Antonii fuit infinitum
" illud imperium, cui totius orae maritimae potestatem
" Senatus decreverat, ut praedones persequeretur ac
" mare omne pacaret (7). ------ *What Neptune's Share
" was, is very plain; whose Empire appears to have
" been like the extensive Authority of Marc Antony,
" who, by a Decree of the Senate, had the Command
" of the whole Sea-Coast, in order to extirpate the
" Pirates, who infested it, and secure the Naviga-
" tion.*" *Thysius* pretends, that, instead of *Antonii*, we ought to read *Pompeii*, which is the reading of the best Manuscripts; and upon this he observes, that *Pompey* was called *Neptunus*, and that several of his Statues were adorned with the Ensigns of That Deity. He is mistaken: There is no doubt but *Lactantius*, who was perfectly Master of *Cicero*, had an Eye to the following Passage of the fourth Oration against *Verres*: " *Postquam Marci Antonii infinitum
" illud imperium senserunt* (8). ---- *After they had felt
" the long continuance of Marc Antony's Authority;*" or to these Words of the following Oration: " Ita se in
" rem, cap. 91.
" isto infinito imperio Marcum Antonium gessisse, ut,
" &c* (9) ----- *Marc Antony behaved himself so ill
" in the long Power he enjoyed, that, &c.*" One of *Vossius's* Sons might have spared the Professor of *Leyden* this false Note; for, in a Book, which was printed thirteen Years before the *Lactantius* of *Thysius*, he observes, that *Thomasius* was very much in the wrong to put *Pompeii*, instead of *Antonii*, in his Edition of *Lactantius*; and proves it by the Authority of *Cicero*, and *Paterculus* (10). I add, that he believes *Florus* meant the same *Antony*, when he says, "Quum ille
" *(Pompeius)*

(1) Vell. Paterc. lib. 2. cap. 31.

(2) See Pierre Matthieu at the end of the Preface to the History of the Peace.

(3) Plut. in M. Antonio init. p. 926.

(4) Id. ib.

(5) Plut. in M. Antonio pag. 924.

(6) Taken from Glandorp. pag. 74, 75.

(7) Lactan. lib. 1. cap. 11. pag. 34.

(8) Cicero Orat. 2. in Verrem, cap. 3.

(9) Id. Orat. 3. in Verrem, cap. 91.

(10) Gerardus Vossius Not. in Vell. Paterculum, pag. 55. Edit. 1639. he cites Cicero Verrina 1, but he should have cited Verrina 2 and 3, ad. II.

ANTONY. 355

(11) Florus, lib. 3. cap. 7. and not cap. 8. as Gerard Voss. cites him.

(12) Plut. in Pompeio.

(13) Dion. lib. 36.

"*(Pompeius)* res in Asia gerens eo quoque præfectum " misisset Antonium, in aliena Provincia inclitus fuit " (11). —— *When Pompey, who commanded in Asia,* " *had sent thither his Lieutenant* Antony, *he was fa-* " *mous in Another's Province*." He shews, that *Florus* has confounded this *Antony* with *Octavius*, who, as *Plutarch* (12) and *Dion* (13) say, was sent by *Pompey* to the Island of *Crete*, when *Metellus* commanded there. There is more ground for this, than for his saying, that the Sirname of *Criticus*, given in *Plutarch* to *Marc Antony*, must be corrected by That of *Creticus*. I know not what Edition of *Plutarch* he made use of; but I find Κρητικὸς in the *Francfort* Edition, 1620, and in That of *Paris*, 1624 I wish he had taken the trouble to examine a Chronological Error, which appears to be in *Paterculus*. This Historian affirms, that there passed but two Years between the Command, which was given to *Marc Antony*, and That, which was given to *Pompey*; and yet *Asconius Pedianus* affirms, that *Marc Antony* obtained it by the Favour of a Consul, called *Cotta*. I enlarge upon this Difficulty in the Article CETHEGUS.

(14) Plut. in M. Antonio init. pag. 925, 926.

[D] *The Encomium*, Plutarch *gives our* Antony, *will be one*.] " He was a worthy, good, Man, says Plu- " tarch (14), and particularly remarkable for his Libera- " lity. He was not very rich, and withal diverted from " the Exercise of his good Nature by his Wife One " Day a Friend of his, who stood in need of Money, " came to borrow some of him. But *Antony*, having " none to lend, ordered his Servant to fill a Silver " Bason with Water, and bring it. The Servant " obeying his Commands, he took the Bason, and " lathering his Face, as if he was going to shave " himself, he sent away the Servant upon another " Errand, and gave his Friend the Bason, desiring " him to make what use he pleased of it. Next Morn- " ing, the whole Family was in an Uproar, and great " Enquiry made after the Bason. But *Antony*, seeing " his Wife in a great Passion, and resolved to put all " her Servants to the Question, acknowledged what " he had done, and begged her Pardon." Ὁμολό- σας συγγνώμην ἔχειν ἐδεήθη (15). *Petita venia id quod erat confessus est.* Plutarch does not justly represent the Character of this Man; he calls him Liberal; whereas he should have made him Prodigal: *Sallust* was not deceived in him. " Marcus Anto- " nius perdundæ pecuniæ genitus, vacuusque curis " nisi instantibus (16). —— Marc Antony, *born to* " *be a Spendthrift, and careless of every thing but the* " *Present*." It must not be dissembled, that *Cicero* denies, what was commonly said of this *Marc Antony*; to wit, that he neither kept an Account of what he received, nor of what he expended. " Audimus " aliquem tabulas nunquam confecisse: Quæ est opi- " nio hominum de Antonio falsa, nam fecit diligen- " tissime (17) —— *We hear, that such an one never* " *kept any Accounts. This was generally reported of* " Antony; *but falsely ; for he kept them very care-* " *fully*."

(15) Id. ib. pag. 926. A.

(16) Sallust. in Fragm. Histor. lib. 3. pag. 446.

(17) Cicero, Orat. 1. in Verrem. cap. 23.

ANTONY (CAIUS) Brother of the foregoing, was a Person of irregular Conduct; insomuch, that his Elder Brother, and He, were much more the worthy Uncle and Father of the *Triumvir*, than worthy Sons of Him, who gave them Life. This *Caius Antony* bore Arms under *Sylla*, in the War against *Mithridates*, and committed many Extortions in *Achaia*; which, with other matters of Blame alledged against him, was the Cause, that the Censors afterwards expelled him the Senate. Nevertheless he was chosen Consul, in preference to *Catiline*, one of his Competitors; but with much less Honour, than *Cicero*; who, notwithstanding all the Plots, which *Caius Antony* and *Catiline* laid to exclude him, was declared Consul with unanimous Consent; whereas *Caius Antony* carried it, but by a few Voices, against *Catiline* (a). It was in this Consulate, that *Catiline*'s Conspiracy was discovered, against which *Cicero* acted with great Zeal. His Colleague had the Command of the Army, which was sent against *Catiline*, and obtained a compleat Victory by his Lieutenant *Petreius*: For, as for himself, either a feigned, or a real, Sickness hindered him from being personally in the Battel. *Dion* says, that it was pretended; and that *Antony*, fearing *Catiline* would discover some very important Secrets against him, would not command in Person (b). After the Victory, he led his Troops into *Macedonia*, and was beaten by the *Dardanians*. He governed That Province Three Years, with so much Violence, and so many Exactions, that the Senate, displeased at his Conduct, sent him a Successor. Upon his Return to *Rome*, He was accused by *Marcus Cælius*; and, tho' *Cicero* undertook his Defence, yet he was convicted and banished. Some say he passed Fifteen Years in the Island of *Cephalonia*; and that his Nephew, *Marc Antony*, who was very powerful in *Rome*, after the Assassins of *Julius Cæsar* had left it, recalled him from his Exile [*A*]. He died some Years after, full of Days and Troubles, and left only one Daughter, whom he saw repudiated, a little after her Marriage, by her Husband *Marc Antony*, the *Triumvir*, on Suspicion of an Intrigue with *Dolabella* (c).

(a) Asconius Pedianus in Orationem Ciceronis in toga candida, contra Anton. & Catilin. in fin. pag. 258.

(b) Dion. lib. 37. ad annum Romæ 692.

(c) See the Remark [G], of the Article FULVIA, and Glandorp. Onomastic. pag. 75, 76.

[*A*] *His Nephew* Marc Antony, —— *recalled him from his Exile*] There are some Difficulties, in relation to the Time of his Re-call, which shall be examined in the Remark [*H*], of the Article of FULVIA.

ANTONY (MARC) One of the *Triumvirs*, generally known by the bare Name of *Marc Antony*, was Grandson of *Marc Antony* the Orator, and Son of *Marcus Antonius Creticus*. Mr *Moreri* is very full on this Article, and therefore I shall take no notice of him. The Mistakes I have collected, on this Head, may find a place in the Article FULVIA, or elsewhere. All that I shall observe here of this *Triumvir* is, that he published a Treatise concerning his own Drunkenness [*A*].

[*A*] *He published a Treatise concerning his own Drunkenness.*] This is a Fact, which modern Writers make no mention of; it is, however, a remarkable one, and to be found in *Pliny*. " Tergilla Ci- " ceroni M. F. binos congios simul haurire solitum " ipsi objicit; Marcoque Agrippæ à temulento scy- " phum impactum: Etenim hæc sunt Ebrietatis " opera. Sed nimirum hanc gloriam auferre Cicero " voluit interfectori patris sui M. Antonio. Is enim " ante eum avidissime apprehenderat hanc palmam, " edito etiam volumine de suâ Ebrietate: Quo patro- " cinari sibi ausus, approbavit planè (ut equidem ar- " bitror) quanta mala per temulentiam orbi terrarum " intulisset. Exiguo tempore ante Prælium Actia- " cum id volumen evomuit, quo facile intelligatur " ebrius jam sanguine Civum, & tanto magis eum " sitiens (1). —— Tergilla *objects to* Cicero, *the Son* " *of* Marcus Cicero, *that he was wont to drink off two* " *Gallons at once ; and to* Marcus Agrippa, *that a* " *drunken Fellow threw a Glass at his Head. These* " *are*

(1) Plin. lib. 14. sub fin. cap. ult.

VOL. I. N° XII. Uuuu

ANTONY.

"are the Works of Drunkenness. Cicero seems to "suffered by His Drunkenness. He vomited forth his
"have disputed the Prize of Intemperance with his "Treatise, a little before the Battle of Actium;
"Father's Murtherer Marc Antony; who, before "which plainly shews, that he was drunk with the
"him, had been very ambitious of it; having even "Blood of Citizens; and, for that reason, the more
"published a Treatise on his own Drunkenness; in "thirsty after it." I wonder Plutarch should take
"which, daring to undertake it's Defence, he plainly no notice of this Piece of Singularity, and that Sueto-
"justifies all the Mischiefs, which the World had nius should not mention it.

ANTONY (CAIUS) Brother of the foregoing, served under *Julius Cæsar*, in the War against *Pompey*, and was forced to surrender himself, with the Troops he commanded in *Illyria*, for want of Provisions (a). After the Death of *Cæsar*, and during his own Prætorship, and the Consulate of his Brother *Marc Antony*, he was sent into *Macedonia* with the Decree of the Senate, which gave *Marc Antony* the Government of That Province. But, whatever Dispatch he could make, he was prevented by *Brutus*, and even fell into his Hands (b). At first *Brutus* treated him honourably, and allowed him the Ensigns of his Prætorship; but, when he perceived, that he endeavoured to corrupt the Army, he put him under an Arrest; and afterwards put him to death, when he was informed of the Proscriptions of the *Triumvirate*, the Murther of *D. Brutus*, That of *Cicero*, &c. *Marc Antony*, having got *Hortensius* into his Power, after the Battle of *Philippi*, sacrificed him to the Manes of his Brother. *Cicero* mentions *C. Antony*, sometimes, in his *Philippics*, but always to his Disadvantage (c).

ANTONY (LUCIUS) Brother of the preceeding, had all the Vices of his Brother, the *Triumvir*, but none of his good Qualities: However he did not want Courage. He was Tribune of the People, in the Year of *Cæsar's* Death, while his Brother *Marc* was Consul, and his Brother *Caius* Prætor. He was Consul, Himself, in the Year of *Rome* 713, and triumphed the first Day of his Consulship over a People of the *Alps*, whom he pretended he had conquered; tho' he had really done nothing worthy of a Triumph, nor exercised any Command in their Country. But *Fulvia*, the Wife of *M. Antony*, and Mother-in law of *Octavius Cæsar*, who then governed all in *Rome*, procured him, by her sole Credit, this Honour. This imperious Woman, desiring to be revenged on *Octavius*, for repudiating her Daughter, excited *Lucius Antony* to take up Arms against him, under pretence of protecting the Inhabitants of *Campania*, whose Lands were assigned to the Soldiers. The Troops, he had assembled, being introduced into *Rome*, by Night, he drove out *Lepidus* one of the *Triumvirs*; and harangued the People, declaring, That, according to his Brother's Intention, he designed to abolish the *Triumvirate*. This Promise filled the City with Joy. He was declared *Imperator*, and marched against *Octavius Cæsar*; but, not daring to keep the Field, he retreated to *Perousa*, where he defended himself, 'till the want of Provisions obliged him to surrender. *Octavius* gave him his Liberty; but what became of him after, is not known (a).

ANTONY (MARCUS JULIUS) Son of the *Triumvir*, and *Fulvia*, found so much Favour with *Augustus*, after the Conquest of *Egypt*, that, by degrees, he was advanced to Employs, and at last to the Consulate, in the Year of *Rome* 744. He married *Marcella*, the Daughter of *Octavia*; and, being by this means become Son-in-law of *Augustus's* Sister, for whom That Prince had a great Esteem, he was the First Favourite after *Agrippa*, the Son-in-law of *Augustus*, and the Sons of the Empress. But he proved ungrateful to his Benefactor, and was one of the first, who debauched his Daughter *Julia*; which, together with some Suspicions of a Conspiracy, occasioned his being condemned to death. Some Historians say, that he killed himself to prevent the Infamy of his Sentence (a). He had studied under the Grammarian *L. Crassitius* (b), and composed a Poem of Twelve Books in Heroic Verse (c), and some Treatises in Prose. It is to Him, that *Horace* addresses the second Ode of his fourth Book. He left one Son very young, whose Name was *L. Julius Antony*. The Emperor banished this Youth to *Marseilles*, under the specious Pretence of keeping him to his Studies. He ordered him very singular Funeral Honours; for he procured a Decree of the Senate, that his Bones should be reposited in *Octavius's* Tomb (d). This was the End of That Ancient and Powerful Family *Antonia*, of which *Tacitus* says, that it had been always Illustrious, but Unfortunate; *Multa claritudine generis, sed improspera* (e). We shall now sum up all Mr *Moreri's* Errors concerning this Family [*A*].

[*A*] *We shall now sum up all Mr* Moreri's *Errors concerning this Family*] I. He ought not to have mentioned this Family under the Letter M, on account of *Marc Ant.ny*: Both He, and his Family, ought to stand under the Letter A. II. He ought not to have said, *That the Family of the* Antonii *was famous among the Nobles of* Rome; for it is plain, that, by this way of speaking, he intended to distinguish it from the *Plebeian* Families: now this distinction is false. The Tribuneship of the People alone, with which *Marc Antony* was invested, at the beginning of the War between *Cæsar* and *Pompey*, proves demonstrably, that the *Antonian* Family was *Plebeian*: for he was made Tribune of the People, without being adopted by a *Plebeian*; there was no Necessity for his imitating *Clodius*, who, to qualify himself for the Office of Tribune, had recourse to such an Adoption (1). I confess the *Antonii* were at first *Patricians*. This appears from the Dignities of the *Decemvirate*, and the Military Tribuneship, conferred upon them, before the *Plebeian* Families

ANTONIA.

Families were admitted to the first Dignities of the Republic. But, whether it were, that the *Antonii*, who appeared with so much Splendor in the seventh Century of *Rome*, did not descend from the same Branch with those, who bore the Sirname of *Merenda*, or whether it were, that they passed, we know not how, from the Rank of *Patricians* to That of *Plebeians*, as has happened to some other Families; it is certain, that their House was *Plebeian* in the Days of *Marc Antony*, the Orator, who first began to raise it. III. It is gross Ignorance to say, that this House *was divided into two Branches, the* Merenda*'s, and the* Marc*'s*. The Word *Marc* is the *Prænomen*, which serves only to distinguish *Persons* ; That, which distinguished the several *Branches*, was called the *Cognomen*, and held the third Place, as *Cæsar, Scipio*, &c. (2). IV. It is not certain, that Q. *Antonius Merenda*, Military Tribune about the Three hundred thirty second Year of *Rome*, was the Son of *T. Antonius Merenda, Decemvir* in the Year 303. V. It is false, that *Livy* makes mention of *M. Antonius Merenda*, Master of the Horse, under the Dictatorship of *P. Cornelius*. He calls him only *M. Antonius*. VI. *Marcus Antonius Creticus* was not killed in a Duel. *Asconius Pedianus* leaves no room for Doubt in this matter. " Indictó, *says he,* Cretensibus bello male se " gesta ibidem periit (3). ———— *He died, after meeting with ill Success in the Cretan War.*" VII. Instead of saying, that *Marc Antony*, the Orator, never wrote down any *of his Orations* ; he should have said, that he never published any (4). VIII. His Answer to those, who asked him the reason of it, is misrepresented ; he did not reply, *that he would not furnish those with Arms, who might be inclined to convict him* of having express'd himself amiss ; he was in no pain for his Words or Phrases ; I mean, of being reproached with Barbarisms, or Offences against the Rules of Grammar ; yet this is what Mr *Moreri* means; as all must own, who understand what an Author means. But *Marc Antony*'s Fear was, lest his Works should convict him of blowing Hot and Cold with the same Breath, and of having confuted, four Years before, what he was then advancing in his Plea. Consult the Remarks [B] and [C] of the Article ANTONY (MARC) the Orator; where I have fully displayed the Reasons, why Lawyers contradict themselves, and maintain one thing to day, and the quite contrary to morrow, according to the different Interests of their Clients. IX. Besides, the Answer, which Mr *Moreri* ascribes to him, is absurd ; for one may write down a Plea, without furnishing the Critics with Arms, provided it be not made public. X. *M. Aquilius* was not condemned upon *M. Antony*'s undertaking his Cause. XI. The Judges did not confess, *That He, who had so often exposed his Life for the Good of the Republic, ought not to lose it so dishonourably*. Had Mr *Moreri* known, that *Aquilius* could, at the worst, have been condemned only to Banishment (5), he would not have given his Style the Colours of Oratory. XII. What a confused contrary way of speaking is it, to say, *That* Marc Antony *was* Consul, Censor *in the Year of* Rome 626, *with* A. Posthumius *in* 657, *with* L. Valerius, *&c.* There is something worse in it, than a confused Style : Falshoods are not wanting. *Marc Antony* was Consul, with *A. Posthumius Albinus*, in the Year 655, and Censor, with *L. Valerius Flaccus*, in the Year 657 (6).

ANTONIA, Eldest Daughter of *Marc Antony* [A], and *Octavia* (a), was a Lady, whose Virtue and Beauty made her the Object of Admiration (b). She was married to *Drusus*, the Son of *Livia*, and Brother of *Tiberius*, by whom she had several Children (c), of which but Three survived *Drusus*, to wit, *Germanicus*, *Claudius*, who was Emperor, and *Livilla*, who was *Tiberius*'s Son's Wife. *Antonia*, yet young and beautiful in her Widow-hood, was courted by several Persons, but refused them all ; an Example of Continency [B], so much the more to be admired, as she lived in a Court exceedingly corrupt. *Tiberius*, whose humour was so stern, had yet a great Regard for this Lady ; which shews, that her Chastity she knew how to join other Virtues, unknown to the chaste *Agrippina*, her Daughter-in-law ; I mean Mildness and Prudence. It was *Antonia*, who discovered to *Tiberius Sejanus*'s Conspiracy

[A] *Eldest Daughter of Marc Antony*] *Suetonius* and *Plutarch* are against me ; the first expressly, and in downright Terms (1) ; the second after an implicit manner : For he only speaks of the Marriage of one of the two *Antonia*'s with *Domitius*, before he mentions the other's Marriage with *Drusus* (2). Now, since *Suetonius* wrote after *Tacitus*, and sometimes seems to refute him ; would it not be better to give Him the preference, and to suppose, that he took the contrary side, only because he was convinced of *Tacitus*'s Error ? Besides, are the Words of *Tacitus* of no weight ? Let every one judge as he pleases ; for my own Part, I have followed *Tacitus*, without pretending to contest the matter with those, who choose to follow *Suetonius*. There are two Passages of *Tacitus*, one in the Forty fourth Chapter of the fourth Book of his Annals, the other in the Sixty fourth Chapter of the twelfth Book of the same Annals, where the Wife of *Domitius* is called *Antonia Minor*. ---- *Antonia the Younger*. I find, that *Lipsius* declares for neither side (3), and that *Glandorpius* prefers That of *Tacitus* to That of *Suetonius* (4). There is a Reason on *Tacitus*'s side, though not conclusive. It may be supposed, that *Drusus*, who, in quality of a Powerful Empress's Son, was one of the greatest Matches of *Rome*, married the eldest of the two Sisters ; but, in answer to this, it may be said, that His *Antonia* was a perfect Beauty. Now this is a Right of Eldership more to the Taste of a young Prince, (nor is it necessary to be a young Prince to have this Taste) than That, which is only founded on the greater Number of Years. It is probable, that *Drusus*, as he was the greater Match, had his Choice ; and, no doubt, he chose the handsomest of the two, whether the elder, or the younger, Sister.

[B] *Antonia, yet young and beautiful in her Widowhood, - - - - was an Example of Continency.*] What is said of her Husband, in relation to his conjugal Fidelity, is yet more surprizing. " Drusum etiam " Germanicum, eximiam Claudiæ familiæ gloriam, " patriæque rarum ornamentum, & quod super om- " nia est operum fuorum pro habitu ætatis magni- " tudine vitrico pariter ac fratri Augusto, duobus rei- " publicæ divinis oculis, mirifice respondentem, con- " stitit usum Veneris intra conjugis charitatem clausum " tenuisse (5). - - - *It was certain,* that Drusus Germa- " nicus, *the singular Glory of the* Claudian *Family, and* " *an uncommon Ornament of his Country, and, what is be-* " *yond all, as famous for Great Actions, in proportion* " *to his Years, as the* Augusti, *his Father-in-Law, and* " *Brother, the two divine Eyes of the Republic, confined* " *his Desires wholly to conjugal Endearments* (6)." Is the remark enough, that, in *Augustus*'s Court, the Emperor's Son-in-law should be contented with one Dish, like a Citizen; and it signifies little to say, that *Antonia* was so young and fair, that *Drusus* knew not where to please himself better. How many Princes, great Lords, and other Persons are there, with whom this Reason is of no force ? But to return to *Antonia*, *Valerius Maximus* continues his Discourse in this manner. " Antonia quoque fœmina, laudibus viri- " lem familiæ suæ claritatem supergressa, amorem " mariti egregia fide pensavit ; quæ post ejus excessum " forma & ætate florens cubiculum socrus pro con- " jugio habuit, in eodemque toro alterius adolescen- " tiæ vigor extinctus est, alterius viduitatis experien- " tia consenuit. - - - - - *The Lady* Antonia, *a greater* " *Ornament to her Family than the Males it pro-* " *duced, repaid her Husband's Love with a remark-* " *able Constance ; for, after his Decease, though still* " *in the Flower of her Youth and Beauty, she was* " *wedded only to the Chamber of her Mother-in-law ;* " *and, in the same Bed, the one's Vigour of Youth expi-* " *red, the other's Experience of Widow-hood grew* " *old.*"

ANTONIA.

Conspiracy [C]; nor was This Prince ungrateful, after a Service of such Importance (d). *Pliny* mentions a very particular Quality of *Antonia*, which is that she never spit (e). He tells us likewise, that she had a Fish, which she was very fond of, and which she adorned with Ear-rings; a Curiosity, which drew many Visitors to her Country Seat (f). This Lady was unhappy in her Family. *Germanicus*, her Son, had indeed all the good Qualities, which could be desired in the Presumptive Heir of the Empire, and was the Darling and Delight of all the *Roman* People; but this only served to heighten *Antonia*'s Affliction, when a sudden Death bereaved her of This Young Prince. This disconsolate Mother was not able to walk as a Mourner, when *Germanicus*'s Funeral was solemnized [D]. Her other Son was so disagreeable, and so brutish, in her Eyes, that she was wont to call him Monster, Rough-Draught of a Man, &c. [E] and made him the Standard of Comparison, whenever she would represent an arrant Blockhead. Her Daughter was a Monster of another kind; she made an Attempt on the Honour and Life of her Husband, and executed it; for she was convicted of Adultery, and of poisoning her Husband. Her own Mother was the Secular Arm, to which she was delivered; who shut her up in a Chamber, where she was starved to Death [F]. The Children of *Germanicus*, whom *Antonia* brought up in her House, gave her no small Trouble. She watched their Conduct; but her Vigilance served only to make her an Eye-Witness of their enormous Crimes. One Day, she surprized *Caligula* with his Sister (g). This Wretch had not yet assumed the *Toga Virilis*; and yet was guilty of Capital Incest. Upon his Accession to the Empire, he decreed all the Honours to his Grandmother *Antonia*, which the Senate had decreed *Livia* (b); but this was only a Start; for he shewed her no Respect afterwards, and even refused her a Private Audience. These Affronts threw her into a Melancholy, which occasioned her Death; and it was even said, that he hastened the

---

" old." *Antonia*'s Chastity found Panegyrists in *Judea*. *Josephus* deserves to be heard: He informs us, that *Augustus* sollicited this Lady to marry again; but she persisted in the contrary Resolution, and preserved an unspotted Reputation in her Widow-hood. The Uncommonness of her Conduct was This. We see great Ladies enough, who live separate from their Husbands, or do not marry a second Time, though courted to it; but do they live without Reproach? Do they give no occasion to censure their Conduct? Here lies the Difficulty, *Hoc opus, hic labor est*. Some scandalous Talkers will say, there are Those, who practise the Maxim, which *Luther* is said to have taught Husbands. *Si nolit Uxor*, said he, *veniat Ancilla*. — — — *If your Wife won't, call your Maid.* This is turning the Tables, and understanding *Luther*'s Expression wrong; which was, *si nolit, si desit maritus, veniat famulus.* — — *If you have no Husband, or if he refuses to comply, call your Servant.* The Words of *Josephus* are as follows: Τιμια δ' ἦν Ἀντωνια Τιβεριῳ εἰς τὰ μαλι̇ςα συγγενεας τε ἀξιωμαςι, Δρεσυ γαρ ἦν ἀδιλφὴ τε ἀυτῇ γυνὴ, καὶ ἀρετῃ τε σωφρον۟, δια γαρ χηρευειν παρημεινεν γαμεν τε ατιςι̇ν τῳ πρεϛ ετερευ, καιπερ τε Σιζἀσε κελευσαντ۟ τινι γαμεισ̓θαι, καὶ λοιδο۟ιων απηλλαξμενον διασωσας αυτῆς τον βιον (7). *Antonia was greatly respected by Tiberius, either because she was related to him, as having been the Wife of his Brother Drusus; or on account of her Continency; for, though she was a very young Widow, she refused to marry again, notwithstanding the Importunity of Augustus; and in this State of Life she preserved an unblemished Reputation.*

[C] *It was Antonia, who discovered Sejanus's Conspiracy.*] *Tacitus* was probably well informed of this Fact; but, unhappily, That Part of his Annals is lost If I am not mistaken, *Josephus* is the only Historian, who relates what share *Antonia* had in discovering this Conspiracy. He deserves Credit, because the Intimacy of *Berenice*, and That of her Son *Agrippa*, with This Lady, and the good Offices she did *Agrippa*, made her known in *Judea*, and induced the *Jewish* Historian to inform himself exactly of what concerned her. Let us believe, then, on his Testimony, that *Antonia* was no sooner informed of *Sejanus*'s Plot, than she wrote all the Circumstances of it exactly to *Tiberius*, who was then in the Island of *Capræa*, whither she dispatched one of her most faithful Domestics with her Letter. This Prince's Consideration for her increased greatly after so eminent a Piece of Service. Ὁ δὲ μαθων τετυ Σηιανον κτεινει καὶ τἐς συντιθιίνας, τᾶντε Αντωνίαν καὶ ωρος ἀξιολογας ἀγων τιμιωτεραν τε ὑπιλαμβανε κατὶ τοις πασι πιθανον (8). *Tiberius, being informed of it, put to Death Sejanus and his Abettors, and had, for the future, a still greater reliance on Antonia, whom before he greatly esteemed.* I shall shew in another Place (9), that *Xiphilinus* occasionally observes, that *Antonia* informed *Tiberius* of certain Matters concerning *Sejanus*.

[D] *This disconsolate Mother was not able to walk as a Mourner, when* Germanicus's *Funeral was solemnized.*] Let us see how *Tacitus* relates the Matter, and the Picture he gives of her in his Reflexions. " *Tiberius atque Augusta publico abstinuere, inferius* " *Majestate sua rati si palam lamentarentur, an ne* " *omnium oculis vultum eorum scrutantibus falsi intel-* " *ligerentur. Matrem Antoniam non apud auctores* " *rerum, non diurna actorum scriptura, reperio ullo* " *insigni officio functam, cum super Agrippinam,* " *& Drusum & Claudium, cæteri quoque consan-* " *guinei nominatim perscripti sint; seu valetudine* " *præpediebatur, seu victus luctu animus magnitu-* " *dinem mali perferre visu non toleravit. Facilius* " *crediderim Tiberio & Augustæ, qui domo non ex-* " *cedebant, cohibitam, ut par mœror & matris exem-* " *plo avia quoque & patruus attineri viderentur* (10). " — — — *Tiberius and Augusta would not appear* " *publickly, thinking it beneath their Majesty to* " *mourn openly; or, perhaps, least the Eyes of the* " *People, examining their Looks, should discover their* " *Dissimulation. I do not find, in any Historians, or* " *Journalists, that Antonia, the Mother, performed* " *any remarkable Part of the Solemnity, tho', besides* " *Agrippina, Drusus, and Claudius, the rest of his* " *Kindred are mentioned by Name; whether it were,* " *that Sickness prevented her, or that her Mind, over-* " *come with Grief, could not support the Greatness of her* " *Misfortune in public View. I rather believe she was* " *hindered by* Tiberius *and* Augusta, *who went not out of* " *their House, that the Uncle and Grandmother might be* " *thought to be equally afflicted with the Mother.*"

[E] *She was wont to call him Monster, &c*] This *Suetonius* informs us of. " *Mater Antonia portentum* " *eum hominis dictitabat, nec absolutum à naturâ,* " *sed tantum inchoatum! ac si quem socordiæ ar-* " *gueret, stultiorem aiebat filio suo Claudio* (11). " — — — *His Mother* Antonia *used to call him a* " *Monster of a Man, not finished by Nature, but on-* " *ly begun! and, whenever she would reproach any* " *one with Stupidity, she was wont to say, he was a* " *greater Fool, than her Son Claudius.*" By this we may judge she was a Woman of Wit and Sense; for your ordinary Women seldom discover, that their Children are stupid; or, if they do, they are not forward, to excuse themselves, and represent them as Changlings, or half-formed Productions.

[F] *She shut her up in a Chamber, where she was starved to Death*] This is another Proof, that she was a Woman of Spirit, who loved her Children

ANTONIA. 359

the Effects of her Melancholy by Poison [*G*]. He paid no Honours to the Deceased, nor assisted at her Funeral (*i*). Probably the Temple of *Antonia*, which *Pliny* alone mentions, took it's Name from this Princess (*H*). She did not live to see the Misfortunes of her Grand-Daughter *Antonia*, whom Mr *Moreri* has mentioned, but not without a Mistake [*I*].

(*i*) Sueton. in Caligula, cap. 23.

no longer, than they were an Honour to her; and preferred the Greatness of a *Roman* Soul to the tender Sentiments of Nature. There were two Traditions concerning the Death of *Livilla*; One, that *Tiberius* caused her to be put to Death; The other, that he pardoned her for the sake of *Antonia*; but that *Antonia* condemned her to be starved to Death (12).

(12) Dion. lib. 58.

[*G*] *Caligula* - - - - *hastened the Effects of her Melancholy by Poison.*] *Suetonius* and *Dion* agree in this Point. " Per istiusmodi indignitates & tædia " caussâ extitit mortis, dato tamen, ut quidam pu-" tant, & veneno (13). - - - - By these *Affronts* and " *Vexations he was the Cause of her Death; not* " *without a Suspicion of having hastened it by Poison.*" *Dion* says nothing of Poison; he only tells us, that this inhuman Wretch, not being able to bear the Reproaches of his Grandmother, obliged her to put an end to her Life (14). I cannot find in what Year this illustrious Lady died; but, since it was in the Reign of *Caligula*, I think her Death may be placed in the Year of *Rome* 792. That of her Husband happened in the Year 744. We may give a near guess at her Age, when she became a Widow, and how long she lived; for she must have been born in the Year of *Rome* 714; since her Mother *Octavia*, who married *Marc Antony* in 713 (15), was delivered of a Daughter, upon his return from *Greece*, the Year following (16). The Poem entituled *Consolatio ad Liviam Augustam de morte Drusi Neronis* (17), represents *Antonia* as very disconsolate, and gives her great Encomiums. We are there informed, as also in *Valerius Maximus*, of *Drusus's* Constancy, and that his last Words called upon his dear Wife:

(13) Sueton. in Antonio, cap. 23.

(14) Dion. lib. 59. See also Sueton. in Caligula, cap. 29.

(15) Calvisius ad annum mundi 3910.

(16) Plut. in Antonio, pag. 930. E. See also pag. 931. D.

(17) It is printed with Ovid's Works, and many take it to be his.

Quid referam de te, dignissima conjuge Druso,
Atque eadem Drusi digna parente nurus?
Par bene compositum, juvenum fortissimus alter,
Altera tam forti mutua cura viro.
Fœmina tu princeps, tu filia Cæsaris: illi
Nec minor es magni conjuge visa Jovis.
Tu concessus amor, tu solus & ultimus illi,
Tu requies fesso grata laboris eras.
Te moriens per verba novissima questus abesse,
Et mota in nomen frigida lingua tuum.

How shall the Muse in feeble Numbers raise
Her Voice, illustrious Lady, to Thy Praise?
A Comfort, equal to great Drusus's Worth!
A Daughter, worthy Her, who gave thy Drusus Birth!
United Hearts in Love! Consenting Pair!
The bravest Warrior HE, and SHE the loveliest Fair!
A Princess born, great Cæsar gave Thee Life;
To him not less, than Jove's imperial Wife.
The sacred Tie consign'd you to His Arms;
And His were All Antonia's blooming Charms.
From Fair to Fair He never learnt to rove;
Thine was his first, and Thine his latest, Love.
On thy soft Bosom he repos'd from Care,
Forgot each Toil and Labour of the War.
His dearest Wife employ'd his latest Breath;
Thy Absence was his only Pang in Death.
Dying, his falt'ring Tongue's uncertain Aim
Call'd on his Wife, and half pronounced thy Name.

[*H*] *Probably the Temple of* Antonia, *which Pliny alone mentions, took it's Name from This Princess.*] He speaks of it in the Catalogue of *Apelles's* Paintings; " Ejusdem, *says he*, arbitrantur manu esse & " in *Antoniæ* templo *Herculeum* aversum: ut, quod " est difficillimum, faciem ejus ostendat verius pictu-" ra, quam promittat (18). - - - *The* Hercules *averted,* " *in the Temple of* Antonia, *is thought to be by the* " *same Hand; that, what was most difficult, the* " *Picture might more truly represent his Face, than* " *promise it.*" A very learned Commentator (19) says, upon this Passage, That he does not know, whether this Temple belonged to the elder, or the younger *Antonia*, nor in what Part of the City it stood.

(18) Plin. lib. 35. cap. 10. pag. 213.

(19) Father Harduoin.

" Cujus illud Antoniæ fuerit, majoris, minorisve, " quove Urbis situ conditum fuerit, incompertum. " Utraque Antonii Triumviri filia, Major Germanici " & Claudii Cæsaris parens: Neronis avia. - - - - " *To which of the* Antonia*'s, the elder, or the younger,* " *it was dedicated, and in what City it was built,* " *is uncertain. Both the* Antonia*'s were Daughters* " *of the Triumvir; the elder, the Mother of Ger-" manicus and Claudius Cæsar: Grandmother of* " Nero." This is to prefer the Opinion of *Tacitus* to That of *Suetonius* (20), and giving the elder to *Drusus*: but, on the other hand, I know not what to make of the Words, *Neronis avia*. I suspect the Printer has, at least, forgot the Epithet *minor*; for, by substituting this Word, we find, that Father *Hardouin* has said something of both the *Antonia*'s; of the elder, that she was the Mother of *Germanicus*, and the Emperor *Claudius*; and of the younger, that she was *Nero's* Grandmother. If no such Word be supplied, there is a manifest Error in this Place, since the Mother of *Germanicus* was not *Nero's* Grandmother. To have recourse to the Adoption of *Nero*, by *Claudius*, would be an ill shift. In another place (21), this Commentator has preferred the Opinion of *Suetonius* to That of *Tacitus*.

(20) *See, above, the Remark* [*A*].

(21) In Plin. lib. 7. cap. 19. Tom. 2. pag. 38.

[*J*] Antonia, *whom Mr* Moreri *has mentioned, but not without a Mistake.*] She was Daughter of the Emperor *Claudius*, by *Ælia Petina*; but born before her Father was Emperor. She married her first to *Cneus Pompeius Magnus* (22), and afterwards to *Faustus Sylla*. She saw both her Husbands die a violent Death. The former was put to Death, by order of the Emperor *Claudius* (23); the latter was massacred, at *Marseilles*, by Ruffians, whom *Nero* had sent thither for that purpose (24). She refused to marry this Prince, who would have taken her to Wife, after the Death of *Pompey* (25). *Nero* put her to Death, upon pretence, that she was concerned in a Conspiracy; I believe it was That of *Piso*. An Historian pretends, that *Piso* was to have carried *Antonia* into the Camp of the *Prætorian* Guards (26). *Tacitus* mentions it, without thinking it very probable (27). He thinks it unlikely, that *Antonia* should have exposed herself to so great Hazard, without the Hopes of becoming *Piso's* Wife. Now there was no room to expect this; for *Piso* was known to be a most uxorious Husband. But *Tacitus* does not stop here; he subjoins a Restriction, according to his Custom; *unless*, says he, *we suppose, that the Desire of Rule in Women is*, of all others, *the most violent*. By this he restores the Probability to *Pliny*'s Account, which he had been labouring to destroy. *Antonia* might have believed, that *Piso* would repudiate his dear Wife, to open a way to the Throne, by marrying the Daughter of the Emperor *Claudius*. " Interim Piso apud ædem " Cereris opperiretur, unde eum præfectus Fenius & " cæteri accitum ferrent in castra, comitante Antonia " Claudii Cæsaris filia, ad eliciendum vulgi favorem, " quod C. Plinius memorat. Nobis quoquo modo tra-" ditum non occultare in animo fuit, quamvis absur-" dum videretur, aut inani spei Antoniam nomen & " periculum commodavisse, aut Pisonem notum a-" more uxoris nisi matrimonio se obstrinxisse: nisi si " cupido dominandi cunctis affectibus flagrantior est " (28). ------ *In the mean time Piso was to wait at* " *the Temple of* Ceres, *from whence the Præfect Fe-" nius, and the rest, were to conduct him to the Camp,* " *accompanied by* Antonia, *the Daughter of* Claudius " Cæsar, *in order to gain the Vulgar to their Party,* " *as C.* Plinius *informs us. I resolved not to stifle* " *this Tradition, true or false; though I cannot but* " *think it absurd, either that* Antonia *should run the* " *hazard of lending her Name to so vain an Enterprize,* " *or that* Piso, *who was remarkable for conjugal Fi-" delity, should engage himself to marry another; un-" less the Desire of Rule be the strongest Affection of* " *the Mind.*" *Moreri*'s Faults are, I. That *Tacitus* calls *Antonia's* second Husband *Cornelius Sulvus*, whereas he calls him *Cornelius Sulla* (29). II. That *Antonia* lived a long time a Widow. Her Husband *Sylla* was killed in the Year 815. *Piso's* Conspiracy broke out in 818. *Poppæa* died the same Year: It

(22) He refered to him this Sirname, voles: Culegula sad taken from him. Dion. lib. 60.

(23) Sueton. in Claud. cap. 27.

(24) Tacit. Ann. lib. 14 cap. 57.

(25) Sueton. in Ner. cap. 35.

(26) Plinius, apud Tacitum. Ann. lib. 15. cap. 53.

(27) Tacit. Annal. lib. 20. cap. 53.

(28) Tacit. Annal. lib. 15. cap. 53.

(29) Annal. lib. 13. cap. 23, (and not cap. 5. as Moreri) and 4°. Morixi i mistaken in citing lib. 14. cap 57. *He should have cited* lib. 14. cap 57. *me has be cited all the Places, which he cares to have cited.*

VOL. I. Xxxx

ANTONIA. ANTONIANO.

is very probable, that *Antonia* was courted soon after; and that her Refusal caused *Nero* to revive the Proceedings against her in particular. Be it as it will, her Widowhood could not be very long, since *Nero*, who caused her to be put to Death, died in the Year 821. In the third Place, the Authors, quoted by Mr *Moreri*, do not say, that *Nero* obliged *Antonia* to kill herself.

ANTONIA, Younger Sister of the preceeding, as well by the Father, as the Mother's Side, will furnish but a small Article. I meet with nothing farther concerning her, than that she was the Wife of *Lucius Domitius Ænobarbus*, and that this Marriage produced one Son and two Daughters; the Son, whose Name was *Cneus Domitius*, was Father to the Emperor *Nero*. We shall speak of the Daughters under the Word DOMITIA; and shew, that Mr *Moreri* is mistaken, in saying, that One of them married *Galba*.

ANTONIANO (SILVIO) a Cardinal, and a learned Man, raised himself by his Merit from a very low Condition; He was of mean Birth, and his Parents so far from being able to breed him a Scholar, that they themselves stood in need of the Charity of others. Some say he was illegitimate; but *Joseph Castalion*, who wrote his Life, has proved the contrary *(a)*. Be That as it will, he was born at *Rome*, in the Year 1540 [*A*]. He made so quick and surprizing a Progress in his Studies, that one can scarce credit the Accounts of it. At Ten Years of Age, he made Verses [*B*] on any Subject, which was proposed to him; which were so good, and so finely turn'd, tho' made *extemporè*, that other Wits could not have composed the like without much Time and Pains. The Trial was one day made at the Cardinal of *Pisa*'s Table, at an Entertainment, which he gave to several other Cardinals. *Alexander Farnese*, taking a Nosegay, gave it to the young Scholar, bidding him present it to That Person of the Company, who should be the next Pope. The Youth presented it to the Cardinal *de Medicis*, and spoke his Elogy in Verse. This Cardinal, who was afterwards Pope *Pius* IV, fancied the Company play'd upon him, and that the Poetry had been prepared before-hand, with much Art, with a Design of making a Jest of him; upon which he seemed to take it amiss; but they solemnly protested to him, that it was made *extemporè*, and desired he would try the Boy himself on any other Subject: He did so, and was convinced of the extraordinary Abilities of the Youth; who enlarged, off-hand, on a Subject, which was proposed to him, in very elegant Verse [*C*]. The Duke of *Ferrara*, coming to *Rome*, to congratulate *Marcellus* II, on his Elevation to the Pontificat, was so charmed with *Antoniano*'s Wit, that he carried him with him to *Ferrara* [*D*], where he appointed him excellent Masters to instruct him in all the Sciences. He was taken from thence by Pope *Pius* IV; who, remembring the Adventure of the Nose-gay, and being now in St *Peter's* Chair, enquired what was become of the young Poet. Finding where he was,

(a) Scripsit Sylvii Card. Antoniani vitam, quem tu n rationibus tum publicarum tabularum testimoniis ab eorum calumniis vindicare conatus est, qui illum à parente minus justa uxore genitum afferebant. *Nicius Erythræus, Pinacoth. I. pag. 167.*

[*A*] *He was born at Rome, in the Year* 1540.] *Nicius Erythræus* makes him to be born at *Rome*: *Romæ, humili loco ——— ortus* (1); but *Toppi* makes him a Native of *Castelli*, in the *Abruzzo*, and gives us an Inscription, made by *Mutius Panza*, in which he is said to be *Castellorum oppidi oriundus* (2). This may only signify, that his Father was of this Place. However it be, I collect from Father *Oldoini* (3), that he was born in the Year 1540, because he tells us, that he died, *August* 16, 1603. *Nicius Erythræus* does not set down the Year of the Century, in which he died, but only, that he died in his grand Climacteric. Monf. *de la Rochepozaü*, in his *Nomenclator Cardinalium*, places his Death on the sixteenth of *August*, 1604. I have chosen to follow Father *Oldoini*.

[*B*] *At ten Years of age he made Verses.*] Father *Strada*, who, with much Politeness, has inserted the Relation of this Adventure in one of his Orations, says, that *Antoniano* was not quite twelve Years of Age (4).

[*C*] *Who enlarged, off-hand, on a Subject, which was proposed to him, in very elegant Verse.*] Father *Strada* informs us, that, while the Cardinal *de Medicis* was considering what Subject he should propose, the Clock struck; upon which he desired him to make Verses on a Clock. The Author has preferred those, which he supposes *Antoniano* made on the Spot; and adds, that the Cardinal of *Trent* presented him with a Chain.

[*D*] *The Duke ——— carried him with him to* Ferrara.] *Antoniano* spoke some Orations there, which have been printed (5), with those, which he pronounced at *Rome*; this inclines me to believe, that he was Professor at *Ferrara*. *Nicius Erythræus* says only, that *Antoniano* taught the Sciences there: Why does he not tell us which they were? The fear of being too tedious is no just Reason for suppressing such Particulars. I have not yet had an Opportunity of consulting the Life of this Cardinal, composed by *Joseph Castalio*; which, no doubt, informs us upon what account he was at *Ferrara*, and in what Year he died, with many other Particulars. Much less can I procure a Book, which Mr *Conrart* sent to Mr *de Balzac*. The Subject was *Italian Discourses of the Philosophical Orator* (6). Mr *de Balzac* despised them: "I allow, *says he* (7), that the Elogium of Cardinal *Dossat*, and Cardinal *Silvio Antoniano* are not amiss, "and that the Author has happily enough imitated "the Parallels of *Plutarch*'s Lives. His long Invective against Nobility is the highest strain of his "Wit: I have observed several fine Strokes in it, "and something of his own Invention, besides what "he has borrowed from others, and particularly from "*Caius Marius*'s Speech in the *Jugurthine* War. "However, I am of Opinion, that, without injuring "his Subject, he might have shortened his Digression. This Common-place Topic, which he has "spun out to such a length, and which he has so "artfully, and so pompously displayed, ought only "to have been touched upon by the Bye. Besides, "that he made himself powerful and dangerous Enemies by it. For it must needs be a great Offence "to the polite World, to prove, that it is no Crime "to be the Son of an Artist, or Rustic."

"*Jerom Ruscelli*, in the seventh Chapter of his "*Rimario*, speaks Wonders of the Talent of our *Silvio Antoniano*, whom, by mistake, he calls *Antonio*, "for *extempore* Poetry. He mentions a Trial, which "was made of it at *Venice*, in the Presence of the "Queen of *Poland**, Cardinal *Trivulcio*, and the "Cardinal of *Ausburgh*. *Antoniano* was not then "above Sixteen. The Princes of *Este* detained him "at *Ferrara*, where he read public Lectures, as the "same *Ruscelli* informs us, in the place quoted." I have this from Mr *de la Monnoie*."

(1) N. F- riche. Pinac. I.
(2) Toppi, Bibl. cen. Napoliet pag. 23).
(3) Oldoini Athen. Roman pag. 62 ;.
(4) Fam. Strada. Prolus. Acad 3. lib 2.
(5) *By de Cere of Joseph Casta- lio, in 1610.*
(6) *See the Dissertations at the end of the Christian Socrates, pag. 10.*
(7) *Ibid.* 470.
* *Bonna Sforza, who quitted Po- land to retire to Bari in I- taly.*

[*E*] *What*

ANTONIANO.

was, he sent for him to *Rome*, and gave him an honourable Post in his Palace. He afterwards made him Professor of Humanity in the *Roman* College. *Antoniano* exercised This Office with so much Reputation, that, on the Day, when he began to explain the Oration *pro Marco Marcello*, he had not only a great Croud of People for his Auditors, but likewise Twenty five Cardinals. He afterwards became Rector of the same College; and, upon the Death of *Pius* IV, the Spirit of Devotion seizing him, he followed *Philip de Neri*, and accepted of the Office of Secretary to the Sacred College, offered him by *Pius* V. He exercised this Employ Twenty five Years, and obtained by it the Reputation of an honest and able Officer. He refused the Bishopric, which *Gregory* XIV would have given him, but not the Post of Secretary to the Briefs, which was offered him by *Clement* VIII, who made him also his Chamberlain, and afterward Cardinal. It is reported, that Cardinal *Alexander de Montalto*, who had behaved a little haughtily towards *Antoniano*, seeing him promoted to the Purple, said, that, for the future, he would never despise a Man in a Cassock and little Band, how low an Object soever he might seem, since, possibly, the Person, whom he had despised, might become not only his Equal, but even his Master. *Antoniano* killed himself by dint of Study; he spent whole Nights in it; which brought a Distemper upon him, of which he died, in the Sixty third Year of his Age. He wrote with so much Ease, that he had never occasion to make any Rasure; and it is said, that he preferred his Virginity all his Life (*b*). See, in one of the Remarks, what relates to his Works [*E*].

Cardinal *Bentivoglio* will furnish me with a large Supplement to this Article [*F*]. I find, that *Antoniano* was one of the Disputants on the Question concerning the Precedency of Patriarchs [*G*].

(*b*) Ex land Niclo Erythio, Pinacoth. l. page 36.

[*E*] *What relates to his Works.*] We have of his, *De Christiana puerorum educatione* —— *Dissertatio de obscuritate Solis in morte Christi* —— *De Successione Apostolica* —— *De Stylo Ecclesiastico, seu de conscribenda Ecclesiastica historia* —— *De Primatu S. Petri* —— *Lucubrationes in Rhetoricam Aristotelis & in Orationes Ciceronis*. —— i. e. *Of the Christian Education of Youth* —— *A Dissertation on the Darkness of the Sun at the Crucifixion* —— *Of Apostolical Succession* —— *Of the Ecclesiastical Style, or of writing Ecclesiastical History* —— *Of the Primacy of St Peter* —— *Lucubrations on Aristotle's Rhetoric, and Cicero's Orations*. —— Several pieces of Verses, some Sermons, Notes and Prefaces on the Romance of *Achilles Statius*, and on the *Terence of Gabriel Faernus* (8), several Letters, &c. He is said to have had a hand in the *Catechism of the Council of Trent* (9). As for his Letters, they are Apostolical Briefs, which he composed while he was Secretary; I shall take notice of them in the following Remark. They are reckoned among the Letters, which the Writers of Anecdotes should make their Extracts from (10). The other Sources are the Letters of the Cardinals *Bembo* and *Sadolet*, Those of *Peter Martyr*, &c. Note, that his Book *De Christiana puerorum educatione*, composed in *Italian*, at the Request of Cardinal *Charles Borromeo*, was printed at *Verona*, by the Care of *Augustin Valerio*, Bishop of the Place, and Cardinal (11).

[*F*] *Cardinal* Bentivoglio *will furnish me with a large Supplement to this Article.*] He says, it was still uncertain, whether *Antoniano* was born at *Rome*; but that there was no doubt of his having been educated there from his Infancy (12). He was placed, by Pope *Pius* IV, in the Service of Cardinal *Borromeo*, That Pope's Nephew; he was This Cardinal's Secretary for *Latin* Dispatches; He attended him to *Milan*, and returned with him to *Rome*. He was made Secretary of the Sacred College; and discharged the Duties of That Post to Admiration. He was admitted to the strictest Intimacy with *Clement* VIII; whose Briefs he composed with so much Eloquence, that That Pope had no reason to envy *Leo* X. the *Sadolet*'s and the *Bembo*'s. He inserted Passages of Scripture in them with great Judgment; for which he was blamed by too rigid a Censor; who said, that it made several of the Pope's Letters favour more of a Monastery, than of the Court of *Rome*, and represented rather the Person of a Preacher, than that of a Sovereign Pontiff. *Che percio alcuni di loro, sappessero più di Claustro regolare, che di corte Ecclesiastica, è representassero quasi la persona d'un predicatore, che un Pontifice* (13). He laughed at this Criticism, and answered, That, if he took the Matter right, there were not too many Scripture-Phrases, in the Letters, which he composed; that, on the contrary, he thought they were not sufficiently filled with them, considering the Quality of the Person, who spake in them, which was That of a Sovereign Pastor of the Church; considering farther, likewise, that they were not prophane Letters, in which a Luxuriancy of Thought and Expression, after the Style of temporal Sovereigns, ought to reign. *Anzi che a lui pareva, che più tosto mancassero in questa parte, havuto riguardo all' essere i Brevi Apostolici scritti dal supremo Pastor della Chiesa, e non lettere profane, che havessero a lussu reggiare con sensi, & parole tratte dalle Secretario de Principi temporali* (14). He adds, that the Briefs of *Sadolet*, and Those of *Bembo*, did not keep up the *decorum*, which the Pontifical Dignity required; and that, in some of his Briefs, *Bembo*, by an Affectation of Latinity, favours, not only of Prophaneness, and a worldly Spirit, but even of Paganism. *Antoniano* was, in his last Sickness, visited by *Clement* VIII, and received from him the Apostolical Benediction. He was naturally modest, of a pleasant Conversation, and a Prudence, which the Court-Spirit had not vitiated (15). He assisted in several Conclaves, and discoursed concerning them with singular Satisfaction; not without making solid Reflexions on the Vanity of human Things. *Men*, said he, *perplex themselves with a thousand Cares, to compass their Ends, but the Providence of God almost always discovers it's Ascendant. Per occasione d'essere stato Secretario del Sacro Collegio tant' anni, s'era trovato egli in molti conclavi, e di quei successi distorrevo con gusto particolare, e monstrava specialmente in quanti modi vi si affaticasse l'industria humana, ed in quanti vi apparisse, e vi prevalisse ordinariamente la providenza Divina* (16). Without doubt he meant to say, that the best concerted Intrigues, and those, which have exercised the Thoughts most, are frustrated, in Conclaves, by unforeseen Accidents. If by this he would insinuate, that the secret Springs of Providence are more particularly discoverable in Those Assemblies, where Popes are elected, he was mistaken; for we see, that, in all the Courts of the World, the Success of the most prudent Politics depends upon I know not what fortuitous Incidents; which may convince us of the Truth of the Proverb, *Man proposes, but God disposes.*

[*G*] *Was one of the Disputants in the Question concerning the Precedency of Patriarchs.*] Read this Passage, taken from a Letter, which *le Paranda* wrote to *Rome*, the eleventh of *December*, 1589. "La causa della precedenza Patriarcale non è ancor venuta à fine, & si tratta tuttavia nella Congregatione delle Ceremonie. Si scrive, & le scritture vanno per *manus*, & si come diffi già il parer della Congregatione è contra la pretenza de gli Arcivescovi, & de Patriarchi. Solamente l'*Antoniano* sostien questa parte, & scrive, & sta sodo. Sara un brau' huomo, se fara tanto che basti, havendo da contrastar con Monsignor Illustrissimo Gesualdo (17).

(8) Nomenclat. Cardinal pag. 178.
(9) See Colomies Bibl. choisi. pag. 36.
(10) Varillas's Preface to the Anecdotes of Florence.
(11) Possevin. Apparat. Sacr. Tom. 2. pag. 405, 443.
(12) Bentivoglio, Memorie overo diario, capitolo 7. pag. 10. Edit. Amstel. 1648.
(13) Id. ib. pag. 111.
(14) Id. ib. pag. 112.
(15) Id. pag. 113.
(17) Id. ib. pag. 157.

ANTONIO.

[17] Lettere de Oio. Francesco Peranda, prima parte, pag. 224. Edit. Venet. 1604.

"do (17). ----- *The Question concerning the Pre-*
"*cedency of Patriarchs is not yet determined, and con-*
"*tinues to be discussed in the Congregation of Cere-*
"*mony. They write, and their Works are in every*
"*one's Hands. And they say the Opinion of the Con-*
"*gregation is against the Pretensions of the Arch-*
"*bishops and Patriarchs.* Antoniano *alone under-*
"*takes their Defence, and writes, and makes a Stand.*
"*He will be a brave Man, if he can support his*
"*Cause against the most illustrious Lord* Gosual-
"*do.*"

ANTONIO (NICOLAS) Knight of the Order of St *James*, and Canon of *Seville*, has done great Honour to the *Spanish* Nation by the *Bibliotheque* of *Spanish* Writers, which he published at *Rome*, in two Volumes, in Folio, in the Year 1672. It is a very good Work in it's kind [*A*]. And, perhaps, no One has succeeded better in Collections of this kind, than Don *Nicolas Antonio*. He was born at *Seville*, in the Year 1617, of a Father, whom King *Philip* IV made President of the Admiralty, established in That City in the Year 1626. Having studied School-Learning, Philosophy, and Theology, in his own Country, he went to study the Law at *Salamanca*, and applied himself chiefly to the Lectures of *Francisco Ramos del Manzano*, who was afterwards One of the King's Counsellors, and Preceptor to *Charles* II. We cannot form a better Judgment of the Progress he made, than from the many Projects he had conceived for the Advancement of Literature, and the manner, in which he had executed part of them, notwithstanding the unavoidable interruption of Affairs, in an Employment, which he had at *Rome*; being Agent-General for the King, his Master, and, besides, concerned in Special Commissions, from the Inquisition of *Spain*, the Vice-Roys of *Naples* and *Sicily*, and the Governour of *Milan*, to negotiate their Affairs at the Court of *Rome*. The Plan of the *Bibliotheque* of the *Spanish* Writers consists of two Parts. The first comprehends all the Authors of That Nation, who lived before the End of the XVth Century; the other Those, who lived after the End of That Century. This latter Part, being ready sooner than the first, was published before it. It appeared at *Rome*, as I have already said, in two Volumes in Folio, in the Year 1672. I cannot tell whether the Author had leisure enough to put the last Hand to the other Part, and to a second Design, no less laborious. He was employ'd upon a Work under the following Title; *Trophæum Historico-Ecclesiasticum Deo veritati erectum, ex manubiis Pseudo-Historicorum, qui Flavii Lucii Dextri, M. Maximi, Helecæ, Braulionis, Luitprandi, & Juliani nomine circumferuntur; hoc est, vindiciæ veræ atque dudum notæ Hispanarum rerum Historiæ, Germanarum nostræ gentis laudum, non ex Germano-Fuldensibus Chronicis, emendicatarum in libertatem & paritatem plena Assertio.──── An Historico-Ecclesiastical Trophy erected to the God of Truth from the Spoils of the Pseudo-Historians, banded about under the Names of* Flavius Lucius Dexter, M. Maximus, Helecas, Braulio, Luitprand, *and* Julian; *that is, The True and Well-known History of the* Spanish *Affairs vindicated, and the Genuine Virtues of our People, not meanly borrowed from the* German *Chronicles of* Fuld, *but restored to their Liberty and Purity*. He had reason to say, that it was not only a Work of vast Extent, but attended likewise with dangerous Consequences (a). For where are Those, who are willing to be undeceived as to Fables, which for a long time have flattered the Vanity of their Nation? To what do not they expose themselves, who venture to stem the Torrent of a Tradition equally fabulous and glorious (b)? Every one knows the Clamour of the *Provençals* upon Mr *de Launoi*'s attempting to cure them of their Errors in relation to *Mary Magdalen* and *Lazarus*. Perhaps Don *Nicolas Antonio* did not presume to meddle with certain pious Fables [*B*], as being very sensible of the Obstinacy of his Countrymen on this Head, and the untractable Temper of the Inquisition. He insinuates,

(a) Immensæ molis, ac forsan invidæ, opus.

(b) See the Remark [D], at the end.

A THOUGHT on the Indexes of Books.

(1) *See the advantage of Character given of it by Mr* Baillet, Tom. 2. *of his Jugemens des Savans,* n. 128. *The Journal des Savans, of* July 6, 1690, *gives us a ’verbiage A nt ic on tius ex licet Work.*

[*A*] *The Bibliotheque of* Spanish *Writers ----- is a very good Book in it's kind* (1).] I have quoted Mr *Baillet*, who has given a Detail of his Excellencies. He has, not without Reason, praised the very Tables of the Book; for they are in a very good Method, and very useful. The Author has wrote a short Preface to it, which shews his good Taste and Judgment. He there introduces the Saying of a *Spanish* Writer, "Indicem libri ab Autore, librum "ipsum à quovis alio conficiendum esse. ── *The* "*Index of a Book should be the Author's own; the* "*Book itself may be wrote by any one else*." The contrary is practised at present; Authors leave the trouble of composing Alphabetical Tables to others; and it must be owned, that they, who are not laborious, and whose Talent lies in a great Warmth of Imagination, are in the right to let others compose the Indexes of their Works; but a Man of Judgment, and Labour, will succeed, in making Tables to his own Writings, much better than a Stranger. There are many Pieces of good Advice to be given in regard to the Composition of these Tables; nor are they mistaken, who look upon them as the Soul of Books.

[*B*] *He did not presume to meddle with certain pious Fables*.] Perhaps I am mistaken; for Mr *Baillet* speaks thus of them; "His Criticism is very

"just and solid in several Places; particularly in what "relates to the fabulous Traditions of the first Ca-
"techists, who planted the Faith in *Spain*, and of
"those false Historians, whom Imposture brought
"forth, for the Delusion of the *Spaniards*, and on
"whom our Author has promised a particular Cri-
"ticism (2)." This would have made me more peremptory, had I not found another Remark subjoined to these Words of Mr *Baillet*; "However,
"there is room to suspect him of too much Indulgence
"for certain vulgar Opinions, which are exploded
"by Critics of the best Taste." Be this as it will, there is no doubt but he would have destroyed the Authority of all the supposed Authors mentioned in his Title (3); nor would he have been the first, who had employed his Pen to this Purpose; for read the following Extract from some Sheets of the Abbot *de la Roque*: "For an Age past, they
"have had the boldness to write *(speaking of* Spain*)*
"and publish false Chronicles, to impose upon the
"Credulity of the Learned, or the Simple; which,
"far from diminishing, increases the Glory of the
"Marquis *d'Agropoli*, who has so justly ridiculed
"and exploded Dexter, the oldest of these false
"Chroniclers, in his *Dissertatione: Ecclesiastica: por*
"*el honor de los antiquos tutelares contra los ficcio-*
"*nes modernas*, printed at *Sarragossa* in 167+ (4).

(2) Baillet, Jugem. des Scavans, Tom. 2. pag. 134.

(3) *See the Remark [D], at the end.*

(4) Journ. des Scavans, *of the 15th* 1687. pag. 11. *See the end of the Remark [D].*

[*C*] *The*

ANTONIO. APAFI.

insinuates, that he had formed the Design of several other Works. But let us not omit That, which he published at *Antwerp*, in the Year 1659, *De Exilio, sive de Pœna Exilii Exulumque Conditione & Juribus*; in folio (c). —— *Of Banishment, or of the Punishment of Exile, and the Condition and Rights of the Exiled*, in Folio.

Thus much I had said of Don *Nicolas Antonio*, in the first Edition. Since That Time, I have been informed, that, being returned to *Seville*, after having studied the Law at *Salamanca*, he shut himself up in the Royal Monastery of Benedictines, where he laboured several Years on the Spanish Bibliotheque, and, for that purpose, made use of the Books of Benedictus de la Serna, *who was, at that time, Abbot of It, and Dean of the Faculty of Theology of Salamanca*; That, *in the Year* 1659, *he was sent to* Rome *by King* Philip IV, *to take care of the Affairs of the Kingdom, as Agent-General* (d) *: That the Cardinal of* Arragon, *Ambassador at Rome, obtained for him, of Pope* Alexander VII, *a Canonship in the Church of* Seville, *the Revenue whereof he employed in Alms and Books*; *That he collected above Thirty thousand Volumes with it*; *insomuch that his Library fell short of none, but the* Vatican; *That, by this Assistance, together with continual Labour, and indefatigable Application, he finished his Bibliotheque of Spain in four Volumes in* Folio (e) —— *That, after he had caused the two first Volumes to be printed, he was recalled to* Madrid *by King* Charles II, *to take on him the Office of Counsellor of the* Crusado, *which he discharged with great Integrity till his Death, which happened in* 1684. —— *That he left no other Estate, besides the vast Library, which he had transported from* Rome *to* Madrid; *on the contrary, that his Executorship was clogged with Debts*; *that his two Brothers, who are Canons of* Salamanca, *and his two Nephews, were not able to get his Bibliotheque of Spain printed, but sent it to Monsieur the Cardinal* d'Aguirre, *who was so generous as to be at the Expence of the Impression himself* [C], *and committed the Care of it to Monsieur* Marti, *his Library-Keeper, who added some Notes in his Eminency's Name.*

I have just seen a little Book, in which I find, that the Jesuits have complained of this Work of Don *Nicholas Antonio* [D].

(c) *Taken from his Bibliotheca Hispanica*, Tom. 2. pag. 118, 119.

(d) Journ. des Sçavans, of the tenth of June, 1697, pag. 420. Edit. Holl.

(e) Ib. pag. 421, 422.

[C] *The Cardinal* d'Aguirre, —— *was so generous, as to be at the Expence of the Impression himself*.] He was the Author's old Friend, and had studied with him in the University of *Salamanca*. The Republic of Letters is extreamly obliged to him for the Expence he was at in printing such a Book, which contains two Volumes in Folio. They were printed at *Rome*, and appeared in 1696. You will find good Extracts from them in the *Journal de Sçavans* (5), and in That of *Leipsic* (6). The Title of the Work is This : " Bibliotheca Hispana vetus, sive Hispanorum qui usquam unquamve scripto aliquid " consignaverunt, Notitia, complectens scriptores " omnes qui ab Octaviani Augusti Imperio usque ad " annum MD floruerunt. Auctore Nicolao Antonio, " Hispalensi Jurisconsulto, Ordinis S. Jacobi Equite, " Patriæ Ecclesiæ Canonico, regiorum negotiorum " in Urbe & Romanâ curiâ Procuratore generali, " demum Matriti consiliario Regio. Opus Posthu" mum. Nunc primum prodit jussu & expensâ Emi" nentissimi & Reverendissimi Domini D. Josephi " Saenz Cardinalis de Aguirre. —— *A Dictionary* " *of ancient* Spanish *Authors, or Memoirs of all those* " *in* Spain, *who have ever, or any where, committed* " *any Thing to writing; comprehending all the Wri*" *ters, who have flourished from the Reign of* Octa" *vian* Augustus *down to the Year* M D. *By* Ni" colas Antonio, *Civilian of* Salamanca, *and Knight* " *of the Order of* St James; *Canon of* Seville, *Agent*" *General for the King and the Inquisition, and last*" *ly the King's Counsellor at* Madrid. *A Posthumous* " *Work*; *now first published by Order, and at the* " *Expence, of the most Eminent and Reverend Lord*, " D. Joseph Saenz, *Cardinal of* Aguirre."

[D] *The Jesuits have complained of this Work of* Don Nicolas Antonio.] A Pamphlet (7) entituled Calumnia convicta, seu Epistola familiaris Cleandri ad clarissimum & eruditissimum virum Evaristum, super Memoriali nuper porrecto, Hispano idiomate, ad Regem Catholicum à Patre Joanne de Palazol Soc. Jesu, nomine & jussu Thyrsi Gonzales ejusdem Soc. Generalis Præpositi. —— *Calumny convicted*; *or a familiar Epistle from* Cleander *to the most famous and learned* Evaristus, *concerning a Memorial, in* Spanish, *lately presented to the Catholic King, by Father* John de Palazol, *a Jesuit, by Order of* Thyrsus Gonzales, *General of the Order*; dated from *Dilingen*, the Twen-

(5) *Of the Months of June and July*, 1697.

(6) Acta Erudit. Lipf. Mens. Jun. & Jul. 1697.

(7) Of *twenty seven Pages in 12mo*.

ty fifth of *June* 1698, informs me, that the Jesuits have represented to the King of *Spain*, that one of the five Propositions of *Jansenius* has been recommended as Catholic in the Work of Don *Nicolas Antonio*. They pretend to be unwilling to attack the Cardinal *d'Aguirre*, who was at the Expence of printing this Work; but it is easy to see that they attack him indirectly. They suppose, that some *Jansenist* has, in this Place, corrupted the Text of *Antonio*. The whole Affair is This: Our Author acknowledges this Proposition of *Prudentius*, Bishop of *Troyes*, for Catholic: " That the Blood of Jesus Christ was shed " for all Believers; but not for those, who never have " believed; who do not now believe; and who never " will believe." *Quod sanguis Christi effusus sit pro omnibus credentibus, sed non pro iis qui nunquam crediderunt, nec credunt, nec credituri sunt*. The Author of the Pamphlet shews, that this Proposition might have been considered as Catholic; and that therefore there was no manner of Reason to suspect the Faith of *Don Nicolas Antonio*, or That of the Cardinal *d'Aguirre*. Note, that his Eminence has declared boldly against the looser Casuists (8); and that this is supposed to be the Reason of the ill Offices the Jesuits endeavour to do him.

It is probable, this will not be the only Complaint brought to the Tribunals against these two Volumes of the *Bibliotheque of Spain*. I have not yet seen them, and I question whether there be a Copy of them in the United Provinces (9); but I am assured, that the Author has declared loudly against the pretended *Luitprand*, and against *Higuera*, who brought him to light; and has fallen foul on *Aubert of Seville*, on the *Chronicles of Dexter*, on *Maximus*, on *Julian*, *&c*. A *Spanish* Jesuit (10) remarks this, in a Work he has published, in favour of his Brethren, at *Antwerp*, Compilers of the *Acta Sanctorum*. It is There I have met with some Passages of Don *Nicolas Antonio* on this Subject. But, since the Marquis *d'Agropoli*, Grandee of *Spain* by a double Title, could not combat these fabulous Historians, without exposing himself to a vexatious Information before the Inquisition (11), as a Writer, who betrayed the Honour of his Country; I cannot suppose the Monks of That Country will ever suffer the Memory of our *Nicolas Antonio* to rest.

(8) *See the several Extracts from his Books, in the Memorial of a Jansenist, which I shall cite in the Article* BELLARMIN, *Remark* [H].

(9) *I write this the* 8*th of February*, 1699.

(10) Anton. Xaramillius, *in Apologia pro Veritate. This Work, translated out of Spanish into Latin, by the Jesuit Pet. Cant. was printed at Antwerp*, An. 1698.

(11) *See the Article* VESPASIAN, *Remark* [D].

APAFI (MICHAEL) Prince of *Transylvania*, was promoted to this Principality in the Year 1661, without his thinking of it. *Ali Bassa*, having forced *Kimin Janos* to quit *Transylvania*, was apprehensive he should not be able to hinder him from returning, and making his Party superior by the help of the Imperial Troops. He resolved, therefore, to set up a Prince in opposition to him, who should be elected by

APAFI.

by the States of the Country, under the Protection of the *Porte*. To this end, he demanded of the Deputies of the Towns of *Transylvania*, whether there were not some great *Transylvanian* Lord, in the Towns, which had submitted to his Arms, worthy of the Principality (a)? They named to him *Michael Apafi*, who kept himself at that time in his Castle of *Ebestfalve*, and had not yet forgot the long Troubles he had suffered among the *Tartars*, from whence he was but lately released, by paying a great Ransom. *Ali* sent for him, without discovering his Design. *Apafi* believed it was to put him to Death [*A*], but durst not refuse to go with the Guard, which was sent for him. His Wife, who was near the time of her Lying-in, was in a mortal Fright, and gave him over for lost. Before he had passed his own Estate, News was brought him, that his Wife was happily delivered of a Son; he knew not whether he ought to rejoice or grieve, at the News: but the *Turks*, who guarded him, and no doubt knew *Ali Bassa*'s Intentions better than he, told him, It presaged a happy Principality to him. *Ali* received him very honourably, and a few Days after procured him to be elected Prince of *Transylvania*. He managed it so, that the Election appeared to be legal; for he caused as many of the Nobility of *Transylvania* to come into his Army, as he could; and told them he wished that They, together with the Deputies of the Cities, would elect a Prince; and promised, in the *Sultan's* Name, to confer the Ensigns of the Principality upon whomsoever they should elect (b). Thus *Michael Apafi* became Prince of *Transylvania*, without any Intrigues, on his part, or Expectation of it [*B*]. He was of Noble Birth [*C*] indeed, but of a quiet Disposition; besides that, his long Imprisonment in *Crim-Tartary* had inspired him with great Humility. *Kimin Janos*, who expected Wonders from his Conjunction with the Imperialists, commanded by the Count *Montecuculi*, found himself disappointed; for, as soon as *Montecuculi* was informed of the Condition of the *Ottoman* Forces, he thought it more convenient to return to *Hungary*, than hazard a Battle. This Retreat gave the *Turks* an opportunity of making great Ravages, and obtaining a Victory in *Transylvania*, which cost *Kimin Janos* his Life, in *January* 1662 [*D*].

His

[*A*] *Apafi believ'd it was to put him to Death*] I give more Credit to this, than to Those, who say he was an ambitious Man. I quote an Author, who was well informed; for he lived at that Time, and had Employments in *Transylvania*, which gave him Opportunities of knowing the bottom of all Transactions (1). Now he relates very ingenuously, that *Apafi* was made Prince of *Transylvania*, without contributing any thing to it himself; and affirms, that he was not an ambitious Man. However, it is a very pardonable Mistake to say, that *Apafi had certain Qualities, which rendred him worthy of a Principality, and an* AMBITION *withal proportionable to the* GREATNESS *of his Soul* (2): For, generally, those who are raised to Elective Principalities, in the midst of Troubles, stirred up by their Competitors, are Men of very aspiring Minds. A *French* Author, who has published an History of the Troubles in *Hungary*, is far from representing *Michael Apafi* as a Prince, who endeavoured to aggrandize himself; for, when he speaks of the Resolution taken by the *Hungarian* Protestants, to confederate themselves with those of *Transylvania*, to maintain their Liberty of Conscience by the Sword; he adds these Words, "The Princess, who was a Woman of a turbulent Spirit, and extremely attached to the Errors of *Calvin*, sollicited this Confederacy very powerfully; whilst her more peaceable Husband employed himself only in Hunting, and in the Conversation of the Learned (3)"

[*B*] *Thus Michael Apafi became Prince of Transylvania, without any Intrigues, on his Part, or Expectation of it.*] Of this I have already spoken in the foregoing Remark. It remains only, that I point out certain Authors, who seem not to have been well informed of the manner of his Election. One of them speaks thus; "In the beginning of the Year 1663, *Kimin Janos* was defeated, and lost his Life. ----- The *Turks*, finding no more Resistance, made themselves Masters of all *Transylvania*, except the Places possessed by the Imperialists. *Michael Apafi*, who had been elected in the Room of *Kimin Janos*, desired a Peace with the *Turks*; and, accordingly, *Hali Bassa* entered into a Treaty with the Baron *de Grez* (4)." This Discourse plainly imports, I. That *Apafi* was at War with the *Turks*, as soon as he was placed on the Throne of *Transylvania*. II. That he was not elected before the Death of *Kimin Janos*, and consequently not 'till the Year 1663. All This is false. He was elected in the Year 1661, during the Life of *Kimin Janos*, and at the Recommendation of *Ali Bassa*: and *Kimin Janos* was killed in the Month of *January* 1662. The Author of the Life of Count *Tekeli* relates (5), by Hear-say only, *that Michael Apafi was raised, by the Turks, to the Principality of* Transylvania, *on his promising a larger Tribute.* Away with this Promise to the same Place with *His other Competitors, who addressed themselves to the Grand Signior*, as the misinformed Mr *Moreri* tells us.

[*C*] *He was of noble Birth.*] Let us hear the Author, whom I have already cited more than once. " Hic (Michael Apafi) erat ex antiquissima magnatum " Familia ortus, pius, sed tam natura, quam propter " diuturnas Carceris Crimensis molestias, plus justo de- " missus ac lenis, ut adepto etiam Principatu nimiæ à " plerisque lenitatis insimularetur (6). ---- *This Prince* " (Michael Apafi) *was of a noble and ancient Family; a* " *pious Man, but, both by Nature, and from the long* " *Troubles of his Imprisonment in* Crim-Tartary, *of* " *too humble and mild a Disposition; insomuch, that*, " *even after he was raised to the Principality, he* " *was reproached by some with too much Lenity.*" These Words, are antiquissima magnatum Familia, sufficiently confute Mr *Moreri*, who says, that *Michael Abasfi* was a *Magistrate's Son* of *Hermanstadt*, *the chief City* of Transylvania. It was certainly on the Credit of His Dictionary, that the Author of the Historical *Mercury* affirmed the same thing (7).

[*D*] *Which cost* Kimin Janos *his Life, in January 1662*.] I have already confuted Him, who said it was in the beginning of the Year 1663. There is another still to be confuted. Sir *P. Ricaut* pretends, that *Kimin Janos*, having been defeated near *Clausemburgh*, resolved, some time after, to try his Fortune *a second time*: That *he gave the Turks Battle, at some Distance from* Presburg; that the Success was a long time doubtful; but that, at last, he was forced to yield to Numbers, and, in the Flight, *was thrown off his Horse by his own Men, and trod to Death*. This Historian remarks, that the *Turks* killed, and took Prisoners, Fifty thousand Christians, in the Battle of *Clausemburgh*; and that, a little before, they declined fighting, because the Emperor's Troops, and those of *Kimin Janos*, were superior to theirs in Number (8). I find nothing of this in my *Transylvanian* Author. He informs me, on the contrary, that *Montecuculi*, and *Kimin Janos*, being advanced beyond *Clausemburgh*, were informed, that *Ali Bassa's* Army was four times stronger than theirs, insomuch that *Montecuculi* declared to *Kimin Janos*, that, considering the ill Condition their Infantry was in, by reason

APAFI. 365

His Son endeavoured to support his Pretensions; but his Efforts were unsuccessful. *Apafi* was obliged to join his Forces with those of the *Turks*, to recover the Places, which the Emperor had possessed himself of in *Transylvania*. The Imperial Garrison of *Clausemburgh* defended itself so long, that the *Turks* and *Michael Apafi* were obliged to raise the Siege with Disgrace (c). Treaties were set on foot for the Evacuation of these Places, but without any Effect; they were forced to come to open War at last (d). The *Turks* were successful in 1663; but, the Year following, they lost the famous Battle of *St Godard*; after which the *Grand Vizier* consented to a Truce of Twenty Years. In the Year 1664, *Apafi* treated with the Imperial Garrisons of *Clausemburgh* and *Zatmar*, who delivered up those two Towns to him (e). He lived under the Protection of the *Porte*, and wholly independant on the Court of *Vienna*, during the Truce between the two Empires. At first he favoured the Malecontents of *Hungary*, without breaking with the Emperor; but at last engaged in an open War for them, and published his Reasons, in a *Latin Manifesto*, addressed to all the Christian Powers [E]. The *Turks* broke with the Emperor, in the Year 1683, and entered *Hungary* with a formidable Army, which penetrated as far as *Vienna*, with all imaginable Ease. But these happy Beginnings were followed by a dreadful Reverse. The *Grand Vizier* raised the Siege of *Vienna*; and from that time there followed nothing but Loss upon Loss, and Misfortune upon Misfortune, on the *Ottoman* side. *Transylvania* fell a Prey to the Imperial Troops; and *Apafi*, instead of asserting the Liberties of *Hungary*, was the Cause of This Kingdom's losing That Shadow of Liberty, which remained to it [F]; for it is now no longer elective, but looked upon as a conquered Country, and, accordingly, is erected into an Hereditary Kingdom. *Apafi* died at *Weissemburgh* towards the end of

(c) *The Governor was called David Rettani. He was a Venetian, and a good Engineer. Vianoli Hist. Veneta, Tom. 2. pag. 669.*

(d) Ex Betlenio, Hist. Rer. Transylvan.

(e) Buno, Not. in Phil. Cluverii introduct. Geograph. pag. 281.

---

(9) Betlenius, pag. 251.

(10) Id. pag. 252.

(11) Id. pag. 284, 281.

(12) Id. pag. 254.

(13) Ricaut. ubi supra, pag. 291.

(14) Pag. 304.

(15) *In the Edition of Amsterdam, in 1686, the Year 1680 is marked on the Top of the Page. This Error may deceive those who do not examine it nearly.*

(16) Book 1. pag. 30.

(17) Pag. 39.

(18) Pag. 32.

son of the scarcity of Provisions, which they had suffered, he could not hazard his Imperial Majesty's Troops (9). *Kimim Janos*, being driven to despair, could hardly refrain from Tears at this Declaration (10); and was forced to return with *Montecuculi* into *Hungary*. He fought no other Battle, but That, in which he was killed; nor did he fight it near *Presburgh*, in *Hungary*, but in the Plains of *Transylvania*, on the Twenty third of *January*, 1662, near a Village called *Hetur* (11). The Historian observes, that about Five thousand Men of *Montecuculi*'s Army perished by Famine and Sickness (12). This Circumstance, joined to that which is observed above, weakens the Credit of what Sir *P. Ricaut* says, viz. that the Emperor's Forces, *and those of* Kimin Janos, *united, formed so fair and numerous an Army, that one would have thought, they were designed not only to defend the Frontiers of Christendom, but even to dispute the Empire of the World with the* Ottomans (13). How can this be, if the *Ottoman* Army was four times stronger? But how can this Victory of the *Turks*, near *Clausemburgh*, which cost the Christians Fifty thousand Men, be credited; how, I say, when there is not a Syllable of it to be found in the History of *Transylvania*? Have the *Turks* their *Gazetteers* at *Constantinople*, who vie with the Christians in framing imaginary Victories?

[E] *And published his Reasons, in a Latin Manifesto, addressed to all the Christian Powers.*] I have a Copy of it by me, printed in the Year 1682, but without Date to the *Manifesto of Michael Apafi*, and as my Edition does not remark the Time of the Publication of That of *Transylvania*, I dare not affirm, that this Prince declared War in 1682; for I find, in the Life of Count *Tekeli* (14), that, in 1681, Apasi *joined him with an Army of* Transylvanians, *and that they both undertook the Siege of* Zatmar. The Author of the History of the *Troubles* of Hungary speaks of That Siege under the same Year (15), and informs us, that *Michael Apafi* made himself Master of the Town (16); that, not being able to reduce the Citadel, he retreated, and lost his Baggage in the Retreat (17); that it was difficult to penetrate into the Cause of this Disgrace (18); that some attributed it to a misunderstanding between Count *Tekeli*, and *Teleki*, who commanded the *Transylvanian* Troops at That Siege; that the latter was accused of making use of bad Powder, which took no effect; and that, according to others, Prince Apasi *would not take the Town himself, on some Advice he had received, that the Grand Signior expected he should put the Place into his Hands: that it is certain, however, that the Bassa, who commanded the* Turks *at That Siege, sent long Memorials to* Constantinople *against this Prince, which obliged* him *to return into his own Country, for fear some Change of Affairs should happen there in his Absence*. Thus this Historian reports the Tittle-tattle of Coffee-house Politicians. The *Historical and Political Mercury* has faithfully copied him (19).

[F] *Was the Cause of this Kingdom's losing That Shadow of Liberty, which remained to it.*] It would be unjust to accuse *Apafi* of Imprudence on this account; for never had any one a better prospect of good Success. The Forces of the Malecontents, alone, had kept the Imperial Troops in play, 'till that time. What might not reasonably be expected, then, from the extraordinary Preparations of the Grand Signior, who had promised Wonders and Mountains to *Tekell*? But, by one of those fatal Conjunctures, by which the Providence of God interposes, from time to time, to confound the best grounded human Hopes, it happened, that *Apafi* not only performed nothing in favour of the Liberty of *Hungary*, but enslaved likewise his own Country. *Sic erat in fatis*. It so happened, that, instead of weakening the House of *Austria*, he raised it from it's drooping Condition; he put it in a capacity of resuming it's Superiority; he ratified it's Claim to the Crown of *Hungary*; and made the *Turkish* Dominions an inexhaustible Fund of good News, for the Confederacy, formed against *France*, during the course of the War. Must it, therefore, be said, that *Apafi* was a hot-headed, rash, Man (20)? By no means, unless all be stiled so, who cannot foresee Events the most contrary to Appearances. Would not the best Politicians have warranted, that *France* would have pushed the Affair on the one side, whilst the *Turks* acted on the other? Who could ever have persuaded himself, that she would continue in Inaction for six successive Years, in the midst of the most favourable Opportunities of aggrandising herself, than ever Nation had? *Apafi*, *Tekeli*, and their Adherents, are very excusable, in not being able to conjecture, that the *French* would chuse to wage War with the Edict of *Nants*, rather than with the House of *Austria*.

What I have said, in relation to the good News, which comes daily to us from *Turky* (21), is no Secret. Our Gazetteers, and other News-writers, give us scarce any Accounts from that Country, but such as are proper to inspire us with Joy. The Murmurs of the People, their Misery, their Vows for Peace; Dissensions in the *Divan*; a Grand Vizier strangled; formidable Factions; Plagues; Fires at *Constantinople*; Rebellions in *Ægypt*, *Arabia*, and *Syria*; and an hundred things of this Nature, which come by the Couriers from *Germany*, sometimes of one kind, sometimes of another; are not these fine Tidings? How many compleat Victories, how many Towns taken, how many Parties defeated, and how many

(19) *Month of May, 1690. pag. 493; but he places the Siege of Zatmar in 1680.*

WHETHER the ill Success of Apafi's Attempt ought to be looked upon as the Effect of Imprudence.

(20) See the Remark [G], of the Article KOTTERUS.

(21) *I wrote this in 1694.*

of *April* 1690 [G]. The *Turks* endeavoured to set up *Tekeli* in his room; but he had not the good Luck to improve to the best Advantage an Incursion he had made into That Country (*f*). The Presence of Prince *Lewis* of *Baden* melted him like Snow before the Sun, if I may use the Expression; nor has he, from That time to the time of my writing this (*g*), given any disturbance to the new Titular Prince of *Transylvania*, the Son of *Michael Apafi*.

(*f*) *During the Campaign of* 1690.

(*g*) *In the Month of February,* 1699.

many successful Incursions into the Enemy's Country, have we not had reason to publish in Summer; and what hopes of Peace have not been given in Winter? Even the raising the Siege of *Belgrade*, in 1693, is represented as an happy Event; since the Imperial Troops had executed their chief Design, which was to hinder the *Ottomans* from making an Inroad into *Transylvania*. I heard a Person say, soon after the Reduction of *Ireland*, that it would have been well to have prolonged the War there, that there might be a sure Fund of new Advantages, both in the East and in the West.

[G] *Apafi died* at *Weissemburgh, towards the end of April,* 1690.] The News-writers differed in the Circumstances of his Death. Some said he died suddenly, in the Assembly of the States of *Transylvania* (22); others, that he died after a long Sickness (23); but all agree, that he died at *Weissemburgh* (24).

(22) *Paris Gazette, of the* 20*th of May,* 1690.
(23) *Mercure Historique, for the Month of May,* 1690. pag 490.
(24) *The Life of Count Tekeli says, at Alba Julia, the same as Weissemburg. Life of Count Tekeli,* pag. 259.

APELLES, one of the most famous Painters of Antiquity, was a Native of the Isle of *Coos* [*A*], and flourished in the Days of *Alexander* [*B*]. He was highly esteemed by This Prince, and the only Person, who was permitted to draw his Picture. He obtained, likewise, another singular Mark of his Favour; for *Alexander*, having sent one of his Mistresses to sit to him for her Picture, and being informed, that *Apelles* was fallen in Love with her, bestowed Her upon him [*C*]. There is room to question, whether *Apelles* abused the Good-Nature of this Great Monarch, as is pretended [*D*]. He was, probably, too good a Courtier, not to know, that a Speech,

[*A*] *Was an Native of the Isle of* Coos.] I find but two Authors, who say so; and one of them must be supposed not to have written what most Editions make him say; but that, instead of these Words, " Apelles eo usque Olympiade CXII provectus ut " plura solus prope quam cæteri omnes contulerit, *he* " *made use of these*," " Apelles Cous Olympiade " CXII picturæ plura solus prope quam cæteri om- " nes contulit (1). ——— Apelles of *Coos, in the* CXII*th* " *Olympiad, contributed, alone, more than all the* " *rest, to the Improvement of Painting*." *Turnebus* was of Opinion, that it ought to be read *Apelles Cous*, and not *Apelles eo usque*. His Supposition has been confirmed by the Manuscript of the *Vatican* (2), by Those of the King's Library, and by That of Mr *Colbert* (3). The other Evidence is *Ovid*, who says,

Ut Venus Artificis labor est & gloria Coi,
Æquoreo madidas quæ premit imbre comas (4).

Thus Venus, rising from her watry Bed,
Immortaliz'd the Coan *Artist's Hand.*

We shall produce in the Remark [*I*], another Passage of this Poet, where some read *Cois*, and others *Cous*. The great number of Authors, who give *Apelles* another Country, induced *le Mazzoni* to defend *Ovid*'s Cause; but, instead of *Cos*, he pretends that the Poet wrote it *Chii* (5). Three Authors of good Credit make *Apelles* a Native of *Ephesus* (6). *Suidas* makes him a Native of *Colophon*, and adds, that the City of *Ephesus* adopted him.

[*B*] *Flourished in the Days of* Alexander.] It cannot be denied, that he was at the height of his Reputation, when That Prince began the Conquest of *Asia*, that is, in the CXI*th* Olympiad. His Adventures at the Court of *Egypt* makes it appear, that he survived *Alexander*. It is a Mistake, then, to say, with *Majoragius*, that he was a Pupil of *Zeuxes*; the Distance of above One hundred and twenty Years between the LXXXIV*th* Olympiad, in which *Zeuxes* flourished (7), and the Reign of the first *Ptolomy*, will not allow it. *Carlo Dati* is the Person, who has taken notice of *Majoragius*'s Mistake. He says, " Non so con qual fondamento Marcento- " nio Majoraggio nel Comento sopra l'Orat di Cicer. " a 11. dicesse che Apelle fosse scolare di Zeusi, " quando tra l'uno e l'altro corse l'eta d'un nomo (8). " ----- *I know not upon what Foundation* Marcan- " tonius Majoragius, *in his Commentary on an O-* " *ration of* Cicero, *makes* Apelles *the Scholar of* " Zeuxes, *since there passed a Century between them.*" His Adventure in the Court of *Egypt* was this: *Apelles* had not the good Fortune to be beloved by *Ptolomy* in the Court of *Alexandria*. A Storm happened to force him into That Port, in the Reign of this King.

A Roguish Fellow, who had a Mind to play him a scurvy Trick, came, and told him, the King invited him to Dinner. *Apelles* waited on him, and, observing the King to be very angry, excused himself, by letting him know, that he came by his Order. The King desired he would tell him, who it was that invited him; but That was impossible; for the Person, who had imposed upon him, was not then in the Room. *Apelles*, upon this, began to draw his Face upon the Wall with a bit of Charcoal, and *Ptolomy* knew him by the very first Lines. " Non fuerat " ei gratia in comitatu Alexandri cum Ptolemæo, " quo regnante Alexandriam vi tempestatis expulsus, " subornato fraude æmulorum plano regio invitatus, " ad Regis cœnam venit, indignantique Ptolemæo & " vocatores suos ostendenti ut diceret à quo eorum " invitatus esset, arrepto carbone extincto e foculo " imaginem in pariete delineavit, agnoscente vultum " plani rege ex inchoato protinus (9)."

[*C*] *Being informed, that* Apelles *was fallen in Love with her, bestowed her upon him.*] *Pliny* relates the Story after this manner; " Alexander ei " honorem clarissimo præbuit exemplo, namque cum " dilectam sibi è paelicibus suis præcipue, nomine Cam- " paspen, nudam pingi ob admirationem formæ ab " Apelle jussisset, eumque tum pari captum amore " sensisset, dono eam dedit. Magnus animo, major " imperio sui: nec minor hoc facto, quam victoria " aliqua; quippe se vicit, nec torum tantum suum, " sed etiam affectum donavit Artifici; ne dilectæ " quidem respectu motus, ut, quæ modo regis fuisset, " nunc pictoris esset. Sunt qui Venerem Anady- " omenen illo pictam exemplari putant (10). ----- " *Alexander honoured him after a very remarkable* " *Manner; for, perceiving that he had fallen in* " *love with his favourite Concubine,* Campaspe, *whom,* " *through Admiration of her Beauty, he had com-* " *manded him to draw naked, he gave her to him.* " *Great as he was in Mind, he was still greater by* " *this Command over himself; an Action This, as much* " *to his Honour as the greatest Victory; for he con-* " *quered himself; nor did he resign his Bed alone,* " *but even his Love, to the Artist; regardless of his* " *Favourite's Lot, who, from being the Mistress of* " *a King, was now to become a Painter's. Some think* " *the* Venus Anadyomene *was drawn from this Ori-* " *ginal.*" *Ælian* relates the same Story; but gives this Mistress of *Alexander* the Name of *Pancaste* (11). The Article of This Prince shall contain a Remark on this Subject (12); as we shall shew, that a Man, who could give the fairest of his Concubines to be drawn stark naked, does not deserve the Encomiums of Continent and Chaste, which have been lavished on him.

[*D*] *There is room to question, whether* Apelles *abused the Good-Nature of this great Monarch, as is pretended.*] *Pliny* may tell us if he pleases, that *Apelles* rendered himself agreeable to this Prince by his Politeness

(1) Plin. lib. 35. cap. 10.

(2) See *Carlo Dati, in his Apostilles on the Life of Apelles,* pag. 104.

(3) See P. Hardouin *on* Pliny, Tom. 5. pag. 264.

(4) Ovid. de Ponto, lib. 4. Eleg. 1. ver. 29.

(5) *Difesa di* Dante, lib. 3. cap. 16. apud Carol Dati, ubi supra, pag. 103.

(6) Strabo, lib. 14. Lucianus, *de Calumn.* Æl. Hist. Anim. lib. 4. cap. 50. *See also* Tzetzes Chil. 8. hist. 197. ver. 193.

(7) *See the Remark* [*A*] *of the Article* ZEUXES.

(8) Carlo Dati, Postille sopra vita d'Apelle, pag. 105.

(9) Plin. lib. 35. cap. 10.

(10) Id. Ib.

(11) Ælian. Var. Hist. lib. 12. cap. 34.

(12) See the *Remarks* [*H*] *and* [*I*] *of the Article* MACEDO. NIA.

APELLES. 367

Speech, so little respectful, as That, which is attributed to him, must displease. The Answer he gave, in relation to Lais, is no Recommendation of his Manners [E]. There has been much Talk of his *Picture of Calumny*; but scarce any one has observed the Blunders, which have been committed in relating the Fact, which was the occasion of this Picture [F]. The Treatise, in which *Lucian* mentions this, is an excellent

ness and Complaisance; but he will scarce persuade those, who know *Alexander*, that a Painter could say to him with Impunity, *Say no more: the very Boys, who grind my Colours, laugh at you*. " Fuit & comitas illi, " propter quam gratior Alexandro Magno erat fre- " quenter in Officinam ventitanti. - - - - - Sed in Of- " ficinâ imperitè multa differenti silentium comiter " suadebat, rideri eum dicens a pueris qui colores te- " rerent. Tantum erat auctoritati juris in Regem " alioqui iracundum (13). - - - - He had a Politeness " of Behaviour, which ingratiated him the more with " Alexander the Great, who frequently visited him " in his Painting-Room. - - - - - - Where Alexander " happening one Day to betray his Ignorance, Apelles, " in an obliging way, desired him to say no more, telling " him the very Boys, who ground his Colours, made " a jest of him: so much Liberty did he take with a " King, otherwise of a passionate Disposition." It is not to be supposed, that *Apelles* could think so harsh an Expression, after what manner soever spoken, would be well taken. Nor is it to be imagined, that *Alexander*, who had been so well educated, and had so good a Genius, could talk so impertinently of Painting, as to deserve to be laughed at by the meanest Apprentice. This is the Opinion of the Learned *Freinshemius*: " Non crediderim in officina " imperitè multa differentem ab Apelle mordaci dicte- " rio repressum fuisse. Nam id neque majestati tanti " regis, neque modestiæ pictoris, hominis non stu- " pidi nec indocti, conveniset; & Alexander, libera- " libus studiis ab extremâ ætate imbutus, etiam de " artibus quas non calleret haud inepte judicare di- " cerat (14)." As for *Megabyzus*, Priest of Diana (15), it would be no such wonder, if *Apelles* had given Him this Advice. And, if we may believe *Plutarch*, it was He, who was censured in this manner by *Apelles*: *Can't you see*, said he to him, *that, while you kept silent, These Boys, who mix the Oker, looked upon you with Respect, on account of the Gold and Purple of your Garments; but that being exposed, when they heard you speak of an Art you did not understand* (16). Another Author says, that it was *Zeuxis*, who spoke thus to Megabyzus (17). I could more easily believe the Liberty, which it is said *Apelles* took with *Alexander*, on another Occasion. *Alexander*, viewing his own Picture, which *Apelles* had just finished, seemed not to admire it as it deserved. A little while after, a Horse was led by, who neighed at the sight of the Horse in the same Piece. *Sir*, said *Apelles* to Alexander, *you would think this Horse was a better Judge of Painting, than your Majesty* (18). But, to give my Thoughts freely, it is all too harsh, too gross, and too brutish, to be ascribed to a Painter, represented, in all other Instances, as a modest, complaisant, and polite Person. A Man must either be on the foot of a Jester at Court, or be such a whimsical, untoward, Humourist, as your great Artists sometimes are: I say, we must have recourse to one of these two Suppositions, to believe, what is said of *Apelles*, not only with regard to *Alexander*, but even with regard to *Megabyzus*, respected on account of his Gold and Purple. *Apelles's* Discourse to *Alexander*, on Occasion of the Horse's neighing, is not so harsh in the Original; but this Sofining does them but little Honour: It is a Blunder; it is gross Ignorance. Let us produce the *Greek*: 'Αλίξανδρῳ δεικνύμενῳ τὴν ἐν Ἐφέσῳ εἰκόνα ἑαυτοῦ τὴν ὑπὸ Ἀπελλοῦ γραφεῖσαν οὐκ ἐπῄνεσεν κατὰ τὴν ἀξίαν τοῦ γράμμα- τος. εἰσαχθέντος δὲ τοῦ ἵππου καὶ χρεμετίσαν- τος πρὸς τὸν ἵππον τὸν ἐν τῇ εἰκόνι ὡς πρὸς ἀληθινὸν καὶ ἐκεῖνον, ὦ βασιλεῦ (εἶπεν ὁ Ἀπελ- λῆς) ἀλλ' ὅγε ἵππος ἔοικέ σε γραφικώτερος εἶ- ναι κατὰ πολύ (19). Alexander, *seeing his own Picture at Ephesus, drawn by Apelles, did not commend the Painting as it deserved; but an Horse being brought, and neighing to the Horse in the Picture, as to a real one; O King (said Apelles) This Horse seems to be a much better Judge of Painting, than you.* *Erasmus* represents the Fact thus: " Apud " Ephesum quum Alexander conspectam effigiem sui

" corporis ad vivum magnâ arte expressam admira- " retur, atque interim fortè equus eductus picto in " eadem tabulâ equo adhinniret, deceptus imitatione, " Apelles, equus, inquit, O Rex, multo melius ex- " pressus est quam tu (20). - - - - *As Alexander was admiring his own Picture, at* Ephesus, *drawn to the like with great Art, an Horse, happening to be brought out, neighed to the Horse in the Picture, being deceived by the Resemblance; upon which* Apelles *said, your Horse, O King, is better drawn than you."* I omit some Circumstances, which *Erasmus* adds, without having found them in *Ælian*. I only observe the Reflexion he puts in the Mouth of the Painter; *Sir, I have succeeded better in painting your Horse, than your Majesty*. This is not the Sense of the *Greek*: a learned Critic has shewed, that the Word γραφικὸς signifies one, who understands Painting; and has by This convinced *Cœlius Rhodiginus*, and *Erasmus*, of misrepresenting the Story (21). I wonder *Pliny* was ignorant of This: He, who takes some Notice of the neighing of the Horse. See, below, the Remark [K].

[E] *The Answer he gave, in relation to* Lais, *is no Recommendation of his Manners*.] She was yet a tender Maid, when *Apelles*, seeing her returning Home from the Fountain, and admiring her Beauty, prevailed upon her to go with him where he pleased. He brought her to an Entertainment, where he was to meet some of his Friends; they laughed at him for bringing with him, instead of a Courtezan, a meer Girl: *Don't trouble your Heads about that*, replied he; *I will manage her so, that, before three Years are at end, she shall have all her Paces to perfection*. Χλευάντων δὲ αὐτῶ τῶν ἑταίρων ὅτι ἀνθ' ἑταίρας παρθέ- νον εἰς τὸ συμπόσιον ἀγάγοι, μὴ θαυμάσητε, εἶπεν, ἐγὼ γὰρ αὐτὴν εἰς μέλλουσαν ἀπόλαυσιν μετ' οὐδ' ὅλην τριετίαν καλὴν δείξω (22). *Irrisus autem à familiaribus, quod meretricis loco virginem adduxisset, nolite mirari*, inquit, *mihi etenim non toto opus erit triennio ut eam ad futuræ voluptatis usum pulchrè doctam instituatamque reddere valeam*. Would not one think the Conversation was concerning an unmanaged Colt, which, in the Hands of an excellent Horseman, would quickly learn all his Airs and Paces? The Reflexion on the Corruption of Those Ages inspires Horror. The Friends of *Apelles* seem even to have surpassed him in Debauchery (23). *Lais* became one of the most famous Courtezans of the Age she lived in. The Painters visited her to take the Model of a fine Neck (24). *Apelles* no doubt copied from the same Original. *"Nemini dubium " esse potest quin hanc ipsam quoque Laidem sibi " veluti in contubernium adsciverit Apelles, quo vi- " vam emendatissimæ formæ imaginem ab animali " exemplo in tabulas suas transfunderet (25). - - - - " Apelles, no doubt, kept this very* Lais *with him " in his House, that he might copy the Resemblance " of a most perfect Beauty from a living Original."*

[F] *Scarce any one has observed the Blunders, which have been committed in relating the matter of the Fact, which was the Occasion of This Picture.*] See how Lucian relates it. The Painter *Antiphilus*, not being able to bear the Favour, which *Apelles* enjoyed with King *Ptolomy*, accused him of being an Accomplice in the Conspiracy of *Theodotus*, Governor of *Phœnicia*. He asserted, that *Apelles* had been seen at Dinner with *Theodotus*, and whispered him in the Ear all the while. He afterwards told the King, that the City of *Tyre* had revolted, and that *Pelusium* was taken, through *Apelles's* means. Yet it was plain, that the Accused had never been at *Tyre*, nor had ever known *Theodotus*, but under the general Quality of Governor of *Phœnicia*. *Ptolomy* was in such a Rage, that, without examining the matter, he was very near putting *Apelles* to death. He considered neither the Accuser, nor the Accused. The former, through Spight and Emulation, might well be suspected of plotting the Ruin of an innocent Person; the latter was too inconsiderable a Person, to be capable of such Attempts; though a Sense of the Obligations he was under to *Ptolomy* had not been sufficient

(13) Plin. lib. 35. cap. 10.

(14) Freinshem Supplem. in Curtium, lib. 2. cap. 6.

(15) Several of the learned think, that Megabyzus was a Name appropriated to the Priest of Diana. Others understand by Megabyzus, in this Place, a great Lord of Persia.

(16) De discrim. Adulat. & Amici, pag. 58. & de Tranquill. Animi, p. 472, 472.

(17) Ælian. Var. Hist. lib. 2. cap. 2. Freinshemius, ubi supra, cites him as having attributed this to Apelles.

(18) Ælian. Var. Hist. lib. 2. cap. 3.

(19) Id. Ib.

(20) In Apophthegm.

(21) Paulus Leopardus Emendationum, lib. 12. cap. 4.

(22) Athen. lib. 13. pag. 588.

(23) Richelet, in Dictionary, under the Word Face, observes, that a Maiden-head is called the Ragoût of Satiety.

(24) Athen. ubi supra.

(25) Junius in Catalogo Artificum, in Apelle, pag. 19.

368 APELLES.

excellent Piece (a). *Apelles*'s Master-piece was the Picture of *Venus*, rising out of the Sea [G]. Some Authors tell us, that the Mistress, whom *Alexander* gave him, sat to him, when he drew this Piece; others, that the Courtezan *Phryne* was the Original. They tell us of another Picture of *Venus*, which he had begun, and which would have surpassed the first, if Death had not prevented him from finishing it [H]. Mr *Moreri* has mistaken one of these Pictures for the other [I], and has misrepresented

(a) It's Title is, Περὶ τοῦ μὴ ῥᾳδίως πιστεύειν διαβολαῖς. Or not lightly to believe a Calumny.

sufficient to stifle in him all ill Designs. The Prince did not consider this. He never enquired, whether *Apelles* had ever been at *Tyre*; he only stormed and swore; and, if one of the Conspirators had not discovered the Wickedness of *Antiphilus*, the Accused had infallibly been put to death. But, when *Ptolomy* was satisfied of the Accuser's Crime, he condemned him to be *Apelles*'s Slave, and gave the latter an hundred Talents. It was upon this Occasion, that *Apelles* drew the fine Picture of Calumny, which *Lucian* has described. It is Pity he did not perceive the monstrous Anachronism he is guilty of in this Relation; for *Theodotus*'s Conspiracy fell out in the Reign of *Ptolomy Philopater*; which did not commence 'till an hundred Years after the Death of *Alexander* (26). Judge then, whether *Apelles* could be alive at that time. One of these two Positions must be laid down; either that *Lucian* speaks of a different *Apelles* from him, who was so much esteemed by *Alexander*; or he confounds some Plot, hatched in the Reign of *Ptolomy Philadelphus*, with the Conspiracy of *Theodotus*. There being no Author, who can give us any Light concerning a Conspiracy, in which Calumny had involved our Painter; it will be Labour in vain to trace *Lucian*'s Error to it's Source. Let us consider only, whether he had any other *Apelles* in view besides Him, who is the Subject of this Article. Now This I cannot conceive; for any one, who knew how to write, would have taken care, in mentioning a Painter, who had nothing in common, besides his Name, with the great and incomparable *Apelles*, not to call him simply *Apelles*. He would have apprized the Reader, that he did not mean the great *Apelles*. Now *Lucian* gives no hint of this; on the contrary, all he says leads us in a direct Line to the great *Apelles*; this, then, is the Person, whom he means. I know, that a learned Man lays a Stress upon the Epithet *Ephesian*, Ἀπελλῆς ὁ Ἐφέσιος. "Ad distinctionem illius Apellis, qui sub Alexandro & Ptolomæo Lagi vixit maximi nominis & artis, Coi Patriâ. Hic autem Patriâ Colophonius: verum Ἔφεσι, id est adoptione, teste Suida, Pamphili Amphipolitæ discipulus (27). ------ To distinguish " him from That Apelles, of great Fame and Art, a " Coan by Birth, who lived in the Time of Alexander, " and Ptolomy the Son of Lagus. Whereas This was a " Colophonian; but, by Adoption, according to Suidas, " a Disciple of Pamphilus of Amphipolis." But I find, that others likewise have given this Epithet to the great *Apelles* (28). Besides which, I can appeal to the Reason contained in the Passage I have cited; for if *Lucian* could give this Epithet to His *Apelles*, because adopted by the Inhabitants of *Ephesus*, tho' born at *Colophon*; I can alledge, that he gave it to the great *Apelles*, born in the Island of *Cous*, but undoubtedly a Citizen of *Ephesus*. Is it probable, a Man of his Fame should settle in That City (where *Alexander* saw, and became intimate with, him) without obtaining all the Privileges of a Citizen? But I have another Proof: *Tollius* allows, that *Lucian* means the same *Apelles* with *Suidas*: now *Suidas* speaks only of the great *Apelles*. This I prove, I. Because he mentions but one *Apelles*. Would he have omitted the Great and Illustrious, to mention only the Obscure and Unknown? II. Because he gives his *Apelles* the Quality of a Disciple of *Pamphilus* of *Amphipolis*, a Quality, which *Pliny* likewise ascribes to the great *Apelles* (29). So that *Lucian*'s Error is evident; and I am surprised, that neither *John Baptist Adriani* (30), nor *Carlo Dati* (31), nor *Francis Junius* (32), nor so many other celebrated Authors, who have spoken of this Treatise of *Lucian*, should perceive it, but should take this Relation to be a real Adventure of the great *Apelles*. *Tollius* very well knew, that the Crime, of which *Apelles* was accused, had relation to the Reign of *Ptolomy Philopater*; but he was not aware, that *Lucian* was deceived; he rather supposed, that *Lucian* had another *Apelles* in view, who was Cotemporary with *Antiphilus*, and Disciple of *Pamphilus*. I cannot

say, in what time *Antiphilus* lived, nor *Ctesidemus*, whose Disciple he was (33); but it is plain, according to *Pliny*, that *Pamphilus* flourished in the Time of *Philip*, the Father of *Alexander* the Great (34).

[G] *Apelles*'s *Master-Piece was the Picture of Venus, rising out of the Sea*.] *Augustus* dedicated it to the Temple of *Julius Cæsar*. The lower Parts of it had been spoiled; and no Hand was able to mend it; Time destroyed the rest; and then *Nero* caused another *Venus* to be drawn by *Dorotheus*, which he substituted in the room of That of *Apelles*. "Venerem " exeuntem e mari Divus Augustus dicavit in delu- " bro patris Cæsaris, quæ Anadyomene vocatur, ver- " sibus Græcis tali opere dum laudatur victo, sed " illustrato: hujus inferiorem partem corruptam qui " resiceret non potuit reperiri. Verum ipsa injuria " cessit in gloriam artificis. Consenuit hæc tabula " carie, aliamque pro eâ Nero principatu subditivit " suo." These are *Pliny*'s own Words, in the tenth Chapter of his Thirty fifth Book. I have recited the Passage, in the Remark [C], where he says that *Alexander*'s Mistress was the Original, from which this *Venus* was drawn. The Article PHRYNE will inform us of a Tradition different from this.

[H] *Death* ---- *prevented him from finishing it*.] If *Calcagnini* could have been prevailed with to give the Testimony of ancient Authors, rather than advance things of his own Head, he would not have affirmed, that *Apelles* voluntarily left his *Venus Anadyomene* imperfect; *the Reason*, says he, *of this Conduct was, that Apelles despaired of finishing it with the same Perfection he had begun it*. " Sed O me " multò Apelle incautiorem! ille enim tanta felici- " tate Veneris emergentis partes superiores expressse, " ut diffisus penicillo reliquas posse absolvere despe- " raverit, atque ita in admirationem posteritatis tabu- " lam inchoastam reliquit (35). ----- *But much " more incantions I, than Apelles! for He had so " happily expressed the upper Parts of Venus rising " from the Sea, that, distrusting his Pencil, he de- " spaired of finishing the rest; and thus left an un- " finished Piece for Posterity to wonder at.*" Carlo Dati, who accuses this Author of advancing several things, without acknowledging from whence he borrows them, produces two other Examples of it. It is certain, that the Words of *Pliny* convict *Calcagnini* of Falshood, as I am going to shew. " Apelles inchoave- " rat aliam Venerem Cois superaturus etiam suam illam " priorem. Invidit more peractâ parte, nec qui succe- " deret operi ad præscripta lineamenta inventus est " (36). --- *Apelles had begun another Venus at Coos, " intending it should excel the former. But Death " obliged him to leave it imperfect; nor was any one " capable of filling up the Outlines of the Work.*" *Cicero* says plainly, in two Places of his Works, that *Apelles* left That *Venus* imperfect (37).

[I] *Mr Moreri has mistaken one of these Pictures for the other*.] Thus he expresses himself: *The finest of all Apelles's Pieces were two Pictures of Venus, one of which, where she was drawn rising out of the Sea, was called Anadyomene; the other was That, which he drew for Those of the Island of Coos, mentioned by Ovid in these Words.*

Si nunquam Venerem Cois pinxisset Apelles,
Mersa sub æquoreis illa lateret aquis.

He quotes *Ovid in Sent*. He should have cited the third Book *de arte Amandi*. You are to know, that *Apelles* did not finish the second of these Pictures; *Pliny* affirms this expressly (38). What Probability is there, that *Ovid*, having two Pictures of *Venus* to alledge, the one finished, the other not, should omit That, and speak only of This? To act thus is to be ignorant of the common Laws of Reasoning. Besides the second Verse is a plain Allusion to the *Venus Anadyomene*, that is, *Rising out of the Sea*. He speaks, therefore, of the first Picture. We know, that the first *Venus* was drawn in this Posture; but we

APELLES.

sented what relates to his Picture of a Horse [K]. No Business was of such Importance, as to oblige *Apelles* to pass a single Day without handling his Pencil; which gave rise to a famous Proverb [L]. The Books, which this great Painter composed on the Art of Painting, are lost (b). It is not known where, or when, he died. One of his chief Excellencies was That of hitting a Likeness to a wonder; insomuch that Physiognomists could form a Judgment, from his Portraits, with as much Certainty, as

---

we know nothing of the Posture of the second. I add, that, if these two Verses of *Ovid* fell from his Pen, as they here represented, he was a bad Reasoner. They must be corrected thus, to become a reasonable Proof of what goes before.

Si Venerem Cois nusquam posuisset Apelles,
Mersa sub æquoreis illa jaceret aquis.

Had not the Coan Artist ------
Drawn Venus, rising, beauteous, from the Main,
Beneath the Waves the Goddess still had lain.

The nicest Critics choose to read *Coüs* instead of *Cois*. I believe they are in the right; though it is plain, that *Apelles* drew his *Venus Anadyomene* for the Inhabitants of the Island of *Coos*; for *Augustus* had it from them, and remitted them in consideration of it the Sum of an hundred Talents of the Tribute, which they were indebted to his Exchequer. They kept this *Venus*, and the *Antigonus* by the same Hand, in the Temple of *Æsculapius*. " Lacter promontorium est Coæ insulæ, in cujus suburbio est ædes " Æsculapii nobilitata Antigono Apelli ----- con- " spiciebatur ibidem quoque ejusdem artificis Venus " Anadiomene (39). Η νυν ἀνακειται τῳ θεῳ " Καισαρι εν Ρωμῃ, τῳ Σεβαστῳ αναθεντος τῳ " πατρι την αρχηγετιν τῳ γενες αυτε. Φασι " δε τοις Κωοις αντι της γραφης εκεινο ταλαν- " των δοσιν γενεσθαι τε προσαχθεν]ῳ φορε " (40). Quæ nunc dedicata est divo Cæsari, Au- " gusto consecrante patri generis sui patronam. Diuit " Cois pro pictura fuisse remissa centum talenta de " imperati tributi summa. ---- Lacter is a Promon- " tory of the Island Coos, in the Suburb of which " is a Temple of Æsculapius, famous for the Anti- " gonus of Apelles ----- the Venus Anadyomene " likewise of the same Artist was to be seen there. " It is now dedicated to Julius Cæsar, Augustus con- " secrating the Patroness of his Family to his Father. " The Coans, they say, were remitted the Sum of an " hundred Talents of the demanded Tribute, in con- " sideration of this Picture." *Pliny* might easily be ignorant, that the *Venus Anadyomene* was drawn for the Isle of *Coos*; no wonder then he should say, that *Apelles's* second *Venus* was designed for Them.

I shall here propose a Doubt, which occurs to my Thoughts on this Occasion: I cannot but think *Pliny* multiplies Beings without Necessity, when he tells us of a *Venus Anadyomene*, and of another *Venus*, which was begun for the Inhabitants of the Isle of *Coos*. The Reason of my Scruple is, that the first *Venus* was perfect only in the upper Parts of the Picture; *Pliny* himself informs us of this, and adds, that no Painter durst attempt to repair the Injury it had suffered (41). Now he never finished the other *Venus*; and no Painter had the Courage to supply what was wanting. This the same *Pliny* informs us of (42). I believe he is the only Author, who makes this Remark concerning two *Venus's* of *Apelles*, defective in the same Parts. Others say this only of the *Venus* of *Apelles* in general; and, whenever they mention this *Venus*, they place her in the Isle of *Coos* (43); now we have seen, that *Augustus* fetched the *Venus Anadyomene* from thence (44). *Pliny*, then, it is probable, has not been over-exact in this matter. I appeal to those, who will take the Pains to examine this small Doubt of mine.

[K] Moreri ------ *has misrepresented what relates to his Picture of an Horse*] Ancient Authors, says Mr *Moreri*, have spoken with great Esteem of an Horse, *drawn so to the Life by Apelles, that the Mares neighed at the sight of it*. I believe no Writer has said this. What *Pliny* informs us of, as to this Matter, is as follows. " Er & equus ejus, sive suit, " pictus in certamine: quod judicium ad mutas qua- " drupedes provocavit ab hominibus. Namque am- " bitu æmulos prævalere sentiens singulorum pictu-

---

" ras inductis equis ostendit: Apellis tantum equo " adhinnivere, idque & postea semper illius experi- " mentum artis ostentatur (45)." The meaning of which is, That *Apelles*, vying with some others, who should paint a Horse most to the Life, and distrusting the Integrity of the Judges, chose to commit his Cause to the Decision of brute Beasts. Horses, accordingly, were led by, who neighed only at *Apelles's* Piece. Some think (46), that the Story in *Ælian* (47), is only a Corruption of this; and that what past between *Apelles*, and the Judges of the Prize, when This Painter preferred the Judgment of a Horse to theirs, was what gave occasion to the Report of his saying to *Alexander*; *Your Horse understands Painting, better than you*. Others think they are two different Adventures (48). For my part, I have already given my own little Opinion; which is, that the Story, vouched by *Ælian*, ought to be looked upon as a meer Fable. *Pliny's* Silence, where so fair an Opportunity presented of speaking his Thoughts, confirms me in this Opinion. Would *Pliny* have been silent concerning the Horse, which neighed at *Apelles's* Door, in the Presence of *Alexander*, and concerning the Inference, which *Apelles* drew from it; Would *Pliny*, I say, have been silent on such a Fact, when he relates the other Adventure, in which *Apelles* appealed, from the Judgment of the Arbitrators, to That of Horses? *Carlo Dati* has observed, that, in neither of these Cases, *Apelles* spoke like an able Painter, since he supposed, that the more Knowledge a Person had, the more he would mistake the Representation for the Object itself. But we must have a care how we apply this Censure to the Adventure, which *Pliny* relates; for *Apelles* did not prefer the Judgment of Horses to That of Men, otherwise than as he perceived, that the Intrigues of his Rivals had corrupted the Judges (49). The Remark of *Carlo Dati* is very just at the bottom. It is easier to deceive *Those*, who do not understand Painting, than *Those*, who do. He quotes *John Paul Lomazzo* (50): And, after him, we might quote Mr *Perrault*, who has well refuted the Consequences, drawn, in favour of the ancient Painters, from their having deceived both Men and Beasts (51).

[L] *Which gave rise to a famous Proverb*] *Pliny* informs us of it; " Apelli fuit alioqui perpetua con- " suetudo nunquam tam occupatam diem agendi, ut " non lineam ducendo exerceret artem, quod ab eo " in proverbium venit (52). ----- *It was an in-* " *violable Rule with Apelles never to pass a Day* " *without exercising his Art, at least by one Stroke* " *of his Pencil; which passed from him into a Pro-* " *verb*." *Carlo Dati* (53) observes upon this, that *Salmasius*, in support of this Proverb, quotes the following Line, as a Verse of *Horace*,

Nulla dies abeat, quin linea ducta superfit.

Let no Day pass, without drawing at least one Line.

Which is neither *Horace's*, nor any other ancient Poet's. He adds, that it has been often the Fate of this Author to trust too much to his Memory. " Non lasciero d'auvertire in questo luogo che *Claudio* " *Salmasio* grandissimo Critico dell' eta nostra, nelle " Dissertaz. Pliniane sopra Solino p. 5. in confermazione di questo proverbio, fidandosi troppo della memoria, come bene spesso egli fece, cita un verso d'Orazio ------ il quale non è (ch' io sappia) nè d'Orazio ne d'altro poeta latino antico, ma forse uno di quei versi proverbiali che vanno per le bocche de gli uomini senza saperfene l'autore. ------ *I shall not omit to apprize the Reader, in this Place, that* Claudius Salmasius, *a very great Critic of our Age, in his Exercitationes Plinianæ on Solinus*, pag. 5. *cites, in Confirmation of this Proverb, and depending too much, as he very often does, on his Memory, a Verse of* Horace ------ *which (to the best of my Knowledge) is neither* Horace's, *nor any other an-*
cient

APELLES. APELLICON. APICIUS.

as if they had been Originals [M]. Witness what he did at the Court of Egypt (c).

(c) *See the Remarks* [B].

"cient Latin *Poet's*; but, perhaps, one of those prover-
"bial *Verses*, which are in every one's *Mouth*, with-
"out the *Author*'s being known."
[M] Insomuch that *Physiognomists* could form a
Judgment, from his Portraits, with as much Certainty,
as if they had been Originals.] The Grammarian *Apion*
tells a Story, to this purpose, so highly improbable,
that one could scarce look upon it otherwise than as a
Fable, though a more credible Author, than this
grand Romancer, had affirmed it. Let us be content
with *Pliny*'s historical Account of the Matter. " Ima-
" ginem adeo similitudinis indiscretæ pinxit, ut (in-
" credibile dictu) Apion Grammaticus scriptum reli-

"querit, quemdam ex facie hominum addivinantem
"(quos metoposcopos vocant) ex eis duxisse aut fu-
"turæ mortis annos aut præteritæ (54). ----- He
"painted so to the *Life*, that a certain *Physiognomist*,
"according to the incredible *Relation of Apion the*
"*Grammarian*, was wont to pronounce, from his Por-
"traits, the Year of the Person's Death, either passed
"or to come." *Pliny* himself cannot conceive, how
any Person should tell, at the sight of a Picture, though
ever so like the Original, at what Age the Person so
painted died, or was to die. The Diviner, no doubt,
enquired, whether the Person was dead or alive.

(54) *Plin.* ubi supra. pag. 210.

APELLES, an excellent Tragedian, under *Caligula*, gained the Emperor's
Favour by the most infamous Means; but, when the Flower of his Youth was past,
he turned Player (a); and still supported himself so well in this Emperor's good
Graces, who would never be without him, not even in Public (b), that he was at last
admitted into the Number of his Counsellors (c). As they were one day standing
near the Statue of *Jupiter*, *Caligula* asked him, *Which of the Two do you think the
greatest*, Jupiter, *or I*? And, because *Apelles* did not answer him so readily, as he
expected, he fell into a violent Passion, and ordered him to be whipt unmercifully;
saying, in a jesting way, that *Apelles* had an agreeable Voice, even in a plaintive
Tone [A]. Some affirm, that he ordered him to be laid in Irons, and turned from
time to time on a Wheel.

(a) Philo. Legat. ad Cajum. pag. 1021.
(b) Dion. lib. 59. pag. 643.
(c) Philo. ibid.

[A] Caligula ----- said ----- that he had an a-
greeable *Voice*, even in a plaintive *Tone*] Suetonius is
my Author. *Inter varios jocos, cum assistens simulacro
Jovis Apellem Tragædum consuluisset, uter illi major*

*videretur, cunctantem flagellis discidit, collaudens sub-
inde vocem deprecantis, quasi etiam in gemitu præ-
dulcem* (1).

(1) Sueton. in Calig. cap. 33.

APELLICON, who bought *Aristotle*'s Library. See the Remarks on the
Article TYRANNION.

APICIUS. There were three *Apicii*, at *Rome*, famous for their Gluttony.
The first lived before the Change of the Republic; the second under *Augustus*, and
Tiberius; and the last under *Trajan*. *Athenæus* means the first *Apicius*, when, having
said, on the Testimony of *Posidonius*, that, at *Rome*, they preferred the Memory of
one *Apicius*, who had surpassed all Men in Gluttony, he adds, that it was the same
Apicius, who had been the Cause of *Rutilius*'s Exile (a). We know, that *Posidonius*
flourished in the Time of *Pompey*, and that *Rutilius* was banished about the Year of
Rome 660. The second *Apicius* was the most famous of the three. *Athenæus* places
him under *Tiberius*, and says, that he laid out prodigious Sums on his Belly; and
that there were several sorts of Cakes, which bore his Name (b). It is He, whom *Seneca* speaks of, in his Ninety fifth Letter, and in the Eleventh Chapter of his Book
de Vita Beata, and in the Treatise *de Consolatione*, which he wrote to his Mother
Helvia, under the Emperor *Claudius*. We find, in the last of these Works, that
This *Apicius* lived in *Seneca*'s time, and kept, as it were, a School of Gluttony, in
Rome; that he had consumed two Millions and a half in good Chear; and that,
finding himself much in Debt, he at last bethought himself of examining into the
Condition of his Estate; and, finding that he had but 250000 *Livres* left, he poisoned
himself, as fearing he should starve with such a Sum. *Dion*, who calls him *M.
Gabius Apicius*, relates the same thing (c), and adds a Particular, which is to be
found likewise in the first Chapter of the fourth Book of *Tacitus*'s Annals; *viz.* That
Sejanus, in his Youth, had prostituted himself to him. *Pliny* calls him *M. Apicius*,
and often mentions the Ragoûts, which he invented (d); *Nepotum omnium altissimus
gurges*. A Book was written on the Subject of his Gluttony, which is cited by *Athenæus* (e). It is not to be doubted, but that This is the *Apicius* of *Juvenal*, *Martial*, and
Lampridius, &c. [A]. The third *Apicius* lived in *Trajan*'s Time. He had an admirable

(a) Athen. lib. 4. pag. 168.
(b) Id. lib. 1. pag. 7.
(c) Lib. 57.
(d) Lib. 8. cap. 51. lib. 9. cap. 18. lib. 10. cap. 48. lib. 15. cap. 8.
(e) Apion *was the Author of it.* Athen. lib. 7.

[A] *This is the* Apicius *of* Juvenal, Martial, *and*
Lampridius, &*c*] I have these Words of *Juvenal* in
view.

— — — — multa videmus,
Quæ miser, & frugi non fecit Apicius - - - - (1).

Now even Apicius *frugal seems and poor,
Outdone by Luxury, unknown before.*
Rev^d Mr R. DUKE.

And These two Verses of *Martial*:

Ipse quoque ad cœnam gaudebat Apicius ire;
Cum cœnaret, erat tristior ille, domi (2).

Apicius, *when invited to a Feast,
Was gay, and chearful, as the merriest Guest;
But, uninvited, when at home he dined,
The gloomiest Mortal, surly, and unkind.*

And That Passage of *Lampridius*, where we read, that
the Emperor *Heliogabalus* often eat Peacocks and
Nightingales Tongues, in imitation of *Apicius*. *Co-
medit sæpius ad imitationem Apicii calcanea camelorum,
& cristas*

(1) Juven. Sat. 4. ver. 23.
(2) Mart. Epigr. 29. lib. 2. *See I bruise E-*pig. 73. lib. 10.

APICIUS.

rable Receipt for preferving of Oyſters; this appeared, when he ſent ſome to *Trajan* into *Parthia*; They were ſtill freſh, when *Trajan* received them (*f*). The Name of *Apicius* was for a long time given to ſeveral Diſhes, and made a kind of Sect among the Cooks. We have a Treatiſe *de Re Culinaria*, under the Name of *Caelius Apicius*, which ſome Critics judge to be very ancient, though they do not take it to be compoſed by either of theſe three *Apicii* (*g*). Some chuſe to call the Author of this Book *Apicius Caelius*. A learned *Dane* is of this Number, who aſcribes this Work to Him, who ſent the Oyſters to the Emperor *Trajan*. This Book was found, by *Albanus Torinus*, in the Iſland of *Maguelone*, near *Montpellier*, who publiſhed it, Twelve Years after, at *Baſil* [*B*]. It had been found elſewhere, near an hundred Years before, by *Enoch d'Aſcoli*, in the time of Pope *Nicolas* V (*h*). There was in the Title-Page *M. Caecilius Apicius*. *Voſſius* (*i*) is of Opinion, that the Author's Name was *M. Caelius*, or *M. Caecilius*; and that he intituled his Work, *Apicius*, becauſe it treated of Cookery. In the Remarks of *Caſaubon* on *Athenaeus*, there are ſome Particulars relating to our *Apicius*

(*f*) Athen. lib. 1. p. 7.
(*g*) Borrichius, Cogit. de variis Linguae Lat. Aetatibus, pag. 18.
(*h*) Platina in Vita Nicolai V.
(*i*) Voſſ. de Analogia, lib. 1. c. 14. pag. 55.

& criſtas vivis gallinaceis demptas, linguas pavonum, & luſciniarum (3). There is another Paſſage in *Juvenal*, in which *Apicius* ſignifies, in general, one who it very expenſive in eating.

- - - *quid enim majore cachinno Excipitur vulgi quam pauper Apicius* (4)?

- - - *what greater Jeſt, Than begging Gluttons, or than Beggar's Feaſts?*
CONGREVE.

It is childiſh, then, in ſome Commentators, to underſtand, here, either the *Apicius* of the firſt Book of *Athenaeus* (5), or Him of the fourth Satire of *Juvenal* (6).

[*B*] This Book was found, by *Albanus Torinus*, *in the Iſland of Maguelone, near Montpellier, who publiſhed it twelve Years after, at Baſil*. He procured it to be printed in 4to, in the Year 1541, and added to it the Treatiſe of *Paul Aegineta, de facultatibus alimentorum*, which he had tranſlated, and the two Books of *Platina, de tuenda valetudine, de natura rerum, & popinae ſcientia*. He tells us, in his Preface, that, having made a Journey to the Iſland of *Maguelone*, twelve Years before, with *Will. Pelliſſier* (7), he had there ſeen a Manuſcript, in which he found, by tracing the Characters, the Title of CAELII APITII DE RE CULINARIA LIBRI X. He was very well pleaſed with this Diſcovery, and procured an exact Copy to be taken of the Work: He immediately found, that it was the Production of an ancient Author. But, the Manuſcript being in great Diſorder, he thought it neceſſary, before he ſent it to the Preſs, to collate it with the Copy of *Venice*; for which he waited a long time. At length it was ſent him; but he found it more imperfect, than That of *Maguelone*. He would have given up all Thoughts of printing this Work, if ſome Men of Learning had not obliged him, by their Complaints, and Importunity, to publiſh it. The ſame Year there was a ſecond Edition of it, in 8vo, publiſhed at *Lyons*, by *Sebaſtian Gryphius*. It was publiſhed at *Zurich*, in the Year 1542, in 4to, with the Notes and Corrections of *Gabriel Humelbergius*. I do not think *Geſner* or *Simler* deſerve Cenſure, for ſaying, that the ſame Work was printed at *Venice*, before *Albanus Torinus* brought it to light. It is pretended, they did not rightly underſtand the Expreſſions of this *Torinus*. *In Bibl. Simlero-Geſneriana dicuntur Apicii libri primum excuſi Venetiis, quod acceptum eſt ex male intellectis Torini verbis in dedicatione.* His Expreſſions are theſe: "Premendum plane cenſebam, donec melioris alicujus exemplaris fieret copia, quod acceptiſſimum eſſe annis ab hinc plus minus quinquaginta Venetiis expreſſum (9). - - - - - *I thought it ought to be ſuppreſſed, 'till I could procure a more correct Copy, ſuch an one as I am informed was printed at Venice, about fifty Years ago*." Though it does not appear, with the utmoſt clearneſs, from theſe Words, that they relate to an Impreſſion of the Work, yet it is excuſable to underſtand them ſo. And, in Fact, a certain Bibliographer affirms, that *Apicius* was printed at *Venice*, in the Year 1503, in 4to. *apud Johan. de Cereto de Tridino* (10). The Heirs of *Andrew Wechel* had ſome Thoughts of printing this Work: *Pignorius* offered them a fair Manuſcript of it by *Velſerus* (11). But it did not go forward. There was an *Apicius*, in the Library of the Dukes of *Urbin*, the

(3) Lamprid. in Heliogabalo, c. 19. pag. 835. See likewiſe cap. 18. pag. 827. & cap. 24. p. 857.
(4) Juven. Sat. 11. ver. 2.
(5) Bernardus Autumnus upon this Paſſage of Juvenal.
(6) Farnaby upon the ſame.
(7) He was Biſhop of Maguelone, i. e. Montpellier.
(8) Joh. Albertus Fabricius in Bibliotheca Latina, pag. 110 Edit. Pat. burg. 1697.
(9) Albanus Torinus in Epiſt. Dedicat.
(10) Merckliuus in Lindenio renovato, p 85.
(11) See the Letters of Reineſius to Daumius, pag. 109.

Characters whereof are like thoſe of the *Florentine* Pandects. It is, at preſent, in the *Vatican*. *Gudius* compared it with the Edition of *Lyons* (12). By the way, *Albanus Torinus* has been ſeverely cenſured for pretending to diſcover the true Air and Taſte of Antiquity in this Author. "Olfaciebam ſtatim autorem "eſſe vetuſtiſſimum, & obſopoeum, qui de re popi-" nali, lingua coquinaria, egregie praeter caeteros "ſcripſiſſet, & qui obſonia delicatius, quam pro ea "aetate qua glandibus veſcerentur homines, confeciſ-" ſet (13). - - - - - *I immediately diſcovered, that he was a very ancient Author, and Maſter of the Art of Cookery, who had excelled all others in writing concerning Eatables, in the Style of the Kitchen; and one who had a nicer Palate at dreſſing a Dinner, than could be expected in that Age, when Men lived upon Acorns.*" *Latinus Latinius* affirms, that a Man muſt be very ſtupid to paſs ſuch a Judgment, and that this pretended *Apicius* is a meer Fool, and a *Barbarian*; ſome of whoſe Diſhes, and Sauces are only fit to fetch the Skin off one's Mouth, and offend the Stomach. "In Latini Latinii Bibl. Profana, ubi "quaedam illius viri docti in Apicium obſervationes "leguntur, ad verba Editoris, ulti in praefat. alt ſe "ſtatim olfeciſſe autorem eſſe vetuſtiſſimum, haec no-"ta occurrit: *Quam vertor ut tuae nares obſtiores "fuerint; Quid enim vetuſtati redolere poſſunt verba "ſemibarbara & ab eo florenti ſaeculo prorſus aliena? "Ego vero, ut quod ſentio paucis expediam, commentum "puto eſſe hominis otioſiſſimi, qui cum illudere poſteris "ejuſdem naris facile ſibi eſſe perſuaſiſſet, mentito no-"mine Apicium credidit venditare poſſe. Sed paſſim oc-"currunt, quibus paene manifeſto prodit ſeipſum autor "ineptus, barbarus, & nullius in ea arte ingenii, aut "guſtus, qui eu interdum conjungat ad ſaporis gra-"tiam, quae uſu docente omnes ſcimus ſummam palato "moleſtiam, nauſeamque ſtomacho, creare ſolere* (14). "- - In Latinus Latinius's Bibliotheca Profana, "*where are ſome of this learned Man's Obſervations on Apicius, we meet with the following Remark on the Editor's Words, in his Preface, where he ſays, that he immediately ſmelt him out to be a very ancient Author. How afraid am I, that your ſmelling is not very good? For what favour of Antiquity is there in Words ſo barbarous, and quite foreign to the Style of that flouriſhing Age. To give my own Opinion briefly, I look upon it to be the Invention of ſome one, who had nothing elſe to do; who, believing he might eaſily impoſe upon Perſons of the ſame Taſte in future Times, thought it would go off under the borrowed Name of Apicius*. But there are numberleſs Paſſages, which diſcover the Author's Ignorance, Barbariſm, and want of Genius and Taſte, in often joining thoſe things together, by way of Reliſh, which we all know, by Experience, are troubleſome to the Palate, and nauſeous to the Stomach." This Judgment of *Latinius* is not amiſs. *Iſaac Grangaeus* had better have conformed to it, than pretended, that the ten Books *de Re Coquinaria*, which go under the Name of *Apicius*, were written by our ſecond *Apicius* (15). I confeſs, the Scholiaſt of *Juvenal* obſerves, that this *Apicius* wrote a Treatiſe of Cookery (16). I own, likewiſe, that *Iſidorus* of *Seville* attributes a like Work to the ſame *Apicius*. "*Coquinae apparatum Apicius quidam primus compo-"ſuit, qui in eo abſumptis bonis morte voluntaria "periit* (17). - - - - - *One Apicius was the firſt, who "wrote a Treatiſe of Cookery, and who, having ſpent "his Fortune in eating, killed himſelf.*" But the Teſtimony

(12) Joh. Albert. Fabricius, ubi ſupra, in Append. p 179.
(13) Alban. Torinus, in Epiſt. Dedic.
(14) Joh. Albert. Fabricius, ubi ſupra, in Append. p 179.
(15) Iſaacus Grangaeus in 4. ver. 23.
(16) Auctor quidam ex earum, qui ſcripſit de juſcellis: fuit enim exemplum gulae. Verus Sch. haſſ. in Juven. Sat. 4. ver. 23.
(17) Iſidor. Hiſpalenſ. Orig. l. 20. cap. 4. apud Joh. Alb. Fabric Bibl. Lat. pag. 132.

VOL. I. 5 A timony

APICIUS.

Apicius (k). I have discovered some Mistakes, on this head, in different Authors (C), which I shall throw together in one single Remark.

stimony of these two Writers is not sufficient to counterpoise the Silence of so many Authors, more worthy of Credit, and who have had unavoidable Opportunities of quoting this Book of *Apicius*. Be it as it will, we are obliged, by all the Laws of just Criticism, to conclude, that, if ever any such Work had been extant, That, which *Albanus Torinus* published, was not It.

[C] *I have discovered some Mistakes, on this Head, in different Authors.*] I begin with Mr *Moreri*; he should not have said, either that the *Apicius*, mentioned by *Seneca*, wrote a Book concerning the *Delicacy of Eating*, or that he hanged himself in *Despair*, when he found he had spent his whole Estate. Mr *Moreri* quotes *Seneca*, *lib. de Consol*. This is too indeterminate, since we have three Treatises of this Philosopher, entituled, *De Consolatione*. He should have cited That, which he addressed to his Mother. It appears from thence, that *Apicius* poisoned himself, upon looking over his Accounts, and finding, that he had but the Sum of Two hundred fifty thousand *Livres* left, all his Debts paid (18), " Ære alie-
" no oppressus rationes suas tunc primum coactus in-
" spexit. Superfuturum sibi sestertium centies com-
" putavit, &, velut in ultima fame victurus, si se-
" stertio centies vixisset, veneno vitam finivit. Quan-
" ta luxuria erat, cui sestertium centies egestas fuit
" (19)! ——— *Oppressed with Debts, he was drove*
" *to the Necessity of looking into his Accounts.* Upon a
" *Computation, he found he should have but One hundred*
" *thousand* Sestertii * *left; and, as if he would have*
" *been driven to the last Extremity of Want, if obliged*
" *to live upon only this Sum, he ended his Days by*
" *Poison. What Luxury was That, which accounted*
" *an Hundred thousand* Sestertii *meer Poverty!*" *Martial* wrote the following Epigram upon this Subject.

Dederas, Apici, bis tricenties ventri,
Sed adhuc supererat centies tibi laxum.
Hoc tu gravatus, ne samem & sitim ferres,
Summa venenum potione duxisti.
Nil est, Apici, tibi gulosius factum (20).

You expended, O Apicius, in eating and drinking, Six hundred thousand Sesterces *; yet an Hundred thousand still remained. Uneasy at this, and to avoid Hunger and Thirst, y u took Poison. This last Draught, O Apicius, was the most extravagant you ever took.*

Not to follow the Author one quotes, as to the particular kind of Death, is a flight Fault; but it is leaving out all the Marvellous of this History, to suppress the Sums this Prodigal had remaining. The Quotation from *Athenæus, lib.* 11, is entirely wrong. Lastly, Mr *Moreri* ought to have known, that there were three *Apicii*, and not have confined himself to one. *Charles Stephens* pretends, that the *Apicius*, mentioned by *Seneca* (21), hanged himself; and that he had published a Book *de Gulæ Irritamentis*, which is to this Day in every one's Hand. No good Critic believes, that the Work, which we have *de re Culinaria*, belongs to this *Apicius*, whom *Seneca* mentions (22). Be that as it will, this was the Foundation of Mr *Moreri*'s Mistake. He found there, that *Apicius* hanged himself; and that he wrote a Book of the *Delicacy of Eating*. He ought to have learned from the same place, that *Apicius* had Two hundred and fifty thousand *Francs* left; for it is a Fact, which *Charles Stephens* has not omitted. *Lloyd* has followed *Charles Stephens* in every thing, except saying, that the Work, *de Gulæ Irritamentis*, is, to this Day in every one's Hands. He has enlarged this Article considerably, by copying what *Lipsius* has observed concerning the three *Apicii*. But he did not know, that the Passage of *Suidas*, concerning the Oysters sent to *Trajan* into *Parthia*, is to be found in *Athenæus*. The Memories of the greatest Men often fail them. *Lipsius* quotes *Athenæus* twice in relation to the *Apicii*, but forgets a third Passage of the same Author, as remarkable, at least, as either of the other two (23). If he had consulted it, he would not have suspected, that the Word *Trajan* was corrupted in *Suidas*. *Hofman* has done little more than copy *Lloyd*; only he has cited more Passages. His Quotations are not al-

ways the truest; for Example, he quotes *Seneca de Consolatione ad Albin*. & *de Consol. ad Elbiam*, as if they were two different Pieces. *Casaubon* (24), makes *Athenæus* say, that several kind of Cakes bore the Name of the first *Apicius*; but it is certain, that *Athenæus* says this of the second *Apicius*; of Him, who lived in the time of the Emperor *Tiberius* (25); Ἐγίνετο καλεῖ τις Τιβερίη χρόνους ἀνὴρ τις Ἀπίκιος, πλουσιώτατος, τρυφητής, ἀφ᾽ ὁ πλακουντῶν γένη πολλὰ Ἀπίκια ὀνομάζεται. *Tiberii saeculo vixit Apicius, vir ditissimus, luxu solutus, à quo complura placentarum genera Apicia nominant.* *DALE-CHAMP* has left an Error in the Translation of *Athenæus*, which might easily have been perceived. It is in the fourth Book, page 168. *Athenæus*, having repeated what *Posidonius* had said concerning the first *Apicius*, a Man infamous for his Gluttony, adds, Περὶ δὲ Ἀπικίου τοῦ καὶ αὐτοῦ ἐπὶ ἀσωτίᾳ διαϐοήτου ἐν τοῖς πρώτοις εἰρήκαμεν; which signifies, that, from the beginning, he meant the *Apicius*, who was also famous for his Gluttony. The *Latin* Translation, therefore, is false. *Antea nos quoque istius Apicii ob immodicum luxum famosi meminimus.* I say this is doubly false; for it does not come up to the Force of the *Greek* Words, and imputes a Lye to *Athenæus*. It is not true, that *Athenæus* had before spoken of the *Apicius*, whom *Posidonius* had mentioned. *Dalechamp* observes, that *Athenæus* spoke, in his third Book, of the *Apicius* now in question, at the beginning of the seventh Page (26). I believe this is false. I say nothing of his citing *Cælius*, *lib.* 5. *cap*. 30 (27). He means *Coelius Rhodiginus*, whose fifth Book has but fourteen Chaapters: He should have cited the eleventh Chapter of the ninth Book (28). This Author says several things, there, of *Apicius*; but if he falsifies, every where else, what he quotes, as he does here a Passage of *Athenæus*, unhappy for Those, who take things upon trust from him. *Athenæus*, according to Him, relates, that *Apicius*, enquiring diligently after a particular kind of Lobsters in *Alexandria*, was informed, that very large ones were taken on the Coast of *Libya*: He immediately set sail thither; and, finding he was sent on a Fool's Errand, he cursed the Country, and resolved never to return thither. *Athenæus* relates no such thing; he only says, that *Apicius* eat a kind of Water-Locusts at *Minturnæ* in *Campania*, which were larger than the Lobsters of *Alexandria*; and, being informed, that there were some in *Africa* of an exceeding Largeness, he sailed thither without Delay, and under great Inconveniencies. The Fishermen, being informed of his Arrival, came and brought him the largest they had taken; and, being assured from them, that there were no larger, he returned to *Minturnæ*, without ever setting Foot on Shore in *Africa* (29).

The modern Author, whom I have cited, was mistaken in saying, that the Manuscript of *Apicius* was found in the Island of *Maguelone*, by *Enoch d'Ascoli*, in the Pontificate of *Nicolas* V. He relies on the Authority of *Leander Albertus*, and on That of *Philip of Bergamo*. " Ut tradit, *ait* (30). Leander Alber-
" tus Bononiensis in Descriptione Italiæ, pag. 267,
" & Philippus Bergomas in Chronici continuatione,
" qui M. Cæcilium appellat. ——— *As we read in* Le-
" ander Albertus*'s Description of Italy*, pag. 267;
" and Philip of Bergamo*'s Chronicle continued, who*
" calls him *M.* Cæcilius." But neither of these Authors mention the Island of *Maguelone*; and it is certain, that the Manuscript was found, in That Place, only by *Albanus Torinus*, in the Year 1529. *Philip of Bergamo*, without any mention of the Place, says only, that, in the time of *Nicolas* V, *Enoch d'Ascoli* found these two Books, *Porphyrion* upon *Horace*, and *M. Cæcilius Apicius*. This he says, under the Year 1454. *Herman Buschius* agrees with him, as to the time. These are the Words of *Leander Albertus*: " Cujus (Enochi Asculani) industria M. Cælius Api-
" tius, & Pomponius Porphyrio in Horatium, circa
" Nicolaum V. Pontif. inventi ac è tenebris in lucem
" vindicati sunt (31). ——— *By whose* (Enoch d'As-
" coli*'s*) *Care* M. Cælius Apitius, *and* Pomponius
" Porphyrion *upon* Horace, *were found, and brought*
" *to light, about the time of Pope* Nicolas V." *Volaterran* affirms, that *Suidas* says, *Marcus Apicius* composed a Book *De Gula*. *Robert Stephens*, a great Copier of *Volaterran*, affirms the same in his *Elucidarium*

APIANUS. APION.

(32) Joh. Albert. Fabricius, ubi supra, pag. 132.

darium Poëticum. They have been both censured: "Vellem locum indicasset, *says our Modern* (32), hoc "enim apud Suidam non reperio.——*I wish they* "*had pointed out the Place; for I find no such thing* "*in Suidas.*"

APIANUS (PETRUS), a *German* Mathematician, in the XVIth Century. I shall add but one Thing to what Mr *Moreri* has said of him; which is, that he is accused of having been a Plagiary from *Roiaumont* [*A*].

[*A*] *Of having been a Plagiary from* Roiaumont.] They, who would swell the Lists of Plagiaries, already published, may, if they please, make use of this Passage of *G. B. Benedetti.* "Hæc omnia tradi- "ta fuerunt & scriptis mandata ab antiquis, & à "recentioribus usurpata, ut facile deprehendi potest "in Erasmo Osualdo, qui omnem fere sui primi "mobilis rationem à Petro Apiano desumpsit; Pe- "trus verò Apianus hæc eadem cum multis aliis Pro- "positionibus à Monte Regio accipiens sibi ipsi ascrip- "sit (1).——*All these things were delivered, and* "*committed to Writing, by the Ancients; and have* "*been usurped by the Moderns; as may easily be seen* "*in* Erasmus Osualdus, *who borrowed the whole* "*Scheme of his Primum Mobile from Petrus Api-* "*anus; who borrowed it, with many other Proposi-* "*tions, from* ROIAUMONT."

(1) Joh. Baptista Benedictus, de Gnomonum umbrarumque solarium usu, cap. 2. fol. 2.

APION, a famous *Grammarian,* and Native of *Oasis,* in *Egypt* [*A*], exercised his Profession at *Rome,* in the Reign of the Emperor *Tiberius* (*a*). No one can deny, that he was a Learned Man [*B*]; and that he had, with great Diligence, traced those Paths of Antiquity, which are the least known, and distinguished himself for the Exactness, and Variety of his Knowledge: But he had all the Pride of a thorough-paced Pedant [*C*]; and spent his Time in Questions of great Difficulty, and little Importance [*D*]. The Emperor *Tiberius* was no Stranger to the Failings of This

(*a*) Suidas in Ἀπίων.

[*A*] APION, *a famous Grammarian, and Native of* Oasis, *in* Egypt.] I cannot conceive why, in *Moreri's* Dictionary, they give us this Grammarian under two Articles, first under the Name of *Apian,* and afterwards under That of *Appion,* without apprizing us, that they are but one Person. I believe no Men of Learning ever called him *Apian;* and I am certain, that they, who pretend to Exactness, never call him *Appion.* Their Reason is, because his Name was borrowed from *Apis,* an *Egyptian* Divinity; and not from *Appia,* a *Roman* Family (1). His Country is strangely mis-spelled by *Moreri;* who has changed it into *Osias.* The Supplement has rectified it. *Suidas* observes, that *Heliconius* had said, that *Apion* was of the Isle of *Crete;* but doubtless he was of *Oasis,* since *Josephus* affirms it; and accuses him of abjuring his Country, in order to pass for an *Alexandrian* (2). This Accusation of *Josephus* would have been of no weight, though he had not exaggerated, and dressed it up in such a Multitude of Words. For *Apion,* in calling himself an *Alexandrian,* after he had been made free of the City of *Alexandria,* did no more, than what several other renowned Professors had practised before. The Sirname of *Plistonices,* which was appropiated to him (3), had an Import very much to his Advantage (4); but it is not known, for what Reason they gave him this Appellation. *Suidas* will have him the Son of a Person, whose Name was *Plistonices.* Ἀπίων ὁ Πλειστονίκου. But, in this Case, the Sirname imports nothing in his Praise. Others say, that his Father's Name was *Posidonius,* Ἀπίων ὁ Ποσειδωνίε (5). It is not impossible, that the Transcribers might have changed Πλειστονίκα into Ποσειδωνίε.

[*B*] *No one can deny, that he was a learned Man.*] *Tatian* stiles him a Man of great Renown, ἀνὴρ δοκιμώτατ@· (6). *Aulus Gellius* speaks of him after the same manner. "Literis homo multis præditus, "rerumque Græcarum plurima atque varia scientia "fuit: ejus libri non incelebres feruntur, quibus om- "nia ferme quæ mirifica in Ægypto visuntur audi- "unturque historia comprehenditur (7).——*He* "*was a Man of great Learning; and had an exten-* "*five Knowledge in Greek Affairs. His Books are* "*well esteemed, in which is contained an Account of* "*almost every thing wonderful and curious in Egypt.*" So much for his Learning; what follows, discovers his talkative and confident Behaviour; "facile atque ala- "cri facundia fuit (8).——*He was of a ready and* "*forward Elocution.*" But let us not incroach on the following Remark.

[*C*] *He had all the Pride of a thorough-paced Pedant.*] *Aulus Gellius* represents him as an errant Braggadocio. "In his quæ audiviste vel legisse sese dicit, "fortasse à vitio studioque ostentationis fit loquacior. "Est enim sane in prædicandis doctrinis suis vendi- "tator (9).——*Concerning those Things, which he* "*pretends to have heard or read, he is more than* "commonly talkative; perhaps through the Vice and "*Desire of Ostentation.* For, in recommending his "*own Opinions, he is a perfect Tradesman.*" *Apion* boasted, with the utmost Assurance, that he bestowed Immortality on those, to whom he dedicated his Works. Never was a Prediction or Promise, more false. Not one of his Books has withstood the Injuries of Time; and, if other Authors had not informed us who he was, his Name and Person had been unknown at this Day: He did nothing, then, in favour of those, whose Names he placed in the Front of his Works. Let us cite the entire Passage from *Pliny.* "Apion quidam Grammaticus, hic "quem Tiberius Cæsar cymbalum mundi vocabat, "quum publicæ famæ tympanum potius videri pos- "set, immortalitate donari à se scripsit, ad quos ali- "qua componebat (10).——*One* Apion, *a Gram-* "*marian, he whom* Tiberius Cæsar *was wont to call* "*the Cymbal of the World, though he had rather seem'd* "*to have been the Drum of public Fame, pretend-* "*ed, that he conferred Immortality on those, to whom* "*he dedicated any Composition.*" Mr *de Tillemont* owns, that he does not understand what *Pliny* means to say of our *Apion* in this Passage (11): And I would make the same Confession, rather than take up with the Explication given by the Supplement to *Moreri.* He boasted, they are the Words of the Supplement, *that he immortalized those, to whom he dedicated any of his Works.* Which made the Emperor *Tiberius* call him *the Cymbal of the World:* Whereupon *Pliny* says, *that he ought rather to be called the Drum of the World, because he always gave a disagreeable Sound.* But first, It is not true, that *Pliny* any where says, that the Emperor called him *Cymbalum Mundi,* because he set such a Value on his Dedications. In the second Place, *Pliny* does not say, that he rather deserved to be called the Drum of the World; he makes use of the Phrase *Publicæ Famæ Tympanum,* which has a particular Force, to represent this Person as a kind of Public Crier, who, by beat of Drum, or sound of Trumpet, publishes to all the Inhabitants of a City, what every one is to be informed of. In the third Place, *Pliny* does not say, that, because *Apion* gave but an unpleasant Sound, he deserved the Appellation of *Tympanum,* rather than *Cymbalum.* Who told the Continuator of *Moreri,* that the Cymbal is more pleasing than the Drum?

[*D*] *And spent his Time in Questions of great Difficulty, and little Importance.*] *Jul. Africanus* calls him the Busiest of all Grammarians; or one, who carried his Enquiries to the utmost Scrupulousness and Nicety: περιεργύτατ@· γραμματικῶν (12). According to *Suidas,* he obtained the Sirname of Μόχθ@·. The Word signifies *Toil,* or hard *Labour,* in this Place, which according to the Conjecture of a learned Man (13), might have crept into *Suidas,* instead of Μόχθ@·. Didymus, *who is sirnamed* Καλκεντερ@· (14), *that*

(1) Vossius de Hist. Græc. pag. 531.

(2) Joseph. contra Apionem, lib. 2.

(3) Plinius, lib. 37. cap. 5. Aul. Gellius, lib. 5. cap. 14. & lib. 6. cap. 7.

(4) Ἀπίων ὁ γραμματικὸς ὁ πλειςονίκης τελαύτησεν, Apion *the Grammarian, who was sirnamed* πλειςονικης *to it is, often* a Conqueror. Clem. Alexandr. Strom. lib. 1. pag. 320.

(5) Jul. Africanus apud Eusebium. Præp. Evang. lib. 10. cap. 10. pag. 497. Justin. Admonit. ad Græcos, pag. 9.

(6) Tatian, apud Euseb. Præpar. lib. 10. cap. 11. pag. 493. D.

(7) Aul. Gell. lib. 5. cap. 14.

(8) Id. lib. 6. cap. 7.

(9) Id. lib. 5. cap. 14.

(10) Plin. in Præfatione Natur. Historiar.

(11) Tillemont's History of the Emperors, Tom. 1. pag. 776.

EXORDS of the Supplement to Moreri. See also so Remark [*E*].

(12) Jul. African. apud Eusebium, Præp. Evang. lib. 10. cap. 10.

(13) Tillemont, ubi supra.

APION.

This Wit: For, though perhaps we do not understand all that this Prince meant (b), yet we may easily perceive, that he took *Apion* for a Romancer, who stunned the World with too loud an Ostentation of his Learning. This Person was Chief of the Embassy, which the People of *Alexandria* sent to *Caligula*, to complain against the *Jews*, who were settled in their City, and with whom they were at great variance. He set out for *Rome*, together with two other Deputies. The *Jews*, on their part, deputed Three (c) of their Body to *Caligula* to justify their Conduct. *Philo* was Chief of the Embassy. *Apion*, animated by That Hatred, which the *Egyptians* had born, time out of mind, to the *Jewish* Nation, accused them of various Crimes; and insisted chiefly on those, which he knew would most exasperate *Caligula* against them; namely, That the *Jews* refused to consecrate Images to him [E], and to swear by his Name; while all the other Subjects of the Empire dedicated Temples and Altars to him (d). One of *Apion*'s Principal Pieces was That *Of the Antiquities of Egypt*. It was doubtless in this Book, that he gave so ample an Account of the Pyramids, that *Pliny* thought him worthy to be ranked among the Twelve Authors, who have treated on this Subject (e). He spoke very disobligingly of the *Jews* in the same Book; nor was he satisfyed with treating them ill on every Occasion, which offered in his Antiquities of *Egypt*; he wrote a Book expressly against them (f). *Josephus* thought himself obliged to confute the malicious Calumnies, with which this Author had loaded them [F]. *Apion* was not alive, when this Answer

---

(b) See Remark [C].

(c) According to Josephus, Antiq. l. 18. cap 10. for Philo, pag. 1041, says that the Jewish Deputies were five in Number.

(d) Joseph. Antiqut. lib. 18. cap. 10.

(e) Plin. lib. 36. cap 12. See also lib. 37. cap. 5.

(f) Justin. Paren. ad Græcos, p. 9. Clem. Alex. Stromat. l. 1. pag. 320.

---

(14), that is to say, *The Man with Entrails of Brass*, had, in the Person of *Apion*, a Disciple, who was his perfect Imitator. *Apion*, as laborious as his Master, had, like him, a Sirname, which expressed this Temper. I think the Disciple had no better Taste, than his Master, in the Choice of his Subjects. *Didymus* composed Treatises on the Place of *Homer*'s Birth, on the True Mother of *Æneas*, and on the Manners of *Anacreon* and *Sappho* (15). His Disciple was so earnestly intent upon tracing *Homer*'s Country and Family, that he had recourse to Magic, to discover them. He thought he had made a wonderful Discovery, when he found, that the two first Letters of the *Iliad*, considered *numerically*, amounted to Forty eight: on this Foundation, he affirmed, that *Homer* deferred, 'till he had finished both his Poems, writing the first Line of the *Iliad*; and then pitched upon a Word to begin with, the two first Letters of which denoted, that both Poems, together, contained Forty eight Books. This favours strongly of the Mysteries of the Caballists. This Man, who was so violent an Enemy of the *Jews*, gave naturally enough into their Dreams, in regard to the mysterious Position of Letters. Be that as it will, let us produce Proofs of the Facts here advanced. "Quærit aliquis quæ sint mentiti veteres magi, cum " adolescentibus nobis Apion Grammaticus prodide- " rit cynocephalim herbam, quæ in Ægypto voca- " retur Osyrites, divinam & contra omnia veneficia: " sed si tota erueretur, statim eum qui eruisset, mori: " seque evocasse umbras ad percontandum Homerum " quanam patria, quibusque parentibus genitus esset, " non tamen ausus profiteri, quid sibi respondisse " diceret (16). ----- *Let any one enquire, if he pleases, after the Fictions of the ancient Magicians; when, in our own Memory, the Grammarian Apion pretended, that the Dog's head Flower, called in Egypt Osyrites, had a divine Virtue, even against all kinds of Sorcery; but, that, if it was wholly rooted up, the Person, who pulled it out of the Ground, would immediately die; and that he had summon'd the Shades, to enquire of Homer, where he was born, and who were his Parents; but that he did not dare to reveal the Answer he had received.*" It appears, by this Passage, that *Apion* himself boasted in his Writings, that he had had recourse to Magic, for a Conference with *Homer*; and that he made a Secret of the Answers, which were made to his Demands. *Pliny*'s Opinion of this Person is very plain. *Seneca* had no great Esteem for him. "Api- " on, Grammaticus, lays he (17), qui sub C. Cæsare to- " ta circumlatus est Græcia (18), & in nomen Homeri " ab omnibus civitatibus adoptatus, aiebat, Homerum, " utraque materia consummata, & Odyssea & Iliade, " principium adjecisse operi suo quo bellum Troja- " num complexus est. Hujus rei argumentum af- " ferebat, quod duas literas (19) in primo versu po- " suisset ex industria librorum suorum numerum con- " tinentes (20). ----- Apion, the Grammarian, " who, in the Time of Caius Cæsar, travelled up and " down Greece, and was adopted in every City, as ano-

" ther *Homer*, pretended, that *Homer*, after having " finished both his Poems, the Iliad, and the Odyssey, " added the first Line to That Work, which comprehend- " ed the Trojan War. The Reason he gave for this " was, because there are two Letters designedly placed " in the first Verse, which denote the Number of the " Books." We learn from these Words, that this Grammarian won the Hearts of all *Greece*; since they received him in all their Cities as a second *Homer*, or as *Homer* himself risen from the Dead. A Man of Learning, and at the same time of Impudence and Pride, imposes upon great Numbers of People by his ostentatious Talk.

[E] *The Jews refused to consecrate Images to him.*] This was the chief Accusation, as *Josephus* particularly relates, in the Place cited by the Continuator of *Moreri*: And, as They were the Jews of *Alexandria*, whom *Apion* had Orders to accuse, it is plain the Question was not what the Jews of *Jerusalem* did, or did not do. And yet, if we may believe our Continuator, this was in reality the Case; nor was it the City of *Alexandria*, which remonstrated against the Jews, but *Caligula* himself, *who complained, that they would not admit his Statue into the Temple of God*. It is true, this Emperor used his utmost Endeavours to have his Statue placed in the Temple of *Jerusalem* (21); but it is equally true, that neither *Philo*'s Embassy, nor This of *Apion*, relates to this Fact. *Philo*, when he so particularly relates the Complaints, and the Questions of *Caligula*, makes no mention of this Statue in the Temple (22). *Caligula* complains, in general, that the *Jews* were the only People, who refused to honour him as a God. *Apion* had already put him out of Temper on this Subject, that he might prevent his doing them Justice in the main Dispute. The Matter in hand related properly to the Priviledges, which the Jews ought to have enjoyed in *Alexandria*: Their Cause was good, and they would have gained it before unprejudiced Judges. But what does *Apion* do? He gives the Cause a different Turn; he renders the *Jews* odious to *Caligula*; he has recourse to Accusations of Impiety, and amuses the Court with captious Points. Thus false Zealots act, at this very Day, to support themselves in a most unjust Authority over Conscience, as well as all other Concerns. This can never be too often repeated.

[F] *Josephus thought himself obliged to confute the malicious Calumnies, with which this Author had loaded them*] Mr *Moreri*'s Continuator commits another Blunder in this Place. *This*, says he, *induced* Josephus, *afterwards, to write the Life and Errors of* Apion. It is not true, that *Josephus* wrote the Life of this Grammarian; and it is speaking very inaccurately to say, *that he wrote his Errors*. These Words naturally suggest this Thought; that *Josephus* wrote a Book of Controversy against *Apion*'s Heresies. The Truth is; Being informed, that several Critics had risen up against his *Jewish Antiquities*, not to condemn the Form, or Stile, of it, but to accuse him of a thousand Fables devised for the Advantage of his Nation; He wrote an Apology; in which

---

(13) Amm. Marcel. in lib. 22. cap. ult. pag. 241.

(15) Seneca Epist. 88. pag. 361.

(16) Plin. lib. 30. c p. 2. sub. fin.

(17) Seneca Epist. 88.

(18) The Manuscript of Lipsius, on those Words Seneca, approves this reading, and pretends that Aponem ia a Manuscript, and a Jack-pudding. Agyria sui & circulatur.

(19) The First Word of the Iliad is Μῆνιν. The Letter μ is 40, the Letter η is for 8.

(20) Compare with this Plutarch. Symposi. lib. 9. cap. 3. pag. 739.

(21) Philo de legat.

(22) Ib. pag. 1041, & seq.

APION. APOLLINARIS.

fwer was written; for the Author makes a Reflexion in it on the Manner of his Death. He affirms, that, after this Man had fcoffed fo much at the *Jewish* Ceremonies, not confidering, his injurious Treatment of the *Jews* in fome Manner reflected on the Ancient Laws of the *Egyptians* (g), he found himfelf feized with a Diftemper, which required Incifions in his Natural Parts, and that, notwithftanding this Remedy, he died in extreme Torture (b). He boafted, that he had called up the Soul of *Homer*, to enquire the Place of That Poet's Birth, and his Family (i). The Titles of Four or Five of his Books are preferved [G].

It is not true, that *Apion* relates, that Euphranor, intending to paint *Jupiter*, went to Athens *to confult a Profeffor, who read Homer to his Scholars ; and that This Painter drew an admirable Portrait of That God from the Defcription, which this Poet gives of* Jupiter, *in the firft Book of the* Iliad (k). This Error, which fell from Father Rapin, in the Firft Edition of his Reflexions on Poetry, was unmercifully cenfured by *Vavaffor* the Jefuit [H].

(g) *Among* et res That of Circumcifion.
(b) Jofeph. lib. 2. contra Apion fub fin.
(i) See Remark [D].
(k) Rapin. Reflex. fur la Poëtique n. 23. pag. 77. Edit. 1674.

which he replied to thefe Cenfures, and the Calumnies, which were publifhed againft the Jews. Half the Apology does not relate to *Apion*, though it is generally quoted, as if it were all againft him. It is cited by Origen, under the Title, *De Antiquitate gentis Judaicæ* (23). ---- *Of the Antiquity of the Jewifh Nation*.

[G] *The Titles of four or five of his Books are preferved*.] I have mentioned his Antiquities of *Egypt*, divided into five Books (24), as alfo his Treatife againft the Jews. I add, that he compofed a Treatife *De Luxu Apicii* (25), ---- *Of the Luxury of* Apicius ; another *De Lingua Romana* (26), ---- *Of the Latin Tongue* : and another *De Difciplina Metallica* (27), ---- *Of the Knowledge of Metals*. Suidas afcribes an Hiftory to him ; wherein he treated of all Nations, ἱστορίαν κατ' ἔθνος, *fcripfit hiftoriam de fingulis gentibus*. The famous Hiftory of the Lyon of *Androcles* is known only from the Relation of *Apion*, who fpeaks of it as an Eye-Witnefs. *Aulus Gellius* relates it after him (28). He is indebted to him for another Obfervation, to wit, the Reafon why the Ancients wore a Ring on the Finger next to the little Finger of the left Hand. *Apion* gave a Reafon for it, taken from fome Anatomical Difcoveries made in *Egypt* (29).

(23) Origen. contra Celfum.
(24) Tatianus apud Eufeb. Prep. pg. 493.
(25) Athen. lib. 7. pag. 294.
(26) Id. lib. 15. pag. 680.
(27) Plinius in Indice, lib. 35.
(28) Aul. Gell. lib. 5. cap. 14.
(29) Id. lib. 10. cap. 10.

[H] *This Error, which fell from Father Rapin ---- was unmercifully cenfured by* Vavaffor *the Jefuit*.] He firft relates the Fact, and then adds : " Guefs, Reader, at the pleafant Blunder of the Reflector, through a Miftake of two Words of this " Commentator (30). Whereas I had faid, *as foon as he came out of the Profeffor's School, he drew the Picture of* Jupiter ; our Reflector, to exprefs thefe Words of Euftathius, καὶ ἀπιὼν ἐγράψεν, *et egreffus pinxit*, tranflated them, *as* Apion, *the Grammarian, wrote*. Where the good Man was much overfeen ; and was not aware, either that the Participle ἀπιὼν is not *Apion*, as That Grammarian calls himfelf ; or that the Verb ἐγράψεν fignifies in this Place, *he painted*, ὁ γράφων καὶ γράφει are taken in the very fame Senfe before, or, laftly, that *Apion, cum difceffiffet*, anfwers to the preceding Verb *παρήν, adftitit*. After all ; if the Reflector had himfelf feen this Paffage of Euftathius, I wonder he fhould thus mifunderftand it, and if he took this Interpretation from fome other, I am yet more aftonifhed, that he fhould pretend to have read Euftathius, fo carefully noting a Paffage, which he had never feen (31).

(30) That is Euftathius.

(31) Remarques fur les nouvelles reflexions touchant la Poëtique, pag. 56. 57.

APOLLINARIS (CAIUS SULPITIUS), a very learned Grammarian, and a Native of *Carthage* [A], lived in the IId Century under the *Antonines*. He had for his Succeffor, in the Profefforfhip of Grammar, *Helvius Pertinax*, who had been his Difciple, and was afterwards Emperor (a). He is fuppofed to be the Author of the Verfes, which are prefixed to *Terence*'s Comedies [B], and contain the Summary of them. There is extant an Epigram, which he compofed on the Order *Virgil* gave to burn his *Æneid* [C]. *Aulus Gellius*, who had ftudied under him, mentions him often with Commendation [D]. I advife the Reader particularly to confult what he has faid

(a) Jul Capitolinus in Pertinace, cap. 1.

[A] *A Native of* Carthage.] I have not met with any ancient Author, who informs me of this ; I fay it meerly on the Authority of fome modern Authors, who have publifhed Collections of Epigrams, or *Catalecta* of the ancient Poets.

[B] *He is fuppofed to be the Author of the Verfes, which are prefixed to* Terence's *Comedies*.] He is among thofe of *Politian*, the 22d of the 22th Book, Edition of Paris, 1526, in 4to.

[2] Hift. des Emper. Tom. 2. pag. 589.

* Gellius, lib. 15. cap. 5.

† Id. lib. 2. cap. 16.

read, in a Letter of *Petrus Crinitus* (1), that Politian had obferved, that thefe Verfes ought not to be afcribed to *Terence*, as is generally believed, but to Sulpitius *Apollinaris*. He adds, that, in a very ancient Manufcript of *Terence*, was to be read this Infcription in Capital Letters over the Summaries, G SULPICI APOLLINARIS PERIOCHA. This Infcription has been of great Weight with the feveral Editors of *Terence*. Mr *de Tillemont* refers us to *Setbus Calvifius* concerning thefe Summaries (2). It is true, *Calvifius* mentions them under the Year 163. But he cites *Suidas* ; and I much queftion, whether he ought to have done fo. Mr *de Tillemont* is not in Fault, if we do not believe there are extant two Pieces more of *Apollinaris*. He * left fome Letters, fays he, and a Writing †, *in which he reprimands another Grammarian, whofe Name was* Cæfellius Vindex.

[C] *There is extant an Epigram, which he compofed on the Order* Virgil *gave to burn his* Æneid.] It is but a fingle Diftich ; and is This :

Infelix alio cecidit prope Pergamon igne,
Et pœne eft alio Troja cremata rogo.

Troy *almoft perifh'd in a fecond Flame*.

Thefe Verfes make us regret the Lofs of others. *Verfus habemus ejus aliquos de Æneide Maronis, qui deperditorum accendunt fitim* (3). Thefe are the Jefuit Brietius's Words. I wonder he does not mention the Summaries of *Terence* ; and more, that *Voffius* fays nothing of our Poet. I confefs, he fpeaks of an *Apollinaris*, whom *Gyraldus* has reckoned among the *Latin* Poets. But, fince This *Apollinaris* lived in *Martial*'s Time (4), it is plain he is different from our Grammarian. Befides, all who are Lovers of Poetry are not Poets : So that we have Reafon to oppofe *Gyraldus*, in giving the Title of Poet to the *Apollinaris* of *Martial*, on account of the Pleafure this *Apollinaris* took in *Martial*'s Poetry. " Eum in poëtis " memorat Lilius, fed non fat firmo argumento ; " nec enim, fi delectaretur epigrammatis, eo & ipfe " fuerit Poëta (5). ---- Lilius Gyraldus *ranks him among the Poets ; but his Reafon is not a fufficient one* ; *for it does not follow, that, becaufe he was fond* " *of Epigrams, he was therefore a Poet*."

[D] *Aulus* Gellius ---- *mentions him often with Commendation* (6)]. He calls him *virum præftantis literarum fcientia* (7), ---- *A Man of remarkable Learning* ; *Hominem memoriæ noftræ doctiffimum* (8), ---- *The moft learned Man of our Times* ; *Virum eleganti fcientia ornatum* (9), ---- *A Man of polite Learning* ; *Virum in memoria noftra præter alios doctum* (10), ---- *A Man fuperior in Learning to all whom we remember*. See the thirteenth Chapter of his twelfth Book. He

(3) Brietius de Poët. Lat.

(4) He addreffes to him the 25th Epigram of the 7th Book.

(5) Voffius de Poët. Lat. pag. 50.

(6) Aul. Gell. Noctes Atticæ. lib. 6. cap. 6, & lib. 13. cap. 16, & lib. 20, cap. 6.

(7) Lib. 6, cap. 17.

(8) Lib. 13, cap. 16.

(9) Lib. 26, cap. 5.

(10) Lib. 18, cap. 4.

VOL. I. 5 B

APOLLINARIS. APOLLODORUS.

said of him in the fourth Chapter of the eighteenth Book: He will there see the true Picture of a Pretender to Learning; and the genteel manner, in which *Apollinaris* ridiculed one of this Character [*E*].

(11) Aul. Gell. lib. 13, cap. 18.

He ascribes to him another good Quality, no less valuable than Learning: Namely, that *Apollinaris* had not That pedantic Stiffness, which makes some censure those magisterially, who take the Liberty of giving their Opinion in Matters, which, perhaps, they do not thoroughly understand. For his Part, He gently admonished the People of their Errors. *Aulus Gellius* gives a remarkable Instance of it. For *Apollinaris*, though he had had ever so little of the Pedant, yet might have used the sharpest Censure on an Occasion, wherein *Aulus Gellius* represents him as behaving with his usual Moderation. It was demanded, in his Presence, who a certain *Cato Nepos* was, whose Name appeared in the Title Page of a Book. A young Scholar took up the Question, and undertook to answer it, but was quite mistaken. It was an Affront to the Professorial Majesty, for a young Man to pretend to answer a Question in the Presence of a Professor of Grammar, without first allowing the Grammarian to give his Opinion; this Pertness was unpardonable; however *Apollinaris* would not set the young Man right, 'till he had first commended him in the civilest Manner. "Tum Apollinaris, ut mos ejus in " reprehendendo fuit, placide admodum leniterque, " laudo, inquit, te, mi fili, quod in tantula ætate " etiamsi hunc M. Catonem, de quo nunc quæritur, " quis fuerit ignores, auditiuncula tamen quadam de " Catonis familia asperfus es (11). ---- *Then Apollinaris, after his usual manner of Reproof, with great Mildness and Candor, replied, I commend you, my Son, that, at these tender Years, though you are ignorant who This M. Cato is, whom we are now enquiring after, you yet seem to have some little Knowledge of the Family of Cato."*

[*E*] *The true Picture of a Pretender to Learning, and the genteel Manner, in which* Apollinaris *ridiculed one of this Character.*] This Pretender boasted in a Bookseller's Shop, that he was the only Man alive, who understood *Sallust*: "For, says he, I do " not stop at the Bark, or Surface of his Thoughts, " but descend to the very Pith and Quintessence

" of them" *Neque primam tantum cutem ac speciem sententiarum, sed sanguinem quoque ipsum ac medullam verborum ejus eruere atque introspicere penitus prædicaret.* *Apollinaris,* assuming the Ironical Manner of *Socrates* (12), addrest himself to my Gentleman with an Air of Respect, and blest himself, that he had so opportunely met with an Oracle, to consult, on a Passage of *Sallust*, the Sense of which he had been asked the Day before, but was not able to give it. He desired to know, what Difference *Sallust* made between *Stolidior* and *Vanior*, when he said, *Cn Lentulus* ----- *perincertum stolidior an vanior* (13). Our Pretender answered, with a scornful Air, that he might propose these Trifles to others; and that he did not give himself the Trouble to examine things which were universally known. By this he plainly discovered his Ignorance with regard to the Question proposed; but, finding himself close pressed, and that the Company began to sneer at him, he took his Leave, pretending he had Business elsewhere. Afterwards *Apollinaris* explained this Passage of *Sallust*; and shewed, that *vanus* signified a *Knave*, and *stolidus* a *Clown*. *Aulus Gellius's* Words deserve to be repeated; they paint this Scene very justly. "Tum ille rictu oris labiarumque ductu contemnsi " à se ostendens & rem de qua quæreretur, & ho- " minem ipsum qui quæreret; Priscorum, inquit, & " remotorum ego verborum medullas & sanguinem, " sicuti dixi, perspicere & elicere soleo, non illorum " quæ procuitata vulgo & protrita sunt. Ipso illo " quippe Cn. Lentulo stolidior est & vanior, qui ig- " norat ejusdem esse vanitatem & stoliditatem. ---- " Then He, drawing his Mouth into a contemptuous " Smile, and pretending to despise both the Question, " and the Person, who asked it, replied; I make it " my Business, as I have already told you, to enquire " into the inmost meaning of obsolete and remote Ex- " pressions; not of Those, which are in every one's " Mouth. He must be more foolish and empty than " This Cneius Lentulus himself, who knows not, that " the same Person was both foolish and empty."

(12) Jactatorem quendam & venditatorem Sallustianæ lectionis irrisit illusitque genere illo facetissimæ dissimulationis, qua Socrates ad Sophistas utebatur.
Gell. lib. 18, cap. 4.

(13) Sallustius, Histor. lib. 12.

APOLLODORUS. A great Number of Persons, of different Professions, and great Merit, have been called by this Name. *Scipio Tetti* (*a*), a *Neapolitan*, composed a Treatise of the *Apollodorus*'s, which was printed at *Rome*, in the Year 1555, with the *Bibliotheca of Apollodorus* translated into *Latin* by *Benedictus Ægius* (*b*). Dr *Thomas Gale* re-touched this Subject above an Hundred Years after (*c*). Mr *Moreri* has given us many Articles under this Name, which stand in need of being revised. He forgot one Illustrious *Apollodorus*, the only Person of the Name, whom I propose to speak of.

(*a*) Moreri calls him Tattius, instead of Tettius.

(*b*) See Nicodemo's Add't' is to the Bibliotheque of Naples.

(*c*) See his Apollodorus, printed at Paris, with other Treatises, in 1675.

APOLLODORUS, a famous Architect, in the Days of *Trajan*, and *Adrian*, was of *Damascus*. He had the Direction of the Stone Bridge, which *Trajan* caused to be built over the *Danube*, in the Year 104; and which passed for the most magnificent of all the sumptuous Buildings of That Emperor. *Procopius* mentions it (*a*); and it is probable, *Apollodorus* left a Description of it in Writing. *Adrian*, who piqued himself on understanding all Arts and Sciences to Perfection, so far as to entertain a Jealousy, and Ill-Will, towards those, who acquired an eminent Reputation in their Professions, had particular Reasons to hate *Apollodorus*; for, as *Trajan* discoursed, One Day, with this great Architect, about some Buildings, which he designed to erect in *Rome*, *Adrian* would needs give his Opinion, and did it, like one, who understood nothing of the Matter (*b*). *Apollodorus* said roughly to him, Go, and paint Citruls *, *As for these Matters, we are now discoursing of, you are intirely ignorant of them.* *Adrian*, in those Days, spent his Time in painting Citruls, or Gourds, and even boasted of it. This Insult of *Apollodorus* cost him dear; *Adrian* never forgot it; and, when he came to be Emperor, took care to be revenged. He would not employ *Apollodorus*; He banished him; and, at last, caused him to be accused of several Crimes, and, upon this Pretence, put him to Death. He was ashamed to acknowledge the true Cause of this Severity. *Apollodorus* had, to his old Offence, added a new Provocation, which touched the Emperor to the quick; he had criticised, and, which is worse, very justly, on a sumptuous Structure, which *Adrian* had caused to be built. This Prince, to shew *Apollodorus* that he did not want his Assistance, sent him a Plan of the Temple of *Venus*, and asked his Opinion of it; but not before the Building was finished. *Apollodorus* wrote to him very frankly, what he thought of the Structure; and found

(*a*) De ædific. lib. 4, cap. 6, pag. 81, apud Tillemont, Hist. des Emper. Tom. 2, pag. 302.

(*b*) Xiphilin. in Hadriano.

* Great Gourds, or Lumps of Flesh.

very

APOLLO. APOLLONIUS.

very essential Faults in it [*A*]; which the Emperor could neither deny, nor repair. This raised the Emperor's Indignation to the utmost, and pushed him upon getting rid of *Apollodorus* (*c*). This last Piece of Ingenuity was much more excusable than the first. Men know not whom they shock, when they reprehend the Ignorance of Those, who would pass for Artists in the Presence of greater Masters. They may chance to affront a Person, whose Subjects they will one Day be [*B*], or whose Favour they may stand in need of. This confirms my Conjecture in relation to the Conversations between *Apelles* and *Alexander* [*C*].

(*c*) Ex Xi-philino in Hadr.

[*A*] *Apollodorus* — — — *found very essential Faults in the Plan of the Temple of* Venus.] He made it appear, by good Reasons, that it was neither large, nor lofty, enough; and that the Statues placed in it were not justly proportioned to the Size of the Temple; *for the Goddesses*, said he, *if they have a mind to rise, and go out of it, cannot accomplish this Desire* (1). An Author of our own has paraphrased this Thought thus. " The Architect *Apollodorus*, see-
" ing some Statues of the Gods in the Temple of
" *Venus*, said; These Gods will do well to continue
" fitting as they are; For, should they stand up, they
" would push off the Roof of the Temple, unless they
" stoop very low; and it will be still worse, if they
" have a mind to go out of it; for, the Doors being too
" low for them, they must be obliged to stoop in an in-
" convenient and indecent Manner (2) " I have some
where read, that the Critics found the same Fault with
the Olympian *Jupiter* of *Phidias*. But others have
built a pious Reflexion on it. Let us hear *Bardin*.
" They say, that *Phidias*, being to make a Statue of
" *Jupiter Olympius*, chose to carve him in a sitting Po-
" sture, and so disproportionate to the Size of the Tem-
" ple, that, if he were to stand up, the Roof would be
" too low for him. Thus we may say, that God en-
" ters our Souls, which are his Temples; but that
" he cannot be contained in them at his full ex-
" tent (3)."

[*B*] *May chance to affront a Person, whose Subjects they will one Day be* (4).] The Relation between *Trajan* and *Adrian* might have warned *Apollodorus* of this: But here lies the Failing of those, who think themselves necessary, and whom an uncommon Capacity introduces into Favour; they imagine it is not necessary to pay their Court to young Princes; and that the great Patron is sufficient. Times change; and they find, that their magisterial Behaviour to all, who speak impertinently before them, in their own Profession, is great Folly.

[*C*] *This confirms my Conjecture in relation to the Conversations between* Apelles *and* Alexander.] I have declared above (5), that I could not persuade myself, that this great Painter would dare to take so gross a Liberty of censuring the young Conqueror, as some Authors pretend. I am very sensible, that They, who excel in certain Arts, are sometimes of such a capricious Humour, that they are not able to contain themselves within the Bounds of Respect, when the Fit is upon them; but I know too, that *Apelles* is said to have been very modest and polite. But the strongest Reason I have for it is this. *Alexander*, the most impatient Man that ever lived, would not have let so scornful a Censure pass unpunished: Now, we do not read, that *Apelles* ever lost the Favour of This Prince. The Argument *à fortiori*, from the greater to the less takes place here. *Adrian* was not so haughty, as *Alexander*, nor was he a King, when he was affronted; yet the Censure of the Architect was a mortal Offence.

(1) Ex Xiphilino, in Hadriano.

(2) Costar. Apolog. pag. 50.

(3) Burdin's Lyceum, cap. 2.

(4) See the Text of the Article AN-TONIA-A O, towards the end.

(5) In Remark [*D*], of the Article APELLES.

APOLLO, a Pagan Deity. Look for PHŒBUS.

APOLLONIUS, of *Perga*, a City in *Pamphylia*, was a famous Geometrician (*a*), in the Reign of *Ptolomy Evergetes*, which reaches from the second Year of the CXXXIIId Olympiad, to the third Year of the CXXXIXth. He studied, a long time, in *Alexandria*, under the Disciples of *Euclid* (*b*), and composed several Books; none of which are come down to us, but his *Conic Sections* [*A*]. It is much esteemed, and several ancient and modern Authors have taken the pains to comment upon, or translate, it [*B*]. Mr *Des Cartes* had no favourable Opinion of it [*C*].

(*a*) Eutocius Ascalonita initio Commentar. in Conica Apollonii, ex Heraclio in vita Archimedis.

(*b*) Pappus in Prooemio ad lib. 7. Mathem. Collect.

[*A*] *Composed several Books, none of which are come down to us, but his* Conic Sections.] Two Books περὶ λόγου ἀποτομῆς, *de proportionis sectione*. Two περὶ χωρίου ἀποτομῆς, *de spatii sectione*. Two διωρισμένης τομῆς, *determinatæ sectionis*. Two ἐπαφῶν, *tactionum*. Two νεύσεων, *inclinationum*. Two τόπων ἐπιπέδων, *planorum locorum* (1). And eight of *Conic Sections*. There can be no doubt, that this last Work contained eight Books; the Author's Epistle Dedicatory to a Geometrician of *Pergamus*, whose Name was *Eudemus*, makes it plainly appear. The Public has not yet seen the last of these eight Books: Only the four first are in *Greek*; the three following have been translated into *Latin*, from an *Arabic* Version. See the following Remark. We find cited the Books of *Apollonius*, *de cochleæ*, *& de perturbatis rationibus* (2). I cannot tell, whether we ought not to ascribe to the same Author the Commentary on the *Phænomena* of *Aratus*, which is attributed by the Ancients to *Apollonius* the Geometrician (3).

[*B*] *Several ancient and modern Authors have taken the Pains to comment upon, or translate, it.*] It is said, that *Hypatia*, the Daughter of *Theon*, wrote a Commentary on the *Conics* of *Apollonius*. We have still That, which *Eutocius of Ascalon* composed on the first four Books of This Work, with *Lemma*'s and *Corollaries*. He promised to comment on the other four also: See his Epistle Dedicatory to *Anthemus*.

We have also (5), to the Number of Sixty five, the *Lemma*'s, which *Pappus* drew up on the *Conics* of *Apollonius*. The Catalogue of the Works of *Francis* *Maurolycus*, printed at *Venice*, informs us, that this ingenious Mathematician wrote a Book entituled, *Apollonii conica elementa libris quatuor & demonstrationibus & lineamentis opportunis instaurata* (6). — — *Apollonius*'s *Principles of Conic Sections, in four Books, and illustrated with Demonstration and suitable Schemes*. *John Baptista Memus* (7), a noble *Venetian*, and Mathematical Professor at *Venice*, translated into *Latin* the four first Books of *Apollonius*; which were printed in the Year 1537 (8). This Translation is of no Value; he did not understand the Subject; and this was the Reason, why he passed over the most visible Faults of the *Greek* Manuscript. " Eos pri-
" mos transtulit, *says* Vossius (9), Joan. Baptista Mem-
" mius; sed infeliciter, eo quod argumentem operis
" non intelligeret: unde non vidit fit manifestas
" Græci codicis mendas, ac sæpe puerilitate alucina-
" tur: sicut monitum Francisco Maurolyco Præfati-
" one in Cosmographiam suam. — — John Baptista
" Memmius *was the first, who translated them*; but *Richardus*,
" *without Success*; since he understood not the Design
" of the Work; whence it was, that he overlooked
" the plainest Errors of the Greek Copy, and is often
" guilty of childish Mistakes; as is observed by Fran-
" cia Maurolycus, *in the Preface to his Cosmography*." *Frederic Commandin* (10) made a new Translation of it, much better than the former, which he published at *Bologne*, in the Year 1566. He added to it a Translation of *Eutocius*'s Commentary, and several Notes. But, having made use of a very faulty *Greek* Manuscript, his Version was not so good as could be wished; for which Reason *Martin Ghetaldus* (11) resolved to trace the Evil to it's Source. He endeavoured of Ragusa.

(1) Vossius de Scient. Mathem. cap. 16, pag. 55, ex Pappo, lib. 7. Mathematicæ collectionis.

(2) Apud Proclum in Euclidem. See the Epitomy of Gessner's Bibliotheque, pag. 71.

(3) See Vossius lib. cap. 32, pag. 116. and de Hist. Græcis, pag. 505.

(4) Claudius Richardus Præf. ad Apollon. Pergæum sect. 10.

(5) In lib. 7. Mathematicæ Collect. Pappi.

(6) Claud. Richardus, ubi supra, sect. 15.

(7) Moreri calls him de Mesines; he undoubtedly believed that he was a Frenchman, which bears this Name.

(8) Claud. Richardus, ubi supra, sect. 15.

(9) Vossius de Scient. Math. pag. 55.

(10) And not Commandon, as Moreri calls him.

(11) He was a Patrician of Ragusa.

APOLLONIUS.

it [C]. Some have thought, that *Apollonius* appropriated the Writings and Discoveries of *Archimedes* to himself [D]. He had a Son, whose Name was *Apollonius*, and who

(12) Ex Voſſio de Scient. Mathem. pag. 434.

ed to correct the Manuſcript according to the Senſe of the Author, and to reſolve the Problems; and by this means believed he had reſtored Life to this ancient Geometrician (12). See the Book, which he entituled *Apollonius redivivus, ſeu reſtituta Apollonii Pergæi inclinationum geometria*, and his *Supplementum Apollonii Galli, ſeu exſuſcitata Apollonii Pergæi tactionum geometriæ Pars reliqua*, printed at *Venice*, in the Year 1607, in 4to. *Claude Richard*, a Jeſuit of the *Franche Comte*, and Royal Profeſſor of Mathematics in the Imperial College of his Order at *Madrid*, in the Year 1642, explained, in his public Lectures, the firſt four Books of *Apollonius*, and, in the Year 1643, four other Books, of which himſelf was the Author, and in which he had ſupplied the other Part of this ancient Geometrician's Work (13). His Explications of the four firſt were printed at *Antwerp*, in 1655, in Folio. He declares that, after having finiſhed theſe two Pieces, he read the *Conics* of *Claude Middorge* (14) with Pleaſure and Admiration, as alſo the Quadrature of the Circle of *Gregory* of *St Vincent*; in which are many things relating to thoſe Books of *Apollonius*, which are wanting. *In quibus* (de quadratura circuli duobus tomis) *præter elementa conica peculiari ordine diſpoſita, innumera prodit, ſicuti Middorgius, quæ ſpectant ad poſtremos quatuor Apollonii libros injuria temporum ſuppreſſos, in lucem revocandos* (15). *Ferdinand* I. Great Duke of *Florence*, propoſed to get ſeveral *Arabian* Manuſcripts, which were in his Library, tranſlated. *John Baptiſta Raimond*, who was the Principal among thoſe, to whom this Prince gave Penſions for this Undertaking, had promiſed to tranſlate *Apollonius*, which was in *Arabic*, in that Library; and ſome Authors have ſaid, that this Tranſlation was finiſhed (16); but nothing of it has been found among his Papers (17). At laſt the Great Duke *Ferdinand* II, and his Brother Prince *Leopold de Medicis*, caſt their Eyes on *Abraham Eccbellenſis*, Profeſſor of the Oriental Languages at *Rome*, and employed him in this Work. By the Aſſiſtance of *Alfonſo Borelli*, Mathematical Profeſſor at *Piſa*, he tranſlated the fifth, ſixth, and ſeventh Books of *Apollonius* into *Latin*. This Tranſlation was printed at *Florence*, in the Year 1661, in Folio, with the Commentary of the ſame *Borelli*; who maintains, in his Preface, that theſe Books are not ſpurious, but the genuine Works of our *Apollonius*. He anſwers the Difficulties of *Claude Middorge*, who imagined, that the three Books, which *Golius* brought from the *Levant* (18), were the Work of an *Arabian*, who conceal'd himſelf under the celebrated Name of *Apollonius*. Father *Merſennus* mentions this Opinion of *Claude Middorge*, but does not approve of it; he believes that the eighth Book of the *Conics* of *Apollonius*, and all the other Works of the ſame Author, as alſo thoſe which *Pappus* has not quoted, are ſtill extant, and actually tranſlated into *Arabic* (19). He produces *Aben Nedin* as his Voucher, who wrote a Book *De Philoſophis Arabibus* (20). i. e. *Of the Arabic Philoſophers*. Obſerve, I. That it was remarked, at the bottom of the Manuſcript of *Golius*, that the eighth Book of *Apollonius* had not been tranſlated into *Arabic*, becauſe it was wanting in the *Greek* Copies, from which the Tranſlation of the others had been made (21). II That the Manuſcript, from which the Tranſlation of *Eccbellenſis* was made, came from the *Oriental* Library, which *Ignatius Neama*, Patriarch of *Antioch*, had left by Will to the Great Duke *Ferdinand* I. (22). III. That *Abalphat Alphabanenſis* is the Author of the *Arabic* Tranſlation, which ſerved *Eccbellenſit* for an Original, and which he made for King *Abicalgiau*, who aſcended the Throne in the Three hundred ſeventy ſecond Year of the *Hegira*. From whence it follows, that this was not the firſt Tranſlation in that Language: for *Gregory Barbebræus* notes, that ſeven Books of the *Conics* of *Apollonius* were tranſlated into *Arabic* in the time of *Almamun*. Now *Almamun* was inaugurated in the Two hundred and third Year of the *Hegira* (23). IV. That *Abalphat* ſtill pretended, that his Tranſlation was the firſt, and that only ſome Fragments of *Apollonius* had been rendred before, from the eaſieſt Places. This would induce one to think, that either he had not ſeen the Tranſlation, which was made in

(13) Cl. Rich. Præf. in Apollon. ſect. 11.

(14) Tres Conicorum libros Claudii Middorgii - - - nova methodo ex Apollonianis fontibus petitos & proprio ingenio appoſite digeſtos. *Claud. Rich. ubi ſupra.*

(15) Id. ib.

(16) As Jerome Lunadorus, in libro de Romana curia. See Borelli, in his Preface.

(17) Abrah. Eccbellenſis, in Præfat. verſionis Apollon.

(18) The 5th, 6th, and 7th of Apollonius's Conic Sections.

(19) Merſennus Præfat. in Apollonii Conica, quæ ſunt in ejus ſynopſi Mathemat.

(20) See Voſſius de Scient. Mathem. pag. 55.

(21) Id. ib.

(22) Borellus, in Præfat.

(23) Abrah. Eccbellenſis, in Præfat.

the time of *Ahmamun*, or that That Tranſlation contained only ſome Fragments of the *Conics* of *Apollonius* (24).

This is what I had to ſay, by way of Comment on the Text of this Remark. I ſay nothing of the *Apollonius Batavus* of *Wilbrord Snellius*, ſeu exſuſcitata geometria *Apollonii Pergæi* περὶ διωρισμένης τομῆς, a Book printed at *Leyden*, 1608, in 4to. I omit, likewiſe, *Vincentio Viviani*, Author of the Treatiſe *De maximis & minimis, geometrica divinatio in quintum librum Conicorum Apollonii Pergæi*, at *Florence*, 1659, in Folio.

(24) Id. ib.

[C] *Mr Des Cartes had no favourable Opinion of it.*] "He was not ſurprized, that others ſhould demonſtrate the *Conic Sections* with more eaſe than "*Apollonius*; becauſe That ancient Author is very te"dious and intricate; and yet all, that he has demon"ſtrated, is, of itſelf, very plain (25)." He com"pared what he had done in Metaphyſics "to the De"monſtrations of *Apollonius*, in which there is no"thing, but what is very clear, and certain, when "each Point is ſeparately conſidered. But, as they "are ſomewhat long, and ſince one cannot readily "perceive the Neceſſity of the Concluſion, without "exactly remembering all that went before, ſcarce "one Man in a City, or a Province, can be found, "who is able to comprehend them: However, on "the Teſtimony of thoſe few, who underſtand them, "and vouch for their Truth, every one gives Credit "to them (26)."

(25) Boillet's Life of Des Cartes, Tom. 2. pag. 39.

[D] *Some have thought, that* Apollonius *appropriated the Writings and Diſcoveries of* Archimedes *to himſelf.*] *Heraclius* affirms, that *Archimedes* was the firſt, who applied himſelf to the Doctrine of *Conic Sections*; and that his Compoſitions on that Subject fell into the Hands of *Apollonius*, who publiſhed them as his own (27). *Eutocius* confutes this by two Reaſons; one is, that *Archimedes*, in ſeveral Parts of his Works, ſpeaks of *Conics* as a Science not new; the other is, that *Apollonius* does not pretend, that he is the Inventor of what he writes; he only ſays, that he has treated the Subject more amply, than had been done by any Author before him (28). This ſeems to me but an indifferent Juſtification of him, as to the Crime of Plagiariſm; for a Man may appropriate the Writings of another to himſelf, though they are not Works, on which the Author pretends to ſay nothing, but what is new. The Honour of explaining a difficult Subject better, than had been done before, is ſufficient to tempt a Man to get into his Poſſeſſion a Work, which may procure him this Honour. This might be the Caſe of *Apollonius*, for any thing that appears in his Apology. There is ſomething farther ſtill; he boaſts ſometimes in the general Summaries of his eight Books, that what he advances is new (29). Judge, then, whether this might not be a powerful Motive to induce him to arrogate ſuch a Work to himſelf. Upon the whole, *Eutocius* defends him but ill; and his beſt Juſtification is the Silence of *Pappus*, his Cenſor, and a Cenſor not a little prejudiced againſt him. Obſerve too, that *Pappus* not only does not accuſe him of Plagiariſm, but expreſsly allows him to be the true Author of the eight Books of *Conic Sections*, though he pretends, that *Euclid* had wrote four Books on the ſame Subject before (30). He defends *Euclid*, againſt *Apollonius*, who had remarked, that this famous Geometrician had ſucceeded very indifferently in a certain Point. He excuſes *Euclid*, by what *Apollonius* himſelf had acknowledged; to wit, that, before the Diſcoveries of *Apollonius*, it was impoſſible to treat clearly on this Subject; the Principles made uſe of before not being ſufficient. He pretends, that *Euclid*, being very good-natured, and modeſt, had confined himſelf to the Diſcoveries of *Ariſteus*, in relation to *Conics*, without either overthrowing, or improving, what the other had begun; and that he had ſtopt, where he found them incapable of carrying him farther; but that he was cautious of ſaying, that this was the Point of Perfection; for he had been to blame in that (31). Note, by the way, that this demonſtrates the Falſeneſs of *Heraclius*'s Pretenſion, that *Archimedes* was the firſt, who wrote concerning *Conics*. *Voſſius* has taken no notice of the

(26) Id. ib. pag. 101.

(27) Heraclius, in vita Apollonii ap. Eutocium, in Comment. in Apollonii Conica.

(28) Eutocius, ibid. See Claud. Richardus, Præf. ad Apollon. ſect. 7.

(29) See the Letter of Apollonius to Eudemus, in the beginning of his 1ſt Book. See likewiſe his Letter to Attalus, at the beginning of the 4th Book.

(30) Pappus in Proœmio, lib. 7. Mathem. Collect.

(31) You will find the Words of Pappus, in the Remark of the Article ARISTEUS, the Geometrician.

APOLLONIUS. 379

who was the Messenger, who presented the second Book of the *Conic Sections* to the Person, to whom the Author had dedicated it (*c*). The *Arabians* have discovered great Ignorance in Chronology, with regard to *Apollonius* [E]. Mr *Moreri* has been guilty of many Blunders on this Head [*F*].

(*c*) *Apollon. Epist. Dedicat.* lib. 2. apud Eutocium.

(32) Vossius, de Scient. Mathem. in Addendis, pag. 434.

(33) Initio Commentarii in Secundum *Συμπόσιον* Archimedis.

(34) Gregorius Baibreus, lib. 3. Chronicor. in Achas, apud Abrah. Ecchellensem Praefat. in Apollon.

(35) Ecchellens. ibid.

the Proofs, which overthrow this Pretension. He observes, as something in justification of *Heraclius*, that *Archimedes* sometimes refers to a Treatise of *Conics*; and That in a Style, which he generally makes use of, in referring to his own Writings (32). He adds, that *Guido Ubaldus* has proved, against *Eutocius*, that *Archimedes* was not ignorant, that *Cones* may be be cut by Planes differently inclined to the Side of the *Cone* (33). But how does this prove the Point in Question? We may allow, that *Archimedes* had wrote an excellent Treatise of *Conic Sections*; but does this imply, that no one before him had treated of this Matter, or that this Work was stolen by the Plagiary *Apollonius*?

[*E*] *The Arabians have discovered great Ignorance in Chronology, with regard to* Apollonius.] They have said, that he lived in the time of *Abaz*, King of *Judab*, and that his Writings on *Conic Sections* induced *Euclid* to write on that Subject a long time after (34). This is so strange a Mistake, that it is surprizing *Ecchellensis* treats it with so much Lenity. He seems unwilling to say, that the *Arabian* Author was mistaken; he only says, that this Chronology is very wide of the common Account. " In his longe vide-
" tur discrepare Gregorias à communi Chronologo-
" rum sententia & opinione, qui Apollonium floru-
" isse scribunt anno periodi Julianæ 4474 — dis-
" crepat præterea ab iisdem Chronologis in ætate Eu-
" clidis, quem Apollonio juniorem agnoscit, ubi illi
" eum collocant in anno periodi Julianæ 4430 (35).
" ——— In this Gregory *seems to differ widely from*
" *the common Sentiment and Opinion of Chronologers,*
" *who write, that* Apollonius *flourished in the Year*
" 4474, *of the Julian Period.* ——— *He dissents like-*
" *wise from the same Chronologers, in relation to*
" *the Age of* Euclid, *whom he supposes to be later*
" *than* Apollonius; *whereas they place him in the*
" 4430*th Year of the Julian Period.*" Ecchellensis leaves us, as it were, at Liberty, to chuse between these two Opinions: He would have done better, to have determined, that the *Arabian* Author was mistaken; for this is most certain. And observe, that his Error is not a Difference of some few Years; *Abaz* began to reign in the Year 3970 of the *Julian* Period. *Ptolomy Evergetes*, in whose time *Apollonius* flourished, succeeded the King, his Father, in the Year 4468, of the same Period. The mistake,

then, is very great, since it includes a Difference of about five Centuries.

[*F*] Mr *Moreri has been guilty of many Blunders on this Head.*] I. He has, simply and absolutely, given our *Apollonius* the Sirname of the *Great Geometrician*: whereas he should have used a Restriction, and contented himself with saying, that his Cotemporaries called him so, on account of his Skill in *Conics*. This is precisely what *Eutocius* of *Ascalon* says of him (36). II. *Moreri* pretends, that this Sirname is the same with that of ὁ Κρίνῳ; which is a great Mistake, treat it as favourable as you please; for, in short, the *Apollonius*, who had the Sirname of Κρίνῳ, was not the Geometrician; he was born at *Cyrene* (37), and never had any Reputation (38). III. *Eutocius* does not treat of *Heraclius*'s Book of the Life of *Archimedes*; he cites it only. IV. To say, That *we have the Treatise of Cones, Conicorum, translated by* John Baptista de Mesmes, *is to be guilty of a Barbarism*, and tends to persuade the Reader, that this *John Baptista* translated the whole Work; whereas he translated only the four first Books. V. It is not true, *that Men of Learning know, that these* (39) *four first Books of* Apollonius *belong to* Euclid *of* Megara (40). VI. No one has said, that *Apollonius* was the Disciple of Eubulides, *a Scholar of* Euclid; and it is not probable, that he ever was; since *Eubulides* applied himself almost wholly to the Sophistry of Logic, and never taught in *Alexandria*, where our *Apollonius* studied under the Disciples of *Euclid*. VII. After having said, that *Euclid* is the true Author of the four first Books of *Apollonius*, ought he to add, that this Author *wrote Commentaries on the four first Books of That Philosopher's* Conics? What Confusion, or rather what Contradictions are here! VIII. It is not true, that *Golius* translated the fifth, sixth, and seventh Books of *Apollonius* out of *Arabic* into *Latin*. Mr *Moreri*, who affirms it, is without Excuse, since he had read in *Vossius* no more than this: *viz.* that *Golius* had brought these three *Arabic* Books from the *Levant*, and that the Mathematics would soon be much indebted to him, especially when these three Books should be printed (41). IX. The *Apollonius*, who was the Master of *Diodorus*, is not the same with him, who is the Subject of this Article. Two more of Mr *Moreri*'s Errors may be seen above (42).

(36) Eutoc. *Ascalon, in Comm. in Conica Apollonii. He hu li' αυ-mony of Getmini, lib. 6. Marbematicorum Præceptionum.*

(37) Strabo, lib. 17. pag. 376.

(38) M. lib. 14. p. 453.

(39) *Note, ab* I Moreri *has said no thing, to which the word* THREE *which makes it an insufferable Jargon.*

(40) See Diogenes Laert. l. 2. n. 111.

(41) Vossius, de Scient. Mathemat. c. 16. p. 55.

(42) In Remark [B], Citations (9) and (10).

APOLLONIUS *Tyanæus*, was One of the most Extraordinary Persons, that ever appeared in the World. I had resolved to make a very long Article of him; but, having seen That, which Mr *de Tillemont* has already given us, I thought it better to employ my time in other Enquiries, than to take a great deal of Pains to say nothing, but what he has said before me, or only to copy him. His Book will pass through more Hands, than this, and every one will more readily consult Him, than My Dictionary. It will be sufficient therefore to advertise my Reader, That, in the second Volume of his Works (*a*), he will find a full and exact Collection of what most remarkably concerns *Apollonius Tyanæus*. However, if but for Form's sake, let me observe, That he was born at *Tyana*, in *Cappadocia*, towards the beginning of the First Century; That, at Sixteen Years of Age, he set up for a rigid Observer of the Rules of *Pythagoras*, renouncing Wine, Women, and all manner of Flesh, wearing no Shoes, letting his Hair grow at full length, and cloathing himself only in Linnen (*b*); that, a little while after, he set up for a Reformer; that he fixed his Residence in a Temple of *Æsculapius*, whither many sick Persons resorted to be cured by Him; that, being come to Age, he gave part of his Estate to his elder Brother; that he distributed another part to his poor Relations, and kept but a very small Share to himself; That he lived six Years without speaking a Word; that, notwithstanding, during this Silence, he quelled several Seditions [*A*], in *Cilicia*, and *Pamphilia* (*c*).

(1) *It was the third City of Pamphylia.*

(2) *Quintill. Declamat. 12. The French have a Proverb, that a hungry Belly has no Ears. The Ancients had such another. See Erasmus's Chiliads. Venter non habet aures. Cato begun a Oration with these Words, Arduum est ad ventrem verba facere, qui caret auribus. — — — It is difficult to persuade the Belly, which has no Ears. The Business was to appease the People, who demanded Corn.*

(*a*) *Pag. 90. Edit. of Brussels.*

(*b*) *Philostr. in Vita Apollon. l. 2.*

(*c*) *Ibidem.*

[*A*] *That, notwithstanding, during this Silence, he quelled several Seditions.*] That, which he put a stop to at *Aspenda* (1), was the most difficult to appease, because the Business was to make those hearken to Reason, whom Famine had driven to Revolt, *fames magistra peccandi, durissima necessitatum* (2). The Cause of this Commotion was, some rich Mens having engrossed the Corn, which occasioned an extraordinary

Scarcity in the City. *Apollonius* stopped this popular Commotion, without speaking one Word. Was there ever a more eloquent, active, and persuasive Silence known! His Talent was very different from That of the Person, whom *Virgil* describes.

Tum pietate gravem ac meritis si forte virum quem
Conspexere, silent, arrectisque auribus astant:

Ille

philia (c): That he travelled, and turned Legiflator; that he pretended to underftand all Languages, without ever having learned them ; to know the Thoughts of Men (d), and to explain the Oracles, which Birds delivered by chirping (e); that he condemned Dancing, and other Diverfions of that kind ; that he recommended Works of Charity (f); that he travelled over almoft all the Countries of the World (g); that, at *Cadiz*, he prevailed with the Intendant of the Country to revolt againft *Nero* (b) [B], and that he died at a very great Age, without it's being certainly known where, or in what manner (i). His Life has been fully related by *Philoftratus* [C]. It contains no doubt a Thoufand fabulous Relations; but, if the Facts were true, we muft not impute them to the Power of Magic. The Pagans very readily oppofed the pretended Miracles of this Man to Thofe of our Saviour [D], and drew a Parallel between them. It is obfervable, that St *Auftin* confeffed, that *Apollonius*, at the worft, was greatly fuperior to the *Jupiter* of the *Gentiles* (k). It cannot be denied, that this Philofopher received very great Honours, both during his Life, and after his Death [E] ; and that his Reputation continued

---

Ille regit DICTIS *animos ac pectora mulcet* (3).

If then fome grave and pious Man appear,
They bufh their Noife, and lend a liftening Ear.
He footbs with fober WORDS *their angry Mood,*
And quenches their innate Defire of Blood.
                              DRYDEN.

Such an one muft *fpeak*, if he hopes to ftop the Fury of a mutinous People. *Apollonius* had no need of Words ; his *Pythagoric* Silence did all that the fineft Figures of Oratory could effect.

[B] *That, at* Cadiz, *he prevailed with the Intendant of the Country to revolt againft* Nero.] " *Philoftratus*, thinks it for his Honour, that he induced " the Governor of *Cadiz*, and the Country about " it, to rebel againft *Nero*; nor did the other Phi- " lofophers make any more fcruple of this than He. " [There being no Inftitution but the Chriftian Reli- " gion, which teaches us to confider Men, not as they " are in themfelves, but in the Order, wherein God " has placed them, nor ever to violate the Fidelity, " which has once been fworn to them (4)]" Mr *de Tillemont* might very well have omitted this moral Reflexion, and indeed the whole Parenthefis. Chriftianity has certainly the moft real and fublime Advantages above all Philofophy ; but, as to the Point here in queftion, I cannot fee that it has had any Right, for thefe thoufand Years paft, to infult the Philofophers. The Chriftians, and They, have been pretty even, on this fcore, for a long time. We may fay of this Engagement, *Never to violate the Faith, which has once been pledged*, what the Poet faid of Chaftity ;

Credo pudicitiam Saturno rege moratam
In terris, vifamque diu - - - - -
Quippe aliter tunc orbe novo cœloque recenti
Vivebant homines (5).

In Saturn's Reign, at Nature's early Birth ;
There was That Thing, call'd Chaftity, on Earth.

For when the World was buckfome, frefh, and young,
Her Sons were undebauch'd. - - - - -
                              DRYDEN.

It continued no longer than the three firft Centuries. Mr *de Tillemont* obferves, that *Apollonius ufed his utmoft Endeavours to raife the whole World againft the Emperor* Domitian (6). He, who wrote this Philofopher's Life, efteems it as an Heroic Exploit in him (7). This Impoftor had mimicked the Son of God in feveral Inftances; but, on the Article of Submiffion and Patience, he pulled off the Mafk ; and, indeed, there was no room for a Parallel on this Head.

[C] *His Life has been fully related by* Philoftratus.] That which *Damis*, originally of *Nineveh*, the *moft devoted to him of all his Difciples*, had compofed, *was properly no more than Memoirs, and ill enough written* (8). They fell into the Hands of the Emprefs *Julia*, the Wife of *Severus*. " She gave " them to *Philoftratus*, who, from them, and by " the help of what he could gather from *Apollonius* " himfelf, and from other Memoirs, compofed the " Hiftory we at prefent have of Him. He men- " tions one *Maximus* of *Eges*, who had written a " Book on *Apollonius*, and one *Marragenes*, who had " written four Books concerning him; but would " have no Credit to be given to the latter (9)." See, in the Remark [*I*], fome other Authors of the Life of *Apollonius*. As for the Life, which *Philoftratus* himfelf compofed, it was firft printed, in *Greek*, at *Venice*, by *Aldus Manutius*, with the Treatife of *Eufebius* againft *Hierocles*. This Treatife was rendered into *Latin* by *Zenobius Accaiuoli*. The Life of *Apollonius* was tranflated into the fame Language by *Allemannus Rhinuccius*, a *Florentine*. The *Latin* Verfion of thefe two Pieces, with feveral Corrections, and fmall marginal Notes of *Gisbert Longolius*, was printed at *Cologne*, in the Year 1532, in 8vo. The *Paris* Edition of all the Works of *Philoftratus*, publifhed by *Frederick Morel*, is better than any of the preceeding Editions; but it were to be wifhed, that fome Perfon well fkilled in *Greek* would correct the *Latin* Tranflation ; he would find many things in it, which require the Hand of a fkilful Operator. See the Remark [*I*].

[D] *The Pagans very readily oppofed the pretended Miracles of This Man to Thofe of our Saviour.*] We need only read a Work of *Eufebius* (10) againft one *Hierocles*, a great Enemy of the Gofpel, in the Reign of the Emperor *Dioclefian*. It appears, that *Hierocles's* Defign, in the Treatife, which *Eufebius* confutes, was to draw a Parallel between *JESUS CHRIST* and *Apollonius Tyanæus*, and that he gives the Preference to the latter. Thefe Words of *Lactantius* confirm what I have faid. " Item, cum facta " *Jefu Chrifti* mirabilia deftrueret, nec tamen nega- " ret, voluit oftendere Apollonium vel paria vel etiam " majora feciffe (11). ——— *Likewife when he would* " *have overthrown the Miracles of* Jefus Chrift, *he* " *could not deny them, he pretended to fhew, that* " *Apollonius had wrought the like, or even greater.*" What Mr *de Tillemont* has obferved is remarkable. " *Apollonius*, fays he (12), by the feeming Innocen- " cy of his Life, and his pretended Miracles, was " one of the moft dangerous Enemies the Church " had in it's Infancy. It feemed, according to his " own Panegyrifts, as if the Devil had fent him in- " to the World, about the fame time that *Jefus* " *Chrift* was to appear, either to counter-balance " his Authority in the Minds of thofe, who fhould " take the Illufions of this Magician for real Miracles, " or that They, who fhould difcover him to be an " arrant Impoftor and Magician, might thereby be " brought to doubt of the Miracles of *Jefus Chrift* " and his Difciples."

[E] *Very great Honours, both during his Life, and after his Death.*] Mr *de Tillemont* juftly reproaches him with not having difclaimed the Style and Title of *God, which his Followers afcribed to him* ; *and if, on certain occafions, he refufed to receive Divine Honours in public* ; it was, fays his Hiftorian, *for fear of Envy* (13). The Inhabitants of *Tyana* built a Temple to other *Apollonius* after his Death (14). His Statue was erected in feveral other Temples (15). The Emperor *Adrian* collected as many of his Letters as he could, and kept them in his fine Palace of *Antium*, with a little Book of This Philofopher concerning the Anfwers he had received from the Oracle of *Trophonius*. This little Book was to be feen at *Antium*, during *Philoftratus's* Life; nor did any

APOLLONIUS. 381

continued as long as Paganism [F]. He left some Works, which have been long since

(16) Philostrat. ubi supra, lib. 8. cap. 8.
(17) Ἡρώων Dio. lib. 77. pag. 878. C. apud Tillem. pag. 219.
(18) Lamprid. p. 123. apud eund.

any Curiosity render this small Town so famous as *Apollonius*'s Book (16). *Antonius Caracalla* had an extraordinary Veneration for *Apollonius*; and built a Temple to him as to an Hero (17). The Emperor *Severus* kept the Image of this Philosopher, in a particular Place, in his Palace, among Those of *Jesus Christ*, *Abraham*, and the best Princes (18). *Aurelian*, having resolved to sack *Tyana*, was prevented by *Apollonius*'s appearing to him in a Vision, and forbidding it; and he not only obeyed this Order of *Apollonius*, but vowed an Image, a Temple, and a Statue to him. *Vopiscus*, in relating this, declares himself his Admirer and Votary, with a Promise to write his Life. The Passage, though somewhat long, deserves a Place here; it being almost all of it a Proof of the Text of this Remark. " Taceri non debet res, quæ ad famam venerabilis viri " pertinet. Fertur enim Aurelianum de Thyanæ civitatis eversione vera dixisse, vera cogitasse: verum " Apollonium Thyanæum celeberrimæ famæ autoritatisque sapientem, veterem philosophum, amicum verum deorum, ipsum etiam pro numine frequentandum, recipiendi se in tentorium ea forma, " qua videtur, subito astitisse, atque hæc Latine, ut " homo Pannonius intelligeret, verba dixisse. *Aureliane, si vis vincere, nihil est quod de civium mortuorum nece cogites. Aureliane, si vis imperare, a cruore innocentium abstine.* *Aureliane*, clementer te age, " si vis vincere. Norat vultum philosophi venerabilis Aurelianus, atque in multis ejus imaginem viderat templis. Denique statim attonitus imaginem " & statuas & templum eidem promisit, atque in meliorem rediit mentem. Hæc ego à gravibus viris " comperi, & in Ulpiæ bibliothecæ libris relegi, & " pro majestate Apollonii magis credidi. Quid enim " illo viro sanctius, venerabilius, antiquius, diviniusque inter homines fuit? Ille mortuis reddidit vitam. " Ille multa ultra homines & fecit & dixit, quæ qui " velit nosse, Græcos legat libros, qui de ejus vita " conscripti sunt. Ipse autem, si vita suppetat, atque " ipsius viri favori usquequaque placuerit, breviter " saltem tanti viri facta in literas mittam: non quo " illius viri gesta munere mei sermonis indigeant, " sed ut ea, quæ miranda sunt, omnium voce prædicentur (19). ------ *We must not omit a Circumstance, which tends to the Honour of this venerable Man. It is related, that* Aurelian *had come to a Resolution, and had declared his Intention, of demolishing the City of* Tyana; *but that* Apollonius *of* Tyana, *an ancient Philosopher of great Renown and Authority, a true Friend of the Gods, and himself honoured as a Deity, appeared to him in his usual Form, as he retired into his Tent, addressed him thus in Latin, so as he be understood by a Native of* Pannonia. *Aurelian, if you desire to be victorious, think no more of the Destruction of my Fellow-Citizens.* Aurelian, *if you desire to rule, abstain from the Blood of the Innocent.* Aurelian, *if you would conquer, be merciful.* Aurelian *was acquainted with the Looks of this venerable Philosopher, and had seen his Image in several Temples. In the Suddenness of his Surprize, he vowed to erect a Temple and Statues to him, and altered his Resolution. This Account I have from Men of Credit; and have met with it in Books in the* Ulpian *Library, and am the more inclined to believe it on account of the Dignity of* Apollonius. *For was there ever any Person among Men more Holy, Venerable, Noble, and Divine, than this Person? He restored Life to the Dead; He did and spoke many Things beyond human Reach; which whoever would be informed of, may meet with Accounts of them in the* Greek *Histories of his Life. I myself propose to write a short Account of this great Man's Actions, if I live long enough, and this Philosopher himself shall permit me; not that his Actions want the Ornaments of my Words; but that such Wonders, as he performed, may be more generally known.*" The Words of *Lampridius*, concerning the manner of the Emperor *Severus*'s Worship, are no less worthy of a place here. He informs us, that, when his had not lain with his Wife the Night before, he began the Day with Acts of Devotion. He went, early in the

(19) Vopisc. in Aurelian. cap. 24.

Morning, into his Oratory, to practise religious Ceremonies in Honour of the Patrons he had made choice of; of which *Apollonius* was one. " Usus " vivendi eidem hic fuit: Primum ut, si facultas esset, id est si non cum uxore cubuisset, matutinis " horis in lararium suo (in quo & divos principes, " sed optimos electos & animas sanctiores, in queis & " Apollonium, &, quantum scriptor suorum temporum " dicit, Christum, Abraham, & Orpheum, & hujuscemodi deos habebat, ac majorum effigies) rem divinam faciebat (20) -- *The same Emperor's manner of Life was This. First, if he was duly prepared, that is, if he had not lain with his Wife, he performed, early in the Morning, religious Ceremonies, in his Chapel, in which he kept the Effigies of the best Emperors, and of Those, who had been the most remarkable for Sanctity; among which was* Apollonius, *and, if we may believe the Historian of his own Times,* Christ, Abraham, *and* Orpheus, *and the like kind of Gods, together with the Effigies of his Ancestors.*" *Eusebius* tells us, that, in his *Time*, there were Persons, who pretended to Inchantments, by invoking the Name of *Apollonius* (21).

(20) Lamprid. in Alexan. Im Severo, c. 29.
(21) In Hierocl. p. 476, 477. apud Tillemont, pag. 220.

[F] *His Reputation continued as long as Paganism.*] Mr *de Tillemont*, who denies this, alledges the Testimonies of *Lactantius*, and *Eusebius*. " From the beginning of the fourth Century, *says* he (22), no " Person whatever worshipped *Apollonius*; it is pretended, that the *Ephesians* still continued to reverence his Statue, under the Name " of *Hercules*, but not under his own; because it " is certain, that he was no more than a mere Man, " and an Impostor." *Eusebius* affirms, likewise, " that, at That Time, scarce any one acknowledged *Apollonius* as a God, or even as an extraordinary and wonderful Man, but only as a meer " Philosopher." Mr *de Tillemont* cites the third Chapter of the fifth Book of *Lactantius*, and the Four hundred sixty eighth Page of *Eusebius*'s Treatise against *Hierocles*. I confess, *Lactantius* supposes, that no one honoured *Apollonius* as a God; For he asks, " Cur igitur, ô delirum caput, nemo Apollonium pro " Deo colit? nisi forte tu solus, illo scilicet Deo dignus, cum quo te in sempiternum versus Deus puniet. ----- *Why therefore, O Madman, does no one honour* Apollonius *as a God? Unless, perhaps, You alone; a worthy Votary of such a Deity, together with whom The True God will punish you for ever.*" But he does not deny, what the Author, whom he confutes, had advanced, that a consecrated Statue of *Apollonius* was still honoured at *Ephesus*, under the Name of *Hercules*: " Simulacrum ejus sub Herculis Alexicaci nomine constitutum ab Ephesiis " etiam nunc honorari (23)." He thinks it sufficient, that *Apollonius* was not honoured under his own, but a borrowed Name; " Ideo alieni nominis titulo " affectavit divinitatem, quia suo nec poterat, nec " audebat. ----- *He, therefore, affected Divinity under a borrowed Name, because he neither could, nor dared, do it under his own.*" This is more subtle, than solid; for, when the *Ephesians* consecrated the Statue, they had no other Intention, than to honour *Apollonius*, and only made use of the Title of *Hercules* ἀποτρόπαιος, or *Alexicacus*, to denote, that *Apollonius* had delivered them from a Plague. It is probable there was no Artifice in this: *Apollonius* did not endeavour to conceal himself under a borrowed Name, for fear his own should raise Scruples in the Minds of the People. Here, then, is a fair Testimony produced by *Lactantius*, in proof of the Worship, which was still paid to our *Apollonius*, in the beginning of the fourth Century. But, with all the Respect due to this Father of the Church, I cannot persuade myself, that the Inhabitants of *Tyana* had discontinued their Veneration, or that the Images of *Apollonius* were removed out of all the Temples (24). I find, in *Eusebius*, that, in his Time, a Report was spread, that many things were performed, by invoking the Name of *Apollonius*. Αὐ] ίκα τῶν νῦν εἰσιν, οἳ περιέργους μηχανὰς τῇ τῦ ἀνδρὸς ἀνακινοῦμενοι προσηγορίᾳ καταεπλυνάτας λέγουσιν (25). Neque vero hodie quoque desunt, qui expertes se dicant ejus nomini invocato magicas inesse virtutes, ad superstitiosa quædam peragenda. He calls them

(22) In Hierocl. peri. In Alexan. Im Severo, c. 29.
(23) Lactan. Divin. Institut. l. 5. c. 3.
(24) See the Passage of Vopiscus, in the foregoing Remark.
(25) Euseb. in Hierocl. p. 541.

APOLLONIUS.

since lost [G]. Mention is made of another Philosopher, called likewise *Apollonius* of *Tyana* [H], who lived in the Reign of the Emperor *Adrian*. I know not of what Sect he was; but every one knows, that our *Apollonius* was a rigid *Pythagorean*. He made such an open Profession of his Belief of a *Metempsychosis*, that he caused a Lion to be adored, under pretence, that the Soul of *Amasis* (*l*) was united to the Body of That Beast (*m*). His Life is translated from the *Greek* of *Philostratus* (*n*) into *French* by *Blaise de Vigenere*, with a very ample Commentary by *Artus Thomas*, Lord of *Embry*, a *Parisian*. It is not long, since an *English* Translation of This Life, with Notes,

(*l*) *A King of Egypt.*
(*m*) Philostr. lib. 5. c. 15.

them magical or superstitious; but there can be no doubt, that many Pagans took them for real Miracles. I find, in St *Austin*, that, in his Time, the Christians were so pressed with the chimerical Parallel between the Miracles of *Apollonius*, and Those of JESUS CHRIST, and by the ridiculous Pretence, that the first equalled, or even surpassed, the latter, that they had recourse to this great Light of the Church for a Solution of this Difficulty. " Sed " tamen etiam ego in hac parte qui PLURIMIS, " quicquid rescripseris, PRO FUTURUM esse " confido, precator accesserim, ut ad ea VIGI- " LANTIUS respondere digneris, in quibus nihil " amplius Dominum, quam alii homines facere po- " tuerunt, fecisse vel gessisse mentiuntur. APOL- " LONIUM siquidem suum nobis & Apuleium alios- " que magicæ artis homines in medium proferunt, " quorum majora contendunt extitisse miracula (26). " ----- On this Occasion, I add my Request, that " you, whose Reply, whatever it be, will be of use " to many, would condescend to exert your utmost Efforts " in refuting the false Pretences of these Objectors, " who would place the Works of OUR LORD on a " Level with the Actions of meer Men. For they " produce against Him Their APOLLONIUS, and " Apuleius, and other Dealers in Magic, whose Mi- " racles they assert to have been greater than His." Then it was, that St *Austin* declared, what you have read in the Body of the Article (27), that *Apollonius Tyanæus* was superior to *Jupiter*; which, by the way, ought to put some modern Divines to the Blush, who will not allow, that the want of the Knowledge of God was a less Evil, than the Worship of the abominable Pagan Deities, who, in St. *Austin*'s Opinion, were even worse than Magicians. 'Quis au- " tem vel risu dignum non putet, quod APOLLO- " NIUM *& Apuleium cæterosque magicarum artium* " peritissimos conferre CHRISTO vel etiam præ- " ferre conantur, quamquam TOLERABILIUS fe- " rendum sit quando illos ei potius comparent quam " Deos suos: multo enim melior, quod fatendum est, " Apollonius fuit, quam tot stuprorum actor & per- " petrator, quem Jovem nominant (28). ----- But " who does not think it even Matter of Laughter, " that they should pretend to compare APOLLONIUS " and Apuleius, and others, skilful in Art Magic, " to CHRIST, and even to give them the Prefe- " rence; though the Comparison of such Persons with " CHRIST is more tolerable, than That of their " Gods: for we must confess, that Apollonius was " much better, than Their Jupiter, as they call him, " the Author and Perpetrator of so many Acts of " Lewdness." The same Father observes, that " the " Pagans, who laughed at the History of *Jonas*, " would have believed a like Adventure to be true, " if reported of *Apuleius*, or *Apollonius Tyanæus*, or " any of Those, to whom they gave the Name of " Magicians, or Philosophers." " *Si hoc quod de* " *Jona scriptum est, Apuleius Madaurensi, vel Apol-* " *lonio Tyanæo, fecisse diceretur, quorum multa* " *mira, nullo fideli auctore, jactitant* ------ *si de* " *istis ut dixi, quos Magos vel Philosophos laudabili-* " *ter nominant, tale aliquid narraretur, non jam in* " *buccis creparet risus, sed typhus* (29). Upon the whole, I find, that, in the beginning of the fifth Century, " *Eunapius* wrote, that *Apollonius* was not " so much a Philosopher, as something between a " God and a Man; and that *Philostratus* ought to " have entituled the History, which he wrote of " him, *The Descent of a God upon Earth* (30). Am I to blame then, in affirming, that *Apollonius*'s Honour continued as long as Paganism?

It remains only, that I answer *Eusebius*'s Authority, by which Mr *de Tillemont* endeavours to support himself. And this is easily done; since it is plain, from the Facts now alledged, that *Eusebius*

gives into an *Hyperbole*, which has not the least shadow of Truth. How can it be true, that, in *Eusebius*'s Time, no one did *Apollonius* the Honour to call him a Philosopher, when *Ammianus Marcellinus*, in the same Century, occasionally speaking of a Fountain, which was near *Tyana*, failed not to remember *Apollonius* with this Elogy, " Ubi amplif- " simus ille Philosophus *Apollonius* traditur natus (31). " ------ *Where the most celebrated Philosopher Apol-* " *lonius is reported have been born*." I should chuse, for the Honour of *Eusebius*, to say, that he was speaking of *Philostratus*; so that his meaning will be, that it is not necessary to refute at large the Dreams of *Philostratus*, since he is an Author of no Repute, and not so much as ranked in the Number of Philosophers. I confess there is some Difficulty in this Explication; but it is plain, that *Eusebius*'s Design was to attack the Phantom of *Philostratus*, and not the true *Apollonius*. Does he not declare, that he had always esteemed *Apollonius* as a learned Man, and allow, that he deserves to be ranked, with all imaginable Honour, among the Philosophers? That he only rejects the fabulous and supernatural Virtues, which *Philostratus*, and some other Panegyrists, ascribed to him, and that, in direct Opposition to *Philostratus*, he will shew, that *Apollonius*, as described by Him, is unworthy to be ranked, not only among the Philosophers, but even among Men of moderate Virtue; So far is he from coming into any Competition with JESUS CHRIST. Μόνην ἐπισκεψώμεθα τὴν τῦ Φιλοσράτυ γραφὴν δι ἧς εὑσυνέμεν ὡς ἐχ ὅτι γε ἐν φιλοσόφοις ἀλλ᾽ ὑδ᾽ ἐν ἐπιεικέσι καὶ μετρίοις ἀνδράσιν ἄξιον ἐγκρίνειν, ἐχ ὅπως τῳ σωτῆρι ἡμῶν Χεισῷ παραπιθέναι τὸν Ἀπολλώνιον (32). *Unam modo pensitemus Philostrati historiam, ex hac enim certis rationibus convincemus Apollonium non inter Philosophos locum, ac ne inter mediocris quidem ac usitatæ probitatis viros dignum sortiri, nedum sit ille Salvatori nostro ratione aliqua conferendus*.

[G] *He left some Works, which have been long since lost*.] He wrote four Books of *Judicial Astrology* (33), and a Treatise *On Sacrifices*, shewing what was to be offered to each Deity (34). This last Piece became very famous: *Eusebius* cites it (35): *Suidas* also mentions it, and adds to it a *Testament*, a *Collection of Oracles and Letters*, and *The Life of Pythagoras* (36). The *Theology*, of which *Eusebius* cites a Passage (37), is perhaps the same Piece, with the Treatise *On Sacrifices*. *Apollonius* wrote a great Number of *Letters*, some of which *Philostratus* has inserted in his History; all of them very short. The *Hymn on Memory* was not composed by *Apollonius*, as Mr *de Tillemont* pretends. In the eleventh Chapter of the first Book of *Philostratus*, pag. 18. I have not met with any such thing, there; but only, that *Apollonius*, at the Age of an hundred Years, had a better Memory, than *Simonides*; and that he often sung the Hymn, which *Simonides* had composed in the praise of Memory. *Suidas* reports this so confusedly, that he seems to say, that *Apollonius* composed This Piece. *König* was deceived by it. See the Forty ninth Page of his *Bibliotheca*. The *Testament*, mentioned by *Suidas* διαθήκη, is, without doubt, the same Book, which *Philostratus* cites in these Words: Καὶ διαθῆκαι δὲ τῷ Ἀπολλωνίῳ γεγράφαται παρ᾽ ἐν ὑπάρχει μαθεῖν ὡς ὑποθειάζων τὴν φιλοσοφίαν ἐγένετο (38). *Apollonius wrote likewise some Memoirs, from whence we may learn how rapturously fond he was of Philosophy*.

[H] *Mention is made of another Philosopher, called likewise* Apollonius *of* Tyana.] *Suidas* is the Author, who mentions him, on the Credit of *Agesiphon*, who wrote a Book concerning Persons of the same Name, περὶ ὁμωνύμων, *de homonymis*. This brings to my Mind, that a learned Man, whom I have already cited (39).

APOLLONIUS. APONA.

Notes, gave great Offence to pious Minds [*I*]. It has been condemned, prohibited, and anathematized, and not without Reason. I take notice of it in my Remarks. Had we what a cotemporary Philosopher, named *Euphrates*, satirically wrote against *Apollonius*, we should be furnished with an ample Detail of Scandal; for, when such Rivals once declare War against each other, they bring many Secrets to Light. *Philostratus* has reason to alledge This *Euphrates*'s Silence, as an Argument to convince those of Calumny, who reproached *Apollonius* with Unchastity, and boldly to maintain, that *Apollonius*, even in the Vigour of his Youth, triumphed over Nature, and always lived in a state of strict Continency (*o*). *Sidonius Apollinaris* has given us a Description of *Apollonius*, which represents him as the greatest of Heroes in Philosophy [*K*]. The Author of this Description does not forget to make his Excuses to the Catholic Church.

(*o*) Philostr. lib. I. cap. 8.

---

(39) Mr de Sallo. See Remark [F], of the Article ALLATIUS.

cited (39), questions, whether the Ancients wrote any Books, like those of *Leo Allatius, de Simeonibus, de Psellis*, &c. He ought not to have questioned it; for, besides *Agrespbon*, we can appeal to *Demetrius Magnes*. Some learned Men would add *Dionysius* of *Sinope*, and *Simaristus*; but they are mistaken. See the Remark [*B*], of the Article DEMETRIUS (MAGNES).

[*I*] *An English Translation of this Life, —— gave great Offence to pious Minds.*] The Author of this Translation proceeded no farther, than the third Book exclusively. If he had done nothing more than translate, there would have been no just Cause of Complaint; but to this Translation he has subjoined a great Number of Annotations, which he borrowed, for the most part, from a Manuscript of the famous *Baron Herbert*, a great Deist, if we may believe many Persons. They, who have read these Annotations, have assured me, that they are full of Poison; that they tend to destroy Revealed Religion, and to bring the Holy Scriptures into Contempt. The Author does not carry on this Design by Arguments, gravely and seriously proposed, but almost continually by prophane Jests, and little Subtilties; so that it was not without Reason, and Justice, that this Book, which was printed in *London*, in the Year 1680 (40), was prohibited under severe Penalties. This new Translator of *Philostratus* was an *English* Gentleman, whose Name was *Charles Blount*. In the Year 1693, he published a Treatise, the Title of which was, *The Oracles of Reason*, and accompanied it with some other small Pieces of the same Stamp. The same Year he died a tragical Death. He was greatly in Love with his Brother's Widow; and pretended, he might marry her without committing Incest; and even wrote a Treatise to prove it; but, seeing no likelihood of obtaining the Church's Consent, he fell into Despair, and killed himself. See the *History of the Works of the Learned* (41). To return: Mr *de Tillemont*, speaking of those, who had wrote the Life of *Apollonius*, stops at *Philostratus*. Let us advance farther. *Nicomachus*, who lived in the Reign of *Aurelian*, wrote the Life of *Apollonius*, on That, which *Philostratus* had composed; *Tascius Victorianus* wrote another upon That of *Nicomachus*. *Sidonius Apollina-

(40) The 7th of the Specifica- tion Year 1680. It must have been concealed for several Years; for it was not condemned till 1693.

(41) Month of November, 1693, pag. 135, 136.

ris wrote a third, and followed the Plan of *Victorianus*, rather than That of *Nicomachus* (42). We read, in *Suidas*, That *Soterichus*, a Native of *Oasis* in *Egypt*, had composed the Life of *Apollonius*. This Author lived in the Reign of *Aurelian*. I cannot imagine on what Ground *Savaron* builds, when he reckons *Plutarch* among those, who had written the Life of our *Apollonius* (43).

(42) Ex Sidonii Apollinaris Epist. 3, lib. 8.

[*K*] *Sidonius Apollinaris has given us a Description of* Apollonius, *which represents him as the greatest of Heroes in Philosophy*.] That every one may judge of this, let us here produce the Words of *Sidonius Apollinaris*. He had written the Life of *Apollonius*; and, sending it to a Counsellor of *Evarigus*, King of the *Goths*, he addresses him after this manner. " Lege virum (fidei Catholicæ pace præfata) in plurimis similem tui, id est, à divitiis ambitum, nec divitias ambientem; cupidum scientiæ, continentem pecuniæ; inter epulas abstemium, inter purpuratos linteatum, inter slabastra censorium: Concretum, hispidum, hirsutum, in medio nationum delibutarum; atque inter satrapas regum tiaratorum myrrhatos, pumicatos, malobatratos, venerabili squalore pretiosum. Cumque proprio nihil esus aut indutui de pecude conferret, regnis ob hoc, quæ pererravit, non tam suspicioni, quam fuisse suspectui: & fortuna regum sibi in omnibus obsecundante, illa tantum beneficia poscentem, quæ magè sit suetus, oblata præstare, quam sumere (44). —— *Read* (*by the Catholic Church's Permission*) *this Life of a Person, in many things not unlike yourself; that is, one courted by the Rich, but not courting Riches; covetous of Science, but moderate in his Desire of Wealth; at Banquets, abstemious; amidst those in Purple, habited himself in Linnen; amidst sweet Ointments and Perfumes, a rigid Censor of Manners; amidst a Race of Fops, rough and unpolished; and amidst perfumed and smooth Courtiers, valuable for his venerable Unattire. And, as he was not indebted to his own Flock either for Food or Raiment, he was the Admiration, rather than Jealousy, of the Countries he travelled over; and, having the Fortunes of Kings ever at his Command, he asked no other Favours, than such as he was wont rather to bestow, when offered, than receive.*"

(43) Savaro, in Sidon. Apollin. pag. 436.

(44) Sidon. Apollin. Epist. 3, lib. 8. pag. 486.

(*a*) Some call him Peter d'Avano.

APONA (*a*) (PETER *of*) in *Latin* PETRUS APONENSIS, or APONUS, one of the most famous Philosophers, and Physicians, of his Times, was born in the Year 1250 (*b*), in a Village situated four Miles from *Padua*. He studied a long time at *Paris*, where he was promoted to the Degrees of Doctor in Philosophy and Physic [*A*]. I cannot tell whether he died very rich; but I have read

(*b*) Jacobus Philippus Tomasinus, Elog. Illustr. Vir. p. 22.

[*A*] *He studied a long time at Paris, where he was promoted to the Degrees of Doctor in Philosophy and Physic.*] *Naudé* takes notice of this, in a Speech, in which he extols the ancient Glory of the University of *Paris*, as much as possible. Let us produce his Words at length, because they incidently inform us, that *Peter* of *Apona* composed That great Work at *Paris*, which procured him the Appellation of *The Reconciler.* " Prodeat tandem *Petrus Aponensis* ab " insigni libro, quem, dum vestras scholas frequenta- " ret, edidit, Conciliatoris nomen adeptus: Cui " latebat in *Italia*, nulli propè cognita, nullis aliis " disciplinis, nullis artibus, nedum propriis, exculta, " nulla denique, vel linguarum cognitione, vel Phi- " losophiæ nitore, decorata Medicina; cum ecce tu- " telaris illius genius, ex *Aponensis* balnei pago, I-

" taliam ab ignorantiæ barbarie, velut alter Camil- " lus *Romam* à *Gallorum* obsidione, liberaturus, di- " ligenter inquirit, ubinam gentium humaniores li- " teræ felicius excolerentur, Philosophia subtilius " traderetur, Medicina purius & solidius edocere- " tur: cumque rescivisset uni *Lutetiæ* hanc laudem " deberi, in eam statim involat, illius gremio totum " se tradit, Philosophiæ, Medicinæque mysteriis se- " dulò incumbit, gradum & lauream in utraque con- " sequitur, utramque postea celeberrime docet, & " post diuturnam annorum moram divitiis vestris " onustus, imo Philosophus, Medicus, Astrologus, " Mathematicus suæ tempestatis præstantissimus, in " patriam suam revertitur, & primus omnium Scar- " dæoni viri gravissimi judicio, synceram Philoso- " phiam, & Medicinam illi restituit. Unde gratitu-

APONA.

read, that he made his Patients pay exorbitant Fees [B]. He was suspected of Magic, and prosecuted on that Account by the Inquisition [C]; and it is probable, that,

" dinis ergo compellandus venit, & à vobis merita
" gratia prosequendus Michael, Angelus Blondus Medicus Romanus, quòd superiori sæculo Aponensis
" vestri *Conciliationes Physiognomicas* elegantioribus
" typis demandare volens, cum vidisset eas à doctore
" vestro, Parisiis, & in Facultate vestra fuisse elaboratas, has idcirco vestri Collegii nomine & auspicio in lucem prodire voluerit (1). —— *Let us next
" produce* Peter *of* Apona, *called* The Reconciler,
" *on account of the famous Book, which he published
" during his Residence in your University. It is certain, that Physic lay buried in Italy, scarce known
" to any one, uncultivated, and unadorned; when lo!
" it's Tutelar Genius, a Villager of* Apona, *destined to free Italy from Barbarism and Ignorance, at
" once* Camillus *freed* Rome *from the Seige of the
" Gauls, made diligent Enquiry, in what part of the
" World polite Learning was most happily cultivated,
" Philosophy most subtily handled, and Physic taught
" with the greatest Purity and Solidity; and, being
" assured, that* Paris *alone laid claim to this Honour, thither he presently flies; gives himself up
" wholly to her Tutelage; applies himself diligently
" to the Mysteries of Philosophy and Medicine; obtains
" a Degree and the Laurel in both; afterwards
" teaches them both with great Applause; and, after
" a stay of many Years, loaden with the Wealth acquired among you, and become the most famous Philosopher, Physician, Astrologer, and Mathematician,
" of his Times, returns to his own Country; where,
" in the Opinion of the judicious* Scardeon, *he was
" the first Restorer of true Philosophy and Physic.
" Gratitude, therefore, calls upon you to acknowledge
" your Obligations to* Michael Angelus Blondus, *a
" Physician of* Rome, *who, in the last Century, undertaking to publish the* Conciliationes Physiognomicæ *of your Aponensian Doctor, and finding, that
" they had been composed at* Paris, *and in your University, chose to publish them in the Name, and under
" the Patronage, of your Society*."

[B] *He made his Patients pay exorbitant Fees.*] We have no account of what he exacted for the Visits he made, in the Place of his Residence; but it is affirmed, that he would not go out of Town to visit the Sick, under an Hundred and fifty *Livres* a Day (2). They add (3), that, being sent for by Pope *Honorius* IV, he demanded *Four hundred Ducats* a Day. Thus we find in the Abridgment of his Life, inserted in the new Edition of *Vander Linden, de scriptoribus Medicis*. *Camerarius* relates the same thing (4), but without naming the Pope, who sent for this Physician. He does not observe the same Silence in relation to the Place, where *Peter of Apona* resided; he says it was at *Bologne*. He mentions, indeed, Pope *Honorius* IV, but says, that the Physician, who exacted so vast a Sum from this Pope, was not *Peter of Apona*. These are his Words. " In the Days of
" our Fathers, there was a Physician of *Florence*,
" whose Name was *Thadeus*, who acquired such a
" Reputation, that, by his Practice out of Town,
" he gained fifty Crowns a Day; and, being sent
" for by Pope *Honorius* IV, received an hundred
" Crowns a Day from him; insomuch, that, at his
" return from *Rome*, he brought away Ten thou" sand Crowns (5)." If he had consulted Chronology, he would not have said *in the Days of our Fathers*: for this Pope was elected in the Year 1285, and died in the Year 1287. *Lancelot de Perouse*, quoting *Ciaconius* (6), says, that this *Thadeus*, a *Florentine*, and Professor at *Bologne*, made the Messengers of Pope *Honorius* IV promise, that he should be paid an hundred Crowns a Day; and adds, that this Journey was worth to him Ten thousand Crowns; but observes, that others write, that *Peter of Apona* had Four hundred Crowns a Day from this Pope (7). He had said, that this *Peter* never went out of Town to Visit a Patient under a Fee of fifty Florins. You will find, in the *Theatrum of Paul Freherus*, that he was Professor of Physic at *Bologne*, and that he was sent for from all parts of *Italy*, though he exacted fifty Florins a Day (8). You will find, likewise, that he bargained, with *Honorius* IV, for the Sum of an Hundred Florins a Day, and that, having cured this Pope, he received a thousand Crowns. These are very different Accounts.

[C] *He was suspected of Magic, and prosecuted on that account by the Inquisition.*] This Suspicion continues still; nay, many do more than suspect, and are even firmly persuaded of it. " The general
" Opinion of almost all Authors is, that he was the
" greatest Magician of his Time; that, by means of
" seven familiar Spirits, which he kept inclosed in
" Crystal, he had acquired the Knowledge of the
" seven liberal Arts; that, like another *Pasetes*, he
" had the Art of making the Money, which he
" had spent, return into his Pocket (9)." The Author, who furnishes me with these Words, adds,
" That it was certain he was accused of Magic, in
" the eightieth Year of his Age (10), and that,
" dying in the Year 1305 (11), before his Trial
" was over, he was yet condemned, as *Castellan*
" reports *, to the Fire; and that a Bundle of
" Straw, or Osier, representing his Person, was publickly burnt at *Padua*; that, by so rigorous an
" Example, and by the fear of incurring a like Penalty, they might suppress the reading of three superstitious and abominable Books, which he had
" composed on this Subject; the first of which was
" the *Heptameron*, now printed at the end of the
" first Volume of the Works of *Agrippa*; the second,
" That, which *Trithemius* calls *Elucidarium Necromanticum Petri de Albano*: and a third, called by
" the same Author, *Liber experimentorum mirabilium
" de annulis secundum 28 mansiones Lunæ* (12)."
These seem to be strong Proofs; yet *Naudé* lays no Stress upon them. He refutes them immediately by observing, that *Peter of Apona* was a Man of prodigious Wit and Learning, in an Age of Darkness; which was sufficient to render him suspected of Magic; being, besides, much addicted to curious and divinatory Sciences. " He was one, *says he* (13),
" who appeared as a Prodigy and Miracle, amidst
" the Ignorance of that Age; and who, besides his
" Skill in Languages, and Physic, had carried his
" Enquiries so far into those less common Sciences,
" that, after having given most ample Proofs, by
" his Writings concerning Physiognomy, Geomancy,
" and Chiromancy, what he was able to perform in
" each of these, he quitted them all, together with
" his youthful Curiosity, to addict himself wholly
" to the Study of Philosophy, Physic, and Astrology; which Studies proved so advantageous to him,
" that, not to speak of the two first, which introduced him to the Favour of all the Popes and
" sovereign Pontiffs of his Time, and acquired him
" the Reputation, which he enjoys at present among
" learned Men; it is certain, that he was a great
" Master in the latter, as appears not only by the
" Astronomical Figures, which he caused to be
" painted in the great Hall of the Palace of *Padua*, and the Translations he made of the Books of
" *Rabbi Abraham Aben Ezra*, added to those which
" he himself composed on critical Days, and the
" Improvement of Astronomy, but by the Testimony likewise of the renowned Mathematician *Regio-Montanus*, who made a fine Panegyric on him,
" in quality of an Astrologer, in the Oration, which
" he delivered publickly at *Padua*, when he explained there the Book of *Alfraganus*." *Naudé* observes afterwards, that *Peter of Apona* was very much addicted to Astrology; whence it is, that many Authors maintain " a quite contrary Opinion to the
" preceding; to wit, that he did not undergo this
" Sentence on the Score of Magic, but because he
" endeavoured to account for the wonderful Effects,
" which often happen in Nature, by the Influences
" of the Celestial Bodies, without attributing them
" to Angels or Dæmons. Which is very evident
" from the Collection, which *Symphorian Champier* *
" has made, of the Passages of his Differences, which
" must not be read without Caution; and from the peremptory Authority of *Francis Picus*, who, speaking of them, says expresly †, Ab omnibus ferme
" creditus est Magus; verum constat quam opposuum dogma ei aliquando tributum sit, quem etiam
" hæreseum inquisitores vexaverunt, quasi nullos esse
" Dæmones crediderit. —— *It was the settled
" Opinion of every one, that he was a Magician:
" but it is certain, that the quite contrary Opinions
" were ascribed to him; since he was even accused of
" Heresy*

Side notes:

(1) Gabriel Naudé, de Antiquitate Scholæ Medicæ Parisiensis, pag. 44, &c.

(2) Cf. Mercklin. in Lindenio renovato. pag. 878.

(3) Id. ibid.

(4) Camerarius, Meditations Historiques, Tom. I. cap. 4.

(5) Id. ibid.

(6) In vita Honorii IV.

(7) Secondo Lancelot da Perugia, l'Hosgidi. Par. II. Disinganno 13. pag. 37.

(8) Freher, in Theatro Viror. Illustr. pag. 1209. Iste est Bernardus Scardonius, lib. 2, classe 9, Historiæ Patavinæ.

(9) Naudé's Apology for great Men accused of Magic, cap. 14, pag. 380.

(10) Tho' it is in *f. lin.* See Remark [F].

(11) This is *literis*; Jul. v. See the same Remark.

* In vitis Illustr. Medicorum.

(12) Naudé, ubi supra, pag. 380.

(13) Id. ib. pag. 382.

(14) This appears from all his Works, and especially in the *Liber Duportatum* of his Conciliator. Ed. ib. pag. 384.

† III. Parte, lib. Cribrat.

† Lib. 2, de Prænot. cap. 7.

A P O N A.   385

that, if he had lived to the End of his Trial, he would have suffered, in Person, what he was sentenced to suffer in Effigie after his Death. We shall relate (c), what his Apologists observe, that His Body, being privately taken out of it's Grave, by his Friends, escaped the Vigilance of the Inquisitors, who would have condemned it to be burnt [D]. He was removed from Place to Place, and at last deposited in St *Augustin's* Church, without Epitaph, or any other Mark of Honour (d). His Accusers ascribed inconsistent Opinions to him; they charge him with being a Magician, and yet with denying the Existence of Devils [E]. He had such an Antipathy to Milk, that the very seeing any one drink it turned his Stomach (e). He died

(c) *In Remark* [C].

(d) Tomasin. Elog. Vir. Illustr. pag. 24.

(e) Mercklinu s, in Lindenio renovato, pag. 879. Freherus, in Theatro, pag. 1103: *He cites* Marcellus Donatus, *and* Math. de Gradibus.

" Heresy by the Inquisition, as one, who opposed the " Doctrine of Spiritual Beings. To which may be " added, that, upon this account, *Baptista Mantuanus* ‖ calls him, Virum magnæ, sed nimium audaciæ temerariæque doctrinæ. ———— One, whose Doctrine was great, but too bold and rash; That *Cassmannus* ‡ reckons him in the Number of those, who ascribed all Miracles to Nature, and that *le Loyer* affirms, in his Apparitions **, that he laughed at Sorcerers, and their Nocturnal Meetings: Whence one would wonder, why the same Authors reckon him frequently among the Inchanters and Magicians; if it were not the Practice of those, who write on such Subjects, so to swell their Books, by copying all they find in Authors, that it is with Difficulty they observe the Precept of the Poet;

‖ Lib. 1. de Patientia. cap. 3.

† *Angelogr.* Parte II. cap. 21. Quæst. 2.

** Book 4, chap. 3.

(15) Horat. Ars Poet.

Primo ne medium, medio ne discrepet imum (15).

All should be uniform and of a Peice.

After this, his Apologist declares, That " he can justify him both from the Crimes of Magic and Atheism, " as well by the Testimony, which the illustrious and religious *Frederick*, Duke of *Urbin*, has been pleased to give to his Merit, by placing his Statue among those of the famous Men, which are to be seen in his Citadel; as also by the public Attestation of the City of *Padua*, which has set up his Effigies over the Gate of it's Townhouse, with those of *Livy*, *Albertus*, and *Julius Paulus*, and with this Inscription on the Base. " Petrus Aponus Patavinus Philosophiæ Medicinæque scientissimus, ob idque Conciliatoris nomen adeptus; Astrologiæ vero adeo peritus, ut in Magiæ suspicionem inciderit, falsoque de hæresi postulatus, absolutus fuerit (16). ———— Petrus Aponus of *Padua*, *very learned in Philosophy and Physic*; *whence he had the Name of* The Reconciler; *and so expert in Astrology, that he was suspected of Magic, and being accused of Heresy, was acquitted.* ———— But, adds he (17), fully to expose the Falshood of these Objections, we may reply to " what *Ludovigius* †† has said of the seven Spirits, which taught him the seven Liberal Arts, that this fabulous Report took it's Rise from what the same *Peter of Apona* ‖‖ affirms, after *Albumazar*, that the Prayers, which are made to God, when the Moon is in Conjunction with *Jupiter*, in the Head of the Dragon, are infallibly heard; and that, having requested for himself, (to use his own Terms) sapientiam à primo, visus est sibi in illa amplius proficere. Upon which account, many Authors justly deride him for so indiscreetly disowning all his Watchings and Labours, and for ascribing his Knowledge wholly to the Superstition of this Prayer; which cannot but be vain, and fruitless, in whatever Sense it be taken. For if you say, it is addressed to the Planets, it is gross Stupidity to believe, that they can hear it; if to God, I would willingly know, whether he was deaf before this Conjunction, or whether he will not hear our Prayers without it, or whether it can force and necessitate him to condescend to the Petitions, which are then made to him. And hence it is, that *John Picus* ‡‡, speaking of this new Solomon, had reason to say, Consulerem Petro isti ut totum quod profecit suæ potius induxstriæ ingenioque acceptum referret, quam Joviæ illi suæ supplicationi. ———— *I would advise this Peter to confess himself indebted, for all his Knowledge, to his own Industry and Genius, rather than to this Planetary Prayer.* It may be said, likewise, in answer to the Proofs, which are brought for the

(16) *This Inscription is* in *Tomasin*, in Elog. Illustr. viror. pag. 23.

(17) Naudé *ubi supra*, pag. 388.

†† Dæmonomagie, Quæst. 16.

‖‖ Differentia CLVI.

‡‡ Lib. 4. adverf. Astrolog. cap. 8.

" three Books, published under his Name, that " they are no less falsely ascribed to him, than many " others are to almost all other great Wits; witness " *Trithemius's* * not allowing them to be genuine, " on account of the many Fables, which have been " forged, in relation to this Author; and his having " said before, in his Catalogue of Ecclesiastical Writers, that he did not believe what was said of the Magic Art of *Petrus Aponensis*, because he had never seen any Book of his on this Subject. " If to this you will farther add the Silence of all the Librarians, and the Confirmation, which *Symphorian Champier* † gives to this Authority of *Trithemius*, when he affirms, that he had never seen any of his magical Books, excepting only some Disputations, in which he treats of it incidentally; I believe nothing can prevent our acknowledging his Innocence, and supposing, with the better Sort, that all the Suspicions of Magic Art, which have been thrown upon him, proceed, as from their true Spring and Original, from the Power, which he attributes to it, in the CLVI Disputation of his *Conciliator*, and from the Predictions, which he might make by Virtue of Astrology; on which, by Length of Time, All These Fables and Chimera's have been grafted; according to the true Observation of *Propertius*.

* Antipoli, lib. 1. cap. 3.

† Tractat. 4, lib. de claris Medicinæ Scriptoribus.

Omnia post obitum pingit majora vetustas *.

* Eleg. 2. lib. 3.

Time magnifies each Object, after Death.

Remark the following Errors of Mr *de Clavigni de Sainte Honorine*. He pretends, that the *Effigies of* Peter of Apona, *made by Order of the Duke of* Urbin, *stands in the Market-Place of* Padua, *with Those of* Livy, Albertus, *and* Julius Paulus, *and that the Inscription contains* Astrologiæ adeo peritus, ut in magiæ suspicionem venerit (18). I. The Statue, under which these Words are inscribed, is not in the Market-Place of *Padua*, but over one of the Gates of the Town-house. *In Una Portarum Prætorii Patavini* (19). II. The Statue, which the Duke of *Urbin* caused to be erected, was not set up in *Padua*, but in the Castle of This Duke. III. The Words, which Mr *de Clavigni* mentions, are not on it's Pedestal. See TOMASINI (20).

(18) Clavigni de St. Honorine, au Ecclef. *des Illustres* Savans pour pels, pag. 101, 102.

(19) Tomas. Illustr. viror. pag. 23.

(20) Ibid.

[D] *The Inquisitors, who would have condemned his Body to be burnt.*] *Peter of Apona*, being accused of Magic and Heresy, died during his Trial, and was buried in the Church of St *Antony*. All the Zealous were scandalized at it: The Inquisitors continued the Process, and, having convicted him, by his Writings, of Impiety, they condemned his Body to the Flames; but, when they could not find it, they ordered his Effigies to be publickly burnt. This is what we read in *Spondanus* (21). But how can we reconcile this with the Inscription, which the Magistrates of *Padua* caused to be put under the Statue of This Physician, and in which they declare, that he was acquitted. *Petrus Romauldus* reports, that the Inquisitors, having publickly read the Sentence of Condemnation against *Peter of Apona*, caused his Effigie to be burnt. He observes likewise, that they could not find his Body; *his Concubine* Marlette *having privately taken him out of his Grave by Night, and hid him a ruinous Sepulchre* (23).

(21) Spondanus Annal. Ecclesiad ann. 1316, n. 8. *He cites* Scardeon. Hist. Patavin. lib. 2, claff. 9.

(22) Ibid.

(23) Ye Romuald, Journal Chronologique. Decemb. 31. *He cites* Bernard Scandero, doubt, Bernard Scardeon.

[E] *They charged him with being a Magician, and yet with denying the Existence of Devils.*] We have seen (24) what Advantage his Apologist makes of this Contradiction; but he ought to have taken notice, that *Bodin* ranks *Peter of Apona* among those Sorcerers, who, to elude judicial Proceedings, maintain, that all that is said of Devils, and Magic, is a Chimera. *Bodin* declares, that he wrote his Book

(24) *In Remark* [C].

of

APONA. APROSIO.

died in the Year 1316, in the Sixty sixth Year of his Age [F]. One of his principal Books was That, to which he gave the Title of *Conciliator*. They tell a very ridiculous Story of him; namely, that, having no Well in his own House, and a Neighbour forbidding his Servant Maid to fetch any more Water at His Well; he caused the Devils to remove his Neighbour's Well into the Street (*f*). He had much better have employed his Devils in making a Well to his own House, and stopping up his Neighbour's, or at least in removing his Neighbour's Well into his own Yard, rather than into the Street.

(*f*) Tomazo Garſoni, Piazza univerſale di tutte le Profeſſioni, diſcorſo 135 fol. 365. verſo.

(2) Bodin's Preface to his Demonomanie des Sorciers, pag. 5. See alſo chap. 5. pag. 71.

of the *Demonomania* of Sorcerers, among other Reaſons, "to ſerve as an Anſwer to thoſe, who endea-
"vour, by printed Books, as far as poſſible, to ex-
"cuſe Sorcerers; inſomuch that it ſeems as if they
"were influenced by the Devil himſelf, to publiſh
"theſe fine Books; ſuch was *Peter of Apona*, a Phy-
"ſician, who endeavoured to demonſtrate, that there
"were no Spirits; and yet it was afterwards affirmed,
"that he was one of the greateſt Sorcerers of *Ita-
"ly* (25)."

(26) Tomaſini, in Elog. Vicor. Illuſtr. pag. 22.

[F] *He died in the Year 1316, in the Sixty ſixth Year of his Age*] So we read, in an Inſcription mentioned by *Tomaſini* (26). If this be true, it muſt be confeſſed, that *Naudé* is miſtaken, when he ſays, that *Peter of Apona*, being accuſed at the Age of eighty Years, died in the Year 1305. *Freherus* ſays the ſame thing, upon the Authority of *Bernardin Scardeon* (27). Let us obſerve, likewiſe, that *Geſner* is miſtaken in

(27) Paulus Freher. in Theatro, pag. 209.

making *Peter of Apona* flouriſh in the Year 1320 (28). *Konig* has copied This Error (29). But Father *Rapin* is much more groſly miſtaken than any of them, when he places him in the ſixteenth Century. "Peter of
"*Apona*, ſays he (30), a Phyſician of *Padua*, who
"flouriſhed under *Clement* VII, debauched his Ima-
"gination ſo far by reading the *Arabian* Philoſo-
"phers, and by too frequent poring on the Aſtro-
"logy of *Alfraganus*, that he was put into the In-
"quiſition on Suſpicion of Magic." *Voſſius* has followed *Geſner*, and makes an Obſervation, which deſerves to be conſidered. He ſays, that *Peter of Apona* ſent his Book *de Medicina omnimoda* to Pope *John* XXII, who was elected in the Year 1316, and held the Chair ſeventeen Years (31). By this we know the Age of This Phyſician. But, if the Year 1316 was That of his Death, the Concluſion is not juſt, nor does it acquit *Voſſius* of an Error.

(28) Geſner, in Bibliotheca, fol. 544.

(29) Konig, Bibl. vet. & nova, pag. 49.

(30) Rapin, Reflex. ſur la Philoſophie, n. 22. pag. 360.

(31) Voſſius de Scient. Mathem. pag. 181.

APROSIO (ANGELICO) born at *Vintimiglia*, on the River of *Genoa*, the Twenty ninth of *October* 1607, was well eſteemed among the Learned, and wrote a great Number of Books. His Family produced ſeveral learned Men (*a*). He was but Fifteen Years of Age, when he entered himſelf in the Order of the *Auguſtins*; where his Abilities procured him the Office of Vicar-General of the Congregation of our Lady of Conſolation at *Genoa* (*b*). When he had finiſhed his Studies, he was thought ſufficiently qualified to teach others; accordingly he taught Philoſophy for Five Years, and afterwards travelled into ſeveral Parts of *Italy*; and, in the Year 1639, fixed his Reſidence at *Venice*, in St *Stephen*'s Convent, where he taught polite Literature (*c*). One thing, which contributed very much to his Renown, was the *Bibliotheque* of the *Auguſtins* of *Vintimiglia*, which was intirely his own Work, and a ſingular Proof of his Love of Books, and the Care he took to underſtand them thoroughly (*d*). He publiſhed a Book concerning this *Bibliotheque*, which is much eſteemed by the Curious [*A*]. Beſides he took great Pleaſure in diſguiſing himſelf under fictitious Names in the Front of his Works. Perhaps he durſt not write, in his own Name, on Matters ſo little conformable to a Religious Life, as the Conteſts

(*a*) See the following Article.

(*b*) Michel Juſtiniani, Scrittori Liguri, pag. 63.

(*c*) Philipp Elſſius, in Encomiaſtico Auguſtiniano, apud Juſtiniani, pag. 67.

(*d*) Raffael Soprani, li Scrittori dell' la Liguria, pag. 21.

[*A*] *He publiſhed a Book concerning this Bibliotheque, which is much eſteemed by the Curious.*] Mr *Morhof* had heard much talk of this Book, but did not know, that it was printed. He mentions it in ſeveral Parts of his *Polyhiſtor* (1), publiſhed in the Year 1688; but always as one, who believed, that this Piece had not yet appeared from the Preſs. It is, nevertheleſs, certain, that the *Bibliotheca Aproſiana* was printed at *Bologne*, in the Year 1673; and that *Martin Fogelius* (2), Profeſſor at *Hamburgh*, had a Copy of it, as Mr *Morhof* might have ſeen in the Catalogue of That Profeſſor's Books; for he cites this Catalogue (3), which was printed in the Year 1678. This is what *Placcius* obſerves in his *Invitatio Amica*, publiſhed at *Hamburgh*, in the Year 1689. He adds, that he has mentioned this Work of *Aproſio* among his Pſeudonymous Pieces (4), and refers us to the Annotations on the Catalogue of *Rhodius* (5). In Effect, he informs us (In the One hundred and fiftieth Page of his Pſeudonymous Pieces, that he was informed, by a Letter from Mr *Magliabecchi* to *Martin Vogelius*, that *Aproſio*, diſguiſed under the Name of *Cornelio Aſpaſio Antivigilmi trai i Vagabondi di Tabbia detto L'Aggirato*, had publiſhed a Book in 12mo, in the Year 1673, intituled *Bibliotheca Aproſiana*, *paſſa tempo Autonnale*. In the Annotations on the Catalogue of *Rhodius*, there is a Doubt raiſed on what *Scaevenius* had ſaid, that *Aproſio* had compoſed a Book entituled, *Bibliotheca Apocrypborum*, in which he reſtored many Pieces to their true Authors (6). The Reaſon of this Doubt is, that the Book, intituled *Bibliotheca Apocrypborum*, is not to be found in the Catalogues of the Works of *Aproſio*, but only the *Bibliotheca Aproſia*. Now it is ſuppoſed, that *Scaevenius* might, by a natural Miſtake, metamorphoſe *Aproſia* into *Apocrypha*. It is ſomething ſtrange, that Father

(1) Pag. 38, 59, 144.

(2) Or Vogelius.

(3) Polyhiſt. pag. 37.

(4) N. 74.

(5) Pag. 27, 28.

(6) See Remark [D].

Oldoini has not mentioned the *Bibliotheca Aproſiana*, *paſſa tempo Autonnale*, ſince he did not publiſh his *Athenaeum Liguſticum* 'till the Year 1680. It is true, he places the *Bibliotheca Aproſiana & Antiquitates Abantiſmilmenſes* among the Works of *Aproſio*; but in ſuch a manner, as to perſuade us, that this Work had never been printed. Mr *Teuſſer*, in the Year 1686, leaves more room for doubt, than for deciding any thing in this Matter (7). Mr *Morhof* obſerves, that Mr *Leti* quotes as an Author, who has cited the ſecond Volume of the *Bibliotheca Aproſiana*. "Pro-
"ducit Idem Leti, ex Abbate Libanoro, pag. 379,
"locum quo totus ſecundus Bibliothecae Aproſianae
"citatur, quo multi continentur ab Hieron. Sava-
"norola manuſcripti libri (8).——*The ſame* Leti *pro-
"duces a Paſſage, from the Abbot* Libanorus, *p. 379.
"where the ſecond Volume of the* Bibhotheca Aproſiana
"*is cited, in which are contained many manuſcript
"Works of* Jerome Savanorola." This Citation of *Leti* is very juſt; and for this, and other Reaſons, I am ſtrongly perſuaded, that *Morhof* does not alledge the *Italia regnante* on the Credit of others, but that he had read it himſelf. How comes it, then, that he does not know, that the *Bibliotheca Aproſiana* was printed at *Bologne*, by the *Manoleſſi*, in the Year 1673, in 12mo? Does not Mr *Leti* poſitively affirm it, in the Three hundred ſeventy ſeventh Page of the fourth Part of his *Italia regnante*, and does he not cite ſufficiently long Paſſages out of This Work of *Aproſio*? He adds, that the Author, having carried on the Relation of his own Life as far as the Two hundred ſixty ſecond Page, mentions afterwards, to the Page 666, ſeveral Authors, who had given in their Works to him (9); and that this firſt Volume contains only the Writers, whoſe Names begin either with the Letters A, B, or C.
He

(7) Catalog. Auctor. Bibliothecar. pag. 18.

(8) Morhof. Polyhiſt. pag. 38.

(9) Narrantes la ſua vita e con l'inſcritti varie curioſità mentovando A. tomo ad A. mici ſuoi. Leti, Ital. Regn. Parte IV. pag. 378.

APROSIO.

tests between the Wits about the *Adonis* of the Cavalier *Marini* [B], or such like Matters [C]. Or, perhaps, he was naturally fond of inventing different Allusions, and in puzzling those, who are eager to unmask a disguised Author. He loved this Employ well enough himself [D]. Be that as it will, if you consult the Authors, who have given us a Catalogue of the *Ligurian* Writers (*e*), you will find, by the Titles of his Works, that he gives himself an hundred fictitious Names, sometimes That of *Masoto Galistoni*, sometimes That of *Carlo Galistoni*, sometimes That of *Scipio Glareano*, sometimes That of *Sapricio Saprici*, and at other times That of *Oldauro Stioppio*, &c. His Life is to be met with in the Work intituled *Bibliotheca Aprosiana*. Several Authors have given him great Commendations; and some perhaps have exceeded the Bounds of Reason (*f*). *He was admitted, among other Academies, into That of the Incogniti of Venice*; as appears by the Book [E] intituled, *Le Glorie de gli Incogniti, overo gli Huomini illustri dell' Academia de' i Signiori Incogniti di Venetia*;—— *The Glory of The Incogniti, or the Illustrious Men of the Academy of the Incogniti at Venice*; where his Elogy appears at large. He was living in the Year 1680, when *Oldoini* published his *Athenæum Lygusticum*.

He believes, that the following Volumes will speedily be printed; but he had been assured, that the second was not; from whence he concludes, that Father *Libanori*, who quotes it, had only seen it in Manuscript (10). This Work of Mr *Leti* was printed in the Year 1676.

[B] *He durst not write in his own Name ---- concerning the Contests between the Wits about the Adonis of the Cavalier Marini*] The Cavalier *Stigliani*, having published the Book of the *Orbiale*, or *The Spectacle*, which is a severe Censure of the *Adonis*, found himself attacked on all sides (11). It appeared plainly, upon this Occasion, how much *Italy* was infatuated with the *Adonis*; They run to this Controversy as it were to put out a Fire: But, among the many Persons, who took Pen in Hand in Defence of the Cavalier *Marini*, none *shewed* more Zeal for the Adonis, nor more Heat against the Enemies of That Poem, than Father Aprosio de Vintimiglia, Hermit of St Augustin (12). He published the *Occhiale Stritolato di Scipio Glareano per risposta al Signor Cavaliere Fra Tomaso Stigliani* (13). - - - - - *La Sferza poëtica di Sapricio Saprici, lo scantonata Accademico Heteroclito, per risposta alla prima censura dell' Adone del Cavalier Marino, fatta dall Cavalier Tomaso Stigliani* (14) — *Del Veratro, Apologia di Sapricio Saprici, per risposta alla seconda censura dell' Adone del Cavalier Marino, fatta dal Cavaliere Fra Tomaso Stigliani.* —— *The Spectacles broke to pieces of Scipio Glareano, in Answer to Father Thomaso Stigliani.* —— *The Poëtical Whip of Sapricio Saprici, in Answer to the Censure of the Adonis of the Cavalier Marini, made by the Cavalier Tomaso Stigliani.* —— *Hellebore &c. An Apology of Sapricio Saprici, in Answer to a second Censure of the Adonis of the Cavalier Marini, made by the Cavalier Tomaso Stigliani.* This Work is divided into two Treatises (15); it was Hellebore given in two Doses. He had wrote against the same *Stigliani*, *Il Vaglio Critico di Masoto Galistoni da Terama sopra il mondo nuovo del Cavalier Frà Tomaso Stigliani da Matera* (16). —— *Il Burato*, Replica di Carlo Galistoni al Molino del Sig. Carlo Stigliani (17). —— *The Poëtical Sieve* &c. and *The Bolting-Cloth* &c. Observe, that *Masoto Galistoni da Terama* is the Anagram of *Tomaso Stigliani da Matera*; and that, instead of putting in the Title in *Trevigi per Girolamo Righettini*, it is put in *Rostoch per Willerno Wallop*, because this *Righettini* was a Bookseller of small Repute. *Aprosio* mentions this in the Hundred and twelfth and thirteenth Pages of the *Bibliotheca Aprosiana* (18).

[C] *Or such like Matters*] I do not think, that the Disputes, concerning the *Adonis* of the Cavalier *Marini*, were more foreign to a Monastic Profession, than the following Works. *Annotationi di Oldauro Scioppio all' Arte degli Amanti dell' Illustrissimo Signor Pietro Michele Nobile Veneto* (19). —— *Lo Scudo di Rinaldo, overo lo specchio del disinganno, Opera di Scipio Glareano* (20). —— *Le Bellezze della Belisa Tragedia dell' Illustrissimo Signor D. Antonio Muscettola, abbozzate da Oldauro Scioppio Ac-* cademico Incognito, Geniale, &c. (21). —— *Annotations of Oldauro Scioppio on The Art of Love of the most Illustrious Signor* Peter Michael, *a Noble Venetian* —— *The Shield of Rinaldo, or the The Undeceiving Mirror, by* Scipio Glareano. —— *A Sketch of the Beauties of* Belisa, *a Tragedy composed by the most Illustrious Signor D.* Antonio Muscettola, *by* Oldauro Scioppio, *of the Academy of the Incogniti*, Geniales &c. There are several such like Compositions among the Manuscript Writings of *Angelico Aprosio*. But it must not be dissembled, first, That there are also among them the Lectures, which he read on the Prophet *Jonas*, in the Church of our Lady *of Consolation* at *Genoa*, in the Year 1649, and 1650 (22). Secondly, That, in the Year 1643, he published the *Italian* Translation, which he had made, of the *Spanish* Sermons of *Augustin Osorius*, under the Name of *Oldauro Scioppio*.

[D] *He loved this Employ well enough himself.*] It is not altogether without Reason, that *Scævenius* relates, that *Aprosio* had wrote a Work, entituled, *Bibliotheca Apocryphorum*, in which he restored several Works to their true Authors; for two Pieces are attributed to one under the Title of *La visera alzata Necatasti di alcuni Scrittori che andarono in Maschera fuori del tempo di Carnevale*, —— *The Visor pulled off from certain Authors, who appeared in Masquerade out of the Time of the Carnival*; the other, which is only a Sequel of the foregoing, is called *Pentecoste di alcuni Autori anonimi è pseudonomi, scoperti per Mantissa della Necataste della visera alzata*, - - - *The Pentecost of certain Anonymous or Pseudonymous Authors, discovered by* Mantissa della Necataste *in* The Visor pulled off. Father *Oldoini* does not inform us, whether these two Pieces were printed, or no; he only says, that *Aprosio* wrote them under a borrowed Name; and by what he quotes in the following Page, *La visera alzata, vevelgata sub nomine* Friani Forbotta, - - - *The Visor pulled off, published under the Name of* Friani Forbotta; we cannot conclude, that they were printed; for he plainly shews, that this *Forbotta* is a different Person from *Angelico Aprosio* (23). It cannot reasonably be doubted, that the two Pieces, which he attributes to our *Aprosio*, are the same with those mentioned in the Journal of *Leipsic* (24). They were printed at *Parma* in 1689. The Name, which appears in the Front, is *John Peter Villani, de Sienne, Academicien Humoriste, Infecond, & Genialis.* It appears, that they were dedicated, in the Year 1678, to Messieurs *Magliabecchi*.

[E] *As appears by the Book*,] It was printed at *Venice* in the Year 1647, in 4to. Father *Labbé* believed, that *John Francis Loredano* was the Author of it (25); but others are of a contrary Opinion, for this among other Reasons, that the Elogy of *Loredano* in this Book is too pompous to be attributed to *Loredano* himself (26). It is thought, that the Verses at the beginning of this Work, and which do not congratulate *Loredano*, as the Author of it, but as the Founder of the Academy of *The Incogniti*, were the Cause of Father *Labbé's* Error.

APROSIO (PAULO AUGUSTINO) a Lawyer, and Member of the *Academy* of the *Apatisti* at *Florence*, was born, at *Vintimiglia*, of one of the chief Families of the Town, and which can boast of having produced Nine Doctors of Law, and One of Physic, from the beginning of the XVIIth Century to the Year 1667. He, whom I here mention, having studied under the Jesuits, at *Genoa*, went to *Rome*, to study the

VOL. I. Nº. XIII. 5 E Law

APROSIO. APULEIUS.

Law. He was admitted Doctor there, in the Year 1449, and afterwards returned home, bought a Collection of curious Books, and retired to a Country House, that he might the more quietly enjoy the Pleasure of reading and composing. He wrote Annotations on the *Belisa* of *D. Antonio Muscetola*, which were printed with the *Bellezze delle medezima abozzate da Oldauro Scioppio*, in the Year 1664. When *Soprani*, from whom I borrow this Article, published his Catalogue of the *Ligurian* Writers, in 1667, our *Aprosio* was preparing a large Moral Treatise, concerning the Overthrow of Capital Vices by their opposite Virtues (a). *Oldoini* informs me, that this Work was printed at *Genoa*, in the Year 1674, and dedicated to the Prince of *Monaco*.

(1) Strage de Vitii capitali trionfati dalle Virtu opposte.

APULEIUS (LUCIUS) a *Platonic* Philosopher, publickly known by the famous Work of the *Golden Ass*, lived in the IId Century under the *Antonines* [*A*]. He was a Native of *Madaura*, a *Roman* Colony in *Africa* [*B*]. His Family was considerable [*C*]. He had been well educated, and had a graceful Person; he had Wit, and Learning; but was suspected of Magic; an Infamy, which to this day does great Injury to his Memory. He studied, first at *Carthage*, then at *Athens*; and afterwards

[*A*] *Lived in the second Century under the Antonines* (1).] *Peter Pithæus* rejecting all Those, who say, that *Apuleius* lived after *Theodosius*, proves, that he lived about the time of *Antoninus Pius*, and some time after (2). This Opinion is supported by such good Reasons, that it is generally embraced. It is plain, that *Scipio Orphitus*, *Lollianus Avitus*, *Claudius Maximus*, and *Lollius Urbicius*, of whom *Apuleius* speaks, as Persons then alive, lived under the *Antonines*. Father *Norris* is mistaken in his Criticism on *Elmenhorst*; he charges him with having acknowledged his Ignorance as to the Time which *Apuleius* lived (3), and refers him to two Passages of *Apuleius*'s Apology; in one of which *Antoninus* is not stiled *Divus*, and in the other mention is made of the Proconsul *Lollianus Avitus*, who was Consul in the Year 144. The Omission of *Divus* is a sufficient Proof, that *Antoninus* was yet living. Father *Norris* would not have been so much mistaken, if the Author, whom he criticises, had not expressed himself as follows: " Quo anno natus (*Apuleius*) non liquido li-
" quet. Verisimiliter tamen possumus adserere eum
" temporibus Antonini Pii Divorumque fratrum vix-
" isse. Meminit enim Lolliani Aviti, Lollii Urbicii
" Pudentis, & Scipionis Orphiti, Coss. qui sub An-
" tonino præcipue floruerunt, summis mactí hono-
" ribus, ut constat ex L. 3. ff. de his qui testamen-
" tis, &c. L. 3. ff. de Decurion (4)." — WHEN
" *Apuleius* lived*, it not currently known; yet it is
" probable, it was in the times of Antonius Pius,
" and his Brothers, who preceeded him. For he
" mentions the Consuls, Lollianus Avitus *, Lollius
" Urbicius Pudens †, and Scipio Orphitus ‖, who
" flourished chiefly under Antoninus, having been ad-
" vanced to the greatest Honours, as appears from
" L. 3. de his qui testamentis, &c." The Passage, in which *Antoninus* is not stiled *Divus*, contains the Reproaches, which *Apuleius* made to his Wife's Son, on his exposing his Mother's Love-Letters. " Hucusque à vobis miserum istum puerum depravatum,
" ut matris suæ epistolas, quas putat amatorias, pro
" tribunali Proconsulis recitet apud virum sanctissi-
" mum Claudium Maximum, ante has Imperatoris
" Pii statuas filius matris suæ pudenda exprobret flu-
" pra, & amores objectet (5). — — — — So far has
" this wretched Youth been spoiled by you, that he has
" not been advanced to recite his Mother's Love-Letters
" before the Proconsul's Tribunal, in the hearing of the
" venerable Claudius Maximus, and even to reproach
" her with her Amours before these Statues of the
" Emperor Antoninus Pius." *Jonsius* is doubly mistaken, when, in order to prove, that *Apuleius* lived in the time, which I assign him, he says, that our Philosopher gives the Elogy of *Divus* to *Antoninus Pius* (6). The Fact is false; and the Consequence drawn from it inconclusive.

[*B*] *He was a Native of* Madaura, *a Roman Colony in* Africa.] This Town, which had belonged to *Syphax*, was given by the *Romans* to *Massinissa*. " Neque hoc eo dixi, quo me patriæ meæ pœnite-
" ret, etsi adhuc Syphacis oppidum essemus: quo
" tamen victo, ad Masinissam regem concessimus,
" munere populi Romani, ac deinceps vetera-
" rum militum novo conditu splendidissima colo-
" nia sumus (7). — — — — *My Meaning is not, that
" I should have been ashamed of my Country, though*

" *we had still continued a Town belonging to Sy-
" phax; after whose Defeat, however, we fell un-
" der the Power of King Massinissa, by Gift of the
" Roman People, and at last became a most flourish-
" ing Colony.*" A little before, he had said, that he was not ashamed, like *Cyrus*, to partake of two different Nations. " De patria mea vero, quod eam sitam
" Numidiæ & Gætuliæ in ipso confinio meis scrip-
" tis ostendisti, quibus memet professus sum — — — —
" Seminumidam, & Semigætulum, non video quid
" mihi sit in ea re pudendum, haud minus quam
" Cyro majori, quod genere mixto fuit, Semimedus
" ac Semipersa. — — — — *As for the Place of my Birth,
" which you have shewn to have been situated on
" the very confines of Numidia and Gætulia, from
" my own Writings, in which I profess myself a Se-
" mi-Numidian and a Semi-Gætulian; I cannot see,
" why I have any more reason to be ashamed of it,
" than Cyrus the Elder had of being of a mixed
" Race, half a Mede, and half a Persian.*" A certain Author, who pretended to set up for a general Censurer, towards the end of the sixteenth Century, falls here into our Hands. After having said, that *Lucian*, under the pretended Form of an Ass, teaches a thousand Impurities he adds, " *Apuleius* hunc imitatus,
" ut vir Græcus se Latine nescivisse ingenue con-
" fessus, in Asino aureo plane rudit (8). — — — *Apu-
" leius, imitating this Writer, and ingenuously con-
" fessing, that, being a Greek, he was ignorant of
" the Latin Tongue, downright brays in his Golden
" Ass.*" First of all, it is not true, that *Apuleius* confesses he does not understand *Latin*: He only says, I. That he did not understand it upon his first Arrival at *Rome*. II. That he learnt it without a Master. In the second Place, it is not true, that he was a *Greek*. *Madaura* was a *Roman* Colony; and, when he would justify himself by the Example of other Poets, he cites the *Greeks* as Strangers, and the *Latins* as his Countrymen. " Fecere tamen & alii talia, & — — — —
" apud Græcos Tejus quidam — — — A P U D N O S vero,
" Ædituus, & Portius, & Catulus (9). — — — *Others
" have done the like, and — — — — A Teian Poet
" among the* Greeks — — — — *but among* O U R O W N
" *Writers,* Ædituus, *and* Portius, *and* Catulus, *&c.*" The Truth is, the *Latin* Tongue was not common at *Madaura*. *Apuleius*, the Son of one of the chief Magistrates, understood nothing of it, when he came to *Rome*. The Son of his Wife *Pudentilla* understood only the *Carthaginian*, and a little *Greek*, which his Mother, who was originally of *Thessaly*, had taught him. " Loquitur nunquam nisi *Punicè*, & si quid adhuc à matre græcissat: Latine enim neque vult neque potest (10).

[*C*] *His Family was considerable.*] His Father's Name was *Theseus*. These Words are our only Authority. " Si, contentus lare parvulo, Thesei illius
" cognominis Patria tui virtutes æmulaveris (11).
" — — — — *If, satisfied with a moderate support, you
" shall emulate the Virtues of your Father Theseus.*" He had exercised the Office of *Duumvir* at *Madaura*. It was the first Dignity of a Colony. " In qua
" colonia patrem habui loco principe Duumviralem
" cunctis honoribus perfunctum (12). — — — *In which
" Colony, I had a Father, who, having gone through
" all inferior Offices, arrived to the Dignity of Duum-
" vir, the principal Post of Honour.*" His Mother, whose

APULEIUS.

wards at *Rome* [D]; where he acquired the *Latin* Tongue without any Affiſtance. An inſatiable Curioſity to know every thing induced him to make ſeveral Voyages, and enter himſelf in ſeveral Religious Fraternities [E]. He would ſee the bottom of their

(13) Id Metim. lib. 2. pag. 115.

whoſe Name was *Salvia* (13), was originally of *Theſſaly*, and deſcended from the Family of *Plutarch*. He ſays this himſelf, at the beginning of his Romance. St *Auſtin* had heard, that *Apuleius* was of a good Family, as appears from his fifth Letter. See, below, the Remark [E], Citation (18).

[D] *He ſtudied, firſt at* Carthage, *then at* Athens; *and afterwards at* Rome] This Gradation is a ſecret to thoſe, who ſtop at the Prologue of his Romance; ſince he makes no mention there of *Carthage*. He is ſatisfied with ſaying, that his firſt Studies were Thoſe of the *Greek* Tongue in *Greece*, and that afterwards he came to *Rome*, where he ſtudied *Latin*, without the Aſſiſtance of a Maſter. " Ibi linguam Atticem " primis pueritiæ ſtipendiis merui, mox in urbe Latia " advena ſtudiorum Quiritium indigenam ſermonem " ærumnabili labore, nullo magiſtro præunte, ag- " greſſus excolui." This Narration is deceitful, and imperfect, and muſt be rectified by other Paſſages of *Apuleius*. Is it at all ſurpriſing, that Authors ſhould relate the Actions of others imperfectly? Do they not ſometimes report their own very confuſedly? Let us produce other Paſſages of our Author. He tells the *Carthaginians*, that, in his Infancy, he ſtudied with them, and that he had begun, likewiſe, to embrace the Platonic Sect among Them. " Sum vobis " nec lare alienus, nec pueritia inviſitatus, nec ma- " giſtris peregrinus, nec ſecta incognitus. ----- E- " nimvero & pueritia apud vos, & magiſtri vos, & " ſecta, licet Athenis Atticis confirmata, tamen hic

(14) Apul. Florilor. pag. 359.

" inchoata eſt (14). ----- *I am no Stranger to* " *you, either as to my Family, my Education, or* " *my Opinions.* ----- *For my Childhood was ſpent* " *among you; you were my Inſtructors; and the Sect,* " *of which I am a follower, though confirmed in it at* " Athens, *was firſt embraced by me here.*" To which he adds; " Hanc ego vobis mercedem, Carthagi- " nienſes, ubique quenſque dependo, pro diſciplinis " quas in pueritia ſum apud vos adeptus. Ubique

(15) Id. ib. pag. 361.

" enim me veſtræ civitatis alumnum fero (15) ---- " *This Acknowledgment, O* Carthaginians, *wherever* " *I am, I pay you, in return for that Inſtruction I* " *acquired among you: I every where acknowledge* " *myſelf the Pupil of your State.*" Some Pages after, he reckons up the Sciences he had ſtudied at *Athens*. " Prima cratera Litteratoris ruditatem exi- " mit: Secunda Grammatici doctrinâ inſtruit: Ter- " tia Rhetoris eloquentiâ armat. Hactenus & pleriſ- " que potatur. Ego & alias crateras Athenis bibi; " Poëticæ commentam, Geometricæ limpidam, Mu- " ſicæ dulcem, Dialecticæ auſterulam, enimvero uni- " verſæ philoſophiæ inexplebilem, ſcilicet nectare-

(16) Id. ib. pag. 363.

" am (16). ----- *The firſt Cup of Knowledge, which* " *we drink at the Hands of our Præceptors, removes* " *entire Ignorance; the ſecond infuſes Grammatical* " *Learning; the third arms us with the Eloquence* " *of the Rhetorician. Thus far many drink. But I* " *drank of ſtill more Cups at* Athens, *the fabulous* " *of Poetry, the Limpid of Geometry, the ſweet of* " *Muſic, the unpleaſant of Logic; indeed the never* " *ſatiating, and truly nectareous, Cup of univerſal Phi-* " *loſophy*." Some will have it, that he ſtudied, at two ſeveral times, in *Greece*; the firſt time, before he ſtudied at *Carthage*, and the ſecond after his Studies in That City. They take no notice of *Rome*; they pretend, that he acquired the *Latin* Tongue at *Carthage* (17): This latter Fact is expreſsly contradicted in the Prologue to the *Golden Aſs*.

(17) He paſſed the firſt Years of his Childhood in Greece, and the following at Carthage, where he learnt Latin without a Maſter. He likewiſe began to learn Philoſophy there. Afterwards he went to Athens, where he ſtudied Poetry, &c. Tillemont, Hiſt. des Emper. Tom. 2. pag. 722.

[E] *And enter himſelf in ſeveral Religious Fraternities.*] He introduces himſelf ſpeaking the following Words, in the third Book of the *Golden Aſs*. " Paveo & fidem ſolide domus hujus operta de- " tegere, & arcana dominæ meæ revelare ſecreta. " Sed melius de te doctrinaque tua præſumo, qui " præter generoſam natalium dignitatem, præter ſub- " lime ingenium, ſacris pluribus initiatus, profecto

(18) Apuleii Metam. lib. 11. p. 204.

" noſti ſanctam ſilentii fidem (18). ----- *I dread to* " *make a full Diſcovery of the Practiſes of this Fra-* " *ternity, and to reveal the Secrets of my Miſtreſs.* " *But I have a better Opinion of you, and your Learn-* " *ing, who, beſides an high Birth, and elevated Ge-* " *nius, know how to guard a Secret inviolably, having*

" *been yourſelf initiated in many Myſteries.*" He concludes his Romance with an account of his Admiſſion into the Religion of *Oſiris*. This Honour was conferred on him at *Rome*. He did not continue long among the Herd of the Initiated, he ſoon raiſed himſelf to the higheſt Degrees. " Deni- " que per dies admodum pauculos, Deus Deûm mag- " norum potior, & majorum ſummus, & ſummo- " rum maximus, & maximorum regnator, Oſiris, non " in alienam quampiam perſonam reformatus, ſed " coram ſuo illo venerando me dignatus affamine, " per quietem præcipere viſus eſt. ----- Ac, ne " ſacris ſuis gregi cætero permixtus deſervirem, in " collegium me Paſtophororum ſuorum, imo inter " ipſos Decurionum quinquennales, elegit. ----- " *Laſtly, in a very few Days after,* Oſiris, *the greateſt* " *of the Gods, appeared to me in a Dream, not in* " *a borrowed Shape, but in his own venerable Perſon.* " ----- *And, that I might not adminiſter his Sa-* " *cred Rites, amidſt the Herd of his Votaries, he* " *choſe me into the College of his Paſtophori, and* " *even appointed me one of his Decurions.*" Before his Arrival at *Rome*, he had been initiated into the Myſteries of *Iſis*; theſe were the firſt Fruits of his recovered Humanity. In the Deſcriptions of theſe Ceremonies he intermixes ſeveral ſublime Sentiments, which are only worthy of the true Religion. As for Example: " Te jam nunc obſequio religio- " nis noſtræ dedica, & miniſterii jugum ſubi volun- " tarium, nam, cum cœperis Deæ ſervire, tunc ma- " gis ſenties fructum tuæ libertatis (19). ----- *De-*

(19) Apol. p. 309, 310.

" *dicate yourſelf immediately to the Obedience of our* " *Religion, and take upon you the voluntary Yoke of* " *Miniſtering in it; for, when you ſhall begin to ſerve* " *our Goddeſs, you will be the more ſenſible of the* " *Fruit of your own Liberty.*" They, who accuſed him of Magic, objected, among other things, that he kept ſomething, I know not what, in a Handkerchief, with a ſingular Superſtition. His Anſwer was: " Vin dicam cujuſmodi illas res in ſudario obvolutas " laribus Pontiani commendarim? Mos tibi geretur. " Sacrorum pleraque initia in Græcia participavi. " Eorum quædam ſigna & monumenta tradita mihi " à ſacerdotibus ſedulo conſervo. Nihil inſolitum, " nihil incognitum dico. Vei unius Liberi patris " ſymmiſtæ, qui adeſtis, ſcitis quid domi conditum " celetis, & abſque omnibus profanis tacite venere- " mini. At ego, ut dixi, multijuga ſacra, & pla- " rimos ritus, varias ceremonias, ſtudio veri, & of- " ficio erga Deos, didici. Nec hoc ad tempus com- " pono, ſed abhinc ferme triennium eſt, cum primis " diebus, quibus Oëam veneram, publice differens de " Æſculapii majeſtate, eadem iſta præ me tuli, & quot " ſacra noſſem percenſui. Ea diſputatio celebratiſ- " ſima eſt, vulgo legitur, in omnium manibus ver- " ſatur ----- Etiamne cuiquam mirum videri po- " teſt, cui ſit ulla memoria religionis, hominem tot " myſteriis Deûm conſcium, quædam ſacrorum cre- " pundia domi adſervare, atque ea lineo texto in- " volvere, quod puriſſimum eſt rebus divinis vela- " mentum (20). ----- *Shall I tell you what kind*

(20) Id. ib. pag. 312.

" *of Things, wrapt up in an Handkerchief, I have* " *entruſted with the Houſe of* Pontianus? *you ſhall* " *be ſatisfied. I was initiated into ſeveral ſacred* " *Rites in* Greece. *Some Tokens and Remembrances* " *of them, delivered me by the Prieſts, I carefully* " *preſerve. What I ſay, is no uncommon, or unknown,* " *Practice. I need go no farther, than you, ye Vo-* " *taries of* Bacchus, *who are here preſent; who are* " *conſcious of what you keep concealed at Home, and* " *adore in private, without any Prophanation. But* " *I, as I have already ſaid, prompted by a Love of* " *Truth, and out of Duty to the Gods, have learned* " *the Myſteries of different Religions, and been ini-* " *tiated in various Rites and Ceremonies. Nor is* " *this a new-invented Apology; for it is now almoſt* " *three Years, ſince, in a public Oration on the Ma-* " *jeſty of* Æſculapius, *on the firſt Day of my Arri-* " *at* Oëa, *I made the ſame Declaration, and reckoned* " *up how many Religions I had been initiated in.* " *This Diſputation is very famous, is commonly read,* " *and is in every one's Hands.* ----- *And can any*
" one

APULEIUS.

their pretended Mysteries. He spent almost all his Estate in travelling [F], insomuch, that, being returned to *Rome*, and having a Desire to dedicate himself to the Service of *Osiris*, he wanted Money to defray the Expence of the Ceremonies of his Reception. He pawned even his Cloaths to make up the necessary Sum (*a*). After this he gained his Livelihood by Pleading: And, as he was eloquent, and subtle enough, he did not want Causes; some of which were very considerable (*b*). But he improved his Fortunes much more by a lucky Marriage, than by Pleading. A Widow, whose Name was *Pudentilla*, neither young nor fair, but who stood in need of a Husband, and had a good Estate, thought him for her Purpose [G]. He was

---

"one be surprized, who has any Remembrance of Religion, that a Man, acquainted with so many Mysteries of the Gods, should lay up at Home some few sacred Trinkets, and conceal them in a Piece of Linnen, which is the purest covering for Divine Things." It is probable, that, if *Apuleius* was a Magician, his Crime was incomparably less, than That of the Magicians of these Times; because he was ignorant, that only bad *Genii* apply themselves to certain Operations, in consequence of the Performance of certain Ceremonies. He believed, with the Platonists, that good *Genii* might do the same (21). I have quoted St *Austin*, in the Text of this Article, who testifies, that *Apuleius* had a religious Dignity, which gave him the Superintendance of the Gladiatorial Shews. *Sacerdos Provinciæ pro magno fuit, ut munera ederet, venatoresque vestiret* (22). Lastly, I find, that our Author had dedicated himself to the Worship of *Æsculapius*, one of the chief Divinities of the *Carthaginians*, and that he had also an eminent Station in His College. "*Principium mihi apud vestras aureis auspicatissimum ab Æsculapio Deo capiam, qui arcem vestræ Carthaginis indubitabili numine propitius respicit. Ejus Dei hymnum Græco & Latino carmine vobis sic canam, jam illi à me dedicatum. Sum enim non ignotus illius* SACRICOLA, *nec recens cultor, nec ingratus* ANTISTES (23). ------ *I shall bespeak your favourable Attention, by reciting an Hymn in Greek and Latin Verse, which I have just dedicated to that God Æsculapius, the tutelar Divinity of the Citadel of your Carthage. For I am no unknown* SACRIFICER *of This God, no recent Worshipper, nor ungrateful* MASTER *of his* CEREMONIES."

[F] *He spent almost all his Estate in travelling.*] This was not the only Cause of the Poverty, into which he fell; he was expensive upon more commendable Occasions; at least he pretended to have been so, when he replied to those, who reproached him with his Poverty. "*Ad istum modum desponsus sacris, sumptuum tenuitate contra votum meum retardabat; nam & viriculas patrimonii peregrinationis attriverant impensæ* (24). ----- *Thus betrothed to Religion, I was unwillingly retarded by the Narrowness of my Circumstances; for the Expences of travelling had weakened the little Strength of my Patrimony.*" Thus he speaks, when he represents the Difficulties he laboured under at *Rome*, in relation to his Admission into the Fraternity of *Osiris*. He had mortgaged himself, as it were, to this mysterious Congregation; he had given his Note of hand; but, as nothing is ever done for nothing, something was to be paid for the Inaugural Ceremonies; and he had not wherewithal to supply the Expence. He was forced, as one may say, to sell his very Shirt; the Divinity, which inspired him, pointed out no other Resource. "*Jamque sæpicule non sine magna turbatione stimulatus, postremo jussus, veste ipsa mea quamvis parvula distractâ, sufficientem corrasi summulam, & idipsum præceptum fuerat specialiter. An tu, inquit, si quam rem voluptati struendæ molireris, laciniis tuis nequaquam parceres, nunc tantas ceremonias aditurus impœnitendæ te pauperiei contaris committere* (25). ----- *Being often prompted, not without great Emotion of Mind, and at last commanded, I scraped together, by making Money of my very Cloaths, mean as they were, a sufficient Sum; for this was particularly required of me. What! says he, would you nor spare your Fringes, if you were in pursuit of your Pleasures, and are you unwilling, when you are to be initiated into such Ceremonies, to encounter a Poverty not to be repented of?*" At that time he ascribed his Indigence only to the Expences of his Travels; but, on another occasion, which I have mentioned, he says he was at great Expences in good Works, such as assisting his Friends, rewarding the Care of those, who had instructed him, and portioning some of their Daughters. He adds, that he should have made no Difficulty to purchase, at the Price of his Patrimony, a thorough Contempt of it; a Contempt, which is a much more valuable Treasure, than a Patrimony itself. This is speaking like a Philosopher indeed. "*Si tamen nescis, be addresses himself to his Accuser* (26), *profiteor mihi ac fratri meo relictum à patre* H. S. *vicies, paulo secus; idque à me longa peregrinatione, & diutinis studiis, & crebris liberalitatibus modice imminutum. Nam & amicorum plerisque opem tuli, & magistris plurimis gratiam retuli, quorumdam etiam filias dote auxi. Neque enim dubitassem equidem vel universum patrimonium impendere, ut adquirerem mihi, quod majus est, contemptum patrimonii. Si, tu know it not, I assure you, that my Father left my Brother and myself an Hundred thousand Sesterces, or little less; which I have something diminished by my long Travels, continued Studies, and frequent Bounties. For I have assisted several of my Friends, and gratified many of my Preceptors; some of whose Daughters I have even portioned. Nor should I make the least Scruple of expending my whole Fortune in acquiring, what is much more valuable, a Contempt of it.*" He had made very solid, and very moral, Reflexions on Poverty (27).

[G] *A Widow,* ---- *neither young, nor fair, but who stood in need of a Husband, and had a good Estate, thought him fit for her Purpose.*] *Apuleius*'s Accuser affirmed, she was sixty Years of Age (28): He had his Design in it; for his Aim was to prove, that the Passion, she had conceived for the Accused, was not Natural, but the Effect of Magic. *Apuleius* made it appear (29), that she was not much above forty Years of Age; and that, if she had past fourteen of them in a State of Widowhood, it was not out of any Aversion to Matrimony, but from her Father-in-law's opposing it: that, at length, a State of Continency had so far impaired her Health, that the Physicians and Midwives agreed, that the best Remedy for the Diseases, which were the Consequence of it, was Matrimony. A Lady, to whom such Advice was given, and who had no time to lose, if she desired to make the best use of her teeming Years, wanted not to be constrained by Magic Art to make choice of a Spouse. This was *Apuleius*'s Argument, and it is of great Force. "*Eo scrupulo liberata, cum à principibus viris in matrimonium peteretur; decrevit sibi diutius in viduitate non permanendum. Quippe ut solitudinis tædium perpeti posset, tamen ægritudinem corporis ferre non poterat. Mulier sanctè pudica, tot annis viduitatis sine culpa, sine fabula, absuetudine conjugis torpens, & diutino situ viscerum saucia, vitiatis intimis uteri, sæpe ad extremum vitæ discrimen doloribus obortis examinabatur. Medici cum obstetricibus consentientibus, penuria matrimonii morbum quæsitum. Malum indies augeri, ægritudinem ingravescere: dum ætatis aliquid superfit, nuptiis valetudinem medicandam* (30). ------ *This Scruple being removed, and, being courted by Persons of the highest Rank, she determined to continue no longer a Widow. For, though she might have supported the Solitude of a single Life, yet the ill State of her Health she could not. This Lady, religiously Modest, and pining, during so many Years of Widowhood, for want of an Husband, was brought almost to Death's Door, through Pains arising from a stoppage of the Matrix. The Physicians and Midwives agreed, that the Distemper was owing to the Want of an Husband; that it increased daily, and gained ground; and that, if she made*"

was not coy; nor was he follicitous to keep his fine Perfon, his Neatnefs [H], his Wit,

Why some Judicial Proceedings are disagreeable to the Fair Sex.

(31) See below, Remark [I].

"*made hafte, Matrimony might cure her.*" Some kind of Proceedings are very unfortunate for the Ladies; where feveral things muft necessarily be revealed to a full Audience, which one would wish to conceal, whether owing to natural or moral Infirmity (31). Had it not been for this Trial, *Apuleius* would never have revealed the Diftemper, with which *Pudentilla* was afflicted, during her Widowhood. However, fhe had this Satisfaction, that, though fhe had fuffered fo much, it was a Proof, that fhe had not had recourfe to the true Remedy. This Confequence was not urged to the Judges; but it was alledged, that fhe had always lived chaftly, and that her Conduct had never been called in queftion.

(32) Apulei, Apolog. pag. 320.

To return to her Age; there is no doubt, that *Apuleius* was younger than She; for fhe had a Son, who had been *Apuleius*'s Companion at *Athens* (32); but I add, that he did not marry without Hopes of having Iffue by her. This he declares, in anfwer to the Reproach thrown on him, of going into the Country to be married. After having replied, that the Reafon of this was to avoid the Expence, which a Wedding in the City would have put them to; he adds, that " the Country is naturally more favourable to Pro- " creation, than the City; and that, to lie down up- " on the Grafs, and under the Shade of Elms, amidft " numberlefs Productions, which fpring out of the " fruitful Bofom of the Earth, cannot but be lucky " to a new married Couple, who defire to have " Children." He fhould have kept this Thought for his *Florida*, I mean for his rhetorical Declamations, in which he gives a Loofe to the falfe Flights of his Imagination. This Paffage fpoils his Apology. It is unworthy of the Judges, before whom he fpoke, and of the Caufe, which he was pleading. " Immo, " fi verum velis, uxor ad prolem multo aufpicatius " in villa quam in oppido ducitur; in folo uberi, " quam in loco fterili; in agri cefpite, quam in fo- " ri filece: mater futura in ipfo maturno fi nubat " finu, in fegete adulta fuper fœcundam glebam. " Vel enim fub ulmo marita cubet in ipfo gremio " terræ matris inter foboles herbarum, & propagines " vitium, & arborum germina (33)."

(33) Ibid. pag. 329.

We fhall fee hereafter (34), that it was declared in open Court, that *Pudentilla* was not handfome; and that her Contract of Marriage contained Claufes, which fuppofed her to be ftill of teeming Years.

(34) In the Remark [I].

[H] *His fine Perfon, his Neatnefs.*] I fhall here give fome touches of his Picture. " At illa obtutum " in me converfa, En, inquit, fanctiffimæ matris " generofa proles. Sed & cætera corporis in- " explicabiliter ad regulam congruentia; inenormis " proceritas, fucculenta gracilitas, rubor temperatus; " flavum & inaffectatum capillitium; oculi cæfi " quidem, fed vigiles, & in afpectu micantes prorfus " aquilino, quoquo verfum floridi fpeciofus, & im- " meditatus inceffus (35).

(35) Metamorph. lib. 2. pag. 115. See alfo lib. 3. pag. 112.

—— But She, turning her " Eyes upon me, faid, behold the worthy Son of the " moft virtuous Salvia; contemplate the juft Propor- " tions of his bodily Parts; his proper Stature, his " moderate Size, and his healthful Afpect; his yel- " low, carelefs, Locks; his Eyes, blue indeed, but " lively, and fparkling, like thofe of an Eagle; " laftly, his beautiful and unaffected Gait."

(36) Accufamus apud te Philofophum Formofum, & tam Græcæ quam Latinæ, proh nefas! difertiffimum. Apolog. p. 275.

His Accufers reproached him with his Beauty (36); his fine Hair; his fine Teeth; and his Looking-glafs. He anfwered to the two firft Particulars, that he was forry the Accufation was falfe. " Quod utinam tam " gravia formæ & facundiæ crimina vere mihi expro- " braffet! non difficile ei refpondiffem, quod Ho- " mericus Alexander Hectori:

'Ούτι ἀπόβλητ' ἐϛὶ θεῶν ἐρικυδέα δῶρα,
'Όσσα κεν αὐτοὶ δῶσιν, ἐκὼν δ' ἐκ ἄν τις
ἕλοιτο.

Munera deum gloriofiffima nequaquam afpernanda: Quæ tamen ab ipfis tribui fueta, multis volentibus non obtingunt.

" Hæc ego de forma refpondiffem. Præterea, licere " etiam Philofophis effe vultu liberali. Pythagoram, " qui primum fefe Philofophum nuncuparit, eum fui " fæculi excellentiffima forma fuiffe: item Zeno-

" nem. —— Sed hæc defenfio, ut dixi, aliquam- " multum à me remota eft: cui, præter formæ me- " diocritatem, continuatio etiam literati laboris om- " nem gratiam corpore deterget, habitudinem tenuat, " fuccum exforbet, colorem obliterat, vigorem de- " bilitat. Capillus ipfe, quem ifti aperto mendacio ad " lenocinium decoris promiffum dixere, vides quam " non fit amœnus ac delicatus, horrore implexus at- " que impeditus, ftupeo tomento affimilis, & inæ- " qualiter hirtus, & globofus, & congeftus: prorfus " inenodabilis diutina incuria, non modo comendi, " fed faltem expediendi & difcriminandi (37). —— " How do I wifh, that thefe heavy Accufations of " Beauty and Eloquence were juft! I fhould, without " Difficulty, reply, as Paris, in Homer, does to Hector.

(37) Ibid. & pag. 276.

- - - - - nor thou defpife the Charms,
With which a Lover golden Venus arms.
Soft moving Speech, and pleafing outward fhow,
No Wifh can gain them, but the Gods beftow.

Pope.

" Thus would I reply to the Charge of Beauty. Be- " fides, that even Philofophers are allowed to be of a " liberal Afpect; that Pythagoras, who ftiled himfelf " the firft of Philofophers, was the handfomeft Man " of his Time; and Zeno. —— But, as I obferved, " I am far from pretending to this Apology; fince, " befides that Nature has beftowed but a moderate " Degree of Beauty on me, my continual Application " to Study wears off every bodily Grace, and impairs " my Conftitution. My very Hair, which I am falfely " accufed of curling, and dreffing by way of Ornament, " is, as you fee, far from being beautiful and delicate; " on the contrary, it is perplexed and entangled, " like a bundle of Flocks or Tow; and fo knotty, thro' " long neglect of combing, and even of difentangling, " as never to be reduced to Order." As to the third Particular, he did not deny his having fent a Powder for the Teeth to a Friend, together with fome Verfes, containing an exact Defcription of the Effects of the Powder. He alledged, that All, efpecially they, who fpoke in public, ought to be particularly careful to keep their Mouths clean. This was a fine Field for Defence, and for turning his Adverfary into ridicule; though, in all Probability, he had given occafion enough for Cenfure, by too great an Affectation of diftinguifhing himfelf from other learned Men. Obferve with how much Eafe fome Caufes are defended, though the Defendant be a little in the wrong. " Vidi ego dudum vix rifum quofdam " tenentes, cum mundicias oris videlicet orator ille " afpere accufaret, & dentifricium tanta indignatione " pronunciaret, quanta nemo quifquam venenum. " Quidni? crimen haud contemnendum Philofopho, " nihil in fe fordidum finere, nihil ufpiam corporis " apertum immundum pati ac fœtulentum; præfer- " tim os, cujus in propatulo & confpicuo ufus ho- " mini creberrimus: five ille culpiam ofculum ferat, " feu cum cuiquam fermocinetur, five in auditorio " differat, five in templo preces allegat. Omnem " quippe hominis actum fermo præit: qui, ut ait " Poëta præcipuus, è dentium muro proficifcitur (38). " I obferved, that fome could fcarce forbear laughing, " when our Orator angrily accufed me of keeping my " Mouth clean, and pronounced the Word Tooth-Powder " with as much Indignation, as any one ever pro- " nounced the Word Poifon. But, furely, it is not " beneath a Philofopher to ftudy Cleanlinefs, and to let " no part of the Body, which is feen, be nafty, or " ef an ill favour; efpecially the Mouth, the ufe of " which is the moft frequent and confpicuous; whether " a Man kiffes another, or converfes, or fpeaks in " public, or fays his Prayers in a Temple. For Speech " is previous to every Action of a Man, and, as an ex- " cellent Poet fays, proceeds from the Wall of the " Teeth." We may make the fame Obfervation upon the laft Head of his Accufation. It is no Crime in a Doctor, of what Faculty foever, to have a Looking-glafs; but, if he confults it too often in dreffing himfelf, he is juftly liable to Cenfure. Morality, in *Apuleius*'s Time, was much ftricter, than at prefent, as to external Behaviour; for he durft not avow his making ufe of his Looking-glafs. He maintains, that

(38) Ibid. pag. 277.

VOL. I. 5 F

Wit, and his Eloquence for some young Girl; he married the rich Widow, chearfully, at a Country-house near Oëa, a Maritime Town of *Africa*. This Marriage drew upon him a troublesome Law-Suit: The Relations of this Lady's two Sons pretended he had made use of Magic, to possess himself of her Heart and Money [*I*]: They

that he might do it, and proves it by several Philosophical Reasons; which, to say the truth, are much more ingenious, than judiciously applied; but he denies, that he really consulted his Looking-glass. " Sequitur de speculo longa illa & censoria oratio, " de quo pro rei atrocitate pœne diruptus est Pudens, " clamitans, *Habet speculum philosophus, possidet speculum philosophus*. Ut igitur habere concedam, ne " aliquid objeciſſe te credas, ſi negaro, non tamen " ex eo me accipi necesse est, exornari quoque ad " speculum solere. —— Plurimis rebus possessu careo, usu fruor: quod ſi neque habere utendi argumentum est, neque non utendi non habere, & " speculi non tam possessio culpatur quam inspectio, " illud etiam doceat necesse est quando & quibus " præsentibus in speculum inspexerim, quoniam, ut " res est, majus piaculum decernis speculum philoso- (39) *Ibid.* pho, quam Cereris mundum profano videre (39). *pag. 282.*

—— Next follows the long and bitter Harangue about the Looking-glass; in which, so heinous is the Crime, *Pudens almost burst himself with bawling out*, A Philosopher has a Looking-glass, A Philosopher is in possession of a Looking-glass. *Suppose* " *I should confess that I have, that you may not believe there is really something in your Objection, if* " *I should deny it ; it does not follow from hence,* " *that I must necessarily make a Practice of dressing* " *myself at it.* —— *In many things, I want the Possession, but enjoy the Use of them. Now, if neither to have a thing be a Proof, that it is made* " *use of, nor the want of it of the contrary: and, as* " *I am not blamed for possessing, but for making use* " *of, a Looking-glass ; it is incumbent upon him to* " *prove farther, at what Time, and in the Presence* " *of whom, I made use of it ; since you determine it* " *to be a greater Crime in a Philosopher to see a Looking-glass, than for the Prophane to behold the Attire* " *of Ceres.*"

Read *Juvenal's* Invective against the Emperor *Otho*, who reckoned his Looking-glass as one of the principal Parts of his Equipage of War.

Ille tenet speculum pathici gestamen Othonis,
Actoris Aurunci spolium: quo ſe ille videbat
Armatum, cum jam tolli vexilla juberet.
Res memoranda novis annalibus, atque recenti (40) *Juven.* Historia, Speculum civilis Sarcina Belli (40). *Sat. 2. ver.*
99.

One holds a Mirrour, pathic Otho's Sheild,
In which he view'd, before he marched to Field
Nor Ajax with more Pride his seven-fold Targe
did wield.

O noble Subject, for new Annals fit,
In musty Fame's Record; unmention'd yet !
A Looking-glass must load th' Imperial Car,
The most important Carriage of the War.
TATE.

By the way, I cannot but think (though I dare not affirm it) that *Apuleius* had his Law-suit in view, when, in one of his Speeches, he described the Contest between *Apollo* and *Marsyas*. He supposes, that *Marsyas* begins with praising his own bushy Hair, his squalid Beard, and hairy Breast ; and then reproaches *Apollo* with extream Neatness: " Marsyas, quod stul-(41) *See the* " titiæ maximum specimen est, non intelligens ſe de-*Application* " ridiculo haberi, priusquam tibiam occiperet inflare, *of this Pas-* " prius de ſe & Apolline quædam deliramenta bar-*sage in the* " bare effutivit ; laudens ſeſe quod erat & coma reli-*Nouvelles de* " cinus, & barba squallidus, & pectore hirſutus, & *la Republ.* " arte tibicen, & fortuna egenus : contra Apollinem, *des Lettres,* " ridiculam dictu, adversis virtutibus culpabat. Quod *Septemb.* " Apollo esset & coma intonſus, & genis gratus, & *1685. Ar-* " corpore glabellus, & arte multiſcius, & fortuna opu-*ticle 7.* " lentus. Risere Muſæ, cum audirent hoc genus " crimina, ſapienti exoptanda, Apollini objectata (41), (42) *Apul.* " & tibicinem illum certamine ſuperatum, velut ur-*Florid. pag.* " ſum bipedem, corio exacto nudis & laceris viſceri-*341.* " bus reliquerunt (42). —— *Marsyas, which was the*

" *the greatest Instance of Folly, not perceiving, that* " *he exposed himself to ridicule, before he began to* " *play upon his Pipe, made an absurd Comparison* " *between Apollo and Himself ; praising himself for* " *his bushy Hair, his squalid Beard, his hairy Breast,* " *his Skill in playing on the Pipe, and his Poverty ;* " *and absurdly reproaching Apollo with the contrary* " *Virtues.* Apollo, *he said, had long Hair, a beautiful Face, and a smooth Body ; that he was a great* " *Scholar, and very rich.* —— *The Muses laughed,* " *when they heard such Crimes, as a wise Man would* " *wish to be guilty of, objected to* Apollo, *and left* " *the poor Piper, overcome in the Contest, like some* " *two footed Bear, mangled and torn, with his Skin* " *stript over his Ears.*" Observe, that *Apuleius* affirms, his Accuser was a huge ill favoured Peasant : " Mihi " istud crede, quamquam teterrimum os tuum mi- " nimum à Thyesta tragico demutet, tamen pro- " fecto discendi cupidine speculum inviseris, & ali- " quando relicto aratro miratere tot in facie tua ſul- " cos rugarum. At ego non mirer, ſi boni conſulis " me de isto distortissimo vultu tuo dicere, de mo- ribus tuis multo truculentioribus reticere (43). —— (43) *Apul.* " *Take this from me ; though That rueful Countenance* *Apol. pag.* " *differs but little from That of* Thyestes *in the Tra-* *284.* " *gedy; yet would you sometimes, for the sake of* " *Information, visit the Looking-glass ; and, leaving* " *the Plow, stand amazed at the many Furrows in* " *your own Face. You will take it in good part, I* " *doubt not, that I mention the Deformities of your* " *Face, but am silent on your more hideous Morals.*"

[*I*] *Made use of* Magic *to possess himself of her Heart and Money.*] *Apuleius* had no need of any great Justification, on the first Article ; for ſince *Pudentilla*, for Reaſons of Health, was reſolved on a ſecond Marriage, before ſhe had ſeen this pretended Wizard, *Apuleius's* Youth, good Mien, fair Speech, Wit, and other Accompliſhments, were more than a ſufficient Charm to ingage this Lady's Affections. He had the most favourable Opportunities of gaining her Esteem ; he lodged for ſome time at her Houſe ; *Pudentilla's* eldeſt Son would abſolutely have it ſo ; and it was He who ſollicited *Apuleius* to marry her (44). *Apuleius* (44) *Apol.* managed his Advantages artfully ; and turned his Ac-*pag. 320.* cuſers into ridicule by Smart and ſurprizing Turns of Wit. " You wonder, ſaid *he*, that a Woman " ſhould marry again, after having been thirteen " Years a Widow ; it is more ſurprizing, that ſhe did " not marry much ſooner. You believe there was " need of Witchcraft, to induce a Widow of her " Age to marry a young Fellow ; whereas, on the " contrary, this is a Proof, that Witchcraft was " unneceſſary." " Cur mulier libera tibi nupſit poſt " annos tredecim viduitatis ? quaſi non magis miran- " dum ſit quod tot annis non nupſerit. —— At enim " major natu non eſt juvenem aſpernata. Igitur hoc " ipſum argumentum eſt nihil opus magia fuiſſe, ut " nubere vellet mulier viro, vidua cœlibi, major " juniori (45)." If the Decree of the Judges had (45) *Ibid.* been founded on a Sentence pronounced, in nearly *pag. 291.* a like Caſe, by the Mother of *Alexander the Great*, it would have been admirable. Ὁ βασιλεὺς Φίλιπ- πος ἥρα Θεσσαλῆς γυναικὸς αἵτιαν ἐχούσης κα- ταεπαρμακεύειν αὐτὸν ἐσπούδασε ἡ ἡ Ὀλυμπιὰς λαβεῖν τὴν ἄνθρωπον ὑποχείριον. ὡς δὲ εἰς ὄ ψιν ἐλθοῦσα, τό, τε εἶδο ἦν εὐπρεπὴς ἐφάνη, καὶ διε- λέχθη πρὸς αὐτὴν ὐκ ἀφυῶς ὐδὲ ἀσυνέτως, Χαι- ρέτωσαν (εἶπεν ἡ Ὀλυμπιὰς) αἱ διαβολαὶ ˙ σὺ γὰρ ἐν σεαυτῇ τὰ φάρμακα ἔχεις (46). —— King (46) Plu- *Philip fell in Love with a* Thessalian *Lady, who was* tarch. in *said to have influenced him by Magic Charms.* Olym-Præcept. pias *contrived to get her into her Power. As soon as* Conjug. pag. *she was brought into the Presence of the Queen, and* 142. B. *not only appeared very beautiful, but spoke with Mo-* See the Re-*desty and good Sense ; away with such Calumnies,* mark [*L*]. *cried* Olympias; *the Magic Charms you employed are* of the Article *all in your own Person.* Thus much for the Con-GRAN-queſt of the Heart. The other Article, which re-DIER. lates to the Money, begets ſome Suſpicion, not of Witchcraft, but of Avarice. It is hard to believe, that this Marriage was not a Sacrifice to Reaſons of Intereſt. But let us not condemn *Apuleius*, without

APULEIUS.

They accused him of being a Wizard (c), not before Christian Judges, as a Commentator pretends that St *Austin* affirms (d), but before *Claudius Maximus*, Proconsul of *Africa*, and by Religion a Pagan. He defended himself with great Vigour: We have his Apology, which he spake before the Judges. It is a very fine Piece (e); and furnishes us with Examples of the most shameful Artifices, that the Villainy of an impudent Calumniator is capable of putting in Practice [K]. It has been observed,

(c) His Accuser was s lled Sicinius Æmilianus. He was Brother to Pudentilla's first Husband. Apul. Apolog. init.

(d) Leon. Coqueus, in August. de Civit. Dei, lib. 8. c. 19, p. 740. Edit. Franc. 1661, in 4to. But he is mistaken. St Austin says quite the contrary.

(e) Augustio ubi supra, lib. 18, cap. 18.

out hearing him. He offers to prove, by his Marriage-Contract, that he had desired nothing of *Pudentilla*, for the present, but only the promise of a moderate Sum, in case he survived her, or had Children by her. He makes it appear, by several of his Actions, how disinterested his Conduct was, and how reasonable it was to demand That Sum from his Wife, which she had promised him. Here he was obliged to make such Confessions in open Court, as *Pudentilla* could very well have dispensed with. He says (47), that she was neither fair, nor young, nor in any respect so tempting, as to induce a Man to have recourse to Witchcraft; and that it ought not to be wondered at, that she had given great Encouragement to such a Person as himself was. " *Quod institui pergam disputare, nullam mihi causam fuisse Pudentillam veneficiis ad nuptias prolectandi. Formam mulieris & ætatem ipsi ultro exprobraverunt, idque mihi vitio dederunt talem uxorem causa avaritiæ concupisse, atque adeo primo dotem in congressu quidem & uberem rapuisse ——— Quamquam quis omnium vel exiguæ rerum peritus culpare auderet, si mulier vidua & mediocri forma, at non ætate mediocri, nubere volens, longa dote & molli conditione invitasset juvenem neque corpore, neque animo, neque fortuna pœnitendum.* (48). ——— *To go on with my intended Defence; There was no Necessity, that I should have recourse to Magic, to induce Pudentilla to marry me. My Accusers have voluntarily reproached her with Age, and want of Beauty; and have taxed me with Avarice, in desiring such a Woman, and with having obtained from her, upon our first coming together, a large and plentiful Settlement.* ——— *Though what Man, of the least Experience, would find fault, that a Widow Lady, of little Beauty, and advanced in Years, who has a mind to marry, should tempt a young Fellow, not contemptible either in Person, Mind, or Fortune, by a large Settlement, and an easy Condition of Life.*" *Pontianus*, the Son of *Pudentilla*, (he tells his Judges) proposed the Marriage of his Mother to him, no otherwise than as an Incumbrance, and as the Act of a Friend and a Philosopher; that is, an Act more becoming a good Friend to *Pontianus*, and a Philosopher, than the staying for a Match, where he might find both Riches and Beauty. *Considere sese, fore ut id onus recipiam, quoniam non formosa pupilla, sed mediocri facie mater liberorum mihi offeratur. Sin hæc reputans formæ & divitiarum gratia me ad aliam conditionem reservarem, neque pro amico neque pro philosopho facturum* (49). He magnifies greatly the Advantages of a Maid, above a Widow. " *How poor soever a fair Maid is,* said he, *she brings you a great Dowry, the Flower and first Fruits of her Beauty, an Heart intirely new. It is with great Reason, that all Husbands set so great a value on a Maidenhead; all other Treasures, which a Woman brings, are of such a Nature, that an Husband may restore them back, if he is unwilling to be obliged to his Wife for them; she may withdraw them; she may recover them at Law; Virginity alone cannot be restored, but remains always in Possession of the first Husband. If you marry a Widow, and she leaves you, she carries away all she brought with her; you cannot boast of retaining any thing, which belongs to her.*" He observes several other Inconveniences in marrying Widows; and concludes, that " *Pudentilla would not easily have been married a second time, if she had not met with, in him, the Temper of a Philosopher.*" *Virgo formosa, etsi sit oppido pauper, tamen abundè dotata est. Affert quippe ad maritum novum animi indolem, pulchritudinis gratiam, floris rudimentum, Ipsa virginitatis commendatio jure meritoque omnibus maritis acceptissima est. Nam quodcunque aliud in dotem acceperis, potes cum libuit ne sis beneficio obstrictus omne ut acceperas retribuere, pecuniam renumerare, mancipia restituere, domo demigrare, prædiis cedere. Sola virginitas cum semel accep-*

ta est reddi nequitur: sola apud maritum ex rebus dotalibus remanet. Vidua autem qualis nuptiis venit, talis divortio digreditur. Nihil affert irreposcibile, sed venit jam ab alio præflorata; certe tibi, ad quæ velis, minime docilis: non minus suspectans novam domum, quam ipsa jam ob unum divortium suspectanda: sive illa morte amisit maritum, ut scævi ominis mulier, & infausti conjugii, minime appetenda; seu repudio digressa est, utramvis habebat culpam mulier: quæ aut tam intolerabilis fuit ut repudiaretur, aut tam insolens, ut repudiaret. Ob hæc & alia viduæ dote auctæ procos solicitant. Quod Pudentilla quoque in alio marito fecisset, si Philosophum spernentem dotis non reperisset (50). This Discourse of *Apuleius* is a noble Field for Reflexions, were there leisure to pursue them; however, in haste as I am to pass on to other Articles, I shall stay to make two Observations; one is, that this Estate, of which the Husband can never be disseized, is a meer Chimera; no Baker, or Butcher, would trust you for Six-pence upon this imperishable Possession. The other is, that *Apuleius* had not considered every Disadvantage of Widowhood. He has said nothing of Widows, who have never had any Children; nor, indeed, was That his Case. A Prebend of *Paris*, who made a trip to *Geneva*, in 1672, with a Design of embracing the Protestant Religion, happened, soon after his Arrival, to single out a young, rich, and handsome, Widow, among other Women in the same Church. He soon found an Opportunity of speaking to her; and, the more he saw her, the more he fancied she would suit his purpose. But, having brought with him from *France*, nothing but the good Plight of Persons of his Profession, and some Insight into the Abuses of Popery, he was repulsed with Scorn. He communicated to me the Secret of his Repulse, and complained less of the Disappointment, than of the manner, in which he was treated (51). I represented ingenuously to him, that he was in the wrong to propose any such thing, considering the present Condition of his own Fortune, and the Circumstances of the Lady. He confessed he was too rich for such a Person as he; *But*, continued he, *much of her Riches must be abated, on the score of her never having had a Child: this alone is a Drawback upon it of Thirty or Forty thousand Livres; at least I should have esteemed her by so much a better Fortune, than I do now, since there is a Presumption of her being barren; especially, when I consider, that my only Brother has no Heirs, and that our Family is in danger of being extinct, if I leave no Posterity.* I would not enter into a farther Dispute with a Man, who had calculated the Matter so nicely. I left him to estimate the Business by himself; and was satisfied with believing, that the Care he had at Heart of preserving his Family had contributed greatly to the opening his Eyes.

(47) Apul. Apolog. pag. 321.

(48) Apol. pag. 332.

(49) Ibid. 330.

(50) Ibid. pag. 352.

Reflexion of a Convert Priest upon a Widow, who had had no Children.

(51) He never talk'd of the Affair, without reserving, Est modus in rebus.

[K] *Furnishes us with Examples of the most shameful Artifices, that the Villany of an impudent Calumniator is capable of putting in Practice*] I shall instance but in one; to shew, that, in all Ages, the Spirit of Calumny has put Men upon forging Proofs by false Extracts from what a Person has said, or written. To convict *Apuleius* of practising Magic, his Accusers alledged a Letter, which his Wife had wrote during the Time of his Courtship, and affirmed that she had confessed, in this Letter, that *Apuleius* was a Wizard, and had bewitched her. It was no hard matter to make the Court believe, that she had written so; for they only read a few Words of her Letter, detached from what preceeded, or followed; and no one pressed them to read the whole. At last *Apuleius* covered them with Confusion, by reciting the whole Passage of *Pudentilla's* Letter. It appeared, that, far from complaining of *Apuleius*, she justified him, and artfully ridiculed his Accusers. These are his Words: You will find, that precisely the same Terms may either condemn, or justify, *Apuleius*, according as they are taken wish, or without, what preceeds them. Βουλομένη γὰρ με δι' ἃς εἶπον αἰτίας γαμηθῆναι,

APULEIUS.

served, that *Apuleius*, with all his Magic Art, could never raise himself to any Post of Authority, though he was of a good Family, had been very well educated, and was much esteemed for his Eloquence (*f*). It was not, pursues my Author, out of a Philosophical Contempt, that he was never in Public Employs; for he thought it an Honour to be invested with the Priestly Office, which gave him the Superintendence of the Public Games; and contended strongly against Those, who opposed the erecting of a Statue, with which the Inhabitants of *Oëa* would have honoured him (*g*). Nothing is more sensible Proof of the impertinent Credulity of the Pagans, than their saying, that *Apuleius* had wrought many Miracles [*L*], that they equalled, or even surpassed, Those of *JESUS CHRIST*. No doubt many Persons took all he had said in his *Golden Ass* for true History. I wonder St *Austin* could be in any Uncertainty about it (*b*), or that he was not convinced, that *Apuleius* intended this Book only as a Romance (*i*). He was not the Inventor of it; the Story is of ancient Date, as Mr *Moreri* discovered in the Words of *Vossius* [*M*]; which yet he did not thoroughly understand. Some Pagans have mentioned this Romance with

---

Side notes (left):

(*g*) Pro statua sibi apud Oëenses locanda, ex qua civitate habebat uxorem, adversus contradictionem quorundam civium litigaret, quod potueros ne lateret ejusdem litis orationem scriptam memoriæ commendavit. August. Epist. 5.

(52) Apul. Apol. pag. 326.

(53) Ibid.

(54) Marcellinus ad Aug. Epist. 4. inter Epist. Augustini. See also the 4*th* Letter of St Augustin, pag. 208.

(55) August. Epist. 5.

(56) Lactant. Divin. Institut. lib. 5. cap. 3. See also St Jerome in Psal. lxxxi.

Side notes (right):

(*f*) St Austin makes this Remark, in his fifth Epistle. See Remark [L.] at the end.

(*b*) Id. de Civit. Dei, lib. 18. cap. 18.

(*i*) Sermone illo Milesio varias Fabulas conferam. Apul. in Prologo.

(57) August. Epist. 5.

(58) Apul. Apolog. pag. 289.

(59) Vossius de Histor. Græc. pag. 517, 518.

γαμηθῆναι, αὐτὸς τοῦτον ἐποίησας ἀντὶ πάντων αἱρείσθαι, θαυμάζων τὸν ἄνδρα, καὶ σπουδάζων αὐτὸν οἰκεῖον ἡμῖν δι᾽ ἐμοῦ ποιῆσαι. νῦν δὲ ὡς μοχθηροὶ ὑμᾶς κακοηθείς τε ἀναπείθουσιν, αἰφνίδιον ἐγένετο Ἀτλάντιος μάγος, καὶ ἐγὼ μεμάγευμαι ὑπ᾽ αὐτοῦ. ναὶ κρω, καὶ ἦλθες γὰρ πρὸς ἐμέ, ὡς ἔτι σωφρονῶ (52). *Being inclined to marry for the Reasons, which I have mentioned, you yourself persuaded me to make choice of this Man, being fond of him, and desirous, by my means, to make him one of our Family. But now, at the Instigation of wicked Men, Apuleius must be informed against as a Magician, and I forsooth am enchanted by him. I certainly love him. Come to me, before any Reason fails me*. He aggravates this kind of Fraud as it deserves. His Words deserve to be engraved in Letters of Gold in a thousand Places, to deter, if possible, all Calumniators in all Countries, and in all Ages, who practise the like Cheats. " Multa sunt quæ sola prolata ca-" lumniæ possunt videri obnoxia. Cujavis oratio " insimulari potest, si ea quæ ex pluribus nexa sunt " principio sui defraudentur, si quædam ex ordine " scriptorum ad libidinem supprimantur, si quæ sinu-" lationis causâ dicta sunt, assseverantis pronunciatione " quam exprobrantis legantur (53). --- *There are many things, which, produced alone, may seem liable to Calumny. Any Discourse may furnish matter of Accusation, if what is connected with foregoing Words be robbed of it's Introduction, if some Things be suppressed at Pleasure, and if what is spoken by way of Reproach to others, for inventing a Calumny, be pronounced by the Reader as an Assertion of the Truth of it.*"

[*L*] *The Pagans pretended, that Apuleius wrought many Miracles*] We should scarce believe, that this had ever been said, if credible Persons did not attest it: But we find, that this Impertinence of the Pagans was such a Cant in St *Austin*'s Time, that this great Prelate was requested to refute it. " Pre-" cator accesserim ut ad ea vigilantius responderem " digneris, in quibus nihil amplius Dominum quam " alii homines facere potuerunt fecisse vel gessisse " mentiuntur. Apollonium siquidem suum nobis & " Apuleium aliosque magicæ artis homines in me-" dium proferunt, quorum majora contendunt exti-" tisse miracula (54). --- *On this Occasion I request of you, that you will exert your utmost Efforts in refuting the false Pretences of these Objectors, who would place the Works of OUR LORD on a Level with the Actions of meer Men. For they produce against him their APOLLONIUS and APULEIUS, and other Dealers in Magic, whose Miracles they assert to have been greater than His.*" St *Austin* contented himself with answering, that, if *Apuleius* had been so great a Magician, he would not have lived in so mean a Condition, as he did, considering his Ambition; That, besides, he had denied the Charge of Magic, which he allowed to be a great Crime (55). His pretended Miracles were spoken of long before St *Austin*; for *Lactantius* expresses his Surprize, that the Author, whom he confuted, had not joined *Apuleius* with *Apollonius Tyanæus*. " Voluit ostendere Apollonium " vel paria, vel etiam majora fecisse. Mirum quod " Apuleium prætermisit, cujus solent & multa mira " memorari (56). --- *He pretended to shew, that Apollonius had wrought as great, or even greater. It is surprizing he should forget Apuleius, who is reported to have wrought many Miracles.*" Apuleius has had the Fate of many other Persons: His Miracles were not spoken of 'till after his Death; his Accusers objected nothing but Trifles against him; or brought the worst Proof in the World of what might have the Appearance of Magic. But I know not how to reconcile St *Austin* with *Apuleius*. The one says, that *Apuleius* could never arrive at any Post of Judicature, ad aliquam judiciariam Reipublicæ potestatem (57). The other boasts, that *he had enjoyed the same Post, which his Father had held*; *who had been* Duumvir, *and had passed through every honourable Employment in the City, where he lived*. " In qua colonia patrem habui loco principe Duum-" viralem cunctis honoribus perfunctum. Cujus ego " LOCUM in ea repub. exinde ut participare CURIAM " cœpi nequaquam degener pari spero honore & " existimatione tueor (58) "

[*M*] *The Story is of ancient Date, as Mr* Moreri *discovered in the Words of* Vossius] Let us first set down his own Words. " *The Metamorphosis of the Golden Ass* is a Paraphrase of what he had taken " from *Lucian*, as *Lucian* had done before from *Lu-* " *cius* of *Patras*, mentioned by *Photius* ----- It " is even probable, that *Apuleius* borrowed, from " the same Source, the very Subject of the Fable, " which he has given his own turn to. For he " understood the *Greek* and *Latin* Tongues very " well." To judge whether Mr *Moreri* deserves Criticism, we must compare what he has said with the Passage of *Vossius*, which was his Original. " De ætate Lucii Patrensis non liquet, nisi quod an-" tiquior credatur Luciano, quippe qui inde com-" pilasse videatur Asinum suum, uti ex Luciano po-" stea asinum suum aureum exscripsit Apuleius. " Nisi is potius eat eodem Lucii fonte sua hausit, " & hoc sanè verisimilius est. Nempe ut Lucium " in epitomen redegit Lucianus, ita paraphrasin Lucii " scripsit Appuleius, fed ille Græcè, hic Latinè (59). " ------ *It is uncertain, when Lucius Patrensis " lived*; *nor is it thought to have been older than " Lucian, who seems to have borrowed from him his " Ass, in like manner as Apuleius afterwards copied " his Golden Ass from Lucian*; *unless perhaps he " copied it from Lucius himself*; *which is most probable. So that, as Lucian epitomized Lucius, Apuleius paraphrased him*; *but the one in Greek, the other in Latin*." It is plain Mr *Moreri* mistook *Vossius*'s Thought, and that he ought not to have said, that *Apuleius*'s Work is a Paraphrase on That of *Lucian*. He should have said, that *Lucius Patrensis* had been abridged by *Lucian*, and paraphrased by *Apuleius*. The Argument, which Mr *Moreri* includes in these Words, *for he understood the Greek and Latin Tongues very well*, is good for nothing. Put this Reasoning into Form, and you will raise this *Enthymema* from it: *He understood the Greek and Latin Tongues very well*; *therefore he took the Subject of this Fable, which he drest up after his own way, from the Fountain-head*; that is to say, *therefore he has not paraphrased Lucian, but Lucius Patrensis*. This *Enthymema* is ridiculous. A Knowledge of the *Greek* Tongue is as necessary in making use of *Lucian*, as of *Lucius*; and the *Latin* Tongue is of no help towards *dressing up in one's own way* a Subject borrowed from *Lucius*. Cannot Mr *de la Fontaine* dress up a Tale of *Ouville* after his own way? It would be of greater Use, than we are aware of, to criticise on the false Logic of Authors. Young Persons,

APULEIUS.

with Contempt [N]. *Apuleius* was extreamly laborious [O], and compofed feveral Books [P], fome in Verfe, and others in Profe; of which but a fmall Part has refifted the Injuries of Time. He delighted in making publick Speeches, in which he gained the Applaufe of all his Hearers. When they heard him at *Oëa*, the Audience cried out with one Voice, That he ought to be honoured with the Freedom of the City (*k*). Thofe of *Carthage* heard him favourably, and erected a Statue in Honour of him (*l*): Several other Cities did him the fame Honour (*m*). It is faid, that his Wife held the Candle to him, whilft he ftudied; but This, I think, muft not be taken literally; it is rather a Figure of *Gallic* Eloquence in *Sidonius Apollinaris*; *Legentibus meditantibufque candelas & candelabra tenuerunt* (*n*). Several Critics have publifhed Notes on *Apuleius* [Q]. I have never met with any modern *French* Tranflation of the *Golden Afs* [R]. This Work ought to be confidered as a continued Satire on the

Perfons, who are born to be Authors, would profit much, and betimes, by fuch Criticifms.

[N] *Some Pagans have mentioned this Romance with Contempt.*] I defire no other Proof of this, than the Letter, in which the Emperor *Severus* complains to the Senate of the Honours paid to *Clodius Albinus*. Among other Elogiums, they had given him That of Learning. The Emperor could not bear, that they fhould give fuch a Character to a Man, who had *filled his Mind with nothing but the Tales and Rhapfodies* of Apuleius. "Major fuit dolor quod "illum pro literato laudandum plerique duxiftis, quum "ille nænis quibufdam anilibus occupatus inter "Milefias punicas Apuleii fui, & ludicra literaria "feneceret (60)." *Macrobius* has configned over all fuch Romances, as *Apuleius*'s *Golden Afs*, to Nurfes. "Vel argumenta fictis cafibus amatorum referta, "quibus vel multum fe Arbiter exercuit, vel Apu-"leium nonnunquam lufiffe miramur. Hoc totum "fabularum genus, quod folas aurium delicias pro-"fitetur, è facrario fuo in nutricum cunas fapientia "eliminat (61). — — *We are furprized to find, that even Apuleius fometimes diverted himfelf with Love-Tales, in which Arbiter cheifly exercifed himfelf. This kind of Fable, which profeffes only to pleafe the Ear, Learning banifhes from her Temple to the Cradles of Nurfes.*"

[O] *Apuleius was extreamly laborious.*] Hear what he fays himfelf, in his Anfwer to his Adverfary, on the Subject of Eloquence. "De eloquentia vero, "fi qua mihi fuiffet, neque mirum neque invidio-"fum deberet videri, fi ab ineunte ævo unis ftudiis "literarum ex fummis viribus dedicus, omnibus aliis "fpretis voluptatibus, ad hoc ævi, haud fciam anne "fuper omneis homines impenfo labore, diuque no-"ctuque, cum defpectu & difpendio bonæ valetu-"dinis, eam quæfiffem (62). — — *As to Eloquence, if I ever had any, it ought not to be thought ftrange or odious, that, from my Youth to this Time, I have endeavoured after it, applying myfelf folely to the Study of Letters, and contemning all other Pleafures, with greater Application of Mind, than perhaps any Man ever did, and even to the Ruin of my Health.*"

[P] *And compofed feveral Books.*] See the Differtation *de Vita & Scriptis Apuleii*, which *Wower* has printed at the beginning of his Edition, and Mr *Fleuri*, the Dauphin Scholiaft, has prefixed to His. It may be faid, that *Apuleius* was an Univerfal Genius: There are but few Subjects, which he has not handled. He tranflated the *Phædo* of Plato, and the *Arithmetic* of *Nicomachus*: He wrote a Treatife *de Republica*; another *de Numeris*; and one *de Mufica*: They quote his *Table-Queftions*; his *Letters to Cerellia*, which are a little too free; his *Proverbs*; his *Hermagoras*; and his *Ludicra*. He mentions the latter himfelf: *Legerunt*, fays he (63), *è Ludicris meis Epiftolium de dentificio, verfibus fcriptum. — — They read, out of my Ludicra, a fhort Epiftle in Verfe, concerning a Powder for the Teeth.* We have ftill his *Golden Afs* in eleven Books; his *Apology*; his Treatifes of *Natural Philofophy*; *de Moral Philofophy*; *de Syllogifmo categorico*; *de Deo Socratis*; *de Mundo*; and his *Florida*. As to his *Letters* to *Cerellia*, I muft not omit the Judgment of a learned Critic (64) on them. He believes, that the Name of *Cicero* ought to be inferted in That Paffage of *Aufonius*, where thefe Letters are mentioned; for *Cicero* was the Perfon, who was reproached with having been too familiar with *Cerellia*, and writing to her too freely. On this Suppofition, we muft read the Paffage in *Aufonius* thus: "Effe Apuleium

"in vita Philofophum, in Epigrammatis amatorem; "Ciceronis in præceptis omnibus exftare feveritatem, "in Epiftolis ad Cerelliam fubeffe petulantiam. — — — "Apuleius *was, in his Life, a Philofopher*; *in his Epigrams, a Lover*; *Cicero's Precepts are all rigidly moral*; *his Epiftles to* Cerellia, *loofe and wanton.*"

[Q] *Several Critics have publifhed Notes on* Apuleius.] *Philippus Beraldus* publifhed very large Notes on the *Golden Afs*, at *Venice*, in Folio, *Ann.* 1504, which were reprinted, in 8vo, at *Paris*, and at feveral other Places. *Godefcalk Stewechius*, *Peter Colvius*, *John Wower*, &c. have written on all the Works of *Apuleius*. *Priceus* has publifhed the *Golden Afs*, and the *Apology*, feparately, with a great many Obfervations (65). The Annotations of *Cafaubon*, and Thofe of *Scipio Gentilis*, on the *Apology*, are much valued. The firft appeared in the Year 1594, and the latter in the Year 1607. The beft Edition of the Book *de Mundo*, is That of *Leyden*, 1591, in 8vo. We are indebted for it to *Bonaventure Vulcanius*. Let me obferve, by the way, that This Treatife is almoft the fame with the Tranflation of a like Work, attributed to *Ariftotle*. The Book *de Deo Socratis* has appeared with the Annotations of *Jofias Mercerus* (66). The Author, whom I quote, will give you a more ample Account of the Editions of *Apuleius* (67). He has made no particular mention of That of *Bafil*, *apud Henricum Petri*, 1560, in three Volumes, in 8vo; nor of That of the fame Town, *apud Sebaftianum Henrici Petri*, 1620; nor of That of *Lyons*, 1614, in two Volumes in 8vo; which perfectly refembles That of *Leyden*, the Pieces of which he particularly fpecifies, placing it in the Year 1614. Perhaps he miftook the *Lugdunum* of *France* (*Lyons*), for the *Lugdunum Batavorum* (*Leyden*).

[R] *I have never met with any modern* French *Tranflation of the* Golden Afs.] If I am not miftaken, *John Louveau* is the Author of the firft old Tranflation: *La Croix du Maine* mentions it, without fetting down the Year, in which it appeared (68). He only fays, that it was printed at *Paris*. It was reprinted, at *Paris*, by *Claudius Micard*, in 1584. One *J. de Montlyard* publifhed a Tranflation of the fame Book, with a Commentary. One of the two Editions, which I have feen, was *according to the Copy*, printed at *Paris* by *Abel l'Angelier*, 1612; the other, at *Paris*, by *Samuel Thibouft*, 1623. The Preface is long; and contains a Criticifm on feveral Errors of *John Louveau*.

I find, that *La Croix du Maine*, and *du Verdier Vau-Privas*, have mentioned a Tranflation, which may very well be older, than That of *John Louveau*. They fay, that *George de la Bouthiere*, of *Autun*, is the Native of *Autun*, rendered the *Metamorphofis*, or *Golden Afs* of *Apuleius* into *French* (69). The one fays, that this Verfion was printed at *Lyons*, by *John de Tournes* and *William Gazeau*, in the Year 1553. The other, that it was printed by *John de Tournes*, in 1516 (70). There is an Error of the Prefs in the laft Date; and it is evident, that, to put the Figures in their right Places, it ought to be 1556: Now, as the fame Author has faid, that the Tranflation by *John Louveau* was printed in the Year 1558 (71), there is Reafon to fuppofe, that it was later than That of *George de la Bouthiere*.

Since the firft Edition of this Dictionary, Part of a Tranflation of the *Golden Afs* has appeared at *Paris*. The *Journal des Spavans* of the ninth of *January*, 1696, mentions it. Monf. the Baron *des Coutures* publifhed, with Notes, in 1698, his *French* Verfion of the Treatife *de Deo Socratis*.

[S] *This*

the Disorders, which the Magicians, Priests, Pandars, Thieves, &c. filled the World with at That time [S].

[S] *This Work ought to be considered as a continued Satire on the Disorders, which Magicians, Priests, &c. filled the World with at That Time.*] This Observation occurs in Mr *Fleuri*'s Annotations. "Tota "porro hæc metamorphosis Apuleiana & stilo & sen- "tentia Satyricon est perpetuam (ut recte observavit "Barthius Adversf. lib. 51. cap. 11.) in quo magica "deliria, sacrificulorum scelera, adulterorum crimi- "na, furum & latronum impunitæ factiones, palam (72) Julius "differuntur (72)." He adds, that Those, who are Floridus, in search of the Philosopher's Stone, pretend to find Comment. it in the Mysteries of the Grand Operation. A Per- Delph. in son, who would take the Pains, and had the requi- Apuleium. site Qualifications (and he must, indeed, have a great many) might draw up a very curious and instructive Commentary on This Romance, and might inform us of several Things, which the preceeding Commentaries, how good soever, have never touched upon. There are some very obscene Passages in this Book of *Apuleius*. It is believed, that the Author has inserted some Episodes in it of his own Invention; and, amongst others, That of *Psyche*. *Horum certe noster ita imitator fuit, ut è suo penu innumerabilia protulerit, atque inter cætera venustissimum illud Psyches Ἐρωτικὸν (73).* This Episode fur- (73) Julius nished *Moliere* with Matter for an excellent Dramatic ubi supra, Piece, and Mr *de la Fontaine* for a fine Romance. pag. 2.

(a) Du Verdier. Biblioth. Franc. pag. 278.

AQUÆUS (STEPHEN), in *French de l'Aigue* *, Lord of *Beauvais* (*a*), in *Berry*, * So the Gashis Native Country, made himself famous by his Military Actions [*A*]; and his Wri- cons call tings, in the Reign of *Francis* I. Not that his Commentary on *Pliny*, which is the Author best of his Works, is good in the Main [*B*]; but it was extraordinary, in those self Stephen Times, for a Gentleman to perform so much. This Commentary was printed in de l'Aigue 1530. Father *Hardouin* was not well acquainted with it's Date [*C*]. nois, in the beginning of

[*A*] *Famous for his Military Actions, and his Writings*.] Father *Hardouin* gives him this Elogium. *Vir* (1) Hardoui- *nobilis in primis, at militia quoque exacta egregie* nus, Præfat. *sordidus* (1). - - - - *A Person very famous, and, after* In Plinium. *War, remarkably sordid.* The Works, he published, are *A singular Treatise concerning the Properties of* (2) Du Ver- *Tortoises, Snails, Frogs, and Artichokes*, at *Lyons*, in dier, Bibl. 8vo (2). Julius *Cæsar's Commentaries on the Roman* Françoise, *Wars*, and other Military Exploits, performed by pag. 278. *him* in *Gaul*, and *Africa*, at *Paris* 1531, in Folio. Le Croix du *Du Verdier* cites this Edition (3). *La Croix du* Maine *points out the Edi- Maine* takes notice of the Edition at *Paris*, in 1539 (4), tion of Paris, but not of That in 1546. We are going to take in 1530. notice of his Commentary on *Pliny*.
[*B*] *His Commentary on Pliny - - - - is not good* (3) Du Ver- *in the main*.] It is more considerable, for it's Size, dier, ubi than it's Learning. The Author corrects only as a supra. Plagiary, and *passes over almost all the difficult Places*. (4) La Croix This is Father *Hardouin*'s Judgment of it. " Com- du Maine, "mentarios scripsit in omnes Plinii libros: Sed mole Bibl Fr. " magis quam eruditione insignes. Nec vero emen- pag. 76. " dationes ulla habet, quam quas à Rhenano mu- " tuatus est: Et ea fere in quibus salebrarum est ali- " quid aut ambagis, solet is, ceu foveam, securus præ- (5) Harduin. " tergredi (5)." He is guilty of the same Fault Præfat. In with several other Writers; he makes use of the Plinium. Property of other Men, without mentioning his Benefactor; and *names him only when he intends to censure him*. *Rhenanus* made this Complaint, in a Letter to a Physician of the Cardinal of *Westphalia*: (6) See the " Hoc mirum, quod quum ex meis castigationibus 50th *Letter* " nonnihil sit adjutus, nusquam tamen mei mentio- *of the Cen-* " nem facit, nisi quoties vult reprehendere (6)." The turia Episto- general Judgment, which he passes on this Work, larum Phideserves to be reported. " In primis ipsum volumen lologicarum, " non est exiguum, ex variis congestum autoribus, *published by* " quod usui pauperculis esse possit, qui non habent Goldast, p. " bibliothecam instructam, puta Aristotelem, & Alber- 106. Edit. " tum de Animalibus, Raphaelem Volateranum, ex 1674. " quo integra ferme capita autor transcripsit bona " fide, hoc est, upa cum ipsis mendis, ne syllaba *a Transla-* " quidem mutata, Cœlium Rhodiginum, Columel- *tion of Cæ-* " lam etiam, Palladiumque, & similes, scriptores. *sar, Edit. of* " Nam hoc præcipue habet studio, citare testimonia *Paris, 1546,* " autorum, qui cum Plinio faciunt, de verbis ipsis mi- *in 12mo.* " nimum sollicitus, quod illi penitus puerile videtur. " In summa liber talis est, qui si non magnopere ju- " vet, excitet tamen literas, & Plinium ipsum vulgo " lectitandum commendet, quæ mihi res in primis grata " est (7). - - - - *In the first Place, it is a bulky* (7) Ibid. " *Volume, compiled from various Authors: (upon which* " *account it may be useful to poorer Students, who* " *have not a well furnished Library) from* Aristotle, " *and* Albertus de Animalibus; Raphaël Volateran, " *from whom the Author has fairly transcribed whole* " *Chapters, not omitting the very Faults, nor alter-* " *ing a Syllable; from* Cœlius Rhodiginus, Columel- " la, Palladius, *and the like Writers. For his chief* " *Aim is, to cite the Testimonies of Authors, who* " *favour* Pliny, *unconcerned as to the Words them-* " *selves, which he thinks deserve the Regard of* " *Boys alone. In short, the Work is such, that, if it be* " *not very entertaining, it may yet promote Learning,* " *and perhaps recommend* Pliny *to a more general* " *Reading which I am particularly pleased with*."
[*C*] *Father* Hardouin *was not well acquainted* (8) Hardou*with the Date of the Edition of* Aquæus's *Commen-* in. Præfat. *tary on* Pliny.] He observes, that *Sigismond Gele-* la Plin. *nius* published a Volume of Corrections on *Pliny*, in the Year 1535; and that, the Year following, *Bætus Rhenanus* published his Work on the same Author; and that, at the end of four Years, our *Aquæus* published his Commentary (8). He must therefore have published it in 1540. Now it (9) See the is certain, that he published it in the Year 1530. 69th *Letter* I suppose Father *Hardouin*'s Mistake proceeded from *of the 3d* his not knowing, that *Gelenius* had twice employed *Book*) *E-* his Pen on *Pliny*, before the Edition of 1635 (9). rasmi's, *pag.* Perhaps the Book of *Aquæus* was later, by five Years, 1957. than the first Corrections of *Gelenius*.

AQUAVIVA (ANDREW MATTHEW) Duke of *Atri*, in the Kingdom of *Naples*, and Son of *Julius Aquaviva*, Count of *Conversano* [*A*], added, to the Splendor of his Birth, an Erudition, which rendered him highly illustrious, towards the End of the XVth, and Beginning of the XVIth Centuries. He was not satisfied barely with studying, and conversing with the Learned; he employed himself in writing Books, and acquitted himself with Reputation; as appears by his Work intituled, *Encyclopædia*; and another, in which he treats of *Moral Virtue* [*B*]. He wrote a Book

(1) See the *History of* Mahom. II. by Guillet, Tom. 2. pag. 373.

(2) See the *Epitaph of* Marullus *addressed to him*, Epigram. lib. 2. pag 16.

[*A*] *The Son of* Julius Aquaviva, *Count of* Conversano.] This Count signalized himself by his Valour, on several Occasions, and commanded the Army of *Naples*, when he was killed in a Skirmish, during the Siege of *Otranto* by the *Turks*, in 1480 (1). His Son, of whom we speak in this Article, was a long time inconsolable for this Loss (2)."
[*B*] *A Work, in which he treats of Moral Virtue*.] One would think, that P. *Jovius* looked upon it to be a *Commentary on* Plutarch's *Treatise of* *Moral Virtue*; and the modern Author of the Annotations on the *Latin Poems of Sannazarius* had the same Thought. " Librum nempe nobilem, cui " *Encyclopædia* nomen, itemque Commentarium in " Plutarchum de Virtute morali (3). - - - - *To wit*, (3) Notæ ad " *an excellent Work, entituled* Encyclopædia, *and a* Sann. Eleg. " *Commentary on* Plutarch, *Of Moral Virtue*." But pag. 189. Ethe Words of *Paul Jovius* are not clear enough dit. Amstel. to determine me to this Sense; I should rather keep 1689. to a more indefinite Idea. He expresses himself thus: " Nemo

AQUAVIVA. AQUINAS.

...likewise *de Re Equestri*. Before he applyed himself with so much Ardour to ...s, he had paid That Debt to Arms, which his high Birth claimed, and had ...ized himself that way; tho' Fortune had been ever averse. He had ...een engaged in two unsuccessful Battles, and was wounded, and taken Prisoner, in both. Study supported him in his Confinement; and he was so happy, as to obtain his Liberty from *Ferdinand*, King of *Aragon*, when *Gonsalvo*, surnamed the *Great Captain*, would have sent him, with other Prisoners, into *Spain*. From that Time, He betook himself to the Pleasures of a private Life, amidst his Books, and in the Company of learned Men, by whom he was highly praised, and honoured [*C*]. He inspired his Brother *Belisarius* with the same Love of Learning, who became likewise an Author [*D*]. Our *Aquaviva* would have been more happy, if he had managed his Estate a little better; but his too great Expences for several Years at last exhausted his Fortunes. He died at *Conversano*, at Seventy two Years of Age; when the *French* Troops, under the Conduct of *Lautrec*, ravaged *Apulia* (*a*) in 1582.

(*a*) Ex Jovio, Elog. Doctor Vir. cap. 73.

"Nemo ex his, qui illustribus orti familiis ætate
"nostra claruerunt - - - - - Andrea Matthæo Aqua-
"vivio - - - - - se luculentius optimis disciplinis ex-
"ornavit; uti præclare constat eo libro nobili pa-
"riter ac erudito qui Encyclopædia inscribitur, &
"de morali virtute Plutarchi plenior liber subtili &
"copioso commentario persimilis ostendit (4). - - - - -
"No one, among those of great Birth, who have flou-
"rished in our Times, - - - - - made a greater Figure
"in the learned World, than Andrew Matthew Aqua-
"viva; as is evident from his excellent and learned
"Book, entitled Cyclopædia, and his larger Work,
"not unlike a subtile and copious Commentary, con-
"cerning Plutarch's Treatise of Moral Virtue." This seems to intimate a laborious Paraphrase on this Work of *Plutarch*.

(4) P. Jovius, Elog. cap. 63. pag. 158.

Since the first Edition of this Dictionary, I have had an Opportunity of discovering, that *Paul Jovius* has expressed himself ill; for this is the Title of the Book of our *Aquaviva*, in the Edition of *Naples* 1526, in Folio. *Commentarii in translationem libelli Plutarchi Chæronei de Virtute Morali - - - - - liber primus. - - - - Commentaries on the Translation of Plutarch of Chæronea's Treatise of Moral Virtue - - - Book the first.* The Title of the *German* Edition, 1609, in 4to, is longer. *Illustrium & exquisitissimarum disputationum libri quatuor. Quibus omnes divinæ & humanæ sapientiæ, præsertim animi moderatricis Musicæ atque Astrologiæ arcana in Plutarchi Chæronei de Virtuti Morali præceptionibus recondita summo ingenii acumine retecta patesiunt, & figuris quæque suis illustrantur, &c. - - - - - Four Books of noble and most exquisite Disputations. In which all the Secrets of divine and human Knowledge, particularly of Music, which commands the Passions, and of Astrology, couched upon the moral Precepts of Plutarch of Chæronea, are very ingeniously discovered, and di-*

"stinctly explained. Neither *Toppi*, from whom I have borrowed this (5), nor *Leonard Nicodeme* make any mention of the Book, entituled *Encyclopædia*.

[*C*] *He was highly praised and honoured by learned Men.*] *Alexander ab Alexandro* dedicated his *Dies Geniales* to him. *Pontanus* dedicated to him his first Book *de Rebus Cœlestibus*, and his Treatise *de Magnanimitate*. *Sannazarius* ingeniously celebrates him for having been (as was since said of Mr *de Montauzier*) a Favourite of *Pallas*, whether under the Name of *Minerva*, or That of *Bellona*.

Favori de Pallas quelque nom qu'on lui donne,
Ou celui de Miverve, ou celui de Bellone.

See the last Elegy of the second Book, towards the end, and the second Epigram of the second Book. As to the Forty fourth Epigram of the same Book, I question, whether it be in praise of our *Aquiviva*, as the Author of the Annotations on *Sannazarius* (6) fancied; it is addressed *ad Neritinorum Ducem*, who, according to *Paul Jovius*, was *Belisarius Aquaviva*, the Brother of *Andrew Matthew*. It seems to me likewise, that the first Elegy of the third Book has no relation to this latter, but to his Father *Julius Aquaviva*. See, in the Author, whom I quote, the Names of several Writers, who have celebrated our *Andrew Matthew*.

[*D*] *His Brother Belisarius - - - - - - became likewise an Author.*] He composed a Treatise *de Venatione*, which he dedicated to his Brother *John Matthew*; another *de Auspicio*; another *de Principum Hiberis educandis*; another *de Re Militari*; and another *de Singulari Certamine*. These Works, first printed at *Naples*, in *Folio*, in the Year 1519, were reprinted at *Basil*, in 8vo, in the Year 1578, by the Care of *Leonclavius*, with the *Manuel Palæolius de Royal Education*.

(5) Toppi Biblioth. Napolet. pag. 14.

(6) Notæ in Sanmaz. pag. 188.

(7) Nicodemo, Addiz. alla Bibl. Napolet. p. 11, 12.

AQUINAS, or **AQUINIUS**, (PHILIP), acquired a great Reputation by his Skill in the *Hebrew* Tongue, which he taught, at *Paris*, in the Reign of *Lewis* XIII; and by his Works, which he published [*A*]. He was originally of *Aquino*, in the Kingdom of *Naples* (*a*), and from thence derived his Name; but he was born in the County of *Avignon*. He was a Convert from the *Jewish* Religion, and had a Pension (*b*) allowed him from the Clergy of *France*. He is mentioned in the Trial of the Marshal d'*Ancre* [*B*]. *Simeon de Muis* has greatly commended him [*C*];

(*a*) I have only his sirname Hearsay.

(*b*) See the Epistle Dedicatory of his Interpretation of the Tree of the Cabala.

[*A*] *He acquired a great Reputation - - - - - by the Works, which he published.*] The Catalogue of them is as follows: *Dictionarium Hebræo-Chaldæo-Thalmudico-Rabbinicum*, fol. printed at *Paris* in the Year 1629; *The Roots of the Sacred Language, ad formam Cubi Hutteriani*, at *Paris*, 1620, 16mo; A Translation, in *Italian*, of *The Apophthegms of the ancient Doctors of the Jewish Church*, collected by Rabbi *Simeon*, Son of *Gamaliel*; The Exposition of *The thirteen Ways, which the ancient Rabbies made use of to explain the Pentateuch*, (1). An Interpretation of *the Tree of the Cabala*, enriched with it's Figure, taken from the ancient *Hebrew* Authors, at *Paris*, at the Expence of the Author, 1620, in 8vo; A Discourse *of the Camp, and Tabernacle of the Israelites*, at *Paris*, by *Tb. Blaise*, 1625, in 4to; *Lateral, Allegorical, and Moral Explications of the Tabernacle, which God commanded Moses to build; of the Priests Vestments, and the manner how they consulted the Rationale of the ancient Law, together with the Form of the Jewish Sacrifices; all*

curiously collected, and faithfully translated from the most learned and ancient Hebrew Authors; a Discourse concerning the Camp of the Israelites; and a Description of the Jewels of the High Priest's Breast-Plate, added at the end of the second Edition, *revised by the Author*; at *Paris*, at the Author's Expence, 1624, in 4to; *Beccbina: Olam, or An Examination of Rabbi Jacob's World; Moral Sentences of the ancient Hebrews, and the thirteen Ways, which they made use of to interpret the Bible*, in 8vo, at *Paris*, by *John Lacquebay*, 1629. *Phil. Aquinatis Hebraicæ Linguæ Profess. Lacrymæ in obitum Illustriss. Cardinalis de Berulle, Parisiis, apud Joannem Bessin*, 1629, in 8vo.

[*B*] *He is mentioned in the Trial of the Marshal d'Ancre.*] This Fact is too singular to be omitted. "*Item*, It is proved, by Informations, as also by the "Deposition of *Philip Aquinas*, formerly a *Jew*, but "now a Christian, whom *Conchini* and his Wife had "sent for to *Moulins*, where the said *Aquinas* was at "the Lieutenant Criminal's House (2), that *Conchini* "and

(1) Printed at *Paris* in 1620. in 4to.

(2) Perhaps he went Tutor there, to Gilbert Gaulmin, who confesses that he had been a Disciple of Philip Aquinas, in rerum MS. librum, suys he, ad libros de Vita Moisis, pag. 30: ex Philippi Dequen Præceptoris olim mei originis disput.

AQUINAS. ARAGON.

him [C]; on the other hand, *Valerian de Flavigni* has spoken ill of him [D]. There was one LEWIS-HENRY AQUINAS, his Cotemporary, who was also well skilled in the Oriental Languages. I cannot tell, whether he was his Son, or his Brother (c). He translated something out of the *Hebrew* into the *Latin* (d) [E]. He had likewise been a *Jew*, and was afterwards a Pensioner of the Clergy. ANTONY AQUINAS, who had been First Physician to *Lewis* XIVth, was Grandson of *Philip*.

(c) Mr Colomiès believes he was his Son.
(d) See Colomiès Gall. Orient. pag. 256.

"his Wife had made use of the Cabala, and the *Jewish* Books. It being to be observed, what this *Aquinas* had farther deposed, viz. that *Conchini*, in the Presence of his Wife, had taken away a Chamber-pot on account of it's Impurity, and removed a Crucifix out of the Room, for fear it should hinder an Effect, which They, *Conchini* and his Wife, expected from reading some Verses of the Fifty first Psalm, *Misereri mei*, in Hebrew: which Reading they caused to be performed by *Aquinas*, in the same Manner as it had been some times performed before them by *Montalto*."

[C] Simeon de Muis *has greatly commended him.*] He expresses himself thus concerning a Verse of the Thirty fifth Psalm: "Cum hic hærerem dubius, "Philippus Aquinas è Judæo Christianus, vir raræ "& exquisitissimæ in Hebraicis literis doctrinæ, & "quem nunquam frustra consulas, forte venit ad me "visendi gratia, & venit quidem optatus. Ille statim "atque de re communicavi, ut singulas Bibliorum "versus imo & voces singulos in numerato habet, "ac tanquam digitos tenet, indicavit locum ex "Esaiæ 66 ver. 13. - - - - *Being at a loss for the "Sense of this Passage*, Philip Aquinas, *a converted "Jew, a Man of uncommon and exquisite Skill in "the Hebrew Tongue, and whom you can never consult in vain, came accidentally to pay me a Visit, "and came opportunely to my wish. For no sooner "had I communicated the Matter to him, but He, "who has every Verse, and even every Word, of Scrip-* "*ture at his Fingers ends, referred me to* Esaiah "66. ver. 13.

[D] Valerian de Flavigni - - - - *has spoken ill of him.*] He was Professor of *Hebrew* in the Royal College, at *Paris*. He ridiculed the Bible of Mr *le Jai* unmercifully, and maintained, that the *Hebrew* Text had been miserably corrupted by *Philip Aquinas* "Tot ac tantis conspurcatum maculis atque "sordibus, obstetricantibus impurissimis manibus Phi-"lippi Aquinatis Avenionensis ex Judæo Christiani, "ut à planta pedis usque ad verticem non sit in "eo sanitas (3). - - - - *Defiled with so many and "great Blots and Filth by the impure Hands of* "Philip Aquinas, *of* Avignon, *a converted Jew, "that, from the Sole of the Foot to the Crown of "the Head, there is no whole Part in it.*"

[E] *He translated something out of* Hebrew *into* Latin.] Read what follows: Commentarius Rabbi Levi filii Gersonis in librum Jobi, seu in V. prima capita, interprete Ludovico Henrico Aquino Lutetiæ. ——— *A Commentary of* Rabbi Levi, *the Son of* Gerson, *on the Book of* Job, *or on the five first Chapters, translated by* Lewis Henry Aquinas, *of* Paris. *Paris, by* Thomas Blaise, 1620, in 4to. Scholia Rabbi Salomonis Jarchi in librum Esther: item excerpta quædam ex Talmudo & Jalcut in eundem librum, interprete Lud. Henr. Aquino. ——— *The Scholia of* Rabbi Solomon Jarchi *on the Book of* Esther; *likewise Extracts from the* Talmud *and* Jalcut *on the same Book, translated by* Lewis Henry Aquinas. *Paris*, 1622, in 4to.

(3) In Epist. de Heptaplis Parisiensibus, apud Colomesium Gall. Orien. pag. 256.

ARAGON (ALPHONSO, fifth of the Name, King of) Sicily. See, under the Word NAPLES, *Alphonso*, first of the Name, King of *Naples*.

ARAGON (JOAN of) the Wife of *Ascanio Colonna*, Prince of *Tagliocozzi*, was the most Illustrious Lady of the XVIth Century. She was born at *Naples*, and descended from the Kings of *Aragon*. The Wits of those Times celebrated her Praises after an extraordinary manner [A]. The Philosopher *Augustin Niphus* was one

The Poetical Deification of this Lady.

[A] *The Wits of those Times celebrated her Praises in an extraordinary manner.*] I have not seen any Dictionary, in which the Article of this Lady is to be met with: It is a Sin of Omission most worthy of Censure; for, perhaps, there never was a Man or Woman in the World, whose Merit has been celebrated by more fine Wits, or in more Languages, than That of *Joan of Aragon*, in the XVIth Century. The Poems, wrote in her Praise, were collected by *Jerom Ruscelli*, and published at *Venice*, in 1555, under the Title of TEMPIO ALLA DIVINA SIGNORA DONNA GIOVANNI d'ARAGONA, fabricato da tutti i piu gentili Spiriti, & in tutte le lingue principali del mondo. ——— A Temple to the Divine Lady *Donna Joanna* of *Aragon*, *erected by the greatest Wits, and in all the principal Languages of the World*. The Poëtical Deification of this Lady was performed with Ceremonies, not unlike Those made use of in the Canonization of Saints. In the first Place, several great Wits, of their own meer Motion, determined to testify their Devotions to this Divinity, and to prepare her a Temple; afterwards, in the Year 1551, the Matter passed into a Decree in the Academy of the *Dubbiosi*, at *Venice*. After several Deliberations and Consultations, on a Question, which was started, to wit, whether this Temple should be jointly dedicated to *Donna Joanna* of *Aragon*, and her Sister, the Marchioness *du Guast*; the Decree imports, That, considering the Opposition anciently made by the Pontiffs to *Marcellus*'s Design of building a Temple jointly to *Honour* and *Virtue*, the Marchioness *du Guast* could have no Part, nor Interest, in her Sister's Temple; except by Means of some particular Interpretations. Not only the Poets, whose Verses *Ruscelli* has collected, but Himself likewise, in the Prose of his Epistle Dedicatory to the Cardinal of Trent, and in his Preface, employs the Terms of Adoration and Divinity; it is true, he adds this Corrective, that the Adoration, paid to this Lady, was only relative, and terminated in the Supream Being, who had conferred so many Perfections upon her. These are his Words. "Questa conos-"cenza ——— ha fatto questi anni à dietro che conos-"cendosi in universale & in particolare da ogni piu "raro giudicio i gran meriti, & il sommo valore, "& la bellezza infinita di corpo & d'animo della Il-"lustrissima & Excellentissima Signora DONNA "GIOVANNA d'ARAGONA, si sieno tutti "i piu begli spiriti di commune consentimento po-"sti à sacrarle un Tempio, come à Donna intera-"mente divina, & la quale, come nobilissima fat-"tura & sembianza del Sommo Iddio, meriti ve-"ramente d' esser con la lingua & col cuore adorata "per immenso honore del fattor suo; potandosi deg-"namente da ciascuno far guidicio, quanta sia infinito "il sapere, il potere, & l' amor verso di noi di chi "così (alla capacita della mente nostra) infinitamente "bella & perfetta & degna d' esser' adorata creatura "habbia potuto, saputo, & degnatosi di voler fare in "questa eta nostra. ——— *This Knowledge ——— has "been the Cause, of late Years, that, the great Me-"rit, Worth, and infinite Beauty, both of Body and "Mind, of the most Illustrious and most Excellent "* DONNA JOANNA *of* ARAGON, *being "universally and particularly known to every one of "the least Judgment, all the Men of Wit unani-"mously agreed to dedicate a Temple to her, as to a "Lady entirely Divine; and who, as being the most "noble Production and Resemblance of the Supream "Being, deserves to be adored with Tongue and Heart, "in honour of her great Creator; every one being ca-"pable of judging of the infinite Wisdom, Power, and "Love*

ARAGON.

one of the forwardeſt in paying his Homage to her. He repreſented her as ſo wonderfully beautiful, and particularized the Perfections of her Body [*B*], in ſuch a manner, that ſome Authors have ſaid he flattered her [*C*], and that Love inſpired him with thoſe high Strains. It has been ſaid likewiſe, that his Quality of Phyſician gave him Privileges, which fired him with Love [*D*]. To me theſe Conjectures appear trifling

" *Love of God towards us, in condeſcending to form*
" *out of our own Species (within the Sphere of human*
" *Capacity) ſo beautiful, perfect, and adorable a Crea-*
" *ture, in this our Age.*" He tells us, in the Preface, that the Subſtance of his whole Collection imports,
" Che queſta gran Donna, come perfettiſſima di corpo
" & d' animo, & come particolariſſima fattura del
" ſommo Iddio, meriti d' eſſere adorata ad honore
" del fattor ſuo. Overo che chiaſcuno partitamente
" l' offeriſce il ſuo voto, à là purita dell' affetto ſuo.
" ——— *That this great Lady, as being moſt per-*
" *fect, both in Body and Mind, and the moſt ſingular*
" *Production of the Supream Being, deſerves to be a-*
" *dored in honour of her Creator; or, that every one*
" *ought, in particular, to offer up his Vows to her,*
" *according to the Purity of his Affection towards*
" *her.*" The leaſt poetical, and the moſt unknown, Languages, were employed in erecting this Temple; as the *Sclavonian*, the *Poliſh*, the *Hungarian*, the *Hebrew*, and the *Chaldaic*; and, perhaps, Mr *de Peireſc* (1) was the only Perſon, in whoſe Favour a like, or a greater, Concourſe of Languages, had ever been employed.

(1) See Remark [C] of his Article.

[*B*] *And particularized the Perfections of her Body.*] *Niphus* dedicated his Treatiſe of Beauty to this Lady; and, to confute the ancient Philoſophers, who maintained, that there is no perfect Beauty in the Univerſe, he alledges, in his fifth Chapter, the Inſtance of *Joan* of *Aragon*. He enters into ſo minute a Detail, in drawing the Picture of this fair one, that, among the great Numbers of Deſcriptions, which the Romances of *Mademoiſelle de Scudery* brought in faſhion, thirty or forty Years ago (2), there is not one, we may venture to ſay, but falls ſhort of his. He is not ſatisfied with deſcribing the Beauties, which are viſible to every Eye, but paſſes to thoſe, *quas ſinus abſcondit*, and to the Proportions between the Thigh and Leg, and between the Leg and Arm. *Ventre ſub pectore decenti, & latere cui ſecretiora correſpondeant. Amplis atque perrotundis coxendicibus, coxa ad tibiam & tibia ad brachium ſeſquialtera proportione ſe habente* (3). In the beginning of this Treatiſe, there is a Letter of Cardinal *Pompeius Colonna* to *Auguſtin Niphus*, vouching for the incomparable Beauty, and great Qualifications, of *Joan* of *Aragon*. Now, no one is ignorant, how far a Cardinal of Quality is a competent Judge, and even a Critic, in theſe Matters, *quàm elegans formarum ſpectator fiet*. Theſe are the Words of his Letter. " Non Vulgo ſpe-
" cioſiſſima quæque exponit natura: noſtro tamen ævo
" parens officioſa ac liberalis, veluti divinitatis æmu-
" la, ut perfectum admirandumque aliquid, Diíſque
" immortalibus quam ſimillimum, gentibus proferret,
" Joannam Aragoniam Columnam procreavit, atque
" ab incunabulis ad hanc uſque ætatem, in qua eſt
" florentiſſima per omnes pulchritudinis & venuſtatis
" numeros, provexit, ut facile principem locum in-
" ter formoſiſſimas vindicarit. Animum præterea ſin-
" gularibus & dotibus & virtutibus inſignivit, *&c.*
" ——— *The finer Productions of Nature are rare, and*
" *uncommon; yet this diligent and bountiful Mother*
" *of all things, in Emulation, as it were, of Divi-*
" *nity, and deſirous of producing a perfect and ad-*
" *mirable Creature, and nearly reſembling the immor-*
" *tal Gods, gave the World* Joan *of* Aragon, *of the*
" *Family of* Colonna, *and added daily new Charms*
" *to her, from Infancy to her preſent Years, in which*
" *ſhe is a conſummate Beauty, and may juſtly claim*
" *the Preference to all other the moſt beautiful Wo-*
" *men. Nature, likewiſe, adorned her Mind with*
" *ſingular Gifts and Virtues, &c.*"

[*C*] *Some Authors have ſaid, he flattered her.*] *Lewis Guyon* cannot be perſuaded, that all the Beauties, which *Auguſtin Niphus* aſcribes to the Princeſs *Joan* of *Aragon*, of the illuſtrious Family of the *Colonnas*, were real: " But, ſays he (4), I fancy he was in
" Love with her, and was drawn into it by having
" ſeen, touched, and handled her, in ſeveral parts of her
" ſick Body, as Phyſicians have a Privilege to do;
" and that, ambitious of obtaining her good Graces,

(2) This is written in 1692.

(3) Niphus pag. 213. Opuſcul. Edit. Pariſ. 1645.

(4) Guyon, Diverſ. Leçons, Vol. 3. lib. 3. c. 12.

" he publiſhed the Book, which he dedicated to her;
" nothing being more likely to gain, either on Wo-
" man or Maid, than a Perſuaſion that their Beauty
" has inſpired us with Love." After which he remarks, " that, if ſo, the Phyſician had forgotten
" the Oath he had taken, upon receiving his De-
" gree, which, among other things, enjoyned him,
" not to luſt after the Maids, or Women, he ſhall
" have under Cure." In the *Table of Matters*, he ſays poſitively, *that Niphus fell in Love with the Princeſs* Joan *of* Aragon, *when ſhe was his Patient.* This is going a little too far; he ought, at moſt, to have ſtopt at a Conjecture. I confeſs, *Niphus*, who was one of the beſt Philoſophers of the laſt Age, was of a very amorous Complexion; ſo far, that neither Age, nor the Gout, could break his Chains, which ſometimes made him act a very ſhameful Part, and even dance to the Sound of a Flute. *Suſceptis liberis, & ſeneſcente uxore, ſeptuagenarius Senex puellæ citra libidinem impotenti amore correptus eſt uſque ad inſaniam, ita ut pleriqne Philoſophum Senem & podagricum ad tibiæ modos ſaltantem miſerabili cum pudore conſpexerint* (5). I confeſs likewiſe, that, being in Love with a Lady of Honour, belonging to *Joan* of *Aragon* (6), he might have a near View of this fair Lady, and warm himſelf, at a ſmall Diſtance, by this great Fire; but it is not certain, that he forgot himſelf ſo far, as to raiſe his Thoughts ſo high. Beſides, as he did not practiſe Phyſic (7), tho' he had taken the Degree of Doctor, it is not probable, that he was Phyſician to this Princeſs; for Perſons of her Quality make uſe, in their Sickneſs, of an experienced, rather than a ſpeculative, Phyſician, who, like *Niphus*, applies himſelf chiefly to the Philoſophical Part; ſo that, upon the whole, I ſhould chuſe to ſay, that, Judgment not being his Talent, he took the Liberty to ſpeak of things he had never ſeen, and to repreſent them according to his own Ideas. What *Lewis Guyon* remarks, that this Princeſs was of the Family of the *Colonnas*, might be true on the Mother's Side; however, he has not expreſſed himſelf as he ought to have done. We have ſeen, that Cardinal *Pompeius Colonna* calls her *Joannam Aragoniam Columnam*; probably becauſe ſhe was married to *Aſcanio Colonna*. Perhaps *Auguſtin Niphus* might have been cenſured upon better Grounds, in relation to the Sixty eighth Chapter of his Treatiſe *de Phyſico*; where, having ſaid, that there was none, in thoſe Times, who deſerved the Name of Happy, but *Joan* of *Aragon*, ſince ſhe was poſſeſs'd of Both the Ingredients of Woman's Felicity, *viz.* Beauty and Chaſtity; he ſpeaks, immediately after, of *Victoria Colonna*, Marchioneſs of *Peſcara*, as a ſhining Example of the Union of Beauty and Chaſtity.

(5) Jovius Elog. c. 92.

(6) Naudæus, in Judicio de Aug. Nipho.

(7) Medicinam licet circitoris inſtar aut perriodeutæ exercuerit, optimè tamen calleatbat. *Id. ib.*

[*D*] *It has been ſaid, likewiſe, that his Quality of Phyſician gave him Privileges, which fired him with Love.*] The Poets, and others, have long ſince made Reflexions on this Privilege of Phyſicians. Thus *Ovid* makes the Amorous *Acontius* ſpeak.

A Remark on the Privileges of a Phyſician.

Me miſerum! quod non Medicorum juſſa miniſtro,
Aſtringoque manus, inſideoque thoro.
Et rurſus miſerum! quod me procul inde remoto,
Quem volumine vellem, forſitan alter adeſt.
Ille manus iſtas aſtringit, & aſſidet ægræ,
Inviſus ſuperis, cum ſuperiſque mihi.
Dumque ſuo tentat ſalientem pollice venam,
Candida per cauſam brachia ſæpe tenet,
Contrectatque ſinus, & forſitan oſcula jungit,
Officio merces plenior iſta ſuo eſt *.

*Ovid. Heroid. Epiſt. 20. ver. 133.

Why ſit I not by your Bed-ſide all Day,
My mournful Head in your warm Boſom lay,
'Till with my Tears the inward Fires decay?
Why preſs I not your melting Hand in mine,
And from your Pulſe of my own Health divine?

But

ARAGON.

(a) See Remark [C].
(b) See Remark [E].

trifling (a). It was not for her Beauty alone, that this Lady was so much admired; her Courage, her Prudence, and Capacity for great Affairs, distinguished her extreamly from other Women of Quality (b). In the Pontificat of *Paul* the IVth, she had a share in the Resolutions, taken by the *Colonna*'s, against the Interests of That Pope. She would have been imprisoned, had it not been in regard to her Sex; but she was only commanded not to stir out of *Rome*. However she dextrously contri-

(c) In 1556. See the Life of the Duke of Alba, and the Remark [I].

ved to make her Escape (c) [E], that she might be the better able to second the Enterprizes of her Son, the Famous *Marc Antony Colonna*, who afterwards acquired so much Honour in the Battle of *Lepanto*. It does not appear, that she was upon good Terms with her Husband at that time; for she was entirely in her Son's Interest: Now there was so great a Misunderstanding between the Father and Son [F], that the latter contributed to the Imprisonment of the former for Crimes of State. Unhappy, that a Lady, of so much Merit, should be at variance with her Husband. This is not so uncommon a Case, as it ought to be, among Persons of her Sex, who are possessed of the greatest Qualities. She shewed a great deal of Constancy, when she lost her Eldest Son, in 1551. What *Aretin* wrote to her, on that Occasion, is mixed with the highest Commendations. See the Sixth Book of his Letters, Page fifth

---

But Oh! these Wishes are all vain, and He,
Whom most I fear, may now sit close by Thee,
Forgetful, as thou art, of Heav'n and Me.
He That lov'd Hand does press, and oft does feign
Some new Excuse to feel thy beating Vein.
Then his bold Hand up to your Arm does slide,
And in your panting Breast itself does hide;
Kisses sometimes he snatches too from thee,
For his officious Care too great a Fee.

                  Mr DUKE.

Remi Belleau, in his Commentary on the second Book of the Amours of *Ronsard*, says, that the Forty sixth Sonnet was taken from this Epistle of *Ovid*. These are the Words of *Ronsard*.

Ha! que je porte & de haine & d'envie
Au Medicin qui vient soir & matin
Sans nul propos tastonner le tetin,
Le sein, le ventre, & les flancs de m'amie.
Las! il n'est pas si soigneux de ma vie
Comme elle pense, il est mechant & fin:
Cent fois le jour il la visite, afin
De voir son sein, qui d'aimer le convie.

Ah! how my jealous Heart, by turns,
With raging Hate, and Envy, burns,
'Gainst Him, who pleads a Doctor's Right
To see my Mistress, Morn and Night;
Who feels her snowy Breast, her Arm,
And handles every secret Charm.
Know you what makes the Doctor pay
An hundred Visits in a Day;
'Tis not as you believe, my Fair,
To guard That precious Life with Care;
But, with a Lover's eager Eyes,
To see your Bosom fall and rise.

But this Difference ought to be observed, that He, whom *Acontius* complains of, was contracted to the sick Person. Without this, she durst not have confest, in her Answer to *Acontius*, that his Rival kissed her but seldom;

- - - - - - Oscula rara
Accipit.

Brantome quotes this Sonnet of *Ronsard*, somewhere in his Memoirs, and says some good Things on the Occasion.

[E] *She was only commanded not to stir out of Rome. However, she dextrously contrived to make her escape.*] The Passage of *Antony Maria Gratiani*, which I am going to produce, contains, in express Terms, the Proof which I want. " Joanna Arragonia, Marci An- " tonii mater, virilis audaciæ femina, quæ virorum " quoque consiliis apud illum habita interfuerat, " continere se domi, neque pedem inde efferre fue- " rat jussa; id enim sic induliserat dignitati ejus pon- " tifex, ne in carcerem duceretur. Ea cum rem spe-

" ctare ad arma bellumque, & primum Pontificiorum " impetum in oppida filii fore intelligeret, vestibus " mane summo commutatis, cum filia & nuru, cor- " ruptis aut deceptis portæ custodibus, egressâ Urbe, " conscensis quos ad id præparaverat equis, protinus " Neapolim aufugit. Pontifex, quanquam deceptum " se delusumque à femina graviter ferebat, acerbius " tamen Hispanis, quorum ea consiliis adminstraren- " tur, irascebatur (8). —— Joan *of* Aragon, *Mother* " *of* Marc Antony, *a Lady of manly Resolution, and* " *who was present at the Consultations held at her* " *Son's House, was commanded to confine herself to* " *her own House; for the Pope, in regard to her Dig-* " *nity, had remitted the Sentence of Imprisonment.* " *This Lady, perceiving that all things tended to War,* " *and being sensible that the first Attack of the Ponti-* " *fical Forces would be upon the Town; in possession of* " *her Son, disguised herself early one Morning, to-* " *gether with her Daughter, and Daughter-in-law;* " *and, bribing, or deceiving the Keepers of the Gates,* " *escaped out of the City; and, mounting Horses, which* " *she had prepared for their Flight, escaped to* Naples. " *The Pope, though vexed to be out-witted by a Wo-* " *man, yet was more angry with the Spaniards, by* " *whose Councils those Affairs were directed.*" It was on occasion of this Escape, and some other Provocations, that the Pope was so much exasperated against the *Colonna*'s, that " he sent a Monitory (9), " to *Joan of Arragon*, by which he forbad her to " marry any of her Daughters without his Consent; " in default whereof, the Marriage, though after " Consummation, should be void (10)."

[F] *There was so great a Misunderstanding between the Father and Son.*] Cardinal *Palavicini* remarks, that *Ascanio Colonna* had offered such Violence to his Creditors, that the *Procurator Fiscal* cited him, to give an Account of his Conduct. *Ascanio*, not appearing, was condemned for Contumacy, and his Lands confiscated. His Son *Marc Antony*, having been a long time at Variance with his Father, took this Opportunity to strip him, by seizing on the confiscated Estates, and driving off the Ministers of Justice, a little before the Death of Pope *Julius* III. *In ipsa rei confectione Marcus Antonius ejus filius, eui cum parente veteres & nunquam satis compositæ controversiæ intercedebant, vim interposuit, eodemque tempore patrem oppidis spoliavit, ab iisque fisci ministros procul habuit* (11). He quitted *Rome* contrary to the Prohibition of *Paul* IV. This Disobedience, together with some former Disturbances, obliged this Pope to publish Letters Monitory against the Father and Son. The Father excused himself, on his being detained a Prisoner at *Naples*, from having endeavoured to excite a Revolt there; the Son alledged, that he had sequestered the Lands into the Hands of *Mendoza*, who could not be dissezed of them, without the Emperor's Order. I am surprized, that *Palavicini* says nothing of *Ascanio Colonna*'s Wife: But since we know, from another Hand, that she was engaged in her Son's Intrigues at *Rome*, and that the Son was at variance with his Father, we may safely suppose, that she was not upon very good Terms with her Husband. *Gratiani* speaks more positively of *Marc Antony*'s scandalous Conduct towards his Father. " Ante omnes, *says he* (12), Colonniorum familia, " magna

(8) Gratian. de Casibus Virorum Illustrium, pag. 322.

(9) On the second of January 1556.

(10) F. Paul's History of the Council of Trent.

(11) Pallavic. Hist. Concil. Tridient. lib. 13. cap. 14. n. 9.

(12) Gratian. ubi supra, pag. 320.

ARAGON.

(d) Of the Edition of Paris 1609.

fifth (d). She had a Sister, who was very handsome even in her old Age, and who had a famous Daughter-in-Law [G].

Every Remark on This Lady's Article might be spun out to a greater Length. For which reason, I shall add, in this Edition, by way of Supplement to what I have already said of her Deification (e), that, soon after the erecting of her Temple by the Care of *Jerom Ruscelli*, a certain Gallant Author dedicated many Statues to it

(e) In the Remark [A].

"magna in civitate pollensque pro illo *(Cæsare)* sta-
"bat, cujus princeps Marcus Antonius cum paulo an-
"te Ascanium patrem, a quo hostili odio dissidebat,
"insimulatum majestatis in custodiam tradendum Nea-
"poli curasset, aliquot oppidis intra fines Romanæ
"Ecclesiæ haud longe ab Urbe imperitabat. ——
"*The great and powerful Family of the Colonna's de-
"clared for Him, whose Head Marc Antony, having,
"not long before, procured his Father, with whom
"he was at irreconcileable Variance, to be imprisoned
"at Naples for Treason, was in possession of some
"Towns within the Territories of the Roman Church,
"not far from the City.*"

[G] *She had a Sister, who was very handsome, even in her old Age, and who had a famous Daughter-in-law.*] A *Spanish* Author speaks of these three Ladies thus: "Que cosas no podrian dezirse en laude y
"exaltation de la hermosissima Duquesa de Tallacoza,
"Donna Joana de Aragon, muger de Sangre Real,
"y en summo grado casta, y buena? Y ainsi de
"Donna Maria su Hermana Marquesa del Vasto? Y
"de Donna Isabel de Gonzaga, su nuera (13). ——
"What Praise may not be bestowed on the most beau-
"tiful Duchess of Tallacoza, Donna Joanna of Ara-
"gon, a Lady of the Blood Royal, and chast and
"good to the highest Degree; likewise of Donna Ma-
"ria, Marchioness of Vasto; and of Donna Isabella
"de Gonzaga, her Daughter-in-law?* Donna Maria of *Aragon*, Sister of *Joanna*, was Wife of *Alphonso d'Avalos*, Marquis del *Vasto*, one of *Charles*
the Fifth's best Generals. *Sorbiere* calls her Marchioness of *Vasco*, and ranks her among the learned Women (14). *Brantome*, who praised her highly, has
placed her among the lasting Beauties; for, after having
repeated the fine things, with which the Grand
Prior of *France* entertained her in a numerous Assembly; *That her Autumn surpassed all the Springs and
Summers then in the Room*, he adds, *and indeed she
was still fairer, and more desireable, than either of
her two Daughters, though both fair and young*: and
the' she was, then, near sixty Years of Age (15). The
Grand Prior (16), *was immediately smitten with her*;
but, though he loved the Mother, yet he took her eldest
Daughter for his Mistress, *por adombrar la cosa.* —— *By
way of a Blind.* After *six Years, or more*, Brantome, &c.
turning to *Naples*, *found her but very little altered,
and still so fair, that he said she could hardly fail of
occasioning a mortal Sin to be committed, either in
Thought, or Deed.* She died at *Chiaia*, in the House
of Don *Garcias de Toledo*, the ninth of *November*,
1658 (17). I do not rememember to have observed, that he ever mentions her Sister. It is true,
he speaks somewhere of the Wife of one *Ascanio Colonna*, who passed for one of the greatest Beauties of
Italy, and whom *Barbarossa* endeavoured to carry off,
in order to make a present of her to the Grand Signior; but he calls her *la Signora Livia* (18) Gonzaga
(19). It is not the same, then, who is concerned
in this Article; though the manner, in which *Augustin Nipbus* has spoken of her Beauty, may create a
Belief, that she was not less likely, than the other,
to prompt *Barbarossa* to such an Attempt. *Thuanus*
has mentioned this *Mary of Aragon*: he says, that
the Island of *Ischia* was chiefly remarkable for having
been the place of this Lady's Retreat. "Dragutes
"—— Ænarium Insulam Arce munitissimam, quæ in-
"ter duas terras saxo imposita est, sed maxime Mariæ
"Arragoniæ Alfonsi Avali Vastii viduæ secessu no-
"bilem, petit (20). —— Dragutes *seeks the Island
"of Ischia, famous for it's strong Citadel, built, be-
"tween two Necks of Land, on a Rock, but chiefly
"for the Retreat of* Mary *of* Aragon, *Widow of* Al-
"phonso d'Avalos, *Marquis of* Vasto." The same
Jerom Ruscelli, of whom I have spoken above, and
who took so much pains to immortalize *Joan of
Aragon*, was at a great Expence likewise in spreading
the Praises of *Mary*. He was not satisfied with using
the liveliest Expressions, his Imagination could suggest,

to set off the Perfections of this Lady, but collected
all the Pieces of Poetry, in which she had been celebrated by the finest Wits of the Times, and printed
them at the end of his Commentary, on a Song of
John Baptist d'Azzia, Marquis *della Terza*. This
Song was written in praise of "(Illustrissima & Ex-
"cellentissima Signora, la Signora Donna Maria d'Ara-
"gonna, Marchesa del Vasto)." —— *The most Illustrious
"and most Excellent Lady, the Lady Donna Maria of
"Aragon, Marchioness of* Vasto." This Commentary of *Ruscelli* was printed at *Venice*, in 1552, in
4to, by *John Griffius*, and contains Seventy three
Leaves. The Marchioness is represented in it as the
Archetype of Beauty, the *Criterium Formæ*; infomuch that, (according to the Commentator) the true
way of knowing, whether other Women are more
beautiful, one than another, is to examine, whether
they resemble her more or less. "Secondo che in
"altre vedra le fattezze del volto & di tutto il corpo
"che habbian somiglianza, ò s'avicino poco ò molto
"à quelle di lei, così giudicare, che le Belleze di
"quelle tali, sieno più ò meno perfette, come del
"Paragon dell' oro habbiam detto. Et da tale es-
"sempio, ò idea, ò più tosto vero Archetipo qui in
"terra della vera Bellezza corporale, formar poi le re-
"gole, le ragioni, le misure, i gradi, & le propor-
"tioni della Bellezza intera e perfetta (21). ——
"*According as, in other Women, you see the correspon-
"dent Lineaments of the Face and Body resemble more
"or less the Beauties of this Lady, to judge from
"thence, that such Women are more or less fair; as
"I have observed of this Paragon of Beauty. And
"from this Copy, or Idea, or rather true Archetype
"on Earth of corporeal Beauty, to form the Rules,
"Reasons, Measures, Degrees, and Proportions, of
"entire and perfect Beauty.*" He makes her no less
beautiful in Soul, than Body; and says, that *Giraldi*
having had the Honour to see her, and hear her speak,
was struck dumb for some time, not knowing whether
she was more desireable for her Beauty, or adorable for
her Wit. "Al cospetto di questa divinissima signora
"condotossi già il Signor Giovan Battista Giraldi
"Cinthio, & contemplando attentissimamente l' una
"& l' altra Bellezza che à gli occhi del corpo, & à
"qui della mente gli si rappresentavano dalla vera
"Bellezza del volto, dalla splendor de gli occhi, dal-
"la soavità della favella, dalla leggiadria & maestà
"del sembiante, & dalla maraviglia de' modi & delle
"maniere veramente angeliche, stette lunga pezza
"tra se stessi attonito, & stupefatto, & dalla somma
"Bellezza del Corpo, che primieramente s' offeriva
"à gli occhi suoi, dovea tosto resolversi, che questa
"fosse da lui da amarsi sopra ogn' altra cosa mortale.
"Poi passando subito col pensiero à quella dell' ani-
"mo, che gli si rappresentava per quei modi & per
"quelle maniere gia dette, si mutava di opinione,
"& risolveasi, che quella sola Bellezza dell' animo,
"dovesse come cosa divina & celeste, con intera hu-
"milta & divotione adorarsi (22). —— *This Signor
"John Baptista Giraldi Cinthio, being conducted to
"the sight of this divine Lady, and attentively
"considering the Charms both of her Mind and
"Body, stood long astonished at the true Beauty of
"her Countenance, the Lustre of her Eyes, the sweet-
"ness of her Voice, the Comeliness and Majesty of
"her Appearance, the Wonderfulness of her Manners,
"which were truly Angelical; and, from the great
"Beauty of her Body, which first struck his Sight,
"immediately thought her worthy of his Love, be-
"yond all other Women. Afterwards, passing in
"thought to the Beauties of her Mind, which appear-
"ed to him in the manner we have already described,
"he changed his Opinion, and determined, that this
"Beauty of the Mind alone deserved to be worshipped
"with perfect Humility and Devotion, as divine and
"cælestial.*" —— Then follows the Madrigal, which
he composed on this Problem.

(13)Joan. de Spinosa, Dialog. in laudes de las Mugeres. fol. 98. verso.

(14) Sorbiere Lettre xv. pag. 73.

(15) Brantome, Dames Galantes, Tom. 2. pag. 243, 245.

(16) Francis of Lorrain, General of the Gallies, Son to Claude, first Duke of Guise. This Journey to Naples was taken in 1559.

(17) Tomaso Costo, Compendio dell' Istoria del Regno di Napoli. Part. 3. fol. 59.

(18) He should have said Julia; we shall speak of her under the Article GONZAGA.

(19) Brantome, Dames Illustr. pag. 283.

(20) Thuan. Hist. ad Ann. 1552. pag. 222.

(21) Ruscelli, Lettura sopra un Sonetto, &c. fol. 57.

(22) Ruscelli, ibid.

[H] *A*

402 ARAGON.

it [H]. The Life of the Duke of *Alba* will furnish me with some new Particulars relating to the Disturbances, which obliged this Lady to fly from *Rome*, in the Year 1556 (f)[I]. She was then very old, according to the Duke of *Alba*'s Historian. She must therefore have enjoyed a long Life; for She died in the Month of *October*, 1577 (g). In the Year 1575, She made a Present to the Capuchins of the Holy Sacrament of the Place, where the Monastery, which they had at *Rome*, was built (b). She was a Benefactress to the Jesuits; for she rebuilt the Church of *St Andrew*, which the Bishop of *Tivoli* made them a present of in the Year 1566 (i). Hitherto I have said nothing of her Genealogy; it is Time I should observe, that she was Daughter of Ferdinand of *Aragon*, Duke of *Montalto* [K], third Natural Son of *Ferdinand* I, King of *Naples*.

(f) See the Remarks [E] and [F].
(g) Tomaso Costo, Compendio dell' Istoria di Napoli, part 3. fol. 168.
(b) See la Ritratto di Roma Moderna, 541, Edit. of Rome 1653.
(i) Ibid. pag. 540.

[H] *A gallant Author dedicated many Statues to it*] He was *Joseph Betuffi*. He published, at *Florence*, in 1566, a Dialogue, entitled, *Le Imagini del Tempio della Signora Donna Giovanna Aragona*. —— *Statues of the Temple of the Lady* Donna Joanna *of* Aragon. The Book consists of an Hundred and twenty one Pages; in which the Praises of several of the fair Sex are artfully intermixed with those of the Goddess of the Temple.

[I] *New Particulars relating to the Disturbances, which obliged this Lady to fly from* Rome, *in the Year* 1556.] The following is an Abstract from the History of the Duke of *Alba*, printed in *Latin*, at *Salamanca*, in 1669, and in *French*, at *Paris*, in 1699. " *Joanna of Aragon*, Mother of *Marc Antony* " *Colonna*, staid behind at *Rome*, ; and the *Caraffa*'s, " who kept her always in Sight, detained her, if I " may so say, as an Hostage. As the Truce, in " some measure, removed their Suspicions, and the " Roads were open, the Duchess went out of *Rome*, " with her two Daughters, on Foot, pretending she " was going to divert herself in a Vineyard, at some " Distance from the Ramparts. Though she was now " very aged, she continued walking, 'till she was out " of sight of the Centinels, who kept the Gates; " after which she got on Horse-back, and mounted " her two Daughters behind two Cavaliers. With " this Equipage, unworthy of her, but very agree- " able to her present Fortune, she fled away to the " Camp. The Duke of *Alba* received her with in- " expressible Joy. As the great Age of this Lady " could give no room for Suspicion, he embraced " her; but contented himself with saluting her two " Daughters, who uncovered themselves out of Re- " spect. I fancy, says he, addressing himself instant- " ly to her, *that I see the famous* Clelia, *who fled, " not from the Enemies Camp in her own City, in- " fluenced by the sole Love, of her Country, but from " the City in the Camp, induced to this Flight by the " force of maternal Affection*. The Duchess was " charmed with the Generosity of the *Spanish* Gene- " ral, and express'd her Sense of it by a thousand " thanks; however, she could not resolve to continue " in the Camp; the Age of her Daughters not per- " mitting her. The Duke consented to it; and " she retired into *Campania*, accompanied by her " Son, and escorted by a Party of Horse, which " the Vice Roy assigned her, out of Respect, not ne- " cessity (23).

We must say a Word or two of the Misfortunes of her Husband. " He was a Prisoner in the Castle of " *Naples*, accused by his own Son of Heresy, and a " Conspiracy against his Catholic Majesty (24); and " when the Duke of *Alba* arrived at *Naples*, in the " Year 1556, he visited him in Prison (25), and heard " all he had to say. —— He comforted the good " old Man as much as possible, and assigned him the " Castle for his Prison; whereas before he had been " confined to a very strait Tower. He relieved the " Distress, to which he was reduced, not only by " giving him Money, but by appointing him an " handsome Pension out of his Son's Estate. —— " However he did not give him his Liberty; the " Accusations against him were supported by too " many Probabilities; and many People thought them " too well grounded. Besides he would have diso- " bliged *Philip*, who kept *Ascanio* in Prison the " remainder of his Days, without, however, de- " priving him of those Advantages, which the Duke " had had the Goodness to grant him."

The Historian remarks, that *this Affair* (26) *was never thoroughly examined into*; and he blames *Noel le Compte*, who accuses the Duke of *Alba* of having rigorously treated the Father of *Marc Antony Colonna*.

[K] *She was Daughter of* Ferdinand *of* Aragon, *Duke of* Montalto.] *Antony*, his Son, succeeded him in the Duchy of *Montalto*, and espoused *Hippolita* of *Rovera*, and afterwards *Antoinette* of *Cardona*, and was the Father of another *Antony*. This latter, fourth Duke of *Montalto*, was married to *Maria de la Cerda*, Daughter to the Duke de *Medina Celi*, and afterwards to *M. Louisa de Luna*. He had several Children, who all died young, except one Daughter, named *Maria*, who was Heiress of the Duchy of *Montalto*, and married, in *Sicily*, to Don *Francis de Moncada*, Prince of *Paterno* (27).

(24) Life of the Duke of *Alba*, Book 4. chap. 19. pag. 382.
(24) Ibid.
(25) Ibid. pag. 342.
(26) *The Accuser* of *Ascanio Colonna*.
(27) *Taken from a Memoir communicated by* Minutolls

ARAGON (ISABELLA of) Daughter of *Alphonso*, Duke of *Calabria*, Son of Ferdinand King of *Naples*, was the Wife of *John Galeazzo Sforza*, Duke of *Milan*. This Duke, before his Marriage, was under the Tuition of his Uncle *Lewis Sforza*; nor was he less so, after he had been married, with great Magnificence [A], to *Isabella* of *Aragon*, in 1489 (a). The Counsels of this Princess, who was as Ambitious as Fair, encouraged him to let the World see he was resolved fully to enjoy all his Rights (b); but he had a strong Party to deal with. The Protector was the most intriguing Man in the World, and the best able to support himself against the just Pretensions of his Nephew. He had fallen in Love with the Princess *Isabella* at first sight; and, as she had been married to *John Galeazzo* only by Proxy, he did not despair of marrying her himself, in exclusion of his Nephew. He discovered his Design to the Princess; assuring her, that she might more certainly depend upon Commanding, if she married him, than if she was the Wife of *John Galeazzo*, his Nephew. This Proposal was rejected with scorn. The Protector was not discouraged; but ordered Matters so, that his Nephew could not consummate his Marriage; and

(a) Corio, Histor. di Milano, parte 6. pag. 879. Edit. 2646. in 4to.
(b) Varillas, Hist of Charl. VIII. lib. 2. pag. 157.

[A] *After he had been married ------ with great Magnificence*.] Read *Tristan Chalcbus*, an Author of those Times (1), in *Nuptiarum Mediolanensium descriptione*. Father *Menetrier* quotes a very long Passage from him, which contains a Description of the magnificent Supper, which *Bergença Botta*, a Gentleman of *Lombardy*, gave to Duke Gale-azzo and his new married Duchess, when he entertained them at his House at *Tortona*. " Each Ser- " vice was ushered in with a kind of an Opera, " which Novelty at that Time rendered agreeable, " rather than the Graces, which have been since " added to these Musical Entertainments (2)."

(1) Konig is grossly mistaken, in making him live in 1672.
(2) Menetrier, Representat. en Musique, pag. 160. & seq.

[B] His

ARAGON.

and to effect this, as was commonly said, had recourse to some Magic Ligature [B]. In the mean time, he caused his own Marriage with *Isabella* to be negotiated at the Court of *Naples*. *Ferdinand* seemed inclined to grant his Request; but the Duke of *Calabria* would never consent to it (c). So that *Lewis Sforza* was obliged to deliver up the Prey to *John Galeazzo*; but he was resolved to be revenged, and destined *Isabella* of *Aragon* to be his Principal Victim. He denied her several things, which flattered either her *Taste*, or her *Diversion* (d), and married a Princess, who thwarted her in every thing. The Young *Isabella* underwent so many Vexations in this Conflict, and kind of Civil War, which is well worth the pains of describing [C], that she sent her Father and Grandfather Word, that, if they did not release her out of this miserable Condition, she should attempt her own Life (e). These Princes were not in a Condition to bring *Lewis Sforza* to Reason, who was instrumental in drawing the French into *Italy*; which overwhelmed the whole House of *Aragon*, which then reigned in *Naples*. He carried his Villiany so far, as to murthur his Nephew (f)[D]. It is in vain

[B] *His Nephew could not consummate his Marriage ---- to effect which he is said to have had recourse to some Magic Ligature.*] *Guicciardin* affirms, that there was such a Report, and that all *Italy* was persuaded of it: " E manifesto che quando " Isabella figliuola d' Alfonso ando a congiugnersi col " marito, Lodovico come la vidde, innamorato di " lei, desidero ottenerla per moglie dal padre: e a " questo effetto opero (cosi fu althora creduto per " tutta Italia) con incantamenti, e con malie, che " Giovan Galeazzo fu per molta mesi impotente " alla consummatione del matrimonio: alla qual " cosa Ferdinando harebbe acconsentito, ma Alfonso " repugno, onde Lodovico esclufo di questa speranza, " preia altra moglie & havutone figliuoli, volto tutti, " i pensieri a trasferire in quegli il Ducato di Milan (3). ---- *It is certain, that, when* Isabella, *the Daughter of* Alphonso, *went to meet her Husband*, Lewis, *seeing her, fell in love with her, and desired her of her Father for himself*; *to which end, as it was then generally believed all over Italy, he so contrived it, by Enchantments and Witchcraft, that* John Galeazzo *was for many Months incapable of consummating his Marriage*; *upon which account* Ferdinand *would have consented, but* Alphonso *refused*; *whence it was, that* Lewis, *being disappointed, and having married another Lady, and had Children by her, employed all his Thoughts to transfer the Duchy of* Milan *to Them*." Mr *Varillas*, as far as I can perceive, does not touch upon this Particular; he only says, that *Lewis Sforza* hindered the Consummation of this Marriage for three Months (4). He proves clearly enough, that the Reason was, because the Parties were kept from each other; for he says (5), that the Father of the Bride thought *himself obliged in Honour* ---- *not to suffer* Lewis Sforza *to keep the new married Couple any longer asunder. That he threatened to complain of it to all* Europe, *and to arm in revenge of his Quarrel*. This was a strange Piece of Malice, and an insufferable Act of Violence in the Protector.

[C] *A kind of Civil War, which is well worth the Pains of describing*.] As *Varillas* seems to have succeeded very well in his Description of this Matter, I believe I shall oblige the Reader with a curious Fragment, by inserting his very Words in this Place. It is a Piece so much the more necessary to this Article, as it serves to discover the Humour, Spirit, and internal Qualities of *Isabella* of *Aragon*. " *Lewis* " *Sforza* gave up *Isabella* to his Nephew ———— " and, to give her a Rival, who should controul " her on every Occasion, he addressed himself to " the Princess *Alphonsina*, Daughter of *Hercules* " *d' Este*, Duke of *Ferrara*. *Alphonsina* resembled " *Isabella* in all things, except in Beauty. Both " were conceited of their Births, and both without " Reason; since they had nothing to reproach each " other with on that Score, and since there was " Bastardy in the Genealogies of both *. They were " both haughty to excess; and their Pride was ow- " ing to a most refined Ambition. They were both " Chaste, more from a Principle of Pride, than Con- " stitution. *Isabella* resolved to marry, and *Alphon-* " *sina* aspired to it, rather to partake of their Hus- " band's Power, than their Beds. Both were Luxu- " rious; and, though both had been educated in Fa- " milies, in which nothing recommended itself so " much as Pasimony, yet they were naturally Pro- " digal, and their Inclinations led them to all pos-

" sible Expences. The Duke of *Ferrara* did not de- " liberate a Moment, whether he should give *Alphon-* " *sina* to *Lewis Sforza*. He had no Dower to " give her; and there was Reason to hope she might " one Day be Duchess of *Milan*. She was there- " fore sent away immediately to *Lewis Sforza*, who " had two Sons successively by her. This Fruit- " fulness made her insult *Isabella*, who had been " delivered a second time only of a Daughter; But " Jealousy had before sowed Discord between them. " *Alphonsina* could not bear the Praises bestowed " on *Isabella*'s Beauty; she looked upon them as a " Reproach to her own Homeliness; nor could *Isa-* " *bella* see with Patience the extrordinary Honours " paid *Alphonsina*, as believing they were due only " to herself. They both lived in the same Palace, " and eat constantly together. They had new Op- " portunities every Day of encreasing their Aver- " sion; and the Courtiers furnished the greatest Part " of them. They paid diligent Court to *Alphonsina*; " because her Husband distributed all the Favours; " and attended in *Isabella*'s Apartment for meer " Form's Sake. She was perfectly distracted at it, " and it was this Solitude, no less than the short " Allowance for her Court, which made her write " to her Father, and Grandfather, that She would " make an Attempt upon her own Life, if they " did not bolder deliver her from this Captivity. On " the other hand, *Alphonsina* was so tired of *Isabella*, " that, to get rid of her, She sollicited her Husband " to make her a Duchess, as he had promised, and " add the Quality of Duke of *Milan* to That of " Administrator of the Duchy (6). *Varillas* had " said, in this very History (7), that *Isabella* had " written to the Duke of *Calabria* her Father, and " to the King of *Naples*, her Grandfather, certain " Letters, the greater Part of which are still ex- " tant (8); in which She complained of her Unhap- " piness, in the most pathetic Terms then in use; " She described it in such lively Colours, as would " have made the hardest Heart relent; She told them " She had made herself a Slave, purely in Obedience " to their Commands; and She threatned to destroy " herself with her own Hands, if She was not im- " mediately set at Liberty.

[D] *He carried his Villiany so far, as to murthur his Nephew*.] I shall again make use of the very Words of *Varillas*. Thus he speaks, under the One thousand Four hundred and Ninety fourth Year, after having conducted his King as far *Pavia*. " *Lewis* " *Sforza*, being persuaded, that it was time to make " away with Duke *John Galeazzo*, his Nephew, " caused, they say, one of those lingering Doses of " Poison to be given him, which produce Symp- " toms of a Consumption and wasting in the Body; " in order to confirm a Report, which was spread " about at that time, that this Prince's Illness pro- " ceeded from the too strong Incitements of his " Wife's Beauty. The Physicians had given him " over, when the King, passing by *Pavia*, where " he lay sick, could not dispense with paying him " a Visit. His Majesty did not speak to him con- " cerning any Business; because *Lewis Sforza* had " earnestly desired to be present at the Interview, " which they durst not refuse him: He only ex- " pressed his Sorrow to see his Cousin German " in so weak a Condition, and endeavoured to " flatter him with some Hopes of Recovery; but " *John Galeazzo*, who found himself a dying,

VOL. I. 5 I and

ARAGON.

404

vain to pretend, that *John Galeazzo* died of over-careffing his Wife [*E*]; the Tradition, which imputes his Death to his Uncle's Ambition, has prevailed. After the *French* had taken *Milan*, the Princess *Isabella* retired to *Naples*, and appeared the most afflicted of all the Princesses her Relations, who were in great Numbers in the Island of *Ischia*, when King *Frederic* was obliged to surrender at Discretion to *Lewis* the XIIth, in the Year 1501 (*g*). She spent a long time in exchanging one Mourning for another; for, in the space of a few Years, she lost her Grandfather, Husband, Father, Brother, Uncle, and Son [*F*]. The only Consolation left her was to see her Persecutor *Lewis Sforza* expiate his Crimes, in *France*, by an hard Captivity, which ended but with his Life. She had yet another Consolation, which affected her perhaps more than the former; which was to see her only Daughter, *Bonna Sforza*, married to *Sigismond*, King of *Poland*; She retired to a Town in the Kingdom of *Naples*, which had been assigned her for her Dower (*h*), where she lived in such a manner, as shewed, that Adverse Fortune had not sunk That Air of Royal Grandeur, in which she had been Educated. She died of a Dropsy; but had time enough to take a Journey of Devotion to *Rome*, in the Pontificat of *Leo* the Xth. She walked on foot to the *Vatican*, followed by a great Number of Ladies, dressed like Brides. The whole Town ran to see this Sight (*i*). It were to be wished, for her Memory's sake, that we could finish her Article here, without an Appendix much to her disadvantage; but we are not Masters of these Things. Her very Panegyrists have made use of the Conclusion we are about to make. This Lady, who, in the Bloom of her Youth, had been so famed for Virtue, gave an handle to Slander in the Decline of her Age, and admitted the Gallantries of *Prosper Colonna*, with

(g) Onftian. de Caflibus Viror. Illuftrium, pag. 41.

(h) Earl; See the laft Remark.

(i) Jovius, Eleg. p. 422.

" and did not doubt but it was owing to the
" Wickedness of his Uncle, laid hold of this Con-
" juncture. He considered not himself; but, calling
" to mind his Son and Daughter, he recommended
" them to the King with a flood of Tears; plainly
" importing, that, if his Majesty did not take par-
" ticular care of them, he foresaw they would be
" poisoned as well as himself. To conclude the
" Tragedy, the Duchess, his Wife, cast herself at
" the King's Feet, as the *Italian* Authors say, who
" are more to be credited in this, than *Philip de
" Commines*, who will have it to be at the Feet
" of *Lewis Sforza*. She was too high spirited to
" act such a Part; and, could she have conquered
" her Pride, she was but too well convinced, that
" her Submission would be all in vain. She did
" not mention her Children, because she supposed
" her Husbands Tears would be effectual in that
" Point: She reserved her's for her Father; and
" the King made her no other Answer, than that
" the Expedition of *Naples* was too far advanced,
" to be left unfinished (9)."

(n) Varillas, ubi supra, pag. 253.

[*E*] *It is in vain to pretend, that* John Galeazzo *died of over-caressing his Wife*.] *Guicciardin* affirms, that this was reported; but gives it as the general Opinion of *Italy*, that this Prince died of Poison, which *Lewis Sforza* had given him. " Fu publicato
" da molti la morte di Giouan Galeazzo essere pro-
" ceduta da coito immoderato, non dimeno si cre-
" dette universalmente per tutta Italia, che e' fusse
" morto non per infermità naturale ne per incon-
" tinentia, ma di veleno: e Teodoro da Pavia uno
" de' Medici Regii, il quale era presente quando
" Carlo lo visitò, affermo haverne veduto segni ma-
" nifestissimi. Ne fu alcuno, che dubitasse che se
" era stato veleno, non gli fusse stato dato per opera
" del zio (10). - - - - - - *that the Death of* John Galeazzo *proceeded from
" immoderate Coition; nevertheless it was universally
" believed by all* Italy, *that he died, not of any
" natural Infirmity, or of Incontinency, but of Poi-
" son; and* Theodore *of* Pavia, *one of the King's
" Physicians, who was present, when* Charles *visited
" him, affirmed, that he had discovered manifest
" Symptoms of it. Nor did any one doubt, that, if
" there was Poison in the Case, it was given him
" by the Contrivance of his Uncle*." *Joviam Pontanus* affirms, that People talked publickly of this a-
bominable Crime of *Lewis Sforza*. " Ludovicum
" Sforciam, qui pubescentem primo, dein adoles-
" centem jam ætatem Joannis Galeatii fratris filii
" Mediolanensis Ducis procuratione hactenus ac pa-
" trocinio tutatus est suo, veneno illum e medio
" sustulisse cives, advenæ, peregrini passim atque
" impune omnes prædicant - - - - - Fora, porticus,
" plateæ, circulique infimorum cujusque generis ho-
" minum nefandi criminis accusationibus - - - - - im-
" precationibus etiam maxime diris plena undique
" circumsonant (11). - - - - - - *Citizens, Foreigners,
" and Travellers, cry out every, and with Impunity,
" that* Lewis Sforza *had poisoned his Nephew* John
" Galeazzo, *Duke of* Milan, *who had been educated
" from his Youth under his Care and Protection*. - - - -
" *The Market-places, Portico's, Streets, and Assem-
" blies of People of the lowest Rank, resound with
" Accusations of this wicked Action, and the most
" dreadful Imprecations on it's Author*." A Crowd
of Historians concur in this, as *Bernardin Corio* (12), *Peter Bembo* (13), *Vianoli* (14), &c.

[*F*] *In the Space of a few Years, she lost her
Grandfather, Husband, Father, Brother, Uncle, and
Son*] *Paulus Jovius* (15) describes this Series of Misfortunes with great Eloquence, but does not always observe Order; for he has placed the Death of the Husband, before That of the Grandfather. As to the Son of our Princess, he says, that *the
French took him away from his Mother, and carried
him into* France, *to make a Monk of him, and that
he died of a fall from an Horse*. " In venatione
" currentis equi lapsu in Heduis exanimatus esse
" nunciaretur. Hunc enim vel invita deposcentibus
" Gallis tradiderat, à quibus cucullati sacerdotis ha-
" bitu in opulenti sacerdotii cœnobium idcirco con-
" jectus fuerat, ne Sforziani Regni legitimæ prolis
" hæres superesset." *Bernardin Corio* gives us a very moving Description of the Sorrow of this Princess, when, all at once, she saw her Husband carried to his Grave, her Son excluded from the Duchy of *Milan*, and the Wife of *Lewis Sforza* on the Throne. " Li suoi fautori cridando duca, visto
" (*Ludovico*) il templo di Divo Ambrosio, e le cam-
" pane in segno de letitia fece sonare, il morto cor-
" po di Giovanne Galeazo anchora essendo nel Do-
" mo scoperto, e quasi universalmente da tutti
" pianto e condolato il miserando e pietoso caso.
" Isabella sua mugliere a Pavia con li poveri fig-
" lioleti vestiti de lugubre vestimenti, come pre-
" gionera si reclude entro una camera, e gran tem-
" po stette giacendo sopra la dura terra, che non
" vide aere. Doverebbe pensare ogni lettore l'acerbo
" caso de la sconsolata Ducissa, e se piu duro il cuore
" havesse de diamante, piangerebbe a considerare
" qual doglia dovea essere quella de la sciagurata e
" infelice mugliere, in uno punto vedere la morte
" del gioventetto e bellissimo conforte, la perdita de
" tutto lo imperio suo, e li figlioletti a canto orbati
" de ogni bene, il patre e fratello con la casa sua
" expulsi dal Neapolitano Reame, e Ludovico Sforza
" con Beatrice sua mugliere nel modo dimostrato
" havergli occupata la signoria. - - - - - *Those of his
" Party saluting him Duke, he visited the Temple
" of St* Ambrose, *and set the Bells a ringing for
" Joy; the dead Body of* John Galeazzo *being yet
" in the House uncovered, and his unfortunate End
" universally*

(10) Guicciard. lib. 1. pag. 27. ad Ann. 1494.

(11) Joviam. Pontan. de Prudentia. lib. 4. init.

(12) Corio, Hiftor. Mediolan. Part. 2.

(13) Petr. Bembus, Hift. Venet. lib. 2. fol. 30.

(14) V.anoli Hiftor. Veneta Part. 2. pag. 20.

(15) Jovius, Elog. lib. 5. pag. 422.

with very little regard to her Reputation [G]. Her Daughter, the Queen Dowager of *Poland*, having retired to the same place, in the Kingdom of *Naples*, followed there the Example of her Mother [H]. So true it is, that Love is the ordinary and almost unavoidable Rock of the Honour and Merit of Women, who have conversed much in the *grand monde*. Sooner or later they split upon it. *Serius ocius fors exitura.* Our *Isabella* died the eleventh of *February*, 1524, as is remarked in her Epitaph, reported by Mr *Misson*, in the second Volume (*k*) of his *Travels into Italy*.

(*k*) *Pag.* 41. 3*d Edition.*

" *universally lamented.* Isabella, *his Wife, with her*
" *poor Children, dressed in Mourning, shut herself up*
" *at Pavia, in a dark Chamber, and lay a long Time*
" *prostrate on the hard Ground. Every Reader will*
" *imagine the melancholy Condition of the disconsolate*
" *Duchess; and, though his Heart be harder than*
" *Adamant, must relent, when he considers what*
" *must have been the Grief of this unhappy Lady;*
" *to behold, at one Instant, the Death of her young*
" *and beautiful Consort; the Loss of all her Power,*
" *and her little Sons, at her Side, deprived of all*
" *their Estate; her Father and Brother, with all*
" *her Family, expelled the Kingdom of Naples; and*
" *Lewis Sforza, with Beatrice, his Wife, possessed,*
" *in the above-mentioned Manner, of the Dukedom.*"

[G] *She gave a handle to Slander in the decline of her Age, and admitted the Gallantries of Prosper Colonna, with very little regard to her Reputation.*] Paul Jovius informs us of this, in the Elogy he made on this Princess: " Ceterum in hac eximie
" virtutis foemina improbae plebis rumor non medio-
" criter pudoris decus perstrinxit, ob id gravior,
" quod cum florente aetate impenetrabilem pudici-
" tiam praetulisset, in ipso demum aetatis flexu Pros-
" perum Columnam sibi cultum, & officium assidue
" tribuentem, saepeque procacem ad urbaniores jocos
" admitteret (16).——— *Yet even this Lady of exempla-
" ry Virtue suffered her Reputation to be not a little
" sullied by common Fame; and the more so, as she,
" who in her Youth had preserved an inviolable Cha-
" stity, in the decline of her Age, admitted the Ad-
" dresses of Prosper Colonna, and often admitted him
" to jest and toy with her.*"

(16) Jovius, *Elog.* p. 424.

[H] *The Queen Dowager of Poland——— followed the Example of her Mother.*] Thuanus reflects more upon the Daughter; than Paul Jovius does upon the Mother; every one may judge of this by comparing the Passages. " Eodem tempore Bona
" Sforzia Sigismundi Augusti Poloniae regis parens
" ———filii pertaesa, Sarmatis relicta, in Italiam
" venit, & honorifice Venetiis excepta est ———
" unde paratam triremem conscendens in Apuliam
" ad Barium navigavit, cujus urbis possessio gentili-
" tio Arragoniae gentis jure dotale & haereditarium
" illi erat. Ibi soluta & dissentiente a priore vita
" ratione postea vixit, consuetudine cujusdem Papa-
" caudae non satis honeste usa, cui & omnia bona
" testamento praeteritis liberis reliquit, & fama ac
" bonis decoctis haud multo post in summa egestate
" & infamia decessit (17). ——— *At the same time*
" Bona Sforza, *Mother of* Sigismund Augustus, *King
" of* Poland, *being tired of her Son, left* Sarmatia,
" *and came into* Italy, *where she was honourably re-
" ceived at* Venice ——— *whence, going on board
" a three-oared Vessel, prepared for her, she sailed
" to* Bari, *of which Town she was in Possession, as
" being her Dower, in right of the House of* Ara-
" gon (18). *There she lead a dissolute Life, con-
" trary to what she had 'till then done, carrying
" on a criminal Correspondence with a young Gallant,
" to whom, in exclusion of her Children, she left all
" her Effects by Will; and, having ruined her Re-
" putation and Estate, died in extream Poverty and
" Infamy.*" This is what *Thuanus* says of the Queen Dowager of *Poland*. Can any thing be added to this Elogy?

(17) Thuan. *Hist.* lib. 16. *ad Annum* 1555. p. 326.

(18) *Mr* Varillas, *in the Life of Lewis* XIII. l. 1. p. 47. *says, that* Lewis Sforza, *finding himself constrained to quit the Dutchy of* Milan, *made over to the* Duchess *Isa*bella *the Principality of* Bari, *and the Principality of* Rossano, *who'd had been proven him in Recompence for having renounced the House of* Aragon *on the Throne of* Naples.

ARAGON (MARY of) Wife of the Emperor *Otho* the Third, and Daughter of a King of *Aragon*, became infamous for her Lewdness; which at last brought her to the Punishment of the Fire. She artfully disguised a young Fellow, whom she was in love with, in Woman's Apparel, and made him pass for her Chambermaid (*a*). We need not ask, whether she used any Moderation; her Temper, and perpetual Opportunities, give us sufficiently to understand, that her pretended Chamber-Maid wanted no Employ, and that she made one in all the Progresses, which the Court took. The Emperor, having discovered this abominable Cheat, was resolved the Empress should have her full share of the Shame; and, for that Purpose, caused the Young Man to be stripped in the Presence of a great many Witnesses, and, upon the flagrant Discovery of his Sex, condemned him to be burnt. He was gracious enough not to punish his Wife, and hoped she would behave her self better for the future; but he was mistaken. She fell desperately in Love with a young Count near *Modena*, and soon declared her Passion to him; for she was in a much properer Station no sollicit, than be sollicited, in Affairs of this kind. The Count, as Chaste, as he was Beautiful, resisted all the Advances, or, to say better, all the violent Attacks made upon him; but, if, in this, he imitated *Joseph*, he had not his good Luck, to come off only with Imprisonment. The Empress complained to her Husband, that the Count had made Love to her, and hoped such Insolence would not go unpunished. The credulous *Otho* ordered the Accused to be Beheaded. But mark, how the Accuser was caught in her turn. The Count, seeing himself condemned, and expecting no Favour, and yet unwilling to reveal the whole Mystery, made his Wife promise she would justify him, in the best manner she could, to the Emperor. She kept her Word, preserved her Husband's Head, and took her Opportunity, when the Emperor administred Justice in a General Assembly, held in the middle of a great Plain, near *Placentia*. She took, I say, this Opportunity of demanding Justice against the Murtherer of her Husband. The Emperor, not knowing who she was, promised to do her Justice to the utmost Rigor of the Law. Upon which the Countess produced her Husband's Head, and offered to prove his Innocency by the Fiery Tryal. Her offer was accepted; a red hot Iron was ordered; she took, and held it in her Hand, as long as they pleased, without being burnt; then boldly demanded the Emperor's Head, as being convicted of the Murther of her Husband: At last she was satisfied with the Punishment of the Empress, whom *Otho* condemned to be burnt (*b*). This happened towards the end of the Xth Century.

(*a*) Secum muliebri habitu circumduxit juvenem, quo cum congrediebatur quotidie, quandoquidem eo pro cubicularia utebatur. ——— *She carried about with her, a young Fellow in Woman's Cloaths, with whom she had daily Opportunities of being familiar; since she made him pass for her Chambermaid.* Munsteri Cosmographia, l. 3.

(*b*) Gotfrid. Viterb. Chron. Parte I. Alb. Krantz Cuspinian. in Othone III. Sigon. apud Maimb. Decadence de l'Empire p. 186.

ARAMONT

ARAMONT.

ARAMONT (GABRIEL) Ambaſſador of *France* to *Conſtantinople*, in the Reign of *Henry* II, was a Gentleman of *Gaſcony*, who acquitted himſelf worthily of his Employ. The Conſtable *de Montmorency*, examining the Overture, which Pope *Paul* III had made, that the only means to recover *Placentia* out of the Emperor's hands was to cauſe the *Turkiſh* Fleet to appear upon the Coaſts of *Naples* and *Sicily*, adviſed the King his Maſter to negotiate with *Soliman* about it. *Aramont* was choſen to tranſact this Affair. He was neither leſs Artful, nor leſs experienced, than *la Foret*, *Rincon*, and *Paulin*, who had preceeded him in This Embaſſy. He made Friends at the *Porte*, who procured him free acceſs, and private Audiences; and he knew ſo well how to turn and wind Matters, that he reconciled *Soliman* to the *French*, who had been greatly prejudiced againſt them. The only queſtion now was, how his Highneſſes Fleet ſhould act: Whereupon *Aramont* returned ſpeedily to *France*, to conſult with his Maſter in what manner the *Grand Signior*'s Aſſiſtance might be moſt uſefully applied. The King and the Conſtable informed him, that they had Intelligence in the Iſland of *Corſica*, and that it might eaſily be taken, if the *Turkiſh* Fleet, and That of *France*, ſhould at once attack it. He ſet out again for *Conſtantinople*, to communicate this Project to the *Grand Signior*; But, landing at *Malta*, was inſtantly requeſted by the Grand Maſter (*a*) to repair to the *Turkiſh* Generals, who had beſieged *Tripoli* in *Barbary*, and employ his Credit, and the Authority of *Henry* the Second, to oblige them to raiſe the Siege. He yielded to their Intreaties, and reached the *Turkiſh* Camp by the time their Batteries were in readineſs to play (*b*). He had ſeveral Conferences with *Sinan Baſſa*, and *Dragut*, in which he remonſtrated to them, that they engaged in an Undertaking altogether oppoſite to the Treaty, which *Soliman* was going to conclude with *France*, ſince his Highneſs had agreed to attack the Emperor only, and that *Tripoli* belonged to the Order of *Malta*. They replyed, That the Knights of *Malta* were perjured Perſons; who, notwithſtanding the Oath they had taken to *Soliman*, when they were treated with ſo much Civility at their Departure out of *Rhodes*, committed continual Hoſtilities againſt the *Turks*; adding withal, that they had Orders to drive them out of *Africa*; and that they could not ſuſpend the Execution of this Order. *Aramont* wanted neither Excuſes nor Replies; and, finding he could not prevail with *Sinan Baſſa*, he reſolv'd to depart with all ſpeed for *Conſtantinople*, if poſſible to obtain from *Soliman*, that *Tripoli* might not be taken. But, as his Credit and Intrigues were not unknown to the Baſſa, he could not obtain Leave to continue his Journey, till after the Taking of *Tripoli*. He ſaved the Lives and Liberties of the *French*, who were in the Place; nor did he decline coming to a Feaſt, to which *Sinan* and *Dragut* invited him after their Conqueſt. *Charles* the Fifth was too politic to overlook this Event; he took occaſion from it to give out, that *France* had contributed to the taking of *Tripoli*. *Henry* the Second did what he could to anſwer this Complaint [*A*]. I have not had time to trace the Negotiations and Adventures of *Aramont* farther. I know, that his Diſpatches were ſometimes intercepted, and that the Emperor made uſe of them to

(*a*) He was a Spaniard, called Omeda.

(*b*) See the Judgment Mr Wicquefort paſſes upon this Conduct, in his Treatiſe of the Ambaſſador, lib. 2. §. 5. pag. 110.

[*A*] *Henry* II. *did what he could to anſwer this Complaint* (1).] The Grand Maſter of *Malta* accuſed our *Aramont* of having induced the Governor of *Tripoli* to capitulate. *Thuanus*, refuting this Accuſation, tells us, that the Conſtable *de Montmorency*, who had all the Power at that time, had charged this Ambaſſador to teſtify to the Grand Maſter the particular Affection, which He, the Conſtable, had for the Intereſts and Proſperity of the Order. This Hiſtorian adds, that he had ſeen Letters, in which the Conſtable expreſſes great Concern at the taking of *Tripoli*; and that his Letters ought not to be ſuſpected of any Diſſimulation, ſince they were written to a Perſon, to whom the Conſtable ſpoke his Thoughts very freely (2). But when *Henry* II. found, that the Emperor's Partizans accuſed the Ambaſſador of *France* of having contributed to this Conqueſt of the *Ottomans*, he diſpatched a Gentleman to the Grand Maſter to complain of the Reports, which were ſpread abroad, and to enquire of him, how *Aramont* had behaved himſelf in That Affair. He declared, that, if he found him guilty of any Miſconduct, he would cauſe him to be puniſhed according to the Exigence of the Caſe; but he deſired, that, if his Ambaſſador was Innocent, the Grand Maſter would give a public Teſtimony of it. The Grand Maſter's Anſwer fully juſtified *Gabriel Aramont*. " Quo in ne-
" gotio nullum officium prætermiſiſſet ut Ordini ea
" in re noſtro gratificaretur, hoc enim a V. M.
" enixe ac religioſe ſibi injunctum. Præterea, ut
" quorum culpa ea clades accepta eſſet certo cunctis
" conſtaret, undique probationes collegimus, & in-
" quiſitione diligenti ſuper ea re habita nihil com-
" perimus quo Aramontium cladi cauſam dediſſe,
" aut deditionis auctorem fuiſſe credi debeat. Quin
" imo ex equitibus captivis — didicimus eum non ſo-
" lum omni culpa vacare, ſed multis beneſactis totum
" ordinem ſibi devinxiſſe, ac proinde non recte nec
" ſecundum rationem factum exiſtimamus ut is rumor
" ſparſus ſit (3). — *In which Affair he uſed his utmoſt
*Endeavours to oblige our Order, as your Majeſty had
* earneſtly and ſolemnly commanded him. Beſides, we
* have collected Proofs from all Sides, to make it ap-
* pear to the World, to whom This Loſs is to be impu-
* ted; and, upon diligent Enquiry into this Matter,
* we find no reaſon to ſuſpect Aramont of occaſioning
* this Loſs, or of adviſing the Surrender. We have
* likewiſe been informed by ſome Captive Knights, that
* he is not only free from all Blame, but that he has
* obliged the Order by repeated good Offices. For which
* reaſon we think this Rumor to be unjuſtly ſpread*."
The King of *France* did not fail to publiſh this Anſwer in all the Courts of *Europe*, to ſhew that his Enemies ſpread Reports right or wrong, without any Foundation, on purpoſe to make him odious. " Eas
" litteras —— poſtea Rex per oratores ſuos paſſim
" publicari juſſit, qua publicatione compreſſis Cæſa-
" rianorum querelis ac rumoribus, evulgata in Gal-
" lici nominis invidiam fama pariter conquievit (4).
" —— *Theſe Letters the King afterwards ordered
* to be publiſhed by his Ambaſſadors; by the Pub-
* lication of which, the Complaints of the Imperialiſts
* being put a ſtop to, the Report, which was ſpread
* to the Diſhonour of the French Name, ceaſed*." This might indeed perſuade ſome, that the Partizans of *Charles* V. were deceived in this Matter; but the Enemies of *France* eaſily excuſed them. When it ſuits our Inclinations, we imagine it allowable to interpret every thing in a certain Senſe, agreeable to a Syſtem, which was once built on very probable Reaſons.

(1) Varillas, Hiſt. de *Henri* II. l. v. 2. p. 198, &c. ad Ann. 1551. See likewiſe *Thuanus*, l. 7. p. 155.

(2) Mr *Briſſac*, who commanded in *Piedmont*.

(3) *Thuan.* lib. 7. ſub fin.

(4) Id. ibid.

ARBRISSEL. ARCESILAS.

to reproach the *French* with their ſtrict Correſpondence with the *Porte* [B]. The Relation of his Embaſſy is in Manuſcript in the Library of Mr *de Lamoignon* (c).

(c) Varillas, Hiſtoire de Henri II. pag. 200.

I have juſt read a Particular, which may ſerve by way of Supplement to this Article. The Golden Iſles in *Provence* were erected into a Marquiſate by Letters of *Henry* II, confirmed by the Parliament of *Aix*; and this Marquiſate *Aramont*, Ambaſſador of *France* to *Conſtantinople*, was inveſted with, and ſeized of, to hold in Fief of the King, with expreſs Orders to build, in theſe Iſles, Caſtles, Towers, and Fortreſſes, to the Expence of Fifty Thouſand Crowns (d).

(d) St Lazare. Hiſtoire de Dignit. Honorar. de France, pag. 400. Edit. of Paris, 1635, in 8vo.

Reaſons. This is without doubt an inexhauſtible Spring of erroneous Judgments; but, provided they are uſeful to us, we are not much in pain about them.

[B] *His Diſpatches were ſometimes intercepted; and the Emperor made uſe of them to reproach the French with their ſtrict Correſpondence with the Porte.*] In a Letter, which *Charles* V. wrote, in the Year 1552, to the Princes and States of the Empire, he expreſſes his wonder, that the Ambaſſador of *France* ſhould pretend to juſtify his Maſter as to the Engagements with *Soliman*: "Have not I, *ſays he*, the "Memorials of *Aramont* drawn up at *Conſtantinople*, "which prove the reality of an Alliance negociated "between the *Porte* and *France* againſt a Chriſtian "Prince?" *Jam quod de communicatis cum Turco conſiliis obiter perſtringit, quaſi abunde purgatum exiſtimet, qua fronte excuſare poteſt? atque penes me habeo Aramontii Gallici legati commentarios Byzantii ſcriptos, & ad regem per Coſtam centurionem quemdam miſſos, qui ſocietatis cum Turcis in Chriſtiani nominis Principem intæ plenam fidem faciunt* (5). Mr *Varillas* obſerves (6), "That the Pope, and "the Emperor, had agreed to accuſe the King of "*France*, in full Council, of an Intelligence with "the Infidels, and to produce thereupon Mr *Aramont's* intercepted Letters, to which a wrong "Turn might eaſily be given, becauſe the Truth "was but half explained." But what occaſion was there for giving a wrong Senſe, ſince *Aramont* undoubtedly negociated a Treaty between *France*, and the *Porte*, againſt the Houſe of *Auſtria*? Was not That alone ſufficient to prove the Intelligence, with

which they would accuſe *Henry* II? The beſt Way, *France* could take, was, not to conteſt the Fact, but to juſtify the Reaſonableneſs of it, by ſhewing, that, where Religion is not concerned, we may make what Alliances we pleaſe. If *Charles* V. had not been always ſupported by good Allies among the Chriſtian Princes, Papiſts, or not Papiſts, he would not have ſtuck at forming Alliances with Infidels; and he would have improved them much better, than *France* did. He was much more cunning, and had greater Abilities than *Francis* I. The *Turkiſh* Fleet, in concert with him, would not have been uſeleſs, as it were with the *French*, who concerted Matters ſo ill, that one is moved to Shame, or Pity, or Laughter, who reads the Hiſtory of thoſe Times. Sincerity had nothing to do in this Caſe. That would have prevented the Emperor from reproaching his Enemy with entering into Alliance with Hereticks and Infidels, when He himſelf was ready to do the ſame, had Maxims of State required it. What would have become then of Thoſe, who could make pathetic Harangues, preſent plauſible Memorials, diſcuſs an hundred fine Common Places? All this muſt have been laid aſide; now this would have been very prejudicial; there would have been no blinding the People, no animating them to any Purpoſe; a thouſand exquiſite Praiſes, and pompous Titles, muſt have been given up.

A Reflection on the Alliances with Hereticks or Infidels.

- - - - - - *accuſat Manilius, ſi rea non eſt* (7).

(7) Juvenal. Sat. 6. ver. 243.

(e) Idem lib. 10. pag. 215.

(6) Varill. Hiſt. de Henri II. liv. 2. pag. 202.

People ſeldom fail to make Reproaches on theſe Occaſions, but when they are guilty themſelves.

ARBRISSEL (ROBERT *d'*.) Founder of the Order of *Fontevraud*. Look for FONTEVRAUD.

ARCESILAS, or ARCESILAUS, one of the moſt renowned Philoſophers of Antiquity, was born at *Pitane* in *Æolia* [A]. He was a Diſciple of the Mathematician *Autolycus*, his Country-man, and followed him to *Sardes*. Afterwards he came to *Athens*; where he was a Diſciple of *Xanthus*, then of *Theophraſtus*, and laſtly of *Crantor* [B]. He learned Geometry under *Hipponicus* (a). He had ſome Inclination

(a) Taken from Diogen. Laert. lib. 4. n. 32.

[A] *Was born at Pitane in Æolia.*] *Diogenes Laertius* is not the only one, who affirms this (1). Read theſe Words of *Pomponius Mela*, in the Chapter, where he deſcribes the Country of the *Æolians*. "Caicus inter Eleam decurrit, & Pitanem illam "quæ Arceſilam tulit, nihil affirmantis Academiæ "clariſſimum Antiſtitem (2). ------ *The River* "*Caycus runs between Elea and That Pitane*, "*where Arceſilas was born, the celebrated Founder* "*of the Academy, which affirmed nothing.*" See alſo *Strabo* lib. 13. pag. 422. in fin. Πιτάνη πόλις Αἰολική ------ ἐκ δὲ τῆς Πιτάνης ἐστὶν Ἀρκεσίλαος (3). *Pitane, a City of Æolia* ------ *Town in Laconia, the Birth-place of This Philoſopher* (4). *Salmaſius* (5), and Mr *Menage* (6), refute him. I cannot tell, whether it is through Inadvertency of the Author, or the Correctors, that *Arceſilaus Pritanæus* occurs in Mr *Gaſſendi* (7); it ſhould have been *Pitanæus*.

(1) Diog. Laert. lib. 4. n. 20.

(2) Pomp on. Mela, lib. 1. cap. 18. pag. 20.

(3) Strabo lib. 13. pag. 422. in fin.

(4) Solin. cap. 7. pag. 22.

(5) Salmaſ. Exercit Plin. pag. 138.

(6) Menag. in Diog. Laert. pag 176.

( ) Gaſſend. Oper. Tom. 1. pag. 18.

(8) Diog. La rt. n. 28, 29.

[B] *A Diſciple of Xanthus, then of Theophraſtus, and laſtly of Crantor* [8].] I am ſurprized, that *Diogenes Laertius*, after having clearly inſinuated, in ſeveral Places, that *Arceſilaus* was a Diſciple of *Polemon*, does not expreſsly ſay ſo in the Life of *Arceſilas*. The following are the Paſſages, where he affirms it. Arceſilas, ſays he, *having left Theophraſtus's School to follow Polemon and Crates, declared, that they were Gods, or the Remains of the Golden Age.* Ἔνθεν καὶ Ἀρκεσίλαον μεταβόντα

παρὰ Θεοφράστου πρὸς αὐτοὺς λέγειν, ὡς εἶεν θεοί τινες ἢ λείψανα τῷ χρυσῷ γένει (9). Hinc & *Arceſilaum, cum ad eos à Theophraſto diverteret, dixiſſe ferunt, illos Deos eſſe quoſpiam, aut aurei ſeculi reliquias.* He obſerves, a little lower, that *Crantor* and *Arceſilas* lodged together, and that *Polemon* and *Crates*, who lodged together with a Citizen, whoſe Name was *Lyſicles*, went and ſupped very often with *Crantor*, and that *Crates* was the Minion of *Polemon*, as *Arceſilas* was the Favourite of *Crantor*. The Tranſlator of *Diogenes Laertius* has confounded all this; for he ſuppoſes, that *Polemon* was the Minion of *Crates*, and *Crantor* of *Arceſilas*. Let us produce the *Greek*: Ἦν δὲ ἐρώμεν⟨⟩, Κράτης μὲν, ὡς προείρηται, Πολέμων⟨⟩, Ἀρκεσίλαο⟨⟩ δὲ Κράντορ⟨⟩ (10). That is: *Erat autem amaſius, ut quidem prædictum eſt, Polemonis quidem Crates, Crantoris autem Arceſilas.* The *Latin* Tranſlation, which no Commentator has cenſured, puts *amator*, where it ſhould have been *amaſius* : There has been no notice taken of the cauſe of the peculiar Signification of ἐρώμενος. Neither has any one obſerved the Contradiction, which follows a little after; for, as the *Greek* orders the Matter, *Arceſilas* is repreſented under the Character of the *Pathic*. Ἀρκεσίλαο⟨⟩ δὲ λων ὑπ᾽ αὐτοῦ (Κράντορος) συνδιῆναι Πολέμωνι, καίπερ ἐρών⟨⟩ (11). *Arceſilaus volens ab illo* (Crantore) *ſe Polemoni commendari, quanquam amatore ſuo.* Let us here reject all the impure and abominable Ideas, which This Author, and many others, ſeem willing to

(9) Id. in Cratete, lib. 4. pag. 240. n. 22.

(10) Id. Ib.

(11) Id. Ib. n. 22.

VOL. I. 5 K

tion to Poetry; and took great delight in reading *Homer* [C]; but his Paſſion for Philoſophy was ſuperior to all others. He ſucceeded *Crates* in the Regency of the Platonic School [D], and introduced new Opinions into it; for he founded a Sect, which was called the *Second Academy*, to diſtinguiſh it from That of *Plato*. He ſtrongly oppoſed the Dogmatiſts; he affirmed nothing; he doubted of every thing; he diſcourſed *pro* and *con*; and ſuſpended his Judgment: *This I do*, ſaid he, *becauſe nothing is*

to ſuggeſt in the like Caſe. When they ſpeak of a Philoſopher, and his Diſciples, they almoſt always obſerve, that he was *fond* (or a *Lover*) of ſuch or ſuch an one. This, I confeſs, may, on ſome Occaſions, be underſtood in a wicked Senſe, but on an hundred others, ought, I think, to be underſtood only of a virtuous and honourable Affection. Among ſeveral Diſciples, One was his Maſter's Favourite. It was He, who was deſigned for his Succeſſor; he, who had moſt Docility, Reſpect, or Genius, &c. Ought this to be expreſſed by the Term ἐρώμενος? But to return to the Fact; The laſt Paſſage, which I cited from *Diogenes Laërtius*, informs us, that *Arceſilas* deſired *Crantor* to recommend him to *Polemon*. The Hiſtorian adds, that *Crantor*, who was ſick, did not take it ill; but, on the contrary, as ſoon as he was recovered, went likewiſe himſelf to *Polemon's* Lectures. Ἀλλὰ καὶ αὐτὸς ὑγιαίνοντα διακεῖν Πολέμωνος (12). *Ipſe quoque, cum ſanus factus eſſet, ſe ad audiendum Polemonem contulit.* This is a Proof, that *Arceſilas* was one of That Philoſopher's Auditors, or Diſciples. He was ſo far ſo, that *Cicero* gives him no other Maſter. " Arceſilas tuus, etſi fuit in diſſerendo pertinacior, " tamen noſter fuit, erat enim Polemonis (13). — " Your Arceſilas, though ſtiff in his Opinions, was " yet one of us, having been a Diſciple of Polemon." *Numenius* aſſigns him ſeveral other Maſters. He makes him ſucceſſively the Diſciple of *Polemon*, *Theophraſtus*, *Diodorus*, and *Pyrrho* (14). He adds, that he learnt of *Crantor* Perſuaſion, of *Diodorus* Sophiſtry, and of *Pyrrho* to turn about like a Weather-Cock, and be nothing at all. Ὢν ὑπὸ μὲν Κράντορος φιλανθρωπικός, ὑπὸ δὲ Διοδώρου ſoφιςικός, ὑπὸ δὲ Πύρρωνος ἀτρεπῶς παντοδαπὸς, καὶ ἴτης καὶ οὐδὲν (15). *Et a Crantore quidem ad perſuadendum callidus, à Diodoro autem ſophiſta, denique à Pyrrhone cum omnem in partem verſatilis ac temerarius, tum etiam nullus eſſe didicit.* He fixed himſelf in the Pyrrhonian Inconſtancy, and wanted only the Name of a *Pyrrhonian*; he was called an *Academic*; a Name which he kept only in reſpect to the Philoſopher *Crantor*, his Maſter, and Lover. Πλὴν τῆς προσηγορίας ἐτύμως Πυρρώνειος ἦν τῆς τάξεως ἀναίρεσιν - - - αἰδοῖ τε ἔφερεν ὑπωμένως λέγεσθαι Ἀκαδημαϊκὸς ἔτι τὸν μὲν τοίνυν. Πυρρώνειον μὲν τῷ ὀνόματι φ, Ἀκαδημαϊκὸς δ᾽ ἐκ ἦν, πλὴν τῷ λέγεσθαι (16). *In Pyrrhone, ſi appellationem excipias, tanquam in omnium everſione acquievit - - - is pro ſua in amatorem obſervantia Academicum ſe vocari adhuc paſſus eſt. Ita qui Pyrrhonicus, excepto nomine, totus erat, idem Academicus præter nomen habebat nihil.* *Numenius* had but juſt before ſaid, that *Arceſilas*, a beautiful Youth, being beloved by *Crantor*, conſtantly adhered to him. Διὰ τὸ καλὸς εἶναι ἔτι ἂν ἐρᾶσθαι τυχὼν ὑφ᾽ ὁρᾷν Κράντορος τῷ Ἀκαδημαϊκῷ προσεχόμενος μὲν τῦτῳ (17). — *Eleganti formâ & commoda adhuc ætate cum eſſet, Crantorum Academicum amatorem nactus, ejus conſuetudine uſus eſt illi quidem.* He adds, that *Menedemus's* Lectures made him a more warm Diſputant; for which he quotes *Timon* (18). Thus we ſee ſeveral Omiſſions in the Liſt, which *Diogenes Laërtius* has left us, of *Arceſilas's* Maſters. I have ſupplied this Defect.

[C] *He took great Delight in reading* Homer.] He preferred him to all other Authors: Every Evening, he read ſome part of him, before he went to Sleep, and, when he roſe in the Morning, he uſed to ſay, *I am going to pay a Viſit to my Miſtreſs* (19), meaning, that he was going to read this Poet. Ἀναλεγόμενος δὲ σπανιώτατον Ὅμηρον εἰ καὶ εἰς ὕπνον ἰὼν παντὸς τι ἀνεγίνωσκεν· ἀλλὰ καὶ ὄρθρου λέγων ἐπὶ τὸν ἐρώμενον ἀπιέναι, ὁπότ᾽ ἂν βουλοιτο ἀναγίνωσκεν (20). *Amplectebatur Homerum maximi ex omnibus, cujus adeo ſtudioſus erat, ut ſemper ante ſomnum ejus aliquid legeret. Mane quoque cum ſurgeret, diceret, ſe ad amaſium ire, cum ſe velle legere innueret.*

[D] *He ſucceeded* Crates *in the Regency of the Platonic School* (21)]. Several Authors place our *Arceſilas* immediately after *Polemon*, without mentioning *Crates*. See a Note of *Aldrobandinus* on a Paſſage of *Diogenes Laërtius* (22), where you will find, that this learned Commentator had no where diſcovered, that *Crates* ſucceeded *Polemon*. You will likewiſe meet with theſe Words of *St Auſtin*: " Moritur Polemon, " ſuccedit ei Arceſilas, Zenonis quidem condiſcipu- " lus, ſed ſub Polemonis magiſterio (23). — Po- " lemon *dies*; to him ſucceeds *Arceſilas*, a Fellow- " Diſciple indeed of Zeno, but under the Tuition of " Polemon." To this Paſſage may be added That of the Fifty ſixth Letter. " Iidem quippe Academici, " qui Platonici, quod docet Auditorum ipſa ſucceſ- " ſio; Arceſilas enim, qui primus occulta ſententia " ſua nihil aliud iſtos quam refellere ſtatuit, quære " cui ſucceſſerit; Polemonem invenies; quære cui " Polemon; Zenocratem; Zenocrati autem diſ- " cipulo Academiam Scholam ſuam reliquit Pla- " to (24). —— *The Academics are the ſame with* " *the Platoniſts, as appears from the very Suc-* " *ceſſion of their Diſciples. For Arceſilas, who firſt* " *taught them to have no Opinions of their own, but* " *to refute every other, you will find to have been* " *the Succeſſor of Polemon; Polemon of Zenocrates;* " *and Zenocrates, Succeſſor, in the School of the Aca-* " *demy, to his Maſter Plato.*" We muſt not here depend upon St *Auſtin's* Authority; for he has not ſtrictly obſerved Exactneſs; and, as he skips over one Step between *Plato* and *Xenocrates* (25), he may have done the like between *Polemon* and *Arceſilas*. I do not inſiſt on his Silence as to *Crantor*, the famous Academic (26), who ſeems to have been the immediate Succeſſor of *Polemon*, and who died before him, and before *Crates* (27). If the Word Succeſſor diſpleaſes you, ſay, that *Crantor* taught in *Polemon's* Life-time. The ſame thing is affirmed of *Crates*; and from hence it comes to paſs, that ſometimes it is ſaid, that *Crantor* ſucceeded *Polemon*; ſometimes, that *Crates* ſucceeded him; ſometimes, that both of them were his Succeſſors; but generally *Crates* is placed after *Crantor* (28). Again; I do not object the Omiſſion of *Crantor* to St *Auſtin*; for I imagine it is wrong to reckon this Philoſopher as *Polemon's* Succeſſor: He died before his Maſter; and I find, that *Lacydes*, the Succeſſor of *Arceſilas*, was the firſt, who reſigned the Succeſſion of his Chair in his Life-time (29). Let us ſay then, that *Crates* alone ſucceeded *Polemon*, and reject this Period of Father *Rapin*: *Crates and Crantor, who were ſucceſſively Heads of* Plato's *School, altered nothing in his Doctrine* (30). He would not have been ſo much miſtaken, if he had named *Crantor* firſt; *Crantor*, I ſay, who died before *Crates*. A celebrated Critic (31), in correcting a Paſſage of *Nonius Marcellus* (32), has ſupplied us with an Authority, which wonderfully favours the Text of this Remark. According to his Correction, we are to believe, that *Lucilius* had ſaid, " Polemon & amavit Craterem, & " huic tranſmiſit ſuam Scholam, quam dicunt. — " Polemon *loved* Crates, *and tranſmitted to him his* " *School, as they call it.*" The Greek of *Diogenes Laërtius* carries the ſame Senſe. Κράτης —— καὶ ἀκροατὴς ἅμα καὶ ἐρώμενος Πολέμωνος. ἀλλὰ καὶ διεδέξατο αὐτοῦ τὴν σχολὴν αὐτῷ (33). *Crates auditor ſimul amaſiuſque* (34) *Polemonis, illiuſque ſcholæ ſucceſſor.* It do not depend on theſe Words of *Cicero*: " Speuſippus autem, & Xenocrates, qui primi " Platonis rationem auctoritatemque ſuſceperant, & " poſt eos Polemon & Crates unaque Crantor, in Aca- " demia congregati, diligenter eis quæ à ſuperioribus " ſuſceperant, utebantur (35). — Speuſippus *and* " Xenocrates, *the immediate Succeſſors of* Plato, *and* " *after them* Polemon *and* Crates, *together with* " Crantor, *taught the ſame Doctrines in the Academy*,

" which

ARCESILAS.

...tain. He attacked with great force whatever the other Sects affirmed [E]; for which

" *which they had received from their Predecessors.*"
They were not positive enough, nor so express, as
this Passage of *Diogenes Laërtius.* Πλάτων ὁ τὴν
ἀρχαίαν Ἀκαδημίαν συστασάμενω, ὁ Σπεύσιπ-
πος καὶ Ξενοκράτης, ὁ Πολέμων, ὁ Κράντωρ, καὶ
Κράτης, ὁ Ἀρκεσίλαω, ὁ τὴν μέσην Ἀκαδημίαν εἰσηγησάμενω (36). ——— Plato, *who founded
the old Academy; after Plato,* Speusippus *and* Xenocrates; *then* Polemon; *after* Polemon, Crantor, *and*
Crates; *to whom succeeded* Arcesilas, *who instituted
the middle Academy.* Casaubon, in his Note on this
Passage, quotes *Galen*, who says, that the Old Academy ended in *Crantes*; and that *Arcesilas*, the Disciple of *Crantes*, founded the lesser Academy (37).
This Commentator is ignorant, who the *Crantes* of
Galen is (38); but it is easily to be seen, either that
the Transcribers have put *Crantes* instead of *Crates*, or that *Galen* himself does not spell the Name
of *Arcesilas*'s Predecessor right. It happens daily,
that the most learned Persons either add, or retrench,
some Letter of the Author's Name, whom they
quote; they intend to name the same Person, whom
others alledge, according to the true Orthography.
I could give an hundred Instances of it, and am surprized, that *Casaubon* makes any Difficulty here. We
must not forget, that he wonders *Galen* has made no
mention of *Crantor*. *Quis vero non miretur omissum
à Galeno Crantorem* (39) *?*

[E] *He attacked with great Force whatever the o-
ther Sects affirmed.*] It would be wrong to pretend,
that he did not justly deserve the Name of an Innovator; but *Diogenes Laërtius* is mistaken, when he
takes him for the first, who introduced the Custom
of Disputing *pro* and *con*. Πρῶτω δὲ καὶ εἰς ἐκά-
τερον ἐπεχείρησε (40). *Primusque in utramque dis-
serere partem aggressus est.* It was the Taste of Socrates; and Plato continued it. We shall quote *Cicero*, who informs us, that *Arcesilas*'s Method of
controverting every thing, which was proposed to
him, was the same with That of *Socrates*; and that
Arcesilas was instructed in *Pyrrhonism* (41) by *Plato*'s
Books, and by the Discourses, which *Socrates* was supposed to have held. " Arcesilas primum, qui Pole-
" monem audierat, ex variis Platonis libris, sermo-
" nibusque Socraticis, hoc maxime arripuit, nihil esse
" certi, quod aut sensibus, aut animo percipi possit:
" quem ferunt eximio quodam usum lepore dicendi,
" aspernatum esse omne animi sensusque judicium,
" primumque instituisse (quamquam id fuit Socrati-
" cum maxime) non quod ipse sentiret ostenderet,
" sed contra id quod quisque se sentire dixisset dis-
" putare (42). ——— Arcesilas, *the Disciple of* Pole-
" mon; *the first, who gathered this Doctrine, chiefly
" from the Writings of* Plato, *and the Discourses of
" Socrates, that there is no Certainty in Objects,
" either of the Sense, or the Mind. This Philosopher
" is said to have had a most graceful manner of speak-
" ing; to have rejected all Judgment of the Mind
" and Senses; and to have been the first, who taught
" his Followers* (*tho'* it had been the constant Practice
" *of* Socrates *before him*) *not to declare their own O-
" pinions, but to controvert those of all others.*" He
says, in another Book, that *Socrates*'s Method, which
had been in a manner disused, was revived by *Arcesilas.* It is in this, that the Innovation of the
latter consists; and therefore the Expressions of *Diogenes Laërtius* are not exact; for it is plain, that a
Philosopher, who professes to dispute every thing,
which is advanced in answer to his Questions, puts
in practice the Method of maintaining both sides of
the Question. Observe these Words: " Is (Socrates)
" percontando atque interrogando elicere solebat eo-
" rum opiniones, quibuscum differebat, ut ad ea quæ
" hi respondissent, si quid videretur, diceret. Qui
" mos, quum à posterioribus non esset retentus, Ar-
" cesilas eum revocavit, instituitque, ut hi, qui se au-
" dire vellent, non de se quærerent, sed ipsi dicerent,
" quid sentirent. Quod quum dixissent, ille contra:
" sed, qui audiebant, quoad poterant, defendebant
" sententiam suam: apud cæteros autem philosophos,
" qui quæsivit aliquid, tacet, quod quidem jam sit
" etiam in Academia (43). ——— *He* (Socrates) *was
" wont, by asking Questions, to make those, with whom
" he discoursed, discover their own Opinions; that,
" if he thought proper, he might reply to their An-
" swers. Which Practice, having been discontinued

" *afterwards, was revived by* Arcesilas *who insti-
" tuted, that they, who would be his Hearers, should
" not ask his Opinion, but declare their own; which
" when they had done, he opposed them; yet his
" Hearers were allowed to defend their own Senti-
" ments. With other Philosophers it was otherwise;
" the Enquirer was silent himself, which is now pra-
" ctised even in the Academy.*" If This Testimony be
not express enough, what think you of This, in which
it is affirmed, that the Academy of *Arcesilas* was
no other, than That of *Plato* ? " Hinc Academiam
" novam appellant, quæ mihi vetus videtur. Siqui-
" dem Platonem ex illa vetere numeramus, qui quis in
" libris nihil affirmatur, & in utramque partem mul-
" ta disserantur, de omnibus quæritur, nihil certi
" dicitur (44). ——— *They call this the New Academy,
" which to me seems to be the Old. For we reckon
" Plato to have been of the Old, in whose Books nothing
" is affirmed, and many things are disputed on both
" sides of the Question; every thing is matter of En-
" quiry, and nothing certainly pronounced.*" I cite,
elsewhere (45), another Passage of no less Force than
this. If any one requires a Scrap of *Greek*, for variety's sake, I can fit him. I have read, somewhere,
that *Epicurus* could not see, without Chagrin, the
great Reputation of *Arcesilas*, the most renowned
Philosopher of those Times; and that he upbraided
him with having acquired a Reputation among the
Ignorant, without drawing any thing from his own
Stock. Τὸ δὲ Ἀρκεσίλαον τὸν Ἐπίκουρον μετρίως
με δοκεῖ ἡ δόξα παρωξύνει, ὡς τοῖς τότε
χρόνοις μάλιστα τῶν φιλοσόφων ἀξατεθέντα (46).
*Arcesilai autem Gloria videretur Epicuro haud medio-
crem attulisse ægritudinem, qui inter ejus temporis
Philosophos maximi fiebat.* It is true, *Arcesilas* did
not set up for Invention. He ascribed to *Socrates*,
Plato, *Parmenides*, and *Heraclitus*, the Honour of
inventing the *Epochè*, and the *Acatalepsia*. Ὁ δὲ
Ἀρκεσίλαω τοιοῦτον ἀπεδέχετο καινολογίας τῆ-
να δόξαν ἀξίαν καὶ ὑποτιθεσθαι τὴν παλαι-
ᾶν, λες ἐλέγχομεν τοὺς τότε σοφιστὰς ὅτι προ-
σεποιεῖτο Σωκράτει καὶ Πλάτωνι καὶ Παρμενίδῃ
καὶ Ἡρακλείτῳ τὰ περὶ τῆς ἐποχῆς ἔσομαι
καὶ τῆς ἀκαταληψίας, οὐκ εὐδαίμων, ἀλλὰ οἱ
ἀναδίδω καὶ βεβαίως αὐτῶν εἰς αὐξηνεν ἐπι-
δόξω ποιήματω (47). Arcesilas *was so far from
any Desire of innovating, or arrogating old Opinions
to himself, that the Sophists of his Times even
reproached him with ascribing to* Socrates, Plato, *and*
Parmenides, *the Doctrines of witholding the Assent,
and Incomprehensibility; not out of Necessity, but to
strengthen, as it were, and confirm them, by inscribing
them to these great Men.* Pray observe, that, by the
Confession of *Diogenes Laërtius* himself, our *Arcesilas*
only rendered the Platonic Method more *Contentious;*
this was all the Change he made in it. Πρῶτος
τὸν λόγον ἐκίνησε τὸν ὑπὸ Πλάτωνω παραδο-
δομένων, καὶ ἐποίησε δι' ἐρωτήσεως καὶ ἀποκρί-
σεως ἐριστικώτερον (48). *Primus orationis genus
quod Plato tradiderat movit effectúque per interroga-
tionem & responsionem contentiosius.* It may, nevertheless,
be said, that he was the first Disturber of the public Peace among the Philosophers; for, besides his
reviving a Practice, which had been almost forgotten,
he pursued the Method of *Socrates* with more Ardor,
than had ever been done before; and shewed himself more eager, more obstinate, and more impatient,
than the first Inventors. And, for this Reason, what
I am going to produce, was said of him. " Non-
" ne jam, quum philosophorum disciplinæ gravissimæ
" constitissent, tum, ut exortus est in optima Repub-
" lica Tiberius Gracchus, qui ocium perturbaret,
" sic Arcesilas, qui constitutam philosophiam ever-
" teret, & in eorum autoritate delitesceret, qui ne-
" gavissent quicquam sciri, aut percipi posse (49). ———
" *Did not* Arcesilas, *like another* Gracchus, *who
" disturbed the Repose of the best of Commonwealths,
" arise to overthrow the established Philosophy, and
" sheltered himself under Their Authority, who denied
" all Knowledge and Perception of Things?*"
Some have enquired into the Reason of *Arcesilas*'s
Conduct; and it was generally ascribed to That warm
Emulation, which grew up between Him and his
Fellow Disciple Zeno. Both had been *Polemon*'s
Scholars (50); and they strove to surpass each other
(51). Now Zeno took part with the Dogmatists;
he

which reason, he was looked upon, in Matters of Philosophy, as a Disturber of the Public Peace (*b*). Some pretend, that, finding no Evidence, which might prevent his floating equally between the Affirmative and Negative, he would write no Books (*c*); but others affirm, that he did write some; and then differ about the Question, whether he published any. Some affirm it, and others say, that he condemned all he had composed to the Flames (*d*). It is observable, however, that he dedicated some Books to *Eumenes*, Prince of *Pergamus*, and to no one else (*e*). We shall see

be laid down Definitions, and Axioms, which Arcesilas *vigorously opposed; and, to gain his Point, did not stick at overthrowing the very Foundation of all Science, and reducing every thing to Uncertainty.* The Passage I am going to cite, gives us this Account, as also of the little Success of his Undertaking (52), tho' supported by the most pleasing Eloquence. " Fuerint illa vetera si vultis incognita: nihil ne est ergo actum quod investigatum est posteaquam Arcesilas, Zenoni, ut putant, obtrectans, nihil novi reperienti, sed emendanti superiores immutationes verborum, dum hujus definitiones labefactare vult, conatus est clarissimis rebus tenebras obducere; cujus primo non admodum probata ratio quanquam floruit, tum acumine ingenii, tum admirabili quodam lepore dicendi, proxime à Lacyde solo retenta est (53)." Others say, that the fear of being nonplus'd by the Objections of certain Persons, who took a pleasure in puzzling the Philosophers, obliged *Arcesilas* to affirm nothing. He placed the *Epoché* before him as a Rampart; this was a Darkness, under favour of which he hoped to escape the Pursuits of the Sophist *Bion*, and the Followers of *Theodoret*, perpetual Sticklers against the Philosophers. *Numenius*, who observes, that *Diocles, the Cnidian,* had adopted this Conjecture, rejects it; and, in my Opinion, not without Reason; for though, by not deciding *pro* or *con*, we may secure ourselves from a thousand perplexing Difficulties, yet we are greatly exposed by so doing; and if, on the one hand, grave and serious Objections, Retortions, and Arguments *ad hominem*, the ordinary and inevitable Rock of the Dogmatists, are the less to be feared; on the other, we are much more exposed to the Raillery and Insults of Banterers. Now it is certain, that *Bion*, the greatest Sneerer of his Time, was less formidable, when he reasoned, than when he turned things into ridicule. Generally speaking, *That* is a very inconvenient Situation, which exposes a Man to Ridicule. *Arcesilas* himself was wont to rally those, who rejected the Testimony of Sense (54). However, let us see the Words of *Numenius*. Οὐ γὰρ πείθομαι, τὰ Κριδία Διοκλέως φάσκοντ᾽ ἐν ταῖς ἐπιζεφομέναις Διαλέξεσιν, Ἀρκεσίλαον φόβῳ τῶν Θεοδωρείων τε καὶ Βίωνος τῶν Σοφιστῶν, ἐπειδήπερ τοῖς φιλοσόφοις, καὶ οὐδὲν ὀκνοῦντ᾽ ἀπὸ παντὸς ἐλέγχειν, αὐτὸν ἐξευλαβηθῆναι, ἵνα μὴ πράγματα ἔχῃ, μηδ᾽ ἂν γε δόγμα ὑπεστὴν προβαλίσθαι πρὸς ἑαυτῷ τὴν ἐποχήν. Τῷ τ᾽ ἂν ἐμοί γε πείθομαι (55). Neque enim Cnidum illum Dioclem audio, qui in suis, ut eas inscripsit, Diatribis, Arcesilam docet, Theodoreorum ac Bionis Sophistæ metu, qui, Philosophis infesti, nullam non eas coarguendi occasionem arriperent, ita sibi, ne quid ab iis molestiæ pateretur, cavisse, ut nec certi quicquam statueret; nam ut sepius effuso atramento, sic illum sese objecta hac assensionis retentione tegere ac tueri. Verum hoc, dixi, ut minus credo.* Note, that one of *Cicero*'s Interlocutors affirms, that *Arcesilas* did not make use of the *Epoché*, in contradiction to *Zeno*, but through a Desire of finding out Truth. *Arcesilam vero non obtrectandi causa cum Zenone pugnavisse, sed verum invenire voluisse sic intelligitur* (56). He says (57) that *Arcesilas* was the first, who discovered, and approved this Proposition; *It is possible, that a Man may neither affirm, nor deny, any thing, in uncertain Matters; and it is the Part of a wise Man so to do. Nemo superiorum non modo expresserat, sed ne dixerat quidem, posse hominem nihil opinari, nec solum posse, sed ita necesse esse sapienti, visa est Arcesilæ cum vera sententia, tum honesta & digna sapiente.* He says likewise, that this Philosopher asked *Zeno, What will be the Consequence, if a wise Man can discern nothing clearly, and if he ought not to admit of any thing, which is not clearly true?* And that *Zeno* answered, *The Consequence will be, that he will clearly*

comprehend some things; and thus will admit of nothing obscure. He was obliged afterwards to give the Marks of those Things, which might be clearly comprehended; but those, which he gave, were contested by *Arcesilas*, who maintained, against him, that Falshood may appear in the same Guise as Truth; and that, consequently, Truth could not be discerned from Falshood. *Zeno* granted, that there was no comprehending any thing, if That, which Is not, can appear to us under the same Form with That, which Is; but he denied the Conformity of Ideas, in regard to that which Is, and that which Is not. *Arcesilas* insisted upon this Conformity. *Incumbit in eas disputationes ut doceret nullum tale esse visum à vero, ut non ejusmodi etiam à falso possit* (58). The Dispute between them turned upon this Point. It had been said before, in this Work of *Cicero*, that the Obscurity of Things, and not Obstinacy, or a Desire of Victory, engaged *Arcesilas* to dispute with *Zeno* (59). I have said, that he carried the Hypothesis of Uncertainty farther than *Socrates*, and I had reason to say so; for he would not so much as confess, with *Socrates*, that he knew his own Ignorance *(I know, that I know nothing).* He suspended his Judgment in every thing, and disputed only to convince himself, that the Affirmative Reasons were no better than the Negative. " Arcesilas negabat esse quicquam quod sciri posset, ne illud quidem ipsum, quod Socrates sibi reliquisset. Sic omnia latere censebant in occulto, neque esse quicquam quod cerni, aut intelligi possit. Quibus de causis nihil oportere neque affirmare quenquam, neque assertione approbare, cohibereque semper, & ab omni lapsu continere temeritatem; quæ tum esset insignis, quum aut falsa, aut incognita res approbaretur, neque hoc quicquam esset turpius, quam cognitioni & perceptioni assertionem approbationemque præcurrere. Huc (rationi quod erat consentaneum) faciebat, ut contra omnium sententias dies jam plerosque deduceret, ut quum in eadem re paria contrariis in partibus momenta rationum invenirentur, facilius ab utraque parte assertio sustineretur (60).* ——— *Arcesilas* denied, *that there was any thing which could be known, not even That Point of Knowledge, which Socrates left himself. Thus these Philosophers thought every thing lay concealed, and that nothing could be either perceived, or understood. Upon which account, they believed, that no one ought to affirm or approve any thing by an Assertion, but restrain himself from giving a rash Judgment; which would then be notorious, when either a false or unknown thing should be assented to; and that nothing was more scandalous, than to suffer the Affirmation, and Approbation, to out-run the Knowledge, and Perception, of a thing. This general Opposition to every Opinion was with this View, that, if the Arguments on both sides of the same Question should be found to be equally strong, the Assertion on both Sides might be the more easily supported.*" It was He, who taught the *Acatalepsia*, or Incomprehensibility of things, more expressly than was ever done before; and carried it to such an Extremity, that *Carneades*, who was able to support it better than He, was obliged to have recourse to some Limitation (61); but it it is certain, that *Arcesilas* only enlarged upon, and unfolded, what the greatest Masters had said before him. " Cum Zenone — Arcesilas sibi omne certamen instituit — earum rerum obscuritate, quæ ad confessionem ignorationis adduxerant Socratem, &, veluti amantes Socratem, Democritum, Anaxagoram, Empedoclem, omnes pene veteres, qui nihil cognosci, nihil percipi, nihil sciri posse dixerunt, angustos sensus, imbecillos animos, brevia curricula vitæ, & (ut Democritus) in profundo veritatem esse demersam, opinionibus & institutis omnia teneri, nihil teneri, nil veritati relinqui, deinceps omnia tenebris circumfusa esse dixerunt (62). ——— Arcesilas opposed Zeno,*

ARCESILAS. 411

see how he has been attacked by a Father of the Church [F]. As he was Master of

"Zeno, induced to it by the *Obscurity of those things*, *which brought Socrates to confess his Ignorance*, as *also Democritus, Anaxagoras*, and *Empedocles, Lovers*, as it were, *of Socrates, and all the ancient Philosophers; who taught, that nothing could be known, perceived, or understood; that our Senses were narrow; our Minds weak; the Course of our Lives short; that Truth* (as *Democritus* said) *lay deep; that all things depended on Opinion, and positive Appointment; that nothing was left to Truth; and that all things were surrounded with Darkness*." It was under the Authority of these great Names, that he attacked the Dogmatists (63). He might have alledged several others, as you may see in the second Book of the *Academical Questions* (64). Nevertheless, *Numenius*, who is passionately transported against him, grounds his Quarrel on the Revolt, which he imputes to him (65). You will find some Strokes of his Indignation in the Description he gives of this Philosopher's Inconstancy. He tells us, "he was a Man, who denied and affirmed the same things; he ran blindfold to the right and left; he gloried in being ignorant of the Difference between Good and Evil; he uttered the first Notion which came into his Head, and immediately overthrew it by a greater Number of Arguments, than he had brought to establish it. He was an *Hydra*, which devoured itself." The Original is more expressive and full. "Ἔλεγε, καὶ ἀντέλεγε, καὶ μετεκυλινδεῖτο λάκλιθεν, καὶ ᾖθεν, ἑκατέρωθεν, ὁπόθεν τύχοι, παλινάγρετος, καὶ δύσκηλος, καὶ παλίμβολος τε ἅμα, καὶ παρρησιχινδυνευμένος, ὀδέν τε εἰδὼς, ὡς αὐτὸς ἔφη, γενναῖος ἂν (66).——Καθέχαιρε τῷ ὀνείδει, καὶ ἡμέρινίω θαυμασῖος, ὅτι μήτε τι αἰσχρὸν ἢ κωλὸν, μήτε ἀγαθὸν, μήτε αὖ κακὸν ἔςι τι, ᾔδει ἀλλ' ὁπότερον εἰς τὰς ψυχὰς πέσοι, τοῦτο εἶπών, αὖθις μεταβαλὼν, ἀντηρπαίεν πλεονάχως, ἢ δὴ ὅσων κατεσκευάκει. Ἦν εἰν ὕδραν τέμνων ἑαυτὸν, καὶ τεμνόμενος ὑφ' ἑαυτῷ, ἀμφότερος ἀλλήλων δυσκρίτως, καὶ τῷ ὄντι ἀσκίτως (67). *Affirmans simul idem, idemque negans, binc, illinc, utrinque, vel undique pedis subito se temereque versans ac revocans, incerti ambigueque sensus, veterator, præceps, atque ut ipsemet, adeo ingenuus est, confitetur, nihil omnino sciens ——— hoc ut probrò jucundissimè frueretur, eoque se nomine mirum in modum circumspiceret, quod quid turpe quidve honestum, quid bonum quidve malum esset, ignoraret: sed potius, ubi quod primum in mentem venerat effutisset, tum repente mutatus, id ipsum pluribus quam ante stabilierat, everteret. Se ipsum igitur ille quasi Hydram secabat & secabatur à se ipso, dum sic in utramque partem loqueretur, ut nec quid sibi vellet intelligeret, nec ullam ipse decori rationem haberet.* On the whole, he acknowledged the Finger of God, in the Ignorance of Man; for he was much pleased with a Verse of *Hesiod*, where it is said, That *the Gods keep human Understanding behind the Veil* (68).

Κρύπλοντες γὰρ ἔχυσι θεοὶ νόον ἀνθρώποισι.
Ignaros hominum suspendunt numina mentes.

[F] *How he has been attacked by a Father of the Church.*] I mean *Lactantius*: He pretends to destroy all Philosophy, by maintaining, with *Socrates*, that we can know nothing, and, with *Zeno*, that nothing is to be believed, but what we know. *Si neque sciri*, says he, (69) *quicquam potest, ut Socrates docuit, nec opinari oportet, ut Zeno, tota Philosophia sublata est.* He confirms his Pretence to the great Number of Sects, into which Philosophy was divided. Each engrossed Truth and Wisdom to it self, and made Error and Folly the Portion of all the rest. So that whatsoever particular Sect we would condemn, we have the Suffrages of all the other Philosophers, who are not of That Sect. You are sure, then, of a Majority, in condemning them all; for each in particular approves your Judgment as to all the rest; and has nothing to oppose, in bar against a general Sentence, but the Testimony it gives it self; in which case it is a Judge in it's own Cause, and consequently unworthy of Credit. See how *Lactantius* destroys all the Sects of the Ancient Philosophy by each other: "They destroy each other, like *Cadmus*'s Brood; not one of them is left alive; and the Reason is,

"because they have, indeed, each a Sword, but no Buckler: They have Arms for an Offensive, but not for a Defensive War. *Pereunt igitur universi hoc modo, &, tanquam Spartiatæ illi* (70) *poëtarum, sic se invicem jugulant, ut nemo ex omnibus restet. Quod eò fit, quia gladium habent, scutum non habent. Si ergo singulæ sectæ multarum sectarum judicis stultitiæ convincuntur, omnes igitur vanæ, atque inanes reperientur. Ita se ipsam philosophia consumit, & conficit* (71). He goes on: "*Arcesilas* observing this, took up Arms against them all, and founded a new Sect of Philosophy, which consisted in not philosophizing at all." *Quod cum intelligeret Arcesilas, Academiæ Conditor, reprehensiones omnium inter se collegit, confessionemque ignorantiæ clarorum Philosophorum, armavitque se adversus omnes. Ita constituit novam non philosophandi philosophiam* (72). From That Time there arose two Parties; one aspiring to perfect Science, the other destroying all Certainty. The first falls to the Ground, if the Nature of Things cannot be known; the Latter is lost, if it can: Supposing their Pretensions equal, still Philosophy must fall, because divided. "If, as I have taught, our miserable State does not admit of any Science, properly speaking, in Man, then *Arcesilas* gains the Victory; but he cannot maintain it; because it is impossible we should not know some things; we should of Necessity perish, if we did not know what is useful or pernicious to Life. *Si autem (ut docui) nulla potest esse in homine interna & propria scientia ob fragilitatem conditionis humanæ, Arcesilas manu vicit. Sed ne ipsa quidem stabit, quia non potest omnino nihil sciri. Sunt enim multa, quæ natura ipsa nos scire, & usus frequens, & vitæ necessitas cogit. Itaque pereundum est nisi scias, quæ ad vitam sunt utilia, ut appetas, quæ periculosa, ut fugias, & vites* (73). After this, *Lactantius* gives us a detail of several Things, which Men know, and insults *Arcesilas*, who could not degrade the rest of the World, without degrading himself; since they might have reply'd to him, *If you prove, that we have no Knowledge, and that consequently we are no Philosophers, neither are you one, for you confess that you know nothing*. So that he cuts his own Throat with the same Dagger, which he employs to kill others. *Quid ergo promovit Arcesilas, nisi quod confectis omnibus philosophis se ipsum mucrone transfixit* (74). *Lactantius* does not blame him in every Thing; he praises him for having discern'd the Folly of those, who believe, that Conjectures about Truth are Science. *Rectè vidit Arcesilas arrogantes vel potius stultos esse, qui putant scientiam veritatis conjectura posse comprehendi* (75): But he does not dwell long on his Praise; he proceeds immediately to the Contradiction, so often objected to the *Pyrrhonians; for this very Reason, that you know nothing, you know one thing*. "*Arcesilas* ——— *introduxit genus Philosophiæ ἀνούσιαςον, quod latinè instabile, sive inconstans possumus dicere. Ut enim nihil sciri posse sciendum sit, aliquid scire necesse est, nam si omnino nihil scias, id ipsum nihil sciri posse tolletur. Itaque qui velut sententiæ loco pronunciat nihil sciri, tanquam præceptum profitetur, & cognitum, ergo aliquid sciri potest.* Huic simile est illud, *quod in scholis proponi solet in afflatæ generis exemplum, somniasse quendam, ne somniis crederet. Si enim crediderit, tum sequitur, ut credendum non sit; si autem non crediderit, tum sequitur, ut credendum sit. Ita si nihil sciri potest, necesse est id ipsum sciri, quod nihil sciatur. Si autem scitur, posse nihil sciri, falsum est ergo quod dicitur nihil sciri posse. Sic inducitur dogma sibi ipsi repugnans, seque dissolvens* (76). *Arcesilas introduced a kind of wavering, uncertain, Philosophy. For, in order to know, That nothing can be known, we must necessarily know something; for if you know nothing at all, this very knowledge, that nothing can be known, will be destroy'd. He, therefore, who gives it as his Opinion, that Nothing is known, professes to know something; something therefore may be known. A-kin to this is That Example of this kind of Philosophy usually propos'd in the Schools; that a certain Person dreamt, that he ought not to believe in Dreams. For if he did believe in them, it follows, that he ought not to believe in them; but if he did not believe in them, it follows, that he ought to believe in them. Thus,*

VOL. I. 5 L "if

ARCESILAS.

of a very persuasive Eloquence, which never wandered too far from the main Subject, and had moreover an happy Talent at answering Objections, he drew a great Number of Disciples to his Auditory [G], though he was severe in his Censures. In general, the World was persuaded of his Integrity; and he filled his Scholars with great Expectations; which made them submit the more readily to his Rebukes, though a little too severe (*f*). Some affirm, that he play'd the Sceptic, only to try his Scholars [H]; and that, after this Probation, he taught them in another manner. He distributed his Money as freely as any Man in the World; and very great things are said of his Liberality [*I*]. He is accused of Vanity, and of affecting Popularity too

(*f*) Diogen. Laert. lib. 4. n. 37.

"*if nothing can be known, we must necessarily know this very thing, that nothing is known. But, if it be known, that nothing can be known, it is false, which is pretended, that nothing can be known. Thus an Opinion is advanc'd, which is repugnant to, and destructive of, itself*". Lastly, *Lactantius* confesses, that, with relation to Physics, there is no such thing as Science, and that it ought not to be so much as sought after. — "Quanto faceret sapientius ac verius, si exceptione facta diceret causas rationesque duntaxat rerum cœlestium seu naturalium, quia sunt abditæ, nesciri posse, quia nullus doceat, nec quæri oportere, quia inveniri quærendo non possunt (77). — *How much more wisely and truly wou'd he have reason'd, if he had said only, that the Causes and Reasons of Heavenly or Natural Things, as being hid, cou'd not be known; since there is no Teacher to instruct us in them; and that we ought not to enquire after them, since no Enquiry will discover them?*

(77) Id. lib. pag. 258.

Let us now make some short Remarks on this Dispute. I. The Argument, he makes use of, to overthrow all the Sects of Philosophy, by each other, proves too much. An Atheist, who should make use of it, at present, to overthrow the Christian Religion, would reason ill; the Christian Sects mutually condemn each other; I grant it; but if you should condemn any one of them in all it's Doctrinal Points, you would not have the Suffrages of all the rest. II. *Lactantius* contradicts himself wretchedly. He confesses, that, if there be no Science among Men, *Arcesilas* gains the Victory; and he pretends to have demonstrated, that we are too frail to attain to Science. Why then does he presently add, that *Arcesilas* loses the Victory, because there are actually several Sciences among Men? III. The Examples he alledges are nothing to the purpose: For, in the Sense, in which the Word is taken in this Dispute, it is not Science, to discern Good from Bad; nor has this kind of Knowledge been call'd in question by the *Acataleptics*. IV. The Charge of Contradiction has less of Solidity in it than of false Lustre; it is rather a Subtilty, than a convincing Reason; good Sense soon unravel the Difficulty. If I dream, that I ought not to believe in Dreams, I am caught in a Trap; for, if I do not believe in them, I do believe in them; and, if I do believe in them, I do not believe in them. Who sees not, that, in this case, the particular Dream, which advises me not to believe in Dreams, must be excepted from all other Dreams? See, in *Sextus Empiricus*, what the Sceptics reply'd to this Objection. V. *Lactantius*'s Concession, as to Physics, was not at all proper to his Design: An Advantage might be drawn from it against his own Cause.

(78) Cicero, de Natura Deorum, lib. 1. cap. 5.

[G] *He drew a great Number of Disciples to his Auditory.*] An Attempt to run down all Science, and to reject not only the Testimony of Sense, but That of Reason too, is the boldest, that ever was form'd in the Republick of Letters. It is like That of the *Alexanders*, and other Conquerors, who would subdue all Nations; It requires much Wit, much Eloquence, much Reading, and deep Meditation. "Si fingulas disciplinas percipere magnum est, quanto majus omnes? quod facere iis necesse est, quibus propositum est veri reperiendi causâ, & contra omnes Philosophos pro omnibus dicere (78). — *If it be a great attainment to be Master of a single Science, how much a greater is it to understand All? which they must necessarily do, who propose to investigate Truth, and to defend All the Philosophers against All the Philosophers*". *Arcesilas* was as fit for such an Undertaking, as a Man could be. Nature and Art had concurr'd to quality him compleatly. He was naturally of a happy Genius, and of a ready and lively Wit (79); his Person and Presence were engaging; he spoke with a good Grace; the Charms of his Counte-

(79) Τὴν Θεόφραςον κινέμενον φαςὶν εἰ πεῖν ὡς ἐυφυῶς καὶ συντεγμένως ἀναλυθείς τῆς διατριβῆς εἰς νεανίσκος. — Theophrastus, *they say, was grieved at his Departure, and said, How ingenious and ready a Youth has left the School.* Diog. Laërt. ubi supra, n. 30. See also n. 17.

nance admirably seconded those of his Voice; he had learnt, under good Masters, all that was most proper to perfect his Natural Abilities; I mean to extend their Force by the Combination of several different Powers. You will find This Detail in *Numenius*; but deliver'd with an odious Turn. *Numenius* did not love *Arcesilas*; yet could not forbear expressing himself thus; Πλὴν τοῖς ἀκούσιν ἤρκεσεν, ὁμῷ τῇ ἀκροάσει ὑπέρδυσωπον ὄνθα θεωμένοις· ἦν ἐν ἀκωμένῳ, καὶ βλεπόμενος ἡδίς᾽. ἐπεὶ τοι προσεσθήσας ἀποδέχεσθαι αὐτῷ τοὺς λόγους ἰούσας ἀπὸ χαλῶ προσώπε τε καὶ σόμαϕ᾽, ἐκ ἄτευ τὴς ἐν τοῖς ὄμμασι φιλοφροσύνης (80). *Yet be engaged the Attention of his Hearers; whilst, as he spoke, they beheld the greatest Dignity of Aspect. For he charm'd both the Eyes and Ears; for which Reason what he said was favourably hear'd, as it flowed from pleasing Lips, attended with a certain Native Sweetness in his Looks*. He says likewise, that *Arcesilas* thunderstruck the Stoics by his various ways of confuting his Antagonists. Let us repeat the whole Passage; it will shew the great Dexterity of our Philosopher, and the great Esteem he had acquired. Οἱ Στωικοὶ δὲ ὑπήκοον ἐκπεπληγμένοι. ἡ μᾶσα γὰρ αὐτοῖς ἐδὲ τότε ἦν φιλολόγῳ, ἐδ᾽ ἐργάτις χάριτων, ὑφ᾽ ἣν ὁ Ἀρκεσίλαῳ, τὰ μὲν ἀπεικρίνων, τὰ δὲ ὑποτίμνων, ἄλλα δ᾽ ὑποσκελίζων, κατεγλωτῆλιζέ το αὐτὸς, καὶ πιθανὸς ἦν. Τοιγαροῦν πρὸς ἐς μὲν ἀντιλέγειν, ἡτζώμενον, ἐν οἷς δὲ λέγων ἦν, καταπεπληγμένων, διεδειγμένον πως τοῖς τότε ἀνθρώποις ὑπῆρχε, μηδεν εἶναι μήτ᾽ ἐν ἔπος, μήτε πάθος, μήτε ἔργον ἐν Εξοχῇ, μηδὲ ἐχρησεν τοσαύτην ὀφθῆναί τοτ᾽ ἂν εἰ τι μὴ Ἀρκεσιλάῳ δοκεῖ τῷ Πιταναίῳ (81). *The Stoics bear'd their things with Astonishment. For their Muse was as yet unskilled, nor Mistress of that Address, by which Arcesilas, variously confuting and baffling Zeno's Arguments, o'rewhelmed them with a torrent of Words, and established his Credit. Thus when They, with whom he disputed, were overcome, and They, before whom he spoke, remain'd astonish'd and confounded, it was evident to the World at that time, that no Opinions were right or wrong, but such as were approved, or condemned, by Arcesilas of Pitane.* The preceeding Remarks might have been sufficient to establish the Merit of *Arcesilas*. But here is a new one. Some one, in *Cicero*, says, that no one would ever have followed This Philosopher's Opinion, if the manifest Absurdity of it had not disappeared under the Eloquence and Dexterity of the Teacher. *Quis ista tam aperte perspicueque & perversa & falsa sequutus esset, nisi tanta in Arcesilâ — & copia rerum, & dicendi vis fuisset* (82).

(80) Numenius, apud Euseb. Præp. Evang. l. 14. cap. 6. pag. 730, D.

(81) Id. ib. p. 733, C.

(82) Cicero, Academ. Quæst. l. 4. cap. 18. fin.

[H] *Some affirm, that he play'd the Sceptic, only to try his Scholars.*] Sextus Empiricus, having said, that *Arcesilas* did not seem to differ from the *Pyrrhonians*; adds, that, if certain Reports were to be credited, he was a *Pyrrhonian* only in Appearance; who, in the main, followed the method of the Dogmatists. The Questions he proposed to his Auditors, to discover whether they had Genius enough to comprehend the Doctrine of *Plato*, made him looked upon as a Philosopher, who affirmed nothing; but he deliver'd *Plato*'s Doctrine, in a Dogmatical way, to Those, in whom he had discovered a found Understanding (83). It is difficult to know whether this Relation be true. See the Dissertations of Mr *Foucher* on the Philosophy of the Academics (84), and the Annotations of *Thomas Aldobrandinus*, to which I refer you (85).

(83) Sextus Empiricus, Pyrrhon. Hyp. typof. lib. 1. c. 33.

(84) Foucher. lib. 1. & 2. & lib. 3. pag. 154, &c.

[*I*] *Very great things are said of his Liberality.*] He did good, and endeavoured to conceal it. Ἐυεργετήσας πρόχειρος ἦν, καὶ λαθεῖν τὴν χάριν ἀντιφρατῷ (86). *Erat ad ferenda beneficia promptus; latere quoque gratiam omni studio quærebat, fastum ejusmodi maxime exhorrens*. This was practising the

(85) Th. Aldobrand. in Diog. Laërt. lib. 4. n. 28.

(86) Diogen. Laërt. lib. 4. n. 37.

Gospel

ARCESILAS.

too much (g). The other Philosophers took a Pleasure in censuring him (h); but did they equal him in Modesty, and a Freedom from Jealousy? Did they exhort their Disciples to hear other Professors? This He did (i). One of his Pupils having signified, that he should chuse to be the Disciple of a certain Peripatetic, he carried him to the Professor, and recommended him to his Care (k). Another time, he expelled a Disciple his School for having affronted *Cleanthes*, in a Verse of a Comedy; and would not restore him to Favour, 'till the Person offended had received Satisfaction (l). The Merit of this Action will appear the greater, when it is known, that *Cleanthes* was the Successor of *Zeno*, who had been *Arcesilas*'s Adversary. This Person was very free from the failing of most Plagiaries; for he declared openly, that he taught nothing but what he had found in Books (m). It is probable he acted thus to give the greater Authority to his Opinions, and to take off the Odium, which the Name of Innovator drew upon him. He had no Inclination to meddle with Politics (n): Nevertheless, when he was appointed to go to *Demetrius* to negotiate some Affairs with King *Antigonus*, in Favour of his Country, he accepted the Deputation. He returned without Success; probably because he never would compliment that Prince, or go to Court, or write Consolatory Letters to him after the Loss of a Sea-Fight (o), as several others had done (p). He had a great share in the Friendship of the Governor of the *Pireum* (q), and received several fine Presents from *Eumenes*, Prince of *Pergamus* (r). He had a very fine Thought concerning Death; for he said, that, of all human Evils, this was the only one, whose Presence is never troublesome to any one, and which makes us uneasy only by it's Absence (s). His Doctrines tended to overthrow all Precepts of Morality; and yet it is observable, that he practised them. The Testimony given him, on this occasion, by the Stoic *Cleanthes*, his Answer, and the other's Reply, are very curious [K]. He was never married (t); though he was of an amorous Constitution; and followed the bent of his Inclinations but too freely, and even to shameful Excesses [L]. He flourished about the CXXth Olympiad (u), and died of a *Delirium*, occasioned by excessive Drinking, at Seventy five Years of Age (x), in the fourth Year of the CXXXIVth Olympiad (y). He boasted of his great Patience during a Fit of the Gout [M]. *Diogenes Laertius* has not given him *Bion* for his Successor: Father *Rapin* imagined this without the least Ground [N]. I have but one Fault to charge Mr *Moreri*

Gospel Precept, before it was declared. " Having " made a Visit to *Ctesibius*, who was Sick, and wanted Necessaries, he dexterously convey'd a Purse of " Money under his Pillow (87)." *Seneca* tells us this. *Arcesilaus, ut aiunt, amico pauperi, & paupertatem suam dissimulanti, ægro autem, & ne hoc quidem confitenti deesse sibi in sumptum ad necessarios usus, cum clam succurrendum judicasset, pulvino ejus ignorantis sacculum subjecit, ut homo inutiliter verecundus, quod desiderabat, inveniret potius quam acciperet* (88). *Plutarch* relates the same Fact more at large, but supposes, that the sick Person was not *Ctesibius*; he calls him *Apelles* of *Chio* (89). Let us add, that *Arcesilas*, having lent some Silver Plate to a Friend, who was to make a Feast, would never demand it afterwards, supposing that it was given, not lent. Some say, that, considering the Necessity of his Friend, he refused to receive it again, when it was returned to him (90).

[*K*] *The Testimony given him, on this Occasion, by* Cleanthes, *His Answer, and the other's Reply, are very curious.*] When once a Man affirms, that there is nothing certain, and that all is incomprehensible, he in effect declares, that it is uncertain whether there be any such thing as Virtue or Vice. Now such a Tenet seems calculated to inspire an Indifferency for Probity and for all the Duties of Civil Life. For which Reason *Arcesilas*'s Adversaries tax'd him with having neglected all those Duties. They pretended, that he lived according to his Principles. But *Cleanthes*, though of a Sect very opposite to This Philosopher, took his part. *Hold your Tongue*, said he to one of these Censurers, *condemn not* Arcesilaus; *he overthrows the Duties by his Words, but establishes them by his Actions.* Παύσαι, ἔφη, καὶ μὴ ψέγε, εἰ γὰρ καὶ λόγῳ τὸ καθῆκον ἀναιρεῖ, τοῖς γοῦν ἔργοις αὐτὸ τίθει (91). *Quiesce*, inquit, *neque vituperes; ille enim etsi verbis afficium tollit, operibus tamen id ponit. Arcesilas* answer'd, That he did not love to be flatter'd: *Is it Flattery*, replied *Cleanthes*, *to maintain, that you say one thing, and do another* (92)? This Repartee is smart enough. Probably he alluded to a Verse of *Homer*, which imports, that Hypocrites and Dissemblers, whose Thoughts are contrary to their Words, ought to be detested as Hell (93). However, at the bottom, This was a great Commendation of the good Life of *Arcesilas*. By the way, there was a Theory in the Doctrine of the rigidest *Pyrrhonians* favourable to Virtue; for, whatever the real Nature of things might be, they taught, that, as to Practice, Men ought to behave according to Appearances. Be that as it will, the true Principle of our Morals depends so little upon the speculative Judgment, which we form of the Nature of things, that nothing is more common, than Orthodox Christians, who live ill, and Free-Thinkers, who live well.

[*L*] *He followed the Bent of his Inclinations — — even to shameful Excesses.*] The good Qualities, mentioned in the Body of this Article, and in the preceeding Remark, were joined, in his Person, with the most criminal Lewdness. So true it is, that Vice and Virtue are sometimes in Alliance. He publickly visited *Theodota* and *Phileta*, two common Women. Καὶ Θεοδότῃ τε καὶ Φιλαίτῃ, Ἠλιαίαις ἑταίραις, συνῴκει φανερῶς (94). *Theodotæ item ac Philetæ, Eliensibus scortis, palam congrediebatur*. The worst is, He was addicted to the Sin against Nature. Φιλομειράκιός τε ἦν καταφερής. ὅθεν οἱ περὶ Ἀρίσωνα τὸν Χῖον Στωικοὶ ἐπικάλουν αὐτὸν φθορέα τῶν νέων, καὶ κιναιδολόγον καὶ θρασὺν ἀποκαλοῦντες (95). *He was fond of Boys, and of an amorous Complexion; insomuch, that the Stoic* Aristo *of* Chios *was wont to call him A Corrupter of Youth, and an impudent Boaster of his unnatural Amours*.

[*M*] *He boasted of his great Patience during a Fit of the Gout.*] Nothing *astonishes me more from those Parts hither*, said he to *Carneades* the *Epicurean*, afflicted to see him in so much Torment, *Nothing*, said he, pointing at the same time to his Feet, and Breast. *Is quum arderet podagræ doloribus, vsitissetque hominem Carneades Epicuri persuasionis, & tristis exiret, mane quæso*, inquit, *Carneades noster, nihil illinc huc pervenit, ostendens pedes & pectus* (96). This was talking like a Stoic, tho' *Arcesilas* was The Antagonist of The Founder of That Sect.

[*N*] Diogenes Laërtius *has not given him* Bion *for Successor. Father* Rapin *imagined this, without the least Ground.*] These are his Words: " *Cicero*, " who knew *Plato*'s Successors very well, says no- " thing of This *Bion*, whom *Diogenes* gives *Arce-* " *silas*

ARCESILAS. ARCHELAUS.

reri with; to wit, his saying, that *Arcesilas* studied under *Xanthus*, and under *Theophrastus*, before he came to *Athens*. I have observed a very gross Error in *Sidonius Apollinaris* [O].

" *silas* for his Successor, and who made himself
" famous by the Vehemency of his Satires, according to *Horace* (97)." The only ground Father *Rapin* can have for what he says, is, that The Life of *Bion* immediately follows That of *Arcesilas*, in the Works of *Diogenes Laërtius*. This Reason is void; since the Author expressly says, That *Lacydes* was the Successor of *Arcesilas* (98), and that *Bion*, being also a Hearer of *Crates*, despised the Opinions of the Academy, and afterwards embraced another Sect (99).

[O] *I have observed a very gross Error in Sidonius Apollinaris.*] He pretends, that, according to *Arcesilas*, who preceeded *Socrates*, God is the Efficient Cause of the Universe, and Atoms the Material Cause of it.

Post hos Arcesilas divina mente patratam
Conjicit hanc molem, confectam partibus illis

Quas atomos vocat ipse leves. Socratica post hunc
Secta micat, quæ de naturæ pondere migrans
Ad mores hominum limandos transtulit usum (100).

Next these, Arcesilas supposed the World
Form'd, by a Mind divine, of lightest Atoms.
The Sect of Socrates succeeded next,
Which, quitting nat'ral Things, applied Philosophy
To polish and inform the Human Mind.

Savaro, without taking notice of this Mistake in Chronology, is contented with observing, that every one ascribes to *Epicurus*, and *Democritus*, the Doctrine, which *Sidonius Apollinaris* attributes to *Arcesilas* (101). This Observation is wrong; for no one ever pretended, that *Democritus* and *Epicurus*, taught, that the Universe was the Work of God.

(97) Rapin. Compar. de Platon & d' Ariftote, parte 4. c. 1. pag. 369.

(98) Diog. Laërt. lib. 4. n. 59 in Lacyde, init.

(99) Id. ib. n. 51, 52. in Bione.

(100) Sidon. Apollin. Carm. 15. ver. 94. pag. 152.

(101) Savaro in hunc locum Sidonii Apollinaris.

ARCHELAUS.

Diogenes Laërtius mentions Four Persons, who bore this Name (a); to wit, ARCHELAUS, the Philosopher (b); ARCHELAUS, the Author of a Description of all the Countries, through which *Alexander* carried his Arms; ARCHELAUS, who described the marvellous Properties of certain things in Verse (c); and ARCHELAUS, the Orator, who wrote a Treatise of Rhetoric. Mr *Menage* adds, to these Four, ARCHELAUS, King of *Cappadocia*; ARCHELAUS, King of *Sparta*; ARCHELAUS, General of *Mithridates*; ARCHELAUS, the Dancer; ARCHELAUS, the Musician; and ARCHELAUS, the Comedian (d). He observes, that *Lucian* mentions the latter in his Treatise, *de conscribenda Historia*; That *Athenæus*, in his first Book, speaks of him, who played upon Instruments of Music (e); and that *Clemens Alexandrinus* mentions the Dancer [A], in the seventh Book of the *Stromata*. He forgot ARCHELAUS the Astrologer (f), and several other *Archelaus*'s, of some of whom I shall speak in the following Articles.

(a) Diogen. Laërt. lib. 2. in Archelao.

(b) *He, who is the Subject of the following Article.*

(c) *See Remark* [C] *of the following Article.*

(d) Menag. in Diogen. Laërt. lib. 2. n. 17.

(e) *See Remark* [H] *of the Article* ABDERA.

(f) Cicero de Divinat. lib. 2. c. 42. *Some Manuscripts have* Η ΑSCHIALUS.

[A] *He observes:—that Athenæus, in his first Book, speaks of him, who played upon Instruments of Music, and that Clemens Alexandrinus mentions the Dancer.*] Mr *Menage* understood the Rules of a just and learned Method of Citation, but he does not observe them upon this Occasion. He should have quoted the first Book of *Athenæus*, in relation *Archelaus* the Dancer; not the seventh of the *Stromata* of *Clemens Alexandrinus*: For, besides that the Right of Seniority does not belong to the latter, we find some Particulars in *Athenæus*, but none in the *Stromata*. *Athenæus* relates, that King *Antiochus* had no Favourite, whom he esteemed more, than *Archelaus* the Dancer (1). This Author had observed, in the same Page, that the Inhabitants of *Miletum* dedicated a brazen Statue to *Archelaus* the Fiddler; if I may be permitted thus to translate Ἀρχελάω τῷ κιθαριστῇ, *Archelai Citharistæ*.

(1) Athen. lib. 1. c. 16. pag. 19.

ARCHELAUS, a *Greek* Philosopher, and Disciple of *Anaxagoras*, was, as some say, of *Athens*, or, as others will have it (a), of *Miletum*. What is very certain, is, that he taught at *Athens*. It is said too, that he was the first, who brought over Philosophy thither [A]. He made but little Alteration in the Doctrine of *Anaxagoras*

(a) Diogen. Laërt. lib. 2. n. 16.

[A] *He was the first who brought over Philosophy to Athens.*] Several Critics have observed, on this Head, the Opposition, which is found between *Diogenes Laërtius*, and *Clemens Alexandrinus*. The one attributes this Translation to *Archelaus*, the other to *Anaxagoras*. Οὗτος (Ἀρχέλαος) πρῶτος ἐκ τῆς Ἰωνίας τὴν φυσικὴν φιλοσοφίαν μετήγαγεν Ἀθήναζε (1). *Archelaus was the first, who brought Natural Philosophy from Ionia to Athens.* These are the Words of *Diogenes Laërtius*: the following belong to *Clemens Alexandrinus*: Οὗτος (Ἀναξαγόρας) μετήγαγεν ἀπὸ τῆς Ἰωνίας Ἀθήναζε τὴν διατριβὴν (2). *Anaxagoras translated the School from Ionia to Athens*. No Person, that I know of, has endeavoured to reconcile these two Opinions, or discover the Origin of this Diversity. To me it seems obvious enough, from what I am going to observe. *Anaxagoras* came a very young Philosopher to *Athens*, and lived there thirty Years (3). It is not impossible, but that his Master *Anaximenes* continued to philosophize in *Ionia* during part of This Interval (4). We may likewise suppose, that *Diogenes*, his other Disciple, succeeded him. Now if *Thales*'s Chair in *Ionia* was not vacant, whilst *Anaxagoras* philosophiz'd at *Athens*, it is false, that he transported *Thales*'s School to That City. Such a Translation supposes, that the Succession failed, upon *Anaxagoras*'s Removal. All that can be said, with Truth, is, that, before This Philosopher read Lectures at *Athens*, no Disciple of the Sect of *Ionia* had taught among the *Athenians*. Perhaps *Clemens Alexandrinus*, and the Authors he followed, meant no more; but did not take the trouble of expressing themselves more exactly. Be That as it will, I think, by *Casaubon*'s good leave (5), that *Diogenes Laërtius* has expressed himself with more Exactness. For you must know, that *Anaxagoras*, leaving *Athens*, retired to *Lampsacus*, where he taught 'till his Death. His Chair in *Lampsacus* was filled by his Disciple *Archelaus* (6), who went afterwards to philosophize at *Athens* (7). *Archelaus*, then, was properly the Person, who transported the School of *Thales* from *Ionia* to *Athens*: This was a true Translation: But it could not be deemed so before; since, perhaps, this School had never been vacant during the time, which past between *Anaxagoras*'s Journey to *Athens*, and his Retirement to *Lampsacus*; or, if it suffered any Interruption, it was speedily repaired by That Philosopher's Return into *Ionia*. It will be in vain to object, that no Writer remains, who has affirmed, that *Diogenes* was the Successor of *Anaximenes*: For I may reply, I. That we have nothing exact in the History of the ancient Philosophers; and consequently, This Silence does not take away the Right of supposing what I do.

(1) Diogen. Laërt. lib. 2. n. 16.

(2) Clem. Alexandr. Stromat. lib. 2. pag. 301.

(3) Diogen. Laërt. lib. 2. n. 7.

(4) *What Diog. Laërt. lib. 2. n. 3. says concerning the time of the Death of Anaximenes is not decisive.*

(5) Casaubon, *on this Passage of Laërtius, censures him, and declares for Clem. Alexandr. Mr Menage does the same.*

(6) Euseb. Præpar. Evang. l. 10. cap. ult. pag. 504.

(7) Id ib.

ARCHELAUS. 415

Anaxagoras (b); he held, with him, that the *Similar* Parts were the Material Principle of all Things, and the Divine Wisdom the Cause of the Formation of Bodies. He also taught, like him, that all Animals, not excepting Men, were produced out of

(b) *See Remark* [C].

do. II. That, *Anaxagoras* having been more famous than *Diogenes*, and having had a Disciple, who continued the Succession; having also, as it is probable enough, survived *Diogenes*; the Succession of the *Ionian* Sect is with more reason continued in him, than in the other. It is very probable, that *Sidonius Apollinaris* associates these Disciples of *Anaximenes*, as two Colleagues, who were the Support of That School.

Quartus Anaxagoras Thaletica dogmata servat:
Sed divinum animum sentit, qui fecerit orbem.
Junior huic junctus refidet collega, fed idem
Materiam cunctis creaturis aëra credens
Judicat inde Deum, faceret quo euncta (8), tulisse (9).

(8) *Tho.*, composed on which Cicero, de Nat. Deor. lib. 1. pag. 46, and St August. de Civit. Dei, lib. 8, cap. 5, *speak of Diogenes of Apollonia, seems that this Diogenes is the Person meant here.*

(9) *Apollin.* Carm. 15, ver. 89.

The Fourth in order, Anaxagoras
Subscribed to Thales' *Doctrine; yet acknowledg'd A* Mind Divine, *Creator of the World.*
His younger Colleague taught, that Air contained The sole Materials of creating Art.

I proceed to other Conjectures. Our learnedest Critics (10) take for the surest Foundation of *Anaxagoras*'s Age, what *Diogenes Laërtius* says; that, at the Time of the Expedition of *Xerxes*, That Philosopher was twenty Years old. From whence they take the Liberty to infer, that, since he lived Seventy two Years, he died in the LXXXVIIIth Olympiad. I shall not dispute this Point. But I have Difficulties to raise against what *Laërtius* says, that *Anaxagoras* began his Journey to *Athens* at twenty Years of Age, and lived in That City thirty Years. It seems very unlikely to me, that he should make choice of the time of *Xerxes*'s Expedition for This Journey, when the *Asiatics* in general did not doubt, but the Republic of *Athens* would be destroyed. However, not to insist on This, let us pass on to stronger Instances. If *Diogenes Laërtius* be right, it must follow, that *Anaxagoras* lived at *Athens* only 'till the second Year of the LXXXIId Olympiad; for *Xerxes*'s Expedition fell out in the last Months of the LXXIVth Olympiad, and the beginning of the LXXVth. But does not *Diodorus Siculus* affirm, that This Philosopher was accused of Impiety, at *Athens*, in the second Year of the LXXXVIIth Olympiad (11)? He destroys, then, the Account of *Diogenes Laërtius*; Yet not without being himself embarassed in another Point; for what will become of the Story, that *Socrates*, after the Condemnation of *Anaxagoras*, became the Disciple of *Archelaus* (12)? What will become of a Fact, which others have vouched, viz. that *Euripides* forsook the Study of Natural Philosophy, and applied himself to the Theatre, on account of the Process against *Anaxagoras* (13)? Could *Socrates*, who was near forty Years of Age, according to the Chronology of *Diodorus Siculus*, at the time of That Trial, stand in need of another Master? Observe likewise, that, according to *Porphyry*, he *began to follow the Philosopher* Archelaus, *at about the seventeenth Years of Age* (14). Had not *Euripides*, who was above fifty Years of Age, at the time of the same Trial, began to write Tragedies 'till That Time? So far was He from delaying it so long, that he wrote one at eighteen (15). To clear up this Matter a little, and find some Method to reconcile these Accounts, we must return to *Diogenes Laërtius*, and quit *Diodorus Siculus*; for, supposing that *Anaxagoras* was accused in the LXXXIId Olympiad, we shall find the pretended Consequences of this Trial, with regard to *Euripides* and *Socrates*, very possible. We may presuppose, that This Poet, having jointly studied Natural Philosophy, and wrote Tragedies, 'till he saw the Danger of *Anaxagoras*, confined his Studies afterwards to the Theatre alone. But what shall we do with *Eusebius*, who tells us, that *Archelaus* succeeded *Anaxagoras*, at *Lampsacus*, before he became a Philosopher in *Athens*? This cannot be true, if *Anaxagoras* lived to the LXXXVIIIth Olympiad; a time, when *Socrates*, a

greater Master than *Archelaus*, had no occasion to submit to his Discipline. Perhaps we ought to suppose, I. That *Archelaus*, having studied some Years at *Athens*, under *Anaxagoras*, assumed the Professor's Chair, upon his Master's retiring from thence. II. That, some time after, he rejoined him at *Lampsacus*, and was his Successor there; and that, afterwards, returning from thence to *Athens*, he entirely transplanted *Thales*'s School thither. It may be proper likewise to suppose, that *Anaxagoras* was accused more than once at *Athens*; and that, having withdrawn into *Ionia* about the Time of the first Trial, he was some time after recalled by *Pericles*, and accused a new after some Years Abode there. We have seen (16), that certain Authors relate, that he was accused by *Thucydides*, the Adversary of *Pericles*, and condemned to Death for Contumacy. Now, after the Banishment of this *Thucydides*, the Authority was in *Pericles*'s Hands for fifteen Years (17); which shews, that *Thucydides* was banished fifteen Years before the Death of *Pericles*. From whence it should follow, that *Anaxagoras* had been condemned for Contumacy, at least fifteen or sixteen Years before the Death of *Pericles*: But, according to *Diodorus Siculus* (18), and *Plutarch* (19), he was accused a little before the beginning of the *Peloponnesian* War; that is, two or three Years before the Death of *Pericles*. We may therefore suppose, that he was twice accused; and, if we place his Return into *Ionia*, and his second Return to *Athens*, in the Interval between these two Accusations; a very considerable Difficulty will be removed by this means. *Socrates* was not a Disciple of *Anaxagoras*, though *Diogenes Laërtius* affirms it (20). I have proved this (21) by a very strong Reason; and can confirm it not only by the Silence of *Plato* and *Xiphilin*, when the Circumstances of the Subject obliged them to mention it, but also by the Silence of the Accusers of *Socrates*, and by the Answers, which *Socrates* made to them. Would they have failed to reproach him with being instructed by a Philosopher, who had been condemned for Impiety? Would not this have rendered him more suspected? Would they have forgot this Circumstance? Would they have been satisfied with reproaching him, in general, that he philosophized like That impious Man? And, if he had actually been his Scholar, would he have replied as he did (22)? Let us conclude, then, that he was no Disciple of *Anaxagoras*. But how can we imagine, that he was not, if we suppose, that *Anaxagoras* did not leave *Athens*, 'till the Time, which *Diodorus Siculus* and *Plutarch* mention. In this case, would not *Anaxagoras* have flourished at *Athens*, when *Socrates* was at the properest Age to chuse him for his Professor; and, if so, can any one conceive, that *Socrates* would attend the Lectures of *Archelaus*, and not Those of This Philosopher? Is it probable, that the former should set up a School at *Athens*, whilst *Anaxagoras* flourished in the same City? Or, if he did, that *Socrates* would prefer his Lectures before Those of *Anaxagoras*? These Difficulties may all be solved, if it be supposed, that this latter was twice banished; and that, in the Time, which passed between the two Condemnations, *Archelaus* philosophized at *Athens*.

There remains one Observation to be made against *Plutarch*. It must not be imagined, that he believed *Anaxagoras* died in the LXXXVIIIth Olympiad (23). For, when he relates the Prodigies, which preceded the Defeat of the *Athenians* at the River Ægos (23); he says, that, according to the Predictions of this Philosopher, a great Stone fell from Heaven. This Misfortune of the *Athenians* happened in the fourth Year of the XCIIId Olympiad. It would be absurd, to suppose, that *Plutarch* meant, that *Anaxagoras* had predicted the Fall of such a Stone twenty Years before: He believed, then, that This Philosopher lived 'till the XCIIId Olympiad. Now this is a great Error. I suspect him much of an Anachronism, in placing the Fall of the Stone in the XCIIId Olympiad. *Pliny*, *Eusebius*, and the *Arundelian Marbles*, confute this. They place This Event in the LXXVIIIth Olympiad (24). Such

(11) Diod. Neuf. lib. 12, cap. 39. pag. 431.

(12) Diog. Laert. lib. 2. n. 19.

(13) *See the Article* EURIPIDES, *in the Text.*

(14) *See the Life of Socrates, by Mr* Charpentier, pag. 5.

(15) Aulus Gellius, lib. 15, cap. 20.

(16) *C.tat.* (14.) *of the Article* ANAXAGORAS.

(17) Pl t. *in* Pericle. pag. 161, F.

(18) Ibid. 12, cap. 39. pag. 433.

(19) Plut. *in* Pericle, pag. 169.

(20) Diog. Laert. lib. 2. n. 19, 45.

(25) *At the end of the Remark* [R], *of the Article* ANAXAGORAS.

(22) *See* Cicero (20), *of the Article* ANAXAGORAS.

(23) Ibid. *Citat.* (13).

(24) Pliny, *in the second Year. See* Cit. (11) *of the Article* ANAXAGORAS. Eusebius, *in the fourth, and see* Arundelian Marbles, *in the 64 Year. See* Hist. *in* Plut. Tom 1, pag. 27.

ARCHELAUS.

of a Terrestrial Matter, Hot and Moist [B]. He applied himself principally to Natural Philosophy, as his Predecessors had done; but intermixed Morality with it a little more than They had done. He was not very Orthodox in this Point; since he maintained, that Human Laws were the Spring and Origin of Moral Good and Evil; that is, He did not admit a *Natural*, but only a *Positive* Right, and consequently believed, that all Actions were indifferent in their own Nature, and became Good or Evil, according as Mankind is pleased to declare them such by certain Laws (c). He wrote a Treatise of Natural Philosophy, according to *Suidas*; and He passed for the Author of some *Elegies*, designed to comfort *Cimon*, who was very much afflicted for the Death of his Wife (d). *Socrates*, the most famous of his Disciples, was his Successor (e). It will be proper to take some Notice of a Poet, whose Name was ARCHELAUS [C]. *Diogenes Laërtius* mentions him; but he is contented with preserving to us the Title of one of his Compositions.

(e) Τὸ δίκαιον εἶναι καὶ τὸ αἰσχρὸν οὐ φύσει, ἀλλὰ νόμῳ. Justum & turpe non natura constare sed lege. *Diog. Laërt. lib.* 2. n. 16.

(d) *Plut. in Cimone.* pag. 481.

(e) Cicero, *Tuscul. lib.* 5. *Diog. Laërt. ubi supra. Clem. Alex. andr. Strom. lib.* 1. *pag.* 301. *August. de Civit. Dei, lib.* 8. *cap.* 2.

Such is the wretched State, in which the so much boasted Ancients have left the History of the Philosophers. A thousand Contradictions throughout, a thousand inconsistent Facts, and a thousand false Dates. Note, that I have not met with any Modern, who confutes those, who place the Death of *Anaxagoras* in the LXXVIIIth Olympiad (25); I say, who confutes them by *Diodorus Siculus*, and *Plutarch*, who both affirm, that this Philosopher was accused a little before the first Year of the *Peloponnesian* War (26).

[B] *He also taught, like him, that all Animals, not excepting Men, were produced out of a Terrestrial Matter, hot and moist.*] The Accounts, preserved to us, of these Opinions, in the Authors, who report them, are so concise, that it is difficult to form any distinct Idea of them. Γεννᾶσθαι δέ φησι τὰ ζῶα ἐκ θερμῆς τῆς γῆς, καὶ ἰλὺν παραπλησίαν γάλακτι, οἷον τροφὴν, ἀνιείσης. Οὕτω δὲ καὶ τὲ ἀνθρώπους ποιῆσαι (27). He taught, that Animals sprung from a warm Earth, which sent forth a kind of milky Substance, by way of Nourishment; and that Men had the same Original. Thus *Diogenes Laërtius* expresses himself. He had said, that, according to this Philosopher's Opinion, the two Causes of Generation were Heat and Moisture (28). He had also explained, how Water, Air, Earth, and Fire, proceeded from these two Principles; but I own, I cannot comprehend the meaning of his Words, and therefore will not be at the Pains of transcribing them. Mr *Menage*, who inserted them in his Commentary, without any Note upon them, seems to have been ignorant of their Meaning. Other Commentators have not been more successful. They leave them to their Native Obscurity. Let us do the same, and have recourse to *Plutarch*, who has said, that, according to *Archelaus*, the infinite Air, the Condensation and Rarefaction of the Air, the one Fire, the other Water, were the Principles of all Things (29). *Justin Martyr* attributes very near the same Opinion to him (30). This seems to me to imply, that he held the Air to be the first Matter, and Fire and Water to be the Elements; but this was not his Opinion, if we may believe St *Austin*; for That Father attributes to him the Doctrine of *Anaxagoras*, concerning the *Homœomeria*, and the Intelligences, which combined them. "*Anaxagoram successit auditor ejus Archelaus: etiam ipse de particulis inter se dissimilibus, quibus singula quæque fluerent, ita omnia constare putavit, ut inesse etiam mentem diceret, quæ corpora dissimilia, id est illas particulas, conjungendo & dissipando, ageret omnia* (31). — *To Anaxagoras succeeded his Scholar Archelaus; who held, likewise, such an Opinion concerning the dissimilar Particles, out of which all things were made, as to allow the Superintendency of a Mind, which, by uniting and dispersing the dissimilar Corpuscles, formed every thing.*" I believe St *Austin* is in the right: for *Simplicius* observes, that *Archelaus*, endeavouring to give an Explication distinct from all others, did nevertheless run into the same Principles with *Anaxagoras*, to wit, an Infinity of similar Particles (32). It is probable, that, as to the first Formation of Animals, they held the same Doctrines. We have seen what *Archelaus*'s Opinion was; This was the Doctrine of *Anaxagoras*: Ζῷα γενέσθαι ἐξ ὑγροῦ καὶ θερμοῦ καὶ γεώδους. ὕστερον δὲ ἐξ ἀλλήλων (33). *Animals sprung originally from Moisture, Heat, and Earth; afterwards from one another.* Since they admitted an Intelligence, which drew the *Homœo-*

meria out of the Confusion, in which they originally were, we must believe, that they supposed, it to preside over the Production of Animals; for, if there be any Creature, the Formation of which stands in need of being directed by a Spirit, it is certainly the Machine of Animals. If what I suppose be true, They have said nothing on this Head, but what may be reconciled with the Holy Scripture; But if they believed, as many others have done, that, in the beginning, Men sprung out of the Earth by the mere Power of Moisture and Heat, &c. they believed the most ridiculous Thing in the World; nor could they know how to answer the Question, why, in succeeding Ages, Men were never seen to be produced the same way. The Question would not have puzzled them in the other Case, since they might have answered, as a Christian would do, that the Intelligence, having once formed Animals, endowed with necessary Parts of Generation, had no need to create any more; the Conservation of the Species being secured by the Instinct of Copulation in Male and Female.

[C] *It will be proper to take some notice of a Poet, whose name was* ARCHELAUS.] He composed a Work on the particular Nature of Things, that is, on the Singularities and Properties, which distinguish them. What has been cited from. it, will not suffer us to doubt, that this was the true Character of the Work. *Diogenes Laërtius* describes it by these Words; Ὁ τὰ ἰδιοφυῆ ποιήσας (34). *Qui quæ cuique rei natura sunt propria, versu prodidit. Casaubon* should not have censured this *Latin* Translation, under pretence, that, according to the Testimony of *Antigonus Carystius*, this Book of *Archelaus* was a Collection of Epigrams, in which the extraordinary and wonderful Properties of things, τὰ παράδοξα, τὰ θαυμάσια (35), are recorded; for this may very well agree with the Title given it by *Diogenes Laërtius*; and, in any Case, the Translator ought not to have given the Title a less general import, than that of the *Greek* Phrase. *Vossius* was not of *Casaubon*'s Opinion; since he has translated the Words of *Diogenes Laërtius* by, *qui carmen fecit de propria cujusque rei natura* (36). The Sense he gives these Words does not seem very just; he understands by them, that *Archelaus* had searched after things, the Nature of which was singular; *quæ propriæ ac singularis naturæ sunt*; as that Goats are never without a Fever, and that they breathe through the Ears, and not the Nostrils. *Auribus capras spirare, non naribus, nec unquam febri carere, Archelaus auctor est* (37). *Athenæus* has cited one *Archelaus*, ἐν τοῖς ἰδιοφυέσιν, and given him the Sirname of *Chersonesus* (38). *Dalechampus* has rendred this *Greek* by, *sua proprinque stirpe genitis* (39); and I wonder *Vossius* has not made use of the same Words in translating this Passage, as in That of *Diogenes Laërtius* (40): He has rendered it *de proprietate naturæ*, and yet believes, that *Athenæus*, and *Diogenes Laërtius*, mean the same Author. This is very probable; though *Antigonus Carystius* tells us, that *Egypt* was the Birth-place of *Archelaus*, who composed Epigrams on the wonderful Singularities of certain Things, and dedicated them to *Ptolomy*. It is possible, that One *Archelaus*, a Native of *Chersonesus*, might pass for an *Egyptian*; it is enough that he dwelt a long time in *Egypt* (41). Mr *Menage*, who pretends, that, instead of ἰδιοφυῆ, it ought to be read δίφυῆ, in *Diogenes Laërtius* (42), seems to me to be mistaken; he founds it on this, that the Scholiast of *Nicander* cites *Archelaus*, ἐν τοῖς δυφυέσι, that is to say, *in libro de iis, quæ sunt ancipitis naturæ.*

(25) *Diogenes Laërtius, lib.* 2. n. 7. *does so. Eusebius places it in the fourth Year of the 79th Olympiad.*

(26) *That is, in the second Year of the 87th Olympiad.*

(27) *Diog. Laërt. lib.* 2. n. 17.

(28) *Instead of ψυχρὸν frigidum, it ought to be read ὑγρὸν humidum. See Mr Menage on this Passage. But, more, that Hermias, in Philosophorum derisione, pag.* 177, *affirms, that Archelaus grew, as Principles of all Things, θερμὸν καὶ ψυχρὸν, Hot and Cold.*

(29) *Plutarch. de placit. Philos. lib.* 1, *cap.* 3. *pag.* 876.

(30) *Just. Martyr. Admonit. ad Græcos, p.* 4.

(31) *Aug. de Civit. Dei, lib.* 8, *cap.* 2. *See also Clem. Alex.* in *Protr. pag.* 43.

(32) *Simplicius, in* 1. *Libr. Physic. Arist.*

(33) *Diog. Laërt. lib* 2. n. 9.

(34) Ibid. lib. 2, n. 17.

(35) *Casaub. in Diog. Laërt. lib.* 2. n. 17.

(36) *Vossius de Hist. Græcis, lib.* 3. *pag.* 329.

Plin. lib. 8. *cap.* 50.

(38) *Athen.* lib. 9. cap. ult. p. 409.

(39) *Dalech. Annot. in Athen. lib.* 766. *Father Hardouin, in Autorum Plinii, pag.* 97, *translates the Words of Athenæus de rebus quæ singulis in locis propria gignuntur.*

(40) *Vossius, ubi supra.*

(41) *There are Examples of this kind. lib.* 14. *pag.* 652.

(42) *Menage, in Diog. Laërt. lib.* 2. n. 17.

ARCHELAUS. 417

naturæ. This Foundation is not solid; for, as the Book of *Archelaus* was not confined to that kind of Singularity, which distinguishes amphibious Animals, produced by the Copulation of Males and Females, of different Species, it is unreasonable to suppose, that the Author made use of a Title confined to this Sense. We should either correct the Scholiast by *Diogenes Laërtius*, or say, that *Archelaus*, having divided his Work into several Treatises, gave a particular Title to each Treatise; for Example, That of Δίφυή to the Epigrams, in which he treats of amphitious Animals. On this Supposition, we may believe, that They, who cite *Archelaus*, *Lib.* I. περὶ ποϊαμῶν, *de fluviis* (43), *Lib.* I. περὶ λίθων, *de lapidibus* (44), cite part of a Work, the general Title of which was Ἰδιοφυή. But I should chuse to say, that another *Archelaus* is meant in these Places. I do not pass the same Judgment on the Citations of *Artemidorus* (45); I believe they relate to the Author of the Ἰδιοφυή.

Let us, here, wonder at the Frailty of human Memory. *Vossius*, in his Treatise of the *Greek* Historians, speaks learnedly of this Author; he sets down what he finds of him in *Varro, Pliny, Athenæus, Antigonus Caryßius*, &c. but remembers nothing of the Matter, when he afterwards comes to treat of the *Greek* Poets; where we read what follows: "Idem (*Archelaus Physicus*) ut ait Suidas, συνέταξε φυσιολογίαν *. Id sic Lilius Gyraldus vertit in 111. Dialogo Poëtis †: *quæ naturæ propria sunt, multis versibus collegit*. Itaque & Archelaum inter Poëtas recenset. Sed addit, Poëtam physicum esse alium ab Socratis magistro. At unde id astruat, non video. Nam Suidas clare ait φυσιολογίαν conscriptam ab Archelao Physico, Socratis magistro. Imò nec video, unde colligat, quempiam Archelaum carmine scripsisse de rerum natura. Saltem ex verbo συνέταξεν, quo Suidas utitur, id colligi nequit. Et Laërtius, cùm dicat tres præterea Archelaos fuisse, non tamen Poëtam in iis memorat (46).——*The same* (Archelaus *the Naturalist*), *according to* Suidas, *composed a Treatise of Natural Philosophy; or, as* Lilius Gyraldus *understands the Greek of* Suidas, *collected in many Verses the Properties of Nature. Therefore he reckons Archelaus among the Poets. But he adds, that the Philosophical Poet is not the same with the Preceptor of Socrates. But how he can prove this, I am at a Loss to know. For* Suidas *expressly says, that the Treatise of Natural Philosophy was composed by* Archelaus *the Naturalist, the Master of* Socrates. *Nay, I cannot conceive, whence he gathers, that any Archelaus wrote of the Nature of Things in Verse. At least it does not follow from the Word* συνέταξεν, *made use of by* Suidas. *And* Diogenes Laërtius, *where he says there were three* Archelaus's *besides, yet mentions no Poet among them*." Behold a very learned Man, who imagines, I. That *Gyraldus* had in view the *Greek* Words of *Suidas*, and not those of *Diogenes Laërtius*, ὁ τὰ Ἰδιοφυή ποιήσας (47): II. That there was no Room to acknowledge a Poet *Archelaus*, different from the Naturalist: III. Nor to suppose, that an *Archelaus* wrote Verses on the Nature of Things: IV. That *Diogenes Laërtius* does not mention any *Archelaus*, who composed Verses. This must surprize us, if we consider it by itself; but it is much worse, when compared with the Three hundred and twenty ninth Page of the Book *De Historicis Græcis*. Mr *Colomies* has corrected the first of these four Faults of *Vossius*, and advanced some good things besides (48); but he is mistaken in supposing, that *Plutarch's* Words, in the Life of *Cimon*, concern *Archelaus* the Poet, for they relate to the Naturalist, to whom *Socrates* was a Disciple. He might have corrected *Gyraldus*, who believed, that *Archelaus*, Author of the Ἰδιοφυή, was a Philosopher. Mr *Moreri* says the same without the least Ground; for a Person, who collects the singular and wonderful Properties of Animals, or Metals, &c. may well be called a Naturalist, or a Natural Historian, but not a Natural Philosopher; unless to the Facts he subjoins the Reasons of them, and a Discussion of their Causes. We do not find, that the Poet *Archelaus* did this. Mr *Moreri* affirms, that *Diogenes Laërtius* often cites him. Say rather, that he never cites him.

ARCHELAUS, First of the Name (*d*), King of *Macedon*, and a Natural Son of King *Perdiccas*, having ascended the Throne, supported himself in it by the most enormous Crimes. His Mother was a Servant of *Alcetas*, the Brother of *Perdiccas* [*A*]; so that, according to the Laws (*b*), he ought to have been himself no more than the Servant of *Alcetas*; but, instead of paying him the Submission he owed him, he caused him to be treacherously murthered. He invited him to his House, promising to restore to him the Crown, which *Perdiccas* had taken from him; he entertained him sumptuously, and, having made him drunk, caused him to be carried out of Town by Night in a close Chariot, with Orders to put him to Death. *Alexander*, the Son of *Alcetas*, was treated in the same manner; He was conveyed drunk in the same Chariot, and murthered, with his Father. *Archelaus* soon after caused his own Brother, the Legitimate Son of *Perdiccas* and *Cleopatra*, and but seven Years of Age, to be put to Death, and thrown into a Well; making his Mother *Cleopatra* believe, that the Child fell in, as he was running after a Goose (*c*). He applied himself diligently to whatever might render *Macedon* formidable; he fortified several Places, caused high Roads to be made; providing himself also with great Quantities of Arms, Horses, and all warlike Stores; exceeding the Kings his Predecessors in these Preparations (*d*). One Thing he put in practice, which They never did; to wit, the fitting out of Fleets, and engaging in Sea-Fights (*e*). He loved Learning and polite Arts [*B*], and had always the greatest Poets, the most famous Painters, and the best Musicians, about him (*f*). He was at a great Expence in having his House painted by *Zeuxes* [*C*], and doubtless was very angry,

[*A*] *His Mother was Servant of* Alcetas, *Brother of* Perdiccas (1).] *Ælian* calls her *Simicha* (2): But, after all, since *Archelaus* was the Son of the King of *Macedon*, it ought not to have been said, that, from the Condition of a Goat-herd, he raised himself to the Throne. Yet this is what *Diogenes* the Cynic affirms, in a Speech of *Dion Chrysostom*. Ἀρχέλαος ἦν Ἀρχέλαος (3). *Caprarius erat Archelaus*. Observe these Words of *Plato*, which inform us, what *Archelaus* ought to have been according to the Laws. Κατὰ μὲν τὸ δίκαιον δοῦλος ἦν Ἀλκέτα, καὶ εἰ ἐβούλετο τὰ δίκαια ποιεῖν ἐδούλευεν ἂν Ἀλκέτᾳ (4). *He was by right the Servant of* Alcetas; *if therefore he would have acted justly, he should have served* Alcetas.

[*B*] *He loved Learning, and polite Arts*.] *Solinus* tells us this (5). I have cited his Words, in the Remark [*N*] of the Article EURIPIDES, at the Beginning. Add to them this Passage of *Ælian*. Ἦν δὲ ἄρα ὁ Ἀρχέλαος ἐραστὴς οὐχ ἧττον ἢ καὶ φιλόμουσος (6). Archelaus *was no less amorous, than fond of Learning*.

[*C*] *He was at a great Expence in having his House painted by* Zeuxes.] *Socrates* plays the Censor upon this Occasion; he says, that this Prince, who had been at such a vast Expence in beautifying his Palace, had been at none at all in adorning his Mind. We know likewise, adds he, that many Strangers make it their Business to go to *Macedon*, to see this Prince's House, but none to see the Prince himself, except

ARCHELAUS.

angry, that *Socrates*, whom he endeavoured to draw to his Court, would never come near him [D]. He might have learnt from him not to be frightned at Eclipses; and he wanted greatly to be set right in That Matter (g). The Esteem he had for *Euripides* is shewn in another Place (b). By the way, his Liberality to ingenious Men was not extraordinary; but this might proceed from his finding them too free in asking [E]. He instituted Sacrifices, and Stage-Plays, in Honour of *Jupiter*, and the Muses; which were celebrated for nine Days together; each Muse had it's Day (i). He sent Chariots with four Horses, which carried the Prizes at the *Olympic* and *Pythian* Games (k). Authors agree as to his being killed, but not as to the Circumstances of his Death, or the Length of his Reign [F]. *Scaliger* himself met

(g) See Remark [D].
(b) In the Article EURIPIDES, Remarks [N], [O], [P], &c.
(i) Diodor. Siculus, lib. 17, cap. 16.
(k) Solinus, cap. 9.

except those he draws thither by his Presents. Now these are Things, which never influence an honest Man (7). I believe he had taken no Pains to conquer his lewd Inclinations, by cultivating the Muses; but I am certain, that he made no mean Progress in adorning his Mind. And, by one of his Sayings, he seems to have made some Progress in Practical Virtue. One of his Courtiers animating him one Day against a Person, who had thrown some Water upon him; he answered, *he has not wetted me, but the Person for whom he took me* (8). Never Philosopher, discoursing on the Privileges of an erroneous Conscience, said a more sensible Thing. All Princes would treat involuntary Faults in this manner, were they but equitable, or if the Interest of the Public would permit the regulating their Practice according to the Ideas of Reason (9). Let us leave this, and return to *Socrates*. In the foregoing Words, he declared several Men of Wit, who went to *Macedon*, only for *Archelaus*'s Sake (10) errant Rascals. Did *Euripides* go thither upon any other Account? Did not the fair *Agathon*, That illustrious Poet, and his Inamorato *Pausanias*, and so many others, go thither purely upon this Account? Οὗτ@- δ' Ἀγάθων - - - - Ἀρχελάω τῷ βασιλεῖ μέχρι τελευτῆς μετὰ ἄλλων πολλῶν συνῆν ἐν Μακεδονίᾳ (11). This *Agathon*, with many others, resided at the Court of *Archelaus*, *'till his Death*.

[D] *Socrates, whom he endeavoured to draw to his Court, would never come near him*] There were two other Persons, whom this Philosopher treated after the same manner; he would neither visit them, nor accept of Presents from them. Ὑπεροφθέντος δὲ καὶ Ἀρχελάου τῆ Μακεδόνθ-, καὶ Σκώπα τῆ Κραννωνίω, καὶ Εὐρυλόχου τῆ Λαρισσαίῳ, μήτε χρήματα προσμένω αὐτῶν, μήτε παρ' αὐτὸς ἀπελθών (12). *In the greatness of his Soul, he despised* Archelaus *the Macedonian,* Scopa *the Crannonian, and* Eurylochus *the Larysæan; nor would ever accept of the Presents, which they sent him, or the Invitation they gave him. Seneca has preserved to us the Excuse, which Socrates made to our Archelaus;* he said, " I will not visit a Man, " from whom I may receive Benefits, without be- " ing able to return them." *Archelaus rex Socratem rogavit, ut ad se veniret: dixisse Socrates traditur, nolle se ad eum venire, à quo acciperet beneficia, cum reddere illi paria non posset* (13). This Answer of *Socrates* has been related by *Marcus Aurelius*, agreeably to the same Sense (14); but *Aristotle* relates it in terms, which are not Philosophical. He supposes *Socrates* to have replied, that It is as great an Affront to confer a Benefit on a Person, who cannot return it, as to injure a Person, who cannot revenge himself. Τῷ γὰρ εἶναι τὸ μὴ δύνασθαι ἀμύνεσθαι ὁμοίως ἐν παθόντι ὥσπερ καὶ κακῶς (15). *Contumeliam esse dixit, non posse referre eum qui accepisset beneficium, perinde ac eum qui injuriam*. This Maxim supposes, that we ought to revenge ourselves on those, who injure us. It is not, therefore, becoming the Morality of a Philosopher, especially such a Philosopher as *Socrates. Seneca* has taken pains to shew, that it was easy for this Philosopher to requite *Archelaus*. Among other things, he says, that the Favours of That Monarch could not have been of equal Value with the Instruction he might have received concerning Eclipses alone, and which would have prevented his falling a second time into such a Consternation, as he was one day in, when the Sun was eclipsed. He shut up his Palace Gates; he caus'd his Son's Hair to be cut off. " Quid " tantum erat acceptarus (*Socrates*) quantum dabat, " si ——— regem in luce media orientem ei rerum " naturam admisisset, usque eo ejus ignarum, ut, quo " die solis defectio fuit, regiam clauderet, & filium

(7) Taken from Ælian, lib. 14. Var. Hist. cap. 17.

(8) Plut. in Apophthegmat. pag. 177.

(9) See, in the New Letters against Maimbourg's History of Calvinism, those, which treat of an erroneous Conscience.

(10) Ælian. Var. Histor. lib. 2. cap. 21.

(11) Schol. Aristoph. in Ranis.

(12) Diogenes Laërtius, lib. 2. n. 25.

(13) Seneca de Benefic. lib. 5, cap. 6, pag. 96.

(14) Marcus Antoninus, τῶν εἰς ἑαυτὸν, lib. 1. n. 25. Note, that he supposes this Affront was made to Perdiccas.

(15) Aristot. Rhetor. lib. 2. cap. 23.

" (quod in luctu ac rebus adversis moris est) tonderet? " Quantum fuisset beneficium, si timentem è latebris " suis extraxisset, & bonum animum habere jussisset, " dicens; Non est ista solis defectio, sed duorum side- " rum coitus, cum luna humiliore currens via infra " ipsum solem orbem suum posuit, & illum objectu " sui abscondit (16). ——— *What Benefit cou'd* Socrates *have receiv'd so valuable as what he wou'd have conferr'd; if he had explain'd the Nature of Things to the mistaken King; who was so ignorant of them, that, upon the day of an Eclipse of the Sun, he shut up his Palace, and (as is practised in Affliction and Adversity) shaved his Son? What an Advantage wou'd it have been to him, had the Philosopher dragged him trembling from his Concealment, and bad him be of good Courage; telling him, This is no Failure of the Sun, but the effect of the Moon's interposing between the Sun and Us, and by that means intercepting it's Light?* Seneca *says, that* Socrates *made this Excuse by way of Irony only* (17), and that, in reality, he refused to go to the Court of *Macedon*, because he would not be abridged of his Liberty. " Via " scire quid verè nolueris? Noluit ire ad voluntariam " servitutem, is, cujus libertatem civitas libera ferre " non potuit (18). ——— *Wou'd you know what in reality he refused? He refused to go to voluntary Servitude; He, whose Liberty a Free State could not bear*." Some say, that *Aristophanes* (19) composed the Comedy of the *Clouds* out of spite to *Socrates*, because *Archelaus, King of* Macedon, *had a better Opinion of This Philosopher than of himself*. Observe, that another fact has been given to *Socrates*'s Answer. It has been said, that he excus'd himself from going to *Archelaus*'s Court, because Bread was at a low Price, and great Plenty of Water at *Athens* (20).

[E] *His Liberality to ingenious Men, was not extraordinary, but this might proceed from his finding them too free in asking.*] *Plutarch* tells us, that " *Archelaus, King of Macedon,* was a little too back- " ward in giving, or making of Presents; which the " Musician *Timotheus* gave him an Hint, by often " repeating, as he sung to his Lute, this satirical " Sentence. *You are too fond of This Son of the " Earth, Silver*. But *Archelaus* immediately repli- " ed, genteely and with a good grace; *And " You demand it of me too fast* (21)". In another Book he relates what I am going to transcribe. A certain Person once, who thought, that nothing was more genteel, than to ask and receive, being at Supper with Archelaus, asked of the King a Golden Cup, out of which He drank. The King commanded his Page to present it to Euripides, who by an accident was then at Table; and, turning to the Person, who had ask'd it, said, " As for you, you deserve to " ask, and be refused, because you ask; but Euripides " deserves to receive, even though he does not ask (22)". Perhaps he set bounds to his Liberality upon a Principle like That of *Charles* the IXth (23); But it is more probable he was of the Taste of Cardinal *Richlieu, who never gave any thing to the Poet* Mainard, *partly* ——— *because he did not love to be ask'd, but would have the Honour of giving of his own meer Motion* (24).

[F] *Authors are not agreed* ——— *As to the Circumstances of his Death, or the Length of his Reign.*] Some say, That, being a Hunting, he was accidentally wounded by his Favourite *Craterus*; and that he died of his Wound (25). Others say, that he was killed by Conspirators, urged on by *Decamnichus*, to commit This Parricide (26). *Quintus Curtius* favours this Opinion. He says, " Quis proavum hu- " jus Alexandrum, quis deinde Archelaum, quis Per- " diccam occisos ultus est? (27) ——— *Who ever revenged " the murther of This Person?* Great-Grand Father " Alexander,

(16) Seneca de Beneficiis, lib. 5.

(17) Ibid.

(18) Ibid. pag. 95.

(19) Charpentier's Life of Socrates, pag. 57. He cites the Commentators on Aristophanes, in argumento illius Comœdiæ.

(20) See Stobæus, Serm. 237.

(21) Plutarch, de Fortuna Alexandri. lib. 2.

(22) Id. de vitioso pudore.

(23) See the Article DAURAT, Remark [F].

(24) Pellisson, Hist. de l'Acad. Françoise, pag. 178.

(25) Diodor. Siculus, lib. 14. cap. 58. I shall cite his Words in the sub Remark.

(26) Aristot. lib. 5. de Republ. cap. 10. I have cited his Words in the Remark [N], of the Article EURIPIDES.

(27) Quintus Curtius, lib. 6. cap. 11.

ARCHELAUS. 419

met with so much Obscurity in these Points, as led him into gross Mistakes (l). Probably *Archelaus* led an impure Life, which occasion'd his Downfal [G]. I have a few Observations to make against *Moreri* [H].

(l) *See Remark* [F].

" Alexander, *of* Archelaus, *or* Perdiccas ?" —— I shall speak farther of This in the following Remark. As for the Length of his Reign, some make it Twenty Four Years (28); others Sixteen (29); others Fourteen (30); and others but Seven (31). This latter Opinion seems to me the most probable: It is That of *Diodorus Siculus* ; and I am surpriz'd at *Calvisius*'s citing this Historian, after having said, that *Archelaus* reign'd Sixteen Years (32). A misinterpreted Passage in *Athenæus* has occasion'd a great deal of Confusion. We read, in the Editions of That Author, that *Pericles* and *Perdiccas* died in the third Year of the *Peloponnesian* War, and that *Archelaus* ascended the Throne immediately after (33). It is impossible *Athenæus* should say this; for his Design is to convict *Plato* of a Mistake; *Plato*, I say, who, in the same Dialogue, where he supposes, that *Archelaus* was then on the Throne, affirms, that *Pericles* died but a little before. It is plain, that his Censor renders himself ridiculous ; and does not know what he says, if he really advances what we read in his printed Works. *Casaubon* justly thinks it strange, that The Translators of *Athenæus* took no notice of so manifest an Absurdity, or could digest so hard a Morsel. *Cum hæc clarissime disputentur ab Athenæo, qui interpretum stomacho non invideat, qui vulgatam loci hujus scripturam adeo ιυσομάχως tulerint* (34) ? For his own part, he confesses himself incapable of it, and, in spite of all the Manuscripts, maintains, that the Copyists of *Athenæus* have omitted a Period in That Place. He seems to me to have guessed very happily at what the Author really said ; Namely, that *Alexander*, King of *Macedon*, who died at the same Time with *Pericles*, was succeeded by *Perdiccas*, who reign'd till the Archonship of *Callias* ; and that *Perdiccas*, dying in That Archonship, *Archelaus* took possession of his Throne. In this Case, *Athenæus* criticises on *Plato*'s Discourse not without some Foundation ; for there is a considerable Interval between the Death of *Pericles*, and the Reign of *Archelaus*. Observe, by the way, that *Casaubon* has answered This Censure (35); but this particular notice, that *Diodorus Siculus*, in assigning to *Archelaus* Seven Years Reign, places his Death in the Second Year of the XCVth. Olympiad, under the Archonship of *Aristocrates*. His Reign, then began, the third Year of the XCIIId Olympiad, under the Archonship of *Callias*. It must be said then, that *Perdiccas* died under the same Archonship. Now, among the Diversity of Opinions concerning the Time of the Reign of This *Perdiccas*, That of *Marsyas* and *Philocorus*, who determined it to Twenty three Years, was made choice of by *Athenæus*, in reasoning against *Plato* : He must, then, have supposed, that *Perdiccas* came to the Crown the same Year that *Pericles* died, that is, in the fourth Year of the LXXXVIIth Olympiad. All this is so strong a Confirmation of *Casaubon*'s Opinion, that, instead of saying his Conjecture is very probable, we may affirm, without Hesitation, that the Period he restores did actually proceed from the Pen of *Athenæus* : And, as it contains the same Words twice or thrice at the end of a Sentence, we may easily apprehend, how the Transcribers might pass it over, and the Reader not perceive the Omission. Most People read to be instructed without Fatigue ; so that they seldom are sensible of an Error in reasoning, which requires some Attention, or Reflexion on what went before ; contenting themselves with saying, *This is obscure*, *This is beyond my Comprehension*. But this brings no Remedy ; The Fault remains still where it was. Critics, and especially Critical Translators, act otherwise. They perceive Mistakes in the Sense ; they endeavour to correct them ; they collate Manuscripts ; and exert their Talent for Conjecture. But in this Passage of *Athenæus*, as *Casaubon* reproaches them, the Edge of their Genius was greatly blunted.

FAULTS of *Scaliger*.

The great *Scaliger* shall be my Proof, that the Genius of the most learned Persons may sometimes be very much confined He did not perceive the manifest Error of the Author, on whom he commented and criticis'd ; and has made This Error the Foundation of a Criticism on *Diodorus Siculus*, to whom he has imputed what is only to be met with in *Athenæus*. To explain This ; *Eusebius* has ranged three Things under the first Year of the LXXXVIIth Olympiad ; The Death of *Perdiccas*, The beginning of the Reign of *Archelaus*, and The beginning of the *Peloponnesian* War. *Scaliger* passes over this, and contents himself with observing, that the first Year of This War is generally placed under the second Year of the LXXXVIIth Olympiad, because, the Rupture falling out towards the end of the Archonship of *Pythodorus*, it was thought it ought to be dated from the Archonship of *Euthydemus* (36), the Successor of *Pythodorus* (37). According to this Usage, he confesses, that the Year of the Death of *Pericles* is the fourth of the LXXXVIIth Olympiad, and the third of the *Peloponnesian* War ; and he cites a *Greek* Passage, which imports, that, in the Year of *Pericles*'s Death, *Perdiccas* King of *Macedon* died also, and *Archelaus* ascended the Throne. He attributes this Passage to *Diodorus Siculus* ; and, accordingly, censures him for an Anachronism of three Years. This proceeds from his supposing, that *Eusebius* is neither mistaken as to the Death of *Perdiccas*, nor the Accession of *Archelaus*. He was ignorant, then, that *Thucydides* had expresly said, that King *Perseus* was living in the sixteenth Year of the *Peloponnesian* War (38). Besides, he was ignorant, that the Words, which he ascribes to *Diodorus Siculus*, belong to *Athenæus* : He knew not, that these Words of *Athenæus* were corrupted; he did not perceive, that they are maimed, and that they ought to be read as *Casaubon* has restored them. Note, that *Salmasius* acknowledges for good Chronology the placing the Death of *Perdiccas*, and the beginning of *Archelaus*'s Reign, in the fourth Year of the LXXXVIIth Olympiad (39). He was ignorant, then, of some things, which he might have learned from *Casaubon* ; but note still more carefully, that, by a favourable Interpretation, one of the Points of my Criticism on *Scaliger* may be eluded, if not confuted. I have observed, that he has censured *Diodorus Siculus* ; which I gathered from these Words : *Diodorus ergo prochronismus fuerit triennii* (40). - - - *Diodorus therefore has anticipated three Years*. They follow the *Greek* Passage, falsely ascribed by *Scaliger* to That Author ; where we also find, that *Perdiccas*, dying in the third Year of the *Peloponnesian* War, was succeeded by *Archelaus*. Now, whereas *Eusebius* affirms, that *Archelaus* ascended the Throne in the first Year of the *Peloponnesian* War, it may be pretended, that *Scaliger* meant no more, than that the Doctrine of *Eusebius* contains an Anachronism or Anticipation of three Years, according to *Diodorus Siculus*. If this be his true meaning, he has not censured this latter Historian ; he was satisfied with suspending Judgment, deciding neither in favour of him, nor of *Eusebius* : It will be a great Pleasure to me, if This Recantation will be allowed to pass. A Critic, who takes Advantage of an equivocal Expression, ought not to omit the favourable Sense ; He shews, by this means, what may be said for, or against, Authors : He sustains alternately the Character of Council for the Plaintiff and Defendant.

(36) *It belongs to the second Year of the 87th Olympiad.*

(37) Scaliger, Animadv. in Euseb. n. 1585, pag. 106.

(38) Thucydides, lib. 6, pag. 341.

(39) Salmas. Exercitat. Plin. pag. 156, 157.

(40) Scaliger, ubi supra.

[G] *Probably* Archelaus *led an impure Life, which occasioned his Downfal*] *Aristotle*, having said, that several Conspiracies have been formed against Monarchs, on Account of their Impurities, immediately alledges the Attempt of *Crateus* (41). This Man never could brook the Dishonour *Archelaus* had done him, in satisfying his brutal Lust upon him. Accordingly a New Affront, which would not of itself have been a just Pretence for Conspiracy, being added to the former, he resolved to get rid of his Master. The Affront was this ; the King had promised him one of his Daughters, and yet married the eldest to the King of *Elymæa*, and the youngest to the Son of *Amyntas*. Reasons of State occasioned this Breach of Promise. Finding himself embroiled in a War with *Sirras*, and *Arrabæus*, he had a Mind to gain over the King of *Elymæa* to his Party. Fearing, on the other hand, that the Son of *Amyntas* would raise Disturbances, he made him his Son-in-law too ; hoping

(41) Aristot. lib. 5 de Republica, cap. 10. pag. 305.

(28) Euseb. in Chron. n. 1585. Helvicus embraces this Opinion.

(29) Calvis. ad Ann. Mundi, 3534.

(30) Petavius, Ration. Tempor. Pars II, lib. 2, sub fin. ex Dexippo.

(31) Diod. Sicul. lib. 14, cap. 38.

(32) Calvis. ad Annum Mundi, 3550, pag. 156, col. 2.

(33) Athen. lib. 5, cap. 18, p. 217.

(34) Casaub. in Athen. pag. 384.

(35) Casaub. ibid. pag. 385.

VOL. I. N°. XIV.

hoping, that this Alliance would keep them united, and produce the same Effect with regard to the Son of *Cleopatra*. Upon this, *Crateüs* gave a loose to his Resentment; but the principal Source of his Hatred proceeded from the Injury he had received in his Body. Ἀλλὰ τῆς γε ἀλλοιευτῆ]ος ὑπήρχεν ἀρχὴ τὸ βαρέως φέρειν πρὸς τὴν ἀφροδισιαςικὴν χάριν (42). Sed *alienationis origo & principium fuit, quod graviter tulisset se ejus libidini ad res venereas fuisse objecutum*. *Hellanocrates of Larissa* joined with him in this Conspiracy on the like Motives; for, having given up the Flower of his Youth to the Passions of *Archelaus*, and perceiving, that This did not avail towards recalling him from Exile, as That Prince had made him hope, he concluded, that his Person had not been made use of, from an Effect of Love, but meerly to dishonour him. Δὶ ὕβριν καὶ ἀ δὲ ἐρωτικὴν ἐπιθυμίαν ἆυτο εἶται τὴν γενημένην ὁμιλίαν (43). *Consuetudinem illam secum esse institutam non propter cupiditatem amatoriam sed propter contumeliam existimavit.* Observe, that *Plutarch* informs us, That *Crateüs*, the Minion of *Archelaus*, killed That Prince (44). *Plato* says the same; but without naming this Murderer, and Catamite; he only says, that the Murderer committed This Crime, in order to seize on the Crown, and that it was wrested from him again in three or four Days by other Conspirators (45). I wonder *Diodorus Siculus* should relate the Death of This King of *Macedon*, and it's Consequences, in a manner so different from This. *Plato* and *Aristotle*, who lived nearer the Time and Place, where these Things were transacted, probably knew the Truth much better than He.

I have observed some Faults in the Commentary of *Gifanius* on this Passage of *Aristotle*. I. This Author affirms, that *Suidas* takes notice, in the Article of *Euripides*, that *Cratevas* took away the Life of his Lover, King *Archelaus* (46). This is not true: *Suidas* mentions *Cratevas* only as a Poet, who, together with *Arribideus*, another Poet, contrived the Death of *Euripides*. II. Instead of saying, that *Plutarch*, in *Alcibiade posteriore*, and *Plato*, in *commentario de rebus amatoriis* (47), have mentioned the Murther of *Archelaus*, The *Alcibiades posterior* should have been ascribed to *Plato*, and The *Commentary de rebus amatoriis* to *Plutarch*. III. It is not true, that *Thucydides*, in his fourth Book, mentions *Archelaus*'s War with *Sirras* and *Arribaeus* (48): He speaks only of the War, which King *Perdiccas*, and *Brasidas*, made against *Arribaeus*, King of *Macedonia*, sirnamed *Lyncestes*. IV. It is false, that *Suidas* has any where placed *Arribaeus* in the Number of the Conspirators against the Life of *Archelaus*; he only says, that the Poet *Cratevas* was assisted by another Poet, whose Name was *Arribaeus*, to destroy *Euripides*. V. He should not have called the first Son-in-law of *Archelaus* King of *Elibaea*, but King of *Elimaea* (49).

[*H*] *A few Observations —— against Moreri.*]
I. It is not true, that *Archelaus* succeeded *Perdiccas*, in the Year of the World 3641. For, according to *Moreri*, This Year of the World answers to the Three hundred fifty first Year of *Rome*. Now This Year of *Rome* answers to the second Year of the XCIVth Olympiad; and we have already seen, that, according to *Diodorus Siculus*, *Archelaus* must have begun to reign in the third Year of the XCIIId Olympiad.
II. It is not true, that *Justin* mentions our *Archelaus*: He, whom he mentions, was Uncle of *Alexander* the Great, and never was King. We need not, therefore, be surprized, that *he does not speak of the time of his Reign*. III. It is not true, that he reckons him among the Sons, which *Perdiccas* had by *Eurydice*: He reckons him among the Sons of *Amyntas* and *Gygea*; Of *Amyntas*, I mean, the Father of *Philip*, and Grandfather of *Alexander* the Great. IV. Neither what *Justin* has said, nor what he has omitted, are a Proof, that he has confounded *Archelaus*, the Grandfather, with *Archelaus*, the Grandson; for he speaks only of an *Archelaus*, who was not the Grandson of our's. V. It is a strange Mistake to place the Death of our *Archelaus* in the CXVIth Olympiad, and to make This Olympiad correspond with the Three hundred sixty fifth Year of *Rome*. VI. It ought not to have been affirmed, that The *Archelaus*, who reigned after *Orestes*, was his Son, and Grandson of *Archelaus*; for, besides that *Eusebius* is little followed in regard to This *Archelaus*, Second of the Name, he does not mention any Degree of Consanguinity. What follows, concerns the Supplement of *Moreri*. There we find, that *Socrates would not come near Archelaus on account of his Tyranny and Inhumanity*. Count This for the VIIth Mistake; for we have seen above (50), that this was not the Reason, which prevented *Socrates* from going to the Court of *Macedon*. The VIIIth Mistake consists in charging *Thucydides*, and *Diodorus Siculus*, with saying, that *Euripides*, being desired to write a Tragedy on the Subject of *Archelaus*, declined it, as being unwilling to describe the Cruelties of This Tyrant. It is very certain, that neither *Thucydides*, nor *Diodorus Siculus* say any thing like this; and I question, whether any good Author among the Ancients gives any Hint of it; Did ever any Prince desire a Tragedy to be wrote *on himself*? Cannot a Court Poet write a Tragedy to please his Master, by omitting the Cruelties of This Master? IX. The Favourite, who killed *Archelaus*, is called *Craterus* in *Diodorus Siculus* (51); This, then, is the Name, which ought to have been given him, and not That of *Crateüs*, or *Cratevas*; since *Diodorus Siculus* is the only Author quoted concerning him. X. For the same Reason, I assert, it ought not to have been said, that he form'd a Conspiracy against *Archelaus*, and that he killed him in revenge for a Breach of Promise. The Continuator of *Moreri* says, that *Archelaus* promis'd his Daughter to this Favourite, and afterwards married her to another. Since he quotes only *Thucydides* and *Diodorus Siculus*; the first of which has not said a Word of this Matter, and the latter relates, that this Favourite wounded his Master inadvertently (52); he deserves a little Censure; for I confess had he quoted *Aristotle*, he would have been sufficiently justified. See the Preceeding Remark. XI. *Diodorus*, whom he quotes, calls Him, who reigned after *Archelaus*, *Orestes* (53): why then are we told, that *This Prince had a Son of the same Name, who succeeded him*? XII. This Historian adds, that *Orestes* was yet a Child, and that he was killed by his Tutor *Æropus*, who afterwards reigned Six Years. Why then do they make him say, that *Archelaus* the Second, Son of *Archelaus* the First, succeeded his Father, and *reigned but four Years; and was kill'd in Hunting, by* Craterus, *one of his Confidents, who afterwards took possession of the Crown; tho' he enjoyed it but Three Days*? So many Words, so many Faults.

ARCHELAUS, King of *Cappadocia*, in the Reign of *Augustus*, was Great Grandson to *Archelaus*, a *Cappadocian* by Nation (a), and General of *Mithridates*'s Army, in *Greece*, against *Sylla*. This General, who had so signalized himself in Defence of the *Piraeum* (b), quitted *Mithridates*'s Party in the second War, and went over to the *Romans*. He left a Son of his own Name, who, upon notice, that the *Romans* designed to attack the *Parthians*, repaired to *Gabinius*, Governor of *Syria*, to engage himself in That Expedition (c). The Senate laid aside the Design, and *Gabinius*'s Army marched to restore the King of *Egypt* (d), who had implored the Assistance of the People of *Rome*, to recover his Crown from his own Daughter *Berenice*. *Archelaus* accompanied *Gabinius* to This War; but, afterwards, left him, to go to *Alexandria*, where he married *Berenice* [*A*]. He did not long enjoy the Crown, which

[*A*] *He married* Berenice.] We shall make an Article of This Princess, and there examine, whether Father *Norris* ought to have said, that she gained over *Archelaus* to her Party, by promising to marry him.
[*B*] *He*

ARCHELAUS. 421

which he acquired by This Marriage; for, about six Months after, he lost his Life (*e*), in a Battel against the Troops of *Gabinius*, in the Year of *Rome* 698 [*B*]. He had obtained from *Pompey* a very honourable Dignity [*C*]; namely the Pontificat of *Comana*, in *Cappadocia* (*f*). His Son *Archelaus* enjoyed it after him (*g*), until *Cæsar* turned him out in the Year of *Rome* 707, in order to give it to another [*D*]. The rest of his Adventures are unknown; except that he was married to a very beautiful Woman, whose Name was *Glaphyra*; and had two Sons by her, one called *Sisinna*, and the other *Archelaus*. The first disputed the Kingdom of *Cappadocia* with *Ariarathes*, who was in Possession of it. *Marc Antony* was made Judge of this Dispute, in the Year of *Rome* 713; and gave it in favour of *Sisinna* (*h*). The Fair Sex had too great an Influence over him, and *Glaphyra* was too beautiful for This Tryal to have any other Issue. Some Historians treat her as a Courtezan (*i*); which makes it the easier to apprehend, why *Marc Antony* gave Judgment in favour of *Sisinna*. But, how probable soever This Calumny may seem, it is not impossible, that the Friendship *Marc Antony* had for That *Archelaus*, who married *Berenice* (*k*), might induce him act as he did. It is not known what became of *Sisinna*; but it is certain, that *Ariarathes* re-ascended the Throne of *Cappadocia*; for *Marc Antony* was obliged to dispossess him a second Time, in the Year of *Rome* 718; and then, conferred the Kingdom on ARCHELAUS, the Son of *Glaphyra* (*l*). This is He, who appears at the Head of this Article. He became very powerful (*m*), and expressed his Acknowledgments to his Benefactor *Marc Antony*, by supplying him with fine Troops during the *Attic* War (*n*). He was so happy, as not to disoblige *Augustus* by it; so that he remained in Possession of *Cappadocia*, and was almost the only Person, to whom so much Favour was shewn (*o*). He assisted *Tiberius*, in the Year 734, to re-establish *Tigranes* in *Armenia* (*p*), and obtained the lesser *Armenia*, and a good Part of *Cilicia*, from *Augustus* (*q*). He fixed his Residence in the Island of *Eleusa* [*E*], near the Coast of *Cilicia*; and, having married *Pythodoris*, the Widow of *Polemon*, King of *Pontus*, he encreased his Power considerably; for, as the Sons of *Polemon* were yet but Infants, he had, without Doubt, the Administration of the Kingdom, jointly with the Queen, their Mother [*F*]. He signalized himself, after an extraordinary manner, in making his Court to *Caius Cæsar*, when sent into the East by his Grandfather *Augustus* (*r*). This proved very fatal to him in the end [*G*]; for

[*B*] *He lost his Life, in a Battle against the Troops of Gabinius.*] This does not agree with the Seventeenth Book of *Strabo*, where we read, that *Ptolomy*, being restored to his Kingdom, put his Daughter, and Son-in law *Archelaus*, to Death. I shall make it appear, in the Article *Berenice*, that *Strabo* is mistaken in this, and that he has contradicted himself. You may boldly pronounce these Words of *Morers* to be false; *Ptolomy, being restored in* 699, *put* Archelaus *and* Berenice *to Death*.

[*C*] *He obtain'd from* Pompey *a very honourable Dignity.*] Father *Norris* says, that the Pontiff of *Comana* was Sovereign of the Place. "Hunc Archelaum Pompeius Sacerdotem Bellonæ, ac Comanorum principem (utraque enim dignitas uni eidemque conferebatur) constituerat, cuivis Dynastæ parem opibus, ex Appiano in Mithridat. p. 252 (1)". — *Pompey appointed This* Archelaus *Priest of Bellona, and Prince of Comana (for both Dignities were conferred upon one and the same Person) A Post, equal in Revenue to That of a Dynast, according to Appian, in Mithridat, p. 252*". We shall examine in another Place, whether this be Right (2).

[*D*] Cæsar *turned him out — to give his Post to another*.] *Hirtius* relates, that *Cæsar* disposed of this Benefice in favour of *Nicomedes*, who made it appear, that he had very just Pretensions to it. " Id homini nobilissimo Nicomedi Bythinio adjudicavit, qui regio Cappadocum genere ortus, propter adversam fortunam majorum suorum jure minimè dubio, vetustate tamen intermisso, sacerdotium id repetebat (3)". — *He adjudged it to an illustrious Person,* Nicomedes *of* Bythinia, *who, being descended from the Kings of* Cappadocia, *justly laid claim to This Priest-hood, which, thro' the misfortune of his Ancestors, had been for a long time lost to his Family*". Father *Norris* affirms, that *Cæsar* confer'd this Dignity on *Lycomedes*, after his Victory over *Pharnaces*; but They, who think fit to consult *Hirtius*, will easily find, that it was disposed of before the Battle. As for the Name of *Lycomedes*, it is to be found in the Editions of *Strabo* (4). It is also certain, that, in *Dion*, we meet with a *Lycomedes*, divested of his Estate by *Augustus*, after the Flight of *Marc Antony* (5), and, perhaps, the Same, whom *Cæsar* raised to the Pontificate of *Comana*: for he reigned

in a Part of *Cappadocia*. The Epithet *Bythinius*, which *Hirtius* makes use of, favours more the Reading *Nicomedes* (6), than *Lycomedes*.

[*E*] *He fix'd his Residence in the Island of* Eleusa.] This we learn from *Strabo*, and *Josephus*. " Post Corycum Eleusa insula est continenti propinqua. Eam Archelaus condidit, ac regiam sibi fecit, cum totam Ciliciam excepta Seleucia esset nactus (7). — *Next to* Corycus *is the Island* Eleusa, *close by the Continent*. Archelaus *fixed his Residence there, after having made himself Master of All Cilicia, except Seleucia*". *Josephus* observes, that *Herod*, having landed at *Eleusa* in *Cilicia*, found *Archelaus* King of *Cappadocia* there (8). It was there that the Envoys of *Herod* received Orders to carry the Letter, which he wrote to *Augustus*. The same Historian observes, that *Eleusa* was called *Sebaste* (10). Might not *Archelaus*, in compliment to *Augustus*, make This Alteration in the Name?

[*F*] *He had, without doubt, the Administration of the Kingdom jointly with the Queen their Mother*.] Father *Norris* positively affirms this (11); I have chosen to make use of an Expression, which imports, not that this Fact is to be found in the Ancient Writers, but that it appears to be very agreeable to Reason. What makes me express my self with some Caution, is, that *Strabo* says nothing more, than that *Pythodoris* lived with her Husband *Archelaus*, during his Life. 'Αυλη δε συνώκησεν Άρχελάω καί συνεμεινεν έκεινω μέχει τέλως (12). *Ipsi* Archelao *nupsit, & cum eo dum is in vivis permansit etiam exegit*. She knew how to command; it is not impossible, then, that she might have governed The Estates of her Children Alone. Γυνὴ σώφρων καὶ δυνατὴ πραγμασιν προςωμάτων (13). *Prudens mulier & præesse rebus gnara*.

[*G*] *This proved very fatal to him in the End*.] I have observed more than once, that Persons, whom we slight, are often destined by Providence to the highest Stations (14). Unhappy for Those, who have treated them with Contempt. Few are so reasonable, as *Lewis* the XII, who said, that a King of *France* ought not to revenge the Injuries done to a Duke of *Orleans*. Our *Archelaus* acted like a Politician: He knew, that *Augustus* loved his Grandson tenderly; And, in all probability, That young Prince was to succeed

422 ARCHELAUS.

for *Tiberius*, recollecting, that he had paid him no Civilities during his Stay at *Rhodes*; and that, on the other side, *Caius Cæsar* had received a thousand Marks of Respect from him, resolved to be revenged, as soon as he found himself Master of the Empire; accordingly he summoned him to appear at *Rome*, and appointed the Senate as Judge [*H*] of the Accusations, which should be brought against him. But Age, the Gout, and, above all, the Indignity of the Treatment he met with, soon broke his Heart, before the Senate had pronounced any Sentence against him. Some believe, that he escaped the Sentence of the Senate, by feigning himself mad [*K*]. He died in the Year of *Rome* 770, and the Fifty second of his Reign; after which *Cappadocia* became

ceed his Grand-father. *Tiberius* was in some kind of Disgrace, in the Island of *Rhodes*, which did not seem to presage him the Empire. *Archelaus* believed he hazarded nothing in neglecting Him, and, besides, had intimations, that it might be dangerous to cultivate his Friendship. He look'd upon all the Honours he paid to *Caius Cæsar* as a sure Fund of Advantages, and Rewards for Life. But he was mistaken; and little considered the Artfulness of *Livia*, in paving her Son's way to Empire. *Caius*, and his Brother, did not live long; and probably she knew the Reason of it. After all, it is often the truest Policy to pay One's court, even when They are in Disgrace, to Those, whom we see in the Road to High Preferment (15). Let us produce Authorities, which inform us of *Tiberius*'s Resentment. "Rex Archelaus, "says *Tacitus* (16), quinquagesimum annum Cappadociâ potiebatur, invisus Tiberio, quod eum Rhodi agentem nullo officio coluisset: Nec id Archelaus per superbiam omiserat, sed ab intimis Augusti monitus, quia florente Caio Cæsare, missoque ad res Orientis, intuta Tiberii amicitia credebatur.—King Archelaus had reigned fifty Years in Cappadocia, being odious to the Emperor Tiberius, to whom he had neglected to pay his Court, when in the Island of Rhodes. Not that Archelaus's omission was the Effect of Pride, but owing to the Advice of Those about Augustus; who thought it not safe for him to cultivate the Friendship of Tiberius, whilst Caius Cæsar was in such high Favour, and had the Command of Affairs in the East.*" *Dion Cassius* says almost the same thing. "Tiberius Cappadociæ regem Archelaum, infensus ei, quia, cum olim sibi is supplicasset, suoque patrocinio usus, cum ab incolis apud Augustum accusaretur, fuisset, Rhodi se neglexisset, ac Caium in Asia venientem officiose coluisset, insimulatum, quasi novis rebus studeret, evocavit Romam (17).—Tiberius, being incensed against Archelaus, King of Cappadocia, who, notwithstanding the Protection he had afforded him, when his Subjects accused him to Augustus, had yet neglected him at Rhodes, and officiously paid his Court to Caius Cæsar, upon his arrival in Asia, cited him to appear at Rome, where he was accused of plotting against the State.*" We learn from this Passage, that *Tiberius* complained, not only of *Archelaus*'s want of Respect, but also of his Ingratitude. The Circumstance of the Place might contribute to exasperate the Emperor; for the Island of *Elœusa*, where *Archelaus* resided, was but Fifteen thousand Paces * distant from *Rhodes* (18).

[*H*] *He summoned him to appear at Rome, and appointed the Senate as Judge*] *Dion* relates this; *Insimulatum, quasi novis rebus studeret, evocavit Romam, ac Senatus judicio tradidit* (19). He was accused of a Crime against the State. *Tacitus* does not seem to be of this Opinion; he intimates very plainly, that *Tiberius* complained only of *Archelaus*'s Incivility, and encouraged him, by Letters from his Mother, to hope, that, by his Presence and Intreaties, he might obtain Pardon. *Ut versa Cæsarum sobole imperium adeptus est, elicit Archelaum matris literis, quæ non dissimulatis offensionibus clementiam offerebat, si ad precandum veniret* (20). This Frankness, with regard to Personal Offences, covered a most dangerous Snare. Either the King of *Cappadocia* did not perceive it, or durst not act, as if he did. He repair'd immediately to *Rome*; was very coldly received by *Tiberius*; and found himself soon after in the hands of Justice. *Ille ignarus doli, vel si intelligere crederetur vim metuens, in urbem properat, exceptusque immiti à principe, & mox accusatus in Senatu* (21). *Suetonius* (22) has spoken of this Action of *Tiberius* only in general Terms. "Reges infestos suspectosque comminationibus magis & querelis

"quam vi repressit: quosdam per blanditias atque "promissa extractos ad se non remisit, ut - - - Ar- "chelaum Cappadocem. ——*Those Kings, whom he "hated and suspected, he repressed by Threatning and "Complaints, rather than by Force. Some, whom he "got into his Power by Soothing and Promises, he "never sent back* —— *as Archelaus the Cappado- "cian.*" I Question whether *Archelaus*, notwithstanding his Age, was not tempted to raise some Commotions after the Death of *Augustus*; for mention is made of One of his Plots (23), which could only relate to That time.

[*I*] *His Age, the Gout, but, above all, the Indignity of the Treatment he met with, broke his Heart.*] Let us hear *Tacitus*. "Mox accusatus in Senatu, "non ob crimina quæ fingebantur, sed angore, simul "fessus senio, & quia regibus æqua nedum, infima "insolita sunt, finem vitæ sponte an fato implevit.— *Being afterwards accused in the Senate, tho' he was not condemned for the Crimes alledged against him, which indeed were fictitious; yet Affliction of Mind, together with Old Age, and a Fate uncommon to Kings, put an end to his Days; whether by a voluntary or natural Death, is uncertain.*" This Historian does not know, whether *Tiberius* killed himself, or only sunk under the Weight of his Misfortunes; but from his Relation it appears, that This Prince was not condemned, and consequently not put to Death. *Dion* will inform us of more Circumstances.

[*K*] *Some believe, that he escaped the Sentence of the Senate, by feigning himself mad.*] *Dion* affirms, that *Archelaus*, bending under the Weight of Years, passed for a Dotard; that, nevertheless, he had all his Senses perfect; but counterfeited the Madman, because he saw no other means of saving his Life (24); that he would yet have suffered Death, had not a false Witness accused him of Threatning Words, and of saying, that, when he should return to his Kingdom, he would shew *Tiberius*, that he did not want Courage. This occasioned Laughter, and diverted *Tiberius* from his Design of putting him to Death. He was so weak, and worn out, that they were obliged to carry him in a Litter to the Senate-House. *Dion* adds, that, for this Time, *Archelaus* escaped Death; but that he died soon after. *Dion* does not contradict the Text of this Remark; for, if the false Witness saved *Archelaus*'s Life, it was only because it was judged, that the Threats of a superannuated, decay'd, old Man, were certain Proofs of a Delirium, of Dotage, and a second State of Childhood, &c. By this it appears, that *Xiphilin* had not the best Judgment, when he suppressed the the feigned Madness of *Archelaus*. This is a Fact which ought not to be omitted by the most concise Writers. *David*, *Brutus*, and others, have successfully put in practice this kind of Dissimulation; They are, therefore, remarkable Adventures, and such as an Abbreviator ought to retain. Let us not omit what *Dion* observes, that *Archelaus* had really been next to an Idiot, some time before; witness *Augustus*'s appointing him a Governor, who was Regent of his Kingdom. I cannot say, whether it was on This Occasion, that he had recourse to the Protection of *Tiberius*. He sued for it, when he was accused by his Subjects: But might they not have represented him as a Fool, at a Time, when he had Reason enough left to desire not to be put under Tuition; and to maintain, that it was out of Malice alone, that his Subjects endeavoured to represent him as unfit to govern? It is difficult to clear up this Matter. The Ancient Historians so accustomed themselves to relate Things only in the Gross, that they afford but little Light into some of the more minute Particulars. Their Method is very good; however, there is an

Art

(15) *This was Pomponius Atticus's Rule. See the Remark [A] of his Article.*

(16) Tacit. Annal. lib. 2. cap. 24.

(17) Dion. lib. 57.

* *Fifteen Miles.*

(18) Strab. lib. 14, pag. 448.

(19) Dion, ubi supra.

(20) Tacit. Ann. lib. 2. cap. 42.

(21) Id. ib.

(22) Suet. in Tiber. cap. 37. See also Eutropius, l. 7.

(23) Philostr. in Vit. Apoll. lib. 1. cap. 7.

(24) Mr de Tillemont, Hist. des Emper. Tom. I, pag. 107, falsely charges Dion, with saying, that Archelaus was acquitted by the Senate, upon his counterfeiting Madness.

ARCHELAUS.

came a Province [*L*]. His Family boasted of a most Ancient and Noble Extraction [*M*]. We shall take some notice of his Posterity in the Article of *Glaphyra*. There is reason to think, that he was Author of some books [*N*]. His Address, in appeasing Herod's fierce Anger against his Son *Alexander*, is a proof of his Abilities on some Occasions (*s*). Some have confounded him with *ARCHELAUS*, the Son of *Herod* [*O*]. I cannot find, that *Eutropius* says, what a modern Author imputes to him, that *ARCHELAUS*, at his Death, bequeath'd his Kingdom to the people of *Rome*; and that *Cappadocia* was reduc'd into a Province by this Title (*t*). Mr *de Tillemont* might have been very certain of a thing, which he seems to doubt of; to wit, that the same *ARCHELAUS*, who was King of *Cappadocia*, obtain'd, by the Favour of *Augustus*, Part of *Cilicia*, and the lesser *Armenia*. Mr *Moreri* has been guilty of several Faults of Omission in this Article. His Continuator has been guilty of but One of Commission; but such an one, as will match with any Four

---

Art of specifying Facts in few Words, and by the by; which would be of great Use, if Writers had the Will, or the Skill, to practise it. One History in *Folio*, might, by the Help of this Art, prevent numberless Disputes, and clear up a great Variety of Particulars, without consisting of above fifty Pages.

[*L*] *After which Cappadocia became a Province*]. *Velleius Paterculus, Tacitus, Dion*, and several others, expressly assert this (25). The proper Terms of the three first are these. " Tib. Cæsar —— ut has ar- " mis, ita auctoritate Cappadociam populo Romano " Stipendiariam fecit (26). —— Tiberius Cæsar —— " *as he reduced these by Force, so by his Authority he* " *made Cappadocia tributary to the Romans*. —— Regnum in Provinciam redactum est (27). —— The " *Kingdom was reduced into a Province*. —— Paulo post " obiit (Archelaus), ac inde Cappadocia quoque Romanorum juris effecta est, Equitique regenda data " est (28). —— *Soon after*, Archelaus *died; from which* " *time Cappadocia likewise became a Roman Province,* " *and was under the Government of a Knight.*" It was *Germanicus*, who executed this Order (29). *Appian* was very much mistaken, in saying, that the Kingdom of *Cappadocia*, was reduced into a Province under *Augustus* (30). Father *Norris*, who corrected this Mistake of *Appian*, has discovered two very considerable Faults in *Riccioli*, one in point of Genealogy, the other in point of Chronology (31). The Words, which he produces from That Author, are these: " Summato Mithridate, creatus est Cappadocum consensu à Romanis Ariobarzanes; tandem Archelao " pronepote mortuo Romæ, Consulibus C. Cælio Rufo & L. Pomponio, ut ait Tacitus, id est anno 84 " ante Christum, desiit regnare in Cappadocia ". —— " Mithridates *being set aside*, Ariobarzanes *was created by the Romans, with the Consent of the Cappadocians; at length*, Archelaus, *his Nephew's Son,* " *dying at* Rome, *in the Consulship of* C. Cælius " Rufus, *and* L. Pomponius, *according to* Tacitus, " *that is, Eighty four Years before* CHRIST, *Cappadocia ceased to be a Kingdom.*" These Words carry the Air of a mutilated Passage: It is no uncommon thing for Printers to omit whole Lines. Be that as it will, *Archelaus* did not descend from *Ariobarzanes*; this is the Genealogical Error of *Riccioli*; and the Consulate of *C. Cælius Rufus*, and *L. Pomponius*, in which he died at *Rome*, fell out in the seventeenth Year of *JESUS CHRIST*; this is his Chronological Error. *Strabo* witnesses in express Terms, that *Archelaus* was not related to *Ariobarzanes*. " Ita " rex ab iis factus est Ariobarzanes, cujus in tertia " stirpe genus defecit. Exinde Archelaus ab Antonio " junctus (32). —— *Thus* Ariobarzanes *was made* " *King by them; whose Race was extinct in the third* " *Generation. Upon which*, Archelaus, *who was of a* " *quite* DIFFERENT FAMILY, *was appointed King by* " Antony." The Error, which *Noldius* imputes to *Jornandes*, is very different from this of *Appian*. He will have it, that *Cappadocia* became a Province in the time of the Emperor *Claudius*, by virtue of the last Will and Testament of *Archelaus* (33). By the way, the Revenues of *Cappadocia* were so considerable, when *Archelaus* died, that *Tiberius* thought himself, by this new acquisition, in a condition to remit one moiety of a Tax, which he had order'd to be levy'd. Regnum (Archelai) *in provinciam redactum est, fructibusque ejus levari posse centesimæ vectigal professus Cæsar, ducentesimam in posterum statuit* (34). He eas'd This Province likewise; and would not exact from it as much as it had paid to the last King (35).

[*M*] *His Family boasted of a most ancient and noble Extraction*] Glaphyra, *the Daughter of the last* Archelaus, *and Wife of* Alexander, *the Son of* Herod, spoke often of her Family, and boasted, that she was descended from *Temenus*, by the Father's Side, and from *Darius*, the Son of *Hystaspes*, by the mother's (36).

[*N*] *There is reason to think, that he was Author of some Books*] *Pliny* seems to intimate this. He quotes *Archelaus* several Times; and it is thought, that, in two Places, he means our *Archelaus*, king of *Cappadocia*. He gives him This very Title in one of these two Quotations: Archelaus, *says he, qui regnavit in* Cappadocia (37); and, as the Discourse there turns upon some Particulars relating to *Amber*, Father *Harduoin* makes no question, but that the same *Archelaus*; is meant in the Seventh Chapter of the Thirty seventh Book of *Pliny*; where one *Archelaus* is quoted concerning the Properties of a kind of Precious Stone (38). Neither does he doubt, that this is taken from the Book *de lapidibus*, cited by *Plutarch* (39). To relate something more certain, I shall point out a Passage of *Pliny*, where *Archelaus* is reckon'd among the Kings, who had written concerning Agriculture (40). I have already mention'd (41) another *Archelaus*, often quoted by *Pliny*.

[*O*] *Some have confounded him with* Archelaus, *the Son of* Herod.] Father *Norris* has convicted *Riccioli* of this Error (42). *Riccioli* had said, that, in the Trial between *Archelaus*, and his brother, concerning *Herod's* Succession, *Tiberius* pleaded his Cause before *Augustus*, and pretends to prove it from this Passage of *Suetonius*: " Civilium officiorum rudimentis Archelaum, Trallianos, & Thessalos varia quosque de " causa, Augusto cognoscente, defendit (43). —— " *He was yet a young Pleader, when he undertook the* " *different Causes of* Archelaus, *the* Trallians, *and* Thessalians, *before the Tribunal of* Augustus." And, as *Velleius Paterculus* informs him, that *Tiberius* left *Rhodes*, to return to *Rome*, in the year 755, he concludes, that *Archelaus* was made Ethnarch in That Year, and not in 751, or before. Father *Norris* shews him, from the Passage of *Dion* quoted above (44), that the Words of *Suetonius* must be understood of *Archelaus*, King of *Cappadocia*. He might have added an Instance, which destroys the Hypothesis of *Riccioli*; to wit, that *Tiberius* defended *Archelaus's* Cause, before he went to *Rhodes*. This is plain from *Dion's* Words; and may clearly be inferr'd from Those of *Suetonius*; who makes *Tiberius's* Defence of *Archelaus* the First in the List of Causes undertaken by Him, when (if I may so speak) he made his first Campaign at the Bar, *civilium officiorum rudimenta*. *Torrentius* is of the same Opinion with *Riccioli*; to wit, that *Suetonius* meant the great Cause of *Archelaus*, the Son of *Herod*: and refers us to *Josephus* (45). But how came they not to perceive, that, in this Case, *Josephus* could not possibly be ignorant of this good Office of *Tiberius*; and, if he knew it, that he could not well have omitted it? I am surpriz'd that Father *Norris*, who makes such frequent and vigorous Attacks upon the Jesuit *Salian*, has spar'd him on this Occasion. This Jesuit fell into the same mistake with *Riccioli*; he has censur'd *Casaubon* for applying (46) the Passage of *Suetonius* to *Archelaus*, King of *Cappadocia*: he represents to him, that the Cause of this Prince was debated in the Reign of *Tiberius*; and maintains, that *Archelaus*, the Son of *Herod*,

ARCHELAUS. ARCHILOCHUS.

Four; it is so very gross [P]. We shall see what it is, in the last Remark of this Article.

Herod, must consequently be understood in this Place; to prove which, he supposes, that JESUS CHRIST staid Two Years in Egypt: For, says he, Tiberius *did not return to Rome in the Second Year of* JESUS CHRIST; *but he was at Rome, when* Archelaus *disputed* Herod's *Succession with his Brother; since he honour'd him with his Protection* (47). Behold how Faults are heap'd upon Faults, when the foundation is ill laid. It is as clear as the Day, that the King of *Cappadocia's* Cause was adjudged by *Augustus*, before *Tiberius* retir'd to the Island of *Rhodes* (48).

[P] *His Continuator has been guilty of but One of Commission; but such an One, as will match with any Four; it is so gross*] He says, that *Scylla* (it is his own Orthography) after having taken the City of *Athens*, kill'd *Archelaus*, General of *Mithridates*'s Army, with his own Hand, at the Foot of the Altar, to which he had fled for Refuge. He quotes *Aulus Gellius*, *lib* 14. It is certain, that *Aulus Gellius* speaks, in the First Chapter of his Fifteenth Book, of a Particular, which the Continuator has mention'd; I mean of an expedient, which *Archelaus* made use of, to hinder the *Romans* from firing a Tower of Wood, which defended the *Pyreum*: We shall see below what it was; but that he has said, that *Archelaus* took Refuge in a Temple, and that *Sylla* kill'd him with his own hand at the Foot of an Altar, is most false. I believe no Author, worthy of Credit, has said this; for it is notorious, that *Archelaus*, having constrain'd *Sylla* to give over attacking the *Pyreum*, and to bend all his Force against the City, had time to retire, when it was taken by assault (49). *Sylla* pursued him, gain'd great Victories over him, and obliged him to make a Disadvantageous Peace. *Archelaus*, finding himself suspected of some Misdemeanors (50), durst not trust *Mithridates*, but went over to *Murena*, who commanded the *Romans*. He was receiv'd with Honour, as *Strabo* has observ'd in more Places than one. Ἣν δὲ ὑπὸ Ἀρχελάῳ υἱεῖ μὲν τῷ ὑπὸ Σύλλᾳ καὶ τῆς συγκλήτῳ τιμηθέντος (51). *This* Archelaus *was the Son of Him, who receiv'd Honours from* Sylla *and the Senate*.

The Secret of preserving his Tower of Wood consisted in causing it to be well rubb'd with Allum. *Quadrigarius*, I think, is the only Historian, who has mention'd this. Others say, that His Tower, and Machines were ruin'd by the Besiegers. It is certain, that Allum has not the virtue *Quadrigarius* speaks of. These are his words. " Tum Sulla conatus est, & tempore magno eduxit copias, ut Archelai turrim unam, " quam ille interposuit, ligneam incenderet. Venit, " accessit, ligna subdidit, submovit Græcos, ignem " admovit, satis fuit diu conati, nunquam quiverunt " incendere: ita Archelaus omnem materiam oblevera " rat alumine, quod Sulla atque milites mirabantur; " &, postquam non succendit, reduxit copias (52). " — Sylla, *upon this, made an Attempt, and hastily* " *drew out his Forces, in order to set Fire to a Tower,* " *which* Archelaus *had built to oppose him. He came,* " *He approached it, He made the* Greeks *retreat; His* " *Men attempted a long Time to set it on Fire; but Ar-* " *chelaus had so daub'd it with Allum, that* Sylla " *and his Soldiers were surpriz'd; and not being able* " *to set it on Fire, he drew off his Forces.*" If the Abbot *de la Roque* had been appriz'd of this Passage of *Aulus Gellius*, he would not have said, " That History " mentions, that *Sylla* formerly undertook to burn a " Tower of Wood, which was defended by one of " *Mithridates*'s Lieutenants, but could not execute " his Design, because it was dawb'd over with a " certain Drug, THE NAME OF WHICH IS NOT " COME TO OUR KNOWLEDGE, and which had the " Virtue to repel the Activity of Fire (53)." Two Things surprize me; The One is, that, since *Quadrigarius* has mention'd so extraordinary an Event, all other Historians should be silent concerning it; The other is, that, since so many Historians have not said a Word of it, *Quadrigarius* shou'd mention it in so express a manner. Facts of this kind strike the mind so forcibly, that an incombustible Wooden Tower would have been the last Thing omitted by an Historian. *Sylla* would infallibly have inserted it in his Memoirs; *Plutarch*, who cites them so often (54), would have met with it in them, and would not have forgotten to mention it. Let us conclude from his Silence, and That of so many other Historians, that the Fact is false. But from whence had *Quadrigarius* this Account? I believe it is impossible to trace the Original of his Error. It is true indeed, that *Plum-Allum* will resist Fire, and will not be consumed by it; but to rub a Tower of Wood with it, and thence to render it incombustible, is a Thing which, I conceive, is impracticable.

ARCHILOCHUS, a *Greek* Poet, Native of the Island of *Pharos* (a), and the Son of Telesicles [A], flourish'd in the XXIXth Olympiad [B]. An uncommon Torrent

[A] *The Son of* Telesicles] This we find, not only in *Suidas*, but in *Oenomaus* likewise, quoted by *Eusebius* (1).

[B] *He flourish'd in the XXIXth Olympiad.*] Authors differ a little in this. *Tatian*, and *St Cyril*, place *Archilochus* in the XXIIId Olympiad (2). *Clemens Alexandrinus* places him the XXth; Others in the XVth, XVIIIth, and XIXth (3). *Cicero* supposes him to have lived in the Reign of *Romulus* (4). *Cornelius Nepos* places him in the time of *Tullus Hostilius* (5). *Herodotus* not only affirms, that he wrote Verses on the Adventures of *Gyges*, and *Candaules*; but that he lived likewise at the same time (6). *Eusebius* makes him flourish in the XXIXth Olympiad. It is easy to reconcile some of these Authors, but not all; for the Revolution, which happened in *Lydia* by the Death of *Candaules*, and the Inauguration of *Gyges*, fell out in the XXVIIth Olympiad (7). The Death of *Romulus* happened in the preceding Olympiad. The Reign of *Tullus Hostilius* takes in the space of time between the first Year of the XXVIIth Olympiad, and the first Year of the XXXVth. *Salmasius*, who was very happy in correcting a Mistake in *Solinus*, did not perceive one of his own. *Solinus* has been rash enough to place the Three Orators of the Family of the *Curio's*, *Archilochus*, and *Sophocles*, in the same Age " Plurimi *says he* (8), inter Romanos " eloquentia floruerunt, sed hoc bonum hereditarium " nunquam fuit nisi in familia Curionum, in qua " tres serie continua oratores fuere: magnum hoc " habitum est sane eo sæculo, quo facundiam præci- " puæ & humana & divina mitata sunt: quippe tunc " percussores Archilochi poetæ Apollo prodidit, & " latronum facinus Deo coarguente detectum; cum- " que Lysander Lacedæmonius Athenas obsideret, " ubi Sophoclis tragici inhumatum corpus jacebat; " identidem Liber Pater ducem monuit per quietem, " sepeliri delicias suas sineret, nec prius destitit, &c. " — Many among the Romans were famous for Eloquence; but This Talent was never Hereditary, except in the Family of the Curio's, in which were Three successive Orators. This was look'd upon as very Extraordinary even in That Age, in which Eloquence was held in great Admiration both by Gods and Men; for, at that time, Apollo discover'd the Murtherers of Archilochus the Poet, and the Robbers were convicted of their Guilt by the Evidence of a God; and, when Lysander the Lacedemonian besieg'd Athens, where the Body of Sophocles the Tragedian lay unburied, Bacchus admonish'd the Chief in a Dream, to suffer his Favourite to be buried; " nor did he desist till, &c." *Salmasius* observes (9), that One of these *Curio*'s lived in the time of *Julius Cæsar*; that *Archilochus* liv'd in the time of *Tarquinius Superbus*; and that *Sophocles* did not flourish till above two Centuries after *Archilochus*. He has reason, then, to laugh at *Solinus*, but is in the wrong to place *Archilochus* in the time of *Tarquinius Superbus*, who reign'd from the third Year of the LXIst Olympiad to the last Year of the LXVIIth: I say, he is in the wrong to place him in this Time, since he, elsewhere, fixes him under the XXIXth Olympiad. *Circiter vigesimam nonam Olympiadem inclaruit Archilochus* (10). Having been guilty of This Error,

ARCHILOCHUS.

Torrent of Scandal was the Characteristic of his Poetry [C]. Terrible was the Power of it; since *Lycambes* hang'd himself, upon a virulent Satire, which *ARCHILOCHUS* wrote against him. The Indignation of this Poet proceeded from a Breach of Promise; *Lycambes*, had promis'd him his Daughter, and afterwards refused her to him. *ARCHILOCHUS* took this so to heart, either because he lov'd the Maid, or that some particular Instance of Contempt had been added to the Refusal, that he diffamed *Lycambes* with all imaginable Virulency. Probably he involved the whole Family in his Pasquinades; for it is said, that the Daughter followed her Father's Example; and some pretend, that three of *Lycambes*'s Daughters died at the same Time of Grief and Despair [D]. Perhaps he revealed some Adventures, equally scandalous, and a Secret to the Public. There seem, at least, to have been some very obscene Passages in his Poem; for it was on occasion of this Satire, that the *Lacedemonians*, taking into Consideration, that the reading such Obscenities was offensive to chaste Ears, prohibited the Verses of *Archilochus*

(11) Scalig. in Euseb. pag. 57, 58. Edit. 1658.

of making *Archilochus*, and the last King of *Rome*, Cotemporaries, he should not have reckon'd Two hundred Years between *Archilochus*, and *Sophocles*; for the Death of the latter fell out in the XCIId Olympiad, or thereabout. Another Great Man (11), has suffer'd himself to be too much led away by the Spirit of finding Fault, when he charges *Herodotus* with having made use of a pitiful Argument, to prove, that *Archilochus* liv'd in the time of *Gyges*; to wit, that *Archilochus* mention'd This King. I confess this Argument would be an absurd One; but it is not true, that *Herodotus* makes use of it; he has only suppos'd it; but drawn no consequence from it. Τῷ καὶ Ἀρχίλοχος ὁ Πάριος κατὰ τὸν αὐτὸν χρόνον γενόμενος ἐν ἰάμβῳ τριμέτρῳ ἐπεμνήσθη (12). *Whom* Archilochus, *who lived at the same Time, mentions in a Trimeter Iambic.*

(12) Herod. lib. 1. c. 12.

[C] *An uncommon Torrent of Scandal ——— was the Characteristic of his Poetry.*] Hence it was that *Horace* considered *Archilochus* as a Madman;

(13) Hor. de Arte Poëtica, ver. 79.

Archilochum proprio rabies armavit Iambo (13).

Rage with Iambics arm'd Archilochus.

ROSCOMMON.

and, when he would give an Idea of the severest kind of Satire, he compares it to That of *Archilochus*.

(14) Id. Epod. 6. v. 13.

In malos asperrimus
Parata tollo cornua
Qualis Lycambe spretus infido gener (14).

— — — *to Rogues a deadly Foe,
I'm still prepared to strike the Blow;
As sharp, as fierce* Archilochus *his Song.*

CREECH.

Ovid, in the same Spirit, uses this Threat;

Postmodo si pergas, in te mihi liber Iambus
Tincta Lycambeo sanguine tela dabit.

*To new Injustice should'st thou still proceed,
The keen Iambi shall revenge the Deed,
And, in thy Wounds, again* Lycambes *bleed.*

(15) Johannes Tortellius Aretinus, in Commentariis de Orthographia; & Jacobus Lanicus, lib. 2. Subseciv. Lect. cap. 4. apud Dionys. Salvagnium Boessium Comment. in Ibin. pag. 25.

This occurs in his Poem *in Ibin*, ver. 51; a Work so full of Scandal, that, they who fancied he wrote it in Imitation of *Archilochus* (15), would be excusable, were it not apparent, from these two Verses,

Nunc, quo Battiades inimicum devovet Ibin,
Hoc ego devoveo teque tuosque modo.

Those Curses, all, on hated Ibis *thrown
By* Battus *Son, accumulated fall
On thy devoted Head.*

that *Ovid* proposed to imitate the Poet *Callimachus*. There are numberless Proverbs, which perpetuate the slanderous Disposition of our Poet; *Archilochia edicta*, ἀρχίλοχον πατεῖς. *Archilochum teris*, &c. The first is to be found in *Cicero*; who made use of it to represent the Edicts, which the Consul *Bibulus* ordered to be fixed up. This poor Consul, not daring to stir out of his House, retained no Shadow

of Authority, but in revenging himself by Pasquinades; in which he displayed the infamous Debaucheries of *Cæsar*, and the vile Practices of his Enemies, in their proper Colours: *In eam coëgit desperationem, ut, quoad protestate abiret domo abditus, nihil aliud quam per edicta nuntiaret* (16). The Edicts, which he published, *Cicero* calls *Archilochia Edicta*; which pleased the People so extremely, that there was no getting through the Press, in the Streets, where they were fixed up; for the People ran in Crowds to read them; which made *Pompey* ready to burst with Spleen. *Archilochia in illum Bibuli Edicta ita populo sunt jucunda, ut eum locum ubi proponuntur, præ multitudine eorum qui legunt, præterire nequeamus, ita ipsi acerba ut tabescat dolore, mihi mehercule molesta, quod & quem semper dilexi nimis excruciant* (17). *Plutarch* speaks thus of these Edicts of *Bibulus*. Βίβλῳ μὲν εἰς τὴν οἰκίαν καταλεισμένῳ ὀκτὼ μηνῶν ἃ περιῆλθεν ὑπατεύων ἀλλ' ἐξέτεμψε διατάγματα βλασφημίας ἀμφοῖν ἔχοντα καὶ κατηγορίας (18). *Bibulus did not stir out of his own house during the eight Months of his Consulship; he only publish'd Edicts, full of Reproaches against them both;* viz. *Pompey* and *Cæsar*. So the Proverb, *Archilochum teris*, I do not believe it signifies, as *Erasmus* imagined, a Slanderer, who treads in the steps of *Archilochus*, or studies his Books; but One, who, having offended *Archilochus*, ought to fear the Destiny of Him, who, having trod on a Serpent, immediately receives a mortal Sting. See what *Lucian* puts into *Archilochus*'s Mouth against a certain Person, who had slander'd him; *Alis cicadam comprehendisti* (19); — *You have taken a Grasshopper by the Wings*; and you will be convinced, that the Explication of *Erasmus*, how conformable soever to *Suidas*'s Sentiment, is false. At the same time I do not deny, that πατεῖν is sometimes taken, as well as *terere*, for *lectitare*. *Aristophanes* says, in his Birds (20), οὐδ' αἴσωπον πεπάτηκας. There are some Epigrams in the *Anthologia*, which give us a very strong Idea of the Calumny of this Poet. *Cerberus* was one of them, is exhorted to keep a stricter Watch than ever, and to take heed of being bit, since *Archilochus* was gone to Hell (21). We shall see in the Remark [G], that he slandered even himself.

(16) Suet. in Cæs. cap. 20. See also cap. 49.

(17) Cicer. ad Attic. Epist. 21. l. 2.

(18) Plutarch in Pomp. pag. 644.

(19) Lucian, in Pseudolog. Tom. 2. pag. 548. See the Article TETTIX.

* [ΤΕΤΤΙΓΑ τὰ πτερὰ συνελαβες. If you press the Grashopper's Wings, it frets and makes a Noise. *So the Poet, whom attacked, is put in a Violent Passion.* Hence Horace, Genus irritabile Vatum. REM. CRIT.]

(20) *This has been communicated to me by Mr de la Monnoie.*

(21) Anthol. lib. 2. c. 25. See also Salmasius, Exercit. Plinian. pag. 394, 395.

[D] *Some pretend, that three of* Lycambes's *Daughter: died at the same time of Grief and Despair.*] I have said, that *Archilochus* took the matter to heart; but his Grief was nothing in comparison to what his Father-in-law, and Mistress, suffered. He gave himself Ease by a bitter Invective, but *Lycambes*, and his Daughters, found their Consolation only in an Halter. *Horace* mentions only the Father's Destiny, and That of the Daughter, who was promised to *Archilochus*.

— — — non res & agentia verba Lycambem;

Nec socerum quærit, quem versibus oblinet atris;
Nec sponsæ laqueum famoso carmine nectit (22).

I match'd Archilochus; *I show'd the Age
His Numbers; but forbore his murth'ring Rage.*

*With no black Lines I daub, no envious Breath
Doth foil Men's Fame, or rhime a Spouse to Death.*

CREECH.

(22) Horat. Epist. 19. lib. 1. ver. 25, 30, 31.

But,

chus [E]. Some have said, that he himself was banished from *Lacedemon* (b); but the Reason they give for it is taken from a Maxim, which he inserted in one of his Poems, *That it is better to throw down one's Arms, than to lose one's Life.* He wrote This in his own Justification (c). His Calumny, which was sometimes an Inconvenience to him in his Affairs [F], and which extended even to his own Person [G], did not deprive him of the Favour of *Apollo*; for, upon his being killed in Battel, the Oracle of *Delphi* drove his Murtherer out of the Temple [H]; nor could it be appeased but by dint of Excuse and Prayer; and even, after this, ordered him to repair to a certain House, and there appease the Ghost of *Archilochus*.

(b) Plutarch. Instit. Lacon. p. 239.
(c) See Remark [C].

But, in the *Anthologia*, we read, that two, or even three, Daughters of *Lycambes* hanged themselves (23). See, in the Article HIPPONAX (24), some Instances of the tragical and mortal Effects of Satire. Let us not omit what a Scholiast on *Horace* observes; to wit, that *Neobula* (so he calls the Daughter, who was contracted to *Archilochus*) did not hang herself on account of her Gallant's Satire, but out of Grief for the miserable Catastrophe of her Father's Life (25). Most Readers will take part with the *Anthologia*; in which *Archilochus* is represented as the immediate Cause.

[E] *It was on occasion of This Satire, that the Lacedemonians - - - - prohibited the Verses of Archilochus.*] *Valerius Maximus* affirms this in express Terms. "Lacedæmonii libros Archilochi è civitate " sua exportari jusserunt, quod eorum parum vere- " cundam ac pudicam lectionem arbitrabantur. No- " luerunt enim ea liberorum suorum animos imbui, " ne plus moribus noceret, quam ingeniis prodesset. " Itaque maximum poëtam, aut certe summo proxi- " mum, quia domum sibi invisam obscenis maledi- " ctis laceraverat, carminum exilio multarunt (26). " - - - - - *The Lacedemonians ordered the Books of* " *Archilochus to be banished from their State, esteem-* " *ing the reading of them to be vicious and immodest.* " *They were unwilling the Minds of their Youth* " *should be tinctured with them, least their Morals* " *should be more injured, than their Genius im-* " *proved, thereby. They therefore punished the greatest* " *of Poets, or next to the greatest, for an obscene* " *Satire on a Family, whom he hated, by banishing* " *his Verses.*"

[F] *His Calumny - - - - - - was often an Inconvenience to him in his Affairs.*] *Pindar* informs me of this particular; for he affirms, that, though *Archilochus* fattened upon Slander, yet was he often put to his Shifts.

Εἶδον γὰρ ἑκὰς ἐὼν τὰ πολ-
λ᾽ ἐν ἀμαχανία
Ψογερὸν Ἀρχίλοχον, βαρυλό-
γοις ἔχθεσιν πιαινόμενον (27).

Vidi enim procul existens saepe in angustiis conviciatorem Archilochum, dum maledicis odiis pinguesceret.

Aretius did not understand this Passage; since he took it to mean, that *Archilochus* was a Gainer by his Calumny, and raised himself by it from a low Estate to Honour and Riches (28). The Word πιαινυσθαι, which signifies *to fatten*, deceived him; he should have remember'd, that, to this Day, *to feed*, or *grow fat*, upon any thing signifies, figuratively, to take an extraordinary Pleasure in it. No doubt *Ovid* had an Eye to this Passage of *Pindar*, when, in his Poem in *Ibin*, he says,

Utque repertori nocuit pugnacis Iambi,
Sic sit in exitium lingua proterva tuum.

*Like His, who first the keen Iambic gave,
May thy abusive Tongue thy Ruin prove.*

We shall see in the Remark [H], that they, who pretend, that Calumny cost *Archilochus* his Life (29), are mistaken.

[G] *His Calumny - - - - - - extended even to his own Person.*] This Poet took such strange Delight in Slander, that, not content to push his Neighbour to pieces, he could not forbear defaming himself (30). For which *Critias* blames him (31); saying, that, had it not been for his own account, we should not have known, that his Mother *Enipone* was a Slave; that meer Poverty forced him to quit the Isle of

Paros, and remove to That of Thasus; that he rendered himself odious there by slandering both Friends, and Foes; that he was extreamly addicted to Women, and very insolent; and, what is worst of all (32), *that he had thrown away his Buckler in Fight.* The Scholiast on *Aristophanes* informs us, that it was in the War against the *Saians*, a People of *Thrace*, that *Archilochus* threw down his Arms, and fled (33). *Aristophanes* has borrowed a Distich of This Poet's concerning this Adventure (34); upon which his Scholiast gives us this Gloss. *Plutarch* repeats the same Verses, and something more.

Ἀσπίδι μὲν Σαίων τις ἀγάλλεται ἣν περὶ θάμνῳ
Ἐντὸς ἀμώμητον κάλλιπον οὐκ ἐθέλων.
- - - - - - - - - - Ἄσπις ἐκείνη
Ἐῤῥέτω· ἐξαῦτις κτήσομαι οὐ κακίω (35).

One of the Saians, perhaps, now prides himself in wearing my Shield; which I unwillingly left behind me, unhurt, amidst the Brier. No matter for the Loss of This Shield; I shall soon purchase as good an one.

Yet our Run-away valued himself more upon being a Soldier, than a Poet.

Εἰμὶ δ᾽ ἐγὼ θεράπων μὲν Ἐνυαλίοιο ἄνακτος,
Καὶ μυσῶν ἐρατὸν δῶρον ἐπιστάμενος (36).

I am a Follower of the God of War, and skilled in the amiable Gift of the Muses.

Alcæus ranged the Posts of Honour after the same manner; he gave the first Place to Arms; and, in describing his House (37), he makes no mention of Books, but of Helmets and Bucklers; all favours of the Arsenal, and not of the Library. Yet it is well known, that he saved himself in Battel by the help of his Heels, and not his Arms. See the Remark [B] of his Article.

[H] *Apollo - - - - drove his Murtherer out of the Temple* (38)] The Name of Him, who slew *Archilochus*, was *Callondas Corax* (39), a Native of the Isle of *Naxos*. The Priestess of *Delphi* drove him out of the Temple, because he had killed a Man consecrated to the Muses. "Ἐκβληθεὶς ὑπὸ τῆς Πυθίας, ὡς ἱερὸν ἄνδρα τῶν μυσῶν ἀνῃρηκώς (40). And yet he had killed him in War, and in fair Combat; as appears more plainly from *Suidas*, than *Plutarch*. For this Reason we cannot suppose, that *Pliny*, upon this Occasion, is sufficiently exact, when he said, in the plural Number, *Archilochi poëtæ interfectores Apollo arguit Delphis* (41). - - - - *Apollo at Delphi accused Those, who had slain Archilochus the Poet.* His Copyer *Solinus*, affecting the Paraphrast, has left himself without excuse; since he has the boldness to say, that this Poet was killed by Robbers; " *Percussores Archilochi poëtæ Apollo prodidit,* & " *latronum facinus Deo coarguente detectum* (42). " - - - - - *Apollo discovered the Murtherers of Ar-* " *chilochus the Poet; thus the Villany of certain* " *Robbers was detected by the Evidence of a God.*" *Eusebius* cites a *Greek* Author, called *Oenomaus*, who gives the Name of *Archias* to the Murtherer of *Archilochus*; " Quare qui Archilochum occidit Archias " à templo quasi scelestus exire ab Apolline jussus " est: musarum enim amicum occiderat (43). - - - - " *Wherefore Archias, who slew Archilochus, was* " *commanded by Apollo to depart from the Temple,* " *as one guilty of Impiety; for he had slain a Friend* " *of the Muses.*" *Galen* has reported the Words of the Oracle.

Μυζῶν

ARCHILOCHUS.

Archilochus (d). And yet this Person had killed him in a fair Combat [*I*]. Iambic Verse was what this Poet excelled in; he was the Inventor of it [*K*], and one of the three Poets, whom *Aristarchus* approved of in this kind of Poetry (e). *Quintilian* places him, in some Respects, above the other two. *Aristophanes*, the Grammarian, was of Opinion, that *Archilochus*'s Iambic Poems, the longer they were, were the finer [*L*]. The Hymn, he composed on *Hercules* and *Iolaus*, was so distinguished, as to be constantly sung three times, in honour of those, who gained the Victory in the Olympic Games (f). Scarce any thing remains of his Works; which, for the sake of Morals, is rather a Gain, than a Loss, [*M*]. They, who speak of several

---

Μυζῶν θεράποντα καθίκτανες, ἐξιθι νηῦ (44).

You have slain a Servant of the Muses; depart from the Temple.

Apollo has been much blamed for acknowledging as a Son of the Muses, and extreamly commending, a Poet, who had written so obscenely. *Oenomaus* reproached This God with This (45): *Origen* and *Eusebius* make use it to shame the Pagans. Τοῦτος προσθῶμεν, says *Eusebius* (46), καὶ δι᾽ ὃν αὐθις ὁ Ἀπόλλων θαυμάζει τὸν Ἀρχίλοχον, ἄνδρα παντοίαις κατὰ γυναικῶν αἰσχρηιθμοζύναις καὶ ἀῤῥηθολογίαις ὡς ἰσ᾽ ἀκούσαι τις σώφρων ἀνήρ ὑπομείνειεν, ἐν τοῖς οἰκείοις ποιήμασι κεχρημένον. Let me add what greatly recommended *Archilochus* to the Favour of *Apollo*; a Poet *so infamous and obscene, that no good Man can bear to hear him*. I omit the Passage of *Origen*; it may be found in his third Book against *Celsus*, in the hundred and twenty fifth Page of the *Cambridge* Edition, 1677.

[*K*] *This Person had killed him in a fair Combat*] I have already observed, that *Suidas* informs us more clearly of this Matter, than *Plutarch*; but I have something to add, which is worth our notice. There is a small Treatise *Of Republics*, attributed to *Heraclides*; in which the Order of the Priestess is to be found, commanding the Murtherer of *Archilochus* to depart the Temple, together with the Murtherer's Answer. This Answer is an inexplicable Riddle in the *Latin* Translation. The Translator supposes, that the Murtherer answered, *I am innocent, for I killed him at a Distance, as the Law commands*. Read the *Greek*, and the Translation of it (47): Ἀρχίλοχον τὸν ποιητὴν Κόραξ ὄνομα ἔχων, πρὸς ὃν φασιν εἰπεῖν τὴν Πυθίαν, ἐξιθι νηῦ. τοῦτον δὲ εἰπεῖν, ἀλλὰ καθαρὸς εἰμι ἄναξ, ἐκ χειρῶν γὰρ νόμῳ ἔκτεινα. *Quidam Corax dictus Archilochum poëtam interfecit. Itaque Pythia ad eum aiebat, exi templo. Cui is respondit, at purus sum Rex, eminus enim, ut lex jubet, interfeci* (Archilochum). A Friend of mine, who is well versed in Philological Learning (48), has confessed to me, that he never heard of an Edict, acquitting Murtherers, who killed at a Distance; and that he did not believe ἐκ χειρῶν signified *eminus*. As he was an intimate Friend of Mr *Gronovius*'s, he consulted him on This Difficulty; and This was the learned Answer of That learned Professor. "Ἐν χειρῶν νόμῳ, locutio est propria in prœliis occi-"forum & occidentium. Quem in illo fervore vel "gladius, vel alia machina deprehendens ad Orcum "mittit, is trucidatur ἐν χειρῶν νόμῳ. Ita omnes "Græci, & præsertim Polybius, ut libro 1. cap. 34. "Καταπαθέμενος σωρηδὸν ἐν χειρῶν νόμῳ διε- "φθείροντο. Ὁ πᾶσιν (49) *illic pugnantes: quod* "*quidem non sufficit, nam & in prælio multi pos-* "*sunt non pugnantes occidi, & tamen* ἐν χειρῶν "νόμῳ. Rursus eodem libro cap. 57. Τάτας γὰρ "αὐταὶ ἀεὶ συνέβαινε διαφθείρεσθαι κατὰ τὰς "συμπλοκὰς τᾶς ἐν χειρῶν νόμῳ περιστεφόντας. "- - - Ἐν χειρῶν νόμῳ *is a Phrase belonging to Those* "*who kill, or are killed, in Battel. Whoever, in* "*the Heat of Battel, is killed by a Sword, or any* "*other Engine, is said to be killed* ἐν χειρῶν νό- "μῳ. *So all the Greek Authors; particularly Po-* "*lybius*, lib. 1. cap. 34. Καταπαθέμενοι, &c. Ca- "saubon *renders it* pugnantes: *which is insufficient;* "*for many may die in Battel, not fighting, and yet* "ἐν χειρῶν νόμῳ. *Again, in the same Book*, cap. "57. Τάτας γὰρ αὐταῖς, &c." There remains no farther Difficulty, after this learned Answer; whereby it appears, that *Corax* meant no more, than that he had killed *Archilochus* in Battel, according to the Laws of War.

[*K*] *He was the Inventor of Iambic Verse*.] This appears from these Lines of *Horace*, in the nineteenth Epistle of the first Book, ver. 23.

- - - - - parios ego primus Iambos
Ostendi Latio, numeros animosque secutus
Archilochi;

I first the Romans keen Iambics taught.
In numerous Smoothness, and in height of Thought
I match'd Archilochus; CREECH.

But yet more clearly from this Passage of *Paterculus*. "Neque quemquam alium cujus operis primus auctor "fuerit in eo perfectissimum præter Homerum & "Archilochum reperiemus (50). - - - - - Homer and "Archilochus alone arrived at Perfection in those "Species of Poetry, of which they were the respective "Inventors." It is certain, that *Iambics* were This Poet's Master-piece. "Ex tribus receptis Aristarchi "judicio scriptoribus Iamborum ad ἔξιν maxime "pertinebit unus *Archilochus*. Summa in hoc vis "elocutionis; cum validis atque brevibus vibrantèsque "sententiæ; plurimum sanguinis atque nervorum; "adeo ut videatur quibusdam, quod quoquam minor "est, materiæ esse non ingenii vitium (51). - - - - *Of* "*the three received Writers of Iambics,* (*in the Opi-* "*nion of Aristarchus*) *Archlochus alone arrived at* "*Perfection. This Poet was Master of the greatest Force* "*of Expression; his Sentences were short and sprightly;* "*in sinews, that many think, if he fell short of any Poet,* "*it was owing to the Defect of his Subject, n.t of his* "*Genius*." *Paterculus*, then, made him the Inventor of Iambics. But he must also have been the Inventor of Epic Poetry, if what is imputed to *Terentianus* be true: "Doctrinæ laudem ei Terentianus tribuit, ut & "Epicorum versuum inventionem, libr. de metris, pag. "86. - Terentianus, *in his Book* Of Metres, *ascribes to* "*him the Praise of Learning, as also the Invention* "*of Epic Poetry*." Thus they speak in the *Thesaurus Fabri*, in the Article of *Archilochus*; but, when we consult the Passage of *Terentianus Maurus*, it is easy to perceive, that the Matter in hand there is the Epode, not the Epic Poem; nor yet would it be certain, that the Passage, which relates to *Archilochus*, declares him the Inventor of the Epode, if This Truth were not learnt elsewhere (52). This Passage might pass for a Citation alledged as an Example of the Epode, spoken of in this Place, which is an *Hexameter* Verse followed by one half of a mat. Pentameter.

Hoc doctum Archilochum tradunt genuisse Magistri,
Tu mihi Flacce sat es.

Lorenzo Fabri observes, that "the *Greeks* for six "hundred Years knew no other than Hexameter "Verse; 'till *Archilochus* taught other kinds with "so much Success, that all began to try their Skill "in Verses of different Measures; which made the "*Greek* Poetry so fine by this Variety of Versifica- "tion (53).

[*L*] *Archilochus's Iambics - - - - - - the longer they were, were the finer*] *Cicero* informs us of this Particular, where he applies it to his Friend *Atticus*'s Letters; "Ut Aristophani Archilochi Iambus, "sic Epistola longissima quæque optima videtur (54). "- - - - - *As the Iambics* of Archilochus *appeared* "*to* Aristophanes, *so the longest of your Epistles seem* "*to me the best*." The same Judgment has been passed upon *Demosthenes*'s Orations.

[*M*] *Scarce any thing remains of his Works; which, for the sake of Morals, is rather a Gain, than a Loss*] The Verses of *Archilochus* afforded no Examples,

several *Archilochus*'s, multiply Beings without Necessity [*N*]. If we had the Dialogue composed by *Heraclides* (g) on the Life of our Poet, we might, in all Probability, find several Particulars in it concerning him; and doubtless we might there find, how he conducted a Colony of *Parians* into the Island of *Thasus* (b). It was some Honour to be chosen for such a Trust.

amples, but what were vitious. He had expressed a deep Sorrow at the loss of his Sister's Husband, who died at Sea. This Tenderness might have been improved to an excellent Lesson; but in him it degenerated into a most pernicious Maxim, *viz.* that he would fly for Consolation to Wine, and other sensual Pleasures, since his Tears could do his Brother-in-law no good, nor his Pleasures harm.

Οὔ τέ τι γὰρ κλαίων ἰάσομαι, ὅτε κάκιον θήσω, τερπωλὰς καὶ θαλίας ἐρέπων (55).

The worst is, that he never scrupled to defame himself, and fill his Poems with a thousand scandalous Reflexions on the Sex. Τῶν ὑπ' Ἀρχιλόχου πρὸς τὰς γυναῖκας ἀτρεπῶς καὶ ἀκολάστως εἰρημένων, ἑαυτὸν παραδειγματίζοντ@ (56). See the use, which *Theodore Beza* makes of this last Sentence in his Notes on the first Chapter of St *Matthew*.

[*N*] *They, who speak of several* Archilochus*'s, multiply Beings without Necessity.*] A Passage of *Eusebius*, misunderstood, occasion'd the mention of an *Archilochus*, an Historian and Chronologer, on whom the Impostor of *Viterbo* had the boldness to father a small Book. Thus *Eusebius* speaks, according to the *Latin* Translation, *Licet Archilochus vicesimam tertiam Olympiadem ——— supputet* (57). It is pretended, that the meaning of this is, that, according to *Archilochus*'s Computation, *Homer* lived in the XXIIId Olympiad. But *Scaliger* has shewed, that the *Greek* of *Eusebius* signifies no more, than that some Authors made *Homer* and *Archilochus* flourish at the same time. *Goropius Becanus* had cleared up this Matter before, in the great and curious Collection relating to *Archilochus*, which he made on purpose to confute the Impostures of *Annius of Viterbo* (58). Thus the pretended Chronologer *Archilochus* comes to nothing. *Vossius* would have done better to have followed this Correction, than to place *Archilochus* among the *Greek* Historians (59). He adds, that *Scaliger* places him in the Reign of *Darius*, the Son of *Hystaspes* (60), without producing any Proof for it. I cannot find in *Scaliger*'s Notes, what *Vossius* imputes to him; neither do I believe he has said any such thing. *Vossius*, having made mention of our Poet *Archilochus*, in another Book (61), under the XXIXth Olympiad, promises another under the XCIVth. But, when we look for him there, we meet with only *An Antilochus*. *Charles Stephens*, *Lloyd*, and *Hofman*, have given us a *Lacedemonian* Poet *Archilochus*, who flourished at *Rome*, in the Reign of *Tullus Hostilius*, and another *Archilochus*, the Son of *Nestor*, who was kill'd by *Memnon* at the Siege of *Troy*. These are all Chimæra's; This last was cal'd *Antilochus*; and there needed but little Attention, to discover, that the Court of the first Kings of *Rome* was no fit Theatre for *Greek* Poets. Most of these last Faults are to be found in *Calepin*.

ARCHIMELUS, a *Greek* Poet, flourished in the Reign of *Hiero*, King of *Syracuse* [*A*]. This appears by the Present, which he received from That Monarch. He had made an Epigram in praise of a prodigious large Ship, which *Hiero* had ordered to be built (a). This Epigram was worth to him above Five thousand Quarters of Corn, which this Prince sent him to the *Pyreum* (b). Behold, then, a Poet, who may be ranked among the Few, who have met with *Admirals de Joyeuse* (c).

[*A*] *He flourish'd in the Time of* Hiero, *King of Syracuse.*] That is about the Year of *Rome* 520, and the CXXXVIth Olympiad. It is probable, that he lived at *Athens*; since this Present of Corn was carried to the *Pyreum*. I wonder *Vossius* could forget this Poet: The Reward of his Epigram makes him remarkable. *Athenæus* has preserved the Eighteen Verses, which were so amply paid for (1). Mr *Catherinot* has not faithfully reported the Circumstances of This Recompence; he says, that (2), Archimelus *was rewarded by King* Hiero *with Thirty thousand Quarters of Corn, for an Epigram of Twenty Verses, written on his Ship.*

ARCHIROTA (ALEXANDER) [*A*] Abbot of the *Olivetans* (a), was of *Naples*. He composed, among other Books, *A Collection of the Actions of the Kings*, mentioned in the Scripture [*B*], and dedicated it to the Queen of *Poland*, *Bonna Sforza*, who resided, then, at *Bari*. In return, she gave him a Pension for Life of Three hundred Crowns *per Annum*. He lived an Hundred and twenty Years (b). *Konig* makes him flourish in 1636, and ascribes to him *A Commentary on the Books of Samuel and Kings*, and *A Treatise on the Vow of Poverty*.

[*A*] ALEXANDER.] *Lancelot of Perousa*, in the Body of his Work, entitled, *Chi l'indovina, e savio — The Soothsayer or Philosopher —* tells us, that This Person's Name was *Alexander*; but in the Margin, and *Table of Matters*, he calls him *Agostino, Augustin*. [*B*] *A Collection of the Actions of the Kings, mentioned in the Scripture.*] This Work was composed in *Italian*. I know not whether it be the same with That entitled, *Discorsi sopra diversi Luoghi della sacra Scrittura ——— Discourses on different Passages of Holy Writ*. The Catalogue of *Oxford* remarks, that it is divided into two Parts; the first of which was printed at *Florence*, in 1581, in 8vo; and the second, in the same City, in 1583, in 8vo. We find, in the same Catalogue, that the Treatise *De Voto Paupertatis, Of the Vow of Poverty*, appeared at *Florence*, in 1580, in 8vo; and that the Author of these three Works was called *Alexander Archirola*. I believe it should be *Archirota*.

ARETIN (CHARLES) was of *Arezzo* in *Tuscany*, as his Sirname testifies (which apply to the other *Aretin*'s). He held a considerable Rank among the Learned of the XVth Century. *Poggius* gives him great Encomiums (a); but they ought to be suspected, because *Charles Aretin* was a great Enemy of *Philelphus*, whom *Poggius* mortally hated. *Philelphus* complains bitterly of our *Aretin*, and represents him as a wicked Man, full of Frauds and malicious Arts (b). This likewise ought to be suspected, as coming from such an Enemy as *Philelphus*; who, being naturally given to slander, became much more so, on account of the Contests he had with some other learned Men. Be that as it will, there are disinterested Persons,

ARETIN. 429

sons, who say, that *Charles Aretin* understood the *Latin* and *Greek* Tongues perfectly well, and that he shewed it by some Translations from the *Greek* (c). He was, besides, a tolerable good Poet [*A*], and wrote *Comedies* in Prose; some Parts of which are inserted by *Albert Eyb*, in his *Marguerite Poëtique* (d). But, what discovers his Abilities most, is, his having been chosen to succeed in the Post of Secretary to the Republic of *Florence*, after the Death of *Leonard Aretin*, in 1443 [*B*]. We do not know the Year of his Death; but Mr *Moreri* is certainly mistaken, when he places it in the Year 1443 [*C*]. The Authors, he quotes, do not say, that our *Aretin* left a Volume of Letters. Some have thought he was the Brother of *John Aretin* (e), of whom we shall speak in his Place. But they are mistaken: He was very ambitious of equalling the Reputation of *Leonard Aretin*, his Predecessor (f).

[*A*] *He was a tolerable Poet.*] This must be understood in regard to those Times; and I question not, with this Restriction, to establish my Text: for thus Mr *de la Monnoie* writes to me: Lilius Gyraldus, *who had seen* Charles Aretin's *Poems, did not find them good; and in Truth, from the Quotations to be seen of them in the Dictionary of* Tortellius, *there is Reason to judge, that they are little worth. Note, that* Tortellius *quotes nothing of Him but Elegiac Verses; but Father* Labbe, * *in two or three Places, cites a Translation of the* Batrachomyomachia, *in Hexameter Verse, by* Charles Aretin.

[*B*] *He was chosen to succeed* Leonard Aretin.] This we have from *Leander Albertus*. " Diem functus est (*Leonardus Aretinus*) anno post C. N. " MCCCCXL, ætatis suæ LXXIV, Florentiæ, " cum illi Reipub. diu à secretis fuisset, & successorem in eo munere habuit Carolum item Aretinum, " & Græcis Latinisque literis eruditissimum, qui etiam ipse quædam de Græciis Latina fecit (1). — *Leonard Aretin died in the Year of Christ* 1440, *aged Seventy four Years, at* Florence; *having been a long time Secretary to That Republic; and was succeeded in That Employ by* Charles Aretin, *a Person well skilled in* Greek *and* Latin, *and who had translated some Pieces out of* Greek *into* Latin". To this Testimony let us add That of *Æneas Silvius*, tho' somewhat long; because it will serve as a Proof of more than one Thing; " Commendanda " est, says he (2), multis in rebus Florentinorum prudentia, tum maxime quod in legendis Cancellariis " non juris scientiam, ut pleræque civitates, sed " oratorium spectant, & quæ vocant humanitatis studia. Norunt enim recte scribendi dicendique artem non Bartolum aut Innocentium, sed Tullium " Quintilianumque tradere. Nos tres ex ea urbe cognovimus, Græcis & Latinis & conditorum operum " fama illustres, qui Cancellariam alius post alium " tenuere, Leonardum & Carolum Aretinos, & Poggium ejusdem reipublicæ civem, qui Secretarius " Apostolicus tribus quondam Pontificibus dictarat " Epistolas. —— *The Prudence of the* Florentines *is to be commended in many things; particularly in the Choice of their Secretaries; in whom they do not require, as many States do, a knowledge of Law, but Oratory and Polite Learning. For they are sensible, that the Art of Writing and Speaking well is not to be learned from* Bartolus, *or* Innocentius, *but from* Cicero. *I have been acquainted with Three successive Secretaries of That City, all famous for their knowledge in* Greek *and* Latin, *and the*

" *Works they have composed; to wit*, Leonard *and* " Charles Aretin, *and* Poggius, *a Citizen of the same* " *Republic, who had formerly, in quality of* Apostolical " *Secretary, dispatched the Briefs of three successive* " *Popes.*" By this Passage the Obscurity, or Error, of another Passage of *Æneas Silvius*, which gave *Vossius* a great deal of trouble, may be corrected. It is this: " Leonardum Aretinum ex te primum " sensi obiisse, qui Latium ornavit literis, quo nemo " post Lactantium Ciceroni proximior fuit. Gaudeo Poggium ejus locum apud Florentinos tenere. " Sed maluissem potius locum non vacasse, ne tanto " splendore caruisset Hetruris (3). —— *You first inform me of the Death of* Leonard Aretin, *who, by his Learning, was an Ornament to* Italy; *and of who, after* Lactantius, *came the nearest to* Cicero. *I rejoice, that* Poggius *succeeds him at* Florence; *but should have been better pleased, that the Post had not been vacant, that* Hetruria *might not have lost so great an Ornament.*" See the Remark [*d*] of the Article ARETIN (LEONARD).

[*C*] *Moreri is mistaken, when he places it in the Year* 1443.] It is certain, that *Poggius* succeeded our *Aretin* in the Employ of Secretary at *Florence*. Now it appears by the Speech, in which he congratulates *Nicholas* the Vth on his Promotion to the Papacy, that he had no Employ at *Florence* in 1447 (4). It must be supposed, then, that *Charles Aretin* was Secretary of *Florence* in 1447: for his Predecessor *Leonard Aretin* died in 1443. But there is a more Demonstrative Proof of Mr *Moreri's* Error. *Poggius*, in a Letter written in the Pontificate of *Nicholas* V, says, that *Charles Aretin* had paid him a Visit; at the same time, when *Nicholas* V. had retired for fear of the Plague, and himself and Family had left *Rome*. Quo primum anno, says he (5), Nicolaus Pontifex quintus, pestis causa, Fabrianum, Piceni oppidum, secessit, cum me ad Terram novam natalem patriam cum familia contulissem, venit eo postmodum rogatus à me, qui Florentinam ob negotia publica adibat, Carolus Aretinus. What lead Mr *Moreri* into a Mistake, was his finding, that (6) *Vossius* does not refute the *German* Author, whom he quotes, and who had said, in his Collections of the Days of Death, and of Nativity, that *Charles Aretin*, the Orator and Historian, died in 1443, at Seventy Four Years of Age. All this agrees so well with *Leonard Aretin*, that, in all Probability, the *German* Author has confounded *Charles* with *Leonard*: However *Vossius* ought to have shewn him his Mistake in relation to the Year of our *Aretin's* Death.

ARETIN (FRANCIS) lived in the XVth Century. He was a Man of great Reading, and understood the *Greek* Tongue. He translated the Commentaries of St *Chrysostom* on St *John*, and twenty of the same Father's Homilies, into *Latin*. He translated also the Epistles of *Phalaris* into *Latin* [*A*]. There is still extant a Treatise of his, *de Balneis Puteolanis*; —— *of the Baths of* Puteoli. *John Antony Campanus*, who was a Favourite of *Pius* II, and *Sixtus* IV, was one of his intimate Friends (a). *Erasmus* did not esteem our *Aretin's* Translations of St *Chrysostom* [*B*]. Some

[*A*] *He translated also the Epistles of* Phalaris *into* Latin.] I have met with several curious Reflexions on these Letters in a Book printed in *Germany*, in 1689 (1); but I must not suppress, that what is only due to *Francis*, is attributed to *Leonard Aretin*. " Latinè emisit Leonhardus Aretinus Florentiæ " MCCCCLXXX. —— *Published by* Leonard Aretin, *at* Florence, 1480". We shall see, in its ARETIN Place (2) that *Leonard* was not living at the Time of That Edition.

[*B*] Erasmus *did not esteem our* Aretin's *Translations.*] He observes, in two Places, the Error, which This Translator is guilty of, in relation to the Word οἵνιγες, in translating the Commentary on the First Epistle to the *Corinthians*. " Quod attinet ad fidem bene reddendi Græca, magis peccatum est ab Aniano, Aretino, & cæteris, quam ab " Oecolampadio, qui magis peccat festinatione quam " imperitia. Versionem Francisci Aretini in priorem " ad Corinth. habemus usque ad cap. 30. Cepi gu-" stum

ARETIN.

Some believe, that our *Francis Aretin* is the same with the famous Lawyer *Franciscus Aretinus*, of the Family of the *Accolti*. But others can scarce believe, that the Translator of some of St *Chrysostom's* Works, &c. is the same *Francis Aretin*, whose Works of Law savour of the grossest Barbarity, without the least Shadow of Knowledge in the *Greek* Tongue. I have some Observations to offer on this Head, which may serve to convince many People, that there is but one *Francis Aretin* in the Case [C]. Be that as it will, let us here speak of *Aretin* the Lawyer. He studied

---

(1) *Præf.* Eccl. 50, lib. 26, pag. 14, &c. See also Epist. 4, lib. 28, pag. 1591.

(4) Pag. 1591.

(5) *Panzir. de Claris legum Interpr.* lib. 2, cap. 103, pag. 243.

(6) Mr de la Monnoie, Remarques MSS.

"stum quam ſuiſt tractaſſet rem, & ecce in ipſo ſtatim limine, quod eſt τον τυϛον καιϛαλας και νομαλ ϑϕεϛως ωατερ αναυνοναν, cineris opinionem vertit pro arrogantia (3).——*As to translating Greek faithfully,* Anianus, *Aretin,* and *others, are more guilty in this respect, than* Oecolampadius, *who offends more thro' Haste, than Unskilfulness. We have the translation of* Aretin *on the first to the* Corinthians, *as far as the 30th Chapter. I immediately perceived how hastily be performed this Work ; for, in the very beginning of it, be renders* οινεις *by* Opinio (Opinion) *instead of* Arrogantia (Arrogance)." He observes, in another Place (4), that *Aret.n* had translated the Commentaries on the First Epistle to the *Corinthians* to the Twentieth Homily.

[C] *I have some Observations to offer on this head, which may serve to convince many People, that there is but one* Francis Aretin *in the case.*] Let us first propose *Panzirolus's* Doubt. " *Liberalibus artibus imbutus, non solum Latinis, sed etiam Græcis literis operam dedisse creditur, & Joannis Chrysostomi in D. Joannem & epistolam primam Pauli ad Corinthios commentaria Latina fecisse; verēor tamen ne la sit* Accolitus, *cum quæ in jure scripsit, illum stylum non oleant, neque ullam ſervent reliquæ Græcæ vestigium (5).——Being a polite Scholar, he is said not only to have studied the* Latin, *but the* Greek *Tongue likewise, and to have translated into* Latin *St* Chrysostom *on St* John, *and St* Paul's *First Epistle to the* Corinthians ; *tho' I much question whether he be the* Accolitus *Aretinus, since what That Author has wrote in the Law does not savour of this Style, nor preserves the least Traces of the* Greek *Tongue.*" Next let us see what Mr *de la Monnoie* writes to me on occasion of this Doubt (6). " *Francis Accolti d' Arezzo,* having written his *Concilia,* and other Works of the Law, in a Stile, " which discovers not only an entire Ignorance of " the *Greek,* but of the *Latin* likewise; I have " been in doubt, as well as *Panzirolus,* whether " This was the same *Francis d' Arezzo,* who has " given us *Greek* Translations, and whose Style is " not inferior to That of most of the *Humanists* of " his time. I knew, that the Lawyer took the " Name of *Accolti,* and the Titles of Doctor and " Knight, whereas the *Humanist* was simply called " *Franciscus Aretinus.* In the mean time, having " lately had the Sight of a Copy of *Francis Philelphus's* Epistles, printed at *Venice,* in Folio, in the " Year 1502 : a very scarce, and much ampler Edition, " than the Others, by Twenty one Books ; I found " a way of resolving my Doubt, upon Reading several of Those Epistles, in which the Author " speaks of one *Francis d' Arezzo,* his Disciple, " equally learned in the Law, and in polite Literature. The Time and Circumstances make it evidently appear, that he is the same, whom *Volaterran,* an almost Cotemporary Writer, mentions, at " the End of his 21st Book. Besides his Law Compositions, his Translations of St *Chrysostom,* of the " Epistles of *Phalaris,* and of Those of *Diogenes* the " Cynic, they attribute to him a Treatise of the " Baths of *Puteoli*; tho' he is not the Author of it, " nor was any farther concern'd, than in dedicating " it to Pope *Pius* the Second, by a Letter conceived in mean Expressions enough. He had also " composed a Book of the Life and Manners of " St *Antonin,* Archbishop of *Florence. Philelphus* " speaks with praise of this Work, in the Twelfth " Letter of his Seventeenth Book. In the Twenty " Eighth Book of Letters of the same *Philelphus,* " there are Six addressed *Francisco Aretino Equiti aurato ac Jurisconsulto,* then Professor of Law " in the University of *Sienna.* In most of these " Letters, he gives him high Commendations, a " great part of which might have been spared. " *Quasi dubitandum sit, says he to him in the First*

" *Letter,* minus tibi esse apud florentissimam istam " Rempub. secunda omnia, qui vir in omni eruditionis ac sapientiæ genere præstantissimus sis, atque ea " virtute præditus, qua non modo ex hominibus hujusce tempestatis nemini cedis, sed potes jure cum " universa antiquitate de laude contendere. ——*As if there were any room to doubt of your Success in That most flourishing Republick; you, who excel in every branch of Learning and Knowledge, and whose extraordinary Virtues not only raise you above the Moderns, but equal you to the most shining Characters of Antiquity.*" It appears by the Third, dated the 8th of *March* 1468, that *Francis* of *Arezzo* was then somewhat above Fifty Years of Age; a Reason he made use of to excuse himself from marrying ; Whereupon *Philelphus* tells him merrily : " *Nam quod ais sentire te debilitatas tibi esse corporis vires, cum sis quinquagenarius, aut paulo amplius, id nulla tibi causa accidit alia, quam quod ætatis robur remiseris, ut, quo tempore tendendus erat arcus, tum eum tu maxime relaxaveris. Quod si eam servasses mediocritatem, quam & Philosophi probant, & ego secutus sum, consuluisses tu sane & posteritati & tibi. —— As to what you plead, that you find your Strength decay'd, being now fifty Years of Age, or upwards, this proceeds from your not having exerted the Strength of your Youth; insomuch, that, when the Bow ought most to have been bent, you gave it the greatest Relaxation. Had you observed That Mediocrity, which the Philosophers approve of, and I have follow'd, it would have been for the Advantage both of your Self and Posterity.*" In the Fourth of the 28th, he enquires after his Studies : *Cæterum cupio ex te nosse quid rerum agas? Non enim satis tuo præstanti ingenio, singularique doctrinæ esse duco, quod doceas leges, & jus civile, nam hæc jam tibi nullius sunt industriæ, cujus memoria divina est potius quam humana. Majora quædam te arbitror meditari, nec enim in eodem semper versaris ludo, itaque fieri non potest, quin aliquid novi semper cudas excudasque. —— I desire you would inform me how you are employ'd? for your great Abilities and uncommon Learning cannot, I think, be satisfied with Teaching the Laws: a Study, which now requires no Industry in you, the memory of which is rather divine, than human: I cannot help believing, that your Thoughts are employ'd on something greater; for, as you do not confine your self to One Branch of Science, you must necessarily strike out something New.* " In the Fifth he desires him to get the " the History of *Ammianus Marcellinus* copied for " him in Parchment. In a Letter of the 29th Book, " he proposes the getting *Demetrius Castrenus,* of " *Constantinople,* entertain'd at *Sienna,* at the Charge " of the Republick, to instruct the Youth in the " *Greek* Tongue. In another Letter of the 31th " Book, he informs him of a Design the Senate of *Venice* had to get him from *Sienna,* and " give him a Chair at *Padua*; and adds, " *Ad hæc ego contra locutus sum, & quæ vera esse novi, & quibus te delectari existimavi, quippe qui non essem oblitus quæ mecum nuper, cum ad Octobrem Senæ fuissem, & de temperamento corporis tui, & de istius cœli, quantum ad te attinet, intemperie locutus fueras. — This Design I opposed, and declared what I knew, and what I thought was agreeable to your Inclinations; for I had not forgot the Conversation, which passed between us at Sienna, in the Month of October, in which you mentioned the State of your own Constitution, and the inconsistency of That Air with your Health.*" What is surprizing in this, is, his saying in the " same Letter, that *Francis* of *Arezzo* was an Enemy " to a barbarous Stile : " *Nec illud ſane præ erendum censui,* Appianum *Alexandrinum esse jam a me magna ex parte Latinum factum, quoniam*

ARETIN.

studied at *Sienna*, about the Year 1443 (b), and afterwards taught the Civil Law there, with such a Vivacity of Genius, that he was nick-named *the Prince of Subtilties*; and that the Subtilty of *Aretin* passed into a Proverb. He signalized himself in Talent chiefly in Disputation; for no one could resist him. He gave his Advice with such Confidence, that he made his Clients sure of their Cause: His Experience did not deceive him; for it was commonly said in Court, Such a Cause is condemned by *Aretin*, therefore it will be lost. He taught also in the Academy of *Pisa*, and in That of *Ferrara*. He went to *Rome* in the Pontificate of *Sixtus* IV, but continued not long there; for he quickly perceived, that the great Hopes he had built on his Reputation would be greatly disappointed. That Pope declared he would willingly give him the Dignity of a Cardinal, were he not loth to injure the Public, by taking so excellent a Professor from his School. When Age would not permit him to exercise all the Functions of his Employ, he was dispensed with from reading of Lectures; but his Salary was continued. Nevertheless he sometimes mounted the Chair; and, though his Lectures had lost their wonted Spirit, yet he had a great many Hearers; which was attributed to his Reputation. One Day, his Scholars being run to a public Shew, he perceived, that there were but forty Persons in his Auditory; and was in such a Passion, that he threw away his Book, and cried out aloud, Aretin *will never explain the Mystery of the Law to so few*. He went away abruptly, and would teach no more. He was naturally severe, and never kept a Servant above a Month or two; for he said, that *those, who were newly hired, served with most Diligence*. He was honoured with the Quality of a Knight; lived always a single Life, and very frugally; which gave him an Opportunity of acquiring a great Fortune. He was no less honoured for his Chastity, than for his Learning. The Reader will be pleased to know the Wife he employed to make his

(b) Pansirol. de Claris Legum Interpret. lib. 2, cap. 103, pag. 249, &c.

"tu nulla barbaria linguæ delectaris. —— *Nor did I think proper to omit, that I had translated into Latin the greatest part of* Appianus Alexandrinus, *because you are displeased with All Barbarism of Style*." Is it then to the Practice of the Age, that the barbarous Expressions of *Francis* of *Arezzo*, in his Writings on the Law, are to be imputed? To me it seems, that there is ground to believe, he industriously affected them; lest, endeavouring to pass for a more Polite Writer, he should not be thought so profound a Lawyer. I have perused some of his Pleadings, which are Barbarism in it self. The CXLIId has been much ridiculed; where, in Consequence of the Agreement, made between *Francis Sforza*, Duke of *Milan*, and *Lewis de Gonzaga*, Marquis of *Mantua*, that, if *Dorothy*, the Daughter of the Marquis, should be found without Deformity of Body, at the Age of Fourteen Years, she should be married to *Galeazzo*, the Duke's Son; he maintains, that the Duke had a Right to demand a Search by the Physicians, who should see, and feel, the Princess stark naked, wherever the Exigency of the Case might require. It appears, however, that this Examination, how grievous soever in the Execution, was demandable by Law; and it was accordingly demanded by the Duke, but refused by "the Marquis."

Having examin'd these Observations of Mr. *de la Monnoie*, I propos'd some other Doubts to him; and he confirm'd his opinion a-new in this manner. *You ought not to doubt in any wise, but that* Francis d'Arezzo, *Translator of some* Greek *Works, and* Francis d'Arezzo, *the Lawyer, whose Comments on the Law, and Pleadings, are extant, are one and the same Author.* Volterran, *who might have seen the Lawyer, allows him, besides his Learning in the Law, a considerable Attainment in the* Belles Lettres (7). Philelphus, *who wrote some Years before, says the same Thing. It appears by the Testimony of the* Epistles, *I have cited to you, that, in his Time, there was one* Franciscus Aretinus, *or* Arretinus *(as he himself, and others, always write) his Disciple, Knight, Lawyer, Professor of Civil Law in the University of* Sienna, *and One, who excell'd in all manner of Literature. I add this following Passage, to these I have already sent you. It is in the First Epistle of the Twenty sixth Book, which is an* Invective against Leodrisio Crivello. "At laudas Franciscum Arretinum, & jure quidem, "sed, ut arbitror, Arretinum. Egisti enim præter "ingenium, & consuetudinem tuam. At meretur "Franciscus Arretinus, cum sit tum Jureconsulto- "rum omnium præstantissimus, tum nullius præclaræ "disciplinæ ignarus. Tamen laudari à te flagitiorum "omnium scelerumque sentinâ dedecorosum est.

"Jubes ab illo ut discam: rectè mones; nam non ab "ipso solum, sed etiam abs te opso, fi quid boni af- "ferre posses, non invitus discerem. Sed cur, quem "tantopere laudas, non item imitaris? Ille prædicat "apud omnes discipulum se meum extitisse, mihique "tribuit tantas laudas, quantis vellem me non carere. "At eft te, inquis, omni doctrina præstantior. Non "eo inficias, neque fero graviter me à multis etiam "discipulis meis superari, id quod fine aliqua mea "laude fieri non potuerit, siquidem hi grati esse vo- "luere. —— *You commend* Francis Arretin, *and just- ly; tho' sure you was asleep, when you did so; for your Disposition and Practice never lead you to Panegyric.* Francis Arretin *deserves Commendation, as being a most skillful Lawyer, and a compleat Scholar. But it is a Disgrace to him to be praised by you, who are a Sink of all Villany and Wickedness. You bid me learn of him: your Advice is good; for I should readily receive Instruction, not only from him, but even from you, were it possible to learn any Good of you. But why do you not imitate a Man, whom you so greatly commend? He publickly declares himself to have been my Disciple, and bestows such Commendations on me, as I wish were due to me. But he excels me, you say, in every Branch of Learning. I confess it, nor am I displeased, that many of my Scholars surpass me; which very Thing cannot but tend in some Degree to my Praise; since They acknowledge themselves indebted to me for it.*" *This Letter is dated the First of* August *1465. At the same time* Janus Pannonius, *who studied, then, in* Italy, *address'd an Epigram to our* Francis d'Arezzo; *the Two first Verses of which were these*:

Francisce, interpres legum, ô Aretine, Sacrarum,
Nec minus Aonia nobilis in cithara.

Learn'd in the Sacred Laws, O Aretin,
Nor less renown'd on the Aonian *Lyre.*

It is certain, then, that this Professor of Civil Law at Sienna, *call'd* Francis d'Arezzo *or* Aretin, *was skill'd in polite Literature; and it is no less certain, that the Name of the same Professor's Family was* Accolti. *You may believe himself: For he subscribes himself at the Bottom of his* 118th *Pleading*, "Decretorum Doctor, Senis ordinariæ legens, & Il- "lustris D. Marchionis Estensis Consiliarius: —— *Doctor of Decretals, Professor at* Sienna, *and Counsellor of the Illustrious Marquis of* Este." *The Times agree.* Volaterran *says, That* Francis Aretin, *Humanist, and Civilian, was at* Rome *in the Pontificate of* Sixtus IV. Francis Accolti *wrote his Hundred and Sixty ninth Plea against the same* Sixtus, *in Favour of*

(7) These are the Words of Volaterran, at the end of the 21st Book, pag. 782. Alexander Imolensis, & Franciscus Aretinus, ambo scriptis excellentibus nuper relictis in memoriâ posteritatis vivent. Franciscus, præter jura, cæteras etiam liberales artes est adeptus, princeps seculi hujus habebatur. Xisti tempore magna expectatione in hanc urbem venit, pauloque post spe frustratus remigravit impari doctrinæ sapientia vitæ que instituto, cum in cœlibatu vixerit, ac operibus inhibuerit, quas cumulatissimas cognatis demum reliquit.

VOL. I.   5 Q

ARETIN.

his Disciples sensible, of how great Importance it is to keep a fair Reputation [D]. Though he had designed his Estate for the Maintenance of a College, yet he left it to his Relations (c). He had a Brother, who became very famous under the Name of BENEDICTUS ACCOLTUS ARETINUS [E]. I shall speak of him in one of the Remarks.

(c) Ibid.

of Lorenzo de Medicis, and the Florentines, whom That Pope had excommunicated for the Murther of the Archbishop of Pisa, and the Imprisonment of the Cardinal, his Great-Nephew. Volaterran *observes, That Francis Aretin, having gone to Rome with great views, stay'd there but a little while, finding that the Success did not answer his Expectation. From whence I infer, that Francis Accolti, who is the same with the Francis Aretin of Volaterran, undertook the more freely to write against Sixtus in Defence of the Florentines, as remembring, that this Pope had let him depart Rome, without acknowledging his Merit. Perhaps, likewise, the Reason of his not marrying was the Hopes he had entertain'd of some Ecclesiastical Dignity, as has been said of the Civilian Jason. There only remains the Doubt, arising from the Difference between the Style of Aretin, the Professor of Law, and That of Aretin, the Translator. It is true This Difference is very great; and, tho' the Translations he has left us are not, indeed, the most elegant Latin, yet, in comparison of his Civil-Law Works, they may be reputed more than Ciceronian. Had he endeavoured (as some Authors to divert themselves have) to* * Burlesque. *write in a Macaronic* * *Style, he could not have succeeded better.* Sunt etiam multi testes, *says he,* Concil. 83 qui viderunt squam bene ire ad molendinum, & ipsum bene molere, & flechariam ligminis bene in puncto. *And,* Concil. 13. Probatur per duos testes nostros, quod ista mulier gessit portaturam capitis secundum habitum nuptarum à sex annis citra. *The whole Book abounds with these Elegancies. The Orthography of the Words taken from the Greek is strangely perverted in it. We there find* Economus, emologatio, cyrothecæ, Grisogonus, emphitheota. *I have insinuated the Reason, which this Lawyer might have, for making use of these barbarisms, viz. that his Brethren did not write, or express themselves, otherwise; if his Language had been more correct, it would not have been understood by those of the Trade. Francis Aretin, or Accolti, which you please, could have express'd himself better; but he loved Money; and, if he had affected to employ the Papinian Style, he might have danced attendance in vain, and would have been generally abandon'd. The same Barbarism reign'd at that Time among the Divines and Physicians. They among them, who first attempted to introduce Politeness, were reckoned neither Divines, nor Physicians, but only Grammarians. They were scarce cured of this Prejudice in the Days of Ludovicus Vives. His Words are worth transcribing.*
" Quæ Lyranus, & Hugo scribunt (*says he,* lib. 1. de
" causis Corruptar. Art.) Theologia est, quæ Erasmus,
" Grammatica. Idem de Hieronymo, Ambrosio, Au-
" gustino, Hilario dicturi, nisi nomina obstarent ; tam-
" etsi hic etiam nescio quid mussant: Quod si Joan-
" nes Picus apologiam suam corrupto illo non scrip-
" sisset sermone, haud quaquam haberetur Theolo-
" gus, sed Grammaticus. Alciatus, Zasius, Canti-
" uncula, Grammatici sunt, cum de jure disputant ;
" Accursius est Jurisconsultus, vel cum interpretatur,
" *quæ,* id est, *&* ; *ait,* id est, *dixit ; seu,* id est, *aut.*
" ------*What* Lyranus *and* Hugo *write is Divinity ;
" What* Erasmus, *Grammar. They would say the
" same of* Jerom, Ambrosius, Austin, *and* Hilarius,
" *did not the Greatness of their Names silence them ;
" tho' even here they mutter I know not what. But if*
" Joannes Picus *had not written his Apology in that
" corrupt Style, he would have been considered, not*

" *as a Divine, but a Grammarian.* Alciatus, Zasius,
" Cantiuncula, *are Grammarians, when they dispute
" concerning Law ;* Accursius *is a Lawyer, when he
" interprets* quæ *by* et ; ait *by* dixit; *and* seu *by* aut."
So that, Sir, there was a Kind of Necessity on Francis Aretin, *the Lawyer, to conform to the Practice of his Time ; and I think these Reflexions, together with the Proceeding, may suffice to persuade you, that he only differs from the Humanists in Point of Elocution.*

[D] *The Wile he employed to make his Disciples sensible, of how great Importance it is to keep a fair Reputation.*] When he found, that the frequent Exhortations he gave them to preserve a good Reputation, availed nothing, he made use of the following Stratagem. Ubi (Ferrariæ) *studiosos ad famam boni nominis conservandam sæpe hortatus, cum nihil proficeret, ridiculum commentum excogitavit, ut quam vim maximum habeat existimatio ostenderet* (8). The Butchers of Ferrara left their Meat all Night in the Shambles. He went thither with his Lacquey before Day, and, having broke open their Boxes, carried off all the Meat. Two of his Scholars, who were reputed the most unlucky, were accused of This Action, and imprisoned. Aretin waited upon Duke Hercules, to desire their Liberty, taking the Fact upon himself. But, the more obstinately he insisted, that He had done it, the more it was believed, that the Prisoners were guilty. For no one durst suspect a Professor, whose Gravity and Wisdom were so well known, of such an Action. The Affair being at last terminated, he openly declared, that he had gained his Point; which was to shew the Weight and Authority of a good Reputation. Quo constantius se facti autorem fatebatur, eo magis qui in vinculis erant rei credebantur, cum ob viri gravitatem nemo id de eo suspicari auderet. Re demum composita, id se Aretinus ad demonstrandum hominis bonæ opinionis auctoritatem fecisse dixit (9). It is well known, that reputed Liars, are never believed, even when they speak Truth. It is quite contrary with those, who pass for sincere Men ; They are believed, even when they lie. See, in Valerius Maximus (10), what a good Opinion once conceived of a Man can do.

(8) Paneir. de Claris Legum Interpret. pag. 250.

(9) Id. ibid. pag. 251.

(10) Valer. Maxim. lib. 3. cap. 7, n. 8.

[E] *He had a Brother, who became very famous under the Name of* BENEDICTUS ACCOLTUS ARETINUS.] He was born in the Year 1415, and, having gone thro' the Studies of Humanity, he applied himself to That of the Law, with so much Ardor, that, in a short Time, he arrived to the Degree of Doctor : and, soon after, by his Public Lectures, and by his Opinions and Advice (11) in difficult Cases, equalled the most famous Civilians of his Time. He did not bid adieu to Polite Learning; but wrote Treatises, which shewed, that this Branch was not indifferent to him. His Dialogue, de præstantia virorum sui ævi, was printed at Parma, in the Year 1692, from the Manuscript, which Mr Maglabecchi produced. During the last Seven Years of his Life, he was Secretary to the Republic of Florence ; where he died, in the Year 1466, in the Fifty first Year of his Age. His Son, Peter, a great Civilian, having been Auditor of the Rota Twenty five Years, was honoured with a Cardinal's Cap by Pope Julius II. He had another Son, whose name was Michael, and who was the Father of Benedictus Accoltus. This Son was Secretary to Clement VII. and afterwards Cardinal (12). See Moreri's Dictionary, at the Word Accolti.

(11) Some of them have been printed.

(12) Taken from the Life of Benedict Accoltus, prefixed to the Dialogue de Præstantia virorum sui ævi.

ARETIN (Guy), a Monk of the Order of St Benedict, lived in the XIth Century. He became famous by discovering a new Method of teaching Music. He published a Book on this Subject, entituled, *Micrologus,* and a *Letter,* which Cardinal *Baronius* has inserted in his Annals, under the Year 1022. He published his *Micrologus,* at the Age of Thirty four Years, in the Pontificate of *John* XX ; and had been three times called to *Rome* by Pope *Benedict* VIII. This Pope had examined the *Antiphonary* of *Aretin,* and was fond of several Things, which he had learned from this Author. *Possevin* gives us this Account of him, in his *Apparatus* (*a*). To say something concerning this Invention of *Guy Aretin,* I must observe, that

(a) Pag. 694.

ARETIN. 433

that it was he, who invented the fix Notes, *ut, re, mi, fa, fol, la*. The Names of thefe fix Notes are faid to be taken from an Hymn, which contains thefe *Sapphic* Verfes.

*UT queant laxis   REfonare fibris
MIra geftorum   FAmuli tuorum
SOLve pollutis   LAbiis reatum* (b).

(b) See Voffius de Mufice, pag. 40.

For this Purpofe, you need only take the firft and fixth Syllable of each Verfe. Some pretend, that the Word *Gammut*, fo common in Mufic, comes from *Guy Aretin*'s having, in making ufe of the firft Letters of the Alphabet, to fpecify his Notes, employed the Letter G, which the Greeks call *Gamma*; and that he did this to fhew, that Mufic came from *Greece* (c). They, who attribute to him a Book againft *Berengarius* are miftaken [A].

(c) Puretiere, at the Word Gammut.

[A] *They, who attribute to him a Book againft Berengarius, are miftaken.*] *Voffius* fell into this Miftake; and thence infers, that he flourifhed in the Reign of the Emperor *Conrad* the Younger; and that, therefore, they, who place him an Hundred Years later, are miftaken (1). The Error, I fpeak of, arofe from hence, that they have confounded *Guy Aretin* with another Monk, whofe Name was *Guitmond*, a Brother of the Convent of St *Leufred*, of the Order of St *Benedict*, in the Diocefe of *Evreux*; who became Cardinal, and Bifhop of *Averfa* in *Italy*. They were very near Cotemporaries; for *Guitmond* died about the Year 1080. He is the Author of Three Books, " De veritate corporis & " fanguinis Chrifti in Eucharistia, adverfus Berenga-
" rium; —— *Of the real Prefence of the Body* " *and Blood of* Chrift *in the Eucharift; againft* Be-" rengarius; which have been printed feparately, and in the *Bibliotheca Patrum* (2). The Caufe I affign for this Error is fo plain, that the fame *Voffius* fays exprefly, in another Place, that, in 1070, in the Pontificate of *Gregory* VII, flourifhed *Guido* or *Guidmont*, born at *Arezzo, Patria Aretinus*, firft a Monk in the Monaftery of St *Leufred*, in the Diocefe of *Evreux*, in *Normandy*, and afterwards Cardinal, and Bifhop of *Averfa*; that, while he was a Monk, he compofed Two Treatifes of Mufic, one in Verfe, and the other in Profe, and is the fame, who wrote Three Books againft *Berengarius* (3).

(1) Voff. de Mufice, pag. 40.

(2) Vide Labbé, de Script Ecclef. Tom. 7. pag 402.

(3) Voff. de Scient. Mathem. p. 95.

ARETIN (JOHN), firnamed *Tortellius*, paffes for one of the learnedeft Men of the XVth Century. He compofed the Life of St *Athanafius* [A], at the Requeft of Pope *Eugenius* IV. He was admitted to the Confidence of *Nicolas* V, whofe Chamberlain he was (a). He was a Man of an agreeable Converfation, and honourably diftinguifhed himfelf from other learned Men, his Cotemporaries, by never difhonouring the Profeffion of Learning by fierce and injurious Difputes. He was chiefly fkilled in the Knowledge of Grammar; as he has fhewn by his Book *De Poteftate Literarum* [B]. *Gefner's Bibliotheca* gives us the Titles of feveral other Works of *Tortellius*, excepting a Lexicon, which he compofed, and which is cited by *Magius* (b). *Laurentius Valla* was much his Friend, and dedicated to him his Books *De Latina Elegantia* [C]. *Voffius*, who affirms (c), that he was the Brother of *Charles Aretin*, would be much miftaken, had he no other Proof for it, than the Words

(a) Jovius Elog. c. 108.

(b) Magius, Mifcel. lib. 2, cap. 14.

(c) Voffius de Hift. Lat. pag. 579.

[A] *He compofed the Life of St Athanafius.*] Paul *Jovius* intimates plainly enough, that *Tortellius* only tranflated it into Latin (1); *Divi Athanafii vitam Eugenio expetenti Latinam fecit.* *Gefner* fays fo more exprefly; *Athanafii Alexandrini vitam ad Eugenium Pontificem in Latinum tranftulit* (2). But *Voffius* allows him much more than the Task of a Tranflator; He makes him the Compiler of it; *Athanafii vitam ex variis, Eugenii poftulato, confarcinavit*; and quotes *Paul Jovius*, and *Volaterran* (3). The Quotation of *Paul Jovius* cannot be altogether exact, as any one may fee by comparing the Words. That of *Volaterran* is not more fo, than the former; thefe are his Words. " Joannes (Aretinus) cognomento " Tortellius, Romanæ Ecclefiæ fubdiaconus, apud " Eugenium quartum fuit. Orthographiam, vitam-" que Athanafii, ac nonnulla alia confcripfit (4). —— " John Aretin, *firnamed* Tortellius, *Subdeacon of* " *the Roman Church, was in the Court of* Eugenius " IV. *He wrote a Treatife of Orthography, the Life* " *of St* Athanafius, *and fome other Works*." *Voffius* affirms, that *Winclelius* has inferted this Life of St *Athanafius* in his *Hagiologia*. He conjectures, that *Tortellius* is the Author of the Life of St *Zenobius*, Bifhop of *Florence*, inferted in the Collections of *Surius*, under the Twenty fifth of *May*. The reafon of this Conjecture is taken from the Circumftances of Time, and from the Name, which the Author of This Life, affumes; to wit, *Joannes Archipresbyter Aretinus*.

[B] *His Knowledge of Grammar is fhewn in his Book* de Poteftate Literarum.] " That, which *Vola-*" *terran* calls *Orthographia*; *Paul Jovius*, a Book " *de poteftate literarum*; *Gefner, Commentarii linguæ* " *Latinæ*; and *Magius, Lexicon*; is but One and " the fame Volume of *Tortellius* in Two Parts; " The Firft of which, which is very fhort, contains
" fome Chapters on the Invention, Number, Figure, " Pronounciation, and Joyning of the Letters of " the Alphabet. The fecond, which is very long, " contains an Alphabetical Catalogue of *Latin* Words, " chiefly taken from the *Greek*, of which he " teaches, or endeavours to teach, the Orthogra-" phy (5)."
[C] *Laurentius Valla dedicated to him his Books* de Latina Elegantia.] From the manner, in which *Gefner* had expreffed himfelf, no One but would judge, that *Tortellius* dedicated this Work to *Laurentius Valla*: Thefe are *Gefner's* words: " Joannes Tor-" tellius, natione Aretinus, Laurentii Vallæ amicif-" fimus, ad quem elegantiarum linguæ Latinæ fex " libros perfcripfit. Nicolai poftmodum pontificis " contubernalis, & ftudiorum ejus intimus comes " (6) —— Johannes Tortellius, *of* Aterzzo, *an in-*" *timate Friend of* Laurentius Valla, *to whom be* " *dedicated Six Books, of the Elegancies of the Latin* " *Tongue. He was afterwards Chamberlain and Con-*" *fident of* Nicolas V, *and an intimate Companion of* " *his Studies.*" Thofe Compilers, who, thro' an Ambition of writing a large Book in a fhort Time, or for any other Reafon, never feek for the neceffary Inftruction beyond the Page in Sight, would eafily commit Three grofs Faults, if they applied their own Conjectures to this Text of *Gefner*. I. They would fay, that *Tortellius* wrote fix Books of the Elegancies of the Latin Tongue, and that he dedicated them to *Laurentius Valla*. II. That, afterwards, he became a Domeftic of Pope *Nicholas* V, and his Oracle of Learning; and that the great Succefs of his Book procured him This Honour. III. That *Nicholas* V. held the Chair in the Year 1420; for, fince *Gefner* places the flourifhing State of *Tortellius* in this time, and common Senfe tells us, that this flourifhing State muft be referred to the time, when *Tortellius* was

(5) Mr. de la Monnoie, Remarques, manufcript.

(6) Gefn. Biblioth. fol. 458, ex Trithemio.

in

Words of *Volaterran*, to whom he seems to refer us. *Volaterran* says nothing of this pretended Brotherhood [D].

Some very good Judges believe, that *Tortellius* was but moderately learned, even for the Age he lived in; but, as he was naturally officious, and held a considerable Post about the Pope's Person, the Wits of those Times gave him great Praises, which some of them retracted afterwards. *Philelphus* was of this Number [E]. I shall observe, in another Place (d), that *Tortellius* was Library-Keeper to *Nicholas* V.

(d) See, in one of the Remarks of the Article NICHOLAS V. the Passage in the Letter of the 26th Book of Philelphus.

in Favour with *Nicholas* V, it follows, that, according to *Gesner*, This Pope sat in the Chair at the time I have said. The Truth is, that he was elected in 1447; and that *Tortellius* had been his Man of Learning, and his Chamberlain, before; when *Laurentius Valla* dedicated his *Elegantiæ* to him. I cannot guess what Mr *Moreri* would be at, in this Article, with his indefinite Citation from *Valerius Andreas*. Why did he not consult *Vossius*, and *Paul Jovius*, who would have furnished him with a Cure for Leanness.

[D] *Volaterran says nothing of this pretended Brotherhood.*] I have very good Reason to call it so; since *Tortellius*, speaking of *Charles* and *Leonard d' Arezzo*, styles them only his Countrymen. *A doctissimis viris nostræ ætatis, & conterraneis meis Leonardo & Carolo Aretinis* *. And, when he mentions *Charles*, he always styles him either *Carolus Arretinus conterraneus meus*, or *Carolus noster Arretinus* †. This was communicated to me by Mr *de la Monnoie*. Let us set down the Words of *Volaterran*, and Those of *Vossius*; and we shall see, whether the latter could build upon the former. "Carolus & Joannes Aretini nobilia temporis illius " ingenia, quorum alter scriba Florentinorum Leo- " nardo successit; Alter Joannes, cognomento Tor- " tellius, Romanæ Ecclesiæ subdiaconus, apud Eu- " genium quartum fuit (7). ------ Charles *and* " John Aretin, *celebrated Wits of That Time*; the " *former of which succeeded* Leonard, *as Secretary at* " Florence; *The latter*, John, *surnamed* Tortellius, " *Sub-deacon of the Roman Church, was retained by* " Eugenius IV" *Vossius* expresses himself thus: " Joannes Aretinus, cognomento Tortellius, Caroli " Aretini, qui post Leonardum Aretinum scriba Floren- " tinorum fuit, frater, Romanæ Ecclesiæ subdiaconus " apud Eugenium IV. ------ præter grande de " orthographia volumen, etiam Athanasii vitam ---- " consarcinavit, ut præter Jovium auctor est Volu- " terranus lib. XXI. Anthropol. ubi & hosce Are- " tinos fratres *nobilia illius temporis ingenia* appel- " lat (8). ------ John Aretin, *surnamed* Tortellius,

* In the 4th Part of his Work, at the Chapter of the Greek T.

† In the second Part, which contains the Words in an Alphabetical Order.

(7) Volaterr. lib. 21, pag. 773.

(8) Vossius de Hist. Lat. pag. 579.

" *Brother of* Charles Aretin, *who succeeded* Leonard " *as Secretary at* Florence, *Subdeacon of the* Roman " *Church, and Domestic of* Eugenius IV. --- *besides* " *a large Volume* de Orthographia ------ *wrote the* " *Life of* Athanasius; *as, besides* Jovius, Volaterran " *informs us*, lib. 21. Anthropol. *where he calls the* " *Brothers,* Aretins, *Celebrated Wits of That Time.*" If they had contented themselves with saying, they were Relations, they might have some good ground for it in these Words of *Philelphus*, " Putabam Ca- " rolum Arretinum rediisse mecum in gratiam. Ita " enim Joannes Arretinus ejus NECESSARIUS tuis " verbis mihi renunciarat (9). ----- *I thought that* " Charles Aretin *had been reconciled to me*; *for so* " John Aretin, *his Relation, informed me from you.*" For though *necessarius* be sometimes taken for an intimate Friend, yet *Philelphus*, and most of the Writers of those times, never used it but in the Sense of a Relation by Blood, or allied by Marriage. I am indebted for this Observation to Mr *de la Monnoie*.

[E] *Philelphus was of the Number of Those, who retracted the Praises, they had bestowed on* J. Aretin.] I shall cite, in the Article NICOLAS V, a Letter of *Philelphus*, dated the first of *August* 1465, in which he greatly commends *Tortellius* for his Skill in *Greek* and *Latin*. But see what the same *Philelphus* wrote, the twenty ninth of *May*, 1473. " Video quosdam nostræ tempestatis homines, qui " cum magnum de se quiddam voluerunt in " arte grammatica profiteri, in maximos errores " devenerunt. E quorum numero principatum " mihi tenere visus est Joannes Tortellius Are- " tinus, qui cum & Græcam & Latinam litteratu- " ram novisse videri vult, u'ramque ignoravisse aper- " tissime declarat (10). ----- *I know several Per- " sons of our Age, who, pretending to great Skill " in* Grammar, *have fallen into the greatest Errors. " Among These* John Tortellius Arretinus *claims the " first place*; *who, at the same time that he would " seem to be versed both in the* Greek *and* Latin *Li- " terature, plainly discovers his Ignorance of both.*"

(9) Philel. Epist. lib. 9.

(10) Mr de la Monnoie supplies me with this.

ARETIN (LEONARD), is more known by This Name, which was given him as he was a Native of *Arezzo*, than by That of *Brunus*, or *Bruni*, which was his Family Name. He was one of the most considerable Men of the XVth Century [A]. He learned *Greek* under *Emanuel Chrysolorus*, as he himself informs us (a); and, his Merit being made known to Pope *Innocent* VII, he obtained of him, though very young, the Place of Secretary of the Briefs, of which he acquitted himself worthily under That Pontificate, and the four following (b). He was afterwards Secretary to the Republic of *Florence* (c), and raised a large Fortune (d), as well, because he always lived a single Life (e), as on account of his Extraordinary Œconomy. He translated some of *Plutarch's* Lives [B], and *Aristotle's* Ethics, from the *Greek* into *Latin*. He composed three Books of the *Punic War*, which may serve to supply some of those, which are wanting in *Livy* [C]. He composed also *an History of the Transactions*

(a) Leon. Aretin. Histor. Rerum Italicar. See also Jovius, Elog. c. 23.

(b) Jovius, ibid. cap. 9.

(c) Leand. Albert. Descript. Ital.

(d) Jovius, ubi supra.

(e) Volaterr. lib. 21, pag. 772.

[A] *He was one of the most considerable Men of the XVth Century.*] Paul *Jovius* says, that *Leonard Aretin* was the first, who restored the Purity of the *Greek* Tongue in *Italy* (1). *Philelphus* allows him great Eloquence, and a great Depth of Genius and Learning (2). *Poggius* (3) and *Laurentius Valla* (4) have ranked him above all his Cotemporaries in point of Eloquence and Learning; but *Floridus Sabinus* is more moderate in his Commendations of him, and gives us no advantageous Idea of his *Latin* (5); in which *Erasmus* seems to agree with him (6). *Æneas Silvius* praises our *Aretin* highly in his Fifty first Letter, and informs us, that the *Florentines* had conferred his Office on *Poggius*. *Vossius* observes, that *Æneas Silvius* and *Leander Albertus* differ in this; the latter saying, in his *Description of* Italy, that *Charles Aretin* succeeded *Leonard* in the Post of Secretary to the Republic of *Florence*. See, above,

the Article (CHARLES) ARETIN (7), where we prove, from *Æneas Silvius* himself, that *Leander Albertus* is in the right.

[B] *He translated some of* Plutarch's *Lives.*] To wit, That of *Paulus Emilius*, That of the two *Gracchi*, of *Pyrrhus*, of *Sertorius*, of *Demosthenes*, of *Marc Antony*, and That of *Cato Uticensis* (8). The Printers have been guilty of a strange Mistake in *Moreri's* Dictionary, in putting (*vers de Plutarque) Plutarch's Verses*, instead of (*vies de Plutarque) Plutarch's Lives.*

[C] *He composed three Books of the* Punic War; *which may serve to supply* ----- Livy.] The two first of these three Books treat of the first *Punic War*, which is wanting in *Livy*. The third treats of the Confusions, into which the *Carthaginians* fell by the Mutiny of the Soldiers, and Revolt of the People; as also of the War against the *Gauls*, and against

(1) Jovius, Elog. cap. 9, pag. 20.
(2) Philelph. Convivor. lib. 2, & Epist. ad eum scripta.
(3) Pogg in Philelph. Invect. 2.
(4) Apud Philelph. Inve t. 1, in Vallam.
(5) Flor Sabinus advers. Calumn. Ling. Lat.
(6) Erasm. in Ciceroniano.

(7) In Remark [B].

(8) Gesner. in Bibl.

ARETIN. 435

Tranſactions of his own Times in Italy [D], That of the Republic of *Florence*, That of ancient *Greece* [E], and That of the *Goths*. But this latter, which procured him great Honour, whilſt it was not known, that he had only tranſlated it from the *Greek* of *Procopius*, drew a kind of Infamy on his Memory (f), when it was diſcovered, after his Death, by the Care of *Chriſtopher Perſona*, that *Procopius*, whoſe Name he had ſuppreſſed, in appropriating his Labours to himſelf, was the true Author of this Hiſtory of the *Goths* [F]. He compoſed ſeveral other Books; a Catalogue of which is to be ſeen in *Geſner's Bibliotheca*; and died, at *Florence*, in the Year 1443, aged Seventy four Years [G]. His Body lies in a Marble Tomb, in the Church of the *Holy Croſs* (g). *Poggius* was one of thoſe, who criticiſed on him [H]. In the Year 1653, Mr *de la Mare*, Counſellor of the Parliament of *Dijon*, publiſhed a Catalogue of *Leonard Aretin's* Books, which he deſigned to have printed. But I believe it was never done. I have heard ſay, that, among the Manuſcripts of the Library at *Oxford*, there was lately found a Copy of *Leonard Aretin's* Letters, in which there were forty, that had never been printed; which, perhaps, may be the Occaſion of a new Edition of them.

(o) Geſn. in Bibl.

(10) Voſſius de Hiſtor. Lat. p. 557.

againſt Thoſe of *Illyria*; Particulars, which are all wanting in the *Roman* Hiſtory (9). *Aretin* has done little more than tranſlate the *Greek* of *Polybius*, though he denies it in his Preface; which is the Reaſon, why *Badius Aſcentius* has placed the Name of *Polybius* at the head of the Work, in his Edition of *Paris* (10).

[D] *He compoſed alſo an* Hiſtory of the Tranſactions *of his own Times in* Italy.] This Work begins with the Schiſm, which was raiſed againſt Pope *Urban* VI, in 1378, and goes down to the Victory obtained by the *Florentines*, in the Year 1440, near *Anglara*.

[E] — *That of ancient* Greece.] This Work reaches from the Generalſhip of *Theramenes*, and *Thraſybulus*, over the *Athenians*, to the death of *Epaminondas*, which comprehends Forty five, or Fifty Years.

(11) Ibid. pag. 558.

(12) *The 116th Chapter of the Elogies.*

(13) *The 9th Chapter of the Elogies.*

(14) Le Gallois, Traité des plus belles Biblioth. pag. 169. Edit. of Paris, 1680.

[F] *It was diſcovered by the Care of* Chriſtopher Perſona - - - - - - *that* Procopius *was the true Author of This Hiſtory of the* Goths.] *Perſona* had determined, according to *Voſſius*, to tranſlate *Agatbias*, when he detected the Inſincerity of our *Aretin* (11). *Voſſius* alledges *Paul Jovius* in proof of this; but it is certain, that *Jovius* makes no mention of *Agathias*, either in the place, where he is cited (12), or in any other (13), where he may be cited; but ſpeaks there expreſly of *Procopius*. I allow, that *Perſona* alſo tranſlated *Agathias*; but the Tranſlation of *Procopius* is what *Voſſius* ought to have taken notice of in the Place, where he mentions the *Plagiariſm* of *Aretin*. So I think it ought to be called, and not *Plagianiſm*, after a modern Author, from whom I ſhall cite the entire Paſſage, becauſe it is full of Errors. He ſays (14), " We are indebted to *David Heſchelius* for the *Greek* " Hiſtory of *Procopius*. *Leonard Aretin* had already " given it in the *Gothic* Language, but ſuppreſt the " Author's Name. But, after *Aretin's* Death, *Chri-* " *ſtopher Perſona* accuſed him of Theft, having him- " ſelf found another Copy of This Hiſtory in the " ſame Language, which he publiſhed under the " Name of it's Author, and thereby convinced *Aretin* " of *Plagianiſm*." What Monſter does he here ſpeak

of? *Procopius* in *Gothic*, publiſhed firſt by *Aretin*, and afterwards by *Perſona*, is ſuch a Chimera, as never was, or ever will be, ſeen. Beſides, it is ſpeaking very inaccurately, to ſay, that *Leonard Aretin* and *Perſona* have given us the Hiſtory of *Procopius*, for they have only tranſlated Part of That Hiſtory. The Printers of *Moreri's* Dictionary have committed a ſtrange Blunder, in ſaying, that *the Hiſtory of the* Goths *was properly but a Tranſlation of* Plutarch.

[G] *And died, at* Florence, *in* 1443, *aged Seventy four Years* (15)] *Leander Albertus* ſays, indeed, that he died at Seventy four Years of Age; but he places his Death in the Year 1440. His Calculation does not agree with *Matthew Palmerius*, who places the Year of the Birth of *Leonard Aretin* in 1370 (16). And, beſides, as I find in *Volaterran*, that our *Aretin* died in 1443 (17), (on the ninth of *March*, according to *Bucholcer*, I chooſe not to follow *Leander Albertus*. I have, above, obſerved (18) the Miſtake of a Modern, who believed, that *Leonard Aretin* was living in the Year 1480.

[H] *Poggius was one of Thoſe, who criticiſed on him*] Theſe Words of *Phileſphus* inform us of it; They are to be found in a Letter, which he wrote to *Lorenzo de Medicis*, the ninth of *May*, 1473. " *Quod eo feci accuratius, quoniam & Leonardus* " *Arretinus familiaris noſter, vir ſane facundiſſimus,* " *adverſus Blondum Flavium multa diſſeruit, & poſt* " *Leonardi obitum Poggius Carolo gratificatus Ar-* " *retino, quem diſſertiſſimi concivis gloria offenderet,* " *libellum etiam contra illius ſcripta contexuit, cum* " *neuter ſuo fit functus officio* (19). - - - - *I have been* " *the more careful in doing This, becauſe both Leo-* " *nard* Aretin, *my intimate Friend, and a very elo-* " *quent Man, wrote many Diſſertations againſt* Blon- " dus Flavius, *and, after the Death of* Leonard, " Poggius, *out of complaiſance to* Charles Aretin, *who* " *was diſguſted at the Reputation of his ingenious* " *Countryman, drew up a Treatiſe likewiſe againſt* " *his Works; when neither of them acquitted them-* " *ſelves well*." This Paſſage was communicated to me by Mr *de la Monnoie*.

(15) Varilliſhes of *Florence*, pag. 102, is miſtaken in making him live above eighty Years.

(16) In Chronico, ad Ann. 1370.

(17) The Printers of Voſſius, pag. 557, have, by miſtake, put CIƆCCCCLXX.

(17) Volat. lib. 21, pag. 772.

(18) In Remark [A], of the Article ARETIN (FRANCIS).

(19) Phileſphus, Epiſtol. lib. 37.

ARETIN (PETER), A Native of *Arezzo*,—renowned for his obſcene and ſatirical Writings, lived in the XVIth Century. They, who deſire to know what the Medal was, which it is ſaid he ſtruck, to inform the World how much the greateſt Princes ſtood in fear of his Satires, may be informed by Mr *Moreri's* Dictionary; in which Medal *Aretin* values himſelf on having laid Thoſe, to whom other Men pay Tributes and Impoſts, under Contribution. This Tradition is ſo general, that he is as well known under the Title of *The Scourge of Princes*, as under the Name of *Aretin*, or That of *Peter Aretin* [A]. He had another very glorious Appellation

given

(1) Aretin, in the ſixth Book of his Letters, fol. 215.

[A] *He was as well known under the Title of the* Scourge of Princes - - - - - - *as That of* P. Aretin.] He boaſted of having This Character all the World over. Read the Letter, which he wrote to *Herſilia del Monte*, a Kinſwoman of Pope *Julius* III, you will find theſe Words in it. " In tanto è manifeſto, " ch'io ſono noto al Sophi, à gli Indiani, & il mon- " do al paro di qualunche hoggi in bocca de la " fama riſuoni: che piu ? i Principi da i popoli tri- " butati di continuo, tuttavia me loro ſchiavo, & " flagello tributano (1). - - - - - - Inſomuch, that it " *is plain I am known to the* Perſians, *the* Indians, " *and every Nation in the World ? Would you have*

" *more ? Princes themſelves, to whom their People pay* " *tribute, are under Contribution to me, who am* " *both their Slave, and their Scourge*." In another Letter, he ſays, that one would ſwear, that Princes paid him Tribute, not that he might praiſe them, but for fear of his Reproaches; adding, that they were Fools for their Pains; for, ſince moſt Great Men were not afraid of the Wrath of God, why, continues he, ſhould they fear my Pen ? *'Impero che la maggior parte de i gran maeſtri non temono l'ira di Dio, e temeranno il furore de la mia penna* (2). This reaſoning is not concluſive: The fear of Men makes us abſtain from a thouſand things, which we

(2) Id. ibid. fol. 120, verſo.

ſhould

VOL. I.   5 R

ARETIN.

given him; the same, with which all Antiquity has honoured the great Merit of *Plato*; to wit, That of *Divine*; *il Divino Aretino* [B]: He has been ſtiled on Medals, *Divus Petrus Aretinus* (a). Some have thought, that he gave himſelf this Title, to ſignify, that he performed the Office of a God upon Earth, by the Thunderbolts, which he darted at the moſt eminent Heads [C]. He boaſted, that his Libels were of more Benefit to the World, than Sermons [D]. He was complimented, in Letters, with having ſubjected more Princes by his Pen, than the greateſt Kings had ever ſubdued by their Arms [E]; and was exhorted to perſevere in this kind of Writing, to the end, that Monarchs might learn to amend [F]. Our Age has produced as bold and virulent Satiriſts, as *Aretin* could be; and yet I believe none of them ever ſettled Contributions in an Enemy's Country. Some miſinformed Writers make *Aretin* paſs for the Author of the Book *De Tribus Impoſtoribus.*

(a) Spizelliuſ Scrutinꝰ Atheiſmi, pag. 19. *afſirms to had ſeen ſome of them.*

ſhould not abſtain from, if we had no other Fear upon us, but That of the Divine Vengeance (3).

[B] *He had a very glorious Appellation, viz.* — — *That of* Divine; il divino Aretino.] It will not be amiſs to ſee *Montagne*'s Opinion of this Elogy: "*Plato*, ſays he (4), had the Surname of *Divine* by "general Conſent, and no one envied him; and "the *Italians*, who boaſt, with Reaſon, of having "generally a more refined Wit, and better Expreſ-"ſion, than other Nations, beſtow it on *Aretin*, "in whom I ſee nothing beyond the common Au-"thors of his Age, except a manner of uttering "loſty, frothy, Bombaſt, or Jeſts, which are inge-"nious indeed, but far-fetched and whimſical; ſo "far is he from approaching That antient Divi-"nity"

[C] *He gave himſelf this Title, to ſignify, that he performed the Office of a God upon Earth*, &c.] I have met with this Thought in an *Italian* Author, quoted by a *German*. "Cur vero ſibi arrogaverit aliorum con-"ſenſu divinitatem, neſcio, niſi forte DEI munus "exercuiſſe dicendus ſit, cum ſumma capita velut "celſiſſimos montes fulminaverit, lingua corrigens "& mulctans quæ ab aliis caſtigari nequeunt (5). "— — —. *Why, with the Conſent of others, he arro-"gated this Title to himſelf; I know not, unleſs, "perhaps, he may be ſaid to have exerciſed the Fun-"ction of a* GOD, *in darting his Thunder on the "higheſt Heads, as on the loftieſt Mountains, cor-"recting and puniſhing thoſe Faults with his Tongue, "which others cannot chaſtiſe.*"

[D] *He boaſted, that his Libels were of more Benefit to the World than Sermons*] He ſays, in his Epiſtle dedicatory to the ſecond Part of his *Raggionamenti*, that " if he does not merit Eſteem on the "Score of his Inventions, yet ought he to receive "ſome Honour for the Service he had done to Truth, "in conveying it into the Chambers and Ears of "great Perſons, to the Confuſion of Flattery and "Falſhood.". He takes notice of what one of Duke *Urbino*'s Ambaſſadors had ſaid, That " if the Mini-"ſters of Princes and Courtiers were rewarded for "their Services, they were obliged for it to the Pen "of *Peter Aretin*." He adds, what another had ſaid; " *Aretin* is more uſeful to human Life, than "Sermons; becauſe Sermons inſtruct only the Ig-"norant; but his Writings reform great Men." Theſe are his Words in *Italian*. " Quando io non "foſſi degno di honor veruno, merce de le inven-"tioni con le quali do l'anima à lo ſtile, merito pur "qualche poco di gloria per havere ſpinto la veri-"ta ne le camere, e ne le orecchie de Potenti ad "onta de l'adulatione, e de la menzogna: e per "non diſfraudere il mio grado, uſero le parole ſteſſe "del Singulare *M. Giamacopo*, Ambaſciadore d'Ur-"bino: non che ſpendiamo il tempo ne ſervigi de "Prencipi inſieme con ogni huomo di Corte, e non "ciaſcun virtuoſo, ſiamo riguardati, e riconoſciuti "da noſtri padroni, bonta de gaſtighi che gli ha dati "la penna di Pietro. E lo ſa Milano, come cadde "de la ſacra bocca di colui, che in pochi meſi mi "ha arricchito di due Coppe d'oro: l'Aretino è "piu neceſſario a la vita humana, che le predica-"tioni, è che ſia il vero eſſe pongono in ſu le "dritte ſtrade le perſone ſemplici, & i ſuoi ſcritti "le ſignorili, & il mio non è vanto, ma un modo "di procedere per ſoſtener ſe medeſimo oſſervato da "Enea, dove non era conoſciuto."

[E] *He was complimented, in Letters, with having ſubjected more Princes by his Pen, than the Greateſt Kings had ſubdued by their Arms*] Thus I have read in a Letter, written to him by *Baptiſta Torniellι* (6).

He tells him, that he merits the Titles *Germanicus, Pannonicus*, &c. as formerly the Emperors took the Names of the Provinces, over which they had triumph'd. " Non ſapete voi, che con la penna vo-"ſtra in mano havete ſoggiogato piu Principi, ch' "ogni altro potentiſſimo Principe con l'arme? La "penna voſtra à qual non mette terrore, à quale non "è formidabile, à chi anche non grata, à chi non "cara, ove ſi moſtra amica? La penna voſtra ſi "puo dir, che v'ha fatto trionfator quaſi di tutti i "Principi del mondo; che quaſi tutti vi ſono tribu-"tarii, & come inſudati. Meritareſte eſſer chiamato "Germanico, Pannonico, Gallico, Hiſpanico, & "finalmente inſignito di quei titoli, quali ſi davano à "gli antichi Imperadori Romani, ſecondo le provincie "per loro ſoggiogate: che ſe quelli ſoggiogavano le "provincee per forza d'arme, & per eſſer piu di loro "potenti, non era gran meraviglia; maggior mera-"viglia, aſſai è, che un privato, inerme, haggio ſog-"giogato infiniti potenti: che l'un potente l'altro, "non e meraviglia. — *Are you not ſenſible, that, "with Pen in hand, you have ſubdued more Princes, "than ever the moſt powerful Monarch did by force of "Arms? To whom is not your Pen a Terror? To "whom is it not formidable? and who is not pleaſed "with it, when it has the Appearance of a Friend? "With your Pen you have, as it were, triumph'd over "all the Princes in the World; who are almoſt all "tributary, and as it were feudatory, to you. You "merit the Titles of* Germannicus, Pannonicus, Gal-"licus, Hiſpanicus; *Laſtly, all the Titles given to "the antient Roman Emperors, according to the Pro-"vinces they had conquer'd; for that Theſe ſhou'd ſub-"ject Provinces by force of Arms, and ſuperior Power, "is no wonder; it is much more ſurprizing, that "a private, unarm'd, Man ſhould conquer number-"leſs, powerful, Men*".

[F] *He was exhorted to perſevere in this kind of Writing, to the end, that Monarchs might learn to amend.*] The Marquis *del Guaſto* ſent him this Exhortation, in a Letter, which he wrote to him with his own Hand (7). He deſir'd no Exemption for himſelf; but that his Faults might be cenſured by *Aretin*; and exhorted him to do it. It is probable he was pretty ſure, he ſhould not be taken at his Word. *Aretin* did not confound his Friends with his Enemies; he only exerciſed his Satire upon thoſe, who neglected to buy it off. " Seguite dico "col ſolito, *ſays the Marquis*, e ſe in me voſtro "amico alcuna coſa men che laudabile conoſcete; "ricordatevi di non laſciar di riprenderla: acciocche "fatto accorto dell' error, come deſidero, lo fugga, "e divenga migliore. Seguite lo ſtil voſtro, che "di nuovo ve ne prego: acciocche, ſe i defetti con "verita ſaranno in altri trovati, ſi vergognino, & "& vergognandoſi, & mendandoſi ſuggano dal vi-"tio alla virtu. Onde i rei divenuti buoni, abbra-"ciati con eſſa virtu, ſi confermino nel bene. Del "che quanto in cio l'humana Repub. ſi avanzi; "lo giudichino quelli, che lo ſanno meglio inten-"der, ch'io no'l ſo eſprimere. — *Follow, I ſay, "your uſual manner; and, if you ſee any thing "faulty even in me your Friend, forget not to reprove "me for it, That I may profit by your Admonitions, "and become better. Perſevere in Satire, I once "more entreat you: that others may bluſh at their "Imperfections; and, by bluſhing, and growing better, "may fly from Vice to Virtue; and, being once re-"formed, may be confirm'd in Good. What Advan-"tages human Society will from hence receive, let "thoſe judge, who underſtand it better, than I am "able to expreſs it.*

(1) *See the Thoughts on Comets, n.* 162, &c.

THE Judgment of Montagne on Aretin.

(4) Montagne's Eſſays, lib. 1. chap. 51, *towards the end.*

(5) Jacobus Gaddius de Scriptoribus non Eccleſiaſticis, Tom. 2. pag. 13, apud Spizellium, in Felice Literato, pag. 112.

(6) *It is in a Collection, publiſhed in* 1548, *at Venice, uporeſſo* Domenico Giglio, *in* 8vo, *at the* 238th P ge *of the firſt Book.*

(7) *It is at the 44th Page of the ſecond Book of the ſame Collection.*

[G] *Some*

ARETIN. 437

bus [G]. I cannot believe, that the Epitaph, mentioned by *Moreri*, was engraved on his Tomb [H], in St *Luke*'s Church, at *Venice*. The Author of this Epitaph, no

[G] *Some misinformed Writers make* Aretin *pass for the Author of the Book* De tribus Impostoribus.] We shall, perhaps, have occasion to examine this Matter more fully, in another Place, and to make it appear, that it is very improbable there ever was [such a Book. The Abbot *Nicaisius*, one of the worthiest Persons of this Age (8), who is acquainted with all the most learned Men in *Europe*, among whom he holds a very considerable Rank, was so kind as to send me, last Year (9), a very curious Dissertation of Mr *de la Monnoie*, his Countryman (10), on the Book *De tribus Impostoribus* *. It is full of very curious Observations, and deserves exceedingly to be printed. Mr *de Beauval* has lately given a small Extract from it (11). The Author shews, by very strong Reasons, that This Book is a meer Chimera. *Grotius* believ'd, but perhaps without Reason, that This very Book had been taken notice of, before *Aretin* was born. He says, that the Enemies of *Frederic Barbarossa* accused him of having composed this Book (12). He should have said, that *Frederic* II was accused of having said, that the World had been deceived by Three Impostors (13). The good Father *Mersennus* pretends, that one of his Friends, who had read the Book in question, had discovered in it the Stile of *Peter Aretin* (14). Meer Cant! Yet one would hardly imagine how much this Notion of Father *Mersennus* has been propagated.

[H] *I cannot believe, that the Epitaph, mentioned by* Mr Moreri, *was engraved on his Tomb*] He does not say positively and precisely, that this Epitaph was engraved on the Tomb of *Peter Aretin*, in St *Luke*'s Church ; but every one must suppose, that this is what he meant ; for he expresses himself after this manner : " He died at *Venice*, where he is " buried in St *Luke*'s Church. This is his Epi- " taph.

Condit Aretini cineres lapis iste sepulto,
Mortales atro qui sale perstricuit.
Intactus Deus est illi, causaeque rogatus
Hanc dedit, ille, inquit, non mihi notus erat (15).

Here Aretin *enterr'd doth lye*,
Whose Satire lash'd both High, and Low :
His God alone It spared ; and why ?
His God, he said, he did not know.

" It is more ingenious in the *Italian* :

Qui giace l' Aretin Poëta Tosco,
Che d' ognun disse malo che (16) di Dio,
Scusandosi col dir' io no'l conoico.

There is nothing in the Thread of *Moreri*'s Narrative, which gives the least Intimation, that these four Verses are not the very Inscription on *Aretin*'s Tomb. It is imposing on every Reader, who has not the Ability to rectify a Mistake by his own Reflexions. It is particularly laying a Snare for Protestants, who, unless they believe with caution, will be apt to infer, that there is no Object so scandalous, which the *Italians* do not admit in their Churches. Several, then, amongst them, might easily believe, on Mr *Moreri*'s Word, that the Patriarch of *Venice* not only suffered an Atheist to be buried in Consecrated Ground ; but also, that the Epitaph of This Atheist was exposed, in the Church, to the View of all the World, in four Verses, which turn the matter into a Jest. For my own part, I cannot believe, that the Corruption and Negligence of the Clergy was ever at such an height, as to suffer Sepulchral Inscriptions of this kind in a Church. I am of Opinion, then, that the Four Verses produced by Mr *Moreri*, are one of Those Satirical Banters, made on the Death of certain Persons, under the Title and Form of an Epitaph. How many of this kind were made on the Cardinals of *Richlieu*, and *Mazarine* ? They, who write the Elogies of Illustrious Men, and who, after the Example of *Paul Jovius*, take a pleasure in relating their Epitaphs, ought always to explain, whether they are Verses actually engraved on their Tombs, or only meer Sallies of Wit. If this Precaution

had been used with regard to *Aretin*, we should not at present read in the *Theatrum* of *Paul Freherus*, and the *Felix Literatus* of *Spizelius* (17), that the four Verses in Question are inscrib'd on the Tomb of this Personage at *Venice* (18). A Divine of *Utrecht* affirms (19), that the Epitaph of *Peter Aretin*, inserted in the Elogies of *Paul Jovius*, and That, which *Pazzi* has reported, testifie, that he was a grand Apostle of Atheism : " *Aretini epitaphium apud Jo-* " *vium in Elogiis virorum doctorum, says he, & al-* " *terum apud Guizeppe Pazzi, indicat qualis & quan-* " *tus Atheismi praco fuerit ; sic enim Pazzi in lib.* " *cui tit.* Continuatione della monstruosa farina, " *Venetiis* 1609. Qui giace l' Aretini poeta Tos- " ca (20), Che disse mal d'ogn'un fuor che di Dio ; " ma si scuso dicendo, no'l (21) conosco. Aliter " *sic* Qui giace estinto quell' amaro Tosco Ch'ogn' " huom vivendo col mal' dir trafisse. Vero e che " mal di Dio giamai non disse, Che si scuso dicen- " do io no'l conosco". Upon this let me observe, first, that *Paul Jovius* does not mention the Epitaph of *Peter Aretin*. How should He, since he died before him ? He mentions That of *Leonard Aretin*, but it contains nothing which in the least reflects on the Faith of the Deceased ; it has nothing to do with Religion. In the second Place, there is no depending on the Two *Italian* Epitaphs ; for they were wrote without Approbation, and were never engraved on the Tomb. They were Sallies of Wit of some Satirical Poet. *Spizelius* has copied the whole Passage of *Voëtius*, almost Word for Word, without citing it (22). Note, that *Lorenzo Crasso* (23) insinuates yet more clearly, than *Moreri*, that the Four *Latin* Verses are inscribed on the Tomb of This Atheist, in St *Luke*'s Church.

Let me here set down a considerable Supplement (24). It is a Custom, among the Catholics, to affix " to some Pillar, or other Place, near the Tomb of " the Deceased, especially if a Person of Reputation, " Funeral Inscriptions, written on Paper. The " Truth is, these Inscriptions are not always ought " to be, in Honour of the Deceased. But, *Aretin* " having been a noted Libertine, it is very possible, " that some Jester convey'd the Epitaph, mentioned " by Mr *Moreri*, and many others, into St *Luke*'s " Church, at the Time of, or after, the Funeral. " Thus the Word of *Ghilini* must be understood, " who has himself likewise explain'd them clearly " enough to the same Effect ; when, after having " said : e sopra il suo sepulchro fu posto questo Epi- " taffio : Condit Aretini cineres, &c. he immediately adds ; sù parimente " appeso alla sua tomba quest' altro, quasi tradotto " d'al suddetto, che va attorno nella bocca fino delle " persone idiote, Qui giace l' Aretin, &c. ------ *This* " *other was hung up likewise at his Tomb, translated* " *as it were from the foregoing, which is That which* " *is most commonly repeated*: Qui giace l' Aretin, &c. The *Italian* Epitaph, as *Ghilini* delivers it, is much correcter, than That in *le Pazzi*, *Voitius*, or *Moreri* ; and I cannot comprehend this latter, when he says, that it is more ingenious, than the *Latin*. Both He, and *Ghilini*, seem to me to be mistaken, in taking the *Italian* for a Transcript of the *Latin*. The contrary, in my Opinion, is the Truth ; and what inclines me to believe so, is, because the *Italian* is to be found in the *New Recreations*, printed at *Paris*, in 1572, in 16mo *, under the Name of *Bonaventure de Periers*, and " the *Latin* is not yet to be met with in any Book so " Ancient ------ There are Faults in the *Italian* Epi- " taph of *Aretin*, produced by *Moreri* and *Voëti-* " *us* ------ The most correct is That, which you read, " in these Terms, in *Ghilini* :

Qui giace l' Aretin amaro tosco
Del sem' human, la cui lingua trafisse
Et vivi, & morti : d' Iddio mal non disse,
Et si scuso, co'l dir, io no'l conosco.

This is so far from weakening my Criticism on *Moreri*, that it rather confirms it.

In

ARETIN.

no doubt, exceeded his Commission. If there was reason to think, that *Aretin* did not *love* God, there was none to say, that he did not *know* him; his Works of Piety plainly testify the contrary [*I*]. I do not believe, that any one Tenet of Atheism is

In the Conversations, which I had, in the Year 1696, with Father *Cornelli*, who accompanied the Ambassador of the Republic of *Venice* to *England*, I ask'd him what he thought of *Aretin*'s Epitaph. He answered, that he did not believe it was such as *Moreri* gives it; and promis'd me to make enquiry. He wrote to me from *Venice*, the 2d of *November* of the same Year, that it was very true, that *Aretin* was buried in St *Luke*'s Church, but that he could not, as yet, discover any thing concerning the Epitaph. He sent me a Passage, taken out of the (25) *Venetia descritta dal Sansovino, coll' additioni del Martiniomi*; which, after informing us, that *Aretin* was interr'd in That Church, says, that he lost all his Reputation after Death, and would have been buried in Oblivion, had not *Ariosto* undeservedly perpetuated his Memory, by crying out in his *Orlando Furioso*; *Behold the Scourge of Princes, the divine* Peter Aretin! " Vi dorme parimente in un deposito posto
" in aria quel Pietro Aretino, il quale fù cognomi-
" nato flagello de' Prencipi, per la licentiosa presun-
" tione della sua mordacissima penna, & il quale
" morendo perde del tutto il nome: pioche essendo
" ignaro di lettere, e operando per forza di natura
" ne' suoi caprici, hebbe dopo morte il meritato pre-
" mio della sua petulantia: conciosia che essendo le
" cose sue reputate dalla Chiesa poco Cristiane, fu-
" rono vietate del tutto à Lettori, e si sarebbe affat-
" to cancellata la memoria, se l' Ariosto burlandosi
" del titolo ch' egli si haveva preso indebitamente,
" non havesse detto nel Furioso;

Ecco il flagello
De Prencipi, il divin Pietro Aretino.

Observe, pray, these Words of Mr Mission; " I can
" scarce believe, what some have affirm'd to me,
" that the severe Epigram, made upon *Aretin*, is
" turn'd into an Epitaph. However, I will, at a
" venture, set down the Copy, which was given
" me of it (26)". It is pity he could never find St *Luke*'s Church open; he went several times thither on purpose to see *Aretin*'s Tomb. If he had seen it, he might easily have decided the Dispute. The Journalist of *Utrecht*, speaking of his Travels, mention the Four Verses, *Condit Aretini cineres*, &c. and declare, that they are engraved on the Tomb of This Satirist. *Cujus sepulchro sequentes versus inscripti esse dicuntur* (27). Once more I believe nothing of it.

[*I*] *His Works of Piety plainly testify the contrary.*] Paul *Freberus* relates, that certain *Italian* Princes, bad Imitators of the Emperor and King of *France*, who brib'd *Aretin* with Presents not to attack them, caus'd an hundred Strokes of a Cudgel to be given him, and that This Punishment had such an Effect, that the Author renounc'd all Defamatory Satires and Libels, and wrote nothing afterwards but pious Books. " Quidam principes Italiæ
" minus sibi convenire existimantes donis eum affi-
" cere, fustibus ad mortem usque cædere per alios
" curarunt, & hoc modo linguam ejus maledicam
" refrenarunt, qui deinceps à scriptis satiricis absti-
" nens sacra scripsit, non sicut priora per Inquisiti-
" onem prohibita (28)". So that he was, with some little difference, in the case of those, whom *Horace* mentions in the First Epistle of the Second Book; ver. 154.

—— vertére modum formidine fustis
Ad bene dicendum delectandumque redacti.

Fear made them civil, and design to write
With Modesty; speak well, and to delight.

CREECH.

I shall mention but Two Circumstances, in which the Cases differ. The first is, that he did not come off with Fear alone; the Cudgel effectually play'd upon his poor Shoulders. The second is, that he did not greatly entertain the World by changing his Stile; He was got out of his Element. Wit distinguishes itself very little, when applied, late, in writing Books of Devotion. This I say, agreeably to the Hypothesis of the *Sieur Freber*, which I shall examine hereafter. But the best of it is, that, in the Opinion of several Persons, the Books he wrote of this kind favour of a true Convert. *It is no Secret, what a thorough Conversion That of the famous* Aretin *was*; *every thing in him was changed, even to his very Name*; *and some pretend, that he succeeded so happily, that it is almost impossible to discover, in the Books of* Partenio Etiro (29), *the least Mark of the old Man, which are so strongly imprinted in the Works of* Pietro Aretino (30). We find, in the Conversations of Mr *Menage*, a Particular, which deserves a Place here. " *Aretin* wrote
" Books of Devotion, which gave occasion to a
" Saying concerning him, *Ubi bene, nemo melius*;
" *ubi male, nemo pejus* —— *Where well, no one,*
" *better; where ill, no one worse*". The following Epigram was wrote on the *Paraphrase of the Seven Penitential* Psalms, *by Peter Aretin*.

Si ce livre unit le destin
De *David* & de l'*Aretin*
Dans leur merveilleuse science,
Lecteur, n'en sois pas empêche,
Qui paraphrase le peche,
Paraphrase la penitence (31).

Start not, that here unite in every Line,
The Fate of David, *and of* Aretin;
He, who before had paraphrased his Sins,
To paraphrase his Penitence begins.

Note, that, in the second Edition of the *Menagiana*, they have omitted the *ubi bene, nemo melius*, and have said, that, in Works of Devotion, the Style of *Aretus* is insufferable; and that nothing can be more mean, than his *Lives of* Christ, *the* Virgin, St Thomas Aquinas; *his* Genesis, *and* Paraphrase on the Psalms; whether we consider the Thoughts, or the Expression. It appears from the Passage of *Freberus*, which I have cited, that the Books of Libertinism, and Those of Devotion, were composed by *Aretin* at different Seasons of his Life; the first before his Conversion, the last after. Mr *Moreri* says, he wrote his pious Works *towards the latter end of his Days*: I question this much; for he says himself, in his Epistle dedicatory of the second Part of his *Ragguionamenti*, that he endeavoured chiefly to write quick, and from his own Stock; and, to prove the Fertility and Quickness of his Pen, he sets forth the Titles of several Works, some on Subjects of Devotion, and others on Matters of Gaiety, which he had composed in a very short time; as His *Psalms*; His *History of* Christ; His *Comedies*; His *Dialogue*; all which were wrote, as it were, in a Day, with a view of proving the Strength of his own Genius. " Tutto e ciancia, eccetto il far tosto, e del
" suo. Eccovi la i Salmi, eccovi la historia di *Christo*,
" eccovi le Comedie, eccovi il Dialogo, eccovi i vo-
" lumi divoti & allegri, secondo i soggetti, &
" ho partorito ogni opera ubasi in un di, è per
" che si fornisca di vedere cio che sa far la dote,
" che si ha ne le fasce, tosto udiransi i furori de
" l'armi e le passioni d'amore, che io doverei lasciar di
" cantare per descriveri i gesti di quel Carlo Augusto."
His Paraphrase on the Penitential *Psalms* was translated into *French*, and printed at *Lyons*, in 1540. His Paraphrase on *Genesis*, with the Vision, in which *Noah* discovered the Mysteries of the Old and New Testament, was printed at *Lyons* in the Year 1540, translated from the *Italian* (32). Who dares pretend, that This Author had, then, renounced his Sins, and of his Libels? However it be, these are the Titles of some of his Works of Devotion. " Specchio delle
" opere

is to be found in his Writings; but, since many of his Libels severely lashed the Disorders of the Clergy, and described, in an impious and libertine Stile, the many Vices imputed to a Monastic Life, no wonder he is made to pass for an Atheist. Add to this, that a Man, who had any Respect for Religion and good Manners, would never have published Dialogues on such Subjects, as *Aretin* made choice of, nor express them in Language so obscene. It is easy to see, that I mean his *Ragionamenti* [K]. They were printed in his Life-time; but it is difficult to discover the

opere di Dio. ---- Parafrasi sopra i sette Salmi. ---- Vita della beata Virgine. ---- Humanita del figliuolo di Dio. ---- Vita di Santo Tomaso d'Aquino. ---- Vita di Santa Catarina Vergine & Martire (33). ---- *A Mirrour of the Works of God.* ---- *A Paraphrase on the seven Psalms.* ---- *The Life of the Blessed Virgin.* ---- *The Human Nature of the Son of God* ---- *The Life of St Thomas Aquinas.* ---- *The Life of St Catharine, Virgin and Martyr.*
  The following is a full Confirmation of what I here advance (34). "Aretin composed his Works of Piety, to exercise his Imagination and to shew, that he was capable of any Thing; to appear likewise the Devotee, and to reap the Liberality of some great Ladies, to whom he sent Copies of this kind of Books. He was not a whit the soberer Man for this; since, after having published his Paraphrase on the seven *Psalms*, and his *Humanita di Christo*, in 1535, he bethought himself, at the end of 1537, of dedicating Those Infamous Postures, which have been so much spoken of, to Baptista Zatti, of Bresse, a Roman Citizen, with a Sonnet at the bottom of each; no less obscene, as M. *Felibien* observes, than the Posture represented. The Epistle dedicatory to This *Baptista Zatti* is in the first Volume of *Aretin's* Letters. It appears also, by the Description, which This Author gives of his own Manners, in the Two hundred and ninetieth Letter of the fourth Volume, dated in *December* 1547, that, though he was, then, in the Fifty seventh Year of his Age *, he led a Life no less licentious, than he had ever done. The Passage, in which he mentions the Interruption he was obliged to suffer in writing This Letter, has something in it very singular (35). ------- We may appeal likewise to the Four hundred and thirty ninth Letter of the same Volume, where it appears, that he made open Profession of a Morality far from scrupulous."
  It is, therefore, a Mistake to pretend, that he composed his pious Works, after he had, by a serious Repentance, renounced his licentious Courses. He composed Works of Piety, and of Libertinism, by turns; being always a debauched Liver, and sunk in Corruption; and if, with regard to Men, he did less Mischief, whilst he exercised his Wit on pious Subjects, than when he employed it on lewd; yet was he more criminal in the Sight of God, on Account of the former Compositions, than the latter. It did not belong to so prophane a Wretch to treat of things sacred. He did them more Injury, by explaining them, with a depraved Heart, and from bad Motives, than if he had openly insulted them. We may apply to him That thundering Censure, contained in these Words of the *Psalmist*.

  But to the Wicked thus saith God,
  How dar'st thou teach my Laws abroad,
  Or in thy Mouth my Cov'nant take ?
  For stubborn thou, confirm'd in Sin,
  Hast Proof against Instruction been,
  And of my Word didst lightly speak.
  When thou a subtle Thief didst see,
  Thou gladly didst with him agree,
  And with Adult'rers didst partake.
  Vile Slander is thy chief Delight,
  Thy Tongue, by Envy mov'd and Spight,
  Deceitful Tales does hourly spread:
  Thou dost with hateful Scandals wound
  Thy Brother, and with Lyes confound
  The Offspring of thy Mother's Bed.
  These things didst thou, whom still I strove
  To gain with Silence and with Love;

  Till thou didst wickedly surmise,
  That I was such a one as thou;
  But I'll reprove and shame thee now,
  And set thy Sins before thine Eyes (36).

I confess, the Generality of Men are not offended at Works of Devotion, composed by Indevout and Prophane Writers; but Persons of nice and delicate Taste are more scandalized at them, than at Pieces, in which such Authors deliver their genuine Thoughts. *Chose one side;* would such Persons say; *be one thing, or other; give not the Printer a Work of Piety to Day, and to morrow a Bawdy Book; we cannot bear such a Farce; since you persist in evil Courses, we had rather you would always appear in your proper Colours.*

  ——— quanto constantior idem
  In vitiis, tanto levius miser, ac prior ille
  Qui jam contento, jam laxo fune laborat (37).

  He that is constant in his vitious Race,
  Runs the same Course, and keeps an equal Pace,
  Is certainly not half so great a Wretch,
  As he, who now rides loose, and now on stretch.
                                  CREECH.

It were to be wished, that no one would presume to write Books of Devotion, without being perswaded of what he says, and without practising it; for to People of Thought and Reflexion it is matter of Scandal to see such Contradiction between the Thoughts and Words, and much more between the Actions and Writings, of such Authors.
  [K] *I mean his* Ragionamenti *.]* They are divided into Three Parts; the last of them, which treats of the Court, and Card-playing, is much more tolerable, than the others. The first treats of the disorderly Practices of Nuns, married Women, and Misses. It is sufficient to say, in general, that the Second is the Spirit and History of *Whoredom*. How abominable soever these Dialogues are, yet are they much less so, than the Book generally ascribed to him, *de omnibus Veneris Schematibus*.
  The following Remark was communicated to me (38): "This Book (*De omnibus Veneris Schematibus* †) which is here ascribed to *Aretin*, and which many perhaps believe to have been composed by him in the *Latin* Tongue, because, out of Modesty, you give it a *Latin* Title, is only a Collection, containing Sixteen lewd Figures, engrav'd by the Famous *Marc Anthony* of *Bologna*, after the Designs of *Julio Romano*, with a Sonnet of *Aretin's* at the bottom of each. He mentions them, in a Letter of the Twenty ninth of *November* 1527, in which he writes to Signor *Cæsar Fregosa*, that he sends him *il libro de i Sonetti e de le Figure lussuriose*. ——— *The Book of Sonnets, and Wanton Figures.* La *Vassari*, and M. *Felibien* after him, have said, that these Figures and Sonnets were Twenty in number. But *Aretin* himself, in his Dedication of them, in 1537, to *Baptista Zatti*, before-mentioned, makes them but Sixteen. There is a Dialogue between *Magdalena*, and *Julia*; the Title of which is, *la Putana errante;* ——— *The Whore-errant;* wherein he treats at length, *da i diversi conjungimenti* ——— *Of the different Ways of C--p--l--t--n,* to the number of Thirty five. This is to surpass four fold the ancient Debauchery;

  Quales nec Didymæ ‖ sciunt puellæ,
  Nec molles Elephantidos libelli, ———
  Sunt illic Veneris novem ‡ figuræ.

  Such Lines, as Harlots never read,
  Nor Elephantis cou'd indite;
                                      Nine

VOL. I.   5 S

ARETIN.

the Year of their first Impression [L]. We have Six Volumes of his *Letters*, which are

Nine Postures Venus there assumes,
To vary the obscene Delight.

"Though the Work has always been printed under "Aretin's Name; yet he disowns it; and says it is "the Work of One of his Scholars, called *le Veniero*. "This he tells us, in his *Capitolo*, addressed to the "Duke of *Mantua*; in which he assures him, that "his Pupil greatly exceeds him in Obscenity.

Ma perch' io sento il presente all' odore,
Un' operetta in quel cambio galante.
Vi mando hora in stil ladro traditore
Intitolata *la Putana errante.*
Dal Veniero composta mio creato,
Che me in dir mal quatro giornate inante.

I add to this a fine Passage of Mr *Chevillier*: "It "was about the Year 1525, that *Julio Romano*, the "most Famous Painter of *Italy*, instigated by the "Enemy of our Salvation, invented Designs, to be "engraved on Copper-Plates. The Subjects of them "are so lewd, that they are not so much as to be "named. Peter *Aretin*, a notoriously infamous Writer, and known in the World for a Profligate and "an Atheist, composed Sonnets for each Design. "*George Vasari*, who relates this, in his Book of the "Lives of the Painters, says, he knows not which "would be most immodest, to cast one's Eyes on the "Designs of *Julio*, or to read the Sonnets of *Aretin*. "*Io non so qual fusse piu o brutto lo spettacolo de i Designi di Giulio all' ochio, o le parole dell' Aretino à gl' orecchi.* 3. *Part. pa.* 302. An Engraver, whose "Name was *Marc Anthony*, ventured to employ his "Tool in engraving these infamous Designs on "Twenty Copper-Plates. Pope *Clement* VII threw "him into Prison; but the Cardinal *de Medicis* saved "his Life. And, as great as *Julio*'s Fame was in Painting, he would have been very severely punished, "if he had not escaped to *Mantua*. It happened "in the Year 1527, that *Rome* was plundered by the "Army of *Charles* V. It was this Engraver's Fortune to lose all his Estate, and be obliged to leave "the Town; soon after which he died. Mr. *Chevillier* adds, that Mr *Jollain*, a Merchant in St *James*'s street in *Paris*, being informed where "some of these infamous Plates lay, which contained "these abominable Designs of *Julio*, and the lewd "Sonnets of *Aretin*, went thither, and bought them "for an hundred Crowns, with a Design to destroy "them; which accordingly he did — He always believed, that They were the Original Plates, engraved by *Marc Anthony*, which he had destroyed "(40)."

(40) Chevillier, *of the Origin of Printing, at Paris, pag.* 224.

[L] *His Ragionamenti were printed in his Life Time; but it is difficult to discover the Year of their first Impression.*] The Preface to the Edition, in 1584, does not suffer us to doubt of the first Fact. The Bookseller, under the fictitious Name of *Barbagrigia*, declares, that "the Author had resolved to "publish his Dialogues, divided into *Days*, after the "manner of *Boccace*," and as they now stand in the Edition I have cited; "But that others had prevented him, and published This Work, against his Will, "and in great Disorder." — — — *Hoggi vi presento di loro una bu. na parte* —— *da me ridotte me la maniera ch' egli le compose, e ne la medesima maniera ch' egli haveva ditterminato di farle la prima volta stampare, s' altri (contra sua voglia) non havessero prima di lui date per mezzo de la stampa in luce assai male acconcie: conciosia cosa che Giornate questo nomasse per seguitare l' alte pedate del gran Giovanni Boccaccio.* I add something still more express to this; and I do it with so much the more Satisfaction, because, at the same Time, I acquit myself of an indispensible Duty towards Mr *Minutoli*, by the Publick Testimony I give him of my singular Esteem, and the great Value I set on the Friendship, with which he honours me. I have consulted This ingenious Professor of *Geneva*; and here present the Reader with an Extract of a Letter, which he communicated to me, and which was sent to him from *Dijon*. "I must now, Sir, "mention to you a Book very opposite to this (41), "to wit, the *Ragionamenti* of Peter *Aretin*: You "desire me to clear up some Points, concerning

(41) *He had been speaking of Mr Ballier's Book, concerning the Worship due to the Blessed Virgin.*

"them. The *Ragionamenti*, or Humorous Dialogues, "of *Aretin* were published before his Death. This "cannot be doubted of; since, in 1551, there appeared an Invective of *Joachim Perion*, a Benedictin Monk, against the Author of the *Ragionamenti*, who did not die till the Year 1556 (42). "*Antonio Francisco Doni*, in the first Part of his "*Bibliotheque*, published in 1550, which contains "only the printed Books, speaks of Two Dialogues, "*Delle Donne* (43), which differ from the *Ragionamenti*, of which he says not a Word, because it is "most certain they were not printed at that time. "As for the Letters, The first Volume alone deserves "to be read, though it contains scarce any thing satirical: The other Five are very flat; you may "take Mr *Menage*'s Word for it, in the *Menagiana*; "who honours them but too much, when he "esteems them for the Stile." In another Letter, Mr *Minutoli* had the Goodness to communicate to me the Two Observations, which he had made, in reading the Letters of Illustrious Men, published by *John Michel Brutus*. He found these Words in a Letter of *John Maludanus* to *Dionysius Lambinus* pag. 369. "Penè me fugerat, quod scribendum in primis fuisse "arbitror. A Perionio editam esse audio orationem "adversus Petrum Aretinum. Periculum est, ne, ut "jampridem principum, ita posthæc & μοναχῶν flagellum esse & nominari velit lacessitus Aretinus. — "*I had almost forgot what I ought particularly to acquaint you with. I am informed, that Perionius has "published an Oration against Peter Aretin. It is "to be feared, lest Peter Aretin, thus provoked, should "become, and desire to be called from henceforth, the "Scourge of Monks, as formerly of Princes.*" There is only the Date of the Day in this Letter; *Nonis Maiis*; but as *Lambinus*'s Answer is dated *Nonis Junsis, anno* CIƆ IƆ LI. it is easy to conjecture in what Year *Maludanus* wrote to him. My Reader will be pleased to find here what *Lambinus*, who was then at *Rome*, thought of *Perionius*'s Harangue. "Perionii orationem in Petrum Aretinum jampridem legeramus, "sed multo non sine risu. Quid enim magis ridiculum excogitari potest quam hominem Benedictinum, Philosophum, Ciceronianum, Theologum, "cum P. Aretino verbis decertare? Omnino suæ existimationi parum consuluisse judicatur; nam quod "arguit illum esse impurum, sceleratum, impium, "quod tum postea? Tales homines non verbis aut "scriptis castigandi, sed legibus & pœnis sunt coercendi. Sed hac de re alias plura. — — — *I had already "read Perionius's Oration against Peter Aretin, but "not without much laughter. For what can be conceived more ridiculous, than for One, who is "a Benedictin, a Philosopher, an Orator, and a Divine, to contest, in Words, with Peter Aretin? He "can gain but little Reputation by such a Controversy; "for, suppose that he proves him to be an impure, "wicked, and impious Fellow; What then? Such Men "are not to be corrected by Words, or by Writing, but "to be restrained by Laws and Punishments. But more "of this hereafter.*"

(42) *See Remark* [N].

(43) *Frehere reckons these two Dialogues among the Works of Aretin, and says nothing of the Ragionamenti. Perhaps these two Dialogues were the first Edition, which was publish'd without the Knowledge, and against the Will, of the Author, and in a different Method from his own.*

As to the Second Part of the Text of this Remark, read what follows; and you will admire the Accuracy and Extent of the Enquiries of the ingenious Gentleman, whom I quote (44). "It is difficult to "determine the exact Time of the first Edition of "the *Ragionamenti*, as well because it is become so "scarce, that it is hardly possible to meet with a Copy "of it, as because the Dialogues, which compose the "Two Parts of this Work, did not appear at the "same Time. The first Part preceeded the other "some Years; but what is certain, is, that they were "both in Print in 1537; the Epistles Dedicatory to "both Parts being inserted in the Edition of the "first Volume of *Aretin*'s Letters, at *Venice*, in *Folio*, by *Francis Marcolini*, in the same Year. The "Title of These *Ragionamenti* has varied. In the "Epistle Dedicatory to the Second Part of These "Dialogues, the Author calls the first *i tre Giorni di "caprici*, and even simply *dialogo*; for this is what "he suggests by these Words, *eccovi il dialogo*, "which nevertheless are not to be found in this "same Epistle, inserted among the Letters of the "first Volume; in which there is a farther considerable Variation. Which is, that, after the Words "*e per non disfraudare il mio grado*, all which follows,

(44) *Mr de la Monnoie.*

ARETIN. 441

are but of little Value [*M*]. His Works of Devotion were not much enquired after (*b*); yet they met with some, who gave them great Commendation (*c*). His Comedies in Prose are much better in their kind. He died about the Year 1556, at the Age of Sixty five Years, more or less [*N*]. It is said, that he fell into so violent a fit of Laughter, upon listening to some obscene Discourse, that he overturned the Chair, on which he sat; and that, in the Fall, he bruised his Skull, and died upon the Spot [*O*]. It was unlucky for him, that he wrote Lampoons against *Peter Strozzi*; for this brave Man threatned to have him assassinated in his very Bed; which so terrified our Poet, that he durst not admit any Person into his House, nor ever stir out of the Doors himself, during *Strozzi*'s stay in the State of *Venice*. For this I shall quote my Author [*P*]. Observe, that This so satirical Poet was lavish of his Praises to excess. We find the most pompous Hyperboles, and extravagant Flatteries, in his Letters to Kings, Princes, Generals of Armies, Cardinals, and other eminent Men: So far are they from carrying the Air of an Author, who makes himself dreaded, or exacts Contributions, that, on the contrary, there appears in them the Meanness of a Writer, who humbly intreats for a Piece of Bread. He employs the most moving Expressions to represent his Poverty, so far as to use the Language of *Canaan*, I mean a Scripture-Cant, as likeliest to raise Compassion, and excite those to Charity, who expect a Reward of their good Works from God. It must not be forgot, that one of the Subjects of his Importunities was the Dowry

of

" as far as è lo sa *Milano come cadde* inclusively, is entirely omitted; instead of which there is: *Usaro le parole cadute della sacra bocca del magno Antonio de Leva, l' Aretino è piu,* &c." Sometimes, instead of *Dialogo*, he says all along, as in his Epistle to his *Ape, il Dialogo de la Nanna & de la Antonia.* Sometimes, as in his Dialogue *della corte*, by his *Nanna* he means the first Part of the *Ragionamenti*, and by *La Pippa* the second. In a letter of the 15th of *May*, 1537, to *Francesco de l' Orme*, he styles both Parts *Dialoghi*, as *Anthony Francesco Doni* likewise does*. It is certain These Dialogues were never entituled *Ragionamenti* by This Author. They bear this Title only since the Edition of the Year 1584. The true Title was *Caprici*. *Perionius* confesses it, in his Invective against *Aretin*. " Scripsit enim, *says he*, atque edidit nefarium librorum quemdam, quem *Capricium* a Caprarum lascivia & libidine inscripsit. ----- *He wrote and published a vile Book, which he called* Caprici *from the Wantonness of* (Capræ) *Goats.* And a little lower; Galli plerique jam Italice sciunt, quo quidem sermone istius *Capricius,* aliique libri, scripti sunt —— *The French almost in general understand Italian, in which* Le Bandel *is mistaken, when, in the Thirty fourth of his Novels, pag. 235. of the first Part, he says, that la Zanina read la Nanna*; They are his own Words: *O sia Raffaella de l' Aretino.* In effect, La *Nanna* and *la Raffaella* are distinct Pieces, and by different Authors. By *La Nanna* should be understood the first Part of *Aretin*'s *Ragionamenti*, and by *la Raffaella,* the Dialogue of *Madona Raffaella,* and *Margareta,* entitled *della bella creanza delle Donne;* which instructs Women in the Arts of Gallantry. It is written by *Alessandra Piccolhuomini,* under his Academical Name of *Stordito Intronato.* This Quotation of *la Nanna* by *le Bandel* serves however to make it appear, that the first Part of the *Ragionamenti* was extant at least from the Year 1535; since, at the end of the same Novel, in which *la Nanna* is quoted, mention is made of *du Bernia,* as being then living, who certainly died in the Month of *May,* 1535; though M. *Baillet* places him after the Poets, who died in 1606. *Il Bernia Vicario Poeta d' Aretino mori apoplectico, says Paul Jovius* in a Letter, of the last of *May,* 1535, to *Ridolfo Pio,* Bishop of *Faience,* afterwards Cardinal of *Carpi,* then Nuncio in *France.* Mr *Menage,* who has made a Chapter expressly of *Bernia,* in the first Part of his *Antibaillet,* has not corrected this " Error."

[*M*] *We have six Volumes of his Letters, which are but of little Value.*] We have already seen the Judgment of a learned Man of *Dijon* on this Subject (45): That of Mr *Menage* may be added to it. " I have read, *says he* (46), all the Letters of *Peter Aretin,* without ever having found any thing in them, worthy of an Extract. There is nothing in them but Stile." One cannot convey a more expressive Idea of a Work, which is barren and dry; like an unfurnished House, or heathy, sandy, uncultivated Ground; for Mr *Menage* knew how to make the most of his Reading, and had an happy Talent at varying his Application of it.

[*N*] *He died about the Year* 1556, *at the Age of Sixty five Years, more or less* (47).] " The Reason " for conjecturing, that *Aretin* died either towards " the end of 1555, or in 1556, is, that, from the " Month of *October,* 1555. (the Date of the Epistle " dedicatory to the last Volume of his Letters), it " does not appear, that he had written any thing; " and that *Ruscelli,* who wrote his *Rimario* in 1577. " mentions *Aretin* therein, as a Person lately dead. " At the Word *Rosa,* in the Vocabulary at the end " of the *Rimario,* he says *Onde il mio Aretino di buona memoria.* That This *Rimario* was composed " in the Year 1557, appears by a Passage, I have " observed from it, above (48), on occasion of *Sil- " vio Antoniano* (49)." *Paul Freberus* is mistaken, in saying, that *Aretin* died towards the Year 1566 (50).

[*O*] *He fell into so violent a fit of Laughter, ---- bruised his Skull; and died upon the Spot.*] " Insandas obscœ- " nitates de meretricibus, ut aiunt, sororibus suis, " cum audiret, ex risu sessum, in qua sedebat, ever- " tisse, occiputque vehementer graviterque ad terram " afflixisse, atque atque allisisse, ut extemplo nequis- " sime interiret. (51)."

[*P*] *I shall quote my Author.*] He is *Remi de Florence.* " Volse Pietro Aretino, *says he* (52), burlare & motteggiare il Sig. Pietro Strozzi, quando " egli diede Marano a Venetiani, e gli fece un Sonetto, che cominciava;

Mentre il gran Strozzi Arma virumque cano, &c.

" Ma il Signor Pietro come huomo valoroso, & che " non voleva sue burle ne suoi motti gli fece intendere, che attendesse ad altro, perche lo farebbe " ammazzare infin nel letto. Onde il povero Aretino, che conosceva il Signor Pietro huomo pio " da farlo che da dirlo, si mise tanto spavento, che " ferrato in casa, ne dando ingresso à persona alcuna, guardava pure se i pugnali piovevano, & meno giorno e notte una vita infelicissima, e per sin " che lo Strozzi stette in paese de' Veneziani, non " ardi mai uscir di casa. ----- Peter Aretin *had a Mind to banter* Peter Strozzi, *upon his delivering up* Marano *to the* Venetians; *and made a Sonnet, which began thus;*

Mean time Great Strozzi, &c.

" But Peter, as a Man of Valour, and who desired " none of his Jokes, gave him to understand, that " he had better mind something else, if he expected to be safe in his Bed. Poor Aretin, who knew " that he was a Man of Deeds, more than Words, was " so frightned, that he kept himself locked up in his House,

ARETIN. ARGYROPYLUS.

of his dear Daughter *Adria* [*Q*]. He took a great deal of Pains to marry her; but saw her so unhappy in this State, that he heartily repented of his Impatience [*R*]. A Fatality too common among Men! for how many things are there, which make us extremely uneasy, before they are accomplished, but much more so after Accomplishment?

"*House, and admitted no one to enter; he even watched to see, whether it did not rain Poignards, and led a miserable Life, Night and Day, during* Strozzi's *Residence in the* Venetian *State, not daring to stir out of his Doors.*" I fancy, when he found himself out of Danger, he behaved like the *Sow, that is washed*.

[*Q*] *One of the Subjects of his Importunities, was the Dowry of his dear Daughter* Adria.] He loved her very affectionately, and had engaged himself to give a thousand Ducats to the Person, who was to marry her. This future Son-in-law was not to be put off to the next Dedication: such an Assignment, which some Authors have put their Creditors off with, would not satisfy him; he articled, that a thousand Ducats should be paid him down, before he gave the Ring to the Bride. *Mille ducati a la promessa da me fatta allo spoſo in contanti, prima che se le dia l'anello* (53). The Gold Chain, which *Aretin* had received from the Prince of *Spain* (54), was forced to go towards the Payment of this Sum. He addressed himself to the Cardinal of *Lorrain* for Assistance in this Necessity. I cannot tell, whether he received any thing from him; but I know, that he was assisted by the Duke of *Florence*. The Bill of Exchange, which That Prince sent him (55), imported, that the Money should not be paid, but on good Attestations that the Marriage was consummated (56). This Condition hastened the Wedding; the Father would have deferred it; for he fancied his Daughter *Adria* was too Young: but this Consideration must now be past by. When she was laid in the nuptial Bed, he said, that She looked like a spotless Victim laid on the sacred Altar: *Per imperiarmi piu l' honore della parola obligata, che il rispetto della etade tenera; consentii, che la innocentia si copulasse co'l sacramento. Ella, nello entrare nel letto, parue una ostia pura, posta ſopra l'altare sacro* (57). It appears, that the Son-in-law did not rigorously exact the Payment of the whole Sum before Marriage; he was satisfied with the Gold Chain, which the Emperor's Son, had given *Aretin*, as Security for what was wanting of the thousand Ducats; but this did not make the Father-in-law a jot the easier; who had a great Desire to keep his Gold Chain; and yet could not get rid of his Daughter, until all the Money was paid: For his Son-in-law refused to take her Home to his own House, without the full Portion.

The Duke of *Florence* was again importuned, and disburst something more (58).

[*R*] *He saw her so unhappy in this State, that he repented of his Impatience.*] It was a very unhappy Match; poor *Adria* was so ill treated by her Husband, that she was obliged to return to her Father (59); but, her Husband promising her better Usage, she was persuaded to a Reconcilement; but was still as unhappy as ever. She was still denied the Power of the Keys; a Power, which never falls to the Petticoat in the Church, but is the Woman's Right in the Management of a Family. She could neither eat, nor drink, but when it pleased others to dispose of the Keys in her Favour: She was perpetually teized about her Dress. Her Husband would not suffer her to wear Jewels, and obliged her to sell a Diamond, which her Father had given her: Thus she was attacked in the most sensible Part; this was tearing her very Heart out. *Aretin* implored for her the Protection of the Duchess of *Urbino* (60). What a Heart-breaking must it be to him, to find himself treated so contemptuously by his Son-in-law, whilst his Fame was spread as far as the Court of *Persia* (61)! What a Domestic Bitter was This amidst the fancied Sweets of a great Reputation! Could it be any Consolation, to consider, that this Brute at the same time despised the Duke of *Florence*, who had earnestly recommended it to him to treat his Wife well? On the contrary this was a new Subject of Confusion to the Person, who had made so ill a Choice of a Son-in-Law. " *Benche en quanto al non fare niſſuna stima " di me simil' cane, non e maraviglia, e ben' da stu- " pire del si poco rispetto che mostra d'havere lo as- " naccio al gran' Duca, la cui benignita mansueta, us- " cendo noi di Pesaro, per il viaggio di Roma, coſi " qual era a cavallo, chiomollo, & dissegli; Se tu " vuoi che non ti si manchi di gratie, tratta la mog- " lie tua, si come di me nata fusse* (62). — *As to " this Brute's little regard for me, it is not to be " wondered at; but it is astonishing that This Ass " should be so wanting in Respect to the Great Duke; " who was so kind, at our Departure from Pesaro to " Rome, as to call him back, when on Horseback, and " ſays; if you expect the Continuance of my Favour, " treat your Wife as if she were my Daughter.*" Note, That *Peter Aretin* had another Daughter, whom he was very desirous of marrying (63).

(53) *Aretin, Letter 145, Book 5. fol. 72. Edit. of Paris 1609.*

(54) *Id. Ib.*

(55) *See the 24th Letter of the same Book. It is dated at Venice, 1548.*

(56) *See the 22th Letter of the 5th Book. It is dated March 1549.*

(57) *Ibid. fol. 102.*

(58) *See the 6th Book of the Letters of Aretin, fol. 121.*

(59) *See the 16th Book of his Letters, fol. 181.*

(60) *His Letter to the Duchess of Urbino is dated from Venice in November 1554.*

(61) *See Remark [A].*

(62) *Aretin, pag. 282, of the 6th Book of his Letters.*

(63) *She was called Austria. See the 21th Letter of the 5th Book.*

ARGYROPYLUS (*a*) (JOHN), a Native of *Constantinople*, retired into *Italy*, while the *Turks* were overturning all *Greece* [*A*]. He was very kindly received by *Cosmo de Medicis*, who made him Preceptor to his Son *Peter*, and his Grandson *Lorenzo* (*b*), and Professor of *Greek* at *Florence*. He testified his Gratitude in a Translation of *Aristotle's* Physics and Ethics. He was attended with a very particular piece of good Fortune in This Work; for *Theodore Gaza*, who had finished a like Translation, threw it into the Fire, that he might not prejudice the Fortune of his good Friend *Argyropylus*. *Gaza* surpassed him in Eloquence, and his Translation would infallibly have eclipsed the other; but, as he was not ignorant of *Argyropylus's* Ambition, and was, besides, a good-natured Man, he made a Sacrifice, which cost him but little; for he was one, who valued neither Praise, nor Money. *Argyropylus's* Conversation disgusted and tired Men of Learning, especially when he took upon him to maintain, that *Cicero* did not

(*a*) And not ARGIRO-PHILUS, nor ARGY-ROPHI-LUS, as in *Moreri*.

(*b*) And not his Nephew, as in *Moreri*.

[*A*] *He retired into Italy, while the Turks were overturning all Greece.*] I dare not say, with *Moreri*, that he retired into *Italy*, after the Conquest of *Constantinople* by the *Turks*; for Two Reasons make me doubt it. One is, *Paul Jovius's* saying, that *Argyropylus* was driven into *Italy* by the same Tempest, which forced *Theodore Gaza* thither (1). Now he observes, that This *Theodore* took refuge there, while *Amurath* shook all *Greece* with his Victorious Arms. *Amurathe Græciam omnem victricibus armis quatiente, in Italiam venit* (2). This inclines me to believe, that *Argyropylus* left his Country before the *Ottomans* had taken *Constantinople*. My second Reason is, because he addressed a Treatise of Consolation to the Emperor of *Constantinople*. To make this a good Argument, it must, I confess, be proved, that

he composed this Piece in *Italy*; and I own I cannot prove this; so that I only offer this Observation, as a motive to keep my Reader in suspence. *Paul Jovius* is to blame, in having neglected Chronology, so much as he has done, in his Elogies; for he might easily have discovered the date of the Offices, Travels, and Deaths, of his Illustrious Persons. This by the way. *Vossius* observes, that This Treatise of *Argyropylus*, his *Monodie*, his Book *de Regno*, and his Parallels between the Ancient and Modern Princes, are in the Library of the most Christian King (3). Mr. *Moreri*, who never saw these Works, affirms, nevertheless, that the Author dedicated them to the House of *Medicis*. Why was he not satisfied with affirming this concerning the Translations of *Aristotle* only? his Guide goes no farther (4).

[*B*] *What*

(1) *Paulus Jovius, Elog. cap. 27. pag. 64.*

(2) *Id. ib. cap. 16. pag. 61.*

(3) *Vossius, de Histor. Græcis, lib. 4, cap. 19, pag. 433.*

(4) *Paulus Jovius, Elog. cap. 27.*

ARIARATHES. ARIGONI. 443

not understand *Greek*. He left *Tuscany*, in the time of a Plague, and went to *Rome*, where he read Lectures on the *Greek* Text of *Aristotle*. His Salary was considerable; but, as he loved good Eating and Drinking, and as his Constitution was able to bear Intemperance, he spent all his Income. So that what has been said of his Gluttony, is not incredible [*B*]. He died of a Fever, which he got by eating too many Melons, at seventy Years of Age (*c*). He discovered great Constancy of Mind, when one of his Sons was killed at *Rome* (*d*). See, concerning the Order, which Pope *Paul* III gave for pursuit of the Murtherers, and for the Funeral of the deceased, the 200th Letter of the Cardinal of *Pavia*, pag. 620. It has been remarked, that he was the first *Greek*, who taught Philosophy in that City [*C*]. He disputed with much Vivacity, and had a very extensive Knowledge. He left a Son, who was an excellent Musician (*e*). The Judgments, which have been passed upon his Translations, differ extreamly [*D*].

(*c*) *T. ken from Paul Jovius, Elog. cap. 27.*

(*d*) *Petrus Alcyonius, in Medicæ Legato priore, pag. 25.*

(*e*) *Obiit relicto filio Isaacio, nobili Musico. Volaterran. lib. 21. p. 776.*

[*B*] *What has been said of his Gluttony is not incredible.*] Let us quote *Paul Jovius*. "Vini & cibi "æque avidus & capax, & multo abdomine ventri- "colus, immodico melopeponum esu autumnalem "accersivit febrem, atque ita septuagesimo ætatis "anno ereptus est (5). —— *Being equally desirous, and* "*capable, of eating and drinking, and having a very* "*large Belly, he got an autumnal Fever by eating too* "*many Melons; and thus was taken off in the Seven-* "*tieth Year of his Age.*" To die of excessive eating is scandalous in any one; much more in Men of Letters. It had been more for the Honour of *Argyropylus* to have died of Hunger. Let us not, however, look upon the enormous Size of his Belly as a good Argument against those, who represent him as a Person of great Abilities: The Event of such a Dispute would be very uncertain. See the Collections, which shall be produced in the Remarks of the Article GORGIAS.

(5) *Jovius, Ibid. p. 65.*

[*C*] *It has been remarked, that he was the first Greek, who taught at Rome*] His Disciple *Politian* is now to be quoted; read these Words of *Hornius*. "Primus ex Græcis Romæ philosophiam professus "fuit Argyropulus, cujus sectatorem se fuisse me- "morat Angelus Politianus, Miscel. cap. 1. eumque "cum literarum Latinarum minime incuriosum, tum "sapientiæ decretorum, disciplinarumque adeo cun- "ctarum, quæ Cyclicæ à Martiano dicuntur, erudi- "tissimum illis temporibus habitum, atque in dispu- "tando acerrimum (6). —— *Argyropylus was the First* "*of the Greeks, who professed Philosophy at Rome;* "*whose Follower Politian was, as he informs us, Mis-* "*cell. ch. 1. as also that, he was not only well versed* "*in the Latin Tongue, but skilled likewise in the* "*Learning of Decretals, and esteemed the greatest* "*Scholar of his Times, in all those Sciences, which by* "*Martian are called Cyclic, and a strenuous Dispu-* "*tant.*"

(6) *Hornius, Historiæ Philosoph. l. 6. c. 6. p. 304, 305.*

[*D*] *The Judgments, which have been passed upon his Translations, differ extreamly*] *Thuanus* observes, that *Perionius*, intending to avoid the Method of *Argyropylus*, fell into another Extreme. He found, that *Argyropylus* had translated *Aristotle* more faithfully, than elegantly; and therefore undertook a Translation, which should please those, who admire good Latin; but, labouring too much at Elegancy of Style, he lay open to the Charge of departing from the Sense of the Author. "Is (*Joachimus Perionius*) cum *Ari-* "*stotelem hactenus a Johanne Argyropylo fideliter po-* "*tius quam ornate versum auribus Latinis propo-* "*nendum statuisset, dum elegantioris stili potius quam* "*veri rationem plerumque Ciceroni suo addictus ha-* "*bet, in contrariam ab Argyropylo reprehensionem* "*incidit* (7). Which Judgment amounts to this: *Argyropylus*'s Translation is faithful, but without Grace or Ornament. Others judge of it quite otherwise; They say there is more of Elegancy, than Faithfulness, in it; and blame him for not translating his Original Word for Word, *according to the Duty of those*, add they, *who translate the Holy Scripture*, and Aristotle. *Aliquot Aristotelis libros convertit magis eleganter quam*

(7) *Thuan. Histor. l. 23. pag 4-2, ad Ann. 1559.*

fideliter, cum in hoc philosopho haud aliter quam in sacris literis verbum verbo reddere oporteat (8). If we consult a Professor of *Louvain*, we shall find this Judgment of *Volaterran* but ill grounded, and that *Argyropylus* confined himself more servilely to *Aristotle*'s Words, than Thoughts; and that his Translation can pass for neither faithful nor elegant. See the words of This Professor: "Superiori sæculo, quidam verba ver- "bis ita admensi sunt, ut sententiam depravarint, non "aliter quam indocti pictores, qui, operosi in cultu effin- "gendo, membra secundum vestem distorquent: quum "Apelles, Parrhasiique, prius nudum corpus effor- "mare, quam amictam superinducere solerent. In. "quorum numero Argyropylum reponas, & Ruffi- "num, alterum interpretem Aristotelis, alterum Gre- "gorii Nazianzeni, de quibus vere id hemistichii dici "potest: Dant sine mente sonum. Fit autem illud "vel ex inscitia, vel ex κακοζηλία quum enim sen- "tentiam apprehendere nequeunt, verba reddunt, "quasi quod ipsi non intellexerint, alius ex illorum "verbis intelligere queat, cum verba non minus ex "sententia vim suam, & significatum accipiant, quam "sententiam constituant. Aliqui rursus fidem existi- "mant à numero verborum non discedere (9). ---- *In* "*the last Age, some Writers so scrupulously adhered* "*to the Words of an Author, as to spoil the sense; like* "*unskilful Painters, who, taking a great Deal of* "*Pains about the Drapery, neglect the Proportions and* "*Symmetry of the Figure: Whereas Apelles, and the* "*Parrhasii, always drew the naked Figure, before* "*they cloathed it.* In the number of these may be ranked Argyropylus, and Ruffinus, *The One a Trans-* "*lator* of Aristotle, the Other of Gregory of Nazi- "anzen; *to whom may justly be applied the Hemistic,* "Dant sine mente sonum; They give a Sound with- "out a meaning. *This proceeds either from Ignorance,* "*or false Emulation; for, when they cannot comprehend* "*the Sense, they render the Words; as if another* "*could apprehend from their Words what They them-* "*selves understand not: whereas Words no less re-* "*ceive their Force and Signification from the Sentence,* "*than constitute the Sentence.* Others again think "*it the business of a Faithful Translator to keep to* "*the very number of the Words.*" Some Learned Men imagine, that *Argyropylus* is here accused of confining himself *verbatim* to the Original, and, where he cannot comprehend his Author's Sense, of having recurred to a jingle of Words without any meaning (10). I question whether this is exactly what *Nannius* aims at. *Huetius* agrees in his Judgment with *Thuanus* (11), and consequently condemns That of *Volaterran*. He condemns *Paul Jovius* likewise, who preferred the Translation of *Gaza* before That of *Argyropylus*, and declares, that, if the first be more Eloquent, the latter is more faithful. *Non efficies quin major quidem eloquentia laus Gazæ, accurate autem interpretandi Argyropylo debeatur* (12). See, above, Remark [*B*] of the Article A C C I A I O L I (DONATO), and wonder at the Diversity of these Opinions.

(8) *Volaterran. lib. 21. pag. 776.*

(9) *Petrus Nannius, Alcmarianus in Collegio Buldianorum apud Lovanienses Latinus Professor, ευφημερον, lib. 1. c. 3. pag. 6.*

(10) *See Mr Baillet, Jugem. des Sçavans, Tom. 4. p. 814. p. 356.*

(11) *Huetius de claris Interpret. pag. 239.*

(12) *Id. ib.*

ARIARATHES. The Name of several Kings of *Cappadocia*. See the Article CAPPADOCIA.

ARIGONI (POMPEIO), Cardinal and Archbishop of *Benevento*, was born at *Rome*, in the Year 1552. During the Time, that he was one of the Consistorial Advocates, he was retained in all the Causes relating to *Philip* II of *Spain*. In the Pontificate of *Sixtus Quintus*, he make a Speech, to shew the Reasonableness of canonizing the blessed *Diego d'Alcala*. He was made Auditor of the *Rota*, in the Year 1591, and Cardinal in 1596, and exercised the Office of Chancellor under *Leo* XI, and *Paul* V. The Archbishoptic of *Benevento* was conferred upon him by This last Pope. He died, the fourth of *April*, 1616, in the *Greeks* Tower near *Naples*, whither he had retired for change of Air. His Body was carried to *Benevento*, where his Nephew erected a Marble Tomb over him, in the principal Church. There are some *Latin* Letters of our *Pompey*, among those of *John Baptista Lauri*, besides the Speech beforementioned, which was printed by *Peter Galesini* (a). As to his *Decisions of the Rota*, they are only Manuscripts in the Cabinets of some learned Men. *Charles Caribari* gave him great Commendations in his List of the Consistorial Advocates (b).

(a) In Libello pro Canonisatione B. Didaci Complutensis. See also Franciscus Pegna, in vita ejusdem Didaci.

(b) Ex Bibl. Romana Prosperi Mandosii.

ARIMANIUS, one of the chief Deities of *Persia*. That Nation was indebted to *Zoroaster* for it's Philosophy; one principal Tenet of which was revived by the *Manicheans*; to wit, That there are two first Principles, one of Good, and the other of Evil. The *Persians* called the Deity, which they acknowledged as the Principle of all Good, and Author of the State, in which Things were first produced, *Orosmades*; and the Divinity, which they acknowledged as the Principle of Evil, and Author of the Corruption, into which the Original Nature is fallen, They called *Arimanius*. They said, that *Orosmades*, having produced the good Spirits, and the Stars, enclosed them in an Egg [*A*]; and that *Arimanius* produced the bad *Genii*, who broke This Egg; from whence proceeded Confusion, and a mixture of Good and Evil. They add, that, at last, after divers Conflicts, in which the Victory would be various, *Orosmades* should totally vanquish *Arimanius*, and destroy him beyond retrieve; which would be followed by a State of great Happiness to Mankind, and by a very commodious Transformation, by which the Bodies of Men would become transparent, and be preserved without any Nourishment (a).

What I have here said is borrowed from an Author, who had it from *Plutarch*, whose entire Passage I shall produce elsewhere (b). It is remarkable, that the King of *Persia*, when *Themistocles* fled to him for Refuge, prayed to *Arimanius*, that he would always influence his Enemies to banish their bravest Men (c). This is a Proof, that the *Persians* considered *Arimanius* as a Divinity, which took a Pleasure only in Evil [*B*]. The same Divinity, doubtless, was meant, when, upon *Darius*'s complaining of the Deity of *Persia*, when he was informed, that the Queen his Wife was dead a Prisoner in the Camp of *Alexander*; he was answered; *With regard to Funeral Honours, &c. you have no reason to accuse the Bad Genius of the Nation* (d). *Your Wife, Your Mother, and Your Children, have lost nothing of their former Fortune, but the Opportunity of seeing your Glory restored by Orosmades* (e). We see, in these Words, the Opposition, which the *Persians* supposed to be between *Orosmades* and *Arimanius*.

(a) Taken from Burnet's Theory of the Earth, lib. 2. c. 10. p. 289, 290. who cites Plutarch de Iside & Osiride.

(b) In Remark [C] of the Article MANICHEANS; and Remark [E] of the Article ZOROASTER.

(c) Plut. in Themist. pag. 126.

(d) The of virgos Asignora. Plut. in Alexandro, p. 682.

(e) Id. ib.

[*A*] *Enclosed them in an Egg.*] I promised, in another Place (1), that I would say something here concerning the Egg, which, according to the Ancient Theology of the Pagans, had been employed in the Production of Beings, when the *Chaos* was reduced. I say, then, that it was the Opinion of the *Phœnicians*, that the *obscure Air*, and the *Chaos*, were the Principle of all Things. This obscure Air is without doubt the same, which others call Night, and to which they attribute the Production of an Egg, out of which proceeded Love, and Human-kind. Τίκτει πρώτιστον νὺξ μελανόπ]ερός ὠὸν (2) This may be ingeniously explained of the Earth, and compared with the Words of *Moses*; by supposing, that the grosser Parts of This obscure and thick Air, subsiding, met with a fat and glewy Substance, with which, incorporating they formed a kind of Slime; which, being hardened, became an habitable Earth (3). Some of the Ancients said, that a Dove, brooding on an Egg, produced *Venus*, or Love. " Verba citat Grotius ex " *Nigidio* in Scholiasten Germanici, ovum mire " Magnitudinis, quod volventes ejecerunt in terram, " atque ita columbam insedisse, & post aliquot dies " exclusisse Deam Syriæ, quæ vocatur Venus (4)." *Lucius Ampelius* pretends it was the Egg of a Fish; *Ovum pisces columbam adsedisse dies plurimos, & exclusisse Deam benignam* (5). By the Egg Dr Burnet understands the *Chaos*, the Holy Ghost by the Dove, and by *Venus* the Earth (6). But I think we should not limit This *Venus*, which came out of the Egg, to the Production of the Earth alone, but understand it of the whole Machine of the World. The Doctor observes, that the Egg was sacred in the Mysteries of *Bacchus*, because of it's Resemblance to That Being, which ingenders and includes every thing in it's self. Ὡς μίμημα τοῦ τὰ πάντα γεννῶντ[ος] καὶ περιέχοντ[ος] ἐν ἑαυτῷ (7). He does not forget to observe, that *Moses*'s Expression relates to the Action of Hens in brooding. " Huic doctrinæ " de Ovo mundano dataque interpretationi tacite fa- " vere mihi videtur *incubatio Spiritus Sancti* in " abyssum, de qua *Moses* in prima telluris productio- " ne, ubi ad ovum manifesto alluditur (8). - - - - " *This Moving (or Brooding) of the Holy Spirit* " *upon the Face of the Waters, which Moses speaks* " *of in the History of the Creation, where he plainly* " *alludes to an Egg, is a tacit Confirmation of This* " *Doctrine of the Mundane Egg, and the Ex-* " *plication I have given of it.*"

[*B*] *The Persians considered* Arimanius *as a Divinity, which took a Pleasure only in Evil.*] If any one is inclined not to grant me this, he may object, that the King of *Persia* was greatly pleased to have gained *Themistocles*; he believed, therefore, the Exile of such Persons to be a fortunate Event for his own Country, and that it was his Interest they should take Refuge in his Court: when, therefore, he prayed to *Arimanius* to inspire his Enemies with a Resolution to banish their bravest Citizens, he demanded a very great Favour of him; and, consequently, he looked upon him as a Principle of Good, upon some Occasions, with regard to the *Persians*. I answer, that This Reasoning is invalid. This Monarch agreed in Opinion with his Divines; he considered *Arimanius* only as a malignant Being; he pretended for the Exile of the great Men of *Greece*, only inasmuch as it was prejudicial to That Country. It was an Action within the Jurisdiction, and to the Taste, of *Arimanius*, as far as it was unjust and pernicious, with respect to the Towns, which banished them. But, as far as it was beneficial to the *Persians*, it was by no means agreeable to him; nor was it under this Notion, that his Assistance was intreated. In a Word, to solve this Objection, it is sufficient to say, that the Affairs of this World being so interwoven with each other, that, generally speaking, one Country profits by the Misfortunes of another, *Arimanius* could scarce effect any thing

(1) Above, Remark [A] of the Article ADAM.
(2) Aristophanes apud Burnetium, Tell. Theor. Sacr. lib. 2. cap. 7. pag. 243.
(3) This is Dr Burnet's Explication, ibid. p. 244.
(4) Id. ib. pag. 259.
(5) Ibid.
(6) Ibid.
(7) Ex Plutarchi Sympos. lib. 2. Quæst. 3.
(8) Burnet's Theory, p. 286.

ARIMINI. ARION.

thing simply and absolutely pernicious; some Advantage would always result from it, either by accident, or otherwise. Now, as He did nothing, but on account of the Evil, which he discovered in it, it could never be pretended, that he was the Principle of any Good. It is true, then, that the Prayer, we are speaking of, is no Proof, that he was considered otherwise, than as a Being, who took a Pleasure only in hurting.

ARIMINI (GREGORY of) See RIMINI.

ARION, a wonderful Horse, and famed in Poetical Story on a different account from *Bucephalus* in the History of *Alexander*. His Origin has been variously spoken of; though all allow it Divine. Some say (*a*), that *Neptune*, being desirous to procure to Men all the Conveniences, which Horses could afford them, struck the Earth in *Thessaly* with his Trident; and immediately out started a couple of Horses; one of which was our *Arion*. Others say, that *Neptune*, disputing with *Minerva*, which of them should give a Name to the City of *Athens*, it was ordered by the other Gods, that which ever of the Two should make the best Present to Men should give a Name to The City. Whereupon, *Neptune* struck the Beach with his Trident, and caused an Horse to issue forth of it [*A*]; but *Minerva* produced an Olive-Tree; and gained the Victory; for it was judged, that Peace, of which the Olive is an Emblem, was better than War, in which the Horse was most useful. Now there are, who pretend, that the Horse, which *Neptune* produced on this Occasion, was named *Arion*. Others say, that This Horse sprung from *Ceres* and *Neptune* (*b*). This Goddess, as she was wandring through the World in quest of her Daughter, met *Neptune*, who made fierce Love to her; but, not being disposed to gratify his Passion, she thought fit to assume the Form of a Mare. This past near the City of *Oncium* in *Arcadia*. *Ceres* in vain endeavoured to conceal herself among the Studd; *Neptune* soon discovered her, and enjoyed her in the Shape of an Horse. She was vext at it at first; but was, afterwards, appeased, and washed herself in a neighbouring River. She had, by this Adventure with *Neptune*, not only a Daughter, whose Name it was not lawful to declare to prophane Persons, but likewise Our Horse *Arion*. There are, who say, that she was in the Form of a Fury, when *Neptune* begot this Horse on her, or that, in effect, a Fury conceived him, from the Act of *Neptune* [*B*]. The Poet *Antimachus*, cited by *Pausanias*, gives him no other Origin, than the Soil of *Arcadia*: But *Quintus Calaber* makes him the Son of *Zephyrus*, and a Harpy [*C*]. However it be, it was believed, that he was brought up by the *Nereids* [*D*], and that, being sometimes harnessed, with other of *Neptune*'s Horses, to the Chariot of That God, he drew him with incredible Swiftness over all the Seas (*c*). He had this peculiar to him, that his Feet, on the off side, were like those of a Man (*d*). *Hercules* mounted him, when he took the City of *Elis*, and afterwards presented him to *Adrastus*. This *Pausanias* informs us of; who adds, that *Antimachus* made *Adrastus* the third Owner of him [*E*]. *Hesiod* represents him as belonging to *Hercules*, in his Combat with *Cygnus* (*e*). *Statius* says, in general, that he served *Hercules* in his Travels, and that, afterwards, the Gods gave him to *Adrastus* (*f*). *Probus* ascribes the whole Honour of This Present to *Neptune* (*g*). Under this

(*a*) Lutatius in Statii Thebaid. lib. 4. v. 43.

(*b*) Pausan. lib. 8. pag. 257.

(*c*) Stat. Thebaid. l. 6. ver. 308.

(*d*) Lutatius, in Statii Theb. l. 6. ver. 302.

(*e*) Hesiod. in Clypeo Herculis.

(*f*) Stat. ubi supra.

(*g*) Probus, in Virgil. Georgic. I.

[*A*] *Neptune, disputing with Minerva - - - - struck the Beach - - - - - and caused an Horse to issue forth of it.*] *Servius* informs us of this, on these Words of *Virgil*.

- - - - - - tuque ô, cui prima frementem
Fudit equum magno tellus percussa tridenti,
Neptune (1).

*And Thou, whose Trident struck the teeming Earth,
And made a Passage for the Courser's Birth.*

DRYDEN.

See likewise *Probus* on the same Passage of *Virgil*.

[*B*] *She was in the Form of a Fury, when Neptune begot this Horse on her; or - - - - - a Fury conceived him by Neptune.*] They are the Opinions of *Apollodorus* and *Hesychius*. These are their Words. Τοῦτον ἐκ Ποσειδῶνος ἐγέννησε εἰκασθεῖσα Ἐριννύϊ κατὰ τὴν συνουσίαν (2). *Ceres, under the Form of a Fury, conceived this Horse by Neptune*. Ἀρίων ὁ Ἵππος Ποσειδῶνος καὶ μιᾶς τῶν Ἐριννύων (3). *The Horse Arion, the Son of Neptune and one of the Furies*. *Bartbius* has confounded This Opinion of *Apollodorus* with That of *Hesychius*. " Unius ex Erynnibus, *says* he (4), sobolem assentitur Apollodoro Hesychius Lexicographus. - - - - " Hesychius *the Lexicographer agrees with Apollodorus, in making him the Offspring of one of the* " *Furies*." This is to make *Apollodorus* say, that *Arion* was foaled by one of the Furies; but he has said no such thing; he expressly observes, that *Ceres* was the Mother of This Horse, and that she had assumed the Form of a Fury, only at the Time of Copulation. *Lloyd* has stolen from *Bartbius* in this Place, without correcting him.

[*C*] *Quintus Calaber makes him the Son of Zephyrus, and a Harpy.*] Behold a second Fault of *Bartbius*, which *Lloyd* has transplanted into his Lexicon, just as he found it. " Intercedit Quintus, *says* Bar- " thius (5), Harpyiæ patronus, cujus fuerit potius " seminio oriundus patre Zephyro, ingratiis etiam " Neptuni. - - - - - - *Quintus Calaber interposes,* " *making him to have been begot upon a Harpy by* " *Zephyrus, against the Will of Neptune*." There " is nothing in That Poet which remarks, that it was with, or without, the Approbation of *Neptune*, that *Zephyrus* and the Harpy produced *Arion* (6).

[*D*] *It was believed, that he was brought up by the Nereids*.] I shall cite only *Claudian*.

Si dominus legeretur equis, tua posceret ultro
Verbera, Nereidum stabulis nutritus, Arion (7).

*To chuse a Master were the Coursers free,
Arion, once the Nereids Care, would be
Subject to thy Command, and court the Whip from thee.*

[*E*] *Adrastus was his third Owner.*] This is true, according to the History, which the Scholiast of *Homer* makes of it, on the Three hundred and forty sixth Verse of the Twenty third Book of the *Iliad*. He says, that *Neptune*, falling in Love with *Erin-*

(1) Virgil. Georgic. lib. 1. ver. 12.

(2) Apollod. Bibl. lib. 3.

(3) Hesychius.

(4) Barth. in Stat. Tom. 2. pag. 899.

(5) Id. lib. 4.

(6) Q. Calaber. lib. 4. ver. 572.

(7) Claudian. Consul. IV. Honorii ver. 555. Lloyd cites this twice.

nys,

445

ARIOSTA. ARISTANDER.

this last Master it was, that *Arion* signaliz'd himself most; he won the Prize of the Race in the *Nemean* Games [F], which the Princes, who undertook the Siege of *Thebes*, instituted in Honour of *Archemorus*, and was the means of preserving *Adrastus* from perishing, with all the other Chiefs, in This famous Expedition. This *Apollonius* testifies in his third Book.

(8) *That is, One of the Furies.* ἦν (8), metamorphosed himself into a Horse, and enjoyed her in *Bœotia*, near the Fountain *Tiphlousa*: that he got an Horse on her, which was called *Apsiau*, because he excelled all others; that he gave him to *Copreus*, King of *Aliartus*; who presented him to *Hercules*; who won the Prize of the Race with This Horse, against *Cygnus*, the Son of *Mars*, near *Trœzene*, and that, afterwards, *Hercules* presented him to *Adrastus*.

[F] *He won the Prize of the Race in the Nemesian Games.*] *Apollodorus*, in his third Book, says, that *Adrastus* was Victor in the Chariot-Race; but *Statius* pretends, that This Prince gave *Arion* to his Son-in-law *Polynices*; and that *Arion* threw his new Driver, and, continuing his Course, outstript all the rest; which did not prevent *Amphiaraus* from carrying the Crown: For, though he did not distance *Arion*, yet it was sufficient, that he carried it from his Competitors, and that *Polynices*, being thrown, could pretend to nothing in virtue of the superior Fleetness of his Horse.

(9) Stat. Theb. lib. 6. ver. 528.

Forsitan & victo prior isset Arione Cygnus,
Sed vetat æquoreus vinci pater: hinc vice justa
Gloria mansit equo, cessit victoria vati (9).

Neptune *forbad, that, in his whirling Car,*
Cygnus the Prize, should from Arion *bear;*
Hence the Steed gain'd the Honour of the Day,
The Prize Amphiaraus *bore away.*

Apollodorus confesses, that *Amphiaraus* carried it in the Chariot Race, ἅρμαʼτι; which his *Latin* Translator ought to have rendered by *curru*, and not *cursu*, as *Barthius* has observed (10). As for the Distich of *Propertius*, which makes *Arion* a speaking Animal, (10) Barth. in Stat. Tom. 3. p. 537.

Qu[id]s & Adrasti fuerit vocalis Arion,
Tristis ad Archemori funera victor equus (11). (11) Propert. lib. 2. Eleg. ult.

—— *such* Arion *was,*
Adrastus' *vocal Horse, who, at the Games*
Sacred to dead Archemorus' *Fame,*
Was crown'd victorious, in the dusty Race.

I do not believe he attributes That Grief to Him, which *Passerat* imagines; The Word *tristis* I take to relate to the fatal Accident of *Archemorus*, for whom These Games were celebrated, and not to the Grief of *Arion*, on finding another Master besides *Adrastus* (12). (12) Nouvelles de la Repub. des Lettres, July 1702, pag. 110.

ARIOSTA (LIPPA), Concubine of *Opizzo*, Marquis of *Est* and *Ferrara*, improved so well the Impressions which her Beauty had made on the Heart of the Marquis, by her Fidelity and artful Management, that, at last, he owned her for his lawful Wife, in the Year 1352. He died the same Year, and left her the Administration of his Estates; of which she acquitted herself very well, during the *Minority of her eleven Children*. From this Lady is descended *The House of Est, which subsists, at this Time, in the Branches of the Dukes of* Modena *and* Rhegio (a). The Author, from whom I borrow this, observes, that *Lippa Ariosta* brought more Honour to her Family, *which was one of the noblest of* Ferrara, —— *than she had taken from it* [A]. The Reader will meet with some Reflexions on This in the Remark, which I subjoin to this Article.

(a) Le Laboureur, Relation du Voiage de Pologne, Part. 3. pag. 375.

[A] *She brought more Honour to her Family — than she had taken from it.*] I have discoursed, in another Place (1), of the singular Efficacy of Marriage. It cannot be sufficiently admired; for, in short, it changes the Nature of the three Distinctions of Time; the *past* is no less affected by it's Influence, than the *present* and the *future*. "Do "you not admire at the force of Custom, and the Au-"thority it has in the World? With three Words, "pronounced by a certain Person, *Ego conjungo vos*, "you privilege a young Man and a Maid to go to "bed together, in fight, and with the consent, of "all the World; and this is called a *Sacrament* "*administered by a consecrated Person*. The same "Action, without these Words, is an enormous "Crime, which disgraces a poor Lady; and He, "who conducts the Affair, is called, an please you, "a Pimp. In the first Case, the Father and Mother "make merry, dance, and conduct their Daughter "themselves to bed. In the other they are at their "Wits 'end, get her shaved, and away with her to "a Convent. It must be confessed that the Law "is a very merry Affair (2)." This is not the *Marvellous* of the Matter: The chief singularity consists in the retroactive Effect. Our *Ariosta* had been a Concubine; her Children were Bastards; this was a Stain to her Honour, and her Family; but all was effaced, washed out, and annihilated, by three Words of the Priest, *Ego conjungo vos*. The Marquis of *Ferrara*, by marrying this Mistress, a little before he left the World, metamorphosed her from a Concubine into an honest Wife, and legitimated her Children. Such Metamorphoses happen daily; and some have pretended, that Children, born

(1) In the Article ALESIUS. Remark [D].

(2) Bussi Rabutin, Lettre 136. Part. IV. pag. 192. Edit. of Holl.

(a) TELMESSUS. See its Article. Plutarch, Arrian, Lucian, Clemens Alexandrinus, and several others, say, that Aristander was of this City.

at a time, when their Father and Mother could not marry for want of a Dispensation, ought to be *legitimated by a subsequent Marriage*; but the Parliament of *Paris* gave Judgment against this Pretence in the Year 1664 (3). It may perhaps be asked, why the Marquis did not comply before the Year of his Death. I answer, that a Fornicator, who finds himself near his end, is more disposed to such a Conduct, than if he were in hopes of living longer. The Checks of Conscience, excited of themselves, or by the Discourse of a Casuist, are more lively at the approach of Death; less Difficulty is then made in passing through a vexatious Ceremony, which may quiet them. Add to this, that a great Lord, solicited to marry by a Mistress, whom he enjoys, may imagine, that she will be a thousand times more obliging, and faithful, while she flatters herself with the Hopes of attaining to the Quality of his Wife, but that, after having attained to it, he will discover her Pride and ill Humour, &c. He may, therefore, think proper to keep her in constant Expectation; but, when he is past Hopes of Recovery, he will think it time to give over this Piece of Management. However it be, some are so severe, that they cannot be reconciled to the Conduct of the Marquis of *Ferrara*, and his Imitators: They would have a Woman, who has dishonoured herself, and been a long time a Scandal to a whole Country, remain all her Life-time in Disgrace; that the Example of her being restored to Honour and Reputation may not serve as an Allurement to other Maids, and, under the like Prospect, conceal from them the Infamy of Concubinage (4).

(3) See the Journal des Savans, for Jan. 12, 1665, pag. 46.

(4) See Remark [D] of the Article ALESIUS.

ARISTANDER, a famous Soothsayer in the Days of *Alexander the Great*, was Native of a certain City in *Asia*, where almost all were born with a Disposition to Prophecy (a). He followed *Alexander* to the Conquest of *Persia*, and acquired

ARISTANDER. 447

quired a wonderful Ascendant over the Mind of This Monarch [*A*], by the great Success of his Art [*B*]. He had been formerly in the same Employ at the Court of King *Philip*; and it was He, who explained That Prince's Dream, after his Marriage with *Olympia*, more to the King's Satisfaction, than any of his Brethren. *Philip* dreamed, that he had sealed the Queen's Belly with a Seal, on which was engraved a Lion,

[*A*] *He acquired a wonderful Ascendant over the Mind of This Monarch.*] It is certain, on the one hand, that, in all the *Macedonian* Army, there was no Soothsayer of such great Reputation and Authority, as *Aristander: Peritissimus vatum* (1). *Cui maxima fides habebatur* (2). *Cui tum plurimum credebatur ex vatibus* (3). It is, on the other hand, most certain, that *Alexander* was very superstitious: *Erat non intactus ea superstitione mentis* (4). *Superstitionis potens non erat* (5). It is easy, then, to conclude, that *Aristander* had a great Ascendant over him. *Quintus Curtius* observes, that This Prince had an implicit Faith in him. "Qui post Darium victum "ariolos & vates consulere desierat, rursus ad super- "stitionem humanarum gentium ludibria revolutus, "ADDIXERAT, explorare eventum rerum sacrificiis "jubet (6). ----- *He, who, after the Conquest of* "*Darius, had left off to consult with Soothsayers and* "*Diviners, relapsing into the Follies of Superstition,* "*commanded* Aristander, *in whom he had an im-* "*plicit Faith, to enquire by Sacrifice the Event of* "*Things.*" If, in any critical Juncture, he was to beg a singular Favour of the Gods, he shut himself up with *Aristander.* With him he shut himself up, to perform the most mysterious and ineffable Ceremonies of Religion. *Plutarch* informs us of this, where he mentions the Preparations for the Battle of *Arbela.* Ἀλέξανδρος δὲ τῶν Μακεδόνων ἀναπαυομένων, αὐτὸς πρὸ τῆς σκηνῆς μετὰ τοῦ μάντεως Ἀριστάνδρου διέτριβεν ἱερουργίας τινὰς ἀποῤῥήτους ἱερουργῶν, καὶ τῷ Φοίβῳ σφαγιαζόμενος (7). *Alexander, whilst the Macedonians slept, performed certain mysterious Ceremonies before his Tent, with* Aristander *the Soothsayer, and sacrificed to* Apollo. *Quintus Curtius* says, that *Alexander,* being much troubled on this Occasion, sent for *Aristander,* to implore the Assistance of the Gods, and that *Aristander,* in his Habit of Ceremony, dictated the Forms of Prayer to him. "Alexander non alias magis territus ad "vota & preces Aristandrum vocari jubet. Ille in "candida veste, verbenas manu preferens, capite ve- "lato prætibat preces regi, Jovem, Minervam, Victo- "riamque propitianti (8)." It is no wonder, that This Prince had such a Value for his Soothsayer; for he did him more service than any of his Generals. By his Assistance he inspired his Army with Hopes and Courage; which greatly contributed to the Success of his Enterprizes. Do but consider This *Aristander* in the Heat of the Battle of *Arbela,* habited in white, and carrying a Branch of Laurel in his Hand, crying out to the Soldiers, that he saw an Eagle pearched on *Alexander's* Head, a certain Pledge of Victory, and that They might see it as well as he. Consider this, and reflect how much this must promote the Victory, without it being necessary, that the Soldiers should really see it? They trusted to the Eyes of the Soothsayer; if they themselves saw nothing, they imputed it to their bad Eye-sight, for the small time they had to look about for such an Object in the Air. "Vates Aristander "alba veste indutus, & dextra preferens lauream "militibus in pugnam intentis avem monstravit, haud "dubium victoriæ auspicium. Ingens rego alacri- "tas ac fiducia paulo ante territos accendit ad pug- "nam (9)." *Plutarch* observes, that *Alexander* lent a helping Hand to his Soothsayers (10), and, least the Event should justify Those, who laughed at *Aristander's* Promise, that the City of *Tyre* should be taken before the end of the Month, he ordered, that That Day, which was the last of the Month, should, for the future, be counted as the Twenty eighth. He would give his Prophet time; who had nevertheless not much exceeded it; for the City was taken upon That Day, if we may believe *Plutarch,* an Author much to be suspected in These Matters. Let us not omit, that no one knew the Art of comforting his Master so well as our *Aristander.* He used very little Rhetoric in recovering him from the most oppressive Melancholy. A Dream served him instead of every thing else, upon these Occasions. *Alexan-*

der, perfectly in Distraction at his having killed *Clitus,* had almost broke his Heart with groaning and weeping. It was feared, he would dye of Sorrow; the Door of his Chamber was forced open; he would hear no Body; but, no sooner had *Aristander* put him in Mind of a Dream, which related to the Death of *Clitus,* and represented to him, that That unfortunate Man was from the beginning predestinated to This End, Our Prince receives immediate and perfect Consolation. Ἀρίστανδρος δὲ τοῦ μάντεως ὑπομιμνήσκοντος αὐτὸν τὴν τε ὄψιν ἣν εἶδεν περὶ τοῦ Κλείτου, καὶ τὸ σημεῖον ὡς δὴ πάλαι καθειμαρμένων τούτων ἔδοξεν ἐκδίδοσθαι (11). *At quum vates Aristander visum illi quod de Clito fuerat ei repræsentatum & prodigium subjiceret, jamdudum hæc in fatis fuisse, ejusque animum relaxare.*

[*B*] *By the great Success of his Art.*] They, who set up for Prediction, are happy, when they serve a Prince, whom the Providence of God designs for great Purposes. A thousand human Reasons induce them to foretel all manner of Success, cost what it will; and they have the pleasure to see the Event justify their Temerity. This was *Aristander's* Case. He ventured to foretel Things at all Adventures; and *Alexander's* good Fortune still saved his Credit. The Prophet had reason to be fond of such a Conqueror; and the Conqueror was excusable in trusting to a Man, who divined so rightly. I have formerly wondered, that *Alexander* should be so superstitious; at present I should wonder, if he had been otherwise; and it is surprizing to me, that his Respect for the Soothsayers was interrupted in the Time of his highest Prosperity (12). He could not be Ignorant, that his good Fortune exceeded the Foresight of his own Prudence, and the Greatness of his Courage. He must, then, necessarily have believed, that an invisible and most powerful Virtue took particular Care of his Affairs: He must, therefore, morally speaking, have been always disposed to cultivate the Favour of That Power, by all those Means, which the Soothsayers suggested to him; I say, the Soothsayers, whom he considered as the proper Judges of the Time, in which Fortune was in a good or bad Humour, and as Arbitrators of the Means to appease This Goddess, and render her propitious. It would be found to be less strange, that certain Princes should slight the Counsels of those, who are Directors of their Devotions: I say, certain Princes, who succeed in their Undertakings, only in proportion to the human Means, which they make use of to render these Enterprizes almost infallible; and who fail of Success, whenever their Prudence has not taken all necessary Measures. They are the *Antipodes* of great Conquerors. But I confess there still remains matter of Wonder in the Case. Could such a Great Soul, as That of *Alexander,* represent God to itself under the Idea, which Superstition gives of him? He had his lucid Intervals; as, when he dismissed one of his Prophets from his Presence, who came to dissuade him from an Attack, for which every thing was prepared; telling him, that *nothing could be more impertinent, in the midst of such Preparations, than a superstitious Soothsayer.* "Si quis, inquit, arti tuæ intentum & extra "spectantem sic interpellet, non dubium quin in- "commodus ac molestus videri tibi possit. Et cum "ille ita prorsus futurum respondisset; censesne, in- "quit, tantas res non pecudum fibras ante oculos "habenti, ullum esse majus impedimentum quam va- "tem superstitione captum (13)? — *Should any One* "*thus interrupt you, whilst busied in your Art, and* "*contemplating the Entrails, I question not but you* "*would think him troublesome and impertinent.* To "*which when the Soothsayer assented: The King ad-* "*ded: Do you think then, that to me, who have such* "*great Things, not the Entrails of Beasts, in view,* "*any thing can be a greater Interruption, than a su-* "*perstitious Diviner.*" The Confidence, which he sometimes had in his good Fortune, hindred him from submitting to the Advice of *Aristander.* He found himself designed for great Things; an Opinion, which is one of the most powerful Springs of Providence;

ARISTANDER.

a Lion. The other Soothsayers, upon this, advised him to have his Wife's Conduct more carefully observed [C]; but *Aristander* maintained, that the Dream signified, that the Queen was pregnant with a Son, who should have the Heart of a Lion (a). She was, then, with Child of *Alexander*. King *Philip* pretended to expound the Dream himself [D], but could make nothing of it. Though *Aristander* had applied himself chiefly to the Interpretation of Dreams; and though he is One of the Authors, who have wrote the most learnedly on This Subject (b), yet he exercised his Talent on all kinds of Prodigies. If News were brought, that a Statue of *Orpheus* had sweated, he would say, that it foreboded, that the Poets would one Day sweat in singing the Victories of *Alexander* (c). If a Swallow fluttered about this Prince, or perched upon his Head, *Aristander* said, it was a Sign of a Conspiracy against the King; which, however, would be discovered (d). If, during the Preparations for the Siege of *Tyre*, Blood, issuing out of a Soldier's Loaf, dismays the King; *Aristander* recovers him, and tells him, since the Blood proceeded from the internal parts of the Bread, it was a fatal Omen to the City, which was to be besieged (e). On another Occasion, he interpreted the Presage of a Raven, which had let fall something on *Alexander*'s Head, and afterwards rested upon a Tower, where it was taken (f). The Entrails of Victims were new Matter of Foresight to This great Soothsayer (g); He explained likewise what the Actions of Men portended [E]. Probably, then, he was

(a) Plut. in Alexand. init. p. 665.
(b) Artemidor. lib. 1. c. 33. p. 30.
(c) Plut. in Alexandro, pag. 671.
(d) Arrian. lib. 1. c. 8.
(e) Q. Curtius, lib. 4. cap. 2.
(f) Ib. c. 6.
(g) Quintus Curtius, lib. 7. cap. 7. Plut. in Alex. pag. 679.

dence; and by That he kept up the Courage of This Soothsayer. "Rex jussum considere felicitati suæ remisit. Sibi enim ad alia gloriam concedere Deos (14). —— *The King sent him back, bidding him trust to His good Fortune, and telling him, that the Gods reserved him for still greater Glory.*"

If any one thinks these Remarks too prolix, let him know, that I have my Reasons for it. My design was to ease another Article (15), which abounds but too much with Matter. Four Articles are read with more Pleasure than One, though That one be shorter than the other four. This obliges me to scatter many Things here and there, which naturally belong to one and the same Subject. What are we not obliged to do to humour a capricious Age?

[C] *Advised him to have his Wife's Conduct more carefully observed.*] Their Reasons were at least as good as Those of *Aristander*; for thus the latter reasoned. *Men do not seal up an empty Box; the Queen must therefore be with Child: since the King has dreamt, that he sealed up her Womb* (16). But hear the Reasons of the other Diviners. *Men do not seal up a Box, when there is no danger, that any Person should open it; it is sealed only as a Precaution against Those, who may approach it. The Queen's Box, then, is in danger, since the King has dreamt, that he sealed up it: The Lyon, engraven on the Seal, signifies the Necessity there is of being upon his Guard. This imports, that the Place is besieged, and begins to think of surrendering; and that, unless a strong and faithful Garrison be kept in it, the Besiegers will quickly enter the Place.* Cicero, to ridicule the Interpretation of Dreams, alledges the different Explications, which were given in much such another Case. "Parere quædam matrona cupiens, dubitans essetne prægnans, visa est in quiete obsignatam habere naturam: ad conjectorem retulit: Negavit eam, quoniam obsignata fuisse, concipere potuisse. At alter prægnantem esse dixit; nam inane nihil obsignari solere (17). —— *A certain Matron, who desired to be a Mother, but was in doubt, whether she was with Child or not, dream't, that her Natural Parts were sealed up. She applied to an Interpreter of Dreams; who told her she could never conceive, as being sealed up. But another assured her she was actually pregnant, since it was not the Custom to seal up an empty Thing.*" But it may be said, that *Aristander* was more successful in his Conjecture, and therefore argued better. I deny the Consequence: a Person may be happier in his Conjectures, without being consequently a Man of more Skill: And might not both Parties have Reason of their side? Does Pregnancy and Chastity always go together? *Olympia* might resemble *Julia* a little, who said, Nunquam nisi navi plena tollo vectorem (18). We are going to see another Explication of this same Dream.

[D] *King Philip pretended to expound this Dream himself.*] Neither *Plutarch*, nor any other Pagan Author informs us of this; but a Father of the Church. I shall set down all he says concerning it; since several things may be learned from it. "Philippus Macedo nondum Pater Olympiadis Uxoris naturam obsignasse viderat annulo. Leo erat signum: crediderat præclusam genituram, opinor, quia leo semel pater sit. Aristodemus vel Aristophon conjectans immo nihil vacuum obsignari, filium & quidem maximi impetus portendi. Alexandrum qui sciunt leonem annuli cognoscunt (19). —— *Philip of Macedon, not yet a Father, dream't, that he had sealed up the Natural Parts of his Wife Olympia. The Seal was a Lion: he believed she would never have a Child; I suppose, because the Lion is but once a Father. Aristodemus, or Aristophon, interpreted the Dream to portend the Birth of a very brave Son. They, who know Alexander, know the Lion on the Seal.*" Hence it appears, 1. That the Seal, applied in a Dream to *Olympia*'s Womb, made her Husband believe, that she would have no Children. There was some ground for this Thought; and we may almost suppose, that *Philip* was One of those Pagans of *Europe*, who, as it is said, had read the Holy Scriptures: I say, this might be supposed, if the Ideas of common Sense did not naturally enough lead to This Prince's Conjecture. But it is certain, that the Word of God represents the Barrenness of Women under This Idea. If the closing of the Womb represents, in Scripture, the Punishment of Sterility (20) inflicted by God, the opening of it represents the Blessing, by which he causes This Evil to cease (21). In the Second Place, it appears, that *Tertullian* made no Reflexion on This Idea, which the Scripture furnishes, and which Nature itself dictates. He considers only the Lyon engraved on the Seal, and believes, that *Philip* built all his Conjecture on That. *Tertullian* supposes wrong in this Place, and concludes ill. It is false, that the Lyon is but once a Father (22): and, besides, would not a Man who thought so, be ridiculous in arguing from it, that he should never have a Child; he ought at least to conclude that he should have One. It appears, in the Third Place, that *Tertullian* had forgot the Name of the Soothsayer, who hit upon the best Explication; he does not know, whether he ought to call him *Aristophon*, or *Aristodemus*. He remembered only the two first Syllables of his Name, and could not properly supply the rest; in a word, he had forgotten the Name of *Aristander*. In the Fourth Place, we see that he was very well satisfied with the Explication of the Dream: It is One of Those, which he alledges, to prove the Excellency of the Soul. Let us finish this Comment, with observing, that, perhaps, King *Philip* contended a long time with his Diviners for the Explication, which he gave of his own Dream; and perhaps *Aristander* said to him, upon this Occasion, what a Musician said, one Day, to the same Prince, in a like Case; *God forbid, that your Majesty should ever be so unhappy, as to understand these things better than myself.* Μὴ γένοιτό σοι οὕτως, ὦ βασιλεῦ, κακῶς, ἵνα ἐμοῦ ταῦτα βέλτιον εἰδῇς (23). *Absit, O Rex, ut eo te infortunio devolvare, ut harum rerum scientia me præ prior.*

[E] *He explained likewise what the Actions of Men portended.*] For Example; he foretold, that *Lysimachus*, one of *Alexander*'s Lifeguard, should attain to Royalty, but not without much Difficulty (24). His Reason was This: *Alexander* being mounted on a good Horse,

(14) Quintus Curtius, lib. 7, cap. 7.
(15) That of Alexander the Great.
(16) Plut. in Alexandro.
(17) Cic. de Divin. lib. 2. cap. 70.
(18) Macrob. Saturnal. lib. 2 cap. 5.
(19) Tertul. de Anima. cap. 46.
(20) Genes. xx. 18.
(21) Ibid. chap. xxx. ver. 22. See also chap. xxix. ver. 31.
(22) See the Notes of Rigaltius on this Passage of Tertullian.
(23) Plut. de discrim. Adulat. & Amici, pag. 67.
(24) Appian. in Syriacis.

ARISTARCHUS.

was the Author of the Book, mentioned by *Pliny*, so full of prodigious Events [*F*]. But, as for the Books of Agriculture, mentioned by *Varro* and *Columella* (*b*), I am apt to believe they were written by another *ARISTANDER*, especially since *Varro* has given the Sirname of *Athenian* to the Author of them. Our *Aristander* survived the King his Master; and his Remonstrances brought the People in good earnest to think of burying him. I know not whether this Particular has been touched upon by any other than *Ælian*, who mentions it in the last Chapter of the twelfth Book of his *Various History*.

Horse, *Lysimachus*, who was not able any longer to follow him on foot, had taken hold of the Horse's Tail, that he might not quit his Master. *Alexander* had, by chance, wounded him in the Forehead with his Lance, and having, for want of Linnen, made use of his Diadem to bind up the Wound, it happened, that the Diadem was stained with Blood: And upon this *Aristander* grounded his Prediction.

[*F*] *Probably he was the Author of the Book, mentioned by Pliny, so full of prodigious Events.*] These are his Words: " Prodigio autem fiunt ex dulcibus acerba poma, aut dulcia ex acerbis; gravi ostento cum in deteriora mutantur ex olea in oleastrum, ex candida uva & fico in nigras: ut Laodiceæ, Xerxis adventu, platano in oleam mutata: qualibus ostentis Aristandri apud Græcos volumen scatet; apud " nos vero C. Epidii Commentarii, in quibus arbores " locutæ quoque reperiuntur (25). ——— *It is a Prodigy,* " *when bitter Apples become sweet, or sweet bitter; it* " *is of dire Portent, when things are changed into* " *worse, The Olive into the wild Olive, or the white* " *Grape or Fig into black; as at Laodicea, upon the* " *Arrival of Xerxes, the Plane-Tree was changed in-* " *to an Olive; with which kind of Prodigies the Work* " *of Aristander, among the Greeks, abounds; among* " *our own Authors, the Commentaries of Caius Epidius,* " *in which we read even of speaking Trees.*" Compare with this the Passage of *Cicero* concerning the Inhabitants of *Telmessus*, mentioned in the Article of That City (26), and wonder at the incredible Facility of the Ancient Pagans in multiplying Prodigies.

(*b*) *Father Hardouin, in Indice Auctorum, takes for the same Aristander Him mentioned by Varro, and Columella, and Him mentioned by Pliny.*

(25) *Plin. lib. 17, cap. 25.*

(26) *Remark [C].*

ARISTARCHUS, a *Greek* Philosopher, and Native of *Samos*, was one of the first, who maintained, that the Earth turned upon it's Center, and described annually a Circle round the Sun [*A*]. He invented one kind of Sun-Dials (*a*). It is not constantly agreed, at what Time he lived. It is only certainly known, that he was born before the Death of *Archimedes* [*B*]. There are extant of his Works only *A Treatise of the Magnitude and Distance of the Sun and Moon*, translated into *Latin*, and commented on, by *Frideric Commandin*, and published with the Explications of *Pappus*, in the Year 1572. Dr *Wallis* published it in *Greek*, with the *Latin* Version of *Commandin*, in 1688, and inserted it in the third *Tome* of his Mathematical Works, printed at *Oxford*, in 1699. The *System of the World*, which appeared under his Name, is a Work of *Roberval* (*b*). We shall remark a Fault, which has crept into the Text of *Plutarch* (*c*).

[*A*] *Was one of the first, who maintained, that the Earth turned upon it's Center, and described annually a Circle round the Sun.*] *Sextus Empiricus*, speaking of the Hypothesis of the Motion of the Earth, intimates plainly, that *Aristarchus* was the chief Inventor of it; for he mentions only Him. Οἵ γε μὲν τὸν τῶ κόσμυ κίνησιν ἀπέλοντες, τὴν δὲ γῆν κινεῖσθαι δοξάσαντες, ὡς οἱ περὶ Ἀρίσαρχον τὸν μαθηματικὸν, ἒ κωλύονlαι νοεῖν χρόνον (1). *They, who denied the Motion of the World, but believed, that the Earth moved, as* Aristarchus *the Mathematician, could easily form an Idea of Time.* Plutarch, intending to clear up a Thought of *Plato*, and, considering with himself, whether That Philosopher did not believe the Motion of the World, adds, That This Opinion was afterwards That of *Aristarchus* and *Seleucus*; and that *Aristarchus* taught it Hypothetically, and *Seleucus* Dogmatically. Ὧς ὕσερν Ἀρίσαρχ@- καὶ Σέλευκ@- ἀπεδείκνυσαν· ὁ μὲν ὑπο]ιθέμεν@- μόνον· ὁ δὲ Σέλευκ@-, καὶ ἀποφαινόμεν@- (2). *Ut postmodo Aristarchus & Seleucus ostenderunt. Sane hoc ille ita ut supponeret tantum, hic etiam pronuntias.* This is intimated, that *Aristarchus* was looked upon as the Author of this Opinion. *Archimedes* intimates the same more plainly. These are his Words: Ταῦτα γὰρ ἐν ταῖς γεγφαμμέναις παρὰ τῶν Ἀσερολόγων διαχρήσας Ἀρίσαρχ@- ὁ Σάμι@-, ὑποθίσεων τινων ἐξιδωκεν γράψας, ἐν αἷς, ἐκ τῶν ὑποκειμένων συμβαίνει τὸ κόσμον πολλαπλάσιον ἦμεν τῷ νῦν εἰρημένῳ· ὑπο]ίθε]αι γὰρ τὰ μὲν ἀπλανῆ τῶν ἄστρων, καὶ τὸν ἅλιον, μένειν ἀκίνηlον. τὰν δὲ γᾶν περιφέρεσθαι περὶ τὸν ἅλιον, καlὰ κύκλν περιφέρειαν, ὅς ἐςιν ἐν μέσῳ τῷ δρόμῳ κείμεν@- (3). ——— Aristarchus *the Samian, confuting these Notions of the Astrologers, laid down certain Positions; from whence it follows, that the World is much larger, than what we just now mentioned; for he lays it down, that the fixed Stars, and the Sun, are immoveable; and that the Earth is carried round the Sun, in the Circumference of a Circle.* Probably the Transcribers have falsified the Passage of *Plutarch*, where we read, that *Aristarchus* pretended, that *Greece* ought to have entered a Process against *Cleanthes* for Irreligion, in believing the Motion of the Earth. Μόνον (εἶναι) ὁ τὸν, μὴ χρίειν ἡμῖν ἀσεβείας ἐπαγγέλλειν, ὥσπερ Ἀρίσαρχ@- ᾤεlο δεῖν Κλεάνθν τὸν Σάμιον ἀσεβείας περκαλεῖσθαι τὸς Ἕλληνας, ὡς κινοῦνla τὸ κόσμυ τὴν ἑςίαν, ὅτι φαινόμενα σώζειν ἀνὴρ ἐπειρᾶτο, μένειν τὸν ἐρανὸν ὑπο]ιθέμεν@-, ἐξελίτεσθαι δὲ καlὰ λοξῦ κύκλῳ τὴν γῆν ἅμα καὶ περὶ τὸν αὐ]ῆς ἄξονα δινυμένην (4). ——— Bring *not an Action of Impiety against us, as* Aristarchus *thought* Greece *ought to have done against* Cleanthes *the Samian for Irreligion, &c.* This is a Conjecture of *Gassendus* (5), and a Correction, which Mr *Menage* adopts as certain. *In verbis Plutarchi,* says he (6), *legendum omnino ὥσπερ* Ἀρίσαρχον *τὸν Σάμιον ᾤεlο Κλεάνθυς δεῖν ἀσεβείας περκαλεῖσθαι τὸς Ἕλληνας.* Amiot did not perceive this Fault.

[*B*] *It is not constantly agreed, at what Time he lived; it is only certainly known, that he was born before* Archimedes'*s Death.*] The Words, I have quoted (7), prove, that, at the latest, our *Aristarchus* could be but cotemporary with *Archimedes*. Now we know, that *Archimedes* lost his Life, when *Syracuse* was taken by the *Romans*, in the First Year of the CXLII Olympiad, during the Second *Punic* War. Observe, that, according to *Plutarch*, quoted above, *Timæus* the *Locrian* lived before *Aristarchus*; for the Sentiment, which he would have explained, is found in *Plato*, as if *Timæus* had spoken it in Conversation. Now, since *Plato* was a Disciple of This *Timæus* (8), and That, after having seen *Egypt*; we must conclude, that, if *Plutarch* has well observed Chronology, *Aristarchus* flourished after *Plato*. We are sure, then, that he did not flourish after *Archimedes*, nor before *Plato*; and I believe it is not easy to fix on any thing more exact. *Blancanus* has placed *Aristarchus* Two Centuries earlier, than *Hipparchus*, and has placed the latter an Hundred Years after the Death of *Alexander*, that is, an Hundred Years after the First Year of the CXIVth Olympiad (9). He believed, then, that *Aristarchus* flourished about the LXXXIXth Olympiad,

(*a*) *Vitruv. lib. 9, cap. 9.*

(*b*) *See Menage, in Diog. Laert. lib. 8, n. 85, pag. 389.*

(*c*) *In Remark [A]. Citation (4).*

(1) *Sextus Empiricus adversus Mathem. pag. 410. Mr Menage in Diog. Laert. lib. 8, n. 85, cites this Passage twice in the same Page, first as Sextus Empiricus's, and secondly as Pyrrho's.*

(2) *Plut. in Quæst. Plat. p. 1006, C.*

(3) *Archimedes in Psammite, pag. 459, apud Menagium, in Diog. Laert. lib. 8, pag. 389.*

(4) *Plut. de facie in Orbe Lunæ, pag. 923, F.*

(5) *Gassend. Phys. sect. 2, lib. 3, cap. 5, pag. 617, Tom. 1, Oper.*

(6) *Menage, ubi supra.*

(7) *In the foregoing Remark.*

(8) *Cicer. de Finib. lib. 5, c. 29, & Tuscul. lib. 1.*

(9) *Blanc. in Mathematicor. Chronol. ad calcem libel de Arist. locis Mathem. pag. 46, 49.*

ARISTARCHUS.

Olympiad, a little after the Birth of *Plato*. This does not agree with the Paſſage of *Plutarch*, which I have alledged. *Simler*'s Opinion agrees with it as little. That Author makes *Ariſtarchus* flouriſh in the Reign of *Artaxerxes Longimanus*, which reached from the firſt Year of the LXXIXth Olympiad to the laſt Year of the LXXXVIIIth (10). *Libertus Fromundus* is yet more oppoſite to *Plutarch*'s Opinion; ſince he knew not whether *Ariſtarchus* preceeded, or followed, *Pythagoras* (11). I believe *Voſſius* (12) would have confuted This Uncertainty by the Authority of *Plutarch*, if he had remembered the Words I have quoted. *John Stadius* believes, that *Ariſtarchus* ſurvived *Archimedes*; for he makes him flouriſh in the CXLVIth Olympiad (13). Note, that *Vitruvius*, naming ſome Mathematicians, who were Inventors, places *Ariſtarchus* in the firſt Rank (14). If this were the Rule to judge by, he muſt be ſuppoſed later than *Philolaus*, and *Archytes* of *Tarentum*.

ARISTARCHUS, a famous Grammarian, was born in *Samothracia*, and choſe the City of *Alexandria* for his adopted Country (a). He was much eſteemed by Ptolomy Philometor, who entruſted him with the Education of his Son [A]. He applied himſelf diligently to Criticiſm, and reviſed *Homer*'s Poems with incredible Exactneſs, but a little too magiſterially; for, whenever a Verſe diſpleaſed him, he treated it as ſuppoſititious [B]. This Edition of *Homer* was much eſteemed, as alſo much

[A] *Ptolomy Philometor entruſted him with the Education of his Son.*] This appears plain in the Words of Suidas. Γέγονε, ſays he (1), κατὰ τὴν ρυς ὀλυμπιάδα, ἐπὶ Πτολεμαίου τοῦ Φιλομήτορος, καὶ τὸν υἱὸν ἐπαίδευσεν. He lived in the CLVIth Olympiad, in the Reign of Ptolomy Philometor, whoſe Son he alſo educated. The Olympiad, which he ſpecifies, anſwers very well to the Reign of This Ptolomy; but This however may be ſaid, that it does not appear, that this Prince had any Sons: Hiſtorians give him but one Daughter, and make his Brother ſucceed him. This Objection is of no force; for, on the one ſide, if the Son, whom he cauſed to be inſtructed by our *Ariſtarchus*, died in his Youth, the Hiſtorians might think, that there was no need of mentioning him; on the other hand, it is a paſſage, that They are all ſilent in the Matter. *Juſtin* gives Ptolomy Philometor a Son; and ſays likewiſe, that Ptolomy, his Uncle, cauſed him to be put to death (2). The learned *Leo Allatius* has not taken notice of this; he will have it, that the Diſciple, which Suidas gives *Ariſtarchus*, was the ſecond Ptolomy *Evergetes*: *Cujus* (Ptolomæi Philometoris) *filium ſecundum Evergetem eradiit, Olympiade CLVI, ut Suidas tradit* (3). This is wrong; the ſecond Ptolomy *Evergetes* was the Brother, and not the Son, of Ptolomy *Philometor*. *Voſſius* was no leſs miſtaken, in believing, that *Ptolomy Philometor* made choice of *Ariſtarchus* for Preceptor to his Son Ptolomy *Lathyrus* (4); he ſhould have known, that Ptolomy *Lathyrus*, or *Latharus*, was the Son of the ſecond Ptolomy *Evergetes*. What Suidas obſerves, that *Ariſtarchus* was a Diſciple of *Ariſtophanes*, the *Byzantian*, does not furniſh a reaſonable Objection; for it is well known, that a very great Error has crept into That Paſſage of Suidas, where we read, that *Ariſtophanes* of *Byzantium* flouriſhed in the XLVth Olympiad; it ſhould be read the CXLVth Olympiad; as *Allatius*, and *Jonſius*, have obſerved (5). "*Ariſtophanis meminit Suidas, in quo obiter Librariorum error in Olympiade notandus eſt. Ipſe namque habet,* Γέγονε δὲ κατὰ τὴν μς Ὀλυμπιάδα, *quæ Hieronymus Wolphius vertit, Vixit Olympiade XLV, cum omnino ſcribendum fit* ρμε*, id eſt, CXLV* (6). - - - - *Suidas mentions Ariſtophanes, in which Author, by the way, a Miſtake of the Tranſcribers, with regard to the Olympiad, deſerves to be taken notice of. For Suidas has it* Γέγονε δὲ κατὰ μς Ὀλυμπιάδα, *which Jerom Wolfius renders by* Vixit Olympiade XLV *[in the XLVth Olympiad]; whereas it ought certainly to be read* ρμε. i. e. 145. The Anonymous Author of the *Deſcription of the Olympiads* places *Ariſtophanes* the *Byzantian*, under this Olympiad. Suidas, in ſaying, that the ſame *Ariſtophanes* was, in his Youth, a Diſciple of *Callimachus*, does not contradict this. Μαθητὴς Καλλιμάχου καὶ Ζηνοδότου, ἀλλὰ τοῦ μὲν νέος, τοῦ δὲ παῖς ἀκούς (7). *A Diſciple of Callimachus and Zenodotus, but of the former in his Youth, of the latter in his Childhood.* A Perſon, who flouriſhed in the CXLVth Olympiad, might have been a Diſciple of *Callimachus*; for That Poet lived 'till the Reign of Ptolomy *Evergetes*, the Son of Ptolomy *Philadelphus*; and we know, that Ptolomy *Evergetes* reigned to the end of the CXXXIXth Olympiad. Now, if *Ariſtarchus* was a Diſciple of *Ariſtophanes* the *Byzantian*, It is pointing out the exact time, in which he flouriſhed, to place him, as Suidas has done, in the CLVIth Olympiad. They, who will weigh theſe ſeveral Particulars, will find ſome Difficulty in aſſenting to this Propoſition: *Ariſtarchus, at the ſame time with Callimachus* (8). The learned *Heinſius* obſerves, that ſome Perſons ſay this (9); and, ſince he does not cenſure them, we may ſuppoſe, that he approves of their Opinion. He would have done better to have condemned it. *Faber* is more to be credited in this, than his Son-in-law: He places *Ariſtarchus* in the Reign of *Ptolomy Philometor* (10). See the Remark [G], where we ſhall prove the Truth of This Opinion, from the Conſideration, that *Crates* and *Ariſtarchus* were Cotemporaries. A Paſſage of *Athenæus* might induce ſome to believe, that our Critic lived under *Ptolomy Philadelphus*; it is, where *Athenæus* relates, that *Ptolomy Evergetes* was one of *Ariſtarchus*'s Diſciples (11). For want of examining the whole, one might be perſuaded, that This *Ptolomy Evergetes* was the Son of *Ptolomy Philadelphus*; but it is certain, that he muſt be taken for *Ptolomy Phyſcon* (12), Brother of *Philometor*. In effect, *Athenæus* ſpeaks of one *Ptolomy*, who wrote Books, and who muſt neceſſarily be the ſame with Him, whom he cites in the twelfth Book (13), and whom he reckons the ſeventh King of *Egypt*.

There are ſtill farther Proofs againſt Mr *Dacier*'s Opinion. It is well known, that *Demetrius Scepſius* (14) lived at the ſame time with *Ariſtarchus*. This *Strabo* teſtifies: Κατὰ τὸν αὐτὸν χρόνον γεγονότες Κράτητί καὶ Ἀριστάρχῳ (15), *æqualis Cratetis & Ariſtarchi.* *Voſſius* did not conſider theſe Words with Attention, when he ſaid, that *Strabo* affirms, that *Demetrius Scepſius* was a Diſciple of *Crates* and *Ariſtarchus* (16). Now This *Demetrius* was Cotemporary with one *Metrodorus* (17), whom *Mithridates* cauſed to be put to death in the Year of *Rome* 681 (18). Judge then, whether One, who flouriſhed under *Ptolomy Philadelphus*, could be cotemporary with This *Metrodorus*. The Death of That *Ptolomy* falls in with the Year of *Rome* 506. Note, that it may be collected from *Diogenes Laërtius*, that *Demetrius* was elder than *Metrodorus*, and, if ſo, there is no reſtoring the Reaſon; for it cannot be ſaid, that I prove too much. Obſerve likewiſe, that the Son of a Diſciple of *Callimachus* was ſtill living (19), when *Strabo* was old enough to aſſiſt at the public Lectures (20). Now, ſince *Strabo* lived to *Tiberius*'s Time, he could not hear the Lectures of the Son of one of *Ariſtarchus*'s Diſciples, if *Ariſtarchus* flouriſhed under *Ptolomy Philadelphus*.

[B] *Whenever a Verſe diſpleaſed him, he treated it as ſuppoſititious*] *Cicero* certifies this in theſe Words: " Si, ut ſcribis, eæ litteræ non fuerunt diſertæ, ſcito " meas non fuiſſe. Ut enim Ariſtarchus Homeri ver- " ſum negat, quem non probat, fic tu (libet enim mihi " jocari) quod diſertum non erit, ne putaris meum " (21). - - - - - *If, as you write, thoſe Letters were " inelegant, be ſure they were not mine. For, as " Ariſtarchus denied thoſe Verſes, which did not " pleaſe him, to be Homer's, ſo I deſire, that what " is not elegant (allow me to jeſt) you would believe " not to be mine.*" To this may be added another Paſſage of the ſame Author: " Niſi forte ſcire vis, me " inter Niciam noſtrum & Vidium judicem eſſe. Pro- " fert

ARISTARCHUS.

much criticised (b). He play'd the Critic upon *Pindar* (c), and *Aratus* (d), and other Poets; and it is not true, that, in order to criticise on every one, without Fear of being censured in his Turn, he had the Address not to publish any thing of his own

"fert alter (ut opinor) duobus versiculis expensum
"Niciæ: alter Aristarchus hos ὀϐελίζει. Ego, tam-
"quam criticus antiquus, judicaturus sum, utrum sint
"τῦ ποιητῦ, an παρεμϐεϐλημένοι (22). — Un-
"less, perhaps, you would know, that I am Umpire
"between our Friend Nicias and Vidius. The one
"acknowledges certain Verses to be genuine, the other,
"like an Aristarchus, condemns them. I, as some
"ancient Critic, am to decide, whether they really
"are the Poet's, or are spurious." It is said, that *Aristarchus* marked, over against the Verses, which he condemned as spurious, the Figure of a *Spit*, from whence it came, that ὀϐελίζειν signifies to condemn. "Translatum ab Aristarcho, qui Homeri carmina in "corpus redegit, atque in libros digessit, versus no-"thos, hoc est adulterinos & subdititios, qui non "videntur sapere venam illam Homericam, ὀϐελίσ-"κοις, id est minutis verubus prænotatis, damnans: "contra, qui viderentur insignes ac genuini ἀσε-"ρίσκοις, id est stellis, illustrans (23). ----- Borrowed from Aristarchus, *who reduced the Poems of Homer into a Body, and divided them into Books;* *condemning those Verses as spurious, which seemed* *not to relish of Homer's Vein, by prefixing an obe-*"lisk, or Spit; on the contrary distinguishing those, "which appeared to be excellent and genuine, with an "Asterisk, or little Star." See *Ausonius*'s Poem, entitled *Ludus septem Sapientum*; where he desires a rigorous Censure of his Poems from *Drepanius Pacatus*. He would be treated, as *Aristarchus* had treated *Homer*, and expresses himself thus:

Mæonio qualem cultum quæsivit Homero
Censor Aristarchus, normaque Zenodoti.
Pone obelos igitur spuriorum stigmata vatum,
Palmas non culpas esse putabo meas (24).

At Aristarchus and Zenodotus polished Homer; so affix the Spits, the Brands of spurious Poets; I esteem them as my Palms, not as my Faults.

It is thought, that he means *Aristarchus* in the last of these two Verses.

Quique Sacri lacerum collegit corpus Homeri,
Quique notas spuriis versibus apposuit (25).

He, who collected the scattered Poems of Homer, and he who branded the spurious Verses.

Charles Stephens, Lloyd, and *Hofman* affirm, in their Dictionaries, that *Ælian* observes, that *Aristarchus*'s Criticisms were so exact, that, whenever he condemned a Verse, as not being *Homer*'s, it was looked upon, of course, as suppositious. *Ælianus* tradit hunc tam castigato fuisse judicio, ut Homeri versus non putaretur, quem ipse non probasset. *Quenstedt* affirms the same thing (26). I do not think *Ælian* says so, and, if he did, he must have been mistaken; for we learn from *Athenæus*, that the Taste of This great Critic (27) was often condemned; some Verses of *Homer*, which he rejected, were still received, and he and his Reasons laughed at. His Confidence alone was sufficient to bring his Judgment in question: He decided, in some Cases, that such and such Verses of the *Iliad* ought to be transferred to the *Odyssey* (28). *Allatius* was not ignorant, that the Criticisms of *Aristarchus* were often censured; and, upon this Occasion, quotes *Athenæus* (29), *Plutarch*, and the Scholiast of *Homer*. He informs us, that the Grammarian *Ptolemy* of *Ascalon* published a Book *de Aristarchi correctione in Odyssæa* (30), and that *Zenodotus* of *Alexandria* was sent for to revise *Aristarchus*'s Criticisms. "Zenodotus alter Alexandri-"nus ideo advocatus est, ut de reprobatis ab Ari-"starcho Homericis carminibus judicium ferret (31)." Idem (Suidas); Ζηνόδοτ@ 'Αλεξανδρεὺς γραμματικὸς ὁ να ἀσις κληθεὶς πρὸς τὰ ὑπ' Ἀριστάρχε ἀθετύμενα τύ Ποιητύ. Nevertheless, he affirms, that Antiquity paid so great regard to *Aristarchus*'s Judgment, that it was believed, that those Verses, which displeased him, were not really *Ho-*

mer's. *Aristarchi porro judicium adeo probavit antiquitas, ut Homeri versus non putarentur, quos ipse non probaret* (32). Does not this betray great want of Judgment? *Elias Vinetus* deserves Censure upon this Occasion: "Cujus (Aristarchi), says he, veteres "tanti fecerant judicium, ut, quem non probaret, "Homeri versum non crederent. Ita Cicero, Suidas, Erasmus (33). ------ *The Ancients had so* *great a Regard for Aristarchus's Judgment, that* *they looked upon whatever Verse he disapproved* *of not to have been Homer's; as we find in Ci-*"cero, Suidas, *and* Erasmus." It is false, that *Cicero* says any such thing (34); he only tells us, that *Aristarchus* took those alone for *Homer*'s Verses, which he himself approved of. Nor does *Suidas* say, what *Vinetus* imputes to him. I can affirm the same of *Erasmus*, in regard to the Place, from whence I have borrowed what has been cited above (35). *Saldenus*, desiring to make some Alteration in the Words of *Charles Stephens*, which I have quoted, has greatly offended against the Reasoning Part. He has not quoted *Ælian*, nor has he affirmed, that *Aristarchus*'s Criticism was exact; he is satisfied with saying, that This Censor believed it so. Thus far all is well; he deserts *Charles Stephens* upon a false Quotation, and will answer but for one thing, which is very probable, to wit, that the Corrector of *Homer* thought himself a very able Man: but here is the Mischief of it: From this advantageous Opinion, which he had of his own Wit, *Saldenus* concludes, that Antiquity received none for *Homer*'s Verses, but such as pleased *Aristarchus*. This is a false Inference. *Grammaticus ille, qui hoc nomen (Aristarchi) gessit, tam castigato se patavit esse judicio, ut Homeri versus nullus haberetur, quem ipse non probaret* (36). *Saldenus* argues; and, to confirm his Argument, he cites us the Words, where *Cicero* says, that *Aristarchus* rejected all the Verses of *Homer*, which were not to his Taste, as suppositious. This Proof is no better, than the Position itself, which was to be proved. I have read, in the Commentary of a modern Author, that *Aristarchus* had so refined and penetrating a Genius for true Criticism, that he was generally called the Prophet, or Diviner, *from his wonderful Sagacity* (37). I have been surprized not to find any Footsteps of this Elogy in a vast number of Writers, whom I have run over, in the Places, where this Grammarian is mentioned. At last I found, in a Note of *Corradus* on *Cicero*'s Epistles, the following Words: Hinc illum (Aristarchum) μάντιν ἐκάλει Παναίτι-ὁ 'Ρόδι@ φιλόσοφ@ διὰ τὸ ῥαδίως καταμαν-τεύεσθαι τῆς τῶν ποιημάτων διανοίας. Athen. lib. 14. (38). I have searched in vain in the fourteenth Book of *Athenæus*. However it be, there is a great Difference between This Quotation of *Corradus*, and That of Mr *Dacier*. The Greek Words sign'fy only, that *Panetius* gave the Name of *Diviner* to our *Aristarchus*; and not that it was the common Style of Antiquity.

Note, that is the Opinion of many, that *Aristarchus* was He, who divided each of *Homer*'s Great Works into as many Books, as there are Letters in the Alphabet, and inscribed each Book with a particular Letter. "*Plutarch. lib. de Homero.* Iliadem & Odysseam Homeri ab Aristarcho Grammatico in numerum librorum divisam ad ordinem & numerum Græcarum literarum. *Eustathius in Iliad.* "A. tradit, Aristarchum & Zenodotum confusum antea Homeri opus digessisse in certos libros, eosque literis distinxisse. Unde non solùm primus tam Odysseæ, quàm Iliadis, liber α vocatur, secundus β & sic deinceps; Verum etiam ipsum opus γράμ-"μα]α nominatur. Et sane verum est, hanc per literas divisionem recentiorem. Nam antiqui nunquam ed usi, ut patet ex Aristotele de Poëtica, Cap. 24. (39). ------ *Plutarch, in his Book de Homero,* *tells us, that the Iliad and Odyssey of Homer were* *divided by Aristarchus, the Grammarian, into a Number of Books, answering to the Order and Number of* *the Greek Letters.* *Eustathius*, upon the first *Iliad*, *informs us, that Aristarchus and Zenodotus digested the Work of Homer, which was before confused,*

own [C]. They, who make him cotemporary with *Pifiſtratus*, are groſly miſtaken [D]. His Reputation continued a long time. *Cicero* and *Horace* employed his Name, when they would deſcribe a too rigid Critic [E]. Some aſcribe to him a Thought, which

" into a certain Number of Books, and diſtinguiſhed
" them by Letters. Whence it is, that not only the
" firſt Books both of the Iliad and Odyſſey are called
" A, the ſecond B, and ſo on; but the whole Work is
" ſtyled Γϱάμμαἴα, The Letters. And indeed This
" Diviſion by Letters is of modern Date. For the
" Ancients never made uſe of it, as appears from
" *Ariſtotle, De Poëtica*, Cap. 24."

[C] It is not true, that, in order to criticiſe on every One, without Fear of being cenſured in his Turn, he had the Addreſs not to publiſh any Thing of his own.] *Saldenus*, under the borrowed Name of *Chriſtianus Liberius*, tells an untruth, when he ſays, " Sic Ariſtarchus Grammaticus nullum non reprehendebat,
" nihil ipſe ſcribens ne ab aliis reprehendi poſſet (40).
" ——— Thus Ariſtarchus the Grammarian cenſured
" every one; but publiſhed nothing himſelf, for fear of
" being cenſured by others." I know not whether he relates it with the ſame Correctives, as in the Work, which he publiſhed in his own Name, in 1688. If he has, Mr *Menage* has not cited him juſtly; for he has dropped an Eſſential Part of the Paſſage, which he reports. Theſe are *Saldenus*'s Words, in the Work, which he publiſhed, in 1688. " Sicuti Ariſtarchus Grammaticus neminem non reprehendebat,
" nihil interim ipſe ſcribens, ne reprehendi ab aliis poſſet
" ut nonnulli volunt: licet alii ſint, ac plerique quidem, qui πολυγϱάφοις ipſum accenſent, ut ſupra
" diximus (41). ——— As Ariſtarchus the Grammarian
" cenſured every one; but publiſhed nothing himſelf,
" left he ſhould be cenſured by others; as ſome will
" have it; tho' others reckon him among the Voluminous Writers; as I have obſerved above" We may add, upon this Occaſion, what Mr *Faber* addreſſed to a Journaliſt (42). *If you had publiſhed any thing of your own, we ſhould be upon the Square; but, as the Caſe ſtands, you play with too much advantage; it is mockery to bett a Farthing againſt a Guinea; I know not who will play with you upon ſuch Terms.*

[D] They, who make him cotemporary with *Piſiſtratus*, are groſly miſtaken.] This is a very ancient Error. *Allatius* cites a long Paſſage (43), in which one of the Commentators of *Dionyſius* of *Thrace* affirms, that *Piſiſtratus* ordered it to be publiſhed over all *Greece*, that They, who brought him any of *Homer*'s Verſes, ſhould receive a Reward, at ſo much *per* Verſe. When he had collected as many as he could, he ſent for ſeventy Grammarians, to each of whom he gave a Copy of this Collection. They were deſired, each of them ſeparately, to range theſe Verſes in the beſt Order they could. After each had done his Beſt, they met again, by *Piſiſtratus*'s Order, and ſhewed their Works to each other. They agreed, unanimouſly, that the Work of *Ariſtarchus* and *Zenodotus* deſerved the preference, and afterwards declared, that *Zenodotus*'s Work ought to yield to That of *Ariſtarchus*. This Story contains This, among other Falſehoods, that *Ariſtarchus* and *Piſiſtratus* lived at the ſame Time. It was eaſy to diſcover this miſtake; yet the Commentators on *Dionyſius* of *Thrace* have perſuaded a great many into a Belief of it. *Euſtathius* has vented it, and, after him, *Genebrard*, and *Jaſon de Nores*. Read this Paſſage of *Allatius*: " Multis
" in *A Iliados* idem aſſerit. Οἱ δε συνθέμενοι ταύτην κατ᾽ ἐπιταγήν, ὥς φασι, Πεισιστράτε τε τῶν Ἀθηναίων τυράννε Γραμματικοί, καὶ διορθωθέντες κατὰ τὸ ἐκριβέστερον, ἐν ἑϐδομήκοντα, καὶ μετ᾽ ἐκ᾿λογῇ ἑνὸς ἐπραχθη. Id eſt:
" Qui vero eam compoſuerunt Grammatici, juſſu, ut tradunt, Piſiſtrati *Athenienſium Tyranni*, & ut hi melius viſum eſt correxerunt; quorum Princeps *Ariſtarchus*,
" & poſt eum *Zenodotus*. Et inferius: Τε δέ Ἀναγελλον τον Ὁμήρε ποίησιν ἐκπλαθεῖσαν ἁρπιχιν ἐποιήσατο Κιναίθω ὁ χῖος. Ἡμνῆσθαι
" τὸ δέ, φασίν, αὐτὸν παμπόλλα δε περὶ τὸν Κίναιθον καὶ πολλὰ τῶν ἐπων ἀυτοῖ ποιήσαντες παρεμβάλοιν. Διὸ καὶ διερρῳδηθησαν
" ἅι Ὁμηρικαὶ βίϐλοι, ὡς ἀναλοσι πεφηλαι. Id eſt:
" Homeri vero poëma diſperſam recitandi principium
" fecit Cinæthus Chius. Verum illam multis modis
" Cinæthi ſectatores depravarunt, multaque a ſe conſcripta carmina inſeruerunt. Quare libri Homerici

" correcti ſunt, ut ſuperius diximus. Gilbertus Genebrardus *Chron*. lib. 2. Piſiſtrati juſſu *Ariſtarchus*
" Homeri rapſodiam recenſuit, & in 24 partes pro
" numero elementorum diſtribuit. Jaſon *de Nores* in
" artem Poëticam Horatii, *Ariſtarchus* miro quodam
" acumine caſtigabat veterum ſcripta, atque ideo colligendis *Homeri* verſibus præpoſitus fuit. In quibus
" vides miros Anachroniſmos. Primus, qui Ariſtarchum ſub Piſiſtrato collocat. Secundus, qui Linæthum Chium aſſerit primum *Homeri* poëma diſperſam recitaſſe. Cum uterque poſt Piſiſtrati tempora floruerit. Cinæthus enim, ſi Pindari Scholiaſtæ credimus, in *Nemeon*, Od. 2. ſub Olympiade
" ſexageſima nona apud Syracuſas *Homeri* carmina
" ἐξερϱαψώδηκε (44). ——— They have deceived many
" others of the Moderns; for *Euſtathius*, on the firſt
" Iliad, aſſerts the ſame Thing. Οἱ δὲ συνθέμενοι οἱ, &c. i. e. The chief of the Grammarians, who diſpoſed and corrected it, by order of *Piſiſtratus*, Tyrant of *Athens*, were *Ariſtarchus*, and after him *Zenodotus*. And a little lower, τᾺ δέ ἀναγέλλειν, &c. i. e. Cinæthus the Chian was the Firſt, who recited the ſcattered Poems of *Homer*. But the Followers of Cinæthus corrupted them ſeveral Ways, and foiſted in ſeveral Verſes of their own. For which reaſon the Books of *Homer* were corrected, as I have ſaid above. Gilbert Genebrard, *Chron*. lib. 2. ſays, that *Ariſtarchus*, by order of *Piſiſtratus*, reviſed the Rhapſody of *Homer*, and divided it into Twenty four Parts, according to the Number of the Letters. *Jaſon de Nores*, upon Horace's *Art of Poetry*, tells us, that *Ariſtarchus* with wonderful Judgment corrected the Writings of the Ancients, and was therefore appointed to collect *Homer*'s Poems. In theſe Paſſages you ſee ſurprizing Anachroniſms. The firſt places *Ariſtarchus* in the Reign of *Piſiſtratus*; The ſecond aſſerts Cinæthus the Chian to have been the firſt, who recited the ſcattered Poems of *Homer*; Whereas both of them flouriſhed after the Time of *Piſiſtratus*. For Cinæthus, if we may believe the Scholiaſt on Pindar, *Nem*. Od. 2. collected together the Verſes of *Homer*, at Syracuſe, in the LXIXth Olympiad.

[E] *Cicero* and *Horace* employed his Name, when they would deſcribe a too rigid Critic] Conſult the Oration againſt *Piſo*, where you will find the following Words: " Verum tamen, quoniam te non Ariſtarchum, ſed Phalarim Grammaticum, habemus, qui
" non notam apponas ad malum verſum, ſed Poëtam
" armis perſequare, ſcire cupio quid tandem iſto in
" verſu reprehendas, Cedant Arma togæ (45). ——— I deſire to know of you, who are not an *Ariſtarchus*,
" but a *Phalaris*, and who, inſtead of affixing a Mark
" to a bad Verſe, purſueſt the Poet himſelf, ſword in
" Hand; inform me, I ſay, what you diſlike in That
" Verſe, Cedant Arma Togæ, &c." The ſame Orator declares, that he was afraid of his Friend *Atticus*'s Nails. *Noſtrum opus tibi probari lator; ex quo avȢiv ipſa pauuiſti, quæ mihi florentiora ſunt viſa tuo judicio. Cærulas enim tuas miniatulas illas extimeſcebam* (46). Thus we ſhould expreſs ourſelves at preſent to denote the Cenſures, which a Reader might mark down in the Margin of a Book, and the *cærulæ miniatulas* of the Paſſage, which I have quoted. *Atticus* was one of thoſe ſincere Perſons, who examine the Compoſitions of their Friends with Strictneſs, and therefore *Cicero* calls him his *Ariſtarchus*. *Quid multa? totum hunc locum, quem ego varie meis orationibus, quarum tu Ariſtarchus es, ſoleo pingere, de flamma, de ferro, (noſti illas* λαμπʒύς*) valde graviter pertexuit* (47). The Verſes of Horace, which I am going to quote, furniſh an Idea, which is a ſtrong Proof of my Text.

Vir bonus & prudens verſus reprehendet inertes
Culpabit duros: incomptis allinet atrum
Tranſverſo calamo ſignum: ambitioſa recidet
Ornamenta: parum claris lucem dare coget:
Arguet ambigue dictum: mutanda notabit:
Fiet Ariſtarchus: nec dicet, Cur ego amicum
Offendam in nugis (48)?

ARISTARCHUS. 453

which others impute either to *Theocritus*, or *Isocrates* [F]. He had several Contests, in *Pergamus*, with *Crates* the Grammarian [G]; and died in the Island of *Cyprus*, at Seventy two Years of Age. He was seized with a Dropsy, and found no better Remedy for this Distemper, than starving himself to Death. There proceeded out of his School to the Number of forty Grammarians [H]. He left two Sons, whose only Merit was their great Simplicity. He, who bore his Father's Name, had been
sold

The prudent Care of an impartial Friend
Will give you notice of each idle Line;
Shew what sounds harsh, and what wants Ornament,
Or where it is too lavishly bestow'd;
Make you explain all that he finds obscure,
And with a strict Enquiry mark your Faults;
With Freedom, Aristarchus-like, will judge *,
Nor for these Trifles fear to lose your Love.
Lord ROSCOMMON.

* This Line is not Lord Roscommon's, but necessary upon the present Occasion.

[F] *Some ascribe to him a Thought, which others impute either to* Theocritus, *or to* Isocrates.] This Saying of *Aristarchus* is upon Record: *I cannot write, what I would; and I will not write, what I can* (49). Mr *Dacier* tells us this, on these Words of *Horace*:

(49) Dacier's Remarks on Horace, Epist. 1. l. 2.

Si quantum cuperem, possem quoque (50).
Did but my Pow'r rise equal to my Will.

(50) Horat. Epod. 1. 1. ver. 256.

The Authors, whom I have hitherto consulted, have not led me to the Source; and my Enquiries have been less successful in this Point, than in That of *Aristarchus*'s Divination. This makes me passionately wish, that Mr *Dacier*, and others like him, would have the goodness to leave off the Practice of not quoting their Authors. Are they afraid, that the Great and Polite World, for whom they labour, should look upon Citations as too pedantic? I can scarce believe, that a Count *de Guiche* (51), for Example, would be displeased to know, where we may find, that *Aristarchus* was the Author of this fine Saying, and was treated as a Prophet. Any Lady, who loves Learning, would be better pleased to know, that *Plutarch*, or *Aristotle*, vouch such a Fact, than, in general, that it is reported. This by the way: To return to our Text; we read, in the Collections of *Stobæus*, that *Theocritus*, being asked, why he did not write, answered, because *I cannot do it as I would and I will not do it, as I can*. Ἐρωτηθεὶς διὰ τί οὐ συγγράφει, ὅτι, εἶπεν, ὡς μὲν βούλομαι οὐ δύναμαι, ὡς δὲ δύναμαι οὐ βούλομαι (53). *Isocrates*, being at Table with *Nicocreon*, King of *Cyprus*, was desired to say something, but would not: and gave this Reason; *What I do know, is not seasonable, and, what may be seasonable, I do not know*. Οἷς μὲν ἐγὼ δεινός εἰμ' ὁ νῦν καιρός· οἷς δὲ ὁ νῦν καιρός, οὐκ ἐγὼ δεινός (52). This puts me in mind of The Thought of *Seneca*: "I never endeavoured to please the People; for they do not approve of what I do know, and I do not know what they do approve of. *Nunquam volui populo placere, nam quæ ego scio, non probat populus, quæ probat populus, ego nescio* (54)."

(51) *We find, in the Continuation of the Menagiana, pag. 6, Edit. of Holland, that this Count, in the midst of the Pleasures and Avocations of the Court, never omitted studying regularly, at least three hours a day.*

(52) Stobæus, Serm. XXI. de cognosc. seipso.

(53) Plut. in Vita Isocr. p. 838. F. See Id. in Symposiac. l. 1. c. 7. p. 613. A.

(54) Senec. Epist. 29. pag. 219.

(55) Suidas in Ἀρίσταρχος.

[G] *He had Contests, in* Pergamus, *with* Crates *the Grammarian* (55)] The Words of *Suidas* are express to this Purpose: Κράτητι τῷ γραμματικῷ συγκαμινῷ πλεῖστα διημιλλήσατο ἐν Περγάμῳ (56). *Cum Cratete Grammatico Pergameno Pergami sæpissime contendit.* By virtue of this Passage, *Casaubon* maintains, that *Crates Mallotes* was not the Antagonist of *Aristarchus*; but another *Crates*, born at *Pergamus* (57). As this *Crates Mallotes* was cotemporary with *Aristarchus*, and very well known to the King of *Pergamus*, it might easily be supposed, that he was the same, who disputed on several Occasions with *Aristarchus*. It is proper therefore to observe, that *Suidas* gives the Sirname of *Pergamenus* to *Aristarchus*'s Adversary. Perhaps he is mistaken; for They, who quote *Crates* of *Pergamus*, represent him rather as an Historian, than Grammarian (58); and it is certain, that Grammar was the chief Study of *Crates Mallotes*. Read this Passage: "*Primus quantum opinamur Studium Grammaticæ in Urbem intulit Crates Mallotes, Aristarchi æqualis, qui missus ad senatum ab Attalo rege, inter secundum ac tertium bellum Punicum, sub ipsam Ennii mortem, quum in regione Palatii prolapsus in cloacæ foramen crus fregisset, per omne legationis simul & valetudinis tempus plurimas ἀκροάσεις subinde fecit, assidueque disseruit, ac nostris exemplo fuit ad imitandum* (59). ------ *It is believed, that* Crates Mallotes, *Cotemporary with* Aristarchus, *first introduced the Study of Grammar at* Rome; *who, being sent to the Senate by King* Attalus, *between the second and third Punic War, about the Time of* Ennius's *Death, and having the Misfortune to fall, and break his Leg, near the Palatine Hill, continued, during the whole Time of his Embassy and Recovery, to read several Lectures, and to hold Disputations; in which he set the Romans an Example worthy of Imitation*." This Passage of *Varro* is generally understood of *Crates Mallotes*. *Crates nobilis Grammaticus, qui fretus Chrysippo homine acutissimo, qui reliquit sex libros περὶ τῆς ἀνωμαλίας; heis libreis contra analogiam atque Aristarchum est nixus* (60). ------ *Crates, a celebrated Grammarian, who relied on* Chrysippus, *a Man of great Subtilty, who left six Books concerning Anomaly; by the help of these Books, he opposed Analogy and Aristarchus*." If *Varro* speaks here of *Crates Mallotes*, it is probable, that *Suidas* mistook the one for the other; I mean, that *Crates Mallotes*, and not *Crates of Pergamus*, was the Rival of our *Aristarchus*. I know not whether the Commentators on *Suetonius* have ever thought of criticising him on a Point of Chronology, which I shall mention. He says, that *Crates Mallotes* came to *Rome* in the Name of King *Attalus*, about the time that *Ennius* died. The Death of That Poet happened in the Year of *Rome* 585. Now He, who reigned at that Time at *Pergamus*, was called *Eumenes*: He began his Reign in the Five hundred and fifty sixth Year of *Rome*, and died in the Year 596, leaving the Tuition of his Son, and the Regency, to his Brother *Attalus*. If *Crates Mallotes*, then, was deputed to the *Romans* by This *Attalus*, Chronology will not allow us to say, that he took this Journey about the time of *Ennius*'s Death. However, *Suetonius* supplies us wherewith to confirm the Opinion of Those, who make *Aristarchus* flourish under Ptolomy *Philometor*, in the CLVIth Olympiad (61). *Eusebius* and *Suidas* are of This Number. *Vossius* has not followed *Suetonius*; for, instead of saying, that *Aristarchus*, and *Crates Mallotes*, were Cotemporaries, he makes *Crates Mallotes*, and *Apollodorus*, the Disciple of *Aristarchus*, Cotemporaries (62). I do not pretend, that this is false: for a Person may be cotemporary both with the Master and the Disciple; but I observe, by the way, that he is mistaken in another Point: He believed, that a Drammatic Piece, which had been translated by *Ennius*, and was called the *Achilles* of *Aristarchus*, had this Name given it, only because That great Critic had corrected it. *Ab hoc & vetus quædam Comædia, quam* Ennius *postea transtulit, dicebatur* Achilles Aristarchi. *Meminit ejus* Plautus (63). *At sic non alia de causâ vocabatur, quam quod ab eo esset emendata.* It is a Mistake. This Piece was a Tragedy of *Aristarchus* of *Tegeas*, cotemporary with *Euripides*. See *Scaliger* (64).

(56) Suidas in Ἀρίσταρχος.

(57) Casaub. in Sueton. de Illustr Gramm. c. 2.

(58) See Vossius de Histor. Gr. pag. 347.

(59) Sueton. de Illustr. Grammat. cap. 2.

(60) Varro, de Lingua Latina, l. 8. init. See also lib. 7. p. 97. See in Voss. ubi supra, several Authorities, which prove, that Crates Mallotes was a Grammarian.

(61) Is answers to the end of the sixth Age of Rome.

(62) Voss. de Arte Gram. l. 1. c. 6. p. 24.

(63) Plaut. in Prologo Pœnuli, ver. 1.

(64) Scalig. Animadv. in Euseb. n. 1561. pag. 103.

(65) Varro, de Lingua Lat. lib. 7. pag. 96.

(66) Id. Ib. lib. 9. pag. 134.

[H] *Forty Grammarians proceeded out of his School*] He may be reckoned the Head of a Sect; witness the Words of *Varro*: "*Relinquitur de casibus, in quo* Aristarchei *suos intendunt nervos* (65). *Hoc in oratione diligentius quam alii ab* Aristarcho Grammatici (66). ------ *It remains to speak of the Cases, in which the Followers of* Aristarchus *exert themselves.* ------ *This Part of Speech they more carefully observe, than the rest of the Grammarians since* Aristarchus." See likewise the
Railleries

ARISTEUS.

sold for a Slave; but the *Athenians* ransomed him (e). I have something to offer against *Moreri* [I].

Railleries of *Herodicus* (67). It appears from *Suidas*, that *Aristarchus*'s School subsisted for some Ages in *Alexandria* (68).

[*I*] *I have something to offer against Moreri.*] I. He suffered himself to be imposed upon by *Vossius*, when he said, that *Aristarchus* was of *Samos* (69). II. Nothing is more impertinent, than to observe, that *Aristarchus* was Cotemporary with *Crates* (70). It is explaining an obscure point by one, which is more obscure, *obscurum per obscurius*. There have been several *Crates*'s; *Diogenes Laërtius* reckons up ter, some Philosophers, others Poets, or Grammarians, or Orators, or Geometricians, &c (71). They did not all flourish at the same time; nor were they all of the same Country; what then can be more insignificant, than to remark, that *Aristarchus* flourished in the Time of *Crates?* The most famous of these *Crates*'s was the Cynic Philosopher. The most natural Sense, therefore, of Mr *Moreri*'s Words is, that *Aristarchus* was Cotemporary with That Cynic: Now this is false; there is a great Interval of Time between them (72). This Censure does not affect *Suetonius*, who says, that *Crates Mallotes* was Cotemporary with *Aristarchus*; for there were few learned Persons in *Suetonius*'s Age, who were ignorant at what time *Aristarchus* lived. III. I believe no one has said, that This Grammarian composed nine Books of *Corrections on the Iliad*, and *the Odyssey*. *Suidas* affirms it of *Crates Mallotes* (73), as *Vossius* observes (74). *Moreri* did not understand *Vossius*'s Words. IV. It is false, that *Ptolomy Lathyrus* was the Son of *Ptolomy Philometor*. V. I believe it to be true, at the bottom, that our *Aristarchus* was living in the CLVIIIth Olympiad; but, since *Eusebius* and *Suidas* make him flourish in the CLVIth, this ought to have been remarked. *Vossius* falsly imputes to *Eusebius* the placing of him in the CLVIIIth (75).

ARISTEUS, the Son of *Apollo* and *Cyrene* [A]. His Article is very imperfect in *Moreri*, who confines himself to the informing us, I. That, by *pursuing Eurydice*, the Wife of *Orpheus*, from place to place, he occasioned her Death, by the bite of a Serpent. II. That the Nymphs, to be revenged of *Aristeus*, killed all his Bees. III. That, *having offered a Sacrifice of Bulls, he recovered what he had lost* (a). IV. That

[A] *The Son of* Apollo, *and* Cyrene] This is the general Tradition; and there are very few Traditions in Mythology more constant than this. Yet *Cicero* mentions another; he says, that the *Greeks* make *Aristeus* the Son of *Bacchus*; and adds, that, in *Sicily*, he was honoured in the Temple of That Deity. He addresses himself to *Verres*. "Quid! "ex æde Liberi Simulacrum Aristei non tuo im- "perio palam ablatum est? ——— Aristeus, qui "UT GRAECI FERUNT, liberi filius, inventor olei "esse dicitur, una cum libero patre apud illos eodem "erat in templo consecratus (1). — — — — *What!* "*was not the Image of* Aristeus *openly taken away* "*from the Temple of* Bacchus *by your Command?* "——— *Aristeus, who being, as the Greeks relate,* "*the Son of* Bacchus, *is said to have invented Oyl,* "*and was consecrated by them in the same Temple* "*with his Father* Bacchus." In another Book, he takes up with the common Opinion, and says, that *Apollo* was the Father of *Aristeus*, the Inventor of Oyl. *Quid Aristeus qui olivæ dicitur inventor Apollinis filius* (2). Let us next speak of *Cyrene*: She was the Daughter of *Hypseus*, King of the *Lapithæ*, who was the Son of *Peneus* and *Creusa* (3). *Creusa* was the Daughter of the *Earth*; and *Peneus* was Son of the *Ocean*. *Cyrene* despised the Employments of other Maidens, and their House-hold Amusements (4), and rising, early (5), was extreamly fond of Hunting, and making great Destruction among the wild Beasts. *Apollo*, encountring her, as she was fighting singly with a Lyon, demanded of *Chiron*, who she was, and whether he might not use force, and enjoy her.

- - - - *Ὀσία*
Κλυ]ὸν χεῖρά οἱ προσενεγκεῖν;
Ἦ ῥα καὶ ἐκ λεχέων
Κεῖρεν μελιηδέα ποίαν (6).

Fas-ne est illustrem manum ei admovere? Utrum & ex stratis tondere mellitam herbam?

Chiron, beginning with an Answer to the last Question, represented, that Lovers ought to make use of the Key of the Heart; that is of soft and tender Words, to persuade the Fair to grant what they request; adding, that, among both Gods and Men, Modesty opposes the Precipitation, with which some fall to downright Enjoyment; and explained himself very nicely upon this Subject.

- - - - καὶ ἐν τε θεοῖς
Τοῦτο κἀνθρώποις ὁμῶς
Αἰδέον τ᾽ ἀμφαδὸν ἀ-
δείας τυχεῖν τὸ πρῶτον εὐνᾶς (7).

Et inter Deos & homines pariter verecundanter aperte postulato dulci frui primum cubili.

"By the way, continues he, it is a visible effect of "your great Civility, that you, who know all "things, should do me the Honour to enquire of "me concerning this Maid's Extraction." This is *Pindar*'s Sense: I pretend not to give a Translation Word for Word; it is sufficient to represent his Thought. Now, if this be his Meaning, who can see, without Indignation, the Liberty, which a *French* Author takes of making him express himself thus? "Is it lawful to see her? May I approach her? "Shall I not be thought rash, if I take her fair "Hand, and gather one of those Vermillion Roses, "which I see painted on her Lips? But the Centaur, smiling, answered him thus: A chast Love, "*Apollo*, ought always to be concealed; and the "Fair Sex, among the Gods, as well as among "Mortals, do not grant their Favours in the Eyes "of the World. Thus is without doubt the Reason, "which makes you speak with so much reserve. A "Lover less chast than you, would not have had "so much Respect; and it is to your own good Manners, rather than to my Instruction, that you owe "this Modesty (8)." This Translation is repugnant to the Original, and inconsistent with itself; for, should we suppose, that *Apollo* did not express himself grosly, but modestly and chastly, *Chiron*'s Answer is ridiculous and contradictory. The Event was, that *Apollo* enjoyed *Cyrene*, without delay, and transported her into *Africa*.

Ὠκεῖα δ᾽ ἐπαιγομένων ἤδη Θεῶν
πρᾶξις, ὁδοὶ τε βραχεῖαι.
κεῖνο κεῖν᾽ ἅμαρ διαίξασεν. Θάλαμον δὲ μίγαν
ἐν πολυχρύσῳ Λιβύας (9).

Celer autem est properantium jam Deorum actis, viæque breves. Illud illa dies peregit. In thalamo autem Libyæ divote auri congressi sunt.

Chiron would have had him say tender things to her, and proceed in a way of honourable Love; but, as *Pindar* observes, *the Gods of the Poets could not away with delays; they dispatched Matters in a trice; they went the shortest Way to work; they boarded briskly, and enjoyed either by fair, or by foul Means.* They took the Romance by the tail (10), and said, with *Boreas* in Love,

Apta mihi vis est (11).

By Force and Violence I chiefly live.

CROXAL.

Cyrene

ARISTEUS.

That *he invented the Secret of extracting Honey, making Oyl, and Cheese* [B]. There are several other Things, which should have been said concerning This Son of *Apollo*; it should have been observed, that he was born in That Part of *Lybia*, where the City of *Cyrene* was built; that he was brought up by the Nymphs; that, having taken a Journey to *Thebes*, he there married *Autonoë*, the Daughter of *Cadmus*; that he had by Her *Actæon*, who was torn in Pieces by his own Dogs; that, after the Death of This Son, he consulted the Oracle of *Apollo*; that, upon the Strength of the Answer, which was given him, concerning the Honours he should receive in the Island of *Cea*, he made a Voyage thither [C]: That, a Plague ravaging all *Greece*, he offered Sacrifices, which put a Stop to it; that, leaving his Family in the Island of *Cea*, he re-passed into *Lybia*; from whence he sailed with the Fleet, which his Mother had

(12) Virgil. Georgic. lib. 4. ver. 355. See also Servius, on ver. 317.

(13) Hygin. cap. 161.

(14) Schol. Apoll. in lib. 2. Argon. v. 502.

(15) Frischlin. in Callimach. Hymn. 2, pag. 397. Edit. Ultraj. 1697.

(16) Apoll. Argon. lib. 2, ver. 502. & seq.

(17) Diod. Sicul. lib. 4, cap. 83, pag. 167.

(18) Pindar. Od. 9. Pyth. pag. 442.

(19) Schol. Apoll. Argon. lib. 2, ver. 500.

(20) Apoll. ibid. lib. 4, ver. 1218. *mentions a Temple of Apollo Nomius.*

(21) Benedictus, in Pindarum ubi supra, pag. 442.

(22) Plut. in Amator. p. 757.

(23) Scholiast. Apoll. in lib. 2. ver. 509.

(24) Apoll. Argon. l. 4. ver. 512, &c.

(25) Id. ib. ver. 1132.

Cyrene conceived, and brought our *Aristeus* into the World. Observe, that *Virgil* (12) and *Hyginus* (13), who make her the Daughter of *Peneus*, follow an Ancient Tradition in this (14). Wherefore we may say, that *Frischlinus* was much in the wrong to blame *Boccace*, and to be ignorant of what They had affirmed. " Constat non recte scripsisse Bocatium, l. 7. Geneal. " c. 28. dum asserit Cyrenem Penei fuisse filiam (15). " ―― *Boccace was certainly mistaken, in asserting,* " *that Cyrene was the Daughter of Peneus.*" *Apollonius* supposes, that she was a Shepherdess, and had resolved to lead a single Life, but that *Apollo*, who carried her away by force, would not suffer her to preserve her Virginity (16).

[B] *He invented the Secret of extracting Honey, making of Oyl, and Cheese.*] *Diodorus Siculus* relates, that *Aristeus*, having learnt of the Nymphs, who nursed him, the Art of curdling Milk, and making Bee-hives, and cultivating Olive-Trees, was the first, who communicated these Inventions to Men. The Conveniences, which they received thereby filled them with so great Acknowledgment, that they paid the same Divine Honours to Him, as they did to *Bacchus*. This Historian adds, that the Nymphs imposed three Names on him, That of *Nomius*, That of *Aristeus*, and That of *Agreus* (17). This agrees well enough with *Pindar* (18). But observe, that he says, that the *Hours* and the *Earth*, to whom *Mercury* carried this Infant, fed him with Nectar and Ambrosia: Others say, that *Aristeus*, having invented the making of Honey, and Oyl, in the Island of *Cea*, and having caused the Winds, which are called *Etesian*, to blow, was surnamed *Jupiter Aristeus* (19), and *Apollo Agreus*, and *Nomius* (20). The Surname of *Nomius* suited him (21), because of the Care he took of his Herds; and That of *Agreus* was proper, because he applied himself to Hunting. The following is a curious Authority for this Interpretation: *They, who take Wolves and Bears in Traps and Gins, put up Prayers to* Aristeus, *because he was the first, who invented the Art of taking them with Snares, and running Nooses.* It is a Passage of *Plutarch*. This is the Original. Εὐχονϊαι δ' Ἀρισαίῳ δολῶνϊες ὀρύγμασι καὶ βρόχοις λύκυς καὶ ἄρκϊος, ὅς πρῶτ@ Θήρεσσιν ἔϊευξε ποδάγρας (22). *Aristeo vota facient foveis altis, aut laqueis positis, qui lupis aut ursis insidiantur, ille feris primus pedicas quia tendere cepit.* The Scholiast of *Apollonius* does not explain the Etymology of these two Names after this manner. He founds That of *Nomius* on *Cyrene*'s having to do with *Apollo*, while she was a Shepherdess, and That of *Agreus* on the Act being performed in the Fields. He adds, that, according to others, the Etymology came from *Aristeus*'s teaching the Shepherds the Art of Tilling and Manuring the Ground. Ἀγρέα καὶ νόμιον, τὸ μὲν, ὅτι ἐν ἀγρῷ ἐμίγη τῇ μητρὶ αὐτῇ ὁ Ἀπόλλων. νόμιον δὲ, ὅτι νεμούσῃ ἐμίγη. οἱ δὲ, ὅτι τὴν καθὰ τὸς ἀγρὸς θεραπείαν τοῖς νομεῦσι εἰσηγήσαϊο (23). The Passage, where *Apollonius* says, that the Inhabitants of *Thessaly* gave these two Surnames to *Aristeus*, contains Particulars, which deserve to be produced here. We there find, that *Aristeus* was brought up in *Chiron*'s Cave, and that, when he was come to Age of Maturity, the Muses gave him a Wife, and taught him Physic, and the Science of Divination, and set him over all their Flocks (24). We find, in another Passage of the same Poet, that he invented Honey, and Oyl (25). He hints, in *Virgil*, that the Pains he had taken in perfecting Agriculture, and feeding of Cattle, had procured him all the Glory he enjoyed.

En etiam hunc ipsum vitæ mortalis honorem,

Quem mihi vix frugum & pecudum custodia solers Omnia tentanti extuderat; te matre relinquo (26).

Lost are the Honours; if my Herd and Plough Honours, which scarce my utmost Toils allow; So wretched is thy Son, so hard a Mother Thou.

He is one of the Deities, whom *Virgil* invokes, when he undertakes to write on Agriculture.

―― et cultor Nemorum, cui pinguia Ceæ Ter centum nivei tondent dumeta juvenci (27).

And Thou, for whom the Cæan Shore sustains The milky Herds, that graze the floury Plains. DRYDEN.

Oppian (28), *Nonnus* (29), the Scholiast of *Pindar*, and *Apollonius*, &c. all agree, in making him the Inventor of Those Things, which I have specified. Some Passages on the same Subject will occur below. The following is One of them, in which the City of *Athens* is made the Place of his Birth. *Oleum & trapetas Aristeus Atheniensis. Idem mella* (30). *By trapetas* are to be understood the Mills for squeezing the Olives (31). Let us not forget, that he invented the Aromatic Gum *Benjamin*. This is asserted by an Ancient Author, quoted by the Scholiast of *Aristophanes* (32), as you may see in the Three Hundred and Fifty fixth Page of *Salmasius*'s Commentary on *Solinus*.

Note, that *Justin* (33) relates, that *Cyrene*, being got with Child by *Apollo, a Deo repleta,* had four Sons, *Nomius, Aristeus, Authocus*, and *Argæus* (34). This is making of the two Surnames of *Aristeus* two Men (35).

[C] *He made a Voyage to the Island of* Cea.] The Greek of *Diodorus Siculus* is εἰς Κῶ νῆσον; and a little after, ἐν τῇ Κῷ. *Rhodoman* translates it *in Co insulam*, and *in Co.* This rendering puzzles the Reader; for it inclines him to believe, that the Greek Historian is speaking of the Island of *Cos*, the Country of the great *Hippocrates*, and not of the Island of *Cea*, as other Authors do, when they speak of *Aristeus*. However, we may be certain, that he means the Island of *Cea*, whether it be necessary to correct the Text, by putting Κέω, instead of Κῷ (36), or that the Rules of Contraction allow us indifferently to make use of Κῶ or Κέω, in speaking of This Island (37). Let us take notice of these Words of *Diodorus*; παρὰ τῶν Κείων τιμαῖς, *de honoribus apud Coos* (38). They shew plainly, that he does not design to speak of the Island of *Cos*. However, let us produce some Authors, who have affirmed, that *Aristeus* settled in the Island of *Cea*; and let us begin with the Commentator *Servius*, on these Words of *Virgil*;

―― et cultor nemorum, cui pinguia Ceæ, &c.

cited above (39). " Aristeum invocat, id est Apol-
" linis & Cyrenes filium ―― hic (ut etiam Sallustius
" docet) post laniatum à canibus Actæonem filium
" Thebas reliquit, & Ceam insulam tenuit primo ad-
" huc hominibus vacuam (40). ―― *He invokes* Ari-
steus, i. e. the Son of Apollo *and* Cyrene. ―― *This*
Aristeus (as Sallust *also informs us) after his Son*
Actæon was torn in pieces by Dogs, left Thebes,
and took possession of the Island of Cea, *which, 'till*
then, had been uninhabited." *Apollonius* informs us, that *Aristeus*, being sent for by the Inhabitants of the *Cyclades*, to put a Stop to the Plague, went from *Thessaly* into the Island of *Cea*.

(26) Virgil. Georg. lib. 4. ver. 326.

(27) Id. ib. lib. 1. v. 14.

(28) Oppian. Cyneg. l. 4.

(29) Nonnus, Dionys. l. 5.

(30) Plin. l. 7. c. 56. p. 99.

(31) Varro de Ling. Lat. l. 4. p. 34.

(32) Ἀριστφάνες ψηϊτον τὴν ἱπϊαελων τῇ στάφϊδι, ἐξ ἕϊέρων δέκαρ καὶ τῷ μαστικη.

(33) Justin. lib. 13. c. 7.

(34) It should be read Αγραως.

(35) See Vossius, de Theolog. Gentil. lib. 1o, pag. 350.

(36) *It is the Opinion of* Voss. *ubi supra.*

(37) *And not, apud* Coos, *as* Rhodoman *has translated it.*

(38) *It is the Opinion of* Salmasius in Solinum, pag. 144, 145.

(39) Citation (27).

(40) Servius in Georg. lib. 1, v. 14.

had given him, to *Sardinia* [D]; that he fixed upon an Habitation there; that he cultivated This Country with great Care; that he banished Barbarity from thence, and civilized the Place; that he visited some other Islands; that the plentiful Harvests, and vast Stocks of Cattle, induced him to stay some time in *Sicily*; where he taught his rare Secrets to the Inhabitants; that, by way of Acknowledgment, they honoured him as a God, especially Those, who cultivated Olive-Trees; that, at last, he went into *Thrace*; that he was admitted there by *Bacchus* into the Mysteries of the *Orgies*; and that, by his Familiarity with That God, he learnt many things, which were useful to human Life; that, having lived there, some time, near Mount *Hæmus*, he disappeared; and that not only the Barbarous People of the Country, but the very *Greeks* instituted to him Divine Honours (*b*). Mr *Moreri* falsly observes, that *Diodorus Siculus* mentions another *Aristeus*, in the Eighty fourth Chapter of the Fourth Book; for That Chapter, and the preceeding, contain what I have now delivered. I am surprized, that we meet with nothing there concerning *Arcadia*, which was one of the principal Stations of *Aristeus* [E]. In the Remarks, you will find the different Opinions of Authors, the Impertinence of some Censures, with other Particulars; nor shall I omit the Astronomical Discovery, which is ascribed to *Aristeus* [F]; nor his worshipping the Dog-Star; nor his Daughter *Macris*

(*b*) Taken from Diodorus Siculus, lib. 4. cap. 23, 84.

Λίπεν δ' ὅγε πατρὸς ἐφετμῇ
Φθίην, ἐν δὲ Κέῳ κατενάσσατο λαὸν ἀξείρας
Παρράσιον (41).

(41) Apoll. Argon. lib. 2. ver. 521.

Commanded by his Sire, the Son obey'd,
And, leaving Phthia, the Parrhasians led
To Cea's Isle.

The Scholiast on this Poet affirms, as I have already observed, that *Aristeus* taught the Art of making Honey, and Oyl, in the same Island. Ἀρισαῖος δὲ ἐν τῇ Κέῳ εὑρὼν τὰ μελισσουρίκα πρῶτος καὶ τὴν τῶν ἐλαιῶν κατεργασίαν (42). We shall see, in the Remark [F], that he established there the Worship of the Dog-Star. *Varro Atacinus* relates, in his Poem of the Argonauts, that, a great Mortality among the Cattle afflicting That Island, *Aristeus* went thither, by *Apollo*'s Direction, and delivered it from That Calamity, after he had sacrificed to *Jupiter Icmæus*. The Winds, and Heats, which occasioned the Mortality, ceased. After *Aristeus*'s Death, the Inhabitants of the Island of *Cea* obeyed an Oracle, which commanded them to place him in the Number of the Gods, and called him *Nomius* and *Agræus*, because of the Service he had done them, by his Industry in feeding their Flocks, and manuring their Lands (43). Be not surprized, to find, in this Place, that he caused the Mortality to cease, by calming the Winds; and to find, hereafter, that he caused it to cease, by raising the Winds: for this ancient Traditions are contrived; one confutes, what the other affirms; one forgets the only Particular, which the other remembers. A compleat Narrative might have informed us, that, by changing the Wind, he restored Health; but They, who knew not how to express the whole, observed only, that the Wind ceased; you must not expect the rest; or, perhaps, that the Wind rose; you are to know no more of it; they will not inform you, that the pestilential Wind ceased, and the healthy succeeded. The Correction, which I have read in *Salmasius*, of a Passage in *Heraclides*, seems to me an happy one; in the mean while I would not swear, that it is not said in the Original, that the Pestilence in the Island of *Cea* proceeded from the Wind. Φθορᾶς οὔσης ζῴων καὶ ζώων διὰ τὸ πνεῖν ἐτησίας (44). A Plague happening on Plants and Animals, occasioned by the Etesian Winds. *Salmasius* corrects the Passage thus. Διὰ μὴ πνεῦσαι τὸ πνεῖν ἐτησίας (45). He prayed to Jupiter, that the Etesian Winds might blow. Which agrees with what I shall observe in the Remark [F].

(42) Schol. Apoll. in lib. 2, ver. 500.

(43) Voss. de Theol. Gentil. lib. 7, cap. 10, pag. 350.

(44) Heraclides, de Politeis, pag. 20.

(45) Salmas. in Solin. pag. 144.

[D] *He sailed - - - - towards* Sardinia.] *Diodorus Siculus* says, that he settled in the Island of *Cea*, after the Death of *Actæon*, and afterwards went into *Lybia*, and from thence to *Sardinia* (46); but others pretend, that his Grief for the Death of *Actæon* gave him such a Distaste for *Bœotia*, and the rest of *Greece*, that he went to reside in foreign Countries (47). They say, it was then, that he led a Colony into *Sardinia*. It is said, that *Dædalus*, having made his Escape from the Island of *Crete*, joined him in conducting this Colony (48); but Chronology refutes this invincibly. *Dædalus* was Cotemporary with *Oedi-*

(46) Diod. Siculus, lib. 4, cap 84.

(47) Pausan. lib. 10, pag. 372. See likewise Silius Italicus, lib. 12, pag. 498.

(48) Id. ib.

pus, King of *Thebes* (49); he could not, therefore, be concerned with *Aristeus*, the Son-in-law of *Cadmus*. However it be, Accounts differ greatly. *Pausanias* says, that a Company of *Lybians* had settled themselves in *Sardinia*, and incorporated with the Natives of the Country, before *Aristeus* came thither; but *Aristotle* relates, that *Aristeus* was the first, who cultivated That Island; and that, before his Time, it served only as a Dwelling to great Numbers of monstrous Birds (50). Consult *Bochart*, who maintains, that This Voyage of *Aristeus* is a Fable (51).

[E] *Arcadia, — was one of the principal Stations of* Aristeus.] For This reason *Virgil* gives him the Epithet *Arcadius*, where he mentions the Invention of new Bees:

(49) Id. ibi.

(50) Aristot. de Mirab. Auscult. pag. 881. Oper. Tom. I.

(51) Bochart. Geograph. sacr. Part. II. lib. 1, cap. 31, pag. 632, 633.

Tempus & Arcadii memoranda inventa Magistri
Pandere, quoque modo cæsis jam sæpe juvencis
Insincerus apes tulerit cruor (52).

(52) Virgil. Georg. lib. 4, ver. 283.

'Tis time to touch the Precepts of an Art,
Th' Arcadian Master did of old impart;
And how he stock'd his empty Hives again,
Renew'd with putrid Gore of Oxen slain.
DRYDEN.

This Art was an Invention of *Aristeus*, and caused him to be honoured as a God in *Arcadia*. "Post eā "(*Cea*) relictā, cum Dædalo ad Sardiniam transitum "fecit. Huic opinioni Pindarus refragatur, qui eum "ait de Cea insula in Arcadiam migrasse, ibique vi- "tam coluisse. Nam apud Arcadas pro Jove coli- "tur, quod primus ostenderit qualiter apes debeant "reparari (53).——*Afterwards, leaving this Island "(*Cea*), he passed over with* Dædalus *to* Sardinia. "Pindar *contradicts this Opinion, who says, that he "passed from the Island* Cea *to* Arcadia, *and there "resided. For the* Arcadians *worship him as* Jupiter; "*because he first taught the Art of repairing the loss "of Bees.*" *Justin* gives *Aristeus* a large Kingdom in *Arcadia*: I shall quote his Words in the following Remark. It is not true, what Mr *Lloyd* affirms, that *Apollonius* makes *Aristeus* go from *Arcadia* to the Island of *Cea*. He has copied this Mistake from *Salmasius* (54).

(53) Servius in Georg. Virg. lib. 1. ver. 14.

(54) Salmas. in Solin. p. 99.

[F] *The Astronomical Discovery, which was ascribed to* Aristeus.] If we consider *Justin*'s Words only superficially, we may be induced to think, that he ascribes the first Discovery of the Solstices to *Aristeus*; but They, who read him with attention, will easily perceive, that he speaks of the rising of the Dog-Star. "Aristeum in Arcadia late regnasse, eumque pri- "mum & apium & mellis usum & lactis ad coagula "hominibus tradidisse, Solstitialesque ortus sideris pri- "mum invenisse (55).———Aristeus *reigned "over all* Arcadia; *and was the first, who taught "Mankind the use of Bees, Honey, and Cheese, and "discovered the rising of the Dog Star.*" The most learned Critics have observed, that it should either be read *Solstitialisque ortus Sideris*, or *Solstitialisque ortus Sirii* (56). Either of these two Readings mean the Dog-Star, as they pretend. It is certain, that This Star had a particular relation to our *Aristeus*.

(55) Justin. lib. 13. cap. 7. pag. 313, 314.

(56) See the Justin, Variorum, of Mr Grævius, on this Passage.

The

ARISTEUS.

Macris [G]. It has been said, that, in reward for the Services he had done Mankind by his Knowledge of all the useful Arts, the Gods placed him among the Stars, and that he was the *Aquarius* of the Zodiac (*c*). The Conformity of his History with That of *Moses* has been curiously and learnedly shewn by *Huetius* (*d*). Almost all that *Lloyd* has added to *Charles Stephens*, on this Article, he has taken Word for Word from the Commentary of *de la Cerda* (*e*); yet without quoting him.

(c) See the Commentary of Germanicus, in Aratæa Phænomena, cap. de Aquario, pag. 118.

(d) Huetius, Demonstr. Evang. Propof. IV. cap. 8. n. 17. pag. 110.

(e) In lib. 4. Georgic. Virgilii.

The Foundation of it was this. The Heats of the Dog-Days had laid waste the *Cyclades*, and produced a Plague, which the Natives intreated *Aristeus* to put a stop to. Upon which, he went into the Island of *Cea*, and, causing an Altar to be built to *Jupiter*, offered Sacrifices to That God: He offered likewise Sacrifices to the pestilential Star, and established an anniversary Worship of it. This produced a very good Effect; for from thence the *Etesian* Winds took their Original; Winds, which continue for forty Days, and which temper the Heat of the Summer:

Καὶ βωμὸν ποίησε μέγαν Διὸς Ἰκμαίοιο.
Ἱερά τ' εὖ ἔρρεξεν ἐν οὔρεσιν ἀστέρι κείνῳ
Σειρίῳ, αὐτῷ τε Κρονίδῃ Διί. τοῖο δ' ἕκητι
Γαῖαν ἐπιψύχουσιν ἐτήσιοι ἐκ Διὸς αὖραι
Ἥματα τεσσαράκοντα. Κέῳ δ' ἔτι νῦν ἱερῆες
Ἀντολέων προτέροισθε κυνὸς ῥέζουσι θυηλᾶς (57).

(57) Apoll. lib. 2. Argon. v. 524.

To *Jove*, the God, who bids the Dews descend,
An Altar on the Mountain's Brow he raised.
To Sirius, then, and Saturn's Son he pray'd.
Etesian Gales hence fan the glowing Earth;
And hence, e'er Sirius lifts his scorching Rays,
The Coan Priests the sacred Rites perform.

Diodorus Siculus does not expresly enough declare, that the *Etesian* Winds were the Effect of *Aristeus*'s Sacrifices (58). He seems to say, that, this Sacrifice having been made about the beginning of the Dog-Star, which falls in with the Season of The *Etesian* Winds, the Plague ceased. But it is certain, he pretends, that the raging Heat of That Star was abated by the religious Acts performed by *Aristeus*. He finds matter of Wonder in it, that the same Person, whose Son was torn to pieces by Dogs, should correct the Malignity of a Star, which is called the Dog. I leave out his *Greek*, and give only the Translation of *Rhodoman*. *Singularem hanc rerum conversionem, si quis penitius examinet, meritò demiretur. Qui enim filium à canibus discerptum vidit, is cœleste sidus canis nomine appellatum, quod hominibus exitium afferre putatur, mitigavit, & mortalibus non paucis auctor salutis exstitit* (59). Other Authors say, in plain and express Terms, that *Aristeus*'s Devotions were the Cause of these Winds. "*Canicula exoriens æstu* "*eorum* (60) *loca & agros fructibus orbabat: & ip-* "*sos morbo affectos pœnas sufferre cogebat, eo quod* "*latrones recepissent. Quorum Rex Aristeus, Apol-* "*linis & Cyrenes filius, Actæonis pater, petiit à pa-* "*rente quo facto à calamitate civitatem posset libe-* "*rare: quem deus jubet multis hostiis expiare Icarii* "*mortem, & ab Jove petere, ut, quo tempore Cani-* "*cula exoriretur, dies quadraginta ventum daret, qui* "*æstui caniculæ mederetur. Quod jussum Ari-* "*steus confecit, & ab Jove impetravit ut Etesiæ fla-* "*rent* (61). — *The Dog-Star, rising with great* "*Heat, destroyed the Fruits of their Ground, and* "*brought a Plague upon the Inhabitants, as a Pu-* "*nishment for their having given reception to Thieves.* "*Their King Aristeus, the Son of Apollo and Cyrene,* "*and Father of Actæon, enquired of his Father, by* "*what means he might remove this Calamity from* "*the State; whom the God commanded to expiate,* "*with many Sacrifices, the Death of Icarius, and to* "*beg of Jupiter, that, at what time the Dog-Star* "*arose, he would send a Wind for forty Days, which* "*should temper the Heat of the Dog-Star. Aristeus obey-* "*ed, and obtained of Jupiter, that the Etesian Winds* "*might blow.*" The Scholiast of *Apollonius* says expresly, that the *Etesian* Winds began to blow upon *Aristeus*'s Prayers. Ὅτι ἐτήσιαι ἐπνεύσαν Ἀρισταίῳ εὐξαμένῳ (62). Consult likewise *Germanicus*'s Commentary on the Phænomena of *Aratus* (63). Let us speak of the Anniversary, which he established. He ordered (64), that, every Year, the Priests of *Cea* should offer Sacrifices, before the rising of the Dog-Star, and that the Inhabitants should arm themselves to observe the rising of This Constellation, and offer Sacrifice to it. Ἐπο-

(58) Diodor. Sicul. lib. 4. cap. 84.

(59) Id. ib. pag. 268.

(60) So it should be read, and not eorum. See Salmaf. in Solin. p. 144.

(61) Hygin. Poët. Astron. lib. 2. cap. 4. pag. 365.

(62) Schol. Apoll. in lib. 2. ver. 500.

(63) German. in Aratæa Phænom. in Aquar. p. 118, 119.

(64) Apoll. lib. 2. ver. 528. you will find his Words, above, Citat. (57).

μοθέτησε γὰρ τοῖς κώοις (read κείοις) κατ' ἐνι-
αυτὸν μεθ' ὅπλων ἐπιτηρεῖν τὴν ἐπιτολὴν τοῦ κυ-
νὸς, καὶ θύειν αὐτῷ (65). *Cicero* says, that they expected to foresee, by observing This Planet, whether the Year would prove healthful, or not. *Ceos accepi-mus ortum caniculæ diligenter quotannis solere servare, conjecturamque capere, ut scribit Ponticus Heraclides, salubrisne an pestilens annus futurus sit* (66). *Manilius* imputes the same to the *Cilicians* (67). I know not whether the Inhabitants of *Calabria*, who offered up Vows to This Star, borrowed This Act of Religion, mediately or immediately, from *Aristeus*:

(65) Schol. Apollon. in lib. 2. ver. 528.

(66) Cicero, de Divinat. l. 1. cap. 57.

(67) Manil. Astronom. lib. 1. p. 13.

—— *sic cum stabulis & messibus ingens*
Ira deum & Calabri populator Sirius arvi
Incubuit, coit agrestum manus inscia priscum
In nemus, & miseris dictat pia vota Sacerdos (68).

(68) Valer. Flaccus, Argon. lib. 1. ver. 682.

So when the Dog-Star o'er Calabria reigns,
And parches with excessive Heat her Plains,
The stupid Peasants, struck with annual Fear,
Assembled in some ancient Grove appear;
In superstitious Rites they pass the Day,
And, as the Priest directs, the Wretches pray.

What Superstition! and yet This was not the most extravagant in Paganism. By the way, the Passage of *Justin*, which I have cited in the beginning of this Remark, will furnish us with an Incident here. Mr *Faber* thought himself the first, who understood it. "*Justin*, says he, does not pretend to say, that "*Aristeus* taught the use of Milk: That would have "been contrary to Truth, and all Antiquity; he "speaks only of the Art of curdling Milk: *Sed* "*ostendisse hominibus qua arte coagulum ex lacte con-* "*fici conformarique possit* (69). Neither does he "pretend, that *Aristeus* invented the use of Honey; "Milk and Honey served to nourish the greatest of "the Gods. *Nam Jupiter, pater ille hominumque* "*Deumque, melle nutritus est & lacte* (70). He "speaks, then, of the Art of curdling Milk with Ho- "ney." *Ergo aliud docuit Aristeus, scilicet coagu-lum fieri ex mixtura, seu, ut Græci vocant, cramate mellis & lactis. Hunc locum à nemine hactenus intellectum arbitror* (71). This Explanation seems to me very ingenious; but the Reasons, on which it is grounded, prove too much; for, if the ancient Tradition concerning the Food, with which *Jupiter* was nourished during his Infancy, prevented *Justin* from saying, that *Aristeus* taught Men the use of Honey, he would not have affirmed, that *Gargoris*, King of the *Cynetes* (72), or *Cunetes*, was the first Inventor of Honey; and yet he has said so plainly, and without leaving room to draw two different Senses to his Words; *Quorum* (*Cunetum*) *Rex vetustissimus Gargoris mellis colligendi usum primus invenit* (73). It cannot, I think, be pretended, that *Justin* paid such a Regard to poetical Traditions, that he was cautious of advancing things, which confute them. A great Number of Authors have said, that *Aristeus* invented Honey; their Words imply so much expresly, and cannot admit of this Signification, *he invented a Mixture of Honey and Milk, which formed a Curd*. It may reasonably, then, be concluded, that *Justin* meant as They did, and that he considered not what the Poets had said concerning *Jupiter*'s Milk and Honey. Observe, by the way, that *Aristeus*'s Inventions consisted sometimes in Mixtures; for he was the first, who taught the *Thracians* to mix Honey with Wine. *Aristeus primum omnium in eadem gente mel miscuisse vino, suavitate præcipua utriusque naturæ sponte provenientis* (74).

(69) Tanaq. Faber. Not. in Justin. l. 13. cap. 7.

(70) Id. ib.

(71) Id. ib.

(72) A People of Spain.

(73) Justin. lib. 44. c. 4.

(74) Plin. l. 14. c. 4. pag. 127.

[G] *His Daughter* Macris,] Very few Authors mention her; but This is *Apollonius*'s Account of her (75). It was She, who set little *Bacchus* upon her knee, after *Mercury* had rescued him from the Flames; and it was she, who fed him with Honey. She lived at that time in the Center of the Island of *Eubœa*: she exposed herself to the Indignation of *Juno*, by the good

(75) Apoll. Argon. l. 4. ver. 1131, & seq.

good Offices she performed to This Child, and was forced to leave the Country, and hide herself in a Cave, in the Island of the *Phæacians*, where she was a great Benefactress to the Inhabitants.

—— Καὶ ϖὸρεν ὄλϖον ἀθέσφαϑον, ἐντακϕαιν.

Et infinitis insularios opibus beavit (76).

(76) Id. lib. ver. 1140.

Let us conclude from hence, that *Aristeus*, Uncle-in-Law to *Bacchus* (77), was much elder than *Bacchus* himself. This does not confute what *Diodorus Siculus* says concerning the Admission of *Aristeus* into the *Orgies*, &c. nor, what others suppose, that he commanded some Troops in *Bacchus*'s Army (78); for Order requires, that the Superiority should ever belong to a Son of *Jupiter*, tho' the Younger Person.

(77) *His uncle the Husband of Antonoë, Sister of the Mother of Bacchus.*

(78) Nonnus, Dionysiacon. lib. 13.

ARISTEUS, the Geometrician, lived before *Euclid*, and composed Works, which met with Esteem. See, below, a fine Passage of *Pappus* [*A*].

[*A*] *A fine Passage of* Pappus.] I term it so, because it informs us of a very curious Particular relating to *Euclid*; which is, that this great Geometrician, (contrary to what *Apollonius Pergæus* had alledged) out of respect to *Aristeus*, and having a particular Esteem for All, who had contributed to the Improvement of the Mathematical Sciences, would not seem to be more expert in the Knowledge of *Conics* than He. I have taken Notice of this before (1). Let us produce the Words of *Pappus*. " *Aristeus* " autem, qui scribit ea quæ ad hoc usque tempus

(1) *In Remark* (D) *of the Article* APOLLONIUS (PERGAEUS), *Citat.* (3).

" tradita sunt solidorum libros quinque, conicis
" cohærentes vocavit - - - - - Euclides autem secutus
" Aristeum scriptorem luculentum in iis quæ de
" conicis tradiderat, neque antevertens, neque volens
" eorum tractationem destruere, cum mitissimus
" esset & benignus erga omnes, præsertim eos qui
" mathematicas disciplinas aliqua ex parte augere
" & amplificare possent, ut par est, & nullo modo
" infensus sed accuratus, non arrogans velut hic
" (*Apollonius Pergæus*) quantum ostendi potuit de
" loco per ejus conica memoriæ prodidit (2).

(2) Pappus, In Proœmio Mathemat. Collect.

ARISTEAS, the *Proconnesian*. Mr *Moreri*, contenting himself with telling us, that he lived in the Time of *Cyrus* [*A*], and that he composed the History of the *Arimaspians*, and *a Treatise of the Origin of the Gods, the whole filled with Fables* [*B*], has omitted what was most singular in This Article. Let us therefore supply it as follows, and say, That This *Aristeas*, dying in his own Country (*a*), was seen, the very same Day, and Hour, reading Lectures in *Sicily*. This Prodigy being several times renewed, and during several Years, obliged the *Sicilians* to build a Temple, and offer Sacrifices, to Him (*b*). *Herodotus* has spoken at large of this Miracle [*C*]. *Pliny* relates, that, in the Island of *Proconnesus*, the Soul of *Aristeas*

(*a*) *The Island of Proconnesus in the Propontis.*

(*b*) *Taken from Apollonius Dyscolus Histor. Commentat. cap.* 2*.*

[*A*] *He lived in the Time of* Cyrus.] This is proved by the Testimony of *Suidas*. Note, that *Cyrus* began to reign in *Persia* in the LVth Olympiad. *Vossius* infers from hence, that *Suidas*, in saying, on the one side, that *Aristeas* flourished in the Lth Olympiad, and, on the other, that This was in the Time of *Cyrus*, has not observed exactness (1). The Anonymous Author, whom *Vossius* has settled the Olympiads, places *Aristeas* in the Lth. This does not agree with what others have said; *viz.* that *Homer* was his Disciple (2). *Tatian* makes him later than *Homer* (3), and was censured for it by *Vossius*, as too favourable, in this Point, to the Good Cause, to wit, that *Homer*'s Age was considerably later than That of *Moses* (4). This Censure seems to me to be but weakly founded; for *Tatian* might justly make use of a Tradition, which was established among the Pagans. It has been said, we see, that our *Aristeas* was the Preceptor of *Homer*; and we read, in *Herodotus*, that *Aristeas* appeared in the World, three Ages after he had composed a Poem (5); so that it was not agreed, that he flourished in the Time of *Cyrus*. Observe, that *Herodotus* was born in the first Year of the LXXIVth Olympiad, and that he does not mention this last Appearance of *Aristeas* as a thing which had lately happened; but on the contrary, intimates, that the Tradition of the *Metapontines*, concerning this Adventure, was of long standing; for he does not say, that they marked the Time of it.

[*B*] *The whole filled with Fables.*] *Aulus Gellius* relates, that, being at *Brundusium*, he saw several Bales of Books exposed to sale, and that he was permitted to purchase as many as he pleased at a low Price; that They were all the Works of *Greek* Authors, who had collected several surprizing and incredible Fables; as *Aristeas*, *Isigonus*, *Ctesias*, *Onesicritus*, *Polystephanus*, and *Hegesias*; that he bought several of them; out of which he made several Extracts, which he inserted in his Work. *Fasces librorum venalium expositos vidimus. Atque ego avide statim pergo ad libros. Erant autem isti omnes libri Græci miraculorum fabularumque pleni: res inauditæ, incredulæ: scriptores veteres non parvæ auctoritatis, Aristeas Proconnesius, & Isigonus Nicaensis, & Ctesias, & Onesicritus, & Polystephanus, & Hegesias. Ipsa autem volumina ex diutino situ squallebant, & habitu adspectuque tetro erant. Accessit tamen, percunctatusque precium sum: & adductus mira atque insperata vilitate, libros plurimos ære pauco emo, eosque omnes duobus proximis mactibus cursim transeo: atque in legendo*

(1) Voss. de Hist. Græc. lib. 4. cap. 2, pag. 433.

(2) Strab. lib. 14. pag. 439.

(3) Tatian. Orat. ad Græcos, apud Voss. ib. lib. 1, cap. 2. pag. 7.

(4) Voss. ib. pag. 6.

(5) Herod. lib. 4. c. 14.

carpsi exinde quædam, & notavi mirabilia & scriptoribus fere nostris intentata: eaque his commentariis adspersi (6). The rest of this Chapter of *Aulus Gellius* is full of Chimerical Narrations, which he had read in Those Authors, or in *Pliny*. You are to know, that the History of the *Arimaspians*, composed by *Aristeas*, was a Poem (7). You will perhaps say, how do we know but the Author wrote it without intending it should be taken for Truth? *Aristeas* had no such Intention. Why do we not judge of the Ancient Poets, as of Him in this Point? I reply, that *Aristeas* had no Intention of diverting his Readers with Reports, which he designed should be looked upon as Fables, because his Aim, in these Stories, was to cure the Incredulity he had observed in the People. No One believed he was a Philosopher; and the Reason was, because he denied having ever been instructed (8). He removed this objection, by pretending, that his Soul had left his Body, and that, taking it's flight towards Heaven, it had surveyed all the *Greek* and *Barbarian* Countries, and finished its Course in the *Hyperborean* Climates. He boasted to have, by this means, discovered the Situation of Places, the Customs of the Inhabitants, the natural Qualities of the Elements, *&c.* and also to have observed the Heavens more exactly, than the Earth. Was not this producing his Tales as so many credential Letters? Did he not, by this, endeavour to establish an Authority, which should give credit to every thing else he had to say? He must, then, have proposed these Facts as true. And they were received as such; for more Credit was given to This Man, than to those Philosophers, who dogmatized without any disguise (9). Note, that *Dionysius Halicarnassensis* observes, that it was not universally believed, that our *Aristeas* was Author of the Books, which went under his Name (10).

[*C*] *Herodotus has spoken at large of this Miracle.*] This is the Sum of his Relation. *Aristeas*, one of the chief Men of the Island of *Proconnesus*, went one Day into a Fuller's House, and died there. The Fuller shut up his Doors, and went and informed *Aristeas*'s Relations of his Death. This News was soon spread all over the City; but, whilst this was the common Discourse, there came one, who affirmed, that he had met *Aristeas* going to *Cyzicus* (11), and that he had spoken with him. His Relations went to the Fuller's House, with Necessaries for his Funeral, but found him not, either dead, or alive. He appeared at the end of seven Years, and composed the Poem of the *Arimaspians*; after which he

(6) Aulus Gellius, lib. 9, cap. 4. pag. 239. *Note, that* Huetius, *in* Demonstr. Evangel. Prop. 9, cap. 141. pag. 1037, *cites this Passage of* Aulus Gellius, *as importing, that what had been said of Aristeas was false. This is not the Thought of Aulus Gellius.*

(7) Herodot. lib. 4. c. 13, 14. Strabo, lib. 1, pag. 15. & l. 13, pag. 405.

(8) Max. Tyrius, Dissert. 22, pag. 223.

(9) Id. ibid. pag. 224.

(10) Dionys. Halicarn. in judicio de Thucyd. cap. 25, pag. 584.

(11) *According to* Plutarch, *in* Romulo, pag. 35, *there were, who affirmed, that they saw him on the Road to Crotona.*

ARISTEAS.

Aristeas was seen to come out of his Mouth, in the Shape of a Raven (c). Others say, that his Soul went in and out of his Body at Pleasure [D]. *Strabo* makes This *Aristeas* one of the greatest Sorcerers that ever was (d). Some say that, to overcome the Incredulity of the People, with Regard to his Doctrine, he persuaded them, that his Soul had travelled into several Countries, separate from his Body (e). Six of his Verses are found in the Treatise of *Longinus* (f). Some others are found in the *Chiliads* of *Tzetzes* (g). He is twice cited in *Pausanias* (b). By the way, They, who pretend, that he was not quite dead, when his Soul was travelling (1), do not much lessen the Wonderfulness of the Prodigy. It is unnecessary to observe, that *Plutarch* laughed at this fine Story (k). *Gyraldus* has been guilty of some Mistakes [E].

he disappeared. Two or three Ages after, he shewed himself to the Inhabitants of *Metapontus* (12) and commanded them to build an Altar to *Apollo*, and to erect a Statue, near it, in honour of *Aristeas* the *Proconnesian*. He told them, that they were the only *Italians*, whom *Apollo* had honoured with a Visit, and that he had accompanied him in That Journey, not in the Shape of *Aristeas*, but in That of a Raven; and, having said this, he disappeared. The *Metapontines* enquired of the Oracle at *Delphi* what this meant: They were answered, that they would do well to obey it accordingly they executed his Orders (13). The Historian testifies, that, in his Time, there was a Statue of *Aristeas* in the Market-Place of *Metapontum*, near the Altar of *Apollo*, surrounded with Lawrel Trees. Let us add to this a Fact reported by *Athenæus*. After the return of *Aristeas* (14), the *Metapontines* dedicated a brazen Lawrel to *Apollo*. This Lawrel having spoken, at the Time when a Dancer of *Thessaly* approached the Market-Place of *Metapontum*, the Soothsayers, who were present, were immediately seized with such Fury, that they tore the Woman in Pieces. Note, that she had received a sacred Present from *Philomelus*, which was a golden Crown of Lawrel; which the Inhabitants of *Lampsacus* had consecrated in the Temple of *Delphi* (15). Note also, that *Æneas Gazæus*, citing the Narrative of *Herodotus*, adds this Circumstance; that the Sacrifices of the *Metapontines* were esteemed to belong in common to *Apollo* and *Aristeas*, as two Deities (16). *Origen* observes, that *Apollo* commanded This *Aristeas* to be honoured as a God by the Inhabitants of *Metapontum* (17). *Meursius* pretends, that *Athenagoras* reproached the *Pagans* with having honoured *Aristeas* in the Island of *Chios*, and with having taken him for the same God as *Apollo* and *Jupiter* (18). Χϊοι 'Αριςεαν τὸν αυτὸν καὶ Διὰ καὶ 'Απόλλω νομίζονῆες (19). Chii *Aristeam*, quem & *Jovem arbitrantur* & *Apollinem*. *Huetius* imagines, with much probability, that, instead Χϊοι, it should be read Κεῖοι, and that the Passage relates to *Aristeus*, the Son of *Apollo* and *Cyrene* (20); for this latter was worshiped in the Island of *Cea* (21). *Suffridus* understands the Passage of *Athenagoras* of this latter (22). *Huetius* shews, that ARISTEUS and ARISTEAS have been often mistaken one for the other (23).

They, who will have all Romances founded on some true Story, may suppose, that *Aristeas*, having counterfeited the dead Man in the Fuller's House, found means to get out, in the Master's Absence, and to convey himself privately out of the Town; and that, having hid himself for some Years, he returned thither again, and produced a Poem, in which he celebrated his Extasies (24); which he was very well pleased should be taken in the literal, and not in the poëtical Sense, in which we understand these Verses of *Horace*:

> Quo me Bacche rapis tui
> Plenum, quæ in nemora aut quos agor in specus
> Velox mente nova (25).
>
> *God of Wine, resistless Pow'r,*
> *Whither will you hurry me,*
> *Full of the Deity,*
> *Transported with a Rage unknown before?*
> *Whither, whither, must I rove?*
> *To what wild Cave, what distant Grove?*
> *Anonym.*

and several others, which *Huetius* mentions (26). I cannot easily agree with him, that *Maximus Tyrius* confirms the Conjecture, to wit, that *Aristeas* did not expect to be understood in a literal Sense (27). *Maximus Tyrius* supposes quite the contrary; as we have seen before (28). As for his Appearance to the *Metapontines*, we may suppose, that an Impostor persuaded them of what *Herodotus* relates; for they were *Pythagoreans*, and consequently believed the Transmigration of Souls.

[D] *Others say, that his Soul went in and out of his Body at Pleasure.*] This was said by *Hesychius Illustrius*, and, after him, by *Suidas*. These are their Words. 'Αρίςεα τὴν Ψυχὴν ἐξιέναι ὅτε ἐβέλοιο, καὶ ἐπανιέναι πάλιν (29). *Aristeæ Proconnesii animam è corpore excessisse, ubi vellet, rursusque rediisse fabulantur*. Τϋτο φασὶ τὴν Ψυχὴν ὅταν ἐβέλοιο ἐξιέναι καὶ ἐπανιέναι πάλιν (30). *Hujus animam, quoties voluisset, exiisse & rediisse dicunt.*

[E] *Gyraldus has been guilty of some Mistakes.*] I. He makes *Strabo* say, that the Eloquence and Address of *Aristeas* were of great Force. *Strabo Aristeam facundiâ & blanditiis vehementer prodidit* (31). This is to understand nothing of This *Greek*, ἀνὴρ γόης ᾒ τις ἄλλος, *second to none in Sorcery*. II. He makes *Herodotus* say, that *Aristeas*, having ordered the *Metapontines* to erect, at the same time, an Altar to *Apollo*, and a Statue to himself, and having at last declared to them, that he was a Raven, was translated before their Eyes. This is misunderstanding *Herodotus's* Relation. I refer you to it (33). III. He says, that *Plutarch* approves of *Herodotus's* Narrative. This is false; *Plutarch* touches upon it but lightly, and makes a remarkable Change in the Circumstances of the Place; and then rejects the whole as a Fable.

ARISTIDES, sirnamed the *Just*, flourished at *Athens* at the same time with *Themistocles*. They were greatly at variance; and it appeared, in their Case, that the being superior to another in Virtue is not always the Means of being so in Reputation [A]. The Vehemence of *Themistocles's Eloquence* made him triumph over the *Justice* of his Rival. It is remarkable, that one of Those, who voted for the Banishment

[A] *The being superior to another in Virtue is not always the means of being so in Reputation.*] This Thought is borrowed from *Cornelius Nepos*; "In his "cognitum est, quanto antistaret eloquentia innocen- "tiæ; quamquam enim adeo excellebat Aristides ab- "stinentia, ut unus post hominum memoriam, quod "quidem nos audierimus, cognomine *Justus* sit "appellatus, tamen à Themistocle collabefactus testula "illa exilio decem annorum mulctatus est (1). ----- "*In Them was seen the Advantage of Eloquence above* "Innocence; for, though Aristides was so remarkably "Virtuous, as alone (at least as far as I can remem- "ber) to have obtained the Sirname of Just, yet, "through the Influence, and by the Vote, of Themi- "stocles, he suffered a ten Years Banishment." Be as honest as you please; if you are not Master of a noisy, blustering, Eloquence, you may depend upon being foiled, though you come in Competition with the basest Fellow of the Town.

ARISTIDES.

nishment of *Aristides*, gave as his Reason the great Reputation for Integrity, which he saw him enjoy [B]. But there is something still more remarkable. This great Man, who so exactly observed the Rules of Equity, in private Affairs, and between Man and Man, did not scruple to prefer the *Useful* to the *Honest*, in Affairs relating to the State [C]. He lived in great Poverty, and gloried in it [D]. He left neither sufficient to portion his Daughters, nor to defray the Expences of his Funeral. The Commonwealth was at the Expence of both (*a*). He was so generous, as not to join with the Enemies of *Themistocles* at a time, when there was Reason to believe they would crush him (*b*): For *Themistocles*, was condemned to Banishment, without *Aristides*'s appearing against him. Authors differ about *Aristides*'s Death (*c*); but *Seneca* has undoubtedly committed a gross Error in relation to it [E]. We shall observe, in the Article ARTEMIDORUS, that a Grandson of *Aristides* gained his Living by telling Fortunes by Dreams.

(*a*) Plut. in Aristide, pag. 335.
(*b*) Ib. pag. 334.
(*c*) He died the fir.ed Year of the LXXVIIIth Olympiad; which was the fourth after the Banishment of Themistocles Cornel. Nepot. in ejus vita.

[B] *One of Those, who voted for the Banishment of* Aristides, *gave as his Reason, the great Reputation for Integrity he saw him enjoy.*] A Citizen of *Athens*, who gave his Vote that *Aristides* should be banished, being asked his Reason by *Aristides* himself, answered very frankly; *I have no Knowledge of the Man; but he displeases me by aspiring to the Sirname of* Just. "*Cedensque animadverteret quemdam scribentem, ut patria pelleretur, quæsisse ab eo dicitur; Quare id faceret, aut quid* Aristides *commisisset, cur tanta pœna dignus duceretur. Cui ille respondit; Se ignorare* Aristidem, *sed sibi non placere, quod cupide elaborasset, ut præter cæteros* Justus *appellaretur* (2)." Thousands think like this *Athenian*, but have not his Candor. Every thing, which excels, displeases them: They have a more favourable Regard for a Common, than a distinguished, Virtue. The Reputation of *Aristides*, which the *Athenians*, one Day, gave such authentic Testimony of, in his Presence (3), has not experienced the Injury of Time, but has preserved itself in all Ages; Read this Passage of *Ausonius*.

(*a*) Id. ib.

(3) See the beginning of Remark [H] of the Article AMPHIARAUS.

(4) Auson. in Mosell. ver. 386. pag. 415.
* *Aristides*.

Nec sola antiquos ostentat Roma Catones:
Aut unus tantum justi spectator & æqui
Pollet Aristides, veteresque illustrat Athenas (4).

Nor Rome alone her ancient Catos *boasts;
Nor He ∗, whose Virtues raised the* Athenian *Name,
Claims the sole Merit, to be Good, and Just.*

[C] *He did not scruple to prefer the* Useful *to the* Honest, *in Affairs relating to the State.*] This is a fresh Example of what we have before (5) observed concerning PUBLIC RELIGION. *Aristides* had made the *Athenians* swear to perform a certain thing, and had himself taken an Oath in their Name. Afterwards he counselled them to act as they should think fit for the Publick Good, and leave the Weight of Perjury to him alone, whilst they themselves took Advantage of the favourable Circumstances, which Fortune presented them. This was his general Maxim, as *Theophrastus* observes: Καθ᾽ ὅλον δ᾽ ὁ Θεόφραϛος φησι τὸν ἄνδρα τοῦτον περὶ τὰ οἰκεῖα καὶ τὰς πολίτας ἄκρον ὄντα Δίκαιον, ἐν τοῖς κοινοῖς πολλὰ πράξαι πρὸς τὴν ὑπόθεσιν τῆς πατρίδος ὡς συχνῆς ἀδικίας δεομένην (6). This Great Man, says *Theophrastus*, *in private Affairs, and towards his Fellow-Citizens, was Justice itself; But, in Affairs, which regarded the Commonwealth, he did many Things not strictly just, in compliance with the Exigencies of the State.* Unhappy Condition of Those at the Helm! The Good of the State requires more than one or two unjust Actions in a Man's Life; perhaps *Aristides* did not come off for an hundred. Observe, that *Cicero* gives us a quite different Idea of him (7).

(5) In Remark [H] of the Article AGESILAUS II.

(6) Apul. Plutarch. in Arist. pag. 334.

(7) Cicero de Officiis, lib. 3. cap. 11. pag. 328.

[D] *He lived in great Poverty, and gloried in it*] He had a very rich Relation, whose Name was *Callias*, who, finding himself publickly accused of not supplying him, wherewith to support Life (8), desired him to declare, before the Judges, whether it was not true, that he never would receive the Sums, he had offered him, at several Times, and whether he had not always replied, that he gloried more in his Poverty, than *Callias* in his Riches; he declared it was true. His Reason was, that there were numbers, who made either a good or a bad use of their Riches, but that it was rare to find a Person, who bore his Poverty with a noble Mind (9). It was a Principle,

(8) The People concluded, from seeing Aristides so ill clad, that he wanted Bread Plut. p g. 334

(9) Id. ib.

then, of Pride, or Singularity, will some say, which made him despise Riches. It is a pleasure to covetous and ambitious Persons to be able to object This to Those, who are not like themselves. But what do they gain by it? If it should be granted, that all Men act from a Principle of self-love, is it nothing to draw one's Glory rather from This Action or Conduct, than from That? And is not This a sufficient Motive to admire the one, and despise the other? *Ælian* relates a Particular, which, at first Sight, seems inconsistent with the notorious Poverty of *Aristides* : He says, that *Those, who were betrothed to his Daughters, refused to marry them after his Death, when his extream Poverty came to be known* (10). He seems to me to be mistaken in this Reasoning: *Aristides*'s Poverty was known in his Life time, but it was known, at the same time, that he was in great Credit. Now the most mercenary and interested Minds think it no disadvantageous Match, to marry the Daughter of a Favourite, in her very Shift, who has many profitable Posts at his Disposal. This might make *Aristides*'s Daughters find Matches in his Life time without a Penny of Portion; but, after his Death, there was no more to hope for; so that they were cast off for want of Money. A Great Wit (11) puts this Judicious Reflexion in the Mouth of a Favourite: *Such a Person would think himself honoured with my Alliance upon equal Terms, and yet thinks he makes a Sacrifice my to Favour, in demanding my Niece.* So true it is, that, when any one courts the Alliance of a Person in great Credit, he considers more his own Advancement, than what Money he may gain by Marriage.

A RIFLEXION on Self love, and on the Desire of marrying the Daughters of Favourites.

(10) Ælian. Var. Hist. lib. 12. c. p. 15.

(11) La Demoiselle des Jardins, in his Extract of the Court of Augustus.

[E] *Seneca has undoubtedly committed a gross Error in relation to his Death.*] *Aristides*, according to him, was condemned to die: All, who met him going to the Place of Execution, sighed, and turned down their Eyes to the Ground, except one Rascal, who spit in his Face. *Aristides* smiled, and said to the Officers, who guarded him; *Advise that Fellow never to open his Mouth so villainously again.* Thus *Seneca* relates the Matter. *Ducebatur Athenis ad supplicium Aristides, cui quisquis occurrerat, dejiciebat oculos, & ingemiscebat, non tanquam in hominem justum, sed tanquam in ipsam justitiam animadverteretur. Inventus est tamen, qui faciem ejus inspueret : poterat ab hoc molestè ferre, quod sciebat neminem id ausurum puri oris. At ille abstersit faciem, & subridens ait comitanti se magistratui, admone istum ne postea tam improbè oscitet* (12). *Lipsius* has very judiciously observed, on this Passage, that *Seneca* has mistaken one Person for another, and has ascribed to *Aristides*, what he should have applied to *Phocion*. It was *Phocion*, who was condemned to die; it was He, who was spit on, as they were leading him to Prison, where he was to drink Poison; and it was He, who, turning himself to the Officers, who attended him, demanded, if none of them would chastize the Insolence of the Fellow (13). *Seneca* has given these Words his own Turn : *Verba noster etiam per argutiolam invertit* (14). Probably this is not the first time he has altered both the Subject and the Words; it were to be wished he were the only Person, who has taken this Liberty. People are very apt to report a good Saying, not as it was spoken at first, but according to the form, which they believe to be the best. That he is deceived in the main, is plain from *Plutarch*'s Account That Historian confesses, that some one had said, that *Aristides* died in exile, but he confutes it (15); what *Seneca* says, may be rejected, then, with much greater Reason, as a Fable. Note, that *Lancelot of Perousa* has not censured this Mistake: perhaps

(12) Senec. Consol. ad Helviam, cap. 13. pag. 785.

(13) Plut. in Phocione.

(14) Lips. in Seneca, Consol. ad Helviam, pag. 783.

(15) Plut. in Aristide, pag. 335.

ARISTO. 461

perhaps he was aware of it, but chose to take it for granted, that he might have ground to maintain, that That Age was extreamly unjuſt, ſince the Senate of Athens cauſed a Man of ſuch eminent Virtues to be put to death (16).

ARISTO, a Native of the Iſle of *Chios*, departed a little from the Sentiments of his Maſter *Zeno*, who was Head of the *Stoics*, as may be ſeen in *Moreri*'s Dictionary, together with ſome of his Doctrines. Not to repeat what is to be found there, I ſhall content my ſelf with obſerving, that the Reaſon, why he rejected Logic and Natural Philoſophy, was, becauſe he judged That Logic was uſeleſs, and that Natural Philoſophy was beyond our Comprehenſion (a). I add, that, having eſpouſed Moral Philoſophy at firſt, he afterwards retrenched much of it: For he would not have People teach any thing concerning the particular Duties of a Huſband to his Wife, or a Father to his Children, or a Maſter to his Servants; but confine themſelves to Lectures upon Wiſdom in general. *Seneca* juſtly blames him for this [*A*]; and ſhews, that particular Precepts, and Sentences, may be of wonderful Uſe [*B*]. *Ariſto* ſaid, that the Nature of God was inconceiveable [*C*]. This induces us to believe, that he abſolutely neglected the Contemplation of Divine Matters. He oppoſed

(16) *See* l'Hoggidi del Padre ſecondo Lancello da Perugia, Tom. 2 pag. 399. &c.

(a) Λέγων τὸν μὲν εἶναι ὑπὲρ ἡμᾶς, τὸν δ' οὐδὲν πρὸς ἡμᾶς. Dicens alterum quidem eſſe ſupra nos, alterum vero nihil ad nos. *Diog. Laert. lib.* 7. n. 161.

[*A*] *He afterwards retrenched much of it:* —— Seneca juſtly blames him for this.] Read theſe Words: "Ariſto Chius non tantum ſupervacuas eſſe dixit naturalem & rationalem, ſed etiam contrarias: moralem quoque, quam ſolam reliquerat, circumcidit. Nam eum locum, qui monitiones continet, ſuſtulit, & pædagogi eſſe dixit, non Philoſophi: tanquam quidquam aliud ſit ſapiens quam humani generis pædagogus(1)." —— *Ariſto the Chian ſaid, that Natural and Rational Philoſophy were not only ſuperfluous, but contradictory; and Moral Philoſophy, the only Branch he left, he curtailed. For he took away the preceptive Part of it, ſaying, it belonged to Pædagogues, not to Philoſophers; as if a Philoſopher were any thing elſe, than a Pædagogue of human kind.*" He confutes him at large in another place (2).

[*B*] *Particular Precepts, and Sentences, may be of wonderful Uſe.*] They ſtrongly affect the Mind, he ſays, when they are contracted in Verſe or in Proſe, and kindle the Seeds of Honour, which are natural to our Souls. "Ipſa, quæ præcipiuntur, per ſe multum habent ponderis: utique ſi aut carmini intexta ſunt, aut proſa oratione in ſententiam coarctata. Sicut illa Catoniana: *Emas, non quod opus eſt, ſed quod neceſſe eſt. Qvod non opus eſt, aſſe carum eſt.* Qualia ſunt illa, aut reddita oraculo, aut ſimilia: *Tempori parce; Te noſce.* Numquid rationem exiges, cum tibi aliquis hos dixerit verſus?

Injuriarum remedium eſt oblivio.
Audentes fortuna juvat.
Piger ſibi ipſe obſtat.

"Advocatum iſta non quærunt: affectus ipſos tangunt, & natura vim ſuam exercente proficiunt. Omnium honeſtarum rerum ſemina animi gerunt, quæ admonitione excitantur: non aliter quam ſcintilla, flatu levi adjuta, ignem ſuum explicat (3). — *Precepts are of great Weight, when they are comprehended in a Verſe, or reduced to a Sentence in Proſe. Such is That of* Cato: Buy, not what is expedient, but what is neceſſary ; *and* What is uſeleſs, is dear at the ſmalleſt Price. *Such likewiſe are theſe, either delivered by an Oracle, or ſeemingly ſuch ;* Improve Time; Know yourſelf. *Do you demand a Reaſon, when ſuch Sentences as theſe are repeated to you?*

Injuries are repaired by being forgot.
Faint Heart never won fair Lady.
Lazy Folks take moſt Pains.

"*Such Sayings want no Advocate. They touch the Paſſions, and operate by the force of Nature. The Seeds of Virtue are implanted in the Mind, and are excited by Precept ; in like manner as a Spark of Fire is kindled, by a Breath of Air, into a Flame.*" He adds, that, ſometimes, they diſcover their Force in the moſt ignorant; and that, *Agrippa*, the Favourite of *Auguſtus*, acknowledged himſelf very much indebted to an Apophthegm on Concord. "Quis negaverit feriri quibuſdam præceptis efficaciter etiam imperitiſſimos? velut his breviſſimis vocibus, ſed multum habentibus ponderis;

nihil nimis.
Avarus animus nullo ſatiatur lucro.
Ab alio expectes, alteri quod feceris,

"Hæc cum ictu quodam audimus, nec ulli licet dubitare, aut interrogare - - - - - M. Agrippa, vir ingentis animi, qui ſolus, ex his, quos civilia bella claros potenteſque fecerunt, felix in publicum fuit, dicere ſolebat, multum ſe huic debere ſententiæ: *Nam concordia parvæ res creſcunt ; diſcordia maximæ dilabuntur.* Hac ſe aiebat & fratrem, & amicum, optimum factum (4). - - - - - *Who will deny, that the moſt ignorant have been effectually ſtruck by certain Precepts ; ſuch as theſe ſhort, but weighty, Sayings,*

Too much of one thing is good for nothing.
A covetous Mind is never ſatisfied with Gain.
The Meaſure you mete to others, expect to have meaſured to you again.

"*We are ſtruck, when we hear ſuch Sayings, nor is there any room for Doubt, or Queſtion.* - - - - - - - *Marcus Agrippa, a Perſon of a great Soul, and the only one, among thoſe, who have roſe by Civil Wars, who was ſucceſsful to the Public Good, was wont to ſay, that he was much indebted to this Saying;* By Concord ſmall Things encreaſe ; by Diſcord the greateſt fall to Ruin. *This, he ſaid, made him the beſt of Brothers and of Friends.*" This ſtrongly confirms a Sentiment of mine in the *Plan of this Work* (5). I obſerved there, that a Sentence, taken out of *Livy*, or *Tacitus*, and delivered, as having formerly been ſerviceable in uniting the Senate of *Rome*, is capable of ſaving a State, &c.

[*C*] *Ariſto ſaid, that the Nature of God was inconceiveable.*] As he gave up Natural Philoſophy, becauſe he could not conceive the Divine Nature, it is probable he quitted Theology for the ſame Reaſon. *Divinarum rerum naturam ſtudioſus videtur fuiſſe, cum iſtud ſæpe jactaret,* quæ ſupra nos nihil ad nos, *ut mirum ſit Ariſtonem Theologos inter hos à Velleio aſcribi.* Theſe are the Words of a Jeſuit, who has given us a Comment on *Cicero*'s Work *de Natura Deorum* (6). He commits a Fault, when he wonders, that *Velleius*, one of the Interlocutors, placed *Ariſto* among the Theologiſts : for This Philoſopher deſerved That Rank as much as Thoſe others, whoſe Opinions *Velleius* has mentioned. This is *Ariſto*'s Doctrine: "Cujus (*Zenonis*) diſcipuli Ariſtonis non minus magno in errore ſententia eſt: qui neque formam Dei intelligi poſſe cenſeat, neque in diis ſenſum eſſe dicat, dubitetque omnino Deus animans nec ne ſit (7). *The Opinion of* Ariſto, *the Diſciple of* Zeno, *is no leſs erroneous ; who thinks, not only that the Form of God is incomprehenſible, but even that the Gods have no Senſe ;* and doubts, whether the Deity has Animal Life, or no." *Minucius Felix* has mentioned the ſame Tenet, and ſaid, that *Xenophon*, and *Ariſto*, perceived the Greatneſs of God by this very Circumſtance, that they deſpaired of ever comprehending It. Socraticus *Xenophon formam dei veri negat videri poſſe, & ideo quærit non oportere ; Ariſto Chius comprehendi omnino non poſſe: uterque majeſtatem dei intelligendi*

(1) Senecæ, Epiſt. 89. pag. 3 6. *See alſo* Epiſt. 94. & Sextus Emp. adverſ Mathem. lib. 7.

(2) Ib. Epiſt. 94.

(3) Id. ib. pag. 387.

(4) Id. ib. pag. 388.

(5) *See* Præfat. apud IX. *at the end of Vol.* IV.

(6) Le'cielopier in Ciceron. de Nat. Deorum lib. 1. pag. 60.

(7) Cicero ib. pag. 60.

ARISTO.

fed *Arcesilas* on the Hypothesis of Uncertainty: But, if any Credit may be given to *Diogenes Laërtius*, Scepticism seems to have been but poorly attacked, and as, poorly defended [D], in those Times. It is said, that *Aristo* was bald, and that his Baldness was the Cause of his Death; the Sun having scorched his Head (*b*). He was voluptuous in his Old Age: *Eratosthenes*, and *Apollophanes*, his Disciples, inform us of this Particular, in *Athenæus* (*c*). I cannot tell, whether it was that he stooped to flatter a Philosopher (*d*), at That time, who was in great Credit at *Antigonus*'s Court (*e*). His Sect continued but a short Time [E]. He was the Author of a Saying, which might render

intelligendi desperatione senserunt (8). A certain Commentator is guilty of a childish Error upon this Occasion: He believes there is a Difference between the Person mentioned by *Cicero*, and him mentioned in the Passage of *Minucius*; I say, he believes it, because he supposes, that *Minucius* is speaking of one, whose Name was *Aristæus*. " Quod Minucius Aristo Chio, " id Cicero de Naturâ Deorum, lib. 1. tribuit Ari- " stoni (9). —— *What Minucius imputes to* Aristæus *the Chian, That Cicero, de Naturâ Deorum, lib. 1, ascribes to* Aristo." *Elemenhorst*, for want of Attention, believed, that the *Aristo* of *Minucius* was a *Dative* or *Ablative*; whereas it is a *Nominative*. By the way, it is not impossible, but that Father *Lescalopier* has imputed That to our *Aristo*, which belongs to *Socrates*. " Celebre hoc proverbium Socrates ha- " buit, quod supra nos, nihil ad nos (10). ------ *It* " *was a celebrated Proverb of* Socrates; *What is above* " *us, is nothing to us." Lactantius* inferred from hence, that *Socrates* despised all Religion. *Ejus viri* (Socratis) *quoties de cœlestibus rogabatur, nota responsio est, quod supra nos, nihil ad nos* (11). Note, that, generally speaking, They, who acknowledge, that the Nature of God is inexplicable, are not to be suspected of neglecting Divine Worship, for it is a Reason with many for adoring God with the greater Humility and Reverence. So that the Observation, made against *Aristo*, has something personal in it, and is founded on it's being well known, that Incomprehensibility was, with him, a Motive of Neglect. I would not positively affirm, that he neglected Religion. I stop at Probability; for, with *Lactantius*'s leave, *Socrates*'s Maxim, which I have just mentioned (12), did not induce That Philosopher to neglect Theology. His Doctrine thereon was as good as could be expected from a *Pagan* (13); and it looks, as if he only desired to set Bounds to human Curiosity, by such Reasons, as our most pious Doctors make use of; namely, that we ought willingly to be ignorant of what God would conceal from us; for there is Danger in such profound Enquiries. " In a Word, " he would not advise a too curious Enquiry " into the admirable Art, with which the Gods have " disposed the Universe, &c. (14)." You will find the rest of this Passage in the Remark [8] of the Article ANAXAGORAS (15), where you will likewise find, that by Cœlestial Things, the Study of which *Socrates* dissuades from, he does not mean matters of Religion, but Astronomy.

[D] *Scepticism seems to have been but poorly attacked, and as poorly defended.*] *Aristo* maintained the Doctrine of *Evidence* against *Arcesilas*; and, seeing a Monster, I mean a Bull with a Womb, he believed his Adversary would draw a very good Argument from thence in favour of *Incomprehensibility*. *Wretch that I am*, cry'd he, *behold here a strong Proof for* Arcesilas (16)! This informs us, that the Dogmatists, in order to maintain, that the Nature of Animals was clearly known, alledged, that the Males and Females of each Species are plainly distinguishable; there being certain Parts so proper to the one, that they are never met with in the other. If they argued after this manner, it is certain, that the Bull, which I have mentioned, served to confute them; but it must be allowed, that they employed a very weak Argument; for the Sceptics did not deny, that, according to Appearances, there was a distinction between the Males and the Females; they maintained only, that it was not known, whether their Nature was such, as it appeared to be. Now it signifies nothing to instance the Example of the Bull in this case. Might they not have replied, *We cannot tell whether it is really a Womb, or not; it may be so only in Appearance. Aristo* asked an *Acataleptic* one Day; *Don't you see That Rich Man, who sits near you?* the other answered, *No: Who has put out your Eyes*, said *Aristo* again (17)? This was a childish Defence;

since the Doctrine of Incomprehensibility does not suppose a Person deprived of the use of Sight. He might have replied to *Arcesilas*; *The Resemblance of a rich Man sitting near me strikes my Sight; nevertheless I do not comprehend certainly, that This Man exists, or what his Nature is.* It is observable, that, among all the Tenets of the Stoics, *Aristo* adhered chiefly to This, *The Wise Man has no Opinion*. There was a Philosopher in his Days, whose Name was *Perseus*, who, to attack him upon this Point, suborned Twin-Brothers; one of which trusted *Aristo* with a Deposit, and the other came, some time after, to demand it; and *Aristo*, being in suspence, was therefore confuted by *Perseus* (18). I can scarce comprehend the meaning of This. Did these Twins resemble each other so perfectly, that it was impossible to know them asunder; or were they as unlike, as generally Twins are? *Diogenes Laërtius* says nothing to this. His Brevity is sometimes so intolerable, that it may be said, we have only ill-digested Extracts of his History of the Philosophers. If these Twins were distinguishable; from whence could *Aristo*'s Suspence proceed? If it was difficult to distinguish them, his Suspence was not to be blamed, and could not be alledged to confute him; for this very suspence was a Proof of his Regard for the Maxim above; *The Wise Man has no Opinion*.

[E] *His Sect continued but a short Time.*] *Cicero* mentions it as One, whose Tenets were lost: " Sen- " tentiæ ------ Aristonis, Pyrrhonis, Herilli, non- " nullorumque, aliorum evanuerunt (19). ------ *We* " *hear no more of the Opinions of* Aristo, Pyrrho, " Herillus, *and some others. Sive, says he elsewhere*, " Aristotelem & Theophrastum ------ sequuti sunt, " five ------ etiam Aristonis difficilem atque ardu- " am, sed jam tamen fractam & convictam, sectam se- " quuti sunt (20). ------ *Whether they followed* " Aristotle *and* Theophrastus ------ *or the difficult and* " *arduous, but now broken and confuted, Sect of* Aristo. Such extravagant Opinions as his could hardly last long; he made no difference between any two things, except Vice and Virtue; and said, that other things were all alike, nor one preferable to another: *His contrarius Aristo Chius præfractus, ferreus, nihil bonum, nisi quod rectum atque honestum est* (21). He went farther, than his Master *Zeno*; for *Zeno* did not deny but there were things distinct from Virtue, which were to be wished for, though they were of no use towards attaining to the Supream Good. This Tenet was far from just, though it was less to be rejected, than That of *Aristo*: For who cannot apprehend, that Health is more to be desired, than Sickness? " Ut " Aristonis effet explosâ sententia dicentis, nihil dif- " ferre aliud ab alio, nec esse res ullas præter virtu- " tes & vitia, inter quas quicquam omnino interesset; " sic errare Zenonem, qui nulla in re nisi in virtute " aut vitio propensionem, ne minimi quidem mo- " menti, ad summum bonum adipiscendum esse dice- " ret. Et quum ad beatam vitam nullum momen- " tum ea res haberet, ad appetitionem autem rerum " esse in his momenta diceret: quasi vero hæc appe- " titio non ad summi boni adeptionem pertineret (22). " ------ *As* Aristo *was mistaken, in saying, that there* " *is no difference of Things, except between Virtue and* " *Vices; so* Zeno *erred, who thought, that nothing, ex-* " *cept Virtue and Vice, had the least tendency towards* " *procuring the Supream Good; yet that Those Things,* " *which had not This Tendency, were to be desired; as* " *if the Accomplishment of This very Desire were not* " *Part of the Supream Good*." It is no wonder, then, that This Sect did not continue long; since *Aristo* himself deserted it at an Age the most favourable to his Maxims. He became a Friend to Pleasures in his old Age (23), when it would have become him much better to have been rigid, and inflexible, *præfractus & ferreus*.

[F] He

ARISTO. 463

render *Aristippus*'s Doctrine less odious, than it generally is [F]. Some Works were ascribed to him, which belonged to *Aristo* of *Cea*, a Peripatetic Philosopher [G]. We shall have some Mistakes of *Vossius* to remark [H].

[F] *He was Author of a Saying, which might render* Aristippus's *Doctrine less odious than it generally is*] He said, that a Philosopher might be of Prejudice to.h's Hearers, who should misunderstand his Words; that, for example, The Followers of *Aristippus* might become dissolute; Those of *Zeno* morose. Is not this to declare, that the Doctrine of These Philosophers did not produce such Effects, but when misunderstood? *Aristo Chius dicere solebat, nocere audientibus Philosophos iis, qui bene dicta male interpretarentur: posse enim afutos ex Aristippi, acerbos e Zenonis Schola exire* (24). He should have added that every Teacher is, therefore, o: liged to avoid ambiguous Maxims, and to prevent false Glosses.

[G] *Some Works were imputed to him, which belonged to* Aristo *of* Cea.] *Diogenes Laërtius*, having given the Titles of several Works of our *Aristo*, adds, that *Panætius*, and *Sosicrates*, ascribe them all, except one, to the Peripatetic *Aristo* (25). He does not say, that This *Peripatetic* was a Native of the Island of *Cea*; but I conjecture, that we ought to suppose him of That Country, because it cannot be understood of *Aristo* the *Alexandrian*, another *Peripatetic* Philosopher, who lived under *Augustus*, and of whom, consequently, *Panætius* could say nothing; for it can be proved, that he was not living in the Six Hundred and Fiftieth Year of *Rome* (26). So that Mr *Moreri* is deceived, when he says, that many have imputed the Works of *Aristo* of *Chios* to *Aristo* of *Alexandria*. The former wrote a Treatise *de Senectute*, which *Diogenes Laërtius* has not mentioned; perhaps it was but part of Another Book. " Hunc librum de Senectute ad te misimus: omnem autem sermonem tribuimus non Tithono, ut Aristo Chius, parum enim esset auctoritatis in fabula, sed M. Catoni seni, quo majorem auctoritatem haberet oratio (27).——*I send you this Treatise* Of Old Age; *The whole Discourse*, to add *the greater Weight to it, I put in the Mouth of Old* M Cato; *not of* Tithonus, *as* Aristo *the* Chian *did*; *for Fable would have added but little Authority to* *it*." Aldobrandinus quotes this Passage of Cicero, as if it should be read *Aristo Ceus* (28); but the best Editions give *Aristo Chius* He is mistaken, then, in pretending, that *Aristo* of *Cea*, the *Peripatetic* Philosopher, was Author of the Book *de Senectute*. He might with more reason have applied this Passage of *Cicero* to Him. " Hujus (Stratonis) Lysias & oratione locuples,

" rebus ipsis jejunior; Concinnus deinde & elegans " hujus Aristo: Sed ea, quæ desideratur à magno Phi" losopho, gravitas in eo non suit. Scripta sanè, & " multa & polita; sed nescio quo pacto autoritatem " oratio non habet (29).——*After* Strato, Lysias " *was copious in words, but, barren of Sense*. His *Dis" ciple* Aristo *was Witty and Elegant*; *but, wanted,* " *what is essential to a great Philosopher, Dignity*: " *He wrote indeed much and politely*; *but, I know not* " *how, what he says wants Weight*." This can only be understood of a *Peripatetic* Philosopher *Aristo*; Mr *Menage* therefore is to blame, in believing, that these *Latin* Words relate to our *Aristo* (30).

[H] *Some Mistakes of* Vossius, &c] He says, that *Aristo* of *Alexandria*, a Peripatetic Philosopher, in the time of *Augustus*, was Author of a Treatise concerning the River *Nile* (31). His Reason is, because *Strabo* observes, that he had seen two Books, in his Time, concerning That River; one of them composed by *Eudores*, and the other by *Aristo* the Peripatetic (32). *But*, continues Vossius, *there having been two* Aristos *of the Peripatetic Sect, one of* Alexandria, *and the other of the Island of* Cea; *Why do I maintain, that he of* Alexandria *composed the Treatise of the* Nile? *because it is more probable, that an Egyptian should write of this River, than an Islander of the Egean Sea.* He destroys This Reason immediately; for he confesses, that it is probable *Aristo* of *Chios*, or He of *Cea*, wrote a Book of the *Nile*; because the Scholiast on *Apollonius* quotes the Opinion of *Aristo* of *Chios*, concerning the Source of This River (33). *He confounds*, adds *Vossius*, Chius *with* Ceus. This Reasoning is not exact. But, This Learned Man may be farther censured, for not knowing the true Reason, why the Treatise of the *Nile*, mentioned by *Strabo*, ought rather to be ascribed to *Aristo* the *Alexandrian*, than *Aristo* of the Island of *Cea*; namely, that *Strabo* speaks of a Book, which was published in his Time. Now *Aristo* of *Cea* flourished a long Time before *Strabo*, as *Vossius* himself acknowledges; for he affirms, after *Diogenes Laërtius*, that *Panæius* and *Sosicrates* (34) ascribed to This *Aristo* almost all the Books, which passed under the Name of *Aristo* the Stoic. *Lloyd* and *Hofman* have copied this long Passage of *Vossius*, word for word, not forgetting even to put *Socrates* instead of *Sosicrates*.

ARISTO (TITUS) a *Roman* Lawyer, in the Reign of *Trajan*, was so Excellent and so Learned a Person, that he ought not to have been omitted by *Moreri*. He was perfectly skilled in Common and Civil Law, in History, and Antiquity [A]. If he did not readily answer to the Questions, which were put to him, it was because he would consider the Matter thoroughly, before he gave his Opinion. He was, besides, an Enemy to Luxury, and free from all Ostentation; one, who sought the Reward of a good Action in the Action itself, and not in the Applause of the Multitude

[A] *He was perfectly skilled in —— Law, in History, and in Antiquity*.] What *Pliny* says upon this (1), and on *Aristo*'s Virtue, is so fine, that I shall not lose one Word of it. " Nihil est illo (Tito Aristone) gra" vius, sanctius, doctius: ut mihi non unus homo, " sed literæ ipsæ, omnesque bonæ artes, in uno ho" mine summum periculum adire videantur. Quàm " peritus ille & privati juris & publici (2)? quantum " rerum? quantum exemplorum? quantum antiqui" tatis tenet? nihil est, quod discere velis, quod ille " docere non possit. Mihi certe quoties aliquid ab" ditum quæro, ille thesaurus est. Jam quanta ser" monibus ejus fides? quanta authoritas? quàm pressa " & decora cunctatio? quid est quod non statim " sciat? & tamen plerumque hæsitat. Dubitat diver" sitate rationum: quas acri magnoque judicio ab " origine causisque primus repetit, discernit, expen" dit: Ad hoc quam parcus in victu? quam modicus " in cultu? Soleo ipsum cubiculum ejus ipsumque " lectum, ut imaginem quandam priscæ frugalitatis, " aspicere Ornat hæc magnitudo animi, quæ nihil " ad ostentationem, omnia ad conscientiam refert: " recteque facti, non ex populi sermone, mercedem, " sed ex facto, petit. —— *So excellent a Person is* Ti-

" tus Aristo, *that not the Life of one Man alone, but* " *Learning itself, and all useful Arts, seem to be* " *greatly endangered in one Man. How skilled is he* " *in every Branch of Law? How versed in Things,* " *in Examples, in Antiquity? Whatever you* " *can desire to learn, he can teach. For my own Part,* " *whenever I would enquire into any abstruse Point, He* " *is my Oracle. How securely may we rely upon his* " *Opinion? What Authority has He? and how becoming is his Deliberation? What is there, which he* " *does not immediately apprehend? yet he generally he* " *sitates. His Doubts arise from the Variety of Rea* " *sons, which may be assigned; all which, with great* " *Judgment, he traces to their Source, distinguishes* " *and weighs. Add to this his great Temperance and* " *Modesty in Dress. I am wont to consider his Bed-* " *Chamber, and his very Bed, as a Kind of Repre* " *sentation of the Ancient Frugality. These Quali* " *fications are set off by a Greatness of Mind, which* " *avoids all Ostentation, and is satisfied with the Con* " *sciousness of having acted well*; *and which seeks the* " *Reward of a good Action, not from the Applause of* " *the People, but from the Action itself*."

[B] *He*

ARISTOTLE.

titude (*a*). He did not profess himself a Philosopher [*B*]; but some of Those, who did, fell very short of him in the Practice of Virtue. He shewed an unparalleled Firmness of Mind in a tedious Fit of Sickness [*C*], and at last desired his Friends to ask the Physicians, whether it was possible for him to recover; and declared, that, if they judged him incurable, he would kill himself; but, if he might escape by suffering his Pains ever so long, he was resolved to live; this he agreed to, at the Intreaties of his Wife, the Tears of his Daughter, and the desire of Those, with whom he conversed (*b*). Pliny, the Younger, who was one of Them, made a good Reflexion upon this, and excellently describes the Tenderness of his Friendship [*E*]. The Physicians gave him good Hopes of his Recovery (*c*). Some affirm, that Aristo attained to a very great Age [*F*]; but the Proof they bring for it is weak enough. He was the Author of some Books [*G*].

(a) See the Proof of this in the Remark [*A*].

(b) Plin. Epist. 22, lib. 3, pag. 67.

(c) Id. ibid.

[*B*] *He did not profess himself a Philosopher.*] His Philosophy was put in practice two Ways; for his Manners were like Those of a true Philosopher; and he did not spend his Life in the Solitude of a Closet, or College, but in the Functions of the Bar. Let us hear Pliny. " In summa, non facile quis quen-
" quam ex istis, qui sapientiæ studium habitu corpo-
" ris præferunt, huic viro comparârit. Non quidem
" gymnasia sectatur, aut porticus, nec disputationi-
" bus longis aliorum ocium, suumque delectat: sed
" in togâ, negociisque versatur: multos advocatione,
" plures consilio juvat. Nemini tamen istorum casti-
" tate, pietate, justitiâ, fortitudine, etiam primo loco
" cesserit (3). ----- Upon the whole, it is not easy to
" draw a parallel between Those, who carry an out-
" side shew of Philosophy, and this Great Man. In-
" deed, he is not a Follower of the Schools, or Por-
" ticos; nor does he entertain the Leisure of others, and
" his own, with tedious Disputations; but is conversant
" at the Bar, and in Business; is helpful to many, as
" an Advocate, to more by his Advice. Yet will he
" give the Preference to none of the Philosophers
" in Point of Chastity, Piety, Justice, and Greatness
" of Mind."

[*C*] *He shewed an unparalleled Firmness of Mind in a tedious Fit of Sickness* (4). " Helay still, and covered,
" in the Height of his Fever, and forbore drink-
" ing, though he had a violent Thirst upon him.
" Miraretis, si interesses, quâ patientiâ hanc ipsam
" valetudinem toleret, ut dolori resistat, ut sitim dif-
" ferat, ut incredibilem febrilem ardorem immo. us
" opertusque transmittat (5)."

[*D*] Pliny ----- *makes a good Reflexion upon this, &c.*] " It is common, he says, to fly to Death
" through an Impetuosity of Spirit; but a great
" Mind, having deliberated whether to live or die,
" weighs the Motives on both sides exactly, and
" by the Weight of Reason is determined to the
" one or the other. Id ego arduum in primis, &
" præcipuâ laude dignum puto. Nam impetu quodam,
" & instinctu, procurrere ad mortem, commune cum
" multis: deliberare vero, & causfas ejus expendere,
" utque suaserit ratio, vitæ mortisque consilium sus-
" cipere, vel ponere, ingentis est animi (6)."

[*E*] Pliny admirably expresses the Tenderness of his Friendship for Aristo.] " He had a passionate Desire to
" retire to his Country-House at Laurentium, and to
" study there; but deprived himself of This Plea-
" sure to keep Aristo Company, who had been sick
" a long time; and he suffered a thousand Dis-

(3) Id. Epist. 20. lib. 1. pag. 66, 67, &c.

(4) See Remark [*E*].

(5) Plin. Epist. 22, lib. 3, pag. 67.

(6) Id. ib.

" quietudes at the Sight of this Object, which
" robbed him of the Leisure, and even Desire of
" returning to his Studies." Let us hear himself. *Diu jam in urbe hæreo, & quidem attonitus. Perturbat me longa & pertinax valetudo Titi Aristonis, quem singulariter & mereor & diligo* (7). This is the beginning of his Letter. He goes on. *Et medici quidem secunda nobis pollicentur: Superest, ut promissis deus adnuat, tandemque me hac solicitudine exolvat. Quâ liberatus, Laurentinum meum, hoc est libellos & pugillares, studiosumque otium, repetam. Nunc enim nihil legere, nihil scribere, aut assiduâ vacat, aut anxio libet. Habes, quid timeam, quid optem, quid etiam in posterum destinem* (8). I cite this whole Passage, as well for the Honour of Aristo, as for That of Pliny the Younger; for there appear in it Marks, of a good-natured Disposition; and it is a Proof, that Virtue has always found a Place of Retreat in Cities, which have been the most corrupted by long Prosperity, followed by tedious and cruel Civil Wars, and the Establishment of Tyranny; which was the Case of Rome at that Time.

[*F*] *Some affirm, that Aristo attained to a very great Age; but the Proof they bring for it is weak enough*] This Proof is taken from Aristo's having assisted at the Pleadings of Cassius; that is, of Caius Cassius Longinus, who was Consul in the Reign of Tiberius. Now they reckon sixty Years between Tiberius and Trajan; and it is certain, that Trajan consulted Aristo in a Point of Law. This is Bertrand's Argument (9). He is confuted from hence; that Cassius lived till the Reign of Vespasian (10) and that, between the beginning of his Reign, and That of Trajan, there are at most but Twenty eight Years (11)

[*G*] *He was the Author of some Books.*] The Pandects make mention of this; and you may see the Titles of them in both the Authors, whom I cite (12). See also Aulus Gellius, who had read, in a Work of Aristo, that all manner of Theft was allowed among the ancient Egyptians, a People famous for the Invention of Arts and Sciences. Id etiam memini legere me in libro Aristonis jureconsulti haudquaquam indocti viri apud veteres Ægyptios, quod genus hominum constat & in artibus reperiendis solertes extitisse, & in cognitione rerum indaganda sagaces, furta omnia fuisse licita & impunita (13). Bertrand supposes it to be a Treatise *Of Theft*, since Aulus Gellius quotes it particularly, as knowing, that Aristo was Author of several Books.

(7) Id. ibid.

(8) Epist. 24, lib. 1, pag. 67.

(9) See Bertrand in Vitis jurisperitorum, l. 2, p. 295, 297.

(10) Pomponius offirms it; see Grotius in Vitis Jurisconsf. l. 2, c. 3, pag. 113.

(11) Grotius, ubi supra.

(12) Bertrand, and Grotius.

(13) Aulus Gellius, lib. 11, c. 18, pag. 302.

(14) Bertrand ubi supra, p. 299.

ARISTOTLE, commonly called the Prince of Philosophers, or The Philosopher, by way of Excellence, was the Founder of a Sect, which surpassed, and at length swallowed, up all the rest (*a*). Not but that It has had it's Reverse of Fortune (*b*) in it's turn; especially in This XVIIth Century, in which it has been violently shaken; though the Catholic Divines, on the one side, and the Protestant, on the other, have run (as to the quenching of a Fire) to it's Relief; and fortified themselves so strongly, by the Secular Arm, against the New Philosophy, that it is not like to lose it's Dominion of a long time. Mr Moreri met with so many good Materials in a Work of Father Rapin (*c*), that he has given a very large Article of Aristotle, enough to dispence with my Assistance. Accordingly, I design not to enlarge upon it as far as the Subject might allow, but shall content myself with observing, in the Remarks, some of the Errors, which I have collected, concerning This Philosopher. I think I have discovered some in Father Rapin's Account [*A*]. It is not a certain, that

(a) Aristoteles, more Ottomanorum, regnare se haud tuto posse putabat, nisi fratres suos omnes contrucidasset. —— Aristotle, like the Turkish Emperors, thought he could not reign in Safety, 'till he had slain all his Brethren. Bacon, de Augment. Scient. lib. 3, cap. 4.

(b) See Mr Launoi's Book, de Varia Aristotelis fortuna.

(c) Comparison of Plato and Aristotle.

[*A*] *I have discovered some Errors in Father Rapin's Account of Aristotle.*] This Remark will be pretty long; I shall therefore divide it.

I. To say that, Aristotle, though he had forsaken his Studies, out of meer Libertinism, and had abused his Tutor's Indulgence for some time, succeeded nevertheless

in

ARISTOTLE. 465

that *Aristotle* exercised Pharmacy in *Athens*, while he was a Disciple of *Plato* (d); nor is it more certain, that he did not. Very little Credit ought to be given to a current Tradition, that he learnt several Things of a *Jew* [B], and much less to the Story

(1) Rapin's Comparison of Plato and Aristotle, p. 3.

(2) Father Rapin does not say, that they make this Remark.

(3) Id. Ib.

(4) Athen. lib. 8. pag. 354.

(5) Ælian. Var. Hist. l. 5, c. 9.

(6) Apud Euseb. Præp. lib. 1, c. 2, pag. 791.

(7) Aristocles Messen. ex. Epist. Epicuri. lib. 5. cap. 9. Athen. l. 8.

(8) Fr. Patricius, Discuss. Peripat. Tom. 1. p. 3.

(9) Plutarch. in Alexandro.

(10) Timæus, apud Suidam, in Ἀριστοτέλης.

(11) Aristocles, apud Euseb. Præpar. lib. 15, cap. 2, pag. 791.

in Poetry; witness the Poem, which he composed on the Death of the Heroes, who were killed at the Siege of Troy (1); is no just way of Reasoning; for, if *Eustathius* and *Porphyry*, who mention This Poem, do not expressly say, that *Aristotle* composed it in his Youth (2), we may imagine, that he wrote it after his return to his Studies; and then this Poem can be no longer alledged as a Proof, of the Progress which he made in Poetry, notwithstanding his Libertine Courses.

II. To say, that, *having by his Debaucheries consumed part of the Estate, which his Father had left him, he listed himself in the Troops of the Republick* (3); is an improper, and a very indeterminate, Way of Expression. If the question were concerning a Person, who was born at *Athens*, or *Lacedemon*, the Expression might be proper enough, but it relates to a Native of *Macedonia*. *Athenæus* knew of but one Author, who had said, that *Aristotle*, having consumed his Patrimony, listed himself; and, finding, that the Profession of Arms was not his Talent, set up to sell Drugs (4). The sole Author of This Story was *Epicurus*. It is very probable, that *Ælian* had it from him (5). *Aristocles*, who rejected it, quotes only *Epicurus* (6). Be this as it will, none of the Authors, whom Father *Rapin* quotes, specify in what Troops *Aristotle* served; and all of them range Matters in this Order. First, *Aristotle* spent his Estate, then he went to the Wars, afterwards he set up a Shop, and at last addicted himself to *Plato*'s Lectures. Father *Rapin* will have it, that he was at the same time both a Druggist, and a Disciple of *Plato*. The Authors, whom he quotes (7), say nothing of this Union of the two Professions. But he ought not, I think, to be censured for this; for it seems probable enough, that *Aristotle*, after he had spent his Estate, *was forced to drive a small Trade in sweet Powder, and Medicines, at Athens, to subsist himself for some time*. This Father *Rapin* says, in relation to the time when *Aristotle* studied Philosophy. *Francis Patricius* goes much farther; he believes, that *Aristotle* was *Plato*'s Disciple till the Age of forty Years, and that he exercised Pharmacy all That Time for a Livelihood. *Satis constat inter omnes ad quadragesimum usque ætatis annum Platonis fuisse auditorem; quo universo tempore pharmacopolii arte nec non etiam medica victuum quæritasse satis est & historiæ & rationi consonum* (8). He adds, that, formerly, Physicians exercised the Apothecaries Trade; and that three Reasons induce us to believe, that *Aristotle* was a Physician. He was of a Family for such a Profession; He composed a Book concerning Health and Sickness; and he excited *Alexander* to the Study of Physic, in which That Monarch acquired no small Skill, both in the Theory, and in the Practice (9). Lastly, *Patricius* alledges the Testimony of *Timæus*. This Historian has spoken very ill of *Aristotle*, and reproached him expressly with shutting up a Shop of most excellent Medicines. Τὸ πολυτίμητον ἰατρεῖον ἀποκεκλεικότα (10). *Qui pretiosam tabernam medicam clausit*. I know not whether I may be permitted to conjecture, that *Timæus* sneered in making use of the Epithet πολυτίμητον. Without which, I cannot see how this Passage of *Suidas* is to be reconciled with what *Eusebius* cites from the same *Timæus*. He gives us a Fragment, in which a Peripatetic answered the Calumnies published against *Aristotle*, and particularly That of the Historian *Timæus*, who had said, that *Aristotle*, in his old Age, shut up his Shop of Medicines, which was grown into Contempt: "Ἡ πῶς ἄν τις ἀποδέξατο Τιμαίου τε Ταυρομενίτου λέγοντος ἐν ταῖς ἱστορίαις, ἀδόξῳ ὄψας αὐτὸν ἰατρεῖον καὶ τὰς τυχούσας, ἐπὶ τῆς ἡλικίας, κλείσας (11). This Passage has been very ill translated; for the Latin Translation makes *Timæus* say, that *Aristotle*, in his old Age, was hired to shut up the Shop of an Apothecary of small Reputation. *Quis Timæum Tauromenitanum audiat dum suis in historiis illum ait affecta jam ætate, neglectis obscuri cujusdam Medici officinæ clandendis fortuos præfuisse*. Is not this an Employ highly worthy of *Aristotle*'s old Age? What Honour to be Porter to an Apothecary, or Physician, scarce known to his next Neighbours!

III. Father *Rapin* (12) tells us, that Clemens Alexandrinus *affirms*, that *Aristotle had Conferences at Athens with a Jew, with a Design of being instructed in the Religion of the Egyptians*. Eusebius *has said the same*; and both believe it on the Testimony of *Clearchus the Peripatetic*. These Words stand in need of being greatly qualified: for, I. All that *Clemens Alexandrinus* affirms amounts only to this, that *Clearchus the Peripatetic* had said, that he knew a *Jew*, who had conversed with *Aristotle*. Κλέαρχος ὁ Περιπατητικὸς εἴδεναί φησί τινα Ἰουδαῖον ὃς Ἀριστοτέλει συντετύχηκε (13). *Clearchus Peripateticus dicit se nosse quemdam Judæum, qui cum Aristotele versatus est*. As for the Place, and Subject, of these Conversations, you must enquire of any one else, rather than of *Clemens Alexandrinus*. II. It is not true, that *Eusebius* affirms any thing upon this Head; he only cites the Words of *Clemens Alexandrinus*. III. *Clearchus*, to whom he directs us, as the first Source, does not say, that *Aristotle* had any Conversation with a *Jew* at *Athens*, but on the contrary, that it was in *Asia* (14); neither does he say, that they discoursed concerning the Religion of the *Egyptians*, or any other particular Subject. I believe, if we had his Book, we should find an exact Account of it, which was cited by *Josephus*, in his fixth Book against *Apion*, to shew, that the *Jewish* Nation was not unknown to the *Greeks*. If Father *Rapin* had consulted the Originals, would he have said, that, to avoid the loss of time, which must *have been spent in travelling into Egypt, which was then believed necessary towards the acquisition of Learning, it is probable*, that *Aristotle was satisfied with being instructed in the Mysteries and Religion of the Egyptians?* Was he not actually travelling in *Asia*, when he had these Conversations, if we may believe *Clearchus?* We shall see, in the Remark [B], whether he deserves Credit.

IV. It is not true, that *Hermias* gave his Sister *Pythias* in Marriage to *Aristotle* (15). See towards the end of the Remark [F].

V. Father *Rapin*'s other Faults, which I have observed, are distributed in the following Remarks.

[B] *Very little Credit ought to be given to a current Tradition, that he learned several Things of a Jew.*] This Tradition has no other Foundation than the above mentioned Passage of *Clearchus*. This Passage would be of no small Authority, did it certainly belong to That *Clearchus*, who was one of *Aristotle*'s most famous Disciples. But, according to all Appearances, it belongs to another *Clearchus*: For, first of all, the Author, quoted by *Josephus*, says, that *Aristotle* met with a *Jew* in his Travels in *Asia*, who had afterwards several Conferences with him, and with some other Men of Letters. ἡμῖν τε καὶ τισιν ἑτέροις τῶν σχολαστικῶν. Learned Men pretend, that, in *Aristotle*'s Time, the Word σχολαστικὸς was not used to signify a Scholar, a Disciple, or a Student (16). However it be, as this Journey into *Asia* cannot be reconciled with *Aristotle*'s History, it is not probable, that one of his Disciples should have invented a Story of This kind, which he himself, and others, knew to be false. It is therefore a more modern *Clearchus*, who supposed this Journey; and he might do it sincerely; for it is well known, that *Solinus* asserts, that *Aristotle* followed *Alexander* in his Wars against *Darius* (17). The anonymous Author of the Life of *Aristotle* (18) says the same thing. II. If it were true, that *Aristotle* had had many Conferences with so able a Man, as He, who is mentioned in the Passage of *Clearchus*, would he have believed, what he says concerning the Origin of the *Jews?* Would he have said, that the *Jews* were descended from the *Calani*, a People of the *Indies*, and that they took the Name of *Jews* in *Syria*, because they possess a Province, which was called *Judea?* That is what *Aristotle* says, in the Passage of *Clearchus*, quoted by *Josephus*. Would his *Jew* have left him in such a childish Error? And should we have found so few Traces of *Judea*, and the *Jewish* Nation, in all *Aristotle*'s Writings, after such full Information, as the

(12) Comparison of Plato and Aristotle, p. 304.

(13) Clem. Alex. Stromat. lib. 1. pag. 304.

(14) Τότε διατρίβοντων ἡμῶν περὶ τὴν Ἀσίαν. Nobis in Asia tum degentibus. It is Aristotle, who speaks, in this Book of Clearchus, de Somno, apud Josephum contra Apionem, & apud Eusebium. Præp. l. 9, c. 5, p. 410.

(15) Rapin's Comparison of Plato and Aristotle, p. 306.

(16) Jonsius, de Script. Hist. Philos. pag. 99.

(17) Cap. 14. apud Jonsium, ib. pag. 100.

(18) Amonius, according to some; Philoponus, according to others. See the Notes of Nunnesius on this Life, n. 44.

ARISTOTLE.

Story of his pretended Conversion to *Judaism*. They, who pretend, that he was born a *Jew*, are much more grosly mistaken [C]. The wrong Pointing of a certain Passage occasioned this Mistake (e). They are deceived, who say, that he was a Disciple of *Socrates* for Three Years successively [D]; for *Socrates* died Twelve or Fifteen Years before *Aristotle* was born. *Aristotle's* Behaviour towards his Master *Plato* is variously related [E]. Some will have it, that, through prodigious Vanity and Ingratitude, he

(e) *See Remark* [C].

the *Jew* might have given him? III. We read, in *Diogenes Laërtius*, that the *Gymnosophists* descended from the *Magi*, and that there were some, who gave the *Jews* the same Original (19). These are two different Facts: As to the first, it is delivered on the Testimony of *Clearchus*, the Disciple of *Aristotle*; but no Authority is produced for the second. Was not This the most favourable Opportunity, and the most indispensable, for quoting *Clearchus* concerning This pretended *Indian* Original of the *Jewish* Nation, mentioned by *Josephus*? If the Book *de Somnis*, in which *Aristotle* speaks of their *Indian* Origin, had been the same *Clearchus's*, who is cited by *Diogenes Laërtius* (20), would he not have been alledged? I pass over *Jonsius's* other Reasons; these three are sufficient to persuade me (21), that *Aristotle* never said what the *Clearchus* of *Josephus* would make him say. I must therefore agree in Opinion with those, who think it wrong in *Cunæus* to treat *Aristotle* so ill for a Piece of Folly, which he never was guilty of. " *Petrus Cunæus* lib. 1. de Repub. Hebr. cap. 4. " Aristotelem falsè nimis & temere perstringit, quod " hic apud Clearchum statuat Judæos ab Indiæ sapi- " entibus esse propagatos: Verba Cunæi hæc sunt, " *Portentosum est & cum summa inscitia conjunctum* " *quod Aristoteles apud Clearchum autumavit, Ju-* " *dæos esse ab Indiæ sapientibus propagatos, sed nomen* " *mutavisse. Quippe philosophos illos, qui apud Indos* " *Callani appellantur, in cava Syria Judæos dici.* " *Pudet me antistatis, adeo hoc nihil est* (22) ---- " *Petrus Cunæus, in Book* 1. *of the Hebrew Republic, Chap.* 4. *censures* Aristotle *too severely and unjustly, for pretending, as cited by* Clearchus, *that the Jews sprung from the Indian Philosophers.* Cunæus's *Words are:* It is monstruous, and attended " with the greatest Ignorance, what *Aristotle*, in " *Clearchus*, conjectures, that the Jews were descen- " ded from the Philosophers of *India*, but had " changed their Name; for that Thos. Philosophers, " who, among the *Indians*, are called *Callani*, in " *Cœlo-Syria* are called Jews." It may be objected, that *Clearchus* was acquainted with the Jew, who had conversed with *Aristotle*; so that he must have been cotemporary with him; but I deny, that *Clearchus* had any Knowledge of him. *Josephus* does not say it; it is *Clemens Alexandrinus*, who adds this Clause; perhaps he quotes by Memory, which is the surest way to pervert a Passage, even as to the most essential Circumstances. See the Carelessness of Translators! He, who translated *Eusebius* (23), renders εἰδέναι by *vidisse*; and the Translator of *Clemens Alexandrinus* is content with *nosse*. It is not a necessary Consequence, that an Author lived at the same time with another Person, because it is said, that he knew one, who had done, or said This, or That; since his meaning might be, that he knew the Books, in which such Persons had said so or so; but when it is said, that an Author had *seen* such or such a one, the Consequence then is plain, that they must have been Contemporaries (24). This admits of no Difficulty; and, consequently, the Translator of *Rufebius* has taken a Liberty, which, by being added to That of *Clemens Alexandrinus*, strangely falsifies the Consequences, which may be drawn from the Passage of *Clearchus*, as cited by *Josephus*. There are Jews, who affirm, not only that *Aristotle* had copied *Salmon's* Works, but that he became likewise a Proselyte of Righteousness (25).

Not satisfied with this, They produce a Letter, which they suppose he wrote to *Alexander* to give him an Account of his Conversion. This Letter you will find in a Work of *Rabbi Gedalia Ben Jachija*, and in the *Modena Theologia* (26) *Judaica* of Mr *Lent*, Professor of Divinity at *Herborn*. Read also this Passage of Mr *Crojus* Father *Bartolocci*, pag. 471, of the first Volume of his *Bibliotheca magna Rabbinica* " relates a Story, void of all probability, which " the *Ravins* tell us of *Aristotle*. Some of them " pretended, that he was born of the Seed of *Israel*,

(19) Diog. Laërt. in Proœmio, n. 19.

(20) *That it is of* Him, *who was the Disciple of Aristotle.*

(21) *Note, that Schoockius, Fabulæ Hamelensis,* part. 2. cap. 12. *alledges, almost Word for Word, the same Observations of* Jonsius, *without citing him.*

(22) Jonsius, de Script. Hist. Phil. pag. 98.

(23) De Præp. lib. 15, p. 410.

(24) *Provided always, that the Witness be sincere.*

(25) Apud Buxtorf citante Konig. Bibl. p. 61.

(26) *This Book was printed at Herborn, in* 1694.

" and descended from the Children of *Cobs*, of the " Tribe of *Benjamin*. Others of them say, that he " was not originally a *Jew*, but that, towards the " end of his life, he embraced their Religion. They " add, that he borrowed all his Philosophy from *So-* " *lomon's* Books, which were found in the City of " *Jerusalem*, when it was taken by *Alexander*, and " that he, afterwards, burnt them, to have all the " Honour of the Wisdom, they contained. They " add farther, that, to justify the change of his " Religion, he wrote a Letter to *Alexander*, which " is inserted entire in That Part of the Great *Biblio-* " *theque*; and in which the *Rabins* make him say, " that Logic is an Iniquity, that Philosophy is " Falshood and Deceit, and that Misery attends " Those, who study it; because that, by means of " the Disputes, which it leads them into, they go " down to Hell (27)." *Selden* quotes Jewish Authors, who have affirmed, first, That, a little before *Aristotle* died, he communicated to his Disciples the Doctrine, which he had learnt from the *Hebrews*, concerning the Immortality of the Soul, and the Punishments and Rewards of a future State. Secondly, That, as to the Points, in which his Doctrine contradicted the Law, he was converted, and became another Man, by the Instructions of the High-Priest, *Simon* the Just (28).

[C] *They, who pretend, that he was born a Jew, are grosly mistaken.*] The Foundation of This Mistake is this. The Ancient Translation of *Josephus* by *George* of *Trebizond* runs thus: *atque ille, inquit, Aristoteles Judæus erat,* instead of *atque ille, inquit Aristoteles, Judæus erat.* Upon this *Marsilius Ficinus* ventured to say, that, according to the Testimony of *Clearchus*, *Aristotle* was a Jew. *Clearchus Peripateticus scribit Aristotelem fuisse Judæum* (29). *Genebrard* fell into the same Mistake. *Ea de causa furiasse Clearchus Peripateticus scribit Aristotelem fuisse Judæum* (30). This *Jensius* informs me of (31). I shall not imitate *Schoeckius*, who has adorned himself with these Spoils, without giving the Honour where it is properly due (32). But, if we understand a Jew by *Religion*, and not by *Birth*, the Source of This Mistake must be searched for higher.

[D] *They are deceived, who say, that he was a Disciple of* Socrates *for three Years successively.*] The Life of *Aristotle*, ascribed to *Ammonius*, or to *John Philoponus*, contains this Error. The Learned *Nunesius*, who wrote Observations on This Life, says, that he met with no one among the Ancients, except *Olympiodorus*, who says, that *Aristotle* had been a Disciple of *Socrates*. He adds, that Cardinal *Bessarion* † fell into the same Mistake, and that *Leonard Aretin*, in the sixth Book of his *Letters*, and *Octavianus Ferrarius*, in his Work *de Sermonibus exotericis*, have shewed the Anachronism.

[E] *Aristotle's Behaviour towards his Master* Plato *is variously related.*] *Diogenes Laërtius* says, that *Plato*, seeing that *Aristotle* had deserted him, said; *He kicks against us, as Colts do against their Dams* (33). *Ælian* explains this Thought of *Plato. The Colt*, he says, *kicks the Dam after being filled with her Milk*: So Aristotle, *having learnt the first Rules and Principles of Philosophy from* Plato, *and, finding himself well fed with the excellent Posture, which his Master had supplied him with, spurred at him, and set up a School, to rival His* (34). Consult *Helladius*, who changes the Ideas a little; for he employs the Comparison of a Horse, which bites his Sire. Ἀριστοτέλης ὁ τῷ πεφυτάτῳ προσάντης ὑπὸ Πλάτωνος ἵππῳ ἐπωνομάζετο. ἐναντιώσεαι δοκῶν τῷ διδασκάλῳ· καὶ γὰρ ὁ ἵππος τοὺς ἑαυτοῦ φίλοις πατέρα δάκνων (35). Aristotle, Head of the Peripatetic School, *was called by* Plato *The Horse, because he opposed his Master; it being common for the Horse to bite his Sire.* But there is still something worse. *Ælian* relates, in another Place (36), that *Aristotle* offended *Plato* by going too magnificently

(27) Journal des Scavans, *of the 14th of July*, 1692, pag. 4*. Edit. of Holland.*

(28) *See* Seldenus, de Jure Naturali, lib. 1, cap. 1, pag. 14, 15. *Edit.* Lips. 1695.

(29) Marsil. Ficin. de Christ. Religione cap. 26.

(30) Genebrardi Chronol. ad Ann. 2672.

(31) Jons. de Script. Hist. Philos. pag. 100.

(32) Schoock. ubi supra.

* Prazi XLII. in Gorgium Platonis.

† Lib. 1. Advers. Calumniatores.

(33) Diog. Laërt. lib. 5, n. 2, in vita Aristot.

(34) Ælian. Var. Hist. lib. 4, cap. 9.

(35) Helladius, apud Photii Biblioth. pag. 1589.

(36) Ælian. lib. 3, c. 19.

ARISTOTLE.

he set up Altar against Altar; that is, erected a School in *Athens*, during *Plato's* Life, and in opposition to him; others say, that he did not set up for a Professor till after his Master's Death. We are told some things concerning his Amours [F], which are not altogether to his Advantage. It was pretended, that his Conjugal Affection was Idolatrous; and that, if he had not retired from *Athens*, the Process for Irreligion, which the Priests had entered against him [G], would have been attended with the same Consequences, as That against *Socrates*. Though he deserved very great Praise, yet it is certain, that most of the Errors concerning him

magnificently habited, by an Air of Raillery, and by talking a little too much; which made *Plato* transfer his Friendship to some other of his Disciples. *Aristotle*, having formed a Party, made use of an Opportunity, which the Absence of *Xenocrates*, and the Sickness of *Speusippus* offered him. These were *Plato's* Sword and Buckler, as we may say. It was easy, in the Absence of these, to insult him. Accordingly he went with a great Number of Disciples to *Plato's* School. The good old Man, being eighty Years of Age, had almost lost his Memory: *Aristotle*, taking Advantage of his Master's Infirmity, put several captious Questions to him, pushed him through every Retreat of his Logic, and proudly triumphed over him. After This Affront, the good Man taught no more in public, but kept at home with his Disciples. *Aristotle* took Possession of his Place: But *Xenophon*, at his Return to *Athens*, finding how things had passed, reprimanded *Speusippus* severely, for having suffered *Aristotle* to take Possession of the School; and gave the Usurper so much Disturbance, as obliged him to quit the Post, and re-established the first Master. If *Aristotle* acted thus, he deserved to be detested; but I believe the Story to be false. His Followers have maintained, that he wanted neither Respect nor Gratitude towards his Master. His having been the Author of another Sect of Philosophy was no Argument, that he was deficient in either. The other *Platonists* would have been in the wrong to have expected him to follow *Plato* in every thing. Did *Plato* add nothing to the Lights, which he received from *Socrates*? However this be, it is affirmed, in the Life of *Aristotle*, that he did not set up a School in the *Lycæum* during his Master's Life-time; and for this Reason, because *Chabrias* and *Timotheus*, who were both of them related to *Plato*, and at that Time very powerful in *Athens*, would not have suffered it. They add, that *Aristotle* erected an Altar to *Plato*, with an honourable Inscription, and that he did not teach in *Athens*, 'till after the Death of *Speusippus*, who succeeded *Plato*. Lastly, it is observed, that he did not take this Employ upon himself of his own mere Motion, but at the Sollicitation of the *Athenians*, who sent Deputies to him for that Purpose. The old *Latin* Translation of This Life of *Aristotle* is sometimes more ample than the Original. As for Example; in the Place, where the Author denies, that *Aristotle* set up a School during *Plato's* Life, the Translation remarks, that it was a Calumny of *Aristoxenus*, and *Aristocles*. The *Greek* has nothing of This. See what *Eusebius* cites from the seventh Book of This *Aristocles*; you will there find a Passage of *Aristoxenus*, which seems to contain This Accusation against *Aristotle*, in general, and somewhat obscure, Terms; and likewise see, that *Aristocles*, having refuted several other Accusations, drops the Cause, as to the Ingratitude of This Disciple (37). So that Father *Rapin* was much deceived (38), when he said, that *Eusebius* justifies him entirely from This Reproach (39). I cannot conceive, why this Jesuit has joined *Ammonius* and *Philoponus*, as two different Apologists, with *Eusebius*; for the Life of *Aristotle*, which he cites, belongs but to one Author; to *Ammonius* according to some, to *Philoponus* according to others.

[F] *We are told some things concerning his Amours.*] There is a strange Complication of Impurities on this Head. His Calumniators report, that He retired to *Hermias*, who commanded in *Atarnus*, a small Town of *Mysia*, near the *Hellespont*; and that *Hermias* had a very criminal Complaisance for him; "Ον οἱ μὲν ταῖς παιδικαῖς γίνεσθαι αὐτῷ (40); *Quem aiii quidem delicias ac lusus ipsius fuisse tradunt*; that he gave him his Daughter, or his Niece, in Marriage; that, finding him to be in Love with his Concubine, he made a Present of her to him (41); that *Aristotle* was so doatingly fond of This Lady, that, having married her, he offered a Sacrifice to Her, like That, which the *Athenians* offered to *Ceres*; and that he testified his Acknowledgment to *Hermias*, by an Hymn, which he composed in his Honour.

My Readers need not be told, that these Calumnies did not proceed from one and the same Pen; some told one Story, some another. One of *Aristotle's* Apologists has observed, that they did not all agree in charging him with one and the same Accusation; but that each Censor came with his particular Satire (42). This, it may be said, is a Sign they did not act in Concert; let me add, that it is a Sign they had no good Proof of any thing; for when a serious Accusation is once proved, all, who write against the accused, eternally reproach him with it. The same Apologist observes, that the particular Accusations, which were drawn up against *Aristotle*, amounted to so great a Number of Crimes, that, if but one of them had been true, he would certainly have been punished by the Judges then in being. His Enemies gave out, among other things, that he had betrayed his Country, and that Letters were intercepted, which he had written to the Prejudice of the *Athenians* (43). To return to *Aristotle's* Wife: some pretend, that it was after her Death, that her Husband offered such Sacrifices to her, as the *Athenians* offered to *Ceres*. Ὁποῖα θύουσιν Ἀριστοτέλη θυσίαν τῇ γυναικὶ τοιαύτην Ἀθηναῖοι τῇ Δήμητρι (44). *Scribit (Lycon Pythagoræus) Aristotelem idem sacrificii genus, quod Cereris ab Atheniensibus fiebat, demortuæ uxori facere solitum*. *Aristocles* answered, I. That *Apellicon's* Books, concerning the Intercourse of *Hermias* with *Aristotle*, fully justified these two Friends. II. That *Aristotle* had sufficiently justified himself as to his Marriage with *Pythias*, in the Letters, which he wrote to *Antipater*. This *Pythias* was the Sister of *Hermias*, and his adopted Daughter. *Aristotle* made it appear, that he did not marry her, 'till after the Death of *Hermias*; that she was a very virtuous Woman, but reduced to so deplorable a Condition, by the Death of her Brother, that he thought himself obliged to marry her out of a regard to *Hermias*.

[G] *The Process for Irreligion, which the Priests had entered against him.*] The Circumstances of this Affair are not known. *Diogenes Laërtius* has only told us (45), that *Eurymedon*, the Priest, accused *Aristotle* of Impiety, on account of an Hymn, which he had composed in Honour of *Hermias*, and an Inscription, engraved on the Statue of the same *Hermias*, in the Temple of *Delphi*. *Phavorinus* imputes the Accusation to *Demophilus* (46). It cannot be conceived by what Quirks of Law the Accusers could draw the least Shadow of a Proof from the Inscription to *Hermias*. It consists of four Verses, which have no Relation to Things Sacred, but are only levelled against the Perfidiousness of the King of *Persia* to This unhappy Friend of *Aristotle*. *Athenæus* informs us, that the Ground of the Accusation, to wit, the Hymn composed for *Hermias*, was unjust, since it was no Religious Poem, nor sacred Piece, as *Demophilus* pretended (47). *Athenæus* adds, that, to give the greater weight to the Accusation, *Eurymedon* had suborned *Demophilus* (48). It is probable, that *Demophilus* was some Person of Quality, and of great Authority in *Athens*. Perhaps he did not see to the Bottom of the Sacerdotal Craft; nor apprehend, that *Eurymedon*, the Priest, desired his Countenance, only to render poor *Aristotle* the more suspected. He expected, that People would Reason after this manner; *If only the Priests had accused* Aristotle, *the Evil might be born withal; their great Piety makes them subject*

VOL. I. 6 B

468 ARISTOTLE.

him are to be looked for in the extravagant Commendations, which have been heaped upon him: As for Example; Is it not a downright Falshood, to say, *That, if* Aristotle *spoke, in his Natural Philosophy, like a Man, he spoke, in his Moral Philosophy, like a God (f): And that it is a question, whether, in his Moral Philosophy, he partakes more of the Lawyer, than of the Priest; more of the Priest, than of the Prophet; more of the Prophet, than of the God (g)?* I shall, in the Remarks, touch upon some Praises bestowed on him, which are still greater than these [H]. Cardinal *Pallavicini* scruples not, in some measure, to confess, That, if it had not been for *Aristotle*, the

subject to be alarmed at the least Thing, which affects Religion: but here is Demophilus, *who is so scandalized at* Aristotle's *Impieties, that he openly demands Justice against him; the Evil must needs be very great.* The Hymn in question is preserved. It is to be found in *Athenæus*, and in *Diogenes Laërtius*; and there is not the least Trace of Irreligion in it. But, doubtless, his Accusers alledged, that *Aristotle* prophaned the use of Divine Hymns, by employing them in the Praises of a Mortal Man. They maintained, that he sung This Hymn daily at his Meals (49). *Aristotle*, not willing to rely on the good Construction, which might be made of his little Poem, retired quietly to *Chalcis*, in *Eubea*, and pleaded his Cause, in writing, at a Distance. *Athenæus* reports some Words of This Apology; but does not warrant them to be really *Aristotle's* (50). *Phavorinus* affirms, in *Diogenes Laërtius*, that *Aristotle* wrote a Speech, at that time, in the Judiciary Style, and that he was the first, who composed such Speeches in his own Cause; or that this was the first time he made them for himself (52). *Nunnesius* affirms, that *Seneca*, *de vita beata*, observes, that *Aristotle* made but This one in his whole LifeTime (52). However it be, his safest way was to plead his Cause at a Distance; for his Accusers were Men, who would never have given him any Quarter, but have set all Engines at Work, till they had found one, which would have done the Business. It was impossible so great a Wit as He should not sometimes laugh at the Impertinence of the publick Worship of the *Athenians*, and speak his Sentiments of Priest-Craft. All, that he had ever said in Conversation, would have been raked up; Witnesses would have been heard; in a Word, he would have been effectually crushed. Besides, who knows, but, at some time or other, a Real Impiety might have escaped him; when, intending to speak only of the immutable Greatness of the Supremely-Perfect Being? *Origen* says, that The Act on of Impiety, which his Accusers would have brought against him, was founded on some of his Doctrines (53). He says, in another place, that it is a Tenet of the Peripatetics, that Prayers and Sacrifices are useless (54). It is probable they built this Doctrine on This false Principle; that infinite Wisdom knows, at all times, what is fit to be done; and that it does not alter it's purpose according to the Desires or Interests of Men; as if the Divinity stood in need of our Prayers, as Notices or Hints, not to do That, which we believe he is prepared to do. Such a Principle, if not rectified by the Lights of Religion, is a real Impiety. *Aristotle* could never have escaped the *Athenian* Priests, if they had held him to This Point. His Answer to those, who demanded the Reason of his Retreat, shews, that he feared, they would find good, or bad, Proofs against him. *I would not willingly be the Cause of the Athenians being guilty of a second Injustice against Philosophy.* The first Injustice was the Death of *Socrates*. Πρὸς τὸν ἐρόμενον διὰ τί απέλιπε τὰς Ἀθήνας, απεκρίνατο ὅτι ι βούλομαι Ἀθηναίος δὶς ἐξαμαρτεῖν εἰς φιλοσοφίαν· τὸ περὶ Σωκράτην πάθω αἰνιττόμενω, καὶ τὸν κατ' αὐτὸν κίνδυνον (55). *Interroganti cur residiquisset Athenas, respondit; quoniam noluisset committere, ut Athenienses bis peccarent in Philosophiam: obscure Socratis mortem innuens, & suum periculum.* He made use of one of *Homer's* Verses, to signify, that it was not safe living in a City, where the Race of Informers never decreased; but one regularly succeeded another. We may reasonably suppose, that he acknowledged himself guilty of having personally offended *Eurymedon*, the Priest of *Ceres* (56), by some Stroke of Raillery; which kindled the Zeal of this Personage, who had suffered the pretended Impiety of the Hymn to lie dormant for twenty Years. It is more dangerous to offend these Gentlemen in their own Persons, than in the Persons or their Gods. See the Remark [R], where we shall relate the Opinions

of some Authors concerning the Cause of *Aristotle's* Flight. I have observed, at the End of the Article, that *Hesychius* affirms, that he was actually condemned, and executed at *Athens*. I use no Hyperbole in the Expression of twenty Years; since *Aristotle* had taught thirteen Years at *Athens*, when the Process for Irreligion obliged him to retire to *Chalcis* (57). He did not return to *Athens*, 'till he had instructed *Alexander*, whose Preceptor he was not, 'till after the Death of *Hermias*.

[H] *I shall touch upon some Praises, bestowed on him, which are still greater than these.*] *Averroes* has said, that, before *Aristotle's* Birth, Nature was incompleat; that, in him, it received it's last Accomplishment, and the Perfection of it's Being; that it could go no farther; that here was the Extremity of it's Power, and the Limits of human Understanding. Another Philosopher has outdone *Averroes*, by saying, that *Aristotle* was a second Nature. Those are *Balzac's* Words, in the Four hundred and fifty ninth Page of the Discourses, which were printed after his *Christian Socrates*. This puts me in mind of the Scruples of an Author, who, seeing that Nature herself subscribed to *Aristotle's* Opinions, durst never doubt of what he had said. *Rectè & hoc Aristoteles, ut cetera; nec possum non assentiri viro, cujus inventis nec ipsa natura dissentit* (58). A *Spanish* Divine says, that, without the particular Assistance of an Angel, or Genius, the Wit of Man cannot penetrate so far into the Secrets of Nature, as *Aristotle* has done (59). He must have believed, then, that *Aristotle* had a good, or an evil, Angel, which instructed him in a thousand things, to which human Understanding could not attain. *William*, Bishop of *Paris*, mentions, " in several Parts of his " Works (60), that This Philosopher had a Familiar " Spirit, who directed all his Actions, whom he " caused to descend from the Sphere of *Venus*, by " sacrificing a strangled Lamb, and some other Ce" remonies." Others have said, that he stood in no need of such Assistance. It was the " Opinion of " the famous Divine *Henry de Assia* (61), that *Ari" stotle* could have acquired as perfect a Knowledge " in Theology, by the Light of Nature, as That, " which was discovered to our first Father, when " he fell asleep in the Terrestrial Paradise (62), or to " St *Paul*, when he was snatched up into the Third " Heaven." A Council, which was held in *France*, under *Philip Augustus*, ordered *Aristotle's* Metaphysics to be burnt. An *English* Doctor, of the Order of St *Augustin* (63), has left in Writing, that it was commonly believed, in those Times, that none but Antichrist should be able thoroughly to understand *Aristotle's* Books; which he would make use of, to convince all those, who should enter into Dispute with him. Let us end this little Collection, with a Passage of *Agrippa*, who informs us, that the Divines of *Cologn* maintained, that *Aristotle* was the Fore-runner of the *Messias*, in the Mysteries of Nature, as St *John Baptist* was, in the Mysteries of Grace. " Dignissi" mus profectò hodie Latinorum gymnasiorum Doctor, " & quem Colonienses mei Theologi etiam divis ad" numerarent, librumque sub prælo evulgatum ede" rent, cui titulum facerent *de Salute Aristotelis* (64); " sed & alium versu & metro de vita & morte Ari" stotelis, quem Theologica insuper glossa illustra" runt, in cujus calce concludunt, Aristotelem ho " fuisse Christi præcursorem in Naturalibus, quemad" modum Joannes Baptista in Gratuitis (65). *A most worthy Doctor of the Latin Schools, and whom* " *my Countrymen, the Divines of* Cologn, *would even* " *exalt to Divinity, and would publish a printed* " *Work Of the Salvation of* Aristotle; *besides another* " *in Verse Of the Life and Death of* Aristotle; *which* " *they have illustrated with a Theological Commentary,* " *at the end of which they conclude, that* Aristotle *was* " *the Fore runner of Christ in Natural Things, as* John

ARISTOTLE. 469

the Church would have wanted some of it's Articles of Faith [*I*]. The Christians are not the only People, who have authorized his Philosophy; the Mahometans (*b*) are little less prejudiced in it's Favour; and we are told, that, to this Day, notwithstanding the Ignorance, which reigns among them, They have Schools for this Sect [*K*]. It will be an everlasting Subject of Wonder to Persons, who know what Philosophy is, to find, that *Aristotle's* Authority was so much respected in the Schools, for several Ages, that, when a Disputant quoted a Passage from This Philosopher, He, who maintained the *Thesis*, durst not say *Transeat*, but must either deny the Passage, or explain it in his own way [*L*]. It is in this manner we treat the

(*b*) See Rapin's Comparison of *Plato* and *Aristotle*, pag. 403.

" John Baptist *was in those of Grace*." To speak impartially, and without any Prejudice, it may be said, that these extravagant Panegyrists do *Aristotle's* Memory more harm than good. These Words of *Tacitus* may, in some respect, be applied to them: " Pessimum inimicorum genus laudantes (66). ——— " *Panegyrists are the worst of Enemies.*" So many just Praises may be bestowed on *Aristotle* (67), that they are inexcusable, who, not satisfied with them, have added others, which are hyperbolical.

Why were they not satisfied with saying, that he dipt *his Pen in good Sense* (68) ? This is what all Philosophers ought to do, if the chief of the Stoics may be believed. Ό Ζήνων ἔλεξεν ὅτι δεῖ τὸν φιλόσοφον εἰς νοῦν ἀποβάπτοντα προφέρεσθαι τὸν λέξιν (69). *Zeno ait mente tinctum proferre Philosophum sermonem debere.* They, who would see a Collection of the Praises given to *Aristotle*, would do well to read George of *Trebizond* (70). *Pererius*, in the first Chapter of the fifth Book *de Principiis ;* *Justus Lipsius*, in the fourth Dissertation of the first Book *Manuductionis ad Philosophiam Stoicam ; Theodorus Angelutius*, in his Answer to *Francis Patricius*, &c.

[*I*] Cardinal *Pallavicini* scruples not, *in some measure*, to confess, That, if it had not been for Aristotle, *the Church would have wanted some of it's Articles of Faith.*] The Author of the new Gospel of Cardinal *Pallavicini* does not fail (71) to make the most of these Words of the nineteenth Chapter of the eighth Book, n. 13. " Di ciò si doveva in gran parte l'obligatione ad Aristotele, il quale se non si fosse adoperato in distinguer accuratamente i generi delle " ragioni, noi mancavamo di molti articoli di fede. —— Great Thanks is due for this to Aristotle, who, *if he had not taken the Pains to distinguish accurately the several kinds of reasoning, we should have wanted many Articles of Faith.*" This Encomium puts me in mind of a Passage of *Nicius Erythræus*, as great a Flatterer of *Aristotle* as any of them: He says, that it was a vain Attempt, in the Subtle and Learned *Patricius*, to oppose the Doctrine of the *Lycæum* ; a Doctrine, which can never be shaken, and which will always triumph over it's Rivals. " Altius Aristotelis " auctoritas radices egit, quam ut cujusquam vim " impetumque pertimescat: viget, semperque vigebit, hominis disciplina ; tantumque quis existimabitur sciæ, quantum ex doctrinæ ejusdam fontibus " haustum, intelligentia comprehensum habuerit ; ac " nemo, cui cor sapiat, non satius esse ducet in iis, " quæ ad Philosophiam pertinent, cum deo, ut ita " dicam, philosophorum errare, quam cum aliis recte " sapere, minorum gentium magistris. Itaque ille, " omnibus in gymnasiis, ad sapientiam properantibus, " dux semper habebitur: ille Theologorum quasi militiæ, adversus religionis nostræ hostes, definitiones, " argumentorum copiam, & alia præclare dicta multa, " tanquam amentatas hastas clargietur, quas illa Theo- " logicis lacertis ac viribus, de cœlo suppeditatis, torqueat ac vibret (72). —— Aristotle's *Authority has taken too deep root, to fear the Attacks of any one. The Doctrine of that great Man flourishes, and will " for ever flourish; and each one will be esteemed " learned, in proportion as he is versed in the Writings of this Philosopher ; and indeed no Man of " Sense, but would chuse, in Matters of Philosophy, " to err with this God of the Philosophers, if I may " be allowed to call him so, than to think right with " Masters of an inferiour Class. For this reason, he " will be the Head of every School, which is in pursuit of true Wisdom ; be will equip our militant Divines, against the Enemies of our Religion, with " Definitions, Arguments, &c. which, as so many " Weapons from Heaven, they may brandish by the " Strength of their Theological Arms.*" To deal fairly, I think myself obliged to say, that Cardinal *Pallavi-*

cini does not advance the Maxim alledged as from himself, nor as an Observation, of which he would inform the World, but only as a malicious Jest of Father *Paul*. He treats this Raillery as impertinent, and says, that the Councils, in which *Substance, Person*, and *Hypostasis*, were so subtily distinguished, were equally exposed to it. In a Word, he does not deny the Fact, and is content to laugh at Those, who laugh at it (73). Father *Paul*, having set down the Decree of the sixth Session, shews what it was that had been censured in it, and, among other things, says, that they, who were versed in Ecclesiastical History, observed, that all the other Councils, put together, had not decided so many Articles, as That single Session, in which *Aristotle* had a great share, in having distinguished between the several kinds of Causes ; and, that, without his Help, we should have wanted many Articles of Faith. *In chi haveva una gran parte Aristotele, coll' haver distinto essattamente tutti i generi di cause, a che, se egli non si fosse adoperato, noi mancavamo di molti articoli di Fede* (74). The Remonstrances of the *Sorbonne*, upon which the Parliament of *Paris* made an Order against Chymists, in the Year 1629, imported, that *no one could oppose the Principles of Aristotle's Philosophy, without interfering with the Scholastic Divinity received in the Church* (75). In the Year 1624, the Parliament of *Paris* banished three Persons, who ventured publickly to dispute against *Aristotle's* Philosophy; and forbad all Persons to vent the Propositions contained in their *Theses*, on pain of corporal Punishments, and to teach any Maxims contrary to ancient and approved Authors on pain of Death (76).

[*K*] *To this Day the* Mahometans ———— *have Schools for This Sect.*] " The Peripatetic Philosophy " is so established every where, that no other is read " in all Christian Universities. Even They, who " are forced to receive the Impostures of *Mahomet*, teach the Sciences no otherwise than " according to the Principles of the *Lycæum*, to " which they are so attached, that *Averrhæs, Alfarabius, Alinahaffar* (77), and several other *Arabian* " Philosophers, often swerve from the Opinions of " their Prophet, that they may not contradict Those " of *Aristotle*, whom the *Turks* have translated into " the *Turkish* and *Arabic* Languages, as *Belonius* " relates (78)." The Author, from whom I borrow these Words, says in another Volume (79), that, according to *Olearius's* Relation, the *Persians* have all *Aristotle's* Works, explained by several *Arabian* Commentators, who are wont to call his Philosophy the Goblet, or Drinking-Cup of the World. " *Bergeron, says be*, observes, in his Treatise of the " *Tartars*, that they had *Aristotle's* Books translated " into their Language, teaching his Doctrine, with " as much Submission, as can be done here, at *Samarcand*, an University of the Great *Mogul*, and " at present the chief City of the Kingdom of " *Usbec*."

[*L*] *Where a Disputant quoted a Passage from This Philosopher, He who maintained the* Thesis, *durst not say* Transeat, *but must either deny the Passage, or explain in it his own Way.*] If any one think fit to contest this Fact, I refer him to several *Courses of Philosophy*, printed in the XVth Century, where This Method is found to have been in use. The Author proves his Thesis, first by Authority, and afterwards by Reason. The Authoritative Proof are Passages out of *Aristotle*. The Answer to the Objections consists also of two Parts. First, Satisfaction given as to the Passages of *Aristotle*, which seem to oppose the Thesis, and which are Authoritative Proofs for the other Party : Afterwards an Answer is given to the Reasons ; but great Care is taken never to say, *I own that*

(66) Tacit. in vita Agric. cap. 41.

(67) *You will find many such, in the Speeches of Coriolanus, and called Aristotelis Laudatio.*

(68) *See the Words of* Suidas, *below, Remark* [*Z*], *at the beginning.*

(69) Plut. in Vita Phocionis, pag. 743. E.

(70) De Comparat. Platonis, & Aristotelis.

(71) Chap. 6. Art. 6. pag. 253.

(72) Pinacoth I. pag 204.

(73) Ma quale sostituzia è quello Scherno, che di ciò si doveva in gran parte l'obligatione ad Aristotele, &c. *See* Rapin's *Reflexions on Philosophy*, pag. 449.

(74) F rber Paul's *History of the Council of Trent.* lib. 2 ad ann. 1546, pag. 276, Edit. of 1629.

(75) Rapin's Comparison *of Plato and Aristotle*, p. 413.

(76) Mercure François, Tom. 10. p. 504.

(77) *It should be Albumassar, or Almuzar baffar.* * Lib. 3. cap. 14.

(78) La Mothe le Vayer, *of the Virtue of the Pagans*, Tom. 5. p. 102.

(79) *The same*, pag. 245.

ARISTOTLE.

the Holy Scriptures in the Divinity Schools. The Parliaments, which have proscribed all other Philosophy, but That of *Aristotle* (i), are more excusable than The Doctors: For, whether the Members of Parliament were really persuaded, as is very probable, that This Philosophy was the best of any, or were not, the Public Good might induce them to prohibit New Opinions, least the Academical Divisions should extend their malignant Influence to the Tranquillity of the State. What is most astonishing to Wise Men, is, that the Professors should be so strongly prejudiced in Favour of *Aristotle*'s Philosophy. Had This Prepossession been confined to his Poetry, and Rhetoric, it had been less wonderful; but they were fond of the weakest of his Works; I mean his Logic, and Natural Philosophy [M]. This Justice however must be done to the blindest of his Followers, that they have deserted him, where he clashes with Christianity [N]. And this he did in Points of the greatest Consequence; since he maintained the Eternity of the World, and did not believe, that Providence extended itself to sublunary Beings. As to the Immortality of the Soul, it is not certainly known, whether he acknowledged it or no [O]. We shall take notice, in another Place, of the long Disputes, which have reigned in *Italy*, on This Subject. In the Year 1647, the Famous Capuchin *Valerian Magni* published a Work concerning the Atheism of *Aristotle*. About One Hundred and thirty Years before, *Marc Anthony Venerius* published a System of Philosophy, in which he discovered several Inconsistencies between *Aristotle*'s Doctrine, and the Truths of Religion. *Campanella* maintained the same, in his Book *de reductione ad Religionem*, which was approved at *Rome*, in the Year 1630. It was, not long since, maintained, in *Holland*, in the Prefaces to some Books, that the Doctrine of This Philosopher differed but little from *Spinozism* (k). In the mean time, if some Peripatetic

that Aristotle *believed so and so*; *nevertheless I deny, that my Thesis, wherein I maintain another Doctrine, is false*. All Endeavours are made use of to give the objected Passages such a Sense, as may agree with the Matter in question. The same Method is still in use among Those of the Church of *Rome*, in the Divinity Schools, with regard to St. *Austin*, and *Thomas Aquinas*.

[M] *The weakest of his Works; I mean his Logic, and Natural Philosophy.*] To be convinced of the Weakness of these Works, we need only read *Gassendus* in his *Exercitationes paradoxicæ adversus Aristoteleos* (80). He says enough there against *Aristotle*'s Philosophy, in general, to persuade every unprejudiced Reader, that it is very defective; but he particularly ruins this Philosopher's Logic. He was preparing likewise a Criticism on his Natural Philosophy, his Metaphysics, and Ethics, in the same way; when, being alarmed at the formidable Indignation of the *Peripatetic* Party against him, he chose rather to drop his Work, than expose himself to their vexatious Persecutions.

Note, that no one pretends to deny, but that, in *Aristotle*'s Logic, and Natural Philosophy, there are many things, which discover the Elevation and Profoundness of his Genius. This we may grant, and, at the same time, judge that *Casaubon*'s *Elogium* on him is somewhat too hyperbolical. " Ego pueros " puto fuisse (socios in Logica) præ divino Aristotele; " & eorum in hoc genere scripta ὕθλον καὶ φλή- " ναφον præ Aristotelis Organo; quo opere omnia " mortalium ingenia (divina aut de rebus divinis sem- " per excipio) longe superavit (81). —— *I look upon* " *the Logicians as Children, in Comparison of the Di-* " *vine Aristotle, and their Writings on this Subject* " *to be Trifles, when compared with* Aristotle's *Orga-* " *num; in which Work he has surpassed all the Wit* " *of Man; divine Subjects ever excepted.* The same may be said of This Passage of Father *Rapin*; " No- " thing appears to have been regular or settled in " Logic before *Aristotle*. This great Genius, fraught " with Reason, and Knowledge, searched so deep " into the Abyss of Human Wit, that he penetrated " all the Secrets of it by his nice Discernment of it's " Operations. This vast Depth of human Thoughts " had never yet been founded: *Aristotle* was the first, " who discovered a new Way of attaining to Science, " by the Evidence of Demonstration, and by proceed- " ing geometrically to Demonstration in the way of " Syllogism, the most finished Production, and great- " est Effort, of human Wit This is, in Miniature, " the whole Art and Method of *Aristotle*'s Logic; " which is so very sure a one, that there can be no " perfect Certainty in reasoning but by this Method, " which is a certain Rule for thinking right on what " ever ought to employ our Thoughts (82)." This

Philosopher's Treatise of Syllogisms may be commended as it deserves, without employing any such extravagant Expressions. There are several very sublime Questions in his Physics, which he discusses, and clears up, in a very masterly Way; but, in short, the main, the Gross, of this Work is good for nothing; *infelix operis summa.* The chief Reason of This Defect is *Aristotle*'s forsaking the Path, which the most excellent Naturalists took, who had philosophized before him. They believed, that all the Alterations, which happen in Nature, are only new Dispositions of the Particles of Matter; they admitted no Generation, properly speaking. This was the Doctrine, which he rejected (83); and, in so doing, was bewildered. For he was obliged to teach, that new Beings are produced, and others destroyed; he distinguished them from Matter; he gave them unheard-of Names, he affirmed, or supposed, things, of which he had no distinct Ideas. Now it is as impossible to philosophize justly without the Evidence of Ideas, as to sail without the Polar Star, or the Compass. To abandon this Evidence is to be beside one's self; it is to imitate a Traveller, who, in a strange Country, should dismiss his Guide; it is to feel one's Way in a strange House by Night without a Candle. Every one knows the many Forms, and Qualities distinct from Substance, which *Aristotle*'s Followers have introduced; he had opened to them This Labyrinth: And if, in the XVIIth Century, Natural Philosophy began to appear again with new Lustre, it was by restoring the Ancient Principles, which he had forsaken, and by recurring to Evidence: In short, it was by excluding the great Number of Entities, of which our Mind has no manner of Idea, out of the Doctrine of Generation, and sticking to the Figure, Motion, and Situation of the Particles of Matter: Things, of which we have a clear and distinct Conception.

[N] *This Justice however must be done to the blindest of his Followers, that They deserted him, where he clashes with Christianity.*] I intend not to enter into Dispute with *Luther*, in behalf of the Divines of *Cologne*: He reproaches Them, and Those of *Louvain* also, with defending, or softening, *Aristotle*'s greatest and most impious Absurdities, by their forced Interpretations. *Aristotelem ipsis in summo esse pretio, & nibil ab eo dictum esse tam absurde vel alienè à nostrâ religione quod non defendant, quod non aliqua interpretatione quantumvis longe petitâ circumvestiant, quò suus ille constet honos atque nominis existimatio* (84). What is not Prejudice capable of!

[O] *As to the Immortality of the Soul, it is not certainly known, whether he believed it or no.*] *Pomponatius*, and *Niphus*, had a great Quarrel on this Subject. The first maintained, that the Immortality of the Soul was inconsistent with *Aristotle*'s Principles; the latter undertook to defend the contrary.

See

ARISTOTLE. 471

patetics may be believed, He was not ignorant of the Myſtery of the Trinity [*P*]. He made a very good End [*Q*], and enjoys Eternal Happineſs [*R*]. He compoſed a very great Number of Books, a great Part of which is come down to us. It is true, ſome Critics raiſe a thouſand Scruples about them. We ſhall ſay ſomething of the Fate of theſe Books, in the Remarks on the Article TYRANNION (*l*). He was extremely honoured in his own City [*S*]; and there were Heretics, who worſhipped His Image jointly with That of JESUS CHRIST. I no where find, that the *Antinomians bore greater Reſpect to This wiſe Pagan, than to the uncreated Wiſdom.*

See the Diſcourſe of *la Mothe le Vayer* on the Immortality of the Soul (85); and *Bodin*, in the fifteenth Page of the Preface to the *Dæmonomania.*

[*P*] *According to ſome Peripatetics,* Ariſtotle *was not ignorant of the Myſtery of the Trinity*.] Emanuel de Moura, diſputing againſt Thoſe, who accuſed *Ariſtotle* of Atheiſm, ſays, I. That a Woman wheedled him to that Degree, that ſhe made him conſult the Oracle of *Apollo* (86). II. That he ordered, by his laſt Will, that the Effigies of certain Animals, which he had vowed for the Health of *Nicanor* (87), ſhould be dedicated to *Jupiter* and *Minerva*. III. That he confeſſes, in the firſt Book *de Cœlo & Mundo* (88). *Se cum aliis obtuliſſe Diis trina ſacrificia, in recognitionem trinæ perfectionis in eis inventæ* (89). *- - That He, and Others, had offered to the Gods triple Sacrifices, in acknowledgment of the triple Perfection found in them.* From theſe Paſſages it is inferred, not only that he believed the Exiſtence of Devils, and was ſuperſtitious, but that he was acquainted likewiſe with a Trinity of Perſons in an Unity of Subſtance; as Salmeron would have it (90); and George Trapezontius before him (91); which laſt wrote a whole Book concerning the Conformity of Ariſtotle's Doctrine with the Holy Scripture. Naudé, from whom I borrow this, obſerves, *That* Emanuel de Moura *evidently miſrepreſents* Philoponus, *who ſays no more, according to the Greek Text, and the Old Tranſlation, which agrees with That of* Nunneſius, *than that* Ariſtotle, *having attained to the Age of ſixteen Years, was adviſed, by the* Pythian Oracle, *to addict himſelf chiefly to Philoſophy* —— Naudé *ſays, that the Three Sacrifices, which he offered to the Gods, and the Knowledge of the Trinity, which many Catholic Doctors aſcribe to him,* "are meer Chimera's, which "owe their Original to what he ſays in his firſt Book *de* "*Cœlo,* ſpeaking of the Trinary Number: Διὸ παρὰ "τῆς φύσεως εἰληφότες ὥσπερ νόμους ἐκείνης "καὶ πρὸς τὰς ἁγιςείας τῶν Θεῶν χρώμεθα "τῷ ἀριθμῷ τούτῳ. That is, *Wherefore, even in* "*ſacrificing to the Gods, we make uſe of this Num-* "*ber, which ſeems to be dictated by Nature herſelf.*
"From which Paſſage nothing more can be inferred, "than that *Ariſtotle* ſays, that, in his Time, they "made uſe of the Number *Three* in Sacrifices; "which is alſo teſtified by *Theocritus.*" Afterwards Naudé obſerves, that Cardinal Beſſarion (93) laughs at Trapezontius *for taking ſo much Pains to prove, from this Text, that* Ariſtotle *had a full Knowledge of the Trinity.* The modern Schoolmen will baſe nothing of theſe Pretenſions. See Piccinardi, Profeſſor at *Padua,* in his *Dogmata Philoſophiæ Peripateticæ.* The *Journal of Italy* mentions it under the Thirty firſt of *Auguſt,* 1674.

[*Q*] *He made a very good end.*] Finding himſelf near his Death, he ſhed a Flood of Tears, and, full of Grief and Hope, implored the Mercy of the Supreem Being. He approved a Sentence of *Homer* extreamly, which ſays, That it does not miſbecome the Gods to aſſume the Nature of Man, to the end that they may enlighten Human Kind. Theſe were Glimpſes of the future Incarnation of the Son of God. "Proditum & illud monumentis eſt, quum "philoſophus hic extrema ſibi ingruere præſenſiſſet, "dolore ac ſpe in lacrymas amplius profuſum pri- "mæ cauſæ miſericordiam intentus implora- "ſe. Quin & Homeri ſententiam ex Odyſſea ve- "hementer approbaſſe, qua non eſſe immortalibus "diis indecorum pronuntiare hominis induere na- "turam, quo ab erroribus ſevocentur mortales. Qua "in re CHRISTI præſenſiſſe adventum auguran- "tur nonnulli ejus viri gloriæ in primis addicti." This we read in *Cælius Rhodiginus* (94). His Authority in Matters of this Nature is good for nothing. Others ſpeak very differently of *Ariſtotle's* laſt Hours. "They ſay, that he died of Vexation, becauſe "he could not comprehend the Cauſe of the Ebbing "and Flowing of the *Euripus.* Upon which ſome Mo- "derns have invented a Fable, which has been greatly "in vogue, viz. that this Philoſopher threw him- "ſelf into the *Euripus,* with theſe Words, *Let the* "Euripus *receive me, ſince I cannot comprehend the* "*Euripus* (95)." *Diogenes Laërtius* quotes an Author, called *Eumelus,* who ſaid, that *Ariſtotle,* having fled to *Chalcis,* poiſoned himſelf there, at ſeventy Years of Age (96). *Apollodorus* ſeems to me more worthy of Credit, who ſays, that This great Man died of Sickneſs, at the Age of Sixty three Years (97).

[*R*] *Enjoys Eternal Happineſs.*] Sepulveda, one of the moſt learned Men of the XVIth Century, made no Scruple to rank him among the Bleſſed, and maintained his Opinion publickly in Writing (98). The Jeſuit *Gretſerus* rebuked him for his Preſumption, but confeſſed, that he was inclined to favour *Ariſtotle* as much as *Sepulveda,* whom he diſapproves only *for his confident manner of Speaking* (99). Add to this, what I have quoted from *Cælius Rhodiginus* (100), and what conſiderable Perſons have obſerved concerning the Reaſon, which obliged *Ariſtotle* to leave *Athens.* Albertus Magnus maintained, that they expelled him thence for his good Qualities: *Propter morum rectitudinem pulſus Athenis* (101); *Gretſer,* in his Diſpute with Sepulveda, about *Ariſtotle's Salvation, does not queſtion, but he intended, by this voluntary Baniſhment, to avoid the Neceſſity, which they would have laid upon him, of paying That Worſhip to Idols, which he believed to be due to God alone* (102). Thus we have, in his Perſon, an illuſtrious Refugee for the true Religion. Origen has given a favourable Interpretation to this Flight of *Ariſtotle* (103); for, in explaining the Precept, which our Saviour gives his Apoſtles, *when perſecuted in one City, to fly to another* (104), he tells *Celſus,* who derided it with his uſual Propheneſs, That Ariſtotle's *withdrawing himſelf, as we have mentioned, was conformable to the Goſpel Morality, and that, being injuriouſly perſecuted, he acted, as* JESUS CHRIST *had adviſed his Diſciples to do* (105).

I have quoted (106) a Paſſage of *Agrippa,* where he mentions a Book *de Salute Ariſtotelis. Voëtius,* who had ſo extenſive a Knowledge of Books, had never ſeen it; but knew pretty exactly the Time of it's Impreſſion. He ſays, in a Theſis, maintained by him on the fifteenth of *December,* 1638, that it was printed at *Oppenheim,* about One hundred and forty Years before, and that *Francis Junius* had ſeen a Copy of it (107). He adds, that one Lambertus Montanus Author, of a Commentary on *Ariſtotle's* Phyſics, (where, in the Year 1486, he is ſtiled Doctor of Divinity) had wrote concerning This Philoſopher's Salvation, and had made it probable from Scripture, and the Opinion of learned Men, that the Stagyrite was ſaved. *Quæſtionem Magiſtralem ſatis acutam ſcripſiſſe, oſtendentem per autoritates ſcripturæ divinæ, quid juxta ſaniorem doctorum ſententiam probabilius ſit poſſit de ſalvatione Ariſtotelis Stagiritæ* (108). You will find, in a Treatiſe *de Pietate Ariſtotelis erga Deum & hominem,* which Fortunius Licetus dedicated to *Innocent* X, and which was approved by two general Inquiſitors, ſeveral Reaſons, by which he endeavours to prove, that *Ariſtotle* is not damned.

[*S*] *He was extreamly honoured in his own City.*] It had been ſaid by King *Philip,* but, at *Ariſtotle's* Requeſt, was rebuilt by *Alexander.* In acknowledgment of ſo great a Benefit, the Inhabitants conſecrated a Feſtival to This Philoſopher; and, when he died at *Chalcis,* in the Iſland of *Eubæa,* they tranſported his Bones from thence; they built an Altar over his Tomb; they called the Place *Ariſtotle's,* and held their Aſſemblies there (109). *Mandeville,* in his fabulous Account of his Travels, ſays, that thus ſubſiſted in his Time, to wit, in the XIVth Century (110).

[*T*] *There*

VOL. I. 6 C

dom [*Y*], nor that *the* Aëtians *were excommunicated, for giving their Disciples* Aristotle's *Categories for a Catechism* (*m*). But I have somewhere read, that, before the Reformation, there were Churches in *Germany*, in which *Aristotle*'s Ethics were read every *Sunday* to the People, instead of the Gospel [*U*]. There are but few Instances of Zeal for Religion, which have not been shewn for the *Peripatetic* Philosophy. *Paul de Foix*, famous for his Embassies and his Learning, would not see *Francis Patricius* at *Ferrara*, because he was informed, that That Learned Man taught a Philosophy different from the *Peripatetic* (*n*). This was treating the Enemies of *Aristotle* as Zealots treat Heretics. After all, it is no wonder, that the *Peripatetic* Philosophy, as it has been taught for several Centuries, found so many Protectors [*X*], or that the Interests of it are believed to be inseparable from Those of Theology (*o*); for it accustoms the Mind to acquiesce without Evidence. This Union of Interests may be esteemed as a Pledge to the *Peripatetics* of the Immortality of Their Sect, and an Argument to abate the Hopes of the New Philosophers; considering withal, that there are some Doctrines of *Aristotle*, which the Moderns have rejected, and which must, sooner or later, be adopted again (*p*). The Protestant Divines have very much altered their Conduct; if it be true, as we are told, that the first Reformers clamoured so loudly against the *Peripatetic* Philosophy [*Y*]. The kind of Death, which

[*T*] *There were Hereticks, who worshipped his Image with That of* JESUS CHRIST, &c.] Read this Passage of Father *Rapin* (111). "The *Carpocratians* were condemned, for placing This Philosopher's Image next to That of JESUS CHRIST, and for adoring him, through an extravagant Zeal for his Doctrine *. The *Aëtians* were excommunicated by the Church, and by the *Arians* themselves, from whom they sprung, for giving *Aristotle*'s Categories to their Disciples, instead of a Catechism †. And the *Antinomians* proceeded to such Excess of Impiety, as to pay more Respect to This wise *Pagan*, than to the *Uncreated Wisdom* ‖." I never was so much convinced, as by this Passage, that This entertaining Writer did not give himself the Trouble of consulting Originals. I confess, *Baronius* says, under the Year, which Father *Rapin* quotes, that the *Carpocratians* had Images, and, among others, That of JESUS CHRIST, (which they said was procured by *Pilate*) That of *Pythagoras*, That of *Plato*, and That of *Aristotle*; and that they paid them the same Veneration as the *Pagans* do to their Idols. But this should not have been alledged: for, besides that *Baronius* no where says, that These Hereticks were condemned on this Account, it does not appear, that They had more Zeal for *Aristotle*'s Doctrine, than for That of the other Philosophers, whose Images they venerated. My Edition of *Baronius* (112) does not contain one Word of what Father *Rapin* mentions under the Year 208: Nor is it possible, that Persons, who sprung from the *Arians*, should be driven from the Communion of the Church, in the beginning of the third Century. It is under the Year 356, that *Baronius* speaks of *Aëtius*: he quotes a long Passage of *Suidas*, in which we find, not that This Heretic gave his Followers *Aristotle*'s *Categories* for a Catechism; but that he explained things to them, according to the Method of *Aristotle*'s *Categories*; meaning, that he was well versed in Logical Disputations and Subtilties. Just, as if, at present, a *Spanish* Schoolman, who undertook to explain a Point of Faith, should follow the Method of the Schools. Could it be said, that he substituted *Aristotle*'s Works in the room of our Books of Religion? To quote *Eusebius*, in the *Twenty seventh Chapter of his History*, is an unwarrantable way of Citation. I do not believe That Author has said one Word of the *Antinomians*.

[*V*] *In some Churches of Germany, Aristotle's Ethicks were read ----- instead of the Gospel.*] I shall quote my Author; he is *Spanhemius*, the Father, in the Secular Oration, delivered by him at *Geneva*, in the Year 1635 (113). "Quin & Philippus Melanchthon, *says* he (114), vir candidissimus testatur diebus Dominicis, variis in locis, pro thematibus Dominicalibus, inde à Karoli M. ætate opera P Guarenfridi, seculo octavo, in Cathedras Ecclesiasticas introductis, Ethica Aristotelis publice populo prælecta, & à se Tubingæ in agro Wirtenburgico audita. - - - - - - Philip Melanchthon, *a Man of great Candor, affirms, that, in several Places, instead of the Sunday Lectures, introduced into the Churches, from the Time of* Charles *the Great, in the VIIIth Century, by the Care of* Guarenfridus, *the Ethicks of* Aristotle *were publickly read to the People, and that he himself had been present at the reading of Them, at* Tubingen, *in the Country of* Wirtemburgh." If another Witness be demanded, and *Magirus* may be admitted, I shall produce him. "Tubingæ quondam Monachus, *says* he (115), pro concione Aristotelis librum Ethicorum explicavit, & vulgo dicebat, quemadmodum Johannes Baptista Baptista Christi præcursor fuit in Theologicalibus, ita Aristoteles fuit præcursor Christi in Physicalibus (116). - - - - - - *A certain Monk, formerly, at* Tubingen, *explained* Aristotle's *Book of* Ethics *publickly to the People; and was wont to say, that, as* John *the* Baptist *was the Forerunner of* CHRIST *in Divine Things, so* Aristotle *was in Natural Things.*"

[*X*] *It is no wonder, that the Peripatetic Philosophy found so many Protectors.*] If All, who have embraced the Philosophy of *Descartes*, had been endued with That wise Moderation, which makes a Man stop, when he has attained to a certain Point; if they could have discerned, what was fit to be divulged, and what kept secret (117), they would not have raised such a Clamour against the Sect in general. The Method of the ancient Philosophers was founded on good Reasons. They had Tenets for the Vulgar, and Tenets for Disciples initiated into their Mysteries. Be that as it will, the applying, or endeavouring to accommodate, *Descartes*'s Principles to the Doctrines of Religion, has been of great Prejudice to His Sect, and retards the Progress of it. This is an almost unavoidable Case. The ancient Fathers complained heavily of the *Aristotelian* Sect (118); and it is almost a general Complaint, that Philosophy does injury to Religion. But, on the other side, it is certain, that Divinity wounds Philosophy: They are two Faculties, which would seldom agree about their just Boundaries, did not the Secular, or Ecclesiastical, Powers, which are always in the Interest of the former, take the necessary Precautions, to reconcile them?

[*Y*] *The first Reformers clamoured loudly against the* Peripatetic *Philosophy.*] Here is another Passage of Father *Rapin* (119): "Nothing did more honour to This great Man's (120) Doctrine in the last Century, than the bitter Invectives of *Luther*, *Melanchthon*, *Bucer*, *Calvin*, *Postel*, *Paul Sarpi* (121), and all Those, who wrote against it, and against the Church of *Rome*. For Their Complaints against *Aristotle* are only because the solidity of his Method gives the Catholics great Advantage in discovering the Subtilty and Artifice of the false Reasonings, which Heresy makes use of to disguise Error, and destroy the Truth." In another Piece, This Author does not speak so much at random, and with so few Proofs. "St *Thomas*, *says* he (122), made use of *Aristotle*'s Method, with so great Success, in explaining the Doctrines of the Church of *Rome*, that *Bucer*, one of the greatest Enemies of our Church, used to say; *Suppress* Thomas's *Works, and I will destroy the Church of* Rome *. It was This Method, borrowed from *Aristotle*, which rendered the Doctrines of our Religion so formidable to all the Innovators of these last Centuries; who, being unable to resist it, endeavoured to cry it down, by declaiming "against

ARISTOTLE. 473

which, in some Respects, does most Honour to the Memory of *Aristotle*, is That, which some have reported; *viz.* that his Vexation at not being able to discover the Cause of the Flux and Reflux of the *Euripus* occasioned the Distemper, of which he died [Z]. Some say, that, being retired into the Island of *Eubœa*, to avoid a Process against him for Irreligion, he poisoned himself (*q*). But why should he quit *Athens*, to free himself from Persecution this way? *Hesychius* affirms, not only that Sentence of Death was pronounced against him, for an Hymn, which he made in Honour of his Father-in-Law, but also that he swallowed Aconite, in execution of The Sentence (*r*). If this were true, it would have been mentioned by more Authors. See the Remarks [G] and [Z].

(*q*) Eumelus, and Diog. Laërt. lib. 5. n. 6.

(*r*) Hesych. in vita Aristot.

The Number of Ancient and Modern Writers, who have exercised their Pens on *Aristotle*, either in Commenting on, or Translating, Him, is endless. A Catalogue of them is to be met with in some of the Editions of his Works (*s*), but not a compleat one. See also a Treatise of Father *Labbé*, intituled, *Aristotelis & Platonis Græcorum Interpretum typis hactenus editorum brevis conspectus*; —— *A short View of the Greek Interpreters of Aristotle and Plato hitherto published*; printed at Paris, in the Year 1657. in 4to. Mr *Teissier* names four Authors, who have composed the Life of *Aristotle*; *Ammonius*, *Guarini of Verona*, *John James Beurerus*, and *Leonard Aretin* (*t*). He forgot *Jerome Gemusæus*, Physician, and Professor of Philosophy, at *Basil*, Author of a Book, *de Vita Aristotelis, & ejus Operum Censura*. — The Life of Aristotle, and a Critique on his Works.

(*s*) In That of Geneva, 1605; and in That of Paris, 1629, procured by William du Val, and which is the best of all.

(*t*) Teissier, Catal. Aut. Bibliothec. pag. 367.

" against the Schoolmen, and chiefly against *Aristotle*, " whose Method they had formerly borrowed, and " which has been adopted in the Schools ever since " St *Thomas*'s Days. The *Anabaptists* were the " first, who began to render the use of Philosophy, " in general, suspected to Those of Their Sect, in " all the Northern Parts, where they had Authority; and to this end they alledged St *Paul*'s Words " to the *Colossians*, in order to interdict it in their " Schools †. *Luther* declared himself with so much " heat against *Aristotle*'s Philosophy, that, in some " Theses, which he maintained at *Heidelbourgh*, in the " Year 1518, he advanced, that they could not reason according to This *Pagan*'s Principles, without " forsaking the Maxims of the Wisdom of Jesus " CHRIST ‖; and took every opportunity, in his " Works, of inveighing against This Philosopher: In " which he was followed by *Zuinglius*, *Peter Martyr*, *Zanchius*, *Melancthon* (123), and all Those, " who have opposed the Doctrines of the Church of " *Rome*: Which made *Melchior Camo*, Bishop of the " *Canaries*, the most eloquent of all the Schoolmen, say, " That the *Lutherans* had a great Contempt for the " Philosophy, which was then taught in the Schools *. " *Calvin* never mentions *Aristotle*, but with all " That Sharpness and Bitterness of Stile, which " his Genius, naturally Violent and Slanderous, inspired him. As did also all Those, who " wrote, in the late Centuries, against the Church " of *Rome*."

† Ex Nicolao Blesslio, in Historia Davidis Georgii. Ex Horn. Hist. Philosoph.

‖ *Qui in Aristotele nude philosophari, prius oportet in Christo judicari.*

(123) *We shall shew in it's proper place, that Melancthon favoured Aristotle.*

* *Nullo apud Lutheranos Philosophiam esse in pretio.* Lib. 9. Locor. Theol. cap. 3.

[Z] *His Vexation, at not being able to discover the Cause of the Flux and Reflux of the* Euripus, *is said to have occasioned the Distemper, of which he died*] This Kind of Death would be a Proof of *Aristotle*'s insatiable Desire to dive into the Secrets of Nature. It would denote an extraordinary Ambition in him to teach Mankind the most hidden Mysteries. And would not this be dying in the Bed of Honour? Would it not be applying himself to his Function, with a firm Resolution to compass his Point, or die in the pursuit of it? I am of Opinion, that they, who have said, that *Aristotle*'s Genius had no other Bounds, than Those of Nature, or that he had been admitted to the most intimate Confidence, and the very Secretaryship of Nature (124), ought to admit of no other Tradition concerning his Death, than That we are speaking of. A Confident, who finds himself disgraced, and a Secret concealed from him in his old Age, ought not to survive such a Misfortune. To speak seriously; I do not believe, that *Aristotle* was Fool enough to die of such a Vexation. *Is it probable, that so considerate a Man, as He, should resolve* — *to give himself up to Vexation and Despair, only because he could not account for the Tide*; *He, who found his Understanding limited in respect to so many other things, of which he was ignorant, without being disquieted at it* (125)?

By the way, Writers often ascribe to *Justin Martyr*, and *Gregory Nazianzen*, what they never said concerning the Death of *Aristotle*. They have not said, that he threw himself into the *Euripus*. *Justin* says only, that *Shame and Vexation, at not being able to discover the extraordinary Effects of Nature, particularly the Ebbing and Flowing of the* Euripus, *broke his Heart.* Οὐδὲ τὴν τῶ Εὐρίπε φύσιν τὸ ὄν]ος ἐν Χαλκίδι γνῶναι δυνηθεὶς διὰ πολλὴν ἀδοξίαν καὶ αἰσχύνην λυπηθεὶς μεῖσεν τῶ βίω (126) *Cum neque Euripi Chalcidici naturam cognoscere posset, unde propter ingens probrum & pudorem in mærorem conjectus morte vitam commutavit.* St *Gregory* does not, in reality, say so much; he is satisfied with not contradicting *Julian*, who had alledged *Aristotle* as an Instance of a Passion for Knowledge, so great, that it was the Cause of his Death. Ἡ κεῖ τὴν Ὁμήρου φιλομαθείαν περὶ τὸ Ἀρκαδικὸν ζήτημα; καὶ τὴν Ἀριςοτέλους φιλοσοφίαν καὶ περὶ οὐδρίαν ἐπὶ ταῖς τῶ Εὐρίπε μεταβολαῖς, ὑφ᾿ ἧς τεθνήκασι (127). *You commend*, in *Homer*, *his eager Enquiry into the Arcadian Question*; *and*, in *Aristotle*, *his Philosophy, and continued Observation of the Flux and Reflux of the* Euripus; *both of whom died Martyrs to their Enquiries.* This is very remarkable, and I question, whether any one has hitherto observed it. Too many, not having a due respect for the Fathers of the Church, are apt to tax them with a blind Credulity. They accuse them particularly of defaming *Aristotle*, in regard to the *Euripus*. But there is reason to think, that *Julian* the Apostate confesses the Fact, which *Justin Martyr* speaks of; for it appears, by the Answer of St *Gregory*, that That Emperor had joined *Homer* with *Aristotle*, as two Instances of a Passion for Knowledge, which had occasioned Death. Now *Homer*, according to the Tradition concerning him, died of Grief, because he could not understand the Answer, which certain Fishermen gave him. We may, therefore, suppose, that *Julian* had adopted a like Tradition concerning *Aristotle*, and the *Euripus*. But, perhaps, he meant no more, than that *Aristotle* had studied the Ebbing and Flowing of the *Euripus*, with such Intenseness of Thought, and meditated so deeply on the Subject, that it destroyed his Health, and brought on him the Sickness, of which he died. This I am inclined to believe was really the Case. It does not appear, that *Eustathius* meant any thing more, where he speaks of the *Euripus* after this Manner. Ἐντάκις τὸ ὅλον νυχθήμερον μεταβάλλει ὁ περὶ Ἐὔβοιαν Εὐρίπος, περὶ ὃν φασὶ διαβρίξανα τὸν Ἀριςοτέλην καταδῦσαι τὸν βίον. *The* Eubœan Euripus *ebbs and flows seven times in a Natural Day*; *during his Enquiries into which,* Aristotle *died.* See the following Passage of Mr *Faber*, in which, after giving the Preachers a rub by the Way, he imputes to *Justin Martyr*, and still more to *Gregory Nazianzen*, what they never said. " Videlicet in Græ- " cia, quemadmodum hodieque fit, oratores sacri, si " tamen tanto nomine illa pulpitorum crepitacula, & " plebeculæ cymbala, cohonestari oporteat, vulgo di- " ditabant Aristotelem, cum illius septenæ in dies " singulos reciprocationis causam non potuisset cog- " noscere, ibi tum misellum sese in Euripum dedisse " præcipitem, & in maximam malam crucem abiisse. " Justinus

(126) Justin. Cohort ad Græcos, pag. 34.

(127) Greg. Naz. Orat. III. p. 79.

(124) Ἀριστοτέλης τῆς φύσεως γραμματεὺς ἦν, τὸν κάλαμον ἀποβρέχων εἰς νῶν. *Aristotle was Nature's Scribe, dipping his Pen in Sense.* Suidas. See, above, the Remark [H] at the end.

(125) Rapin's Comparison, &c. pag. 310.

AN APOLOGY for Justin Martyr, and Greg. Nazianzen.

ARISTOTLE. ARIUS.

"Justinus cognomento Martyr, & Gregorius Nazianzenus, qui primi, aut inter primos, hanc fabulam olim in scripta sua retulerunt, id vel studio Philosophiæ Christianæ (ita enim isti Græculi Christianismum vocare solent) fecere; dum videlicet insanientem veterum Græcorum sapientiam obscurandam & premendam existimarunt; vel fortasse etiam, (quidni enim veris locus sit?) priscæ historiæ ignoratione. Nam ex Eumolpi, Apollodori, Favorinique scriptis, quæ illa etiam tempestate superfuisse scimus, facile didicisse Boni Viri poterant, rem longe se secus habuisse, quam prodiderunt (128). —— *In Greece, as is done even at this Day, the Sacred Orators, if this Name be applicable to those noisy Haranguers of the Mob, commonly gave out, that* Aristotle, *when he could not discover the reason, why the* Euripus *ebbed and flowed seven times in a Day, took it so to Heart, that he threw himself headlong into That River.* Justin Martyr, *and* Gregory Nazianzen, *who first adopted this Fable in their Writings, did it for the sake of the Christian Philosophy, as They love to stile Christianity; being, forsooth, of Opinion, that the pretended Philosophy of the ancient Greeks ought to be eclipsed, and kept under; or, perhaps, through Ignorance of ancient History. For the good Men might easily have learned from* Eumolpus, Apollodorus, *and* Favorinus, *whose Writings we know were extant at that Time, that the Matter was quite otherwise, than as they have related it.*"

Gyraldus had fathered it upon them before, and made a pious Reflexion upon the whole. I. He says, that *Justin Martyr* affirms, that *Aristotle* died, because he could not discover the Cause of the Ebbing and Flowing of the *Euripus*. II. That *Procopius* has said the same, in the fourth Book of his History. III. That *Gregory Nazianzen*, having observed, that *Homer*'s not knowing how to resolve a Question proved fatal to him, immediately contemns *Aristotle*'s Philosophy, with regard to the Variation of the *Euripus*, which was the Cause of his Death. IV. That the *Greek* Commentator on That Father relates, that the Philosopher cast himself into That Arm of the Sea, with these Words, *Let the* Euripus *receive me, since I cannot comprehend the* Euripus. Ἐπειδὴ Ἀριστοτέλης οὐκ εἷλε τὸν Εὔριπον, Εὔριπος ἐχέτω τὸν Ἀριστοτέλην· *Postquam Aristoteles non prehendit Euripum, Euripus habeat Aristotelem* (129). V. That from hence we may conclude, that Fortune has been unpropitious to the impious, not only in the true, but also in the false Religions.

ARISTOTLE, a famous Architect in the XVth Century, was of *Bologne*, and of the Family of the *Alberti* (*a*). One of the most remarkable things related of him, is, that he could transport an entire Stone Tower from one place to another [*A*]. *John Basilides*, Great Duke of *Muscovy*, sent for him (*b*), and employed him in building of several Churches. There are Names, which are difficult to be supported. That of *Aristotle* is one of them. Yet we meet with above Thirty *Aristotles* [*B*].

[*A*] *He could transport an entire Stone Tower from one Place to another.*] *Jonsius* cites two Testimonies, *Beroaldus*, and *Matthew Palmerius* (1). The first expresses himself thus: "Non diu est, quod Aristoteles civis noster, mechanicus longe omnium præstantissimus, turrim ex sede sua movit, motamque arte mechanica in alium haud longe distinctum locum transportavit. Non est mendacio locus, cum adhuc supersint qui vidêre (2). —— *It is not long ago, that our Countryman* Aristotle, *the most excellent of Mechanics, moved a Tower from it's Place, and transported it, by Mechanic Art, to a Place not far off. The Truth of this is vouched by several, who were Eye-witnesses of it.*" These are the Words of *Palmerius*: "Aristoteles Bononiensis Architectus insignis habetur, qui lapideas turres integras illæsas subjectis fundamento lapidibus ad alium traduxit locum (3). —— Aristotle *of* Bologne *is famous for Architecture; who transported Stone Towers, entire and unhurt, from one place to another, placing Stones under the Foundation.*"

[*B*] *We meet with above thirty* Aristotles.] See the Dissertations of *Jonsius de Historia Peripatetica*; and you will find Twenty one *Aristotles* in the first of them. The Author believed, at that time, that he had summed them all up (4); but he found, that Knowledge increases with Years. For, when he published his Treatise *de Scriptoribus Historiæ Philosophiæ*, he had eleven *Aristotles* more to add to the former. He had likewise something more to say of some of the Twenty one. What has been related in the preceeding Remark, is one of these Additions.

ARIUS, the Head, and Founder, of ARIANISM, a Sect which denied the Eternal Divinity, and Consubstantiality, of the WORD, lived in the IVth Century. He was born in *Africa* near *Egypt*. *Eusebius*, Bishop of *Nicomedia*, much in Favour with *Constantia*, Sister of the Emperor *Constantine*, and Wife of *Licinius*, contributed greatly to the Propagation of this Heresy (*a*). He was a Man of a ready Wit, a true Court-Bishop, in short, perfectly well qualified to make the Fortune of a new Doctrine. He took *Arius* into his Protection; and brought him into favour with *Constantia*. For it has been always thought, that unless Women concern themselves in the Interests of a Sect, it can never make any considerable Progress. *Arius*'s Party visibly gained Ground: There were Bishops, who publickly embraced it: Disputes were frequent in the Cities; and sometimes from Words they came to Blows: It was absolutely necessary, that the Emperor should remedy This Disorder. This he did, by convening the Council of *Nice*, in which the Doctrine of *Arius* was condemned in 325. This Heresiarch was banished by the Emperor, who, likewise, ordered his Books to be burnt; and prohibited them under Pain of Death [*A*]. Some pretend, that *Arius*, having abjured his Heresy in the Presence of the Council,

[*A*] *The Emperor —— prohibited his Books under Pain of Death*] *Socrates* gives us the Letter, in which *Constantine* ordered, that All, who should find any Book composed by *Arius*, and not burn it, should be immediately punished with Death. Ἐκεῖνο μέντοι περασόμεθα, ὡς εἴ τις σύγγραμμα ὑπὸ Ἀρείου συνταγὲν φωραθεῖν κρύψας, καὶ μὴ εὐθὺς προσενεγκὼν πυρὶ καταναλώσῃ, τούτῳ θάνατος ἔσται ἡ ζημία· παραχρῆμα γὰρ ἁλοὺς ἐπὶ τῷδε κεφαλικὴν ὑποστήσεται τιμωρίαν (1). *Illud etiam denuntio, quod si quis Librum ab* Ario *compositum occultasse deprehensus fit, nec eum statim oblatum igne cumbusserit, mortis pœnam subibit.* I do not remember to have read any Author, who has remarked this strange and surprizing Extravagance of *Constantine*. He is satisfied with banishing this Arch-Heretic; he does not condemn those to Death, who adhered to *Arianism*; and yet threatens with Death Those, who should conceal any of *Arius*'s Works. Was there ever a wider Disproportion between Punishments and Crimes? May not a Man be very Orthodox, and yet curious enough to see what Heretics can say for themselves, and to preserve scarce Books, as those generally are, which are condemned to the Flames? And yet, if an Orthodox

ARIUS. 475

cil, avoided the Sentence of Banishment [B]; but others assert, that he suffered Exile [C], and that the Emperor did not recal him 'till Ten Years after [D] (b). They contend, that some had induced That Prince to believe, that *Arius* was Orthodox at the bottom. They add, that *Constantine*, being confirmed in this Opinion by the Profession of Faith, which *Arius* presented to him, wrote in his Favour to the Bishops, who were assembled at *Jerusalem*, for the Dedication of the Temple; That the Bishops, who still remained in That City, when *Arius* arrived with the Emperor's Letter, were for the most part concealed *Arians*; so that they did not fail to declare his Doctrine Orthodox, and to re-admit him to the Communion of the Church; That, to compleat the Triumph, they were of Opinion, that *Arius* ought to be re-established in *Alexandria*, where he had received the first Strokes of the Church's Anathema; And that, as St *Athanasius*, who was it's Patriarch, and *Arius*'s grand Adversary, was in Exile, they believed, that, in His Absence, it would be no difficult matter to re-instate *Arius* in the Communion of the Church of *Alexandria*; But that they were deceived; and that the People would never re-admit him; That *Constantine*, being informed of the Continuance of the Troubles, cited *Arius* to *Constantinople*, and prevailed upon him to subscribe the Formulary of *Nice*; That, afterwards, he sent him back to the Bishops, who were then assembled at *Constantinople*; I say, sent him back to them, to be received into the Communion of the Church, in That Imperial City; That He, who was then Bishop of *Constantinople*, would never give his Consent to it, though it was represented to him, that *Arius* had signed all that was required of him; That, notwithstanding, *Eusebius* procured, that the Sacrament of the Church should be administred to his Friend in the great Church of *Constantinople*; That he conducted him thither in a kind of Triumph, attended by a great Number of his own Party; but that, as they drew near the Great Square, *Arius*, pressed by a natural Necessity, retired in haste to a Public House of Office, and died immediately, all his Bowels gushing out, together with his Liver and Spleen, in the Year 336 (c). Some very Learned Men reject this Chronology [E]. *Arius*'s Sect did not die with him; it subsisted a long time, and with Credit, in several Parts of the World. It cannot sufficiently be wondered at, that a Minister, who passes for a Learned Man, should be ignorant of so notorious a Fact

---

Orthodox Christian had been found with a Book of *Arius* in his keeping, though upon such a Principle, he would have been immediately hanged; whilst one, who made open Profession of *Arianism*, was suffered to live. What more ridiculous? Not to say, that it is a Contradiction to let Heretics live, and yet forbid them, on pain of Death, to keep the Books of their Founder. To this may be added, that *Arius*, and some Bishops, his Adherents, being banished, their Conversation was still more dangerous, than the reading of their Books. How came it then, that They, who should converse with these Exiles, were not threatned with the Punishment of Death?

[B] *Some say, that Arius —— avoided the Sentence of Banishment.*] *Baronius* affirms, on the Credit of St *Jerom*, that *Arius* made a shew of Repentance; and that, having subscribed to the Council of *Nice*, he was admitted to the Peace of the Church by That Council, and was not banished. It cannot be denied, but that St *Jerom* says, that *Arius* made his Peace with the Council of *Nice* (2); but much greater Credit is due to the Letter of That Council, than to the Opinion of a single Person, who lived after That Time. In This Letter is set forth how *Arius*'s Opinions had been examined, and condemned; but as to what had been acted against his Person, and what became of him, they forbear to mention it, that they might not be thought to insult him in his Disgrace. Would they have spoken thus of One, in whose Recantation they had acquiesced? The learned *Henry Valesius*, reasoning on This Letter of the Council, commends their Moderation, because they did not anathematize *Arius* by Name, but Those in general, who taught such and such Heresies; and because that, instead of soliciting the Emperor to banish the Heretics, they expressed their Concern at their Banishment (3).

[C] *Others assert, that he suffered Exile.*] *Sozomen* is of this Number; for he affirms (4), that *Arius* was recalled, a little after the Separation of the Council. Ἄρειος ἐπὶ τὴν ἐξορίαν ἀπαγόμενος ἀνακλήθη (4). *Non multo post Synodum Nicænam Arius ab exilio revocatus est.* The Submission of the two Bishops, who were deprived of their Churches, is a Proof of *Arius*'s Banishment. I mean *Eusebius*, and *Theognis*. *Philostorgius* informs us, that these two Prelates were banished by *Constantine*, three Months after the breaking up of the Council (5); and affirms, that they obtained their Recal, three Years after. Now they obtained it by submitting to the Decisions of the Council in a Writing, which they sent to the Bishops; wherein they took notice, that He, who was the Principal in these Disputes, had been recalled from his Banishment; and that it would be absurd to pretend, that, after His Reconciliation, They could not make their own Innocence appear (6). Thus we have two Facts cleared up; one, that *Arius* was banished; the other, that he made his Peace with the Bishops, and that he obtained his Recal, before *Eusebius* and *Theognis* procured theirs; which fell out, according to *Philostorgius*, in 328; whose Opinion agrees very well with the History of those Times. It is false, then, that *Arius* was not recalled before the Year 335.

[D] *That the Emperor did not recal him 'till ten Years after.*] Father *Maimbourg* has followed This false Chronology. We have already proved Him to have been in an Error.

[E] *He died in the Year 336 —— very learned Men reject this Chronology.*] *Valesius* proves, that *Arius* was not living at the time of the Council of *Jerusalem*, which received Letters from *Constantine*, concerning the Reconciliation of some principal Members of *Arianism*. "Arius Hæresiarches diu ante Synodum Hierosolymitanam e vita excesserat; ut certissimis argumentis probavi in libro secundo Observationum Ecclesiasticarum, Capite II (7). — Arius *the Hæresiarch died long before the Council of Jerusalem, as I have proved by invincible Arguments in* the second Book *of my Ecclesiastical Observations. Ch.* II. It was not, therefore, *Arius*, the Arch-Heretic, who was recommended to This Council by *Constantine*, and who found the Bishops, assembled at *Jerusalem*, so favourable to him. In the mean time, *Socrates* says expressly, that the Council, which was transferred from *Tyre* to *Jerusalem*, for the Dedication of the Temple, received *Arius* and his Adherents into the Communion of the Church, by virtue of Letters from *Constantine*, which testified, that He was persuaded of the Orthodoxy of *Arius*, and *Euzoius*. Ἄρειον μὲν καὶ τὰς περὶ αὐτὸν ἐξίζεσθαι τοῖς βασιλικοῖς γράμμασι πειθαρχεῖν λέγοντες, δι' ὧν ἐδηλώκει αὐτοῖς πεπεῖσθαι περὶ τῆς πίστεως Ἀρείου καὶ Εὐζωΐου (8). *Arium quidem una cum sociis in communionem recipiunt, obtemperare se dicentes Imperatoris literis, quibus certiores ipsos fecerat fidem*

ARIUS.

a Fact [F]. He was ignorant likewise of another no less evident; for he pretends, that no Penal Laws were enacted against This Sect [G]. Another Thing, which he has advanced, has not a little perplexed him; for great Advantage has been made of what

se Arii & Euzoii penitus perspectam haberet. Constantine had sent the Confession of Faith, which *Arius* and *Euzoius* had presented to him (9), to the Bishops, assembled at *Jerusalem*; and St *Athanasius* plainly says, that the Synod of *Jerusalem* received *Arius* and his Followers into it's Communion. Γράφοντες δεῖν δέχθηναι Ἄρειον καὶ τὲς σὺν αὐτῷ (10). *Scribentes suscipiendos esse Arium & Socios. Valesius* solves the Difficulty, by saying there were two *Arius*'s; one the Arch-Heretic; the other his Follower; they had both been excommunicated by *Alexander*, Bishop of *Alexandria*. He, who presented a Confession of Faith, with *Euzoius*, to *Constantine*, and was reconciled by the Council of *Jerusalem*, was not the Arch-Heretic, but the Other *Arius*. *Valesius* proves this, not only by Reasons, which shew, that the Arch-Heretic was dead long before the Year 335, but also by the Petition of *Eusebius*, and *Theognis*. These two Bishops implored Pardon, protesting their Innocence, in the Year 328, and alledged, that the Head and Author of these Controversies was reconciled and restored. This could not be said of That *Arius*, who was re-united to the Church, by the Synod of *Jerusalem*; for the Petition, or Confession of Faith, which He, and *Euzoius*, presented to *Constantine*, a little before That Synod, that is about the Year 335, testifies, that they were then in Exile and excommunicated. The sudden Death of *Arius*, in which the Orthodox have found so many Mysteries, happened after the Council of *Jerusalem*. It follows, then, that The *Arius*, who died in this manner, was not the Heresiarch, and that they have transferred to one Point of Time what happened at another Conjuncture. It is strange there should be so little Order, and Exactness, in Ecclesiastical History; one cannot ascertain *Arius*'s Exile, the Duration of it, and such like Particulars, but by arguing from different Facts, some attested by This, others by That Author. One good Historian might suffice to give the Thread of the principal Events, though all the rest were lost.

[F] *Arius's Sect did not die with him*; *it subsisted a long time*, —— *a Minister, who passed for a learned Man, was ignorant of so notorious a Fact*.] See what he says: " I am persuaded, that *Arianism* never " made a great Party in the World. It is true, se- " veral Bishops made profession of it; but this He- " resy did not spread among the People (11)." What he says elsewhere, is much stronger; for he asserts, that *Arianism* only passed through the Church like a Torrent. It cannot be pleaded, in his excuse, that This is one of those Errors, which escape by Surprize, and through want of Attention; for he remarks this Fact as fundamental and essential to his System. His Opinion, on the one side, is, that Heresies against the Mystery of the Trinity are fundamental and damnable; and, on the other, that GOD has never suffered such kind of Heresies to continue long, or make any considerable Figure in the World. " GOD, says he (12), cannot permit " large Christian Societies to fall into damnable Er- " rors, and persist A LONG TIME in them; at " least, to judge by Experience, we cannot believe " it possible, since such a thing never yet happened." Mr *Nicolle* was the first, who read him a Lecture on the Words of the Hundred and forty ninth Page. This he did without Bitterness, or Insult, in these Terms: " What Mr *Jurieu* says, is very true, if un- " derstood of the great Blaze of *Arianism*, which " passed, indeed, like a Flash of Lightning: But " it is less exact, when applied to the Times, which " succeeded. Though the Church had recovered " it's former Splendor in most Parts of the World, " yet there were several considerable Bodies, as the " *Vandals* in *Africa*, the *Goths* in *Asia*, in *Italy*, in " part of *France*, and in *Spain*, who openly professed " *Arianism*, and where the Controversy was suf- " ficiently enough cleared, for the People to take part " in it (13)." Mr *Pellisson* came next to the Charge, in this manner. " Those *Arians* gave him some " Trouble, as well as the *Phanatics* and *Socinians* of " these Times, and Those, whom he calls *Photini-*

" *ans* of *Poland*, and *Transylvania*. Some Remains " of Modesty hindered him from associating himself " with them, in one and the same Church. He " found the means to get rid of them, without enter- " ing upon This Discussion, or calling in Master " Workmen, to know whether the Foundation was " ruined wholly, or but in part. He does not pre- " tend, he says, to comprehend, in This one exten- " sive Church, Any but Those Societies, which form " a visible Body. The *Arians*, it seems, never be- " came a Body, at least a *Great* Body, (and this a- " gainst the Faith of all History, which every where " mentions their Communion, their Assemblies, their " Βασιλικαι, or Churches, as wholly distinct from " Those of the Orthodox). The *Phanatics*, the " *Socinians*, the *Photinians* of these Times, have not, " as yet, any regular Assemblies, or Polity, or Union " with each other. They are, therefore, of no Ac- " count. But if, for the Punishment of our Sins, " and unhappy Divisions, GOD should permit these " common Enemies to multiply, and to regulate " and form themselves into a Body, they are, then, " agreeably to his own Principles, upon the same " Foot with others; and there will be no Difficulty " in supposing, that a Man may be saved among " them (14)." The Author, in reply to Mr *Nicolle*, confesses, " That the *Arians* formed a GREAT Body, " but maintains, that they continued but a very short " Time, *and that* GOD *suffered their Communion* " *to perish, because it did not preserve the Funda-* " *mental Truths* (15)." A third Censor has arisen, who maintains, like the two former, that *Arianism* was not only of great Extent, but also of conside- rable Duration, and that it was an Heresy, which spread among the People. See the Book, entituled, *Janua Cælorum reserata* (16). The Author makes it appear (17), that *Arianism* subsisted above Three hundred Years in splendor; that it was, for almost two Ages, the established Religion in *Spain*; that it was on the Throne in the East, and West, and that it reigned in *Italy*, *France*, *Pannonia*, and *Africa*. Never was Author driven from one vexatious Conse- quence to another more vexatious, as was the Au- thor of the System, by the pretended *Carus Lare- bonius* (18). He plainly shews him, that, if GOD never suffered *great Christian Societies to run into damn- able Errors, and continue in them long*, and if GOD destroyed Arianism, *because it did not preserve the Fundamental Truths*; it necessarily follows, I. That the Errors of the Church of *Rome* are not damnable. II. That *Mahometanism* has preserved the Funda- mental Truths. The Author of the System pretends, that *Mahometanism* is not a Sect, which arose from Christianity, and therefore that he has nothing to do with it's Extent or Continuance. These are Ob- jections, which the utmost Chicanery can never an- swer. The Synods cannot pretend Ignorance, and yet they have never censured this Doctrine of the System; though it fully justifies the Church of *Rome*, and consequently convicts the Reformed of being Schismatics.

[G] *He pretends, that no Penal Laws were enacted against this Sect*.] Let us cite a fine Passage of the *Preservative against a Change of Religion*. The Mi- nister, of whom I speak, published this Book, whilst he was in *France* (19), and opposed it to the Catho- lic Exposition of the Bishop of *Condom*. See what he says at the eleventh Page (20). " The Church has " suffered Persecutions, but never exercised any " She has had the upper Hand of *Paganism*, as *Pa-* " *ganism* has had of her; but never returned her like " for like. She did not employ the Authority of " the *Constantines*, and the *Theodosius*'s, to embrue " the Temples of the false Gods with the Blood of " their Worshippers, as the *Pagans* did the Swords " of their *Nero*'s, *Maximin*'s, *Decii*, and *Dioclesian*'s, " to drench the Earth with the Blood of Christians. " One must be very little versed in the History of the " Church, to be ignorant, that, in all the Contests " she had with the *Arians*, *Eutychians*, and other " Heretics, she made use only of Exhortations, Au- " thors, Councils, and such like Arms." The Au-

what he says concerning the Faith of the Fathers, who preceeded the Rise of *Arianism* [H]. This Sect has been, by turns, Persecuting, and Persecuted [I], and fell at last by the Way of Human Authority [K]. I scarce meet with any Author, who does not esteem it a Crime in *Arius*, that he put his Opinions into Verse, to be sung by his Disciples. Both the Matter, and the Form, of the Poem, which he intituled *Thalia*

(21) Pag. 354, of the Supplement.

thor of the *Philosophical Commentary* had reason to wonder, that a Professor of Divinity, who passed in *France* for a Man well versed in Ecclesiastical History, should betray such Ignorance as this (21). But he was still more astonished, that, after Father *Thomassin* had set this Matter in the clearest Light, another *French* Writer, addressing himself to the Bishop of *Meaux*, should say, " One thing I must tell you, " my Lord, That, throughout ancient and modern " History, all Acts of Violence, exercised by Princes " on the Score of Religion, have ever been looked " upon as Spectacles of Horror, and that the Names " of such Princes are never mentioned, even to " this Day, without Execration." I add here the Reflexion of the Commentator. " What! Are the " *Constantine*'s, the *Theodosius*'s, the *Honorius*'s, the " *Marcian*'s, the *Justinian*'s, who put in Execution " so many Penal Laws against Sectaries, who con- " demned to Death those, who persevered in Pagan " Idolatry, in *Manicheism*, &c. and even those, who " read, or were in possession of, the Books of He- " reticks; are These, I say, Names, which are never " mentioned, at this Day, without Execration? How

(22) Ibid. p. 355.

" will he prove this (22)?" The Divine, who published the *Preservative*, has, it seems, studied Ecclesiastical Antiquity better, since his Transplantation into *Holland*. He has there learned to refute Toleration, by the Authority of the *Constantines*, the *Theodosius*'s, and the *Charlemagnes*. " *Paganism*, says

(23) Droits de deux Souverains, pag. 280.

" he (23), would have been still in being, and three " parts of *Europe* would still have been *Pagan*, if " *Constantine*, and his Successors, had not made use " of their Authority to abolish it." In *France* he took it very ill, that the Secular Power should be made use of: and in *Holland* he takes it very ill, that it should not be imployed. And now, after this, who dares pretend, that, by changing of Climate, one does not change Opinion?

(24) Horat. Epist. 11, lib. 1, v. 27.

Cœlum, non animum, mutant, qui trans mare currunt (24).

They, that beyond-sea go, shall sadly find,
They change their Climate only, not their Mind.
CREECH.

There is a local Faith, and a temporary Faith, which have not yet been mentioned in the Division of the *Genus* into it's *Species*. See the Remark [H], of the Article St AUGUSTIN.

[H] *Great Advantage has been made of what he says concerning the Faith of the Fathers, who preceeded the Rise of Arianism.*] He maintained, in his Pastoral Letters, that Those Fathers did not believe an Equality of Persons in the Trinity; and that they admitted a Temporal Generation of the WORD, which had conferred on the *Second Person* his entire and perfect Existence. It is plain, that this Opinion differs in nothing from *Arianism*; and that it overthrows the Eternal Trinity of Persons. The Bishop of *Meaux* pressed Mr *Jurieu* so home upon this Point

(25) In his Avertissemens.

(25), that he obliged him to break the Silence, to which he had reduced him on some other Points: But his Reply did him more harm, than his Silence could have done; he was forced to contradict himself, and retract several Things, and still got nothing by it. The Bishop returned to the Charge; drove his Adversary before him, and obliged him to enter the Lists no more: So that, among the most distinguishing Elogies, which were bestowed on this Prelate, it was not forgot, that he had stopped the

(26) See the Speech, made by Mr Bruyere, when he was admitted a Member of the French Academy.

Mouth of the most daring Critic of the Age (26). Mr *Jurieu* was scarce got out of the Bishop's Hands, when he fell into those of *Carus Larebonius*, who shewed him, that if the Fathers of the three first Centuries held That Opinion of the Trinity, and the Generation of the WORD, which he imputes to them, it must necessarily follow, that neither the Heresy of the *Arians*, nor That of the *Socinians*, were Damn-

able, or Fundamental (27). It must be carefully remarked, that the Victories, gained over this Minister, concern only his particular Opinions, and in no wise the Doctrine of his Church; of which *The History of the Works of the Learned* (28) advertised the Public. This is no Foreign Matter; it belongs of right to a *Critical Dictionary*; for it is false in Fact, that the Heresy of *Arius* was implicitly taught by the Fathers of the three first Centuries. It is something strange, that Mr *Jurieu*, having considered *Arianism* in so many Lights, should always view it in the wrong. It would be more difficult to find a Fencer, who could never hit a Bull. *Taurum toties non ferire difficile est* (29). We must not omit, that, as to the Matter of Fact, in relation to the Penal Laws of *Constantine*, and the Continuance and Extent of *Arianism*, the Authors, I have already cited, have shewn him his Error very civilly, and without having recourse to the Insults, and hard Language he himself would have made use of, in the like Case, against an Adversary.

(27) See the Janus Celorum referens, pag. 119, &c.

(28) For the Month of May, 1692, Article 9, pag. 393, &c.

(29) See Trebellius Pollio, in the Life of Gallienus.

[I] *This Sect has been, by turns, persecuting, and persecuted.*] It cannot be denied, that the Orthodox were the Aggressors; for we have seen, that *Constantine* banished the Ringleaders of *Arianism*, and threatened those with Death, who should not burn all the Writings of That Arch-Heretic: but it is certain, that *Constantius*, his Son, and *Valens*, who raised *Arianism* to the Throne, treated the Orthodox with more Rigor, than *Constantine* had done the *Arians*. Upon all other Occasions, the latter seem to have been of a more tolerating Spirit, than the former: and it is a Thesis, which the Philosophical Commentator has undertaken to prove, in the Supplement to his Work (30). Among other Reasons, he alledges this; that, at the time, when *Recaredus* extirpated *Arianism* in *Spain*, the Catholic Bishops were much more numerous than the *Arian*, though the *Arian* had been the *predominant* Religion, for near Two hundred Years before: A strong Presumption, that the Catholics were but little molested.

(30) The 30th and 31st Chapters.

[K] *And fell, at last, by the way of human Authority.*] *Mariana* passes lightly over the Rigors, which *Recaredus* must needs have exercised, and excuses them from hence, that the Case required Severity, and that the People were not displeased with it. " Contigit " autem Recaredo, quod haud scio an regum ulli, " ut religione permutanda, quod propemodum ne- " cesse erat, motus existerent, sed neque diuturni " admodum neque graves; & severitas animadver- " sionis non modo invidiosa non esset, quia necessa- " rio suscipiebatur, sed etiam popularis, &, cum bo- " nis omnibus, tum infimo cuique gratissima (31).—— " *It happened to Recaredus, as to scarce any other* " *King, that, though the Change of Religion, in his* " *Dominions, which was almost necessary, was at-* " *tended with some Disturbances, yet were they nei-* " *ther of long Continuance, nor of ill Consequence;* " *and so far was the Severity, which he exercised* " *upon this Occasion, from being odious, that it was* " *popular, and pleasing, not only to good Men, but to* " *the meanest of the People.*" The Author, beforementioned, observes, that, if the Complaints, which the *Arians* made, had been preserved to us, it is probable we should find in them a very long Detail of Acts of Violence; and that, after all, it was purely by Accident, that *Arianism* was ruined, without Persecution: For, as *Mariana* says, since Punishments were not made use of, then, with any Necessity required, we must conclude; I. That, if they were not often put in practice, it was because the *Arians* were not obstinate. II. That, had the Difficulties been ever so great, yet they would have been reduced, either by fair, or foul Means, to a Compliance (32). By the way, This Author (33) is guilty of a very gross Contradiction, into which Writers, who undertake to speak of *Conversions*, are apt to fall. They lay it down, as a general Maxim, that Obstinacy is the Character of Heresy; and yet, to cover the Violence of

(31) Mariana, lib. V, cap. 14. Consult the Supplement to the Philosophical Commentary, pag. 373.

(32) Supplement to the Philosophical Commentary, p. 375, 376.

(33) Ibid. pag. 277.

ARIUS. ARMINIUS.

Thalia, have met with Censure [L]. There might perhaps be some Prepossession in This. A Modern Author, who favoured This Heretic's Opinions, has wrote some Treatises to shew, that the Fathers of the three first Centuries held the same Opinions [M]. He was at no great trouble to compile Passages; for he found them ready collected to his Hand in the *Dogmata Theologica* of Father *Petavius*. Two *English* (d), and one *French* Divine (e), have wrote an Apology for the Ancient Fathers against Him.

(d) *Gardiner, and Bull.*

(e) *Mr le Moine, Professor at Leyden.*

of the Converters, they tell us, that the Conversions were made with ease; and from this Facility draw a Proof of the Heresy of those converted. For the true Church, say they, is not so easily deserted; the Resistance, which the *Arians* made to King *Recaredus*, was so weak, and short, that this alone is enough to shew, that they contended for Falshood, and not for Truth, which alone is able to govern reasonable Minds, and inspire them with Fortitude (34).

(34) *Thomassin, de l'l'Unité de l'Eglise, pag. 449.*

[L] *Both the Matter, and the Form, of the Poem, which he intituled* Thalia, *have met with Censure.*] There has been great Reason to condemn Heresies; to pity Those, who profess them in good earnest, and to abominate those, who teach them, without believing them; for such Teachers are Monsters of Ambition, and Wickedness: but I cannot conceive, why it should be imputed as a Crime peculiar to heretical Teachers, that they make use of Methods suited to the Capacities of the Ignorant, in instructing them according to the false Lights of their Consciences. "After *Arius* had forsaken the Church, he formed " a Design of composing several Songs for Seamen, " Travellers, and Those, who work at the Mill; he had " also set such of them to Tunes, as he thought were " proper to affect his Followers, according to their " different Dispositions, endeavouring, by the Me- " lody of These Songs, to infuse his Impiety into the " most ignorant and stupid among the People ―― " But his *Thalia* was much more celebrated, than his " other Works. He borrowed the Title, and Mo- " del, of it from an ancient Poet, called *Sotades*. ― " This Burlesque Poet affected so wanton a Style in " his Song, and the Numbers of it were so effemi- " nate, that the *Pagans* themselves treated him with " the utmost Contempt; nor is this at all aggravated " in the words of St *Athanasius*; since the most un- " chaste Poets, and They, who write most licentiously, " blush at the Impurity of the Songs of this Infa- " mous Author. It was in imitation of this Poet, " that *Arius* gave his Work the Name of THALIA; " which properly signifies a Banquet, and Assembly " of young People, or a Song made to be sung in " Those kind of Feasts (35)." Afterwards Mr *Hermant* cites a very long Passage of St *Athanasius*, in which *Arius* is called *an I know not what* Sotades; *ridiculous even to the* Pagans *themselves* ― and an Heretic, *who had no emulation for any thing, but the ridiculous Discourses of* Sotades (36). In the same Place we meet with the beginning of the *Thalia*, and another Fragment, which contains the Heresy of *Arius* concerning JESUS CHRIST. One cannot but condemn the ridiculous and insufferable Pride, which appears in the *Exordium* of the *Thalia*; but, once more, let us condemn *Arius* for being an Heretic, and not, upon this Supposition, for having put a Formulary of his Belief into Verse; otherwise we must allow Heretics and Infidels to condemn the Orthodox, not only for professing the true Gospel, but likewise for singing, besides the Psalms of *David*, several Hymns and Canticles, whose Verses and Airs may chance to resemble the most prophane and wanton Songs of an Opera. To speak in general, it is fitter, that every one, be his

(35) *Hermant's Life of St Athanasius, lib. I, cap. 13, pag. 61.*

(36) *Ex Orat. II, contra Arianos.*

WHETHER we are to condemn Spiritual Hymns and Songs, which are set to the same Airs with prophane Ballads.

(a) *This Word in Dutch signifies Old Water, and from hence the Name of Arminius's Country is the Titles of his Books is Veteraquina.*

Religion what it will, should sing Pious, than wanton and satirical, Songs. The Sailor, and the Miller, under the Misfortune of being *Arians*, did better to sing their Catechism, than their Amours. To say, that the *Pagans* themselves laughed at *Arius*'s Songs, is alledging a very weak Reason; for I believe the *Gentiles* made no great difference between the *Arians*, and the *Orthodox*, but hated them both alike; the *Arians* were no more favourable to *Pagan* Idolatry, than the Orthodox. I cannot tell whether Mr *Hermant* had Reason to say, *that the* Pagans *themselves treated* Arius *with the utmost Contempt as a ridiculous Fellow*. For the words, which he cites a little after, shew plainly, that it was *Sotades*, and not *Arius*, whom St *Athanasius* meant, when he said, that he was ridiculous to the *Pagans* themselves. I say it, and repeat it; it is allowable to compose pious Verses in the same Metre, and of the same Measure, with the Songs of an Opera; consequently one might compose Hymns to the *Sotadic* Measure. The Evil does not lie in this Conformity; it is rather in the Handle, which is given to Scoffers to laugh at Psalmody. I set aside the Subject of the Poetry. And, to let the Protestants, in particular, see what Judgment they ought to make of the Invectives against the *Thalia* of *Arius*, they must be informed of what Father *Maimbourg* published concerning the Psalms, translated into Verse by *Clement Marot*. He speaks as ill of them, as of the *Thalia* of *Arius*. What he says of the *Thalia*, is to be found in the Eighty first Page of the first Tome of his History of *Arianism* (37). What he says of the Psalms, in his History of *Calvinism* (38), is This: "These " were the Psalms, which they sung at That time; " to which *Beza* afterwards added the rest of the " Psalter; and which were set to Tunes of a soft and " effeminate Air, which have nothing in them of the " Devotion and Majesty of the Music of the Catholic " Church." We cannot deny what *Varillas* says (39), that the Airs were taken from the best Songs of the Times. See Jeremiah de Pours, *in his second Book of Divine Melody*, pag. 577. It is not without Reason, that I alledged the Songs of an Opera, as my Example: I would insinuate, that we should carefully avoid imitating the Airs of a Ballad in Spiritual Songs; otherwise Religion is too much exposed to Contempt and Laughter; as appears by the Book, which the Author of the *Court Bishop* so much ridicules (40). It is a Collection of Spiritual Songs, composed by a Jesuit, and by Father *Martial de Brive*, a Cordelier, and set to the most burlesque Ballad-Tunes; I fancy the *Thalia* of *Arius* might vie with the Impertinence of This Collection, printed with the Approbation of two Doctors of Divinity.

(37) *Tom. I. pag. 81, Edit. of Holl.*

(38) *Pag. 99.*

(39) *Varillas, History of Heresy, Book XXI, pag. 49. ad Ann. 1559.*

(40) *See his third Dialogue, pag. 86, &c. Edit. of Holl.*

[M] *A Modern Author* ―― *wrote some Works, to prove, that the Fathers of the three first Centuries held the same Opinions.*] His Name was *Sandius*. What he wrote on this Subject is entituled *Nucleus Historiæ Ecclesiasticæ*, in 1668, in 8vo. The same Book was much enlarged in the Year 1676, in 4to. *Appendix addendorum, confirmandorum, & emendandorum, ad Nucleum Historiæ Ecclesiasticæ, cum responsionibus ad Gardinerum*, in 1678, in 4to.

ARMINIUS (JAMES) Professor of Divinity at *Leyden*, was born at *Oudewater* (a) in *Holland*, in the Year 1560 [A]. His Father died during his Infancy; and he was indebted for his first Instructions to a good Priest, who had relished the Opinions of the Reformed, and who, to avoid being obliged to say Mass, changed his Abode often. He followed his Studies at *Utrecht*, when Death bereft him of his

[A] *He was born in the Year* 1560.] *Bertius* amuses himself with giving the Year of *Arminius*'s Birth two Characters, which no doubt he thought worthy of Reflexion. He observes, that *Philip Melancthon* died in That Year, and that the *Conference of Poissy* was held in the same Year, in which the Protestant Deputies pleaded the Cause of two Thousand one Hundred and Ninety Churches, who humbly sued to the King for Liberty of Conscience (1). To say nothing of his Calculation, which, perhaps, is not the most exact; It is mistaken as to the Year; the *Conference of Poissy* began in the Month of *September* 1561. Begin the Year either at *Easter*, or on the first of *January*, you will never justify *Bertius*.

(1) *Bertius, in Orat. Funebr. Jacobi Arminii.*

[B] *He*

his Patron. This Loss would have plunged him into great difficulties, if he had not fortunately met with assistance from his Countryman, *Rodolphus Snellius*, who brought him with him to *Marpurgh*, in 1575. Scarce was he arrived there, when he received the News that *Oudewater* was pillaged by the *Spaniards*. This News threw him into a deep Melancholy; nor could he forbear returning into *Holland*, to be himself a Witness of the State of things there; but, finding, that his Mother, Sister, Brothers, Relations, and almost all the Inhabitants of *Oudewater*, had been put to the Sword, he returned to *Marpurgh*, travelling all the way on Foot. Having heard, that an University was founded at *Leyden*, he soon returned to *Holland*, and studied in this new Academy with so great Application and Success, that he acquired a very particular Esteem. In 1582, he was sent to *Geneva*, at the Expence of the Magistrates of *Amsterdam*, to perfect his Studies in the Colleges there, where he chiefly followed the Lectures of *Theodore Beza*, who at that time expounded the Epistle to the *Romans*. He had the misfortune to displease some of the Principal Members of the Academy, by publickly maintaining the Philosophy of *Ramus*; and That with much heat; and even teaching it in private; for this he was obliged to retire, and went to *Basil*, where he was received with Applause. He read public Lectures there [B], and acquired such Credit, that the Faculty of Divinity would have given him the Degree of Doctor without any Expence. He modestly declined the Offer, and returned to *Geneva*, where, finding the Adversaries of the *Ramists* somewhat cooled, he moderated his own heat likewise. He had a great desire to see *Italy*, and particularly that he might hear the Philosophical Lectures of the famous *James Zabarella*, at *Padua*. He satisfied This Curiosity, and passed six or seven Months in his Travels; after which he returned to *Geneva*, and from thence to *Amsterdam*, where he found he had been sufficiently censured in relation to his Journey into *Italy* [C], which had a little cooled the Affection of the Magistrates, his Patrons

[B] *He read public Lectures at Basil.*] "The Professor *James Grynæus* came often to them, and gave him great Commendations. Nor did he scruple, in maintaining a Thesis, to refer it to Him to answer Those Objections, which seemed the strongest; and was wont upon those Occasions to say, *Let my Hollander answer for me*. *Salent Basileæ feriis vindemialibus doctiores studiosi publicè in- terdum in Academia exercitii gratiâ aliquid extra or- dinem ducere. Eam laborem Arminius noster haud in- vitus suscepit, laudatus id à reverendo viro D. Jacobo Grynæo, qui etiam lectiones ipsius præsentia sua aliquoties cohonestavit: idem quoque in disputationi- bus publicis, si quid gravius proponeretur, aut dignus vindice nodus occurreret, non est veritus, honoris causâ Arminium nostrum media in studiosorum turba sedentem citare, & (ut Grynæi candorem agnoscas) dicere, Res- pondeat pro me Hollandus meus* (2). Note, that he observed in him a Spirit too much inclined to refine upon things, and that he gave him very good Advice thereupon. *Bertius* is not the Author, who informs me of this, but *Philip Pareus*. He relates, that *Theodore Beza* advised one of his Friends to restrain the Subtilty of his Genius, as what Satan had often taken advantage of to delude great Persons. "Do not ingage yourself, continued *Beza*, in vain Subtilties; and, if sometimes certain new Thoughts arise in your Mind, approve them not, without first examining them to the bottom; how pleasing soever they may be at the first View. *Calvin* gave me this Advice; I have followed it; and have found the benefit of it." *Sicut magnopere in hortor, ut Dei dona in te collata omni studio excolas: ita cum te ἀγχινοία, non vulgari donatum esse videam, quâ sæpe ad maximas decipiendas vires non territo conatu Satanas est abusus, velim te diligenter cavere, ut nullis inanibus argutiis te ipsum irreties, & quoties nova quædam tibi in mentem veniunt, diligenter illa, quantum- libet in initio tibi illa arriserunt, excutere, priusquam approbes. In omnibus denique istis prompto & alacri ingenio tibi concesso modereris. Ego quidem certè per Dei gratiam non prorsus hebes de hoc ipso à magno illo viro beatæ memoriæ JOHANNE CALVINO ad- monitus ita facere statim ab initio studui, cum ad sacra studia me totum converterem. Neque me hujus consilii unquam pœnituit: nec, ut spero, pœnitebit* (3). *Philip Pareus* had the Original of This Letter of *Theodore Beza*; and he adds, that "*JAMES GRYNÆUS* had given the same Advice to *ARMINIUS*, the Founder of the New *Pelagianism*, at the time when he studied Divinity at *Basil*; as *Grynæus* himself had informed him." *In quam sententiam clarissi- mum & sequacissimum JACOBUM ARMINIUM, novi Pelagianismi instauratorem in Belgio, cum juvenis*

operam daret S. Theologiæ in Academia Basiliensi, gra- viter quoque admonitum fuisse à venerando sene D. JA- COBO GRYNÆO, cujus memoria sit in benedic- tionibus! Ipsemet mihi, quando ad pedes ejus in Rauricâ discentium Synagogâ sederem, narravit (4). If any one accuses me of inserting these Passages at length, only as Helps to swell out a large Book, he will betray a want of Judgment; for they are very fit to suggest useful Reflexions to several Persons, and very necessary for some Readers. Remember *St Paul's* Maxim, *Knowledge puffeth up* (5); but take notice, that there is another Talent which *puffs up* yet more. A Man of an unbounded Memory, and Reading, applaudes himself on his Knowledge, and grows proud; but he prides himself, and presumes much more, when he fancies he has invented a new Method of explaining, or treating, Matters. We do not esteem ourselves so much Proprietors of That Knowledge, we have drawn from Books, as we do of an Explanation, or Doctrine, of which we are the Inventors. It is for such Inventions that we feel all the Force of Paternal Love and Tenderness. It is here we find the most bewitching Charms; it is This, which blinds us; it is This, which makes us lose Ground. This is a Rock, of which young Persons of a subtle Wit cannot be too frequently warned.

[C] *He had been sufficiently censured in relation to his Journey into Italy.*] Among the several Epidemical Distempers of the Human Mind, I know of none more blameable, and productive of bad Effects, than the Practice of giving the Reins to Suspicion. It is a very slippery Road. We are soon got a great Way from the Place we set out from. We easily pass from one Suspicion to another; we seldom stop at *Possibility*; we run forward to *Probability*, and to the greatest *Probability*; and, presently after, That which passed only for Probable, is reported as certain and incontestable: and in a little time, This pretended Certainty is spread over a whole Town. Great Cities are more subject to This Disorder, than others. It was reported, in *Amsterdam*, that "*Arminius* had kissed the Pope's Toe, whom he had seen only in a Croud; that he had contracted an Intimacy with Jesuits, whom he had never heard of; that he had made himself known to *Bellarmine*, whom he had never seen; and that he had abjured the Reformed Religion, for which he was prepared to die." These Reports were all false; and yet They made an Impression on the Minds of the Magistrates, who supported This young Man. Let us hear the Author of his Funeral Oration. "*Inter damna (itineris Italici pœnebat)* quod in amplissimi Senatus Amsterdamensis offensiunculam ob id factum tunc temporis in-

(2) *Id. ibid.*

(3) *Beza, apud Philippum Pareum, In vita Davidis Pareï, pag. 57. See also a Letter of the same Beza, among those of Arminius, pag. 26, Edit. 1684.*

(4) *Philippus Pareus, Ibid.*

(5) *1 Cor. viii. 1.*

VOL. I. 6 E "currisset,

ARMINIUS.

trons and *Mecenas*'s. He easily justified himself with Persons of Understanding; but there were some weak and suspicious Spirits, who could not get over this Stumbling-Block (b), till he had made the whole Church sensible of his fine Talent at Preaching; by the means of which he regained the Love and Esteem of all the World. His own Colleagues paid Homage to his Understanding, and confessed, that his Sermons were useful and instructive even to Them. *Martin Lydius*, Professor of Divinity at *Franeker*, judged him a proper Person to answer a Writing, in which the Doctrine of *Theodore Beza*, concerning Predestination, was opposed by some Ministers of *Delft*. *Arminius*, in compliance with his Request, undertook to refute This Work; but, during the Examination, and whilst he was ballancing the Reasons on both sides, he went over to the Opinion, he was to refute, and even carried it farther than the Ministers of *Delft*. He condemned, with Them, the Supralapsarian *Beza*, and afterwards acknowledged no other Election, but That, which was grounded on the Obedience of Sinners to the call of God by JESUS CHRIST. He was brought into trouble for This at *Amsterdam*; he was accused of departing from the received Doctrine; but the Authority of the Magistrates suppressed This Contest. He was advanced to the Professorship of Divinity, at *Leyden*, in the Year 1603; and it was with no small difficulty he obtained his Dismission from Those of *Amsterdam*. After he had removed the ill Impressions, which had been given of his Doctrine, he was admitted Doctor of Divinity at *Leyden* (c), and installed in the room of the Professor *Francis Junius*. He had exercised his Ministry in the Church of *Amsterdam* fifteen Years. The Disputes about *Grace* soon after grew hot in That University; and the States of the Province were obliged to appoint Conferences between Him and His Adversaries. He was summoned several times to the *Hague*, and went thither to give an account of his Doctrine. This Contest, his great Application to Business, and the Vexation to find his Reputation sullied by several Calumnies (d), impaired his Health in such a manner, that he fell into a Distemper, of which he died, the nineteenth of *October*, 1609 [D], with great Sentiments of Piety and Patience (e). It were to be wished he had made a better use of his Knowledge [E]; for, tho' his Intentions probably were good, yet it may be said, that he innovated

(b) *Infirmi quidam fratres factum illud perpetuo infectari, & in circulis suggillare. Bertius in Orat. Funebr. Jac. Arminii.*

(c) *He was the first, on whom this Title was solemnly conferred in the University of Leyden. Bertius, ubi supra.*

(d) *Not on account of his Morals, but for his Opinions.*

(e) *Taken from his Funeral Oration, spoken by Peter Bertius.*

" currisset, suffundentibus frigidam quibusdam, quos " omnino præstitisset judicia in ipsius reditum sus" pendere. Hinc ergo, sumpta occasione, spargebatur " in vulgus, illum Pontificis soleam deosculatum, " quem non nisi in conserta turba, ut reliqui spe" ctatores, vidisset, nec soleat bellua honorem istum " nisi Regibus ac Principibus deferre : Jesuitis ad" fuevisse, quos nunquam audivisset : Bellarmino in" notuisse, quem nunquam conspexisset : Religio" nem orthodoxam abjurasse, pro qua paratus esset " ad sanguinis usque profusionem decertare (6)."

[D] *The Vexation to find his Reputation sullied — — — — impaired his Health, and brought him into a Distemper, of which he died, the nineteenth of* October, 1609.] There is reason to think, that this Vexation contributed more to his untimely Death, than any thing else. It was a bad Leaven, which soured the peccant Humours, and which complicated his Distemper a thousand Ways. " Quum in" domita mali pertinacia ipsi quoque arti (Medicinæ) " faceret opprobrium : Altius enim defixa quam ut " evelli posset, nova indies excitabat symptomata, fe" bres, tussim, hypocondriorum extensionem, expi" randi difficultatem, oppressionem à cibo, laboriosos " somnos, atrophiam, arthritidem; nullamque ægro " pausam vel requiem concedebat : accessere postea " dolores in intestinis, ilio, & colo, cum obstructione " nervi optici sinistri, & ejusdem oculi obfuscatione. " — — — — *The Stubbornefs of his Disease baffled all " the Art of Medicine*; *for, being past cure, it every " Day brought on new Symptoms*; *Fevers, a Cough, " an Extension of the Hypochondria, Difficulty of " Breathing, Oppression of Food, restless Sleep, Con" sumption, and Gout* ; *nor had he any respite from " his Distemper*; *afterwards he felt Pains in his in" testines, with an Obstruction of the left optic Nerve, " and a Dimness in the left Eye* (7)." Sometimes he was heard to sigh, and cry out, as formerly the Prophet did, *Wo is me, my Mother, that thou hast born me a Man of Strife*, &c. Let us produce a long Passage of *Bertius*. " Quid mirum, si commo" tus fuerit famæ suæ, salutis, & laborum dispendio; " quum neque viro bono quicquam fama sua sit an" tiquius, neque Christiano salute, neque S. Theo" logiæ doctori petitis ex scriptura demonstrationi" bus ? Oppressio, inquit Siracides, *insanire facit sa" pientem*. Eadem huic dolorem, ex dolore morbum " conciliavit, ex morbo mortem. O tetrum, & vi" perinum, exque imo tartaro excitatum malum !

" Quoties illum ex Propheta privatim etiam cum " gemitu exclamantem audivimus! *Væ mihi, mater " mea, quare genuisti me virum discordiæ in uni" versa terra ?* *Nec fœneravi, nec fœneravit mihi " quisquam*; *& tamen omnes maledicunt mihi*. Re" vocavit tamen seipse ad rationis & tranquillitatis " septa (8). --- *What Wonder, if the loss of his Reputa" tion, his Health, and his Labour, affected him*; *since " a good Man sets the greatest Value on his Fame, " a Christian on his Health, and a Divine on Proofs " fetched from Scripture ?* Oppression, says the Son " Sirac, maketh a wise Man mad. *It was This very " Thing, which first afflicted him*; *Affliction next " impaired his Health*; *and at last a Distemper killed " him*. *O Thou Black, Poisonous, and most Hellish " Evil ! How often have we heard him exclaiming " to himself, with a Sigh, in the Language of the Pro" phet* : *Wo is me, my Mother, that Thou hast born " me a Man of Strife, and a Man of Contention " to the whole Earth ! I have neither lent on Usury, " nor Men have lent to me on Usury*; *yet every " one of them doth curse me*. *However, by the " help of Reason, he recovered his Peace of Mind."* This we cannot reflect on, without deploring the Vanity of human Things. We look upon Stupidity as a great Misfortune; and Fathers, who are not blind to the Dulness of their Sons, are sensibly afflicted at it : They want to discover in them a great Genius, a sublime Understanding; and, if they find them thus qualified, their Joy is inexpressible. This is to wish we know what. *Arminius* had much better have been an errant Blockhead, than so great a Wit; for the Honour of giving his Name to a Sect, which makes a Figure in the World, and which has produced able Men, was but a chimerical Good, in comparison of the real Evils, the Vexations, the Pains, and Bitterness, which he felt in his Life-time; which shortened his Days; and which he had escaped, had he been but an ordinary Divine, a little Wit, or a Blockhead; in short, had he been One of That Class of Men, of whom it is proverbially said, *He will broach no Heresies**. *Juvenal* would have alledged an Example of this kind in his Tenth Satire, if there had been Religious Disputes in his Times, which had caused the Death of one of the Disputants.

[E] *It were to be wished he had made a better use of his Knowledge.*] I mean, that he had governed himself by St *Paul*'s Rule. This great Apostle, inspired

(6) *Bertius in Orat. Funebr. J. Arminii.*

(7) *Bertius, ubi supra, fol. **ij, verso.*

(8) *Id. Ibid. fol. **, verso.*

* *A Proverb in France, to denote a dull Wit.*

ARMINIUS. 481

innovated without necessity, and under Circumstances, in which his Innovation proved a Source of Disorders, which ended in a Schism. He left seven Sons, and some Daughters, and a great number of Disciples, who continued the Dispute so warmly, that it was thought necessary to have recourse to a National Synod. They were condemned in it; but did not submit, and soon formed a seperate Sect, which still continues, and which, by Degrees, has engaged itself in several other more considerable Errors. The *Moreri* of *Amsterdam* mentions some of the Authors, (*f*) who give an account of this famous Quarrel. I add to them the Histories of *Triglandius*, and *Boxhornius*, and a new Work of a Professor of *Tubingen* (*f*). This grand Dispute produced Multitudes of Books on both Sides. A Professor of Divinity at *Cologne*, disguised under a fictitious Name (*g*), gives a List of them according to the order of Years, in a Work, which he intituled *Pacificatorium dissecti Belgii.* I question

(f) Johan. Wolfgangus Jæger. His Work is intituled Historia Ecclesiastica sæculi XVII. The first Decad was printed in 1692.

(g) Ægidius Afhackerius. He assumed the Name of Salomo Theodorus. See Val. Andreas, Bibl. Belg. p. 22.

spired by God, and immediately directed by the Holy Ghost in all his Writings, raised to himself the Objection, which the Light of Nature forms against the Doctrine of Absolute Predestination; he apprehended the whole Force of the Objection; he proposes it without weakening it in the least. *God hath Mercy on whom he will have Mercy, and whom he will he hardeneth* (9). This is St *Paul's* Doctrine; and the difficulty, which he starts upon it, is This; *Thou wilt say then unto me, why doth he yet find fault? For who hath resisted his Will* (10)*?* This Objection cannot be pushed farther: Twenty Pages of the subtilest *Molinist* could add nothing to it. What more could they infer, than that, upon *Calvin's* Hypothesis, God wills Men to commit Sin? Now This is what St *Paul* knew might be objected against him. But what does he reply? Does he seek for Distinctions and Qualifications? Does he deny the Fact? Does he grant it in part only? Does he enter into Particulars? Does he remove any Ambiguity in the Words? Nothing of all this; he only alledges the Sovereign Power of God, and the Supream Right, which the Creator has, to dispose of his Creatures as it seems good to him. *Nay then, O Man, who art thou that repliest against God? Shall the Thing formed say to him that formed it, why hast thou made me thus* (11)*?* He acknowledges an Incomprehensibility in the thing, which ought to put a stop to all Disputes, and impose a profound Silence on our Reason. He cries out, *O the Depth and the Riches both of the Wisdom and Knowledge of God! how unsearchable are his Judgments, and his Ways past finding out* (12)*!* All Christians ought to find here a definitive Sentence, a Judgment final and without Appeal, in the Dispute about *Grace*; or rather they should learn, from this Conduct of St *Paul*, never to dispute about *Predestination*, and immediately to oppose This Bar against all the Subtilities of Human Wit, whether they arise of themselves in meditating on This great Subject, or whether others suggest them. The best, and the shortest, Way is early to oppose this strong Bank against the Inundations of Reasoning, and to consider this definitive Sentence of St *Paul* as Those Rocks, immoveable in the midst of the Waves, against which the proudest Billows beat in vain; They may foam and dash; but are only broken against Them. All Arrows, darted against this Shield, will have the same Fate, as That of *Priam*.

Sic fatus Senior, tellumque imbelle sine ictu Conjecit; rauco quod protinus ære repulsum, Et summo clypei nequicquam umbone pependit (13).

This said, his feeble Hand a Javelin threw; Which, flutt'ring, seemed to loiter as it flew: Just, and but barely, to the Mark it held, And faintly tingled on the brazen Shield. DRYDEN.

Thus ought Men to behave, when the Dispute is between Christian and Christian. And, if ever we think proper to exercise our Wit on Points of this Nature, we ought at least to found a Retreat betimes, and retire behind the Bank I have just mentioned. Had *Arminius* acted thus, as often as his Reason suggested to him Difficulties against the Hypothesis of the Reformers, or whenever he found himself called upon to answer any Disputants, he would have taken a perfectly Wise and Apostolic Course, and employed

(9) Rom. ix. 18.

(10) Ibid. ver. 19.

(11) Ibid. ver. 20.

(12) Ibid. chap. xi, ver. 33.

(13) Virgil. Æneid. lib. 2, ver. 544.

the Lights of his Understanding just as he ought to have done. If he believed there was something too harsh in the received Doctrine; or, if he found it an ease to himself to adopt a less rigid Opinion, he might have enjoyed his particular Notion; but then he should have been content to have enjoyed it in Silence; I mean, without disturbing the Rights of Possession; since he could not do this, without raising a dangerous Storm in the Church. His Silence would have saved him a great deal of Trouble; and he should have remembered the old Apologue.

Sed tacitus pasci si posset Corvus, haberet Plus dapis, & rixæ multo minus invidiæque (14).

But, could the talking Crow in quiet eat, His Envy had been less, and more his Meat. CREECH.

See the Remark [D] of the Article HALL (JOSEPH).

But, say some, *would he not have been a Prevaricator, and unworthy of the Ministry, if he had neglected to instruct his Auditors, whom he believed to be ingaged in a false Doctrine?* I answer; That two capital Reasons would have excused his speaking out: one was, that he did not believe the Hypothesis, which he disapproved, to be contrary to Salvation; the other, that his new Method was useless towards removing the principal Difficulties, which occur in the Doctrine of Predestination. We may grant, that the least Truth, absolutely speaking, deserves to be proposed, and that there is no Error so inconsiderable, which it is not better we should be cured of, than retain; but, when the Circumstances of Time and Place will not permit any Novelties to be proposed, be they ever so true, without occasioning a thousand Disorders, in Universities, in Families, and in the State itself; it is infinitely better to leave Things as they are, than undertake to reform them: The Remedy is worse than the Disease. Our Conduct in this Case should resemble That towards certain sick Persons, to whom no Physic can be administred, without stirring several bad Humours, the agitation of which would be more pernicious, than the Coagulation (15). I except one Case; *viz.* where the saving of Souls is concerned, and the snatching them out of the Jaws of the Devil; for, in this case, Charity will not suffer us to stand idle, how great soever the Commotions may be, which by this means are accidentally raised: we must submit the Consequences to the Care of Providence. Upon this foot, *Arminius* was no ways obliged to oppose the common Doctrine; he did not believe, that any one endangered his Salvation, by following the Hypothesis of *Calvin*. Let us consider the other Circumstance, which rendered him inexcusable. To a System, full of great Difficulties, he substituted another System, which, to speak truly, involves no less Difficulties, than the former. One may say of his Doctrine, what I have observed of the Innovations of *Saumur* (16). It is better connected, and less forced, than the Opinion of Mr *Amyraut*; but, after all, it is but a palliative Remedy; for the *Arminians* have scarce been able to answer some Objections, which, as they pretend, cannot be refuted on *Calvin's* System; besides, they find themselves exposed to other Difficulties, which they cannot get over, but by an ingenuous Confession of the

(14) Horat. Epist. 17, lib. 1, v. 50.

(15) Expediebat quasi ægræ suscipique Reipublicæ requirere quocumque modocunque ne vulnera curatione ipsa rescindentur. ---- It was expedient for the Commonwealth, sick and wounded as it were, to rest any how; lest the very Cure should tear open it's Wounds. Florus, lib. 3. cap. 23.

(16) See Remark [E], of the Article AMYRAUT.

I question whether his Catalogue be compleat. It is difficult not to omit some in such a number of Pieces. As to the Works of *Arminius* [F], see our last Remark.

the weakness of human Reason, and the Consideration of the incomprehensible Infinity of God. And was it worth while to contradict *Calvin* for this? Why was *Arminius* so very difficult at first, when, at last, he was obliged to fly to This Asylum? Why did he not begin here, since here he must come sooner or later? He is mistaken, who imagines, that, after entering the Lists with a great Disputant, He shall be allowed to triumph, only for some small Advantage, which he had over him at first. An Athletic, who throws out his Antagonist in the middle of the Race, but has not the Advantage of him at the End, is not entituled to the Palm. It is the same in Controversy; it is not sufficient to parry the first Thrusts. Every Reply, and Rejoinder, must be satisfied, and every Doubt perfectly cleared up. Now this is what neither the Hypothesis of *Arminius*, nor That of the *Molinists*, nor (17) *See Mr Jurieu, in his Judgment on the rigid and Latitudinarian Methods of explaining the Doctrine of Grace.* That of the *Socinians*, is able to do (17). The System of the *Arminians* is only calculated to gain some few Advantages, in Those Preludes to War, in which the forlorn Hope is sent out, to skirmish; but, when it comes to a general and decisive Battle, This Detatchment must retire, as well as the rest, behind the Intrenchments of Incomprehensible Mystery.

[F] *The Works of* Arminius] These are the Titles of them: "Disputationes de diversis Christianæ " Religionis capitibus. --- Orationes, itemque Tracta- " tus insigniores aliquot. --- Examen modestum li- " belli Guilhelmi Perkinsii, de Prædestinationis modo " & ordine, itemque de amplitudine gratiæ divinæ. " ------ Analysis capitis IX. ad Romanos. ---- Disser- " tatio de vero & genuino sensu cap. VII. Epistolæ " ad Romanos. ----- Amica collatio cum D. Fran- " cisco Junio de Prædestinatione, per litteras habitæ. " ---- Epistola ad Hippolytum à Collibus, &c. ----- " i. e. *Disputations on the several Heads of the Chri-* " *stian Religion*. ------ *Orations, together with some* " *more remarkable Tracts*. ----- *A Modest Examination* " *of a Book of* William Perkins, *concerning the Man-* " *ner and Order of Predestination, and concerning the* " *Extent of Divine Grace*. ----- *An Analysis of the* " *ninth Chapter to the Romans*. ---- *A Dissertation* " *concerning the true and genuine Sense of the Seventh* " *Chapter of the Epistle to the Romans*. ---- *A* " *Friendly Conference with* Francis Junius *concerning* " *Predestination, held by Letter*. ------ *An Epistle to* " Hippolytus à Collibus, *&c.*"

ARNAULD, a Noble and Ancient Family of *Auvergne*. It is above Two Hundred Years, since a Daughter of this House was married to a Lord *de la Fayette*, the Grandson of Him, who was Marshal of *France* under *Charles* VIth. About the Year 1480, HENRY ARNAULD married *Catherine Bariot*, a Kinswoman of Him, who was Counsellor in the Parliament of *Paris*, and Master of the Requests in the Reign of *Lewis* XI (*a*). Soon after this Marriage, He settled at *Riom*, whither he was invited, with several other Persons of Merit, by Peter de Bourbon, Count of *Beaujeu* [*A*], who kept his ordinary Residence there. This Prince was married to *Anna* of *France*, Daughter of *Lewis* XI, who had an absolute Power over the Mind of her Brother *Charles* VIII, and was Regent during his Minority. *Henry Arnauld* insinuated himself into the Esteem of the Count and Countess of *Beaujeu*. He was made Master of the Horse to the Count, and Governor of the Town and Castle of *Hermant*. It was the Place of his Birth, and about eight Leagues distant from *Riom*, on the Frontiers of the *Marche* of *Limousin*, near *Ussel*. This Government was continued to him by the Constable of *Bourbon*, Son-in-Law to the Count *de Beaujeu*. The Office of Master of the Horse was also continued to him. He did great Service to the Constable, by causing his Horses to be shod backwards (*b*), when *Francis* I, who considered him as a Rebel, sent a Guard to take him. They, supposing by the Horses Tracks, that he was gone quite the contrary Way from the Place, where he had concealed himself, lost their time in searching for him where he was not. *Henry Arnauld* had contracted a very strict Friendship with *Florimond de Robertet*, Secretary to the Count *de Beaujeu*, and afterwards Secretary of State under *Francis* I; and it was wholly his own fault, that he did not procure a very advantageous Match for his Son, by the Generosity of this Friend; but he would return one Act of Generosity by another [*B*]. He left two Sons *John* and *Anthony*. The first died without Children: In the Parish Register of the City of *Riom*, in the Year 1542, he is stiled Commander of *Hermant*. His younger Brother, ANTHONY ARNAULD kept up the Family. His first Wife was *Margaret Mosnier-Dubourg*, a near

(*a*) *From Him descend Mr Bariot, Marquis of Mouffy, and Mrs Bariot, Countess of Honneüil and Masy.*

(*b*) *We find in the Galanteries des Rois de France, printed in Holland, in 1694, pag. 289, of the first Tome, that the Family of Arnauld was stripped of all for this Stratagem.*

[*A*] *He was invited to* Riom, *with several other Persons of Merit, by* Peter de Bourbon, Count *of* Beaujeu.] In *Riom* are yet to be seen the Houses of *Montboissier, Montmorin, Chazeron, Florat, Chasteaugay, Mariliac, Dubourg, Duprat, Forget*, and *Robertet*; who were all chief Officers, and Favourites, of the Count and Countess of *Beaujeu*, and of their Son-in-Law, the Constable of *Bourbon*; by whom they were all successively advanced to the chief Dignities of the Sword, and of the Gown (1). Thus you see by what Accident it happened, that so many *Auvergnates* appeared at the Court of *France* in the highest Posts, under *Charles* VIII, *Lewis* XII, and *Francis* I. The Countess of *Beaujeu* had drawn them out of their Province, and had put in their Power to make their own Fortunes. Had it not been for her, they might all have died in obscurity; their great Talents would never have shone beyond their own Country. Conclude from hence, that the particular Glory of a Province, at certain times, depends wholly on Patronages of this kind. You will find a Supplement to this in the Continuation of the *Menagiana*, pag. 304, and 305, of the Edition of *Holland*.

[*B*] *He would return one Act of Generosity by another*.] The Affair was this: *Florimond de Robertet*, leaving *Montbrison*, his native Place, settled at *Riom*, and became Secretary to the Count *de Beaujeu*. He governed him absolutely; as he afterwards did *Charles* VIII, and *Lewis* XII, after the Death of the Cardinal *d'Amboise*; and lastly, *Francis* I, to whom he was Secretary of State. He had such an Affection for *Henry Arnauld*, that, when he left *Riom*, to reside at the Court of *Charles* VIII, he took all his Children along with him, except his Eldest Daughter *Jane de Robertet*, whom he left at *Riom* with the Wife of *Henry Arnauld*, designing, that they should marry her to their Eldest Son *John Arnauld*, when she came of Age. But the Guardians did not think their Son a Match good enough for her; so they married her to the richest young Man of *Riom*, whose Name was *Amable de Ceriers*, the Son of one *Mariliac* (2).

(1) *Taken from a Memoir, inserted in the Mercure Galant of December, 1693, pag. 42.*

(2) *Taken from it about Manus.*

[*C*] He

ARNAULD.

a near Relation of the Chancellor of That Name, Sister of the famous *Annas Dubourg*, Counsellor in Parliament, and of *John Dubourg*, Lieutenant-Criminal of *Riom*. He had but one Son by This Marriage, viz. JOHN DE LA MOTTE-ARNAULD, whom *Thuanus* mentions with so much Praise in his History; and who, at the Head of a Troop of Horse, of which he was Captain, shut himself up in the Town of *Ussoire*, which held for the King against the *League*, and maintained the Siege of it a long time with the Lords of *Chabanes*, and of *Chazeron*; after which he made a vigorous Sally at the Head of thirty Troopers, and killed the Count of *Randam* (*a*) with his own Hand, who was Chief of the League in *Auvergne*. The Death of This Person occasioned the raising of the Siege, and the winning of a Battle, which was fought some time after, and which secured all *Auvergne* to *Henry* IV, on the same Day, and in the same Year, that he gained the Victory in the Battle of *Yvri*. The Father of this *John Arnauld* had followed the Profession of Arms from the beginning. He had raised a Company of Light-Horse, and was in several Actions. But *Catherine de Medicis*, knowing him to be an able and faithful Person, made him her Attorney-General, and the King's Attorney in the Presidial Court of *Riom*, which, at that time, had above forty Leagues of Extent (*d*). He distinguished himself greatly in these two Employs. In all the Acts remaining of him, he styles himself Lord of *la Motte*, *Chantegrenelle*, *Fontainebleau*, *Pessac*, and *Bonnefilles*, all Fiefs, and Castles, not above half a League from *Riom*. His second Wife was *Anne Forget*, Daughter of the Steward of the Houshold to the Constable of *Bourbon* (*e*). He lived to the Age of an Hundred and One Years, and died at *Paris*; whither Queen *Catherine de Medicis* had called him. He was buried in the Church of *St Sulpice*, and in the first Chapel, that had been built in it, of which he himself was the Founder. The Title of the Foundation imports, that he had the Office of Auditor of the Accompts, and Comptroller-General [C], and that he was Lord of *Corbeville* near *Paris*. From his second Marriage proceeded twelve Sons (*f*), one of whom was ANTHONY ARNAULD: I shall mention him in a separate Article; ISAAC ARNAULD, who was Intendant of the Finances: DAVID ARNAULD, a Captain, who was killed at the Siege of *Jerzeau*; LEWIS ARNAULD, Receiver-General of the Finances at *Riom*; another LEWIS ARNAULD, the King's Secretary at *Paris*; and PETER ARNAULD, who was the youngest of the twelve Brothers, and who distinguished himself most in the Profession of Arms. He was Marshal of the Camps, and Armies, of King *Lewis* XIII; Governor of Fort *Lewis*, and Colonel of the Regiment of *Champaigne*. He it is, of whom the Sieur *de Pontis* makes such honourable mention; who ventures to equal him to the most famous Commanders among the *Greeks* and *Romans*. He says, that he understood the Ancient Military Discipline the best of any Man, and made his Soldiers strictly observe it, who loved him even to Adoration. *Isaac Arnauld*, above-mentioned, was the Father of another ISAAC ARNAULD, who was Governor of *Philipsburg*, and Camp Master to the Carabineers, one of the bravest Men, and finest Wits, of the Age: He is celebrated in the Works of *Voiture*. His Sister was married to *Manasses de Feuquiers*, who commanded the King's Army before *Thionville*, in the Year 1639 (*g*).

(*c*) *Madam de Senecey, Governess of the King, was his Daughter.*

(*d*) *The Presidial Courts of Queret, of Clermont, and of Aurillac, were not as yet dismembered from it.*

(*e*) *Mons. Forget, Secretary in the Reign of Henry IV, was of the same Family.*

(*f*) *The Historical Description of the Life of Mr Arnauld, Doctor of the Sorbonne, mentions only eight Sons, which John Arnauld had by two Wives, pag. 2, Edit. of Liege, 1702.*

(*g*) *Taken from a Memoir, communicated to the Author of the Mercure Galant, December 1693.*

[C] *He was Auditor of the Accompts, and Comptroller-General.*] Since the first Edition of this Work, I received a small Memoir, written by one of the principal Genealogists of *Europe*; in which I find as follows: " *Anthony Arnauld*, Sieur *de la Mothe*, and " *Villeneuve*, His Majesty's Attorney in the Seneschal's Jurisdiction of *Auvergne*, at *Riom*; Solicitor-General to the Parliament in 1568, and 1570; afterwards Auditor of the Accompts at *Paris*, and Attorney-General of *Catherine de Medicis*; was ennobled, in *December* 1577, by the Title of Auditor " of the Accompts. He was the Son of *Henry Arnauld*, Bailiff of the Town of *Harmant*, in *Auvergne*, and of *N. Colonges*. He had married " *Anne Forget*, Daughter of *John Forget*, Sieur *de Bidoigne*, the King's Attorney in *Auvergne*, and of " *Jane Godinet*; and he died at the Age of an Hundred and One Years, about the Year 1591. See " the Memoirs of *Sully*, Tom. IV. fol. 27." Read also the Continuation of the *Menagiana*, pag. 305, *Dutch* Edition.

ARNAULD (ANTHONY) (*a*) Advocate in the Parliament of *Paris*, the Son of another *Anthony*, whom I have mentioned in the preceeding Article, acquired a wonderful Reputation by his Eloquence. *Henry* IV, intending to shew the Duke of *Savoy* the Parliament, made Choice of a Day, when *Arnauld* was to plead a fine Cause (*b*). He gave this able Man a Breviate for Counsellor of State. The Queen *Mary de Medicis* made him her Advocate-General, and would have made him her Secretary of State; but he declined this Office, and told her Majesty, *he could do Her more Service, in quality of Advocate, than if he was Secretary of State*. This Fact is intimated in his Epitaph [*A*]. One Day the Advocate-General, *Marion*, was so well

(*a*) *Konig calls him Marc Anthony. The Letter M, which He, and Others, met with before Anthony, in some French Books, in which it stands for Maitre, or Monsieur, was, probably, the Cause of this Mistake.*

(*b*) *The Question concerning the Punishment due to Slanderers. See in Matthieu's History of Henry IV. Tom. I. pag. 455, an Argument on this Subject.*

[*A*] *He refused to be Secretary of State —— This Fact is intimated in his Epitaph.*] Mr *le Maitre*, Grand-Son, and God-Son of *Anthony Arnauld*, the Advocate, was Author of the Epitaph. They, who would read it, need look no further than this Page 1 and They, who have no such Curiosity, may pass it over.

Passant, du grand Arnauld revere la memoire.
Ses vertus à sa race ont servi d'ornement,
Sa plume à son pais, sa voix au Parlement,
Son esprit à son siecle, & ses faits à l'histoire.
Contre un second Philippe Usurpateur des lis
Ce second Demosthene anima ses écrits,
Et contre Emmanuel arma son éloquence.

well satisfied with hearing him plead, that he took him home in his Coach to Dinner, and seated his Eldest Daughter *Catherine Marion* near him. After Dinner, he took him aside, and asked him what he thought of his Daughter; and, being answered, that she seemed to him a Lady of great Merit, he gave her to him in Marriage (c). One of the most famous Causes, which *Anthony Arnauld* ever pleaded, was That of the University against the Jesuits, in the Year 1594. We shall see hereafter how he was rewarded for it [*B*]. Some say, that he published a Book in 1602, to prevent their Re-call [*C*]. But, foreseeing, that they would return, and become formidable, he endeavoured to suppress it. He had been Counsellor and Attorney-General to Queen *Catherine de Medicis*. They, who have reported, that he was of the Reformed Religion, have reported a very great Falshood [*D*]. He had Twenty

(c) *Taken from the Memoir, in the Mercure Galant, for December. 1693.*

Il vit comme un neant les hautes dignitez,
Et preféra l'honneur d'oracle de la France
A tout le vain éclat des titres empruntez.

*Paſſenger, whoe'er thou art, revere the Memory
Of the Great* ARNAULD.
*His Virtues were the Ornament of his Family,
His Pen of his Country, His Voice of the Parliament,
His Wit of the Age, and his Actions of History.
Against a second* Philip, *Usurper of the* Lilly,
This second Demosthenes
*Animated his Writings;
And arm'd his Eloquence against* Emmanuel.
*He despised the highest Dignities,
And preferr'd the Honour of being
The Oracle of* France
To all the vain Splendor of borrowed Titles.

[*B*] *How he was rewarded for it.*] He sent back the Present, which the University had ordered him: He would have it said, that so famous a Cause was pleaded *gratis*. The University drew up an Act in the most authentic Form, by which it engaged itself not to an eternal Acknowledgment, not only to himself, but to his Posterity. These are the Terms of the Decree: "Quapropter, cum Consultorum diser-
"tiſſimus & Disertorum consultiſſimus D. ANTONIUS
"ARNALDUS, in Foro Pariſienſi spectatus à multis
"annis Patronus, pro Defensione juris Academici
"—— tantopere desudarit: & longa comptaque Oratione, quæ Doctorum manibus teritur, probarit
"—— Cumque idem pro Defensionis laboribus &
"Patrocinii jure oblatum sibi ab Academia honorarium remiserit, quatuitamque suam operam esse
"voluerit; ne apud Nos ingrati animi culpa resideat,
"placuit Rectori, quatuor Facultatibus, & singulis
"Nationibus, ut perpetua tanti beneficii memoria
"publicis Tabulis consignatis & testata apud posteros exstaret, huicque Sacramento se omnes Academiæ Ordines obstringerent, se ea officia, quæ à
"bonis clientibus fido Patrono solent deferri, omnia
"IN ILLUM EJUSQUE LIBEROS ac posteros
"studiosè collaturos, nec eorum unquam honori,
"commodis, famæque defuturos (1). —— *Wherefore,
"since the most famous Lawyer,* ANTHONY ARNAULD,
"*many Years a celebrated Advocate in the Courts
"of* Paris, *has so greatly exerted himself in Defence of the Rights of the University; and proved,
"in a long and beautiful Oration, which is in the
"Hands of the Learned,* &c. *And, whereas the
"said Lawyer has declined accepting the Present, sent
"him by the University, in consideration of the Pains
"of his Defence, and as justly due to his Patronage;
"and desires to bestow his Labour gratis: Therefore,
"least the Imputation of Ingratitude should rest upon
"us, it hath pleased the Rector, the Four Faculties,
"and every Order, that the Memory of so great a
"Benefit shall be preserved upon Record to Posterity,
"and that every Member of the University shall oblige himself, by an Oath, to discharge every Instance of
"Duty, usually paid by good Clients to a faithful
"Patron, to* HIM *and his* CHILDREN, *nor ever to
"be wanting to their Honour, Advantage, and Fame.*"
You will find This at large in the Preface of a Book printed at *Large*, in 1699, and entitled " *Causa* Arnaldina, seu Antonius Doctor & Socius Sor-
"bonicus à censura Anno 1656, sub nomine Facultatis Theologicæ Pariſienſis vulgata, vindicatus.
"—— *The* Arnaldian *Causes, or* Anthony Arnauld,

(1) *Præfat. Cauſæ Arnaldinæ,* pag. XCVII.

" *Doctor and Fellow of the* Sorbonne, *vindicated from
" the Censure, published, in* 1699, *in the Name of
" the Faculty of Divinity at* Paris."

[*C*] *He published a Book, in 1602, to prevent their Re-call.*] It is a small Book, entituled, *Le Franc & Veritable Discours*. Father *Richeome* refutes him, in his Apologetical Complaint, in which he refutes likewise the Jesuits Catechism, which appeared at the same Time, and came from the Pen of *Stephen Pasquier*. I have read a Particular, in the Remarks on the Catholic Confession of *Sancy* (2), which I shall here transcribe: "The Advocate *Arnauld* re-
" turned no Answer; not that the Book entituled,
" *The Truth defended* (3), had stopped his Mouth;
" but because he perceived, that the Interest of the
" Jesuits with *Henry* IV would carry it in the end
" against all the Reasons, which could be alledged
" for establishing the Decree of their Banishment. In
" effect, the poor Man was so much afraid, that
" he had gone too far in his little Book, that I
" have seen a Copy of it, wherein an able Man
" of those Times had made the following Observa-
" tion with his own Hand. *This Book (The Free
" and True Discourse) composed by Mr* Anthony Ar-
" nauld, *their good Friend*: And a little lower, *The
" Copies suppressed by the Author*."

[*D*] *They, who have reported, that he was of the Reformed Religion, were greatly mistaken.*] The Author of the *Amphitheatrum Honoris*, disguised under the Name of *Clarus Bonarſcius*, which is the Anagram of *Carolus Scribanius*, his true Name, speaks of the Advocate *Anthony Arnauld* as a known *Calvinist*. The *Imago Primi sæculi Soc. Jesu* does the same. The Author of the Apology of *John Chatel* says, pag. 205, that the Name of *Arnauld* comes from ἀρνύμαι, which signifies to *deny* or *apostatize*, and that it approaches near to That of *Antichrist*, in which is found the Name of the Beast. And, p. 206, *A worthy Minister of him, to whom a Mouth is given, speaking great Things and Blasphemies*, Rev. xiii. (4). *Du Pleix* had related the same Falshood, but retracted it publickly. He had said, in the first Edition of his History of *Henry* IV, speaking of the Trial, which the Jesuits had with the University of *Paris*, in 1564; " That *Anthony Arnauld* making a
" Profession of *Calvinism*, the Choice, which the
" Agents of the University had made of him, was
" esteemed highly scandalous and unbecoming." But thus he recants. " *Anthony* Arnauld, *a most eloquent
" Man, was Council for the Plaintiff* (5). *I for-
" merly believed, upon false Information, that he
" was a Protestant; but, in truth, he never was. He
" left behind him most virtuous Children, and most
" zealous for the Catholic Religion*." It is strange, that an Historian, who was none of the meanest, could be deceived, as to the Religion of so famous a Lawyer, who had taken the whole Parliament to witness of his Catholicism, in the same *Plea*, which gave *Du Pleix* occasion to speak of him. This is what he says in That *Plea*. " If perhaps They, and
" Their Favourers, have the Impudence to assert,
" that the *Sorbonne* was Heretical in the Year 1554,
" when it published This Decree against Them:
" Just as they have the Assurance to give out, among
" the Women of their Congregations, that all, who
" prosecute This Cause, are Heretics, sprung either
" from *Geneva*, or from *England*. If I myself, who
" speak, were not known to have been brought up,
" from my Infancy, in the Royal College of *Navarre*; and if my Profession, so notorious, and
" my Admission into both public and honourable
" Employs, in the Years 80, and 85, did not too
" manifestly secure me from their Impostures; they would

(2) Book II, chap. 6, pag. 535.

(3) *The Author of the Remarks had said,* p. 574, *that* Richeome, *under the Name of* Francis de la Montagne, *had answered, in 1594, a* Book, *entituled* La verité Defenduë.

(4) *Taken from the Question curieuse ſi Mr* Arnauld *est Heretique,* pag. 13.
i. e. A curious Enquiry, whether Mr Arnauld *be an Heretic.*

(5) *That is, the University.*

ARNAULD. 485

Twenty two Children by his Marriage with *Catherine Marion* (d) [E], and died about the Year 1618. Observe, that one of his Daughters reformed the Abbey of *Port-Royal* [F].

He acquitted himself at the Bar, " with so much Honour (e), and in so extraor-
" dinary

" would no doubt pretend, that I came from thence
" likewise to plead against them." Experience convinced him, and convinces to this Day, that he was
mistaken, in fancying himself sheltered from their
Impostures; for, besides the Writers I have cited,
there have lately arisen two new Accusers; the first
is Father *Hazart*; the second, though the Name
he gives himself be a fictitious one (6), produces a
Letter from a Gentleman, whose Name is Mr *de
Heucourt* (7), who affirms, that the Father of Mr *Arnauld*, Doctor of the *Sorbonne*, was born, and died,
a Huguenot. I have reason to say, that Father *Hazart* has renewed the Accusation; for these are his
Words, " The Recantation of Mr *du Pleix* does not
" affect me, nor debar me of the Liberty of taking
" his first Sentiment for the Legitimate Issue of his
" best Information, and the second as the Offspring
" of his Complaisance for the Relations of the Sieur
" *Arnauld*, who had Credit enough, at that Time,
" to gain over, or oblige, an Author, to any thing
" of This Nature (8)." It was replied, that one
must be of a very perverse Spirit " to prefer, what
" an Historian acknowledges he had said on false
" Suggestions, to what he asserts, as certain and
" indisputable, upon better information. Were
" there many Persons of so wicked a Character,
" the Prejudice, which an Historian might do by
" publishing, from bad Memoirs, Falsehoods to the
" Dishonour of his Neighbour, would be irreparable,
" since his Recantation would signify nothing (9)."
It is but flying to Father *Hazart*'s Answer. " See, by
" the way, concludes he, how well Mr *du Pleix* is re-
" warded for having been so partial to the Jesuits. This
" shew how much they love him, whilst they make
" him have so little Conscience, as that, having
" said nothing but the Truth, when he affirmed,
" that the Advocate, who pleaded against them, was
" an *Huguenot*, he should notwithstanding retract
" this afterwards, and establish a Lie out of meer
" Complaisance." I know not (10) of any Reply,
which has been made to the Challenge of Him, who
published Mr *d'Heucourt*'s Letter: The Summons
was very pressing; for thus the Author addressed
himself to Mr *Arnauld*: " This Letter, the Original
" of which is put into my Hands, to be sent to you,
" absolutely requires you to produce the Certificate
" of your Baptism; for the Jesuits, your Enemies,
" are not, it seems, the only Persons, who reproach
" you with being born a Huguenot." But the Publisher
of this Letter was greatly confounded, when the World
was informed, that Mr *d'Heucourt* disclaimed it.

The Public has seen This in the Journal of Mr
Basnage (11), and in a Book, which has appeared
since the first Impression of this Article; I mean the
Abridged History of the Life and Writings of Mr *Arnauld*.
Observe how the Author treats this Matter, in the
Seventeenth and Eighteenth Pages. " We shall not
" here lose time in confuting the impertinent Author
" of the *Important Advice to Mr Arnauld, &c.* wherein
" an Extract is produced of a pretended Letter of the
" Marquis *d'Heucourt*, to prove, that Mr *Arnauld*
" and his Father were born *Calvinists*. All this is down-
" right Imposture. For not only the Extract of the
" Certificate of Baptism, which the Adviser required
" might be produced, is at Hand, but also an Instru-
" ment in Form under The Marquis's Hand, dated
" from *Brompton*, near *London*, the 4/14th of May,
" 1692, wherein he declares, that he knows nothing
" of it, that the Letter never came from him, and
" that it is a Piece maliciously and falsly composed."
It is very probable, that one of our Advocate *Arnauld*'s Brothers turned Huguenot (12); for one, who
must have known this very well, has informed me,
that Madam *de Feuquiers* (13), and Madam *d'Heucourt*, her Sister, who were This Advocate's Nieces
by the Father's Side, were of the Reformed Religion
to their Death. The same Person informed me likewise, that ISAAC ARNAULD, Minister of *Ro-
bel*, and Author of a Book, entituled *The Contempt of
the World*, was of the same Family with Mr *Arnauld*.
This Work was printed more than once; for the Edition of *Rouen* in 1637, imports, that it had been
Revised, Corrected, and Augmented with three other
Treatises by the same Author; to wit, *Virtuous Resolutions; Of the Obedience due to the King; and Meditations on old Age*.

[E] *He had Twenty Two Children by his Marriage.*——] The Name of the Eldest was *Robert*;
The same, who became so famous by the Name of
ARNAULD d'ANDILLI: See the following
Article. The second died Bishop of *Angers*, in the
Month of *June*, 1692. His Name was HENRY
ARNAULD; who had acquired a great Esteem
under the Name of the Abbot of *St Nicholas*, before
he attained to the Mitre. Being at *Rome*, he saved,
by his Dexterity and Courage, the Honour and Estate
of the *Barberini*, from the Attempts of the Creatures
and Relations of Pope *Innocent* X. In acknowledgement of which, the Prince of *Palestrina*, and the
French Cardinals, *Anthony* and *Charles Barberini*, not
only caused a Medal to be struck, and his Picture to
be drawn, which they hung up in all their Houses,
but erected likewise a Statue to him in their Palace
at *Rome*, with an Inscription, which *Fortunatus* had
composed for *St Gregory* of *Tours* (14). He died in
the Odour of Sanctity in his Diocess at *Angers*; which
he had never left for near Forty four Years that he
was Bishop of it. CATHERINE ARNAULD,
the Eldest Daughter of *Anthony*, was married to Mr
le Maitre, one of his Majesty's Council, and Master of
the Accompts at *Paris*, by whom she had *Anthony le
Maitre*, the Famous Advocate, and *Isaac le Maitre*
of *Sacy*, known by his Translation of the Bible, by
That of the Imitation of JESUS CHRIST,
the Life of *Dom. Barthélemi des Martyrs*, and
his sacred Poems. ANGELICA ARNAULD,
another Daughter of *Anthony*, perpetual Abbess of
Port-Royal in the Fields, reformed That Abbey on the
same Foot with That of *Clairvaux*, and made it Elective and Triennial. Five of her Sisters, with their
Mother, took the Religious Habit in this Convent, and
led a very austere Life there till their Death (15).

Observe, that, in the *Abridged History* of the Life of
Mr *Arnauld*, pag. 20, it is asserted, I. That he was
the Twentieth and last of the Children of *Anthony Arnauld*, and of *Catherine Marion*. This does not a-
gree with the Memoir (16), which I have quoted, II.
which gives them Twenty Two. II. That, when
the Father of so many Children died, *there were but
Ten of them alive, Four Sons, and Six Daughters*.

[F] *One of his Daughters reformed the Abbey of*
Port-Royal.] The Name of *Port-Royal* makes so
much noise, the *Arnaulds* are so much concerned in
it, and the Particulars of all this so little known, that
I may well suppose the Curious will receive with pleasure any Information on this Subject. For this Reason I believe it will not displease my Reader, if I
here insert what I have read in a printed Case (17).
Pieces of this kind are seldom known to many Persons.

" *Port Royal* is originally a Monastery of *Bernar-
" din* Nuns, six Leagues from *Paris*. One of Mr
" *d'Andilli's* Sisters was made Abbess of it, in the
" beginning of this Century, when she was but Ele-
" ven Years of Age. This was a common Abuse at
" that time; from which God drew great Good.
" For, at the Age of Seventeen Years, God inspired
" her with so earnest a Desire to reform her Abbey,
" tho' there were none, either Men or Women,
" reformed in the whole Order of the *Cistertians*,
" that she resolved and performed it with ease enough,
" God giving an extraordinary Blessing to her good
" Designs. She banished all Property from thence;
" all the Nuns, after her Example, bringing into the
" common Stock what they had before in their private
" Possession. She established an exact recluse Life, per-
" petual Abstinence, the Office of the Night, Fast-
" ings, Labour, and Silence, according to the
" Rules of *St Benedict*. And it was this Odour of
" Sanctity, like the Perfume of the Spouse, which
" drew her Sisters, Nieces, and her Mother likewise,
" in their turns, to this House. The Design of so
" perfect a Reformation, undertaken so courageously,
" and executed so happily, acquired her so great an
" Esteem with the whole Order, that, when she was
" but Twenty seven, or Twenty eight, Years of Age,
" she was chosen to reform the famous Abbey of *Mau-
" buisson*,

"dinary a manner, that no Person since, except his Grandson Mr *le Maitre*, "has been known to appear there with so much Reputation and Dignity. His "House was continually filled with Princes, and great Lords, who came to consult "him about their most important Affairs, and he was every where held in such Ve- "neration, that, after his Death, they were forced to expose his Body for some "time on a Bed, to satisfie the People, who pressingly demanded it." They are mistaken, who impute to him an Apology for *Phalaris* [G].

"*buisson*. She past Four or Five Years there; which "obliged her to leave to her Sister, who was after- "wards called *Mother Agnes*, the Care of her House "of *Port-Royal*, as her *Coadjutrix*. It was about this "time, and while she was at *Maubuisson*, that she saw "St *Francis de Sales*, who was come to *Paris*, to "found there an House of the Visitation. She sent "to desire he would visit her, and put herself under "his Conduct; and it appears by this Saint's Letters "what an Esteem he had for his dear Daughter the "Abbess of *Port-Royal*."

The Author of the *Factum* adds, that the Widow of *Antony Arnauld*, Mother of This Abbess, had a strong Desire to become a Nun, under the Conduct of her own Daughter; and that, as God had inspired her with this Desire, about the same time that the Abbess was advised to transfer her Monastery of the Fields to *Paris*; "She bought a very fair and large "House, and Gardens, in the Suburbs of St *James*, "which she bestowed on the Abbess, Convent, and "Nuns of *Port-Royal*, that they might settle there; "which they actually did, having, at a great Expence, "put the House at *Paris* into the Condition it is at "present in, by the Blessing of God on their Charity "and Disinterestedness. There it was, that this "happy Mother of so many pious Children took her "own Daughter for a Mother, consecrating herself "to God by a Religious Profession to live under her "Discipline: And, having done so for the space of "fourteen or fifteen Years, with very edifying Fer- "vour and Humility, she had the Consolation, before "her Death, to give her Blessing to six Daughters, "and six Grand-Daughters, who were all in the "Monastery, and all Nuns, except one, who died "young, and had been only a Pensioner." Lastly, it appears by This *Factum*, that the Abbess of *Port-Royal* was Incumbent for Life, and one of her Sisters *Coadjutrix*; but that both of them, having only the good of their House in view, willingly parted with their Titles, and settled a triennial Election. Mr *d'Andilly* obtained the necessary Permission from the King, tho' it deprived him of the Means of keeping this Abbey always in his own Family. Add to this what we shall observe in his Article.

[G] *They are mistaken, who impute to him an Apology for* Phalaris.] The Words of Father *Abram*, which I am going to cite, have a visible Relation to our *Arnauld*. "De Phalaridis Agrigentorum Ty- "ranni immani crudelitate supervacaneum fuerit di- "cere, cum & pleni sunt aliorum libri, & ipse se "nefarium, immanem, & sceleratissimum in epistolis "sæpe fateatur. Unus inventus est Arnaldus, qui "non ita pridem orationem dicam, an nugas? de "ejus laude conscripserit. Videlicet ex eodem cala- "mo Phalaridis Apuleiique laudatio & Societatis no- "stræ criminatio manavit, ut quibus se similem esse "mallet, liquidius ostenderet. ———— *It will be su-* (19) Abram. "*perfluous to say any thing of the monstrous Cruelty* in Clowon. "*of* Phalaris, *Tyrant of* Agrigentum, *since other Au-* Onat. Tom. "*thors have given a full Account of it, and* Pha- 1. pag. 103. "laris *often acknowledges himself to be monstrously* "*wicked in his Epistles*. Arnauld *alone is found,* "*who lately wrote an Oration in his Praise. From* "*the same Pen flowed the Panegyric of* Phalaris *and* "Apuleius, *and the Accusation of our Society; that* "*the Author might more plainly shew, whom he would* "*resemble*." The Mistake is a gross one; for the Author of the Apology for *Phalaris* was an *Arnauld* of *Provence*. See the Remark [M] of the Article EPICURUS.

ARNAULD d'ANDILLI (ROBERT), Eldest Son of the preceeding, was a Person of great Merit. See his Elogy in *Moreri*'s Dictionary, and in the *Illustrious Men* of Mr *Perrault*. He married Mademoiselle *de la Broderie*, the Daughter of Him, who had been so long Ambassador in *England*, and Grand-Daughter to a Sister of the Chancellor *de Silleri*. This Marriage produced five Daughters, all Nuns at *Port-Royal*, (the Eldest of which, Sister *Angelica* of St *John*, passed for a Prodigy of Wit, Knowledge and Virtue) and three Sons. The Eldest is the Abbot ARNAULD, Commendatory * Abbot of *Chomes* (*a*), who, after having (*c*) He died * One, who born Arms a long time in the King's Service, in the Regiment of his Cousin *Isaac* in February, enjoys a Be- *Arnauld*, Camp-Master of the Carabineers, retired to his Uncle, the Bishop of *An-* 1699. nefice in *gers*. The second is HENRY ARNAULD, Lord of *Luzancy*, who passed his Commen-dam. Life in Solitude. The third is SIMON ARNAULD, Marquis of *Pompone*, formerly Minister and Secretary of State, and still a Minister of State, known by his (*b*) Mem-ir Embassies into *Holland* and *Sueden* (*b*). Mr *Arnauld d'Andilly* was sent early into the of the World. He had several Employs, which attached him to the Court, and to an At- Mercure tendance on the deceased King; but he never suffered himself to be corrupted by Galant, for the bad Air, which is usually breathed in such Stations [A]. The Difference he had 1693. with the President *de Grammond*, who had mentioned him, in his Latin History, otherwise than he ought to have done, may be seen in the Collection of his *Letters*. They, who forged the Romance of the Assembly of *Bourg-Fontaine*, denoted by the Letters A. A. one of the pretended Accomplices of the Design, which was supposed to have been taken there, of introducing *Deism*; and, when they perceived, that these Letters could not belong to Mr *Arnauld*, the Doctor, they applied them to

[A] He never suffered himself to be corrupted by the bad Air, which is usually breathed in such Stations.] "He was a *Frenchman*, who, all the time he lived "at Court, in *Paris*, and in the Country, had the "best established Reputation, and was the most ge- "nerally talked of for his Piety and Probity: there "being no one, who would not willingly subscribe "to what a famous Author wrote of him above fifty "Years ago, *That he was never ashamed of the Gospel* "*Truths, nor made an Ostentation of the Practice* "*of it's Precepts*." This is what we find in the fourth *Factum* of *Jansenius*'s Great Nephews (1). (1) At the Where we likewise find (2), "That, before he for- 12th Page. "sook the World, and during his Residence at Court, (2) At Page "he dedicated his whole Genius for Poetry to the 18. "Honour of his Saviour, and to the Design of giving "a Relish for the Christian Truths; for he had not "as yet retired from the World, when he wrote (3) See, be- "his Poem (3) on the Life of JESUS CHRIST, and low, the Re- "his Stanzas on the Noblest and most Edifying mark [C], "Truths of Religion." Citation (9).

[B] The

ARNAULD. 487

to another Person, to wit, *Arnauld d'Andilli*, as was at last fairly explained (c). But the Author of the *Facta*, or Cases, of *Jansenius*'s Great-Nephews, made it appear by solid Reasons, that the second Application of the two A. A. was absurd [*B*]. Mr *d'Andilli* retired to the Monastery of *Port-Royal* in 1644, where he passed the Remainder of his Life in a continued Application to Works of Piety. He composed several Books there (d), which the Public received favourably, and which are so numerous, that they make eight Volumes in Folio (e). He died there on the 27th of *September* 1674, in the Eighty sixth Year of his Age (f).

He lost his Wife in the Year 1637. *Balzac*'s Reflexion on this Loss is worth knowing [*D*].

[*B*] *The second Application of the two A. A. was absurd.*] I shall not repeat all the Reasons alledged to prove this; I shall only remark, that it is observed, among other things, that he had been present in all the Expeditions, which King *Lewis* XIII made, both before, and after, the Time of the chimerical Cabal of *Bourg-Fontaine* (4), "to quell Those of his "Subjects, whom their false Religion had engaged "in Rebellion (5). These were Occasions, continue "they (6), of enflaming more and more his Zeal "for the Catholic Religion, by the Aversion, which "these kind of Wars inspire against Heresy; but it "was not the way to become a Divine, having "never studied Theology, as he could not have "done, to sustain the Part, which they make the "Authors of the Fable of *Bourg-Fontaine* act. He "knew as much of Religion, as a Man of great "Parts could learn of it, from his Catechism, from "pious Books, from the Conversation of holy Persons, from reading the Word of God, and hearing "it preached; but the less he knew of what was "taught in the Schools, the more incapable was he "of raising Doubts concerning the Truth of our "Mysteries (7), having accustomed himself early to "captivate his Understanding to the Divine Authority, which is visibly lodged in the Church; and "sure never any Person was farther from cavilling with God, or pretending, by his weak "and self-conceited Reason, to comprehend what "we ought to believe with Faith and Humility."

[*C*] *He retired to the Monastery of Port-Royal.*] Let us continue to quote the fourth *Factum*. "It "was to Port Royal in the Fields, that he retired in "the Year 1644; whither his Nephews, the Advocate Mr *le Maitre*, and one of his Brothers, "who was a Soldier, had retired five or six Years "before, when there were yet no Religious "there; for it was not 'till the Year 1648, that "the House of *Paris* obtained leave of the Archbishop to send Part of their Religious to their Country House." My Reader may choose between the Author of this *Factum*, and Mr *Richelet* (8), who says, that Mr *Arnauld d'Andilli* made his own House of *Pompone* his Retreat. I am satisfied with confronting these two Authorities; and pass on, with Pleasure, to cite what you are now going to read; because it contains some of Those Particulars, relating to the Lives of great Men, which so many are curious to know. "*Arnauld d'Andilli* ---- served the King "and the State twenty Years. As a Reward of his "Services, he had a Pension of Eight thousand

"Livres settled on him, which were afterwards reduced to fix; with this he retired to *Pompone*, a "Village seven or eight Leagues distant from *Paris*, "where, forsaking the Vanities of the World, and "leading a truly Christian Life, he composed several Works: *His Letters, and a Poem on the Life "of* JESUS CHRIST (9). ------ *Josephus*'s History of the Jews, the Works of *S*t Theresa, and "Those of Davila, translated, are the Fruits of his "Solitude. ---- The best of his Translations is "That of *Josephus* (10). Some time after it had been "published, *Richelet* went, one Day, to see him at "*Pompone*; after some Discourse, the Conversation "fell on the manner of Authors composing. "And, knowing that *Richelet* was particularly acquainted with the famous *D'Ablencourt*, he asked "him, how many times That excellent Man revised each Piece before he gave it the Publick : "*Richelet* replied *six times*; and I, replied Mr *Arnauld, revised the History of* Josephus *ten times* ; I "*carefully corrected the Stile of it, and polished it "more than any of my other Works*. *Arnauld d'Andilli* ---- in his Retirement, after seven or eight "Hours Study, every Day, used to divert himself "with the Pleasures of the Country, and, above all, "others, with That of pruning his Trees. He had "generally so good Fruit, that, every Year, he sent "Presents of it to Queen *Anne of Austria*; and That "Princess was so well pleased with it, that every "Season she desired to have some." This Application to Gardening, and *philosophizing* profoundly on the Nature *of Trees*, is attested by Mr Perrault, in his *Illustrious Men*, pag. 143, Edition of Holland.

[*D*] *Balzac*'s *Reflexion on this Loss is worth knowing.*] What he wrote concerning it is much for the Honour of our *Robert Arnauld*, and his Family. "The News of Madam *d'Andilli*'s Death affected "me sensibly. I interest myself in all the good and "bad Success, of a Family which ought to be dear "to *France*, and which arose for the Honour of "the *French* Name. But I pity our Friend particularly, who, having never had any unlawful Passion, loses all his Mistresses, and Pleasures, at "once, in his Wife. He is, nevertheless, so well "skilled in the Christian Doctrine, and has so many "learned Men of his Family about him, that he "needs no Stoic Philosophy, nor any foreign Assistance, to defend himself against the Attacks of "Fortune. All Reason, all Preach, all Persuade, in "That Family, and, One *Arnauld* is worth a Dozen "*Epictetus*'s (11)."

ARNAULD (ANTHONY) Doctor of the *Sorbonne*, Son of *Anthony Arnauld* the Advocate [*A*], was born at *Paris*, the sixth of *February*, 1612, being the twentieth Offspring of his Father's Marriage with *Catherine Marion*. He studied Humanity and Philosophy

[*A*] *Son of* Anthony Arnauld *the Advocate.*] This Descent is undoubtedly the Origin of the great Hatred of the Jesuits towards Mr *Arnauld*, and of Mr *Arnauld* towards the Jesuits. The Author of the *Question Curieuse* (1) does not absolutely deny this, since he speaks in this manner. (2) : "Mr *Arnauld* was "born the sixth of *February*, in the Year 1612. His "Father was Mr *Anthony Arnauld*, so famous as the "Bar, and known in the History of the Jesuits, by "the famous Plea, which he made against them, for "the University of Paris, in 1594. ----- For the "Reason, which I have mentioned, Mr *Arnauld* was "born with a second original Sin, which no Sacrament could efface; and, the Crime of the Plea having "made the Father a *Calvinist*, and Minister of *Antichrist*, in the Minds of the Jesuits (3), though a "good Catholic, and a good Christian, every where

"else, the Son, in their Opinion, must necessarily "be born a Child of Wrath, and be yet worse than "a Heretic, before he could be a Christian." One of the Protestant Authors, who wrote against *Maimbourg*'s History of *Calvinism*, believed, that Mr *Arnauld*'s Aversion to the Jesuits proceeded from Education. These are his Words (4). "I have "formerly compared him to *Hannibal*, too obstinately persecuted by the *Romans* (5). I cannot tell "whether I may not compare him to the same Han-

VOL. I.   6 G   "nibal,

Philosophy in the College of *Calvi* (a), and afterward began to study the Law; but he was soon taken from this Study, and turned to That of Divinity, by the Care of his Mother, seconded by the Abbot of St *Cyran*. After this Determination, he applied himself to study in the College of the *Sorbonne* (b), and went through a Treatise of Grace under Mr *l'Escot*: But, not finding This Professor of the *Sorbonne*'s Lectures conformable to the Doctrine of St *Paul*, he resolved to study This Point in St *Austin* himself, and preferred This Father's System to That of Mr *l'Escot*. This he testified publickly in a Probation Thesis, which he maintained, in the Year 1636, in order to be admitted to his Degree of Bachelor (c). He employed an *Interval of Two Years*, which, according to *the Laws of the Faculty at* Paris, *must pass between the Probation, and the Licence*, in hard Study; after which, he began the Acts of his Licence, *about the Easter of the Year* 1638, and continued *them till* Lent 1640. He went thro' the Act of *Vesperies* the eighteenth of *December* 1641, and, the Day following, received the Doctor's Cap. While he was a Licentiate, he composed, and publickly taught, *A Course of Philosophy* (d). At the end of this Course of Philosophy, which he taught at *Paris*, in the College of *Mans*, he caused Theses to be maintained, wherein he gave a remarkable Instance of his Integrity, Docility, and Humility [B]. He was ordained Priest in the *Ember Week of September*, of the Year 1641, and celebrated his first Mass on *All Saints Day*, *of the same Year, after a Retirement of Forty Days*——*He had began his Licence, without any design of becoming a Member of the Sorbonne*——*He would have been satisfied with enjoying the Rights of Hospitality, which gave him the liberty of lodging in the House* (e). But *The principal Doctors pressing him to think seriously of entring into it, and promising him, that, provided he would read a Course of Philosophy, no notice should be taken of the Circumstance of Time, he undertook the Affair without any regard to the Obstacles, which lay in his way, to wit, that, while he was performing the Acts of his Licence, the Time, in which the Statutes prescribed that the Course of Philosophy should be gone thro'*, was elapsed——*The two Years of this painful Work being ended, he petitioned the House, that they would admit him to the Proof of his Course, and deliberate on the Honour he demanded of being received into That illustrious Body*. Mr *l' Escot* found an Opportunity at this time of being revenged on him. *As he had not taught his Penitent Cardinal* Richelieu *to forgive, He had himself learned of his Penitent never to forgive* (f). He prevented Mr *Arnauld*'s Admission into the

"nibal, promising his Father, in his tender Years,
"that, as soon as he should be of Age to bear Arms,
"he would wage War against Those mortal Ene-
"mies of his Country. It is well known, that Mr *Ar-*
"*nauld* is the Son of the famous *Anthony Arnauld*, Ad-
"vocate in the Parliament of *Paris*, who pleaded so
"eloquently, for the Universsity, against the Jesuits,
"in the Year 1594, and who omitted nothing to
"persuade the Judges, that they ought not to be
"tolerated in the Kingdom. This Action rendered
"him as odious to the whole Society, as the whole
"Society was to him, or more. It is very pro-
"bable, that he inspired the same Sentiments, with
"regard to the Jesuits, into his Sons; it is very cer-
"tain, at least, that in this they have not degenera-
"ted from the Virtue of their Father."

[B] *He gave a remarkable Instance of his Integrity, Docility, and Humility*] "At the end of the
"Course of Philosophy, which he taught in the Col-
"lege of *Mans*, in the Universsity of *Paris*, he made
"several of his Scholars maintain Theses: Among
"whom, was the Sieur *Barbey*, since a famous Pro-
"fessor of Philosophy in the same University, and
"Mr *Wallon de Beaupuis*, an Ecclesiastic of *Beau-*
"*vais*, a Person of great Piety, who is still alive,
"and has delivered this Fact in Writing. This latter
"maintaing his Thesis, on the Twenty fifth of *July*,
"1641, Mr *de la Barde*, a learned Priest of the Ora-
"tory, and at that Time Canon of the Cathedral
"Church at *Paris*, took up the Dispute, and pressed
"his Arguments so home, that the Professor was
"obliged to come in to the Assistance of his Scholar.
"But he was himself so hard pressed by the illu-
"strious Disputant, that he found himself unable to
"Reply. It had been easy for him to have got off
"by some Distinction or other, as Professors often do.
"But this did not agree with his Sincerity, and Love
"of Truth. He told him, therefore, publickly,
"and without Ceremony, that he believed him
"to be in the right; that his Opinion appeared,
"in His Judgment, to be the most true, and that
"he himself would follow it for the future. He
"was as good as his Word: for, about three Years
"after, This same Disciple being to perform his Pro-
"bation-Lecture in the *Sorbonne*, for his Degree of
"Bachelor, he desired Mr *Arnauld* to compose his

"Thesis for him. He did so, and laid down the
"contrary Opinion to That in his own Philosophi-
"cal Theses (6)." An essential Part is wanting in
This Narrative. We are not told what Opinion
Mr *Arnauld* had maintained, when he confessed his
Error, upon the strong Objections of his Opponent.
Let us supply this, and say, that the Thesis, which
Mr *de la Barde* attacked, was this: *Ens synonymè convenit Deo & creaturæ* (7). The Author of the Narrative judges right, when he says, that this Action of Mr *Arnauld* was Great before God, and Rare among Men, and that That, which proceeds from Integrity of Heart, from a constant and uniform Love of Truth, from a Greatness of Soul, which is above the Desire of Victory, and the Fear of lessening a Reputation, - - - - - *is always great* (8). But he seems to me to treat the Solutions, which may be given of Their Arguments, who maintain, that the Idea of Being is not applicable, synonymously, to God and his Creatures, with a little too much Disdain. I formerly examined this Dispute, which is very famous in the Schools, and was of Opinion, that They, who deny the *Univocation of Being*, have the Crowd, the Many, on their Side;

- - - - - - - - - illos
Defendit numerus, junctæque umbone phalanges (9);

but not the most solid Reasons; wherefore I chose the Opinion, which they oppose. I have maintained it often in public Disputations, but never found, that any Objection of Difficulty was proposed to me. My Adversary presently flew to the common Objection, that *God is a Being* κατ' ἐξοχὴν, *a self-existent Being, Infinite, and supremely Perfect; whereas the Being of Creatures is only precarious*. I found no manner of Difficulty in this Objection; for the very Rudiments of the Doctrine of *Universals* instruct us, that the Ideas of the *Genus* are entirely distinguished from the *Specific* Properties, by an Abstraction of the Mind. But had I known, that Mr *Arnauld*, having once been of this Opinion, had renounced it in Disputation, I should have suspected, that there were some Difficulties in it, which I had not met with in any of the *Spanish* School men, whom I had examined. Let us remember, that it has been observed, that he was not necessitated to alter his Opinion. This im-

ports

ARNAULD.

the Society of the *Sorbonne* [C]. He had not the same Credit after the Death of the Cardinal: But, if he had the mortification to see this young Doctor admitted into That Society, in the Year 1643, He did not fail to promote his Exclusion, when an Opportunity offered. The Book concerning *Frequent Communion*, published by Mr *Arnauld* in 1643, greatly displeased the Jesuits. They represented it, both in their Sermons, and in printed Books, as fraught with the most pernicious Doctrines. The Controversy about *Grace*, which grew warm at that time in the University of *Paris*, served only to foment the Animosities between the Jesuits and Mr *Arnauld*. This Doctor strongly defended *Jansenius*, both by refuting the three Sermons of Mr *Habert*, and the Apology of this Preacher for them, and by replying to Mr *le Moine*, Professor of the *Sorbonne* (g), and some others. There was no room for a Judicial Censure, till he published Two *Letters* on an Adventure of the Duke *de Liancour*, a great Friend of the *Port-Royal* [D]. Two Propositions were found in the second of these Letters, which the Faculty of Divinity condemned in the Year 1656. Mr *Arnauld* was at the same time declared excluded from the Faculty. There were many Irregularities in the Proceedings against him [E]. He had not appeared publickly for several Years before; for, from the time that he had been cited to *Rome*, on occasion of the Disputes about his Book concerning *Frequent Communion*, the Queen-Mother being with difficulty prevailed upon to revoke the Orders she had given him to depart immediately, *he passed his Time*, either absconding here and there, or in Solitude at Port-Royal. This retired Life continued near twenty five Years, till the Peace of *Jansenism*, concluded in 1668. Mr *Arnauld* was included in This Peace; and, accordingly, went to pay his Duty to the King, and the Nuncio, and appeared as much as he pleased in Public, till 1679, when he voluntarily quitted the Kingdom, being informed, that his Enemies rendered him suspected to the King (h). It is not doubted, but he has lived ever since in the *Low-Countries*; tho' he has discovered himself but to a very few of his trusty Friends. He was put to Trouble at *Liege* in the Year 1690 [F]. The Reflexion, which was made on This Enterprize, deserves

ports, that he did not find his first Tenet indefensible; but only, that the *Analogy of Being* seemed to him a better Doctrine, than the *Univocation*. *Eruditos discipulo sub validissimorum argumentorum mole fatiscente* (10), *suppetias venit Magister, diuque cunctatus, non cedendi necessitate coactus, sed veritate & veritatis amore victus, victum se ultrò professus est, & à sententia sua discessurum publicè sponondit. Promisit stetit*, &c. (11).

[C] *Mr l'Escot prevented Mr Arnauld's Admission into the Society of the Sorbonne.*] There were but two Doctors, who opposed Mr *Arnauld's* Request: "They alledged Statutes, and Custom, which required, that the *Course* should be performed before the *Licence*. And, as to this Difference, which was to be decided by a Plurality of Voices, they were of Opinion, that Cardinal *Richelieu*, Patron of the *Sorbonne*, should be appealed to, as Judge of what was against the Laws and Liberty of the House; and it would have been a Crime, at that Time, to have refused such a Judge. Monsr. Hardivilliers, Archbishop of *Bourges*, and Mr *Habert*, Doctor of Divinity, of the Church of *Paris*, were deputed to him (12). — The Cardinal did not judge it proper, that the Society should do any thing against their Statutes and Customs. But it was not so much a Zeal for the Orders and Rules of the House, which made him act in this manner, as the Knowledge he had of the strict Union between Mr *Arnauld*, and Mr *de St Cyran*; as Resentment, because Mr *Arnauld* had not sought his Protection, during his Licence; and, lastly, as the Influence, which Mr *l'Escot* had on his Penitent, the Cardinal. For This Doctor was One of the Two Opposers, and, as I have observed, had conceived a strong Prejudice against Mr *Arnauld*, from a meer Spirit of Jealousy, and Revenge. It was certainly more honourable for Mr *Arnauld* to be excluded the Society in this manner, than received into it, as most others are. He was, however, admitted after the Cardinal's Death; the *Sorbonne*, as well as other Societies, having, then, recovered it's Liberty (13)." Mr *l'Escot*, "made himself amends some time after, by getting him excluded both the House, and Faculty, by the Censure of 1656, of which He was the Promoter, together with Mr *le Moine*, who succeeded him, both in his Chair, and his Opinions (14).

[D] *He published two Letters on an Adventure of the Duke de Liancour, a great Friend of the Port-Royal.*] This Duke sent his Grand-Daughter to be educated at *Port-Royal*, and kept the Abbot *de Bour-*

zeys in his House. In the Year 1655, he came to Confession to a Priest of St *Sulpice*, his own Parish, who declared, "that he could not give him Absolution, unless he promised to break off all Commerce with Those Gentlemen, to withdraw his Grand-Daughter from the *Port-Royal*, and dismiss The Abbot. —— Thus Affair making a great Noise at *Paris*, and all over *France*, Mr *Arnauld* was desired to publish a Letter, in Justification of this Lord. —— A great Number of Answers being published to this Letter, Mr *Arnauld* thought himself obliged to refute the Calumnies, with which they were filled, by publishing a second Letter, in which he answered nine of those Pieces (15)."

[E] *There were many Irregularities in the Proceedings against him.*] "Commissioners were appointed in Mr *Arnauld's* Cause, who were his declared Enemies, against whom he had written on these Subjects, and who were known by every one to have been the most zealous for his Ruin; and all the Representations he could make thereupon signified nothing (16). All the Doctors of the Community of St *Sulpice*, against whom Mr *Arnauld's* Letter was written, were so unjust as to continue his Judges, notwithstanding his Exceptions; whereas they wanted only a little Honour to have made them voluntarily decline it, since God even in Lay-Tribunals (17)." You will find several other Irregularities, Innovations, Contraventions to the Order, always observed on these Occasions, and Violations of Natural Right, in the Protest of Mr *Arnauld* against the Faculty (18).

The Book, which was printed at *Leige* in the Year 1699, under the Title of *Causa Arnaldina*, may serve as a compleat Account of the Proceedings of the Divines of *Paris*, and the Substance of his Doctrines, which they censured. Several Pieces are collected in This Work, which Mr *Arnauld*, and his Party, published at that Time, to support the Justice of his Cause.

[F] *He was put to Trouble at Leige in the Year 1690.*] Six Superiors assembled to issue out Canonical Warrants against him. These were the *Guardian* of the *Franciscans*, the *Guardian* of the *White-Friars*, the *Sub-Prior Vicar* of the *Augustins*, the *Rector* of the Jesuits, the *Vicar* of the *Dominicans*; and the *Prior* of the *Jacobins*. They stiled him One *Arnauld*; but, with submission, This did no Honour to their Communities; It was either an Ignorance unpardonable in Men of Letters, or an Affectation of Contempt unbecoming Persons, who are

ARNAULD.

deserves the Consideration of Those, who govern (i). He continued his Exploits of the Pen against the Jesuits with great force to his Death, as he did for some time against Those of the Reformed Religion; but a Minister, who was the most exposed to his Attacks, had recourse to a Stratagem, in the Year 1683, which put a stop to his Incursions on the Protestant Party. I mean the Author of the ESPRIT DE MR ARNAULD [G]. We might give a long List of Falshoods in point of Fact relating to This Doctor; but we shall content our selves with mentioning a Few of them. It has been pretended, that he was born an *Huguenot* (k). He has been

(i) *See Remark [A], of the Article* BOSSU (JAMES).

(k) *See Remark [D], of the Article* ARNAULD (ANTHONY) *the Advocate.*

---

are dedicated to the Service of the Altar, and who make Decrees concerning the Faith. No Man of Letters can say, without exposing himself to the Laughter of the Learned, *One* Scaliger, *One* Sirmond, *One* Petavius, *One* Salmasius, *One* Grotius, *One* Selden, and (if the Question be about a Doctor of the *Sorbonne*) *One* Arnauld. The Disputes, in which this latter was engaged, have made so much Noise, and are remarkable for so many great Exploits on both sides, that all Men of Letters, who should but think themselves suspected of being ignorant of them, would have reason to oppose the four following Lines of *Virgil* to Suspicions so injurious.

Quis genus Æneadum, quis Trojæ nesciat urbem,
Virtutesque, virosque, aut tanti incendia belli?
Non obtusa adeo gestamus pectora Pœni,
Nec tam aversus equos Tyria sol jungit ab urbe (19).

(19) *Æneid. lib.* 1, *ver.* 569.

Who has not heard ———
The Name and Fortune of your Native Place,
The Fame and Valour of the Phrygian Race?
We Tyrians are not so devoid of Sense,
Nor so remote from Phœbus' Influence.

DRYDEN.

Be this as it will, I cannot forbear producing here the Decree of the six Regulars of *Leige* (20); the Latinity of it is so exquisite, that it may serve to unbend my Reader a little. " Nos infra scripti Superiores Conventuales Regularium in Civitate Leodiensi, certiorati de Conventiculis, quæ habentur " apud CERTUM ARNOLDUM, doctrinam suspectam " spargentem, censemus D. Vicarium charitative " certiorandum, ut similia Conventicula dissipare, & " prohibere non dignetur, etiam cum dicto Arnoldo " conversationes. Datum in Conventu Minorum " hac 25. Augusti 1690. Ad quem effectum commisimus R. P. M. Ludovicum Lamet, Priorem " Dominicanorum, ad nomine nostro accedendum " D. Vicarium, & exponendum intentionem nostrum. " —— *We, the underwritten Conventual Superiors* " *of Regulars in the City of Leige, being certified of* " *Meetings held at* ONE ARNAULD'*s, a Spreader* " *of suspected Doctrine, are of Opinion, that the Vicar* " *be charitably certified, that he would condescend to* " *disperse and prohibit such Meetings, and even all* " *Conversation with the said Arnauld. Given at a* " *Meeting of the Minors this Twenty fifth of* August " 1690. *To which effect we have commissioned Father* " Lewis Lamet, *Prior of the Dominicans, to go, in* " *our Name, to the Vicar, and declare to him our* " *Intention.*" The Author of the *Question Curieuse* says indeed, that Father *d'Iserin* had boasted of having a *Commission*, or *Permission*, from *his Highness the Bishop of* Leige, *to cause Mr* Arnauld *to be arrested wherever he should find him in his Diocess* (21); but he treats it as an egregious Lye (22).

(20) *This Story is told at the 228th Page of the Question curieuse.*

(21) Ibid. pg. 198.
(22) Ibid. pg. 200.

[G] *I mean the Author of the* ESPRIT DE MR ARNAULD.] An hundred things may be said of This Work; but, as it is probable, I shall have other Occasions of mentioning it, I shall confine myself here to a very few Observations. The Author of This Book had published a Work, which met with great Success. They, who had the Care of the Impression, at the Hague, entituled it, *The Politics of the Clergy* of France. They are Dialogues, in which there is a great deal of Beauty and Politeness, but little Solidity of Argument, and very little Caution in the vending of several Facts, which are notoriously false. Monsr *Arnauld* refuted this Book (23) in a little too contemptuous a way, and in a manner so much the more disobliging, as he manifestly convicted his Adversary of

(23) *In an Apology for Catholicks, printed in* 1681.

having argued very weakly, and published several Untruths. He began with another Book of the same Author (24); and seemed inclined to reply to the Apology for the Morality of the Reformed concerning the *Inamissibility* * of Grace: In a Word, the Author of the *Politics of the Clergy* fore-saw, that he was like to have such an Adveriary in Mr *Arnauld*, as would never allow him any Respite, nor ever pass by a Contradiction, a false Reasoning, or false Matter of Fact. This by no means agreed with one, who was determined to publish a great many Books, and who seldom gave himself the Trouble of revising what he had once written. He gave himself up to the Fire of his Imagination; and This was an inexhaustible Fund to him of false Logic, and gross Contradictions. He considered with himself, in what manner he might best prevent Mr *Arnauld* from sticking thus in his Skirts, and judged, that none could be more effectual, than to attack him personally; I mean, to impute all manner of personal ill Qualities to him. He executed this Design with all imaginable Passion, and, being in the full Carreer of Scandal, he stuck at nothing; he cast about to the Right and Left, to find still more subject for Satire; so that we may apply to him, in regard to Slander, what was said of *Voiture*, in respect to Love; he extended it *from the Scepter to the Sheepbook, from the Crown to the woolen Cap*. Mr *Arnauld*, not thinking proper to engage with a Person, who fought with such Weapons, resolved to be absolutely silent in relation to the Reformed; and thus, what the whole Society of the Jesuits could not compass, one single Minister contrived, and executed successfully; I mean the Secret of silencing This Doctor. This was not the only Advantage, which the Author of the *Esprit de Mr Arnauld* drew from his Satire; he struck such a terror into an hundred other Authors, who would have attacked him, and into several other Persons, to whom he was not the most agreeable, that they were afraid of drawing his Indignation upon them. This ought not to surprize us; for, in short, there are few Families, which may not be reproached with some Adventure (25), or who have not some Enemies malicious enough to publish some scandalous Story or other, especially if they can privately get it printed. The *Esprit de Mr Arnauld* seems to promise Publication to every little scandalous Story, which may be sent by the Post; whether it concerns a private Person, as Father *Soulier*, or a public Minister, as the late Mr *Colbert*.

A young *Jansenist*, considering the Effect of this Satire, compared Mr *Arnauld* to the ancient City of *Troy*, which the bravest Warriors, and a thousand Ships, could not conquer; but which fell by the Artifice of a Deserter, and a wooden Horse.

Talibus insidiis, perjurique arte Sinonis,
Credita res, captique dolis -----
Quos neque Tydides, nec Larissæus Achilles,
Non anni domuere decem, non mille carinæ (26).

With such Deceits he gain'd their easy Hearts;
Too prone to credit his perfidious Arts.
What Diomede, *nor* Thetis' *greater Son,*
A thousand Ships, nor ten Years Siege had done,
False Tears, and fawning Words, the City won.

DRYDEN.

" It is true, added *he*, this Comparison will not " hold in all Points; for the *Esprit de Mr Arnauld* " does not resemble the wooden Horse, which had " the chief Captains of the Army in it's Belly (27); " but rather Those Ships, which, by *Hannibal*'s Ad- " vice, were provided with earthen Pots, filled with " Serpents."

(24) *Entituled,* A Preservative against a Change of Religion.

* *Impossibility of losing.*

(25) *The Spaniards have a Proverb; No ay generacion, do no aya puto ó ladron.*

(26) Virgil. Æn. lib. 2, ver. 195.

(27) Huc delecta virum sortiti corpora furtim Includunt cæco lateri, penitusque cavernas Ingentes, uterumque armato milite complent. Id. ibid. ver. 18.

ARNAULD. 491

been reckoned One of the Cabal of *Bourg-Fontaine* [H]. He has been made to go to Nocturnal Witch-Meetings [I]: He has been sent to command the Troops of the *Vaudois* [K]: He has been advanced to the Post of Squire to the *Goliah Peter Jurieu*

" Serpents." See *Cornelius Nepos* in the Life of That *Carthaginian* General.

[H] *He has been reckoned one of the Cabal of* Bourg Fontaine.] *Du Plessis's* Calumnies, with regard to the Father, are nothing in comparison to the Falfhood, which Mr *Filleau*, the King's Advocate in the Presidial Court of *Poictiers*, published concerning the Son, in the Year 1654: for there is no doubt, that he reckoned Mr *Arnauld* in the Number of the feven Doctors of the Assembly of *Bourg-Fontaine* (28). The Case, in short, was this: Mr *Filleau*, publishing a *Judicial Relation*, in the Year 1654, of what had passed at *Poictiers*, on occasion of the new Doctrine of *Jansenism*, declared, that an Ecclefiastic had assured him, that, in a Conference, which feven Persons had held at *Bourg-Fontaine*, in the Year 1621, They had consulted about the Means to abolish Christianity; that This Ecclefiastic had himself been one of the feven; that, some time after, he broke with the other six, only one of whom was then living, and whose Names were (J. D. V. D. H.) (C. J.) (P. C.) (P. C.) (A. A.) (S. V.) By certain Circumstances, attending this Narrative, and by the Character of certain Books, which we are given to understand were published purely in execution of the Engagements entered into at *Bourg-Fontaine*, every one believed, that the Letters of the first Name denoted *John du Verger de Hauranne*, Abbot of St *Cyran*; Those of the second *Cornelius Jansenius*, Bishop of *Ypres*; thofe of the third *Philip Cospian*, Doctor of the *Sorbonne*, Bishop of *Nantes*, and since of *Lisieux*; thofe of the fourth *Peter Camus*, Bishop of *Belley*; thofe of the fifth *Anthony Arnauld*, the Subject of this Article; and thofe of the sixth *Simon Vigor*, Counsellor in the Great Council. Mr *Filleau* affirms, "That it was resolved, in this Assembly, to attack the two Sacraments, which are the most frequented by Adults, " to wit, Those of Penance, and the Eucharist; " and the Means, proposed for attaining this end, " was, to introduce a difuse of them; not by dif" covering any direct Design of making them lefs " frequented, but by rendering the Practice of them " fo difficult, and clogged with Circumstances fo " incompatible with the Condition of the Men of " Those Times, that they should remain in a manner " inaccessible, and that, by this difuse of them, " founded on fuch plaufible Appearances, All Belief " in them would by degrees be loft." The Public thought, that This was pointed at Mr *Arnauld*, becaufe of his Book of *Frequent Communion*, and that therefore Mr *Filleau* certainly meant him, by the fifth of those dangerous Conspirators against the Christian Religion, marked (A. A.) (29).

As we are not concerned, in this Place, to examine into the Truth, or Falfhood, of this Conspiracy, I shall content myself with faying, that Mr *Arnauld* looked upon this as one of the highest Excesses of Calumny, that had ever been known, and that, in particular, he perfectly cleared himself from the Accusation of being found in the Conference of Thefe Deists (30). For he made it appear, that, having been born in 1612, he could be but nine Years of Age, when it was pretended, that this Conference was held. This Juftification is fo strong, that not only the Silence of the Accufer, but even the formal Confeffion of one of the Accufer's Friends, made it appear, that nothing could be replied to it. On the other fide, Father *Meynier*, pretending, that Mr *Filleau*'s Account of the Conference of *Bourg Fontaine* contained nothing but what was very certain, confeffes, " that Mr *Arnauld* had given " convincing Proofs, that he was not of this Af" fembly; but, *adds he*, he is deceived, in believing, " that *Anthony Arnauld* is the Perfon meant by the " Letters A. A. I affure him, in behalf of the Au" thor of the Judicial Relation, that Those Letters " denote Another, who is yet living, and is too " good a Friend of Mr *Arnauld*'s to be unknown " to him (31)." Mr *Pafcal*, who was then writing the Provincial Letters, preffed the Jefuits to name the private Betrayer of the Conference, the fix Doctors, who had affifted at it, and particularly the Perfon denoted by the Letters A. A. and who, tho'

not Mr *Arnauld* himself, was too intimate a Friend of his to be unknown to him. But thefe Challenges were difregarded; and it is but a few Years fince, that a very famous Jefuit of *Antwerp* declared to the Public, that This Friend of Mr *Arnauld* was his own Brother *Arnauld d'Andilli* (32). This has been already confuted. See the Remark [B] of the Article ARNAULD d'ANDILLI.

[I] *He has been made to go to Nocturnal Witch-Meetings.*] I cannot tell in which of the two Affemblies Mr *Arnauld* would rather have been prefent, That of *Bourg-Fontaine*, or That, which the late Mr *Maupas*, Bishop of *Evreux*, has fomewhere fpoken of. " It is certain, that he affirmed to feve" ral Perfons, that he had been informed by a con" verted Wizard, that he had feen Mr *Arnauld*, " and a certain Princefs of the Blood (33), at " Nocturnal Witch-Meetings, and that Mr *Arnauld* " had made a very fine Speech to the Devils (34)." If he must have a chofen between thefe two Extreams, and if the Speech might have tended only to excite the Devils to fome Amendment of Life, I make no doubt, but the Doctor would much rather have harangued in this Meeting, than have given his Opinion in the Charter-houfe of *Bourg-Fontaine*, for the Abolishment of Christianity, and the Propagation of Deifm.

It were to abufe the Patience of my Readers to expofe the ridiculoufnefs of this Tale, which this Prelate related to feveral Perfons; it is one of Thofe Falfhoods, which Mr *Arnauld* thinks no one ought ever to give himfelf the Trouble of confuting. Thefe are his Words (35): " The Increfs of Honour may " be confidered two Ways; either with regard to " the Calumny itfelf, which poffibly may be very " heinous, of with regard to Thofe, who, being " once prepoffeffed with it, may afterwards have a " very ill Opinion of the Perfon calumniated. It " is properly the latter Confideration, which obliges " a Man to defend himfelf; for, how enormous fo" ever it be in itfelf, it may fafely enough be flight" ed, if it is of fuch a Nature, that no fober Perfon " will give Credit to it. As for Example; what the " late Mr *de Maupas*, Bishop of *Evreux*, had for" merly faid, that he was told, by a converted Wi" zard, that Mr *Arnauld* had been at their Noctur" nal Meetings, and that the Devils had admired the " Speech he made to them, was in itfelf an horrible " Calumny; in the mean time, if any impertinent " Fellow had inferted this in a Libel, would any one " have the Doctor give himfelf the trouble of con" futing it; and, in default of this, would there be " any Reafon to fuppofe, *that it was the Impoffi" bility of anfwering it, which forced him to be filent, " and that he had, in Effect, confeffed it* ? "

[K] *He has been fent to command the Troops of the* Vaudois.] This Falfhood has little more of Probability in it, than the former. There have been, of late, Manufcripts, which pofitively affirm, that the *Arnauld*, who is at the Head of the *Vaudois*, is Mr *Arnauld*, Doctor of the *Sorbonne*, who has at laft declared himfelf, and does Wonders in Savoy, at the Head of the Troops of That Party (36). It would be a very furprizing Metamorphofis, if, at the Age of Seventy eight Years, a Doctor of the *Sorbonne*, who has employed his whole Life in Study, and who has wrote fo much againft the Proteftant Clergy, fhould himfelf become a Minifter militant, and exchange his Pen for a Sword, and a brown Musket, endeavouring to make *Arnauld*'s Carabineers ftill more talked of, than Thofe of One of his Uncles, very well known to the *Rochellers*, under the Reign of *Lewis* XIII (37). The late Bifhop of *Leige* was told, at his own Table, That Mr *Arnauld* had abjured the Catholic Faith at Boilleduc, *and that he was married there* (38). The greateft part of Thofe, who are called Zealots, fear nothing more than the Orthodoxy of Thofe, whom they accufe. They do not imitate God, *who defires not the Death of a Sinner, but that he may be converted, and live*. They would have the Perfon, they have once accufed, apoftatize in good earneft; and are angry, that he does not go over to the Enemies Party, to make their Accufations good. They would much rather

VOL. I. 6 H

ARNAULD.

Jurieu [L]. It has been said, that he was banished from *France* [M]; and that He wrote the Apology for the Catholics only to recover his Benefice [N]. Several Books

rather another should damn himself, than that themselves should pass for notorious Calumniators. See what a Modern Author says upon this (39).

[L] *He has been advanced to the Post of Squire to the Goliah Peter Jurieu.*] They, who place Mr *Arnauld* at the Head of the *Vaudois*, certainly affront him less, than They, who represent him as Squire to the *Goliah Jurieu*. This the Bishop of *Malaga* did, in his *Catholic Complaint*, by applying, as well as he could, to these two famous Writers, a Thought of St *Bernard*, in relation to *Peter Abelard*, and *Arnauld* of *Bresse* (40); which gives him an opportunity of drawing this Conclusion: " Isti qui modo surrexe-" runt, novus Golias, & ejus armiger, PETRUS " scilicet, & ARNALDUS, facili negotio exter-" minabuntur. — *They, who have lately arisen, The new* " *Goliah, and his Armour-Bearer, to wit,* PETER, *and* " ARNAULD, *will be easily exterminated.*" The Public has seen the Letter, which Mr *Arnauld* wrote to This Prelate, wherein he tells him, that his Highness (41) must needs have been strangely imposed upon, to be told " that Dr *Arnauld* was Squire to Mr *Jurieu,* " the Goliah of the Protestants against the Catholic " Party; for, *continues he,* if your Highness had " known This *Arnauld,* you could not have been " capable of so great an Error in Judgment, as to " take Two of the most declared Enemies in the " World to be of the same Party, and to mistake " Him, who has zealously supported the Cause of the " Church against That Minister, for his Associate and " Confident in the cruel War, which he wages a-" gainst the Church." It is certain, that the two Authors, who have been taken, the one for a *Goliah*, and the other for his Squire, are both so far from being such, that it is not more false, that Mr *Arnauld* assisted at the Conference of *Bourg-Fontaine,* or at the Nocturnal Meetings of the Wizards, than that he is the Squire of the *Goliah Peter Jurieu.* Nothing, then, can be more cold, or more remote from Truth, than the Allusions borrowed from the Passage of St *Bernard*.

This is what the pretended *Goliah* has reproached the Author of the *Catholic Complaint* with, no less than the pretended Squire. " If This Bishop, *says he* " (42), had been of a discerning Taste, his violent " Invectives would not have turned upon the silly " Allusion to the Names of *Arnauld* of *Bresse,* and " *Peter Abelard*; meaning, that Monsieur *Arnauld* " is the Successor of *Arnauld* of *Bresse,* and the Mi-" nister *Peter Jurieu* of *Peter Abelard.* He would " not have called That Minister the *Goliah*-Enemy of " the Church, and *Arnauld* his Squire. That *Ar-*" *nauld* and This Minister are too much at variance, " to conspire together: Besides, Mr *Arnauld* is of a " fitter Age, Size, and Strength, to be the *Goliah,* " than the Squire. This He also pretends to, and no " one will dispute the Honour of it with him."

I must here note a small Defect of Memory in Mr *Arnauld.* He complains (43), that, after the weak Comparison of *Arnauld* of *Bresse* with *Arnauld* of *Paris,* and of *Peter Abelard* with *Peter Jurieu*, they make the Bishop of *Malaga* say, that This Doctor was the *Goliah* of the Party, and the Minister his Squire. We have seen, that he has been made to say quite the contrary.

[M] *It has been said, that he was banished France.*] A Doctor of the *Sorbonne* (44), a *Savoyard* by Nation, maintained, in a Book intituled *Reasonable Prejudices against Jansenism,* printed at *Geneva* in 1686 (45), that Mr *Arnauld* had been banished *France* by the King's Order. The following Words, in the Advertisement to the Reader, import this: *I thought I could not speak the whole Truth, without blaming the Conduct of this old Puritan, who, by the Justice of the most Christian King, is a Fugitive in Holland.* It is, nevertheless, certain, that he voluntarily quitted the Kingdom; and it cannot be doubted, after the Letters, which he wrote, in 1679, to the Chancellor, Mr *le Tellier,* and to the Archbishop of *Paris,* printed in the first Volume of the *Esprit de Mr Arnauld,* in the Year 1684. So that it is strange, that, two Years after, the Abbot *de Ville* should be ignorant of a Truth, exposed to public View, in a Satire, for which there has been so great a Demand. But it is

yet more strange, that, in the Year 1690, Mr *Arnauld* should be obliged to get These two Letters printed, in order to confute Those, who *published every where, that he was a Rebel to his King, and that he had been banished France, as a turbulent Fellow* (46). I believe the Author of the *Esprit* has reported a no less Falshood, in maintaining, *That he was expelled Flanders.* Tho' this good Man, continues he (47), *thinks his Adventures are unknown, yet we have certain Intelligences, that he was expelled the Netherlands by order of The Governour.* The Term *Chaser*, which the Author of the General Criticism on *Maimbourg's* History of *Calvinism* makes use of, is a little equivocal. They have reported, says he (48), that Mr Arnauld's *House was a Rendezvous of discontented Persons; that caballing and factious Conferences were held there, that they prepared Memoirs there for the Court of* Rome; *in a word, they have gained their Point, which was to expel him* * *with the rest of the Cabal.* This means no more, than that they procured certain Orders to be sent to Mr *Arnauld,* which were the cause that he made choice of a Retreat in a foreign Country.

[N] *He is said to have wrote an Apology for the Catholics, only to recover his Benefices.*] Mr *Jurieu* was grossly mistaken, when he said, that Mr *Arnauld* had wrote the Apology for the Catholics, in hopes of being restored to his native Country, that he might peaceably *enjoy his Estate, and Benefices* (49), and that the fear of having *his Benefices confiscated* engaged him in some false Steps. This could not be better refuted by a Geometrical Demonstration, than by the public Declaration, which Mr *Arnauld* made, *that he never had a Benefice*; for it can never enter into the Mind of a reasonable Man, that a Doctor so jealous of his Reputation, as he is, and who could not expect to escape the most mortifying Confusion, if he falsly denied, that he ever had a Benefice, when he really had enjoyed one, should venture to publish such a Falshood in a printed Work. We need, then, only cast our Eyes on these Words of Mr *Arnauld,* to be demonstratively convinced of his Adversary's Falshood. " The seditious manner, *says he* (50), in which they " presumed to speak of the Affairs of That Country, " obliged the Ambassador of his *Britannic* Majesty to " demand of the *States* a Condemnation of the most " Vehement of their Libels, to which they were " pleased to give the Title of *Esprit de Mr Arnauld,* " tho' perhaps I am the least ill treated in it of a great " Number of Persons, whom they pull to pieces, " without their having any relation to me, but what " is either Ridiculous or Imaginary; having almost " nothing to reproach me with, but secret Intentions, " often grounded on manifest Falshoods: As, when " they say, that it was not out of Regard to Religion, " that I wrote the Apology for the Catholics, but up-" on a Prospect of Interest, and for fear of losing my " Benefice; I, who, all the World knows, " have none." Thus he speaks, in a Letter dated the Twentieth of *October* 1684. He speaks no less positively in a Work printed in 1689. " As for the " Book falsely entituled *Esprit de Mr Arnauld,* he (51) " never had any thoughts of answering it; for, it " having been sent him some time after it appeared, " in opening each Volume in several places, he met " with such things, as sufficiently acquainted him " with This Minister's Genius; for instance, That " idle Calumny (52), that they suffered the Children " of Quality of twelve or thirteen Years of Age, " who studied Humanity at *Port-Royal,* to read the " *Socinian* Books; and another no less ridiculous, " tho' less heinous; that Mr *Arnauld,* who has " no Benefice, and who never sought any, " wrote the Apology for the Catholics to preserve " his Benefices. He concludes from hence, that so " passionate and unreasonable a Calumniator, being " unworthy of Credit, deserved no answer, and " from that time till now he never read a word in " the Book, before your *Defence* appeared (53)." So that what the *Latins* express by the Proverb, *Cantherius in porta,* has happened to the Author of the *Esprit de Mr Arnauld:* He has stumbled at the very Threshold.

Note, That Mr *Arnauld* had once a Canonship in the Cathedral of *Verdun,* when he began his Licence in

---

(39) *General Criticism on Maimbourg's History of Calvinism, pag. 584, second Edition.*

(40) *Father Maimbourg has play'd upon the same equivoc. I Name of Arnauld of Bressia, in his Decad. dl I' Empire; and Theoph. Raynauld has wrote a Book, entituled, Arnaldus de Brixia redivivus in Arnaldo de Lutetia. ... i. e. Arnauld of Bresse revived in Arnauld of Paris.*

(41) *This Title was given him, because he was a Natural Son of Philip IV of Spain.*

(42) *Religion of the Jesuits, p. 59.*

(43) *Morale Pratique, Tom. 3. pag. 773.*

(44) *He is called Abbé de Ville. See Nouvelle de la Republ. des Lettres, for July 1686. Art. 8.*

(45) *The Title imports, that it was at Cologne, by Abraham du Bois.*

(46) *Quest. Curieuse, pag. 212.*

(47) *Esprit de Mr Arnauld, Tom. 1. pag. 38.*

(48) *Lettres V.*

* *le CHASSER.*

(49) *Esprit de Mr Arnauld, Tom. 1. pag. 34. 36. 44.*

(50) *The second Addition to the Apology for the Catholics, p. 14.*

(51) *It is off Himself that Mr Arnauld speaks.*

(52) *See the Refutation of this Story in Mr Arnauld's Dissertation on the pretended Happiness of the Pleasures of Sense, printed in 1687.*

(53) *Tom. III, de la Morale Pratique.*

ARNAULD. 493

Books have been ascribed to him, which he never wrote [O]. I shall take notice of some of them; and I doubt not but many others may be pointed out. His Silence has

(54) Præfat. Cauſæ Armaldinæ, p. vii.

(55) Ibid. pag. xix.

PERPETUITÉ de la Foi.——*Perpetuity of the Faith*. A Diſpute between Meſſ. *Arnauld* and *Claude*.

(56) *See, be-him, Remark* [9].

(57) A. B. R. D. L. D. P. *that is,* Abel Rotolp, de la Deveze, Paſteur. *He was formerly Miniſter at* Caſtres, *and now at the Hague*.

(58) That is, according to the Bookſeller's anticipated Date; for I believe the Book came out in 1665.

(59) Acta Eruditorum Lipſienſ. 1683, pag. 639.

(60) Acta Eruditorum Lipſ. Ibid. *But in* 1613, pag. 442. *they affert it.*

in the Year 1638 (54), but he quitted This Benefice a little before he received Deacons Orders in the Year 1641 (55).

[O] *Several Books have been aſcribed to him, which he never wrote.*] I shall divide this Remark into four Sections.

I. Without obſerving the Order of Time; As the firſt Falſhood in relation to the Books aſcribed to him, I ſhall mention That, which regards *The Perpetuity of the Faith*. For This Book has given occaſion to the moſt famous Diſpute, that was ever raiſed between the *Roman* Catholics and Proteſtants. Mr *Claude*, who was Advocate for the latter, has gained the greateſt Honour by it, that ever Miniſter gained: And Mr *Arnauld*, who was principal Advocate for the former, perhaps never exerted the whole Force of his Genius with more Application, than on this Occaſion. All that vaſt Wit, Eloquence, Reading, and Logic, can furniſh of ſhining and ſtrong, appeared on both ſides in the Courſe of the Diſpute; Each Party claims the Victory; nor can all the Pains and Expence, which the *Port-Royal* has been at, to procure a great Number of Atteſtations from the *Levant*, avail any thing againſt the Perſuaſions of the Reformed, touching the Faith of the Chriſtians of Thoſe Parts, with regard to the Euchariſt. The Ignorance, which reigns among Thoſe Chriſtians, the ill Character of the *Greek* Nation, Time out of Mind, in Point of Sincerity, the mercenary Subſcriptions, of which they are thought capable (56), &c. enervate, in the Eyes of Proteſtants, all the Atteſtations, which the *Port-Royal* has produced. But this does not prevent the Controverſy's being looked upon (ſetting aſide the Prejudices of Party) as one of the moſt memorable and glorious Tranſactions of Mr *Arnauld's* Life. I had reaſon, then, to begin this Remark with the firſt Exploit of this great Conteſt.

I could wiſh, that the Author, who has given us a good Abridgment of the Life of Mr *Claude* (57), had, with the utmoſt Exactneſs, noted the Epoch of This War, ſince Mr *Claude* has not dated the Preface of his firſt Book. This Defect may deceive ſeveral Perſons; for example, I have Mr *Claude's* firſt Anſwer, printed at *Paris*, by *Stephen Lucas*, in 1672. The Title does not inform me, whether it be the firſt or ſecond Edition; and, in the firſt Line of the Preface, I find, that the Diſpute had been depending about Four Years, and that it was a Year ſince the Manuſcript, which had been communicated at that time to Mr *Claude*, was printed. Till I have better information, I find myſelf almoſt invincibly inclined to paſs this ſlight Judgment, that the *Perpetuity of the Faith* was printed the firſt time, in the Year 1671. In ſaying This, I am aware, that One is often miſtaken in Conjectures of this kind, when the requiſite Date is not prefixed to the Prefaces. My Edition of the *Perpetuity of the Faith* is the Fourth, and is of the Year 1666; but I am informed by it of the Date of the firſt; for I find, at the bottom of the Abſtract of the Licence, that the firſt Edition of This Book was finiſhed the fifteenth of *July* 1664. Mr *Claude's* firſt Anſwer ſeems to me to be of the Year 1666 (58). The Author of his Life, not thinking exact Dates neceſſary in an Abridgment, was the Occaſion, that the learned Men, who wrote the Journal of *Leipſic*, to the great Benefit of the Republic of Letters, and with much Honour to their City, which may juſtly be called the *Athens* of *Germany*, were miſtaken with regard to the firſt Writings of this Miniſter. They pretend, that his firſt Anſwer to the *Perpetuity of the Faith* was printed, before he ſerved the Church of *Montauban* (59); but the Truth is, The Firſt and Second were both printed at the ſame time, after the firſt had been handed about, for four or five Years, in Manuſcript, and after he had left *Montauban*. But to return to the Fact;

Mr *de la Devoze* does not affirm, that the *Perpetuity of the Faith* is a Work of Mr *Arnauld*; but is ſatisfied with ſaying, that he is ſuppoſed to have been the Author of it. The Journaliſts of *Leipſic* keep within the ſame Bounds (60); but, in the Supplement of *Moreri*, in which is a very long Article of CLAUDE, taken in part from the Abridgment of his Life, it is

poſitively affirmed, that Mr *Arnauld* is the Author of the *Perpetuity of the Faith*. In the mean time, the moſt common and probable Opinion aſcribes This Work to Mr *Nicolle*, the Three large Volumes of the *Perpetuity defended* to Mr *Arnauld*, and the General Anſwer to the ſecond Book of Mr *Claude* to Mr *Nicolle*. The *Queſtion curieuſe* ſays nothing poſitively of it; becauſe the Catalogue, which we find in it, of the Writings of the Gentlemen of *Port-Royal* againſt the Proteſtants, does not diſtinguiſh Thoſe of Mr *Nicolle* from Thoſe of Mr *Arnauld*.

Obſerve, that the firſt Volume of the *Perpetuity defended* was printed in the Year 1669, and that the Author, having heſitated for a Year, whether he ſhould anſwer Mr *Claude's* Book, began to do it in *January* 1667, and finiſhed The firſt Volume in *June* 1668 (61). Obſerve alſo, that It is aſcribed to Mr *Arnauld* in ſome of the Approbations at the Head of the Work. This is ſufficient to remove all uncertainty.

II. The Author of the *Eſprit de Mr Arnauld* aſcribes the ſecond Volume of the *Moral Pratique* to This Doctor, but gives no manner of reaſon for it. Mr *Arnauld* gave him the Lye publickly. " It is cer- " tain, *ſays* he (62), that Mr *Arnauld* is not the Au- " thor of the *Moral Pratique*. The Jeſuits have " aſcribed it to him —— on the Faith of Mr *Jurieu* " only; a Perſon decried for his Falſhood and " Lying, and who alone aſcribes This Book to " Mr *Arnauld*, as he does many other Pieces, in " which every one elſe knows he never had the leaſt " ſhare." From That time the Accuſer never endeavoured to juſtify what he had ſaid; ſo that Equity muſt judge it to be a falſe Imputation. The Proofs muſt needs be very difficult, ſince the Biſhop of *Malaga* ſpeaks but doubtfully of it, on the ſole Authority of Mr *Jurieu*; for he ſays (63): *modo fit* ARNALDUS, *ut innuit* PETRUS JURIEU *in ſuo* SPIRITU.

— IF ARNAULD *be the Perſon, as* PETER JURIEU *intimates in his* SPIRITUS. The Author of the *Defence of the new Chriſtians*, who is thought to be Father *le Tellier*, one of the beſt Pens of the Order, was more deciſive, than the Prelate, though he ſeems to have no other Authority than Mr *Jurieu*: For which Mr *Arnauld* gives him a ſmart Reprimand, and accuſes him *of judging raſhly*; *which wounds Charity and Juſtice, if the Circumſtances of it be well conſidered. The only Reaſon*, adds he (64), *why you make him the Author of it, is the Teſtimony of a Man, who, in your own Eſteem, is unworthy of Credit, and ſo notorious for his Falſhoods, that he is only fit to call the cleareſt Truths in queſtion, when he advances them.*

III. The Journal of *Leipſic* aſcribes *The Lawful Prejudices againſt the* Calviniſts to Mr *Arnauld* (65). Yet, according to the general Opinion of Thoſe, who are beſt informed in theſe Particulars, Mr *Nicolle* is the Author of it; and the Abbot *de Ville* aſcribes it to him by Name (66), in the Preface of the Book beforementioned; where he retorts on the Gentlemen of *Port-Royal* the Prejudices, which they made uſe of againſt the Reformed. The Proof, which the Gentlemen of *Leipſic* employ, is not a good one; for, tho' the Biſhop of *Condom*, and He of *Grenoble*, give their Approbation, in One and the ſame Act, to the *Prejugez Legitimes*, and three other Books, one of which is certainly Mr *Arnauld's*, yet they do not ſuppoſe, that the others are ſo too. They were joined together, becauſe they came all four from the *Port-Royal* at the ſame time. Theſe four Books; are the *Prejugez Legitimes—Lawful Prejudices*; the *Reponſe Generale à M. Claude,—General Anſwer to Mr Claude*; the *Renverſement de la Morale,—Overthrow of the Morality*; and the ſecond Volume of the *Perpetuité defendue,—Perpetuity defended*.

IV. In the Year 1669, A Work called *A Defence of the Church*, againſt Mr *Claude's* Book, intituled, *A Defence of the Reformation*, was printed at *Antwerp* (67). The Journaliſts of *Leipſic* conjectured, that it was a Piece of Mr *Arnauld's* (68); but it came from another Hand, viz. from *Peter d'Antecourt*, a Religious of *St Genevieve*, and Chancellor of the Univerſity of *Paris*, as another excellent Journaliſt informs us (69).

(61) *See the* Preface.

THE ſecond Tome of the Morale Pratique—Practical Morality.

(62) Letter of a Divine, on the Defence of the new Chriſtians, pag. 2.

(63) Catholic. Quer m. lib. pag. 103.

(64) Morale Pratique, Tom. III. pag. 36.

FAKTOEN Legitimes—Lawful Prejudices.

(65) Acta Eruditorum. Ann. 1683. pag. 438, 450, *and in the* Index, p. 561. Ann. 1690. pag. 595.

(66) *Py miſtake he calls him* Nicol. which is unjuſtly a criticed, ſays *le*, to Mr *Nicol*, one of the moſt popiſh Writers of *Port-Royal*.

THE Defence of the Church.

(67) 77. *the Page imports, at* Cologne, *for* Peter Marteau.

(68) Acta Eruditorum Anni, 1690, pag. 18, *and in the* Index, pag. 611. (69) Hiſtory of the Works of the Learned, *Aug.* 1689, pag. 514; *September*, 1689, pag. 34.

I paſs

ARNAULD.

has been imputed to a false Reason [P]. Some have given him Spectacles, and a faithless Servant [Q]. The chief Works, written by him, since his quitting France, relate to the System of Nature and Grace, by Father Mallebranche; the *Philosophical Sin*; the Practical Morality of the Jesuits; and some Propositions of Mr *Steyaert*. In this last Book, he vigorously attacks Father *Simon*, in defence of the New-Testament of *Mons*, and in relation to the Inspiration of the Sacred Writers, and the Translations of the Scripture into the Vulgar Tongue [R]; as also in favour of the Attestations

(70) Papebroch. Elucid. Histor. Actor. in Controversia Carmelitana, pag. 135.

(71) Printed at Cologne, by Van Bülning, 1698. It contains 5. Pages in 12mo.

* Refutation of a Book of Father P. Annat, &c. pag. 7.

I pass by an Error of the Jesuit *Papebroch*; which is That of ascribing the Books, which have appeared under the Name of *Petrus Aurelius*, to Mr *Arnauld*. *Petrus Aurelius vero nomine est Antonius Arnaldus* (70). I know not what to say to a Fact, which I have met with in a Pamphlet (71), intituled, *A Defense of the Mandate of my Lord the Bishop of Arras, of the thirtieth of December, 1697, against a Libel intituled, The ancient Heresy of the Jesuits renewed, &c.* The Author of the Defence pretends to prove, that the *Jansenists* have acknowledged the Authority of the Church in determining the Sense of a Book. And This is what he says at the Twenty fourth Page; "Among several, whom I could produce, I shall content myself with one Author, who may serve instead of all the rest. It is Mr *Arnauld*, the Head and Oracle of *Jansenism*. After having, in the fourth Part of the Apology for the Nuns of *Port-Royal*, exceeded all that ever has been said against the Infallibility of the Church, in ascertaining the Sense of Books; and, in a new Work, in defence of the Apology, and others of his Writings, being reduced to an Impossibility of justifying himself from the Reflexion cast upon him, that his Arguments tended to destroy the Certainty of Tradition; he found himself necessitated, in spite of himself, to make this important and decisive Acknowledgment, which ruined, in a few Lines, all his Labours for so many Years. *There are certain Matters of Fact*, says this Writer *, *from which the Truth of a Doctrine must necessarily be concluded: And these are They, which contain the Tradition of the Church. For instance; from the Fathers having unanimously taught, that such a Doctrine is Matter of Faith, it follows, that This Doctrine is Matter of Faith —— and thus it is plain, that the Church being infallible in the Decision of Doctrines, she is likewise so in the Decision of such Facts, as necessarily follow from Those Doctrines, and which are the necessary means, by which she attains to the Knowledge of the Truths of Faith.* Thus far Mr *Arnauld*." This is clear and express. It is positively affirmed, that The Apology for the Nuns, and the Confutation of one of Father *Annat*'s Books are two of our Doctor's Pieces. I do not pretend to deny it; though, on the one side, the Stile of the Apology seems to me more correct than His, and on the other, less lively, and less vehement. This Apology is a pretty large *Quarto*, divided into four Parts, and printed in 1665. Observe, by the way, the Fate of Disputes: It scarce ever happens, in supporting an Opinion, that we are at full Liberty to make use of Maxims, which are purely universal. We have some other Opinions to manage, which oblige us to Restrictions; but This is a very inconvenient Restraint; for The Adversary makes his Advantage of our Exceptions. This supplies him with Arguments *ad hominem*, and gives him great Advantage; and it is, generally, by this Means, that he recovers himself, after he has been fairly thrown. The *Jansenists* are an Example of This in the Apology for the Mandate of the Bishop of Arras. I would willingly see how they will get off. Both Parties are Sufferers in this Affair. The Infallibility of the Church cannot be maintained as to Facts; and, unless this be admitted, one is exposed to a thousand Inconveniences. As to the Book *des deux chefs qui n'en font qu'un*; —— *Of two Heads, which make but one*; I shall speak of it in another Place. It is a Work falsely ascribed to Mr *Arnauld*. This Imputation is in an anonymous Piece, printed in the Year 1688, and supposed to be Father *le Tellier*'s. The Title of it is *An Apologetical Letter for Mr* Arnauld, &c. It would be more reasonable to say, that the Doctrine itself, *of the two Heads which make but one*, was maintained by the Doctor of the *Sorbonne*, in the Preface to his Book of *Frequent Communion*; but even This wants Proof. See the *Abridged History of his Life* (72).

[P] *His Silence has been imputed to a false Reason.*] The Difficulties proposed to Mr Steyaert make it appear, that the Author of the *Voyage to the World* of Des Cartes had not exactly consulted the Period of Time, as to the Quarrel between Mr *Arnauld* and Father *Mallebranche*, when he said, that the first engaged in it purely to have a Pretence for not answering two Books, which had appeared against him, one composed by a Minister, and the other by a Jesuit. It must be confessed, that the Public is scarce yet recovered from the Astonishment, which the first Year's Silence of this Doctor raised with regard to these two Books; but it is certain, whatever the subtile and polite Traveller to the New World may say of it, that he was engaged with Father *Mallebranche*, before the *Esprit de Mr Arnauld*, and the Observations of Father *le Tellier*, appeared (73). I must not dissemble, that the Reasons Mr *Arnauld* gave for this Silence pleased some; but they are very far from pleasing all Readers. I have already cited a Passage, which relates to these Reasons (74); here is another; "As for Mr *Jurieu*, he is become so famous all over *Europe* for Slander and Calumny, that he is no longer able to hurt Those, whom he attacks. I know that two Persons, both Protestants, have wrote to Mr *Arnauld* about him, as a Man decried among his own Party, and whose Passions have made themselves ashamed of him; and that they have offered to send him Memoirs, which would discover what he is. But it is no wonder Mr *Arnauld* did not take them at their Word, or that he would not throw away his Time in writing against a Man formidable only by Abuse and Slander (76)." He immediately produces some Facts, which he pretends were nothing but monstrous Calumnies, published by This Minister. The Reasons he gives for his Silence, as to Father *le Tellier* (77), have satisfied but few Persons.

[Q] *Some have given him Spectacles, and a faithless Servant.*] The Writings published on a Correspondence by Letter between a pretended *Arnauld*, and a Professor of *Douay*, contain Matters, which may be thought *à propos* to a Work of this kind; however I shall only observe the manner, in which Mr *Arnauld* refutes the Complaint imputed to him of having been robbed by his Servant, and being scarce able, by reason of his great Age, to read a small Character. *How could I complain of a Servant*, says he, *who robbed and betrayed me; I, who never had any, but what were very faithful, and who have had none at all for twelve Years past, since I left Paris* (78). In a Note on Mr *de Ligny*'s Letter, it is said, *That Mr* Arnauld *never made use of Spectacles, and that he could read the smallest Character as easily as the largest*. These are little Particulars, which deserve to be communicated to Those, who are curious in the History of illustrious Persons. As to the Intrigue of the False *Arnauld*, it is one of the finest Comedies, has ever been acted; and had as much Success as the Authors could expect. Perhaps there is no Instance of a Mortality, which, in so short a Time, swept away so many Professors in an University, as This Affair did in That of *Douay*; perhaps no Discharge ever cleared the Ranks so well. This may serve to put us in Mind of these Words of the *Psalmist*; *And Thou shalt renew the Face of the Earth*.

[R] *He vigorously attacks Father* Simon, *in Defence of — The Inspiration of the Sacred Writers, and the Translations of the Scripture*.] I have elsewhere (80) produced two Propositions of the Jesuits, which were censured by the Faculties of Divinity of *Louvain* and *Douay*. They are Propositions, which seem to limit or qualify the Inspiration of the Scriptures. Upon this, Mr *Simon* took part against the Censors (81), and was refuted

(72) Pag. 85, &c.

(73) See the Difficulties proposed to Mr Steyaert, Part 2. page 59, &c.

(74) Above, Citat. (53).

(75) It is at the 23-th Page of the *3ˢ Tome of the Morale Pratique*.

(76) Differtation on the pretended Happiness of the Pleasures of Sense, pag. 12.

(77) Morale Pratique, Tom. III, p. 266, 267.

(78) Première Plainte, pag. 9.

(80) In the Article Father ADAM, a little before Citation (9).

(81) See Chap. 21, 24, of The Critical History of the New Testament.

ARNAULD. 495

Attestations of the *Greeks* [S], &c. ———— He died in the Night between the eighth and ninth of *August* 1694, Aged Eighty two Years, six Months, and two Days. At this great Age, he received two signal and uncommon Favours from Heaven; for the Sickness, of which he died, continued but a Week, more or less, and never prevented his saying, or hearing, Mass, and rehearsing his *Breviary* almost *at the ordinary Hours* (*l*). His Agony was mild, calm, and short. On the other Hand, he had as great strength of Mind, and Memory, and wrote as well the last Year of his Life, as at forty or fifty Years of Age. These are Blessings, which rarely attend learned Men. Some few Months before his Death, he wrote four Letters against Father *Mallebranche* (*m*), and one to his old Friend Mr *du Bois*, full of *Reflexions on the Eloquence of Preachers* (*n*). The Public has seen these last Works, and found no signs in them of a declining Judgment. Mr *du Bois* did not long survive either his Admission into the *French* Academy, or the reading of these Reflexions, from which he might have learned, that he understood nothing of St *Austin*'s Rules concerning the Eloquence of the Pulpit (*o*). I question whether the Public will ever see what Mr *Arnauld* wrote, about the same time, in Favour of Mr *Boileau* [T]; I doubt not but his Letter to him is admirable. There

(*l*) Abridg'd History of Mr *Arnauld*, pag. 279.

(*m*) See the Journal des Sçavans, of the 28th of June, 1684.

(*n*) Abridg'd History, pag. 294.

(*o*) What he has said on this Subject, is to be found in the Preface to his French Translation of some Sermons of St Austin. See the Journal des Sçavans, of the 7th of June, 1694.

---

refuted by Mr *Arnauld*, from page 113, to page 236, of the *Difficulties proposed to Mr Stepaert*. He defended himself in his *New Observations on the Text and Versions, of the New Testament* (82), from Page 33, to 91. Many Things may be learned, by exactly comparing the Reasons of the one with Those of the other. It is well known, that, of all the Catholic Writers, Mr *Arnauld* was the Man, who most learnedly and solidly supported the Usefulness of the Translations of The Scripture. What he said, as to the Reason of the thing, on this Subject, is admirable: And what he has said as to Fact; I mean, to shew, that, in the Intention of the Church, the Laity were never excluded from reading the Word of God in the Vulgar Tongue, is fine and curious; but if you read Mr *Simon*'s Answer (83) attentively, you will not know what to think as to the Church's Opinion in This Matter. The Sentiments of Doctors, the Judgments of Universities, and Mandates of Prelates, in a Word, the public Acts alledged on both sides, form such a strange Variety, and especially when we examine the Motives and Principles laid down by Those who condemn, and Those who allow of, the reading the Translations, that, upon the whole, the People, according to the Church's Intention, ought to be both forbid, and permitted, to read the Holy Scriptures. There are few Facts, which may be more easily reduced to historical Pyrrhonism, than This Question; *Does the Church disapprove, or approve, the reading of the Scripture, in the Vulgar Tongue, by the Laity?* How strange is it, that no positive Decision can be given of this Question, either in the Negative or Affirmative? Should not a Body, which boasts of Infallibility, be more uniform in it's Proceedings? Mr *Arnauld* would, with the Torrent of his Eloquence and Learning, carry away a great Number of Readers to a Belief, that the Church of *Rome* was calumniated, when it was so often reproached with prohibiting the Laity the reading of the Word of God; I say he would induce them to believe this, did not Mr *Simon* oppose his Banks to These Torrents. Thus, in the same Communion, one Doctor defeats the Labours of another: The common Enemy makes his Advantage of this, and has reason to cry out;

Sæpe, premente Deo, fert Deus alter opem.

Oppress'd by One, Another God befriends.

[S] ———— *As also in favour of the Attestations of the Greeks.*] I have observed before (84), that the Protestants despised them, as things easily obtained from That mercenary Nation. "Emendicatis undique " per Legatos Regios, Consules, Missionarios, Græ- " culorum hac de re testimoniis, a quibus nihil non " pretio extorqueas (85). — *Attestations of the Greeks, " of whom Money will buy any thing, having been " begged up and down by Ambassadors, Consuls, and " Missionaries.* Mr *Arnauld* produced several Attestations from *Greek* Priests, to shew, that, in this Point, they followed the Doctrine of the *Romish* Church; but it is, nevertheless, true, that most of them were obtained by Money. Mr *Wheeler* affirms, that, in his Travels thro' *Greece*, he spoke with several *Papas*, whom Mr *de Nointel*, Nephew of Mr *Arnauld*, endeavoured to corrupt in " this manner (86)." Here are two Evidences of the Fact I had asserted. Note, that Mr *de Nointel* was not Mr *Arnauld*'s Nephew. They call him so there, in all probability, from having read, in Mr *Claude*'s Answer (87), that Mr *de Pompone*, Nephew to Mr *Arnauld*, and at that time Ambassador in *Sueden*, had procured him Materials. However it be, Mr *Simon* confessed, that there were even Catholics, who did *not rely on this great Number of Attestations* (88), and he assigns the reason of their Doubts. Mr *Arnauld* examines all this with extraordinary Zeal, and gives the Sum of what he had replied to *Spanhemius*, in his Apology for the Catholics (89).

[T] *What Mr* Arnauld *wrote in Favour of Mr Boileau*.] The Criticism on the tenth Satire of *Boileau* (90), falling into Mr *Arnauld*'s Hands, put him upon "writing a Dissertation, in the form of a Let- " ter, in which he undertook the Defence of the " Satire, with That Force of Wit, and Style, which " never failed him: The Party for the Ancients was " proud of it; and this occasioned *Boileau*'s writing " Those fine Verses on Mr *Arnauld*, in which he " prefers the Apology, which This Doctor wrote, for " his Satire to all the Honours he enjoyed, and even " to That of being the King's Historiographer. ———— " The rigid *Jansenists*, or the Rigorists, were not " pleased with this last Piece of Mr *Arnauld*. What ! " a Doctor, grown grey in serious and grave Dis- " putes, to write, at above Eighty Years of Age, of " Poetry, Women, and Romances! How unbecom- " ing ! The Party were vexed at it, and whispered, " that their Head demeaned himself. Poetry, as " they represented it, was a frivolous Art, which " ought not to have employed the Thoughts of so " great a Genius for a Moment. This came to *Bol- " leau*'s Ears; upon which he set about his Poem *Of " the Love of God*, to shew, that Poetry can reach " the most sublime Subjects." These Particulars have been communicated to me by a Person of great Wit and Learning (91), very well known to *Boileau*. Let us here produce a Passage, in the tenth Epistle of This great Poet, where he addresses himself to his own Verses.

Mais des heureux regards de mon Astre étonnant
Marqués bien cet effet encor plus surprenant;
Qui dans mon souvenir aura toûjours sa place:
Que de tant d'Ecrivains de l'Ecole d'Ignace
Etant, comme je suis, ami si declaré,
Ce Docteur toutefois si craint, si reveré,
Qui contre Eux de sa plume épuisé l'énergie,
Arnaud, le grand Arnaud, fit mon apologie (92).
Sur mon tombeau futur, mes Vers, pour l'énoncer (93),
Courés en lettres d'or de ce pas vous placer.
Allés jusqu'ou l'Aurore en naissant void l'Hydaspe,
Chercher, pour l'y graver, le plus précieux jaspe.
Sur-tout à mes Rivaux fachés bien l'étaler.

But observe the still more surprizing Effect of the happy Influence of my wondrous Star; an Effect, which shall ever hold it's Place in my Memory; that, being a declared Friend, as I am, to so many Writers of St Ignatius's

(82) Printed at Paris, in 1695, in 4to.

(83) In the New Observations on the Text, and Versions, of the New Testament, from pag. 465, to pag. 584.

(84) In Remark [O], n I, immediately after Citat. (56).

(85) Spanhem. Strictur. in Expost. Epist. Cosdom.

(86) Biblioth. universelle, Tom. XI, pag. 445.

(R*) Claude's Answer to *Perpetuity Defended*, Book IV, chap. III, pag. 4, 8.

(88) In his Critical History of the Faith of the Levant.

(89) Difficulties proposed to Mr Stepaert, Par 6, pag. 275, 276, &c.

* Boileau inserted it in his Edition of 1713. This Piece has appeared in all the subsequent Editions.

(90) It is his Satire against Women.

(91) Mr Maain, Advocate in the Parliament of Paris.

(92) Mr Arnauld wrote a Dissertation, in which he inserts the several Beauties and it is in his last Will.

(93) It is that in the Edition of the wits, published in June Town of the United Provinces.

VOL. I. 6 I

There is another Happiness to be considered in his Life, which surpasses Those I have observed; to wit, his having always been very exact in the Practice of the Exercises of Piety, which his Priesthood required of him; and, what is yet more difficult, his abstaining, in his very Youth, from sensual Pleasures, and ever preserving a Purity of Manners, without Taint or Blemish (*p*). It does not appear, that his Adversaries ever attacked him on this Head; tho', in point of Orthodoxy, they have endeavoured to defame him all manner of ways. If the reading of bad Books could produce the same Effect in the Minds of all young Persons, as it did in his, it would not be amiss to recommend it to them [*U*]. The Protestations he has made of his Adherence to the true Faith, and of his Zeal for God, appear in several parts of his Works, particularly in the *Spiritual Testament* [*X*], which he made, the sixteenth of *September* 1679, wherein he calls God to witness with what Dispositions he engaged in writing such and such Books. The Court of *Rome* did, at last, acknowledge his Merit [*Y*]; and it was purely his own fault, that he was not a Cardinal. It is unnecessary to observe, that he opposed all relaxation of Morality, and that he was always a Teacher and Director of Austerity. It appeared, indeed, that he swerved a little from the strait Path, in an Affair, which gave occasion to a *Factum*, or Case, of Mr *Des-Lyons* [*Z*]. Note, that the Place, where he died, is unknown. It is believed to

---

tius's *School, This Doctor, so ever dreaded, and revered, who exhausts the whole Force of his Pen against them,* Arnauld, *I say, the Great* Arnauld, *writes my Apology. My Muse, inscribe this Event in Letters of Gold on my future Tomb. Fetch from the distant East, where* Aurora, *rising, salutes the* Hydaspes, *the most precious* Jasper, *to engrave it. But be particularly careful to display it to my Rivals.*

[*U*] *If the reading of bad Books could produce the same Effect in the Minds of all young Persons, as it did in his, it would not be amiss to recommend it to them.*] This is his own Account of this Matter. "I remember to have formerly read (when I " was very young) in a Book, entituled, if I re-" member right, *The Muses Rally'd*, something very " wicked on this Subject. The Poet glories in " having obtained, what he could not ask without a " Crime; and the Reason he gives for obtaining his " Desire is altogether abominable. It was, Because, " *says he*, the Lady had too solid a Judgment, not to " look upon *Those old Stories of Honour, which arise* " *in the Brains of married Men and Mothers, as* " *meer Chimeras*. I am certain, that what is here " in *Italic* was in His Verses. For I was so greatly " shocked at it, that it has ever since remained in my " Mind. Thus Poet, then, must have supposed, " that nothing but the Consideration of Honour " could have prevented This Lady's satisfying his " Desires; and that she had got over This Conside-" ration by the Force of Reason (94)."

[*X*] *His Spiritual Testament*] I have a Copy of it, published at *Liege*, in 1696. There is a Preface to it; in which the preceeding Edition is disclaimed.

[*Y*] *The Court of* Rome *did, at last, acknowledge his Merit*] Pope *Clement* X, having read some of Mr *Arnauld's* Works, commended them extremely, and declared, that the Author would do him a great Pleasure, if he would send him Copies of them, or deliver them to his Nuncio (95). Cardinal *Altieri*, who had shewed the Pope these Books, could not sufficiently commend the Author, and often concluded his Praises with this honourable Testimony: Mr Arnauld *has done the Church great Service; it were to be wished, that Death would never deprive us of such a Man.*—— De Ecclesia opt. me meritus est Arnaldus; optandum esset, ut talem virum mors illi nunquam eripturâ esset (96). The Esteem and Affection of *Innocent* XI for This Doctor is not unknown to the Public. See the Letter, which he caused to be written to him by Cardinal *Cibo*, the second of *January*, 1677; it is printed at the end of the Letter, which Mr *Arnauld* wrote to the Bishop of *Malaga*, the second of *December*, 1688. There is also a Letter of Mr *Favoriti*, That Pope's Secretary, dated from *Rome* the third of *April*, 1680, which contains great Commendations of him, and lively Expressions of the Pope's Grief, on account of the Persecutions of Mr *Arnauld* (97). He had an Intention of promoting him to the Purple; and it was wholly the Doctor's Fault, that it was not done, " De Arnaldo in purpuratorum Procerum " Ordinem adlegendo aliquando Sanctitatem suam co-" gitasse, etsi certum est & pluribus notum, nollem " tamen hic commemorare, nisi Eminentissimus Car-" dinalis intimorum Romanæ Aulæ consiliorum testis " locuples, id nuper Parisiis evulgasset, asseruissetque " per unum Arnaldum stetisse quominus is Eminen-" tissima illa dignitate ornaretur (98). —— *Though* " *the Intention of his Holiness to have made* Arnauld " *a Cardinal be certain, and known to many, yet I* " *should have taken no Notice of it here, had not* " *a very Eminent Cardinal, who is perfectly acquainted* " *with the Councils of the Court of* Rome, *of late* " *publickly declared it at* Paris, *and asserted, that* " Arnauld *might, if he pleased, have been invested* " *with That high Dignity."* Alexander VIII, who had a great Kindness and Esteem for Mr *Arnauld*, before he was Pope, did not alter his Dispositions, after he was raised to St *Peter's* Chair. He granted him some Favours, and would have done him many more, if he had lived longer, and Mr *Arnauld* had given him Opportunities of doing it (99).

Take notice, that the Bishop of *Malaga* caused almost all the Copies of the first Edition of his *Quærimonia Catholica* to be burnt, as soon as he understood, that, without his Privity, Mr *Arnauld* was called an Heretic in it. He, who burnt the Copies with his own Hand, gave a formal Attestation of this (100).

[*Z*] *He swerved a little from the strait Path, in an Affair, which gave occasion to a* Factum, *or Case, of Mr* Des-Lyons.] A Niece of Mr *Des-Lyons*, Doctor of the *Sorbonne*, and Dean of *Senlis*, dexterously engaged Mr *Arnauld* in a Conduct, not altogether to his Honour. She sued her Father; and *Arnauld* patronized her in the Suit as much as possible. This did not become a rigid Casuist. Besides, she was so whimsical in her Devotions, and of so wrong a Turn, that Mr *Arnauld* had but little of That Faculty, which is called *The Discernment of Spirits*, when he suffered himself to be deceived by This Hypocrite. Mr *Jurieu*, who had heard of the *Factum* of Mr *Des-Lyons*, passionately desired to procure a Copy of it, and applied several Times to a Person, who might have lent it him. He chiefly employed the Bookseller's (101) Intercession, who printed his *Justification of the Morality of the Reformed*, at the *Hague*, in the Year 1685. This was applying himself to a proper Person; for, if any one could have obtained it, it was doubtless This Bookseller: but The Person, who had the *Factum* in his Hands, would never part with it to a Writer, whom he knew disposed to draw from it whatever new Matter he could for Insult, and Invective. He was not ignorant, in what manner This Author poisoned every thing, whom the Business was to pull Mr *Arnauld* to pieces. Observe the Artifice of Mr *Jurieu!* Having failed this way, he would persuade the Public, that he set no Value on the Advantage he might have made of This *Factum*, and had even been so moderate, as voluntarily to renounce it. These are his Words: "To convince the World, that " we are not very sollicitous in enquiring after every " thing, which may serve to render Mr *Arnauld* " odious, we omit all that the *Factum's* of Mr *Des-Lyons* " might have supplied us with against him (102)." There are several Falshoods in Prefaces, which pass for

ARNAULD. 497

to be a Village in the Country of *Liege*. It is still less known, where he was buried; and this is one point of Conformity, which his Friends have observed, between His Fate, and That of *Moses* (*q*). He desired, that his Heart might be carried to *Port-Royal* (*r*). This was accordingly done; but Mr *Santeüil's* Verses on this Subject raised a furious War [*A A*]; which gave great Diversion to several Persons. There was

(*q*) *See the Abridg'd History of his Life, pag. 303.*

(*r*) *Perrault's Illustrious Men, p. 57.*

for venial Sins, not only at the Bar of the Republic of Letters, but even at the Bar of the Church; but This can plead Privilege at neither of These Tribunals. The Jesuits did not let the *Factum* of Mr *Des-Lyons* fall to the Ground; they maliciously weighed the Circumstances of it, and drew Matter of much Reflexion and Raillery from it. See a Piece, which is supposed to have come from Father *le Tellier*, and which appeared in the Year 1688, entituled; *An Apologetical Letter for Mr Arnauld, written to an Abbot, a Friend of His, on three of the last Books, which were written against That Doctor.* I. *The Esprit de Mr Arnauld.* II. *Observations on the New Defence of the French Translation of the New Testament printed at Mons.* III. *An Answer of Mr Des-Lyons, Doctor of the Sorbonne, Dean and Prebend of Senlis, to Mr Arnauld's Letters.*

[*A A*] *Mr* Stanteüil's *Verses on this Subject raised a furious War.*] The Ladies of *Port-Royal* received Mr *Arnauld's* Heart, "with all imaginable Transports of Joy, and deposited it in the most honourable Place they could think of. The Heart being "thus disposed of, an Epitaph was wanting. No "Person was thought more capable of writing one, "than Mr *Santeüil.*——— As the Business was of a "delicate Nature, the Nuns considered, that they "must take Mr *Santeüil* at an Advantage. For this "Purpose, they invited him to come and pass a "few Days at *Port-Royal*, with one of his Brethren, "who was it's Superior (103); and, during his "Abode there, he composed the following Verses.

(103) *History of the Troubles, caused by Mr Arnauld, after his Death; or, The Quarrel between Mr Santeüil and the Jesuits, pag. 5, Edit. 1696.*

Ad Sanctas rediit sedes ejectus & exsul:
Hoste triumphato, tot tempestatibus actus,
Hoc patria in placido, hac sacrâ tellure quiescit,
Arnaldus, veri defensor, & arbiter æqui.
Illius ossa memor sibi vindicet extera tellus;
Huc cœlestis amor rapidis cor transtulit alis,
Cor nunquam avulsum, nec amatis sedibus absens (104).

(104) *Ibid. pag. 40.*

Mr *de la Fémas* gave this *French* Translation of it.

Enfin, après un long voyage,
Arnauld revient en ces saints lieux:
Il est au *Port* malgré les envieux,
Qui croyoient qu'il seroit naufragé.
Ce Martir de la verité
Fut banni, fut persecuté,
Et mourut en terre étrangere;
Heureuse, de son corps d'être depositaire,
Mais son cœur toûjours ferme, & toûjours innocent,
Fut porté par l'amour, à qui tout est possible,
Dans cette retraite paisible,
D'où jamais il ne fut absent (105).

(105) *Ibid. pag. 41.*

In *English* thus.

Here rests in hallowed Earth, secure from Spight,
Arnauld, great Arbiter of Truth and Right;
Arriv'd in Port, and landed safe on Shore,
The Foe subdued, and the wild Tempest o'er.
Tho' in some distant Land his Bones be laid,
His Heart, on rapid Wings by Love convey'd,
Enjoys the dear Retreat, from which it never stray'd.

No sooner were these two Pieces printed together, and dispersed in the World, but the Jesuits complained of Mr *Santeüil's* Proceedings.——— He turned a deaf Ear to them, flattering himself, that the Murmurs, then raised, would insensibly die of themselves (106). But, finding himself attacked in a Piece, supposed to be sent out of the Country (107),——— he began to think of making Satisfaction. "He was Thunder-struck, "and ran immediately to the Jesuits College, to

(106) *Ibid. pag. 7.*

(107) *Enituled*, Santoilius Vindicatus.

"beg Pardon in the most humble and moving "Terms, conjuring all Those he met with not to "undo him; that he had always been a Friend "to the Society, and that the Epitaph in question "was not His, but had been forged in his Name "by his Enemies, to ruin him with the Jesuits. "They replied, that they wished what he said were "true, but that bare Protestations were not sufficient; and that he must undeceive the Public by "an authentic Confession; which they required of "him, as an Barnest of his Sincerity. He promised all they would have him; but the Difficulty "was how to perform his Promise (108)." The Flattering Panegyric, which he wrote, on their Society, did not serve his turn (109); they perceived, "the little "Artifice, he made use of, to elude his Promise; "they treated him as a double Dealer, and a Knave; "in a Word, he found himself overwhelmed with "Epigrams, which came pouring upon him from "all Parts; and in which the young Jesuits of the "College, whom he somewhere calls *Pubes Jesuitica Sagittaria*, had no small Share. On the other "hand, the *Jansenists* took no less Offence at his "Cowardice, than the Jesuits at his Insincerity; and "they gave him Marks of it, in a Piece in Burlesque Verse, which they published against him, "and which begins,

(108) *History of the Troubles, caused by Mr Arnauld, after his Death.*

(109) *Ibid. pag. 10.*

Santeüil, ce renommé Poëte, &c.
Santeüil, *That far fam'd Bard*, &c.

"Thus he found himself sadly out in his Reckoning, and perceived, that, by endeavouring to keep "fair with all the World, he had disobliged all." Having thoroughly considered the whole Affair, He resolved to sacrifice the *Jansenists* to the *Jesuits*, and made an humble Confession of his Fault to These, by Letter; but This would not satisfy them; they demanded a Recantation (110). He was pestered with Epigram upon Epigram, which he received Day after Day (111). He wrote a Letter to Father *la Chaise*; in which he interpreted some Terms of the Epitaph in the softest Manner he could. The Answer, he received from this Jesuit, encreased his Disquiet (112). He was obliged to think of a second Apology (113). The *Tenderest Point, and That, in which all the Difficulty lay, was his having said of Mr Arnauld*;

(110) *Ibid. pag. 11.*

(111) *Ibid. pag. 14.*

(112) *Ibid. pag. 17.*

(113) *Ibid. pag. 20.*

———— Ictus illo fulmine *(Vaticano)*
Trabeate Doctor, jam mihi non amplius
Arnalde, saperes.

"That is; *If you had been struck with the Thunder of* "*the Vatican, I should absolutely have disclaimed you.* "Now this was saying nothing at all. The Jesuits "would have had him put *Sapies*, instead of *Saperes* "(for all was brought to the Test, before the Copies "were printed off). To have put *Sapies* would have "been to have declared Mr *Arnauld* excommunicated and condemned. One of his Friends, with "whom he advised about it, gave him a Hint for "finding out a *Medium* between *Saperes* and *Sapies*; "which was to put *Sapias*, which might equally be "taken in the sense of the other two Words; but he "found, that he could not give up the *Saperes*, "without offending the *Jansenists.* At last, after "long Deliberation, he resolved to please each Party "as near as possible. He got two kinds of Copies "printed; in some of which was *Sapias*, for the "Jesuits; telling them, *vivâ voce*, that he took it in "the sense of the *Sapies*; and *Saperes* in the others, "to please the *Jansenists.*" To this he added an Explanation of some other Parts of the Epitaph. But he neither satisfied the Jesuits, nor the *Jansenists.* The latter published a very bitter Piece against him (114), and the latter attacked him no less vigorously. At last Father *Commire* entered the Lists. He had lain by hitherto, as a Body of Reserve, "but at last appeared

(114) *Frituld, Santoilius Vindicatus, See the History of the Troubles, &c. p.*

was a great Clamour raised against the Jesuits, for procuring an Order, that Mr *Perrault* should be obliged to suppress the Sheet, in which he celebrated Mr *Arnauld*, in his Collection of the Portraits and Elogies of the Illustrious Men of the *French* Nation [*BB*]. I must not forget the Esteem, which this Doctor of the *Sorbonne* gained with

"peared in the Field of Battle; and, to break off a Dispute, which there was no end of, and to prevent Mr *Santeüil* from so often contradicting himself, he seized him, and put a Gag in his Mouth, which has ever since been very troublesome to him. I mean the *Linguarium*, which all the Learned ascribe to This great Poet (115)." A Poet of the University, and no Friend to the Jesuits, entred the Lists, and wrote a Piece enntituled *Santolius pendens, Santeüil on the Gibbet*. It is One of the best, which appeared during This long Poetical War. I think Three Accounts have appeared of this Quarrel: I have not seen the first; That, which I have quoted, is the second: The third is of the Year 1697, and posterior to the Death of Mr *Santeüil*: It contains the Letters, which were written to This Poet by several Jesuits, and differs from the second in some Circumstances.

(115) Ibid. pag. 33.

It is certain, that This Quarrel made a great noise; for which reason the Author of the Relation thought himself obliged to make use of this Preamble (116). "It is the Fate of Those, who have occasioned great Troubles in their Life-time, to occasion others after their Death. That of *Alexander* did not extinguish the War in *Asia*; on the contrary, it broke out again with greater fury, thro' the Ambition of his Lieutenants, who long disputed the Crown. Something like this happened to Mr *Arnauld*; if it be proper to compare a Doctor with a Conqueror. His Death, which seemingly ought to have put an end to all the Troubles, he had occasioned in his Life-time, on the contrary raised new ones. Every one knows, in how unworthy a manner the *Jansenists* exclaimed against an Holy Abbot (117), for explaining himself too freely on this Occasion, and saying, with regard to the great Head of a Party, which fell in the Person of Mr *Arnauld, Happy is He, who has no other than* JESUS CHRIST. This was what the first News of Mr *Arnauld*'s Death produced. But, his Heart being afterwards carried back to *France*, could not re-enter it without scattering still farther Seeds of Dissention, by the Quarrel, which it occasioned between Mr *Santeüil* and the Jesuits." Many will here recollect a Complaint of *Balzac* against Father *Goulu*'s Epitaph (118); but if the Jesuits, on the one side, might say, that the very Tomb of Mr *Arnauld* insulted them, the *Jansenists* might exclaim, on the other, that They did not suffer this Divine to rest even in his Grave.

(116) Ibid. pag. 3, 4.

(117) *The Abbot de la Trappe*.

(118) *See Remark* [M], *of the Article* P. GOULU, *General of the Bernardine Mendicants*.

Et ce n'est pas assez de paier en la vie,
Il faut encor paier au dela du trepas (119).

Even Death from farther Payment cannot save;
The Debt must be discharged beyond the Grave.

(119) *These are two Lines of the Opera, which was acted in 1674, entituled, as I take it,* Le Triomphe d'Alceste. -- *The Triumph of* Alcestes.

[*BB*] Mr Perrault *was obliged to suppress the Sheet*, &c.] The following Passage we meet with in a Letter, published in the Year 1697 (120). "Mr *Perrault*, of the Academy, has presented the Public with a Book intituled, *The Elogies of the Illustrious Men of this Reign*. Mr *Arnauld* and Monsr. *Pascal* justly had a Place in it. *Baptiste*, and *Moliere*, hold their Rank in it, as illustrious Persons of their kind: The Book was printed by Authority; the Portraits engraven. It was to have been published four Months ago; but the Fathers Jesuits have applied so strongly to the higher Powers, that they have ordered the Author and Bookseller to retrench Monsieur *Arnauld* and Monsieur *Pascal*'s Articles, and suppress their Elogies. —— Monsieur *Arnauld* was one of the greatest Men of This Age: He did the Church service in opposing *Calvinism*, and defending the Faith of the Eucharist. He lived and died in the Communion of the Church, and in perfect Obedience to the Holy See, which would certainly have rewarded his great Deserts, if the profound Humility of This learned Person had not several Times made him refuse one of the most eminent Dignities of the Church. *Moliere* lived impiously, and died excommunicated, like a Reprobate: In

(120) *Letter of a Lady of Quality to an old learned Lady*, pag. 24, 25.

the mean time Monsieur *Arnauld* is struck out of the Number of Illustrious Men, and *Moliere* holds his Rank among them." Such Reflexions were made all over *France*, and in foreign Countries; and what *Tacitus* said, on the Statues of *Cassius* and *Brutus* not appearing at *Junia*'s Funeral, was not forgot on this Occasion; *Præfulgebant Cassius atque Brutus eo ipso quod effigies eorum non visebantur* (121). —— *Cassius and Brutus outshone the rest for this very Reason, because their Statues were not exposed.* This Thought was applied to Mess. *Arnauld* and *Pascal*. The Verses, which were made on this Occasion, have been spread all the World over; for they have been inserted in the *Nouvelles Historiques & Politiques*, printed every Month at the *Hague*. Let us add, that several were of Opinion, that the Jesuits did not act over prudently in this Affair; since the surest way to draw the Eyes and Attention of the Public on These two famous Persons, was to oblige Mr *Perrault* to suppress their Elogies and Portraits. This Conduct served only to enhance the Merit, which it strove to efface; it led directly to the Passage of *Tacitus*; and could only occasion Exclamations, and Censures, in favour of the Persons suppress'd, and against the Instruments of their Suppression. But all are not agreed as to the supposed Imprudence in this Point. Skilful Persons have maintained, that the Faction, which all along opposed Mr *Arnauld*, did nothing but what favoured of the justest and most refined Policy. What! say they; do you think *Tiberius* did not foresee the Reflexions, which would be made, on his not exposing the Statues of *Brutus* and *Cassius*, among so many others, in a Funeral Ceremony? He knew the Advantage, which their Absence might give them; but thought the Inconvenience greater in letting these two Assassins of *Julius Cæsar* appear among the Images of his Family; this would have been in some measure vindicating their Memory; and it was not his Interest to make the least step that way. There is no question, but the Jesuits likewise foresaw the Advantage, which Mr *Perrault*'s suppressing the Elogies of these two great Men would give them. But, all things considered, they thought this would be a much less Inconvenience to themselves, than the giving the opposite Faction room to make their Advantage of Mr *Arnauld* and Mr *Pascal*'s appearing, with Privilege, on the Theatre of Illustrious Men. By procuring them to be struck out, they armed themselves with a new Act, which might be useful in the Course of the Process: They kept them in Disgrace; and prevented any one's alledging the Licence, obtained by Mr *Perrault*, as a Proof of their being restored; but, what was more considerable, the Public was prevented from imagining, that the Jesuits had not the same Credit as formerly. The Public would scarce conclude, that, if the Characters and Elogies of These two Gentlemen had full liberty to appear in a privileged Book, it was because the Jesuits had no Inclination to make any Opposition to it. It would be much more natural to think, that it was out of their Power to prevent it. Now such an Opinion is to be guarded against; the Effects of it may be of ill Consequence; for the Influence of Reputation is of great Efficacy, either in advancing or retarding Events. Who knows not, that, in Matters of Trade, a Merchant, who passes for rich, and is not so, is generally more successful, than One, who is really rich, but passes for poor? All other Conditions of human Life are the same in this respect. If it be Imprudence to engage in certain things, it is still greater Imprudence to abandon them, after having once engaged in them. Upon the whole, Honour and Glory are here both concerned. This Principle is no less active in the Wars at the Bar, than in those properly so called (122). Lastly, every one knows, that, in all Suits of great Importance, each Party provides against all the Proceedings of the other. Good Policy, then, required, that They should not, by their Silence, acquiesce in any Proceedings of the *Jansenists*. They were to guard against Epitaphs, and the Authors of Elogies, the better to maintain the grand Process, and support

(121) Tacit. Annal. Lib. III, in fine.

(122) *Marcellus multa magnis ducibus ficut non aggrediunda, ita semel aggressis non dimittenda esse dicendo, quia magna fame momenta in utramque partem fierent, tenuit ne incepto abiremur. —— Marcellus confirmed him in his Understanding, by saying, that, many things, as they ought not to be undertaken by great Generals, so, when once undertaken, are never to be dropped.* Titus Livius, lib IV, Decad III.

ARNGRIMUS. ARNISÆUS.

Mr *Des Cartes* [*CC*]. I have heard some, who were admitted to an Intimacy with him, say, that he was of great Plainness of Manners, and that, unless some Question was proposed to him, or some Information desired, he said nothing out of the Road of common Conversation [*DD*], or which might create a Suspicion of his being a learned Man; but, when he was obliged to answer Those, who put him upon some Point of Learning, he seemed to be quite another Man; he said an hundred fine Things, with all the readiness imaginable, and had a particular Gift of making himself intelligible to the meanest Capacity. I propose, in part of my Work (*s*), to insert a Letter, which it is supposed the King wrote to him, in the Year 1678. By the way, They, who were the occasion of his resolving on a voluntary Exile, lost more than they gained by it; for he never wrote against them in *Paris*, but religiously observed the Conditions of Peace; till seeing himself driven by force out of the Kingdom, he published a great number of Pieces, which have done the Jesuits no small Prejudice (*t*). It is pretended, that he became the Apostle of *Jansenism* in *Holland* [*E E*].

(*s*) *See Remark* b [*A*] *of the Article* TPRES.

(*t*) *See the Abridg'd History of his Life, pag. 179.*

port the Discussion of the Problem, or *Curious Enquiry, whether Mr Arnauld be an Heretic*; a strange Question indeed, and which some *Roman* Catholics affirm, and others deny daily, with Impunity. This shews, there is a Source of Anarchy in the State of Man, which can never be wholly rectified. It is chiefly to be seen in Ecclesiastical Bodies; for, since the Church of *Rome* has not the Secret of determining between the Affirmative and the Negative, what other Church can ever expect to have it? Other Churches have not, like That, Tribunals, which are acknowledged to be infallible. They are not governed with such an Air of Authority, and high Reputation, as That is. It is, therefore, less to be wondered at, that the Protestant Ministers accuse each other of Heresy in printed Books, than that a Doctor of the *Sorbonne* should be torn to pieces, as an Heretic, by the Faction of the *Molinists*, whilst three Popes honoured him with their Friendship, Esteem, and Praises, and the most famous Prelates set their solemn Approbations at the Head of his Works. It is near sixty Years, since this Dispute began (123); and there is still as much room as ever to deny or affirm. Protestant Controversies are not of such long Continuance. They are generally adjusted after three or four Pamphlets of a Side, and the Reputation of Orthodoxy, which they would take from each other, is secured to both. But even this smells a little of *Anarchy*, and of That State of Nature, in which the Aggressor has nothing more to fear, than the Resistance of the Attacked, and not the Punishment of a common Judge: Bodies Politic are not subject to such Disorders. No one is permitted to call another Knave, or Rascal; Thief, Traitor, Murderer, Prostitute, or Liar (124). Reputation is here something better fixed.

For the rest, the Suppression, enjoined Mr *Perrault*, hindered not, but that the Copies of his Book, published in *Holland*, contained the Elogies of Messieurs *Arnauld* and *Pascal*. It only occasioned some small Confusion in the figuring the Pages, which the Edition of *Holland* has set right.

[*CC*] *The Esteem, which Mr Arnauld gained with Mr Des Cartes.*] He was the Author of four Objections against This Philosopher's Speculations; and they are judged by all to be the solidest, that have been proposed against That Work. Mr *Des Cartes* himself gave this Judgment of them: see his *Life* composed by Mr *Baillet* (125). I must observe, that Mr *Arnauld* had taught *the same Philosophy at Paris, with That of Mr Des Cartes, before the latter had published his first Essays* (126). So that he was as falsely called a *Cartesian*, as a *Jansenist*. Read what follows: " He had fetched his Opinion of *Grace* " from the Source; that is, from *St Austin*'s Works, " before ever the Book of Mr *d'Ypres* appeared.

(123) *This work wrote in 1699.*

(124) *This must be understood with regard to publick Accusations.*

(125) *Baillet's Life of Des Cartes, Tom. 2. pag 174, &c. See also Pemole's Illustrious Men, pag. 57, 58.*

(126) *Id. ib. pag 144. See also pag. 328.*

" He had publickly maintained them, in the Presence " of Bishops, four or five Years before That Prelate's " Book was published (127). He had embraced " them without so much as knowing, that *Jansenius* " was writing on *Grace* ———." Scarce did he know, that there was such a Man, as *Jansenius*, in the World (128).

[*DD*] *He said nothing out of the Road of common Conversation.*] This must be understood with some Restriction; otherwise it cannot be reconciled with what we find in the Account of his Life; we there meet with some Hours of Conversation after Meals, " in which much was to be learned from him; be- " cause, being qualified for Reflexion, he always made " such as were very solid, either on human Events, " on the Conduct of Life, on the Rules of Morality, " or on Matters of Learning, and public Affairs. " These Conversations were often employed in peru- " sing new Books; and he always judged so rightly " of them, that the Opinion he gave (tho' rarely " with a decisive Air) was decisive of itself, and with- " out Appeal. His Memory, as things were read or " spoken in Company, supplied him always with " something of what the best Authors had said on " the same Subject: And it was surprizing to hear " him repeat a great number of *Latin*, and *French*, " Verses, which he had read only in his Youth, or " several Years before. He was a Master of the *La- " tin* Poets, and applied the finest Passages of them " with great Justness, and a great Presence of Mind, " according as occasion offered in Conversation (129) " Let us say, then, that his Conversation was plain and vulgar, only when he was with Persons, who were not intimate with him, or who did not engage him by their Questions to exert his Talents.

(127) A-bridged History of Mr Arnauld, pag. 35.

(128) Ibid. pag. 32.

(129) Ibid. p. 28, 288.

[*E E*] *It is pretended, that he became the Apostle of* Jansenism *in* Holland] There appeared a small Book (130) in the Year 1698, in which it is affirmed (131), that Mr *Arnauld* " having wandered for some time " in the Catholic *Netherlands*, at last took Refuge in " *Holland*. Mr *Neerkassel*, Bishop of *Castoria*, and " Apostolical Vicar in the United Provinces, received " him as a Man of God, and lodged him in his " Nunnery of *Delft*; where Mr *Arnauld* lived some " Years without being known to any, but his inti- " mate Friends. In this Place he governed the Mind " of That Prelate absolutely, who took great delight " in recommending all the young Divines, in whom " he discovered any Genius, to Him for Instruction. " His most constant Companions were Mr *de Codde*, " the present Archbishop of *Sebasta*, and Successor of " the Bishop of *Castoria* in the Apostolical Vicarship; " Mr *van Huyssen* - - - - So that *Jansenism* in *Holland* " proceeded, properly speaking, from the Nunnery " of *Delft*, about the Year 1689.

(130) *Intituled Memoirs concerning the Progress of Jansenism in Holland.*

(131) *Pages 3, and 5.*

ARNGRIMUS, a learned Man, and a Native of *Iseland*. Look for JONAS.

ARNISÆUS (HENNINGUS) born at *Halberstadt*, and Professor of Physic in the University of *Helmstadt*, was a Philosopher, and Physician, very much esteemed towards the beginning of the XVIIth Century. His Political Works are in great Repute, in which he has established a Tenet directly opposite to That of *Althusius* [*A*]. He was invited to *Denmark*, and went thither; where he had the Honour to be

(1) *See the Article* ALTHUSIUS.

[*A*] *He established, in his Political Works, a Tenet directly opposite to That of* Althusius (1).] For he maintained, that the Authority of Princes ought never to be violated by the People. See his Book *de Authoritate*

VOL. I.   6 K

ARNISÆUS. ARNOBIUS.

(a) Witte, in Diario Biogr. ad Ann. 1635.

be the King's Counsellor, and Physician (a). The University of *Helmstadt* lost greatly by this Retreat [B]. It is falsely pretended, that he was Professor at *Jena* [C], and that he left his Library to the University of That Place. It might have been said, without a Falshood, that he read Lectures in the University of *Francfort* on the *Oder*, before he read Any in That of *Helmstadt* (b). He had travelled into *France* and *England* (c). He died in the Month of *November* 1635 (d). I shall give the Titles of several of his Works [D].

(b) Arnisæus, Præf. libror. de Jur. Majest.

(c) Id. ib.

(d) Witte, ubi supra.

ritate Principum in populum semper inviolabili, printed at *Francfort*, in the Year 1612. See also his three Books *de Jure Majestatis*, printed at the same Place in 1610, and his *Prælectiones Politicæ*, printed also at *Francfort*, in the Year 1615. He did not finish this last Piece, which however appeared to be very fine. *Opus præclarum, sed imperfectum* (2). He gave a Catalogue of Those, who have maintained, that the Sovereignty resided in the People; a most pernicious Doctrine, in the Opinion of *Boeclerus*, and the Hinge of Rebellion. *A fatali hoc & pestilenti errore — suspensa est omnis illa rebellandi licentia, quam variis vocabulis præscribunt* (3). *Boeclerus* adds, that it is a deplorable Consideration, that there are very great Men in This List, and remarks the different Passions, which lead them to take this Side. " *Patronos & Præcones nefariæ philosophiæ recen-* " *suit Arnisæus principio libri de auctoritate prin-* " *cipum in populum semper inviolabili.* Fuisse in illis " *magnos viros, dolendum: quorum aliquos animus* " *arrogans, elatus, indomitus, ad fingendam & prin-* " *gendam libertatem stoico supercilio forte impulerit:* " *alios metus oppressionis & tyrannidis eo evibraverit,* " *ut potestatem civilem bene constitutam negarent,* " *nisi populo subjiciatur: nonnullis commentitiæ sa-* " *pientiæ species placuerit, ut tali tanquam terricu-* " *lamento reges, ne in tyrannidem elaberentur, reten-* " *tatos cuperent* (4). — *Arnisæus, in the begin-* " *ning of his Book,* Of the Inviolable Authority of " Princes over the People, reckons up the Patrons " and Preachers of the contrary wicked Doctrine. *It* " *is melancholy to consider, that there are many* " *great Men among Them; some of whom, perhaps,* " *were prompted, by an Arrogant, Elate, Unconque-* " *rable Disposition, to conceive and describe Liberty* " *with all the Pride of Stoicism; others were driven,* " *by the fear of Oppression and Tyranny, to deny any* " *Government to be well constituted, which is not* " *subject to the People; and some were pleased with* " *a kind of pretended Philosophy, which taught them,* " *that Kings should be kept in Awe, least they de-* " *generate into Tyrants.*" If such a Catalogue were to be made in this present Year 1699, it would be much larger; for the Doctrine of the Supream Authority of the People is of late grown into Fashion. *Grotius* praises a Political Piece of *Arnisæus* very highly (5).

[B] *The University of* Helmstadt *lost much by His Retreat.*] This is testified by *Conringius*, who styles *Arnisæus, æternum Juliæ Academiæ & incomparabile ornamentum* (6), — *The Perpetual and Inimitable Ornament of the* Julian *Academy.* " *Vir incompara-* " *bilis, says he, in another Book* (7), *à quo civilis* " *philosophiæ in Academia Julia, ut alibi nusquam,* " *fuit exculta, & simul Imperii quoque, ut aliarum* " *Rerum publicarum veterum recentiumque, historia* " *etiam sparsim quidem, accurate tamen satis est* " *inculcata* — *illius in Daniam discessu simul u-* " *trumque hoc studiorum genus fuerit heic quasi* " *consepultum.* — *An Incomparable Man; who*

(2) Bosius de comparanda Prudentia Civili, n. 2.

(3) Boeclerus in Grot. de Jure Belli & Pacis, lib. I. cap. 3. n. VIII. pag. 236.

(4) Id. ib.

(5) Grot. de Imperio Summar. Potestatum circa sacra, cap. III. n. 8.

(6) Conring. de Civili Prudentia, cap. 14.

(7) Id. in Dedicat. Exercitat. de Rep. Imper. German.

" *cultivated Politics in the University of* Helmstadt, " *beyond what it had ever been elsewhere; and, at* " *the same Time, inculcated the History of the Empire,* " *as also of other Republics both ancient and modern,* " *accurately enough, though scattered here and there.* " — *By his Departure to* Denmark *both these* " *kind of Studies were at once buried in this Uni-* " *versity.*"

[C] *It is falsely pretended, that he was Professor at* Jena.] This we find in an Edition of a Work of *Bosius, de comparanda prudentia civili.* But This Edition was disclaimed by *Bosius's* Widow. See the Advertisement, which she inserted at the beginning of this Book, when she published it free from the Errors, which disfigured the former Edition.

[D] *The Titles of several of his Works.*] Besides the Poetical Treatises, which I have already mentioned (8), he wrote a Book *de Subjectione & Exemptione Clericorum* — *Of the Subjection and Exemption of the Clergy*: Another *de potestate temporali Pontificis in Principes* — *Of the Temporal Authority of the Pope over Princes*: Another *de Translatione Imperii Romani* — *Of the Translation of the* Roman *Empire*: Another *de Republica* — *Of Civil Society*: Another *de Jure Connubiorum* (9) — *Of the Rights of Marriage*: The Title of another is *Doctrina Politica in genuinam methodum, quæ est Aristotelis, reducta & ex probatissimis quibusque Philosophis, Oratoribus, Jurisconsultis, Historicis,* &c. *breviter comportata & explicata* (10) — *Political Institutes reduced to* Aristotle's *Method, and briefly compiled and explained from the most approved Philosophers, Orators, Lawyers, Historians,* &c. He wrote also on Physic: His *Observationes aliquot Anatomicæ* — *Some Anatomical Observations*; were printed at *Francfort* in the Year 1610, in 4to. His Dispute *de Lue Venerea cognoscenda & curanda* — *Of the Knowledge and Cure of the Veneral Disease*; was printed the same Year at *Oppenheim*, in 4to. I do not know the date of the first Edition of his *Disquisitiones de partus humani legitimis terminis*; — *Enquiries into the lawful Bounds of Human Birth*; nor of his Books *de Preservatione à Peste* — *Of a Preservative against the Plague*: *de Hydropum essentia & curatione* — *Of the Essence and Cure of Dropsies*: *de apoplexia & epilepsia cognoscendis & curandis* (11) — *Of the Knowledge and Cure of the Apoplexy and Epilepsy.* As for his Philosophical Writings, we are to know, that he wrote Annotations on *Crellius's* Logic: *Epitome Metaphysices ad mentem Aristotelis* — *An Abridgment of Metaphysics according to the Principles of* Aristotle: *De constitutione & partibus Metaphysicæ* — *Of the Constitution and Parts of Metaphysics*: *Vindiciæ pro Aristotele de subjecto Metaphysicæ & Natura Entis* — Aristotle *vindicated on the Subject of Metaphysics, and the Nature of Being*: *Disputationes* VIII *Metaphysicæ* — *Eight Metaphysical Disputations*: *Epitome doctrinæ Physicæ* — *An Epitome of Natural Philosophy.*

(8) In Remark [A].

(9) See the Diarium Biograph. of Witte ad Ann. 1635.

(10) See Lendenius renovatus, pag. 390.

(11) Witte, ubi supra.

ARNOBIUS, Professor of Rhetoric, at *Sicca*, in *Numidia*, towards the end of the IIId Century, was brought over to the Profession of Christianity by Dreams (a). He applied himself to the Bishops for admission into the Church; but They, remembring how violently he had always opposed the true Faith, distrusted him, and, before his admission into the Number of Catechumens, would have him give Proofs of his Sincerity [A]. To satisfie them, he wrote a Book against the *Gentiles*, wherein

(a) See Remark [A].

[A] *The Bishops — before his Admission into the Number of Catechumens, would have him give Proofs of his Sincerity.*] St *Jerom* furnishes us with these Particulars. " *Arnobius Rhetor, says he* (1), *clarus in Africa habe-* " *tur: qui quum in civitate Siccæ ad declamandum* " *juvenes erudiret, & adhuc Ethnicus ad credulitatem* " *somnii compelleretur, neque ab Episcopo impetra-* " *ret fidem quam semper impugnaverat, elucubravit*

(1) Hieron. in Chronico Eusebii ad Ann. II. Olymp. 276.

" *adversus pristinam religionem luculentissimos libros,* " *& tandem velut quibusdam obsidibus pietatis fœdus* " *impetravit.* — *Arnobius is a famous Rhetorician* " *of* Africa; *this Person taught Oratory in the City of* " Sicca, *and was converted from Heathenism by* " *Dreams; but being distrusted by the Bishops, as ha-* " *ving hitherto opposed the Faith, he wrote an excel-* " *lent Work against his former Religion, and, at last,*
" upon

ARNOBIUS.

In he very powerfully confuted the Absurdity of their Religion, and the Ridiculousness of their false Gods. He employed all the Flowers of his Rhetoric, and displayed much Learning, in it; but, as he had a laudable Impatience to be admitted into the Body of the Faithful, He made a little too much haste in composing this Work [B]; which is the true Reason, why It is not so justly and beautifully disposed, as could be wished. The worst is, that, not having a full Knowledge of the Christian Truths, he vented very dangerous Errors [C]. It is not known what became of him afterwards, nor at what time he died. His Work contains *Seven Books,* and

---

" *upon giving these Hostages of his Sincerity, was admitted to the Peace of the Church.*" He was looked upon as an Enemy, who had a Mind to enter into a Treaty of Peace; but, before the Conclusion of it, they expected Security for his good Behaviour; Hostages were demanded, and he gave them: These were Seven Invectives against the *Pagans*: He was afterwards looked upon as a good Brother; and received into the Peace of the Church.

[B] *He made a little too much haste in composing this Work.*] Let us Comment upon this by a Passage of Baronius. " Quod verò opus illud, ut inter Fideles admitteretur, quasi fidei suæ vadem festinus absolvit; hinc planè est quòd in eo (ut ait Hieronymus) fuisse visus est inæqualis & nimius, & absque operis sui partitione confusus. Rursum verò quòd nondum plenè esset scientia rerum Christianarum imbutus, utpote cùm non solùm non fuerit baptismate illustratus, sed nec in Ecclesiam inter catechumenos acceptus; venia dignus est, si aliquibus nævis visus est commentarius ille respersus (2). ——— *The Reason of That Inequality, Prolixity, and Confusion, which St Jerom observed in This Work, which he wrote as a Pledge of his Faith, in order to be admitted among the Faithful, was the haste, with which he composed it. Again, if this Commentary be interspersed with some Errors, the Author may in excuse say, that he had not as yet a full Knowledge of Christianity, having neither been enlightened by Baptism, nor received into the Church among the Catechumens* (3)."

[C] *He vented very dangerous Errors.*] We have just seen, that Baronius imputes the Heterodoxy of the Seven Books of *Arnobius* to the Precipitation, with which they were written: For the Author could not defer writing them, 'till he had leisure to be better instructed in all the Points of the Christian Faith. The Annalist would have us excuse the Errors of *Arnobius,* as being of no Consequence; but it is certain, that the Inquisition would, at this Day, condemn Those to be burnt, who should publish such Doctrines. I own, we ought to make great Allowances for *Arnobius;* but it is no less true, that his Opinions concerning the *Origin* of the *Soul,* and the Cause of *Natural Evil,* together with some other capital Matters, are very pernicious. This I have observed elsewhere (4). In regard to our Mysteries, he might have pleaded what *Persius* confesses with Regard to Poetry, which he ventured to write, before he understood his Subject.

Nec fonte labra prolui Caballino:
Nec in bicipiti somniasse Parnasso
Memini, ut repentè sic Poëta prodirem.
Heliconidasque, pallidamque Pyrenen
Illis remitto, quorum imagines lambunt
Hederæ sequaces. Ipse semipaganus
Ad sacra Vatum carmen affero nostrum (5).

I never did on cleft Parnassus *Dream,
Nor taste the sacred* Heliconian *Streams;
Nor can remember when my Brain inspired
Was by the Muses into Madness fired.
My Share in pale* Pyrene *I resign,
And claim no part in all the mighty Nine.
Statues, with winding Ivy crown'd, belong
To nobler Poets, for a nobler Song:
Headless of Verse, and hopeless of the Crown,
Scarce half a Wit, and more than half a Clown,
Before the Shrine I lay my rugged Numbers down.*

DRYDEN.

Read here Mr *Du Pin*'s Judgment. " It is plain he was " not as yet thoroughly instructed in the Mysteries of " our Religion. He attacks the Religion of the " *Pagans* more solidly, than he defends That of the " *Christians.* He discovers the Folly of *Paganism* " more happily, than he proves the Truth of Chri" stianity. But this ought not to be thought strange; " for it is common to all new Converts, who, being " as yet full of their own Religion, are better able to " detect the Errors and Folly of it, than to display " the Proofs and Excellency of That, which they " embrace (6)." I meet with no Author, who speaks so tenderly of *Arnobius*'s Errors, as Dr *Cave.* He says, that, perhaps, there are Doctrines in him something different from the True Faith. " Dogmata quædam " habet FORSAN minus Catholica, quæ homini è " Gentilium tenebris recens erumpenti, & nondum " Christianæ fidei elementis satis instructo, condonanda " sunt (7). ——— *He advances some Doctrine:* perhaps " *not altogether Catholic, which may be pardoned in " one but just emerged from the Darkness of* Paganism, " *nor yet fully instructed in the Elements of Christian " Faith.*" This is carrying the Indulgence much farther, than was done in the Preface to the Edition of *Leyden* in 1651, where it was thought sufficient to say, that *Arnobius* swerved *a little* from Orthodoxy. " Aliis in locis à veritate Christiana NONNIHIL rece" dit. Sed hoc condonandum illi, qui ex Ethnicismi " tenebris recens ad veritatem Christianam pervenerat. " Idem huic Autori evenit, quod ix solet, qui ex " carcere tenebricoso in lucem perducti visum adhuc " dubium habent (8). ——— *In other places,* he recedes " *a little from Christian Truth. But he is excuseable " in this, being then but just arrived from the Darkness " of Heathenism to Christian Truth. Our Author's " Case is the same with Theirs, who, being brought out " of a dark Dungeon into Light, cannot immediately " distinguish Objects with certainty.*" Once again; let us excuse This Father, but not be so simple, as to call the Doctrines, he advanced, by the soft Name of *Small Errors.* If we consider them right, they merit the same Treatment as would be given them, at this Day, if any Doctor should at present advance them. It must be owned, without a Cavil, that a Modern Author read a good Lecture to his Censor upon this Subject. Let us hear him. " Mr *Jurieu* weighs " *Arnobius*'s Errors in a false Balance. He judges of the Do" ctrine by the Persons, and not the Persons by the " Doctrine. One and the same Error alters it's Na" ture, according to the Circumstances of Place, and " Time. It is monstrous Heresy, according to the " Subject in which it is found, and the Age in which " it reigns. This Partiality of Mr *Jurieu* appears " in all his Disputes against the present Sectaries, in " whom he pardons nothing; at the same time that " he carries his Indulgence for the Fathers to a prodi" gious Excess ——— (9). The respect we have for " Persons should not make us respect their Errors, " when they are capital. So, all occasions of the " like Nature, we should call *A Spade, a Spade,* &c." Mr *Jurieu* willingly excuses *Origen*'s Errors, on account of his great Zeal; but, if any Modern should presume to put us off with the Dreams of the Ancients, Mr *Jurieu* would not think himself obliged to bear with them. " If These visionary Notions " be Heresy and Impiety, which change Hell into " a Purgatory, and by this means destroy the Dread " of Eternal Punishment, and the Fear of God, why " ought they to be suffered in *Origen* (10)? " The Tenderness, with which Mr *Jurieu* speaks of " St *Hilary*'s, and St *Jerom*'s Errors, is certainly " not edifying." He excuses them, by saying they are Mistakes, and Oversights. " But, should a Divine " of this Age think fit to maintain the same Opinions," Mr *Jurieu* would think himself obliged to call them Extravagancies, and Impieties. " What a notorious " Partiality is This! The same Things, which are " Extravagancies, and Impieties, in our Age, are " only excusable Mistakes, and Oversights, in the " IVth

---

(2) Baronius ad Ann. 302. n. 67. pag. 733.

(3) Mr du Pin is of this Opinion. He composed, says he, (Biblioth. des Auteurs Ecclef. Tom. I. pag. 203.) when he was but a Catechumen, VII Books.

(4) Consult the Table of This Dictionary, at the Word ARNOBIUS.

(5) Persius, in Prologo.

(6) Du Pin, Biblioth des Auteurs Ecclef. Tom. I. Col. 2. Edit. of Holland.

(7) Gulielmi Cave Histor. Literatæ pag. 112.

(8) Præf. Arnobii in Edit. Lugd. Bat. 1651.

(9) Sanrin, Examen de la Doctrine de Mr Jurieu, pag. 681.

(10) Id. ib. pag. 683.

and not *Eight*, as was believed for some time [D]. They have been commented on by learned Men, and printed several times [E].

" IVth Century. Why so (11)?" This Author pretends to have discovered the source of these double Weights. Let us hear him again (12). " Mr *Jurieu* " forgives them Those Errors, as light and trifling " Faults, which, in Persons of our own Age, would be " Infernal Heresies. It is common for us to shew " great Respect, and an high Esteem, for Those, " who have had the happiness to live several Centuries " before us; tho' we discover in them all Those " Weaknesses, and bad Qualities, which we cannot " suffer in the Moderns. If we cannot esteem the " Ancients, we think ourselves at least obliged to " love them; and, by judging with Christian Cha" rity, to put the most favourable Construction we " can upon their Words. Whereas, on the contrary, " we glory in an enflamed Zeal against our Cotem" poraries; we forgive them nothing, but are lavish of " our *Anathema*'s against them. And yet, the Inte" rests of Religion once preserved, Charity should " rather be exercised towards the Living, than Those, " who have been dead for several Ages past. The " Charity, we have for These, costs us little; be" cause their Merit does not excite our Jealousy and " Envy, nor do we consider them as our Rivals. But " we must mortify Self-love not a little, to judge " charitably of an Adversary, who speaks and writes " against us, and whose Reputation eclipses our " Glory; and this is a Sacrifice, which we do not " easily make. As Mr *Jurieu* had no Quarrel against " *Origen*, and as he has personal Enemies in the *Soci*" *nian* Party, no wonder, if he has more indulgence " for the former, than the latter."

[D] *Seven Books, and not Eight, as was believed for some time.*] Every one knows, that the Title of the small Work of *Minucius Felix* is *Octavius*. It is found, in several ancient Manuscripts, joyned with the Books of *Arnobius*, which occasioned it's passing for One of His; and, without doubt, the Word *Octavius*, taken for *Octavus*, misled many a Reader. Let us cite the following Words of Mr *du Pin*. " This " Book (13) passed a long Time for the *eighth* Book " of *Arnobius*; for, being found in an ancient Ma" nuscript of the *Vatican*, with the Seven Books of " *Arnobius*, it was four times printed under That " Name *, without any one's knowing it's true Au" thor. The learned Civilian *Baudouin* was the first, " who discovered This vulgar Error, and caused This " little Treatise, with a learned Preface, in which " he restores it to it's proper Author, to be separate" ly printed at *Heidelberg*, in the Year 1560. Now, " tho' the Honour of having made the first Discovery " be due to This famous Civilian, yet, Thirty three " Years after, *Ursinus*, causing *Arnobius*'s Works to " be printed at *Rome*, whether he had not seen *Bau*" *douin*'s Edition, or would assume the Honour of " This Remark to himself, separated *Minucius*'s Book " from Those of *Arnobius*, without any Intimation " that it had been done before, thus ascribing to him" self the Honour of the Discovery (14)." We find much the same thing in the Preface (15) to the *Minucius Felix*, printed at *Leyden* in the Year 1652. We there find likewise, that, almost at the same time that *Francis Baudouin* made it appear, that the pretended *eighth* Book of *Arnobius* was the Work of *Minucius Felix*, another Critic had some Suspicion of the Mistake. " Eodem fere tempore id ipsum " suboluit etiam Hadriano Junio (16). — *About the* " *same time* Hadrian Junius *began to suspect the same* " *Thing*." This is not exact: It should have been said, that *Francis Baudouin* was not the first, who discovered it; for He did not publish what he knew of the Matter, till four Years after another had communicated This Thought to the Public. His *Minucius* appeared in the Year 1560. Now we find the following Passage concerning this Matter, in a Piece, which *Hadrian Junius* published in the Year 1556. " Arnobio, qui septem duntaxat adversum gentes libros " edidit, octavus accrevit, quum sit Minucii Felicis " Octavius, ab interlocutorum uno ita vocitatus, nova " ratione obliterandi auctoris (17). — *An Eighth* " *Book was insensibly tacked to the seven Books of* Ar" nobius *against the* Gentiles, *which was indeed the* " Octavius *of* Minucius Felix, *so called from one of* " *the Interlocutors; a new Way of concealing the Au*" *thor*." The following Year, *Baudouin* was not

cured of the common Error; for he cited the Treatise of *Minucius* as the *eighth* Book of *Arnobius*. " Sic " ille apud Arnobium Cecilius Christianos dictitat cum " coënunt infantis occisi sanguinem lambere (18). — " Horribilis profecto est oratio Cecilii illius leguleii " Romani qui apud Arnobium libro octavo hæc ad" huc Christianis objicit (19). — *Thus the* Cecilius " *in* Arnobius *pretends, that the Christians, when* " *they come together, drink the Blood of a murthured* " *Infant*. — *It is a shocking Speech of That* Cecilius, " *the Roman Lawyer, who, in the eighth Book of* " Arnobius, *still charges the Christians with This* " *Practice*." *Lewis Carrio* ascribed to *Junius* the Honour of being the first, who had restored the *Octavius* to it's True Author; and, in a Book, which he published, at *Paris*, in the Year 1583, he speaks thus. " Illi (Minucio) Octavum adversus gentes " librum Junius noster in Animadversis suis princeps " jam olim vindicavit (20). — *Our* Junius, *the First,* " *who made the Discovery, had before, in his Animad*" *versions, restored the eighth Book against the Gen*" *tiles to it's True Author,* Minucius Felix." Read these Words of Mr *Joly*: " Minutii Felicis vetustis" simi scriptoris Christiani dialogus elegantissimus " contra idolorum vanitatem tam diu pro octavo " Arnobii adversus gentes libro habitus est, quia Mi" nutius eum sub nomine Octavii protulerat, donec " à Francisco Balduino Jurisconsulto, anno 1560, " Arnobio abductus, & genuino Autori redditus est, " veluti Nicolaus Rigaltius in præfatione ad eundem " Minutium observavit (21). — *The most elegant* " *Dialogue of* Minucius Felix, *against the Vanity of* " *Idolatry, was so long thought to be the eighth Book* " *of* Arnobius, *adversus* gentes, *because he had in*" *scribed it* Octavius; *till* Francis Baudouin, *the* " *Lawyer, took it from* Arnobius, *and restored it to* " *the true Author, as* Nicolas Rigaltius *observed in* " *the Preface to the same* Minucius." Here are two learned Men, who were ignorant, that *Junius* was before-hand with *Baudouin* in the Discovery of the true Author of the *Octavius*. However I think Mr *Joly* had no reason to place This Book in the List of the *Pseudonymous*. He pretends, that, in publishing it, the Author disguised himself under the Name of *Octavius*: I think it were better to say, that *Octavius* is the Title of the Book, and not the supposed Name of it's Author. It would be improper, to say, that *Plato*'s Dialogues were published under the False Names of the Persons, from whom they are entituled. *Minucius Felix* imitated *Plato*: he would have his Dialogue carry, for it's Title, the Name of The principal Interlocutor.

[E] *His Works — have been printed several times*.] If I had the necessary Books, I would give an exact account of the Editions of *Arnobius*; but I must give up this Design, and confine myself to some critical Observations on Those, who have given us Catalogues of these Editions. The Author of the Preface to the *Arnobius*, printed at *Leyden*, in the Year 1651, says, I. That the first Edition of This Father is That, which *Francis Priscianensis*, a *Florentine*, published at *Rome*; but does not say in what Year; a Fault of Omission, which cannot be excused. II. That *Sigismund Gelenius* altered several things in this Edition, not by the Assistance of Manuscripts, but by trusting to the Conjectures of his own Genius. III. That *Theodore Canterus*, in publishing *Arnobius* with Additions, complained of *Gelenius*'s Boldness. IV. That *Godescale Stewechius* laboured with Success on This Father. V. That *Elmenhorst* added to his Commentary the *various Readings*, collected as well from the Manuscripts, and the Edition published at *Rome*, in the Year 1542, from an ancient Manuscript of *Francis Sabæus* (23), as from the Edition of *Fulvius Ursinus*. VI. That *Desiderius Heraldus* published Annotations on the Seven Books of *Arnobius*. I have three things to offer against all this: In the first Place, the List of the Editions is very imperfect; in the second Place, the Edition of *Rome*, 1552, is the same with the First, though it be mentioned here as different from it. In the third Place, it is not true, that the Annotations of *Desiderius Heraldus* followed the Edition of *Elmenhorst*. The latter is of the Year 1610, and *Heraldus*'s Edition appeared at *Geneva*, in the Year 1597, and at *Paris* in the Year 1605.

Let

ARNOLDUS.

(24) It is at the 20th Page, Col. 1. of the first Tome of his Bibliotheque Edit. Holl.

(25) I make use of the Edition of Holland.

(26) Pocciantius de Scriptor. Florentinis, pag. 69.

(27) Ludov. Carrio Emendat. lib. I. cap. 9. fol. 18. Mr Du Pin affirms it, pag. 110, Tom. I. Biblioth.

Let us now examine Mr *du Pin's* List (24). I obferve, in the firft Place, that the proper Names in it are very much difguifed (25). There we find *Canrerus*, inftead of *Canterus*; *Hermenborftius*, inftead of *Helmenborftius*; *Stevochins*, inftead of *Stewochius*. Befides, I obferve, that he mentions one *Theodorus Prifcianenfis*, as the Printer of the firft Edition. This is certainly a miftake. We have feen, that the *Florentine Francifcus Prifcianenfis* was the firft, who publifhed the Works of *Arnobius*. Now he was no Printer. *Pocciantius* does not give him this Appellation; he only makes him a good Philologift, and Author of fome *Italian* Books (26). I am perfuaded, that *Fauftus Sabæus*, Library Keeper of the *Vatican*, communicated the Manufcript to him, from which the Edition of *Rome* was printed, in 1542. In the Preface of the Edition of *Leyden*, it was wrong to make a Diftinction between the Edition of *Francifcus Prifcianenfis*, and That, which was publifhed from the Manufcript of *Sabæus*. Note, that *Lewis Carrio* is of Opinion, that the Manufcript of *Arnobius*, which is in the Library of the King of *France*, is That, which was employed in the firft Edition (27). He imagines, that, becaufe it was dedicated to *Francis* I, the Manufcript was likewife fent him. In the third Place, I obferve, that it is not true, that the feven Books of *Arnobius* were printed with the Notes of *Heraldus*, in 1583; nor that the Edition of *Hamburgh*, in 1610, ought to be diftinguifhed from That before-mentioned; I mean from That, which was accompanied with the Commentary of *Elmenhorft*.

Laftly, I obferve, that *Stewechius* did not publifh an Edition of *Arnobius*, at *Duäy*, in the Year 1634; his Edition is of *Antwerp*, in 1686, and he had been dead a long time, when his *Electa in Arnobium* were reprinted at *Duäy*, in the Year 1634. *Cum paratitlis feu Summariis Leandri de Sancto Martino*. You will find a like Miftake at Citation * of the Remark [D], where Mr *Du Pin* fays, that *Erafmus* publifhed *Arnobius* in 1560; whereas He died in 1536. Let us take fome Notice of Father *Labbé* (28). He thinks the Edition of *Leyden* a very good one; but wonders, that The Undertakers of it, did not infert the *Arnobianus Criticus* of *Meurfius*, which was printed at *Leyden*, in the Year 1598, *cum Hypercritico Minutiano*. He would at leaft have had them take Notice of it. They, who fhould retort upon him, that he himfelf ought to have remembered the *Eclogæ ad Arnobium of Julius Cæfar Bulenger* (29), would not have the fame Reafon; for That Book is of no ufe, either in correcting the Text of *Arnobius*, or in unfolding the literal Senfe; it is nothing but a Series of Quotations, explaining fome Thoughts of *Arnobius*. The fame Jefuit reflects upon the great *Salmafius*, for promifing a Commentary on This Author, and not keeping his Word. *Salmafiani autem illi Commentarii tamdiu expectati, tam fæpe ejus amicorumque literis promiffi atque jactati, in fumum tandem ventofque evanuerunt* (30). I believe fuch a Piece of *Salmafius* would have made finer Difcoveries, than his learned Commentary on the Treatife of *Tertullian de Pallio*.

(28) Labbé, Differt. de Scriptor. Ecclef. Tom. I, pag. 105.

(29) Printed at Touloufe, in 1612, in 8vo.

(30) Labbé, ubi fupra.

ARNOLDUS (NICHOLAS) Profeffor of Divinity at *Franeker*, was born at *Lefna*, a City of *Poland*, the Seventeenth of *December* 1618. His Mother being left a Widow, when he was but three Years of Age, took all imaginable Care of his Education, and dedicated him to Learning. He went through his Humanity Studies in the College of *Lefna*, under *Comenius*, among other Regents, who at that time read his *Janua Linguarum* to his Scholars. He was ordained *Acolyth* (a), in the Synod of *Oftrorog*, at Fifteen Years of Age, and, in this Station, accompanied *Orminius* (b), for two Years, in vifiting the Churches of *Poland*; after which, he was fent to *Dantzic*, in the Year 1635, and there applied himfelf to the Study of Eloquence and Philofophy. He fometimes experienced the ill Humour of *John Botfac*, who was grieved, that a young Man of fuch Hopes fhould be a *Calvinift*. In the Year 1638, he returned into *Poland*, and ftudied *Sermonary Theology**, under the Direction of *Orminius*, and, a Year after, was fent to *Podalia*, to be Rector of the School of *Jablonow*. Having exercifed This Employ during three Months, he difcharged the Minifterial Functions at the Houfe of a great Lord (c) for two Years fucceffively. It being obferved, that his Talents might be of great Ufe to the Church, it was thought proper to give him an Opportunity of improving them in the moft famous Univerfities. He began his Travels in the Year 1641, and came firft to *Franeker*, where he made a great Progrefs under his Countryman *Maccovius*, and under *Cocceius*. The Year 1643 he fpent in the Univerfities of *Groningen*, *Leyden*, and *Utrecht*, and foon after returned to *Franeker*; where he applied himfelf to ftudy *French* and *Englifh*. The following Year he went over into *England*; but, finding it impoffible to get to *Oxford*, the Roads being ftopped by the King's Forces, or by Thofe of the Parliament, he went on Foot to *Cambridge*; but could hear no Divinity Lectures there, the Profeffors being all under Confinement in *Trinity* College. Being on his Return to *Franeker*, he applied himfelf to Preaching, even in *Dutch*; and his Sermons were fo well relifhed, that, in hopes of retaining him in *Friefland*, they diffuaded him from revifiting *Poland*. He was judged very capable of the Miniftry by the Claffical Synod of *Franeker*, who had examined him; and the Praifes they gave him induced a young Gentlewoman of That Country to accept of him for a Hufband [A]. He was married to her in the Year 1645, and foon after

(a) The Reformed Churches of Bohemia retained this Part of Ancient Difcipline. — An Acolyth is an Under Deacon, the loweft Order of Priefts.

(b) Superintendant of the Churches of Great Poland.

* A Syftem of Divinity compiled from Sermons.

(c) Johannes de Potock Potocki, Succamerarius Terræ Halicienfis.

[A] *The Praifes they gave him induced a young Gentlewoman of That Country to accept of him for a Hufband.*] This we are informed of by the Author of his Funeral Oration. "Fecit paulo poft, *fays he* (1), tanta omnium laus, ut nobiliffima in Friffia Virgo Remigia à NITZEN facilis in conjugale ejus rueret amplexus anno 1645. —— *Soon after, This general Approbation induced a Noble Lady of Friefland*, Remigia of NITZEN, *readily to meet his Embraces in Wedlock, in the Year* 1645." This Lady was to be commended for preferring Reputation and Merit to Riches. There are other Examples of Matches of this Nature; for it is certain, that many Proteftant Divines, recommended only by the

Credit of their Eloquence, or Learning, have married to great Advantage, and rendered themfelves very confiderable by the Rank of the Family, into which they have married. The great Probability, that they may, fooner, or later, be raifed to diftinguifhed Benefices, or confiderable Profefforfhips, may have contributed towards it. Be this as it will, the Wife of our *Arnoldus* is to be commended. She died in the beginning of the Year 1652, and left no Children. In the Year 1653, he married again to the Widow of an Advocate of *Leewaerden*, whofe Name was *Anne Pybinga*, the Daughter of a Burgo Mafter of *Franeker*, who brought him nine Children, five Sons (2) and four Daughters, and furvived him. He

(1) Marckius, in Orat. Funebr. Arnoldi, p. 32.

(2) The fecond and third were Twins. See the Programma of the Rector of the Univerfity. It is printed before the Orat. Funebr.

VOL. I. 6 L

after had an Invitation from the Church of *Beetgum*. He served it faithfully and constantly, till the Year 1651, without listening to the Invitations addressed to him from other Churches; but, That Year, he complyed with the Instances of the States of *Friesland*, who chose him to succeed *Cocceius*, as Divinity-Professor at *Franeker* (d). He discharged This Office with great Abilities 'till his Death, which happened on the Fifteenth of *October* 1680, after a tedious Sickness, in which he gave several Marks of his Piety, and Resignation to the Orders from above (e). I shall mention some Journies which he took after his Promotion to the Professorship [B] of Divinity; and shall not forget the Books, which he published [C].

He had but three Sons, and one Daughter, living, when he died (3).

[B] *Some Journies, which he took after his Promotion to the Professorship.*] In the Year 1652, he paid a Visit to his Relations at *Lesna*, and passed a Month pleasantly with his Uncle by the Mother-side, *Martin Gertichius*, Minister of the Place, and famous for several Works. He travelled again, in the Year 1656, in the Retinue of the four Ambassadors Extraordinary, which the States General sent to the King of *Sweden*, and to the King of *Poland*. Their Excellencies would have him for their Preacher, and were very well pleased with the Sermons he made, either in *Dutch, German,* or *Polish*, as occasion required. This Journey lasted two Years. In this time *Arnoldus* gained the Esteem of *Stephen Corycinsky*, Chancellor of *Poland*, *John Oxenstiern*, Great Marshal of *Sueden*, *Douglas*, General of the Troops, and the Elector of *Brandenburgh*, who offered him the Post of Public Preacher. In the Year 1666, he was deputed to *Heidelberg*, to persuade *Spanhemius* to accept of a Professorship of Divinity in the University of *Franeker*, but returned without Success.

[C] *The Books, which he published.*] I omit the Diligence, with which he collected and methodized the Works of *Maccovius*, which he put to the Press; of an *English* Book of *Jeremiah Dykes* (4); but I shall mention his Confutation of the Catechism of the *Socinians*; his *Anti-Bidellus*; his *Anti-Echardus*; his Book against *Brevingius*; his Apology for *Amesius* against *Eberманнus*, Defender of *Bellarmin*; his Theological Disputes on select Subjects; his Commentary on the Epistle to the *Hebrews*; his *Lux in tenebris*; and what he published against *John Amos Comenius*. Read this Passage of his Funeral Oration concerning these Works: " Quis est qui non - - - - " prædicet Raccovianæ Catecheseos, in qua religionis " dicam an impietatis Socinianæ plenissimum est com-

" pendium, curatissimam refutationem, quæ supra " fidem impiis seductoribus molesta, doctis grata est? " Cujus non laudem meretur tum Anti-Bidellus, quo " Pneumatomachi furorem, & fatuam Comenii (5) lu- " cem extinxit; tum Anti-Echardus, cujus conquisitum " & male colligatum fasciculum ita dissolvit, ut disso- " lutarum scoparum hactenus retinuerit nomen? Imo " quem non in mille detorsionum tenebris ineffa- " biliter delectat doctissimarum illa vindicarum lux, " quam publico toties recusam dedit, & cujus ope " tuta Ecclesia errorum evitat devia? Sed ne in hoc " quidem labore acquiescere potuit, qui in Ecclesiæ " voluit consumi bonum. Brevingii ab eo tempore " feliciter demolitus est tribunal, Erbermannum Bel- " larmino adversus Amesium suppetias ferentem con- " fodit, &c. (6). ——— *Who does not extol the ac- " curate Confutation of the Raccovian Catechism, " which is the fullest Compendium of the Religion, " or rather Impiety, of the Socinians; and which " is, beyond Expectation, irksome to those impious " Seducers, but highly acceptable to the Learned? " Whose Praise is not due to the Anti-Bidellus, in " which he extinguished the Rage and false Light " of the Socinian Comenius; next the Anti- " Echardus, which so ruins That Author's Miscel- " laneous and ill-connected Fardel, that it still " retains the Name of The Broom pulled to pieces? " In short, who is not inexpressibly pleased, in the " Darkness of a thousand Turnings and Windings, " with the Light of those learned Vindications, " which he so often published, and by the Help of " which The Church avoids the devious Paths of " Error? But he did not stop here; he desired to lay " himself wholly out for the Good of the Church. " From that Time the Tribunal of Brevingius was " happily demolished, and Erbermannus, who assisted " Bellarmin against Amesius, wholly vanquished in " Dispute, &c.*" Thus you have some ANTI's not in Mr *Baillet*'s List.

ARODON (BENJAMIN d') a *German Jew*, Author of a Book full of Precepts for the Ladies. It was translated from the *German* into *Italian*, by Rabbi *Jacob Alpron*. This Translation was printed at *Venice*, in the Year 5412, according to the *Jewish* Calculation (a), after it had been carefully corrected by Rabbi *Isaac Levita*. This Book is filled with Observances, not only in regard to Cleanliness of Body, but likewise with respect to the Practice of Prayer, and good Works. The Observances of the first kind contain several Niceties and superstitious Regularities; and there is sometimes a great deal of *Rigour* in Those of the second [A]. This will be more fully seen in the Remark, which accompanies This Article.

[A] *There is sometimes a great deal of Rigour, in the Observances of the second Order.*] For Example; " The Husband and Wife must not speak a Word " in the Act of Conjugal Duty, and entertain only " pious Thoughts, without any Consideration of the " Pleasure, and in pursuance only of the Divine Will;" and they are assured that, " If they act other- " wise, their Children will be born deformed, lame, " dumb, or squint-ey'd." " Ogni persona deve esser " auvertita tanto l'huomo, come la donna, nel tem- " po che si congiungono insieme, non devono par- " lar, nè haver niun cattivo pensiere, ne debbano " scoprirete li loochi occulti è vergognosi, perche " quelli che parlano in quel tempo che se congiun- " gono insieme, quella creatura che viene conceputa " in quell' istante, riuscisse dal ventre della madre " con qualche מקרה ò zoppo, ò muto, ò guercio, " ò simili mancamenti, ò del tutto distrutto, è mal " conditionato ——— non devono haver intentione " in quell' istante alli piaceri ma solo per adempir " il voler divino (1) ——— ambidoi devono pensar " in quell' instante che questo non lo fanno per il " lor giovamento & adempir il precetto ——— ogn' " huome da bene fa quello, che deve pensare in " quell' instante, perche si deve pensar solo à pen- " sieri santi è pii (2)." This Precept is both very refined, and very rigid. See what is said, in the *News from the Republick of Letters* (3), concerning a Book of Mr *Yvon*, a Minister of the *Labadists*. Such great Purity in this kind of Pleasure is rather to be wished, than hoped, for; nevertheless, the *Casuists* are to be commended, for insisting upon it, and endeavouring to introduce Purity, where the Passion of Brutal Lust has but too much sway. Had our Rabbi believed, as the Church of *Rome* does, that Marriage is a Sacrament, he could not have required more Holy Dispositions from the Married, than Those he demands. He imposes upon them at once the Law of *favete linguis* ⁎ (4), the Observation whereof the *Pagans* recommended in their greatest Mysteries, and That of *sursum corda* †, which the ancient Church never forgot to prescribe in the Celebration of it's most solemn Ceremonies. In a word, it is certain, that, had he received the Doctrine of *Jesus Christ* with a true Faith, and been animated with the Spirit of Grace, he could not have given Advice more worthy of Evangelical Purity. This ought to shame the looser *Casuists*, who are so common among Christians.

Note,

ARRERAC.

Note, that the Precepts of This *Rabbi* do not at all agree with the Advice of Physicians; who pretend, that a Child, conceived under Distraction of Mind, I mean under serious, grave, and spiritual Thoughts, will be simple, foolish, and weak (5). They give very different Advice to Those, who desire Children (6); but any Man of tolerable Sense must grant, that They lead Mankind into a very bad School of Chastity; Their Precepts are calculated only for Those, who would confine every thing to Animal, Earthly, Sensual, and *Epicurean* Life. We must go to our *Rabbi's* School, if we would learn to demean ourselves, in this part of our Duty, like Creatures endowed with a Spiritual Soul, and not deserve the Censure;

(c) See Remark [C] of the Article ASSI-SA (Francesco d').
(6) See Roderic de Castro, de Natura Mulierum, lib. 3. cap. 5.

O curvæ in terras animæ, & cœlestium inanes (7)!
O sordid Minds, of Heavenly Thoughts devoid!

(7) Persius, Sat. II. ver. 26.

We shall the better comprehend how excellent and sublime the Morality of This *Jew* is, if we remember, that it is directly opposite to the Maxims of Those Doctors of Impurity, who have filled their Poems with so much Wantonness. These dangerous Poisoners are far from advising Silence; and it is This, which furnished a Modern with a Confirmation of the Interpretation he has given of the Words of a *Greek* Poet, which contain a Description of the Grotto of the Nymphs. As for the agreeable *Murmurings*, says he (8), mentioned by *Homer*, they are without doubt the obliging Words of Lovers, the *ohi me cor mio* (Oh! my Heart!) of the *Italians*; the ζωή καὶ ψυχή (My Life and Soul!) of the *Greeks*; and the *alma de mi alma* (Soul of my Soul!) of the *Spaniards*; *such as attend upon the most favourable Privacies, and which made the most knowing, of all the Poets, in the Art of Love, to say;*

(8) Hexameron Rustique, IV Journée, p. 212, &c.

Accedant questus, accedat amabile murmur,
Et dulces gemitus, aptæque verba joco *.

* Ovid. de Arte Amandi, lib. II. ver. 723.

And, whilst in Bliss together you expire,
Let Sighs, and gentle Murmurs, fan the Fire.

Hear what he says in another Place;

Et mihi blanditias dixit, dominumque vocavit,
Et quæ præterea publica verba juvant †.

† Id. Amor. Lib. III Eleg. 6. ver. 21.

She lisp'd soft Flatt'ry, my Desires to move,
And try'd the Force of Words, to kindle Love.

I will not inform you, that the Term juvare is altogether Erotic, and consecrated to the last Delights of Love, which are again expressed, as well as the Murmurs, in these two Verses of the same Author;

Me voces audire juvat sua gaudia fassi,
Utque morer, me, me, sustineamque roget ‖.

‖ Id. de Arte Amandi, Lib. II.

Give me the Girl, who dies upon the Kiss,
In Murmurs soft, expressive of the Bliss;
Who courts my Stay; whose Beauties never cloy,
Inspire new Raptures, and revive the Joy.

——— The famous Epithalamium of the Emperor *Gallienus*, *which* Trebellius Pollio *perfers to Those of an hundred other Poets, who all exercised their Pens on the same Subject, wonderfully expresses these soft and obliging Murmurs, and the Caresses, which are inseparable from them. It is said, that, holding the Hands of two of his Brother's Children, when he married them, he pronounced these Verses of his own Composition;*

Ite, ite, o pueri, pariter sudate medullis
Omnibus inter vos, non murmura vestra columbæ,
Brachia non hederæ, non vincant oscula conchæ.

Now go, my Children! prove the Toils of Love;
In Murmurs soft surpass the cooing Dove;
Cling, like the Tendrils of the curling Vine;
And close each Kiss, as sticks the Shell-fish, join.

It is difficult to conceive any thing more pathetic, or passionate, on this Head. To be diametrically opposite to These false Doctors, the Bane of Youth, is no small Praise; it is a just Presumption, that the Morality, which one advances, is of admirable Purity. Add to all this the judicious Answer of the famous Mr *Drelincourt* to a Bishop, who had made an Observation altogether unbecoming, I will not say a Person of his Character, but even a Layman, which was, not over fond of a wanton Stile. These are Mr *Drelincourt's* Words (9); "Instead "of washing out, with his Tears, those ways of "speaking, that the Virgin *Mary* is the Spirit and "Life of *Christians*, he defends them with a Rail-"lery, which would better become Those, who "tread the Stage. You Gentlemen, says he, Pastors "of the Protestant Church, who have your dear "Counterparts, not so much inseparable accidents of "your Substance, as Bone of your Bone, and Flesh "of your Flesh, nay, who are but one Flesh in two "Persons, use indeed much more endearing Terms to "Those Souls of your Souls, Those Lives of your Lives, "Those Lives of your Hearts and Souls, Those Souls of "your Lives and Hearts, than the World knows of; for "you are Those Spiritual Persons, who judge the whole "World, nay the very Angels, and with much more "Reason the Romanists, without being subject to be "judged by any. I know not whence he had his In-"formation, and shall not answer for the Expressions "of Those, who have Wives by stealth. But a "grave Person, who lives in a chaste Marriage, "does not study such extra-agant Rhetoric." The Prelate replied in a manner so Burlesque, that nothing could exceed it (10).

(9) Drelincourt's Avant-coureur de la Replique à Mr le Camus, Evêque de Belley, pag. 36, 37.

(10) See his Answer to the Avant-coureur of Mr Drelincourt, pag. 156.

ARRERAC (JOHN d') Counsellor in the Parliament of *Bourdeaux*, towards the end of the XVIth Century, is Author of a Book, which I shall take notice of below [*A*].

[*A*] *He is Author of a Book, which I shall take notice of below* (1) It is entituled *La Philosophie Civile & d'Etat, divisé en l'Irenarchie & la Polemarchie.* ——— *Civil and Political Philosophy, divided into Irenarchy and Polemarchy;* and was printed at *Bourdeaux,* by *Simon Millanges,* in the Year 1598, in 8vo. It consists of two Volumes, only the first of which I have seen (1). The Author gives us this Idea of it (2). " I have borrowed my Subject from the " Laws of the first Book of the Pandects, which " the Doctors universally despise, either because " They do not understand them, or because they " look upon them as of but little use toward Chi- " canery, of which they are more Slaves, on " account of the Gain they hope from it, " than Lovers of Virtue and Honour. This Book " is so rich and fruitful of excellent Laws, that I " am much mistaken, if I do not prove in mine, " that it contains the greatest Part of the Laws of " Nature, and of both Moral and Civil Philosophy, " together with the Order of the *Roman* Magistracy " and Jurisdiction. I have added to this first Book " the two first Titles of the second, upon which " I have discoursed of the Rights of Jurisdiction, as " well according to the *Roman* Policy, as our own " *French* and Ecclesiastical Law; and of This Law " of Nature; *quod quisque juris in alium statuerit,* " *ut ipse eodem jure utatur.*" This relates to the first Tome, or the *Irenarchy,* that is, *State of Peace:* what follows concerns his *Polemarchy,* or *State of War.* It is a small Volume, containing, in four Books, *the Qualities and Perfections of the General of an Army, the Artifices and Stratagems of ancient Commanders, the Uses to be made of Occurrences in War, and the Way to preserve a Victory, after it is obtained* (3). This Author had read much, and is not sparing of his Quotations; but, generally speaking, he says but little on each particular Subject, which gives him room to treat of a great Number. He frequently attacks the most celebrated Lawyers, as *Accursius, Alciatus, Budæus, Cujacius, &c.* and, from Time to Time, he makes uncommon Observations.

(1) It contains 722 Pages.
(2) J. d'Arrerac, Epistle Dedicatory to the Cardinal de Joyeuse.
(3) Ibid. pag. 2.

ARRIA. ARRIAGA.

ARRIA, the Name of some *Roman* Ladies, whom I shall mention in the Remarks of the Article PAETUS.

ARRIAGA (RODERIC d') a *Spanish* Jesuit, was born at *Lucrona*, the Seventeenth of *January*, 1592. He entered into the Society on the Seventeenth of *September*, 1606, and taught Philosophy, with great Applause, at *Valladolid*, and Divinity at *Salamanca*; and, being informed, by Letters from the General of The Order, that it would be more for the Glory of God, that some *Spanish* Jesuits should go into *Bohemia* (a), to teach the sublimer Sciences there, he offered himself for This Employ. He arrived at *Prague* in the Year 1624. He taught Scholastic Divinity there for the space of thirteen Years, and was Director-General of the Studies twenty Years successively, and Chancellor of the University for twelve Years. He solemnly received the Cap of Doctor of Divinity, and acquired much Reputation. The Province of *Bohemia* deputed him three times to *Rome*, to assist there at the general Congregations of the Order (b). He was several times intreated to return into *Spain*, but to no purpose. He was very much esteemed by *Urban* VIII, *Innocent* X, and the Emperor *Ferdinand* III. He died at *Prague* on the Seventeenth of *June* 1667 (c). He published several Books [A], in which he discovered much Subtility, and Wit. He seems to have succeeded much better in confuting what he denied, than in defending what he affirmed; and it is pretended, that thereby he became a Favourer of *Pyrrhonism*, tho' he always declared, that he was no *Pyrrhonist* [B]. It would certainly be the highest Injustice to suspect him of the least Prevarication, or of betraying the *Dogmatists*; for, if, on one hand, he exerted all his Strength in confuting a great number of Opinions; he employed it on the other, in supporting the Opinions, which he had embraced: It was easy to see, that he acted with Sincerity, and exerted himself to the utmost; and, if his Proofs are weaker than his Objections, the blame must be laid on the nature of the Things. The Diligence, with which he confuted the Subtilties, which have been invented by the Schoolmen, to prove, that two contradictory Propositions are sometimes true, and sometimes false [C], is a sufficient Demonstration, that he was passionately in the Interest

[A] *He published several Books.*] A Course of Philosophy, in one Volume; and a Course of Divinity, in eight Volumes. The Course of Philosophy, printed in Folio, at *Antwerp*, in the Year 1632, has been reprinted several times. The Edition of *Lyons* is augmented. The first and second Volume of his Course of Divinity were printed in the Year 1643; the Third and Fourth in the Year 1644; the Fifth in the Year 1649; the Sixth in Year 1650; the Seventh and Eighth in the Year 1655. They are All in Folio, printed by *Balthazar Moret*, at *Antwerp* (1). He had The ninth Volume in hand, when he died: It was That *de Jure & Justitia* (2). Don *Nicolas Antonio* makes *Arriaga* the Author of a Book, *De Oratore*, printed at *Cologne* in the Year 1637, and of The Brevis Expositio Literæ Magistri Sententiarum, cum Quæstionibus quæ circa ipsam moveri possunt, & Autboribus qui de illis disputant.—— A Brief Exposition of the Letter of the Master of the Sentences, with the Questions, which may be started thereupon, and the Authors, which controvert them; printed at *Lyons*, in the Year 1636, in 8vo, after other Editions (3); but, as Father *Sotuel* does not mention These two Books, tho' the first was ascribed to This Jesuit by *Alegambus*, there is reason to believe, that Don *Nicolas Antonio* is mistaken.

[B] *It is pretended, that thereby he became a Favourer of* Pyrrhonism, tho' he always declared, that he was no Pyrrhonist.] This is the Opinion of Mr *de Villemandy*: "Sunt alii, says he (4), qui periculosius "adhuc sollicitant (sacratiora fidei dogmata) cujus- "modi Arriaga suis in disputationibus Theologicis; ni- "hil enim moliuatur ut aliorum quorumcunque "placita reflexionibus & objectionibus suis destruam, "ipsi autem nihil sere adstruunt — Celebris est inter "Romanenses Scholasticos Rodericus ille Arriaga— "Is multis Volum. Fol. & Philosophiam & Theolo- "giam est persecutus; jam autem singula quæque sic "tractat ut aliorum seré omnium opiniones variis "rationibus infirmare studeat, suas autem levissime "suffulciat. Si ex hac methodo ingenii conditio "dijudicetur, vere Pyrrhonius potest haberi; cum ta- "men placita sua quantum potest firmet, iisque con- "stanter inhæreat, non potest legitime eo nomine do- "nari (5) — There are some, who yet more dangerously "shake the most sacred Articles of our Faith, such as "Arriaga, in his Theological Disputations; for they "take a great deal of Pains to overthrow the Opi- "nions of others, but establish nothing themselves——

"This Roderic Arriaga is famous among the Roman "Catholic Schoolmen. He treats of Philosophy, and Di- "vinity, in many Folio Volumes; but handles them in "such a Manner, that he endeavours to weaken the "Opinions of almost all others by a Variety of Argu- "ments, but makes but a poor Defence of his Own. "If the Author's Way of Thinking may be judged of by "this Method of Proceeding, he is a thorough Pyrrho- "nian; but, when he labours to establish his own "Opinions, he cannot fairly lay claim to This Appella- "tion." It may be affirmed, that, if the Reading this Jesuit's Writing inclines us to think him a *Pyrrhonist*, it is purely by Accident, and against his Intention; for he is as Dogmatical as any One, and as zealous to confirm his Decisions; but, whether thro' the Weakness of human Understanding, or the Difficulty of the Subjects, he found himself in the Case of a great numbers of Authors, who can discover the weak Side of a Doctrine to admiration, but never where the Force of it lies. They are like Those Generals, who destroy the Enemy's Country with Fire and Sword, without being able to put their own Frontiers in a Posture of Defence. Mr *Ancillon* thought This Jesuit "very singular in his Way of Writing, and "much freer than others, who, thro' a base Servi- "tude, dare not forsake the Opinions of the Writers "of Their Society, and who scrupulously follow "them as infallible —— Reporting the Opinion of "*Vasquez*, he says plainly, that, in the main, he "lays but little stress on Father *Vasquez*'s Solutions "(6). Mr *Ancillon* adds, "In reading *Arriaga* and "*Oviedo*, I have observed, that, when one of these "two Jesuits maintains the Affirmative of a Propo- "sition, the other maintains the Negative; which "is not very usual among the Doctors of the *Romish* "Religion in general, and which I have seldom ob- "served, except in *Cornelius à Lapide*, and *Estius*." It is no uncommon thing for the Jesuits to confute each other on a great number of Questions, as well in Philosophy, as School-Divinity. Witness *Suares* and *Vasquez*.

[C] *The Subtilties of the Schoolmen, to shew, that two contradictory Propositions are sometimes true, and sometimes false.*] He has very well distinguished These Sophisms: See his second Disputation on the Summulæ of Logic (7). I have seen some Professors very much puzzled, when these Objections were made to them; which, in truth, ought only to pass for Cavils, unluckily invented by Persons of too much leisure,

ARSENIUS.

Interest of the *Dogmatists*, against the *Pyrrhonians*. He gave up most of the received Opinions of the Schools in Points of Natural Philosophy, such as the Composition of the *Continuum*, Rarefaction, &c. and therefore undertook to defend The Innovators in Philosophy (d). It is pity so refined and penetrating a Genius had not had a better Notion of right Principles; for he might have carried them very far. A small knowledge in Hydrostatics would have discovered to him the reason of a Phænomenon, in the Explanation of which he took a great deal of Pains to no purpose. His Efforts, and his Zeal in this Matter, make it lamented, that he ran with such force out of the right Way.

(d) *In the Preface to his Course of Philosophy.*

leisure, but who never pretended, like *Heraclitus*, that one and the same thing effectually is, and is not. They only intended to exercise their Wit. Observe, that *Aristotle* does not believe, tho' *Heraclitus* said this, that he really thought so. Ἀδύνατον γὰρ ὑπ-
〈Greek passage〉 — *It is impossible for any One to think, that the same Thing is and is not, as some believed Heraclitus to have affirmed. For it is not necessary we should believe every thing we say.*

(f) *Aristot. Metaphys. lib. III, cap. 3. pag. 667. G.*

[D] *The Reason of a Phænomenon, in the Explanation of which he took a great deal of Pains to no purpose.*] The Phænomenon was, that a Piece of Timber, which is lighter than Water, does, nevertheless, not float on the Water, with regard to it's whole bulk, or thickness. A Beam, floating in a River, lies partly under, and partly above, the Water. This cannot be explained according to the common Principles of Gravity and Levity, and hence proceeded the Vanity of the Efforts of *Arriaga* (9). The new Philosophers find no difficulty in this. See the System of Mr *Gadrois*.

(9) *Arriaga Disputat. 4. de Generat. Sect. 5, de Element. Subsect. VI. pag. 519.*

ARSENIUS, a Deacon of the *Roman* Church, famous for the Nobility of his Family, but much more for his great Learning, and Piety, was chosen by Pope *Damasus* to be sent to the Emperor *Theodosius*, who wanted a Preceptor for his Son *Arcadius*. He came to *Constantinople* in the Year 383, and was very well received by the Emperor, who was offended, one Day, both at the Disciple and the Master, because he found the latter standing, and the other sitting, at his Lesson. He ordered, that his Son, tho' he had already been declared *Augustus*, should stand uncovered, while *Arsenius* instructed him, and lay aside the Marks of Imperial Dignity during That time. *Arsenius*, employing all his Endeavours to accomplish his Disciple in Learning and Virtue, found himself at last obliged to add Chastisement to Censure. Young *Arcadius* was so incensed at it, that he desired one of his Officers to rid him of his Preceptor (a). The Officer advertised *Arsenius* of it, who retired privately into the Deserts of *Ægypt*, where he passed several Years with the Anchorets of *Scetis*, in the most fervent and austere Exercises of Devotion. He died there at the Age of ninety five Years [A]. *Theodosius*, hearing with grief of *Arsenius*'s Retreat, ordered him to be sought for every where, without being able to discover him (b). There are some Faults in *Moreri*'s Dictionary relating to this Article [B]. I have met with some likewise in other Writers [C]. Several

(a) *Taken from the Month of Baronius, ad Ann. 383, n. 22, 23. He cites Metaphrastes under the 19th of May, and Sozomen under the 19th of July.*

(b) *Flechier his History of Theodosius, pag. 273, 274.*

[A] *He died there at the Age of Ninety five Years.*] Hear how Mr *Arnauld d'Andilli* (1) divides this long Life of *Arsenius*. He says, that, "He passed forty "Years in the Court of the Emperor *Theodosius*, "forty in *Scetis*, ten in *Troche*, which is above "*Babylon*, over against the City of *Memphis*, three "in *Canopus* of *Alexandria*, and two in the same "Town of *Troche*, whither being returned he fi-"nished his Course in the fear of God." This Expression, *He past forty Years in the Court of Theodosius*, is very improper; for, unless we will find a notorious Error in it, it must be taken in this Sense; He was forty Years old, when he quitted the Court of *Theodosius*. In effect, to take it in the proper and natural Signification of the Words, *Arsenius* must have lived to above One hundred and twenty Years of Age. His Age, at the time when he went to *Constantinople*, upon being chosen Preceptor to *Arcadius* by *Damasus*, ought to have been added to the Ninety five Years. This Pope would not have chosen a young Man of twenty: Besides, *Theodosius* reign'd but about sixteen Years, and he did not receive *Arsenius* 'till the fourth Year of his Reign.

[B] *There are some Faults in Moreri's Dictionary.*] I. *Arsenius* could not have been sent to *Theodosius*, in the Year 383, to be Preceptor to *Arcadius* and *Honorius*, since *Honorius* was not born before the Year 384. *Baronius* had remarked this Fault to Those, who wrote the Life of *Arsenius*, and ascribed it to one, who knew, in general, that *Theodosius* had two Sons; *aliquis quod sciret duos fuisse Theodosio filios, adjecit Homorium* (2). This Error remained in the Life of *Arsenius*, written by Mr *d'Andilli* (3), who quotes *Rufinus* (4) as his Authority. II. I confess, that *Baronius* (5), on the Credit of the *Lives of the Fathers*, says (6), that *Arsenius* was Godfather to the two Sons of *Theodosius*; but this does not agree with *Rufinus*, who says, that they

(1) *D'Andilli's Lives of the Fathers Solitary, p. 204.*

(2) *Baron. ad Ann. 383, n. 22.*

(3) *It is in the IId Tome of the Lives of the Fathers Solitary, by Arnauld d'Andilli, p. 1. 8, of the Edit. in 8vo. of 1676.*

(4) *Lib. III, n. 37.*

(5) *Ad Ann. 395, n. 26.*

(6) *Part II, pag. 36.*

were put into *Arsenius*'s Hand *presently after their Baptism* (7). Besides, *Baronius* himself has observed, that it is a Mistake in the Life of *Arsenius*, when it is said, that he was sent by *Damasus* to be Preceptor to *Arcadius* and *Honorius*. The latter was not yet born; and the other was but about eight Years old. And it is not probable, that *Arsenius* continued at the Court of *Theodosius*, 'till the Time that *Honorius* stood in need of a Preceptor. III. Mr *Flechier* says plainly, that *Theodosius* ordered *Arsenius* to be searched for throughout the whole Empire. It is very improbable then, that *Arsenius* did not leave the Court 'till after the Death of *Theodosius*, in the Year 395. I say, this is very improbable, tho' it be advanced as a certain Fact, in the first and third Volume of The Dictionary. IV. He should have suppressed the Circumstances, which Mr *Flechier* had expressly remarked, to wit, that the Officer, whom *Arcadius* employed to kill *Arsenius*, gave This Preceptor notice of it. The Supplement to the Dictionary supposes, that *Arsenius* was divinely forewarned of it. V. *Arcadius* was not associated to the Empire at five Years of Age, but at the Age of seven or eight; as *Baronius*, and *Flechier* observe. " *Erat tunc Arcadius annum ætatis agens octavum, " natus nimirum sub consulatu Gratiani quarto & " Merobaudis, triennio ante Theodosii patris Impe-" rium* (8). —— *Arcadius was then eight Years " of Age, having been born in the fourth Consul-" ship of Gratian and Merobaudes, three Years be-" fore the Accession of his Father Theodosius to the " Empire.*" VI. *Socrates* should not have been quoted; for what he says of *Arsenius*, has scarce any relation to the Article of the Supplement. However, if any, the Twenty third Chapter of the third Book should have been alledged.

[C] *Some Mistakes in other Writers.*] *Matthias*, in his *Historical Theatre* (9), supposes perpetually, that

(7) *Apud Arnauld d'Andilli, ubi supra.*

(8) *Baron. ad Ann. 383, n. 22.*

(9) *Pag. 713. Edit. Amstel. 1668.*

ARSENIUS.

(c) See the first Volume, printed at Paris, in 1677.

Several of *Arsenius*'s Actions, and Sayings, are to be found among the *Apophthegmata Patrum*, published by Mr *Cotelier* (c).

that *Arsenius* was Preceptor to *Honorius*, as well as to *Arcadius*, and That at the same Time. He does not consider, that *Honorius* was not born, when *Arsenius* was sent to *Theodosius*, to instruct *Arcadius*: He never so much as dreamt, that *Honorius*, being nine Years younger than his Brother, was very unfit to assist at the Lectures, which were read to *Arcadius*, during the Life of *Theodosius*. Observe this Circumstance well; because *Metibias* was not ignorant, that *Arsenius* absconded before the Death of the Emperor; for he remarks, that *Theodosius* ordered him carefully to be searched for. He quotes the Twenty third Chapter of the fourth Book of *Socrates*, where nothing of what he says is to be found. He adds, that *Arcadius*, after the Death of his Father, was informed where *Arsenius* lay concealed, and sent to desire his Pardon for what had passed, and his Holy Benediction. *Doujatius*, being carried away with the Stream, joins *Honorius*: with *Arcadius* (10). *Charles Stephens* knew our *Arsenius* only under the Quality of *Patrician*; and supposes him not to forsake the Court, but only his Estate, to go into a Monastery, being admonished by a Voice from the Clouds, commanding him to fly, and live in Silence and Peace. *Hofman* has added to this only the Post of Preceptor to *Arcadius*. *Lloyd* has suppressed the whole Article. Observe, that *Nicephorus*, the Son of *Callistus*, affirms, that *Theodosius* appointed *Arsenius* Preceptor to his Sons (11).

(10) Arsenius, non ille Arcadii & Honorii Preceptor.-- Arsenius, not the Preceptor of Arcadius, and Honorius. Doujatius Prænot. Canon. p. 429.

(11) Nicephor. Histor. lib. XII, cap. 23.

ARSENIUS, Patriarch of *Constantinople* in the XIIIth Century, was a Native of That City. He was educated in a Monastery of *Nice*, and was likewise Superior of it: But he renounced This Dignity to addict himself wholly to a Monastic Life, either in the Monasteries of *Apolloniade*, or Those of Mount *Athos*. He was taken from this way of Life, in the Year 1255, by the Emperor *Theodorus Lascaris*, who made him Patriarch of *Constantinople*. Four Years after, the same Emperor, before his Death, declared him one of the two Preceptors of his Son *John*. The other Preceptor was *George Muxalon*; who, discovering Designs very contrary to the true Interest of the Young Prince, gave *Arsenius* a dislike to his Employment, which was the cause of his returning to a Monastic Life. But, in the Year 1261, when the *Greeks* had recovered *Constantinople*, under the Conduct of *Michael Palæologus*, *Arsenius* was recalled to resume the Patriarchate, and fill That See, from which the Patriarchs had been excluded for above fifty Years. The next Year, the Emperor *Michael Palæologus* caused the Eyes of *John Lascaris*, Son of the Emperor *Theodorus*, to be put out. *Arsenius*, offended at so barbarous an Action, committed on his Pupil, excommunicated *Michael*, who, to disperse these Ecclesiastical Storms, assembled a Council, and, on false Accusations, caused *Arsenius* to be deposed, and banished him to the Island of *Proconnesus*. He lived a long time in This Exile; but it is not certainly known in what Year he died. He was a good Man, but wholly unqualified for Business (a). He is an Author [A].

(e) Taken from Cave's Historia Literaria Scriptor. Ecclef. p. 725.

[A] *He is an Author.*] He wrote a *Nomo-Canon*, or Collection of Canons, divided into One hundred and forty one Titles, to each of which he adds some Articles or Heads of the *Imperial* Laws. It is inserted in *Greek* and *Latin* in the *Bibliotheque* of Canon-Law, published by Messieurs *Justel* and *Vœl*. We have also the Testament of *Arsenius*, published in *Greek* and *Latin*, by Mr *Cotelier*, in the second Volume of his Monuments of the *Greek* Church (1).

(1) Cave's Histor. Literar. p. 726. Doujat. Prænot. Canon. pag. 429.

ARSENIUS, Archbishop of *Monembasia*, or *Malvasia*, in the *Morea*, in the XVIth Century, passed for a learned Philologist. He was an intimate Friend of *Paul* III, and wrote very elegant Letters to him; in one of which he complains of the little Affection of the Church of *Rome* for the *Greek* Nation [A]. He submitted to the Church of *Rome*, which made him so odious to the *Greek* Schismatics, that *Pachomus*, Patriarch of *Constantinople*, excommunicated him; and the *Greeks* reported, that *Arsenius*, after his Death, was *Broukolakas*, that is, that the Devil hovered about his Corps, and re-animated him (a). We have some Works of His [B].

(a) See Guillet, Lacedemon Ancienne & Nouvelle, p. 527, and Crusius in his Turco-Græcia.

[A] *He complained of the little Affection of the Church of Rome for the Greek Nation.*] See the Words of Mr *Guillet*. " *Arsenius* wrote some elegant Letters to Pope *Paul* III, which are still extant. In one of them he complains much of the " little Affection the Church of *Rome* has for the " *Greek* Nation, in that it hath not raised any of " them to the Dignity of Cardinal. *Paul* was made " Pope in the Year 1535 (1). If this Complaint be taken for general, *Arsenius* is guilty of a Falshood; for it is certain, that Cardinal *Bessarion* was a *Greek*: we must, then, believe, that *Arsenius*'s Reproaches were like Those of *Musurus*. The latter complains bitterly, that not one *Greek* had a Share in the numerous Promotions, which *Leo* X. had newly made (2). *Paul* III. was elected Pope in the Month of *October*, 1534.

(1) Guil. Lacerd. Anc. & Nouv. pag. 327.

(2) See the Article MUSURUS.

I have been informed by Mr *de la Monnoie*, " That no Letter of *Arsenius* to That Pope is to be " found, except That, which serves as a Dedication " to the *Scholia* of *Euripides*. It is there he complains, that, among so many Cardinals of all Nations, there are not, at least, two or three *Greeks*. " Καίτοι ἰδ᾽ ἀποτυχὲς ἦν ἵνα ἢ δύο τῶν Ἑλλήνων ἐν τοσούτοις πασσοδαποῖς ἐναριθμεῖσθαι τῶν Καρδιναλίων." Nothing is more useful, or necessary, than to have recourse to the Fountain-head.

[B] *We have some Works of his.*] A Collection of *Apophthegms*, printed at *Rome*, in *Greek*: Another Collection of *Scholia* on seven Tragedies of *Euripides*, printed at *Venice*, 1534. He says, in his Epistle Dedicatory to Pope *Paul* III, that he had composed it in the Isle of *Candy*, at *Venice*, and at *Florence*. See the *Bibliotheque* of *Gesner*.

ARSENIUS, A *Greek* Monk, wrote a Letter against *Cyrillus Lucar*, Patriarch of *Constantinople*, which was published in *Greek* and *Latin*, at *Paris*, in the Year 1643, with the Acts of the Council, wherein *Parthenius*, Patriarch of *Constantinople*, caused the Confession of This *Cyril* to be condemned in the Year 1642. Every one
knows,

ARSINOE. 509

knows, that the Confession of *Cyril* was conformable to the Opinions of *Geneva*. Mr *Claudé* maintained (a), that This Condemnation was a spurious Piece. The Catalogue of the Library of *Oxford* has confounded *Arsenius*, Author of the *Nomo-Canon*, with our *Greek* Monk.

(a) Claudé's Answer to Mr Arnauld, lib. III, cap. 22, p. 478.

ARSINOE. There have been several Queens of This Name. Mr *Moreri* has mentioned the Principal, not without some Mistakes. He is a little too short on *Arsinoe*, the Sister of *Cleopatra*: We shall make amends for this Brevity in the Article PTOLOMY AULETES (a).

(a) Remark [A].

ARSINOE, the Wife of *Magas*, King of *Cyrene* [A], dishonoured herself by her Lasciviousness. A little before *Magas* died, he contracted their only Daughter *Berenice* to the Son of *Ptolomy*, King of *Ægypt*. Immediately after his Decease, *Arsinoe*, who was not pleased with this Contract, considered how to break it. She caused *Berenice*, with the Kingdom of *Cyrene*, to be offered to *Demetrius*, Brother of *Antigonus* (a). This Offer was accepted: *Demetrius* immediately embarked, and had so favourable a Passage, that he soon came to the sight of *Berenice*. He was a handsome Man, and valued himself the more upon it, as he soon perceived the Impression, which his Beauty had made on the Heart of *Arsinoe*. He neglected the Daughter, to make himself more acceptable to the Mother: He treated the Soldiery with Contempt; in short, he rendered himself so odious, that the whole People turned their Thoughts on the Son of *Ptolomy*. It was resolved to make away with *Demetrius*; and the Means of doing it were concerted with *Berenice* (b). Ruffians were set to murther him, at a Time when he had appointed to lie with *Arsinoe* [B]. This Lady, hearing her Daughter's Voice, who stood at the Door, and commanded them to spare her Mother, covered her Gallant's Body with her own, as well as she could; but her Endeavours were in vain. He lost his Life; after which the Marriage of *Berenice* with the Son of *Ptolomy* was consummated (c). *Justin*, if I mistake not, is the only Historian, who informs us of this: I am surprized at it; for an Action of this Nature highly deserved to be taken notice of. What is still more strange, is, that no one informs us what became of *Arsinoe*, nor whence she sprung, nor what became of *Berenice*; and, so far from any one's relating, that *Ptolomy Evergetes*, the Son of *Philadelphus*, married her, it is on the contrary affirmed, that he married *Cleopatra* (d). Note, that *Ptolomy Evergetes* had a Son, called *Magas* (e), from whence it may be conjectured, that his Wife's Father's Name was *Magas*, as *Justin* reports. I shall remark some Errors of Mr *Moreri* [C], and one of Mr *Menage* [D].

(a) He was King of Macedon.
(b) This may be inferred from the Words of Justin.
(c) Taken from Justin, lib. XXVI, cap. 3.
(d) See Mattathias Theatr. Histor. pag. 363. He cites an Author; but we find in Josephus Antiq. lib. XII, cap. 4, that the Wife of Ptolomy Evergetes was called Cleopatra.
(e) Plut. in Agide & Cleomene, pag. 820.

[A] *The Wife of Magas, King of Cyrene.*] In the Editions of *Justin*, he is called *Agas*; but good Critics have observed, long ago, that it must be read *Magas*; they add, that *Pausanias*, *Pollianus*, and *Athenæus* call him so (1). It may be objected, perhaps, that He, whom *Pausanias* mentions, was not the Husband of our *Arsinoe*; for He was Brother, by the Mother's side, of *Ptolomy Philadelphus*; whereas the Husband of *Arsinoe* was the Brother of *Ptolomy Evergetes*. This is the History of *Magas*, according to *Pausanias*. He was the Son of *Berenice*, and of *Philip*, a Macedonian of mean Extraction. *Eurydice*, *Antipater's* Daughter, having been married to *Ptolomy*, the Son of *Lagus*, carried This *Berenice* into *Ægypt*; who lay with *Ptolomy*, and, among other Children, brought him *Ptolomy Philadelphus*, who reigned after his Father. She caused the Government of *Cyrene* to be given to her Son *Magas*; who married *Apama*, the Daughter of King *Antiochus*, and had a great Difference with *Ptolomy Philadelphus*. This is the *Magas* of *Pausanias* (2). Is it not plain, then, may any one say, that This cannot be the *Magas* of *Justin*, who was married to *Arsinoe*, and who died about the time that the Son of *Pyrrhus* was restored to the Kingdom of *Epirus* (3). The Critics may reply, that *Magas*, King of *Cyrene*, having reigned fifty Years (4), he might very well have lived till the Restoration of the Son of *Pyrrhus*, which the best Chronologers place in the Year of *Rome* 493 (5), which was the Twenty fifth of the Reign of *Ptolomy Philadelphus*. So that, instead of saying, as is commonly done, that *Justin* (6) speaks of *Ptolomy Evergetes* in his Twenty sixth Book, it must be asserted, that he speaks of *Ptolomy Philadelphus*; and that it is to him that he gives *Magas*, King of *Cyrene*, as a Brother: that, if he calls *Arsinoe* the Wife of *Magas*, it is no proof, that His *Magas* differs from This of *Pausanias*; since the same King of *Cyrene* might have been successively married to *Apama*, the Daughter of *Antiochus*, and to our *Arsinoe*. By the way, the Wars, wherein he was engaged against *Ptolomy Philadelphus*, according to *Pausanias*, agree very well with the *Magas* mentioned by *Justin*. "Rex *Cyrenarum Agas decedit, qui, ante infirmitatem,* Berenicen unicam filiam, ad finienda cum Ptolomæo fratre certamina, filio ejus desponderat (7). ——— Agas, King of *Cyrene, died, who, before his Weakness, had betrothed his only Daughter Berenice to the Son of his Brother Ptolomy, in order to put an End to all Contests*." I confess, this does not seem to agree with the *Magas*, mentioned by *Athenæus*; for he was one, who, enjoying Peace, was immersed in Pleasure and Idleness, and grew so fat with eating, that his very Grease choaked him (8). But this Objection is not unanswerable; may not a Prince, in the space of fifty Years Reign, be engaged in some Wars, and live afterwards in a long Repose?

(1) See the Commentary on Justin, in the Edition of Grævius, at Leyden, 1683.
(2) Pausanias, lib. I, pag. 6.
(3) Justin, lib. XXVI, cap. 3.
(4) Athen. lib. XII, pag. 550.
(5) See Calvisius ad Ann. Mundi, 3690.
(6) See the Index of the Justin of Grævius; and observes, that Bissilius, in Decade IV Ruinarum Illustrium, pag 1534, supposes, that Justin speaks of one Agas, Brother to Ptolomy Evergetes.
(7) Justin, lib. XXVI, cap. 3.
(8) Athen. lib. 12, pag. 550.

[B] *Ruffians were set to murther him, at a Time when he had appointed to lie with Arsinoe.*] The *Jesuit Bisselius* thought this Circumstance matter of Admiration. "Adulteris autem, *says he* (9), *duobus* illis, Berenicæ filiâ mœchæ conscia, tensæ per dispositos percussores ita funt insidiæ (quod mireris) ut in ipso flagrantis sceleris ardore deprehensis supervenientes adulteræ filia, mœchique conjunx, *Berenice* pro thalami nefandi foribus subsistens, &c. — *The Two Adulterers* (*which is surprizing*) *were so betrayed into the Hands of* Assassins *by* Berenice *the Daughter, who was conscious of the Intrigue, that, in the very Ardor of their enormous Guilt,* Berenice, *the Daughter of the Adulteress, and betrothed to the Adulterer, surprizing them, and standing at the Door, &c.*" But neither the Circumstances of Time, nor Place, have any thing wonderful in them. It was easy to observe, when *Demetrius* went to *Arsinoe*'s, Chamber, and it was the most plausible Opportunity that the Conspirators could take.

(9) Bisselius, Ruinar. Illustrium Decade IV, pag. 1536. Justin says, Cui (Demetrio) cum in lectum socerus convenisset, percussores immituntur.

[C] *Some Errors of Mr Moreri.*] I. This way of expressing himself is not exact; *Magas gave his Daughter* Berenice *in Marriage to* Ptolomy: The *Latin* says *Berenicem* ——— *filiam desponderat* (10). *Betrothed his Daughter* Bernice. *Moreri's* Words conceal a Fact, which is not unravelled in the Sequel of his Narrative; to wit, that *Berenice* continued with her Father and Mother. Quite a different thing was intended, where we read, that he was given in Marriage to the Son of a King of *Egypt*. That he might not therefore mislead his Readers, he should have

(10) Justin, ubi supra.

have used the word *desponders* in the strictest Sense. This Observation is small in itself; but the Application of it may be of Importance to Those, who Translate. They can never too scrupulously follow This Rule: to wit, that they should avoid equivocal Expressions, and all that may hinder the Reader from entertaining the Ideas best suited to the Nature of each Subject. II. It is not true, That *Justin* says, that our *Arsinoe* was Daughter of *Antiochus Soter*. III. Nor, that her Husband's Name was *Magus* (11). IV. Nor, that this pretended *Magus* was the Son of *Ptolomy Lagus* (12). V. Nor, that she obliged her Daughter to marry *Demetrius*. VI. Nor, that she had a Design of setting the Crown on his Head. VII. Nor, that she was deposed. Can we sufficiently censure so bold a Liberty? This Narrative is at pleasure, without any Authority. And yet he quotes his Author. I know, that, in taking an Historian of so little Judgment, as *Justin*, for a Guide, there is a Necessity of supplying several Circumstances; but then notice should be given, that they are supplied, and not imposed on us as a Translation of *Justin*. I have often said, that this Abbreviator had but little Judgment; and I am certain, that *Trogus Pompeius* would exclaim a thousand times against him, did he but know in what a sad Condition his Work is left by this Epitomizer. He would lose himself in the Errors of his Abbreviator. Almost all the *Antiochus*'s, the *Ptolomy*'s, and the *Antigonus*'s, appear in his History without their Marks of Distinction: It is uncertain, whether he speaks of the Father, or the Son, or the Grand-Son; and it must be guessed at for the most part: He has not taken the Trouble to tells us, whether This Marriage of *Berenice* was consummated or no. A fine Question, you will say! And yet he ought expresly to have affirmed, or denied, it; for it is not improbable, that One, who observed, with Joy, that he was beloved by the Mother, should readily agree, to defer his Marriage with the Daughter. You will answer me, perhaps, that *Justin* gives *Arsinoe* the Title of Mother-in-Law to *Demetrius*: *nimis placere socrus cœperat*: but I reply, that, after this, he gives *Berenice* the Title of *Virgin*; *quæ res suspecta primo virgini*; and, consequently, one of these Phrases overthrows the other; which is a shrewd Suspicion, that he does not employ his Terms in the most exact Sense: *Justin*'s Index, in the Edition of Mr *Gravius*, gives *Berenice* only the Title of Betrothed (13). However that be, *Justin*, and many other Epitomizers, never consider, that Abridgments ought to resemble Pygmies, who have all the Parts of a perfect human Body, tho' each of them in Miniature. Contract the Parts of a Narration in an Abridgment as much as you please, but cut off none. Let us reckon Mr *Moreri*'s contradicting himself for the eighth Fault. He will have it here, that *Berenice*, the Wife of *Ptolomy Evergetes*, was the Daughter of *Magus*, and yet affirms elsewhere (14), that she was this *Ptolomy*'s own Sister.

[D] *I shall observe an Error of Mr Menage*] It is in his Annotation on these Words of *Diogenes Laërtius*: Δημητριν τῶ πλευσαντ[ ]ις Κυρηνην, ἐπι πλέον τεραθηναι λέγεται (Ἀρκεσιλα῀) (15). *Demetrium qui Cyrenem* (16) *navigavit amasse plurimum dicitur* (*Arcesilaus*). "I do not wonder, says "Mr *Menage*, that This Philosopher, who was so "fond of young Boys, should fall in love with *De-* "*metrius*, whose Beauty seems to have been very "extraordinary, and was, at last, fatal to him, for he "was killed in the Embraces of his Mother-in-law." *In noverca concubitu cæsus est.* *Justin*, cited by Mr *Menage*, gives no Authority for saying, that *Arsinoe* had such a Relation to the Minion of *Arcesilaus*. It had been much better for him to have taken notice of the Faults of the *Latin* Interpretation (17).

ARTABANUS, the Son of *Hystaspes* [A], and Brother of *Darius* I, of That Name, King of *Persia*, is represented to us, by *Herodotus*, as a wise Man, who always opposed those pompous Expeditions, which were so fatal to the *Persian* Monarchy (a). He was not of Opinion that *Darius* ought to attack the *Scythians* (b); and much less that *Xerxes* should ingage himself in a War with the *Greeks*. *Herodotus* has preserved to us the solid Reasons, on which his Advice was grounded [B], and the Judgment he gave on the prodigious Army both for Sea and Land Service, with which *Xerxes* prepared to pass from *Asia* into *Europe* (c). The Difficulties, which *Artabanus* represented to him, made the King choose to send him back into *Persia*, to command there in his Absence, rather than have his Attendance in the Expedition (d). The Event demonstrated how judiciously, and faithfully, he had advised. He did not however always preserve This Fidelity; for he conspired against *Xerxes*, and slew him (e); and afterwards drew in *Artaxerxes*, the Son of *Xerxes*, to make away with his Brother *Darius*: he drew him into it, I say, by making him believe, that *Darius* was the Murtherer of *Xerxes*. But *Artaxerxes* discovered the Truth soon after, and killed *Artabanus* as he was pulling off his Cuirass (f). *Diodorus Siculus* differs from *Justin*, as to the manner of *Artabanus*'s being punished for his Crime (g). We shall see, in the Remark [B], how This Prince reasoned on Dreams, and upon the Duration of human Life.

[A] *The Son of Hystaspes.*] I cannot imagine where Mr *Moreri* had read, that *Artabanus* was *a Native of* Hircania. The two Authors he has quoted (1) say nothing like it. *Ctesias* makes the Father of *Artabanus* to have been a Favourite of *Cambyses*, named *Artasyras*, who, at first, favoured the Usurpation of the *Magus*, and afterwards the Design, formed by the seven great Lords, to expel the *Magus* (2).

[B] *Herodotus has preserved to us the solid Reasons, on which his Advice was grounded* (3).] One would think *Herodotus* had made it his Business to do Honour to *Artabanus*'s Prudence and fine Sense. He never indulges his Imagination more, than when he makes This Prince argue. *Xerxes*, after putting himself into a great Passion, and violently abusing him, submitted to his Reasons, and thought no more of the Expedition; but two Dreams, one upon another, pushed him on to prosecute it (4). He went to *Artabanus*, and told him his Dreams; adding, withal, *I will try whether you will have the like*; *take my Robes, sit on my Throne, lie in my Bed*. *Artabanus* answers, That he was not worthy of so much Honour; and then reasons very judiciously upon Dreams, saying, That, if there be any thing Divine in these Dreams of *Xerxes*, his Majesty had Reason to think, that he should have the like; "for what could we "think, if a God, who had a War at Heart, and "came at Night to injoin it some Monarch, who "had resolved to live in Peace, should not appear, "and give the same Orders, to his first Minister of "State, when nothing less can make it certain whe- "ther this God does indeed desire the War? But, "continues he, do not imagine, that it is therefore "necessary I should take your Habit, and lie in your "Bed. That *I know not what to call it*, which "appeared to you in a Dream, is not so ignorant a "Being, as to mistake me for you, by seeing me "dressed in your Robes; and, if he does not think "fit to address himself to Me, your Garments will "no more influence him to do so, than my own." *Xerxes* would be absolutely obeyed: *Artabanus* dreamed in Conformity with his Master, and opposed the War no longer, but became the Promoter of it, though he remained greatly diffident of the Success (5). If these Things were true, ought we not to conclude, that they had for their Author That Spirit, which was a Liar and a Murtherer from the beginning; for *Xerxes* was threatened with great Disgrace,

ARTABANUS.

(6) *Id. ib. cap. 14.*

Disgrace, if he desisted from That Enterprize (6). At another Time, *Artabanus* reasoned, in a very uncommon manner, on the Shortness of human Life; a Subject, which had caused *Xerxes* to weep, at the Sight of his numberless Army (7). "We live but too long, *says he*; our Life, short as it is, is long enough to turn our Brain, and make us often wish for Death, as an easy Refuge from the Miseries that overwhelm us. If Life is, nevertheless, seasoned with an agreeable Relish, it is an Argument, that God is envious of human Happiness."

(7) *Id. ibid. cap. 46. See Remark [L]. of the Article PERICLES, at the End.*

Would not the *Greek* Philosophers have said of this way of thinking, as *Pyrrhus*, upon his viewing the *Roman* Army: *The Order of Battle of these Barbarians*, said he, *and their Manner of encamping, have nothing of the Barbarian in them* (8)? *Christianity* only can rectify this. It is to be observed, that *Herodotus* was very well acquainted with the Vanities, and Miseries, of Mankind; but he affected a little too much to trace the Causes of them in the Envy, or Malignity, of the Gods. *Plutarch* has condemned him for it (9).

(8) *Plutarch. in Pyrrho, pag. 393.*

(9) *See Remark [K], of the Article PERICLES, at the words the End.*

ARTABANUS I, King of *Parthia*, the seventh from *Arsaces*, Founder of the Monarchy (*a*), was the Son of *Priapatius*, and Brother of *Phrahates* and *Mithridates* [*A*], who had all three reigned successively over the *Parthians*. He succeeded his Nephew *Phrahates*, and died soon after of a Wound in the Arm, which he received in the War he made against the *Thogarians* (*b*).

(*a*) *About 230 Years before CHRIST.*

(*b*) *Justin, lib. 42. c. 2.*

[*A*] *He was the Son of Priapatius, and Brother of Phrahates, and Mithridates.*] Mr *Moreri* makes him the Son of *Phrahates* I, and Uncle to *Phrahates* II; but these are two incompatible Relations; for *Phrahates* II was the Son of *Mithridates*, who was Brother to *Phrahates* I; how then could a Son of *Phrahates* I be Uncle to *Phrahates* II? This is the Reason, why, though *Justin* gives *Priapatius* but two Sons, I have given him a third, namely, *Artabanus* I. When Authors explain themselves ill, we must take this Liberty with them. *Justin* relates two Things (1). I. That *Priapatius*, dying in the Twenty fifth Year of his Reign, left two Sons, the elder of whom, named *Phrahates*, reigned before his younger Brother *Mithridates*. II. That *Phrahates*, the Son of *Mithridates*, reigned after his Father, and that his Paternal Uncle *Artabanus* was his Successor (2). How confused is this! He mentions *Mithridates*, and *Phrahates*, as the only Sons of *Priapatius*, and yet intimates, that he had another, since, otherwise, *Artabanus* could not be Paternal Uncle to *Mithridates's* Son. I have, in vain, searched for a Solution of this Difficulty, in several Commentators on *Justin*, and also in the Notes of the last *French* Translator (3).

(1) *Justin, lib. 41. c. 5.*

(2) *Id. lib. 42. cap. 1, 2.*

(3) *He takes the Title of Monsieur D. L. M. His Translation was printed at Amsterdam, 1694, from the Paris Edition of 1693.*

ARTABANUS II, King of *Parthia*, when he was only King of the *Medes* [*A*], was called by the *Parthians*, to reign over them, in Exclusion of *Vonones*, whom they had sent for to *Rome*, and whom *Tiberius* had very freely granted them (*a*). *Artabanus* was of the Race of the *Arsacidæ* as well as *Vonones*, and had this farther Advantage, that he was not become obnoxious to That People by a *Roman* Education (*b*). The first Battle was fortunate to *Vonones*; but he came off so ill in the second, that he was forced to fly into *Armenia* [*B*]. The victorious *Artabanus* would not let him rest there; and, as *Tiberius* had not promised *Vonones* the necessary Protection (*c*), he was forced to quit *Armenia*, and retire to *Silanus*, Governor of *Syria*. This contributed greatly to secure the Crown on the Head of *Artabanus*, which he received about the Seven Hundred and sixty ninth Year of *Rome*, and sixteenth of the Ist Century. However, he was not easy at the Continuance of his Rival in *Syria* (*d*); for the Communication of Intelligence, being quick and easie, kept up the Spirit of Faction: He therefore sent an Embassy to *Germanicus* to renew the Alliance between them, and insisted, at the same time, that *Vonones* should be obliged to leave *Syria*. The Success of This Embassy is not known; but it is certain, that, after the Death of *Germanicus*, the King of the *Parthians* grew very haughty towards the *Romans*, and cruel to his own People (*e*). He was so elated with his good Fortune in the Wars he had waged with several neighbouring Nations, that, without any regard to *Tiberius*, whose grey Hairs he despised, he seized upon *Armenia* [*C*], and

(*a*) *Joseph. Antiq. lib. 18. cap. 3.*

(*b*) *Tacit. Annal. lib. 2. cap. 2.*

(*c*) *Id. lib. cap. 4.*

(*d*) *Id. ib. cap. 58.*

(*e*) *Id. lib. 6. c. 31.*

[*A*] *When he was only King of the Medes.*] *Moreri* and *Hofman* have both said, that *Tacitus* makes him King of the *Dacians*. This is what That Historian never dreamed of; he only says, that *Artabanus* had been educated among the *Dahæ*: *Artabanus Arsacidarum è sanguine apud Dahas adultus excitur* (1). There is a great deal of Difference between the *Dahæ* and the *Dacians*; and he must have his Thoughts otherwise employed, (to say no worse,) who could believe, that a *Parthian* Prince had been educated near the *Danube*.

[*B*] *Vonones — his Competitor came off so ill in the second Battle, that he was forced to fly into Armenia.*] Mr *Moreri* has published two other Falsities. He has made *Vonones* obtain two Victories over the *Parthians*, who yet had the better of his Competitor but once (2); and he attributes one Defeat of *Artabanus's* Army to *Vitellius*; a Defeat, I say, followed by other Losses of *Artabanus*, towards the Year 36. But I. It is false, that *Vitellius* defeated the Troops of this King of the *Parthians*; II. It is certain, that the Mischief *Vitellius* did him, by Intrigues and Money, was not 'till after other Losses. Mr *Hofman* also ascribes two Victories to *Vonones*, and one to *Vitellius*, which, he says, was the Cause of *Artabanus's* abandoning *Armenia*. A Mistake; yet infinitely more excusable, than what this Writer has committed after *Lloyd* and *Charles Stephens*, in saying, that *Artabanus*, being a great Enemy to *Tiberius*, seized upon *Armenia*, and was killed by a *Persian* Soldier, whose Name was *Artaxerxes*; after whom there were no more Kings of the *Parthians*, but only of *Persia*. A prodigious Anachronism! See the Article ARTABANUS IV.

(1) *Tacit. Ann. lib. 2, cap. 3.*

(2) *Joseph. Antiq. lib. 18. cap. 3. Tacit. ibid.*

[*C*] *Without any regard to Tiberius — he seized upon Armenia.*] It is impossible to be more insulted, than This Emperor was by *Artabanus*; who no sooner perceived, that his Invasion of *Armenia* was an Injury, which *Tiberius* did not revenge, but he attacked *Cappadocia* (3). But what can be more severe, than the Letters he wrote to him? Let us here *Suetonius*; "Quin & Artabani Parthorum regis laceratus est literis, parricidia & cædes & ignaviam & luxuriam objicientis, monentisque ut voluntariâ morte maximo justissimoque civium odio quam primum satisfaceret (4). —— He was also flung with Letters from Artabanus, King of the Parthians, reproaching him with his Indolence, Luxury, Murthers, and Parricides, and advising him, by laying violent Hands on himself, to give immediate Satisfaction to the extream Hatred, and just Resentment of his Subjects." There was, certainly, some personal Aversion in the Case; for *Artabanus* behaved very civilly, and even very humbly, towards *Tiberius's* Successor. Let us hear *Suetonius* again. "Artabanus Parthorum rex odium semper contemp- "tumque

(3) *Dion, lib. 58, sub. fin.*

(4) *Suet. in Tiber. cap. 66.*

VOL. I. 6 N

ARTABANUS.

and gave it to his Eldeſt Son *Arſaces* [D]. He ſent to demand all the Treaſures, which *Vonones* had depoſited in *Syria* and *Cilicia* (*f*), and, in rodomontade, gave out, that, if all that *Cyrus* and *Alexander* had been poſſeſt of were not reſtored to him, he would come and take it by force. The Malecontents at Court deputed private Meſſengers to *Tiberius*, deſiring him to ſend them *Phrahates*, the Son of King *Phrahates* (*g*). This was readily granted; and, when it was known, That this Prince, endeavouring to live after the manner of the *Partbians*, to which he had been a long time diſuſed, had fallen ſick, and was dead, *Tiridates*, who was of the Houſe of the *Arſacidæ*, and nearly related to *Phrahates*, was ſubſtituted in his Place. Another Adverſary was at the ſame time ſtirred up againſt *Artabanus*, namely *Pharaſmanes* King of *Iberia*. *Artabanus* was worſted from this Quarter; for, after his Son, King of *Armenia*, had been poiſoned, his other Son *Orodes*, whom he had ſent into *Armenia*, was defeated there by *Pharaſmanes*. Some time after, he was beaten there himſelf, and being obliged to advance towards the Provinces, which *Vitellius*, Governor of *Syria*, threatened (*h*), there remained no Obſtacle to hinder *Mithridates*, Brother of *Pharaſmanes*, from becoming King of *Armenia* (*i*). This Loſs of *Artabanus* was ſoon followed by a greater. *Vitellius*, by his Money and Intrigues, obliged him to quit That Country, and retire into *Hircania*, where he was reduced to live upon what he could get by Hunting (*k*), while *Vitellius* put *Tiridates* in Poſſeſſion of his Kingdom. But ſo powerful a Party was formed againſt the new King, that it was no hard matter for *Artabanus*, who was recalled, to compel ſo weak a Prince as *Tiridates*, to retire (*l*). This happened in the thirty ſixth Year of the Iſt Century. *Artabanus*'s former Pride was now ſufficiently mortified: He courted the Friendſhip of *Caligula* (*m*), and when he found that his Deſign of carrying the War into *Syria* (*n*), was in danger of miſcarrying thro' the Diligence of *Vitellius*, he agreed to an Interview with this *Roman*, and to a Treaty of Peace, the Conditions of which were to the Advantage of *Caligula*. Ten Years after, he was depoſed, and forced to retire to *Izates*, King of *Adiabene* (*o*), by whom he was received in a moſt generous manner, and not with bare Compliments. For *Izates* negotiated the Matter with the *Parthians*, in ſuch a manner, that he obliged them to ſet him again upon the Throne; and *Cinnamus* himſelf, who had been advanced in his Room, was the Perſon, who replaced the Diadem upon his Head. There is Reaſon to believe, that *Artabanus* died a little after; but whether by the Treachery of *Gotarzes* his Son, or Brother [E], or otherwiſe, is uncertain.

" tumque Tiberii præ ſe ferens, amicitiam Caligulæ
" ultro petiit, venitque ad colloquium legati conſu-
" laris, & tranſgreſſus Euphratem aquilas & ſigna Ro-
" mana Cæſarumque imagines adoravit (5). —— Ar-
" tabanus, King of the Parthians, always diſcovering
" an Hatred and Contempt of Tiberius, induſtriouſly
" ſought the Friendſhip of Caligula, and came to con-
" fer with the Conſular Embaſſador; and paſſing over
" the Euphrates, he paid Adoration to the Roman
" Eagles and Standards, and to the Images of the Cæ-
" ſars." *Dion* remarks, that *Vitellius* obliged *Artabanus* to ſacrifice to the Statues of *Auguſtus* and *Caligula*, and to give his Children for Hoſtages, after having agreed to the Treaty of Peace, which he preſcribed to him (6). This ſhews *Joſephus* to be miſtaken, in believing the Interview between *Vitellius* and *Artabanus*, with all it's Conſequences, to have happened under *Tiberius* (7). According to Him, it was to *Tiberius*, that *Darius*, the Son of *Artabanus* (8). was ſent as an Hoſtage, with rich Preſents, and a Giant, a *Jew* by Nation, and *Eleazar* by Name, who was ſeven Cubits high.

[D] *He gave* Armenia *to his Eldeſt Son* Arſaces.] Thus *Tacitus* and *Dion* name him. *Joſephus* calls him *Orodes* (8), confounding one of *Artabanus*'s Children with the other. His Son *Orodes* was not King of *Armenia*, but was ſent thither to revenge the Death of his elder Brother *Arſaces*, and had like to have been killed in the Attempt; for having, in the Battle, engaged perſonally with *Pharaſmanes*, King of *Iberia*, he was dangerouſly wounded, but not killed, as was immediately given out, to the great Diſcouragement of the *Parthians* (9), and as *Joſephus* has ſince affirmed, in his *Jewiſh* Antiquities (10).

[E] *Artabanus died —— by the Treachery of* Gotarzes, *his Son, or Brother*.] The manner, in which the exact Mr *de Tillemont* expreſſes himſelf, is fallacious. *Artabanus*, ſays he (11), *died ſoon after, by the Treachery of* Gotarzes, *his Brother, according to* Tacitus, *or rather his Son, as* Joſephus *affirms*.

Every Reader will imagine, from theſe Words, that *Joſephus* ſays, that *Artabanus* was put to death by his Son *Gotarzes*, when not a Syllable is to be met with to this Purpoſe. So far from it, he mentions *Artabanus* as dying of a Diſtemper, and ſucceeded by his Son *Varadanus*, whoſe Succeſſor he makes to be *Artabanus*'s other Son, *Gotarzes*. It is ſtrange, that *Tacitus* and *Joſephus* ſhould agree ſo little in the main Circumſtances of Matters ſo near their own Time! The latter gives *Artabanus* a peaceable Death, and ſeveral Sons: The former makes him periſh with his Wife and Son by the Treachery of his Brother; which ſeems to import, that *Artabanus* had but one Son. One cannot tell which ſide to take, conſidering that *Tacitus* is not wholly free from Contradiction. Firſt, he will have *Gotarzes* to be the Brother of *Artabanus*; a little after he makes him the Brother of *Bardanes*, and intimates very clearly, that *Bardanes* was the Son of *Artabanus*; for he repreſents him in a great Rage with the *Seleucians*, not ſo much becauſe they did not ſubmit to him, as becauſe they had been Rebels againſt his Father. *In quos, ut patris ſui quoque defectores, ira magis quam ex uſu præſenti accenſus* (12). Who is this Father, if not *Artabanus*? I ſhould be almoſt tempted to believe, that this *Artabanus*, mentioned by *Tacitus* (13), was the Son, who had already ſucceeded, or who was to ſucceed King *Artabanus*, and that *Gotarzes*, another Son of King *Artabanus*, murthered this Brother, to make his own way to the Throne, and, for the greater Security, involved the Mother and Son in the ſame Deſtruction with the Father. This Conjecture clears all Contradictions. But there are other Differences between *Joſephus* and *Tacitus*. The latter makes *Gotarzes* die a natural Death, and gives him *Vonones* for Succeſſor, and his Son *Vologeſes* after him (14). *Joſephus* makes *Gotarzes* periſh by the Treachery of his Subjects, and his Brother *Vologeſes* to be his immediate Succeſſor (15).

ARTABANUS III, King of the *Parthians*, Succeſſor, and perhaps Son, of *Vologeſes*, whom *Suetonius* mentions as a great Friend of *Nero* and *Veſpaſian*, lived in the Reign

ARTABANUS. 513

Reign of the Emperor *Titus*. This is what *Zonaras* informs us of after this manner (a). He says, that an *Asiatic*, whose Name was *Terentius Maximus*, pretending to be *Nero*, prevailed with some of his own Countrymen, and a great many other Persons towards the *Euphrates*, to believe it, and at last retired to *Artabanus*, King of the *Parthians*, who, being then displeased with *Titus*, received the Impostor very kindly, and prepared to re-inthrone him [*A*].

(a) Zonaras in Tito ad Ann. Cyriter, 80.

[*A*] *Received the Impostor very kindly, and prepared to re-inthrone him.*] Although there were more than one conterfeit *Nero*, yet few will believe this *Terentius Maximus* to have been any other, than the Impostor, mentioned by *Suetonius*. And, if it be objected, that the latter did not appear 'till twenty Years after the Death of *Nero*, that is, in the seventh Year of *Domitian*; it may be answered, that *Zonaras* is not incapable of confounding one Reign with another; and that, after all, it must be something surprizing, that, in so short a time, two Impostors should meet with so great Encouragement in the same Country, or, if they did, that they should not both be recorded by the Historian, who speaks of One of them, as of a singular Adventure. The Impostor, mentioned by *Suetonius*, was very powerfully protected by the *Parthians*. " Cum post viginti " annos adolescente me extitisset conditionis incertæ " qui se Neronem esse jactaret, tam favorabile no- " men ejus apud Parthos fuit, ut vehementer adjutus " & vix redditus sit (1). ―――― *Twenty Years after* " *the Death of that Emperor, when I was a Lad,* " *a Person, of unknown Condition, gave out, that* " *he was Nero, and was so strongly supported in his* " *Pretensions by the Parthians, that he was defeated* " *with great Difficulty.*"

(1) Sueton. in Neron. sub. finem.

ARTABANUS IV. was the last King of the *Parthians*; for *Artaxerxes*, a *Persian* by Nation, having deprived him of his Crown and Life in the Year 229, took upon him the Title of King of *Persia*, which his Successors continued as long as That Monarchy lasted. The Reign of *Artabanus* had been glorious enough, and had given some Trouble to the *Romans*, who were not at all behind hand in making suitable Returns. He was so imprudent as not to keep upon his Guard, while the Emperor *Severus* ravaged the Neighbouring Countries; and was taking his Rest under the Security of a Peace, when he found the *Roman* Forces on a sudden pouring in upon his Dominions. All that he could do was to save himself with a small Guard (a). The City of *Ctesiphon*, in which he kept his Residence, was plundered, and all his Treasures and Moveables fell into the Hands of the Enemy (b). But this foul Play was nothing in comparison of the perfidious Trick, which *Caracalla* played him. This Emperor sent Ambassadors to him with rich Presents to demand his Daughter in Marriage, and alledged an hundred fine Things, which would result from That Alliance, to the Honour and Advantage of both Nations (c). *Artabanus* at first rejected the Proposal, foreseeing no Concord in This Marriage, considering the Difference of Language and Customs, between his Daughter and a *Roman* Emperor. At last *Caracalla*'s repeated Instances, his Oaths, his Protestations of Love for his future Empress, obtained the Father's Consent. But, all this while, *Caracalla* was meditating such a Scene of Villany, as may be taken for the Model, or at least the rough Draught, of the St *Bartholomew* of *Catherine de Medicis*. He marched with his Army into the Country of the *Parthians*, and was every where received as the King's Son-in-Law; and, upon his advancing towards the Capital, *Artabanus* went out to meet him, accompanied with an infinite Number of his People. The *Parthians* thought of nothing but shewing their Joy, in Feasting, Singing, and Dancing, when *Caracalla* gave the Signal to his Soldiers to fall on This unarmed Multitude. They killed as many of them as they pleased, there not being any in a Condition to resist. *Artabanus* had much ado to save himself. From that Day *Caracalla* did nothing but plunder and burn; till, tired with his Ravages, he returned into *Mesopotamia*, where he was assassinated. *Artabanus*, being eager to revenge the Injury which he had suffered, marched with all possible Expedition against the *Roman* Army, which had elected *Macrinus* in the room of *Caracalla*. The Battle, having continued two whole Days from Morning till Night, was renewed upon the Third, and, in all probability, would have lasted till one or other Army had been quite destroyed, if *Macrinus* had not found means of acquainting *Artabanus* with the tragical End of *Caracalla*, and of declaring, that he himself disapproved what had passed, and was willing to restore all the Prisoners and Booty then in his Possession, and to live in Peace with him. *Artabanus* accepted these Offers, and a Peace was concluded between Him and the New Emperor in the Year 217. He was the first, who took upon him the Title of The Great King, and wore a double Diadem [*A*]. His evil Destiny

(a) Herodian. lib. 3. cap. 9.

(b) In the Year 210, according to Calvisius.

(c) Herodian. lib. 4. cap. 10, &c.

[*A*] *He was the first, who took upon him the Title of the Great King, and wore a double Diadem* (1).] I have cited my Author, and it is very true, that *Herodian*, in the place cited, has these Words: Ἀρτάβανον τε τὸν πρότερον καλέμενον τὸν μέγαν βασιλέα, καὶ δυσὶ διαδήμασι χρώμενον ἀποκτεῖναι (2). *Atque Artabano, qui rex magnus primus appellatus est, duplicique diademate utebatur, necem intulisse*. But I believe his Meaning is, that, before *Artabanus* IV, no King of *Parthia* assumed this Title of The Great King; and he would be much mistaken, if he should say absolutely, that he was the first Prince, who called himself so; it being certain, that the ancient Kings of *Persia* used This Style, as appropriated to themselves. See the Twenty fourth Verse of *Æschylus*'s *Persians*, and *Stanley*'s Observations upon It. He quotes the Testimonies of *Dion Chrysostome*, Orat. 3. of *Josephus*, in *Antiquit*. lib. 11. cap. 6. of *Herodotus*, lib. 8. and lib. 5. of *Xenophon*, in *Expedit*. lib. 1. of *Aristides*, in *Romæ Encomio*. of *Suidas*, in μέγας βασιλεὺς. Mr *du Rondel* informed me of This Passage of *Stanley*. We may add, to these Authors, *Plato*, in *Gorgia*, pag. 321. C. *Plutarch*, in *Vita Cimonis*, pag. 485. E. *The Book of Esther*, cap. xvi. ver. 1. Read also the Panegyric of *Isocrates*, and you will find in it the Complaint of That Orator against the *Greeks* of his Time, who, in their common Discourse, gave the pompous Title of

(1) Herodian. lib. 2. cap. 2. pag. 217.

(2) Id. ibid.

ARTABANUS.

Destiny raised him up a formidable Enemy in the Year 226; I mean That *Artaxerxes*, who maintained his Rebellion with such Courage and Success, that, in three Years Time, he put an end to the *Parthian* Monarchy.

of The Great King to the Monarch of *Persia*. Οὑ' βασιλέα τὸν μέγαν αὐτὸν προσαγορεύομεν, ὥσπερ αἰχμάλωτοι γεγονότες (3). Do we not call him *the Great King, as though we were his Captives*? Note, that the Kings of *Persia* were not the first, who assumed this Title. The Kings of *Assyria* had used it, as may be collected from the eighteenth Chapter of the second Book of *Kings* (4), where we find the Words of the Ambassadors of *Sennacherib*. I remember the Answer, which Father *Goulu* made to a Criticism upon a Passage of his Translation of *Socrates*'s Apology. Let us first produce the Words of the Critic. "*Je ne sçay de quoy l' accuser; si ce n' est d' une ignorance volontaire, en un passage de son Apologie de Socrates, où il lui fait dire:* Je m'assure que quand se seroit le Grand Seigneur, & non pas une personne de basse condition, qu'il préféreroit une nuit semblable à celle-là à toutes les nuits & à tous les autres jours de sa vie, &c. *Je voudroy bien luy demander si ce Grand Seigneur n'est pas le Turc; & si c'est lui, comment Socrates en pouvoit parler, si ce n'estoit par prophétie, puis qu'il n'y peut pas avoir huit cent ans que les Ottomans ont commence leur Tyrannie, & qu'il y en a plus de treize cens du siècle de Socrates au leur, à conter depuis l'année quatriesme où il est nay dans la soixante & dixseptiesme Olympiade* (5). — *I am at a loss how to charge him, except with wilful Ignorance, in a Passage of the Apology of Socrates, where he makes Socrates say:* I am persuaded, that, were he the Grand Seigneur, and not a Person of mean Condition, he would prefer a Night like That before all other Nights and Days of his Life, &c. *I would fain know of him whether this Grand Seigneur be not the Turk; and, if he be, how Socrates could speak of him, except by way of Prophecy; since the Turks began their Empire not quite Eight hundred Years ago, and the Age, in which Socrates lived, was above Thirteen hundred before That, reckoning from the fourth Year (in which he was born) of the LXXVIIth Olympiad.*" Here follows the Refutation of this Criticism. "*Un habile Homme m'auroit épargné une réponse, en ne me faisant pas une demande si sotte. Mais, Patience; répondons à cet ignorant. Ouy, Paladin* (6), *le Turc est aujourd'hui celui qu'on nomme Grand Seigneur. Mais, du tems de Socrates, c'étoit le Roy des Perses, qu'on appelloit de la sorte, & qu'on se nommoit point autrement. Aux autres Rois, dit Suidas, on donne le titre des Etats & des païs qui sont de leur Obeïssance, & pour ce on dit le Roi de Macedoine, & le Roi des Lacedemoniens. Celui des Perses se qualifie simplement le Grand Roi, ou le Grand Seigneur,* μέγας βασιλεύς, μέγας δεσπότης. *Et, comme il portoit le titre de Grand Seigneur, ses Sujets prenoient la qualité d'esclaves, & sa Cour s'appelloit la Porte, ses Courtisans oἱ ἐπὶ θύραις βασιλέως, ceux qui estoient à la porte du Roi. L'Empereur de Turcs lui a succédé au Titre de Grand Seigneur, aussi bien qu'en la meilleure partie de ses Roïaumes, & en la forme de son Gouvernement. De façon que, sans revelation & sans prophétie, Socrates a pu parler du Grand Seigneur, de quoi le Paladin ne l'à pu reprendre sans decouvrir son ânerie. Mais, de le renvoier à Herodote, à Thucydide, & aux autres bons Auteurs, pour apprendre la vérité de ce que je dis, ce seroit à moi péne perduë. Car le pauvre malheureux confesse qu'il n'a point de livres, ni d'argent pour en acheter; & à péne ceux qui ont des Bibliotheques lui voudroient confier les leurs: & puis, il n'y entend du tout rien. Je me contenterai donc de l'envoier étudier l'Histoire des Turcs au bout de pont neuf; où les colporteurs estallent leurs images, à fin que, sans qu'il lui coûte rien, il apprenne dans les Cartes, où les Empereurs des Turcs sont figurez en taille douce, depuis quel temps les Ottomans sont devenus Grand Seigneurs, s'il y a 800 ans, comme dit le Paladin, ou bien si c'est depuis trois siecles feulement* (7). — *A Man of tolerable Sense would have spared me an Answer, by not asking so foolish a* "*Question. But, Patience; let us answer this ignorant* "*Fellow. Yes, most renowned Don Quixote, the* Turk "*is at this Time called the* Grand Seignor. *But,* "*in* Socrates's *Time, the King of* Persia *was called* "*so, and by no other Name. Other Kings, say* Suidas, "*take their Titles from the Dominions and Coun-* "*tries under their Obedience; and therefore we say,* "*the King of* Macedonia, *and the King of the* "Lacedemonians. *The* Persian *Monarch calls him-* "*self only the Great King, or the Grand Seignor,* "μέγας βασιλεύς, μέγας δεσπότης. *And, as he* "*bore the Title of Grand Seignor, his Subjects took* "*upon them the Quality of Slaves, his Court was* "*called the Port, and his Courtiers* οἱ ἐπὶ θύραις "βασιλέως, *They who stood at the* King's *Gate.* "*The Emperor of the* Turks *has succeeded him in* "*the Title of Grand Seignor, as well as in the best* "*part of his Dominions, and in the Form of his* "*Government. So that* Socrates *might speak of the* "*Grand Seignor, without Revelation or Prophecy;* "*and our Don's Criticism does but discover him to* "*be an arrant Ass. But it would be loss of Time* "*to refer him to* Herodotus, Thucydides, "*and other good Authors, for the truth of what I* "*say; because the poor unhappy Creature confesses* "*he has no Books, nor Money to buy any; and they,* "*who have Libraries, will hardly trust him with* "*the use of them, nor does he understand any thing* "*at all of the Matter. I shall content myself there-* "*fore with sending him to study the History of the* "Turks, *at the Foot of the* Pontneuf, *among the* "*Printsellers, where, without any Charge, he may* "*learn, from the Prints of the* Turkish *Emperors,* "*how long it is since the* Ottomans *became* Grand "Seignors, *whether Eight hundred Years ago, as* "*this* de la Mancha *Knight pronounces, or only* "*Three hundred.*" I have copied this long Passage, that the Reader, at a small Expence, and without consulting the Pieces of this famous Controversy of the General of the *Feuillans*, may see the coarse, rude, Manner of the Paper Wars of Those Times (8). But we must not let pass the Legerdemain of Father *Goulu*, who, not finding his Account in μέγας βασιλεύς, cunningly adds μέγας δεσπότης as the Words of *Suidas*. This will never acquit him with learned Readers: it only serves to impose on the Ignorant, and brands him with Forgery in the Opinion of all others. Upon the whole, the Criticism upon his *Grand Seignor* appears to be just.

To conclude; The Pride of Eastern Monarchs was not so well flattered with the lofty Title of King of *Kings*, as with That of The Great King; for we see, that *Artabanus* IV, to enhance his former Character, caused himself to be styled the Great King, rather than continue That of King of Kings, which he had received from his Predecessors. In *Pompey's* Time, This was commonly given to the King of *Parthia*; and, if *Pompey* did not observe This Form in writing to him, it was from a Regard to those other Kings, who were come to pay him Homage (9). *Phrabates* assumed it in a Letter, which he wrote to *Augustus* (10). *Suetonius* has given it to the King of *Parthia*, who was Contemporary with *Germanicus*, in the Place, where he mentions the Sorrow, which was expressed for the Death of That illustrious *Roman*. "*Regulos quosdam barbam posuisse, & uxorum capita rasisse ad indicium maximi luctus.* Regum etiam Regem & exercitatione venandi & convictu Megistanum abstinuisse, quod apud Parthos justitii instar est (11).*" — Several "*petty Kings had their Beards taken off, and their* "*Wives Heads shaved, as a Mark of the deepest Mourn-* "*ing. The* King of Kings *also abstained from* "*Hunting and Feasting with his Nobles, which, among* "*the* Parthians, *is like shutting up the Courts of* "Justice, *in some public Calamity.*" I do not wonder at *Artabanus's* Taste, when I consider, that the Title of King of Kings had been much more common, than That of the Great King. The Title of King of Kings was given to *Agamemnon* (12). *Diodorus Siculus* affirms, that *Osmanduas* and *Sesostris* were so styled, the one in his Epitaph (13), the other in Inscriptions on Pillars (14). Both had reigned gloriously in *Egypt*. The same Title was given to *Cyrus*

---

(3) Isocrates in Panegyr. pag. 96. See the Article AGESILAUS II. Citat. (38).

(4) Verses 19, and 28.

(5) Discours d'Aristarque à Nicandre sur les foutes de Phyllarque, p. 120, 121.

(6) *He makes use of this word, because he had to do with* lavertsac, *against whom a Satire had appeared intitled,* La defaite de Paladin Javersac, *i. e.* Javersac the Knight-Errant defeated. *See his Article.*

(7) Achates à Palemon pour la Defence de Phyllarque, pag. 43.

(8) I. a. 1628.

(9) Plut. in Pompeio, p. 639. C.

(10) Dion. lib. 55. ad ann. 748, pag. 636.

(11) Sueton. in Caligula, cap. 5.

(12) Cicer. Epist. 14. lib. 9. ad famil. p. 31. Livius, lib. 45. c. 27.

(13) Diodor. Siculus, lib. 1. cap. 4.

(14) Id. ib. cap. 55.

ARTABAZUS. ARTAVASDES.

in his *Epitaph* (15); and also to *Tigranes*, King of *Armenia* (16). The Holy Scriptures apply it to *Nabuchodonosor* (17). Note, that the Kings of *Persia*, who succeeded the Kings of *Parthia*, continued to style themselves Kings of Kings. See *Sapor*'s Letter to *Constantius*, in *Ammianus Marcellinus* (18), and the Annotations of *Valesius* on That Place. See also *Trebellius Pollio*, in the Life of *Aurelian*, and the Notes of the Commentators. Some Authors will have it, that the Emperors of *Constantinople* carried this Title still farther. *They bore, in their Atchievement of Arms, four* B*'s, termed in Heraldry* Fusils *(19), which stood for* βασιλεῦ βασιλέων βασιλεύων βασιλεύει, *that is to say, King of Kings, reigning over Kings:* Let us note, by the way, that the giving the Title of King to a tributary Prince was out of pure Pride.

ARTABAZUS, the Son of *Pharnaces*, commanded the *Parthians*, and the *Chorasmians*, in the Expedition of *Xerxes* (a). It was He, who, after the Battle of *Salamis*, escorted the King his Master as far as the *Hellespont* with 60000 select Soldiers (b). As soon as *Xerxes* was passed into *Asia*, *Artabazus* returned back, and, in his way, thought himself obliged to punish the City of *Potidæa*, which had cast off the Persian Yoke on the News of their ill Fortune. He besieged it a very long time, without being able to take it, by reason of Innundations, arising from tempestuous Weather. He was more fortunate in the Siege of *Olinthus*. He disapproved the Resolution taken to leave *Mardonius* in *Europe* (c), and it was wholly against his Advice, that *Mardonius* engaged in the Battle of *Platea*, which was so fatal to the *Persians*. *Artabazus*, who had foreseen what happened, preserved the 40000 Men, whom he commanded, and with much Prudence brought them back into *Asia* [A]. Mr *Moreri* shews no Discernment in this Matter. See the Remark.

[A] *Preserved the Forty Thousand Men, whom he commanded, and with much Prudence brought them back into* Asia.] Mr *Moreri* says, that *Artabazus* gathered together the broken Remains of the Army. This is not understanding the Author, whom he quotes. *Herodotus* plainly informs us, that *Artabazus* kept these Forty Thousand Men apart as a Body of Reserve, and that, when he was going to lead them to Battle, he perceived, that *Mardonius* was routed, and fled another way. If *Mardonius* had survived the Loss of That Battle, he would not have failed to have said, in his Vindication, that *Artabazus* had sacrificed him; but he had either been a Spectator only, or a Run-away; that, having given his Advice against the Battle, he had contributed what lay in his Power to the Loss of it, in order to raise a Trophy to his own Prudence. *Artabazus* would not have been the only Person, who, by such a Conduct, had maintained the Opinion he had given in a Council of War. It is a strange Oversight to say, as Mr *Moreri* does, that the *Greeks* lost That Battle. And The Siege of *Potidæa*, naked and unfurnished of all manner of Circumstances, what does it do there? Of what use is it to a Reader?

ARTAVASDES I, King of *Armenia*, Son and Successor of That *Tigranes*, who was conquered by *Lucullus* and *Pompey*, in the War with *Mithridates*, betrayed the *Romans* basely, in the Expedition of *Crassus* (a); for, after having been to wait upon That General with 6000 Horse, and promising him a Supply of 40000 Men, he broke his Word, and excused himself on Pretence of the War he was obliged to maintain in his own Country against the *Parthians* (b). *Crassus*, finding himself abused, threatned very severely (c), but was not in a Condition to punish This Treachery; on the contrary, *Artavasdes* had a great Share in the Rejoicings, which were afterwards made, at the Court of the King of *Parthia*, for the Destruction of the *Roman* Army. He had fixed the Marriage of his Sister with *Pacorus*, the Son of *Orodes*, King of the *Parthians* (d), and was at the Court of *Orodes*, during the excessive Joy occasioned there by so great a Victory. He saw a thousand Diversions full of Insults on the *Romans*; he was present at their Feasts and Comedies, and heard *Euripides*'s Verses applied to the Disaster of *Crassus*, whose Head was brought in upon the Stage, while the *Bacchantes* of That Poet was represented. This gave *Plutarch* occasion to say, that *Orodes* understood *Greek*, and that *Artavasdes* composed Tragedies, Orations, and Histories [A], some of which were preserved to his own Time. I take This *Artavasdes* to have been the same, who deceived *Marc Antony* [B]. He persuaded him to turn his Arms against

[A] *Artavasdes composed Tragedies, Orations, and Histories.*] Here is a *Greek* Poet and Historian, who has been forgot by *Vossius*, as a Poet, but not as an Historian (1) tho' *Mallinc*r*ot* places him in his Collection of Historians never before taken notice of. *Mallincrot* observes, that *Appian* has cited the History of our *Artavasdes*, but has differed a little as to the Author's Name. He adds, that he was the first Prince of That Name, who reigned in *Armenia* (2). This may be true, altho' the Conjecture of several Critics on a Passage of *Justin* should be good. They pretend, that we ought to read *Artavasdes*, and not *Ortoadistes*, in the second Chapter of the Forty second Book. So that there must have been a King of *Armenia* called *Artavasdes*, in the time of *Mithridates* the Great, King of *Parthia*. This *Mithridates* was deposed, and succeeded his Brother *Orodes*, who obtained That memorable Victory over the *Romans*. Our *Artavasdes*, indeed, reigned at the same time with *Orodes*; yet nothing hinders, but he might have begun to reign before him, and his Father *Tigranes* be dead before the deposing of *Mithridates* the Great; in which Case *Artavasdes* might have been at War with the latter. It is true, that, to make *Justin* agree with *Plutarch* (3), and *Dion* (4), it must be supposed, that His *Mithridates* the Great is the *Phraates*. These make to reign in the Time of *Tigranes*.

[B] *I take this* Artavasdes *to have been the same, who deceived* Marc Antony.] My Reasons are these; He, who betrayed *Crassus*, was the Son of *Tigranes*, as *Dion* affirms (5). He, who deceived *Marc Antony*, was the Son of *Tigranes*, as *Josephus* says (6), whose Testimony, if there were occasion for it, might be confirmed by *Strabo*, who not only affirms, that He, whom *Marc Antony* punished for his Perfidy, reigned after *Tigranes* (7), but also that he was His Son (8). So then He, who deceived the *Romans* in the Time of *Crassus*, is the Same, who deceived them in the Expedition of *Marc Antony*. Mr *Moreri* did not understand it so; He would have us acknowledge Two *Artavasdes*'s. Had he stopt here, his Opinion would not have been thought so strange; but what follows can never be enough wondered at. He will have it, that One of These *Artavasdes*'s was He, who composed Histories and Poems, and that the other was He, whom *Marc Antony* led in Triumph to *Alexandria*, in the Year of *Rome* 720. He says, that the latter left a Son of his own Name, the same, perhaps, mentioned by *Plutarch*, who had

516　ARTAVASDES.

(e) *He was called Artavasdes.*

(f) Dio, lib. 49. Strabo, lib. 11. pag. 361, 366. Plutarch. in Anton. pag. 933.

againſt the King of *Media* (e), and by that means engaged him in an Enterprize, which had a very bad Iſſue, and in which he never ſeconded him (f). *Marc Antony*, deferring his Revenge till a more convenient Seaſon, diſſembled for the preſent; but, two Years after, *viz.* in the Seven Hundred and twentieth Year of *Rome*, he uſed ſo many Artifices and fine Promiſes, that at laſt he drew him to a Conference, and then, keeping him Priſoner, loaded him with Silver Chains [C], and led him in Triumph to *Alexandria*. *Artavaſdes*'s Wife and Children were alſo forced to adorn *Marc Antony*'s Triumph. They were all led in Chains of Gold, through the midſt of the People, to *Cleopatra*; but neither Promiſes nor Threats could prevail on them to fall on their Knees before her, or make Supplications to her: they called her only by her Name, which was the occaſion of their being more ſeverely treated. Some time after, *Artavaſdes* was put to Death, and his Head ſent to the King of the *Medes*. It was *Cleopatra*, who ſent him This Preſent upon her return to *Alexandria*, after the loſs of the Battle of *Actium* (g). She fancied, That this Head would induce the King of *Media* to enter into a ſtricter Alliance with *Marc Antony* againſt *Auguſtus*. We ſhall find, in the following Article, what became of the Sons of *Artavaſdes*. He had a Daughter, married to King *Dejotarus* (b).

(g) Dio, lib. 51. See Remark [G] Citation (11).

(b) Cicer. ad Attic. Epiſt. 22. l. 5.

(9) Plutarch *does not ſay, that he had much, or ſo much, Wit.*

(10) Strabo, lib. 11, ſub finem.

(11) See Tacitus, Ann. lib. 2. c. 3.

(12) Id. ib.

had ſo much Wit (9), *and betrayed* Craſſus. What Blundering is here! *Craſſus* was betrayed in 701; He, who betrayed him, was actually King of *Armenia*; how then could he be the Son of a King of *Armenia*, who was dethroned in the Year 720? Mr *Moreri* remarks, that This dethroned Prince *died ſome time after in Priſon*. This is forgetting a very eſſential Circumſtance; for he was killed. 'Αρτάβιδν σνπάκτ]ον]Θ- τῶ Ἀκ]ίακα πολίμω (10). ------ *He was taken off upon the breaking out of the War of* Actium. *Cleopatra*, according to *Dion*, was returned to *Alexandria*, from the Battle of *Actium*, when this Murther was committed (11). He adds, that he left a Son named *Artavaſdes*. No ſuch thing; his eldeſt Son, who ſucceeded him, was called *Artaxias*; his other Son *Tigranes*. And as to That other *Artavaſdes*, who, according to Mr *Moreri*, quoting *Tacitus*, ſoon loſt *Armenia*, which *Tiberius* had given him, he was not the Son of the former, but the third, or fourth, King after him. It is moreover falſe, that *Tacitus* ſays, that *Tiberius* gave him *Armenia*. What he ſays is this; " Dem juſſu Auguſti impoſitus Arta-
" vaſdes, & non ſine clade noſtra dejectus. Tum C.
" Cæſar componendæ Armeniæ deligitur: Is Ario-
" barzanem origine Medum ob inſignem corporis
" formam & præclarum animum volentibus Armeniæ
" præfecit (12). ------- *Afterwards, by* Auguſtus's *Order*, Artavaſdes *was ſet over them, who laſt not his Kingdom, without the Defeat of our Forces.*
" Then C. Cæſar *was appointed for the ſettling Armenia. He pitched upon* Ariobarzanes, *of Median extraction, and excellent Endowments both of Body and Mind, to be their King, whom the Armenians very willingly received.*" Laſtly, what Mr *Moreri* ſays, that *Auguſtus* ſent a Son of *Agrippa* thither, who was ſoon dethroned, is very falſe: for *Caius Cæſar*, the Son of *Agrippa*, was not ſent into *Armenia* 'till after the Deſtruction of the laſt *Artavaſdes*. Nor was he ſent to take it for himſelf, but only to ſettle That Kingdom: accordingly he placed *Ariobarzanes* on the Throne, and afterwards continued to viſit the Eaſt with a Magnificence becoming the preſumptive Heir to the whole *Roman* Empire. If one would endeavour to commit Miſtakes, is it poſſible to make more than Mr *Moreri* has done, who has been guilty of ſeven or eight in ſixteen Lines? Mr *Hoffman* makes but three, in this Article. He ſays, I. That *Artavaſdes* aſſiſted *Craſſus* againſt the *Parthians* (13). II. That *Tiberius* gave *Armenia* to another *Artavaſdes*. III. That *Auguſtus* had before given it to *Artabazus*, the Son of *Agrippa*, who was ſoon depoſed. Mr *Lloyd* has ſuppreſſed this whole Article, tho' it ſtood very fair in *Charles Stephens*.

[C] *Marc Antony* ------- *loaded him with Silver Chains.*] *Dion* remarks, that the Choice of this Metal was to avoid diſhonouring Royal Majeſty with Chains of Iron (14). *Paterculus* ſays, that, in order to render them more honourable, they were made of Gold. " Catenis, ſed ne quid honori deeſſet, aureis " vinxit (15). ------- *He ordered Chains to be put on, " but, that they might be as honourable as poſſible, they " were of Gold.*" The ſame Ceremony had been uſed to *Darius* (16). But what ſhall we ſay to Mr *Ryck*, who treats a Fact, advanced by *Lewis d'Orleans* to reconcile *Paterculus* with *Dion*, as a meer Fiction (17)? The Fact is this; that *Artavaſdes* was loaded with Silver Chains in Priſon, and with Chains of Gold on the Day of Triumph. Mr *Ryck* maintains, that neither of theſe two Hiſtorians have mentioned either Priſon or Triumph, and therefore can never admit of any ſuch Reconciliation. But yet it is very true, that *Dion*, in the ſame Page, where he ſpeaks of Silver Chains, mentions alſo thoſe of Gold, which were put upon *Artavaſdes*, and his Family, on the Day of Triumph. The Slips of Memory are ſometimes very ſurprizing.

(13) Charles Stevens *ſays ſo too*.

(14) Dio, lib. 49. circa finem.

(15) Patercul. lib. 2. cap. 82.

(16) Curt. lib. 5. cap. 12. Vide ibi Freinſhemium.

(17) Ryck, Animadv. ad Tacit. Ann. lib. 2. cap. 3. pag. 28, 29.

ARTAVASDES II. was eſtabliſhed King of *Armenia* by *Auguſtus*. Between the Death of *Artavaſdes* I, and this time, had preceeded *Artaxias*, *Tigranes*, and the Children of *Tigranes*. *Artaxias*, the Eldeſt Son of *Artavaſdes* I, had made his Eſcape, when his Father was put in Chains (a); but not before he had endeavoured to maintain himſelf on the Throne, with his Troops, and the Towns, which had proclaimed him King, after his Father was taken (b). He had the Misfortune to be beaten by *Marc Antony*, and then took Refuge among the *Parthians*, by whoſe Aſſiſtance he reigned at laſt in *Armenia* (c); but, upon the Complaint of his Subjects, and their Requeſt to have his Brother *Tigranes*, who was educated at *Rome*, *Auguſtus* ordered *Tiberius* to depoſe *Artaxias*, and confer the Kingdom on *Tigranes* (b). *Artaxias* was murthered by his own Subjects, before the Approach of *Tiberius* [A], ſo that he had no

(a) Joſeph. Antiq. lib. 15. cap. 5.

(b) Dio, lib. 49.

(c) Arſacidarum vi ſeque regnumque tutatus eſt. Tacit. Annal. Lib. 2. cap. 6.

(d) Dio, lib. 54.

[A] *Artaxias was murthered ------ before the Approach of* Tiberius.] *Dion*, who informs us of this Circumſtance, is miſtaken in the Name; for he calls him *Artabazes*, inſtead of *Artaxias* (1). *Tacitus* imputes the Death of *Artaxias* to the Treachery of his Relations; *occiſo Artaxiâ per dolum propinquorum* (2); but *Horace* aſcribes it to the Valour of *Tiberius*.

------ *Claudi virtute Neronis*
Armenius cecidit (3).

By brave Tiberius's *Arms* Armenia's *Monarch fell.*

This is no wonder! Poets know too well how to give an agreeable turn to Events: Every thing, in their Hands, becomes Matter of Panegyric, and furniſhes Flowers to crown Princes with. *Joſephus* ſays only, that *Artaxias* was depoſed by *Archelaus*; and *Tiberius* (4). *Suetonius*, without mentioning *Artaxias*, contents himſelf with obſerving, that *Tiberius* placed *Tigranes* on the Throne. " Ducto ad orientem exer-
" citu regnum Armeniæ Tigrani reſtituit, ac pro Tri-
" bunali diadema impoſuit (5) ------ *Leading the " Army into the Eaſt, he reſtored the Kingdom of " Armenia to* Tigranes, *and on a Throne inveſted him " with*

(1) See Lipſius on Tacit. Ann. lib. 2. c. 3.

(2) Tacit. ibid.

(3) Horat. Epiſt. 12. lib. 1. v. 26.

(4) Joſeph. Antiq. lib. 15. cap. 5.

(5) Suet. in Tiber. c. 9.

ARTAVASDES. 517

so hard Task to instal *Tigranes* (*e*). This happened in the Year of *Rome* 734. Neither *Tigranes*, nor his Sons, enjoyed their Royalty long (*f*); they gave place to *Artavasdes* II [*B*], whose Reign was also short (*g*). *Augustus*, who had advanced him, being made acquainted with the Confusions of *Armenia*, dispatched thither his Grandson *Caius Cæsar*, to compose them. This young Prince made *Ariobarzanes* their King, with Universal Satisfaction.

(6) Παρεχωσαν, ar-mis subjugavit, recepit, ad deditionem compulit.

(7) Scaliger in Euseb. pag. 170.

(8) *He calls him* Artabanes *by mistake, in imitation of* Dion. *Fratre ejus Artabane, says he, regni insessore ab Armeniis occiso.* — *His Brother Artabanes, who had usurped the Throne, being killed by the Armenians.*

(9) Redacta *Armenia* in potestatem populi Romani, regnum ejus *Artavasdi* tradidit. — *Having reduced Armenia under the Power of the Roman Empire, he made Artavasdes their King.* Tacit. lib. 2. cap. 96.

FAULTS of *Moreri's* Supplement.

"*with the Diadem*." The Term *restored* does not seem properly applied, because *Tigranes*, who was the younger Brother of *Artaxias*, had never been in possession of the Crown of *Armenia*; nor could he have any Right to it during the Life of his Elder Brother. *Scaliger*, who very rightly observed the Mistake of *Eusebius*, in using an Expression, which implies the Conquest of *Armenia* by *Tiberius* (6), when the *Armenians* desired nothing more, than to have *Tigranes* for their King: I say, *Scaliger*, who so justly censures this Impropriety of *Eusebius* (7), ought himself to have avoided The *restituit* of *Suetonius*, and not given *Artaxias* the Title of Usurper (8). There is another Impropriety, or Mistake, in *Eusebius*, and in his Translator St *Jerome*, which has not been noted by *Scaliger*. They affirm, that *Tiberius* seized on *Armenia*, παρεσχηατο, *occupavit Armeniam*: Now he only gave the *Armenians* the Master they desired. It is also certain, that he inthroned him, and put the Diadem upon his Head, and, if there had been occasion for it, would have assisted him with his Forces; how comes it then, that *Scaliger* says, *Armenia* was given to *Tigranes* without any Act of *Tiberius*? What does he mean in maintaining, that St *Jerom*, when he affirms, that *Tiberius* seized on *Armenia*, *occupavit*, ought to have believed, that it belonged already to the *Romans*? I confess I understand nothing of this Logic. But why does he not condemn *Paterculus*, as well as These two Fathers of the Church? *Paterculus*, tho' an Historian, flatters *Tiberius* like a Poet, and has complimented him upon having reduced *Armenia* under the Power of the *Roman* Empire (9). This is not his only Error; he calls Him *Artavasdes*, whom *Tiberius* crowned King of *Armenia*, when his true Name was *Tigranes*.

[*B*] *Tigranes and his Son — — gave place to Artavasdes II*] Here the Authors of The Supplement to *Moreri* have been no less faulty, than *Moreri* himself. I omit their asserting, that our *Artavasdes* was the Son of *Artaxias*, and consequently the Nephew of *Tigranes*: There is nothing of this in the second Book of *Tacitus's* Annals, the only Author whom they have quoted; but let that pass. They add, that the Sons of *Tigranes* were stiled Kings by *Tiberius*, and that Artavasdes II, their Cousin, succeeded *him* after to the Crown, by the Order of the same Emperor. *Tacitus*, their only Evidence, confutes them; for he expressly

says, that all this was done by *Augustus*. Instead of affirming with them, that the *Romans* took Arms against this *Artavasdes*, and at last destroyed him, his Words are, *non fine clade nostra dejectus*, which rather signify the contrary, that he was deposed in spite of the *Romans*, who supported him, and by the Defeat of their Succours. See the Article ARTAVASDES, King of *Media*. Lastly, they say, that *Tigranes*, the Uncle of our *Artavasdes*, *was beheaded at Rome*, *under the Emperor* Tiberius. This is absurd; for the Installing of *Tigranes*, whom they would have to be the Uncle of *Artavasdes* II, was performed in the Seven hundred thirty fourth Year of *Rome*, and his Reign lasted but a very short time. The Execution of *Tigranes* under *Tiberius* happened in the Year 789: So that, according to these Gentlemen, That Prince must have lived above fifty Years after he was deposed, and attained to such an Age, as would not have escaped the Observation of the Historian, who mentions the Indignity of his Death. It is to be observed, that *Tigranes*, created King of *Armenia* in the Year 734, had been taken Prisoner, together with his Father, by *Marc Antony* in 720, and was then a Youth full grown (10). Observe also, that, a little after his Coronation, he married his Children to one another (11), according to the Custom of those Nations. But, what is yet more observable, He, whom *Tiberius* caused to be put to Death, was *Herod's* Grandson. *Josephus* tells us, that *Alexander*, the Son of *Herod*, had, by his Wife *Glaphyra*, the Daughter of *Archelaus* King of *Cappadocia*, two Sons, one of whom, named *Tigranes*, reigned in *Armenia*, and was impeached before the *Romans* (12). This without doubt was He, of whom *Tacitus* speaks in this manner. "Ne *Tigra*nes quidem Armenia quondam potitus, ac tunc reus, nomine regio supplicia civium effugit. — Not even *Tigranes*, who had been King of *Armenia*, when accused and sentenced as a Criminal before the *Romans*, could escape Punishment on account of his Royal Dignity (13)." Mr de *Tillemont's* Conjecture, that This *Tigranes* was King of the lesser *Armenia*, which *Augustus* had given to *Archelaus* (14), might be admitted, if it could be reconciled with *Josephus*, who says, that the Descendants of *Alexander* and *Glaphyra* reigned in the greater *Armenia*. Ἡ δε Ἀλεξάνδρου γενεά τῆς μεγάλης Ἀρμενίας ἐβασίλευσε (15).

(*f*) Nec Tigrani deunctum nomen Imperium fuit, nec libertà ejus. Tacit. ubi supra.

(*g*) Id. ib.

(10) See Josephus, lib. 15. cap. 5.

(11) Tacit. Annal lib. 2. cap. 3.

(12) Joseph. lib. 18. c. 7.

(13) Tacit. cap. 4o.

(14) Hist. des Emper. Tome I. not. 11. sur Tibere.

(15) Joseph. de Bello Jud. lib. 2. c. 19.

ARTAVASDES, King of *Media*, was attacked by *Marc Antony*, at the Sollicitation of another *Artavasdes*, King of *Armenia*. This Enterprize proved very fatal to *Marc Antony*; and, as he believed himself betrayed by the Adviser of it, he turned all his Rage against him, and entered into an Alliance with the King of *Media*. He gave him part of *Armenia*, as soon as he had taken it from the other *Artavasdes*, and cemented This Peace by the Marriage of his Son *Alexander* with *Jotape*, Daughter to the King of the *Medes*. The Troops, with which he supplied him, made him victorious over the *Parthians*, and over *Artaxias*, the Son of *Artavasdes*, King of *Armenia*; but, as soon as he recalled them, and detained those which his Ally had lent him, This Prince, unable to resist his Enemies, fell into their Hands. *Dion* relates this under the Seven Hundred and twenty first Year of *Rome* (*a*). It is probable he was not long a Captive, and that he was the same King of *Media*, to whom *Cleopatra* sent the Head of *Artavasdes*, King of *Armenia*, in the Seven Hundred and twenty fourth Year of *Rome* (*b*). The Supplement to *Moreri* is here very erroneous [*A*].

(*a*) Dio. lib. 49.

(*b*) Id. lib. 51.

[*A*] *The Supplement to* Moreri *is here very erroneous.*] We find there I. *That this* Artavasdes, *King of* Media, *Son and Successor of* Darius, *maintained a vigorous War both against* Artavasdes, *King of* Armenia, *and against* Pompey: II. *That he was at last defeated by the* Parthians, *and that he took Refuge at* Rome *under* Augustus, *who conferred on him the lesser* Armenia, *instead of* Media, *which he had lost.* *Plutarch* is quoted, and *Dion* in his Forty ninth Book. But, to confute this the retrograde way, by one obvious Remark; Does not the bare citing *Plutarch* look like bantering the World, and resolving to assert Falsities with Impunity? For who would not much rather give over criticising, than read two great Volumes in Folio, to discover the Truth of one inconsiderable Fact? It is certain, *Dion*, in his Forty ninth Book, no where says, that This *Artavasdes* fled to *Rome*; nor that *Augustus* made him a Present of the lesser *Armenia*. I know of no Author, who says so. I find indeed, in *Tacitus*, that *Augustus* ordered one *Artavasdes* to reign in *Armenia* after the Son of *Tigranes*; but not that it was to make him amends for *Media*. It is likely, That they, who wrote the third Volume of *Moreri*, have made use of this Passage of

Tacitus

Tacitus for a double Purpose; on the one side, to assert, that *Tiberius* gave *Armenia* to an *Artavasdes*, the Son of *Artaxias*, and Nephew of *Tigranes* (1); and on the other, that *Augustus* conferred it on *Artavasdes*, the deposed King of *Media*. Lastly, how careless is it to say, that he maintained a vigorous War against the King of *Armenia*, and against *Pompey*? This War against the King of *Armenia* had no such need of being vigorously maintained, considering that the Treachery of That Prince to *Marc Antony*, was later than the War, which *Pompey* made in That Country, by about Thirty Years. Nor have I observed, either in *Plutarch*, or *Appian*, that any *Artavasdes*, King of *Media*, was attacked by *Pompey*: I find only, in *Appian*, that *Pompey* subdued *Darius* King of *Media* (2).

ARTAXATA [*A*] was the Capital City of *Armenia*, on the River *Araxes*. *Hannibal* was the Person, who not only drew the Plan, but also surveyed the Building of it, at the Request of *Artaxias*, King of *Armenia*, to whom he retired after the Defeat of *Antiochus* (a). We may be sure, that a Situation, made choice of by so able a General, was very advantagious [*B*], both in time of War and of Peace. This City was burnt by *Corbulo*, in the Eight Hundred and eleventh Year of *Rome* (b). That great Captain would not have proceeded to such Extremity against the Inhabitants, who brought him the Keys of their City, upon his first investing it, if the Laws of War had not made it absolutely necessary [*C*]. For so great a City could not be kept without a great Garrison, which he could not spare without weakening his Army to such a degree, as must have disabled him from any farther Enterprize; And, to have abandoned it in the Condition he found it, would have been giving up both the Glory and Advantage of the Conquest. He resolved therefore to raze it, and was encouraged thereto by a great Miracle [*D*], *si credere dignum est*. The City was covered all on a sudden with a thick Cloud, from whence issued abundance of Lightning, while the Sun continued to shine all round it to the very Compass of the Walls. Some time after, This City was rebuilt by *Tiridates*, who called it *Neronea* in Honour of *Nero* (c), from whom he had received at *Rome* a thousand Civilities, upon his going thither to pay him Homage in the Year of *Rome* 819.

[*A*] ARTAXATA.] *Plutarch* observes, that this City took it's Name from That of King *Artaxas*, (or *Artaxias*), to whom *Hannibal* proposed the Building of it (1). What Mess. *Lloyd* and *Baudrand* note, that *Tacitus* calls it *Artaxia*, is not true; for he calls it constantly *Artaxata*. What they add, that *Strabo* names it *Artaxiasata* (2), is not accurate; for this is plainly insinuating, that he calls it nothing else, or, at least, that it is the principal Name he gives it. Now it is certain, that he commonly calls it *Artaxata*, and only once observes, that it was also called *Artaxiasata*. *Pineda* had reason to alter Ἀρταξίασωτα to Ἀρταξίασατα in *Stephanus Byzantinus*, who doubtless used the Expression of *Strabo*, since he quotes him. It is certain, at least, he never called This City *Artaxia*, as *Ortelius* falsely affirms both of Him, and of *Tacitus*. The Omission, which *Pineda* accuses this *Stephanus* of, is indeed inexcusable; for that *Hannibal*, a Refugee in *Armenia*, observing a very advantagious Situation, advised the Prince, whose Guest he was, to build a City there, and took upon himself the Direction of the Work, is a Circumstance, which ought not to have been suppress'd in a Dictionary of Cities. I am inclined to believe, that *Stephanus Byzantinus*, having *Strabo* before his Eyes, when he composed the Article of *Artaxata*, did not overlook what he found there concerning *Hannibal*; but that his Epitomizer, a Person of much less Judgment, ought to be charged with this Neglect, which *Pineda* so justly complains of. There is, perhaps, no Work, which requires more Discernment, or a better Taste, than the abridging a large Book (3). I cannot forbear making this Remark, because I am myself daily perplexed by the Negligence of Abreviators; while by their means I meet with Difficulties and Obscurities in an hundred Places, which probably were intelligible in the Authors, whom they have abridged. See what Mr *Gronovius* observes of the Authors of the *Synopsis Criticorum* (4).

[*B*] *It's Situation was very advantagious*] *Strabo* informs us, that *Artaxata* was built in a Place, where the River made a *Peninsula*; so that the Walls were surrounded with the River, in form of a Circle, wanting but little of being perfect. His Translator entirely mistakes his Meaning, and is justly reprimanded for it by *Pinedo* (5). If the Version only be consulted, we must believe this City to have been without Walls, except in the Place, where the River did not surround it; *Cinctâ muri loco flumine, nisi qua isthmus est*. — *It was encompassed by the River instead of a Wall, except only at the* Isthmus. The *Greek* tells us quite another story; Τὸ τεῖχ(ο)· κύκλῳ πϵϱιϐάλληται τὸν πολαμὸν πλὴν τῷ ἰσθμῷ. — *The Wall was surrounded by the River in form of a Circle, except only at the* Isthmus.

[*C*] *It was burnt by* Corbulo, — *which the Laws of War made absolutely necessary*] The more we consider the inevitable Consequences of War, the more we shall detest Those, who are the Causes of it. Here is *Corbulo*, who reduced a great and fine City to Ashes, and made an infinite Number of Women, Children, and old Men, miserable, who never did him any Injury. Inquire of Those, who understand the Trade of War best, whether he did well, they will tell you, he did very well; and that, in case he had not acted so, he must have been esteemed a very weak General, for the Reasons alledged by *Tacitus*: " *Artaxatis ignis immissus* " *deletaque & solo æquata sunt, quia nec teneri* " *sine valido præsidio ob magnitudinem mœnium*, " *nec id nobis virium erat quod firmando præ-* " *sidio & capessendo bello divideretur, vel si in-* " *tegra & incustodita relinqueretur, nulla in eo uti-* " *litas aut gloria quod capta essent* (6). —— Artaxatis *was burnt down, and razed to the Ground, because* " *so large a City could not be defended without a* " *strong Garrison, which was not to be spared out* " *of an Army, but just sufficient for carrying on the* " *War; and, to leave it entire, and ungarrisoned,* " *would have been throwing away both the Honour,* " *and Benefit, of taking it.*" The Insults, which a General suffers, when he leaves his Conquests without putting them out of a Condition to hurt him, or keeps them to the too great weakening of his Army, make him so despicable, that, to maintain his Reputation, one of the main Springs of War, he must give occasion to no such Insults. So that it is by a fatal and an unhappy Necessity, that the hard Laws of War oblige us to deprive an Enemy of That, which can be of no Advantage to ourselves.

[*D*] *And was encouraged thereto by a great Miracle*.] *Tacitus*, with all his great Wit, has swallowed the Marvellous with as much Relish, as Those of meaner Capacities are used to do such fort of Dainties. Doubtless the Inhabitants of *Artaxata* endeavoured to comfort themselves on the Destruction of their City, among other Reasons, by some Miracle, which might assure them, that the Gods were displeased with it; and therefore every thing, which could be represented in this Light, was easily believed. But what Notions they had of this Matter we want some Historian of theirs to inform us of. The *Romans*, on their Part, did not want Persons, who knew how to turn the Tables in favour of their Country. For this Particular we are obliged to *Tacitus*. " Ad- " jicitur Miraculum velut numine oblatum, nam " cuncta

ARTAXIAS. ARTEMIDORUS.

" cuncta extra tectis hactenus sole industria fuere, quod mœnibus cingebatur ita repente atrâ nube coopertum fulguribusque discretum est, ut quasi insensantibus Deis exitio tradi crederetur (7) —— Heaven itself seemed also to appear in it by a Miracle; for, while all without the Walls continued to enjoy the brightest Sunshine, all within was so suddenly covered with a black Cloud, darting forth Lightning on all Sides, that the City was thought to be marked out for Destruction by the Anger of the Gods."

ARTAXIAS I, King of *Armenia*, while he was only one of the Generals of *Antiochus* the Great, made a Partition of *Armenia* between himself, and another of That King's Generals [A]. That Prince suffered them both to enjoy their Sovereign Authority (a). They took Advantage of his Complaisance; and, when he was defeated by the *Romans*, they submitted to the Victors, and obtained from them the Title of King (b); after which, They endeavoured to inlarge their Dominions, as much as they could, at the Expence of their Neighbours. *Tigranes*, who made himself so famous in the Wars of *Mithridates*, whose Daughter he had married, was descended from *Artaxias*. *Plutarch* relates, that *Hannibal*, being retired to *Artaxias*, after the Defeat of *Antiochus*, gave him a great deal of good Advice; and that, having found out a Place, which no account was made of, very proper for building a City, he drew a Plan for it, shewed *Artaxias* the Ground, and persuaded him to build it. *Artaxias* was very much pleased with the Proposal, and desired *Hannibal* to undertake the Direction of the Work. His Request was complied with, and hence arose a large and beautiful City, which, in Honour of the Founder, was named *Artaxata* (c). This is all I find, in the two Authors, quoted by The Supplement to *Moreri* (d): As to his rebelling against his lawful Prince, upon a Confidence in the Friendship of the *Romans* (e), I find no shadow or trace of it, any more than of his practising all possible Methods, to maintain himself in his Usurpation, or of his dying in Prison under *Antiochus Epiphanes*. These are meer Chimeras, without the least support from any Quotation.

[A] *He made a Partition of* Armenia *between himself, and another of the Generals of* Antiochus *the Great*] In the Editions of *Strabo*, he is called Θαεσιάδης in one Place (1); and Ζαριάδρις, or Ζαϕριάδρις, in another (2). It was easy for those, who had the Direction of these Editions, to have inserted the same Word every where; and I wonder *Casaubon* has made no Remark upon this, since he has made some, which are not more material.

ARTAXIAS II, King of *Armenia*, Eldest Son of *Artavasdes*, as we have already said (a), was proclaimed King by his Father's Army [A], upon his Father's being taken Prisoner with his Queen, and other Children (b). This Eldest Son endeavoured to support himself against *Marc Antony*, and gave him Battle; but was defeated, and forced to fly into the Country of the *Parthians*. He returned some time after into *Armenia*, and reigned there. This was undoubtedly after the taking of *Artavasdes*, King of *Media*: For, before the *Parthians* took That King (c), they were beaten by him, and *Artaxias* bore a share in the Disgrace. He disgusted his Subjects in such a manner, that they impeached him at *Rome*, and desired his younger Brother *Tigranes* for their King (d). *Augustus*, having this *Tigranes* in his Custody, sent him to them, and ordered *Tiberius* to in-throne him. But *Artaxias* was murthered by his Relations, before the arrival of *Tiberius*.

[A] *He was proclaimed King by his Father's Army*] The Continuators of *Moreri*, or *Tacitus*, say, that it was *Marc Antony* who placed *Artaxias* upon the Throne; but which nothing is more false. They add, that *Artaxias*, having been defeated, was sent into Exile among the *Parthians*. Which is another Mistake; for he retired thither himself for Refuge. If *Marc Antony* had been in a Condition to have banished him after his Victory, he would not have sent him to the *Parthians*, but have brought him bound Hand and Foot to *Alexandria*.

ARTAXIAS III, King of *Armenia*, was the Son of *Polemon*, King of *Pontus*, and was named *Zeno*. He took such a pleasure, from his Infancy, in imitating the Customs of the *Armenians*, that he thereby gained the Affections of the Nation. So that *Germanicus* thought he could not cast his Eye on a fitter Person, to supply the Place of *Vonones*, whom the *Armenians* had driven out. He went therefore to *Artaxata*, and, in the presence of all the People, gave the Diadem to This *Zeno*, in the Year of *Rome* Seven Hundred and seventy one. At the same instant, the Assembly proclaimed him *Artaxias*, after the Name of the Capital City. *Tacitus*, who informs us of all these things (a), mentions his Death under the Year Seven Hundred and eighty eight (b).

ARTEMIDORUS, He, who wrote *on Dreams*, was a Native of *Ephesus*; nevertheless, in That Book, he gives himself the Sirname of *Daldianus*, in Honour to the Country of his Mother [A]. But, in his other Books, he continues to call himself The *Ephesian*.

[A] *He gives himself the Sirname of* Daldianus, *in Honour to the Country of his Mother*.] *Ephesus*, *says he*, of which Place I have, in the Title of several of my Books, declared myself a Native, is sufficiently renowned of itself, and has been justly celebrated by many able Pens; but the small Town of *Daldis* (1), has hitherto remained in obscurity for want of Panegyrists. I am resolved therefore

ARTEMIDORUS.

Ephesian. He lived under *Antoninus Pius*, as he informs us himself, where he says, that he knew an Athlete, who, having dreamt, that he had lost his Sight, obtained the Prize (*a*), in the Games, which That Emperor ordered to be celebrated. No Author ever took more pains on a useful Subject, than *Artemidorus* has done upon a very trifling one [B]. He was not contented to buy up all that had been written on the Explication of Dreams, which amounted to several Volumes [C], but he spent many Years

"fore, since it happens to be my Country by my
"Mother's Side, to acknowledge my Obligations to
"it in this manner." This would be more liable to a Suspicion of Vanity, had it been delivered with more Formality and Method; but this Author expresses himself with so much Ingenuity, that it seems rather to have been the manner of That Age to use these Words with different Ideas from what they would now be understood to import. Τὴν δὲ ἐπιγραφὴν μὴ θαυμάσης ὅτι Ἀρτεμιδώρου Δαλδιανοῦ καὶ οὐχὶ Ἐφεσίου ἐπιγέγραπται. ἔπερ πολλὰ τῶν ἤδη εἰς ἄλλας πραγματείας πεποιημένων μοι βιβλίων. τὴν μὲν γὰρ Ἔφεσον συμβέβηκε καὶ αὐτὴν δι' ἑαυτὴν περιώνυμον εἶναι καὶ πολλῶν ἀξιολόγων κηρύκων τετυχηκέναι. Δαλδία δὲ, πόλισμα Λυδίας, καὶ ἀσφοδρᾳ ἀλλόγιμον. διὰ τὸ μὴ τοιούτων ἀνδρῶν τετυχηκέναι, ἀγνοεῖτ τὸ μέχρι εἰς ἐμὲ μεμένηκε. διὸ δρεπήσεα ὅσιν μοι πατρίδι πρὸς μητρὸς ταύτα ἀποδίδομι αὐτῇ (2). Wonder not, tho', in the Title of this Book, I call myself *Artemidorus the Daldian, and not the Ephesian*, as my other Works have it. For Ephesus has had the good Fortune, not only to be famous in itself, but also to be highly complemented by many eminent Persons. While Daldia, a little Place in Lydia, and not very considerable, for want of such Patrons, continues yet unknown. Therefore, as this is also my Country, since I owe it to my Mother, I thus repay the Debt." *Rigaltius* ought to have kept to this Reason, and not have sought for two others: one of which is, that *Apollo* inspired *Artemidorus*, in the City of *Daldia*, with the Design of interpreting Dreams; the other is, that, there having been another *Artemidorus* of *Ephesus*, the Interpreter of Dreams ought not to have used the Title of *Ephesian*, which was already in the Possession of another (3). This last Reason, though the worst of the two, was nevertheless adopted by a Man of Learning (4). *Artemidorus* himself confutes it beyond Contradiction, since he declares, that he styled himself the *Ephesian*, in a great Number of Books. So that he did not then think of preventing his being confounded with *Artemidorus* the Geographer. Without doubt he was much better known by the Title of *Ephesian*, than by That of *Daldian* (5).

[B] *In treating of Dreams, he made choice of a very trifling Subject.*] If our own Experience be not sufficient to convince us, that, generally speaking (6), there is nothing more confused, than the Ideas, which we call Dreams, we need only consider this Author's own Maxims, to be persuaded, that his Art does not deserve the Attention of a wise Man. There is no Dream, which *Artemidorus* has not explained, but will bear a quite different Interpretation, with the same probability, and with, at least, as natural Resemblances, as Those, on which That Interpreter proceeds. I say nothing of the Injury done to Intelligences, to whose Direction we must necessarily impute our Dreams, if we expect to find in them any Presage of Futurity. What a way of instructing do we ascribe to them! How unworthy of their Knowledge and Gravity, and, in a Word, of such Beings as they are! If they cannot instruct us better, how great is their Ignorance! And if they will not, how great is their Malice (7)! Might not one entreat them, a thousand times, of his good Angel, as well as of his evil Genius, in the Words of Æneas,

Quid natum toties crudelis tu quoque falsis
Ludis imaginibus (8)?

Ah, cruel Mother, such Deceits to use,
And with delusive Forms thy Son abuse!

What I am most surprised at, is, that *Artemidorus* should take so much Pains to establish a Doctrine, which might give him so much Vexation: For must

he not be afraid of dreaming, what his Art might represent to him as ominous? He had found, by his Studies, that, when a Traveller dreams he has lost the Key of h's House, it is a Sign that some Body has debauched his Daughter (9). If *Artemidorus* had dreamt such a Dream, while he was abroad, would he not have believed there was a fine Trade driving at Home? Could this Knowledge have been agreeable to him? Or had he not much better have been without it? He tells us, that, having dreamed, his Wife had insulted him (10), he was much troubled the next Day, when he perceived a Man coming towards him, who was not his Friend. Observe how, by Virtue of his Onirocrify, he turned an imaginary Evil into a real one.

The Objection, which I have just hinted, and which I ground on the Notions the Christian Doctors give us of the Angelical Natures, seems very strong to me, on a Supposition of the Truth of these Notions; but, if we establish a different System, and which has no repugnancy to the Possibility of things, That Objection is much weakened. That is, if we believe there are Spiritual Beings, not only more limited than Man in certain Respects, are to the manner of making themselves understood, but even more fickle and capricious. How can we tell, whether they do not love to divert themselves at our Cost, and make us run after Enigma's, in which they mix something puerile and frivolous, on purpose to make the Scene more ridiculous? How do we know but we serve to divert them, as Beasts do us? And perhaps, when they would correspond with us, they may meet with such Difficulty, in the Motion of our animal Spirits, as may render the Attempt impracticable? See the Remark [D] of the Article MAJUS. Be it as it will, Reason gives us a sufficient Caution against establishing any such Art, and shews all Pretence to it to be a most vain and chimerical Undertaking.

[C] *He bought up all that had been written on the Explication of Dreams, which amounted to several Volumes.*] I have already expressed my Astonishment at some Persons, who have laboured hard to convince themselves of the pretended Science of Dreams. I should not wonder, that several, who call themselves Diviners, should boast of being Masters of it; they may maintain themselves by it, and, not having any Faith themselves in the Art they profess, may but be great Gainers by the Dreams of others, without being at all disquieted with their own. But I cannot judge thus of *Artemidorus*, nor of several other grave Authors, who have written on the Interpretation of Dreams (11). They were themselves the first deceived. Those, named by *Rigaltius* (12), are as follows, *Artemon Milesius, Antiphon, Apollodorus Telmiffensis, Apollonius Attaleusis, Aristander Telmiffensis, Aristarchus, Alexander Myndius, Cratippus, Demetrius Phalereus, Dionysius Rhodius, Epicharmus, Geminus Tyrius* (13), *Hermippus, Nicostratus Ephesius, Phœbus Antiochenus, Philocborus, Panyasis Halicarnasseus, Serapion, Strato*. These, according to *Rigaltius*, were all prior to *Artemidorus*. *Tertullian* names only some of them, when he says (14), "Quanti autem commentatores & assirmatores in "hanc rem, Artemon, Antiphon, Strato, Philocho-"rus, Epicharmus, Serapion, Cratippus, & Diony-"sius Rhodius, Hermippus tota Sæculi literatura.
"—— How considerable are the Commentators and "Authors on this Subject, Artemon, Antiphon, Stra-"to, Philochorus, Epicharmus, Serapion, Cratippus, "Dionysius Rhodius, and Hermippus, *the whole* "*Learning of the Age.*" *Andrew Schot* adds, to some of those beforementioned, *Astrampsychus, Cassius Maximus, & Dionysius Heliopolita* (15). He says, that *Artemidorus* has quoted these two last; but, as to *Cassius Maximus*, I do not see, that *Artemidorus*, who has dedicated the three first Books of his Work to him, speaks of him otherwise, than as a Man, who was curious in this Science (16), and might be

ARTEMIDORUS. 521

Years in travelling up and down to get acquainted with Fortune-tellers. He kept a continual Correspondence with Those in the Towns and Assemblies of *Greece*, in *Italy*, and in the most populous Islands; and he collected every where all the old Dreams he could hear of, and the Events, which it was said they had (*b*). He despised the Reflexions of those grave and supercilious Persons, who treat all Pretenders to Predictions as Sharpers, Impostors, and Cheats [D]; and, without regarding the Censures of these *Cato*'s, he frequented those Diviners several Years. In a word, he devoted all his Time and Thoughts to this Science of Dreams, and thought his great Labour had enabled him to warrant his Interpretations by Reason and Experience [E]. He took great care to instruct his Son in the same Science, as appears by the two Books, which he dedicated to him. So eager a pursuit after these Studies is the less to be wondered at, when we consider, that he believed himself under the Inspiration and Direction of *Apollo* (*c*). He intreats his Readers very seriously neither to add to, nor diminish from, his Book, and makes a kind of Adjuration to them thereupon, in the Name of the All-seeing Eye of Providence, which watches over all things [F]. He dedicated his three first Books to one *Cassius Maximus* [G], and the other two to his Son. They were printed, in *Greek*, at *Venice*, in the Year 1518. In the Year 1603, *Rigaltius* published them at *Paris*, in *Greek* and *Latin*, with Notes. The *Latin* Translation, he made use of, was That published by *John Cornarius*, at *Basil*, in the Year 1539. *Artemidorus* wrote a Treatise of *Auguries*, and another of *Chiromancy*:
But-

(*b*) Ibid. Pref. pag. 3. See also lib. 5. pag. 252.

(*c*) Id. sub fin. lib. 2. pag. 161.

---

(17) Lib. 2. circa fin. pag. 161.

be Master of it in a little Time (17). And, as for *Dionysius Heliopolita*, I have not met with him at all in *Artemidorus*. *Pappus*, of *Alexandria*, might certainly be named, who, we are assured by *Suidas*, wrote on the Interpretation of Dreams. See, above, the Article of ACHMET. Among the Moderns, there was one *Joshua Abrech*, who promised Wonders in the Title of his Book. I know nothing more of him, than what is to be met with in *Vander Linden* (18), and in *Theophilus Spizelius* (19). His Work was printed in the Year 1607. We shall mention *Junianus* MAJUS in his Place (20). It just now comes into my Memory, that *Lysimachus*, the Son of a Daughter of *Aristides*, got his Living by interpreting of Dreams in the Streets. Μνημονεύων Ἀειετείδου συγγενείων τὸ μάλα πενιᾷ Λυσίμαχον, ὃς ἱαυτὸν ἐκ πίνακός τινος ὀνειροκριτικῆ, παρὰ τὸ Ἰακχεῖον λεγόμενον καθεζόμενος ἔζωσεν (21). *We may remember Lysimachus, the Grandson of Aristides, by his Daughter, who was so poor, that he sat near a public Place, called* Jaccheum, *interpreting Dreams, out of a Dream Book, for a Livelihood.* He was reduced to this through Poverty. But had he turned Cobler, and mended old Shoes, instead of delivering himself to his Customers out of this sort of Dream Almanack, he had brought less Discredit on the Memory of his Grandfather.

[D] *He despised the Reflexions of those grave and supercilious Persons:* —— *who despise the Pretenders to Predictions.*] These Criticisers are sometimes in the wrong, and, on such Occasions, it is best to go on our Way, without regarding their Censures. But was this *Artemidorus*'s Case? Was he much less to blame than they, who, in imitation of *Catullus*, unreasonably ridicules the sage and experienced Advice of old Age, as the Reproof of ill natured Greybeards?

Vivamus, mea Lesbia, atque amemus,
Rumoresque senum severiorum
Omnes unius æstimemus assis (22).

Let's live and love, my Lesbia,
*Regardless, while we're young and gay,
Of all that stern old Age can say.*

Sober Readers will easily judge of all this: I leave it to their Thoughts, and will content myself with setting before their Eyes *Artemidorus*'s own Words. Τοῦτο δὲ καὶ σφόδρα διαβέβλημαι τῶν ἐν ἀγορᾷ μαντέων, οὓς δὴ προσίζανας τε καὶ γόηας καὶ βωμολόχους καλοῦσιν οἱ σεμνοπροσωποῦντες, καὶ τὰς ὀφρῦς ἀνεσπακότες, κατὰ φρόνησας τῆς διαβολῆς ἔτεσι πολλοῖς ὡμίλησα (23.) — *Particularly when the Practisers in Divination were driven out of the Market-Place, and treated as Beggars, Jugglers, and Buffoons, by those, who knew how to affect grave and supercilious Countenances, in defiance of this contumely, I corresponded with them many Years.*

(18) De Script. Medici.

(19) Specim. Biblioth.

(20) See his Article, and the beginning of the Remark [H], of the Article ALEXANDER AB ALEXANDRO.

(21) Phalereus in Socrate, apud Plutarch. sub fin. vit. Aristid. pag. 335.

(22) Catull. Epigr. 5.

(23) Artem. in Præfat. pag. 3.

[E] *He thought his Labour, in the Science of Dreams, had enabled him to warrant his Interpretations by Reason and Experience.*] Let us hear what he says himself. Ἀεὶ τὴν πεῖραν καὶ κανόνα καὶ μάρτυρα τῶν ἐμῶν λόγων ἐπίσταμαι. Ἐγὼ μὲν ἐν πάντῃ μὲν ἤδη διὰ πείρας ἐλήλυθα τῷ μηδὲν ἄλλα πράττειν ἀεὶ δὲ καὶ νυκτὸς καὶ μεθ' ἡμέραν πρὸς ὀνειροκρισίαν εἶναι (24). —— *I always appeal to Experience, as the Rule and Demonstration of what I advance. For, by studying Onirocrisy Day and Night, and doing nothing else, I have arrived at an universal Experience.*

[F] *He made a Kind of Adjuration to his Readers, in the Name of* —— *Providence, which watches over all Things.*] " If any one, *says* he (25), thinks he " can add any thing new to my Book, let him keep " it to himself, as properly his own. This is fair; " if he finds, that I have said too much, he may take " only what he likes, and leave the rest." Τὰ λοιπὰ τῶν βιβλίων μὴ ἐξαίρειν ϑεῶν ἱππότην καὶ φύλακα πάντων νομίζων τὸν Ἀπόλλωνα. Expunging nothing of my Works, as he knows there is a God, who observes all Things, and that Apollo is our Protector. He was afraid of your foul Play, often practised, of turning Authors topsy-turvy, either by Abridgments, or Interpolations.

[G] *He dedicated his three first Books to one* Cassius Maximus.] *Rigaltius* can find no such Person, *and perhaps,* says he, *we ought to read* FABIO *or* TATIO MAXIMO; *for* Julius Capitolinus *makes mention of one* Gavius Maximus, *who was Præfect of the Prætorium, for twenty Years, under the Emperor* Antoninus, *and who had* Tatius Maximus *for Successor*. However it be, The Patron *Artemidorus* addressed himself to was a *Phenician* by Nation (26), a great Orator, and of so ready a Wit, that he was able to understand an Author perfectly without reading him through (27). *Andrew Schot* calls him *Cossinus Maximus*, and distinguishes him from *Cassius Maximus* (28). Two Faults for one, without counting That of the Remark [C] (29). I do not know whether any one has thought of reading *Claudius Maximus* instead of *Cassius Maximus*. Under the Emperor *Antoninus Pius*, there was a Proconsul of *Africa*, whose Name was *Claudius Maximus*. The charge of Magic, against which *Apuleius* defended himself, was brought before this Proconsul. It appears, from several Passages in his Plea, that this *Claudius Maximus* passed for a learned Man, and one who was curious in Philosophical Learning. " Bene quod apud te, Maxime, causâ agitur, qui pro " tuâ eruditione legisti profectò Aristotelis περὶ " ζώων γενέσεως, περὶ ζώων ἀνατομῆς, περὶ " ἱστορίας multijuga volumina: præterea problemata " innumera ejusdem, tum ex eâdem sectâ cæterorum " in quibus id genus varia tractantur. —— *It is happy for me, that I am to plead my Cause before thee,* " O Maxime, *who art so learned, as to have read the* " *numerous Volumes of* Aristotle, *on the Generation of* " *Animals, on the Anatomy of Animals, and on History; besides his great Work of Problems, and several others, of the same Sect, treating on various* " *Subjects of This kind.*" Thus he speaks at Page 115.

(24) Id. lib. 2. sub fin. pag. 161.

(25) Id. ib.

(26) Id. ib.

(27) Id. in Præfat. p. 4.

(28) Andr. Schott. in Senec. Contrav. IX.

(29) Citation (13).

But we have no Remains of them [H]. *Tertullian* has not taken notice of him in That Paſſage, where he quotes ſeveral Onirocritic Authors (d); but *Lucian* does not forget him, tho' he names but two Writers of This Claſs (e).

115. A little after, he addreſſes him in this manner; "Audiſti, Maxime, quorum pleraque ſcilicet legeras "apud antiquos philoſophorum. —— *The greateſt* "*part of what thou haſt heard, O Maximus, thou* "*haſt read thyſelf amongſt the ancient Philoſophers.*" Elſewhere (30) he ſays to him; "Multa fando, Maxi- "me, audiſti, & plura legendo didiciſti, non pauca "experiendo comperiſti; —— *Many things, O Maxi-* "*mus, haſt thou heard in Diſcourſe, more haſt thou* "*learned by Study, and not a few haſt thou diſcovered* "*by Experience.*" And again (31); "An quod multo "præſtabilius eſt, tua doctrina, Claudi Maxime, tua- "que perfecta eruditione fretus, contemnam ſtultis "& impolitis ad hæc reſpondere. —— *Much rather* "*had I rely, O Claudius Maximus, on thy great* "*Learning, and deſpiſe giving any Anſwer to the ig-* "*norant and illiterate.*" He ſeems alſo to have been at firſt a Philoſopher by Profeſſion, but to have raiſed himſelf by his long military Services. "Erras —— "ſi eum fortunæ indulgentiâ non ex philoſophiæ cen- "ſurâ metiris: ſi virum tam AUSTERÆ SECTÆ, "tamque diutinæ militiæ non putas amiciorem eſſe "coërcitæ mediocritati quàm delicatæ opulentiæ (32). "—— *You are miſtaken —— if you think, the Fa-* "*vours of Fortune have more weight with Him, than* "*the Dictates of Philoſophy; or that a Perſon of ſo* "AUSTERE *a* SECT, *and ſo old a Soldier, will not* "*rather take the Part of contented Mediocrity, than* "*of effeminate Opulence.*"

[H] *He wrote a Treatiſe of* Auguries, *and another of* Chiromancy; *but we have no Remains of them.*] *Vander Linden* falſely affirms, even in his Edition of, *Merklinus,* that *Aldus* has printed them in *Greek,* that *Cornarius* tranſlated them into *Latin,* and that *Rigaltius* publiſhed them in both theſe Languages (33). We muſt ſearch a little higher for the Original of this Miſtake; nor will the Inquiry be uſeleſs; it may ſerve to let thoſe, who write Abridgments, ſee, into what a Multitude of Errors they are apt to lead their Readers. *Geſner* had ſaid; "Artemidorus ——ſcrip- "ſit de ſomniorum interpretatione libros 4. item de "auguriis & manuum inſpectione. *Suidas.* Hujus "autoris quinque libros Aldus Græcè excudit (34). "—— Artemidorus —— *wrote four Books of the In-* "*terpretation of Dreams, and alſo of Auguries, and* "*of Chiromancy. Suidas. Five Books of this Author* "*are printed in* Greek, *by* Aldus." He had obſerved, afterwards, that theſe five Books were only concerning Dreams. See how *Simler* has abridged this Text. "Artemidorus ——ſcripſit de ſomnio- "rum interpretatione lib. 4. Item de auguriis & "manuum inſpectione. Eos Aldus Græcè excudit. "—— Artemidorus —— *wrote four Books of the In-* "*terpretation of Dreams. Alſo of Auguries, and Chi-* "*romancy. Theſe Aldus has printed in* Greek." Is This abridging, or miſinterpreting, an Author? It looks more like the latter than the former.

ARTEMISIA, Queen of *Caria,* and Daughter of *Lygdamis* [*A*], accompanied King *Xerxes,* in Perſon, in his War with the *Greeks* [B]. She was a Woman of great Capacity, and perfectly Maſculine Courage. So that, happening to be poſſeſt of Sovereign Authority, as well by being Widow of the late King, as on account of the Minority of her Son (a), during the Preparations of *Xerxes,* ſhe took this occaſion to ſignalize herſelf, and voluntarily engaged in That famous Expedition. She diſtinguiſhed herſelf in it very particularly both by her Counſel and Conduct. The Reaſons, on which ſhe grounded her Advice, againſt engaging in the Battle of *Salamis* (b), were extremely juſt. She ſaved herſelf very artfully in That Battle; for, ſeeing herſelf purſued by an *Athenian* Ship, without any hope of eſcaping, ſhe attacked a *Perſian* Ship, commanded by *Damaſithymus* King of *Calyndus,* with whom ſhe had a quarrel, and ſunk him (c). This made Thoſe, who were in chace of her, believe, that her Veſſel was of their own Party [C], and ſo quit the Purſuit. By good fortune for her, not one of *Damaſithymus*'s Men was ſaved. So that ſhe got rid of an Enemy, without the leaſt ſuſpicion of having deſtroyed him; and eſcaped being taken, with the honour of having ſunk a *Greek* Ship. *Xerxes* was much miſtaken on this occaſion; for he cryed out, that *his Men had behaved themſelves like Women, and his Women like Men* [D]. He intruſted her with the Government of his Children, the young Princes of

[*A*] *She was Daughter of* Lygdamis] *Herodotus* does not ſay, what *Moreri* fathers upon him, *viz.* that *Lygdamis* was King of *Halicarnaſſus* (1). He only ſays, that *Artemiſia* was of *Halicarnaſſus,* by the Father's ſide, and of *Crete* by the Mother's Side. If the ſame Hiſtorian had not declared, that *Lygdamis,* who aſſiſted *Piſiſtratus,* and to whom, after *Piſiſtratus* was re-eſtabliſhed in *Athens,* he gave the Command of the Iſle of *Naxos,* was a Native of That Iſle (2), I ſhould have taken him for our *Artemiſia*'s Father, or Grand-father. *Blancardus,* in his Edition of *Harpocration* (3), has continued the Error of Thoſe, who went before him, *viz. Damis,* for *Lygdamis* (4). *Valeſius*'s Annotations point out the proper Correction, which *Gronovius* has actually made, upon publiſhing *Harpocration,* in the Year 1696.

[B] *She accompanied King* Xerxes, *in Perſon, in his War with the* Greeks (5).] *Suidas* ſays, it was againſt the *Perſians* ſhe took Part (6); that this Paſſage may, perhaps, have been mangled; for That piece of Wit of *Xerxes,* mentioned immediately after, by *Suidas,* that *the Men were become Women, and the Women Men,* would be unintelligible, if *Artemiſia* had been in the *Greek* Army, where the Men fought like Lions. *Mauſſac* ſuppoſes, that *Suidas* wrote, as it is in *Harpocration,* κατὰ τὰ Περσικά (7). In the Perſian War.

[C] *She made thoſe, who chaſed her, believe, that her Veſſel was of their own Party.*] *Herodotus* has forgot a very eſſential Circumſtance, for want of which his Narration loſes much of it's Probability. He ought to have told us, as *Polyænus* has done, that *Artemiſia* cauſed her *Perſian* Colours to be taken down (8). *Polyænus* makes her follow the Conduct of Thoſe Pirates, who hoiſt all ſorts of Colours, according as they have occaſion. When ſhe gave Chace to a *Greek* Ship, ſhe hung out *Barbarian* Colours; but, if a *Greek* Ship purſued her, ſhe diſplay'd *Greek* Colours. He has turned the Engagement of this Queen ſo many Ways, that he makes three or four different Actions of it, and tells us of a Spindle and Diſtaff, ſent by the King of *Perſia* to a Captain of a Ship, which there is no making Senſe of, ſince the Ship, which *Artemiſia* engaged with, was ſunk, and all the Men in her loſt.

[D] *Upon her Account,* Xerxes *cried out, that his Men had behaved themſelves like Women, and his Women like Men.*] Let us ſee what *Herodotus* ſays: Ἔξεξαν δὲ εἶπαι λέγεται πρὸς τὰ φαιζόμενα, οἱ μὲν ἄνδρες γεγόνασί μοι γυναῖκες, αἱ δὲ γυναῖκες, ἄνδρες (9). *Xerxes, upon hearing this Account, is reported to have cried out,* "My Men are become "Women, and my Women Men." To this let us add, what *Juſtin* ſays: "Artemiſia regina Halicar- "naſſi, quæ in auxilium Xerxi venerat, inter pri- "mos duces bellum acerrimè ciebat, quippe ut in "viro muliebrem timorem, ita in muliere virilem "audaciam cernere (10). — Artemiſia, *Queen of* "Halicarnaſſus, *who joined her Forces with* Xerxes, "appeared

ARTEMISIA.

of *Persia*, when, according to her Advice, he quitted *Greece* to return into *Asia*. The *Athenians* were so incensed at a Woman's making War against them, that they promised a great Reward for the taking *Artemisia*, and ordered all their Captains of Ships to endeavour it (d). Her Statue was erected at *Lacedemon*, among those of the *Persian* Generals, in the Portico, built with the Spoils of That Nation (e). The Stratagem she used, to make herself Mistress of *Latmus*, is as much to be commended upon the Principles of *Machiavelism*, as to be condemned upon Those of Christianity. She placed her Troops in Ambuscade, and then went in a devout Procession, with Eunuchs, Women, Trumpets, and Drums, to celebrate the Feast of the Mother of the Gods, in a Wood, which was consecrated to her, near That City. The Inhabitants, charmed with this Zeal, ran thither to admire her Piety; and, in the mean time, *Artemisia*'s Army took Possession of the Town (f). These great Qualities did not preserve her from amorous Foibles [E]. She was passionately in Love with a Native of *Abydos*, whose Name was *Dardanus*, and was so enraged at his slighting her, that she put out his Eyes while he slept (g). The Gods, to punish her, caused her Passion to grow yet more violent; insomuch that being advised by the Oracle to go to the Promontory *Leucas* (h), the Refuge of Lovers in despair, she went thither, took the Leap, but did not recover it. She was buried in that Place. Many Writers preposterously confound her with the *Artemisia* I am going to mention [F].

[E] *Her great Qualities did not preserve her from amorous Foibles.*] All Heroines are not like *Agrippina*, who overcame the Weakness of her own Sex, by imitating the Fortitude of the other. "A grippina, æqui impatiens, dominandi avida, virilibus curis fœminarum vitia exuerat (11). Agrippina, impatient of an Equal, and eager for Rule, by manly Thoughts put off the Woman's Weakness." *Semiramis*, who was ambitious and warlike to the highest Degree, was prodigiously lascivious. It is observed, that most great Warriors are of an amorous Complexion: Of which the mystical Commentators may give *Homer* the Honour, for so naturally describing the Intercourses of *Mars* and *Venus*; but I believe this is not so generally true, in the Case of Women, who seem best secured against the Follies of Love by the Pursuits of Ambition.

[F] *She is preposterously confounded with Artemisia, the Wife of Mausolus.*] It seems *Pliny* is guilty of this Fault; for he says, that *Artemisia*, the Wife of *Mausolus*, gave her Name to the Herb called *Parthenis* (12). Now, since the Herb *Artemisia*, (which we call *Mugwort*,) is mentioned by *Hippocrates*, and the Wife of *Mausolus* was not born till after *Hippocrates*; *Pliny*, in That Passage, has mistaken one *Artemisia* for the other. If one of them gave her Name to the Herb *Mugwort*, it must be the Daughter of *Lygdamis*, the great and couragious *Artemisia*, who accompanied *Xerxes*. Mr *Chevreau*, to whom I owe this Remark against *Pliny*, observes, that *Leo Allatius*, from whom he has it, has, with Reason, censured *Robert Stephens*, for saying (13), *That Artemisia, the Wife of Mausolus, signalized herself in Xerxes's War against the Grecians* (14). Mr *Chevreau* has remarked the same Mistake in the *Historical Theatre of Christian Matthew*: he adds, *That it was not without Reason, that Pliny, in the Passage alledged, gave Mausolus the Title of Rich.* I find, indeed, This Epithet in *Du Pinet*'s Translation; but not in the *Pliny* of Father *Hardouin*: And I find, that *Pliny*, in another Place (15), describing the Magnificence of the *Mausoleum*, says only, that *Mausolus* was a petty King of *Caria, Cariæ regulus*. Father *Hardouin* endeavours to help out his Author, by suggesting, that all the Kings of *Caria* assumed the Name of *Mausolus*, as all the Kings of *Egypt* did the Name of *Ptolomy*; and, therefore, that *Artemisia*, the Wife of *Mausolus*, to whom *Pliny* imputes the Vanity of giving her Name to an Herb, is She, who lived in the Time of *Xerxes*: But he must give me leave to say, that, in this Case, his Author would be very liable to censure on another Account; namely, for characterizing a Queen by a Title, which must have been common to her with all the other Queens of That Country. Father *Hardouin* grounds his Conjecture on a Passage, where the two *Artemisia*'s are stiled Queens of *Caria* (16). I shall pass by this reasoning of his, and observe, that *Tzetzes* is a little puzzled (17). According to him, one of the *Artemisia*'s was the Wife of *Mausolus*, and the other the Wife of *Hecatomnes*; the first of whom he makes the Companion of *Xerxes*. Now all Authors agree, that She, who built a magnificent Tomb for her Husband, was the Daughter of *Hecatomnes*, and Wife of *Mausolus*; and that the *Artemisia*, who joined the *Persians* against the *Greeks*, was the Daughter of *Lygdamis*. The great *Scaliger* will not pass Muster here: He has too apparently taken the one for the other (18), and That in a Place, where it was not easy to make such a Mistake: For it is in the Abstract of a Book, the Author whereof has declared, in plain Terms, that he speaks of one *Artemisia*, the Daughter of *Lygdamis*, who took up Arms against the *Persians* (19). *Scaliger*, suppressing all these particular Descriptions, has substituted That of the Widow of *Mausolus*, which can only be applied to That Queen of *Caria*, who so much honoured the Memory of her Husband. This celebrated Writer has led another great Man into an Error, having occasioned *Valesius* to affirm, that, after the Death of *Mausolus*, *Artemisia*, seeing herself slighted by *Dardanus*, whom she loved, put out his Eyes, and, finding herself afterwards still more in Love, went to take the *Leucadean* Leap, by which she lost her Life (20). By comparing This Passage with That of *Scaliger*, it plainly appears, that the one is a Transcript of the other. This stumble of *Valesius* in so Even a Road, and the Difference he observes between *Theopompus*, who makes *Artemisia* die of Grief for the Loss of her Husband, and *Ptolomy*, the Son of *Hephæstion*, who makes her die for Love of another Man, as *Valesius* pretends, are so much the more amazing, as he had, but two Lines before, quoted the seventh Book of this same *Ptolomy*, to prove, that *Artemisia*'s Father's Name was not *Damis*, but *Lygdamis*. *Balthasar Bonifacius*, who gives the same false account of the Wife of *Mausolus* (21), confesses he took it from *Scaliger*. *Habemus confitentem reum: The Criminal pleads Guilty.* And it may be properly said of this Way of propagating Faults,

— dedit hanc contagio labem,
Et dabit in plures: sicut grex totus in agris
Unius scabie cadit, & porrigine porci:
Uvaque conspecta livorem ducit ab uva (22).

*Infections, from one single Cause begun,
Soon spread their Poison, and thro' Numbers run.
So, one Sheep touch'd, none of the Flock escape:
And the whole Bunch rots from one smitten Grape.*

Mr *Menage*, having said a great many fine Things of *Artemisia*, the Wife of *Mausolus*, and particularly of the Honour done her, in proposing her as a Model of conjugal Love, goes on in this manner: *Yet Ptolomy, the Son of Hephæstion* —— *says, that Artemisia was so smitten with the Love of one Dardanus, &c.* And, having repeated the whole Story, he proceeds thus: "There were two *Artemisia*'s, both Queens of "*Caria*, as *Suidas* informs us; She, who was married "to *Mausolus*, and another more ancient: and, if this "Story be true, it is most probable, that it happened "to the first *Artemisia*, and that This *Ptolomy*, the "Son of *Hephæstion*, in applying it to the Wife of "*Mausolus*,

ARTEMISIA

(23) Menag. Obfervat. fur Malherbe, pag. 53.
"*Maufolus*, was miftaken (23)." The Conjecture of this learned Man is very juft; but he was in the wrong in charging *Ptolomy* with fixing this Adventure on the Wife of *Maufolus*. *Sarafin*, introducing Mr *Menage* in the Dialogue, upon the Queftion, *whether a young Man ought to be amorous*, makes him fay, that *Artemifia*, the fame *Artemifia* who was fo afflicted for the Death of her Husband, *who drowned herfelf in Tears, and reproached the Stars, which could not help it,*

(24) Sarafin's Works, pag. 252.
With all that Rage can make one fay,
When Reafon flies, and gives it way (24),

(25) See the Nouveaux Dialogues des Morts, 2. part. p. 175. Dutch Edit.
fe'l, at laft, in Love with *Dardanus*, and that the moft profeffed *Coquette would be afhamed of the Paffion of That Queen*. Upon this he quotes what *Scaliger* fays; fo that we fee one, or rather two, ingenious Men, Mr *Sarafin* and Mr *Menage*, deceived by the learned *Scaliger*. The witty Author of the *New Dialogues of the Dead* has made That *Artemifia*, who lamented her Husband fo much, in Love with a young Man (25).

It would be too tedious to point out all thofe, who have confounded the two *Artemifia*'s. *Revifius Textor* (26), and the Authors of the *Thefaurus Fabri* are of This Number. *Olivier*, who wrote a Commentary on *Valerius Maximus*, is alfo one of them; though he knew, that *Strabo* and *Herodotus* did not agree about the Genealogy of The *Artemifia*, whom they mention (27). He innocently imagined, that one of the two muft be in the wrong, and never dreamed, that they fpoke of different Perfons, and were both in the right. It is true, Mr *Hofman* gives two Articles of *Artemifia*; but, in the firft, he has huddled together confusedly, what fhould have been diftinguifhed under the two different Heads; and he is doubtful, whether the Wife of *Maufolus*, and the Daughter of *Lygdamis*, are not one and the fame Perfon. Befides, he quotes *Vitruvius* for Facts, which he never once mentions. Mr *Lloyd* led him the way in That falfe Quotation from *Charles Stephens*, which he has not corrected; And from whom he has very furprifingly pirated the whole Article of That *Artemifia*, who followed *Xerxes*; which Article was very correct.

(26) In Offician.

(27) Valerius Maximus Variorum, edit. 1655.

(a) Strabo, lib. 14. pag. 411. Suidas in Ἀρτεμισία.

ARTEMISIA, Queen of *Caria*, the Daughter of *Hecatomnes* (a), Sifter and Wife of *Maufolus*, immortalized herfelf by the Honours fhe paid to the Memory of her Husband. She caufed a very magnificent Tomb to be built for him, in *Halicarnaffus*, which was called *Maufoleum*, and was one of the feven Wonders of the World; from whence the Appellation of *Maufoleum* has ever fince been given to all fumptuous Structures of this kind. *Pliny* has left us a particular Defcription of this ftately Monument (b). It may be feen in *French* in the Hiftory of Mr *Chevreau* (c), and in the Supplement to *Moreri*. *Artemifia* lived but two Years after her dear Husband (d), who died without Children (e), after he had reigned twenty four Years, towards the End of the CVIth Olympiad [A]. She died of Grief and Melancholy (f) [B], before the *Maufoleum* was finifhed (g). It is faid fhe mixed her Husband's Afhes with Water, and drank them, that fhe might ferve him for a living Tomb (h). It muft not be forgot, that fhe caufed excellent Panegyrics to be made on him, and propofed a Prize of great Value for him, who fhould acquit himfelf beft (i). *Theopompus* obtained it. They fay, that his Mafter *Ifocrates* was one of the Orators, who entred the Lifts [C]. *Theodectes* of *Phafelides*, who was another of the Competitors, compofed a Tragedy called *Maufolus*, which had better Succefs, than his Profe. Nor muft we forget, that, inftead of Lamentations and Tears, in which moft Writers bury

(b) Plin. lib. 36. cap. 5.
(c) Lib. 7. cap. 7.
(d) Diodor. Sicul. l. 16.
(e) Strabo, l. 14. p. 471.
(f) See Remark [D].
(g) Plin. lib. 36. cap. 5.
(b) A. Gell. l. 10. c. 18. V. Maxim. lib. 4. c. 1.
(i) A. Gell. ibid. Plutarch. in Vita Ifocr.

[A] *Maufolus, her Husband, died — towards the End of the CVIth Olympiad.*] Moft Editions of *Pliny* make *Maufolus*, King of *Caria*, die in the fecond Year of the Cth Olympiad, according to the beft Manufcripts, has fixed his Death to the fecond Year of the CVIth Olympiad, and the Four hundred and fecond of *Rome*. *Obiit Olympiadis centefima fexta anno fecundo; Urbis anno 402*. Mr *Chevreau* obferves, that *Ufher* judged this Paffage of *Pliny* to be corrupted, and that *Maufolus* died in the fourth Year of the CVIth Olympiad, *Anno Mundi* 3651 (2). This agrees very well with thefe Words of Father *Hardouin*: "*Quid quod & Diodorus non ad Olympiadis cvi annum alterum Maufoli obitum, fed ad quartum refert*, lib. 16. ver 435 (3). — But *Diodorus* places the Death of *Maufolus*, not in the *fecond*, but *fourth*, *Year of the CVIth Olympiad*: and with the Duration of the Reigns of Thofe, who fucceeded *Maufolus*, till *Alexander*'s Expedition. See the Remark [A] of the Article ADA. It is certain, that *Maufolus* was dead, and *Artemifia*, who did not furvive him above two Years, living, when *Demofthenes* made an Oration for the Liberty of the *Rhodians*. Now he fpoke this Oration in the fecond Year of the CVIth Olympiad, as may be collected from *Dionyfius* of *Halicarnaffus* (4). *Maufolus*, then, died in the laft Year of the CVIth; and the anonymous Author, who defcribed the Olympiads, was miftaken, in placing *Maufolus*'s Funeral Oration, by *Theopompus*, in the firft Year of the CIIId Olympiad. *Valefius* has committed the fame Miftake. *Hæc Artemifia in funere Mariti agones celebravit Olympiade cIII* (5). — *This Artemifia folemnized her Husband's Funeral with Prize Contefts in the CIIId Olympiad*. They, who, after the Example of *Calepin*, Mr *Lloyd*, and Mr *Hofman*, &c. would refer us to the feventh Book of *Herodotus*, for an Account of the *Maufoleum*, can never have rightly confulted the Chronological Tables, which muft be very falfe indeed, if the Death of *Maufolus* be found in them, before That of *Herodotus*.

[B] *She died of Grief and Melancholy.*] We have feveral great Authorities for this Fact, no lefs than a

(1) Plinius, lib 36. c. 5. pag 280, & cap. 6. pag. 288.
(2) Chevr. Hift. du Monde, lib. 7. cap. 3.
(3) Harduin. in Plin. Tom. 5. p. 280.
(4) Dion. Halicarn. Epift. de Æftat. de Script. D. mofth.
(5) Valef. Not. in Hippocrat. Lexicon, pag. 93.

Theopompus, a *Cicero*, and a *Strabo*. *Theopompus*'s Account is very full. "Ἠν φησι Θεόπομπος φθινάδι νόσω ληφθεῖσαν διὰ τὴν λύπην ἐπὶ τῷ ἀνδρὸς καὶ ἀδελφῷ Μαυσώλω, ἀποθανεῖν (6). *Who is faid*, by *Theopompus*, *to have died of a wafting Diftemper*, *contracted through Grief for the Lofs of* Maufolus *her Husband*, *and Brother*. That of *Cicero*. "*Artemifia illa, fays he* (7), *Maufoli Cariæ Regis uxor, quæ nobile illud Halicarnaffi fecit fepulchrum, quamdiu vixit, vixit in luctu, eodemque etiam confecta contabuit. Huic erat illa opinio quotidie recens, quæ tum denique non appellabatur recens cum vetuftate exaruit.* — *That Artemifia, the Wife of Maufolus of Caria, who built The famous Monument at Halicarnaffus, lived in Sorrow, and pined away with it to Death. To her, the fame Sentiment was always new, which was then only not efteemed new, when quite worn out with Age.*" It is almoft certain, *Cicero* was ignorant, that *Artemifia* furvived her Husband but two Years; otherwife he would not have ufed fuch Expreffions as fignify a very long Sorrow. But let us fee what *Strabo* fays: Φθίσει δ᾽ ἀποθανεῖσαν διὰ πένθος τοῦ ἀνδρὸς (8). *She died of a Confumption, through Grief for her Husband.*

[C] *They fay Ifocrates made a Panegyric on him.*] I have quoted two good Vouchers (9); and can add a Third, of great Weight, which is *Theopompus*: He publickly boafted of having carried the Prize from his Mafter *Ifocrates* (10). But I am not ignorant, that *Suidas*, without mentioning *Ifocrates*, the *Athenian*, fpeaks of another *Ifocrates*, Difciple and Succeffor of the former, and born either at *Heraclea*, or *Apollonia*, on the *Euxine* Sea. *Suidas* fays, it was He, who difputed the Prize of Eloquence with *Theodectes*. *Theopompus*, and *Erythreus* (11). This latter was of *Naucratis* in *Egypt*, which will make *Aulus Gellius* guilty of a Miftake, in the Place, where we read, that *Theopompus*, *Theodectes*, and *Naucrites* difputed That Prize (12). *Naucrites* is not the proper Name of One of Thofe Competitors; it is only his Name derived from the Town, where he was born, a little altered; for it fhould have been *Naucratites* (13). *Olivier* names them *Theopompus*, *Theodotes*, and *Naucrates* (14). But, if

(6) Apud Harpocrat.
(7) Cicer. Tufculan. 3. The Paffage is wrong quoted in Val. Max. Variorum. T. 4. lib. 4. Reprinted in Rouen. A. Gellius is twice quoted not the Particle non, which makes it intolerable Nonfenfe.
(8) Strabo, lib. 14. pag. 452.
(9) Plutarch. in Vita Ifocrat. A. Gellius, lib. 10. cap. 18.
(10) See Eufebius Præp. Evang. l. 10, cap. 3. pag. 464.
(11) Suidas in Ἰσοκράτης.
(12) A. Gell. lib. 10. cap. 18.
(13) Moreri and Hofman have it Naucrites.
(14) Olivier, in Val Max. pag. 395. Edit. Lugd. Bat. 1655.

ARTEMISIA. ASCLEPIADES.

bury *Artemisia* during her Widowhood, there are those, who affirm, that she made some very heroic Conquests [D].

(15) Suidas in Ἰσοκράτης.

(16) Photius in Biblioth. cod. 1:6. p. 332.

(17) Cicero de Orat. lib. 3. & in Oratore.

(18) Dion. Halicarn. in Judicio de Isæo, p. 228.

(19) Quintil. lib. 3. c. 6, init.

If *Aulus Gellius* is to be preferred before *Suidas*, as in my Judgment he ought to be, then we must own, that the latter is mistaken in the Place, where we read, ἅμα τῷ Ἐρθραίῳ Ναυκράτην δὶνηγωνίσαιο (15); he contended with *Erythræus*, the Naucratian. *Photius* favours *Aulus Gellius*, by saying, that *Naucrates* of *Erythrea* was one of *Theopompus's* Competitors (16). On one side, or the other, they have mistaken the proper Name for the Name derived from the Town. Observe, that *Cicero* (17), *Dionysius Halicarnassensis* (18), and *Quintilian* (19), speak of One *Naucrates*, a Disciple of *Isocrates*. However, *Amiot* has translated the Passage of *Plutarch* in a quite different manner from *Wolfius*, and *Xylander*: according to These, *Isocrates's* Panegyric on *Mausolus* was lost; but, according to *Amiot*, it was preserved. *Isocrates*, says he, contended for the Prize, which Queen Artemisia instituted on account of the Tomb of her Husband Mausolus; and the Oration, which he made in Praise of the deceased, is still extant. Without doubt the different Manner of Accenting has produced These different Translations: some read τὸ δὲ ἐγκώμιον ὁ σώζεται, but this Panegyric is not preserved; others read τὸ δὲ ἐγκώμιον ὃ σώζεται, and this Panegyric is there preserved. See what sport Fortune makes with Manuscripts: one single Point, either taken away, or added, or altered, turns the Affirmative into the Negative.

(20) *That de Libertate Rhodiorum*, at page 78 of his Works; Edit. Genev. 1607. folio.

[D] *There are some, who affirm, that she made some very heroic Conquests.* I say nothing of *Demosthenes's* Oration, which has been quoted before (20), though it is certain, from the manner of That Orator's expressing himself, that *Artemisia* was not represented in *Athens* as a disconsolate Widow, pining away, and neglecting the Affairs of her Kingdom, to confine her Thoughts wholly to the Memory of her Husband. The *Athenians* considered her as a Woman in a Condition to make herself feared; for one of the Arguments, which *Demosthenes* had to confute, was drawn from the Motions which *Artemisia* might make, if the *Athenians* should espouse the Interests of the *Rhodians*. But I leave this, to pass to something more close to the Point. *Vitruvius* tells us, that, after the Death of *Mausolus*, the *Rhodians*, disdaining, that *Caria* should be governed by a Woman, attempted to dethrone her (21). Their Design was defeated by a Stratagem of *Artemesia's*, which was presently followed by another, executed by herself, in Person, with so much Vigour and Success, that, in a very short time, she made herself Mistress of *Rhodes*. She caused two Statues in Brass to be erected there, as a Trophy of her Victory; one of them represented the City of *Rhodes*, the other *Artemisia* marking That City with a hot Iron. *Vitruvius* adds, that the *Rhodians* never durst remove This Trophy from it's Place, (for That was a thing forbidden by their Religion), but They encompassed it with a Building, which concealed it from public View. Does this look like the Conduct of a disconsolate Widow, entirely employed in sighing and groaning, and so lavish of Life, as to sacrifice it to sorrow in two Years Time? It is in vain to pretend, that *Vitruvius* speaks of the other *Artemisia*: I am sensible Mr *Chevreau* has thought so (22); but there are two incontestable Arguments to the contrary. For, I. the *Artemisa* of *Vitruvius* was the Wife of *Mausolus*; and, II. she possessed herself of a City, which was not built 'till the Time of the *Peloponnesian* War, when *Xerxes* and *Artemisia* were no longer in Being. Ἡ δὲ νῦν πόλις ἐκτίσθη κατὰ τὰ Πελοποννησιακὰ ὑπὸ τῶν αὐτῶν ἀρχιτεκτόνων, ὡς φασιν, ὑφ' οὗ καὶ ὁ Πειραιεὺς (23). *that now is, was built in the Time of the Peloponnesian War, they say, by the very same Architect, who built the Piræum.* It is not, therefore, without Reason, that *Vitruvius* makes both the *Artemisias* Commanders of Armies, and Women of Martial Spirit, ἄμφω δὲ στρατηγητίδας, γυναίας αὐροσέτρεις. What can we think of Authors, who give us such inconsistent Accounts of one, and the same, Queen? One Person, greatly obliged by her, might be sufficient to make the World believe, that her Grief for her Husband was the Cause of her Death. Writers would repeat it an hundred Times, from one to another, not only as a Rarity, but also, as an Example worthy of Imitation. The most singular Embellishments are given, sooner or later, to such sort of Traditions.

(21) Vitruv. de Architect. lib. 2. cap. 8.

(22) Chevreau, lib. 7. cap 3. p 34.

(23) Strabo, lib. 14. pag. 45.

(24) Tzetz. chil. 12. ver 665. hist. 455.

(a) *Φλιάσιος*, a Polion. Diog. Laert. de Vitis Philosoph. l. 2. in Menedemo, circa init. p. 155. Edit. Amst. 1692.

(b) Id. Ibid.

(c) Id. ibid. pag. 159. n. 137.

(d) Id. Ibid. pag. 153. n. 126.

(e) Id. ib. p. 8. 159. n. 137.

(f) Id. Ibid.

(g) Id. Ibid.

ASCLEPIADES, a Native of *Phlia* (a) in *Peloponnesus*, made a great Figure among the ancient Philosophers. He was a Disciple of *Stilpo* (b), and brought over *Menedemus* to the same School; *Menedemus*, I say, with whom he contracted such an intimate Friendship (c), that it might, perhaps, be compared to That of *Pylades*, and *Orestes* [A]. After having studied together under *Stilpo*, at *Megara*, they went to *Elis*, where they conferred with the Disciples of *Phædon* (d). They were both very poor, and forced to earn their Living with the Sweat of their Brows [B]; however, they found Time for their Studies, and became great Philosophers. *Menedemus* was younger than his Friend (e); but they had no Regard to the Difference of their Age, when they came to a Resolution of marrying. Their Design was to live and keep House together, even after quitting their State of Celibacy. To this end they judged it necessary to choose their Wives, with a Precaution most likely to secure their domestick Quiet, and believed this End would be answered in a Family, where there was a Mother and her Daughter, both marriageable. *Menedemus* married the Mother, and *Asclepiades* the Daughter (f). The latter being dead, *Menedemus* surrendered his Wife to his Friend, and married a rich Maid; but would have *Asclepiades's* Wife continue Mistress of the House. It was no hard Matter for him to find out a good Match; because he had the chief Authority in the Town, where he lived (g); I mean *Eretria*, the Place of his Birth. *Asclepiades* died there very old (h). He had lived very temperately, amidst the great Plenty of his Friend's Table (i), and bore the Misfortune

(h) Id ibid. n. 138.

(i) Συνήσας τῷ Μενεδήμῳ σφόδρα εὐτάκτως ἀκων ... He lived with Menedemus very fawningly in the midst of great Opulence.

---

(1) Diogen. Laert. lib. 2. n. 137.

[A] *His Friendship for Menedemus might be compared to That of Pylades and Orestes.* These are the Words of *Diogenes Laertius*: Φιλία τε ἦν μάλιστα (Μενεδήμῳ) ἐκ δήλον ἐκ τῆς πρὸς Ἀσκληπιάδον συμπνοίας, οὐδέν τι διαφερέσης Πυλάδου φιλοστοργίας (1). — *Menedemus was remarkable for his Friendship, as appeared from his Conjunction with Asclepiades, no way inferior to That of Pylades with Orestes.* After this, our Author says, that *Archepolis*, intending to make them a Present of a considerable Sum, his Generosity was of no service to them; for a laudable Disagreement happened between them, about the taking last, and, as they could not settle this Point, neither of them took any thing.

[B] *Both he, and his Friend, were forced to earn their Living with the Sweat of their Brows.* They hired themselves, as Labourers, to a Mason. *Asclepiades* was not so much ashamed of it, as *Menedemus*; he did not value who saw him, naked (2), carrying up Mortar to the Top of the House; but *Menedemus* hid himself, when he saw any Body pass by (3). *Athenæus*, who says nothing of this, tells another, yet more remarkable, Story. "The *Areopagites*," says he (4), called *Menedemus*, and *Asclepiades*, "two young Students in Philosophy, and very poor," "to be summoned before them, and demanded of "them, How come you to be so fat? you have no "Estate, you follow no Employment, but spend all "your

(2) It should be understood of no being clothed, but of being in a short Vestment in hot Weather.

(3) Diogen. Laert lib. 2. n. 137.

(4) Athen. lib. 4. c. 13, pag. 168.

ASCLEPIADES.

fortune of losing his Sight very patiently [C]. His Death did not extinguish the Friendship *Menedemus* had for him [D]. When I have said, he was a Disciple of *Stilpo*, it is needless to observe, that he flourished some little time after the Death of *Alexander*. He had a Son, who behaved himself so very ill, that *Menedemus* turned him out of Doors, without so much as speaking to him, which proved the Means of reclaiming the young Debauchee (k).

ASCLEPIADES, a Native of *Prusa* in *Bithynia*, was one of the most famous Physicians of Antiquity. He was cotemporary with *Mithridates*, as appears by his refusing to go to his Court, in spite of all the great Promises which were made him to procure This Visit (a). He could not be prevailed on any farther, than to send a Prescription (b). He was the Head of a new Sect (c); and found out the Method of making Wine serviceable in the Cure of Distempers (d). This Practice, and the use of cold Water, which he allowed his Patients (e), brought him into great Esteem (f). Having cured a Person who was going to be buried [A], he acquired an incredible Reputation; but the Wager, which he laid against Fortune, made him be cried up with yet

"*your Time in hearing the Philosophers?* Please to send for such a Miller, replied the two Scholars. He was sent for, accordingly; and, when he came, declared, that they came, every Night, into the Mill to grind, and had two Drachmas for their Labour. The Judges, admiring their Conduct, honoured them with a Present of Two hundred Drachmas. They would have been punished, if they had not declared the Means of their Subsistence.

[C] *He bore patiently the Misfortune of losing his Sight*] I make no question but these Words of *Cicero* relate to our *Asclepiades*: " Asclepiadem " ferunt non ignobilem, nec inexercitum Philoso- " phum, quum quidam quæreret, quid ei cœcitas at-

" tulisset, respondisse ut puero uno esset comita- " tior (5)." The Loss of my Eyes, *said our Philosopher*, procures me this Advantage, that I never go alone, I have always a Boy extraordinary in my Retinue.

[D] *His Death did not extinguish Menedemus's Friendship for him.*] Having been informed, that his Servants refused Admittance to one, who had been a Favourite of *Asclepiades*, he commanded them to let him in. *Know,* says he (6), *that though* Asclepiades *is in his Grave, he opens my Door for him*. This Favourite came afterwards to dine with *Menedemus*.

[A] *He cured a Person who was going to be buried.*] This is what *Pliny* says of it: Summa autem (fama est) *Asclepiadi Prusiensi* — *rulato è funere hominem & servato* (1). — Asclepiades, *the Prusian*, ——— *gained the highest Reputation, by ordering a Person to be carried back again, who was going to be buried, and curing him*. He observes, elsewhere, that this sort of Resurrection was necessary to establish the Reformation, which was then made, in the Practice of Physic; and that it is not to be imagined, that so great an Innovation was introduced, without some very considerable Motives. " Magna auctori- " tate, nec minore fama, cum occurrisset ignoto fu- " neri relato homine ab rogo atque servato, ne quis " levibus momentis, tantam conversionem suctam exi- " stimet (2)." *Celsus* mentions this admirable Cure only by the By. " In vicino sæpe quædam notæ " positæ non bonos sed imperitos medicos decipiunt; " quod Asclepiades sciens, funeri obvius, inclamavit, " eum vivere qui efferebatur (3). — *Some Symp- " toms are so alike, as to deceive the ignorant, tho' " not the judicious, Physician; it was from this Skill, " that* Asclepiades, *meeting with a Funeral, pronoun- " ced the Body to be alive.*" But *Apuleius* has enlarged on the Circumstances of it, without forgetting, that the Heirs were not very well pleased with *Asclepiades*, for maintaining, that the Man was not dead. " Asclepiades, *says he* (4), inter præcipuos " medicorum, si unum Hippocratem excipias, cæ- " teris princeps, primus etiam vino opitulari ægris " repperit: sed dando scilicet in tempore; cujus rei " observationem probe callebat: ut qui diligentissime " animadverteret venarum pulsus inconditos, vel præ- " claros. Is igitur, cum forte in civitatem sese reci- " peret, & rure suo suburbano rediret, aspexit in " pomeriis civitatis funus ingens locatum, plurimos ho- " mines ingenti multitudine qui exequias venerant cir- " cumstare, omnes tristissimos & obsoletissimos vestitu. " Propius accessit, ut etiam incognosceret, more " ingenii humani, quisnam esset; quoniam percon- " tanti nemo responderat. At vero ipse aliquid in " illo ex arte deprehenderat. Certe quidem jacenti " homini ac prope depositio Fatum abstulit. Jam " miseri illius membra omnia aromatis perspersa, " jam os ipsius unguine odoro delibutum, jam jam " pollinctum, jam cœnæ paratum, contemplatus eum " diligentissime quibusdam signis animadvertit, etiam " atque etiam pertractavit corpus hominis: & inve- " nit in illo vitam latentem. Confestim exclama- " vit, vivere hominem, procul ergo faces abigerent, " procul ignes amolirentur; rogum demolirentur, " cœnam feralem à tumulo ad mensam referrent.

" Murmur interea exortum, partim medico creden- " dam dicere; partim etiam irridere medicinam. Po- " stremo propinquis etiam hominibus invitis, quod " ne jam ipsi hæreditatem habebant, an quod ad- " huc illi fidem non habebant, ægre tamen ac dif- " ficulter Asclepiades impetravit brevem mortuo " dilationem. Atque ita vespillonum manibus " extortum, velut ab Inferis, postliminio domum " reculit, confestimque spiritum recreavit: confe- " stimque animam in corporis latibulis delitescen- " tem quibusdam medicamentis provocavit. — " Asclepiades, *the Prince of Physicians,* next to Hip- " pocrates, *was the first, who used Wine as a Medi- " cine. But he took care to give it on proper Occasions, " which he very well understood, from his diligent " Attendance to the Indications of the Pulse. As he " happened one Day to return from his Country House " to the City, he saw in the out-skirts a very large " Funeral, with a great Multitude of People surround- " ing the Body, all very sorrowful, and in mourning " Habits. He drew near out of Curiosity, according " to Custom, to learn whose it was, those he had in- " quired of not having satisfied him. His Skill found " an opportunity of making a great Discovery. With- " out doubt he saved the Life of a Man, supposed to be " Dead, and whose funeral Rites were almost all per- " formed. The poor Wretch was already bestrewed " with Spices, his Face perfumed, his Body anointed, " and the Funeral Entertainment prepared; when " Asclepiades, *observing him attentively, and carefully " examining the Body, found by his Art some Signs of " Life in it. He immediately cried out, that the Body " was alive, that they might throw away their Torches, " extinguish the Fire, demolish the Funeral Pile, and " remove their Feast from the Tomb to the Table. The " Company murmured; some were for believing in the " Doctor, others ridiculed the Profession. At last, " though the Heirs opposed it, either because they were " in Possession of the Inheritance, or had no Faith " in the Physician, with great difficulty* Asclepiades " *obtained a short Reprieve for the dead Man. And " so having rescued him from the Undertaker's Hand, " he had him brought Home again, as it were from " the infernal Regions, and immediately, by the Vir- " tue of his Medicines, revived his Spirits, and re- " covered the scattered Remains of Life.*" The Story of the Woman, that was twice carried to be buried, will not be amiss in this Place. She was brought to Life, without the Assistance of Medicine; but her Husband was not overjoyed at it. The Story is this. " A Woman in a Village of *Poitou* had a severe " Illness, at the end of which she fell into so deep

ASCLEPIADES.

yet greater admiration [B]. He engaged to renounce the Title of Physician, if ever he should be sick, and won the Wager; for he died by a Fall, at a very great Age. It was at *Rome* he became so famous. He came thither to teach Rhetoric (g); but, not finding That Employ profitable enough, he applied himself to the Practice of Physic; and, not being acquainted with the Remedies then in use, he took occasion to condemn them, and invent new ones. He contrived easy Methods, and such as any one might use without the Help of a Physician. This made them very acceptable; and all the World ran to him, as to one sent from Heaven [C]. One Thing, which favoured his gaining so great a Reputation, was the foolish Credulity of That Age as to the Magic Virtue of certain Plants; for it being easy to demonstrate, that most of those Virtues were chimerical, it was no hard Matter for *Asclepiades* to destroy all the Credit of the ancient Prescriptions [D]. He held, that the Soul was not distinct from Matter (h). He composed several Books, which are all lost. *Pliny*, *Celsus*, and *Galen* have quoted some of them. He had also many famous Disciples (i). *Pliny's* Niceness seems to be carried too far; he could not bear, that a Man, who had only studied Physic for Profit, should be allowed to give Rules of such

(g) Id. Ibid.

(h) See Tertullian, in his Book de Animâ, cap. 15.

(i) See their Names in the 46th Letter of Reinesius to Rupertus, pag. 395.

consequence

" deep a Lethargy, that her Husband, and those a-
" bout her, believed her dead. They wrapped her
" up only in Linnen, according to the Custom of
" poor People in That Country, and had her carried
" out to be buried. As they were going to Church,
" one of her Bearers went so close to a Bush, that
" the Thorns pricked her, and roused her from her
" Lethargy. Fourteen Years after, she was dead a-
" gain, at least supposed so. As they were carrying
" her to the Grave, and coming near the old
" Place, the Husband cried out, two or three times:
" *Pray keep a little farther off the Bush* (5)."

(5) Montaigne, p. 117, 118. of the first Dutch Edition.

[B] *The Wager, which he laid against Fortune, made him be cried up with yet greater Admiration.*] I do not believe, that the most pretending Quacks, of our Days, dare lay any such Wager, especially if they were obliged to deposit a Sum of Money. However, I am persuaded, that the Reader will not be displeased to find *Pliny's* Text here: " Summa autem
" Asclepiadi Prusiensi (fama est) ———— maxime
" spontsione factâ cum fortunâ, ne medicus credere-
" tur, si unquam invalidus ullo modo fuisset ipse:
" & victor, supremâ in senectâ lapsu scalarum ex-
" animatus est (6). ———— Asclepiades, *the Prusian,*

(6) Plinius, lib. 7. c. 37. pag. 58, 59.

" *gained the highest Reputation,* ———— *chiefly by*
" *staking his Credit, as a Physician, against his ever*
" *being sick himself: he carried his Point, and died,*
" *in extream old Age, by a Fall down Stairs.*" It was a surprizing Temerity in Our Physician; but the good Fortune, in not being belied by the Event, appears, to me, yet more extraordinary. I observe, that, in some things, he was a meer Quack. He administred Wine in some Distempers, and boasted so much of his Remedy, that he said, the Power of the Gods was hardly equal to That of Wine. *Asclepiades utilitatem vini aquari vix Deorum potentiâ pronunciavit* (7).

(7) Id. lib. 23. cap. 1. pag. 251.

[C] *All the World ran to him, as to one sent from Heaven.*] We may conceive, from the Words of *Pliny*, an Idea of the Ascendant some Physicians have, even in our Days. " Torrenti ac meditatâ quotidie
" oratione blandiens, omnia *(remedia)* abdicavit: to-
" tamque medicinam ad causam revocando, conje-
" cturæ fecit, quinque res maxime communium auxi-
" liorum professus abstinentiam cibi, alias vini, fri-
" cationem corporis, ambulationes, gestationes: quæ
" cum unusquisque semetipsum sibi, præstare posse
" intelligeret, faventibus cunctis ut essent vera quæ
" facillima erant, universum prope humanum genus
" circumegit in se, non alio modo, quam si cœlo
" emissus advenisset (8). ———— *Soothing the People*

(8) Id. lib. 26. cap. 3. pag. 444.

" *every Day with a fluent and premeditated Oration,*
" *he banished all Medicines: and, reducing the whole*
" *Art of Physic to the Test of Reason, he proved it*
" *to be but conjectural. Five Things, of most common*
" *Benefit, he held to, Abstinence from Meat, at other*
" *Times from Wine, the use of the Flesh-Brush, the*
" *Exercise of Walking, and of Riding: Which, as*
" *every one believed he could prescribe for himself such*
" *Remedies as these, and as it is natural to wish*
" *those Things true that are most easy, made all Peo-*
" *ple flock to him, as to one sent from Heaven.*"

[D] *Most of the Magic Virtues of Plants being chimerical, it was easy for* Asclepiades *to destroy the Credit of ancient Prescriptions.*] It is the Nature of Man to run into Extremes. Shew him but some Truths, and he shall believe all the Falsities you think proper to couch under them. Undeceive him but

of some Falsities, by evident Demonstration, and he shall question the Truth of every Thing. Thus, by exploding the Impertinence of the Remedies called Magical, *Asclepiades* was enabled to overthrow even those Things, which might be better grounded. *Pliny* very naturally describes this Inclination for Extremes, so remarkable in Human Nature. " Super omnia,
" *says he* (9), adjuvere eum (Asclepiadem) Magicæ
" vanitates, in tantum evectæ, ut abrogare herbis
" fidem cunctis possent. Æthiopide herbâ amnes ac
" stagna siccari conjectâ, tactu clausa omnia aperiri.
" Achæmenide conjectâ in aciem hostium, trepidare
" agmina, ac tergâ vertere. Latacen dari solitam â
" Persarum rege legatis, ut quocunque venissent om-
" nium rerum copiâ abundarent, ac multa similia.
" Ubinam istæ fuere, cùm Cimbri Teutoniqúe terri-
" bili Marte ululárent, ut clausa Lucullus tot reges
" Magorum paucis legionibus sterneret? Curve Ro-
" mani duces primam semper in bellis commerciorum
" habuere curam? Cur herclè Cæsaris miles ad Pharsa-
" liam famem sensit, si abundantia omnis contingere
" unius herbæ felicitate poterat? Non satius fuit Æ-
" milianum Scipionem Carthaginis portas herbâ pate-
" facere, quam machinis claustra per tot annos qua-
" tere? Siccentur hodie Æthiopide Pontiæ paludes,
" tantumque agri suburbanæ reddatur Italiæ. Nam
" quæ apud eundem Democritum invenitur compo-
" sitio medicamenti, quo pulchri bonique & fortu-
" nati gignantur liberi, cui unquam Perfarum regi
" tales datæ? Mirum esset profectò, hucusque pro-
" vectam credulitatem antiquorum, saluberrimis or-
" tam initiis, si in ullâ re modum humana ingenia
" novissent, atque non hanc ipsam medicinam ab As-
" clepiade repertam, suo loco probaturi essemus eve-
" ctam ultra Magos etiam. Sed hæc est omni in re
" animorum conditio, ut à necessariis orsa primò,
" cuncta pervenerint ad nimium. — — — — — — *The*

(9) Id. Ibid. cap. 4. pag. 446.

" *greatest Assistance,* Asclepiades *received, was from*
" *the Magical Superstitions, which were carried to*
" *such an Height, as made it easy to abolish all Sort of*
" *Faith in Plants. That the Æthiopian Plant would*
" *dry up Lakes and Rivers, if thrown into them, and*
" *force open Doors, or the strongest Securities, by the*
" *Touch of it. That the Achæmenian Plant, by being*
" *cast at the Enemy, would make their Troops tremble,*
" *and turn their Backs. That the Plant, called Latace,*
" *used to be given by the Persian King to his Em-*
" *bassadors, that they might always be sure of Plenty,*
" *wheresoever they went: and many more of this Na-*
" *ture. But where were these Virtues, when the Cim-*
" *bri, and Teutoni, thundered at their Gates, and*
" *when Lucullus, with a few Forces, overthrew so many*
" *Kings of the Magi? Or why were the Romans, in*
" *their Wars, so careful, in the first Place, to secure*
" *their Supplies? How came Cæsar's Soldiers to fall*
" *short of Provisions at Pharsalia, if one Plant only*
" *could make plenty? Would Scipio Æmilianus have*
" *lain, so many Years, battering the Walls of Carthage,*
" *with his Engines, if he could have forced open the*
" *Gates with a Plant? Let the Æthiopian Herb*
" *dry up the Pontine Lake at this Day, and restore to*
" *Italy so great a Tract of lost Land. Did ever That*
" *Composition of Medicine, reported by the same Author*
" Democritus, *to have been so serviceable towards beget-*
" *ting handsome, dutiful, and fortunate Children, pro-*
" *duce any such Effect in any one of the Persian Kings?*
" *It would be wonderful indeed, that the Credulity of*
" *the Ancients, which at first had some reasonable*

VOL. I.   6 R   " *Foundation,*

ASCLEPIADES.

consequence to Mankind [E]. *Suidas*, who has confounded our Physician with one *Asclepiades*, a Grammarian of *Myrlea*, has been reproved for it by Mr *Moreri* agreeably to the Observations of *Vossius*. Therefore I shall mention it no farther, but content myself with pointing out the Causes of it. I shall only remark the Mistakes of some other Authors [F]. Those of Mr *Moreri* are not very considerable

---

[10] Id. lib. 29. cap. 1.

[11] Id. lib. cap. 3. pag. 445.

[12] Jonsius de Script. Philosoph. pag. 167.

[13] Pineo, in Stephan. Byzant. pag. 470, n. 15, & pag. 757.

[14] Athen. lib. 10. 456.

[15] Casaub. in Athen. pag. 769.

"Foundation, should be stretched to such a Pitch, if human Nature knew how to observe a Medium in any thing ; or, if this very Reformation in Physic, introduced by Asclepiades, had not been carried, as we shall shew in it's proper place, to a greater height of Extravagance, than even That of the Magi. But such is the Imperfection of our Minds, that, though we set out reasonably, yet we carry every thing to an Extreme." Father *Hardouin* repeats this in the Place, where *Pliny* describes the great Power, which certain Physicians had gained over the People, at the same time that they mutually condemned one another's Practice. —— "Hinc illæ, says he [10], circa ægros miseræ sententiarum concertationes, nullo idem censente ne videatur accessio alterius. Hinc illa infelicis Monumenti inscriptio, turba se medicorum periisse. Mutatur jam quotidie toties interpolia, & ingeniorum Græciæ flatu impellimur. Palamque est, ut quisque inter istos loquendo polleat, imperatorem illico vitæ nostræ necisque fieri. —— Hence arise these wretched Wranglings of Physicians about their Patients, no one caring to come into the Sentiments of another, for fear it should look like giving him the Preference. Hence That unlucky Epitaph, The Distemper he died of was the Number of his Doctors. *The Art is always changing, by such daily Innovations, and the Wits of Greece turn us which Way they will. And we see, that every one of them, who has a Talent for talking, presently assumes over us the Power of Life and Death.*"

[E] *Pliny—could not bear, that such a Man should be allowed to give Rules of such Consequence to Mankind.*] His Words are remarkable. "Id solum possumus indignari, unum hominem è levissimâ gente, sine opibus ullis orsum, vectigalis sui causâ, repente leges salutis humano generi dedisse, quas tamen postea abrogavere multi [11]. —— *This one Thing is enough to raise our Indignation, that one of so very mean an Extraction, and of no Fortunes, should, for his own Profit only, so suddenly take upon him to give Rules of Health to Mankind, which, by the Way, were afterwards exploded by several of his Successors.*"

[F] *The Mistakes of some other Authors, concerning Asclepiades, &c.*] *Meursius* has been reprimanded for taking *Asclepiades* of *Myrlea*, and *Asclepiades* of *Nicæa*, for two different Persons. "Malè Meursius hunc Myrlæanum & Nicenum tanquam duos distinctos recenset [12]. — *Meursius has erroneously distinguished this Asclepiades the Myrlæan, and Nicæan, into two different Persons.*" *Jonsius* affirms it to be a Mistake, and that the same *Asclepiades*, who was born at *Myrlea*, and whose Family was of *Nicæa*, is indifferently sirnamed *Myrlæanus*, and *Nicæus*. *Pinedo* fell into the same Error with *Meursius* [13]. In the List of Authors, quoted by *Athenæus*, *Asclepiades* of *Myrlea* is understood to be meant in these Words of the tenth Book: Ἀσκληπιάδης ἐν τοῖς τραγῳδουμένοις [14]. *Dalechamp* has translated them, *Asclepiades libro de iis quorum nomine editæ sunt tragædiæ.* —— Asclepiades, in his Book of those, in whose Names have been published Tragedies. *Casaubon* censures him for This, and makes it appear, that the Title of That Work was not of the Masculine Gender τραγῳδούμενοι, but of the Neuter Gender τραγῳδούμενα, and that *Plutarch* also has quoted it so [15]. He does not say where the Quotation is to be found. But, to supply This Defect, I shall observe, that it is in the Life of *Isocrates*, as we shall see presently. He might have added, that the same Work of *Asclepiades* is quoted in the Neuter Gender, by *Stephanus Byzantinus*, and by *Photius*, as we shall make appear by and by. This Critic understands That Work of *Asclepiades* to have treated of the great Actions, which served the Tragic Poets for their Subject-matter. I am altogether of the same Opinion, and take *Dalechamp* to be mistaken. The *Latin* Translator of *Plutarch* has also misunderstood the Title of That Book ; for these Words of *Plutarch*, Ἀσκληπιάδης ὁ τὰ τραγῳδούμενα συγγράψας,

he has thus rendred, *Asclepiades tragœdiæ scriptor* [16]. —— Asclepiades, *a Writer of Tragedy*. This shews clearly enough, without consulting exactly what follows [17] in the Translation, that he took *Asclepiades* for a Tragic Poet. *Andrew Schot* makes the same Slip in his Translation of *Photius*. *Photius* speaks thus. Ἀσκληπιάδης δὲ τὰ τραγῳδούμενα συγγράψατο [18]. *i. e.* according to *Andrew Schotus*, *Asclepiades, qui Tragœdias scripsit.* —— Asclepiades, *who wrote Tragedies*. But it is all a Mistake ; the *Asclepiades*, there mentioned, is not represented to us as such an Author. Observe, by the way, that he was the Disciple of *Isocrates*, from whence you may judge of the time, in which he lived. *Pinedo* understood the Sense of the Word τραγῳδούμενα better than the Translator of *Plutarch*, and has rendred Ἀσκληπιάδης ὁ τὰ τραγῳδούμενα γράψας ἐν ἓξ βιβλίοις [19] ; *Asclepiades qui de rebus in Tragædia decantatis sex libros scripsit*. —— Asclepiades, *who wrote six Books of those Things, which have been made the Subject of Tragedies*. These Greek Words are taken from *Stephanus Byzantinus*, where he informs us, that the *Asclepiades*, who composed those six Books, was of *Tragilos*, a City of *Thracia*. *Casaubon* should have censured *Dalechamp*, for imagining, that *Athenæus* means *Asclepiades* of *Myrlea*, in the Passage above cited. *Gesner* has fallen into the same Error [20]. *Stephanus Byzantinus* would have justified such a Censure. You will find in *Pinedo* two grand Mistakes : I. He says, that *Asclepiades* of *Myrlea*, a Disciple of *Apollonius*, was a Grammarian, who taught at *Rome*, under *Pompey* the Great, and had lived, in his Youth, at *Alexandria*, under *Ptolemy* IV. II. He proposes it as a Question, whether he is the same *Asclepiades*, who taught Grammar in *Turditania*, a Province of *Spain* [21]. On the first Head, I must observe to him, that a Man, who had lived under *Ptolemy* IV, and had taught at *Rome*, in *Pompey's* Time, would have been a Prodigy ; for between the last Year of That *Ptolemy*, and the Death of *Mithridates*, who was vanquished by *Pompey*, there are no less than an Hundred and forty Years. On the second, I may only observe, that *Strabo* plainly says, that *Asclepiades*, of *Myrlea*, taught Grammar in *Turditania* [22]. The Sieur *Pinedo* had observed it himself, in another Place [23]. How comes he then to make a Query of it ?

Let us examine, in two Words, an Observation of Father *Hardouin*. He says, that *Asclepiades*, of *Prusa*, was a Friend of *Cicero*, and proves it from a Passage of the first Book *De Oratore*. He quotes only a little part of it [24] ; but this is the whole Passage. "Neque verò Asclepiades is, quo nos medico amicoque usi sumus, tum quum eloquentiâ vincebat cæteros medicos, in eo ipso quod ornatè dicebat, Medicinæ facultate utebatur, non eloquentiâ [25]. Nor did Asclepiades, *who was both my Friend and Physician, though he excelled all other Physicians in the Art of Speaking, make no use of his Eloquence, but only of his Physic.*" We ought to observe, that it is not *Cicero*, who speaks, but the Orator *Crassus* : *Asclepiades* therefore was the Friend and Physician of *Crassus*, and not of *Cicero*. Besides, *Cicero* makes *Crassus* speak thus in the Year of *Rome* 662 [26], and mentions *Asclepiades* as then dead. This furnishes us with an Objection against *Pliny*, for saying, that *Asclepiades*, gaining but little by the Profession of Eloquence, turned Physician in the Time of *Pompey* [27]. It is certain, that, in 662, *Pompey* was but a young Lad. See the following Remark, Number IV.

Jonsius supposes, that there were two *Asclepiades's* of *Myrlea* ; that the first was a Disciple of *Apollonius*, the Grammarian, and Author of a Book entituled φιλοσόφων βιβλίων διορθωτικά, *Philosophorum librorum emendationes* [28]. --- *Emendations of the Books of the Philosophers* : And that the second wrote some Books concerning Grammar and Grammarians [29]. I cannot conceive upon what he can found this Distinction. The best Thing he can say for it is, that *Asclepiades*, of *Myrlea*, refuted, in his Grammar, a Sentiment

[16] Plut. in Vita Isocrat. pag. 837. C.

[17] *Which confirms, that he took Tragœdiæ Scriptor, not for one who treats of Tragedy, but for a Writer of Tragedies.*

[18] Photii Biblioth. Cod. 260, pag. 1456.

[19] Steph. Byzant. verbo τράγιλος.

[20] Gesner in Biblioth. fol. 97.

[21] Pineda, in Steph. Byzant. pag. 757.

[22] Strabo, lib. 3. pag. 108.

[23] Pineda, in Steph. Byzant. pag. 479.

[24] Eloquens Medicus *dicitur Cicerone*, lib. 1. de Orat. pag. 283. qui se eo modo dico & amico usum esse gloriatur. *Harduinus* in Indice Auctor. Plinii, pag. 99.

[25] Cicero, de Orat. fol. 61. C.

[26] See Fabricius, in Vita Ciceronis, ad Ann. urbis 662.

[27] Plin. lib. 26, c. 3.

[28] Jonsius, de Script. Hist. Philos. pag. 167.

[29] Id. ib. pag. 205.

Sentiment

siderable [G]. There was another *Asclepiades*, a famous Physician, under the Emperor *Adrian* [H].

Sentiment of *Dionysius* of *Thrace*. " In isto opere " Dionysii Thracis de partibus Grammaticæ senten- " tiam refellit, teste Sexto Empirico (30). —— In " That Work, he confutes an Opinion of Dionysius, " the Thracian, concerning the Parts of Grammar, " as Sextus Empiricus witnesses." This *Dionysius*, according to *Suidas*, taught at *Rome* in *Pompey's* Time, and had been a Disciple of *Aristarchus*. It must therefore follow, you will say, that the *Asclepiades*, who refuted him, was not He, who was a Disciple of *Apollonius*. I grant the Consequence; but I suspect some small Mistake in *Suidas*. It seems to me, that a Disciple of *Aristarchus* (31) would have been too old to teach in the Time of *Pompey* (32). I am therefore of Opinion, that *Dionysius* of *Thrace*, the Disciple of *Aristarchus*, did not live till *Pompey's* Time. In which case it would be possible, that *Asclepiades*, a Disciple of *Apollonius*, might confute him; for this *Apollonius*, having been Keeper of the *Alexandrian* Library, after *Eratosthenes* (33), who died in the Beginning of the CXLVIth Olympiad (34), might very well be cotemporary with *Aristarchus*, and have Disciples at that time cotemporary with those of *Aristarchus*. Consequently there is no necessity for finding out another *Asclepiades*, the Confuter of *Dionysius* of *Thrace*, younger than *Asclepiades*, the Disciple of *Apollonius*. I cannot tell why *Vossius* acquiesces so readily with *Suidas's* joining the Character of a Disciple of *Aristarchus* with That of Professor at *Rome* in *Pompey's* Time (35). He is justly censured for saying, that *Asclepiades*, of *Alexandria*, wrote a Book about the People of *Attica*, and quoting the Scholiast of *Aristophanes* to prove it. *Asclepiades Alexandrinus* * τὺς κατὰ δῆμον ἄρχοντας consignavit, ut autor Scholiastes Aristophanis in nubes (36). *Jonsius* shews him, that the Scholiast says no more, than that *Asclepiades* called the Demarchs τοὺς κατὰ τὸν δῆμον ἄρχοντας (37).

[G] *Those of Mr* Moreri *are not very considerable*] I. The Ancients do not ascribe the History of *Alexander* the Great, quoted by *Arian*, to *Asclepiades* of *Myrlea*, as he affirms. II. His saying, *Strabo* adds, *that* Asclepiades *of* Myrlea *had taught Grammar in* Spain, is making *Strabo* father the other Particulars, which *Moreri* had mentioned before. But this is groundless. III. He questions, without any manner of Reason, whether the Relation to *Spain* concerns another *Asclepiades*; for *Strabo* affirms it expresly of *Asclepiades* of *Myrlea*. IV. He ought not to have asserted so positively, that *Mithridates* was at War *with the* Romans, when he endeavoured to get *Asclepiades* the Physician to his Court; for we have seen, above (38), that *Cicero* speaks of This Physician as of one, who was not alive in the Year of *Rome* 662. at which time *Mithridates*, strictly speaking, had not made War with the People of *Rome*. This shews, that Mr *Moreri* might well be mistaken, in affirming, that *Asclepiades was in esteem at Rome in the Time of Pompey the Great* —— *that is to say, when That great Man was at the Head of the Republick*. Does he not place the Birth of This *Pompey* on the last Day of *September*, of the Year of *Rome* 648? How will he reconcile this with the Passage in *Cicero*, where *Asclepiades* is mentioned? I know very well, he may shelter himself under the Authority of *Pliny*, and that *Jonsius* may be brought in for a Second. But how comes *Pliny* to be of more Credit than *Cicero*? And can he be sure, that *Jonsius* is not mistaken? " Asclepiades Medicus quidam *bebold a quidam very ill employed: This* Asclepiades *is too famous to deserve so slighting an Epithet* (39). " Prusiacus " in Bithynia Philophysicus cognomine sub Pompeio " M. vixit teste Strabone lib. 12. (40). —— *Asclepiades*, a certain Physician of *Prusa*, in *Bithynia*, *firnamed* Philophysicus *(from his Love of Philosophy), lived under* Pompey *the Great, as* Strabo *testifies in Book* 12." But I find nothing more in the twelfth Book of *Strabo*, than that *Asclepiades*, of *Prusa*, was a Physician (41). Father *Hardouin* has quoted *Strabo* (42), to prove this Point as well as *Jonsius*. V. The *Asclepiades*, mentioned by *Plutarch* in the Life of *Isocrates*, was not a *Tragic Poet* (43), as Mr *Moreri* affirms.

[H] *There was another* ASCLEPIADES, *a famous Physician, under the Emperor* Adrian.] He was of the same City as the former (44), and flourished under *Trajan*, *Adrian*, and *Antoninus*: he was made free by one *Calpurnius*, and obtained the Rights of a *Roman* Citizen, and several other Privileges. We learn all this from an Inscription: See the Letters of *Reinesius* (45). He wrote several Books about the Compositions of Medicines, both Internal, and External (46).

ASPASIA of *Miletus*, Mistress to *Pericles*. We shall give her History in the Remark [M] of the Article PERICLES.

ASPASIA of *Phocea*, Mistress to *Cyrus* the younger. We shall give her History in the Remark [C] of the Article of That Prince.

ASTYANAX, the only Son of *Hector* and *Andromache* [A], gave the *Greeks* Uneasiness in the midst of their Victories, tho' he was then but an Infant. Being hindred, by contrary Winds, from returning home after the Destruction of *Troy*, *Calchas* declared, they ought to throw *Astyanax* headlong from the Top of the Walls, because, if he lived to Man's Estate, he would not fail to revenge the Death of his Father, and even exceed him in Valour. Whereupon *Ulysses* went to search for him; and having found him, notwithstanding all the care his Mother took to hide him, he executed the Sentence *Calchas* had pronounced (a). Others say, that *Menelaus* was the Executioner (b). Others attribute his Death to *Pyrrhus* alone, without intimating, that the *Greeks*, or *Calchas*, had judged it necessary (c). However it be, the Poets, and Writers of Romances, found means to restore him to Life again, or rather to make him escape out of the Hands of the *Greeks* [B].

[A] *He was the only Son of* Hector *and* Andromache.] *Homer* affirms This expresly; for, without question, they, who translate Ἐξαίρετόν ἀγαπητὸν the Scholiast understands it. The Grief of *Andromache*, in the Twenty second Book of the *Iliad*, plainly shews, that she had only This Son. *Hector* gave him the Name of *Scamandrius*, and the *Trojans* called him *Astyanax*, because *Hector* was the sole Defence of the City (2).

[B] *The Poets, and Writers of Romances, found means to restore him to life again, or rather to make him escape out of the Hands of the* Greeks.] They have said, that the same Son of *Hector*, whose Name was *Astyanax*, or *Scamander*, was called, also, *Francion*, and that from him the Kings of *France* are derived (3). The *Manetho* of *Annius* of *Viterbo* makes *Francus*, the Son of *Hector*, King of the *Celtæ*, that is, of the *Gauls*. The Forger of That Piece, in his Notes, cites *Vincent* of *Beauvais*, who says, that This *Francus*, retiring among the *Gauls*, after the Destruction of *Troy*, became so great a Favourite of the King, that He married his Daughter, and succeeded him in his Crown. I do not find, In *Manerbo* (4), what *Du Pleix* quotes from him, viz. that *Francus* succeeded *Rhemus*, King of the *Gauls*, whose Daughter he

ATHENAGORAS.

he had married (5). Neither do I find it in the Commentator upon *Manetho*. *Du Pleix* adds, that *Trithemius*, alledging at his *Authority*, Hunnibaud, *who lived under Clovis I. and who names, for his Authors, Dorac, and* Wasthald, two Scythian *Historians*, says, that *Hector* had two Sons, one of which, called *Astyanax*, or Scamander, perished at the taking of Troy, the other, named Laodamas (6), *or Francion, escaped out of the Enemies Hands, and fled, with a great Number of Trojans, into Pæonia, which was afterwards called Pannonia; and that, being kindly received by the King of the Pæonians, he settled in that Country,* on the Frontiers of *Scythia*, and there built the City of *Sicambria*, where he, and his Posterity, reigned, 'till the Days of King *Antenor*, who was killed by the *Goths*, Four hundred and twenty Years before CHRIST. The Violences of the *Goths* obliged the *Trojans*, or *Sicambrians*, to retire into *Germany*, where they divided themselves into two Branches: one of which, afterwards, founded the *French* Monarchy among the *Gauls*; the other remained in *Germany*, and there founded *Franconia*, or *Eastern France*. What Chimæras are these! Mr *Moreri*, not considering, that the Authors of these Legends are charged with a sufficient Number of Falsities, fathers upon them others, which they never advanced. He ascribes to *the false* Manetho, *and to other Authors of that Stamp,* the making Francion, *or* Francis (7), *the Son of* Hector, *the first King of the* Gauls. But they are so far from saying This, that they affirm, that the King of the *Gauls* gave him his Daughter. Besides, how thoughtless is it to describe *Andromache* only as the Mother of his *Francion,* and never once to mention her undoubted Son *Astyanax!* These are two Faults in *Moreri*; to which we shall add a third. He says, that *Astyanax* was thrown down, headlong, from the Walls, by order of *Ulysses*, and quotes for it *Virgil*'s *Æneid*. Now this Poet has said nothing like it in all his Works.

ATHENAGORAS, an *Athenian* Philosopher, flourished after the middle of the IId Century: He was a learned Man, and very zealous for Christianity. All Which appeared from the Apology, which he addressed to the Emperors *Marcus Aurelius Antoninus*, and *Lucius Aurelius Commodus*. This happened, according to *Baronius* (a), in the Year 179; or, according to Mr *Dodwell* (b), in the Year 168. It is no easy matter to give a Satisfactory Proof, that the last Opinion is more probable, than the first [A]. I find all agree, that *Athenagoras* was deputed by the Christians to the Imperial

[A] *He presented —— his Apology in the Year 179, —— or in 168. —— It is not easy to prove, that the last Opinion is more probable, than the first.*] Many Reasons are alledged on both sides. These are Mr *Dodwell*'s (1). The Apology of *Athenagoras* is addressed to two Emperors, to whom the Author gives the Titles of *Armeniacus, Sarmaticus, & quod maximum est, Philosophis.* This is applicable to *Marcus Aurelius*, and to his Brother *Lucius Aurelius*, but not to his Son *Lucius Aurelius.* He was never called Philosopher; And the second Apology of *Justin* shews That Title to have been common to *Lucius Aurelius*, and to his Brother, *Marcus Aurelius.* Hunc Titulum cum Marco Lucium verum habuisse communem constat è secundâ Apologiâ *Justini* (2). Father *Pagi*, Dissertat. Hypat. pag. 216. makes use of the same Argument, and quotes *Eusebius*, lib. 4. cap. 12. Now this *Lucius Aurelius* died towards the end of the Year 169. So that the Apology must have been presented before That time. I wave the particular Reasons, which induced Mr *D.dwell* to make choice of the Year 168 for the *Epocha of* This Work. It is objected against him, that the Complement of *Sarmaticus* cannot belong to *Lucius Aurelius*, who died before the *Sarmatæ* were attacked; but he answers, that this might be a Slip of the Transcriber, instead of That of *Paribicus*, which was given to the two Brothers, together with That of *Armeniacus*, after the War of *Armenia* (3). He adds, that the profound Peace, on which *Athenagoras* congratulates the Emperors (4), cannot agree with the time of *Marcus Aurelius*, and his Son reigning together. He makes no answer to the chief Objection: and yet something may be said to it, as will appear presently. We must not forget his Observation, that *Athenagoras* intimates, that his Apology was made in the same Olympiad, that *Peregrinus* burnt himself (5). This Action of *Peregrinus*, according to Messieurs *Dodwell*, and *de Tillemont* (6), belongs to the Year 165; but *Scaliger* places it in the Year 166 (7). He grounds his Notions on this, that *Peregrinus* exhibited this Spectacle during the Celebration of the Olympic Games. He is of opinion, that *Athenagoras*'s Work was presented to the Emperors in the same Olympiad: His Reason is, because *Peregrinus* threw himself into the Fire three Years before the Death of *Lucius Verus*, one of Those Emperors. This Argument is preferable to Mr *Dodwell*'s, grounded on the Words of *Athenagoras*; for they note only the Place, and not the Time, of this Man's burning himself. Περὶ τὴν Ὀλυμπίαν (8); *Near the City* Olympia. See Mr *de Tillemont* (9). The Proof, drawn from the profound Peace of the Empire, is of such a Nature, that it serves both Parties: Cardinal *Baronius* makes use of it, to shew, that the Apology could not have been presented under the Reign of *Marcus Aurelius*'s Brother, nor in any other Time, but in 179 (10). Mr *de Tillemont* does not rightly understand This Cardinal's Argument, since he represents him as inferring, *that This Apology must have been written in the Year* [176, *or*] 177, *because it intimates, that the Empire was then in profound Peace* (11).

These are the principal Reasons of Those, who pretend, that the Apology of *Athenagoras* was not presented before the Year 177, which was That of the Promotion of *Commodus*, the Son of *Marcus Aurelius*, to the Dignity of *Augustus* (12). They maintain, that He, who is associated with *Marcus Aurelius*, in the Inscription of the Apology, was the Son, and not the Brother of That Emperor; and prove it from the Words, which compare these two Princes to God the Father, and God the Son. " Ipsa quidem oratio longè validius nobis præbet argumen-" tum. *Vos quidem*, subjicit Vir disertus, *in summa* " *Imperii Majestate adeo conjunctis animis orbem re-* " *gitis*; ut inde Cœlestii etiam Regni contemplationem " *animo quis complecti queat. Ut Vobis enim Patri* " *& filio in potestate sunt omnia, regno in Vis di-* " *vinitus collocato, (Regis enim Anima,* inquis Spiri- " tus Propheticus, in manu Dei *est) sic uni Deo &* " *Filio ejus, hoc est Verbo, subjecta sunt omnia.* Nullus " hic est cavillationibus locus: Imperatores non tan- " tum alloquitur, sed etiam comparationem instituit " duos inter terrenos Reges, quibus omnia humani- " tus loquendo parebant, ac summum Cœli & Terræ " Dominum, qui simul cum suo Unigenito Imperii " Orbis universi habenas moderatur (13). —— The pag. " Apology itself furnishes us with a much stronger " Argument. Your Imperial Majesties, *says the learn-* " *ed Author*, govern the World with such perfect " Harmony, as in some sort resembles That of the Co- " lestial Government. For, as the supream Power on " Earth is, by the Grant of Heaven, (*the Life of* " *Kings,* as the Prophet says, *being in the Hand* " *of God,*) committed to your Majesties, Father, " and Son; so the supream Power of the Universe " is lodged in one God, the Father, and his Son, the " Word. Here *is no room for Controversy: be not* " *only addresses the Emperors, but also makes a Com-* " *parison betwixt two earthly Kings, to whom all* " *things, humanly speaking, are subject, and the su-* " *pream Governor of Heaven and Earth, who, together* " *with his only begotten Son, commands the Universe."* See how strongly Mr *de Larroque* has stated this Argument. Mr *de Tillemont* has seconded it with another Passage. "*Athenagoras*† tells Those two Princes, " he wishes, *that the Son may succeed the Father;* " ἵνα παῖς παρὰ πατρὸς διαδέχηται τὴν βα- " σιλείαν. [He speaks, therefore, to a Father, and " " a Son,

perial Court, and that he actually presented their Apology [B]; but there is Room to

" a Son, of whom the first only governed the Em-
" pire, though the other might have the Title of
" Emperor; that is to say, to *M. Aurelius*, and his
" Son *Commodus*, and not to two Brothers, who
" reigned in Conjunction. It is yet clearer in ano-
" ther place †, where he says, *All is submitted to*
" *your Majesties, to the Father and the Son*: ὡς
" ὑμῖν παῖρὶ καὶ ὑιῷ πάν]α κεχείρω]αι which
" Father *Pagi* ‖ had no other way of getting over,
" but by saying, that *Athenagoras* will have *Lucius*
" to be the Son of *M. Aurelius*, though he was
" only his Brother, purely to make a more exact Al-
" lusion to the two Persons of the Trinity, the Fa-
" ther, and the Son (14)." Father *Pagi* has made
use of an Evasion, in this Place, which is not likely to do much Mischief. He had better have said,
that *Athenagoras* was not ignorant, that *Lucius Au-*
relius had married the Daughter of *Marcus Aurelius*,
and that, therefore, as he addressed himself to the
Father-in-law, and Son-in-law, he might justly consider them as Father, and Son. It is thus, in effect,
that Father *Pagi* has answered this Objection (15).
He observes, also, that Mr *Toinard* is of the same
Sentiment. The other Passage, which Mr *de Til-*
lemont quotes, is not conclusive: we may understand it in this Sense: *We put up our Prayers*
for your Empire, that the Son may recieve it from
the Father, as Justice requires. Περὶ μὲν τῆς
ἀρχῆς τῆς ὑμεῖτέρας εὐχόμεθα, ἵνα παῖς μὲν
παρὰ παῖρὸς καθὰ τὸ δικαιότατον διαδέχηθαι
τὴν βασιλείαν (16). This Thought is very reasonable, whether we suppose the Apology addressed to
Marcus Aurelius, and his Brother, or to *Marcus Au-*
relius, and his Son. It is a Prayer, which, according to *Baronius*, does not respect *Commodus*, who
was, already, associated in the Empire, but his Descendants. It is a Wish, that *Marcus Aurelius*'s Family
might always possess the Imperial Dignity, according
to the Order of lawful Succession, in a direct Line.
Note, that Father *Pagi* quotes this Prayer as a Proof,
that the Son of *Marcus Aurelius* was not yet Emperor. I shall, in another Place (17), confute the
Inference, which is drawn from what *Athenagoras*
has said of one *Alexander*.
  We may conclude two things from all this: First,
That the Foundation of the Controversy is, that one
side makes the Brother of *Marcus Aurelius*, the other
his Son, to be his Partner in the Empire. Secondly,
That their Arguments, on both sides, are far from con-
clusive, since the Dispute continues yet undecided.
Scaliger (18), Father *Labbé* (19), Father *Pagi*, Mr
Dodwell, Mr *Chevreau* (20), &c. are for the Brother:
Suffridus Petri (21), *Baronius*, *Petavius* (22), Mr du
Pin (23), Mr *de Larroque*, Mr *de Tillemont*, and se-
veral other learned Men, are for the Son.
  Let us observe, by the way, a Mistake of *Grotius*.
Floruit Athenagoras, says he (24), *circa ann. Christi*
190, *at ex libri inscriptione apparet*. This is not
just; for, *Marcus Aurelius* being dead in the Year 180,
the Title of a Book, dedicated to him, can never prove,
that the Author flourished towards the Year 190.
  [B] *It is agreed, that Athenagoras was deputed* ——
to the Court —— *and that he actually presented their*
Apology; but there is Room to doubt of these Facts.]
These are the Words of *Baronius*. " *Orientis quo-*
" *que Ecclesias eâdem esse clade vexatas*, LEGATIO
" *pro illis ab Athenagorâ Christianensi* —— *tunc*
" *Imperatores* SUSCEPTA, & *Apologia pro eisdem tunc*
" *scripta ac dictis principibus* OBLATA, *manifestam*
" *certamque fidem faciunt* (25)." —— *That the Eastern*
" *Churches were under the same Persecution, the* DE-
" PUTATION, *then* UNDERTAKEN, *on their Behalf,*
" *by Athenagoras, the Athenian, to the Emperors,*
" *and the Apology composed for them, and* PRESENTED
" *to those Princes, sufficiently demonstrate*." Father
Labbé expresses himself as fully. " LEGATIONEM
" SUSCEPIT *pro Christianis inter annum* 165 ——
" & *annum* 170 —— *non desunt tamen qui anno*
" *dumtaxat* 177 OBLATUM *librum illum Imperato-*
" *ribus asserant* (26). —— HE UNDERTOOK *a* DE-
" PUTATION *for the Christians, between the Year*
" 165, *and* 170. *But there are some, who affirm, he*
" *Apology was not* PRESENTED *till the Year* 177."
Mr *Moreri*, translating this Passage of Father *Labbé*,
uses these Words. *He presented an excellent Apology*

for the Faithful to the Emperor Marcus Aurelius Antoninus. —— *He had been Deputy at Rome for the*
Christians, from the Year 165, *to* 170. He did not
rightly understand his Original; for the Words of Father *Labbé* do not signify, that the Deputation of
Athenagoras lasted from the Year 165, to 170, but
that it happened in some part of That Interval.
They, who know the frequent Journies of the *Roman*
Emperors in those Days, would never venture to expose themselves, by affirming, that This, or That, Person
was deputed to them at *Rome*, without being very
well assured of it. It must be allowed therefore, that
Mr *Moreri* has quitted his Guide a little too unad-
visedly, in determining both the Duration and Place
of this Deputation; when Father *Labbé* has not
said one Word of either. Mr *Dodwell*, who conjectures, that *Athenagoras* discharged this Deputation
(27), upon the Return of the Emperor *Lucius Verus*
to *Rome*, to triumph there (28), is not in the least
concerned in this little Criticism, in Regard to his determining the Place; because he has not done it,
without a very learned Deduction of proper Circumstances. But I can hardly agree with him, that
This Christian Philosopher did really ever discharge
this Deputation at all.
  My first Reason is taken from the Silence of all
the Ancients. Is it possible, that such a Deputation,
which the Circumstance of the Time, the Merit of
the Deputy, and the Strength of the Apology presented to the Emperors, must have made so memorable, should never be once mentioned by any one
Author? In the second place, It does not seem probable, that, when the Christian Name was so hated
and persecuted, *Athenagoras* should present himself
at the Imperial Court, as deputed by That Body, or
that he should obtain Audience there, and even deliver to the Emperors a long Writing, in which,
notwithstanding his respectful Moderation, he represents the *Pagan* Religion in so ridiculous and scandalous a Light, as would have been most likely to have
inflamed the Rage of the Persecutors. I shall add,
that the Title of This Writing, the strongest Proof
that can be urged against me, is, in my Opinion, no
Proof. Ἀθηναγόρου Ἀθηναίου φιλοσόφου Χριστιανοῦ
πρεσβεία περὶ Χριστιανῶν: *The Deputation of* Athenagoras *the* Athenian, *the Christian Philosopher, in*
behalf of the Christians. This is the Title of the
Piece. But, you may, if you please, observe, I. That
some Manuscripts, after πρεσβεία, add ἢ ἀπολογία, *or Apology* (29); and that others, instead of
πρεσβεία, read ἀπολογία. II. That the Word
πρεσβεία not only signifies an Embassy, or Deputation, but also an Address, or Petition; Τὴν
πρεσβείαν *non modo Legationem, sed & Depreca-*
tionem at Supplicationem apud Græcos significare no-
tum est (30). III. That the Title of *Embassy* is not
given to an Embassador's Speech, but to the whole
Account of his Negociations. So that it would be
very improper to take the word πρεσβεία here for
Embassy. Lastly, I observe, that Mr *de Tillemont*
expresses himself differently from other Writers. *It*
appears plainly, says he (31), *that the Faith was then*
persecuted in the East, seeing Athenagoras *was obliged*
to compose an Apology there, under the Title of A Legation *for the Christians, which he address'd to both the*
Augustus's. He does not mention any Journey, or
Deputation, or the presenting of any Apology to the
Emperors; he speaks only of a Piece composed in the
Author's Country, and address'd to *Marcus Aurelius*, &c.
Every body knows the difference between a Writing
actually given into the Hands of a Monarch, and a
Writing only address'd to This Monarch. I confess, Mr
de Tillemont's Authority seems here to be very good:
for he lays it down as a Rule, not to extend the Testi-
monies of Authors beyond what they clearly im-
port; And he keeps himself scrupulously within the
limits of his Proofs. From whence I infer, that he
found no manner of ground for This Deputation of
Athenagoras, nor for the actual presenting of his
Apologetical Writing.
  To reduce what I think of this matter into a narrow Compass, I am not ashamed to own, that I take
Athenagoras to have been like those modern Writers,
who, without stirring out of their Studies, have spread
Pieces of their own composing all the World over,

VOL. I.   6 S   under

ATHENAGORAS.

to doubt of these Facts; and we may with a great deal of probability believe the same Thing of This Writing, which was known to be true of an infinite Number of Petitions of the Protestants in *France*, which have been printed without ever being presented to the Prince [C]. I cannot imagine on what ground *Athenagoras* is said to have been a Priest (c). It is something surprizing, that he should be unknown to *Eusebius*, St *Jerome*, and to almost all the other Fathers; for we find him no where quoted, except in a Work of St *Epiphanius* [D]. He was not entirely clear from Heterodoxy [E]; but, this excepted, the two Pieces, which we have of his, are very valuable (d).

(c) Father Labbé, Dissert. de Script. Eccles. Tom. I. pag. 6 &c. affirms it, and so does Moreri.

(d) The other is a Treatise de Resurrectione.

The under the Title of *A Petition of the Protestants presented to the King*. They, who shall read these Compositions an hundred Years hence, will not question but that they were actually presented; but we know better. We know, there was handed about, in 1680, a printed Piece, which had all the Air of a Petition, actually presented to the King of *France* by Those of the Protestant Religion (32). An infinite Number of People in foreign Countries, and in the Provinces remote from *Paris*, believed it. Yet I am credibly informed, that it never was presented, and it is certain, that the Deputies of the Churches, who drew it up, disowned the Publication of it. There appeared in Print another such Piece, during the Conferences at *Ryswick*, in the Year 1697, which was handed about without being owned; but which, may one Day be placed among authentic Acts, since it does not appear from the Petition itself, that it was not actually delivered into the Hands of *Lewis* XIV. Without doubt the Primitive Christians acted in the same manner. They composed Writings, addressed to the Emperors, and published them, in hopes that some of the Copies might come to the Hands of Those Princes, and incline them to put a stop to their Persecutions, by shewing the Accusations to be false. To conclude, I am perswaded, *Athenagoras* did, in the IId Century, what *Calvin* did in the XVIth. *Calvin*, lurking in a little Chamber at *Basil*, dedicated his *Christian Institution* to *Francis* I, which neither He, nor any Body else, ever pretended to him.

It ought not to be concealed, that, the very Day I finished this Remark, I communicated it to Mr *Cockburn* (33), who offered immediately to consult Mr *Dodwell* upon it. He has done me the favour to communicate to me the Answer he received, which is full of excellent Learning, in support of Arguments, brought in favour of the Sentiment I have now been opposing. These Arguments have some Weight. The Letter of That learned Man deserves to be printed, and I would willingly have inserted it here, if I had had his Permission; but, not having That, I ought also to deprive myself of the Liberty of the Dispute.

[C] *An infinite Number of Petitions of the Protestants in* France, *have been printed without ever being presented to the Prince*] The Public is so well apprized of this, that it were a very needless Task to go about to prove it. But, as for what concerns the Petition, which was handed about in the Year 1680, I have reason to believe, that my Readers will imagine I have gone too far, in denying, that it was ever presented. Therefore it is but just, that I should give my Reasons. I begin, by distinguishing this Petition from several others, which were drawn up at different Times; and I say it is the same, which was confuted by a Priest, called *Seulier*. The Answer, which he gave to it, was printed without his Name. This Answer is mentioned in Page 6 of *The last Efforts of oppressed Innocence*, and in Page 305 of the *History of the Edict of Pacification* (34), and in Volume III of the *History of the Edict of* Nantes (35). In this last Book is also found a Summary of This Answer, as of a Writing, whose Author was unknown. This Historian of the Edict of *Nantes* affirms (36), that the Petition was presented, and adds, *It happened, I know not how, that, some time after, it was printed, and publickly dispersed abroad*. I believe he is mistaken, and that it was printed and dispersed, before it could be presented. Now after it had appeared in public, to be sure the King never received it. See, in the Life of Mr *du Bosc*, how the Council was offended, because the Deputies of The Protestants had published a Petition, which they had presented, but which the King had not yet answered (37). This Prince *was so displeased with the printing of This Petition, that he condemned it without seeing it, and ordered two of the Deputies to be* clapt into the Bastile (38). This passed about the Year 1671. How is it probable then, that, nine Years after, that is to sa., at a Time, when things were much worse, the Deputies of the Churches durst publish a Petition, after having presented it to the King, and before the receiving his Answer? The Author of the History of the Edict of *Nantes* might elude this, by maintaining, that the Missionaries got the Petition of the Protestants printed. This, though possible, is against all Probability. But here is a Fact which is more home to the purpose. In a very little time, after This Petition was seen in public, Mr *Jurieu* composed a Book, wherein he speaks of it only as of a Petition, THAT WAS DESIGNED *to be presented* (39). Does he not deserve more Credit in such a Point, than the Historian of the Edict of *Nantes*, who did not write 'till many Years after This Event? Upon observing the Difference between these Writers, I caused three of the chief Deputies of the Churches to be consulted, and particularly Him, who passes for the Author of the Petition. The Answers, which I received from them, agree perfectly in this, that they do not remember whether it was presented or not. They excused their Forgetfulness, by reason of the great Number of Affairs, which then passed through their Hands, and the long, and very troublesome, Time, that has elapsed since. I have no reason, then, to fear, that any reasonable Person will accuse me of Rashness, in taking up with this Opinion; for, besides the Proofs I have alledged, I remember, that the freshest, and, as it were, original Tradition, was, which Mr *Jurieu* has also followed, that the Petition was published without ever being presented by the Deputies.

[D] *We find him no where quoted, except in a Work of St* Epiphanius.] We must even correct the Text, to make out this Quotation of him: Τί ἓν ὁ Διάβολ. Λέξεῖαι; ἀντυπμα περὶ τὴν ὕλην ἔχων, καθάπερ ἐλέχθη, ὅ Ἀθηναγόρας, γενόμενον ὑπὸ τῷ Θεῷ (40). *What then shall we understand the Devil to be?* A Spirit conversant about Matter, *as it has been said*, O Athenagoras! *created by God*. This is what the Editions of *Epiphanius* say; and, according to this, it ought rather to be understood of another *Athenagoras*, who had been introduced, as one of the Speakers, in the Dialogue, from which *Epiphanius* gives some Extracts. Now it is a Dialogue, composed by *Methodius* against *Origen*, and in which *Methodius* is one of the Interlocutors. But the Critics have very justly conjectured, that, instead of ὣ Ἀθηναγόρας, we ought to read τῷ Ἀθηναγόρᾳ, *by Athenagoras* (41).

[E] *He was not entirely clear from Heterodoxy*.] He admits two sorts of bad Angels; the one comprehends those, whom God created, and who acquitted themselves ill in the Commission, which was given them, to govern Matter, and to preside over the Production of Forms; the other comprehends those, which the former begot by carnal Conversation with Women: It comprehends, I say, the Souls of Giants, who were begot by This Copulation (42). *Suffridus Petri* observes, that *Athenagoras* supports his Hypothesis by two Passages of Scripture, which he has misunderstood. "Testimonia sunt potissimum duo, "sed male intellecta, quibus niti videtur Athenagoras (43). — *The principal Authorities, which Athenagoras seems to build upon, are two, but both misunderstood*." He misunderstands, and misapplies, much in the same manner, That Passage of the Gospel, which condemns those, who repudiate one Wife to marry another; for he makes use of it to condemn second Marriages, which he calls, without mincing the Matter, a specious Adultery. "Ἡ οἷ. τις ἐτίχθη, μύνων, ἢ ἐφ᾽ ἑνὶ γάμῳ. Ὁ γὰρ δεύτερ., εὐπρεπής ἐςι μοιχεία. Ὃς γὰρ ἂν ἀπολύσῃ, φησί, τὴν γυναῖκα αὐτῦ, καὶ γαμήσῃ ἄλλην, μοιχᾶται·

(32) See the following Remark.

(33) He is a Scotchman, a Doctor of Divinity, the Author of some English Books against Bourignonism.

(34) Of the Holland Edition 1682. The Sieur Soulier is Author of this History, and has not put his Name to it. He has owned himself Author of the Answer to the Petition. Ib. pag. 305.

(35) Lib. 16. pag. 404, and the following.

(36) Ibid.

(37) Life of Mr du Bosc, pag. 81.

(38) Ibid.

(39) See the Derniers Efforts de l'Innocence opprimée, p. 6.

(40) Epiphan. advers. Hæres. n. 64. p. 544. Tom. I.

(41) Pauleus Leopardus, Emendat. lib. 19. c. 9. Petavius in Epiphan. advers. Hæres. 64. n. 22. p. 260, 261.

(42) Athenag. p. 227, & seq.

(43) Suffridus Petri in Atheneag. Apolog. p. 218.

ATHENAGORAS.

The Stile of them is good, and *Attic* enough, but a little too much clogged with Parentheses, and Transpositions. They have been printed a great many times, as may be seen in Mr *du Pin*, who has, nevertheless, forgot some Editions [F]. I shall mention a Romance

(44) Athenag. p. 298.

ὅτε ἀπολύσει ἐπιτρέπων ἧς ἔπαυσέ τις τὴν παρθενίαν, ὅτε ἐπιγαμεῖν. ὁ γὰρ ἀποτερῶν ἑαυτὸν τῆς προτέρας γυναικὸς, καὶ εἰ τέθνηκε, μοιχὸς ἐςὶ παρεγκεκαλυμμένῳ, παραβαίνων μὲν τὴν χεῖρα τῷ Θεῷ, ὅτι ἐν ἀρχῇ ὁ Θεὸς ἕνα ἄνδρα ἔπλασε καὶ μίαν γυναῖκα (44). Let every one either continue in the same State he was born in, or content himself with once marrying. For a second Marriage is but a specious Adultery. For the Scripture says, Whosoever shall put away his Wife, and marry another, committeth Adultery. Neither permitting the putting away of Her, whose Virginity has been enjoyed, nor the marrying of another. And whosoever quits his first Marriage, although his Wife be dead, is in some measure an Adulterer, by exceeding God's own Appointment, who, in the Beginning, made one Man, and one Woman. You see he imposes the same Law on all Men, which God prescribed to the chief Priest alone; if they will marry, it must be only with a Maid (45). He is not contented, that they have their Virginity themselves, but will also have them choose none but Virgins for their Wives. But this is erring consistently; Because, if second Marriages were criminal, it would be criminal even for a Bachelor to marry a Widow, and every time he discharges the matrimonial Duty would be committing a fresh Crime. For this would be causing his Wife to sin, and, according to the Rules of Morality, whosoever causes others to sin sins himself. The same may be said of a Maid, who should marry a Widower. *I don't know*, says Mr de *Tillemont* (46), *Whether the Expression* ⁎ *which* Athenagoras *uses concerning the Prophets, at a time, when the Extasies of* Montanus *began to trouble the Church, may not give ground to suspect, that he was engaged in That Party. However, neither* Scultetus, *nor Mr* du Pin, *I have observed That Place to be liable to any bad Construction.* I do not find, that there is the least Reason to suspect him of Montanism on this Account. How many of the Orthodox are there, who believe, that the ancient Prophets were in Extasies, and that their Tongues, or their Pens, were the Instruments of the Holy Ghost? What then could they find fault with in these words of Athenagoras? Νομίζω καὶ ὑμᾶς —— οὐκ ἀνοήτως γεγονέναι οὔτε τῶν Μωσέως, οὔτε τῶν Ἡσαΐου καὶ Ἱερεμίου καὶ τῶν λοιπῶν προφητῶν, οἳ κατ᾽ ἔκςασιν τῶν ἐν αὑτοῖς λογισμῶν κινήσαντ[ος] αὐτοὺς τοῦ Θείου πνεύματος, ἃ ἐνηργεῖτο ἐξεφώνησαν· συγχρησαμένου τοῦ πνεύματ[ος], ὡσεὶ καὶ αὐλητὴς αὐλὸν, ἐμπνεύσειας (47). *I suppose that even you* —— *are not ignorant of the Transactions either of* Moses, *or of* Isaias, *and* Jeremias, *and the rest of the Prophets, who, by an Extasy of Thought, the Divine Spirit moving them, spoke as they were inspired; the Spirit operating on them, in like manner as the Musician on his Flute.* It is true, the Comparison of the Holy Ghost with one, who plays on a Flute, is mean, but the Foundation of it is right.

A REFLEXION on the *Jewish* High-Priest not being allowed to marry unless with a Virgin.

What I have said of the Law, which was prescribed to the High-Priest of the *Jews*, suggests a Conjecture, which I shall venture to publish in this Place. The Primitive Christians, who declared so strongly against second Marriages, were perhaps engaged in That Opinion from this Consideration, that there ought to be greater Perfection under the Evangelical, than under the *Mosaic* Law; so that Lay Christians ought to observe all the strictest Regularity, which was in use among the Ecclesiastics of the Synagogue. In effect, it seems, that, in some respects, all Christians are appointed to the Priesthood (48). If, then, it was thought fit to forbid the High Priest of the *Jews* rather than a Widow, on purpose that This Prohibition might remind him of his strict Obligation to Purity, may it not be thought reasonable to subject all Christians to the same Condition? Thus, perhaps, some might say: Perhaps also, the original Design of This moral Restriction might be totally to remove the Abuses of That kind of *Polygamy*, which Divorces had made frequent. The Men of false Wit would deserve something more than to be laughed at, should they attack this Injunction up-

on the High Priest. *The Law, prescribed to him,* would these Jesters say, *ought to command something mortifying to his Pleasures; whereas, on the contrary, it obliges him to the most delicious Relish of them, and not to take up with a second-hand Dish. The Rest of the People may make shift with the leavings of others: He only is taught to be nicer, and of a daintier Palate.* Poor insipid Raillery! for it is in reality a Slavery, not to have the liberty of marrying where we please; and how many sensual Persons, in a full Liberty of Choice, would prefer a Widow before any other Mistress? But, besides, is it not meer Blindness, not to see the Wisdom of the Lawgiver in this Prohibition? Did not This Law warn the great Pontiff to abstain, more than others, from the least Irregularities? For, if a Woman ceased to be worthy of him, the moment she left aspiring to That supreme Degree of Perfection and Honour, which she might have attained by preferring a chast Widowhood before a second Marriage; if the sole want of This height of Virtue, if, I say, this sole want, which is not so much a real Fault, as a bare Privation of distinguished Merit, was sufficient to make her unworthy to marry with the High-Priest, was not this a Proof, that God required of him a more exact Conduct? Read these Words of a great Man: " Quin & illa ad declarandam insigniem vitæ mundiciem pertinent, quod si quis de stirpe Aaron teneatur profluvio sanguinis, vetatur ad sacerdotis mensam accedere sacrifque vesci panibus: item quod quicunque vitio maculâve corporis essent deformati, submoventur à sacris ministeriis: rursus quòd ipse pontifex jubetur virginem suæ gentis ducere, à viduâ, repudiatâ, ac prostitutâ, abstinere. Non statim quod plebi licet, licet & sacerdoti: multitudini multa conceduntur, à sacerdote summa requiritur puritas in omni vitæ portione (49). —— *Now these Things are intended to point out a more particular Purity of Life, That, if any of the House of* Aaron *be taken with an Hæmorrhage, he should not be permitted to come to the Priest's Table, or to taste of the consecrated Bread: Also, that such as were defective, or deformed, in their Bodies, should be incapable of the Priesthood: Again, that the High-Priest himself is commanded to abstain from a Widow, a Wife divorced, and a Prostitute, and to marry, if at all, to a Virgin of his own Nation. Not every thing, that is lawful for the People, is also lawful for the Priest: Many things are allowed to the Multitude, but from the Priest is required the strictest Purity in every Station of Life.*" The same Spirit reigned in the Christian Discipline, even at the time, when married Persons were not excluded from the Priesthood (50); for it not excluded Those, who had married either two Wives successively, or a Widow, or who had been dishonoured by the Adultery of their Wives; and, if This dishonour happened to them in the Time of their Priesthood, they were obliged either to free themselves from it by a Divorce, or abdicate their Character. " Verba synodi Neocæsar. cap. " 8. hæc sunt: si cujus uxorem adulterium commisit, cùm esset laicus, evidenter fuerit probatum, " hic ad ministerium ecclesiasticum admitti non potest. Quod si in clericatu eo jam constituto adulteravit, dato repudio dimittere eam debet: si vero " retinere ejus consortium velit, non potest suscepto " ministerio persrui. cap. si cujus, 34. distin. (51).—— *In Chap. 8. of the Council of* Neocæsarea, *are these words: If it proved, by good Evidence, that the Wife of any Layman has committed Adultery, he cannot be admitted to the Ecclesiastical Function. But, if the Wife of a Priest commit Adultery, he must divorce her: or, if he will retain her, be must renounce his Ministry.*" See Mr *Morin's* Dissertation, or the Abstract given of it in the *News from the Republic of Letters* (52).

[F] *Mr* du Pin *has forgot some Editions of* Athenagoras.] His List is very large (53), but not every where rightly pointed, in the Edition of *Amsterdam* (54). This confounds our Understanding. He has not taken Notice of the Edition of *Oxford*, nor That of *Leipsic*: The first appeared in the Year 1682, in

marginal notes:

(45) Levit. xxi. 13, 14.

(46) Tillemont, ubi supra, pag. 759.

⁎ Athenag. Leg. p. 9, d.

† Scult. pag. 52. Du Pin, Tom. I. p. 315.

(47) Athenag. pag. 72, 74.

(48) See 1 Pet. ii 5, 9.

(49) Erasmus in Ecclesiaste,l. 1. pag. 45, 47.

(50) See Duaren de Sacris Ecclesiæ Minist. ac Benefic. lib. 4. cap. 2. pag. 386.

(51) Id. ib. pag. 387.

(52) For the Month of July, 1684, Art. 6, pag. 517.

(53) See the first Tome of his Nouvelle Bibliotheque printed in 1686.

(54) I speak of that, as not having That in of Paris.

a Romance, which appeared under the Name of *Athenagoras* [G]. If I could have consulted the Dissertation, published by Father *le Nourry* (e), it would have furnished me, without doubt, with some good Materials for this Article; but his Work is not yet come to our Hands (f), tho' it was printed in the Year 1697. I have seen some account of it in the *Journal des Sçavans* (g), and in the *Acta Eruditorum* of *Leipsic* (h).

in 12mo, by the Care of Dr *Fell*, Bishop of *Oxford*; and the latter, in the Year 1684, in 8vo, by the Care of *Adam Rechenberg*. They are both of them in *Greek* and *Latin*, with Notes. Neither has he mentioned the Commentary of *Kortholt* on the Works of *Athenagoras*. This Piece was printed at *Kiel*, in the Year 1675, in Folio, and was inserted, with Additions, in the Edition of *Justin Martyr*, of *Athenagoras*, &c. at *Leipsic*, in 1686. Note, that *Guy Gauffart*, Prior of St *Foi*, at *Coulommiers*, published a *French* Translation of the Apology of *Athenagoras*, and subjoined the Annotations of *Suffridus Petri*. This was printed at *Paris*, in 8vo, in the Year 1574. *Du Verdier Vau-Privas*, who is my Author for this (55), mentions a *French* Translation of two Pieces of *Athenagoras*, done by *Arnauld du Ferron* (56), but does not say when, or where, it was printed (57).

[G] I shall mention a Romance, *which appeared under the Name of* Athenagoras.] According to Dr *Cave*, we have, hitherto, only seen the *French* Translation of it, printed at *Paris*, by *Daniel Guillemont*, in the Year 1612, with this Title: *Of the true, and perfect, Love, written, in* Greek, *by* Athenagoras, *an Athenian Philosopher, containing the chaste Loves of* Theogonus *and* Charida, *of* Pherecides *and* Melangenia. *Martin Fumée*, Lord of *Genillé*, was Author of This Translation, and sent it, in the Year 1569, to Mr *de Lamané*, Secretary of the Cardinal of *Armagnac*. It was found among the Papers of *Bernard* of *Sanjorry*, who published it in the Year 1612 (58). Consult *Huetius* (59), who speaks largely of This Book, and who supposes, that *Philander* is it's true Author. He informs us, that This *Fumée* boasted, that he had procured the *Greek* Original, by the means of *Lamani*, Protonotary of the Cardinal of *Armagnac*.

Note, that the Edition, mentioned by Dr *Cave*, and which he had seen in the Library of *Vossius*, is not the first. I have one, printed at *Paris*, by *Michael Sonnius*, in 1599, 12mo. The Title differs but very little from That, which we have seen above (60). The Preface is of *Bernard* of *Sanjorry*, and dated from *Castres*, the first of *October*, 1596. It informs us, that *Sanjorry* being almost Seventy, had found, among his Papers, a Copy of This Work, which he had got transcribed from That, which had been sent to Mr de Lamané, and, that he had desired *Monsieur* de Fonbouzart, *who was going to Court, about some Affairs of his own, to do him the Favour to carry this Work with him, and to take the Trouble of communicating it to some Printer, as he passed through Paris*.

ATHENÆUM [A], was a public Edifice in *Rome*, built by the Emperor *Adrian* [B], to serve for an Auditory to the Learned, and to those who chose to recite their

[A] ATHENÆUM.] This Name comes from *Minerva*, in *Greek* Ἀθηνᾶ, The Goddess of all polite Arts, and Sciences. It was thought fit, that an Edifice, built in favour of the Learned, should bear the Name of That Goddess. Some have thought, it was a Temple, consecrated to her; but *Aurelius Victor* does not give us That Idea of it. "Gymnasia, says he (1), speaking of the Emperor *Adrian*, "Doctoresque curare occœpit, adeo quidem ut etiam "ludum ingenuarum artium, quod Athenæum vocant, "constituerit. —— He began to shew a great Regard *to Exercises, and Professors, in all learned Arts and Sciences, insomuch, that he built them Schools, which are called the Athenæum.*" Other Historians, who speak of this Edifice, represent it only as a Place for Lessons, Declamations, and Lectures. "Ad Athenæum audiendorum & Græcorum & La- "tinorum rhetorum vel poëtarum caussa frequenter "processit. —— *He frequently went to the Athenæum, to hear the* Greek, *and* Latin, *Rhetoricians and Poets*." *Lampridius* speaks thus of *Alexander Severus*. This Passage is quoted in *Calepin*, a little after having said, that the *Athenæum* was consecrated to *Minerva*, and that the Poets, and other *Greek* Writers, brought their Works thither, as the *Latin* Authors brought theirs into the Temple of *Apollo*. Judge by this of the Exactness of Those, who composed, or corrected, That great Dictionary. *Cruquius* makes use of the same Division; he sends the *Latin* Poets to the Temple of *Apollo*, and the *Greek* to the Temple of *Minerva*, which he calls *Athenæum* (2). But let us go on in observing what the Ancients have said of the Place in question; "Cum Pertinax "eo die processionem quam ad Athenæum parave- "rat, ut audiret Poëtam, ob sacrificii præsagium "distulisset (3). —— *When* Pertinax, *by reason of some ill Omen in the Sacrifices, put off the Procession he intended to have made, that Day, to the Athenæum*." Another says, that *Gordian*, the Emperor, had declaimed, in the *Athenæum; ubi adolevit, in Athenæo controversias declamavit* (4). *Philostratus* says, that the Sophist *Adrian*, who was in great Esteem at *Rome*, had no sooner declared, that he would make a Declamation, than the Senators, Knights, and every body, flocked to the *Athenæum*. Δρόμῳ ἵχωσιν ἐς τὸ Ἀθήναιον ὁρμῆς μεςοὶ (5). *They ran to the* Athenæum *with great eagerness*. Let us add these Words of St *Jerom*: *Quando omne Athenæum Scho- lasticorum vocibus personabat* (6). —— *When the whole* Athenæum *rang with the Voices of the Professors*: And those of *Sidonius Apollinaris*: *Dignus omnino quem plausibilibus Roma foveret ulnis, quoque recitante crepitantis Athenæi subsellia cuneata quaterentur* (7). —— *Worthy, in the highest Manner, of the greatest Applauses* Rome *could give, and to shake the crowded Seats of the ecchoing* Athenæum *with his Repetitions*. The Etymology, *Dion* gives us, is a new Argument against Those, who have taken the *Athenæum* for a Temple of *Minerva*: he says, that the Place was so called, from the Exercises of the Learned, there performed, ἀπὸ τῆς ἐν αὐτῷ τῶν πεπαιδευμένων ἀσκήσεως (8). He informs us also, that the Consul assembled the Senate, in the *Athenæum*, when he understood, that the *Prætorian* Cohorts had seized the Murderers of *Pertinax*. The Objection, which might be drawn from the Senate's never meeting but in Places consecrated by the *Augurs*, does no way balance the Reasons, which prove, that the *Athenæum* was not a Temple of *Pallas*. To conclude, They, who pretend, that the first Place, which was called *Athenæum*, was a Building in *Athens* (9), will have much ado to prove it. Good Mr *de Marolles* has a very wrong Notion of This Word; for, in his Translation of *Aurelius Victor*, he says, that *Adrian* invited *learned Men from all Parts; as if he intended to transplant Athens to Rome*.

I shall observe, occasionally, that, in the City of *Athens*, the Rhetoricians, and Grammarians, met in the Temple of the Muses, upon Trials of Skill. Ἀνδρες παρὰ τὸ τέμενος τῶν Μουσῶν ἔνθα ποιηταὶ καὶ ῥήτορες καὶ τῶν γραμματικῶν οἱ παῖδες ποιοῦνται ποιοῦνται τὰς ἐπιδείξεις. *He leads away to the Temple of the Muses, where the Poets, Rhetoricians, and Grammarian Scholars often resort to shew their Parts*. Thus speaks an Author of the VIth Century of the Practice in his time; I mean *Zachary*, of *Mitylene*, in his Book *de Mundi opificio*. See the Three hundred thirty ninth Page of the eleventh Volume of the *Bibliotheca Patrum*, printed at *Paris* in the Year 1644.

[B] *Built by the Emperor* Adrian.] This I have proved by the Passage of *Aurelius Victor*: *Casaubon* has also very good Reason to laugh at *Theodorus Marsilius* (10), whom he treats roughly enough, without naming him. This Author spends a great many Words, in his Commentary on *Persius*, to prove, that the

ATHENÆUM. ATHENÆUS. 535

their Works in Public. It appears from the beginning of *Juvenal*'s Satires, that these sort of Lectures were very frequent, and that *Fronto* lent his House and Gardens to those Poets, who had a mind to recite their Verses before a numerous Audience (*a*). Many others were also willing to lend their Houses for the same Purpose (*b*); but, unfortunately for the Poets, these Favours were often very expensive [C]: for He, who was to read his Work, was to fit up the Room, and pay the Hire of the Seats. It is very probable, that the Emperor *Adrian*, who loved and understood the Sciences, had This View, among others, in building the *Athenæum*, viz. to free Authors from these great Incumbrances. Without doubt This Place served also for a College (*c*); for it was not only used for reciting of Compositions, but likewise for reading of Lectures. I find too, that the Senate sometimes met there (*d*). The Name of this Place has been applied, in a general Sense, to signify all kind of Universities, or Seminaries of Learning, appropriated to the teaching of Languages; for they are called in *Latin Athenæa*. Some are also of Opinion, that Libraries have been called *Athenica* (*e*).

(*a*) *Frontonis platani convulsæque marmora clamant, Semper & assiduo ruptæ lectore columnæ.*

(*b*) *Stella, in Martial. Epig. 6. l. 4. Titinnius Capito, in Pliny, lib. 8. Epist. 12. Quadratus, in Arrian's Epict. lib. 3. cap. 23.*

(*c*) See Remark [*A*].

(*d*) *Ibid. towards the end.*

(*e*) *Salmas. in Trebell. Pollion. de triginta Tyrannis.*

(11) Vossius *de Imitat. pag. 36.*

the *Athenæum*, and the Temple of *Apollo Palatinus*, were one and the same. *Vossius* (11) has repeated the same Accusation against him, and has given him, for an Accomplice, Father *Raderus*, on the seventieth Epigram of the tenth Book of *Martial*. He might have added *Savaron* for a second Accomplice, who, by these Words of *Horace*,

hired House, but cannot forbear saying, that *Vossius* maintains it without any ground, since the Testimonies, he alledges, mean nothing less, than what he pretends. The first Passage, he quotes, is That of the Dialogue *de Causis corruptæ Eloquentiæ*, where we have just now met with *domum mutuatur*, which signifies a borrowed, and not an hired, House. The second is of *Juvenal*, in these Words:

WHETHER the Poets repeated in a hired House. Errors of *Vossius*.

(12) Horat. Sat. ult. lib. 1. ver. 37.

------ hæc ego ludo,
Quæ nec in æde sonent certantia judice Tarpâ (12);

*These idle Lines shall ne'er in Judgment come
Before the learned Audience of Rome;*

understands, that *Horace* would not have his Verses read in the *Athenæum* (13). He gives This Interpretation as the very Words of an ancient Scholiast. *Lipsius* makes use of the same Authority, though he confesses, that another ancient Scholiast understands there by *ædem* the Temple of *Apollo Palatinus* (14). If That learned Man had remembered the Passage of *Aurelius Victor*, he would not have preferred the Interpretation of the first of these Scholiasts to That of the latter (15). See the Article TARPA, in it's Place.

[C] *These Favours were often very expensive:*] The Author of the Dialogue *de Causis corruptæ Eloquentiæ* is my Evidence, where he says, *Domum mutuatur, & auditorium exstruit, & subsellia conducit, ut beatissimus recitationem ejus eventus consequatur*. ------ *He borrows a House, builds an Auditory, and hires Seats, that his Repetitions may meet with the most favourable Reception*. *Juvenal* will serve for a second Witness, where he threatens the Poets with the Mortification of not finding any Great Man, who will re-imburse them the Expences they have been at.

(13) Savar. in Sidon. Apollon. Ep. 14. lib. 9.

(14) Lips. Epist. 48. Centur. 3. ad Belgas.

(15) See Vossius de Imitat. p. 61.

cum jam celebres notique Poëtæ
Balneolum Gabiis, Romæ conducere furnos
Tentarent (17).

*When now the celebrated Wits, for need,
Hire Bagnios, to the Cryer's Trade succeed,
Or get their own, by baking others Bread.*
        CHA. DRYDEN.

which denote only the dismal Poverty of the Trade, which had almost forced the Poets to become Bankrupt to the Muses, and to seek their Living by some mechanic Employ, as one may call That of a Bath-Keeper, a Baker, or a Cryer. The third Testimony is taken from these Words of the same *Juvenal*:

(17) Juven. Sat. 7. v. 3.

Nemo dabit regum quanti subsellia constent,
Et quæ conducto pendent anabathra tigillo,
Quæque reportandis posita est orchestra cathedris (16).

*With no kind Patron now the Poet meets,
To pay the Hire of Pulpit and of Seats.*

I do not deny, but they sometimes repeated in an

Ipse facit versus, atque uni cedit Homero
Propter mille annos; &, si dulcedine famæ
Succensus recites, Maculonis commodat ædes (18).

*Himself writes Verse, which he to your's prefers;
And only yields to Homer's for their Years:
But, to your Share to try what Fame will fall,
Any great Man will lend an empty Hall.*

It is so plain, that, neither in this, nor in the foregoing Passage, are Poets said to have hired the Chamber, where they recited their Verses, that it is unaccountable how such Mistakes should escape the Sight of the learned *Vossius*. Observe, that they are found in a Book, which was printed in the Author's Life-time (19), the Title whereof is, *De Imitatione cum Oratoriâ tum præcipuè poëticâ, deque Recitatione Veterum*. This latter Subject has been amply treated by *Cresollius*, in his *Theatre of the ancient Sophists*.

(16) Juven. Sat. 7. ver. 45.

(18) Juven. Sat. 7. ver. 38.

(19) At Amsterdam 1647, with the Institutiones Poeticæ.

ATHENÆUS, a *Greek* Grammarian, born at *Naucratis* in *Ægypt*, flourished in the IIId Century [*A*]. He was one of the most learned Men of his Time; he had read

[*A*] *Athenæus ------ flourished in the IIId Century.*] *Faber* has censured *Helvicus*, who, in quoting *Suidas*, places *Athenæus* in the Reign of *Antoninus Pius* (1). Here are two Faults, for *Suidas* makes him flourish under *Marcus Aurelius*, though he does not deserve to be copied in this, since *Oppian*, who dedicated a Poem to the Emperor *Caracalla* (2), died before *Athenæus*. *Helvicus* ought not then to have placed *Oppian* fifty Years after him. *Faber* reproves him for this Mistake, and maintains, that *Athenæus* lived at the same time with *Herodian*, who finished his History in the Year 238. It is certain, *Athenæus* places himself after *Oppian*, in point of Time. Καὶ τὸν ὀλίγῳ πρὸ ἡμῶν γενόμενον Ὀππιανὸν τὸν Κίλικα (3). *And Oppian, the Cilician, who lived a little before our Time*; says he, speaking

of several Authors, who had treated of Fishing. Without doubt it will be objected, that he elsewhere says (4), that he knew the Poet *Pancrates*, who received some Present from the Emperor *Adrian*: But This raises no great Difficulty; it is sufficient to suppose, that This *Pancrates* was very young, at That time, that he lived eighty Years, and died before *Athenæus* had attained to the twentieth Year of his Age. You will find, by this, that the latter might very well have lived 'till the Reign of *Gordianus*. If Mr *de Tillemont* had recollected the *Greek* Passage of *Athenæus*, which I have quoted, The Age, which he thought due to This Writer, would have appeared still more surprizing to him; for he supposes him *very aged*, by imagining only, that his Work was written after the Death of *Commodus*; and the Reason, he

(1) Tanaq. Faber Epist. 63. lib. 1. p. 211, 212.

(2) Who was killed in 217.

(3) Athen. lib. 1. p. 13.

(4) Id. lib. 15. p. 677.

VOL. I.   T 6

ATHENÆUS.

(a) See the Preface of Casaubon on Athenæus.

read so much, and had so good a Memory, that he may justly be called the *Varro of the Greeks* (a). Of all his Works [B], there remains only That intituled the *Deipnosophists*, that is to say, *the Sophists at Table* (b), where he introduces a number of learned Men, of all Professions, who converse with various Subjects, at the Table of a Roman Citizen, called *Larensius*. There is an infinite Variety of Facts and Citations in this Work of *Athenæus*, which makes the reading of it very pleasant to Those, who have skill enough to love Antiquity from a rational Motive. But, without doubt, the learned Men, who were cotemporary with the Author, did not judge of this Work so favourably, as we do in this Age. Those learned Men could consult the Originals, and there find most of the things, which *Athenæus* presented them with; for which Reason they considered his Book in a bad Light, as nothing else but a tedious Collection from others. But, for our part, who can come at but a very few of the Authors referred to by *Athenæus*, and have no other Opportunity of meeting with a hundred particular Curiosities, mentioned by him, but in his Collection, we look upon it as a very precious Treasure: we regard it with a favourable Eye, and transfer to the Author all the Esteem we have for the Rarities recorded by him, which are indeed become such, only because the Books, out of which he took them, are lost. For this same Reason, such a Compiler, whom our Age might not esteem in the least, would be greatly admired a thousand Years hence, if there should happen, in the Republic of Learning, such Revolutions as destroyed most of the Works of the ancient *Greeks* and *Romans*. We cannot answer, that nothing like this will ever happen again. Let us, then, not blame those, who compile; they labour perhaps more usefully for future Ages, than the Authors, who borrow nothing from others. We find, in the *Deipnosophists* of our Author, a great many Touches of Slander, Fragments of scandalous Reports, and obscene Stories. No Book has been worse treated by Transcribers, than This of *Athenæus* [C]; all the Editions we have of it are very imperfect [D]. Somebody made an Abridgment of This Work [E]. Mr *Moreri* could

(e) Tillemont, Hist. des Emper. Tom. 2. p. 809.

he gives for it, is, *That Athenæus had known the Poet Pancrates, famous in the Time of Adrian* (5). He finds no Fault with *Suidas*, who placed him under *Marcus Aurelius*; tho' he ought to have censured him, in consequence of the *Greek* Passage above-mentioned. I would not have it pretended, that it is not *Athenæus*, who boasts of having known the Poet *Pancrates*, but that they are the Words of *Callixenus*, the *Rhodian*, whom he had quoted a little before. This Supposition will not pass. *Casaubon* perceived plainly, that these are not *Callixenus's* Words, in the Book of *Athenæus* (6); but he has omitted a very strong Reason for proving this Point. It is, that the Passage in question begins thus; *Since I have mentioned the City of Alexandria*. Now *Callixenus* would never have spoken thus, in a Work of his own, concerning That very City (7). It is therefore *Athenæus* himself, who makes use of these Words, after having finished the Relation of what he had borrowed from *Callixenus*.

(6) Casaub. in Athen. pag. 958.

(7) Ἐν τοῖς περὶ Ἀλεξανδρείας. In iis libris de Alexandria mercurii Alexandrini. Atben. lib. 15. p. 676.

(8) Ibid. lib. 5. pag. 211.

(9) Voss. de Hist. Gr. p. 232.

(12) Athen. lib. 1. c. 13. in fine.

[B] *Of all his Works.*] One was *concerning the Kings* of Syria, as himself informs us (8). *Vossius* ascribes to him another, *concerning Illustrious Men, and Generals of Armies, who had fought Duels* (9). He grounds his Opinion on these Words of the fourth Book. Ὅτι δὲ καὶ οἱ ἔνδοξοι καὶ οἱ ἡγεμόνες ἐμονομάχουν καὶ ἐκ προκλήσεως τοῦτ᾽ ἐποίουν, ἐν ἄλλοις εἰρήκαμεν (10). *But that Illustrious Men, and Generals of Armies, have fought Duels, upon Challenges, we have in another Place discoursed.* This Subject would be very proper for a particular Treatise, but it might also be inserted as an Episode in another Work, and chiefly by an Author, who ran so much Ground in a little Time, and who loved Rhapsody so well, as *Athenæus*. Therefore *Vossius's* Opinion is not very certain.

[C] *No Book has been worse treated by Transcribers, than This of Athenæus.*] The Omissions, Transpositions, and false Reasonings, are not to be numbered. These are Faults of the Transcribers; but, as to the loss of part of the Work, there is no Reason to lay That to their Charge. The two first Books, the beginning of the third, and most part of the last, are wanting. To supply this loss as well as possible, they have printed the Abridgment of what was lost, together with what was preserved entire; for, as I shall shew presently, we have still an Abridgment of the whole Work.

[D] *All the Editions we have of it are very imperfect.*] The first is That of *Aldus Manutius*, in the Year 1514. *Marcus Musurus*, a *Greek* by Nation, assisted him with his Care and Skill. However, for want of good Manuscripts, and a due Exactness in

correcting it, there remains an infinite Number of Faults in their Work. The *Basil* Edition of *John Valderus*, in Folio, which followed next in the Year 1535, by the Care of *James Bedrot*, and *Christian Herlinus*, was little better. *Natalis Comes* ventured to translate *Athenæus* into *Latin*. His Learning is very well known. It appears by his Mythology, that he had read and studied much; but, as he was ignorant in Criticism, it is certain, that his Translation is most wretched. It is the first that was published. "Ante omnes alios (nam de Sanga Romano vereor ut credendum sit Paulo Jovio) Latinum fecit Athenæum (11). Quamvis rumor spargeretur Sangam patritium Romanum, virum, ut aiunt, eximiæ doctrinæ id præstitisse (12)." *Casaubon* does not cite the Place, where *Paulus Jovius* says this: It is in the Book *de Piscibus Romanis*. These are the Words: *Sanga Romanus, Poëta lepidus, cujus beneficio Athenæum Latinum legimus* (13). But these five last Words are left out of the *Basil* Edition, in 1561, by *Henry* and *Peter Perna*: which shews, that *Paulus Jovius* had corrected his Mistake. *Dalechamp*, a famous Physician, published a second, which exceeds That of *Natalis Comes*, and might have been much better than it is, if the Author had met with less Practice. But, as he kept close to his Profession, and spent only the leisure Hours, his Patients left him, on *Athenæus*, he has not done all that might be expected from him, though for near thirty Years he dedicated all his spare Time that way (14) And thus it remained ever since. The Edition of *Dalechamp*, the *Greek* on one side, and the *Latin* on the other, with the Volume of *Casaubon's* Annotations, is the best *Athenæus* extant. The Abbot of *Marolles* has translated this *Greek* Author into *French*. I do not question but he followed the *Latin* Translation as his only Model, and has committed many Mistakes. I know nothing of this Work, but from the *Journal des Sçavans* (15). It is in 4to, and was printed at *Paris*, in the Year 1680. It is the first *French* Translation from the Original, and the last Performance of the Translator. I have been informed, that it sold so well, that it is very scarce at the Booksellers, and bears an excessive Price. As to what has been said concerning a Translation by *Sanga*, see, above, Citation (11), (12), and (13).

[E] *Somebody made an Abridgment of This Work.*] *Casaubon* confesses ingenuously, that This Abbreviator is unknown to him, and that he can neither tell his Name, nor Country, nor the Age he lived in (16). However, he places him above Five hundred Years before himself, and is very certain he ought to be placed before *Eustathius* (17), because *Eustathius* has,

(11) Casaub. Præf. Animadv. in Athenæum.

(12) Dalechamp. Ep. Dedic. Athenæi.

(13) P. Jovius de Piscibus Romanis, cap. 51. pag. 104. E. dit. 1531, ex Officina Frobeni.

(14) Ex Præfat. Casaub. in Athenæum.

(15) Of May 1680.

(16) Casaub. Animadv. in Athen. init.

(17) Id. in Præfat. & in Animadv. p. 3.

ATHENÆUS. ATRAX.

could not forbear saying something of it, but was grosly mistaken [F]. All that he has said of *Athenæus*, and of two other Persons of the same Name, is erroneous [G]. See the last Remark of this Article.

(18) Id. in Animadv. pag. 1, 2.

has, upon several Occasions, made use of the Abridgment of *Athenæus*, in Preference to the Original, which led him into some Errors (18). *Casaubon* fancies, that this Abbreviator was some Grammarian, who undertook the same thing on *Athenæus*, which *Hermolaus* had done on the Work of *Stephanus Byzantinus*, for which, in some Respects, he deserved to be commended for his Learning, and in others, to be condemned for his want of Exactness (19). The Manuscripts of *Athenæus* were very much corrupted, even when this Abridgment was made. This is proved by two Reasons: There appears several Faults in the Abridgment, answering to those in the Manuscripts: And the Abbreviator confesses, that he passes over several things, because they were corrupted (20). *Casaubon* had a Manuscript of the Abridgment (21), which *David Hoeschelius* sent him: It wanted the first Book, and part of the second; so that they had retrenched from the Beginning of it almost all that had been inserted in the Editions of *Athenæus*, to supply what was lost from the Original of the *Deipnosophists*.

(19) Ibid. pag. 3.

(20) Id. in Præfat.

(21) Id. Animadv. init.

[*F*] *Mr Moreri* —— *was grosly mistaken*] These are his Words: Athenæus *composed a Work of the* Deipnosophists, *in fifteen Books, which* Hermolaus *of* Byzantium *abridged, according to* Suidas. I pass by his Sin of Omission: No doubt he ought to have told us, whether That which is extant be the Work itself, or only the Abridgment he is speaking of. We shall only take notice of his Sins of Commission. I. It is false, that *Hermolaus of Byzantium* abridged *Athenæus*. II. It is false, that *Suidas* says so. III. It is false, that *Suidas* mentions any Abbreviator of the *Deipnosophists*. At first I took *Casaubon* to be the Cause of this Mistake, I mean a very innocent Cause; for who would ever imagine, that any one could stumble at these Words? " Putum confectam Constantinopoli ante " annos quingentos & amplius hanc epitomen ab ali- " quo Grammatico, qualis fuit Hermolaus Byzanti- " us, auctor eorum Excerptorum, quæ hodie pro " Ἐθνικῶν Stephani libris in doctorum manibus ver-" santur (22). —— *I suppose this Epitome was com-* " *posed at Constantinople, above Five hundred Years* " *ago, by some such Grammarian, as* Hermolaus *of* " Byzantium, *who is the Author of Those Extracts*, " *which now pass among the Learned, for the original* " *Work of* Stephens's *Ethnics.*" But afterwards I found, that it was *Charles Stephens*, who deceived Mr *Moreri*. I think *Volaterran* is the first, who falsely makes *Suidas* say, that *Hermolaus of Byzantium* had abridged *Athenæus*. This Fault of *Volaterran* was taken notice of in the Edition of *Athenæus*, in 1535, as may be seen, without consulting That Edition, if we cast but an Eye on *Gesner's Bibliotheca*. How easy soever it was to avoid the same Error, since *Gesner* observed it, yet it is certain, that *Charles Stephens*, *Lloyd*, and *Hofman*, are fallen headlong into it; and they assure us, which is worse, that we have no other *Athenæus*, but the Abridgment of *Her-*

(22) Ibid. pag. 3.

molaus of Byzantium: Opus, quod ad nos fanè haud-quaquam integrum pervenit: ejus epitome ab Hermolao Byzantio TANTUM *relicta: Authore Suida.*

[*G*] *What has been said* —— *of two other Persons of the same Name, is very erroneous.*] These are *Athenæus* the Historian, and *Athenæus* the Philosopher. Mr *Moreri* says, that the first *Athenæus wrote the History of Semiramis*, and that this History is to be found in the second Book of *Diodorus Siculus*, and that *Muretus* has copied it, without citing the Author. It is easy to see, that these Words contain I know not how many Contradictions. Is it usual for an Historian to crowd into a small Corner of his Work all that another Historian has wrote on a long Reign, a Reign fruitful of Events? Could such a Critic, as *Maretus*, include the whole Life of *Semiramis* in one of his short Chapters (23)? This is absurd. He ought, therefore, to have expressed himself. In this, or some such manner: Diodorus Siculus *relates an Action of Semiramis, and quotes an Author, whose Name is* Athenæus. *Muretus mentions the same Action, without quoting any Author.* To conclude from hence, that this *Athenæus* had composed the History of *Semiramis*, and ought consequently to be ranked among the Historians, is going a little too fast: According to this Rule, *Seneca* must have wrote the History of almost all the great Men in the World; for there is scarce one of them, who is not recorded by him, for some memorable Action, or Sentence. This may be said against *Vossius*, who, at a venture, places Him, whom *Diodorus Siculus* mentions, in the Number of Historians; but he has taken care not to say, positively, that the same *Athenæus* wrote the History of *Semiramis*. As to *Athenæus*, the Philosopher, it is false, that *Strabo*, cited by Mr *Moreri*, says, that he taught *Aristotle's* Philosophy at *Rome*; that, being returned home again, he was accused of a Design to form a Republic, and that he was taken into Custody. This is what *Strabo* says of him (24). " *Athenæus*, a Pe-" ripatetic Philosopher, a Native of *Seleucia*, in " *Cilicia*, had a Share in the Government, and was " a Demagogue in his Country for some time. Af-" terwards he became an intimate Friend of *Mu-*" *rena*, and fled with him, upon the Discovery of " *Murena's* Conspiracy against *Augustus*. He was " taken in his Flight; but the Emperor, not finding " him guilty, set him at Liberty. *Athenæus* re-" turned to *Rome*, and to those, he first met with, " repeated these Words of *Euripides*:

"Ἥκω νεκρῶν κευθμῶνα καὶ σκότου πύλας Λιπών.

From Death's wide Caverns, and Hell-Gates, I come.

One can hardly guess at the Original of these Mistakes of Mr *Moreri*; for it seems more difficult to corrupt things in this Manner, than to deliver them as they are found.

(23) *It is the 17th of the 16th Book*, Variarum Lectionum. *Moreri has cited it, but it is in his Article of* Athenæus *the Physician.*

(24) Strabo, lib. 14. pag. 461.

(a) Steph. Byzant. verbo Ἄτραξ.

(b) Strabo, lib. 9. pag. 303.

ATRAX, or ATRACIA (a), a City of *Thessaly* (b), on the River *Peneus*, had it's Name from *Atrax*, the Son of *Peneus*, and *Bura*, who was it's Founder (c). It must have been considerable, since the Poets have sometimes made use of the Epithet *Atracian*, to signify *Thessalian* [A]. *Pliny* places the *Atracians* amongst the People of *Ætolia* (d); but we must not from thence infer, that he would be understood to speak of them, as different from the Inhabitants of the City *Atrax*, which he assigns to *Thessaly* (e). The Divisions of Nations, and Boundaries of Provinces, have often been altered; so that the same District, which belonged, at one Time, to *Ætolia*, might, at another, be esteemed part of *Thessaly*. The River *ATRAX*, whose Mouth opened into the *Ionian* Sea (f), passed thro' the Country of the *Atracians*.

(c) Steph. Byzant. ubi supra.

(d) Plinii Histor. Nat. lib. 4. c. 2.

(e) Ibid. c. 8.

(f) Ibid. lib. 4. cap. 2.

(1) Ovid. Met. l. 12. ver. 209.

(2) Prolet Elatera, ib. ver. 89.

(3) Antonin. Liber l. Metam. c. 17.

[*A*] *The Poets have sometimes made use of the Epithet* Atracian, *to signify* Thessalian.] *Cæneus*, who was killed in the Quarrel between the *Centaurs* and *Lapithæ*, at the Wedding of *Pirithous*, is called *Atracides*, by *Ovid* (1); not to represent him as the Son of *Atrax*; for he had a little before called him the Son of *Elatus* (2); but, in general, as a *Thessalian*. I am not unaware, that some Authors (3) say, he was the Son of *Atrax*. The same Poet calls the Wife of *Pirithous* only *Atracis*.

Define mirari posito quod candida vino
Atracis ambiguos traxit in arma viros (4).

No wonder Beauty so's a Centaur warms,
And makes him quit the Nuptial Cup for Arms.

In another Place, he gives her proper Name *Hippodamia*; but he adds to it the Epithet *Atracis*.

(4) Ovid Amor. lib 1. Eleg 4. v. 7.

An

ATTALUS. ATTICUS.

An fera Centauris indicere bella coëgit
Atracis Hæmonios Hippodamia viros (5)?

Offended Beauty cruel Wars can wage;
The Centaurs felt the Force of Female Rage.

Valerius Flaccus describes her by the Words *Atracia Virgo* (6).

We cannot suppose *Ovid* takes her to be the Daughter of *Atrax*; this would prove too much. For then *Cæneus* must also have the same Father; whereas he makes him the Son of *Elatus*, and does not say one Word of *Cæneus* being Brother to the Bride; an unpardonable Omission, if he had understood him to be Brother-in law to *Pirithous*.

I take it, that *Apuleius* imagined, that *Atracis* was the proper Name of the Wife of *Pirithous*; for, as he wrote in Prose, he would not have called her by That Name, if he had thought it only a figurative and poetical Expression. *Sic instar Atracis*, says he (7), *vel* (read *&*) *Pirithoi dispectæ disturbatæque Nuptiæ. Beroaldus* very well understood it of *Hippodame*, (or *Hippodamia*,) Wife of *Pirithous*; but when he adds, that she was called *Atracis*, because she was the Daughter of *Atrax*, who was the first Inventor of Magic amongst the *Thessalians* (8), he affirms, what he ought to have proved; for we no where find, that *Atrax* established Magic. It is very true, Magic has been called *Ars Atracia* (9); but this means no more, than *Ars Thessalica*, and signifies only Magic in general, because *Thessaly* was famous for That Art (10). We are to understand in the same Sense These Verses of *Valerius Flaccus*:

Quamvis Atracio lunam spumare veneno
Sciret, & harmoniis agitari cantibus umbras (11).

Tho' by Thessalian *Arts the Moon be stain'd,*
And calls up Spirits by his Magic Strains.

The Scholiast of *Statius* is the only one, if I am not mistaken, who has said, that *Atrax* was the Father of *Hippodamia*. It is thus I would correct the Word, *Hippocatæa*, and not, as *Barthius* makes it, *Hippocrateæ* (12). The Scholiast of *Homer*, on the Twenty first Book of the *Odysse*; *Eustathius*, on the same place; and *Hyginus*, at *cap.* 23; say, that the Wife of *Pirithous* was called *Hippodamia*, and was the Daughter of *Adrastus*. I do not know whether the Genitive Ἀδρηκῷ might not have been changed into Ἀδράσου. If this was the Case, *Atrax*, the true Name of the Father of *Hippodamia*, would be lost in That of *Adrastus*. The Transcribers have made Mistakes ful as great as This. I shall give an Example, not foreign to our Subject. All the Manuscripts of *Lycophron*, at present, read ἁρπαγας λυκες, Rapaces Lupos, *Ravenous Wolves* (13); this signifies the Argonauts; but the Copy, which *Stephanus Byzantinus* made use of, read ἀτρακιας λυκες (14), *Atracenses lupos*, that is, *Thessalian Wolves*. It is thus *Eustathius* has cited this Place of *Lycophron* (15).

What *Barthius* pretends, that *Atraciæ oræ*, in *Propertius* (16), signifies a very distant Place, and that *Catullus* has used the Word *Atracis* in the same Sense (17), is not very ingenious. Some Critics, in *Catullus*, read *Ataris*, a River in *Gaul*, instead of *Atracis*, a River in *Greece*; but, however that be, we ought to understand literally the Words of *Catullus* and *Propertius* (18). As to the Supposition of *Barthius*, that they allude to the Art of Magic, it is altogether ridiculous.

ATTALUS, the Name of some Kings of *Pergamus*. See PERGAMUS.

ATTICUS (TITUS POMPONIUS) has the Character of one of the most honourable Men in ancient *Rome*. He behaved himself so prudently, that, without forfeiting his Neutrality, he preserved the Esteem and Affection of the Two contrary Parties [*A*]. The intimate Friendship, which he had for *Cicero*, did not hinder his having a very strict Union with *Hortensius*; and he brought Those Two Rivals in Eloquence not only to forbear all mutual Reflexion, but even to keep up a good Understanding [*B*]. He never had the least Difference, either with his Mother, or his

[*A*] *He preserved the Esteem and Affection of the two contrary Parties*] He sent Money to the Son of *Marius*, who was a declared Enemy to the Republic; and insinuated himself so far into *Sylla's* Favour, that this *Roman* General would always have him near him, and did not take it ill, that *Atticus* excused himself from following him to *Rome*, on account of his resolving to observe a Neutrality (1). " Noli, oro " te, inquit Pomponius, adversum eos me velle du- " cere, cum quibus ne contra te arma ferrem, Ita- " liam reliqui (2) ——*Ask me not, says* Pomponius, *" to go against those, whom because I would not fol- " low against you, I left* Italy." He kept himself quiet in *Rome*, during the War between *Cæsar* and *Pompey*; this was not displeasing to *Pompey* (3), but extremely pleasing to *Cæsar*. After the Death of the latter, he sent Money to *Brutus*, when the Party for Liberty began to grow weakest, and did a thousand good Offices to the Wife and Friends of *Marc Antony*, when his Party seemed ruined beyond all Recovery. *Marc Antony* was not ungrateful; for, though he exerted a furious Hatred against all the Friends of *Cicero*, yet he wrote, with his own Hand, a very obliging Letter to *Atticus* (4). He afterwards promoted the Marriage of *Atticus's* Daughter, with *Agrippa*, the Favourite of *Augustus* (5). Lastly, notwithstanding the cruel Divisions, which broke out between *Marc Antony* and *Augustus*, our *Atticus* maintained himself in both their Friendships. One of them (6) never set out any where, without sending him a particular Account, by Letter, of what he was doing, what he was reading, and where he was going: and, when he was at *Rome*, he wrote almost every day to consult him on some Question; the other (7) acquainted him with all his Affairs. Without doubt it was difficult to preserve, at the same time, the Friendship of two such Antagonists. "Hoc " quale sit facilius existimabit is, qui judicare poterit, " quantæ sit sapientiæ eorum retinere usum benevo- " lentiamque, inter quos maximarum rerum non so- " lum æmulatio, sed obtrectatio tanta intercedebat, " quantum fuit incidere necesse inter Cæsarem atque " Antonium, cum se uterque principem non solum " urbis Romanæ, sed orbis terrarum, esse cuperet (8). " ——*What this was, be is best able to judge, who " is sensible of the great Prudence, requisite to pre- " serve the Correspondence and Friendship of those, who " were not only Competitors for the greatest Things, " but such Enemies to one another, as* Cæsar *and An- " tony must necessarily be, when each of them aspired " to be the Emperor, not only of* Rome, *but of the whole " World.*"

[*B*] *He brought* Cicero *and* Hortensius ——*to keep up a good Understanding.*] They, who are sensible, how much an Emulation in Eloquence influences and stirs up the other Passions, will conceive no mean Idea of the Conduct and Merit of a Man, who knew how to keep the Peace between the two most famous Orators of Antiquity. It was not sufficient, that *Pomponius Atticus* could insinuate himself agreeably into People's Affections; he must also have some remarkable Qualities to deserve so great an Esteem. What I am going to quote, is, therefore, very proper to describe his Merit. " Utebatur intime Q. Hor- " tensio, qui iis temporibus principatum eloquentiæ " tenebat, ut intelligi non posset uter eum plus dili- " geret Cicero an Hortensius, & id quod erat difficil- " limum, efficiebat ut inter quos tantæ laudis esset " æmulatio, nulla intercederet obtrectatio, essetque " talium virorum copula (9). ——*He was very in- " timate with* Quintus Hortensius, *who, at that " Time, was acknowledged supreme in Eloquence, so that " it was hard to say which loved him must,* Cicero *" or* Hortensius; *and, what was most difficult of all, " he*

ATTICUS. 539

his Sister [C]. He always behaved himself generously to his Friends, and opened his Purse to them in their Necessities. This he could well afford; for, besides the great Fortunes, which fell to him by Succession [D], he found ways to lay out his Money to a very great Advantage. The Troubles, which arose at *Rome*, between the Parties of *Cinna* and *Sylla*, made him resolve, in his Youth, to go to *Athens*, where he lived a long time. He was so very much beloved by the *Athenians* [E], that the Day he left their City was, in some Manner, a Day of Mourning. He loved Learning extremely, and had, in his Family, several Librarians (a), and very good Readers. He had always something read at his Table, even when he entertained his

(a) See, below, Citation (38).

" be brought it about, that, between these two so
" great Rivals, there was not only no Contention, but
" even an Union."

[C] *He never had the least Difference either with his Mother or his Sister*] When he was Sixty seven Years of Age, he lost his Mother, who was ninety Years old, and had a Sister near the same Age with himself. He declared, at his Mother's Funeral, that he had never any Occasion to seek her Reconciliation, and that there never had been any Quarrel between his Sister and himself. " Hoc ipsum verè glorian-
" tem audierim in funere matris suæ, quam extulit
" annorum 90, cum esset septem & 60, se nunquam
" cum matre in gratiam rediisse, nunquam cum sorore
" fuisse in simultate, quam propè æqualem habebat;
" quod est signum aut nullam unquam inter eos que-
" rimoniam intercessisse, aut hunc eâ fuisse in suos in-
" dulgentiâ, ut quos amare deberet irasci eis nefas
" duceret (10)." —— *This I heard him deservedly*
" *glory in, at the Funeral of his Mother, whom he*
" *buried at ninety Years of Age, being sixty himself,*
" *that he had never stood in need of her Pardon, or*
" *been at Variance with his Sister, who was about the*
" *same Age with himself: which is a Sign, either*
" *that there was no Complaints among them, or else*
" *that he had so great an Indulgence for his Family,*
" *as to think it a Sin to be angry with those be ought*
" *to love.*" I do not mention this Circumstance of Time to swell my Book, or to fill up a Sheet of Paper: every one sees it is essential to this Remark; for, if the happy Temper of *Atticus* appears here to be so very singular, it is chiefly on account of the Number of Years he passed with his Mother and Sister without the least Broil. It is pity the History did not add how he lived with his Wife. Mr *Cornelius Nepos* should not boast at all on This Head (11); and this may create some Suspicion, that his Conduct, or Patience, could not signalize themselves so much in This respect, as towards his Mother and Sister, who perhaps, on their Part, contributed very much to That good Agreement, and did not oblige him to make great Advances. The Matter, on this Supposition, would lose much of it's Singularity with regard to *Atticus*, but, taking it all together, it would not be less, but rather more extraordinary. See, in the following Remark, that *Atticus* kept always in Favour with an Uncle, whose Temper was so humoursome, that no other of his Relations were able to bear it. Let us return to the Wife of *Atticus*. It is strange, that *Cornelius Nepos* should say nothing of her, neither good nor bad, and that we must have recourse to other Authors to know that her Name was *Pilia*, and that *Atticus* married her in the Year of *Rome* 697 (12). He was far from young; he was Fifty three Years of Age. He had made no great haste to inlist himself in That Warfare. We may collect from one of *Cicero's* Letters (13), that *Pilia* loved her Husband; for, as to That other Passage (14), from which some have concluded, that she had Thoughts of a Divorce, it is plain it ought to be read other-ways, and only signifies, that she was threatned with the Palsy. Mr *Sarazin* affirms, in his Translation of the Life of *Pomponius Atticus*, that the City of *Athens* erected also Statues to *Pilia*, the Wife of *Atticus*: but it is evident, he made use of a bad Edition; for you must not read *Pilia* in *Cornelius Nepos*. *Atticus's* Marriage was too long after his Return from *Athens*, for the *Athenians* to think of erecting Statues to his Wife. Would *Cornelius Nepos* have been so senseless as to speak of the Statues of *Pilia*, without saying who she was? The Family, *Pilia*, makes no manner of Figure in the ancient History of *Rome*.

[D] *The great Fortunes, which fell to him by Succession.*] *Quintus Cæcilius* was his Uncle by the Mother's Side. He was a Man of an insupportable Temper; but *Atticus* humoured This perverse Spirit of his so well, that he kept in his Favour, without any Interruption, to the very last. He found his Account in this Compliance; for *Cæcilius* made him his principal Heir, and left him near a Million of Money. *Atticus's* own Patrimony was about Two Hundred Thousand Li. res. *In Sestertio vicies quod a Patre acceperat* (15). In short, *Cæcilius* having adopted his Nephew by Will, it became necessary for *Atticus* to take upon him from that time the Name of *Q. Cæcilius Pomponius Atticus*. Let us see what *Cornelius Nepos* says of the peevish Temper of this Uncle. " Habebat avunculum Q. Cæcilium equitem Roma-
" num, familiarem L. Luculli (16), divitem, difficil-
" limâ naturâ, cujus sic aspertitatem veritus est, ut
" quem nemo ferre posset hujus fine offensione ad
" summam senectutem retinuerit benevolentiam: quo
" facto tulit pietatis fructum: Cæcilius enim moriens
" testamento adoptavit eum, hæredemque fecit ex
" dodrante. Ex qua hæreditate accepit circiter
" centies L L S. (17). —— He had an Uncle by
" the Mother's Side, named Q. Cæcilius, a Roman
" Knight, an intimate Friend of L. Lucullus, rich,
" and extremely ill-natured, whose Temper he was so
" fearful of offending, that, though no Body else could
" please him, he kept in Favour with him to the last;
" by which means he reaped the Fruit of his Dutiful-
" ness for Cæcilius, at his Death, adopted him in
" his Will, and made him his Heir to three Parts in Four.
" He made of this Inheritance about 100000 Sestercer."

[E] *He was very much beloved by the Athenians.*] He had carried thither the best part of his Effects, and, both by Loans and Presents, very much obliged the City of *Athens* (18). They were not ungrateful, but complimented him with all sorts of public Honours. He refused the making him a Citizen, and the erecting a Statue to him; but, after his Departure, they erected several. There was a very great Concern shewn at his leaving them. " Quo factum est
" ut huic omnes honores quos possunt publice habe-
" rent, civemque facere studerent, quo beneficio ille
" uti noluit: quod nonnulli interpretantur, amitti
" civitatem Romanam, alia adscita. Quamdiu affuit
" ne qua sibi statua poneretur restitit, absens prohi-
" bere non potuit — Tranquillatis autem rebus
" Romanis remigravit Romam —— Quem dies sic
" universa civitas Atheniensium prosecuta est, ut la-
" crymis desiderii futuri dolorem indicaret (19). —
" For which reason, they studied to heap on him all
" possible public Honours, and were desirous of making
" him a Citizen; but he declined This Favour; some
" think, because this new Freedom would have taken
" away his Privileges, as a Citizen of Rome. Whilst he
" continued there, he would never suffer any Statue
" to be erected to him, but, when he went away, he
" could not prevent it — The Distractions of his Coun-
" try being composed, he returned to Rome — Which
" Day the whole City of Athens did so strictly ob-
" serve, that they expressed, by their Tears, the great-
" ness of the Loss they were going to suffer.*" He spoke the Greek Language so perfectly well, that one would have taken him for an *Athenian* (20). Some think his Sirname of *Atticus* came from thence. *Volaterran* affirms it, as a thing related by *Cornelius Nepos* (21); but he is mistaken. The Abbot *St Real* says, that *Atticus* called himself so, because he was very learned in Greek, and lived most of his Time at Athens (22). He has been told, that he ought only to have said, on account of the long Stay he made at Athens, in his Youth; since it is certain, that he lived most part of his Life in Italy, or Epirus, where he had an Estate, as appears by his Life, written by Cornelius Nepos, and by several Passages in *Cicero's* Letters (23).

[F] *He*

(10) Corn. Nepos, in Vita Attici, cap. 17.

(11) Corn. Nepos, in Vita Attici, cap. 17.

(12) See the third Epistle of Cicero ad Quintum Fratrem, lib. 2. and Fabricius in the Life of Cicero ad annum urbis 697.

(13) The 13th of the 9th Book to Atticus.

(14) Of the 7th Epistle of the 16th Book to Atticus.

(15) Corn. Nepos, c. 14.

(16) Valer. Maximus, lib. 7. c. 8. n. c. says, that Cæcilius us had promised to make Lucullus his Heir, and that, having deceived him, his Corpse was dragged through the Streets.

(17) Corn. Nepos, c. 5.

(18) Ibid. cap. 2.

(19) Ibid. cap. 3. & 4.

(20) Ibid. cap. 4.

(21) Volaterr. lib. 18 pag. 666.

(22) Remarks on Cicero's Epistles to Atticus, in the Bibliotheque Universelle, Tom. 20. pag. 78.

(23) The Author of Bibliotheque Universelle, ibid.

VOL. I. 6 U

ATTICUS.

his Friends [F]. He never had a Thought of advancing himself above the Rank he was born to, which was That of a Knight. He might have attained to great Offices in the Republic; but he chose rather to decline them [G]; because, in the Corruption, which then reigned, he could neither obtain, nor exercise, them legally. He never had a Law-Suit in his Life. He never impeached any one, nor seconded Those, who did. The Emperor *Augustus* was related to him; the manner of the Relation was thus. *Atticus* had married his Daughter to *Agrippa*. That Marriage produced a Daughter, whom *Augustus* betrothed to *Tiberius* almost as soon as she was born (*b*). I believe the Wife of *Atticus* was of no great Family (*c*). He deserves a Place in the List of good Authors [H]. He attained to the Age of Seventy seven Years almost without knowing what Sickness was. He had lived for Thirty Years together without any occasion for Physic. At last he fell sick, and, for Three Months, his Distemper was but slight, but, afterwards, his Pains were excessive. He sent for his Son-in-Law *Agrippa*, and two other Persons, and declared to them, he was resolved to put an end to his Life by abstaining from all Nourishment; he desired them to approve of his Resolution, and not oppose it, since all their Exhortations would be in vain. *Agrippa*, however, employed both his Prayers, and his Tears, to prevail with him to live, but all to no purpose. After two Days Abstinence, his Fever ceased, and his Pains were much abated; yet *Atticus* persisted in his Resolution, and died three Days after (*d*). This was in the Year of *Rome* 721. He is fallen, in our Times, into

(*b*) Nata est Attico nepti ex Agrippa, cui virginem filiam collocarat. Hanc Cæsar vix annıculam Tiberio Claudio Neroni Drusilla nato privigno suo desponsit. --- Atticus had a Granddaughter, by Agrippa, whom had married his Daughter. Cæsar, when she was scarce a Year old, betrothed her to Tiberius Claudius Nero, who was born of Drusilla, by his Son-in-law. Corn. Nepos in Vita Attici, cap. 19.

(*c*) See Remark [C] towards the end.

(*d*) Ex Cornelio Nepote, in Vita Pomponii Attici.

[F] *He had always something read at his Table, even when he entertained his Friends.*] If he had kept an open Table for all sorts of Guests, this Custom of Reading would have been very disagreeable to a great many People; but he invited none, but those of his own Taste. "*Nemo in convivio ejus aliud* "*acroama audivit quam anagnosten* ---- *Neque un-* "*quam sine aliqua lectione apud eum cœnatum est,* "*ut non minus animo quam ventre conviva delecta-* "*rentur, namque eos vocabat quorum mores a suis* "*non abhorrerent* (24). --------- *No Body heard* "*any other Music at his Entertainments, but Reading.* "*Nor did any Body eat with him, without something* "*being read; so that his Company were entertained in* "*their Minds, as well as Bodies; for he invited those* "*only, who were of the same Taste with himself.*"

[G] *He might have attained to great Offices in the Republic, but he chose rather to decline them.*] This was certainly the strongest Proof he gave of his Virtue. There was no attaining to Offices in those Times but by ill Practices; nor could they be exercised according to the Rules of Justice, and for the public Good, without running the Hazard of some Violence from a great many ill Persons. He chose therefore rather to live in a private Condition, than to purchase Dignities at the Price of his Conscience. How good and rare is this! If all the World were of *Atticus*'s Mind, there would be Room to apprehend a State of Anarchy; but we may sleep very quietly on this Score: there never will be wanting a Number of Persons, corrupt enough to accept of Employments, upon any sort of dishonest Terms, greater than the Number of Places to bestow on them. I have been told, that a Person, who had travelled all his Life-time, answered those, who made a Jest of his unsettled Temper, that he would willingly have fixt in some Town or other, if he could but have found one, where Power and Credit were in the Hands of honest Men. Another Traveller, happening once to declare, that he would ramble no longer, than till he could meet with a Town governed by Men of the most Merit, was answered, YOU WILL DIE THEN IN YOUR TRAVELS. "*Honores non petiit cum ei paterent prop-* "*ter vel gratiam vel dignitatem; quod neque peti* "*more majorum, neque capi possent conservatis legi-* "*bus, in tam effusis ambitus largitionibus, neque geri* "*è republica sine periculo, corruptis civitatis mori-* "*bus* (25). ----- *He declined all public Offices, tho'* "*both his Interest and Authority were great enough to* "*have got him any Thing: Because they could neither* "*be applied for, according to the Custom of his An-* "*cestors, nor procured, without breaking through the* "*Laws by excessive Briberies, nor discharged with* "*Integrity, even under the Sanction of the Govern-* "*ment, without very great Danger, from so general* "*a Degree of Corruption.*" Compare with this what was said, above, in the Article of ALEXANDER ab ALEXANDRO.

[H] *Atticus deserves a Place in the List of good Authors.*] He composed Annals, wherein he observed an exact Chronology, and cleared the Genealogies of the *Roman* Magistrates in the plainest Manner that could be. This Work comprehended seven Centuries; from whence we may easily conjecture, that it principally concerned the *Roman* History. I say *principally*; for no doubt but the Author, in his Chronological Series, gave an abstracted Account of several other States. *Cicero* puts it beyond all Question: "*Cognoscat etiam, says he* (26), *rerum gestarum &* "*memoriæ veteris ordinem maxime scilicet nostræ* "*civitatis: sed & imperiosorum populorum & regum* "*illustrium: quem laborem nobis Attici nostri levavit* "*labor, qui conservatis notatisque temporibus nihil* "*cum illustre prætermitteret, annorum septingento-* "*rum memoriam uno libro colligavit.* ----- *Let him* "*be well acquainted with the Chronological Order of* "*the Customs and Actions of Antiquity, chiefly of our* "*own City, but also of other considerable States, and* "*illustrious Princes: which will now become an easier* "*Work, by the Pains our Atticus has taken, who, by* "*an exact Observation and Distinction of Times, with-* "*out omitting any Thing remarkable, has included an* "*Account of Seven hundred Years in one Book.*" These Annals seem to have contained a kind of Chronological Tables. "*Habuit iste liber Attici & nova* "*mihi quidem multa, & eam utilitatem quam requi-* "*rebam, ut explicatis ordinibus temporum uno in* "*conspectu omnia viderem* (27). ---- *This Book of* "*Atticus had indeed many Things new to me, and* "*such a Conveniency as pleased me, by digesting the* "*Order of Times in such a manner, that I could see* "*every thing at one View.*" I have already said, that *Atticus* observed the Genealogical Order very exactly: I shall add here, that he wrote particular *Treatises on some Families*, and composed Inscriptions, of four or five Verses each, to be placed under the Portraitures of eminent Persons; and that his Talent was much admired in expressing so many things in so few Words. "*Attigit quoque Poëticen, credimus, ne ejus expers* "*esset suavitatis. Namque versibus qui honore rerum-* "*que gestarum amplitudine cæteros Romani populi* "*præstiterunt expoluit, ita ut singulorum imaginibus* "*facta magistratusque eorum non amplius quaternis* "*quinisque versibus descripserit, quod vix credendum* "*sit tantas res tam breviter potuisse declarari* (28). --- "*Moris etiam majorum summus imitator fuit anti-* "*quitatisque amator, quam adeo diligenter habuit* "*cognitam, ut eam totam in eo volumine exposuerit,* "*quo magistratus ornavit. Nulla enim lex, neque* "*pax, neque bellum, neque res illustris est populi* "*Romani, quæ non in eo suo tempore sit notata, &,* "*quod difficillimum fuit, sic familiarum originem* "*subtexuit, ut ex eo clarorum virorum propaginea* "*possimus cognoscere. Fecit hoc idem separatim in* "*aliis libris, ut M. Bruti rogatu Juniam familiam a* "*stirpe ad hanc ætatem ordine enumeravit, notans* "*qui a quo ortus, quos honores, quibusque tempori-* "*bus cepisset. Pari modo Marcelli Claudii de Mar-* "*cellorum; Scipionis Cornelii, & Fabii Maximi de* "*Corneliorum, & Fabiorum, & Æmiliorum quoque,* "*quibus libris nihil potest esse dulcius eis qui aliquam* "*cupiditatem habent notitiæ clarorum virorum* (29). "----- *He attempted something also in Poetry; very* "*likely, that he might be no Stranger to it's Harmony.* "*For*

(24) Corn. Nepos, c. 24.

(25) Ibid. cap 6.

(26) Cicero in Oratore.

(27) Idem, in Bruto.

(28) Corn. Nepos, cap. 18.

(29) Ibid.

ATTICUS. ATTILA.

into the Hands of a very severe Censor [*I*]; but he has not been left undefended against the Rigour of these Censures [*K*]. We have something to correct in Mr *Moreri's* Dictionary [*L*]. I forgot to mention, that *Atticus* was of the Sect of *Epicurus* (*e*), and that we may defy the most zealous Defenders of That Doctrine, which holds it impossible, that Men, without the Belief of a Providence, can equal in Virtue Those, who acknowledge a *Jupiter*, a *Neptune* &c. to shew a better Man, than *Atticus*, among the greatest Bigots of Paganism.

(*e*) See Gassendus de Vita Epicuri, lib. 2. cap. 6.

"For he is described, in no more than four or five Verses, under each Picture of some of the most famous Romans, all the Offices and Actions, for which they had been eminent, and expressed so many Things in so few Words, as it is scarce to be credited. —— He was also a strict Imitator of the Customs of his Ancestors, and a Lover of Antiquity, which he so perfectly understood, that he wrote a full Account of it, in the same Work, which he composed concerning Magistrates. For there is not a Law, a War, a Peace, or any one remarkable Thing relating to the Roman People, which he did not mention in it, together with the Time when each happened. And, what was most difficult of all, he has so nicely traced the Original of Families, that it is easy to see from what Stocks our great Men are derived. He composed particular Pedigrees in other Books; one for the Junian Family, at the Request of M. Brutus, from the very Beginning of it, in exact Order, down to our Times, remarking every Branch, from whence sprung, what Honours, and in what Times, each had enjoyed. In like manner, he obliged Marcellus Claudius with the Genealogy of the Marcelli, and Scipio Cornelius, and Fabius Maximus, with those of the Cornelii, the Fabii, and the Æmilii; which Book, afford the greatest Pleasure imaginable to such as are curious to know the Particulars concerning eminent Men." It is pity these Books are lost; they would clear up a very great Number of Difficulties. I say nothing of the *History of Cicero's Consulship*, which *Atticus* had wrote in the *Greek* Language (30), and in a plain Style (31).

[*I*] *He is fallen, in our Times, into the Hands of a very severe Censor.*] It is the Abbot of St *Real*. See the Book entitled *Cesarion, ou Entretiens divers*. It was printed at the *Hague*, from the *Paris* Edition in 1685. It is divided into four Days, the third of which contains a very severe Censure on *Pomponius Atticus*, and his Panegyrist *Cornelius Nepos*. I have been informed, that the Author of This Work persisted in the same Sentiments, and that it appears by the Remarks he has added to the Translation of the two first Books of *Cicero's Letters* to *Atticus*. That Translation is mentioned in a Book very well known (32), and I have always wondered, that the Booksellers of *Amsterdam* did not counterfeit it; for I don't question but much may be learned by reading This Work.

[*K*] *But he has not been left undefended against the Rigour of these Censures.*] In the Year of 1686, there appeared a little Book in *Holland*, entitled, *Le retour des pieces choisies, ou bigarrures curieuses*, which, amongst other Things, contains an Apology for *Pomponius Atticus* against the Attacks of *Cesarion*. The Author of the Apology conceals his Name; but it is no Secret, that it was the late Mr *Reinssant*, his most Christian Majesty's Cabinet-keeper of Medals. The *News from the Republic of Letters* (33) enlarged on this Piece of Mr *Reinssant's*, in such a manner as was not pleasing to the Abbot of St *Reale*.

[*L*] *We have something to correct in Mr Moreri's Dictionary.*] I. It is false, that *Cicero* married *Atticus's* Sister. It was *Cicero's* Brother, who married her. II. He ought not to have mentioned

the Ties of Friendship, occasioned by This Marriage; since *Cornelius Nepos* observes very particularly, that *Atticus* had more kindness for *Cicero*, than for his Brother-in-law *Quintus Cicero*. "Erat nupta soror Attici Q. Tullio Ciceroni, easque nuptias M. Cicero conciliarat, cum quo à condiscipulatu vivebat conjunctissimè, multo etiam familiarius, quam cum Quinto, ut judicari possit plus in amicitia valere similitudinem morum quam affinitatem (34). ------ *Atticus's Sister was married to* Q. Tullius Cicero; *the Match was made by* M. Cicero, *with whom he had lived in the greatest Intimacy from the Time of their being Schoolfellows, and much more familiarly, than even now with* Quintus; *whence we may judge, that Friendship is not so much governed by nearness of Relation, as by Similitude of Manners.*" *Pomponia*, the Sister of *Atticus*, did not always live well with her Husband (35); so that she was not very fit to tie the Knot of Friendship between her Husband, and Brother. III. *Cicero* did not dedicate a Volume of his Letters to *Atticus*; it should have been said, that he kept a continual Correspondence with him by Letters, and that we have a Collection of the Letters, he wrote to him, divided into sixteen Book. *Cornelius Nepos* mentions it (36), and says, that they comprehend the History of those Times, and, in some sort, a Prophecy of what was to follow. "Ut nihil in iis non appareat, & facile existimari possit prudentiam quodammodo esse divinationem. Non enim Cicero ea solum quæ vivo se accidèrunt futura prædixit, sed etiam quæ nunc usu veniunt cecinit ut vates. —— *That nothing was omitted in them, and it may be truly said, that his Judgment was, in some sort, prophetical; for* Cicero, *like a true Prophet, did not only foretel what would happen in his own Time, but also what is now come to pass in ours.*" IV. It is carrying the Point too far, to say, That Atticus had no other Servants, but such as were fit to read to him. It was sufficient to have said, that he had several ingenious Domesticks, who could read, and write, very well, and bind Books; and that every one of his Footmen could do This (37). *Cornelius Nepos* says no more of it; Who, therefore, in the XVth Century, would take upon him, to make twenty times as much of it? Has he not expressly observed, that, besides his Domesticks, who might be Readers, and Librarians (38), *Atticus* had others, all very well instructed, and born, and bred, in his House? "In ea (familia) erant pueri literatissimi, anagnostæ optimi, & plurimi librarii, ut ne pedissequus quidem quisquam esset qui non utrumque horum pulchre facere posset. Pari modo ARTIFICES CETERI quos cultus domesticus desiderat apprime boni. Neque tamen horum quemquam, nisi domi natum domique factum, habuit (39). —— *He had, in his Family, very learned Youths, excellent Readers, and many of them Librarians, and every one of his Lockeys had both Qualifications. He had, also,* OTHER ARTIFICERS, *most skilful in their kinds, for all domestic Uses; and every one of them born, and educated, in his House.*" The first, and third, of these four Mistakes, are not in the *Holland* Edition.

(30) Ibid.
(31) *Cicero*, Epist. 7. lib. 2. ad Atticum.
(32) *In the 2. tb Tome of the Bibliotheque Universelle*, p. 73. See also *the Journal des Sçavans fr* Febr. 12, 1691.
(33) *Of Dec.* 1686. Artic. 4. p. 1405.
(34) Corn. Nepos, c. 5.
(35) See *Cicero's* Ep.l. to *Atticus*, l. 5. Epist. 1.
(36) Cap. 16.
(37) *We find the Names of some of these Domesticks of* Atticus, *in the Epistles* Cicero *wrote to him*.
(38) *This Word means both Persons transcribing, and making up of Books, or binding them, according to the manner of those Times.*
(39) Corn. Nepos, c. 13.

ATTILA, King of the *Huns*, sirnamed *the Scourge of God*, lived in the Vth Century. He may be reckoned among the greatest Conquerors, since there were but few Provinces in *Europe*, which did not feel the Weight of his victorious Arms. He would not grant the Emperor *Theodosius* a Peace, on any other Condition, than of becoming his Tributary [*A*]. The Battle, he lost in *Champagne* (*a*), in the Year 451

(*a*) In Campis Catalaunicis.

[*A*] *He would not grant the Emperor* Theodosius *a Peace, on any other Condition, than of becoming his Tributary.*] According to the rodomontado Maxim, *That we ought to give Things an honourable Name*, what the Emperor was obliged to pay, every Year, to *Attila*, was not called a Tribute, but a Pension. These are the Words of a modern Author. "He forced the Emperor *Theodosius*, the younger, shamefully to beg a Peace of him; neither could he obtain it, without buying it, by paying him down Six thou-
"sand

ATTILA.

451, did not weaken him to such a degree, but that he soon found himself in a Condition to proceed to ravage *Italy*; and, if the Prayers of Pope *Leo* had not stopped him, he would infallibly have taken the City of *Rome*. We must not believe what is reported of the Apparition of an old Man standing with a naked Sword in his Hand by St *Leo's* side, and threatning *Attila*. This King of the *Huns* was of a small Stature (*b*); but That did not hinder his striking a Terror into the most couragious, by his lofty Carriage and fierce Countenance. He knew very well how to join Craft with Force [*B*]. Superstition was one part of his Politics [*C*]. He was an artful, subtle, Dissembler, wise in Council, and daring in Execution, cruel to his Enemies, but merciful enough to those, who submitted to him in the Posture of Supplicants. He is also said to have made it a Point of Honour, to keep his Faith inviolably with those, whom he had once received into his Protection (*c*). He would not suffer extravagant Flatterers (*d*). The most common Opinion about the Manner of his Death is, that he was suffocated, by a Bleeding at the Nose, on his Wedding Night [*D*]. We shall relate in another Place (*e*), how greatly he was courted by HONORIA.

(*b*) Maimbourg Hist. de l'Arianisme, Tom. 3. pag. 5. ex Jornande, cap. 25. & à Paulo Diacono in Miscell. lib. 15.

(*c*) Maimbourg supra. See Remark [*E*].

(*d*) See the Article MARULLUS of Constantinople.

(*e*) In the Article HONORIA.

———

"sand Pound Weight of Gold *, and obliging him-
"self to pay him One thousand more every Year †: So
"that the Emperor of the East, whatever Recourse
"he had to the specious Title of Pension, to save
"his Honour, became Tributary to the *Huns* (1)."
The same Author relates, that " *Attila*, having seen
"a Picture, in the Palace of *Milan*, which repre-
"sented an Emperor on his Throne, with the *Scy-
"thians*, in Chains, at his Feet, ordered it to be
"taken away, and another put in it's Place, wherein
"he himself was drawn, sitting on a Throne, sur-
"rounded with Emperors, loaden with Bags of Gold
"and Silver, which they emptied at his Feet, in a very
"submissive Posture; intending to shew thereby, that,
"as he had obliged *Theodosius* to pay him Tribute
"seven or eight Years before, he would force the
"Emperor *Valentinian* to do the same, to save his
"Life, and the miserable Remains of his Em-
"pire (2)."

[*B*] *He knew very well how to join Craft with Force*] This appears by the Intrigue, which he managed in his Expedition against the *Gauls*. He endeavoured to disunite the *Romans*, commanded by *Ætius*, from the *Visigoths*, under their King *Theodoric*. For this Purpose he sent Word to the Emperor *Valentinian*, that he had no Thoughts of committing any Acts of Hostility against the Subjects of the Empire, that he only intended to chastise the *Francs*, and the *Visigoths*, whereof the former had been so audacious as to invade the Territories of the Empire, and the latter were only Slaves to *Valentinian*. At the same time he let *Theodoric* understand, that he had made the King of the *Vandals* believe, that he came into *Gaul* against the *Visigoths*: but, that it was only a Pretence to deceive the Emperor; that his true Design was to divide the Empire, between the *Huns*, and the *Visigoths*, and that he would fall upon *Italy*, if *Theodoric* would attack the *Gauls* (3). *Valentinian* and *Theodoric* easily discovered this Snare, and jointly repulsed This crafty Conqueror. "Homo subtilis,
"antequam bella gereret, arte pugnabat, cætera epi-
"stolas blandimentis oppleverat, studens fidem adhi-
"bere mendacio (4)." —— *An artful Man, before
"he engaged in a War, he fought with the Weapons
"of Policy, he filled his Letters with Compliments,
"the better to cover his Dissimulation.*"

[*C*] *Superstition was one Part of his Politics*] "He found means to possess the Minds of his Sol-
"diers with a superstitious Belief, that he had some-
"thing in him divine, on which his good Fortune
"depended; for, whether he believed it himself,
"or rather only pretended so, he made them be-
"lieve, he had found the Scymitar of *Mars*, who
"was worshipped by That People, and that the Fates
"had promised the Empire of the World to Him,
"who should be possessed of That fatal Sword (5)."
This is one of the most prevailing Stratagems, that a General of an Army can make use of, to manage, and move, his Soldiers, by the Springs of a mysterious Superstition, which fills them either with Resolution, or Fear, according as the Case requires; with Resolution, when there is occasion for Fighting, and with Fear, when they are inclinable to Mutiny. It is very well for a Soldier to be persuaded, that his General has a Guardian Angel, who delivers him out of all Danger (6). *Attila* was superstitious himself: "Religioni persuasionibusque de Diis à suâ gente
"susceptis usque ad superstitionem addictus (7)." ——

"*Addicted much to Religion, and a Belief in all the
"Notions of his Country, concerning the Gods, even to a
"Degree of Superstition;*" for, a little before the Battle of *Chalons*, " he consulted his Diviners, who told him,
"that, in truth, they could discover nothing advan-
"tageous to the *Huns*, from all their Observations,
"but that the Enemy's General would be killed
"in the Battle. This was enough to deceive *Attila*;
"he imagined, the Death of *Ætius* was certain,
"and that, the Obstacle being thus removed, his
"Way would be open to the Conquest of the Em-
"pire. He did not value the Loss of his Soldiers,
"being fully persuaded, he should always have a suffi-
"cient Number left, provided he survived That
"Great Commander (8)." But he was deceived, for *Ætius* was not so much as wounded in the Battle."

[*D*] *He was suffocated, by a Bleeding at the Nose, on his Wedding-Night*] It is reported, that, after Pope *Leo's* Prayers had prevailed with him to spare the rest of *Italy*, he returned into *Pannonia*, laden with the Spoil, and that, though he had a great Number of Concubines, yet he would take one more, who was the Daughter of the King of the *Bactrians*. She was a perfect Beauty; and he loved her so passionately, that he would honour her with all the Ceremonies of Marriage, and give her the first Rank among his Wives. He kept his Wedding with great Solemnity; but he drank so much, and afterwards heated himself so excessively, in the Embraces of his new Wife, that, being at last fallen asleep, he was taken with a Bleeding at the Nose, which suffocated him. "Ildico puella ei fuit præ cæteris
"gratissima, Bactrianorum regis filia mira pulchri-
"tudine & incomparabili venustate, cujus amore
"succensus eam primariæ uxoris loco habere con-
"stituit. Comparatis pro regia dignitate nuptiis, per
"omnem intemperantiæ licentiam in conjugali con-
"vivio sibi indulsit, Baccho ac Veneri corpus ita
"ea nocte confecit, ut, inter dormiendum supino cor-
"pore, profluvio sanguinis è naribus continuo suf-
"focatus interierit (9). —— *A Virgin, named* Ildico,
"*charmed him above all the rest, Daughter of the
"King of the* Bactrians, *and an incomparable Beau-
"ty, with whom he was so passionately in Love, that
"he determined to give her the first Place among
"his Wives. The Nuptials being solemnized suitably
"to the Royal Dignity, he gave himself up to all
"possible Intemperance: at his Wedding Feast, and so
"inflamed his Body, that Night, with the Excesses
"of both Bacchus and Venus, that, as he lay sleep-
"ing on his Back, a Bleeding at the Nose suddenly suf-
"focated him.*" This Story would All be probable enough, if they had not added, that *Attila* was then One hundred and twenty four Years of Age. It is hard to believe, that, at such an Age, a Man should be capable of so great Excesses with the Fair Sex. A *Friesland* Historian has alledged this Fact, in favour of the Histories of his own Nation, which make their Kings very long lived. He does not borrow it from *Bonfinius*, but from *Michael Ritbius*. " His adde testimonium Michaelis Rithii, qui libro
"de regibus Hungariæ primo scribit, Atthilam Ita-
"lica præda opimique spoliis onustum in Panno-
"niam se recepisse, uxoremque superduxisse regis
"Bactrianorum nomine Milzoth, etsi plures alias ha-
"beret in matrimonio, eumque cum nuptiales epulas
"apparatissime celebrasset, liberius solito crapulatum
"in

ATTILA. ATTILIUS.

by the Sister of *Valentinian* III. His Life was written, in the XVth Century, by an Italian Refugee in *Poland*, named *Callimachus Experiens*. Others have wrote it since [*E*].

It is said, he was ambitious of abolishing the *Roman* Language, and establishing his own in its stead [*F*].

(10) Bernard. Furmerius Annal. Phrisicor. lib. 3. cap. 9. pag. 243.

" in cubiculum se recepisse, erumpentque è naribus " sanguine in os dormientis ext.actum esse, anno " ætatis suæ 124, regni sui 44. Si tantam ætatem " in hoc libidinoso tauro Scythico credimus, cur non " & eamdem Frisiis accidere potuisse censeamus (10)?

—— To these we may add the Testimony of Michael Rithius, *who, in his first Book of the Kings of Hungary, says, that* Attila, *loaden with the Spoils and Wealth of Italy, retired into Pannonia, and married a Wife, named* Miloth, *of the Family of the King of the* Bactrians, *though he had already a great many others: and that, celebrating his Nuptial Entertainment, with the greatest Solemnity, he drank so much harder than usual, that, after he got to bed, a Bleeding at the Nose seized him, as he slept, and suffocated him, in the One hundred and twenty fourth Year of his Age, and the Forty fourth of his Reign. If this lustful Scythian Bull could attain to so great an Age, why might not the same Thing happen in our Country of* Friesland ?" Lastly, some have related, that *Attila* did not die in this Manner; but that his new Wife, who did not love him, finding him drunk, and fast asleep, like another *Holophernes*, stabbed him with a Knife (11).

(11) Maimb. Hist. de l'Arianisme, Tom. 3. pag. 35. ann. 453, ex Cassiodoro.

[*E*] *Others have wrote it since.*] Nicholas Olahus, Archbishop of *Strigonium*, wrote the Life of *Attila*, much more fully than *Callimachus Experiens*. He composed it, while he was Counsellor to Mary of *Austria*, Governess of the *Netherlands*. You read, in it, the Speech, which *Attila* made to his Army, a little before the Battle of *Chalons*. That Speech is formed on all the common Places, as appears by the marginal Notes. *Sambucus* has inserted This Work of *Olahus*, and That of *Callimachus Experiens*, in his Edition of *Bonfinius*. The Sieur *Otrokocsi* (12), who published a Book on the Origin of the *Hungarians*, makes ample mention of *Attila*, chiefly taken from the Relation of *Priscus*, who had accompanied the Ambassadors sent by *Theodosius* to This King of the *Huns*, in the Year 448. He draws divers Observations from That Relation,

(12) He is a Protestant Divine, an Hungarian Refugee. His Book, intituled Origines Hungaricæ, was printed at Franeker, in 8vo, in 1693.

to shew, that *Attila* was a very honourable Person: He does not forget the Reproaches, which That Prince caused to be made to the Emperor *Theodosius*, on the Eunuch *Chrysaphius*'s endeavouring to engage *Edecon*, *Attila*'s Envoy at the Court of *Theodosius*, to murder his Master. This Envoy pretended to undertake it for a great Sum of Money, which was promised him; and afterwards discovered all to *Attila*. The Money was brought, and the Plot proved; the King of the *Huns* complained of it to *Theodosius*, in a grand Manner, and with an Air suitable enough to the Character given him, of Easiness to his Suppliants, and Steadiness to his Word. " Supplicibus propè ad " mollitiem facilis, & qui in fidem semel receptos " in perniciem usque suam tueretur (13). —— *Easy, almost to a Degree of Weakness, to his Suppliants, and a Protector of those, whose Cause he had once undertaken, even to his own Prejudice.*"

(13) Callim. Experiens.

[*F*] *It is said, he was ambitious of abolishing the* Roman *Language, and establishing his own in it's stead.*] I have met with this, in a Piece of *Alcyonius*, where *John de Medicis*, who was Pope *Leo* X, is introduced speaking these Words. " In Bibliotheca " nostrâ asservatur Liber incerti autoris Græcè scrip- " tus de reb. à Gotis in Italiâ gestis: in eo memini me " legere Attilam regem post partam victoriam tam " studiosum fuisse Goticæ linguæ propagandæ, ut " edicto sanxerit ne quis linguâ latinâ loqueretur, " Magistrosque insuper è suâ provinciâ accivisse, " qui Italos Goticam linguam edocerent (14). —— *In our Library is preserved a Book, of an uncertain Author, written in* Greek, *concerning the Adventures of the* Goths *in* Italy, *in which I remember to have read, that King* Attila, *after his Conquest, was so set upon propagating the* Gothic *Tongue, that he prohibited the speaking* Latin, *by an Edict, and sent for Masters from his own Country to teach the* Italians *this new Language.*" In the Article of the Emperor CLAUDIUS (15), you will find some Collections, concerning the Zeal of several Princes, for the Language of their Country.

(14) Petrus Alcyonius, in Medice Legato posteriore, fol. h iij, verso.

(15) *Remark* [*A*].

ATTILIUS, a *Latin* Poet, lived, according to all appearances, in the Beginning of the VIIth Century of *Rome*. *Volcatius Sedigitus* has given him the fifth Place among the Ten Comic Poets. Yet he was but a mean Author; his Stile was as hard as Iron (*a*), not only according to *Cicero*'s Taste, but even according to *Licinius*'s, who had nothing near so delicate an Ear as *Cicero*. The Translation of *Sophocles*'s *Electra* by *Attilius* was good for nothing; and yet *Cicero* judged it worth the Reading (*b*). *Suetonius* observes, that some Passages were taken out of it to be sung at *Julius Cæsar*'s Funeral, because they were applicable to the Murtherers of That Emperor (*c*). *Casaubon* and *Torrentius* have in vain altered That Passage of *Suetonius* [*A*]. They have only given an Example of the Confusion, which Criticism may sometimes occasion.

(*a*) *See Remark* [*I*] *of the Article* ACCIUS, *at the beginning*.

(*b*) *See the same Remark*.

(*c*) Sueton. in Cæsare, cap. 94.

[*A*] *Casaubon and Torrentius have in vain altered That Passage of* Suetonius.] *Casaubon*, having found, *Ex Electra Attilii alia ad similem sententiam*, in all the Copies of *Suetonius*, was, nevertheless, of Opinion, that This *Attilii* ought to be changed for *Attii*. " Sic emendavimus, *says he*, corruptam omnium li- " brorum lectionem Attilii. —— *We have thus corrected the corrupt reading of* Attilii *in all the Books.*" *Torrentius* is not satisfied with putting out *Attilius*, in favour of *Attius*: he puts out *Electra* also, upon Pretence, that *Suetonius* has mentioned but one Piece of *Attius*, intituled, *Armorum judicium*, like That of *Pacuvius*, which he had but just quoted. The Reason *Torrentius* gives for his Emendation, is, that the Manuscripts vary extremely, as to the Name of This Poet, but that the greatest Number of them have *Accius*, or *Attius*. Thus we see the Critics do not agree on the Readings of the Manuscripts, which is a Matter of Fact. *Casaubon* confesses, he found *Attilius* every where. *Torrentius* says, on the contrary, that he met with *Attilius* but seldom. *Peter Crinitus* complained, that the Grammarians had put *Accius*, instead of *Attilius*, in That Passage of *Suetonius* (1). But let us come to something of more Substance. Though *Casaubon* has not given us his Reason for changing the Text, we

(1) P. Crin. de Lat. Lat. c. 14.

need not doubt but it was the same with That of *Torrentius*. Now *Torrentius*'s Reason is this: He did not remember to have read any thing concerning the *Electra* of *Attius*, nor concerning a Poet, whose Name was *Attilius*. It is not so surprizing, that a learned Man should suffer himself to be hurried away to the Denial of a Fact, upon so weak a Principle as This, as that two such excellent Critics should be ignorant, that *Cicero* mentions the *Electra* of *Attilius*; that he treats *Attilius* as a very harsh Poet; that *Volcatius Sedigitus* speaks handsomely of him, in *Aulus Gellius*; and that *Varro* quotes him in his fifth and sixth Books of the *Latin* Tongue (2). I say nothing of *Crinitus*, nor of *Gregory Gyraldus*, who have remembred him in the Lives of the *Latin* Poets, by such Tokens, that the latter has falsely charged *Cicero* with calling him a Tragic Poet (3). I shall not meddle with the Complaints, which have been made against those, who alter the Reading of Manuscripts, according to the Model of their own Understandings. This would be entering upon That Subject very unseasonably, considering the great Services, which *Casaubon* has done to the Republic of Learning, by his vast and judicious Erudition. *Torrentius*'s Merit is not of so high a Stamp; but it, has it's Value, which I would not in the least depretiate.

(2) See Ressnelius Var. Lect. lib 3, cap. 3, pag. 379. apud Sueton. Crevis. in Cæsare, cap. 94.

(3) Vossius, de Poët. Lat. pag. 7.

ATTIUS.

ATTIUS. AUBERI. AUBERTIN.

ATTIUS (LUCIUS) a Tragic Poet. *See* ACCIUS.

AUBERI (N.) Author of an History of Cardinal *de Richelieu* [*A*], and of Cardinal *Mazarin*; see the Journal *des Sçavans* (a). If some particular Reason does not hinder me, I shall always make use of such a Reference as This, when the Book to be referred to is easily to be met with, and only contains the Life of a Person in a very compendious manner.

(a) *For the 14th of March, 1695, pag. 115, & seq. of the Holland Edition.*

[*A*] AUBERI, *Author of an History of Cardinal* de Richelieu.] It was printed at *Paris*, in Folio, in the Year 1660, with two other Volumes, containing *Letters, Instructions*, and *Memoirs. Anthony Bertier*, Bookseller of *Paris*, who printed them, had collected the Pieces contained in the two latter, with great Care; but he represented to the Queen Mother, *That he durst not publish them, without her Majesty's particular Authority and Protection, because there were several Persons in favour again at Court, whose past Conduct not having been regular, and appearing very much to their Disadvantage, in those Memoirs, would certainly occasion him a great deal of Trouble.* Go on, said the Queen to him, *finish your Work without Fear, and make Vice so much ashamed, that nothing but Virtue may shew it's Face in France* (1).

(1) LaCaille, *History of Printing, p. 285, 286.*

AUBERTIN (EDMUND) in *Latin Edmundus Albertinus*, Minister of the Church of *Paris* in the XVIIth Century, was a very learned Man. He was born, at *Chalons* on *Marne*, in the Year 1595. He was received into the Ministry at the Synod of *Charenton*, in the Year 1618, and appointed to the Church of *Chartres*, from whence he was transferred to *Paris* in the Year 1631 (a). He wrote, properly speaking, only one Book [*A*], but acquired more Reputation by That one, than other Learned Men have done by printing an hundred Volumes. The Subject of this Work is the Controversy of the Eucharist. It appeared in the Year 1633, under the Title of the *Eucharist of the ancient Church*. The Agents of the Clergy of *France* complained of Mr *Aubertin* before the King's Council [*B*], and obtained a Warrant to take him into Custody, for having stiled himself Pastor of the Reformed Church of *Paris*. This Process was dropt; the Time was not yet come to push these sort of Matters too far (b). Whether the merit of the Piece, without the assistance of This Accident, made it sell so well, or that People concluded it must be excellently well done, because the Clergy chose to attack it by way of the Secular Arm; it is certain, the Author had reason to be contented with the Success of his Book [*C*].

(a) *Preface of his Book* de Euchâristia, *written by David Blondel.*

(b) *I have heard, that, after this, for some Expression he used in the Pulpit, the Court suspended him from preaching for two or three Years.*

This

[*A*] *He wrote, properly speaking, only one Book.*] For the Essay, which he published on St *Augustin*, to shew, that the Sentiments of That Father, concerning the Eucharist, were not conformable to Those of the Church of *Rome*, but to Those of the *Protestants* (1), ought only to be looked upon as a small Specimen of the Book, which he published in Folio, in 1633. I say this after the learned *Blondel*. " *Augustinum quem obtorto collo in partes trahere conabatur Perronius abducenti fortiter extorsit*, vindi- " *catumque in Dei castra feliciter reduxit*. Hoc in- " *signi virtutis Specimine dato*, & tirocinio, si licet " *dicam*, *posito, de patrum universorum causâ asse- " renda serio cogitans, Antiquæ Ecclesiæ Eucha- " ristiam nobis accuratiore studio repræsentavit* (2).— " *He rescued St* Austin *out of the Hands of* Perron, " *who had forced him into his Service, entirely a- " gainst his Meaning, and brought him back again to " his Post, in the true Cause of God. Having given " this glorious Specimen of his Zeal, and, as it were, " his first Essay on the Subject he was considering, " the Vindication of the Fathers, he has since more " fully described the Eucharist of the ancient Church."* I never saw the Observations he wrote, out of respect to the Abbot of Marolles, on a Book of Mr de la Milletiere, *who pressed him for an Answer to some difficult Questions*; but I have been told, it is a Book of Two hundred and Twenty six Pages, which was printed in the Year 1648, concerning the Controversy of the Eucharist. The Abbot of *Marolles* mentions it in the List of the Presents he had received from Authors.

(1) *This Book was printed in the Year 1646; the Title of it is, Conformity of the Belief of the Church with That of St* Augustin, *on the Sacrament of the Eucharist; it contains above 500 Pages in 8vo.*

(2) *David. Blondellus*, in Præf. libri Albertini de Eucharistiâ.

[*B*] *The Agents of the Clergy of* France *complained of him before the King's Council.*] They represented, in their Petition, that Mr *Edmund Aubertin*, Minister of the pretended Reformed Religion at *Charenton*, had caused a Book to be printed, wherein he took upon himself the Title of *Pastor of the Reformed Church of* Paris, and addressed his Preface to the Faithful of the Reformed Church of the said City of *Paris*; and that, in the Approbation of This Book, the other Ministers of *Charenton* stiled themselves Pastors of the Churches of the Isle of France, Champagne, and Country of Chartres; and, in their Subscriptions, wrote themselves Maistrezat, and Drelincourt, *Pastors of the Reformed Churches of* Paris, and Dallié (3), *Minister of the Holy Gospel of the said Church*. The same Agents complained, that, in the Title of the Book, the Cardinals *Bellarmine* and *Du Perron*, were called *Adversaries of the Church*. The King ordered, that *Aubertin should be seized, and imprisoned in the Bishop's Fort, if he could be taken*; and, if not, that *he should be summoned by the public Crier, with a short three Days Warning, that his Effects should be seized, and inventoried, according to the Decree, in order to proceed to his Trial*; and that the said *Maistrezat, Drelincourt, and Dallié, should be summoned to appear in Person to be heard, and interrogated, on the Facts mentioned in the Petition*. His Majesty commanded the Ministers, *and others professing the pretended Reformed Religion, to use the Titles given them by the Edicts, and no others, forbidding them to call the Catholics Adversaries of the Church* (4). This Arret was given in the King's Privy Council, the fourteenth of *July*, 1633 (5). The Author of the History of the Edict of *Nantes* informs us (6), that this *Affair, which made much Noise to little Purpose, was ended almost as soon as it was begun, and produced, for that time, only some verbal Prohibitions* (7). He adds, That *the Book was the greater in request for it, and that the Success encouraged the Author to revise and enlarge it, and to treat the Subject compleatly in a large Latin Volume, which did not appear 'till after his Death, and the unsuspected Catholic Doctors never durst confute it Paragraph by Paragraph*.

(3) *They have mistaken the true Names of Maistrezat and Dallié.*

(4) *See* Remark [*B*] *of the Article* BOCHART (MATTH.) *towards the end.*

(5) *It is in the Collection obtained for the Affairs of the Clergy during the Agency and Pursuit of the Sieurs, the Abbot* de Palmpont, *and the Prior* de Mousliers.

[*C*] *He had reason to be contented with the Success of his Book*.] We have just now shewn the Judgment passed upon it by the Author of the *History of the Edict* of Nantes. He only followed That of Mr *Daillé*, the Son, whose Words are these: " The Name of " Mr *Aubertin* is immortal, here below, and will live " for ever in That great and incomparable Work of " *The Eucharist*, which remains to this Day, superior " to all the Attacks of Those of the other Communion; " not one of whom has dared to oppose him fairly, " or undertake him Face to Face, if we may so say. " Even They, who pass among them for the Pillars " and Heads of the Party, could only give him " some indirect Blows, according to the Rules of this " new

(6) Tome 2, pag. 534.

(7) *This ought not to be understood of the Private Actions carried on in the Arrest of the 14th of July, 1633.*

AUBERTIN. 545

This obliged him to revise, enlarge, and complete it, with so much Application, that he seems to have made it his whole Business and Study. He composed his new Book in *Latin*, but had not the Satisfaction to see it published. After his Death, it was printed at *Deventer*, by the care of *David Blondel* (c). When this Book began to be forgot, there arose a Quarrel between *Messieurs de Port-Royal*, and Mr *Claudé*, which made known the Name of *Aubertin*, and the Character of his Work [D], to a great many Persons, who had never heard of it before, or remembred it no longer. Mr *Claudé* had a thousand Occasions to mention the Merit of This Book [E]. Mr *Aubertin* died at *Paris*, the fifth of *April* 1652, aged Fifty seven Years. He was exposed, in his Agonies, to the Insults of the Curate of *St Sulpice* [F], and, in spight of his drowsiness, which was one of the principal Symptoms of his Distemper, he had his Mind free enough to declare, when That Missionary questioned him, that he died in a full Belief of the Truths he had always professed. He had had much Access to the Duke *de Verneuil*, who was at that time Abbot of *St Germain des Prez*. That Prince would often have him at his Table: He found him very entertaining, of an Universal Conversation, well skilled in the Culture of Fruit-Trees, and Flowers, in Music, &c. One of Mr *Aubertin*'s Sons was Minister of *Amiens*.

(c) *In the Year 1641. It is a Folio, with near 1000 Pages in two Columns.*

(8) *Life of Mr Daillé, pag. 28.*

"new Art, which they have invented, and which "the Despair of their Cause has made them put in "practice, under the specious Name of a Method of "Prescription (8)." Mr *Daillé* means here the Divines of *Port Royal*, who, in their Book of *The Perpetuity of the Faith*, instead of opposing Mr *Aubertin*'s whole Work, have only combated his History of *The Innovation of Faith*: Neither have they done this, by opposing Facts to Facts, but Arguments only. See the second Chapter of the first Book of Mr *Claudé*'s great Answer, wherein he shews, that the Author of *The Perpetuity of the Faith* attacked Mr *Aubertin*'s Book *in an oblique and indirect manner.*

WHAT Judgment th Port Royal makes of Aubertin.

[D] *A Quarrel between Messieurs de* Port Royal, *and Mr* Claudé, *made known the Name of* Aubertin, *and the Character of his Work*] The Author of *The Perpetuity of the Faith*, out of this great Work of our Minister, attempts only to confute the History of the Innovation. This gave occasion enough to produce on the Stage the Name and Work of *Aubertin*. See here a Passage in *The Perpetuity of Faith*. "Au- "bertin also, perceiving, that there was no way

(9) *He means the Supposition of Blondel, that Transubstantiation was never thought of 'till a long time after Berenger.*

"to maintain a Notion so evidently ridiculous (9), "thought it necessary to alter The Plan. Observe, "then, in what View we ought to consider, what- "ever this Minister, who unhappily spent his Life "in searching, among the Writings of the Ancients, for "all possible Helps towards obscuring the Truth, has "found most plausible to prove so great a Degeneracy "from the ancient Faith, which he is obliged to make "out, that he may not himself pass for an Innova- "tor." Mr *Arnauld* has treated him much more

(10) *In the Preface of the Perpetuity defended.*

unhandsomely, though he confesses (10), that it is greatly to be wished, that *some ingenious Person would undertake to confute the Books of the new Ministers, and, amongst others, That of* Aubertin, *and Those of Mr* Daillé. He maintains, "That *Aubertin*'s Work "is very contemptible; that This Minister was a Man "of low Parts; a mean Critic, without any loftiness "of Style, or Judgment; who had read much, be- "cause That required only Eyes and Leisure, but "who had read without Penetration, or Understand- "ing; who does not distinguish between good "and bad Reasons; who exclaims every Moment "on the weakest Proofs; who has corrupted com- "mon Sense, by the Habit of repeating always the "same Absurdities, and who, far from *having ob- "tained a fair Victory over the School of* Rome, "*has only discovered the Weakness of the* Calvi-

(11) *Perpetuity defended, lib 1, cap. 1, p. 5.*

"nists (11)."

PLAN of Mr *Aubertin*'s Book.

[E] *Mr* Claudé *had a thousand Occasions to mention the Merit of This Book.*] In favour of Those, who, without any Trouble, than That of reading this Article, desire to know Mr *Aubertin*'s Plan, I shall copy these Words of Mr *Claudé*. "Mr *Au- "bertin*'s whole Book is a Body of Controversy on "the Subject of the Eucharist, which is divided "into three Parts. In the first, he considers it from "the Holy Scriptures, and from Human Reasoning. "He produces his Passages, and his Arguments, he "confutes the Answers, which are made to them; he "relates the Passages and Arguments of Those of the "Communion of *Rome*, and answers these, and al- "most every Thing else, which has hitherto been said

"considerable in This Controversy. In the second, "he examines the Belief of the Church, for the first "fix Centuries, by an exact Discussion of all the "Passages on both sides; and he makes it appear, "that Transubstantiation, and the Real Presence, "were unknown Doctrines in all That time. In the "third, he gives the History of the Introduction "of Those Doctrines (12)." Mr *Claudé* had already said, in his first Answer, that Mr *Aubertin*, after having examined to the Bottom all the Questions concerning the Eucharist, "By the Holy Scriptures, and "by Reasoning, and having obtained a fair Victory "over all the Subtilties of the School of *Rome*, "examines very particularly all the Passages of the "Fathers, which have hitherto been produced on this "Subject by both sides; thus discovering, to all the "World, the alteration the Church of *Rome* has "made, by perpetually comparing the ancient and "new Doctrines: To which he adds the History "of the Rise and Progress of Transubstantiation, "and the Real Presence (13)."

(12) *Mr Claud´'s Answer to Mr f-nao. ll's Book, lib 1, chap. 2, pag. 25.*

(13) *Claud´'s Answer to the second Treatise, chap. 1.*

[F] *He was exposed, in his Agonies, to the Insults of the Curate of St* Sulpice] At nine o' Clock in the Evening, he came to the sick Man's Door with the Bailiff of *St Germains*. The Mob, to the Number of Forty, followed him with Arms. He knocked at the Door, and pretended to be the Physician, in order to gain Admission. As soon as the Door was opened, the whole Troop rushed violently into the House, affirming, That the sick Person desired to make his Abjuration before a Priest; but that he was hindered, which was the Reason of their coming to deliver his Conscience from such Slavery. The eldest Son of the agonizing Minister defended the Stairs, as well as he could, but, at last, to hinder the Mob from breaking the open Chamber Door, it was agreed, to let the Curate and *Bailiff*, only, come into the sick Person's Chamber. The Cries and Shoutings of their Guard, recovered Mr *Aubertin* a little out of his Lethargic State, so that he declared, very distinctly, his Perseverance in the Reformed Religion. The Curate and Bailiff went out, and had much ado to make the Mob retire; who, in a little Time after, returned again, crying out, That the Curate and Bailiff had been forced out of the House; and would have broke and plundered it, if two Persons of Note had not intreated them to desist. " *Viciniam non latuit ex- "trema hæc calamitas, quæ pii viri spirans adhuc "spolium cujusvis illudere parati injuriæ exponebat.* "*Lamentabili ista occasione infeliciter usus præfer- "vidi sed tumultuosi zeli vir Joannes Jacobus Olle- "rius, Basilicæ S. Sulpicii Curatus, & Sodalitatis "quæ de propaganda fide dicitur primipilus, &c.* (14) "—— *The whole Neighbourhood were witnesses of "this extreme Violence, which exposed to the insults "of his Enemies the yet breathing Remains of the pious "Man. He who unhappily made use of this melan- "choly Occasion, was* John James Ollerius, *a Man of "too hot and tumultuous a Zeal, Curate of the Church "of St* Sulpice, *and Chief of the Society de propa- "ganda* Fide, &c." Can any one think of this, without remembering That pathetic Expostulation of *Lucretius*?

(14) *David Blondellus, Præfat. Latini de Eucharistie de Eucharistie.*

T.ntum

AUBIGNÉ. AUDEBERT.

Tantum Religio potuit suadere malorum?

What can escape Religion's hot-brained Zeal?

*Tristius haud illo monstrum nec sævior ulla
Pestis & ira Deûm Stygiis sese extulit undis* (15).

*Monsters more fierce offended Heav'n ne'er sent,
From Hell's Abyss, for human Punishment.*
DRYDEN

It will not suffer Men even to die quietly. After having tormented them all their Life-time, it lays Snares for them, even in the Height of a Distemper, which robs them of the use of their Reason. It takes advantage of those Moments, when the Soul is as sick as the Body, and where

Claudicat ingenium, delirat linguaque mensque (16);

Reason grows weak, delirious Thought and Speech.

(15) Virgil. Æn. lib. 3. ver. 214.

(16) Lucret. l. 3. v. 454.

AUBIGNÉ (d')———

I have read, in the *Mercure Galant*, for the Month of *January* 1705 (1), That *John d'Aubigné was Favourite and Chancellor to* Jane d'Albret, *Queen of* Navarre, *and Mother of* Henry IV, *and in great Favour with That Prince; that he died at* Geneva, *after having left his Prince, on his renouncing his Religion; that he was then in the Posts of Admiral of* Britany, *Governour of* Oleron, *and* Maillezais, *and Gentleman of the Bed-chamber to the King; that we have now remaining of his, an* History of France, *much commended, both by his Cotemporaries, and Successors, for it's Impartiality; that it is esteemed a Master-Piece in History; and that some Authors set as great a Value on it, as on* The Celebrated History of Thuanus; *that, according to the Remark of Otto, he let drop his Pen, when he came to the Death of That great Prince* (2), *and could proceed no farther; that This History is in two Volumes in Folio; that it was revised, and carefully corrected, by himself, and printed on very fine Paper, and with a beautiful Letter, at* Maülezais, *where he was Governour; that his Son* Constant, *Vice-Roy of the* American Islands, *whither he went in* 1643, *was Father to* Madam Maintenon, *and the* Count *d'Au-* bigné *lately deceased,* Knight of the King's Orders, *and Governour of* Berry (3). In the *Mercure Galant* for the Month of *February* 1705 (4), the Christian Name of *d'Aubigné* is corrected, from *John* to *Agrip-pa*. His *universal History* is also said to be in three Volumes, the last being very scarce, and printed at London. His *Life* is said to be written by himself with great Exactness, *and a Manuscript of it to be at* Paris, *of his own Hand-writing, a very curious Piece.* The Marquis *de Tigny,* Brother to the Bishop of *Noyon,* is Head of the eldest Branch of the Family of *Aubigné.* He is Father to the Count *d'Aubigné,* to whom the King has given the Royal Regiment (5).

(1) Mercure Galant, Jan. 1705, pag. 233, & seq.

(2) Henry IV.

(3) He only left a Daughter, who is married to the Duke of Noailles.

(4) Mercure Galant, Febr. 1705, pag. 207.

(5) Ibid. Jan. 1705, p. 232, 233.

AUDEBERT (GERMAIN), President in the Election, or Court, of *Assessors* of Subsidies in *Orleans*, was a Man of much Merit, and a good *Latin* Poet, in the XVIth Century. He was *Alciatus's* Disciple at *Bolonia* for some Years, and returned from *Italy* so well pleased with the Country, and the People he there conversed with, that he employed his whole skill in Poetry in the Description of *Rome*, of *Venice*, and *Naples* (a). These three Poems have been inserted in the first Volume of the *Deliciæ Poëtarum Gallorum* of France. We shall see, below, in what manner the *Venetians* rewarded his Description of their City. He composed other Poems, which would very probably have been published, if his Son, who was Counsellor in the Parliament of *Britany*, had survived him long enough (b). *Scævola Sammarthanus* has composed the Elogium of our *Audebert* with his usual Eloquence. He gives him the most essential Qualities of a good Man. Mr *Moreri* has faithfully reported the substance of This Elogy. I question not but he was ignorant of the advantagious Consequences, which the *Protestants* have drawn from That Chapter of *Scævola Sammartbanus*, to justify one of their most famous Ministers from an horrid Accusation. We can never sufficiently deplore Mens Malice or Ignorance, when we remember, that *Theodorus Beza* was accused of an abominable Crime, on so frivolous a ground as his Epigram, *de sua in Candidam & Audebertum benevolentiâ*. Mr *Maimbourg* renewed This Accusation in his History of *Calvinism*. He is very fully refuted by an examination of the Piece it self, without forgetting to strengthen the Apology from the great Merit of *Audebert* (c). *Theodorus Beza* had already made use of This Argument [A]. Mr *Graverol*, the Minister, had a design of publishing the Epitaphs of This illustrious Magistrate, in a *Latin* Dissertation, which he published about That time (d); but received them too late. He has communicated them to me, and this is a very convenient opportunity to publish them [B]. The History of our *Audebert* may be seen there, such

(a) Sammarthanus, Elog. lib. 2.

(b) Reliêtis, præter ea quæ commemoravi Poëmata, silvarum aliquot libros, qui lucem expectare potuerant ab ejus Hærede, &c. He left, besides tho' e I have mentioned, several Poems called Sylvæ, in several Books; which was expected to have been published by his Heir, &c. Sammarthanus, Elog. lib. 2.

(c) Jurieu's Apology for the Reformed, Part 1, pag. 143, & seq.

(d) De Juvenilibus Theod. Bezæ Poematiis, Amstel. 1683. in 8vo.

[A] *His great Merit was made use of in Justification of* Beza ———— *who had already made use of This Argument.*] It is in his second Apology against *Claudi de* Saindes. He says, that, when he composed the Epigram, *Audebert* was then Advocate in the Parliament of *Paris*. This is his *Latin*; " Quid-" quum eò usque proveheris ut meam cum honestissi-" mo viro, & jam tum in Senatu Parisiensi Advo-" cato, quem vocant, nunc vero in civitate Aureli-" ensi magnâ cum dignitate versanti, amicitiam & " familiaritatem summam ac nefarium & execrandum " illud scelus transferas, quod à nobis ne nominari " quidem sine horrore potest, à vobis autem in vestris " illis gurgustiolis, ut omnes norunt, pro ludo & " joco ducitur, quis te ipsum vir honestus non exe-" cretur (1)? ———— *What, when you are transported* " *to such a Pitch, as even to construe my most intimate* " *Friendship and Familiarity, with a Man of the high-* " *est Honour, at that time Advocate, as the Title is,* " *in the Parliament of* Paris, *and now in great Dig-* " *nity at* Orleans, *into so wicked and abominable a* " *Crime, as I cannot so much as mention without* " *Horror, though it serves you in your Cells for* " *Jest and Sport, must you not be detested by all* " *good Men?* "

[B] *This is a very convenient Opportunity to publish the Epitaphs of* Audebert.] Not to let it slip therefore, I shall insert here, word for word, what the Person above mentioned has wrote, and sent me.

" I beg your favourable Acceptance of the true " Copy I send you, of the Epitaphs of *Germain Au-* " *debert*, and of his Son. If I had received them " at the time they were promised me, I would have " added them to the small *Latin* Apology of *Theo-* " *dorus Beza*, which a special Occasion obliged me " to publish. Such an authentic Piece alone seems " to me capable of putting an end to the abominable " Calumny, which has hitherto been charged on the " the Memory of That excellent and religious Man, " whatever evasion may be invented to elude it's " Force, and you will do a signal Piece of Service " to Truth, by presenting the Public with This new " Vindication of him.

" Here lies Messire *Germain Audebert*, Native of " This City of *Orleans*, Prince of the Poets of his " Time, who, for his Virtue only, was ennobled
" with

(1) Beza Op rum, Tom. 1, pag. 30.

AUDEBERT. AUDIGUIER.

such as an Historical Dictionary ought to give it. The Sieur *Konig* has split this Author into Two [C]. *Sammarthanus* is not the only Person, who has wrote This great Man's Elogy [D].

"with all his Posterity, by the Most Christian King
"of *France* and *Poland*, *Henry* III, and made a
"Knight. And, to crown his Honours, his Ma-
"jesty gave him two Golden Flowers-de-luces, to be
"born on a Chief in his Coat of Arms, for their ad-
"ditional Ornament. He was also made a Knight by
"our Holy Father Pope *Gregory* XIII, and by the
"Doge and Republic of *Venice*; the latter also sent
"him into *France*, by their Embassador, the Order
"of St *Mark*. And, notwithstanding all these great
"Honours, he continued still to act as an Assessor
"in That Jurisdiction for the space of fifty Years;
"so great a Lover was he of his Country. In
"consideration of which, his said Majesty, having
"created and appointed a President, and a Lieu-
"tenant, in each Court of Subsidies in *France*, he
"exempted the said Messire *Germain Audebert*, and
"would have him preside and preceed both the one
"and the other. He wrote three Books of the
"City of *Venice*, one of *Rome*, one of *Naples*, and
"two of *Sylvæ*: He died in the Year 1598, the
"Twenty fourth of *December*, aged about eighty
"Years.

"And, under the same Marble, lies Messire *Ni-
"cholas Audebert*, one of the King's Counsellors in
"his Court of Parliament of *Britany*, Son of the
"said Messire *Germain Audebert*, a great Imitator of
"his Father's Virtues, who died five Days after his Fa-
"ther, in the Forty second Year of his Age. May
"their Souls rest among the Blessed.

*Audebertorum, Germani Patris, & Nicolai filii
    Tumulus.*

Audebertorum si quis depingere laudes
Cogitat, ille sibi nihilo plus explicet, ac si
Insane sapiens solum illustrare laboret.
Parcendum verbis igitur, vanoque labori.
Sit dixisse satis, situs hic jacet Audebertus,
Et pater, & gnatus patris cito fata secutus.
Nominat hæc quisquis sinceri nomina linguâ
Virtutum & laudum gazas simul eruit omnes:
Quas qui nescierit communis luminis expers
Credatur furvis semper vixisse sub antris.

The Tomb of the Audeberts, Germain the Father, and Nicholas the Son.

To gild with Verse the Audeberts *Renown,*
You might illuminate the Sun as soon.
Words are but lost on such transcendent Fame,
'Tis all summ'd up in one great Word, their Name.
Who this repeat, their Virtues amply praise;
Ignorance of This Ignorance itself betrays.
The Audeberts *lie here, Father and Son,*
Scarce parted in their Deaths, and in their Tomb
but One.

"These three Epitaphs are found written in Let-
"ters of Gold, on a Black Marble, affixed to the
"Wall of the Gallery, in the Church-yard of the
"Church of the Holy Cross of *Orleans*, about sixty
"Paces in the Gallery, as you enter on the Left-
"Hand. They have been copied word for word
"from the Original, by a Person to be depended
"on."

Here ends the Copy of Mr *Graverol*'s Letter.
We may conclude, from what is said of the Office of *Audebert*, in the first of these Epitaphs, that Mr *Jurieu* is mistaken, when he says, that *Audebert* died

after having gone through all the great Offices of the long Robe (2). *Sammarthanus* might have saved him from this Slip; for he expressly observes, that *Audebert* was so modest, that he contented himself with an Office very much below his Merit. "Nec sibi
"quidquam, *says he* (3), de solitâ modestiâ detraxit,
"contentus ea quam apud suos jamdudum exercebat
"vectigalium indictionumque præfecturâ, humili
"fortasse illâ & obscurâ, si hominis dignitatem respi-
"cias, sed quam eo tantum animo susceperat, ne nul-
"lam Reipublicæ partem attigisse, sibique soli vixisse
"diceretur. —— *Nor did he abate any thing of his*
"*usual Modesty; for he contented himself to continue*
"*the Office, he had a long Time before enjoyed, of Pre-*
"*sident in the Court of Assessors of Taxes and Sub-*
"*sidies; mean, indeed, and obscure with regard to his*
"*Dignity, but which he chose to discharge, that he*
"*might not be said to throw up all concern for the*
"*Public Service, and to live for himself only.*"

[C] *Konig has split this Author into Two.*] He gives us one *Germanus Audebertus*, and one *Aurelius Audebertus*. For the first he refers us to the Hundred and ninty first Page of *Sammarthanus*'s Elogies; and he says of the second, that he composed three Poems in the Year 1603. *Scripsit Venetias, Romam, Parthenopen, carmine, An.* 1603.—*On* Venice, Rome, *and* Naples. This Date is a new Mistake; since *Audebert* died in the Year 1598. It is true, Those three Poems were printed at *Hanau* in 1603; but This was not the first Edition. We may see, by this, that it is not so easy to compose a Dictionary of Authors, as some may think. They, who are ignorant of the Chronology of Editions, and the Difference of Christian Names, or Those of the Country, are very liable to Mistakes. *Germanus* is *Audebert*'s Christian Name, and *Aurelius* is his Name from his Country. What is most to be admired is, that Mr *Konig* refers us to an Author, whom he had not seen himself: For, if he had taken the Pains to cast his Eye on the place of *Sammarthanus*, which he quotes, he would there have seen, that it was *Germanus Audebertus*, who composed the three Poems on *Venice, Rome,* and *Naples: Venetias, & Romam, & Parthenopen —— ea carminis majestate descripsit —— He described the Cities of* Venice, Rome, *and* Naples, — *in such beautiful Poetry.* — When we send a Reader to consult an Author, it is but reasonable to set the Example, and consult him first ourselves.

[D] *Sammarthanus is not the only Person, who has wrote* Audebert's *Elogy.*] An Advocate of the Council, who called himself in *Latin Rodolphus Botereius*, has praised *Audebert* magnificently, in his History of *France* (4). He does not forget the Honours, which the Pope, and the Republic of *Venice*, paid him; but, whereas the Epitaph ascribes the Honour *Audebert* received from the Court of *Rome*, to *Gregory* XIII, He attributes it to *Gregory* XIV. He mentions the Place, where the Ambassador of *Venice* conferred on him the Knighthood of St *Mark*, and before what concourse of People. "Gregorius XIV, ac Veneti
"illum civitatis jure & equestris ordinis dignitate do-
"narunt: effusius Veneti, qui per Oratorem suum in
"suburbano Tybure Gentiliaco, assidente spectaculo
"& convivio longa corona hominum literatissimorum,
"Audebertum torque aureo Divi Marci insignive-
"runt.—— Gregory XIV, *and the* Venetians, *pre-*
"*sented him respectively with the Priviledges of their*
"*City, and the Order of Knighthood. But the* Vene-
"tians *more remarkably, who, by their Ambassador at*
"Gentilly *near* Paris, *at a public Feast, and before a*
"*large Assembly of learned Men, invested* Audebert
"*with the golden Collar of the Order of St* Mark."

(2) Jurieu's Anctory sur the Reformed, Part 1, pag. 145.

(3) Sammarth in Elogiis.

(4) Botereius, lib. 5, pag. 46., & seq. ad Ann. 1598.

AUDIGUIER (N. d')

Author of several Books [A], much read, when first published, but now not taken notice of, flourished in the beginning of the Reign of Lewis

[A] *Author of several Books.*] He published *The true and ancient Usage of Duels,* which was printed at *Paris,* by *Peter Billain,* in 1617. It is a Book of Five hundred thirty two Pages, in 8vo, and deserves a Place in Libraries. He published also some *French* Poetry, — *Gregory* XIV, *The Amours of* Lysander *and* Calista*, Those of* Arisander, *and* Clitonice, Flavia, Minerva, &c. These were Romances, which had a great run

VOL. I. N°. XVIII.   6 Y

AUDIGUIER. AVENTINE.

Lewis XIII. The Sieur *Sorel*, having said, that the Author of *Polyxena* (a) might one Day produce something better, unless he had AUDIGUIRE's ill Fortune, adds, that they both of them fell by the Hands of Those they took to be their Friends (b). "I believe, says he, elsewhere (c), *Audiguier* was a Man of Wit; but he was more of the Soldier, than the Scholar, as appears in all the Dedications of his Books, where he is almost always speaking in a military way: They say also, that, to express his negligent Air in writing, he one Day said, by way of Bravado (d), that *he made his Pen with his Sword*. Some say he received this Repartee, that *then it was no wonder he wrote so ill*; but This is too satirical. Undoubtedly This Boast has a great deal of Beauty, and deserves a Place amongst the *French Apophthegms*." D'*Audiguier* had a Nephew, who passed for the Author of the Translation of *Stratonice*, an *Italian* Romance; but it was believed, that *Malleville* was the real Author, and had made him a Present of it, as *being his particular Friend* (e). There was one d'AUDIGUIER, an Advocate in the Parliament of *Paris*, who published some Pleadings (f). I do not know, whether he was the same with the Nephew, who was *Malleville's* Friend; but I am certain, he lived in the XVIIth Century (g); and I believe This Nephew was the Author called *Audiguier, junior*, and who published, among other Works, *Eromené*. From a Passage, cited below, I am induced to believe, that our *d'Audiguier* was killed in the Year 1630 [B].

(1) *Note, that Sorel has criticised the text first, in his Remarks on the Berger Extravagant, chiefly in the 13th Book of the 1st Remarks.* run (1). He translated into *French* the *Spanish* Novels of *Michael Cervantes*. *Sorel*, in a Work published a long time after his *Berger Extravagant*, passes this Judgment on our Author. " I do not think, *says he*, that we ought absolutely to despise the Sieur d'*Audiguier*, Author of the *Adventures* of *Lysander* and *Calista*. Though he had not much Learning, he wrote in very sprightly and clear Style for That Time, as we see in several Romances, and some Letters, and Translations, which he was the Author of. His first Work, which he called the *Soldier's Philosophy*, was a little too much upon the Gasconade; but he improved himself so much by translating *Cervantes's Novels*, and a Book of *Rodriguez*, of *Christian Perfection*, that we may allow him to be one of our best Translators. His last Work, called *The Amours of Aristander and Cleonice*, was none of the worst of his Time (2)."

(2) *Sorel, Bibl. Franç. pag. 261.*

[B] *From a Passage — I am induced to believe, our d'Audiguier was killed in the Year 1630.*] This Passage is taken from one of *Balzac's* Letters, dated the twentieth of *August* 1630. D'*Audiguier* is not named in it, there being nothing but Asterisks, instead of the Person's Name; but, however, I make no doubt but it was The Author, whose Article I have here given. I take his Character to be very justly drawn in the following Words (3). "Yet it is better to be innocently merry in the *Hotel de Venice*, than to lose one's Life in the *Temple Marspès*, as poor * * did. I lament him, on account of his Misfortunes, and manner of Death, and am sorry he had not time to think of his Salvation, or to ask Pardon for his Sins. But to imagine, that one of the great Lights of *France* is extinguished, or that we have lost one of our most considerable Men, I knew him too well to conceive so high an Opinion of him. He was truly a Man of Spirit, and had some Flights of Fancy, that would have passed off agreeably enough, if they had not been printed. But he is not to be mentioned among our Modern Authors, or in a Collection of the Poetry of these Times. However, he set no Value at all on his Courage, and other military Virtues, but piqued himself entirely on his Abilities in speaking and writing. He had so great a Conceit of his Merit this way, that, for my endeavouring, one Day, to cure him of this troublesome Symptom, he never forgave me to the Day of his Death."

(e) *Pelisson, Histoire de l'Academie Franç. pag. 292.*
(f) *Marolles, Memoires, p. 41.*
(g) *Marolles, Denombrement des Auteurs, pag. 407.*
(3) *Balzac's Letters, Book 3, Lett. 42, p. 38-, 388, Tom. 1. of Balzac's Works, Edit. of Paris by Joly, 1665, in 2 Vols Folio.*

AVENTINE (JOHN), famous for his *Annals of Bavaria*, flourished in the XVIth Century [A]. He was of mean Birth, the Son of an Inn-keeper of *Abensperg* in *Bavaria* [B]. He studied first at *Ingolstadt*, and afterwards in the University of *Paris*, under *Faber Stapulensis* and under *Josse Clicton*. Being returned into *Germany*, in the Year 1503, he stayed some time at *Vienna*, where he taught, in his Chamber, Eloquence and Poetry. He went from thence into *Poland*, in the Year 1507, where he publickly taught the *Greek* Grammar at *Cracow*: He returned into *Germany*, and passed some time at *Ratisbon*, from whence he went to *Ingolstadt*, in the Year 1509, where he explained some Books of *Cicero*. As he was esteemed a very ingenious Man, he was sent for to *Munich*, in the Year 1512, to be Preceptor to Prince *Lewis* and Prince *Ernest* (a). He travelled with the latter of these two Princes (b). After this, he undertook to compose the Annals of *Bavaria* [C], and was

(a) *They were the Sons of Albert the Wise, Duke of Bavaria.*
(b) *See the History of Bavaria of the Sieur la Blanc, Tom. 3, pag. 414, 415.*

[A] *He flourished in the XVIth Century.*] He was born in the Year 1466, and died in 1534. Whence *Vossius* very justly infers, that *Genebrard* is mistaken, in making this Historian flourish in the Year 1366 (1). Father *Gaultier* followed *Genebrard's* Fault. In the Epitome of *Gesner's Bibliotheca*, the Death of *Aventine* is falsly placed in the Year 1529.

[B] *He was of mean Birth, the Son of an Inn-keeper of Abensperg in Bavaria.*] *Jerom Zieglerus* says, That this Man's Name was *John Thurmair*, and that from thence it comes, that *Leonard* of *Eck*, in an Epigram, gives the Name of *Thurniomarthus* (2) to *John Aventine* (3). He adds, That the Name of the Annalist of *Bavaria* was *Aventinus*, because the ancient Name of *Abensperg* was *Aventinium*. The Emperor *Antoninus*, continues he, calls it in his Itinerary *Abusina*. Mr *Bullart* did not well understand This: *The City of Abensperg*, says he (4), *is sufficiently celebrated in the Roman History, but principally by the Emperor Antoninus, who, in his Itinerary, calls it* Aventinium. This Author would find it very difficult to prove, that This City was sufficiently famous in the *Roman* History. The learned *Lambecius* believed it would be found to have had no other Name than That of *Abusina*, which is given it in the *Itinerary of Antoninus*; and for this reason blames the Author of the Annals, for not having called himself *Abusinensis*. *Patria ejus fuit* Abusina, *unde falsò, cum se nominare debuisset* Abusinensem, *cognomine usus est* AVENTINI (5). But would That Name have founded as agreeably as That of one of the Hills of *Rome*?

[C] *He undertook to compose the Annals of* Bavaria.] He had a Pension for it, and began it a little before the Death of the Emperor *Maximilian*. The Work consists of seven Books, and extends to the Year 1533. *Vossius* observes all these Things: "Annales Bojorum libris 7 reliquit —— Terminatur ejus historia anno CIↃ IↃ XXXIII. Extremis Maximiliani temporibus jam cœperat historiam suam scribere auspiciis & liberalitate fruens Guilielmi & Ludovici, Bavariæ ducum,

(1) *Vossius de H.P. Lat. pag. 655.*
(2) *Τυρνιομάρθος.*
(3) *Ziegler us in Vita Jo. Aventini.*
(4) *Bullart, Academie des Sciences, Tom. 1. p. 147.*
(5) *Lambec. Comment. Cæsar. lib. 2. cap. 6. pag. 4-1, in Not. Margin. n. 3. apud Maurium Epomymol. pag. 91.*

AVENTINE. 549

was encouraged to it by the Assurances, the Dukes of That Name gave him, of bearing all his Charges. He omitted nothing that might answer the Expectation of his Masters; he consulted the Records of *Germany* as carefully as possible, and applied himself wholly to That Work. He did not lose his labour; for he acquired by it a great Reputation. In the Year 1529, he received an Affront, which troubled him all the rest of his Life. He was taken out of his Sister's House, at *Abensperg*, by Force, and imprisoned. No One ever knew the true Reason of This Violence, which would have been carried yet farther, if the Duke of *Bavaria* had not taken this learned Person under his Protection. The invincible Melancholy, which possessed *Aventine* ever after This Affront, was so far from making him resolve to continue the single Life he had lead to the Sixty fourth Year of his Age, that it rather, perhaps, put him upon Thoughts of Marriage. This new Inclination was not so strong, but it gave him Time to consult the Holy Scriptures, and his Friends, what was best for him to do. He met with nothing but Counsels full of Uncertainty [*D*]; and therefore found it necessary to resolve this Question for himself, which he accordingly did in favour of Marriage [*E*]. There remained nothing more to do, but to seek out a Match, which he was so imprudent as to leave to a crafty old Woman, who deceived him basely [*F*]; for she brought him a Woman of the Country of *Suabia*, who had three great Imperfections; for she was poor, ugly, and peevish; which gave him an opportunity of making many Experiments [*G*]. After his marriage, he hired a House at

---

(6) Vossius, de Hist. Lat. pag. 655.

" ducum, qui patri suo Alberto successerunt anno
" 1508 (6). ——— *He left the Annals of the Bavarians*
" *in seven Books* ——— *His History ends at the Year*
" 1533. *He began it about the latter End of the*
" *Reign of* Maximilian, *under the Auspices, and*
" *Generosity, of* William *and* Lewis, *Dukes of* Bavaria,
" *who succeeded their Father* Albert *in* 1508." These Annals did not appear before the Year 1554. They were published by *Jerom Zieglerus*, Professor of Poetry in the University of *Ingolstadt*: But, as he confesses himself in the Preface, he left out the Invectives relating to the Clergy, and several Stories not at all material to the History of *Bavaria*. " Multa fine dubio emendasset (*Aventinus*,) pleraque
" forsitan mutasset etiam, si per fata licuisset ———
" Invectivas quasdam contra Ecclesiasticas personas,
" item fabulosas narrationes nihil quidquam ad historiam facientes non fraude sed judicio omisimus (7).

(7) Zieglerus in Præf. Cisneri, shews, in his Preface, that if Aventine had lived, he would not have altered what Zieglerus pretends he would have altered.

" ——— Many Things, without doubt, Aventine him-
" self would have corrected, and many, perhaps, entirely
" changed, had Fate given him Leave ——— Some
" Reflexions upon Ecclesiastical Persons, and also fa-
" bulous Relations, not at all material to the History,
" I have taken the Liberty, on mature Deliberation,
" without the least ill design, to omit." The Precaution of *Zieglerus*, and his Sincerity in owning the Mutilations, did not tally together; for this Confession excited the Curiosity of the Protestants, and put them upon searching for what had been suppressed; and they sought so diligently for a Manuscript of These undismembered Annals, that at last they found it. It was published at *Basil*, in the Year 1580, by the Care of *Nicholas Cisnerus*. The Title of This Edition is *Johannis Aventini annalium Bojorum libri* VII. *ex autenticis manuscriptis codicibus recogniti, restituti, auctis diligentia Nicolai Cisneri*. *Cœffeteau* could not forbear shewing his Anger at the Edition of *Cisnerus*. See what he says: Aventine *is an Author not to be credited in these Ecclesiastical Matters, having no other aim in his Annals, than to dishonour the Clergy; and he is particularly exceptionable in the History of* Gregory VII. ——— *The Incontinency of his Pen, in these Matters, was the Cause that* Zieglerus, *who first published him, retrenched many of his lying Narratives, and Invectives against the Clergy, in That Impression*; *but the Protestants, who turn their Ears from the Truth, to listen to Fables, not being able to bear This Correction, have republished These Annals with all their Filth* (8).

(8) Cœffeteau's Answer to the Modesty of Iniquity of the Sieur du Plessis, pag. 673.

[*D*] *On the Subject of his Marriage, he met with nothing but Counsels full of Uncertainty*.] This is what Mr *Bullart* relates concerning the Answers he received from Books. " *Socrates* left him in Suspence, by his Advice formerly given to a young
" Man, under the same Irresolution. *Marry, or not*
" *marry, you will be sure to repent either of the one*
" *or the other*. He would have needed no other
" Council, if he had taken That of *Diogenes*, who
" told young Persons, *that it was too soon to marry*; and
" old ones, *that it was too late*. Euripides soothed
" his Inclination, by remarking, *That a Wife is a*
" *great Comfort to her Husband, in Sickness and Ad-
" versity*, but discouraged him with several other

" Sentences, he has elsewhere pronounced, against
" That Sex (9)." This is a meer Romance, and only begging an Opportunity to shew a little Commonplace Readings for the Life of *Aventine* says expressly, that he examined only some Passages of Scripture, for and against Matrimony, with two of his Friends; *Sæpius multos locos ex sacris literis suadentes & dissuadentes matrimonium protulit*.

(9) Bullart, Acad. des Sciences, pag. 148.

[*E*] *He concluded for Marriage*.] Let us hear the same Mr *Bullart* once more. " *Aventine*, being
" tired with consulting both the Dead and the
" Living, and hoping to find a Wife to his Wishes,
" cried out on a sudden; *I am old, and have need of*
" *a Companion to assist and take care of me in the*
" *Infirmity of my Age*." So says Zeiglerus; *Senectutem suam omnino considerans, tandem prorumpens in hæc verba dixit,* " *senex sum, mibi ministrari opus est*." His Conclusion was according to the Rule of Logic, *Conclusio sequitur debiliorem partem*. ——— *The Conclusion follows the weaker Part*. On one side, his Books and his Friends advised him to deliberate all his Life-time; on the other, his Infirmity counselled him to marry. By his Conclusion he took the weaker Side. But, had he not two Children in few Years, and This in spite of the Ugliness, and Brawls, of his Devil of a Wife, which could be no Provocatives That way? He was wrong, then, to say, he wanted a Wife for the Infirmity of his Age: He had much more need of one for the Remains of his Youth.

[*F*] *Who deceived him basely*.] His Historian has not done him Justice here; for see how he expresses himself: " Duxit Suevam, morosam mulierem, il-
" lepidam, & omnino pauperem, deceptus ab anu
" quadam, quæ ei illam ut famulam saltem addux-
" erat. ——— *He married a* Suabian, *ill natured, disagree-
" able, and poor, a certain old Woman having de-
" ceived him, by bringing her to him, at least, for
" a Servant*." The old Woman did not bring him this *Suabian* for a Wife, but only for a Servant. Wherein, then, did she deceive him ? *Zieglerus* ought to have told us; for, if we take his Account right, the old Woman is very excusable, and the old Man not to blame. It is very likely, that, being resolved to marry, and having lost too much Time already, considering his Age, he took the first Female that came to hand, which was his own Servant; and so became a fit Subject to increase the List of the *Colletets*, and of all such as have married their Servants (10).

(10) See the Menag ana, pag. 252. and the Remark [*E*,] of the Article BRISEIS.

[*G*] *His Wife gave him an Opportunity of making many Experiments*.] " Having surmounted all Obstacles, and decided all Doubts, by his Marriage,
" he had nothing more to do, but to meditate on
" his new State of Life, and to consider which
" was the easier Task, to bear with the Expence
" of a Wife that is poor, or with the Pride of one
" that is rich ; to be secure in an ugly one, that
" is a Temptation to no body, or to have the
" Trouble of guarding a handsome one, that is a
" Temptation to every Body. As his Wife was,
" at least, as bad as *Socrates's Xantippe*, That great
" Philosopher's Example might also give him Consolation

550 AVENTINE.

at *Ratisbon*, and afterwards was called to *Ingolstadt*, in 1533, to be Preceptor to the Son of one of the Duke of *Bavaria*'s Counsellors (c). He was desirous of bringing his Wife thither, and for that purpose made a Journey to *Ratisbon* in the *Christmas* Holidays, where he arrived very ill of a Distemper, which had seized him on the Road by the way, of which he died the Ninth of *January* 1534, aged Sixty eight Years. He left but one Daughter, who was not above two Months old (d). He was buried there in the Church of St *Hemeran*, where his Epitaph gives him the Encomium of a good Catholic (e). But the Jesuits have discovered, by their Inquiries, that, under the Mask, he was a good *Lutheran* [H]. It is by This, that Those of the Church of *Rome* endeavour to weaken the force of his Evidence against the Conduct of the Popes, and the bad Lives of the Priests; for the *Protestants* have quoted *Aventine*'s Annals

(e) Leonardus ab Eck.

(d) He had but one Son.

(e) Taken from his Lives written by Jerom Ziegler. It is prefix'd to his Annals.

---

(11) Bulart, Acad. des sciences, pag. 148.

(12) Conringius, de Rebus (quid. apud Magirum, Epon. mol. Critic. pag. 90.

(13) Rara est adeo concordia formæ, Atque pudicitiæ, So seldom Chasty and Charms agree. Juv Sat. 10. ver. 297.
Lis est cum formâ magnâ pudicitiæ. —— Beauty and Modesty are fir'd at first. Ovid. Ep. 16. v. 288.

(14) Fastus inest pulchris, sequiturque superbia formam. — Beauty's attended by its Haughtiness, Pride. Ovid. Fastor. lib. 1. v. 419.

(15) Ita istæ solent quæ viros subservire sibi postulat à dote trentæ fœces —— The Haughtiness of large Dowries demands victory Isthean Subjection from the Husband. Plaut. in Menech. Act. 1, Sc. 2, ver 16. See the Electra Plautina of Philip Pireus, at the Word Contagium.

(16) Magno Periculo custoditur quod multis placet —— It is very dangerous keeping what liness will make me easy. Horat. Publius Sy. rus.

"tion (11)." Certainly This learned *German* was extremely disappointed; he thought to get into a safe Harbour, and to shelter himself from a thousand Inconveniencies, but exposed himself to a continual Storm, even tho' his Wife had been rich and handsome; but she had nothing for her Portion, and a quarrelsome Disposition. "*Aventinus vir doctus, magni judicii integritatisque, sed fortunâ admodum tenui, quam corrupit ulterius ductâ uxore rixosâ & malorum morum, ut cum duobus malis paupertate & uxore malâ ipsi fuerit conflictandum* (12). —— *Aventine was a learned Man, of great Judgment and Integrity, but little Fortune, which was made yet less by a quarrelsome, cross-grain'd Wife; so that he had two great Evils to contend with, Poverty, and a scolding Wife.*"

We shall, perhaps, do him Justice, if we suppose, that he did not marry this Wife without having seriously considered all Inconveniencies. She could not deceive him as to her Ugliness, so long as he had Eyes. She was brought to him as a Servant, so that he could not think her rich. These two Defects, therefore, he could be no Stranger to, her want of Beauty and Fortune. Nor ought this Knowledge to condemn him for Imprudence; for it might promise to exempt him from a thousand Inconveniencies. As he had read much, he knew the general Maxims of the Ancients, on the Discord between Beauty and Chastity (13), and on the Pride, which attends Beauties (14), but perfectly possesses Fortunes (15). These Maxims are taught in the College, and there are a thousand occasions to apply them every Day; which makes them remain strongly imprinted in the Memory, and This increases the Fear of experiencing the Truth of them, when once we come to run the hazard of them. It is very probable, then, that *Aventine* considered, that by marrying a handsome young Wife, he should expose his Forehead to a shameful, and very uneasy Disgrace. Without doubt he knew, that Beauty did not exclude a very sincere Resolution of Chastity; but, on the other Side, he imagined, that it makes it very difficult to execute This Resolution. The Courtships, which are almost unavoidable in such a Case, are of wonderful Force, to conquer the strongest of these Resolutions. When he considered his Age, he could not but be still more alarmed: His Sixty fourth Year added to his Fears; and, perhaps, he might reflect with himself; *If these things happen where the Wood is yet green, what can be hoped for, where It is quite dry? A young Man is not exempt from This Misfortune, and how should I avoid it, who am old?* And yet, as natural as it is to fear these real Evils, in the Case of an old Husband, who has a handsome young Wife; it is much easier to avoid These, than imaginary ones. I mean, that such a Husband has more reason to fear the Torments of his own Jealousy, than the Disloyalty of his Wife. It happens oftener, that a Man is jealous of his Wife, without a Cause, than that she is dishonest, without his suspecting it. There is, then, some likelihood, that *Aventine* was more distrustful of himself, than of a handsome Wife, and that he argued with himself thus: *I grant she may be really chaste; but am I sure I shall not be so weak as to suspect her, when I perceive how agreeable she is to my Friends and Neighbours, and They to her* (16). *Let my Jealousy be ill grounded as one would wish, it's Stings and it's Torment will still be the same. The safest Way is to run no Hazard, but marry This Servant, whose Homeliness will make me easy; for*

—— casta est quam nemo rogavit:

The Nymph may be chaste, that never was try'd.

If she should be ill inclined, where could she find Gallants? Besides, as she is poor, I shall have no reason to fear she will be imperious: This will preserve my Authority, and secure me from Noise and Contradiction. Do not I know what the ancient Poets have said (17)? If we suppose he considered the Matter thus, we shall find him more unfortunate, than imprudent: For, in short, the Reasons, which determined his Choice, are specious and plausible; but we must, at the same time, suppose, that the third Defect was not known to him, and that his Servant had the Wit to hide her peevish, muttering, morose, scolding Humour. She took care not to discover it; for she quickly perceived, that her Master was resolved to marry at any rate, and, without doubt, it was not long before he gave her some Intimations, that he would not look for a Wife out of his own House. As it is wrong to judge by the Event, let us not condemn him for Imprudence, because his Marriage was unhappy. The wisest are caught in it. *Cato* was deceived by his own Arguments, in a like Case (18). In a Word, two things must be known, before we can say, that *Aventine* was imprudent: I. That he did not weigh the Reasons before mentioned, on both sides. II. That, by marrying a young, rich, and beautiful Wife, he would not have met with so many Vexations, as by marrying his Servant. These are the two Sources of rash Judgments; Persons are condemned, without knowing either the secret Motives, which, upon due Deliberation, determined them, or what would have happened if they had made a contrary Choice.

[H] *The Jesuits have discovered, that, under the Mask, he was a good* Lutheran.] I say under the Mask, for as he was buried in a Catholic Church, with the usual Ceremonies, and that the Character of *Veræ Religionis amator,—A Lover of the true Religion*, is inserted in his Epitaph, we cannot suppose, that he had ever declared openly for the Protestants, not so much at the Point of Death, in That decisive Moment, which takes away all Pretences for Dissembling. It is true, also, that the Stile of his History is altogether *Roman Catholic*, if Those Places be excepted, where he speaks so freely against the Tyranny of the Popes, and the Immorality of the Clergy (19) It ought not to be thought strange, then, that Mr *Du Plessis* objects him to Those of the Church of *Rome*, as an Evidence, who was of their own Religion. Mr *Du Plessis* was ignorant of the secret Memoirs, which Father *Gretzer* had published. See here a Passage of That Jesuit: "*Addit Plessæus Invectivæ Aventinianæ hanc clausulam; hæc quidem licet professione Romanus, plura furte, si licuisset, dicturus.* Professione Romanos, "*hoc est Catholicus, non fuit Aventinus, sed hæreticus; cujus criminis ut alia probanda desset, id tamen satis superque liqueat ex Epistolâ Melanchthonis ad Aventinum quam ex ipso Autographo recitavi, lib. 2. contra Calvinianum replicatorem, cap. 19.* (20) —— *Plessis*, to *Aventine*'s *Invective, subjoins this Clause*; He has said thus much, notwithstanding he was of the *Romish* Persuasion, and probably would have said much more, if he durst. *Aventine was not of the* Romish, *i. e.* Catholic, *Persuasion, but an Heretic; this Crime might be proved upon him, if there were no other Evidence of it, from an Epistle of* Melanchthon *to Aventine, which I have given from the Original itself, "lib. 2. against the* Calvinistic *Author of the Reply, "chap. 19.*" *Coeffeteau* did not know This Circumstance; nevertheless he positively asserts, that *Aventine* was an Heretic: He says (21), "As for *Du* "*Plessis*

(17) One of them has said, Spontàm fine deo non habet à loquendi libertatem —— A Wife, without a Portion, has not the Liberty of Speech. And Plautus says, in Aulular. Act. 3. Sc. 5, v.r. Quæ indotata est ess in potestate est viri, Dotatæ mactant & malo & damno viros —— She that has no Portion is at the Mercy of her Husband; but be, that marries a Fortune, must be at the Mercy of his Wife.

(18) See Remark [I], of (19) *Contra Arrianæ*, at the Beth'em of Du Plessis Tom. 2, pag. 167.

(19) See Rivetus, in his Apologia Creffeteau, in Beh't of Du Plessis pag. 167.

(MARCUS).

(20) Orèsferi. in Examplar, mine Myster. Du Plessis. cap. 45 pag. 354.

(21) Coiffeteau's Answer to the Mystery of Iniquity, p. Plessis 676.

AVENTINE.

Annals a thousand times, to shew the Disorders of the Church. The other Writings of this Author have very few of them been printed [*I*]. Mr *Moreri* has succeeded very indifferently in this Article [*K*].

" *Plessis* making *Aventine* of the *Romish* Profession, we will never agree to it: His Language discovers him, and throughout his Annals he shews how his Passion transports him against the Holy See. Therefore, to cut him short, all that they object against us, from him, is not worth a Chesnut Leaf, and I judge him no more worthy of an Answer, than the Impostor *Benno*, by whose Memoirs he wrote the Life of That Pontiff (22)." *Aventine* has been treated as a *Lutheran* Author, in the List of prohibited Books; *Fromondus*, however, does not believe him to have been an Heretic, but only one, who, like *Erasmus*, speaks too freely against the Irregularities of the Monks. " Liberrimæ enim linguæ (hæreticæ dicere non ausim, neque puto) & plane Erasmicæ in Monachorum & Ecclesiasticorum vitia fuit A*ventinus*. Plus etiam nimio favens Schismaticis, & parum integra fide res Rom. Pontificum prodidisse perhibetur, ideoque meruit in classe auctorum cautè legendorum ab Indice expurgatorio recenseri (23). — — — *Aventine was a very free Declaimer, (a Heretic I dare not say, nor do I think he was,) and*, like Erasmus, *lashed the Vices of the Monks and Clergy*. He is also said to have shewn too much Favour to the Schismatics, and to have betrayed the Cause of the Popes, through *want of Zeal, and therefore deserved a Place in the Index Expurgatorius, among the Authors, who are to be read with Caution*." Men of the greatest Memory often forget what others remember commonly enough. I am going to give an Example of it. *Conringius* had forgot, that They, who published *Aventine*'s Annals at *Ingolstadt*, had retrenched what did not appear agreeable to the Notions of a good Catholic (24). He says (25), " Libri ejus post mortem demum ab ipsis pontificiis Ingolstadii sunt editi, ut hinc appareat primos saltem editores non improbasse quæ ibi reperiuntur. — — — *After his Death, his Books were, at last, published at* Ingolstadt, *by the Popish Party, which shews, that the first Editors, at least, found nothing there, but what they approved of*." He confesses, that *Aventine* held a Correspondence, by Letters, with several Protestants, and with *Melancthon* by Name, and that he inclined to their Side, which did not hinder him from dying in the *Romish* Communion. " Vixit superiori sæculo quando maxima illa sacrorum mutatio fieret, & multa pontificiæ religionis dogmata improbavit. Per literas familiaritatem coluit cum Protestantium nonnullis, & cum Philippo quoque Melanchthone : Reperire tamen non potui reliquisse eum penitus Ecclesiam Romanam utut in Protestantes videatur propensior : Vixit enim & mortuus est in illa Ecclesia, sepultusque Reginoburgi in Monasterio S. Emerani ceremoniis pontificiæ Ecclesiæ usitatis (26). — — — *He lived in the last Century, when That great Revolution happened in Religion, and disapproved of many of the Papal Doctrines. He corresponded, by Letters, with several of the Protestants, and particularly with* Philip Melancthon. *Yet I could never find, that he had absolutely renounced the* Romish *Church, how much soever he might seem more inclining towards the Protestants* : *For he lived, and died, in That Church, and was buried at* Ratisbon, *in the Monastery of St* Hemeran, *with the usual Romish Rites and Ceremonies*." I observe, that *Aventine*'s Fate may justly be compared with That of Father *Paul*.

[*I*] *The other Writings of this Author have very few of them been printed*.] *Vossius* observes, that *Aventine* informs his Readers, in the Two hundred and thirty sixth Page of his Annals (which is the Three hundred and forty fourth in the Edition of 1580) that he had published the History of *Oëtingen*, a City of *Suabia*; *publicatæ à se historiæ Utinensium meminit* (27). *Gesner* has not mentioned This History. He speaks only of a *Grammar*, published by *Aventine*, in the Year 1519, and of a Book concerning the manner of counting on the Fingers, published at *Ratisbon*, in the Year 1532; to which the Author had subjoined the Summary of a great Work, which only required the Assistance of a *Mecænas* for its Publication. This is the Title of the Book, printed in 1532. *Numerandi per digitos manusque (quin etiam loquendi) veterum consuetudinis Abacus, sive Explicatio ex Bedâ cum picturis & imaginibus, unà cum capitibus rerum quibus illustrabitur Germania ab Aventino, modo contingat benignus Mecænas*. *Gesner* gives an exact Account of This great Work of *Aventine*; whereby it appears, that the same Author had formed a very fine and large Plan, to illustrate the Antiquities of *Germany*. The general view alone of the Subjects, which he undertook, is sufficient to create Astonishment. See the Letter, which he wrote to *Vadianus*, in 1530 (28). He intended very soon to have published such another *Chronicle*, as That of *Eusebius*; an *Ecclesiastical History* from the beginning of the World to his own Time; some *ancient Grammarians*, a *Greek* and *Latin* Dictionary, *Annotations on* Claudian (29), &c. But it is not known what is become of These Works. To comprehend how he could be able to go through with so many Writings, we must know, that he began to study by break of Day, and oftentimes returned again a little after Supper, and continued 'till Midnight (30). As he broke the Ice for Those, who have treated of the Antiquities of *Bavaria* (31), it is no wonder, they have discovered Faults in his Annals (32). He would have found more in theirs, if they had lead him the way, as he has done them. *Lambecius* has corrected him in many Things (33).

[*K*] *Mr* Moreri *has succeeded very indifferently in this Article*.] I. He is excusable for placing *Aventine* under the Letter I, in his first Edition; but a Repetition of the same Fault is unpardonable. He could not be ignorant of the general Complaint of his having ranked his illustrious Persons according to their *Christian* Names. Why, then, was not the Occasion of This Complaint avoided in the following Editions? II. *Aventine* was born in the Year 1466, and not in the Year 1460. III. Having once committed This Mistake, as *Aventine* died in the Year 1534, he ought not to have given him Sixty eight Years of Age. He should have committed one Mistake more, and made him live Seventy four Years; because, for want of adding this second Mistake to the first, he has left an intolerable Blunder, in reckoning but Sixty eight Years from the Year 1460 to the Year 1534. IV. It is not true, that *Nicholas Gesner* published *Aventine*'s Annals. He ought to have said *Nicholas Cisner* (34). V. To say, that *Nicholas Cisner* published these Annals, with Additions, is very improper; for This seems to imply, that he had added, to them, something of his own. But This he has not done. His Performance was only This: He published These Annals after a Manuscript of *Aventine*, Passages, which had not been castrated; so that his Edition is more ample, than That of *Zieglerus*, because it contains all Those, which *Zieglerus* had suppressed. The Words of *Vossius*, which *Moreri* has stumbled at, would not have deceived an attentive Reader : They intimate clearly enough, that *Cisner* only restored to *Aventine*, what had been taken from him. *Annales Boiorum libris* vii. *reliquit : quos ex authenticis Codd. restituit & auxit Nicolaus Cisnerus* (35). *Vossius* was a little to blame in not mentioning the caitrated Edition: had he done That, what I have now quoted would have been much clearer. VI. A Priest, as *Moreri* was, acts but a strange Part, when he calls *Nicholas Cisner*'s Additions *considerable*; since Those Additions consist only of Invectives against the Popes, and the *Romish* Clergy. VII. The *other Pieces*, which *Aventine* left, are not Those, which Cardinal *Baronius* did not esteem very *Orthodox*. It was against the *Annals of Bavaria*, That Cardinal was so much incensed. VIII. He ought not to have quoted *Baronius* T. IX. *Anni* A. C. 772 (36); for This looks as if *Baronius* had written, at least, nine Volumes upon this one Year 772.

Marginal notes (left column):

(22) *Gregory* VII.

(23) Libert. Fromondus, in libro de Orbe Terræ Immob. pag. 24, 25.

(24) *See Remark* [C].

(25) Conringius apud Magirum, Eponymol. Critic. p. 90.

(26) Id. ib.

(27) Vossius de Hist. Lat. pag 655.

Marginal notes (right column):

(28) *It is the* 49*th of the Century published by* Goldast.

(29) See Gesner, Bibliotch. fol. 386.

(30) Zieglerus in ejus Vitâ.

(31) Conringius, apud Magir. Eponymolog. Crit. p. 90.

(32) Brunnerus, in his Annals of Bavaria, cri-tic, ex hin officio. See Zeisler de Histor. p. 134.

(33) Lambec. Commentar. Biblioth. Cæsi Lib 2, cap. 1, 2. See Magir. Eponymol. pag. 91.

(34) In the Holland Edition, it is Nicholas Gesner.

(35) Vossius de Hist. Lat. pag. 655.

(36) Vossius, the only Author that Moreri has quoted concerning A*ventine*, might also have a preferred him from what he tells, who thus cites this one place, ex T. IX. ad Ann 772.

AVERROËS.

(e) See all his Names, in Remark [C].

AVERROËS (a), one of the most subtile Philosophers that appeared among the *Arabians*, was of *Corduba* (b), and flourished in the Twelfth Century [A]. He had an extraordinary esteem for *Aristotle*, and commented upon his Works so very learnedly, that he was called The *Commentator* by way of Excellency. It has been thought wonderful, that, *without knowing any Thing of Greek, he could penetrate so well into the Sense of the Original*; and it is believed, not without reason, that, *if he had known That Language, he would have perfectly understood Aristotle's Thoughts. Qui Græcè nescius feliciter adeò mentem Aristotelis perspexit, quid non fecisset si Linguam scisset Græcam* (c)? This some learned Men say; but others affirm, that he has interpreted *Aristotle* very indifferently [B], not only for want of Learning, but also of Capacity. He was Professor in the University of *Morocco* [C], and became very skilful in Physic; but he understood the Theory of it better than the Practice [D]. He is looked upon as the Inventor

(b) *It is falsly said in the Lindenius Renovatus, that Corduba is a City of Arabia.*

(c) Vossius de Philosophorum sectis, pag. 90. See Kockerman's Works in the Remark [I].

[A] *He flourished in the XIIth Century.*] I see no other Proof of it than this; that his two Sons were seen, by Ægidius, at the Court of *Frederic Barbarossa* (1). "Ætatem ex co colligimus quod " Ægidius Romanus in nono Quotlibeto refert se " duos ejus filios vidisse in aulâ Frederici Barbarossæ. " Is vero regere cœpit Anno CIƆCLII. ac impe- " ravit Annos XXXVII. —— *The Age he lived in " may be gathered from hence, that Ægidius, in " his ninth Quodlibet, affirms he saw two of his " Sons at the Court of* Frederic Barbarossa: *Who " began his Reign in the Year* 1152, *and reigned " thirty seven Years*. These are *Vossius*'s Words in the One hundred fourteenth Page of his Book *de Philosophià*, chap. 14. See also the seventeenth Chapter of his Treatise *de Philosophorum sectis*, page 91, where he proves, by the Evidence of the *Conciliator*, and of This *Ægidius*, that *Averroës* flourished in the Year 1150, he refers us to the *Quodlibets* of *Ægidius*, lib. 2. *Quæstione de unitate intellectûs*. *Reinesius* observes, that the Death of *Averroës* is placed in the Five hundred ninety fifth Year of the *Hegira*, which is the Eleven hundred ninety eighth of the *Christian Æra* (2). I wish Mr *Konig*, who refers us to *Reinesius*, had not placed This Death in the Year 1225. He ought to have referred us to *Hottinger*, and to have rectified him; for That learned *Swiss*, having said, after *John Leo*, that *Averroës* died in the Six hundred and third Year of the *Hegira*, makes That Year answer to our Year 1225 (3). This is a great Mistake; it answers, Part of it, to our Year 1206, the other Part to our Year 1207 The *Bibliotheca Rabbinica* of *Bartolocci* says, that *Averroës* flourished from the Year 1131, to the Year 1216, which was That of his Death; that his Commentaries on *Aristotle's* Philosophy were finished at *Sev.lle*, in the Year 1187, and that Those on his Metaphysics were written in the Year 1192 (4).

[B] *Some of the Learned affirm, that he has interpreted* Aristotle *very indifferently - - - - for want of Learning*.] This was the Opinion of *Ludovicus Vives*. " Nomen est commentatoris nactus, *says* he (5), ho- " mo qui in Aristotele enarrando nihil minus expli- " cat, quam eum ip∫um quem suscepit declarandum. " Sed nec potuisset explicare etiam si divino fuisset " ingenio, quum esset humano, & quidem intra " mediocritatem Nam quid tandem adferebat, quo " in Aristotele enarrando po∫set esse probe instructus? " Non cognitionem veteris memoriæ, non scientiam " placitorum priscæ disciplinæ, & intellegentiam " sectarum, quibus Aristoteles pa∫sim scatet. Itaque " videas eum pessime philosophos omneis antiquos " citare, ut qui nullum unquam legerit, ignarus " Græcitatis ac Latinitatis, pro Polo Ptholomæum " ponit, pro Prothagorâ Pythagoram, pro Cratylo " Democritum, libros Platonis titulis ridiculis inscri- " bit: & ita de iis loquitur, ut vel cœco perspicuum " sit literam eum in illis legisse nullam. At quàm " confidenter audet pronuntiare hoc aut illud ab " eis dici, &, quod impudentius est, non dici : Quum " solos viderit Alexandrum, Themistium, & Nico- " laum Damascenum: Et hos, ut apparet, verso in " Ara‘icum perversi∫sime ac corruptissime. Citat " enim eos nonnunquam, & contradicit, & cum " eis rixatur, ut nec ipse quidem, qui scripsit " intelligat. Aristotelem verò quomodo legit, non " in sua origine purum & integrum, non in lacunam " Latinam derivatum, non enim potuit linguarum " expers, sed de Latino in Arabicum transvasatum. " —— *He has gained the Name of Commentator, tho'*

" *he is very far from explaining his Author* Aristotle, " *or deserving That Title. This would have been " too great a Task, for one of an extraordinary Genius, " much more for him, who had but a moderate one, " nay, to say the Truth, a mean one. For what Qua- " lifications had he for undertaking a Commentary " on* Aristotle ? *He had no Knowledge of Antiquity, " nor of it's several Doctrines, and Sects, with " which* Aristotle *every where abounds. So that you " find him cite all the old Philosophers in such a " wretched Manner, as proves he never could have " read one of them. Through his Ignorance of Greek and " Latin, he puts* Ptholomæus *for* Polus, Pythago- " ras *for* Prothagoras, Democritus *for* Cratylus, *and " miscalls the Titles of* Plato*'s Books very ridiculously; " and speaks of them so, that even a blind Man " may see he had never read a Letter of them. But " what a prodigious Degree of Assurance is it, for " him to pronounce, that such a Thing is said by " them, or, what is still more shocking, that such a " thing is not said by them: when he had seen on- " ly* Alexander, Themistius, *and* Nicolas Damascenus : *and these only in blundering* Arabic *Translations. For " he sometimes cites them, and contradicts them, and " raises such Controversies with them, as he himself " does not at all understand But how does he read " Aristotle ? not pure and entire in the Original, " nor even in his first Debasement in a* Latin *Tran- " slation, for he understood neither of these Languages, " but degenerated again out of* Latin *into* Arabic." He afterwards proves the Inability of this Interpreter of *Aristotle*, by an Example (6. See *Cœlius Rhodiginus*, who, in general, says almost the same thing (7). We must not trust to Father *Rapin*, who makes him say This of *Avicenna* (8) For That Jesuit did not always quote from the Original. However, what he is going to say is by no means contemptible: " As " *Averroës* understood nothing of *Aristotle*, but by " an unfaithful Translation, he fell himself into such " terrible Misconstructions of his Sense, that *Bogolin*, " a Philosopher of *Verona*, *Zimara*, and *Mantinus*, " understook, *in vain, to correct him* (9)."

[C] *He was Professor in the University of* Morocco.] It was under the third King of the Race of the *Almohades*, after the Expulsion of the *Almoravides*. Read this Passage of *Reinesius*: " Quem " *Averroëm* adpellant vulgo scholæ, ejus nomen inte- " grum est Abual-Walid Mohammed, ebn Achmed, " ebn Mohammed, ebn Roshd: Docuitque in Aca- " demia Maroccana auspiciis Jacobi, tertii ex Al- " mohadis, post ejectos Almoravidas, regis (10). — " *The true Name of Him, who is called, in the Schools*, " *Averroës, was* Abual-Walid Mohammed, ebn Ach- " med, ebn Mohammed, ebn Roshd : *And he taught " in the University of* Morocco, *under the Reign " of* James III, *of the* Almohades, *after the Ex- " pulsion of the* Almoravides."

[D] *He became very skilful in Physic; but he understood the Theory of it better than the Practice.*] His principal Work in Physic is That, which is called *Colliget*. He there treats of This Science in general; and it cannot be amiss to give here a Piece of the Preface : " Ex præcepto *nobilis Domini Avdelach Sempsi*, " qui pro consilio suorum Philosophorum Avolait " & Avenchalit injunxit mihi ut conscriberem opus, " quod Arabico sermone totam Medicinæ Scientiam " contineret, ad approbandum judicandumve sen- " tentias veterum, collegi hoc opus Colliget, id est, " Universale, sic inscriptum propter ordinem doctri- " næ observandum, qui paulatim ab universalibus " ad

AVERROËS.

Inventor of an Opinion both very abfurd, and very contrary to *Chriſtian* Orthodoxy [E], but which, neverthelefs, made fuch a formidable Progrefs among feveral

(11) Præf. Averrois apud Geſnerum, in Biblioth. fol. 101.

" ad particularia procedit. In hoc enim libro uni-
" verſales regulas inchoavi, & deinceps favente Deo
" alium librum de iis quæ particularia funt inſtituum,
" &c. (11) —— *At the Command of my noble Lord*
" *Audelach Sempſe, who, by the Advice of his Phi-*
" *loſophers, Avoſait and Avenchalit, obliged me to*
" *undertake a Work, in the Arabic Language, which*
" *ſhould comprehend the whole Science of Phyſic, that*
" *I might judge and approve of the Opinions of the*
" *Ancients. I have compoſed this Work* Colliget, *that*
" *is, Univerſal: So entitled, on account of the Or-*
" *der to be obſerved in Teaching, which proceeds by*
" *degrees from Univerſals to Particulars. For in this*
" *Book I have given ſuch Rules as are Univerſal;*
" *and hereafter, if Providence permits, I ſhall write*
" *one concerning Particulars, &c.*" To make it plain, that he valued himſelf for his great Skill in Phyſic, it will be ſufficient to obſerve, that *he was a Rival*
of the great Avicenna, *and ſo great an Enemy*
to him, that he avoids naming him in his Writings:
Avicennæ Medici æmulus & inimiciſſimus fuit, ut eum nominare in ſuis Libris vereatur (12): his Affectation in this Reſpect is very evident. This Affectation was undoubtedly the Reaſon, why, in confuting a Doctrine maintained by *Avicenna*, he attacked it only as the Sentiment of *Galen*. I ſpeak of the Doctrine, which aſſerts, that the Animal Spirits, which cauſe Joy are bright, and Thoſe, which cauſe Melancholy, black. Mr Petit has taken notice of this Affectation of *Averroës*. " Nunc quibus mentis penetrationibus Averrois hanc Aviſennæ opinionem impugnet, videamus: quamquam eo loco directe Aviſennam non petit, ſed Galenum, ſpontaneum melancholicorum metum ab humoris, qui in iis abundat, nigredine repetentem; verum quæ ibi Galeno
" objicit, pari impetu in memoratam Aviſennæ opinionem redeunt (13). —— *Let us ſee now what*
" *Arguments* Averroës *brings againſt this Opinion*
" *of* Avicenna*; though he does not there directly at-*
" *tack* Avicenna, *but* Galen, *who aſcribes the ſpon-*
" *taneous Timorouſneſs of melancholy Perſons to a*
" *black Humour abounding in them, and what he*
" *there objects againſt* Galen *falls with equal force*
" *on this Opinion of* Avicenna." *Averroës*, either on purpoſe, or through forgetfulneſs, has behaved in a quite contrary Manner, with regard to *Avempace;* for he names him as the Author of a Remark, which he might have read in *Philoponus* (14). This is only by the by. Now, that he was more learned in the Theory, than the Practice, he himſelf confeſſes, as Mr Petit obſerves. " Averroës fatetur de ſe ultro
" in ſeptimo eorum librorum, quos *Colliget* vulgus
" appellat, cap. 6. Ego, inquit, non Rudui et Scien-
" tiæ (Medicinæ) ut videar mihi in ea eſſe ſuffi-
" ciens: Et alibi negat ſe in eorum numero eſſe qui
" ægris remedia adhibent (15). —— Averroës
" *makes this Confeſſion of himſelf, in the ſeventh of*
" *theſe Books, commonly called* Colliget, *and I*
" *have not, ſays he, ſtudied This Science (of Phyſic)*
" *in order to make myſelf perfect in it: And, elſe-*
" *where, he denies himſelf to be in the Number of*
" *thoſe, who adminiſter to the ſick.*" This Paſſage of Mr Petit is much more exact, than theſe Words of *Voſſius*. " Aver-roës Cordubenſis, cognomento
" Commentator, medicus non tam practicus, quam
" theoreticus. Fuit medicus Maroliini regis (16).
" —— Aver-roës of Corduba, *firnamed* the Commentator, *a Phyſician, not ſo much in Practice,*
" *as in Theory. He was Phyſician to King* Memarolinus." The laſt Words weaken, inſtead of confirming, the former; for, to be a Prince's Phyſician, requires great Practice. I ſay nothing of *Memarolini* (17), which was not a proper Name, but a Name of Dignity, and conſequently not fit to be joined with the Word *regis*. *Merclelinus* was not aware of This, when he ſaid, *Videtur Medicus*
fuiſſe regis Miramamolini (18) —— ——
He ſeems to have been Phyſician to King Miramamolinus. Symphorian Camper was the Original of This Error; he had ſaid, that *Averroës* lived at *Corduba*, in the Time of King *Miramalinus, tempore*
Miramalini regis apud Cordubam (19). Obſerve, that the Phyſicians of *Paris*, great Favourers of Phlebotomy, would not eaſily agree, that *Averroës* was not

much ſkilled in the Practice of Phyſic; for it is ſaid, that his Example contributed much to extirpate an Error, which they diſapproved. Read theſe Words of *Stephen Paſquier*. " How many Ages have we
" practiſed Phyſic, with the Notion, that Children
" ought not to blooded, 'till fourteen Years of
" Age, and that bleeding of them before That Time
" was not a Cure, but certain Death? A Hereſy,
" which we ſhould have lived in to this Day, if
" it had not been for *Averroës*, the *Arabian*, who
" ventured to make the firſt Experiment of it on
" a Son of his own, about ſix or ſeven Years of
" Age, whom he cured of a Pleuriſie (20)."

[E] *He is looked upon as the Inventor of an Opi-*
nion, both very abſurd, and very contrary to Chriſtian
Orthodoxy.] I think it would be more proper to ſay, that he has cleared and explained it, and, by maintaining it with more application than ever, has given a kind of new Life to it; for the ſame *Pomponatius*, who affirms, in his fourth Chapter, that it is a Monſter forged by *Averroës;* Figmentum & Monſtrum eſt Averroï confictum (21); has alſo ſaid, in the third Chapter, that *Themiſtius* and *Averroës*
taught the ſame thing. " Averroës itaque & ut
" exiſtimo ante eum Themiſtius concordes poſuere
" animam intellectivam realiter diſtingui ab anima
" corruptibili, verum ipſam eſſe unum numero in
" omnibus hominibus, mortalem vero multiplicatam (22). —— Averroës *therefore, and, I think,*
before him Themiſtius, *maintained an intellectual*
Soul really diſtinct from the corruptible Soul, that
the former was only One in all Mankind, but the
Mortal One as numerous as the Individuals." The Jeſuits of *Coimbra* go higher; for they will have it, that *Theophraſtus* underſtood the Doctrine of his Maſter *Ariſtotle* in this Senſe. " Occurrit alia ſententia
" exiſtimantium in diſciplina Ariſtotelis ponendam eſſe
" unam duntaxat animam intellectricem, ſive unum
" intellectum qui omnibus hominibus aſſiſtat, ut ſolis
" lumen univerſitati. Sic enim Ariſtotelem interpretati funt ejus diſcipulus & Scholæ ſucceſſor Theophraſtus, Themiſtius, Simplicius, Averroës, aliique
" non pauci, etſi non omnes eodem modo de hujuſmodi intellectu locuti fuerint (23). —— *There*
occurs another Opinion of Thoſe, who, according to
the Doctrine of Ariſtotle, *maintained only an intellectual Soul, or one Intellect, which ſerves all Mankind, as the Light of the Sun does the Univerſe.*
For ſo has Ariſtotle *been interpreted by his Scholar, and Succeſſor in his School,* Theophraſtus, *by*
Themiſtius, Simplicius, Averroës, *and others, tho'*
they have not all expreſſed themſelves alike, concerning
this Intellect." They add, that ſeveral Moderns have owned, that, according to *Ariſtotle's* Hypotheſis, the Underſtanding of all Men is one and the ſame Subſtance. " Hoc quidem Argumentum per-
" movit etiam ad prædictam Intellectus unitatem in
" Ariſtotelis doctrinâ aſſerendam non paucos è re-
" cenſioribus peripateticis in quibus ſunt Thom. An-
" glicus, Achillinus, Odo Jandunus, Mirandulanus,
" Zimara, Vicomercatus, & quidam alii (24). ——
" *This very Argument induced many of the modern* Peripateticks *to aſſert this Unity of the Intellect, according to the Doctrine of* Ariſtotle, *amongſt whom*
are Thomas Anglicus, Achillinus, Odo Jandunus,
Mirandulanus, Zimara, Vicomercatus, *and others.*"
But that ſome among Theſe Moderns will have it to be, in all Men, as an affiſtant Form, others as a conſtituent Form. The latter is the Opinion of *Mirandulanus* (25), and of *Achillinus* (26). But obſerve here a Miſtake like This of *Pomponatius*. The Jeſuits of *Coimbra* elſewhere aſcribe the Invention of the Unity of the Intellect in All Men to *Averroës*. This will appear the more ſurpriſing, when the Words are ſeen, which precede Thoſe, where they affirm it.
" Secunda (*ſententia*) fuit Avicennæ 9. Metaph. cap.
" quarto, & in lib. Natur. part. 5. Avempace in epi-
" ſtola de lumine, & Græci cujuſdam Marini cujus
" mentionem facit hoc loco Philoponus, ajentium in-
" tellectum agentem eſſe ſubſtantiam quandam ſepa-
" ratam, quam Avicenna Cholcodæam nuncupabat.
" Idem placuit Averroï in libello de beatitudine ani-
" mæ, cap. 5 & in epitome Metaph. tractatu 4. qui
" errori errorem ſubnectens, aliorum veſtigia ſecutus,
" unum,

several *Italian* Philosophers, that it became necessary to condemn it by the Pope's at the bottom. It is impious, because it leads to a Belief, that the Soul, which is properly the Form of Man, dies with the Body (33), it is absurd, because (33) *Ser Remark* [H] *towards the End.* nothing can be more senseless, than to maintain, that two Men, who are directed by their respective intellectual Operations to kill each other, have the same Soul? What can be imagined more chimerical, than that two Philosophers, one of whom affirms, and the other denies, the same Thesis, at the same time, are but One only Being, as to the Intellect? We will examine what an Adversary of *Pomponatius*, advanced against This Extravagancy.

" unum omnium hominum finxit communem intel-
(27) Conim- " lectum, ut alibi retulimus (27). ----- *The second*
bricensia In " [*Opinion*] *was That of* Avicenna, *in his* Metaphy-
lib. 3, de A- " sics, *lib.* 9. *chap.* 4. *and in his Book de* Natur.
nima, cap. 5. " *Part* 5. *of* Avempace, *in his Epistle* de Lumine,
Quæst. 1. " *and of* Marinus, *a certain Greek, mentioned here*
Artic. 1. " *by* Philoponus; *who held, that the acting Intellect*
pag. 226. " *is a certain separate Substance, which* Avicenna
" *calls* Cholcodæa. Averroës *is of the same Senti-*
" *ment, in his Book de* Beatitudine Animæ, *chap.* 5.
" *and in* Epitome Metaphys. *Tractat.* 4. *who, adding*
" *Error to Error, in imitation of others, has pretend-*
" *ed, that there is but one Intellect, in common to*
" *all Men, as we have elsewhere related.*" That
is to say, That the Unity of the Intellect is a
Fiction, which *Averroës* has added to the Errors of
others; yet nevertheless it is plain, this Fiction does
not at all differ from the Doctrine they attribute to
Avicenna, &c. We must remember, that, according
to *Averroes*, the Intellect of Men is the lowest De-
(28) Com- gree of Intelligences, and occupies the lowest Place
mentator ip- of the Universe (28). " Esse mentium infimam
se Comm. " omnium, & unicam. Nam sicut coelestis globi
10, l. 3, de " singuli singulas habere mentes videntur, ita &
Anim ponit " orbis hic inferior unam, ut ipse vult, habet, quæ
ipsam esse " non hujus hominis sit, vel illius: Sed humanæ
ultimam " speciei mens sit, & dicatur, ut speciei unicæ uni-
Intelligen- " cus sit intellectus in hoc orbe inferiori, ut pleri-
tiarum. " que intelligunt, ubique totus compingi (29). —
Pompon. de " *It is One only, and That the lowest of Intelligences.*
Immortalitate " *For, as each of the celestial Orbs seems to have it's*
Anim. cap. " *particular Intellect, so has this inferior Globe*
4, pag. 11. " *it's Intellect, which he will have to be One,*
(29) Cælius " *and not appropriated to This, or That Man: but to*
Rhodigin. " *be the Intellect of the whole human Species, that*
Antiq. Lect. " *there may be to One Species One Intellect, in this*
lib. 3, c. 2. " *lower Orb, as most understand it, that the whole*
pag. 109. " *is contained every where.*" Be this as it will,
these Jesuits, in confuting this pretended Unity of
the Intellect of all Men, attack This Philosopher
only; so much do they, at least, esteem him the
chief Defender of This Chimera. They observe,
that Scotus *had said, that* Averroës *became wor-*
thy to be excommunicated by human Races, and
that others say, that his Doctrine is such a dread-
ful Monster, that the Forests of Arabia *never pro-*
duced a greater. " Hæc Commentatoris seu com-
" mentitoris potius de unitate intellectûs sententia
" adeo stulta est, ut meritò Scotus in 4 d. 43 q. 2.
" dixerit dignum esse Averroem qui ob has ineptias
" ex hominum communione averruncetur. Alii vero
" hoc ejus figmentum monstrum vocârint quo nul-
" lum majus Arabum sylvæ genuerint. Certè hoc
" unum sat esse debuisset ad eos coarguendos qui
(30) Conimb. " filium Rois tanti faciunt, ut ejus animam Aristo-
In lib. 2, de " telis animam esse dicant (30)." The last part of
Anima, cap. this Passage informs us, that, among other Elogies,
1, Quæst. 7. *That of having* Aristotle's *Soul was given to This* Ara-
Art. 2. pag. bian. The Jesuits of *Coimbra* will have it, that to
60. confute this, it is sufficient to consider only the
Doctrine of the Unity of the Intellect. But This
Observation is false; for, as several of the Moderns
have owned, This Doctrine is only an Inlargement
and Explication of *Aristotle*'s Principles. I could
prove this by many Remarks, but shall content myself with this, that, according to the Hypothesis of our
Philosopher, the Multiplication of Individuals can
have no other Foundation, than Matter; from
whence it follows, that the Intellect is but One, since
Aristotle makes it separate and distinct from Matter.
Viderunt Aristotelem *simpliciter probare intellectum*
(31) Pom- *possibilem esse immixtum & immaterialem* (31). This
ponatius de is the Observation of *Pomponatius.* " Quod vero
Immortal. " unicus sit intellectus in omnibus hominibus sive
Anim. c. 4. " possibilis ponatur, patere potest ex eo quoniam apud
pag. 7. " Peripateticos est celebrata propositio, multiplicatio-
" nem individuorum in eadem specie non posse esse
" nisi per materiam quantam, ut dicitur 7 & 12 Me-
(32) Ibid. " taph, & 2 de Anima (32). —— *But that the In-*
pag. 8 " *tellect in all Men is but One, or may be supposed so,*
" *appears from hence, that the Peripatetics have a*
" *celebrated Maxim, that the Multiplication of Indivi-*
" *duals can be only by Matter and Quantity, as is said*
" *in* 7 *and* 12. Metaph. *&* 2. de Anima." But
how much soever This Opinion of *Averroës* may be
grounded on *Aristotle*, yet it is impious and absurd

First, He confutes it, as it supposes, that the Intellect is not in Man, and afterwards, as it supposes that all Men have but one and the same Intellect. On the first Point, he enquires why an Intellect, which ought to unite it's Operation to That of the Man, in the most intimate Manner possible, should think it a Dishonour to unite itself with the Organs, to compose with them one Individual (34)? You will easily apprehend the (34) Antonius Sirmondus de Immortalitate Animæ adversus Pomponatium & Assectas, p. 268. intimate Union there mentioned, if you take notice, that, according to the *Averroïsts*, the Soul of Man is not capable of Understanding without the help of This assisting Intellect. This Intellect then must supply, by it's Operation, what the Soul of Man wants; and consequently our intellectual Acts depend on two Principles, whereof one is only passive and defective, the other is active and perfect. These two Principles therefore concur and terminate in the same effect; and consequently the Action of the Intellect of the *Averroïsts* unites it self, in a most intimate manner, with the Soul, which understands. But this difficulty is not great; for the Union objected is not more intimate, than That of the Operation of God, with the Operation of the Creature, according to the Doctrine of Co-operation; and yet it does not follow from hence, that these two Causes must be personally united. The Author pretends to obviate this Answer, by saying, That the Operation of the Intellect of the *Averroïsts* is immanent and particular, which cannot be said of the Co-operation of God (35); but this may (35) Id. Ib. pag. 369. easily be answered; so that his Disputation is not so victorious as to the first Point, as it is with regard to the second; for observe how he presses *Averroës: That Intellect, of which you speak, is either God, or a Creature. If it is God, I ask this Question, Does he act within or without himself? If without himself? what a Monster would not an Operation of the Understanding be, which is placed without the Intellect, and in another Person* (36). This proves too (36) Quid hoc peranti intellectio ve extra intellectum consistat & quidem toto ab ea distincta supposito? Id. ibid. pag. 370. much; for from hence it must be inferred, that the Divine Intellect cannot produce an Act of Intelligence in the Soul of Man, without producing the same in itself. Now This is false and absurd. The other Branch of the Question reduces the *Averroïsts* to the last Extremity. If God forms in himself the Acts of Intelligence, which are in Man, how many Errors must he entertain? " Sed neque
" intra Deum contineri potest (*intellectio*) quod im-
" mensos in eum errores toties inveherit, neque enim
" opinione suâ fallerentur homines; neque etiam
" prorsus ulla valeret excusatio, quin prima ac sum-
" ma veritas à se ipsa monstrosè deficeret, si assig-
" nanda ipsi essent, si in sinu ejus & complexu re-
" ponenda quæcunque esse possunt falsa hominum
" judicia (37). —— *Neither can it* [the Intellect] *be* (37) Id. Ib.
" *contained within God, since it must produce in him*
" *such prodigious Errors, as often as Men are deceived*
" *in their Opinions; nor can any Salvo be found*
" *sufficient to explain, how the supream Truth can*
" *avoid degenerating from itself in a monstruous*
" *Manner, if it must be charged with, and made*
" *to entertain, all those false Judgments, to which*
" *Men are liable.*" If they answer, that this Intellect is created, the Author replies, that a Creature does not seem sufficient to regulate so effectually all human Souls at the same time (38). Besides that (38) Id. Ib. p. 371, 372. the contrariety of Opinions, which reign among Men, cannot lodge together in one single Understanding.
" Quomodo in unam & eandem intelligentiam si-
" mul cadet contrarietas illa opinionum & senten-
" tiarum, quam toties in hominibus experimur, cum
" unus ait, alter negat de eodem idem? Quæ ea-
" dem quæstio impedire potest adversariorum in res-
" ponsione

AVERROËS. 555

Pope's Authority [F]. This Opinion is, That there is an Intelligence, which, without

" ponsione jamjam explosa de intellectu divino. ———
" How can That Contrariety of Opinions, and Notions,
" which we so often observe among Men, concerning
" one and the same Subject, ever subsist in one, and
" the same, Intellect? Which very Objection shews
" also the Absurdity of That long exploded Notion of
" the Divinity of This Intellect." This last Objection has the same force against Those, who affirm, that This Intellect is God. Thus is also Spinozism invincibly confuted (39). It is remarkable, that the Author owns all the strength of his Objection to consist in his having proved, that the Operation of the Intellect of the Averroïsts on the Souls of Men is inherent (40). But I think, there is no Reason for them to allow, that he has proved This Point. As to what remains, he declares, that he should have nothing to say against Averroës's Sentiment, if That Philosopher had only spoke of the Operation of the Divine Intellect, considered as the first Cause. " Restat ergo, ut suum istud somnium integrum Averroës somnii loco & mendacii
" haberi sinat, aut certè interpretetur ipse de actione
" intellectûs divini, quâ parte non intellectûs quidem præcisè, sed est prima causa, in omnes
" causarum secundarum, adeoque inferiorum intelligentiarum effectus ex virtute sua inhærens aliquid
" (41). ——— An ita possit accipi, non disputo, illud
" contentus ostendisse, quòd nisi quid simile sonet
" ejus doctrina, inanis ac stulta sit, si quid autem
" simile, ne pilum quidem nobis adversantem habeat (42). ——— It remains therefore, that Averroës must either give up this whole Chimerical Notion of his for a Dream, and a Fiction, or interpret
" it of the Act of the Divine Intellect, not as it is
" the Intellect, but the first Cause operating on all
" second Causes, and consequently in some Degree influencing by it's Agency the Effects of inferior Intellects. — Whether or no it can be so explained,
" I shall not undertake to dispute, being content
" with having shewn, that, unless his Doctrine be
" construed after some such manner as this, it is
" empty and absurd, but, if it be so construed, I have
" nothing to object against it." He tells us, That he has not meddled with the Objections, which Thomas Aquinas started against the Hypothesis of This Arabian. You may find it perfectly confuted in a Work of Mr Du Plessis Mornay (43).

It is surprizing, that such great Genius's, as Aristotle and Averroës, should invent so many Chimera's concerning the Intellectual Faculty; and yet I will venture to say, that the Superiority of their Parts was the very Cause of it. It was by their great Penetration, that they discovered such Difficulties, as obliged them to leave the common Road, and despise many other ways, where they did not meet with what they sought. The most certain Knowledge they had of the Nature of the Soul was, that it is capable of thinking successively of a thousand things; but, how it reduced this Capacity into Action, they could not comprehend: The Operation of Objects, their Species, their Images in the Brain, as much refined as you please, nothing of all this seems sufficient to give the Soul an actual Intelligence. See with what Force Father Mallebranche confutes all that has been said of the Manner of our knowing things (44). He could find no other Expedient, but to assert, that we see them in God, and that the Ideas are not produced in our Souls. Some ancient Philosophers have said, that God is the general Intelligence of all Spirits; that is to say, that he publishes Knowledge on them, as the Sun does Light on Bodies. Read these Words of the Jesuits of Coimbra: " Prima sententia fuit
" Alexandri libro secundo de Anima, cap. 20. & 21.
" existimantis intellectum agentem esse intellectum
" universalem omnium conditorem, hoc est Deum;
" quod etiam Platonis dogma libro sexto de republicâ fuisse creditur, qui intellectum agentem nostros animos cœlitus irradiantem comparavit soli,
" ut ex Themistio hoc in lib. refert divus Thomas
" 1 part. quæst. 79. articulo quarto. In eundem errorem lapsus fuit Priscianus Lydus asserens, intellectum agentem non esse partem animæ, sed mentem primam atque divinam, vel Ideam boni (45).
" ——— The first was the Opinion of Alexander, in
" his second Book de Anima, cap. 20, 21, who held
" the acting Intellect to be the universal Intellect,

" the Creator of all things, i. e. God; which is al-
" so esteemed to be the Doctrine of Plato, in his sixth
" Book de Republicâ, where the acting Intellect, irradiating our Minds, is compared to the Sun, as
" St Thomas relates from Themistius, in this Book,
" Part I, Quæst. 79, Art. 4. Priscianus Lydus is
" fallen into the same Error, in asserting, that the
" acting Intellect is not part of the Soul, but the supream and divine Mind itself, or Idea of Good."
When a Subject is very obscure, it is no wonder, that the greatest Philosophers speak of it a little out of the way, and on Suppositions not easily to be apprehended. Now there cannot be a more difficult Subject, than This of the Formation of Thought. It is, perhaps, more so, than That of the Original of the Soul. This is giving a great way; for it is a very wise Reflexion Bartholin makes on a Story reported of St Anselm. This Archbishop of Canterbury, finding himself near Death, at the Age of Seventy six Years, is said to have begged a short Respite, that he might finish a very obscure Inquiry, he had begun, into the Original of the Soul (46). If he had obtained Seventy six Years more, says Bartholin, I doubt he could scarce have made an end of so obscure a Question. Valdè dubito, si vel totidem annos quos vixerat illi addidisset Deus vitæ arbiter, ad finem quæstionis dubiæ unquam potuerit pervenire (47). Observe, that most of the Cartesians teach, that, as there is none but God, who can give Motion to the Body, so there is none but God, who can modify the Spirits. They except Those Actions of the Soul, which are criminal. But, as to all what we call Sensation, Imagination, Passion, Memory, and Idea, They pretend, that God is the efficient and immediate Cause of these, and that the Action of Objects, or the Motion of our Animal Spirits, is only the occasional Cause. This Opinion is but an Extension of That attributed to a famous Interpreter of Aristotle, and which Mr Du Plessis Mornay confutes by specious Reasons, but such as our Cartesians would not embarass themselves with. Let us see something of what he advances: " As to the Opinion of A-
" lexander (Aphrodisiensis) who maintains, that there
" is an universal acting Intellect, which impresses
" the possible Intellect, i. e. every one's Capacity, and reduces it into Action, most of the
" Reasons produced above, against Averroës, will
" hold, also, against him. But, because, by this
" acting Intellect, he seems to mean God himself,
" there is this yet farther to be objected, That God,
" who is all Good and all Wise, would not imprint
" on our Understandings the Follies and Vices we
" find in it, neither would he leave it in so much
" Ignorance and Obscurity, as we feel in it, but
" conquer in all Men That Contagion, which This
" Body brings with it; and, though he should not inspire or influence so many things to the one,
" as to the other, according to the several Capacities of This rasa Tabula, This blank Paper, yet
" he never would produce in any such a World of false
" Images, as every Man may perceive within himself. Farther, This Influence must either be continual, or interrupted. If continual, we should
" understand all that our Imagination could represent to us without Trouble or Application: If interrupted, we could not, of ourselves, understand any thing whatsoever, nor will when we
" would. Now, on the contrary, we find it difficult to apprehend some things, and are forced to
" overcome the Ignorance of our Understanding,
" as it were, Step by Step; and there are others,
" which we can apprehend as soon as they offer
" themselves, and whenever we please (48)."

[F] *Which made such a formidable Progress — that it became necessary to condemn it, by the Pope's Authority.*] I have reported, in another Place (49), the Words of one of the Bulls of Pope Leo X, which was approved in the Lateran Council. I shall add here, that Raimond Lully made great Instance to Pope Clement V, to condemn Averroës's Commentaries on Aristotle; and that he endeavoured to engage Philip the Fair, King of France, to do the same. He represented These Books as full of pernicious Errors, and such as will lead young Persons, by Degrees, to Impiety: He prayed, petitioned, and wrote a Book on this Subject, but found both

the

VOL. I. 7 A

AVERROËS.

without multiplying it self, animates all the Individuals, of Human Species, so far as they exercise the Functions of the reasonable Soul. There is scarce any Book, of *Averroës*, which discovers better Sentiments, than That, which is intituled *Destructiones Destructionum contra Algazelem* [G]. Very disadvantageous Reports have been spread of This Philosopher's Religion [H]; for he is said, not only

(50) Theoph. Raynaudus, Erotem. de malis ac bonis Libris. n. 340, pag. 200, loquens Charles Bouille, in the Life of Raimondus Lullius.

the Pope, and the King of *France*, deaf to all his Sollicitations (50). At present, there is no Occasion to desire this, or to pray, that, at least, this Philosopher may be prohibited from passing for an Oracle ; for his Authority is now void, and no Body waites time in reading him ; but some Centuries have been much infatuated with his Doctrine. Read what follows. " Congruentior & exauditu facilior fuisset " petitio, pro qua nunc, (quæ Dei benignitas est,) " non est satsgendum. Nimirum ne Averroës ora- " culi loco esset in Scholis : Quod cùm superiore " sæculo, & paucis anterioribus, invaluisset, præser- " tim in Italia, ut Canus, *lib.* 10, *de locis, cap.* 5, " notavit ; occasio fuit magnorum in oris illis erro- " rum, & inutilis diligentiæ, qua aliqui non minùs " in pervolutando Averroë collocabant operæ, quàm " in sacris literis ponant, qui iis maximè delectan- " tur : Nec fidei minùs Averroi tribuerunt, quàm " optimi quique fideles Canonicis scriptoribus : Quod " indignissimum fuisse, nemo non videt. Nunc A-

(51) Id. ib.

" verroës in scholis depontanus evasit (51). —— *It* " *had been a properer Petition, and much easier to* " *have been obtained, though now, thank God, we* " *have no occasion for it, That Averroës should not* " *pass in the Schools for an Oracle : for his being* " *so esteemed in the former Age, and some few pre-* " *ceeding ones, especially in* Italy, *at* Canus *in lib.* " 10, *de Locis, cap.* 5, *has observed ; occasioned, in* " *these Parts, great Errors, and an useless Industry,* " *some having taken as much Pains in turning over* " *Averroës, as the greatest Divines ever bestowed on* " *the Holy Scriptures themselves: Nor have the Ca-* " *nonical Writers met with greater Faith from the* " *most zealous, than* Averroës *has from his Followers:* " *which all must agree to have been a high Indignity.* " *But now* Averroës *is quite exploded the Schools.*" *Ludovicus Vives* complained very much of the Authority, which This *Arabian* Professor had obtained. " Quem Philosophi de nostrâ Scholâ, qui post eum " scripsere, ita sunt amplexati, ut penè authoritate " Aristoteli adæquarint, nec solum qui longo post " intervallo vixerunt, sed qui illius quoque ætate : " Quod factum est & ignorantiâ meliorum, & ad- " miratione mercimonii linguâ & sensûs peregrini :

(52) Lud. Vives, de Causâ corrupt. Artium, lib 5. pag. 167.

" Ut gratiam ei conciliaret apud primos novitas, a- " pud posteros vetustas (52). —— *Who is so highly* " *esteemed by the Philosophers of our Schools, who* " *have wrote after him, that his Authority has been* " *almost made equal to That of* Aristotle, *not only by* " *Those, who have lived long after him, but even by* " *Those of his own Time ; which has happened* " *through Ignorance of better Writings, and out of a* " *Humour of admiring such as are foreign, both in* " *Language and Sentiments. So that be came into*

(53) Clavigny de Sainte Honorine, of the Use of suspected Books, pag. 48, 49.

" *Favour with the former Ages for his Novelty, and* " *with the latter for his Antiquity.*" He observes here a remarkable piece of good Fortune: Some lucky Genius's please at first for their Novelty, and at last for their Antiquity. Let the Reader examine, if he pleases, this reasoning of a Modern. " We need

(54) *I find nothing more of it in* Paul Jovius, Elog. Viror. bellicâ virtute illustr. lib. 4, pag. 334, *than that* Bajazet II, Peripatetici Averroes opinionibus obnectabatur, *so as much debighted with the Opinions of A-* verroes, *the Peripatetic.*

" not wonder to see, that Men have had so much " esteem for *Averroës*, since *Cardan's* Father, who " dealt in Magic, assures us, that the Devils them- " selves have admired his Doctrine, and that *Ba-* " *jazet* diverted himself with it, in his greatest " Pains of the Gout ; which is as great a Proof of " it's Merit, as it's being admired by the Intel- " ligences (53)." If what relates to *Bajazet* is " of no better Credit than the rest, I question it much (54). In respect to *Cardan*'s Father, it ought to have been said, that one of the Spirits, which appeared to him, professed himself to be an *Averroist*, and not that *Averroës* was admired by the Intelligences ; and it ought to have been added, that *Cardan* himself insinuates, that This Story of his Father was fabulous. " Ille verò palam Averroïstam se pro-

(55) Cardanus de Subtilit. lib. 9, pag. 682.

" fitebatur. Hæc seu historia seu fabula sit ita se " habuit. Quod fabula videatur satis Argumento " esse debet quod, &c. (55) —— *He openly professed* " *himself an* Averroïst. *This is a true Relation of*

" *this Story or Fable. But that it is a Fable, suffici-* " *ently appears from hence, that,* &c."

[G] *No Book of* Averroës *discovers better Sentiments, than his* Destructiones Destructionum contra Algazelem.] Or rather, *Destructorium Destructorii*. The *Arabic* Title is, *Hahapalah Altahapalah* (56). In This Piece, *Averroës* confutes the Metaphysical Opinions, which *Algazel* had maintained against the Philosophers. Most of These Opinions of *Algazel* are very pernicious ; for Example, he denied, what the Philosophers held, that the World is the Work of God, that God is an Agent, that he is a One, Simple, and Incorporeal, Being, and that there cannot be two uncreated Natures (57). Since *Averroës* takes the part of the Philosophers in all these Propositions, it cannot be denied, but that he labours in favour of Orthodoxy. In Father *Rapin's* Opinion, it is one of his best Pieces (58). But, on the other side, can This good Cause receive any great Service from such a Defender, who denies the Possibility of the Creation, and maintains, that all spiritual Beings are eternal, and that God does not know particular things, nor extend his Providence over the Individuals of this World (59) ?

(56) *See* Reineseus, Epist. 11, ad Hofm. pag. 33.

(57) *See* Gesner's Bibliotheca, fol. 100 verso.

(58) *See* Rapin's Reflexions on Philosophy, n. 30, pag. 363.

(59) *See* Possevin's Bibliotheca Selecta, lib. 12, cap. 36.

[H] *Very disadvantageous Reports have been spread of This, Philosopher's Religion.*] You will find, in *Moreri's* Dictionary, that, according to His Opinion, *Christianity* was an impossible Religion ; that *Judaism* was a Religion of Children, and that *Mahometism* was a Religion of Swines; and that he afterwards cried out, *Moriatur anima mia morte Philosophorum* ; that is, *Let my Soul die the Death of the Philosophers*. Behold, how he has imitated *Balaam*, who said, *Let me die the Death of the Righteous, and let my last End be like his* (60). Mr *Moreri* does not exactly relate his Opinion concerning Christianity ; *Averroës called it*, says he, *an impossible Religion, because of the Mystery of the Eucharist*. It is certain, that This Philosopher did not speak so obligingly of it, when he reflected on the Practice of the Communion of *Rome*. Read these Words of Mr *Daillé*, which he addressed to Father *Adam* : " The wise " Men of the World have not excused you this " strange Belief, any more than the *Jews* ; witness " the Words of the Philosopher *Averroës*, which " Cardinal *Du Perron** relates, on the Credit of *Sarga*, " one of the Fathers of your Society ; *that he found* " *no Sect worse, or weaker, than That of the Chri-* " *stians, who, themselves, eat, and break to pieces, the* " *God, whom they adore* (61)." Before I go any farther, I shall make two Remarks against This learned Minister. I. That Cardinal *Du Perron* is not, properly, the Person, who relates these Words on the Credit of one of Father *Adam's* Fraternity ; he only relates them, as cited by Mr *Du Plessis* ; for it is This latter, who alledges, on This Subject, what the Jesuit *Scarga* observes concerning the Sentiment of This *Arabian* Philosopher (62). II. That, instead of *Sarga*, he should have said *Scarga*. We shall here relate a Passage of another Minister : " If we should " receive the holy Sacrament kneeling, ------ we " should be a Scandal, and a Stumbling-block to " the Weak : But we should give the Infidels occasion to blaspheme the sacred Name of God, and " to have an Abhorrence for Christianity. For we " cannot forget the sad Example of the *Pagan* Philosopher †, who, having seen the Sacrament eaten, " which had before been adored, said, *That he had* " *never seen a more foolish, or more ridiculous Sect,* " *than That of the* Christians, *who adore That, which* " *they eat* ; and for that reason this unhappy Man " cried out, *Let my Soul be with Those of the Philo-* " *sophers, since the* Christians *adore what they eat* (63)" The same Minister alledges, elsewhere, a Passage of *Cicero*, very agreeable to This Sentiment of *Averroës* (64). " Ecquem tam amentem esse putas, qui illud " quo vescatur, Deum credat esse (65). ---- *Hast* " *who do you think is so senseless, as to believe, that* " *what he eats is God* ?" *Cicero* spoke thus, on account of giving the Name of *Ceres* to Corn, and That

(60) Numb. xxiii, 10.

* Du Perron, de l' Eucharist. lib. 3, cap. 29, p. 973.

(61) Da Ill'e's Reply to Father *Adam*, and to Cardinal *Richelieu*, Part I, chap. 16, pag. 116.

(62) *Du Plessis's* Treatise of the Sacrament, pag. 1106.

† Averroës.

(63) Drelincourt. Dial. 9, *against the Missionaries* on the Service of the Reformed Churches, p. 305, 306.

(64) Id. Dial. 6, p. 236.

(65) Cicero de Nat. Deor. lib. 3, cap. 16, pag. 619.

AVERROËS. 557

only to have despised the *Jewish*, and the *Christian*, but also the *Mahometan*, Religion, which was what he outwardly professed. Several Authors have taken the Pains

(66) Id. ib. — That of *Bacchus*, to Wine: "Cum fruges Cererem, "vinum Liberum dicimus, genere nos quidem fer- "monis utimur usitato (66). —— *When we call* "*Corn Ceres, and Wine Bacchus, we use them only* "*as customary Expressions.*" Father *Lescalopier* confesses, that This illustrious *Pagan* is very rational, when he argues in This manner, in regard to *Ceres*,
(67) Lescalopierus in Cic. de Nat. Deor. pag. 622. — and *Bacchus*; "But, *adds he* (67), it is an extra- "ordinary Wisdom, under Christianity, to eat what "we believe to be God, and we look upon Those "as guilty of a most senseless and stupid Infidelity, "who do not take the Words of *Jesus Christ*, *This* "*is my Body*, literally, and who, by way of Ridi- "cule, object to us these Words of *Cicero*. *Amen-* "*tissimæ ac solidissimæ infidelitatis damnamus hæ-* "*reticos homines, qui Christi Domini, hoc est ipsius*
(68) Id. ib. — "*veritatis, planissima disertissimaque verba*, &c. (68).— "Illud Academicum sublato cachinno procaciter usur- "pant, Academicorum, non Fidelium nepotes: *Ec-* "*quem tam amentem esse putas qui illud, quo ves-* "*catur, Deum credat esse?* At cum Apostolo Catho- "lici respondemus: *Nos stulti propter Christum*;
(69) Id. ib. — "*utinam vos sitis prudentes in Christo* (69). ------ "*They, who reproach us with This Academic Jeer,* "*are the Descendants of the Academics, and not of* "*the Faithful.* Who, think you, can be so mad, as "to take That, which he eats, to be God? *We Ca-* "*tholics answer, with the Apostle,* We are Fools "for Christ's sake, *would to God ye were wise in* "Christ." It is not our Business to examine here- into the Merits of these Reflexions; we are only considering the Sentiments of *Averroës*. I observe, that *Vossius* has only spoken in general of this Philosopher's Contempt of the *Christian Religion*; he has not considered it in particular, as arising from Transubstantiation. "Quam parum viderit tantus "Philosophus in verâ & unicâ salutis viâ, arguit il-
(70) Vossius de Philosophor. Sectis, cap. 17, pag. 91. — "lud quod diceret, malle se animam suam esse cum "Philosophis, quam cum Christianis (70). ---- *How* "*little so great a Philosopher understood of the true* "*and only Means of Salvation, is evident from his* "*saying, That he had rather his Soul were with the* "*Philosophers, than with the Christians.*" Some say, that *Averroës* was born a Christian, but that he first turned Jew, and afterwards Mahometan. *De Chri-*
(71) Anton. Sirmondus, de Immortal. Animæ, pag. 29. — *stiano Judæus, de Judæo factus est Mahumetanus* (71). Others say, that he wrote against the three great Legislators, *Moses*, Jesus Christ, and *Mahomet*; and that he supplied the Materials of the Book *de*
(72) Claud. Berigardus, In proœmio Circuli Pisani, pag. 5. — *tribus Impostoribus* ----- *of the three Impostors* (72). Others observe, *That he never believed there were any Devils* (73); and that therefore *Cardan* does violence to his Doctrine, *when he introduces an Evil Spirit, who calls himself one of his Disciples and Fol-*
(73) Naudé's Apology for great Men, pag. 320. — *lowers* (74). Nothing can be pronounced with greater Warmth, than This Sentence, or Wish, of *Erasmus*; Utinam prodisset ingens illud opus adversus Averroïn impium, καὶ τρὶς κατάρατον (75) — Wou'd to God, That great Work were once published against the
(74) Cardan. de Subtilit. lib. 19, pag. 682. — impious, and thrice accursed, *Averroës*. He wrote this to one, who had informed him, that his great Book against *Averroës* was printed. " Alterum magnum "opus sectum in libros sex & quadraginta ex Peri- "pateticâ disciplinâ confecimus adversus Averroëm,
(—) Erasmus, Epist. 20, lib. 10, pag. 532. — "quod etiam excusum est (76). —— *The other great* "*Work, containing Forty six Books, on the Doctrine* "*of the Peripatetics, we have composed against Aver-* "*roës and it is now printed.*" How comes it, then,
(76) Ambrosius Leo, Epist. ad E. ralm. *This Letter is the 28th of the 10th Book, among those of Erasmus, pag. 531.* — that *Erasmus* wishes for the Publication of it? Is it not a Sign, that in answering his Friends, he had not always their Letters before him, and so forgot some Particulars in them? Be it as it will, his Wish puts me in mind of one of *Petrarch's* Letters, where- in he exhorts a learned Divine to confute *Averroës*, That mad Dog, who barks so furiously against Jesus Christ. *Petrarch* adds, that he had made some Collections for such a Work: but, that he neither had the Leisure, nor Knowledge, which was requi- red for it. He calls the Silence of so many great Men, on this Occasion, impious; and desires that the Work, which he exhorts his Friend to compose, may be dedicated to himself, though he should happen to be in his Grave. "Extremum quæso, ut "cum primum perveneris, quò suspiras, quod citò

"fore confido, contra canem illum rabidum Aver- "roëm, qui, furore actus insando, contra Dominum "suum Christum, contraque Catholicam Fidem "latrat, collectis undique blasphemiis ejus, quod ut "scis, jam coeperamus, sed me ingens semper, & "nunc solito major occupatio, nec minor temporis, "quam scientiæ, retraxit inopia, totis ingenii viribus "ac nervis incumbens, rem à multis magnis viris "impiè neglectam, opusculum unum scribas, & mi- "hi illud inscribas, seu tunc vivus ero, seu interim
(77) Franc. Petrarcha, Epistolâ ultimâ Libri sine titulo, pag. 656. — "ablero (77). —— *My last Request is, that, as soon as* "*you are settled to your wish, which I hope you will* "*be very shortly, you will undertake, with your whole* "*Strength, what has hitherto been so impiously ne-* "*glected by so many great Men, a Work against That* "*mad Dog* Averroës, *who, transported with an im-* "*pious Rage, barks against his Lord* Christ, *and* "*against the Catholic Faith, wherein the World may* "*see a full Collection of all his Blasphemies, which,* "*you know, I had begun myself, but have been pre-* "*vented, by a continual Interruption of Business, now* "*greater than ever, and by want of Leisure, as* "*well as of Ability. Which Work I beg you will* "*dedicate to me, whether living or dead, at the* "*Time of it's Publication.*" Let us also quote Mr *du Plessis* 's *Aristotle* is said by many to have had but little Religion, and his Interpreter, *Averroës*, none
(78) Du Plessis Mornai, *of the Truth of the Christian Religion*, cap. 23, fol. 258, verso. — "at all —— (78). We all know how particularly "*Averroës* presses the Eternity of the World, and "an Universal Intellect, which can never be con- "sistent with Piety (79)."

To finish This Picture of *Averroës*'s Irreligion, we must not forget the Touches, which may be given it, from his Hypothesis concerning the Soul of Man. It is certain, he did not admit of any Rewards, or
(79) Id. Ib. fol. 259. — Punishments, after this Life; for, to speak properly, he taught the Mortality of the Human Soul. I am sensible, he acknowledged, that the Understanding was of an eternal Nature, and never died: But then, in this Respect, he did not consider it as a Substance appropriated to every Man; and, consequently, tho' he confessed, that the first Cause of the Intellectual Operations of *Peter* and *Paul* subsisted after their Death, yet, nevertheless, he believed, that all that had particularly belonged to *Peter* and *Paul*, as well to the Body, as the Soul, ceased to live, when they died. So that he denied Heaven and Hell. *Vossius*, who very well understood This Doctrine, ought not to have charged it absolutely on *Mirandulanus*, since That Au- thor does not adopt it as true in itself, but only as
(80) See, above, Remark [E, Cit. Of (13)], *where I have quoted from the* Jesuits *of Coïmbra*. — a lawful Intepretation of *Aristotle*'s Words (80). Durst any one have declared, in Print, for an im- pious Opinion, which must expose him to the Fires of the Inquisition? The Passage of *Vossius*, which I am go- ing to quote, will serve to shew, that the most learned Writers do not always distinguish as they ought to do. Sometimes they impute to a Philosopher, not what he absolutely believes, but what he says must be believed, in consequence of the Opinions of *Ari- stotle*, or of some other Founder of a Sect. "Bisa- "riam jubet considerare hominis intellectum (*Aver- "roës*), ut est intellectus, & ut est forma, quam "obtinet, dum nobis unitur. Priori modo sit eum "à morte nostrâ superesse, quippe æternum: nec "dare homini essentiam, sed uniri illi per operatio- "nem suam phantasmatum interventu. Hanc sen- "tentiam etiam sequitur Antonius Mirandulanus "evers. singul. certam. lib. xxxii. sect. 1. & lib. "seq. sect. ii. & vi. Similiterque Cardanus; quem "propterea reprehendit, ac refellit Cæsar Scaliger
(81) *It should be* cccxvii. — "Exercit. cccvi (81), sect. 30. Et sanè ea sen- "tentia Scripturis è diametro aversatur; ut quæ "suam cuique animam, sua etiam à morte præmia,
(82) — "& poenas adscribat (82). —— He (*Averroës*) *con- "siders the Intellect of Man in two Lights, as it is*
(82) Vossius de Origine & Progressu Idololatriæ, lib. 3, cap. 42, p. 952. — "*the Intellect itself, and as it is the Form, which* "*is produced by it's Union with us. In the first* "*respect*, he says, *it survives us, being eternal; nor* "*does it make the Essence of a Man, but it only uni-* "*ted to him in it's Operation, by the Intervention of* "*Ideas. This Opinion is also followed by* Antonius "Mirandulanus, evers. singul. certam. lib. 32. sect. 1. "& lib. 33. sect. 2. & 6. *And also by* Cardan, *who* "*is animadverted on, and confuted by* Cæsar Scaliger "Exerc.

AVERROËS.

Pains to translate his Works into *Latin* [*I*]. I was in hopes, that, before This Article went to the Press, I should have had the Pleasure of consulting the Volume, where Don *Nicholas Antonio* has spoken so very amply of *Averroës*; but find myself disappointed of it, and confined to the Abstracts only of the Journalist of *Paris*. You are going to see what I take from thence. "*Averroës*, of *Corduba*, was in-
"structed, by his Father, in the Knowledge of the Law, and in the Religion of his
"Country. He was excessive fat, tho' he allowed himself but one Meal a day; He passed
"all his nights in the study of Philosophy; and, when he found himself tired, diverted
"himself with reading some Book of Poetry, or History; He was never seen to
"play, or seek any other Amusement. The Errors he was accused of gave occa-
"sion for a Sentence, which deprived him of his Estate, and obliged him to recant.
"After his Condemnation, he took a Voyage to *Fez*, and returned afterwards to
"*Corduba*, where he continued, till, at the earnest request of the People, he was
"recalled to *Morocco*, where he passed the remainder of his Life, and died in
"1206 (*d*)." The Journalists of *Leipsic* intimate, That Don *Nicolas Antonio*, in this part of his Work, made great use of a Book of *John Leo*, published by *Hottinger* (*e*). So that, as to This I can go to the Fountain Head as well as He. I find, therefore, in this Work, that the People of *Corduba* raised *Averroës* to two high Offices, which his Father and Grandfather had enjoyed [*K*]: They were Those of Chief Justice, and

(*d*) Journal of the Learned of the 2d of July, 1697. pag. 475. Edit. of Holland.

(*e*) Acta Eruditi. Lipsi. 1697. pag. 305.

"*Exerc.* 306. *sect.* 30. *And indeed this Opinion is*
"*directly opposite to the Scriptures, which assign to*
"*every one his own respective Soul, and his own*
"*respective Rewards and Punishments after Death.*"
[*I*] *Several Authors have taken the Pains to translate his Works into Latin.*] Here is a Passage of *Huetius*, which will inform us of the Names of some of These Translators, and at the same time of a Mistake of *Scaliger*. "Vix ullos Averroïs Arabi-
"cos codices in Europa reperiri posse putabat Sca-
"liger, solamque conversionem ab Armegando Bla-
"sio, Jacobo Mantino, Johanne Francisco Burana,
"Abrahamo de Balmis, Vitale Nisso, Calo Calony-
"mo, Johanne Bruyerino Campegio, Paulo Israë-
"lita, aliisque adornatam in lucem venisse. Ego
"tamen his viris manibus Arabicum Averrois li-
"brum, ex oriente huc olim à Postello devectum;
"quod miror Scaligerum fugisse, Postello olim a-
"micitiâ, & literariâ consuetudine conjunctum. Eo
"libro continentur in Logicam, Rhetoricam, & Poë-
"ticam commentaria; quæ ad Jacobi Mantini, &
"Abrahami de Balmis interpretationem à me expen-
"sa, fidem eorum & artem apertè mihi compro-
"barunt (83). ----- Scaliger *believed, that there was*
"*scarce such a Thing as an Arabic Copy of Averroës,*
"*to be met with in all Europe, and that we had*
"*nothing more than the Translations of him, by*
"Armegandus Blasius, Jacobus Mantinus, Johannes
"Franciscus Burana, Abrahamus de Balmis, Vitalis
"Niffus, Calus Calonymus, Johannes Bruyerinus
"Campegius, Paulus Israëlita, *and others. But I*
"*myself have seen an Arabic Averroës, in a Style,*
"*formerly brought hither, out of the East, by Po-*
"*stellus; and which one would wonder that Scaliger*
"*should never hear of, who was his intimate Friend*
"*and Correspondent in Learning. In this Book are*
"*contained the Commentaries on Logic, Rhetoric, and*
"*Poetry; which, upon my Examination of it, along*
"*with the Translations of* Jacobus Mantinus, *and*
"Abrahamus de Balmis, *has convinced me both of*
"*their Fidelity and Ability.*"
Note, that certain Rabbins have translated some of *Averroës*'s Works into *Hebrew* (84). It is proper to observe here, what we meet with in *Possevin*. That Jesuit affirms, That They, who were so fond of This *Arabian* Philosopher, could only read him in pitiful Translations, before the Edition, which *John Baptista Bagolin* got printed at *Venice*, by the *Junta*'s in the Year 1552 (85). *That* Edition, continues he, *cannot be worth much; for, as to one part of Ave-rroës Works,* Bagolin *made use of a Translation of a Jew, named* Jacobus Mantinus: *and, as for the other part, the preceeding Translations were made use of, and even Those, which* Niphus *and* Zimara *had never corrected in their Labours on* Averroës. The Translator *Mantinus* followed the Steps of *Abraham de Balmis*, who had succeeded very indifferently. So that we cannot promise ourselves, that a Translator who had such bad Guides, has rightly expressed the Original: And, as *Bagolin* did not understand any thing of *Arabic*, he could be no judge of Those Translations (86). I am going to copy a long Pas-

sage of *Kerkerman*, where he wishes, that God would raise up a Translator, who might deliver the Works of *Averroës* from the gross and obscure Barbarity of former Interpretations. Then would appear the great Services, which This *Arabian* has done to Philosophy. "Quid & quantum Universæ Phi-
"losophiæ *Averroës* iste profuerit, tum clarum per-
"spectumque haberemus, si quem nobis Deus virum
"excitaret, qui *Latinam* ejus versionem ab ista, qua
"scatet undique, molesta barbarie liberaret, & stylo
"*Latino* saltem mediocri & intelligibili in gratiam
"Philosophiæ studiosorum verteret. Ad quam rem
"illa, quæ nuper *Avicennam Arabicum* nitidissimis
"typis dedit clarissima Typographia *Medicea* pluri-
"mum adjumenti adferret, si lingua *Arabica Aver-
"roëm* ederet, atque ita occasionem viris ejus linguæ
"peritis faciliorem præberet barbaræ versionis emen-
"dandæ, & ad intelligentiam traducendæ: alias cer-
"tum est, *Averroëm* à multis neglectum iri, à qui-
"bus legeretur diligenter, nisi tam multis locis non
"intelligeretur. In Posterioribus Anal. apparet sin-
"gularem operam præstitisse & immortalitate dig-
"nissimam; Et Epitome Logicæ, quam scripsit, lau-
"datissima est ob varias causas, ut & Logica ejus
"quæsita. Nemo tam interpretum veterum videri
"potest proximus *Aristotelis* menti atque hic *Arabs*
"(87). ------ *How much all Philosophy is indebted to* Averroës, *can then only be known, when God shall raise up a Genius, who will free our* Latin *Translations of him from the unintelligible Barbarisms every where to be met with, and render him in That Language, in a Style, at least tolerable, and intelligible, for the Use of Students in Philosophy. To this purpose, the late beautiful* Medicean *Edition would greatly contribute, if* Averroës *were also printed in* Arabic, *which would give an easy Opportunity to the Learned, in That Language, to correct That barbarous Translation, and make it intelligible: otherwise it is certain,* Averroës *will be neglected by many, who would read him very diligently, if he was not unintelligible in so many Places. In the latter Part of the* Anal. *it appears, he has performed an excellent Work, and such as deserves to be immortal: His Epitome of Logic is much admired, and his Logic greatly sought after. None of the ancient Interpreters seem to hit the Sense of* Aristotle *so happily as this* Arabian." I doubt there are not many Persons at this time of Day, who would make such a Wish, or ground such fair Hopes on a compleat Translation of *Averroës*'s Works, or give him such great Commendations.

[*K*] *The People of* Corduba *raised* Averroës *to two high Offices, which his Father and Grandfather had enjoyed.*] His Grandfather was one of the most famous Lawyers of his Time; he passed for a second *Malich*, who was One of the four greatest Casuists of the *Mahometan* Religion; *unus ex quatuor primariis Juris Muhammedorum Canonici Interpretibus* (88); and was moreover a learned Divine. It was He, whom the People of *Corduba*, shaking off the Yoke of their Prince, and desiring to have the King of *Morocco*

(83) Huetius, de Claris Interpretibus, p. 185.

(84) See the Bibliotheca Rabinica of Father Bartolocci, Tom. 1, pag. 13, & seq.

(85) Possevinus, Bibliooth. Select. lib. 12, cap. 16, pag. 43, Tom. 2.

(86) Id. Ib.

(87) Kckermannus in Præcognitis Logicis, Tract. 2, cap. 2, & 32, pag. 103.

(88) Hotting. Biblioth. Theol. lib. 2, cap. 3. pag. 272.

AVERROES. 559

and of Chief Priest. He was very capable of discharging them, by his great Knowledge in the Law, and in Theology. After the Study of These two Sciences, he applied himself to Natural Philosophy, Physic, Astrology, and Mathematics. Whilst he held the Offices before mentioned, the King of *Morocco* sent Deputies to him, to offer him That of Judge of *Morocco*, and of all *Mauritania*, and on condition that he should continue all the Posts he was possessed of in *Spain*. This Proposition pleasing him, he went to *Morocco*; but, having settled Judges there as his Substitutes, he returned to *Corduba*. Wonders are related of his Patience, Liberality, and Mildness [*L*]. He referred all Criminal Causes to his Lieutenant, and never gave his Opinion in them. So many good Qualities did not hinder him from having many Enemies, who thwarted him extremely, and accused him of Heresy; which brought upon him many troublesome and grievous Consequences [*M*]: however, he was honourably delivered

Morocco their Master, deputed to That Monarch to negotiate That great Affair. He obtained, of him, all the Favours he asked, in behalf of Those Mutineers, and returned to them, loaden with Presents, and Compliments, having been created Chief Priest, and Chief Judge of the Kingdom of *Corduba*. He died, after having enjoyed These Dignities a very long time, and left a Son, who was a Lawyer, and was preferred to the same Posts, by the Votes of the Inhabitants of *Corduba*. This Election being confirmed by the King of *Morocco*, our Lawyer found himself invested with a high Character. We find, that the Authority of his Offices extended over all *Andalusia*, and the Kingdom of *Valencia*. His Life was long, and pleasant. After his Death, his Offices were conferred on his Son *Averroès*, by the Votes of the People (89). It is remarkable, that, at the Request of several great Persons, who implored his Clemency in favour of *Ibnu Saïgb*, a famous Physician, who was detained in Prison for the Crime of Heresy, he set him at Liberty; during which Proceeding, *Ibnu Giulgiul* said, *The Father of* Averroès *does not know, that he has a Son, who will be a greater Heretic than This* (90). And he was not deceived in it.

[*L*] *Wonders are related of his Patience, Liberality, and Mildness.*] There were several Persons, among the Nobility and Learned Men at *Corduba*, who hated, and opposed, him. As he was one Day reading a Lecture, in the Auditory of the Civil Law, a Servant of one of his Enemies came and whispered something in his Ear, which made him change Colour: but he answered only *Yes, Yes*. The next Day the same Servant returned to the Auditory, asked his Pardon, and confessed, before all the Students, that he had abused *Averroès* grosly by whispering in his Ear: He answered, *God bless you, for declaring, that I am provided with Patience*. He gave him afterwards a certain Sum of Money, with this Advice, *Do not That to others, which you have done to me*. Though he was rich, both by his Marriage, and by his Offices, yet he was always in debt, because he was very liberal to learned Men, who were necessitous, whether they loved, or hated, him. One Day, as his Friends reproved him for distributing his Wealth amongst his Enemies, he said to them, " Unhappy Men, as you are, you do not know, that to do " good to one's Relations, and Friends, is not an " Act of Liberality; a Man is inclined to That by " the Dictates of Nature: to be liberal, is to communicate our Substance to our Enemies; and, since " my Riches have not been acquired, either by my " Ancestors, or myself, by Merchandise, or Art, or " Arms, but by the Profession of Virtue, is it not reasonable, that I should dispose of them in Acts of Virtue? I find, that I have not misplaced them, for they " have converted my Enemies into Friends (91)." Add to this, what I have said concerning his Sobriety, his Vigilancy, his Application to Study, &c (92). He would not consent, that his youngest Son should be advanced to the Honours, which were offered him at the Court of *Morocco*: and he was so far from rejoicing at the Respect, which was shewed to That young Man, the Design of which was to please the Father, that he was troubled at it in good earnest (93). What piry is it, that so many Virtues, and so many good Qualities, were not accompanied with Orthodoxy, but on the contrary attended with the most enormous Errors! The Writings of his Adversaries pretend not to defame him for any Thing, but his Heresy, and the Panegyrics of his Admirers are founded only on his Virtue and Learning, &c. " Hic à mul-

" tis laudatus, à nonnullis vero aliis vituperio affectus est
" - - - Adversarius ejus scripsit epistolam, quâ vituperabatur Averroës, eum de hæresi infamando, & alius
" scripsit aliam laudando èum de nobilitate, justitia
" & doctrina: quæ quidem epistolæ sunt longissi-
" mæ (94). ——— *He was commended by many, and condemned by others.* ——— *One of his Enemies wrote a severe Letter against* Averroès, *defaming him on account of Heresy; and another Person wrote one in Commendation of him for his Honour, Justice, and Learning: These Letters are very long.*"

[*M*] *His Enemies accused him of Heresy; which brought upon him many - - - - grievous Consequences*] Several of the Nobles and Doctors of *Corduba*, and particularly the Physician *Ibnu Zoar*, envied him, and resolved to prosecute him for Heresy. They procured some young Persons to desire of him a Lecture in Philosophy; he agreed to it, and, *in That Lecture, discovered to them his Philosophical Belief. Inter legendum autem suam Philosphæm fidem detexerunt* (95). They caused an Information of it to be drawn up by a Notary, and accused him for an Heretic; which Information, being signed by an hundred Witnesses, was sent to *Mansor*, King of *Morrocco*. That Prince, upon sight of it, became incensed against *Averroès*, and said aloud; *It is evident This Man is not of our Religion: Hunc nostræ legis non esse patet*. He caused all his Effects to be confiscated, and condemned him to keep within the *Jews* Quarters. *Averroès* obeyed: but, going sometimes to the Mosque to say his Prayers, and being one Day chased from thence by the Children with Stones, he retired from *Corduba* to *Fez*, where he kept himself concealed. But, in a few Days, he was discovered, and imprisoned; and they sent to *Mansor*, to know what should be done with him. That Prince assembled several Doctors of Divinity, and Civil Law, and enquired of them what Punishment such a Man deserved? Most of them answered, That, as an Heretic, he deserved Death; but some represented, that it was not proper to execute This Punishment on a Person, who was chiefly known from his Character of a Civilian, and a Divine; Because, said they, *the World will not understand it to be the Condemnation of an Heretic, but of a Civilian and a Divine: And the Consequence will be*, I. *That the Infidels will not embrace our Faith, to the Discouragement of our Religion*. II. *Complaints will be made, that the African Doctors seek opportunity to take away one another's Lives. It would be better to make him retract before the Gate of the great Mosque, where he shall be asked, if he repents: Our Advice is, that, if he repents, your Majesty should pardon him; for there is no Man on Earth that is without a Fault. Mansor* was pleased with this Counsel, and gave Orders to the Governor of *Fez* to put it in Execution. Accordingly, our Philosopher was conducted, on a *Friday*, to the Gate of the Mosque, at the Hour of Prayer, and placed bareheaded on the highest Step, where all Those, who entred into the Mosque, spit in his Face. Prayer being ended, the Doctors, with the Notaries, and the Judge, with his Assistants, came, and asked this miserable Wretch, if he repented of his Heresy: he answered in the Affirmative; whereupon he was sent back, and continued at *Fez*, where he read Lectures in the Civil Law. *Mansor*, having permitted him, some time after, to return to *Corduba*, he accordingly went thither, where he lived miserably, being deprived of his Estate and Books. In the mean time, the Judge, who had succeeded him, acquitted himself so ill in his Office, and Justice, in general, was so badly administred in That Country,

that

AVERROËS.

(f) Taken from a Book, De Viris quibusdam illustribus apud Arabes, translated by John. Leo Africanus, and published by Hottinger, in chap. 3. of the 2d Book of his Biblioth. Theol.

delivered from them before he died. His Answer to a young Gentleman, who desired him to bestow his Daughter on him, is curious enough [N]. A very remarkable Story is told concerning the effect of an Imprecation he pronounced against his youngest Son [O]. He composed a great many *Amorous Poems*; which, when he grew old, he threw into the Fire *(f)* [P]. I cannot tell from whence *Du Verdier Vau-Privas* borrowed these Words: *Averroës was broke by a Wheel placed on his Breast.*

You

that the People groaned under it. *Mansor*, being willing to redress This Grievance, assembled his Council, where he proposed to re-establish *Averroës*; and, most of the Council being of the same Opinion, he sent him an Order to come immediately to *Morocco*, to take upon him again his Station of chief Magistrate. *Averroës* departed forthwith, with all his Family, and passed the rest of his Days at *Morocco* (96), where he was buried without the *Curriers Gate* (97), and where his Tomb and Epitaph were to be seen a very long Time after (98).

(96) Ibid. pag. 276, & seq.

(97) Ibid. pag. 279.

We ought not to forget his Answer to Those, who asked him about the State of his Soul during This Persecution. *That State,* said he, *both pleased, and displeased me: I was pleased with being discharged from the troublesome Functions of Judicature, but I was displeased at being oppressed by false Witnesses.* He added, *I have never wished to be restored to my Office, nor have I accepted it again without my Innocence being first cleared* (99).

(98) Ibid.

(99) Ibid. pag. 278.

[N] *His Answer to a young Gentleman, who desired him to bestow his Daughter on him, is curious enough.*] " Give me her, says this Gallant, *and I will give* " *you her weight in Gold.* O domine *Judex,* da mihi " in uxorem filiam tuam, & quanti eam ponderave- " ris itidem aurum tibi tradam (100). Can you tell, " answered *Averroës,* whether my Daughter be hand- " some, or homely? do you know whether you " shall like her? The other replied, *I have seen her* " *Copy,* I mean her Brother (101). *I am afraid,* " said *Averroës, your too great Heat is hurrying you* " *into a blind Bargain* (102). The young Man went away ashamed, and never had the Courage to make a second Attack. That Daughter was afterwards married by her Father to a Relation of the King of *Morocco* (103). When I said, that *Averroës's* Answer was curious, I had an Eye to two things; in the first place to the Circumstances, and in the next to the Obscurity of the Translator. I suspect the Passage to be wrong rendred. He was not well acquainted with the *Latin* Tongue: for, in all probability, there was some better Turn in the *Arabic* words, than what he has given us in the Translation; and therefore the Learned, who are curious, will like to have the Examination of this little Fact proposed to them. It is something very extraordinary to meet with a Gallant, who will barter his Gold, weight for weight, against a Maid he never saw. The Price must rise very high, even in *Spain,* where People are much leaner, than in many other Countries. *Averroës* would have done well to have asked the Gallant this Question; *Do you know whether my Daughter be small, or lusty?* This had been a very material Consideration; because, in the second Case, the Price must be higher, and yet the Value lower. According to our Customs, nothing would be more wonderful, than a Gallant, who had never seen the Daughter of the chief Magistrate of the place, where he lived: but, amongst the *Mahometans,* nothing is more common: they do not permit their Daughters to shew themselves at the Windows and Doors of their Houses, nor to run about from one House to another, and receive Visits every Day. And yet it is certainly remarkable, that this noble *Corduban* (104) should know no better, than by Conjecture, whether *Averroës's* Daughter was handsome. These are some of the Circumstances, to which I had an Eye.

(100) Ibid. pag. 275.

(101) Comperationem ejus vidi, fratrem scil. ejus. Ibid.

(102) Timeo te cam non cognovisse ob impetum tuum. Ibid. pag. 276.

(103) Ibid.

(104) Juvenis quidam ex nobilibus civitatis. Ib. d. p. g. 2 c.

[O] *A very remarkable Story is told, concerning the Effect of an Imprecation he pronounced against his youngest Son.*] The following Quotation, which composes this Remark, loses most of it's Beauties in a Translation. It is observable from it, that *Averroës* wished rather to see the Death of his Son, than his disobedience, and that, thereupon, he uttered an Imprecation, which That young Man outlived but ten Months. This long *Latin* Passage is not taken from *Hottinger;* for I find it more correct in another Author. " De Verrois carminum efficacia, hanc " historiam historicus Arabs refert : Quadam die eo " existente cum amicis quibusdam, colloquentibusque, " ingressus est filius ejus cum aliquibus sociis juveni- " bus, quos cum animadvertisset Averroës, protulit " duo carmina, hujus sensus : Rapuerunt pulchritu- " dines tuæ capreolo pulchritudinem suam, donec " miratus est omnis pulcher in te : Tibi est pectus " ejus, & oculi ejus, & stupor ejus ; Verum cras " cornua sua patri tuo eruet. Post quæ dixit, Sit " maledicta peregrinatio : quando eram juvenis, ali- " quando patrem meum puniebam : Nunc autem Se- " nex filium meum punire non possum. At deum " deprecor, ut priusquam videam aliquid contra vo- " luntatem meam, eum mori faciat. Sicque prius- " quam transirent menses decem filius ejus mortuus " est, & major solus remansit, qui judex opinionis & " sectæ effectus est (105). ——— *Of the Power of* " *Averroës's Poetry, an Arabic Historian relates this* " *Story. One Day, as he was conversing with cer-* " *tain Friends, his Son came in with some of his wild* " *Companions, which Averroës taking notice of, spoke* " *two Verses to This Effect. Thy own Beauties could* " *not content Thee, thou hast stript the wild Goat* " *of his Beauties, and They, who are as beautiful as* " *thyself, admire thee. Thou hast got his wanton* " *Heart, his letcherous Eyes, and his senseless Head,* " *but to morrow thou shalt find thy Father will have* " *his pushing Horns. After which he said, cursed be* " *all Extravagancies : When I was young, I sometimes* " *punished my Father : Now I am old, I cannot punish* " *my Son. But I beg of God to deprive him rather of* " *Life, than suffer him to be disobedient. Accordingly,* " *within ten Months, his Son died, and the eldest* " *only remained, who became a Defender of his Opi-* " *nion and Sect.*" *Bartholin,* who furnishes me with this Passage, unreasonably imputes the great Effect, we are speaking of, to the Philosopher's Verses, which ought only to be imputed to the Imprecation pronounced by *Averroës* in Prose. Compilers have collected many Examples of the Effects of such Imprecations (106).

(105) Tho. Bartholinus, de Medicis Poeticis, pag. 105, 106.

(106) See Camerarius, in his Historical Meditations, Tom. 3. Book 5, chap. 6. and Tom. 3. Book 2, chap. 15.

[P] *When he grew old, he threw his amorous Verses into the Fire.*] His Speech, which accompanied This Act, is full of wise Reflexions. *A Man,* says he, *will always be judged by his Words ; and, if I have spoken ill, I will not discover my Folly : If my Verses pleased any One, He would take me for a wise Man, and I do not acknowledge that I am so.* You see here a good Character. *Averroës,* having committed a Fault, was willing to repair it; and equally declined both the Approbation, which he thought he did not deserve, and the Censure he feared he might deserve. His Love Verses would have met with a numerous Set of Admirers, who would have blessed his Memory, and even adored it. *Ovid* and *Catullus* are Examples of this. But he desired none of their Praises. Others would have thought it very indecent, that such a great Person, such an excellent Lawyer and Philosopher, should have wrote Love Verses. But he has prevented their Censure, by taking Care, that no One should read what he had composed on such a Subject. All his other Poetical Works are lost, except a very small Piece, wherein he declares, that, *when he was young, he was disobedient to his Reason ; but, when he was old, he followed it* : Upon which he forms this Wish : *Would to God I had been born old, and that from my Youth I had been in the State of Perfection.* This seems to me to be the true Sense of these Words of *John Leo* (107). *De suis quidem Carminibus tantum duo reperiuntur ad verbum significantibus :* " Inobe- " diens enim fui voluntati meæ juvenis, ac, quando " tempus cum calvitie senectutempe agitavit me, tum " parui voluntati meæ. Utinam natus fuissem senex, " & in juventute absolutus (108)." What Wish could be more becoming a Philosopher?

(107) Hottinger. Bibl. Theolog. pag. 278.

(108) In Juventute absolutus. Perhaps the Translator put in Italic stead of ab, and so it might be transposed Exempt from Youth.

Let us now relate what *Averroës* did, in regard to the amorous Verses of another Writer. There

was

AVERROËS. 561

You will find them in a Chapter, which he entitles, *Of several Learned Men, Ancient and Modern, who have died miserably* (g). I was surprized to find so very little Notice taken of this famous Philosopher, in the Oriental Library of Mr d'Herbelot [Q]. There was reason to believe, that a Man, of such a vast Knowledge in Arabic Learning, would have produced a thousand fine Things concerning the Doctrines and Fortune of *Averroës*; but, instead of this, we meet with a Brevity, which is amazing, and so far from instructing us in what we want to know, that it rather confounds what we knew before.

(g) *Is the 26th of the 2d Book of his Diverses Leçons.*

was, at *Corduba*, a Philosopher, Physician, and Astrologer, whose Name was *Abraham Ibnu Sahal*, who, by the Caprice of his ill Fortune, fell in Love, and fell to writing Verses, without considering the Doctoral Dignity. *Postea ob disgratiam suæ fortunæ amore captus, & dignitate doctorum postposita cœpit edere carmina* (109). The *Jews*, his Brethren in Religion, advised him not to publish Those wanton Verses. He returned them a prophane Answer in Poetry. Whereupon they applied to the Authority of the Magistrate; and, as *Averroës* was the chief Judge of the Country, they addressed themselves to him. They represented to him, that This *Abraham* had corrupted the whole City with his Poetry, particularly the Youth of both Sexes, and that nothing else was sung at Nuptial Entertainments. *Averroës* was angry with Our Poet, and forbad him to proceed in such Compositions, under such Penalties as the Case should require, or the Judge think proper. Being told, that This Prohibition did not put a stop to the *Jew's* Vein of Poetry, and desiring to know the Truth of it, he sent a Person, he could trust, to the Poet's House, who returned with this Report: *I found no Body at his House, but your eldest Son, writing out some of his Poems.* He added, *There is not in all Corduba a Man, Woman, or Child, who has not learned some of the Verses of Abraham Ibnu Sahal.* Upon this, *Averroës* proceeded no farther: *Can one single Hand*, said he, *stop a thousand Mouths?* Observing one Day at a Bookseller's, that the *Alcoran* was sold but for a Ducat, and that the Poems of This *Jew* went off at one word for ten Pistols (110), he cried out, *This City will soon be destroyed, for I have seen the People's Contempt for holy things, and their fondness for such as are dishonest and forbidden.* " *Tunc dixit Averrois, omnibus adstantibus*, Scitote, " hanc Civitatem mox ruituram, quoniam vidi po- " pulum, quæ ad fidem pertinent, vilusse: atque " prohibita, atque inhonesta grata extitisse, majorisque fecisse. Et sicut dixerat successit: Non adhuc " elapsis quinquaginta annis Christicolæ oppugnarunt " Cordubam, & multas alias civitates (111)." — *And* " *as he said, so it happened;* for, in less than fifty " *Years, the Christians took This, and several other* " *Cities.*" From hence it may be gathered, that some Vices prevail in all Countries, Religions, and Ages. The *Mahometans* of *Spain* acted the same part, in the XIIth Century, which a great many *Christians* of *Paris* have done in the XVIIth. If they are to buy Mr *Godeau's Psalms*, they will cheapen a long time, and never bargain, unless at a very low Price; but, for the *Satirical Parnassus*, they will never make one Word, but give whatever Price the Seller shall ask. Let us also observe, that we find Examples of good Actions in each Country, Age, and Religion. If *Christians*, in these latter Ages, have burnt their prophane Poems, their Love and wanton Verses (112), *Averroës* did the like, under the Profession of *Mahometism;* I say, under the Profession; for it is suspected, that inwardly he was of no Religion at all (113). His Prediction of the Miseries of *Corduba* does not prove the contrary; for it is natural enough to believe, that so great a Degree of Degeneracy, and Corruption of Taste, as to occasion a Contempt of what is esteemed Holy, and a Fondness of what is thought dishonest, must necessarily throw a City into very great Disorders.

[*Q*] *I was surprized to find so very little Notice taken of This famous Philosopher, in the Oriental Library of Mr d'Herbelot.*] First, It is surprizing, that, in this Work, the Author has not placed Our Arabian Philosopher under the Name, which has been given him by all western Nations, I mean That of *Averroës*. I grant, that This is not the true Name, but One very much corrupted by Confusion of Dialects: But have we not sufficient Reason to continue This Name in our Dictionaries, since he was

scarce ever called by any other in This western Part of the World. If it be thought more proper to give This Philosopher's Article under the *Arabic* Name, in it's true Orthography, Notice, at least, should be given of it, under the Word *Averroës*; and, consequently, *d'Herbelot*, by not doing so, is guilty of a very material Omission. In the Body of his Work, we find neither *Averroës*, nor *Aben Roës*, nor *Aben-Roïs*. We are obliged, therefore, to have recourse to the Index, which is not very agreeable. But what is to be found there? *Averroës* (114), with a Reference to Pages 303, 719, 815? At Page 303, we find only, that *Averroës* was one of those Philosophers, who believed, that the World was Eternal. At Page 815, we find only, that *Mohammed Al-Gazeli* believed, that *Averroës's* Principles were *very contrary to Those of the Mussulman's*. But, at Page 719, we find the Article of our Philosopher, under the Word ROSCHD. That Article does not contain twenty Lines; the latter half of which is this: " *Averroës* was the first, who translated *Aristotle* out " of *Greek* into *Arabic*, before the *Jews* made their " Translation; and, for a long time, we had no " other Text of *Aristotle*, than That of This great " Philosopher's *Arabic* Translation, who, afterwards, " added to it very ample Commentaries, which St " *Thomas*, and the other Schoolmen, made use of, " before the *Greek* Originals of *Aristotle*, and of his " Commentators, were known to us (115)." I find here many things, to which I can give no Credit; for I observe it to be the Opinion of learned Men, that *Averroës* was far from being Master of the *Greek* Tongue (116). I know, farther, that the Caliphs *Almanzor, Abdalla*, and *Almemon*, who preceeded *Averroës* some Centuries, caused a great many *Greek* Books to be translated into *Arabic* (117). This, therefore, makes it improbable, that *Averroës* was the first Translator of *Aristotle* into *Arabic*, even though we should suppose him sufficiently skilled in *Greek*. *Alpharabius*, who flourished in the Xth Century, found *Aristotle's Physics* in *Mesopotamia* (118). He is also generally esteemed the Translator of *Aristotle's Analytics*, according to Mr d'*Herbelot* (119). *Rigord* says, That a Council, held at *Paris*, in the Year 1209, condemned some of *Aristotle's* Books to be burnt, which were explained in the Colleges, and had been lately brought from *Constantinople*, and translated out of *Greek* into *Latin*. " Delati de novo " à Constantinopoli & à Græco in Latinum transla- " ti (120)." This does not agree with Mr *d'Herbelot*, because it proves, that, about the Time, that *Averroës* died, they made use, at *Paris*, of a Translation of *Aristotle* from the *Greek*. It is certain, that, before the middle of the XIIth Century, *Aristotle's* Philosophy was taught in the University of *Paris*. See the Complaints of St *Bernard*, related by Mr *de Launoi* (121). This same Passage of *Rigord* shews, that the *Greek* Books of *Aristotle* were in *France*, in the time of *Averroës*. Lastly, if with somebody would name me any Translators of *Aristotle*, and *Averroës's* *Arabic* Commentary, who lived between *Averroës* and *Thomas Aquinas*. All the *Latin* Translators of This *Arabic* Philosopher, that are come to my Knowledge, are later than That Angelical Doctor. I would not be understood to reject what I have read in some Authors, that the Emperor *Frederic* II, who flourished before the Time of St *Thomas*, and after *Averroës*, caused the Books of This *Arabian* to be translated into *Latin*. This may be inferred from these Words of *Cuspinian:* " Libros multos ex Græco & ex Ara- " bico Latinos fieri curavit, inter quos & Aristotelis " voluminis fuerunt & multa Medicorum (122). — " *He procured many Books to be translated out of* " *Greek and Arabic, into Latin, among which were* " *Aristotle's Works, and many others, in Physic;*" and from This Passage of *Wolphgang Hungerus*, in his Notes on *Cuspinian* (123). " Curavit quoque ea " fieri translationes operum Aristotelis, & scriptorum " Medicinæ

(109) Hotting. Biblioth. Theol. pag. 288.

(110) Prædictus emptor nihil respondens, sed manus crumenæ imponens decem aureos numeravit & prosolvit, & librum accepit, & in pace recessit. . . . *The Buyer said nothing, but put his Hand in his Pocket, and told out ten Pistoles, and took the Book, and went away contented.* Ib. p. 290.

(111) Ibid.

(112) Pic. Mirandulanus did it; *see the End of the Remark* [D], *of the Article* ADONIS. *Petrarch had a Mind to do so; See Mr Baillet's Judgment on the Poets,* Tom. 5. pag. 24. *He reported, that he had wrote both P* oems. *See his first and Letter of the eighth Book of his Familiar Letters, pag. 278.*

(113) *See the Remarks* [H] *and* [M].

(114) *It is an Error of the Press.*

(115) *D'Herbelot's Biblioth. Orient. pag. 719, col. 1.*

(116) *See above, pag. 383, Citations* (5) *and* (9).

(117) *See Father Rapin's Comparison of Plato and Aristotle, p. 403, 404. See also Mr d'Herbelot's Biblioth. Orient. p. 546.*

(118) *Rapin's Comparison of Plato and Aristotle, p. 404.*

(119) *Herbelot's Biblioth. Orient. pag. 337.*

(120) *Rigordus in vita Philippi Augusti apud Launoium de varia Aristot. Fortunâ, pag. 6.*

(121) *Launoius, ib. d. cap. 3. pag. 24, & seq.*

(122) *Cusp. in Fred. II. init. p. 419.*

(123) *Hungerus Annotat. in Cuspin. pag. 150.*

"Medicinæ ex lingua Græca & Arabica, qui in "hunc ufque diem in fcholis lectæ funt, atque eti- "amnum leguntur; & Bononiam eafdem mifit, "ut Academiæ offerrentur, quod ejus ex Epiftolis "apparet. —— *He caufed Thofe Tranflations to be* *made of the Works of* Aristotle, *and other Writings* *in Phyfic, out of the Greek and Arabic Languages,* *which have been read ever fince in the Schools, and* *are in ufe at this Time; and fent them to* Bononia, *as a Prefent to That Univerfity, as appears from his* *Letters*." See alfo the Chronicle of *Carion* (124,) where he fays expreſsly, that This Emperor caufed to be tranflated the *Almageft* of *Ptolomy*, and feveral Works of *Ariftotle, Galen, Avicenna,* &c. (125); you will find the fame Names in the *Theatre* of *Mathias* (126), under the Quotation of the feventh Book of *Aventine's* Annals, and of the Chronicle of Ca-

(124) Pag. 480.
(125) Pet cer in Chronic. Carion, lib. 5, pag. 684.
(126) Pag. 956.

rion. I do not know how it happens, that *Averroës* is not named; however, I take him to have been one, amongſt the Authors, tranflated, by the Care of This Emperor. But, as I faid before, I fhould be very glad to know the Names of the Perfons employed in thefe Tranflations. One thing is worth remarking, in Mr *Herbelot's Bibliotheque,* which is, that the *Mahometans* look upon the Doctrine of Thofe who, admitting a Firft Mover, maintain alfo, that the World is eternal, as mere Atheiſm (127). This Doctrine is afcribed to the moſt famous Philofophers, who have flouriſhed among the *Arabians,* to *Averroës,* to *Avicenna*, and to *Alpharabius* (128). The Chriſtians generally pafs the fame Judgment upon This Doctrine, which, certainly, can never be fupported, without treating the Holy Scripture as a Fable.

(127) Herbelot. Bibl. Orient. pag. 537, col. 2.
(128) Id. Ib. & pag. 303, col. 1.

AUGE (DANIEL *d'*), in Latin *Augentius,* was born at *Villeneuve-l'Archevêque,* in the Diocefe of *Sens* in *Champaigne* (*a*). He lived in the XVIth Century, and was efteemed for his Learning and Writings [*A*]. He was appointed, in the Year 1574 (*b*), to the Office of his Majefty's *Greek* Profeffor in the Univerfity of *Paris,* which was vacant by the Death of *Lewis le Roi* (*c*). He had been Tutor to the Son of That *Francis Olivier,* who was Chancellor of *France*. This appears from the Epiftle Dedicatory of a Book to *Antony Olivier,* Biſhop of *Lombés,* and Uncle to his Pupil (*d*). It is dated at *Paris,* the Firſt of *March* 1555. I am not certain as to the Time of his Death; I only know, that *Francis Parent,* his Succeffor in the *Greek* Profefforſhip, entred upon That Office in the Year 1595 (*e*).

(*a*) La Croix du Maine, Biblioth. Franç p. 68.
(*b*) Du Breul, Antiquitez de Paris, pag. 566.
(*c*) Ibid.
(*d*) It is the Poem of Sannazarius, intituled, De Morte Chriſti Lamentatio. Dan. d'Auge printed it at Paris, with his Notes, in the Year 1557, in 4to.
(*e*) Du Breul, Antiquit. de Paris, p. 566.

[*A*] *He was efteemed for his Writings*] They are *A Confolatory Oration on the Death of Meffire* Francis Olivier, *Chancellor of* France, printed at *Paris* in 1560; *Two Dialogues of Poetic Invention, of the true Knowledge of the Art of Oratory,* and *of the Fiction of Fable,* printed at *Paris,* in 1560; *A Difcourfe on the Arrêt of the Parliament of* Dole *in Burgundy, concerning a Man accufed and convicted of being a* Were-wolf † (1); *The Inftitution of a Chriftian Prince,* tranflated from the Greek *of* Synefius, *Biſhop of* Cyrone, *with an* Oration on true Nobility, *tranflated from the Greek of* Philo Judæus, *printed, at* Paris, in 1555; *Four Homilies of St* Macarius, *the* Egyptian, printed at *Paris,* and afterwards at *Lyons,* in 1559; *An Epiftle to the Noble and Virtuous Youth,* Anthony Thelin, *Son of the Noble* William Thelin (2), *Author of the Book intituled,* Divine Effays, *wherein is ſhewn the true Patrimony and Inheritance, which Fathers ought to leave their Children*. This Epiftle is printed at the beginning of the *Divine Effays,* at *Paris,* in 1565. He revifed and corrected them. He publiſhed alfo *A Tranflation, into* French, *of the moſt beautiful Sentences, and Forms of Expreffion, in* Cicero's Familiar Epiftles, printed at *Paris,* in 1556 (3). This is all I find in *la Croix du Maine,* and in *du Verdier*. I do not meet with any mention of the Notes on the Poem of *Sannazarius,* which I have fpoken of, in the Body of this Article.

† One who is fo d to transform himfelf into a Wolf.
(1) Le Croix du Maine, Biblioth. Franç. pag. 68.
(2) Honeſt a Gentleman of Auvergne.
(3) Du Verdier, Bibl. Franç. pag. 248.

Of all the Works of *Daniel d'Auge,* I efteem moſt curious the Difcourfe on the Arrêt, which condemns the Were-Wolf. *Bodin* fays, This Arrêt was paſſed by the Parliament of *Dole,* the eighteenth of *January,* 1583, againſt *Giles Garnier* of *Lyons,* and was printed at *Orleans,* at *Paris,* and at *Sens*. He relates the *principal Circumftances*. "Namely, That "the faid *Garnier,* on *St Michael's* Day, in "the Shape of a Wolf, did feize upon a young "Girl of ten or twelve Years old, near the Wood "of *Serre,* in a Vineyard of *Châtenoy,* about a "quarter of a League from *Dole,* and there killed, "and tore her, as well with his Hands, refembling "Paws, as with his Teeth, and eat the Fleſh of her "Thighs and Arms, and carried fome to his Wife: "That, in the fame Form, a Month after this, he "took another Girl, and killed her, and would "have eaten her, if he had not been prevented by "three Perfons, as he himſelf confeſſed: That, fifteen Days after, he ftrangled a young Child of "ten Years of Age, in a Vineyard of *Gredifans,* "and eat the Fleſh of the Thighs, Legs, and Belly: "And that, in the Shape of a Man, and not of "a Wolf, he killed another little Boy, of the Age "of twelve or thirteen Years, in the Wood of the "Village of *Perouſe,* with a Defign to have eaten "him, if he had not been hindered, according to "his own Free Confeffion. He was condemned to "be burnt alive, and the Arrêt was executed (4)."

(4) Bodin, Demonomanie des Sorciers, Book 2, cap. 6, pag. 218, Edit. of Lyons, 1598, 8vo.

St AUGUSTIN, one of the moſt illuſtrious Fathers of the Church, was born at *Tagaſte* in *Africa,* the Thirteenth of *November,* 354. His Father, whofe Name was *Patricius,* was but a mean Citizen of That Place; his Mother was named *Monica,* and remarkable for her Virtue. Their Son had no Reliſh for Learning [*A*]. However, his Father put him to it againſt his Inclination, refolving to advance him in this way, and fent him to ſtudy *Claffical* Learning at *Madaura*. At the Age of Sixteen, he took him from thence, and fent him to ſtudy Rhetoric at *Carthage*. St *Auguſtin* went thither towards the end of the Year 371 (*a*). He made a great Progrefs in the Sciences,

(*a*) Du Pin's Hiſtory of Eccleſiaſtical Authors, Tom. 3, pag. 138.

[*A*] *He had no reliſh for Learning*.] By the Picture St *Auguſtin* himſelf has drawn of his Youth, it appears, that he was what we call a *Rake*: *He ſhunned the School as the Plague;* he loved nothing but Gaming and public Shews; *he ſtole all he could from his Father; he invented a thouſand Lies to avoid the Rod, which they were obliged to make uſe of, to puniſh his Licentiouſnefs* (1). *Furta etiam faciebam de cellario parentum & de menſa, vel gulâ imperitante, vel ut haberem quod darem pueris ludum ſuum mihi, quo pariter utique delectabantur, tamen vendentibus. Fallendo innumerabilibus mendaciis & pædagogum & magiſtros & parentes, amore ludendi, ſtudio ſpectandi nugatoria, & imitandi ludicra inquietudine*. This confutes what *Leo Allatius* affirms; "That St *Au-*

(1) Auguſt. Confeſſ. lib. 1, cap 19.
What were St Auguſtin was learned, and an Author, from his Youth.

"guſtin, at twelve Years of Age, had read and un- "derſtood all *Ariſtotle's* Books, relating to Logic "and Theory, of himſelf, without the Affiſtance of "any Maſter; and that, at the fame Age, he had "compoſed fome excellent Writings, to difcover and "confute the Errors of feveral Authors (2)." The Writer, who took upon him the Name of *Chriſtianus Lupus,* has faid the fame thing (3). Mr *Baillet* confutes them both very folidly, by St *Auguſtin's* Confeffions, and difcovers the Cauſe of their Miſtake. "Let us believe, *fays he* (4), that They, who gave "the firſt Occafion for This Miſtake, read *Twelve* "inſtead of *Twenty,* in the Place, where St *Auguſtin* "fpeaks of it. This Saint acknowledges *, that he "was near Twenty Years of Age, when a Treatife

(2) In Apib Urbanis, p. 146. apud Baillet of Famous Children, p. 59.
(3) Chriſt. Liberius, de ſcrib. & Inp. libris, pag. 178, apud Baillet, ibid.
(4) Baillet, ibid. pag. 60, 61.
* Confeſſ. of lib. 4. c. 16.

AUGUSTIN.

Sciences, but gave himself up to Debauchery with Women [B]. He had a mind to read the Holy Scriptures; but the Simplicity of the Style disgusted him: he was yet too great an Admirer of the Pagan Eloquence, to have a Taste for the Bible. He had, in general, a great Desire to discover Truth; and, being in hopes of finding it in the Sect of the *Manicheans*, he engaged in it, and maintained most of it's Doctrines with much Fervency. Having lived some time in *Carthage*, he returned to *Tagaste*, where he taught Rhetoric with so much Applause, that his Mother was congratulated upon having so admirable a Son. This did not hinder the holy Woman from being extremely afflicted on account of her Son's Heresy, and Debauchery. He returned to *Carthage* in the Year 380; where he taught Rhetoric with a great deal of Reputation. It was at this time he fixed his Incontinency, which had been rambling after various Objects: He took a Concubine, to whom he kept very constant, and had, by her, a Son, whom he named *Adeodatus*, the Gift of God, and who had very good Parts [C]. He became a little wavering in his Sect, because he could meet with no satisfactory Answer to the Difficulties he had to propose [D]: however,

" of *Aristotle* fell into his Hands, called *The Ten Categories*, which he had often heard mentioned, at *Carthage*, with great Applause. ----- He read it alone, and understood it perfectly well: so that afterwards conferring about it with Those, who said, they had learned it with much Pains from excellent Masters, who had not only explained it to them in Words, but also by Figures, drawn on the Sand, he found he had comprehended it as well by himself. He says also, that, at the same Age, he read, and understood, without any Help, all Books of the Liberal Arts, which he could meet with. He says the same thing of the Mathematics, and particularly of Geometry, Music, and Arithmetic.

[B] *He gave himself up to Debauchery with Women.*] He began very early: for, at sixteen Years of Age, he followed the Dictates of That unruly Passion; " Ubi eram, (*says he*), & quam longè exulabam à deliciis domus tuæ, anno illo sexto decimo ætatis carnis meæ, cum accepit in me sceptrum, & totas manus ei dedi vesaniæ libidinis, licentiosæ per dedecus humanum, illicitæ autem per leges tuas (5)? ------ *Where was I, and how long was I banished from the Delights of thy House, in That sixteenth Year of my Flesh, when I submitted to it's Empire, and gave myself up entirely to all it's violent Lusts, which disgrace our Natures, and are sinful by thy Laws?*" He spent That Year in Idleness, because his Father not being then able to provide for his Expences at *Carthage*, was by degrees making up a Sum sufficient to send him thither. The Joy of This good Father was remarkable, upon discovering, as he was bathing with his Son, an uncommon Forwardness of Nature (6). He could not forbear acquainting his Wife with the News; and had the Pleasure of fancying himself already a Grandfather, upon seeing his Son would so soon be fit to make him one. ------ *Quinimo ubi me ille pater in balneis vidit pubescentem, & inquieta indutum adolescentia, quasi jam ex hoc in nepotes gestiret, gaudens matri indicavit* (7). St *Augustin*'s Mother, instead of being pleased, was very uneasy at it; she feared the ill Effects of it, and therefore made him very serious Remonstrances to abstain from the Sex, and particularly from Adultery: " Secreto memini ut monuerit cum solicitudine ingenti ne fornicarer, maximeque ne adulterarem cujusquam uxorem. Qui mihi monitus muliebres videbantur, quibus obtemperare erubescerem (8). ------ *I shall never forget how earnestly she cautioned me against Fornication, and particularly against Adultery; which I looked upon as such womanish Advice, that I was ashamed to follow it.*" But he took no notice of these good Exhortations; for he contracted such a strong Habit of Incontinence, that, even after he had renounced *Manicheism*, and prepared himself for Baptism, he took a new Concubine in the Room of *Adeodatus*'s Mother, 'till the Wife, he was to marry, should attain to a fit Age (9). for which he was to wait near two Years (10). It is remarkable, that, in the Dispute between St *Augustin* and *Alypius*, on Marriage and Celibacy, *Alypius*, instead of persuading St *Augustin* to live single, suffered himself to be persuaded to marry. *Alypius* had led a very chaste Life; tho', in the beginning of his Youth, he just stolen a Taste of those forbidden Pleasures, but recovered This Slip betimes. *He dissuaded St Augustin from Matri-* mony, as an Obstacle to the Design they had formed *to live together in the Study of Wisdom.* " Prohibebat me sine Alypius ab uxore ducenda, causans nullo modo nos posse securo otio simul in amore sapientiæ vivere, sicut jamdiu desideraveramus, si id fecissem (11)." *St Augustin confessed to him ingenuously, that it would be impossible for him to contain himself,* and alledged to him the Example of some married Sages, who had been faithful to God and their Friends. He added, *that there was a great Difference between Those transient Pleasures, which Alypius had tasted, and since forgot, and Those, which he* (Augustin) *had made habitual to him, which would also become more engaging under the fair Cover of Marriage.* *Alypius* was so touched with this Discourse, that he resolved to be married himself: *That I may know,* said he, *by Experience, what St Augustin has found more charming than Life itself.* " Cum me ille miraretur, quem non parvi penderet, ita hærere visco illius voluptatis, ut me affirma rem quotiescunque inde inter nos quæreremus, cœlibem vitam nullo modo posse degere, atque ita me defenderem, cum illum mirantem viderem, ut dicerem multum interesse inter illud quod ipse raptim & furtim expertus esset, quod pœne jam nec meminisset quidem, atque ideo nulla molestia facile contemneret, & delectationes consuetudinis meæ, ad quas si accessisset honestum nomen Matrimonii, non eum mirari oporteret cur ego illam vitam nequirem spernere. Cœperat & ipse desiderare conjugium nequaquam victus libidine talis voluptatis, sed curiositatis. Dicebat enim scire se cupere, quidnam esset illud sine quo vita mea, quæ illi sic placebat, non mihi vita, sed pœna videretur (12)." However, neither of them did ever marry, but over lived very chastly.

[C] *He took a Concubine,* ----- *and had by her a Son, whom he named* Adeodatus, *the Gift of God, who had very good Parts.*] Without doubt my Reader will be pleased to find something here, concerning This Bastard; and therefore I shall inform him of what I have met with in Mr *Baillet*. " *Adeodatus* was but fifteen Years of Age, when his Father was baptized; but he was then so forward, and had made so uncommon a Progress in Knowledge, that he excelled many Persons of ripest Years, and several even of Those, who had got a Character in the World for their Gravity and Learning. About the same time St *Augustin* composed a Book, by way of Dialogue, intituled, *Of the Master: Adeodatus* and himself, are the two Personages of This Dialogue; and he takes God to witness, that all, he makes his Son say in That Work, is entirely his own, though he was then but *fixteen* Years of Age. St *Augustin* adds, That he had seen yet more wonderful Things in This Child, than what we have related. Lastly, in spite of his own great Firmness of Soul, he owns, he was astonished at the Prodigy of his Son's Parts. *Adeodatus* received the Sacrament of Baptism, together with his Father, and died soon after (13)."

[D] *He could meet with no satisfactory Answer to the Difficulties he had to propose.*] St *Augustin* had a penetrating Wit; he was a Rhetorician by Profession, and understood Logic. It is easy for a subtile and eloquent Disputant to form Doubts, and make Replies. It must not then be wondered at, that he embarrassed the *Manichean* Doctors; any

more

(5) Confess. lib. 2. cap. 2.

(6) *It was against Decency, among the Pagans themselves, that a Son and a Father should bathe in the same Place. See* Cicero de Offic. lib. 1, cap. 35. Val. Max. lib. 2, cap. 1, n. 7. Plutarch. in Catone majore, p. 348.

(*) August. Confess. l. 2. cap. 3.

(8) Ibidem.

(9) Ibid lib. 6, cap. 15.

(10) Ibid. cap. 13.

(11) Ibid. cap. 12.

(12) Id. ib.

(13) Baillet, des Enfans celebres, pag. 61. ex Aug. Confess. lib. 9. cap. 6.

AUGUSTIN.

however, he did not forsake their Opinions, but waited for better Explications. His good Mother *Monica* went to him at *Carthage*, to endeavour to draw him from his Heresy and Luxury; nor did she despair, tho' she found, that her Remonstrances were, then, to no Purpose. He wanted a new Theatre, for displaying his Learning, and resolved to go to *Rome*; and, that he might not be diverted from this design, he embarked without communicating it either to his Mother, or to his near Relation *Romanian*, who had maintained him at School (b). He taught Rhetoric at *Rome*, with as much Applause, as at *Carthage*: so that *Symmachus*, Prefect of That City, understanding, that they wanted, at *Milan*, an able Professor in Rhetoric, appointed him to That Employ, in the Year 383. St *Augustin* was very much esteemed at *Milan*; he made a Visit to St *Ambrose*, and was kindly received by him. He went to his Sermons, not so much out of a Principle of Piety, as That of a Critical Curiosity. He wanted to know if That Prelate's Eloquence deserved the Reputation it had obtained. It pleased God to make this the Means of his Conversion: St *Ambrose*'s Sermons made such an Impression upon him, that St *Augustin* became a Catholic in the Year 384. His Mother, who was come to him to *Milan*, advised him to marry, that he might effectually forsake his former Irregularities. He consented to the Proposal, and sent his Concubine back into *Africa*; but, as the Wife, designed for him, was so very young, that he was to wait two Years before he could marry her, not being able to resist his Natural Inclinations so long, he relapsed to his usual Incontinence. At length, the reading of St *Paul*'s Epistles, the Sollicitations and Tears of his Mother, and the good Discourses of some Friends, procured for him the finishing stroke of Grace; he felt himself a good Christian, ready to forsake all for the Gospel; he left off teaching Rhetoric, and was baptized, by St *Ambrose*, on *Easter*-Eve in the Year 387. The following Year, he returned into *Africa*, having lost his Mother at *Ostia*, where they were both to have embarked (c). He was ordained Priest in the Year 391, by *Valerius* Bishop of *Hippo*; Four Years after, he became Coadjutor to That Prelate, and did very considerable Services to the Church by his Pen and his Piety, until his Death, which happened the Twenty eighth of *August* 430 (d). The particulars of his Episcopal Life and Writings would be superfluous here; They may be found in *Moreri*'s Dictionary, and in Mr du Pin's Bibliotheque; and if Those Gentlemen had not too lightly passed over St *Augustin*'s irregular Life, I might wholly have dispensed with this Article: But, for the better Instruction of the Public, it is proper to discover both the Good, and the Bad, of Great Men. The Approbation, which Councils and Popes have given St *Augustin* on the Doctrine of Grace, adds greatly to his Glory; for, without That, the *Molinists*, in these latter Times, would have highly advanced their Banner against him, and pulled down his Authority. We have shewn elsewhere (e), that all their Politics could scarce keep them in decorum, and prevent their attacking him indirectly. It is certain, that the Engagement, which the Church of *Rome* is under, to respect St *Augustin*'s System, casts her into a Perplexity, which is very ridiculous [E]. The *Arminians*, not having the same Measures to keep, deal very sincerely with This holy Father of the Church

(b) *His Father died about the Year 372.*

(c) *Taken from the Ecclesiastical History of John le Sueur, Tom. 3. ad Ann. 388. pag. 484, & seq. Edit. in 12mo.*

(d) *Du Pin, Biblioth. des Ant. Eccl. Tom. 3. p. 158.*

(e) *Above, in the Remarks [C] [D] and [L] of the Article ADAM (JOHN) the Jesuit: where you will see the various Judgments passed upon St Augustin. See also Etat de la Faculté de Théologie de Louvain, in 170x pag. 207.*

---

more than that he puzzled several Catholic Doctors, and that the weak Answers, which they returned to his Objections, confirmed him in his Heresies. He confesses, that, to his cost, he had gained a thousand Victories in these Engagements: so true is it, that every Orthodox Person ought not to engage himself in Disputes; and that, unless he has to do with an Heretic of his own Strength, he can do nothing, humanly speaking, but harden his Adversary. "Quædam noxia victoria pœne mihi semper in disputationibus proveniebat, differenti cum Christianis imperitis; quo successu creberrimo gliscebat adolescentis animositas, & impetu suo in pervicaciæ magnum malum imprudenter vergebat (14). ——— *In disputing with unlearned Christians, I had almost always the ill Fortune to get the better of them; which frequent Success still added fresh Fuel to the Heat of my Youth, and hurried me headlong into That greatest of Mischiefs, Obstinacy.*"

[E] *The Engagement of the Church of Rome to St Augustin's System casts her into a Perplexity, which is very ridiculous.*] It is manifest to all Men, who examine Things without Prejudice, and with sufficient Abilities, that St *Augustin*'s Doctrine, and That of *Jansenius*, Bishop of *Ypres*, are one and the same; so that we cannot, without Indignation, behold the Court of *Rome* boasting to have condemned *Jansenius*, and yet preserved St *Augustin* in all his Glory. These are two Things altogether inconsistent. More than This, The Council of *Trent*, in condemning *Calvin*'s Doctrine of Free Will, did necessarily condemn That of St *Augustin*: For no *Calvinist* ever denied, or can deny, the Concurrence of the human Will, and the Liberty of the Soul, in the Sense which St *Augustin* has given to the Words Concurrence, Co-operation, and Liberty. There is not a *Calvinist*, but acknowledges Free Will, and it's Use in Conversion, if That Word be understood according to St *Augustin*'s Idea's. Those, condemned by the Council of *Trent*, do not reject Free Will, but as it signifies a Liberty of Indifferency. The *Thomists* reject it also under That Notion, and yet pass for very good Catholics. See another Comical Scene! The Physical Predetermination of the *Thomists*, the Necessity of St *Augustin*, That of the *Jansenists*, and That of *Calvin*, are all one and the same thing at the Bottom; and yet the *Thomists* disown the *Jansenists*, and both of them think it a Calumny to accuse them of teaching the same Doctrine with *Calvin*. If one might be suffered to judge of another's Thoughts, here would be great Room for saying, that Doctors are, in this Case, great Comedians, and are only acting a Part, and that They cannot but be sensible, that the Council of *Trent* either condemned a meer Chimera, which never entered into the Thoughts of the *Calvinists*, or else, that it condemned, at the same time, both St *Augustin*, and the Physical Predetermination. So that, when they boast of having St *Augustin*'s Faith, and never to have varied in the Doctrine (15), it is only meant to preserve a Decorum, and to save the System from Destruction, which a sincere Confession of the Truth must necessarily occasion. It is a great Happiness for some Persons, that the People never trouble themselves to demand of them any Account of their Doctrine, and that they have not a sufficient Capacity for it. They would, otherwise, oftener mutiny against Doctors, than against Tax gatherers. They would

(14) *August. de duabus Anim.*

(15) *M. Basnage shews plainly, that in the Council of Trent, and elsewhere, the Church of Rome decided against St Augustin, and against it's Common History of the Religion of the Reformed Churches, Tom. 2. pag. 452, & seq.*

AUGUSTIN.

Church [F]. A Learned *French* Critic may make use of terms as respectful as he pleases, yet he cannot hinder us from discovering, that he heartily despises St *Augustin*'s Commentaries on the Scripture [G]. If Mr *Claude*, who condemned This Father's

WHETHER Ecclesiastical Doctors have any reason to stand in fear of the Capacities of the People.

would say to them; *If you do not know that you deceive us, you deserve to be sent to the Plough for your Stupidity; and, if you do know it, you deserve to be shut up within four Walls, with Bread and Water, for your Wickedness.* But there is nothing of this to fear; the People are content to be led on in the usual Road; and, if they were inclinable to enquire a little farther, they would not be able to discuss such Points; Their Business does not permit them to acquire a sufficient Capacity.

[F] *The* Arminians - - - - - - *deal very sincerely with This holy Father of the Church.*] They might have perplexed the World, as well as the Jesuits; but they thought it much better to give up St *Augustin* wholly to their Adversaries, and to acknowledge him for as great a Predestinarian (it is a Term much used among them) as *Calvin*. Without doubt the Jesuits would have done the same, if they durst have condemned a Doctor, whom the Popes and Councils had approved.

[G] *A learned French Critic - - - - - heartily despises St Augustin's Commentaries on the Scriptures.*] I mean Mr *Simon*: See his *Critical History of the Old Testament* (16), wherein the chief Encomium he gives This Father is, that he knew his own Insufficiency. "He has very well observed, *says* "*he* (17), the Qualifications necessary to make a "good Interpreter of the Scripture; and, as he was "a modest Man, he freely confessed, that he him- "self wanted most of them; therefore we ought "not to wonder, if sometimes we find but little "Exactness in his Commentaries on the Scriptures. "—— He soon acknowledged, that the Undertaking, "to answer the Manicheans, was above his Strength. "*In Scripturis exponendis tyrocinium meum sub tanta* "*sarcinæ mole succubuit*." I confess, that Mr *Simon* does not quote *Peter Castellan*, without blaming him. But, as he wrote in *France*, was it not necessary to use all This Caution? "I cannot approve, "*says he* (18), of the Heat of *Peter Castellan*, Grand "Almoner of *France*, who accuses St *Augustin* with "too much Liberty, in reproaching him *with having* "*been only in a Dream*, when he explained the Holy "Scripture." They, who wrote against him, knew very well how to object to him the little Agreement there is between the Esteem he would seem to have for St *Augustin*'s Writings, and the Judgment he really makes of them; and they have taken this Occasion to draw a very disadvantageous Picture of This Father. "No other Idea, *say they* (19), can be for- "med of the Blessed St *Augustin*, than That of a De- "claimer, who says all that comes in his Head, "whether to the Purpose, or not, provided it agrees "but with a certain *Platonic* System, which he had "formed of the Christian Religion; One, who "loses himself every Moment in the Clouds, and "suffers himself to be carried away by cold "Allegories, which he delivers for Oracles; in short, "of One, who had none of Those Qualifications, "which an Interpreter of the Holy Scriptures ought "to have." Of all this they give fome very strong Examples. Mr *Simon*, in his Reply, has not much troubled himself to defend St *Augustin*. It is easy to see, he had not this at Heart: He pays some Regard to Decency, but much more to his Desire of confuting his Adversary (20). It may be observed, in several Places of his Writings, to be his Opinion, that, since St *Augustin* makes no Difficulty to forsake the *Greek* Fathers on the Subject of Grace, there is no Reason to follow him, in Preference to Those *Greek* Fathers. This Pretence would answer very well, if there was but room to urge it: But, since St *Augustin*'s Doctrine, on Grace, has been approved of by the Church, it must follow, that all Doctrine, opposite to That, is to be rejected; and therefore whatever may be found in St *Chrysostom*, which favours *Molinism*, as a particular Tenet, and at least implicitly branded by the authentic Approbation given to St *Augustin*. This is the Perplexity I mentioned above, which exposes the Church of *Rome* to a sort of Ridicule. I shall relate *Castellan*'s Words; they are remarkable, and his Life is not a very common Book in this Country: "Ut divum *Augustinum* contra

(16) Book 3, chap. 9.

(17) Ibid. p. 397, 398.

* Lib. 1, Retract. cap. 18.

(18) Hist. Critique du vieux Test. pag. 399.

(19) See the Book entitled The Sentiments of some Divines of *Holland*, on the Critical History of the Old Testament, pag. 337, & seq. *and the Defence of those Sentiments*, pag. 348, & seq.

(20) See the Answer to those Sentiments, pag. 2, & seq. *and the Answer to the Defence*, p. 193, & seq.

"hæreticos de hominis Christiani Justificatione dis- "putando, proxime ad divi *Pauli* sententiam acces- "sisse fatebatur, ita linguarum ignoratione somniasse "frequenter atque etiam desiraste sacra explicando "asseverabat: cumque bonarum artium magis non "ignorans quam peritus dici posset, non satis ido- "neum esse judicebat cui de artibus differenti le- "gendo tempus transmitteretur qui minime otio a- "bundaret. Eam quoque still *Augustiniani* ansra- "ctuosam sinuositatem esse, & sermonis omni ele- "gantia vacui impuritatem addebat, ut ab homine "liberaliter in literis educato citra fastidium legi "vix posset (21). —— *As he confessed, that St Au- "gustin, in his Disputation against the Heretics, con- "cerning Christian Justification, comes the nearest "of any to the Sense of St Paul; so he affirmed, that "by his Ignorance in Languages he has been often "in a Dream, or even out of his Head, in his In- "terpretation of the Scriptures; and that, as he may "rather be said not to have been a Stranger to Arts, "than a Master of them, it is but last Time to those, "who have not a great deal to spare, to listen to "him, in his discoursing in those Subjects.* Farther, "*that St Augustin's Style is so rough and tedious,* "*and not only void of all Elegance, but even very* "*incorrect, that it must nauseate a Reader of a learned* "*Education.*"

Since the first Edition of this Dictionary, I have seen the Explication, which Mr *Simon* has given, to stop the Complaints of the *Jansenists*. My Intention, says he (22), *was not to diminish, in the least, the Au- "thority of St Augustin, whom I have always acknow- "ledged to be the most able Divine of the Western "Churches, and to have deserved the great Elogies, "which so many Popes have given him —— I agree, "that the Church assures us, that Those, who have "taught Theology with Art and Method, have taken "St Augustin for their Master and Guide. These are "the Words of the Roman Breviary; but they do not "mean, that Those Masters of Theology, who followed St "Augustin in the manner of treating This Science, "are obliged never to depart from the Opinions of That "learned Bishop; nor that Those same Opinions are Ar- "ticles of Faith, nor lastly, that the other Fathers are "to be forsaken, when they do not entirely agree with him. "The Church teaches us, in the same Lessons of the Bre- "viary, speaking of St John Chrysostom*, That all "the World admires his Way of interpreting the sacred "Books, according to the Letter, and judge him worthy "of what was believed of him, viz. that St Paul, whom "he particularly honoured, dictated several things to "him. I always had the highest Veneration for Those "two great Men, who are to this Day the Admira- "tion of the Eastern and Western Churches; but, in ex- "plaining certain Passages of the Scripture, about which "St Augustin and St Chrysostom differ, I thought I "might follow St Chrysostom's Interpretation, when- "ever it seemed the most literal. This Difference, "which no way affects our Fundamentals, does not "hinder them from agreeing together in the essential "Points of our Belief. Speaking of St Augustin, in my "History of the Commentators, I might indeed have been "more cautious in my Expressions; and I have even "mentioned some Things, said of him by Cardinal Sa- "dolet, which seem too severe. But I never designed to "oppose the Doctrine of This holy Doctor, who confuted "so powerfully the Heretics of his Time. He adds, "That he proposed Cardinal Gasper Contarini for his "Guide, who judged, that there was a certain Medium "to be observed between Those, who, under pretence of "being Enemies to the Lutherans, came too near the "Heresy of Pelagius; and Those, who, having some "Tincture of St Augustin's Writings, instead of imita- "ting his Modesty and his Charity, preached very "puzzling Doctrines to the People, which they did not "understand themselves, nor could any way explain but "by running into Paradoxes.* "I believed, *continues* "*he,* that I could not do better, than to imitate "That great Cardinal, in my Answer to the Divines "of *Holland*, who had objected against me, that the "Tradition of the Church was not constant and cer- "tain; by producing, for an Example, the Doctrines "of Grace, and of Predestination, in which the "Church

(21) Petr. Gasland. in Vitâ Castellani, pag. 44, 45.

(22) Simon's Preface to the New Observations on the Text and Versions of the New Testament, printed at Paris, 1695, in 4to.

* Interpretandi rationem & inveniendi sententiae sacrorum explanationem omnes adhibere videantur, numque exstimant cui Paulus Apostolus quem ille mirifice coluit scribenti & prædicanti multa distincte videantur. Brev. Rom.

ther's Approbation of Penal Laws in Matters of Conscience, had lived but three or four Years longer, he would have exposed himself to a severe Censure [H].

A Phy-

" Church had followed and authorized St *Augustin*'s
" Explanation, notwithstanding he differed, they say,
" from all the other Fathers, both *Greek* and *Latin*,
" who went before him. I observed to them, that This
" difference was only in some Points, which had
" never been determined as Articles of Faith, and
" in some Passages of Scripture, which might very
" well admit of different Interpretations; and there-
" fore that the Church ought not to be accused of
" Inconstancy in Tradition." This needs very little
Examination to discover it to be a Mask or Colour,
which can only deceive very ignorant Persons: For,
pray tell me, whence come the most material Controversies? Is it not from a Difference in explaining
some Passages of Scripture? Why then do you make
use of the Idea of This difference, to shew us, that
St *Chrysostom* and St *Augustin* differ in nothing essential? Is it only an accident, and nothing material
to the Doctrine of Grace, to know in what the
Power of a Sinner consists, and what is the Essence
of his Liberty? Is it not rather a fundamental Part
of This Doctrine? If then these two Fathers are directly opposite in their Explication of the Nature of
Free-will, it is certain, their Difference is in Essentials, and the Church cannot adopt the Hypothesis of the one, without rejecting That of the other.
Otherwise it must be said, that she embraces a Truth
without condemning the opposite Error; for, in
short, though it were possible, that both of them may
be mistaken, yet it is impossible, that both their Opinions should be true: Therefore, either They, who
follow St *Chrysostom*'s Explication, or They, who follow St *Augustin*'s Doctrine, must be in an Error. Here,
again, we may observe the great Perplexity of the
Church of *Rome*. She is forced to approve both
those who hold that Grace does all, and those who
hold that Grace does nothing, in obtaining our Assent; some of her Doctors, on the one side, teach,
That we form this Assent ourselves, with full Liberty to refuse it: on the other, That Grace produces this Assent, without leaving us the least Liberty to refuse it. The one, or the other, teaches an
Error, which does not turn upon a Trifle, but on a
Point of very great Consequence. And yet the
Church of *Rome*, with her pretended Infallibility,
lets this whole Matter pass without Censure. If
she condemns *Jansenism*, she is obliged to declare,
at the same time, that she does not condemn St *Augustin* (23); this is to undo, with one hand, what
is done with the other. Observe, by the way, these
words of Mr *Simon*; *The Difference — was only
in some Thing), which have not been determined as Articles of Faith.* This is to say, that, provided an
Error affects only some Points, which have not
yet been determined as Articles of Faith, the Person,
who propagates it, may still be an Orthodox, and a
very good Christian; I say, observe this Privilege of
an erroneous Conscience. Observe also, that, though
it were lawful to dissent from St *Augustin*'s Opinion,
before the Doctrines of Grace were determined in the
Time of that Father; it does not follow, that, after
those Determinations, the Writers of the XVIIth
Century are at liberty to return to St *Chrysostom*'s O-
pinion; for here is a substantial Remark of a Divine,
whom Mr *Simon* can by no means suspect: " In the
" Disputes concerning Grace, Election, and Pre-
" destination, less Regard is to be paid to the ancient
" Fathers, who lived before the *Pelagian* Heresy,
" than to those, who came after: And much less to
" the *Greeks*, than to the *Latins*; notwithstanding
" that these came after That Heresy —— But, among
" the *Latins*, whose Authority, we have already ob-
" served, is to be preferred to That of the other Fa-
" thers, Divines agree, that St *Augustin* is he, on
" whom we ought most to rely: For not only all
" the Fathers, and all the Doctors, who came after
" him, but the Popes themselves, and the Councils
" of other Bishops, have held his Doctrine, con-
" cerning Grace, for Certain and Catholic: and
" they have ALL BELIEVED it a sufficient Proof of
" the Truth of an Opinion, that This Saint had
" taught it (24)."

[H] *If Mr* Claude —— *had lived three or four Years, he would have exposed himself to a severe Censure.*] I have two things to shew; the one, that

Mr *Claude* blamed St *Augustin* for approving the Penal Laws against Heretics; the other, that, if he had
lived three or four Years longer, he would have been
censured for censuring St *Augustin*.

I. To prove the First, I need only recite some
Expressions of Mr *Claude*, in a Letter, which was made
public. He confesses, That St *Augustin had an admirable Understanding, a happy and fruitful Imagination, discovering, almost on every occasion, great
Piety, Justice, and Charity*: But he adds, *There
is one thing, which tarnishes his Memory extreamly,
viz. that, after having expressed Sentiments of Mildness and Charity, in regard to Proceedings against
Heretics, his Disputes with the Donatists so very
much inflamed him, that he became quite another Man,
and turned Advocate for Persecution* (25).

II. The Acts of the Synod of the *Walloon*
Churches of the United Provinces, held at *Amsterdam*
in the Month of *August*, 1690, demonstrate, beyond
controversy, the second thing I am to prove; for
This is one of the Propositions, which That Assembly
condemned, *The Magistrate has no right, by Virtue
of his Authority, to suppress Idolatry, and hinder the
Progress of Heresy.* I say, This Proposition is one of
Those, which the Synod *solemnly and unanimously declares false, scandalous, pernicious, and equally destructive of Morality and Religion*. The Synod *prescribes, prohibits, and condemns them as such, forbidding all Persons, Ecclesiastic and Secular, under the
severest Censures, to utter them either in Pulpits,
or in private Conversations —— And most expresly
commanding all Consistories, within their Jurisdiction,
to redouble their Pastoral Care and Vigilance, in proportion to the Danger, which threatens their Flocks,
to suppress, without Distinction, or Complaisance, all
who shall be found guilty, by refusing private Persons the Holy Sacrament, and by suspending the Ministers from their Offices till the next Synod, calling
in two Pastors of the Neighbouring Churches to join in
That Sentence* (26). Some may object, that if Mr
Claude had been living, at the Time of holding this
Synod (27), perhaps They would not have condemned
This Proposition. I can say nothing at all to this: but,
be it as it will, there is no denying, but that his
Opinion has been anathematized. For it is evident,
that St *Augustin* only maintains, that Magistrates
ought to suppress Heretics, by making them liable
to certain Penalties. Now the Synod of *Amsterdam*
establishes This so strongly, that it puts the contrary
Proposition in the number of pernicious Errors,
for which it orders the Laity to be excommunicated,
and the Clergy suspended. Therefore it has approved the same Doctrine, which Mr *Claude* condemned in St *Augustin*: and the Opinion of Mr
Claude lies under the Anathema of This Synod.

If Mr *Claude* was surprized, that St *Augustin* should
be such a Turncoat in his Opinion, others wonder
yet more, that the *French* Refugee Ministers (28)
appear to be so too. For, whereas St *Augustin* changed
his Opinion, upon observing the good Success of
the Emperor's Laws, in suppressing a Schism; these
Refugee Ministers have changed their Opinion, while
the Ruin of their Churches, by the Authority of
the Sovereign, was quite fresh in their Memory, and
the Wound still bleeding. If they had been asked,
while the Edicts of Persecution were pouring on
their Party, what they thought of the Conduct of
a Prince, who inflicted Penalties on Those of his Subjects, who desired only the Liberty of serving God
according to their Consciences, they would have
answered, that it is unjust; and yet, as soon as they
are come into another Country, they have pronounced their Anathema against Those, who condemn the
use of Penal Laws, in order to suppress Errors. This
should serve for an Example of the Instability of human Things; and may furnish matter for much moral Reflexion.

He, who was the Promoter of These Synodical Decisions, had been a Deserter in Opinion; but it was,
in some Measure, by a special Privilege, and by a
prophetic Dispensation, from which others could draw
no Consequence. His *Politics of the Clergy*, his
Perservative, &c. had highly condemned the use of
Penal Laws in Matters of Religion. He had amply
discussed This Point, in his Answer to the History

of

AUGUSTIN.

A Physician of *Paris* has published a very singular Remark; he pretends, that This great Saint could bear a great deal of Drink, and would sometimes make free with it, but without getting drunk. We shall produce his Reasons, as well as Those of a Journalist, who confutes him [*I*]. I shall not say much of the Editions of *Calvinism*; at least, he had given to understand, that he was desirous of confuting effectually the Advocates for Penal Laws. It is true, he had pulled down with one hand, what he endeavoured to build with the other; and fell into an unfortunate Contradiction, which exposed him to terrible Mortifications from several Writings, which were published against him; but, in short, all this was not sufficient to shew, that he had expressly declared on both sides of the Question. It was only in consequence of the Revelations, which he thought he had received from, above, about the approaching Ruin of Popery: I say, it was only in consequence of these, that he exerted himself against Those, who did not believe it lawful to extirpate Sectaries by the Authority of the Secular Power. He imagined These Persons had picked a personal Quarrel with him, and were conspiring against his Explication of the *Apocalypse* (29). The Clergy of *France* have made great use of St *Augustin*'s Reasons, to justify the Conduct of the Court towards the Reformed. All that St *Augustin* published on this Subject has been ordered to be printed by itself, translated into elegant *French*. A Protestant has published a Confutation of it, in the third Part of the *Philosophical Commentary* on these Words, COMPEL THEM TO COME IN. See (30) the Reflexions, which have been made on the Prejudice, done to the good Cause, by the Authority of This Saint. It has been wondred at, that Mr *Poiret* should endeavour to excuse him. See the *History of the Works of the Learned*, for the Month of *May*, 1692, pag. 358; and for the Month of *August* of the same Year, pag. 552.

[*I*] *A Physician — pretends, that This Saint could bear a great deal of Drink — but without getting drunk. We shall produce his Reasons, as well as those of a Journalist, who confutes him*] The Physician, I am speaking of, is Mr *Petit*. The Chapter, where he treats of this, is entituled, "Videri B. Augustinum non invalidum potorem fuisse (31). — *That St Augustin seems to have been a hard Drunker.*" He immediately lays down, for the Foundation of his Assertion, these Words of *Augustin*: "Ebrietas longe est à me: misereberis, ne appropinquet mihi. Crapula autem nonnunquam surrepit servo tuo; misereberis, ut longe fiat à me (32). — *Drunkenness is far from me; thou wilt have Mercy on me, Lord, that it may not come near me. The* Crapula *surprizes thy Servant sometimes; thou wilt pity him, that it may go far from him.*" This seems to be a sort of Contradiction; for, the Crapula being the Effect of Drunkenness, how can any one confess, without contradicting himself, that he never drinks to the Degree of Drunkenness, and yet that he is sometimes overcome by the *Crapula*? Mr *Petit* shews, by the Authority of *Aristotle*, that the *Crapula* is the last Stage of Drunkenness, that it is the Head ach, which remains, when sleep has dissipated the Vapours of the Wine, and when a Man, who has been drunk, recovers his Understanding, and is no longer under the Alienation of Mind, which deprived him of his Senses. He confirms this by a Passage of *Pliny*, and by some Verses of the Poet *Alexis*; and This is his Method of clearing up this seeming Contradiction. He supposes, that *This great Saint had a very strong Head, and was able to drink a great deal of Wine, without losing the Use of his Reason, but not without being incommoded by it next Day*. Quid id esset cerebro ac mentis firmitate ut posset in eadem vini quantitate, quæ multos ad insomiam redigeret, rationis usum conservare (33). Upon this Foot, a Man may justly say, that he is never drunk, though, on some Occasions, he finds himself punished with the *Crapula*, for having drunk too much; and he ought to acknowledge this to be an Imperfection, which stands in need of the Mercy of his heavenly Father. "Sic "nobis dubitatio illa vanescit, vindicaturque Augu- "stinus à turpitudine eorum, qui rationem suam vi- "no obruere non dubitant: non tamen à culpâ "omnino, ipso judice, qui tantum vini hauriret, "inde ut crapulam aliquando incurreret, nec posset

"sui inter pocula temperare, quin nimio potu in- "terdum valetudini suæ incommodaret. Quâ de re "ibi misericordiam Dei imploratſ (34). *Thus we shall make this Difficulty vanish, and vindicate St Augustin from the beastliness of Those, who make no Scruple to intoxicate their Senses with Wine; nor yet leave him intirely innocent, because of his drinking, by his own Correction, so much as to cause a* Crapula, *and not having that Guard upon himself in his Cups, to prevent drinking more than his Health would bear. On which account he implores the Mercy of God.*" Mr *Petit* excuses St *Augustin*, from the Nature of the Climate, where he lived, and from the Custom of the *Africans*, and proposes this Objection to himself. It is probable, that this great Man's Practice was agreeable to the Advice he gave to others: Now *he recommends the living on Herbs and Bacon, and drinking two or three Glasses of Wine, without Water. Duæ vel tres vini meracæ potiones propter diligentiam valetudinis sumptæ cum obsequiis & lario laudantur* (35). The Answer is, *That it is probable St Augustin did not so strictly practise This Rule, but that he might sometimes transgress it among his Friends, and those whom he invited to his Episcopal Table. Velim & mises illud concedis, non minus probabile; non ita hunc regulæ illi adhæsum vixisse, ut non cum vinî modum nonnunquam inter amicos, & mensæ episcopalis hospites, bibendo excederet* (36). For, otherwise, it must be concluded, that he lived only on Herbs and Bacon, which cannot be supposed, without monkish Stupidity. *Quid putare cucullata reret dementia* (37).

Let us see what Mr *Clasen* has answered to this *strange Paradox of* Mr *Petit*: For so he calls this Assertion (38). He is for reading "the whole Chap "ter of the Confessions, from whence the Passage is "taken (39)." We shall find, "That St *Augustin* there "represents his own Disposition, with regard to eat- "ing and drinking, and declares, that he had learn- "ed of God not to seek after Aliments, any other- "wise than as after Medicines, and to use both "alike". He says, "that, according to this Principle, "he is always upon his guard against Pleasure, "when he satisfies the Cravings of Nature; that he "is in a continual War with himself, by Fastings, "and Abstinence; that he frequently reduces his "Body into Subjection, and continually hears the "Voice of GOD crying to him; *Ne graventur corda "vestra in crapula & ebrietate* (40). *— Let not "your Hearts be overcharged with Drunkenness and "Debauch.*" Mr *Consin* asks, "Whether a Bishop, "who lived in This manner, can be suspected to have "drank sometimes to excess?" He assures us, "no Di- "stinction is to be made here; that St *Augustin* never "drank more than Necessity required; and that, "therefore, when he said, *Crapula autem nunnun- "quam obrepit servo tuo*, he takes the Word Crapula "in another Sense (41). Besides That of *Aristotle*, "wherein it signifies the Heat and Pain caused by "Wine, taken to excess, it is capable of two more, "at least; according to one of which, it is taken for "an Excess of eating; and, according to the other, "for the Pleasure itself of eating and drinking. "St *Augustin* did not use it in the first Sense; for "he was as far from eating, as from drinking, to "excess. So, then, he could only understand it "in the second Sense, and confess, that, though "he endeavoured to be continually on his Guard "against the Temptation of Pleasure, which places "itself, as it were, in Ambuscade, at the Entrance "of the Aliments, necessary to allay Hunger and "Thirst, and to maintain Health; yet he sometimes "suffered himself to be surprized by it. This Sur- "prize happens to the most perfect, to Those, who "mortify their Bodies, and nourish them only with "Fastings and Abstinence." Mr *Ceasa* confirms this, by producing several Testimonies of *Possidius*, concerning St *Augustin*'s Sobriety. I think he would have done well to have given good Authority for the two Significations of the Word Crapula, which he has added to That, so well proved by Mr *Petit*. It

Editions of St *Augustin*'s Works [*K*]. Several of his Treatises have been translated into *French*.

It belongs to my Readers to decide this Dispute: I content my self with giving them the Arguments on both Sides. I shall only add, that I have consulted several Dictionaries, without being able to find there the least Appearance of the Signification, in which the Word *Crapula* will have the Word *Crapula* used in this Place. I have even met with some Physicians, who maintain, that Drunkenness and *Crapula* signify the same thing; and that *They, who pretend to make any Difference between them, raise idle Contentions about Words. Qui differentiam inter Crapulam & Ebrietatem fingunt λογομαχᾶσι. Fœs. pag.* 353. *Dist. num.* 475 (42). It is certain, that, in *Cicero*, the Phrases *Crapulam edormire, Crapulam exhalare,* mean the same thing as the *French* Words *cuver son vin* (43), i. e. *to sleep one's self sober. Plautus* uses, in the same Sense, *Crapulam amovere* (44), *Crapulam edormire* (45), *Crapulam edormiscere* (46). It is also well known, that, at this present time, the *French* Word *Crapula* is more odious than That of *Ivresse, Drunkenness*; for it signifies the highest Degree of Drunkenness. It is, as *Furetiere* observes, *a shameful and continual Debauch with Wine, or other intoxicating Liquors. Crapuler,* adds he, *means, to drink without ceasing, to be continually, and filthily, drunk.* The Dictionary of the *French* Academy confirms these Interpretations. But there is no consequence to be drawn from one Age to another, as to the Sense of Words. Use makes it vary prodigiously. There was certainly a Distinction between Drunkenness and *Crapula,* both in *Aristotle*'s, and *St Augustin*'s Time. This appears clearer from The Passage of the Father of the Church, than from That of the Philosopher. The Question is, to know wherein this Difference consisted, in the Time of *St Augustin*. Without doubt, if Mr *Petit* had replied to Mr *Cousin* (47), he would have shewn a great deal of Learning, and I believe would not have forgot, that Authors, who, like *Aristotle,* treat a Subject dogmatically, confine themselves very strictly to Genus and Species, and observe the Propriety of Terms, designed to signify the Distinction of each Species, or the different Degrees of one and the same Quality; but Poets and Orators soon lay aside This Exactness: they either introduce, themselves, a greater Liberty of Words, or else conform to That established by public Custom, which uses, indifferently, on a thousand Occasions, Those Expressions which the Doctors so nicely distinguish.

[*K*] *I shall not say much of the Editions of St Augustin's Works.*] We meet with a List of them in Mr *du Pin* (48), which is neither so large, nor so exact, as That published by the Journalists of *Leipsic* (49). But, since it is very easy to consult Those Authors, it would be superfluous to copy them here. I shall only say, that the best Edition of This Father's Works is That printed at *Paris*, by the Care of the *Benedictine* Monks of *St Maur*. It is divided into ten Volumes in Folio, as some others are: but there is a new Order, or Disposition, in each Tome. The Ist, and IId, were published in the Year 1679, the IIId, in 1680, the IVth, in 1681, the Vth, in 1683, the VIth, and VIIth, in 1685, the VIIIth, and IXth, in 1688, and the Xth, in 1693. This last Volume contains the Writings of *St Augustin* against the *Pelagians*.

There came out, *A Letter from the Abbot* ** *to the R R F F. Benedictines of the Congregation of St Maur, on the last Tome of their Edition of St Augustin* (50). The Author of This Letter pretends, that their Design was to favour *Jansenism*, and that the Proofs he gives of it are very convincing. I have heard, that This Letter perplexes the *Benedictines* so much the more, because it has made some Bishops call them to an Account for their Conduct, and threaten to forbid the Reading of This Edition of *St Augustin* in their Dioceses.

These learned Fathers have given an Explanation of this Matter, and cleared themselves to the Public from this Aspersion. See the Letter of a Divine to one of his Friends, on the Libel, entitled, *A Letter of the Abbot* **** *&c.* It was printed the Twenty second of *February,* 1699, and contains Eighty eight Pages in 12mo; but it did not determine the Dispute. There came out a Memorial of a Doctor of Divinity, addressed to My Lords, the Prelates of France, on the Answer of a Benedictine Divine to the Letter from a German Abbot (51), and the Author of This Memorial maintains, That all the Accusation of the *Benedictines* is just, and that the Answer of Those Fathers is insufficient. He takes notice (52), that they sent from *Rouen* to *Paris* a second Answer to the *German* Abbot, and that Father *de St Marthe* was very ready to father it. The *Benedictines* replied; but could not silence their Adversaries. Some other Writings were published *pro* and *con*; but I cannot give the Particulars, because I have met with but few of them: I have seen a little Book, called, *The Conduct of the Benedictines on the attacking of their Edition of St Augustin*. It contains Seventy nine Pages in 12mo, and was printed in the Year 1699. Among other things, we are told there, I. That, before they had published any thing in their own Defence, *a Writing was addressed to them from an unknown Person — who took care to disperse it all over Paris, before be sent them any Copy* (53). II. That The Title of this Piece was, *A Letter from a Commendatory Abbot, to the Reverend Fathers, the Benedictines of the Congregation of St Maur.* III. That, as the Letter, which the *German* Abbot wrote against these Fathers, was called, *The German Benedictine,* they called This, *The Little Benedictine*; and all the World owned, that the younger was not inferior to the elder. IV. *That the Author, from the beginning to the end, only personated, and spoke the Language of the Jansenists, in order to be the better understood by the B B* (54). V. That *The Little Benedictine* exasperated, and stirred up the Party; who, from that Moment, resolved to defend the new *Augustin*, and that the Abbot *du Guet* went to the Abbey to offer his Pen to the Congregation of *St Maur* (55). VI. That *The Little Benedictine* had not long made it's Appearance, before another smaller, and more agreeable one, came out, on a sudden (56), entitled, *The Letter of a Benedictine, not reformed, to the Reverend Fathers, the Benedictines of the Congregation of St Maur,* and came from the same Hand as the *Little Benedictine*. VII. That the *Benedictines* were deliberating, when *a fourth Benedictine appeared, which was so serious, as to make one believe, that it was really produced in a Cloister.* It's Title was, *A Letter of a reformed Benedictine of St Dennis, in answer to the German Abbot, the Commendatory Abbot, and the Benedictine not Reformed* (57). VIII. That the first Answer of the *Benedictines* came from *St Dennis,* and was attributed, by all the World, to Father *Lamy*: It is entituled, *A Letter from a Divine to one of his Friends, on the Libel, called, A Letter from the Abbot* *** *to the Reverend F. F. the Benedictines, &c* (58). IX. That there appeared another Answer, unexpected, which Father *St Marthe* bragged he had written in less than two Days: the Title of it is, *Reflexions on the Letter from a German Abbot* (59). X. That it is universally agreed, that the best thing, which has been wrote on the Affair of This Edition, is That, entitled, *A Memorial of a Doctor of Divinity, addressed to my Lords, the Prelates of France, on the Answer of a Divine among the Benedictines, to a Letter from the German Abbot* (60). XI. That a Man, more learned, than polite, handed about a Manuscript against Father *St Marthe,* and called it, *St Marthe a bad Divine, and a good Jansenist* (61); That the Manuscript of This learned Man was followed by another Manuscript of some melancholy Author of a very bad Taste, entituled, *Antimony, by way of Preservation against the Calumnies of Father St Marthe* (62); and that This last Manuscript was succeeded by another attributed to a Jesuit: it is called, *Vindiciæ Petavii* (63). XII That, in the Book entituled, *A Solution of divers Problems,* and ascribed to Mr *du Guet,* the *Jansenists* undertake the Defence of the *Benedictines* with an high Hand (64). XIII. That there appeared a third Answer of the *Benedictines* (65), called *Vindiciæ Editionis S. Augustini à P P.B B. adornatæ*; which preceeded most of these Writings I have been naming, and that it is little more than a Translation of Father *Lamy*'s Answer, and is publish'd under a borrowed Name, *&c.* (66).

I have

I have also seen a Piece attributed to Lamy; 'Tis a Complaint of the Apologist for the Benedictines, to the Prelates of France, on the Defamatory Libels, which are dispersed against That Religious Society, and their Edition of St Augustin; together with a Summons to the Authors of Those Libels to appear before the Archbishop of Paris; and on account of the Process, which was entered against the Benedictines, on their Edition of St Augustin. All this contains Eighty eight Pages in 8vo. The Author, having demanded of the Prelates the Punishment of their Adversaries, takes notice that *The Difficulty* — *is to find out those unquiet and seditious Spirits, who have attacked the Benedictines* (67). *It is not so great as may be imagined*, adds he; *it is true, they take care not to set their Names to their Libels: But the R. R. F. F. the Jesuits take so much pains to claim the Merit of them, and discover themselves by other means, in so many places of these seditious Writings, that they cannot possibly be mistaken, unless People take a Pleasure in deceiving themselves.* He, then, proposes his Conjectures, and, after some general Considerations, he gives *something more particular and decisive* (68). " And now, says he, as to the Letter of the German " Abbot, if these Fathers had not discovered them- " selves by their Air, Voice, Accent, Principles, " and Doctrine, yet it is a Fact, which no Body, at " this time of day, contests, or denies, that Father " Langlois, a Jesuit of the College of Lewis le Grand, " is the Author of it: and certainly That good Fa- " ther could not expect, that the World should be " ignorant of it, since the Book was sold public- " ly enough, even in the College. As for the " other Libels, such as the Letter of the Commen- " datory Abbot, and That of the Monk not Reformed, " besides our knowing, that they made Presents of " them every where, and raised Trophies in them to " their pretended Victories; how many times have " they, there, taken the Pleasure to characterize, " name, and declare themselves to be our Adver- " saries. It is proper, my Lords, to let you see in " what Shapes and Colours they shew themselves : " I shall use their own Words ; Consider, says one " in these Letters, what the Jesuits do: They, whom " you may suspect to be your Adversaries. Take them " for your Model in this Matter. They answer every " thing." After having made a Collection of a great many more Characters, he goes on thus ; " I think, " from all these Descriptions, it cannot be doubt- " ed, but that they are Jesuits: But it will be " said, they are only a small number of particular " Persons. I grant it: We know they must be only " some particular Persons; for a whole Society was " never yet known to have, all of them, a Hand " in the Writing of one and the same Letter. But " is there not some reason to attribute These Writings " to a whole Body, when That Body generally speaks " and talks of them with Pleasure and Approbation? " Nay, when they boast of, and distribute them by " way of Presents, and in a triumphing Manner, as " all the World knows the Jesuits have often done " in respect to These Letters. In a word, my Lords, " how scandalous soever the Writings of any parti- " cular Persons of a Society may be, there is ground " to attribute them to the whole Society, when the " Superiors take no care to suppress them; or, if " That be not in their Power, when they do not " shew by some public Act, that they disapprove " them; or when they do not make a Reparation " to the Parties offended, as notorious and public " as the Injuries and Calumnies have been. It is " by this Rule, that the scandalous Piece called, *The* " *Comedy of the Monks*, has been always looked upon " as a Work of the Society of the Jesuits; in which " almost all the Religious are treated with an Indig- " nity and Derision, which would hardly be par- " doned in the most furious Heretic. It has been, " I say, justly attributed to the whole Body, altho' " composed and acted by their young Scholars; be- " cause it doth not appear, that the Superiors ever " made any Satisfaction for it, or any just Amends " (69)." After this he shews, that it belongs to the Archbishop of *Paris* to determine this Difference (70); and he summons his Adversaries to appear personally at That Tribunal, *and to prove their several Accusations, on pain, if they fail in any of them, of being condemned as Slanderers, and their Libels judged Defamatory* But, not to give them an opportunity of abusing This Citation, as too loose and uncertain for want of a Time prefixed, and yet not to be too pressing upon them, we give them two Months from the Day that our Citation shall be published at Paris (71). Lastly, he shews, what the State of the Question is; and afterwards, in the drawing up of the Process, he refutes several Things published against the Benedictines.

I dare say, that the Archbishop of *Paris*, and even a National Council, would be puzzled in the Determination of such a Cause as This is; for, besides the Questions of *Jansenism* being full of Equivocations, Two powerful, and very learned Communities, who have each their Friends and Enemies, can cut out work enough, and start Incidents to Eternity. The best Expedient, when such Disputes are on foot, is to have recourse to the Secular Power, as to a God in a Machine, who may come, and cut the Knot. This is what has happened in This Dispute. The King ordered the Chancellor to write a Letter to the Archbishop of *Paris*, to put a Stop to This Controversy, and to forbid the Parties to publish any Thing farther about it (72). But, be this as it will, it must be said of the *Benedictines*, that they took the most reasonable Method of all, as well to shew their own Integrity, as to stop the Course of the Libels. They demanded a regular Proceeding, where their Accusers should be obliged to declare their Names, and to prove their Accusations according to Law. Without this no good issue can be expected; for, even in the worst Causes, They, who have the liberty to plead only at the Tribunal of the Public, by anonymous Pamphlets, find it always in their Power to be haughty, insulting, and clamorous, whilst there are Writers and Printers A Private Man, whether he be in the right, or the wrong, is soon silenced, if his Pieces do not sell; he cannot go on with them, without being at the charge of the Press, which is beyond his Abilities. But this Inconveniency can never affect such rich and powerful Communities, as Those of the *Benedictines*, and Jesuits.

They are going to print This Edition at *Amsterdam*, in a smaller Character, which will be sold much cheaper than That of Paris (73). There was a design to print with it the Critical Notes of a learned Map, who conceals himself under the Name of *Joannes Pherecponus* (74); but I understand since, that the design is altered, and that Those Critical Notes will be printed separately, with the Commentary of *Ludovicus Vives*, on the Work *de Civitate Dei*, &c. There was some reason to fear, that the *Roman* Catholics would be displeased with it; and therefore they will be left at full Liberty to buy, or leave These suspected Notes. They will be in a separate Volume, and all *St Augustin's* Work, exactly conformable to the Edition of *Paris*, will be sold either with or without them.

AULNOI (MARIA CATHERINA LE JUMEL DE BERNEVILLE Countess d') so famed for her Writings [*A*], was the Wife of *Francis de la Motte*, Count d' *Aulnoi*. She died his Widow in the Month of *January* 1705. Her Mother, whose second Husband was the Marquis *de Gadaigne*, died at *Madrid*, where she enjoyed a considerable Pension, which King *Charles* II. had given her, for the great Service she had done That Nation, while she was at *Rome*. *Philip* V. continued this Pension. The Countess d'*Aulnoi* left four Daughters (a).

[*A*] *She is famed for her Writings.*] The first, she published, is entituled *A Journey into Spain*. She went thither with the Queen of *Spain*, the first Wife of *Charles* II. Her other Works are, *Memoirs of the Court of Spain*, which has had three Editions in *France*, and one in *Holland* ; *Memoirs of the Court of England* ; *Hippolito*, *Earl of Douglas* ; *The History of John de Bourbon*, *Prince de Carency* ; *The Earl of Warwick*. These are so many little Romances, which have been universally read. She has also published several *Tales of the Fairies*, and a Paraphrase on the *Miserere* (1).

AURAT,

AURAT. AURELIANUS.

AURAT, or **D'AURAT** (JOHN) in Latin *Auratus*. See DAURAT.

AURELIANUS (LUCIUS DOMITIUS) *(a)*, Emperor of *Rome* in the IIId Century, was one of the greatest Warriours of Antiquity. It is not certain where he was born [*A*]; but it is agreed, that his Extraction was very mean, and that his Mother, who made it her Business to foretel Events, was a Priestess of the Sun *(b)*. He was of a good Stature, handsome, robust, and of a very lively Genius *(c)*. He loved Action, Wine, and good Chear *(d)*; but not Women *(e)*: He observed Discipline exactly, and caused others to observe it with the utmost Severity [*B*]. One Thing was observed in him: he continued poor amidst the very great number of Offices

(a) The Emperor Claudius, writing to him, calls him only Valerius Aurelianus. Vopiscus in Aurel. cap. 17.
(b) Id. ibid.
(c) Id. cap. 46.
(d) Id. c. 4.
(e) Id. c. 6.

[*A*] *It is not certain where he was born*] *Vopiscus*, having related three Opinions (1), adds, *That it usually happens, that the native Place of Persons, meanly born, is uncertain*. He gives this reason for it: *Because they generally tell a lie on that occasion, and adopt some Place of greater Note, which they pretend to be That of their Birth, in order to recommend themselves to Posterity, in a brighter Light, by the Splendor of the Place of their Nativity. Eventi quidem ut de eorum virorum genitali solo nesciatur qui humiliori loco nati, plerique solum genitale confingunt, ut dent posteritati de locorum splendore fulgorem* (2). I believe there is another Cause, which contributes yet more to it; I mean the number of the Places, which contend for the Honour of producing famous Persons. They take the Advantage of the uncertainty of the Fact, and, hoping never to be effectually disproved, They vainly, and without any grounds, report, that They are born in such and such a Place. From hence came the Disputes about *Homer's* Country. I grant, with *Vopiscus*, that our principal Inquiry into the Characters of great Princes, is not to know where they were born, but how they have governed: *Nec tamen magnorum principum virtutibus summa scienda est, ubi quisque sit genitus, sed qualis in republ. fuerit*. Nevertheless, as we are naturally very inquisitive to know the time and place of the Birth of Great Men, I think an Historian is obliged to make all possible inquiry to satisfy his Readers in This Point; and that they have a right to complain of the Negligence of a great number of Writers, who have been wanting in this Particular (3).

[*B*] *He observed Discipline exactly, and caused others to observe it, with the utmost Severity*] We may add, that he had the good Fortune to see, that This Severity did not make the Soldiers mutinous, but only fearful of neglecting their Duty. Without doubt it was good Fortune; for sometimes Generals have as much reason to fear the Consequences of too great a Severity, as those of too great Lenity. *Aurelian* found it very right, to punish rigorously, and without remission. " *Militibus ita timori fuit, ut sub eo postequam semel cum ingenti severitate caftrensia peccata correxit, nemo peccaverit. Solus denique omnium militem, qui adulterium cum hospitis uxore commiserat, ita punivit, ut duarum arborum capita inflecteret, & ad pedes militis deligaret, eademque subito dimitteret, ut scissus ille utrinque penderet. Quæ res ingentem timorem omnibus fecit* (4). — *He was so much feared by the Soldiers, that, whosoever of them once felt the great Severity of his Correction, for breach of Orders, never offended again. He was, in short, the only Commander, who ever punished so terribly the Crime of Adultery, committed, by a Soldier, with the Wife of the Person, upon whom he was quartered: The Tops of two Trees were bent down to each other by Violence, and, being fastened to the Feet of the Criminal, were let go again, and so tore him in halves. This struck them all with very great Terror.*" You see, by this Quotation, he used the same sort of Punishment in the Case of a Soldier's committing Adultery with the Wife of his Host, that *Alexander* inflicted on the Traitor *Bessus*, who killed King *Darius*. Nothing can be finer, than *Aurelian's* Orders, concerning the Soldiers Duty. St *John Baptist* could not have laid them under a greater Number of Restrictions, had he been ever so particular (5). *Aurelian* would not suffer them to touch any Fruit, nor to take of the People any Salt, Wood, or Oil, nor to transgress the Rules of Chastity. Would not one think, that he had a Design to introduce the Monastic Discipline into the Army?" *Hujus epistola militaris est ad vicarium suum data hujusmodi: Si*

(1) *Ortus, ut plures loquuntur, humili, familia obscuriori; ut nonnulli Dacia Ripensi. Ego autem legisse memini auctorem qui eum Mæsia genitum prædiceret. Most say he was born at Sirmium, of an obscure Family; some in Dacia Ripensis. And I remember to have read an Author, who declares, he was born in Mæsia.* Vopiscus in Aurel. c. 3.
(2) Id. ib.
(3) *See Remark [A] of the Article* ROTTERDAM.
(4) Vopisc. in Aurel. cap. 7. pag. 434.
(5) Luke iii. 14.

" *vis tribunus esse, imò si vis vivere, manus militum contine. Nemo pullum alienum rapiat, ovem nemo contingat, Uvam nullus auferat, segetem nemo deterat: oleum, sal, lignum, nemo exigat: annona sua contentus sit. De præda hostis, non de lacrymis provincialium, habeat: arma tersa sint: ferramenta lamiata — alter alteri quasi servus obsequatur: à medicis gratis curentur; aruspicibus nihil dent: in hospitiis caste agant; qui litem fecerit, vapulet* (6). — He wrote thus to his Lieutenant. *If you would continue your command, or even your Life, keep strict Discipline among the Soldiers. Let not one of them steal a Chicken, touch an Egg, pluck a Grape, or damage the standing Corn; or make any Exactions of Oil, Salt, or Wood, but make every man content himself with his Allowance. Reward them by the Spoil of our Enemies, but not by the Tears of our Friends and Subjects: Let their Arms be clean; their Swords and Spears sharp; — let them serve one another; let the Physicians attend the sick and wounded, gratis; let the Priests take nothing of them for their Sacrifices; let them live chastly in their Quarters; and let Him, who breeds Quarrels, run the Gantlope.*" He was so rigid, that the Emperor *Valerian*, who had a singular Esteem for him, durst not put his Son under his Direction, for fear That young Prince, who was inclined to be wild, should too far experience the Austerity of such a Master: For which reason, he chose for him a more gentle Governor. Read the Answer he gave to the Consul *Antoninus Gallus*, who would have That Office conferred on *Aurelian*? " *Culpas me familiaribus literis quod Posthumio filium meum Gallienum magis quam Aureliano commiserim: quum utique & secerioi & puer credendus fuerit & exercitus: nec tu id diutius judicabis, si bene scieris quanta fit Aureliani severitatis. Nimius est, multus est, gravis est, & ad nostra jam non facit tempora. Testor autem omnes deos, me etiam timuisse nequid etiam erga filium meum severius, siquid ille fecisset, ut est natura pronus ad ludicra, sævius cogitaret. Hæc epistola indicat quantæ fuerit severitatis, ut illum Valeriani etiam timuisse se dicat* (7). — *You blame me, in your Letters, for chusing to put my Son. Gallienus under Posthumius, rather than under Aurelian; when the Youth, as well as the Army, requires his Severity of Discipline; but you would be no longer of This Opinion, if you knew but Aurelian's extreme Rigour. His Punishments are too frequent, too great, and heavy, and no way proportioned to the Usage of these Times. And I call the Gods to witness, I am afraid he should execute some dreadful Sentence, even upon my Son, if he should misbehave, as he is naturally idle.* This Epistle shews he was so extremely severe, that *Valerian* himself was even afraid of him.*" We must not forget *Aurelian's* Strictness to his Domestics. *"He caused those, who had neglected their Duty, to be whipt in his Presence; and be delivered up several of his own Servants to public Justice, to have them punished for their Faults. He caused one of his Maid Servants to be put to Death, for committing Adultery with one of his Lacqueys.* — *Servos & ministros peccantes coram se cædi jubebat, se plerique dicunt, causa tenendæ severitatis: ut alii, studio crudelitatis. Ancillam suam, quæ adulterium cum servo suo fecerat, capite punivit. Multos servos è famila propria, qui peccaverant, legibus audiendos judicio publicis dedit* (8)." *Most ascribe all this to his strict Method of Discipline; but some, to the natural Cruelty of his Temper. Valerian* was in the right to say, that such a Man was too severe for the Age he lived in. *Ad nostra jam non facit Tempora!*

(6) Vopisc. in Aurel. cap. 7. pag. 434. & 440.
(7) Id. ib. cap. 8. pag. 438, 440.
(8) Id. ib. cap. 4. pag. 583.

AURELIAN.

Offices, which were conferred upon him [C]. He had so strong an Inclination to draw his Sword, that the Soldiers gave him the Sirname of *Sword in hand*, to distinguish him from a Captain of the same Name [D]. He made such a Slaughter in Combats, that he killed Forty eight *Sarmatians* in one day; and the number *Thousand* was made use of to count the mortal Blows, which he had given the Enemy (*f*). This became the Subject of Songs and Ballads (*g*); he received from these the same Honours, as the first King of the *Jews* (*h*), and deserved it much better: For it was not pretended, that *Saul* killed, with his own hand, the Thousand Enemies, whose Slaughter was ascribed to him in the Songs; but This was literally understood of *Aurelian*. He was adopted by *Ulpius Crinitus*, one of the greatest Men of those Times (*i*): The Emperor *Valerian*, who managed That Affair (*k*), made him Lieutenant to the same *Crinitus* (*l*), who was General of the Frontiers of *Illyricum* and *Thracia* (*m*), and appointed him Consul in the Year 258. These Rewards, and some others, were rendred yet infinitely more agreeable, by the Encomiums and particular Marks of Esteem, with which the Emperor conferred them [E]. We

---

[*f*] Vopisc. ibid. cap 6.
[*g*] Id. ib. & cap. 7.
[*h*] 1 Sam. xviii. 7.
[*i*] Vopisc. in Aurel. cap. 14.
[*k*] Id. ib. cap. 15.
[*l*] Ibid. cap. 10.
[*m*] Ib. cap. 13.

[A] He was only fit for the Sect of the Montanists. The Christians of the succeeding Ages would have found him too rigorous; and how many Casuists, at this Day, would say of his Morals, as they do of Those of the Fathers, that they are too strict, and that This bitter and rough Physic does not agree with our Sick? What military Men, or even grave Citizens, think it worth while to punish the Familiarities of their Men and Maids? The general Punishment, for their Faults of this Nature, is to turn them away. Nay, sometimes Masters are so kind, as to marry them to each other. Observe, that History mentions but one of *Aurelian's* Servants, who was punished for her Lasciviousness. It is a Sign, that such Transgressions were very rare in his Family, which is a Matter of wonder, considering what we see every Day, and that a General, or an Emperor, must necessarily have a great many Slaves of both Sexes.

[C] *He continued poor, amidst the very great Number of Offices, which were conferred upon him* (10).] The Emperor, his Master, testified This Virtue, when he charged the Public with the Expence, which the Consulate, he promised *Aurelian*, would require. "Consulatum cum eodem Ulpio Crinito in annum "sequentem a die undecimo Calend. Juniarum, in "locum Gallieni & Valeriani, sperare te convenit "sumptu publico. Levanda est enim paupertas eorum hominum, qui diu reipublicae viventes, pauperes sunt, & nullorum magis (11). — *You may expect the Consulship, together with* Ulpius Crinitus, *for the next Year, from the* XI *of the Cal. of* June, *in the Room of* Gallienus *and* Valerianus, *and that your Expences shall be born by the Public. For no sort of Poor deserve That Regard so much, as Those, who have long served the Public, and yet are poor.*" The Historian, who furnishes this Passage, produces the Letter, which the Emperor wrote to him his Pleasure, as to what should be given to the new Consul. "Aureliano, cui consulatum detulimus ob PAUPERTATEM, qua illi magnus est caeteris major, dabis ad editionem Circensium aureos Antonianos trecentos, &c. (12). — "To *Aurelian, whom we have made Consul on account of his POVERTY, which makes That great Man still greater, you are to present Three hundred pieces of Gold, of Antoninus's Coin, for his Expence in exhibiting the Circensian Shows.*" Some have said, that "*the Poverty of* Aurelian *obliged* Valerian *to order* Ulpius Crinitus *to adopt him.* "Memini me in quodam libro Graeco legisse — Mandatum esse Crinito a Valeriano, ut Aurelianus adoptaretur, idcirco praecipue quod pauper esset (13)." It is remarkable, that, when he was Emperor, he used a great deal of Moderation in doing good to his Friends: Perhaps, from his long Habit of contemning Wealth, and the Opinion he had, that moderate Riches were sufficient for a great Man: Perhaps, also, because he would not irritate the People by excessive Profusions; for Subjects are not pleased to see their Prince bestow his Treasures and Favours on his Friends, in an extravagant manner. *Vopiscus* tells us, That "*this Emperor chose to observe a Medium, which should take away the Inconveniencies of Poverty, without substituting Those of Envy.* "Amicos suos honeste ditavit & modice, ut miserias "paupertatis effugerent, & divitiarum invidiam pa-

"trimonii moderatione vitarent (14)." He adds, That "*he would not suffer any Person to wear Silk Cloaths, of which he gave them an Example, and subjected his own Wife to This Law; for, when she desired, at least, one Silk Suit, he answered her, God forbid, that Thread should cost as much as Gold. For, at that time, a Pound of Silk was worth a Pound of Gold.* — Vestem holosericam neque ipse in vestiario suo habuit, neque alteri utendam dedit. Et quum ab eo uxor sua peteret, ut unico pallio blatteo serico uteretur, ille respondit, *Absit ut auro fila pensentur*: libra enim auri tunc libra serici fuit (15)." See Mr *de Tillemont*, who has observed the little Agreement between This Fact, and certain things reported by the same Historian, or others, concerning This Emperor's Luxury (16). But we must not forget, that the Cloaths of his Domestics were no richer, after his Advancement to the Throne, than before (17); and that he granted the Senators the Liberty of wearing the same Habit with himself (18).

[D] *The Soldiers gave him the Sirname of* Sword in Hand, *to distinguish him from a Captain of the same Name.*] What a proper Distinction is This to flatter the Pride of a brave Warriour? I shall relate the Words of *Vopiscus*: "Gladii exerendi cupidus. "Nam quum essent in exercitu duo Aureliani tribuni, hic, & alius qui cum Valeriano captus est, huic signum exercitus apposuerat *manus ad ferrum*, ut si forte quaereretur quis Aurelianus aliquid vel fecisset vel gessisset, suggereretur, *Aurelianus manu ad ferrum*, atque cognosceretur (19). — *Remarkably fond of drawing his Sword. For there being in the Army two Tribunes, both named* Aurelian, *this, and another, who was taken Prisoner with* Valerian, *the Soldiers called him* Sword in Hand, *by way of Distinction: so that, when it was asked, which* Aurelian *had done any thing, the Answer, which meant him was,* Aurelian Sword in ' Hand."

[E] *The Emperor conferred them with Encomiums, and particular Marks of Esteem.*] I am going to relate them; for they contain the considerable Services, which *Aurelian* had done to the Empire. "Valerianus Augustus Celonio Albino praefecto urbi. Vellemus quidem singulis quibusque devotissimis Reipub. viris multo majora deferre compendia, quam eorum dignitas postulat, maxime ubi honorem vita commendat. Debet enim quid praeter dignitatem pretium esse meritorum. Sed facit rigor publicus, ut accipere de provinciarum oblationibus ultra ordinis sui gradum nemo plus possit. Aurelianum fortissimum virum ad inspiciendа & ordinanda castra omnia destinavimus: cui tantum inesse laboris, quae ab omni Republica, communi totius exercitus confessione, debetur, ut digna illi vix aliqua vel nimis magna sunt munera. Quid enim in illo non clarum? quid non Corvinis & Scipionibus conferendum? Ille Liberator Illyrici, ille Galliarum Restitutor, ille dux magni totius exempli. Et tamen nihil possumus addere tanto viro ad muneris gratiam quam patriae sobria & bene gerenda Respub. Quare sinceritas tua, mi parens charissime, supradicto viro efficiet, quandiu Romae fuerit, panes militares mundos sedecim, &c. (20) "Valerianus Caesar, *to* Ceionius Albinus, *Prefect of the City. It is our Desire to distinguish those, who*

[9] Id. ib. pag. 439.
[10] See the List of them in Vopiscus, cap. 10.
[11] Id. Ib. c. 2, pag. 445.
[12] Ibid. cap. 12.
[13] Ibid. cap. 15.
[14] Ibid. cap. 45. pag. 553.
[15] Id. ib. pag. 540.
[16] Tillemont. Hist. des Emper. Tom. 3. p. 1074, 1075.
[17] Vopisc. in Aurel. cap. 1.
[18] Ibid. cap. 49.
[19] Id. Ib. cap. 6, pag. 426.
[20] Id. ib. c. 9, p. 440.

VOL. I. 7 E

572 AURELIAN.

We do not find, that *Aurelian* made any Figure under the Emperor *Gallienus*; but, under *Claudius*, he held the principal Posts, and commanded the Army with so much Glory, that, after the Death of That Emperor, all the Legions concurred to set him on the Throne (*n*). This happened in the Year 270. A little while after, he came to *Rome*, and, after establishing his Authority, he marched towards *Pannonia*, where the *Goths* had made an Irruption (*o*). He gave them Battle, and obliged them to repass the *Danube*, and to desire a Peace. After this, being informed, that the *Marcomans*, the *Juthungi* (*p*), and some other Nations, had resolved to carry the War into *Italy*, he marched against them, and overthrew them in a general Engagement, near the *Danube*. He killed many of them, as they repassed That River, and hindred the rest from returning into their Country, by shutting them up in the *Roman* Dominions. The want of Provisions, and many other Inconveniencies, which obliged them to desire a Peace of him, did not inspire them with such a Submission, as he expected. Their Deputies assumed so high an Air, that he dismissed them very haughtily; for, imagining he had cut off the Retreat of their Army, he concluded they could not escape him. But he was mistaken: The Enemy disengaged themselves, and, marching before him, entered into *Italy*, where they made great Ravages round about *Milan*. He could not follow them with Speed enough; for his Army was heavier than theirs. They defeated him by Surprize near *Placentia* (*q*), and, if they had understood the Military Art, as well as he, they might have ruined the Empire after such a Victory; but, as they knew not how to make use of their Advantage, and did not march close, he defeated them in several Rencounters, and reduced them to nothing (*r*). During This War, the Books of the *Sibyls* were consulted at *Rome*: I shall mention some Circumstances of it, which shew the Religion of *Aurelian*, and the Irreligion of his Flatterers [F]. It is likely he pursued the Enemy as far as *Germany*, where he was obliged to stop some time to repulse the *Vandals*, who had passed the *Danube*. He defeated them, and forced them to beg a Peace, which he was very willing to grant them (*s*). He returned to *Rome* full of Resentment, for the Seditions, which had been raised there, and punished them with extreme Cruelty (*t*). This was his predominant Vice; and it was for the sake of this, that many have refused to rank him

---

" *who have deserved well of the Commonwealth,*
" *with greater Rewards, than are suitable to their*
" *Rank, especially where their whole Life will justify*
" *their Distinction. For, besides what is due to their*
" *Station, there is also something due to their extraor-*
" *dinary Merit. But the public Exactness requires,*
" *that none should receive, out of the Revenues of the*
" *Provinces, any more than is allotted to the Degree*
" *of his Dignity. We have appointed That brave Man,*
" *Aurelian, to inspect and direct our Incampments,*
" *to whom both we, and the Commonwealth, are so*
" *greatly indebted, that no Rewards can be thought*
" *too great, or even worthy, of him. What has he*
" *not performed? What could the Corvini and Scipio's*
" *have done more? He is the Protector of Illyricum,*
" *the Restorer of the Gallia's, a General, great in*
" *every Action. And yet we can assign to so extraor-*
" *dinary a Man no other publick Reward, than the*
" *frugal and regular Administration of the Common-*
" *wealth allows. Be it your Care, therefore, my beloved*
" *Cousin, to furnish him, during his stay at Rome, with*
" *sixteen fine military Loaves, &c*." *Valerian* wrote thus to the Prefect of *Rome*: and here follows part of his Letter to *Aurelian*: " *Ego de te tantum,*
" *Deo favente, spero quantum de Trajano, si vive-*
" *ret, posset sperare Respub. Neque enim minor*
" *est* (21), *in cujus locum fidemque te legi. Con-*
" *sultatum cum eodem Ulpio Crinito in annum se-*
" *quentem à die undecimo Calend. Juniarum, in lo-*
" *cum Gallieni & Valeriani, sperare te convenit*
" *sumptu publico.* ——— *I hope for as great things*
" *from you, under the Favour of Heaven, as the*
" *Commonwealth might have expected from Trajan,*
" *had he lived. Nor is He an unfit Match for you, to*
" *whom, both in Office and Friendship, I have de-*
" *signed you for a Partner You may expect, there-*
" *fore, the Consulship, together with* Ulpius Crinitus,
" *for the next Year, from the XI of the Cal. of* June,
" *and your Charges shall be born by the Public.*"
Here is also the Speech, which *Valerian* made to him, in the Presence of the Army, and the Court: " *Gra-*
" *tias tibi agit, Aureliane, Resp. quod eam Gotho-*
" *rum potestate liberasti. Abundamus per te præda,*
" *abundamus gloria, & his omnibus quibus Romana*
" *felicitas crescit. Cape igitur tibi pro rebus gestis*
" *tuis coronas murales quatuor, coronas vallares quin-*
" *que, coronas navales duas, coronas civicas duas,*
" *hastas puras decem, vexilla bicolora quatuor, tu-*
" *nicas ducales russas quatuor, pallia proconsularia*
" *duo, togam prætextam, tunicam palmatam, to-*
" *gam pictam, tunicam profundum, sellam ebo-*
" *ratam. Nam te consulem hodie designo, scrip-*
" *turus ad senatum, ut tibi deputet scipionem, de-*
" *putet etiam fasces. Hæc enim imperator non so-*
" *let dare, sed à senatu, quando fit consul, accipere*
" (22). ——— *The Commonwealth returns you thanks,*
" *Aurelian, for freeing her from the Insults of the*
" *Goths. By your Victories we abound in Spoil,*
" *we abound in Glory, and in every thing else, which*
" *can contribute to the Prosperity of Rome. Accept,*
" *therefore, for your great Services, four Moral*
" *Crowns, five Rampire Crowns, two Naval Crowns,*
" *two Civic Crowns, ten polish'd Spears, four Stan-*
" *dards of two Colours, four military Buff Suits,*
" *two Proconsular Cloaks, and the Robe of State,*
" *the Robe embroidered with Palms, the rich Trium-*
" *phal Robe, a Suit to wear under Armour, and the*
" *Ivory Chair. For I this Day appoint you Consul,*
" *and will write to the Senate to send you the Staff*
" *and Fasces, the Insignia of your Office: which are*
" *never given by the Emperor, but always by the Se-*
" *nate, to the new Magistrate.*"
The first, of these three Passages of *Vopiscus*, contains one thing well worth Observation, and which does not at all agree with our common Notions of the Disorders of the Empire. We fancy, that, after the Soldiers took upon them to create, and kill, their Emperors, there was nothing but Oppression, and Tyranny, in the *Roman* Provinces. This was not always true: we see here, that *Valerian* managed the public Expences, in Ease to the Provinces, with more Precaution, than is this Day used in Christian Kingdoms.

[F] *Some Circumstances, which shew the Religion of* Aurelian, *and the Irreligion of his Flatterers.*] The Consternation was very great in *Rome*, upon hearing, that the *Marcomans* were entered into *Italy*, and made great Ravages there [23]. Some Seditions followed upon it, which made *Ulpius Syllanus*, Chief of the Senate, propose to consult the Books of the *Sibyls*: but some Senators opposed it, alledging, that, under so brave a Prince as *Aurelian*, there was no occasion to inform themselves of the Will of the Gods. This Difference of Opinions causing the Consultation of those Writings to be deferred, it became necessary for *Aurelian* to interpose. He wrote, therefore,

AURELIAN. 573

him among good Princes; and, according to the Saying of *Dioclesian*, he was much fitter to command an Army, than to be an Emperor [G]. However, we must take notice, that his sanguinary Disposition did not hinder him from being beloved by the People: His Liberality, and the care he took to maintain Plenty, and to punish Misdemeanors, caused his Cruelty to be forgot [H]. Having punished the Seditious, and

therefore, to the Senators, that "*he wondered they should hesitate about a Matter of That Nature, just as if they were deliberating in a Christian Church, and not in the Temple of all the Gods.* — — Mitror vos, patres sancti, tamdiu de aperiendis Sibyllinis dubitasse libris, perinde quasi in Christianorum Ecclesiâ, non in templo deorum omnium, tractaretis (24)." He pressed it very earnestly; he promised to defray the necessary Expences, and for that purpose sent orders to his Treasurer; "*for*, added he, *it is no Disgrace to conquer by the Divine Assistance : it was thus our Ancestors began and ended several of their Wars.* Neque enim indecorum est diis juvantibus vincere; sic apud majores nostros multa finita sunt bella, sic cœpta (25)." So that *Syllanus* had reason to say to *Aurelian's* Flatterers, that This great Man both honoured and trusted in the Gods, and that their Assistance never disgraced brave Men. "Meministis P. C. me in hoc ordine sæpe dixisse jam tum, quum primum nuntiatum est Marcomannos erupisse, consulenda Sibyllæ decreta, utendum Apollinis beneficiis, interveniendum deorum immortalium præceptis: recusasse vero quosdam, & cum ingenti calumniâ recusasse, quum adulando dicerent, tantam principis esse virtutem, ut opus non sit deos consuli, proinde quasi & ipse vir magnus non colat, non de diis immortalibus speret. Quid plura ? audivimus literas quibus, rogavit opem deorum, quæ nunquam cuiquam turpis est ut vir fortissimus adjuvatur (26). — *Venerable Fathers, You have often heard me, in this Place, on the first News of the Invasion of the Marcomans, give my Opinion for consulting the Sybilline Oracles, for making use of Those Favours of Apollo, and for attending to the Will of the immortal Gods. This some Persons opposed, and with great Abuse opposed ; insisting, with their Flattery, that such was the Virtue of our Prince, as made all Application to the Gods unnecessary. As if this great Prince himself did not worship, and trust in, the immortal Gods. Why should I say more ? we have heard his own Letters, wherein he desires their Assistance, which the bravest of Men need never be ashamed of.*" After receiving *Aurelian's* Letter, there was no farther delay; the Senate caused the Books of the *Sibyls* to be consulted, which occasioned a long Train of Devotions (27). Observe, by the way, how much the Maxim of *Ajax* is esteemed by some Persons (28). We have Flatterers here, who imagine we never need have recourse to the Assistance of Heaven, but when we distrust the Valour and Prudence of the Princes of this World. I shall add here two Proofs, that *Aurelius* was not of this Opinion: "Credo adjuturos Rom. Remp. Deos qui nunquam nostris conatibus defuerunt (29). — *I trust the Commonwealth will be assisted by the Gods, who have never once failed to prosper our Arms.*" This he wrote, when he found himself perplexed by the long Resistance of *Zenobia*. He acknowledged, in another Letter, that his Victories were a Present from the Gods. "Unde apparet nullam mihi à Diis immortalibus datam sine difficultate victoriam (30). — *From whence it appears, that the Gods have given me no Victory, without Trouble.*" It is true, he added, that these Presents were always attended with a thousand Difficulties. It is the Fate of all things: it is not Virtue alone, which must be acquired by the Sweat of our Brows; it holds equally true of all other good things. Sic diis placitum. — *Such is the Will of Heaven.*

Τῆς δ' ἀρετῆς ἱδρῶτα θεοὶ προπάροιθεν ἔθηκαν
᾿Αθάνατοι, μακρὸς δὲ καὶ ὄρθιος οἶμος ἐπ' αὐτήν.
Καὶ τρηχὺς τὸ πρῶτον (31).

*Closely the Gods their fav'rite Virtue keep,
Nor make her known to Men on Terms too cheap.*

*Long is the Passage to her blest Abode ;
Steep and discouraging at first the Road.
Barr'd are all Passes, all Access denied,
To those, who take not Labour for their Guide.*

In this sense, there are no Free-Gifts; and we must confess, that this Will of Heaven is founded in Goodness; for our Joy in acquiring any good Thing is heightened by the Pains it cost us.

[G] *His Cruelty hindered many from ranking him among good Princes; and, according to the Saying of* Dioclesian, *he was much fitter to command an Army, than to be an Emperor.*] *Vopiscus* will inform us of these Particulars: "Et Aurelianum quidem, says he (31), multi neque inter bonos, neque inter malos, principes ponunt, idcirco quod ei clementia, imperatorum dos prima, defuerit. Verconius Herennianus præfectus prætorio Dioclesiani, teste Asclepiodoto, sæpe dicebat, Dioclesianum frequenter dixisse, quum Maximiani asperitatem reprehenderet, Aurelianum magis ducem esse debuisse quam principem. Nam ejus nimia ferocitas eidem displicebat. — *There are many, who will not allow Aurelian to be ranked either among good or bad Princes. They deny him the first, for his Want of Clemency, That principal Jewel in a Crown.* Verconius Herennianus, *Commander of the Guard to* Dioclesian, *as Asclepiodotus relates, often affirmed it to be a frequent Saying of Dioclesian, when he reproved Maximinian for his Roughness, that Aurelian was cut out for a General, but not for a Prince. For he did not like his too great Austerity.*" These words of *Dioclesian* were the words of a good Judge; for he used to say, That there is nothing more difficult, than to reign well (33), and he perfectly understood the Reasons of This Difficulty. You will find them in *Vopiscus* (34); an Author, who observes, that, in so great a number of *Roman* Emperors, there were reckoned but very few good ones (35); and who commends the Jest of a Buffoon, *That all the good Princes may be painted on a Ring.* — "Vides quæso quam pauci sint principes boni, ut bene dictum sit a quodam mimico scurra Claudii, hujus temporibus, *In uno annulo bonos principes posse perscribi atque depingi* (36)."

[H] *His Liberality, and the Care he took to maintain Plenty — caused his Cruelty to be forgot.*] The manner, in which he punished the Seditious, which were raised in *Rome*, during his Absence, so much exceeded the bounds of a just and necessary Severity, that it tarnished his Reputation, and rendered him very odious: "Magnum illud, & quod jam fuerat, & quod non frustra speratum est, infamiæ tristioris ictu contaminavit imperium. Timeri cœpit princeps optimus, non amari, quum alii dicerent, periodendum talem principem, non optandum; alii bonum quidem medicum, sed mala ratione curantem (37). — *He stained the Glory of This great Reign, both what it had already gained, and was still like to gain, by one sad Blot of Cruelty. This excellent Prince began to be dreaded, instead of beloved: and some said, such a Governour was not to be endured, much less desired; others, that he was a good Physician, but practised too rough a Method of Cure.*" The People did not long continue This Hatred: they were soon mollified by the Distributions of Bread, Flesh (38), and Oil (39), and such other Kindnesses, which they enjoyed under His Government. They were still such, as in the time of *Juvenal*, and formed no other desires, beyond Those of Bread, and public Shows: Nothing could be more gay, than They were, provided they had their Bellies full.

— Jampridem ex quo suffragia nulli
Vendimus, effugit curas. Nam qui dabat olim
Imperium, fasces, legiones, omnia, nunc se

Continet,

(24) Idem, cap. 20, pag. 463.

(25) Idem, cap. 20. pag. 464.

(26) Idem, cap. 19. pag. 459, 460.

(27) Idem, cap. 20.

(28) See Remark [E] of the Article AJAX the Son of Telamon.

(29) Vopisc. cap. 16.

(30) Idem, cap. 38.

(31) Hesiod. Opera & Di.s, ver. 287.

(32) Vopisc. cap. 44. pag. 532, 533.

(33) Id. Ib. cap. 43.

(34) Ibid.

(35) Idem, cap. 42.

(36) Id. Ib. pag. 529.

(37) Idem, cap. 21, pag. 467.

(38) Idem, cap. 35.

(39) Idem, cap. 48.

AURELIAN.

(a) Vopisc. cap. 22.

and composed all Disorders at *Rome* (u), he undertook an Expedition into the East against *Zenobia* (x). He presently ended This War by taking That brave Princess. I say, he ended it presently, though he found, by the way, many Enemies to give Battle to, and many strong Places to reduce. We have seen, elsewhere (y), what hindred him from ruining *Tyana*. He exposed himself so much, when he besieged *Zenobia*, in the City of *Palmyra*, that he received a Wound from an Arrow (z). He defeated the *Persians*, who came to the Assistance of the Besieged; and acquired such a Reputation by the Conquest of all *Zenobia's* Dominions, as cannot be expressed (aa). In his return towards the *West*, he understood, that the *Palmyrenians* had revolted. This News made him return into *Syria*, and he was got to *Antioch*, before they heard he was coming (bb). He punished *Palmyra* with an excessive Cruelty; for he put all to the Sword (cc). He was yet at *Carræ* in *Mesopotamia*, when he was informed of the Revolt of the *Egyptians*: He marched against them with his usual Success and Expedition; he defeated their Leader, took, and put him to Death, and so subdued *Egypt* in a very little time (dd). His desire of re-uniting the *Gauls*, *Spain*, and *Britain*, which had been usurped by *Tetricus*, made him return into the *West*. He gained a Victory near *Chalons* on the *Marne*, which decided the matter; the rather, because *Tetricus* surrendred himself during the Battle (ee). He returned to *Rome*, and triumphed over *Zenobia* and *Tetricus* with an extraordinary Pomp (ff). He repassed into *Gaul*, and, being informed, that the Barbarians were entred into the Country of the *Vindelici* (gg), he marched thither immediately, and dislodged them. From thence he passed into *Illyricum*; and, judging, that there was no possibility of preserving *Dacia*, which *Trajan* had made a Province of, beyond the *Danube*, and which had been lost under *Gallienus*, he withdrew from thence the Troops and the Inhabitants, and settled the latter in part of *Mæsia* and *Dardania*, which he converted into a new Province (hh). He had a fine Army in *Thracia*, which he designed to lead, after the Winter, against the *Persians*, when he was killed by one of his Generals (ii). This happened in the Month of *January*, 275. We know the great Actions of his Life only in general; but, if we knew the Particulars of them from such exact Descriptions as are now used in relating Battles, and Conquests, we should admire him beyond expression.

(40) Juven. Sat. 10. ver. 77.

Continet, atque duas tantum res anxius optat,
Panem, & Circenses (40).

Now, free from Care, Those Slaves the People live,
No longer plagued with Votes to sell, or give.
That mighty People, whom the World obey'd,
Whose Voices, Consuls, Armies, Emp'rors made;
Now Liberty's no more, are sunk so low,
Their whole Ambition asks but Bread and Show.

It was by these means, This Emperor made himself beloved by the Multitude. Read the Letter, which he wrote to the Overseer of the Provisions: " *Aurelianus Augustus Flavio Arabiano præfecto annonæ.* " *Inter cœtera, quibus diis faventibus Romanam* " *Rempub. juvimus, nihil mihi est magnificentius* " *quam quod additamento unciæ omne annonarum* " *urbicarum genus juvi: quod ut esset perpetuum,* " *navicularios Niliacos apud Ægyptum novos, &* " *Romæ amnicos posui. Tiberinas extruxi ripas:* " *vadum alvei tumentis effodi, dils & perennitati* " *vota constitui, almam Cererem consecravi. Nunc* " *tuum est officium, Arabiane jucundissime, elabo-* " *rare, ne meæ dispositiones in irritum veniant. Ne-* " *que enim populo Rom. saturo quicquam potest esse* " *lætius* (41). ――― *Aurelianus Cæsar to Flavius Ara-* " *bianus, Præfect of the Provisions. Among the* " *Services, which by the Favour of the Gods I have* " *done to the Commonwealth, I esteem none greater* " *than That of making an Addition of one twelfth* " *Part more to all the City Provisions. Which that* " *I might perpetuate, I have built proper Vessels to* " *Egypt, for navigating in the Nile, and at Rome,* " *for the Tyber. This I have also new embanked;* " *and deepened the Shallows of the swelling Channel.* " *I have performed all holy Rites to the Gods, to* " *Eternity, and to All Bountiful Ceres. It is now* " *your part, most agreeable Arabianus, to put my De-* " *signs in Execution. Nor can any Thing give me so* " *much pleasure, as to see the Roman People supplied* " *with Plenty.*" He had a design to settle a perpetual Distribution of Wine, and had taken measures for it (42). It is said, that the Commander of his Guards dissuaded him from the execution, by saying, that, if *Wine was given to the People, they must also have Geese, and Fowls. Si & vinum populo Romano damus, superest ut & pullos & anseres demus* (43). Such Largesses, as These are sufficient to cause the spilling of some Persons Blood to be forgot. Though *Aurelian* had caused his Sister's Son, or Daughter, or both, to be put to Death, for frivolous Reasons (44); though he had rashly inflicted capital Punishments (45); all this was not able to make him lose the Affection of a People, whom he fed so plentifully, and cloathed so handsomely (46). Besides, his Severity put a Stop to several Disorders, which were very odious to the People. He extirpated all Informers, Extortioners, public Bloodsuckers, and such sort of Vermin. " *Quic-* " *quid sane scelerum fuerit, quicquid malæ conscien-* " *tiæ, vel artium funestarum, quicquid denique fa-* " *ctionum, Aurelianus toto penitus orbe purgavit* (47). " ――― *Item quadruplatores ac delatores ingenti severi-* " *tate persequutus est: tabulas publicas ad privatorum* " *securitatem exuri in foro Trajano semel jussit.* " *Amnestia etiam sub eo delictorum publicorum de-* " *creta de ex exemplo Atheniensium: cujus rei etiam* " *Tullius in Philippicis meminit. Fures provinciales* " *repetundarum ac peculatus reos ultra militarem* " *modum est persequutus, ut eos ingentibus suppliciis* " *cruciatibusque puniret* (48). ――― *Whatever Crimes* " *whatever Iniquities, or pernicious Arts, whatever* " *Factions appeared, all these Aurelian totally extir-* " *pated.* ――― *He also punished all Informers, and* " *Sharers of Confiscations, with exceeding Severity:* " *and once burnt all the public Accounts in* Trajan*'s* " *Market-Place, for the Security of Those concerned* " *in them. He decreed also a general Indemnity for* " *all Offences against the State, after the Example* " *of the Athenians: which is mentioned by* Cicero " *in his Philippics. The Robbers of the Provinces,* " *who were guilty of Extortion, Bribery, or Em-* " *bezzling the Public Money, he treated with more* " *than military Rigour, and made them undergo the* " *most cruel Tortures and Punishments.*" He enlarged the Circumference of *Rome*, and restored the ancient Bounds of the Empire (49). By this show of Grandeur the People suffer themselves to be decoyed. He applied himself to reform Abuses; he limited the Number of Eunuchs, because they were risen to too high a Price (50). He prohibited the keeping any Concubines, who were of a free Condition (51). To conclude, it was a Pleasure to the *Roman* People to see This Emperor make himself feared by the Senate: Perhaps That Assembly was grown a little too haughty; but, be it as it will, I imagine it was thought proper, that the Senators should

AURELIAN.

expression, and think the Complaint of *Junius Tiberianus* extremely just [*I*]: For, in short, *Aurelian* carried the War from *East* to *West*, with the same ease as we do now from *Alsatia* into *Flanders*. He was much lamented, and had most magnificent Monuments erected in Honour to him. They deified him [*K*], and built him a Temple. It is remarkable,

---

should be taught how to behave, by such a Master, as School-Boys under the Correction of a Pedagogue. *Populus autem Romanus eum amavit, Senatus & timuit* (52). *Senatus mortem ejus graviter tulit, gravius tamen Populus Romanus, qui vulgò dicebat Aurelianum pædagogum esse Senatorum* (53).

[*I*] *The Complaint of* Junius Tiberianus *was extreamly just*.] What, said he, shall a *Thersites*, a *Sinon*, and other Monsters of Anquity, be known to us, and to our Posterity ; and shall they not know *Aurelian*, a most illustrious Prince, and a most severe Emperor, who restored the whole World to the *Roman* Name? Heaven grant this Madness may never happen. Hereupon he engaged *Flavius Vopiscus* to undertake That Emperor's History, and promised him all the Memoirs the Library of *Trajan* could furnish. I shall relate That Historian's own Words: "Quæsivit à me *(Junius Tiberianus)*
" quis vitam *Aureliani* in literas retulisset. Cui ego
" quum respondissem, neminem à me Latinorum,
" Græcorum aliquos lectitatos, dolorem gemitus sui
" vir sanctus per hæc verba profudit : *Ergo Ther-*
" *sitem, Sinonem, cæteraque illa prodigia vetustatis,*
" *& nos bene scimus, & posteri frequentabunt : di-*
" *vum Aurelianum, clarissimum principem, severissi-*
" *mum imperatorem, per quem totus Romani nomini*
" *orbis est restitutus, posteri nescient? Deus avertat*
" *hanc amentiam. Et tamen, si bene novi, ephemer-*
" *ridas illius viri scriptas habemus, etiam bella cha-*
" *ractere historico digesta, quæ velim accipias, &*
" *per ordinem scribas, additis quæ ad vitam perti-*
" *nent. Quæ omnia ex libris linteis, in quibus ipse*
" *quotidiana sua scribi præceperat, pro tua sedulitate*
" *condisces. Curabo autem ut tibi ex Ulpia bibliotheca*
" *& libri lintei proferantur. Tu velim Aurelianum*
" *ita ut est, quatenus potes, in literas mittas* (54).
" — He (Junius Tiberianus) asked me *who had wrote*
" *the Life of* Aurelian. *I answered, I had read it in*
" *some Writings of the Greeks, but not in any of La-*
" *tins, on which That excellent Man expressed his*
" *Concern in this pathetic Complaint:* What, shall
" a *Thersites*, a *Sinon*, and such other Prodigies of
" Antiquity be kown to us, and our to Posterity ; and
" shall they not know the Divine *Aurelian*, the
" most celebrated Prince, the strictest Emperor, who
" restored the whole World to the *Roman* Name?
" May Heaven avert such Madness. And yet, if I
" am not mistaken, we have the Journals of This
" great Man in Writing, and also his Wars, digested
" in historical Method, which I would have you
" take, and copy in order, and insert in their pro-
" per Place, whatever relates to his Life. You will
" find the Particulars by a careful perusal of this
" Journal, which is wrote in Books made of Lint,
" and contains the Minutes of each Day's Transa-
" ction, set down by his own Command. I will
" take care they shall be sent you out of the *Ulpian*
" Library. Do you write such a History of *Aure-*
" *lian*, as may describe him to the Life, as near as
" you are able." Observe, that *Vopiscus* spoke thus about thirty Years after the Death of *Aurelian* : I say, observe This as a Proof either of the Ignorance, or Negligence, of the *Latins* of those Times. None of them had yet published any thing of the great Actions of This Prince, the Restorer of the Empire, *Orbis restitutor*, as he is called on a Medal. He did not expect This Disgrace, when he took care to have a daily Register kept of the Series of his Exploits (55).

[*K*] *He was much lamented.* —— *They deified him*] Those very Men, who put him to Death, erected a magnificent Tomb for him, and consecrated a Temple to him (56) ; for they discovered, that they had been brought into That Conspiracy, by a horrid Piece of Villany. We shall show what That was. *Aurelian* had threatned his Secretary *Mnestheus*; who, giving himself over for lost, as he well knew the Threats of This Prince would be put in Execution (57), resolved to be beforehand with him, and made several Persons believe, that *Aurelian* designed putting Them to Death. He shewed them a List,

wherein he had put himself, and exhorted them to save their Lives. They were all Persons, who had either incurred *Aurelian's* Displeasure, or had Reason to believe, that, by the Importance of their Services, they stood very well in his Favour, and had nothing to fear (58). All those Persons plotted against his Life, and put it in Execution But having afterwards discovered the Secretary's Fraud, they were the most zealous to honour *Aurelian*. *Mnestheus* was exposed to the wild Beasts, and care was taken to preserve the Memory of That Punishment on This Emperor's Tomb (59). The Soldiers would not confer the Empire on any of those, who were concerned in his Death, but applied to the Senate for a new Prince, and for the Deification of *Aurelian* (60). The Senate would not take upon them to create an Emperor, but as for the divine Honours which the Army desired for *Aurelian*, they were decreed without any delay. *Tacitus* (61), who first gave his Opinion in the Senate, made a very fine Speech, which the Reader will be glad to find here, since it contains a just Abstract of *Aurelian's* most splendid Actions, and is embellished with some curious Sentiments. " Rectè atque ordine consuluissent dii immortales
" P. C. si boni ferro inviolabilis extitissent, ut lon-
" giorem ducerent vitam ; neque contra eos aliqua
" esset potestas iis qui neces infandas tristissima mente
" concipiunt. Viveret enim princeps noster Aurelia-
" nus, quo neque utilior fuit quisquam. Respirare
" certe post infelicitatem Valeriani, post Gallieni ma-
" la, imperante Claudio cœperat nostra Respublica :
" at eadem reddita fuerat Aureliano toto penitus or-
" be vincente. Ille nobis Gallias dedit, ille Italiam
" liberavit : ille Vindelicis jugum Barbaricæ servitu-
" tis amovit. Illo vivente Illyricum restitutum est,
" redditæ Romanis legibus Thraciæ. Ille (proh pu-
" dor) Orientem fœmineo pressum jugo in nostra
" jura restituit : ille Persas insultantes adhuc Vale-
" riani nece, fudit, fugavit, oppressit. Illum Sarra-
" ceni, Blemyes, Axomitæ, Bactriani, Seres, Hiberi,
" Albani, Armenii, populi etiam Indorum, veluti
" præsentem penè venerati sunt Deum. Illius donis
" quæ à Barbaris gentibus meruit, refertum est Capito-
" lium : quindecim millia librarum auri ex ejus li-
" beralitate unum tenet templum, omnia in urbe fa-
" na ejus micant donis. Quare P. C. vel deos ipso
" jure convenio, qui talem principem interire passi
" sunt, nisi forte secum eum esse maluerunt. Decerno
" igitur divinos honores : id quod vos omnes existimo
" esse facturos. Nam de imperatore deligendo ad eun-
" dem exercitum censeo esse referendum. Etenim in
" tali genere sententiæ nisi siat quod dicitur, & electi
" periculum erit, & eligentis invidia. *Probata est*
" *sententia Taciti* (62). — *Venerable Fathers : It*
" *would have been happy for Mankind, if the im-*
" *mortal Gods had been pleased to make all good*
" *Men invulnerable, and longer lived ; that no vile*
" *Attempts of the Wicked, to destroy them, might*
" *have their Effect. Then had our Prince* Aurelian
" *been still living, than whom there never was a*
" *greater. After the Misfortunes of* Valerian, *and*
" *the Mismanagements of* Gallienus, *it is true, our*
" *Commonwealth began to take Breath under the Em-*
" *peror* Claudius ; *but it was* Aurelian, *who restored*
" *her, by conquering the whole World. It was he,*
" *that recovered the* Gallia's : *It was he, that freed*
" *Italy : It was he, who shook off the Barbarian Yoke*
" *from the* Vindelici. *To his Life we owe the*
" *Restitution of* Illyricum, *and the* Thracia's *to the*
" *Roman Empire. To his Life we owe the Recovery*
" *of the East from the Oppression (O shameful!) of*
" *a Woman. By his Arms the* Persians, *triumphing*
" *for the Death of* Valerian, *were routed, subdued,*
" *and inslaved. The Terror of his Arms have made*
" *him almost adored as a present Deity, by the* Sa-
" racens, *the* Ethiopians, *the* Axomites, *the* Bactrians,
" *the* Seres, *the* Heberi, *the* Albani, *the* Armenians,
" *and* Indians. *He has filled the Capitol with the Pre-*
" *sents made him by the* Barbarians ; *He has given*
" *to one Temple* 15000 *Pounds of Gold, and all the*
" *rest have shared of his Liberality. We justly, there-*
" *fore,*

AURELIAN. AUREOLUS.

remarkable, that there was no Deity for which he shewed more Zeal, than for the Sun [L]. He left but an only Daughter, whose Grandson was yet living in the Time of *Dioclesian* (kk). He was a Senator much reverenced for his Virtue, and had been Proconsul of *Cilicia*. We must regard as fabulous, what *Abulpharagius* says, that Aurelian *upon making Peace with* Sapor, *King of* Persia, *gave him his Daughter in Marriage* (ll). It is also pretended, that he sent him some *Greek* Physicians, who taught the *Persians Hipprocrates*'s Physic (mm). Note, he never employed any Physicians in his Sickness, and scarce ever made use of any other Remedy than Abstinence (nn). To conclude, it was a Happiness for the Christians, that such a bloody Prince did not undertake Their Extirpation. I confess one of the Persecutions of the Church is placed under his Reign; but some Historians never once mention it, and those who do agree it was short (oo). Before I make an end of this Article, I must take notice of a Distinction which *Vopiscus* has made, and which very few Persons are capable of making [M]: *Such*, says he (pp), *was the End of* Aurelian, *a Prince more necessary than good*. What we find in *Angeloni*, concerning some pieces of Marble found in the time of Pope *Urban* VIII, upon levelling the place where *Aurelian* had built a Temple, on Mount *Quirinal* (qq), gives a very great Idea of the Magnificence of That Edifice.

" fore, O *Venerable Fathers, may expostulate with
" the Gods themselves, for suffering the Murder of
"* Aurelian, *unless it was their Pleasure to receive
" him amongst them. I therefore decree to him all
" divine Honours: in which I hope to meet with
" your unanimous Concurrence But as to the Election of an Emperor, I think we ought to refer
" That to the Army. For should we undertake it,
" and our Nomination not be complied with, the
" Elected would be in Danger, and the Electors in
" Disgrace.* The Opinion of *Tacitus* was approved." The same *Tacitus* being elected Emperor some Months after (63), began his Reign by ordering four Statues to be erected to *Aurelian*, one of Gold in the Capitol, and three of Silver in other Places; and that every Body should have the Picture of That great Prince. The three Silver Statues were dedicated, but not That of the Capitol. " In eadem oratione Aureliano
" statuam auream ponendam in Capitolio decrevit:
" item statuam argenteam in Curia, item in templo
" Solis, item in foro divi Trajani. Sed aurea non
" est posita: dedicatæ autem sunt solæ argenteæ.
" In eadem oratione cavit, ut si quis argento publice
" privatimque æs miscuisset, si quis auro argentum,
" si quis æri plumbum, capital esset cum bonorum
" proscriptione. —— Addidit, ut Aurelianum omnes
" pictum haberent (64). —— *In the same Speech he
" decreed to* Aurelian *a golden Statue, to be erected
" in the Capitol; also a Silver one in the Court,
" another in the Temple of the Sun, and a third in
" the Market of* Trajan. *Only the Silver Statues
" were dedicated; that of Gold was never erected.
" He, in the same Speech, decreed, that whoever should,
" either publickly, or privately, adulterate Silver
" with Copper, or Gold with Silver, or Copper with
" Lead, should suffer Death, and Forfeiture of Estate.
"* —— *He added, that all should be obliged to have
" the Picture of* Aurelian.*"

[*L*] *There was no Deity for which he shewed more Zeal than for the Sun.*] It seems to me that his first Education was the Cause of That Worship; for it is likely, that his Mother, who was Priestess of the Sun, inspired him from his Youth with a particular Devotion for That Deity (65). However it be, we find, that when he thanked *Valerian*, on his appointing him Consul, he made use of these Words: *Dii faciant & Deus certus Sol ut & Senatus de me sic judicet* (66). —— *May the Gods, and that undoubted Deity the Sun, grant, that the Senate conceive the same Opinion of me.* A learned Man pretends (67), that he spoke thus in a Letter (68), *as if the other Gods were doubtful, and the Sun only certain.* It is pretended, that, in the Battle which he won against *Zenobia*'s Forces, near *Emesa*, he was assisted by a Deity, who encouraged the Soldiers, and made the Infantry support the Cavalry, which was ready to fly (69). As soon as he entered victorious into *Emesa*, he went to the Temple of the Sun: *Statim ad templum Heliogabali tetendit, quasi communi officio vota soluturus*, and found there the same Figure of the Deity, who had favoured him in the Battle. Wherefore he *founded some Temples in That Place* (70), and afterwards built the Temple of the Sun in *Rome* (71). He also caused the Temple of the same God to be rebuilt in *Palmyra*. Here are the Orders, which he dispatched for That Purpose; I shall relate them, because they discover to us both This Prince's Cruelty, and his Devotion for the Sun. " Aurelianus Augustus Celonio Basso. Non oportet
" ulterius progredi militum gladios. Jam satis Palmyrenorum cæsum atque concisum est. Mulieribus non pepercimus, infantes occidimus, senes jugulavimus, rusticos interemimus: cui terras, cui urbem deinceps reliquemus? Parcendum est iis qui remanserant. Credimus enim tam paucos tam multorum suppliciis esse correctos. Templum sane Solis, quod apud Palmyram aquilifer legionis tertiæ cum vexilliferis & draconario & corniclinibus atque linteonibus diripuerunt, ad eam formam volo quæ fuit, reddi. Habes trecentas auri libras è Zenobiæ capsulis: habes argenti mille octingenta pondo. De Palmyrenorum bonis habes gemmas regias. Ex his omnibus fac cohonestari templum: mihi & diis immortalibus gratissimum feceris. Ego ad senatum scribam, petens ut mittat pontificem qui dedicet templum (72). ---- Aurelianus Cæsar *to* Ceionius Bassus. *It is time to sheath our Sword. The* Palmyrenes *have sufficiently felt it's Edge. We have spared neither Women nor Children, we have put both the Aged and the Husbandman to the Sword. To whom, then, shall we leave the Lands, to whom the City? We must spare the rest. The few, who remain, will, undoubtedly, remember the Punishment of so many. The Temple of the Sun, at* Palmyra, *which the Standard Bearer of the third Legion, with his Ensigns, and Colours, and Trumpets, and Fifes, demolished: I will have rebuilt after the same Model. You have, of* Zenobia's *Treasure, Three hundred Pounds of Gold, and Eighteen hundred Pounds of Silver, You have, of the* Palmyrenes *Effects, the Crown of Jewels. With all these, erect a Temple; and you will perform a Work, not only most grateful to me, but also to the immortal Gods. I will write to the Senate, to send a Chief Priest to consecrate it.*"

[*M*] Vopiscus *has made a Distinction concerning* Aurelian, *—— which few Persons are capable of making*] The Faults of *Aurelian* were serviceable, the State stood in need of them, but, in *Vopiscus*'s Opinion, it does not follow from thence that he was a good Emperor. This is the Language of a Man who is careful not to confound things. A great Number of Persons are ignorant of this Distinction. They look on That as a truly, and absolutely, good and just Reign, which has prevented, or removed, some great Evil; and if once they fancy that a Government is unjust, they look on it as truly, and absolutely, bad, without regarding the necessary Advantages the Public receives from it.

AUREOLUS (PETER) a *Franciscan* Friar, and since Archbishop of *Aix*, was one of the most subtil and famous Divines of his Time. He flourished about the end of the XIIIth Century, and the beginning of the XIVth. He was born at
Verberie

AUREOLUS. 577

Verberie on the *Oise*, and his Name was *Oriol* (a); but as he is only known by the Latin Name which he gives himself, I place him here, without imitating *Moreri*, who refers us from *Aureole* to *Oriol*. That Reference would be more pardonable, if we found in his Article of *Oriol*, all that might be reasonably expected from an Historian, who cites the Life of that illustrious Archbishop of *Aix* (b); but this he falls very short of. Nor can I supply his defect, for I do not believe, the Work, which contains the Life of *Aureolus*, is any where to be met with in all the United Provinces. What I can say is only this ; *Aureolus* was Professor of Divinity in the University of *Paris* (c): they appropriated to him the Title of *Doctor facundus* (d). He was Provincial of *Aquitain*, when he was made Archbishop of *Aix* (e), and did not live long after he was raised to that high Dignity [*A*]. It has been said that he that he was promoted to the Rank of a Cardinal. He had a very penetrating Understanding, but was too fond of distinguishing himself by new Opinions [*B*]. It is pretended, that he maintained the Impossibility of the Creation [*C*]. The Dominicans had a formidable Adversary in him, and caused him to be refuted with much Spirit, by

(a) Labbe, Dissert. de Scriptor. Ecclef. Tom.2. pag. 183.

(b) Placed, as he says, before the Commentaries of Oriol, on the Master of the Sentences, printed at Rome in the Year 1595.

(c) Labbe, ubi supra, pag. 184.

(d) Id. ib.

(e) Bellarm. de Script. Ecclef. pag. 365.

[*A*] *He did not live long after he was raised to the Dignity of Archbishopric of Aix.*] The Archbishopric of *Aix* was conferred on him in the Year 1321 ; and we find that *James de Concos de Broirez*, a Dominican, was installed in the same Archbishopric the tenth of *July*, 1322 (1). It must follow, then, that the Twenty seventh of *April*, which was the Day of *Aureolus*'s Death (2) belongs, at farthest, to the Year 1322. Behold the Negligence of Those Times: They were contented to note the Day, in which an Archbishop died, and never troubled themselves about the Date of the Year.

[*B*] *He was too fond of distinguishing himself by new Opinions.*] This is a very dangerous Character ; a Rock much to be feared: we scarce ever find, that those, who have Wit and Learning enough to raise strong Objections against the common Opinions, have Judgment enough to stop at a proper Time, and to discern what is not worth the Trouble of a Reformation. Here is a Passage, where those Sort of Persons are well represented, and our *Aureolus*, in particular, by Name. " Ex hac classe, insignia " ingenia duo, Durandus, & Aureolus minus bene " audiunt, quod ingeniis, quibus valebant plurimum, " indulferint in plerisque ; & novas cudere, ac com- " minisci opiniones, communem tramitem fine causâ " deferendo non dubitarint. Estque haud dubie ar- " gumentum judicii minus exquisiti, nec fatis ma- " turi, vel emuncti, ferri facilè, & abfque urgenti " ratione, extra viam : ita ut quamvis res de qua " agitur, ad scholæ tricas merè pertineat, nec inde " dispendium ullum doctrinæ fidei, vel fan's, ac " puris moribus fit timendum, tamen consultissimum " fit, quando manifesta ratio non urget, ab ante- " riorum placitis non discedere (3). ---- *Of this* " *Class two great Scholars,* Durandus *and* Aureolus, " *have suffered most in their Characters, for using* " *their Extraordinary Talents so freely, on all Oc-* " *casions, and leaving the common Road, for no other* " *Reason, than only to invent, and start, new Opi-* " *nions. And it is certainly a Sign of a weak Judg-* " *ment, not sufficiently improved and corrected, to be* " *easily, and without just cause, led out of the* " *Way: So that even when the Question is only a-* " *bout scholastic Niceties, and can do no possible Da-* " *mage, either to our Faith, or our Morals, yet the* " *wisest Method is, not to leave the old Maxims, unless* " *upon very satisfactory Grounds.*" And yet, it must be confessed, that the Innovators (4), and confounding Wits, are sometimes necessary ; for what considerable Progress could be made without them? Should we not fall asleep, under Pretence, that every thing has been found out already, and that we must acquiesce in the Opinions of our Fathers, as in their Lands, and their Son? The Disputes, and the Confusions, which are raised by bold, ambitious, and rash Men, may be, in themselves, as great an Evil as you please ; but they are highly useful in respect to the Sciences, and the Improvement of the Mind. This may be said even of Civil Wars. A very honest Man affirms it of the Civil Wars, which ravaged *France* in XVIth Century. He says, they refined either the Genius or the Language of some ; they cleared the Judgment of others ; they served either for a Bath to wash ; or a Curry-Comb to scrape off their Dirt. Here are his Words ; both the Thoughts, and the Expressions, deserve citing in this Place. " Ut sæpe res adversæ inex-

" pectatis bonis locum faciunt, ita in hac publica, " & omnium maxima calamitate res autor dari potest, " quibusdam ingenium evasisse limatius, acumen per- " spicacius, judicium resecatius, os mundius, scripta " purgatiora, prorsus ut agnoscere liceat, ærumnarum " procellas, quibus æstuavimus his esse balneas quæ " sordes eluerunt, aliis strigilem quæ squamam de- " tersit, quibusdam uredinem, quæ absumpsit quic- " quid luxurians & inutile. Denique fi quis verè " æstimet, nunc demum intelligimus, etam, quæ Rei- " publicæ tempestas fuit, privatim, & paucuIis esse " cotem qua acuitur, & faculam qua accenditur quic- " quid in singulis est optimum (5). ---- *At Mis-* " *fortunes often occasion unexpected Benefits, so this* " *public and heaviest of Calamities, may have been* " *the Cause of polishing the Wit, clearing the Un-* " *derstanding, pruning the Judgment, refining the* " *Language, or purifying the Style, of some Persons;* " *so that the Storms of Affliction, whose fury has have* " *felt, must be owned to have served, as Baths to wash* " *away Spots, Curry Combs to scrape off Dirt,* " *or Blasts to consume what was useless and luxuriant.* " *And to judge of it rightly, we may now, at last,* " *perceive, that the public Misery has proved a pri-* " *vate Happiness, and either sharpened, as a Whet-* " *stone, or kindled as a Torch, all manner of Excel-* " *lencies in particular Persons.*" In truth, the Public might very well be without such Curry-Combs, Files, or Whetstones, as some may please to call them. Doubtless it is better to want those Advantages, than to pay so great a Price for them. It is better to continue sick, than to be cured by a Remedy so terribly dear. However it be, our Doctor here was resolved to follow no Body's Opinion in his Commentary on the *Master of Sentences* ; and on the other side no Body followed he: All took a Pleasure in opposing him ; some compared him to *Ismael*; *Quorm* (Petrum Aureolum) *Antoninus ait * i ita scrip-fisse in librum sententiarum, ut quia manus ejus contra omnes qui jam antea scripserant, etiam manus omnium contra eum fuerint* (6).

[*C*] *It is pretended, that he maintained the Impossibility of the Creation.*] The Knowledge I have of this Matter is very small, for I can only assure you, that *Theophilus Raynaudus*, after having rejected some Reasons of *Averroës* as very weak, adds, that the Arguments, on which Aureolus so ill employed his Learning, to shew the Creation to be impossible, amount to the same thing. " Eodem recidunt argu- " menta quibus Aureolus apud Capreolum in 2. d. 1. " q. 2. *in argumentis contra quartam*, parum faeli- " citer ingenium exercuit, ut probaret creationem " esse impossibilem. (7). ------ *These Arguments* " *are in* Capreolus, *2. d. 1. q. 2.* in his Arguments " *against the fourth.*" Observe particularly, that he had never read *Aureolus*, nor knew any thing of his Doctrine, but as he found it represented in his Adversary *Capreolus*. This puts me under a new Necessity of groping here in the Dark : But yet I believe I shall not be mistaken in the Conjecture I am going to make. I suppose that *Aureolus* did not directly, and absolutely, affirm, that the Creation was impossible, for that would have been broaching an Opinion very repugnant to the *Romish* Faith. He maintained only, that, for such and such Reasons, he should have held it impossible, that a Being could be made out of nothing, if Faith did not teach him, that the Words, which the Scripture uses concerning the first Formation of the World, must be understood to signify

(1) Labbe, Dissert. de Script. Ecclef. Tom. 2. pag. 184.

(2) Id. ib.

(3) Theoph. Raynaudus, Erotem. de malis ac bonis Libris, n. 430, pag. 230.

(4) Id. not in tie deal mean to a turn attempt necessary Reformation.

(5) Carolus Paschalius, de optimo genere Elocutionis, pag. 124.

* Anton. tit. 24, c. 8, §. 2.

(6) Spondan. ad Annum, 1333, n. 10, pag. 464.

(7) Theoph. Raynaud. in Theol. Naturali, Dist. 8. n. 334, pag. 1039.

578 AURIEGE.

by one of their best Pens [D]. I shall say something concerning his Writings [E]. You will find the Time of his Death in the Remark [A].

signify a Creation, properly so called. Having once covered himself with this Shield, he might safely exert the whole Strength of his Genius, to prove the Impossibility of the Creation; he only ventured upon a Philosophical Dispute, in which he did not fear that he should want Cavils and Subtilties. I make no question but they, who read this, and have a Copy of *Capreolus* in their Studies, will be so curious as to consult him, to know whether this great Antagonist of *Aureolus*, faithfully lays down the whole State of the Question. There are a great many, who, on such an Occasion, would say, they are confuting a Doctor, who maintains the Impossibility of the Creation, and would exaggerate the pernicious Consequences of that Doctrine, without ever intimating, that the same Doctor preserves the Orthodox Opinion, and submits the most subtil Arguments which the Light of Nature affords him, to the Authority of Tradition. I know, that, in another Case, *Aureolus* behaved himself in the very same manner, as, I suppose he has done with respect to the Creation; which makes my Conjecture more probable. He said, that *nothing but the Authority of the Saints could make him believe, that Transubstantiation is a true Change of the whole Bread, into the whole Body of our Lord.* I have read this in a Book of Dr *Allix*. *Petrus Aureolus Romana Ecclesiæ Cardinalis hoc profitetur*; *propter solas authoritates Sanctorum teneo, quod Transubstantiatio est verus transitus & conversio totius panis in totum corpus Domini. in 4. dist. 11. q. 1. a. 2.* (8).

[D] *The Dominicans caused him to be refuted — by one of their best Pens.*] It was by the same *Capreolus*, whom I have just before mentioned. Consult his Commentary on the *Master of the Sentences*. " He " there attacks briskly, *and levels his whole Force* " *against the Commentary of* Aureolus, *on the same* " *Master.* — Quæ (Commentaria Aureoli) in suis " in easdem sententias Commentariis sæpius excussit " exagitavitque Joannes Capreolus (9)." He insinuates, that the false Interpretations which *Aureolus* made, and which served him for Principles to draw odious Consequences from, had not always their only Foundation in the Obscurity of his Understanding, but were in some measure owing also to his Passions. I have this only from Father *Baron*, who expresses himself thus: " Memini me Capreolum nescio quo ex quæ- " stionibus in primum sentent. loco legere, soluto " quodam argumento Aureoli, quo ad grande aliquod " impium, & absurdum ex falsa interpretatione so- " litæ sententiæ rem deduxerat, hæc modestè ad- " junxisse Capreolum: ea nostra responsione patet " hanc objectionem Aureoli profectam esse ex per- " *verso intellectu, quidquid sit de affectu* (10). — " I remember C-preolus, *somewhere in his Questions* " *on the first Book of the Sentences, after refuting an* " *Argument of* Aureolus, *which by a false Interpre-* " *tation of our Opinion, had established something* " *monstrously impious and absurd, thus modestly adds:* " *From our Solution it appears, that the Objection of* " Aureolus, *proceeds from a depraved Understand-* " *ing, whatever might be his Disposition.*" Note, That *Constantius Sarnanus*, a *Franciscan*, and a Cardinal, wrote a Book, wherein he pretends to reconcile *Aureolus*'s Opinions, with those of *Capreolus* (11). He endeavoured to shew the same Agreement between the Doctrines of *Thomas Aquinas*, and those of *Scotus* (12). Just in the same manner some have pretended to discover a good Understanding between *Plato* and *Aristotle*. This is either trifling with Readers, or ridiculing, without designing it, those whom they endeavour to reconcile. Such a Peace is dishonourable to both Parties, and the Mediators might fear some severe Expostulations, is they, who first began the Quarrel, should return again into the World. They would be apt to say, *What, do you pretend that we only dispute about Words, and that we agree in the same Doctrines, without perceiving it; our Passion so strongly prepossessing us, that we*

understand not what we are saying? *This is a Satire all over, we will have no Peace on such ignominious Conditions. Among with your Projects of Re-union; we had rather continue the War, than see it ended at the Expence of our Learning and Understandings.* Observe, that there are some Instances, where the hottest Controversies are only the Effects of a Misunderstanding; but I do not think we can judge so of *Thomism* and *Scotism*, nor consequently of the Difference between the *Scotist Aureolus*, and the *Thomist Capreolus*.

[E] *I shall say something concerning his Writings.*] Those who have spoke of them, observe so little Exactness, that they neither distinguish between those Writings, which are yet remaining, and those which are lost; nor between those which have been printed, and those which never were. Father *Labbe* (13), who complains of this Neglect, too common among Bibliographers, promised to repair it amply; but he died without publishing his large Work, of which the Dissertation, I have quoted, was but a Specimen (14). He observes, that the *Breviarium Bibliorum of Aureolus, sive Epitome universæ sacræ scripturæ juxta literalem sensum*, was printed at *Venice*, in the Year 1571, and at *Paris* in the Year 1585 (15), by the care of *Stephen Nouellet*, Doctor in Divinity, of the Faculty of *Paris*; and that the *Commentaries on the four Books of Sentences*, were printed at *Rome* in, in folio, the Year 1595, and dedicated to Pope *Clement VIII*, by Cardinal *Constantius Sarnanus* (16). He rejects what Father *Maracci* reports in his *Bibliotheca Mariana*, that the Treatise of *Aureolus de Conceptione immaculata B Virginis*, was printed at *Toulouse* in the Year 1314: he says, perhaps that Writing was composed in that Year, or printed in the Year 1514.

Let us make some small Remarks on all this. I. The Catalogue of the *Oxford* Library mentions the *Epitome totius S. Scripturæ*, printed at *Strasburg* in the Year 1514. Father *Labbe* did not know of that Edition: nor *Gesner* neither. *Gesner*'s Epitome, published in the Year 1583, does not take notice of any of *Aureolus*'s Books which had been printed: but observe, that our *Peter Aureolus* is there very falsly distinguished from *Petrus de Verberia, dictus Aureoli*. II. It is not true that the Commentaries on the four Books of Sentences, were printed at *Rome*, in the Year 1595. *Bellarmin* affirms, that he saw only the Commentary on the first of those four Books, and that it was printed at *Rome*, in the Year 1596 (17). The Catalogue of the *Oxford* Library, and that of the Archbishop of *Reims*, place in that Year, the Edition of *Aureolus*'s Commentary on the first Book of Sentences, and they place in the Year 1605, the Edition of the Commentary on the three following Books, with the *Quodlibets*. All this makes two Volumes in Folio, printed at *Rome*, the first in 1596, in the *Vatican*; the last by *Zanzetti*, in the Year 1605. I wonder that *Bellarmin* had no knowledge of the printing of the last Volume. This is something stranger, than to see in *Moreri*, that *we have several Editions of the Commentaries of* Aureolus*, on the Master of the Sentences*; *but that this of* Rome *of* 1595*, is the most correct*. Where could he shew those several Editions? Would he have dated That of *Rome* as he did, if he had known what I have said above? III. I must needs say Father *Labbe* has been too favourable to Father *Maracci*, who could believe that there were Books printed in the Year 1314. Does not all the World know that Printing was not used in *Europe*, tell about the Middle of the XVth Century? What then was the Jesuit *Oldoini* dreaming on, when he boasted of having seen the Treatise of *Aureolus, de Conceptione Virginis Mariæ*, printed at *Toulouse* in the Year 1314? *De Conceptione Virginis Mariæ Librum, qui habetur M. S. Tolosæ in Collegio Fuxensi, & excusum vidimus Tolosæ anno* 1314 (18).

(8) Pet. Allix, Præfat. Historica de Dogmate Transubstantiationis. pag. 66.

(9) Labbe, ubi supra, pag. 184.

(10) Vincentius Baronius, Apologet. lib. 1. §. 2. p. 240.

(11) Oldoini Athen. Roman. p. 176.

(12) Id. ib.

(13) Labbe, ubi supra.

(14) *See the Preface of his Dissertatio de Scriptoribus Ecclesiasticis.*

(15) Oldoini, in Athen. Rom. pag. 532. *makes it* 1581.

(16) Ibid. pag 533. *says the same thing.*

(17) Bellarm de Scriptor. Ecclesi. pag. 385.

(18) Oldoini, Athen. Roman. pag. 533.

AURIEGE, or rather ARIEGE [*A*], a River in *France*, has it's Source in

[*A*] ARIEGE.] It is so called in the Countries through which it passes. In the old Maps it is called *Arregia*, and *Areia* in a Manuscript Martyrology of the Monastery of *Moissac*. There is in that Manuscript the Passion of St *Antonin*, who was martyred at *Pamiès*, and it is affirmed there, that the Bark wherein

AURIEGE. AURISPA.

(e) *It is a Lordship situate, was erected into a Marquisate, for the late Mr Dassion, elder Brother of Messr. de Bonrepaux, Ambassador of France to the Court of Denmark, and afterwards in Holland.*

in the Mountains which limit the County of *Foix* towards *Roussillon*. It passes by *Tarascon*, *Foix*, *Pamiès*, *Barilles*, *Bonac* (a), *Saverdun*, *Sainte-Gabelle*, and *Haute-Rive*, and falls into the *Garonne* at *Portet*, a long League above *Toulouse*, after having received the Waters of the River *Lers*, on the Right, and Those of the *Arget*, and of the *Leze* on the Left [*B*]. The *Ariege* is rapid and full of Fish, and also very good to drink; but it is only navigable from *Haute-Rive*. Du Bartas praises it much [*C*]. See also the Passage of *Bertrand Helias*, related by *Papyrius Masso* (b).

(h) *Papyrius Masso de Ilum. Gall. pag. 412.*

(1) *Hadrian. Valesius in Notitia Galliæ. pag. 26.*

wherein his Body was laid, passed through That River into the *Garonne*. " Per fluvium qui Areia dicitur, " ad Garonnam usque perveniens fluvium navicula " (*in qua corpus Antonini mart. à Gentilibus necati*) " inde alium qui Tarnis dicitur inveniens fluvium, " inde retrogrado cursu per Tarnin intravit in Avario- " nis alveum (1). — *The Boat* (in which was the Body " of *Antoninus*, the Martyr, murdered by the Gen- " tiles) *coming along the River Areia, as far as to " the Garrone, and there finding another River, called " Tarnis, returned in a retrograde Course along the " Tarnis, into the Channel of the Avario.*" Hadrian *Valesius*, from whom I have this, has censured Those who call it *Auriege*, and treated *Papyrius Masso* very ill for naming it *Aurigera*. " Fluvius est vulgo di- " ctus *Ariege*, quibusdam corruptè l'*Auriege* : à Mas- " sono (2) prisci ejus fluvii nominis ignaro *Aurigera* " novo ac ridiculo nomine nuncupatus (3). —— *The " River is commonly called* Ariege, *by some corruptly* " l'Auriege; *by* Masso, *who was intirely ignorant of* " *the ancient Name of This River, it is ridiculously* " *called* Aurigera." Mr *Baudrand* believes that the true *Latin* Name of that River is *Alburacis* (4). I wish he had quoted some good Author. *Sanson* calls it *Lauriegue* in a Map which he published in the Year 1675 (5). But most of the proper Names in it are so disfigured, that we ought to suppose them to be faults of the Engraver. Mr *Moreri* has very pleasantly imagined that the *Auriege* and *Lauriege* are the two Names by which it is called. He forgets the true one? and does not dream, that the two Names he mentions, are but one and same; one of them expressed without the Article, the other with the Article. His mistake is just the same as if he had said, that the River running by *Paris*, is called *Seine* and *Laseine*. I know many Authors make a jest of a Writer who takes them up for Errors of this Nature, and pretend to be above those Trifles: But they are vain Pretenders, who want a fair Mask to cover either their Ignorance, or their Idleness, or their ill Taste, or their Incorrectness. If a City or River were only mentioned occasionally in a Piece of Wit, the faults which those Gentlemen call Trifles would be excusable. But the Case is very different, when those Faults concern the chief Subject of the Book. That which is only an insignificant Nicety in the Writings of a Divine, will sometimes be a capital Fault in a Geographer, or in the Author of a Dictionary. I remember *Papyrius Masso* has called it *la Riege*. See afterwards the Remark [*A*] of the Article GARONNE.

[*B*] *After having received on the Right, the Waters of the* Lers, *it receives those of the* Arget, *and the* Leze, *on the Left*.] *Moreri* deserves a small Censure here: He says, that the *Auriege*, *having received the* Lers, *the* Arget, *and the* Leze, *falls into the* Garonne. This signifies plainly, that the Mouth of the *Lers* is above the Mouth of the *Arget*, and that the entrance of the *Leze*, is between the two others. Nothing can be more false. The *Arget* comes into the *Ariege*, near *Foix*, and there is eight or nine Leagues distance between *Foix* and *Sainte-Gabelle*, which is very near the Mouth of the *Lers*. " Ler- " tius vero in Aurigeram labitur prope Templum " S. Gauvillæ (6). — *The* Lers *falls into the* Auriege, " *near the Church of St* Gabille." The *Leze* has it's Entrance three or four Leagues below That of the *Lers*. *Coulon* might have taught *Moreri* the Order of those Entrances. Note, he observes, that the *Auriege is called by the Latins,* Aurigera (7) *and the Larger*, Argentigera (8) *and that the One produces*

(6) *Papyr. Masso, Descript. Flumin. Gall. p. 470.*

(7) *Coulon, Rivers of France, Tome 1. pag. 483.*

(8) *He had stone laid the Arget, which is the true Orthography.*

Gold, the Other Silver (9). Perhaps he had taken these Remarks from *Olhagaral*, who wrote as follows: *And what shall we not say of the* Lers, *with his Flux and Reflux* (10) ? *Of the* Auriege, *and of the* Arget, *Rivers with Gold and Silver Banks ? Does not this witness the hidden Treasures in the Bowels of Those Mountains* (11) ?

[*C*] *Du Bartas praises it much.*] See here the third Sonnet of his *Nine Pyrenean Muses*, presented to the King of *Navarre* (12).

(9) *Note, that Bertrand Helias, Historian Fuxensium, lib. 1. related some curious Circumstances concerning that Gold. Papyr. Masso, Descript. Flum. Gall. pag. 412. quotes his Words.*

(10) *See concerning this admirable Phænomenon, the 3d day of the 1st Week of Du Bartas, pag. 284.*

(11) *Peter Olhagaral, Preface of the History of Foix, Bearn, and Navarre.*

(12) *Du Bartas, in the Appendix of the first Week, page 934.*

(13) *Since Du Bartas's Time, this has been remedied.*

Fleuve d'or & de flot & de nom & de sable,
Riche en grains, en pastel, en fruits, en vins, en bois,
Auriege au viste cours clair ornement de Foix,
Qui rend par ton tribut Garonne navigable,
Fille de si grand Mont, qui cache, espouvantable,
Son front dedans le Ciel, qui chenu tous les Mois,
Depuis le bord du Su jusqu'au bord Escossois,
Ne void autre plus grand à sa grandeur semblable ;
Clair flot, je te feroy par un discours facond
Plus riche que Pactol, plus que le Nil second :
Plus loin que l'Ocean on orroit tes eaux bruire :
Fier, on t'egaleroit aux fleuves les plus Grands :
On te verroit au Ciel comme le Po reluire,
Si je voyoy tes bords repurgés de brigans (13).

Auriege, *thou noble River, known to Fame
For thy bright Waves, and for thy Golden Name.
Thy Borders every Scene of Plenty shew,
Who pours her Horn, where'er thy Waters flow.
Foix to thy rapid Course owes all it's Pride ;
And deep Garonne it's navigable Tide.
A mighty Mountain is thy awful Sire,
Whose tow'ring Head does to the Skies aspire,
Hoary with Loads of everlasting Snows,
Nor, e'en from Pole to Pole, an Equal knows.
O would the Muse assist thy darling Theme,
In loftiest Notes, I'd sing thy Crystal Stream.
With their just Praise, thy mantling Waves should smile,
Rich as Pactolus, fruitful as the Nile.
Far as loud Ocean can be heard to roar,
Should ev'ry Murmur eccho from thy Shore.
Thy curling Surge should prouder Floods out-vy ;
And like the Po resplendent reach the Sky.
Cou'd I thy Banks from ambush'd Rogues release,
And make the Traveller taste thy Stream in Peace.*

See also the seventh Sonnet, you will find this in the beginning of it :

François, arreste toy, ne passe la campagne,
Que nature mura de Rochers d'un costé,
Que l'Auriege entrefend d'un cours précipité :
Campagne qui n'a point en beauté de compagne (14).

(14) *Du Bartas, ibid. pag. 936.*

Stay, great Navarre, *nor leave these charming Plains,
Where far above all Rival, Beauty reigns.
Rocks, Nature's Walls, the distant Prospect close ;
And all around the hasty Auriege flows.*

AURISPA (JOHN), a Native of *Noto* in *Sicily* (a), was one of the most Learned Men of the XVth Century. He understood the *Greek* and *Latin* Languages; he was a good Orator, and wrote very well, for those Times, both in Prose and in Verse. It is said that he was honoured with the Poetical Crown in *Italy*. He was Secretary to Pope *Nicolas* V, who gave him great Proofs of his Esteem, by

(a) *The Name of this Town in Latin is Netum.*

VOL. I. N°. XIX. 7 G presenting

presenting him with two rich Abbies [*A*]. He entertained a long Correspondence, by Letters, with *Philelphus,* and his Name is celebrated by *Laurentius Valla, Antonius Panormita,* and several other famous Authors. He retired to *Ferrara,* and lived there to a great Age, honoured with the Esteem of the Lords of that Country [*B*], which proved very advantageous to him; for he did not only subsist, but also grow rich by their Liberality (*b*). What he composed is at present very hard to be met with [*C*].

[*A*] Nicholas V, —— *presented him with two rich Abbies.*] He gave him That of *St Pelip de Grandi* (1), the Thirty first of *May,* 1449. and that of *Ste Marie de la Roccade* (2), in the Year 1451. *Aurispa* had a Law Suit for this last Benefice, with one who had it bestowed upon him by *Alphonsus,* King of *Naples.* See *Rocchus Pirrus,* in the Two hundred and twenty fifth Page of his Account of the Church of *Syracuse* (3).

[*B*] *He retired to* Ferrara, *and lived there to a great Age, honoured with the Esteem of the Lords of that Country*] I prove all this from a Passage of *Gyraldus.* " Johannes Aurispa Siculus, *says he* (4), orator in aliquo poëtarum ordine reponi potest, quippe " qui Græcè & Latinè probè doctus esset, carmina " tamen ejus quæ ipse legi nescio quid Sicularum " gerrarum habere videntur: fuit enim eo tempore " quo nondum exquisitæ literæ in lucem redierant. " Vixit autem Ferrariæ ad summam senectutem, in " pretio habitus à nostris principibus, qui & eum lo" cupletem reddiderunt: ab hoc ferunt Cistarellum " familiam originem duxisse. —— John Aurispa *of* " Sicily, *the Orator, deserves some sort of Place among* " *the Poets, being very learned in Greek and Latin,* " *though his Poems, which I have read, contain I* " *know not what old Wives Tales: for he wrote in* " *the obscurer Ages of Learning. He lived at* Ferrara, " *to a great old Age, esteemed by our principal Fa-* " *milies, who made him rich; the Family of* Cista" *rella is said to owe it's Rise to him.*"

[*C*] *What he composed, is at present very hard to be met with*] These are the Books ascribed to him: *A Translation of* Archimedes; the *Translation of* Hierocles's *Commentary on the Golden Verses of* Pythagoras; *and that of a Consolatory Treatise of* Philicus *to* Cicero. *Gesner's* Epitome mentions these three Pieces, without saying whether they were ever printed. It is certain, that *Aurispa's Hierocles* was printed at *Basil,* by *Henry Peter,* in 8vo, in the Year 1543 (5). *Gesner* cites part of the Preface, by which it appears, that it was wrote when the Author was already eighty Years of Age (6). In the Library of *Gabriel Naudé,* there was a Manuscript, entituled, *Comparatio de præsidentia Hannibalis Carthaginensis, Alexandri Magni & Scipionis Majoris Romani apud superos, ex Græco in Latinum conversa ab Aurispâ Oratore ad Baptistam Senatorii & Equestris Ordinis Civem Romanum* (7).

AUROGALLUS (MATTHEW) a Learned Man of the XVIth Century, and Professor of three Languages in the University of *Wittemberg* (*a*); was born in *Bohemia.* He had made a curious Collection of the best Books of Antiquity, and was not contented to esteem them, as many others do, who endeavour to procure themselves a Name by their numerous Libraries, but loved also to read them. I have seen an Epistle Dedicatory (*b*), wherein he is exhorted to publish the Physician *Aëtius,* Nineteen Books of Natural History composed by an unknown Author, the Hymns of *Callimachus,* the Orations of the Ten *Athenian* Orators, and several other *Greek* Manuscripts, brought from the *Levant* to *Bohemia* by the Baron *Bobuslas* of *Hassensteyn,* which came to his hands *cognationis & studiorum hæreditario jure,* as next Heir both in Kindred and Learning. It seems to be inferred, from Those *Latin* words, that he was related to That Baron. There are some Books of his remaining [*A*]. He died in the Year 1543 (*c*), and had been a great Assistant to *Luther* in the Translation of the Bible.

[*A*] *Some of his Books are remaining.*] I do not know whether there are any more besides *Compendium Hebrææ Chaldææque Grammatices,* printed at *Wittemberg,* in 8vo, in the Year 1525, and at *Basil,* in the Year 1539; and *De Hebræis Urbium, Regionum, Populorum, Fluminum, Montium, & aliorum locorum Nominibus Liber, è veteri instrumento congestus,* printed at *Wittemberg,* in the Year 1526, and at *Basil,* in 1539, in 8vo (1). That second Edition was enlarged by the Author.

AUSONIUS, in *Latin Decius,* or rather *Decimus Magnus Ausonius,* one of the most excellent Poets of the IVth Century, was of *Bourdeaux* (*a*), and the Son of a Famous Physician [*A*]. He was educated with a very particular Care; the whole Family

[*A*] *He was the Son of a famous Physician*] Whose Name was *Julius Ausonius.* He was a Native of *Bazas,* and settled at *Bourdeaux* (1). His Wife's Name was *Æmilia Æmia,* and was the Daughter of *Cæcilius Argicius Arborius,* who fled into *Aquitain,* after a Proscription, which had deprived him of all the Estate he had in his Country (2). This *Arborius,* having fixed himself in the City, called *Aquæ Tarbellorum* (3), married a virtuous Woman, of little or no Fortune, whole Name was *Æmilia Corinthia Maura.* From this Marriage proceeded one Son, and three Daughters. The Son was the same *Æmilius Magnus Arborius,* who taught Rhetoric at *Toulouse,* and was took such a very particular Care of the Education of our Poet (4). One of the Daughters was married to *Julius Ausonius,* and brought him four Children, of which the Poet *Ausonius* was the second. You will find all this, and what follows, in his *Parentalia,* or in his *Epicedion in Patrem.* This *Julius Ausonius* was a Man of very great Merit; and, if he was like the Picture which his Son has left of him, he was a Remnant of the Golden Age. There was the greatest Uniformity imaginable in his Conduct.

He offered, gratis, the Assistance of his Art, to all who desired it: He studied to keep up the good Opinion others had of him; but never judged favourably of himself.

Judicium de me studui præstare bonorum;
Ipse mihi nunquam, judice me, placui (5).

It is from others I must seek Applause,
For my own Judgment always damns my Cause.

He had an Aversion for Law-Suits; he neither increased his Estate, nor diminished it; he never was either Witness, or Informer, against any Person's Life (6), he was neither envious nor ambitious; he thought Swearing and Lying were both alike; he never was concerned in any Conspiracy, Plot, or Cabal; he religiously observed the sacred Laws of Friendship; he made Happiness to consist not in possessing what one would have, but in not wishing for what Fortune did not give:

Felicem

AUSONIUS.

Family interested themselves in it (b), either because his Parts were very promising, or because the Scheme of his Nativity had prognosticated, that he should attain to great Honours [B]. He made a surprizing Progress in Learning, and at the Age of Thirty Years was appointed to teach Grammar, in *Bourdeaux* (c). Some time after he was promoted there to the Office of Professor of Rhetoric (d). He acquired so great a Reputation in This Employ, that he was invited to the Imperial Court to be Preceptor to *Gratian*, Son of the Emperor *Valentinian*. He made himself very agreeable both to his Pupil and his Pupil's Father, and received from them such Rewards and Dignities, as made him a very eminent Example of *Juvenal*'s Maxim, *That when Fortune pleases, a Rhetorician may become a Consul* (e). He was, in effect, raised to the Consulship by the

(b) See the Poems of Ausonius, entituled Parentalia.
(c) Auson in Præf. ad Syagrium.
(d) Id. la Professor. n. 24, p. 187.
(e) Si fortuna volet fies de Rhetore Consul Juven. Sat. 7. ver. 197.

Felicem scivi, non qui, quod vellet, haberet:
Sed qui per fatum non data non cuperet (7).

Happy is he, who can his Wish restrain,
Not he, who can that anxious Wish obtain.

He did not endeavour to discover other Mens Secrets; he did not invent false Reports against his Neighbour's Reputation; but if he knew some prejudicial Truths, he concealed them.

Non occursator, non garrulus, obvia cernens,
Valvis & velo condita non adii.
Famam, quæ posset vitam lacerare bonorum,
Non finxi: & veram si scierim, tacui (8).

I shunn'd, with Caution, the officious Tale;
Saw what was bare, but ne'er withdrew a Veil.
I never forg'd, to urge another's Fate,
False Facts; nor did I those I knew relate.

He never thought, that not committing a Fault was a Matter of Merit; he preferred Morality before the Laws; that is, if I mistake not, he did a good Action, because it was good, and not because it was conformable to the Laws.

Deliquisse nihil nunquam laudem esse putavi,
Atque bonos mores legibus antetuli (9).

In want of Fault, I never Merit saw;
Nor Virtue, in Obedience to the Law.

He kept his Marriage Vow exactly, during the Forty five Years he was married (10); and if he had the Pleasure to see what he wished come to pass, it was not by too great an Indulgence of Fate, but because he set such strict Bounds to his Wishes.

Non quia fatorum nimia indulgentia: sed quod
Tam moderata illi vota fuere viro (11).

Nor did he this to Heav'ns Indulgence owe;
But to his limiting his Wish so low.

He was compared to the ancient Sages of *Greece*; and imitated them in the most difficult Point, which was to practise what they taught; he endeavoured much more to lead the Life of a wise Man, than to discourse like one:

Quem sua contendit septem sapientibus ætas:
Quorum doctrinam moribus excoluit:
Viveret ut potius, quam diceret arte sophorum,
Quamquam & facundo, non rudis ingenio (12).

To rival Greece *in Wisdom's School he sought,*
More wisely acting what the Sages taught;
Supreamly wise, he chose not to excel
So much in speaking, as in living well.

And yet he was eloquent in *Greek*, though not in *Latin*;

Sermone impromptus Latio: verum Atticæ linguæ
Suffecit culti vocibus eloquii (13).

He studied with Success the Arts to speak,
Tho' not in Latin, *yet in nobler* Greek.

(7) Id. ibid.
(8) Id. ibid.
(9) Id. ibid.
(10) Ibid. pag. 300.
(11) Id. in Parental. cap. 2, pag. 110.
(12) Id. Ib.
(13) Id. in Epiced. pag. 298.

We need not wonder, then, if, after his Death, he was honoured with this Elogy, *He imitated no Body, and is imitated by no Body.*

Inde & perfunctæ manet hæc reverentia vitæ,
Ætas nostra illi quod dedit hunc titulum:
Ut nullum Ausonius, quem sectaretur, habebat:
Sic nullum, qui se nunc imitetur, habet (14).

So good a Life met with a due Regard;
This great Encomium was it's just Reward.
As he cou'd find no Copy to pursue,
So he found none could copy what he drew.

He was honoured with some illustrious Offices, without having the Trouble to exercise them; and died at ninety Years of Age, without being sensible of any Decay. He walked without a Staff, and found no sort of Defect.

Curia me duplex, & uterque senatus habebat
Muneris exsortem, nomine participem (15).

Both Courts, both Senates, my Relation claim,
Excuse my Presence, but inrol my Name.

Ipse nec affectans, nec detractator honorum,
Præfectus magni nuncupor Illyrici (16).

I neither sought for, nor despis'd, a Name,
So Prefect of Illyricum *became.*

Nonaginta annos baculo fine, corpore toto
Exegi, cunctis integer officiis (17).

Ninety Years Load without a Staff I bear,
My Body active, and my Senses clear.

He composed some Works of Physic in *Latin*, which *Vindicianus* (18), and *Marcellus* (19), have honourably mentioned. *Scaliger* affirms, that he was the Emperor *Valentinian*'s Physician, before his Son was chosen *Gratian*'s Preceptor (20): but I have found no Proof in *Ausonius*.

[B] *The Scheme of his Nativity had prognosticated, that he should attain to great Honours.*] *Cæcilius Argicius Arborius*, his Grandfather, by the Mother's side, understood Astrology, and had calculated This Nativity; he kept it private, but his Daughter discovered it. *Ausonius* informs us of these Particulars himself.

Tu cœli numeros, & conscia sidera fati
Callebas, studium dissimulanter agens.
Non ignota tibi nostræ quoque formula vitæ:
Signatis quam tu condideras tabulis;
Prodita non unquam. Sed matris cura retexit
Sedula, quam timidi cura tegebat avi (21).

Thy Art from conscious Stars our Lives can date,
And in Heav'ns Aspects read the Book of Fate.
There all my future Fortunes didst thou trace,
And in thy Schemes the pleasing Secret place.
But what the Grandsire with such Care conceal'd,
The curious Mother's prying Eye reveal'd.

He adds, that *Arborius*, meeting, from time to time, with the Frowns of adverse Fortune, and lamenting his Son,

(14) Id. in Parental. cap. 1, pag. 110.
(15) Id. in Epiced. pag. 298.
(16) Id. Ib. pag. 302.
(17) Ibid. pag. 303.
(18) See 'caliger, in Vita Ausonii.
(19) Marcell. in Epist. præfixi lib. de Medica. & cap. 25, ejusd. libri.
(20) Scalig. in Vita Auson.
(21) Auson. in Parental. cap. 9. pag. 117.

(f) *And not in the Year 382, as Vinetus affirms, in his Notes on Ausonius's Thanks.*

(g) *See Remark [F].*

(b) *Auson. in Parental. cap. 9.*

(i) *Albertus Petrus Rubenius, Differt. de Vitæ Fl. Mallii Theodori, pag. 81.*

the Emperor *Gratian*, in the Year 379 (f), after having gone through other very considerable Offices; for, besides the Dignity of Quæstor, with which he was honoured in the Life of the Emperor *Valentinian*, he was created Prefect of the *Prætorium* in *Italy*, and in *Gaul*, after the Death of That Prince (g). The Thanks which he gave to the Emperor *Gratian*, for his Promotion to the Consulship, is an excellent Performance. The time of his Death is not certainly known; but it is beyond question, that he was living in the Year 388, and even in the Year 392, and that he lived to a great Age [C]. He had married a Wife of a good Family who died young (b). He had some Children by her, and did not marry any more. He was much esteemed by the Emperor *Theodosius*, and some believe That Monarch conferred on him the Dignity of a *Patrician* (i). They found this on a Letter, which appears, in most Editions, at the beginning of *Ausonius*'s Works. Nothing can be more obliging than That Letter: Some Critics judge it to be supposititious; but they cannot deny that This Emperor very much esteemed *Ausonius*'s Poems, and exhorted him to publish them; for this appears by a Preface which is incontestably That Poet's own. There is an extreme inequality in his Works, either because his Muse was a little too inconstant; or because some Pieces have been inserted in his Poems, which he had but rough drawn, or because some particular Reasons obliged him to permit the Publication of some Verses, which he had not time to polish. Generally speaking, there is something harsh in his Manner, and in his Style; but it was rather the Defect of the Age, than of his Genius. They who are good Judges of Poetry can easily see, that if he had lived in *Augustus*'s time, his Verses would have equalled the best of that time, so much Delicacy and Wit appears in most of his Writings. Though the general Opinion makes him a Christian, yet some learned Persons believe he was not one [D]. If they ground their Objection either on some lascivious Verses

(22) *Id. ib. pag. 118.*

Son, who died at thirty Years of Age, comforted himself, under his Afflictions, with the Expectation of those Dignities, which the Stars had promised to his Grandchild.

Dicebam sed te solatia longa fovere;
Quod mea præcipuus fata maneret honos.
Et modo conciliis animarum mixte piorum
Fata tui certè nota nepotis habes.
Sentis quod quæstor, quod te præfectus, & idem
Consul, honorifico munere commemoro (22).

Pleased with the Honours Fate for me design'd,
No longer thy own Griefs distract thy Mind.
Ev'n now thou smil'st among the Dead, to see
This full Accomplishment of Fate's Decree:
To see me thus adore thy pious Shade,
A Quæstor, Præfect, and a Consul made.

Observe, that he supposes his Grandfather's Soul, even in the Abode of the Blessed, was sensible of the Accomplishment of the Horoscope, and of the particular Dignities which our Poet had obtained at the Emperor's Court. He is less Orthodox in another Place; for he there questions, whether any thing of us remains after our Death.

(23) *Id. in Professoribus, cap. 1, in fine, pag. 243.*

Et nunc, sive aliquid post fata extrema superest,
Vivis adhuc, ævi quod periit meminens;
Sive nihil superest, nec habent longa otia sensus,
Tu tibi vixisti: nos tua fama juvat (23).

And now if after Death there ought remains,
In thy blest Shade sweetest Remembrance reigns.
Or if the Grave no farther Prospect give,
Yet thy past Life, will make thy Fame still live.

(24) *Id. in Clarit Urbibus, cap. 7, pag. 237.*

(25) *And not in the Year 391, as Vinetus affirms in this Place of Ausonius. He is more ex-ift in the Life of Ausonius, is there has it the Year 388.*

(26) *Baron. ad Ann. 394, n. 72, pag. 884.*

(27) *Auson. Oratione actione, pag. 709.*

I cannot tell whether those, who say he was a Pagan, have ever quoted this Passage, as a Proof of their Opinion.

[C] *It is beyond question, that he was living in the Year* 392, *and that he lived to a great Age.*] He speaks (24) of the Punishment of the Tyrant *Maximus*, whom *Theodosius* cut off, in the Year 388 (25). *Baronius* proves, that *Paulinus* dedicated himself to a Monastic Life in his Retirement at *Nola* in the Year 394 (26). It was but few Years after the devout Life he had led in *Spain*, and which *Ausonius* had blamed. This makes us judge, that our Poet was living in the Year 392. Whence it follows, that he lived to a great Age, for he was already old when he was made Consul in the Year 379 (27). Add to this, that there was but very

little difference between his Father's Age, and his own (28); but he survived his Father, who died at Ninety Years of Age.

(28) *Auson. Epist. 1.*

[D] *Some learned Persons believe he was no Christian.*] *Vossius* is of That Number. He says (22), "*Poëta fuit gentilis, quemadmodum ex Paulino liquet: ut quæ Christum celebrant perperam illi sint tributa.* — *He was a Heathen Poet, as appears from* Paulinus: *So that Those Poems, which celebrate Christ, are falsely ascribed to him.*" Father *Briet* affirms the same thing, he only gives *Vossius*'s Expressions another turn. "*Ex Paulino certum est eum Ethnicum fuisse, quare opera Christiana huic adjudicari solita, sine dubio alterius sunt* (30). — *It is certain from* Paulinus, *that he was an Ethnic, and therefore those Christian Compositions usually ascribed to him, must, undoubtedly, to be of another Hand.*" *Borrichius* goes further, for he affirms, that *Ausonius* often incurred *Paulinus*'s Censure, because of his Paganism. "*Religione Ethnicus, Eisque à* Paulino *amico, sed Christiana Sacris dedito identidem objurgatus* (31). — *Paullinus discipulus Ausonii quem colebat ut præceptorem, sed ut aversum à Christiana religione subinde increpabat, quemadmodum ex opere ipsius liquidam est* (32). — *In Religion a Heathen, and on That Account reproached by* Paulinus, *who was his Friend, but had been converted to the Christian Faith.* — Paulinus, *a Scholar of Ausonius, whom he much honoured as his Master, but now and then blamed for his Aversion to Christianity, as is evident from his Works.*" All this shews, that even great Authors do not always take the trouble of going to the Fountain Head, but sometimes stop at the first Testimony they meet with. Those, who consult St *Paulinus*'s Works, find nothing there to persuade them, that *Ausonius* professed Paganism; and since *Paulinus* no where uses any pressing Exhortation to him to be baptized, they conclude, he had already professed the Gospel. They conclude yet it more certainly from those express Words they meet with there,

(29) *Auson. Epist. 1.*

(30) *Briet. de Poët. lib. 4. pag. 50.*

(31) *Borrich. Differtat de Poët. pag. 73.*

(32) *Id. ib. pag. 74.*

Non reor hoc Sancto sic displicuisse Parenti (33).
Mentis ut errorem credat, sic vivere Christo (34).

I hope my holy Tutor now will find
The Christian Faith, no Error of the Mind.

So that the Reading of St *Paulinus*'s Works proves the very Reverse of what *Vossius* and some others have affirmed; it demonstrates *Ausonius*'s Christianity, as *Lilius Gyraldus* acknowledges. "*Christianus quidem Ausonius fuit, ut ex ejus Versibus, & item* Paulini *ejus discipuli facilè colligimus* (35). — *Ausonius was indeed a Christian, as appears from his*

(33) *That is Ausonius.*

(34) *Paulinus in Epistol. defina as Ausonium in fine.*

(35) *Gyrald. Hist. Poët. Dial. 10, pag. 524.*

AUSONIUS.   583

Verses that he composed [E], or on the manner in which he condemned the Solitude of *Paulinus*, or on the intimate Friendship he preserved with the Pagan *Symmachus*, they

"his Verses, and also from his Scholar Paulinus."
It is therefore without Foundation that some would take from This Poet, what appears in Praise of JESUS CHRIST in his Collection of Verses. Nay, tho' we should take from him the *Carmen Paschale*, which begins with

Omnipotens solo mentis mihi cognite cultu,

as some Critics would take from him the *Oratio Paschalis, versibus Rophalicis*, yet there would be enough left in his Works to confute Those, who affirm he was a Pagan. Now see of what Consequence it is to apply to some among the Moderns, rather than others, when one is not willing to be at the Pains to run to the Fountain. If *Vossius* had addressed himself to *Baronius*, he would have avoided the Fault he has committed, and so would They who copied it. He could never have believed, after reading *Baronius*, that St *Paulinus* gives the least Proof of the pretended Paganism of our Poet *Ausonius*; for That learned Cardinal relates the respectful Answer of St *Paulinus*, and makes it appear, that *Ausonius*'s Thoughts, on That Friend's Retreat, does not differ from Those, which worldly Christians form, daily, when they see a young Man of Quality renounce all the Enjoyments of the World, to dedicate himself to a Monastic Life (36). It is pretended, that *Ausonius* thought some Misanthropic Humour, or Malady like That of *Bellerophon*, made *Paulinus* retire from the World, and renounce the Muses (37).

*Tristis, egens, deserta colit: tacitusque pererrat
Alpini convexa jugi: ceu dicitur olim
Mentis inops, coetus hominum, & vestigia vitans,
Avia pertustrasse vagus loca Bellerophontes* (38).

Deserts, or Alpine *Hills*, *shall be his Haunts,
His dire Attendants, Silence, Grief, and Want*:
*There, like Bellerophon, disturb'd in Mind,
Far shall he fly all Footsteps of Mankind.*

Thousands and Thousands of Christians might have made the same Judgment; it must therefore be but an impertinent Proof of Paganism. Without doubt *Arnisæus*, and the *French* Author, whom he quotes, were Christians, and yet they judged, like *Ausonius*, of the love of Solitude; they discovered, clearly enough, that they imputed the Retirement of the Founders of Monks, to a melancholy Humour. "Medici inter signa morbi melancholici referunt, si quis quærat solitudinem, aut si quem tristis agat mœror, torvave severam fronte, vel à lætis sociorum cœtibus arceat; & Gallicus quidam non inconcinnus scriptor, ejus ordinis fuisse censet Franciscum, Dominicum, aliosque Eremitas, aut Anachoretas, qui contra naturæ præscriptum politicis societatibus se subtraxerunt, in eremos, instar Endymionum, sese abdiderunt, & quo melancholica ingenia maxime afficiebantur, novum vitæ genus, affectatæ religionis pallio vestitum, considerunt (39). ——— The *Physicians* esteem it a Sign of a Melancholy Disorder, to seek Solitude, or to be given up to Grief, to have a stern, sour, Countenance, or to fly good Fellowship; and a judicious *French* Writer is of Opinion, "that This *Class* will take in Franciscus, Dominicus, and other Hermits, or Anchorets, who, against the Law of Nature, have withdrawn themselves from human Societies, and hid themselves in Wildernesses, like Endymion, and afterwards covered, under the Cloak of Religion, that new Kind of Life which They affected only out of a melancholy Disposition." *Baronius* has not forgot to observe, that *Ausonius* was educated by two Nuns, who were his Aunts (40). This is a Proof that he was of a Christian Family. Now, Christianity being upon the Throne in those Times, and Paganism exposed to Disgrace and Persecution, it seldom happened that a Christian turned Pagan. Since, then, *Ausonius* was educated from his Infancy in Christianity, we ought to believe he professed it all the Days of his Life; for nothing is more absurd than the Thought of *Giselinus*, who says, That *Claudian* and *Ausonius*, being prevailed upon by the Authority and Eloquence of *Symmachus*, abjured the Christian Faith, and plunged themselves again into Idolatry (41). He pretends to prove this by the

Testimony of St *Augustin*, and by the great Friendship *Symmachus* expressed in his Letters to them. The Jesuit who confutes this, shews, that St *Augustin*, without mentioning *Ausonius*, said only, that *Claudian* had been addicted to Paganism (42); this is not affirming he had ever once been a Christian. And as for what concerns *Ausonius*, he is justified as well by the Silence of the Emperor *Gratian*, and of St *Paulinus*, as by their Kindnesses. We might add, that the Reason, borrowed from the Friendship of *Symmachus*, is the weakest in the World: they were not united by the Conformity of Religion, but by the love they both of them had for Learning.

It cannot be denied, but that Mr *Baillet* embraces the Opinion of those who pretend, that *Ausonius* was a Pagan, I say it cannot be denied, when we consider his Words. "These are Defects, which he ought to have made up by some good Qualities, and by Maxims and Sentiments drawn from Morality, as the best Poets of Antiquity took care to do before him. But, as he lived among Christians, he was afraid, perhaps, that he might be mistaken for one of them, if his Opinions, in Morals, had been found agreeable to theirs (43)." It is certain, that the best Maxims of Morality are found in *Ausonius*'s Works, and particularly the Apophthegms of the ancient Sages of *Greece*. What can be a finer Piece of Morality, than his Description of *Vir bonus* (44)?

[E] *He composed some lascivious Verses.*] Scaliger the Father, found some of *Ausonius*'s Epigrams so filthy, that he thought Fire only was able to purify them. "Nonnulla (epigrammata) adeo fœda atque detestanda ut neque scriptore neque auditore digna, non in spongium incumbere merita sint, sed solis si ignis expiari posse videantur (45). ——— Some (Epigrams) *are so detestably obscene, that they deserve neither Writer nor Reader, and, instead of the Spunge, they seem to me to merit no other Purification than That of the Flames.*" I wonder he says nothing against the Obscenities of the *Cento nuptialis*, which have principally excited the Indignation of several other Authors. Here is a fine Passage of Mr *Baillet*: "It were, at least, to be wished, that some body had expunged the abominable *Cento*, that wicked Piece of Patchwork, which he made up of several half Verses of *Virgil*, on Subjects purely *amorous*. It is with much Justice, that the University of *Paris* complained, Forty Years ago, of the Malice of This Poet, in making *Virgil* speak in so very lewd a manner; who of all the Poets of Antiquity was most celebrated for his Chastity *. And Father *Briet*, a Jesuit, has carried his Zeal yet further †, when he represents this Action of *Ausonius* to us as an Outrage highly penal; declaring it to be as great a Piece of impudent Assurance, as of scandalous Obscenity, to make such a Misapplication; and that there was something rather diabolical than human in That pernicious Art of perverting Things, and changing good into bad, to lay Snares for the Innocence and Integrity of Youth (46)." And because many Persons will be glad to read Father *Briet*'s own Words, I am going to copy them. *Centones ejus Virgiliani non tantum impurissimi sunt, sed & impudentissimi, quibus castissimos versus, libidinosæ affinxit materiæ, opere, quod plus dæmonem, quàm hominem sapiret, adolescentium pudicitiæ insidiantem.* *Ausonius* wrote That Piece at the Instance of the Emperor *Valentin an*, who had composed such another. He excuses him himself on That Order, and observes, that a Prince cannot express any sort of Command more absolute, than That of a Request. He found himself much perplexed; for, in writing a wicked Poem, he exposed himself to the Accusation of grossly sacrificing his Reputation to Flattery; and by writing a better Poem than That of the Emperor, he was like to be condemned for his Insolence, in having the Assurance to be more witty than his Master. He affirms, I. That he observed such a Medium, that, without pretending to outdo *Valentinian*, he wrote a Poem not inferior to his. II. That he had the Advantage of pleasing him, and not having conquered him, he did not incur the Disgrace, which a Victory might have drawn upon him.

This

VOL. I.   7 H

AUSONIUS.

(b) In Epist. ad Solom. Pantherum. they are grossly mistaken. These are, however, the most specious Reasons which have been alledged. *Ritterhusius* looked upon That Friendship as a great Prodigy (k). *Scaliger's*

This is the Language of a cunning Courtier. But to do This Poet all the Justice, which the Delicacy of his Wit and Pen here deserves, we must hear his own Words. " Piget Virgiliani carminis dignitatem tam jo- " culari dehonestasse materia; sed quid facerem? jussum " erat, quodque est POTENTISSIMUM IMPERANDI " GENUS, rogabat qui jubere poterat, S. imperator " Valentinianus, vir meo judicio eruditus: qui nup- " tias quondam ejusmodi ludo descripserat, aptis " equidem versibus & compositione festiva. Experi- " ri deinde volens, quantum nostra contentione prae- " celleret, simile nos de eodem concinnare praecepit. " Quam scrupulosum hoc mihi fuerit, intellige. Ne- " que anteferri volebam, neque posthaberi: quum " aliorum quoque judicio detegenda esset adulatio " inepta, si cederem: insolentia, si ut aemulus emine- " rem. Suscepi igitur similis recusanti: feliciterque *(47) Auson. in Praefat. Cent. Nup-tial. p. 500, 501.* " & obnoxius gratiam tenui, nec victor offendi (47). " ------ *I am ashamed to have disgraced the Dig- " nity of Virgil's Poetry on so jocular a Subject: But " what could I do? I was commanded to do it, and, " which is* THE MOST ABSOLUTE SORT OF COM- " MAND, *I was desired to do it, by him who could " have commanded it, even by his Sacred Imperial " Majesty* Valentinian, *a Prince, in my Judgment, " truly learned: who had, himself, treated a Nuptial " Subject after the same ludicrous Manner, in very " apt and witty Poetry. Desiring therefore to try, " how far he should excel, in this our Trial of Skill, " he commanded me to undertake the Work. You will " readily imagine I had a very nice Task. I was " neither willing to excel, nor be excelled: if I " fell short, it would look, in the Judgment of others, " like Flattery: if I out-did, it would seem Insolence. " I undertook it, therefore, with an Appearance of Un- " willingness: and, by a happy Course, I kept in Favour " as an Equal, and offended not as a Superior"* If it were true, that the *Cento nuptialis* of the Emperor *Valentinian* was not inferior to that of *Ausonius,* it must be said, that This Monarch was not unskilled in Poetry; and besides, as he was grave, and of exemplary Chastity, it may serve much for *Ausonius's* Justification. ' Omni pudicitiae cultu domi castus, " & foris, nulo contagio conscientiae violatus ob- " scenae, nihil incestum: hanque ob causam tan- " quam retinaculis petulantiam fraenarat Aulae rega- *(48) Amm. Marcell. lib. 30, cap. 9* " lis (48). ------ *He observed the strictest Chastity, " at home and abroad, and avoided all Obscenity and " Pollution: and thus bridled, by his Example, the " Licentiousness of his Court."* So great an Example may clearly prove, that the most severe and chast Persons give way sometimes to witty Performances, wherein the Descriptions of the chief Nuptial Ceremony abound with too much Looseness and Obscenity; for there is no question to be made, but this Piece of Poetry of the Emperor *Valentinian* was very wanton. The Subject required it, being Matrimonial, which is always treated in a merry Vein. " Nup- *(49) Auson. in Praefat. Cent. Nup-tial. p. 500, 501.* " tias quondam ejusmodi ludo descripserat (*Valenti- " nianus*) aptis equidem versibus, & compositione " festivâ (49). ------ *He (*Valentinian*) had himself " treated a Nuptial Subject after the same ludicrous " Manner, in very apt and witty Poetry."* We may *(50) See the Art. cic* be well assured that the Emperor's Verses were no less amorous than Those of the Emperor *Gallienus* (50). *(51) See Mr Flechier in tre Life of Theodosius, pag. 52.* It must be acknowledged then, that *Ausonius* deserves some excuse, because he wrote his Nuptial Cento by way of Imitation, and at the request of his Master, one of the most grave and chast Emperors that ever was, and, besides, a great Follower of the most pure Christian Doctrine (51). So that if he had not allowed of a Toleration (52), it would have been said of him, that he wanted no Talent, which becomes the most Orthodox Monarchs. I only remark this to shew, that Those, who place *Ausonius* among *(52) Amm. Marcell. lib. 30, cap. 10, & ibi Valesius.* the *Pagan* Poets, under pretence that he wrote such a lascivious Piece of Poetry as that *Cento Nuptialis,* do not give Things a thorough Examination. Without doubt he is to blame; I do not pretend to excuse him. I only say, that this Fact is not a Proof of Paganism, nor sufficient to give any just Suspicions, that he was not a very Orthodox Christian. I prove this from the Circumstances of it. I mean, from the Emperor's Character, who

commanded him to compose such a Writing, and approved it. How many Christian Poets are there, whose Works are more lascivious than this *Cento Nuptialis?* Many of them must be degraded from the Name of Christians, if we follow the Maxim of *Gyraldus,* " Christianus quidem Ausonius fuit ----- " sed petulantior tamen & lascivior quam ut inter *(53) Gyrald. Hist. Poet. Dial. 10, p. 514.* " Christianos numerari dignus sit (53). ------ Auso- " *nius was indeed a Christian, but so loose and las- " civious, that he deserves not to be named among " Christians."* Without going so far as *Italy,* is there not an *Epithalamium* in the Works of a Poet at the *Hague,* which, for Obscenity, does not yield to the *Cento of Ausonius* (54). I address this prin-*(54) See Ba-sium 20, five Epithalamium of John Secundus, p. 203.* cipally to *Ritterhusius,* who looked upon the Conduct of *Ausonius,* as monstrous: I mean, that a Poet, who was a Christian, both in Practice and Profession, should write lasciviously: " Illud impri- " mis apud me monstri instar habet, hominem Chri- " stianum, &, ut apparet, non nomine tantum; " sed e pectore & moribus, adeo saepe lasciva at- " que improba scribere potuisse, ut nisi nomen Au- " sonii esset adscriptum, Bilbilitanum poëtam le- *(55) Conrad. Ritterhus. Epist ac So-lom. Pan-therum.* " gere putes (55). ------ *To me it appears particular- " ly monstrous, that one, who is a Christian, and " that, as it seems, not in Name only, but also in " Morals and Disposition, could write such wicked " and lascivious Verses, that if the Title did not " shew them to be* Ausonius's*, you would think you " was reading* Martial." He is not satisfied with the Excuse the Author made on the Purity of his Life,

Lasciva est nobis pagina, Vita proba est.

My Book is wanton, but my Life is chast.

(56) See Re-mark [D] of the Article VAYER. I relate this Excuse at length, in another Article (56). Let us observe, that *Ausonius* was so sensible that he should be blamed, that he endeavours to justify himself at the beginning, in the middle, and at the end, of That small Poem. We have seen what he said at the beginning, we shall see in another Place *(57) Ibid.* (57), what he said at the end: It remains only to observe, what he said in the middle. Know then, that after having described the Wedding-Feast, the Procession of the Bride and Bridegroom, the Wedding Presents, the Complements of the Company; and having modestly enough represented the first Discourse of the married Couple, he stops there, and advertises his Readers, that what he had to say more, not being covered with a Veil, it was their part to decline going any farther. " Hactenus castis auribus " audiendum mysterium nuptiale, ambitu loquendi, " & circumitione velavi. Verum quoniam & sescen- " ninos amat celebritas nuptialis, verborumque petu- " lantiam notus vetere instituto ludus admittit, cae- " tera quoque cubiculi & lectuli operta prodentur, " ab eodem auctore collecta: ut bis erubescamus, " qui & Virgilium faciamus impudentem. Vos, si " placet, hic jam legendi modum ponite, caetera *(58) Auson. Nupt. pag. 523, 514.* " curiosis relinquite (58). ------ *Thus far I have " veiled the Nuptial Mystery with many Words, and in " long Descriptions, for an Entertainment to modest " Ears. But, because the matrimonial Solemnity re- " quires some smutty Mirth, and Custom has autho- " rised these loose Descriptions, the remaining Secrets " of the Chamber and Bed, will be given you by " the same Author; who must blush again and again, " for imposing upon* Virgil's *Words so impudent a Mean- " ing. You that please may stop here; and leave the " rest to those who are more curious."* He has reason to say, that what he calls *Imminutio* (59), will be *(59) That is, The Deflo-ration.* described in very obscene Terms. *Moreri* has been the most indulgent of all Men: *There are some Pieces,* says he, *which* Ausonius *composed in his Youth, wherein he complies too much with the Liberty of the Age he lived in.* This Censure is not rigid enough, and supposes a Falsity; for certainly *Ausonius* was not young when he composed the Nuptial Cento. I do not speak of the Verses which he made on a handsome Slave, whose Name was *Bissula,* and who had been adjudged to him for his Share of the Plunder, after a great Victory obtained in *Germany,* in the

Year

AUSONIUS.

Scaliger's Mistakes [F], and the principal Editions of Ausonius [G], will be the Subject of

Year 368; for we do not know to what Degree of Licentiousness he carried Them; They are lost, and we may only conjecture, that They were very free, since he requires Readers who had drunk hard.

— — — — — admoneo, ante bibas.
Jejunis nil scribo: meum post pocula si quis
Legerit, hic sapiet (60).

He who would relish our lascivious Page,
Must first with flowing Cups his Taste engage.

This does not agree at all with what remains of this Poem; there is nothing obscene either in the Words or Thoughts; we must conclude therefore, that the greatest Part of it is lost. A certain Commentator, without thinking of this, has proved the same thing by another Argument. He Remarks, That this Poem is too short at present, to suppose it ever could have had so large a Preface as we now find prefixed to it (61); and consequently it must have been much longer, when the Author finished it, than we now have it. However, *Ausonius*, who was then past the Heat of Youth, described, in all likelihood, the Charms of his Slave with a pretty deal of Freedom: She appeared so agreeable to him from the first Moment, that he presently set her at Liberty (62).

[F] *These are Scaliger's Mistakes.*] I. He believed, *Ausonius* was raised to the Office of Prefect of the *Prætorium*, in the Emperor *Valentinian*'s Life (63). This is not true, *Ausonius* declares that he owed this Office solely to the Emperor *Gratian*. " Tot gra- " dus nomine Comitis propter tua incrementa con- " gesti, ex tuo merito, te ac patre principibus, quæ- " situra communia, & tui tantum Præfectura benefi- " cii (64). — So many Honours heaped upon me, " at being your Præceptor, on account of your own " Proficiencies, and great Merit, by both Emperors, " your Father and yourself, the Quæstorship your joint " Gift, but the Præfectship your own single Favour." II. Scaliger believed, without Reason, that there was a Mistake in the *Theodosian* Code, where mention is made of *Auxonius*, Præfect of the *Prætorium* (65). He would have it read *Ausonius*, and not *Auxonius*. He would not have required such a Correction, if he had observed, that the Person, concerned in that place of *Theodosius*'s Code, died about the Year 371, and that *Ausonius* enjoyed the Consulship in the Year 379, and lived yet many Years after. III. He would have all the Laws addressed to *Antonius*, Præfect of the *Prætorium*, to be corrected, and that *Ausonius* should be read in those Places, and not *Antonius*. This is wrong, for it is certain, that *Ausonius* was honoured with the Office of Præfect of the *Prætorium* of *Italy*, in the Year 376, five Months after the Death of the Emperor *Valentinian*, and that his Son *Hesperius* was given him for his Colleague (66). We know, also, that *Antonius* was made Præfect of the *Prætorium* of *Gaul*, about the same time. *Antonius* remained in the same State the following Year; *Ausonius* and his Son, discharged the Præfectship of *Italy*, and *Antonius*, that of *Gaul*; but, in the Year 378, *Antonius* was Præfect of the *Prætorium* in *Italy*, and *Ausonius* and his Son, were Præfects in *Gaul*, and so continued 'till the Year 380. You will find the Proofs of all this, in the Author quoted in the Margin (67). IV. Scaliger believed, that *Ausonius* spoke of himself in these two Verses:

Aut Italum populos, Aquilonigenasque Britannos
Præfecturarum titulo tenuere secundo (68).

Latians, and farthest Britains too obey
Th' appointed Præfect's delegated Sway.

It is a Mistake: The Poem, wherein these two Verses are, was composed in the Life-time of the Emperor *Valentinian* (69). Now *Ausonius* was not Præfect of the *Prætorium*, 'till after the Death of that Prince (70). V. There is no crediting what *Scaliger* affirms, That *Ausonius*, after his Consulship, enjoyed the Office of Proconsul of *Asia*, and that of Vicar of the Diocese of *Africa* (71). We find, indeed, one *Auxonius*, that was Vicar of the Diocese of *Asia*, in the Year 365, and another *Auxonius*, that was Pro-

consul of *Asia*, in the Year 381 (72). But this is nothing to *Scaliger*'s Opinion. VI. He mistakes the Uncle for the Grandfather, in these Words. " Hoc " tanto viro nascitur Burdegalæ Decius Magnus Au- " sonius nomine avi materni, cognomine patris (73). " — *Of so great a Man was:* Decius Magnus " Ausonius *born at Bourdeaux, taking his Name* " *from his Grandfather, by the Mother, his Sirname* " *from his Father*." *Ausonius*'s Grandfather, by the Mother, was called *Cæcilius Argicius Arborius*; he left a Son, whose Name was *Æmilius Magnus Arborius*. So that *Scaliger*'s Mistake is plain. VII. He says, that *Hilaria*, and *Julia Cataphronia*, who had made a Vow of Virginity, were *Ausonius*'s Aunts, by the Mother (74). This is only true with regard to *Æmilia Hilaria*, for the Nun *Julia Cataphronia*, was his Aunt by the Father (75).

[G] — *and the principal Editions of* Ausonius.] *Gesner*, and his Abbreviators, affirm, That *Aldus* is the first who published this Poet. They do not say in what Year, but, if they mean the Edition of *Venice*, in 1517, they may easily be confuted; for besides, that *Aldus* was not then living, Mr *Van Beughem* affirms, that *Ausonius* was printed at *Milan*, in 1490 (76), and, since that, at *Venice*, in the Year 1496, with a Preface, by *George Merula* (77). The Edition of *Basil*, 1523, by *Valentine Curio*, is sufficiently known: That of *Lewis Mireus*, printed at *Lyons*, by *John de Tournes*, in the Year 1557, is preferable to all the former. The Bibliographers mention it, but I do not see that they take any notice of That which *Ducheri* published ; in praise of which, *Nicolas Bourbon* made four Verses, which may be seen on the reverse of the Title of the Edition of *Lyons*, by *Sebastian Gryphius*, 1549. I say nothing of *Plantin*'s Edition, 1568, with the Notes of *Theodorus Pulman*. That of *Joseph Scaliger*, at *Lyons*, by *Anthony Gryphius*, in 1575, with a very learned Commentary, under the Title of *Ausonianæ lectiones*, eclipsed all the former. Every Body knows, that *Elias Vinetus* is one of the Commentators who has bestowed most Pains on our Poet's Works. He was Teacher of Classical Learning at *Bourdeaux*, and being pressed, by several Persons of that City, to publish an Edition of their famous Countryman, he endeavoured to oblige them, but found no Manuscript of *Ausonius*, in the Libraries of *Bourdeaux*, so that all he could do, was to compare the Editions together. He restored and corrected several Passages, and while he was preparing his Commentaries, to give the Reasons of his Criticisms, he caused *Ausonius*'s Works to be printed, as he had corrected them. His Friend, *James Goupil*, had the Care of this Edition, which is that of *Paris*, 1551. Some Years after *Vinetus* recovered a Manuscript, found near *Lyons*, and which gave him much Light; and as that left him but little Excuse to those who pressed him to print his Notes, he published the Poem *de Claris Urbibus* at *Poitiers*, together with his Commentary, in the Year 1565. He sent a Compleat Copy of *Ausonius*'s Works to *Anthony Gryphius*, who had desired it of him, and engaged to print it immediately; but that Edition not appearing, he was persuaded to make use of the Press, which was set up, in the mean Time, at *Bourdeaux*. He therefore gave another Copy to *Simon Millanges*, who began to print it at *Bourdeaux*, in the Month of *February* 1575, and finished it by the beginning of Summer, in the same Year. At the same time came out the Edition of *Gryphius*; but, for want of Paper, *Millanges* could not print off *Vinetus*'s Commentary. It was not printed 'till four Years after *Millanges*'s Edition of *Ausonius*'s Works (78). Therefore, to speak properly, it ought not to be said, that the best Edition of *Ausonius*, is that of *Bourdeaux*, with the Commentaries of *Elias Vinetus*, in the Year 1575. *Præ reliquis verò laudanda locu- lenta Ausonii Editio, cum commentariis viri docti Eliæ Vineti vulgata, Burdigalæ A.* 1575. *& post ejus obitum A.* 1590, 4. (79). For, as I have said before, those Commentaries did not appear 'till 1580. *Moreri* has been exact in this Point; he is only mistaken, in saying *Vinetus* was of *Xaintes*; the Word *Santo* signifies nothing here but *Saintongeois*, one of the Country of *Saintoinge*. The Library of the Archbishop of *Reims* (80), mentions an *Ausonius*, printed by

AUSONIUS. AUSTRIA.

of two Remarks below; and I shall not forget to observe the Mistake of *Trithemius*, who pretended that *Ausonius* was Bishop of *Bourdeaux* [H].

by *Millanges*, at *Bourdeaux*, with the Commentaries of *Elias Vinetus*, in the Year 1575. I imagine that this Mistake proceeds from applying the Date 1575, to all the Pieces bound together, which only suits with *Ausonius*'s Works, at the beginning of the Volume. *Borrichius* is in the Wrong to say, I. That the Edition of *Vinetus*, is one of the best. II. That *Vinetus* has commented upon *Ausonius*'s Poem *de Urbibus* (81). Does not this look as if he had wrote no Commentaries on the other Poems of *Ausonius*? The best Edition of this Poet, is that of *Amsterdam* 1671; but I have elsewhere observed (82), that the Title falsely promises, that they have there inserted all the entire Notes of *Mariangelus Accursius*.

I shall give a Supplement to all this, in the Article MARTELLIUS (HUGOLIN), at the End of the Remark [A]. Not having Father *Lacarry*'s Book (83), I am forced to content myself with what I find of it in the *Journal des Sçavans*. "The double Prefect-ship of *Ausonius*, which gave *Scaliger* so much "Trouble, is here clearly explained. We find that, "in the Year 378, *Ausonius* was Prefect of the *Prætorium*, in the *Gauls*, and in *Italy*, with his Son "*Hesperius*; but he was not Prefect in *Italy*, any "longer than 'till about the Month of *July*, at which "time one *Antonius* was appointed Prefect of the "*Prætorium* in *Italy*, as he is said to have been in "the Code. So that the Prefectship of *Ausonius* and "*Hesperius*, in *Italy*, was interrupted by *Antonius*; "but he enjoyed it again, together with his Son, "in 379, and continued, with him, that in the "*Gauls*, without any interruption, during the Years

"378, and 379 (84)." This Hypothesis, and Chronology, are not agreeable to the Sentiment of *Rubenius*, before related. If I had Father *Lacarry*'s Book, I might, perhaps, be able to determine which of them has explained this Matter with greatest Accuracy.

[H] *Trithemius pretended that* Ausonius *was Bishop of* Bourdeaux.] *Trithemius* affirms, That this Bishop was very learned in the Scriptures, and as remarkable for his Piety as his Learning, and that he flourished under *Maximus*, in the Year 310, and did some handsome Things, with St *Martin*, St *Ambrose*, and St *Jerom*, in the Synod, which That Prince caused to be held at *Tryers*. What a heap of Fables are here! *Vinetus* observes, that some Persons will have it, that *Ausonius* was canonized. He says also, that the Inhabitants of *Angoulême* honoured one *Ausonius*, amongst their chief Saints, who was, as they say, their first Bishop, and he does not think it impossible, but that the Poet *Ausonius*, upon being elected Bishop by the Inhabitants of *Angoulême*, might have accepted that Dignity (85). A Manuscript Chronicle of *Angoulême*, says, that *Ausonius*, a Disciple of St *Martial*, and Bishop of *Angoulême*, suffered Martyrdom, when the *Vandals* ravaged *Gaul* (86). *Alteserra* confutes this, by observing, that a Disciple of St *Martial* could not be living in the beginning of the IVth Century, when the Irruption of the *Vandals* (87) happened. However it be, our *Ausonius* is represented in very various Lights. Some say that he was not so much as a Christian; and others, that he is in the Catalogue of the canoniz'd Saints.

AUSTRIA (Don JOHN of), Natural Son of the Emperor *Charles* V, was born, at *Ratisbon*, the Twenty fourth of *February* 1545. A Gentlewoman of *Ratisbon*, whose Name was *Barbara BLOMBERG* (a), was willing to pass for his Mother [A], to save the real Mother the Scandal she must necessarily have undergone in being

[A] *Barbara Blomberg was willing to pass for his Mother.*] *Famianus Strada* says, that Cardinal *de la Cueva* revealed this Secret to him (1). That Cardinal had learned it from the Infanta *Clara Eugenia*, to whom *Philip* II, who concealed nothing from her, had discovered it. This Prince always pretended to the World, that *Barbara Blomberg* was the Mother of *Don John*. "Eodemque loco habitam à Philippo "Rege scenæ pariter inserviente (2). ——— *And was* "*treated as such by King* Philip, *who likewise kept* "*up the Pretence.*" The Sacrifice which that Lady was willing to make of her own Reputation, to that of a great Princess, is nothing near so great as may be imagined: It is thought a Scandal to pass for a private Gentleman's Mistress; but how many Ladies glory to be Mistresses of Kings and Emperors? I have said that this Sacrifice was made in favour of a great Princess: *Strada* informs me of it. "Joannem Au-"striacum non ex Barbara Blomberga uti creditum "ad eam diem, sed ex longe illustriori ac Plane "Principe femina procreatum: cujus ut famæ par-"ceretur prætentam fuisse aliam à Carolo Cæsare.——— "*John of* Austria *was not born of* Barbara Blomberg, "*as was then believed, but of a much more illustrious* "*Lady, and even a Princess, to save whose Reputation,* "*That other was only pretended by* Charles *the Emperor.*" The same Historian remarks, that *Don John* was twice deceived, as to his Mother, and never informed of the Truth. He first believed himself to be the Son of *Magdalen Ulloa*, and afterwards of *Barbara Blomberg*. How happy and vigilant soever he was to discover the most secret Intrigues of the Enemy, he could never unravel this domestic Mystery. "Ha-"bet profecto unde minus sibi de sua sagacitate pla-"ceat humanum ingenium, quando tantus princeps, "atque intima quæque vel in hoste rimari solitus, "domi suæ, suorumque ignarus adeo vixerit obierit-"que, ut bis in matre deceptus, semper alienam co-"luerit, nunquam suam (3). ——— *It is indeed enough* "*to make the human Understanding less proud of it's* "*Sagacity, to see that so great a Prince, who could* "*penetrate into the closest Secrets of the Enemy, should* "*yet live and die so ignorant of his own Birth, and* "*of what so nearly concerned him, that he was twice* "*mistaken in his Mother, and could never discover*

"*where to pay his Duty right.*" I wonder that Father *Strada* says nothing of a third Person, who passed for *Don John*'s Mother. The Author of a learned Dissertation, printed in 1688 (4), speaks with great Praise of *Catharine de Cordonna*, born at *Naples* in the Year 1559. She went into *Spain*, with her Cousin the Princess of *Salerno*, in the Year 1559, and, by her Virtue and Piety, acquired the esteem of *Philip* II, in such manner, that he commanded *Rui Gomez*, Prince of *Evoly*, Governour of *Don Carlos*, and *Don John*, to take care of This Lady. *Rui Gomez* took her home to his House, and, upon observing her admirable Prudence, desired her to undertake the Government of his Family, and to assist him in the Education of the two Princes. She acquitted herself of that Trust with all the care imaginable, and *Don John* always honoured her as his Mother. The Author of the Dissertation makes a Remark on that word: *Before we go any farther,* says he (5), *we ought to clear that Saint from an abominable Calumny, by which some abusing that word, would insinuate as if she was the true Mother of John of* Austria. *Strada of Rosberg seems to have given occasion to that supposition, by describing that Prince's Mother, in his Genealogy of the House of* Austria, *only by the Name of* Catharine. *But the chast and mortified Life which* Catharine de Cordonna *always led from her Infancy, could not leave Room for such a Suspicion.* He adds several other Reasons to justify *Catharine de Cordonna*, and ends the Remark with these Words: *It was another more illustrious Person* (who was the Mother of *John of* Austria) *and whom our Saint* (6) *had also known, as the Historian of her Life observes*; *but who, for weighty Considerations, was never discovered.* Let us add to all this a Passage of Mr *Varillas*. The secret of the Birth of *John of* Austria, says he (7), *was never rightly discovered, and whether the too high quality of his true Mother required all these Precautions*; *or that more care was taken to avoid the Scandal, than the Sin*; *it is certain that* Charles *only discovered to* Quichade *whose Son* John of Austria *was*: *and that he ordered him to let him pass for his own Son, till his Imperial Majesty, in resigning his Dominions to* Philip II, *informed him that he was his natural Brother.* This Moderation of Mr *Varillas* is more to be commended,

AUSTRIA. 587

being publickly known to be so. The Child was carried into *Spain*, before he was a Year old [B]; the Emperor charged *Lewis Quixada* with this Commission, whom he had several times experienced to be very well qualified for keeping a Secret (b). He ordered him to let the Child be brought up by his Wife *Magdalen Ulloa*, without giving any body room to suspect who was the Father. *Quixada* served his Master in This, with all the Fidelity imaginable, for he did not only keep the Secret inviolable, but had also an extraordinary Care of *Don John*'s Education. *Charles*, upon his Death Bed, discovered, to his Son *Philip*, that he was the Father of the young Lord whom *Quixada* educated at *Villagarsia*, and charged him to acknowledge him for the future as his Brother, and to treat him in that Quality. *Philip* did not perform this Order till two Years after [C], but then he did it in a very genteel Manner. He caused *Don John* to be educated with *Don Carlos*, and *Alexander Farnese*. Those three Princes were almost of an Age, but *Don John* was much the finest, both in Person and Parts. *Philip* was displeased at the aversion he found in him to an Ecclesiastical Character, for which his Father had designed him. And much less at a Frolick of That young Lord, in taking a Journey to *Barcelona*, without the King's leave, accompanied with a great number of young Gentlemen, to go to the War of *Malta*. But the Letters he received from the King, before he embarked, put a stop to that Voyage. He so readily obeyed the Order, he had received to return, that he, in some measure, appeased *Philip*'s anger by so immediate a Compliance; and he entirely recovered his Favour, by making the first Discovery to him of *Don Carlos*'s Machinations. There was but very little Friendship between Those two young Princes [D]. A little while after, *Don John* was sent to the Kingdom of *Granada* against the *Moors*, and signalized himself in that War. He was declared *Generalissimo* of the League against the *Turks*, and, in that Post, gained the famous Battle of *Lepanto*, in the Year 1571. After which he took the City of *Tunis*, and That of *Biserta*, and returned triumphant into *Italy*, attended by *Amidas*, King of *Tunis*, whom he had made Prisoner. He had left a Garrison in *Tunis* against *Philip*'s Order, and there was already a Rumour of conferring upon him the Title of King of *Tunis*, by the Interposition of the Pope. The King of *Spain* was not at all pleased with these continual Successes; the Idea which he formed to himself of that young Prince's Ambition made him uneasy (c). He sent him to command in the *Netherlands*; but ordered him to pacify those Provinces: He had not a Mind to have him there at the head of an Army. Being thus prejudiced against him, he easily believed all Reports which could give him room to suspect his Brother's Conduct; and some say, that, to increase the Misunderstanding, means were used to inform him, that *Don John* was going to be married to Queen *Elizabeth* (d). To cut the Matter short, I shall just observe, that *Escovedo*,

(b) Quem expertus erat arcanorum celantissimum, Strada, decad. 1, lib. 10, pag. 612.

(c) Quod Philippo suspicionem intendit istum victoriarum cursu juvenem non diu laturum privatam fortunam & regna jam re rogare alienum. --- quando invasit Philippus animum, to suspect, that so young a Conqueror would be too much elated with his Victories, to be long satisfied with a private Condition, and that his next Step would be to importune him for some Kingdom. Id. ib. pag. 617.

(d) See Remark [F].

---

mended, than the Liberty taken in the second Edition of the *Menagiana*, in declaring plainly, that *Don John* of *Austria* was born of his Father's own Mother. What gave occasion to this, was an excellent Saying of *Charles* V. It seems upon cancelling an unjust Privilege, which he had granted, He said, *I had rather deface my Hand-Writing, than my Conscience*. Upon which we find, in the second Edition of the *Menagiana*, pag. 422, the following Gloss. *What a tender Conscience is here, for one who was so great a Cheat all his Life, and, if scandal may be believed, did not scruple to lie with his own Sister, while* Barbara Blomberg *served as a Screen to this incestuous Commerce, by passing for the Mother of* Don John *of Austria*.

[B] *The Child was carried into* Spain *before he was a Year old*.] *Brantome* tells another Story, which I will relate in the Remarks of the Article BLOMBERG; and which ought not to be believed to the Prejudice of *Strada*.

[C] *Charles* V *discovered, to* Philip II, *that* Don John *was his Brother, and charged him to acknowledge him as such --- which he obeyed but --- till two Years after*.] The Application of an Historian to the principal Matters, makes him sometimes not discover a Slip in Calculation. Here *Strada* affirms, that *Don John* was born the Twenty fourth of *February* 1545; that his Father died the Twenty first of *September* 1558; that *Philip* acknowledged *Don John* two Years after the Death of his Father; that he caused him to be educated with his Son *Don Carlos*; and that These two Princes had not yet attained to their fifteenth Year, *annum quartum decimum nondum supergressi*. If *Strada* had reckoned right, he would have made it above fifteen Years. It cannot be pretended that the Year 1547. was That of the Birth. I confess that Mr *Moreri* vouches it, but it cannot be the Opinion of *Strada*, since, by placing the Death of *Don John* on the first of *October* 1578, he makes him Thirty three Years of Age. So then there is no fault

of the Press in the number 1545. The Author of the Dissertation on the *Hemina* (8) places the Birth of that Bastard on the fourteenth of *February* 1545, and his Death about the first of *October* 1578, *in the Army near* Namur; and censures the Genealogy of the House of *Austria*, which makes him die at *Bruges* in the Twenty fifth Year of his Age. He also censures Father *Strada*, for having placed the Death of *Don John* in the Month of *December*: but we read, in express words, in *Strada*, *Kalendis Octobris* (9). Mr *Varillas* is not to be credited, when he says, *That* Philip II, *let eleven Years pass, before he performed his Father's Orders, and that* John *of* Austria *was already twenty Years of Age, when his Catholic Majesty bethought himself to acknowledge him for his Brother* (10). According to this Calculation he would have been twenty four Years old. Let us remember that he was sent *Generalissimo* to the Kingdom of *Granada*, in the Year 1569 (11). According to Mr *Varillas*, therefore, *Philip* II must have begun, by that important Office, to acknowledge him for the Natural Son of *Charles* V. This would be judging very wrongly of that Prince, to impute to him such a precipitate Conduct.

[D] *He made the first discovery of* Don Carlos*'s Machinations: there was but little Friendship between Those two young Princes*.] I shall relate one particular that is mentioned in *Brantome*. It is said that *Don Carlos* "having discovered something of moment to "*Don John*, he revealed it to the King of *Spain*, who "always loved him the better for it, though he rewarded him but very indifferently afterwards; and "*Don Carlos* hated him so much for it, that they "generally quarrelled, so that once he called him "Bastard, and Son of a Whore; to which he "returned this Answer, *Si yo lo soys mos yo tengo* "*padre mejor que vos*; *Yes I am so, but I have a* "*better Father than you*; and they were like to have "come to blows about it (12).

(8) Pag. 187.

(9) Strada, Decad. 1, lib. 10, pag. 611.

(10) Varillas's History of Francis I. Book 13, pag. 389.

(11) Moreri says 1570.

(12) Brantome's Lives of Foreign Captains, Tom. 2, pag. 117, 118.

VOL. I. 7 I [E] *Escovedo*,

AUSTRIA

Escovedo, Don *John*'s Secretary, having been sent to *Madrid*, by his Master, to sollicite the Succours which were a long time expected, was killed there [E]. Don *John*, upon this, found himself to be in Disgrace; and his vexation, to see himself sacrificed to the Contempt of the Enemies, for want of Supplies to make head against them [F], threw him into a Distemper, of which he died the first of *October* 1578 (e). It was even believed that he was poisoned [G]. He did indeed recommend his supposed Mother, and his supposed uterin Brother, as also his Domesticks to King *Philip*, but durst not mention to him his two Natural Daughters (f) [H].

His Elogy may be seen, among those of several other Warriors, in a Book composed by *Primo Damaschino*, and printed at *Rome*, in the Year 1680, under the Title of *La Spada d' Orione stellata nel Cielo di Marte*. But if you are desirous to see the Particulars of the Complaints made against his Conduct, with many of his intercepted Letters, you need only read the Summary *Discourse of the just Causes and Reasons, which obliged the States General of the* Netherlands, *to provide for their Defence against* Don John *of* Austria. It is a very curious Manifesto printed at *Antwerp*, by *William Sylvius* the King's Printer, in the Year 1577. See also the Manifesto published by Prince *John Casimir*, Count Palatine of the *Rhine*, in the Year following, to justify his Expedition.

[E] *Escovedo*, Don *John*'s *Secretary, being sent to* Madrid — *was killed there*.] Mr *le Laboureur* says, that he had read some Memoirs written by Mr *Peirese*, which make *Escovedo die after his Master*: and that Mr *du Vair*, who had been told that Particular, *in a familiar Conversation with* Antonio Perez, related it to Mr *de Peirese* (13). This deserves to be examined. Perhaps I shall compose an Article for *Escovedo*, wherein I shall treat of this more amply, and we shall see whether it was before or after *Don John*'s Death, that the Designs, which he and the Duke of *Guise* had formed, were known at the Court of *Spain*. *Philip* II was not so much in the wrong as was imagined; and *Don John* would have been able, in a little time, to have cut him out more work than the *Dutch*. He was no truer, in respect to his Sovereign, than the Duke of *Guise*. But it must be owned, that the jealous Humour of *Philip*, and his mysterious Politics, was the chief Cause of inspiring his Family with those rebellious Thoughts. "Multi fal-
"lere docuerunt, dum timent falli, & aliis jus pec-
"candi suspicando fecerunt (14). — *Many Persons*
"*have put others upon cheating them, by their fear-*
"*fulness of being cheated, and have occasioned, by their*
"*Suspicions, the very Thing they suspected.*"

[F] *He saw himself sacrificed to the Contempt of his Enemies, for want of Supplies to make head against them*] Thus the King of *Spain*, as great a Politician as he was, chose rather to lose the *Netherlands*, than not to satisfy the Jealousies, and other hidden Passions, which disquieted his Soul. It is to this that the *Dutch* are as much, or more, indebted for their Liberty, than to their good and wise Conduct. There are few great Affairs but what owe their Success as much, at least, to the Misconduct of one of the Parties, as to the Prudence of the other. There was no great difficulty to draw *Philip* II into the Snare, as soon as his Jealousies were discovered. *Strada* fancies, that the Prince of *Orange* wrote about *Don John*'s Marriage, with the Queen of *England*, to one of his Friends at *Paris*, and the promise which the Bridegroom made of Liberty of Conscience to the Protestants, on purpose to increase King *Philip*'s Suspicions: he thought that his News would not fail to be known by the *Spanish* Ambassador. "Quin ad hanc
" quoque suspicionem Regi confirmandam haud sane
" dubitaverim aspexisse Orangium, scriptis ad ami-
" cum litteris in Galliam, quibus Joan. Austriaci,
" atque Angliæ Reginæ conjugium significabat: ad-
" debatque, pro suâ in eam rem operâ, spem sibi
" ab Austriaco, factam liberæ per Belgium Religio-
" nis. Id, quod à Varga, Hispano apud Gallum
" oratore in arcana cujusque intento, sollicitè admoni-
" tum ferunt Philippum Regem (15). — *I make*
" *no doubt, but the Prince of* Orange *had an Eye to*
" *the confirming this Suspicion of the King's, in the*
" *Letters he wrote to a Friend in* France, *intimating*
" *a Marriage between* John *of* Austria, *and the Queen*
" *of* England : *and adding, that* John *had promised her,*
" *so far as in him lay, a Liberty of Conscience through*
" *the whole United Provinces. This* Varga, *the Spanish*
" *Ambassador in* France, *who was always on the Watch*
" *for Secrets, is said to have met with, and to have*
" *sent a particular Account of it to King* Philip."

[G] *It was believed* — *that he was poisoned.*] You will find here both Accounts, of *Strada* and *Brantome. Ex Mœrore contabuit,* says *Strada* (16) · *An vero ad hoc quo satis extingui potuit, venenum aliud cujusquam dolo subjectum fuerit (namque in defuncti corpore extitisse non obscura veneni vestigia affirmant qui viderunt) equidem nihil ipse statuerim.* He died of Grief: But whether, to dispatch him more effectually, any Poison was given him, for those who saw the Body, affirm there were very evident Signs of Poison,) I will not take upon me to determine. *That poor Prince*, says *Brantome* (17), *did not long enjoy that great Glory and Praise, for he, who had so often sought Death in the hard Field of* Mars, *died in a soft Bed, as if he had been a Favourite of* Venus, *and not a Son of* Mars. *It was said that he died of a contagious Distemper, which the* Marchioness *of* Avré, *with whom he was in love, had given him, but this is not generally said, not even in* Spain: *for it is thought that he was poisoned with perfumed Buskins.*

[H] *He durst not recommend to* Philip II, *his two Natural Daughters*] Don *John*, the handsomest Prince of his Time, was also very Gallant and Complaisant. Judge whether he was not a lucky Man. He got a Daughter at *Madrid*, and another at *Naples*. She at *Madrid* was called *Anne*, and her Mother was a Person of the first Quality, and a perfect Beauty, "Ex Mariâ Mendoziâ splendidissimi generis formæque " elegantissimæ puellâ (18). — *Of Mary* Mendoza, " *a young Lady of a most noble Family, and incompa-* " *rable Beauty.*" The same Lady who had brought up *Don John* (19), brought up this Bastard-Child likewise privately till she was seven Years of Age, and then put her into a Nunnery. *Philip* II took her from thence, and sent her to *Burgos*, where she became perpetual Superior of the *Benedictine* Nuns. *Don John*'s other Daughter's Name was *Joan*: her Mother was a Lady of *Sorrento*, whose Name was *Diana Phalanga*, and after she was brought up to seven Years of Age, by her Father's Sister, the Duchess of *Parma*, she was put into the Nunnery of St *Clara* at *Naples*, where, having lived twenty Years, she was afterwards married to the Prince of *Butero*. Those two Daughters of *Don John* died almost in the same Day, in the Month of *February* 1630. He had caused them to be brought up so privately, that he did not doubt but that the King was ignorant of the whole Secret: nor had he trusted it to his great Friend the Prince of *Parma*, who did not know any Thing of those Bastard Children, but, from the Duchess his Mother, a little before the Death of *Don John. Eas Regi incompertas crediderat: quippe occultè adeo cautèque educatas, ut Alexander ipse secretorum ejus planè omnium particeps filiarum alteram ignoraret: alteram non ob Austriaco sed à Margaritâ matre haud pridem nosset* (20). The Author of That Prince's Life, printed at *Amsterdam* in 1690, will have it, that Don John *discovered his Amours with the Fair* Mendoza, *and the Birth of his Daughter* Anne, *to his dear Nephew Prince* Alexander Farnese, *because, both living at the same time, in the* Spanish *Court, they observed each other very narrowly, and because they were too good Friends to hide any* Thing

AUSTRIA. AUTON. AZOTUS. 589

Expedition. He got it printed, at *Newstad*, in *High-Dutch* and *Latin*. There was another *Don John* of AUSTRIA [*I*], in the XVIIth Century, who made a considerable Figure in the World. He was the Son of *Philip* IV, by a Comedian [*K*].

Being from each other. But, says he, *being well perfuaded, that the declaring of a Crime is a Crime, he had made a Secret of his Amours with Diana to him* (21). This is giving *Strada* the lie without Grounds, or Proof, and it is affigning a Reason for that Prince's Silence, which proves too much.

[*I*] *There was another Don John of* AUSTRIA, *in the* XVIIth *Century*] He was the Natural Son of King *Philip* IV, of *Spain*, and was born in the Year 1629 (22). He was legitimated in the Year 1642, and no body paid the Complement of Congratulation upon it to *Philip* IV, with fo much forwardnefs as *James Panzirola*, the Pope's Nuncio (23). The King's Love for that Child was the moft tender imaginable. In the Year 1642 he declared him *Generaliffimo*, both by Sea and Land, in the War againft *Portugal*, and, fome Years after, he fent him into *Italy*, againft the Rebels of *Naples* (24). The laft Expedition having proved very fortunate, inclined that King to give the fame *Don John* a Commiffion to reduce the revolted *Catalans* to their Duty. After this he fent him to command in the *Netherlands*. That Poft did not contribute greatly to *Don John's* Glory; that which he acquired by raifing the Siege of *Valenciennes*, vanifhed away by the ill Succefs which attended him in other Places; and efpecially by the lofs of the Battle of the *Dunes*, which was foon followed by the lofs of *Dunkirk*. He was no lefs unfortunate, in the War of *Portugal*, after the Peace of the *Pyrenes*; for the Army, which he commanded, was entirely defeated; and he fell into Difgrace, and received Orders, from the King his Father, to retire to *Confuegra* (25). He had no fhare in the Government after the Death of That Prince; the whole Adminiftration was in the Hands of the Queen-Mother, and the Jefuit *Nidhard*. They would have removed him, under the fpecious pretence of fending him into the *Netherlands* to oppofe the Arms of *France*; but he difcovered their Cunning, and would not go thither, pretending to be fick. The Court, being offended with That Conduct, made him retire to *Confuegra* (26). He did not forget himfelf in That Retreat, but managed fo well the Difcontents of thofe, who were incenfed at the great Favour fhewn to Father *Nidhard*, that, at laft, This Jefuit was forced to withdraw. He went from *Spain* to *Rome*, and from That Time *Don John's* Affairs went better, 'till at laft he was recalled to Court (27), and had the chief Direction of the Government. He died the feventeenth of *September*, 1679, after Twenty three Days Sicknefs (28). Some faid he had been poifoned. " Vi fono perfone, che " afficurano che foffe un colpo ufcito dalla mano del- " la *Reg. Mad.* è del Cardinal *Nitardi*, coll' affiften- " za de' fuoi partigiani (29). ———— *There are fome who affirm, that the Blow came from the Hands of*

" *the Queen Mother, and Cardinal Nitardi, by the* " *Affiftance of their Parts.*" Others have faid, that he was fo much troubled at the King's Marriage, with the Daughter of the Duke of *Orleans*, that it was the Caufe of his Death; and yet, according to the common Opinion, he was the chief Promoter of That Marriage (30). I remember to have read, in fome Gazette, of the Year 1678, that the Marquis of *Agropoli*, being fufpected of having wrote a Comedy againft *Don John*, was banifhed to *Oran*.

[*K*] *Son of* Philip IV, *by a Comedian*.] All the World knows, that *Ph. lip* IV was very much addicted to the Love of Women He difcovered that Inclination very early, and he had a Governor, who was fo far from holding him up, in fuch a flippery way, that he contributed to his Fall. It was the Count *d'Olivarez*; who was alfo fubject to That Paffion himfelf, and for That Reafon, as was as for the better fecuring to himfelf the Adminiftration of Affairs, encouraged the lewd Temper of his young Prince: he was in hopes, that, under the Reign of his Pupil, he fhould have the greateft Offices of the State, and he forefaw, that if the Monarch fhould lead a voluptuous and effeminate Life, he could exercife them with much more Authority: And befides, that his own Debaucheries would have a much freer Courfe under a Mafter whom he fhould only imitate. This Management of his had the defired Succefs. *Philip* IV afcended the Throne at fixteen Years of Age, in the Year 1621, and left the Care of the Kingdom to the Count-Duke, *d'Olivarez*, who neglected no means of continuing the Indolence of That Monarch. He invented new Diverfions, and brought to *Madrid* the moft compleat Company of Comedians that could be formed in *Spain*. They acted before the King in the Year 1627. There was an Actrefs among them, whofe Name was *Calderona*, that pleafed him very much. She was not very handfome, but extreamly genteel and engaging, and had a charming Voice. The King no fooner faw her on the Stage, but he fell in Love with her, and ordered her to be brought to his Chamber: He faid he had only a Mind to hear her fpeak nearer him. As foon as the Count-Duke received This News, he managed the Meeting, and caufed the Actrefs to be introduced at Night into his Majefty's Chamber. She did not return from thence 'till the next Day, and then left the Prince fo much in love with her, that he declared her his Favourite. She was but fixteen Years of Age. After that they met frequently, fhe proved with Child, and was delivered of our *Don John*. But, after her lying-in, fhe broke off That Commerce (31), and fhut herfelf up in a Nunnery, and took the Habit of a Nun, with the Benediction of the Pope's Nuncio (32).

AUTON (JOHN d') a Gentleman of *Saintonge* (*a*), Abbot of *Angle* (*b*), of the Order of St *Auguftin*, lived under the Reign of *Lewis* XII. He was kept in waiting at Court, on purpofe to write the private Hiftory of That Prince (*c*). This Work he actually performed, and it was printed at *Paris*, in the Year 1615, in 4to, by *Theodore Godfry*. It extends only from the Year 1506, to 1508 (*d*). We find there fome Verfes which the Author had dedicated to his Sovereign (*e*).

AZOTUS, a City of *Paleftine* near the Sea, one of the five *Satrapies* of the *Philiftines* (*a*). There they kept the Chief of their Idols, called *Dagon*, which fell down and broke before the Ark which they had taken from the *Jews*, and placed in the Temple of that Idol (*b*). It does not appear, that the *Jews* fubdued This Place before the Reign of *Uzziah* King of *Juda* (*c*) [*A*]. It was taken from them by *Tartan*,

[*A*] *It does not appear, that the Jews fubdued this Place before the Reign of Uzziah.*] Look as long as you pleafe, in the eleventh and fifteenth Chapters of *Jofhua*, to which *Moreri* refers, you will not find, that *Jofhua* conquered the City of *Azotus*. Nor is it truer, that Thofe of the Tribe of *Judah*, conquered it in the Time of the *Judges*: The Author, who affirms it, and quotes the firft Chapter of the Book of *Judges* (1), has no grounds for it. That which deceived either *Moreri*, or the Author whom he followed, is, that, in the fifteenth Chapter of *Jofhus*, This City feems to be in the Dividend of the Tribe of *Judah*. But he ought to have remembered, that they reckoned, in thofe Dividends, both what was already conquered, and what was, afterwards, to be conquered. It appears plainly, from the third Chapter of *Judges*, that the five Governments of the *Philiftines*, and confequently this of *Azotus*, were

AZOTUS.

Tartan, General of the Army of *Sargon* King of *Affyria*, as *Isaiah* tells us (d), who lived in that time. Some time after it was besieged by *Psammitichus* King of *Egypt*, and it was one of the longest Sieges ever heard of: for they lay before this Place Twenty nine Years, before they could take it (e). It was ruined, in all probability, by the *Egyptians*, since the Prophet *Jeremiah* mentions it only as the remainder of a City (f). It was considerable in the Wars of the *Maccabees*; and the taking of it was not the least of *Jonathan*'s Exploits. The Enemies he had defeated retired thither, and shut themselves up in the Temple of *Dagon*. He ordered it to be set on Fire, so that they perished in the same Flames which consumed the Temple and City (g). We read, in the *Acts of the Apostles*, that when St *Philip* had baptized the Eunuch of Queen *Candace*, he was *caught away by the Spirit of the Lord, and was found at Azotus* [B]. Prophane Authors have mentioned this Place as the chief Trading City of the *Arabians* (h); and it's Inhabitants must necessarily have made a considerable Figure, since *Strabo* has placed them in the List of the four Nations which were intermixed with the *Cælosyrians*, and the *Phœnicians*, the two principal People, according to him, which possessed *Syria* (i). *Stephanus Byzantinus* pretends, that the Founder of *Azotus* was one of those Fugitives who came from the *Red-Sea* into *Palestine*, and that he gave the Name of his Wife to the City which he built; which name signified a She-Goat. Mr *Bochart* has rejected all this (k). St *Jerom* says, That, in his time, *Azotus* was still a considerable Town [C].

were not conquered by *Joshua*. God himself, when he represented that This Conqueror was too old to finish That War, places these same five Governments among the Countries, that remained to be conquered (2). This discovers another Mistake of *Moreri*: *Joshua*, says he, *subjected it first to the Hebrews, towards the Two thousand five hundred and eighty sixth Year of the World, and it was afterwards one of the five Satrapies of the Philistines.* Was it not so before *Joshua's* Time, by the Testimony of God himself?

[B] *Was found at* Azotus (3).] *Moreri* pretends it was in This City, that St *Philip* was taken away. If he had read the eighth Chapter of the *Acts*, which he quotes, he would not have ventured to have said so.

[C] *St* Jerom *says, that, in his Time,* Azotus *was still a considerable Town* (4).] These are his Words, *Usque hodie insigne oppidum Palæstinæ...... A considerable Town in Palestine to this Day*. Mr *Baudrand* will have it, that having been anciently an Episcopal City, under the Archbishopric of *Cæsarea*, it became afterwards a meer *Municipium* in St *Jerom*'s Time. *Olim Episcopalis sub Archiepiscopo Cæsareensi, postea municipium tempore S. Hieronymi* (5). He must excuse my saying, that this Change was certainly the very Reverse. For what could have ruined the Bishopric of *Azotus*, between the Time it's of Erection and the Age of St *Jerom*?

BABELOT,

BABELOT. 591

B.

BABELOT, Chaplain to the Duke of *Montpensier*, distinguished himself so much by his Cruelty, during the Civil Wars of *France*, under *Charles* IX, that he has acquired a very considerable place in History. It ought not, therefore, to be thought strange, that I should bestow on him this Article. He was a *Franciscan* Friar, who left the Monastery to follow " the Army, out of his implacable Hatred " to the *Calvinists* (a). He had so little Regard to his Character " and Profession, that instead of saving the Lives of those whom the Fortune of " War reduced to the Mercy of *Montpensier*, that he earnestly sollicited him to put " them to death; and could not endure that any of them should be pardoned [*A*]. " This Thirst after the Blood of the *Calvinists*, which the two first Wars could not " allay, grew more raging in the third, when the Prince's (b) Soldiers being infor- " med, that *Babelot* had imprudently shut himself up in *Champigni* (c), gave such a " furious Assault to that place that they took it (d). The pleasure of finding them- " selves Masters of the Person whom they looked upon as their Executioner, made " them more human to the Inhabitants of *Champigni*. Those they pardoned, and " discharged all their Revenge on *Babelot*. They hanged him on an extraordinary " high Gibbet (e) [*B*]; and if they gave him time to prepare himself for Death, it " was only to have leisure to reproach him for his Cruelty. The Vengeance which " the Duke of *Montpensier*, who loved him, took for his Execution on the *Calvinists*, " when Chance, or Weakness, put any of them into his Hands, caused for some " Weeks an *unfair War* (f) between the two Parties. The Soldiers of *Brissac* cut " the Throats of the Garrison of *Mirebeau*, though they had capitulated in due " Form; and *d' Andelot* treated that of *St Florent* in the same manner." Here was a Man altogether destinated for the Destruction of the *Huguenots*, since, even after his very Death, he occasioned the Slaughter of many of them. *Brantome* believed him guilty

(a) *I only translate here the Words of Varillas, History of Charles IX. Tom. 2, pag. 147.*

(b) *He meant the Person of Conde, Chief of the Protestants.*

(c) *A Town in Poitou, which belonged to the Duke of Montpensier.*

(d) *In 1568.*

(e) *It is a great chance, if his Fraternity have not placed him in the number of their Martyrs.*

(f) *That is, They gave no more Quarter.*

[*A*] *He earnestly sollicited the Death of the Cal*vinists, *and could not endure that any of them should be pardoned.*] *Brantome* deserves to be heard. " When they brought him, *(says he* (1), *speaking of " the Duke of* Montpensier) *any Prisoners, if it was* " a Man, he only said to him, at first sight, *My* " *Friend, you are a* Huguenot, *I recommend you to* " *Monsieur* Babelot. *This Monsieur* Babelot was a " learned *Franciscan* Frier, who governed him very " him very peaceably, and never stirred from him " to whom the Prisoner was no sooner brought, " but, after a short Examination, he was immediate- " ly comdemned to death, and executed."

[*B*] *He was hanged on an extraordinary high Gibbet.*] This puts me in Mind of what *Galba* did to a Man, who endeavoured to save himself from Death, by pleading his Right of a *Roman* Citizen; he caused him to be fastened to a Cross, very well whitened, and much higher than the rest: This was to honour the Quality of the Criminal, and give him a little Comfort; but all this might rather look like Mockery. " Tutorem quod pupillum cui substitutus hæres " erat veneno necasset cruce affecit, implorantique " leges & civem Romanum se testificanti, quasi sola- " tio & honore aliquo pœnam levaturus, mutari, " multoque præter cæteras altiorem & dealbatam " statui crucem jussit (2). ———— *A Guardian, who had* " *who had poisoned his Ward, whose Heir he was,* " *being condemned to be crucified, and pleading the* " *Privileges of a Citizen of* Rome, *to alleviate and* " *make his Punishment more honourable, he ordered* " *him a Cross painted white, and much higher than* " *the rest.*" I do not know what were the Motives to Those, who made choice of a more exalted Gibbet for the Monk *Babelot*; perhaps they designed only to excite a greater Attention to the Fantasticalness of the Characters of That Man, without any Allusion, or Regard to the Practice of Antiquity. See *Justin* (3) concerning *Maleus*, a General disgraced by the *Carthaginians*, *qui filium cum ornatu suo, in altissimam crucem in conspectu urbis suffigi jussit;* — *who commanded his Son to be hanged, in his finest Dress, on an exceeding high Cross, in the full View of the City*; and *Silius Italicus* (4), concerning *Regulus*:

(1) Brant. Memoires, Tom. 3, p. 281.

(2) Suet. in Galba, c. 9.

(3) Justin, lib. 18, cap. 7.

(4) Silius Italicus, l. 2. ver. 343.

--------- Vidi cum robore pendens
Italiam cruce sublimis spectaret ab altâ.

High *from th' exalted Cross he saw, unmoved,*
His Country, he so faithfully had loved.

Haman, in the Book of *Esther,* had prepared, for *Mordecai,* a Gibbet fifty Cubits high. Sometimes the excessive Height of the Gibbet, has been intended to expose the Sufferer to the View of a greater Multitude of People. See the Remark [*C*] of the Article OTHO III. I shall observe, by the way, that Those, who compare This Cross of *Galba* to That which *Verres* ordered for *Gavius* (5), are not exact; for all that was remarkable in the latter was, that it was not erected in the Place where the Inhabitants of *Messina* used to crucify Malefactors, but on That Side, which looked towards *Italy*. It was thus *Verres* chose to insult over the Sufferer, who declared himself a *Roman* Citizen; *He shall look,* said he, *from the Top of his Cross, towards* Italy, *and towards his House.* " Quid attinuit cum Ma- " mertini more atque instituto suo crucem fixissent " post urbem in via Pompeia, te jubere in ea parte " figere quæ ad fretum spectaret, & hoc addere quod " negare nullo modo potes, quod omnibus audien- " tibus dixisti palam, te idcirco illum locum deli- " gere, ut ille qui se civem Romanum esse diceret, " ex cruce Italiam cernere ac domum suam prospi- " cere posset. ———— *What did it avail, when the* " *Custom of the* Messinians *was to crucify their Ma-* " *lefactors behind their City, in the* Pompeian *Way,* " *for you to command the Cross to be erected on That* " *Side next the Sea, and to add, what you cannot* " *possibly deny, what you declared openly before all* " *the People, that you therefore chose That Place,* " *that he, who called himself a Citizen of* Rome, " *might, from his Cross, behold* Italy, *and cast a* " *Look towards his House.*" It is this last Circumstance which *Cicero* has chiefly insisted upon (6); though *Lactantius*, who had no occasion for That Paticular in the Subject he was treating on, makes him only consider the Indignity of That Punishment in general (7).

(5) Torrentius *has done it; see his Comment. in* Sueton. Galb. c. 9.

TORRENTIUS *has mistaken the Meaning of a Passage in* Cicero.

(6) Cicer. in Verr. 7.

(7) Lact. Instit. Divin. lib. 4. c. 18.

[*C*] Brantome

VOL. I.   7 K

BABYLAS

Guilty of another sort of Crime, that is, of inspiring his Master with the Brutality of causing Women to be ravished [C].

[C] Brantome believes him guilty ----- *of advising the Brutality of causing Women to be ravished*] The Duke of Montpensier used to recommend his Prisoners to his Guidon, *Viro bene vasato & bene mutoniato,* ---- *A Man extreamly well hung and provided.* Brantome describes this very freely, and adds as follows: "This is the Punishment of Those " poor Huguenot Ladies, invented by Monsieur de " Montpensier, which I am apt to believe might be " taken, by Monsieur Babelot, from Nicephorus (8), " where he says, that the Emperor *Theodosius* took " away, and abolished, a Custom, long used in *Rome,* " that is, if any Woman was taken in Adultery, " the *Romans* did not punish her by preventing the " Repetition of her Crime, but by the greatest Pro- " vocations of her Lust ; for they shut the Criminal " up in a narrow Lodge, and then suffered her " impudently to take her Fill of Letchery with eve- " ry Body that came, the most nasty and filthy. The " Manner was for those lewd and whoring Fellows " to be furnished with certain little Bells, all the " Time they were in company with the Lady, " which, by their tinckling, and ringing, might " not only discover what they were doing, to Those " who were passing by, or listening, but also sig- " nify, that This Punishment was accompanied with " Shame and Ignominy. What Ignominy! which " they cared much for! Truly this was a very abo- " minable Custom which That wise Emperor abo- " lished, as the Historian *Nicephorus* relates : in whom " possibly Monsieur *Babelot* found it, and caused it " to be copied by this brave *Guidon* (9)."

BABYLAS, one of the most celebrated Martyrs of the ancient Church, was made Bishop of *Antioch* in the IIId Century, under the Emperor *Gordian* (a). He governed his Church as a good and holy Prelate ought to do, and after having worthily discharged his Function about Thirteen Years, he obtained the Crown of Martyrdom towards the Year 251, during the Persecution of *Decius.* Some say, he was actually put to Death for the Christian Faith (b); and others say that he died in Prison (c). All agree, he desired to be buried with his Chains (d). It is pretended, that his Relics silenced one of *Apollo's* Oracles. St *Chrysostom* has more than once displayed all his Eloquence to celebrate the Memory of St *Babylas*: It is pity he was not sufficiently informed of the Facts which he advanced. He supposes that this Martyr was put to Death for denying a Criminal Emperor an Entrance into the Church [A]; and he speaks of that Emperor's Crime like one who had but little consulted History [B]. Neither did he so much as know what was said of That Prince's

[A] *St Chrysostom* ------- *supposes that this Martyr was put to Death, for denying a criminal Emperor an Entrance into the Church.*] It is certain, that *Babylas* died in the Reign of the Emperor *Decius*; and therefore, if *St Chrysostom*'s Account were true, it must have been *Decius* that was excluded from entring into the Church; but it does not appear, that *Decius* was ever at *Antioch* in the whole Time of his Reign. Baronius advances, without proof, that *Decius* went into *Syria*, in the Year 253, to make War against the *Persians*, and that it was then that *Babylas* would not suffer his Church to be prophaned by the Presence of such an Emperor (1). This neither agrees with Chronology nor History, nor with the Prudence of the Bishop of *Antioch.* The best Chronologers place the Death of *Decius* in the Year 251 (2). No good Historian says that *Decius* was in the *East,* to make War with the *Persians,* It is true, the Acts of St *Laurence* (3) affirm, that This Emperor went to make War against the *Persians,* and that he took from them the Country of *Babylon, Assyria,* all *Persia, Hircania,* and even *Bactriana,* and that he died at *Rome,* being possessed with a Devil a little after the Martyrdom of St *Laurence* (4); but those Acts are without Authority, and full of Faults (5). Father *Noris* does not scruple to say, that all That War of *Persia* is a meer Fable (6). With regard to the Prudence of St *Babylas,* we may say, that it would not have suffered him to resist a *Pagan* Emperor. *It was not agreeable to the Conduct of the Church, for St* Babylas *to attempt hindring him from coming into it, if he had come thither, as a* Pagan, *to commit some Violence ; for the Church had not, nor exercis'd, any Power over any, but those that were of the Number of her Children, and she patiently suffered the Insults of Persecutors.* Thus speaks the Author of the Life of *Tertullian,* and of *Origen* (7). Mr *de Tillemont* confirms that Remark. Upon those Occasions, says he (8), *the Church defended herself only with Prayers, and with a peaceable and humble Patience, with which she suffered the Insults of Persecutors.* We find, in a Sermon, ascribed to St Chrysostom*, *that St* Roman *of* Antioch opposed a Pagan Governour from entring into the Church; but it is a very extraordinary Thing, and the Fact is by no means certain. He observes also, that all the Terms, which St *Chrysostom* makes use of, shew, that the Prince, whom St *Babylas* opposed, was a Christian. So that it cannot be true, that this holy Man resisted *Decius,* and yet he died under the Empire of *Decius*: St *Chrysostom,* therefore, must be allowed to have fallen into a Mistake, in saying, That St *Babylas* suffered Death for having denied the Entrance of his Church to an Emperor.

[B] *— and he speaks of that Emperor's Crime, like one who had but little consulted History.*] He relates, that a certain People being in War with This Emperor, desired to make an end of it, and to confirm the Peace *by all the strongest and most inviolable Ties that were known among Men*; that the Agreement *was made and confirmed by Oath on both sides*; that those People being willing to shew their Enemies that they acted sincerely, persuaded their King to give his own Son as an Hostage to the Prince with whom they had concluded the Peace; that what followed made it appear, that instead of being *deposited, as they intended, in the Hands of a Friend, he was put into the Mouth of a Lyon*; since that Prince, *having no regard either to the Youth of the Son of his Allie, or to the inviolable Sanctity of the Oath which he had taken, or to that all-seeing Eye of the Divine Justice for the punishing of Crimes — with his own Hand, cut the Throat of him whom he ought to have protested as a sacred Depositum, and as the indissoluble Tie of the Alliance* (9). This, says St *Chrysostom,* was the Crime of That Prince, whom St *Babylas* treated in the following manner. " That " great Prelate, on this occasion, perfectly imitated the " Zeal of *Elias,* and of St *John*; for he did not con- " sider, that he was then to resist not only a Prince, " or a common King, but him that was Master of a " great Part of the Earth, who had a very powerful " Army, and whom all things seemed to conspire to " make dreadful to him. He was not dazzled with " all this outward Splendor — but that very Splen- " dor serving only to represent to him, in the same " Moment, the Supream Majesty of that King whose " Minister he was — he stept boldly to that *Crimi-* " *nal Prince,* in the midst of his Guards, stopt him " with his Hand against his Breast, represented his " Crime to him, and forbad him, in the Name of " God, from entring into the Assembly of the Faith- " ful (10)." It is needless to observe, that St *Chrysostom* uses the most lively and pathetic Figures of his Rhetoric, in the Relation of these Facts (11): one may easily think so, that knows (and who is ignorant of it?) he was a great Preacher, and spoke to a People full of Respect and Zeal for the Name of St *Babylas* (12). But is he not to be pitied for having employed

BABYLAS.

Prince's Submission to the severe Discipline of St *Babylas* [C]. We may point out the general Grounds of some of his Mistakes [D]. All this will be treated of in the Remarks,

employed so many Ornaments, and so powerfully exerted his Imagination and Lungs, on such Falsities? For what can be more chimerical, than to suppose People, who were Enemies to the *Romans*, should persuade their King to deliver his Son for an Hostage into the Hands of their Emperor? If any People did this, without doubt they were the *Persians*. But it is very certain they did nothing like it, during the Episcopacy of St *Babylas*. I question very much whether any *Roman* Emperor ever killed, with his own Hand, a young Prince, delivered to him as an Hostage, after the Conclusion a Peace: But it is absolutely false, that one of the Emperors, under whom St *Babylas* enjoyed the Bishoprick of *Antioch*, was ever guilty of so barbarous a Perfidy. I do not question, in the least, but that St *Chrysostom* erred very innocently; because he did not only affirm those Errors in the Pulpit, but also in a Piece he wrote against the Gentiles (13). If he could promise himself that his Auditors would forgive him for insisting upon a false and pious Tradition, he could not have expected the same Favour from the Enemies of the Christian Name. He therefore believed himself, that what he asserted was true.

[C] *St Chrysostom did not know what was said of that Prince's Submission to the severe Discipline of St* Babylas.] St *Chrysostom* has supposed, that St *Babylas* had to do with a Monarch, who punished with Death the holy Resistance that was made against his entring into the Church. The Falsity of this Fact has been sufficiently detected, by shewing that St *Babylas* died in the Reign of *Decius*, and that *Decius* had not met with any Resistance at the Door of the Church of *Antioch*. Here is another Proof of the same Falsity. The Predecessor of *Decius* was *Philip*: And it was to him that St *Babylas* is thought to have refused the Entrance of his Church, nor considering him as an Emperor, but as a Christian, who ought to submit to the Rules of Discipline and Penance. Now it is pretended, that This Emperor submitted to Those Laws, and that he behaved himself towards the Prelate of *Antioch*, much in the same manner as *Theodosius* has since done towards St *Ambrose* at *Milan*. *Eusebius* relates, That the Emperor *Philip* was desirous to assist at the public Prayers on *Easter*-Eve; but that the Bishop would not suffer him to come into the Church, before he had obliged him to confess his Sins, and place himself among the Penitents; which the Emperor performed with all the Marks of a sincere Piety, and Fear of God (14). *Eusebius* relates this only on a meer Hear-say, and neither names the Place of this great Event, nor the Prelate, who had the Honour of it. It is very strange that such things should have been so confusedly known. We even find some very learned Men, who will not allow the Emperor *Philip* to have been a Christian. But however it be, we must not separate the Courage of *Babylas*, and the Submission of *Philip*, as St *Chrysostom* has done: they must either be both received, or both rejected. There are some Historians that speak of it with greater exactness than *Eusebius*. The Chronicle of *Alexandria* observes, that the Empress was condemned to do Penance, as well as the Emperor her Husband: It adds, that St *Babylas* made use of this Severity, because *Philip* had killed the Emperor *Gordian*'s Son (15). Note, that *Erasmus*, deceived by St *Chrysostom*, remarks the great Difference, as to the Success, between the Courage of St *Babylas*, and that St *Ambrose*. " *Babylæ*, says he " (16), parum feliciter cessit quod Imperatorem " impia cæde funestatum templo prohibuit; imo fe- " liciter cessit ipsi qui præsulis autoritatem suâ morte " confirmavit. At Ambrosio cessit feliciter, qui sum- " ma constantia suam tuens autoritatem, ipsum etiam " Cæsarem Christo lucri fecit. —— Babylas *had but* " *ill Fortune in denying his Church to an Emperor,* " *polluted with Blood, or rather had good Fortune in* " *confirming his Episcopal Authority by his Death.* " *But Ambrose had better Fortune, in not only main-* " *taining his Authority, with the greatest firmness, but* " *also bringing over the Emperor to Christ.*" And in another place: " Ambrosius Episcopus Mediola- " nensis ausus est Theodosium Cæsarem, ob crudelem " ac præcipitatam in Thessalonicenses sententiam,

" à templi limine secludere, postque sævas objurga- " tiones, post indictam satisfactionem in pœnitentium " classem relegare —— Tentavit idem Babylas An- " tiochenus Episcopus adversus regem innocentis ho- " micidio pollutum, & intersectus est (17). —— Am- " brose, *Bishop of Milan, had the Courage to shut* " *the Church Door against the Emperor Theodosius,* " *for his cruel, and hasty, Sentence against the People* " *of* Thessalonica, *and after severely reproaching him,* " *and enjoining him a suitable Atonement, to place* " *him among the rest of the Penitents* —— *Babylas,* " *Bishop of Antioch, attempted the same Thing* " *against an Emperor guilty of Murder, but lost his* " *Life by it.*"

[D] *We may point out the general Grounds of some of his Mistakes.*] We have just now seen that it was said, St *Babylas* grounded his Conduct on *Philip*'s perfidious Murder. The Emperor *Gordian*, under whom he was Prefect of the *Prætorium*, had intrusted him with his Son: after *Gordian* was dead, *Philip* designing to reign in his stead, killed the young Prince committed to his Care. St *Babylas* knowing him guilty of such an execrable Murther, would not admit him into the Church: *Decius* revenged the Affront put upon *Philip*; and put *Babylas* to Death for it. This we find in the Chronicle of *Alexandria*, as it had been related by *Leontius*, Bishop of *Antioch*, in the Year 348. He did not perfectly understand *Philip*'s Conduct, but came much nearer the Truth than St *Chrysostom*. The Emperor *Gordian*, under whom *Philip* was Prefect of the *Prætorium*, had no Child to trust with any Body, for he had none at all. So that *Leontius* must quite mistake the matter, in saying that *Philip* killed the Son, in order to succeed That deceased Emperor. The Truth of this Fact is this: *Philip*, taking the Advantage of the Emperor *Gordian*'s Youth, caballed in such manner that he caused himself to be declared his Colleague and Guardian. The Factions were revived, that of *Gordian* was worsted: *Philip* caused him to be deposed, and afterwards to be killed (18). The Misrepresentations of this Fact increased in time. *Leontius* said, that *Philip* killed the Son of his Emperor, the same Son of whom That Emperor had committed to his Care. This is already one step out of the way; and a direct departing from the Truth. St *Chrysostom* affirms, that *Philip* killed the Son of a Prince, with whom he had concluded a Treaty of Peace, the same Son this Prince had deposited, as a Pledge of his Friendship, and of his sincere Desire, to live in perfect Harmony with him. This is a second false Step; and is going a great way towards the Mistake of *Leontius*. This last Author says, that *Decius* caused *Babylas* to be put to Death, to punish his Insolence toward *Philip*. Those who knew the Aversion that *Decius* had for *Philip*, such an Aversion as was believed to have been the Cause of *Decius*'s persecuting the Christians, found this Assertion of *Leontius* to be very absurd. They corrected it, therefore, by supposing, that *Philip* himself caused St *Babylas* to be put to Death (19); thus have they corrected one Fault with another, and unhappily deceived St *Chrysostom*. They have disappointed him of some Reflexions, which he might have had an Opportunity of setting off with the Ornaments of his Eloquence, to repel the Insults of the Pagans, and display the Glory of the Evangelical Ministry. The Humiliation of an Emperor, at the word of a Bishop, would have supplied St *Chrysostom* with some fine Thoughts; it is pity he did not know it. See how he expresses himself, in the Resistance of St *Babylas*: " Where- " as, *says he* (20), the Priests of the false Deities " are more Slaves to the Emperors, than to their " Gods, and attend their Worship only for fear " of those Princes, to whom the Devils are also in- " debted for the Honour and Adoration paid them " by Men; on the contrary, this great Bishop of *An-* " *tioch*, has demonstrated, by punishing the Empe- " ror himself, in a manner very sensible to a reason- " able Man, and as much as he was permitted to " do, according to the Extent of the Power of the " Church, that the Priests of the Religion of JESUS " CHRIST, are Slaves to no Body on Earth; and " that they ought to be so jealous of that holy Ex- " altation,

594 BABYLAS.

(e) *See the Lives of Tertullian and of Origen, p. 757.*

(f) *See Remark [E].*

Remarks, as also the Request which it is pretended, *Apollo* made to the Emperor *Julian*, concerning the Relics of St *Babylas* [E]. This Martyr has the Honour of having obtained three great Victories over the Pagan Emperors, two in his Lifetime, and the third after his Death (e). The First is, the Advantage he gained over *Philip*, by obliging him to keep without the Church in the Condition of a Penitent: The Second is, That he had over the Persecutor *Decius*, when he chose to prepare himself to suffer any thing for the Faith, rather than to do any thing unbecoming his Episcopal Function: The Third is, That which his Ashes obtained, over the Oracle of *Apollo* near *Antioch* (f). Mr *Chevreau* has not been very exact in speaking of the Martyrdom of St *Babylas* [F]. We shall examine This more particularly below.

[E] *It is pretended, that Apollo made a Request to the Emperor* Julian —— *concerning the Relics of St* Babylas.] There was, near *Antioch*, a Temple and an Oracle of *Apollo*, in a Place called *Daphne*. Here Superstition and Debauchery strove which should outdo each other. It was the Rendezvous of Lovers, and their Mistresses: others went thither to pay their Devotions; and, in all probability, many pursued both those Ends, at one and the same Time. *Gallus*, the Brother of *Julian* the Apostate, was no sooner declared *Cæsar*, but, to put a stop to this double Disorder, he built a Church in the place, and ordered the Tomb of *Babylas* to be brought thither. It is said, that, upon this, *Apollo* returned no more Answers. The Tomb of this Martyr was the Cause of it, and not the Interruption of the Sacrifices: For, upon receiving the Sacrifices, in the Reign of *Julian*, the Oracle still continued silent; and when *Julian* went himself to consult it, he was told, that the dead Bodies, which incumbered that Place, shut the Mouth of the Oracle. The Emperor applied this only to St *Babylas*'s Tomb, and therefore ordered it to be taken away. The Christians of *Antioch* brought it into the City. There was a Procession of Persons of all Ages, and both Sexes, who sung a Song of Triumph all the way (21), repeating, for the Chorus of their Song, the Confusion of those who adore Idols, from *Psalm* XCVII. Ἐξήρχον δὲ τῶν ψαλμῶν τοῖς ἄλλοις, οἱ τότες ἀκειζοντες, καὶ ξυνετάχει τὸ πλῆθ⊕- ἐν συμφωνία καὶ ταύ- την τὴν ῥῆσιν ἐπᾷδον ἀσχυθησας πάντες οἱ προσκυνοῦντες τοῖς γλυπτοῖς οἱ ἐγκαυχώμενοι τοῖς εἰδώλοις (22). Those who were skilful in singing, presided in the Song, and the People answered, in Chorus, and repeated this Verse, "Confounded are all "they who worship graven Images, and glory in "Idols." We might conclude, *à fortiori*, from this History, that the Birth of JESUS CHRIST imposed Silence on all the Oracles of Paganism; if we did not otherwise find, from the Confession of *Sozomen*, that this Oracle of *Apollo* gave Answers 'till the Empire of *Constantius*, in whose Time *Gallus* obtained the Dignity of *Cæsar*. The Objection seems yet stronger against Those who do not acknowledge any diabolical Operation, in the Oracles of the Pagans. But see what Mr *Van Dale* answers: He supposes, that the Priests of *Apollo*, being unwilling to be so nearly observed by the Christians, who came thronging to *Babylas*'s Tomb, invented an Answer which might oblige the Emperor to take away the Tomb of That Martyr. Those Priests feared nothing so much as the Eyes of the incredulous, and concluded, they should never be able to hide their cunning Practices from People who would be so curious to discover them, as the Christians. Perhaps, also, the blind Superstition of these Priests persuaded them, that it would be a very religious Act, to get removed, from the Neighbourhood of their Temple, a Tomb of a Christian Martyr, so much reverenced by the Enemies of their Gods. "Christiani, quibus repleta erat Antiochia, aliique e-

(21) *It was about 40 Stadia, that is 5000 Paces.*

(22) *Sozomen Hist. Eccles. lib. 5. cap. 20.*

"jusdem religionis aliunde advenientes, visitabant "quotidie sepulchra Martyrum, atque inprimis qui- "dem Babylæ. Sub quo prætextu suum loca illa "ita frequentarent, cum subreperent etiam huic O- "raculo oculisque emissitiis omnia perlustrarent, ut "sic detegerent imposturas ac præstigias ibi exerci- "tas, neque id ferrent ea tempora, ut vi expellere "eos inde possent Antistites: illi sub prætextu à "mortuis purgandi locum Dis sacratum, cum Ba- "bila aliisque, Christianos inde removere nitebantur. "Nihil enim magis aut citius detegere valebat An- "tistitum ejusmodi imposturas, quam continuus con- "cursus publicæque Panegyres, ob ludos aut festa "publica ibi celebranda: si quarumcumque sectarum "Philosophis, eorumve sequacibus ad illa pateret acces- "sus (23). —— *The Christians, with whom Antioch* "*abounded, and those of the same Religion, coming* "*thither, from other Places, daily visited the Tombs* "*of the Martyrs, and, above all, That of St Babylas.* "*By which means, as they had an Opportunity of* "*observing the Oracle, and of prying into every* "*Thing which passed, in order to detect the Frauds* "*and Impostures there carried on, the Priests not* "*having Power enough, in Those Times, to drive* "*them from thence by Force, endeavoured to get them* "*removed, with Babylas, and others, under the Pre- "*tence of clearing, from the Pollution of dead Bo- "*dies, a Place, which was consecrated to their Gods.* "*For the Jugglings of the Priests were like to be* "*as readily, and as fully, detected by these conti- "*nual Assemblies, and public Commemorations, on* "*account of celebrating there Rejoicings and Festival* "*Solemnities; as if they were laid open to the strictest* "*Examination of all the several Sects of Philosophers.*"

[F] *Mr* Chevreau *has not been very exact in speaking of the Martyrdom of St* Babylas.] See what he says of it: "*Babylas, Bishop of Antioch, suf- "*fered Martyrdom, with his three Children, for* "*not permitting Numerian to see the Ceremonies* "*of the Christians, adding, That a Man polluted* "*with Blood, and with the Sacrifices of Idols, could* "*not enter into the Church; or, as Suidas says,* "*That he would not suffer the Wolf to enter into* "*the Sheepfold of the Lord* (24)." I. *Babylas* had no Children; He should therefore have said, that three Brothers of his, who were yet Children, or very young, suffered Martyrdom with him (25). II There is above thirty Years between the Death of *Babylas*, and the Reign of *Numerian*. III. The ancient Writers do not ascribe to That Martyr Mr *Chevreau*'s Expression. We must confess, that the Undertaking of a General History is very difficult Matter. Mr *Chevreau* was a learned Man; he knew the Defects of those who went before him in That Design; he took a long time for his Work; and yet - - - - - As he is yet alive (26), and, notwithstanding his Age, enjoys a perfect Health of Body and Mind; therefore I do not doubt but he will publish a new Edition, yet more curious than the preceeding (27). I hoped that Mr *Chevreau* could not have taken amiss those little Critical Notes we have just now seen; and, as I had all the Esteem for him, which is due to his great Merit, I would have suppressed them, if I had thought they would have made him uneasy: But I thought that he was above being concerned at so trifling a Matter. I fancied he would have applied to himself what I said in my first Preface, and he was certainly one of those Authors, who need not have been alarmed at little Losses (28). I was therefore surprized, at his unexpected Resentment, and heartily troubled for having made him so. There are some Persons of great Note, who can be my Witnesses, that when I wished him a yet longer Life than he had already enjoyed (29), I did it, not only

(23) Van Dale, de Oraculis, pag. 442. *See the Nouvelles de la Republ. des Lettres for March 1684, pag. 15, 16.*

(24) Chevreau's Hist. of the World, lib. 4, cap. 4, pag. 400, of Vol. 2. Edit. of Holland, 1687.

(25) Lives of Tertull. pag. 738.

(26) This was wrote in 1694.

(27) *He has actually published a new Edition of his Hist. at the Hague, 1698, with several Additions and Corrections, but has also altered nothing in this Passage concerning Babylas.*

(28) *See the Specimen of this Dictionary, towards the End of the fourth Paragraph.*

(29) *He died Febr. 15. 1701, aged 87 Years and some Months. See the Journal of Trevoux for March and Apr. 1701, pag. 241. Dutch. Edit.*

BABYLON. 595

only in regard to his being the Ornament of his Age, but also out of the Desire I had, that he might find, in this second Edition, the greatness of my Respect for him, and the Explanation of a thing, which had been expressed in an ambiguous manner. I am apt to think, that this Ambiguity was the chief Cause of his Discontent: he thought, that the pointed Line, *and yet ---- had some Poison in it*. 'Tis a Gap, which his own Imagination filled with disobliging Ideas; and I was desirous, he should know, that, according to my sincere meaning, That *Hiatus* was left only as a general Representation of the Impossibility of avoiding Faults, in a Work containing abundance of minute and particular things, even though an Author be ever so learned.

But, to come to the Point, Mr *Chevreau* himself acknowledges the Solidity of my first Remark; since he confesses (30), *that it had been better to have put three Brothers, who were as yet Children, to take a way all Equivocation, and that he ought to have explained himself more clearly, than several Authors, who expressed it so before him*. As for the Expressions, which I said the ancient Authors did not ascribe to St *Babylas*, Mr *Chevreau* quotes *Georgius Syncellus*, and *Paulus Diaconus* (31); but can these Authors be called ancient, with respect to the time of the Martyr we now treat of? Did not they live towards the end of the VIIIth Century? Lastly, he quotes several Writers, most of them modern, who have said, that *Babylas* was slain by *Numerian*, and repeats these Words of Mr *Tillemont* (32); *We must confess, that the History of St Babylas is embarassed with many Difficulties, beyond our Capacity to surmount*. I agree, that all this may serve to excuse Those, *who are not exact in their account of the Martyrdom of St Babylas*; but it will always be allowable to remark, where Care is not taken to chuse such Expressions, as are the most exact we can meet with.

(30) Chevreau, Part. 2. pag. 321, Dutch Edition.

(31) Ibid. pag. 321.

(32) Ibid. p. 329, 330.

I am very well satisfied, that Mr *Chevreau* has found Faults in my Book. Any one, who has not the fourth part of his Learning, may find a great many in it. If he had given some Examples of what he has said, in general, concerning those *essential Faults against our Language, and concerning those mean, burlesque, obscure, and perplexed Expressions* (33), I should think myself obliged either to dispute the Point, or submit to the Accusation: and I should very willingly do the latter, if I could be made sensible of the least Reason for it imaginable: But, since he has pointed out nothing, I may be allowed to take That part of his Book for general and loose Reflexions (34). He charges me, particularly, with a kind of Contradiction, about a Man, *who had been*, as he says, *my Idol a long time* (35). I am sure he would have omitted this, if he had seen how I have justified myself on that Point, in my *Reflexions on a Paper, entituled, The Judgment of the Public, &c.* And, as for using *Words, which*, he says, *nice Ears cannot endure* (36), the Reader may see, in an Explication, at the end of this Book, what I have to answer to That; I should be glad to deserve all that he says, by way of retorting, to the Period, which ends with *and yet ---- (37)*. And I should think myself very happy, if I could be excused, for this Reason, that it is impossible, or next to impossible, to avoid committing a great many Faults, in such a Work as this. I do not believe I should ever have engaged in this Dictionary, if I had foreseen, that all my Care was to avoid Mistakes could not have secured me from making a great many, and very gross ones too.

To conclude, I must desire my Readers to consult the learned Work of Mr *de Larroque* (38), printed at *Leyden*, in the Year 1688, under the Title of *Matthæi Larroquani Adversariorum Sacrorum Libri tres*. See the 79th, and following Pages.

(33) Ibid. pag. 320.

(34) Compare this with the end of the Remark [C] of the Article ROY.

(35) Chevreau, Part. 2, pag. 320.

(36) Ibid.

(37) Ibid. p. 330, 331.

(38) Daniel Larroquanus Matthæi filius.

BABYLON. *Moreri*, and his Continuators, have collected so many things concerning this City, that, to make this Article of any reasonable length, I should be obliged to repeat most of their Observations: So that, to spare the Public the distaste of finding the same things in different Dictionaries, I shall confine myself here to a Fact, which they have not touched upon. I do not examine whether what they relate so be exact as it ought to be. The Inhabitants of *Babylon* pretended, that their City was very ancient; they counted Four hundred seventy three Thousand Years from the first Observations of their Astrologers to the coming of *Alexander*, as *Diodorus Siculus* informs us (*a*). Others, keeping to a round number, say, that the *Babylonians* boasted of having preserved, in their Archives, the Observations, which their Astrologers had made on Nativities, for the space of Four hundred and seventy Thousand Years [*A*]. From hence we ought to correct a Passage of *Pliny* [*B*], which some Authors make use

(*a*) Lib. 11. pag. 118 Edit. Rhodomani.

[*A*] *The Babylonians boasted of having preserved Observations, made by their Astrologers, ———— for the space of Four hundred and seventy thousand Years.*] We shall only quote two Passages out of *Cicero*. " Contemnamus etiam Babylonios, & eos qui e Caucaso " cœli signa servantes, numeris & motibus stellarum " cursus persequuntur. Condemnemus, inquam, hos " aut stultitiæ, aut vanitatis, aut imprudentiæ, qui " cccclxx. millia annorum, ut ipsi dicunt, monu- " menta comprehensa continent (1). — *We must " also despise the Babylonians, and others, who have " made Observations of the Stars, from Mount Cauca- " sus, and attempted to trace their Number and Mo- " tion: We must despise them, I say, either for their " Ignorance, their Vanity, or their Inconsiderateness, " in affirming, that their Records take in Four hun- " dred and seventy Thousand Years.*" Let us see how he laughs at this in another Place. " Quod aiunt " cccclxx millia annorum in periclitandis experiun- " disque pueris quicunque essent nati, Babylonios " posuisse fallunt. Si enim esset suscitatum, non es- " set desitum. Neminem autem habemus autorem " qui aut fieri dicat, aut factum sciat (2). — *It " must be a wretched Mistake, to say, that the Baby- " lonians employed Four hundred and seventy Thou- " sand Years, in calculating the Nativities of all " the Children, who happened then to be born. If this " were true, they would certainly have continued " the same Trade to this Day. But we have no good " Author, who either affirms their practising it at " present, or knows any thing of their having done so " for that Space of Time past.*"

(1) Cicero de Divinat. lib. 1, cap. 19.

(2) Id. Ibid. lib. 2, cap. 46.

[*B*] *From these Astronomical Observations of the Babylonians we ought to correct a Passage of Pliny.*] These are his Words; " Epigenes apud Babylonios " 720 annorum observationes syderum coctilibus late- " ritiis inscriptas docet, gravis auctor imprimis: qui " minimum, Berosus & Critodemus, 480 annorum. " Ex quo apparet æternus literarum usus (3). — *Epigenes, an Author of great weight, tells us, that the Babylonians had Observations of the Stars, for Seven hundred and twenty Years, recorded on Bricks*: Be- rosus *and* Critodemus, *who make the least of it, say Four hundred and eighty Years.*" He had said, a little before, that he believed the *Assyrian* Letters had been perpetual, or that the *Assyrians* had always made use of Writing, *Litteras semper arbitror Assyrias fuisse* (4). We ought, therefore, to look upon the Testimonies, he borrows from *Epigenes* and *Berosus*, concerning the Astronomical Observations, recorded by the *Babylonians*, as Proofs of his Opinions; for the Conclusion, he draws from those Testimonies, is the same with the Opinion he had laid down a little before: " Ex quo apparet, *this is his Con- " clusion*, æternus litterarum usus. — *From whence " it appears, that the Use of Letters has been perpe- " tual.*" Now there is nothing so absurd as his Reasoning, if he is supposed to speak according to the present Readings of the Manuscripts and Editions of his Books. *Epigenes*, a credible Author, affirms, that the Observations of the *Babylonian* Astrologers comprehend Seven hundred and twenty Years. Those, who give them the least Extent, as *Berosus* and *Critodemus*, assign them Four hundred and eighty

(3) Plin. lib. 7, c. 56.

(4) Mr Perizonius deserves it ought to be read Assyriis. See his Dissertatio Philologica de Originibus Babylonicis. They are some of these which were maintained in the Mouth of April, 1694.

VOL. I.   7 L   eighty

596 BABYLON.

use of improperly, either to confute the antiquity of *Babylon*, or for other Purposes. This a learned Professor of *Leyden* has lately observed (*b*), and I wonder it has not been taken notice of sooner. *Aristotle* knew, without doubt, that the *Babylonians* boasted of having a Series of Astronomical Observations, comprehending a prodigious number of Centuries. He was desirous to inform himself of the Truth of This by means of *Callisthenes*, who was in *Alexander*'s Retinue, but found a great mistake in the Account; for it is pretended, that *Callisthenes* assured him, that the Astronomical Observations, he had seen in *Babylon*, comprehended no more than 1903 Years. Simplicius reports This, and borrows it from *Porphyry* (*c*). If *Callisthenes* has computed right, it must be agreed, that, after the Deluge, Men made very great haste to become Astrologers; for, according to the *Hebrew* Bible, there is but Two thousand Years to be found from the Flood to the Death of *Alexander*. There is reason to question what *Simplicius* reports; and it is remarkable, that all the ancient Authors, who have ascribed the building of *Babylon* to *Semiramis*, have no other Authority, than That of *Ctesias*, whose Histories abounded in Fables (*d*). And, therefore, we see, that *Berosus* very much blames the *Greek* Writers for affirming, that *Semiramis* built *Babylon*, and adorned it with most beautiful Structures (*e*). The Supplement to *Moreri* quotes *Quintus Curtius*, in relation to the Immodesty of the *Babylonian* Women. It may be added, that This Lewdness was very ancient. *Jeremiah*'s Letter, inserted in the Book of

eighty Years. Therefore the use of Letters has been perpetual, and I have reason to believe, that it has always been practised in *Assyria*. It is thus *Pliny* argues, in his Natural History, as we now have it: It is thus, I say, he argues, after having observed, that *Cadmus* brought the Use of Letters into *Europe*, and that the Invention of them, in *Egypt*, was said to have happened fifteen Years before the Reign of *Phoroneus*. A Fool, a drunken Man, or a Dotard, could scarce have been Author of such a Heap of Contradictions. It must, therefore, necessarily be supposed, that this Passage is not in it's original State: And it is greatly to be wondered, that a Thousand learned Criticks should have examined these Words, without perceiving such an inconsistent piece of Logic in them, as might make them suspect, that the Passage was corrupted. *Scaliger*, *Vossius*, Sir *John Marsham*, and Mr *Dodwell*, have so little mistrusted it, that they have taken it for the Foundation of the Conclusions, which they would draw concerning the Age of *Berosus* (5), or against the Antiquity of *Babylon* (6), or for other Purposes (7). Father *Harduin* has corrected part of this Passage; but it was not to rectify *Pliny*'s Reasoning; for, if this had been his principal Motive, he would have corrected all: It is Mr *Perizonius* (8), who has fully discovered the whole Matter, and proved the Corruption of the Text (9). He has demonstrated, that the Number of a *Thousand* must be added as well to the Account of *Epigenes*, as to That of *Berosus*; and then *Pliny*'s Argument would stand thus; that, according to the Testimony of *Epigenes*, the Observations of the *Babylonian* Astrologers comprehended Seven hundred and twenty Thousand Years; and, according to the Testimony of those, who, like *Berosus* and *Critodemus*, give them the least extent, Four hundred and eighty Thousand Years. And *Pliny* is certainly in the right, upon the Supposition he makes, that these Testimonies are authentic, to conclude, that the beginning of the *Assyrian* Letters is impossible to be found. Now, when a thing is so ancient, that the Original of it is beyond finding out, we may, without any scruple, affirm it, as *Pliny* has done, to have been perpetual. But would any one venture to call it so, when the Proofs given of it's Antiquity leave it much later than several Things, whose Beginnings are known? This must have been *Pliny*'s Case, had he wrote what we find in his Work at this Time. Consider well what he has said concerning *Cadmus* and *Phoroneus*.

Father *Harduin*'s Correction deserves a distinct Explanation. He mends *Pliny*'s Text thus: " E diverso Epigenes apud Babylonios CCCCLXX annorum " M observationes siderum coctilibus laterculis inscriptas docet —— qui minimum, Berosus & Critodemus, CCCCXC annorum. —— On the contrary, " *Epigenes tells us, that, amongst the Babylonians, there were celestial Observations for Four hundred and seventy Thousand Years, inscribed on Bricks.* —— *Berosus and Critodemus, who make the least of it, say Four hundred and ninety Years.*" On one side, he puts Four hundred and seventy Thousand, instead of Seven hundred and twenty; and, on the other,

Four hundred and ninety, instead of Four hundred and eighty. He builds on Manuscripts, as to the last Correction, and on the Authority of *Cicero*, as to the first (10). It is true, he says, by the way, that the Passage itself, in *Pliny*, seems to require the first Correction. " Certè annorum millia locus iste " postulare videtur, non annos (11). —— *Certainly* " *This Place requires the reading Thousands of Years,* " *instead of Years.*" This looks as if he was sensible, how bad a Reasoner *Pliny* is made by the common Reading. But, if a Thousand be added to the Four hundred and eighty of the common Reading, we fall into another Difficulty; for, then, *Berosus* allows Four hundred and eighty Thousand Years to the Observations of the *Babylonian* Astrologers; and yet we know, that, when he mentions the great Care of the *Babylonians*, in preserving the Memory of several natural and historical Matters, he speaks but of a Hundred and fifty Thousand Years. Βηρωσσὸς ἐν τῇ πρώτῃ τῶν Βαβυλωνιακῶν φησὶ γενέσθαι αὐτὸν κατ' Ἀλέξανδρον τὸν Φιλίππου τὸν ἡλικίαν, ἀνάγραφα δὲ πολλῶν ἐν Βαβυλῶνι φυλάσσεσθαι μετὰ πολλῆς ἐπιμελείας ἀπὸ ἐτῶν που ὑπὲρ μυριάδων ιε' πεντεκαίδεκα χρόνον, περιέχειν δὲ τὰς ἀναγραφὰς ἱστορίας περὶ τοῦ οὐρανοῦ, καὶ θαλάσσης, καὶ πρωτογονίας, καὶ βασιλέων, καὶ τῶν κατ' αὐτοὺς πράξεων (12). —— *Berosus, in his first Book concerning the Babylonians, says, he himself was born in the Time of Alexander, the Son of Philip; and that there were Inscriptions, preserved, with great Care, at Babylon, comprehending above a Hundred and fifty Thousand Years: and that these Inscriptions contained Accounts of the Heavens, and of the Sea, of the Originals of Things, of Kings, and their Transactions.* It must be confessed, that this Passage equally proves these two things: The one, That the Number Four hundred and eighty, or Four hundred and ninety, ought to be struck out of *Pliny*'s Text; The other, That Four hundred and eighty Thousand must not be put in the room of it, but rather a Hundred and fifty Thousand. And yet it might admit of some Cavil: It may be objected, that *Berosus*, being better informed of the Fact, found Four hundred and eighty Thousand Years, and inserted That Calculation in a Book, which *Pliny* followed. It might also be objected, that the Numbers, in the Passage quoted by *Eusebius*, have been corrupted. However it be, I should chuse to retain the Correction of Father *Harduin*, only with the Alteration, as to *Berosus* and *Critodemus*, of an Hundred and fifty Thousand, instead of Four hundred and ninety.

I shall observe, by the way, that *Vossius* has not been careful enough, in relating what concerns *Berosus*, in the Passage of *Pliny*, which is the Subject of this Remark. He pretends, that *Pliny* says, *Berosus* wrote the History of what had passed during the Space of Four hundred and eighty Years. I quote *Vossius*'s own Words. " Plinius, Lib. vi, Hist. " Nat. Cap. LV, (*He should have said Lib. vii, Cap.* " LVI.) refert Berosum tradere memoriam quadringentorum annorum & octoginta (13). —— Pliny " reports, that Berosus has given a History of Four " hundred

BABYLON. BACAOVIUS.

of *Baruch*, touches something of it, but in an obscure manner, and wants a Commentary, taken out of *Herodotus* [C].

"*hundred and eighty Years*" Compare them with the Passage of *Pliny*, and you will find how wide they are from the Truth. Whom shall we trust?

[C] *Jeremiah's Letter, concerning the Immodesty of the Babylonian Women, wants a Commentary, taken out of* Herodotus.] This is *Jeremiah's* Text: "The Women also, with Cords about them, sitting "in the Ways - - - - but if any of them, drawn "by some that passeth by, lie with him, she re- "proacheth her Fellow, that she was not thought "as worthy as herself, nor her Cord broken (14)." To understand this right, we must have recourse to *Herodotus*, who informs us, That there was a Law at *Babylon*, which obliged all the Women of the Country to seat themselves near the Temple of *Venus*, and there to wait for an Opportunity of lying with a Stranger (15). They were all forced to go through this Ceremony once in their Lives. The rich sat in their Coaches, and had a great number of Domesticks to attend them: The others had only certain Ranks, which were separated from each other with Cords (16), but in such a Manner, that there was Liberty to go in and out, that Strangers might pass freely in the Intervals, and make choice of her, who best suited their Taste. When they had made their Choice, they cast Money into her Lap, and led her aside, in order to enjoy her. They put up a Prayer for her to the Goddess of the Temple (17). These Women were not suffered to refuse any Stranger, nor the Money given them, how small soever was the Sum. They were obliged to follow the first Stranger, who threw them Money. Observe, that these Sums were appointed for Religious Uses. Γίνεται γὰρ ἱερὸν τοῦτο τὸ ἀργύριον (18). *This Money is held sacred.* After the Performance of the Act, they might return to their Houses; the Devotion, or Expiation, which the Goddess required, was accomplished.

(14) *The Book of Baruch in the Apocrypha, chap. 6.*

(15) Herod. lib. 1, c. 19.

(16) *I am forced to paraphrase a little, to make* Herodotus *the better understood, who has not been particular enough in his Explanation.*

(17) *This was* Venus *the Babylonians called her* Mylitta. Herod. lib. 2, cap. 199.

(18) Ibid.

Those, who were beautiful, or agreeable, were soon dispatched, and relieved from Duty; but the ugly waited long for the propitious Hour to satisfy the Law. Some were so unfortunate, that three or four Years waiting did not end their Noviciate. Καὶ γὰρ τοιαύτα καὶ τριςαιτία μετέξέτεραι χρόνον μίνουσι (19). *Some wait three or four Years.* This removes all Obscurity from *Jeremiah's* Words. Each of these Women were kept in a little Cell, bound about with Cords, and did not come out but by breaking the Cord; after which, they insulted over those, who were yet in the Inclosure. We may apply to those, who were taken out but late, these Lines of *Catullus*:

Tam gratum mihi, quàm ferunt puellæ
Pernici aureolum fuisse malum,
Quod zonam solvit diu ligatam (20).

*Dear as the Golden Apple, in the Race,
Which check'd the flying* Atalanta's *Pace.
Nor sought she Gold, but seiz'd the specious Bait,
With Joy to end her tedious Virgin State.*

Who can sufficiently bewail the monstrous Alliance, preserved by Paganism, between the Worship of the Gods, and the most filthy Passions? It might justly have been called *The easy Devotion*, if the Comedy had contained more Acts and more Scenes, and if there had not been a disadvantageous Mixture for the ugly; for three or four Years Patience was an hard Penance for one single Rencounter. *Martin del Rio* retracted what he had said, on the Words I have quoted from the Book of *Baruch*. He thought they were to be understood of certain Ligatures practised to make themselves loved. See his *Magical Disquisitions* (21).

(19) Ibid.

(20) Catull. Epigr. 2.

(21) Lib 3, Part 1, Quest. 9, pag. 13.

BACHOVIUS (REINIER) was born at *Cologne*, in the Year 1544. You may find his Life, among those of the Civilians of *Germany*, in *Melchior Adam*. I shall not repeat what *Moreri* has taken from him: I will only give an account of the Persecutions, which *Bachovius* suffered, at *Leipsic*, for his *Calvinism*. At first he was only suspected, and they were satisfied with keeping him out of all public Employs; but, the Times altering, he obtained the Office of a Senator, and afterwards, in the Year 1585, That of an *Echevin*, and, in three Years more, That of Consul. The Elector, *Christian* I, dying in the Year 1591, *Bachovius* was urged to profess *Lutheranism*; and, because he would not, they compelled him to relinquish his Offices. He would not hearken to the advice given him to retire, though the danger of a Prison was represented to him; he thought his Flight would give his Enemies a Handle to pronounce, that he esteemed himself guilty: But, in the Year 1593, he was obliged to give way to popular Commotions, and leave *Leipsic*. He went first to *Servestæ*, and, the Year after, into the *Palatinate*, having lost almost all his Effects. He met with a kind Protector in the Person of the Elector *Palatine*, and enjoyed several profitable and honourable Offices at *Heidelberg* till his Death, which happened the Twenty seventh of *February* 1614 (a). He published a Book, which discovered more of the Divine, than of the Civilian [A]. He left, among other Children, *Reinier* or *Reinhard* BACHOVIUS, whom he saw promoted, from the Professorship of Politics, to That of Civil Law, in the University of *Heidelberg*. This Son obtained a great Name among the Civilians of the XVIIth Century [B]. He was particularly remarkable

(a) *Taken from* Melchior Adam, *in the* Volume *of Civilians.*

[A] *He published a Book, which discovered more of the Divine, than of the Civilian.*] It was a sort of a Commentary on the famous *Heidelberg* Catechism. *Melchior Adam* speaks thus of it: "*Propagan- "dæ veritatis evangelicæ studio edidit Catechesin "Palatinatus, testimoniis Sacræ Scripturæ ac sen- "tentiis patrum, qui primis quingentis à Christo nato "annis in Ecclesia Dei claruerunt, exornatam & illustra- "tam, cum epitome vitæ eorundem patrum, & metho- "dica narratione de Conciliis, quorum Canones in "illo Catechetico libello citantur* (1). — *Out of a sin- "cere Desire for the Propagation of Evangelical Truth, "he published the Catechism of the Palatinate, adorned, "and illustrated, with the Testimonies of sacred Scrip- "ture, and Opinions of the Fathers, who were fa- "mous, in the Church, for the first five Centuries "after* CHRIST, *with an Epitome of the Lives "of those Fathers, and a Methodical Account of* "the Councils, *whose Canons are cited in That Ca- "techism.*"

(1) Melch. Adam in vitis Jurisc. p. 472, 473.

[B] *Reinier or Reinhard Bachovius — obtained a great Name among the Civilians*] *Conringius* calls him, *Disciplinæ juridicæ æternum decus* (2). — *The perpetual Ornament of the Civil Law. Vinnius* says he is, *subtilissimus Jurisconsultus, non tam suæ sententiæ adstructor, quam destructor alienæ* (3). — *The most able Civilian, not so much in advancing Opinions of his own, as in overthrowing those of others.* Another says, *Eo in his, quæ ad solidam nostri juris interpretationem faciunt, acutiorem vix tradit prior ætas* (4). — *The former Age scarce produced a greater Interpreter of the Civil Law.* Lastly, the Compliments of *accuratissimus, subtilissimus, acutissimus, inexorabilis Censor* (5). - - - *The most accurate, most able, judicious, most severe Censor*, are commonly given to him. The Elogy, *Vinnius* gives him, agrees

(2) Conringius, de autoritate juris publ. in Germania apud Magirum Eponym. p. 99.

(3) Vinnius, cap. 11, de Pact. n. 9.

(4) Hahn, in Disæc. Observ. ad Wesenbecium apud eundem.

(5) Schutz, apud eundem.

598 BACHOVIUS. BACON.

remarkable for his skill in confuting, with great Subtilty, whatsoever he undertook to oppose (b). He was wavering on the Point of Religion; for he said, in confidence, to a *Lutheran* Professor (c), that, if he might be permitted to read private Lectures of the Civil Law at *Strasburg*, he would leave his Professorship of *Heidelberg*, and remove to *Strasburg*. He declared, that he detested the Doctrine of absolute Predestination, and that he believed the Corporeal Presence of JESUS CHRIST in the Sacrament of the Lord's-Supper, tho' he knew not the manner of it. The Person, to whom he discovered this Inclination, communicated it to the Magistrates of *Strasburg*, who ordered him to be assured he should be welcome. *Bachovius* removed to that City, with his Library; but, not finding a maintenance there (d), he returned to *Heidelberg*, where his Friend found him under great Vexation and Sickness, in the Year 1629 (e).

(b) *See Remark* [B].

(c) *His Name was* Tabor, *and he was esteemed a great Civilian.*

(d) *Vitæ præsidiis destitutus religionem omisit. —— Being disappointed of a Livelihood he quitted that Religion. Præsidium in Mausoleo Taboris.*

(e) *Taken from Præschius in Mausoleo Taboris.*

agrees but with too many Persons: There are too many Writers, and Men of great Reasoning, who have had Success in proving their own Doctrine, but yet can entirely demolish That of others. Men, who engage in Disputes, are commonly stronger in the Offensive, than in the Defensive. See what an Elector of *Cologne* said concerning the Quarrel between the *Cordeliers* and *Jacobins*. Father *Paul* relates it. See the fourth Book of his History of the Council of *Trent*, Page 309 of Mr *Amelot de la Houssaie*'s Translation.

BACON (ROGER) An English *Franciscan*, lived in the XIIIth Century. He was a great Astrologer, Chymist, and Mathematician. It was this, undoubtedly, which occasioned him to be suspected of Magic. There runs a Tradition among the *English*, that This Fryar made a Brazen Head, which answered all his Questions [A]. *Selden* rejects this as a childish Fable [B], and observes, that no Historian has mentioned it, and that *Bale*, who had defamed *Roger Bacon*, recanted, and honourably repaired That Injury. *Francis Picus* says, That he read, in one of *Bacon*'s Books, "That a Man might become a Prophet, and fore-tell things to come by means of "the Looking-glass, *Almuchefi*, composed according to the Rules of Perspective; "provided he used it under a good Constellation, and first brought his Body into an "even and temperate State by Chymistry (a)." This is agreeable to what *John Picus Mirandulanus* has maintained, That *Bacon* only busied himself with Natural Magic (b). This Fryar sent several Instruments, of his own Invention, to Pope *Clement* IV (c). Several of his Books have been published: *Specula Mathematica & perspectiva, Speculum Alchemiæ, De mirabili Potestate Artis & Naturæ, Epistolæ cum Notis*, &c. In all probability, he did not perform any Thing by compact with the Devil; but has only ascribed to Things a surprizing Efficacy, which they could not naturally have. Consequently, there is reason to say, that his Writings contain a great deal of Superstition [C]. He was very much infatuated with Judicial Astrology.

(a) *Francisc. Picus, lib. 2. de Prænotione, cap. 1. & lib. 7. cap. 7. cited by Naudé, Apology for Great Men, pag. 490.*

(b) *Joh. Picus in Præfat. Apologiæ, cited by Naudé, ibid.*

(c) *Naudé, ibid. p. 493.*

[A] *He is said to have made a brazen Head, which answered all his Questions.*] *Mayer* remarks, That *Roger Bacon* is commonly introduced upon the Stage, in Comedies, as a great Magician, and that "the "common Report is, that he, and his Fellow-Monk, "*Thomas Bungey*, wrought seven Years to forge "This Head, to know, from it, if there might not "be some means to inclose all *England* with a thick "Wall and Rampart? Upon which it gave them "an Answer, which however they could not rightly "understand, because, not expecting to receive it so "speedily, they were taken up in other things, "than listening to the Oracle (1)." These are popular Stories, which do not deserve to be recorded. The like are told of *Albertus Magnus* (2).

[B] *Selden rejects this as a childish Fable.*] These are his own Words: " Istiusmodi caput ex ære " conflatum ab eruditissimo Rogero Bachone est " in ore nostratis vulgi, sed non sine injuria in " illius Mathesin, quam summam & à dæmonum " præstigiis puram monstrarit satis illius opera quot- " quot nos legisse contigit, & quidquid adversus eum " uti magum seu γενηθμανζιν ʃ. Balæus inscitia " dicam, an in optimas artes malitia, editione cen- " turiarum prima satis incogitanter effutierat, id bene " monitus omne non modo retractavit, verum in ea " quæ tali & tanto viro digna sunt postrema recog- " nitione etiam prudenter commutavit. Nec quod " hanc vulgi famam adstruat, habent Annales nostri "(3).—— *Our common People are full of a Story "of a brazen Head, made by the most learned Roger Bacon, very much to the Prejudice of his Mathematical Knowledge, which all his Works, which "I have had an Opportunity of reading, demonstrate "to have been very compleat, and intirely clear from "diabolical Jugglings: and whatsoever*]. Bale, *either "of Ignorance, or Malice to those excellent Studies, "had, in the first Edition of his Centuries, very "inconsiderately thrown out against him, as a Ma-* " gician, *or Necromancer, he has, on better Advice, "in his last Edition, not only retracted, but also wisely substituted, in it's Place, what becomes the Character of so great a Man. Nor is there any Authority in our History for That common Report."* John Dee, *an English Philosopher and Mathematician, wrote an Apology for Roger Bacon. He mentions it in the Epistle dedicatory of his* Propædeumata Aphoristica de præstantioribus quibusdam naturæ virtutibus. *See* Naudé, *in the Four hundred eighty eighth Page of his Apology for great Men.*

[C] *His Writings contain a great deal of Superstition.*] Martin del Rio, *who, of all Men in the World, in these Matters, is least prodigal of his Absolution to Persons suspected, clears Roger Bacon of Magic, and is contented to make him only a superstitious Author.* " Alchindus, *says he* (4), Rogerius " Baconus, & Geber Arabs, multis scatent supersti- " tiosis; ideo vetitæ lectionis etiam hos putarim. —— " Alchindus, *Roger Bacon, and* Geber, *the Arabian, "abound in Superstition, and therefore, in my Opinion, ought not to be read."* John Wierus *is not so favourable; for he puts Roger Bacon, Petrus Aponensis, Anselmus Parmensis, Cicchus Asculus, and some others, in the same Class; whereas* Martin del Rio *treats the three last, I have named, as true Magicians, and puts* Bacon *only in the number of the Superstitious.* " Ab hoc numero removeo, ut de- " moniacos magos, Picatricem Hispanum, Anselmum " Parmensem, Cicchum Esculanum, Petrum de Abo- " no, & Corn. Agrippam, & Paracelsum —— ho- " mines partim atheos, partim hæreticos (5). —— "*I exclude from this Number, as diabolical Magicians,* Picatrix *the* Spaniard, Anselmus Parmensis, " Cicchus Esculanus, Petrus de Abono, Cornelius " Agrippa, *and* Paracelsus, —— *Men partly Atheists, " and partly Hereticks."* As for the rest, Wierus *agrees perfectly with him; that is, he took* Petrus Aponensis, Anselmus Parmensis, *&c. for Practisers of infernal*

(1) *Maierus, Symbol. aureæ Mensæ, lib. 10. pag. 453, cited by Naudé, Apology for great Men, pag. 431.*

(2) *See, above, Remark [F], n. 2, of the Article* ALBERTUS (MAGNUS).

(3) *Selden de Diis Syris Syntagm. 1, cap. 2, pag. 38.*

(4) *Disquisit. Magicar. lib. 1, cap. 3, pag. 22.*

(5) *Ibid.*

Aſtrology [D]. ———The Letter, which he wrote to Pope *Clement* IV, and which is now in the Library of *Lambeth,* together with great Encomiums on the Holy Scriptures, mentions a very odd Project; for he there exhorts That Pope to confirm, by Apoſtolical Authority, and to recommend to the whole Church, the Method he had found out to teach every Body *Hebrew, Latin, Greek,* and *Arabic,* in a very few Days. He pretended, that the Laity ought not only to read the Scripture, but alſo to underſtand the Originals [*E*]; and he averred, that his *Univerſal Grammar* was earneſtly wiſhed for, and had been confirmed by ſeveral Prophecies.

Infernal Magic. " Superiorum magorum nugamen-
" ta itidem inſulsè ſequuti ſunt Appion Grammati-
" cus. Julianus Apoſtata, Robertus Anglicus apud
" Helvetios miſere mortuus, *Rogerius Bacbon,* Petrus
" Aponenſis Conciliator dictus, Albertus Teutonicus,
" Arnoldus de Villanova, Anſelmus Parmenſis, Pi-
" catrix Hiſpanus, vel author libri ad Alfonſum ſub
" Picatricis nomine, Cicchus Aſculus Florentinus, &
" plerique alii obſcurioris nominis ſcriptores, deplorati
" certe ingenii homines. Qui quum ſe magiam tra-
" dere pollicentur, non niſi aut deliramenta quædam
" nulla ratione ſubnixa, aut ſuperſtitiones piis omni-
" bus indignas congeſſerunt (6). ——— *The Tricks of*
" *former Magicians are fooliſhly followed by* Appion
" *the Grammarian,* Julian *the Apoſtate,* Robertus An-
" glicus, *who died miſerably in Switzerland,* Roger
" Bacon, Petrus Aponenſis, *called the Reconciler,* Al-
" bertus Teutonicus, Arnoldus de Villà Novà, Anſel-
" mus Parmenſis, Picawix *the Spaniard, or the Au-*
" *thor of the Book under his Name to King* Alphonſus,
" Cicchus Aſculus *the Florentine, and ſeveral other*
" *Writers of obſcurer Names, Men of deſperate Minds:*
" *Who, inſtead of the Magic they pretend to be Ma-*
" *ſters of, have only heaped together either ſome idle*
" *Dreams, without any Foundation of Reaſon, or Su-*
" *perſtitions unworthy the Attention of all pious Per-*
" *ſons."*

[*D*] *He was very much infatuated with Judicial*
Aſtrology.] John Picus maintains, that the Book, entitled *Speculum Aſtrologiæ,* which treats of the Lawful and Unlawful Authors, who wrote upon Aſtrology, is a Work of *Roger Bacon* (7). That Book
was condemned by Gerſon (8), and by *Agrippa, as*
exceedingly ſuperſtitious (9). Francis Picus (10), and
many others, have condemned it, becauſe the Author
maintains in it, *with ſubmiſſion to better Judgments,*
that the Books of Magic ought to be carefully pre-
ſerved, becauſe the Time draws near, that, for certain Cauſes not there ſpecified, they muſt neceſſarily be
peruſed, and made uſe of on ſome Occaſions. Naudé
adds, *That* Roger Bacon *was ſo much addicted to*
Judicial Aſtrology, that Henry de Haſſia, Gulielmus
Pariſienſis, Nicolas Oreſmius ———— *were obliged to*
inveigh ſharply againſt his Writings and all the Vani-
ties of Aſtrologers (11).

[*E*] *He pretended, that the Laity were not*
obliged to read the Scriptures, but alſo to underſtand
the Originals.] As I have not read his Letter, I
cannot ſay whether he relies upon this Argument:
That a private Perſon, who underſtands neither the
Greek nor *Hebrew* Language, is obliged to depend
on the Fidelity and Capacity of Tranſlators: Which,
it may be ſaid, is but a weak Foundation, and not
to be truſted, to build our Salvation on. However
it be, his Pretenſion is ſufficiently extravagant, and
contains Impoſſibilities. This is the Judgment of

the Author, who mentions this Letter. " Inter Scrip-
" tores 13 ſeculi, qui a Whartono pro Scripturis &
" ſacris vernaculis adducuntur, comparet *Rogerus*
" *Bacon,* cujus epiſtolam de laudibus S. Scripturæ
" ad Clementem IV. bibliothecæ Lambethanæ tenet.
" O ſervat autem, Autorem illum portentoſa quædam
" & impoſſibilia in prolixa illa epiſtola comminiſci.
" Non enim tantum neceſſarium eſſe docet, ut om-
" nes Chriſtiani ſacram Scripturam tanquam fidei ſuæ
" fontem & regulam perfectè ſciant, ſed etiam fontes
" Hebraicos & Græcos ab omnibus conſulendos aſ-
" ſerit. Et quamvis incredibile videatur, ut ſinguli
" Chriſtiani linguarum iſtarum notitiam ſibi compa-
" rare poſſint, id tamen Baconus factu perquam fa-
" cile eſſe perſuadere ſuis Lectoribus cupit, impri-
" mis cum ſe Grammaticam, quandam univerſalem
" inveniſſe glorietur, cujus ope intra pauciſſimos dies
" quilibet linguam Hebraicam, Græcam, Latinam,
" & Arabicam, addiſcere queat; & ut omnes, quod
" legunt, etiam intelligant, ſe opus quoddam ma-
" nuductorium ſeu præliminare ad promovendam S.
" Scripturæ intelligentiam editurum ſpondet, enixe
" Pontificem orans, ut artificium ſuum, ſummis
" omnium votis expetitum, & frequentibus vati-
" ciniis confirmatum, Apoſtolica autoritate confir-
" met & univerſæ eccleſiæ commendet, unde in-
" numera in eccleſiam beneficia redundatura mini-
" me dubitat (12). ——— *Among the Writers of the*
" *XIIIth Century, who are produced, by* Wharton,
" *in favour of tranſlating the Scriptures, and Di-*
" *vine Services, into our own Language,* Roger Bacon
" *is credited, whoſe Epiſtle, to* Clement IV, *on the Praiſes*
" *of Sacred Scripture, is now in the* Lambeth *Li-*
" *brary. But he obſerves, that this Author, in that*
" *long Epiſtle, has projected ſomething very monſtrous*
" *and impracticable. For he boldly it to be neceſſary*
" *for all Chriſtians, not only to underſtand perfectly*
" *the Sacred Scripture, as the Fountain and Rule*
" *of their Faith, but alſo to be able to conſult the*
" Hebrew *and* Greek *Originals. And, though it*
" *may ſeem incredible, that every Chriſtian ſhould be*
" *able to attain the Knowledge of thoſe Languages,*
" *yet* Bacon *would perſuade his Readers, that it may*
" *very eaſily be done, eſpecially ſince he pretends to*
" *have invented an univerſal Grammar, by the help of*
" *which any one may, in a very few Days, make him-*
" *ſelf Maſter of* Hebrew, Greek, Latin, *and* Ara-
" bic; *and, that all, who read, may underſtand, he*
" *promiſes to publiſh an Introductory Work, to make*
" *the Sacred Scripture more eaſily underſtood, earneſt-*
" *ly deſiring the Pope, that This Invention of his,*
" *ſo very much wiſhed for by all, and confirmed by*
" *ſeveral Prophecies, might be eſtabliſhed by his Apo-*
" *ſtolical Authority, and recommended to the whole*
" *Church, to which he is ſure it will bring innu-*
" *merable Advantages."*

BACON (FRANCIS), Lord High Chancellor of *England* under King *James* I, was one of the greateſt Men of his Age, and one of thoſe, who beſt underſtood the Imperfections in the Philoſophy of that Time. He ſtudied hard to find out a Remedy for them, and formed very fine Plans for their Reformation [*A*]. The Public received his Works very favourably. A compleat Edition was made of them at *Franc-*
fort in Folio, in the Year 1665. The *Journal of the Learned* did not mention it without beſtowing great Encomiums upon this illuſtrious Chancellor (*a*). The Trea-
tiſe *De Augmentis Scientiarum,* which was reprinted at *Paris* in the Year 1624, is one of This Author's beſt Productions [*B*]. His *Moral and Political Works,* tranſlated into French

[*A*] *He formed very fine Plans for their Refor-*
mation.] See what Mr *Baillet* has ſaid of them, in the firſt Volume of the Life of Mr *Des Cartes* (1), and what *Gaſſendus* has ſaid in particular of *Bacon's* Logic (2).

[*B*] *The Treatiſe* De Augmentis Scientiarum — *is one of This Author's beſt Productions.*] See here what *Coſtar* laid of it to *Voiture: I have lately read*

the Books, which Chancellor Bacon *wrote about the Ad-*
vancement of Sciences, in which I found a great many
admirable Things (3). He afterwards gives Inſtances of ſome of thoſe Things, and by his Choice ſhews his good Taſte; for indeed they are all fine and great Thoughts. I have been informed, that *Bacon's* Works were principally made uſe of by *Coſtar,* and that he took from thence the Ground, or Baſis, of his Collections;

BACON. BACOUE. BADIUS.

French by *Baudouin*, sold so well, that they had a Run of several Editions. *His Life of Henry* VII, *King of England*, is very much esteemed (*b*). By labouring so hard for the Republic of Learning, *Bacon* neglected his Domestic Affairs, in such a manner, and plunged himself into so many Expences, that he died very poor. We shall produce two Authorities on this Subject [*C*]. His Death is placed on the Ninth of *April* 1626. He lived Sixty six Years.

lections; that is, having found some Thought in *Bacon*, which pleased him, he wrote it down, and, when he met with any thing, that related to it, in other Books, he added it to that Leaf; after which he needed no other Index, or Common-Place.

[*C*] *We shall produce two Authorities for* Bacon's *Poverty.*] The first I am indebted for to the *Bibliotheque Universelle*; for the second, to the *Sorberiana*. The *Bibliotheque Universelle* informs me, that *James Howel* says, in a *Letter* (4) dated the *Sixth of January* 1625 (5). —— " That Chancellor *Bacon* " died so poor, that he scarce left enough to bury " him; which made *Howel* say, That, though he had " a great Genius for Learning, he had no great Judg- " ment of Things. However, he imputes this " Chancellor's Poverty either to his Contempt of " Riches, or excessive Liberality. *Howel* says, That, " a little before his Death, he wrote a mournful Let- " ter to the King, wherein he implored his Assistance, " *For fear he should be reduced in his old Age to Beg- " gary, and be obliged to study only how to live, in- " stead of living, according to his Wish, only in order " to study.* Expressions, which seem as low to our " Author, as those of another Letter, which he had

" wrote before to the Prince of *Wales*, were pro- " phane. He told That Prince, *That he hoped, as the " Father had been his Creator, the Son would be his " Redeemer* (6)."

Let us see, now, what *Sorbiere* says : " *Bacon*'s *Na- " tural History*, at *Paris* 1631, translated, or rather " epitomized, by *Peter Amboise* Esq; *Sieur de la Ma- " delaine* The Translator has added an Account of " That Chancellor's Life, and, at the end, a Transla- " tion of his *New Atlantis*. Those few excellent " Remarks, I have seen, make me wish greatly for " an intire and faithful Translation. Mr *Boswel* tells " me, he had a particular Intimacy with this extra- " ordinary Man, who left him in his Will all his " Papers, which was the only one, which was execu- " ted out of a vast Number of Legacies, which he " gave by way of Pleasantry. He bequeathed Four " hundred thousand Livres to an imaginary College, " which he had given the Plan of, in his *New Atlan- " tis* (7)." This Account does not seem to say, that *Bacon* died poor; it rather insinuates, that he died not a little whimsical (8): But, if you consider it closer, you will find there is a Sign of Indigence in it.

BACOUE (LEO), born at *Casteljaloux* in the lower *Guienne*, forsook his Family Religion, which was That of the Reformed, and became a *Franciscan*. He attained afterward to the Prelacy, and was made Bishop of *Glandeve*. My Author observes, That Father *Leo Bacoue* is the only converted *Huguenot*, who was promoted to Episcopacy under the Reign of *Lewis* XIV (*a*). This Fryar published a *Latin Poem on the Education of a Prince*, about the time that the *Dauphin* was to have Preceptors. He re-printed it at *Paris* in the Year 1685. The *Journal des Sçavans* mentions it, the following Year (*b*).

BADIUS (JODOCUS), firnamed *Ascensius*, because he was born in the Borough (*a*) of *Assche* near *Brussels*, was in much Esteem for the great number of Books, which he printed and commented. He was born in the Year 1462. He performed his first Studies at *Ghent*; he continued them in *Italy*, and made a great progress in the *Greek* Language at *Ferrara*, under *Baptista Guarini*. He settled at *Lyons*, and taught the *Latin* and *Greek* Tongues there as well in public as in private. Afterwards he removed to *Paris*, and set up a Printing-House there, which gained him great Reputation [*A*]. From thence came forth several Classic Authors, with his Explications and Notes [*B*]. He bestowed the same Pains on some Modern Authors, as *Petrarch*, *Politian*, *Laurentius Valla*, *Baptista Mantuanus*, &c. He published also some Books of his own both in Prose and in Verse (*b*) [*C*]; and it is agreed, by good Judges, that, if his Domestic Cares had not obliged him to write as much, or more, for Gain, than for Glory, he would have succeeded much better than he did [*D*]. *Erasmus* happened

[*A*] *He set up a Printing-House, at* Paris, *which gained him great Reputation*.] Father *du Moulinet* informs us, That *Jodocus Badius* was the first, who brought into *France* the round Characters; and that, before him, all the *French* Printers made use of the *Gothic* Characters. *About the Year* 1500, *he came from* Italy *into* France, *as well to teach* Greek *in* Paris, *as to set up a very fine Printing-House there, which he called* Prælum Ascensianum, *Ascensius's* Press (1). Father *du Moulinet* forgets, that *Badius* stopt a very considerable Time at *Lyons*, before he came to *Paris*. See the Remark [*H*]. As for the rest, Mr *Chevillier* has proved, against That Father, That *Printing in* France *did not begin with* Gothic *Letters*, *and that Roman Letters were used there, before* Badius's *Time* (2); And farther, that tho' *a great Number of His Editions were printed in a good Letter* —— *He printed several also in* Gothic (3). [* *Gabriel Naudé*, in the seventh Chapter of his *Addition to the History of* Naude XI, pag. 317, and 318, of the Edition of 1630, pretends, that it was The *Workmen*, who, less desirous of Honour than Profit, introduced the *Gothic* Characters; but I know not how he understands This; since many of the old Editions, which we have in *square Letters*, are

no less charged with Abbreviations, than the *Gothic*, which succeeded them. REM. CRIT.]

[*B*] *He printed a great many Classic Authors, with his Explications and Notes.*] *Valerius Andreas* gives a List of them, wherein we find *Horace*, *Persius*, *Terence*, *Juvencus*, *Theocritus*, *Sallust*, *Valerius Maximus*, *Quintilian*; *Aulus Gellius*, and several Treatises of *Cicero*. " Commentarii verò, sive fa- " miliares enarrationes, circumferuntur, in Horacium " *Flaccum*, &c (4). —— *There are also handed about " Commentaries, or familiar Explanations, on* Horace, " &*c*." The List of *Suertius* is still larger, and mentions *Ovid*, and *Seneca*'s Tragedies (5).

[*C*] *He published some Books of his own, both in Prose, and in Verse.*] *Valerius Andreas* mentions these following: *Psalterium B. Mariæ*, *Epigrammatum liber*, *Navicula stultarum mulierum*, *De Grammatica*, *De conscribendis Epistolis*, *Vita Thomæ à Kempis*.

[*D*] *If his domestic Cares had not interrupted him, — he would have succeeded much better than he did*] *Erasmus* speaks very freely of this; " Nec in- " felicitèr omnino cessit conatus Badio; adest illi fa- " cilitas non indocta, felicius tamen cessurus, nisi curæ " domesticæ, reique parandæ studium, interrupissent " otium

BADIUS. 601

happened to compare him, in some things, to *Budæus*; and it can scarce be credited, what a Clamour was raised at *Paris* against That Comparison [*E*]. Those, who place *Badius*'s Death in the Year 1526, are mistaken [*F*]. He was incumbered with a very great Family, and it is said, in his Epitaph, That, in all probability, the Number of his Children would have equalled That of his Books, had he made as early a beginning in the one, as he did in the other [*G*]; but that he had been much longer an Author, than a married Man. I would not warrant This to be exactly true [*H*].

His

" *otium illud Musis amicum, hujus laudis candidato* " *necessarium* (6). —— *Nor was Badius's Attempt* " *unsuccessful: his Manner is easy, and not unlearned:* " *But he would have succeeded much better, if his* " *domestic Cares, and Endeavour for a Maintenance,* " *had not interrupted that Quiet, which the Muses* " *require in one, who writes for Fame.*" He passes the same Judgment in one of his Letters (7). " *Aliis* " *liberum erit de Badio judicare quod volunt; ego* " *semper illum habui in eorum numero, quorum nec* " *eruditionem, nec ingenium, nec eloquentiam possis* " *contemnere: tametsi non dissimulo illum longe ma-* " *jorem fuisse futurum, si fortuna benignior otium ac* " *tranquillitatem studiorum suppeditasset.* ——*Others* " *may judge as they please of* Badius: *for my own part,* " *I have always esteemed him in the number of those,* " *whose Learning, Understanding, and Eloquence, are* " *by no means contemptible: though I cannot deny but* " *these would have appeared to much greater Advan-* " *tage, if an easier Fortune had allowed his Studies* " *a greater Tranquillity.*" *Brixius,* after having given a very mean Idea of *Badius,* says, he studied much more for Gain, than to become Eloquent. " *Scio* " *Badium non esse prorsus ἄμουσον. Verum qualis* " *qualis est talem se certe hominibus nostris hacte-* " *nus probavit, ut quoties a doctis sermo inter do-* " *ctos incidit de Badio plane ἰδιώτης λόγῳ. Illi,* " *quod non inficiaris, quæstus tantum non eloquentia* " *scopus est* (8). ——— *I know* Badius *is not* " *altogether unlearned. But, let him be what he will,* " *the Appearance he has hitherto made in the learned* " *World is such, that, whenever Men of Learning* " *speak of others of their own Class, not a Syllable* " *is mentioned of* Badius. *It cannot be denied but* " *that his Aim was Gain, and not Eloquence* "

[*E*] *Erasmus compared him* —— *with* Budæus*; and it can scarce be expressed, what a Clamour was raised, at Paris, against That Comparison.*] *Brixius,* who was *Erasmus*'s Friend, wrote to him a Letter on This Subject, part of which I have quoted. He told him plainly, That the learned Men of *Paris* were very angry to find, that he had, in some measure, preferred *Badius* to *Budæus.* " *Quo major indig-* " *natio nostrorum omnium animos subit, quod hic* " *in opinione, justâ de causâ quum sint, existimunt* " *illum abs te non tantum* Badio *collatum, sed &* " *postpositum. —— Ea una commissura adeo nostris* " *omnibus invidiosa est, ut multorum tibi benevolo-* " *rum animos à tui studio abalienarit, ob id quod* " *existimant* Budæum *cum* Badio *commissum perinde* " *esse ac si quis* Achillem *cum* Thersite *committeret* " (9). —— *All our People have conceived so much the* " *greater Indignation against you, to find one, for whom* " *they have so just a Value, not only compared, but* " *even postponed, by you, to* Badius. —— *This one Compa-* " *rison has so disgusted every Body here, that it has* " *drawn off a great many of your Well-Wishers from* " *the Respect they had for you, who look upon your* " *comparing* Budæus *with* Badius *to be just like* " *matching* Achilles *with* Thersites." *Erasmus* justified himself, and made it appear, that he had very evidently given *Budæus* the Superiority. He wondered they had not perceived it in *France*; or, if they had, how they came to make such an out-cry, and compose so many satirical Verses. *Demiror isthic esse doctos, qui hæc non videant, & si vident, magis etiam demiror esse qui vociferentur, qui maledicis Versiculis rem dignam existiment* (10). This Affair became so much talked of, that it reached the Ears of *Francis* I. " *Si verus est rumor, sic fremunt amici* Budæi*, quasi* " *in cineres patris ac matris illius imminxerim. Cla-* " *mant ô Cœlum! ô terra!* Budæum *cum* Badio *?* " *Clamant me invidere gloriæ* Budæi*, meque multis* " *epigrammatis dilacerant.* —— *Causâ delata est &* " *ad Regis cognitionem. Volenti cognoscere diffidii* " *causam, dictum est* Budæum *me taxasse in loco* " *quodam, eo me offensum quæsisse vindictam, eum-* " *que cum* Badis *contulisse* (11)." ——— *If Report*

" *speaks true, the Friends of* Budæus *are as much in-* " *censed, as if I had offered the greatest Indignity to* " *the Ashes of their Father and Mother. They cry* " *out to Heaven and to Earth, What !* Budæus *with* " Badius! *They charge me with envying* Budæus's " *Glory, and lash me with their many stinging Epi-* " *grams.* ——— *The Matter is brought even to the* " *Knowledge of the King. To whom, on Inquiry into* " *the Cause of this Dissention, they pretend, that* Bu- " dæus *has somewhere censured me, which has pro-* " *voked me to take This Revenge, by comparing him* " *with* Badius." If *Erasmus* designed to honour *Badius* by That Comparison, he was very much mistaken; for this poor Man was wounded to the Heart, every time Complaints were made of the Injustice done to *Budæus.* It had been better for *Badius,* if *Erasmus* had not thought of him. The offence was removed in the second Edition.

[*F*] *Those, who place his Death in the Year* 1526, *are mistaken.*] *Swertius* was content to say, that he found *Badius* had lived to the Year 1526 (12). This indeed leaves it doubtful, whether or no he lived beyond that Year; but he does not pretend to affirm, that he did not live beyond it. *Konig,* instead of expressing himself thus cautiously, affirms, that *Badius* died in the Year 1526. And others have said it after him. But let us consider a little *Brixius*'s Letter, which I have quoted; it was written in the Year 1528, and mentions *Badius* as living. *Valerius Andreas* says nothing at all concerning his Death. *Moreri* places it about the Year 1529, or 1530. But he is mistaken; for it is very well known, that *Erasmus* rejoiced, in a Letter of the Month of *September* 1530, (13), that the current Report about the Death of *Badius* was not true: And we have an Edition of the Epistles of *Longolius,* published by *Badius* in the Year 1533. *Gesner* observes, in his *Bibliotheca,* printed in the Year 1545, that *Badius* had been dead about ten Years. He was not dead, when the Book of *Alphonsus à Castro,* against Heresies, was printed at *Paris*; for *Badius* was one of those, who printed it in the Year 1534 (14). The Title Page of *Peter Lombard,* in *Epistolas Pauli,* has these words: *pro hæredibus Jodoci Badii* 1535, *Mense Decembri* (15). So that he was not living in the Month of *December* 1535.

[*G*] *The Number of his Children would have equalled those of his Books, had he made as early a Beginning in the one, as he did in the other.*] This Thought was the Subject of the following Epitaph, composed for him.

Hic, liberorum plurimorum qui parens,
Parens librorum plurimorum qui fuit,
Situs *Jodocus* Badius est *Ascensius.*
Plures fuerunt liberis tamen libri,
Quod jam senescens cœpit illos gignere,
Ætate florens cœpit hos quod edere (16).

Here lies Jodocus Badius Ascensius,
Father of many Children,
Author of many Books:
His Books were more numerous than his Children,
Because he commenced Author very early,
Father very late.

This is not the Epitaph, now to be seen on the Tomb of *Jodocus Badius,* in the Charnel-House of the Collegiate Church of *St Benedict* at *Paris* (17), where he was buried (18). If we may rely upon the Truth of these Lines, he followed the Maxim of most of the Learned, and married late. See the Book entituled *Valesiana* (19).

[*H*] *He had been much longer an Author, than a married Man* —— *I would not warrant this to be exactly true*] The *Sieur de la Caille* is the Cause of

this

BADIUS.

His Son *Conradus* BADIUS was born at *Paris*, and settled at *Geneva*. He became a very good Protestant, and demonstrated it in the *Koran of the Cordeliers*. He translated the first Book of it, and compiled the second, and adorned both with Marginal Notes, which are very severe. He was both a Printer and an Author, and made some Attempts in *French* Poetry. He wrote something of this kind against *Nostradamus* (*e*). Three of his Daughters were married to famous Printers [*I*]. I was a long time at a Loss to know, what a certain Modern Author means, by seeming to charge *Henry Stephens* with having censured *Jodocus Badius* [*K*]. I have nothing to say concerning one *Conradus* BADIUS, who died, with all his Family, of the Plague at *Orleans*, where he was Minister, in the Year 1562 (*d*), and was a Friend of *Theodorus Beza* from his Youth (*e*).

Mr *Chevillier*, who collected several Elogies on *Jodocus Badius*, asserts, that he had been Professor of Belles Lettres *in the University* of Paris, *and afterwards in the City of Lyons, where he read the Poets in Public* (*f*).

There is certainly a Mistake in the Title of One of the Books, which *Valerius Andreas* ascribes to him [*L*].

(c) Du Verdier Vau-Privas, Biblioth. Franç pag. 237.
(d) Beza, History of Churches, lib. 6, pag. 249.

(e) Ant. Fayus in Vitâ Theod. Bezæ, p. 45.
(f) Chevill. Original of Printing at Paris, pag. 137.

---

(20) History of Printing, pag. 72, 73.

this Doubt: he says, That *Badius*, at his Return from *Italy*, taught several Gentlemen in *Lyons*, *and composed, and printed, a great many good Books, at the House of* John Trechsel, *Printer at Lyons, whose Daughter,* Thesis Trechsel, *he married* ----- (20). It was to him, continues this Author, that the learned Robert Gaguin, *the twentieth General of the Order of the* Trinitarians, *who knew his Merit and Capacity for Correcting the Press, wrote to print his Works, as appears by the Letter of That General to him, prefixed to his Epistles in Quarto, in the Year* 1498. *This obliged* Badius *to go to* Paris *about the Year* 1499, *or* 1500, *after the Death of his Father-in-law, both to teach the Greek Tongue there, and to restore the Art of Printing, which began to decline.* It appears from this Passage, that *Badius* was a married Man in 1500. He was then but Thirty eight Years of Age; therefore it cannot be said, that he deferred his Marriage 'till he was old; *jam senescens carpit illas gignere*: And yet his Grandson, *Henry Stephens*, affirms it: for *Henry Stephens* is the Author of That *Latin* Epitaph, and of a *Greek* Epitaph, which turns on the same Thought. " *Jodoco* Badio elegantissimis

(21) Almeloveen de Vitis Stephanorum, pag. 28.

" hisce Epitaphiis parentavit ex filiâ nepos Henricus " Stephanus, quæ propter elegantiam non potui non " adscribere (21). ------ Henry Stephens *his Grandson, by his Daughter, paid his Duty to* Jodocus Badius *in these elegant Epitaphs, which, for their Beauty, I could not forbear transcribing.*" The Epitaphs may be seen in *Henry Stephens* Book, *de Artis Typographicæ Querimoniâ*. Mr *Almeloveen* has published both of them, with another of the same Author in *Latin*, in his curious Dissertation *De Vitis Stephanorum*.

[*I Three Daughters of J.* Badius *were married to famous Printers*.] *Catherine Badius*, a Daughter of *Jodocus*, was married to *Michael Vascosan* (22). *Perrette Badius*, another Daughter of *Jodocus*, was the Wife of *Robert Stephens* (23). *Jane Badius*, the other Sister, married *John de Roigny* (24), *who made use of the Mark of his Father-in-law, and yet the Prelum Ascensianum on his Editions for above Twenty five Years* (25). *Perrette* understood *Latin*, which she learnt, either by her Father's teaching her, as Mr *Almeloveen* believes (26), or by hearing People speak it in her Husband's House. Each of these Opinions is probable: Those who are of the latter, may take it from this, that a Sister of *H. Stephens*, Daughter of *Perrette Badius*, learned *Latin* without the Assistance of a Grammar, and only by use. For *Robert Stephens*'s House was always full of People, who spoke nothing but *Latin*; so that the very Maid-Servants acquired That Language. See the Epistle Dedicatory of *Henry Stephens*, prefixed to *Aulus Gellius*, where you will find these words, directed to his Son: " Aviæ tuæ eorum quæ " Latinè dicebantur (nisi rarius aliquod vocabulum " intermisceretur) haud difficilior erat intellectus, " quàm si dicta sermone Gallico fuissent. Quid de " superfluite forore mea, amita autem tua, nomine " Katharina, dicam? Illa quoque eorum quæ Latine " dicuntur interpretem non desiderat: multa vero & " ipsa eodem loqui sermone potest; & quidem ita " (licet nonnunquam impingat) ut ab omnibus intel- " ligatur. Unde illi hæc Latinæ linguæ cognitio? " Artem certè Grammaticam haud magistrum habuit, " nec ahus illi hac in re quam usus præivit. --- *Your* " *Grandmother understood as readily what was spoke* " *in Latin, except now and then some uncommon Ex-*

" *pressions, as she did her own Mother-Tongue. Your* " *Aunt* Katharine *also, the only Sister I have now* " *living, never needed an Interpreter for that Lan-* " *guage. She even spoke it pretty well herself, and,* " *though not without some Slips, yet so as to be easily* " *understood Nor was she taught this by Grammar,* " *but only by use.*" He explains what he means by this use, *viz.* that the Printers and Correctors of *Robert Stephens* spoke nothing but *Latin*.

[*K*] *I was a long time at a Loss to know what a certain modern Author means, by seeming to charge* Henry Stephens *with having censured* Jodocus Badius.] This perplexity was occasioned for want of understanding a Period of the Sieur *de la Caille*; which, I think, I have, at last, apprehended. That Period runs thus: " Here is his Epitaph, inserted by *Henry Stephens* in his Book *de Artis Typographicæ Querimonia*, printed by the same *Stephens* " in 1569, wherein are several Complaints addressed " to the said *Badius*, both in *Greek* and *Latin* (27)." At first I thought it meant, that *Henry Stephens* had reproached *Badius* very much, both in *Greek* and *Latin*, for having spoiled the Trade: But, considering that he was his Grandson, and finding nothing against *Badius* in the *Querimonia Artis Typographicæ*, which Mr *Almeloveen* has published, I could not tell what to think. Mr *Almeloveen* having assured me, that he had cut nothing off from the *Querimonia*, occasioned my reading the whole Period over again; upon which I now apprehend, that these words, *both in Greek and Latin*, most probably relate, not to *Complaints*, but to *Epitaph*. At last I have had an Opportunity of consulting the very Work of *Henry Stephens* (28). I found in it, I. A Preface in Prose, against the Ignorance of Printers. II. A Poem, wherein Printing is introduced, complaining of it's decay. III. The Epitaphs, both in *Greek* and *Latin*, and some in *Latin* only, of some learned Printers. But I could no where meet with any Complaints, either against *Badius*, or addressed to him; so that this Passage of the Sieur *la Caille* is a Riddle to me, if it is not a mistake. It is not to be wondered, that dead Languages, which admit of such a Variety of Transpositions, should be so obscure to us; when our own will not a little puzzle us, by altering the usual Order of the Words.

[*L*] *There is certainly a Mistake in the Title of One of the Books, which* Valerius Andreas *ascribes to him*.] He makes him Author of a Work, entitled, *Navicula stultarum Mulierum* (29), but notes neither the Place, nor Time, of the Impression: he is satisfied, in regard to this, with copping the Catalogue of *Swertius*. I have been informed (30), that *Badius* published, in 1513, a Book, entitled, *Navis stultifera Collectanea ab Jodoco Badio Ascensio variis carminum genere, non sine eorundem familiari explanatione, constata*. It is probable, that the Book, which *Valerius Andreas* mentions, is the same with This; or, at most, that it differs only as a Part from the Whole. I am opinion, likewise, that the Work, published by *Badius*, in 1513, is taken from That, which is entitled, *Navis Narragoniæ*, written by *Sebastian Brandt* (31). Native of *Strasbourg*, Professor of Law, and a good Poet for those times, *viz.* the End of the XVth Century. See, in *Gesner's Bibliotheque* (32), what the *Navis Narragoniæ*, or *Navis stultorum*, is.

(27) La Caille, History of Printing, pag. 74.

(28) Mr Almeloveen wrote lately his Books so obliging, sent me the Artis Typographicæ Querimonia.

(30) By Mr de la Costre, a Dutch Minister.

(31) Or Titio.

(32) Gesner, Biblioth. fol. 593.

---

(22) La Caille, History of Printing, pag. 102.
(23) Ibid. pag. 96.
(24) Ibid. pag. 105.
(25) Chevill. History of Printing, p. 138.
(26) Almeloveen, ubi supra.

(29) See Remark [*C*].

BADUEL

BADUEL.

BADUEL (CLAUDIUS) in Latin *Baduellus*, lived in the XVIth Century. He was of the Reformed Religion, as appears from his *Latin* Translation of some *Sermons of John Calvin*, which he published at *Geneva*; as also from the *Acts of the Martyrs*, which he printed in *Latin*, at the same Place, in the Year 1556 (a). I am very certain, he taught the *Belles Lettres*, in the College of *Nimes*; for we find, among his printed Works, *Oratio ad instituendum Gymnasium Nemausense de Studiis Literarum*; and another Piece, intituled, *de Collegio & Universitate Nemausensi*. He wrote well in *Latin*, and was a good Orator, a good Father, and a good Christian. These two last Qualifications appeared very plainly in his *Epistola paraenetica ad Paulum filium de vero Patrimonio & Hæreditate, quam Christiani Parentes suis Liberis debent relinquere*. I refer you, for the Titles of his other Books, to the *Epitome of Gesner's Bibliotheque*: But I shall say something of a *Discourse* he published *on the Marriage of Men of Learning* [A]; and I shall shew, that the Epitomizers of Gesner have been guilty of some Omissions; for they take no Notice of *Baduel*'s having composed, in *Latin*, a Funeral Oration on the Lady *de St Veran* (b). The Catalogue of the *Oxford* Library ascribes to him some *Notes on the Apocrypha*, printed at *London*, in the Year 1660.

(a) Frisii Epitome Bibl. Gesneri, p. 150.
(b) She was Daughter of the first President of the Parliament of Toulouse. This Funeral Oration, translated into French, by Charles Rozel, was printed at Lyons, in 1546. See the Bibliotheca of du Verdier.

[A] *I shall say something of a Discourse he published on the Marriage of Men of Learning*] This is the Title of it: *De Ratione Vitæ studiosæ ac literatæ in Matrimonio collocandæ & degendæ*. It was printed at *Lyons*, by *Sebastian Gryphius*, in 1544, in 4to, and at *Leipsic* in 1577, and 1581 (1). This last Edition contains One hundred forty three Pages, in 8vo. A Professor at *Leipsic*, whose Name was *Gregory Bresman*, has added a Preface, very much in Commendation of the Author, and his Book. I is certainly a very judicious Performance, and full of excellent Morality. *Baduel* dedicated it to Mr *de Mascencal* (2), first President of the Parliament of *Toulouse*. He sets off, in it, the Excellency of Matrimony, and shews the Disorders which usually attend a single State; and refutes those, who object, that Matrimony is inconvenient to Men of Learning, by interrupting their Studies, and not allowing them the Liberty of applying wholly to their Books. He tells us (3), he had made choice of this State himself, and gives some Advice to those, inclined to follow his Example, for the chusing a proper Wife, very earnestly exhorting to join the Pleasures of an agreeable Marriage with the Profession of Letters. He says, that *William Bigot*, a Person well skilled in Physic and Philosophy, had promised a Treatise to prove Matrimony necessary; that is, according to the Sentiment of *Baduel*, in order to a perfect Enjoyment of Health. " Gulielmus Bigotius, " says he (4), qui in Medicis ac Physicis diligenter " versatur, summam harum rerum habet scientiam, " aliquando promisit se de conjunctione Matrimonii " usuque ejus necessario scripturum. Necessarium (o-" pinor) intelligit, sine quo homo non potest vale-" re. Itaque eam partem Naturæ, conjugium ad " bonam Corporis constitutionem appetendis, nos ei " explicandam relinquemus: in quo valde prudenter " faciet, si eam commoditatem ex legitima uteris " conjunctione, ejusque moderati consuetudine, pe-" tendam esse doceat: & ea incommoda ostendat " quæ ex liberis illis ac dissolutis scortationibus hu-" manis corporibus multa & magna afferuntur.----" *Therefore this Part of Nature*, says he, *which re-" quires Matrimony, in order to a healthful Consti-" tution, I shall leave him to explain: In which " he will do very prudently, if he demonstrates this " Advantage to arise from a lawful and moderate " Use of Copulation; and at the same time describes " the many, and great, Disorders, the Body must be " subject to, from a licentious and dissolute Course of " Venery*." To give a just Idea of this Work, I shall borrow the Words of a Professor of *Leipsic*, who procured a second Edition of it. He remarks, that nothing is more necessary in the Conduct of Life, than to consult the Rules of Prudence: but that there are few Persons, who think of doing this, even in the Question concerning Matrimony, which is the most difficult of all to determine with Judgment (5). The Impatience of Youth hurries us into it, without listening to any Advice, but That of Passion or Interest, &c. and yet the false Steps, which are made in it, are entirely irreparable. " Plerique vigentis A-" dolescentiæ annis, addit he (6), cum ineft maxima " consilii imbecillitas atque imperitia, cœco quodam " amoris impetu commoti ac fervore juvenili inflam-" mati, ante implicantur conjugio, quàm quod illud " vitæ genus sit judicare potuerunt. Multi, formæ " venustate allecti, plures dotis magnitudine ines-" cati, neque pauci splendore generis fascinati, his " autoribus & consuasoribus agunt omnia. ------" Quos, meo quidem judicio, satius erat, cum ani-" mis suis considerantes illud *Publii Syri*, *deliberan-" dum est diu, quod statuendum est semel*; & hoc " item alterum, *Deliberare utilia*, *Mora est tutissi-" ma*; diu secum multumque deliberare, atque ad " naturæ suæ rationemque vitæ institutum consilium " conferre omne, præsertim cum in deligendo ma-" trimonio, si quid errorís acciderit (accidit autem " sæpissimè) non quod aliis in rebus facere in promp-" tu est, cum quis fortè fe errasse intelligit rationem " & consiliorum mutationem instituere cuiquam sit " integrum: sed aut stultitiæ pœnam luere, aut ne-" gligentiæ culpam præstare oporteat sempiternam. " ----*Most Persons, in the Prime of their Youth, " and before they are at Years of Discretion, pushed " on by a juvenile Heat, and the blind Passion of " Love, hurry into Matrimony, before they can make " any Judgment of That State of Life. Many are cap-" tivated with the Charms of Beauty, more with those " of Fortune, and some with the Splendor of a " Family, and are led by no other Views but those.* " --- *Who, in my Opinion, would do much better, by " considering That Saying of* Publius Syrus; We ought " long to deliberate on what we can determine but " once; and That other, To deliberate on Questions " of Importance, is the most safe Delay; to " deliberate again, and again, and consult their own " Tempers, and the Nature of That State, in the most " particular Manner; because, if we commit any Mistake " in marrying (which is too often the Case), we can-" not remedy it, as we do those in other Matters, by " changing our Methods and Counsels; but must sit " down by what we have done, and either do Pe-" nance for our Folly, or continue our Fault of Care-" lessness, as long as we live." It being therefore so necessary, and at the same time so unusual, to enter, with Prudence, into This State, it was thought of signal Service to the Public, to reprint *Baduel*'s Book, which contains the best Instructions in the World, and particularly advises to apply, by earnest Prayer, to the Holy Ghost, for Assistance. The Author of the Preface holds it necessary to begin with this, when we deliberate on a Point so nice and hazardous. " Qui hanc vitæ conjugalis viam ingres-" suri sunt, operam ante omnia dabunt, ut Deum " sibi consiliarium, atque in rei tam arduæ consul-" tatione, atque affectione moderatorem, piâ ac re-" ligiosâ nominis divini imploratione afciscant. ----" de quâ unius & trini Dei, in coëundo conjugio ar-" denti invocatione diligenter facienda, præter com-" plura alia prudentiæ & circumspectionis & cau-" tionis in hoc vitæ genere constituendo, præcepta " sedulò tenenda, piè, sapienter, & eruditè admo-" dum in hoc quem tibi, Lector benevole, de alie-" no largientes offerimus, Libello disseritur. ---- *They, " who enter upon This Way of conjugal Life, should " first of all endeavour, by Devotion and Prayer, to " prevail with God to be their Counsellor and Con-" ductor in so difficult an Affair. ------ Concerning " which earnest Application to the triune God, be-" sides several other Rules of Prudence and Circum-" spection to be constantly observed in this State of " Life, the Book, which I present the Reader with, " at another's Expence, does piously, prudently, and* " *learnedly*

(1) It was this made Mr Konig falsly believe, that Baduel composed it in 1581. See his Biblioth. Vetus & Nova.
(2) Ad Joh. Mascencalium.
(3) De Ratione Vitæ studiosæ in Matrim. collocand. pag. 3.
(4) Ibid. p. 47, 48.
(5) In deliberatione de contrahendo Matrimonio, quæ est unum omnium difficillima. Greg. Bresmanus Præf. ad Lector.
(6) Gregor. Bresmanus, Præfatione ad Lector.

BAGNI.

(γ) *Inferior Lieutenant in the Seneschalship of Provence, in the Jurisdiction of Arles. See the Bibliotheque de la Croix du Maine, pag. 134. and that of du Verdier, pag. 532.*

" *learnedly treat.*" This Work of *Boduel* has been translated into *French*, by Guy de la Gard (7): but, if he has not succeeded better in his Translation of the Book, than he has in That of the Title, it cannot be very valuable. He intitles his Version, *A very useful Discourse of the Dignity of Matrimony, and the virtuous Conversation of Men of Learning.* It was printed at *Paris*, in 1548, in 8vo.

BAGNI (JOHN-FRANCIS) lived in the XVIIth Century. He was raised to the Dignity of a Cardinal by Pope *Urban* VIII, in the Year 1629, on the Recommendation of *France* (a). Mr *Moreri* speaks of him very largely, but not without committing Mistakes, which it will be proper to take Notice of [A]. This Cardinal went through more Employs than Mr *Moreri* mentions, as will appear in our Remarks. One thing has been said of him, in the *Sorberiana*, which is false on several Accounts [B]. He had a Brother, who was called the Marquis of

(a) *Memoirs of the Cardinal Richelieu, at the beginning of the Year 1630.*

[A] *Mr Moreri speaks of him —— and commits Mistakes, which it will be proper to take notice of.*] He says, I. That Cardinal *Bagni* was of the House of the Counts *de Guidi*. This is pretending, that the Name of his Family was *de Guidi*: But he should not have separated the Name of *Guidi* from That of *Bagni* or *à Balneo*. *Naudé* never divides them. II. That he was born the fourth of *October*, 1573. This does not agree with an Author, whose exactness is infinitely more to be depended on, than That of *Moreri* (1). This Author places the Death of Cardinal *Bagni* on the Twenty fourth of *July*, 1641, and makes him Seventy six Years old. So that, consequently, he was born in the Year 1565. III. That *Clement* VIII sent *Bagni* into *France*, to congratulate *Henry* IV, on his Marriage with *Mary de Medicis*. This is not true. Mr *Moreri* did not understand *Thomasin*, whom he quoted. He might read, in this Author, that Cardinal *Aldobrandini*, Legate of *Clement* VIII, in *France*, as well on the Account of the Marriage of *Henry* IV, as of the Peace with *Savoy*, had *John-Francis Bagni* in his Retinue. And here is the whole Amount of this pretended Deputation. IV. *Moreri* multiplies *Bagni's* Nunciatures beyond the Truth: He will have it, that he was twice sent Nuncio into *France*, once under *Gregory* XV, and once under *Urban* VIII; and farther, that *Gregory* XV sent him Nuncio into *Flanders*. *Thomasin* does not go so far, but is satisfied with saying, that *Bagni* was sent to *Paris* by *Gregory* XV, in the Quality of Nuncio-Extraordinary; and that he went from *Paris* into *Flanders* to act there as Ordinary Nuncio. *Gassendus* does not go so far as *Thomasin*; he says, that *Bagni*, going as Nuncio to *Brussels*, passed through *Paris*, and saw there, *incognito*, all that was to be seen. *Transiit sub id tempus* (that is, in the Month of *July*, 1621). "*Parisiis memoratus supra Vicelegatus à Balneo, Pontificis Nuncius* DESTINATUS *in Flandriam, qui cum vellet singularia quæque in urbe spectare, sed tamen quasi* INCOGNITUS, *commodum profecto convaluit Peireskius, qui ipsum varie deduceret ad eruditos, and Musea, ad opera omnia rariora* (2). —— *About the same time, the Vicelegate Bagni, beforementioned, passed through Paris, to go to Flanders, being appointed Nuncio there by the Pope, who desiring to see, incognito, every Thing remarkable in that City*, Peiresc *was luckily so well recovered, that he introduced him successively to all the learned Men, and shewed him the Libraries, and every Thing that was curious.*" I know very well, that he was Nuncio in *France*; but it was at another time. The same *Gassendus*, speaking of the illustrious Men, with whom *Peiresc* was become acquainted, in the Year 1614, says This of our *John-Francis Bagni*. "*Unus fuit* Joannes-Franciscus Vidius à Balneo, Patracensis Archiepiscopus, & per ea tempora Avenionensis Vicelegatus. Singularis enim deinceps necessitudo intercessit, seu donec ille Avenione degit, seu cum est versatus perillustris Nuncius tam apud principes Belgarum, quam apud Regem Christianissimum, feu postquam factus est Cardinalis raræ ac spectatæ virtutis* (3). —— *One was* John-Francis Guidi Bagni, *Archbishop of* Patras, *and then Vice-legate at* Avignon. *There was a particular Intimacy between them, not only during his Residence at* Avignon, *but also while he was Nuncio-Extraordinary both to the States of* Holland, *and to the most Christian King, and after he was made Cardinal for his great and singular Virtue.*" It is most certain, that *Bagni* was twice Nuncio; for *Naudé*, who was a long time his Domestic, and Library-Keeper, speaks thus to him in the Dedication of his *Coups d'Estat*: "My Lord, since

(1) *Baillet's Life of Des Cartes, Tom.* I. *pag.* 219.

(2) *Gassend. in Vita Peireskii, lib.* 3. *ad Ann.* 1621. *pag.* 289.

(3) *Ibid. pag.* 251.

" you are now at *Rome*, enjoying the Honours due " to your Deserts, and That Quiet, which you have " merited by so happy a Conduct in your public " Employs, while you have been seven times Go- " vernour, once Vice-legate, and twice Nuncio, I " did not think, &c." He was sent Nuncio to *Brussels* by *Gregory* XV, and into *France* by *Urban* VIII. *Thomasin* and *Moreri* are both in fault; they could not give a right Account of one of the clearest matters in the World. It was during his being Nuncio in *France*, that *Bagni* was raised to the Cardinalship. *Gassendus* says, that, in the Spring of the Year 1631, he passed through *Provence*, in his Return to *Rome*, and that he went to see his old Friend Mr *de Peiresc*. "*Vere novo Cardinalis à Balneo, utraque suâ Legatione functus, & accepto Parisiis purpurato pileo, Romam rediit* (4). —— *In the beginning of the Spring, Cardinal* Bagni, *having discharged both his Nunciatures, and received the red Cap at* Paris, *returned to* Rome." He brought the learned *Gabriel Naudé* along with him. He continued in his Station of Nuncio at *Paris*, for above a Year after his Advancement to the Cardinalship, and was particularly concerned in reconciling the Differences between the Queen-Mother and Cardinal *Richelieu* (5). A Manuscript Memoir of Mr *Baudrand* says, I. That he was not made a Cardinal at the Recommendation of *France*, *though we are told so in the History of the Ministry of Cardinal* Richelieu; *but meerly by the Pope, as* Nuncio *of the Holy See, which is a Favour frequently conferred on those, who are* Nuncio's *in* France, *and* Spain, *and at the* Imperial *Court.* II. That there is a Mistake in those words of *Gassendus*, which I have quoted (6): *accepto Parisiis purpurato Pilco Romam rediit.* "The Pope " doth not send the Red Hat to the Cardinals, which he " makes, but they are obliged to come and receive " it at *Rome*; for the Pope sends only the *Calot* by " a Courier, and afterwards the Red Cap by one of " his Chamberlains. So that Cardinal *Richelieu* and " Cardinal *Mazarin* never had the Red Hat, be- " cause they never went to *Rome* after their Pro- " motion. For above One hundred and twenty Years " past, the Pope has never sent the Red Hat to " any but the Cardinal *Infants*, into *Spain*, which " was a particular Favour in respect to his Brother " the King of *Spain*." All this is very curious: but yet Mr *Baudrand* should not have censured *Gassendus's* words, since they do not signify, that the Cardinal received the Red Hat; but only that he received the Red Cap. *Gassendus* says *Pileo*, not *Galero*. It is said, that *Paul* V departed from the Custom, introduced by *Sixtus* V: and That, in favour of the Duke of *Lerma*, to whom he ordered the Cardinal's Hat and Ring to be given, at *Madrid*, in 1618; this Duke being seventy Years old (7). See the eleventh Chapter of the fifteenth Book of *Pallavicini's History of the Council of* Trent.

[B] *One Thing has been said of him, in the* Sorberiana, *which is false on several Accounts.*] It is pretended, that, at the sight of the Thirty seven Volumes of the Councils, printed at the *Louvre*, he cried out, *I wonder there should be still any Heretics in* France. *What Christian from henceforth can be any thing but a Catholic?* Sorbiere admires this Thought: "Op- " time Cardinalis Banius, ut Gallia Nuncius, says *be,* " dum 37 Vol. Concil. cerneret typis regiis impressa " aiebat: Miror unde jam in Gallia hæretici sint, " quis enim hypothesium Christianarum servans po- " test non esse Catholicus (8)? It is false, That this Cardinal ever saw Those Thirty seven Volumes: He died in the Year 1641, and That Edition of the Councils came out in the Year 1644. But, if he had said, what is ascribed to him, he must have very much betrayed

(4) *Ibid. l.* 4. *ad ann. pag.* 307.

(5) *See the History of Cardinal Richelieu, by* Aubery, Vol. I. *pag.* 264, 279. *Edit. of* Holl. 12mo.

(6) *Above, Citation* (4).

(7) *Mercure Galant, for* Apr. 1706, *pag.* 209.

WHETHER the Councils in 37 Volumes are able to convert Heretics.

(8) *Sorberiana, pag.* 12. *Edit. of* Holland.

BAGNI. BAIUS.

of BAGNI [C], and was General of the Pope's Troops in the *Valteline*, in the Year 1624.

betrayed his Judgment. For nothing can be so improper the Conversion of Hereticks as a Work of many Volumes, as Thirty seven Volumes of the Councils. Of Ten thousand Protestants, there will scarce be found two, who can read a Page in That Edition of the *Louvre*, and among those, who understand *Latin*, the greatest part have neither the Inclination, nor the Patience, to undertake so vast a reading. The Inconveniency would not be remedied by Translations into the Vulgar Tongue; for who, among the Ignorant, would not lose themselves in such a Sea as This? Without the Grace of GOD, and the Power of Education, the reading of the Councils would make an hundred Times more Infidels than Christians. There is no History, which affords more matter of Scandal, nor a more shocking Scene of Passions, Intrigues, Factions, Cabals, and Frauds, than This of the Councils (9). Those, who published the *Menagiana*, forgot a good Jest, which I have heard several times, in the *Mercuriales* of Mr *Menage*. A witty Man is quoted there, who when he heard say, " Such a " one was condemned in such a Council, cried, It " was a sign he did not know how to cabal so " well as his Adversaries, or had not the same support " from the secular Arm." Can Those, who know the Religion of *Serberie*, be well edified by his *Optime*?

(9) *See Remark [B] of the Article* NESTORIUS.

[C] *He had a Brother, called the Marquis of Bagni.*] Mr *Baillet* assures us, that This Marquis was the Brother of Cardinal *John-Francis Bagni*, and that, having quitted the Sword, he advanced himself, in Ecclesiastical Dignities, even to That of the Cardinalship, to which he was promoted in the Year 1657 (10). He had been Nuncio in *France* all the time of the Pontificate of Innocent X, and the two first Years of Alexander VII. —— He died at Rome, the Twenty third of August, 1663, aged eighty Years (11). Mr *Baillet* thinks it likely, that Mr *Des Cartes* went to see him in the *Valteline*: He grounds his Conjecture on This Marquis's being addicted to the Study of Natural Philosophy (12). The Truth is, *Des Cartes* was not only well known to Cardinal *John Francis Bagni*, but also much respected by him (13). The *French Mercury* says, " That the Marquis *de* " *Bagni*, to whom his Holiness had given the Com- " mand of h s Forces in the *Valteline*, was known to " be a Partisan of *Spain*, descended from the Family " of the *Colonna's*, altogether *Spanish*, chief of the " *Gibelins* in *Romagna*, and who had always been a " Pensionary of *Spain*, having, as such, accompanied " the Constable *Colonna*, in his Journey into *Spain*, " four Years ago (14)."

(10) Baillet's Life of Des Cartes, Tom. 1, pag. 162.
(11) Id. ib. p. 219, 120.
(12) Ibid. pag. 139. *See also* pag. 161.
(13) Ibid. pag. 243, 254, 300, 301, 302.
(14) Mercure Francois, Tom. 10, p. 179, ad Ann. 1624, quoting the Venetian Gazettes.

(a) *He is more known by this Latin Name, than by that of de Bay, which was his true Name.*

BAIUS (a) (MICHAEL), Professor of Divinity at *Louvain*, was born at *Melin* in the Territory of *Aeth*, in the Year 1513. He distinguished himself so much by his great Progress, and prudent Conduct, during his Studies at *Louvain*, that, from the Station of a Scholar, he was promoted to That of Principal of the College of *Standonck* (b). Having been three Years in That Office, he applied himself to teach Philosophy; and, after six Years spent in Those Lectures, he obtained the Place of Principal of the Pope's College in the Year 1549 (c). In the same Year he was made *Licentiate* in Divinity. Two Years after he took his Doctor's Degree, and was appointed *Regius* Professor of Scripture. In 1563, he was one of the Divines sent by the King of *Spain* from *Louvain* to *Trent* [A]. He was admired in That Council. He obtained the Deanry of St *Peter* at *Louvain*, in the Year 1575. At the end of Three Years he was promoted to the Dignity of Conservator of the Privileges of the University (d). His Epitaph imports, that he was Chancellor of the same University, and Inquisitor-General in the *Netherlands*. He was a very learned Man, and no less eminent for his Morality, Piety, and Modesty, than for his Parts and Learning (e). He had read over St *Augustin*'s Works nine times (f): He composed several Works in Divinity [B], which discovered That Reading (g), and which contained, as was pretended, a great number of Propositions, condemned by Pope Pius V [C]. He wrote also some Books of Controversy against Those of the Protestant

(b) *It is the Name of the Founder.*
(c) *I correct* Valerius Andreas *thus, for his number,* c13.13.xcv, *is a most absurd Fault of the Printer.*
(d) Ex Valer. Andreæ Biblioth. pag. 670.
(e) *See Remark* [H].
(f) Swert. in Athen. Belg. Valer. Andreas.
(g) *See Remark* [E].

[A] *The King of Spain sent him from Louvain to Trent.*] See, in Cardinal *Palavicini*, all the Springs, which retarded or advanced the Deputation of *Michael Baius* (1). The Writer of *Commendon*'s Life has past over this slightly, and with too much Flattery (2); but the Author of the History of the Council unravels all *Commendon*'s Intrigues very clearly, and gives him only what belongs to him. This Nuncio, being at *Brussels*, in the Year 1561, took notice of the Differences, which had happened at *Louvain*, on account of some particular Notions of *Baius* and *Hessels*, concerning the Doctrine of Free-will, That of Good-works, and some others. These two Doctors had kept Silence a long time, in consideration to those who had given them that Advice; but hearing that, at the Sollicitation of the Franciscans, the Sorbonne had condemned eighteen Propositions, and being exhorted by their Disciples to defend their Cause, they prepared themselves accordingly. *Commendon* put a Stop to This Paper-War, not by his fine Discourses, as *Gratiani* affirms, but by writing such Letters to the Pope, as occasioned him to give order to Cardinal *de Granvelle* to enjoin them Silence (3).

[B] *He composed several Works in Divinity.*] He published some of them, the Titles whereof are these, as I find them in *Valerius Andreas*: *De Meritis Operum libri II. De prima hominis Justitia & Virtutibus impiorum libri II. De sacramentis in genere contra Calvinum. De forma Baptismi.* All these Treatises were printed together at *Louvain* in the Year 1565. The Next Year these following were printed there; *De Libero Hominis Arbitrio liber I.*

(1) Palavic. Hist. Concil. Trident. lib. 15. c. 7.
(2) Anthony Maria Gratiani, Life of Cardinal Commendon, translated by Mr Flechier, pag. 151.
(3) Palavic. Hist. Concil. Trident. lib. 15. c. 7.

De Charitate, Justitia, & Justificatione, libri III. De Sacrificio liber I. De Peccato Originis liber I. De Indulgentiis liber I. De Oratione pro defunctis liber I.

[C] *Which contained, as was pretended, a great Number of Propositions condemned by* Pius V.] I say, as was pretended; for the Fact is not yet settled, and I find *Michael Baius* is very far from granting, that he taught what was imputed to him. " However, " *says he* (4), among those Propositions (5), there " were some very different from our Sentiments; " others which we never maintained, nor meddled " with, in any Sense, but all, or, at least, most, " of them, were turned, and expressed, in such a " malicious Manner, that the very Form of them " alone might make them appear suspicious, especially " in the Opinion of those, who had not purposely " studied these sorts of Questions." This is the old Game of the ODIUM THEOLOGICUM: That Passion, which occasioned a Proverb long ago, finds Heresies where-ever it pleases; it frames such artificial Extracts, and so proper to exasperate the People, that it transforms, into pernicious Heresies, That, which, when considered with it's Principles, Restrictions, and Applications, is not so much as heterodox. This Passion is contagious: A Physician, who affects to set up for an Informer, from a Motive of Zeal only, finds himself all on a sudden possessed with the Sacerdotal Spirit; he produces unfair Extracts; he divides what he should join, and joins what he ought to divide, and gives the Propositions such a turn, as is proper to make them appear most shocking

(4) *In his Letter to* Cardinal Simonetta *cited by* Gery, *Apology for the Censures, p. 42.*
A METHOD of extracting Propositions out of a Book that one would have censured.
(5) *He speaks of those which the Franciscans shewed to Cardinal* Granvelle, *and which were afterwards sent to* Rome. *See the Apology for the Censures, pag. 42, 43.*

BAIUS.

stant Religion [*D*]. He paid such a Respect to the Pope's Censure [*E*], that, tho' he did not believe, he had taught any Heterodox Doctrines, yet he would not suffer the Books to be reprinted, which were pretended to contain the censured Propositions (*b*). *Valerius Andreas* has committed several Mistakes in speaking of That Censure [*F*]. We are promised a New Edition of the Works of *Michael Baius*. It will contain several Pieces never yet printed. The Editor will illustrate it with many Theological and Historical Notes. He has compared the Editions of This Author's Works with the Manuscripts to be met with in the best Libraries. There was a Report, that *Michael Baius*, to be revenged on the Jesuits, who, he believed, had promoted the Censure of his Doctrine, employed all his Credit in *Louvain* to cause the Doctrines of *Leonard Lessius* to be censured there (*i*). It ought not to be forgot, that the Bull of *Pius* V was very tender of his Honour [*G*]. His last Will was a Proof

(*b*) Val. Andreas, in Biblioth. pag. 671.

(*i*) See the Apology for the Censures passed on the two Universities, published by Mr Gery in 1688.

ing to the Consciences of the Judges. The Physician *Francis Blondel* will soon afford us an Example. This is not the only Injustice observed in Persons possessed with This Passion: Their double Weights and Measures give us another Instance of their Wickedness. Desire their Censure against their Inquisitors; shew them, ever so plainly, the Justice of your Cause; they will either turn a deaf Ear to it, or pay you with Nonsense. It is Then, that their Charity suffers all, and excuses all.

[*D*] *He wrote some Books of Controversy against those of the Protestant Religion.*] The same *Valerius Andreas* supplies us with the following Titles; *Responsio ad Quæstiones Phil. Marnixii de Ecclesia Christi, & Sacramento Altaris,* at *Louvain,* 1579. *Apologia pro Responsione contra Objectiones ejusdem de veritate Corporis Christi in Eucharistia,* at *Louvain,* 1581. *Epistola de Statutum Inferioris Germaniæ unione cum iis qui se desertores Romanæ Ecclesiæ vocant, & de Juramento quod eorum jussu à Clero & Monachis exigitur,* at *Louvain,* and at *Cologne,* 1579. He wrote also a Letter *de juramento jussu Ducis Alenzonii Antverpiæ in prætori concepti & comprobato.*

[*E*] *He paid a great Respect to the Pope's Censure.*] To comment rightly on this Text, I will make use of the Words of the Sieur *Gery,* Bachelor in Divinity. "This pious and learned Doctor, says he, " speaking of Baius (6), at the Time of his greatest " Reputation, saw, all of a sudden, a Bull appear a- " gainst Seventy six Propositions, which the Sollicitors " of That Censure imputed all to him, tho' some of them " were none of his, others were turned in a malicious " Manner to make them obnoxious, and some others, " which the Bull itself acknowledged, might be main- " tained in a Catholic Sense. They were not satisfied " with sending to *Louvain,* in the usual Form, in " 1570; but a second Publication was made of it " nine or ten Years after; and they affected to have " it done by a Jesuit, in 1580; whom the Society " had without doubt sollicited, to make a Shew of " their Credit. What did *Baius* do; and what did " the Faculty? Nothing else but humbly submit, " and, for Peace sake, and the Edification of the " Faithful, suppress all the Justifications, Expli- " cations, and Representations, which they might " have made." However, it must not be supposed, that *Baius* wrote nothing in his Justification: His Letter to Cardinal *Simonetta* (7) proves the contrary; for he shews there, that Dr *John Hessels,* and himself, had put into Cardinal *Granvelle's* Hands their Answer to certain Propositions, which he had communicated to them. The *Scotists* forged these Propositions, to cry down Those two Doctors, and presented them *to some dignified Persons,* without either naming *Hessels,* or *Baius.* If I was to be asked the Reason of their desiring to cry down these two Professors, I should answer, that it was because they had introduced a Method of Study, which had the Appearance of an unpleasant Novelty. "Af- " ter the Explication of the *Master of the Sen- " tences,* they were for reducing the Study of Di- " vinity to the Holy Scriptures, and to the Wri- " tings of the ancient Fathers (8)," and principally to those of St *Augustin.* This " was not pleasing " to Persons possessed with quite different No- " tions, and particularly to those, who, not being " willing to trouble themselves with much Study, " think it better to follow the Opinions already re- " ceived by the Majority, than to be at the Pains " of establishing new ones, on the solid Foundations " of Scripture: And these Persons imagined, it was " with design to point at, and reflect upon, them,

(6) Gery's Historical Apology for the two Censures of Louvain and of Douay, pag. 26, Edit. of Cologne, 1688.

(7) The Sieur Gery, p. 40, produces part of it, which he translated from the Latin, which is printed in the Facti of the University of Louvain, p. 356.

(8) Gery, Apology for the Censures, pag. 40, 41.

" whenever, in Lectures or Disputes, any Sentiment " was advanced different from theirs, or any thing " taught contrary to the Maxims they had long " received from certain Authors." *Baius* was not satisfied with writing This Letter (9), but sent an Apology for his Opinions to the Pope, in the Year 1569.

[*F*] *Valerius Andreas has committed several Mistakes, in speaking of the Censure, of* Pius V, *of* Baius (10).] I. He reports it for a Certainty, that the Bull of *Pius* V, against the Seventy six Propositions, was confirmed by *Gregory* XIII. In the New Edition of *Baius,* this will be shewn to be false (11). II. He asserts, that most of Those Seventy six Propositions were extracted out of *Baius's* Books. The contrary will be proved in the New Edition. III. He contents himself with saying, that the Bull of *Pius* V was published at *Louvain,* the seventeenth and nineteenth of *April,* 1570. But, besides that, he should have said the sixteenth of *November;* he is guilty of some Omissions. He does not say, that the Bull was published either by the Pope's or Cardinal *Granvelle's* Order, but by the Order of the Duke *d'Alba,* and by That of the Synod of *Mechlen.* This was irregular, since the Pope had commissioned Cardinal *Granvelle* to notify the Bull to the Divines of *Louvain,* in such manner as he should judge most convenient. However, *Valerius Andreas* should have expressed who Those were, who gave order for the Publication of the Bull. He ought also to have observed, that, on the Days he mentions, I mean the seventeenth and nineteenth of *April,* Michael Baius declared his Opinion, in publick, upon the condemned Propositions. His Recantation was extorted from him by wicked Practices. The new Edition will treat of all these things. IV. He says, that some credible Persons told the Pope, that some Divines of *Louvain* were writing an Apology for the condemned Propositions. It will be shewn, by the Testimony of *Toletus,* that they were false Informers, who reported these things to the Pope. V. He asserts, that *Gregory* XIII. condemned the same Propositions anew. This will be made appear to be false. VI. He places the Death of *Baius* on the sixteenth of *December;* whereas it happened on the sixteenth of *September* (12). I do not repeat, what I have already observed, concerning the wrong Chronology of his Printers (13). I ought not to add his making *the Year* 1551, the first of *Baius's Regius* Professorship of Divinity: He is not mistaken; but the Epitaph of *Baius* was not grounded upon This Date, since it mentions That Professorship to have continued forty Years, two Years more than the Calculation of *Valerius Andreas* requires. These Bulls against *Michael Baius* may have been multiplied, by some Persons, beyond the Truth, by making no Difference between condemning a Doctrine, and publishing another Person's Condemnation of That Doctrine. In this Sense, indeed, it may be truly said, that *Gregory* XIII condemned the Seventy six Propositions; for he not only inserted, in a Bull of his own, the Constitution of *Pius* V, declaring, that he found it in the Pope's Register, and that an entire Obedience ought to be paid to it; but he commanded also, that his Bull should be solemnly published at *Louvain,* by the Jesuit *Toletus,* in the Year 1580. M.*rilion,* great Vicar of *Mechlen,* notified That of *Pius* V to the Divines of *Louvain,* in 1567: And, in the Year 1570, he notified it to them again, with a little more Formality.

[*G*] *The Bull of* Pius V *was very tender of his Honour.*] The Letter of *Baius,* which has been quoted (14), adds, " that, after many long Sollicitations, " which

(9) It is quoted in the Bibliothèque Universelle, Tom. 14, pag. 198, as being printed at the end of Baius's Apology at Rouen, 1666.

(10) Valer. Andreas, in Fastis Academicis Studii Lovaniensis.

(11) What I say here, and in the Body of the Article, concerning the new Edition of Baius's Works, is taken out of a Memoir, which fell into my hands, and which comes from good Authority.

(12) He has done it in the Bibliotheca Belgica.

(13) To the Citation (c).

(14) Above, Citation (7).

BAIUS.

Proof of his great Charity [H], for he left all his Estate to the Poor (k). He founded a College at *Louvain*, and dedicated it to St *Augustin* (l). He died the Sixteenth of *September* 1589, aged Seventy seven Years, and was buried in the Pope's College, of which he had been a long time Principal. His Nephew *James* B A I U S, Doctor of Divinity, caused a Monument to be built for him with a fine Inscription (m). This Nephew followed his Uncle's steps. He was made Doctor of Divinity in the Year 1586 (n). He was often deputed for the Affairs of the University of *Louvain*, and executed his Commissions with great Prudence and Ability (o). He was Dean of St *Peter*'s in the same City, and *Regius* Professor of the Catechism (p). He published some Treatises [I]. He gave all his Estate to the Founding

(k) Swert. in Athenis Belg. pag. 503.

(l) Id. ib.

(m) This will find it in Swertius ubi supra.

(n) Valer. Andr. Bibl. Belg. pag. 401.

(o) Swert. ib. p. 355.

(p) Valer. Andr. ibid.

---

(15) Palavicin. Histor. Conc. Trident. lib. 15. cap. 7. says, Septuaginta novem Baii Positiones.

(16) Gery, Apology for the Censures, p. 43.

(17) Ibid. pag. 44.

(18) Palavicin. Histor. Conc. Trident. lib. 15. cap. 7. n. 12.

(19) In Remark [E] of the Article ANGLUS (THOMAS).

A BULL *of the Pope, wherein the placing of the Words caused an Obscurity, which was increased by the Omission of a Comma.*

(20) St Amour's Journal, Part. 2. pag. 64. cited in the Biblioth. Universelle, Tom. 14. pag. 201. See also the Difficulties proposed to Mr Steyaert, Part. IX pag. 18. and the new Edition of Baius's Works, Part. II pag. 235. & seq.

" which began from the Pontificate of *Pius* IV,
" they obtained, at last, a Bull of *Pius* V, dated the
" first of *October*, 1567, which condemns Seventy
" six (15) Propositions (16)." It is true, he who
brought the Bull, by Commission from Cardinal *Granvelle*, declared publickly, in the Assembly of the
Faculty of Divinity at *Louvain*, that the first sixty of
those Propositions were taken out of the Writings of
Baius (17); but, in short, the Bull did not name
him; and besides, the Condemnation was expressed
very tenderly, since it allowed, that some of those
Propositions were capable of a favourable Construction. Cardinal *Palavicini* informs us, that, in order
to treat *Baius* with the greater Tenderness, Pope *Pius*
V was contented with causing his Bull to be privately
notified to the University of *Louvain*, by the Bishop of *Mechlen*; but that *Gregory* XIII, finding the
Evil was not remedied, judged it necessary to make
a solemn Publication of it, and deputed his Preacher,
the Jesuit *Francis Toletus*, for that Purpose, who did
not oblige *Baius* to a public Recantation, or put
him to any Disgrace. " Hic studuit Baium remo-
" vere à pravis illis opinionibus, cohortatus, ut se-
" dis Apostolicæ judicio acquiesceret : & perpaucis
" colloquiis id obtinuit, privata illius retractatione con-
" tentus: atque hoc pacto Bajus non solùm illæsus
" perstitit, sed ipsius etiam nomini verba Diplomatis
" pepercere ; quin per illud ejus errores manum tam
" mitem experti sunt, ut vix viderentur errores, cùm
" aliquæ ex proscriptis positionibus, nullis certis in
" hac exceptione adnotatis, dicerentur posse sustineri
" in aliqua minùs propria significatione (18)." — *He
" endeavoured to bring off Baius from his erroneous O-
" pinions, advising him to acquiesce in the Judgment
" of the Holy See : This he accomplished after a few
" Conferences, and was content with his private Re-
" cantation : And, by this means, Baius not only conti-
" nued free from Trouble, but escaped being so much as
" mentioned in the Pope's Bull. Nay, his Errors
" were, in That, so very tenderly handled, that they
" scarce seemed to be Errors ; since some of the Con-
" demned Propositions, without particularly excepting
" any of them, are therein declared to be capable of
" being maintained in a less obvious Sense.*" We have
observed, in another place (19), the Inconveniency
of censuring a heap of Propositions, in such a general
and loose manner, that the *respectivè*, in the Conclusion, cannot enable us to make any Distinctions. The
Bull of Pope *Pius* V had this Inconveniency; and,
besides, left the Reader uncertain, on another account ; for, without particularizing any thing, it affirmed, that, among the condemned Propositions,
there were some, which might be maintained, in
some certain Sense. This was the least that the Bull
permits ; and there could be no question, but it permits this ; but it might be pretended, that it permitted much more. The placing of the Words produced this perplexing Obscurity ; a Comma was omitted :
This Omission made the Words capable of two very
different Constructions ; and That was the occasion of
much Contest. See the *Latin* I am going to quote,
and admire the Turns and Chances of Controversies.
" Quas quidem sententias strictè coram nobis exami-
" ne ponderatas, quanquam nonnullæ aliquo pacto
" sustineri possint in rigore & proprio verborum sen-
" su ab auctoribus intentâ hæreticas, erroneas, sus-
" pectas, temerarias, scandalosas, & in pias aures of-
" fensionem immitentes, respectivè & præsentium au-
" toritate damnamus (20). ——— *Which Propositi-
" ons, after having passed our strict Examination, al-
" though some of them may in some sort be defended
" in the literal and proper Sense of the Words, and in
" which the Authors intend them to be understood,
" we condemn them respectively, by the Authority of*

" *these presents, as heretical, erroneous, obnoxious, præci-
" pitate, infamous, and offensive to pious Ears.*" That,
which the Pagans called the Sport and Caprice of
Fortune, is not excluded from this Sanctuary : the
pretended infallible Oracle of *Rome* does not remedy the Mischief. After having taken a great deal
of trouble to concert all the Syllables of his Answer,
he may see, that his Transcriber, or Secretary, by
forgetting one *Comma*, shall be the Cause of the Damnation of an infinite Number of Persons. Nay, farther, the *Comma* will do nothing there, whether
you place it after *possint*, or not ; the Equivocation
still remains There is no Rule, either in Writing,
or Printing, by which a *Comma* after *possint* must
necessarily confine what follows to the Word *dam-
namus*. The most correct Books, which furnish numberless Instances, where *Commas* placed, as this might
be, after *possint*, do not at all hinder, but what follows, from such a *Comma* to the next succeeding
one, may relate to the Word *possint*, or any Word
so situated.

[H] *His last Will was a Proof of his great Charity*]
The Apologist for the Censures of *Louvain*, and
Douay, lets this Virtue of *Michael Baius* against the
pretended Miracles of *Lessius*. " It is a great Miracle, *says* he (21), to see so much Humility,
" accompanied with such great Parts and Learning,
" that even *Toletus* could not forbear giving him
" the following Character, which is preserved in
" *Louvain* by Tradition : *Michaele Baio nihil doctius,
" nihil humilius,* — *Nothing can be more learned, or
" more humble, than* Michael Baius. It is a great
" Miracle, to see so much Submission and Patience,
" as appeared in his Conduct, in regard to the
" Pope's Bull. It is a great Miracle, to see a holy
" Priest, whose many Studies and Occupations have
" not abated his Piety ; and who melts into Tears
" at the Altar, from a lively Sense of the Sanctity
" of our Mysteries. Lastly, it is a great Miracle,
" to see so much Charity for the Poor, extending
" so far, as to desire no other Heirs, and which,
" for their sakes, stifles all Sentiments of Nepotism ;
" how just soever they might be, in him. This
" will make *Baius* always dear to Posterity ; whereas a Reputation, supported only by an artificial
" Pretence to Miracles and Wonders, without Foundation, will soon be lost, and vanish away in
" Smoak." Cardinal *Palavicini* reports, that *Com-
mendon*, giving an account, to the Cardinal of *Mantua*, of the State, in which he found the University
of *Louvain*, in the Year 1561, observes to him,
that *Michael Baius*, and *John Hessélius*, had taught
some Novelties on Free-will, and that they were
two Persons very remarkable for their Learning, and
good Lives (22) ; that *Ruard Tapper* had taken Umbrage at their Union, and thought they valued
their Learning too much, though they were otherways very modest and virtuous ; " But, *adds* he,
" every one places his Pride in the Art he professes,
" and bears other things very easily. *Compertum sibi
" esse Ruardam in Theologicis disciplinis præclarum,
" dum is, in illa Academia docens, in his duobus adhuc
" ætate juvenili observaret infaustam conjunctionem
" ingenii & audaciæ, solitum esse dicere se nonnisi
" schisma ab illis expectare, & Theologicam lauream
" diu ipsis diffusiise : eos profectò videri scientiæ
" suæ nimis amantes, quamvis alioqui probos &
" modestos : & hæc ille verba sapienter usurpavit,
" digna quæ à nobis repetantur ; sed cujusque superbiis in ea arte quam profitetur sita est, cætera
" facile suffert (23).*"

[I] *James Baius published some Treatises.*] A Panegyric on the Arrival of the Archduke *Albert*, and the Infanta of *Spain* : Catechismus, sive Institutionum

(21) Gery, Apology for the Censures, pag. 37, 38.

(22) Erant ambo & scientiâ & exemplo vitæ conspicui. Palavic. Hist. Conc. Trident. lib. 15. cap. 7. n. 7.

(23) Id. ib. n. 9.

VOL. I.   7 O

BAIUS

ding of a College [K], and died the fifth of October, 1614 (q). ——— The new Edition of the Works of *Baius*, which I mentioned as a thing to come, has appeared since the first Impression of this Dictionary [L], and been condemned at

num Christianæ Religionis libri IV, and *De Venerabili Eucharistiæ Sacramento & Sacrificio Missæ, libri III*. (24).

[K] *He gave all his Estate to the founding of a College*] *Swertius* asserts, I. That *James Baius* left the Administration of his Estate to his Nephew *Giles Baius*, Doctor and Professor of Divinity, and that he charged him to apply it intirely to the founding of a College, for young Persons of his Country. II. That *Giles Baius*, in obedience to his Uncle's Will, called BAIANUM. III. That this College had been built but few Years; he takes notice in what place. *Osseculus patrini desiderio, augustissimum* (Collegium) *ab hinc paucis annis extruxit e regione Pædagogii Falconis* & BAIANUM *meritò indigetatur* (25). But *Aubertus Miræus*, who could not be ignorant of what *Swertius* had wrote upon it, affirms only, that he had read somewhere, that *James Baius* had designed the Foundation of a College, for the Reception of young Students in Divinity. *De altero Collegio Sacrarum Literarum studiosis adolescentibus pariter alendis pié prudenterque cogitasse scriptum invenimus* (26). Thus Writers deliver themselves, when they can only praise a Man for the good Intentions, which as Author, whom they have read, ascribes to him: For, when they know They have been actually executed, they expresly mention it. *Aubertus Miræus*, therefore, knew nothing of the building of the *Collegium Baianum*. Now this Ignorance of so notorious a Fact is something prodigious, in such a Man, as This, who so well knew his own Country, the *Spanish Netherlands*.

[L] *A new Edition of the Works of* Baius *has appeared since the first Edition of this Dictionary*] This is the Title of it: *Michaelis Baii celeberrimi in Lovaniensi Academiâ Theologi Opera: cum Bullis Pontificum, & aliis ipsius causam spectantibus, jam primum ad Romanam Ecclesiam ab conviviis Protestantum, simul ac Arminianorum, cæterorumque hujusce temporis Pelagianorum imposturis vindicandam, collecta, expurgata, & plurimis quæ hactenus debuerant opusculis aucta: studio A. P. Theologi. Coloniæ Agrippinæ, sumptibus Balthasaris ab Egmont & sociorum*, M.DC.XCVI. It is a pretty large *Quarto*, divided into two Parts. The first contains, besides those Writings of his, which were already printed, six or seven Pieces of *Baius*, which had never been published. The second conuits almost intirely of such, as now make their first Appearance, and relate to the Censure of some of *Baius*'s Propositions. One of these is a Chronological Narrative of the Proceedings in that Cause, and was wrote by him, who had the Care of This Edition. This Narrative informs us, among other things, that *Michael Baius* was induced to form his Method of teaching Divinity, on the Scripture, and on the Fathers, and chiefly on St *Augustin*, for two Reasons (27). The first was, because the Protestants of the *Netherlands* boasted to have the Scripture, and the ancient Fathers, on their Side. The second, because many Catholic Writers (28), deserting the Hypothesis of St *Augustin*, came extremely near That of the *Pelagians*. *Ruard Tapper*, and *Tiletan*, Professors of Divinity at *Louvain*, approved this new Method of *Baius*, as soon as they heard of it, after their return from the Council, in the Year 1552: And it is affirmed, that *Ruard* cried out one Day, *What Devil brought this Doctrine into our School, in our Absence?* This was the beginning of a furious Storm against *Baius*; the *Franciscans*, especially, tell foul upon him. The respective Guardians of *Nivelle*, and of *Ath*, sent eighteen Articles to the Faculty of Divinity at *Paris*, in the Year 1560, and desired their Judgment upon them. That University condemned them all, some, to the Number of three, as false and contrary to the Scripture; and the rest as heretical. *Baius* made Remarks on This Censure, and had a Mind to communicate them to some Doctor at *Paris*, but he gave over That Design, when he saw it impossible for him to obtain a Copy of this Decree of the *Sorbonne* (29) He communicated them to the Provincial of the *Franciscans*. He shews plainly, that the *Sorbonne* had censured, as Heretical, what

was visibly contained in St *Augustin*. The Year following, a List was presented, to Cardinal *Granvelle*, of the Propositions extracted from the Writings of *Baius*, as was pretended; and yet some of those Propositions were contrary to his Opinions; others he had never disputed for, or against; and most of them were drawn up so artificially, that the very turn of the Expressions might make them suspected either of Falsity or Heresy (30). The Cardinal communicated them to *Michael Baius*, who returned an Answer not now to be found. The same Cardinal received Orders to impose Silence on the Parties; and by This means the Quarrel was composed: But it was renewed in the Year 1564; for *Tiletan* endeavoured to obtain the Censures of the Universities of *Spain* against *Baius*'s Writings (31), and he sent Extracts of them to *Pius* IV, that they might be condemned. Other Extracts were added to These, and sent to *Pius* V, who issued a Bull, the first of *October*, 1567, wherein he condemned Seventy six Propositions. This Bull was neither published, nor fixed up, but was only read to *Baius*, and to the particular Faculty of Divinity at *Louvain*, the Twenty ninth of *December*, 1567, by *Maximilian Morillon*, Vicar-General of the Archbishop of *Mechlen* (32). This Vicar-General being required to give a Copy of This Bull, he refused it. He declared, that he had Orders to prohibit all the printed Books, out of which most of the Seventy six Propositions were said to have been extracted. The Dean of the Faculty represented, That, for great Reasons, it was very necessary, that the Books of *Baius* should not be prohibited; neither were they. This Doctor wrote to the Pope, the eighth of *January* 1569, and sent him an Apology, wherein he made it appear, that he had not taught those Seventy six Propositions, and that most of them, if understood in a certain Sense, were true, and the very Doctrines of St *Augustin*. The Answer, which the Pope returned him, the third of *May*, the same Year, contained an Exhortation to submit to the Censure. *Baius* was extreamly surprized, when That Letter of *Pius* V was delivered to him, to see himself treated like a Rebel, who had incurred the Punishment of Excommunication and of Irregularity. He requested *Morillon* to be absolved from This Sentence, but could not obtain it, without abjuring the Articles, which the Bull had condemned. *Summopere autem miratus est Baius secum agi ac si suas vindicias & apologiam scribendo Pontifici, in eum fuisset rebellis, ac Excommunicationis & Irregularitatis censuras incurrisset: à quibus cùm peteret absolvi, Morillonus absolutionis beneficium ei impertiri noluit, quin prius Articulos per Bullam confixos ejuraverit* (33). From that time every Body was suffered to inveigh against This Doctor, as if he had really taught those Seventy six Articles; they exclaimed against him in their Sermons, and in their Lectures: He bore this Opposition very patiently; but, in the Year 1570, he was advised, by three Bishops (34), to vindicate himself. He explained himself, therefore, on these Matters, in his Auditory of Divinity, and declared, that, among those Seventy six Propositions, there were some, which deserved to be condemned, but which he had never maintained; that others were maliciously drawn up, which he did not admit of, in the bad Construction that might be put upon them, though otherwise they were very capable of a sound Interpretation. *Carpit in Scholis Theologorum quid circa hujusmodi Articulos sentiret, cum multâ humilitate ac modestiâ, aperire: declarans nonnullos ipsorum esse falsos ac jure confixos, sed à se nunquam traditos: alios esse arte ac dolo confictos, qui pravum sensum pati possunt, quem nunquam tenuit, licet & in sano intelligi quoque facilè possent* (35). In the Month of *June* of the same Year, 1570, the Bishops of the *Netherlands* held a Council at *Mechlen*, wherein, at the Instance of the Duke d' *Alba*, they engaged to cause the Bull of Pope *Pius* V to be solemnly published at *Louvain*, and to be signed by all the Professors of Divinity. The Commission for it was given to *Morillon*, who performed it the fifteenth of *November*, the same Year. However, he could not

BAIUS.

at *Rome* by the Congregation of the *Index*. It contains many inftructive Particulars, and feveral things, which would carry the makers of Reflexions a great way. The Remark, which I fhall give, concerning This Edition will make a good Supplement to this Article. The Editor was very ill treated by Father *Dez*, a Jefuit, in a Work compofed on purpofe to defend the Church of *Rome* againft the injuries he had done it (*r*).

(*r*) Quibus cirundcevatis Bain notperus ceitare

not obtain the figning of the Formulary, which required the Approbation of the Cenfure of the Seventy fix Propofitions. The Faculty of Divinity of *Louvain* imagined this to be fome Snare laid for them, and, though they were affured, by a Letter, from the Bifhop of *Boifleduc*, and the Bifhop of *Ghent*, that there was no Defign to furprize them, it does not appear, that ever they agreed to That Signing: But, the following Year, a Decree was made, importing, that the Seventy fix Propofitions fhould be held for condemned, and that all the Members of the Faculty fhould abftain from teaching them, and that all the Books, wherein they fhould be maintained, fhould be taken away from the Students in Divinity (36). It is to be obferved, that *Morillon* did not deliver any Copy of the Bull, which he thus folemnly notified. This gave occafion to fome to maintain, that it was not authentic, or, that, having been furreptitiously obtained, it would be revoked. Others maintained the contrary with great Heat. Pope *Gregory* XIII, being follicited by the *Spanifh* Ambaffador, in his Mafter's Name, and by Father *Toletus*, in the Name of fome Divines of *Louvain*, to apply a fpeedy Remedy to Their Difputes, formed a Conftitution the Twenty eighth of *January*, 1579, wherein he inferted the Bull of *Pius* V, without approving, or confirming, the fame, and without condemning the Seventy fix Propofitions anew; he was contented to fay, that he had found it among the Records of his Predeceffor, and to order, that Credit fhould be given to it. He fent the fame Father *Toletus* to *Louvain*, in the Year 1580. This Jefuit there folemnly notified the Conftitution of *Gregory* XIII, and afked *Baius*, whether he condemned the Seventy fix Articles, or not. *Baius* anfwered, *I condemn them according to the Intention of the Bull* (37). All the Doctors, Licentiates, Bachelors, &c. declared, that they fubmitted to That Bull. *Toletus* informed *Baius*, in fome Converfation, which he had with him, that he was accufed of teaching his Difciples, privately, the Doctrines, which *Pius* V had condemned. *Baius* denied it, and defired to undergo all manner of Punifhments, if That Accufation could be legally proved. But, no Steps being made towards it, *Toletus* promifed to give a good Teftimony of him at the Court of *Rome*, and declared it was falfe, that the reading of *Baius*'s Writings was forbidden. He propofed to him the figning of a Formulary, which was very hard; but, however, *Baius* did it to procure fome eafe to himfelf. He was obliged to own, under his Hand, that he had taught many of the Seventy fix condemned Articles, and that they were condemned in the Senfe, in which he had taken them. " Ei præfcripfit (*Toletus*) quandam Confeffionis formulam, in qua fateri " debuit multos ex damnatis 76 Articulis à fe " traditos, ac eo fenfu profcriptos quo eos docuif- " fet; cui formulæ optimus hic Doctor, undique la- " ceffitus ac calumniis obrutus, ut tandem pace ali- " quâ frueretur, fubfcripfit die vigefimâ quartâ Mar- " tii hujus anni 1580 (38)." He wrote a Letter to the Pope, wherein he declared the Calumnies fpread againft him, for the Space of twelve Years concerning thofe Articles, and defired a Copy of the Bull of *Pius* V. This was granted him, in *June*, 1580. Father *Horantius* wrote a Piece againft him, the fame Year. He complained of two things; one was, that *Baius* had anfwered *Philip de Marnix* too civilly (39). *Conquerens* 1. *quòd ejus epiftolæ Marnixio fcripta ni- mis benignæ fuiffent* (40). The other, that *Baius* had affirmed, according to the Doctrine of St *Auguftin*, that the Scripture only is to be confulted, in order to judge of the Church. 2. *Quod Baius Auguftinum fecutus dixiffet judicium de Ecclefia effe ex fola Scriptura petendum* (41). *Baius* juftified himfelf, in a Letter, which he prefixed to his Apology againft *Philip de Marnix*, in the Year 1581. He was difturbed again in the Year 1585; for his Enemies accufed him to the Pope's Nuncio, and required, that he fhould be examined on certain Articles,

which they had drawn up againft him (42). It is not known, whether he underwent This Examination.

The Author of this Chronological Narrative takes a prodigious deal of Pains to prove to us, that Mr *Leidecker*, and fome other Minifters are in the wrong to conclude, from That Bull of *Pius* V, that the Church of *Rome* has condemned the Doctrine of St *Auguftin*, and favoured the new *Pelagians* (43). It feems to me, that he fhews clearly enough the Invalidity of That Bull, the Difhonefty of thofe, who made the Extracts, the Negligence of That Pope, and the Precipitation, wherewith he condemned thofe Propofitions, before he had examined the Works, from whence it was pretended, that they had been taken, &c. This Negligence appeared alfo from the Rules of Grammar not being obferved in That Bull (44). It may be alledged, that *Urban* VIII, in his Bull againft the Book of *Janfenius*, publifhed in the Year 1642, confirmed the Bull of *Pius* V and That of *Gregory* XIII. But the Author anfwers, that *Urban* VIII, did not confirm thofe two Bulls, but upon the Suppofition of Facts, which were falfe, and that therefore his Confirmation was void. " Quandoquidem ergo " *Urbanus* eas non confirmaverit, nifi fuppofendo " quæ falfa funt; ex ifta confirmatione nullum ro- " bur accedit iftis fuorum Predeceflorum Confitu- " tionibus: quod enim in fua origine vitiofum ac " nullius roboris eft, ratihabitione non fit validum, " vel, ut jura loquuntur *, *Quod initio vitiofum eft*, " *non poteft tractu temporis convalefcere: nec firmatur " tractu temporis, quod jure ab initio non fubfiftit* (45). " ------ Since therefore *Urban* did not confirm them, " but upon Suppofitions, *which were falfe*; *fuch a Confirmation could add no Authority to the Conftitutions of his Predeceffors: For what is originally " void, and of no Force, can never be made good by " fubfequent Ratification; or, as the Law fays*, What " is void from the Beginning, can never become " valid by any Courfe of Time; nor does long Ufage " confirm any thing, which did not legally fubfift from " the firft." This Pope being deceived by *Francis Albizzi*, Affeffor of the Holy Office, and Penfionary of the Jefuits, imagined, that the Bull of *Pius* V had been attended with all due Formality, and had been confirmed by That of *Gregory* XIII. Thefe were two falfe Suppofitions; for *Pius* V did not caufe his Bull to be fixed up, or to be folemnly publifhed, at *Rome*: And, as for Pope *Gregory*, he was fatisfied with faying, that he found it among the Records of his Predeceffor. *Urban* VIII, therefore, was made to affirm a Falfity, by inferting, in his Bull, that the Articles, condemned by *Pius* V, had been condemned anew by *Gregory* XIII: and, to conceal the Knowledge of This Impofture from the People, care was taken to leave the Conftitution of *Gregory* XIII out of the Bull of *Urban* VIII, tho' the Bull of *Pius* V was inferted in it. " Animadvertendum eft quod *Urbanus* VIII in Bulla " fuperius memorata enunciaverit quidem à *Gregorio* XIII confirmatam fuiffe *Pii* V Conftitutio- " nem, articulofque in ea confixos denuò fuiffe dam- " natos. Verùm hæc *Urbani* VIII Bulla apertè falfi " ea faltem in parte convincitur, ficut & ab *Joanne " Sinichio Lovaniensis* Academiæ delegato *Romæ* con- " victa eft, ex ipfomet *Gregorii* XIII Diplomate, " in quo nihil de ifta confirmatione, aut de iterata " hujufmodi articulorum difpunctione habetur. Ne " autem id innotefceret, *Albizzius*, Jefuitarum ftipendiarius, qui Bullam *Urbani* VIII confcripfit, " in ea quidem *Pii* V Bullam integram inferuit, " fed non *Gregorii* XIII Conftitutionem, ex qua " fingulis patuiffet ejus mendacium, & quam falfo in " Bulla *Urbani* dicatur *Pii* V Bulla à *Gregorio* XIII " confimata, profcriptique in ea articuli iterum à " *Gregorio* XIII prohibiti: cum *Gregorius* XIII dun- " taxat teftificetur tenorem Bullæ, quam inferit, effe " planè conformem tenori Bullæ, quam in *Pii* V " regiftro invenit; & ifti tenori eam fidem adhiben- " dam,

BALBUS.

(46) Ibid. pag. 242.
" dam, quæ ipfius Bullæ protographo debetur (46).
"———— It is to be obferved, That Urban VIII, in
" his Bull before-mentioned, declared, that the Con-
" ftitution of Pius V had been confirmed by Grego-
" ry VIII; and that the Articles, therein condemned,
" had been condemned anew. But This Bull of Urban
" VIII afferts a Falfity, at leaft in this Refpect,
" as was proved by John Sinnichius, Deputy for the
" Univerfity of Louvain, at Rome, and from the Bull
" itfelf of Gregory XIII, wherein not a Syllable of
" That Confirmation, or of a fecond Condemnation of
" Thofe Articles, is to be found. But, that this might
" not appear, Albizzi, Penfionary of the Jefuits,
" who drew up the Bull of Urban VIII, inferted in
" it indeed the Bull of Pius V, but not the Con-
" ftitution of Gregory XIII, which would have dif-
" covered his whole Fraud, by fhewing how falfely
" he had made the Bull of Urban declare, that the
" Bull of Pius V was confirmed, and that the pro-
" hibited Articles were again prohibited by This Con-
" ftitution of Gregory XIII; when This Pope only
" teftifies therein, that the Tenor of the Bull, which
" he inferts, is exactly conformable to the Tenor of
" the Bull, which he had found in the Regifter of

" Pius V; and that the fame Obedience ought to be
" paid to it, which was due to the Original." All
this is much more proper to fhew the Artifices ufed
in the Condemnation of Books, than to confute
Mr Leidecker; for, in fhort, for one Roman Catholic,
who believes Baius to be innocent, there are above
a thoufand, who believe him juftly condemned; and
therefore the Church of Rome may, with much likelihood, be accufed of holding This Doctor's Opinions
for Heretical, which are moft agreeable to St Auguftin's
Doctrine. This ought to make the Fate of fome Men
pitied. Though Paffion, Irregularity, and Injuftice,
appear manifeftly in the Proceedings ufed againft
them; yet, in the Opinion of the Majority, they
will be fuppofed guilty. A Judgment againft their
Doctrine is fufficient to fecure the Prejudices of the
Public. The Adverfary will enjoy the Fruit of his
Frauds and Intrigues; he will conftantly engage the
Folly of the People on his Side, who generally pre-
fume in favour of Tribunals.

A great Work of Baius is promifed (47), if this
new Edition goes off well. This will be his Commentary on the Mafter of the Sentences, and his Explication of David's Pfalms.

(47) In Præfat.

BALBUS. This Name makes fuch a Figure in the Ancient *Roman* Hiftory, that it is ftrange the Hiftorical Dictionaries fhould pay fo little Regard to it [*A*]. If I endeavour to repair their Fault, it is chiefly in refpect to *Lucius Cornelius* BAL-BUS, who was Conful in the Year of *Rome* 714, and who had a Nephew, whom I fhall mention either in the Text, or in the Remarks, as occafion offers. This Conful was born at *Cadiz*. He fignalized himfelf by his great Courage in the Wars, which the *Romans* carried on in *Spain* againft *Sertorius*, and againft the *Lufitanians*; info-much, that *Pompey*, being very well fatisfied with his great Services, declared him a *Roman* Citizen. *Lucius Gellius* and *Cn. Cornelius*, who were Confuls a little time after, made a Law, that all thofe, whom *Pompey*, with the Confent of the Council of War, had made Citizens of *Rome*, fhould be actually fo efteemed. By this means *Balbus* entered into full Poffeffion of his Freedom of *Rome* (a). He took upon him the Prænome of *Lucius* from one of thofe two Confuls, and the Name of *Cornelius* from the other [*B*]. He was fo much efteemed in *Rome*, that he had the Friendfhip of the greateft Men of the State, as of *Pompey*, *Craffus*, *Cæfar*, and *Cicero*, and was adopted by *Theophanes* (b), who was very particularly beloved and regarded by *Pompey*.

(a) See Cicero in Oratione pro Cornelio Balbo, & ibi Manuelum & Nicolaum Abramum.

(b) Cicero lib. & Epift 7. ad Attic. lib. 7.

The ORIGINAL of the Surname Balbus. Whether Ch. Stephens has rightly applied it to the Atilii.

(1) Michael II, of That Name, who was Emperor of Conftantinople, from the Year 810 to 826.

(2) Lewis III, of That Name, who was alfo King of France, and who died in 8-9.

WHAT Name thofe, two Confuls, who obtained the Freedom of Rome, gave themfelves.

[*A*] *The Hiftorical Dictionaries have paid but little Regard to this Name.*] They are prodigioufly barren on the Word *Balbus*. *Charles Stephens* remarks, that it was the Surname of the *Atilii*, and that the firft of This Family, who was called *Balbus*, was fo called, becaufe he ftammered; and that afterwards his Pofterity preferved This Sirname. It is very likely, that This Appellation had the fame beginning, in feveral Families, as it is certainly on the fame Account, that, in all Countries, fo many Perfons are named *White*, &c. And fince there has been an Emperor of the Eaft (1), and another of the Weft (2), who had both of them the Sirname of *Balbus*, or *Stammerer*, from That Defect in their Speech; Why fhould it feem ftrange, that, in the time of the Roman Common-wealth, a like Defect introduced This Sirname into feveral illuftrious Families? It is not, therefore, for This, that *Charles Stephens* deferves to be criticifed, but becaufe he miftook the *Atelii* for the *Atcii*, or *Atii*, and becaufe he expreffed himfelf in fuch a manner, as if the *Atilii* had no other Sirname but This: whereas they have had, among them, thofe of *Regulus*, *Serranus*, *Calatinus*. Nay, there was one *C. Atilius Balbus*, Conful in the Year of *Rome* 508, and 518, which is, perhaps, the caufe of *Charles Stephens*'s Error. Mr *Lloyd* ought to have been fatisfied with correcting This Article; but he thought it fitter wholly to fuppref it; in Imitation of Thofe Chirurgeons, who, inftead of curing the Wound, cut off the whole Limb: Or, as Difputants ferve an Objection, when they find themfelves upon pretty much the fame Terms with *Alexander*, in refpect to the *Gordian* Knot. Mr *Hofman* neither cured, nor cut off, but retained the Article as he found it in *Charles Stephens*.

[*B*] *He took upon him, in refpect to ———— the two Confuls, the Prænome of* Lucius, *and the Name of* Cornelius.] It was the Cuftom of *Rome*, that Thofe, who obtained their Freedom, took upon them the Name of him, who procured them That Honour. It was for This Reafon, that the Hiftorian

Theophanes, and his Pofterity, bore the Name of *Pompey*. It may be afked, *Why then did not Cornelius Balbus alfo take the Name of* Pompey? My Anfwer is, Becaufe he chofe rather to ground his Right on a Law, than on the Kindnefs of That General. The Law, I fpeak of, is That made by the Confuls *L. Gellius*, and *Cn. Cornelius*, with the Confent of the Senate, in the Year of *Rome* 682. It imported, that all Thofe, on whom *Pompey* had conferred the Freedom of *Rome*, with the Approbation of the Council of War, fhould be reputed Citizens of *Rome*. " Nafcitur, Judices, caufa *Cornelii* ex eâ lege quam " *L. Gellius*, *Cn. Cornelius*, ex Senatus fententia tu- " lerunt; quâ lege videmus ratis effe fanctum, uti " cives Romani fint ii, quos *Cn. Pompeius* de con- " filii fententia fingillatim civitate donaverit (3). — " *The Caufe of* Cornelius, *Judges*, *is founded on* " *That Law*, *which* L. Geilius, *and* Cn. Cornelius, " *by Decree of the Senate*, *enacted*; *which we fee* " *has folemnly confirmed Thofe*, *as Citizens of Rome*, " *to whom* Pompey, *with Confent of his Council*, " *had refpectively given That Privilege.*" *Balbus*, looking upon Thofe two Confuls as the true Authors of the Honour he enjoyed, took the Prænome *Lucius* from the one, and the Name *Cornelius* from the other. This is much more likely, than what *Manutius* fays, *That*, *though Balbus had been made a Roman Citizen by* Pompey, *yet he was neverthelefs obliged for That Freedom to* Cornelius Lentulus, *whofe Prænome*, *and Name*, *he took*, *according to Cuftom* (4). He conjectures alfo, that This *L. Cornelius Lentulus* is the fame, who was Conful, the firft Year of the Civil War, that is, in the Seven hundred and fourth Year of *Rome*. To conclude, we learn from hence, that Cardinal *Baronius* made too long an Enumeration of *Titus*'s Favours to *Jofephus*, when he notes particularly, that, befides the Right of a Citizen, he alfo conferred on him the Name of the Family of *Flavia* (5). For, in the firft place, it was *Vefpafian*, and not *Titus*, who made him a Citizen (6); and, after that, the Name *Flavius* was given him of courfe.

(3) Cicero Orat. pro Balbo.

(4) Manut. in Argumento Orat. pro Balbo. See alfo the Note on this into Bo 1: Cicero's Epiftles to Atticus, pag 8. Edit. Grav. Where there feems to be an Error of the Prefs.

(5) Baron. ad. ann. 56. n. 12.

(6) Jofeph. in Vita fua.

[*C*] *Capitolinus*

BALBUS.

Pompey. It is on account of this Adoption, that *Capitolinus* names him *Balbus Cornelius Theophanes* [C], when he says, that the Emperor *Balbinus* affirmed, that he was descended from him (c). The Prosperity of *Balbus* raised him up Enemies, who commenced a Law-Suit against him about his Freedom: *Crassus, Pompey,* and *Cicero,* pleaded his Cause (d), and gained it. He found himself much perplexed during the War between *Cæsar* and *Pompey*; for he had great Obligations to both. It appears, that he gave the preference to *Cæsar,* but in such a manner, that he endeavoured to bring Matters to a Reconciliation (e). *Velleius Paterculus* remarks it as a great Temerity, that *Balbus* was so bold, as to go to *Pompey*'s Camp, to gain over the Consul *Lentulus,* who was considering at what Price he should sell himself (f). It was by this means, adds he, that *Balbus,* tho' a *Spaniard,* opened his way to the Triumph, the Pontificate, and the Consulship. *Pliny,* indeed, observes, that *Balbus* was made Consul, and that he was the first Foreigner, who obtained That Dignity (g); but, as for the Honour of a Triumph, he says it was another *Cornelius Balbus,* a Nephew of This, who obtained it, with the *Roman* Freedom, the first of all Foreigners (h). We shall see wherein *Paterculus*'s Fault consists. These two *Cornelii Balbi* were so rich, that the Uncle, at his Death, left Twenty five *Drachmas* to each *Roman* Citizen (i), and the Nephew caused a new City (k) to be built at *Cadiz* (l). The Uncle wrote a *History of* Julius *Cæsar,* in the form of a Journal (m). It was, undoubtedly, he, who contracted so very strict a Friendship with *Pomponius Atticus* [E]. Some have confounded *Cornelius Balbus* with *Cornelius Gallus* [F]. We shall shew, that *Vossius* was

[C] *Capitolinus names him Balbus Cornelius Theophanes.*] I give you this Author's words: "Familiæ vetustissimæ, ut ipse (*Balbinus*) dicebat, "à Balbo Cornelio Theophane originem ducens, "qui per Cn. Pompejum civitatem meruerat, quum "esset suæ patriæ nobilissimus, idemque historiæ "scriptor (7)." — *Of a very ancient Family, as he* "(*Balbinus*) *himself affirmed, derived from* Balbus "Cornelius Theophanes, *who was made a Citizen* "*of* Rome *by* Cn. Pompey, *being of a noble Rank* "*in his own Country, and also an Historian.*" Casaubon imagines, that This is to be understood of the Historian *Theophanes,* born at *Mytelene,* in the Island of *Lesbos* (8). *Vossius* (9), Mr *de Tillemont* (10), and several others, are of the same Opinion. I believe they are mistaken, and it is better to understand here the adopted Son, than the Father. *Cornelius Balbus* was the Son of *Theophanes* by Adoption. The three Titles, which *Capitolinus* made use of, belong to him, and the last only belongs to *Theophanes.* If I am told, that *Balbus* was not of noblest Rank in his own Country, I answer, No more was *Theophanes* in *Mitylene.* It is true, *Strabo* affirms, that *Theophanes* had a share in the public Offices, and that he became the most Illustrious of all the *Greeks* (11). But This does not help us to confirm the words of *Capitolinus*: *Strabo* does not ascribe to him Antiquity of Family, or Nobleness of Blood, which raised him above all the other *Mitylenians*; and This is the Point in question, in *Capitolinus.* So that the Objection signifies nothing, since it would prove too much: And it is enough for me, that *Balbus*'s Enemies did not deny, but that he was of a very honourable Family. *Hunc in eâ civitate, in quâ fit natus, honestissimo loco natum esse concedis* (12). It is likely, they would not acknowledge all he ascribed to himself hereupon. There is another Objection to be feared. *Balbus* was Consul, and *Theophanes* was not: Whence comes it, then, that *Capitolinus,* who remarked his Quality of Historian, forgot That of Consul, much more proper, than the other, to set off the Nobility of *Balbinus*? I answer, that *Capitolinus* is not a Man, from whom much Accuracy, and Judgment, is to be expected. The worst, which may come of it, would be to say, that he applied *Balbinus*'s Pretensions wrong, and that he thought, that *Cornelius Balbus Theophanes,* from whom That Emperor said he was descended, was the same *Theophanes,* of the Island of *Lesbos,* whose chief Glory was That of having been an Historian. I would not absolutely reject this Conjecture; Men of better parts, than *Capitolinus,* might have taken the one for the other in that place; but I rather choose to say, that he knew *Balbus,* of *Cadiz,* was Author of an History.

[D] *I shall mention wherein Paterculus's Fault consists.*] These are his words; "Tum Balbus Cornelius excedente humanam fidem temeritate ingressu "castra hostium sæpiusque cum Lentulo collocutus, "Consule dubitante quanti se venderet, illis incre- "mentis fecit viam quibus non Hispaniensis natus, "sed Hispanus, in triumphum & Pontificatum assur- "geret, fieretque ex privato Consularis (13). —— "Cornelius Balbus, *by an incredible Rashness, entring* "*into the Enemies Camp, to gain the Consul* Len- "tulus, *whose particular Friend he was, treated* "*several times with him, who was, for some time,* "*considering what Price to ask for his Treachery.* "*By this means,* Balbus *cleared the way to these Pre- "ferments, whereby, though he was not only born* "*in* Spain, *as several* Romans *and* Italians *were,* "*but also of Natural Spaniards* (14), *yet he obtained,* "*in* Rome, *the Honour of a Triumph, and the Pontifi- "cate; and, from a private Person, became at last a* "*Consul.*" I shall say nothing of This Action of *Balbus,* which *Cicero* has greatly celebrated in the places I quote (15). I will only dwell a little on *Paterculus.* Either he says nothing to the purpose, or he affirms, that *Balbus* was raised to the Consulship, as well as to the Honour of a Triumph, and to the Dignity of Pontiff; and it would be in vain to deny This under pretence, that he did not say, & *Consulatum,* as this seems to be the most natural Expression, to signify, that *Balbus* was made Consul: I shall not take upon me to prescribe Forms to one, who spoke so politely, as That Author did; he had his Reasons for altering the turn of his Phrase, when he came to mention the Consulship. But he was mistaken in the Thing, and confounded the Uncle's Honours with Those of the Nephew. That *Balbus,* who negociated with *Lentulus,* in the beginning of the Civil War, is the Nephew, as appears by *Cicero*'s Letters, which I have quoted. It was *Balbus* the Nephew, who triumphed over the *Garamantes,* the first Stranger honoured with a Triumph, as we learn from *Pliny* (16); but it was *Balbus* the Uncle, who was the first Stranger honoured with the Consulship, as the same *Pliny* informs us (17). These two *Balbus*'s were distinguished, at *Rome,* by the Title of *Major,* given to the Uncle, and That of *Minor,* to the Nephew. I wonder, that *Salmasius,* who distinguished the Honours of both very well, did not take notice of this Fault of *Paterculus* (18).

[E] *He contracted a very strict Friendship with Pomponius Atticus.*] This cannot be denied, when we consider, that *Atticus,* having resolved to end his Life by starving himself, sent for his Son-in-law, and L. *Cornelius Balbus,* and *Sextus Peducæus,* to declare to them his final Resolution (19). I think, I have read, in one of *Cicero*'s Letters, that *Balbus* was one of those, who were often entertained at *Atticus*'s Table (20). Which would prove, that he delighted in hearing good things read (21).

[F] *Some have confounded* Cornelius Balbus *with* Cornelius Gallus.] It is in relation to a Fact, which is far from honouring his Memory. They make him die in the Act of Venery (22). Without doubt, the first Occasion of this Mistake, was an Error of the Press. *Cornelius Gallus* had been put in the List of those, who died in that Condition, on the Authority of *Pliny* (23); and the Printer using a B, for a G, caused several to mistake the one for the other. I find this Error in several Editions of

VOL. I. Nº. XX.   7 P

BALBUS.

was in the wrong to censure *Savaro* [G]; that *Lloyd* and *Hofman* deserve some Censure [H]; that *Paulus Manutius* is not entirely excusable [I]; that *Glandorpius* multiplies Persons of this Name unnecessarily [K]; that the distinction of the greater and

of *Tiraquellus*'s Commentary on the Matrimonial Laws.

[G] *Vossius was in the wrong to censure* Savaro.] Whilst he was taking notice of a Fault, which he believed he had found in *Savaro*'s Commentary on *Sidonius Apollinaris*, he himself was mistaken (24). *Savaro* had affirmed, that *Balbus*, to whom *Sidonius Apollinaris* ascribes the Journal of *Julius Cæsar*'s Life (25), is the same with *Balbus Cornelius Theophanes*, of whom *Julius Capitolinus* says, in the Life of *Balbinus*, *That he had obtained the Roman Freedom by* Pompey's *Favour, and that, moreover, he was the most Noble of his Fellow-Citizens, and an Historian*. *Vossius* refutes this Pretension of *Savaro*, I. Because *Balbus*, Author of the Journal, was an intimate Friend of *Julius Cæsar*, as appears by *Suetonius* (26), and by *Aulus Gellius* (27); whereas *Theophanes* was an intimate Friend of *Pompey*, which was made a Crime of to his Posterity, as *Tacitus* observes, in the sixth Book of his Annals. II. Because *Theophanes* was a *Lesbian*, and wrote in *Greek*, and *Balbus* lived at *Rome*, and wrote in *Latin*.

If I had a mind to be over-critical, I might object to these Reasons, I. that the same *Balbus*, who was one of *Cæsar*'s intimate Friends, was also one of *Pompey*'s Friends; and so far honoured with his Confidence, that *Pompey*'s other Friends were jealous of him (28). It is true, that the Conjunction, which was then between *Pompey* and *Cæsar*, having permitted *Balbus* to cultivate the Friendship of the latter, without failing in what he owed the former, it was at last found, that *Cæsar*'s Favours were superior to Those of *Pompey*: Nevertheless, *Balbus* obtained leave of *Cæsar* not to follow him against *Pompey*, and retired to *Rome* during the Civil War (29). It is true, also, that he was *Cæsar*'s Agent there, and that, by endeavouring to bring Matters to an Agreement, he did not appear altogether free from Partiality. But, after all, it is not sufficient, in order to make a just Opposition between *Balbus* and *Theophanes*, to say, on the one side, as *Suetonius* does, that *Balbus* was an intimate Friend of *Julius Cæsar*, and, with *Aulus Gellius*, that *Balbus* was one of *Cæsar*'s Agents at *Rome*, during his Absence; and to say on the other side with *Tacitus*, that *Theophanes* had been one of *Pompey*'s intimate Friends and that *Tiberius* imputed it as a Crime to *Theophanes*'s Posterity: For, considering That Emperor's capricious Humour, he was like enough to persecute a Family, under pretence, that it had obtained the Freedom of *Rome* by *Pompey*'s Favour. Now This would be true in a literal Sense, as to *Theophanes*, though he should be confounded with *Cornelius Balbus*; since it is not only certain, that *Pompey* conferred That Freedom upon him, but also that he pleaded for him, when they brought it into question, and loaded him with Favours. So that *Vossius*'s first Reason is not good. II. I might say, in the second place, that the *Theophanes*, whom *Vossius* means, lived at *Rome*, as well as *Balbus* ; and since there have been *Romans*, who have wrote Histories in *Greek*, it does not follow, that *Balbus* is not *Theophanes*, because *Theophanes* wrote in *Greek*. Nay, how do we know, whether the *Balbus* in question be not the *Cornelius Balbus*, whose eighteenth Book, of the 'Εξηγητικῶν, *Macrobius* has quoted (30)? *Simler* does not doubt it (31).

But, without trifling on Disputes, which may be charged with too scrupulous a Preciseness, here is the *jugulum causæ*, and the decisive Point, in three words. *Vossius* imagined, that *Savaro* confounded *Cornelius Balbus*, with *Theophanes*, born in the Island of *Lesbos*, and Author of an History of *Mithridates*'s War. But he has not done this. He has only confounded him with the *Theophanes*, mentioned by *Capitolinus*, and who differs very much from Him of *Lesbos*, though he has This in common with him, that He also received his Freedom of *Rome* from *Pompey*. Now there is nothing more reasonable, than to take the *Theophanes* of *Capitolinus*, for the *Cornelius Balbus* of *Suetonius*, and for the *Balbus* of *Sidonius Apollinaris*; for it is certain, that the same *Cornelius Balbus*, born at *Cadiz*, and honoured with the Freedom of *Rome*, by *Pompey*, was, by the Recommendation of the same *Pompey*, adopted by *Theophanes* of *Lesbos* (32) : after which, according to Custom, he named himself *Lucius Cornelius Balbus Theophanes*, as *Paulus Manutius*, and *Corradus*, have observed; the former in his Argument of *Cicero*'s Oration for the same *Balbus*; and the latter in his Notes on *Cicero*'s Epistles to *Atticus*: And both of them have taken this *Balbus* for the Historian *Cornelius Balbus Theophanes*, mentioned by *Capitolinus*. So that, if there had been any Fault to be found with This, *Vossius* should have censured Those learned *Italians*, rather than *Savaro*, who came a long time after them.

[H] *Lloyd* and *Hofman deserve some Censure*] I say nothing of *Charles Stephens*; he has been a little too dry on our *Cornelius Balbus*; but what he mentions of him is not ill chosen. *Lloyd* has cut off some Words from it, which were not superfluous, *viz.* That we still have *Cicero*'s Oration for This *Balbus*: for they are two very different Facts, the one that *Cicero* pleaded such a Cause, and the other, that we still have his Plea; and it is in the latter Case, that the Readers are mostly interested. Mr *Hofman* lengthens the Article (33), to inform us, that there was another *Cornelius Balbus*, of *Lesbos*, sirnamed *Theophanes*, that is, to teach us a Falsity. *Lucius Cornelius Balbus Theophanes* is no way different from Him, who was of *Cadiz*, and who is the Subject of this Article.

[I] *Paulus Manutius is not entirely excusable*] I have already touched upon some of his Mistakes; here are yet two more. The one is in his Argument of *Cicero*'s Oration for *Cornelius Balbus*, and in the Notes on That Passage of the Oration, where mention is made of the Adoption of This *Balbus*. He there says, most falsely, that *Theophanes* was one of *Pompey*'s Freed Men (34); for it was not his Liberty, but his Freedom of *Rome*, which *Pompey* gave *Theophanes*. " Quid Magnus hic noster, *says Cicero*, qui cum " virtute fortunam adæquavit : nonne Theophanem " Mitylenæum scriptorem rerum suarum in concione " militum civitate donavit (35)? —*What did our* Pom- " pey *do, who loves to join Fortune and Virtue to-* " *gether : did he not, in an Assembly of the Soldiers,* " *present* Theophanes *of* Mitylene, *the Writer of his* " *History, with the Freedom of the City?*" The other Mistake of *Manutius* is in referring us, among other Authorities, to the seventh Book of *Pliny*, chap. 43 (36), concerning the Triumph of *Cornelius Balbus* the Younger, Nephew to him we are speaking of ; for *Pliny*, in that Place, speaks only of the Uncle's Consulship. One may easily be mistaken in such Cases as these. Father *Harduoin*, on the same Place of *Pliny*, refers us to a Passage of *Paterculus* (37), where he only speaks of *Balbus* the Nephew.

[K] *Glandorpius multiplies Persons of this Name unnecessarily*.] He ought not to have produced three Consuls called *L. Cornelius Balbus*. It is to multiply Beings without necessity. He says, the first is *Balbus* the Elder, whose Consulship he places in the Year of *Rome* 713. The second is *Balbus* the Younger, for whose Consulship he says nothing particular, contenting himself to set down the Words of *Paterculus*. The third is one *L. Cornelius Balbus*, who, he says, was made Consul for some Days, towards the end of the Year, by *Augustus*, and *Marc Antony*, and had such a vast Estate as to be able to bequeath Twenty five Drachma's to each Citizen of *Rome* (38) The Truth of it is, These three Consuls make but one ; for *Balbus*, the Uncle, is the same with Him whose Consulship was of so short a Continuance. Do but consult *Dion Cassius*. To ascertain this Consulship, Father *Harduoin* says wittily, That *Balbus* was Consul under the Consulship of *Cn. Domitius Calvinus*, and of *C. Asinius Pollio*, in the Year of *Rome* 714. *Consul sic fuit, quontam ita necesse est dicere*, Cn. Domitio Calvino *secundum*, C. Asinio Pollione *Coss. Anno Urbis* DCCXIV (39). To conclude, if *Glandorpius* had known any thing of the Passage of *Pliny* (40), where *Balbus* the Elder is called Paternal Uncle, *Patruus*, of *Balbus* the Younger, he would not have descended to the Quotation of such a bad Authority as That of *Volaterranus*, to inform us, that one

BALBUS. 613

and lesser Consulship is chimerical [L]; and that *Moreri* committed several Faults [M], though his Article of *Balbus* is very short and dry.

I shall say but little of some other *Balbus*'s, mentioned by ancient Authors. *Lucius Lucilius* B A L B U S, Disciple of *Mucius Scævola*, and Preceptor of the famous *Servius Sulpitius*, was an excellent Lawyer. He flourished about the Year of *Rome* 670. *Cicero* says, that *Sulpitius* exceeded his Master [N], who, by the Addition of a mature Judgment to his Learning, was something flow, whereas his Disciple was quick and expeditious. *Balbus*'s Writings are lost, to which perhaps his Disciple *Sulpitius* did not a little contribute, by inserting most of them in his own (*n*). We must not, as *Glandorpius* has done, confound this *Balbus* with *Quintus Lucilius* B A L B U S the Stoic Philosopher, one of *Cicero*'s Interlocutors in the Books *de Natura Deorum* (*o*). *Publius Octavius* B A L B U S was Cotemporary with *Cicero*, who praises him for his Knowledge in the Civil Law, for his Wit, and Probity, and for many other good Qualities (*p*). *Cicero* gives as good a Character of *Lucius Octavius* B A L B U S, who lived at the same time (*q*). It is likely, that one of these two was the *Octavius Balbus*, of whom *Valerius Maximus* reports, that, having saved himself, through a Back-door, from the Cruelty of the Triumvirs, and hearing, that they were killing his Son in his House, he returned back again, and caused himself to be put to Death (*r*). *Appian* reports the Matter somewhat differently (*s*).

one of those *Balbus*'s was the Son of the other's Brother.

[L] *The Distinction of the greater, and lesser, Consulship is chimerical.*] Observe, a little, to what Extravagancy of Thought Men are subject. There are some, who, from these Words *Plinj*, *Fuit & Balbus Cornelius Major Consul*, have fallen into the Chimera of two Degrees of Consulship, and pretended, that *Balbus* was made Great Consul, or First Consul (41). It was easy to see, that *Major*, in This Passage, does not relate to *Consul*, but to the Name. Cornelius Balbus, *the Elder*, was *Consul*.

[M] *And that Moreri committed several Faults.*] I. It is only with an *it is said*, that he reports, that *Cornelius Balbus* composed a *Journal*, or *Ephemeris*, of what happened daily to *Cæsar*. If he had known, that *Sidonius Apollinaris* mentioned That Journal, as a Book, which was extant, and also commended it (42), he must have rejected. That *it is said*. Some will have it, that *Symmachus* spoke of This same Book, when he wrote to his Friend: " *Si impar est* " *desiderio tuo Livius, sume Ephemeridem C. Cæ-* " *saris decerptam Bibliothecæ meæ ut tibi muneri* " *mitteretur.* Hæc te origines, situs, pugnas, & " *quidquid fuit in moribus aut legibus Galliarum* " *docebit* (43). ----- *If Livy does not fully satisfy* " *your Desire of having the History of ancient Gaul,* " *you need only take Cæsar's Ephemerides, which I* " *made you a Present of out of my own small Li-* " *brary. This will explain to you the Origin, Si-* " *tuation, Battles, Customs, and Laws of the Gauls.*" But others pretend, that *Symmachus* means only the *Memoirs Cæsar* had wrote himself, and which we still have under the Title of *Commentaries on the Wars of Gaul* (44). It is, nevertheless, true, that he wrote other Memoirs, under the Title of *Ephemeris*, as we learn from *Servius*. Why might not *Symmachus* speak of the latter? II. The Advice he gives, to take care not to confound This Author with one of the same Name, surnamed Theophanes, who was of Lesbos, as *Savaro*, and others have done, contains two Faults. We have shewn the first, in justifying *Savaro* from the Censure of *Vossius*. The second consists, in supposing, that there was an Historian, born in the Island of *Lesbos*, whose Name was *Cornelius Balbus Theophanes*; than which nothing can be more false. The Historian *Theophanes*, born at *Mitylene*, in the Island of *Lesbos*, was from *Cn. Pompeius Theophanes*, because *Pompey* had conferred the Freedom of *Rome* upon him; but he never added the Name of *Balbus*, or *Balbus Cornelius*, to That of his Family; and there is reason to be surprised, that *Vossius* should make such a Slip, as to say, that the Historian *Cornelius Balbus Theophanes*, mentioned by *Julius Capitolinus*, was *Theophanes* the *Lesbian*, who wrote the War of *Mithridates* (45). III. But again, Why must we take care not to do as *Savaro* did? It is because *Cornelius Balbus* dwelt at *Rome*, and because *Theophanes* was of *Lesbos*. Are not these two Attributes incompatible in the same Subject, and can a better Proof be required, for a personal Distinction? See how Errors grow: *Moreri*, designing to abbreviate *Vossius*'s Proof, made it incomparably worse, than it was. IV. He goes on thus: *I think he is the first, whom Cicero defended against an Accusation, for taking, unjustly, the Title of a Roman Citizen.* Besides, that the Expression is so far from being clear (46), that one would think, by it, that the Cause of the Person in his own Words, than from mine. Read, therefore, what follows. " *Cum dicendi causâ duobus peri-* " *tissimis operam dedisse* (Servius) L. Lucilio Balbo, " *C. Aquilio Gallo, Galli hominis acuti & exercitati* " *promptam in agendo & in respondendo celeritatem* " *subtilitate diligentiæque superavit: Balbi docti & e-* " *ruditi hominis in utraque re considerantam tardi-* " *tatem vicit, expediendis conficiendisque rebus. Sic* " *& habet quod uterque eorum habuit, & explevit* " *quod utrique defuit* (47). ---- *At he* (Servius) *had* " *learned to plead under two excellent Masters, sc.* " *Lucilius Balbus, and C. Aquilius Gallus, he ex-* " *celled his ingenious and experienced Master Gallus's* " *great readiness in speaking and replying, by his* " *Subtilty and Diligence; and his learned and judi-* " *cious Master Balbus's deliberate Consideration of* " *every thing, by his Expedition and Dispatch. So* " *that he both had, what each of them had, and* " *made up, what each of them wanted.*"

BALBUS, BALBI, or BALBO (JOHN) a *Dominican* Monk, flourished in the XIIIth Century. He understood *Greek*, a rare thing in those Days, and much more *Latin*, than all his Fellow Monks together. He was as much esteemed for his good Life, as for his Knowledge, and some have treated him as a Saint [*A*]. It was for this reason his Image was placed in St *Thomas*'s Church at *Pavia*. The Title of his Works may be seen in *Moreri*, who, instead of referring us to *Vossius*'s Book on the

[*A*] *Some have treated him as a Saint.*] This appears from the following Passage. " *Non vi hà man-* " *cato chi lo riponga nel numero de' Beati, e come* " *tale fi vede dipinto nel Tempio di S. Tomaso di* " *Pavia, in luogo eminente vicino al soffitato* (1). ---- " *There have not been wanting those, who have placed* " *him in the Number of Saints, and he may be seen* " *painted, as such, in the Church of* St Thomas, *at* " *Pavia, in a high Place near the Ceiling.*"

[*B*] *Let*

BALBUS.

the *Latin* Historians, would have done well to remark, that *John Balbus* is far better known by the Name of *Joannes de Janua*, or *Joannes Januensis*, than by any other. We shall observe why he went by This Name, and examine whether he be the same with *Jacobus de Voragine* [B]. We shall make but One Remark for all This, and for what may follow from it.

[B] *Let us see why he went by This Name, and whether he be the same with* Jacobus de Voragine.] *John Balbus*, a noble *Genoese*, was called *Januensis*, or *de Janua*, because he was of *Genoa*. He says himself, in his *Catholicon*, at the Word *Janua*, that he was of a City called *Janua*, which City is no other, than *Genoa*: From *Luitprandus*'s Time it was rather called *Janua*, than *Genoa*: either to insinuate more clearly, that *Janus* was the Founder of it, or in regard to the Reason, mentioned by *John de Janua*, namely, that this City is the Gate of *Provence*, *Lambardy*, and *Tuscany*. He informs us, in the same Place, that he was called *Frater Johannes Januensis de Balbis*, and that he had wrote some other Books. At the end of the *Catholicon*, he says, that, after several Years of great Labour, he finished it on the Day of the Nones of *March*, which is the seventh Day of *March*, 1286.

WHETHER *Joannes de Janua*, and *Jacobus de Voragine*, are one and the same Author.

(2) Oudin, Supplement. de Scriptor. Eccles. pag. 501.

Mr *Oudin*, formerly a Monk of the Order of the *Præmonstratenses*, and at present associated with the Protestant Church, to the great Satisfaction of the Party, which has great Reason to think itself happy, in gaining so great a Man, and expects many fine Pieces from his Pen; I say, Mr *Oudin* pretends, that *Jacobus de Voragine*, Author of the *Golden Legend*, and *Johannes de Janua*, Author of the *Catholicon*, are only one and the same Person (2). His Reason for it is, that all agree they both lived at the same time, were both *Dominicans*, both of *Genoa*, and therefore both called *Januensis*. So that it was an easy thing, for those, who saw the Name of *Januensis*, at the beginning of several Manuscripts, preceeded by the Letter *J*, being the initial one of the Christian Names *Joannes*, and *Jacobus*, to ascribe them sometimes to *Jacobus Januensis*, and sometimes to *Joannes Januensis*; which must make two Authors of one.

But I must beg leave to tell him, that his Conjecture receives a severe Blow from the Enumeration, which the Author of the *Catholicon* has given of his Works, at the Word *Janua*; for, though there might have been a great Distance of Time, from his ending the Article *Janua*, to his finishing the *Catholicon*, yet it is not at all likely, that, if he had wrote any Books, during that time, he would have omitted adding them to the rest in That Article, upon closing That Dictionary. And therefore it may be supposed, that the Catalogue, which he gives under the Word *Janua*, is of the Year 1286, in which he put the last Hand to the *Catholicon*. Now it is certain, that *Jacobus de Voragine* published an *Italian* Translation of the Bible in the Year 1270. What likelihood is there, that, sixteen Years afterwards, upon mentioning the Books he had given the Public, he should forget one of so new an Undertaking, and, in all respects, so remarkable, as the Translation of the Scriptures into the Vulgar Tongue? It is not at all probable, therefore, that *Jacobus de Voragine* should be the Author of the *Catholicon*. However, we shall not determine this Point, but wait for the Information of the Learned, and particularly of Mr *Oudin*. Dr *Cave* also chuses to suspend his Judgment of it (3).

(3) Cave, de Script. Eccles. pag. 750.

This is what I said, in the Specimen of my Dictionary, but now I can speak, in a more positive manner, against Father *Oudin*'s Conjecture: I have, for my Foundation, several good Reasons, from a very able Hand (4). Here is the Extract of a Memoir, which came from *Dijon*. "I believe, it may be clearly decided, that *Joannes de Genoa* ought by no means to be confounded with *Jacobus de Voragine*. The first, who is the Author of the Dictionary, entitled *Catholicon*, was never cited by the Name of *Jacobus*. The second, who is Author of the *Golden Legend*, was never cited by the Name of *Joannes*. The first is always called *Joannes de Jarud*, or *Januensis*, because he was, undoubtedly, of *Genoa*, of the Family of the *Balbi*. The second, whose Family is unknown, is generally called *Jacobus de Voragine*, very rarely *Jacobus Januensis*, and then we either understand *Archiepiscopus*, or else suppose that he was called so, by reason of the small Distance between the Borough of *Liguria*, called

(4) From the learned Mr de la Monnoye.

Voragine, the Place of his Birth, and *Genoa*. The first was only a *Dominican* Monk. The second was raised to the Archbishopric of *Genoa*. All Authors, and the *Dominicans*, among others, have constantly distinguished the Names, the Country, and the Works, of These two Writers. This is carefully observed, by *Leandro Alberti*, in his Description *della riviera de Genoua di Ponente*. *James Bracelli*, a *Genoese*, who wrote in the Year 1431, and is Author of a little Book, *De claris Genuensibus*, makes no mention, there, of *Jacobus de Voragine*, because he was not of *Genoa*: but he speaks, in it, with Praise of *Joannes Balbus*, the Author of the *Catholicon*, to whom he would not have failed to have given the Stile of Archbishop of *Genoa*, if he had enjoyed it, as he must have done, according to the Opinion of Those, who confound him with *Jacobus de Voragine*."

Simler is so far from confounding two Authors in one, that, on the contrary, he has made three of one; for he speaks of *Joannes de Janua*, of *Joannes Januensis*, and of *Joannes Balbus*, as of three different Authors (5). He is farther mistaken, in writing *Baldus* for *Balbus*, a Fault, which *Quenstedt* followed, in his Treatise of the Country of Illustrious Men (6). *Martinius* also gives into This Fault of Multiplication. It is in the Catalogue of the Dictionaries he consulted to make his own: at the beginning of his *Lexicon Philologicum*, printed at *Bremen*, in 1623, and afterward at *Francfort*, in 1655, and reprinted at *Utrecht*, in the Year 1697. He mentions the *Catholicon*, which was finished the Day of the Nones of *March* 1286, and quotes the very Words, at the end of the Dictionary of *Joannes de Janua*. Immediately after, he names a *Summa quæ vocatur Catholicon*, published by Brother *John de Janua*, and printed at *Venice*, in 1487. It is plain, that they are only two different Editions of one and the same Book, and that the first ought no less to be ascribed to *John de Janua*, than the second. *Martinius* would not have failed doing it, had he known what is in the Article *Janua*, in the *Catholicon*, finished in 1286.

MULTIPLICATIONS of *Joannes de Janua* into several Authors.

(5) Epitome Biblioth. Gesneri.

(6) Pag. 307.

I find it is not yet rightly agreed, who was the Author of the Dictionary, first entituled *Catholicon*. Mr *du Cange* ascribes it to our *John de Janua*, and says, that neither *Papias* nor *Ugutio*, who had made some Compilations before, used This Title (7): But *Borrichius*, who wrote afterwards, and has seen Mr *du Cange*'s Preface, undertakes to maintain, nevertheless, that *Papias* is the Author of the *Catholicon*, and that he finished That Work, in the Year 1286 (8). He had found it affirmed in That Preface, that *Papias* did not flourish in the Year 1050, as *Trithemius* will have it, but in 1053, as the Chronicle of *Albericus* justifies: and yet he lays it down, as a certain Fact, that *Papias* finished his Dictionary, in 1286 He ought either to have refuted Mr *du Cange*, or, at least, to have observed, that he was mistaken. This Proceding, and Silence, serve only to puzzle the Reader. However, it is a strong Presumption against *Borrichius*, to see, that he places the Conclusion of *Papias*'s Dictionary exactly in the same Year, 1286, that *Joannes de Janua* finishes his *Catholicon*. The above-quoted Memorial assures me, that *Papias* did not write the *Catholicon*, which was finished in 1286, and that *John Balbi* is the first, who made use of the Word *Catholicon* for the Title of a Dictionary.

OF the Book, entitled *Catholicon*.

(7) Du Cange, Præfat. Glossar. Lat.

(8) Borrich. Append. de Lexicis Græcis & Lat. at the end of his Analecta ad Cognit. de Ling. Lat. 1692.

It was a long time ago, that *Bartbius*, without having consulted the Manuscript Chronicle of *Albericus*, judged, that *Papias* was more ancient, than he was supposed to be. *Platina* delivers it for certain, that he lived in the Time of Pope *Innocent* III; that is, in the beginning of the XIIIth Century, which agrees with *Trithemius*. *Barrichius* places him at the end of the XIIIth Century. But *Barthius*, in the third Chapter of the third Book of his *Adversaria*, placed him under the Reign of *Henry* II (9), because This Author carries the List, which he gives, under the Word *Ætas*, of all the Princes of the past Age, no further than *Henry*, whom he calls *minorem*, which he would not have done, if there had already

THE Age of *Papias*, according to *Barthius*.

THE Neglierence of the Continuators. Complet.

(9) He died in the Year 1024 [?] See Barthius Recip. st. nns to trace in it.

already been more than two Emperors of the Name of *Henry*. It is true, that *Bartbius* raises a Suspicion, which, generally speaking, is justified by the prodigious Neglect of Those, who continue, or enlarge, Compilations. This is, that; perhaps, *Papias* left the Article *Ætas* just as he found it in some old Dictionary, without continuing the Catalogue down to his own Time. Thus we find, in the Chronicle of the Abbot of *Ursperg*, in one Place, that the Author was at *Rome*, in the Year 1102 (10); in another, that he was very young, *in minori ætate*, in the Year 1198, and in another, that he was made an Abbot, in the Year 1215. If the Continuator had cleared up the Matter, with respect to his Additions, we should not have met with so much Confusion.

(10) See Vossius de Hist. Lat. lib. 2. cap. 57. and Bellarm. de Script. Ecclef. p. 335. *falsly accused by Zeiller, de Hiftor. pag. 155. of having believed the Number* 1102 *to be falsified.*

BALDUS, a famous Civilian in the XIVth Century, was the Son of *Francis Ubaldus* [*A*], a Physician of *Perugia*. He studied under *Bartolus*, and, being but fifteen Years of Age, he proposed such a puzzling Objection to him, that he required time to consider of it; and the Answer to it was not given till the next Day. So that those, who say, *Baldus* began his Studies very late, are grosly deceived [*B*]. A little after his promotion to the Degree of Doctor, he maintained some Theses, which *Bartolus* opposed for five Hours together, without being able to obtain the Victory. He often pleaded Causes against *Bartolus*, and there arose such an Emulation between them, as soon degenerated into Hatred. This cannot be doubted, when we see, that *Baldus* made it his endeavour to eclipse the Reputation of his Master. What has been said, that, upon consulting the *Pandects* of *Pisa*, on occasion of a Dispute which they had, concerning the reading of a Law, *Baldus* was convicted of several Falsifications, and that he was punished for them in an ignominious manner, ought to pass only for a Fable [*C*]. He taught at *Perugia*, and Cardinal *de Beaufort* was his Scholar there, who was afterwards Pope *Gregory* XI. He was called to *Padua* about the Year 1378; but left That University, when *Galeazzo Visconti*, designing to re-establish That of *Pavia*, drew thither, by the power of his Money, the ablest Professors

[*A*] *He was the Son of Francis Ubaldus.*] Observe, then, that *Baldus* is the Christian Name of This Civilian, and *Ubaldus* his Sirname. *Moreri* calls him, besides, *Peter*; which is confounding the elder Brother with the younger. *Petrus Ubaldus* was the third Son of the Physician *Franciscus Ubaldus*, and was a good Civilian. And so was his Brother *Angelus Ubaldus*. See *Pancirollus*, in the seventieth, and following Chapters, of the second Book *De claris Legum Interpretibus*.

[*B*] *Those, who say,* Baldus *began his Studies very late, are grosly deceived.*] It is reported, that he was forty Years of Age, when he began to study the Civil Law, and that *Bartolus* having said to him, *tarde venifti Balde. —— You come late Baldus. Baldus* answered him, *citius recedam. —— I shall return the sooner* (1). *La Mothe le Vayer* has lengthened *Bartolus's* Speech, and makes him say, *You come late*, Baldus, *you will be an Advocate in the other World. Sero venis Balde, eris advocatus in alio sæculo*. I do not believe, that, if *Bartolus* said this, he intended any Allusion to *Cato's* Jest, That Censor, to deride *Isocrates's* School, said, *That the Scholars grew old in it, that they might exercise their Eloquence in Hell, at the Bar of* Minos (2). This Story, about *Baldus*, has no Foundation. *Pancirollus* proves, that, at the Age of fifteen Years, he started a very puzzling Objection to the famous *Bartolus*; that, at the Age of seventeen Years, he read public Lectures: and that, four Years after, he wrote a Book *de Pactis*, and another *de Constitutо* (3). These are the words of That Writer: " Opinioni " Bartoli adeo argutè contradixit, ut ille argumenti " acumine perterritus respondere non potuerit, com- " mendatoque juvene tempus ad solvendum petiit, & " sequenti mane respondit. Deinde 17 annum in- " gressus solenni interpretatione difficillimam legem " publicè Baldus explicuit, unde fabulosum est quod " vulgò fertur, Baldum quadragenarium ad legum " studia accessisse (4). —— *He objected so ingeniously " to the Opinion of* Bartolus, *that he was surprized " with the Force of the Argument, and could not solve " it, but, commending his young Opponent, desired some " time to answer his Objection, which he accordingly " did the next Day. Afterwards, upon entring into " his seventeenth Year,* Baldus *explained a very difficult Law in a solemn Lecture, whence That common " Report must be fabulous, that* Baldus *was Forty " Years old, when he first began his Studies on the " Civil Law.*" The Civilian *Zasius* reports the same Story on the Credit of *Paul Citadin*; but *Tiraquellus* rejects it as a Fable (5). " Adducerem, *says* he (6), " quod de Baldo vulgo dicitur —— nisi scirem hæc " esse commentitia & prorsus fabulosa, ut ex iis con- " stat quæ supra diximus. —— *I should mention what " is commonly reported of* Baldus, —— *if I did not " know it to be only an Invention, and a Fable, as " appears from what I have already said.*" Mr *Baillet* observes, that *La Mothe la Vayer*, and Father *Bartoli*, seem to have adopted This Opinion, as of a Fact well attested, — *and not a Story made at random*. He refers to President *Tiraquellus*, and to the eighth Chapter of the Elogies of *Paulus Jovius* (7). He cites *la Mothe le Vayer*, Letter 32, pag. 420, and *Bartoli*, Car. Hom. lit. pag. 248. I never read, that *Tiraquellus* was *President*. *Paulus Jovius* observes, that *Baldus's* Parts were not only forward, but lasting: " Præcoci ingenio penè puer, non ad optimum " modo frugem, sed rarissimo etiam naturæ dono ad " longam senectutem pervenit (8). —— *A Youth of " almost too early a Wit, and which yet not only pro- " duced excellent Fruit, but also, by an uncommon " Gift of Nature, continued even to a good old Age.*

[*C*] *What is said* - - - - - - *that he was convicted of several Falsifications, and punished for them - - - - ought to pass only for a Fable.*] Some say, the Disgrace, which he received, obliged him to exile himself, and to say, as *Scipio Africanus* did, that his ungrateful Country should not supply him with a Grave: *Publica traductum patria excessisse ferunt, & abeuntem Scipionis Africani verba protulisse, ingrata patria ne ossa quidem mea habebis, ac in voluntario exilio senem defunctum fuisse* (9). Others say, that he was condemned to be marked with a hot Iron on the Forehead, and that *Bartolus* protected him. *Jason* had heard of it; but he was very much in the wrong to immortalize This *Hear-say* in his Works. Such Reports should never be so far honoured, but in these two Cases; the one, when they are extreamly probable; and the other, when they are to be branded with a Note of Reprobation; that is, refuted and hissed at. In this latter case, it is very useful to mention such Traditions, because nothing is more proper to make one suspect the Reports of Fame, than to shew the foolish and ridiculous Credulity of foregoing Ages. To prove demonstratively, that *Jason's Hear-say* is a Fable, there needs no other reason than this. *Jason* knew it only by Hear-say; if the thing had been true, he would have read it in an hundred Places. *Baldus* lived a very long time with great Honour: He wrote Books; he consulted whom he thought fit; he had some formidable Opponents and Adversaries. We may be perfectly assured, that, if he could have been reproached with an Infamy, it would have been done in more than one Book. It is there, that *Jason*, and all the World, would have learned This Disgrace. It is the Misfortune of learned Men, who make themselves eminent, and write much, that, sooner or later, they will be publickly reproached with the least Faults of their Youth. If other Authors become their Enemies, they must expect satirical Romances, rather than the Discretion of an Adversary. Thus *Pancirollus* should have apologized for *Baldus*; he should have expressly

BALDUS.

fors he could meet with. A quick Repartee, which *Baldus* made, the firſt time he appeared in the College of *Pavia*, cauſed him to be admired [*D*]. He had a formidable Colleague there, whoſe Name was *Philip Caſſolus*. This was a Man of an excellent Memory, and great Parts; but the good Opinion he had of his own ſufficiency having put him upon giving a Challenge, he was overcome, and his Glory ſacrificed to That of *Baldus* [*E*]. The Death of *Philip* did not free his Competitor from trouble; for there was ſuch a warm Emulation between the Profeſſor, who ſucceeded him, and *Baldus*, that they introduced the ſhameful and pernicious Cuſtom of bribing Auditors by Supplications. *Baldus* raiſed a great Fortune [*F*]. He compoſed a great many Books, and there is no probability of his having ſtudied but two Hours in a Day [*G*]. He muſt not be produced as an Inſtance of an Author without Faults; had he only had That of contradicting himſelf, he would fall very ſhort of Perfection; but he had a great many others [*H*]. The Excuſes he made for his Contradictions deſerve to be conſidered [*I*]. He died the Twenty eighth of

(10) Pancirolli. Ibid. pag. 202.

expreſsly, and openly, made uſe of this Obſervation, and not have only ſaid; "Quæ omnia falſa eſſe & " alii potius eveniſſe non dubito, cum nulla de hoc " certa extet auctoritas, & eum Ticini deceſſiſſe con-" ſtet (10). *All which I conclude to be falſe, and ra-" ther to have happened to ſome other Perſon, ſince we " find no good Authority for it, and are certain, that " he died at Pavia.*"

(11) Ibid. pag. 203.

[*D*] *The* Quick Repartee, *which* Baldus *made* ——— *cauſed him to be admired*] He was of a ſmall ſize, ſo that, as ſoon as he appeared in the Auditory, they cried out, *Minuit præſentia famam*, --- *His Preſence leſſens his Fame.* He anſwered, without altering his Countenance, *Augebit cætera virtus*, --- *Virtue will enlarge every Thing elſe.* Pancirollus adds, *Quo dicto omnibus ſui admirationem injecit* (11). ——— *Which Reply made him much admired by all.*

(12) Id. ib.

[*E*] *The* Glory *of* Caſſolus *was ſacrificed to That of* Baldus] *Caſſolus* had engaged himſelf to anſwer, upon the Spot, all Queſtions propoſed to him concerning laſt Wills. The Day and Hour were appointed to make good this Challenge. The Aſſembly was numerous: *Baldus* ſtood up, and propoſed a Queſtion, which *Caſſolus* could not anſwer. *Baldus* was obliged to ſhew the Law in Queſtion. Judge whether the Challenger was mortified. "Philippus, qui, ut " memoriâ cæteris anteceſſebat, itâ ſuperbo titulo " Doctorum Doctor vocabatur, ingenio fretus, ſe ex " omnibus ultimarum voluntatum quæſtionibus ex " tempore reſponſurum profeſſus eſt. Statutâ ad " dicendum die, cum in magnâ expectatione eſſet, " ſurgens Baldus interrogavit, Ubi in jure cautum " reperiretur, parem non eſſe ejus, qui non vult, " ei, qui non poteſt, conditionem. Ad primam in-" terrogationem hæſitante Philippo, cum Baldus de " propoſita quæſtione legem oſtendiſſet, magnam " gloriam retulit (12). ——— Philip, *who, as he excelled all others in Memory, ſo alſo was called by the proud Title of Doctor of Doctors, depending upon his Abilities, undertook to ſatisfy extempore all Queſtions concerning laſt Wills. The Day appointed being come, and great Expectation raiſed,* Baldus, *ſtanding up, asked, Where it was, that the Civil Law had provided, that the Caſe of him, who would not, ſhould be eſteemed quite different from That of him who could not. Philip being puzzled at the firſt propoſing the Queſtion,* Baldus *produced the Law required, and gained great Glory.*"

(13) Ibid. pag. 204.

[*F*] Baldus *raiſed a great Fortune.*] The Opinions he gave only on the Point of Subſtitution, brought him in above Fifteen thouſand Crowns: "De jure " reſpondendo immenſam pecuniam coëgit, qui ex " ſolis ſubſtitutionum ſpeciebus plus quindecim millia " aureorum lucratus fuiſſe traditur. Aliunde præ-" tereà ex innumeris aliarum ſucceſſionum crimi-" numque cauſis & contractibus perampla opes " accuſavulit (13). ——— *He got a prodigious Sum of Money by his Practice in Law, ſo that one only Article of Subſtitutions is ſaid to have procured him Fifteen thouſand Crowns. Beſides innumerable Cauſes of other Succeſſions, and criminal ones, and Contracts, by which he heaped up immenſe Riches.*" He had ſeveral Lands, and lived in a pleaſant Country-Houſe near *Pavia,* from whence he came on his Mule to the Auditory. Pancirollus adds (14), *Domus vetuſtate vitiata adhuc hodie pro re memoranda oſtentatur.* ------ *The Ruins of the Houſe are ſtill ſhewn as a Curioſity.*

(14) Pag. 205.

[*G*] *There is no probability of his having ſtudied but two Hours in a Day*] Pancirollus, containing this, re-

lates, among other Things, that *Baldus,* going a Journey, which hindered him from ſpending ſo much of his Time in reading, as he was uſed to do, ſaid, *At every Step of my Horſe's Foot, I loſe a Law out of my Head.* — *Quit gradus equus ambulabat, tot leges ſibi excidere querebatur* (15). It is a Sign he had acquired, and ſtill retained his Knowledge, by much reading.

(15) Ibid.

[*H*] *But he has a great many Faults.*] He advances a thouſand Things ſingular, and contrary to the Opinion of other Civilians, and without quoting any Law: they are only his own Fancies: He quotes Laws nothing at all to the Purpoſe. he treats of many things quite out of their Order: he is too barren on the eſſential Part, and too prolix on the uſeleſs: He anſwers Queſtions no Body ever asked: and anſwers nothing to what every Body asks: He confounds himſelf by his own Subtilties, and gives himſelf too much liberty: The Vivacity of his Wit is the Cauſe of the want of Uniformity in his Opinions. "Cum " parum ſibi conſtans ſæpenumero contrarius reperi-" tur, id tamen non levitate, ſed ingenii ſubtilitate " eveniſſe Paulus Caſtrenſis autumat (16). ——— *His Inconſiſtencies, and very often downright Contradictions,* Paulus Caſtrenſis *thinks to be owing not to the Levity, but Subtilty, of his Parts.*" Thoſe, who have a quick Imagination, have commonly but a ſhort Memory; and this is the Reaſon why they do not remember, when they conſider a Queſtion in one view, that formerly they maintained it in another ſenſe. They contradict themſelves without knowing it. Add to this, that a ſubtle Wit eaſily invents Arguments to prove and diſprove the ſame things. But it is a great Defect not to be capable of ſuſpending the Effects of This Subtilty, till the Mind is perfectly ſettled.

(16) Ibid. pag. 203.

[*I*] *The Excuſes he made for his Contradictions deſerve to be conſidered.*] He ſaid, that our Underſtanding alters, and that he therefore argues one Day after one manner, and another Day after another. I believe he reſerved to himſelf, *in petto,* the Privilege, which he attributed to Legiſlators. The Biſhop of *Pavia* asked, one Day, why the Laws were ſo changeable; *Baldus* anſwered him, that the ſame things become either lawful, or unlawful, according to the Times. In time of War ſome things are permitted, which are forbid in time of Peace: Therefore Juſtice enjoins all things, which become proper to the Times; ſuch a Conduct is proportioned to the preſent Circumſtances, therefore it is juſt. Thoſe, who make Laws, imitate Phyſicians, who permit, order, and forbid, the ſame things, according to Times and Seaſons; theſe are what they obſerve. *Ipſe quoque ſe excuſat, quòd Intellectus, qui ratiocinatur, non ſemper ſit idem, ſed varius; & Epiſcopo Ticinenſi ſæpe interroganti, cur totius Leges mutarentur, reſpondit, flagrante bello permittitur, quod pacis tempore non licet, id ita juſtum eſſe, quod cuique ſuo tempore expedit, exemplo enim medicorum tempora & legum latoribus diceba obſervari* (17). This was *Baldus's* Anſwer; and This is either implicitly, or explicitly, the Principle, on which Authors argue, who confute themſelves, when they are to diſpute againſt two ſorts of Enemies. *This Propoſition is true and good, this Day, while I diſpute againſt* Pelagius*; in a Year's Time it ſhall not be ſo, if I am to diſpute againſt* Calvin. See what has been ſaid, above, concerning the Contradictions of Advocates, and the Apology *Cicero* makes for them (18). I remember to have read, that certain Controverſiſts, not being able to deny, but that the Church commands certain things, which

(17) Ibid.

(18) In the Remarks [*B*] and [*C*] of the Article ANTONY (MARC) the Orator.

BALDUS. 617

of *April* 1400 [*K*]. His Death was something Tragical: He had a little Dog, which he loved very much, and plaid with, and kissed very often. In one of these Caresses he was bit by the Lip, and the Dog, being mad at that time, communicated a subtle Poison to the Body of *Baldus*, which had no effect for a long time; but at last it produced the *Hydrophobia*, or Dread of Liquids, and caused an incurable Distemper (*a*). *Baldus* lived Seventy six Years (*b*), and left two Sons, who proved good Civilians (*c*). *Zenobius*, the Eldest, was Bishop of *Tiferno* (*d*).

(*a*) *Taken from Pancirollus de claris Leg. Interp. l. 2. c. 70, pag. 201, & seq.*
(*b*) *P. Jovius, Elog. cap. 8, pag. 27.*
(*c*) *Pancirol. ibid. p. 203.*
(*d*) *Ibid.*

which do not seem agreeable either to Scripture, or to the Primitive Church, have maintained, that they were nevertheless just and true, because the Holy Spirit, who guides the Church, inspires her in every Age with such Interpretations, as are most proper for the good of Souls. "Scripturas esse ad tempus adap-" "tatas & varie intellectas, ita ut uno tempore secun-" "dum currentem universalem ritum exponeretur," "mutato ritu iterum sententia mutaretur (19). Non" "est mirum si praxis Ecclesiæ uno tempore inter-" "pretatur Scripturam uno modo, alio tempore alio;" "nam intellectus currit cum praxi (20). ——— *That* "*the Scriptures are adapted to the Times, and to*" "*be variously understood, so that they shall be ex-*" "*plained at one time, according to the Universal*" "*Usage then prevailing; if this Usage comes to alter,*"

(19) *Nicolaus Cusanus, Epist. 2. ad Bohemos.*
(20) *Idem, Epist. 7.*

" *so must the Interpretation.* ——— *It is no wonder* " *if the Practice of the Church interprets the Scrip-* " *ture at one time in one way, at another time in* " *another; for the Understanding goes along with the* " *Practice*" I love this plain dealing.
[*K*] *He died the Twenty eighth of April, 1400.*] His Epitaph confirms it; so that *Bellarmin* is deceived in placing the Death of *Baldus* in the Year 1400 (21). *Trithemius*, who placed it in the Year 1423, asserted a Falsehood; but Mr *Moreri*, who said, that, according to *Trithemius*, the Death of *Baldus* ought to be placed in the Year 1423, was not in the wrong. The *Dutch* Edition of his Dictionary ought not to have made the Correction of 1403, instead of 1423.

(21) *Bellarm. Script. Ecclef. pag. 352.*

BALDUS (**James**), one of the best *Latin* Poets *Germany* produced in the XVIIth Century, was born at *Enfisheim*, in 1603. He turned Jesuit in the Year 1624. He taught Rhetoric and Literature for six Years; he was a Preacher many Years, and preached also at the Court of the Elector of *Bavaria*, and acquired an extraordinay Reputation by his Poems. There were none, even among the Protestants themselves, but praised them in a singular manner [*A*]. One of his last Works was his *Urania victrix, seu Animæ Christianæ Certamina adversus illecebras quinque sensuum corporis sui*. Pope *Alexander* VII was so pleased with it, that he sent his Medal in Gold to the Author. Father *Baldus* consecrated it to the Blessed Virgin [*B*]. Some Senators of *Nuremberg* disputed which of them should have his Pen [*C*], and it is said, that He, to whose share it fell, kept it in a Silver Case. This Poet died at *Neubourg* the Ninth of *August*, 1668. His Poetry is of a miscellaneous kind; and consists of *Panegyrics, Treatises of Morality, Pieces for the Stage* [*D*], *Pieces of Devotion, Sylvæ, Odes, &c* (*a*).

(*a*) *Taken from Sotuel, Biblioth. Script. Soc. Jesu p. 356.*

[*A*] *Even the Protestants* ——— *praised his Poems in a singular Manner.*] Father *Southwell* expresses himself upon this, in these terms: "Ipsis Aca-" "tholicis etiam adeo placuerunt, ut publico typo" "eum Horatium Germanum nominare non dubita-" "rint. ——— *The Non-Catholics were so pleased*" "*with them, that they did not scruple to name him,*" "*in print, the German Horace.*" If I am not mistaken, this is grounded on a Letter of *Barlæus*. Father *Baldus*, having seen the Verses *Barlæus* had wrote in Praise of the Duke of *Bavaria*, wrote a very obliging Letter to him, and sent him a Volume of his Poems. *Barlæus* returned him Thanks for it, with great Complements, and said to him, among other things: "Restituisti nobis lyram neglectam diu" "& intermissam, ut jam merito vocari possis lyrico-" "rum scriptor, aut potius Bojorum fidicen lyræ, ut" "ad Horatii verba alludam (1). ——— *You have*" "*restored the Lyre a long time neglected and unstrung,*" "*so that you may now be justly called a Lyric Wri-*" "*ter, or rather Master of the Bavarian Lyre, that*" "*I may allude to the Words of* Horace." This Letter was written the first of *March*, 1644. The Jesuit was then Rector of the College of *Munich* (2).
[*B*] *He consecrated a Medal of* Alexander *VII to the Blessed Virgin.*] This is what *Southwell* says of it. "Hanc vero Jacobus Deiparæ Virgini anathe-" "ma appendit, ut palam faceret cui Palladi ipse"

(1) *See the 467th Letter of* Barlæus, *pag. 911. See also the 487th, written to the same* Baldus.
(2) *See the Table of* Barlæus's *Letters.*

" suos labores consecraret (3). ——— *This Medal,* " James *consecrated to the Virgin Mother of* Christ, " *that it might shew who was his Minerva, and Pa-* " *troness of all his Labours.*"
[*C*] *Some Senators of* Nuremberg *disputed which of them should have his Pen.*] "I do not know, *says* " Mr *Baillet* (4), whether he, who preserved it in a " fine silver Case, made on purpose for it, did " not commit a Sacrilege; because it seems to me, " that Father *Baldus* had consecrated it to the Holy " Virgin, and that his Intention was, that it should " be hung up on one of her Images, or over one of " her Altars, as *Lipsius* had formerly done in a like " Fit of Devotion."
[*D*] *His Poetry* ——— *consists of Pieces for the Stage.*] There is one of them, which bears this Title: *Poesis Osca, sive Drama Georgicum de Belli malis & Pacis bonis carmine antiquo, Attellano, Osco, Casco* (5). How rustic soever this Piece, and the Osque and Casque Gibberish, in which it was composed, may seem, yet I do not question, but that it cost the Author both more Time and Wit, than a grave Piece in good *Latin*. We must be cautious therefore of believing, that it was printed at *Munich*, in the Year 1617, as Father *Southwell* asserts. *James Baldus* was not capable of executing such an Undertaking at the Age of fourteen Years.

(3) *Sotuel, Biblioth. Soc. Jes. pag. 356.*
(4) *Judgm. on the Poets, Tom. 5. n. 1507, pag. 42.*
(5) *Compare this with the Dialogue of* Mariangelus Accursius *which I have mentioned in the Remark* [*F*] *of his Article.*

(*a*) *His Great Great Grand-Father left the Name of* Cantagallina, *an illustrious Family of* Perugia, *from which he was descended, and took this.* Fabr. Scharloncin. *See below, Citation* (*e*).

BALDUS (*a*) (**Bernardin**), Abbot of *Guastalla*, born at *Urbino*, in the Year 1553, was one of the most learned Men of his time. He made such great Progress under his first Tutors, that he found himself able to translate the *Phænomena* of *Aratus* into *Italian* Verse, while he was yet but a young Scholar. His Father, perceiving by these early Trials, that he had a very promising Son, sent him to *Padua* in the Year 1573 [*A*]. Bernardin studied *Homer* there under Emanuel Margunius (*b*), and

(*b*) *He was of* Candia, *and Professor of the* Greek *Tongue at* Padua.

[*A*] *His Father, perceiving his Capacity, by these early Trials* ——— *sent him to* Padua.] Correct, by this, a Fault of *Nictus Erythræus*. I am sure he had no Intention to lessen the Fame of our *Baldus* in any thing, and yet he did lessen it very much; but it was done inadvertently, and for want of observing the order of Time. He has said, that after the Lectures of Margunius (1), *Baldus* thought himself sufficiently

(1) *Not* Margunius, *as it is in* Erythræus.

BALDUS.

and, by himself, almost all the other *Greek* Poets, and understood them very well. He composed a Book at *Padua* concerning *Machines of War* (c), which made his Name fly beyond the *Alps*, and increased his desire of understanding *French* and *High Dutch*; for he thought it was a piece of good Manners to learn the Language of those, whose Affection he had acquired. He became Master of those two Languages with a great deal of Ease. He was forced to leave *Padua* on account of the Plague, and, being returned to *Urbino*, he applied himself for five Years to *Frederic Commandino*, an excellent Professor of Mathematics, and learned of him all the parts of That Science. He was extremely sorry for the Death of That learned Man; and, having applied himself to write his Life, this drew him into a design to write those of all the *Mathematicians*. He laboured twelve Years about it. The *Commentaries*, which he published in 1582, on *Aristotle*'s Mechanics, discovered his Capacity in that sort of Knowledge. To unbend his Mind in those difficult Studies, he wrote a Poem in his Mother-Tongue concerning the *Art of Navigation*. *Ferdinand de Gonzague*, Prince of *Molfetta*, and Lord of *Guastalla*, being a great Lover of Mathematics, would have our *Baldus* near him. In That Court he began to write on *Vitruvius*, and composed the Book, *De verborum Vitruvianorum significatione*. A Fit of Sickness having hindred him from taking a Voyage into *Spain* with his Master, he employed the leisure Time, the absence of *Ferdinand de Gonzague* gave him, in writing a very Methodical *Treatise of the Court* (d), and several other Works [B]. He was made Abbot of *Guastalla* in 1586, without ever once asking it; and, from that time, he applied himself wholly to the Study of the Canon-Law, the Fathers, and Councils, and the Oriental Languages, without excepting the *Arabic* [C]. Having composed five Books, *De nova Gnomonice*, in the Year 1595, he translated, in the following Year, the *Chaldee Paraphrase on the Pentateuch*, and enlarged it with Commentaries; after which he translated the Book of *Job*, and the *Lamentations of Jeremiah*, from the *Hebrew*, and added *Notes* to them. He spent some spare Hours in explaining a Plate, which is at *Eugubio* [D], on which there are some old *Tuscan* Inscriptions. He began

sufficiently able to translate some *Greek* Poems into his Mother-Tongue: "Apud quem tantum profecit, "ut eo duce & cercum quodammodo lucente obscu- "rissima Græcorum quorundam poëtarum loca pene- "traverit - - - - - - Quamobrem eâ est incensum animi "alacritate atque fiduciâ, ut ausus sit poëmata Græca "in nostrum sermonem convertere (2). — *Under* "*whom he made such Proficiency, that, by his Instru-* "*ction, and, as it were, shewing a Light, he was able* "*to understand the most difficult Passages of certain* "*Greek Poets* — *This gave him so much Spirit* "*and Courage, as to attempt the Translation of some* "*Greek Poems into our Language.*" He had translated a Poem of *Aratus* before he went to *Padua*. [B] *He wrote several other Works.*] This Remark shall only contain the Titles of some of our *Baldus*'s Writings; I mean those, which have not been mentioned in the Text of this Article, whether the Author composed them during his Master's Voyage, or at any other time. I say, then, that he translated *Heronem de Automatis & Balistis*; the *Paralipomena of Quintus Calaber*, and the *Poem of Musæus*; and wrote a Book of Mathematical Paradoxes; another, *de Scamillis imparibus Vitruvii*; another, *de Firmamento & Aquis*; another on the Description of the Temple by *Ezekiel*; another, *De Historia scribenda Legibus*; another, of the Antiquities of *Guastalla*; the Life of *Frederic*, and that of *Gui Ubaldus*, Dukes of *Urbino*; *Oeconomia Trop logica* in *S. Matthæum*; several *Latin* and *Italian* Poems, among which That, intituled *Desphobe*, is an Imitation of the *Cassandra* of *Lycophron*. The following Remarks will give the Title of some of his other Books. I shall observe here, that *Nicius Erythræus* has reason to say, that the Description of the Temple is a very difficult Matter, but he was in the wrong to take *Jeremiah* for *Ezekiel* "Jerosolymitani templi — descriptionem, *says he* (3), "per Hieremiam literis consignatam & traditam, rem "involutam & multis difficultatibus obsessam, evolvit, "illustravit, atque hominum intelligentiæ aperuit. — "*The Description of the Temple of Jerusalem, left us,* "*in writing, by Jeremiah, a Subject obscured and at-* "*tended with many Difficulties, he cleared and illu-* "*strated, and made universally intelligible*"

[C] *He applied to the Study of the Oriental Languages, without excepting the* Arabic] He studied it at *Rome*, with *John Baptist Raimondi*, and also the *Sclavonian* Tongue, with so much Application, that he was almost a Stranger to all manner of News. Romæ dum viveret fere nescivit quid gereretur in aulis: Arabicæ enim linguæ cum *Jo. Baptista Raimondo* diligentissimus studuit, & arcana industria Sclavonicæ,

quam perfectè callebat (4). He translated the *Geographical Garden* of an anonymous Author out of *Arabic*, and composed a *Dictionary* of that Language. He believed, that this unknown Author lived towards the end of the XIth Century. If *Marc Velserus* had lived, he would have caused the Translation of that Geographical Work, and the other Writings of *Baldus*, to be printed (5).

[D] *He took pains in the explaining of a Plate, which is at* Eugubio] *Scbouckius*, having but a confused Notion of this Work of *Bernardin Baldus*, ascribed another to him, which is none of his. "E sterquilinio "Anniano Bernardinus Baldus nuper collegit Antiqui- "tates Etruscas anno 1637. Florentiæ evulgando "volumen typis perquam elegantibus cujus hæc in- "scriptio: *Etrujcarum antiquitatum fragmenta qui-* "*bus urbis Romæ aliarumque gentium primordia,* "*mores & res gestæ indicentur, à Curtio Inghira-* "*mio reperta Scornelli prope Vulterram anno salutis* "M D C XXXVII. *Etbrufco vero* cIↃ cIↃ cIↃ cccc xcv "(6). — *Bernardin Baldus lately collected the Antiqui-* "*ties of* Tuscany, *out of some Rubbish at* Annium, "*in the Year* 1637, *and published a Volume at* "Florence, *in a very neat Character, with this Title* ; "*Some Fragments of the Antiquities of* Tuscany, "*shewing the Origin of the City of* Rome, *and of* "*other States, together with their Customs and* "*Transactions, found by* Curtius Ingharamius, *at* "Scornelli, *near* Vulterra, *in the Year of Christ,* 1637, "*of* Tuscany, 3495." How could a Man, who knew that *Baldus* died in the Year 1617, commit such a Mistake? What is the more surprizing, is, that the same *Scbouckius*, after speaking in this Manner, at the Sixty seventh Page, speaks, as he ought to do, in the Two hundred and seventeenth Page. "Si- "mili ratione egit Bernardinus Baldus, vir cætero- "quin longè doctissimus, annis abhinc ferme quin- "quaginta evulgando suam quasi divinationem in ta- "bulam Æneam Eugubinam linguâ Etruscâ veteri "perscriptam, simul abutendo operâ Marci Velseri "viri cæteroquin judiciosissimi (7). — *Such was* "*also the Conduct of* Bernardin Baldus, *otherwise ex-* "*tremely learned, who, about fifty Years ago, upon* "*publishing his Conjecture upon a Copper-Plate, en-* "*graved in the old* Tuscan *Language, at the same* "*time reflected upon the Work of* Marcus Velserus, *a* "*Man otherwise very judicious.*" Why then did he not correct his Mistake? Perhaps he had forgot it, as it happens but too often to those, who are fond of writing much. They can hardly maintain that Character, without copying, in haste, whatsoever they find in all manner of Books. See what *Scbarfencbius*

BALDUS. BALESDENS.

began a very great Work in the Year 1603, I mean *A Description of the World*. His Plan was no less Historical than Geographical, and extended to the least Boroughs of which the Modern Writers have said any thing. He finished the whole Work, as to the Matter [E], but put only part of it in Order. He died the Twelfth of *October* 1617, after having laboured under a great Rheum for forty Days (e) [F]. He was extremely laborious [G], without Ambition, or Vain-glory, always ready to excuse other Mens Faults, which he grounded on a very good Reason [H]; very devout, not only for a Mathematician, but also for a Churchman [I].

(e) *Taken from a Letter of* Fabricius Scharloneius *ad illustrissimum & reverendissimum dominum* Lælium Ruinum, *Epis. copum Balneoregiensem, ex-Nuntium Apostolicum ad Poloniæ regem. See also* Nicius Erythræus, Pinacoth. I. pag. 4. *and the Funeral Oration of* Baldus, *by* Marc Ant. Virgilius, *not printed in* 1607, *as Mr* Teissier *says, Bibl. p. 223, but in* 1637.

nus says concerning this Work of *Baldus*. " Tabulam Etruscam Eugubinam interpretatus fuit : in ea autem divinatione, ut ajebat, subcisivas unius mensis horas consumpsit. —— *He explained a Tuscan Plate of* Eugubio : *and spent, in those Conjectures, as he said himself, the spare Hours of one Month.*" Our *Baldus* is mentioned in the new Edition of the *Eponymologium of Magirus*, only to let us know, that he published a Book, in the Year 1637, the very same that *Schoockius* ascribes to him. Is not this an admirable Choice?

[E] *He finished the Description of the World, as to the Matter.*] These are the Words of his Historian. " Totum opus ad umbilicum perduxit : non digessit " tamen universum, quatuor, aut, ni fallor, quinque " tantum tomi fuerunt ordine alphabetico dispositi. " supereßent septem aut octo disponendi, quantum " ex chartarum & fasciculorum mole conjicere licet. " —— *He brought the whole Work to Perfection ; but had not adjusted, I think, above four or five Volumes of it in alphabetical Order ; there might be such as seven or eight more to be digested, as near as one could guess from the Quantity and Heaps of Papers.*" I do not believe, the List, *Fabricius Scharloneius* has given of our *Baldus*'s Works, is imperfect ; but, according to the ill Custom of most of those, who give such sort of Lists, he does not distinguish the Books, which have been printed, from those, which have not (8). I have not transcribed the whole List.

(8) *See, above, the beginning of Remark* [E] AURELUS.

[F] *He died —— after having laboured under a great Rheum for forty Days.*] I thought I might thus translate *Scharloncinus*'s Words: *Posteaquam dies 40 vehementi Distillatione vexatus fuisset.* *Vossius* understood a *Catarrh*, by *Distillatio*, and he is not in the wrong to pretend, that these two Words are synonymous. That of Rheum seemed to me the most proper ; because a *Catarrh* seldom continues so long as forty Days. *Moreri*, by a great Mistake, construes this an Apoplexy of forty Days.

[G] *He was extremely laborious.*] He would rise at Midnight to study, and read while he was eating. " In studiis sic assiduus fuit ut sæpe & legeret & " comederet. S. Augustini de civitate Dei inter " prandium evolvit ; statim à noctis meridie dum et " vires firmiores essent ad lucubrandum surgebat " (9). —— *He was so earnest in his Studies, that he often both eat and read. He thrice went thro' St Augustin's Book* de Civitate Dei, *during the Times of his dining: So long as his Constitution held good, he rose at Midnight to his Studies.*" He reckoned an *Euclid*, translated into *Arabick*, one of his Books of Recreation. *A prandio Euclidem Arabicè editum, vel Libellum aliquem Germanicum, aut*

(9) *Scharloncinus in Vita* Baldi.

Gallicum in manus sumebat (10). *After Dinner he used to take into his hand an Arabic Euclid, or some high Dutch or French Book.* Happy are those, who can take so much Pains, without impairing their Health.

(10) Id. ib.

Felices quibus ista licent, miramur & illos,
Et nostri misereamur.

Happy are they whose Studies never tire ;
Ourselves we pity, while we them admire.

[H] *He was always ready to excuse the Faults of others, which he grounded on a very good Reason.*] If we knew the Insides, said he, of those, we take for the best of Men, we should find not one, but who deserves Correction. *Facile parcendum esse dicebat iis maximè qui in re levi impegissent, quoniam si quos censemus optimos, nudos conspiceremus, nullum eorum non judicaremus multis dignum verberibus* (11): This may seem too far stretched : Perhaps it were better to keep to Cardinal *Mazarin*'s Maxim. He said, *That the greatest Men were like Beasts for Sacrifice, which, though never so nicely chosen, had always something bad, when their Entrails were examined* (12). I remember, on this Occasion, a Passage of Father *Rapin*, which I thought very judicious the first time I read it. It is a Thought he makes use of, by way of Apology, for *Cicero*. There are, says he (13), *certain things at the bottom of the Souls of the greatest Men, which, if they could be perceived, would shew them to be as weak as others* —— *and often times the Reputation of those, we so much admire, does not proceed so much from their Art in displaying their good Qualities, as from That of hiding their bad ones, and not suffering themselves to be seen into.*

A REFIXION *on hidden Faults.*

(11) Id. ib.

(12) *See the Preface of* Mr Chanut's *Memoirs.*

(13) *In the Comparison of* Demosthenes *with* Cicero.

(14) *Thus I translate* obesa bus fellis omnibus facierum facie: *bat : Which Words, perhaps, mean only, that* be offeciated *every* Holyday. *but it cannot be dened, I say, is contained in the Latin Words of* Scharloncinus.

[I] *He was very devout, not only for a Mathematician, but also for a Churchman.*] He fasted twice a Week ; he communicated every Holy-Day (14), and was very charitable to the poor. His Mother said, that, when he was but a Year old, he did not only look upon the Altars and Images with Joy, but also with Veneration (15). *With Joy,* I do not question for it is usual for Children to leap at the Sight of Guildings, Ornaments, and Images : but, as for *Veneration,* That is another thing ; they have at most but mechanical Motions, just as they are used. Our *Baldus* died well fortified with all the Sacraments of the Church, and in the Arms of Friars. *Spiritum Deo reddidit Sacramentis Ecclesiæ omnibus ritè munitus* (16). *Quemadmodum sanctissimè vixerat, ita etiam sanctissimum in complexu cucullatorum patrum extremum vitæ spiritum edidit* (17).

(15) Scharlon. ibid.

(16) Id. ib.

(17) Nic. Erythræus Pinacoth. 1, pag. 7.

BALESDENS (JOHN), Advocate in the Parliament of *Paris*, and in the Council, was born at *Paris*. He was admitted into the *French Academy* about the Year 1647, in the room of *Malleville*; and, if he had not given up his Pretensions to Mr *Corneille*[*A*], he had succeeded *Mainard*, who died before *Malleville*. The Chancellor *Seguier* was his *Mecænas* (a). He published several Works, of which he was not the Author [B]. I think he lived till towards the Year 1676 (b). I have not found

(a) *See* The History of the French Academy, pag. 230, 238.

(b) *The State of France, in 1686, places* Balesd ns in *the List of the dead Academists, between* Conrart *and des* Marets : *Conrart died in September,* 1675.

[*A*] *He gave up his Pretensions to Mr* Corneille.] See what the Historian of the *Academy* says of it. " Mr *Corneille* was afterwards received in the place " of Mr *Mainard*. Mr *Balesdens* had also been pro-" posed, and, as he had the Honour to belong to the " Chancellor, the *Academy* said That respect for it's " Protector, as to depute five of it's Members to him, " to know whether both Persons proposed were equal-" ly agreeable to him. The Chancellor assured them " he would leave the Society entirely at their Li-" berty ; but, when they began to deliberate on their " Choice, the Abbot of *Cerisy* presented them with " a Letter from Mr *de Balesdens*, full of a great many

" Compliments to them, and to Mr *Corneille*, to " whom he desired they might give the Preference, " protesting that he paid him this Honour, as his due, " on all Accounts. The Letter was read, and " commended by the Assembly : and he (1) was " afterwards received into the first Vacancy, which " was That of Mr *de Malleville* ; but I do not find " on what Day ; for, since that Time, the long and " frequent Indispositions of the Secretary of the Aca-" demy have left great Vacancies in the Regi-" sters (2)."

(1) Mr Balesdens.

(2) Pellisson Hist. de l'Acad. Franç. pag. 230, Edit. 1672, in 12mo.

[B] *He published several Works, of which he was not the Author.*] Mr *Pellisson* gives this List of all that

BALESDENS. BALMIS.

found his Name in the *Petition of the Dictionaries*; and yet it ought to be there, according to the *Menagiana* [C]. He had lived in the College of *Harcour* [D].

that *Balesdens* published (3). "He translated the Book entituled, *The Penitent Sinner's Looking glass*; and, among other Manuscripts, which he had collected, he gave the following to the Public: *Cartesudium Logicæ, seu Logica memorativa, vel Poëtica, R. Patris Thomæ Murnor, cum notis & conjecturis. Rudimenta cognitionis Dei & sui, Petri Seguierii Præsidis insulati. Elogia clarorum virorum Joannis Papirii Massonii*, in two Volumes. *Gregorii Turonensis opera pia, cum Vitis Patrum jui temporis*, in two Volumes. *The Acts of the Conveyance of Dauphiné, made to the Crown of* France. *A Treatise of Brandy, by Mr* John Bronaut, *the King's Physician*. He published, also, Æsop's *Fables, corrected by himself, in* French, *for the King's Instruction, with Maxims Political and Moral*." Mr *de Marolles* says, That *Balesdens* gave him "several Letters in a figurative Style, without mentioning a very great Number of others, of which he proposed to make several Volumes, there was such a prodigious Number of them (4)."

[C] *His Name ought to have been in the* Petition of the Dictionaries, *according to the* Menagiana.] In Effect, these Words are found there: *the first Sample of my Poetry*, says Mr *Menage, was the* Petition of the Dictionaries. *I was looking for Rhimes to finish it.* Mr du Puy *sent me* Claquedent *to Rhime to* Baleident (5). Mr *Menage* had the best Memory in the World; but yet he might mistake one thing for another, even in those, which personally concerned him. I do not believe, that he asked for the Rhime in question, to finish his *Petition of the Dictionaries*; for That incomparable Satire was finished before *Balesdens* came into the Academy. He was not admitted before the Year 1647, or 1648; and That *Petition* was finished about the Year 1642: I shall prove it from the History of the Academy. Mr *Pellisson* relates, that Mr *Menage* suppressed That *Petition, after be had made it*: He goes on thus; "It remained above ten Years concealed among his Papers, 'till a Person, who had them all in his keeping, suffered himself to be robbed of it, by a Person not unknown to us, who soon gave several Copies of it (6)." Mr *Pellisson* had said, in the same Page, That "a Printer had lately published *this Petition*, in a small Form, with many Faults, *and that* it had since been more correctly printed, in Quarto." Without doubt he means, by This more correct Impression, the Edition of Mr *Menage's Miscellanea*, which appeared in the Year 1652. However it be, the Year 1652 is the Date of Mr *Pellisson's* Book; and consequently the *Petition of the Dictionaries* was finished in 1642 (7). It might be said, that, when Mr *Menage* was tired with keeping That Piece, which he had suppressed, and was resolved to publish it himself, among his other Poems, he designed to enlarge it, by introducing the new Members of the Academy; and that, if *Balesdens* is not among them, it is because the Rhime, which Mr du *Puy* sent, did not please, or was too difficult to come in there. Upon this Supposition, Mr *Balesdens* was obliged to his Name, for escaping the Lash, in the *Petition of the Dictionaries*, and That Name, so untractable, with respect to rhiming, produced a much more favourable Effect, than Those of *Tuttuanus* (8), and *Earinus* (9): But I do not think, there is any room to make this Supposition; for the *Petition*, printed in the Year 1652, does not contain the Name of any one Member, admitted into the Academy, since the Year 1640; and yet there were some among those new ones, who lay open to Mr *Menage*, as much as he could desire. Was good Mr *du Rier* a Translator without Reproach?

[D] *He lived in the College of* Harcour.] Mr *de Marolles*, who informs me of this, adds, That *Balesdens's* Landlord was *a good Man, whose Name was* le Landex, *since Doctor of Divinity, and Uncle to the two Mazures, Curates of St Paul, one after another* (10). He says, *That* Balesdens *was, at That Time, of a merry Humour, and of a diverting Conversation*.

BALMIS (ABRAHAM *de*) a *Jewish* Physician, born at *Lecci* [A], in the Kingdom of *Naples*, flourished at *Venice* in the Beginning of the XVIth Century. He composed a *Hebrew* Grammar [B], printed at *Venice* in *Hebrew* and *Latin*, by *Daniel Bomberg*, in the Year 1523. He translated into *Latin* several Commentaries of *Averroës* on *Aristotle*, as also some Works of *Avem Pace*, and wrote a Book of his own, *De Demonstratione*, and another *De Substantia Orbis*. See *Gesner's Bibliotheca*, and the *Bibliotheca Rabbinica of Bartolocci*. We must not forget, that he taught in the University of *Padua* (*a*), and that he took a much greater Pleasure in confuting what was advanced by others, than in laying down any thing certain of his own [C].

[A] *He was born at* Lecci.] You will find these Words in *Gesner's Bibliotheca*: "Ibidem (1) hic author natum se scribit in Litio civitate agri Salentini quæ à Brundusio Hydrunto & Graia Gallipoli 24 milliaribus distat, eodem in loco sita ubi olim Rudiæ patria Ennii, ex reliquiis Rudiarum nacta originem (2). — There this Author writes, *that he was born in* Litium, *a City of the* Salentines, *which is distant from* Brundusium, *from* Otranto, *and* Græcian Gallipoli, *Twenty four Miles, situated in the same Place, where* Rudiæ, *the Native Place of* Ennius, *formerly stood, and was built with the Ruins of* Rudiæ." I wonder, that neither *Toppi*, nor *Leonard Nicodemo*, have mentioned him, in the *Bibliotheca Napoletana*.

[B] *He composed a* Hebrew Grammar.] He intituled it *Mikne Abraham*, that is to say, *Abraham's Possession*. Father *Bartolocci* is mistaken, when he says, that *Daniel Bomberg* translated it into *Latin* (3). If he had consulted the Preface, he might have seen, that *Daniel Bomberg* caused That Translation to be made by others. First of all, he employed the Author himself, and ordered him to make his Translation literal. This Strictness was observed for some time. Afterwards the Author used a greater Freedom, in order to have some Elegancy: After his Death, *Calonymos*, who finished the Translation, took infinitely more Liberty, and *Bomberg* did not oppose it (4). This shews, that *de Balmis*, was no longer living in the Year 1523. Mr *Simon* says, that the Translation of That Grammar is *word for word, and very barbarous* (5); that, *in truth, there is but little Method, in That Author, but that otherwise he shews great Erudition*, and that, *in a great many Places, he corrects the Errors of the Grammarians, who wrote before him* (6). *Huetius* gives a very faithful Account of the *Latin* Translation (7). He says, that *de Balmis* began it, and that *Calos Calonymos* finished it; that the first rendered it barbarous, and more obscure, than the Original; and that the second, thinking to avoid the Defects of the other, ran into the opposite Extream.

[C] *He took a much greater Pleasure in confuting ------ than in laying down any Thing certain of his own.*] *Munster* makes this Reflection on him. "Abraham de Balmis, *says he* (8), nihil aliud agere mihi visus est quam veterum doctrinam perpetuo convellere atque impugnare, magis in infectando occupatus quam in docendo. At in dubium tantum vocare priscorum præceptiones, cum interim nihil certi statuas, non docere est sed ridere. ——— Abraham de Balmis *seems to me to do nothing but continually attack, and oppose, the Doctrine of his Predecessors, being more taken up with conjuring, than with teaching. But, to weaken the Authority of the old Maxims, without establishing something new in their room, is not the way to instruct, but to turn every thing into Jest.*"

BALTHASAR

BALTHASAR. 621

BALTHASAR (CHRISTOPHER) was a Man of Learning and Merit, in the XVIIth Century. He applied himself principally to the Study of Ecclesiastical History, and This Application gave him a very great Disgust for the *Romish* Doctrines, and a great Desire to embrace the Protestant Religion. He had a considerable Post in the *Presidial* of *Auxerre* (a), and, because he must either resolve to quit that, or still keep his Religion, he was for some time in doubt which part to take: But, at last, Conscience got the better, and obliged him to leave *Auxerre*, his Estate, Office, Relations, and Friends, and go to *Charenton*, where he was publickly received into the Reformed Church. He persevered in it to his Death, and edified his Brethren as well by his good Life, as by his Conversation. The Expences he was obliged to be at in *Paris* being too great for the Circumstances he was in, and his Conversion exposing him too much in such a City as That, he considered, that it would be better for him to retire into some Province, and was very well pleased to find himself invited to go to *Castres* by a young and rich Counsellor of the *Bipartite Court of the Edict* (b), who lodged him in his House, and allowed him a reasonable Pension. This Counsellor thought himself very fortunate in having a Learned Man with him, who might teach him a great many fine things by his Instructions and Conversation. But Mr *Balthasar*, desiring to labour for the Public, would have all his time at his own disposal, and for that reason he took leave of his Counsellor. His Design was favoured by the National Synod of *Loudon* in the Year 1659; for That Assembly granted him a Pension of Seven hundred and fifty Livres, to be paid by all the Churches of *France*, according to the Repartition, which was made of them (c). Before That Synod was held, he had prepared a good number of Dissertations on material Points against Cardinal *Baronius* (d). He gave four or five of them to a Minister of *Castres*, who was one of the Deputies of the Province of *Upper Languedoc* and *Upper Guienne*. They were presented to Mr *Daillé*, Moderator of That National Synod, who, of all the Ministers, was best able to judge of the Goodness of those Pieces. Mr *Daillé* was very well pleased with them, and gave all the Company a very advantageous Character of them. He brought them to *Paris*, where it was hoped they would have been printed; for they were thought to deserve Publication. But the Event made it appear, that no Measures were, or could be, taken for it. The Author, who was very old, and afflicted with the Stone, happened to die; Mr *Daillé* died also; and, after this, the Church of *Castres* wrote several Letters to recover those Dissertations, but they could not so much as learn what was become of them. Mr *Balthasar* left some others not quite finished, and many Collections, most of which consisted of separate Notes, wherein he had set down the Authorities and Testimonies he was to make use of against Cardinal *Baronius*. It is pity, that all this should remain in a Chest, in the Possession of I know not who (e). Mr *Balthasar* wrote very well in *Latin*; his Panegyric on Mr *Fouquet* is in a fine Style. This is all that I have seen of his, and I cannot tell whether he published any thing else. If he had been less scrupulous about his Language, he might have made a quicker Progress in his Censure on *Baronius*. However, I believe what has been said of his Scruples about his *Latin*, is something Hyperbolical [*A*]. What is reported of his Credulity in Witchcraft seems to me more likely [*B*].

(a) *It was That at the King's Advocate.*

(b) *His Name was Mr au Faur.*

(c) *It was at the Request, and Recommendation, of the Synod of Upper Languedoc, and of Upper Guienne. He enjoyed already a Pension of 300 Livres. See the Acts of the National Synod of Loudon, in the Synodicon of M. Quick, Tom. 2, pag. 572.*

(d) *He gave them the Title of Distribæ. His Work was in Latin.*

(e) *Taken from a Memoir, communicated by Mr de la Devéze, heretofore Minister at Castres, and now at the Hague.*

[*A*] *What has been said of his Scruples about his Latin is something Hyperbolical.*] Among several Pieces, the Abbot *de Marolles* published in the latter Part of his Life, there is one, which contains the *Names of Those, who had presented him with their Books, or honoured him with their Compliments, in an extraordinary Manner.* There we find the following Words: "*Christopher Balthazar*, who had made so "many Collections, with his own Hand, for several "manuscript historical Treatises. He designed to "compose some Animadversions on the Annals of "*Baronius*; but went a little too late about it, and "had not yet formed his Stile, intending to polish "it yet farther, after too elegant a Manner, inso- "much, that he could not write one whole Page "of his Book in a Day, though he was above Sixty "three Years of Age." If the Abbot *de Marolles* had dated the Time, which he pointed at, we had known at what Age Mr *Balthasar* obtained a Pension from the Synod of *Loudon*.

[*B*] *Notice has been taken of his Credulity in Witchcraft.*] The same Abbot *de Marolles* supplies me with the whole Commentary on This Text. The Passage is somewhat long, but I will not abridge it: What will not serve for one Purpose, may serve for another. "Let us return now into our Closet, where "one day, in a Company of learned Men, were "Mr *Balthasar*, who is so skillful in the Know- "ledge of History, and Mr *de Sorbieres*, whose "Affability and Learning deserve also much Com- "mendation: The one, from being a Catholic, had "embraced the pretended Reformed Religion (1), and "the other, from being a Protestant, was returned "to the Catholic Church. Whereupon, the first be- "ing taken to task, on account, that the Motives "of his Change could not be comprehended, con- "sidering his great Knowledge, said, he was induced "to it, from a Belief, that there was more Purity, "and Simplicity, in the other Communion, than "in ours: That it had re-established the Holy Liber- "ty of the Gospel, under the mild Yoke of Faith "in our Lord's Promises; and that it had taken "away all Abuses, and Superstitions, to place, in their "room, a Worship agreeable to the Usage of the Pri- "mitive Church. All the Parts of his Answer were "disputed; but That proving ineffectual, the Dis- "course was turned to other Matters; and from the "Number of Stories told of Sorcerers, and Appari- "tions, which would scarcely be credited by Children: "whereby it appeared, that he, who had shewn "himself such an Enemy to Superstition, admitted "it, in some Measure, by a sufficient Credulity for "these Things; besides that, having explained him- "self on the vain Predictions of Astrologers, he dis- "covered plainly, that he adhered but too much to "them, as well as to Those of *Nostradamus*, in his "Centuries, than which nothing in the World can "be more gross. This was the Judgment of the "whole Company, in which was present the Abbot "*Talman* (2), a Man of fine Parts, Mr *Baudeolt* (3), "Abbot of *Massai*, and the Abbot of *Verdus*, who "have so intirely shook off all popular Errors, with "Mr *de la Herpiniere* of *Blois*, so rational, in all "his

(1) *The Memoirs of the Abbot de Marolles were printed off the 5th of January, 1656. Mr Balthasar had therefore made his Abjuration in 1655, at least.*

(2) *He ought to have said Tallemant.*

(3) *He ought to have said Bourdelot.*

BALZAC.

" his Sentiments, Mr *de Marſay le Boſſu*, Governor
" of *Gien*, whoſe great Knowledge is accompanied
" with a noble Elocution, and ſome others, whereof
" one only endeavoured to maintain the Opinion,
" which had been rejected (4)." [4] *The Abbot de Marolles's Memoirs,* pag. 276.

BALZAC, a small Lordſhip in *Angoumois*, on the River *Charante*, is famous for having given it's Name to, and been a long time the Reſidence of, one of the moſt Eloquent Writers of the XVIIth Century [*A*], namely, the famous Mr *de BALZAC*. His Name was *John Lewis Guez*, and he was the Son of *William Guez*, a Gentleman of *Languedoc* [*B*], who was very deſerving, and who, having devoted himſelf early to the Service of *Roger de Bellegarde*, Mareſchal of *France*, and Governor of the Marquiſate of *Saluces*, conducted ſeveral Affairs with a great deal of Prudence. Before he was Twenty ſix Years of Age, he was ſent to the Court of *Philibert Emanuel*, Duke of *Savoy*, about ſome Negotiations of Conſequence, which he managed very ſucceſsfully, and gained the Eſteem of This Prince. Some time after, he was Governor to the Son of the Mareſchal *de Bellegarde*: This young Lord was killed in the Battle of *Coutras*, in the Year 1587 (*a*). The Father died in the Year 1579 (*b*). So that *William Guez*, having loſt theſe two Patrons, found a third in the Duke *de Epernon*, who deſired to have him near him. His Services proved very conſiderable on ſeveral troubleſome Occaſions. *Henry IV*, having obſerved with what Addreſs, Integrity, and Steadineſs, This Gentleman diſpatched the Affairs, on which the Duke *de Epernon* ſent him to Court, would willingly have retained him in his Service (*c*); but found him more inclined to a Country Life, than to That of the Court, with which his Virtue would not eaſily ſuit. This good Gentleman fixed himſelf in the Province of *Angoumois*, where he died the Twentieth of *September*, 1650, at the Age of an Hundred Years [*C*]. He had married a Gentlewoman of the Family of *Neſmond*, with whom he lived Sixty four Years in perfect Concord (*d*). He had by her, among other Children, the Famous Mr *de Balzac*, whom I am going to mention. See the *Latin Elogy of William Guez*, compoſed by Mr *de Girac*, and printed at the end of the *Chriſtian Socrates*. I have taken from it what has been juſt now read, to which I add; I. That *William Guez* did ſo much reſemble Father *Narni*, that, the firſt time Mr *de Balzac* ſaw That famous Preacher, he *thought his Father had diſguiſed himſelf in a Capuchin's habit* (*e*). II. That, among ſeveral other Virtues of *William Guez*, Don *Peter de St Romuald* praiſes the Magnificence, which he ſhewed in the Structure of the Caſtle of *Balzac*, and in That of his Houſe at *Angoulême* (*f*). That Houſe was *furniſhed with ſuch exquiſite Rarities, and particularly Pictures and other Ornaments*, that the Queen Mother, *Mary de Medicis*, would lodge no where elſe during her abode in *Angoulême*. III. That one of his other Sons was called Mr *de Rouſſines* (*g*). IV. That he had a Daughter, who is very often mentioned by Monſieur de Balzac [*D*].

(*a*) Father Anſelm's Hiſtory of the great Officers, pag. 194.

(*b*) Id. ibid.

(*c*) See the Choice Letters of Balzac, p. 364. Edit. of Holland.

(*d*) She lived 'till the Year 1653. See the 15th Letter of Balzac to Conrart, Book 3.

(*e*) Balzac, Letter 27, to Chapelain, lib. 3.

(*f*) St Romuald, Three Chronol. ad Ana. 1627.

(*g*) Mr de Balzac wrote the 4oth Letter of the 8th Book to him.

[*A*] *It is famous, for having given it's Name . . . . to one of the moſt eloquent Writers of the XVIIth Century.*] I cannot tell what *Moreri* builds upon, when he ſays, that Thoſe of the Family of *Guez* have enjoyed the Name of the Lordſhip of *Balſac*. I. Firſt of all, he ought to have known, that *Balzac* is the Name of This Village, and *Balſac* That of the ancient Family of *Balſac d'Entragues* (1). II. Secondly, none but *John Lewis Guez* uſed the Name of *Balzac*; his Father always retained the Name of his Family (2); and if, after the Death of *John Lewis*, ſome of his Relations called themſelves *Balzac*, I do not believe it came to Mr *Moreri's* Knowledge. In ſhort, what has been ſaid by ſome Perſons, " That, if Mr *de Balzac* had not taken the " Name of his Lordſhip, his Family Name is the " Head of his Works would have prevented his " great Succeſs in the World, and that People would " not have conceived ſo favourable an Idea of his " Letters, if they had been entituled *Monſieur Guez's* " *Letters*; and that it is believed, the Name of *Balzac* being taken for That of a Noble and Ancient " Houſe, ſufficiently known, procured him the more " Reſpect (3);" this, I ſay, is partly probable, and partly very falſe. It is probable, that ſuch a plain Name, as That of *Guez*, might have prejudiced an Author in the Title of a Book (4); but it is very falſe, that *John Lewis Guez* put the Name of *Balzac* in the Title Page of his Books, to avoid this Inconveniency, and to make People believe, that they came from a great Lord; This was the thing, which *Sorel* would be at, with his confuſed, and perplexing Expreſſions. Once again, this is falſe: for *John Lewis Guez* had taken the Name of *Balzac*, before he thought of printing his Letters. I cannot apprehend how it happened, that Mr *Menage*, who cauſed This Author's Poems, and *Latin* Letters, to be printed, where we ſee, both in the Title, and at the Top of every Page, the Name of *Joannis Ludovici Guezii Balzacii*, ſhould ſay, that they bear the Name of *Joannis Ludovici Guezaei Balzacii* (5). I ſhould think, that the Printer of the *Anti-Baillet* put *Guezaei* inſtead of *Guezii*, if I did not ſee the ſame Fault, in a very correct Edition of Mr *Menage's* Poems (6).

[*B*] *Balzac - - - - - was the Son of* William *Guez, a Gentleman of* Languedoc.] Sometimes Mr *de Balzac* repreſents his Extraction, in ſuch a manner, as to give us an high Idea of it. He ſays, *That Thoſe, to whom be has the Honour of being related, have founded Monaſteries in ſeveral Parts of the Kingdom, and that* Angoulême *and* Toulouſe *are proud of the Marks of their Piety* (7). He tells us, in another Place, that the Great Grand-father of his Great-Great Grand-father was preſented with three Pariſhes, in *Languedoc*, by the Counteſs *Alix* (8). *Theophilus* gives us a quite contrary Idea of Mr *de Balzac*'s Family.

[*C*] *Who died at the Age of an hundred Years.*] I have made uſe of a round Number, after Mr *de Girac*, whom I have quoted; but I ought to rectify the Matter a little, by means of a Letter of Mr *Guez*, to his Son, ſigned *Guez*, and dated the twentieth of *November* 1642 (9). *He was then entered into the Eighty ninth Year of his Age.* He could not therefore be an hundred Years old, the twentieth of *September*, 1650, which was the Day of his Death. That Letter is a preſſing Exhortation to publiſh ſome Manuſcripts, but, above all, the Apologies againſt *Phylarchus*.

[*D*] *He had a Daughter, who is very often mentioned by* Mr de Balzac.] She was married to Mr *de Campagnolle*, who died Captain of the Guards, at *Montauban*, and who was the Brother of a brave Man, whom *Thuanus* ſometimes mentions (10). That Captain of the Guards left a Son, who was killed at the Seige of *Lens* (11), and a Daughter, who is the Lady of CAMPAGNOLLE, ſometimes mentioned in Mr *de Balzac*'s Letters (12). He ſhews much Fondneſs for That Niece, and gives good

(1) Sorel's Knowledge of good Books, pag. 28, Edit. of Holland, and Menage, Anti-Baillet, Tom. 1, pag. 4, obſerved it.

(2) Anti-Baillet, ib.

(3) Sorel's Knowledge of good Books, pag. 28, cited in the Judgment of the Learned, Tom. 1, pag. 454.

(4) See the Preface of the New Letters againſt Maimbourg's Hiſtory of Calvinism, and in the 2nd Letter, pag. 64, a Paſſage of the Mercure Galant in the Letters of the Chevalier d' Her . . . .

(5) Menage, Anti-Baillet Tom. 1. p. 4.

(6) Is the Index: It is the Edition of Wetſtein at Amſterdam, 1687.

(7) Balzac, Miſcellan. Works, Diſc. 14.

(8) Choice Letters, pag. 367.

(9) Ibid. pag. 362. Edit. of Holl.

(10) See the Latin Poems of Balzac, pag. 112, in Iſaac.

(11) See the Volume of Letters to Conrart, Book 5, Letter 3.

(12) See the 6 & 16 Letter of the 10th Book, and the 42d of the good 9th.

good Advice for her Education. See his *Choice Letters*, Page 157, and the Forty sixth, Forty seventh, and Forty eighth Letters of the seventh Book, in the Edition in *Folio*. I have found a Passage, in a Letter of *Costar*, which concerns the Lady of *Campagnolle*. *At* Balzac, says he (13), *you will see a Niece, beautiful and ingenious, who very well understands true gallantry from false, and who wants nothing but a little more of your Esteem*. This he wrote to *Voiture*. I have seen another Book, in which there is something, which may relate to This Lady. It is there said, that *Langlade* (14), one of Those, whom Cardinal *Mazarin* employed most in his secret Negotiations, had, before he came to Court, fallen in Love with a young Lady in the Country, called Mademoiselle de Campagnol (15). " He " did not dare to propose Marriage to her; but he " had exacted a Promise from her, not to marry, " and engaged himself to let her know, when his " Fortune should be in a Condition to make her " happy. He trusted *Gourville* with his Engagement to This young Lady, and, told him, with some " Discontent, that he did not think his Fortune was " sufficient to pretend to This Alliance, having, in " all, but Forty thousand Crowns. *Gourville* bid " him not trouble himself about That, but go, with " all Satisfaction, and conclude his Marriage, promising to give him as much more. Upon this " Assurance *Langlade* departed, and gave a great deal " of Joy to *Mademoiselle de Campagnol*, by shewing " her he had not forgot her. They were married, and " *Langlade* returned to *Paris*, with his new Wife, " where they found *Gourville* had taken a fine House " for them, and furnished it splendidly. He gave " *Langlade* That fine Furniture, with a great Quantity of Plate and Jewels for his Wife, besides the " Forty thousand Crowns; and Madam *de Parville* " (16) took great Care to shew this Country Lady " all the *Beau Monde*. This new married Couple " lived a long time together, in mutual Satisfaction."

(13) *See the 20th Letter of the Entretiens des Voiture & Costar*, pag. 249.

(14) *Gallantries of the Kings of France*, Tom. II. pag. 239, *Edition of* Brussels, 1694.

(15) Ibid. pag. 242.

(16) *She was a Mistress of Gourville's*.

BALZAC (JOHN LEWIS GUEZ *Sieur de*), was born at *Angoulême*, in the Year 1595 [*A*]. He acquired an extraordinary Reputation very early. There was so lively an Imagination, so much Eloquence, and so many uncommon Thoughts, in the Letters, which he wrote in his younger Years, that those, who saw them, were charmed with them, and praised them every where: So that, being in the Service of the Cardinal *de la Valette* (a), he soon became known, and esteemed at Court; insomuch, that Cardinal *Richelieu*, to whom he had wrote several times, did him the honour to answer him very obligingly. This Answer was printed with *Balzac*'s Letters, the first Edition whereof is of the Year 1624. He thought himself in the way of a very great Fortune [*B*]; his Letters sold so well, that they had a Run of several Editions. They were praised beyond measure; but not with the unanimous consent of all Readers. Some contradicting Spirits started up, either excited by Envy, which is most likely, or from a discovery of the weak Passages of *Balzac*'s Works. These Dissentions, having reigned for some time in Conversation, became a public War in the Year 1627, and one of the most cruel, that ever was known of this kind. It was begun by a young Monk, who wrote a little Book, intituled, *The Conformity of Mr Balzac's Eloquence with That of the greatest Persons of the past and present Times*. Tho' this Piece was not printed, yet it went almost as publickly from Hand

(a) Sorel, Biblioth. Franç. pag. 121 of the 2d Edit.

[*A*] *He was born at Angoulême, in the Year* 1595.] I have not met with this in any Book, but observe, how I have inferred it from two Letters of Balzac. He mentions, in one of these two Letters (1), the Thanks he had given to Mr *Spanheim*, in 1649, for the fine Oration, which he had received from him, and *which had revived in him a Passion, which Fifty three Years had taken from him*. Without doubt, That Oration was his Funeral Oration on Frederic Henry, Prince of *Orange*: it may be supposed, that he received it in the Year 1648; for he was not quick in answering; he was, therefore, Fifty three Years of Age, in 1648, and must consequently be born in 1595. In the other Letter, dated the fifteenth of *October*, 1637 (2), he speaks of a Piece, which he composed, at seventeen Years of Age, and says, that it was full Twenty five Years, since his writing it. So that he was Forty two Years of Age, when he wrote That Letter, and consequently must be born in 1595. St *Romuald* places his Birth in the Year 1598. *For he was*, says he, *Twenty eight Years of Age, in* 1626 (3); but he forgot to prove This Reason. I do not deny, but I have found a Passage, which proves, that *Balzac* was born in 1596. I quote it in the Remark [*B*].

The small Piece, he composed, at seventeen Years of Age, is worth a Digression. He owns, that, in writing it, he committed both a Fault, and a Folly, and excuses himself, the best he can, on his Youth, and on *his composing it in Holland, without designing to publish it in print* (4). He took it very ill, that *Heinsius* revived that Fault. I have already observed (5), that this is an inconveniency, to which Authors, any thing famous, are very liable: They generally happen into some Paper Quarrel, which causes their Antagonists to search out, carefully, every little Fault of their Youth, to reproach them with in public. I do not wonder, that some have believed, that, at This Time, *Balzac* would not have refused to make his Fortune in *Holland*, under the Profession of an *Huguenot*. Before I read the Piece, I am mentioning, I took it to be a rash Judgment; but I have altered my Opinion, since Mr *Minutoli* favoured me with a Transcript of That Writing (6). He had a printed Copy of it, of the Edition, which *Heinsius* caused to be published, at *Leiden*, in the Year 1638. The Title of it is, *A Political Discourse on the State of the United Provinces* of the Netherlands, *by I. L.* D. B. *a French Gentleman*. It is a Pamphlet of four or five Pages, subscribed, at the end, *John Lewis de Balzac*. This Work is very fine, full of Wit and Thought; but I am well assured, that *Baudius*, who was in a public Office at *Leyden*, and who received a Salary from the States of *Holland*, would not have decided so stron ly for the Justice, wherewith the States threw off the Yoke of *Philip* II, nor have fought for such high Compliments for *Holland*, nor such cutting Invectives against the *Spanish* Government, nor, in short, such studied Maxims, in favour of Liberty of Conscience. So that it is very excusable to suspect, that the *French* Gentleman, perhaps, founded the Business, by That flying Sheet, and that, if the Republic, struck with Admiration of so fine a Pen, and so well affected, had offered a good Post, the Author, of seventeen Years of Age, would have preferred it before his Country, and his Catholicism.

Mr *de Balzac* took his Journey into *Holland*, in the Year 1612. *Theophilus* was his Fellow-Traveller, whom, if we may believe Father *Goulu*, *he, at the same time, played a very scurvy Trick* (7), which occasioned the Misunderstanding between That Poet and *Balzac*. The terrible Letter, which *Theophilus* printed against him, contains a Charge of two, or three, unpleasant Adventures: *I do not speak*, says he, *of the plundering of Authors*; *Doctor Baudius's Son-in-law accuses you of another sort of Theft*. - - - - *I do not repeat my having formerly drawn my Sword to revenge your being cudgelled*.

[*B*] *He thought himself in the way of a very great Fortune*.] It is very pleasant to hear him relate the Reasons of his great Hopes. Read, then, the second Story, which he tells, in his *Entretiens* (8): it concerns himself. Among other things, you will find there the Proof of what I have said, concerning the Elogies, given to his Letters, even before they were printed. He tells us, That the Bishop of *Luçon*, being

(1) *It is the 14th of the 1st Book to* Conrart: *the Thanks to Mr Spanheim are in the 10th of the 9th Book*.

(2) *It is the 10th of the 3d Book to* Chapelain.

(3) St *Romuald, Chron. Abridgment, ad Ann.* 1598.

A WRITING *published by Balzac, at 17 Years of Age*.

(4) *The 10th Letter to* Chapelain, *Book* 3.

(5) *See above, at the End of the Remark* [C] *of the Article* BALDUS.

(6) *He is Master of a great number of such scarce Pieces, which he always took great care to collect.*

(7) *Letters of Phylarch. Part.* I. pag. 257.

(8) Entret. 2. pag. 132, *Edit.* 12mo.

VOL. I. 7 S

Hand to Hand, as if it had been in Print, and no Body was ignorant, that a *Feuillant*, called Brother *Andrew*, was the Author of it [C]. Mr *de Balzac* defired it might be publickly confuted; which was performed in the Apology, publifhed by *Ogier* in 1627 [D]. The General of the *Feuillans*, whofe Name, at that time, was Father *Goulu*, took Brother *Andrew*'s Caufe in hand; and, under the Name of *Phyllarchus* (*b*), wrote two Volumes of Letters againft *Balzac*, with an extraordinary Heat, as I fhall relate in his Article. This Quarrel was the occafion of a great many Books (*c*), and raifed fuch a Storm, as almoft overwhelm'd Mr *Balzac*, as well becaufe of the Artifices of his Enemies, as becaufe he had given fome hold to his Critics, by fome very dull Hyperboles, vain Sallies, and ticklifh Propofitions. He let this Storm blow over, without anfwering his Adverfary [E]. Upon whofe Death, which happened in the Year 1629, a Calm enfued. The Public began to recover from the prejudices, they had fuffered themfelves to be poffeffed with againft Mr *Balzac*, who, making a good

(*b*) *Tho. this.* f. t. *of the ret, he wrong of his State to his quality, also of General of the Feuillans.*

being recalled from his Exile (9), careffed him extreamly, and complimented him as an illuftrious, rare, and extraordinary, Perfon, and that, Living invited him to Dinner, one Day, he faid, to a great many Perfons of Quality, at Table with him, Here's a Man (that Man was then but Twenty two Years of Age) to whom we muft do good, when it lies in our Power, and we muft begin with an Abbey of Ten thoufand Livres a Year. *Is it poffible to conceive a finer beginning?* Many would have been lent him upon this, at Rome, and Wagers laid on his future Advancement Neverthelefs, Matters went no farther. Cardinal Richelieu *did not remember what the Bifhop of Luçon has faid.* This puts me in mind of a Paffage of the *Menagiana:* " Monfieur *de Balzac* af- " pired firft to be a Bifhop. Afterwards he defired " only to be an Abbot; but he did not fucceed in " either. He even writes, in one of his Books, that " he fhould never be an Abbot, unlefs he himfelf " fhould be the Founder of the Abbey (10)."

(10) Page 190.

[C] *A little Book was publifhed againft him — whereof a Feuillant, called Brother Andrew, was the Author*] He was of *Mans*; he reconciled himfelf afterwards to Mr *Balzac*, and went to fee him, at *Anguuléme* (11). Mr *Balzac* entertained him magnificently, and contracted a cordial Friendfhip with him, which continued as long as they lived (12). He wrote feveral Letters to him, wherein he ftyles him, *The Reverend Father Don Andrew de St Dennis*. See, particularly, one of the Differtations, printed with the *Chriftian Socrates*, in the firft *Entretien*, and, among the *Latin* Letters, the Poem, entitled, *Iter fperatum*, preceeded by a Letter, wherein *Balzac* relates the Change of That Monk with much Joy, and makes ufe of this fine Exclamation, a *Parody* on *Virgil* (13),

(11) St Romuald, Contin. Chron. Ademari ad Ann. 1627.

(12) *See his Concern for the Interefts of Father Andrew, in the 18th and 18th Letters of tom. 2. Book 1. to Conrart, written in the Year 1653.*

O fuperi tanton' placuit concurrere motu
Æterna pofthac mentes in pace futuras?

(13) *Virg. Æn. lib. 12. ver. 503.*

*Jove, could'ft thou view, and not avert thy Sight,
Two jarring Authors join'd in cruel Fight,
Whom Leagues of lafting Love fo fhortly fhall unite.*
DRYDEN.

(14) Page 268.

Another *Latin* Letter, which preceeds This (14), informs us, that Brother *Andrew*, who, accoording to *Voiture*'s Expreffion, had been the *Helena* of That War, having heard, that Mr *Balzac* was dead, lamented, and praifed him. But, after this, being informed, that the News was falfe, he became a good Friend of the fuppofed deceafed, and therefore made it appear, that he was not in the Cafe of This Sentence:

(15) Horat. Od. 24. l 3.

Virtutem incolumem odimus,
Sublatam ex oculis quærimus invidi (15).

*We flight that Virtue we enjoy the moft;
And never know it's Value, 'till 'tis loft.*

This Circumftance muft not be forgot, that This Friar, who was then Prior of the Convent of St *Martin*, near *Orleans*, had no fooner heard of Mr *Balzac*'s dangerous Sicknefs, than he affembled all his Monks to pray with him for the fick Perfon (16). The latter, being recovered, gave an Incenfe Pot for the Altar of their Church, of Four hundred Livres Value, and an annual Revenue to fupply it continually with Per-

(16) *Preface to the Balzac's Works, and the Relation of his Death.*

fumes. If *Moreri* had mentioned the evident Marks Mr *Balzac* gave of his fincere Reconciliation with Brother *Andrew*, and with Father *Garaffe*, there would not have been found fo great a Want of Judgment in this Place of his Dictionary. *He was efteemed, from the firft, as the moft eloquent Man in France. This Reputation raifed him a great deal of Envy,* and the Quarrel he had, toward the Year 1627, with Father Goulu, General of the Feuillans, and others, is fufficiently known. All the World, however, was perfuaded of Mr *Balzac*'s Sincerity, and Generofity, who died, as he had lived, very much of a Chriftian. What a ftrange leap, from the Year 1627, to the Year 1654, in fo few Lines! And, befides, what fignifies, *That Sincerity, and That Generofity, which every Body was, however, perfuaded of?* Was That the Bufinefs in Hand? The Queftion was, only to know, whether *Balzac* was a good, eloquent, and orthodox Author.

[D] *This Piece was refuted, ------ in the Apology, publifhed by Ogier, in 1627*] There have been various Reports, about the true Author of That Work. Some believed, that he, who fathered it, was really the Author of it: Others, that he only lent his Name to a Piece, compofed by *Balzac* himfelf. Here is what Mr *Menage* fays of it: " Prior " *Oger* anfwered thofe Books of Father *Goulu*, a- " gainft Mr *Balzac*, in a Piece he intituled, Mr Bal- " zac's *Apology* (17), which is a Book, wrote with " fome Learning and Elegancy. But *Oger* furnifhed " only the Learning: The Elegancy was, altogether, " Mr *Balzac*'s own. I have heard Mr *de Racan*, " and Mr *de Gomberville*, fay fo feveral Times, who " had feen Mr *Balzac* intent on That Work. And " I have read, elfewhere, that Mr *de Balzac*, fpeak- " ing of That Work, declared, that he him felf was " the Father of it, and *Oger* only the God-father; " that he had fupplied the Silk, and *Oger* only the " Canvas (18)." In all Probability, the publifhing this Report made the Sieur *de la Motte-Aigron* fear fuch another Fate, which he endeavoured to prevent, by declaring, in the Preface to his Anfwer to *Phyllarchus*, that the Advice he had received from feveral Places, that they would give his Book a Mafter, obliged him to advertife all his Readers, *That he was no Roger, who fought under the Arms of Leo*; that he had not the Complaifance of thofe, who father other People's Children; that he could not endure to have his Books made for him; and that, for this, he was no more obliged to his Friends, than to the greateft Strangers in the World. He tells us, in the fame Place, that his Preface, on *Balzac*'s Letters, had been very falfely afcribed to others. This will be feen more particularly in his Article (19).

[E] *He let this Storm, raifed againft him by Father Goulu, blow over, without anfwering his Adverfary*] I confefs, that, at this very time, he took Pen in Hand to compofe his *Relation* to *Menander*: but That Piece was not printed till a long time after. The reafon of This Conduct appears from thefe Words of *Balzac*'s Twenty third *Entretien*. " You may remem- " ber the cruel Perfecution kindled againft me above " twenty Years ago. At that time an Angel from " Heaven would not have been heard, if he had come " down to plead my Caufe. The Faction was too " ftrong, and too paffionate, to allow the Public to " form a right Judgment. God be thanked, the " Storm is over, and, after it, fucceeds a Calm. The " Face of Things being changed, it is to be hoped " that Right will alfo take place again." The Author

BALZAC.

a good use of his Disgrace, and also of the indifferent Success of his *Prince* [F], retired to his Country-House, where he not only refined his Thoughts and Style, but his Heart also, and there preserved, by his Epistolary Correspondences [G], and the Pieces, he from time to time published, the Reputation of very great Merit, and of the best Pen in *France*. However, it must be confessed, that his Style seems too much laboured, and the turn of his Thoughts sometimes too much affected, and seldom natural: but, tho' his Letters have not that easy Air, and that happy Sprightliness

---

(20) Menage, Remarks on Ayrault, p. 252.

thor, finding himself importuned anew to publish his Defence, complied with it. *Menander*, to whom he addresses his Relation, is *Mainard* (20). Though that Relation contains a Defence of some of the Passages, which Father *Goulu* had criticized, yet it is rather a general Answer, than a continued and compleat Refutation of the two Volumes of *Phyllarchus*. *Balzac* also vindicated some Passages, which a Doctor of *Louvain*, and a Doctor of *Bezançon*, had censured

(21) See the Pieces, added at the End of the Christian Socrates.

(21). I find there is a Fault in his Calculation. It appears by his Twenty seventh *Entretien*, that he did not resolve to publish his Apologies, till above twenty Years after the Persecution he had suffered from *Phyllarchus*. And yet, it is most certain, that the Volume of his Miscellaneous Works, of which the Discourse to *Menander* makes a very considerable part, was printed in the Year 1645, and his Bookseller says in it, That the Author could not refuse the Publication of it, at the repeated Instances of his Father, who was Ninety one Years of Age. If you compare Mr *Guez's* Letter, which I have mentioned in the Remark [C] of the foregoing Article, with That Advertisement to the Reader, you will find, that the Resolution of printing the Apologies against *Phyllarchus* was taken in the Year 1644. How can this agree with the Twenty seventh *Entretien*?

[F] *He made a good Use of the indifferent Success of his Prince.*] The Author's Friends had promised This Work as a Master-Piece, which would silence all Critics: especially those, who accused *Balzac* of being incapable of writing any thing but Letters. The Event did not answer these Expectations: That Book added nothing either to *Balzac*'s Reputation, or Fortune, and raised him some trouble from the *Sorbonne*.

(22) Balzac's Letter 43, l. 8. Entretien, 13, p. 182.

Though the Marquis *d'Aytona* had caused it to be burnt at *Brussels* (22); it was yet mentioned, with the utmost Contempt, in an Answer of the Abbot of *St Germain*, as a Book *suppress'd by the Censure of the Doctors, and the Sentence of the Judges, a Month after it's Birth*. Mr *Pellisson* relates, that, in the Year 1636, *Balzac* read some part of his *Prince*, which he then called the Minister of State, to the French Aca-

(23) History of the French Academy, pag. 221, & 167.

demy (23). This would make one believe, that, at first, he had only a Mind to write the Cardinal's Panegyric. But it is certain, Mr *Pellisson* was mistaken. The *Prince* was printed in the Year 1631. This Book was to have been followed by two others; the latter of which was called the *Minister of State*. Some observe, that, in his *Prince*, he praises the Cardinal more than the King. (See the Thirty seventh Page of the fifteenth Volume of the *Bibliothèque Universelle*.) But this is false. We find, in the eighth Book of This Author's Letters, the Answer the Faculty of Divinity wrote to him, to signify, that they were satisfied with his offers to alter what they had found worthy of Censure. The *Latin* Letter, he wrote to a Father of the *Christian Doctrine*, concerning This Process of the *Sorbonne*, is admirable. It is in the Hundred eighty seventh Page of his *Epistolæ selectæ*, in the Edition, of *Paris*, 1651, in 12mo.

Observe, That some Persons have affirmed, that this Work was one of the Author's best Performances. *It is thus, Sir, that you yourself have practised it in your Prince, and in your Relations to Menander, which are the two great Miracles of your Art, and the highest Pitch of Heroic Eloquence*. Thus says *Costar*

(24) Richelet's Letters, pag. 97.

in his Defence of *Voiture*. Mr *Richelet* says, in his Remarks on some Letters, *That the Prince, and the Aristippus, are two of the most Eloquent Pieces of* Balzac (24). If a Judgment of the Merits of *Balzac*'s *Prince* was to be made by the Number of Editions, it would be very advantageous: "At first came out "two Editions in *Quarto*, at the same time; then "another in the same form, but in smaller Chara-"cters, and full of Faults, which I believe was "printed at *Niort*, or at *Poitiers*. Afterwards, there "was one in 8vo, pretty good, though pirated.

"After that, came out That of *Bouillerot*, in 8vo also, "but corrected; and lastly the Edition in 12mo, of "*Courbé*." These words are taken from a Letter, Mr *du Rondel* did me the Honour to write to me the tenth of *May* 1698. I am going to quote another part of it. "I have lately bought, *says he*, the "*Prince*, of the first Edition, wherein I found, with "unspeakable delight, what Mr *de Balzac* had writ-"ten, and what he afterwards altered and cut off: "and it was on this occasion, that I first rightly ap-"prehended what *Scaliger* meant by his *detrahendo fe-*"*cit auctiorem*. *Balzac*, by cutting off five or six Pas-"sages, suppressed Faintness, re-animated Weakness, "increased his Strength, and recovered the Atten-"tion, which was just forsaking the Reader." I make use of an Edition in 4to, of the Year 1632. The place, where it was printed, is not set down; but doubtless it was at *Rouen*. I have seen one, in a small 8vo, printed at *Paris* by *Tousainte du Bray*, 1632. It is called, in the Title, *The second Edition corrected*. Mr *Perrault*, who so highly commended *Balzac*'s *Aristippus* (25), said nothing advantageous of his *Prince*. He only takes notice, that this Piece appeared after the Miscellaneous Works. I flatter myself he will not take it amiss, if I observe, that he is mistaken. For the Miscellaneous Works did not appear till a long time

(25) Perrault's Illustrious Men, pag. 176.

after the *Prince* (26). Let us conclude with a Passage of *Gabriel Naudé*: "Quibus omnit us velut coronidem "accessisse ferunt Billaci, Viri Clarissimi, Princi-"pem, Gallicè modo pumice diligentur expolitum. "Verum enimvero, quoniam ipse liber post meum "è *Gallia* discessum typis suit demandatus, ut prop-"tereà nondum in manus meas pervenerit; varia-"que, ut audio, ac prorsus ancipiti judicorum "alea fuit acceptus: hoc solum de illo pronunciare "possum, quod fuit ab antiquis in simili occasione "ex formula usurpatum, *Non liquet* (27). — To "all which, they say, is added, as a finishing Piece, the "*Prince of the most famous* Balzac, *now represented* "*in the finest French Polish*. *But, as that Book was* "*not printed till after my leaving* France, *and as it* "*therefore not yet come to my Hands, and has been,* "*I hear, very differently received: I can only say* "*this of it, as some of the Ancients did on a like* "*Occasion*, It does not appear."

(26) The Licence for printing his Prince, is dated the 18th of Sept mb. 1631; and the Approbation is dated the third of October following. The Miscellaneous Works were printed in the Year 1647.

(27) Naudæus, Bibliogr. Polit. p. 47.

[G] *He kept up Epistolary Correspondences.*] This Correspondence was so great, that it over-powered Mr *Balzac*. For, besides that he composed with extreme Difficulty, he knew, that his Letters would be shewn to every body, and must therefore be very exact. See how he describes his own Case in this respect. "He receives all the bad Compliments of "*Christendom*, to say nothing of the good ones, "which give him yet more trouble. He is per-"secuted, he is killed, with the Civilities, which "come to him from the four Quarters of the "World; and last Night there lay fifty Letters on "the Table in his Chamber, which required An-"swers; and those eloquent ones, and such as might "be shewn, copied, and printed ——— (28)." He says in another place (29), "At this very time I am "speaking to you, there lie a Century of Letters "on my Table, which wait for Answers: I owe "some to crowned Heads." As he was the first in *France*, who acquired a great Name by this sort of Writings, he obtained the Title of the great *Epistolizer*; and this he sometimes gave himself. *Sciat se dignum fuisse invidiâ magni Franciæ Epistolarii* (30). — Let him know he has drawn upon him-self the Envy of the great Epistolizer of *France*. The first Letters, he published, were not near so good as those he wrote after his Retirement; and yet the latter did not sell any thing like the former. *Sorel* had reason to make this Observation (31); and the Critic *Maimbourg* was not to blame for repeating it (32). This shews the capricious Humour of the Public.

(28) Balzac, Entretien, 7.

(29) The seventh Letter of the fifth Book, to the Volume to Conrart. See also the Choice Letters, pag. 15. and the Letters to Chapelain, pag. 81, Edit. of Holland.

(30) Select Epistles, pag. 288.

(31) Sorel, Biblioth. Franç. pag. 135.

(32) Preface to the New Letters on Maimbourg's History of Calvinism.

[H] His

BALZAC.

Sprightlinefs, which shines in those of *Voiture*; yet they are very pleasing, and have a certain lively and serious Gaiety, almost inimitable [H]. There appear also, in all his Writings, a great many Touches of Learning, well chosen, and well applied. In a Word, one cannot sufficiently admire, considering in what condition he found the *French* Tongue, how he could open his way to such a neatness of Style. It must not be wondered at, that his Writings favour of Labour. Elevation, and Grandeur, was his principal Character; which cannot be attained without Meditation. In all probability, future Ages will do his Works Justice, for the long Discredit, they suffered, by means of some Critics: Which did not hinder a great number of very excellent Judges from persevering constantly in their first Admiration (*d*). He was a good *Latin* Poet; and his *Latin Letters* shew, that he wrote That Language in very great Purity. If he had many Enemies, who wrote against him [*I*], he had, on the other side, a very great number of Friends, and Admirers (*e*); and there were few Persons of Merit, either *French* or *Foreigners*, who, in travelling through *France*, did not take the Pleasure of making him a Visit [*K*]. He was one of the forty Members of the *French* Academy [*L*]. Cardinal *Mazarin* endeavoured

(*d*) *See what Mr Menage said of him in Balzac's Eloge, quence, Menagiana, pag. 112, 113, 114. See also Mr Perrault in Balzac's Elogy.*

(*e*) *The great* DESCARTES *loved and esteemed him very much. See his Life by Mr Baillet, Vol. I. pag. 139, & seq.*

[*H*] *His Letters ------ have ------ a certain lively and serious Gaiety, almost inimitable.*] Let us hear what *Richelet* says (33). "*Balzac* does not "make a Complaint, which has not in it something "witty, new, and eloquent. — He had a pleasing "sprightly Melancholy: This appears in his Letters, "and he never speaks of it without charming the "Heart, and inspiring Delight. ——— He discovers "there a certain Melancholy full of Charms, which "engages more than all the Gaiety in the World."

[*I*] *He had a great many Enemies, who wrote against him.*] The Chancellor *Seguier*, having prevented the Publication of a Book composed against *Balzac* in 1636, received, a little while after, a Letter from that Author (34), which contains the following Words: "So long as there are none but these Pen-"Gladiators, who present themselves for Licence to "appear in print, be not so sparing of the Prince's "Favours, but abate a little of your Severity. If "it was a new thing, perhaps I should not be displeased with the Suppression of the first Libel, "which should abuse me: but since there are as "many of them, as will make a small Library, I am "very well pleased to see the Number increased, "and I take delight in raising a monumental heap "of Stones, which Envy has cast at me, without doing me any harm." Among those, who wrote against him, besides the Persons already mentioned, we may reckon *Daniel Heinsius*, who answered, with some sourness, the Criticisms, which *Balzac* had made on the *Herodes Infanticida*. See the Thirty fifth *Entretien* of *Balzac* upon this, and the Twenty fifth Letter of the first Book of *Chapelain*, and the twentieth of the second Book. *Salmasius*, who was *Heinsius*'s Enemy, and *Balzac*'s Friend, appeared in this Dispute, and adjudged the Victory to his Friend: but a Minister of *Languedoc*, whose Name was *Croi* (35), took arms against *Balzac* in favour of *Heinsius*: and yet, a little while after, he wrote very sharply against *Heinsius*; but it was indeed on other matters. *Nicolas Bourbon*, of the *French* Academy, is also one of the Number. See what the Historian of the Academy says of it (36). We must not forget *Costar*, who, thinking, that *Balzac* had, by way of Jealousy, engaged Mr *de Girac* to criticize *Voiture*, addressed to him the Defence of *Voiture*, and stuft it full of stinging Raileries. The Blow was felt, and the matter came at last to an open War. And *Costar* threw off the Mask. See how Mr *Girard* reproaches him for it in the Preface to *Balzac*'s *Entretiens*. There are some Facts in the *Menagiana* very proper to be inserted here. "Mr *de Balzac*, after having obliged Mr *de Girac* to write in *Latin*, against the Letters of *Voiture*, engaged also Mr *Costar* in the Defence of *Voiture*, and to write against Mr *de Girac*: this was to procure to himself the Praises of both "Parties. I passed through *Mans* in my return to "*Paris*, at the same time that the *Defence* was finished. "Mr *Costar* gave me two Copies of it, the one to be "sent to Mr *de Pincbesne*, Nephew to Mr *Voiture*, "and the other to Mr *Conrart*. He told me, that "he would willingly submit it to any Alterations, "either by adding, or diminishing. One of the "Copies was communicated to Mr *Balzac*, who "sent some Corrections; but, in the mean while, "the Work was printed. And, as his Corrections "came when the Impression was finished, an Account "was sent him, that they were received too late; "and the Book appeared such as it was, which "gave him some Uneasiness (37)." I pass over the biting Expressions bestowed on *Balzac*, in the *Hexameron Rustique*. See the Complaint, which Mr *Menage* makes, for having been introduced in it, to act a Part against Mr *Balzac* (38). I omit also what passed between Mr *du Moulin*, and him; for it was on a slight skirmish of Controversy, wherein each Party was complimented. Other Disputes proceeded from it, which were more malignant (39); but, as far as I can remember, Mr *Balzac* received only this little Blow in it; *Vir ingenio compto & Gallicæ eloquentiæ laude clarus Balzacus, sed in religionis negotio plusquam infans*. ——— *Balzac* famous *for his fine Understanding, and but French Eloquence, but in Matters of Religion ignorant below the Capacity of a Child*. Mr *du Moulin* gave it him in the Epistle Dedicatory of his Answer to *Petra-Sancta*. No notice was taken of it, as if the Insult was not known. See the eleventh Letter of the second Book to *Chapelain*. I should be too tedious, if I should undertake to speak of one *de Vaux* (40), and all the other Adversaries of *Balzac*.

(33) *Richelet, Lett. p. 81, 82.*

(34) *It is the 43d of the 3d Book of the second Part of the Choice Letters.*

(35) *He is the Author of the Anonymous Answer to Balzac's Letter and Discourse on a Tragedy of Heinsius, entitled, Herodes Infanticida; which Answer was printed at Geneva (tho' the Title doth not mention it) in 1642.*

(36) *Pag. 269, Edit. 1672. See also the 28th, and 36th Letter of the second Book to Chapelain.*

(37) *Menagiana, pag. 166, 167.*

(38) *Ibid. pag. 323.*

(39) *The Jesuit Sylvester à Petra Sancta having written sharply against du Moulin's Answer to Balzac, was paid in the same Coin, by du Moulin and Rivetus.*

(40) *He published the Tomb of the French Orator.*

[*K*] *There were few Persons ——— who ——— did not take the Pleasure of making him a Visit.*] This was a great Incumbrance to him, as appears by these words of his seventh *Entretien*. "Some troublesome "Persons come here sometimes, from above an hundred "Leagues distance, and that on purpose, if they "may be credited, who are almost the Death of "him, beginning with their first Compliment, that "his great Reputation, and the Celebrity, which he "has given to the Place of his Abode, have obliged "them to come and see A Person so well known, "and A Village so renowned; so that he ought "not to take amiss so just and obliging a Curiosity. "Some Days fince, one of these curious Persons "began his Harangue with, *The Respect and Veneration, which he always had for him, and for the Gentlemen his Books*. Nothing can be more Historical than this; by which you see how far the "Style of Compliments may be carried." They were not only learned Men, who went to see him, but great Lords also, and I am much deceived, if the Count *de Pigneranda* did not do him that Honour, when he passed through that Country, in his Return to *Spain*. Mr *Balzac* informs us with Pleasure, that the same Count had reproached him for the ardent Zeal of his Pen, in the Defence of the Honour of *France*. This we find in the Letter, wherein he confutes the current Report, that he had composed a Manifesto for the Prince of *Condé*, in 1651 (41).

(41) *It is printed at the end of the Christian Socrates.*

[*L*] *He was one of the forty Members of the French Academy*.] Mr *Pellisson*, having related, from the Register of the Academy, that, on the thirteenth Day of *March*, 1634, Mr *de Boisrobert* produced a Letter, which he had wrote, on his own Authority, to Mr *de Balzac*, to acquaint him, that, if he should request of the Society, by Letter, to be admitted among them, it would readily be granted. I say, Mr *Pellisson*, having related this, adds, *That he did not find in the Register what followed upon it; but that undoubtedly Mr Balzac was, upon his Answer, admitted, a little while after, into the Academy* (42). Mr *Balzac* did not find Mr *Pellisson* a faithful Historian

(42) *History of the Academy, pag. 221.*

in

BALZAC.

endeavoured to recall him to Court (*f*). Queen *Christina* was very kind to him, and defired him to write to her (*g*). The greateft Lords of the Kingdom gave him, in his Defert (*h*), many Marks of their Efteem (*i*). His greateft Excellency was, that he not only lived and died in his Retreat as a good Man, but alfo as a good Chriftian. While he was living, he fet a-part Eight thoufand Crowns of his Eftate for Pious Ufes (*k*). He caufed two Chambers to be built for him, in the Convent of the Capuchins of *Angoulême* [M], where he often refided (*l*). It was there that he compofed his *Chriftian Socrates*. He fpoke fome very fine things on his Death-bed, and, by his Will, ordered himfelf to be buried in the Hofpital of *Our Lady of the Angels* in *Angoulême*, at the Feet of the Poor, that were buried there (*m*). He bequeathed twelve thoufand Livres to that Hofpital, and left a Fund, of an hundred Livres a Year, to be given every two Years as a Prize to him, who, in the Judgment of the *French Academy*, fhould beft compofe a Difcourfe on a Pious Subject (*n*). He died the eighteenth of *February* 1654 [N]. The Sieur *Morifcet*, a Canon of *Angoulême*, made his Funeral Oration, and another *Morifcet*, Brother of the former, and Advocate in the *Prefidial* of the fame City, caufed a Difcourfe to be printed in Praife of the Deceafed (*o*). An Edition of all *Balzac*'s Works was publifhed at *Paris*, in the Year 1665, in two Volumes in *Folio*, with a Preface of the Abbot *Caffagnes*, a Member of the *French* Academy. Confult the *Illuftrious Men* of Mr *Perrault*, and you will find there an Elogy of *John Lewis Guez*.

in this matter: He acknowledges, that Mr *Boifrobert* had exhorted him feveral times to write a complimentary Letter to the Academy, and had even threatened him from the Cardinal, if he fhould refufe to write That Compliment: But he declares, that he wrote no Anfwer, and that, about five or fix Months afterwards, he had an Account of his being made a Member of the Academy, and of his Name having been feen in the Sun of the little honeft Man, Mr *de la Peyre* (43). From whence he concludes, that, if a Letter had been prefented, as from him, to the Academy, it was a falfe one. This is what he wrote to Mr *Conrart*, the Twenty fecond of *September* 1653. It is not known, what anfwer he received from him to clear the matter: but it appears by a Letter of the third of *November*, of the fame Year, that Mr *Conrart* had undeceived him. One would almoft fufpect, that Mr *Conrart* had fatisfied him, that he had feen the very Original of That Compliment under his own Hand; from whence he muft conclude, that the greateft Wits do not always remember the Letters they have written fome Years before. What is unqueftionable is, that Mr *de Balzac* took himfelf to be a true and abfolute Academift; for the Regifter of the fourteenth of *April*, 1636, teftifies, that he *read fome part of his Prince in the Academy* (44); and it has been proved by his printed Letters, that he " fent fome of his " Works to Monfieur *du Chatelet*, defiring him to " read them in the Academy, and to accompany " them with fome of his Words, which, he faid, " would not only fuffice to excufe him to them for " the Thanks, but alfo for the Speech, which he " owed them (45)." He had juft before faid, " That " the Honour which the Academy had done him, " to admit him into their Body, without obliging " him to go to *Paris*, were two fingular Favours " at one time." I remember two Paffages in his Letters, wherein he acknowledges the Gentlemen of the Academy for his Brethren. The firft is in the fixteenth Page of his Choice Letters, and the laft in the Ninty fifth Page of his Letters to *Chapelain*.

[M] *He caufed two Chambers to be built for him in the Convent of the Capuchins of Angoulême.*] I have not read any where, but in the *Menagiana*, that he had a Defign to put on the Habit of that Order. " Mr *de Balzac* was fo affected with Devotion, that he " entered into a Convent of the *Capuchins*, where he " had a Mind to put on their Habit. Neverthelefs, " he did not die there (46)." Perhaps he defired, like many others, to die in the Habit of St *Francis*.

[N] *He died the eighteenth of* Feb. 1654.] The Lift of the Academifts, printed at the end of the fecond Edition of *The Hiftory of the Academy*, makes Mr *de Balzac* live 'till the Year 1657, fince, in that Year, it names *Hardouin de Perefixe*, Archbifhop of *Paris*, as his Succeffor. On the contrary, the Lift of the deceafed Academifts, printed at the end of the *State of France*, of the Year 1680, mentions Mr *de Balzac* as dead a confiderable time before the Year 1654; fince it places him before *Baro* and *Baudouin*, who died before the Year 1651. If Mr *Pelliffon* had been concerned in the fecond Edition of *The Hiftory of the Academy*, two Faults, which I have quoted, would not have been feen in the Lift; one whereof relates to the time, when *Balzac* died, the other to the Perfon that fucceeded him, who is not Mr *de Perefixe*. Moreover, Mr *de Perefixe* was not Archbifhop of *Paris*, in the Year 1657. But Mr *Pelliffon* has not examined thefe Particulars. Mr *Baillet*, who, without doubt, believed the contrary, is very excufable, for having thought, that, on fuch an Authority, he might place the Death of *Balzac* in the Year 1657 (47). As to the Day of his Death, *Moreri*, St *Romuald* (48), *Henningus de Witte* (49), Mr *Perrault*, and feveral others, fay it was the Twenty eighth of *February*. But the Perfons, whom I have confulted, informed me, that it was the nineteenth of *February*, according to the Contract made with the *French* Academy, concerning the Fund that *Balzac* left it, and according to a Manufcript Letter of the Sieur *Morifcet*. Laftly, it was the eighteenth of *February*, if we may rely on thefe two things: the one is, that, in the Preface to *Balzac*'s Works, it is affirmed, that the Account of his Death was written the very next Day after: the other is, that this Account is dated the nineteenth of *February*, 1654.

BANCK (LAURENCE) a Native of *Norcopin* in *Sweden*, was Profeffor of the Civil Law, in the Univerfity of *Franeker*, for the fpace of fifteen Years (*a*). He gained fo great a Reputation, while he was a Student there, that, upon his Return thither from his Travels into *France*, *Italy*, *Spain*, &c. the Civil Law Chair was prefented to him, together with a very good Salary (*b*). He died the thirteenth of *October* 1662 (*c*). I fhall mention his Works below [*A*], and particularly an Edition, which he publifhed, of the famous Book of *Taxes of the Romifh Chancery* [B]. It is a Work fufficiently curious to be confidered a little more

[A] *I fhall mention his Works below.*] He publifhed, at *Franeker*, in 1649, a Book intituled, *de Tyrannide Paparum in Reges & Principes Chriftianos*. Seven Years after, he publifhed *Roma triumphans, feu Inauguratio Innocentii X*. As to his Pieces, *De Bancae Ruptoribus*; *De Duellis*; *De Confiliis & Confiliariis Principum*, &c. (1) I cannot afcertain their Dates.

[B] —— *and an Edition, he publifhed, of the Taxes of the Romifh Chancery.*] I have related, in another Place (2), feveral things concerning thefe Taxes, and particularly mentioned the Edition of them, publifhed by *Pinet*, in the Year 1564. I have obferved alfo, that *d'Aubigné* quotes the Edition of *Paris*, in 1520. This is not the firft, as fome have imagined; for the Edition

BANCK.

628

more particularly, and deserves our making some Reflections on it, as well to rectify what we have already said of it elsewhere (d), as to illustrate what several other Authors have written about it, who have not explained themselves with due exactness.

(d) In Remark [B] of the Article PINET.

(3) It is in Latin and Dutch, in 8vo. See Preface, and p. 730.

Edition of *Bois-le-duc*, 1664 (3), shews, that this Book was printed at *Rome*, in the Year 1514, and at *Cologn* (4), in 1515 : and was entituled *Regulæ, Constitutiones, Reservationes, Cancellari, S. Domini nostri Leonis Papæ decimi, noviter editæ & publicatæ*, and

(4) By Gosvin Colinius.

that, in fol. 67, it has these Words : *Taxæ Cancellariæ, per Marcellum Silber, alias Franck, Romæ, in Campo Floræ, Anno M.D.XIV, die XVIII Novembris impressæ, finiunt feliciter. - - - - - The Chancery Taxes, printed by Marcellus Silber, alias Franck, at Rome, in the Campus Floræ, the eighteenth of November, 1514, is happily completed*. This is attested by two of the *Echevins* of *Bois-le-duc*, together with the Town-Clerk, who had collated, Word for Word, this Edition of *Rome*, with That published by *Stephen du Mont*, Bookseller at *Bois-le-duc*, in the Year 1664, and entituled, *Taxæ Cancellariæ Apostolicæ, & Taxæ Sacræ Pænitentiariæ*. In this last we find (5) the Passage, quoted by *d'Aubigné*, from the *Paris* Edition, in 1520 (6): *Absolutio pro eo qui matrem, Sororem, aut aliam conjanguineam vel affinem suam, aut commatrem, carnaliter cognovit, gr.* v. *Absolutio pro eo qui Virginem deflorarit, gr.* vi. (7). ——— *The Absolution of him who has lain with his Mother, Sister, or other Relation, either in Consanguinity, or Affinity, is taxed at Gr.* v. *The Absolution of him who has deflowered a Virgin, Gr.* vi. This is also to be met with in the Edition of *Franeker*, in 1651 (8). I am surprized it should be wanting in the Edition of *du Pinet*, entituled, *Taxe des Parties Casuelles de la Boutique du Pape*. This is in *Latin* and *French*, with Notes added by the Editor. He was greatly to blame, in not mentioning on what authentic Copies he formed his Edition; for it differs from the others, both in the order of Matters, and in the Denomination of Monies. This mentions only *Tournois, Ducats*, and *Carlins*; and the others only *Gros*: at least the Ducat and Carlin is very rarely mentioned. *D'Aubigné* affirms (9), that the *Paris* Edition says, *The Murder of a Father, or Mother, is rated at one Ducat, and five Carlins*: but, in the Edition of *Franeker* (10), and in That of *Bois-le-duc* (11), it is, " *Absolutio pro eo qui interfecit patrem, ma-*
" *trem, sororem, uxorem - - - - - g.* v. vel vij (12).
" *The Absolution of him, who has murdered his Father,*
" *Mother, Sister, Wife, - - - - - - - - at g. v. or vij.*"
I say, I am surprized, that this Article of Incest should be missing in the Edition of *du Pinet* (13), in which we find more enormous Articles; These, for instance ; " *Absolutio à lapsu carnis super quocun-*
" *que actu libidinoso commisso per clericum, etiam*
" *cum monialibus, intra & extra septa monasterii, aut*
" *cum consanguineis vel affinibus, aut filiâ spirituali,*
" *aut quibusdam aliis, sive ab unoquoque de per se,*
" *sive simul ab omnibus absolutio petatur cum dis-*
" *pensatione ad ordines & beneficia, cum inhibitione,*
" *tur.* 36. duc. 3. *Si verò cum illis petatur ab-*
" *solutio etiam a crimine commisso contra naturam,*
" *vel cum brutis, cum dispensatione, ut supra, &*
" *cum inhibitione, turon.* 90. duc. 12. carl. 16. *Si*
" *verò petatur tantùm absolutio à crimine contra na-*
" *turam, vel cum brutis, cum dispensatione, & inhi-*
" *bitione,* turon. 36. duc. 9. *Absolutio pro moniali,*
" *quæ se permisit pluries cognosci intra & extra septa*
" *monasterii, cum rehabilitate ad dignitates illius or-*
" *dinis, etiam abbatialem,* turon. 36 duc. 9. *Ab-*
" *solutio pro concubinario, cum dispensatione ad or-*
" *dines & beneficia,* turon. 21. duc. 5. carlin. 6 (14).
" - - - - - - - - *The Absolution and Pardon of all Acts*
" *of Fornication committed by a Cleric, in what*
" *manner soever, whether it be with a Nun, with-*
" *in or without the Limits of the Nunnery, or*
" *with his Relations, in Consanguinity, or Affinity,*
" *or with his God-daughter, or with any other Wo-*
" *man whatsoever; and whether also the said Absolu-*
" *tion be given in the Name only of the Cleric him-*
" *self, or of him jointly with his Whores, with a*
" *Dispensation to enable him to take and hold his Or-*
" *ders, and ecclesiastical Benefices, and with a Clause*
" *also of Inhibition, costs Thirty six Tournois, and*
" *nine or three Ducats. And if, besides the above,*
" *he receives Absolution from Buggery, and the Crime*
" *against Nature, although committed with brute*

" *Beasts, with the Dispensation and Clause of Inhibi-*
" *tion, as before, he must pay ninety Tournois, twelve*
" *Ducats, and six Carlin's. But, if he only receives*
" *Absolution from Buggery, or the Crime against Na-*
" *ture, and committed with brute Beasts, with the*
" *Dispensation and Clause of Inhibition, he pays only*
" *Thirty six Tournois, and nine Ducats. A Nun,*
" *having committed Fornication several times within*
" *and without the Bounds of her Nunnery, shall be*
" *absolved, and enabled to hold all the Dignities of her*
" *Order, even that of Abbess, by paying Thirty six*
" *Tournois, and nine Ducats. The Absolution of him,*
" *who keeps a Concubine, with Dispensation to take*
" *and hold his Orders, and ecclesiastical Benefices,*
" *costs Twenty one Tournois, five Ducats, and six*
" *Carlin's* (15)." I conjecture, that *du Pinet* followed the Edition, which the Protestant Princes inserted amongst the Causes of their rejecting the Council of *Trent*, and which was entituled, *Taxa Sacra Pænitentiariæ* (16). Mr *Heidegger* recites some Pieces of it, which exactly agree with the Edition of *du Pinet* (17) It is observed by some, that there is an Epitome of the *Taxes of the Romish Chancery*, at pag. 603, *& seq.* of a Work entituled, *Luculenta Deductio Causarum recusati Concilii Tridentini à Protestantium Germaniæ Principibus publicatarum*, and at the beginning of a Book of *Hunnius de Indulgentiis*, and at pag. 216, *& seq.* of *Musculus*'s Common Places (18). The Author of the Book, entituled *Simonia Curiæ Romæ*, printed in 1612, has inserted in it this Passage of the said *Common Places* (19). Compare this with the Remark [*A*], of the Article TUPPIUS.

We shall say something of the Edition, published by *Laurence Banck*. It was printed at *Franeker*, in the Year 1651, in 8vo. He says, he consulted the most ancient Copies, both printed and Manuscript ; and, by comparing them Word for Word, supplied from those, which were most perfect, what was wanting in the others. He made use of the Edition of *Cologn*, in 1523, of that of *Wittemburg*, in 1538, of that of *Venice*, in 1584 (20), and of a Manuscript, which had been communicated by *John Baptist Sibon*, a *Bernardin* Friar, and Reader of the College at *Rome*. By this means he enlarged this Edition, something beyond any of the former. He added a sort of *Glossary*, or Notes, to explain the difficult Terms. He also subjoined a small Piece, in *Italian*, containing the Taxes in Use, under Pope *Innocent* X ; and explained the Value of Money, according to the Usage of that Time. His Notes have been of great Service to the Author of the Remarks, added to the Edition of *Bois-le duc*. Note, that, in the Preface of this here, it is observed, that the Inquisitors have put the *Tax of the Chancery* in the List of condemned Books. " *Nascentem suffocare conati sunt ipsi Authores, &*
" *in Indice Librorum prohibitorum, ex Patrum Con-*
" *cilii Tridentini authoritate, Hispaniarumque Regis*
" *& ducis Alban.* decreto, *Leodii* anno 1570 edito,
" *inter primæ Classis Authores atro calculo notarunt*
" (21). ——— *The Authors themselves endeavoured*
" *to stifle it in the Birth, and branded it among the*
" *Works of the first Class, in the List of prohibited*
" *Books, published at Liege, in the Year 1570, by*
" *the Authority of the Fathers of the Council of Trent,*
" *and by the Decree of the King of Spain, and Duke*
" *d'Alva.*" I have not This Edition of the *Index Librorum prohibitorum*. That, which I make use of, and which was copied from That of *Madrid*, in 1667, in Folio, places, only under the third Class, *Praxis & Taxa Officinæ Pænitentiariæ Papæ, ab Hæreticis depravata* (22) : Observe, that it is only condemned on the Supposition of it's having been corrupted by Hereticks ; and the *Index*, published at *Rome*, by Order of *Alexander* VII, uses the same Words with this of *Spain* (23). But let them suppose as much as they please, that it has been corrupted by Hereticks, the Editions of it, which cannot be disowned, as That of *Rome*, in 1514 ; That of *Cologn*, in 1515 ; Those of *Paris*, in 1520, in 1545, and in 1625 (24) ; and Those of *Venice* (25), one in the sixth Volume of the *Oceanus Juris*, published in 1533, the other in the fifteenth Volume of the same Collection, reprinted in 1584: These Editions, I say, are more than sufficient

BANDEL. 629

ficient to justify the Reproaches of the Protestants, and to cover the Church of *Rome* with Confusion. Our *Laurence Banck* was ignorant of almost all these Editions, I have particularized, as also of That of *Francfort*, in 1612, in 4to (26). *Rivet, Voëtius, Hottinger*, and several other, *Helluones Librorum*, great Readers, have falsely believed, that the Edition of 1520, was the first (27); for they have principally urged this Edition against the *Roman* Catholics, who would not allow, that ever the *Taxation of the Chancery* had appeared by Authority. *Voëtius* relates, that, in 1633, a Chancellor of *Bois-le-duc* declared he would abjure his *Catholicism*, if any one could shew him those Abominations, which the Protestants had quoted, as from the *Taxes of the* Romish *Chancery*. Application was made to *Rivet*, who lent his Copy of the *Paris* Edition, in 1520 (28). *Voëtius*, in giving this Account, takes Occasion to exhort, very pathetically, the Library-keepers of Protestant Universities, to preserve and buy up the authentic Copies of this Work. " Quia autem, *says he* (29), " hic *Taxæ Pænitentiariæ* mentio facta, moneo exemplaria pauca hodie haberi posse (quâ & quorum " arte facilè prudentiores conjiciant;) aliqua tamen " in manibus nostrorum superesse editionis Parisiensis " 1520, in 4º, apud Tussain Denis. Edita etiam est " Venetiis, cum quamplurimis aliis Tractatibus in " *Oceano Juris*. Addo, rem & librum à Pontificiis " passim negari, ubi ita usu venit, ut nostri, allegando illam Taxam, mendacii & calumniæ suspecti " fiant, imò & arguentur. Accidit anno 1633, ut " quis J. Consultus idemque Senator Sylvæducensis, " desertionem & rejectionem Papatus mineretur, (more ipsis non insolito,) si quidem tam abominanda, " qualia ex Taxâ nostri referunt, demonstrari possent. " Ut amplissi. & consult. huic Viro ex asse satisfierent, " quæsitum apud exemplari (30), me de etiam à me " postulatum est. Quod cum mihi ab ipsis pontificiis editum nullum esset, petii commodato à celeberrimo Theologo Andreâ †Riveto. Ante biennium " alibi concertatione inter nostros & Pontificios quosdam oborta super eâdem hâc Taxâ, denuo consultus, commonstravi Bibliothecam D. Riveti, in quâ " certo scirem exemplar edit. Parif. 1520. haberi; " quippe quod ipse ante annos aliquot manibus & oculis meis usurpaffem, & Fratribus Sylvæducensibus " ex summi illius Theolog. concessione aliquamdiu " usurpandum misissem. Velim hâc occasione obstatos omnes publicos Reformatarum Scholarum, " Ecclesiarum, Politiarum, Bibliothecarios, exemplaria illa, si quæ in ipsorum potestate sint, capsis " inclusa diligenter custodiant, ne à plagiariis auferantur; aut, si non sint, hoc agant, ut à privatis " five Bibliopolis, sive Viris literatis, prece aut pretio " quovis redimant. —— But, *since I have been mentioned the* Poenitentiary *Fees, I must take notice, that there are but few Copies of it now to be met with, (by whose means, and what Contrivance, is not difficult to be conjectured,) though we have some of the* Paris *Edition, in 1520, in 4to, by* Tussain Denis, *still remaining in our Hands. It was also published at Venice, with several other Tracts, in the* Oceanus Juris. *I must add, that both the Fact, and the Book, are denied by the Papists, insomuch that when we cite those Fees, we are not only suspected, but even accused, of Forgery and Calumny. It happened in the Year* 1633, *that a certain Civilian, and Counsellor of* Bois le-duc, *engaged (by an usual Bravo) to renounce Popery, if those Abominations could be proved, which our Protestants quoted from those Fees. In order to give full Satisfaction to this honourable and learned Person, great Inquiry was made for a Copy of it, and, among others, Application was made to me. As I had not an Edition by me, which was published by the Papists, I borrowed one of That celebrated Divine,* Andrew Rivet. *About two Years after, being consulted again, upon another Dispute between our People, and some of the Papists, concerning these Fees, I shewed them the Library of* Rivet, *where I knew there was a Copy of the* Paris *Edition,* 1520; *having myself pe-*

" *rused it, some Years before, and sent it, by the Favour of that great Divine, to be perused, for some time, by the Fraternity of* Bois-le-duc. *I would take this Occasion earnestly to intreat all public Library-keepers of Protestant Seminaries, Churches, and Societies, who have any of these Copies in their Custody, to take particular Care and secure them in their Cases, out of the Reach of Plagiaries; and those, who have not any of them, to make it their Business to procure such as are to be met with in private Hands, either of Booksellers, or Men of Learning, at any Rate.*"
I take the *Romish* Controvertists, who have not a Word to say against the Authority of the Edition of *Rome*, or That of *Paris*, to be under great Perplexity. This appears from the Answers of Abbot *Richard* to the *Prejugez* of Mr *Jurieu*. This Minister had published the *Abominations of the Tax of the Chancery* (31). The Abbot replies, that these were only particular Facts, which had never been *authorized by the Laws and Canons of the Church of* Rome (32). We find, indeed, *continues he* (33), that [Mr *Jurieu*] relates " these Taxes from an old Book of the *Romish* Chancery. But is it not extremely ridiculous, to endeavour to pass upon the World a Book of Taxes for Laws and Canons? Would it not be making a Jest of all Civil Law, to insert Tables of Taxes into the Code, and reckon them in the Number of Laws? Would not this be doing great Honour to the Gentlemen concerned in them? Let Mr *Jurieu*, therefore, inform himself, what are the Laws and Canons of the Church of *Rome*; and let him know, in the mean time, that these old Taxes of the Chancery of *Rome* are not only of no Authority in the Church, but have always been regarded by her with Horror. The *Taxes of the Chancery* began but under the Pontificate of *John* XXII, about the Year 1320; and the *Taxes of the Pænitentiary* appeared only towards the Year 1336, under *Benedict* XII †; and both were immediately suppressed, and ever afterwards ranked in the Number of prohibited Books, according to the Remark of Mr *du Mont*, who printed them in the Year 1664; which sufficiently shews the Church of *Rome*'s Abhorrence of those Taxes, and that the is far from proposing, or observing, them for Rules, as Mr *Jurieu* would make us believe she has done. Let him therefore consider, that the Acts of the Officers of the Court of *Rome* are but particular Acts, and not at all the Acts of the Church." This Answer is far from sufficient; for, in the first place, the Church of *Rome* has never shewn, by the Suppression of these Taxes, that she has had them in Abhorrence. They have been printed thrice at *Paris*, twice at *Cologn*, and twice at *Venice*; and some of these Editions have been published since *Claude d'Espence* exclaimed publickly against the Enormities of this Book. We have seen, that the Inquisition of *Spain*, and That of *Rome*, have condemned it only as they suppose it to have been corrupted by Heretics. I must add, in the second place, that the Suppression of such a Work is not a sure Sign of disapproving the Rules it contains. This may only signify, that they repented of the Publication of it, as it gave so fair a Handle for the Heretics to reproach the Court of *Rome*, and to wound the Church of *Rome* through the Sides of the Pope. These ought to be esteemed Mysteries of State, *Arcana Imperii*, not to be divulged (34). Are there not Persons of the same Opinion as to Ceremonies (35)? I pass by many other Considerations, which a Controvertist might alledge against Mr *Jurieu*'s Adversary; but I shall not content myself with observing, that *Claude d'Espence* exclaimed, very loudly, against the Abomination of these Taxes (36); I must also observe, that the Protestant Controvertists cite This, in all their Disputes, and that the *Spanish* Inquisition would have this Passage expunged from That Doctor's Book (37). Note, that the Inquisition of *Rome* has condemned *Laurence Banck*'s Edition of the Taxes (38).

BANDEL (MATTHEW), born at *Castro-novo* in *Lombardy*, flourished in the XVIth Century (a). He was a *Dominican*. *Moreri* (b) has repeated the greatest part of what *Vossius* had said of him; but he ought to have added some other curious matters of Fact, and not to have omitted two Circumstances, which were taken notice of by *Vossius*: One of which is, That the Translation of *Egesippus* is in *Italian*;

BANDEL.

Italian; The other, that the Inhabitants of *Fermo* caused the Harangue, which *Matthew Bandel* made in praise of their City, in the Year 1513, to be placed among their Records (c). Here follow some Supplements. This Friar, being at *Mantua*, contracted a very strict Friendship with *Julius Cæsar Scaliger*, which continued all his Life-time, and which he carefully cultivated in *Guienne* [*A*]. He was some Months Bishop of *Agen*, and there he composed, in the *Italian* Tongue, the Histories, or the Gallant Novels, which made him so famous. I have quoted them in the Remark [*M*] of the Article LEO X. and in the Remark [*I*] of the Article MAHOMET II. They are each of them dedicated to some Person of his Acquaintance (d). The Twenty first of his Second Part is dedicated to *Lucretia de Gonzague*, to whom he had been Preceptor (e). He dedicated another to his Friend *Scaliger*. They have been translated into *French*, and we must say a word about the Judgment, which the Translator made of them [*B*]. The Catalogue of *Thuanus*'s Library (f) informs me, that the three first Parts were printed at *Lucca*, in the Year 1554, in *Quarto*, and the fourth at *Lyons*, in the Year 1573, in *Octavo*. I wonder, that Mr *Menage* did not place this Monk in the Catalogue of Ecclesiastics, who have composed Love Verses (g) [*C*].

(c) Voss. de Hist. Lat. pag. 677.

(d) See Remark [*A*].

(e) See that Lady's Article.

(f) In pag. 408, of part 2.

(g) It is at the end of the Anti-Baillet.

[*A*] *He contracted a Friendship, with Julius Cæsar Scaliger, --- which be cultivated --- in Guienne.*] This would scarcely be known, but from these Words: "Eodem tempore Mantuæ degebat Matthæus Bandellus insuper Dominicanus, vir eloquentissimus, & optimus, qui postea per aliquot menses Episcopus Aginnensis fuit, & Mantuæ Marium Æquicolam sumina observantia coluit, atque ibi cum Julio Cælare arctissima amicitiæ necessitudine conjunctus fuit, quam ab eo tempore, ad supremum usque vitæ diem, in Aquitania perpetuavit. Is, quum unam historiarum suarum, quas Aginni Etrusca lingua Boccatium imitatus conscripsit Julio dedicaret, eum non solum Scaligerum agnoscit, sed etiam illustrissimum vocat in epistola dedicationis. Et quum in quatuor tomis ingentibus, singulas singulis summis, & nobilissimis, ac generosissimis viris dedicaverit, neminem eorum majori honore, quam Julium affecit, quum aliquot ex illis illustres vocare nulla fuissset invidia (1). ---- *At the same Time lived, at Mantua, Matthew Bandel, a Dominican, a very eloquent, and excellent Man, who was afterwards, for some Months, Bishop of Agen, and, at Mantua, professed a great Esteem for Marius Æquicola, contracting also there a most intimate Friendship, and Familiarity, with Julius Cæsar Scaliger, which he continued afterwards, in Guienne, to the Day of his Death. He dedicated to him one of his Novels, which he wrote in Italian, in Imitation of Boccace, and calls him Illustrious Scaliger, in his Epistle dedicatory. And, though he dedicates every particular Novel, in all the four great Volumes, to so many several Persons of the highest Rank, yet he honours none of them more remarkably than Scaliger, though calling some of Those illustrious was far from a being Compliment.*" *Lucretia de Gonzague* wrote two Letters to Father *Bandel*, which intimate to us, that he was advanced to some Preferment. The first (2) shews, that he was in *France* (3), the second that he was in *Guienne*: In the first he is called *Reverendo patre*, but, in the other, he is stiled *Monsigner P. Bandello*, and he is congratulated on his new Dignity. There is no Date of the Year to it. He was not yet a Bishop, when *Julius Cæsar Scaliger* wrote him a Letter (4), on the Death of *Fracastorius*. The Mother (5), *Bandel* returned him, is dated *Bassanui* 22 *Novemb.* 1553.

(1) Joseph Scaliger. in Confutatione Fabulæ Burdoniæ, p. 269, 270.

(2) Letter of Lucretia de Gonzague. Venice 1552.

(3) Page 63.

(4) Pag. 56. of his Letters, Edit. of Leyden, 1600.

(5) Letter 5, among those of Julius Cæsar Scaliger.

(6) Printed at Paris, in 1561; and reprinted, the same Year, at Antwerp.

[*B*] *His Novels have been translated into French. --- Here is the Judgment the Translator made of them.*] Observe, that of all, that the first six were done into *French*, by *Peter Boisteau*, and the other by *Belleforest*. The Advertisement to the Reader, prefixed to the first Volume (6), contains these Words: "Desiring also that you would not to take it ill, if I have not confined myself to the Stile of *Bandel* for his Phrases seemed so harsh to me, his Expressions so improper, his Discourse so ill put together, and his Sentences so barren, that I chose rather to new-mou'd his Work, and put it into another Form, than to be such a superstitious Imitator, having only taken the Subject Matter of the History, as you will easily discover, if you have the Curiosity to compare my Style with his." Observe here a Fact, which is pretty curious. *Belleforest*, working on the Thirty seventh Novel, was seized with such a Remorse of Conscience, that he resolved to leave off his Translation. "I will here lay down my Pen, says he (7), and leave, from henceforth,

(7) P. Pelotreau, 'Traité Bibliothèques, Tom. III. 134, 135, 136. Edit. Paris, 1664.

these Subjects, which are capable of being turned every way, and may serve as Lessons of Instruction to some, and, to others, as Examples, to incourage them in their Follies and Wildness; for what I have done of it, at this time, was rather to gratify a Friend, than out of any Desire to be accessary to the Publication of any Thing of this kind. Not that Age exempts me from speaking merrily and jocosely; but, whatever may be concealed under them, that may colour the too soft, and tender, Expressions, necessary to be used in describing Amours, there are different times for these Merriments: And, besides, I have other Designs of greater Consequence than *Bandel*'s Histories, or the Amours of Those, who, by their Example, should deter us from following our sensual Appetite so far, as to become, at last, the Entertainment of Posterity, by the Memory of our Follies. This King (8), then, shall put an End to my Undertaking, and make me, from henceforth, take my Leave of all prophane Subjects, unless, sometimes, a more solid History should enliven my Spirits, and a longer Discourse should encourage me still to go on with this Author, whom I have rather adorned and amplified, than followed, or imitated." To excuse what is past, he adds this Remark. "I do not write Love Stories out of Laciviousness, but as one, who laughs at Fools, and those, that are vainly transported with, and suffer themselves to be conquered by, their Lusts; and accuses Adulterers, detests the Infamous, abhors Murtherers, and is sorry, that there are such senseless Men in the World, who sacrifice their Lives for so short a Pleasure, as the Ease of the Body. In fine, I praise Virtue, and condemn Sin, wishing, that, as I myself have taken warning, by these Examples, so I may see others put an End to their Folly, by the Amendment of their Lives. If any Body takes more Delight in the merry Stories, that are in *Bandel*, let him divert himself with them as much as he pleases: As for me, (as I have said) I give him up my Share of it, and leave him also the Happiness and Honour he may receive from thence, by enriching this dry Author, and also our Language, with the natural Sweetness of his Eloquence (9)." See here a *French* Layman, who scruples to translate, what an *Italian* Monk had wrote about Love. But this Scruple did not continue long; for *Belleforest* finished That Translation, and even added some Supplements to it.

(8) Henry VIII, King of England.

(9) Belleforest, ibid. pag. 65.

[*C*] *Mr Menage has not placed him in the Number of Ecclesiastics, who composed Love Verses.*] *Bandel* wrote some, and was congratulated for them, by his Friends. See *Julius Cæsar Scaliger*'s Epigram, *de Bandelli amoribus Thusca lingua decantatis* (10), and the four Verses I am going to transcribe:

Dum teneros loquitur dulcis Bandellus amores,
Ipse sui oblitus tela remisit amor.
Seu canit Aonium fontem fontisque sorores,
Fonti ipsi ex illo lactea vena fluit (11).

*While sweet Bandellus paints Love's various Charms,
The list'ning God lets fall his useless Arms.
Or, if of Helicon we hear him sing,
His flowing Wit supplies the Muses Spring.*

The Catalogue of *Nicolas Heinsius*'s Library (12) informs me, that the *Canti* XI, &c. *dal Bandelli*, were printed, at *Agen*, in the Year 1545, in 8vo.

(10) You will find it in the Article [*B*].

(11) Just. Cæsar Scaliger in Poesiboribus, p. 327, part 2.

(12) In pag. 270, part II.

BANDOLE

BANDOLE. BANGIUS. BARANZAN.

BANDOLE (ANTHONY de), Advocate in the Parliament of *Provence*, published a French Tranſlation of *Xiphilinus*, at *Paris*, in the Year 1610, in *Quarto*. He alſo printed, in the ſame City, in 1609, in *Quarto*, a Parallel between *Cæſar*, and *Henry* IV, prefixed to *Cæſar's Commentaries*, tranſlated into *French*, and commented on by *Vigenere*.

BANGIUS (THOMAS), Doctor and Profeſſor of Divinity in the Univerſity of *Copenhagen*, was born in the Year 1600 (a). He finiſhed his Studies in Humanity in the College of *Ottenſee*, in the Iſland of *Funen*, and, about the Year 1621, he went to *Copenhagen*, where he continued his Studies with great Succeſs. *Gaſper Brochmand*, Profeſſor of Divinity, and Biſhop of *Sealand*, made him Preceptor to his Son. *Bangius* was, at the ſame time, Preceptor to *Chriſtian Friis*, eldeſt Son of the Chancellor of *Denmark*. Having continued that Employ above five Years, he obtained a Penſion of the King, and went to *Roſtock*, from whence he returned to *Copenhagen*, upon the Emperor's Troops advancing towards the *Baltic* Sea. He finiſhed his Courſe of Divinity under Profeſſor *Brochmand*, and then went to *Franeker*, where he learned *Rabiniſm* and *Chaldaiſm* under *Sixtinus Amama*, by whom he was much eſteemed. He afterwards ſtudied at *Wittemberg*, where he received a Letter, in the Year 1630, from the Rector, and Council, of the Univerſity of *Copenhagen*, offering him the Profeſſorſhip of the *Hebrew* Tongue. He deſired to be excuſed, as not being learned enough to acquit himſelf worthily of that Office: But, being adviſed by Profeſſor *Brochmand*, who was then Rector, not to refuſe what was offered him, he accepted of it, upon condition that he might be permitted to imploy the Income of that Poſt in ſtudying the *Arabic* and *Syriac* Languages, for ſome Years, under *Gabriel Sionita* (b). This being conſented to, he went to *Copenhagen*, and, in the Month of *September* 1630, he took poſſeſſion of the *Hebrew* Profeſſorſhip, and afterwards was made Doctor in Philoſophy. He diſcharged this Duty, to the Advantage and Improvement of the Students, till the Year 1652, when he was promoted to the Profeſſorſhip of Divinity, vacant by the Death of *Brochmand*. He was made Doctor of the ſame Faculty in the Year 1653, in the King and Queen's Preſence. Three Years after, the Office of Library-Keeper of the Univerſity was conferred upon him, and he performed the Dedication of the Church of the *Trinity*, by a *Latin* Sermon (c). Being taken ill, the eleventh of *October* 1661, his chief Care was of the Concerns of his Soul: He Confeſſed himſelf, and Communicated the ſixth Day of his Sickneſs, and died the Twenty ſeventh of the ſame Month (d). He married, in 1638, the Daughter of a Senator, by whom he had fourteen Children, eight Sons and ſix Daughters. His Writings teſtify his Learning [*A*].

[*A*] *His Writings teſtify his Learning.*] He was an Author before he was a Doctor: for, in the Year 1627, he publiſh'd an Expoſition of a Paſſage of *Jeremiah* (1). His *Vindiciæ locorum Geneſ.* xlviii. 16. *Geneſ.* lvi. 1. *Pſalm* xix. 1. appeared in the Year 1630. The Year following, he publiſhed *Fontium Iſraëlis Trias*, *Jona*, *Michæa*, *Ruth*; and in the Year 1634, his *Exercitatio Glottologica*, *de Ortu Linguarum*. His *Exercitationes octo literariæ antiquitatis* appeared in the Year 1638. The two Books, *Obſervationum Philologicarum*, appeared two Years after. The *Hermes & Pan Hebraicus*, *quo vivum abſoluti Hebraici Lexicographi exemplum proponitur*, was printed in 1641 (2). The *Phoſphorus Inſcriptionis hieroſymbolicæ*, *quo Stellæburgum regium Haſnienſe illuſtratur*, came out in the Year 1648, and was followed, the Year after, by the *Tropæum protevangelicum*, *quo ex Scriptis Pontificiorum oſtenditur veram eſſe lectionem*, Ipſum conteret tibi caput, & ſoli Chriſto convenire. The *Exercitatio elenchtica de Nephilimis*, *Gigantibus vulgo dictis*, *oppoſita Jacobo Boulducco* was a Work of the Year 1652; and the *Oliva Sacræ pacis repurgata*, a Work of the Year 1654; and the *Cœlum Orientis & priſci Mundi*, a Work of the Year 1657. I do not mention the Titles of ſome other Works, which have not been omitted in the *Funeral Programme*, nor by *Albert Bartholin* (3). Some of the Books, whoſe Titles I have mentioned, are only Orations, of which Number is the *Oliva Sacræ pacis repurgata*. This, however, has obtained a Place for the Author in the Catalogue of the Reconcilers of Religion (4), and has been wholly inſerted in the *Irenicorum Tractatuum Prodromus*, by *John Duræus*, or rather Dury.

BARANZAN (REDEMPTUS), a *Barnabite* Fryar, was one of the firſt, in the XVIIth Century, who ventured to quit the Path of *Ariſtotle's* Philoſophy. *La Mothe le Vayer* ſays, that *he may be placed among the firſt Wits of our Age* (a), and that the Works of his Youth entitle him to it [*A*]. He adds, that this honeſt *Barnabite* had many times promiſed him, but always under the good pleaſure of God, That he would appear to him again, *if he ſhould depart this Life*. He did not keep his word, *Providence having ordered otherwiſe*; and he verified the Sentence of a *Latin* Poet.

Qui nunc it per iter tenebricoſum,
Illuc unde negant redire quemquam (b).

[*A*] *He may be placed among the greateſt Wits of our Age; the Works of his Youth intitle him to it.*] Doubtleſs he means the Book *De novis Opinionibus Phyſicæ*, printed, at *Lyons*, in the Year 1619. *Konig* mentions two of This Fryar's Works. *Edidit*, ſays he, *Uranoſcopiam & campum Philoſophicum*, ann. 1620 (1). — *He publiſhed two Pieces, one called* Uranoſcopia, *the other* Campus Philoſophicus. I have had, in my Hands, a Copy of the *Campus Philoſophicus*, printed, at *Lyons*, in the Year 1619. It contained but one Volume, and treated only of Logic, very much in the manner of the *Peripatetics*: but the Approbation, annexed, gives me to underſtand, that This Volume is but the firſt Part of *Baranzan's* Courſe of Philoſophy, and that the general Title of That Courſe is, *Summa Philoſophica Annecienſis*; which confirms what I have ſaid, that That Author taught in *Anneci*.

[*A*] Volaterran

Who now does Death's benighted Way explore,
From whence the wand'ring Soul returns no more.

I shall mention, in another place (c), some Persons who have made such Promises. Baranzan was of Verceil: He taught Mathematics and Philosophy in the City of Anneci in Savoy. Naudé, in the Seventy ninth page of the Instruction, which he published in 1623, concerning the Society of Rosicrusians, mentions him as then dead.

BARBARUS (FRANCIS), a Noble *Venetian*, was a famous Man in the XVth Century. He was not only very learned, but also very skillful in the managing Affairs of Government. He was no less a Statesman, than a Man of Letters, as he made appear in all the public Employs, with which he was intrusted; and principally when he was Governor of *Brescia*. The Vigilance, Steadiness, Tractableness, and other great Virtues, wherewith he defended That City against the Forces of the Duke of *Milan*, commanded by the famous *Picinin*, cannot be sufficiently admired. He had Enemies within, and without, the Town, and conquered them all. The Divisions were very great in the City: the *Avogadri*, and the *Martinenghes*, were the Heads of two opposite Factions; he engaged them, by his Eloquence, to unite, and act in concert, for the Public Good. The length of the Siege, or Blockade, caused a Famine in the Town, and the Famine caused the Plague; and yet, under all these Obstructions, he had the happiness to frustrate all Attempts of the Enemy, for three Years, and force them to retire. This happened about the Year 1439 (a). Some Authors believe, that our *Francis Barbarus* is he, who wrote a Book *de Re Uxoria*, some *Letters*, and some Orations. It is the opinion of *Volaterran* (b), who adds, that he had been a Disciple of *Chrysoloras*, and that he forgot all his *Greek* in his Old-age. *Volaterran* might perhaps be under some Mistake [A]. *Francis Barbarus* died in the Year 1454 (c).

[A] *Volaterran might perhaps be under some Mistake.*] These are the Grounds of my Suspicion. I find, in *Vianoli*, that *Francis Barbarus*, who so successfully defended the City of *Brescia*, was the Father of *Zachary*, and That *Zachary* was the Father of *Hermolaus Barbarus* (1). I find, in *Gesner's* Bibliotheca, that *Francis Barbarus*, Author of the Book *de Re Uxoria*, translated the *Lives of Aristides* and *Cato* from the *Greek* of *Plutarch*, and dedicated them to his Brother *Zachary*. I find, in *Volaterran* (2), that *Hermolaus Barbarus* was Nephew (3) of That *Francis Barbarus*, who defended the City of *Brescia*: *Volaterran* had mentioned this *Francis Barbarus*, in the Seven hundred and seventy third Page, and, among other things, had said of him what follows: " He understood the *Greek* Tongue well, but, as " I have heard his Relation, *Hermolaus Barbarus*, say, " he forgot it quite in his Old-days. *Hic postremo* " *senescens, uti ab Hermolao ejus necessario accepi,* " *literarum Græcarum, quas pr.bè tenebat, erat omnino* " *oblitus.*" The other Particulars, which *Volaterran* has related of This *Francis Barbarus* are, that he had been a Disciple of *Chrysoloras*, that he had written a Book *de Re Uxoria*, some *Orations*, and some *Letters*, and that he acquired a great Reputation in defending the City of *Brescia*. *Dum Brixia Prætor esset, eam urbem à Philippi ducis obsidione magnâ cum laude liberavit.* This gives room to suspect, that *Volaterran* has promiscuously joined together what belongs respectively to the Father and Son. The Passage of *Gesner* testifies, that *Francis Barbarus*, Author of the Book *de Re Uxoria*, and Translator of the *Life of Aristides*, was the Brother of *Zachary Barbarus*. Now, according to *Vianoli*, *Zachary Barbarus* was the Son of him, who defended *Brescia*, and Father of *Hermolaus*: it should be said, then, that he, who defended *Brescia*, had a Son, whose Name was *Francis Barbarus*, who wrote the Book *de Re Uxoria*, and translated the *Lives of Aristides* and *Cato* out of the *Greek* of *Plutarch*, and who was Uncle of *Hermolaus Barbarus*. According to this, *Volaterran* attributes certain Things to the Father, which belong only to the Son. Moreover, he, who defended *Brescia*, might have had a Brother, whose Name was *Zachary*, to whom he had dedicated his two Translations; and then *Volaterran's* whole Mistake would consist, in not having known, that *Francis Barbarus* was the Grandfather of *Hermolaus*. If I had the Works of *Francis Barbarus*, probably, I might find some Circumstances, which would decide the Question. But, for want of that Advantage, I desired Mr *de Larroque* to clear my Doubt; and this was his Answer: " Mr *Joli* proves (4), that the Au- " thor of the Book *de Re Uxoria* was the Grandfa- " ther of *Hermolaus*, and that he published it about " the Time of the Council of *Constance*; for *Poggio* " and *Paul Vergerio* mention That Book, in some " *Letters*, dated from the City of *Constance*: *Poggio's* " *Letter* is written to *Guerini* of *Verona*, and That " of *Vergerio* to *Nicholas Leontinus*. They praise " *Francis Barbarus* for having written so well con- " cerning Marriage, though he was very young, " and not married himself. He dedicated the Tran- " slation of the *Lives of Aristides* and *Cato* to his " Brother *Zachary*, and died in the Year 1454: " Mr *Joli* distinguishes two *Daniel Barbarus's.*" Note, I have been told, that this Preface of Mr *Joli*, which I have quoted, contains several Elogies of the Author of the Book *de Re Uxoria*, and clears up a great many Things, that concern learned Men.

Gesner and *Vossius* quote a Letter of *Andrew Brentius*, by which one may learn, that *Francis Barbarus*, Grandfather of *Hermolaus*, and Father of *Zachary*, had composed and translated many Books. " Nimirum in te omnia Francisci Barbari patris vi- " tutum lumina elucescunt: cui certe multum La- " tina lingua debet, tot tantisque ab eo libris partim " compositis, partim conversis, à quo minime dege- " nerat Hermolaus filius, te tanto patre non indig- " nus (5). — For, in you, all the Virtues of your Father " *Francis Barbarus shine in their brightest Lustre: to* " *whom, undoubtedly, the Latin Tongue is greatly in-* " *debted, on account of so many Books, some composed,* " *and others translated, by him; and from whom Her-* " *molaus, a worthy Son of so great a Father, does* " *not at all degenerate.*" It is very certain, by the Testimony of *Hermolaus* himself (6), that his Father's Name was *Zachary*; so that *Philip de Bergamo* was much mistaken, when he made him the Son of *Francis Barbarus*, and Grandson of *Zachary*: *Francisci Barbari filius, Zachariæ Barbari nepos* (7). *Moreri*, as well here, as in a thousand other Places, translates *Nepos* by *Nephew*, which is a very gross Fault. They, who pretend to write good *Latin*, use *Nepos* only to signify Grandson: They, who are not so scrupulous in their *Latin* Style, use, indeed, the Word *Nepos* for *Nephew*, but they commonly add, *ex fratre*, or *ex sorore*, to take off the Equivocation; if they say *Nepos* only, they mean *Grandson*.

BARBARUS.

BARBARUS (HERMOLAUS), Grandson of the foregoing, was one of the moſt Learned Men of the XVth Century. He was born at *Venice*, the Twenty firſt of *May*, 1454 (*a*). He made ſuch great, and ſpeedy, Proficiency in his Studies, that he began to write Books at the eighteenth Year of his Age [*A*]. The public Employs, wherein he was very early engaged, did not prevent his earneſt application to Learning [*B*]. He was ſent, by the *Venetians*, to the Emperor *Frederic*; and to his Son *Maximilian* King of the *Romans*; and This Deputation was ſo far from putting a ſtop to his Pen, that it ſupplied him with matter to exerciſe it; for he did not only publiſh the Speech [*C*], which he delivered before thoſe two Princes, at *Bruges*, in the Year 1486, but he wrote alſo a Treatiſe of the Agreement of Aſtronomy with Phyſic; I ſay, he wrote it the ſame Year, as he went through the City of *Cologne* in his way to *Mentz*, at the deſire of *Theodoric Flas*, a Phyſician of *Nuis* (*b*). As he underſtood *Greek* very well, he undertook the moſt difficult Tranſlations, and began with a celebrated Paraphraſt on *Ariſtotle*; I mean *Themiſtius*. Afterwards he undertook *Dioſcorides*, whoſe Text he corrected as well as he could, and made a Tranſlation of it; to which he added a very learned Commentary. It is ſaid, that he alſo attempted two of the moſt difficult Treatiſes of *Plutarch* (*c*): I cannot tell whether That Tranſlation was ever publiſhed. He had a deſign to tranſlate all *Ariſtotle's* Works [*D*]; and he ſays, in one of his Epiſtles Dedicatory, that the Execution of that Deſign was a great way advanced. He had an extraordinary Facility in writing Verſes, and it is pretended, that he compoſed above Twelve thouſand [*E*]. But, of all his Works, there is none, which gained him ſo much Reputation, as That, which he perform'd on *Pliny*. He corrected near Five thouſand Paſſages of That Author, and occaſionally reſtored Three hundred in *Pomponius Mela* (*d*). This noble Work has been criticiſed [*F*], as well as his other Books

(*a*) Geſner. in Biblioth. fol. 243, ex Trithemio.

(*b*) Geſner. in Bibl. fol. 317.

(*c*) De Iſide & Oſiride & cur Oracula deſierunt. Geſner. in Libl.

(*d*) Hermol. Barbarus in Præfat. ad Alexandrum VI.

[*A*] *He began to write Books at the eighteenth Year of his Age*] Geſner tells us ſo; *Ab octavodecimo ætatis ſuæ anno ſcribere exorſus multa elegantiſſima opuſcula compoſuit* (1). *Voſſius* intended the ſame thing: but, becauſe his Printer forgot two Letters, it occaſioned Mr *Teiſſier* to ſay, that *Hermolaus Barbarus began to write at Twenty two Years of Age* (2). This is his Tranſlation of theſe Words of *Voſſius*, *Ab anno ætatis duo vigeſimo ſcribere orſus fuit* (3). And thus you ſee the Errors of Printers are ſometimes of great Conſequence. It is plain, that *Voſſius* had written *duodevigeſimo*: So that two Letters, ſuppreſſed in this Word, have robbed an Author of four Years Glory. Mr *Teiſſier's* Fault may be ſeen in the One hundred fifty ſeventh Page of Dr *Cave's Appendice*.

[*B*] *His public Employs - - - - did not prevent his earneſt Application to Learning.*] We muſt underſtand this with ſome Reſtriction; for it is certain, that thoſe Employs muſt have interrupted his Studies. " *Honores, ſays* he (4), *in republica geſſi multos & " magnos: quâ fide, quâ opinione, quâ gratiâ, non " dixerim. Placet quidem impendiſſe annos penitus " duodecim, ſed octo reipub. continuos: totum id " tamen tempus literis ferè periit. — I have di- " ſcharged many, and great, Truſts in the Common- " wealth; with what Fidelity, Reputation, and Fa- " vour, I ſhall not pretend to ſay. I have been en- " gaged in them full twelve Years, eight of which " have been entirely ſpent on the Public: And the " whole Time was almoſt quite* loſt *to Learning*."

[*C*] *He publiſhed a Speech*] It was dedicated to *Caronde let*, who was then Chief Secretary to the King of the *Romans*. The Author confeſſes, that he does not publiſh it exactly as he delivered it; but he declares, at the ſame time, that he gives it entirely as he had prepared it. If he did not ſpeak it as it was compoſed, it was, becauſe the Courtiers deſired him to be ſhort, and to come ſpeedily to the main Point. They were not ignorant, that the Study of polite Learning flouriſhed at that time in *Italy*, and that the Ambaſſadors from That Country took a Pleaſure in making long Speeches, ſet off with all the Ornaments of Rhetoric. Nay, *Hermolaus* was obliged to reduce the two Speeches, which he, and his Colleague had prepared, into one; and, as the Abridgment, and the Reduction, were to be made in the Space of an Hour and a half, judge of *Hermolaus*'s Preſence of Mind, which happily overcame all Theſe Difficulties. " *Obſecro ne mirere ſi qua leges in hoc* " *libello quæ tunc dicta non fuerunt. Nec enim ad-* " *didi nunc ea, ſed detraxi tunc, admonitus ab au-* " *licis exemplo quam limen attigi ne longus eſſem,* " *ambitioſa reciderem, optima quæque dicerem, pa-* " *tientiſſimis omnino, ſed occupatiſſimis tamen Prin-* " *cipibus, parcerem. Amputavi ſubitò confiſſo multa.*

(1) Geſn. Biblioth. fol. 317.

(2) Teiſſier's Additions to the Elogies of Thuanus, Tom. I. p. 354.

(3) Voſſius de Hiſt. Lat. pag. 622.

(4) Herm. Barbar. Epiſt. 11, lib. 12, inter Politian. Epoſtolas.

" *Conſiderans hoc & æſtimans quòd ſeſqui- " horam antequam Principes adiremus ſignificatum " nobis fuerit non duas orationes ſeorſum, ut cogi- " tabamus & paraveramus, ſed unam dubbus jun- " ctim habendam & recitandam eſſe* (5). - - - - *Be " not ſurprized if you meet with ſome Things here, " which were not delivered. They are not now added, " but were then ſuppreſſed, being adviſed, by the Cour- " tiers, as ſoon as I appeared, not to be long, to cut " off all Flouriſhes, to ſpeak only to the material " Points, and to favour, as much as poſſible, Princes, " who, though they had a great deal of Patience, yet " had very little Leiſure. I immediately cut off ma- " ny Things. - - - - - Conſidering, and providing for " this alſo, that we were told, about an Hour " and half before we were to be admitted into the " Preſence, that we muſt not deliver two ſeparate " Speeches, as we expected, and had prepared, but " put both of them into one.*"

[*D*] *He had a Deſign to tranſlate all* Ariſtotle's *Works.*] See what he ſays in the Preface to his *Pomponius Mela* (6). " *Vocant nos majora quædam ſtu- " dia, urgemuſque noſtrum illud vetus omnes Ari- " ſtotelis libros in latinum vertendi exponendique " propoſitum. Quod ſi ad exitum perduxero* (nam " *bona ejus pars jam pridem perfecta eſt*) non dubito " *futurum, quin de reliquo in literis labore gratia " mihi fiat. - - - - I am intent upon greater Studies, " and am carrying on the old Deſign of tranſlating " into* Latin, *and commenting on, all* Ariſtotle's *Works.* " *Which if I can bring to Perfection, as a great* " *Part of it is already done, I do not doubt but the* " *learned World will thank me for all the reſt of* " *my Time, ſpent in their Service.*" His Tranſlation of *Ariſtotle's* Rhetoric was publiſhed after his Death. See the following Article.

[*E*] *He had an extraordinary Facility in writing Verſes; and had compoſed above Twelve thouſand.*] Among other Pieces of Poetry, he wrote a Poem of Six hundred Verſes, which bears the ſame Title with a Piece, written by his Grand-father *Francis Barbarus*, I mean, *de Re Uxoria*; but the Subſtance of them is very different. *Francis Barbarus* preſcribes Rules as well to thoſe, that would marry, as to thoſe, that are already married (7): he is to be very particular, that he has a Chapter *de coïtus ratione*. *Hermolaus* confines himſelf to this Queſtion, *Whether a wiſe Man ought to marry* (8)? and concludes for the Negative.

[*F*] *That noble Work, on* Pliny, *has been criticiſed*] It has been pretended, that he had too much indulged his Conjectures and Memory. *Pintianus* uſed him very rudely upon it. Thoſe, who pardon him the Defects of his Memory, do not forgive the Inſtances of his Temerity; but declare, very freely, that he has undertaken to correct many things, which were no Faults,

(5) Herm. Barbarus Epiſt. ad Carondeletum, inter Epiſtolas Politiani 45, lib. 12.

(6) Apud Geſner. Biblioth fol. 317, verſo.

(7) See the Titles of the Chapters of his Work in Geſner's Biblioth. fol. 240, verſo.

(8) Geſn. Bibl fol. 317.

BARBARUS.

Books [G]. He was Embassador from the Republic of *Venice* to Pope *Innocent* VIII, when the Patriarch of *Aquileia* died. The Pope immediately conferred That Patriarchate upon him. *Hermolaus* was so imprudent as to accept of it, without waiting for the Approbation of his Superiors [H], though he could not be ignorant, that the Republic of *Venice* had made Laws, to forbid all Ministers, sent from thence to the Court of *Rome*, to accept any Benefice. *Hermolaus*'s Excuses, grounded on the Pope's having compelled him to embrace the Prelacy, were not listened to. The Council of Ten signified very roughly to him, to renounce the Patriarchate, and that, if he did not, his Father should be degraded from all his Dignities, and

Faults, but only surpassed his Understanding. It is true, that, in several Editions of *Pliny*, great Regard has been had for *Hermolaus*'s Corrections, since they have been inserted in the Text; but it was said, long ago, that this pretended Physician of *Pliny* had given him more Wounds, than he had cured. Let us see how Father *Hardouin* expresses it. " Ipse " (*Hermolaus*) in iis quæ attigit, sæpè nimium con- " jecturæ, memoriæ etiam plus quam hominem de- " ceat, tribuit: uti paulo acerbius eam ob rem in- " vectus in eum Pintianus olim exprobravit. Sed " concessâ facile veniâ μνημονικῶν ἁμαρτημάτων, " quod minus mirum sit memoriam excidere aliqua- " rum rerum, quam constare omnium : at non ve- " niâ dignus æque, cum neglectis veterum exem- " plarium vestigiis, & priscarum ante se editionum " securus, plurima pro arbitrio, eruditè magis quam " cautè ac verè, mutavit, vel planè pessumdedit : " cum plurima ex iis quæ castigavit, non errata illa " sint, sed parum intellecta. Tantum nihilominus " auctoritati Barbari subsecuta ætas eruditionique " tribuit, ut conjecturas illius, ceu totidem κυρίας " δόξας, in contextum inseruerit, unde eliminandæ " à nobis variis argumentis fuere. Sensit jamdudum " hanc labem operi Pliniano illatam auctor Epigram- " matis, alias haud perelegantis, in Commentarios à " Stephano Aquæo editos, de quibus agendum mox " erit. Sic enim ille :

Dum facere Hermoleos medicinam Barbarus optat
Non paucis lacero vulneribus Plinio,
Perlæsum gravius conjecta vulnerat arte:
Nec minus incauta plurima turba manu.
In tantum ut Latio jam deploratus abiret,
Ob multa in Stygias vulnera fessus aquas, &c.

" Felicior aliquanto SIGISMUNDUS GELE- " NIUS, qui uno duntaxat archetyporum præsi- " dio, collatis inter se exemplaribus, non pauca re- " stituit, quæ Hermolao latuerant (9). —— *He* (Her- " molaus) *in his Corrections, gives often too much* " *Liberty to Conjecture, and to Memory a great deal* " *more than any Man ought to do*; *for which Pintia-* " *nus has a little too severely reproved him*. *But his* " *Faults of Memory are very excusable, since it is* " *much less to be wondred at the letting slip some* " *things, than the retaining all*: *but he is not so easi-* " *ly to be pardoned, for slighting all old Manuscripts*, " *and former Editions, and boldly altering, in an ar-* " *bitrary Manner, with more Learning than Caution* " *and Truth, and sometimes plainly defacing*: *since* " *a great many of his Emendations appear where there* " *were no Faults, but only his own Misunderstand-* " *ings*. *And yet the succeeding Age paid such a regard* " *to the Authority, and Learning, of* Barbarus, *that* " *they inserted his Conjectures as so many authentic* " *Glosses into the Body of the Text, which have cost us* " *a great many Arguments to remove*. *This Injury*, " *done to* Pliny, *was observed by the Author of an Epi-* " *gram, otherwise not very elegant, on the Commen-* " *taries published by* Stephanus Aquæus, *of which we* " *shall presently speak*. *Thus he*,

While Barbarus, and other Quacks, pretend
The mangled State of Pliny's Text to mend:
Their Art so much in blind Conjecture deals,
It boldly gives ten wounds for one it heals.
That thus defac'd he flies the Latian Light,
And gladly seek Repose in Realms of Night.

" SIGISMUNDUS GELENIUS *used a* " *much more successful Method, who, by the sole help* " *of Manuscripts, which he collated, has restored a*

" *great many Places, which Hermolaus passed by*." I have let down this long Passage, the better to convince Mr *Varillas* that he was mistaken in a Matter, which was pretty well known. But yet, I am very well satisfied, that *Hermolaus*'s Work on *Pliny*'s Natural History deserves Admiration, considering the great Number of Authors he was obliged to consult, and the little time he had for it. He says, he performed it in twenty Months: He broke the Ice for others; he found *Pliny* in a very bad Condition, and like a Land that had lain waste a long time, or a House infected with the Plague, or haunted by Hobgobblins. *Hæc erant in Plinianis codice flagitia, propter quæ non parum multis divinum opus tanquam senticetum, imo vero quasi pestilens aut lemuribus infame domicilium vitabant. Ea nos Græcis & Latinis auctoribus perlectis omnibus lucubratione viginti mensium revellere ac publicare curavimus* (10). As to *Volaterran*'s Notion, that it was an Undertaking little suitable to the Character of *Hermolaus Barbarus*; *opus impar ejus dignitates & vitæ instituto* (11), it has been very justly condemned, as well because *Hermolaus* had entred upon it before he was a Churchman, as because it were to be wished, that many other Prelates would commit the like Faults. *Utinam sic a multis ejus dignitatis atque instituti peccaretur* (12). *Vossius* adds another Reason, which is, that *Pliny* did not make him neglect the Episcopal Functions ; witness his Sermons, still preserved in Manuscript at *Padua*. I should rather chuse to say, that, since the *Venetians* would not suffer him to accept that Dignity, he could not neglect the Patriarchal Functions in favour of *Pliny*. Note, that, having published that Work in the Year 1492, he added an Appendix to it, which he calls *Secundæ castigationes*, and which is dated at *Rome*, the thirteenth of *January*, 1493.

[G] *As well as his other Books*.] His Translation of *Themistius* is not just, if we may believe *Vossius*. " Ipse ille Themistius ab Hermolao Barbaro, dum nimium studet elegantiæ, tantâ conversus est libertate, " ut sæpissimè longè aliud dicat quam senserit Themistius (13) : —— Hermolaus Barbarus, *while he* " *too much studied Elegancy, took such liberty in tran-* " *slating* Themistius, *that he often said those Things* " *which* Themistius *was very far from meaning* :" And he has shewn, in the Translation of *Aristotle*'s Rhetoric, that he did not understand *Greek* well enough, if we rely on *Francis de Epishen* (14). It is objected, that he was so full of *Pliny*, that he too often made use of his Words in the Translation of *Dioscorides*: This Translation has been often criticized by Marcellus Virgilius. *Dectè quidem & eleganter transtuli, sed (ut nonnullis videtur) nimis ad imitationem Plinii, quam dum ubique sequitur à Dioscoridis verbis aliquando recedere videtur*. Marcellus Virgilius, qui post Hermolaum eosdem libros transtulit, plerumque interpretationem ejus carpit (15).

[H] Hermolaus *was so imprudent as to accept of the Patriarchate of* Aquileia, *without waiting for the Approbation of his Superiors*] I know of no Body, who has related the Fact better, than *Peter Bembus*; for which reason it cannot be improper, or disagreeable to all those, who have not that History, to see here what he says of it. " Eo mortuo Innocentio " Patriarchatum (sic enim appellant) Aquileiensium " —— Hermolao Barbaro, legato apud se Veneto " attribuit. Quod ubi civitas intellexit, tametsi Her- " molaus ad Senatum scripserat, coactum se à Ponti- " fice vestem senatoriam mutavisse : quoniam tamen " sacerdotiis cooptari cives Veneti, qui legati Romæ " essent, lege prohibebantur ; graviter tulit, ausum " illum contra leges patrias facere. Auxit ejus rei " magnopere invidiam, quod antea ex Hermolai li- " teris, quas ad Senatum de Barbi morte dederat, " more institutoque majorum comitiis senatoriis præ- " judicium

BARBARUS. 635

and soon after see his Estate confiscated. They were inflexible: *Zachary Hermolaus* made use of all imaginable Means to obtain the Consent of the Republic to the Patriarchate of his Son; but, not being able to gain his Point, he died of Grief [*I*]. His Son followed him soon after: Some say, that Grief also was the Cause of his Death [*K*]; but it is more likely, that he died of the Plague. *Pierius Valerianus* has placed him at the head of his *Unfortunate Learned Men*. He seems to me to run an extravagant Length, in saying, that it is not certainly known, whether *Hermolaus Barbarus* was ever buried [*L*]. This great Man died at

" judicium Patres fecerant, cujus ipsi civis nomen ad
" id adipiscendum sacerdotium Innocentio commen-
" darent. Itaque deceptos in eo sese, ac propè de-
" lusos querebantur. Erat omninò Hermolaus, propter
" ejus summam in literarum atque optimarum ar-
" tium studiis præstantiam, magnum apud exteras
" nationes nomen, apud suos quidem certè maxi-
" mum: nam ad doctrinæ singularem opinionem
" etiam vitæ perpetuam innocentiam adjunxerat. Si-
" mul is multum patris opibus, & gratia, qui summo
" proximum in civitate magistratum gereoat, mul-
" tum clientelis, necessitudinibus, propinquitatibusque
" pollebat. Quibus tamen in rebus omnibus satis
" sibi præsidii non habuit: cum pluris à Patribus una
" legum charitas, majestasque, quam ullorum civi-
" um omnibus aucta nominibus dignitas, atque ca-
" ritas, fieret. Decemviri enim literas ad eum se-
" verè scriptas dederunt; mora omni, excusatione-
" que sublata, sacerdotium repudiaret: id si non
" faceret, patrem magistratu remoturos, & bona
" ejus publicaturos præ se tulerunt. At pater, per-
" spectâ civitatis voluntate, omnibus tentatis rebus,
" cum jam eam flecti & leniri posse diffideret,
" ægritudine animi est mortuus. Filius non multò
" post Romæ, edikis Plinianis castigationibus, im-
" mensi propè laboris opere, privatus plebeio mor-
" bo periit. Eum vitæ finem Hermolaus habuit,
" omnium ex sua civitate, qui ante illum nati es-
" sent, Latinorum & Græcorum literis planè doctissi-
(16) Bemb. " mus (16). —— *Upon his Death, Innocent gave*
Hiſtor. Ve- " *the Patriarchate (as it is called) of Aquileia, to*
netæ, lib. 1. " *Hermolaus Barbarus, Embaſſador for the Venetians*
fol. 18 verſo. " *at Rome. Which, when the Senate underſtood, not-*
" *withſtanding Hermolaus had ſignified to them by*
" *Letter, that he had not made this Exchange of his*
" *ſenatorial Robes, without being compelled to it by*
" *the Pope, the Venetian Laws not allowing any of*
" *their Citizens, who are ſent Embaſſadors to Rome,*
" *to accept of any Eccleſiaſtical Preferments, they*
" *were much incenſed, that he ſhould dare to infringe*
" *the Laws of his Country. What farther heightened*
" *their Diſpleaſure was, that, upon the News the Se-*
" *nate had received, by Letters from Hermolaus, of*
" *the Death of Barbus, they had, in their Aſſembly,*
" *according to ancient Cuſtom, made choice of a Per-*
" *ſon, whoſe Name they were to recommend to Inno-*
" *cent, to ſucceed in That Patriarchate. Therefore*
" *they looked upon themſelves as deceived, and in*
" *ſome Meaſure tricked by him. The Reputation of*
" *Hermolaus was very great in foreign Nations, on*
" *account of his extenſive Learning; and greateſt of*
" *all in his own; the Integrity of his Life being as*
" *extraordinary as his Knowledge. The Wealth and*
" *Intereſt of his Father, whoſe Office in the Republic*
" *was next to that of the Venetian Magiſtrate, the Num-*
" *ber of his own Dependants, Friends, and Relations,*
" *were great Advantages to him. But yet all theſe*
" *put together were not ſufficient to protect him: ſince*
" *the ſingle Conſideration of the Value and Authority*
" *of their Laws was of more weight with the Senate,*
" *than all the Excellencies, which any of their Citi-*
" *zens could poſſibly attain. The Council of Ten*
" *wrote ſeverely to him, that, without delay or excuſe,*
" *he ſhould renounce his Eccleſiaſtical Dignity; and*
" *threatened to degrade his Father, and confiſcate his*
" *Eſtate, in caſe of Refuſal. The Father, finding the*
" *fixed Reſolution of the Senate, which he had, in*
" *vain, tried all poſſible means to ſoften and divert,*
" *died of Grief. The Son not long after, having pub-*
" *liſhed his Corrections of Pliny, a Work of immenſe*
" *Labour, died at Rome in a private Station, and of*
" *a vulgar Diſtemper. This was the End of Hermo-*
" *laus, who, for his Learning in Latin and Greek, was*
" *the moſt extraordinary Perſon Venice had ever pro-*
" *duced.*"

[*I*] *His Father —— died of Grief.*] We have just now seen, that *Bembus* asserts it. The thing is likely enough; for he was an ancient Man, and enjoyed one of the chief Posts of the Republic. Such an hard Experience of the Decay of one's Credit in one's old Age, and to the Prejudice of a famous and dearly-beloved Son, is generally a fatal Blow. *Zachary Barbarus* died in the Year 1492, much resigned to the Decrees of Providence: He was in the seventieth Year of his Life: He was much lamented, and his Funeral-Pomp was very magnificent. See the Letter, which *Hermolaus* wrote to his Friend *Antonius Calvus* (17). "Accedit quod septuagesimum (17.) It is
" ingressus annum, quamdiu in familia nostra vixit *the 32d of*
" nemo; quod functus omnibus honoribus; quod re- *the 12th*
" publica incolumi; quod liberis honesto loco posi- *Book of those*
" tis; incredibili desiderio & amore civitatis excessa, *of Politian.*
" frequentia funeris tanta (ut audio) quanta in cive
" nunquam. —— *We muſt add, that having entred*
" *into his ſeventieth Year, to which none of our Fa-*
" *mily ever before arrived; that having attained all*
" *the higheſt Honours; that having ſeen the Republic*
" *in abſolute Security; that having placed his Children*
" *in honourable Stations, he died extreamly lamented*
" *and beloved by all, and was attended, I am told,*
" *at his Funeral, by ſuch Numbers, as no Citizen*
" *ever had been before.*"

[*K*] *Some ſay, that Grief alſo was the Cauſe of his Death.*] *Volaterran* affirms it: "Romæ decessit ex
" animi dolore exacerbante quod orator à Venetis
" missus, præter ejus autoritatem Senatus, Patriar-
" cha Aquileiensis ab Innocentio fuerat creatus, ac
" proptereà contumax & exul (18). —— *He died at* (18) Volat.
Rome through exceſs of Grief, becauſe, being ſent lib. 21, pag.
thither Embaſſador by the Venetians, and made 777.
Patriarch of Aquileia, by Innocent, without their
Conſent, he was therefore declared a Rebel, and an
Exile." I am fully persuaded, he died, being accounted a Rebel, and an Exile; for he always took upon himself the Title of Patriarch, notwithstanding the strict Orders he had received from his Sovereign to renounce the Patriarchate; but I believe he died of the Plague, and not of Grief. My Reason is, I. That, from the time of his Disgrace to his Death, he was engaged in a Work, which required a great Composure of Mind, and a perfect State of Health (19). II. That *Peter Crinitus*, who lived at (19) Vix.
that time, declares, That *Hermolaus* died of the *The Correc-*
Plague (20). He does not relate it in general, but *tion of Pli-*
adds a very particular Circumstance, which is, that *ny.*
Picus Mirandulanus, having heard at *Florence*, that (20) Crinit.
Hermolaus was sick of the Plague, sent him an Anti- de honeſtâ
dote with all Speed; but the Messenger came too Diſciplinâ,
late. *Paulus Jovius* reports the same Fact. "Morè lib. 1. c. 7.
" ante diem irrepsit, & pestilenti quidem morbo
" properats, adeo ut quod à Pico Politianoque Flo-
" rentiâ laboranti per dispositos equos mitteretur
" miræ potestatis antidotum, veneni celeritate præ-
" verteret (21). —— *Death approached before-* (21) Jovius
" *hand, being haſtened by a Peſtilential Diſtem-* Elog. c. 36.
" *per, which made ſuch quick Diſpatch, that the*
" *famous Antidote, which was ſent him with all poſſi-*
" *ble Expedition from Florence by Picus, and Poli-*
" *tian, came too late.*" So that I can easily believe what *Hermolaus Barbarus* says of himself, That he bore his Disgrace without Uneasiness, and was even pleased with an Injury, which gave him an entire Leisure for Study (22). His Friends were afraid he (22) See the
would sink under his Disgrace, and his Enemies *31ſt Letter of*
declared so every where. It was undoubtedly by means *the 12th*
of these latter, in order to rob him of the Honour of *Book of thoſe*
his Constancy and Tranquillity, that what was owing *of Politian.*
to a contagious Distemper, was ascribed to Grief. See, in the Remark [*F*], what I quote out of *Alcyonius*.

[*L*] *Pierius Valerianus* —— *ſays, that it is not certain, whether* Hermolaus Barbarus *was ever buried.*] I say once more, that *Pierius Valerianus* seems to run an extravagant Length, in saying, that this Patriarch, dying in Poverty, and forsaken, was depri-

VOL. I. 7 X ved

BARBARUS.

at *Rome*, in the Year 1493. He expresses, in his Letters, a great Resignation, and Tranquillity of Mind, in regard to the Treatment, he had received from his Country (*e*). I do not believe, he can be said to have been a Cardinal [*M*]. It is reported, he had recourse to the Devil, to know the Sense of a *Greek* word [*N*], made use of by *Aristotle*. We must not forget, that *Laurence de Medicis* gave him some *Testimonies* of a singular Esteem [*O*]. Mr *Varillas* has given us a very entertaining and elaborate Account of *Hermolaus Barbarus*, but he is mistaken in many things, and oftener than from *Moreri* [*P*].

I shall ved of Burial: "Ob susceptum inconsulto Senatu "suo Aquileiense sacerdotium exsul factus, & de "possessione ejectus, vitam inopem aliquandiu traxit, "Alexandri Pontificis summi sportula quodammodo "sustentatus: paucis verò post mensibus pestilentia "contactus, desertus ab omnibus, infeliciissimo mor-"tis genere oppressus est; quique laudatione, & elo-"quentia sua innumeros aetatis suae homines illustra-"verat, & funere, & honore sepulchri ita defrauda-"tus est, ut ubi sepultus, quòve hominis cadaver "conjectum fuerit, ignoretur (23).——*Being exiled,* (23) Pier. *and deprived of his Estate, for accepting the Patri-* Valerian. de *archate of Aquileia, without consulting the Senate,* Literatorum *he lived very poor for some time, and was in some* Infelic. *measure maintained by the Charity of Pope Alexan-* pag. 9. *der. In a few Months after, he was taken with the Plague, and, being forsaken by all, died in the most wretched manner; and he, who, by his Eloges and Eloquence, had so highly honoured a great Number of his Cotemporaries, was so far denied both a Funeral and Grave, that, where his Corps was thrown, or buried, no Body can tell.*" Paulus Jovius, who wrote after Pierius Valerianus, does not only say, that *Hermolaus Barbarus* was buried, but also mentions the Place of his Burial. "Scilicet ut nimis "severa patria optimi civis ossa non haberet, quae "sub colle hortorum ad Flumentanam portam sepul-"chro condita è Campo Martio ab erudita Romana (24) Jovius "juventute salutantur (24).——*But that his cruel* Elog. c. 36. *Country might not have the Remains of so excellent a Citizen, they were buried under the Hill of the Gardens, near the Flumentan Gate, where they are visited by the Roman Youth from the Campus* (25) Roche-*Martius.*" Mr *da la Rochepozai* (25), and Father pozai in No-Oldoinus (26), point out the place of his Sepulture more menclat. clearly: they place it at *Santa Maria del Popolo*. If Cardinal. *Valerianus* had only said, that the Fear of the Plague (26) Oldoi-caused those, who should have assisted the Patriarch ni, in A-(27), to forsake him, he would not have fallen into then. Ro-This Hyperbole. mano.

[*M*] *I do not believe, he can be said to have been* (27) See, *a Cardinal.*] Pierius Valerianus is far from affirming below, the it; he says some things, that are too inconsistent with Passage of it; but does Paulus Jovius, who has so clearly con- Alcyonius. tradicted him as to the burying place of *Hermolaus Barbarus*, say, that this Patriarch had obtained a Cardinal's Cap? Not in the least: he only says, that he was designed for that Dignity. "Tulisti "quippe aequo animo suffragiorum severitatem, quum "ex eo tamen pari merito tibi purpura pararetur. (28) Valeri- "Sed mors ante diem irrepsit (28).——*Thy even* an. de Litte- *Mind received the cruel Sentence unmoved, and* rat. Infel. *such appeared thy great Merit, that it was just* pag. 9. *about being rewarded with the Purple. But Death approached before hand.*" The Author of the *Nomenclator Cardinalium* reports, that *Trithemius*, followed in this by Pierius Valerianus, and several others, assert, that *Hermolaus Barbarus* attained to the Cardinalship. As to himself, he affirms nothing, but contents himself with these words, *Cardinalis designatus, sed ut fertur nondum evulgatus.*——*Designed a Cardinal, but, as it is said, not declared.* Vossius quotes the Franciscan, *John Riosche*, who asserts (29) In (29), that *Hermolaus Barbarus* was made a Cardinal Compendio (30) Father Hardouin affirms the same thing (31). Historico.

[*N*] *It is reported, he had recourse to the Devil,* (30) Voss. de *to know the Sense of a Greek Word*] This Word H. L. Lat. is so essential to the Peripatetic Natural Philosophy, pag. 621. that, without first fixing the Sense of it, there is no understanding what *Aristotle* meant, concerning (31) Praef. in the Nature of Body. I speak of the Word ἐντελέ- Pl. n. χεια, which some *Latinists*, not being able to find a better, have at last rendered by That of *perfectibabia*. Peter Crinitus speaks as if *Hermolaus* himself had boasted of That magical Consultation, and as if he had said, that the Answer was given with such a weak Voice, that he could make nothing of

it. "Et revera perexilis vocula daemonum & exigua "est, quod olim noster quoque Venetus Hermolaus "dicebat, vocem se daemonis praetenuem & pene "subsibilantem audisse, qua ille, de Aristotelis forte "entelechia interrogatus, sibi ipsi & Georgio Pla-"centino respondisset (32).——*And, indeed, the* (32) Crinit. *Voice of Devils is soft and low, as our Hermolaus,* de honesta *of Venice, formerly said, that he heard the Devil* Disciplina, *answer a Question, he, and George Placentinus,* lib. 6. c. 11. *had put to him, concerning the Entelechia of Ari-stotle, in a faint and whispering sort of Voice.*" I believe I have gone to the Source of this Fact, by quoting Peter Crinitus: Most People (33) quote (33) Father only Bodin's *Daemonomania*, where I have not yet Rapin's Re-met with this Transaction of Hermolaus (34). Some flections on quote Maurolius, who mentions it in his Treatise *de* Philosophy, *Entelechia*. To conclude, some pretend, that *Bar-* pag. 350. *daeus* is the Inventor of *Perfectibabia*: You will find Teissier, E-these Words in *Du Verdier Vau-Privas, And even* log. Tom. 1. *Those, who intended to praise him, have said of him,* pag. 853. Est foeliciissimus quidem, sed audaciissimus in novan- (34) I have dis vocabulis——*He is very happy indeed, but very* not had lei-*bold, in coining new Words*; *as when he rendered Ari-* sure to look *stotle's* Entelechia *by the Word* Perfectibabia (35). Page after Note, that several Persons maintain, that *Cicero* has Page for very ill translated that Word of *Aristotle* (36). this, but I

[*L*] *Laurence de Medicis gave him some Testi-* met with it *monies of a singular Esteem.*] He went to meet him, in the places notwithstanding his ill State of Health, and received where it was him very magnificently at his Country Seat: "Cum most likely "Hermolaus Barbarus Reipub. Venetae nomine lega- (35) De Ver- "tiones forte pro Italiam obiret, & ad urbem Flo- dier, Biblio- "rentiam obiter accederet, Laurentius Medicis (qui oth. Franç. "Florentinam Rempublicam non minore tum con- pag. 472. re- "silio, quam fortuna gubernabat) statim tanto viro porting what "cum amicis pluribus (ut fit) obviam procedit: ni- said of Bar- "hil veritus, quod aegros pedes haberet, ac formidi baeus. "doloribus vexaretur. Tum in Cajana villa (quam (36) Joannes "infinito propè sumptibus aedificabat) honorificen- Ferrerius "tiissimè illum accepit: simulque tanti hominis inge- Pedemonta- "nio, & doctrina singulari provocatus, eam quoque nus confutes "liberalissimè studiorum nomine illi obtulit, cum them in the "insigni atque instructiissima bibliotheca, quam ad Treatise de "exemplum Philadelphi mira tum industria para- Entelechia. "verat, ut in eo quasi Musarum secessu simul cum "Pico Mirandula honestioribus disciplinis, ac philo-"sophiae sacris pro arbitrio incumberet. In quo "Hermolaus Barbarus (ut homo maximè humanus) "libenter se dixit & studiorum causâ, & Laurentii "merito talem animum agnoscere: villamque ipsam, "si per publicas curas liceret, excipere (37).—— (37) Petrus *As* Hermolaus Barbarus, *who happened to be charged* Crinitus de *with some Embassies, from the Republic of Venice,* honesta Dis-*to Italy, took the City of Florence in his Way,* ciplinâ, lib. *Laurence de Medicis, who then governed the Flo-* 11, cap. 9. *rentines with no less Prudence than Success, went* pag. 40. *out to meet so extraordinary a Man, with a great Number of his Friends, as the Ceremony is: Not at all regarding, that he had the Gout in his Feet, and was in great Pain. Then he receiv-ed him very honourably at his Villa Cajana, which he had built at an infinite Expence: and, at the same time, in respect to his great Abilities, and extraordinary Learning, he offered him the Use of it, for the pursuing his Studies, together with a large and curious Library, which, in Imi-tation of Philadelphus, he had collected with sup-sing Industry, in order to enjoy this Retreat of the Muses, together with Picus Mirandulanus, in the Pursuit of Learning and Philosophy. Which kind Of-fer,* Hermolaus Barbarus, *as he was perfectly com-plaisant, readily replied he should be glad to accept, not only for the sake of his own Studies, but also in regard to his Highness's great Favour, if his public Commissions would have given him leave.*"

[*P*] *Mr* Varillas *has given a very entertaining and elaborate Account of* Hermolaus Barbarus; *but he*

I shall cite a Passage of *Alcyonius*, which will shew, that our *Hermolaus* congratulated himself on his Disgrace, and that he never studied with so much application, as after his Country had used him ill [*Q*].

he is mistaken in many things, and oftner than Moreri.] He says (38), L That *Hermolaus Barbarus* was esteemed, at *Venice*, the most remarkable of all the Nobles for the Profession of the highest, and nicest, Gallantry. II. That no Body ever saw him study, or that no Books were to be seen in his Chamber, or Closet. I question the first of these things, and the second I hold to be false. III. That, having undertaken the most laborious Task, then known, in the Republic of Learning (this was the Correction of *Pliny* (39), he made use of the Authority of Manuscripts, and that of The *Greek* and *Roman* Writers, who had treated on the same Subjects; and that, *in such Places, where those two Assistances failed him, he made use of his own Conjectures; with so much Probability and Success, that not one of them have been rejected.* See the Confutation of this, in the Remark [F]. IV. *That it was by this ingenious Method he discovered, that Pliny was born at Como, and that he composed a Dissertation about it, which convinced all those who read it.* Of all the Authors I have consulted for a List of *Barbarus*'s Works, I have found none, who ascribes to him any such Dissertation. It is true, that, in his Preface to *Pliny*, he seems to prefer the reading *Catullum congerronem meum*, before That of *Catullum conterraneum meum*, whereby he eludes a very strong Argument, which is taken from That Passage, to prove, that *Pliny* was of *Verona*. It is true also, that, independently from the reading *Congerronem*, which he will neither absolutely admit, nor reject; he declares, that *Pliny* was of *Como*, and not of *Verona*; but he does not enlarge upon this; he contents himself with three Lines: This therefore cannot be called a formal Dissertation. Now, though *Varillas* were in the right, as to this Point, yet he tells a great Falsity; for there is scarce any learned disinterested Critic, but always adjudged *Pliny* to those of *Verona*. "Causam dudum adjudicarunt Veronensibus eruditi, inter quos præcipui Polycarpus Palermus singulari opere de Plinii patriâ, & Scaliger in Euseb. Chron. pag. 190 (40). — *The Learned have long since adjudged the Cause to the City of Verona, among whom the principal are Polycarp of Palermo, in a particular Treatise on Pliny's Country, and Scaliger on Euseb. Chron. pag. 190."* Very probably the misunderstanding *Paul Jovius*'s Words deceived *Varillas*. "Novocomensis C. Plinium secundum civem suum ab imperitis individiose surreptum erudita præclaraque sententia reddidisti (41). — *Your great Judgment did restore to Novocomum her Citizen C. Pliny II. whom the illiterate had robbed her of."* V. He tells us, in the *Secret History*, That the prodigious Desire *Barbarus* had to remedy the Disorders in *Physic*, made him attempt *Dioscorides in the same manner, as he had done* Pliny. Which is to confound the Order of Times. *Barbarus* lived so short a time after the Publication of his Work on *Pliny*'s Natural History, that he formed no new Designs; he had Books enough to finish; and I do not doubt but that he had begun with *Dioscorides*, before he applied himself wholly to *Pliny* (42). VI. *Hermolaus*'s Friends advised him quietly to enjoy the Honour, which he had acquired by his *Pliny*, and his *Dioscorides*; but he himself told them, he must translate what *Themistius* had left us on *Aristotle*, and be performed *what he had proposed.* Here is a new Anachronism: the Translation of *Themistius* is one of the first that *Barbarus* published. "Themistii Peripatetici Paraphrases in aliquot Aristotelis Libros admodum adolescens Latinas effecit (43). — *He translated the Paraphrase of Themistius the Peripatetic, upon some Books of Aristotle, when he was very young."* He dedicated it to *Sixtus* IV, who had been dead eight Years, when he published his Notes on *Pliny*. VII. *Hermolaus did the Republic Justice, against his own Interest, and confessed, that they had Reason to be against him. He intreated the Pope to confer the Benefice on Him, who should be presented to him by the Ambassador of Venice; and expressly declared, that he would not have it, if he must purchase it at so great a Price, as the Displeasure of his Citizens.* This seems to be a meer Romance: We have seen already (44), in the Passage of *Peter Bembus*, that *Hermolaus*'s Father would never let go his hold, and that he only endeavoured to soften the Republic. It is certain also, that the new Patriarch always preserved his Title, and did not submit to his Temporal Superiors. VIII. I do not know where *Varillas* read, *That the only Means, for Hermolaus's Cure, was to send him right Bezoar, and that there was some of it in a Vessel of Agate at Florence, which the Soldan Caitbay had presented to Laurence de Medicis Peter Crinitus*, who ought to know it as well as any Body, says, that the Antidote belonged to *Picus Mirandulanus*, who knew the Composition of it. " Pharmacon contra pestem quod ille sibi si quando incidisset asservabat diligentissimè, curat ut Romam quàm celerrimè ad Hermolaum devehatur. Dicebat autem Picus illud ipsum ex oleo scorpionum linguisque aspidum, & aliis ejusmodi venenis, confectum (45). — *The Remedy for the Plague, which he carefully kept for his own Use, whenever he should meet with that Misfortune, he dispatched to Hermolaus, at Rome, with all possible Expedition. Picus said, it was a Preparation from Oil of Scorpions, Tongues of Asps, and other Books of that kind."*

Mr *Moreri*'s Faults consist in saying, I. That the Senate did not approve the Choice, which *Innocent* VIII made of *Hermolaus Barbarus*, for the Patriarchate of *Aquileia*. II. That *Hermolaus Barbarus* published *Pliny*'s Natural History. The Senate would have no less disapproved the Election of another Person; and the Republic was not displeased for what *Innocent* VIII had done in favour of *Hermolaus Barbarus*, but because the Pope pretended to dispose of the Patriarchate without consulting them, and because *Hermolaus* had acknowledged the Pope's pretended Right, in accepting of that Dignity, against the Laws of his Country. He published his Corrections on *Pliny* without *Pliny*'s Text (46).

[*Q*] *A Passage of Alcyonius will shew, that Hermolaus — never studied with so much Application, as after his Country had used him ill.*] Here is the Passage: it is Cardinal *John de Medicis* (47), who speaks. " Exsilium igitur Barbaro non solum calamitatem detraxit, sed etiam dignitatem auxit, quod quidem ita constanter, moderateque ferebat, ut facetissimè jocaretur Musas illud sibi à patria impertraslè, quoniam ægrè ferrent hominem suis sacris initiatum ambitione vulgarium honorum distineri, & plebeis occupationibus impediri. Itaque plura scripsit biennio exsul quam XX. ante annos cum patria frueretur & honoribus illius florentissimus effet, recognitionem erratorum Plinianii codicis, explanationem librorum de anima Aristotelis, cum tamen ante ejusdem Philosophi libros talis argumenti in Latinum convertisset, & XVI. libros de ratione differendi, veteres Peripatetici organon eos appellant; & V. Rhetoricos & unum Poëticum, octoque Dioscoridæ Medicos, quos alio etiam opere instruxerat quod Corollarium inscribebat. Adjecerat quoque pulcerrimam expositionem ad libros analyticos posteriores Aristotelis ante in Latinum tralatos (48). — *Exile, therefore, not only eased him from Trouble, but advanced him in Dignity; and he bore it with such Constancy and Moderation, that he used to jest, and very pleasantly call it a Favour, which the Muses had obtained for him, from his Country, in order to prevent one, initiated in their Mysteries, from being otherwise taken up, and interrupted with popular Ambition, and pusne Employments. Therefore he wrote more, in the two Years after his Banishment, than he did in twenty Years before, when he was in Favour with his Country, and in fullest Enjoyment of it's Honours; namely, a Correction of the Errata of Pliny, an Explication of Aristotle's Books of the Soul, which he had before translated into Latin, as also his sixteen Books of The Art of Reasoning; the Peripatetics call them Organon; and five Of Rhetoric, and one Of Poetry, and the eight Books Of Physic of Dioscorides, enlarging them with a Work, which he calls a Corollary. He had likewise added an excellent Commentary on the latter Books of Aristotle's Analytics, before translated into Latin."* This seems to refute what I have advanced above (49); but, her; if you confider it attentively, it does not; for, befides that there might be fome want of Exactnefs in this Enumeration of *Alcyonius*, it is certain, that part of the Writings, which he particularizes, are rather a Revifion, or a more ample Expofition, of what *Hermolaus* had already performed, than a quite new Undertaking; and it appears plainly, that *Diofcorides* had paft through his Hands before his Exile, and before the Correction of *Pliny's* Text. It is a Confirmation of what I have faid againft *Varillas*. Farther, it ought to be obferved, that the Writings, in this Lift, were not publifhed before the Death of the Author, who, therefore, could not be advifed to take his Eafe, on account that his *Pliny*, and, afterwards, his *Diofcorides*, had acquired him fufficient Honour. We fhall now fee, that *Alcyonius* obferves, that thefe Works of *Barbarus* were preferved in Manufcript, in a Library. "Et hæc quidem omnia (50) adhuc diligentiffimè affervari vidi à fratribus illius cum, fedecim abhinc annos (51), Venetiis Bibliothecam illius excuterem, atque incredibili fum lætitia elatus cum cognovi doctiffimi amiciffimique hominis elucubrationes non intercidiffe, quod ne eveniffet magnopere verebar, cum in fuburbano Olivierii Caraphæ Collegæ mei ex peftilentia obiiffet, & domeftici intimique familiares fugâ faluti fuæ confuluiffent, omniaque tanquam bona caduca in medium reliquiffent. Sed ejus generis fcripta ab interitu & furto vindicata fuiffe narrabant Zanoteli cujuldam operâ, quem ille habebat ad manum (52). —— *And all thefe I found were ftill very carefully preferved by his Brothers, upon my examining his Library at Venice, about fixteen Years ago; and it was an exceeding great Pleafure* " to me, to underftand, that the Lucubrations of this learned and friendly Man were not loft, as I apprehended they had been, on his dying of the Plague, at the Country Houfe of my Colleague Oliveri Carapha, and being forfaken by his Friends and Domeftics, for fear of Infection, and leaving all his Papers and Things in fuch Confufion, and without an Owner. But they informed me, that thefe Writings were preferved by the Care of one Zenoteles, who attended him." I cannot deny, but that *Barbarus*, in the Epilogue of his Corrections on *Pliny*, does promife an Edition of *Diofcorides*: "Scire oportet, fays he (53), annotamenta hæc —— Diofcoridi quoque prope diem emittendo profutura: —— *It will not be improper to hint, that thofe Annotations —— will alfo be of Service in an Edition of Diofcorides, which I fhall fhortly publifh.* " But I ftill infift, that *Varillas* has not diftinguifhed the Times. A Work of this Author, on *Diofcorides*, had been feen, before he publifhed That on *Pliny*, and after he had given a Paraphrafe of *Themiftius*. See what follows: " Primum quidem dum Themiftii nobis paraphrafin atque id juvenis adhuc tam eleganter Latine loquentem producit: mox edito in Diofcoridem corollario tam variam ac recondidam doctrinæ rerum omnium fupellectilem depromit: poftremum Plinio —— fuccurrit (54). —— He *firft publifhed an elegant Latin Tranflation of the Paraphrafe of* Themiftius, *while he was very young: afterwards, by publifhing his Corollary on* Diofcorides, *he difcovered an inexhauftible Fund of Learning: in laft of all, he undertook the Affiftance of* Pliny."

(50) *The Work on Pliny, publifhed by the Author himfelf, fhould have been excepted.*

(51) *Alcyonius fuppofes that Cardinal John de Medicis faid this about the Year 1512.*

(42) *Alcyon. in Medice Legato priore.*

(52) Herm. Barbarus in Monito ad Lector. ad calcem caftigat. pag. 522.

(54) Jo Oporinus Fp. dedicat. Caftigat. Herm. Barbari in Plin.

BARBARUS (DANIEL), Great Nephew to the preceeding, was efteemed for his Learning. He publifhed a Commentary on the Five *Predicaments* of *Porphyry*, in the Year 1542. Two Years after, he publifh'd a Commentary on the Three Books of *Ariftotle's* Rhetoric to *Theodectus*, which had been tranflated into Latin by *Hermolaus Barbarus*. He had faid, in a Letter to *Gefner*, that he hoped fpeedily to publifh feveral Works of *Hermolaus* (a). We are indebted to him for the Edition of the Dialogues of *Speron Sperone*.

(a) *Taken from Gefner, Bibl. p. 196, verfo.*

BARBARUS (DANIEL), of the fame Family as the preceeding, was Patriarch of *Aquileia*, and famous for his Learning. He had much addicted himfelf to Mathematics and Philofophy, before he was dignified in the Church; but, after his Promotion to Epifcopacy, he applied himfelf wholly to the Study of Divinity. He was fo prejudiced in favour of *Ariftotle*, that he would willingly have taken an Oath of Fidelity to him, had he not been a Chriftian (c). He was Embaffador of *Venice* in *England*, when Pope *Paul* IV named him Coadjutor to the Patriarch Grimani (b). He was one of the Fathers of the Council of *Trent*, and expreffed there a great Zeal for the Pope. He voted ftrongly againft thofe, who defired the Communion in both Kinds (c). He died in the Year 1569, aged Forty one Years (d). He had publifhed feveral Works [A], and doubtlefs, if he had lived longer, he would have publifhed many more (e).

(a) *Taken from Thuanus. lib. 46, pag. 942.*

(b) Palavic. Hift. Conc. Trid. l. xvi. cap. iv, n. 22.

(c) Id. lib. xviii. cap. iv. n. 4, ad An. 1562.

(d) Voff. de Scient. Mathem. pag. 355. Thuanus, l. xlvi. pag. 942.

(e) Thuanus ibid.

[A] *He had publifhed feveral Works.*] A Commentary on *Vitruvius*, which was printed at *Venice*, in the Year 1567. La *prattica della perfpectiva*, printed at the fame Place, in the Year 1559, and in the Year 1568 (1). *Catena Græcorum patrum in quinquaginta Pfalmos latinè verfa*. *Aubertus Miræus* (2), *Moreri, Teiffier* (3), *Konig, Paul Freberus* (4), &c. afcribe to him the Commentary on the Five *Predicaments* of *Porphyry*, and the Commentary on *Ariftotle's* Rhetoric, which I mention'd in the preceeding Article: But, as the firft of thefe Commentaries was printed in the Year 1542, and the fecond in the Year 1544, it is evident they are not the production of our *Daniel Barbarus*, who was born in the Year 1528 (5). *Freberus*, by a very ftrange Miftake, fays, that our *Daniel Barbarus*, who died in the Year 1569, at 40 Years, of Age, had obtained the Patriarchfhip of *Aquileia* from Pope *Innocent* VIII. to whom he was fent Embaffador from *Venice* (6).

(1) Voff. de Scient. Mathemat. pag. 355, & 425.

(2) De Scriptor. Sæculi XVI.

(3) Teiffier, Addit. to Thuanus, Tom I. p. 354.

(5) *According to Thuanus and Voffius.*

(f) Freber. ibid.

BARBARA, Wife of the Emperor *Sigifmond*, was the Daughter of *Herman* Count of *Cilia* in *Hungary*. *Sigifmond* had been taken by the *Hungarians*, and placed under the Guard of two young Gentlemen, whofe Father he had put to Death. While he was under their Guard, he perfuaded their Mother to let him efcape. This point was not gained without having made a great many Excufes to her, for the Death of her Hufband, as well as a great many Promifes. Among other things, he promifed her to marry the Daughter of the Count of *Cilia*, a near Relation of this Widow; and he performed that Promife (a). She proved the moft extraordinary Woman, that ever was feen. She had no manner of fhame for her lewd Life. Nor did her great Singularity confift in this; there have been but too many Princeffes, who have fhewn no Regard for what the World fhould fay of them, with refpect to their Impudicities. What made her

(4) Freh. Theat Vir. illuftr. pag. 165.

(a) Æneas Silvius in Addition. ad Anton. Panormitam de dictis & factis Alphonfi. l. iii. n. 44. p. 690.

BARBARA.

her so extraordinary, was Atheism [*A*], which is almost without Example among Women. She did not believe there was either Heaven, or Hell [*B*], and laughed at those Religious Persons, who renounced the Pleasures of Life, and mortified their Bodies. *Sigismond* found himself also ill married upon other accounts; for his Wife *Barbara* plotted, with some great Lords of *Bohemia*, to drive him out of the Kingdom, and to marry another Husband. He discovered the Plot, and condemned the Empress to perpetual Imprisonment. When he was dead, she was set at liberty (*b*); and, as she had Thoughts of marrying again, some body represented to her the Example of the Turtle-Dove, which lives single all her life, after the death of her first Mate. But she answered, *If you would propose to me the Example of Beasts, Let it be That of Pigeons and Sparrows* (*c*) [*C*]. She grew old at *Gratz* in *Bohemia*, without forsaking her Debaucheries (*d*), and died there about the Year 1451. The *Bohemians* buried her very magnificently at *Prague* in the Tomb of their Kings, as *Bonfinius* affirms in the seventh Book of the third Decad. *Prateolus* does not forget her in his Alphabetical Catalogue of Heretics, which makes him very ridiculous; for she did not forge any new Doctrine, nor set up her self as the Head of a Sect; She fell into the Impieties, which are common to all times. In all Countries, profane and impious People have always ridiculed those, who, out of a Principle of Religion, undertake the Task of mortifying the Flesh, instead of following the inclination of Nature (*e*).

(b) Ex Mathis, Theat. Histor. in Sigismundo, pag. 998.

(c) Æneas Silvius, ubi supra, n. 5, pag. 56.

(d) Cretii in Bohemia in vita turpi & fœdâ libidinibus cenienuit. Aleat. . 1, ibid.

(e) Barbara —— flutras app l1abat virgines quæ pro Christi nomine passæ fuissent, proptereâ quod voluptatis gaudia non gustâssent. Prateolus, pag 85.

[*A*] *What made her so extraordinary, was Atheism, which is almost without Example among Women.*] I am not ignorant of what has been lately published in a Satire on that Sex, which, in my Opinion, is Mr *Boileau*'s Master-Piece. In this new Piece, Impiety itself is made one of the Irregularities of Women;

Dans le sexe j'ai peint la pieté caustique.
Et que seroit-ce donc, si Censeur plus tragique
J'allois t'y faire voir l'atheisme établi,
Et non moins que l'honneur le Ciel mis en oubli ?
Si j'allois t'y montrer plus d'une Capanée,
Pour souveraine loi mettant la destinée,
Du tonnerre dans l'air bravant les vains carreaux,
Et nous parlant de Dieu du ton de Des-Barreaux ?

Justly I've shewn the Sex's flaming Zeal.
What if still blacker Crimes I should reveal,
The Female Atheist's gigantic Pride,
Trampling on Heav'n and Hell with impious Stride;
A bold Capaneus in a Woman's Form,
Daring the Heights of Providence to storm;
Defy it's Laws, disown it's sovereign State,
And substitute that senseless Idol, Fate;
To brave the dreadful Thunder's threatning Tone,
And speak of God as Des-Barreaux has done?

But all this may be true, though there be not above four, or five Women, in *France*, fallen into those impious Maxims. I am willing to own, that this Prodigy is become something less extraordinary, since Women do not pretend to be so ignorant as formerly. It will require a certain Proficiency in false Metaphysics, to sink the Mind into this unhappy abyss of Irreligion. However it be, I am very much of Opinion, with the Author of the *Thoughts on Comets*, that Women do not deserve to be censured upon such an account. " Atheism is not their Vice:
" they make it a Virtue not to enter into deep Reason-
" sonings; so that they stick to their Catechism, and
" are much more inclined to Superstition, than Im-
" piety; they are great Followers of Indulgences and
" Sermons, and so much possessed with a thousand
" Passions, that fall, as it were, to their lot, that they
" have neither the necessary time nor capacity to call
" in question the Articles of their Faith (1)." It is certain, they will sooner find the Secret of reconciling Passions and Religion together, even in *Molinosism* itself, than the Expedient of believing nothing.

[*B*] *She did not believe there was either Heaven or Hell.*] See the Picture *Bonfinius* has left us of this Woman; " Barbaram Imperatricem ea tempestate
" Græci diem obiisse ferunt, indomitæ libidinis muli-
" erem, quæ inter adulteros publicè vitam duxit,
" prostitutoque pudore viros sæpius petiit quam pe-
" teretur. Quum ab omni religione destituta foret,
" superos ac inferos esse negabat: religiosas ancillas,
" jejunis aut orationi recuisque divinis intentas, gra-
" vius increpabat, nullis asseverans molestiis ac inedia

" corpus esse macerandum: immo laute pascendum,
" in deliciis & voluptatibus alendum, & post mortem,
" cum nihil superfit, nullam deorum animorumque
" curam esse subeundum (2). ——— *The Greeks relate,*
" *that the Empress Barbara died about that Time, a*
" *Woman of insatiable Lewdness, who spent her Life*
" *publickly among Adulterers, and, laying aside all*
" *Modesty, sollicited the Men much oftener than they*
" *sollicited her. Having thrown off all Religion, she*
" *denied there was either God or Devil: She severely*
" *chid her Maids, who were devoutly inclined, and*
" *spent their time in fasting and praying, and other*
" *religious Exercises, affirming, that the Body ought*
" *not to be mortified, or made uneasy, but much ra-*
" *ther indulged and gratified in the most luxurious*
" *manner; and that, as there was no such thing as a*
" *future State, it was needless to be concerned about*
" *Gods and Spirits.*"

[*C*] *If you would propose to me, said she, the Example of Beasts, let it be that of Pigeons and Sparrows.*] It is one of the finest Common-Places of Mortality, to shew Man his Disorders, by comparing them with the Regularity of Beasts; Men tear each other to pieces; Man is a Wolf to Man (3); but Beasts of the same Kind do not fight with each other. It is by this means that *Horace* endeavoured to make the *Romans* ashamed, who engaged themselves in Civil Wars: *The Wolves and Lyons*, says he, *do not do so*. He supposes his Objection to be so strong, as to reduce those, against whom he urges it, to a shameful Silence.

Neque hic lupus mos, nec fuit leonibus
Unquam, nisi in dispar, feris.
Furorne cœcus, an rapit vis acrior ?
An culpa ? responsum date.
Tacent, & ora pallor albus inficit,
Menteque perculsæ stupent (4).

Nor Wolf, nor Lion preys upon his Kind:
And shall we Man a greater Savage find ?
Well may the Question turn the Monster pale,
And make the faultring Sense it's Office fail.

Juvenal made use of the same Morality in his fifteenth Satire, *ver.* 159.

Sed jam serpentum major concordia : parcit
Cognatis maculis similis fera : quando leoni
Fortior eripuit vitam leo ? quo nemore unquam
Expiravit aper majoris dentibus apri ?
Indica tigris agit rabida cum tigride pacem
Perpetuam, sævis inter se convenit ursis :
Ast homini, &c.

But Serpents now more Amity maintain :
From spotted Skins the Leopard does refrain :
No weaker Lion's by a stronger slain :
Nor, from his larger Tusks, the Forest Boar
Commission takes his Brother Swine to gore :

(1) Some Thoughts on Comets, n. 147, pag. 421.

(2) Bonfinius, Rerum Ungaricar. Decad. III. lib. vii. pag. 344, 345.

T H E Inconveniences of a System of Morality form'd on the Conduct of Beasts.

(3) Homo homini lupus. Erasm. Adag. chil. 1, cent. 1, n. 70, p. 43.

(4) Horat. Epod. 7.

VOL. I. 7 Y *Tyger*

> Tyger with Tyger, Bear with Bear, you'll find
> In Leagues offensive and defensive join'd.
> But lawless Man, &c.   TATE.

Mr *Boileau* has very well translated the *Latin* of those two Poets, and joined other Examples to it (5).

> Voit-on les loups brigans, comme nous inhumains,
> Pour detrousser les loups, courir les grands chemins?

> Un aigle sur un champ pretendant droit d'aubeine
> Ne fait point apeller un aigle à la huitaine:
> Jamais contre un renard chicanant un poulet
> Un renard de son sac n'alla charger Rolet.
> Jamais la biche en rut n'a pour fait d'impuissance
> Traîné du fond des bois un cerf à l'audience:
> Et jamais Juge entre eux, ordonnant le congrés,
> De ce burlesque mot n'a fait ses arrêts.

> Who sees the High-way Wolf in ambush lye,
> To rob his Brother Wolf in passing by?
> When does the Eagle on the Eagle prey,
> By setting up a Claim to waif and stray?
> When does the Fox, whom constant Thefts maintain,
> For Poultry stoln his Brother Fox arraign?
> When does the rutting Hind a Suit commence,
> And prosecute the Stag for Impotence?
> When does the Judge, assign'd to try their Cause,
> With bandy Orders stain the sacred Laws?

Though this is a very fine and pathetic Common-Place, yet it hath it's Foible: For, first, it may be eluded by turning it into a Jest; and, in the second place, it may be seriously opposed by the Maxim;

Nil agit exemplum litem quod lite resolvit (6).

> That Argument but little Force displays,
> Which, solving one, another Doubt will raise.

that is to say, It may be retorted, and, by turning the Tables, the Moralist may lose his Advantage. I do not pretend to approve of those, who oppose Jests to Arguments; but I say, it is a very great Disadvantage to an Argument, to be able to be turned into Ridicule by those, who love jesting. Let us prove this by an Example. Suppose any body had undertaken to persuade Mr *de Bautru*, that it is better to chuse an old Mistress, than a young one, and had quoted the place of *Pliny*, where it is said, *That the Rams are fonder of old Ews than young ones*; would he not have been confounded by this Answer, given him with a Sneer (7), *That is, because Rams are Rams* (8). A *Roman* Lady made use of the like Thought, on somebody's wondering why the Females among Beasts did not desire the Male, but when they had a Mind to become Mothers. The Lady answered, *It is because they are Beasts*. Simile dictum Populiæ Marci filiæ, quæ miranti cuidam quid esset quapropter aliæ bestiæ nunquam marem desiderarent nisi cum prægnantes vellent fieri, respondit, bestiæ enim sunt (9). Was not this a confounding Stroke? So much for the first Inconveniency. The other is not less considerable; for, in short, a Man, who is to be sent to learn his Duty in the School of Beasts, will tell you, that he desires no better Doctrine. "For there, *says* he, I "shall learn to determine Right by Force: The "stronger Mastiff does not scruple to rob the weaker "of his Share. What is more common than to see "Dogs fighting together? Do not Chickens attack "one another in sight of their common Mothers? "Do not Cocks fight together so cruelly, that many "times the Battle does not cease before the Death of "one of the Combatants? Do not Pigeons, the Symbol of Meekness, come very often to Blows? "What can be more furious, than the Engagement "of Bulls? Does not Force decide their Right in their "Amours."

> ------ Ignotis perierunt mortibus illi
> Quos Venerem incertam rapientes MORE FERARUM
> Viribus editior cædebat ut in grege TAURUS (10).

> No Pen their Histories did e'er relate,
> If so in promiscuous Love have met their Fate,

> Cut off by some superior Lover's pow'r;
> As the Herd Bull no Rival can endure.

> Illi alternantes multa vi prælia miscent
> Vulneribus crebris: lavit ater corpora sanguis,
> Versaque in obnixos urgentur cornua vasto
> Cum gemitu: reboant silvæque & magnus Olympus:
> Nec mos bellantes una stabulare, sed alter
> Victus abit, longeque ignotis exulat oris
> Multa gemens, ignominiam plagasque superbi
> Victoris, tum quos amisit inultus amores,
> Et stabula aspectans regnis excessit avitis (11)

> The stooping Warriors, aiming Head to Head,
> Engage their clashing Horns; with dreadful Sound
> The Forest rattles, and the Rocks rebound.
> They fence, they push, and pushing loudly roar;
> Their dewlaps and their sides are bath'd in Gore;
> Nor, when the War is over, is it Peace;
> Nor will the vanquish'd Bull his Claim release:
> But, feeding in his Breast his ancient Fires,
> And cursing Fate, from his proud Foe retires.
> Driv'n, from his native Land, to foreign Grounds;
> He with a gen'rous Rage resents his Wounds;
> His ignominious Flight, the Victor's Boast,
> And, more than both, the Loves, which unrevenged be lost.
> Often he turns his Eyes, and with a Groan
> Surveys the pleasing Kingdoms, once his own.
>   DRYDEN.

"Shall I not learn the most unnatural Barbarity in "the School, where you send me? Do not some "Beasts devour their young Ones? Shall I not learn "Incest there?

------ sed enim damnare negatur
Hanc venerem pietas, coëuntque animalia nullo
Cætera delectu, nec habetur turpe juvencæ
Ferre patrem tergo: fit equo sua filia conjux,
Quasque creavit init pecudes caper, ipsaque cujus
Semine concepta est ex illo concipit alea.
Felices, quibus ista licent: humana malignas
Cura dedit leges, & quod natura remittit
Invida jura negant (12).

> But Piety this Passion must allow;
> All Creatures else promiscuous Love pursue.
> Bulls know no shame their Daughters to bestride;
> The willing Filly makes her Sire a Bride;
> The wanton Goat does his own Kids enjoy;
> Nor to the Bird are his own young Ones coy.
> O happy these! while Man by Nature free,
> To envious Laws gives up his Liberty.

"Shall I not learn there to seize on every thing that "lies within my reach, that I may lay up Provisions like the Ant?

------ sicut
Parvula, nam exemplo est, magni formica laboris
Ore trahit quodcunque potest atque addit acervo
Quem struit, haud ignara ac non incauta futuri (13).

> Great Heaps to raise, learn from the little Ant;
> See her vast Stores, to guard from future Want.

"Shall I not free myself from the hard Slavery, which "torments so many People, and makes them break "out into these pathetic Complaints?

> Que vôtre bonheur est extrême,
> Cruels lions, sauvages ours,
> Vous qui n'avez dans vos amours
> D'autre regle que l'amour même!
> Que j'envie un semblable sort!
> Et que nous sommes malheureuses
> Nous de qui les loix rigoureuses
> Punissent l'amour par la mort (14)!

BARBERINI. BARCLAY.

How exquifite your Blifs appears,
Cruel Lions, favage Bears;
Whofe Loves no other Rule confines,
But that which Love itfelf enjoins!
How envied is your happy Fate!
How wretched is our flavifh State;
Whofe rigid Laws, againft all Senfe,
Make Love a Capital Offence!

It cannot therefore be denied, but that the Examples, which the School of Brutes affords, of all manner of Irregularities, do fomething weaken the moral Reflections I have mentioned in the beginning of this Remark: For, fince Divinity affures us, all Beafts are free from Sin, it cannot be faid, that fome are grown diforderly for a Punifhment of their Faults, and that others have been preferved regular for a Reward of their Virtue. So that whatever they do is equally regular; and, if any one fhould afk, as *Sigifmund's* Widow did, *Why will you rather have me imitate the Turtle-Dove, than the Pigeon, or the Sparrow?* You can give no good Anfwer, without confulting the Grounds of Morality, as much as you would be obliged to do, if you did not at all make ufe of the Example of the Turtle-Dove. What Anfwer would Mr *Boileau* give to a Sophift, who fhould maintain, that his *rutting Hind* is a very falfe Comparifon? For, to make it good, it muft be fuppofed, that this Brute is capable of being in the fame Condition with thofe Women, who fue a Man *for Impotency*. Now can a Hind be in fuch a Cafe? Does fhe engage her Faith to a fingle Stag? If one fails her, does fhe not find others? Mr *Boileau's* biting Invective, and Satire, would be well grounded in a Country, where there were no Laws of Marriage; but it is very certain, that, in fuch a Country, Men would no more be fued for Impotency, than Stags, nor condemned to fhew their Manhood by a *Congrefs*, in purfuance of an Order of Court.

What I have faid does not at all leffen my Belief, that the moral Obfervations, I am fpeaking of, are very proper to affect moft People. Therefore I do not blame *Francis de Sales*, who propofed the Elephant for an Example of Chaftity; and I condemn the Anfwer of the Emprefs *Barbara* A thoufand things might be faid on this Subject. The Actions of Brutes are, perhaps, one of the moft profound Myfteries, on which our Reafon can be exercifed; and I am furprized, that fo few Perfons perceive it. But let us relate the Words of *Francis de Sales*: " The Elephant, *fays he* (15), is one of the " moft unwieldly, but, at the fame time, the worthieft " and moft fenfible of the whole Brute Creation. " I fhall fay one word of his Chaftity; he never " changes his Female; he very tenderly loves the " Mate he has once chofen; but yet he cohabits " with her only every third Year, and then not " above five Days, and fo privately, that he is " never feen in the Act: On the fixth Day, he " makes his Appearance, and, in the firft place, goes " directly to fome River, and wafhes his whole " Body, nor returns to the Herd before he is purified. Is not this a fine, and a chafte, Difpofition " of fuch an Animal, and a good Example to married People, not to fet their Affections on their " Senfuality and Pleafure, but, as foon as thofe " Gratifications are over, to wafh their Heart and " Affections, and purify themfelves as fpeedily as " poffible, that they may afterwards have their " Minds at full Liberty, for the Performance of " Actions more pure and exalted? *&c*." What he fays of the Elephant is taken from *Ariftotle* (16). *Pliny* (17), and *Ælian* (18). *Claud. Spenceæus* in his Treatife *Of the State of Widowhood*, where he fpeaks of *Monogamy*, had remarked this of the Elephant, and given it, together with that of the Turtle-Dove, for eminent Examples of Modefty and Chaftity to Chriftians.

(c) Introduction to a devout Life, part 3. c. 39.

OF the Chaftity of the Nuptial Bed.

(16) Ariftot. Hift. Anim. lib. 5. c. 15.
(17) Plin. lib. 8. c. 5.
(18) Ælian. Hift Anim. lib. 8. c. 17.

BARBERINI (FRANCIS), one of the beft Poets of his Time, was born in the Year 1264, at *Barberino* in *Tufcany*. His Mother being a Native of *Florence*, he went and fettled in that City, where the Profeffion of a Civilian, but, above all, the beauty of his Poems, made him very confiderable. Moft of his Works are loft. That, which was intituled *The Precepts of Love* [A], had a better deftiny. It was printed at *Rome*, in the Year 1640, and adorned with fine Cuts. It was done by the Care of *Frederic Ubaldini*, who took that occafion to court the higher Powers; for the Houfe of *Barberini*, which was defcended from this Poet, enjoyed the Papacy at that Time. At the beginning of This Work he placed the Author's Life and fome Elogies; and, becaufe there were feveral obfolete words in thofe Verfes, he added a Gloffary to explain them, and clear, or prove, the Senfe of them, by the Authority of cotemporary Poets (a).

(a) Taken from the Acta Eruditorum, in §. 74 of Vol. I. of the Supplements, pag. 349.

[A] *His Poem entitled*, The Precepts of Love *was preferved*.] This is equivocal; one might imagine that this Poem was a School of Coquettry, like that of *Ovid, de Arte amandi*; but it would prove a very great Miftake. There is nothing more Moral than this Poem of *Barberini*. It contains nothing but Rules, which teach thofe their Duty, who fix their Love on Glory, Virtue, and Eternity (1).

(1) Acta Eruditor. pag. 340, of the Ift Vol. of the Supplements.

BARCLAY (WILLIAM) a Learned Civilian in the XVIth Century, was of *Aberdeen* in *Scotland*, and of a very good Family [A]. Though he had been in favour with Queen *Mary Stuart*, he could not make his Fortune at the Court of the King of *Scotland*, the Son of that Princefs. This made him refolve to retire into *France* in the Year 1573 (a); and, though he was near thirty Years of

(a) The Life of John Barclay, prefixed to the Argenis, has it the Year 1571.

[A] *He was of a very good Family*.] Namely, That of *Barclay*, which is related to all the great Families of *Scotland*, as appears by a Patent, from King *James*, printed before the *Argenis*. I make ufe of the Word *Patent*, becaufe it is not a meer Letter, written to the Duke of *Lorrain*, as Mr *Menage* affirms (1), but a Letter, fealed with the great Seal of the Kingdom, and addreffed to all Perfons, in the ufual Form, *To all to whom thefe Prefents fhall come, Greeting*. Mr *Menage* is very excufable in his Miftake; but he, who caufed this Superfcription, *Epiftola Jacobi Scotiæ Regis, Carolo Lotharingiæ Duci*, to be placed before King *James's* Atteftation, is guilty, either of unpardonable Fraud, or Ignorance. He ought to have read That Writing, fince he caufed it to be printed, and prefixed to a Book (2). There is not a Line in it but will fhew, that it was not a Letter written to the Duke of *Lorrain*. The *Italian* Tranflator of the *Argenis* (3) tells us, That the Relations of the Lady *Malleville* would not agree to her Marriage with *William Barclay*, before they had feen Proofs of the Nobility he had boafted of. He adds, That this vexed *Barclay*, only on account of the amorous Impatience, with which he was tranfported; for he was obliged to wait for the Arrival of a Certificate, before he could tafte the Pleafures of Enjoyment. He goes on, and fays, That, *when the Relations of the fair Lady faw the Royal Atteftation, they were the firft, who haftened the Confummation*. It is impoffible to forbear wondering, when we find thefe things in the fame Page with the King of *Scotland's* Certificate; for This Prince declares,

(1) Menage, Remarks on the Life of Ayrault, pag. 228.

(2) It is printed before the Argenis.

(3) His Name is Francefco Pona; he wrote the Life of John Barclay, and prefixed it to his Tranflation of the Argenis.

of Age, yet he went to study the Civil-Law at *Bourges*. Some time after, he there took his Doctor's Degree [*B*]; and as he had a great deal of Wit, and applied himself very much to Study, he soon made himself capable to teach the Civil-Law. His Uncle, the Jesuit *Edmond Hay*, procured him a Professorship in that Science, in the University of *Pontamousson*, by the Credit he had with the Duke of *Lorrain*, who had lately founded that University. That Duke did not only confer the chief Chair on *Barclay*, but made him also one of his Counsellors of State, and Master of Requests of his Palace. In the Year 1582 (*b*), *Barclay* married a Gentlewoman of *Lorrain* (*c*), by whom he had a Son, who became a Famous Man, and was the innocent cause of his Father's falling out with the Jesuits. This young Man had so much Wit, that they used their utmost endeavours to get him into their Order. His Father was angry with them for it; and they with him in their turn, and did him so many ill Offices with the Duke, that they obliged him to leave *Lorrain*. He went to King *James* at *London*, who offered him a place in his Council with a very good Salary; but he refused those Offers upon account of the condition annexed to them, which was to embrace the Religion of the Church of *England*. In the beginning of the Year 1604, he returned into *France*, and accepted the Professorship of the Civil Law, which was offered him by the University of *Angers*. He taught there with great Splendor [*C*], till his Death, which happened towards the latter end of the Year 1605 [*D*]. He was buried at the *Franciscans* (*d*). He published some Books [*E*], and

(*b*) *See Remark* [*A*], *of the following Article*.

(*c*) *Her Name was Anne de Malleville*.

(*d*) *Taken from Mr Menage's Remarks on the Life of Peter Ayrault, pag. 228, &c. seq*.

declares, expresly, that *Barclay* had a Wife already (4); and this is farther certain, from the Date of the Attestation (5). That Date is above a Month after the Birth of *John Barclay*, the Son of *William*, and of the Lady *Malleville*. Judge how the amorous *William Barclay* was obliged to delay his Joy, by waiting for a Certificate —— The Author of *John Barclay's* Life, in *Latin*, was in the same Error. He says, The Attestation was required, that he might prove himself a Person of Quality to his future Spouse. *Cum Anna de Malavilla contracturus nuptias ex Scotia regias literas accersivit, quibus ingenuæ nobilitatis titulos futuræ sponsæ appropriaret*.

[*B*] *He studied the Civil Law at Bourges — — and there took his Doctor's Degree*.] *Cujacius* presided at That Act (6). It is a great Falsity to say, that *Barclay's* Marriage did not interrupt his Studies, and that, having continued them, after his Wedding, from a Scholar he became a Doctor, and, from a Doctor, a Professor of the Civil Law: *Lequale (non ze) non rompendo il bel filo de gli studii di lui, successe che di scholare ch' egli era, passato al grado del Dottorato, ricevè una lettura principale di Leggi* (7).

[*C*] *He taught, at Angers, with great Splendor*.] "He went to his Lectures, attended by his Son, "and two Servants, dressed in a magnificent Robe, "with a great Chain of Gold about his Neck (6)."

[*D*] *He died towards the end of the Year 1605*.] Mr *Moreri*, being deceived by *Nicius Erythræus*, and others, has put down the Year 1609, instead of the Year 1605. He believed, with Reason, that our *Barclay* went to teach the Civil Law, at *Angers*, in 1604; and he found, in *Nicius Erythræus*, that This Professor lived five Years after taking Possession of That Place. "*Ab "Andibus optimis conditionibus evocatur, ut in ipso- "rum gymnasio primariam Juris Civilis cathedram ob- "tineret, ubi cum jam quinquennium docuisset est mor- "tuus* (9). — — *He was invited, by the University of "Angers, on advantageous Terms, to accept the prin- "cipal Chair of the Civil Law, which he enjoyed "five Years, and then died*." It was natural to conclude, that he did not die, *'till about the Year* 1609. But the *Italian* Author is mistaken, since, besides the Authority of Mr *Menage*, I can alledge this Reason; *William Barclay* was dead before the Differences between *Paul* V, and the *Venetians*, were ended. "*Ac- "cendebant hominem & pietate & jam senecta liberio- "rem illæ turbæ quas multi ominabantur, cum Pon- "tifex in Anglum Venetosque districtus, illum qui- "dem jam à sacris nostris alienum acerbare, hos au- "tem alienare videbatur. Sed tam pium conatum "intercepit fœlix & in Christo obitus*. —— *The Di- "sturbances, which many foresaw, from the Pope's "Violence against England and Venice, which seemed "to exasperate the former, already alienated from "our Communion, and to alienate the latter, stirred "up the good Man, whose Piety, and old Age, had "given him a greater Degree of Freedom. But a "happy, and truly Christian, Death prevented his "pious Design*." This we find in the Preface to the Book *De Potestate Papæ* (10). The Differences between the Pope, and the Republic of *Venice*, were ended in the Year 1607. The Sieur *Witte* being, perhaps, deceived only by *Moreri*, has placed the Death of *Barclay* in the Year 1609 (11).

[*E*] *He published some Books*.] Among others, *Prœmetio*, on the Life of *Agricola*, and a Commentary on the Title of the *Pandects de Rebus Creditis & de Jurejurando*. He published it in the Year 1605, at *Paris*. But the two Pieces, which made the most Noise, were the Treatise of the Papal Power, and That of the Regal Power. The Title of the first is, *De Potestate Papæ, an & quatenus in Reges & Principes sæculares jus & imperium habeat*. The second is entitled, *De Regno & Regali potestate adversus Buchananum, Brutum, Boucherium & reliquos Monarchomachos*. He published this latter Work at *Paris*, in the Year 1600, and dedicated it to *Henry* IV. The other did not come out of the Press before the Death of the Author, who durst not even say, that he was writing such a Work. "Et qui- "dem *de Regno* libros quibus popularem ambitum "exagitabat nulla dissimulatione conscripsit. Sed hoc "opus (*de Potestate Papæ*) secreto congressus est, 'cum "tunc aliquid Pontifici negare hæresis censeretur "(12). — — — *He never dissembled the writing his "Book, of* The Regal Power, *wherein he lashes po- "pular Ambition. But this Work (Of the Papal "Power) he undertook privately, the denying the Pope "any thing being, then, esteemed Heresy*." He undertook these two Pieces, when he saw the Disorders of the League, the Subjects in Arms against their King, and the legitimate Possessors of the Throne declared, by the Papal Bulls, to have forfeited their Crown. *Lorrain*, where he was advantageously settled, followed the Stream, and approved the Revolt of Subjects, and the Attempts of the Court of *Rome* against the Temporalities of Princes. He remained firm in his Principles; for he had learned them in a good School; neither must it be questioned, but that the Seditions of the *Scots* had been, in this Respect, his chief Catechism. Nothing is more proper to make the Republican Maxims hated, than to see, that they have produced Troubles, which have destroyed the Religion one believes to be the true one, and dethroned a Queen, by whom one was beloved. However it be, the Professor of *Pontamousson* shewed an uncommon Steadiness: Most Persons alter their Principles as they change their Country and Interests; as for him, he preserved those Maxims in *Lorrain*, which he had in *Scotland*, though the Situation of Affairs was entirely reversed. The Authority of the People, advanced above the Royal Power, served, in *Scotland*, for the Ruin of Popery, and, in *France*, for the Ruin of the Protestants. Notwithstanding all this, *Barclay* did not change his Opinion: He had found it unjust in *Scotland*, where it promoted the Catholic Religion, and found it no less unjust in *France*, where it promoted the same Religion. It is a Rarity to meet with so much Constancy in a Doctor; but those, whose Principles turn like Weather-cocks, are every where to be found. I have said, that *Barclay* durst not

(4) *In Lotharingii confedisse, ibique affinitatem generis moribusque suis non indignam contraxisse. That, being settled in Lorrain, he had married a Wife, not at all unsuitable either in Family or Virtue*.

(5) *The* 19*th of March*, 1582. *Moreri, ubi supra at the* 28*th*.

(6) Menage, *ubi supra*.

(7) Franceschi Pona, *ubi supra*.

(8) Menage, *ubi supra*, pag. 231.

(9) Nic. Erythr. Pinacoth. III, pag. 76. Paul Freher. in Theatr. p. l. 1535, *makes him to contract Letters for Jesus &c. Yes it. He quotes* Imperialis *and* Thomasin.

(12) Witte, in Appendice Diarii Biographici.

(12) In Præfat Operis de Potestate Papæ.

The League did not alter *Barclay's* Hypothesis concerning the Independence of Kings.

(13) Mr Menage, Remarques sur la Vie d'Ayrault, p. p. 228, *alledges this Passage, to shew, that Perkins Barclay, the Son of William, was born in* 1582.

BARCLAY.

and one among the rest, wherein he refuted some Authors, who, tho' of different Religions, did yet agree in Republican Maxims in favour of Religion [F]. He had an aversion for the *Calvinists* [G]; which Spirit of Bitterness was probably occasioned by the Condition he saw his Country in, when he was forced to abandon it for the sake of his Catholic Religion (*e*).

not own he was writing against the Maxims of the *Italians*; but this ought only to be understood of the time of the Continuance of the League; for, when it was defeated, he no longer made a Mystery of his Work, but sent it to the Press, and dedicated it to *Clemens* VIII (13). But he took it away again from the Printer, and kept it near ten Years, during which time, he added a great deal to it, but cut off much more. He was making all the haste he could to finish it, on the Apprehension of the Differences, which were likely to happen, between the Pope, and the *Venetians*; but Death hindered him from putting the last Hand to his Work (14).

[*F*] *He refuted some Authors, who, though of different Religions, yet agreed on Republican Maxims, in favour of Religion.*] He refuted two Protestants, *Buchanan*, and *Hubert Languet*: And also *Boucher*, one of the Curates of *Paris*, and a very violent Leaguer. This Man submitted the Sovereign Authority to the People, for the good of the Catholic Religion; the others did the same thing for the good of the Protestant. So that they were all three united in the general Thesis, and all three Adversaries to *Barclay*.

[*G*] *He had an Aversion for the* Calvinists.] This appears by his Writings. Read these Words of Mr *Menage:* "He was a great Enemy to the *Calvinists* "and *Lutherans*. In his Commentary on the Title "in the *Digests de Rebus creditis*, he says, speaking "of *Doneau*, Doctor-Regent of the Civil-Law in the "University of *Bourges*, *Hugo Donellus unus ex præ-* "*ceptoribus meis: vir civilis Disciplinæ peritus, sed* "*malus, quia hæreticus Calvinista* (15). —— Hugo "*Donellus, one of my Preceptors, to be admired for* "*his Learning in the Civil Law, but to be abhorred* "*for his Calvinistical Heresy.*"

BARCLAY (JOHN), Son of the foregoing, was born at *Pontamousson*, the Twenty eighth of *January*, 1583 [*A*]. The Jesuits of That Town, under whom he studied, were so charmed with his Wit, that they used their utmost Endeavours to draw him into their Society. I have already said, that this was the reason of his Father's going to King *James*, who was lately come to the Crown of *England*. He brought his Son along with him; his Son I say, who was already an Author [*B*], and had some new Works ready for the Press: He had published a Commentary on the *Thebais* of *Statius*, in 1601 (*a*), and he published a Latin Poem on the Coronation of King *James*, and the first part of the *Euphormio*, in the Year 1603. Those two Pieces pleased his *Britannic* Majesty very well, who loved and understood Learning. *John Barclay* dedicated to him That beginning of the *Euphormio*. He returned into *France* with his Father, who would not leave him with King *James*, for fear That Prince, who would willingly have retained him, should engage him to abjure the *Romish* Faith. He continued at *Angers*, till his Father's Death; after which he went to *Paris*, where he married [*C*], and went soon after to *London*. He was there in the Year 1606, and

[*A*] *Was born at* Pontamousson, *the Twenty eighth of January*, 1583.] I have blindly followed Mr *Menage*, but reserved to myself the Liberty to rectify him here by himself. He mentions, at Page 228, what I have taken for the Text to This Remark, and afterwards affirms, at Page 232, that *John Barclay* died the twelfth of *August*, in the Year 1621, aged Thirty nine Years and six Months. He must therefore be born in the beginning of the Year 1582. This is confirmed by another Fact, related by Mr *Menage*. In the Year 1603, *John Barclay* dedicated the first Part of the *Euphormio* to the King of *England* (1), and declares, in the Apology for the *Euphormio*, that he was but Twenty one Years of Age, when he caused that first part to be printed (2). An Author, who is but twenty Years and some Months old, does not use to say, that he is but Twenty one Years of Age; he expresses himself only in that manner, when he is in his Twenty second Year. *Barclay* was, therefore, full Twenty one Years old, in 1603; and consequently was born, not in the Year 1583, but in 1582. So that, if his Birth-day were the Twenty eighth of *January*, his Father's Marriage must be placed in the Year 1581, and not, as Mr *Menage* would have it, in the Year 1582. The same Consequences will follow from what he says (3), that *Barclay*, being but nineteen Years of Age in 1601, printed a Commentary on *Statius*. He remarks, that he, who wrote the Life of *John Barclay*, printed before the *Argenis*, is strangely deceived in saying, that *John Barclay was born at Aberdeen* (4). If he was mistaken in the Place of his Birth, he was not mistaken in the Time, which, he says, was the Twenty eighth of *January*, 1582. We read, under the Effigies of *John Barclay*, in the Frontispiece of the *Argenis*, that he was born the Twenty eighth of *January*, 1682: And thus the Engravers deceive us, as well as the Printers.

[*B*] *He was an Author very early.*] We have seen already, that, at nineteen Years of Age, he published a Commentary on *Statius*; he deserves, therefore, to be inserted in the next Edition of *Baillet's Famous Children*; but he would deserve it yet more, if his true Age had been known to *Nicius Erythræus*: for, in that Case, he must have been an Author at fifteen Years. And, indeed, *Erythræus* says, that *Barclay* was but Seventeen Years of Age, when he wrote a Poem on King *James's* Coronation; that is to say, in 1603. *Annum tum agebat Joannes decimum Septimum cum de Regis inauguratione elegantissimum carmen edidit, maximo verborum sententiarumque splendore illuminatum; quod lectum Rex adeo probavit, ut &c.* (5). At that rate, he must have been but fifteen Years of Age, when, in 1601, he published a Commentary on the *Thebais* of *Statius*. Let us observe, here, a new Mistake of That *Italian* Author, which proved contagious to *Moreri*, and so contagious, that it has produced another. Mr *Moreri* was not contented with saying, that *Barclay* was but seventeen Years of Age, when King *James* was crowned, but he has converted the printed Poem of This Author into a Speech delivered on that Occasion. *Paul Freherus* places *John Barclay's* Birth in the Year 1585, and the Panegyric on the Coronation in the seventeenth Year of his Age (6).

[*C*] *He went to Paris, and there married.*] "He "married *Louise Debonnaire*, Daughter of *Michael* "*Debonnaire*, Treasurer of the old *Bandes*, and of "*Ursina Denisat*. —— He went afterwards, with "his Wife, into *England*, where he had, by her, "two Sons and a Daughter (7)." He did not marry at *Rome: Moreri*, who says so, did not, in the least, understand his *Nicius Erythræus*, who would easily have informed him, that *Barclay* escaped from *England*, with his Wife and Son, and retired to *Rome*, where she brought him another Son. *Ibi Barclaius ex uxore quam habebat masculam prolem suscepit. Sed aliquanto post — clam ex Anglia una cum uxore & filio se fugâ surripuit, ac Romam venit* (8). —— *Romæ novam ex uxore suâ masculam prolem accepit, ac civis una* Urbem

and it was then, that he came acquainted with Mr *de Peiresc*. He had lately published the History of the *Gun-Powder-Treason*. It is a Pamphlet of Six Leaves *(b)*, printed at *Amsterdam*. In the Year 1610 *(c)*, he published, at *London*, an Apology for the *Euphormio*, and his Father's Treatise *De Potestate Papæ* [D]. In the Year 1612, he printed a Book at *Paris*, intituled *Pietas* [E]. It is an Answer to Cardinal *Bellarmin*, who had wrote against *William Barclay*'s Book of the Papal Power. Two Years after, appeared the *Icon Animorum*, which he published at *London*. From whence he went, in the Year 1616, to *Paris*, where he was presented, by his good Friend Mr *de Peiresc*, to Mr *du Vair*, Keeper of the Seals. He went afterwards to *Rome*, being invited thither by Pope *Paul V*, where he published a Book of Controversy, intituled *Parænesis ad Sectarios*. He received a great many Favours from Cardinal *Bellarmin*, though he had written against him. He died at *Rome*, the twelfth of *August* 1621 *(d)*, while his *Argenis* was printing in *France (e)* [F]. His body was carried into the Church of St *Onuphrius* upon the *Janiculum*. His Son erected a Marble Monument for him, in St *Laurence*'s Church, on the way to *Tivoli (f)*: We shall give the Reason, in the Remarks, why his Widow caused her Husband's Busto to be taken from thence [G]. Many believe, that *John Barclay* made Profession of the Protestant Religion in

Urbem nostram auxit (9). *Maffeo Barberini*, who was afterwards Pope *Urban* VIII, was God-father to our *Barclay*'s new Son (10). In Reading these Words of *Erythræus*, one would never imagine, that *Barclay*'s Wife did not come to *Rome*, 'till four Years after her Husband: and yet *Gassendus* affirms it to be true. Read the Place, where he mentions the good Offices, which Mr *de Peiresc* did the Husband, in the Year 1616, and the Wife and Child in 1620. *Præterea fuisse Peireskio non minorem circa Barclaii uxorem, filium, & Jo. Ludovicum Debonarium uxoris germanum, cum* QUARTO *post* ANNO *profecti Romam ad illum sunt* (11). If Mr *Menage* had well considered these Words of *Gassendus*, he would not have said, that *Barclay* went to *Rome*, in the Year 1617, and that his Wife, his Son, and his Brother-in-law, came to him there, in the Year 1619 (12). He adds, that *Barclay*'s Son came to *Paris* with his Mother, in the Year 1652; that *he made no great Figure*; that he composed *Latin* Verses; and that, at the same time, he printed there, a *Latin* Elogy. *Erythræus* speaks of *Barclay*'s Widow, as of a presumptuous and haughty Woman: See, below, the Remark [G]. In the *Latin* Life of *John Barclay*, it is falsly said, that he married *Louise Debonnaire*, after having been employed in several Embassies by King *James*.

[D] *He printed his Father's Treatise De Potestate Papæ.*] If we believe Mr *Menage* (13), the printing That Book lost him great Part of the King of *England*'s Favour. I cannot apprehend from whence this should come, since this Book strongly confutes the Pretensions of the *Ultramontanes*, and particularly *Bellarmin*'s Arguments, and stoutly maintains the Independency of Kings. Could any thing be written more agreeable to King *James*? I conjecture, that *Gassendus*'s *Latin* (14) has deceived Mr *Menage*; and this convinces us yet more effectually, how difficult it is to write very clearly in *Latin*. Upon examining the Passage more closely, it will appear, that the Author does not affirm, that the Book, concerning the Pope's Power, displeased King *James*; but it may very easily be so understood, without some Attention. The Jesuits did not believe, that the printing of That Book had displeased the King of *Great Britain*: But, on the contrary, they reproached *John Barclay* for having put it in the Press with That Prince's Consent, and with the Corrections of the *English* Divines.' *Neque vero nisi ejus* (Regis) *nutu patris tui librum à Britannici Evangelii ministris ad libidinem deformatum, Londini typis excusum* (15). Mr *Menage* has not rightly marked the Year of the Impression. That Work was printed in the Year 1609. The Congregation of the *Index* condemned it the same Year, by their Decree of the ninth of *November*.

[E] *He printed a Book at* Paris, *which he intituled* Pietas] Here is the remaining Part of the Title: *Sive publicæ pro regibus ac principibus, & privatæ pro Gul Barclaio parente, vindiciæ contra Bellarminum*. The Letter of *Eudæmon-Joannes*, which I have quoted, testifies, that *Barclay* took a Journey to *Paris* for the printing of That Work, to do more Service to the Protestants of *England*: for it was said, "that

" he thought he should be less suspected of Intel-
" ligence with the Enemies of the Church, if he
" published That Work out of *England*." *Ac nunc quoque non dissimili consilio te Lutetiam è Britannia demigrasse, ut cum & coram apud viros principes, & scriptis apud cæteros, Ecclesiæ causam calumniis tuis traducares, tamen quanto majora locorum intervalla ab Rege disjungereris, hoc longius abesse à suspicione fraudis* (16). This is one of the most cunning and common Touches of the ODIUM THEOLOGICUM. Those, who are at a loss to answer the Objections, raised against the Common Doctrines, fall upon the Persons, who propose those Objections: They brand them as so many false Brothers, who are in League with the Adversaries, and only retain the outward Profession of Orthodoxy, to enable them to do greater Execution.

[F] *He died* ------ *while his* Argenis *was printing in* France.] His good Friend, Mr *de Peiresc*, to whom he had sent the Manuscript, took care to find him a Printer, at *Paris* (17). The first Edition of This famous Book is That of *Paris*, 1621. It has been translated into several Languages, as *French*, *English*, *Italian*, *Dutch*, &c. *Nicius Erythræus* observes, that it was translated into *Italian* to satisfy the Curiosity of the Women. Hearing that this Book was very much cried up, they expressed a great Desire of knowing the Contents of it. " Eadem ingenii fæcunditate peperit egregium illud opus, *Argenidis* nomine, quod & argumenti novitate, & verborum splendore, ac rerum varietate, tantum commendationis habuit, ut mulierum etiam, quæ illud miris in cœlum laudibus efferri audiebant, ad cognoscendum, quid illud afferret, studia commoverit; ideo ut quidam quo animum illis expleret, in *Italicum* sermonem illud convertisset (18). ---- *The same Fruitfulness of Genius produced that celebrated Work, entitled the* Argenis, *which, for the Novelty of the Subject, the Beauty of the Language, and Variety of Matter, was so universally admired, as to raise, even among the Women, a Curiosity to know what it contained; so that, in order to gratify them with an Opportunity of reading it, some Person translated it into* Italian. Mr *de Peiresc* caused the Author's Effigies to be placed in the Title of the Book, with the following Distich, which he desired *Grotius* to compose (19).

Gente *Caledonius*, *Gallos* natalibus, hic est,
Romam Romano qui docet ore loqui.

His Birth in France, *his Name in* Scotland *shines: The* Roman *Tongue he ev'n at* Rome *refines.*

[G] *We shall give the Reason, why his Widow caused her Husband's Busto to be taken from thence.*] *John Barclay*'s Tomb was near the Gate of the Church-yard, over-against which Cardinal *Francis Barberini* had erected another, for his Preceptor *Bernard William*. Both Tombs were exactly alike. *John Barclay*'s Widow, being offended at so perfect a Resemblance, would have demolished her Husband's Tomb; but, not being able to do That, she would,

BARCLAY.

in *England* [H]: He denied it publickly [I]. His Books of Controversy had no great Success: the others had many Admirers [K], and have not wanted Censurers [L]. As to the Fortune he made at *Rome*, it is variously related. Some say,

would, at least, have his Marble Busto taken from it, and brought to her House. Her Pride could not endure, that her Husband, who was Illustrious by his Birth, and more so still by his Wit and Learning, should be there parallelled with a pitiful Pedagogue. "Quod uxor Barclaii mulier tumido, "ut ajebant, animo atque elato, cum vidisset, sta- "tim viri sui imaginem ex sepulchro illo, quod to- "tum demoliri non posset, detrahi jussit, ac domum "suam afferri; quod acciperet indigne, cum cui ipsa "nupta fuisset, generis splendore clarum, sed inge- "nii & eruditionis fama clariorem, cum homine ob- "scuro, ac nullius fere ingenii, &, ut ipsa dicebat, "pædagogo, componi (20)."

[H] *Many believe, that* John Barclay *made Profession of the Protestant Religion in* England.] The Jesuit *Eudæmon-Joannes* lays it to his Charge, that, while he lived at the Court of the King of *England*, he either actually was, or at least passed for, a Heretic. He adds, that it was said, This Prince made use of him, to translate his Preface concerning the Oath of Allegiance into *Latin*, and to carry it to several Princes. "Nam te quidem aliquot annis in "aulâ ejus Regis ita versatum ferunt ut hæreticus "aut planè esses, aut haberere quidem certè. Cui "nonnullam etiam Latinè reddendâ, deferendique "ad Principes præfatione ejus monitoriâ operam abs "te navatam memorat (21)." *Erythræus*, not daring to say, positively, that *Barclay* was a Heretic in *England*, or, at least, that he professed Heresy, does yet declare it as the Opinion of all the Papists of that Country, that King *James* made use of *John Barclay's* Pen to compose the Book, entituled, *Funiculus triplex, & Cuniculus triplex.* These are his Words: "Utrum autem, apud regem, incor- "ruptam catholicam religionem semper conserva- "rit, vel saltem, si non animo, specie tenus hære- "ticorum se erroribus obtinierit, incertum est mihi: "illud autem certum, catholicorum omnium in An- "glia fuisse opinionem, Regem illum in eo libro, "cui titulus est *Funiculus triplex, & Cuniculus tri- "plex*, componendo usum fuisse Barclaio adjutore "atque magistro (22)." I know of no body, who has been more decisive on this Question, than *Imperialis*. He says, plainly, that *Barclay* embraced the Religion of the *Church of England*, and afterwards abjured it; but, that they were so little perswaded of the Sincerity of his Conversion at *Rome*, that, after his Death, they caused the Inscription, and the Statue, which his Son had put upon his Tomb, to be taken away (23). *Paul Friberus* attributes this to the Jesuits: "Statuam & inscriptionem quam ejus "demortui gloriæ filius in templo S. Laurentii extra "muros erexerat, patres Soc. Jesu sublatam & dele- "tam voluerunt (24)." —— *The Jesuits ordered "the Inscription and Effigies, which his Son had de- "dicated to his Memory, in St* Laurence's *Church- "yard, to be taken down and demolished."* The Truth of it is hard to be known: It is possible, something was found among his Papers, or elsewhere, which might discover, that he was a Protestant in his Heart, and occasion this Resentment shewn against his Tomb. It is possible, on the other side, that the Vanity of his Wife might be the only Cause of the disordering of his Tomb; and that this might give occasion, to such as are fond of Conjectures, or of idle Comments on Town-talk, to find a Mystery in it, and some private Process of the Tribunal of the Inquisition.

[I] *He denied it publickly.*] We must either lay aside the most certain Maxims, by which we judge of Facts, or acknowledge, that *John Barclay* did not renounce the Catholic Profession in *England*. He declares publickly, that he was born, and always continued, a Catholic (25), and that, though he had accepted of an Office from King *James* (26), he never conformed to the *Church of England*, nor absented himself from the Catholic Assemblies. *I was constant*, says he, *at the latter*. He calls to witness the *French* and *Spanish* Embassadors, and their Fathers Confessors, *why were also mine*, says he. Here is something of yet greater force. He appeals to King *James*, of whom he boasts to have obtained the Pri- vilege not to be disturbed in his Catholic Religion. King *James* was yet living, when *Barclay* published these Particulars: the Embassadors, to whom he appealed, were not all dead. How can it be thought therefore, that he declares a Falsehood? He vindicates himself from another thing, which had been laid to his Charge; That of having been the Author, or Promoter, of a terrible Libel, which appeared against King *James*, as soon as *Barclay* left *England*. Lastly, he makes a Recantation of certain Doctrines, in the Book, which he had written against Cardinal *Bellarmin*. He does not forget to mention, that he went away with the Royal Permission. *Neque furtum mei feci: impetrati regis pace publicè cum familia à Britanniæ oris solvi.*

[K] *The others had many Admirers.*] See, in the Works of Sir *Thomas Pope-Blount* (27), and Mr *Baillet* (28), several fine Encomiums made on *Barclay*. The following, if it were true, would without doubt be the greatest of all, in respect to the Dignity of it's Author. It is reported, that Cardinal *Richelieu* was continually reading the *Argenis*, and that from it he took all those Counsels, and Political Expedients, with which he put *France* into so advantageous a Situation. *Ad immortalitatem Barclaii una sufficiet illius Argenis, quam Richeloeus ævi nostri miraculum assiduus, ut ajunt (29), versabat manibus, habebatque quasi præceptricem ac directricem illius regiminis, quo deinceps Galliam venerabilem juxta terribilemque gentibus cæteris fecit (30).*

[L] *And have wanted not Censurers.*] We have seen the Distich under *Barclay's* Picture, composed by *Grotius* (31). It is a great Compliment on that Author's *Latin* Stile. However his Style has not been approved by every Body. "The Anonymous Author of "the little Book, entituled *Censura Euphormionis,* "printed at *Paris* in 1620, speaks of the Style of "the *Euphormio*, in these terms: *& quod miretur aliquis; latinitas quoque ipsa Romanas aures peregri- "nitate radit, & veteris saporis imbutam palatum "offendit.* —— *And what is very surprizing, even "the* Latin *of it sounds like a foreign Language to "a Roman Ear, and is shocking to those, who have "any Relish for the Elegancies of Antiquity.* It is thought, to mention this by the way, that *Seton*, a *Scotchman*, was the Author of that little Book. *Joseph Scaliger*, in his Three hundred and eleventh Letter to *Charles Labbè*, does not speak at all more favourably of That Satire of *Barclay*. *Quanti Euphormionem Barclæi faciam ex eo cognoscere potes, quod vix sex folia ejus legere potuerim.* —— *What an Opinion I have of* Barclay's Euphormio, *you may guess from this, that I have scarce been able to read six Leaves of it.* Thus speaks the Original of 'that Letter, which I have seen in *Charles Labbè's* Hands; for, in the Edition of *Scaliger's* Letters, there is an Asterisk in the stead of *Euphormionem Barclæi.* He gives much the same Account of it in his *Scaligerana secunda*: *There is a Pedant at* Angers, *who wrote a Satyricon, which seems at the beginning to promise some thing, but in the Conclusion makes out nothing at all* (32). *Peter Mesuier*, a Canon of *Vezelai*, answered the Book entituled *Censura Euphormionis*, by another, entituled *Censura censuræ Euphormionis*; but this Answer was so very indifferent, that, in all probability, it made *John Barclay* himself write an Apology for his *Euphormio* (33). But, as it has been already observed, *John Barclay* was but Twenty one Years of Age, when he published the first Part of that Satire. His *Argenis*, which was written in his riper Years, is better done. And, if he, who wrote *John Barclay's* Life, printed before the *Argenis*, may be believed, Cardinal *Richelieu* very highly esteemed that Performance. I shall conclude with remarking, that a *Benedictine*, named *Bugnot*, who taught Rhetoric in the Abbey of *Tiron*, composed *Latin* Notes on that Work, which were printed "at *Leyden* in 1664, with the *Argenis* (34)."

This is the Harvest of the learned Mr *Menage*; I shall endeavour to gather up some Gleanings after him, and begin with these Words of *Balzac*: "An Academist "of *Rome*, a Confident of the formidable *Scioppius*, know- ing

BARCLAY.

say, that *Maffeo Barberini*, who loved him very well, having been created Pope, was a great Benefactor to him, and conferred a good Benefice upon his eldest Son, and the Office of his Holiness's Chamberlain (g). Others say, that he was forced to amuse himself with the culture of Flowers, to divert the Concern he was under, on seeing himself so little advanced (h) [M]. But it is certain, that he died before *Barberini* was elected Pope. He attempted some Things in Poetry, and several good Judges commend the *Latin* Verses, we have of his, as very extraordinary (i). His Works have been confusedly mentioned in *Moreri*'s Dictionary [N]. He was revising his *Euphormio*, in order to reprint it. He left behind him the *History of the Conquest of Jerusalem* (k), and some Sheets of the *History of Europe* (l). It could not, with any Truth, be said, that King *James* sent him Embassador to the Courts of the Emperor, King of *Hungary*, and Duke of *Savoy* [O]. He makes no mention of it himself, when he describes the

"ing the Friendship, that was between Mr *Barclay*, "and myself, and the Love I had for his *Argenis* "in order to moderate, as he said, the Violence of "my Passion, offered to shew me in that new Hi- "story, which we had then in Manuscript, Fifteen "hundred Improprieties, upon a fair Computation, "besides innumerable other Faults, and strange "Phrases (35)." *Sorel*, an Enemy of *Balzac*, passed much the same Judgment on the Style of the *Argenis*. "As for the *Argenis*, says he (36), if it's *Latin* "is esteemed, I am of a quite contrary Opinion; "for there are an infinite number of new Words in "it, which were never current in *Rome*, insomuch, "that, if *Sallust* were to return into the World again, "he would be at a loss to understand them." He pretends, that, *in this, he only follows the Opinion of the most learned, who have some of them even gone so far as to say, That* Barclay*'s Language was rather French, than Latin* (37). He is not content with censuring the Style, but also condemns the Oeconomy of the Work itself, and is no less severe on the *Euphormio* (38). "It is, says he (39), an "History of a Person of mean Quality, but it is "extreamly silly. —— What gave this Book so "great a Run was it's being in *Latin*, and the Ra- "rity of seeing a modern Romance in that Lan- "guage; but it has never been considered, that it "is lucky for the Author, that he did not write it in "a Vulgar Language, because there is now no "notice taken, that he does not understand how to "make each of his Persons speak agreeably to his "Character, which is the Grace of a Satire. In- "stead of this, he affects pedantic Expressions, and "makes a Footman speak like a Schoolmaster, who "understands *Greek* and *Latin* History; so that, all "this considered, together with the lowness of the "Adventures, the Satire of *Euphormio* appears to "be the Work of a School-Boy, just beginning to "learn Wit (40)." When he grew old, he was not quite so severe in his Censure; but he continued his Dislike to the *Euphormio* (41). *That Satire*, says he (42), *was wrote in Latin by John Barclay, and translated into French by John Berault, Doctor of Physic, of the Faculty of Paris; there is a good deal of Learning in it, with some touches of Satire on several Vices of the Age; but the Method of it is not the most ingenious, and agreeable, that one has ever invented.* We have already seen what *Scaliger* thought of the *Euphormio*: This is the Judgment he passes on the Style. *There are a great many Faults in it, which every Body does not know: as there are Gallicisms in* Beza*'s Poetry* (43). We must not forget, that this Book had the same fate with the Treatise of the Pope's Power; it was condemned by the Inquisition. The Decree orders the expunging some Parts of it: but *Nicius Erythræus* says, That the Booksellers were forbid to sell it, and all particular Persons to keep or read it; and that, before this Order, he had read some Part of it. *Partem Euphormionis degustavi tum, cum nondum lata lex erat, ne bibliopola cuipiam liceret cum vendere, aut cuiquam domi habere ac legere* (44). Let these Words be well considered, and compared with some others in Page 77. It is surprising, that the Court of *Rome* should shew so little regard to the Congregation of the *Index*: We shall see, that *John Barclay* was very graciously received at *Rome*, and most liberally supplied with every Thing, by the Bounty of the Pope, on account of the Reputation he had acquired by his *Euphormio*. "Romam venit, "ubi cum Pro eo quod ex EUPHORMIONE, quem "ediderat, celebratum ejus nomen esset, est ab om- "nibus humaniter exceptus, & à Paulo V, qui tum "Romanam Ecclesiam Pontifex administrabat, bonis "omnibus, quibus sponte se exuerat, amissis, in victu, "vestitu, ac cæteris omnibus ad vitam necessariis, mag- "nifice ac liberaliter habitus (45). Mr *Menage* has found a Fault in the Epistle Dedicatory of the *Argenis* (46). *Barclay*, addressing himself to King *Lewis* XIII, tells him, That the Prince, of whom he was born, deserved in his Life-time the Sirname of *Le Grand*, the Great, which was not conferred upon him till after his Death. *Eo es parente genitus, qui vel confessione hostium, sæculi sui summus Magni cognomen ferre vivus debuerat, quod vos modestius extincto adsidistis* (47). This is a Fallity: for *John Barclay*'s Father, decicating his Book *de Regno*, to *Henry* IV, in the Year 1600, gives him the Title of *Henricus Magnus*. Mr *Menage* confesses, that he owes this Observation to Mr *Balzac*.

[M] *Some will have it, that he was under a Concern on seeing himself so little advanced.*] The Author of the *Italian* Translation of the *Argenis* confesses, that the Favours of *Paul* V, and *Gregory* XV, were no way proportionable to the Merit of *John Barclay*, whether it be, says he (48), *that Fortune is pleased to persecute Virtue every where, or that the Pope thought, that Poverty was the true Mother of Knowledge* (49). He insinuates, that *Barclay* was no good Oeconomist, and that his generous Temper, and numerous Family, reduced him pretty low. *hoi dunque si tratteneve il Barclaio con facolta non poco angaste rispetto in numerosa famiglia, e gli suoi spiriti generosi.* In some *Latin* Verses, where he introduces his Wife, who causes her Picture to be drawn, *Barclay* says he had but two Sons. In his *Latin* Life, those Verses are quoted, to prove, that he had two Sons and one Daughter. What Judgment is here!

[N] *His Works have been confusedly mentioned in* Moreri*'s Dictionary.*] I. I have said already, in the Remarks [B] and [C], that this Author has converted a Piece of Poetry into a Speech; II. And that he has falsly placed the Scene of *John Barclay*'s Marriage at *Rome*; III. And his Birth in the Year 1586. IV. He is in the wrong to think, that *Barclay*'s *Satiricon Euphormionis* contains five Books. Properly speaking, it contains but two, for the third is only an Apology for the other two; the fifth is not *Barclay*'s, but *Morisot*'s; and the fourth is not built on the Model of the foregoing. It is the Book, which the Author entituled, *Icon animorum*. V. *Moreri* knew nothing of this, since he spoke of That *Icon animorum*, as of a distinct Work from the five pretended Books of the *Satiricon Euphormionis*. VI. If I am not mistaken, *John Barclay* published no other Pieces against the Protestants, but only the *Parænesis ad Sectarios*, which he carried ready finished into *Italy*, and printed it at *Rome*, as soon as he arrived there. And yet, *Moreri* tells us, that *Barclay* published some Books against the Protestants, during the melancholy and solitary Life he led at *Rome*, amidst the Favours of *Paul* V, and of his Successor *Gregory* XV. The *Parænesis ad Sectarios* was printed in the Year 1617. *Gregory* XV was not elected till the Year 1621. VII. He adds, that *Barclay* published also, at that time, the *Icon animorum*. This is false. That Work was printed at *London* in 1614, two Years before the Author went to *Rome*.

[O] *It could not with any Truth be said, that he was sent Embassador.*] A Writer of Panegyrics, or Lives, is too apt to make use of great Words. If a Prince appoints any Body to carry a Packet of

BARCLAY. BARCOCHEBAS.

the Life he led with King *James* (m); and all that can be made of it, in my opinion, is, that this Prince might make use of him to transmit, to foreign Princes, some Copies of the Book, he composed for their common Interests, against the Pretensions of the Court of *Rome*. His *Euphormio* and *Argenis* have been translated into *French* [P].

(o) *The Duke of Savoy's Name was Charles Emanuel.*

(51) *In the Life of Barclay, before the Argenis.*

of Importance, you will soon see the Dispatch of a Courier, converted into an Extraordinary Deputation; or even into a real Embassy. I am willing to believe, that, if the Presents, which King *James* made to several Princes, as an Author, were intrusted to *Barclay*, it was not as to a meer Bearer; it is likely, that the King, who knew his Merit, made that Commission agreeable to him; but, after all, That Message makes so little Noise; that it is a Jest to say; " Illius (Regis magnæ Britanniæ) nomine legationes obivit ad Rodolphum Imperatorem, ad " Matthiam Pannoniæ Regem, & ad (50) Emma" nuelem Philibertum ducem Allobrogum (51). — " *He was sent Embassador, by that King, to Rodol-*

" *phus the Emperor,* Matthias *King of* Hungary, " *and* Emanuel Philibert, *Duke of* Savoy."
[P] *His* Euphormio *and* Argenis *have been translated into French.*] I have already quoted *Sorel* (52), who observes, that the *Euphormio* was translated into *French* by *John Berault*: I must add, that this Translation was printed at *Paris*, in the Year 1640, in 8vo, and that it was preceeded by two others, the Authors of which, *for fear of keeping too superstitiously to the Letter, have left the Work at least as difficult as they found it* (53). *Berault* has subjoined a Key, and Commentary, to his Version. The Translation of the *Argenis* was printed at *Paris*, by *N. Buon*, in 1624, in 8vo; but the Author of it is not named.

(m) *Barclaius in Præf. Parenet. ad Sectarios.*

(72) *Above, Citat.* (30).

(53) *See the Advertisement of the Bookseller, before the Translation of Berault.*

(a) *That is, Son of the Star. He applied to himself the Prophecy of the Book of Numbers, chap. xxiv. ver. 17. There shall come a Star out of Jacob.*

BARCOCHEBAS, or *Barcochab* (a), excited innumerable Disorders in *Judæa*, by his Impostures, and drew a dreadful Calamity upon his Nation under the Reign of *Adrian*. He was a *Jew*, who declared himself to be the *Messias*, and found a famous Rabbi, who favoured That impious Pretension (b). This false *Messias* suited himself surprizingly to the Prepossessions of That miserable People; he spoke of nothing but Wars, Battles, and Triumphs; and the first Lesson of his Gospel was, that they ought to rebel against the *Romans*. He had so much the less Trouble to inculcate This Doctrine, because he took his time, when the Zeal of Religion had thrown the *Jews* into a violent Rage against the Emperor. That Prince had newly established a Colony near *Jerusalem* (c), where he had settled Idolatry. The *Jews* looked upon this as an intolerable Abomination, and a prodigious Prophanation of the Holy Places; on account of which they were very inclinable to rebel. Some pretend, that Circumcision was forbidden them [A]: this was to force their Consciences. The *Talmud* alledges another reason for their taking up Arms [B]. Their Impostor is said to have made use of the same Trick, which *Eunus* had practised in *Sicily*, to make the Slaves revolt; that is, he kindled Straw in his Mouth, that he might be thought to vomit Fire [C]. He fortified himself in several places; but he chose the City of

(b) *His Name was* A K I- B A. *See his Article.*

(c) *Which he called* Ælia Capitolina, *after his own Name and of* Jupiter Capitolinus, *to whom he raised a Temple to be built there.*

[A] *Some pretend, that Circumcision was forbidden them.*] *Spartian* imputes their rising to that Prohibition: *Moverunt ea tempestate & Judæi bellum quod vetebantur mutilare genitalia* (1). ——— The *Jews* at that time broke out into Rebellion, because they were denied the Liberty of Circumcision. It is not unlikely, that the circumcising of their Children was forbidden them, since we read in *Modestinus*, that they obtained from *Antoninus Pius* the Liberty of doing it; they had been disturbed on that account, and were obliged to have recourse to the Emperor's Justice. *Circumcidere Judæis filios suos tantum, rescripto Divi Pii permittitur: in non ejusdem religionis qui hoc fecerit, castrantis poena irrogatur* (2). The Decree, which they obtained, seems to say, that sometimes they circumcised Children not born of their Sect. This was forbidden them on the Penalties established against Castration.
[B] ——— *The* Talmud *assigns another Reason for their taking up Arms.*] It is reported, that the *Jews* had a Custom to plant a Cedar on the Birth of a Son, and a Pine on that of a Daughter; and to make the Bridal-bed of the Wood of those Trees, when their Children married. It is added, that, in a Journey, which the Emperor's Daughter made into *Judæa*, some part of her Chariot happening to break, her People cut one of these Cedars, and brought it to her; that the *Jews*, not being able to bear this, rose up in Arms, and killed those, who had cut down that Tree. The Emperor, understanding, that the *Jews* were revolted, marched in great Wrath against them, and extirpated them. " Ob crus carpenti vastata est " *Bethara*. In more fuit ut cum nasceretur infans " plantarent cedrum, cum infantula, pinum; cumque " nati contraherent matrimonium, ex iis conficerent " thalamum. Die quadam transiit filia Cæsaris, & " confractum est ei crus carpenti. Cedrum istiusmo- " di exciderunt atque ad eam attulerunt. Insurre- " xerunt in eos Judæi atque eos occiderunt. Rela- " tum est Cæsari rebellare Judæos. Profectus ille " in eos iracundus, excidit totum cornu Israëlis (3)." The *Jews* would be altogether inexcusable, if they

(1) Spart. in Vita Adriani, cap. 14.

(2) Modestinus Libro Regularum, apud Casaubon in Spartian. Adrian. cap. 14.

(3) In Tra-Etatu Tal-mudico Babyl. *Sanhedrin* fol. 5. apud Joh. à Lent, de judæorum Pseudo-Messis, p. 7.

revolted on so flight an occasion as this. These poor People do not even know how to tell a Lie to their Advantage. What Ignorance is it to give the Emperor *Adrian* a Daughter! To conclude, Pines are Trees, which grow too slowly (4) to serve for a Bed, by that time a Daughter will be ready to share it with a Man; and many of them would have deserved to be pitied, if they had been obliged to wait for a Husband, 'till their Pines were grown to a sufficient Size.

[C] *Barcochebas is said to have made use of the same Trick with* Eunus ——— *that is, he was thought to vomit Fire.*] This we learn from St *Jerome*. " Tu " videlicet flammeus, immo fulmineus qui in loquen- " do fulminas. Atque ut ille Barchochebas auctor " seditionis Judaicæ stipulam in ore succensam anhe- " litu ventilabat, ut flammas evomere videretur (5). " ——— *Thou hast not only the command of* Fire, *but* " *also of* Thunder, *in thy Words. And as* Barcochebas, " *that Ringleader of the Jewish Rebellion, kindled* " *Straw in his Mouth, and ventilated the Flame with his* " *Breath, that he might be thought to vomit it.*" Here is a Man, whose Words were Fire and Flame, not only in a figurative, but literal, Sense. As for *Eunus*, see what *Florus* says of him: " Syrus quidam " nomine Eunus (magnitudo cladium facit ut memi- " nerimus) fanatico furore simulato dum Syriæ deæ " comas jactat, ad libertatem & arma servos quasi nu- " minum imperio concitavit; idque ut divinitus fieri " probaret in ore abdita nuce, quam sulphure & igne " stipaverat, leniter inspirans flammam inter verba " fundebat (6). ——— *A certain Syrian, named* " Eunus *(the prodigious Slaughter he occasioned makes* " *me mention him) counterfeiting a divine Inspiration,* " *while he pretends to brandish a Lock of Hair of the* " *Syrian Goddess, he excited the Slaves to assert their* " *Liberty, and take up Arms, as it were by the Com-* " *mand of the Gods; and that he might prove his Com-* " *mand from Heaven, having artfully conveyed into his Mouth some* " *Fire and Sulphur, in a Nutshell, he gently breathed* " *out the Flames as he spoke.*" This is an Example to shew Sovereign Princes, how dangerous those Persons

(4) *It may be said of them,* Tarda venit seris factura nepotibus umbram. Virg. Georg. *lib* 2. *v*. 58. *A sullen Tree At leisure grows for late Posterity.* Dryden.

(5) Apologia 2. adversus Ruffinum.

(6) Florus, *lib.* 3. *c.* 19.

VOL. I. 8 A

of *Bitter* for his place of Arms, and the Seat of his Empire. It is said, that, to try the Courage of his Followers, he required them to cut off one of their Fingers, and on the Remonstrances, which were made him, he left off that Test, and made use of another Invention [D]. He ravaged a great number of places, and massacred a Multitude of Persons: He was particularly barbarous towards the Christians [E]. The Emperor, being informed of these Violences, sent some Troops to *Rufus* Governor of *Judæa*, with Orders for the immediate suppressing this Sedition (*d*). *Rufus*, in obedience to this Order, exercised a thousand Cruelties, but yet could not obtain his End. The Emperor was forced to re-call *Julius Severus*, the greatest Captain of those Times, from *England*, and commit to him the whole Conduct of That War (*e*). This General gained his Point against the *Jews*, without giving them a general Battle. He attacked them after another manner, as well because of their great number, as also because he saw them fight like desperate Men. He chose therefore rather to charge them separately, to cut off their Provisions, to shut them up, and straighten them (*f*); and at last, all was reduced to the Siege of *Bitter*, in the eighteenth Year of *Adrian* (*g*). The great number of *Jews*, who threw themselves into that City, was the cause of their making a very long Defence, and being reduced to great Extremities by Famine (*b*). After the taking of that place, the War was not quite ended, but did not continue long: *Barcochebas* perished in it (*i*), and the *Jews* have not failed to invent some Fables about it [*F*]. The manner, in which *Adrian* dispersed the Remains of that unhappy Nation, was very cruel [G]. But all the Stories,

(*d*) Euseb. Hist. Eccles. lib. 4, c. 6. pag. 118.

(*e*) Xiphilin. in Adriano.

(*f*) Id. ibid.

(*g*) About the Year of CHRIST CXXXIV.

(*b*) Euseb. ubi supra.

(*i*) Id. ib.

(12) Joh. à Lent, de Pseudo-Messiis, pag. 14, ex Echa Rabbati.

---

sons are to a State, who pretend to Inspiration. This last enthusiastic Impostor raised an Insurrection of above Sixty thousand Men, and gave the *Roman* People a great deal of Trouble.

[D] *It is said that he tried his Followers, by obliging them to cut off a Finger, — and that he made use of another Invention.*] It is reported, that he drew Two hundred thousand Men after him, who had cut off one of their Fingers, to make Proof of their Courage. The wise Men, not approving such a Mutilation, deputed some Persons to him, to know how long he would thus mangle the *Jewish* Nation, *usque quo tute Judæos mancos efficies?* He answered, *How then would you have me try their Strength?* They replied, *That he should enroll none, but those, who could pull up, with their Hands, a Cedar from Mount* Libanus. He took their Counsel, and found Two hundred thousand Men more, who gave this proof of their Strength (7). You will say, these are *Jewish* Fables. It is true, and as such I relate them; and, for that Reason, they belong the more properly to this Dictionary.

[E] *He was particularly barbarous towards the Christians.*] Indeed he made a great Slaughter of the Gentiles, but he did not force them to renounce their Religion. He play'd the part of a Converter, only towards the Christians; I say of a *Dragooning* Converter, and, perhaps, worse (8); for he condemned all those to Death, who would not forsake JESUS CHRIST, and load him with Curses. *Justin* Martyr has complained of this: *Proxime namque bis Judaico Barcochebæ defectionis Judæorum dux & princeps, solos Christianos ad gravia supplicia nisi Christum abnegarent & maledictis incesserent, protrahi jussit* (9). *David Gans* does not deny, but that those of his Nation spilled whole Torrents of Blood (10). I am even of Opinion, that he represents their Executions much more dreadful than they actually were. He pretends, that, in the City of *Alexandria* alone, they killed above Two hundred thousand Persons, and that, in the Island of *Cyprus*, and the parts adjacent, they did not leave one Man alive. *Tunc Judæi Bitterrenses unxerunt eum (Barcocheban) & elegerunt ipsum in regem super se, jugum Romanorum abjicientes. Occiderunt ex Romanis & Græcis qui in Africa innumerabiles instar arenæ maris, similiter fecerunt Ægyptiis: incolæ urbis Alexandrinæ etiam ex Romanis interfecerunt ultra bis centena millia. Qui in Cypria, occiderunt omnes plane gentes vicinas, ut ne superstes quidem remaneret.* See what will be said hereafter (11), concerning the omission of a Common Form in *Adrian's* Letters. O religious Wars, how horrible are your Cruelties!

[F] *The Jews have not failed to invent Fables on the Death of Barcochebas.*] They say, that, after the taking of *Bitter*, *Barcochebas's* Head was brought to the Emperor *Adrian*, and that he asked *who had killed him?* and that he ordered the Soldier, who replied, *It was I*, to go and fetch the Body. The Soldier, being come to the Place, found a Serpent round *Barcochebas's* Neck. The Emperor having viewed the Body, said, *If this Man had not been killed by his own God, who could have hurt him* (12)?

[G] *The Manner, in which Adrian dispersed the Remains of that unhappy Nation.*] I have a great deal of Reason to make use of the Word *Remains*; for the Number of *Jews*, who perished in that War, is not to be expressed. The Abbreviator of *Dio* relates, that they had fifty Fortresses, and Nine hundred and eighty five very considerable Boroughs, razed; that they had lost Five hundred and eighty thousand Men in Battles and Inroads, and that the Number of those, who perished by Famine, Sickness, and Fire, is infinite: So that almost all *Judæa* remained without Inhabitants (13). Let us now see what was done with those, who happened to survive so great a Desolation. " An incredible Number of " all Ages and Sexes * were sold at the same Price as " Horses, in a very famous Fair, called the Fair of " the *Turpentine Tree* †. Wherefore the *Jews* had " an Abhorrence for that Fair. ----- Those, who " could not be sold there, were brought to *Gaza* ‡, " and exposed to Sale in another Market, established " there by *Adrian*, and which, the Chronicle of " *Alexander* says, is yet called *Adrian's* Market. " Those, they could not sell in *Palestine*, were transported into *Egypt* ‡, where they perished by Shipwrecks, and by Famine, or were killed by the Pagans. -------- When the War was ended, *Adrian* prohibited the *Jews*, by an Edict publickly fixed up **, from returning to *Jerusalem*, on pain " of Death ††, and Guards were purposely placed " there, to hinder them from entering it ††. That " Law denied them even the Liberty of coming " near it, or of being in any Place, where they might " have a Sight of it ‡‡. *Tertullian* *, and St *Jerom* †, go yet further, and extend That Prohibition all over *Judæa*; and the *Jews* seem to agree to it, when they speak of the Fast, which they " instituted on account of That Decree, whereby " their Fathers had been forbidden to come into the " Country of *Judæa* †." The Author, of whom I borrow This Passage, with all it's Quotations (14), makes a Remark on the Fair of the *Turpentine-Tree*. He observes, that " St *Jerom* says ‡, in a cer- " tain Place, that *the Jews were sold*, at *Abraham's* " Tent, where is kept, *says he*, an annual Fair, " very much frequented. This is not difficult to " be granted, for, in the Place, where *Abraham* had " lived, in the Valley of *Mamre* [near *Hebron*], and " where he entertained three Angels, there was re- " maining, in the IVth Century a Turpentine-Tree, " which the People of the Country said had been " there from the Creation of the World." See the Remark [G] of the Article ABRAHAM: Let us return to the Calamity of the *Jews*. Some Authors say, that *Adrian* caused their Ears to be cut off, and transported them into *Spain* (15). It is very

(7) In Midrasch Rabbeta Megillot fol. 6", apud Joh. à Lent, ubi supra, pag. 10, 11.

(8) *I wake use of a perhaps, because several Parisians maintain, that the Judaico Barcochebæ defectionis Judæorum dux & princeps, solos Christianos ad gravia supplicia nisi Christum abnegarent & Death, would have been a less Cruelty, than what was committed in France, by the Dragoons in 1685.*

(9) Justin. Apologia pro Christianis ad Antoninum Pium.

(10) David Gans, Germine Davidis ad Ann. 840. millenarii quarti, apud à Lent, p 9.

(11) In Remark [*I*].

(13) Xiphil. in Adriano.
* Hieronym. in Jerem. cap. 31. pag. 342. *b*.
† Chronic. Alex. pag. 596.
‡ Id. Ibid.
‡ Hier. in Zach. cap. 11, p. 272. *d*.
** Id. in Is. cap. 6, pag. 31. *d*.
†† Euseb. Hist. Eccl. lib. 4, cap. 6, & Demonstr. Evang. lib. 2, cap. 3*b*. pag. 71. *a*.
Justin. Apol. 2, p. 84, *b. c*. Dial. pag. 234. *a*.
‡‡ Justin. pag. 84. *b*. Sulpic. Sev. lib. 2. pag. 749.
II Euseb. Hist. Eccles. lib. 2. in Is. lib. 3. p. 227.
* Apol. cap. 21, p. 20, *d*.
† In Judic. cap. 13. pag. 225. cap. 6, pag. 12. In Daniel. cap. 9, pag. 593. *d*.
‡ Scaliger. Isag. lib. 1. cap. 6, p. 45.

(14) Tillemont, Hist. des Emper. Tom. 2, pag. 501, 502, 503.
‡ In Zachar. cap. 8. pag. 262.

(15) Apud à Lent, de Pseudo-Messiis, pag. 17.

BARCOCHEBAS.

Stories, the Rabbins tell on this Subject, are not to be credited [*H*]. This War cost the *Romans* a great many Lives (*k*). If I mention in the Remarks several Facts, which concern this War, it is because the Article of *Hadrian* refers to them, and there was a necessity of shortening, as much as possible, That Emperor's Article, by means of This Reference. The Jewish Authors suppose, that *Adrian* was personally in that War [*I*], that he besieged and took the City of *Bitter*, and that he disputed, with a Rabbi, about the Doctrine of the Resurrection of the Dead [*K*]. This Fact is very curious; And will be found in the Remarks.

Eusebius

(*k*) *See Remark* [*E*].

very likely, that Part of the Idolatries, which That Emperor established in the new City of *Jerusalem*, did not begin 'till after the Destruction of *Bitter*, and the Death of *Barcochebas*. It was one of the most sensible Shocks, which that unhappy Nation ever had to sustain. *Adrian*, knowing their Abhorrence for Swine, caused one of Marble to be set up over the Gate, which led to *Bethlehem* **. He made use of the Stones of *Solomon's* Temple ††, for the Building of a Theatre, and several Pagan Temples. Two of his Statues, and some Idols, were set up in the Place, where That Temple stood ‡‡. The Statue of *Jupiter* was set up in the Place of our Saviour's Passion. This is what St *Paulinus* affirms ‡‡: but, according to St *Jerom* *, *Jupiter's* Statue was set up where JESUS CHRIST rose from the Dead, and That of *Venus*, where he died. The Cavern, where he was born, was profaned by the Temple, and infamous Worship, of *Adonis* †. See Mr *de Tillemont*, to whom I am indebted for these Particulars (16).

[*H*] *All the Stories, which the Rabbins tell on This Subject, are not to be credited.*] They say, that the Slaughter was so great in *Bitter*, when the *Romans* made themselves Masters of it, after a Siege of three Years and a half, that the Horses marched up to the Mouth in Blood (17). They add, that the Blood made so strong a Current, that it carried Stones, of the Weight of four Pounds, along with it, and ran for the Space of four Miles into the Sea. Now *Bitter* was four Miles from the Sea. *Adrian* had a Vineyard-plot eighteen Miles long, and as many wide; (it is the Distance from *Tiberias* to *Zipporis*) where he made a Fence or Partition with the Bodies of those, who were killed in *Bitter*: For he would not suffer them to be buried, nor were they buried 'till the Reign of his Successor. There were two Rivers in the Valley of *Jadaim*, running on different Sides of it (18); the Rabbins computed, that the Water made but two thirds, and the Blood the other third, of those Rivers. For seven Years the Gentiles had no need to dung their Vines, they were so richly manured with the Blood of the Jews. The Blood carried away Stones with it of an immense Magnitude, and entered forty Miles into the Sea: *Quinimo sanguis rapiebat secum petras magnitudinis quadraginta modiorum, donec ad quadraginta milliaria usque in Oceanum fluerit* (19). Three hundred Skulls of Children were found on one Stone. There are, in these Rabbinical Expressions, some touches of the Style, which *Rabelais* makes use of, to represent the Valour and Prowesses of his *Garagantua* and his *Pantagruel*. But let us relate one more Story concerning the Slaughter of *Bitter*. In That City there were Four hundred Colleges, and in each College Four hundred Masters, each of which had Four hundred Disciples, or Scholars in his Class. In the first Attack, the Scholars made use of their Writing Pens (20), to kill their Enemies; but, after the Place was taken, they were packed up with their Books and thrown into the Fire. *Ista pubes principio hostes impetum facientes graphiis suis confodiebat: cum vero bi prævaluerent, urbem cepissent, involverunt puerulos illos cum libris suis, eosque igne sic cremarunt* (21). The Jews say, that *Adrian* destroyed twice as many People of their Nation, as *Moses* brought out of the Land of *Egypt*, and they esteem him a greater Persecutor of them, than either *Nebuchadnezzar*, or *Titus* (22). One of their best Chronologers affirms, that the Loss, which their Nation sustained in the time of *Nebusaraddan*, or in the Time of *Titus*, does not come up to That, which they sustained under the Reign of *Adrian*; for the *Talmud* says, that Four Millions of Persons perished at *Bitter*, *quadringentas myriadas*. Nevertheless, there is, in the Ritual of the Jews, a Hymn for the ninth Day of the Month *Ab*, being That of the Date of *Adrian's* Edict, which prohibited their

setting Foot in *Judæa*: I say there is an Hymn, wherein *Nebuchadnezzar* and *Adrian* are equally represented, as two great Scourges of their Nation. That Hymn names them often, but speaks only once of *Vespasian* and *Titus*; it mentions Four hundred and eighty Synagogues burnt by *Adrian*. " Recordare Domine qualis fuerit Adrianus, crudelitatis " consilia amplexus, consuluit idola se pervertentia. " Et sustulit, combussitque quadringentas & octo- " ginta synagogas (23). ----- *Remember, O Lord,* " *the Sin of Adrian, who, following the Counsels of* " *Cruelty, and listening to Idols, which perverted* " *him, destroyed, and burnt, Four hundred and eigh-* " *ty Synagogues.*"

[*I*] *The Jewish Authors suppose, that Adrian was personally in That War.*] *Eusebius* says expressly, that the Emperor sent some Troops to the Governor of *Judæa*, to chastise the Revolt of *Barcochebas*, and never mentions That Prince's going thither afterwards in Person. The Abbreviator of *Dio* speaks only of the Generals, who were sent into *Judæa* by *Adrian* (24). He remarks, that, during That Emperor's Stay in *Egypt* and in *Syria*, the Jews, who were discontented at the Building of Ælia *Capitolina*, durst not stir, but appeared in Arms openly, as soon as he was gone. He adds, that *Adrian* sent, against them, the best of his Generals, and particularly *Julius Severus*. This was a proper Place to say, whether he was present, in Person, when the Rebels were punished; and yet That Writer mentions nothing of it: From whence it seems to follow, that *Adrian* did not at that time go into *Judæa*. But, not to conceal any Thing, it must be owned, that *Dio* makes a Remark, which intimates, that *Adrian* was present in That War. He says, that the *Romans* lost so many Men in it, that This Emperor, writing to the Senate did not use the common Preamble, *Si vos liberique vestri valetis bene est, ego quidem & exercitus valemus*. ---- *If you, and your Children, are well, it will give me cause to rejoice; I have the Pleasure to assure you of my own Health, and That of the Army*. One would think, that a Prince, who begins his Letter with These Words, must be present in the Army; and if he is not, he ought not to make Use of That Compliment, neither in time of Prosperity, nor in Time of Adversity. It does not, therefore, seem likely, that *Dio* would have made This Observation, if he had thought, that *Adrian* was near *Rome*, or very far from the Army, when he wrote to the Senate. This Objection may be easily answered; for, in the first Place, it may be said, that *Adrian's* Absence was the very Occasion of his not using That Form; from whence it would follow, that *Dio* did not rightly apprehend all the possible Causes of That Omission, when he ascribed it only to the Loss, which the *Roman* Army had suffered. It may be said, in the second Place, that an Emperor, who is a great way from his Army, might very well make use of That Form, in a Letter, wherein he acquaints the Senate with the good News, which his Generals have wrote to him. In fine, it might be maintained, against *Dio*, that the Victory, obtained over the Jews, was so compleat, and did so effectually remove all Possibility of a new Insurrection, that, tho' the *Roman* Army had sustained great Losses, there was room to write to the Senate, according to the Style, commonly used in the News of Prosperity. It is possible, therefore, that This Writer might make a wrong Observation.

[*K*] *And, that he disputed with a Rabbi about the Doctrine of the Resurrection of the dead.*] This Fable says, that the chief Difficulty, objected by *Adrian*, was, that the Parts of a dead Body were dispersed in a thousand Places. He was answered, that there was a small Bone in our Body, which was incorruptible, and that God would restore our Body again out of That little Bone. The Jews pretend, that

** *Hieron. in Chron.*

†† *Euseb. Demonstr. lib. 8. cap. 3. pag. 406.*

‡‡ *Iter Burd. p. 43. a. Sulpic. Sever. lib. 2. pag. 149.*

‡‡ *Epist. 11. p. 134, 135.*

* *Epist. 13. pag. 102.*

† *Paulin. Epist. 11. p. 134, 135.*

(15) *Tillemont, Hist. des Emper. pag. 503.*

(17) *See the Book Echa Rabbati super Thren. 11. v. 2. apud Noldium de Vita & Gestis Herodum, pag. 453.*

(18) *In Tractatu Talmudico Giffin, apud à Lent, p. 16.*

(19) *Ibid.*

(20) *An Instrument wherewith they used to write in these times.*

(21) *Tract. Giffin. apud eundem à Lent, p. 23.*

(22) *See Jo. à Lent, pag. 14.*

(23) *Apud eumdem à Lent, pag. 18, 19.*

(24) *Xiphilin in Adriano.*

WHAT the Jews report of a little Bone called LUZ, which they say is in the Back of Man.

BARCOCHEBAS. BARDE.

Eusebius supposes, that *Adrian* intrusted this War to his Lieutenants (*l*). It is at least very certain, that *Adrian* did not command his Uncle *Trajan*'s Troops in *Judæa* during the Rebellion of *Barcochebas*. *David Gans*, the Jewish Historian, is very much mistaken in affirming it (*m*). Some say, that there were two *Barcochebas*'s, one under *Titus*, the other under *Adrian*; and that the first, having failed in the Test required of him, was killed as an Impostor, and a false *Messias*. Upon his declaring himself to be the *Messias*, a Passage of Scripture was alledged to him, which imports, according to the Jewish Exposition, that the *Messias* will be able to discern, by the Smell, whether a Person accused be Innocent or Guilty (*n*) [*L*], and it being found, that this pretended *Messias* had not a Nose good enough to make that distinction, he was put to Death. This Opinion is not much followed (*o*).

that a celestial Dew will soften That Bone, and make it grow, in the same Manner as a little Leaven raises the whole Mass, or, as a Grain of Wheat shoots into the Ear. *Osiculum illud dicunt rore quodam cælesti molliendum & extendendum ad instar fermenti quod in totam se messem diffundit, vel quemadmodum granum aliquod tritici in cristam se exporrigit* (25). *Adrian* would not believe any thing concerning the Incorruptibility of That Bone; but the Rabbi, with whom he disputed, made a Trial of it; and it resisted every thing, Fire, Water, the Hammer, &c. Here is a long Passage of *Manasses Ben-Israel*. " Ajunt in spina dor-
" si aliquod ossiculum esse, quod nunquam pereat: ex
" isto ossiculo solo post interitum & annihilationem om-
" nium aliarum partium, dicunt, hominem instaura-
" tum, restitutumque iri, in resurrectione mortuo-
" rum; juxta illud, quod in Beresit Raba Paras. 28.
" legitur; Adrianus (cujus ossa comminuantur) quæ-
" sivit ex R. Jeosuah filio Hanina, unde Deus bene-
" dictus germinare faciet hominem in futuro sæculo?
" respondit ille, ex — lux, seu ossiculo spinæ. Rur-
" sus alter, unde nosti hoc? da mihi illud, inquit
" ille, ossiculum, & te docebo: contudit illud in
" mola, sed non tusum est; conjecit in ignem &
" non conflagravit; conjecit in aquam, & non attri-
" tum est; imposuit incudi, malleoque cecidit; sed
" ne hilum comminutum est: Imperator Romanus,
" sive quod rideret resurrectionem mortuorum, sive
" quod audiverat aliquod incorruptibile ossiculum esse
" in corpore humano, cupiditate ejus sciendi; vel
" quia, uti verisimilius est, hæsitabat ob difficultates
" eas, quas jam recensuimus, quæsivit ex R. Jeosua
" filio Hanina, unde, vel quomodo restituerentur
" mortui, quorum membra tam longe, lateque dis-
" persa essent ac dissipata ? Respondit illi R. Jeosuah,
" ex ossiculo spinæ dorsi, appellato lux, quod incor-
" ruptibile est. Qui cum non posset facile adhibere
" fidem, experimento ei ostendit ita esse. Hæc opi-
" nio, si quid antiquis credimus, non improbabilis
" est. Istud enim ossiculum tale est, ut nequeat in-
" terire, quamvis hodie nullus sit, qui illud noverit.
" Sunt qui arbitrentur, Davidem hujus osficuli men-
" tionem facere, cum ait, Custodiens ossa ejus, unum

" ex iis non consumptum est. Psalm xxxiv. 21. (26).
" ——— *They hold, that there is in the Spine of the
" Back a little Bone, which never perishes: and that
" from this little Bone only, after Death and Annihi-
" lation of all the other Parts, the whole Man will
" be renewed, and restored in the Resurrection of the
" Dead. According to what we meet with in Beresit
" Raba Paraf.* 28 *; Adrian (whose Bones I wish may
" all be annihilated) asked Rabbi Jeosuah the Son of
" Hanina, from whence the human Body was to spring
" up again for a future State. To which he an-
" swered, from Lux, or the little Bone of the Spine.*
" The other replied, how do you know that? I will
" take that Bone, says he, and shew you: he tried to
" grind it in a Mill; he threw it into the Fire; he en-
" deavoured to dissolve it in Water; he attempted
" to break it on an Anvil with a Hammer; but all to
" no purpose; it remained still the same: The *Roman
" Emperor*, either in order to ridicule the Resur-
" rection of the Dead, or to be satisfied of the Truth
" of what he had heard of the Incorruptibility of a
" little Bone in the human Body, or which is most
" probable of all, being puzzled with the Diffi-
" culties we mentioned, urged *R. Jeosuah*, the Son of
" *Hanina*, with this Question. Whence, and by what
" means, shall the Dead be restored, whose Bodies
" have been dispersed over the Face of the whole
" Earth? *R. Jeosuah* answered him, From the little
" Bone of the Spine, called *Lux*, which is incorrup-
" tible. The Truth of which being doubted, he
" demonstrated it by Experiment. This opinion, if
" we have any Faith in Antiquity, is not improba-
" ble. For That little Bone is of such a Nature, that it
" cannot be destroyed, though there is no Body now
" who knows it. Some have believed, that *David*
" had regard to this Bone, when he said, *Thou pre-
" servest his Bones, one of them shall not perish.
" Psal.* xxxiv. 21." These doting Fools should have said, that this little Bone is the true Seat of the Soul.
[*L*] *The Messias will be able to discern by the smell whether a Person accused be Innocent or Guilty.*] Compare this with what will be related in the Remark [*C*] of the Article DEMOCRITUS.

BARDE (JOHN *de la*), Counsellor of State, Marquis *de Marolles*, on the River *Seine*, was Embassador of *France* in *Switzerland*, in the Reign of *Lewis* XIV. He had been chief Deputy of Mr *de Chavigni*, Secretary of State (*a*). He assisted at the Conferences of *Munster*, as a Minister of the Second Rank, and some Endeavours were used to have him complimented with the Title of Excellency, but without any Success [*A*]. He had then been named Embassador

[*A*] *Endeavours were used to have him complimented with the Title of Excellency, at the Treaty of Munster, but without Success.*] Mr *de Wicquefort* reports it, and adds, that the Plenipotentiaries of *France* made their first attempt on the Nuncio, who answered, that he would not do it (1). They pressed him to give Mr *de la Barde* that Title, and the first Visit. The Reasons he gave for his Refusal were, That *he would not set an Example, which no body would follow,* nor make Mr *de la Barde useless, who was very serviceable to the Assembly.* He would indeed have made him useless, because, if he had done him the Honour which was desired, he must have put him under a Kind of Necessity of requiring it from all the other Embassadors, and of not appearing any more if they had refused him, as it would infallibly have happened. The *Venetian* Embassador imitated the Nuncio; and so *la Barde was obliged to be satisfied with the Honours they were willing to do him.* He *desired the Emperor's*

Ministers at Osnabrug to distinguish him from the other Ministers of the second Rank, and since they could not treat him as an Embassador, not to treat him as a Resident; and provided he was treated in the third Person after the Italian Manner, he should not pretend to the place of Honour in Visits or Conferences. And indeed he could expect no great Distinction, at Munster, or Osnabrug, by virtue of his Credential Letters for the Swiss Cantons. Mr *de la Barde* complained of an *Italian* Writer, for misrepresenting this matter, and, to convince him, affirms, that the Plenipotentiaries of *France* always treated him as an Embassador, and that they could do no otherwise, since the King's Patent, and all the Letters from Court, gave him that Character. " Avauxius ac Ser-
" vianus hunc haud secus ac seipsos invicem ha-
" buere; neque aliter poterant, cùm regio diplomate
" atque omnibus Regis atque Mazarini ad se atque
" ad alios litteris legatus esset appellatus. Id eo
" accuratius

BARDE. BARLETTA.

sador to *Switzerland*. He served *France*, with great Faithfulness, and Ability, in the whole course of that Embassy. He wrote the *History* of France in *Latin*, from the Death of Lewis XIII, to the Year 1652. That History was long expected, as a Master-piece [*B*]: It was printed, at last, in the Year 1671 (*b*), and well received by the Public. The Style of it is good; the Narrations are without Flattery, and shew a great Knowledge of the Intrigues of the Cabinet. The Author has Latinised his Name by That of *Labardæus*. The *Latin* Names, he gives to others, would puzzle the Reader, had he not taken care to place the *French* Names in the Margin. He had made a *French* Translation of this *History*, which, in the opinion of some good Judges, was very much inferior to the original *Latin* (*c*). " As he was very learned, in Matters " of Divinity, he also wrote a Book of Controversy, in *Latin*, against the " Opinion of the Protestants, concerning the Eucharist (*d*) [*C*]." The *Dutch Gazettes* have informed us, that he died in the Year 1692, being ninety Years of Age. The Addition I would make to the Remark [*C*] of this Article, will be found below, [*D*].

(a) *Labardæus*. Hist. de Rebus Gallicis, lib. 4. pag. 189, ad Ann. 1646.

" accuratius mihi dicendum fuit, quod homo qui-
" dam Italicus eâ de re secus scripsit ex alienâ lubi-
" dine, atque invidiâ in Labardæum: nam id illi
" ipsi tribuere nolim, qui in hujuscemodi rebus eti-
" am supra verum aliis favit, hos cùm Residentes,
" aut ad minores Principes absque ullo Titulo missi
" essent, Legatos nihilo secius appellando (2). ----
" D'Avaux and Servien *regarded him as their Equal*;
" *nor could they indeed do otherwise, since his Royal*
" *Credentials, and all the King's and Mazarine's*
" *Letters, both to himself, and other Ministers,*
" *stiled him Embassador. It was necessary to be the*
" *more particular in this Affair, because it has been*
" *misrepresented, by a certain Italian Author, out of*
" *Envy and Prejudice to* la Barde: *For it cannot be*
" *ascribed to his Manner of writing, which inclines*
" *to the other extream, and gives the Title of* Em-
" *bassador to Residents, and such as are sent with-*
" *out a Character to inferior Princes*."

[*B*] *His History* of France *was long expected, as a Master-Piece.*] " Mr *de la Barde* is preparing a " *Latin* History, which is to shew, that *France* has " either it's *Sallust* or it's *Virgil*." This is what Father *le Moine* thought proper to intimate to the Public, in his *Treatise of History*.

[*C*] *He wrote a Book of Controversy, in* Latin, *against the Opinion of the Protestants concerning the Eucharist.*] This puts me in mind of what I have heard his Grandson, the Abbot of *Brion*, Canon of *Notre-Dame* at *Paris*, say, *viz*. That he applied himself several Years, with great diligence, to examine the Opinion of some Fathers about That Question, and to compose a large Volume of great Learning; but, all of a sudden, it came into his Head to destroy that great Work, so that one

Morning he threw all he had wrote upon that Subject into the Fire.

[*D*] *Here is what I would add to the Remark* [*C*] *of this Article.*] This relates to his Book of Controversy. In a Manuscript Letter of his, to one of his Friends, dated from *Solothurn, March* 3. 1663, we find these words. " Libellum ad te de " re seriâ, imò divinâ, mitto, quo tibi otii mei, " sicuti prius negotii, ratio constet: in eo Latinitatem " nostram ne quæsiveris, quam de divinis scribendi " atque disputandi genius vix patitur. —— *I send* " *you a Treatise on a serious, and indeed a divine,* " *Subject, that I may shew you the manner of my* " *spending my leisure Hours, as I have formerly* " *done in respect to my busy ones: you must not look* " *for Purity in our* Latin, *it being scarce consistent* " *with these Divinity Discourses and Disputations.*" His Friend answers him a little time after in this manner. " Restat ut de opusculo tuo Theologico " gratias agam; in hoc solitam elegantiam tuam " desideravi; neque verò tu argumenti severitatem " excusa: quid enim est tam contumax, quod ni- " tescere, quid tam horridum, quod poliri ameni- " tate istâ tuâ non possit; sed nimirum ingeniis " Helvetiis scribebas. —— *I must not forget to thank* " *you for your Piece of Divinity, in which I ex-* " *pected to have found your usual Elegance: the na-* " *ture of the Subject is no excuse: for what is there* " *so obscure as not to be illustrated, what so rough* " *as not to be polished, by your fine Pen: but you* " *wrote to* Helvetian *Understandings*." This Answer is dated the 19th of the same Month. These Passages will fix the Time of this Book of Controversy to this Year 1663.

BARLETTA (GABRIEL), a Dominican Monk, distinguished himself towards the end of the XVth Century [*A*], by a manner of Preaching much more becoming a Buffoon, than a Minister of the Gospel. He was born at *Barletto* (*a*), in the Kingdom of *Naples*. Henry *Stephens* is not the only Person, who exclaimed against his manner of Preaching (*b*), full of mean Explications, only proper to expose our most venerable Mysteries to contempt; some Roman Catholics have not spared *Gabriel Barletta* on this Head [*B*]: And this Censure does

(a) *In Latin* Barulum.

[*A*] *He distinguished himself towards the end of the* XV*th Century.*] *Altamura*, in his *Bibliotheque* of the *Dominicans*, places *Barletta* in the Year 1470; from whence it appears, that *Possevin* was mistaken only 200 Years. " (1), Neapolitani regni, Apulus, Ordinis autem " Dominicani, Theologus & concionator utilis, cum " floreret anno 1270. —— Gabriel Barletta, *of* Apu- " lia, *in the Kingdom of* Naples, *of the Dominican* " *Order, a Divine, and able Preacher, flourished in* " *the Year* 1270." He adds, that his Sermons were printed several times, before the Edition of *Venice*, 1571.

[*B*] *Some Roman Catholics have not spared him.*] *Theophilus Raynaud*, under the Name of *Petrus à Vallis Clausa*, wrote sharply against *Barletta*, and reproached him particularly for his impertinent Answer to this Question, *How the Woman of* Samaria *knew that* JESUS CHRIST *was a Jew? See*

knew it, says he, *by the Circumcision*. It must be confessed, that this Critic was not so exact as he ought to have been; for he does not only forget to mention the two other marks, whereby, as *Barletta* says, That Woman knew JESUS CHRIST to be a *Jew*; but he also makes *Barletta* say, that she saw our Lord was circumcised; but it is certain *Barletta* did not express himself in that manner: " Prima ad habitum quem portabat —— secunda " quia Nazaræus in cujus capite novaculum non as- " cendit —— tertia ratio ad circumcisionem: nullus " alius populus erat circumcisus. —— *The first Mark* " *was that of his Habit* —— *the second, his never* " *having had his Head shaved, as being a* Nazarene " —— *the third, his Circumcision: no other People* " *were circumcised.*" It would signify nothing towards the Justification of this Critic, to say, that what he imputes to *Barletta* may be inferred from his words: for what a Man says ought never to be

(1) Possevin. Apparat. Sacr. Tom. 2. fol. 521, apud Altamur. p. 518. *This Fault is not to be found in the Edition of Cologne*, 1607. *It is there*, pag. 610, cum floreret Ann. 1470.

(*b*) *See the* Apology *for* Herodotus, *where many Strokes of* Barletta *may be found*.

confounded

BARLETTA. BARLEUS.

does much greater Service and Honour to the Catholics, than the Pains the *Dominicans* take to justify This Preacher [C]. His Sermons were printed at *Venice*, in the Year 1571, in Two Volumes in 8°. The First Volume contains the *Lent* Sermons: the Second contains the Sermons on the *Advent, Pentecost, Whitsunday, Ascension,* and other *Festivals* (c). He was yet living, when the *Turks* took *Otranto,* in the Year 1480 (d). Some of his Friends undertook to justify him, by denying him to be the Author of the Sermons, which passed under his Name [D].

(c) Possevin. Apparationem. To r.st. pig. 610.

(d) Altamer. Biblioth. Ordin. Prædicat p.175.

A RULE which those ought to follow, who impute certain things to an Author.

confounded with the Consequences, which may be drawn from what he says. How many things escape not only an Orator, but also an Author, whereof he does not perceive so much as the most immediate Consequences? It is very possible therefore, that this Critic, by imputing to him those Consequences, imputes to him what he never thought of. So that, if a Man will be an exact and faithful Critic, he must prescribe this Rule to himself: "Censure the very "words themselves, which are obnoxious, and reli-"giously forbear either to add or suppress a Tittle. "Shew the Authors the Consequences, which proceed "from them, but do not assert, that they have seen "and admitted those Consequences; wait for what "they will reply, when they are told, that they "follow naturally, and necessarily, from what they "have said." I cannot believe, that *Barletta* could ever have arrived at such a heighth of Impudence and Extravagance, as to utter the *impudorata blasphemia,* which his Critic imputes to him, in such fine *Latin*. It is enough to accuse him of not knowing what he said with his third Mark. I shall therefore leave his Critic to *Altamura's* Anger. "Pessimè "igitur à Valle Clausâ falsavit calumniaturus Barlettæ "sententiam exscribendo respondit Samaritanam "cognovisse Christum esse Judæum videndo eum "esse circumcisum. Ubi fraudulento silentio præ-"terivit duas priores rationes, &c (2) —— Valle "Clausâ, *in order to* si..y Barletta's *Opinion, has* "*most abominably* re..cited *it, and made him say,* "*That the Woman of Samaria knew Christ to be* "*a Jew, by seeing he was circumcised. Where he* "*unfaithfully suppresses the two former Reasons before* "*given,* &c." Another of his Sermons was censured with greater exactness. In that, the Question is, why the Holy Ghost deferred his coming into the World for ten Days. *Barletta* ascribes this to the fear of being served in the same manner as the Son of God was, and makes the Dispute between the Father and the Holy Ghost to end only by this expedient. The Holy Ghost brought himself to take the Appearance of Wind and Fire, that he might not run any hazard among Men. What can be said meaner, and more unworthy of the Divine Majesty?

(2) Altamer. pag 519.

[C] *The Dominicans take a great deal of Pains to justify this Preacher.*] To begin with the Sermon on the *Pentecost,* I observe, that *Altamura* is so far

from owning, that there is any thing in it worthy of Censure, that, on the contrary, he finds it represents the Obstinacy of Mankind with wonderful Art, and is very much surprized at this rash Accusation of so eminent a Preacher. "Tanti nominis, *says he* (3). "concionatorem, tantoque cum fructu verbum Dei "disseminantem, ut adhuc vigeat ad perpetuum tur-"ti viri decus commune in Italia proloquium. *Nostra* "*prædicare, Qui nescit Barlettare* (4). —— *So emi-* "*nent and edifying a Preacher, that to his immortal* "*Honour it continues a Proverb in Italy, to this Day,* "*He who knows not how to imitate Barletta,* "*knows not how to preach.*" As for the main part of the other Objection, he answers it very poorly; for he pretends, that, according to *Barletta,* the Woman of *Samaria* knew by JESUS CHRIST's Garment, and his Hair, that he was a *Jew*; from whence, in arguing, she drew this Consequence, that *he was circumcised.* Once more, the shortest and best way is to say, that this poor Preacher did not know what he said with his third Mark: he had not known whereabout he was, had he taken it for a Subject to reason upon.

(3) Id Ibid.

(4) He had already said this in p.y. 195, with a long Train of pompous Elogies.

[D] *Some understood to justify him, by denying, that he was the Author of the Sermons, which passed under his Name.*] Leander *Albertus* pretends, that, in his Youth, he knew the ignorant Person, who forged those unworthy Productions, which went under the famous Name of *Barletta* (5). It is much to be wondred, that the new Author of the *Bibliotheca* of the Order, has not alledged this reason in Justification of his Brother; some would be apt to say he durst not make use of it, because what Leander *Albertus* had said was known to be false. But, whether it be so or not, it is at least very certain, that there are some impertinent Things in the Writings, which are incontestably ascribed to *Barletta.* We have seen the Censure of Father *Reynaud. Moreri* is in the wrong to maintain, That *several Protestant Authors have made use of his pretended Sermons, to ridicule the Catholics, and that, among those,* Henry Stephens *is one of the first:* for I dare be positive, that the Sermons, from whence *Henry Stephens* took his Railleries, are none of those, which *Leander Albertus* imputes to an Impostor. The Dispute between the Father and the Holy Ghost is one of *Henry Stephens's* Gaieties; now *Altamura* acknowledges, that *Barletta* is the Author of it.

(5) Alberti Descript. Ital. p. 370.

BARLEUS (MELCHIOR), a Native of *Antwerp,* a *Latin* Poet in the XVIth Century, and Son of *Lambert Barleus,* who was Keeper of the Records of *Antwerp,* above Forty Years, was educated under good Masters, and testified by several Writings, both in Prose and in Verse [A], the Progress he had made. One of his Brothers, whose Name was *James,* left his Country for his Religion, and made his Escape into *Holland,* where, after having been Regent of the second Class, in the College of *Leyden,* he was called to the *Brill,* to be Rector of the College there. *Gaspar Barleus,* elder Brother of *Melchior* [B], succeeded in the Office of Keeper of the Records, which his Father had; but, when *Antwerp* was again brought under the Yoke of the *Spanish* Government, he left his Country, and retired into *Holland.* He carried his eldest Son along with him, who was yet in the Cradle (a), and of whom I shall speak in the following Article.

(a) Taken from Gaspar Barleus Funeral Oration spoken at Amsterdam, L. John Arn. Corv hist, Jan. 18, 1648.

[A] *He published several Writings, both in Prose and in Verse.*] These are the Titles of them; Brabantiades libri 5. & Antwerpia Encomium. De Diis Gentium libri duo, in Elegiac Verses, at *Antwerp* in 1662 (1). De raptu Ganymedis libri tres (2), & Bucolica, at *Antwerp* 1572. A Speech *De vita humana;* cum adjuncto carmine, *De Rerum humanarum vicissitudine,* ad Gasparem fratrem, at *Antwerp* 1566 (3). Historia de Domus Austriacæ Eminentia (4).

[B] *Gaspar* Barleus *was elder Brother of* Melchior.] I make no doubt but *Valerius Andreas* has taken this *Gaspar* for him who was Professor at *Amsterdam,* and whose *Latin* Verses were so much cried up. If he

(1) Valerius Andreas Bibl. Belg. pag. 669.

(2) Cuperus colic., in Oratiun ori Gaspar. Barlæi.

(3) Valer. Andreas, ubi supra.

(4) Curverus ibid.

has, he was grossly mistaken: That Professor was *Melchior's* Nephew, and not his Brother. If it be said, in order to excuse *Valerius Andreas* on this account, that he does not make the Mistake, which I have supposed, yet he would be in the wrong on another: for when an Author is described by his Relations, those ought never to be made use of, who are unknown either in the Commonwealth of Learning, or in the World; and consequently these words of *Valerius Andreas, Melchior Barleus, Antverpiensis, Gasparis frater,* would be impertinent, if they were meant of *Melchior's* Brother; because that Brother, though he taught at *Bommel,* is an unknown Person. *Moreri* has committed the same Fault with *Valerius Andreas.*

BARLEUS.

BARLEUS (GASPAR), Nephew of the foregoing, was Professor of Philosophy at *Amsterdam*, and one of the elegant Latin Poets of the XVIIth Century. He was born at *Antwerp* in the Year 1584 (a). His Father, who was a Protestant, fled into *Holland*, when the Duke of *Parma* had made himself Master of that City. He staid three Years in *Leyden*, after which he was called to *Bommel*, to be Rector of the College there. He enjoyed that place seven Years, and then died, having designed his Son *Gaspar* for the Ministry of the Holy Gospel. This *Gaspar* studied eight Years in the College of the Province of *Holland* at *Leyden*, and, being afterwards received into the Ministry, he served a Country Church near the *Brill*. *Bertius*, being advanced from the Office of Sub-Principal to the Principalship of that College, thought no Person so fit to succeed him as our *Barleus*. His Recommendation was successful; *Barleus* was made Sub-Principal, and, some time after, Professor of Logic, in the University of *Leyden*. He concerned himself so far in the Disputes of the *Arminians*, that he was removed from all his Offices, when the opposite Party had fully triumphed in the Synod of *Dort*, in the Year 1618. *Barleus* began, then, to study Physic, and, in two Years time, thought himself fit to commence Doctor. He took his Degree at *Caën*; but scarce ever practised at all. Some young Persons desired him to read Lectures to them in Philosophy, and polite Learning; and, as it was what he had been used to, he resumed this Employment, and regained a great Character for it, even in the University of *Leyden*. The Magistrates of *Amsterdam*, having erected a famous School in the Year 1631, offered him the Professorship of Philosophy. He accepted, and discharged it very honourably until his Death, which happened the fourteenth of *January*, 1648 (b). He was a Man of great Merit. There is extant a Volume of Speeches, which he pronounced on several Subjects, and which are not only commendable for the Style, but also for the Turn, and frequent Touches, of Wit. Poetry was his chief Talent: His Muse was very copious and lofty (c). There scarce happened any great Subject during his Life, on which he did not bestow some pompous Encomium, if he was not prevented by Reasons of State [A]. Cardinal *Richelieu*, and Chancellor *Oxenstiern*, were not forgot: much less did he pass by the Conquests and brave Exploits of *Frederic Henry* Prince of *Orange*. Queen *Mary de Medicis*, and the magnificent Reception she met with at *Amsterdam* (d), gave *Barleus* occasion to exercise his Eloquence. He published some very sharp Pieces of Controversy, against the Adversaries of *Arminius* [B].

That

(a) By the Epistle Dedicatory of his Letters, it appears that he was born *February* the 12th.

(b) Taken from his Funeral Oration made by John-Arnold Corvinus. The Diarium of the Sieur Witte places his Death in 1647.

(c) See the Pieces that Barnehius cites in his Dissertat. de Poet. p. 140.

(d) In 1637.

[A] *There scarce happened any great Subject, during his Life, on which he did not bestow some pompous Encomium, if he was not prevented by Reasons of State*] I make use of this Restriction, because I have read in *Barleus*'s Letters, that he refused to write a Poem on the Coronation of the Emperor *Ferdinand* III, which had been requested of him. He considered, that he had to do with suspicious Persons, who would not fail to stigmatize him as a Pensionary of the House of *Austria*: besides, after having so highly celebrated the Victories of *Gustavus* over the Emperor, he did not see how he could compliment *Ferdinand*, on any great Honour acquired in making War with the *Swedes*. He is an honest Poet! How many of his Profession get over these Scruples! They have a two-handed Pen ; they do not only prepare Panegyrics for the conquering Party, be it who it will, but also, after the Event, make Verses for both Parties (1). I do not question but that there are Poets in *Italy*, who have complimented, or will compliment, both the Dauphin, and Prince *Lewis* of *Baden*, on the Campaign of 1693. These are the Words of *Barleus*: "Literas accepi Vienna, quibus petitur uti laudatione "aliqua velim prosequi Coronationem Ferdinandi ter-"tii Imperatoris. Ego si sapiam abstinebo ab illa "laudatione religiosissime. Quamquam enim ea pos-"sem scribere quæ ad laudes Imperatoris faciant, nec "Reip. nostræ adversentur, tamen prout sunt nostra-"tium ingenia, judicarent me beneficio obstrictum "Austriacis. Scimus Cæsarem non quidem aperto "Marte nos petere, sed per latus Hispani nobis gra-"vem esse. Laudavi etiam non ita pridem Gusta-"vum Sueciæ Regem, ejusque adversus Cæsarem "bella probavi. Jam ut laudem Ferdinandum ter-"tium ob gesta adversus Suecos feliciter bella, à pru-"dentia mea impetrare non possum. Non sum ambi-"dexter, sed ab omni adulatione alienissimus. Cu-"perem obsequi petitioni illustrissimi Legati, sed hoc "cavendum ne dum foris benè, domi male audiam. "Forte nimis sum meticulosus, sed & illud certum "illam Cæsaris laudationem à me profectam calam-"niæ suspicionibusque oportunam fore (2). — *I* "*received Letters from Vienna, desiring I would* "*compose something in Honour of the Coronation of* "*the Emperor* Ferdinand III. *But I think it pru-* "*dent to decline this Task entirely. For though I* "*might pay a Compliment to the Emperor, without* "*the least Prejudice to our Commonwealth, yet such* "*are the Suspicions of our People, that they would be-* "*lieve me to be bribed by the House of* Austria. *We* "*know the Emperor does not persecute us directly,* "*but only by means of the* Spaniard. *Besides, I* "*have congratulated* Gustavus, *King of* Sweden, *on* "*his War with the Emperor. And I cannot think it* "*consistent with my Reason, to compliment* Ferdi-"nand III, *on the very same Occasion. I scorn to* "*play a double Part, and have the greatest Aversion* "*to Flattery. I should be glad to obey the Request of* "*the most illustrious Embassador, but must take care* "*that, while I am esteemed abroad, I am not ill* "*thought of at home. Perhaps I am too scrupulous,* "*but undoubtedly an Encomium on the Emperor, com-* "*posed by me, would give room for Suspicions and Re-* "*flexions.*" *Barleus*'s Fear was not without Foundation; and, if Reason would not suffer him to write the Panegyric of *Ferdinand* III, because *Holland* was at War with the House of *Austria*, and an Author should not blow hot and cold, Prudence no less advised him to forbear that Elogy. Those, who believed him a Friend to the *Arminians*, would have defamed him as an Enemy to God and the State, and would not have been content with declaring him such, both in private and in public. To conclude, if all the Heroes, he celebrated, paid him as well as Cardinal *Richelieu* (3), he had no reason to say, that the Culture of *Parnassus* is That of an ungrateful Soil.

[B] *He published some very sharp Pieces of Controversy against the Adversaries of* Arminius.] In the Year 1615, he published a Piece at *Leyden*, entituled, *Bogermannus* ἐλεγχόμενος, *sive Examen Epistolæ dedicatoriæ quam sub ad pietatem illustrium Ordinum Hollandiæ & Westfrisiæ notis præfixit* Joannes Bogermannus *Ecclesiastes Leowardiensis: in quo etiam Crimina à* Matthæo Slado *impacta* Erasmo Roterodamo *diluuntur*. The Year following he published a little Book, the Title whereof was, *Dissertatiuncula in quâ aliquot*

(1) Compare this with what Macrobius, Saturnal. l. 2, cap. 5, pag. 337, says of a Man who had taught two Ravens, the one to congratulate Augustus, and the other to congratulate Marc Antony.

(2) Gaspar. Barlæus, Epist. 334, pag. 668: the Letter was wrote in the Year 1636.

(3) If we believe a certain Cardinal in the case Som-coco Linneri Son's criania, pag. 42.

That Wound was never healed: He was looked upon all his Life time, as a Favourer of that Sect [C], and many Persons murmured against the Magistrates of *Amsterdam*, for entertaining such a Professor. All his Proceedings were narrowly watched, and not the least Favour shewn him. He was terribly exclaimed against, for some Verses he had made on the Book of a Rabbi [D]. After his Death, his Letters were published in Two Volumes (e); but the *Sextus Empiricus*,

aliquot Patriæ Theologorum & Ecclesiasticorum male sana consilia & studia justa orationis libertate reprehenduntur. There was too much tartness in that piece, and it was too severe on the Preachers; for he pretends (4), that *Holland* afforded, "Viros Prædicatorii ordinis vocales plus satis, qui ad scribendos salutiferos libros inepti, ad prædicandum Christi sapientiam elingues, tamen ad obtrectandum cum Magistratibus, tum dissentientibus circa res religionis symmistis, diserti sint & copiosi. — *Preachers louder than they need to be, who have neither Pen to compose good Books, nor Tongue to deliver the Doctrines of Christianity, but can find both in the most full and eloquent manner to defame not only Magistrates, but also their own Fraternity, who differ from them in matters of Religion.*" In the following Page he says, "Si templa aliquot Hollandiæ peragrare libeat, Theologos quamplurimos in spermologos, concionatores in convivatores, pacis præcones in factionum principes & schismatis faciundi buccinatores transformatos mirabere, nec tam reformatæ amplius, quam pessimis aliquorum moribus deformatæ religionis antistites esse jurabis. —— *If you look into some of the Churches of Holland, you will be surprized to find several Divines transformed into idle Praters; Preachers into Slanderers; and the Messengers of Peace into Ringleaders and Trumpeters of Faction and Schism: insomuch that you would be apt to regard them as Priests of a Religion, not reformed, but deformed by the badness of their own Morals.*" This is a most violent Insult on those, whose Character ought to have obliged him to treat them with Respect. This Invective was immediately translated into *Dutch*. I cannot well tell whether it was in this Dissertation, that he called one *Vincent Drielenburch*, who had set up for a Prophet, by the Name of *Nebulo*; but either in this, or some other, Writing, he made use of that opprobrious Expression; which exasperated that Person to such a Degree, that he published a Book, wherein he calls *Barleus* a Knave and a Rascal, *Nebulonem & Scelestum*, and engaged to give an Hundred Livres to the Deaconry of *Leyden*, and to deliver himself up into the Hands of Justice, that his Punishment might be exemplary, if it could be proved, by solid Reasons, that he was a Knave, *Nebulo. Vincentius etiam Drielenburch suis prophetandi partibus non desuit, nam anno superiore à Gaspare Barleo in scripto quodam Nebulonis nomine designatus, id adeo Propheticæ suæ dignitati patevit esse injuriosum, ut edito nec scripto eundem Barleum scelestum & Nebulonem nominaret, &c.* (5). A little while after, there came out a Book, which pretended to prove this Charge against *Drielenburch*, by ten incontestable Reasons. He answered those ten Reasons, and flew out extremely against *Barleus*. The latter composed a *Remonstrance to the States-General* during his Exile. It is dated from *Francfort*, in the Month of *August*, 1620, and intituled, *Fides imbellis, sive Epistola parænetica ad illustrissimos & potentissimos Fœderatarum Provinciarum Ordines*. It is a Piece very well written, wherein the sad Consequences of Persecution, and the Rights of Conscience, are very pathetically represented. You will find it in the *Præstantium & Eruditorum Virorum Epistolæ* (6).

[C] *He was looked upon, all his Life-time, as a Favourer of the Arminian Sect.*] It is certain, that, after he was restored in the University of *Leyden*, he did not break off his Correspondence with the Arminians. His Hundred and fifty sixth Letter informs *Uytenbogard*, that *Polyander*, Professor of Divinity at *Leyden*, had discovered to his Friends, that all the Moderation, which appeared in the Writings, published by the Faculty of Theology, against the *Arminians*, came from himself: *Quicquid mollius leniusque scriptum reperitur in specimine, à se profectum esse, reliqua aspersora collegarum esse* (7); but that he desired the *Arminians*, who were made acquainted with it, would keep it secret, because it would expose him to the Indignation of his Colleagues. *Rogavit me obnixè per D. Vossium intermittatem, tibis uti scriberem, ne si fortè hæc*

res ad aures vestras pervenerit, ejus in responso vestro meminisse velitis, ne collegarum suorum invidiæ ac odiis, quorum jam semina jacta, majer objiciatur (8). The following Letter testifies, that one of *Polyander's* Colleagues reproached him for having told this to *Barleus*, an Enemy of the Church: *Tu hoc dixisti Barleo, quem scis esse hostem Ecclesiæ, qui illud ipsum ad Uytenbogardum, & Episcopium perscripturus est.* These Letters were written in the Year 1630. It appears, by *Barleus's* Letters, that he was always of the Opinion of the *Remonstrants*.

[D] *He was exclaimed against, for some Verses he had made on the Book of a Rabbi.*] *Manasses Ben-Israel*, one of the most learned Men among the *Jews*, in the XVIIth Century, published a Book on the Creation, in the Year 1634. *Barleus* made an Epigram upon it, and, according to Custom, suffered it to appear at the Head of the Work. He declared too plainly, that he preferred a good Life before the Truth of speculative Doctrines. A Divine of *Deventer*, made a mighty bustle about it; he published a Piece, wherein he maintained, that the Epigram was full of Blasphemies, and that the Author of it was a *Socinian*. Nay, there was a Design to bring the Matter before the States of *Holland*, to convict *Barleus*, and all the *Arminians*, of *Socinianism*. *Consilia agitari uti Libellus iste Censoris ordinibus Hollandiæ exhibeatur ut appareat Barleum & Remonstrantes esse Socinianos* (9). *Barleus* defended himself with Heat, and was very angry. He maintained, that his Words were maliciously interpreted, and even falsified, that they might the better colour the Arts they made use of, to find such a Meaning as he had never thought of. "*Epigramma quoddam meum* ------ *quæsitis & perversis detorsionibus malignè interpretatur.* Dicit illo epigrammate contineri varia quæ Ecclesiæ perniciosa, religioni Christianæ probrosa, & in Deum ac Dominum nostrum Jesum Christum impia sunt. Socinianismum adhæc autori epigrammatis impingit, &c. ------ Censor pessima fide voculam è carmine sustulit, & suam substituit, *maneamus pro vivamus*. Sensus affingit versibus meis de quibus ne per somnium quidem cogitavi (10). ------ *He maliciously interprets a certain Epigram of mine* ------ *by far-fetched and unfair Constructions. He says, that Epigram contains several Things destructive to the Church, opprobrious to Christianity, and blasphemous to* GOD, *and our* LORD JESUS CHRIST. *He also charges the Author of it with Socinianism, &c.* ------ *This Censurer has unjustly suppressed an Expression of mine, and substituted one of his own,* maneamus, *instead of* vivamus. *He construes my Verses in such a Sense, as I never once dreamed of.*" He protested that he was no *Socinian*, that he never had been one, and that he detested the Doctrines of the *Socinians*. He added, that some would be glad to have him a *Socinian*, that their Hatred of him might find a larger Field of Triumph. *Non sum Socinianus nec fui unquam, imo hostis sum istorum dogmatum acerrimus. Vellent quidam me esse qui expendas in me odii materiam sollicitè quærunt* (11). If that Judgment were false, it was, however, not unlikely; for those who engage in Controversies about Doctrines, accuse their Adversaries of so many things, that, commonly speaking, nothing can mortify them more, than to appear quite different from their Representations. However it be, it was lawful for *Barleus* to repulse the Calumny; but he ought not to have made such stinging Verses against the Divine of *Deventer*, that perhaps *Archilochus* would not have exceeded them. That Divine's Name, in short, was *Vedelius*, and his Book entituled *Deus Synagogæ*. A Professor of *Utrecht* (12) second him in that Attack, by a Piece called *Vorstius redivivus*, which *Vedelius* took care to get printed. *Vossius* believed, that *Barleus* fell sick, by laying the Insults of those two Antagonists too much to Heart. See what he wrote to *Grotius* the fifteenth of *December*, 1637. "Collega Barleus jam tertium mensem laborat quartanà. Metuitur ei à *μαραημῶ*.

Empiricus, which was expected from him, never appeared. He has shewn how able he was to write History, by the *Relation of what passed in Brasil*, during the Government of Count *Maurice of Nassau*. He published that History in the Year 1647. Strange Reports were raised about his last Sickness [E], and about his Death [F]; but the Truth of it is hardly to be known: There is but little Credit to be given to Reports of this Nature; for it is notorious, from an hundred Examples, that, if an Author has distinguished himself ever so little, Fame does very much magnify the Personal or Domestic Disgraces, which befal him: And those, who are acquainted with the whole Secret, are commonly Persons too nearly concerned to publish what may occasion the least Disreputation.

(13) *The Event did not confirm this Conjecture. The like are made every Day, that prove false.*

(14) *This is a true Gallicism. C'est celui de l'Entrée.*

(15) Epist. præst. & eruditor. Virorum, pag. 76. Edit. in fol. 1684.

(16) Rochus Honerdius in Epist. ad Barlæum, ibid. p. 795.

(17) *In the Sorberiana*, pag. 3, 38. Edit. of Holland, 1694.

(18) *Doubtless it is a Fault of the Press. Perhaps the Author had written Silloniset; for, besides the false that Vedelius put a Name to the Piece, it is very Vid: ... supposed, ... in the Note.*

" Ut convalescat, non videtur idem fore qui quondam
" (13). Afflixit valetudinem opere properando quod
" nunc excuditur. Est hoc de ingressu (14) reginæ
" matris in urbem nostram, & honore pompæ ei
" exhibito. Typis prodibit augustis, plurimis exorna-
" tum picturis. Atque hoc quod dixi non dissimu-
" lat apud amicos. Sed multum metuo ne morbum
" hunc inde contraxerit, quod nimis ad animum re-
" vocaret quæ adversus eum scripta sunt à Doct.
" Vedelio, & Mag. Schoockio (15). - - - - - - - *My*
" *Colleague,* Barleus, *has been afflicted with a Quar-*
" *tan these three Months. He is in some Danger of*
" *a Consumption. If he recovers, he will scarce ever*
" *be the same Man again. He destroyed his Health,*
" *by applying so closely to the Work, which is now*
" *printing. The Subject is the Entry of the Queen-*
" *Mother into our City, and her magnificent Recepti-*
" *on. It will appear in a very fine Latter, and a-*
" *dorned with several Copper-Plates. He owns, among*
" *his Friends, the Account I have now given. But I*
" *much fear, that his Distemper is rather owing to his*
" *laying too much to Heart the Calumnies published*
" *against him by Dr* Vedelius, *and Mr* Schoockius."
I believe, that most of *Barleus's* best Friends found
him too much concerned for the Censure of his Epigram; for they advised him to despise his Critics,
whom they lashed severely. " Tibi sum auctor ut
" eos posthac præteritione mulctes. Acerrima vin-
" dicta est contemptus: in malam rem homines ad
" civilia ingenia vexanda natos. Ex Epigrammate
" scilicet quo Manassen Judæum non proscindis con-
" vitiis, totus in te Theologorum ordo asperatus om-
" nem Hæreticorum sentinam in caput tuum infun-
" det. - - - - - - Si verpum, apellam, recutitum eam-
" dem dixisses, & virum, ut videtur, non malum
" poëticis scommatibus exagitasses, palmarium meruis-
" les. - - - - - - Si quid mihi apud te est fidei crabro-
" nes istos iterum dico posthac negliges. Acrius enim
" post repulsam instant, & ubi excusseris venenum
" omne in aculeos advocant tanquam ipsi læsi (16).
" - - - - - - *I desire you would, for the future, repay*
" *them with Neglect. Contempt is the most galling*
" *Method of Revenge; and fittest to be used against*
" *those, who are born to defame modest Merit, and*
" *prove a Pest to Mankind. Because your Epigram*
" *does not load* Manasses *the Jew with Reproaches,*
" *the whole Order of Divines are angry, and bespatter*
" *you with all the Filth, which Heresy ever produced.*
" *- - - - - If you had called him a circumcised Wretch,*
" *and abused him, though he does not seem to deserve*
" *it from you, with poetical Slander, you would have*
" *been admired. - - - - - - - If I have any Influence*
" *over you, I again beg you would despise these Hor-*
" *nets. For a Repulse only makes them return to the*
" *Charge with greater Fury, and, if you shake off their*
" *Venom, they only prepare to sting you with all their*
" *Vengeance, as though you were the Aggressor.*" *Bar-*
leus's Epigram, which was the Cause of so much Stir,
would have found a place here, if it had not lately
been inserted in a little Book, which is in every body's
Hands (17). I am surprized to find in it but a very
small part of *Barleus's* Verses against *Vedelius*; but
I wonder yet more, how *Sorbiere* could think, that he
Passage, which he mentions, shews the Author scoffed
at both Religions. These are *Sorbiere's* Words: " Cùm
" Vedelius nomen suum in priori scripto analytico
" epigrammatis Barlæani restituisset (18) ait

- - - - - - quid tenebroso
Calumniator prave delites antro,
Et exoleta sæve tergiversator
Arcessis orco monstra perditæ sectæ?
Cur versipellis Sarmatæ malas voces

Portenta fidei, exsibilata Senensis
Commenta verbis africas serenatis?

" Quæ sane nec Calvinianis satisfacere nec aliis, sed
" utriusque religionis ludibrio habitæ poëtam merito
" suspectum reddidere (19). - - - - - *Because* Vedelius
" *had suppressed his Name in his first Piece, against*
" Barleus's *Epigram, he makes him this Reply,*

Why starts the Slanderer, in his darksome Den,
The hellish Maxim of the worst of Men?
Why brings he back that cursed Sect to light,
Long since condemn'd to everlasting Night?

" *which can neither be agreeable to the Calvinists,*
" *nor the others, but justly renders the Poet suspected*
" *of ridiculing both Religions.*" A Man must be mad
or drunk to judge so; for the Verses, which we have
just now read, are the most severe that can be made
against *Socinianism,* and no Body can testify more
earnestly, than *Barleus* has done, how much he detested to be suspected of that Heresy. This Author's
Prose, which *Sorbiere* has quoted a little before, thunders full as violently against that Sect.

[E.] *Strange Reports were raised about his last Sick-*
ness.] I have heard say, that he thought himself to
be made of Glass, and that he was afraid of being
broke to pieces, when any body came near him.
Others have told me, that he fancied himself Butter,
or Straw, and durst not come near the Fire. This is
inconsistent with his Funeral Oration, spoken by *Cor-*
vinus, Professor of Law; for it is there affirmed,
that he read a Lecture to his Scholars the Day before he died, and that he was going to read another,
when a Faintness seized him, from which he never
recovered. *Id quod dolemus, eo accidisse momento quo*
se parabat ut juventuti sibi commissæ docendo debitum
præstaret officium (20). " Antecessit quidem eum
" morbus cum quo luctabatur subinde, non tamen
" tantus quin aliquomodo consuetis adhuc sufficeret
" laboribus. Audiveram eum, pridie diei quo eum
" mors invasit, discipulis docentem: audivissem ea-
" dem qua occidit, nisi ipsi eum abstulisset, ita ut
" accepimus, plurimis hodie exemplis fere epidemica
" lypothymia. —— *He had before laboured under an*
" *Indisposition, which now and then afflicted him,*
" *but not so severely as to hinder him from going on*
" *with his usual Employments. His Pupils had been*
" *at Lectures with him the Day before he died, and*
" *were to have gone again the next, if a sudden*
" *Fainting, as I have been informed, which, by fre-*
" *quent Instances, was become almost epidemical, had*
" *not carried him off.*" It is very remarkable, that
he had a little before made use of the same Precaution: " Inopinate eum extinxit, UT NOBIS RELA-
" TUM, Lipothymia. Inde factum ut eum extin-
" ctum ante audiverimus, quàm morti esse propin-
" quum morbus prænuntiaret. - - - - *A sudden Faint-*
" *ness, as I have been told, carried him off. So that*
" *we heard of his Death, before any Distemper had*
" *discovered him to be in Danger.*" Observe, that
Corvinus had just before addressed his Speech to the
Disciples of the deceased. And can any one think
he would have told them falsly to their Face, that they
afflicted at one of his Lectures, the Day before his
Death?

[F.] *And about his Death.*] *Morbesius* reports, that
Barleus died in a Well, and that it is not known,
whether he fell into it accidentally, or threw himself
into it. *Misero fato periit, puteo submersus, an sponte,*
an casu, incertum, de morte ejus jam supra divimus.
It is thus he speaks, in the Three hundredth Page
of his *Polyhistor*. Doubtless he refers us to Page 155,
when

(19) *Sorbe-*
riana, p. 39.

(20) Corvinus in Orat. Funeb. Barlei.

BARLEUS. BARLOW.

when he says, that he had already mentioned This Death: But, in the One hundred fifty fifth Page, he does not a'cribe it either to an Accident, or to a premeditated Design, but affirms, that *Barlæus* became mad, and cast himself into a Well; and quotes the Sixty fourth Letter of *Sorbiere*. "Eo nonnul-" lorum excrescit è fiducia nimia ambitio, ut fini-" stro aliorum judicio in extrenam incidant insa-" niam. Quod Barlæo accidit, qui ob prælatum sibi " Spanhemium in maniam incidit, seque ipsum in " puteo suffocavit, quod de eo Sorbierius refert *Epist.* " 64. extatque apud Duportum *Musarum subcisivæ-*" *rum, Lib.* 1. de eo Epigramma (21). ——— *To such* " *an Extream are some Persons burried by Pride and* " *Self-conceit, that a Disappointment from the Judg-*" *ment of others shall throw them into Madness. This* " *happened to* Barlæus, *who, on account of the Pre-*" *ference being given to* Spanheim, *fell into a Distra-*" *ction, and drowned himself in a Well*; This is re-" lated *by* Sorbiere, Epist. 64. lib. 1. *And there* " *is an Epigram upon it in* Duport's Musæ Subci-" sivæ, lib. 1." This Quotation is very false, for here is what *Sorbiere* says. "The Death of *Bar-*" *læus*, of which you desire the Particulars, is not " of that Importance (22), though he was a very " worthy Man; for there will always be found a " greater Number of excellent Poets than Physi-" cians. When I was at *Amsterdam*, they spoke va-" riously of his Death, as if Melancholy had hastened " it. It is true, that, having composed a *Funeral* " *Oration*, in Verse, on the Death of the Prince of " *Orange*, and Dr *Spanheim* having spoke one in " Prose, he bore the Inequality of their Reward " very impatiently: For, as *Salmasius* said, very plea-" santly, they made a great Mistake, in giving the " Trooper's Pay to the Foot Soldier, and That " of the Foot Soldier to the Trooper. *Barlæus* " had but Five hundred Livres, and the other " had Five hundred Crowns." There is nothing about *Barlæus's* Death in the *Sorberiana*. We find there, indeed, that, according to the common Report, *Barlæus* was subject to some Fits of Lunacy: " Ferebatur intervalla quædam minus lucida habere, " nec aberat conjectura oculorum qui non bene sanam " cerebri particulam indicabant. ——— *He was said to* " *have Intervals of Phrensy, and that a Wildness* " *about the Eyes discovered his Brain was not right.*"

(21). Morhof. Polyhist. p. 155.

(22) *That is, of the same Importance with that of* Walton *and Vossius, noted before.*

BARLEUS (LAMBERT), Brother of the foregoing, was born at *Bommel* in *Guelderland*, in the Year 1595 (a). He was *Greek* Professor in the University of *Leyden*. Before That, he had been Teacher of the Second Class in a College at *Amsterdam* [*A*], and, before he taught that Class, he had been Minister of the Baron *de Langerac*, the *Dutch* Embassador in *France* (b). He was called to *Leyden* to fill up the place of *Jeremiah Hoelzlin*, and a new Addition was made to that Office; for it was given him with the Title of Professor in Ordinary (c), which is attended with several Advantages. He made his Inauguration Speech, *De Græcarum Literarum Præstantia ac Utilitate*, the Twenty second of *October*, 1641. In 1652, he published the *Timon of Lucian*, with several Notes, which have nothing very extraordinary, or profound, in them, but may be useful to Youth. He died the sixteenth of *June*, 1655 (d). His Commentary on the *Theogony of Hesiod* was printed in 1658.

(a) Witte in Diario Biographico.

(b) Corvinus in Orat. Funebri Gasp. Barlæi.

(c) See the Epistle Dedicatory of his Timon of Lucian.

(d) Witte, Diar. Biogr.

[*A*] *He had been Teacher, of the second Class, in a College, at* Amsterdam.] The *Dutch* give the Title of *Conrector* to the Teacher of this Class. That is to say, *The Rector's Assistant*. They call the Teacher of the first Class *Rector*. He has an Inspection over the other Teachers.

BARLOW (THOMAS), Bishop of *Lincoln*, in the Reign of *Charles* II, was a very learned Man. He was a long time Professor of Divinity in the University of *Oxford*, and it has been suspected by a certain Person, that he was removed from thence for being too Orthodox [*A*]. He was very zealous against Popery, as he demonstrated by his Writings [*B*]. He had a large Collection of Books, and was a Man of great Reading. He died in the Year 1690, or thereabouts. Some small Pieces, which were found among his Papers, have been published since his Death. He has been confounded with *William Barlow* [*C*], Bishop of *Lincoln*, who flourished under King *James* I, and also died under that Prince.

[*A*] *It has been suspected, by a certain Person, that he was removed from the University of* Oxford *for being too Orthodox.*] This certain Person is a famous Minister, and Professor of Divinity, at *Groningen*; in a Word, it is *James Alting*. He says, in a Letter dated the thirteenth of *March*, 1670, That Dr *Barlow* was lately advanced to the Bishoprick of *Lincoln*, on purpose that he might be removed from the University, where he taught the Orthodox Faith (1); for, adds he, the *English* are much inclined to *Pelagianism* and *Socinianism*: And, on this Occasion, he mentions a Book, *De Unione & Communione cum Christo*, the Author of which is named *Sherlock*.

[*B*] *He was very zealous against* Popery, *as he demonstrated by his Writings.*] When there was so much Discourse about *Titus Oates*, and the horrible Conspiracy, which he discovered, This Bishop published a Book, wherein he maintained, against all Evasions, that it is an Article of the *Roman* Faith, that the Pope may depose Sovereigns, and give their Dominions to others. This was a very good way to shew, that he designed to do the Papists some Prejudice; for, of all the Means likely to stir up the Zeal of the Nation against them, there is none can do it more effectually, than to shew, that they are always ready, from a Principle of Conscience, to take up Arms against Protestant Princes. The Book, which *Barlow* published on That Subject, was immediately translated into *French*, and published under this Title: *An Historical Treatise on the Subject of Excommunicating and Deposing of Kings*: at *Paris*, by Claude Barbin, 1681 (2).

[*C*] *He has been confounded with* William Barlow.] The two Authors, who have added some Supplements to the Treatise of *John Deckherrus, De Scriptis Adespotis*, are fallen into this Error. *Deckherrus* had said, that the Jesuit, who wrote, in *English*, against King *James*, concerning the Apology for the Oath of Allegiance, was refuted by Mr *Baclo*, Bishop of Lincoln. One of his Friends (3) informed him, by Letter, that This Prelate's Name was not *Baclo*, but *Thomas Barlow*: "Is si placet est *Thomas* " *Barlovius* magni apud Anglos nominis, & de no-" stratibus optime meritus. Optandum foret videre " aliquando ἀνέκδοτα ipsius, quorum magnam in " instructissima sua Bibliotheca copiam habet, & nu-" perrime uno & altero opusculo præsertim contra " Curiam Romanam magnum litteratis desiderium " excitavit. Historia ejus de conspiratione contra *Ja-*" *cobum Angliæ Regem*, vulgo *The Gun-powder Trea-*" *son*, non ita pridem publicum vidit. ----- *His* " *Name is* Thomas Barlow, *who is very famous in* " *his own Nation, and deserves very well of ours.* " *It were to be wished he would present the World* " *with his Manuscript Pieces, which are very nume-*" *rous, and, by a late Taste or two of which, chiefly* " *against*

(1) Jac. Alting. Oper. Tom 7. pag. 391.

(2) *I was not advertis'd that the Place of Edition is* Rotterdam.

(3) Paulus Vindingius. See the Epistle of Scripti Adespotis pag. 355. Edit. 1681.

BARNES.

" *against the Court of Rome, be has greatly excited
" the Curiosity of the Learned. His History of the
" Conspiracy against James King of England, common-
" ly called The Gun powder Plot, has been lately
" published.*" The Letter, from which I have taken
these Words, was written, at *Strasburg,* in 1681. It
is plain therefore, that Mr *Deckherrus*'s Friend imagined, that the Bishop of *Lincoln,* who had wrote,
for King *James,* against a Jesuit, was yet living.
Now this is a great Mistake. It was in the Year
1609, that King *James* made use of the Pen of
Dr *Barlow,* Bishop of *Lincoln,* against *Robert Parsons,*
an *English* Jesuit. If That Doctor had been yet
living, in the Year 1681, his Age must have been
a Circumstance very extraordinary, and those would
have been inexcusable, who should have mentioned
his Learning, and his Books, without taking notice
of his great Age. It will be to no purpose to use
any Evasions, or urge, that some learned Men live
an hundred Years; since it is very well known,
that the Name of the Bishop of *Lincoln,* who wrote
for King *James,* was *William,* and not *Thomas.* I
do not know whether an hundred Years would have
been sufficient for *Thomas Barlow* to be living in
1681, and to have been a Bishop in the Year 1609;
for it is very rare to be a Bishop, in *England,* before the Age of Thirty five or forty Years. The
Author of the *Nouvelles de la Republique de Lettres,*
who took a small Review of Mr *Deckherrus*'s, and
Mr *Vindingius*'s Faults, did not only overlook this,
but, which is worse, adopted it (4).

(4) *See de Scriptis A- desportis,* pag. 372.

BARNES (ROBERT) (a), Professor of Divinity, and Chaplain to *Henry*
VIII [A], King of *England,* was sent, by his Master, into *Germany,* in the Year
1535 [B]. He conferred forthwith with the Protestant Divines, on the Subject of
the Divorce : He had afterwards some Audiences of the Elector of *Saxony,* and
joined with the *English* Embassadors, who proposed to that Elector an Alliance against
the Pope, and who desired, that *Henry* VIII might be associated in the League
of *Smalcald.* They gave hopes of a Reformation in *England*; but, at the bottom,
their only aim was to obtain an approbation of their Master's Divorce, and a
Politic Alliance to give the Emperour more Trouble, who threatened to revenge
the Injury done to his divorced Aunt. They carried back an Opinion of the
Divines of *Wittemberg,* which was not altogether favourable for them [C]; but
they suppressed the Conclusion, when they presented it to the King. That part
which

(a) *See Remark* [A].

[A] *He was Professor of Divinity, and Chaplain to King Henry* VIII.] He was mentioned by these Titles, in the Credential Letters, which the King, his Master, gave him, in order to his Negotiation in *Saxony*; and those Letters are dated from *Windsor,* the eighth of *July,* 1535 (1). His Christian Name does not appear, in those Letters, before That of *Barnes.* In *Germany* he gave himself the Name of *Antony Amarius,* though his true Name was *Robert Barnes.* When he dedicated his *Lives of the Popes* to the King of *England,* in the Year 1535, he signed R. *Barnes,* Doctor (2). It appears, in a Preface of *Luther* (3), that *Barnes* concealed his Name, and his Title of Doctor, in *Wittemberg,* for fear of the Persecutors. *Melanchthon* calls him D. *Antonius* Doctor, or D. *Antonius,* in a Letter, which he wrote to the King of *England,* the thirteenth of *March,* 1535 (4).

[B] *He was sent, by his Master, into Germany, in the Year* 1533.] The Preface, which I have quoted, informs me, that *Barnes* resided at *Wittemberg,* about the Year 1530, and that he did even lodge in the House of *Luther.* "Quis ante annos decem hoc de-
" cus in Barnesio quæsivisset, & quod Christus ipse
" in eo nobiscum versatus esset? domesticum enim
" & commensalem habuimus (5). — *Who, ten*
" *Years ago, would have expected this Honour from*
" *Barnes, and, that Christ himself, in him, should*
" *make his Abode with me? For he both lodged and*
" *boarded with me.*" *Barnes* might have lived in *Germany* 'till the Year 1535, and might have received Credential Letters there, from *Henry* VIII, to negotiate with the Elector of *Saxony.* Upon This Supposition, the Author of the History of the Reformation of *England* might very well say, "That, at
" last, while the Bishop of *Hereford* was at *Smalcald,*
" that is, in the Year 1536, *Barnes* was sent, by
" That Minister, into *England,* where he was very
" well received by *Henry,* and entertained by *Cromwell* (6)." I say, upon This Supposition, this Account would be exact; for all that Mr *de Seckendorf* alledges against it, is, that *Barnes* came from *England* into *Germany,* in the Year 1535, with a Commission from *Henry* VIII (7). He was therefore returned into *England,* before the Bishop of *Hereford* sent him thither, and therefore the Message he was sent on, by That Prelate, ought not to be taken for his Return Home. But can it be proved, that the Credential Letters were not sent to *Barnes* into *Germany,* and that he himself was sent into That Country? Yes, it may: *Seckendorf* proves it from the Records, which have furnished him with many good Pieces: "Veneret Wittembergam (Reg. x. fol. 99.
" n. 42.) verno hujus anni 1535 tempore, Doctor
" EX BRITANNIA ab Henrico Rege MISSUS (8). —

"There came, to *Wittemberg,* in the Spring of the
" Year 1535, a Doctor from *England, sent by Henry* VIII." *Melanchthon* confirms the same thing in *Greek;* for he made use of That Language to inform his good Friend *Camerarius,* that there was an Envoy from *England,* who spoke of nothing but of the King's second Marriage, and who said, that *Henry* VIII cared but little for the Affairs of Religion. "Ἥλθε δὲ πρὸς ἡμᾶς ξένος τις σεμνότατος ἐκ
τῆς Βρετανίας, μόνον διαλεγόμενος περὶ τοῦ
δευτέρου γάμου τοῦ βασιλέως, τῶν δ᾽ εἰς ἐκκλη-
σίας πραγμάτων ἡ μέλως, ὥς φησι, τῷ βασιλεῖ (9). But, though we are not allowed to make the Supposition before mentioned, yet we may nevertheless hold Dr *Burnet*'s Account to be true. That Historian says only, that the Bishop of *Hereford* sent *Barnes* into *England:* he does not deny, that *Barnes* was returned thither before.

[C] *He, and his Colleagues - - - - carried back an Opinion of the Divines of* Wittemberg, *which was not favourable for them*] Dr *Burnet* gives the Particulars of it very exactly: " Their first Sentiment
" of this Matter, *says he* (10), was, that the Ordi-
" nances of the Levitical Law were not moral. - - - -
" Afterwards they altered their Opinion, when the
" Question had been a little more agitated; but they
" never agreed, that a Marriage, already consumma-
" ted, could be disanulled, and they confirmed them-
" selves more and more in this last Opinion, so that
" they condemned the King's two Marriages." He mentions this under the Year 1530. Not that he was ignorant, that This Opinion was given in 1536; but he did it, without doubt, to shew his Reader, all at once, the different Opinions of the Divines on the Divorce of *Henry* VIII. Mr *Seckendorf* thought so: for when he remarks, that the Opinion of the Divines of *Wittemberg* is to be found in the *History of the Reformation of the Church of England,* in the Collection of Records, and Original Papers, among those belonging to the Year 1530, he adds this Parenthesis *(forte per occasionem).* " Annus &
" dies responso huic non est adscriptus, & *Burnetus* illud inter alia anni 1530 *(forte per occasionem)*
" retulit. Lib. II. fol. 94 (11). - - - - - *This Opinion is without Date, and Burnet has related it*
" *(perhaps occasionally) among the Transactions of the*
" *Year* 1530. Book II. pag. 94." The Bishop of *Meaux* did not know, that the Decree of *Wittemberg* was of the Year 1536. He speaks only of *Melanchthon*'s Opinion, as to That Year, and does not criticise Dr *Burnet,* for having placed the Answer of the Divines of *Wittemberg,* in the Year 1530 (12). Mr *Seckendorf* observes, that the Copy of That Answer, which he read in the Archives of *Weimar,* is

(1) See *Seckendorf,* History of *Lutheranism,* lib. 3. pag. 110. in the *Additions.*

(2) Id. In *Supplementis ad Indicem* l. n. 10.

(3) That which he prefixed to the *Relation of the Martyrdom of Barnes,* inserted in the *seventh Volume of his Works.* See *Seckendorf,* lib. 3. pag. 262.

(4) It is the 61th of the 29 *Book.*

(5) *Luther apud Seckendorf,* lib. 3. pag. 262.

(6) *Burnet*'s Hist. of the Reformation, Book 3. pag. 689.

(7) *Seckendorf,* lib. 3. pag. 262.

(8) Id. ibid.

(9) *Melanchthon, Letter* 170, *of the 4th Book,* dated the 11th of *March* 1535.

(10) *Burnet*'s Hist. of the Reformation, Book 2. pag. 220. ad Ann. 1536.

(11) *Seckendorf,* lib. 3. pag. 112.

(12) *See the History of the Variations,* lib. 7. n. 58.

which muft have been difagreeable to that Prince, was in the Conclufion (b). The Conduct of *Barnes* pleafed the King of *England* very well; for which reafon he was employed to cultivate a Correfpondence with the Princes of *Germany*. He was fent feveral times to thofe Courts; and, among other Negotiations, he was the firft who was employed in the Treaty of Marriage with Anne of Cleves [D]. He was a good *Lutheran*, and made no Secret of it in his Sermons; for, in the *Lent* Seafon of the Year 1540, he confuted the Sermon, which Bifhop *Gardiner* had preached againft the Doctrine of *Luther*. He took *Gardiner*'s own Text, and taught a quite contrary Doctrine to what that Prelate had eftablifhed concerning Juftification: he even attacked that Bifhop perfonally, after an indecent manner, and jefted on the Name of *Gardiner*. *Gardiner*'s Friends complained to the King about it, who ordered, that *Barnes* fhould give him Satisfaction for it; that he fhould fign certain Articles, and make a Recantation in the Pulpit. All this was performed, but in fuch a manner, that Complaints were made, that in one part of his Sermon he had the Subtilty to maintain what he had retracted in the other. Upon thefe Complaints the King ordered him to be fent to the Tower, from whence he never returned but to fuffer Death in the midft of Flames [E]; for the Parliament condemned him as an Heretic, without giving him leave to make his Defence. A little before his Death, he declared his Belief, rejected Juftification by Works, the Invocation of Saints, &c. and defired that the King would go about a good Reformation (c). The freedom of his Tongue had brought him into many Troubles a long time before. In *Wolfey*'s Profperity, he preached fo ftrongly at *Cambridge* againft the Luxury of the Prelates, that every body might eafily guefs he defigned it againft That Cardinal. *This occafioned his been fent for to* London, *where he came off* - - - - - *by the Sollicitations of* Gardiner *and* Fox, *by means of abjuring fome Articles propofed to him.* "Afterwards he was imprifoned again on new Accufations, and then every one "believed he would be burnt. But he made his Efcape, and retired into *Ger-*
"*many,*

(b) Seckendorf Hift. Lutheranifmi, lib. 3. pag. 110. & feq.

(c) Taken from the Hiftory of the Reformation of England, wrote by Dr Burnet, Bifhop of Salifbury, lib. 3. pag. 689. & q.

is longer than That, which is to be found among Dr *Burnet*'s *Original Pieces*. Here is the Paffage, which was fuppreffed by the Embaffadors of *Henry* VIII. "Etfi "confentiamus cum Dominis legatis fervandam effe "legem de uxore fratris non ducenda, manfit tamen "inter nos controverfum quod legati ftatuunt difpen-"fationi locum non effe, nos vero putamus effe illi "locum. Neque enim ftrictius obligare nos lex po-"teft quam Judæos: fi autem lex difpenfationem "admittit, vinculum matrimonii utique fortius eft "quam lex illa altera de uxore fratris. —— *Although* "*we agree with their Excellencies the Embaffadors,* "*that the Law, which prohibits the marrying a Bro-*"*ther's Wife, is to be obferved, yet we differ in this,* "*that they hold this Law cannot be difpenfed with,* "*and we think it may. For we cannot be under a* "*ftricter Obligation to the Law, than the Jews* "*were; and, if the Law admits of a Difpenfation,* "*the Tie of Matrimony is more binding than that* "*other Law concerning the Brother's Wife.*" Mr *Seckendorf* conjectures, that the Embaffadors fuppreffed That Paffage, that their Mafter might ftill entertain Hopes, that the Divines of *Wittemberg* would at laft approve his fecond Marriage.

This Thought is very reafonable: and, in general, thofe Divines might very juftly fuppofe, that there are Acts, which ought not to have been executed, and which yet, being once executed, ought to be maintained. But, I confefs, I cannot well apprehend how the beginning and end of their Opinion can be reconciled. They own, on the one fide, that the Ordinances of the Levitical Law are Divine, Natural, and Moral; that no Law can be made in Oppofition to them; and, that the Church has always judged, that a Man's Marriage with his Brother's Widow is inceftuous. "Hoc manifeftum eft, & negare "nemo poteft, quod lex tradita Levit. xviii. 20. "prohibet ducere fratris uxorem, &c. fed divina, "naturalis, & moralis lex eft intelligenda tam de vivi "quam de mortui fratris uxore, & quod contra hanc "legem nulla contraria lex fieri aut conftitui pof-"fit (13):" and, on the other fide, they maintain, that This Levitical Law may be difpenfed with: *Legati ftatuunt difpenfationi locum non effe, nos vero putamus effe illi locum*. If it may be difpenfed with, *Henry* VIII ought to have believed, that he was lawfully married to *Catherine* of *Aragon*. But, if it is Indifpenfable, Divine, Natural, and Moral, and fuch, in a Word, as will admit of no contrary Authority; laftly, if the Church has always adjudged, that a Marriage, not conformable to This Law, is inceftuous, then *Henry* VIII ought to have looked

(13) *Apud* Seckendorf, pag. 112. Burnet's Hift. Reform. in Collection of Records, Part 1. l. 2. n. 35.

upon his Cohabitation with *Catherine* of *Aragon* as no other than Inceft, and therefore immediately he ought to have abftained from it, and the Divines of *Wittemberg* ought to have made no Doubt, whether they fhould approve, or difapprove, his Divorce. The Maxim, *That there are things, which ought not to have been done, which, when once they are done, ought not to be undone*, could have no place here, fince the Queftion was about the Continuation of an Inceft. Thofe, who love Scandal, and want an Opportunity to recriminate, would not eafily agree with the Obfervation of Dr *Burnet*, "That if, in the Conduct "of the *Saxon* Divines, there does not appear the "Cunning, the Policy, and the Diffimulation, of the "Court of *Rome*, yet there appears in it, at leaft, "the Candour, the Sincerity, and good Confcience, "of the Apoftolic Times (14)." For my own Part, I had rather fuppofe, that they did not reafon confiftently, than that they defigned to have the Pleafure of reflecting on the Pope's Difpenfation, and at the fame time the Policy of carrying it fair to *Charles* V, and the Interefts of his Coufin the Princefs *Mary*: but an Adverfary, who loves to give things a malicious Turn, might, by way of Reprifal, pafs a fevere Judgment on the Conduct of thofe Divines (15).

(14) Burnet, Hift. of the Reformation, lib. 2. pag. 229.

(15) *See the* Bifhop *of* Meaux's Hift. of the Variat. l. 7. n. 57.

[D] *He was employed in the Treaty of the Marriage with* Anne *of* Cleves.] This was a Misfortune to *Barnes*: "Becaufe the King being not well pleafed "with that Marriage, fpared neither the Author nor "the Inftruments of it." This is what the Bifhop of *Salifbury* affures us (16). *Luther* has touched on another Circumftance; he fays, That the true Caufe of the King's hatred for *Robert Barnes*, was the Liberty, wherewith that Doctor diffuaded him from repudiating *Anne* of *Cleves* (17). Mr *Seckendorf* pretends, that Dr *Burnet* obferves the fame thing (18): I queftion it much; for I have not met with it in his *Reformation of England*.

(16) Hiftory of the Reformation, lib. 3. pag. 689. ad Ann. 1540.

(17) In Præfat. Revelation. Martyrii Barnefii apud Seckendorf. l. 3. p. 262. a. 13.

[E] *He was fent to the* Tower, *from whence he never returned, but to fuffer Death in the midft of Flames*.] The Relation of his Martyrdom was fent from *England* into *Germany*. Mr *Seckendorf* found it in the Archives of *Weimar*, tranflated into the *German* Language (19). *Luther* publifhed it (20), and added a Preface to it, wherein, among other things, he praifes *Barnes*'s Modefty. "He was not "ignorant, *fays he*, of the Failings of *Henry* VIII, "nor did he diffemble them among his Friends; "but every where elfe he fpoke of that Prince in "very refpectful and honourable terms (21)."

(18) Ibid.

(19) Ibid. n. 24

(20) *It is inferted in Vol. VII. of his Works, Edit. of* Altorf, f. 422.

id. ibid.

(21) Ibid. n. 25.

[F] *There*

BARNES. 659

"many, where he applied himself wholly" to the Study of the Bible, and of Divinity. He made so great a progress in it, that he became very considerable both among their Doctors, and Princes. When the King of *Denmark* sent Embassadors into *England*, he ordered, that *Barnes* should accompany them (*d*), or rather that he should be one of them (*e*). The Bishop of *Salisbury*, whom I quote in the Margin, might easily be justified in a Point, for which he is criticized (*f*). There are at least two Books published by *Barnes* [*F*].

[*F*] *There are at least two Books published by Barnes.*] The one contains the *Articles of his Beliefs*; the other is the *History of the Popes*. The first was printed in *Latin* with a Preface of *Pomeranus*, at whose House *Barnes* lodged at that time. It was printed in the *German* Language, at *Nuremberg*, in the Year 1531. It contains nineteen *Theses* according to *Luther's* Principles, and several Proofs taken from the Scripture, and the Fathers. The other Book was printed at *Wittemberg* in the Year 1536, with a Preface of *Luther*: It contains the Lives of the Popes from St *Peter* to *Alexander* III, and is dedicated to the King of *England*: The Author wrote the Epistle Dedicatory the tenth of *September* 1535. He treats the Popes very ill; and promises to continue their History down to his own Time (22) Mr *Seckendorf* is of opinion, that this Book deserves a second Edition (23), and has inserted the Preface of it in his Indexes, because, *says he*, it is very difficult to be met with, and may be reckoned for lost. *Quia Liber ipse rarissimè invenitur, & pro deperdito haberi potest* (24). It is certain, however, that a new Edition of it was published at *Leyden* in the Year 1615, which contains also the Lives of the Popes, written by *John Bale*, and which is not yet very scarce.

(*d*) Id. ib. pag. 683.

(*e*) Fox mentions this last Opinion, which seems doubtful to Dr Burnet, ibid. p. 683.

(*f*) See Remark [*B*].

(22) Ex Scholiis sive Supplementis Seckendorfii ad Indicē I.

(23) Recudi meretur. ib.

(24) Id. in Indice III, ad Ann. 1536.

BARNES (JOHN), in *Latin Barnesius*, an *English Benedictin* Monk, was one of those *Roman Catholics*, who, following the Examples of *Erasmus, Cassander, Wicelius, Modrevius,* Father *Paul*, and many others, made all their life-time Profession of the Catholic Religion, though they observed a great many abuses in it, which they heartily wished to see reformed. He wrote a Book against *Mental Reservations*, which was not at all pleasing to the Jesuits [*A*], though he dedicated it to Pope *Urban* VIII. His *Catholico-Romanus pacificus* is full of such things as cannot be relished by those, who are called good Papists [*B*]. Doubtless he desired to bring the two Churches as near one another as ever he could. The Court of *Rome* was very much displeased with him for it. This poor Man, of unexceptionable Morals (*a*), being at *Paris*, was apprehended [*C*], and stript of the Habit of his Order, to be carried into *Flanders* bound on Horseback. He was afterwards sent to *Rome*, where he remained in the Prison of the Inquisition, till he was removed into That of Lunatics (*b*). In this latter Station he ended his Days, being most certainly worthy of a better fate. He was a professed Monk of the Convent of the *Benedictins* of *Douay*, and had been Superior there (*c*); but, being not able to agree with the Monks of his Order, he retired into *France*, and did not obey the Summons of the *Benedictins*, requiring

(*a*) See Remark [*B*].

(*b*) See the French Mercury, Vol. XIV. pag. 336.

(*c*) Ibid. Vol. XII. pag. 752.

[*A*] *He wrote a Book against Mental Reservations, which was not at all pleasing to the Jesuits.*] It was printed at *Paris* in the Year 1625, under the Title of *Dissertatio contra Æquivocationes*: it was printed in *French* the same Year, and in the same place, under the Title of, *Traité & Dispute contre les Equivoques*. The Approbation of the Faculty of Divinity says, that *John Barnes* was *Doctor of Arts, of Sacred Theology,* and *Professor of* the *English Mission,* and first *Assistant for the Congregation of* Spain, and is dated the thirteenth of *July* 1624. The Author's Epistle Dedicatory is dated from *Paris* the thirteenth of *January* 1625. So that Father *Theophilus Raynaud* is mistaken, when he says, that *Barnes* was carried to *Rome*, and imprisoned under the Pontificate of *Paul* V. I shall relate his own Words, for they inform us of something concerning This poor *Benedictin*. "Joannes Barnesius Jesuitis admodum infensus, ob nonnullas suspiciones de compertâ illis vitâ suâ, eo loco fuit apud Paulum V, ut eum tanquam novæ fidei fabrum per Albertum Austriacum è Gallia abductum, & è Belgio Romam avectum judicaverit carcere dignum; donec emoto cerebro inter fatuos pone S. Pauli minoris ædem sacram fatuari desiit cum aliorum periculo (1). — John Barnes, *a great Enemy to the Jesuits, from some Suspicions he had of their having discovered his Manner of Life, was seized in* France *as a Heretic, by* Albert *of* Austria, *and carried through* Flanders *to* Rome, *where he was condemned by* Paul V, *to be imprisoned; till, becoming distracted, he was removed to the* Hospital *of* Lunatics *behind the Church of* St Paul *the Minor, where he ceased to do mischief by his Madness.*" This Passage was quoted by *Edward Brown*, in the Eight hundred twenty sixth Page of his *Appendix* to the *Fasciculus rerum expetendarum*, printed at *London* 1690. See the following Remark. We read in the *French Mercury* (2), That this honest *Benedictin believed, that the Jesuits hated him mortally, after the Printing of his Book of Equi-*

(1) Theophil. Raynaudin Theologia antiqua de veri Martyrii adæquate sumpti notione. *This Book was printed at* Lyons *in* 1656, *under the Name of* Leodegarius Quintinus. *The Passage which I quote out of it, is* pag. 174 *of his* Appendix Apopompæus.

(2) *In Vol.* XII, *p.* 752.

vocations; that *Doctor* Gamaches *(who was accounted one of the most able Divines of his Time) refused to give his Approbation of it, when requested of him*; and that he wrote that Book whilst he was Confessor in the Convent of *Chelles* (3).

[*B*] *His* Catholico-Romanus pacificus *is full of such Things as no good Papist can relish.*] It was printed at *London* in 1690, in the *Appendix* of the *Fasciculus rerum expetendarum.* The Author of the *Appendix* informs us, that he had seen three *Manuscripts* of This Work of *Barnes*; and he quotes these words of *John Basier,* Professor of Divinity. "Bonus ille Irenæus (4) tametsi vitæ inculpatæ & famæ integræ fuit, mediâ Lutetiâ correptus, suo habitu exutus, & quadrupedis instar barbarum in modum alligatus ad equum, & ita vehementissimè avectus primo in Flandriam, deinde Romam, ibi in Inquisitionis barathrum, deinde in maniacorum ergastulum erat detrusus (5). — This good Irenæus, *though of an unblameable Life, and unspotted Reputation, was arrested in the middle of* Paris, *stript of his Habit, and tied upon a Horse, more like a Beast than a Man, in a very barbarous Manner, and so carried away by violence, first into* Flanders, *and then to* Rome, *where he was thrown into the Dungeon of the Inquisition, and afterwards into the Receptacle of Lunatics.*"

[*C*] *He was apprehended at* Paris.] They would have sent him away the same Day he was taken, if the Captain of the Watch had not been so impatient, as the Father Procurator of the *Benedictins* of *Douay* was. But this impatient Person was forced to acquiesce till next Day, and then Father *Barnes* was carried in a Coach to *Vilette*, where two *Benedictins* waited to go along with him, and with the Guards, who were ordered to carry him to *Cambray*. He was bound on a Horse, and delivered to the Governor of *Cambrays*, who sent him to the Castle of *Waerden* (6). Father *Theophilus Raynaud* was in the wrong to speak of Orders from *Albert* of *Austria*; for

(3) Mercure Franç. Tom. XII, p. 751.

(4) *That is, the Benedictin Barnes.*

(5) Brown, in Append. Fasciculi Rerum expetend. *He quotes* John Basier, Diatribe de antiquæ Ecclesiæ Britannicæ libertate, Brugis impress. 1656.

(6) French Mercury, Vol. XII. pag. 753.

VOL. I.   8 D

quiring him to return to *Douay*, or to retire into some other of their Monasteries. He lodged at *Paris* near the College of *Navarre*, afterwards in the College of *Burgundy*, and lastly in the House of the Prince of *Portugal*, where the Captain of the Watch arrested him the fifth of *December* 1626. He was writing an Answer to the Book intituled, *Apostolatus Benedictinorum in Anglia*, wherein he would have inserted his particular Opinions about the Discipline of the Church (*d*). Father *Theophilus Raynaud*, concealing himself under a fictitious name, wrote against his Treatise of Equivocations [D].

Perhaps it will be entertaining to the Reader, to find here the reason, why *Barnes* was an Enemy to the Jesuits [E]: I mean the reason, which they have published.

(*d*) Ibid.

for That Archduke was dead a long time before *Barnes* was apprehended. I have quoted This Jesuit's Words in the first Remark.

[D] Father *Theophilus Raynaud*, *concealing himself under a false Name, wrote against his Treatise of Equivocations*] I speak of the Book entitled, *Splendor veritatis moralis, seu de licito usu Æquivocationis, pro Leonardo Lessio, adversus Joannem Barnesium Anglum Monachum*. It was printed at *Lyons*, in 1627, in 8vo: The Author takes the Name of *Stephanus Emonerius*. I have a stronger proof of it, than That, which *Placcius* formed out of two Passages of Father *Alegambus* (7). in one of which it is said, that *Theophilus Raynaud* composed, *sub nomine alieno*, the Treatise, of which I have just now given the Title (8); and in the other, that he concealed himself under the Name of *S. Emonerius* (9). This is my Proof. Father *Abram* says, in his Treatise *de Mendacio* (10), that *Theophilus Raynaud* acknowledged the Book of *Emonerius*, entituled *Splendor veritatis moralis*, for one of his Works, and that he may easily be discovered in it. *Mirror te hunc pro Theophili partu agnoscere,* — *I wonder you should take this for one of* Theophilus's *Productions*: thus says one of Father *Abram's* Interlocutors; the other answers: "Quid ni vero agnoscam cùm illum in suis " Mortalibus suum esse fateatur (11)? Quem si abdi- " caret, nullo tamen negotio patrem vel ex ipsa " filii facie cæterisque corporis lineamentis 'agnoscere " possemus,

Sic oculos, sic ille manus, sic ora ferebat.

" *Why not, when he owns it himself in his Moral* " *Works? And if he should disown it, it were easy* " *to find him out to be the Father, from the Resem-* " *blance it bears to him in every part of it,*

The Eye, the Hand, the Face exactly like.

Here is a Passage of *Theophilus Raynaud*, which shews, that he acknowledged the Confutation of *Barnes* to be his Work, and that this *Benedictine* was yet living in the Year 1650. " Dixi ego sane in præfatione " operis de Æquivocatione, adversus Caëtani ger- " manum, bipedum omnium effrontissimum, Joan- " nem Barnesium Anglum, qui vicenario carcere, in " quem curante summo Pontifice reclusus est, nec- " dum deterfit multiplicis adversus Deum, & Reli- " gionem Catholicam, ac S. Benedicti familiam, " malignitatis rubiginem ---- Societatem Jesu, &c. " (12). — *I have said, in my Preface to that* " *Work on* Equivocation, *against* Caëtan's *own Bro-* " *ther, the most hardened Wretch living; who, by* " *twenty Years' Imprisonment under the Jurisdiction* " *of his Holiness, has not worn off the least Particle*

" *of the Canker of his abundant Virulency against* " *God, the Catholic Church, and the Family of St* " *Benedict* ---- *that the Jesuits, &c.*"

[E] *This is the Reason, why he was an Enemy to the Jesuits.*] On his Return from *Spain* into the *Netherlands*, he assisted at one of their public Disputations, wherein the Respondent proposed his *Quodlibetal* Thesis thus : *An Joannes, in Hispania infamis, possit hic in Belgio absque peccato infamari.* That is to say, *Can John, being infamous in* Spain, *be innocently defamed in the* Netherlands*?* Such Cases of Conscience have been examined by *Soto, Molina,* and several other Writers; but in a general manner, though with the Addition of some particular Circumstances. Those Generalities were not kept to in the Disputation, at which *John Barnes* assisted ; for the Question was reduced to such precise Terms, by denoting in a particular Manner the time, and place, that he believed they meant him personally, as that he would never be persuaded to the contrary, though they made very humble Protestations to him, that they had no such design. He resolved to revenge himself, and make choice of the Subject of Equivocations. *Theophilus Raynaud* relates this, when he mentions the Answer, which he wrote against that Book of *Barnes*. " Ad singularia locorum ac tem- " porum adjuncta, illis in oris persamiliaris, difficultas " restricta est. ---- Clara locorum designatione peti- " tum se ratus Barnesius, bellum indixit inconcilia- " bile Societatis Jesu Doctoribus; nec se ullis un- " quam vel contestationibus, vel mollibus ac propè " supplicibus verbis, flecti passus est, ut nihil minus " quam de eo notando cogitatum esse, in eo Thesium " programmate ac proloquio, persuaderetur (13). " ---- *The Difficulty was urged with particular Cir-* " *cumstances of Time or Place, according to the Cu-* " *stom of their Disputations.* ---- Barnes, *thinking* " *himself pointed at by the Place, which was named,* " *declared perpetual War against the Jesuit Doctors;* " *nor could he ever be prevailed upon by any Eviden-* " *ces, or the most candid and even humble Declara-* " *tions, to believe, that there was not the least Thought* " *of aiming at him in the Discussion of that Thesis."* He does not forget to say, that *Barnes* was condemned to perpetual Imprisonment; and that, having lost his Senses, he was removed to the Hospital of Lunatics; " Barnesium, ob periculosas novitates, " carceri esse mancipatum, postea autem emota " mente, in satuorum ergastulo Transtiberino, (vulgo " gli Pazzarelli) conclusus est; ubi anno 1643, " erat superstes (14). — Barnes, *for his pernicious* " *Innovations,* — *was thrown into Prison, and* " *afterwards, running distracted, was removed to the* " *Madhouse on the other side the* Tyber, *(commonly* " *called* gli Pazzarelli,*) where he was living in the* " *Year* 1643."

BARON (PETER), Professor of Divinity in the University of *Cambridge* in the XVIth Century, was a Frenchman born (*a*). He excited some troubles in that University, by certain Doctrines, which he delivered there, in the Year 1590. It was pretended, that his Opinions came very near those of the *Pelagians, Whitaker, Tindal, Chadderton, Perkins, &c.* opposed them in their Sermons, Lectures, and Books ; but, at first, they spared their Adversary's Name, because of his great Age. Perceiving afterwards, that he continued to dogmatize, and that he maintained an heterodox Hypothesis in his *Summa trium de Prædestinatione Sententiarum* ; *Whitaker* formally declared himself his Antagonist, and refuted his *Summa*. The Matter was brought before Queen *Elizabeth*, and the Archbishop of *Canterbury*. A Convocation of Prelates, and Doctors of Divinity, met at *Lambeth*: *Whitaker* was summoned to appear there, who maintained the common Opinion with so much Strength, that it became gloriously triumphant. That of *Baron* was condemned, and nine Articles (*b*) were drawn up, the twentieth of *November* 1595, which

BARON. 661

which were received in the University by Public Authority. *Baron* was dismissed, and returned into *France*: which restored Peace to that University (c). Some *(c) Alting. Ibid.* think, that he was used too severely [*A*]. We shall see the Titles of some Works of this Professor [*B*].

[*A*] *Some think, that he was used too severely.*] The Extracts of a Book of *Thomas Fuller*, which Mr *Des Maizeaux* has been so kind as to send me, shall be my Commentary on this place. That Book is an History of the University of *Cambridge*, and is to be met with at the end of *The Church History of Great Britain, from the Birth of Christ till the Year* 1648.

(1) Margaret Countess of Richmond, Mother of Henry VII, built some Colleges at Cambridge, and founded two Professorships of Divinity, one at Oxford, and another at Cambridge. Those who enjoy those Professorships, and the Salary annexed to them, are called Margaret Professors. John Tisher, Bishop of Rochester, was the first who enjoyed that at Cambridge: Erasmus was the second, and Baro the fourteenth. This Marginal Note is Mr Des Maizeaux's.

(a) Fuller's Hist. of the University of Cambridge, ad Ann. 1596.

" A Contest happened between Mr *Chadderton* " (afterwards Master of *Emanuel* College), and Dr " *Baro*, Margaret Professor (1), about some hetero- " dox Opinions, vented by the same *Baro*, both in " his Readings and Print, (*viz.* in his Commentary " on *Jonah*, and Book *de Fide*).

" Whereupon the Doctor procured Mr *Chadder-* " *ton* to be called into the Consistory, in the Pre- " sence of the Vice-Chancellor, Dr *Hauford*, Dr *Har-* " *vey*, and Dr *Legge*, where he utterly denied, that " he had ever preached against the Doctor, but he " propounded these Questions as erroneous and false.

1. *Primus Dei amor non est in natura fidei Justificantis.* — The principal Love of GOD is not in the Nature of justifying Faith.

2. *Fides Justificans non præcipitur in Decalogo.* — Justifying Faith is not commanded in the Decalogue.

" Many Papers, in *Latin,* passed between them, " and at last they were conceived to come nearer to- " gether.

" The end of *Peter Baro's* triennial Lectures began " to draw near: now, although Custom had made " such Courtesy almost a Due, to continue the same " Professor, where no urgent Reasons to the con- " trary were alledged, yet the University intended not " to re-elect him for the Place, meaning fairly to cut " him off just at the Time, (which would be the less " Pain and Shame unto him,) when his Years should " be expired (2). He himself was sensible of it, " and, besides, he saw the Articles of *Lambeth*, lately " sent to the University, and foresaw, that Subscrip- " tion thereto would be expected from, yea imposed " on, him, to which he could not condescend, there-

" fore resolved to quit his Place. So that this his " Departure was not his free Act, out of voluntary " Election, but That whereunto his Will was neces- " sarily determined; witness his own reply to a Friend, " requiring of him the Cause of his withdrawing: " *Fugio*, saith he, *ne Fugarer.* —— *I fly for fear I* " *should be driven away.*

" Some conceive this to be hard Measure, which " was used to one of Dr *Baro's* Qualifications: for, I. " He was a Foreigner, a *Frenchman*, *Turpius ejicitur* " *quam non admittitur hospes*. II. A great Scholar; for " he that denieth Learning in *Baro*, (so witnessed in " his Works,) plainly affirmeth no Scholarship in " himself. III. An inoffensive Man for Life and " Conversation; seeing nothing of Viciousness could " be charged upon him, which otherwise, in his " Contest with Mr *Chadderton*, had been urged a- " gainst him. Lastly, an aged Man, coming hither " many Years since, (when the Professor's Place as " much needed him as he it,) and who had painful- " ly spent his Strength in the Employment. Others " alledged, that, in such Cases of Conscience, there " is no Plea for Courtesy, and that *Baro*, as he was " a Stranger, had brought in Doctrines to the infect- " ing the University, the Fountain of Learning and " Religion, and therefore Archbishop *Whitegift* de- " signed the removing him from his Place (3). *(3) Id. Ibid. p. 145, & seq. Edit. of Lond. 1655.*

This is, Sir, (they are Mr *Des Maizeaux's* Words) *what Fuller says; and I chuse to translate him literally, though not so well, rather than run the hazard of deviating from his Sense.* He takes notice, that all the *English* wrote *Baro* constantly, or *Baroe*, and that, in Original Writings, the Doctor signed *Baro*; from whence it might be concluded, that I should have called him *Baro*, and not *Baron*, unless it be said, that he latinized his Name, when he signed *Baro*, and that the *English* called him according to the *Latin* Termination. That which is certain, is, that the Name of *Baron* is much more used in *France*, than that of *Baro*, which is not altogether unknown nei- ther, witness the Continuator of *Astrea* (4). *(4) See the History of the French Academy, pag. 321.*

[*B*] *Here are the Titles of some of* Baron's *Works.*] *Prælectiones* 39, in *Jonam*, printed at *London*, in 1579. *Summa trium Sententiarum de Prædestinatione. De Præstantia & Dignitate divinæ Legis.*

BARON (VINCENT), in Latin *Baronius*, a Monk of the Order of St *Dominic*, was much esteemed in the XVIIth Century, for several Books, which he published. He had the Famous *Theophilus Raynaud* for his Antagonist, and I do not know whether the Desire of encountring so famous a Champion, might not make him take, for that Jesuit's Work, what was really not so. He sometimes has acknowledged himself mistaken in his Conjectures on that Head. The Works of Father *Baron*, which are come to my knowledge, are, a Book, *on Justification, against the Doctrine of the Calvinists*; a *Moral Theology*, divided into three Parts [*A*], and an *Apology for his Order* [*B*]. In his Moral Theology, he has treated on the principal Matters in dispute between the *Dominicans* and the Jesuits. He was a famous Preacher. Here

[*A*] *He composed a Moral Theology, divided into three Parts.*] The first is designed against the Doctrine of Probability, *adversus Laxiores Probabilistas* (1). He therein confutes *Caramuel*, who had wrote four Letters against the Dissertation, which *Fagnano*, Dean of the Prelates of *Rome*, had inserted in his Commentaries on the Canon-Law. *Fagnano* maintains strongly, that an Opinion, which is thought less probable, ought never to be preferred before that, which is thought more probable. *Caramuel* confuted him, and was confuted by our *Vincent Baron*. Father *Theophilus Raynaud* was refuted by the same Work, in relation to an Opinion of *Suarez*, condemned by *Clement* VIII. *Suarez* had maintained, that Confession might be made by Letters: Father *Theophilus* contrived some Expedients to defend his Brother against the Pope's Censure, and Father *Baron* wrote against those Expedients. He, at the same time, fell upon the *Jansenists*, since he maintained, against *Wendrokius*, " That sometimes, though very " rarely, there happen Cases, wherein there may be " an invincible Ignorance, as well of the Law of Na- " ture, as of a positive Law (2)." In the second

(1) Journal des Sçavans, March 8, 1666. pag. 194.

(2) Ibid. pag. 198.

Part, he attacks *Amadæus Guimenius*, and is not satisfied with maintaining, that the loose Opinions, which are imputed to the *Dominicans*, are not their true Sentiments; he shews also, what Judgment ought to be passed on those Opinions. He acknowledges, in his Preface, the wrong Notion he had entertained in composing his Work: He thought, that *Amadæus Guimenius* was but a fictitious Name, which Father *Theophilus* had given himself (3). In the third Part he treats of Liberty, and of the *Media Scientia*; and he maintains, that the Fore-knowledge of GOD has no other Foundation, than his Decrees; and that this Fore-knowledge is so far from destroying Man's Liberty, that, on the contrary, it establishes it (4). This must not be taken for a Paradox; for whoso- ever should say otherwise, would not follow the Definition of Liberty, which ought to be given in the System of Physical Predetermination: It is by virtue of the different Ideas of Liberty, that the Dispute may be spun out, and the Reader so deluded, as not to be able to judge of the ill Success of his Cause.

(3) Ibid. Apr. 12. 1666, p. 36.

(4) Ibid. June 21, 1666, pag. 257.

[*B*] —— *and an Apology for his Order.*] It is a *Latin* Work, like the foregoing: It is an Answer to the

Here is a Memoir, which came into my hands since the first Edition of this Work (a). "Father *Vincent Baron* was born at *Martres*, in the Diocess of " *Rieux* in *Gascony*. He entred into the Order of *Dominican Friars* at *Toulouse* " in the Year 1622. He taught Divinity for several Years, with applause, in " the Convent of the same City, and was Prior there, as he was likewise at " *Avignon*, and in the General Novitiate of the Suburb of *St Germain* at *Paris*. " He was Definitor for his Province, in the General Chapter held in the Year " 1656. Where he presided at the *Theses* dedicated to Pope *Alexander* VII, which " gained him the esteem of all the City, and of the whole Order. He was in " the Assembly, when the Pope sent to tell the Definitors, and the Fathers of " the Chapter, that he was under the greatest Concern to see so deplorable a " loosness in Christian Morality, which had been introduced into it by certain " new Casuists, exhorting them to compose another System, agreeable to the " Doctrine of St *Thomas*. This engaged Father *Baron* to undertake those Pieces " he composed on that Subject. He was again elected Provincial, and after- " wards the Father General sent him Commissary into *Portugal*, on Affairs of " Importance, wherein he was so successful, that the Queen, the Court, and all " the Monks, gave testimony of his Merit by a public Act. He returned to " *Paris* to the General *Novitiate*, and died there the Twenty first of *January* 1674, " being seventy Years old. Besides several *Latin Poems*, which he left as a " sample of his capacity in Literature, he published the Books, which I shall " mention below [*C*]." You will find a very honourable Passage concerning him in the Historical Apology for the Censures of *Louvain* and *Douay* (b). The Congregation of the *Index* was not favourable to him [D].

(a) *By the means of Mr* Pinsson des Riolles.

(b) *Published in* 1688. *by Mr* Gerv. *Bacholm of Divinity: this Passage is at p.* 213.

the cruel Invective of Father *Theophilus Raynaud*, entituled, *De immunitate Cyriacorum à Censuris*, and to him, who pretended to shew, that it is well if the tenth Part of all the Works, which are ascribed to *Thomas Aquinas*, be really his. Father *Baron* enters the List also, with Mr *de Launoi*, who maintained, that many Passages of the Fathers, cited in a Treatise of *Thomas Aquinas*, against the *Greeks*, are forged. This *Dominican* was not contented to write an Apology for his Order, he made also their Panegyric (5). [*C*] *He published the Books, which I shall mention below.*] What I am going to transcribe is contained Word for Word in the Memoir, from which I have taken the Addition to this Article. *Theologia Moralis*, Paris, 1665, two Volumes in 8vo. *Primus Tomus ejusdem correctus, Editio secunda* 1667, in 8vo. *Libri Apologetici contra Theophilum Rainaudum*, Paris, 1666, two Volumes in 8vo. *Mens sancti Augustini & Thomæ de Gratia & Libertate*, 1666, in 8vo. *Ethica Christiana*, Paris, 1666, two Volumes in 8vo. *Responsio ad Librum Cardenæ*, Paris, in 8vo. *Heresy Convicted*, Paris, 1668, in 12mo. *Panegyrics on the Saints*, Paris, 1660, in 4to. The Book entituled *Ethices Christianæ septemdecim loci*, composed against one *Matthew Moya*, who had taken the Name of *Amadæus*, was censured at *Rome*, by the Intrigues of Cardinal *Nizard*, who was offended at it; and *Capisucchi*, the Master of the sacred Palace, who had approved of it, was turned out, and Father *Hyacinthus Libelli*, since Archbishop of *Avignon*, was put in his Room. *Capisucchi* was afterwards re-instated, and, since that, made a Cardinal. I do not find, in this List of the Works of Father *Baron*, the *Exercitatio*, which Mr *de Launoi* refutes with surprizing Sharpness, in one of his Letters, the fourteenth of his fifth Part. See the Remark [*P*], of the Article of (J O H N *de*) L A U N O I, at the beginning.

Two or three Months after I had received this Memoir, the following Account was sent me. " Apo-

(c) Journal des Sçavans, March 7. 1667. p. 92.

" logia pro sacra congregatione Indicis ejusque Secre- " tario & Dominicanis, contra Petri à Valle clausa " Libellum famosum inscriptum, *de Immunitate Authorum Cyriacorum à Censura*; Romæ, typis —— " M.DC.LXII, in 4o. Advertat lector præter inau- " mera errata ex prælo passim sensum & stylum au- " ctorum mutantia, addita nonnulla necessaria sermo- " ne simplici, & multa adjecta convitia : has autem " labes tollet secunda editio. —— *An Apology for the " sacred Congregation of the Index, and their Se- " cretary, and for the Dominicans, against a Libel of " Petrus à Valle Clausa, under the Title of* The Ex- " emption of Ecclesiastical Authors from Censure. " Printed at Rome, 1662, in 4to. *The Reader is " to take notice, that besides innumerable Errors of the " Press, which every where disturb the Sense and " Stile of the Author, there are some material Things " added in plain Language, and much Scandal : but " these Imperfections will be corrected in a second Edi- " tion.* This second Edition was published at *Paris*, " by *Simon Piget*, in the Year 1666, in two Volumes, " divided into five Books. The first printed at " *Rome*, at the Instance of Cardinal *Capisucchi*, then " Master of the sacred Palace, who approved it, oc- " casioned the removing of the same *Capisucchi* from " his Office, by *Alexander* VII, a great Friend to " the Jesuits. It was also put into the Index, the " Twenty eighth of *February*, 1664."

[*D*] *The Congregation of the Index was not favourable to him.*] Here is an Extract of their Decree, of the Twenty seventh of *September*, 1672. *Duo primi Tomi operum Fr. Vincentii Baronii, inscripti Theologiæ moralis Summa bipartita, prohibentur : tertius vero præfati auctoris suspenditur donec corrigatur : ultimi autem duo Tomi ejusdem Auctoris, scilicet quartus & quintus, quinque libros apologeticos continentes, pariter prohibentur* (6). See the End of the preceeding Remark.

(6) *See Father Papebroch, Respons. ad ex hibit. Errorum, p.* 285.

BARONI.

BARONI (LEONORA), an *Italian* Lady, one of the best Singers in the World, flourished in the XVIIth Century. She was Daughter of the Fair *Adriana* of *Mantua*, and was so admired, that a great many fine Wits made Verses in her Praise. There is a Volume of excellent Pieces, in *Latin*, *Greek*, *French*, *Italian*, and *Spanish*, printed at *Rome*, under the Title of *Applausi poëtici alle glorie della Signiora Leonora Baroni* [*A*]. Those, who desire to know the particular Perfections

[*A*] *There is a Volume of Pieces, in her praise, under the Title of* Applausi poëtici alle glorie della Signora Leonora Baroni.] *Nicius Erythræus* (spoke of this Work, when he said, " Legi ego, in Theatro " Eleonoræ Baronæ, cantricis eximiæ, in quo omnes " hic Romæ, quotquot ingenio & poëticæ facultatis " laude præstant, carminibus, tum Etruscè tum La- " tinè scriptis, singulari ac prope divino mulieris illius " canendi artificio tanquam faustos quosdam clamo- " res & plausus edunt ; legi, inquam, unum Lælii " (Guidiccionis) Epigramma, ita purum, ita elegans, " &c. (1). —— *I have read, in the Theatre of Leono- " ra Baroni, the celebrated Singer, wherein all the " Wits and Poets, here at Rome, have, in Italian and*

(1) Nic. rythr Pin coth. II, pag. 129.

BARONIUS. BARTAS. BARTHIUS.

Perfections of her singing, may read the Account given by a good Judge, who had heard her sing [*B*]. It is from him I have borrowed this Account.

" and Latin *Verses, complimented and applauded her divine Skill in singing: I have read, I say, one Epigram of* Lælius Guidiccio, *so beautiful and elegant, &c.*"

[*B*] *They may read the Account given by a good Judge, who had heard her sing.*] " She is endowed with fine Parts; she has a very good Judgment to distinguish good from bad Music; she understands it perfectly well, and even composes; which makes her absolutely Mistress of what she sings, and gives her the most exact Pronunciation and Expression of the Sense of her Words. She does not pretend to Beauty, neither is she disagreeable, nor a Coquet. —— She sings with a bold and generous Modesty, and an agreeable Gravity. Her Voice reaches a large Compass of Notes, and is exact, loud, and harmonious; she softens and raises it without straining, or making grimaces. Her Raptures and Sighs are not lascivious; her Looks have nothing impudent, nor does she transgress a Virgin Modesty in her Gestures. In passing from one Key to another, she shews sometimes the Divisions of the enharmonic and chromatic Kind, with so much Art and Sweetness, that every body is ravished with that fine and difficult Method of singing. She has no need of any Person to assist her with a *Theorbo*, or a Viol, one of which is necessary to make her singing complete; for she plays perfectly well herself on both those Instruments. In short, I have had the good Fortune to hear her sing several times, above thirty different Airs, with second and third Stanzas, composed by herself. I must not forget to tell you, that, one Day, she did me the particular Favour, to sing with her Mother and her Sister: Her Mother played upon the Lyre, her Sister upon the Harp, and herself upon the *Theorbo*. This Consort, composed of three fine Voices, and of three different Instruments, so powerfully transported my Senses, and threw me into such Raptures, that I forgot my Mortality, and thought myself already among the Angels, enjoying the Felicity of the Blessed."

I have taken this from a Discourse on *Italian* Music, printed with the Life of *Malherbe*, among other Treatises at *Paris*, in 1672, in 12mo, at the end of which are these Words: *This Discourse was composed by Mr Maugars, Prior of St Peter de* Mac, *the King's Interpreter of the* English *Language, and, besides, so famous a Performer on the Viol, that the King of* Spain, *and several other sovereign Princes of* Europe, *have wished to hear him.*

BARONIUS (DOMINIC), a *Florentine* Priest and Preacher in the XVIth Century, wrote vigorously against the Church of *Rome*, and concurred with the *Vaudois* in *Piedmont* to maintain Orthodoxy; but, at last, he was esteemed a false Brother, because he maintained, that, in time of Persecution, it was not necessary to make outward Profession of the Truth [*A*]. *Celsus Martinengue*, Minister of the *Italian* Church of *Geneva*, wrote against him on that Subject, and Replies were made on both sides. These Books are become very scarce, I know not for what reason. Our *Baronius* composed a Mass according to his own Fancy, which he thought likely to reconcile the Differences betwixt the two Religions; but he found himself disappointed; for the Protestants rejected his Project (*a*).

(*a*) *Taken from the Ecclesiastical History of the Vaudois, composed by* Peter Giles, *chap.* 10, *pag* 61, *&* seq. G.neva 1644.

[*A*] *He maintained, that, in Time of Persecution, it was not necessary to make outward Profession of the Truth.*] He did not therefore deserve the Name of *Antinicodemite*, which *Peter Giles* gave him; but rather That of *Nicodemite*. Let us see in what manner That Historian speaks of him. " *Dominic Baronius, says he* (1), *was a Florentine*, a Popish Priest, and a Preacher of Repute, and who, in less dangerous Times, had shewn some Zeal for the true Religion, almost wholly embracing it, and condemning almost all the Papal superstitious Constitutions, except only some few Particulars, which though he retained, yet he treated them so ambiguously, that it could hardly be known what was his Opinion of them, as appears in several *Italian* and *Latin* Treatises composed by him, and particularly in That of human Constitutions, wherein he shews what may be admitted, and what ought to be rejected. In that Book, among several great Errors, which he condemns in the " Popish Church, he says of the Mass ——." I do not set down the Passage, which *Peter Giles* alledges; but here is what follows that Quotation: " He wrote, in the same Stile, concerning the other " Popish Superstitions: But, for all this, he endea- " voured to persuade, that, in very dangerous Times, " and Places, People might dissemble outwardly what " they thought of such Errors, and even go to Mass, " provided they constantly retained the Truth in- " wardly, and did not heartily concur in any of " those Errors. He said, that, in such Times, and " Places, the Minister of Truth ought to make it " his Business to shew his Disciples the Tares, and " to teach them how to discern them from the good " Grain, and to make them hate the Tares, and " love the Wheat with all their Heart: But, as to " the outward Profession, that he ought to let the " Lord work his Pleasure, without exposing himself, " and others, to great Dangers. — *Celsus de Martinengue* — confuted, by a notable, and long, " Treatise, all the Reasons *Baronius* alledged in " Support of his Opinion; and Replies were made " on both Sides for some Time. And *Baronius*, " thinking himself able to reconcile the two Reli- " gions, reformed the Mass, in order, that, agree- " ably to what he had laid down, People might go " to it with a good Conscience; and sung it himself, " according to his own Reformation, and acted in " the same manner, in several other Points, thinking, " by that means, to please every Body, by trim- " ming. But his Proceeding was condemned by a " great number of the truly Faithful, not only by " Words and Writings, but also by their Actions, " since they chose rather to part with their earthly " Goods, and this temporal Life, than to shew any " outward Consent to Popish Idolatry, and errone- " ous Superstitions (2)."

(1) Peter Giles's History of the Churches of the Vaudois, chap. 10, pag. 62.

(2) Id ibid. p.g 64. See also p. 246.

BARTAS (WILLIAM DE SALUSTE *Seigneur du*) A *French* Poet. See SALUSTE.

BARTHIUS (GASPAR), one of the most learned Men, and fruitfullest Pens, of his Time, was born at *Custrin* in the Country of *Brandenburg*, the Twenty second of *June* 1587 (*a*). His Family was of an ancient Nobility [*A*]: His Father, *Charles Barth*, Professor of the Civil Law at *Francfort* on the *Oder*, Counsellor to the Elector of *Brandenburg*, and his Chancellor at *Custrin*, died the sixth of *February* 1597, at *Halberstad*, from whence his Widow withdrew to *Hall* with her

(*a*) Hulsemannus in Concione funebri, apud Freher. Theatr. Viror. illustr. pag. 1546.

[*A*] *His Family was of an ancient Nobility.*] There are but few Gentlemen of Quality, and few great Lords, who can shew a more ancient Original than *Barthius*. One of his Ancestors signalized himself

her Children; *Gaspar* was sent to *Gotha*, afterwards to *Eisenach*, and, after that, to several Universities of *Germany*, and *Italy* (*b*). He became so learned in a little time, that his Childhood was admired by great Men [*B*], and he composed several Books while he was a beardless Boy [*C*]. He had a wonderful Facility in making Verses [*D*]; and also published a great many [*E*]. He learnt the living

(*b*) Hulsemannus, *ib.*

self in the War against the *Vandals* in the Retinue of the Emperor *Lewis* the *Debonair*, in the Year 856. He was a *Bavarian*; he commanded the Cavalry, and was killed in That War, as *Cyriacus Spangenbergius* observes (1). The Grandfather of *Barthius* was one of the chief Gentlemen of *Bavaria*: he went and settled in the Circle of the *Upper-Saxony*, where he bought several Estates, and, in the Year 1545, he was honoured by the Emperor, and the States of the Empire, with many noble Titles. "Avus idem noster, ne in his terris minor esset "gentilibus suis alibi viventibus, à Carolo quinto, Con"silio & Senatus-consulto omnium Imperii statuum "tum Spiræ præsentium, ex integro Cæsareæ Ma"jestatis & sacri Imperii auctoritate utriusque nobilis "& miles Tornearius declaratus est, omniaque liberæ "& veræ nobilitatis privilegia accepit, cum singulari "integritatis, doctrinæ, & strenuitatis testimonio, anno "Christiano M. D. XLV (2). —— *That the Rank* "*of my Grandfather, in this Country, might not be in*"*ferior to That his Family held in other Places, he* "*was knighted, and declared Noble, both by the Em*"*peror* Charles V, *and his Council, and by Decree* "*of all the States of the Empire, then assembled* "*at* Spires, *and received all the Privileges of a free* "*and true Nobility, with a particular Testimony of* "*his Integrity, Learning, and Courage, in the Year* "1545." He enjoyed the Office of Chancellor at the Court of *Albert* of *Brandenburgh*, Elector of *Mentz*, Archbishop of *Magdeburg*, and Cardinal. One of his Ancestors, whose Name was *Herman*, was Grand Master of the *Teutonic* Order, towards the end of the XIIth Century (3). The old Annals make mention of him: *Munster* speaks of him in his Cosmography; and the Catalogues of the Grand Masters of That Order, even those composed by *Jerom Megiserus*, do not forget him. Others of the same Family are to be met with in the Relations of Turnaments, and in the Collections of the Coats of Arms of principal Noble Families of *Germany*. The Father of *Gaspar Barthius* had several Brothers (4), who all died without Children (5). One of them had been Master of the Horse to some great Princes, and did not want Learning (6). *Barthius* says, that he shall be the last of his Family: *Superstes nunc ego omnibus paterni mei nominis familiam meam universam mecum rebus humanis brevi educam* (7). You see him in the Front of several of his Works, with the Title of *S. R. Imperii Eques*. The Thoughts of his Family dying with him was extreamly afflicting, and lay very much at his Heart: He often considered this melancholy Subject; which makes me believe, that he was very easily comforted on the Death of his Wife. She was barren, and likely, according to his reckoning, to outlive his Virility; for, otherwise, he would not have spoken in the manner we have seen. But, when he least suspected it, his Wife died. He soon took another, to see whether he could avoid the hard Fate, he had so much feared, of being the last of his Family. He looked upon himself no longer an useless Load on the Earth; this might be proper to call himself, while he despaired of having any Offspring. He had the Happiness to beget Sons and Daughters by a second Marriage; but he forgot to correct the Places of his Commentary, where he appears to be out of Hopes of leaving a Successor. If he did not care to correct his Manuscript, he ought, at least, to have added something, at the end of it, concerning his second Marriage being more fruitful than the first. If I am asked, How I came to know, that his first Wife was not dead, when he complained of being the last of his Name? My Answer will be, That I infer it from this small Calculation. *Barthius*'s Funeral Oration informs me, that he became a Widower in the Year 1643, and that his Mother died at *Hall*, the Twenty second of *January* 1622. Now she had been dead but eighteen Years, when he made his Complaints: "Ego inutile ferè pondus "terræ omnibus mei nominis mortalibus superstes "supervivo integro octodecennio (8). - - - *I am almost* "*an useless Load on the Earth, having outlived all* "*my Family full eighteen Years, and being the last* "*of my Name.*" His first Wife must therefore have been alive at that time.

(1) In Annalibus Saxonicis, cap. 100, pag. 138.

(2) Barthius in Statium, Tom. II. pag. 1026.

(3) Id. ibid.

(4) Barthius *says, at pag.* 1026, 1027, *of his* Commentary on Statius, *in the space of a few lines, that he had six Paternal Uncles, and that his Grandfather left six Sons. This is inconsistent.*

(5) Illiberes omnes—— excesserunt. *Ibid. pag.* 1027.

(6) Ibid. pag. 1025.

(7) Ibid.

BARTHIUS's causless Fear of dying without Posterity.

(8) Id. ibid. pag. 126.

[*B*] *His Childhood was admired by great Men.*] If I am allowed to extend the Word Childhood a little farther than usual, my Text will be very true; since *Scaliger* set a great Value upon the first Productions of *Barthius*. "Cujus virtutem juvenilem "ac cordatos ausus Josephus Scaliger *suspexit* adeo, ut "divinationis instar hanc illi de Barthio vocem exci"disse compertum sit, *natum esse adhuc unum æter*"*nitati ingenium, quod si ad maturitatem perveniret,* "*literas aliquandiu vivere posse* (9). - - - - - *Whose* "*juvenile Capacity, and judicious Performances,* Jo"seph Scaliger *so greatly amired, that, in a sort of* "*prophetic Spirit, he declared thus concerning* Bar"thius, that there was now one Genius more born "for Eternity, and, if this should live to Maturity, "Learning might survive some time longer." *Daumius* says, that some learned Men were not ashamed to learn of This young Scholar: "Eo adolescenti uti do"ctore non erubuerunt Taubmannus, Siberus, Schmi"dius. Quæ Gruteri aliorumque apud exteros vi"rorum de eo tum lata fuerint judicia, domi eorum "literæ asservatæ partim, partim lectæ, docent (10). "- - - - - - - - Taubmannus, Siberus, *and* Schmi"dius, *thought it no Disgrace to be taught by This* "*Youth. The Judgment, which* Gruterus, *and other* "*Foreigners, passed on him, may be seen in their* "*Writings, either published, or in their own Hands.*" Another learned Person, who had been *Barthius*'s School-fellow, speaks thus of him: "Novi - - - - "ante annos ferè quinquaginta pueri præstabiles "minas, cum sub Wilkii p. m. manu essemus "*συσχολασαὶ*: novi ante hos XLIII. annos Wite"bergæ adolescentem florentem gratia apud non"nullos, θαυμαζόμενον ἄνω κάτω ab æqualibus "(11). - - - - - *I knew him* - - - - - - *almost fifty* "*Years ago, a very promising Lad, when we were* "*Schoolfellows, under* Wilkius: *I knew him, about* "*Forty three Years ago, a Youth in great Esteem a*"*mong some, and much admired by those of his own* "*Age.*"

(9) Spizelius in Templo Honoris reserato, pag. 381.

(10) Daumius Epist. 14. ad Reinesium.

(11) Reinesius Epist. 15. ad Daumium, pag. 46. *This Letter is dated* Jan. 14. 1651.

[*C*] *He composed several Books, while he was a beardless Boy*] Mr *Baillet*, who has placed him in his Catalogue of *Famous Children*, will give us the most particular Account of him. He informs us, "That, at twelve Years of Age, *Barthius* turned "the Psalter of *David* into all sorts of *Latin* Verses; "and that, in the same Year, he published other "Poems in the same Language; *and that* the Col"lection of Silvæ, Satires, Elegies, Odes, Epigrams, "and Iambic Verses, which he caused to be printed "at *Wittemberg* in the Year 1607, comprehends all "the Poetry he composed from the thirteenth to the "nineteenth Year of his Age (12)." We have it from himself, continues Mr *Baillet* (13), "That, be"ing yet but in the fixteenth Year of his Age, he "wrote a Treatise, or Dissertation, by way of Letter, "on the Manner of reading *Latin* Authors usefully, "by beginning with those from *Ennius* to the end "of the *Roman* Empire; and continuing them, from "the Expiration of the *Latin* Tongue, to the Critics "of these latter Times, who have restored the an"cient Authors *. It is a Performance, which the "Author says cost him but Twenty four Hours; "but it is so close, and so full, that it shews *Bar*"*thius* must, even at that Time, have read a pro"digious deal; and that this Reading was so far from "being indigested, or confused, that it was accom"panied with a perfect Judgment, *&c.*" To this may be added, that he was but eighteen Years of Age, when he composed a Commentary on the *Ceiris* of *Virgil*, which was printed at *Amberg*, in the Year 1608, and contains much Learning.

(12) Baillet, Famous Children, p. 297, 298.

(13) Ibid. pag. 296.

* It is to be found in the 50th Book of his *Adversaria*.

[*D*] *He had a wonderful Facility in making Verses.*] *Barthius*, having observed, that *Statius*, in some Measure, congratulated himself on having spent but two Days about the *Epithalamium* of *Stella*, which contains Two hundred seventy eight Hexameters, adds, that *Statius* did not expose himself to the Censure of

BARTHIUS.

living Languages, and made it appear, by his Translations out of *Spanish* and *French* [F], that he was not contented with a superficial Knowledge of them. It is surprising to find, what a number of Authors he must have read, from his *Adversaria*, and Commentaries on *Statius* and *Claudian*. Most Critics are satisfied with reading Prophane Authors; but this was not enough for him; he acquired also a great Knowledge of Ecclesiastical Authors, especially those, who lived in the middle Ages. His constant application to Books obliged him to relinquish all manner of Business, and to lead a retired life at *Leipsic* (c). He resolved early to disengage himself intirely from the World, and the Study of Prophane Authors, in order to apply himself only to the great Affair of Salvation [G]. He put this design in execution in the latter Years of his Life; and it appears, by his *Soliloquia*, published in 1654, that his Thoughts were deeply engaged on Eternity [H]. He died the seventeenth of *September* 1658, a little above Seventy one Years of Age (d). The Manuscript Works he left behind him [I], those which were printed

(14) Nam fuit hoc vinofus: in hora sæpe ducentos, Ut magnum, versus dictabat, stans pede in uno. He, turning on his Heel, wrote, in one Hour, Two hundred Verses, good ones to be sure. Hor. Sat. 4. l. 1.

(15) Barthius, in Stat. Tom. I. pag. 7.

(16) Spizelius in Templo Honoris, pag. 382.

(17) Id. ib. p. 386, 387.

(18) See the Bibliotheque of the Spanish Writers, Vol. I. pag. 403, 413, Vol. II. pag. 212.

(19) Judgment of the Learned. Tom. I. pag. 542.

(20) Daumius in the Preface to Barthius's Commentary on Statius, dated March 15, 1664.

of *Horace* (14), since he did not make Two hundred Verses in an Hour, as That Poet did, whom *Horace* ridiculed (15). " I find a great Hyperbole, continues he, in That Criticism, though I am not " ignorant what it is to make a great many Verses " in a little time; for, in three Days time, I translated " into *Latin* the three first Books of the *Iliad*, " which Translation contained a little above Two " thousand Verses."

[*E*] *And also published a great many.*] For, besides those mentioned in the Remark [*C*], he published a Poem at *Francfort*, in 1623, entituled *Zodiacus vitæ Christianæ; Satyricon, pleraque omnia veræ Sapientiæ mysteria singulari suavitate enarrans*. It is divided into twelve Books. In the same Year, and Place, he published *Epidorpidum ex mero scazonte libri III. in quibus bona pars humanæ sapientiæ metro explicatur*. His Epigrams, divided into thirty Books, and dedicated to King *James*, appeared under the Name of *Tarræus Hebius* (16). The four Books *Amabilium Anacreonte decantati*, were printed in the Year 1612. He wrote a Paraphrase on *Æsop's Fables* in Verse, a Translation of *Musæus* also in Verse, and a Poem on *Leander* (17). I do not believe his Translation of *Quintus Smyrnæus*, in Verse, was ever published. He speaks of it in the Five hundred eighty fourth Page of the third Volume of his *Statius*.

[*F*] *He composed Translations out of* Spanish *and* French.] I do not know, that he translated any thing out of the latter Language, besides the Memoirs of *Philip de Comines*, which he put into *Latin*. He had much more Inclination for the *Castilian* Tongue, as he has shewn in several Places; and Don *Nicolas Antonio* was not ignorant of the Praises, which he bestowed on the *Spanish* Books (18). I know but two *Spanish* Books, translated into *Latin* by *Barthius*; one is the *Celestina*, the Author whereof was unknown to him; the other is the *Continuation of the Diana* of *Montemajor*. Here is the Title, which he gave to the Translation of the *Celestina*. *Pornoboscodidascalus Latinus. De lenonum, lenarum, conciliatricum, servitiorum, dolis, veneficiis, machinis plusquam diabolicis; de miseriis juvenum incautorum qui florem ætatis amoribus inconcessis addicunt, de miserabili singulorum periculo & omnium interitu*, at *Francfort* 1624. He added some Notes to his Translation. The *Spanish* Author of That Work, or of That Tragi-Comedy, was *Rodericus Cota*. The Continuation of the *Diana* of *Montemajor*, translated by *Barthius*, is the Work of *Gaspar Gil-polo*. *Barthius*'s Translation was printed, at *Hanow*, in 1625, under the Title of *Erotodidascalus, seu Nemoralium libri V*. Mr *Baillet* says (19), That he also translated the *Pornodidascale* of *Aretin* into *Latin*. Without doubt, it is the same Book, which *Daumius* speaks of in these Terms: " Reliqua " quæ ------ Barthius publicavit ex indiculo Colloquio P. Aretini *de las Damas* ex Hispanico ab " ipso translato, & à nobis recuso nuper, adjecto cognoscere poteris (20). ---- *The rest* ---- *which* " *Barthius published from* Aretin's *instructive Dialogues,* " *On Ladies of Pleasure, translated by him out of* " Spanish, *and revised by us, will appear from the Work* " *itself here subjoined.*" You may conclude from hence, that This *Latin* Translation of *Aretin*, was not made from the Original, but from a *Spanish* Translation.

[*G*] *He resolved early to disengage himself intirely from the World*, ----- *to apply himself only to his Salvation.*] Having said, that his Mother had some Fore-sight of her Death, three Years before she died,

and that he survived That good Mother eighteen Years, in perfect Health, except a Weakness in his Sight (21), he adds; " Cupio autem cœpta scribendi " laboribus demum aliquando defungi, & totum me " Christo dedicare, quam rem sæpius jam orsum habetenus infinita bellorum & bellicorum tumultuum " exactionumque impedimenta hactenus suspenderunt. " ----- *My Desire is to quit, at last, all farther* " *Thoughts of writing, and dedicate myself intirely* " *to* Christ, *which I have already very often attempted, but have hitherto been prevented by the Interruption of Wars, and Tumults of Wars, and* " *other Hardships.*" To know at what Time he spoke thus, one need only remember, that his Mother died in the Year 1622. See the end of the Remark [*A*].

[*H*] *His Thoughts were deeply employed on Eternity.*] Here is the Testimony, which *Theophilus Spizelius* has given of him: " Sacrum nimirum ad Deum " sinceramque pietatem Barthius meditabatur accessum, plurimis piè literatorum ac Deo sacratorum " hominum exemplis incitatus. Quo de imprimis " testatur insigne SOLILOQUIORUM OPUS, extremis vitæ temporibus à Barthio publicatum, flagrantissimis ad Deum suspiriis oppido plenum, & " vel Augustino scriptore dignum, quod etiam hemiplecticus quotidiè revolvere, & per priorum meditationum vestigia denuò cogitationes suas cœlo " immittere, consuevit; quinimò divinum amorem, " quem intimis fibris semel imbibisset, continuis " precum ejaculationibus animum jugiter atque roborandum putavit, quousque è sacræ pariter ac literariæ solitudinis diversorio, anno ævi nostri octavo & quinquagesimo, ætatis vero septuagesimo primo emigravit (22). ----- *Barthius was studying* " *to make his Approaches to God, and true Piety,* " *being incouraged to it by the Examples of many of* " *the piously Learned, who had devoted themselves to* " God. *This his admirable Piece of* Soliloquies *particularly demonstrates, being published by him in* " *his latter Years, and abounding with the most fervent Ejaculations to* God, *worthy of* St Augustin " *himself, and which* Barthius, *though lame of one* " *Side with the Palsy, used every Day to turn over,* " *and by pursuing the Thread of his former Meditations, to send his Thoughts again to Heaven. He* " *made it his Business to nourish and strengthen incessantly that divine Love he had established in his* " *Heart, by the continual Exercise of Prayer, 'till he* " *departed from this sacred and learned Retreat in* " *the Fifty eighth Year of our Century, and the Seventy first of his Age.*"

[*I*] *The Manuscript Works he left behind him.*] *Daumius* has informed the Public, that there were found, among this Author's *Adversaria* (23); some *Notes*, and third Volumes of his *Adversaria* (23); some *Notes*, and *Glossaries* on the Writers of *Palestine*, published by *James Bongars*: *Benedictus Paulinus Petrocorius de Vitâ* S. Martini, *&* Paullinus Pelleus *cum* Tertulliani Jona, Juretique *& Barthii animadversionibus*; XXI Books of *Epigrams*: XII Books of *Anacreontics*: *The Zodiac of the Christian Life*, corrected and enlarged in several Places: several other *Poems*, most of which had never been printed, and the rest had been corrected: *Glossaries* on *Valerius Maximus*, and on the *Epistles* of *Pliny the Younger*. *Daumius* declares, that, if the Cruelty of the Times, entirely prejudiced against Literature, will permit it, and if, by the Liberality of some *Mecenas*, any Benefit may accrue by

it

(r) Spizelius, in Templo Honoris reservato, pag. 383.

(d) Witte, Diarium, Biogr.

(21) Barth. Commentar. in 'statium. Tom. II pag. 826.

(22) Spizel. Templo Honoris, p. 384, 385.

(23) Daumius, in Pref. Comment. Barthii in Statium.

printed [K], those which were burnt together with his House [L], and those which he is known to have wrote, but are lost no body can tell how [M]: I say all these Works make such a prodigious bulk, that it is scarce possible to conceive they could be performed by one Man. I do not know whether any, who have lived to turn grey in the dust of a Registry Office, ever wrote so much as this Author has done. There is a Story published, which had better have been suppressed, concerning a Tour, it is pretended, he made into *Holland* with a fair Lady [N]. Some learned Men have complained of the printing of That Story,

(24) Id Ib.

it to his Heirs, all those Works may one Day be printed. *Si diritas permittat temporum politioribus heu Musis prorsus insensrum, fructusque si aliquis Mæcenatum benignitate ad relictos τῦ μακαρίτε hæredes sit redundaturus* (24). I have not heard, that any of those Manuscripts have ever stirred out of his Heirs Hands, except the *Paulinus Petrocorius de Vita S. Martini*, which *Daumius* took Care to get printed in the Year 1681. The Booksellers will not catch at that Bait as they did formerly, when *Barthius* touched their Honour, by declaring, in a Preface, that he had a very great Number of Books, which waited only for the Courtesy of the Booksellers, to appear in public (25); and that they should be printed, as soon as he could meet with an industrious Bookseller to undertake it (26). This produced a very speedy Effect, as to some of his Works, and a flower one as to others: but, nevertheless, most of these Books were printed, when that Preface was mentioned in the *Bibliotheque Universelle*. Let us see in what Terms it was done; the Passage deserves to be set down; it contains a Criticism somewhat satirical, but grounded on Reason. " There is a Preface before it, mentioning " the Titles of some Books, which the Author pro- " mised to bestow on the Public, but few of which " have been printed (27), because he found no Book- " sellers, as he himself observes (28), who had the " same Zeal, as himself, for the Advancement of Li- " terature. But, if all his Works were like this, it " it may be pronounced, that we have lost little " more than a great many Quotations of no great " Use. Not but that there might be some good " Things in them, as well as in this: But they are, " as it were, hid under so great a Number of Pas- " sages of the Ancients, that it requires a great " deal of Patience to find them out (29)."

(25) "equentur deinceps, uti quidem Typographorum comitas erit. *Bartho. Præf. in Rutili Itinerar.* it is dated Octob. 24, 1622.

(26) Expectant Editionem, si follertem Typographum nacti fuerimus. *Id. ib.*

(27) It is certain that the best part of them is printed.

(28) He does not observe this in that Preface.

[K] *Those which were printed.*] I will only here take notice of the chief of them: A great Volume in Folio, entituled *Adversaria*, divided into sixty Books. *Quibus ex universa antiquitatis serie omnis generis loci tam Gentilium quam Christianorum scriptorum illustrantur & emendantur, cum ritum, morum, legum, formularumque observationes & elucidationes, cum undecim indicibus, vii auctorum, iv rerum.* At *Frankfort*, 1624. The Author has shewn in it a surprising Degree of Memory, Reading, and Learning; it is pity we cannot say as much of his Clearness, and Judgment. He left two other Volumes of *Adversaria* of as large a Size, without reckoning his having revised and corrected the first. *De quo Adversariorum Tomo secundo jam tertio, aterque enim jam peractus est, primo etiam recensito in iis & amotis nebulis quas illi induxere livor voluit* (30). The whole contains a Hundred and eighty Books. Let us proceed to some other Titles. *Galli confessoris Christianæ doctrinæ compendium, seu forma Constantiæ habitus; C. Barthius recensuit & Animadversionum libros adjecit;* Francfort, 1623, in 8vo, *Pburbadius contra Arianos cum animadversionibus. Guil. Britonis libri Philippidos cum notis. Claudiani Ecdicii Mamerti de Statu Animæ, libri III. cum Animadversionibus;* Cygneæ, 1655, in 8vo. *Æneæ Gazæi Dialogus de Immortalitate Animarum, cum Zacharia Mityleneæo Philosopho Christiano, Græcè & Latinè,* Leipsic, 1655, in 4to. *Barthius* published a new Translation of *Æneas Gazæus*, as to *Zachary*, both which Works he adorned with Notes. *Soliloquia rerum Divinarum;* Cygneæ, 1654, in 4to. A large Volume of Notes on *Claudian*, printed in the Year 1650, in 4to. And three large Volumes upon *Statius*, printed in 1664, in 4to. He was not well pleased with That Edition of *Claudian*, because the Printer had not made use of a good Corrector (31). It is pity that there is no Table of Matters, nor, in general, any Index. His Commentaries on *Statius* are very free from that Fault.

(29) Bibl. Universelle, Tom. V, p. 310, in the Extract of Rutilius's Itinerary.

(30) Barthius in Statium, Tom. I. pag. 110. *See also the Preface of Daumius.*

(31) Id. ib. pag. 454.

[L] *Those, which were burnt, together with his House.*] It was a Country-house, which was burnt by the Carelesness of the Farmer, or some such other Person, who inhabited it. " Cum villa nostra urbana " non bello, non latronum manu, sed perfidi incolæ " temeritate conflagravit (32). ——— When my " Country-house was burnt down, not by the Misfor- " tune of War, or the Violence of Robbers, but by the " Audaciousness of the treacherous Inhabitant." It is, without doubt, That which *Daumius* calls *Incendium Sellerbusanum*, which happened in the Year 1636. " Etiam nonnulla flammis, *says be* (33), incendio " Sellerhusano, anno M.DC.XXXVI. abjumta periere. " ——— Some also perished in the Flames, in the " Fire of Sellerhuse, in 1636." By this Misfortune, *Barthius* lost his *Index Appulejanus* (34), all that he had wrote on *Tertullian* (35), his *Index* on *Thucydides,* &c. " In quo scriptore (Thucydide) per bellicos hos " trienniales motus & excessiones ingens damnum ac- " cepimus, *indicem* enim tam in auctorem quam Scho- " liasten (qui recentior tamen est quam vulgo atten- " tur) confeceramus, is cum parte Bibliothecæ periit " (36). Flammæ ——— ingens scrinium manu " mea scriptis chartis effertum, simul abstulerunt: & " sic perierunt mihi multa juvenilia & puerilia scripta " (37). ——— *In which Writer* (Thucydides) *by the* " *Disturbances and Removes, which War has occasioned* " *for three Years together, I have met with great* " *Loss; for I had made an Index, both to the Author* " *and his Scholiast,* (*who is much more modern, than* " *be is generally esteemed,*) *this perished with part of* " *my Library. The Flames ——— destroyed a great Desk* " *full of my Manuscript Works all together; and so* " *went many of my childish and youthful Productions.*" He says, that his Library had been already twice plundered, when the Fire made that new Havock. *Adesse Bibliothecæ non pessumis miris modis duabus vastationibus depopulatæ, & uno incendio vix dimidiatim ereptæ* (38).

(32) Id. Ib. Tom. III. p. 1398. *He had said, in the ninth Page of the first Tome, Flammæ non ab hoste sed domestico scelere meæ turn manssoni injeciæ. ——— My House was set on fire, not by hostile, but domestic Wickedness.*

(33) Ibid. &c. p. 1398. *of the third Volume, where he joys, Notæ nostræ in integrum seri Tertullianum ——— Our Notes upon almost all Tertullian.*

(34) Barth. in Statium, Tom. I. pag. 6. & passim alibi.

[M] *Those, which were lost, no body can tell how.*] *Daumius* says, that, after the Author's Death, they looked in vain for his Commentary on St *Augustin De Civitate Dei,* his Book *De Superstitionibus Veterum,* his Treatise *De dubiis Scriptoribus,* his *Characters,* and several other Writings of that Nature. *Barthius* quotes very often the Books I have just now mentioned, and gives an advantageous Idea of them. It is very likely, considering the Nature of their Subjects, that they were none of the worst of his Works. He had begun a great many others, to which he referred his Readers, as if they had been already printed. See the *Index Autorum* of his *Statius,* at the Word *Barthius.*

(36) Tom. M, p. 305.

(37) Ibid. Tom. I. pag. 9.

(38) Ibid. Tom. II, p. 372.

[N] *There is a Story published, concerning a Tour, it is pretended, he made into* Holland, *with a fair Lady.*] Mr *Colomies* mentions it on the Authority of *Isaac Vossius*. He was very much to blame to print such Stories, which he had only met with in Conversation. Every body knows, that they, who like to entertain a Company pleasantly, are furnished with a great many little Stories, to which they add such Circumstances as they think proper, to make them more singular and diverting. They would not take this Liberty, if they knew, that what they say would be printed. However it be, the Story runs thus: " Mr *Vossius* ——— told me one Day, that *Barthius,* " being come from *Germany* to *Harlem,* to see *Scriveri- " us,* he brought a very fine Lady along with him; " and that *Scriverius* had no sooner seen her, but " he found the means to make *Barthius* drunk, that " he might entertain the Lady with more Liberty; " which succeeded according to his Desire. Never- " theless, he could not do it so well, but that *Bar- " thius,* being recovered from his Drink, had some " Suspicion of what had past; which increased in such " a manner, that he carried the Lady back again in
a great

Story, and pronounced it a Fable [O]. *Barthius* had two Wives (e). He married the first in the Year 1630, and the second in the Year 1644. The first died in the Year 1643, without bringing him any Children. The second bore him a Son and three Daughters, and survived him (f). He happened to be four times in besieged Towns, and came off without any other loss, than only once of his Cloaths and Arms (g). He complained of having been ill used by *Vossius* [P]. He took *Scaliger*'s Part very warmly against *Scioppius* [Q], but was no Friend to the Learned *Reinesius*. The latter had discovered too many of his Faults, not to make him angry [R]. It was impossible that an Author, who wrote so many things, and with so much Precipitation, could escape the judicious Censure of *Reinesius*. It has been pretended, that it was not always for want of Memory, that

" a great Rage, and suffered her to be drowned in
" the *Rhône* (39)." It must not be denied, that *Bar-*
" *thius* had a bad Reputation, as to his Morals. One
" of his best Friends confesses it; but he maintains,
" that this was ill-grounded. " De moribus quæ in-
" vidi nugati sunt quorumque causa ego ignotum meo
" malo abhorrebam, rem aliter quindecennali hac cum
" eo conversatione comperi. Adeo quicquid de eo
" dixerunt scripserantque ego hactenus prorsus credere
" abnui, cujus intima nescio an æque uli patuerint
" (40). - - - - - - - *As to the Vices, which have been*
" *maliciously objected to him, and on account of which*
" *I had an ill Opinion of him before I knew him, to*
" *my own Disadvantage, I have found, by fifteen Years*
" *Conversation with him, that he is intirely clear*
" *of them. So that I have hitherto absolutely contra-*
" *dicted all the Stories, which have been told, or*
" *wrote, about him, and I believe no body knows*
" *him so intimately as I do.*"
[O] *Some learned Men have complained of the print-*
ing of that Story, and pronounced it a Fable.] See here what *Morhofius* has said of it : " Quibus (Colomesii
" opusculis) adjicitur libellus Gallico sermone, cui ti-
" tulus *A Collection of Particulars*, in quibus multa de
" eruditis familiariter à Vossio aliisque suppeditata,
" laudato semper autore, vir ille effusivit, quæ insig-
" nis sane temeritas fuit. Multa tamen in his sunt
" mendacia, quale illud de Casparo Barthio horren-
" dum, qui contubinam suam Rheno suffocaverit,
" quod ejus cum Scriverio amores deprehenderit (41).
" - - - - - - *To which* (Colomesius's Works) *is added*
" *a small Piece in French, entituled*, A Collection
" *of Particulars, wherein, with the highest Indiscre-*
" *tion, he blabbed out several Stories, familiarly told*
" *by Vossius, and others, of learned Men, always re-*
" *membering to name his Author. Among these are*
" *a great many Lies, such as that horrid one about*
" *Gasper Barthius's drowning his Mistress in the*
" Rhine, *on account of an Intrigue he had discovered*
" *between her and Scriverius.*"
[P] *He complained of being ill used by* Vossius.] Few Persons had cause to make the like Complaint ; for never was so learned a Man, as *Vossius*, more complaisant or modest to those he censured. However, let us see *Barthius*'s Complaint at length. " Quo loco vir doctiff. (42)
" pulcrè etiam de *Lutatio* judicat doctum esse lectu-
" que dignum Exegeten, præter quidem glossemata.
" Sanè longè melius & compertius, quam nuper Jo-
" annes Gerhardus Vossius, qui Lutatium ex Servio
" & Higinio compositum dicere ausus est maximam
" partem. Qui doctissimus homo cum alio nos loco
" perperam (ut clara res est, & demonstratam jam
" no..s alibi) ineptiarum & absurditatis, nunquam à
" nobis læsus, & ab invidia planeque egregiè ineptis
" Thrasunculis incitatus, insimulare ausus sit, meritò
" utriusque notæ hic habebitur, cum ea Commenta-
" riis Lutatianis insint, quorum nec centesimam par-
" tem Servianæ & Higinianæ Commentationes vin-
" dicare possint. Idem præstantissimus vir incogitate
" eodem loco scribit Lutatium à Lindebrogio primum
" editum (43). - - - - - - *In, which Place That learned*
" *Man also judges favourably of* Lutatius, *that his*
" *Comment and Glosses are full of Learning, and*
" *worth reading. And, indeed, much more truly and*
" *justly, than* John Gerard Vossius, *who boldly af-*
" *firmed, that* Lutatius *had borrowed the greatest part*
" *of his Performance from* Servius *and* Higinius. *This*
" *most learned* Vossius *has also, in another place, with*
" *equal Injustice,* (as *I have demonstrated elsewhere,)*
" *taken the Liberty to accuse me, who never offended*
" *him, of Impertinence and Absurdity, on the Instiga-*
" *tion of some envious Boasters, who are themselves*
" *remarkably impertinent ; by which he has, deserved-*

" *ly, drawn upon himself both those Accusations, since*
" Servius *and* Higinius's *Commentaries cannot lay*
" *claim to a hundredth part of what is contained in*
" *those of* Lutatius. *The same excellent Man has also*
" *hastily asserted, in the same Place, that* Lutatius
" *was first published by* Lindebrogius."
[Q] *He took* Scaliger's *Part very warmly against* Scioppius.] Three Books, wrote against that great Man's Enemy, are ascribed to him ; and his Name was found out by way of Anagram, in That of *Tarræus Hebeius Nobilis à Sperga. Resoluto Anagrammate Gasperis Barthii Berolinæi confirmat Excellentissimus Geisserus de Mutatione Nominum. Exemplar. dec.* 1. n. 5.
(44). The first of those three Books is entituled *Cave canem, de Vitâ, Moribus, Rebus gestis, Divinitate Gasparis Scioppii Apostatæ Satyricon*, Hanov. 1612, in 12mo. The second, *Scioppius excellens ; in laudem ejus & sociorum pro Josepho Scaligero & omnibus probis Epigrammatum libri III. ex triginta totis hinc inde collecti.* It is printed with the first. The third, *Amphitheatrum Sapientiæ*, Hanov. 1613, in 8vo. See *Rhodius* in the place which I have quoted, and *Placcius*, in the 262d Page of his *Pseudonymous Writers*.
[R] Reinesius *discovered too many of his Faults not to make him angry.*] They were such Faults as an ingenious Man could not have defended ; they were Faults which deserved Condemnation, which is so much the more shocking and provoking. " A. Cl.
" Barthio quem tu tantum non in cœlum effers, &
" quem sua defensurum esse scribis nihil indigni ini-
" quive expecto, tam licet ipsi in meis, si quando
" lucem adspicient publicam, (lenta autem res est, &
" fortasse incumbent in spongiam, ut olim illius Ajax)
" quàm in ipsius mihi licere visum est experiri ; non
" existimo autem Soli obtocuturum esse. Sunt enim
" pleraque, quæ nunc quidem produxi, adeo certa li-
" quidaque, ut nisi temere litigare velit, ne calamum
" quidem contradicturus mihi tingere debeat. Per-
" pende, quæso, mi carissime NESTERE, ἄντω σπάθας,
" ubicunque ab eo dissentio : maximè verò examina,
" quæ cap. 8, *lib.* 2. quo ejus in Plinium Valerianum,
" dictum Empericum, illas emendationes producun-
" tur, trado & miraberis hominis doctissimi manife-
" stissimas inscitias, frustrationes, & puerilia ταερμά-
" μαλα, audaces etiam conjecturas in autorem non
" intellectum invectas deprehendes magno numero.
" Istas si quis præfractè tueri præfumserit, eum ne
" sani quidem capitis esse dixero ; Barthium autem
" mecum fore & visurum, me quamvis indigno in-
" dice, id quod verum est nullus dubito ———— *I ex-*
" *pect no other than a handsome Behaviour from* Bar-
" thius, *whom you cry up so to the Skies, and affirm*
" *to be about publishing a Defence of his Writings.*
" *He may try the Proof of my Works, if ever they see*
" *the Light, (which will require some time first, and,*
" *perhaps, they may come to the Sponge at last, as*
" *his* Ajax *did)* as *I have done in Respect to his ;*
" *I do not suppose he will rail at the Sun. For a great*
" *many things, I have advanced, are so clear and cer-*
" *tain, that he can never contradict them, except for*
" *the sake of Contradiction. Examine, I beg of you,*
" *my dearest* Nesterus, *without Prejudice, the places*
" *where I differ from him, but especially* cap. 8, lib. 2,
" *where his Emendations on* Pliny Valerianus, *called*
" *the Empiric, are considered. I there shew, and you*
" *will be surprized to see, the most manifest Ignorance,*
" *Mistakes, and childish Notions, and bold Conjectures,*
" *and Misunderstandings of the Author, in great Num-*
" *ber. If any one should obstinately presume to defend*
" *these, I shall think him mad ; but I do not doubt*
" *but* Barthius *will agree with me, and see the Truth,*
" *however unworthy I am to shew it.*" These are the Words of *Reinesius*, in a Letter which he wrote to
Nesterus,

that *Barthius* contradicted himself [S]. It is no wonder his Memory, how strong soever it might be, should often deceive him, considering his method of composing his Books [T]. He made no Collections, and scarce ever corrected what he had once written.

(1ˢᵗ) It is the 6th. *Nesterus*, the Thirty first of *March*, 1638 (45). See also his fifteenth Letter to *Daumius*.

[S] *It has been pretended, that it was not always for want of Memory, that Barthius contradicted himself*] " Some have observed, that, when he gives (46) Baillet, Judgm. Tom. III. pag. 404. " his Judgment, he falls now and then into Contradictions, for want of Memory (46)." *Daumius* pretends, that those, who took notice of that sort of Contradictions, knew nothing of *Barthius*'s Designs. " He wrote, *says he*, all that came into his Mind, " this Day one thing, and to morrow another, on " purpose that, when he should look over them again, " some time or other, those Contradictions might " engage him to examine things more nicely, and " give him a better Opportunity to correct, or con- " firm, what he had written. Memini in publicis a- " licubi Disputationibus diversæ sententiæ ejus loca " exagitata fuisse. Sed auctores scopum scriptoris nescio " an vel per transennam viderint. Novi enim, hoc " consilio, eoque fine, Barthium ea, quæ in mentem " sibi venerant, in chartam conjecisse, etiam diversis " diverso tempore sententiis, ut quandoque ad ea re- " vertenti illa diversitas ampliorem de veritate cogi- " tandi suppeditaret materiam, occasionemque longè " commodiorem retractandi vel stabiliendi quod scrip- " serat. Id quod fine capitis vi Libri undecimi & (4ᵗʰ) Daum. Epist. 14. ad Reinesium, pag 37. " alibi sæpius testatur (47)." See how *Reinesius* has confuted this Apology (48).

[T] *It is no wonder his Memory ———— should fail him, considering his Method of composing his Books.*] We (48) Rein. Epist. 14. ad Daumium, pag. 45. must hear his own Words. " Puto jam tale quid " supra notasse. Non enim potest, ut, nullis peni- " tus rebus adjuti, omnium strictam memoriam ha- " beamus. Omnino enim aliter nos commentamur, " quam solent homines etiam litteratissimi, dum au- " ctores legunt, excerpentes quædam atque ea de- " inde excerpta in Silvam Observationum, eam porro " Silvam in Commentaria redigentes. Nunquam tale " quid factum à nobis est : Sed ut cuique auctori e- " narrando benè facere volumus, arrepto illi Animad- " versiones hoc genus imputamus, solius memoriæ be- " neficio nixi, quam marginalibus nonnunquam prius " Notis instruimus, dum cum libris veterihus Edi- " tiones comparamus. Cætera omnia è calamo flu- " unt elegante & minuto literarum ductu. Nec un- " quam scriptio repetitur : nec ullis lituris cruciatur: " quarum nec decem aliquas hactenus hi Commenta- " rii agnoverint (49). - - - - - - *I think I have before* (49) Barth. in Statyrn. Tom III. pag. 462. " *observed some such thing. For it is impossible for* " *me, who use no sort of Assistance, to have a perfect* " *Memory of every thing. For my Method of comment-* " *ing is quite contrary to that commonly used by the* " *most learned Men, who, in reading Authors, take* " *Notes all along, and then afterwards reduce those* " *Notes into a Collection, and that Collection into* " *Commentaries. I have never done any thing like* " *this : But, as I would do Justice in explaining each* " *Author, I ascribe these sorts of Observation to every* " *one respectively, by the sole Strength of my Memo-* " *ry, which is sometimes first directed by Marginal* " *Notes, made on my comparing the several Editions.* " *Every thing else flows from my Pen in a small and* " *exact Letter. Nor do I ever write any thing over* " *again, or blot out what I have once wrote. These* " *Commentaries have not hitherto met with ten In-* " *stances of this Kind.*" I do not know whether it is right to boast of such a thing ; I think the Public deserves more Respect.

BASINA, Wife of *Childeric* King of *France*, and Mother of the Great *Clovis*, had been married to a King of *Thuringia*. *Childeric* being forced to leave his Dominions, because his Lewdness had so exasperated the People, that he had reason to (a) About the Year 460. fear the worst from them, fled (a) to the King of *Thuringia*. He was received by him with all manner of Respect ; without doubt *Basina*, who was a very beautiful Princess, entertained him admirably well. Experience has always shewn, that those lascivious Princes, who are expelled their Country, do not renounce their Gallantries in the place of their Retreat. *Childeric* was an Example of it: He fell in Love with *Basina* ; and, finding her not cruel, he made no scruple to pursue the matter so far as to enjoy the Wife of that same Friend and good Neighbour, who furnished him with a place of Refuge [A]. He engaged her in so close an Amour, that she could never after quit it. The *French* recalled (b) Gregor. Turon. Hist. Franc. lib. 2. cap. 12. *Childeric* eight Years after they had expelled him (b). *Basina* could not be easy with that Prince's Absence. She left her Husband, and went to *Childeric* ; and, when he asked the cause of her Visit, she answered, ingenuously, that it was her Love of him [B] ; and that if she had known any Prince beyond the Seas, who could have

[A] *Childeric made no scruple - - - - - - to enjoy the Wife of that same Friend - - - - - - who furnished him with a place of Refuge*] There would be ground enough to believe it, though the Historians had not related it. Would *Basina* have run after *Childeric*, if she had not loved him, and talked with him the Pleasures of Love? But we have the Testimony of Historians : These Words are to be found in the Author of the *Atchievements of the Kings of France*, in the seventh Chapter. " Dum fuit in Toringia " cum Basina Regina uxore Bisini Regis ipse Childe- " ricus commixtus est. ———— *While he was in Thu-* " *ringia*, Childeric conversed criminally *with Queen* " Basina, *the Wife of King* Bisinus." *Aimonius* relates the same thing in the eighth Chapter of the first Book, " Dicebatur idem princeps consuetudinem Stu- " prs cum ea habuisse, cum exularet. ———— *The same* " *Prince was said to have continued an adulterous* " *Commerce with her in his Exile.*" *Rorico* is more expressive : I will quote him in the following Remark.

[B] *She answered him ingenuously, that it was her Love of him.*] According to *Gregorius Turonensis*, in the twelfth Chapter of the second Book of the History of the *French*, the Answer was thus expressed : " I very well know that you are an useful and vali- " ant Man. It is on this account, I am come to " live with you : for, be assured, that if I had " known of any Body, in the Provinces beyond the " Seas, who could have been more useful to me " than yourself, I would have gone and desired to " have lived with him." The Abbot of *Marolles*, who thus translated the Text of *Gregorius Turonensis*, adds a Remark to advertise us, that *Basina*'s Meaning, in this Discourse, *is equivocal*. This is not unlikely : I do not believe that *Childeric* had given any proofs of his Military Valour in *Thuringia* : So that the Valour, which *Basina* spoke of, might be of another nature, and more useful to a Queen than a Martial one ; and I am tempted to believe, that, both in *Gregorius Turonensis*, and in *Rorico*, we ought to read *virilitatem & viriliorem*, instead of *utilitatem & utiliorem*. The Equivocation will still remain. *Basina* answers, *I know your Virility, and that y-u are a very brave Man.* Those words are better connected than the following. *I know yes are an useful and valiant Man.* Let no body object the Immodesty of these words, *I know your Virility* ; is there not as much in a Woman's saying to her Gallant, *I know your usefulness?* However it be, Here is the Latin of *Gregorius Turonensis*: " His regnantibus si- " mæ!

BASINA. 669

have been more agreeable to her, she would have gone to him. *Childeric* was charmed with this discourse, married *Basina*, and had a Son by her, who was a very brave Prince, and embraced the Christian Faith. If this Woman's Conduct was worse than That of *Helena* [C], That of *Childeric*, all Circumstances rightly considered, was not better than That of *Paris*. Father *le Cointe*'s excuses are but very trifling [D]. The Author of the *Galantries of the Kings of France*, relates the Visions of *Basina*'s Bridegroom better than Mr *de Cordemoi* [E].

Since

(1) Apud du Chesne, Tom. I. pag. 696.

(2) Ibid. pag. 727.

" mul Basina relicto viro suo ad Childericum venit.
" Qui cum sollicite interrogaret quâ de causâ ad
" eum de tantâ regione venisset, respondisse fertur,
" *Novi*, inquit, *utilitatem tuam quod sis valde stre-*
" *nuus, ideoque veni ut habitem tecum. Nam no-*
" *veris, si in transmarinis partibus aliquem cogno-*
" *vissem utiliorem te, expetissem utique cohabitationem*
" *ejus.* At ille gaudens eam sibi in conjugio copu-
" lavit." The anonymous Author of the *Gesta Regum Francorum* (1), *Fredegarius* (2), and the Monk *Rorico*, relate *Basina*'s Answer in the same manner as *Gregorius Turonensis*: only *Rorico* has explained it much better, and expresly said, that the Discourse of that Woman was full of Lewdness. Which is so far from weakening my Conjecture concerning *virilitatem & viriliorem*, that it strongly confirms it. These are the words of *Rorico*: " Basina quoque
" Sisini regis uxor, apud quem latuisse praemonstra-
" vimus Childericum, saepius relicto viri thoro con-
" sortium nostri Regis est experta. Quamobrem &
" eum nec multo post in Franciam est sequuta, cu-
" piens loco uxoris habitare cum eo. Quam Chil-
" dericus cum insperate conspexisset, & ad quos usus
" de tam longinqua provincia ad eum properasset
" inquireret, illa postposito pudore muliebri, ut erat
" nimis luxuriosa, tale fertur dedisse responsum:
" quoniam novi utilitatem tuam & pulchritudinem,
" & quod sis habilis & strenuus, è domo veni ut
" habitem tecum, nam si in extremis terrae finibus
" utiliorem te cognovissem, & hunc nihilominus ex-
" petissem. Complacuit regi mulieris sermo facetus, & eam gaudens sibi sociavit in uxorem (3).
" ------ Basina also, the Wife of King Sisinus,
" with whom, we have before shewn, that Childeric
" had taken refuge, often left her Husband's Bed to
" share that of our King. For which reason, not
" long afterwards, she followed him into France
" desiring to live with him as his Wife. Childeric
" being surprized at so unexpected a Visiter, and de-
" siring to know the Cause of her Undertaking so long
" a Journey, she, laying aside all female Modesty, as
" being of too amorous a Constitution, returned this
" Answer: It was because I know you useful and even
" necessary in the furthermost Parts of the Earth, I would
" have gone to him. The King was much taken with
" her pleasant Answer, and married her with much
" Satisfaction." This whole Relation of *Rorico* shews, that this Woman did not compliment *Childeric* as a brave Warrior, but as a compleat Champion in Love.

(3) Roric. de Gestis Francorum, lib. 1. pag. 802, in the first Vol. of du Chesne's Edition.

[C] *Her Conduct was worse than That of Helena.*]
To give every Body their Due, I ought to say here, that this pretty Comparison is none of my own; I find it in a modern Writer (4). " Basina, *says he*, *the Mo-*
" *ther of Clovis*, was not contented to prostitute
" her Honour to *Childeric* I, who fled for Prote-
" ction to her first Husband *Bisinus*, or *Basinus*,
" King of *Thuringia*; but did worse than *Helena*,
" who at least would be carried away, whereas this
" Woman came into *France* of her own Accord,
" and with so much confidence, that she durst tell
" *Childeric*, that, if she had known a braver Man,
" and worthier of her Love, she would have gone
" to him to the end of the World."

(4) In la Mothe le Vayer, Tom. X. pag. 342. Letter 43.

[D] *Father* le Cointe's *Excuses are but very trifling.*] He takes it ill, that *Aimonius* should say, that *Childeric* married *Basina* before the Death of her first Husband (5). He pretends, that *Aimonius* is the first who said it, and loaded the Birth of *Clovis* with such an Ignominy. He adds, that this Historian is not to be credited, considering the Distance of the Time he lived in, and his Prepossession against the *Merovingians*. He brings two other Reasons, one that the *Germans*, who were the Stem of the *French*, did not permit Adultery; the other, that, if *Childeric*

(5) Le Cointe Annal. Ecclest. Francorum, Tom. I. pag. 94.

had married another Man's Wife, he would have exposed himself to the same Danger, which forced him to leave his Kingdom eight Years before. From all which Considerations he chuses rather to believe, that *Basina*, not being able to endure the ill Treatment she received from her Husband, fled into *France*, and that she did not marry *Childeric* before she had certain News of her Husband's Death. He remarks, that others say she was divorced, and that therefore, under Paganism, nothing hindered her from marrying a second Husband. He refers us to *Robertus Cenalis* (6). Let us examine a little into this Dispute. In the first place, I say, that, if the Silence of the Authors, who preceeded *Aimonius*, is a good reason, it must no longer be said, that the King of *Thuringia* abused his Wife, or that he divorced her, or that he was dead before *Childeric* married her. These are Facts mentioned by none of the ancient Authors. In the second place, does not *Gregorius Turonensis* say, that *Basina* left her Husband, and that her first Answer to *Childeric* pleased him so well that he married her? Is not this almost saying in express terms, that she was *Childeric*'s Wife before her first Husband was dead? In the third place, the Passage out of *Tacitus*, which Father *le Cointe* alledges to prove, that the *Germans* disapproved Adultery, shews, that *Childeric* was exempted from the General Law (7); for whatever was the real Motive of the Woman's coming to him, she declared it was grounded on that Prince's Valour: Besides, the Punishment of Adultery was left to the Husband's Choice, and *Basina* was no longer in her Husband's Country. Not to observe, that Laws are seldom made for Sovereigns. Lastly, *Childeric* had nothing to fear from the Mutiny of his Subjects upon this account; he married a Stranger who was come to seek him: What harm could this do the *French*? I own that they had revolted eight Years before; but then they were alarmed, one for his Daughter, another for his Sister, &c. for *Childeric*, at that time, gave himself up to debauchery in a very violent Manner (8). The Affair of *Basina* did not at all concern them; would they have ever thought of breaking the Reconciliation by espousing the Quarrel of a King of *Thuringia*?

(6) Lib. 1. de Re Gallica, Periocha 12.

(7) *This is the Passage of Tacitus; Severa illic matrimonia, nec ullum morum partem magis laudaveris, nam prope soli barbarorum singulas uxoribus contenti sunt. exceptis admodum paucis qui, non libidine, sed ob Nobilitatem, pluribus nuptiis ambiuntur. Paucissima tam numerosâ gente adulteria quorum poena praesens & Maritis permissa. Ibere Marriages are very first, and no part of the Customs is more commendable. For they are almost the only People who content themselves with one Wife, except only to some few, who are indulged with more than one, and that not for their lust, but their Nobility. Adulteries are very rare among them, and it is always left immediately to the Husband to be punished at the Discretion of the Husband.*

(8) *When they were reproached for their Seditions, they justified their Reason, Quia fine lege adulterabatur, his not res. Bic ub is unjustly violated or Duplices. De Gestis Francor. l. 7.*

[E] *The Author of the Galantries of the Kings of France, relates the Visions of Basina's Bridegroom better than Mr de Cordemoi.*] These are his words:
" It is reported, that having intreated *Childeric* not
" to lie with her on the Wedding-Night, she sent
" him three times into the Court-Yard of his Palace,
" desiring him to observe, without fear, the Visions
" which should appear before him; and that, by her
" occult Science, he was entertained the first time with
" Unicorns, Lions, and Leopards; the second time
" with Bears and Wolves; and the third time with
" Dogs and Cats; from whence he concluded, that
" those various Animals presaged the Diversity of the
" Manners and Customs of the Race, which was to
" proceed from their Marriage. It will be so much
" the more readily believed, that this report is only
" a Fable invented at pleasure, if it be observed,
" that the ardent Passion, which that Queen had for
" *Childeric*, would, in all probability, never have
" permitted her to lose so much time, which she
" knew how to pass more pleasantly, than to lie in
" Bed alone, while her Lover was entertained with
" those pretended Apparitions (9)." It cannot be denied, but that the Reason he alledges to confute that old Story has some force; but it would have had much more, if *Basina*'s forwardness itself did not make it too probable, that the Ardour of her Passion had already received some considerable Relief. After what had passed between them, neither *Childeric* nor she were like to pay much regard to the Marriage Ceremony, or to defer their Embraces till the Nuptial Solemnity had authorized them: And for that reason *Basina* might well let him rest till the following Night. Mr *de Cordemoi* pretends, that *Basina*

(9) Ga'antries of the Kings of France, Tom. I. pag. 5.

was

BASINA.

Since the first Edition of this Work, I have read what Father *Daniel* has published, against those, who say, that *Childeric* was expelled by his Subjects, that he was recalled at the end of eight Years, and that the Queen of *Thuringia* came after him, &c. This Author thinks, *That what* Gregorius Turonensis *has wrote upon it, is nothing more than an Abstract, or Abridgment, of some Romance current in his time* (c); and that the Visions, Childeric *is pretended to have had on his Wedding Night, and which have been added to the Story of* Gregorius Turonensis, *have the Air of a Romance*, as well as the rest (d). I shall mention the Quarrel commenced with *Pâquier*, and the Answer returned to his Criticism [F]: From this Remark, it will appear, that Disputes occasion many Faults to be committed, as well of the Heart, as of the Understanding.

(c) *Father Daniel, Dissert. II, on the History of France, pag. 425, Edition of Paris, 1696.*
(d) *Id ibid. pag. 426.*

[F] *I shall mention the Quarrel commenced with* Pâquier, *and the Answer returned to his Criticism.*] Let us first relate *Pâquier's* Words: " Our ancient " Writers place *Clovis* among the Legitimate, but do " not consider, that, in their Account of his Life, they " affirm the quite contrary. They all agree in this, " that *Childeric*, having been expelled the Kingdom " for his Extortions and Cruelties, retired to *Thu-* " *ringia*, where, having been honourably received by " the King, he fell in Love with his Wife Queen " *Basina*: insomuch, that being afterwards recalled " by the *French*, he carried her away, and married " her, violating thereby the Law of Nations, and of " Hospitality; and yet the Great *Clovis* was born of " that Marriage (11)." Let us see, in the next place, the Censure of Father *Garasse*: He says, " *That* Pâ- " *quier* adding something of his own to the fabulous " Report of the ancient Chroniclers, *sets forth, that* " *Childeric*, having fled for shelter to the King of " *Thuringia*, fell in Love with his Wife, and ravished " her, and carrying her into *France* married her in " contempt of every Thing sacred (12)." He goes on thus (13), " *Master* Pâquier might have despised " such Dreams, and learned from *Paul Æmilius*, " and *Gregorius Turonensis*, the falsity of this Narra- " tion; and the Sieur *Du Pleix* has related it very judi- " ciously in the Life of *Childeric* —— (14). The an- " cient Chroniclers of *France* never judged or dream- " ed, that *Clovis* was a Bastard, for having married " *Basina*, or any other *Thuringian* Woman; for if " he married *Basina*, he might have learned of the " *French* Historians, that she came herself into *France*, " after the Death of her Husband the King of *Thu-* " *ringia*, and married *Childeric* her second Husband, " from which true and lawful Marriage *Clovis* was " born." Let us pass to the Answers returned to *Garasse*. First he was censured for having opposed *Gregorius Turonensis* to Mr *Pâquier*, *who yet* —— *forms his Doubts on that Author's Words* (15). They were quoted and confirmed by the Testimony of *Aimonius* — *who seems in some things to go farther than he*; for he remarks, that *Basina* forsook her Husband, *Priori objecto viro* (16). Then to the Testimony of those two Historians was added That of *Nicolles-Gilles*. These are his Words, in the sixteenth Page of the Life of *Childeric*: " During the time that *Childeric* " was with *Basinus*, King of *Thuringia*, he fell in " Love with his Wife, whose name was *Basina*; " and after he was recalled to his Kingdom, the said " Queen *Basina*, who doted very much on him, " forsook the said *Basinus*, King of *Thuringia*, her " Lord and Husband, and came to *Childeric*, who " forgetting the former Kindnesses which he had " received, married her, by whom he had *Clovis* " the first Christian King of *France* (17)." It was observed, that *Richard* of *Vassebourg* authorizes this Opinion in his Antiquities of the *Belgic Gaul*, and that *all our modern Historians follow it*. But it was thought sufficient to quote *Belle-Forest*, who said, " That *Childeric* determined to marry, but in so do- " ing he appeared very ungrateful to his Host, the " King of *Thuringia*, whose Wife he debauched and " married, without troubling himself for the wrong " done to *Basinus*, or the Reproach that he might " receive for it (18)." At the Conclusion it was said, that all the Authors, who have been quoted, " are as authentic, and judicious as your (19) Logi- " cian *Du Pleix*, who lent you his Whim in this " Passage, to authorize your want of Judgment." The mistake was not forgotten, which *Garasse* made, when he said, that *Clovis* married *Basina* (20). It was called both " an impious and malicious Igno- " rance; for by that means he would make the " first Christian King of *France* more abominable " than those brutish *Ethiopians*, who, as S: *Jerom* " says against *Jovinian*, defiled their Mothers Bed " without any Distinction (21)." Instances of the like Abominations were quoted there, with many Exaggerations, and long Declamations.

This Dispute shews us part of the Corruptions, which prevail in most Writings of this Nature. The Apologist passes over one of the Faults which had been censured: He does not justify *Pâquier*, nor does he own, that he was rightly accused as to that Article; I mean the Rape of *Basina*. Our ancient Chroniclers have not mentioned it, and therefore *Pâquier* aggravated *Childeric's* Ingratitude: he made Additions, which were both fabulous and scandalous. The Authority of *Gregorius Turonensis* might well be alledged against him, and nevertheless his crafty Apologist supposed, that this Historian had only been alledged, in relation to the other parts of *Basina's* Adventures, and on that Supposition founded the most insulting Reproaches. Here are already three great Corruptions; not to acknowledge That Part of the Remarks of a Critic, which is good and just; to dissemble That, which is favourable to him in his Quotations; and to apply intirely, with much noise, to That only which may be turned into a disadvantageous Sense. Here is another Irregularity: *Garasse* censured some Faults, and committed others in his Censure. *Gregorius Turonensis* was not and against him in different Respects; he made no distinction, but quoted him in a general manner, and placed him between *Æmilius* and *Du Pleix*. Ought he not to have given him the first Rank? He perplexed himself wretchedly about a pretended Marriage of *Clovis* with *Basina*. This was done heedlessly: It appears plainly, that a Hurry of Mind, and a Distraction common enough among Authors, made him write contrary to what he thought; the Sequel of his Discourse evidently shews he did not believe that *Clovis* was the Husband of *Basina*. Yet *Pâquier's* Apologist falls violently upon that Passage: he takes it to be a capital Crime: His Zeal for the first Christian King of the *French* grows warm, and he calls the Figures of Rhetoric to his Assistance. Is this to act honestly? His Adversary had shewn him an Example of a like Corruption; for he had very wrongly armed himself with the Appearance of a great Zeal for the Honour of the Nation, on account of their first Christian King. He had preferred a Kind of Impeachment for a Crime of State, very unjustly, since, except the Rape, *Pâquier* had only followed our ancient Histories, and modestly represented their Consequences. How shameful is it, that Authors should be suffered to take the Liberty to engage Sovereign Princes in their petty Quarrels?

It is much more useful to make Readers sensible of these Faults in Writers, than to criticize Historical Falshoods: and therefore I hope what I have just now observed will meet with Approbation.

(10) *History of France, Tom. I. pag. 128, ex Fredeg. Scholast. cap. 12.*
(11) *Pâquier, Recherch. de la France, lib. 6, c. 44. pag. 588.*
(12) *Garasse Recherch. des Recherch. pag. 60.*
(13) *Id ibid. pag. 61.*
(14) *Id. Ibid. pag 63.*
(15) *Defence of Stephen Pa'quier against the Impostures and Calumnies of Garasse, lib. 2. §. 4. p. 160.*
(16) *Ibid. pag. 161.*
(17) *Ibid. pag 163.*
(18) *Ibid. pag. 164. Nota, the Author observes, that* Ronsard *confirms that Opinion in Book 4. of his Francisade, and that* de Serres *calls that an Illegitimate Marriage.*
(19) *The's Words are spoken to* Garasse.
(20) *Defence of Pasquier against Garasse, p. 166.*
(21) *Ibid. lib. 3. §. 2. p. 426, 427.*

SOME Examples of the Frauds of Authors.

BASNAGE. 671

BASNAGE (BENJAMIN), the Son of *N. Basnage*, Minister of *Norwich* in *England*, and afterwards of *Carentan* in *Normandy*, was born in the Year 1580. He devoted himself to his Father's Profession, and was also Minister of *Carenian*; nay he continued so all his Life, though other more considerable Churches, and particularly that of *Rouen*, desired to have him for their Minister. He considered his first Church as his Spouse, from whom nothing but Death could divorce him; and therefore he would not make use of the liberty, which the National Synod of *Charenton* had given him, in the Year 1623 [*A*]. He assisted in that Synod, as a Deputy of the Province of *Normandy*. In the Year 1631, he was again named by that Province to assist in the National Synod of *Charenton*; but the King forbad him to go thither, and took his Church from him. He was presently after restored to it, and obtained leave to sit in that Synod, as a Deputy of *Normandy*. The Remonstrances, made to his Majesty by that Assembly, produced this good effect. He had given such Proofs of his Capacity and Prudence, that he was elected Moderator of the National Synod of *Alençon* in 1637. This Assembly wanted a Moderator, furnished with many Talents; for they had very nice Matters to handle. The Disputes about Universal Grace had made a great noise; it was to be feared, that a Theological War would break out in the Reformed Churches of *France*, more formidable than a severe Persecution; Mens minds were already very much heated, and prepossessed. This Synod settled Matters on a right foot, to which the Prudence and Conduct of the Moderator very much contributed. He was associated with the Moderator in the National Synod of *Charenton* in the Year 1644. This Assembly deputed him to the Queen-Mother, who gave him some Marks of her Esteem. He had a great number of Disputes with the Controvertists; he wrote against the Church of *Rome*, and they against him (*a*). His *Treatise of the Church* was much esteemed (*b*): He undertook a *Work against the indiscreet Votaries of the Holy Virgin*, which remained imperfect. He died at Seventy two Years of Age, in 1652, which was the Fifty first Year of his Ministry. He left two Sons, who made his Name very Illustrious, both upon their own, and their Childrens, account [*B*]. It must not be forgot, that he was deputed to King *James*, and that, by That Prince's leave, he went into *Scotland*, where he did great Service to the Churches in their Temporal Interests. King *James*'s Letter of Leave styles him *Deputy from all the French Churches*. He is often mentioned in the *Synodicon in Galliâ Reformatâ*; but That Work, being in *English*, does not always observe the true Orthography of proper Names [*C*], which sometimes produces Confusion.

(*a*) Lescrivain, and Draconis are the chief who wrote against *bim*.

(*b*) *If I am not mistaken, it was printed at Rochel, in the Year 1612.*

[*A*] *He would not make use of the Liberty of quitting his Church, which was granted him by the Synod of* Charenton, *in* 1623.] The Provincial Synod of *Normandy* had permitted him to leave his Church; That Church had appealed about it to the National Synod, and That Appeal was rejected by the National Synod of *Charenton*, in the Year 1623. However our *Benjamin* did not leave his Church.

[*B*] *He left two Sons, who made his Name very Illustrious, both upon their own, and their Children's, Account.*] The eldest, *ANTONY BASNAGE*, was born in the Year 1610, and followed his Father's Profession, and was Minister at *Bayeux*. He signalized himself by his Constancy and Courage in the last Persecution; the Prison of *Havre de Grace*, into which he was put at the Age of Seventy five Years, did not shake his Resolution. When the Edict of *Nantz* was repealed, he was set at Liberty, and fled into *Holland*: He died at *Zutphen*, in the Year 1681, aged Eighty one Years. He left a Son, whose Name is *SAMUEL BASNAGE*, Sieur *de Flottemanville* (1), who had been Minister with Him of the Church of *Bayeux*, and is at present at *Zutphen*. He is one of the most learned Ministers, who left *France*. He had already published a Book in *Latin* (2), which is a Continuation of the Critical Observations on the Annals of Cardinal *Baronius*, which *Casaubon* had begun. He is now writing an Ecclesiastical History (3). I have wrote the Article of the other Son of *Benjamin Basnage*.

[*C*] *He is often mentioned in the* Synodicon *in* Galliâ Reformatâ, *which does not always observe the true Orthography of proper Names.*] For Example, in the Ninety fourth Page of the second Volume of the *Synodicon in Galliâ Reformatâ*, mention is made of the Deputies of *Charenton, Sainte Mere & le Val de Serre*. It ought to have been said, *Carentan, Sainte Mere Eglise, & le Val de Serre*. In the Seventy fifth Page *Benjamin Basnage* is stiled Minister of *Charenton*; and, in Pages 259, and 274, Minister of *Quarentin*; and, in Page 322, Minister of *Sainte Mere*. It should be *Sainte Mere Eglise*;

and it ought to have been observed, that *Carentan* and *Sainte Mere Eglise* are two Places, which made but one and the same Church among those of the Reformed Religion. They had, indeed, each of them a distinct Place of Worship; but, as one was looked upon as annexed to the other, there was but one Pastor, and one Consistory for both. At Page 89, it is said *the Conference of Constantine*, instead of *the Conference of the Cotentin*. These are Faults of Orthography, which may confound Readers, and make them think, that there were Churches, in *Normandy*, called *Sainte Mere, Charenton*, and *Quarentin*. A Person, who should be employed by Booksellers to make Additions to a Geographical Dictionary, might imagine he had made a considerable Discovery, by finding those three Parishes in a Country, where the Geographers had not yet perceived them. Faults are like Sparks of Fire; That, which is at first but an Alteration of a Letter, becomes sometime a Complication, or Heap of monstrous Falsities. It must be remedied early, *principiis obsta*. Here are also Mistakes of another Nature. The Author of the *Synodicon* makes mention (4) of one *Peter Basnage*, Son of *Anthony*, and Grand-son of *Benjamin*, and says, that this *Peter Basnage* had no Church in the Year 1637. This is a Mistake. *Anthony Basnage* had but two Sons; the eldest called Mr *de Flottemanville*, who was born in the Year 1638. The younger was named *Francis*, and followed the Profession of Arms, and died in the Year 1685. The same Author takes (5) Mr *Basnage*, Minister of *Rotterdam*, to be the Son of *Benjamin Basnage*; but he is only his Grandson. These small Faults, which I find myself obliged to discover for the Instruction of Readers, do not hinder me from believing, that Mr *Quick's* Work (6) is very curious and useful, and that all the Reformed of *France* are very much obliged to him for the Pains he has taken to make such an ample and exact Collection of their Synods, and for the long Preface, which he has added to it.

(1) *He was born in* 1638.

(2) *Intituled* De Rebus Sacris & Ecclesiasticis Exercitationes Historico-criticae, Ultrajecti. 1692, *in 4to.*

(3) *He has already published three Volumes of it, in folio, entitled*, Annales Politico-Ecclesiastici Annorum DC. XLV *a* Caesare Augusto ad Phocam usque. *They were printed at Rotterdam, for* Leers, *in* 1706, *and dedicated to the States General in* 1706. *He promises to continue this Work*.

(4) *Page* 385.

(5) *Page* 497.

(6) *An English Minister, who, in* 1692, *published, at London, the* Synodicon in Galliâ Reformata; *or, the Acts, Decisions, Decrees, and Canons, of the seven last National Councils of the Reformed Churches of France, a Volumes in Folio.*

VOL. I.   8 G   [*A*] *If*

BASNAGE.

BASNAGE (HENRY), Son of the foregoing, was born at *Ste. Mere Eglise* in Lower *Normandy*, the sixteenth of *October*, 1615. He was one of the most able and eloquent Advocates of the Parliament of *Normandy*, into which he was admitted in the Year 1636. There was no considerable Cause, which he was not employed in. He went to *Paris*, with the Deputies of the Province of *Normandy*, on account of the * Tax called *Tiers & Danger*: It was he, who drew up the Memorial of the Province, and who was made choice of to defend That Cause. At the request of the Marquis *de Matignon*, he took another Journey to *Paris*, to regulate the Shares of the Succession with the Marquis *de Seignelay* (*a*); and it is well known, that he would have been concerned in the general Review of the Common Laws of *France*, if the Project, formed about it, had been put in execution (*b*). In the Year 1677, he was nominated Commissioner for the Affairs of Religion, and worthily discharged that Trust. He was equally successful in Consultations, and Pleadings; and has made it appear, that he could prove as good an Author, as an Advocate. The *Common Law of Normandy*, which he published with very ample Commentaries in the Year 1678, was so much valued, and sold so well, that a Second Edition of it, in Two Volumes in Folio, was published in the Year 1694. At the same time was printed a third Edition of his *Treatise of Hypothecæ, or Pledges*. And, notwithstanding his great Age, the Author had the care of those Editions: his Judgment and Understanding continued unimpaired. This is very rare, and happens only to those, who have had both a lively Imagination, and a strong Head; which was his Character. His Religion did not hinder those, who were at the Head of the Parliament, and the rest of the most considerable Members of that illustrious Body, from having a great Esteem, and a particular Kindness, for him. He received all manner of Civilities from M. *de Monthelon*, first President of *Rouen*, to whom he dedicated his *Common Law of Normandy* in the Year 1694. He died at *Rouen*, the twentieth of *October*, 1695, aged eighty Years and four Days. If he had not the pleasure of seeing his Children in his old Age, yet it was a great Comfort to him to hear of the Honour, which they acquired in Foreign Countries by their excellent Writings [*A*]. He had also the Satisfaction to know, that his Son-in-Law, Mr *Bauldri*, Professor of Sacred History at *Utrecht*, had made himself very much esteemed by his Lectures, and by a learned Commentary on the Treatise of *Lactantius de Mortibus Persecutorum* (*c*).

* It is a Tax which the Gentry pay once in every King's Reign, for Forests and Woods.

(*a*) He had married the Marquis of Matignon's Sister-in-law.

(*b*) Some Persons of Credit have been told, that M. le Tellier, Promoter of that Project, had nominated Mr Basnage for one of the Executors.

(*c*) Printed at Utrecht, in 8vo, in the Year 1692.

[*A*] *If he had not the Pleasure of seeing his Children ---- yet he heard of the Honour, which they acquired, in foreign Countries, by their excellent Writings.*] His eldest Son, *JAMES BASNAGE*, was but a little above Twenty two Years of Age (1), when the Church of *Rouen* desired him for their Minister, in the Room of Mr *le Moyne*, in the Year 1676. He served that Church with much Applause from that time, 'till the Revocation of the Edict of *Nantz*. Then he retired into *Holland*, and settled at *Rotterdam*, where he is Ordinary Minister (2). The *Latin* and *French* Books, which he has already published, and chiefly his admirable Answer to the Bishop of *Meaux*, have fully justified those, who promised his History of the Church would be a very compleat Work; which has been yet farther made good by the Publication of the Work itself (3). His other Works are the *Examination of the Methods proposed by the Assembly of the Clergy of France, for the Re-union of Protestants to the Church of Rome*, printed, at *Cologn*, in 1684. *The Epistle of St Chrysostom to Cæsarius the Monk, together with three Epistolary Dissertations*, printed, at *Rotterdam*, in 1687, and reprinted in 1694. *The Holy Communion, or a Treatise on the Necessity and Means of communicating worthily*, printed, at *Rotterdam*, in 1687, and several Times since. *A Treatise on Conscience, with Reflexions on the Philosophical Commentary*, printed, at *Rotterdam*, in 1696. *The History of the Jewish Religion, from* JESUS CHRIST, *to the present Times, by way of Supplement to* Josephus, actually printed, at *Rotterdam*, in five Volumes in 12mo.

His younger Brother, HENRY *BASNAGE*, Sieur *de Beauval* (4), was admitted Advocate in the Parliament of *Normandy*, and pursued his Father's Steps; but the Troubles, on account of Religion, made him rather choose to retire into *Holland*, than to follow a Path so glorious in the Eyes of the World. He was very young, when he published a little Piece on the *Toleration of Religions*, which was wrote with a great deal of Spirit and Judgment. He has acquired, and is daily maintaining, an immortal Reputation over all *Europe*, by publishing the *History of the Works of the Learned*. The Disputes he had with Mr *Jurieu* often interrupted him in That Work, and produced several very lively and sharp Pieces, on both Sides. His Correction of *Furetiere's Dictionary*, which he has improved with several Additions and Emendations, and an infinite Number of Examples, taken from more polite *French* Writers, is a Work of very great Use. He is again actually revising it.

Though these Gentlemen are yet living, there is a Necessity of mentioning them, to prevent their being continually mistaken the one for the other, as has been already done in some Books. See the Remark [C] of the foregoing Article, and this Passage of the *Bibliotheque Universelle*: Wherein it is shewn, that the Author of the History of the Journals is not very well acquainted with Messieurs *Basnage*. "I "have already said, that this Work (5) is very ne- "cessary; but I must add, that it would be much "more so, if he, who wrote it, had been better in- "formed; for he has committed several Mistakes, "which discredit the whole, 'till they be corrected. "For Example, speaking of the *History of the Works* "*of the Learned*, which is known to be wrote by "Mr *de Beauval* the Advocate, he says, that a *French* "Refugee Minister is the Author of it, and that his "inserting in the Title Page, *By Mr B*** *Doctor* "*of the Civil Law*, is only to conceal himself the "better: That This Minister, and Author of That "Work, is the same, who wrote against the Bishop "of *Meaux*, and against *Baronius*, confounding, at "this rate, three very different Persons. It is true, "we may very well excuse him on this Article; for "it is very rare to see one single Family produce "so many famous Authors; and they, who are not "well acquainted with every Branch of it, may very "easily confound them (6)." This Reflexion is both ingenious and judicious.

(1) He was born at *Rouen* in 1653.

(2) Those who have the Direction of Churches are so called, to distinguish them from other *French* Ministers, who reside in the Towns of *Holland*.

(3) It was printed in Nov. 1698, in 2 Vols in Fol. See the History of the Works of the Learned, 1698, pag. 381, & 500. And the Journal of Utrecht, Tom. IV. pag. 24.

(4) He was born at *Rouen*, Aug. 7, 1656.

(5) That is to say, M. Christiani Junckeri Dresdensis Historicum de Ephemeridibus seu Diariis Eruditorum.

(6) Bibliotheque Universelle, Tom. XXII. p 427, 423.

BASTA

BASTA. 673

BASTA (NICOLAS), by Nation an *Epirote*, was a good Officer of Horfe in the *Spanish* Service in the *Netherlands*, where the Duke *d'Alba* brought him in the Year 1567 (*a*). He fignalized himfelf in the Defeat of *la Noue* before *Engelmunfter* in 1580 (*b*). The Duke of *Parma* gave him a very honourable Teftimony [*A*], four Years after, by fending him to the Affiftance of the Elector of *Cologne*. His Father, whofe Name was *Demetrius*, had born Arms forty Years in the Service of the Houfe of *Auftria* (*c*). He was undoubtedly related to *George Bafta* [*B*], which is fufficient to prevent the Cenfure of thofe, who might perhaps be apt to blame me for publifhing this Article. When a Perfon deferves a place in a Dictionary, he in fome meafure opens the Gate to his Relations. Let this be obferved once for all.

[*A*] *The Duke of* Parma *gave him a very honourable Teftimony*] It is this: "Hunc (*Blafium Capi-* "*ficcum*) & Nicolaum Baftam veterem Epirotarum "equitum ductorem Coloniam mittens Alexander, "Colonienfibus refcripferat, deletlos a fe fuiffe ftre- "nuos adeo gnarofque militiae viros ut horum con- "filia, fi occafio fe daret, tuto ipfe fequi paratus "effet (1). ----- Alexander, *fending Him* (Blafius "Capifuccus) *and* Nicolas Bafta, *the old Epirote Gene-* "*ral of Horfe to* Cologn, *wrote thus to the Inhabitants*, "*that they were Perfons chofe by him for fo remark-* "*able a Courage and Skill in War, that, if he had* "*Occafion, be himfelf fhould think it the fafeft Courfe* "*to follow their Direction.*"

[*B*] *He was undoubtedly related to* George Bafta.] Some fay he was his Brother (2), and obferve, that four famous Hiftorians (3) have afcribed a glorious Action of *George* to *Nicolas*; it is the Succour thrown into *la Fere* in the Year 1596. *Bouterouc* has not been guilty of That Fault; he very rightly gives the Name of *George* to him, who performed That Action (4). Few Warriors will confent to fuch Affignments of Glory, and brotherly Love feldom reaches fo far. The anonymous Author, who publifhed the Hiftory of the Archduke *Albert*, in the Year 1693, gives the Name of *Nicolas Bafta* to him, who brought a Convoy of Provifions into *la Fere*.

BASTA (GEORGE), a famous General, in the beginning of the XVIIth Century, was originally of *Epirus* (*a*), but born in a Village called *la Rocca*, near *Tarentum*. He commanded a Regiment of *Epirote*, or *Albanefe*, Horfe, when the Duke of *Parma* took Poffeffion of the Government of the *Netherlands* in the Year 1579; and he perfected himfelf in the Military Art under fo great a Mafter as That Duke, who, foon difcovering *George Bafta*'s Merit, made him Commiffary General of the Horfe in the Year 1580 [*A*]. There was no confiderable Enterprize, in which he did not affign him a principal part. During the Siege of *Antwerp* in 1584, he had Orders to keep the Field, to hinder any Succours from entring into the Place; and, in 1588, having reinforced the Troops, which befieged *Bonn*, he contributed very much to the taking of that Town (*b*). In the Year 1590, he followed the Duke of *Parma* into *France*, to the Affiftance of the League; and, in the Year 1592, he had the command of the Rear-guard during the firft Retreat (*c*). He was alfo concerned in the Expedition of Count *Charles* of *Mansfeld*, in *France*, in the Year 1593 (*d*). After which, he went to make fome Campaigns in *Hungary*, and returned into the *Netherlands*, where, in the Year 1596, he was charged with a very difficult Commiffion, which he executed very much to his Honour (*e*); this was to throw a Supply of Provifions into *la Fere*, then befieged by *Henry* IV. Never was more Conduct, Secrecy, and Diligence, feen, than he made appear on that occafion. But, without doubt, the beft Theatre of his Exploits was *Tranfilvania* and *Hungary*. In the Year 1601, he obtained a fignal Victory over *Sigifmund Battori*, who had caufed himfelf to be elected Prince of *Tranfilvania*. The Imperialifts loft fcarce 300 Men; but *Battori* loft above 10000 Men, 110 Colours, 40 Pieces of Cannon, and all the Baggage of his Army. The Town of *Claufemberg* was befieged foon after, and forced to yield to the mercy of the Conqueror. *Bafta* rid himfelf of a troublefome Rival, who had fhared the Honour of that Day with him, I mean the *Waiwode* of *Walachia*, whom he caufed to be killed in his Tent, on fufpicion of his holding a private Intelligence with the *Turks*. The Year following, he quite ruined the Affairs of *Battori*, by the taking of *Biftric*, and the Defeat of *Mofes*, Prince of the *Sicules*: So that *Battori*, humbly defiring a Peace, renounced all his Pretenfions, and was fatisfied with obtaining the Quality of a Baron of *Bohemia*, by way of Favour. In the Year 1603, *Bafta* again defeated the Army, which *Mofes* had raifed, and perhaps he would have forced the broken remains of it in *Temefwere*, if the approach of the Winter had not hindered him from befieging that Place. The Severities, he exercifed, the following Year, againft the Proteftants of *Tranfilvania*, did the Emperor great Injury. He caufed the like to be practifed in *Hungary* by the Count *de Bel-joieufe*, which

made

[*A*] *The Duke of* Parma ----- *made him Commiffary General of the Horfe.*] I fhall take this Occafion to obferve, that, in thofe Times, That Office was but of a new Creation in the *Netherlands*. That Duke *d'Alba* brought it thither from *Italy* in the Year 1567, where it lately owed it's Birth to *Ferdinand Gonzague*, Governor of the *Milaneze*. The Duke *d'Alba* conferred it on *Anthony Olivera*, defcended from That *Martin Olivera*, whom Don *Pedro*, King of *Caftile*, had fent for from *France*, to ferve againft the *Moors* of *Granada* (1). *George Bafta* difcharged That Office very well, and it was, during his ficknefs at *Caudebec*, that the Cavalry, falling off from the good Difcipline, under which he had kept it, did not perform it's Duty fo well in the Attack, which the Royalifts made, upon the Duke of *Parma*, in 1592 (2).

[*B*] *The*

674 BASTA. BATHYLLUS.

made *Stephen Boſtkai* take up Arms, who ſoon found himſelf ſtrong enough to obtain a Victory over the Imperial Troops, which That Count commanded. *Baſta* could only repair this Loſs in part; for if, on the one hand, the Siege, which he laid to *Caſſovia*, diſengaged the Count *de Bel-joieuſe*, he was, on the other hand, obliged to raiſe it (*f*). In 1605, he had the Vexation not to be able to hinder the *Turks* from making themſelves Maſters of *Gran* (*g*); but he had at leaſt the comfort, by his Encampment near *Comorra*, both to become an invincible Barrier againſt them, and to charge them advantageouſly, upon their going to take their Winter Quarters. The Peace, which was made with the *Turks*, the Year following, and the little time he lived afterwards, ſilenced the Hiſtorians as to any farther Account of his Exploits [*B*]. He was honoured with the Title of a Count (*b*). Some ſay the *Turks* never had any Advantage over him [*C*]. We muſt not forget, that he is an Author [*D*], and in very great Eſteem [*E*].

(*f*) Ex Thuano.
(*g*) Mercure Franç. Tom. I.
(*h*) Strada, Dec. 2, l. 3.

[*B*] *The Peace ------ and his Death ------ ſilenced the Hiſtorians, as to any farther Account of his Exploits.*] *Bonifacio Vannozzi*, in a Letter dated in *January*, 1608, ſays, that two Letters, wrote by *G. M. Praga*, the Seventeenth and Twenty fourth of *December*, 1607, informed him of *George Baſta*'s Death (3). I fancy that this *G. M. Praga* had been Secretary to this General. He lamented the Loſs of this Maſter, and commended the Kindneſs, which Count *Charles*, and the Counteſs his Mother, ſhewed him (4). I take notice of this, only to ſhew that this General did not die without lawful Iſſue. The Advice, which was given to *G. M. Praga*, makes me think, that he had a Mind to write the Hiſtory of his Maſter: That Advice is very good. *Vannozzi* repreſents to him, that, if a Man deſires not to paſs for a Flatterer, he muſt undertake the particular Hiſtory of ſome famous Action, in which the Perſon, whoſe Life he writes, had the principal Part. He points to one, as to *George Baſta*, and adds, that, by managing it in this manner, he would have an Opportunity of repreſenting the glorious Actions of a Man, without ſeeming to affect it. The great Advantage of this Method is, that it does not oblige an Hiſtorian to ſpeak of the Imperfections of his Hero; whereas an entire Hiſtory of his Life requires, that he ſhould be repreſented, not only with his Virtues, but his Vices too. Now how commendable ſoever a Perſon may be, he is not without his Faults; and ſometimes the bad Qualities are as numerous as the good. He quotes, on this Account, what *Livy* ſays of *Hannibal*: " Alcuni per fuggir'ill nome d'adulatore, tanto ambi-
" to, quanto dannato, ſi danno à ſcriver' un' attion
" publica, ò un tal membro di eſſa, nella quale habbia
" parte principale colui, di cui noi intendiamo iſto-
" riar l'attiani e la vita: verbi grazia, volendoſi porre
" in Carta la vita del ſig. Co. Baſta, ſi potrebbe pig-
" liare à diſcriuer' un' accidente della guerra d'Un-
" gheria, ſiaſi il tumulto e la Seditione de Ribelli,
" od altra impreſa, nella quale S. E. haveſſe hauuto
" parte principale: & coſi diſſimulatamente metterſi
" à dir delle ſue prodezze, con molto propoſito, e
" fuor di ſoſpetto; che hoggi dì per lo più non ſi
" leggono vite e narrationi di Grandi, che non ha-
" biano del fauoloſo: E per cotali ſcrittori ſon tenuti
" à dire il vero, e fuggir la Menzogna: Stando che,
" coſì non fuſs' egli, non vi ſia alcuno tanto lauda-
" bile, che non habbia i ſuò Nei: Onde ſaggiamente
" Livio, dopo una gran diceria à favor d'Annibale,
" chiuſe il periodo coſi; Æquabant vitiis virtutes:
" Perche, come perliſſimo Maeſtro ſapeva, che non
" fi poteva, ne doueva tralaſciar' indietro i cenni de'
" vizi, del deſcritto per vertuoſo (5)." He takes notice, that *Hannibal*, who had but one Eye, blamed the Painter, who gave him two, and recompenced

(3) Vannozzi, Miſcellaneous Letters, Vol. 3. pag. 189.
(4) Ibid. pag. 190.
(5) Id. Ibid. p. 191, 192.

him who drew him in Profil (6). This ſhews, that he would not have any Body tell a palpable Lie in his Favour; but was very well pleaſed with thoſe, who found out the Art of hiding his Imperfections. *Vannozzi* afterwards hits upon a *Latin* Precept, which is very fine: " *Conuien dunque*, *ſays he* (7), ut veritas
" ante oculos habeatur, gratia, atque odiis poſthabi-
" tis; melius eſt enim Hiſtoricum, & Politicum, ſi
" non ſert ratio temporum, ab Hiſtoria ſcribenda ab-
" ſtinere, quam eam turpiter mentiendo, & adulando,
" quod pleroſque factitaſſe Flavius Vopiſcus ſcripſit,
" maculare. Republicæ enim intereſt, nequid om-
" nino niſi quod ſit compertum & exploratum in lu-
" cem exeat, *&c.*" This means, that, if the Times will not allow of ſpeaking the Truth, it is better to forbear writing Hiſtories, than to tell Lies; for the Public is concerned, that whatever is printed be true. He concludes with another Rule: *To praiſe but little, and to blame ſtill leſs. Seniamo la Lettera,* ſays he (8), *con quel moraliſſimo Detto : Lauda parcè,* *& vitupera parcius.* This was well worth a Digreſſion; which I ſubmit to the Judgment of all diſcerning Men.

[*C*] *Some ſay the Turks never had any Advantage over him.*] Let us hear *Strada*. " Militari ſcientiâ
" clarum quem è Farneſianâ Scholâ ſupremum Cæſa-
" rei exercitus Ducem vidimus in Parnoniâ ex Otho-
" manicis copiis perpetuò victorem (9). — *Famous*
" *for his military Knowledge, who, from the Duke*
" *of Parma's School, became chief General of the Im-*
" *perial Army, and was always victorious over the Ot-*
" *toman Forces in Pannonia.*"

[*D*] *He is an Author.*] His *Maeſtro di Campo generale*, was printed at *Venice*, in the Year 1606, and his *Governo della Cavalleria leggiera*, at *Francfort*, in 1612.

[*E*] *And in very great Eſteem.*] See here what *Naudæus* ſays of him in his Treatiſe of Military Study; " In equeſtris militiæ diſciplina quatuor ſeu duces ſeu
" tribuni communiter proponuntur, quorum de ea re
" lucubrationes tanquam abſolutiſſimæ omnium ſibi
" calculos & approbationem conciliarunt; ſcilicet
" Georgius Baſta qui ſummus mandatorum curator in
" Belgico Regis exercitu, & Cæſarianarum deinde
" copiarum ductor ſummo cum imperio fuit. ——
" *In the Military Diſcipline of the Cavalry, four*
" *Commanders or Captains are commonly propoſed,*
" *whoſe Lucubrations on this Subject are univerſally*
" *approved, and eſteemed the moſt complete; namely,*
" *George Baſta, who was Commiſſary general in the*
" *King's Army in Flanders, and afterwards Gene-*
" *raliſſimo of the Imperial Forces.*" The three others are *Ludovicus Melzius*, *Flaminius à Cruce*, and *Johannes Jacobus Walheuſius.*

(6) Ibid. pag. 192.
(7) Ibid.
(8) Ibid.
(9) Strada, Dec. 2. l. 3.

BATHYLLUS, a young Man of *Samos*, paſſionately beloved by *Anacreon*, who mentioned him often in his Verſes [*A*]. Among the remaining Odes, which we have of that Poet, there is one (*a*), wherein he draws the Picture this beautiful Youth.

(*a*) It is the 29th.

[*A*] *Anacreon ------ mentioned him often in his Verſes.*] *Horace* obſerves it: Theſe are his Words,

Non aliter Samio dicunt arſiſſe Bathyllo
  Anacreonta Tejum;
Qui perſæpe cava teſtudine flevit amorem
  Non elaboratum ad pedem (1).

Thus for Bathyllus did Anacreon burn,
And in looſe Verſe his amorous Paſſion mourn.

(1) Horat. Epod. 14.

Andrew Schottus ſhews an unaccountable piece of Madneſs in quoting theſe Verſes of *Horace*, to prove that *Mæcenas* loved the *Pantomime Bathyllus*, of whom I ſhall ſpeak hereafter (2). *Charles Stephens* was not leſs miſtaken, when he ſaid, that *Bathyllus*, the Darling of *Anacreon*, is the ſame with the *Pantomimus*, mentioned in theſe Words of *Juvenal*, *molli ſaltante Bathyllo* (3). Is not this as much as to ſay, that *Juvenal* and *Anacreon* were Cotemporaries?

(2) Andr. Schot. ad Senec. Contr. Præf lib. 5. pag. 484. Edit. Th. de Juret.
(3) They are in Satire V. ver. 63.

[*B*] Poly-

BATHYLLUS.

Youth. His Description is not confined, like those of our Romances, to the visible parts; but extends also to those concealed; which is the reason that Madam *le Fevre* could not fill up all the places of her Translation, but was forced to leave whole Lines with Afterisms. This same *Bathyllus* had been loved by *Polycrates*, Tyrant of *Samos*, who caused a Statue to be erected to him [B], in the Attitude of a Man singing, and playing on the Lyre. *Chabot* was mistaken in calling him *Pantomimus* [C]. Mr *le Fevre*, in endeavouring to excuse *Anacreon*'s dissolute Life, has published some things, which were not very well known [D].

[B] *Polycrates — — — who caused a Statue to be erected to him*] Some think, that *Juvenal* speaks of it, when, addressing himself to the Gods, he says,

— ut video, nullum discrimen habendum est
Effigies inter vestras, statuamque Bathylli (4).

Barthyllus' Statue at this rate may prove
Thy equal Rival, or a greater Jove.

Others read *Vagelli*, instead of *Bathylli*. That Statue of *Bathyllus* was in the Temple of *Juno*, at *Samos*, before the Altar. *Apuleius* has given a very particular Description of it (5).

[C] *Chabot is mistaken, in calling him Pantomimus.*] *Hic Bathyllus*, says he (6), *Samius fuit Pantomimus Anacreonti in maximis deliciis*. Very probably his Error proceeds from the Idea he had of another *Bathyllus*, to whom the Title of *Pantomimus* very well agrees, as shall be seen hereafter.

[D] *Mr le Fevre, in endeavouring to excuse Anacreon's dissolute Life, has published some things, which were not very well known.*] I will here perform the Promise I made in the Remark [G], of the Article ANACREON. This is the most proper Place for these Things. They would have made That Poet's Article too long; but I shall find room enough in this of *Bathyllus*. I say, then, that, as Mr *le Fevre* could not be Ignorant, that our Poet's Love for *Bathyllus* passed for mere Sodomy, and that *Polycrates*'s Jealousy of *Smerdias* made a great Noise, it is unaccountable how he could say, "We do not read, that *Anacreon*'s Pleasures were Matters of Scandal, nor that his Gaieties were e'er complained of (7)." What he observes, in another place, is much more reasonable. He says, that more scandalous Passions have been seen in the Auxiliary Troops of *France*, than *Anacreon*'s Amours. His Latin Description of them is too fine to be translated: "An id potius amet quod patrum noftrorum memoria in copiis Auxiliaribus vidit Gallia?

Serica cum Dominam ducebant vincla capellam,
Cui nitidum cornu multo radiabat ab auro,
Et segmentatis splendebant tempora vittis.
Illa rosa & myrto fertisque recentibus ibat
Altum vinctâ caput, dilectæ conscia formæ (8).

"Or would be rather pursue those Amours, which were observed by France among the Auxiliary Forces, in the Memory of our Fathers?

Their Mistress Goat in silken Cords was led;
Her gilded Horns their Rays of Glory spread;
Her Temples with the finest Ribbons bound,
Her Head with Myrtles, and with Roses crown'd,
Proudly she tript, and scarcely trod the Ground.

This is a Piece of secret History, the Circumstances whereof, it is likely, several Readers will enquire into; a She-Goat, the Mistress of an *Italian* General, and led in Pomp with the Ornaments of a jointed Baby. It is impossible to carry farther, by the most strained Constructions, the

Novimus & qui te transversa tuentibus hircis (9).

We know who did your Business, &c.
And what the Goats observed with leering Eyes.

Mr *le Fevre* was brought into trouble for This Discovery: "It is not proper, *says he* (10), that People should know, that I made the Verses about the *Crowned Goat*. Your Father, to whom I formerly told the History of the She-Goat, mentioned in the Dedication of *Anacreon*, and who is not igno-

"rant in what manner I was treated in the Sanhedrim, will tell you my Reasons." Here is something which will facilitate an Enquiry into this Fact. The Duke *de Nemours*, having besieged *Lyons*, in the Year 1562, "was obliged to retire, being forsaken by Three thousand *Italians*, who deserted for want of being paid at the appointed Time. Their living had been so licentious, that the Country People knew no better Remedy, than to burn all the She-Goats of the Places, thro' which they passed (11)." I chuse rather to quote *Varillas*, than *d'Aubigné*, who informs us, "That the Duke of *Guise*, having a Mind, that the Duke *de Nemours* should command at the Siege of *Lyons*, *Tavannes* caused the Army to disband, and disgusted the *Italians*, by saying, that he could not lead Men to War, who forced Children and She-Goats; a thing so well known in the Country, that the Peasants left not one She-Goat alive, after their Departure (12)." The same Historian says, that the Baron *Des-Adrets*, leading his Men to fight against the Count *de Suze*, made no other Speech but this, "See there the Murderers of Women and Children, and the Lovers of She-Goates; let us fall on (13)." Doubtless *d'Aubigné* knew this by fresh Tradition, and had read an Historian, who had named the Chiefs of those infamous Soldiers, and who says, that *Tavannes*, being either little satisfied with the Arrival of the Duke *de Nemours*, who was to command the Siege, or hoping for no good Success from it, retired into *Burgundy*; that afterwards the Duke *de Nemours* "marched directly into *Dauphiné*, where several Actions were performed (14); but, *continues he*, the Duke *d'Anguejol*, complaining of his Pay, retired at That Time, except six Companies, which accompanied *Nemours*, under the Command of *Brancaccio*. Those *Italian* Troops, sent and paid by the Pope, did much harm wherever they passed, and plundered the very Shoes of the poor Lazars they met with, and were, besides, so villainous and detestable in their Lives, that they brought She-Goats along with them to make use of, for their more than brutish Filthiness; which was the Cause that, afterwards, the Peasants killed, and threw into their Laystalls, the She-Goats in all the Places through which they passed." The Author of the *History of the remarkable Things which happened in France, from the Year 1547, to the beginning of 1597*, relates the same things. "During these Transactions, *says he* (15), the Sieur *de Tavannes* came from *Burgundy*, within three Leagues of *Lyons*, with a Design to storm the City; but he was too far off, although he had then with him above Five thousand Men, besides Three thousand *Italians*, in the Pope's Pay, commanded by the Count *d'Anguejol* (16). These *Italians*, who were the greatest Pilferers in the World, carried a great many Goats with them, and brutishly copulated with the Beasts, &c. (17)" It appears by all these Authors, that this happened in the Year 1562. But here is a Writer, who mentions other Circumstances. "The History of *France*, *says he* (18), tells us, That the Duke of *Nevers*, coming from *Italy* into *France*, to assist the King, whose Crown the House of *Guise* endeavoured to invade, under pretence of Religion, brought from thence Two thousand Goats, covered with Caparisons of green Velvet, with broad Gold Galoons. It does not give us room at the same time to doubt, what use these Goats were for; it tells us, that they were Mistresses for him, and all his Officers." That Duke *de Nevers*, is, without doubt, *Lewis de Gonzague*, who married *Henrietta de Cleves*, the fourth of *March*, 1565. Now we do not read, that he went from *Italy* into *France*, with a Body of Troops, in the Year 1562. He was *Lieutenant General in the Marquisate of Saluces, and the rest of* Piedmont, belonging to *France*, and he received Orders to draw out those warlike Troops, which were there kept

676 BATHYLLUS.

[marginal notes left column:]
(19) Varillas, Hist. of Charles IX. Tom. II. pag. 102, Dutch Edit.
(20) Id. ib. pag. 103.
(21) Davila's Hist. of the Civil Wars of France, lib. 4. pag. 283.

(a) Athen. lib. 1, c. 17.
(b) Suidas in Πυλάδης. Athen. l. 1, cap. 17.
(c) Athen. ib. Plut. Symp. lib. 7, c. 8.

[main text:]
in reserve (19); and having discharged, with the Money the Pope sent him, *part of the Pay due to his Soldiers, he drew out of his Government about Thirteen thousand Men,* entered into Dauphiné, raised the Blockade of *Lyons,* besieged and took *Mâcon,* and went to join the Duke of *Anjou,* in *Champagne* (20). See *Davila,* in the fourth Book of his History (21). One of these two things must be true: either those Goats were seen twice in *France,* or they were not seen in the Army of *Lewis de Gonzague*: But however that be, *d'Artagnan's* Memoirs certainly offend against Chronology; for, in the time of the Duke of *Nevers's* Expedition, the House of *Guise* did not attempt to usurp the Throne. The Protestant Historians, who speak of these Goats in the Year 1562, say nothing like it about the Duke of *Nevers's* Troops, in 1567 (22). Now no Body can be ignorant, that their Silence in this Matter is of great Moment.

BATHYLLUS of *Alexandria* (a), a Freedman of *Mæcenas,* and very much beloved by him [*A*], invented, together with one *Pylades,* a new way of representing all sorts of *Dramatic* Pieces in Dances. This Invention was called the *Italian Dance* (b) [C], and comprehended *Tragedy, Comedy,* and *Satire.* Not that it was a mixture of them, but that both these *Pantomimes* preserved the Character of each kind in the performance of their Play. They differed in this, that *Bathyllus* excelled in the Comic [D], and *Pylades* in the Tragic part (c). The Emulation, which prevailed between them, formed two Sects of long continuance: each of them left some Scholars, who endeavoured to make their School famous, and to perpetuate the Name of their Master (d); for the Followers of *Bathyllus* were called *Bathylli,* and those of *Pylades* were called *Pyladæ.* Both of them preserved the Methods and Characters of their Masters. The Dances of the latter were grave, and proper to excite the great Passions of Tragedy; and those of the former were merry, and suited with amorous Adventures and comical Subjects. They were such Provocatives to Lust, and gave such irresistible Temptations to the

[right margin notes:]
(22) D'Aubigné, Tom. I. l. 4, cap. 1, 2, p. 34. The History of Reims title Thou., La Popelinière, True and Perfect History of the Troubles, Book 3.
(d) Seneca, Nat. Quæst. lib. 7. c. 32. See Salmas. in Carinum Vopisci, Voss. Instit. Poet. lib. 3, cap. 38.

[A] *He was a Freedman of Mæcenas, and much beloved by him.*] See the Scholiast of *Persius,* on these words of the fifth Satire,

Tres tantum ad numeros Satyri moveare Bathylli,

and consider this Passage of the Fifty fourth Chapter of the first Book of *Tacitus's* Annals: "indulseratque ei ludicro Augustus dum Mæcenati obtemperat effuso in amorem Bathylli.——Augustus encouraged these Diversions, in complaisance to Mæcenas's Fondness for Bathyllus." Consult *Dion* also, in the Fifty fourth Book, and *Seneca* in the Preface to the fifth Book of *Controversies.*

[B] *He and Pylades were Inventors of a new manner of representing Dramatic Pieces in Dances.*] *Suidas* says expressly, that *Augustus invented the Dance of the Pantomimes, Pylades, and Bathyllus being the first, who introduced it* (1). Every body is sensible, that *Suidas* means, that *Augustus* was the first, who authorized, and established the Invention of those two great Dancers (2). In the Greek of That Author it is Βακχυλίδες. This fault remains in the *Suidas* of *Æmilius Portus,* though *Lipsius* had corrected it (3); when he rectified two Passages of *Seneca,* one of which had, *Bathyllo Mæcenate* (4), instead of *Bathyllo Mæcenatis,* and the other, *Si Pantomimus essem, Pantillus essem* (5), instead of *Si Pantomimus essem, Bathyllus essem.* *Zosimus* agrees with *Suidas* (6): he places, among the Causes of the Destruction of the *Roman* Empire, the Introduction of the Dances of the *Pantomimes* under *Augustus,* which were unknown before, and of which *Pylades* and *Bathyllus* were the Authors. *Athenæus,* where he speaks from himself, names only *Bathyllus,* but when he quotes *Aristonicus,* he also mentions *Pylades* (7). It is true, that, to find this in his Text, we must correct one word of it, as *Salmasius* has very well done. The Greek runs thus, Τατον τὸν Βαθυλλον φησὶν Αριστόνικ@. καὶ Πυλάδης, ἐ ετί καὶ σύγγραμμα περὶ ὀρχήσεως, τὴν ιταλικὴν ὄρχησιν συϊστασθαι ἐκ τῆς κωμικῆς, &c (8). We must read Πυλάδην, and translate the words thus, "Aristonicus ait, Bathyllum hunc & Pyladem qui librum de saltatione scripsit, Italicam saltationem composuisse ex comica, &c.——Aristonicus *says, that this Bathyllus and Pylades, who wrote a Book on Dancing, invented the Italian Dance from the Comic, &c.*" There is no likelihood that, since so many other Writers had made *Pylades* partaker of the Honour of the Invention, or conferred it altogether upon him, he himself should have ascribed it all to his Rival in a public Piece. This Passage of *Athenæus* has served the same Critic to correct *Suidas* (9). The words of *Suidas* signify, that *Pylades* wrote concerning the *Italian* Manner of Dancing, which he had invented, that is, concerning the Comic, Tragic, and Satiric Dancing (10). *Wolfius* and *Æmilius Portus* understand it so, because they found no fault in these words: Έγραψε περὶ ὀρχήσεως τῆς ιταλικῆς ἥτις ὑπ' αὐτῷ εὑρέθη. περὶ τῆς κωμικῆς καλουμένης ὀρχήσεως καὶ τῆς σατυρικῆς. *Salmasius* pretends, that, instead of περὶ τῆς κωμικῆς, it must be read ἀπὸ τῆς κωμικῆς, and so on; which signifies, that *Pylades* wrote a Book concerning the *Italian Dance,* which he had invented and formed out of the Comic, &c. It is certain, that, by this means, *Suidas* would say a thing, which *Athenæus* relates positively. Let the Readers judge whether it might not be true, that *Pylades's* Book treated in particular of the three ancient Sorts of Dances, and of That, which he had substituted in the Room of those three, which was necessarily different from each of them, though perhaps it retained them all intirely.

[C] ——— *which was called the* Italian *Dance.*] I chuse rather to express myself thus, than barely to say, that *Pylades* and *Bathyllus* invented the Art of representing a *Dramatic* Piece by Dancing, and the Action of the Hands. I am not ignorant, that many Authors speak of it as of a thing, which began first under *Augustus:* for, besides the Authorities quoted in the foregoing Remark, it is certain, that *Suidas* says, somewhere, *That at this time* (that is, under This Emperor) *the Dance of the Pantomimes was introduced, unknown before,* ἔτω πρότερον ἔσα (11). *Zonaras* also places the Establishment of it under *Augustus* (12). But, because *Salmasius* made it appear, that the Custom of acting Dramatic Poetry by the Motion of the Feet and Hands was much ancienter than *Bathyllus* and *Pylades* (13), it is better to say, that they only perfected That Art, and practised it after a new Manner. He believes, that, before their Time, the *Pantomimes* performed their Dances and Gestures while Tragedy or Comedy was representing, and that these two Men were the first, who discharged all the Actors, and introduced Dancing only on the *Orchestra* (14). I shall observe elsewhere (15) with what new Entertainments *Pylades* enriched the Art he professed. *Lipsius* believed himself to be the first, who discovered *Augustus* to be the Inventor of That Dance (16). This Discovery, as we have seen, is not very fortunate.

[D] *Bathyllus excelled in the Comic Part.*] *Athenæus* (17), and *Plutarch* (18), inform us of the difference, which was in this Respect between these two Dancers. It may be very well inferred from these words of *Seneca* the Father: "Quidam melius equitem patiuntur, quidam jugum, & ut ad morbum te meum vocem, Pylades in comœdia, Bathyllus in tragœdia, multum à se aberant (19).——*Some can best bear a Trooper, some a Yoke, and, to instance in my own Distemper,* Pylades *in Comedy, and* Bathyllus *in Tragedy, differ widely from each other.*" The Sequel of the Discourse proves, that the Design is to shew, that a Person is not equally fit for different Parts. But, though each of these *Pantomimes* had

[left lower margin notes:]
(1) Suidas in ὀρχηστής
(2) See Zosimus, lib. 1.
(3) Lipsius in Tacit. Ann. lib. 1. pag. 63.
(4) Controv. Præf. lib. 5.
(5) Præf. lib. 3. Epist. tom.
(6) Zosim. lib. 1.
(7) Athen. lib. 1. c. 17, pag. 20.
(8) Salmas. in Carinum Vopisci, pag. 811. Edit. Lugd. Bat. 1671.
(9) Id. Ibid. See Vossius Instit. Poet. lib. 2. pag. 180.
(10) Suid. in Πυλάδης.

[right lower margin notes:]
(11) Suid. in Ἀθηνοδώρος.
(12) Zonaras, lib. 1.
(13) Salmas. in Carinum Vopisci.
(14) Ibid. p. 830, 831.
(15) In the Article of this PYLADES.
(16) Lips. in Tacit. Ann. lib. 1.
(17) Lib. 1. c. 17.
(18) Sympos. lib. 7. c. 8.
(19) Epitom. lib. 3. Præf.

BATHYLLUS. BAUDERON. 677

the female Spectators, that I dare not say of them, in my Mother Tongue, what *Juvenal* did in Latin [*E*]. The *Romans* divided themselves into Parties, on account of these two famous *Pantomimes*, and it seems, that the Friends of *Bathyllus* had once the Honour of causing *Pylades*, to be banished (*e*). The kindness of *Mæcenas* for *Bathyllus* may authorize This conjecture, with submission to *Macrobius* [*F*]. See what we shall say in the Article of PYLADES. Mention is made of *Bathyllus* in the eighth Fable of the fifth Book of *Phædrus*. The Author of *Moreri*'s Supplement has given a very proper account of This *Pantomime*; but his Quotations are wrong; for the Citation from *Plutarch* concerns only a small part of the Article, and That from *Lucian* has two great Defects; one is, that the Book *de Pantomimi Scena*, to which the Reader is referred, is a Chimera; the other; that the Treatise *de Saltatione*, where *Lucian* has said many things of *Pantomimes*, does not particularly mention *Bathyllus* and *Pylades*. I believe I have discovered the Origin of this wrong Quotation.

(*e*) Dion. lib. 54.

had their Excellencies and Perfection, as I have observed, yet they both undertook Tragedy and Comedy. *Bathyllus* was not the only one, who acted Plays, wherein some Persons were to be represented in great Motion, as the *Pans*, and the Satyrs feasting with *Cupid*; it appears, that *Pylades* signalized himself by representing a Feast, given by *Bacchus* to the *Bacchantes* and Satyrs (20). *Vossius*, who appropriates such a Subject to *Bathyllus* (21), had not sufficiently regarded the learned Dissertation of *Salmasius*.

[*E*] *I dare not say, in my Mother Tongue, what* Juvenal *did in Latin.*] To shew how indecent this would be, see here *Juvenal*'s words in the sixth Satire.

Cheironomon Ledam molli saltante Bathyllo
Tuccia vesicæ non imperat: Apula gannit
Sicut in amplexu: subitum & miserabile longum
Attendit Thymele, Thymele tunc rustica discit.

One sets a dancing Master cap'ring high,
And raves and pisses with pure Extacy:
Another does with all his Motions move,
And gapes and grins, as in the Feat of Love:
A third is charmed with the new Opera Notes,
Admires the Song, but on the Singer dotes:
The Country Lady in the Box appears,
Softly she warbles over all she hears;
And sucks in Passion, both at Eyes and Ears.
DRYDEN.

Father *Tarteron*, the Jesuit, suppressed this *Latin* in his new Edition of *Juvenal* (22), which he translated into *French*. He also suppressed some other Passages, for the Reasons, which he alledges in his Preface. Thus much by the by.

[*F*] *It seems the Friends of* Bathyllus - - - - - - *caused* Pylades *to be banished : The Interest of* Bathyllus *may authorize This Conjecture, with Submission to* Macrobius.] He says, that *Pylades* incurred *Augustus*'s Indignation, because the Dispute between him and *Hylas*, who had been his Scholar, had raised a Sedition among the People. The answer ascribed to *Pylades* by *Macrobius*, Sir, you are ungrateful, let them concern themselves with our Quarrel (23), is the same with That mentioned by *Dion*, who reports, that this *Pantomime*, being recalled from his Exile, and reproved by *Augustus* for his Quarrels with *Bathyllus*, made answer, *It is to your Advantage*, Cæsar, *that we amuse the People, and hinder them from giving attention to other matters.* Συμφέρει σοι, Καῖσαρ, περὶ ἡμᾶς τὸν δῆμον ἀποδιατρίβεσθαι (24). *Expedit tibi*, Cæsar, *populum nobis tempus consumere*. Let who will take *Macrobius*'s Part against *Dion*: as to myself, I prefer the latter; and I think it most probable, that it was not in *Hylas*'s, but in *Bathyllus*'s Favour, that the Emperor was angry with *Pylades*. In the Article of the latter, we shall see the Opposition between *Dion* and *Suetonius*.

[*G*] *The Supplement of* Moreri *makes a wrong Quotation concerning* Bathyllus. - - - - - - - *I believe I have discovered the Origin of it.*] *Salmasius* quotes *Lucian* several times, who wrote a fine Treatise of Dancing. Among other Passages, he quotes That, which contains the Description of the Equipage of a *Pantomime*, if I may be allowed the Liberty of That Word, to express all the Instruments made use of in Dancing. Now, before he quotes those of *Lucian*, he has these words, *Lucianus; de Pantomimi Scenâ & apparatu*: By which, he does not mean to denote the Title of a Book, but only the Matter of a certain Passage he is going to quote. However, Mr *Hofman* was deceived by it; for, after having mentioned part of what relates to *Pylades*, in the Book of *Salmasius*, he refers us to *Lucian de Pantomimi Scenâ & appar.* and, as he puts these words in *Italic*, it is not to be questioned but this proved a Trap, into which the Continuator of *Moreri* fell headlong.

(20) See the two Greek Epigrams mention'd by Salmasius in Carinum Vopisci, p. 835.

(21) Vossius, Inst. Poët. lib. 2. pag. 281.

(22) At Paris 1689.

(23) Καὶ ἅμα φησὶ χαρίεσαι Βασιλεῦ Ἰασον αὐτοῖς περὶ ἡμᾶς ἀσχολεῖσθαι. Macrob. Saturn. lib. 2. c. 7. in fine.

(24) Dion. lib. 54. ad Ann. 7164 pag. 610.

BATHYLLUS, a *Latin* Poet, cotemporary with *Virgil*. See, in the Supplement of *Moreri*'s Dictionary, what is recorded of him. We have only to add this Circumstance to it, that the second Paper, *Virgil* caused to be posted up, began with the Distich, which *Bathyllus* had appropriated to himself, and that the next words were, *Hos ego versiculos feci*, &c. *Giraldus*, who is a Modern Author, ought not to have been quoted, but *Virgil*'s life by *Donatus*. I cannot tell where *Charles Stephens* found his *Bathyllus*, an excellent Tragic Poet, who did not succeed so well in Comedies.

BAUDERON (BRICE), a *French* Physician, born at *Parei*, in the Country of *Charolois*, flourished towards the end of the XVIth, and beginning of the XVIIth Century. He applied himself with great success to the Composition of Medicines, and published a *Pharmacopœia* [*A*], which has acquired a very great Authority. It

[*A*] *He published a* Pharmacopœia.] It was printed several times. *John de Renou* has observed, that the second Edition is of *Lyons*, by *Bennet Rigaud*, in 1596: and that the third is of *Lyons*, by *Peter Rigaud*, in 1603 (1). He says also, that he had seen, in the third, the Fault he had censured. Note, he makes this Remark, in a Book, printed in the Year 1623, wherein he answers a Complaint of the Son of *Bauderon*, and exhorts him to be " more diligent another time, in examining and correcting more particularly the Writings of his Father; in order to render them more clear and intelligible to those of his Profession, instead of confounding and making them more obscure (2)." From hence we may infer two Things: one, that our *Bauderon* was not *the* Author living in 1623; the other, that his *Pharmacopœia* had been published with Additions by his Son. It was translated into *Latin*, by an *Englishman*, whose Name was

(1) Renou, Antidotaire, lib. vi. c. iv. pag. 39, of the French Translator, Edit. of Lyons, in 1637.

(2) Ibid. See the Article RENOU.

BAUDIER. BAUDIUS.

(a) *See at the beginning of his Praxis, &c. the French Version of John Baptist Verjus, of Mascon.*

It is in French. He settled at *Mâçon* (a), and practised Physic there many Years. It is from this place he dates the Preface of a *Latin* Book, he caused to be printed at *Paris*, in the Year 1620 [B], wherein he tells us, he was eighty Years of Age, and had practised Physic 50. He was not living in the Year 1623 (b).

(b) *See remark [A].*

(3) *Mercklini Lindenrenovatus, pag. 133.*

was *Philemon Holland*. This Translation was printed, with some other Pieces of the same Kind, at *London*, in the Year 1639, in folio, and at the *Hague*, in 1640, in 12mo (3).

[B] *He caused to be printed at Paris, in 1620, a Latin Book.*] It is in 4to, and contains Eight hundred Forty nine Pages. The Title is, *Praxis in duos Tractatus distincta: in priore agitur de Febribus essentialibus, tam simplicibus, quàm compositis, confusis, erraticis, malignis, ac pestiferis, & symptomaticis, in genere & specie curandis: in posteriore, de Symptomatis & Morbis internis, à Capite ad pedes usque.*

BAUDIER (MICHAEL), a Gentleman of *Languedoc*, lived in the Reign of *Lewis* the XIII. He published several Books, which procured him the Character of a Copious, and Laborious, Author, and sold very well. I know of no other than the following Books: *Inventory of the General History of the* Turks (a): *The History of the Seraglio: That of the Religion of the* Turks: *That of the Court of the King of* China: *The Life of Cardinal* Ximenes: *The Life of the Cardinal* d'Amboise: *The Life of the Marshal* de Toiras: *History of the Ministry of* Romieu: *The* Piedmontois *Soldier's relation from the Camp of* Turin *of what passed in the Campaign of* Italy, *in the Year* 1640.

(a) *The 2d Edition is of Paris 1620, in 4to.*

BAUDIUS (DOMINIC), Professor of History in the University of *Leyden*, was born at *Lisle* the eighth of *April* 1561. He began his Studies at *Aix la Chapelle*. His Father retired thither with his Family during the Cruelties of the Duke *d'Alba*, and died there in the Year 1576. A little time after, *Baudius* went to continue his Studies at *Leyden*, where he staid but eight Months, and went afterwards to *Ghent*, whither his Mother had retired, and from whence she sent him to *Geneva*, where he studied Divinity, and performed all the Exercises of a Student in that Science. In the Year 1583, he returned to *Ghent*, where he continued his Studies of Divinity under *Lambert Daneau*; then he went to *Leyden*, where, having applied himself fifteen Months to the study of the Civil Law, he was made Doctor of Law in *June* 1585. Some days after, he followed the Ambassadors, which the States General sent into *England*, and became acquainted with several Persons of Note, and particularly with the famous Sir *Philip Sidney*. He was admitted one of the Advocates of the *Hague* the fifth of *January* 1587, and, being very soon weary of the Bar [A], he went to travel into *France* [B], where he continued ten Years [C]. He found good Friends, and great Patrons, there: *Achilles de Harlai*, first President in the Parliament of *Paris*, was one of the latter, and caused him to be admitted an Advocate in the Parliament in the Year 1592 (a). In 1602, *Baudius* went into *England*, with *Christopher de Harlai*, whom *Henry the Great*,

(x) *The Life of Baudius, which I shall quote hereafter, says 1591, but it appears, by his 23d Letter of the 1st Century, that it was in 1592.*

[H] *He was soon weary of the Bar.*] Being a Walloon, he could not speak Dutch well enough to plead with Success; besides he stood in need of an Employ, which would furnish him with ready Money, and That is not to be expected from the Profession of an Advocate, till after many Years. Add to this, that he a little fed himself with the Vain hopes of Court Preferment; and lastly, that he was born a Poet, which, of all things in the World, gives the least relish for the knotty Subtilties of the Bar. See the Advice *Lipsius* gives him to persevere with Patience (1).

(1) *In a Letter dated Oct. 1. 1587, among those of Baudius in Cent. IV Ed. 1. of Leyden, 1650.*

[B] *He went to travel into France.*] He had a good Opinion of himself, and fancied, that he might obtain a public Character to travel honourably. He imagined, that the States would send him to the King of *Navarre*, if his Friends should request it of them. He communicated his Thoughts to *Lipsius*, who was then Professor in the University of *Holland:* The Answer, which he received from him, taught him handsomely to know himself better, " Prioribus " (*literis*) agebas de legatiuncula ad Navarrenum: " quo fundamento, mi Baudi, aut qua spe? Nun- " quam id factum, & ut in tua persona novum ex- " emplum Ordines instituant, cave credas. Tu hoc " & alia mereris, sed male res humanas nosti, si me- " rita in his talibus appendis potius quam fortunam. " ———— Hoc unum te moneo ne præcipitem te " tuorum vota, pia, sed improvida, qui ad lapsum " sæpe impellunt dum cogunt festinare. Ne sperne " honores, sed nec avide appete, & qui eo minorem " te putant quia cares, tu eos habe pro minutis " (2). ———— You mention, in your former Letters, the " Deputation to the King of Navarre, but on what " Foundation, my Friend, and with what Hopes?

(2) *Lipsius, in a Letter dated to his Month of Sept. 1588. It is the 23th among those of Baudius, Cent. IV.*

" There has not been hitherto any Instance of such a " Deputation, and I would not have you think the " States will now begin to appoint one in your Fa- " vour. You deserve indeed this, and a great deal " more, but you are little acquainted with the World, " if you think Fortune has not a greater Share in " these Things than Merit. ———— One thing I " would advise you, not to give too much ear to the " Persuasions of Friends, which though well intended " are yet unseasonable, and who, by spurring on too " fast, are often the Occasion of a Fall. Neither " despise Honours, nor court them too eagerly: And, " if any think the worse of you, for not being pos- " sessed of them, you ought to think as meanly of " them." This is a very wise Answer; *Seneca* could say nothing more judicious. *Baudius* was never the better for this good Advice: We shall see, in the Remark [C], that he continued all his Lifetime infatuated with Deputations and Embassies.

BAUDIUS'S Infatuation with the Quality of Deputy. *See Remark* [C].

[C] ———— *where he continued ten Years.*] He testifies, in some of his Letters, that he designed to end his Days there, provided he could meet with a tolerable Maintenance. " Ægrè enim ægrè Gal- " liam desero, nec deseram, nisi desertus ab omni " ἀυτάρκιᾳ (3). ———— Ego hic aut alibi in hoc regno " sedem exilii circumspicio: ignoscat mihi genius " patriæ, plane non tenetor reverterundi desiderio (4). " ———— *I have no Thought of leaving France, nor* " *will I leave it, unless all manner of Hope first* " *leaves me.* ———— *I will either here, or in* " *some other part of this Kingdom, find out a Place* " *of Exile: my Country must pardon me, for I have* " *indeed not the least Desire of returning.*" He alledges several Reasons to *Thuanus*, why he did not intend to return into *Holland*, and he makes use of this

(3) *Baudius Epist. 7. Centur. 1. pag. 21. is dated from Caen, July 1. 1591.*

(4) *Id. Epist. 8. ejusdem Cent. p. 22.*

BAUDIUS. 679

Great sent thither Ambassador (b). This *Christopher* was the only Son of the first President. At last *Baudius* settled at *Leyden*, being made Professor of Eloquence there in *May* 1602. After the Death of *Merula*, he read Lectures on History: and was allowed to do the same on the Civil Law. In the Year 1611, the States divided the Office of their Historiographer between him and *Meursius* (c), and, in consequence thereof, he wrote the *History of the Truce* (d). That Work is well penned. *Baudius*'s Style was very polite, as appears by his *Letters*. His Friends published a great Number of them after his Death, and, from time to time, others have been added to them in the new Editions. He was a great Latin Poet [D]: the Verses we have of his leave no room to doubt it. He composed several kinds of them, and in great Numbers: and they have born many Editions. He

Some Facts concerning Baudius's Abode in France, &c.

this as the strongest; That he could not leave *France*, while he hoped for any Thing there. "Nos
" ---- qui vix non pervulgata ad bonam mentem
" adspiramus non magis illic ad res tractandas idonei
" censemur quam ὄνοι λύρας; vultures togati om-
" nia virtutis præmia possident bonis de præsidio deje-
" ctis, vel (quod deterius est) viri Mercuriales, quibus
" quam bene conveniat cum genere literatorum disci-
" mus magno nostro malo. Denique (quæ ratio
" maxima est) non possum à vobis divelli quamdiu
" speculæ locum videro (5). ----- *We* ---- *who
" quit the common Road, in our Search of Goodness,
" are esteemed there as unfit for Business, as an Ass
" to be a Musician; The Vultures of the long Robe
" are in Possession of all the Rewards of Virtue, in
" exclusion of the Good, or (which is worse) The
" Men of Business and Traffic; whose Disposition towards
" Men of Letters I know by sad Experience*. Lastly,
" (which is the strongest Motive), I cannot be torn
" from you, whilst I have the least Hope remaining."
He was too happy to return into a Country, which he spoke so ill of. He desired *Thuanus* to get him into the Family of the Prince of *Dombes* (6); and I believe he made the same Request to *Scaliger* (7). He was recommended to a worthy Gentleman, who, besides his Diet, allowed him Eight hundred Livres a Year (8), and, by that means, he found an Opportunity to insinuate himself into the Acquaintance of all the most illustrious Persons in the Parliament of *Paris*, which was then sitting at *Tours*. He wrote, from *Caën*, to *Thuanus*, that he was about a Work like That of *George Cassander* (9). I cannot say, whether any Body ever placed *Baudius* among the Reconcilers of Religion. He endeavoured to cause *Lipsius* to be invited to *Paris*, and was very much vexed, that this Affair was neglected; for he found a great Disappointment in it. He desired to see his Native Country again, without being at the Expence of the Journey, and in such a manner as might do him Honour, and afford him a Pretence to give himself some Airs: He hoped to be deputed to fetch *Lipsius*: Was there not reason enough to be vexed that they should be so backward at *Paris* to send for That great Man? " Lipsio equidem omnia sum-
" ma cupio, & ob honorem hominis, & ob amorem
" literarum. Sed tamen mei potissimum commodi
" ratio à me ducebatur, cum tam ambitiosis flagi-
" tationibus hoc agebam, ut huc evocaretur. Sua-
" debat enim voluntas, & rerum mearum status ur-
" gebat, ut in patriam excurrerem: quod ut sine
" sumptu meo & cum nonnulla dignitate fieret, bella
" occasio evenisse videbatur, si quod spe ac votis
" præceperam, publico nomine ad eum accersendum
" Legatus forem (10)." When he wrote this to *Thuanus*, his Affairs were in a bad Condition (11); he kept in the Country, because his Purse was too low to maintain him in *Paris*. The following Letter (12) to the same, was wrote in Prison: He says, That no Body would be bail for him, and That, without it, Mr *Seron*'s good Office, at whose Recommendation the Judges had been favourable to him, would be intirely useless. In 1597, he was at *Paris*, full of too presumptuous Pretensions. The Envoy of the United Provinces was so ill, that it was thought he could not recover. *Baudius*, flattering himself with the Thoughts of succeeding him, wrote immediately to *Scaliger*, and desired his Assistance to procure him the Character of Envoy of the States General to *Henry* IV (13). *Scaliger* returned him almost the same Answer that *Lipsius* had done about ten Years before (14). In the Year 1598, *Baudius* wrote to the two Envoys of *Holland*, at the Court of *France*, most humbly beseeching them to procure him some Employment in his Country's Service (15). In the

Month of *July*, of the same Year, he was in Prison for bailing another inconsiderately. *In carcerem conjectus sum nullum ob flagitium, sed ob inconsultam spopondendi temeritatem* (16). In the Year 1602, he went into *England*, with *Christopher de Harlai*, as his Secretary and Counsellor, and as a learned Man. *Profectus sum in Angliam ut si sim à consiliis, à secretis, ab interioribus studiis* (17). The same Year he went into *Holland*, where he was made Professor. This is all his Letters have informed me of concerning his Abode in *France*. He thought himself so fit for an Embassy, and had so strong an Inclination this way, that his Professorship at *Leyden* could not cure him of That Passion. Above all, he would fain have been appointed to congratulate *Henry* IV, in the Name of the States General, upon the Report, that This Prince had been elected King of the *Romans* (18). " Si qua occasio aperiretur, ut ex-
" tra ordinem publico nomine in Galliam legari pos-
" sem, multum felicitati meæ gratularer. Sed hæc
" ægri somnia sunt, ut & rumor ille qui pervagatur
" de Gallo designato Rege Romanorum. Quid si
" tamen ita esset, cum inest in incredibili fuga ve-
" ritas, & in verisimili mendacium, non disconveni-
" ret magnificentiæ Illustrissimorum Ordinum, mitti
" qui publicam lætitiam secunda Oratione testaretur
" (19). ------ *I should think myself very happy, if
" I could meet with an Opportunity of being sent Em-
" bassador Extraordinary into* France. *But these are
" only a sick man's Dreams, as well as the Report
" of the* French *King being elected King of the* Romans. *But, if it should be so, as we sometimes
" find incredible things to be true, and probable things
" to be false, it would not be unbecoming the Magnificence of the High and Mighty States to testify
" the public Joy on this Occasion by a complimenting
" Embassy*." In the Year 1607, he went into *England* to present his Poems to King *James*, and he had a great Notion of getting himself to be deputed to That Prince by the States General. For this Purpose he desired Mr *Vander Myle*, *Barnevelt*'s Son-in-law, to recommend him to his Father-in-law; and did not question but that *Barnevelt* would invent some Pretence for this Deputation. But, not succeeding in this, *Baudius* was resolved to pursue his Design at all Events, and so undertook That Journey with no other Character than That of his own Deputy. " Si amplissimi Ordines aliquid huic mortali
" mandare dignarentur quod nostra vox deferret ad
" aures Regis, forte nihil admitterent cujus eos pœ-
" nitere posset, & mihi tum gaudio tum honori esset
" reip. causa legari, nec Baudii negotium omittere.
" ---- (20) Sin frustra mecum hæc blanda somnia
" meditor ibo à me legatus (21). ------ *If the Illustrious States would vouchsafe to charge me with
" a Compliment to the King, perhaps they would do
" nothing they need be ashamed of, and it would be
" both a Pleasure and an Honour to me, to represent
" the Republic, and, at the same time, not to neglect my
" own private Affairs.----But, if I only flatter myself
" with vain Hopes, I will go my own Embassador.*"
[D] *He was a great Latin Poet.*] See the Judgment *Borrichius* (22) and *Morhosius* (23) pass on his Poems. The first Edition is not of the Year 1607 (24), but of the Year 1587: He dedicated it to *Petrus Regemorterus*. This Epistle dedicatory is the second of *Baudius*'s Letters. He had published a Book of *Iambics*, by itself, dedicated to the Cardinal de *Bourbon* (25). He dedicated some of his Poems to the King of *England*, and some others to the Prince of *Wales*, in the Edition of the Year 1607, and he went over Sea to make his Present to his two Patrons. He had the cruel Mortification to return Home without receiving the Value of a Farthing from

VOL. I. 8 I those

He died at *Leyden*, the Twenty second of *August* 1613 (e). He had some mortifications in the latter Years of his Life [E]. He was none of those warlike Doctors in

those two Princes; all he gained, by That Journey, was to become their Creditor, which was not worth his Expences. Here follow his Grievances and Complaints (26). "Arbitror te ex indicio famæ factum "esse certiorem, me superiori mense Augusto transfretasse in magnam Britanniam, cujus & Monarchæ "de manu in manum tradidi Salisberiaci Poëmata "mea, quorum minus malum carmen heroicum ejus "honori inscribitur. Duo vero Gnomarum Iambicarum libri dedicati sunt Principi Britanniarum, "quicum horam amplius unam familiariter sum collocutus. Sed hæc fine stetit omnis regia liberalitas, "nec teruncio factus sum propensior, ut vel meo "exemplo liquere possit, magnos terrarum dominos "posse perdere, non donare. Interim non pœnitet "suscepti itineris, nisi quod te non offenderim. "Nam & habeo reges debendi reos, & olim fors "fuat intelliget

Ἦ ἄτην, ὅ τ᾽ ἄεισον Ἀχαιῶν υἷες ἔτισι.
Durabo, & memet rebus servabo secundis.

" - - - - I suppose you have heard, that, in August "last, I crossed the Sea into Great Britain, to whose "King I presented my Poems, at Salisbury, with my "own Hand, the most tolerable Copy of Heroics being inscribed to him. The two Books of moral Sentences, in Iambics, were dedicated to the Prince "of Wales, with whom I had the Honour of above "an Hour's familiar Conversation. But the Royal "Generosity reached no farther, nor was I one Brass "Farthing the better for it, so true is it, from my "Example, that great Princes can ruin, instead of "rewarding. However, I do not, in the least, repent of my Journey, except only in not meeting "with you. For I have now those Princes in my "Debt, and perhaps they will some time or other "remember

How wrong to slight the bravest of the Greeks!
We must with Patience wait for better Times.

[E] *He had some Mortification in the latter Years of his Life*] He was obliged to sollicit a long time for an Augmentation of his Salary, though they could not be ignorant of the grievous Persecutions he suffered from his Creditors. He desired only to be admitted into the Sect of the *Millenarians*, that is, that his Salary might be raised to a thousand Gilders (27) which was hardly granted him, after many mean Sollicitations, when *Scaliger's* Pension was divided among several other Professors. "Multis collegarum aucta "sunt stipendia, quo nomine illis gratulor non invideo: "sane omnes videntur quasi facto agmine concurrisse ad cernendam hæreditatem & legenda spolia "maximi virorum Josephi Scaligeri (28). Læsus "esse videor quod præteritis comitiis nulla sit habita Baudii ratio nec in augendo peculio, nec in "causa ordinariatus, quum tamen multi collegarum "etiam plura obtinuerint quam ausi erant sperare (29). " - - - - *Many of my Colleagues have had their Stipends augmented, for which I congratulate, and not envy, them: Indeed they seem to have flocked together on Purpose to enter upon the Inheritance, and divide the Spoil of the greatest of Men,* Joseph Scaliger. *I think I have been very ill used, in not being taken notice of by the last Assembly either as to increasing my Salary, or making mine a Professorship in Ordinary, when several of my Colleagues have obtained even more than they could expect.*" Nay, at that very time, poor *Baudius* was the last, who was thought of, though he alledged, that he had contributed as much as any Body to That great Man's coming into *Holland* (30), At last his Stipend was raised, but they forgot his repeated Instances on another Account: he was left Professor extraordinary, though he had sollicited a long time for a Place among the ordinary Professors, that he might enjoy the right of Suffrage in the Assemblies of the University, without which he could not have any share in the Perquisites arising from Promotions " Intellexi hesterna die ex sermone nostri "Heinsii herois, habitam esse Baudii rationem in "supplemento peculii. Quo nomine plurimum me "Collegio Curatorum, in primis autem benevolentiæ

"tuæ debere confiteor. Sed si eadem opera in ordinem redactus essem, nulla ex parte beneficium "claudicaret. Nisi forte honorificentius est quoc extra ordinem nobis ob sedulam in pu`lico munere "obeundo curam ac diligentiam præmium sit decretum, quam si adscriptus essem manipulo Ordinariorum. Mihi quidem judicia bonorum & optimæ voluntatis conscientia potior est omni prærogativa sententiæ dicendæ: tamen aliquid dandum "est famæ, & publico hominum errori (31). - - - - *I understood yesterday, from the Discourse of our great* Heinsius, *that some Regard has been had to the augmenting my Salary. On which Account I own myself very much obliged to the College of Curators, but must of all to your particular Kindness. If by the same means I could have been ranked among the ordinary Professors, the Favour would have been perfect in every Respect. Unless it be thought more honourable to decree me an additional Reward as Professor extraordinary, on account of my great Care and Diligence in the Discharge of my Office, than if I had been listed among those in ordinary.*" *Baudius* was not grown the wiser for *Lipsius's* Advice. " I value the Esteem of good " Men, *says he*, and the Testimony of my Con- " science, more than the Privilege of giving my " Voice; but some Regard must be had to Fame, " and popular Error." Thus Men love to flatter themselves, and deceive the Public: They would enjoy Honours, and the glory of despising them, at the same time. " It is not, that we ourselves value, *say* " *they*, such a Degree of Honour, or such a Prero- " gative, which makes us sollicit for it; but, be- " cause the Vulgar will despise us, if we cannot ob- " tain it." But what had *Lipsius* said to *Baudius?* " Look on those as the lowest sort of People, who " shall despise you, because they do not see Fortune " favour you." If *Baudius* had made use of this wife Maxim, would he have said, that some Regard must be had to popular Opinions? To leave this moral Digression, our Professor attained the Right of voting before his Death: He was ranked, at last, in the Class of Professors in ordinary (32); but, by the Maxim, *Turpius ejicitur quam non admittitur hospes*, it had been better for him, if he had not been received into it; for he was degraded from it; and because, during That Suspension, he had taken Place of a Professor in ordinary at a Funeral, he was severely reprimanded in a full Academical Council, where he was cited to appear for several other Reasons (33). I say nothing of the Injunction he received, not to pronounce the *Speech* he had prepared against the Scholars of *Leyden*, who had, in a seditious Manner, committed many Disorders (34). He was also forbid to publish it. But it was published afterwards, and is a very good Piece. I have not hinted, that they took from him the Professorship of the Civil Law (35), and that the Academical Council declared to him, on his Admission into the Body of the ordinary Professors, that he should take Place last of all (36). He would not submit to That Sentence, but alledged his common Topic again, that some Regard ought to be had to the Errors of the People. " Fortiter contemno & Stoica firmitate con- " coquo ineptias illas & concertationes de loco, quum " ad rectam rationem & ad serium ac severum judi- " cium rem exigo. Sed obsecundandum est populo " & scenæ, cujus calculo magni sæpe viri ex ejus- " modi inanibus vel æstimantur vel depretiantur (37). - - - - *I heartily despise, and, with the Firmness of a Stoic, am intirely unconcerned at those Follies and Contentions about Place, upon a strict and serious Consideration of the Matter according to right Reason. But we must suit ourselves to the present Taste and Times, according to which these Trifles have very often a great Share in advancing or blasting the Characters of Great Men.*" This is down right declaring, that he did not regulate his Conduct by right Reason, duly considered, but by popular Follies, duly considered. Let us pass to other Matters: his ill Husbandry made him fall into Poverty, and under the Hands of his Creditors, so as to occasion, in his Person, some Disgrace to the University: For he was put under Guardianship, as incapable of the Administration of his Estate. " Ut liberer ab impe-
" riosa

in the Cabinet, who will neither have Peace nor Truce, and who treat, as ill affected to their Country, all those, who do not reject the Offers and Offices of the Mediators of Peace, as a dangerous Poison, and a fatal Snare. He earnestly exhorted the States to make a Truce with *Spain*. It is true he durst not put his Name to the two Speeches he published on that Subject (*f*). It is also true, that those two *Speeches* [*F*], and the Verses he made upon *Spinola*, excited great murmurings [*G*]. This pacific humour only regarded the State; for he was otherwise no Enemy to Poetical Quarrels: he maintained them with so much violence, that I do not believe, that the most famous Heathen Poets, for the bitterness of their Invectives, such as *Archilochus*, and *Hipponax*, could ever heap up more abuses, or make a more exquisite choice of vilifying Expressions. He principally employed them against the declared Enemies of the great *Scaliger*. They could not bear any Contradiction, and the most Cunning Man would have found it a very difficult thing to stop their Mouths. So that there was a reciprocal Shooting, and alternate

(*f*) *He published one under the name of* Latinus Pacatus, *and the other under that of* Julianus Roebecius.

---

(38) Epist. o. Cent. IV. dated June 13, 1613.

" riosa auctoritate Curatoris homo jam quinquage-
" nario major, nec, ut opinor, ætatis vitio delirus,
" aut ad agnatos & gentiles remittendus ----- de-
" decus vero publicum fuerit nos in hoc regno li-
" bertatis administratione bonorum prohiberi quasi
" rebus nostris superesse non possimus (38). ---- *That
" I may be freed from the Arbitrary Power of a Guar-
" dian, who am now above fifty Years old, nor yet,
" I think, superannuated, or in such a State as to
" need being put under the Care of my Relations and
" Friends.* ----- *But this is a very public Disgrace,
" to be debarred the Administration of my own Af-
" fairs, in a Nation of Liberty, as if I had lost my
" Senses.*" We shall mention hereafter his keeping a Mistress, which made him the Jest of all the Country. In a Word, this poor Man went through so many Vexations, that he says, in one of his Letters (39), he would have put an end to his Life, if God had not ordered us to keep our Station here, 'till he calls us from it. His Courage and drinking kept him up. He was not surprized, when the Faction of his Colleagues threatened to expel him from the Chair of the Civil Law, or to oblige him to Silence by the great Noise the Scholars should make (40). Was it not better to live like a Hermit, than with such Colleagues?

(39) *It is the* 29*th of the* IV*th Century, p. 496.*

(40) Epist. 68 Cent. III. p. 408, 411.

[*F*] *The two Speeches, he made on the Peace, --- excited great Murmurings.*] We should rather say, they had like to have ruined him; for Prince *Maurice* was made to believe, that he was abused in it, and a Report was spread, that the Embassador of *France* had bribed the Author, with a good Sum of Money, to write concerning the Truce. *Baudius* was obliged to write both to the Prince, and his Secretary, in his own Justification; and to deplore his ill Fortune for exposing him to a Crowd of malicious Calumniators, or false Interpreters of his Words (41). " Sup-
" pose, *said he*, I have not had a sufficient Know-
" ledge of every particular Fact, to be able to ad-
" vise what is most expedient for our Country;
" does it therefore follow, that I must appear to have
" acted like an ill Subject in freely speaking my Senti-
" ments in such a Republic as ours?" " Quod si
" per imprudentiam factum est, ut à recte suadendo
" mens aberraverit, quandoquidem pleraque τῶν
" καθ' ἕκαστα me latent, circa quorum cognitionem
" recti consilii norma gubernari non potest: saltem
" nihil fecisse arbitror præter officium boni civis,
" si in regno ac domicilio libertatis, quæ fide suæ
" præsidio secura conquiescit, ausus sum uti felici-
" tate temporum, quibus & sentire quæ velis, &
" quæ sentias fidenter effari liceat (42)." In all Countries, there are but too many Persons, who think no Body can differ from them on State Affairs, without being bribed by the Enemies of their Country. There are others of better Understanding, who know very well, that a Man may have a great Zeal for the Public Good, and, at the same time, be of an Opinion quite contrary to theirs; but yet make People believe, that such an Opinion favours of Treason: they must do it to make others afraid to contradict them. Whether it proceeds from the Jealousy of the Ignorant, who think, that there is no right way but their own (43), or from the Art of cunning Men, who make others believe what they do not believe themselves, a Man is equally to be pitied, when he finds himself exposed, as *Baudius* was, to the Fury of Slanderers.
" Illud in universum obtinet, *says he*, vitio huma-

(41) *See Letters 1, 3, and 4 Cent. III.*

(42) Epist. 4 Cent. III. pag. 320.

(43) Hominem imperito nunquam quidquam iniustius, Qui nisi quod ipse facit nihil rectum putat. Terent. A. d Iph. act 1. sc. 2. Mr *Morus,* Præf. Notar. in Nov. Test. *says, that instead of* imperito *it should be* simido. to. *It is certain, that, in the Matter here in question, there are no such false and rash Judges, as the half-Learned.*

" næ malignitatis, ut nihil tam commode dicatur à
" viris alicujus famæ & existimationis quin læva in-
" terpretatione depravari possit. ----- Quid porro
" absurdius eo genere hominum qui me rumoribus
" distulerunt, quasi redemptus essem pretio ab am-
" plissimo Præside & Legato Jeanninio ut scilicet
" inanes logos pro insigni liberalitate rependerem, &
" succenturiarer doctor umbraticus viro in summis
" rebus trito ac subacto (44)? ----- *It is univer-
" sally true, such is the Malice of Mankind, that the
" best Thing which can be said by Men of Character
" and Reputation is liable to Misconstruction.* ------
" *But what can be more absurd, than the loading me
" with this Calumny, as if I had been bribed by the
" illustrious President, and the French Embassador,
" in order, it seems, to repay them empty Words for
" their great Liberality, and for me, who am only
" an obscure Doctor, to be added as an Assistant to
" one, who has been so thoroughly versed and em-
" ployed in the greatest Affairs?*"

(44) Epist. 3. Cent. III. pag. 319. *See also* pag. 321.

[*G*] *And the Verses which he made for* Spinola.] The Marquis of *Spinola* went into *Holland* before there was any thing concluded, either about a Peace or Truce. *Baudius* printed a *Poem* in Praise of That Marquis; but he suppressed the Copies of it, 'till the Business, which brought him thither, should more plainly appear. He only gave some of them to his most intimate Friends. " Mitto tibi exem-
" plum carminis quo gratulatus sum Marchioni Spi-
" nolæ, quam in hanc regionem illius ergo adveniret.
" Curavi, ut vides, illud typis excudendum. Sed ex
" consilio amicorum hactenus asservavi intra penetra-
" lia Vestæ, nec communicavi nisi cum paucissimis in-
" timæ admissionis. Certe non est visum consultum, ut
" ipsi traderetur. Non quod illic quidquam sit indig-
" num constanti vero vel bono cive: sed quia non vide-
" tur, &c. (45). But yet it was known, that this Poem was printed; and the Author was like to have been banished for it. He escaped that Punishment, only because there were some equitable Persons among those, who examined that Piece of Poetry. *Penè mihi stetit exilio hæc editionis festinatæ temeritas, nisi sanior pars inspectis carmine me omni culpa liberasset* (46). A great many others would have pronounced, that no Body could praise That Marquis, without being a Traitor to the State, and a Pensioner of the Court of *Spain*. *Pravo & sinistro ingenio nati sunt qui crimen & pœnæ perduellionis scelus putant, si quis assurgere audeat in laudem hostis. Tales multos alit hæc ætas, & quidem inter eos sunt qui sedent ad clavum reip. sub quorum maxillis edendum* (47). They would, at least, have appeared, outwardly, of Opinion, that whoever does not speak, or write, according to their Inclinations, and prejudiced Notions, must necessarily be a Traitor: And this it is not to consider, that Reason has different Faces, and does not appear in the same Light to all sorts of Understandings. There were even particular Excuses for *Baudius*: He was a good Poet, and could not avoid thinking on all remarkable Subjects; the Marquis of *Spinola's* coming into *Holland*, was a Subject of that Nature; it was, therefore, very possible, that *Baudius* made Verses on that Marquis, only to exercise his Muse on a noble Matter, without any ill Thoughts against the State. This was not only very possible, but also very probable. Besides, the Expectation of some Pistoles, as a Reward for some Verses, is very consistent with the most perfect Loyalty. The worst that could be said of him, was, that he

(45) Epist. 86. Cent. II. pag. 287.

(46) Ibid. pag. 288.

(47) Ibid. *See also Letter* 95. *Cent. II. p.* 302.

alternate Broadsides, between the University of *Leyden*, and the College of *Antwerp* [*H*]. I have not found, that *Baudius* makes any mention of his Children; but I know that he left his last Wife big with Child (*g*), and that he was at least twice married [*I*], and that this was not the most unexceptionable part of his Life.

Wine he had not the Zeal of the Times, that is, such a Temper of Mind as to take Fire, and startle at the very hearing the Word *Spaniard*. He kept his Affections cool, and wished well to the Public calmly, and without Passion, and only according to Reason. " Ego " tamen si lentum hoc negotium sperato pacis eventu " concludetur, ut ex intimis sensibus voveo, non " dubitabo virum (*Marchionem Spinolam*) affari, & " quidquid hujus est muneris meque omnem ipsi of- " ferre, salvo jure patriæ libertatis (48). ——— But if " this tedious *Treaty* ends in a *Peace*, as I heartily " wish it may, I shall make no Scruple to apply to him, " (the *Marquis Spinola*,) and offer all the Service " I am capable of, consistently with the Liberty of my " Country." But the Public has occasion for quite another Disposition, That of an artificial and blind Hatred. Discourses, which feed this Passion, are at least Appurtenances of Maxims of State, *Arcanorum Imperii*.

[*H*] *There was a reciprocal Storm, and an alternative Assault, between the University of* Leyden, *and the College of* Antwerp.] See the Book entituled, *Væ Victis, lusus Rhetorum advaticorum adversus Leydenses eructationes, munerario Godefrido Vrancken*. It is the true Name of a Jesuit, mentioned by *Alegambus* (49); and yet he ascribes the *Væ Victis* to the Jesuit *Maximilian Habbeque* (50). It was printed in the Year 1609. There is mention made in it of a Writing, which I have not seen, published, the Year before, by the Jesuits of *Antwerp*, against one *Schlaffius*. It would require a long List, to give the Titles of all the Pieces, printed at that Time, in the *Spanish Netherlands*, against the Professors of *Leyden*, and in *Holland*, against the Jesuits. *Baudius* was one of those, whom the Jesuits attacked after the most cruel Manner. He is terribly lashed in the *Væ Victis*. *Scribanius* did not spare him in the Year 1607, in his *Dominici Baudii Gnomæ Commentario illustratæ*. *Baudius* did not deny, but that he had wrote too passionately against the Jesuits, and seemed to be troubled for it; he hoped also, that Persons of Candor would not take rigorously, what he had only expressed according to poetical Licence. Here is what he wrote to *Swertius* (51): " Utinam rebus integris, te monitore & " consiliario essem usus! liber noster, si non melior, " saltem securior & latioribus auspiciis existet in lu- " cem. Multaque nimis licenter effusa, vel privatis " laribus inclusissem ne temere erumperent, vel, quod " tutissimæ cautioni genus est, tardipedi deo com- " misissem. Nunc post culpam admissam serio ringor, " verum haud gravate veniam impetraturus confido " apud elegantioris notæ judices & benignos rerum " æstimatores, qui non abrepti præjudiciis aut lect- " um studiis, in causæ cognitione diligenter expen- " dent, quantum publicis legibus ac moribus licentiæ " Poëtarum concedatur. ——— Ante omnia & vellem & " fuerat melius, non religiose unctos. Nec pruden- " tissimo consilio factum esse confiteor, quod tela " strinxerim in universam Sotericorum sodalitatem. " Sunt enim ex iis multi, quos ob doctrinam & vir- " tutis ac probitatis indolem revereor atque obser- " vo. ——— I *wish I had asked your Advice, before I* " *had taken one Step. My Book, if not with Improve-* " *ments, would, at least, have been published with* " *greater Pleasure and Security. Many things, too* " *freely touched, would either have been kept still* " *private, or, which is the safest Way, committed to* " *the Flames. I now heartily repent of my Fault,* " *but hope to meet with no small Favour from Judges* " *of the highest Rank, who estimate things fairly, and* " *without being influenced by Prejudice or Party, will* " *carefully consider, what Allowances our Laws and* " *Customs always make to poetical Licence.* ——— *A-* " *bove all I wish, and it had better, I never had* " *meddled with the Jesuits*. Nor was it prudent to " attack their whole Society. For there are a great " many of them, whom, for their Learning, Virtue, " and Probity, I reverence and esteem." In another Letter, wherein he owns, that his Stile was too passionate, he hopes, that the Rage, which his Enemies express against him, will excuse him with equitable Persons. He goes on, and says, " I have just " now read a Book, published against me, which is " altogether interwoven with ridiculous Lies, though " the Title seemed only to promise the Pen of a " Friend (52)." *Serio pœnitet quædam nimiæ acerbi- tatis foras erupisse, quæ domi continuisse, & vellem & fuerat melius.* ——— *Verum ut rem natam intelligo, non erit mihi sollicite causa dicenda apud æquos judices. Ipsa enim adversariorum procacitas & convitia sine more effusa largam materiam mihi præbent non tantum ad sperandam absolutionem, sed ad consequendam laudem moderationis ac modestiæ. Vidi enim & evolvi hesterna die à capite ad calcem librum in me conjectum,* &c (53). Several Reasons shew, that the Book he had just read, was the Commentary in *Gnomas* (54). Now that Commentary was a Work of *Scribanius* (55), and yet *Baudius* ascribes it to *Rosweide*, with so much Persuasion, that he declares, nothing can alter that Belief: *For*, says he, *this resembles the other Writings of that Jesuit, like two Drops of Water*; *there appears the same Genius, Humour, Stile, and Character.* We may conclude from hence, by the way, that the best Judges of Stile may be mistaken in their Opinion of this sort of Likeness, and in the Consequences they draw from thence, as to Authors of Books. *Non possum demoveri ab ea sententia quin existimem ac prorsus persuasum habeam, editorem hujus præclari fœtus esse Patrem Heribertum Rosweidum. Nam non ovum ovo, nec aqua è puteo tam similis est aquæ, quam liber iste refert nobis indolem, genium & characterem aliorum librorum, qui ab eodem Patre sunt expositi* (56). What is remarkable in it is, that *Baudius*, who feared to find, in the Commentary on his *Gnomæ*, the Infirmities of which he knew himself guilty, had, as he said, the Comfort to find nothing in it, but such Falsities as were notorious to all those, who knew him. *Verebar ne curiosus alienarum populorum observator, ea mihi ex vero objiceret, quæ seriò conscientiam remorderent, & diligentius vivendi necessitatem imponerent. Nunc quæ de me inclementer dicit, pleraque talia sunt, ut risum non bilem moveant iis qui me norunt, nec ad alios judices provocandum habeo, quàm qui oculis & sensu communi non destituuntur* (57). It is commonly the Fault of Satirists; they are too sparing in the Article of Spy-Money; they impute Crimes which are false, and omit those which are true. *Baudius* disowns the *German* Author, who had made his Apology in the Chair, against the Commentator on the *Gnomæ*. " Quidam parasitaster par- " vulus è Germania huc advenians, me multum recla- " mante, impetravit à Senatu nostro Academico, ut " sibi liceret publice pro mea dignitate scilicet adver- " sus illum declamare. Ac ne quid ad summam fini- " sterlitatis deesset, aut ut caput unctius referret, " etiam orationem illam in vulgus edendam curavit. " Testari possum ex animi sententia, mihi factum istud " vehementer displicuisse. Satius enim erat me de- " seri ab omni patrocinio, quam à tam infirmo tibi- " cine causam nostram sustentari (58). ——— *A certain insignificant Sycophant coming hither from Germany, obtained leave of our University, in spite of all I could say to the contrary, to make a Declamation in my Defence, against that Author. And that he might completely shew his Awkwardness, or make a sprucer Appearance, he has published that Oration. I can truly say, I am exceedingly displeased with this Performance. For it is much better to be destitute of all Defence, than to take up with so poor a one as this.*" I must further observe, that the Invectives, *Baudius* seems most to repent of, are those which relate to Princes and crowned Heads. He did not spare even the King of *France*, who was an Ally of the Republic. *Sed horrifica dictu sunt quæ in Lojolitas, in editorem Amphitheatri, in impurissimum Schoppium stringimus. Atque utinam hoc sine sese cohibuisset styli nostri procacitas. Sed in Pontificem, in Philippos, in Archiduces, in partium duces, evomit virus acerbitatis suæ, nec parcit ipsi Liligero regi* (59).

[*I*] *He was at least twice married.*] He speaks of his Wife's Death, in a Letter of the tenth of *March,* 1610 (60), and he writes the Twenty first of *February*, 1613, that he was married again. *Opinier jam te*

BAUDIUS.

Wine and Women were the two Rocks, on which his Reputation was shipwrecked [K]: This

(61) Epist. 3. Cent. IV.

te ex fama audiisse me choro maritorum iterum esse adscriptum (61). I have not had time to look over every Letter, Page by Page, so that I cannot tell whether he mentions the Time, when he married his first Wife, or whether he had any Children by her, or not: but I know, that this Wife had Children by another Husband: for *Baudius* mentions a Son, and a Daughter of his Wife (62), and complains also of the Daughter's ill Houswifry (63). Perhaps the Son-in-Law, which *Theophilus* gives to this Professor, might be this bad Houswife's Husband. It may be also, that, for want of Attention, *Theophilus* calls him Son-in-law, who was only *privignus*, the Wife's Son (64). The Author of the *Væ Victis* observes, that *Baudius* had no Children.

(62) Epist. 8. Cent. IV. pag. 486, & alibi.

(63) Epist. 22. Cent. III. p. 344.

(64) See above, at the end of the Remark [A] of the Article BALZAC (f. L. Guez de).

Natura quamvis liberos neget tibi
Effœte BURDI, nec tibi BAUDI, tua
Similes parentis Hecuba filios creet (65).

(65) In Epicitha‹ i mate pag. 13.

*Tho' sterile Burdius no Offspring knows;
Nor Hecuba, whom for his Wife he chose,
To Baudius his Infant Likeness shews.*

[K] *Wine and Women were the two Rocks, on which his Reputation was shipwrecked.*] Since this Remark will be somewhat long, I shall divide it into Sections.

I. As to the first, he confesses the Fact: See three fine Passages on that Subject, at the Head of his Letters, extracted from his own Letters. I only relate the first and second. "Concurrunt omnes, *says*

(66) In Epistola quædam ad Curatores Academiæ, It is the 33d of Cent. III. of Edit. of 8vo, the Passage is at pag. 362.

" *he* (66), non dicam ut ille Satyricus, augures, ha-
" ruspices, sed quidquid est ubique hominum curio-
" sorum, qui in aliorum acta tam sedulo inquirunt,
" ut ea fingant quæ nunquam fuerunt, nihil inveniet
" quod in nobis carpere possit livor, quam quod ic-
" terdum ad exemplum prisci Catonis liberalius in-
" vitari nos patimur, nec semper constistimus intra
" sobrietatem veterum Sabinorum. Huic quoque pec-
" catulo indies moderari conamur, & pulchre proce-
" dit. —— *I defy, not only as the Satirist says, Au-*
" *gurs, and Soothsayers; but also all inquisitive Per-*
" *sons whatever, who pry so industriously into other*
" *Peoples Affairs, and forge Facts which never hap-*
" *pened, to discover, if they can, any thing in my*
" *Character, worthy of Censure, except my now and*
" *then indulging a little too freely, after the Ex-*
" *ample of old Cato, and breaking through the Rules of the Sabines. And even this small Fault*
" *I am every Day endeavouring to mend, and have*
" *gained a good deal of Ground.*" He expresses this with a better Grace, in the second Passage: " Ma-
" lignitas obtrectatorum nihil aliud in nobis sugillare
" potest quàm quod nimis commodus sim conviva-
" tor, & interdum largius adspergor flore Liberi pa-
" tris (67). —— *The most malicious can accuse me of*

(67) Epist. 26 Cent. III. p. 35?.

" *nothing but being too good a Companion, and some-*
" *times tasting a little too freely of the Favours of Fa-*
" *ther Bacchus.*" Since he has confessed his Fault, there is no occasion to produce Scriverius as a Witness against him, who supposes, that Charon, having given *Baudius* his Choice, either to remain in the other World, or to return into this, on condition to drink Water, and take his first Wife again, *Baudius*

(68) See Dominici Baudii Amores, pag. 14.

chose the former (68). Here is already something relating to the second Head; Scriverius would not have made such a Supposition, if *Baudius* had lived well with his first Wife.

II. Never had any Man less need to be comforted than he, when he lost her. His good Friend Heinsius could not forbear being merry upon it, both in Prose and in Verse, which he addressed to him; he wrote to Grotius on the same Subject, and told him, That our Age did not come short of That, which had seen *Xenophon* make an end of his Sacrifice, notwithstanding the News of his Son's Death: nor of That, which had seen *Q. Martius* go from the Burial of his Son to the Senate. "*Baudius, says he to him,* made
" himself drunk the Day he buried his Wife, and
" left nothing to do for the Comforters; he had effe-
" ctually administered to himself, before their coming,
" all the Consolation it was possible for them to think
" of. The emptiness of his Purse is much more
" grievous to him, than the Vacancy he has met
" with in his Bed. I have helped him to some Money,
VOL. I.

" which has revived all his Spirits; for, instead of That
" melancholy Air, and those down-cast Looks, which
" appeared in him, as if his Wife had been still living,
" I say, instead of that great Sadness, I perceived him
" raised all at once to a sort of Gaiety." *Baudius noster*
es ipse quæ uxorem extulit die vinum gustare voluit ——
omnia solatia quæ exulceratis adhiberi mentibus solent
ipse occupavit. Nihil amici in luctu reliquit quod vel
imputare illi possent —— *Stabat antea demissa vultu*
ac tristi: uxorem ejus vivere adhuc credidisses (69).
Vix spes melior affulsit, respirare cœpit, & constan-
ter multa de fragilitate vitæ disputare: nemo funus
esse in ædibus existimasset (70). All these Pieces of
Heinsius are diverting. But this Insensibility was not
the greatest Fault *Baudius* committed, in relation to
that Sex. We shall see, presently, more unlucky Incidents.

(69) Ibid. pag. 12, 13‹.

(70) Ibid.

As soon as he came into *France*, he stopped so long at *Caen*, that there was a Report he was detained there by a Mistress. *Non posse me binc à muliercula*
divelli quam impotenti amore deperam (71). He denied it, and said, that the Dangers, which he had met with in the Journey, were the Cause of so long a stay. He said also, that, in spite of the Oppressions of the Professors, he might, at least, have taught the Civil-Law at *Caen*, if he had not engaged himself elsewhere. He gives a very bad Idea of That University, as to the Faculty of the Civil-Law. " Timu-
" erunt sibi Juridici Professores ne ego —— eos de
" imperitiæ possessione dejicerem. —— Præses de quo
" retuli verbis acribus homines istos castigavit eosque
" assimilavit Draconi Hesperidum hortorum. Tenes
" quorsum. Quid multa? frementibus miseriis istis
" leguleis partim odio religionis, partim conscientia
" Inscitiæ suæ, perfectum est ut qui Leidæ gradum
" accepissent, legitime promoti videantur (72). ——
" *These Professors of Civil-Law were afraid that I*
" —— *should dispossess them of their Ignorance.* ——
" *The President, I told you of, severely reprimanded*
" *them, and compared them to the Dragon, who watched*
" *the Hesperian Gardens. You know on what Account.*
" *In short; notwithstanding the Opposition of those*
" *wretched half Civilians, partly from the Quarrel*
" *of Religion, and partly from the Consciousness of*
" *their own Ignorance, it was established, that they, who*
" *had taken their Degree at Leyden, should be allowed*
" *as regular.*"

(71) Epist. 16. Cent. I. pag 36.

(72) Epist 23. Cent I. pag 44. See also his Poem In tres Juris Perverters, ibid. p. 35›

Scriverius believed, that Lipsius meant *Baudius*, when he wrote to Barclay, in the Year 1599. "Scri-
" bit ad me, queritur, fed parum aperte, & ulcus
" aliquod sermonum eâ veste tegi equidem odoror.
" Si leve curatu, parum est: sin pravum aliquod &
" ϕυσίωδον (insanabile) doleo causâ præclari inge-
" nii quod sese (ah temere, ah stulte) in barathrum
" & præceps dedit. *Quis illigatum te triformi Pe-*
" *gasus expediet Chimærâ?* Sed meliora opto (73). ——
" *He writes to me, and complains, but with*
" *so much Reserve, that I suspect some Ulcer at the*
" *bottom. If it may be easily healed, the Matter is*
" *not great; but if it be of a malignant Kind, and*
" *incurable, I shall be sorry for the sake of so inge-*
" *nious a Man, that he should, foolishly, and incon-*
" *siderately, throw himself headlong into such a Pit.*
" *Where will you find a Bellerophon to extricate you*
" *from this monstrous Chimæra? But I hope better*
" *Things.*" This favours of a Man drawn into, or deeply engaged in, an unhappy Intrigue.

(73) See Amores Baudii at the begnning.

To end with the worst part, I shall anticipate the Order of Time, and here observe, that he had made a Promise of Marriage, which he did not keep. ——
When he found himself a Widower, and pressed both by his Poverty and Constitution, to seek another Wife, he charged two of his Friends to inform him of the Circumstances of his former Mistress, and declared to them, that, if she was rich, he was ready to marry her before any other. He did not question but that he was still beloved by her. " Veteribus
" amoribus meis ex animo volo, nec ullam præopta-
" verim, si ad cæteras dotes accedit etiam copiofus
" imber qui olim per impluvium defluxit in sinum
" *Danaes.* —— Nisi molestum sit, velim aliquid
" temporis impartiare disquisitioni, quo loco res ejus
" fitæ sint. Nam quin vivat nostri memor, & non
" immunis amorum, nullus dubito (74). The Answer he received, was a Proof that he had too good an Opinion of himself: the Lady declared, she did not love great Drinkers. *Baudius* apprehended her meaning,

(74) Epist. 22. Cent. III. p. 345, dated June 1. 1610.

8 K

This exposed him to Contempt, and Public Laughter. His very Friends made smart

meaning, and his Conscience was eased by that Refusal; for he made a Scruple of breaking his Promise; but now he found himself free, since she would not accept of him. "Etsi sincero affectu nympham illam prosequor, tamen magis liberandæ fidei religione, & veterum repromissorum ultro citroque stipulatarum memoria adductus sum, ut consortium ejus ambire non dedignarer, quam formæ lenocinio, vel divitiarum conditione (75). —— Gaudeo me bona cum nymphæ ejus gratia liberatum esse nexu veteris promissi, καὶ δυσλύτου συναλλάγματ[Ο], cujus adhuc me nonnulla incessebat superstitio (76)." It is remarkable, that all these Scruples of Conscience did not hinder him from annexing a Condition to the Design of executing his promise. Which Condition was, that his former Mistress should be rich (77), or else he would not marry her; and, to soften what might be too hard in this Resolution, he added, that, in this, he only considered her Interest; for, said he, *would it not be very injurious to her, to bring me Children, who could expect no other Inheritance from us, but Poverty and Hunger?* "Tu vero me tacente satis intelligis quam parum ex usu utriusque foret, τὸν πενίαν καὶ τὴν πεῖναν (78), infelici contubernio invicem sociari. Quocirca nisi tam bene fundatum sit patrimonium amicæ, quam unice diligo, ut sine notabili incommodo nostris difficultatibus mederi queat, in rem communem est ut aliud mihi subsidium prospiciam. Quod ne in eam partem velit interpretari, quasi quidquam detrimenti ceperit amor ille pristinus, quo juvenculam forma & ætate florentem sum complexus, testor ex animi sententia me hoc ejus causa facere, ne liberos educemus in spem egestatis atque esuritionis (79)."

He made his Addresses elsewhere, *viz.* to one, whose Name was *Sophia*, in whom he found nothing good but her Riches. She had a very brutish Father, from whom he received a thousand Hardships; and she seconded her Father for some time, and complained of having been stolen: Very probably, she had been taking a Ramble for some Days with *Baudius*, which was then a piece of Gallantry in that Country. *Baudius* thought this Complaint very ridiculous, and most likely to stain *Sophia*'s Reputation; and he said, by way of Allusion to *Fimbria*'s Process against *Scævola*, that she had nothing to complain of, except that the Weapon was not thrust up to the Hilt. "Nihil habet quod de nobis queratur, nisi forte velit eam intentare accusationem quam adversus Scævolam —— quod scilicet non totum telum corpore receperit (80)." *Sophia* was pacified, and seemed to disapprove her Father's Brutality. *Baudius* was in Raptures at this, and spoke of nothing but Marriage, though he knew very well, that this Mistress had no other Merit but a good Portion. The last Obstacle was removed, which was a Promise of Marriage, *Baudius* had made to a prostituted Servant, whose hold him on his Promise (81), and I believe, that, after this, the Marriage with *Sophia* was consummated. The following Passages prove This Lady's ill Qualities, and her Father's Brutality. "Hesterna die gravier apud Rectorem questus sum de —— Renovavi etiam veteres offensas quod me in causa desipientis Sophiæ allocutus esset tanquam vitæ iratum, & candidatum patibuli. Sed Sophiam istam suis moribus ulciscendam permitto, si quidem rata habet quæ barbarus parens in me rustice & inciviliter designavit: nam contrarii rumores ad me deferuntur. Nonnulli dicunt eam honorifice & amice de nobis loqui: quod si ita est, recte & ordine facere ipsam arbitror, καὶ γὰρ τοῖς λωίον εἶν, & tunc paratus sum omnium præteritorum memoriam fideli amnestia ex animo delere, καὶ μὴ μνησικακεῖν. Sin talia flagitia probat, nunquam eam sermone fuero dignatus. Sunt enim qui dicant me ab ipsa proscindi tam cruentis convitiis, quasi crimen sit quod vivam (82). —— *Yesterday I complained heavily to the Rector concerning* —— *I even ripped up former Grudges, and accused him of having treated me, in the Affair of the foolish Sophia, as One angry with Life, and a Candidate for the Gallows. As for Sophia, I leave her to the Punishment of her own Manners; if she indeed approves of the just and uncourteous Treatment I have met with from the Brute her Father; for I have been told the contrary. Some say, that she speaks, respectfully and friendly of me; if This be true, I think she behaves with justice and decency; and I am then ready to forget every thing past. But, if she approves of such vile Treatment, I will never condescend to speak to her more. For I am informed by some, that She reproaches me with such bitterness, as if it were a Crime, that I am alive.*" Behold a good-natured Man! he had already shewn, that he was easy to be pacified. "Reversus domum —— optata omnia comperi de mea *Sophia,* quæ me absente ancillam lecti & arcanorum sociam misit ad patrem scitatum —— super nostra majestate, an durius accepissem plenam familiaritatis repulsam, an æra bestia factus essem, amissa voluntate revertendi. Ego vero oculum mihi exsculpi malim, quam pati ut tam opima conditio elabatur e manibus (83). —— *Returning home, I found every thing relating to my Sophia just as I could wish: She had sent her Chamber-Maid and Confidant to her Father, to enquire —— concerning My Majesty; whether I resented her absolutely denying to admit of my Familiarity, and whether I was so furiously enraged, as to resolve never to return. For my own part, I would sooner lose an Eye, than miss so fair an Opportunity of being happy.*" This Good nature would be less shameful, were it not for the Poverty, to which *Baudius* was reduced, and the great Estate of His *Sophia.* We meet with the following Words, in the Ninety fifth Page of the *Dominici Baudii amores,* and in the first Letter of the IVth Century, Page 479. This Letter was written the Twenty first of *July* 1612. "Plerique putant hanc labem non alia conditione deletum iri, quam si insulsum pecus uxorem duxero, cui præter Sophiæ nomen nihil adest humani cordis. An ideo pereundum erat Pompeio magno, si Lucullus non esset luxuriosus? Ego invitam cogere non possum ut velit esse conjux invicti Jovis, & tanti non est ut vel illi, vel furioso parenti supplicem. Dos tamen non esset adspernanda, nisi marita foret, & posset absque muliebri capite contingere. Postquam —— reversus fuerit, persuasu amicorum decretum est mihi jacere novissimam aleam, & exquirere an mecum lege fidelis καὶ ἀδόλου ἀμνησίας pascisci velit. Paratus sum ex animi sententia conceptis verbis jurare μὴ μνησικακεῖν: dum & ipsa levitatis culpam agnoscat, & parentis furias non approbet. Si tergiversabitur, relinquam illam ulciscendam suis moribus, & aliam consortem invenero, quæ melius intelliget suam felicitatem. —— *Many think I can never wipe off this Disgrace, but by marrying This Foolish Creature, who has nothing of Human, but The Name of Sophia. Would Pompey the Great have been ruined, if Lucullus had not been luxurious? I cannot compel her, against her Will, to be the Wife even of* Jupiter *himself; and it is not worth my while humbly to sue either to Her, or her mad-brained Father. Her Fortune, I confess, is not despicable, could it be obtained without marrying, and having the Woman into the bargain. When he returns, I have resolved, by the Advice of my Friends, to make one Effort more, and try, whether we can come to terms of Agreement, on condition of forgetting every Thing past. I am ready, on my part, sincerely to swear an eternal Oblivion; provided She acknowledges her own Levity, and does not approve of the injurious Treatment of her Father. If she shall refuse to comply with this Offer, I will leave her to the Punishment of her own Manners, and look out for another Wife, who shall better understand her own Happiness.*" Some Days before he had more Courage. He had a good Opinion of himself: He says, in the same Letter, that he is not so exhausted, but he may yet obtain a Woman of Merit, though he has been so foolish, as to pay a long Courtship to an impertinent *Xantippe.* "Non adeo exarui ex amoribus & humoribus, ut bona mes sapienti fæminæ vendi tare non possim, etiamsi tam insipienter circa Sophiam deliraverim, ut mihi Socratica fides objecta sit (84)." He was resolved to make a fresh Attempt; but was so much disgusted at This foolish Creature, and her brutish Father, that he almost wished

smart Jests upon it, which have been printed. Nevertheless, we must not believe

ed to be again refused. "Heri mihi Heinsius noster
" adfuit, & rogatu meo adductus, partim sua sponte
" incitatus, recepit in se munus colloquendi serio cum
" Festo Hommio περὶ τῆς Σοφίας. Is tenet cla-
" vum imperii, & patris animum habet in sua manu.
" Sed summa cum æquitate exspecto quemlibet even-
" tum, & prope est ut malim repulsam, ita me tædet
" & contumeliarum parentis, & insulsorum filiæ mo-
" rum, quæ præter nomen non possidet micam sa-
" lis (85). ——— *Our Friend Heinsius was with me
" yesterday, and has undertaken, partly at my Re-
" quest, and partly of his own meer Motion, to talk
" seriously with Festus Hommius about Sophia. I
" am little sollicitous for the Event; nay I almost wish
" to be refused, so tired am I of the Father's contu-
" melious Behaviour, and the folly and stupidity of
" the Daughter, who has not common Sense, and is a
" Woman only in Name.*"

We are now come to the most disgraceful Scene of All. *Baudius* kept a Concubine for some time. She was a Servant-Maid, who was common to several Students, and who, finding herself with Child, fathered it on *Baudius* alone. She insisted likewise, that he had promised her Marriage, and summoned him before the Judges, to oblige him to perform his Promise. This Affair was both matter of Scandal and Laughter; but they, who know the World, will easily believe, that it occasioned more of the latter, than the former. *Baudius's* Superiors could do no less than disgrace him, by suspending him from his Office. The Raillieries, to which he found himself exposed, made him take a Journey to *Ghent*. "In-
" ter alias causas quæ me moverant ut in viam me
" darem hæc fuit non infima, ut prudenti absentia
" subterducerem me ab importunis conjugii disparis
" congratulationibus, quibus cottidie aures meæ cir-
" cumsonabantur (86). ——— *Among other reasons,
" which induced me to take a Journey, This was not
" the least, that, by prudently absenting myself, I
" might avoid the Congratulations on an unequal Match,
" with which I was perpetually teized.*" He seemed to question, whether This Servant-Maid was with Child; but he was afraid, that, if she should lye-in, she should swear the Brat to Him; for which reason he desired his Friends to order it so, that such a Slut as she should not be admitted to take her Oath; and offered voluntarily to do whatever the Laws of Humanity required; that is, to take care of the Child, which should be born: but he thought it hard to be obliged to it. "Periculum enim est in mora, nam
" propinqua partitudo appetit, siquidem paritura est,
" nam permulti dubitant num sit gravida, quod si est,

Sublimi feriam sidera vertice.

" Cuperem inferi mandato, non esse illi scorto pub-
" lice diffamatissimo deferendum jusjurandum tem-
" pore partionis, nec habendam fidem in designando
" parente tam multorum capitum.

Cum suis vivat valeatque mœchis,
Quos simul complexa tenet trecentos.

" Ego nihilominus sponte mea incitatus faciam quod
" officium humanitatis injungit. Sed cogi Baudium
" non decet, non opportet, à tam prostituti pudoris
" scorto (87). ——— *Delays are dangerous;
" for she is near her Time, if she be really with
" Child, which many doubt of; if so,*

I'll strike my Head against the Stars.

" I could wish it were inserted in the Mandate, that
" This most infamous Prostitute be not allowed to give
" her Oath at the time of her Delivery, and that
" no credit be given to her in pointing out the Father
" of the many-headed Offspring.

Will fare the Jade, with her three hundred Sparks.

" However I am willing to do every thing, which
" the Laws of Humanity require. But Baudius ought
" not to be compelled by so shameless an Harlot." However, he chose rather to keep Another's Child, than desert a human Creature, and comforted himself with the Reflexion, that it would be a Proof of his Manly Vigor; and that hereafter it would be no Prejudice to his future Wife *Sophia*, who should be a Field, for the Cultivation of which he would from thenceforth reserve his whole Strength. "Ut ut res cadet, nihil mihi evenire potest tristius
" aut deterius quam quod animo præcepi, & mecum
" ante peregi. Nempe futurum, ut perjurio caput
" alliget, & ὑποσολιμαῖον obtrudat heroi Baudio.
" Quid tum postea? Malo agnoscere alienum, quam
" fœtum humanum non ali. Testimonio erit me
" marem esse, & viri munia posse fungi. Nihil
" inde abradetur in posterum meæ Sophiæ, cujus ar-
" vo familiari reservabitur

Quidquid in arte mea possum promittere (88).

" ——— *However, nothing can happen to me
" more unfortunate, than what I suspect, namely, that
" This Jade will perjure herself, and obtrude a Ba-
" stard upon the Hero Baudius. But what then? I
" had rather father Another's Brat, than suffer an
" human Creature to perish. Besides it will be a
" Proof of my Manhood, and Ability to perform the
" Duties of an Husband. My Sophia will not here-
" after find she has lost any Thing by it; for the
" Culture of whose Field shall be reserved*

All I can promise in the Tilling-Art.

He wrote This the Twenty ninth of *March* 1612, when it was reported, that the Servant-Maid was ready to lye-in. "Fertur esse, ἐν ὀδύνῃ, sed nul-
" lus credo,

——— Licet illi plurima manet

Lacryma.

" Sunt enim, quibus non potest persuaderi, eam esse
" gravidam, & ego quidlibet credo cadere posse falsi-
" moniæ, fraudis, & malitiæ in tam profligatam,
" perditam, atque infestabilem fœminam. ——— *She
" is said to be in labour; but I give no credit to it,
" notwithstanding all her Tears; for some will not
" be persuaded she is with Child; and I can easily
" believe so profligate, abandoned, and detestable, a
" Woman capable of any Falshood, Cheat, and wicked
" Contrivance.*" He did not deny, but that he had promised the Girl Marriage; but pretended, that such a Prostitute, as she, did not deserve to enjoy the Benefit of the Laws: He did not believe, that any Faith ought to be kept with this Kind of Heretics; for he recollected, that he had read so in the *Code*; but, as he could not cite the place, he desired *Grotius* to put his Advocate upon producing That Law, in order to put a stop to the Proceedings of his Doxy. And, as This Girl's Pretensions was the only Thing, which hindered *Baudius's* Mistress from signing the Marriage-Contract, he desired his Friend to dispatch the Matter. "Domum reversus audivi nun-
" cium perquam optabilem de meis amoribus. Om-
" nia eveniunt ex animi sententia, nec quidquam
" deest ad votorum summam, nisi ut eximam scrupu-
" lum de pollicitatione matrimonii cum exoleto isto
" propudio, labe & tabe meæ famæ & exstimationis.
" Hanc tu pestem ac perniciem si amolitus fueris pro
" dignitate muneris quo fungeris, & pro scortatore
" qua merito vales plurimum, solidiorem capies glo-
" riam, quam

——— Dirum qui contudit hydram,
Notaque fatali portenta labore subegit.

" Tam viles personæ, tam diabolares victimæ publi-
" carum libidinum, non sunt dignæ observatione
" legum, ut memini aliquando legere in corpore
" Juris, sed locus non occurrit memoriæ. Quæso
" te, ut hisce literis perlectis continuo cures accersen-
" dum advocatum vander Werven, qui legem hor-
" rendi carminis dictet, cujus obnunciatione fulmi-
" nari possit fatalis illa fundi nostri calamitas. Hoc
" ego beneficium tanti faciam, ut nemini plus in vita
" sim unquam debiturus. Sed maturas oro, nam
" amanti & animo cupienti nihil satis festinatur (89).
" ——— *Returning home, I received the most
" agreeable News in relation to my Love Affair. Every
" thing is as I could wish, nor is any thing*

" wanting

lieve All that the fatyrical *Scioppius* has publifhed on this laft Head [*L*]. Some Tempers

" *wanting to the Completion of my Defires, but to re-*
" *move the Scruple about my Promife of Marriage to*
" *That Proftitute, the Stain of my Character and Re-*
" *putation. If, by the Dignity and Authority of*
" *your Function, you can rid me of This Plague, you*
" *will gain more Honour, than He,*

Whofe Toil the Dire, Portentous, Hydra quell'd.

" *Such Infamous Wretches, fuch Diabolical Victims*
" *to Public Luft, deferve not the Regard of the Laws;*
" *as I remember to have read fomewhere in the Code,*
" *though the Paffage does not at prefent occur to my*
" *Memory. I defire you, upon the Receipt of This*
" *Letter, to fend for the Advocate* Vander Werven,
" *who, by reciting the dreadful Denunciation, may*
" *terrify This Creature, who gives me fo much Diftur-*
" *bance. But be as expeditious as poffible; for Love*
" *is impatient of Delay.*" This is what he wrote on the Twenty eighth of *March*. He was not clear of the Affair in the Month of *June*: the Girl was yet in hopes of being married to him either by fair or foul Means; and *Baudius* durft not appear before his Miftrefs, during this Suit with his Concubine. " Hoc
" nifi fundamentum præftruatur, non finit θυμός
" ἀγήνωρ, ut viam affectem ad meam Divam, quæ
" non intelligit fua bona: nec ideo tamen demove-
" bor ab amandi propofito, quamdiu fpes aliqua fupe-
" rerit expugnandi ferreum iftud pectus (90). - - - -
(90) Epift. " *Till This Foundation be laid, my Pride will not fuf-*
96. Cent. " *fer me to approach my Goddefs, who does not under-*
III. p. 408, " *ftand her own Good; yet will I perfift in my Refolu-*
dated June " *tion of paying my Addreffes to her, whilft there is*
11, 1612. " *any hope of conquering that ftubborn Breaft.*" He was inclined to enter into Articles with the Girl, and defired *Grotius* to draw them up; hoping, that the Creature, intimidated by his Threatnings, would fign the Agreement. " A tuo difceffu nec patrem
" τῆς ἀτόφου Σοφίας allocutus fum, nec me conve-
" niendum curavit Mercurii mater, nifi quod audio
" eam adhuc pafcere ebriofas, futiles, & furiofas fpes
" de matrimonio.

- - - - - - - fed prius Appulis
Jungentur capreæ lupis.

" Quid mihi autor es ut faciam ? expectem litis even-
" tum ? hoc fpiffum eft amanti, cujus animo nihil fatis
" feftinatur. Quanquam hifce nugis jam longum
" valedixi, faltem inducias pepigi. Cuperem ad me
" mitti per hunc ipfum nuncium formulam tranf-
" actionis, quam ipfe conceptifti. Spero me effecturum
" injecto metu majoris malitatis ut cupide fubfignet,
(91) Ibid. " & voluntariam condemnationem fubeat (91). - - - -
" *Since your Departure, I have not once fpoke to the*
" *Father of the foolifh Sophia, who, I am informed,*
" *ftill entertains vain hopes of the Match. But, fooner*

The Goat fhall mix with The Appulian Wolf.

" *What would you advife me to do? To wait the*
" *Event of the Suit? The Impatience of a Lover can-*
" *not bear delay: though I have bid a long Adieu to*
" *thefe Follies, at leaft have made a Truce with them.*
" *I could wifh you would fend me by the Bearer of*
" *This The Articles of Accommodation, which you*
" *yourfelf have conceived. I hope, by threatning her*
" *with fomething worfe, to prevail upon her readily to*
" *fign Them, and fubfcribe her own Condemnation.*"
The Affair was yet undecided in the Month of *July*
(92) See Let- following (92), and *Baudius* thought it very ftrange,
ter 97, of that This Slut was not banifhed out of the Country.
Cent. III. " Tot Juftitiæ Antiftites unicam maleficam Circen,
*pag. 473, " quæ meos fenfus venenavit, amoliri non poffunt,
well often, " faltem ut Lædam contagione fua, & ædes meas
of Cent. IV, " noxia vicinitate, non intellet (93). - - - *So many*
p. 470. " *Difpenfers of Juftice cannot rid me of One mif-*
(93) Epift. 1. " *chievous* Circe, *who bewitched my Senfes; nor even*
Cent. IV. " *prevent her from infefting* Leyden *with her Conta-*
" *gion, and my Houfe with her baneful Neighbourhood.*"
He refolved, that fhe was fuffered to continue his Neighbour, that the Indignity of fo many Affronts might force him to retire elfewhere. *Video hoc agi*
" *ut contraverfiis haud tolerandis ἄκοντα θυμῷ adigar*
" *ad difpiciendam pedum viam, & quærendam haud*
(94) Ibid. " *ingloria atque inopis exilii fedem* (94). At laft he

put an end of the Affair, not by a Sentence of the Judges, but by way of Accommodation, on the Twentieth of *October* 1612. He conceded as little as
poffible ; *redemi me captum quam potui minimo* (95) ; (95) Epift.
after which he was foon married. He wrote to 28. Cent. IV.
Peter Rubens (96), that he was very well fatisfied
with his Wife. I do not know, whether he changed (96) It is
his Mind; but, however it be, This Marriage was Letter 3, of
of no long Continuance. *Baudius* died the Twenty Cent. IV,
fecond of *Auguft* 1613, being reduced to a miferable pag. 483,
Condition by a *Delirium*. *Delirio ac Vigiliis conti-* 21, 1613.
nuis miferè attritus, omnique tandem robore exutus
(97). His beft Friends laughed at his Follies in Love. (97) In VI-
One of them propofed him as an Example to all In- ta ejus.
continent Perfons, and exhorted them to reftrain their Paffions by the moft auftere Remedies, rather than indulge them like *Baudius*:

Quifquis es, exemplo tanti moveare mariti,
Parce libidinibus luxuriofe tuis.
Addita fit potius lafcivo fibula membro,
Ut vindicta tuam tranfeat ifta domum (98). (98) Scrive-
rius in Epi-
taphio Bau-
Whoe're Thou art, a Slave to Joys of Senfe, dii, p. 235.
Let This Example teach thee Continence. Baudii A-
Wou'dft Thou avoid vindictive Fortune's Frown, morum.
Let the ftrong Button keep the Rebel Member
down.

See the Collection, entituled *Baudii Amores*, pub-
lifhed by *Scriverius*, in the Year 1638. You will find there, at page 77, *A Cento Virgilianus* of *Daniel Heinfius*, " ad Dominicum Baudium, qui poftquam
" ignarus cum ancilla, cum qua tum alii, tum plu-
" rimi fcholaftici confuerant, aliquamdiu congeffus
" effet, folus præter expectationem prole ab ea eft
" donatus —— *to* Dominic Baudius, *who, after hav-*
" ing correfponded with a Girl, who was common to
" feveral Students, had alone a Child unexpectedly
" fathered upon him."
No doubt, fome will fay, it would have been better to have pointed out, in the Margin, where thefe Things are to be found, than to produce fo many Paffages of This Author; but many others will be glad not to be at the Trouble of looking for them. It is to pleafe the Lazy, whofe number was never fo great as in This Age, that I have taken the Pains to collect Thefe Paffages of *Baudius*. Let no one complain, that I difturb the Afhes of the Dead; for I fay nothing but what *Baudius's* Friends have publifhed, and what other Authors have informed the Public of feveral
times. See *Spizelius* (99), who cites a Book, which (99) Theo
I would willingly have confulted : It was printed in philus Spi
the Year 1675 (100). zelius in I
felice Lite
[*L*] *We muft not believe all that the fatyrical* Sci- rato, p. 11
oppius *has publifhed on This laft Head.*] He fpeaks
too ill of him, to deferve credit ; the moft infamous (100) Spe
Pimping, and Magic, are the Exploits, which he men Bibli
attributes to him. His *Latin* Words cannot modeftly fophiftaruy
be rendered into *Englifh*: The Original is This : Gadenenfi
" Baudius Parifiis, ubi multis annis in concubinatu fum- um, publ',
" ma cum fœmina & velut *quadruplataris* filium dece- ed by Schel
" bat, vixit, non tantum magiæ deditus, incantatoribus vig d.
" & fortilegiis ædes fuas aperuit, & concubinæ fuæ
" filiolam ad peragenda nefaria facra commodavit,
" Dæmoniumque de thefauris reconditis, imprimifque
" de Petronio utrum is alicubi integer exftaret, con-
" fuluit ; fed etiam amicis quibufdam majorem quan-
" dam ingenii divinitatem præferentibus ejufdem con-
" cubinæ filium, puerum non inelegantem, turpiffi-
" mus leno proftituit, ut cum poftea tumentibus pueri
" marifcis fcelus propalatum iri metueret, quo minus
" eum veneno connubernales tollerent, minimè impe-
" divit, actumque jam de miffello puero fuerit, nifi
" unius contubernalium acumine expediti fuiffent,
" anicula, quæ morbo mederi fciret, inventa. Nec
" nequaquam à me fingi, neminem paulò humanio-
" rum Parifiis ignorare puto (101)." The General (101) A1
Senfe of which is as follows; that " *Baudius*, living phot ides
" many Years in a State of Fornication at *Paris*, con- Scioppius
" verfed with Magicians and Enchanters, and con- pag. 166.
" fulted the Devil about hidden Treafures, and par-
" ticularly whether *Petronius* was any where to be
" found entire ; and that, having proftituted the Son
" of his Concubine, and being in danger of being
" difcovered,

BAUDIUS. 687

Tempers are exposed to the hazard of losing a good Name. It cannot be denied, that *Baudius* was of an amorous Complexion: He was but a Student in Divinity, when he fell in Love with a Girl, who lodged at the Professor *Lambert Danœus*'s House (*h*). The Remarks will inform us farther of This Affair. He was too free in his Opinions, and even in his Discourse, and had not the Prudence to accommodate himself to the Prejudices of the Times; This could not but create him Enemies, and expose himself to the ill Effects of their rash Judgments (*i*). He consulted Platonic Ideas too much; which is the reason, why he was a little too much scandalized at the Disputes, which were raised in *Holland*. He foretold the ill Consequences of them, some of which proved false, and others true. He thought They would occasion an Alteration in the Government; in This he was mistaken [*M*]; he believed they would create a Schism; In this he judged right [*N*]. They, who published his *Letters*, have procured more Delight

(*h*) See his 26th Letter Cent. II. pag. 224.

(*i*) See Remark [M].

---

(102) See Lett. 79, of Baudius, Cent. II. p. 276.

"discovered, by some Marks of the Injury he had "done him, he would have suffered him to be poiso- "ned, had not an Old Woman been found, who "undertook to cure the Child." If These things were so well known at *Paris*, as *Scioppius* affirms, how came it, that the First President appointed *Baudius* to be his Son's Secretary in an Embassy? *Scioppius* invented This, or had it from ill-grounded Stories, and divulged it in revenge for the abusive Language, which *Baudius* had given him, even before The *Scaliger Hypobolimæus* appeared (102).

[*M*] *He thought They would occasion an Alteration in the Government; in This He was mistaken.*] We must hear Himself: He declares, that, were it not for Conscience, and Religion, he would have retired elsewhere long before, and that the violent Disputes of the Divines, and many other Disorders, made him fear, that the Work of the Reformation would be very much endangered by them. " Nisi me in his locis " conscientiæ scrupulos, & religionis vinculum atti- " neret, jampridem captum esset augurium de mi- " grando, nec Leida spes meas includeret. Quan- " quam non pessime mecum agitur. Sed nec ea no- " stri ratio habetur, quam opportuit. Theologorum " etiam nostrorum dissidentes, & virulentæ concer- " tationes, odia fratrum, quæ ne morte quidem fini- " untur, aliaque nostræ militiæ flagitia, penè effici- " unt ut & illud superbum nomen reformatæ religi- " onis, & ipsâ causâ incipiat mihi esse dubiæ sanita- " tis. —— Præsagit mihi animus imminere his Pro- " vinciis fatalem rerum commutationem, & ex inte- " stinis vitiis rediturum aliquando veteris imperii de- " siderium. Suspectus sum multis, & charus accep- " tusque non paucis, quod voce & stilo passim in- " culco subditorum obsequia in legitimos Principes, " & pleno ore decanto veras laudes Archiducum (103).

(103) Epist. 72, Cent. III. p. 431, 433; dated March 9, 1610.

" —— *Did not a Scruple of Conscience, and the Tie " of Religion, detain me, I had e'er now departed " in a good Hour, nor had Leyden any longer been " the Object of my Wishes. Though my Condition " here is far from being the worst. But I do not " meet with proper Regard. Besides, The virulent " Disputes of Our Divines, the Animosities among " Brethren, which Death itself cannot put an end to, " and Other Enormities of our Warfare, induce me " to suspect, that the proud Name of Reformation, " and the Cause itself, is but short-lived.* —— *I fore- " see a fatal Alteration in the Affairs of These Pro- " vinces, and am apprehensive, that the Intestine Di- " visions, which reign among us, will make the Peo- " ple wish for the ancient Government. I render my- " self suspected to Many, and acceptable to not a Few, " by inculcating, both in Conversation and Writing, the " Obedience of Subjects to their Lawful Princes, and " celebrating the true Praises of the Arch-Dukes.*" I question not, but *Baudius* proposed the Doctrine of the Obedience of Subjects, which he mentions, with too much Indiscretion, and Confidence; so that it is no wonder, if he was hated by several People. He was so bold also, as to insert This Doctrine in a public Thesis; and it is observable, that his Academical Superiors did not oblige him to expunge it, but only ordered him to inform the Youth, that they should not embrace such Opinions inconsiderately. " Quærit primum ex me, an statuissem præsidium " & auctoritatem suffragii commodare defendendis " corollariis periculosæ aleæ plenis, ut est disputare " in ambas partes, An religio sit de substantiâ reipub- " licæ, & negare fas esse subdito privatoque homini " ob causam religionis arma sumere contra Principem,

" & id generis alia. Respondi, causam non videri " cur in hoc atrio libertatis non sit fas absque per- " vicaciâ sentire quæ velis, & quæ sentias expromere. " Tamen rogatus ut admonerem juventutem ne te- " mere & absque delectu talibus axiomatis assensum " præberet, significavi me facturum (104). —— *He " first asked me, whether I had resolved to under- " take the Defence of dangerous Propositions, such as " the Question, whether Religion be essential to a State, " and the Assertion, that it is unlawful for a private " Man, and a Subject, to take up Arms against his " Prince, for the sake of Religion. I replied, that " I saw no reason, why, in This Seat of Liberty, a " man might not, without the Imputation of Perverse- " ness, think as he pleases, and speak as he thinks. " However, being desired to admonish the Youth, not " to assent to such Propositions rashly, and without Ex- " amination, I promised to do so.*" Never was Man fitter to gain himself Enemies by the Liberty of his Tongue, and his Maxims, than *Baudius*: " We " make War, *said he*, with the most powerful Prin- " ces of the World, and yet we are under the " Correction of an hundred petty Rulers: *Bellum " gerimus contra potentissimos Mundi Monarchas, & ser- " vire cogimur istis minutioribus satrapis* (105). See the Liberty he takes of censuring the Divines, who had condemned *Vorstius*, without hearing him. Observe the ill Consequences, which, he says, must follow, if these Gentlemen are suffered to decide concerning the Honour and Merit of others, on meer Presumptions, Suspicions, and Hear-says. " Evadet " ista effrænis audacia in optimi cujusque deforma- " tionem, & præjudiciis, suspicionibus, rumusculis, & " susurris, tantum licentiæ permittitur, ut famæ & " fructu dignitatis exuantur viri doctrinâ meritisque " spectabiles. Sed de negotio fratrum, & sacrati gre- " gis, dabitur alias opportunior differendi locus (106). " —— — *This unbridled Liberty, will blast the " Reputations of the best of Men, if Men of Learn- " ing and Merit must lose their Characters upon Pre- " judices, Suspicions, Rumours, and Whispers. But I " shall have a better Opportunity of considering the " Business of the Brotherhood, and sacred Herd.*" Once again, He was very fit to gain himself Enemies, and I am not surprized, that so many heinous Calumnies have been spread concerning him. In the Year 1609, he took a Journey into *Flanders*. During his Absence, a Thousand Stories went about, that he was gone to change his Religion, that he was already provided of a good Benefice, that he had turned Monk, and an hundred other things of this Nature, which gave occasion to the Thirty third Letter of the IIId Century. He was in such dread even of the Absurdities of Common Fame, that he wrote This Letter to Two of the *Curators*.

[*N*] *He believed they would create a Schism; in this he judged right.*] He built his Conjecture on the great Animosity, which he observed on both Sides. The Points in dispute seemed to him capable of being accommodated, provided The Combatants would but hear each other with a charitable Disposition. It was therefore the Disposition of the contending Parties, which made him fear they would come to a total Rupture. He was upon the Spot; and could see, in what Manner *Gomarus*, and his Friends, on one side, and *Arminius*, with his Adherents, on the other, mixed their private Passions with the Interest of their Doctrines. He declared freely, that the *Spaniards* and *Hollanders* would sooner agree together, than These two Ecclesiastical

(104) Epist. 99, Cent. III. pag. 471.

(105) Epist. 82, Cent. II, pag. 278.

(106) Epist. 33, Cent. III, pag. 362.

VOL. I.   8 L   Factions

light and Usefulness to the Readers, than Honour to his Memory. They are politely written [O], and are full of Wit; but he commends himself too much in them; He appears too Poor [P], too Importunate to his Friends, too Craving, too Vain, too Selfish, and too Irregular. This is to apologize for the Age, he lived in, of which he complained so much. It is partly by These Faults, that several learned Men render themselves contemptible in the Places, where they live, whilst they are the admiration of Those to whom they are known only by their Works. Notwithstanding the Length of This Article already, I cannot forbear subjoining here a very remarkable Particular; to wit, that *Baudius* had undertaken

Factions. Here follow his own Words: I set them down, that I may not be thought to deliver my own Opinions under his Name. I am in this, and many other Places, a bare Transcriber. " Utinam omnes nostri muneris & ordinis pari voto ac studio in eandem mentem conspirarent! Sed facilius conveniet inter Belgas & Hispanos, quam inter fratres, ubi semel in contentionem exardescere cœperunt. Omnino res erumpet in schisma, nisi foritibus consiliis huic malo occurratur. - - - - Si spiritu docilitatis & Christianæ caritatis ducerentur duces (ut sic dicam) partium, confectum negotium esset. Sed utrinque videre est magnos animorum motus, manifestam concursationem, ut suffragatores sibi concilient, denique mentem contentionis studiosiorem, quam indagandæ noscendæque veritatis:

Iliacos intra muros peccatur & extra.

" Sed ob Atridarum culpas supplicium ferunt Achivi: & Academia pessimi odoris est non solum apud extraneos, verum etiam apud nostros cives (107). " - - - - - O! that *All of our Function and Order would unanimously conspire in Opinion*! *But sooner will the Hollanders and Spaniards come to an Agreement, than The Brethren, when once they have began to grow warm in Controversy. The Affair will end in a Schism, if The Evil be not provided against with the utmost Prudence and Caution.* - - - *Were the Leaders of each Party (if I may so call them) governed by a Spirit of Teachableness and Christian Charity, the Business would be done. But, on both Sides, we see great Animosity, a manifest Struggle who shall gain the most Converts, and a Temper of Mind more disposed for Contention, than the Discovery of Truth;*

Alike in Guilt Besieger, and Besieg'd.

" *The Greeks suffered for the Offences of the Sons of* Atreus; *and the University stinks in the Nostrils not only of Foreigners, but even of our own Countrymen.*"

[O] *His Letters are written politely.*] We read in the *Scaligerana* as follows: " Baudius a une Stile non Ciceronien, mais du temps de Domitianus: je garde toutes les Lettres de Baudius. - - - - - - Baudius *writes in a Stile, not Ciceronian, but such as was practised in the Time of* Domitian: *I keep all his Letters by me.*" Scaliger, therefore, thought them elegant, and good. It does not appear, that *Baudius*'s Style is properly That of any Age of Latinity.

[P] *He appears too Poor.*] It was not so much the Honour of being the States Historiographer, as the Salary of That Office, which made him sollicit for it so earnestly. He put off his Creditors, 'till the Payment of his Pension of Historiographer; That Time never came; and They would be no longer put off in That manner; insomuch that he was reduced to Great Streights. " Flagitantium importunitas efficit me morosiorem, quam naturæ meæ Genius, & amicitiæ tuæ reverentiæ patiatur. Assiduæ enim obtundor à molestia Creditoribus, quorum nomina rejicio in spem obtinendi ejus muneris; sed tamdiu lactasti sunt hoc palpo, ut ulterius produci non possint (108). - - - - - - - - *The Importunity of my Creditors sowres my Temper more than my natural Disposition, and the regard I have for your Friendship, allow of. I put off the payment of what they demand by the hopes of obtaining That Post; but They have been so long wheedled with This Pretence, that they are resolved to be put off no longer.*" When he said, that his Estate feared neither Thieves, Fire, nor other Calamity,

Non incendia, non graves ruinæ,
Non facta impia, non dolos veneni,
Non casus alios periculorum;

and that It resembled That of *Bias* (109); The Application was not more ingenious, than true: He spoke like an Historian, and not like a Rhetorician. At last came his Pension of Historiographer; but it was only as a drop of Water to a Thirsty Man: He foresaw it, and had been told of it; wherefore he wanted another Remedy, *viz.* a rich Wife. " Si possem in nassam matrimonii illicere fœmininum aliquod opime dotatum (agnosco heic facundiam supplementi chronicorum) non aspernarer dona deorum. Sed ad eam spem aspirare non audeo, quamdiu mihi certamen erit cum hydra molestorum flagitatorum (110). - - - - - - *Could I but prevail upon some very rich Lady to marry me, I should be thankful to Heaven for the Blessing. But I dare not entertain such an hope, whilst I am combating with an Hydra of importunate Duns.*" Let us add to this what he wrote to his Patron *Vander Myle.* " Recte dicebas nuper, nihil aliud posse locare in solido, & ad portum bonæ spei appellere quassatam ratem Baudii, quam opimam aliquod conjugium: sed procax istud genus divitum ac fortunatarum mulierum spernit viros fama meritiique celebres, nisi censu quoque censeantur (111). - - - - - *What you said, the other Day, is very true, that nothing but a wealthy Match can secure, and bring Home safe, poor* Baudius'*s scattered Vessel; but the Misfortune is, your moneyed Ladies despise Men, even of the greatest Reputation, who have not as much Money, as Merit.*" But no Relief came time enough: In vain did he beseech the Curators, with the most moving Expressions, to deliver him from the hard Persecution of his Creditors. " Humanitatis tuæ genium adjuro atque obtestor per Deum immortalem, per sua Christianæ Charitatis, per vinculum sanctæ fidei, & quidquid apud gentes venerandum & antiquum habetur, impone tandem optatum finem diuturnæ expectationi; neu me patere longius versari inter sacrum & saxum, sub ictu Creditorum, qui meas aures assiduè molestis vocibus circumsonant, ut defœcato animo studia doctrinæ tractare nequeam (112). - - - - - *By the Eternal God, by the Laws of Christian Charity, by the Bond of Holy Faith, and by whatever The World esteems Venerable and Sacred, I adjure, I beseech your compassionate Nature, to put, at length, a wished for Period to my tedious Expectation; nor suffer me any longer to continue in this Perplexity, under the Lash of Creditors, who are perpetually dunning me, and interrupting my Studies.*" He was left to their Mercy; and, except his Person, they seized on all that was in his House. The Jesuits of *Antwerp* knew it, and insulted him upon it. Read but these Verses, taken from the Thirty seventh Page of the *Væ Victis!*

Pauperior Codro Catti nil continet arca.
Qui pote? Jam dicam: Baudæus in ære tabernæ
Totus erat, (nosti quam pocula sæpe salutet)
Caupo tulit lectos, sedes, mensasque, abacosque,
Et chlamydem & vestes, ollas, ignemque, focumque;
Nil Baudæus habet, secum tulit omnia Caupo.
Nec sat erat. Quid ages Baudi? Venderis & ipse?
Accipe Caupo libros, vetulas has ferto papyros,
Museum atque oleum, laternam & lampada sume;
Sit modo liber adhuc Baudæus obire popinas.

The Poverty of Codrus *is his Fate:*
You ask, how so? attend, while I relate.

Baudius

BAUDIUS. BAUDOUIN.

undertaken a Work, designed to effect a Coalition of Religions [*Q*]: A Work, which, besides other Talents, required a great Share of Piety, as he himself assured *Thuanus*, in communicating to him his Design. You will find his own Words below.

Baudius *had run up a long Tavern-Score;*
(That Baudius lov'd his Glass, you knew before)
The cruel Vintner, when he cou'd not pay,
Carried Beds, Tables, Chairs, and All away:
Yet All too little: what remains there yet?
Say, Baudius! *Shall your Person pay the Debt?*
No! — *Landlord, take my Books: if That won't do,*
Away with Lamp, and Oil, and Papers too:
But at his Liberty let Baudius *move,*
From Tavern still to Tavern free to rove.

Scriverius, Baudius's good Friend, says little less, than the Jesuits.

(113) *I take the meaning of this to be, that* Baudius *married a Widow with three Children.*

En, cum jure trium natorum ducitur uxor (113);
Et simul in barathrum præcipitatur amans.
Sic labuntur opes: fic nil stipendia profunt;
Pensio sic domino sæpe negata suo.
Pallia sic alius, Cajæque monilia servat:
Æra fugant inopem sic aliena famem.
Profilit & duris urgens in rebus egestas:
Pignora stant, vacua non redimenda manu (114).

(114) Scriverius, in Baudii Amoribus, p. 135.

A Wife, *at length, behold! The Lover gains,*
And thence the Right, Three Children give, obtains;
Yet, cruel Fate! to Prison dragg'd must go:
Thus there's an End of Wealth, and Pension too.
Rich Cloaths and Jewels, once the wealthy Dame's,
Transferr'd from Caia, *now Another claims.*
Whilst pressing Want, with meagre Look, stands by,
And, unredeemable, his Pledges lie.

[*Q*] *He had undertaken a Work, designed to effect a Coalition of Religions.*] What he says of it himself, is This. "Jampridem animo concepi opus, & tra-"ctatu arduum, & usu maxime necessarium, quod "ipsum olim aggressus is, de quo nuper multus "nobis sermo fuit, Georgius Cassander. Hic, ta-"metsi nihil dicas, tamen auguror animo quid co-"gitationi tuæ occurrat; esse nimirum rem tantæ "molis, ut eam vix mente completsi possim, nedum "facultate consequi. Fateor equidem ad hanc pro-"vinciam deligi par esse hominem instructum om-"nibus ingenii ac doctrinæ copiis. Opus insuper

"multiplici inquisitione, varia librorum supellectile,
"plurima rerum memoria, &, quod familiam ducit,
"pietate. Sed utilitatis magnitudo, & penuria ta-
"lium virorum, debet etiam ad hunc honestissimum
"laborem mediocres viros invitare, ut, si a spe per-
"ficiendi absint, saltem præclaræ voluntatis conscien-
"tia perfruantur. Ego mihi conscius sum quam
"parum possum, sed aggrediendi studium probis
"omnibus me probaturum non despero. Deum certè
"confido piis conatibus adfuturum, in quem preci-
"puè intuens, id oneris tollere decrevi. Quod si
"saltem effecero, ut aliorum scribendi studia exci-
"tentur, qui digne hanc spartam exornare possint,
"nihil est quod me non assecutum esse existimem
"(115). — *I have, a long time, conceived the De-*
sign of a difficult, but very necessary, Work, which (115) Baudii Epist. ad J. A. Thuan. apud Colemesii Opusc. pag. 41, 42.
was undertaken, likewise, by George Cassander:
He, I mean, of whom we had, lately, so much
Discourse. Here, I guess at your Thoughts, before
you declare them; namely, that the Work is of so
extensive and difficult a Nature, as scarce to be
comprehended, much less executed, by me. I confess,
The Undertaking requires a Person of the greatest
Ability and Learning, much Enquiry, many Books,
a great Memory, and, above All, a pious Disposition.
But the great Usefulness of It, and the Scarcity
of Persons so qualified, is sufficient to engage Men
of moderate Talents in so generous an Undertaking;
that, if They cannot flatter themselves with the
Hopes of Success, They may, at least, enjoy the
Consciousness of a worthy Intention. I am sensible
of my own Inability; but I do not despair of ap-
proving my Intentions to All Good Men. At least,
God, I doubt not, will assist my Endeavours; in
Confidence of whose Favour, I have determined to
undertake the Task. And if I can but excite others
to employ their Pens more successfully on the same
Subject, I shall have obtained the Utmost of my
Wishes." Colomies adds: "Opus, animo, ut puto,
"conceptum, nunquam prodiit. Hinc patet, cur Bau-
"dium Georgii Cassandri Asseclam in Gallia Orien-
"tali * dixerim, quod multis perobscurum, nec im-
"merito, videbatur (116). — *This intended Work* * Pag. 124.
was, I think, never published; which is the Rea- (116) Colomesii Opusc. pag. 42.
son, why, in the Gallia Orientalis, *I call* Baudius
The Page of George Cassander; which to many
seemed obscure, and not without Reason."

BAUDOUIN (*a*) (FRANCIS), in *Latin Balduinus*, a famous Civilian, was born at *Arras*, the first of *January*, 1520. He studied Six Years in the University of *Louvain*; afterwards he was some time with a great Lord (*b*), at the Court of *Charles* V; and then went into *France*, where he acquired the Friendship of the most Learned Men (*c*), and, among others, That of *Charles du Moulin*, at whose House he lodged (*d*). The eager Desire of being acquainted with the most famous Ministers, induced him to travel into *Germany* [*A*]: He saw
Calvin

(a) *He is called likewise* Balduinus, Baldouin, Baudouin. *See the Cabal Chimerique, pag. 250, Edit. 2. He wrote himself, in French,* Baldoin.
(b) *The Marquis de Bergue.*
(c) *Of* Budæus, *of* Bassif, *&c*
(d) *Ex Valerio Andrea, Bibl. Belg. p. 232. This is also to be found in* Baudouin's *third Reply to* Calvin, fol. B. 5.

[*A*] *The eager Desire of being acquainted with the most famous Ministers.*] This is the only Fault, which the Roman Catholics could impute to Him; if we may believe his Elogist, *Papyrius Masso*. I have carefully perused That Author, to discover whether *Baudouin* ever forsook the outward Profession of the Church of *Rome*. But I find nothing, which can persuade me of it; for His becoming acquainted with *Calvin*, and *Bucer*, to learn, from their own Mouths, the Reason of their Separation, is no Sign, that he was a Protestant. It was meer Curiosity, and, at the most, but a kind of Distrust, which signifies nothing, unless it be added, that, having heard the Reasons of These Reformers, he found them so good, that he came over to Their Side. Now *Masso* is so far from saying this, that, on the contrary, he tells us, that *Baudouin* disapproved of their Reasons. "In "Germaniam profectus à defensoribus novæ sectæ "intelligere voluit, quas ob causas à Romana & ve- "teri Ecclesia decessissent ----- quorum opiniones "*Non Probans*, Bucerum tamen & Melanchthonem "aiebat sibi ob modestiam placuisse: Calvinum dis-
"plicuisse propter nimiam vindictæ & sanguinis si-

"tim quam in eo deprehendisset (1). ----- *He* (1) Papyr. Masso, Elog. Parte II, p. 156, 157.
travelled into Germany, *to learn from the Defen-*
ders of the New Sect, for what Reasons they had
separated from the Roman *and* Ancient *Church.* ---
And, though he did not approve of Their Notions,
yet he commended Bucer *for his Modesty, but was*
displeased, he said, with Calvin, *for That Thirst*
after Revenge and Blood, which he discovered in
him." He says, I confess, that there was, former-
ly, an Intimacy between *Calvin* and *Baudouin* (2). (2) Famill-iaris quondam sui. Id. ibid. p. 262.
But does this imply, that the latter had been a *Hu-*
guenot? May not the Reader imagine, that they were
acquainted at College, before *Calvin* became The
Head of a Party? You may tell me, that Chronology does not allow of This: I reply, that you are
much to blame, if you desire to be understood only by Those, who are acquainted with the Nativities of several Persons, and will take the Trouble of
arguing from Thence. Your Duty is to express *Bau-*
douin's Abjuration in such clear Terms, that any
Reader may see it from your Book alone, without
the Help of Memory, or Reflexion. I go yet farther, and maintain, that Those very Persons, who
should

BAUDOUIN.

Calvin at *Geneva*, Bucer at *Strasburg*, and others in other places. Being returned to *Paris*, he was invited to *Bourges*, to be Professor of Civil-Law [B]; and he discharged This Office with so much Honour, that he made his Colleague *Duaren* jealous of him (e). At the end of Seven Years, he left That Professorship, to teach the Civil-Law at *Tubingen* (f), whither he was invited; but, being informed, in his Journey, that *du Moulin* designed to return to that University, he stopped at

should remember, that *Calvin* was at the Head of a Sect, before *Baudouin* left the College, will not find any thing, which looks like an Abjuration, in the *familiaris quondam sui*; for, by explaining These Words by other Passages of *Papyrius Masso*, They will fix upon this Sense of Them: *Baudouin*, having assured *Calvin*, that he sincerely enquired after the Truth, had several Conferences with him, in which his Wit, Docility, and Sagacity, so charmed *Calvin*, that He made a Friend of This Heretic, even before he was fully convinced of the Truth of his Doctrine. Their Intercourse continued a long time; for two Years are not too long for solving the Difficulties, which *Baudouin* might propose. *Calvin*, who hoped to gain over, and wished it passionately, caressed him very much, and opened his Heart freely to him. At last This Prey escaped him: *Baudouin*, not finding all his Objections answered, would not embrace the new Doctrine. This is the Sense, which might be given to the Words of *Papyrius Masso*. He should not, therefore, have expressed himself in a Manner, so apt to mislead the Reader.

Moreri is yet more to blame; for he cannot justify himself, by alledging the Privileges of an Elogist. He declares, by the Title of his Book, that he acts the Part of an Historian: he could not, therefore, allow himself the Liberty, which *Masso* might pretend to, under the favourable Title of *Elogium Francisci Balduini*. *Masso*, intending to write the Elogy of a famous Civilian, might say, "I thought it allowable in disguise what is disadvantageous to the Memory of my Heroe." A bad Excuse, and a continual Source of Illusion, and Falshood! But, after all, it comes better from a Panegyrist, than an Historian. What shall we say, then, to *Moreri*, who contented himself with these Words; "He had the Curiosity to visit *Calvin*, and the other Heads of the Protestants. It is said also, that he was inclined to go over to their Party, but, that the reading of a Piece of *George Cassander* hindered him from it (3). He had contracted a Friendship with *Calvin*, but it was of no long Continuance." So far from finding the Abjuration of Popery in these Words, it appears clearly from them, that *Baudouin* never abjured the Church of *Rome*. Where is then The Historical Sincerity, and Perspicuity, which require, that, if all other Books were burnt, the History alone of a Man should plainly inform every Reader whether he said, or did, such a thing? The Fault, which I censure, is, therefore, very great, if it be true, that *Francis Baudouin* changed his Religion: It will, therefore, appear enormous to Those, who know, that he changed his Religion at least seven times. Read the public Reproof, which he received for it; it is not expressed in general Terms, but attended with Circumstances. "*Ejectum te, Balduine, & excommunicatum ab omnibus piis, quicumque in Gallia aut Germania nomen tuum audierunt, negare non potes. Septies his viginti annis religionem mutasti. Non sepius fere serpentes pellem mutant. Educatus es apud tuos in Flandria Papistice. Postea Genevæ Christianam Religionem professus es: eoque nomine aliquoties ad corporis Christi communionem accessisti: Inde Lutetiam profectus Papisticum habitum recepisti. Mox Genevam reversus, & in Calvini contubernio, mensa, familiaritate, mensis multos commoratus, iterum Evangelici nominis factus es. Postea Biturigibus ad Papisticam Idololatriam, tanquam canis ad vomitum, rediisti. Inde Argentoratum profectus, Evangelicum te professus es: cum Petro Martyre vixisti. Cœnam Dominicam in Gallorum Ecclesia amplius decies participasti. Mox Heidelbergam delatus confessioni Gallicarum Ecclesiarum, sub qua paulo ante cœnam Dominicam duodecies sumpseras, hostis factus es, & Hessusianis te partibus dedisti. Tandem in Galliam reversus, quartum Papista factus es. Horum si quid falsum aut fictum sit, volo ut mihi oculos eruas:* aut, ut calumniatorium tuum supplicium imitemur, crura mihi suffringas (4). ------ *You cannot deny, Baudouin, that All Good Men, either in France or Germany, who had heard of your Name, passed Sentence of Excommunication on you. In the Space of twenty Years last past, you have changed your Religion seven times. Serpents scarce oftener cast their Skins. You was educated a Papist, in Flanders, your Native Country. Afterwards, at Geneva, you made Profession of the Christian Religion; under which Name you sometimes partook of the Communion of the Body of* CHRIST. *From thence going to Paris, you turned Papist again; afterwards, returning to Geneva, and being many Months intimately acquainted with* Calvin*, you became once more an Evangelic. Some time after, at Bourges, you returned to Popery, as a Dog to his Vomit. From thence going to Strasburg, you professed yourself a Protestant; and conversed with* Peter Martyr. *You received the Sacrament more than ten Times in The French Church. Not long after, at Heidelburg, you declared War against the Confession of the Gallican Church, under which, but a little before, you had twelve times communicated, and went over to the Party of The Hessusians. At last, returning to France, you embraced Popery for the fourth Time. If This be not All true, I give you leave to pull out my Eyes, or (to imitate your own Punishment for Calumny) to break my Legs.*" These Words are taken from a long Letter, written to *Baudouin*, in the Year 1564. The same Computation had been already mentioned to him in the Year 1562, and with very curious Circumstances; for he was put in mind, I. That, having desired to be admitted to the Holy Sacrament in the *French* Church at *Strasburg*, he had made a long Declaration of his Faith in the Presence of the Assembly. II. That, during his Abode at *Geneva*, he had made some public Discourses on Matters of Religion. "*Verbosissimam fidei tuæ confessionem publice in templo non infrequenti hominum conventu magna & confidenti voce pronuntiasses, ut ad sacræ Cœnæ & corporis Christi communionem recipereris ---- in publica (ut vocant) congregatione confessique pastorum & doctorum hominum tanquam Saul inter Prophetas verba de rebus sacris faceres* (5). ------ *You bad pronounced, with a loud and assured Tone of Voice, in a full Church, before a large Congregation, a very long Confession of your Faith, in order to be admitted to the Communion of the Eucharist. ----- You discoursed of divine Matters, like Saul among the Prophets, in a public Congregation (as they call it) and Assembly of Pastors and learned Men.*" I have read this in a Letter, which *Francis Hofman* is said to have been the Author of. Observe, that he is deceived in the Circumstance of Time; for he supposes, that *Baudouin* made his first Abjuration of Popery at *Strasbourg*; This is false; he did it, there, the third time. The Protestants gave him the Sirname of *Ecebolius*, to signify, that he changed his Religion as often as his Linnen; and they quarrelled so often with him for it, in their Writings, that no One can pretend Ignorance of it (6). See the second Volume of the Disputes of *Votius*, page 780.

[B] *He was invited to Bourges, to be Professor of the Civil-Law.*] We shall touch on a second Fault of The Writers, who speak of him: They scarce ever distinguish at what time he was provided with such, or such Offices. Mr *Menage*, who avoided This Fault, observes, that *he was Professor of the Civil-Law, at Bourges, from 1549 to 1556* (he should have said, from 1548 to 1555), *and that he received the Doctor's Cap, there, from the Hands of* Eguinarius Baro (7). The Ceremony of This Reception was performed the twelfth of *March* 1549, as Mr *Catherinot* informs us (8). He adds, that, in the Year 1553, the Wages of *Francis Duaren* amounted to Nine hundred and twenty Livres, Those of our *Baudouin* to Three

BAUDOUIN.

at *Strasburg*, where for a Year he read Civil Law Lectures. Afterwards he went to *Heidelberg*, where he was Professor of the Civil-Law and History near five Years, till he was sent for by *Anthony de Bourbon*, King of *Navarre* [C], who made him Tutor to his Bastard. He carried his Disciple to *Trent*, and, understanding,

Three hundred and fifty, and Those of *Hugh Doneau* to Two hundred and thirty. I observe This, to convict *Papyrius Maffo* of a Falshood, who says, that *Baudouin*'s Wages were as good, as Those of his Colleagues. " Accerfitur à Biturgibus ad docendi " munus suscipiendum, futurus Collega Baronis, & " Duareni Jurisconsultorum, accepturusque de publico " honorarium QUANTUM illis daretur (9). - - - - " *He was invited, by the People of* Bourges, *to take " upon him a Professorship, in conjunction with Baro " and* Duaren, *Lawyers, upon a Promise of a Stipend " equal to what his Colleagues received.*" I have shewn, elsewhere (10), that he is guilty of Another Falshood. Mr *Catherinot* remarks, under the Year 1549, *That Baudouin was for some time suspected of Heresy, as having been a Disciple of* John Calvin *at* Geneva *and Commensal of* Charles du Moulin, *at* Paris. He says also, that, in 1556, *Baudouin* wrote against *Duaren* about Benefices, and that *Duaren* called him, in Contempt, *Balbin*. *See*, continues he, *his Picture, in a Letter of* Duaren, *of the thirteenth of* June 1555. I give some Extracts of This Letter in another Place (11). *Note*, that, during his Stay at *Bourges*, he held a Correspondence with *Calvin* by Letters, and assured him, that he was a good Protestant in his Heart (12). He was upbraided with having suborned a rich Widow at *Bourges* (13), and having left That University, without taking Leave of his Landlord (14). I only mention these Things, that some Circumstances may be seen of the Profession, which our *Baudouin* exercised in the University of *Bourges*. Mr *Menage* affirms, that, in 1556 (15), he made, there, the Funeral Oration of *Equinarius Baro*, whose Enemy he had been, if we believe *Duaren* (16). " Duarenus tantam juvenis (Bal- " duini) gloriam non ferens, nunquam se Balduino " æquum præbuit (17). - - - - - Duaren *was so jea- " lous of young* Baudouin's *Reputation, that he " never was a Friend to him.*" I shall farther observe, that the Date of his Call to the Professorship of *Bourges* discovers a Mistake of Mr *Bullart*. He says, that This learned Man *was gone to* Geneva, *to hear, from the Mouth of* Calvin *and* Beza, *the Reason, which had obliged them to forsake the Church of* Rome (18). He acknowledges, that This Journey preceded the Time, wherein *Baudouin* was made Professor at *Bourges*. He ought, then, to grant, that *Baudouin* made it before the Year 1549, and consequently, when *Beza* was not yet a fit Person to be consulted on Those Matters. It is certain, I. That *Beza* was yet a Papist, and at *Paris*, when *Baudouin* cried up *Calvin's* and *Bucer's* Letters in all Companies (19). II. That *Baudouin* was gone from *Geneva*, before *Beza* went thither (20). This supplies us with a strong Proof of the Falshood, contained in these Words of *Varillas* (21): " Calvin, who pretended to raise him " by the same Ways, that *Beza* had gained Repute " in the Party, invited him to *Geneva*, received him " in his House, admitted him into the Intrigues of " the Consistory, and made use of him several Years " as a Secretary. But, whether *Baudouin's* Humour " was extremely fickle, as the *Calvinists* reproached " him afterwards, or that he discovered, that *Cal-* " *vinism* was but a refined Hypocrisy, as he declared " in a satirical Apology; he went from *Geneva* to " *Heidelberg*." *Beza* was not yet of the Protestant Religion, when *Baudouin* received so many Marks of Friendship from *Calvin*. *Baudouin*, after he had received Them, did not go to *Heidelberg*, but returned into *France*, and was seven Years Professor at *Bourges*. I confess, that, after This, He went again to *Calvin* at *Geneva* (22), but he did not stay long there; he suffered a severe Reprimand there, and testified his Repentance; he went soon after to *Strasburg*, by *Calvin's* Advice, and did not teach the Civil-Law at *Heidelberg*, 'till after he had taught it at *Strasburg*. " Quum illa Bituricensis conditio eum " gravaret (ostentatio enim, qua sola pollet, evanue- " rat, ut spei & votis minimè satisfaceret) non du- " bitavit huc se recipere : & quum undique liberis " eum convitiis exagitarint, qui prius amici fuerant, " humaniter à me impetrata venia admissus fuit. Feci " quidem quod necesse erat, ut severa objurgatione " correctus lapsus sui fœditatem agnosceret. Servi- " liter assensus est, & adulatoriè meis se consiliis re- " gendum permisit. Argentinam profectus nomen " dedit apud Pastorem & Seniores Gallicanæ Eccle- " siæ (23). ——— *Being displeased with his Situation " at* Bourges, *which by no means answered his vain- " glorious Expectations, he made no Scruple of retir- " ing hither; and, notwithstanding the Reproaches, " which, on all sides, were cast on him by* Those, *who " had formerly been his Friends, I received him kind- " ly. By a severe Reproof, which was necessary, I " brought him to acknowledge the Foulness of his Apo-* " *stacy. He servilely complied, and flatteringly gave " himself up to be governed by my Advice. Yet, going " to* Strasburg, *he went over to the Pastor and Elders " of the Gallican Church.*" Thus you see how *Varillas* informed himself of Things, which he pretended to speak of.

[C] *He was sent for by* Anthony de Bourbon, *King of* Navarre] Some say, that he was, then, in *Lorrain*, in the Retinue of Prince *Casimir*, Son of *Frederic*, Count Palatine (24). Others, that he was returned into *France*, with *the Heir of the Count* Palatine, *who came to* compliment *Charles IX, on his Accession to the Crown* (25). But All this does not so much as touch upon the Intrigue, which *Beza* mentions. He says, that, after the Death of *Francis* II, They, who feared to lose their Authority, in the Court of *France*, endeavoured chiefly to induce the King of *Navarre* to return back to the *Romish* Communion (26). They engaged him to send an Embassador to the Court of *Rome*, in hopes either to recover his Kingdom, or to obtain Another from the Catholic King, by the Pope's good Offices. On the other hand, They gave him Hopes, by suborn'd Persons, that The Protestants of *Germany* might unite in his Favour, and assist him in recovering the Crown of *Navarre*; especially, if means could be found out to reconcile the Religions. They mentioned a Professor of *Heidelberg* to him, whose Name was *Baudouin*, who was a fit Person to negotiate such Matters. He sent for him into *France*; he conferred with him; and, judging him fit to find out the means of An Agreement in Religion, he set him to work; and, after some rough Draughts, prepared at *Paris*, he sent him back into *Germany*, and charged him, by Name, to consult with *Cassander*. This Intrigue, designed to break off the Conference of *Poissy*, did not effect it. The Ministers had already assembled there twice, when *Baudouin* returned with a Project of Union, printed at *Basil* (27). He was reprimanded for returning too late : He found, that the Bishop of *Valencia*, who had promised him a Professorship of Civil-Law, had changed his Mind. All, that he could obtain, was to be Preceptor to the King of *Navarre*'s natural Son. He went to *Paris*, and gained Esteem by his Lectures, in which he joined Civil-Law with History; but he lost his Reputation on the Publication of the Book against the Treaty for a Reconciliation of Religions, which he had brought from *Germany*. He undertook to write against *Calvin*, in his own Defence; the Consequences of which we shall see below.

Varillas may be said, in the main, to confirm this Account of *Beza*. He says, that " *Baudouin* went " from *Geneva* to *Heidelberg*, where he was Professor " of the Civil-Law; 'till, *Cassander* having inspired " him with the Desire of re-uniting all Religions, he " thought it best to begin with *France*, where he ex- " pected to find the least Opposition. He came to " *Paris*, where he communicated, to the Cardinal " of *Lorrain*, the famous Consultation, which the " same *Cassander* had drawn up for the Execution of " his Project. The Cardinal received it with so " much the more Joy, as he foresaw, that, though " it should not produce all the Effect, which it's Au- " thor expected, yet it would, at least, set the Pro- " testants at Variance, and divide the Ministers of " the Assembly of *Poissy*, by the Overtures of Agree- " ment, which it would suggest to the most mode- " rate among them (28)." *Varillas* had said just before,

VOL. I. 8 M

standing, that *Anthony* was dead of a Wound, which he had received at the Siege of *Rouen*, he returned with his Pupil into *France*, and found his Estate and his Books plundered (g). He returned to his own Country, whither he was invited, to teach the Civil-Law in the University of *Doüay* [D]. He was promised great Advantages,

fore, that, by this means, *Baudouin* became Preceptor to the King of *Navarre*'s natural Son. He tells us, afterwards, how the Ministers got " clear of the " Difficulties, which *Baudouin* had thrown in their " Way. But, *continues he* (29), They would not " have disentangled themselves so easily from *Bau-* " *douin*'s second Difficulty, if Fortune had not fa- " voured them. He had persuaded the Cardinal of " *Lorrain* to send for the most famous Lutheran Pro- " fessors of the *Palatinate*, and the Dutchy of *Wir-* " *temberg*, to introduce them into the Conference, " where, he was sure, they would be more zea- " lous against the *Calvinists*, than against the *Catho-* " *lics* ; and that, by this means, besides the Pleasure " of setting the Hereticks together by the Ears, their " Quarrels would make them ridiculous to the Court, " where their Doctrine was before admired ; and the " People, who thought them uniform, understand- " ing, that they had quarrelled among themselves, " would so suddenly change the Esteem they had " for them into Contempt, that no *Frenchman* would " leave the Communion of the Church for the fu- " ture. It must be confessed, that the *Catholics* never " received more wholesome Advice, than This of " *Baudouin*; and, if it had been put in practice with " as much Diligence, as was requisite in so delicate " an Intrigue, all the Evils, which the Conference " of *Poissy* produced, afterwards, would have been " prevented. And, indeed, the Ministers, who were " not ignorant of their Adversaries most private Ma- " xims, having discovered what *Baudouin* had " proposed to their Disadvantage, were transported " against him with all the Excess of Passion, which " Indignation, Spite, Jealousy, and Fury, can in- " spire, when animated by a false Zeal, and hidden " under so specious a Cover."

Note, That *Varillas* is mistaken, when he says, that *Baudouin* carried *Cassander*'s Consultation to the Cardinal of *Lorrain* : For it was not made 'till three Years after (30). I shall give, below (31), the Title of The Work, which he carried, and shall observe (32), that he was employed to mediate an Ecclesiastical Agreement with the Prince of *Condé*.

[D] *He was invited, to teach the Civil-Law in the University of* Doüay.] The Marquis de *Bergue*, and several other great Lords of the *Netherlands*, engaged *Maximilian de Bergue*, Archbishop of *Cambrey*, to manage matters so, that This Professorship of Civil-Law might be procured for *Baudouin*. They desired to make use of his Advice in Matters of State and Religion (33) ; for they knew his Opinion was, that the Laws against the Sectaries ought to be mitigated (34). " Nam Balduinus in ea erat sententia, ut ve- " terem Edictorum severitatem leniendam profitere- " tur, affirmaretque, retinere eâ ratione facilius " auctoritatem neque veteres consuêsse, neque iis, " quæ tunc erant, temporibus, posse (35). — For " *Baudouin was of such an Opinion, as to declare,* " *that the ancient Severity of the Edicts ought to be* " *mitigated, and to affirm, that Our Ancestors neither* " *did, nor could, in those Times, support the Autho-* " *rity of the Church by such means.*" So that there is reason to believe, that he returned to *Paris*, because he would not be engaged, by the Duke of *Alba*, in the cruel Proceedings then in agitation. " Ac ne forte quæsitor reis datus capitalibus senten- " tiis provincialium suorum subscribere cogeretur (36). " — *And least, by being appointed to enquire into* " *the Guilt of the Accused, he should be obliged to join* " *with those of his own Province, in pronouncing Sen-* " *tence of Death on Them.*" The Male-contents of the *Netherlands* promised themselves great Things from his Counsels, since, besides the Principles, which I have already mentioned, he was a Person of great Address, and perfectly knew the World: " Ut in " Belgium venit, magnum sui expectationem omni- " bus fecit. Solers animo, obsequendi gratiâ, & ci- " vili congressu, nec minus oth•ni comitate, ad inge- " nia principum vitam instruxerat. Nec enim novo- " rum hominum deliramenti sectabatur, & rursus in " religione scrupulum oderat. Humaniusque credebat, " iniquitati temporum cedere, pietatifque integrita-

" tem in paucis violare, quam vim adferre turbatis " conscientiis, quas in contaminatis hominibus nulla " unquam supplicia eluunt (37). - - - - - - *Upon his* " *Arrival in the Netherlands, great Expectations* " *were raised of him. He was a compleat Courtier ;* " *he never gave into the Follies of Upstarts ; nor was* " *a Bigot to Religion Besides which, he thought* " *it more becoming a Man to give way a little to the* " *Iniquity of the Times, and rather to recede from* " *the strict Laws of Piety in a few Instances, than to* " *offer Violence to disturbed Consciences, which, in* " *Persons infected with them, no Punishment can ever* " *wash out.*" The Author, whom I quote, had observed, that *Baudouin* had been very well known to *Lewis* of *Nassau*, at *Heidelberg*. The third Apology of This Civilian informs us, that the Prince of *Nassau*, who had been his Auditor at *Strasburg*, had lately caressed him much in the *Netherlands* (38). Let us add to this, that he was esteemed by *William*, Prince of *Orange*. " Francisco Balduino, jurisconsulto " egregio, pacis Ecclesiasticæ studioso, magni facto à " Principe Arausionensi Wilhelmo, aliisque Belgarum " proceribus, qui & opera ejus usi sunt, cur credi " non debeat, nihil causæ est (39). - - - - - - *I see* " *no reason, why we should not give Credit to* Francis " Baudouin, *an excellent Civilian, who studied the* " *Peace of the Church, and was highly esteemed by* " *William, Prince of* Orange, *and others of the Nobi-* " *lity in the Low-Countries.*" It is *Grotius*, who says this, and who affirms, that That Prince, and other great Lords of the *Netherlands*, consulted *Baudouin*. It was in their first Proceedings against *Spain*. He was present in the first Assemblies of *Breda* ; and they employed him to draw up the Writing, in which they demanded, of the Duchess of *Parma*, the free Exercise of their Religion. He shewed, that Religion cannot subsist without An Outward Exercise, and that it requires This, as a necessary Support, and Nourishment (40). The Author, who informs me of this, observes, that *Baudouin* had been recalled from his Exile, by the Archbishop of *Arras*. *Ab exilio per Archiepiscopum Atrebatensem (it should be Atrebatensem) revocatus* (41). To understand This, The Reader must know, that, finding himself accused of Heresy, he left his Country, and that, after his Flight, a Sentence of Proscription was pronounced against him (42). It was revoked, when they recalled him, in order to consult with him on the State of Affairs in the *Netherlands*. Note, that the Author, who speaks of the Archbishop of *Arras*, does not relate the Thing, as he ought : The Chronicle of *John Francis le Petit*, to which he refers, will tell us the Circumstances of it better : " *Francis Baudouin* - - - - " *having before been banished from* Arras *for his* " *Religion, was sent for by the said Lord, Prince* " *of* Orange, *from* France, *to consult him on the* " *Difficulties, which then occurred ; who, after his* " *Banishment, was revoked by the Chamber of* " Artois, *at the Instance of the Archbishop of Cam-* " *bray, went to the said Prince, in the City of* " Brussels ; *where, having conferred with him, and* " *and the other above-mentioned Lords, he drew up* " *a Discourse, in the Form of a Proposal, concern-* " *ing the Then Religious Troubles, which was sent* " *to the King of* Spain, *directed to his own Person,* " *wherein are contained the true Means of prevent-* " *ing all Insurrections, and extirpating Sects, and* " *Heresies* (43)." This Discourse is preserved entire, in the Chronicle of *John Francis le Petit*. It is solid, and very judicious. This Chronicle says, that " *Bau-* " *douin* luckily hit upon the true Remedy of the " Troubles, which the King, and his Council, might, " of late, have known to be so."

Let us remark, by the way, that the Writers, who speak of him, are in the wrong to say, that from the *Netherlands* he went to *Paris*. They should have said, that he did not go to *Paris*, till he had fled to *Geneva*, where he embraced the Protestant Religion (44). He boasted, that, for the Profession of the Gospel, he had suffered Exile, and the loss of all he had : but some affirm, that his Mother sent him all that he could pretend to of his Patrimony,

BAUDOUIN. 693

Advantages, and was very courteously received by the Duke of *Alba*, on the Eve of That Day that Count *Egmont* was imprisoned: but, fearing to be chosen one of the Judges of Those Persons, whom they had a mind to put to Death, he desired leave to be absent for some Days, under pretence of fetching his Wife, and his Library; and, having obtained it, he returned to *Paris*, where he stayed. He read there public Lectures on some Parts of the *Pandects*, with the Applause of a Crowd of Auditors (*b*). He accepted the Professorship of Civil-Law, which was offered him by the University of *Bezanſon*; but, understanding at his coming there, that the Emperor *Maximilian* had forbid That University to erect This Professorship, he would read no Lectures there, though he was sollicited to do it. He returned to *Paris*, where he followed the Advice of *Philip de Huraults* (*i*), which was, to teach the Civil-Law in the University of *Angers*. This He did near four Years, and till the Duke of *Anjou*, who was proclaimed King of *Poland*, sent for him to *Paris*, at the time, when the *Poliſh* Embaſſy was received there [*E*] (*k*). He was designed for the Professorship of Civil-Law in the University of *Cracow*

(*b*) See Remark [*K*].
(*i*) The Duke of Anjou's Chancellor.
(*k*) Taken from Papyrius Maſſo, ubi ſupra, pag. 258, & ſeq.

---

(45) Calvin. Reſponſ. ad Balduin. ſub fin. p. 370, Tractatuum Theolog.

(46) Brother of William, Prince of Orange.

(47) Nicol. Burgund. ubi ſupra, pag. 68.

(48) Taken from Nicolas Burgund. pag. 67, 68.

ny. " Fortunis exutum fuiſſe negant conterranei & " familiares : quia extra Cæſaris ditionem à matre & " cohæredibus permiſſum fuit ſumere quantum ex " hæreditate, ſi integra fuiſſet ejus conditio, perve-" nire ad eum poterat: ut ne quidem aſſis jacturam " fecerit. Et aliquando coram homini gratulatus " ſum, quòd tam facilè recuperaſſet, quod ſibi crede-" bat periiſſe (45). -------- *His Countrymen and* " *Acquaintance deny, that he was ſtripped of his For-*" *tunes : ſince, when he was out of the Emperor's Power,* " *his Mother, and Co-heirs, allowed him to take as* " *much of his Patrimony as he could have claimed,* " *had it remained entire ; ſo that he did not loſe a ſingle* " *Farthing : And I myſelf have perſonally congratula-*" *ted him upon the eaſy Recovery of what he looked* " *upon as l ſt.*" Obſerve, pray, a want of Exactneſs in *Papyrius Maſſo*. He ſays nothing of the Journey, which our *Baudouin* took into the *Netherlands*, at the Sollicitation of the great Lords, who would remedy the Diſorders, which The too great Severity of the Penal Laws, againſt the Sectaries, produced daily. He ſpeaks only of a Journey taken, during the Government of the Duke of *Alba*. This is to forget the principal Thing, and to reduce the Affair to but a ſmall part of it. What I have quoted from *Valerius Andreas*, *Nicolas Burgundius*, and ſeveral others, and which is a very conſiderable Part of *Baudouin*'s Life, ought to be referred to the Year 1564, under the Government of the Ducheſs of *Parma*. It was in That Year, that *Caſſander* and *Baudouin* were conſulted by the Malecontents. The one, viz. *Caſſander*, was named by the Count *de Horn*, and the other by Count *Lewis* of *Naſſau* (46). It was believed, that Theſe two Men were capable of accommodating the Differences of Religion. The Prince of *Orange* promiſed great things to *Francis Baudouin*, and not only deſigned to procure him a Profeſſorſhip of Civil-Law, in the Univerſity of *Louvain*, or in That of *Doüay*, but alſo a Seat in the Privy-Council. *Baudouin*, returning into *France*, with a Promiſe to come back again into the *Netherlands*, at a proper Time, received many Preſents from That Prince. Count *Lewis* of *Naſſau* preſſed him ſeveral times to keep his Word, and endeavoured to dazzle him with the Splendor of Dignities : *Imminentium Honorum blanditiis allicere* (47). But *Baudouin* thought he ſhould not find his Account in the Buſineſs he had promiſed to undertake ; all his Friends adviſed him not to concern himſelf in it, and he was in hopes of a better Reward for the Pains he took to reconcile the *Bourbons* with the *Guiſes* (48). Theſe are Particulars, which deſerved to have been touched upon by *Papyrius Maſſo*; and yet he has not ſaid a Word of them; but, inſtead thereof, tells us, That the *Spaniards* offered him the Profeſſorſhip of Civil-Law, in the Univerſity of *Doüay* ; that They promiſed him a yearly Penſion of Six thouſand Florins, and a ſhare of Fifty thouſand Florins, in the Confiſcation of the Eſtates of Thoſe, who ſhould be proſcribed ; and that The Duke of *Alba* received him civilly, *&c*. It would appear very ſtrange, that the *Spaniards* ſhould honour a Man in this manner, who had favoured the Prince of *Orange*'s Deſigns, if we did not remember *Baudouin*'s Inconſtancy, I mean, his extream Readineſs at changing Sides. The Hiſtorian, whom I quote, having mentioned a fine Diſcourſe of the Prince of *Orange*, adds, that it was the Fruit of *Baudouin*'s Converſations. " Nemini mirum videri debet, tan-

" tam in illo principe eluxiſſe cognitionem Philoſo-" phiæ ; ex Balduini colloquiis hauſerat (49). ----- " *No One ought to think it ſtrange, that This Prince* " *diſcovered ſo great a Knowledge of Philoſophy ; he* " *acquired it by converſing with* Baudouin." I ſhall obſerve, in another Place (50), what he did in relation to the Maſſacre of *Paris*. [*E*] *The Duke of* Anjou ------ *ſent for him to* Paris, *at the time, when the* Poliſh *Embaſſy was received there*.] *Baudouin* was this Prince's Maſter of the Requeſts (51): He gained the Favour of the *Poliſh* Embaſſadors, by converſing with Them, and publiſhed a Diſcourſe *de Legatione Polonica*, dedicated to *John Zamoski* (52); it is thought he would have gone into *Poland*, the Spring following, if he had not died. This is all that *Papyrius Maſſo* tells us of the Matter. Let us, therefore, look upon moſt of what is related by Mr *Bullart*, as fabulous Hyperboles. " It was, ſays he (53), during *Baudou-*" *in's* Abode at *Angers*, that the *Poliſh* Lords, who " came to offer Their Crown to *Henry*, Duke of *Anjou*, " arrived in *France*. A Perſon of Ability was wanting, " to receive This ſumptuous Embaſſy, and to anſwer " it. It was a material Point to return Thanks for " This Offer, without depreſſing the Royal Dignity " that was offered : It was requiſite to ſpeak both like a " King, and a grateful Man. No Perſon in *France* was " found better qualified to undertake this, than the pru-" dent BAUDOUIN. The Duke of *Anjou* having " ſent for him to *Paris*, This great Man appeared " in the Halls of the *Louvre* among the chief Per-" ſons of the State : He was Interpreter to That fa-" mous Embaſſy : He was no leſs applauded for the " Excellency of his Anſwer, than the famous *Za-*" *moski* for That of his Speech ; and he made himſelf " ſo conſiderable to Thoſe Illuſtrious Embaſſadors, that " it was reſolved to ſend him into *Poland* to ſettle " That Crown on the Head of the new King, and to " diſpoſe That Nation to receive him: but his laſt " Sickneſs, which ſeized him at the ſame time, de-" prived him of That Honour, and the Duke of *An-*" *jou* of the Hopes he had of re-eſtabliſhing the Uni-" verſity of *Cracow* by his Means." Nothing could happen more glorious, than This, to a Profeſſor of *Angers*: How comes it then, that one of his beſt Friends does not mention it, in the Elogy, which He conſecrated to him ? No good reaſon can be aſſigned for it, unleſs we ſay, that it is falſe ; for it is againſt all probability, that he ſhould be ignorant of ſuch a thing, if it really happened. Writers of Elogies may be permitted to make uſe of a more figurative, and flattering, Language, than Hiſtorians : but neither Lying, nor Amplifications, ſuch as change the Nature of an Adventure, ought any more to be allowed Them, than Hiſtorians : ſo that it may be ſaid, that Mr *Bullart* is guilty of an inexcuſable Exceſs. *Thuanus*, who has exactly related what concerned the *Poliſh* Embaſſadors, their Speeches, and the Anſwers, which were made to them, ſays nothing of our *Baudouin* (54). It is always the Biſhop of *Poſnania*, who ſpeaks, and a Chancellor, who anſwers him: *Biraque*, Chancellor of *France*, replied, when They harangued *Charles IX. Chiverni*, Chancellor of the Duke of *Anjou*, returned an Anſwer, when They harangued This Duke, and when They read to him the Act of his Election. If any other ſpeaks beſides, it is, *Nicolas Chriſtopher Radzievil*, on the *Poliſh* Side (55), and *Paul de Foix*, for

(49) Nicol. Burgund. Hiſt. Belg. pag. 131. ad Ann. 1564.

(50) In the Article CHARPENTIER (Peter).

(51) Menag. Remarks on the Life of P. Ayrault. pag. 185.

(52) He was one of the Poliſh Ambaſſadors.

(53) Bullart. Acad. des Sciences, pag. 229.

(54) Thuan. lib. 57. init.

(55) Id. ib. pag. 47.

Charles

BAUDOUIN.

Cracow (*l*), and it is thought he would have followed the new King into That Country, if Death hath not prevented him. He died in the Arms of his only Daughter [*F*], in the College of *Arras*, at *Paris*, the Twenty fourth of *October*, 1573 (*m*) [*G*]. This is the Sum of what *Papyrius Maſſo*, *Valerius Andreas*, *Aubertus Miræus*, *Bullart*, and ſeveral others, relate of him. It is very ſtrange, that they ſhould ſo boldly ſuppreſs all that relates to his changing of his Religion (*n*). One can hardly infer from their Narratives, that he lived once in the Proteſtant Communion. *Moreri* has, either through Ignorance, or Diſſimulation, omitted the ſame Things. But, in requital, he enlarges on the Quarrel between *Calvin* and *Baudouin*. It was a very ſharp one [*H*]. *Beza* came into it with a little too much

(*l*) Thuan. lib. 57. pag. 47.

(*m*) Papyr. Maſſo, Elog. Part II. pag. 261.

(*n*) See Remark [*A*].

(56) *Id. ib.* pag. 49.

(56) *Charles* IX (56). My Remark would be of leſs weight, if *Thuanus* had made no manner of mention either of *Zamoski*, or *Baudouin*. But we find, that he ſpeaks of them both; and after this Manner: He ſays, That Speech of *Zamoski* was printed; but that it was not known, whether it had been ſpoken; *In eandem rem edita, an habita ſit incertum, Oratio luculenta a Joanne Zario Zamoſcio* (57): and he adds, that *Baudouin* cauſed another Speech to be printed, addreſſed to *Zamoski*. Is not This plainly giving us to underſtand, that *Baudouin* was not choſen to interpret That *Polander*'s Speech, and to anſwer it in the Preſence of the whole Court? What can be ſtronger againſt Mr *Bullart*'s Narrative?

(57) Id. ib. pag. 47. Note, that the Pages are very ill marked here in Thuanus, Edit. of Francfort, 1625.

[*F*] *He died in the Arms of his only Daughter*] Her Name was *Catherine*. She was twice married; "her firſt Huſband was *John de Sauzay*, Sieur de "*Sainte Ouanne*, in *Poitou*; and her ſecond Huſ- "band was *Adam le Changeur*, Sieur du *Cotau*, in "*Berri* (58)." She was born at *Heidelberg* (59). Her Mother's Name was *Catherine Biton*; and was of *Bourges*. She was the Widow of *Philip Labbé*, Great Grand father of Father *Labbe* a *Jeſuit*, when ſhe married *Baudouin* (60). She had ſome Children by her firſt Huſband, who, with their Grand-mother, were ruined by their Step-father, as *Calvin* relates it. "Ipſum minimo ſuppuiſſe eſſe clamant Biturigum, "qui ſuos privignos, ſimul cum eorum avia, ſpoliave- "rit (61). — *The Inhabitants of Bourges cry out, "that he had but little Affection for his Children-in- "law, having ruined them, together with their "Grand mother.*" Our Civilian was more deſirous to leave a Daughter behind him, than a Son, becauſe he feared *Cicero*'s Deſtiny, whoſe Son inherited nothing of his Father's Eloquence. *Percontanti mihi mallette filiam, quam filium habere, minime* (62) *inquit, Roma enim Ciceronis filium non agnoſcebat loquentem* (63).

(58) Menag. Remarks on the Life of Ayrault, pag. 158.

(59) Papyr. Maſſo, Elog. pag. 261.

(60) Menag. Ibid.

(61) Calvin. Tractat. Theolog. pag. 370.

(62) It ſhould be limo for minime makes a contrary Senſe to Malſo's meaning.

[*G*] *He died the Twenty fourth of October* 1573] And not the eleventh of *November* 1572, as *Valerius Andreas* ſays. *Thuanus* places his Death on the eleventh of *November* 1573; Mr *Menage* on the Twenty fourth of *October* 1574; and yet he makes him but Fifty three Years, nine Months, and Twenty four Days, old, though he had placed his Birth on the firſt of *January* 1520. Theſe two Faults proceeded from *la Croix du Maine*.

(63) Papyr. Maſſo, Elog. Part II. pag. 261, 262.

[*H*] *The Quarrel between Calvin and Baudouin was very ſharp*]. I mentioned the Origin of it (64), when I ſaid, that *Francis Baudouin* diſperſed a little Book concerning a Re-union of Religions, whilſt the Conference of *Poiſſy* was held. It was an anonymous *Latin* Diſcourſe, compoſed by *Caſſander*, and entituled, *De officio pii ac publicæ tranquillitatis vere amantis viri in hoc religionis diſſidio.* When it was known at *Geneva*, that *Baudouin* deſigned to prejudice the Reformed by This little Book, it was thought proper to lay him open to the Public. For which reaſon, *Calvin*, in refuting This Piece, which he imputed to *Baudouin*, laſhed him ſeverely. His Refutation is entitled, "Reſponſio ad verſipellem "quendam mediatorem, qui pacificandi ſpecie rectum "Evangelii curſum in Gallia abrumpere molitus eſt. "— *An Anſwer to a certain turn-coat Mediator, "who has endeavoured to break off the right Courſe "of the Goſpel in France*." It is in the Volume of *Calvin*'s *Opuſcula*, pag 351, and the following. *Baudouin* defended himſelf, by publiſhing a Work, for which he had obtained a Licence in the Year 1557; he revised it, and added an Appendix to it (65). In a Word, it was His *Ad leges de famoſis libellis & de calumniatoribus, commentarius,* printed, at *Paris*, by *Andrew Wechel*, in the Year 1562, in 4to. *Calvin*'s Reply appeared in the Field ſoon after with a

(64) In Remark [*C*].

(65) See Remarks on the Life of Calvin, Art. I. pag. 202. 2003; and Calvin's Anſwer to Baudouin, init.

ſtrong Reinforcement (66); for it was accompanied with ſeveral Pieces compoſed by good Pens; beſides which, They publiſhed The Letters, which This Deſerter had written at ſeveral times to *Calvin*. "Reſpondit "quoque Joannes Criſpinus ejus conterraneus, & "perpetuus, quoad ejus fieri potuit, amicus. Ad- "juncta ſunt quorundam inſignium virorum ſcripta, "quibus perpetua iſtius improbitas, ſumma impuden- "tia, & extrema inſcitia ita manifeſte redarguitur, "ut ne nunc quidem poſſit ignorantiam ſuam diffi- "teri. Additæ ſunt denique ipſius literæ variis "temporibus ad Calvinum ſcriptæ, ut horrenda illa "defectio, ipſius apoſtatæ teſtimonio, apud omnes "bonos ſanciretur (67). —— Johannes Criſpinus, "likewiſe, his Countryman, and, as far as he could "be ſo, his Friend, anſwered him. There were "added, likewiſe, Pieces by ſome of the beſt Hands, "in which his perpetual Diſhoneſty, conſummate Im- "pudence, and extream Ignorance, are undeniably "proved. Laſtly there were added His Letters, written "at different Times to Calvin, as a Satiſfaction to all "good Men of his horrid Apoſtaſy.*" The Nature of this Collection will be more exactly known, if I give the Title of it here; which is This: "Joannis Cal- "vini reſponſio ad Balduini convicia. Ad leges de "transfugis, deſertoribus & emanſoribus, Franciſci "Balduini epiſtolæ quædam ad Joannem Calvinum "pro Commentariis. Franciſci Duareni J. C. ad "alterum quendam Juriſc. epiſtola, de Franciſco "Balduino. Antonii Contii J. C. admonitio de fal- "ſis Conſtantini legibus, ad quendam, qui ſe hoc "tempore Juriſconſultum Chriſtianum profitetur. De "officio tum in Religione, tum in ſcriptionibus, reti- "nendo, epiſtola ad Franciſcum Balduinum Juriſ- "conſultum. Ad legem III. C. Impp. de Apoſtatis, "Joannis Criſpini Commentarius ad Juriſconſultos. "—— *John Calvin's Reply to the Calumnies of Bau- "douin. Some Epiſtles* of Francis Baudouin to John "Calvin, *by way of Commentaries on the Laws rela- "ting to Deſerters, and Vagabonds. An Epiſtle of "Francis Duarenus* J. C. *to another Civilian, con- "cerning Francis Baudouin. An Advertiſment of "Anthony Contius* J. C. *concerning the Spurious "Laws of Conſtantine, to one, who, at this time, "profeſſes himſelf a Chriſtian Lawyer. Of the Duty, "to be obſerved, both in Religion and Writings, An "Epiſtle to Francis Baudouin, the Civilian. The "Commentary of Joannes Criſpinus on the III. C. "Imperial Law, concerning Apoſtates, addreſſed to "the Civilians.*" This Collection, containing an Hundred and ſeventeen Pages, was printed in the Year 1562, in 4to. *Baudouin* compoſed a ſecond Anſwer, which was printed at *Paris*, and at *Cologne*, in the Year 1562. *Calvin*, not thinking fit to refute it, publiſhed a Piece, of but One Page, wherein he informed the Public, that he would Anſwer This Adverſary no more (68). It is there, that he reproaches him with having violated the Laws of Hoſpitality, by ſtealing ſome Papers, which might be of Service to him in his perfidious Attempts. "Antequam reſ- "pondeo, *ſays he* (69), monendi ſunt lectores nihil "hac monedula eſſe furacius, ut hac parte fratrem "ſuum patruelem Antonium Balduinum ſuperet, cui "ob furandi ſolertiam, cognomen Ablativi à condiſ- "cipulis inditum fuit. Tanta fuit mea erga ipſum "facilitas, ut quicquid erat in bibliotheca mea char- "tarum liberè, me abſente, excuſſerit. Subripuiſſe "quæ in rem ſuam fore putabat, non aliunde peten- "da eſt luculentior probatio, quàm ex ejus ſcripto, "in quo ſe bellè prodidit. Certe feles ejus & hoſpi- "talitas hic deprehenditur (70). ------ *Before I "reply, I muſt inform the Reader, that nothing is "more pilfering, than this Jackdaw, in which reſ- "peet he exceeds his paternal Uncle, Anthony Bau- "douin,*

(66) Epiſtolæ, Reſponſa, ad Balduini Convicia &c. is for the moſt Volume of his Opuſcula; as for inſtance, ſecond Piece which is publiſhed a- gain? Pag douin, the it was uſed after it.

(67) Beza ibid. p. 207.

(68) It is very plain in the Volume of his Opuſ- cula; as for the ſecond Piece which is publiſhed a- gain? Pag douin, the it was uſed after it.

(69) Cal- vin Præfat. Reſponſio- nis ad Bal- duini con- Oper. To II.

(70) See V les. Andr Bibl. Belg pag. 214.

BAUDOUIN.

much bitterness, even in the Opinion of several of his own Party [*I*]. It cannot be denied, that *Baudouin* was of a very inconstant, and fantastical, Humour.

He

(71) Commentarius de statu resp & religionis in regno Galliæ, Tom. I. fol. 169. ad Ann. 1561.

"douin, who, for his cunning in thieving, was nick-
"named by his School-fellows The Ablative. He had
"such easy access to me, that, in my Absence, he had
"the Liberty of turning over all the Papers in my
"Library. That he pilfered what might be of Use to
"him, is evident from his Writings, in which he
"has finely betrayed himself. Here his Fidelity, and
"Observance of the Laws of Hospitality, plainly ap-
"pear." Beza supplied his Place, and replied to
Bauduin's second Piece, who speedily published a
third Apology against them. It appeared in the Year
1564, and the Title of it is, " Pro Fr. Balduino re-
" sponsio ad Calvinum & Bezam, cum refutatione
" Calvini de scriptura & traditione (71). - - - - - - - -
" An Apology for Francis Baudouin, and a Confuta-
" tion of Calvin concerning Scripture and Tradition."
The Preface, which *Baudouin* composed on *Optatus*,
in the Year 1563, may be counted for the fourth
Piece. It was translated out of *Latin* into *French* by
Peter Veil, who prefixed it to his *French* Translation
of *Optatus*, printed at *Paris*, in the Year 1564.

This Account affords us Matter for Censuring a
Protestant Writer. He mentions the Intrigues relating to the Writing of *Cassander*, and adds, that
Baudouin, not having been called by the Catholics,
nor by the Reformed, to the Conference of *Poissy*,
discharged all his Spleen against the Ministers, and
published some Libels against *Calvin*, and *Beza*, and
that They answered him. *Publicis scriptis infectatus
est Calvinum & Bezam, qui edito responso ad illius
probra respondent, & illum mendacii, perfidiæ, atque
impietatis reum esse instituunt demonstrare* (72). This
is to declare him the Aggressor; which is false: So that
This Author is not as faithful, and exact, as he
should have been.

(72) Id. ib.

[*I*] *Beza came into it with a little too much bitterness, even in the Opinion of several of his own Party.*]
The Piece, which he published concerning it, is in
the second Volume of his Works (73). Here is a small
Extract of the Letter, which *Sainte Aldegonde* wrote
to him in the Year 1566. " Statueram præterea
" certiorem facere te quàm hic sinistrè plerique inter-
" pretentur libellos istiuc ultro citroque tum in Bal-
" duinum tum in Heshusium scriptos, ex eoque ho-
" mines malevolos gravem Evangelicæ veritati con-
" ciliare invidiam. Sed quoniam audivi te harum re-
" rum ab aliis esse factum certiorem, volui ab hoc
" argumento supersedere. Rogo tamen, observanda
" in Christo parens, ut vel in harum regionum gra-
" tiam, in quibus non modo cum hypocritis eo no-
" mine nobis est colluctandum, verumetiam ab aper-
" tis hostibus gravia multa perpetienda, (qui suam
" tyrannidem in contentiones nostras derivant) non
" graveris stylum quàm modestissimè in Evangelicæ
" veritatis Apostatas ac adversarios temperare. Non
" quidem quod parcendum illis censeam, qui nullum
" non lapidem movent, quò nos in invidiam gravio-
" rem vocent, sed ne (dum illis pro merito respon-
" detur) quod suis illi vanissimis erga nos maledictis at-
" que calumniis nequeunt consequi) nempe ut Evan-
" gelii lucem obruant, ejusque sectatores apertis ve-
" ritatis hostibus excarnificandos tradant) id ipsum
" nostris, etsi justissimis ac verissimis, non tamen, uti
" plerique existimant, Evangelica mansuetudine dig-
" nis, vel accusationibus, vel responsionibus, adeptos
" se esse glorientur. Id si feceris, uti omnino statu-
" isse te audio, & nos magna invidia levar;s, & illis
" ipsis perfidis Apostatis turpem maledicentiæ notam
" inustam relinqueris. Itaque ut sacias, vehementer
" hic omnes Evangelii studiosi (qui te plerique ut
" parentem amant & colunt, reverenturque ut Præ-
" ceptorem) etiam atque etiam te rogant (74).
" *I had determined likewise to have informed you of
" the Misconstructions, which several here put upon
" the Pieces written on both Sides, both against Bau-
" douin, and Heshusius, and that ill-disposed Persons
" conceive from hence a Prejudice against The Gospel-
" Truth But, bearing, that you are already ac-
" quainted with it, I thought I might be dispensed
" with from entring upon this Subject. Yet, O vene-
" rable Father in* CHRIST, *I intreat you, for
" the Sake of This Country, in which we are not
" only necessitated to contend with Hypocrites, as such,
" but have many Evils to suffer from professed Ene-
" my, who impute their own Tyranny to Our Divi-
" sions, that you would be pleased to temper the Keen-*

(73) Pag. 201, & seq.

(74) Philippus Mar nixius, Epist. ad Theod. Bezam. It is the Geneva among Beza's Letters, pag. 205, 206, Tom. III. Oper.

" *ness of your Style, and write with as much Modera-
" tion, as possible, against Apostates, and the Ene-
" mies of the Christian Faith. Not that I think they
" deserve to be spared, who leave no Stone unturned to
" increase the Odium against us; but that, by answer-
" ing them as They deserve, we should give them an
" Opportunity of boasting to have obtained That, by
" Our Accusations, or Answers (which, though ever
" so just, and true, are, by many, thought not worthy
" of the Gospel Mildness) which They cannot effect by
" their ill-grounded Calumnies and Reproaches; I
" mean, The Extinction of the Gospel-Light, and The
" Persecution of it's Followers by the avowed Enemies
" of Truth. If you do This, as I hear you have deter-
" mined to do, you will both free us from a great
" Odium, and leave the shameful Brand of Calumny
" on These perfidious Apostates. This All, who are
" Lovers of the Gospel, here, most earnestly intreat
" of you, whom They Love and Honour as a Father,
" and revere as a Teacher*" It appears from these
Words, I. That other Person had already informed
Beza of the Prejudice, which the passionate Writings, that had appeared against *Baudouin*, did to the
Reformed. Ill-disposed Persons took an Occasion from
them to render the Reformation odious. II. That he
was most humbly desired, for the future, to take off
the Edge of his too sharp Pen, if it were only in
Favour of the Reformed of the *Netherlands*, who
had, on this Occasion, not only the Hypocrites (75),
but also declared and violent Enemies, to deal with.
III. That it was to be feared, that True and most
just Answers, but void of Christian Meekness, would
accomplish That, which The Impudence of Calumniators endeavoured in vain to effect, *viz.* That The
Light of Truth should be extinguished, and it's Professors suffer a cruel Persecution. IV That, if *Beza*
condescended to This Advice, as it was said he was
resolved to do, he would free the Church of *Christ*
from a great Odium, and the Apostates would remain
branded with Calumny. He answered *Sainte Aldegonde*, That, if He alone had been abused, he should
no more have been moved at it, than if he had heard
a Dog bark in the *Indies*: But, Religion being concerned in it, he thought he was obliged to treat
The Infamous Apostate, who had calumniated it, according to his Desert; and that he regarded but little
the Scruples of moderate Men. *The impudent Lies of
That Calumniator,* says he, *must affect them as much,
as the Vigor of Our Replies.* Every One may see,
that it is necessary I should set down his own Words;
for many may imagine, I pervert the Sense of them.
Here they are: " Superest ut ad extremam tuam Epi-
" stolam paucis respondeam. Balduinum & Heshufi-
" um nonnulli vellent moderatius à me fuisse repre-
" hensos. Ego verò cuperem istos æquè affici im-
" pudentissimis eorum conviciis in homines innoxios
" contortis, ac justis nostris defensionibus. Quid non
" enim is in optimum illum & innocentissimum Dei
" servum jaculatus est fœdus illi Apostata ? in me
" verò quid non dixit ? Et tamen Deus mihi testis
" est in animam meam, non multò magis me, si res
" mea privata ageretur, ista petulantia commoveri po-
" tuisse, quàm si in his regionibus versans audivissem
" canes in India latrare. Sed quum per nostrum la-
" tus viderem Gallicas omnes Ecclesias ab isto con-
" ductitio rabula confodi, & tanquam seditiosos accu-
" sari, quotcunque istorum latronum telis corpora
" sua non objecerunt, ut tacere necesse fuit, nisi &
" Christi causam & regiam majestatem prodere ma-
" luissem, peccavi scilicet, quòd ejus calumniis sic
" respondi, ut & ipsum sycophantam suis coloribus
" depingerem, & causæ nostræ bonitatem probarem.
" Itaque quod ad illum attinet, non dissimulo me
" nullum peccatum agnoscere, & moderatos istos
" nihil morari. De Heshusio, quoniam aliud argu-
" mentum tractabam, fateor causam illam potuisse ali-
" ter agi. Sed singularis illa istius hominis & inscitia
" & audacia in hos veluti scopulos me adegit, ubi
" tamen spero me naufragium non fecisse (76).
" *It remains only to answer your last Letter in few
" Words. There are, who could wish I had reproved
"* Baudouin *and* Heshusius *with more Moderation.
" And I cannot help wishing, these Persons were equal-
" ly affected with the impudent Calumnies They have
" vented against innocent Persons, as with My Just
" Defence. For what has not This base Apostate
"* thrown

(75) I believe he means the Anabaptists.

(76) Theod. Beza, Epist. VII, pag. 209.

VOL. I.   8 N

BAUDOUIN.

He was, with respect to Universities, what certain Persons are in relation to Mistresses, who run from one Fair to Another, *and from Shore to Shore in the Sea of Love.* It is very probable, that, when he lived at *Bourges,* in the Romish Communion, he had more affection for the Protestants, than when he communicated with Them at *Heidelberg.* It may also be suspected, that he neither liked Popery, nor Calvinism, nor Lutheranism, and that he would have new-modelled Them, and perhaps many other Sects, to form A New One out of Them. What is certain, is, that he aimed at a Re-union of Religions (*o*). On the other hand, it cannot be denied, that he had very fine Parts, an Extensive Knowledge (*p*), an admirable Memory, and an Eloquence so much the more persuasive, as he was a handsome Man (*q*), and had a strong, and pleasing, Voice (*r*). We are not to think, therefore, that there is any exaggeration in what has been said of his

" *thrown out against That best and most innocent Servant* " *of* GOD? *What has he not said against Me? And* " *yet* GOD *is my Witness, that, were it only my own* " *private Concern, This Insolence would scarce move* " *me more, than if I should, in this Country, bear the* " *barking of Dogs in the Indies.* But, when I am " *sensible, that the whole Gallican Church is woun-* " *ded through my Sides, by this barking Brawler,* " *and That All, who resist the Attacks of these Rob-* " *bers, which ought to be done, if we would not be-* " *tray the Cause of* CHRIST, *and the King's Ma-* " *jesty, are accused as seditious, I have offended,* " *forsooth, in so answering his Calumnies, as to paint* " *the Sycophant in his proper Colours, and prove the* " *Goodness of Our Cause. Therefore, as to Him, I* " *will not dissemble, that I am conscious to myself of* " *no Fault, and that I disregard these moderate Men.* " *With regard to* Hesthusius, *as I was, then, hand-* " *ling another Argument, I confess the Cause might* " *have been otherwise managed. But the singular* " *Ignorance and Impudence of the Fellow drove me* " *upon these Rocks, upon which, however, I hope I* " *have not made Shipwreck.*"

I shall make but two Reflexions on This Answer. In the first place, it is undeniable, that Readers give some reason to believe, that they are more offended at the Bitterness of an Apologist, than at That of the Aggressor. Let a Writer defame all the World, the Dead, the Living, Sovereigns, Subjects, his Brethren in Religion, The Adversaries of his Party; let him exercise This Trade several Years successively, and become more malicious, and satirical, as he grows old; I confess, that The Reader perceive it, and blame him for it: but if, at last, This Man happens to be very ill treated by Those, whom he has provoked, you will hear an hundred times more Complaints against Them, than against Him. His very Enemies think it strange, that he was not treated with more Moderation. They have read, with pleasure, what was published to his Disadvantage; and yet they will not stick to say, that he ought to have been spared. This is an Effect of the immoderate Inclination Men have for censuring others. Some People are pleased to approve of nothing. But let us not judge so of those Moderate Persons, whose Opinion is mentioned by *St Aldegonde.* Doubtless, They were yet more offended at the satirical Audaciousness of *Baudouin,* than at the Invectives of those, who confuted him; but they could have wished, that slandering had been the Character of the Enemies of the True Religion, and that They, who defended it, had distinguished themselves by Wisdom, and a moderate Style. They hated a satirical Disposition, which mixes Defamation with Reason, in which Personal Injuries predominate; and They could not detest it without some uneasiness, whilst it was common to their Enemies, and their Friends. Wherefore, They wished, as well for This, as for some other Reasons, that it were one of the distinguishing Characters of the Catholic Writers, and that the Protestants would not, by adopting it themselves, free them from this Brand of Infamy. I observe, in the second place, That *Beza* indulged his Imagination too far; for, if the Book, which he wrote against *Baudouin,* were the only One left us, we should not only take This Civilian for a most infamous Rascal, but also for an Author without any Wit, Learning, or Merit. He has, therefore, given a deceitful Description of him; since it cannot be denied by those, who have read what *Baudouin* has written, and what others have said of him, that he was a Man of very great Parts. An Author may be excused,

on account of the Infirmity of Human Nature for not allowing his Enemy to be Learned, Eloquent, and Ingenious. But, if he be permitted to conceal These Truths, he ought, at least, to abstain from denying Them. The Passion, which an Author shews, in the Works, he composes against the Enemies of his Religion, may proceed, sometimes, from a great Zeal; wherefore it must be said, that Anger is equivocal between Temper, and Devotion. But I cannot see, how the Haughtiness of a Writer can be reduced to an Evangelical Principle. I call *Haughtiness* the Contempt he expresses for his Adversary, and the Affectation of treating him as the most wretched of Authors; though the contrary be notoriously true, and is evident from his Employments, and Writings. I could wish not to have found, in the History of the Reformed Churches, that *Baudouin* died a wretched Pedant (77). Such an Expression ought not to have fallen from the Pen of *Beza,* who was then Professor of Divinity, and formerly Professor of Greek. He should have left so unpolite, and contemptuous, a Way of treating Those, who instruct Youth, to the Gentlemen of the Sword. He should not have affronted a Profession, which was of the same kind with his own. If it be said, that he did not place *Baudouin's* Pedantry in his being a Professor, but in his personal Defects, this is to say nothing at all; since This Civilian did not want Politeness, and knew how to converse with great Men, and enter into their Intrigues (78). An eager Desire of treating him with Contempt induced *Beza* to say, that, when he was proposed to the King of *Navarre,* in 1561, to be employed by him, That Prince did not know, that there was such a Person, as *Baudouin,* in the World (79). This is one of Those Things, which Authors advance at Random, and which they cannot justify afterwards. *Baudouin* affirms, that he was recommended to That Prince by the Queen of *Navarre* (80), to whom he had the Honour to pay his Duty, on the Wedding-day of That Queen's Daughter with That Prince (81). He affirms, that the Favour, and Good-will, of This Princess confirmed the Choice, which was made of him, for the Professorship of Civil Law, at *Bourges.* This is very probable; for, as she was Duchess of *Berry,* and promoted the Interest of Learning, there was no attaining to any Preferment in That University without her Concurrence. How was it possible for *Beza* to confute *Francis Baudouin,* on This Point? Some will, perhaps, say, that Zeal for Religion sometimes induces Divines to treat a Man, whom they refute, with the greatest Contempt, and as a wretched Author; for They think it expedient for the good of the True Church, that her Sons should be persuaded, that none but ignorant Men oppose her. I answer, that a Zeal, which should occasion a Conduct, so contrary to Sincerity, Reason, and Justice, and yet more to the strict Morality of JESUS CHRIST, can never pass but for a very blind Zeal. I will not mention the Inconveniencies of such a Conduct. It may be said to such Men: *You may easily defend your Cause, since you acknowledge, that it is so weakly attacked; your Triumphs are no sign, that you fight for the Truth.*

I must make yet another Observation. Sainte *Aldegonde* did not give all the necessary Advice; he forgot one, which was very material: He did not advise the returning an Answer to *Baudouin's* Third Apology. I know, that, in Matters of Right, a Man need not be so nice, as to leave none of his Adversary's Works unanswered. In a second Reply, Things may

his Auditory [K]. He eat, and drank, but little; and he took great Pains (s). He did not approve, that Hereticks should be put to Death (t); and reproached *Calvin* very much, on account of *Servetus* (u). He was no Colleague of *Cujacius*, as some affirm [L]. I shall say something concerning his Writings, and of his being accused of *Plagiarism* [M]. Note, That *Theodorus Beza* says, that he died, gy againſt either

may be set in the best Light, which can be given them; and, then, a Man may promise himself, that the intelligent Reader will not think it strange, if he does not enter the Lists again: But, in Matters of Fact, relating to personal and defamatory Accusations, the Aggressor must never be silent first; for, if he does not reply to the Apologies of The Accused, it is a Sign, that he wants Proofs, and that he is forced to stop at the Opposition of a meer Negative. *Baudouin*'s Third Answer is full of giving the Lye, and recriminating; and contains some Facts in Vindication of himself; so that *Beza* ought not to have left it unanswered; he should have been put in mind to support his first Reply by a new Piece in Justification of the former. In these kind of Quarels, He, who quits the Field, loses the Battle: Both Plaintiff and Defendant are obliged to answer every new Reason, alledged against them, tho' they were to publish twenty *Cases* in their own Defence. Take notice of the Epithet *new*, which I make use of; for, if the Accuser, for example, or his Friends for him, should multiply Writings continually, repeating the same Things, only with some small Alterations as to the Form, and never answering either the Matters of Fact, or the Reasons of the Accused, the latter may keep a profound Silence; his first Apology is sufficient, 'till, among the Multitude of *Cases*, published by his Adversary, One be found, containing something new.

[K] *What has been said of his Auditory.*] Bishops, Counsellors, and Gentlemen of the Sword, appeared there. *Sammarthanus* affirms This, as having seen it. " Homo, *says he* (82), facundissimus, ipsoque oris " ac totius corporis habitu non injucundus, ex hi- " storiarum & civilis disciplinæ conjunctione, suis " prælectionibus gratiam & venerem asserebat. Ac " eum quidem sæpe vidimus hoc splendido summæ " doctrinæ apparatu, Lutetiæ profitentem, cum ad " ejus auditorium permulti primæ notæ homines, " episcopi, senatores, equites, libenter & maxima fre- " quentia confluerent. ----- *He was a most eloquent* " *Man, of a pleasing Aspect and Deportment; and* " *set off his Lectures by a Mixture of History and* " *Civil Law. I have seen him often, with This* " *splendid Equipage of Learning, in the Professor's* " *Chair at Paris, attended by many Persons of the* " *first Rank, Bishops, Senators, and Gentlemen of* " *the Army, who crowded to hear him.*"

[L] *He was no Colleague of Cujacius, as some affirm.*] *Beza* is one of them. " It is a shameful " thing for you, *says he* to him, to reflect upon *Cal-* " *vin*, as being of an Humor incompatible with others, " *natura ἀκοινώνητος* for you have rendered your- " self intolerable to all your Colleagues, wherever " you came. If you deny it, *Duareu, le Conte, " Cujacius, Hotman,* &c. will convict you of the " contrary (83)." *Baudouin* replied, that *Cujacius* was his Successor at *Bourges*, but not his Colleague, and that They had never seen each other. " Cu- " jacius Balduino in Scholâ successit: collega nun- " quam fuit, imo alter alterum nunquam vidit. Per " literas aliquando collocuti sunt, sed tam amice ut " nihil magis. Imo Cujacius Balduinum rogavit in " illud suum collegium ut rediret. Si nobis non cre- " dis, Cujaciam interrogato (84). ----- *Cujacius* " *succeeded Baudouin in That School: he was never* " *his Colleague; nay, They never saw each other. They* " *corresponded sometimes by Letter, but with the ut-* " *most Friendliness. Cujacius even entreated Bau-* " *douin to return to his College. If you do not be-* " *lieve me, ask Cujacius himself.*"

[M] *I shall say something concerning his Writings, and his being accused of Plagiarism.*] In his Twenty third Year, he commenced Author; for, in 1542, he published, at *Louvain, Leges de re rustica, item Novella Constitutio prima de hæredibus & lege Falcidia Justiniani,* which he had translated from the Greek, and accompanied with a Commentary (85). This was reprinted, the following Year, at *Basil* (86), by *Oporinus,* with a large Book of *Anthony Garron.* In

1545, he published, at *Paris, Prolegomena de Jure Civili*; and, in 1546, *Commentarii in libros IV. Institut. Juris Civilis Justiniani Imperatoris.* His Commentary on the Laws of the twelve Tables was printed several Times. The third Edition is of *Basil,* 1557, in 8vo, by *Oporinus,* who printed, at the same time, his *Juris Civilis Catechesis,* and his Commentary *ad Edicta veterum Principum Romanorum de Christianis,* a Work, wherein he maintains Toleration, and which, for That Reason, was censured by *Claude de Sainctes* (87). I omit several other Books of Civil-Law, published by This Author. But the following Particular must not be omitted: I find in Mr *Menage,* that, " At the Request of the " *Prince of Condé*, he wrote a *Treatise of the means* " *of attaining to a good Reformation in Religion.* " This Treatise having been published by a Carme- " lite, who had left his Order, and who added much " of his own to it, *Baudouin* complained of This Pro- " ceeding to the Prince of *Condé.* The Prince banished " The Monk from his Court, and gave *Baudouin* leave " to defend himself. On this Permission, *Baudouin* " wrote his *Advice on the Reformation of the Church,* " in *Latin,* and afterwards in *French:* and his *An-* " *swer to a Preaching Calumniator, in French* (88)." In *Baudouin*'s Third Answer, it appears, that, by order of the Queen-Mother, he went to see the Prince of *Condé* in Prison, and conferred with him about the reconciling of Religions, and that he was commanded to write a Book concerning This Conference, which was renewed after That Prince was set at Liberty. The composing of This Work hindered him from carrying a Letter to the Duke of *Guise* (89). Neither ought I to forget, that his *Constantinus, sive de Constantini Imperatoris,* printed at *Basil,* in the Year 1556, was put in the *Index Librorum expurgandorum,* and that he passes for the Author of a Book, which was printed at *Strasbourg, Sub Christianorum Jureconsultorum nomine contra Duareum,* in the Year 1556; but he disowned it (90). In *Gesner*'s Epitome, Another Work is ascribed to him, which belongs to Another *Baudouin; Non bujus, sed Petri Balduini, sunt* (91). It is Notes on *Tully*'s Offices. It was He, who translated an History of Poland into French, written, in Latin, by *John Herbart* of *Fulstin, Castellan of Sanoc.* This French Translation was printed at *Paris,* in 4to, without the Translator's Name (92). He disguised himself sometimes *under the Name of* Peter de la Roche, Petrus Rochius (93), *and called himself* Atrebatius, *by way of allusion to* J C. Trebatius *and to his Country* (94).

As for the Plagiarism, which was laid to his Charge, read what follows. " Pudendum est, & nimium il- " liberale illud plagium, quod ipse insciari non po- " test, de annotationibus in Justiniani Institutiones " Brecthano præceptori suo surreptis. Omitto quæ " non modo Ferretus & Othomanus, quorum fortas- " sis familiaritate tum abutebatur ex vetere illa for- " mula τὰ τῶν φίλων κοινά, sed etiam maximi " ipsius inimici Baro, & Duarenus, optimo jure ex " istius centonibus repetunt. Omitto etiam turpis- " simorum erratorum Centurias, quas Contius & ipse " Juris Interpres in istius Constantino, quamvis exi- " guo libello, annotavit (95). ----- *He cannot deny* " *That Ungenerous Plagiarism, in his Annotations* " *on* Justinian*'s Institutes, which he stole from his* " *Master* Brecthanus. *I omit what not only Ferre-* " *tus, and* Othomanus, *whose Friendship perhaps he* " *abused, from that old Maxim, that among Friends* " *All Things are common, but what even his* " *greatest Enemies,* Baro *and* Duaren, *have a just* " *claim to, in his* Cento's. *I omit, likewise, the* " *Centuries of most scandalous Errors, which* Contius, " *who was himself an Interpreter of Law, remarked in* " *his* Constantine." That *Contius,* mentioned by *Beza,* was Professor of Civil Law at *Bourges,* and was called *Antony le Conte.* Hotman is also mentioned in This Passage. He was One of *Baudouin*'s Adversaries, and treated him with the utmost Contempt (96).

He

698 BAUDOUIN. BAUTRU.

either in the prosecution of a Law-Suit, or of Vexation, because Another was preferred before him to follow the Duke of *Anjou* into *Poland* (x). Many Reflexions might be made on the Oddness of his Fortune [*N*].

(x) Theod. Beza in vita Calvini, ad Ann. 1561, pag. 281.

He even called him *Hermaphrodite*; and it seems he took this Word in it's natural Sense; though elsewhere he takes it figuratively (97). " Uxor (inquis), " *be speaks to* Papyrius Masso, mihi nulla est, nec " unquam fuit. Nec mirum, Massone: siquidem Balduint præceptoris tui similis es, quem omnes di- " cebant esse Hermaphroditum (98). - - - - - *You say* " *you have no Wife, nor ever had. This is not to* " *be wondered at in* Masso; *for you are like your* " *Preceptor* Baudouin, *who was said, by All, to be* " *an* Hermaphrodite." He pleases himself with saying, that *Cujacius* slighted *Baudouin*: " Cum omnes " sciant quod prædictus Cujacius non fecerit unquam " numerum de Balduino plus quam de suis veteribus " ocreis (99). - - - - - *When All knew, that the afore-* " *said* Cujacius *made no more account of* Baudouin, " *than of his old Boots.*" Mr *Menage* observes, and wonders at it, that *Cujacius* never mentioned *Baudouin* (100). We have seen, that he wrote very obliging Letters to him (101).

(97) Tu es Hermaphroditus in negotiis status, sicut fuit Balduinus in negotiis religionis. - - - - *You are an Hermaphrodit in Matters of State, as Baudouin was in Matters of Religion.* Id. ib. pag. 284.

(98) Id. Ib. pag. 281.

(99) Id. ib. pag. 269.

(100) Menage's Remarks on the Life of *Ayrault*. pag. 158.

(101) *Above, Citat.* (84).

[*N*] *Many Reflexions might be made on the Oddness of his Fortune.*] He was a Man of Wit, Learning, Eloquence, and Dexterity: He was a handsome Man; and he understood the Intrigues of the Court: Some of These Qualities, which I have specified, were very eminent in him. Great Princes employed him, several times, in Matters of Consequence, which put him in the way to Preferment; and yet he could never advance himself much, and, I think, did not die very rich. How many Persons, inferior in every thing to This great Civilian, rise very high, attain to great Offices, maintain themselves in them, acquire a good Name, great Riches, and much Authority? They have nothing shining in them; They do not excel in any thing, nor have any eminent Qualities: In vain do we look for That, in Them, which excites Admiration; we shall sooner find it in other Persons; who, nevertheless, continue always in a mean Condition, how often soever they have had a favourable Opportunity of raising themselves. Most of Those, who consider This Train of Human Affairs, find something in it, which displeases, and vexes them; and They discharge their Spleen on what They call the Injustice or Blindness of Fortune. They seldom hit the true Reason of it; and consider but little Another Cause, which oftener produces This, than They imagine. They ought to know, that Eminent Qualities will not raise a Man to the Height, which they seem to promise, unless They be seconded by some other Qualities, or not crossed by certain Defects; for, not being seconded, or being crossed, they are an Insufficient Cause, and, consequently, according to the Laws of Mechanism, They must fail of their Effect. Now This is the Case of many of Those, who are Men of Great Parts: They want certain Things, with which These noble Talents would perform Wonders, and without

The Effect of the Proportions and Disproportions between the Qualities of one, and the same, Man.

which They can neither advance, nor support, Them. The Qualities of These Persons are not well sorted; there is not That Harmony, and Proportion, between Them, which ought to be: So that, instead of assisting, They ruin one another. It is, therefore, no wonder, if a Man does not raise himself, and even if he miscarries, with such an Equipage. As for Those, who attain to a great Fortune, and maintain themselves in it, without having any Eminent Qualities, it is not to be wondered at. There is such a Concert, or such a Proportion, between Their good and bad Qualities, that they reciprocally support each other, and form thereby a compleat Principle, which is sufficient for the Production of a Thousand profitable Adventures. It is with This, as with Machines; for, how coarsely soever they be made, They will play better, if their Parts are ranged, and proportioned, as They ought to be, than the most admirable Machine would do, if some Pieces were taken from it, or if some were added to it, which did not correspond with the rest. " It is not enough to " join, to a Knowledge of the World, That of Books, " much Wit, and Eloquence, and several other Eminent Qualities; if, otherwise, you are unpolite, " capricious, indiscreet, lazy, timorous, selfish, subject to mean Jealousies, presumptuous, incapable " of following a tedious Business, inconstant, fitter " to begin an hundred new Projects, than to support " the Fatigue of carrying on the same Business for " some time; I say, if you are a Man of such a " Stamp, and if, notwithstanding your great Qualities, you do not raise yourself, do not blame Fate, " the Iniquity of the Age, or the Malignity of your " Neighbours; but blame yourself for it: impute " the Cause of it to the Disproportion between the " Qualities, which have been allotted you." I reckon *Francis Baudouin* among Those, who are in this Case. Note, that some Persons, among Those of this Stamp, do themselves Justice: They know the Mixture, which renders all their fine Talents useless; and, if they murmur, it is not against their Neighbours, but against their own Temper, and against Nature, which counter-balances whatever Qualification she had given them for rising in the World. However, I do not intend to comprehend, in This Hypothesis, a great Number of Particular Cases, in which the Causes of a Bad, or Good, Fortune are altogether External; I mean, that They, who, notwithstanding their eminent Qualities, remain in Obscurity, have had no favourable Opportunity of raising their Condition, and that They, who have attained to great Preferments, without any Merit, have found themselves in such an active Whirl of Circumstances, that They have had no Occasion to second it, and that their Incapacity was no obstacle in their Way. But remember, that *Baudouin* did not want Opportunities: They were often thrown in his Way.

BAUTRU DES-MATRAS (Maurice), chief Lieutenant of the Provostship of *Angers*. His Sons, and Grandsons, have made his Name very famous, as shall be shewed.

BAUTRU DES-MATRAS (John), Son of the foregoing, was an Advocate in the Parliament of *Paris*, and One of the best of them; for *Anthony Loisel*, in his Dialogue about Advocates, speaks of him in this manner; *Bautru had a higher Flight, than They all; I do not say, that he was more Learned, than any of Them, but his Tongue was better hung, and, if I may say so, more* Angevin (*a*). *William* and *René* BAUTRU DES-MATRAS were his Brothers. *William*, Counsellor in the Great Council, and *Great Reporter* of *France* (*b*), was Father of the famous Mr *Bautru*, of the *French* Academy, of whom we shall speak hereafter. *René*, Assessor in the *Presidial* Court of *Angers* [*A*], and Mayor of *Angers* in

(a) La Croix du Maine, pag. 200, *speaks of him in praise, and says, that he died the 23d of August, 1580, aged 42 Years.*

(b) Ex Nagii nomine Gallicis vitam Pe Ærodii, 176.

[*A*] *René, Assessor in the Presidial Court of* Angers.] Doubtless *Dambrun* spoke of Him, on occasion of a Woman (c), who was said to be possessed with Devils. She had two Devils, says he (2), one named *Beelzebub*, and the other *Astareth*. The first is a true Devil, a great Enemy of the *Hugue-nots*, who hates every Body, and would have beat

" *Monsieur Matras* of *Angers*, if he had not taken " up a Cudgel, and said to him, *Beelzebub*, you " Rogue, if you play your tricks with me, I will beat " you like a Devil. —— The Clergy of *Angers* " would have these two Devils to be first examined " by the Church; one of the Judges of the Town " said, that their Honour was concerned in it; and, " in

(1) Matths Prulin's of Poem ...

(2) Claude F. Catholic...

(3) chap. 2.

Pag. 35.

2

BAUTRU. 699

in 1604, was Father of *Charles*, Canon of *Angers*, known by the Name of PRIOR DES-MATRAS, and Author of some Treatises of Divinity (c) [B]. I think it is the same Prior *des-Matras*, who was so famous for his witty Sayings [C], that he came but little short, in them, of Mr *Bautru* of the *French* Academy.

(c) Ex Menag. ibid.

" in order to examine these Spirits, he began to speak " *Latin*, and *Matras* to speak *Greek*." See the Remark [B] of the Article GRANDIER.

[B] *Author of some Treatises.*] Here is what Mr *Menard* says of him, in his List of the Writers of *Angers*. " *Carolus Bautru, Presbyter, Doctor Theologus, & Professor, Ecclesiæ Mauricianæ Andegavensis Canonicus, maximi ingenii scientiarumque dotibus excellens, familiaque inter clarissimas præcipua. Scripsit de sanctissimo Eucharistiæ Sacramento tractationem, brevi publicandam, quam vidimus. Interea typis exposuit disputationem ad articulum quartum quæstionis* 76. *tertiæ partis Summæ Theologicæ Sancti Thomæ, utrum tota quantitas dimensiva corporis Christi sit in hoc Sacramento*, Andegavi, apud Antonium Hernault, 1638 (1). "—— *Charles Bautru, Priest, Doctor and Professor of Divinity, Canon of* Angers, *a Man of great Wit and Learning, and of a very noble Family. He wrote a Treatise concerning the Sacrament of the*

(1) Apud Menag Annotations on the Life of Peter Ayrault, pag. 177.

" *Eucharist, shortly to be published, which I have seen. In the mean time he put to the Press a Disputation on the Fourth Article of the Seventy sixth Question of the Third Part of St* Thomas's *Summary of Divinity*, Whether the whole dimensive Quantity of " the Body of *Christ* be in the Sacrament. Angers, " *for* Antony Hernault, 1638."

[C] *He was famous for his witty Sayings.*] Mr *Cousin* observes (2), that Mr *Menage's* Memory supplied him with many witty Sayings, which he had learned in his Youth, and that the best of them were those of the Prior Bautru des Matras. This shews, that, in Mr *Cousin's* Judgment, the Prior is to be preferred before the other *Bautru*, as to witty Sayings: for he could not be ignorant, that Mr *Menage* had as well learned Those of *Bautru* the Layman, as those of *Bautru* the Ecclesiastic. The *Menagiana* shews us, that Mr *Menage* had improved much more in the School of the first, than in That of the other.

(2) Journal of the Learned, August 11, 1692, pag. 544.

BAUTRU (WILLIAM) Count *de Serrant*, Counsellor of State in Ordinary, Introductor of Embassadors, Embassador to the Archduchess in *Flanders*, and the King's Envoy in *Spain*, *England*, and *Savoy*, was of *Angers* (a), and Son of *William Bautru*, Counsellor in the Great Council (b). He was one of the finest Wits of the XVIIth Century. He was, above all things, admired for his Jests, and smart Repartees [A]; and we find, in the Writers of his Time, a thousand Marks of his great Reputation. One of them (c) says; *He is a Man, who makes part of his Philosophy to consist in admiring but very few things, and who, for these fifty Years, has been the Delight of all the Ministers and Favourites, and generally of all the great Men in the Kingdom, and was never their Flatterer.* He was admitted into the French Academy at the beginning of it's Foundation; he could not well be forgotten, being so well known to the Cardinal *de Richelieu*. His Marriage with Martha Bigot, Daughter of a Master of the Accompts of *Paris*, did not prove a very happy one. (A fine Subject for Common-Place and Reflexions!) [B] A Son proceeded from

(a) History of the French Academy, pag. 347. Edit. 1673.

(b) Menage, Remarks on the Life of William Menage, pag. 376.

(c) Costar's first Vol. of Letters, pag. 120.

[A] *He was particularly admired for his Jests, and smart Repartees.*] I desire no other Proof of it, than the Turn of the Poet St *Amant*, in laughing at Those, who loved silly Jests, and Quibbles:

Si vous oïez une équivoque,
Vous jettez d'aise vôtre toque,
Et prenez son sens malautru
Pour un des beaux mots de Bautru (1).

When Pun ambiguous you bear,
With transport you applaud the Joke:
'Tis wond'rous fine, I vow and swear;
A better Bautru never spoke.

(1) St Amant, in the Poem entituled, The Paltry Poet, pag. 228.

The *Menagiana* would supply me with strong Proofs, if I stood in need of them: Mr *Bautru* is to be found in every Page of it; and we are told, in the Preface, " That, besides the witty Sayings of Mr *Menage*, " there are Others to be found there, and particular" ly Those of the Famous Mr *de Bautru*, whom he " knew perfectly well; for he had been his great " Friend, and had seen and conversed with him very " familiarly" *Costar's* Letter, which I have quoted (2), contains several Things, whereby one may discover Mr *Bautru's* Genius. He had the Inspection of the *Gazette* (3), and it is to him, that the Advertisement of the *Gazetteer* of *Cologne* imputes what was too favourable to Cardinal *Mazarin* in the *Paris Gazette* (4).

[B] *His Marriage —— did not prove a very happy one. A fine Subject for Common places!*] Since, what I am going to say, was printed at *Paris*, with Privilege, I may, doubtless, publish it in *Holland*, without fear of incurring the Censure of Judicious Persons. " Mr *de S*——— (5) was the Son of Mr *de " Bautru*: and, though they lived together, where " Mr *de Srigneley* lives at present, yet neither of " them owned themselves as Father, or Son. Mr " *de Bautru* said, that he would own Mr *de S*——— " for his Son, provided he was a good Man; per-
VOL. I.

(2) It is the 50th of the 1st V. l.

(3) Menagiana, p. 328, in Edit. 1. of Holl.

(4) Printed in 1642. See, the t. Pages 33, 45.

(5) I. Edit. 2. of Paris, they have put Serrant at length.

" haps he had some reason to question whether he " was so or not. The violent Suspicions, which he " had, of his Wife's Disloyalty had induced him to " prosecute her at Law, and to be revenged of her. " And, indeed, he caused his Servant to be seized, " whom he accused of having had intelligence with " his Wife, and procured him to be condemned " to be hanged, at his first Trial: The Servant appealed, and was only condemned to the Galleys, " because he made it appear, that Mr *Bautru* had " done himself justice, and had used him cruelly. " This Affair having made a great noise, Mr *de Bautru* resolved to laugh at it, as well as others, " and would say sometimes: If the *Bautru's* are " Cuckolds, they are not Fools. His Wife would " always be called *Madam de Nogent*, notwithstanding " her Marriage (6), saying, that she would not be " called *Madam Bautru* by Queen *Mary de Medicis*, " who could, then, hardly pronounce *French* right." This is what I find in the second Edition of the *Menagiana*; in which they have adjusted This Passage, which was not intelligible in the First Edition. But, since this Lady's Name has been written after the *Italian* Pronunciation, it is easy to see why the refused to bear it. Quibbling prevailed at that time, and she was exposed to Raillery by various Allusions to the Word *trou* (Hole).

If Wit could secure a Man from Cuckoldom, which so many People dread, and so many call a Trifle, Mr *de Bautru* would have been exempted from This Disgrace; but Wit, Courage, a noble Mien, and even the Royal Dignity, are no security against it. This Disgrace has something common with Death; but there is this difference; Death spares no Crowned Heads; and there are every where very virtuous Queens. Notwithstanding this difference, the same Common-place of consolation ought to make an infinite Number of People submit to both these Accidents with Patience. A Poet, who was a Philosopher endeavours, very nobly, to inspire an indifference for Death, by this Reason : " Good " Kings, The most formidable Monarchs, the " Greatest

(6) I do not understand This; for, to make it Sense. The Lady, must, I think, have been called Mademoiselle, or Madam de Nogent, when she married Mr de Bautru. Now this is not at all likely for Mr de Bautru had a Brother, who went called Mr de Nogent, which however, that That Lordship did not come into their Family by Mr de Bautru's Marriage.

8 O "Greatest

BAUTRU.

from it, (viz.) *William* BAUTRU, Count of *Serrant*, Chancellor to the Duke of *Orleans*, and Husband of *Mary Bertrand*, Daughter of *Macé Bertrand*, Lord *de la Bafiniere*, and Treafurer of the Exchequer. From this Marriage proceeded two Daughters, *Margaret* and *Mary Magdalen*. The firft was married to the Marquis *de Vaubrun*, her Uncle, *a là mode de Bretagne*, as fhall be faid hereafter (d): The fecond was married to *Edward Francis Colbert*, Count *de Maulevrier*, Lieutenant-General of the Armies of *France*, and Brother to Mr *Colbert*. The *Menagiana* informs me, that the Grandfather of thefe two Ladies died, being about Seventy Years of Age

(d) *See the following Article, Citat. (a).*

" Greateft Warriors, the fineft Genius's, the Inven-
" tors of Arts, and the moft Subtle Philofophers,
" are dead; and fhall you, an inconfiderable private
" Man, a Slave to a thoufand fhameful Paffions,
" complain, that Death will not fpare you?

Lumina fis oculis etiam bonus Ancu' reliquit
Qui melior multis quam tu fuit, improbe, rebus.
Inde alii multi reges, rerumque potentes
Occiderunt magnis qui gentibus imperitarunt.
Ille quoque ipfe, viam qui quondam per mare magnum
Stravit, iterque dedit legionibus ire per altum,
– –
Lumine adempto animam moribundo corpore fudit.
Scipiades belli fulmen, Carthaginis horror,
Offa dedit terræ proinde ac famul' infumus effet.
Adde repertores doctrinarum atque leporum,
Adde Heliconiadum comites, quorum unus Homerus
Sceptra potitus eadem aliis fopitu' quiete eft.

Ipfe Epicurus obit decurfo lumine vitæ,
Qui genus humanum ingenio fuperavit, & omnis
Præftrinxit ftellas exortus uti ætherius fol.
Tu vero dubitabis, & indignabere obire
Mortua quoi vita eft prope jam vivo, atque videnti,
Qui fomno partem, &c (7)

(7) Lucret. lib. III. fub. fin. *See Bernier's Abridgment of Gaffendus, Tom. VII, pag. 27, Edit. 1684.*

But, more to comfort thee, – – – – –
Confider, Ancus perifh'd long ago,
Ancus, a better Man, by much, than Thou.
Confider, Mighty Kings, in Pomp and State,
Fall, and ingloriously fubmit to Fate.
Confider, even He, That mighty He,
Who laught at all the Threatning of the Sea,
That chain'd the Ocean once, and proudly led
His Legions o're the fetter'd Waves, is dead.
Scipio, That Scourge of Carthage, now the Grave
Keeps Pris'ner, like the meaneft common Slave.
Nay, Greateft Wits, and Poets too, that give
Eternity to others, ceafe to Live.
Homer, their Prince, That Darling of the Nine,
(What Troy wou'd at a fecond Fall repine
To be thus fung?) is nothing now but Fame,
A lafting, far diffus'd, but empty, name.
Nay, Epicurus Race of Life is run,
That Man of Wit, who other Men out-fhon,
As far at meaner Stars the mid-day Sun.
Then, how dar'ft Thou repine to dye, and grieve,
Thou meaner Soul, thou dead ev'n whilft alive;
That fleep'ft and dream'ft the moft of Life away, &c.
CREECH.

Let us fay the fame to Thofe inconfiderable private Perfons, who are vexed at the Intrigues of their Wives: " You torment yourfelves for a Thing, " from which the moft powerful Monarchs, the " greateft Warriors, the fineft Wits, and the moft " learned and zealous Doctors, are not exempted. " What are You, that you fhould be more nice, " than they? learn, by thefe great Examples, to " bear your Misfortune patiently."

Give me leave to fay, by the by, that our *Malherbe* made ufe of *Lucretius*'s Thought, in the Epitaph of a Prince.

Je fuis poudre toutes fois,
Tant la Parque a fait fes loix

Egales & neceffaires,
Rien ne m'en a fu parer:
Aprenez, ames vulgaires,
A mourir fans murmurer.

In common Duft, a Monarch once, I lye;
Such is th' impartial Law of Deftiny.
Ye Vulgar Souls, when Fate's Decrees require,
Learn hence, without a murmur, to expire.

On occafion of this Paffage of *Malherbe*, Mr *Menage* mentions the Epitaph of *Margaret* of *Auftria*, which ends thus:

At vos plebeio geniti de fanguine, quando
Ferrea nec nobis didicerunt fata, nec ullis
Parcere nominibus, patientius ite fub umbras.

You, who of bafe Plebeian Clay are made,
Since Death, impartial, ftrikes the greateft Head,
Refign, contented, to the fatal Blow,
And go, with patience, to the Shades below.

Johannes Secundus is the Author of This Epitaph. Mr *Menage* made a Parody of *Malherbe*'s Verfes on occafion of an Epic Poem (8). I fhall alfo obferve, by the way, that the like Morality has been made ufe of, to teach all Men, that they ought not to complain of being fubject to Death. It has been reprefented to them, that the greateft Cities are deftroyed; and are They fo unreafonable, as to think it ftrange, that Man fhould dye! " Ex " Afia rediens, cum ab Ægina Megaram verfus navi- " garem, cœpi regiones circumcirca profpicere. Poft " me erat Ægina, ante Megara, dextra Piræeus, " finiftra Corinthus: quæ oppida quodam tempore " florentiffima fuerunt, nunc proftrata & diruta ante " oculos jacent. Cœpi egomet mecum fic cogitare: " Hem, nos homunculi indignamur, fi quis noftrum " interiit, aut occifus eft, quorum vita brevior effe " debet, cum uno loco tot oppidum cadavera pro- " jecta jaceant (9). —— *Returning out of* Afia*, as I* " *failed from* Ægina *toward* Megara*, I began to* " *furvey the Countries around me. Behind me was* " Ægina*, before me* Megara*, on my Right* Piræeus*,* " *on my left* Corinth *: which Cities, formerly the moft* " *flourifhing, now lye in Ruins. I began to reflect* " *with myfelf: What! Shall fo inconfiderable a* " *Creature as Man, whofe Life ought to be ftill* " *fhorter, complain of being Mortal, when, at one* " *view, we behold the Ruins of fo many Cities?*". *Taffo* has copied this Thought very well.

(8) *See his Obfervation on Malherb pag. 521.*

(9) *Servii Sulpicii piﬅ. ad Ciceronem. It is the of the 4th Book ad familiaris, 193, 194.*

Giace l'alta Cartago; à pena i figni'
De l'alte fue ruine il lido ferba:
Muoiono le città; muoiono i regni;
Cuopre i fafti, e le pompe, arena ed herba;
E l'huom d'effer mortal par che fi fdegni:
O noftra mente cupida e fuperba! (10).

(10) *Jerufalem of Taffo, Canto*

Here lofty Carthage lies: the poor Remains
Of it's proud Ruins fcarce This Shore retains.
Cities muft die; Kingdoms to Death muft yield,
Their Pomp concealed in Duft, and Herbage of the Field.

And grudge we Death, to thefe Examples blind?
How covetous, How proud, The Human Mind!

Confult the thirtieth Dialogue of *Balzac*, and you will find there a fine Imitation of this Thought in Latin Verfe: but you will not find thefe Words of *Rutilius* there:

BAUTRU. 701

Age (e), and, properly speaking, without Confession [C]. He was no Bigot [D], and had been very much afflicted at his Wife's Disloyalty [E].

Non indigemur mortalia corpora folvi;
Cernimus exemplis oppida poffe mori (11).

Repine no longer at Mortality;
Example teaches, that even Cities die.

Nor these Verses of *Ausonius*:

Miremur periiffe homines? monumenta fatifcunt,
Mors etiam faxis marmoribufque venit (12).

What wonder, if the Human Frame decay?
Death sweeps the Monuments of Art away.

Scarron, who turned every thing into Burlesque, made, as every one knows, a fine Sonnet upon this Thought. It begins thus:

Superbes monumens de l'orgueil des humains,
Pyramides, tombeaux, dont la vaine structure,

The last six Verses run thus:

Par l'injure des ans vous êtes abolis,
Ou du moins la plufpart vous êtes demolis.
Il n'est point de ciment que le tems ne diffoude:
Si vos marbres fi durs ont fenti fon pouvoir,
Dois-je trouver mauvais qu'un mechant pourpoint noir,
Qui m'a duré deux ans, foit percé par le coude?

Ye Tombs, and Pyramids, that brave the Sky,
Proud Monuments of Human Vanity!
By Time destroy'd, in Ruins now Ye lye.
No Cement can refift it's mighty Power:
If Time the strongest Marbles can devour;
Should I complain, that a vile Doublet black
Betrays, in Two Years Wear, full many a Crack?

Let us not forget Authors of a low Rank: They, and first of all myself, ought to make some use of This Morality: The Faults, which escape us, are pardonable, because the most famous and learned Writers, as the *Scaliger*'s, the *Salmafius*'s, have committed many over-fights. If such Authors are often mistaken, Those of a mean Rank, in the Commonwealth of Learning, ought not to be ashamed of their Mistakes, any more than other Nations were ashamed of being overcome, after the downfall of *Carthage* (13). *Post Carthaginem vinci neminem puduit* (13): This is what I have said, in the Plan of this Dictionary (14). Observe, that it must not be pretended, that I contradict, here, what I said there, and which I had enlarged on another place (15), that great Authors are most subject to commit Faults. This is very True in certain Respects; and, yet, their Mistakes may serve for a Comfort, and Excuse, to Vulgar Writers. But an ill use ought not to be made of them; we must endeavour to aim at Perfection.

[C] *He died, properly speaking, without Confession.*] The *Menagiana* affords me the Proof of this: " Mr

" *de Bautru* was about Seventy seven Years of Age, " when he died. He came often to see me, two or " three Years before his Death, on the Days that " I held a Conference at my House. I was at one " of my Friends, when word was brought me, that " he was fallen into an Apoplectic Fit. I ran to " see him; but he had already lost his Senses. Fa-" ther *de Harrouys* was sent for to confess him. " When they told him what he was come for, he " said to him, with a troubled Voice, Father, I " do not know you, neither do you know me, and " yet I must tell you the most secret Things that I " have done. I faw him die —— He died, as it " were, without speaking, and even without Con-" fession. He confessed himself, indeed; if Con-" fession may be made by an Interpreter. As he was " stammering, a Footman explained to the Confef-" for what his Master would say. I leave you to " think, what a Confession This was (16)." If the Question should be asked, Why his ordinary Confessor was not sent for? it may, perhaps be answered, *Because he had none.* It is probable, that he was one of Those, who put off the Sacrament of Penitence to their last Hours.

[D] *He was no Bigot.*] This may be inferred from what I have just now said, that there was no Acquaintance between him, and the Confessor, who prepared him for Death. But can any thing be more express than the Testimony of his Son? " After the Death of Mr *de Bautru*, when they " were about selling his House, they found his " Chapel out of order and in decay. It is no won-" der, said Mr *de S* —— (17), for Mr *de Bautru* " neglected his Chapel, as much as he took care " of his Kitchen and Library." If he preferved an outward Appearance, it was only for the Sake of Decency: *Being retired to St Lazarus's, some One gave him That Part of the Passion to meditate upon, which he thought would affect him most; and he fixt his Thoughts on the three Dice;* that is to say, on the Place, where it is said, that the Soldiers cast Lots for our Saviour's Garment. *He loved Gaming much* (20).

[E] *He was very much afflicted at his Wife's Difloyalty.*] See, in the Remark [B], how he sued his Wife, and the severe Punishment, which he caused to be inflicted on his Servant, her Accomplice. Is not This to be very sensible of the Disgrace of his Forehead? But, on the other side, he soon laughed at it, as others did, and would say sometimes, *If the Bautru's are Cuckolds, they are no Fools* (21). It was the most cunning expedient he could chuse (22); for, if such a Jester, as he was, had appeared serious, sullen and melancholy, he would have been very much laughed at. And, when all is done, he might jeft upon it at his Ease, since he had not connived at the Fault; it is only a voluntary Cuckoldom, which may justly be reproached, either seriously, or in jeft. *It is somewhat surprizing,* says Mr Menage (23), *that, for forty or fifty Years, Mr de Bautru should have filled all Europe with his Jests, and witty Sayings, whilst there were so many things to say against him.* Risum fecit, sed ridiculus fuit. *I do not know where I have read this: Assurance goes a great Way* (24).

BAUTRU (NICOLAS) Brother of the foregoing, was known by the Name of Count *de Nogent* [A]. He had five Children by his Marriage with *Mary Coulon*, Sister

[A] *He was known by the Name of Count de Nogent.*] This Count was one of *Sorbiere*'s Patrons, as appears by the twentieth Letter of That Author, wherein he intreats him to improve, to his Advantage, the Elogy, which he had made on Cardinal *Mazarin*. This appears yet better by the Eighty first Letter, where he thanks him for the Money, which his Eminence had gratified him with. I quote these Letters, that They, who desire to know Men by public Testimonies, may satisfy their Curiosity. They may also see the Forty seventh Letter. The *Menagiana* contains some curious Things concerning the Count *de Nogent.* " He came to *Paris* with but " Eight hundred Livres yearly Rent; and he had " an Hundred and fourscore thousand, when he died.

" The first Day he appeared at Court, he carried " the King on his Shoulders through a watery Place " in the *Tuilleries*. Monsieur *de Nogent* was an admirable Man at reviving a languishing Conversation. Being one Day in the Circle of the Queen-" Mother, *Anne of Austria*, and perceiving the Conversation flag, and that the Queen-Mother, and " the Ladies, among whom was Madam *de Guimene*, " had been silent for some time; breaking Silence, " and addressing himself to the Queen, Madam, said " he, is it not a very odd thing in Nature, that " Madam *de Guimene* and myself should be born in " one Day, and but a quarter of an Hour after each " other, and that she should be so Fair, and myself " so Black (1)?" They, who have the Address, which

BAUTRU. BEAUCAIRE.

Sister of *John Coulon*, Counsellor in the Parliament of *Paris*; I. ARMAND BAUTRU, Count *de Nogent*, the King's Lieutenant in *Auvergne*, Master of the Wardrobe, and Marshal *de Camp*, who was killed in 1672, as he was passing the *Rhine* on Horseback [B]. His Body was found, fifteen Days after, in the *Rhine*, three Leagues below *Tolhuis*, where the *French* crossed That River. This Count had married *Diana Charlotte de Caumont de Lausun*, Sister to the Marquis *de Lausun*, who has been Captain of the Life-Guards, and Governour of *Berri*, and had the Honour to be betrothed with Mademoiselle *de Mompensier*, Daughter of *Gaston* of *France*, Duke of *Orleans*, and Grand-daughter of *Henry* the Great. II. NICOLAS BAUTRU, Marquis *de Vaubrun* [C], Lieutenant-General of the King's Armies, and Governour of *Philippeville*. He married *Margaret Bautru* (*a*), and was killed in 1675, in the Battle, which was fought beyond the *Rhine*, a few Days after the Death of Marshal *de Turenne*. III. LEWIS BAUTRU, called the Chevalier *de Nogent*, Colonel of Horse. IV. MARY BAUTRU, Wife of *Rene de Rambures*, Marquis *de Rambures*: From this Marriage proceeded a Son, in whose Person the Family of the *Sires de Rambures* ended, as to the Male Issue. V. CHARLOTTE BAUTRU, Wife of *Nicolas d'Argouge*, Marquis *de Rannes*, Cornet of the Light-Horse of the Guard, and Colonel-General of the Dragoons of *France* (*b*). He was killed in *Germany*, in the Month of *July* 1678 (*c*). He was Lieutenant-General. His Widow married again with *John Baptist Armand de Rohan*, Prince of Montauban, Son of *Charles de Rohan*, Duke of *Mombazon* (*d*).

which he had, of reviving a languishing Conversation, are a great Help in the World; for, since, in the very Circles of the Queens of *France*, they are apt to fall into a kind of Drowsiness, which is almost as troublesome to the Company, as a Calm to Seamen: one may very well think, that a great many other Assemblies are subject to This Inconveniency. Is it not, therefore, very agreeable, that somebody should be always ready to revive the Company, that it may not be said, as Those Ladies in the *Menagiana* did, *It rains Weariness, as fast as it can pour?* But I wonder how the Count *de Nogent*, endowed with This Virtue, could be so weak, as Mr *Menage* represents him to be, against the Attacks of *Angeli*. "One Day, at the King's Dinner, *Angeli* said to "the Count *de Nogent*, Let us be covered; This "is of no Consequence to us. The Count *de No-* "*gent* was so vexed at it, that it did not a little "contribute to his Death (2)." In the first Edition This was said of Mr *de Bautru*, the Count *de Nogent*'s eldest Brother. It is true, that, instead of saying, that it contributed much to his Death, it is only said, that he was very much troubled at it It were to be wished, that Mr *Menage* had corrected the *Menagiana* himself.

[*B*] *Armand Bautru* − − − − − *was killed in* 1672, *as he was passing the* Rhine.] The News Writers of those Times informed the Public (3), *That They,*

who believed the Count *was drowned, without having been wounded, and that his Horse was the Cause of his Death*, were mistaken; since, after his Body was found, it *was discovered, that he was killed by a Musket-shot in the Head.* They published also, that his Body *was buried in the great Church of* Zevenart. In the Year 1686, the Marquis *de Biron* married a Daughter of This Count *de Nogent*.

[*C*] Nicolas Bautru, *Marquis de* Vaubrun.] It is He, of all the Family, who seems to have been most familiar with *Sorbiere*: That Author's printed Letters witness it; as also his Relation of a Journey to *England*. From the Letter, which he wrote to him, the eighth of *August*, 1657 (4), we learn, that This Marquis was Colonel General of the *Carabiniers of France*, and of an extraordinary Valour, but that it did not hinder him from being fond of good Books: "I wait, *says he to him*, for the Happiness "of seeing you again at *Paris*, the next Winter, "in That Chamber of the *Louvre*, where I have "found you so often reading *Tacitus*, whilst the o- "ther Courtiers were imploying the Morning in "powdering their Hair, and tying their Knots of "Ribbons." He was a very active Officer: His Disputes with the Count *de Lorge*, after the Death of Marshal *de Turenne*, had like to have proved very fatal to the *French*.

BEAUCAIRE DE PEGUILON (FRANCIS), in Latin *Belcarius Peguilio*, Bishop of *Metz*, was a very learned Man in the XVIth Century [*A*]. He descended from one of the most ancient Families of the *Bourbonnois*, and was one of the first Gentlemen of his Country, who applied themselves solidly to the Study of Literature. The Progress, which he made in it, induced *Claudius of Lorrain*, first Duke of *Guise*, to choose him for Preceptor to his second Son, the Cardinal of *Lorrain*. Beaucaire succeeded so well in this Employ, that he received many Praises for it from the Court of *France*, which he did not expect. He went with the Cardinal of *Lorrain* to *Rome*, where he conferred with *Paul Jovius*, Bishop of *Nocera*, which did not hinder him afterwards from confuting That Prelate's Historical Mistakes. At his return from *Italy*, the Cardinal of *Lorrain* procured him the Bishopric of *Metz* [*B*]: He carried him afterwards to the Council of *Trent*; and it was before That

[*A*] *He lived in the* XVI*th Century.*] According to *Kon g.* he was alive in the Year 1625. *Res Gallicas,* says he, *anno* 1625, *in literas redegit*. − − − − − *In the Year* 1625, *he wrote an History of the* French *Affairs.* Which is false. It is true, his History was printed at *Lyons*, in the Year 1625, but it had been written a long time before. The Bibliographers often commit such Mistakes.

[*B*] *The Cardinal of* Lorrain *procured him the Bishopric of* Metz] Some say, that he only kept This Bishopric for the Cardinal. The Reader will not be displeased to find, here, the Account, which *Theodorus Beza* gives of the whole Matter. "At "that same time (1), *says he* (2), *Charles of Lor-* "*rain*, Cardinal, and Bishop of *Metz*, the greatest

"Enemy, that our Religion had, resigned the Bi- "shopric of *Metz*; at which Those of the Refor- "med Religion greatly rejoiced. But, as it was "not at all likely, that such a Man, being the most "Ambitious and Covetous of any of his Rank in "the World, should voluntarily resign such a noble "Preferment, it was immediately discovered, that "this Hypocrite had only resigned his Title of Bishop, "as making a Conscience of holding so many Cro- "siers in his Hands, and reserved, in the mean "time, all the Temporalities to himself. This Ti- "tular Bishop's Name was *Peguillon*, one of his "Protonotaries, a Man of some Learning, but little "skilled in Divinity, who, being accompanied by "two other Bishops, viz. of *Toul* and *Verdun*, both "like

BEAUCAIRE. 703

That famous Assembly, that *Beaucaire* delivered the Speech [C], which is at the end of his thirtieth Book *(a)*; for you must know, that he wrote an History of his own Times in *Latin*, which is much esteemed. He began it, when, in the Year 1568, he had resigned the Bishopric of *Metz* to Cardinal *Lewis* of *Lorrain* [D], and was retired to his Country-Seat, called *la Chrete*, in *Bourbonnois*. He brought it down from the Year 1462, to the Year 1567, and left off writing it, in the Year 1588. He was, then, in his Seventy fifth Year *(b)*; for he was born the Fifteenth of *April* 1514 *(c)*. He designed to continue it *(d)*; but it is probable, the Infirmities of Old-age prevented him. He did not intend to publish this Work [E]; for he feared he had spoken such Truths, as might raise him dangerous Enemies. It was *Philip Dinet*, Sieur *de St Romain* (e), who, having found This History in the Author's Library at *la Chrete*, caused it to be printed, at *Lyons*, in the Year 1625 *(f)*. It is said, that *Beaucaire* died the Fourteenth of *February* 1591 *(g)*. He was a very fit Person to draw up the Decisions of a Council [F]; for he knew how to manage the Terms so well, that all the Disputants, that were to be satisfied, were pleased with it. The manner of his voting, one Day, concerning Episcopal Authority, displeased

---

(a) Taken from the Preface to The History of Lewis XI, by Varillas.
(b) Belcarius, in fin. lib. XXX.
(c) Id. in Præfat. Historiæ.
(d) Id. in fin. lib. XXX.

(e) He had been the Duke of Longueville's Governor, and afterwards his Envoy in Swisserland, at several Times.
(f) In the Bookseller's Advertisement.
(g) Spondanus, ad Ann. 1566, n. 34.

" like himself, came to *Metz*, and alarmed a little
" those of the Reformed Religion, who thought they
" were come as Inquisitors, with some great Power,
" to persecute them, which made many of them ab-
" sent from the City. But GOD diverted this Storm;
" and *Peguillon* was contented to publish a little
" Book in *Latin*, concerning Sanctification, and the
" Baptism of Infants, which was soon after answer-
" ed: So that Those, who had absented themselves,
" returned without any Molestation. But These Bi-
" shops gained a Nick-name by it, which was given
" them by those of their own Religion, who fir-
" named them the *Lent Bishops*, because, said they,
" they are as meagre as *Lent*, having only a small
" Pension, assigned them on the Bishoprics, of which
" they enjoyed the Titles, but the Cardinal the Pro-
" fits." See the Remark [D].

[C] *He delivered a Speech before the Council of Trent.*] He spoke it on the Day, which the Fathers of the Council had chosen to give Thanks to GOD for the Battle of *Dreux* (3). The two Historians of That Council acknowledge This Prelate's Eloquence (4); but *Pallavicini*, who does not give such a long Extract of the Speech, is more prolix on the Praises of the Orator, than Father *Paul*, and remarks also, that *Beaucaire* had lost his Nephew in That Battle. " Belcarius Episcopus Metensis vir eloquen-
" tia præclarus victorum laudes celebravit magnifica
" oratione ad Synodum, publicæ felicitati gratulatus
" in luctu domestico, quippe qui Gilbertum Belca-
" rium sui fratris filium amiserat in conflictu, atque
" hæc omnia eleganti quam scripsit historiæ consig-
" nata posteritati tradidit (5). - - - - Beaucaire, *Bishop*
" *of* Metz, *a Man of great Eloquence, celebrated the*
" *Praises of the Victors, in a pompous Oration before the*
" *Council, congratulating the Public Felicity amidst Do-*
" *mestic Affliction: for he had lost his Nephew,* Gilbert
" Beaucaire, *in the Battle: All which he delivered down*
" *to Posterity in an Elegant History, which he wrote."*

[D] *In the Year* 1568, *he resigned the Bishopric of* Metz *to Cardinal* Lewis *of* Lorrain.] When Cardinal *Charles* of *Lorrain* made This Bishopric over to him, he reserved the Right of Reversion to himself; *Regressum, ut Romani Pragmatici vocant, sibi exceperat* (6). But he did not make use of this Right for himself. The Bishopric of *Metz* remained in *Beaucaire*'s Hands from the Year 1555, 'till 1568 (7). It is falsely said, in the Advertisement to the Reader, before his History, that he went to *Trent*, with Cardinal *Lewis* of *Lorrain*, to whom he resigned his Mitre. It is certain, that he resigned it to him (8); but he followed Cardinal *Charles* of *Lorrain* to *Trent*. He was at *Rome*, in the Month of *November*, 1555, when the Pope gave him his Bull for the Bishopric of *Metz*. This I infer from his saying, that he admired the Eloquence, with which That Pope represented the Episcopal Duties to him. " Mense No-
" vembri Paulus me Pontificatu Metensi cedente Lo-
" tharingo Cardinale donavit, ac quum illi gratias
" agerem, me mei officii admonendo, & commissum
" populum commendando, facunda in primis & satis
" prolixa oratione respondit, ut tam expeditam in
" homine tene & in multis negotiis versato eloquen-
" tiam admirarer (9). *After he had resigned it,* he retired Home, and, to employ his leisure Hours, wrote a Commentary on the *French* Affairs. " Quum
" - - - - - post decimum tertium ex quo id munus
" suscepissem annum, Metensi pontificatu defunctus-

" essem, eoque cessissem, & me ab hominum fre-
" quentia subducens in Christianum fundum (10) pa-
" ratum senecturi jam dudum inter nostros Boios flu-
" diorum meorum domicilium secessissem, ne om-
" nino otiosum vitæ extremum tempus traducere vi-
" derer, commentarios rerum Gallicarum scripsi (11)."

[E] *He did not intend to publish This Work.*] He declares so himself " Hos (Commentarios) me
" editurum non profiteor; lateant in Christiana (12)
" nostra bibliotheca, donec tuto exire possint: vere
" nec in cujuisquam gratiam aut odium scripsisse con-
" firmo (13). - - - - *I have no Intention to publish*
" *them: let them rest in my Library of* la Chrete,
" *'till they may safely come abroad; I declare, that*
" *I wrote them impartially, and with a strict regard*
" *to Truth."* This he says in his Preface; and here is what he says in the Conclusion of his Work: " Maturo judicio ne in multorum odia incurreremus,
" veritas enim odium parit, ut inquit poëta Comi-
" cus, non statim edendos judicavimus. - - - - - *Upon*
" *mature Consideration, to avoid giving Offence to*
" *many, since, as the Poet says, Truth gains us Ene-*
" *mies, I thought proper to defer the Publication of*
" *of Them."* He is very violent against the Protestants; but it is not in that Respect, that the Fear of offending several Persons made him resolve not to publish it.

[F] *He was a very fit Person to draw up the Decisions of a Council.*] Father *Paul* mentions the Difficulty, which the Fathers of the Council found themselves in, on the Question about Marriage. " The first
" Chapter concerning Abuses, importing the Re-
" establishment of the Banns, ordered by *Innocent* III,
" - - - - - was touched and retouched several times,
" - - - but always so unsuccessfully, that the last Cor-
" rection was the worst. Among other things, a
" Point, already agreed upon, was altered; which
" was, That all Marriages, made in the Presence
" of three Witnesses, should be valid. And, in-
" stead of one of the Witnesses, it was said, That
" all Marriages, contracted without the Presence
" of the Priest, should be void; which raised
" the Ecclesiastic Order infinitely. - - - - - - I
" have not found in my Memoirs, who was the
" Author of This great Advantage, nor many other
" Particulars, which I would not have failed to men-
" tion, if I had known them. In the mean while,
" I must not rob *Francis de Beaucaire*, Bishop of
" *Metz*, of the Honour, which is due to him:
" for it was He, who, seeing the Impossibility of
" reconciling such different Opinions, gave This
" Decree the Form it now bears, which really ad-
" mits of several Senses, but suits admirably well
" with the various Opinions about That Matter (14)."
We find the following Words in the Annals of *Spondanus*: " In quo decreto ad formam reducendo quæ
" probaretur & in sessione promulgaretur, cum patres
" valde perplexi essent, Franciscus Belcarius Episcopus
" Metensis, vir pius doctusque & acumine ac maturitate
" ingenii præstans, eum composuit quæ publicè con-
" spicitur, cæteris comprobantibus (15). - - - - *In the*
" *forming of which Decree the Form, which should*
" *be approved of, and promulged in the Session, when*
" *the Fathers were under great Perplexity,* Francis
" Beaucaire, *Bishop of* Metz, *a pious, learned,*
" *and ingenious Prelate, drew up That, which*
" *is publickly seen, with the Approbation of the*
" *rest."* If any one should say, that a Person, who
could

---

(3) January 9, 1563.
(4) See Father Paul, lib. vii.

(5) Lib. 19. cap. 10. n. 5.

(6) Belcar. lib. xxvi, n. 6.
(7) Ibid. sub fin. lib. 30.
(8) Id. ibid.

(9) Id. lib. xxvii, n. 6. ad Annum 1555.

(10) His Country Seat called la Chrete.
(11) In Præfat.
(12) Of la Chrete.
(13) In Præfat.

(14) Hist. of the Councill of Trent, lib. viii. ad Ann. 1563. pag. 730.
(15) Spondan. ad Ann. 1563. n. 39.

VOL. I. 8 P

pleased the Flatterers of the Court of *Rome*; insomuch, that the Cardinal of *Lorrain* censured him for it [*G*], and denied, that he had ever been his Disciple. I refer the Reader to *Moreri* for some other things which I omit. I believe there is an Exaggeration in That *great Number of Books*, which he ascribes to *Beaucaire*, and some Confusion in the Titles, which he sets down [*H*]. Cardinal *Pallavicini* praised *Lewis* XIII for permitting a Book to be dedicated to him, in which the Alliances of *Francis* I with the *Turks* are very freely censured (*b*). That Book is the History of *France*, composed by our Bishop of *Metz*. He had a Brother, whose Name was JOHN, who was educated with the Constable of *Bourbon* (*i*), and who had a Son killed in the Battle of *Dreux*, and a Daughter married to *Sebastian* of *Luxembourg*, Viscount *de Martigues* [*I*].

(*b*) Pallavic. History of the Council of *Trent*, lib. v. chap. I, n. 3.

(*i*) Belcari us, in Pref

could draw up a Decree so perspicuously, that every Reader might know, that such and such things are condemned in it, and that only such a thing is formally approved in it, would be a fitter Man to draw up the Decisions of a Council than *Beaucaire*; This is my Answer. I agree, that such a Man would be more proper for this Business, if Synodical Assemblies could, or would, sacrifice Political Interests to Truth, and Integrity: But, because They, who compose These Assemblies, have not Virtue enough to act only in favour of Justice, or Faith enough to hope, that a good Cause will be sufficiently protected by GOD, without the Assistance of Politics, there are no fitter Persons for their Purpose, than those, who know how to draw up Acts full of Ambiguities, and such as may satisfy the opposite Parties. However, it cannot be denied, that the Bishop, of whom I speak, was a fit Tool for the Pope; since That Council designed to displease none of the School Factions. "Who will not admire the Prudence of this Council? We are told very ingenuously (16), that the Members of it resolved to contrive their Decisions in such a manner, and to chuse and adapt their Words so, as not to prejudice, in the least, the different Opinions of the Schools, about which the Catholic Doctors were otherwise very much divided. We are farther told, that it concerned the Prudence of the Council not to expose the Church to new Troubles, by the Disputes, which would have been raised among Divines, if their Doctrine had been discussed, and censured; and that it appears, that it is one of the Articles, on which the Pope had particularly insisted; not having intimated his Inclination for any particular Thing, but for the managing of the Schoolmen's Disputes, that he might not thwart any Opinion without Necessity, and in order to re-unite all the Catholic Forces against the Sectaries. *This was practised so exactly*, says our Author, *that one may see, by the very Words, of which the Definitions are composed, that the Fathers of the Council have been scrupulously exact, in finding out Terms, which should not prejudice any of Those Opinions.* If Father *Paul* had said This, such a Discourse would have been taken for a Satire on the Court of *Rome*: But it is Cardinal *Pallavicini*, who says it; and, consequently, it must be believed to be true (17)."

THE Spirit of the Council of *Trent*.

(16) That is to say, in a Book, written by a Doctor of the *Sorbonne*, name *Suevas*, and printed at *Paris* in 1615, concerning the *Sufficiency of Attrition*.

(17) *Taken from the* Nouvelles de la Repub. des Lettres, Febr. 1686, Art. I. pag. 127.

[*G*] *The Cardinal of* Lorrain *censured him for it.*] Cardinal *Pallavicini*, having said, that the Bishop of *Metz* declared, that he believed, that Bishops received their Authority immediately from GOD, and that they were not meerly the Pope's Delegates, and that the Pope's Power is not unlimited, adds, that, in this, he went beyond his Bounds, *hac in re plurimum ille cancellos transgressus est* (18). "It was suspected, *continues he*, that the Bishop, and the Cardinal of *Lorrain*, juggled, and acted in concert; but the Cardinal, in order to remove These Suspicions, declared, that he had never been *Beaucaire*'s Scholar, and censured him before the Embassadors of *France*, and twelve Bishops." *Fama erat, hunc Episcopum Lotharingi magistrum fuisse: & sane intimam cum eo familiaritatem exercerbat, atque ejus operâ nobilem illam Sedem acceperat. Unde suspicio fuit, eos concorditer se gessisse, & textum à discipulo obscurè propositum fuisse dilucidatum à magistro interpretationis suæ claritate. Sed Cardinalis, hujusce famæ conscius, Gualterio negavit* * *se unquam Beauqueri discipulum fuisse; eum quidem à se agnosci virum maximæ literaturæ, sed minimi consilii. Nec abstinuit, quin illum castigaret coram duobus Gallis Oratoribus, & duodecim Episcopis* (19). They, who know the Spirit of a Court, which was the Soul of this Cardinal's whole Conduct, will not build much on what he said, when he found, that he was called in question for *Beaucaire*'s Opinions. He was willing to make use of him in sounding the Business, in order to see whether any thing could be done to please the *Gallican* Church, but, afterwards, was as ready to disown him, when he knew that the Court of *Rome* was offended at it. After all, *Beaucaire* was, perhaps, a Man of no great Conduct, as we may suppose This Cardinal declared. This is but too common among studious Persons.

(18) Pallavic. lib. xix, cap. 6, n. 5. pag. 284.

* Littera Gualterii ad Borromæum. 7 Decembris & sequentibus 1562.

(19) Acta Paleotti apud Pallavicinum, ibid. n. 6.

[*H*] *There is some Confusion in the Titles, which* Moreri *sets down.*] He says, that *Beaucaire composed a Treatise of Children, that die in their Mother's Womb, ---- and a Treatise against the* Calvinists] This is to declare plainly, that the first of these two Treatises does not oppose the Tenets of the *Calvinists*; which is false; for it is designed to oppose the Opinion, which they have, that the Children of the Faithful are sanctified in their Mother's Womb; and, therefore, that, though they die without receiving Baptism, they are, nevertheless, saved. The Passage of *Theodorus Beza*, which I have alledged before (20), informs us, that this Book of *Beaucaire* was answered. An anonymous Author replied to This Answer; his Reply was printed at *Paris*, in the Year 1567, in 8vo (21), with the first Treatise of *Beaucaire* (22), and some others. Properly speaking, the two Books, mentioned by *Moreri*, are but one and the same Book. *Spondanus* remarks, that *Beaucaire* published his Dissertation against the Tenets of the *Calvinists*, concerning the Sanctification of Children in their Mothers Womb, in 1567; but what I have said before, shews plainly, that This Book had appeared before That time, and a little after *Beaucaire*'s Instalment in the Cathedral of *Metz*. Now he obtained That Bishopric in the Month of *November*, 1555, as I said in the Remark [*D*]. So that it must be said, that *Beaucaire* prepared a second Edition of his Treatise, and that he did not publish it till the Year 1567. He inserted some Letters in it, which were intercepted at *Châlons*, on *Marne*, during the Conference of *Poissy*. These Letters were written by *Taffin*, and *Theodorus Beza*. *Taffin*, Minister of *Metz*, had consulted the Ministers of the Conference of *Poissy*, on the Question, Whether Children, baptized by a Woman, should be re-baptized. He was answered, That some Persons, of great Judgment, did not believe that it ought to be done, and that, therefore, they had thought fit to refer the Discussion of That Point to the Church of *Geneva*, and to That of *Zurich* (23). *Moreri* says, that the History of *France*, by *Beaucaire*, begins with the Year 1460, and ends with the Year 1580. But, had he consulted the Authors, whom he quotes, *Spondanus* (24) would have informed him, that it begins with the Year 1462, and ends with the Year 1566; that the Author promised, indeed, to continue it, if GOD gave him Life for it, but that the Effect of this Promise did not appear, though the Work was not published till about forty Years after *Beaucaire* had finished it. The Catalogue of the *Bodleian* Library commits the same Fault with *Moreri*: I do not wonder at it, since the Bookseller's Preface contains This Error.

(20) *In R mark* [*B*].

(21) *The T tle of it* Anonymi Antapolog contra Ap logiam, M tensium n nistrorum nomine scriptam, everfione sanctificat nis Calvi ane.

(22) *Th Title is* C tra Calvi anorum d ma de sa ctificatio infantium uteris m trum.

(23) Cla de Saint *Answer the Apo of* Theo rus Beza *cited by* teolus, leach. H ref. pag. 98.

(24) A Ann. 15 n. 34.

(25) Bel rius's *H* lib. 28, 37.

[*I*] *His Brother* JOHN —— *had* —— *a Daughter married to* Sebastian *of* Luxembourg.] *Beaucaire* speaks of This Marriage, and says, that Queen *Mary Stuart*, the Wife of *Francis* II, procured him for her Niece, whom she greatly loved (25). *Le Laboureur* confirms this. "*Sebastian* of *Luxembourg*, *says he* (26), partly out of Inclination, and partly in hopes of gaining the Affection and Favour of Queen *Mary Stuart*, married *Frances* (27) *de Beaucaire*, Daughter of *John S. de Peguillon*, and Maid of Honour to the said Queen, who loved her entirely for her good Qualities. He had an only Daughter by her, whose

(26) *A to* Castel Tom. I 829, 8

(27) *H Uncle, should k best, cal* Mary, 23, n. Mr le boureur *ing bette formed, her so wife, in ther Ph*

BEAULIEU.

"Estate she managed with as much Care and Prudence, as she had shewn in the Education of This "great Heiress (28)." *Brantome* had not forgot this; for, in the List of the Ladies, who were eminent in the Court of *Catherine de Medicis*, he places *Madam de Martigues, formerly called Mademoiselle de Villemontois, a great Favourite of the Queen of Scotland* (29). Mr *le Laboureur, Tom. I, pag. 318*, says, that the Lady *de Villemont..* was *Mary de Beaudore*, Daughter of *John*, Lord of *Puy Gaillar*, Seneschal of *Poitou*.

BEAULIEU (LEWIS LE BLANC Sieur de) Minister, and Professor of Divinity at *Sedan*, in the XVIIth Century, was a Man very commendable for his Learning and Virtue. A great many Theological Theses were maintained under his Direction, and collected into one Volume, after his Death, and printed in *England*. The Public was so well pleased with them, that This Edition was soon sold off, and Another published in the same Country, in the Year 1683 (*a*). If he had not been a *Frenchman*, a Preface would have been prefixed to the first, or second Edition, giving an Account of the Author's Life; for the *French* are very apt to let the History, or the Life, of a Kinsman, famous for his great Parts, and learned Works, fall into oblivion. The Impossibility I find of fixing the Time, and Place, of the Birth of *Lewis le Blanc*, the Time of his Promotion to the Ministry, and to the Professorship of Divinity, and other Historical and Chronological Circumstances, must be imputed to such a Negligence. I can say nothing more, than that he died in the Month of *February* 1675, and that he was well beloved by the Marshal *de Fabert* (*b*), one of the greatest Wits of his Age. Some of his Sermons were printed at *Sedan*, in the Year 1675. It is not in them, that the brightest Merit of the Author is to be looked for, but in his Theses, wherein he treats, with a wonderful Clearness [*A*], and great Penetration, the most important Matters of Divinity, and applies himself chiefly to remove the Misunderstandings, which have so greatly multiplied Controversies. He lays down the true State of the Question; he clears up things that are ambiguous, and makes it appear, that many Disputes, which are thought to be real, are only Disputes about Words. It is scarce credible, how much this Method prejudiced a great many ignorant Persons against him [*B*]. They imagined, that he endeavoured to bring back the Reformed to the Communion of the Church of *Rome*. They, who knew his Virtue, and Piety, did not suspect any such thing of him; nor they, who were capable of judging right of his Theses: But many People in the remote Provinces knew him no otherwise, than as they had been told, that he shewed, that, in some things, the Divines of both Parties did not so much differ from each other, as was believed. These Gentlemen, being unwilling to lessen the Subjects of Division, which they would rather have increased, or being accustomed to interpret things ill, or rashly believe those, who give a bad Turn to the Actions of their Neighbours, looked upon Mr *de Beaulieu* as a false Brother, who was promoting the great Design of re-uniting both Churches [*C*], which the Cardinal *de Richelieu* was so fond of. This Professor's Penetration obliged him to

[*A*] *He treated the most important Matters with wonderful Clearness.*] Because Mr *Nicolle* will be sooner believed, than myself, I shall quote a Passage of his *Lawful Prejudices against the Calvinists*. "One of "their Professors of *Sedan*, whose Name is *Lewis le "Blanc*, has particularly signalized himself on this "Subject, in his *Theses of Justification*. That Pro- "fessor, who justly deserves the Praise of having an "extraordinary clear Head, and of being a very fit "Man to unravel Questions, which are perplexed "by the different use of Terms, examines, in his "Theses, the chief Differences between the Catho- "lics and Protestants, on this Head, and concludes, "on all the Articles, that The Catholics are in the "right, and The Protestants only contrary to them "in Words (1)."

[*B*] *This Method prejudiced a great many ignorant Persons.*] They are not only weak Men, who have entertained Suspicions against Mr *Beaulieu:* See here what an ingenious Minister has published; "I re- "spect Mr *le Blanc's* Memory; but the concern for "Truth obliges me to remark, what no one is ig- "norant of, namely, that This Divine wrote after "a manner, which made his Orthodoxy much sus- "pected. Thinking to clear up Matters, to remove "useless Disputes, or Those, which turn only on "Words, and to take away all Equivocations, he has "extremely straitned the Space, which separates us "from the Church of *Rome*. He has reduced the "most important Controversies almost to nothing: "And, by This Conduct, as also by his great Mild- "ness, and the strong Inclination, which he always "shewed for Peace, he has given many Persons occa- "sion to rank him among the *Latitudinarians* (2). "—— The famous Mr *le Blanc* de *Beaulieu*, for "whose Memory I have otherwise a great Venera- "tion, is not a Divine, whose Pen is to be borrow- "ed, to describe the Opinion of the Reformed, "about controverted Matters with the Papists. —— "He was a little too Neutral in the Quarrel, which "we have to decide with Them (3)." *Hæc ille* (Le *Blanc*, pag. 796, n. 56.) *qui laxus nimium est controversiarum quas tractat arbiter, quo factum ut nimium partium adversarum conciliationi intentus, à communi via Reformatorum sæpe discesserit* (4).

[*C*] *It was believed, he was promoting the great Design of re-uniting both Churches.*] These false Suspicions increased, when a certain Report was spread abroad, That the Marshal *de Turenne*, being very fond of re-uniting both Religions, had consulted the Professor of *Sedan*, and received a Letter from him, which was shewed to all the Ministers, in order to surprize them. This Report was not altogether groundless; for Mr *Jaquelot* says, that, in 1672, the Agent, who was employed in This Affair, came to Vassi, in Champagne ———— *with a Confidential Letter, signed Lewis, and a Letter from Monsieur de Turenne, to Mr de Beaulieu, Professor of Divinity at Sedan, and which That Professor's Answer to Mons. de Turenne, ———— and the Signatures of the Pastors of Picardy and Champagne, whom he had visited*; but he adds, that This Answer did no Injury to Mr de Beaulieu's Reputation (5). *Note*, that he produces (6), an Act of the Synod of the *Isle of France*, which justifies the Ministers, who had signed. The Piece, in which he mentions these things, is a Letter against Mr *Benoit*, Minister of *Delft*, who did not fail to answer it; and who, among other Remarks, made this, that the Signatures of the most innocent Ministers contained This Restriction; "And I promise to contribute to "it, as much as lies in my power, with a safe Con- "science (7)." He adds, that this last Clause, "taken "from

BEAULIEU.

to avoid certain Terms, commonly received, which he found somewhat inconvenient. He did it, particularly, as to the Doctrine of the Certainty of Salvation. This gave Mr *Arnauld* an occasion to quarrel with him [D]. Mr *de Beaulieu* had no Children; his Widow, who was a very understanding and virtuous Woman, shewed an Heroic Constancy in the last Persecution (c). She could never be forced to make any Abjuration; so that, after many Vexations, which she endured, she died without betraying her Profession in the least. Mr *le Blanc*, Counsellor in the Presidial of *Sedan*, Brother to Mr *de Beaulieu*, endeavoured twice to make his Escape into *Holland*, after his Abjuration, but was taken in the Way, and brought back again into his Country. *The King forgave him the Punishment of the Gallies, to which he had been condemned for designing to leave the Kingdom against the Prohibitions* (d).

Mr *de Beaulieu* has been very often cited, in the Quarrel between two *French* Ministers, who disputed, among other things, about the Principle of Faith. What I cite out of their Writings, may serve to discover his Opinions, and Character [E], and,

(c) *Mr Quick speaks of it in his Prolegomena to the Synodicon in Gallia Reformata.*

(d) *Remarks on the Confession of Sauri, pag. 555. Edit. 1699.*

" from Mr *de Beaulieu*'s Letter, was a Snare laid for
" the Simplicity of good Souls. — — — It is certain,
" that Three sorts of Persons were concerned in This
" Project. I. Ill-minded Persons. II. Plain and
" honest Men. III. Wise and clear-sighted Persons,
" but dazzled, either with the seeming Usefulness of
" the Thing, or with the Name of Mr *de Beaulieu*,
" a Man of great Merit, but of too Apostolic a Sin-
" cerity, to distinguish himself from the Craftiness of
" the Marshal *de Fabert*, an old Courtier, and who
" did not scruple to deceive People (8)." There is
a small Mistake here; for the Marshal *de Fabert*
had been dead above seven or eight Years, before This
Project was set on foot. Monsr. *de Turenne* was the
Promoter of it.

(8) Id. ibid. *pag. 41.*

[D] *This gave Mr Arnauld an occasion to quarrel with him.*] He accused him of having renounced the Opinions of the *Calvinists* in four Points of the Doctrine of the Certainty of Salvation (9). Mr *de Beaulieu* published a particular *Thesis* on This Subject, in Answer to Mr *Arnauld*. The latter replied after his Adversary's Death (10): *A Disciple, and intimate Friend*, of the deceased, answered Mr *Arnauld*'s Reply (11). I have compared The Disciple's Answer and Mr *Arnauld*'s Reply together, but could not determine which was right, or which was wrong; They are properly Questions of Fact, about which a thousand Equivocations, and all the Art of Disputation, may be used on both Sides. A Man must have more leisure, than I have, to examine This thoroughly. Nevertheless, I believe, if Mr *de Beaulieu* had written his Apology himself, his Cause would have been better defended.

(9) *Arnauld's Overthrow of The Morality, cited by Peter Jurieu; Justification of the Morals of the Reformed, Book IV. chap. xiv. pag. 40 &c. Edit of the Hague 1685.*

(10) *In his Book intituled, Calvinism convicted anew, c. 19.*

(11) *See the Justification of the Morals of the Reformed, Book VI. chap. xiv. pag. 36.*

[E] *What I quote out of their Writings, may serve to discover his Opinions, and Character.*] Let us begin with a Passage of Mr *Saurin*: He had just said, That Mr *le Blanc*'s Name *is not so much authorized, as famous, among us* (12); and here is what he adds: What Mr *Jurieu* mentions of Mr *le Blanc* " is more " fit to cry down his Doctrine, than to give it cre- " dit. For Example. Is it not a new way of defend- " ing the Authority of the Scripture, and the Truth " of the Christian Religion, to say *, *That it is ne- " cessary, that That, which is the first Principle of " Faith, should not be proved by itself, nor by another " Principle: and yet, that the Principle of Faith " should not be an evident Thing, because, as in Hu- " man Sciences, there are certain Principles, which " are the first, on which all others depend, which " neither depend on themselves, nor on other Princi- " ples, so it is with the Doctrine of Faith. They, " who know the A, B, C, of the Art of Thinking " and Reasoning, know also, that a Proposition, " which is not self evident, and is not mediately, or " immediately, demonstrated by another self evident " Proposition, cannot be a Principle of Science, or " of Faith, nor so much as pass for a true Proposi- " tion, whilst it remains in That Obscurity. — Mr " *Jurieu* adds, after Mr *le Blanc*, *That, though the " Scripture*, that is to say, the Divinity of the Scrip- " ture, *be not self evident, it ought not to be conclu- " ded, therefore, that it is not the first Principle of " Faith, and that it ought to borrow it's Authority " from elsewhere* (13). These Words neither agree " with right Reason, nor the Word of GOD. The " Divinity of the Scripture is evident by it's Cha- " racters —— Mr *de Beaulieu* reasons no better, " when he answers the Objection, which the Ene- " mies of Christianity make against the Holy Scrip-

(12) *Saurin's Examination of Mr Jurieu's Theology, pag. 260.*

* *Page 24, col. 1.*

(13) Id. ib. *pag. 261.*

" tures in this manner. *As for those impertinent " Questions, which are asked us, How do you prove, " that the Apostles wrote their Books by Divine In- " spiration? We answer, That they require an unjust " thing of us*; viz. *that we should demonstrate a " thing, which is not to be demonstrated. We, there- " fore, confess freely, that we cannot demonstrate it, " that is to say, prove and demonstrate it Mathema- " tically; But we deny, that it follows from thence, " that Those Books cannot be the first and certain " Rule of Faith, because it is the Property of the " Principles of Faith not to be evident* (14)." See, in Mr *Saurin*'s own Book how he confutes These Maxims.

We must insert Mr *Jurieu*'s Answer here. " It " is a curious Thing, *says* he (15), to see how Mr " *Saurin* uses Mr *de Beaulieu*, whom he calls, else- " where, a most Excellent Man. But, here, because " he is of Mr *Jurieu*'s Opinion, and of That of " the whole Church, concerning the Evidence of " the Principle of Faith, he must needs be a Man " of no very sound Orthodoxy; he favoured Popery, " and Arminianism; he was a great Latitudinarian; " he saved as many Persons as he could; he propo- " sed such Absurdities, that he deserved to be sent " back to his A, B, C; and it is imprudent to own " one's self his Disciple The Truth is, we can hard- " ly believe our own Eyes. Here we may perceive " what advantage the Living have over the Dead, " as the Wise Man tells us: Such a one pulls the " dead Lion by the Beard, who durst not have come " within a thousand Paces of him, if he had been " alive. —— They, who knew the late Mr *de Beau- " lieu*, know, that he was the most reserved Man " in the World in speaking his own Opinions; A " faithful Historian of Those of others, but most re- " served as to his own: giving his Resolution only " on notorious things, and such as were owned by " all Divines. So that, unless he had been out of " his Wits, it is not to be imagined, that he would " have explained his Mind about such nice Proposi- " tions, had he not been persuaded, that he followed " the common Road. How could a Man, who " made it his Study to know the Opinions of all " Divines, and who seldom declared his own, be ig- " norant of a Matter of Fact, known to Mr *Saurin*, " who never saw but the Outside of great Libraries? " Or, was Mr *de Beaulieu* so foolish, and so wicked, " as to establish an Impiety, of which he was the " Author, as a public Opinion? Whom does Mr " *Saurin* hope to persuade of this? They, who have " read the first Part of this Work, about the Mat- " ter of Fact, will be ashamed of Mr *Saurin*'s Rash- " ness: Since they will see, that our Orthodox Di- " vines, since *Calvin*, have spoken as Mr *de Beau- " lieu* did; and that, in This, and almost in every " thing else, he is but an Historian. But does not Mr *de Beaulieu* advance here hard Things, about this Question, which are peculiar to him? For Ex- ample *; *That the Proofs, which are alledged for " the Divinity of the Holy Scriptures, are not of the " Nature of Those, which are called* de Fide, *in the " Schools*; *that they are not drawn from any Princi- " ple, or Rule, of Faith, and that, by themselves, " they cannot make an Article of Faith*. Has any " Body said so? Yes; It has been said, *Calvin* has " said it in stronger Terms; he calls Those, who " build Faith on the Characters of the Scripture (16), " foolish and impertinent." These Proofs are not of Those, which are called *de Fide* (17). —— " The " other

(14) Id. *pag. 262.*

(15) *Jurieu's Defence of the Doctrine of the Church, p. 372, 373.*

* *Disput. Tom. IV de S. Scriptura* N° 9.

(16) *Jurieu ubi supra p. 378, 3*

(17) *Jurieu ibid. pag 381.*

BEAULIEU.

and, consequently, will not be superfluous. Some are persuaded, that there is great Misunderstanding in This Contest [F]. His Doctrine concerning the Efficacy of Baptism was also censured. See the Book, which I quote (e), printed at *Amsterdam* in 1695. See, I say, the fifth Leaf of the Preface, and the Treatise, which makes the Conclusion of it. See also Mr *Saurin*, pag. 522, 550, &c. of his Examination of Mr *Jurieu's* Theology. To conclude, I have just now discovered, that Mr *de Beaulieu* was born at *Plessis Marli* (f), where his Father was Minister, and that he died at the Age of Sixty Years, and six Months.

" other Accusation against Mr *de Beaulieu* *, of being " a Latitudinarian, *of enlarging the Way to Salva-* " *tion, and of saving as many Persons as he could*, is " also ridiculous, since it is inconsistent with the " Doctrine, which Mr *Saurin* lays to his Charge. " He was rigid as to the Doctrine of Grace, and " believed, that the Holy Ghost produced the Cer- " tainty of Faith, without Means, as we have seen. " —— This Accusation —— is entirely grounded on " his explaining the State of some Controversies " otherwise than they are commonly understood. " But, if he should be deceived, it would only be a " meer Error of Fact; for he never favoured any re- " laxed Opinion, nor established the Indifferency of " Religions, nor a general Toleration of all Sects, " as Mr *Saurin* does." Let us end with Mr *Saurin's* Reply. " I speak of Mr *de Beaulieu* with all the " Esteem and Respect, which he deserves; and I " put a great Deference between him, and Mr *Ju-* " *rieu*; not for the reason, which Mr *Jurieu* sup- " poses, that is, because the one is dead, and the " other living; but because the living does not re- " semble the Dead in every thing. Nevertheless, I " observe Mr *de Beaulieu's* Faults as Those of a great " Man. This I may do. I do not send him back " to his A, B, C, as Mr *Jurieu* accuses me of do- " ing, two or three times. I say only, That *Those,* " *who know the A, B, C, of the Art of Thinking, and* " *Reasoning, know also, &c* (18) This is certain, " and may be said by Those, who are persuaded " (19). I do Mr *de Beaulieu* no wrong in calling " him a Latitudinarian. He was not so in the " odious Sense, which Mr *Jurieu* puts upon the " Word, in taking a *Latitudinarian* for a Kind of " Atheist. But he was so, in some Degree. The " manner, in which he explains the State of some of " our Controversies, with the Papists, and other " Sectaries, about Justification, the Certainty of Sal- " vation and other matters, is a Proof of it: And " our Learned and Sincere Divines do not deny it." Since Mr *Jurieu* replied nothing, I end the Remark here.

[F] *There is great Misunderstanding in This Con-* *test.*] Consider well the above-mentioned Words of Mr *de Beaulieu* (20). They inform us, that he believed the Inspiration of the Holy Scriptures could not be *Mathematically demonstrated.* Let us compare That with This Answer of Mr *Saurin*. " If, by Mathe- " matical Demonstration, Mr *le Blanc* understands " such a Demonstration, against which Flesh and " Blood can make no Objection, I acknowledge, " that the Divinity of the Scripture cannot be Mathe- " matically demonstrated: but, notwithstanding, it " may be Morally demonstrated, so as to remove all " doubts, which is manifestly contrary to Mr *Ju-* " *rieu's* Principles (21)." The comparing of these two Passages shews, that Mr *de Beaulieu*, and Mr *Saurin*, teach the same Thing in the main. They both own, that the Divinity of the Scripture cannot be Mathematically proved: But you will say, does not Mr *Saurin* maintain, That it may be proved by Moral Demonstration? I own it; but I should be very much mistaken, if he could prove, that Mr *le Blanc* did not teach the same Thing. I am sure, That great Divine never denied, that the Proofs of the Divinity of the Scriptures are as strong as Moral Demonstration. He had no Interest in denying it; for, because a Man owns, that a thing cannot be proved by Mathematical Demonstration, it does not follow, that, if he argues well, he must acknowledge, that it cannot be Morally demonstrated. Let us farther shew the Misunderstanding of This Dispute. Mr *Saurin* fancies, that, according to the Principles of his Adversary, the Proofs of the Divinity of the Scripture do not exclude all Manner of Doubt. This is full of Equivocation. His Adversary does not pretend, that They, who perceive the weight and force of Those Proofs, ought still to entertain some doubt; he does not deprive them of full Certainty, and entire Persuasion. He pretends only, They do not see, that the contrary is impossible; as it appears to be in Things, which have been Mathematically demonstrated. It happens daily, that we are fully convinced of a Thing, and have not the least doubt about it, though we know, that the contrary is possible. A Traveller, lodging in an Inn, the Master of which he never knew, eats, without fear, what is set before him; He knows very well, that his Meat may be poisoned, and that there is no Metaphysical, Physical, or Moral Contradiction, in supposing, that his Meat has been mixed with Poison, by chance, or out of Malice. He is not ignorant, that such things have been done; nevertheless, he is persuaded, that he ought not to fear any thing in This Case; He eats with a full Persuasion, that he shall not be poisoned. We have still less doubt, when we eat at a Friend's House; and, yet, we are convinced, that it is possible, the Meat may be poisoned. Therefore a Divine must not be censured for saying, that we are perfectly convinced of the Truth of the Doctrine, which our Pastors declare to us, though the Reasons, on which they ground them, do not prove to us, that it is impossible the thing should be otherwise. Let us remember, that Mr *Saurin* gives up all Pretention to Geometrical Proofs; He is satisfied with Moral Demonstration, against which Flesh and Blood only can raise any Objections. Now This is exactly his Adversary's Doctrine; They quarrelled therefore for they knew not what. Mr *Jurieu* declares, that he has not said any thing, which can imply, that he excludes Conviction of Conscience (22); he maintains, that he has laid down, that the Characters of Divinity, which appear in the Revelation, Are able to produce a Kind of Certainty in a Man, who has any Equity, and is not prejudiced, without the Assistance of the Spirit of GOD. But, first of all, there are no Men in the World, who are not prejudiced. All, who are not yet converted, are full of the Prejudices of the Flesh. Besides, we do not require I know not what Certainty; but a Certainty, which surpasses all Certainty, even That of Sciences grounded on Demonstration (23). —— Surely, Those Characters are not such as can produce, in a well-disposed Mind, a Certainty of Speculation equal to the Certainty of Geometrical Sciences (24). —— He says, first, That there are none of Those well-disposed Minds in the World, before Grace. II. That a Man, of Equity, and no Prejudices, might obtain a Kind of Certainty of the Divinity of the Scriptures, even without Grace. III. That the Certainty, which we require, is a Certainty, which surpasses That of Geometrical Demonstration (25)." Observe farther, That Mr *Jurieu* declares, that he meant, " that Those internal and external Characters, placed " and ranged, by the Arts of Logic and Rhetoric, in " the Works of our learned Men, by laying down, " at first, self-evident Principles, and leading the " Mind from one Conclusion to another, make a " better Proof to Reason, than common Moral Demonstration; But that These same Characters, " nakedly proposed, and without Art, do not make " up Moral Demonstration, especially to the illiterate, who must be led by the Hand, and are not " able to understand several Things, which require " Study and Penetration. Most of our simple and " illiterate People never consider attentively That " Demonstration, which is called Moral. But These " same Characters, put together, which do not make " up Moral Demonstration to the Mind, especially " in the common Sort of People, form a Proof of " *Sentiment*, which is beyond all Exception, and " which is as lively as the Impression of the Sun on " the Eyes (26)." Thus these Gentlemen are at last of the same Opinion: The one does not pretend to any Mathematical Demonstration, nor the other neither.

ther. The latter is for Moral Demonstration, which the other grants him. The most plausible thing, which can be said in Mr Saurin's Favour, is, that, at first, Mr Jurieu did not well explain his Opinion, and that he seems not to have explained it, but by contradicting himself, according to custom. I believe also, that, when he began to meditate on this Subject, he did not very well know the Nature of Moral Demonstration. He formed too great an Idea of it; and This was, probably, the Reason, why he durst not say, that the Proofs of the Divinity of the Scripture amounted to such an high Degree of Evidence. If he had known the true Nature of This Kind of Demonstration, he would have less exposed himself. Moral Demonstration does not lie, like Geometrical, in an indivisible Point; It has a greater compass, and extends, from a Great Probability, to a very Great Probability. These are it's bounds, and, consequently, there is a great way to go from the Place, where our Proofs begin to be called Moral Demonstration, to the place, where they begin to be called Physical, or Metaphysical, or Geometrical, Demonstration. Perhaps, That, which deceived Mr Jurieu, was his seeing, that the Certainty, and Evidence, with which we know, that there was such a Man as Julius Cæsar, such a Republic as Rome, &c. does not pass for Science, but for Human Faith, for Opinion, and, at most, for the Effect of Moral Demonstration; and, because he did not see, that the Inspiration of the Scripture could be proved by as convincing Reasons, as Those, which prove, that Cicero existed, he feared to say, that there was Moral Demonstration for This Inspiration. If he entertained such a Thought, he did not know the true Nature of Things; for it is not true, that the Foundation of the Certainty and Evidence, with which we know, that there was a Roman Republic, is meer Moral Demonstration, nor that our Persuasion in that Respect is an act of Human Faith, or Opinion: It is Science properly so called; it is the Conclusion of a Syllogism, whereof the Major and Minor are clearly and necessarily true Propositions. There is at least Physical Demonstration in it. The School Philosophers were not ignorant of This. " Ille actus non est fidei, sed scientifi-
" cus; innititur enim non humano testimonio, sed
" repugnantiæ physicæ, qua video non potuisse tot
" homines convenisse ad mentiendum. —— Ille as-
" sensus oritur à duobus principiis, quæ non patiun-
" tur dissensum. Primum est hoc: *impossibile est
" tot homines tot sæculis convenire ad mentiendum.*
" Secundum est: *hoc dicunt tot homines tot sæculis*
" (27). —— *This Act is not of Faith, but scientifi-
" cal; for it depends not on human Testimony, but
" Physical Contradiction, by which I see, that so many
" Men could not conspire in a Lie. —— This Assent

" arises from two Principles, which demand our As-
" sent: The first is: It is impossible so many Men
" should, for so many Ages, agree in a Lye. The
" second is: This is affirmed by so many Men for so
" many Ages." However it be, Mr Jurieu explained himself better at last.

Let us take notice of Mr Saurin's Remark, That, " if, by Mathematical Demonstration, Mr le Blanc " understands a Demonstration, against which Flesh " and Blood can raise no Objection, he acknow- " ledges, that the Divinity of the Scripture cannot " be mathematically demonstrated." It were to be wished, that we had a general Rule to distinguish the Objections, which proceed only from Flesh and Blood; for each Christian Sect ascribes the Objections, which are made by Others, to That Principle, and so the Ball is tossed back again, and the Disputants are so far from deciding a Controversy, by maintaining, that a Doctrine is only opposed by Difficulties, suggested by Flesh and Blood, that it is an everlasting Dispute, whether a Difficulty, or an Objection, proceeds from such a Principle. I add, that there are some Truths, against which the most prejudiced, and most passionate, Men will not dispute, though it be never so much their Interest to oppose them. Porphyry, a great Enemy of the Christian Religion, and a great Zealot for Paganism, did not deny certain matters of Fact, alledged by the Christians. The Interest of his Cause required, that he should deny them; for it is a very great Advantage, in a Dispute, to reject both the Matters of Fact, and the Consequences of them. Mr Saurin, who is fully persuaded, that the Objections, which the Reformed alledge against the Church of Rome, do not proceed from Flesh and Blood, knows very well, that, when the Question is about some Miracle, wrought by Relicks, They deny the Fact, and add, That, though the Miracle should be certain, it would not prove the worshiping of Relicks to be lawful. So that, according to the best Laws of Disputation, carefully observed by the Orthodox, Porphyry might have thought himself obliged not only to deny the Consequences of the Facts, alledged by the Christians, but the very Facts themselves. Flesh and Blood, I mean his Prejudices, and Passions, might lead him to it; for the more things we require our Adversaries to prove, the more we puzzle and tire them. How comes it, then, that That Enemy of JESUS CHRIST did not deny certain Facts alledged by the Apostles? Is it not because they could be supported by much clearer Reasons, than Those, which he alledged for what he denied? I decide nothing: it will suffice to say, that sometimes Flesh and Blood lay down their Arms, and submit to a Light, which does not please them.

BEAUMONT (FRANCIS de) Baron Des-Adrets, was one of the Noblemen of France, whose Courage and Military Actions made the greatest Noise in the Religious Wars, under the Reign of Charles IX. He was of Dauphiné, and had learned the Profession of Arms in Piedmont, which was the best, and most famous, School of War in that Age. It is pretended, that the Desire of revenging himself of the Duke of Guise, who had been against him in a Law-Suit (a), made him declare for Those of the Protestant Religion (b). They add, that Catherine de Medicis wrote a Letter to him to excite him to Revenge, and even that she permitted him to make use of the Huguenots, that he might the better ruin That Duke's Authority in Dauphiné. The Duke of Guise, Governour of That Province, had made la Mothe Gondrin his Lieutenant there: he was his Creature, and a Gentleman of great Courage (c). Des-Adrets, judging, that he could not begin his Undertakings more successfully, than by ridding himself of That Gentleman, practised upon some People in Valence, and managed his Intelligence in such a manner, that la Mothe Gondrin, overwhelmed by the Sedition, which was raised in That City, was stabbed, there, in cold Blood. So that Valence was the first Town, which the Baron made himself master of, and where his Dignity was increased; for, whereas he was before Colonel of the Legionaries of Lyonnois, Dauphiné, Provence, and Languedoc (d), he was chosen, the next day after the Sedition (e), Administrator of Affairs, till the Prince of Condé's farther Declaration. From That Time, he over-ran all the Country, and, understanding, that the Protestant Party had made themselves Masters of Lyons, he went thither, and assumed all the Authority to himself [A], without much inquiring,

[A] *He assumed, at Lyons, all the Authority*] Notwithstanding the Pains Varillas took to trace all the Steps of Des-Adrets, he was mistaken as to the Government of Lyons. He always built on This Foundation, that, as soon as That City declared for the Reformed, the Prince of Condé sent Mr de Soubise to

ring, whether it would be acceptable. With Five hundred Men, he defeated the Three thousand, which *St Vital* brought with him into the Neighbourhood of That City, to ravage the Country; he ransacked *le Forez*, secured *Grenoble*, where he compelled the whole Parliament to go and hear a Protestant Sermon; he plundered and burnt the great Charter-House; seized on *Pont St Esprit*; entered, like Thunder, into the Country of *Avignon*; and had, doubtless, taken the chief City of it, to treat it as the Pope's Troops had treated the City of *Orange*, had he not been informed, within a League of *Avignon*, that the Catholics had made themselves Masters of *Grenoble*. He marched That way immediately, and spread such a Terror among the Catholic Troops, that *Maugiron*, who commanded them, fled into *Savoy*, and durst not return into *Dauphiné*. *Grenoble* was soon reduced under our Baron's Power, who treated That City more kindly, than they had reason to expect. He was much more barbarous in other Places [*B*], which he seized by main Force, and where he exercised great Cruelties by way of Reprisals [*C*]. The Victory, which he obtained, against the Count *de Suz*, at *Vaureas*, made him Master of *Orange*, and of the County of *Venaissin*, and made *Avignon* tremble a second time. He defeated all the Pope's Troops; he entered into *Provence*; and overthrew all that appeared against him. Nevertheless, there were some Disappointments, or private Jealousies, which made him fail of relieving *Cisteron*. This Disgrace was followed by some others: The Duke of *Nemours*, after the ill Success of the Siege of *Lyons*, won two Battles against the Baron *Des-Adrets*; but durst not engage with him a third time; and

(1) Varillas's History of *Charles IX*, Tom. I, pag. 183.

(2) Id. pag. 213.

(3) See d'Aubigné, Tom. I, pag. 203, and Beza, Eccles. Hist. lib. xi, pag. 222, &c.

(4) Varillas, pag. 200.

(5) Maimb. Hist. of Calvin. p. 273.

(6) Supplement to Moreri's Dictionary.

(7) Beza Ibid. pag. 221, and Ibid 12, pag. 255, & seq.

(8) Allard's Life of *Des-Adrets*, pag. 43, and 39, cited by Maimb. Hist. of Calvinism.

(9) A *brave Man, whose Name was* Monceclas.

(10) Sc. Varillas, Charl. IX, Tom. I, pag. 212.

(11) All id, ubi sup.

(12) At *Mornac*, in the Court of of *Venaissin*.

(13) Castelnau, Memoirs, lib. iv. cap. 2.

to be Governour there (1): for, when he speaks of the first Discontent of *Des-Adrets*, he says, *it proceeded from the News, that* Soubise *was entered into* Lyons (2). This supposes, that, after having commanded there for some time, he left That Post, and that *Des-Adrets* succeeded him, but that *Soubise* was sent thither again to the Exclusion of his Successor. This Historian is mistaken; The first, who commanded in the City of *Lyons*, after it had declared for the Cause, was the Baron *Des-Adrets* (3): *Soubise* was not sent thither, but when he was thought to be a fitter Man for That Post, than the Baron; and he continued in it 'till the Peace. *Varillas* would have known this Gradation, had he considered well his own Words: "*Des-Adrets, says he, ---- approaching* Lyons, under Pretence of bringing a speedy Succour to the Calvinists of That great City, who had luckily seized upon it, flattered them so, that he persuaded them to join him, and to write to the Prince of *Condé*, that they should be very well pleased to have him for their Governour (4)." I add, that *Maimbourg* (5), and his Copier (6), are mistaken, when they say, that *Des-Adrets* seized on *Vienne*, and *Grenoble*, before he seized on *Lyons*. It is certain, that the first thing he did, after having made himself Master of *Valence*, was to hasten to *Lyons*, which he knew the Protestants had seized, three Days after the Sedition of *Valence* (7). Mr *Allard* did not know This Fact: he places the Expedition to *Lyons* after the Conquest of *Vienne*, which, as he says, happened after the Reduction of *Grenoble* (8).

[*B*] *He was very barbarous in several Places.*] For example; he treated the Garrison of *Montbrisson*, which had surrendered at Discretion, very cruelly. They represented to him, in vain, the Laws of Humanity; he would divert himself with seeing Those miserable Soldiers precipitated: they were brought to the Top of the Platform, above the Tower. Those, who had not the Courage to precipitate themselves, were cast down headlong; and not so much as their Chief (9) was pardoned. Only one Soldier was saved. Twice he took a run from one end of the Platform to the other, as if he designed to leap farther, but stopt short on the brink of the Precipice. *Des-Adrets* said to him, with a sharp Tone, It was enough to have twice founded the Ford; the Soldier replied, boldly, *That he would give him four times to do it*. These Words softened the Baron's ill Humour in such a Manner, that he gave the brisk Fellow quarter, who durst make use of his Jests in such a pressing Extremity (10). Some say (11), that the Biron's Soldiers, as barbarous as their General, received Those, who were thrown down from the Tower, with horrid Cries, and Shouts, on the Points of their Halberts, and Pikes. *Castelnau Mauvissiere* relates, in this Manner, the Cruelty, which he pretends *Des-Adrets* used in another Place (12). "About "Two hundred Catholics, *says he* (13), who had "compounded to surrender the Town, retired into "the Castle, thinking, that the Capitulation would

"be kept. Nevertheless, the Baron *Des-Adrets* caused "them to be thrown down headlong from the Top "of the Castle, notwithstanding the public Faith, "which was sworn, saying, That it was to revenge "the Cruelty, committed at *Orange*. Some of Them, "who were thrown down out of the Windows, "from a very great Heighth, laying hold of the "Bars, the said Baron *Des-Adrets*, very unhumanly, "caused their Fingers to be cut off. One of Those, "who were precipitated, falling down from the Top "of the Castle, upon a great Rock, "chanced to take hold of a Branch of a Tree, which "he would not let go: they shot, and threw many "Stones, at him, but could not hit him. The Baron, "wondering at it, saved his Life; and he escaped, "as it were by a Miracle. When I was in *Dauphiné*, I went to see the Place with the Queen-"Mother: He, who was saved, was still living near "That Place." D'*Aubigné* ascribes the taking of *Mornac* to *Mouthrun*, Lieutenant of *Des-Adrets*, and observes, that *Montbrun* endeavoured, in vain, to moderate the Slaughter; that one of Those, who were thrown down, "continued hanging on some "Branches, and that some Soldiers having shot at "him, without wounding him, *Montbrun* saved him, "and made him serviceable to him (14)." He says also, that Those of *Orange* "placed several dead "Bodies on Floats, and let them go down the River "*Rhone* to *Avignon*, with these Words written on "their Breasts, *Toll-Gatherers of* Avignon, *stop not* "*these Tormentors; for they have paid Tribute at* "*Mornac*." All these Facts are taken from *Beza*'s Ecclesiastical History (15), which shews plainly, that *Des-Adrets* was not the Author of what was done in *Mornac*. So that the Supplement to *Moreri* must be corrected by This, as well as the Memoirs of *Castelnau*, and *Maimbourg*'s History of *Calvinism*.

[*C*] *He was cruel, by way of Reprisal.*] Here we must take notice of a great Falsity of *Maimbourg*. After having mentioned the Cruelties of *Des-Adrets*, he adds these Words; "There were indeed some "Catholics, who, being justly incensed at so many "horrid Crimes, abused the Right of Reprisals, and "treated them almost in the same Manner, of their "own Authority; but there were but few, who perished so (16)." He supposes, then, that *Des-Adrets* began to excercise These Barbarities, and that the Catholics only followed his Example, and made use of them by way of Reprisals. But this is either gross Ignorance, or prodigious Insincerity; for Historians, least suspected of Partiality towards those of the Protestant Religion, confess ingenuously, that the Cruelties, which were exercised at *Orange*, preceeded Those of *Des-Adrets*. Do but read *Varillas*'s History of *Charles IX* (17), and you will find there, that, before the Leaps of *Mornac* and *Montbrisson*, the Catholics had exercised the most enormous Cruelties at *Orange*, and particularly That of precipitating People from the Tops of Rocks, or on Pikes and Halberts. See the Article SERBELLON (FABRICIUS), where I mention These strange Barbarities

(14) D'Aubigné, Hist. Univ Vol. I. pag. 207.

(15) Pag. 12, p. 272.

CONTRADICTION of Maimbourg.

(16) Maimb. Histoire of Calvinism, lib. iv. pag. 275. Ed. in Holl.

(17) Tom. I, p. 203, 204.

and found it more proper to use Artifices, to induce This formidable Leader of the Protestants to change sides [D]. They endeavoured to prevail upon him by Promises, and Threats [E]; they shewed him, that he had great Enemies in his Party [F]: At last, they staggered him in such a manner, that his Conduct became more and more suspected by the Prince of Condé, and the Admiral. The Conclusion was, that they secured his Person [G], at Romans, the Tenth of January, 1563 (f). He did not come out of Prison, but by the Treaty of Peace, which was concluded the

(f) Varillas, History of Charles IX.

Barbarities. *Castelnau*, whom I have already quoted, makes use of this memorable Reflexion; "Indeed it "seemed, that, by a Judgment of GOD, the Cruel- "ties were reciprocal on both sides; and *Orange* "was thought to be the Foundation of Those, which "were committed by the *Huguenots*, in cold Blood, "in *Dauphiné*." Let us not forget the Baron's Answer to his Officers, when they represented to him the Injustice he was going to commit, and the Evils, which it might draw on their Party. "He replied, with a Face, whose natural Defor- "mity was much increased by Fury, that the Pu- "nishment, which he was going to inflict, was ne- "cessary to stop the Cruelty of the Catholicks, and "that, in order to reduce them to the Laws of a "fair War, which they had first violated at the taking "of Orange, it was necessary they should know, "that the Calvinists could wage a cruel War, as well "as themselves (18)." *Varillas*, who *ridicules These two Excuses*, could not confute him as to these Words, which they had first violated at the taking of Orange, since he had already observed, of himself, "that the "Baron heard of the Cruelties, committed at *Orange*, "with those inward Transports of Joy, which a "bloody Man is capable of, when an unexpected "Accident gives him an Opportunity of committing "all manner of Excesses, without being reproached for "having been the Aggressor (19)." I refer my Reader to the Answers, which *Des-Adrets* made to *d'Aubigné*, who asked him, one day, three things: "Why he "had committed some Cruelties so ill becoming his "great Valour? Why he had forsaken a Party, to "which he was so much indebted? and, then, why "he had no Success in any thing, since he had for- "saken That Party, though he had acted against "it (20)?" He answered, to the first Point, "That "no body commits a Cruelty in returning one; "that the first are called Cruelties, and the second "Justice. Having, thereupon, made an horrible Dis- "course, of above Four thousand Murthers, commit- "ted in cold Blood, and of the Invention of unheard "of Torments, and chiefly of the Leaps of *Mascon*, "where the Governour taught the very Children to "see the *Huguenots* die without Pity, he said, that "he had served them something like it, having Re- "gard to the Time past, and to the Time to come: "with Respect to the Time past, not being able to "endure, without great Cowardice, the tearing in "pieces his faithful Companions; and, as for the Time "to come, there were two Reasons, which no Cap- "tain can disapprove; the one, that the only Means "to put a stop to the Cruelties of an Enemy, is to "return them the like (21); whereupon he men- "tioned Three hundred Horsemen, sent back, some "time ago, to the Enemies Army, on Waggons, "having each of them a Hand, and a Foot, cut off, "to change a merciless War into a courteous one." All his other Answers are full of Sense; to which I refer my Readers as I have said already, contenting myself to observe, here, I. That These Leaps of Mascon are to be found in the Article of That City. II. That our Baron justified himself more faintly to the Duke de Nemours, than to *d'Aubigné*. See the following Remark.

[D] *The Duke de Nemours used Artifice.*] If we may believe *Varillas*, the Duke *de Nemours* prevented *Des-Adrets*, by writing a Letter to him, *desiring him to treat two Italian Soldiers, who were fallen into his Hands, as Prisoners of War* (22). But *Beza* says, the Baron wrote first to the Duke, to desire him to set at Liberty two *Italian* Soldiers (23). There is no question but that *Varillas* is mistaken; for *Des-Adrets's* Letter, set down at length in *Beza's* History, begins with the Request of the Liberty of Those two *Italian* Soldiers. *Varillas* has committed another Fault, for he does not faithfully report the Substance of That Letter: he pretends, that the Baron *imputed the Necessities of Vaureas, Boulenne, and Pier- relate, to the Necessity of obliging the Catholics to a*

fair War with the *Calvinists*, whom they hanged as fast as they took them; and that he added, that, after having obtained this Point, so necessary to his Party, that he could hardly find any Soldiers before, he observed exactly the Military Laws, which had learned in Piedmont. There is nothing like This in *Des-Adrets's* Letter; he only confesses, that, at *Pierre-late* and *Boulenne*, two Towns, which he had taken by Assault, he could not, to his great Grief, with-hold the Soldiers from taking their Revenge on Four or Five hundred Men, whom they found there. His Apology does not consist in alledging just and necessary Motives of his Cruelties, nor in saying, that, having attained the end, for which he had committed them, he desisted from them; he only denies them; and he does it, as *Beza* observes, *in a very faint and soft Stile*. *Varillas* says truly, that the Duke *de Nemours*, apprehending by That Letter, that *Des-Adrets* was discontented, caused a Conference to be proposed to him, which was accepted.

[E] *They endeavoured to prevail with him by Promises.*] They wrote very civilly to him (24), and, after having represented to him, that the way, he took, would infallibly lead him to a Confiscation of Body and Estate, they tempted him with a Promise of the Collar of the Order, and with That of a Company of fifty Men at Arms, with the Sum of an Hundred thousand *Livres*; and, if he chose to live out of the Kingdom, they engaged themselves to send him the Sum of an Hundred thousand Crowns. The Duke *de Nemours* used all manner of Promises and Flatteries, when he conferred with *Des-Adrets*.

[F] *They represented to him, that he had great Enemies in his Party.*] The Marshal *de Brissac* communicated a Letter of the Admiral to him, which he had received in the following Manner. *Soubise*, who suspected *Des-Adrets*, had acquainted the Admiral with it; the Soldier, who carried the Letter, was intrusted with an Answer to it; but, instead of carrying it to *Soubise*, he brought it to the Marshal *de Brissac* (25) Here are the Contents of it, as far as they relate to This Baron; "As to what you write "to me, concerning the Baron *Des-Adrets*, every "Body knows him to be what he is; but, since he "has, hitherto, served so well in This Cause, "we must bear his Insolence a little; for it is to "be feared, that his Insolence may be changed into "Fury. Wherefore my Opinion is, that you use "your Endeavours to bring him to a Conference, "and bear with him as much as you can."

[G] *They secured his Person.*] Here is a Passage of *Castelnau's* Memoirs. "The Duke *de Nemours*, know- "ing *Des-Adrets* to be a good Captain, and a Per- "son of great Credit and Reputation, thought it "more expedient for the King's Service to gain "him over, than to oppose him by Force; which "he did so dexterously, with fair Promises, and "smooth Words, (as being a very persuasive Prince, "and who always knew how to prevail upon Men "by his winning Address) that the *Huguenots* never "had, since, a greater Enemy in That Country, than "This Baron, who began, from that time, to con- "trive Mischief against them. The *Huguenots*, be- "ing very vigilant, had notice of it; for they had "Spies every where. Which was the Reason, why "the Baron *Des-Adrets*, being gone to *Valence*, "was taken Prisoner by *Mouvans*, (by Advice of "Cardinal *de Chatillon*, and of the Sieur *de Cursol*, "since made Duke of *Usez*,) who sent him to *Ni- "mes*, where he was in very great Danger, and "would hardly have escaped with Life, had it not "been for the Peace; by Virtue of which he was "set at Liberty (26)." See the twelfth Book of *Beza's Ecclesiastical History*, where the Detention of *Des-Adrets* is mentioned at large. "After divers In- "terrogations and Answers —— Peace intervening, "he was released, and sent to his House, without any "Absolution or Condemnation." These are *Beza's* Words (27).

[H] He

the same Year; and then he professed his first Religion; and, afterwards, bore Arms against the other; but without any Success or Glory [H]; for which he is not the only Person, who has given very bad Reasons (g). This General shewed no longer the same Vigilancy, Activity, Intrepidity, and Presence of Mind, which had been admired as Prodigies, whilst he served the *Cause*. All Those great Qualities, and the Victories, which he obtained over the Papists, did not hinder the Protestants from looking upon him as a *Goliab*, who *dishonoured the Battles of* Israel, by his barbarous Conduct [I]. He *died without Honour, in an ignominious Old-Age, equally despised by both Parties* (b); much unlike That Baron *Des-Adrets, Quantum mutatus ab illo!* who had been dreaded as far as *Rome* (i); for they were apprehensive there, that

(g) *See Remark* [H].

(b) Maimb. Hist. of Calvinism, pag. 275. *See Rem.* [K].

(i) Brantome's Elogy of Monluc.

[H] *He served in the Catholic Party, without any Success, or Glory.*] See, here, what is to be found in the same Historian. "Being fallen so low, He (28) went yet farther, since; having born Arms against Those of the Reformed Religion, as well in *Dauphiné*, as in other Parts of *France*, being Colonel of a Regiment of Foot, in which he got nothing but Shame, with such a loss of his Reputation, that he was never since employed, but remained in his House, a Spectator of other Men's Miseries (29)." *D'Aubigné* says, that he was defeated, when the Army of the Duke of *Deux Ponts* entered *France*, in the Year 1569 (30). He says, elsewhere (31), that, at *Lyons*, at the return of the King of *Poland*, an Usher refused Admittance to *Des-Adrets*; and it was on this Occasion, that He asked him the three Questions, mentioned before (32). He desired to know of the Baron, why he had so little Success in the Catholic Armies. "Child, *answered be, with a Sigh* (33), nothing is too hot for a Captain, who has no more Interest in the Victory, than his Soldiers: With the *Huguenots*, I had Soldiers; and, since, I have had none but Merchants, who think on nothing but Money: The others feared nothing, and were full of Revenge, Passion, and Honour; I could not keep in the Reins of the first; but the latter have worn out my Spurs." To speak the Truth, These Reasons are very weak; and, to confute them invincibly, it would be sufficient to refer the Readers to the great Number of general, and particular, Battles, in which the Protestants Troops were beaten. What! were not the Papist Soldiers *full of Revenge and Passion?* Did they not hear continually their Priests, who exhorted them to take Vengeance of the *Huguenots*, for their plundering and prophaning of Churches? is there any thing, which inspires more Fury, than such Discourses? What shall we say of the Decrees (34), "which permitted all manner of Persons, and even ordered all Communities to fall upon the *Huguenots*, at the ringing of the Alarm-Bell, to pursue them strenuously every where, and to kill them without Mercy, as so many wild Beasts, mad Dogs, and Wolves, that destroyed all the Kingdom: So that, through the Crimes of one Party, and the Revenge of the other, there was nothing to be seen, in all the Provinces of *France*, but Burnings, Blood, and Slaughter, and a Thousand frightful Images of Death?" Could the Catholic Soldiers be free from Passion and Revenge amidst such dismal Objects? Was it more necessary to use Spurs for them, than Reins for the *Huguenots? Monluc* and *Tavanes*, and several other Commanders of the same Party, make it appear, that it was the Baron *Des-Adrets*'s own Fault. At the Bottom, he did the Protestants more wrong, than he thought: and the Bishop of *Meaux* knew how to take advantage of the Disposition, he ascribed to them, of having been full of Passion, and Revenge (35). But here is another Reason more fit, than That which he gave to *d'Aubigné*. "Never any Man acquired so great a Reputation in so short a Time; and never any great Commander lost it sooner: For the Duke *de Nemours*, who was sent against him, and who could not defeat him by open Force, had no sooner brought him over to his Party, but they represented him as the weakest, and most unfortunate, Officer, of the Royal, and Catholic Party. Not but that he had always the same Valour, and Experience; but there is a great Difference between fighting for, and against, one's King. For every thing is permitted in a Revolt; and a Commander shews himself such as he is; whereas, in the Service of his Prince, he must appear such as he ought to be; and he is more subject to Military Discipline. In effect, the Baron

Des-Adrets was as furious, as valiant; he signalized himself more by the Terror of his Arms, than by the Reputation of his Conduct; and he made more Noise, than other Men of his Quality, because he was more cruel, and dreadful. In the King's Army, they would not have suffered his Fury; and the Law of Reprisals was so punctually observed, that both Parties were obliged to keep Faith, and to wage a fair War (36)." Though it be my Interest to find Faults in Authors, since They are so many Materials for my Work, I am truly concerned, that so judicious a Person, as Mr *le Laboureur*, should have published such bad Reasoning. Ask him, Why *Des-Adrets* was a great Commander during his Protestantism, and a very pitiful Officer in his Catholicism? He will answer you; it is *because, in a Revolt, a Man does all that he can do; but, in a lawful War, all that he ought to do.* There was never a more false Maxim, or more injudiciously applied, than This; since it is certain, that, in a Civil-War, the King's Party acts with more Boldness, and Confidence, than the Other: For the rebellious Party, finding itself sufficiently odious, will not begin the Breach of Military Discipline, the Violation of Capitulations, Slaughters in cold Blood, against the public Faith, &c. It is the Prince's Party, which gives itself more Liberty, in that respect, pretending to have only to do with People convicted of Felony, and actually under Sentence of Death: It seldom makes a fair War, but when the other Party resolves to use Reprisals. At least, Matters stood so in the Religious Wars, under *Charles* IX, and, consequently, This Maxim was very ill applied. Besides, I wonder, that Mr *le Laboureur* did not take notice of the Passage of *Brantome*, which he quoted a little after. That Passage is a Parallel between our Baron, and *Monluc*, wherein, though *Brantome* makes the latter a little less cruel, than the other, he says, nevertheless, that they might be compared in all things; *both very brave, and valiant, both very capricious, both very cruel; both Companions in* Piedmont*; and both very good Captains.* According to Mr *le Laboureur*'s Maxim, *Des-Adrets* would never have acquired the Reputation of a great Captain, if he had always served his Prince: Why, then, did *Monluc* acquire That Reputation, or why did he preserve, and perfectly maintain, it, even when, according to Mr *le Laboureur*, a fair War, and the Law of Reprisals, were punctually observed? Why then did *Des-Adrets* lose all his Reputation, since That of *Monluc* was not lessened?

[I] *The Protestants disapproved of ——— his barbarous Conduct.*] Besides what has been already said on this Subject (37), I shall observe, here, that it was said, *that he taught his Children to be cruel, and to bathe themselves in Blood* (38). *The eldest, who was afterwards a Catholic, was very busy in the Massacre of Paris.* He died at the Siege of *Rochel*, with Contrition for the great quantity of Blood, that he had shed. The Protestants are little concerned, whether This Hear-say of *Brantome* be true, or not; for They were the first, who condemned This Baron's cruel Disposition (39). But every Body is concerned not to suffer the Licence of Him, who published the Supplement to *Moreri*'s Dictionary: He says, *That, after a great Slaughter,* Des Adrets *made his two Sons bathe themselves in the Blood of the Catholics.* Father Maimbourg supplied him with This Gloss (40). Both of them should be told, that they ought not to take so great a Latitude in their Paraphrases. Their Witness, grounded on a Hear-say, made use only of the Word *Blood.* What right had they to pretend, that he spoke of *Human Blood?* Do not Butchers contract an Habit of Cruelty, by the effusion of the Blood of Beasts?
A Writer,

(28) *That is, The Baron Des-Adrets.*

(29) Beza, Hist. Eccles. l b xli. pag. 307.

(30) D'Aubigné, Tom. I. pag. 403.

(31) Ibid. pag. 215.

(32) *In Remark* [C].

(33) D'Aubigné, Tom. I. pag. 217.

A PASSAGE *of D'Aubigné criticised.*

(33) Maimbourg, Hist. of Calvinism pag. 276.

(35) *See Mr* de Meaux's Hist. of the Variations, lib. x. n 39.

A CRITICISM *on a Passage of Mr Le Laboureur.*

(36) Le Laboureur, Addit. to Castein. Tom. II. pag. 23.

(37) *In Remark* [B].

(38) Brantome's Apology of Monluc.

(39) *See* Beza's Hist. Eccel. lib. xi. pag. 221.

THE Supplement to *Moreri*'s Dictionary criticised.

(40) Hist. of Calvinism, pag. 274.

BEAUMONT.

that he would fit out a Fleet, to pay the Pope a Visit. We shall speak of his Children in one of our Remarks [K].

Here is a Supplement, which I borrow from a Work, which I have read since the first Volume of This Dictionary was printed off. The Baron Des-Adrets, being but fifteen Years of Age, was One of the Two hundred Gentlemen of *Dauphiné*, who were in the Army, which *Odet du Foix*, Lord of *Lautrec*, commanded in *Italy*, in the Year 1527 (k). He signalized himself every where. In 1532, he obtained the Standard of the Company of *the Lord Depuy S. Martin*, Lieutenant in the Government of *Provence* (l). He had some Dispute with *George d'Urre de Venterol*, to whom That Company was given *in the Year* 1537, *and who* hindered him from obtaining the Lieutenancy (m). This displeased him *so much, that he protested he would serve no more, and retired to his Father in* Dauphiné. Some time after, he went to *Turin*, to his Uncle *Boutieres* (n), General of the Army of *Piedmont*, *who left him the Conduct of some Legionaries of That Province, which made part of the Garrison of the Town.* He continued *in this Employ till the Disgrace of Boutieres, which happened in* 1544, *and which obliged the Uncle and Nephew to retire into* Dauphiné (o). A long Sickness hindered our Baron, above three Years, from bearing Arms. He had a Troop of Horse under the Marshal *de Brissac*, Lieutenant-General for the King in *Italy* (p), and was afterwards made *Colonel-General of the Legionaries of* Dauphiné (q). He received three Wounds, at the Siege of *Vulpian*, in the Year 1555. The Charge of Colonel of the Legionaries of *Provence, Lyonnois,* and *Auvergne,* was given him; and he led them, with those of *Dauphiné*, to the Duke of *Guise*, at *Turin*, in the Year 1557 (r). He lost his Baggage, and his Liberty, at the taking of *Moncalve*, in the Year 1558 (s), and accused *Pequigni*, who was Governour there, of the Loss of that Town. He cited him before the King, and lost his Cause [L]. His Resentment, for

(k) Allard's Life of the Baron Des-Adrets, pag. 3, 4.
(l) Ibid. pag. 7.
(m) Ibid. pag. 9.
(n) Brother to Des-Adrets's Mother.
(o) Allard, Ibid. p. 10.
(p) Ibid. pag. 12.
(q) Ibid. pag. 14.
(r) Ibid. pag. 16.
(s) Ibid. pag. 19.

A Writer, who quotes an Author, should keep religiously to his Expressions, and not commit the Sophism. *à dicto simpliciter ad dictum secundum quid.* Let him conjecture, if he pleases; but he ought not to give his Conjectures as matter of Fact.

[K] *We shall speak of his Children in one of our Remarks.*] *Brantome,* whom we have quoted concerning the eldest, says, That there was a younger, who was the King's Page; but *Beza* will tell us more Circumstances about him. "The greatest Evil, says "he, speaking *of This Baron* (41), was, that, grow- "ing worse and worse after this, he forsook the Re- "formed Religion, and carried his Children to Mass; "the eldest of which, having been bred up in *Ger-* "many, during the Troubles at the Court of the "Elector *Palatine,* became, soon after, one of the "most vitious young Men in *France;* but GOD "did not let him live long. The other two were "Twins, and were born at *Geneva* during the Trou- "bles, to one of which *John Calvin* was God-Fa- "ther." Mr *Allard* relates, that He, who had been the King's Page, and of whom he mentions a very bold Action, "was involved in the Massacre on "St *Bartholomew's* Day (42). *Davila* says, in his "fifth Book of the Civil-Wars of *France,* that the "two Sons were called, the one Colonel *Montaumor,* "and the other Colonel *Rowray,* and that one of "them was killed in the Massacre on St *Bartholomew's* "Day. The other died of Sickness (43)." Let us relate the bold Action of the Page. "The King "ordered him one Day to call his Chancellor; This "Page found him at Dinner; and, having told him, "that the King would speak with him, and the "Chancellor having answered, that, after he had "dined, he would go and receive the King's Orders: "*How!* said the Page, *will you defer one Moment,* "*when the King commands you?* And, thereupon, he "took one end of the Table-cloth, and threw all "that was upon it to the Ground. This Story was "told the King by the Chancellor himself, and his "Majesty, laughing, said only, that the Son would "be as violent and passionate as the Father (44)." Observe, that this Writer has not well apprehended these Words of *Davila*. "Nel Medezimo Palazzo (45), "furono amazzati Teligni genero dell' Amiraglio, "Guerchi suo luogotenente —— i Colonelli Mon- "taumar, e Rourai, il figliuolo del Barone de S. Adrets, "e tutti quelli della sua corte (46). —— *In the Pa-* "*late Medezimo, were killed* Teligni, *the Admiral's* "*Son-in-law;* Guerchi, *his Lieutenant* —— *the Co-* "*lonels* Montaumar *and* Rourai, *the young Son of the* "*Baron de* S. Adrets; *and all these in his own Court.*" He does not pretend to speak of two Colonels, that were the Sons of our Baron, nor is it well known, whether, by his Baron *de S. Adrets,* he meant ours. If he did, I fancy he was mistaken. Let no one object

(41) Beza's Hist. Eccles. lib. xii. pag. 307.

(42) Allard, Life of Des-Adrets, pag. 82.

(43) Id. Ib. pag. 9., 91.

(44) Ibid. pag. 82.

(45) *That is,* The Admiral's House.

(46) Davila, lib. v p 272. Edit. of Venice, 1630.

these Words of *d'Aubigné;* "The Marquis *de Rosnel,* "Brother of Prince *Porcian,* was killed by *Buffi d'* "*Amboise,* and the Son of the Baron *Des-Adrets,* "about a Law-suit, which he had with his Cousin- "German (47);" for the meaning of them is, that *Buffi d'Amboise,* and the Son of That Baron, killed *Rosnel.*

Mr *le Laboureur* said, in 1658, that the Family of *Beaumont* was extinct (48). I have been informed, by Mr *d'Hosier,* by means of a Friend, that *Susanna de Beaumont,* Daughter and Heiress of our Baron *Des-Adrets,* was married to *Cæsar de Vaucerre,* Lord of *Teis,* and *St Desier,* in *Dauphiné.* Their Posterity continues to this Day. Mademoiselle *Des-Adrets,* who died Maid of Honour to the Duchess of *Orleans,* after the Year 1680, and who had been a Protestant, was descended from This *Susanna.* Her Brothers were the Marquis *Des-Adrets,* who is Captain of a Ship, and the Chevalier *Des-Adrets,* who was *Aide de Camp* of the Marshal Duke of *Noailles,* when he was killed at the Siege of *Roses,* in *June,* 1693. He had been Captain of a Ship; but was cashired, because he would not assist at the Lectures, which Mr *Renaude,* Engineer of *Marine,* read at *Brest,* by the King's Order.

I shall insert here the Addition, which I published at the end of the first Volume of this Dictionary. It contains these Words: *I have just now received* (49) *the Life of our Baron Des-Adrets,* composed by Mr *Allard, wherein Mr le Laboureur's Mistake is thus laid open.* "The Family of *Beaumont* is not extinct, "as Mr *le Laboureur* believed, speaking of the Baron "*Des-Adrets,* in his Additions to the Memoirs of "*Castelnau.* It continues still in the Branches of *Pom-* "*pignon* in *Languedoc,* of *Bresset,* in *Auvergne,* of "*Autichamp,* and of *St Quintin,* in *Dauphiné.* It "is true, that That of Baron *Des-Adrets* ended in "two Daughters, the eldest of which, whose Name "was *Susanna,* was twice married; the first Mar- "riage was with the Lord of *Tarvanas,* in *Piedmont;* "and the second with *Cæsar de la Vausserre,* to whom "she brought the Seat of *Des-Adrets.* The other's "Name was *Esther,* Wife of *Antony de Saffenage,* "Lord of *Iseron* (50)."

[L] *He cited* Pequigni *before the King, and lost his Cause.*] I shall set down Mr *Allard's* Narrative. "The Baron, having accused *Pequigni* of the Loss "of the Town, and of his Liberty, and Baggage, "pretended, that he ought to endemnify him for "the Damage he had sustained: For this end, he "summoned him before King *Francis* II, who had "succeeded *Henry* II, where he maintained his Cause "admirably well, and said, that *Pequigni* suffered "the Enemy to enter without Opposition; that he "might easily have defended the Breach, since it "was but small, and the number of those, who re- "solved

(47) D'Aubigné, Tom. I. lib. I. c. 4. pag. 456.

(48) Le Laboureur, Addit. to Castelneau, Tom. I. pag. 24.

(49) *In the Month of* Sept. 1696, *by the Care of the oblieging* Mr Pinsson des Rioloes.

(50) Allard's Life of Des-Adrets, pag. 1, & 2.

BEAUMONT. 713

for it, againſt the Houſe of *Guiſe* was managed by *Catherine de Medicis* (t), and had the Conſequences, which we have already ſeen. The Author, whom I quote, gives a very particular Account of it, as alſo of This Baron's Actions, which he performed after his Return to the King's Party. He makes them more conſiderable, than other Hiſtorians do; but he owns, that this brave Captain was ſuſpected of Intelligence with the Huguenot Party, that he was impriſoned, that he juſtified himſelf [M], and received Orders to raiſe a thouſand Foot, which he conducted to *Turin* (u). He was there during the Maſſacre on St *Bartholomew's* Day. He ſoon returned into *Dauphiné*, and, *ſeeing the ſmall Account they made of him, he retired to* la Frette (x), *in the* Graiſivodan (y). He refuſed to ſign the Formularies of the League, in the Year 1577 (z). He went to compliment the Duke of *Maienne*, at *Grenoble*, in the Year 1581 (aa), and performed, there, an Act of his ancient Valour [N]. He accompanied *la Valette*, who was ſent into *Dauphiné* againſt *Leſdiguieres*, in the Year 1585 (bb). *At laſt, being tired with ſo many Fatigues, oppreſſed with Age, and extreamly diſguſted with the World, he retired again to* la Frette, *where he lived a Year with viſible Marks of his Return into the Boſom of the Church. He died, therefore, a true Catholic, after having made his Will, the Second of* Febr. 1586, *and was buried in a Chapel of the Parochial Church, which belonged to his Houſe* (cc). The Reader will not be diſpleaſed to ſee the Titles, which he gave himſelf, whilſt he was at the Head of the Proteſtants of his Province [O], nor to know, that his Countenance diſcovered the Fierceneſs of his Temper [P].

(t) *Mr Allard, ibid. produces this Queen's Letter.*
(u) Ibid. pag. 81.
(x) Ibid. pag. 83.
(y) *It was one of his Houſes.*
(z) Ibid. pag. 84.
(aa) Ibid. pag. 87.
(bb) Ibid. pag. 89.
(cc) Ibid. pag. 90.

(cr) Ibid. pag. 19, 20.

" ſolved to paſs through it, very inconſiderable;
" that, if he denied it, he would make him con-
" feſs it in a Duel. This Diſpute appeared ſingu-
" lar to the Court; and theſe two Enemies had
" ſome Friends among the Great Ones, who hin-
" dered the Deciſion of it for ſome time. It went,
" nevertheleſs, in favour of *Pequigni*, by the Credit
" of the Houſe of *Guiſe*, which began to be very
" great in *France*; and they were forbid to attempt
" any thing againſt each other, on the Penalty of
" being puniſhed as guilty of High-Treaſon: Where-
" upon, the Baron was ſo enraged, that he ſwore
" he would be revenged on the *Guiſes*; and This
" was the Reaſon, why he embraced, afterwards,
" the Proteſtant Party: This is what *Thuanus* ſays;
" and it is agreeable to Truth (51)."

[M] *He was ſuſpected of Intelligence with the Huguenot Party, was impriſoned, and juſtified himſelf.*] At his Return into *Dauphiné*, after the Battle of *Moncontour*, " he was obliged to retire to his

(5*) Ibid. pag. 75.

" Houſe, becauſe *Gordes*, Governor of the Province,
" had conceived a great Hatred againſt him (52).
" It is thought, that he ſuſpected him of being ſtill
" inclined to the Huguenot Party, and even of ha-
" ving favoured the Armament, which was made,
" near *Geneva*, by Count *Lodowick* of *Naſſau*, and
" of holding Intelligence with him. —— Whatever
" there was in it, it is certain, that *Gordes* made
" but little account of him; at which the Baron
" murmured highly, and made ſome Complaints,
" which were ſomewhat bold, and even raſh; which
" coming to the King's Ear, *Gordes* received Orders
" to cauſe him to be arreſted; which he did. He
" was carried to *Grenoble*, and from thence to *Lyons*,
" and impriſoned in *Pierreciſe*. At firſt, he was

(53) Ibid. pag. 76.

" thought a loſt Man, and ſo much the more,
" becauſe Letters were intercepted from Princes,
" and the Admiral, in his Favour, and becauſe
" the chief Heads of the Proteſtants interceded for
" his Liberty (53)." He obtained it by the Peace, which was concluded in the Month of *January*, 1571 (54). He appeared before the King *in his*

(54) Ibid. pag. 77.

" Council. " There he declared, that, being innocent,
" he ſupplicated his Majeſty to ſuffer him to re-
" nounce the Benefit of the Edicts of Pacification,
" made in favour of thoſe, who had acted againſt
" his Intereſts, under Pretence of Religion or Policy;
" that he had never done any thing, for which he
" might be blamed; but that, if any Perſon was ſo bold
" as to maintain, that he was criminal in any reſ-
" pect, he was ready to make him deny it, Sword
" in Hand, if his Majeſty would be pleaſed to per-
" mit it. The King anſwered him, That he was per-
" ſuaded of his Innocence, and good Intention;
" that he had never queſtioned his good Conduct,
" and Zeal for his Service; that he was extreamly
" ſatisfied with him; that he always believed his
" Intentions were good, and other things of that
" Nature, of which he deſired his Majeſty to grant

(55) Mr Allard has publiſhed this Act, p. 79, No. 21.

" him an Act: Which was willingly done. It is in
" the Regiſter of the Chamber of Accompts (55)."

[N] *He performed, at* Grenoble, *in* 1581, *an Act of his ancient Valour.*] The Duke de *Maienne* " be-

" ing at *Grenoble*, in 1581, the young *Pardaillan*,
" Son of *la Mothe Gondrin*, (ſpoke haughtily and in-
" juriouſly of the Baron *Des-Adrets*, becauſe of the
" Loſs of his Father at *Valence*. The Baron was
" informed, in his Retirement, what Terms he made
" uſe of, and alſo, that he ſaid, if he met him, he
" would abuſe him: Which obliged him to come
" to *Grenoble*, where, having waited upon the Duke
" of *Maienne*, and having been kindly received by
" him, he ſaid, ſeveral times, and alſo in the Pre-
" ſence of *Pardaillan*, that he had left his Solitude,
" and was returned into the World, to ſee if any
" One bore him any Grudge, and to give him Sa-
" tisfaction; that his Sword was not ſo ruſty, nor
" his Arm ſo weak, or his Strength ſo much impaired
" by Age, but that he was able to give Satisfaction to
" all thoſe, who had any Complaint againſt him.
" *Pardaillan* neither ſaid, nor did, any thing, that
" might give occaſion for a Quarrel; ſo that *Des-
" Adrets* retired again, being ſatisfied with this laſt
" Bravery (56)."

(56) Ibid. pag. 87, 88.

[O] *The Reader will ſee the Titles, which he gave himſelf, whilſt he was at the Head of the Proteſtants of his Province.*] They are as follows: " *Francis de Beaumont*, Lord *Des-Adrets*, Gentleman in Or-
" dinary of the King's Chamber, Colonel of the
" Legionaries of *Dauphiné*, *Provence*, *Lyonnois*, *Lan-
" guedoc*, and *Auvergne*, Governor, and Lieutenant
" General for the King in *Dauphiné*, and my Lord
" the Prince of *Condé's* Lieutenant in the Chriſtian
" Army, aſſembled for the Service of GOD, the Li-
" berty and Deliverance of the King, and the Queen-
" Mother, the Preſervation of their States and Gran-
" deur, and of Chriſtian Liberty in the ſaid Coun-
" tries (57)." In the Chamber of Accompts of

(57) Ibid. pag. 28.

Grenoble, " there are ſeveral Ordinances drawn up
" in his Name - - - - wherein he takes That Qua-
" lity upon him, and, in others, he calls himſelf,
" *Chief Governor of the Companies aſſembled for the
" Service of* GOD, &c. There are ſome, which are
" thus directed; *To all the True and Faithful Sub-
" jects of the King, our Sovereign and Natural Lord,
" aſſociated in the Confeſſion of the Reformed Churches,
" and Well-wiſhers to the Peace and Tranquillity of
" this Country of* Dauphiné, *Greeting, and Peace
" through our Lord* JESUS CHRIST (58)." Was

(58) Ibid. pag. 29.

he not a very fit Perſon to uſe ſuch Language? Was he not a new Apoſtle, well qualified to imitate St *Paul's* Evangelical Salutation?

[P] *His Countenance diſcovered the Fierceneſs of his Temper.*] *Thuanus*, who obſerved him ſo nicely, at *Grenoble* (59), in the Year 1572, that he was able to

(59) Thuan. de Vita ſua, lib. 1. pag. 1165.

delineate him by Memory, ſo as any one might know him again, gives this Deſcription of him : " Erat
" jam totus canus, ſed cruda adhuc ac viridi ſene-
" nectute, Oculis truculentis, naſo aquilino, facie ma-
" cilenta, ſed ruboribus interfuſis, ut lutum Languine
" maceratum, quod in P. Corn. Sulla obſervatum eſt,
" ori inſperſum diceres, de cætero corporis habitu
" proſus militari (60). - - - - - *He was now quite*

(60) Id. ib.

*grey-headed, but of a vigorous and robuſt old Age;
* *he had fierce, ſparkling, Eyes, a ſharp Noſe, a
* *lean Viſage, but fluſhed; ſo that you would ſay,*

"as was observed in P. Corn. Sulla, that his Face | "for the rest of his bodily Constitution, it was al-
"was sprinkled with a Mixture of Dirt and Blood; | "together military."

BEAUNE (RENAUD de) Archbishop of *Bourges*, and, afterwards, of *Sens*, in the Reign of *Henry* IV. See SAMBLANÇAI (WILLIAM).

BEDA (NOEL), Doctor of Divinity in the University of *Paris*, was the greatest Clamourer, and the most mutinous and factious Man, of his Time. He was a *Picard* (*a*), and lived in the Reign of *Francis* I. He declared himself a sworn Enemy to all those, who designed to make Learning flourish again (*b*); and it was on this score, that *Erasmus*, and *Faber Stapulensis*, incurred his Indignation. He pretended to have found a great many Heresies in the Paraphrases of *Erasmus*, and published a Book on that Subject. *Erasmus* justified himself, and, accusing him in his Turn, convicted him of a great number of Calumnies [*A*]. *Beda*, instead of proving, that he had been no Calumniator, or, instead of confessing, that he had not rightly apprehended his Adversary's Meaning, had recourse to the Art of Caballing: He read *Erasmus*'s Books over again; he made new Extracts out of them, as unfaithful as the former [*B*], and gave them to be censured by the Faculty of Divinity; where his

(*a*) Erasm. Supputat. Errorum Bedæ, fol. 22.

(*b*) Beza's Hist. Eccl. lib. I. p. 2.

[*A*] *Erasmus convicted him of a great Number of Calumnies.*] See the Book entituled, *Supputationes Errorum in censuris Natalis Bedæ per Erasmum Roterodamum.* It was printed in the Year 1527. The Reverse of the Title page will inform you, that *Erasmus* found One hundred eighty one Lies, Three hundred and ten Calumnies, and Forty seven Blasphemies, in a pretty small Book of his Censurer; and This, without dealing rigorously with him; for he was spared in many things, which deserved to be taken notice of. "Ac ne quis quæratur iniquam
" supputationem, non imputavimus illi tam multa
" indocte, stulte, & fine mente dicta. Non impu-
" tavimus tam multas propositiones, quas in censuris
" omisit, &c (1). ----- *And, lest any one should*
(1) Erasmus " *think my Computation unfair, I have not charged*
in the Reverse of the " *him with many things, unlearnedly, foolishly, and*
Title-Page of " *inconsiderately, advanced. I have not imputed to*
Errorum in " *him the many Propositions, omitted by him in his*
Censuris Be- " *Censures, &c.*" A Man of Honour, and Conscience,
dæ. would have made it his chief Business to vindicate himself against such kind of Lies; but *Beda*, and Those like him, find their Account better in repeating their first Accusations an hundred times over, just as if nothing had been answered to Them. If *Erasmus* may be credited, his Adversary's Book displeased *Francis* I so much, that he prohibited the Sale of it. "Importeret & infeliciter edito libro sic debac-
" chatus est in me, ut Rex Christianissimus mox, ubi
" rem cognovit, vetuerit codices divendi, haud du-
(2) Erasm. " bie vetiturus excudi, si tempestive monitus fuisset (2).
Epist. 73. " ----- *He raised so against me, in a weak and un-*
lib. xix. p. " *fortunate Work, that the most Christian King, being*
892, dated " *informed of it, immediately prohibited the Sale of*
Nov. 1527. " *the Book, and, no doubt, would have put a Stop*
See also Ep. " *to the printing of it, had be had timely Informa-*
14. lib. 20. " *tion.*" The Book, which *Beda* published, at the
pag. 974. & same time, against *Faber Stapulensis*, was likewise
Epist. 4. lib. prohibited; nevertheless, the Copies of these two
24. p. 1287. Books were suffered to be dispersed. "Urit homi-
" nem, quod liber, quem in Jacobum Fabrum scrip-
" serat, edicto regio suppressus est, etiamsi non est
(3) Id. Epist. " suppressus (3). ----- *He is nettled at the Royal*
62. lib. 19. " *Edict, which suppresses his Book against* James Fa-
pag. 877, " *ber, though, in Reality, it be not suppressed.*" "Nec
dated Nov. " jussus premere præstit, sed elusit Regis edictum, cu-
30, 1527. " rans ut in Germaniam spargeretur, & istic clam di-
(4) Id. Ep. " straheretur (4). ----- *Though commanded to suppress*
71. lib. 39. " *the Book, he did not obey, but eluded the King's*
pag. 886. " *Edict, contriving to have it dispersed, and private-*
See also E- " *ly sold*, in Germany.
pist. 14. lib. I shall set down, here, a Passage of Mr *Chevillier*'s
20. Book about the Origin of Printing at *Paris*. "*Fran-*
" *cis* I --- was so exasperated against Dr *Noel Beda*,
" who had refuted the Paraphrases and Annotations
" of *Erasmus*, and against the Faculty, who had ap-
(5) That of " proved, and caused his Book to be printed (5),
Beda against " that, the Doctor, being gone to the Court about
Erasmus. It " some Business of his Society, was kept Prisoner
was printed " there for a whole Day, not obtaining his Liberty,
at Paris, by " but on Condition to appear whenever it should
Jodocus Ba- " be required, and a Letter under the Privy-Seal
dius in 1526, " was sent to the Parliament, dated from *Amboise*,
in f[olio]. " the ninth of *April* 1526, whereby they were or-
" dered to put a Stop to the Sale of *Beda*'s Book.

" I have read, in a Copy of the Registers of that
" Court, a Letter of *Jodocus Badius*, wherein he
" says, that he had printed Six hundred and fifty
" Copies of This Book, many of which had been
" sent into *Spain, Italy, Germany*, and *England*;
" that he had about fifty compleat Copies left, and
" promised not to distribute them (6). ---- More- (6) Chevil-
" over, *Lewis de Berquin*, a private Lutheran, and lier's Origin
" and a Friend of *Erasmus*, with whom he held of Printing
" Correspondence by Letters, presented twelve Pro- at Paris,
" positions out of *Beda*'s Book, pretending they con- pag. 174.
" tained some Impieties, and Blasphemies, and re-
" quired, that the Faculty should be obliged to con-
" demn, or prove them by the Holy Scripture. The
" King heard this Accuser favourably; and, the tenth
" of *July* 1527, he sent the Propositions, by the
" Bishop of *Bazas*, to the Rector, whom he ordered
" to cause them to be examined by the four Facul-
" ties assembled together, and not by the Doctors
" of Divinity only, *quæ in hac materiâ suspectos*
" *habebat*, as the Register of the Faculty says, ---
" I find no written Account of what the Judgment
" of the four Faculties was (7)." Take notice, that (7) Ibid.
" the Divines of *Paris* had rendered themselves so pag. 175.
" much suspected of Passion and Anger, that the
" King would not permit them to be Judges in
" This Cause, without joining with them the three
" other Faculties. It will not be amiss to see in what
" manner he bridled These Zealots: Here is an Extract
" of the Letter, which he wrote to the Parliament,
" the ninth of *April* 1526. "And, because we are
" duly informed, that the said Faculty, and their
" Agents, write indifferently against every Body,
" slandering their Honour and Reputation, as is done
" against *Erasmus*, and may endeavour to the like
" against others, We command you - - - - to write
" immediately to Those of the said Faculty, or their
" Deputies, and to forbid them - - - - to write,
" compose, or print, any thing whatsoever, either
" in general, or in particular, before it has been
" revised and approved by you, or your Deputies,
" and debated in a full Court (8)." These Regula- (8) Ibid.
tions did not continue long, though they seemed p. 179, 180.
worthy of a general and perpetual Establishment.

[*B*] *He made new Extracts out of them, as unfaithful as the former.*] The more he found himself convicted of Calumny, the more he endeavoured to ruin him, whom he had calumniated. He, therefore, resolved to try, whether, by producing the same Accusations a-new, under a Form somewhat different, he might not make a better Advantage of them. "Urit
" hominem - - - - quod ego respondens & meam
" innocentiam & illius impudentiam sic omnibus ob
" oculos posui, ut in speculo non possit evidentius.
" Itaque prorsus animo gladiatorio parat vindictam,
" non se purgans, quod non potest, sed easdem ca-
" lumnias alia specie rursus ingerens. - - - - Habet
" sexcentas propositiones è paraphrasibus deceptas ---
" eas ut narrant ad Facultatem defert, & in aliquot
" jam audio pronunciacum. Sed quomodo proponit
" artifex? Omittit quæ rem explicant, quæ calum-
" niam excludunt: addit de suo quæ faciunt ad ca-
" lumniam: proponit velut à me dicta hoc tempore
" quæ dicuntur ab Evangelistis aut Apostolis, & ad (9) Erasm.
" Ecclesiæ primordia pertinent (9). ---- *He is vexed,* lib. 19.
" Epist. 62.
" to 827.

BEDA.

his fiery Temper, and his factious and violent Declamations against the Novelties of those Times, and against Those, who were not zealous enough to suppress them, gave him a kind of tyrannical Sovereignty [C]. This he abused in such a manner, that, at last, they were obliged to give him up to the Secular Power, which,

to

" *to find my Innocence, and his own Impudence, represented, in my Answer, as faithfully, as in a Glass. He, therefore, prepares, with the Fury of a Gladiator, to take his Revenge, not by vindicating himself, which is out of his Power, but by repeating the same Accusations under another Form. ------ He has selected Six hundred Propositions out of my Paraphrases. ------ he presents them, they say, to the Faculty; and, as I am informed, Judgment is given upon some of them. But how does This crafty Fellow propose them?* He omits whatever tends to explain the Matter, or to remove Scandal: *he adds of his own what contributes to Calumny: he proposes, as if advanced, at present, by me what was said by the Evangelists, or Apostles, and related to the Infancy of the Church.*" Beda omitted none of the knavish Tricks of an unfaithful Maker of Extracts. He suppressed what was proper to justify the Accused Person, and to discover the Calumny: He added what would strengthen his Accusations; he turned to one Sense what had been said in another. There is nothing more easy, than to cause an innocent Opinion to be condemned by such Artifices: See the Seventy third Letter of the nineteenth Book of *Erasmus*. He contrived another Artifice; for he made choice of some Heads of Accusation, and, having put them into *French*, he sent them to the Court, to incense the Great Men, the Women, and all *France*, in general, against *Erasmus* (10). He had already alledged the Title of King of *France*, which *Erasmus* gave to the King of *England*, in dedicating a Book to him (11); I say, he had already alledged it, to render this poor Author odious at the Court of the Most Christian King I do not know, whether any one told him to his Face, that he was very much in the wrong, not to endeavour, before all things, to justify himself; and that it was disgraceful to leave *Erasmus*'s Lists unanswered, such Lists as convicted him plainly of gross Errors, and shameful Calumnies. "*Quum meæ supputationes ob oculos omnium posuerint hominis inscitiam cum pari malitia conjunctam, non cogitat de purgando, sed articulos aliquot decerptos ex acervo calumniarum & Gallicè versos misit in aulam regiam. ---- Nunc eosdem articulos vobis ingerit, scilicet in ordinem digestos, ut novi videantur, perinde quasi nihil sit responsum* (12). ------ *Though my Computations plainly discovered the Ignorance and Malice of the Man, yet he never thinks of justifying himself, but, selecting some Articles out of an Heap of Calumnies, he turns them into* French, *and sends them to Court* ------ *Now he repeats the same Articles to you, drawn up in such an Order, that They may appear new, as if they had never been replied to.*" He should have answered This without having recourse to so many unfair Practices. Perhaps *Erasmus* was the only Person, who reproached his Adversary with This. "*Nisi* Beda *prorsus diffideret suæ causæ, responderet saltem ad quædam loca tam impudenter calumniosa vanaque, ut res manibus, quod aiunt, sentiri possit. Nunc, hoc omisso, quod in primis curatum oportuit, vim parit, concitat facultatem, ut articulorum turba, suffragiis, & autoritate, me opprimat* (13). ------ *Did not Beda entirely distrust his own Cause, he would at least reply to some Passages, so impudently scandalous and false, that the thing may be felt, as the Proverb has it. But, having omitted This, which was his principal Concern, he now prepares Force, and stirs up the Faculty, to oppress me by a Multitude of Articles, by Votes, and by Authority.*" I say, *Erasmus* was perhaps the only Person, who reproached him after this Manner; for, commonly, They who are not concerned in the Injustice of an Inquisitor, govern themselves by the Rule of *Thinking more, than Speaking.*

[C] *His factious Behaviour ---- gave him a Kind of tyrannical Sovereignty, in the Faculty of Divinity.*] I do not know, whether any thing is more difficult, than to obtain an equitable Judgment, in a Process of Doctrine, against such a Man as *Beda*. He was naturally violent; he indulged this violent Disposition with the greater Licence, as he covered himself with the fair Pretence of the Interest of Truth: He boldly defamed his Adversaries in his Books: He called moderate Persons base Prevaricators, which was a good means to oblige part of the Judges to side with him against their Consciences; for there is no pleasure in exposing one's self to be defamed by the Assessors of an Inquisition: In a word, it was the ready way to tyrannize over the Faculty of Divinity. Here is the most faithful Description, which can be seen, of the manner, how a Man of *Beda*'s Stamp may extort an Academical Decree, a Synodal Sentence, &c. *Michael Angelo* never painted more to the Life. "*In omni consessu semper fuerunt, qui studiis & improbitate rerum summam sibi vindicarent, nec temere sit, ut melior pars vincat. Per illos primùm res privatim decernitur, mox excluduntur integriores, adhibentur idonei, præfatio commendat concordiam, adduntur minæ; bic,* inquiunt, *apparedit, qui sint* Lutheranæ *factionis. Si quis dixerit aliquid æquius, mox audit à frementibus,* Lu*thero pejor. Sunt ingenia modesta, quæ malunt quiescere, quàm cum talibus contentionem suscipere. Sunt qui in gratiam privatam deflectant à sua sententia: sunt qui metuant aut sperent aliquid, eoque premant quod judicant optimum: sunt qui non intelligant, quod nude proponitur: sunt qui iisdem affectibus excæcati sunt, quibus* Beda: *sunt quos utcunque sanos clamor ac tumultus aliorum, ita ut sit, agit in furias. Ita non sit, sed extorquetur senatusconsultum. In quo prodendo rarius qui extorserunt admiscent affectus suos, aliis vel inscitis, vel conniventibus. Et hoc dicitur collegii decretum* (14). ------ *In every Assembly, there have been Men, who, by dint of Industry and Dishonesty, gain a Superiority over the rest; nor is it without cause, that the better Part prevails. Every Thing is first determined in private by these Men: afterwards Those of Integrity are excluded; such, as are for their Purpose, only admitted: they begin with recommending Unanimity, and end with Threats; Now, say they, we shall discover, who are of the* Lutheran *Faction. If any one delivers himself with more Moderation, than usual, presently it is murmured, that he is worse than* Luther. *There are moderate Tempers, which chuse to be quiet, rather than contend with such Persons: Others there are, who sacrifice their Opinion to private Favour: with some, Hope or Fear prevails, and induces them to stifle what they judge to be best: Some do not understand what is nakedly proposed: others are blinded by the same Passions with* Beda: *There are, who, though sound of Mind, are driven to a Kind of Madness by the Clamour and Noise of Others. Thus a Decree is not made, but extorted. In the framing of which, They again, who have extorted it, intermix their own Passions, the rest either not perceiving, or conniving at it. And This is called A Decree of the Faculty.*" What he says in the fourth Fol. of his *Supputatio Errorum in censuris Bedæ*, is, likewise, a true Picture. "*Deligantur Deputati ad id idonei, quos optant ii, quorum autoritas vel improbitas vincit in collegiis, in quibus frequenter, quod ait* Livius, *major pars vincit meliorem, nonnunquam minor sed importunior superat & majorem & meliorem. Allegatur Relator. Decernitur. Interim cum scribis res est. Et hinc insulciuntur quædam obiter, quæ vel non sentiuntur, vel dissimulantur.* ------ *Deputies are afterwards pitched upon, proper for the purpose, who are chosen by Those, whose Authority, or Knavery, has acquired a Superiority in the Colleges; in which, as* Livy *observes, The greater Part prevails over the Better, and sometimes the Less, but more importunate, conquers the Greater and Better. An Informer is appointed. A Decree is drawn up. In the mean time Scribes are employed. Hence some things are frequently repeated, which are either not perceived, or are connived at.*" That, which is to be lamented, is, that the Management, described in this Passage, is put in practice, even when the Question is to condemn what deserves it most. See the Complaints made against the Censure of a Book of *Mary d'Agreda* (15). Observe, that our *Beda* accomplished his Design:

(10) Idem. Epist. 1, lib. 19, pag. 85.

(11) Ibid. Epist. 3, lib. 24, pag. 130.

(12) Id. Epist. 72, lib. 19, pag. 886.

(13) Id. Epist. 72, lib. 19, pag. 892.

(14) Erasmus, Epist. 72, lib. 19, pag. 889.

(15) *In Remarks* [C], *of the Article* MARY D'AGREDA.

VOL. I. 8 S sign:

to punish him for his high Offences, condemned him to make the *Amende honorable*, and to confess, at the Gate of the Cathedral Church of *Paris*, in the Presence of a great Number of People, that he had spoken against the King and the Truth. He was, moreover, condemned to Banishment (*c*). This happened in 1535. He had very much opposed the Design, which *Francis* I had, to cause the *Sorbonne* to give a favourable Opinion for the Divorce of *Henry* VIII. He was not in the wrong in the main; for all, that was done to corrupt some Universities in *France*, was a true Mystery of Iniquity; but he ruined his Cause by his Passionate Behaviour, and his mutinous Carriage [*E*]; and even involved himself in the

(*c*) Beza, Ibid. p. 25.

sign: The Faculty of Divinity censured *Erasmus*'s Book, the Twenty seventh of *December*, 1527. It is true, This Censure was not made public till four Years after (16).

(16) See Chevillier, Of the Origin of Printing at *Paris*, pag. 173.

[*D*] *He was condemned to make the Amende honorable.*] *Bartholomew Latomus*, who was then at *Paris*, wrote this News to *Erasmus*. " Beda tuus " fecit emendam, ut vocant, honorabilem, cum hac " confessione quod contra veritatem & Regem loquu- " tus esset, quæ verba ante ædem divæ Virginis " magno populi concursu præeunte præcone palam " pronunciavit: ne forte Lutheranum illum fuisse " putes. Sed tamen detinetur adhuc in carcere, de- " trudendus in Monasterium aliquod, ut ferunt, ubi " & quando Regi visum fuerit. —— *Your* Beda *has* " *made the Amende honourable, as they call it,* " *with this Confession, that he had spoken against* " *Truth and the King; which words he pronounced* " *openly at the Door of the Cathedral of the blessed* " *Virgin, with a Cryer preceeding him, and before a* " *great Concourse of People: This I inform you of,* " *that you may not think he was a Lutheran. How-* " *ever, he is still kept in Prison, to be thrust into* " *some Monastery, they say, where and when the* " *King pleases*." This Letter of *Latomus*, dated the Twenty ninth of *June* 1535, is the Twenty seventh of the Twenty seventh Book of *Erasmus*.

[*E*] *He spoiled his Cause by his passionate Behaviour*] Messieurs *de Bellai*, who concerned themselves extreamly in the good Success of *Henry* VIII's Divorce, speak very ill of *Beda* in their Letters. " I " have never yet seen This King (*of England*), nor " those that are in Credit with him, in so fair a way, " as they are at present in; to which what your Di- " vines have done has wonderfully contributed, ac- " cording to the Advice, that is come from the Em- " bassadors. But there is one *Beda* of That Number, " who is a dangerous Person; and there would be " no need of having many such in a good Com " pany." This is what *John du Bellai,* Bishop of *Bayonne*, wrote from *London* to Mr *de Montmorency*, the Twenty ninth of *December* 1529 (17). His Brother, *William du Bellai*, wrote to *Francis* I, the ninth of *June*, 1530, that *Beda* had committed great Disorders in the Assembly of the Faculty. " During " which Discourses, *says he,* and whilst their Beadle " was collecting the Names and Opinions of the De- " liberators, to see what the Opinion of the Majority " was, one of the said Gentlemen, our Masters, " stood up, and took the Roll out of his Hand, and " tore it; and thereupon, they all arose in great " Disorder and Tumult, some beginning to cry out, " that they had done and spoke enough about it, and " that the greatest and soundest Party was of Opinion " to deliberate no more about it, without writing to " you, Sir, and to the Pope In this manner the " Company departed; and the King of *England*'s " Embassadors, who were walking in a Gallery, see- " ing them come out in such disorder, and with " such a noise, and hearing all the Discourse, which " passed between them, retired very much displeased " to their Houses, putting a very ill Construction " upon this Business. And they told me, they knew " very well heretofore, what were the secret Practi- " ces of *Beza*, and his Accomplices, to render the " Consultation such as they had found it (18)." *Du Bellai* adds, I. That, at his Request, the first President sent for *Beda*, *Barthelemy, Tabary, and some other Ringleaders of this Discord and Faction,* and made them promise, that they would meet again the next Day. II. That the same first President " made " the said *Beda* come to him in the Church of our " Lady, *about another Circumstance,* and remonstrated " to him his Abilities, and the Inconvenience, to which " he might put *the King*, and was so urgent with

(17) See the Hist. of the Divorce of *Henry* VIII, by Mr le Grand Tom. III, p. 421.

(18) Ibid. p. 455, 406.

" him, that he swore expresly, not only not to hin- " der the King's Letters from being obeyed, but to " use his Endeavour, as if it were for his own Life, to " make the thing pass without noise or scandal (19)." III. That, though, " at first, he would not *trust* " *too much to this Promise,* forasmuch as, notwith- " standing another Promise formerly made to the " great Master, *the said* Beda had begun his Faction, " without which the Business might have been deter- " mined without any trouble to the King. Never- " theless, seeing the first President would trust *to* " Beda *for it, he* (du Bellai) *would not write again* " *to the King about it.*" The Letter of the fifteenth of *August* of the same Year is curious. *Du Bellai* informs Mr *de Montmorency*, I. That the Business " had been carried on by such wicked Intrigues, " that, *says he,* I have often seen the King's Business " in danger to suffer greatly by it; and I assure you, " that, if I had not daily made use of the Assistance " of the first President, who, besides the Authority " of his Place, has great Credit with the said *Beda,* " and his Accomplices, such an inconveniency would " have happened by the Attempt of a foolish, I dare " not say an ill, Man, that the Ability of a thousand " wise Men would hardly have remedied it without " extraordinary Trouble; and perhaps any other " Judge, not infected with the Persuasion, which I " perceive in the said President, that the before men- " tioned *Beda,* when he speaks Theologically, is " infallible and impeccable, would have called That " a Mortal Sin, which the said President can hardly " believe to be a Venial Sin: However, the King " has appointed Commissioners to enquire into the " Abuses and Insolencies of the said *Beda,* and his " Accomplices." II. That the *English* Embassadors had obtained an Order, from *Francis* I, to the Beadle of the Faculty of Divinity, *to give an authentic Duplicate of some Act signed with* Beda's *own Hand*; and that they had addressed themselves to the King, because to have it " by the leave of the Faculty, was " to go back to A, B, C, considering the Tyranny here- " tofore usurped by the said *Beda,* and his Adhe- " rents." III. That the first President (20) " is so " much persuaded of the Sanctity of *Beda*, that he " cannot believe the Faults he sees in him, which " are such, to speak the Truth, that, if I had com- " mitted such myself, and had a dozen Heads, I " should have deserved to lose them all; as any Body " may see, that will read the Legend, which the " two Presidents, *le Viste,* and *Povellot,* will make " of them. Nevertheless, My Lord, I do not con- " clude, that the said *Beda* is the only wicked Per- " son; for he has Companions enough, that would " be glad to give the King occasion to do some- " thing hastily against them, to acquire the Name of " Martyrs with the Mob. I have often heard of " their malicious Undertakings under the Title and " Colour of Honesty and Hypocrisy; but I could " never have believed the tenth Part, if I had not " seen it (21)." These words are worth their weight in Gold; for they wonderfully represent the Character of many of those turbulent Zealots, who cause a thousand Disorders in a State, by the desire they have to domineer over the Multitude, and who willingly expose themselves to Persecution, that the People, interesting themselves in their Disgrace, may make an Insurrection, and finish what their Intrigues have begun. The Bishop of *Bayonne*, in his Letters to Mr *de Montmorency,* confirms the greatest Part of what his Brother had written; " The Business of the " King of *England*, *says he* (22), was proposed at " *Paris*, after it could be deferred no longer; *Beda* " played the Devil there, and the Assembly broke up " without coming to any Conclusion; the King will " have them begin again, and, if it be necessary, to " send

(19) Ibid. pag. 468.

(20) It was Lizet, *whom* Beza *derided so much. William du Bellai represents him here as a weak Person, and unfit for its Office to boot.*

(21) Le Grand's Divorce of *Henry* VIII, Tom. III, pag. 473.

(22) In a *Letter, dated* June 1, 1530, apud le Grand, ubi supra, pag. 489.

BEDA. BEDELL.

the Crime of Perjury. He had much Credit with the first President *Lizet* (*d*), a Man much more fit to act the part of a bad Controvertist, as he did before his Death, than to be at the Head of the first Parliament of *France*. *Beda* was one of the chief Promoters of the Death of *Lewis de Berquin*, as we shall relate in the Article of That Protestant Martyr. In general, there was no one in *Paris*, who shewed more Violence against Those, who are called Hereticks, than himself (*e*); and This is the reason, why *Beza* (*f*) ascribes the Punishment, which was inflicted on *Beda*, of being *confined to Mount St Michel, where he died the eighth of* January, 1537 (*g*), rather to the just Judgment of God, than to That of Men. He had been Principal of the College of *Montaigu*. You will find, below, the Titles of his Works [*F*].

" send him the said *Beda*. —— I was told, that the Gentlemen of the Faculty were gone into the Conclave, to re assume the Business relating to the King of *England*, *Beda*, *Bartelemy*, and their Adherents, being the Authors and Promoters of it, who, after so many Alarms on their Part, as you have heard, have no sooner been out of the Presence of their Dean —— but they have, of their own paramount Authority, undertaken to break what was generally done and concluded in so great an Assembly (23). —— You know, my Lord, that I formerly told you, that *Beda* was suspected of a Design to get the Register falsified by the Beadle; and I would not give him time to increase That Suspicion, rather than lessen it (24)." By These Strokes of the Pencil we may know the true Character of This Personage.

[*F*] *The Titles of his Works*.] *De unica Magdalena contra Jacobum Fabrum & Jud cum Clichtoveum*, at Paris 1519 *Contra commentariis ejusdem Fabri in Evangelia & Epistolas libri II. & contra Erasmi paraphrases liber I.* at Paris 1526. *Apologia adversus clandestinos Lutheranos*, at Paris 1529. *Apologia pro filiabus & nepotibus Annæ contra eumdem Faorum*. He is thought to be the Author of the *Restitutio in integrum benedictionis cerei paschalis* (25).

BEDELL (**WILLIAM**), Bishop of *Kilmore*, in *Ireland*, was born in the Year 1570, at *Black Nottey*, in *Essex*. He studied at *Cambridge*, where he took his Bachelor's Degree, in the Year 1599. He left That University to exercise the Ministry at *St Edmondsbury*, in *Suffolk*, which he did very zealously, without any Interruption, 'till he was made Chaplain to the Embassador, whom King *James* sent to the Republic of *Venice* (*a*). During his eight Years abode at *Venice*, *Bedell* contracted a very intimate Friendship with Father *Paul*, and, when he returned into *England*, he brought the famous *Mark Antony de Dominis* along with him, as also several Manuscripts, of Father *Paul*'s, and, among others, *The History of the Council* of *Trent*. He returned again to *St Edmondsbury*, and, amidst the Functions of the Sacred Ministry, he translated into *Latin* The *History of the Interdiction*, and That of the *Inquisition*, which Father *Paul* had given him; and dedicated them to the King. He translated, also, the two last Books of *The History of the Council*. In the Year 1615, he was provided with a considerable Benefice, in the Diocese of *Norwich*, which he possessed twelve Years, applying himself very much to his Duty, and caring but little to make a noise in the World. He was so little known, that no one could give any Account of him to *Diodati*, a Divine of *Geneva* [*B*]. Nevertheless, his Reputation reached into *Ireland*, where, with a general Consent, he was nominated to the Headship of *Trinity* College (*b*). He would not accept of This Place, without the Command of his Superiors; and, being commanded to do it by King *James*, he joyfully obeyed, and discharged the Duties of That Employment to Admiration. Two Years after, he was promoted to the Bishoprics of *Kilmore* and *Ardagh*, in the Province of *Ulster*, being, then, in his Fifty ninth Year (*c*). He found These two Dioceses in great Disorder, and was very active in reforming Abuses. He began with the Plurality of Benefices, and, to set a good Example, he resigned the Bishopric of *Ardagh*, and kept only That of *Kilmore*. He made some Regulations as to

[*A*] *Bedell contracted a very intimate Friendship with Father* Paul.] The Intimacy, which This Famous *Venetian* Divine had with *William Bedell*, was without any reserve; he discovered his Heart to him, which was more imbued with the Faith of the Reformed Churches, than with That of the Council of *Trent*. Nothing, perhaps, more clearly evinces Father *Paul*'s reformed Faith, than the Particulars, which Dr *Burnet* published in the Life of our Bishop of *Kilmore*: I shall speak at large of it in another place (1). I shall only observe here, that Father *Paul* assisted *Bedel* in learning the *Italian* Language, and that *Bedell* helped the other to learn the *English* Tongue Father *Paul* confessed, that he received from him some other Instructions, which were more considerable: See, hereafter, the Remark [*H*]. I add, that *Bedell* translated the Liturgy of the Church of *England* into *Italian*; and that he had the Liberty of conferring with Father *Paul when*, and *as often as he would*, even when none but Persons known to him were suffered to come near him, by reason of the wounds, which That Father had received (2).

[*B*] *No one could give any Account of him to Diodati.*] What I say here would be no Encomium of a Person of little Merit; but, as to our *Bedell*, who was an able Divine, and a Minister, who performed his Office so worthily, one cannot say of him, that he was little known, without extolling to the Skies, at the very same time, his Modesty, Humility, Disinterestedness, and several other truly Pastoral Virtues, and very rarely to be found. Where are there Churchmen of great Abilities, who do not endeavour to make a Noise in the World, but chiefly to reach the Ears of Princes, and Favourites? Let us set down Dr *Burnet*'s Remark: " *Diodati*, says he " (3), That famous Divine of *Geneva*, being come " into *England*, could meet with no one, who " could give him any tidings of him, though he was " very well acquainted with the Clergy. He was " much surprised, that such an extraordinary Man, " so much admired in *Venice*, so cordially cherished " by Persons of the greatest Merit, should be so " little known in his own Country: he had lost all " hopes of seeing him, when, meerly by accident, " he met him in the Streets of *London*, where they " expressed their great Surprize and Joy to each " other. *Diodati* presented him afterwards to " the learned Dr *Morton*, Bishop of *Durham*, whom " he informed of the particular Esteem, which Fa- " ther *Paul* had for him; and That Prelate gave " him a very favourable Reception."

[*C*] *He*

BEDELL.

to Refidence: He was very zealous for the Converfion of the *Roman* Catholicks, and, thinking, that nothing could contribute more to it, than a Tranflation of the Scriptures into the *Irifh* Language [C], he caufed it to be undertaken. This Bufinefs met with many Obftacles. He expreffed a great Zeal for the Re-union of the *Lutherans* and *Calvinifts* [D]. He did not approve of Thofe, who made ufe of a paffionate Stile againft Popery [E], and did not think them fit to undeceive Thofe, who erred. He took a quite different Method: He was a Man of an Apoftolic Charity;

[C] *He fet on foot a Tranflation of the Scriptures into the* Irifh *Language.*] He had learned That Language; "and, though he was too old to fpeak it, "yet he underftood it fo well, that he made a com-"pleat Grammar of it, which, it is faid, was the firft "that ever was made (4)." In favour of the new Converts, "he caufed the Common-Prayers to be "read every Sunday in *Irifh*, and affifted at them "himfelf. —— The New Teftament, and the Liturgy, had been already tranflated into *Irifh*; but, "judging, that the Old ought no longer to remain "untranflated, he fought for fome one, who was "Mafter of that Language, to tranflate it (5) ; —— "and, cafting his Eyes upon one *King*," aged about feventy Years, he put him into Orders, provided him with a Living, and defired him to fet about it. This Perfon, not underftanding the Oriental Languages, was obliged to tranflate it from the *Englifh*; His Work was revifed by *Bedell*, who, after having compared the *Irifh* Tranflation with the *Englifh*, compared the latter with the *Hebrew*, with the LXX, and with the *Italian* Verfion of *Diodati*. When This Work was finifhed, he refolved to be at the Charge of the Impreffion; but his Defign was ftopped: Advice was given to the Lord Lieutenant, and the Archbifhop of *Canterbury*, that it would be a fhameful thing for a Nation to publifh a Bible, tranflated by fuch a defpicable Man, as *King* was (6). There was a Clergyman, who obtained the Benefice of This old Man, and thruft *him out of it with Ignominy and Violence* (7). He was not only deprived of it, but alfo attacked in his Reputation. "It is ufual, *fays* Dr *Burnet* (8), for thofe, who commit an Injuftice, to "juftify it by another, to load their Adverfaries "with Calumnies, and frequently to repeat their Ac-"cufations, in order to prepoffefs the People againft "them, and to opprefs them fo much, that they "may not be able to obtain any Redrefs, that entire-"ly fink under fuch a weight of Malice" *Bedell* ufed all his endeavours to prevent the Oppreffion of This poor Tranflator, and prepared Matters to have the *Irifh* Bible printed in his own Houfe; but the Troubles followed; and he did not live long enough to execute his Refolution. The Manufcript was not loft; for, *by the Diligence of the famous Chriftian Philofopher*, Mr *Boyle* (9), *they were printing of it*, when Dr *Burnet* publifhed the Life of our Bifhop (10).

[D] *He expreffed a great Zeal for the Re-union of the Lutherans and Calvinifts*] He was not contented to impart his Thoughts by Letters to Mr *Durry*, *but did alfo affift him in the Expence, he was obliged to be at, to negotiate this Union, and gave him an annual Penfion of Twenty five Piftols, which he paid regularly to his Correfpondent in* London (11). This Mr *Durry*'s Name in *Latin* is *Duraeus*: The pains, he took, to execute his Project of Re-union, are almoft incredible. I believe, without making much hafte, he took as many Journies, as the Jefuit *Matthieu*, who was called *The Poftillion of the League*. They may be compared in fome things; but they differ in many others. One was the Minifter of a League, which was already formed, and which, being actually in Arms, had none but violent Defigns. The other was the Minifter of a meer notional Confederacy, which was only to be built on the Moderation of Men. So that it is no wonder, if one of them rode Poft, and the other travelled at his leifure. There is, among the Treatifes, which *Duraeus* publifhed in 1662 (12), *William Bedell*'s Opinion on the Queftions, which the Undertaker of the Re-union had propofed to the Divines. This Prelate made it appear, that he was fit for fuch an Undertaking. A great Number of *Lutherans*, being fettled at *Dublin*, refufed to communicate with the Church of *Ireland*. They were fummoned before the Archbifhop's Council; They anfwered, that the *German* Divines did not find, that the Prefence of JESUS CHRIST in the Eucharift was taught, conformably to their Doctrine, by the Church of *Ireland*. The Archbifhop fent them to the Bifhop of *Kilmore*; who gave them fuch a folid Anfwer, that the *German* Divines, who faw it, advifed the *Lutherans* of *Dublin* to communicate with the Church of That Place. Dr *Burnet* fays upon This, that the Church of *England* have given *no pofitive Definition of the manner how the Body of* CHRIST *is prefent in the Sacrament* : So that Men *of different Opinions may practife the fame Worfhip, without being obliged to declare themfelves, and without any Prefumption, that they all againft their Belief* (13) I have always heard it faid, that there would be no better way to prevent Schifms, and Difputes, than to avoid Particulars, and to allow of as General Formularies as may be.

[E] *He difapproved of thofe, who made ufe of a paffionate Stile againft Popery.*] He preached one Day, among other things, as follows: "Give me leave, "my Brethren, to fpeak my Thoughts freely; I "am very fenfible, it will difpleafe many Perfons; "but That fhall not hinder me from difcharging my "Confcience; and I hope Men of Underftanding "will not take it amifs. I have long ago been of "Opinion, that the manner, in which many Per-"fons treat their Adverfaries, in their Writings, "and in their Sermons, deferves Cenfure; They "give a loofe to their Pens, and Tongues, and what "they fay is only a Series of Calumnies, and in-"jurious Language; They think they have done "Wonders, when they imitate their Enemies, or "when they furpafs them in them in That Way, in "which He, who does the beft, does, really, the "worft; they endeavour to juftify their Proceedings "by the Text; *Anfwer a Fool according to his Folly, "without confidering the other Text, Anfwer not a "Fool according to his Folly, leaft thou become like "unto him.* But they are, fometimes, the more in-"excufable, becaufe, not underftanding their Ad-"verfaries Opinion, or, at leaft, difguifing, and making "it more unreafonable, than it is, the Proofs, which "they bring, have nothing that is folid, and con-"fift only in judicious Words about ambiguous "Terms, which each Party takes in a different "Senfe (14). —— Let us not envy the Papifts, and "other Heretics, the Glory of outdoing our Adver-"faries in railing: becaufe the more one excels in "this Art, the more one is remote from the great "Pattern of Charity, who fays, *Learn of me, for I "am meek and lowly in Heart* (15). - - - - - It is not "with fharp and cutting Expreffions, but with folid "Reafons, that Error is to be confuted. - - - - - - - "It is our Duty to confound Error, not to cavil, or "to rail. It is faid, that *Alexander*, having heard "one of his Soldiers fcoff at his Enemy *Darius*, re-"primanded him fmartly in thefe Words; *Friend, "I lifted thee to fight againft* Darius, *and not to treat "him unworthily, as you do* (16). But, in truth, "JESUS CHRIST, our Captain, is but little obli-"ged to Thofe, who treat their Adverfaries in this "manner; and it is very probable, that, if he was yet "on Earth, he would fay to them; *Preachers of my "Gofpel, I am willing you fhould refute Popery, and "that you fhould oppofe my Enemy Antichrift, and "all the Sects, which fight under his Banner; but I "have not called you to give them ill Words*. Thefe "are my Sentiments concerning the manner, in which "we ought to treat Thofe of the *Romifh* Commu-"nion: Perhaps they do not conform to the Practice "of *Luther*, *Calvin*, and fome other great Men. "But our Conduct muft not be regulated according "to the Example of others: They were Men; and "perhaps they had the failure of too warm a "Zeal (17)."

This is a fmall part of the Extract, which is given us of This Sermon, in This Prelate's Life. He, who gave it, informs us, that This Sermon was preached a little after the Difference, which happened in the Houfe

(4) Ibid. pag. 119.

(5) Ibid. pag. 120.

(6) Ibid. pag. 124.

(7) P. 125.

(8) P. 129.

(9) P. 131.

(10) *That is, in the Year* 1685.

(11) Burnet, *in the Life of* William Bedell, pag. 132.

(12) *This Book is entituled* Irenicorum tractatuum Prodromus.

(13) Burnet, ubi fupra, pag. 133.

(14) *This touches upon the two greateft Faults of Thofe, who manage Controverfies. The one is, that they would raife too much at it; to Adverfaries ; the other is, not faithfully to ftate the Opinions, which they refute : They diffemble the ftrong Reafons of the oppofite Party; they ftick to falfe Interpretations, &c.*

(15) *Thefe Words of* JESUS CHRIST *were the Text on which the Bifhop preached.*

(16) *I believe the Bifhop miftakes one for another: It was Memnon, a General of* Darius, *who faid fo to a Soldier, that flandered* Alexander. Plutarch Apophth. pag. 174. But, at the Ancients are not always uniform in applying this kind of Sayings to the fame Perfons, the Bifhop might, perhaps, have read what he fays.

(17) Burnet's *Life of* William Bedell, p. 145, 147.

BEDELL.

Charity; and it was his kind Usage of the Papists, which, with the special Protection of GOD, saved him from their Fury [F], when they made such a Massacre in *Ireland*, in the Year 1641. His House, where several Persons had taken Sanctuary, was spared for two Months; and, at last, when the Papists resolved to employ Force against Those Persons, they had such a Regard for him, as to desire him to send them away; which if he did not, they declared, that they had Orders to seize him. But he chose rather to give himself up to the Discretion of the Rebels, than to put those out of his House, who came for Refuge there. So they took him Prisoner, with his two Sons, and brought them, with those few Persons, that were in his House, to the Castle of *Lochwater*. He had the Liberty to preach in his Prison; and, a little while after, he was set at Liberty, with his two Sons, by an exchange of Prisoners. He was carried to the House of an *Irish* Minister, and died within a few Days (*d*), with the most Christian Dispositions, that a true Prelate can have. His End answered the good Life he had led; he was the greatest Example, that these latter Ages can parallel with the holy Pastors of the Primitive Church (*e*). The *Irish* Catholics, whose Hatred for the Protestants, and Spirit of Rebellion, inspires them with more Fierceness, than the Nature of their Climate, and Education, admired his Virtue, and gave him very signal Marks of their Respect, on the Day of his Burial [G]. His Learning was great [H]; and he would have testified it to the Public by a greater Number of Books [I], if he had printed all Those, which he composed. They were almost all lost; for the Rebels scattered his Papers, and his whole Library. He was Seventy two Years of Age, when he died, and was yet very vigorous; neither did he use Spectacles (*f*).

House of Commons in *Ireland*, where there were many Papists. Dr *Burnet*'s Judgment upon it is well worthy of attention. He gives us, says he (18), *such a fine Method of handling Controversies, that the Advice will, I think, be found to be as extraordinary, as it is little practised.*

[*F*] *It was his kind usage of the Papists, which saved him from their Fury.*] Their Bitterness, (I make use of the Bishop of *Salisbury*'s Words) was not strong enough to resist the Sweetness, which he had shewed on all Occasions, and which made them say very often, that He should be the last *Englishman*, who should be driven out of *Ireland*. He *was the only Person in the County of Cavan, who was not disturbed in his House, nor in the Church-yard, or Church, which were full of poor persecuted People* (19). When the Rebels sent him Word to dismiss all those, who sheltered themselves under his Roof, he added, *That, as he had done good to several People, and had not disobliged any Body, they had more regard for him, than for any Englishman in Ireland* (20). See the following Remark.

[*G*] *The Irish Catholics ------ gave him very signal Marks of their Respect, on the Day of his Burial.*] The titular Bishop of *Kilmore* had taken possession of the Bishopric: It was necessary to desire his leave, that Bishop *Bedell* should be buried in his Churchyard: He alledged, at first, that it was holy Ground, which ought not to be prophaned by such Burials; but, at last, he granted all that was desired, and, accordingly, on the ninth of *February*, 1642, " the " Body of the deceased was buried near that of his " Wife, as he had desired in his Life-time. On this " sad Occasion, the *Irish* would pay him extraordi-" nary Honours; The Chief of the Rebels drew up " his Troops, and made them accompany the Corps " in great Ceremony, from Mr *Sheredan*'s House, to " the Church yard of *Kilmore*; They would also have " had Mr *Clogy* (21), perform the Office, according " to the Liturgy of the Church of *England*; but, " though the Gentry would have paid him this Com-" pliment, it was not thought fit to make use of it, " for fear of stirring up the Rage of the Mob, which " was already too much exasperated. When the " Body was laid in the Ground, they fired a Vol-" ley, and cried out in *Latin*, *requiescat in pace ul-" timus Anglorum,* ⸺ *Peace be with the last of the " English*; and, indeed, they had very often pro-" tested, that they had more Consideration for *Be-" dell*, than for any of the other *English* Bishops, " and that he should be the last that should be remo-" ved from them (22)."

[*H*] *His Learning was great.*] Father *Paul* declared, that he had learned more from *William Bedell*, in all the speculative, and positive, parts of Divinity, than from any other Person he had conversed with (23). This same Father had read the New Testament in *Greek*, with so much Exactness, that he had made Notes upon each Word; but he found, by *Bedell*'s Criticisms, that he had not well understood certain Passages; and was very much pleased to learn the true Sense of Them, which This learned *Englishman* shewed him (24). *Marc Antony de Dominis* desired the same Doctor to examine the ten Books of his *Ecclesiastical Republic*. " *Bedell* corrected many Mis-" applications of Scripture, and many Quotations of " the Fathers, in it; for That Prelate, being alto-" gether ignorant of the *Greek* Tongue, must needs " have committed a great many Faults;" the Number of which was so great, that *Bedell* could not correct them all (25). He observed some Mistakes, in the Works of the learned *Usher*, Archbishop of *Armagh*. " They were neither many, nor of any great Mo-" ment; but, because they did not answer the un-" common Exactness of That great Man, he thought " he was obliged to point them out to him: which " he did; and the Archbishop received his Censure " with his usual Mildness, and Humility (26)." He studied much, " and chiefly the original Text of " Scripture, of which he had so often read the " *Hebrew*, and the *Greek* of the LXX, that he had " them as fluent as the *English* Translation (27)."

[*I*] *He had composed a greater Number of Books.*] I have said, in the Body of this Article, that he published a *Latin* Translation of some of Father *Paul*'s Works. I must observe, at present, that *Marc Antony de Dominis* was much better satisfied with *Bedell*'s Translation, than with That of *Newton*. The latter translated the two first Books of *The History of the Council of Trent*; and the other translated the two last (28). *Bedell* published a Book of Controversy in the Year 1624, and dedicated it to the Prince of *Wales*. This Book was a Confutation of some of *Wadsworth*'s Letters. This *Wadsworth*, Fellow Student, and Chamber-Fellow of *Bedell*, was provided with a Benefice in the same Diocese with *Bedell*, and was sent into *Spain*, about the same time, that *Bedell* was sent to *Venice* (29). I say, he was sent into *Spain*, in the same quality of Chaplain, and to teach the Infanta English, when her Marriage had been agreed upon with King *James*. He suffered himself to be persuaded to forsake his Religion and his Country, and published some Letters, containing the Motives of his Change (30). *Bedell* confuted them. It is believed, that his Answer had some Effect on *Wadsworth*'s Heart, though it did not induce him to make an outward Profession of the Reformed Religion. It is thought so, because the Son of this new Catholic came to *Bedell* at *Kilmore*, and told him, " That his " Father had ordered him to return him Thanks for " the Pains he had taken to instruct him; that he " read his Book continually, and he had heard him " say sometimes, after the reading of it, that he would " make his escape." *Bedell* mentions a Discovery, which was made, of the Number of the Beast, in the Inscription of a *Thesis*, dedicated to Pope *Paul* V (31). It was found, that the numeral Letters of these Words, *Paulo* V. *Vice Deo* made 666; but he does not pretend

pretend to be the Author of the Difcovery: However he was fo (32), and he did Father *Paul*, and other Divines of the Republic of *Venice*, a very great Pleafure, when he communicated it to them (33). He wrote a very long Treatife on thefe two Queftions ; *Where was the Reformed Church before Luther ; and what was the Fate of Thofe, who died in the Bofom of the Church of* Rome, *before the Reformation ?* He was refolved to publifh it ; and the Learned Archbifhop *Ufher* often preffed him to it: The *Irifh* Rebellion occafioned the Lofs of This Work (34), *and of a great Collection of critical Expofitions on different Paffages of the Scripture*, together with his Sermons, and learned *Paraphrafes on all the Epiftles and Gofpels of the Day, according to the Liturgy of the Church of* England (35). The *Irifh feized on them, and the other Manufcripts, whereof there was a great Cheft full; only his great Hebrew Manufcript was fortunately taken out of the Hands of thefe profane Men, and is preferved in the Library of* Emanuel *College. This good Luck happened by means of an* Irifhman, *whom he had converted, who, mixing with the Rebels, brought away This Manufcript, and fome other Books, with him.* One would be apt to believe, that it is the fame, which is mentioned in the Twenty fifth Page. Now it is faid there, that *Bedell* bought, of Rabbi *Ley*, chief *Chacham of the Synagogue ---- the fine Manufcript of the Old Teftament, which he gave to* Emanuel *College; though he had a great Value for it; for it is faid, that it coft him it's Weight in Silver.*

BEGAT (JOHN), Counfellor in the Parliament of *Dijon*, was deputed to *Charles* IX, in the Year 1563, to prefent an Addrefs to His Majefty, againft the Edict, which granted the Proteftants the Exercife of their Religion, after the firft Civil-War. The States of *Burgundy* were refolved not to fuffer the Affemblies of the Proteftants, notwithftanding That Edict ; and, to make the Court approve of it, *Begat* was fent thither, who fpoke vigoroufly on That Subject. Afterwards he publifhed an Apology, wherein he pretends to fhew, by feveral Arguments, that Two Religions ought not to be fuffered in one State, and that Toleration is offenfive to GOD, and againft the Public Peace. The Proteftants publifhed a Writing againft it (a) [*A*].

[*A*] *He publifhed an Apology ---- the Proteftants publifhed a Writing againft it*] I have not yet feen any Catalogue of Authors, who make any mention of This Work of *Begat*'s which made me refolve to find it out: befides, we fhall fee, in this Article, the little Regard, they had then in *France*, for the Royal Authority. The Province of *Burgundy* did not only refufe to comply with the King's Pleafure; but decided, after a mature Deliberation, in the Affembly of the States, that they would not obey his Will. When fuch things as thefe are reprefented to the *French*, fince the Revolution, which happened in *England*, in the Year 1688, they know not what to fay, and could wifh, that the Proofs of thefe Recriminations were no where to be found. I have the Remonftrance of *Begat*, in *Latin*, printed at *Cologne*, in the Year 1564. It is entitled, *Refponfum conventus trium ordinum ducatus Burgundiae de edicto pacis nuper in caufa religionis factae, ad Chriftianiffimum Galliarum Regem, Carolum Nonum*, anno 1563. I wonder it fhould be fo little known ; for it was tranflated into feveral Languages, as I have juft now feen, in the *Paradoxical Mifcellanies* of *Peter de St Julien*. The Paffage is fo curious, that it deferves to be produced entire. "To fpeak of a more " recent Affair, when the Parliament of *Burgundy*, " affembled at *Dijon*, deputed Mr *John Begat*, Coun" fellor in the fame, to lay before the King the " Reafons, why That Court had not proceeded to " the Publication of the Edict of *January* (1), (where " the faid *Begat* fpoke fo well, and fo learnedly, " that no other Remonftrance was better received " in our Time: which may be judged fo, becaufe " the fame *French* Remonftrance has been tranflated " into *Latin, Italian, Spanifh*, and *High Dutch*) it " happened, that the faid *Begat* fell into private Dif" courfe with the Chancellor de *l'Hôpital*, on the " fame Subject ; and, as the Counfellor infifted up" on the Privileges of *Burgundy*, and faid, that the " King had fworn, and promifed, to obferve them, " the faid Sieur de *l'Hofpital* (as knavifh, as a Chan" cellor) replied, that it did not belong to Subjects " to act againft their King *ex fponfu* (they were his " Words) ; and that all Contracts of Sovereign Princes " with their Subjects bind them no longer, than " they think fit (2)."

BELLAI, an illuftrious and ancient Family in *Anjou*, which has produced fome great Men. See, in *Moreri*, a long Series of the Genealogy of the *du Bellai*'s, and a pretty large Account of the Perfons of That Name, who have moft diftinguifhed themfelves. I fhall avoid Repetitions, as much as I can, in fpeaking of *William du Bellai*, and of his Brother *John du Bellai*: I mean, that, as far as can be done, I fhall omit what *Moreri* has already mentioned.

BELLAI (WILLIAM du), Lord of *Langei*, was Son of *Lewis du Bellai* (a), and of *Margaret de la Tour-Landri*. He did *Francis* I great Services, both by his Courage, and Parts ; he was no lefs a good Captain, than an able Negotiator ; and his Pen was as good, as his Tongue, and his Sword. His Dexterity in penetrating into the Intrigues and Defigns of his Enemies, by his Spies, was furprizing. See, in *Moreri*, what Brantome faid of him, and add to it, what I relate below [*A*]. He was

[*A*] *His Addrefs, in penetrating into the Defigns of his Enemies, was furprizing: add to it what I relate below.*] *Francis de Billon* obferves, that the Lord of *Langey* never began the Execution of any Military Undertaking, before he had made ufe of his Pen to difcover the State of things (1). He reports, afterwards, thefe Words of *Charles* V. *Langey's Pen has fought more againft me, than all the barbed Lances of* France (2). He commends This Lord's Secretaries very much ; for, after having fpoken of a Perfon, who offered Two thoufand Crowns of Gold, in vain, for a Copy of a Letter, which a Cardinal had written to *Francis* I, he adds, that This " Perfon went away confounded, as having prefumed, " that he had to do with fuch good Merchants, as Thofe " of the late Marquis *du Guaft*, whom a Secretary " of the famous *Langey* (whofe Name was *Landry*, " by the Help of Money, founded to the very Bot" tom of their Thoughts: which he did out of Af" fection to a Mafter, who, in Cafe of Neceffity, " had a voluntary Sacrifice made him of the Hearts " of his Secretaries, and other Gentlemen: Hence " it is, that The Saying, *Langey's* Education, is full " ufed in many Places, to his Praife, and to put " *Frame* in Mind of the ferviceable Perfons of his " Time (3)." If the Author, who has fpoken fo much of the great Effects of the Pen, and alledged fo many Examples of it, had known what I have now quoted, he would have adorned his Work, entituled *Arma Anferina*, with it (4).

[*B*] *He*

BELLAI.

was one of the chief Springs, which moved some Universities of *France* to vote according to the Passions of *Henry* VIII, King of *England*, when That Prince resolved, by way of Divorce, to quit his Wife, and be at Liberty to marry *Anne Bullen*. It was the Interest of *France* to favour the King of *England*, in this Matter; for the divorcing of Queen *Catherine* was an Affront to the Emperor, and a Pleasure to *Henry* VIII. This Affront on the one Side, and Pleasure on the other, were very proper to form a strict Alliance between the King of *England*, and *Francis* I; which was the reason, why *William du Bellai* used his utmost Endeavours in Favour of *Henry* VIII. He was sent several times to the Protestant Princes of *Germany*: He dexterously warded off the Blows, which were aimed at him there, in relation to the Severity, with which his Master punished Heretics [B]. He was made a Knight of the Order, and Lieutenant General in *Italy*. He had composed *An History of his own Times* [C], in *Latin*, divided into *Ogdoades* (*b*), and, afterwards, by the King's Order, he translated it into *French*: Somebody stole this Work; so that the Public has been deprived of it, except some Fragments, and three or four Books, which MARTIN DU BELLAI, the Author's Brother, inserted in his Memoirs [D]. You will see, in the Remarks, what Judgment *Montagne* passed on This

(b) La Croix du Maine imagined, falsly, that William du Bellai had wrote a Book, entituled Ogdoades, which was different from his History of France.

[B] *He dexterously warded off the Blows, which were aimed at him in relation to - - - - the Punishment of Heretics.*] See the Substance of his Speech in the ninth Book of *Sleidan*: It was not possible to make a more artful Apology, than That, which he made for the Punishment, which *Francis* I, had inflicted on some of his Subjects, who had embraced the new Opinions. But *Langey's* Conversations were, at least, as artful as his Speeches; he conferred with the Doctors, and consest to them, that, on divers Points, the Opinions of the King, his Master, did not much differ from Those of a Book, which *Melanchthon* had published (5). Father *Maimbourg* was very angry, upon this Occasion, with *Sleidan*. "How is it possible, *says he* (6), that the Lord *du Bellai* (7) could have said so false a thing and so contrary to all Probability? He, who, in the beginning of That same Year, had followed the King *in a famous Procession, where That Prince shewed so much Zeal for the Catholic Religion*, and, after which, he caused six Men, convicted of Lutheranism, to be burnt alive, with a slow Fire. One might as well ask, how can a cunning and dexterous Embassador make use of any Disguise, when he desires to obtain things of great Importance, which a sincere Acknowledgment would infallibly make him lose?" Father *Maimburg* confesses (8), that *du Bellai* declared, that They, who were punished in *France*, were such as the Protestants of *Germany* would not acknowledge. The same Jesuit does not censure *Sleidan* for having said, that *du Bellai* protested the King his Master had not declared against Lutheranism, by the Punishment, to which he had condemned some of his Subjects, and that none but malicious Calumniators could be guilty of so extravagant an Assertion. "*Illum animadvertisse quidem in soae ditionis quosdam*: sed hoc ad ipsorum injuriam nullam pertinere, tametsi male, oh dicant quam illos è medio sustulit ipsorum quoque causam veluti prœjudicio quodam condamnasse: rogat autem ne tam ineptis calumnis moveantur (9)." Father *Maimbourg* must therefore have believed, that The Embassador spoke in this Manner: Now what can be said more contrary to Sincerity, more false, and more unlikely? Was it not notoriously known, that, at *Paris*, they gave no more Quarter to the Lutherans, than to the Zuinglians? See what has been said, on all this, against Father *Maimbourg*, in the Critical Answer to his History of *Calvinism* (10). We have, here, an Article of the Religion of Sovereigns, and of the Embassadors Catechism; which is, That Heresy ought to be persecuted at Home, and caressed in foreign Countries, in order to stir up a Civil War in a State, which it is their Interest to weaken, or in order to make an advantageous Alliance. It is the Embassador's Trade to act according to the Doctrine of Equivocations; and it should have been chiefly invented for them. But, to go on, *Sleidan*'s Honesty has been displayed in it's full Lustre by Mr *Seckendorf*. He quotes *William*, and his Brother *John du Bellai's* Letters, written to *M. Lanchthon*; wherein they assured him of the good Sentiments of *Francis* I (11). Nay, he quotes a Letter, which That Prince wrote to the League of *Smalcalde*, to excuse the Punishments in

question (12). The Confederate Princes were plainly imposed upon; and were made to believe many things, to hinder them from coming to an Accommodation with *Charles* V. A Modern Historian (13) observes, that *William du Bellai*'s Discourse to the Faculty of Divinity at *Paris*, assembled to deliberate on the Divorce of the King of *England*, was all a Cheat; and why should he have been more sincere to the Prejudice of *Francis* I, in *Germany*?

[C] *He composed An History of his own Times in Latin.*] *Scævola Sammarthanus* was much mistaken, when he said, that This Work was the History of *France*, from the beginning of the Monarchy, to the time of the Author. *Historiam de rebus Gallicis ab ipsa imperii origine ad sua usque tempora, tum Latinè tum Gallicè, gravissìmo stilo persecutus est* (14). If he had read the Prefaces, he would not have said so; for *William du Bellai* declares, in express Words (15), That his Memoirs begin with the Infancy of *Francis* I. He adds, that he had, at first, prefixed to them, by way of Introduction, a Discourse about the Origin of the *Gauls*, and *French*, and the Reduction of Those two Nations into one, which threw off the Roman Yoke; but that, afterwards, he laid aside That Discourse, and enlarged it so much, that he made a separate Work of it, and one of the seven *Ogdoades*, which made up his History. He treated, in That *Ogdoade*, I. Of the Antiquity of *Gaul* and *French*; II. Of the Division of *Gaul* and *France*; He gave, there, a Geographical Description, and reconciled the Modern Names with the Ancient, as well as he could; III. Of the Laws and Customs, as well Military, as Political, and of the Offices, and Dignities. He accommodated the Time past to the present, as well, and as near, as he could (16). *Martin du Bellai* does no less clearly condemn *Scævola Sammarthanus*. "My deceased Brother, *say he* (17), *Messire William du Bellai*. - - - - had composed seven *Latin Ogdoades*, which he translated, by the King's Order, into our Vulgar Language, wherein might be seen, as in a clear Glass, not only a Picture of the Occurrences OF THIS AGE, but also a wonderful Dexterity of Writing, according to the Judgment of the most Learned." If it had been a compleat History of the Monarchy, would he have recommended his Brother's Memoirs by the sole *Occurrences of this Age*, and by the Stile? Note, That the Work of the Antiquity of the *Gauls*, and *French*, is so full of Fables, that one would think the Author did not so much design to write a History, as to forge a Romance. *Non Francogalliæ historiæ, sed Amadisicarum fabularum instituisse tractationem videtur.* Thus *Francis Hotman* speaks of it, at the end of the fourth Chapter of his *Francogallia*.

[D] *Of which there remain - - - - three or four Books, which MARTIN DU BELLAI - - - - inserted in his Memoirs.*] He was both a Soldier and an Author, as well as his Brother. He was Knight of the King's Order, Captain of the fifty Men of Arms of his Ordinances, and his Lieutenant-General in *Normandy*. He left some Memoirs, which reach, from the Year 1513, when he came to Court, to the Death of *Francis* I. "They are, says he (18), Memoirs both of Peace and War, of which I can partly speak as an Eye-witness; for I was personally

BELLAI.

This Book [E]. The Prologue contains very important Pieces of Advice to Historians, and very solid Reflexions on the Indignities, which are offered to History [F]. It is through a palpable Mistake, that a Book, concerning Military Discipline,

" sonally present, in several Places, on this, and the " other, side of the *Alps*; and, as for the rest, I " could have certain Advice from those, who were " present." Of the ten Books, which make up This Work, there are but three, which belong to *William du Bellai*, if we may rely on the Title-page, on the Preface of *Martin du Bellai*, and on the Title of the Prologues of the *Ogdoades*: But, if we consider the Running-title, and the particular Title, which is at the Head of each Book, we shall find, that the fifth, sixth, seventh, and eighth, Books belong to *William du Bellai*, and that the first, second, third, fourth, ninth, and tenth, belong to *Martin*. That, which belongs to *William*, is taken from the fifth *Ogdoade*, and reaches from the Year 1536, to the Year 1543 (19). The whole Work of *William* consisted of seven *Ogdoades*: but the first did not relate to *Francis* I; It treated of the Antiquities of the *Gauls* and *French*, &c. as I have already observed (20). The other six were designed for That Monarch's Reign. The ten Books, which remain, written partly by *William*, and partly by *Martin*, were printed at *Paris*, in the Year 1569, in Folio, by the care of *René du BELLAI*, Baron *de la Lande*, Son-in-law of *Martin*. Some quote an Edition of *Paris*, in *Folio*, in the Year 1572. I have seen one, which was printed off at *Paris*, the twentieth of *October* 1587, in Folio, by *Peter de Voirnir*, the King's Mathematical Printer, and was sold by *Peter de Fuilleur*. *Du Chesne*, in his *Bibliotheque* of the Writers of the History of *France* (21), says, that there is a *Geneva* Edition, in 8vo, 1594; but he says nothing of That of *Rochel*, 1573, in 8vo. *Hugh Surceu* translated This Book into *Latin*, and published it at *Frankfort*, in *Folio*, in the Year 1574. *Martin du Bellai* died at *Glatigni*, the ninth of *March*, 1559 (22). He had married *Isabella Chenue d'Yvetot*, and, by This Marriage, he became Prince of *Yvetot* (23).

[E] *What Judgment* Montaigne *passed on This Book.*] These are his Words (24). " It is always pleasant to " see things, written by those, who have experienced " how they ought to be managed; but it cannot be " denied, that a great want of That Freedom, and " Liberty, of writing is evidently discovered in Those " two Lords, which is conspicuous in the old *French* " Writers, as in the Sire *de Joinville*, Domestic " Servant of *St Lewis*, *Eginard* Chancellor of *Charlemagne*, and, of later Memory, in *Philip de Comines*. We have, here, rather a Plea for King " *Francis* against the Emperor *Charles* V, than an " History. I do not believe they have altered any " thing as to the main; but they make a Trade of " judging of Events, often against Reason, to our " Advantage, and of omitting all that is ticklish, in " the Life of their Master; witness the removal " of Messieurs *de Montmorency* and *Brion*, which is " here forgotten; nay, the very Name of Madam " *d'Estampes* is not to be found in it. Private " Actions may be concealed; but, to pass over in " Silence, what every Body knows, and Matters, " which have produced such public Effects, and " of such great Consequences, is an inexcusable " Fault. In short, to have a full Knowledge of " King *Francis*, and of the Things, which happened " in his Time, you must look elsewhere if you will " believe me. The Advantage, which may be " reaped from the reading of This History, consists " in the particular Account of the Battles, and Warlike Exploits, wherein These Gentlemen were " present, in some private Sayings, and Actions, of " some Princes of their Time, and in the Practices, " and Negotiations, conducted by the Sieur *de Langey*, where there are many things, which deserve " to be known, and Discourses, which are not " vulgar." If *Moreri* had read the Memoirs of these Gentlemen, one might very well say, that he knew but little how to judge of Books: for he says, the Stile of *William du Bellai* is *pompous, and magnificent; and such as Persons of Quality ought to write in*. First of all, it is certain, that the Stile of This Illustrious Person is not pompous and magnificent; it is incorrect; and it does not appear, that the Author took any pains about it; besides it is full of broken *Latin* Terms; which shews, that the Author does himself Justice, when he declares, that he had no regard to the Perfection of the Stile. In the second place, Persons of Quality do not write in a pompous Stile; It is not by this Character, that one may discover, whether an Author be a Person of Quality, or not: A professed Rhetorician, or preaching Monk, write an hundred times more pompously, than a Courtier.

[F] *The Prologue of his Ogdoades contains very important Pieces of Advice to Historians, and very solid Reflexions on the Indignities, offered to History.*] There never was more occasion to attend to This, than at present; but the worst of it is, that most of those, who are guilty of the Faults, censured by *William du Bellai*, do not commit them through Ignorance. It is Malice, Animosity, or the Desire of pleasing the People, and of getting Money by it, which engage Writers to falsify their Relations. Whatever may be the Cause of This Disorder, I shall set down a long Passage of This Author. He observes, very judiciously, That it is necessary, that They, who are acquainted with Affairs, be speedy in publishing Them; for, otherwise, it becomes too difficult to trace things back to their Original. " Slowness in History, *says* " *be* (25), is of so much the more dangerous Consequence, because the Lives of Mortals are short; " and, if nothing be committed to writing by those, " who know, and remember, the Affairs of their " Times, They, who come after, though they are " Masters of a good Stile, and use Diligence, cannot write with certainty, and agreeably to the " Truth. This we may, already, have observed in " some of the last preceeding Years, of which to " speak truly, and at large, is a difficult Matter, " partly through the Negligence, and partly through " the Rashness of the Historians themselves, who, " nevertheless, complain, that they have not Materials, worthy of their Studies, and Labour; but " they would have done better, both for themselves " and us, if they had written nothing, rather than " have published under the Title of an History, a " Parcel of fabulous and lying Stories, of which we " have, at this Day, a greater Plenty, than we " have of true Histories. I have read, in some Chronicle (which I believe some will think to be a " Dream) that a King of *France*, after Dinner, " chased a Stag from *Compiegne* to *Laudun*, which is " about 100 Leagues. Every one knows, that the " virtuous, and praise-worthy, Prince, *Charles*, Duke " of *Orleans*, after he had been thirty Years a Prisoner in *England*, for the Service of the Crown of " *France*, at last returned home, and died, loaded " with Years and Honour: yet we read, in more " than twenty Authors, that he was beheaded at " *Paris* for High-Treason. Did not the last King of " *Scotland* die in a Battle against the *English*, in the " Year 1514? and yet I have read, that he returned " Victorious, and Triumphant, into his own Kingdom. I avoid Prolixity, in recounting a great " Number of these Lies, which are certainly published only through the Rashness, Carelessness, and " Indiscretion, of Those Historians, and Writers of " Chronicles, who, oftentimes, deliver That for " certain, which they first heard, without having " any regard to the Credibility of the Person, who " related it to Them; or else by setting down what " is commonly reported among the People; which, " generally, has very little Truth in it: from whence " it proceeds, that Readers, who are better informed, are not very willing to believe other good " ancient Authors, thinking that they wrote after " the same manner. Thus, in another Case, Cardinal *Bessarion* (26), seeing so many new Saints canonized at *Rome*, whose Lives he knew, and did " not approve of; *These new Saints*, said he, *make " me very doubtful and scrupulous with respect to what " is said of the Ancient ones*. And I wish the Masters of Chronicles would be quiet, or else give " Names to their Books, answerable to the Contents, and that Those, who are able and willing " to speak the Truth, were so zealous for the Honour and Glory of their Country, as to write in their

BELLAI.

Discipline, is ascribed to *William du Bellai* [G]. I believe he is the Author of the other Works, which are ascribed to him [H]; but I do not think they were ever printed. I except *The Epitome of the Antiquities of Gaul*, which was printed, with some other small Pieces, in the Year 1556. *La Croix du Maine* assures us, that William

" their own Language, what they have seen, or
" heard, from credible Persons. Then the Men of
" Letters might enrich their Stile, and make it ele-
" gant, without the Trouble of searching the Truth
" amidst so many Lies, Contradictions, and Incon-
" sistencies, which are published by the said Writers
" of Chronicles, who foolishly depend upon the Hear-
" say of the first Person they meet with."

[G] *It is through a palpable Mistake, that a Book, concerning Military Discipline, is ascribed to* William du Bellai.] *Du Verdier* ascribes This Book absolutely to him; but *la Croix du Maine* gives us to understand, that he is not sure of it: He neither notes the Year, nor the Place, where it was printed, but says only, That *the Instruction of the Military Art is to be found printed under the Name of the said Sieur* de Langey. *Du Verdier* is more exact; he gives the Title in this Manner; *Instructions about War, extracted out of the Books of* Polybius, Frontinus, Vegetius, Cornazan, Machiavel, *and several other good Authors, by Mess.* William du Bellai, *&c. printed at Paris, 4to, and 8vo, by* Michael Vascosan, 1553. *Brantome was fully persuaded*, that the same Book had appeared under it's Author's own Name: " The Book, *says he* (27), which *Monsieur de Langey* wrote concer-
" ning the Military Art, shews him to be a better
" Captain, than That, which *Machiavel* wrote on
" That Subject, does him: It was a foolish thing
" for the latter, who did not know what War was,
" to compose a Book about it; just as if a Philoso-
" pher should write a Book of Hunting, as *le Fouil-
" lou* did." It is easy to prove, by the Book it-self, that *William du Bellai* is not the Author of it. The Author of the Work was but a *Gendarme* in the Company of the Sieur de Negrepelisse, in the Year 1528. He was at the Siege and taking of Trouja, under Monsieur de Lautrec: he retired to Barletta, a Town of Apulia, after he came out of Prison; for he had been taken Prisoner, when the Company, in which he served, was defeated, in the Retreat, which the Marquis *de Saluffes* made from before *Naples*. He says all these things himself in his Book: Now nothing of all this can agree with *William du Bellai*. He was a great Lord in the Year 1525, when the Queen Regent sent him into *Spain* to *Francis* I. He was, in 1527, one of those, who were present at the Judgment, given against *Monsieur de Bourbon* (28). The King sent him the same Year into *Italy*, with Money, to the Confederate Princes, and to promote the Interests of the League with Pope *Clement* VII. He was sent into *England* in the Year 1529, and 1533. He was, then, Gentleman of the King's Chamber. Being Governour of *Turin*, in the Year 1537, he was sent into *Germany* to demand a Diet, in which the Pretensions of the Emperor, and of the King of *France*, to the Duchy of *Milan*, might be discussed. He was not therefore commanded, the same Year, *in Quality of a Captain of a Company of Foot Soldiers, to assist the Sieur de* Roberval *in making himself Master of the Valleys of St* Martin, *and* Lucerne. Now the Author of the *Military Discipline* says, towards the end of the second Book, that he received such an Order: It is, therefore, most certain, that the Lord *de Langey* did not compose That Book. These are such demonstrative Reasons, that he, who makes use of them (29), does not think it necessary to add this; " If Mess. *William du
" Bellai* was the Author of it, he would not praise
" himself (30)' for having a perfect Knowledge of
" War, and Learning, nor call himself, speaking in
" the third Person, my Lord *of Langey* (31), as
" *Mumbrin Poseo* (32), an *Italian* Translator, and
" the last *French* Correctors, have very well obser-
" ved; Moreover, the *Sieur de* Langé, who forgets
" himself but little, or not at all, in his Memoirs,
" and who curiously quotes the Places, where he
" was, makes almost no mention of himself in all
" That Expedition, undertaken by *Monsieur de Lau-
" trec.*" Let us not be contented with knowing only, that This Work was ascribed to a Person, who was not the Author of it, but let us know the Reason of this Mistake, and the true Father's Name.

Raimond de Pavie, *Sieur de Forquevauls*, a Gentleman of *Gascogne*, is the Author of This Work. He communicated a Copy of it to *William du Bellai, as to his good Lord and Friend, and to whose Judgment he had first submitted it*. This Copy was found among the Papers of That Lord (33); This is the Origin of the Mistake. If the Author's Kinsmen had acquainted the Public with the Truth of This Fact, before *Naudé* published his *Syntagma de studiis militaribus* (34), it is probable, That *Syntagma* would not have retained the common Error, which we find in these Words: " *Qui* (Erricus Romus) *nunc in Tellica
" Valle sub Christianissimo Rege catarorum præfectus,
" idem omnino facit, quod quondam in Alpinis Peda-
" rinis* Guilielmus Bellajus Langæus, *eodem munere
" detungens, fecerat, cum is etiam libris de re militari,
" quos postea* Mambrinus Roseus Italicè, *& omnes
" terme populi sua lingua reddiderunt, ob summam
" ejusmodi librorum, qui ab expertis & celeberrimis
" nostra & patrum memoria ducibus conscripti fuerunt,
" utilitatem* (35). —— *W—* (Henry de Roban) *now
" Marshal de Camp in the* Vendôme, *under the most Chri-
" stian King, does the same, which was formerly done by*
" Bellai, *Lord of* Langey, *having published A Trea-
" tise of Military Affairs, which afterwards* Mam-
" brinus Roseus *translated into Italian, and all other
" Nations into their respective Languages, on account
" of the great Usefulness of such Kind of Books, which
" have been written, in our own and our Fathers Me-
" mories, by experienced and famous Generals.*" *Naudé* is moreover mistaken, in supposing, that the Books in question were printed during the Life of *William du Bellai.* He seems to value That Work much. His Judgment was therefore different from That of a Commentator on *Onosander*, of whom the Baron *de Forquevauls* complained in this manner: " This *Mi-
" litary Discourse* is indeed a necessary Work, and
" useful to those, who profess the Trade of War,
" and which will continue a long time esteemed, and
" prized, in the Hands of the most Understanding
" Men, in spite of the Slanders, and contrary Opi-
" nion, of a Modern Author, who, in his Annota-
" tions on the *Military Art of* Onosander, a *Greek*
" Writer, strives to despise one, with whom this Au-
" thor is not to be compared, in this Science, though
" he wrote more like a Doctor than a Soldier, du-
" ring the leisure, and idle Time, which the good
" Table, and the Amours of a certain Abbot with
" his Wife, afforded him (36), and though he has
" extracted his Commentaries from divers Authors,
" whereas the Text of him, whom I am speaking
" of, was conceived on Horseback, and written,
" *Sword in Hand*, by the Sieur *de Forquevauls* (37)." What was *la Croix du Maine* thinking of, when he said, That the Constable, *Anne de Montmorency*, passed for the Author of the Book in question (38)? Did he not know, that the Constable, was a Man of no Learning or Reading, and was not able to write? Let us see from whence his Doubt proceeded: " It
" is, *says* he, because, in reading that Book, I found,
" that the Author of it praises Messire *William du Bel-
" lai*, Lord of *Langey*, very much, and recommends
" him for his Learning and Skill in Wars which
" makes me believe, that he is not the Author of it,
" but that those Memoirs were found in his Library;
" without the Name of him, who wrote them, and
" that it was presupposed it was his own Work, be-
" cause he had promised to write some Memoirs. I
" do not assert, that he is the Author of them, nei-
" ther do I deny it." If he had read the Work well, he would have found stronger Proofs, than That, which he draws from the Praises given in it to *William du Bellai.*

[H] *I believe he is the Author of the other Works, which are ascribed to him.*] See the Catalogue of them in the *French Bibliotheques* of *la Croix du Maine*, and *du Verdier*. Some of the chief of them were, perhaps, never finished: It is probable, *la Croix du Maine* gave That for a perfect Work, which the Author only promises in the Prologue of the *Ogdoades*.

VOL. I.   8 U   [I] Le

BELLAI.

(t) La Croix du Maine. Biblioth. Franç. pag. 239.

William du Bellai was born about the Year 1498, at *Glatigni*, in *le Perche* (t). I believe he is mistaken, as to the Time [*I*].

[*I*] La Croix du Maine *assures us, that he was born, in* 1498, *at Glatigni* —— *I believe he is mistaken as to the Time.*] After having said, Page 139, that *William du Bellai was born in the Year* 1498, *or thereabouts*, he places his Death, in the following Page, on the ninth of *January*, 1543, at the Age of Forty seven *Years, or thereabouts.* Would a Man, ever so little exact, say so? Would he not place, either 1496, on one side, instead of 1498, or 45 on the other, instead of 43? But this is not the chief thing. Brantome observes, that *Langey died, not very old, and might have lived longer* (39). Can any one speak thus of a Man about Forty four Years of Age. Moreover, Cardinal *du Bellai* was Sixty eight Years of Age, when he died (40); now he died in 1560; he was, therefore, born in the Year 1492. It cannot, then, be said, that *William du Bellai* was born in the Year 1498; for he was older than his Brother, the Cardinal (41). I have just now discovered, that he died in his Climacterical Year. *Rabelais* observes it, in the Twenty first Chapter of his third Book, after having said, that he died the tenth of *January* 1543. The Author of the Remarks on the *Confession of Sanci* gave me notice of this Passage.

(39) Brantome's Illustrious Frenchmen, Tom. I, pag. 384.

(40) Teissier, Additions to Thuanus, Tom. I, pag. 184.

(41) Sammarth. in Eulog.

BELLAI (JOHN *du*), younger Brother of the foregoing, was a Man of great Merit. He concurred, with his elder Brother, in favouring the Passions of *Henry* VIII, and decoying the Protestants of *Germany*, in order to serve *Francis* I, whose Affairs required, that a Quarrel should, at any rate, be fomented between the Emperor, and *England*, by the Divorce of *Catherine* of *Arragon*, and that the Confederates of *Smalcalde* should be amused with Lies, about the pretended Inclination of *Francis* I, to give the *Lutherans* some Satisfaction. This Conduct would have been more inexcusable in *John du Bellai*, who was a Bishop, than in his Brother *William*, who was a Lay-man; I say it would have been more inexcusable, if That Bishop had not been also an Embassador, and a Statesman (a). The Definition of Persons, invested with That Character, is well known. Let us add, that it is not unlikely, that *John du Bellai* had a sincere Desire, and even some Hopes, of a Reformation, and that, upon this Prospect, he sincerely encouraged *Melancthon* to come into *France*; for he inclined, for some time, towards *Lutheranism*, and even reformed himself privately as to the Article of Celibacy, by a Marriage of Conscience, which he contracted [*A*]. He was Bishop of *Paris*, when, in 1534, he was sent to *Rome* to soften Matters, in relation to the King of *England*; but he had no good Success, and could not hinder the Pope from fulminating an Excommunication against *Henry* VIII. He was promoted to the Cardinalship, by Pope *Paul* III, in the Year 1535, and died, in 1560, at *Rome*, where he had retired, after the Death of *Francis* I. He was a Man, who would willingly have quitted the Mitre, and Crosier, to take the Helmet, and Sword [*B*]. If it be true, that he condemned

(a) He was Bishop of Baionne, in the Year 1532, when Francis I. sent him Embassador into England.

[*A*] *He reformed himself privately, as to the Article of Celibacy, by a Marriage of Conscience.*] *Brantome* affirms it, in this manner; " I have heard a " Lady of great and ancient Quality say, That the " late Cardinal *du Bellai*, being Bishop and Cardinal, " had married Madame *de Chatillon*, and died married; this she said, discoursing with Monsieur *de Manne*, of *Provence*, of the Family of *Seulal*, and Bishop of *Frejus*, who had attended the said Cardinal fifteen Years at the Court of *Rome*, and had been one of his private Protonotaries; and, happening to speak of the said Cardinal, she asked him, Whether he had never told, and confessed to him, that he was married? Monsieur *de Manne* was much surprized at this Question. He is yet living, and can tell whether I assert a Lye; for I was there. He answered, That he had never heard him, or others, say so. Well then, I tell you so, replied she; for there is nothing more true, than that he was married, and died really married to the said Lady *Chatillon* (1)." This Lady was the Widow of Mons. *de Chatillon*, who was wounded before *Ravenna*, and who died of his Wounds at *Ferrara* (2). He had been in great Credit in the Reign of *Charles* VIII. His Widow, young and fair, was chosen Lady of Honour to the Queen of *Navarre*, and gave her the good Advice which That Queen mentioned in her *Hundred Novels*. Admiral *de Bonivet* crept into This Princess's Bed through a Trap-Door, but he got nothing there but a scratched Face (3). The Queen would have complained of this Attempt to her Brother *Francis* I, if the Lady *Chatillon* had not given her " This good Advice, which is one of the finest " and wisest, and the most proper to avoid Scandal, " that could have been given, even by a first President " of *Paris*; and which shewed, nevertheless, that the " Lady was as Cunning and Crafty in such Mysteries, " as Wise and Discreet; and therefore it is not to " be doubted, that she kept her Marriage with the " Cardinal very private. —— I believe, that the " Cardinal, her said Husband, who was one of the most Learned, Eloquent, Wise, and Prudent, Men " of his Time, had taught her to speak so well, and " give such good Advice. —— I think, the said " Cardinal *du Bellai* might have done it; for, at that " time, he inclined much to *Luther's* Doctrine and " Religion (5)."

[*B*] *He would have quitted the Mitre and Crosier to take the Helmet and the Sword.*] *Brantome* shall be my Witness again. He says, that, when *Charles* V so haughtily braved the King of *France*, at *Rome*, it was a Misfortune for *Francis* I, not to have any Embassadors there, that were Swords-men (6). " And " yet, had it not been, *continues he*, for Cardinal " *du Bellai*, who was as quick, and hasty, as any " Military Man, (and indeed he looked like one; for " he was qualified for any thing, and one of the " greatest Men, both for Learning, and War) things " had not gone well there, and the King had been " much disgraced. Which makes me think, that " there never were any Gown-men, who deserved " more to be Embassadors on all Occasions, than This " Cardinal (as he has demonstrated in many Embassies, before he was a Cardinal, in *Italy*, *Germany*, and *England*), and the Bishop of *Dax*, of the House of *Nouailles*, in *Limosin*, who served our Kings worthily in That Station, in *England*, and at *Venice* (where I have seen him), and afterwards at *Constantinople*. I will not wrong many other worthy Persons of their Character, whom I have seen in such a Station; but, in my Opinion, Cardinal *du Bellai*, and the Bishop of *Dax*, have surpassed them all; for they could as well have made use of their Swords, as of their eloquent Tongues: And, indeed, an Embassador is as often obliged to treat of Affairs relating to War, as of State Matters." *Thuanus* (7) and *Sammarthanus* (8) have observed, that This Cardinal removed the Fear of the *Parisians*, who were in dread of *Charles* the Fifth's Army, and that he prepared all things for a vigorous Defence, having caused the City to be fortified. *Moreri* has said the same, but with little Exactness;

(1) Brantome's Lives of the Gallant Ladies, Tom II, pag. 153.

(2) Idem, pag. 154.

(3) Ibid, pag. 155.

(4) Ibid.

(5) Idem, pag. 156.

(6) Id Eloge of Francis I, of Tom. I, of his Memoirs, pag. 246.

(7) Thuanus Histor. lib. 26, p. 538.

(8) Sammarth. in Eulog. pag. 13.

BELLAI. BELLARMIN.

condemned *Anne du Bourg* [C] to be burnt, his Vote muſt have been given at a Diſtance; for he was at *Rome*, when the Trial of *Anne du Bourg* was ſet on foot.

Exactneſs: He will have it, that *John du Bellai* did theſe things, when *Charles* V. entered into *Provence*, in 1537, and that the King, quitting his Capital, left This Cardinal there, and made *him his Lieutenant-General, to provide for the Security of* Picardy, *and* Champagne. Here are two Miſtakes: The Irruption of *Charles* V into *Provence* happened in the Year 1536; That, which put the *Pariſians* in fear, and occaſioned him to order their City to be fortified, happened likewiſe in the Year 1536 (9); but it concerned *Picardy*, and not *Provence*. It is That, which *Charles* V cauſed to be made by the Count of *Naſſau*. *Thuanus* (10) refers the Care of Cardinal *du Bellai*, for the City of *Paris*, only to the Invaſion of *Champagne*, in the Year 1544. But he is miſtaken.

(9) Mezerai, Abridg. Chron. ad Ann. 1536.
[10] Thuan. ubi ſupra.

[C] *It has been ſaid, that he condemned* Anne du Bourg.] This is to be found in Mr *Teiſſier*. Many blamed him, ſays he (11), *for being the firſt, who condemned* Anne du Bourg *to be burnt alive; for which Reaſon, ſay they*, GOD *took him out of this World, forty Days after the Execution of This Illuſtrious Martyr*. The Calculation would not be right, according to the Annals of *Spondanus*, who places This Cardinal's Death on the ſixteenth of *February* 1560 (12); for we find, elſewhere, that *du Bourg* was executed the Twenty third of *December* 1559 (13). The Author, whom Mr *Teiſſier* quotes, ſays, that This Cardinal died the ſixteenth of *February*, and fifty Days after *du Bourg*. His Calculation is leſs remote from the Truth, than That, which Mr *Teiſſier* imputes to him; neverthelſs, it is not exact; and therefore This Obſervation is chimerical.

(11) Additon to the Elogies, Tom. I, pag. 1·4. He quotes Contiuat. Sleid. per Michael Lunpórd. lib. 2. He ought to have ſaid Lundorpium.
(12) Spond. Annal. ad Ann. 1560, n. 34.
(13) Bezs, Hiſt. Ecclef. lib. 3. pag. 248.

BELLARMIN (ROBERT), an *Italian* Jeſuit, was the beſt Writer of his Times, in Matters of Controverſy. He was born at *Monte Pulciano* (a), in the Year 1542, and admitted among the Jeſuits in the Year 1560. His Mother, *Cynthia Cervini*, was Siſter of Pope *Marcellus* II. He was ordained Prieſt, at *Ghent*, by *Cornelius Janſenius*, in 1569, and, the Year following, he taught Divinity at *Louvain*. He was the firſt Jeſuit, who taught this Science in That famous Univerſity, and he did it with extraordinary Succeſs. Having lived ſeven Years in the *Netherlands*, he returned into *Italy*, and, in 1576, he began to read Lectures on Controverſy, at *Rome*; which no Jeſuit had yet done in That City. He acquitted himſelf ſo well, that *Sixtus* V, ſending a Legate into *France*, in the Year 1590, gave him *Robert Bellarmin*, as a Divine, who might be very uſeful, if any Diſpute about Religion ſhould happen to be diſcuſſed. He returned to *Rome*, ten Months after, and was ſucceſsfully promoted to ſeveral Offices, either in the Society, or at the Pope's Court, till, in the Year 1599, he was honoured with the Cardinal's Hat. It is ſaid, that they were forced to threaten him with an *Anathema*, to make him accept of That Dignity. Three Years after, the Archbiſhopric of *Capua* was given him, which he reſigned, when, in the Year 1605, the new Pope (b) would have him near his Perſon. He was employed in the Affairs of the Court of *Rome*, till 1621. Then he left the *Vatican*, and retired to a Houſe of his Order, where he died, the ſeventeenth of *September*, in the ſame Year 1621. In his laſt Sickneſs, he was viſited by Pope *Gregory* XV, whom he entertained with the Compliment of the *Centurion* [A], *Lord, I am not worthy, that thou ſhouldeſt come under my Roof*. He charged the Jeſuit *Eudemon-Johannes* to teſtify publickly, that he died in the ſame Faith, which he always profeſſed, and maintained with his Pen (c). It appears, that, on the Day of his Funeral, he was looked upon as a Saint [B]. It is certain, that no Jeſuit did more Honour to his Order, than He, and that no Author maintained the Cauſe of the Church of *Rome*, in general, and That of the Pope in particular, better than He. The Proteſtants knew it very well [C]; for moſt of their learned Divines wrote
against

(a) *A Town of* Tuſcany.

(b) *To wit*, Paul V.

(c) *Taken from the* Bibliotheque, *compoſed by* Alegambus.

[A] *He entertained Pope* Gregory XV *with the Compliment of the Centurion.*] Suppoſing, as he did, that the Pope is the Vicar of the Son of GOD, he did not ſee, in the Application of this Paſſage, all the Prophanation, which others ſee in it; and, perhaps, he thought he ſaid nothing but what was very pious. *Alegambus* relates This as a fine Circumſtance of *Bellarmin's* laſt Hours. " Inviſit eum decumbentem Gregorius XV Pontifex Max. ac bis per-" amanter amplexus ſacrum ſe pro ejus valetudine " facturum promiſit. Ipſe Chriſti Vicarium obſe-" quioſiſſime reveritus uſurpavit illud Centurionis, " *Domine, non ſum dignus ut intres ſub tectum me-* " *um* (1). ---- *Pope* Gregory XV *viſited him, as* " *he lay ſick, and, twice embracing him very lovingly,* " *promiſed him, he would pray for his Health.* Bellar-" min, *out of profound Reſpect to the Vicar of* " CHRIST, *addreſſed him in the Words of the Cen-* " *turion*, Lord, I am not worthy, that thou ſhouldeſt " come under my Roof." The *Spaniſh* Embaſſador, who made uſe of the ſame Words of the Centurion to a Prince, whom he looked upon as an Heretic, cannot be ſo eaſily excuſed. *Balzac*, who alledges this Example to his Cenſor, blames it at the ſame time. " What would he have ſaid of the Compli-" ment of That *Spaniſh* Embaſſador in *England*, who " received a Viſit of King *James*, with theſe Words " of the Maſs: *Domine, non ſum dignus ut intres ſub* " *tectum meum* (2)?"

(1) Alegambus, Biblioth. Script. Societ. Jeſu, pag. 409.

(2) Diſcours I, *to Cardinal* Bentivoglio, *in the ſequel of the Chriſtian* Socrates, pag. 442, 443.

[B] *It appears that, on the Day of his Funeral, he was looked upon as a Saint.*] The *Swiſs* of the Pope's Guard were poſted round the Coffin, to keep off the Crowd, who endeavoured to throw themſelves on the Corps, to touch and kiſs it. All that he had made uſe of, was taken away, and diſtributed to thoſe, who deſired to have Relics of Them for devout Purpoſes. " Adverſus undam populi concur-" ſantis ad oſculum tactumque ſacri pignoris adhi-" bere oportuit Helvetios è ſtipatoribus Pontificiis. " ------ Quicquid rerum in uſu habuit raptum di-" ſtractumque in poſtulantes eſt ad venerationem (3)." When *Bellarmin* reſigned his Archbiſhopric of *Capua*, the whole City was greatly afflicted at it: Some kiſſed his Garment; others rubbed their *Roſaries* devoutly againſt it; and every one preſſed for his Bleſſing (4). Theſe are Preludes of Worſhip, which may, in time, be followed by a Canonization in Form. It is pretended, that he foretold ſome things, and wrought ſome Miracles (5); and, becauſe, after his Death, the Odour of his Sanctity was rather increaſed than diminiſhed, the Congregation of the Rites was ordered, a-new, in the Year 1674, to proceed to the neceſſary Informations concerning his Life, and Miracles, to the end, that, if there be occaſion, he may be beatified (6).

(3) Alegambus, Biblioth. Script. Soc. Jeſu, pag. 409.

(4) Alegambus, ibid.

(5) Idem, pag. 410.

(6) Sotuel, in Bibliotheca Scriptor. Societ. Jeſu, pag. 722.

[C] *No Author maintained the Cauſe of the Church of* Rome *better than He. ----- The Proteſtants knew it very well.*] " They grant, that he
" is

BELLARMIN.

against him for the Space of forty or fifty Years. Their Professors, Lectures, and Theses, made his Name resound every where; *Ut litius Hyla, Hyla omne sonaret (d)*. He was atacked on all Sides, and his Adversaries did not forget to examine, whether he had not contradicted, and afforded Weapons against, himself [*D*]. It is the Subject of a Book, which must needs have perplexed him not a little. There are some indiscreet and rash Men to be found every where; and therefore it is no wonder, if some Protestant Writers have published Falshoods against *Bellarmin*, of which his Party took Advantage [*E*]. There is no great Inconvenience in this, when unknown Writers

(d) Virgil. Eclog. 6, ver. 44.

"is the most subtle Enemy of the Truth, that has hitherto undertaken to oppose it: That *Demetrius*, the Silver-smith, spoken of in the nineteenth of the *Acts of the Apostles*, did not use so much Art in working his little Silver Shrines of *Diana*, as this cunning Artisan of Error did, in re-building the Palaces, and Altars, of Superstition: Which has given occasion to compare him to That *Marcion*, of whom *Tertullian* says, that, Dedecus suum ingenio obumbrat, qui cum causa ubique ferè pessimas tueatur & impiorum dogmatum patrocinio verissimum se Satanæ atque Antichristi satellitem præbeat, agit tamen ingenio, ut speciosis coloribus inducat omnia, & distinctionum præstigiis, & umbris, eludat ea quæ solidissimâ veritate constituta sunt (7). —— He has the Address to disguise the badness of his Cause; and, though he generally undertakes to defend the worst, and, by patronizing impious Tenets, shews himself a true Minister of *Satan*, and Antichrist, yet he has the Art of giving a specious Turn to every thing, and, by subtle Distinctions, of eluding what is built upon the strongest Reason." Be sure not to believe what *Alegambus* says, viz. That *Beza* owned, that *Bellarmin* had overthrown all the Protestant Authors. *Nec ipsi hujus causâ sunt dissiteri, ex quibus Theodorus Beza, unus hic liber, ajebat, nos omnes hum. proturbat* (8). It is a Jest to alledge such things, without quoting the Book, where they are to be found. On such Occasions, the very Line, or, at least, the Page, ought to be quoted, otherwise every one will take such an Assertion for an ill-grounded Hear-say. I am fully persuaded, that *Beza* had not such a good Opinion of *Bellarmin*, and that, if he had, he would never have owned it. *Alegambus* says another thing, the Falshood whereof is not so obvious; which is, That a new Lecture was founded at *Cambridge* and *Oxford*, to confute *Bellarmin*. " In Angliæ Academia Cantabrigiensi primum, mox etiam in Oxoniensi, nova prælectio instituta est, ad controver- " sias Bellarmini, si possent, resellendas (9)."

[*D*] *It has been examined, whether he has not contradicted himself*.] A Minister of *Lithuania*, whose Name was *Andrew Crastovius*, composed a Work intituled, *Bellum Jesuiticum* (10), in which he objects to the Jesuits Two hundred and five Contradictions. Sometimes *Bellarmin* does not agree with the other Jesuits, but most frequently *Bellarmin* confutes himself, in That Book.

I have said elsewhere (11), that he was reproached with having made use of, and opposed, the same Principles, according as he was to dispute either against the Protestants, or against the Enthusiasts. Here are some Particulars concerning that sort of Contradiction. " Some, being willing to excuse *Bellarmin's* Contradictions, and want of Memory, have said, that the great number of Persons, who had a Hand in the Fabrick of This Work, I mean, of his Writings, like the Builders of *Babel*, introduced this Confusion, for want of Understanding one another: But Those of his Communion are so far from taking this for an Excuse, that they reject it, as injurious to him: *Fuligati*, who wrote his Life, says, that he never employed an *Amanuensis*. —— I believe, the true Cause of *Bellarmin's* Contradictions, is, that the present necessity of attacking, or defending, is a more powerful Object, than any other; he cared but little, whether he was consistent with himself, or not, provided none should believe, that he agreed with his Adversaries (12). —— *Bellarmin* has often verified This Observation in his Books of Controversy; When he disputes against the *Libertines* and the *Schwenckfeldians*, about the necessity of the Scripture, he speaks like a Protestant. And, when he disputes against the Protestants, on the same Subject, he argues like a *Schwenckfeldian*. If he

(7) Ancillon's Critical Miscellanies of Literature, Tom. I, pag. 348. See also Whitaker, in the Preface to his Treatise de Scripturâ.

(8) Alegamb. Bibl. Soc. Jesu, pag. 411.

(9) Id. Ibid.

(10) It is a Book in 4to, of 161 pages, printed at Basil, in the Year 1594.

(11) In Remark [B], of the Article ANTONY (MARC), *the Orator. Citat. (7).*

(12) Ancillon's Critical Miscellanies of Literature, Tom. I, pag. 352.

"undertakes to confute the *Pelagians* about the Perfection of Works, he makes use of all the Arguments of those, whom he calls *Calvinists*: If he has to do with the *Calvinists*, he makes use of the Reasons and Distinctions of the *Pelagians*. If he writes against the *Anabaptists* concerning the Baptism of Children, he proves it by the Scripture: If he disputes with Us about Tradition, the Baptism of Children is one of the Points, which seems to him to prove the necessity of it, and of which the Scripture does not speak after a convincing manner, as he says. This puts me in mind of the Comparison, which I have seen somewhere, of *Bellarmin* with a certain *African*, whose Name was *Leo*, whom he himself compares to That Amphibious Bird of *Æsop*, who was sometimes a Bird, and sometimes a Fish; a Bird, when the King of Fishes exacted a Tribute; and a Fish, when the King of Birds exacted it. Ut Leo quidam Africanus in Granatensi Regno natus, & postquam subjugatum est illud Regnum, in Africam profugus, de se fatetur, si Afros vitio aliquo notari sentio, me Granatæ natum profiteor; si Granatenses malè audiant, mox Afer sum; Bellarminus certè multò quàm ille elgantius aviculam illam imitatur, qui nimirùm respondet, Tom. I. Controv. l. 1. c. 7. Patres secutos esse septuaginta Interpretum Editionem; Idem. Tom. I. Controv. l. 1. c. 20. de 3. Esdræ agens, ait Patres secutos esse Hebræos, & tamen illud alterum, notate, quanta vi verborum efferat. Negari (inquit) non potest. Ipse tamen id ipsum loco posteriori negat (13). —— Thus *One Leo Africanus, born in the Kingdom of Granada, but who, upon the Reduction of That Kingdom, fled into Africa, confesses of himself*; *If I hear the Africans charged with any particular Vice, I profess myself a Native of Granada*; *if the People of Granada are reproached, presently I am an African*. *Bellarmin certainly imitates That Bird with more Elegance, than He*; *when he replies, Tom. I Controv. l. 1. cap. 7. that the Fathers followed the Edition of the Septuagint*; *whereas, Tom. I. Controv. l. 1. c. 20. treating of the third Chapter of* Esdras, *he says, the Fathers followed the Hebrew*: *and yet observe how strongly he asserts the former*; *It cannot be denied, says he: yet he himself denies it in the latter Place*."

[*E*] *The Protestant Writers published Falshoods against* Bellarmin, *of which his Party took Advantage*.] The Jesuit *John Argentus* makes mention, in the Apology of his Order, of four Libels newly come out against the Society, the third of which is levelled directly against *Bellarmin*, and relates many things, which had caused, attended, or followed, his Death. Nevertheless, This Cardinal was yet living. Doubtless, *Theophilus Raynaud* meant This Libel, when he said, that, Twenty five Years before (14), a Book was published in *Germany*, wherein *Bellarmin* was accused of having killed many Children, to hide his Incontinence (15). It was said, moreover, that the Cardinal, being at last moved to Repentance, had gone to *our Lady of Loretto*, to see whether he could expiate his Crimes; but that the Priest, to whom he had confessed them, was seized with so much Horror, that he commanded him to be gone; which shews *Bellarmin* into a Despair, of which he died soon after. This is the Substance of That Libel. *Bellarmin* read it, and laughed at it. Doubtless, he made many Reflexions on the Book, which asserted his Death. *Theophilus Raynaud* thought, that Father *Gretser* had given himself a needless Trouble in refuting these kind of Stories, and that they did great Prejudice to the Protestants (16); for one might learn from thence what Judgment was to be made of the pretended Letter of St *Udalric*, which says, that Six thousand Children's Heads were found in the Wells of Pope *Gregory* II, after

(13) Id. Ib. pag. 354.

(14) This Collection does not agree with the Year 1610, the Date of the Raynaud's Book, and with what there Jesuit says, that Bellarmin laughed at That Label.

(15) Th. Raynaud's Hoplotheca, §. 2, Serie 166, 167.

(16) It appears from the Bibliotheca of Alegambus, that Gretser published Vindiciæ pro Cardinalis Bellarmini criminationibus & insectis Lutherani Magisterii Ernesti Zephirii, Ingolstadii, 1611, and Congratulatio Bellii famosi adversùs illustr. Cardinalem Bellarminum, transslated into High Dutch, by Father Conrad Vetter, 1615.

BELLARMIN.

Writers commit this Fault; but, when Professors of Reputation impute to This Cardinal what he never taught, they injure their Cause, and expose themselves to great Mortifications. A Professor of *Sedan*, who has been very much talked of in *Holland*, is guilty of this Fault. It is remarkable, that *Bellarmin* did not follow the Doctrine

NECES-
SARY Qua-
lifications
for a good
Jesuit.

after he had driven away the Priests Wives. "Hæ-
"reticis, vel ad unam horam vagum mendacium,
"in lucro ponitur. Revera tamen ex hoc menda-
"cio deceffit illis haud exiguum. Siquidem inde
"deprehensum eft, qua fide ex horum mendaciloquo-
"rum majoribus quispiam, ex commentitia S. Udal-
"rici Epiftola, fex millia capitum infantilium, intra
"puteum Gregorii fecundi, cùm is uxores facerdo-
"tibus abftuliffet, reperta dixerit. Non eft enim
"ovum ovo fimilius, quàm hoc de Bellarmini infan-
"ticidiis fcriptum, & illa S. Udalrici Epiftola de cæ-
"dibus per Clericos & Sacerdotes fcortatores, adver-
"fus quam fubdititiam S. Antiftitis Epiftolam, & ipfe
"Bellarminus l. de Cleric. cap. 22. & Baronius anno
"591. aliique certarunt." It is no ways neceffary, that the Falfities, publifhed againft *Bellarmin*, fhould have a retroactive Effect on the Story of the Six thoufand Childrens Heads; but it is certain, that no better Service can be done to the Jefuits, and in general to any Party, which one undertakes to defame, than to publifh Calumnies, which may eafily be confuted. It is worthy of Obfervation, that, among fo many Perfons, poffeffed with an unconquerable Itch of publifhing Satires, fo few have the Art of poifoning them as they ought. Moft of Thofe, who attempt it, are ignorant, that, in order to fucceed well in it, that is, to direct the Blow right, a Man muft religioufly obferve thefe two things: One is, to advance nothing but what may be proved; and, above all, to abftain from Accufations, which may eafily be confuted: The other is, not to maintain obftinately what has been once confuted. I had forgot a third Advice, which is, carefully to diffemble one's Paffion, and to hide the Appearances of it. I own, that a Man, who acts quite contrary to thefe Rules, finds but too many Perfons, in his Party, who greedily fwallow down all that he fays; but it is This very thing, which does a great Prejudice to their Caufe; becaufe the other Party grows angry, and looks upon their Adverfaries, from whom fo many Satires, fo greedily fwallowed, proceed, as Men deftitute of Reafon, Equity, and the Affiftance of Grace. Thefe are not Reflexions at random, but grounded upon Experience. See how Father *le Tellier* takes advantage of fome Stories, which are fpread abroad without knowing whether they be true or falfe. Read what follows:
"For Example: What will it avail the Jefuits of
"*China* to have been the firft, and almoft the only
"Perfons, who fubmitted, and without the leaft Re-
"fiftance, to the Apoftolical Vicars, as foon as they
"appeared there in 1684; fince, notwithftanding
"this, their Enemies publifhed again, in the laft Sum-
"mer, by the Pen of their Secretary, the Gazetteer
"of *Holland*, that the Holy Father was extreamly
"angry with the Jefuits, becaufe they would not
"acknowledge the Bifhops, whom he fent to *China*?
"Can it be queftioned, but that, fome Years hence,
"This Lye will appear again in it's turn on the
"Stage? Likewife, what will it avail the Jefuits of
"*Germany* to have an Atteftation, figned by four of
"the Elector *Palatin's* chief Counfellors, all Prote-
"ftants, wherein they teftify, that the Hiftory of
"the Jefuit, counterfeiting a Voice from Heaven,
"to deceive That Prince, and to animate him to
"the Deftruction of Herefy, is a meer Fable? Will
"this Atteftation hinder fome good Proteftants,
"who fhall continue the Jefuitical Hiftory, from
"making, fome time or other, a Chapter about
"This chimerical Adventure, on the Credit of the
"Gazetteer of *Holland* (17)?"

Is it not ftrange, that the Author of the *Religion of the Jefuits* had rather follow his blind Paffion, than make a good ufe of this Paffage of Father *le Tellier*? So far from it, that he brought the Apparition of the *Palatinate* again on the Stage; and omitted nothing to make his Readers reject the Atteftation of the Elector *Palatin's* Proteftant Counfellors (18). I have it from very good Hands, that he blamed the Minifter a Refugee, who inferted This Atteftation in his Abridged Hiftory of *Europe* (19). Such Perfons fpoil the Trade, they take in hand. They

(17) A Defence of the new Chriftians, *Part I*, *§ 19.* 29. *Edit. of Paris*, 1687.

(18) The Religion of the Jesuits, printed at the Hague, 1610, pag. 77. See Remark *(P)*, of the Article LOYOLA.

(19) Month of August, 1696, pag. 260.

fhould leave Satire to moderate Writers, who would compofe them in a more dexterous and perfuafive Manner.

[F] *A Profeffor of* Sedan —— *is guilty of this Fault.*] He maintained fome Thefes, in the Year 1674. concerning the Power of the Keys, and charged Cardinal *Bellarmin* with having faid, " That a contrite Man, full of Faith, and defirous to be reconciled with GOD, perifhes eternally, except he can get a Prieft to reconcile him before Death. WHICH I NEVER READ, *added he,* WITHOUT ASTONISHMENT AND INDIGNATION (20)." This implies, that he had often read thefe words in *Bellarmin*; and yet they are not to be found in That Author. The Guardian of the *Irifh Capuchins* (21) difputed againft thefe *Thefes*, and complained, at firft, very vehemently of the wrong, which was done to *Bellarmin*. He continued the Difpute with the fame violence, and confounded the Profeffor. This was not all. When the Difpute was ended, the King's Attorney *prefented his Petition againft the faid* Profeffor for (22); the Confequence of which was, that the Author of the *Thefes* made his Recantation in Writing, which was figned by him, and three other Minifters. No one has any reafon to think it ftrange, that fuch an Accident fhould be mentioned in a Dictionary of this Kind; for it would avail nothing, for the future, to be filent about it. And, though I fhould have the Difcretion not to fay any thing of it, it would not be lefs known in *Holland*, where the *Journal of the Learned* is in every Body's Hand. Four Years ago, every one might have read, there, the Subftance of what I have juft now related; and befides, that *the Authentic Proofs of Mr* Jurieu's *Recantation*, (for it was he, who compofed, and maintained, thefe *Thefes*) *are three Certificates* produced by the *A*bbot *de Cordemoi*; one was made *by the King's Attorney at Sedan, the other by the Count* de la Bourlie, *Governour of the fame City,* and the laft by Father *Nicolas d' Hibernie, A Capuchin* (23). I have read thefe three Certificates, in the Book of the Abbot *de Cordemoi*; they are dated in the Year 1689. It may eafily be imagined, that this Difgrace afflicted thofe of the Proteftant Religion, and pleafed the *Roman* Catholics.

It is againft my Will, that I am forced to make an Addition to this Remark, in This Edition; but Mr *Jurieu* having publifhed fomething very outrageous againft me on this Subject, it will be proper to produce, here, both his Words, and my Reply. "The "great blank, which remains in the laft Pages of this "Sheet, is a Temptation to me, which I cannot "refift, to alledge a notable Example of the Trifles, "and the Malignity, which This Book is faid to be "full of. The Cafe is this: Mr *Jurieu*, in a public "and printed Difpute, quoted a Paffage out of *Bellarmin*, wherein through the Slip of the Author's "Pen, or the Printer's Miftake, inftead of *attritus*, "there was *contritus*; which made *Bellarmin* fay, "That a Man, weeping, penitent, and *contrite*, was "damned, if he did not receive the Sacerdotal Abfolution: Whereas *Bellarmin* faid, that a Man, "grievoufly bemoaning his Sins, through a Senfe "*of Attrition*, was damned, if he did not receive "the Church's Abfolution. This moved a Monk to "make a great Clamour, Mr *Jurieu*, in a Time of "Perfecution, granted him, what he would have "granted him any where elfe, even in a Country, "where the Proteftant Religion had been the prevailing Religion: that is, he acknowledged, that "there was a Fault in the printed Copy, proceeding "either from the Author's Hand, or from the Printer, and that *Bellarmin's* Opinion was fuch as the "Monk faid. Any fincere Perfon would have owned "as much in *Amfterdam*, or *London*. Is this a Story, "which, after having been printed in feveral Satires, "deferved to pafs, through a third and fourth Impreffion, into a Book, which was defigned for Immortality? Can any thing be more mean, or pitiful? There is therefore both Malice, and Meannefs, in it (24)." Thefe are Mr *Jurieu's* Words; and, in the following manner, I confuted them. "I find,

(20) Thefes de poteftate clavium, p. 21, cited by the Abbot de Cordemoi, Letter to the New Catholics, p. 117.

(21) Hermand called Father Robert.

(22) Certificate of the Sieur Rambour, the King's Attorney at Sedan, cited by the Abbot de Cordemoi, ubi fupra, p. 128.

(23) In the Abftract of a Letter from the Abbot de Cordemoi to the Catholics of the Diocefe of Arquert, in *Xaintonge*, printed in the Journal of the 24th of April, 1690, pag. 277, Edition of Amfterdam.

(24) Jurieu's Judgment of the Publick on the Critical Dictionary, p. 46, 47.

"find, that *Bellarmin*'s Bufinefs fticks in his Sto-
"mach: I do not wonder at it; but Prudence fhould
"not have fuffered him to make an Addition of it
"at the end of his Work. Silence had been beft.
"The lefs certain things are ftirred, the lefs they
"are troublefome. What I have faid of That Affair
"is no Example of *Trifling and Malignity*. Without
"it, I fhould have ill performed the Duty of an Hi-
"ftorian; fince the Original Defign of my Work
"was to obferve the falfe Accufations, to which the
"Perfons, of whom I was to fpeak, may have been
"expofed. If I had omitted This in the Article of
"*Bellarmin*, might it not have been juftly faid, that
"I was Partial, and that I omitted Things, which I
"could not preted to be ignorant of? I borrowed it,
"not from a Satirical Book, as he falfely fays; but
"from a Book of Controverfy, and from the *Jour-
"nal of the Learned*. I do not examine the Turn,
"which he takes, to cover his Fault; I only defire
"my Readers to have recourfe to my Dictionary, in
"order to compare the Pieces, which are produced
"there, with his Reflexions. By this Comparifon it
"will appear, how much Nature fuffers in him,
"when he is obliged to perform fome Act of Hu-
"mility, and Sincerity. I am not furprized at it;
"for, when a Bow has been always bent one way,
"it is very difficult to bend it the contrary way, at
"the firft undertaking. It is the fame thing with
"the Fibres of our Brains (25)."

(25) Refle-
xions on a
Pamphlet,
entituled,
*Judgment of
the Public*,
&c. pag. 15.

Moft of my Friends thought, that I had too much
neglected to make ufe of my Advantages: *Opportunities*, fay They, *have not failed you, but you have
been wanting to Them*; *and a Man ought to avoid
this Reproach, in a Paper War, no lefs, than in a
true War*. Why did you not fully expofe This Author's *Subterfuges*? Could you not have confounded
him by fuch and fuch *Reflexions*? I excufed myfelf
with the moft proper means to put an end to this
Difcourfe; which was by faying, that fuch Obfervations fhould not be fquandered away in a loofe Sheet;
and that it was better to referve them for another
Edition of my Dictionary. I have confidered the
matter, fince, more than once, and have found,
that the beft way is to leave my Readers to reflect on
this little Incident. It will not be difficult for them
to compare all the Pieces of This Procefs together,
nor to difcover, in Mr *Jurieu*'s Apology, the grimaces, and contortions, of a Man, who fuffers the
rack. After all, it belongs to the Abbot *de Cordemoi*
to refute This Apology. It is my Bufinefs, rather
to be the Hiftorian, than the Author, of the Reflexions, which This Quarrel may afford.

[G] *Bellarmin did not follow the Doctrine of the
Jefuits concerning Predeftination*] He was a good
Thomift, and no ways a *Molinift*. But, how great
foever his Authority was among his Brethren, he had
but few Imitators. The fmall number of *Anti-Moli-
nifts*, in That great Body, was, neverthelefs, of fome
ufe. I cannot better explain his Thought, than by
fetting down the words of the Author of the Hiftory
of the Congregation *de Auxiliis*. "We fometimes
"meet with Men of an extraordinary Genius, who
"have acquired Credit, and have made themfelves
"neceffary to their Society; and who, raifing them-
"felves above the Fears and Confiderations, to which
"others think themfelves obliged to yield, teach the
"Truths, which they have learned from good Stu-
"dies, more freely, not being able to refolve to
"betray their Confciences, or to act againft their
"Knowledge. The Society bears with them, and
"fuffers this little Revolt, becaufe they know how
"to make it ferviceable to their Party, and turn it
"to their Advantage and Glory; befides they know,
"there is no danger, that fuch an example fhould
"be followed by a great number, and caufe a Schifm
"in the Schools of the Society. Nay it is for their
"Grandeur, and agreeable to their Principles, to
"have grave Doctors of all Opinions, as it may pro-
"mote their Capital Doctrine of Probability. No
"one knows what may happen. Things may take
"a quite contrary Turn; and, if the Society fhould
"find themfelves obliged, (at leaft in fome Provinces)
"to change their Opinion about Grace, as they did

"in *France* about the Pope's Authority, it would
"not be confiftent with their Dignity to look for
"grave Doctors elfewhere, on whofe Authority
"they might ground their Change. Among the
"Divines, of whom I fpeak, we may reckon Father
"*Tiphaine*, fo famous for his two Works, *De ii,,e-
"ftafi*, and *De Ordine*, and the Author of the *Lee-
"fis*, which was maintained at *Rome* in 1674, whofe
"Opinions concerning Predeftination, and Grace,
"are altogether agreeable to Thofe of St *Auguftin* (26),"
I have fet down this Paffage at length, not only becaufe it may be inferred from it, that *Bellarmin* was
very much confidered in his Order, and that he knew
it well, but alfo by reafon of a certain Salt, with
which thefe words are fprinkled, which is very proper to excite many Notions.

(26) *Al-hegaril hiftory
of the Con-
greffions de
Auxiliis*
p.g. 81.

[H] *He did not favour loofe Principles of Morality,
or the Expreffions of Indifcreet Zealots* —— *in the
Litanies*.] The Patrons of This Morality did not approve of the Delay of Abfolution; but Cardinal *Bellarmin* "preached, before fome Popes, the neceffity,
"and ufefulnefs, of this Delay; and his Sermons are
"fo full of this Doctrine, that it plainly appears, he
"laid it much to heart, and put it in practice very
"carefully. One may fee fome very fine Paffages,
"extracted out of them by Cardinal *d'Aguirre*, in
"his eighth and tenth Differtations on the third
"Council of *Toledo* (27)." He, who fupplies me
with thefe words, is a *Janfenift*, who publifhed a
Memorial, containing, I. *A Summary Deduction of the
Origin and prefent State of the Doctrinal Difputes in
the Netherlands, and of the true means to put an end
to them*: II. *A fuccinct Anfwer to the three Accufations of* Janfenifm, Rigorifm, and Novelty (28). He
fays, that the "Learned and Pious Cardinal *Bellar-
"min* might have paffed for an Innovator, as well as
"for a Rigorift, if he had done, in thefe times,
"what he did on divers occafions for the Re-eftablifh-
"ment of Difcipline, and for the Reformation of
"Abufes. The Alterations he made in his Archi-
"bifhopric of *Capua*; the Order, which he fettled in the
"Bifhopric of *Monte-Pulciano*, which he governed
"fome Years, in the Abfence of the right Bifhop; the
"Advice, which he gave Pope *Clement* VIII. for
"the Reformation of the Church; That, which he
"addreffed to his own Nephew, Bifhop of *Theana*,
"for his Conduct, and for the Adminiftration of his
"Diocefe; the Sermons, which he preached in the
"Apoftolic Palace, and in the two Churches, I have
"already named, are fo many witneffes of the holy,
"and neceffary, Novelties, which he endeavoured
"to introduce, and of which he made the Obligation
"known. —— Every one knows, that it is chiefly
"upon This (29) that the Accufation of Novelty was
"firft formed. But, if it be an Innovation, Cardi-
"nal *Bellarmin* cannot be cleared. For he made
"fuch Alterations in the Litanies of the Holy Vir-
"gin, as would, now-a-days, make Thofe exclaim
"greatly, who are fo lavifh in beftowing the Epithet
"of *Innovator*, and That of *Enemy to the Worfhip
"of the Holy Virgin*, that nothing is more common,
"in their Writings, than thefe kind of Accufations
"againft the moft Catholic Perfons, and Thofe, who
"are moft truly devoted to the Worfhip of The Mo-
"ther of God. But this moft Pious and Learned
"Cardinal cannot be accufed of Novelty in This,
"without accufing Pope *Paul* V of it, by whofe
"Order he made thofe Alterations. He gives an ac-
"count of it in a Preface, wherein he fays, *That be
"has retrenched feveral Verfes of the Litanies of our
"Lady of* Loretto, *becaufe they were too metaphori-
"cal, fuch as thefe,* TURRIS EBURNEA, HORTUS
"CONCLUSUS, *and the like*; *and that be bad omitted
"others, becaufe, though they may admit of a good
"Senfe, they are fufceptible of an harfh one, from
"whence the Enemies of the Church take occafion to
"blafpheme, fuch as thefe are:* MARIA, DEI ET
"HOMINUM MEDIATRIX, INTERCEDE PRO NO-
"BIS; AB OMNI PECCATO LIBERA NOS DOMINA;
"*and others of that nature. For fuch kind of Invo-
"cations feem to attribute to the Holy Virgin what
"is proper to* JESUS CHRIST *as* GOD."

(27) Me-
morial, &c.
See the Ci-
tations follow-
ing.

(28) Printed
at Delft, by
Henry van
Rijn, 1696.
It contains
28 Pages in
4°.

(29) To wit,
the correct-
of fome Ex-
preffions,
which fcan-
dalize the
Heretics; as
fome in the
Pfalter, af-
cribed to St
*Bonaven-
ture*, which
feem to a-
fcribe to the
Holy Virgin
what be-
longs only to
God, or to
JESUS
CHRIST,
ibid. p. 20.

[H] *What*

BELLARMIN.

periors, in suffering some things to be altered in his Writings, and altering some Passages himself, concerning the Efficacy of Grace, does not hinder him from being, in the main, an *Augustinian* Doctor [*I*]. He brought himself into Trouble, almost for the same Reasons, which so much embroiled the Abbot *de la Trappe* with the Monks [*K*].

Some

[*I*] *What was altered in his Writings —— concerning the Efficacy of Grace, does not hinder him from being an* Augustinian *Doctor.*] Let us illustrate this by a Passage taken out of a *Jansenist* Book. "There is reason to believe, that the Doctrine of This Cardinal, on This Point, was, originally, very agreeable to St *Augustin*'s Notions, which he sent his Controversies to be printed in *Germany*, and that it was one of the Opinions, which his Brethren of That Country took the Liberty to alter, *in hopes*, says the Author of his Life, *to do more good among Hereticks*. I do not fear making a rash Judgment, in attributing this Alteration to Father *Gregory* of *Valentia*, That famous Martyr of the *Molinian* Grace. He was at *Ingolstadt*, whilst they printed *Bellarmin*'s Controversies there; and he caused some *Theses* to be maintained there, in the Year 1584, which are, perhaps, the first of the Society, in which this new Invention of the *Scientia Media* appeared, which he thinks to be necessary in order to defend Human Liberty against the new Hereticks. I will not deny what is said of the Heroic Patience of Father *Bellarmin*, for which the Author of his Life commends him on This Occasion: yet it appears, by the Revision he made of his Work, in 1608, that he found it had been too much softened, or rather too much corrupted, in relation to the Efficacy of Grace. And This Author of his Life, after having praised his Modesty, and his Humility, in suffering the Alterations of some of his Opinions, testifies, that, on the other side, he firmly stood to Those, which he believed to be either of Faith, or very much authorized in the Church *: *It cannot be conceived*, says he, *how inflexible he appeared on such Occasions, as was plainly seen by what happened in relation to what he had taught, in his Books, concerning Predestination, the Assistance of Divine Grace,* &c. That is, They could never make him change his Opinion in relation to Free-Predestination, which makes, as he says, Part of the Faith of the Church; nor concerning Grace, which he believes to be efficacious, not meerly by the Event, nor because it pleases the Will to consent to it; but by itself, and of it's own Nature: Which he positively says to be agreeable to St *Augustin*'s Doctrine, and also to the Holy Scriptures. This he had always at Heart: And the Congregation *de Auxiliis*, which was just broke up, and where he had heard the *Dominicans* maintain the true Influence of Grace, of itself, with so much Solidity, caused, without doubt, some Remorse of Conscience in him, for having had a Patience, so prejudicial to Truth, in permitting his Sentiments to be altered upon This Subject; or in having altered them himself, by virtue of the Promise, which he had made, when he was admitted among the Jesuits, to follow the Opinions of the Society, as it's Constitutions obliged him to do. That which is certain, is, That he corrected, not all that was to be corrected, the Society being too far engaged to abandon him, but some Passages, in which it did not appear, that he acknowledged any other manner of Operation in Grace, than That, which is called *Objective*, and *Moral*; he will have it known on the contrary, that he admits of an effective, and physical, Operation: Voluntatem moveri per gratiam etiam efficienter & physice; Deum aspirare voluntati bonum desiderium, afflare initium bonæ voluntatis: quæ aspiratio sive afflatio physica actio est & Deo propria ‡. —— *That The Will is influenced, likewise, Effectively and Physically, by Grace; That* GOD *inspires the Will with good Desires, or inspires the first Motions of good Inclinations; which Inspiration is a Physical Operation, and proper to* GOD. This he repeats several times: *For fear*, says he †, *that any one should imagine, that we only admit of a Moral Influence on the Will by Grace.*" The *Jansenist* Author, having quoted some other Passages of The same Work of *Bellarmin*, concludes thus: "By all this it appears sufficiently what we should have found in

"*Bellarmin*, if his Work had not been altered by "other Hands; and what That blind Obedience "can do, which the Jesuits promise to yield to the "Society, when they are received into it ; even "in relation to the Doctrine of the Church. But "it appears also, that the first and last Opinions of "*Bellarmin* were for the Doctrine of Grace, efficacious by itself, and that the Engagement, which "he was under to the Society, not having permitted him to expunge all that had been inserted in "his Works without his Knowledge, nor to alter "the Foundation of the Opinions, which they had fathered upon him, yet he could not forbear giving "Testimony to the Truth before his Death, knowing well, that he had said enough to overthrow "all that remained in his Works, contrary to St *Augustin* (30)." Let us observe, that *Robert Abbot* strongly attacked *Bellarmin* in relation to the Alterations in the new Editions of his Works (31).

[*K*] *He brought himself into Trouble, almost for the same Reasons, which so much embroiled the Abbot* de la Trappe *with the Monks.*] *Bellarmin* wrote a Book *de Gemitu Columbæ*, wherein he says, That one of the Things, which ought to make pious Souls lament and groan, is the great Remissness, into which some Religious Orders are fallen. Bitter Complaints have been made of This, as of a biting Invective (32). But the Cardinal has not wanted Apologists, who have maintained, that what he complained of, is but too true; and that the want of Reformation is so visible in divers Places, that They, who live in this Disorder, and do not perceive it, verify the Maxim, *Sensibile juxta ac multo magis intra sensum positum non facit sensationem* (33). Let us quote a Passage of *Theophilus Raynaud*: " Audivit Bellarminus asper & mordax, quia in libro de Gemitu Columbæ fontem unum lacrymarum proposuit, Religiosorum aliquorum Ordinum laxationem, quam homo ille spiritu barytono uspiam cerni insciatur, & utinam vel in speciem vere insiciaretur. Sed tanti fuit, Bellarminum mordere quoquo modo. Nam esse aliquas Religiones laxatas, & quibus reformatio sit necessaria, res est adeo nota, ut nemo nisi cœcus non videat, ait Major *in.* 4. *d.* 38. *q.* 23. Sed non est novum aliquos ita cœcutire, præsertim in causa propria, ut notum est ex eo exemplo quod recitat Nider *lib.* 2. *de Reform. Relig. cap.* 9. Episcopi ex ordine collapso assumpti, qui, audiente ipso Nidero, pertinacissime insiciatus est, suum Ordinem esse collapsum, & reformatione egere, quantumvis (inquit Nider), luce foret clarius toti mundo, contrarium esse verum (34). ------ Bellarmin *was taxed with Calumny and Invective, because, in his Book* de Gemitu Columbæ, *he makes one Source of Tears to be the Decay of Discipline in some Orders; the truth of which This Author* (He, who complained of *Bellarmin*'s *absolutely denies; and I wish he could with reason deny it, even as to Appearances. But it was worth while to attack* Bellarmin *at any rate. For, that some Religious Orders have relaxed Discipline, and stand in need of Reformation, is so notorious, that no one, that is not blind, but sees it, as* Major *says, in* 4. *d.* 38. *q.* 23. *But it is no uncommon Thing for People to be thus blind, especially those that are in the Case; as appears from the Instance, alledged by* Nider, lib. 2. de Reform. Relig. c. 9. *of a Bishop, taken from a fallen Order, who, in the hearing of* Nider *himself, obstinately denied, that his Order was fallen, and stood in need of Reformation, when* (says Nider) *it was as clear as the Noon-Day, that the contrary was true.*" The Pseudonymous *Philadelphus de novo lacu*, who wrote a Treatise *de modernis Jesuitarum moribus*, tells us, that it is questioned, whether *Bellarmin* be the true Author of the *Gemitus Columbæ* (35). This doubt seems to me very unreasonable; for This Treatise came out whilst That Cardinal was living, and was inserted in the Collection of his Works. Observe, that the Dominican *Gravina*, is one of Those who wrote against this *Gemitus*. See the Remark [*B*] of the Article KELLER.

[*L*] *Some*

(30) *Gety's Apology*, p. 177, 178.

(31) Rob. Abbotus, de suprema potestate Regia, *Præl.* II, Art. III.

(32) *The Author of this Complaint is a Monk, against whom the Jesuit* Baeza *said something,* lib. 4. de Jesu figurato, cap. 1, n. 32. *See* Theophilus Raynaud, Erotemata de malis ac bonis libris, pag. 112.

(33) Theoph. Raynaud. ibid.

(34) Id. ibi.

(35) See pag. 108, of *Mr* Mayer's *Dissertation;* De Bellarmini fide ipsa Pontificia dubia. See below, Citat. (67).

* Sin verò dogmata ipsa fidei, &c. e'us in operibus censurà notabantur, dici non potest quàm stantem se immutabilemque præberet. Clarè id agnitum est in his quæ evenere circa editas opiniones de prædestinatione, de auxiliis divinæ gratiæ, &c. lib. 2, cap. 5.

‡ Recognit. oper. Bellarm. Ingolstad. 1601, p. 36.

† Pag. 97.

BELLARMIN.

Some have thought, that he did great Prejudice to the *Roman* Catholics, by his Books of Controversy [L], because the Objections of the Heretics are to be found in them. An ingenious Man, not being able to find *Bellarmin*'s Works in any Bookseller's Shop in *Italy*, suspected that they were forbidden to be exposed to Sale, for fear the Opinions, which the Author confuted, should be known [M]. The whole Body of Controversies, published by this Cardinal, comprehended, at first, three Volumes in Folio; but they were divided into four, in the Edition of *Cologne*, 1615, because

---

[L] *Some said, that he did great Prejudice to the Roman Catholics by his Books of Controversy*] Father *Theophilus Reynaud* confesses, that some have thought, that, perhaps, it might be very expedient to suppress Cardinal *Bellarmin*'s Controversial Books, as well because the Heretics may easily make a wrong use of them, taking what is for their Turn out of them, and leaving the rest, as because the Catholics may be deceived by them, for want of understanding the Answers to the Objections. Some have thought, that Cardinal *du Perron* was of This Opinion; and, perhaps, they were not mistaken: Nay, it is said, that he openly declared it in Conversation, not considering the Consequences of it. But, when he came to know, that he was charged with judging in this manner of *Bellarmin*'s Books, he strongly denied it. *Doctissimus Card. Perronius cum hoc sibi calumniosum copiosè & validè illud detersit, ut refertur in ipsius Bellarmini vita* lib. 2. cap. 7 (36)

(36) Theoph. Raynaud, de bonis ac malis libris, pag. 223.

He wrote a Letter to That Cardinal, wherein he confuted this Accusation with all his Industry and Strength. This Letter, dated from *Rome* the tenth of *February* 1605, is in the Life of *Bellarmin*, composed by *Fuligatti*, and in the Dissertation of Mr *Mayer*, whom I quoted before (37), who informs us, that Cardinal *Bentivoglio* protested he had heard Cardinal *du Perron* pass this Judgment on *Bellarmin*'s Controversies. *Sanctè testari — — — so ex ipsius Cardinalis* Perronii *ore propriis hoc excepisse auribus de Bellarmini Controversiis judicium* (38). The Collector of the *Perroniana* had not heard him say the same thing, or else he did not think fit to mention it; for here is all he says: "Cardinal *Bellarmin* has a very fine and clear Wit. He has treated very well of the Sacraments *in genere*; nothing can be better. But we cannot say the same of the Treatise *de Eucharistiâ*. When he found any Subject already well scanned, and examined, by others, he explained it wonderfully well by the beauty and clearness of his Wit; but, when he found a Subject intricate and much confuted, he lost himself in it (39). He often made use of the Translations of the *Greek* Fathers, without having recourse to the *Greek*: I wonder at it, since he understood it very well. Among other Books, he makes use of the *Præparatio Evangelica* for praying to the Saints, and quotes it, in *Latin*, from the Translation of *Trapezuntius*, which is very different from the *Greek*, and which contains a Clause, not at all to be found in the *Greek*." That my Readers may judge of all this, I have set down here the Passage of Cardinal *Bentivoglio*. "Tale era il concorso generale intorno alle sue controversie (40) benche non riesceno mai tanto uniformi i giudizi, che non vi stano ancora di quelli frà i più dotti Cattolici, è più versati in materie simili, che haverebbono qualche volta desiderato di vederlo stringere, ed abbater con forza maggiore alcuni argomenti heretici, e con maggior pienezza riportare quei tanti, e sì manifesti vantaggi, che poteva dargli in ogni questione la Dottrina Cattolica: meco più d'una volta in Francia mostrò d'aver questo senso particolarmente il Cardinal Perrone, quel gran Cardinale, quel ch'e stato l'Agostino Francese del nostro secolo: del resto lo riconoscevaancor egli un per de più dotti, e più eminenti, e più benemeriti scrittori, che havesse havuto la Chiesa ne i tempi nostri (41). — — — Such was the general Opinion of his Controversial Writings; though the Judgments passed on them were not so uniform, but there were still some among the more learned Catholics, who wished to have seen him combat some Heretical Arguments more forcibly, and with more ease to obtain those so great and manifest Advantages, which the Catholic Doctrine might have given him on every Question. Cardinal* Perrone, *in particular, declared to me,*

(37) In Citat. (35). See pag. 184, &c. of that Dissertation.

(38) John Frider. Mayer, ibid. pag. 192.

(39) Compan.lla Synt. de libris probis, cap. 4. Art. 9, juxta est ab almost after the jam manner: Bellarminus, controversias says he, h et impostate plurimum illustravit, claros, non in ei pars, magn.s in labore, sed modus in talmen in inventione.

(40) That is to say of Bellarmin.

(41) Memorie ovro diarii del Card. Bentivoglio, pag. 121, 122, Edit Amstel. 1648.

"more than once, in France, that this was his Opinion; That Great Cardinal, who was the French Augustin of our Age; yet even He acknowledged him for one of the most eminent and most deserving Writers, which the Church has had in our Time."
By this it appears, that the Censure was reduced to This, that *Bellarmin* had not always confuted the Reasons of the Heretics with all the Strength and Victory, which the Goodness of his Cause might have supplied him with. Observe, that some Protestants confess, that he sets down their Reasons and Objections honestly enough. Mr *Heidegger* praised him among others things, "quod non perinde malignus atque Jesuitæ alii, Valentia imprimis, Vasques, Becanus, Maldonatus, &c. meliore ut plurimum fide adversariorum suorum argumenta allegavit, & amantior quam illi veritatis, sicubi erravit, prudens scienique errare non videtur (42). — — — That, being more candid, than the rest of the Jesuits, particularly Valentia, Vasques, Becanus, Maldonatus, &c. he generally represented the Arguments of his Adversaries more impartially; and that, as he appeared to have a greater Regard, than They, to Truth, if he was mistaken, his Errors do not seem to be voluntary."* Let the Reader judge as he pleases of the Narrative of the Dominican *Vincent Baron*. That Monk engaged in Controversies, and disputed sometimes with Protestant Divines. He affirms, that he heard one of them say, that *Bellarmin* had done them a very great Piece of Service, by putting their Divinity into good Order, and by giving more force to their Arguments, than they had in their Writers. Whereupon Father *Baron* praises *Bellarmin*'s Plain-dealing, but without forgetting to say, that he had throughly confuted the same Reasons of the Protestants, which he had represented with all their Force (43). He adds, that he had heard say, in That Cardinal's Justification, that, in his Dispute about Mysteries, the Arguments of those, who attack are more easily apprehended, than the Arguments of those, who reply. "Hoc solum adjunxerim quod in defensionem Bellarmini me aliàs audivisse memini, mysteria fidei hoc habere, quòd, cùm superent captum rationis humanæ, faciliora sunt sensui argumenta quæ impugnant, quàm responsa, quæ defendunt (44)." This is to tell us plainly, that Complaints were made, that *Bellarmin* proposed the Objections of the Heretics better, than he confuted them. I shall examine, in another Place (45), whether They, who are so honest as to set down fairly the Arguments of their Adversaries (which but few Persons do), behave answerably to the Spirit, which prevails, more or less, in all Communions, of not permitting the Sale of Heretical Books.

(42) Heidegger Papatus, p. 312.

(43) Baronius Apolog. lib. 4. Sect. 4, pag. 162, 164.

(44) Id. ib. pag. 162.

(45) In Remark [G], of the Article CHRYSIPPUS.

[M] *An ingenious Man — — suspected, that they were forbidden to be exposed to sale, for fear of making known the Opinions, which They refuted.*] The ingenious Person, whom I mean, is Sir *Edwin Sandys*. See what he says: "I protest, it was never in my Power to find *Bellarmin*'s Works, or Those of *Gregory de Valentia*, or any other of that Nature, in any of the Booksellers Shops. But, instead of them, I found infinite Heaps of Invectives, and Declamations, every where; which made me conjecture, that they were designedly suppressed, and kept within the Inclosures of the Monasteries, least, by the free and common reading of them, wherein the Author must of necessity have alledged the Arguments, and Tenets of the Protestants, some Flower might be smelt, and some Fruit, or Seed, of the Protestant Religion might be tasted. I leave it to more sagacious Persons to enquire whether this Conjecture of mine be true, or not (46)." Let us add King *James*'s Words. "Fama proditum est, nescio quibus verum, libros controversiarum Bellarmini in Italia non permitti vulgo, propterea quod objectiones ejus nimis "validæ"

(46) Survey of the State of Religion, pag. 224, Edit. in 12mo. 1642.

BELLARMIN. 731

because seven new Treatises were added to the first Volume, whereof the last is the Revision, and Correction, which the Author made, of all his Works [N]. It is thus, that the Writers of the *Bibliotheque* of the Jesuits have explained themselves ; but This is not exact [O]. Besides this Body of Controversies, he composed many other Books, which amount to three Volumes in Folio, in the Edition of *Cologne*, 1617 *(e)*. Some of his *Sermons*, and many of his *Letters*, have been published since his Death *(f)*. His Life has been written by four, or five, Authors [P] ; the last, if I am not mistaken, is *Daniel Bartoli*. The rash Judgment, *Scaliger* passed on *Bellarmin*, cannot be sufficiently condemned [Q].

Though this Jesuit had eagerly maintained the Pope's Power over the Temporalities of Kings, yet he displeased *Sixtus V*, and had the Mortification to see his Work inserted in the *Index* of the Inquisition [R]. What he wrote on the same Subject

---

"validæ sint, responsiones autem nimis debiles (47).
"—— *It is reported, with what Truth I cannot* "*say, that the Controversial Works of* Bellarmin *are* "*not permitted to be publickly sold in Italy, because* "*his Objections are too strong, and his Answers too* "*weak*."

[N] *The Revision, and Correction, which the Author made, of all his Works*] I have read a curious Particular in Mr *Chevillier*, which I shall relate here with great Pleasure. "This Cardinal, seeing, that "he had Controversies were printing in divers Places, "and that many Faults were left in them, thought "he ought to endeavour to remedy this Evil. He "made such an exact Copy of his Book, and corrected "it so well, that there remained not one Error in the "Manuscript ; and he gave it to a Bookseller of "*Venice*, to have a most exact Impression of it. But "it happened quite contrary to his Hopes. The "Printer neglected this Edition so much, that it proved the most faulty of all. This famous Author, "being vexed at it, took Pen in Hand to acquaint "the Publick with it, after having seen, that That "Impression, being accounted an Original one, had "carried the Evil into a second, and had also much "infected the fair Edition of *Ingolstadt*, to which it "served for a Model. He published his Book, entitled, *Recognitio Librorum omnium Roberti Bellarmini*, wherein he inserted a *Correctorium*, which "shews all the Faults of That Edition of *Venice*, and "was printed in octavo, at *Ingolstadt*, in the Year "1698. He complains, in the Preface, pag 125, "that, in above forty Places, the Printer makes him "give a Negative, for an Affirmative, Answer, and "an Affirmative for a Negative. And the *Errata*, "which he made, fills Eighty eight Pages. *Et quod* "*gravissimum est (animadverti) suprà quadraginta* "*locos ita esse corruptos, additis vel detractis nega*-"*tibus particulis, vel alio modo immutatis, ut contra*-"*rium omninò sensum contineant, quod certè summo me* "*dolore afficit* —— *tamen quoniam animadverti non* "*paucos errores editionis primæ Venetæ in Editionem* "*secundam Venetam, & in Ingolstadiensem ex Venetâ* "*expressam, transiisse, ideò in Correctorio notavi Li*-"*bros, Capita, Paragraphos, Columnas, Literas, &* "*Versus* (48)." *Note*, that This *Correctorium* was, at first, printed at *Rome*, in the Year 1607, and that, in the Year 1596, the Author, causing his controversial Works, revised, and enlarged, to be printed at *Ingolstadt*, had acquainted the World, that he did not acknowledge the preceeding Editions for his, not that they contained any Opinions, which ought to be disapproved, but on account of the Faults of the Impression, as he told *Possevin*, in the Year 1598 (49).

[O] *What the Writers of the Bibliotheques of the Jesuits have said of the Correction of his Works, is not exact* (50). I find, in a Work, printed in the Year 1608 (50), that, before That Year, *Bellarmin*'s Controversies had appeared, in four Volumes. The first Edition in three Volumes, in Folio, is of *Ingolstadt*, 1586. The following Year, they were reprinted again, at the same Place, in *Octavo*. A new Edition was made of them in the same City, in 1588, and another in the Year 1590. The first Edition, in four Volumes, is of *Venice, apud Minimam Societatem*. An *Appendix* of several particular Treatises was added to it (51). It must be said, then, that *Alegambus*, and his Continuator, are not exact, since they give us That of *Cologne*, 1615, for the first Edition, in four Volumes. They say also, that the first Edition of the first *Tome* came out in the Year 1581, That of the second in the Year 1583, and That of the third in the Year 1592. This is contrary to *Possevin*'s

Relation, and wants Exactness on another Account ; for They should have named the Place, where those pretended first Editions were made.

[P] *His Life has been written by four or five Authors*.] Mr *Teissier* reckons up nine of them, and ranges them in this manner ; 1. *Daniel Bartoli* ; 2. *Didacus Ramirez* ; 3. *Jacobus Fuligatus* ; 4. *Georgius Robertifonus* ; 5. *Johannes Morinus* ; 6. *Marcellinus Cervinus* ; 7. *Petrus Morinus* ; 8. *Sylves*[?]. *Petra Sancta* ; 9. *Tarquin. Galluccius* (52) But we must reduce the Number ; *James Fuligattis, John Morin* (53), *Peter Morin* (54), and *Sylvester Petra Sancta*, ought to pass only for one Historian of *Bellarmin* : for the three last have only translated the *Italian* Work of *Fuligatti* ; and, if *Petra Sancta*, who translated it into *Latin*, made some Additions to it, he ought not, therefore, to be considered as one of the Historians. If *George Robertusson* wrote This Cardinal's Life, ought he not to appear, in his Place, in the Body of Mr *Teissier*'s Book ? But he no where appears there. We meet with only one *Georgius Robertsorus* there, who was Author of the Life of *Robert Rollocus*, a *Scotch* Divine. *Note*, that *Tarquin Galluccius* did not compose *Bellarmin*'s History, but only his Funeral Oration. Mr *Mayer* gave a more exact List (55) : he quotes the Life of *Bellarmin*, written by *James Fuligatti*, and printed at *Rome*, in the Year 1624, in 4to ; *Daniel Bartoli de vita Bellarmini*, at *Rome* 1618 (56), in 4to ; *Marcellinus Cervinus de vita & mortibus Bellarmini*, at *Sienna* 1622, in 8vo ; *Didacus Ramirez in vita Bellarmini ex variis authoribus concinnata* ; & *Nicolao Antonio in Bibliotheca Hispana memorata* ; And the Account *de pio obitu Bellarmini ex literis Eudæmono-Johannis*, printed at *Dilingen*, in the Year 1621. He quotes also *Gallutius, Alegambus, Sebastiani Badii de ira Roberti Cardinalis Bellarmini* (57) ; the Elogies of *Eusebius Sarrini*, a *Florentin* Abbot of the Order of *Citeaux* à *Ughelli*, in the Four hundred fifth Page of the sixth Volume of the *Italia Sacra* ; *Imperialis* ; *Andrew du Saussay* ; & *Nicius Erythræus*. He forgot *Edward Coffin*, an *English* Jesuit, who wrote a Book *de morte Cardinalis Bellarmini*, printed at *St Omer*, in the Year 1623, in 8vo : he disguised himself under these two Letters C. E (58). *Note*, that *Didacus Ramirez* was a *Spanish* Jesuit, who died the eighth of *April* 1647 (59).

[Q] *The rash Judgment Scaliger passed on Bellarmin cannot be sufficiently condemned*.] Let him say, as much as he pleases (60), that *if any One would give him a Bellarmin, he would not accept of it*, and that he would take care not to lose his Time in reading such an Author, who writes ill, *quod male scripsit non legam, nec male bonas horas collocabo*. But he is inexcusable in saying, that *Bellarmin* did not believe any thing of what he printed, and that he was a meer Atheist (61) ; that it is to usurp GOD's Right who is the only Judge of Thoughts, and he who searches the Reins and the Hearts. It is to set a bad Example, and to authorize the fury of those, who said, that *Calvin, Beza*, &c. preached against their Conscience, and had no Religion.

[R] *He had the Mortification to see his Work de Pontifice Romano inserted in the Index of the Inquisition*.] From This Fact Mr *Arnauld* draws a good Argument *ad hominem* against those, who preach up the Authority of the Congregation of the *Index*. We find, says he (62), that *Bellarmin*'s Work *de Romano Pontifice* "was proscribed by *Sixtus V*, because he "judged, as well as those, to whom he had given "it to be examined, that it had done great Prejudice "to the Pontifical Dignity, by saying, that the "Power, which they pretended, that J. C. gave to "his

VOL I. 8 Y

ject against *William Barclay* was treated still worse in France [S]. Among all the *Roman* Catholics, who have wrote against him, none has so fully discovered the weak Parts of his Works, as *John de Launoi* [T]. We shall mention two of *Bellarmin's* Thoughts, which shew, that he loved Peace, and that he was not pleased with the Ambition of the Cardinals [U]. The Protestants have taken notice of one thing, which he says, concerning the Merit of Works, viz. That *Because of the Uncertainty*

(63) Fuligatti, and Petra Sancta, *in the Life of Bellarmin.*

" his Vicar, on Earth, over the Temporalities of
" Kings, is not direct, but only indirect; and it
" was for this reason, that, these Books *de Romano*
" *Pontifice,* were inserted among the Prohibited.
" This is what these two Jesuits (63) give us to un-
" derstand, somewhat obscurely, to induce us to be-
" lieve, that this proceeded not so much from the
" Pope, as from *Bellarmin's* Enemies, who had per-
" suaded him to it: *Doctrina Bellarmini autoritatem*
" *illam* MINUI, *quam Christus Dominus Vicario suo*
" *in terris dedit ad Ecclesiæ dignitatem firmitatem-*
" *que; idque fieri in opinione ipsius circa Dominium*
" *temporarium, quod Pontifici competit item* IN RES
" TEMPORARIAS. By which These Authors under-
" stand the Power, which it is believed, at *Rome,*
" the Pope has, to depose Kings; as appears by the
" following Page, where *Bellarmin's* Book against
" *William Barclay* on this Subject of deposing Kings
" is called: *Tractatio de Potestate Pontificis* IN RES
" TEMPORARIAS, *adversus Gulielmum Barclaium.*
" So that it was not for want of having understood
" *Bellarmin's* Doctrine right on this Subject, that
" he received the Affront of having his Books put
" among the condemned Writers; but because That
" Pope was not satisfied with the indirect Power,
" which he gave him, over Kings, and would have
" a direct one. And this continued as long as That
" Pope lived. For these same Authors acknowledge,
" that it was not, till after his Death, that the Car-
" dinals expunged them *ex indice probroforum scrip-*
" *torum.* Pray, Sir, tell us, whether you think,
" that any Jesuit will own, that it would have been
" a mortal Sin to read *Bellarmin's* Books *de Romano*
" *Pontifice,* during the Life of *Sixtus* V, and that,
" if a Priest had done it, he would have deserved *to*
" *be deprived, by a Sentence, of the Power of preach-*
" *ing, confessing, and directing Souls?"*

(64) Pag. 377, & seq.

Consult the Dissertation of the famous Mr *Mayer,*
de fide Bellarmini ipsi Pontificis ambigua, printed at
Amsterdam 1697, and you will find, there (64), a
long Passage of *Fuligatti,* and some others. Consult
also the second Tome of the *French Mercury;* it will
inform you " That, towards the end of the Year
" 1586, when the first Book of the Controversies of
" *Bellarmin* was brought into *France,* of the Impres-
" sion of *Ingolstadt, Stephen Michel,* a Bookseller of
" *Lyons,* being at *Paris,* joined with another Book-
" seller in publishing That Book; which they began
" to do; and, notice thereof being given to the
" King's Attorney-General, he caused one and twenty
" Sheets, already finished to be seized, and forbad
" them to continue the printing of it: It was on ac-
" count of the third Controversy, where he treated
" *de Summo Pontifice,* and where he attributed an in-
" direct Power to the Pope over Emperors, Kings,
" and Sovereign Princes, and divers other things a-

(65) *French Mercury,* Tom. II, pag. 32.

" gainst the temporal Sovereignty of Kings (65)."
One may therefore say of the *medium,* which *Bellarmin* observed, between the *Ultramontain* Canonists, and
the Doctors of the *Sorbonne,* what *Herennius Pontius* declared in relation to the Conduct of his Son,
who saved the Lives, but not the Honour, of the
Roman Soldiers. *Ista quidem sententia ea est, quæ neque amicos parat, neque inimicos tollit, servare modo*

(66) Titus Livius, lib. 9, Decad. I.

quos everterunt inveneris (66) —— *It is an Opinion,
which neither gains you Friends, nor loses you Enemies,
barely to preserve Those, whom you exasperate against
you by Ignominy.* Thus Jesuit observed a mean which displeased the Court of *Rome,* without pleasing the Court of *France.* It is the common fate of moderate Opinions; they neither procure you Friends, nor appease your Enemies, and they leave you for a mark to the two Factions, which place themselves in the opposite Extreams.

[S] *What he wrote on the same Subject against* W. Barclay, *was treated still worse in* France] I mean his *Tractatus de potestate summi Pontificis in Tempora-
libus adversus Guilielmum Barclaium,* printed at *Rome* in the Year 1610. Mr *Mayer* observes, that King *James* wrote against This Treatise, and that the Se-

nate of *Venice,* and the Parliament of *Paris,* condemned it. He gives us, in *Latin,* the Decree of That Parliament, and refers us to the Continuator of *Thuanus* (67). He says also, that This Work of *Bellarmin* wanted but little of being burnt at *Paris* by the Hands of the Common Executioner: " Faces jam
" accendebat carnifex, ut poenas à scripto & scriptore
" sumeret, nisi Reginæ animus, & iteratis & non de-
" sinentibus Jesuitarum deprecationibus fractus, illas
" extinxisset (68) —— *The Executioner already be-*
" *gan to light the Fire, to punish The Work and it's*
" *Author, had not the Disposition of the Queen, in-*
" *fluenced by the repeated and incessant Intreaties of*
" *the Jesuits, extinguished it."* See the second Tome of the *French Mercury,* and you will find, these (69), the Substance of the Remonstrance of Mr *Servin,* the King's First Advocate, and the Decree of the Parliament (70), in these Terms: " The Court forbids all
" Persons, of what Quality and Condition soever, on
" the Penalty of High-Treason, to receive, retain,
" communicate, print, cause to be printed, or to ex-
" pose to sale the said Book. And enjoins those,
" who shall have any Copies of the said Book, or
" know any Persons, who have, to declare it speedi-
" ly to the Ordinary Judges, that diligent search
" may be made after them, at the Request of the
" Substitutes of the said Attorney-General, and that
" the Guilty may be proceeded against, as is requi-
" site (71)."

(67) Jo. Frider. Mayer, S. Reg. Majest. Suecicæ Germaniam Suecicæ Consiliarius in Sacris Primarius, Doct. & Profess. Theolog. & Ecclesiæ Humour-genesis ad D. Jacobi Pastor, D sertati f e ipsis Pontificiis dubiis, pag. 180.

(68) Id. ib. pag. 183.

(69) French Mercury, pag. 33, & seq.

(70) Novemb. 26, 1610.

[T] *No One has so fully discovered the weak Parts of his Works, as* John de Launoi.] Mr *Mayer* will inform you fully of This, in his Book. See also the Remark [I] of the Article LAUNOI (JOHN).

(71) French Mercury ib. pag. 36.

[U] *He loved Peace, and had not learnt the Am-
bition of the Cardinals.*] Peter de St *Romuald* says, that the most excellent of all *Bellarmin's* Works, " treating of Controversies, was proscribed at *Rome,*
" and inserted in the Index of Infamous Books. ——
" Which he bore, *adds he,* with the same Patience,
" as he suffered the Contradictions of a certain Car-
" dinal, in the Conclave, saying to those, who
" wondered at it, that an Ounce of Peace was worth
" more than a Pound of Victory. Being also asked
" (perhaps on account of that Cardinal) how it hap-
" pened, that there were so few Cardinals in the Ca-
" talogue of the Saints; it is, *said he,* because they
" aspire to be Most-Holy: A smart Answer for those,
" who know what these Words signify in *Italy; per-
" che vogliono esser sant' ssimi* (72)." The meaning of which is, that the Desire of being made Pope hinders the Cardinals from acquiring Holiness, though That Desire be a longing after the Title of Most Holy Father. The *Critical Miscellanies* of Mr *Ancillon* inform me, that Mr *Godeau,* " wrote *Bellarmin's*
" Elogy, *says,* that one of his usual Sayings was, that
" the Cardinals are not Holy, because they would
" be Most Holy, that is to say Popes, who are cal-
" led Most Holy Fathers: An Opinion, which he
" had from his Uncle *Marcellus* II, who cried out,
" one Day, at Table, *Non video quomodo qui lo-
" cum hunc altissimum tenent salvari possint* (73), I
" do not see how those that are seated in St *Peter's*
" Chair can be saved (74)." The Respect, which I have for the Memory of the late Mr *Ancillon,* a Man of much Piety and Learning, is not inconsistent with the Liberty I am going to take. I do not find an exact Connexion between the Cardinal's Thought, and That of the Pope. *Bellarmin's* Intention was, not to say, that a Pope can hardly be saved, but that the Desire of being made a Pope attaches the Cardinals in such a manner to earthly Things, and unjust Intrigues, that they can make no Progress in the Way of Holiness. But Pope *Marcellus* II had not this Thought; he only considered the Obstacles, which a Man, who is actually Pope, meets with in the way of Salvation. So that *Bellarmin's* Jest does not seem to me to be part of his Uncle's Inheritance. If it be objected against me, that a Pope stands in need of as many Intrigues to perform the Part, which he acts in the World, as a Cardinal to attain to the Pontificate;

(72) Peter de St Romuald, Chronol ad Ann. 1621, p. 416, 417.

(73) Onaphrius in Marcello II. apud Arcell. ibid. p. 329.

(74) Ancillon's Critical Miscel. Tom. I, pag. 328.

BELLARMIN. 733

certainty of our own Righteousness, and for fear of Vain-Glory, the surest way is to put our whole Trust in the alone Goodness and Mercy of GOD (g). Neither have they forgot what he preached at *Louvain*, in 1571, on the Excellency of the Bible. They *make use of it to confute all, that he has said since, in his Works, against the Perfection and Sufficiency of the Scripture* (h). The Book, which supplies me with these Words, contains many solid and curious Remarks concerning *Bellarmin*. I find in it, that This Cardinal, *might, perhaps, have been Pope, if he had not been a Jesuit* [X] ; *for* Henry IV told the French Cardinals, *who went to the Conclave, after the Death of* Clement VIII, *that he should be very glad if* Bellarmin *was made Pope* (i). I have read also, that *the same Jesuit acquired the Esteem of* Henry IV, *whilst he was at his Court, whither he was sent with Cardinal* Henry Cajetan (k), *and that it is certain, the best of his Works is*

"cate ; I shall answer, that it is another Question, and that it is to exceed the Limits, which ought to be put to the Sense of the Words, which *Bellarmin* made use of. I go further, and maintain, that, though the same Cardinal had said, on some other Occasion ; *That Popes are so far from deserving to be canonized, that they can hardly keep themselves from Hell* ; it cannot be pretended, that the *Italian* Words, which you have seen before, are the Copy of his Uncle Pope *Marcellus*'s Exclamation. That Exclamation puts me in mind of the Sally of a *Frenchman*, who heard somebody praise the Piety, and moral Severity, of *Innocent* XI, in the Year 1689. " The Catholic " Church, *said* he, has no need of such a Pope ; it " were better for her to have a Sovereign Pontiff, " who understands the Art of aggrandizing himself, " and of taking hold of all Opportunities, according " to the Politics of the most refined Courts. The " Greatness, and Majesty, of the Catholic Church, " require a Head, not endowed with the Virtues of a " Priest, but with the Talents of a cunning Politician. " They require a Head, who has the Courage to " damn himself, for the Good and Increase of his " Dominions ; this is the way to perform the Of- " fice of a good Shepherd, who gives his Life for " his Sheep ; this is to devote one's self for the Re- " public, better than *Codrus*, and the *Decii* did (75). " A scrupulous, and devout Pope, like good *Adrian* VI, " is only fit to let the Temporals of the Church " perish (76), which are so advantageous for the Main- " tenance of the Spirituals." Such was This *Frenchman*'s Discourse.

[X] *He might, perhaps, have been made Pope, if he had not been a Jesuit.*] He had more Votes, than any of the rest, in the first Scrutiny of the Conclave of *Leo* XI (77) ; nevertheless, they did not think of him, then, in earnest. It was in the following Conclave (78), that they looked upon him as a fit Man to be Pope, and that they endeavoured to procure him the Pontificate ; but Cardinal *Aldobrandini*'s Faction made this Design miscarry. *Bellarmin*'s Virtue, and the too great Power of the Jesuits, were the two chief Considerations, which hindred him from succeeding *Leo* XI. " *Aldobrandino* ——— fuggiva. —— Bellar- " mino come Giesuita scropoloso, è che tal volta " haveva improvato molte attioni di *Clemente* " *Zio*, è di lui stesso (79). —— Haveva *Bellarmino* " grand' amici per esser egli di letteratura, è bontà " singolare, mà l'esser Giesuita, è di conscienza de- " licata, lo rendevano poco amabile, apprello molti, li " quali mossero ogni pietra, per rovinarlo. —— Fù " rinovata, è sparsa per tutto la memoria del dis- " gresso dato à *Bellarmino* da *Sisto* V, che gli fece " prohibire l'opera sua *de potestate Papæ* : furono dis- " corse al vivo tutte le conseguenze, che potevano " deviare dall' etaltatione di un Giesuita ; & insomma " s'adopromò in maniera, che s'aquietò affatto il tut- " to (80). —— Aldobrandino ——— fled away. " Bellarmin, *as a conscientious Jesuit, and who had of- " ten disapproved of many Actions of* Clement, *his " Uncle, and of* Clement *himself.* —— Bellarmin *had " great Friends, on account of his Learning, and sin- " gular Goodness ; but his being a Jesuit, and of a " tender Conscience, rendered him disagreeable to many, " who left no Stone unturned to ruin him.* —— *The " Memory of* Bellarmin's *Disgrace with* Sixtus V, *who " prohibited his Book* De Potestate Papæ, *was revived, " and spread every where : Every Consequence, which " might hinder the Promotion of a Jesuit, was tho- " roughly discussed ; and they employed their Interest " in such a manner, that the whole Affair was dropped.*" Let us set down, here, a Passage of Mr *Ancillon*. " I have always heard say, that the Court of *Rome*

" will take care not to place a Jesuit in the Papal " Chair, and that *Europe* ought not to desire it ; be- " cause they would infallibly make themselves Ma- " sters of the Holy See ; insomuch that all the other " Orders might look upon themselves as excluded " from it for ever, and that by this means they would " make their Power, which is already very great, " almost infinite and boundless : If we believe those, " who write on this Subject, it seems this Maxim is " not new in the Court of *Rome*. They have di- " strusted the Jesuits a long time, and are on their " guard against them, in this respect ; and we read, " in the Life of *Bellarmin* himself, that *Clement* VIII, " speaking of That Cardinal, who had already made " himself famous, said, *Dignus, sed Jesuita est* (81)." We have a Proof, here, of the rash Judgments, which are only grounded on first Appearances. If you do not examine things thoroughly, and if you consider only the first Impressions, which they make on the Mind, you will imagine, that, in order to obtain a Dignity, it is a very great Advantage to belong to a very powerful Body ; but, if you take the pains to reflect, you will find almost an invincible Obstacle in This very Thing. Within these ten Years (82) we have seen two Examples of this. Nothing contributed so much to exclude the Cardinal of *Furstemberg* from the Archbishopric of *Cologne*, and the Cardinal of *Bouillon* from the Bishopric of *Liege*, as their being recommended, and protected, by the Court of *France*, whose Power was superior to That of other States. Refer to This what I have said in Remark [H], of the Article INNOCENT XI, and remember the Thought of *Florus*, *ipsa sibi obstat magnitudo.* I have already applied it, on a quite different Occasion (83). *N.te,* That Monf. *Godeau* observes, " that *Baro- " nius,* having made some Overtures to *Bellarmin* " of the Thought, that he, and some other Cardinals, " had of making him Pope, he received the Proposal " as an Injury, was downright angry at it, and re- " solutely answered, that, if the taking up of a Straw " from the Ground could make him Pope, he would " not stoop to take it up (84)." I wonder that Mr *Ancillon* has not spoken of the solemn Vow, which *Bellarmin* made, of not desiring the Papal Dignity, which he did not defer, should be conferred upon him. He engaged himself not to enrich his Relations. These are the Terms of his Vow : " Die 24 Septembris anno 1614, " fer. 6, in domo Novitiorum S. Andreæ degens, & " exercitiis spiritualibus vacans, matura præhabita de- " liberatione in sacrificio Missæ, cum sumpturus es- " sem S. Dom. nost. corpus, votum vovi Domino in " hæc verba : Ego Robertus, Cardinalis Bellarminus, è " Societate Jesu religiosus professus, voveo Deo om- " nipotenti in conspectu B. V. Mariæ, ac totius cœ- " lestis curiæ, quod si forte, quod non cupio, & " precor Deum, ut non accidat, ad Pontificatum as- " sumptus fuero, neminem ex consanguineis vel af- " finibus meis exaltabo ad Cardinalatum, vel tem- " poralem Principatum, vel Ducatum, vel Comita- " tum, vel quemcunque alium titulum, neque eos " ditabo, sed solùm adjuvabo, ut in statu suo ci- " vili commodè vivere possint. Amen, Amen (85). " —— On the Twenty fourth of September, *in the " Year* 1614, *being in the House of the Novitiates " of* St Andrew, *and intent upon spiritual Exercises, " after mature Deliberation in the Sacrifice of the " Mass, and being about to receive the Body of our " Lord ; I made a Vow to* GOD *in the following " Words :* I Robert, Cardinal Bellarmin, *a professed " Religious of the Order of* JESUS, *vow to Al- " mighty* GOD, *in the Sight of the blessed Virgin " Mary, and the whole Heavenly Choir, that if, " which I do not desire, and wish to* GOD *may never " happen,*

BELLARMIN.

is his Book de Scriptoribus Ecclesiasticis *(l)*. I wish I had not met with these two Facts there; for they are not true [*Y*]. The Inscription, which was put under this Cardinal's Print, imports, that he had preserved his Virginity, and his Baptismal Innocency, and that he had never told a Lie *(m)*. When he was dying, he bequeathed one half of his Soul to the Holy Virgin, and the other half to JESUS CHRIST *(n)*. He was so patient, that he suffered Flies, and such small Insects, to be very troublesome to him [*Z*]. He let them alone, saying, that they had no other Paradice, than the Liberty to fly, and light, where they pleased. He was a Man of a small Stature, and of a mean Outside; yet he discovered the Beauty of his Wit in his Face *(o)*. He expressed himself with Clearness, and premeditated the Words, which were to represent his Thoughts, so exactly, that no Rasures appeared in his Writings *(p)*. His *Hebrew* Grammar is pretty well esteemed; though it is thought, that he had but an indifferent Knowledge of That Language *(q)*: some say, that he was quite a Stranger to *Greek (r)*. I do not believe the Pope ever

" happen, I should ever be elected Pope, I will never
" raise any of my Family or Kindred to the Purple,
" Temporal Principality, Duchy, Earldom, or any o-
" ther Title; nor will I enrich, but only assist them
" to live comfortably in their Civil Capacity. Amen.
" Amen."

[*Y*] *Ancillon advances two Facts concerning Bellarmin, which are not true.*] Every one knows, that Cardinal *Cajetan*, Legate of *Sixtus* V, in *France*, made it his chief Business to cause *Henry* IV to be excluded from the Crown. It was not at the Court of That Monarch, that *Bellarmin*, That Legate's Chaplain, acquired the King's *Esteem*; for he was not there; he was at *Paris*, among the *Leaguers*, and used his utmost Endeavours for the Interest of the Rebels. This is what the Ministers have not failed to object; Read this Passage of *Drelincourt*; " Whence comes it, that Those of the Protestant Re-
" ligion were in the King's Camp, whilst *Bellarmin*,
" *Panigarola*, and such Persons, were at *Paris*,
" preaching up Sedition, and the Pope sent some
" Legates to authorize the *League*, and to throw
" Oil into a Fire, which he ought to have ex-
" tinguished with his Tears, and his own Blood (86)?" As for what concerns the Treatise of the Ecclesiastical Writers, it is a good Work in it's kind; but it is far from being *Bellarmin's* best Book. There are several Treatises in his Volumes of Controversies, which discover his Wit, Learning, and Capacity, more nobly. Twenty small Pieces, every one as good as That, *de Scriptoribus Ecclesiasticis*, would not have raised him to the Degree of Honour, which he deserved for the Form alone, in which he cloathed his Body of Controversies: for see, here, the Commendation which a Learned *Englishman* gave him, on this Subject: " Vir erat, haud inficior, admirandæ industriæ,
" doctrinæ, lectionis stupendæ, Bellarminus: qui ut
" primus, ita solus, immanem illam molem, & im-
" mensum chaos controversiarum, stupendâ ingenii
" dexteri felicitate, artificio singulari, excoluit, in or-
" dinem redegit confusum prius, accuratâ diligentiâ,
" & multorum annorum studio, eleganter expolivit:
" præripuit ille palmam secuturis omnibus, & sibi
" desponsatam vel destinatam cuicunque laudem ab-
" stulit. Nam ab illo, qui tractant hodie Contro-
" versias, ut ab Homero Poëtæ, sua omnia ferè mu-
" tuantur (87). - - - - Bellarmin *was, I confess, a
" Man of surprizing Industry, Learning, and Reading*;
" *the first, and only Person, who, with Abilities,
" and Diligence, happily polished, and reduced into
" Form, the immense Chaos of Controversies. In this
" be surpassed All that came after him, who, in
" treating such Subjects, borrow almost every thing
" from him, as the Poets do from* Homer." Considerable Faults have been observed (88), in the Treatise, which *Colixtus*, and Mr *Ancillon*, pretend to be the best of all This Jesuit's Writings. See *Bosius*, in the second Chapter of his *Introductio in Notitiam Scriptorum Ecclesiasticorum*, with Mr *Crenius's* Notes. *Labrun*, says he (89), *omnium, quos Bellarminus edidit, optimum vocat* D. Calixtus, *tractatu de conjugio Christorum, sectione* 202. If we may believe Father *Labbe*, the first Edition of This Book of *Bellarmin* is of the Year 1617 (90). Father *Sirmond* took great care of it, as the Author had desired him (91). Several other Editions were made of it, which the Printers spoiled extreamly; but, at last, a very correct one was published at *Paris*, by Cramoisi, in the Year 1658, in 8vo. Father *Labbè*, who revised the Proofs,

formed the Plan of a Work upon it (92), which some very good Judges take for the best he composed. I mean his *Dissertatio de Scriptoribus Ecclesiasticis*; which was printed, at *Paris*, in two Volumes, in 8vo, in the Year 1660. The Authors of the *Bibliotheque* of the Jesuits knew nothing of the first Edition of This Treatise of *Bellarmin*; one of them, viz. *Alegambus*, mentions none, and *Sotuel* mentions only That of *Cologne* 1622, in 8vo. A new one was made in the same City in the Year 1684, in 4to; and the Continuation, which *Andrew de Saussai* published, in the Year 1665, was joined to it. *Bellarmin's* Omissions were very considerable, as appears by the Supplement of Father *Oudin*, which was mentioned in the *News from the Republic of Letters*, in the Month of *April*, 1686.

Remark a Mistake of *Bosius*. He says, there is no trusting to *Bellarmin's* Judgment about the *Greek* Writers, because he did not understand the *Greek* Language; and that This Ignorance, which appeared in his other Books, was most conspicuous in the Treatise of the Ecclesiastical Writers, as *Casaubon* observed. " Græcarum Litterarum prorsus ἀμύητον
" fuisse sicut omnia illius scripta, sic eximiè hic liber
" novissimè ab eo profectus, Casaubono judice exer-
" citat. 16. sect. 150. ostendit, ut proinde judiciis
" illius de Græcis scriptoribus satis tuto fidi non pos-
" sit." *Bsius* had just before said, that the first Edition of This Work of *Bellarmin* is of the Year 1616 (93). How could he believe then, that *Casaubon* had spoken of it, in that manner, in a Book, which was printed in the Year 1614? But, after all, will you say is it true, that *Casaubon* spoke of This Work; for, in this Case, *Bosius's* Error will be very inconsiderable? I answer, there is a great probability, that he had This Treatise of *Bellarmin* in view. There is an Edition of *Cologne* 1613, set down in the Catalogue of *Oxford*: and I have seen one of *Lyons*, 1613, in 4to, Revised and Corrected by the Author. So that This Work was plainly enough hinted at, in That Passage of *Casaubon*, where it is said, that it was the last Book of *Bellarmin*, which appeared; we may, therefore, affirm, that Father *Labbe* is mistaken, in placing the first Edition of it in the Year 1617.

[*Z*] *He suffered Flies - - - - to be troublesome to him*.] This deserves to be set down in *Fuligatti's* own Words. " Inter insignes Bellarmini virtutes, alii po-
" nunt miram ejus in perferendis vexationibus pa-
" tientiam, quam Jacobus Fuligattus laudat sequen-
" tibus verbis: Culices, modicellas aviculas, sicut &
" alia parva naturæ incommoda, velut à DEO tra-
" ditas ad exercitium patiendi, vultu adeò miti per-
" ferebat, ut nec ipse opposita manu, nec exciente
" ventulum aliquo, eas conaretur abigere. Aliquando
" Clementi Merlino R. rotæ auditori, dum sermones
" familiares, ut fit post negotia decisa, sererent, re-
" tulit, se nocte ejus diei, qui est Catharinæ virgini
" sacer, adeò ad renes à bestiolis quibusdam nequam
" ac damnificis morsu fuisse vexatum, ut magno sensu
" conversus ad CHRISTI, præpendentis à cruce Domini,
" simulacrum dixerit: ò Domine, si hoc quicquid est
" damni, quod certè parum est, mihi tantum af-
" fert molestiæ, æcquænam erunt supplicia damnato-
" rum? si apud gehennam impios manent tormenta
" tàm ærumnosa, nec, precor, in eâ me præjicias, æte-
" nim impar eis iisdem sustinendis. Cardinalis Cres-
" centius addit, Bellarminum ita sè patientiæ velut
" victimam destinasse, ut muscas à vultu ne depelle-
" ret

BELLEAU. BELLFOREST.

ever sent him to *Louvain*, to put an End to the Disputes of *Michael Baius* there, or to make a Report of them at *Rome* [*A A*]. So many Persons have attacked him, and so many have defended him, that Catalogues have been made of both. The List *of his Defenders was composed by* Beraldi, *an Italian* (*s*).

(s) Baillet, Tom. I, of the Anti's, pag 81, 82.

(94) Antrae as Carolus, Memorab. Eccleiast. pag. 533.

" ret quidem, tametsi adisse nimium essent, sicuti " Romae in ceju silent; cùmque hoc mirarentur, qui " aderant, ipse Jupiter, Haud aequum esse, ajebat, " perturbare animantes illos, quibus non utique su- " peresset paradisus alius, quàm volitandi libertas, ac " potestas, ubi malunt, commorandi (94). —— Among " the remarkable Virtues *of* Bellarmin, others place " his wonderful Patience, in enduring Vexations, " which *James* Fuligatti *celebrates in the following* " Words: He considered Gnats, a little flying Insect, " and other small Vexations, which Nature throws " in our Way, as sent by GOD, to exercise our " Patience; and he suffered them so calmly, that he " neither endeavoured to drive them away with " his own Hand, nor permitted any one else to do " it. In a Conversation, once, as is usual after the " Fatigue of Business, with *Clemens Merlinus,* Au- " ditor of the *Rota,* he told him, that, on the Eve " of the Festival of St *Catherine,* he was so tor- " mented with the biting of pernicious Insects at " his Reins, that, through the Acuteness of the Pain, " turning to the Figure of our Saviour on the Cross, " he cried out, O Lord! If This trifling Affliction " gives me so much uneasiness, what must the " Damned endure? If such dreadful Misery awaits " the Wicked in Hell, O! never throw me into it, " for I shall be unable to support it. Cardinal *Cre- " scentius adds,* that *Bellarmin* had so devoted him- " self to Patience, that he would not drive the Flies " from his Face, though they were extremely trou- " blesome, as is usual at *Rome*, in hot Weather; " which when the Standers by expressed their Won- " der at, he mildly told them, It was unjust to di-

" sturb those little Creatures, whose only Paradise " is the Liberty of flying, and resting, where they " please." It is certain, there is a way of spinning out Consequences from the Evangelical Precepts, or Counsels, which leads almost necessarily to That Patience, which is attributed to *Bellarmin*; but nevertheless Reason shews us, that it is no ways likely, that JESUS CHRIST, or his Apostles, in recommending to us so expressly the Contempt of the Conveniencies of Life, intended to forbid us the right of freeing ourselves from the Vexation of Bugs, and of driving away a Fly, which is troublesome to us.

[*A A*] *I do not believe the Pope ever sent him to* Louvain *to put an End to the Disputes of* Baius, *or to make a Report of them at* Rome.] Mr *Leydecker* says, I. That *Bellarmin* was sent thither to inform himself of Those Disputes, and to pacify them; or, at least to give the Pope an Account of them. II. That he acquitted himself very well of This Commission, and that, after having heard *Michael Baius*, he returned to *Rome*, very angry for having found, that he treated, as Pelagian Doctrines, several Opinions of the Schoolmen, which were *Bellarmin's* own (95). I can find no trace of this Deputation in the Writers of This Jesuit's History; and I know, that he made but little Noise, when he went to *Louvain*. He acquired his first Reputation in the seven Years, that he taught Divinity in That Place (96); and, as he was in *Augustinian* as to the Points in dispute between *Baius*, and his Antagonists, it is not at all likely, he was ever angry with That Doctor, for the Reason, which Mr *Leydecker* mentions.

(95) Melch. Leyd-cker, Disput. Historico-Theologica II, de vario Jansenia-rum fato. See the Preface to the Edition of the Works of Baius, 1696, and pag. 213, of Part II.

(96) Nicius Eryth. Pinacoth. I, pag. 85.

BELLEAU (REMI), a *French Poet* of the XVIth Century, was born at *Nogent le Rotrou*. I shall not say much of him; for *Moreri* has already observed almost all that I could have collected. This Poet turned the Odes of *Anacreon* into *French*, and deprived them of *a great part of their Beauty*, if we may believe some Authors (*a*); but others maintain, that he equalled the Original, and that, if he had loved drinking as well as *Anacreon* did, he would have out-done him. Do not trust too much to This Encomium; for it is taken from a piece of Poetry, made by *Scævola de Sainte Marthe*, in praise of the *French* Translation, of which I am speaking (*b*). *Pasquier* thinks, that, in point of *Gaiety*, *Belleau* was another Anacreon *in his Time* (*c*) [*A*]. He acted one *of the chief Parts* in the *Cleopatra*, and the Rencounter of *Jodelle*, when they were acted before King *Henry*, at *Paris*, in the Palace of *Reims* —————— and in the College of Boncour (*d*). He died in 1577, and in his fiftieth Year (*e*). He commented on the second Part of the Amours of *Peter Ronsard*.

(a) Teissier, Addit. Tom. I, pag. 404, Edit. 1° 6. He quotes the end *P*. I of Cola, pag. S 9.

(b) Sammarthanae Elog. lib 3, pag. 13, 14.

(c) Pasquier, Recherch, lib. 7, cap. 7, pag. 622.

(d) Id. ibid. pag. 623.

(e) Thuan. lib 64, pag. 204.

(1) Du Chesne, A ntiqua of Towns of France, pag. 2, 6.

[*A*] *Belleau, according to* Pasquier, *was another* Anacreon *in his Time*.] This was also the Opinion of *Andrew du Chesne*. "The Country of *Perche*, " *says he* (1), produced This genteel and learned " Poet, among others, in the Reign of *Henry* II, " whom I look upon as another *Anacreon* of our

" Age, in Matters of Gaiety: I mean, *Remi Belleau*, " whose Design was to imitate *Sannazarius* in his " Works. For, as the *Italian Sannazarius* made the " Shepherds of his *Arcadia* speak in Prose, in which " he placed all his *Tuscan* Poetry; so our great " *Belleau* has done the like in his Pastorals."

BELLEFOREST (FRANCIS de), was born in the Month of *November*, 1530, near *Samatan*, a Town of the Country of *Cominges*, in *Guienne* (*a*). He was but seven, or eight, Years of Age, when his Father died: His Mother, finding herself without an Estate, did all she could to keep him some time at School. He was educated some Years in the House of the Queen of *Navarre*, Sister to *Francis* I. He studied, afterwards, at *Bourdeaux*, under *Buchanan, Vinetus, Salignac, Gelida*, and some other learned Men; then he went to *Toulouse*, to study the Civil-Law there; but his Genius made him apply himself to quite another thing. He trifled away his time in making French *Verses, to please the Ladies*, and, having spent *seven or eight Years among the Delights of the Nobility*, and in the trifles of Gallantry, he went to *Paris*, where he attended the Professors Lectures, and contracted a strict Acquaintance with divers learned Men, and even insinuated himself into the Company of several Persons of Quality (*b*). He gained little, or nothing, by all This; insomuch, that, if the Booksellers had not bought the Productions of his Pen, he had not had Bread to eat. Study was his Inheritance; and he was one of those Authors, who maintain their Families by dint of their Pens: His best Friends tell us, that, by the Blessing of GOD on the Labour of his Hands, he maintained

(a) La Croix du Maine, Bibl. Franc. pag. 85.

(b) Du Verdier Van Privas, Biblioth. Fr. p. 366, 367.

VOL. I.   8 Z   his

BELLEFOREST.

his Family by his Books [*A*]. And, therefore, it is no wonder, if he wrote such a great Number of Books (*c*), and undertook to write upon so many different Subjects, which were beyond the reach of his Abilities: He was obliged to follow the Direction of the Booksellers, and to turn himself every way, according to the Taste of the Public; that is, according as certain Books, good or bad, sold well. It is said of him, *That he had Moulds, in which he cast new Books with great Expedition* (*d*). He died at *Paris*, the first Day of *January*, 1583, and was buried in the *Franciscans* Church, as he had desired in his Will (*e*). *Thevet*, who was not a more considerable Author, boasted publickly, that *Belleforest* made him a public Reparation, on his Death-bed [*B*]. They had been much embroiled together. La *Popeliniere* speaks very ill of these two Authors [*C*]. *Ghilini* has committed a great many Faults in a short Elogy of *Belleforest* [*D*]; and, if he had been as ill informed in every thing else, his Works would be of no value.

(*c*) *You will find a large List of them in the Bibliotheque of la Croix du Maine, and in That of du Verdier Vau-privas.*

(*d*) *Du Haillan, Epist. Dedicat. prefixed to The History of France, Edit. of* 1584.

(*e*) La Croix du Maine, ubi supra, pag. 91.

[*A*] *His best Friends tell us ------ that he maintained his Family by his Books.*] Du Verdier Vau-Privas (1) declares himself *Belleforest*'s intimate Friend, and Admirer. *I received*, says he, *as much Satisfaction from our Correspondence by Letters, as I was afterwards sorry for his Death. ------ His Name will be immortal among Men, so long as the World endures, by reason of the fine Works, which he composed.* Now see how he speaks of his Friend's Fortune. *Belleforest was intimately acquainted with Ronsard, Baïf, Belleau, Vigenere - - - - Chopin, the Ornament of the Palace of Paris, and many others; he was caressed by Princes, beloved by the Nobility, and esteemed by all the virtuous Men of this Kingdom; but his Fortune was so mean, that he lived only by his Study; and the Labour of his Hands and Mind, being bless'd with, and supported by, the Divine Grace, relieved the Necessities of his Family.*

[*B*] Thevet - - - - *boasted publickly, that* Belleforest *made him Reparation, on his Death-bed.*] There is nothing more dishonest than This Man's Proceeding. He glories in the Humility, which his Adversary expressed to him, on his Death-bed; and yet he abuses him, as much as he could have done, before their Reconciliation. These are his Words: "There are some, who, having no more Learning than *Munster*, have, nevertheless, been so bold as to scrawl after him, and new-mould him; which is the second Head, on which I ground my Complaint against Those, who, not having been much farther than the Smoak of their Chimnies, their Stoves, or Cottages, dare, in the mean Time, persuade themselves, that there is no Spot of Ground, but what they have ferreted: but it is only in Imagination. To cover their too presumptuous Undertakings, they have stollen, here and there, as much as they could; and, sometimes, they have cut off small Pieces from the Discourses, which they have castrated: So that most of their huge Books are only composed of patched Pieces, which have so ill a Grace, that, by what I can hear, they serve only to wrap up Butter, and Sugar. I am sorry *Belleforest* was so indiscreet as to patch up *Munster*'s Cosmography. I question not but some will think, that what I say of it proceeds from a Spirit of Revenge, and that, having been provoked by him, I intend at present to pour out the Fury of my Anger upon him. God shall be my Witness: And, truly, if he had offended me more than he did, I would not satirize, and speak ill of, a dead Man. Besides, at the end of his Life, acknowledging the Wrong, which he knew he had done, in printing those Books, wherein, against his Conscience, he aspersed the Characters of good Men, and of those, who patronized and supported them; he sent for me, and, in the Presence of two Doctors of the *Sorbonne*, and of his Physician, and Bookseller *Gabriel Buon*, after having kissed my Hands, he confessed publickly, that he felt his Conscience burthened for the blame he had laid on me; for which he asked my Pardon several times. As for me, I desired him, the best I could, not to think any more of it; forasmuch as we are all Men (2)."

[*C*] La Popeliniere *speaks very ill of these two Authors*] I shall set down, somewhat at length, what he has said of them, and I hope, it will not displease those, who love to see things in the original Authors, and who would find it difficult to procure the Author, whom I quote. " These two Men,

(1) Biblioth. Franc. pag. 367.

" sometimes Friends, and sometimes Enemies, have deserved the worse of Learning, as they were unworthy to treat of it. Nay, they were as destitute of Wit, Judgment, Memory, and all the Qualifications of a good Genius, as they were supplied with Boldness to interpret ill, and write worse, what they never understood. And, because some hasty Travels of the one, and the Itch of Writing, which possessed the other, made their Essays acceptable to the Vulgar, who neither will, nor can, take time to examine things well; they set up for Scriblers, at such a rate, that all the Printers of *Paris*, preferring their mean Capacity to all Judicious Works, strove to buy up, publish, and make them appear to all the World. And, tho' they were never well instructed in their Youth, nay, without any considerable Experience of the things of this World, and, moreover, poor and destitute of all the Means, which the most knowing Men have always called the Wings of Virtue; yet these universal Wits have passed through all Professions. There is no Language, or Science, but what they have prophaned. Nay, they have scribbled Histories, Particular, and Universal, according to their foolish Fancies. How can one help it? As all Seasons are attended with certain Accidents, which bring evil to All, and good to none, the Causes whereof are unknown to us, and cannot be imputed to the Faults of Men: So there have always been, and ever will be, certain private Men, in all States, who, being only fit to confound and spoil every thing, undertake nothing, but what will prejudice others, and profit no Body. These Men are like Itching, the Forerunner of a Sickness to Those, who are troubled with it. Their Hands itched; they could not forbear writing; not for the Public Good, but for their particular Profit; which they kept up with the wretched Labour of their unruly Pens. So that I have often lamented, that, *France* being so well provided with good Writers, such low Genius's, who can boast of nothing but an assiduous, and useless, Labour, should find People, who will throw away their Time in reading their Nonsense, their Annals, Histories, and Universal Geographies, contrived, formed, hatched, and published in their solitary Dens. Those, who do not take the Pains to inform themselves of the Particulars of the World, and chiefly to observe the Course, and Issue, of each Man's private Actions, cannot believe, how much prejudice *Belleforest* and *Thevet* have done to Youth, and, consequently to the State; explaining abundance of Passages so ill, and many times in a quite contrary Sense; corrupting, and falsifying, Matters; and taking many things for granted, which they had ridiculously fancied in their own weak Brains. Without mentioning a World of other Impertinencies, wherewith they have patched up their silly Writings. Neither of the two *Cato*'s would in this have excused *Belleforest*, (though he boasted to have written as much as St *Augustine*) if Poverty made him speak like a Jay, that is, like a Beast. For he has shewed himself too brutish on all accounts towards Posterity (3)."

[*D*] Ghilini *has committed a great many Faults, in a short Elogy.*] What he said of our *Belleforest* contains, in all, but Twenty two Lines. These are his Errors: He takes *Cominges* for a City of *Gascogne*: he affirms, that *Belleforest* published several Works in *Latin*, and, among others, *The Annals of France* in two Volumes; *The History of nine Kings of France*, whose

(2) H. wet's Munster in Munster Villi pag. 100. 2.3. *Life of him in 12°1, in 12mo.*

(3) Popeliniere's History of Histories, pag. 459.

BELLEY. 737

whose Names were Charles: The Universal History, or an Abridgment of Cosmography. All this is false: These Works, and all the other Books of This Author, were written in *French. Gbilini* adds, that there is a *Catalogue of the Illustrious Men,* who have made themselves famous, in Monasteries, both by their Learning, and their Actions, and *An History of the Holy Martyrs,* in three Volumes, written by This Author. But there is no manner of likelihood, that This Catalogue was ever printed. *La Croix du Maine* never saw it; and he knew only, that *Belleforest* mentions it in the Hundred ninety third Leaf of his Cosmography. *Du Verdier Vau-Privas,* an intimate Friend of *Belleforest,* says nothing of This Catalogue; and no one is ignorant, that Authors refer to Works, which they have not yet made Public. The same *du Verdier* informs us, that "The Life, "*Passion,* and Burial of St *Dionysius,* the *Areopagite,* "and of his Companions, who were his Fellow- "Martyrs, collected out of divers Authors, by the "late *John,* Doctor of Divinity, great Prior of the "Abbey of St *Denis* in *France,* and done into *French*

"by *Belleforest, is printed* in the Third Volume of "the History of the Lives and Deaths of the "Saints (4)." This is the notable ground, on which *Belleforest* by Gilbini, not as a Translation, but as an Original. He attributes also the Translation of St *Cyprian's* Works to him. If he had consulted *Vau-Privas,* he would have read there, that This Writer translated only some Treatises of St *Cyprian* (5), and that all the Works of That Saint were translated by *James Tigeou.* Lastly, Gilbini is somewhat to be blamed for not knowing the Year of *Belleforest's* Death, and for placing it about the Year 1603. As for the excessive Praises, with which he crowns This Author's Memory, They might be reckoned among his Faults, were it not that many other Writers might lead him into This Profusion. I shall quote but one of Them. *René de Lazinge,* speaking of *Belleforest,* says, *He is a Man of great Reading, who is not ignorant of any Thing, which is left confused in Antiquity, the Passages of which he clears up with great Care, and in good Language* (6).

BELLEY, a City of *France,* and Capital of the Province of *Bugei,* is *very ancient, since the Episcopal See was established there in the Year* 412 (a). Consult the Dictionary of *Moreri,* and add to it what follows: "The Diocese of *Belley* "has four Towns, six large Boroughs, and more than Two hundred Villages, "being extended ten Leagues in Diameter (b). The Dignity of a Prince of the "Empire is added to That of Bishop of *Belley*; a Title, which was given by the "Emperors to the Archbishop of *Bezançon,* and his three Comprovincials, or Suf- "fragans, *Basil, Lausanne,* and *Belley.* The Sovereignty of the City of *Belley,* "and it's Territory, which is pretty wide, belonged to the Bishop. But he was "deprived of it gradually, by a powerful and neighbouring Prince, under the "Disguise and Appearance of Protection. There are still extant, in the Archives "of the Church, several Excommunications issued on this Occasion, and many "others of Opposition, and Resistance; but, in these Cases, Right is on the side "of Power (c)." Since That Time the Revenues of the Bishopric have greatly decreased; for "it's largest Possessions consisted in the Rights, which This Rebel "Lordship has usurped, and which were confined almost wholly to the City (d)." This is what I borrow from a Work of Mr *Camus,* Bishop of *Belley,* published in 1644; in which he deduces these Facts, with some Observations, in order to refute a Monk, who had spoken disrespectfully of This Bishopric [A]. I find, in *Guichenon,* that *John de Passelaigue,* Bishop of *Belley,* obtained of *Lewis* XIII, in 1635, "a Confirmation of all the Privileges, granted to the Bishops of *Belley,* by the "Emperor *Frederic* ——— excepting however the Regale, and the coining of "Money (e)." This *John de Passelaigue* succeeded *John Peter Camus,* who began to govern This Diocese in the Year 1609, and who found many Disorders in the Convents [B], particularly in That of St *Sulpice.* I shall take Occasion to remark the

[A] *Some Observations, in order to confute a Monk, who had spoken disrespectfully of This Bishopric*] This Monk had written a Book, entitled *The Anti Camus.* At the Thirty ninth Page were These Words. *It is very strange, that a little neglected Bishopric behind the Alps, whose Name is scarce to be met with in the Archives of the Church, and whose Pastor, for want of Employment at home (his District is so small) goes about preaching, like a Franciscan, should pretend, not only to equal, but to exalt itself above the Popes, to abolish their Order, and reform their Regulations.* "The Diocese is not so small, replies Mr Camus "(1), but I can name to him five Archbishoprics, "and more than Twenty five Bishoprics, in *France,* "of smaller Extent; more than twelve of which the "sole Provinces of *Languedoc* and *Provence* can furnish. I will prove to him twenty Archbishoprics, "and an Hundred and twenty Bishoprics, in *Italy,* of "smaller Extent, than the Diocese of *Belley.* — It is "not behind the Alps, if you do not consider the "Alps on the Side of *Italy,* in like manner, as, "with regard to us, the Archbishopric of *Turin* is "laid behind the Alps. Though it were in the Alps, "Would it be the less considerable? How many "noble Archbishoprics, and Bishoprics, are there in "this Great World of Hills? *Ambrun, Tarantaise,* "*Grenoble, Guyenne* (2), *Maurienne, Syon, Lausanne,* "*Constance, Basil, Arles, Ivreé*; All Dioceses of "Note, Churches Famous, and celebrated for their "Antiquity and Extent. —— I will prove to him "that the Antiquity of the Diocese, which he calls "so small, is more than a thousand Years, and that

"there are, in *France* alone, more than thirty or "forty Bishoprics of later Date. — Bishoprics are "not to be measured by their Revenues: otherwise "a Curacy of *Sicily,* which I could name, and "which has but One Cure, with Thirty thousand "Crowns *per annum,* would be a large Archbishopric (3)." Here are some particulars, which will gratify the Curiosity of several Readers, though they are not necessary to the Article of *Belley.*

[B] *John Peter Camus found many Disorders in the Convents of the Diocese of* Belley.] The following is part of the Description, which he gives of these Disorders. "There was An Abbey (4) of Monks, "richly founded, whose Abbot was an Huguenot "Captain, a married Man, and Governor of a "neighbouring Fortress, who kept the whole Country, of the "try about him in Awe and Fear (5)."

He took it into his Head to keep a Stud in the Convent, and "having collected a great Number of "Mares, which are very large and fine in *Bresse,* he "sent for Stallions from *Spain* and *Germany,* and "large Asses from *Auvergne* which are of an enormous "Size, in order to produce Mules by their Mixture with the Mares, according to the Method established in This Stud. —— The Church, which "was as large as a Cathedral, served as a Repository "for Hay, Straw, and other Forrage, necessary for "the Sustenance of these Animals, during four or "five Months of the Winter, that the Earth is all "covered with Snow. The Monks had but just the "Liberty of part of the Choir about the Altar, to "sing the Service in, where they continued to do it

the pious Fraud, which was published concerning the Foundation of This Monastery [C].

" it with Negligence enough. In the Abbot's House
" were several Huguenot Soldiers, with their Trulls
" (a Baggage inseparable from the pretended Refor-
" mation of Those of the fifth Gospel); and there
" they said their Prayers, sung their Psalms, and
" lived, in short, a merry Life, like Reapers at
" Harvest, Grape-gatherers, or Conquerors, when
" they divide the Spoils of their Enemies. ——— The
" pretended reformed Abbot, to stop the Mouths of
" the Monks, and prevent their Complaints, aug-
" mented their Prebends, or Canonical Portions,
" and, thro' Artifice, and worldly Prudence, caressed
" them extreamly, admitting them to his Table in
" the Citadel, where he entertained them like an
" Abbot and a Captain, supporting them in their
" Humours, and protecting them against all the
" neighbouring Nobility. The Intimacy became so
" great, that they styled him *Our Abbot*, and He
" Them *My Monks*, and said *My Abbey*, when he
" spoke of their House.

" You are not to think, that the Monks spent
" their Time in catechising the Soldiers, Governors
" of the Stud, and their Companies, which might have
" been formed into another Stud of Rational Brutes.
" ——— This Convent became *A Church Militant*:
" for you might see Monks a-hunting with Soldiers,
" each with his Musket on his Shoulder: the
" Monks never stirred abroad but upon large Horses,
" and the better according to the Permission and In-
" dulgence of the Abbot, always well armed, with
" Sword and Pistol, and often with Carbine: they
" were seen every Day traversing the Country in
" This Equipage; insomuch, that it might be said
" of them, as of the *Sbulamite*, in the Canticles,
" that they were Choirs of Warriours, and Batallions
" of Choristers (6).

*This fine Management continued eight or nine Years.
The Bishop sometimes threatned to inform the Parliament, or the King's Governor, or Lieutenant, of it,
in order to put a Stop to such scandalous Proceedings:
but the Monks, on the one side, made themselves whiter
by their Exemptions and Privileges, than their Habits;
and, on the other, threatned him with the Power of
the Abbot, who, as a formidable Scourge, kept the
Nobility, Church, and People of the Country, in awe.
And, as a Proof of his Violence, and Power, he went
so far, as even to make an Attempt on the Person of
the Governor, who had a Man slain at his Feet, after
the Manner related in the French Mercury. ——— The
King, to punish this Attempt, commanded the Citadel
to be razed; and the Tyrant was turned out of it, as
well as of his Abbey; and afterwards, retiring among
the Huguenots of Languedoc, from whence he sprung,
he was assassinated by Those of the same Party, and his
nearest Relations, during the Siege of* Montauban. *The
Abbey was put into the Hands of a Professed Abbot of
the same Order, who, at least, removed the Scandal of
the Stud* (7).

*At the Foot of the same Hill, is a Convent of Nuns,
of the same Order: of whom the above-named Monks
call themselves the Fathers; and are indeed so; for
they have the Direction and Visitation of them. Here
are no traces, or footsteps, of a Cloyster, nor any
kind of Regulation. It is a General Landing Place to
all Companies; a true Watering-Place of* Africa: *and
surprising Intercourses are there carried on, under the
Pretence of Relation and Consanguinity. Whenever
The Captain-Abbot, mentioned above, came, with the
Officers of his Regiment, to see his Stud, he went
down to pay a Visit to the Monastery of the Valley,
where he was received with great Respect; and we
may suppose, that he made them fine Exhortations from
the ninth Verse of the seventh Chapter of the First to
the* Corinthians. *That there was a perpetual Intercourse of Conversations, and Familiarities. ——— A continual Flux, and Reflux, of Companies; the Great
entered, the Small went out: The Gate was open to
All, without respect to Sex, or Age. ——— In short,
Confusion reigned there; and the Wound became so desperate, for want of Judgment and Discretion, that
Licentiousness was there taken for Innocent Freedom,
and Liberty in supplied the Place of Liberty* (8).

*In vain did the Bishop publickly exhort, and remon-
strate, again and again, against these Abuses.* " At
" last, he gave them to understand, that he was
" bound in Conscience not to suffer these Irregulari-
" ties any longer; since the Council of *Trent* had
" ordered the Bishops and Ordinaries to see that the
" Nuns keep their Vows, whatever Privileges their
" Orders might lay claim to: Having apprized them
" of this; do but hear the Vanity and Presumption
" of Two Reverends, who, at different Times, had
" had the Conduct of this Blessed Flock; and who
" expresly opposed This Reformation: the first re-
" plied, that the Council of *Trent* had been held
" by Bishops, and, consequently, that they were
" not bound to obey it, because their Order was
" privileged, and exempt from the Jurisdiction of
" Bishops, and that the Councils of Monks were
" their General Chapters. The Other, mere artful,
" alledged, that This Council having consisted but
" of [*trente*] *thirty* Bishops, though there had been
" forty or fifty, it could have no Place in the Uni-
" versal Church, of which the Monks made the
" most illustrious Part, the most perfect and com-
" pleat, as being in a State of Perfection. There
" was One Nun, of a fine, I know not whether of
" a good Wit, who, being *prepossessed* (not to say
" *prompted* *) by these excellent Tutors, or rather
" Fathers, replied, one Day, to the Remonstrances
" of *M. D. B.* My Lord, You seem to me resolved
" to broil us all *alive*, though we have not deserved
" it. To which He replied readily, but coldly: My
" Sister, you plainly shew, by your Discourse, that
" you are very *lively*, and but little *dead* to your-
" self. I mean very little mortified: for, as The
" Fish, which is yet alive, leaps from the *Gridiron*,
" and tumbles among the Coals, which a dead
" one does not do: So those Nuns, who are not
" well dead to the World, and whose Passions are
" alive, and often vivifying, chuse rather, like *Sa-
" lamanders* and *Pyrakdes*, to live amidst the Fire
" of Conversation, according to the Thought of St
" Bernard, who compares a Monk, conversing with
" the World unhurt, to the Miracle of the three
" Children in the Furnace, than to remain enclosed
" within a *Grate* †, crucified with JESUS CHRIST,
" their Spouse. So little able were *M. C.* the Abbot,
" who succeeded the Captain, and all the Superiers
" of the Order, either to confine, or reform, these
" good Ladies, of whom, out of Decency and Mo-
" desty, I shall say no more, leaving the rest to the
" Imagination of the Reader, who, from what has
" been said, may form conjectures of what is hid
" under the Curtain of Silence (9)."

*The Book, from whence I borrow These Frag-
ments, has not been omitted by Mr* Baillet, *in his
curious List of* ANTI'S, *any more than the* ANTI-
HERMITE, *and* ANTI MOINE, *of the same Mr* Camus. *He says of the two latter, that they shared so
in the fate of the rest of this Author's Works, that it
is scarce known, that there ever were such Books. If
they continue running on, with the same Precipitation,
as hitherto, to Annihilation, the Memory of them will
very soon be effaced; and it will be difficult to preserve
even their Names in Booksellers Catalogues* (10). *This
is equally applicable to That entitled, The Anti* Basilic,
in answer to the Anti Camus, *by* Olenix *of* Bourg-
l'Abbé, *I have, therefore, reason to believe, that
the long Extracts, I have given of this Work, will be
more agreeable, than if I had made use of a Reference, which would have been useless to the greatest
Part of my Readers.*

*It will be proper to take notice of some Instances
of Neglect in the Narrative of Mr* Camus. *I. He
does not Name the Huguenot Abbot, nor the Citadel, of which he was Governor. I supply this Defect, and say, that he speaks of* Peter d'Escodeça, *Lord
of* Boisse, *Baron of* Pardaillan, *Colonel of Horse
of the Regiment of* Champagne, *and Governor of the
Citadel of* Bourg *in* Bresse. II. *He was of* Guienne,
and not of Languedoc. III. *The Disorder, he was
guilty of, shall, if you please, continue eight or nine
Years, but not in Sight of Mr de* Bellei, *who was not
consecrated Bishop, till the Year* 1609. *Now the Citadel of* Bresse *was razed in the Year* 1611 (11). IV.
*The King, at that time, was not, as yet, out of his
Minority;* V. *And it cannot be said, that the Governor committed all these Outrages under the Minority
of* Lewis XIII.

[C] *The pious Fraud, which was published concerning the Foundation of This Monastery.*] " The An-
" cient

BELOY.

"cient Manuscript Chronicle of *Savoy* — imports, that *Amé*, the second of the Name, First Earl of *Savoy*, and Lord of *Bugey*, made a Vow to found an Abbey in his Estates, in order to obtain Issue; after which he had a Son, called *Humbert*, who falling sick, and being in danger of dying, before the Accomplishment of the Vow, his Father built, and founded, the Abbey of St *Sulpice*, in *Bugey*, at the Persuasion of the Countess of *Savoy*, his Wife." The Words of the Chronicle are These.

It happened one Night, that the Countess, as she lay in Bed, sighed several Times: The Earl enquired the Reason of it. Sir, said she, *I fear the loss of our Son* Humbert. *Why so?* replied He. *Because*, said the Lady, *you have made a Vow to our Lord to found an Abbey, in case* GOD *grants us Issue, and you have forgotten to perform it, and seem not to care for it. Then the Earl replied; Doubt not, but I will, shortly, accomplish it,* GOD *willing. Then he sought for a proper Place; and, finding it, he built a fine Abbey on a Mountain, situated in* Bugey, *under the Name of the Confessor, St* Sulpice; *which he properly endowed, and established an Abbot, and Monks, to praise* GOD *for the Issue he had granted him.* Paradin, in his * History of *Savoy* *, has exactly followed the Manuscript Chronicle of *Savoy*; and adds, that, when the Abbey was finished, and the Vow accomplished, the young Prince of *Savoy* recovered; placing the Time of this Foundation before the Year 1118 (12). *Guichenon* refutes all this very solidly: he says, that he found, in the Archives of St *Sulpice*, that, in the Year 1130, " Fifteen Monks, of the Order of *Citeaux*, and one *Bernard*, who was their Superior, went to the Mountains of *Bugey*, by Permission of *Hugh*, Abbot of *Pontigni*, with a Design of doing Penance there, and leading an austere Life; and that *Amé*, the first Earl of *Savoy*, who was preparing to go to the Holy Land, in order to engage their Stay, granted them *Letters, and Privileges*. — As to the Occasion of the Foundation, it is certain, that the Historians of *Savoy* are mistaken, in publishing, that it was after the Birth of the young Earl *Humbert*, Son of the said *Amé* — for the Grants of Earl *Amé* import the direct contrary; the first of which, dated at *Yenne*, in the Presence of *Pontius*, Bishop of *Belley*, and *Humbert*, Bishop of *Geneva*, has these Words: *Igitur quicumque ista legerit, & audierit, hoc donum me fecisse cognoscat, tempore quo in montanis fratres hospitando retinui, scilicet antequam de uxore mea Mattildi nomine, liberos aliquos procreassem*; i. e. *Be it known to all, who shall read, or hear, these Presents, that I bestowed this Gift, at the time, when I entertained the Brotherhood in the Mountains; that is, before I had a Child by my Wife:* and the second: *Noverit omnis tam extraneus, quam propinquus, hanc meam donationem fecisse, antequam de uxore mea, Mattildi nomine, liberos aliquos procreassem*; i. e. *Be it known to All, Strangers as well as Natives, that this Grant was made before my Wife* Matilda *had brought me any Children* (13)."

I cannot persuade myself, that Chance, or Ignorance, produced the Falshood, which *Guichenon* has refuted. It is rather the Effect of the Artifice of the Ecclesiastics. They bring Water to their Mill whatever way they can; and, to encourage the Great to build Monasteries, or give pious Donations, they forge Instances of Fruitfulness, or Recovery, or some other temporal Advantage, which they ascribe to a Liberal Piety.

BELOY (PETER de (a), Advocate-General in the Parliament of *Toulouse*, had not yet this Employ, when he wrote for the Rights of the King of *Navarre*, against the *League*. If he had been a Protestant, he would have done nothing, in This, but what had been very natural, and required no extraordinary Virtue; but, as he was a *Roman Catholic* (b), and at *Paris*, when he published That Work against the *League*, he ought to be looked upon with some Admiration. That Work is entituled, *A Catholic Apology against the Libels, Declarations, Councils, and Consultations, made, written, and published, by the Leaguers, Disturbers of the Peace of the Kingdom of France, who have taken up Arms, since the Decease of Monsieur, the King's only Brother;* by E. D. L. I. C. It came out in the Year 1585, and was translated into *Latin* [A]: The Writers of the *League* called it an infamous *Libel* [B], and the Author found himself exposed to a severe Persecution [C]. He was a learned Civilian,

[A] His Catholic Apology *was translated into* Latin] I have seen two Translations of it in That Language. One of them, if we believe the Title, was printed, at *Paris*, by *James Petit Chou*, 1586. In the other, we find neither the Place of the Impression, nor the Printer's Name; but the Title is longer than in the Original; and there is an Advertisement of the Translator.

[B] *The Leaguers called it an infamous Libel*] See the Book, entituled, *An Answer of the true French Catholics to the Advertisement of the English Catholics for the Exclusion of the King of* Navarre *from the Crown of* France. The Edition, which I make use of, is of the Year 1589. On the back of the Title-page, you find a Catalogue of the *Diffamatory Libels*, at which That Answer is levelled: The Catholic Apology *by* Beloy *is the Third of Those Libels*. I have seen a particular Answer to the chief Heads of That Work of *Beloy*, which passes for a Piece of *Bellarmin*'s. The Author calls himself *Franciscus Romulus*. He neither attacks his Adversary, about the Genealogy of the House of *Bourbon*, nor about the Bastardy, which was objected to *Henry* IV, by reason of his Mother's Marriage with the Duke of *Cleves*; nor about the Dispute of the Preference of the Uncle to the Nephew; but reduces all to Religion, and to the Foundation of the Bull, which declared the King of *Navarre* to have forfeited the Succession, and to be uncapable of reigning, only on account of his Heresy. The first thing, which *Franciscus Romulus* undertakes to shew, is, that the Author of *the Apology* was no Catholic, as he boasts himself to be, but a meer Heretic, or perhaps an Atheist. *Nos igitur, ut ejus vestigiis insistamus, demonstrabimus primum Auctorem Apologiæ falso sibi Catholici nomen assumere, cum aut hæreticus, aut fortasse etiam Atheus sit* (1). This it is to be over-fond of certain particular Doctrines, which, at the bottom, are not essential to Religion. They, who are fond of these particular Doctrines, impudently maintain, that whoever opposes them is a False Brother, a Prevaricator, a Spy, a Traytor, and, to say all in a Word, an Atheist. In all Communions, there are some such opinionated Persons, without excepting the Protestants, who have quitted *France*. *Bellarmin* may serve to shew them their Illusion; for He, whom he accused of Heresy, and whom he suspected of Atheism, always professed the Catholic Religion, like a very good Man. Here is a Passage of *Anthony Arnauld*: " Who wrote That outrageous Answer " against the *Catholic Apology*, but the Jesuits, " who industriously published the most false and " scandalous Things imaginable against the Person, " and Rights, of his present Majesty (2)?"

[C] *He found himself exposed to a severe Persecution.*] *Cayet* relates, that, at the time of his writing his Book (3), they drew up a Parallel between the chief Writer of the Royalists, and the chief Writer of the Leaguers (4). He means *Peter Beloy*, and *Lewis d' Orleans*. It was said, " that both of them " published their Books without their Names; He, " who wrote for the League, was more eloquent, " but a Calumniator; He, who wrote for the King " of *Navarre*, was more learned, and a true *Frenchman*. The Writer of the League, contrary to the " Royalist, was first rewarded for his Writings, and " was made Advocate-General in the Sovereign Court " of the Kingdom, during the Power of the League;

lian, and a Man of great Reading. He had already published some other Books [D]. Du Plessis Mornai acknowledges him for the true Author of the *Catholic Apology* (c). I shall produce the Fragment of a Letter, which will be a good Supplement to This Article [E].

I add, to what I have already said, the true Duration of his Imprisonment. Cayet is satisfied with saying, that it lasted more than two Years (d); but Beloy relates, that it continued four Years. I shall produce his Words, which will serve as a Supplement to the List, I give, of his Works [F].

" and since he has met with much Trouble and Vexa-
" tion. ---- But He, who wrote in defence of the
" Majesty of Kings, had Trouble and Afflictions, and
" was imprisoned in the beginning. In the Year 88,
" (5) he was clapt up in the Jail belonging to the
" Parliament (6). After the Death of the Duke of
" Guise, he was removed, and strictly kept in the
" Bastile for two Years; and, having found means
" to escape, he fled to *St Dennis*, where he found
" Monf. *de Vic*, Governor for the King, who re-
" ceived him, presented him to his Majesty; and,
" for a Recompence of his Troubles, he is at this
" Day Advocate-General in one the Parliaments of
" this Kingdom (7)." The Fate of these two Authors, was, therefore, an Image of what was said
to *the Rich Man* (8); but it was an imperfect one;
for *Lewis d' Orleans* prospered again, after having
endured some Fatigues, much more inconsiderable,
than what he deserved, by reason of his furious Rebellions.

[D] *He had already published some other Books.*] La Croix du Maine mentions the four following: *A Declaration of the Right of lawful Succession to the Kingdom of Portugal, belonging to the Queen-Mother of the Most Christian King,* at *Antwerp,* and at *Paris,* 1582, in 8vo. *A Panegyric or Remonstrance for the Seneschal and Judges* - - - - *of Toulouse, against the King's Notaries, and Secretaries of the said City,* at *Paris,* 1582, in 4to. *A Verbal Petition for the above-said Lords, and Officers of Toulouse, containing an Apology for, and Defence of, the Advertisement, published in the Name of the Doctors Regents of the University of Toulouse,* at *Paris,* 1583, in 8vo. *A brief Explication of this present Year 1583, according to the Gregorian Calendar,* at *Paris,* 1583, in 8vo. La Croix du Maine adds, that a Work of the same *Beloy* was printing at *Paris,* in 1584. viz. *A Computation of the Times since the Creation of the World, 'till 1583, divided into two several Columns;* and that he would speak, in another Place, of the Latin Works of This Author. The Catalogue of the Bodleian Library mentions two Books; *Petri Beloii variorum Juris Civilis, liber 4. & Disputatio de successione ab intestato, &c.* at *Paris,* 1583, and *the Collation of the Edicts of Pacification with the Explication of the said Edicts,* at *Paris,* in 1600, in 8vo. *Beloy* is Author of a *Commentary* on the *Edict,* which ordered the *uniting* of the King's Patrimony to the Crown-Lands, at *Toulouse,* 1608, in 8vo.

[E] *A Fragment of a Letter, which will be a good Supplement to this Article.*] Here you have what the Author of the Notes on the Confession of *Sanci,* and on the *Catholicon,* was pleased to write to me: " I have a Book, which might have given you much
" Light concerning the famous Civilian, Peter Beloy:
" The Title of it is: *A Reply to the Answer, which
" the Leaguers have published against the Examination,
" which was drawn up, of their pretended Discourse con-
" cerning the Salic Law of France,* 1587. There is
" in it an ample and fine Genealogy of *Peter Beloy,*
" in honour of That Learned Man, and which
" proves him a Gentleman of a Family originally
" of *Bretagne,* and transplanted into *Languedoc,* and
" elsewhere: but the most singular thing, I find in
" it, is, that it appears, that *Peter Beloy* was already
" Prisoner in the 1587; and, consequently, that it
" was King *Henry* III, who caused him to be im-
" prisoned, in complaisance to the *Guises,* who ac-
" cused him, moreover, of being a Shuffler, and a
" Heretic, and who had already caused him to be
" accused, the foregoing Year, before the King, by
" a Bishop, —— whom I suspect to be C. *Roze,*
" of having wrote the Book, for which, *Thuanus* in-
" forms us, that *Francis le Breton,* who was the Author
" of it, was hanged, in 1586. It appears, there,
" also, that *Beloy* was of a Family, whereof all the
" Members, and particularly himself, had always
" been good Catholics; that, at the Age of Twenty
" one Years, he was named Regent of the Univer-
" sity of *Toulouse,* by the University itself, and by
" the Parliament: that, afterwards, after having per-
" formed the Function of an Advocate, four or five
" Years, at *Toulouse,* he was made Counsellor in the
" Presidial of That City, with Marks of a most ho-
" nourable Distinction by the Parliament of *Paris;*
" and that, what had given an Advantage against
" him, at *Paris,* to his Enemies, the Leaguers, was,
" that, during this long Abode, which he was obliged
" to make there, as a Deputy of his Brethren, to the
" Court (9), his Zeal for his Prince, and his Coun-
" try, had moved him to oppose several ill Designs
" of the League. Moreover, I must observe, that,
" since it is certain, that he was already a Prisoner,
" in 1587, there is no Reason to say, that he was
" not imprisoned 'till 1588. Mr *Menage* has quoted
" a Discourse at the opening of one of the Settings
" of Parliament, spoken by *Peter Beloy,* in the Year
" 1609 (10)." The Author of this Letter has inserted part of these Facts in the second Edition of
his Notes on the Confession of *Sanci* (11), and he
observes one thing, which I ought not to omit;
which is, that our *Beloy* was born in the City of
Montauban (12), and that his three elder Brothers
were killed in the King's Service against the Huguenots.

[F] *This Remark will serve as a Supplement to the List —— of his Works.*] The Epistle Dedicatory (13) of his Exposition of *Daniel's Seventy Weeks* contains these Words. " Finding myself at Leisure,
" during the last Summer, I was pressed, and almost
" compelled, by my Friends, to look over again,
" and review, part of *The Computation of Times* (14),
" which I formerly drew up in the Prison of the
" Bastile of *Paris,* where I was confined during the
" four Years Tyranny of the League, in order to
" the Publication of This Essay." Conclude from this, that he would have published other Works of this Nature, and the more from his calling this little Dissertation on *Daniel's Weeks, The first Essay of his Historical Discourses.* We must, therefore, add this Dissertation to the Catalogue of *Beloy's* Works. It is entituled, *An Exposition of the Prophecy of the Angel Gabriel, touching the seventy Weeks, described by the Prophet Daniel, in the ninth Chapter of his Prophecies,* by Mr *Peter de Beloy, &c.* at *Toulouse,* 1605, in 8vo. The following have, likewise, been omitted. *Of the Origin and Institution of several Orders of Knight-hood, as well Ecclesiastical as Secular,* dedicated to Monseigneur the Dauphin of Viennois, Duke of Bretagne; at Montauban, for Dennis Haultin, 1604, in 8vo. *An Arrêt of the Parliament* of Toulouse, pronounced in Appeal as of a Grievance reprehended by Father John Journé, *a Monk of the Order of St Dominic, and Provinciel of the said Order in the Province of Toulouse, on the Proceeding against him, ordered by the Bishops of Condom and d' Aure, containing The Pleading on this Affair,* by Mr Peter de Beloy, *Counsellor and Advocate-General of the King in the said Parliament,* at *Paris,* according to the Copy printed at *Toulouse,* in 1612, in 8vo (15).

BELOT,

BELOT. BEMBUS.

BELOT (N.), Advocate in the King's Privy-Council, under the Reign of *Lewis* XIII, published a Book, which gave occasion to place him, with little Honour, in the famous *Petition of the Dictionaries* [*A*]. He undertook to prove, that our Language ought not to be made use of in learned Works, alledging, among other Reasons, that the communicating the Secrets of Sciences to the People has produced great Evils. He promised another Work [*B*], wherein he was to shew the Particulars of That Proof.

[*A*] *He published a Book, which gave Occasion to place him - - - - in the famous* Petition of the Dictionaries.] Mr *Pellisson* makes mention of it: "At that "time, if I am not mistaken, the Sieur *Belot*, Ad-"vocate, dedicated also a Book to the Academy, "which I could not find, and which is not men-"tioned in the Registers, entitled, *An Apology for "the Latin Tongue*; and it was That, which gave "occasion to This fine Passage in the *Petition of the "Dictionaries*.

"La pauvre langue Latiale
"Alloit être trouſſée en male,
"Si le bel Advocat Belot, &c (1)."

(1) Pelliſſon's Hiſtory of the French Academy. p. 195, 196.

What Mr *Pelliſſon* means by *& cætera* contains eleven Verses, which are these;

Du Barreau le plus grand ſalot,
N'en euſt pris en main la defenſe,
Et protegé ſon innocence.
En quoy, certes, & ſa bonté,
Et ſon zele, & ſa charité,
Se firent d'autant paroiſtre,
Qu'il n'a l'honneur de la connoiſtre;
Semblable à ces preux Chevaliers,
Ces Paladins Avanturiers,
Qui, deffendant des Inconnuës,
Ont porté leur nom juſqu' aux nuës.

Thy Language, Latium, *ill had fared;
But* Belot, *Advocate prepared,
Thy Patron ſtands, Thy ſtrong Defence,
And vouches for Thy Innocence.
In truth,* Belot'*s a generous Friend,
A Tongue, he knows not, to defend.
Like thoſe adventurous Knights of old,
Don* Quixots *ſo renown'd and bold;
Who, fighting for a Fair unknown,
Great Proweſs have in Combat ſhewn.*

I have That Book, which Mr *Pelliſſon* could not find; and I am going to say something of it; for it muſt be but little known, since, in the Year 1650 (2), it escaped the moſt curious Enquirers. The Title of it is: *An Apology for the Latin Tongue, againſt the Preface of Monſieur* de la Chambre, *in his Book of new Conjectures about Digeſtion, dedicated to Monſieg-*

(2) It was at the Time that Pelliſſon was writing the Hiſtory of the Academy.

neur Seguier, *Chevalier, Chancellor of* France It was printed, at *Paris*, in the Year 1637, in 8vo, and contains about eighty Pages, including the Epiſtle Dedicatory, the Preface, &c. The Author ſays (3), that he was forced to publish it, and tells the occaſion of it. "You muſt know, that Monſieur *de la "Chambre* —— having obliged me to give him my "Opinion concerning his firſt Treatiſes, my Free-"dom made me find Fault with him as to the Lan-"guage; and, having, nevertheleſs, continued to "write in *French*, he thought himſelf obliged to "prefix a Preface to his Book, entituled, *New Con-"jectures about Digeſtion*, in favour of our Language, "againſt the *Latin*, which, being addreſſed to me, "under the Name of Reader, I found myſelf ob-"liged to anſwer it by this Apology, which my "Friends got out of my Hands, by making uſe of "the Authority of ſuch Perſons, as might command "me to give it to the Public (4)." At the end of his Book, he added the Letter, which he wrote *to the Gentlemen of the French Academy*.

(3) In the Preface.

(4) Belot, Preface, fol. A. ii.

[*B*] *He promiſed another Work*] Note, that he would have Mr *Seguier* intereſt himſelf in This Cauſe for political Reaſons. *The Welfare of the State*, ſaid he, *and That of Religion are concerned in it*. According to his Account, the ancient *Romans* ſuffered by having uſed the vulgar Language in every thing. "Such are the Effects, which the Secrets of the "Learned, unſeaſonably diſcovered to the People, "have produced among the *Romans*, and whereof "the Example would be as dangerous to our Mo-"narchy, as it was prejudicial to That Empire. I "omit the fine Conſiderations, which might be drawn "from each Science, and which would make it more "clearly appear, of what Moment it is to keep "them ſecret, or, at leaſt, not to declare them but "to ſuch Perſons, as may be qualified for it. You "will find matter of Wonder, and Aſtoniſhment, in "in a Treatiſe of Politics, which I have enti-"tuled, France, *or The perfect Monarchy*, when you "come to conſider, that the Knowledge of Philo-"ſophy, imparted to the People, has produced ſo "many Buſy-Bodies, and Sophiſters, the Knowledge "of Divinity ſo many Heretics, and Atheiſts, That "of Morality ſo many Hypocrites, and falſe Virtues, "and That of Phyſic (becauſe 'tis profeſſed in our "Language) ſo many Quacks, and Murtherers, who "kill more Men than the Plague, and the War, "both together, and who have no other way of "livelihood, than That of killing ſo many People "with Impunity (5)." It is not uſeleſs to preſerve the Memory of ſuch falſe turns of the human Mind; They are Poiſons, which may ſerve as Remedies.

(5) Belot's Apology, pag. 28, & ſeqq.

BEMBUS (PETER), a noble *Venetian*, Secretary to *Leo* X [*A*], and afterwards Cardinal, was one of the beſt Writers of the XVIth Century; though it muſt be agreed, that he made himſelf ſometimes ridiculous, by an affected way of making uſe only of ancient *Latin* Words [*B*]. His Hiſtory of *Venice* was very much cenſured

[*A*] *He was Secretary to* Leo X.] He wrote a great many *Letters* for That Pope; he was handſomely rewarded for them; and, beſides, he had the Honour of being looked upon as the Author of all Thoſe Letters; for they came out under his Name, and with Thoſe, which he had wrote for himſelf. The latter are divided into ſix Books, and the others into ſixteen. *Leo* X had another Secretary, who was as great a *Puriſt* as *Bembus* (1). He made choice of them before he came out of the Conclave, where he was promoted to the Papacy (2). Mr *Graverol*, the Advocate, would have publiſhed, with ſome Notes, the Letters, which they wrote for That Pope, if an untimely Death had not put a ſtop to That Work.

[*B*] *Made himſelf ſometimes ridiculous by an affected way of making uſe only of ancient Latin Words.*] "How many Follies has the Affectation of making

(1) It was James Sadolet, conſtantly afterwards Cardinal.

(2) Bembus, Hiſt. rerum Venetar. in fine.

"uſe only of *Cicero*'s Words, and of what is called "pure Latinity, cauſed certain *Italian* Authors to "commit? Who would not laugh to hear *Bembus* "ſay, that a Pope was elected by the Favour of "the Immortal Gods, *Deorum immortalium benefi-"ciis?*" I take theſe Words from the Author of the *Art of Thinking* (3). Before him, *Juſtus Lip-ſius* had judiciouſly, and pleaſantly, criticized *Bembus's* Latinity (4). He blames him, among other things, for having ſaid, that the Senate of *Venice* wrote to the Pope; *Put your Truſt in the Immor-tal Gods, whoſe Vicar you are on Earth: — ut fidat Diis immortalibus, quorum vicem gerit in terris*. After this, we ought not to wonder, that he made uſe of the Word *Godeſs*, ſpeaking of the Holy Virgin. It is in a Letter (5), where Pope *Leo* X reproaches the Inhabitants of *Recanati*, for having given bad Timber for the Building of our Lady of Lor. etc.

(3) Art of Thinking, Part III, chap. 19, pag. 366.

(4) Lipſius, Epiſt. 57, Centur. II, Miſcellan. pag. 177.

(5) The 1-ſt of the 8th Book.

censured by *Lipsius*, upon That Account. It has been also criticized by others, with respect to Sincerity (a). His Letters have not been more spared [C]. He began betimes to run the hazard of being an Author [D]; and he was very successful in it; for his *Azolani* had an extraordinary Run (b). He was much taken notice of at the Courts of the Duke of *Ferrara*, and of the Duke of *Urbino*, which were then the most polite of That Country, and the Rendezvous of the finest Wits (c). He publickly testified his Gratitude for the Esteem, with which the Duke and Duchess of *Urbino* honoured him, for he wrote a Book in their Praise (d). He was a good *Italian*, and *Latin*, Poet; but he was justly censured for having published some loose and obscene Poems [E]. He is one of Those, who have been accused of having spoken

Loretto, and commands them to furnish better, least, says he, it should seem, that you deride us, and the Goddess herself; —— Ne tum nos, tum etiam Deam ipsam, inani lignorum inutilium donatione, lusisse videamini. The Words, which Christianity has consecrated, as, *fides, excommunicatio*, seem barbarous to This Writer; he chooses rather to make use of *persuasio* for *fides*, and of *aqua & igni interdictio* for *excommunicatio*. *Lipsius* finds some other Faults in him, as some *Italicisms*, and also some *Solecisms*. The same *Lipsius*, in his Notes on the ninth Chapter of the first Book of his Politics, comprehends, in a few Words, what he had more amply shewed in the above-cited Letter. Among other things, he says; "Cum tam curiosè à verbis sibi caverit, repe- "rio alibi, quae non dicam Tullana non sint, sed "vix Latina." —— *Notwithstanding his great Care in the Choice of his Words, I meet with some, which are not only not Ciceronian, but scarce Latin.* The Phrase *afferre naves*, which he criticizes, would be more pardonable in a *Dutchman*, because the same Word in *Dutch*, which signifies *to bring*, signifies also *to carry*, which creates sometimes very pleasant Expressions from *Dutchmen*, who begin to speak *French*. The History of *Venice*, which *Lipsius* criticized so much as to the Stile, appeared, to our Mr *Balzac*, the Work of a mean Wit, and of a dry and grovelling Author (6).

[C] *His Letters have not been more spared.*] His Friends have been challenged to shew any one of them, that do not grossly trespass against *Grammar*, and that is not remarkable for some egregious Childishness, and moreover without any Solidity. "Ut cae- "teram carminum ejus obscoenitatem taceam, quid "ejus epistolis ineptius, & quidem illis quas Ponti- "ficis maximi nomine & de rebus maximis scripsit, "& ad viros maximos? Mentiar ego cum *Scipione* "*Gentili* *, & luam gravi poena, pi vel unam mihi "in tot illis voluminibus Epistolam ostendant ama- "tores ejus, quae non insigni aliquo vitio Gramma- "tico laboret, aut puerili aliqua ineptia conspicua "sit & demonstrabilis. Ne quid de rebus ipsis atque "scientiis dicam sapientiae inanissimis, & mire lan- "guidis, & (repetendum est enim, quod ejus pro- "prium nomine est) ineptis (7). ———— *To say no-* "*thing of the other Obscenities to be met with in* "*his Verses, what can be more trifling, than his* "*Letters, even Those, which he wrote, in the Pope's* "*Name, in Affairs of the greatest Importance, and* "*to the greatest Men? Let me pass for a Lyar with* "*Scipio Gentilis, and suffer great Punishment, if* "*his Favourers can shew me but one Letter in so* "*many Volumes, which does not somewhere remark-* "*ably offend against Grammar, or is not conspicuous* "*for some childish Impertinence. I say nothing of* "*the Subject Matter of them, and That surprizing* "*Emptiness, and (I must again repeat it, as being* "*peculiar to him) That Impertinence.*"

[D] *He ventured betimes to run the Hazard of being an Author.*] During the three Years (8) he was in *Sicily*, a Scholar of *Constantine Lascaris*, Professor of the *Greek* Tongue, at *Messina*, he composed a *Latin* Treatise *de Monte Ætna*, which was printed in 1495 (9). Being returned home to his Father, he followed him some Years after to the Court of *Hercules d' Est*, Duke of *Ferrara*. He made himself beloved, and respected, there; and it was at this time, that he wrote his *Azolani*. They are Discourses on Love, so called, because it is supposed, that they were made in the Castle of *Azolo*. He was, then, but twenty six Years of Age (10). This *Italian* Book had great Success, both among Men and Women; one would have past for a Novice in *Italy*, who should have been a Stranger to

it. "Eos libros tanta hominum, mulierum etiam, "medius fidius, approbatione, & tanquam plausu ex- "ceptos recentes esse meminimus, ut extemplo cunctâ "eos Italia cupidissimè lectitarit, atque didicerit.. ut "non satis urbani aut elegantes ii haberentur, quibus "Asulanae illae disputationes essent incognitae (11)." It has been printed several Times. One *John Martin*, Secretary to Cardinal *de Lenoncourt*, made a *French* Translation of it, which he published in the Year 1545.

He translated it from the *Italian* Edition of the Year 1540, which had been preceeded by three or four others, since That of the Year 1515; and he observes this, to prevent any Person from wondering at the Differences, which were between his Translation, and the Original, printed by *Aldus*, in the Year 1515 (12). "If they please to consider, says he (13), "that *Bembo's* Work has been three or four times re- "printed since That Time, and that the said Signior "*Bembo* has cut off some things from it, which seem- "ed superfluous to him, and also that the last Im- "pression (which I have followed,) is of the Year "1540, made, (as it is to be supposed) by his Au- "thority, and Permission; my Opinion is, that they "will not say, that I have wronged the Author in "any thing." This was of some use to *Gaffarel*, who, finding himself censured for employing his Pen in Matters ill-becoming a Clergyman, excused himself by the Authority of divers Examples; and by name, That of the *Azolani* of Cardinal *Bembo* (14). It might have been objected to him, that That Work was composed by a young Gentleman, who was not yet engaged in the Ecclesiastical State; but he might have replied, that the Author published a new Edition of it, after his Cardinalship.

[E] *He has been censured for having published some loose and obscene Poems.*] We have seen already (15) what *Lanzius* reproaches him with; here is a Passage of *Scaliger*: "Petrus Bembus elegiaco (carmine) "cam partem corporis humani celebravit, sine qua "nulla obscoenitas foret. Legatur ejus Elegia, cujus "initium :

Ante alias omnes, meus hic quas educat hortus,
Una puellares illicit herba manus :

"quod poëma merito vocare possis obscenissimam ele- "gantiam, aut elegantissimam obscenitatem. Unius "& quadraginta distichorum est (16). ———— Peter "*Bembus celebrated, in Elegiac Verse, That Part of* "*the Body, without which there would be no Obsce-* "*nity. Read his Elegy, which begins thus :*

Of all the Plants, which in my Garden grow,
This must the Female Touch desires to know.

"*which Poem may deservedly be called The Most Ob-* "*scene Elegance, or The Most Elegant Obscenity. It* "*consists of Forty one Disticha.*" *Thuanus* and *Menage*, shall serve as new Witnesses; the former by these Words; "Illius (Bembi) multa licentiosius, ut "temporum nequitia & domini cui serviebat mores "ferebant, scripta extant (17); ———— *There are ex-* "*tant several loose Compositions of the same Bembus,* "*which are owing to the Vice of the Times, and the* "*Manners of the Master, whom he served.*" And the latter by this Remark: "If it was true, "that *John della Casa* was excluded from the Car- "dinalship for his Poem, Cardinal *Bembo* was more "fortunate than He; for the licentious Verses, which "he wrote in his Youth, and which are yet more "licentious than Those of the *Capitolo del Forno*, did "not hinder him from being made a Cardinal (18)."

[F] ———— *and*

BEMBUS. 743

spoken of the Word of GOD with great Contempt [F]. Perhaps he only found fault with the Stile of it. Authors differ about the Sex of his Children [G]; but they agree, in saying they were illegitimate, and three in Number. One of his Letters informs us, that his two Grandmothers lived a hundred Years [H]. He died in the Year 1547 (e), in his Seventy seventh Year (f). Speron Sperone says, he set a great Value on the Knowledge of Languages [I]. If this Article be short, it is because *Moreri* has spoken at large of Cardinal *Bembo*.

Upon the Death of his Mother, he wrote a very fine confolatory Letter to his Father BERNARD BEMBUS. He says in it, that she had lived Forty eight Years with her Husband, in a Concord, which no Complaint had ever interrupted [K]; and he seems to be very much afflicted for the Loss of This good Mother. He

[F] —— *and for having spoken of the Word of* GOD *with great Contempt.*] I can go back no farther, than a *German* Author, whose Name is *Thomas Lanzius*, who published several Speeches, for, and against, the Nations of *Europe*. He says, without quoting any Body (19), that *Bembus* advised a Friend not to read St *Paul*'s Epistles, for fear of spoiling his Stile. " Advertite, auditores, inepti hominis impietatem cum pari stultitia conjunctam. Is siquidem " Epistolas omnes Pauli palam condemnavit, easque " deflexo in contumeliam vocabulo Epistolaceias est " ausus appellare, cum amico autor esset ne illas attingeret, vel, si coepisset legere, de manibus ejiceret, si " elegantiam scribendi & eloquentiam adamaret (20). " — — *Obferve, Gentlemen, the equal Impiety and Folly of the Man. He openly condemned All* St Paul's *Epistles, and contemptuously dared to stile them Epistolets, advising a Friend not to meddle with them, or, if he should begin to read them, presently to throw them by, if he loved Elegance of Stile, and Eloquence.*" Others pretend, that, having heard, that *Sadolet* explained the Epistle to the *Romans*, he said to him; Let these Fooleries alone, they do not become a grave Man: *Omitte has nugas, non enim decent gravem virum tales ineptiae* (21). We shall see, in another place (22) a Story, which was spread abroad, which would induce one to think, that he did not believe the Immortality of the Soul.

[G] *Authors differ about the Sex of his Children.*] *Moreri* gives him two Sons and a Daughter; but *Imperialis* observes, that *Bembus* kept a Concubine all his Life-time, by whom he had three Daughters (23). It is certain, that *Bembus* had a Son, whose Name was *Torquato*, to whom *Manutius* dedicated his *Virgil*. I do not question but that *Imperialis* is mistaken; for *John della Casa*, who wrote the Life of *Bembus* with great Application, says expresly, that his Mistress had two Sons by him, to wit, *Lucilio* and *Torquato*, and a Daughter, whose Name was *Helena*, who was married to *Peter Gradenigue*. He remarks also, that This Mistress was a fine Woman, and that *Peter Bembus*, a well shaped, polite, gallant, and courteous Man, was greatly beloved in all Companies. During his Abode at *Ferrara*, Duke *Hercules d'Este*, and *Lucretia Borgia*, the Wife of *Alphonsus d'Este*, shewed him a particular Friendship (24).

[H] *One of his Letters informs us, that his two Grandmothers lived a hundred Years.*] This Letter being short, I shall set it down at length (25): It appears by it, that *Bembus* would willingly have sacrificed these two old Women to the Life of his deceased Brother. " Petrus Bembus Herculi Scrotio. Avias ambas meas effoetas, deploratasque foeminas, & jam pro-
" pe centum annorum mulieres, mihi fata reliquerunt: unicum fratrem meum juvenem ac florentem " abstulerunt, spem & solatia mea. Quomobrem quo " in moerore sim ipse facile potes existimare. Reli-
" qua ex meis intelliges. Heu me miserum! Vale. " Id. Jan. 1504. Venetiis. — Peter Bembus to " Hercules Strozza. *Fate has left me both my Grand-
" mothers, wretched old Women, and now almost an " hundred Years old: but it has robbed me of my only " Brother, in the Flower of his Youth, my Hope and " Consolation. You may, from hence, easily guess at " my Affliction. The Rest my People will inform you " of. Farewel. Venice. The Ides of January, 1504.*" He was much more affected with his Mother's Death. See the Remark [K].

[I] *He set a great Value on the Knowledge of Languages.*] So far as to prefer it before the Marquisate of *Mantua*. " Jo so nulla per rispetto à que gloriosi: " ma quel poco che io ne so delle lingue, non lo cangierei al Marchesato di Mantoua (26). ——— I am

" not vain of my Knowledge in any Language; but the " little I know of them I would not exchange for the " Marquisate of *Mantua*." A Writer of Dialogues makes no scruple to ascribe to his Interlocutors, what they never said; and therefore I set no great reason to believe, that *Peter Bembus* was really of This Opinion, having no other Proof for it, than This Author's Dialogue. Some have quoted *Speron Sperone*, as if *Bembus* had only mentioned his Talent of writing in *Latin* (27); but it is certain, from the Words that I have cited, that *Bembus* spoke, in general, of the Knowledge of Tongues: And it must not be imagined, that he pretended to exclude the *Greek*, which he had learned in *Sicily* under *Lascaris*, so far as to write it very well (28).

[K] *His Mother had lived Forty eight Years with her Husband, in a Concord, which no Complaint had ever interrupted.*] These are his Words: " Cum duae " essent causae quibus maximè commoveri debui ad " luctum, una quod me parente optima meique amantissima orbatum viderem; altera, quod te privari lectissima prudentissimaque conjuge, cum qua " duodequinquaginta annos SINE ULLA QUERELA " concordissimè vixisses, tibi patri meo acerbissimum " atque luctuosissimum putarem futurum; harum " duarum causarum altera me abs te levari sentiebam, &c (29). ———— *Tho' I have two Reasons to " be afflicted; the One, The Loss of the best and " fondest of Mothers; the Other, The extream Concern, which must affect you, O my Father, at being " deprived of the choicest and most prudent of Wives, " with whom you have lived Forty eight Years, in " the utmost Concord; yet you yourself afford me Relief from one of these Occasions of Sorrow, &c.*" This Letter, dated from *Urbino*, the Twenty second of *November*, 1509, is a great Elogy of the Mother, and an illustrious Testimony of her Son's Affection. It deserves to be read from the beginning to the end. *Bernard Bembus* had already some Grandsons. His Wife had lived near seventy Years. There is another Letter of *Peter Bembus*, wherein he shews his Brotherly Affection; for he gives there a lively Representation of his Sister's Unhappiness, that he might obtain some Remedy for That Lady's Misfortunes from the Patriarch of *Venice*. She was married to a Man, who gave himself over to all manner of Lewdness, and who bestowed that Affection, which was due to his Wife, on Prostitutes. " Marcelli ejus mariti meretricio amore animus turpiter " abalienatus (30). De Marcello etiam spero fore, " ut cum se ille meretricia consuetudine plenâ infamiae, plena calamitatis, liberatum per se solutumque facere animo atque pacto cognorit, tibi gratias agat, quod illum belluarum more sine pudore, " fine lege, fine ullo officio degentem, ad hominum " vitam rationemque traduxeris (31). ——— *As for " Marcellus, I am in hopes, that, when he comes " seriously to reflect, that you have freed him from the " Infamy and Danger of a Life spent among Harlots, " he will return you thanks for bringing him over " from a brutal, shameless, and irregular, Conduct, " to the Life and Reason of a Man.*" He abused her horribly, without being moved to pity by her Patience, and Silence, and by That Modesty, whereby she endeavoured to bring him back to his Duty. " Nolo tibi commemorare quot aut quantas indig-
" nitates Antonia soror universum biennium pertu-
" lerit, dum prudens atque optima mulier, humanitate, pudore, continentia, labore etiam summo suo, " quodque in hujusmodi rebus solet esse difficillimum, " taciturnitate, viri improbitatem, perditissimosque " mores placare, ac flectere in melius, cupit (32). " —— *I forbear to recount to you the many Indig-
" nities*

VOL. I.   9 B

BEMBUS.

He was blamed for having followed the Custom of Flatterers, with whom the Merit of the living always exceeds That of the dead; for he published, that *Paul* III, was more learned, than *Leo* X. It is worth while to see how he justified himself [*L*]. After the Death of *Navagier*, in 1530, the Council of Ten pitched upon Him to write *The History of the Republic of* Venice (g) [*M*]. His Age of sixty Years would have made him decline This Trouble, had he not been more willing to incommode himself, than not to do this Service to his Country (h). I must say a Word of the Design, it is pretended he had, to refuse the Cardinalship [*N*]. His Historian enlarged on this Point, and did not fail to say, that his Narrative would pass for a Fable, with many Persons, who judge of their Neighbours by themselves. He has nobly expressed This Common-place [*O*], as will be seen below (i); and I shall examine it more at large, in the last Remark of this Article.

(g) Bembus Epist. 25. lib. 3. pag. 302.
(h) Id. init. Histor. Rerum Venet.
(i) Citat. (40).

"nities my *Sister* Antonia *has suffered for full two Years; whilst That prudent, and best of Women, endeavours, with Complaisance, and Modesty, with Patience, and even the greatest Pains, and (what is uncommon in such Cases) with Silence, to reform the abandoned Morals of her Husband, and bring him back to the right way*." This is a finer Letter, than the other; it is dated from *Urbino*, the seventh of *July*, 1510, which occasions a small Difficulty; for it is supposed there, that *Bembus*'s Mother was yet living: "Curandum tibi certè est ne Soror mea, ne Pater, ne Mater, ne universa nostra familia - - - securè tandem ac planè liberè irrideamur (33). - - - - *It is certainly incumbent on you to take care, that my Sister, Father, Mother, and whole Family, be not, securely, and with Impunity, made the Subject of Mockery and Derision*." And we have seen, that he wrote a Letter of Consolation to his Father, upon his Widowhood, in the Month of *November*, 1509. It were to be wished, that so many Letters of great Men were not wrong dated (34).

(33) Id. ib.
(34) See Remark [*B*], of the Article AMMONIUS (ANDREW).

[*L*] *It is worth while to see how he justified himself from the Charge of Flattery*.] When, in 1535, he published the Letters, which he had written in the Name of *Leo* X, he dedicated them to *Paul* III, and declared him much more learned, than Pope *Leo* X was. "Eas autem ad te, Paule, potissimum literas mitto; quia Pontifex maximus es, ut Leo decimus fuit, & in optimarum artium disciplinis multo, quam ille, habitus doctior. Vera enim fateri omnes non solum honestè possumus, sed etiam debemus —— *I, therefore, dedicate these Letters to you*, Paul, *because you are Pope, as was* Leo X, *and esteemed more learned, than He. For we not only may, but ought, to confess the Truth*." This Elogy was looked upon as exorbitant; *Bembus*'s Character, and the Remembrance of the great Favours he had received from *Leo* X, were not to be seen in it. "Esse nonnullos, qui me in laudando Paulo Pont. Max. longius progressum esse putent, quàm aut mei mores, aut summa in me Leonis X officia, aut veritas omnino ipsa postularit (35). - - - - *Some there are, who think that I have gone further in commending Pope* Paul, *than my own Character, or the Favours I received from* Leo X, *or than even Truth itself demanded*." He answered *Mussa*, who gave him Notice of This Censure, That he had only given the Preference to *Paul* III, as to Literature, which the Domestic Misfortunes of *Leo* X had hindered him from making any great Progress in; that he had taken care not to judge which of the two surpassed the other in Prudence, Firmness, Temperance, Goodness, and Liberality; that it was not difficult to know; that *Paul* had more Learning, than the other; that he had never failed to acknowledge the Favours of *Leo* X, though he was less indebted to him for his Fortune, than to *Julius* II. "Tametsi mediam plus partem earum quæ habeo fortunarum omnium Julius secundus Pont. Max. cui nunquam inservivi, contulit (36). - - - - *Tho' Pope* Julius II, *whom I never served, conferred on me more than half the Fortunes I possess*."

(35) Bembus, Epist. 8c, lib. 6, pag. 702.
(36) Id. ib. pag. 702.

[*M*] *He was pitched upon to write the History of the Republic of* Venice.] They would have him to begin it, where *Sabellicus* had ended it (37), and continue it down to his own time. This Interval comprehended Forty four Years (38). He did not complete it; for he ended his Work at the Death of *Julius* II. This History is divided into twelve Books, and was printed at *Venice*, in the Year 1551, and reprinted, the same Year, at *Paris*, by *Michael Vascosan*, in 4to. It was afterwards printed at *Basil*, with the other Works of *Bembus*, in three Volumes, in 8vo, in the Year 1567. Neither He, nor any one else, could reap any Benefit from *Andrew Navagier*'s Labour, who had a like Commission, and who, at his Death, had ordered all his Writings to be burnt (39). We have seen, in the Remark [*B*], what Judgment was passed on the History written by *Bembus*.

(37) About the Year 1486.
(38) Bembus, in it His of *Julius* II. Verum Book.
(39) Id ibid.

[*N*] *It is pretended, he had a Design to refuse the Cardinalship*.] *Morèri* speaks of it at large; but he has not discovered the Beauties, with which *John della Casa*, whom he copies, has adorned That Narrative. This Historian of our *Bembus* declares, he is not ignorant, that several People will reject this Part of his Narrative; and That, since most Men judge of others by themselves, it will not be believed, that *Peter Bembus* sincerely despised a Degree of Honour, which almost every one judges to deserve the most passionate and earnest Wishes; but that, as for himself, who writes, whilst things are yet fresh in Memory, and whilst part of the Actors are yet living, he ought not to be suspected of an Imposture; but that, after all, he is not afraid of the Appearances of Falshood, which attended the Truth he was about to publish, remembering very well, that the Fault of Those, who venture to advance Untruths in History, is as great, as the Fault of Those, who dare not speak out the Truth. I do not represent the Beauties of the Original, any more than *Morèri*; and therefore I shall set down the Author's own Words for the sake of those, who understand *Latin*. "Non sum nescius multos fore, qui nostræ orationi hac in re parum fidei habeant: plerique enim omnes, quid de aliena voluntate credendum sit, de sua conjecturam faciunt: itaque incredibile multis visum iri intelligo, Bembum id verè atque ex animo aspernatum esse, quod omnes ferè summa cupiditate expetendum atque optabile esse existiment; tametsi scribimus hæc recenti hujus facti memoria, multisque, qui in agendo adfuerunt, superstitibus, quos mendacii atque impudentiæ nostræ conscios ac testes habere cur velimus causa nulla est. Sed quoniam par eorum peccatum esse censemus, qui mentiri in historia audent, atque eorum, qui dicere verum reformidant; mendacii speciem, verum cum dicturi essemus, non horruimus (40)." I find myself obliged to say here, that I am none of Those, of whom *John della Casa* foresaw the Incredulity. I have seen so many Characters in *Peter Bembus*'s Letters, not only of an honest Man, and a generous and assiduous Friend, but also of a learned Person, who preferred the Calmness of a retired Life, which permits an entire Consecration to the Muses, before the Vanities and Pomps of a Court, that I can easily imagine, he wished in earnest not to be a Cardinal.

(40) Joannes Casa, in vita Petri Bembi, pag. 150, Collect. Battesti.

[*O*] *His Historian says, that this will pass for a Fable with Those, who judge of their Neighbours by themselves; and as he has nobly expressed This Commonplace.*] It is what we have seen in his *Latin* Words; and, consequently, there remains only for me to prove, that there is a Common-place in them; which I shall easily do. One of the Difficulties, which attend the writing of History, is, that the Readers are apt to look upon the noblest Actions, of which they find themselves incapable, as so many Lies: This has been observed long ago. "Ac mihi quidem, *said* Sallust (41), - - - - in primis arduum videtur, res gestas scribere; primum, quod facta dictis exæquanda sunt; dehinc, quia plerique, quæ delicta reprehenderis, malevolentia & invidia dicta putant, ubi de magna virtute, atque gloria bonorum memores, quæ sibi quisque facilia factu putat, æquo animo accipit, supra, veluti ficta, pro falsis ducit. - - - - - *For my own Part, I look upon the writing of History to be the most difficult Task; first, because the Actions and Stile must correspond; then, because*

(41) Sallust. in Proœm. belli Catilin. pag. 6, 7.

BEMBUS. 745

"because most Readers think, when you find fault, it is through Malevolence and Envy; and because, when you celebrate the remarkable Virtue and Glory of good Men, what each Man thinks he could with ease have performed himself, he admits to be true, but, what is above his Capacity, rejects as false." Pericles had already made the same Observation concerning Those, who hear a Funeral Oration. "The Praises, said he, which the Auditors think themselves capable of deserving, are not subject to be criticised; but, if they exceed their Strength, they render them envious and incredulous, and are looked upon by them as Fiction, and a Piece of Flattery." *Eatenus tolerabiles sunt alienæ laudes, quatenus scipium quisque parem arbitratur alicui illarum assequendæ: quibus vero imparem, iis invidet, fidemque non habent* (42). The Foundation of all this is, that every one is apt to measure other Men's Actions by his own. "*Quæ volumus & credimus libenter, they are Julius Cæsar's Words* (43), *& quæ sentimus ipsi, reliquos sentire speramus.* —— *What we desire, and willingly believe, and what we ourselves think, we hope are the Sentiments of others.*" Nothing is more easy, than to deceive Those, who never deceived others, and nothing is more difficult than to draw those into a Snare, who have always acted fraudulently (44). The Reason, both of This Facility, and This Difficulty, may easily be guessed at. A good, plain, and sincere, Man does not suspect any Inclination to Deceit; and for That Reason, he acts without much Precaution; but a Knave, thinking, that others are like himself, keeps on his Guard against all the Artifices, which he knows he should make use of on the like Occasions. It is usual to judge disadvantageously of Those, who mistrust every thing, and who readily believing all the ill Reports, which are spread concerning their Neighbours, deny, or question, or put an ill Construction on, the best, and the most laudable Actions, which they hear of. What *Phædrus* said of certain Persons, who take the Descriptions or Censures of Vice for personal Affronts, may be applyed to them; *Are you so imprudent*, said he to them, *as to reveal the Secrets of your Hearts in such a manner?*

Suspicis ne si quis errabit sua,
Et rapiet ad se, quod erit commune omnium,
Stulte nudabit animi conscientiam (45).

Others had already made use of This Thought. *Cicero* had said; "*Neminem nomino; quare irasci mihi nemo poterit, nisi qui ante de se voluit confiteri* (46). —— *I name no body; no body, therefore, can be angry with me, but He, who is resolved to betray himself.*" St *Jerom* said; "*Quando sine nomine contra vitia scribitur, qui irascitur, accusator est sui* (47). —— *Since we write against Vice, without pointing out the Offenders, He, who takes it ill, is his own Accuser.*" It is therefore pretended, that These credulous Men, with regard to Slanders, who are, otherwise, incredulous as to the Praises of their Neighbours, shew, thereby, the bad State of their Minds, their Disposition to Evil, and their Inability for what is Good. *Faber* made use of this Common-place against Those, who pretended, that he had acted contrary to Piety, in maintaining, that the Passage of *Josephus*, relating to JESUS CHRIST, is spurious. *They will make it appear*, says he, *that Impiety seems but a Trifle to them, if they accuse others of it without Reason.* "Si quis tamen aliter judicaverit, & meum scribendi consilium in crimen detorserit, is, ut ait ηδικώτατος poëta.

Stulte nudabit animi conscientiam.

"Quemadmodum enim & recte & vere olim pronunciavit Amphis,

Ὅστις ὁμνύοντι μηδὲν πείθεται,
Αὐτὸς ἐπιορκεῖν ῥᾳδίως ἐπίσαται.

"Sic non minus vere dici potest, Qui ob rem nullam alios impietatis insimulant, eos satis aperte ostendere quam leve peccatum existiment tam dirum scelus (48)." The two *Greek* Verses of this Passage have a very fine Sense; they signify, that He, who will not believe his Neighbour's Oaths, will easily be guilty himself of Perjury: which is much like these Words of *Tertullian* to a Maker of rash Judgments; *si potes ista de aliis credere, potes & facere.* —— *If you can believe these things of others, you are capable of doing them yourself.* One of Those, who wrote against *Marc Antony de Dominis*, laid a great Stress upon This Common-place. "Hic aliud argumentum adducam, quo ostendam, conscientiam tuam & fidem meritò nobis & cordato cuivis suspectam esse debere. Nosti, opinor, Oratoris dictum, cujus veritatem quotidiana experientia declarat: *Ut quisque pessimus est, ita de aliis pessimè suspicatur.* Qui fastu tumet, superbos; qui divitiis inhiat, avaros; qui sanctitatem fingit, hypocritas; qui dolos versat, proditores; qui nulla fide & conscientia est, conscientiam pensi non habere unà secum omnes existimat (49). —— Si Vigilantinus, qui nullos castos ex Clero credebant, bene objicit Hieronymus, satis ostenduit quàm sanctè vivant, qui malè de omnibus suspicantur; certè satis conscientiam tuam, quam jactas puram, quam sit tetra & impia ostendis, qui de Scriptoribus Romanis, Parisiensibus, mo!ernis, antiquis, Græcis, Latinis, Imperatoribus Christianis, Summis Pontificibus antiquissimis, Conciliis generalibus plenissimis, sex Christianis sæculis, tetra & impia non suspicaris modò, sed certissimè affirmas, ubi ne levissima quidem justæ suspicionis umbra est (50). ---- *I will here produce another Argument, to shew, that we, and every honest Man, ought to suspect your Conscience and Faith. You know, I presume, the saying of the Orator, the Truth of which is confirmed by every Day's Experience, The worse a Man is himself, the more apt he is to suspect others. The haughty Man suspects every one else of Pride; The covetous Man, of Avarice; the Pretender to Sanctity, of Hypocrisy; the Trickster, of Knavery; and the Man of no Faith or Conscience, of the want of both ----* If St *Jerom* objects, *with reason, to the Vigilantians, who believed none of the Clergy were chast, that They, who suspect ill of others, shew how boldly themselves live; surely you betray the Impiety and Foulness of your Conscience, whose Purity you boast; when, without the least Shadow of just Suspicion, you not only suspect, but confidently affirm, base and impious Things of of the Roman Authors, Parisian, Modern, Ancient, Greek, Latin, Christian Emperors, Ancient Popes, the fullest General Councils, and the six Christian Centuries.*"

Observe, that there is no Subject, on which the *Roman* Catholics have made more use of this Common-Place, than That of Continency; for they have affected to say, that Those, who accuse the Clergy of not observing it, and Those, who think the Observation of it to be almost impossible, are lascivious Men, who judge of others by themselves (51). The Jesuit, who wrote against *Thuanus*, under the false Name of *Joannes Baptista Gallus*, was so audacious as to say, that That great Man, having the Reputation of loving Women, easily believed, that other Men had the same Fault, and alledged *Nero* to him. "Quod de Nerone ferunt, qui cum perditissime & impariffime viverit, castum esse posse neminem censebat (52). —— *As they report of Nero, who, being himself addicted to the most scandalous Debaucheries, believed no Man could be chast.* Ostendunt, continues he, ajebat S. Hieronymus, de hæreticis agens, quam castè vivant, qui benè de aliis sentire aut loqui nequeunt. ὄσεις ἀπαβαλεις διαιρεομενος ἀπασίας. —— St *Jerom*, treating of Heretics, said, *They shew, how chastly they live, who cannot think, or speak, well of Others: They measure others by their own Impurity.*" The *Greek* is quoted as out of *Gregory Nazianzen*. What is alledged of *Nero*, is to be found in *Suetonius*, and in stronger Terms. "Ex nonnullis comperi, *says the Historian* (55), persuasissimum habuisse eum neminum hominum pudicum, aut ulla corporis parte purum esse: verum plerosque dissimulare vitium, & calliditate obtegere: ideoque professis apud se obscœnitatem, cætera quoque concessisse delicta. ---- *I have been informed by some, that he was fully persuaded, that no Man was chast or pure in any part of his Body; but that many only dissembled Vice, and artfully concealed it: for which reason, when any one made Profession of Obscenity before him, he allowed him every other Vice.*" If I add to all this a cruel and impudent Invective of *Scioppius* against *Theodorus Beza*, it is only to confute it. He asserts, that the reason, for which That Minister suspected pested the Falsity of the History, which we read in the eighth Chapter of St *John*, is, because it is said there, that JESUS CHRIST remained alone with the Woman, who was accused of Adultery (54). " Talia Beza, qui in octavum caput Johannis affirmat, " sibi mulieris in adulterio deprehensæ historiam suf-" pectæ fidei ac veritatis esse, quòd CHRISTUS dica-" tur solus cum sola fœmina remansisse: sibi nempe " conscius, quid solus ipse cum Candida sua sola agere " consueverit: qui, sicut Spartani, quòd Martiales ac " bellatores essent, omnes Deorum dearumque imagi-" nes atque statuas hastatas faciebant, tamquam Deos " omnes virtute bellica præditos existimarent; ita " ipse propter suam libidinem & impudicitiam, CHRI-" STUM quoque Sanctum Sanctorum, &c (55). ---- " *Such is* Beza, *who, on the eighth Chapter of St* " John, *affirms, that he suspects the Truth of the* " *Story of the Woman taken in Adultery, because* " CHRIST *is said to have been left alone with the* " *Woman: being conscious to himself of what went* " *to pass between him and his* Candida, *when alone* " *together: And, as the* Spartans, *worshippers of* " Mars, *and Warriours, made the Statues of all their* " *Deities armed with Spears; so this Man, being* " *himself lubidinous and immodest, supposes* CHRIST, " *the Holy of Holies*, &c." Never was Satire so ill grounded as This; for it is true, indeed, that the History of This Woman was suspected by *Beza*; but it is no ways for the reason, which *Scaliger* alledges: *Beza* gives several reasons for it; and, if he observes, that JESUS CHRIST was left alone with The Woman, it is not because such a Circumstance contains a Motive of some dishonest Suspicion, but because the thing itself does not agree with the Sequel of the Text, and does not seem probable (56).

(54) *The Franciscan* Feuardentius *had already published the same Lie, in the 13th Chap. of the 4th Book of his Theomach a Calvinistica*, p. 164.

(55) Scioppius, in Scaligero hypobolimæo, fol. 15. verso.

(56) *See the Notes of* Bezas *on the 7th Chap. of St* John.

BEME, Murtherer of Admiral *de Chatillon*, on St *Bartholomew's* Day, would not deserve a Place in This Dictionary, were it not, that many Persons, knowing a Man by some very enormous Crime, desire to know what became of him afterwards, and of what species of Death he died. Now they cannot well satisfy their Curiosity, without much Trouble, when the Person in question is of mean Rank; wherefore, it must be a great Pleasure to them, when a Book is put into their Hands, whereby they are enabled to satisfy themselves immediately. Let thus much be said, once for all, in regard to such like Articles. BEME, then, a *German* by Nation [A], educated in the House of the Duke of *Guise*, made himself the chief Executioner of the Massacre, which was resolved upon against the Admiral (a). It was *Beme*, who, as soon as the Chamber Door was broke open, asked him, *Art thou the Admiral?* And, knowing by his Answer what he had asked, he run his Sword through his Body, and then gave him a great cut, with his Back-sword, over his Face. It was He, who answered the Duke of *Guise*, enquiring *If the Business was done*, that it was done, and who threw the Body, by the Duke's Order, out of the Window. He was taken in *Xaintonge*, by the Garrison of *Bouteville*, in the Year 1575. He promised a great Ransom, and to cause *Montbrun* to be released, whom the Catholics had taken in *Dauphiné*. The Desire alone of saving *Montbrun*, kept *Beme* from being put to Death; wherefore he was in great fear, when he heard, that *Montbrun* was executed; He bribed a Soldier, *who saved him on a good Horse, with a Pistol at his Saddle Bow*. *Bertanville, Governor of the Place, finding, that he was escaped, mounts on a cropt Horse alone, and overtakes* Beme, *and the Soldier; and, having no other Weapon but a Sword, makes at both of them*; the Soldier would not wait for him; but *Beme* cried out to him, *Thou knowest that I am a dangerous Fellow*, and fired his Pistol; the other, answering, I will not suffer thee to be so any longer, thrust his Sword up to the Hilt into his Prisoner's Belly. Thus d'*Aubigné* relates the Fact (b). *Beza* says much the same (c) [B]; but we shall see below, that *Thuanus* relates the Matter with other Circumstances [C]. *Mezerai* calls This Murtherer *N. Dianovitz-Besme* (d).

(a) Thuan. lib. 42. pag. 1075.

(b) D'Aubigné, Hist. Tom. II. lib. 2. cap. 16. p. 749.

(c) Beza, Hist. Eccles. lib. 10. pag. 479.

(d) Mezer. Tom. III. in fol. pag. 380. Edit. 1685.

[A] *He was a German by Nation*] He was born in the Country of *Wirtemberg*, and it is said, he was the Son of One, who had been intrusted with the Artillery (1). The Author of the Book, *de furoribus Gallicis* (2), observes, that it was said, that the Cardinal of *Lorrain* had married one of his Bastards to *Beme*. He calls him always *Benstus*: It is probably a Fault of the Printer for *Bernestus*. *Cavriana*, whom I shall quote below, says, that This Person had been Page to the Duke of *Guise*, the Father.

[B] *He was slain by* Bertanville ------ *Beza says much the same*] Let us relate what he says; for it contains some other Circumstances. Speaking of the Defeat of the *Reiters* (3), commanded by *Thoré*, Son of the Constable *Anne de Montmorency*, he says, that *Clervant* was taken Prisoner there; " And had " it not been for the Credit of divers Lords his Rela-" tions (and because, about the same, *Beyme*, one of " the chief Murtherers of the Admiral, as well for " That, as for other Reasons greatly beloved by the " Duke of *Guise*, had been taken by Those of the " Reformed Religion near *Ponts* in *Poictou*) (4) he " would hardly have saved his Life. ------ Some " time after, he was conducted to *Paris*, and much " carried about, to try if they could exchange him " for *Beme*; but, though he was in very great Dan-" ger of his Life, being desired to agree to That Ex-" cnange, he generously answered, that he would " never consent to be exchanged for such a detestable " Murtherer; and GOD favoured him so much, " that, having been put to ransom ------ he was " at last set at liberty, and, *Beme*, thinking to make " his Escape from the Castle, where he was a Priso-" ner, was retaken, and cut in pieces, as he deser-" ved, except that it was not done by the Hands of " a Common Executioner (5)." *Cavriana*, having said, in his Discourses on *Tacitus*, that *Beme* shot the Admiral with a Pistol, adds that This Murtherer was killed in the same manner, some time after, as he was returning from *Spain*. *Fu pochi anni dapoi venendo d'Espagna con somigliante spezie di morte del suo fatto premiato*. This Account is not so clear, and so particular, as it should be; but some other Writers have cleared up the Matter.

[C] *Thuanus relates the Matter with other Circumstances*.] He says, that *Beme*, returning from *Spain*, whither the Duke of *Guise* had sent him to buy Horses, or, under That Pretence, to renew the Correspondence, which the late Cardinal of *Lorrain* had kept up with *Philip* II, was taken near *Jarnac*; that he offered his good Offices to release *Montbrun*, and a very considerable Sum; but that his Proposals were not regarded, and that, on the contrary, Those, who had taken him, sollicited the *Rochellers* to buy him of them for a thousand Pistoles, and afterwards to punish him with the utmost Severity for the infamous Murther of the Admiral; that the *Rochellers*, for fear of reprisals, and by the Counsel of *la Noué*, rejected these Offers; that *Bretoveville*, Governor of *Bouteville*, being unwilling to ransom such a Prisoner, and fearing, that, if he should put him to Death, he would set an example, which might be attended with ill Consequences, found out an expedient; which was to suborn a Soldier to supply *Beme* with the

(1) *The Life of Admiral Coligny*, pag. 129.

(2) *He disguised himself under the Name of Ernestus Varamundus Frisius.*

(3) *In* 1575.

(4) *He should have said* Xaintonge.

(5) Beza, Hist. Eccles. lib. 16, pag. 479.

BENCIUS. BENEDICTIS.

the means to escape. This Soldier, and *Beme*, made their Escape accordingly; but they fell into the Ambuscades, which *Bretouville* had laid for them, and *Beme* was killed with several Stabs (6). *Mezerai* relates the Matter much in the same manner (7): He says, that the Consistory of *Rochel* would have given a thousand Crowns for That Prisoner, to have punished him publickly; but the Wisest, and *Bertoville* (8) *Governour of the Place* (9), apprehended a Retaliation.

Peter de St Romuald says, " that the *Rochellers* de- " sired to have *Beme*, at the Persuasion of *la Nouë*, " fired to have him to a severe and shameful " Death; *and that* Beme, *being mortally wounded by* " Bertoville, *and afterwards killed by the Soldiers*, " was, at last, sent to the Baron *de Rosnë*, at his " great Sollicitation, who caused him to be honour- " ably buried at *Engolesme*: *and that* the Soldier, " who had endeavoured to favour his Escape, being " grievously wounded, came off with a Ransom, and " was banished the Place (10)."

BENCIUS (FRANCIS), an *Italian* Jesuit, was born at *Aquapendente*, in the Year 1542 [*A*]. He studied the *Belles Lettres* at *Rome*, under *Marc Antony Muretus*, and made so happy a Progress under the Lectures of this Great Rhetorician, that he became one of the most excellent Orators of That Time. He was likewise a very good *Latin* Poet. There is something very surprizing in the Manner, in which it is said he came to a Resolution of taking the Habit of a *Jesuit* [*B*]. He taught Rhetoric for many Years, at *Rome*, in the College of the Society, and died there, the sixth of *May*, 1594 (*a*). He had three Brothers, who were likewise Jesuits (*b*): His Father was yet alive in the Year 1590 (*c*). You will find, in *Moreri*, the Titles of some of his Works; I shall confine myself to his Speeches [*C*].

[*A*] *He was born at* Aquapendente *in the Year* 1542.] The Elogies, extracted from *Thuanus* by Mr *Teissier*, inform us, that *Bencius* was born in a Village of *Tuscany*, called *Aquapendente*, *which was the Patrimony of his Father* (1). The *Latin* Words of *Thuanus* are, *Patrimoniali Etruriæ oppido, cui Aquapendenti nomen, natus* (2). The Word *oppidum* being equivocal, and signifying sometimes a Borough, sometimes a Town, it must not here be taken for a Village, but a Town. I know not whether *Thuanus* had reason to say, that the Father of *Bencius* was Lord of it. *Alegambus* says no such thing; and it is not usual with That Author to suppress what may enhance the Birth and Riches of the Writers of his Order.

I have two reasons for fixing the Birth of *Bencius* to the Year 1542: the one is, that he died in the Year 1594: This is attended with no difficulty; the other is, that we find in *Alegambus*, that he died in the Fifty second Year of his Age. *Alegambus* is a little confused in his Figures; however I was of Opinion there was no Error in This; but I am surprized, that, in making The *Errata* of his Work, he did not rectify the following. *Annos natus* xx, *in Societátem est ascitus*. xv Cal. *Junii, anno Christi* MD.LXX (3). —— *Anno Salutis* MD XCIV, *migravit e vitâ, ætatis suæ* LII, *postquam venit in Societatem* XXVII (4). He says, that *Bencius*, having become a Jesuit in 1570, at the Age of twenty Years, was in the Fifty second Year of his Life, and Twenty seventh of his Profession, in 1594. These Computations destroy each other. *Nicius Erythræus* is more confident; for, having once said, that *Bencius* became a Jesuit at the Age of twenty Years, he allows him Fifty two Years of Life, and Thirty two of Jesuitism (5).

[*B*] *There is something very surprizing in the manner of his coming to a Resolution of taking the Habit of a* Jesuit.] They, who would read the Particulars of this Adventure, may consult *Alegambus*, and *Nicius Erythræus*. They will there read of nocturnal Apparitions, of a Crucifix, and many other things. I shall only observe, that *Nicius Erythræus* goes farther, than the other Author. The latter is satisfied with telling us, that, from the Image *Bencius* first confessed himself, which was to some of the Jesuits, he took it into his Head, that he should one Day be of their Order (6): but, according to *Nicius Erythræus*, he thought he heard, during his Confession in the Church of the Jesuits, a Voice, which pronounced these Words: *You shall also be, one Day, of the Number of these Religious* (7): *Alegambus*, as I have already observed, does not extenuate what advances the Credit of his Society. It is probable, therefore, *Nicius Erythræus* has here expressed himself hyperbolically: the Fact, in passing from Mouth to Mouth, was exaggerated before it reached the Ears of This Writer.

[*C*] *I shall confine myself to his Speeches*.] Some of them were printed separately; and Manuscript Copies of others were handed about. These Copies became imperfect, in proportion as they multiplied. This made the Author resolve to publish an Edition of his *Speeches* in 1590 (8). He dedicated it to Cardinal *Ascanio Colonna*. He published likewise the same Year a Collection of *Latin Poems*, and dedicated it to Cardinal *Francis Sforza*. His *Speeches*, to the Number of Twenty six, are accompanied with a short Dissertation *de Stylo & Scriptione*, and contain, among other Pieces, the funeral Oration of *Muretus*, That of *Alexander Farnese*, Duke of *Parma*, and That of Cardinal *Alexander Farnese*. The *Poems* are divided into four Books. They were reprinted with the *Speeches*, at *Ingolstadt*, in the Year 1599; and there are added to them Two *Dramatic Poems* of the same Author (9), which had been published separately. The Edition of *Cologne*, for *John Kinchius*, in 1617, in 12mo, contains all This. It is pretty correct; but the Paper and Character are very bad. The Publisher has not added the Poem in *Hexameter* Verse, entituled, *Quinque Martyres*, or the five Martyrs, in which *Bencius* has celebrated the Martyrdom, which Five Jesuits suffered in the *Indies*, in 1583. This Work, divided into six Books, was printed at *Venice*, in the Year 1591, and dedicated by *Benedictus Georgius* to Cardinal *Octavio Aquaviva*, Nephew of *Claudius Aquaviva*, General of the Jesuits. I have the Edition of *Antwerp*, in 1602, in 12mo. The Author sets off the Simplicity of History with Poetical Fictions, of which he gives the Reader notice: *Si qua visa, & quæ speciem habent miraculi, inserta sunt, factum est, ut Poeticum Artificium Historiæ simplicitati mederetur*. Relations in Prose have often need of the same Advertisement.

Mr *Teissier* affirms, that *Nicius Erythræus* says, that This Jesuit *translated* Aristotle's *Rhetoric so well, that it is difficult to find a more perfect Work of the Sort* (10). I have not met with This in *Erythræus*'s Elogium of This Jesuit: I only find, that *Muretus* dedicated his *Latin* Version of *Aristotle*'s Rhetoric to *Bencius*, and that the latter read Lectures on the same Work (11).

BENEDICTIS (ELPIDIO *de*), had a good Share in the Esteem and Affairs of Cardinal *Mazarin*. He was his Secretary during his Nunciature in *France*, and afterwards his Agent at *Rome*. He acquitted himself so well of That Employ, that the Cardinal praised his Fidelity and good Conduct, in his last Will, and recommended him to the Most Christian King. This Recommendation was not fruitless; for the Abbot *Benedictis* was declared Agent of *France* at *Rome*, and loaded with Riches. He was ordered, by the Cardinal's Heirs, to cause a sumptuous Funeral Service to be performed for him in the Church of *St Vincent* and *St Anastasius*, which had been his Eminence's Parish. He performed it admirably well,

VOL. I. 9 C and

and published a Description of This Funeral Pomp (a). He was ordered to cause a Funeral Solemnity to be performed for the Queen-Mother (b), with all manner of Pomp, in the Church of *St Lewis*, which is That of the Nation; he performed it like a Man, who perfectly understood these sort of Ceremonies. The Description of These Funerals is to be seen in a Book, which he published (c). He wrote another, which is an authentic Monument of his Zeal for the Honour of his Benefactor; for, having been informed, that a Book was handed about, which strangely defamed Cardinal *Mazarin*, he published a Collection of divers Memoirs in *Italian*, which he thought proper to confute That Satire. He enlarged it soon after, and added some Political Reflexions to it. He translated the Treatise of the Prince of *Conti*, concerning the *Duty of Great Men*, into Italian. I ought not to forget the *Chronological Tables*, which he published. Those who have seen the House and Garden, which he caused to be built near *Rome*, or who have read the Description, which he gave of them, under the Title of *Villa Benedicta Literaria*, must grant, that he understood Architecture, and knew how to adorn and embellish a House. He is the Author of the Decorations, which are to be seen in a Chapel, dedicated to *St Lewis*, in the Church of the same Saint, which Chapel he caused to be built almost from the Foundation (d).

BENI (PAUL), Professor of Eloquence, in the University of *Padua*, from the Year 1599, 'till his Death, which happened in the Year 1625, was one of the most copious Writers, that flourished in his Time. He was a *Greek* by Nation [A], as it has been lately said; and was not born at *Eugubio*, in the Duchy of *Urbino*, as many Persons affirm. He lived a long time among the Jesuits; but he left their Society, because they would not permit him to publish a Commentary on *Plato*'s *Feast* : The Obscenity of the Subject obliged them to refuse him the Permission he desired. The Reputation, which his Works procured him, moved the Senate of *Venice* to choose him to succeed *Ricciboni*, in the Chair of Eloquence; but he did not answer the Hopes, which were conceived of him. He tired his Auditors with long, wordy, Discourses, void of Matter, and pronounced in a languid manner, which, together with some other Reasons (a), and the pleasing manner, in which his Colleague, *Vincent Contarini*, delivered his Learning, made his Auditors desert so fast, that, sometimes, there were not so many Persons in his School, as are required for the signing of a Contract (b). This did not discourage him from his Study, nor lessen his extraordinary Application to his Books, and his Pen. One may easily be convinced of this, by the great number of Books, which he gave the Public, wherein there is, doubtless, a great deal of Learning and Wit. He singly maintained a Quarrel against the Academy *della Crusca* [B], with such Success, as rendered him formidable to many Authors [C]. The Respect, they have, at *Padua*, for the Memory of *Livy*, did not hinder our *Paul Beni* from attacking That Historian with the utmost Vigor (c). Consult *Moreri*'s Dictionary; for I only mention what he has omitted.

[A] *He was a Greek by Nation.*] I was surprized to find This affirmed in the *History of the Works of the Learned* (1), and, in order to know, which of the two said so, The Author of That Journal, or the Author of the Book, mentioned by Him, I consulted the Life of *Tasso*, and found these Words in it (2); "All "the Learned Men in *Italy* ------ have followed "*Paul Beni*'s Opinion unanimously. That Learned "*Greek*, transplanted into *Italy*, made it appear, in "an elaborate Comparision of the Poems of *Homer*, "*Virgil*, and *Tasso*, that the modern Poet had comprehended all the Beauties of the two Ancient in "his Work, without imitating their Faults." I thought it was a Mistake; for I knew, that *Tomasini*, and *Lorenzo Crasso*, affirm, that he was born at *Eugubio*; and he calls himself *Eugubinus*, in the Titles of some of his Books, and In the Inscription, which he desired might be put on his Tomb; and, therefore, I followed This Opinion in the first Edition of This Dictionary. But I have been freed from my Error by the Abbot *de Charnes*, and That in such a Manner, as engages me to think myself happy in having said, that I esteemed and honoured him very much. He supplied me with a Passage, which does not permit me to doubt, that our *Beni* was born in *Candia* (3). It is true, He was but a Child, when he came into *Italy*.

[B] *He singly maintained a Quarrel against the Academy della Crusca.*] Every Body knows, that the *Italian Dictionary* of That famous Academy of *Florence*, is a Work of great Importance; "Which was, "doubtless, the reason, why, as soon as it appeared, "it met with almost as many Critics, as Readers. "Among others, *Beni* did not cease to cry down "This Work, and to declame against the Authors of "it, as so many Monopolizers of the *Italian* Language: He undertook to make it appear, that they "had neither Ability, nor Authority, requisite to "decide in such a Manner. The Book, which he "published on That Account, was printed at *Padua* "in the Year 1613, in *Quarto*, under the Title of "*Anti-Crusca*, ò vero, *Il Paragone della Lingua Italiana, nel qual si mostra chiaramente que l'antica* "*sia inculta e rozza, à la moderna regola*, &c (4). ------ "The Gentlemen of the Academy chose to answer "him with the Pen, instead of proceeding against "him any other way. But, if we may believe *Tomasini*, This Method, which was, besides, the longest, "and the most perplexing, did not succeed to their "Honour. For it occasioned a furious Reply from "*Beni*, who produced it as a Defence of the *Anti-* "*Crusca*. He published it under the Title of *Il Cavacanti*, ò vero, *la Difesa del Paragone della Lingua Italiana*, &c (5). ------ The End of This "Combat was so glorious for *Beni* (in the Opinion "of *Tomasini*) that he obtained the Victory over all "the Academy *della Crusca*, and was proclaimed Defender *of the Italian Tongue* (6)." Let us see the Words of *Tomasini*. "Adversus Academicos Cruscantes, & Dictionarium Italicum ab iisdem editum, "Anti-Cruscam condidit. Cui cum respondissent "Academici, cumulatè libro iisdem altero sub Cavalcantis nomine satisfecit, seque à variis eorumdem "jurgiis validè adeo vindicavit, ut toto orbi clarissimus acerrimusque Italici Idiomatis Defensor fuerit "acclamatus (7)." It is said, that he obtained as great a Victory over The Gentlemen some time after, in defending *Tasso* against their Censures (8).

[C] — *which rendered him very formidable to many Authors.*] He was summoned to appear at *Rome*, on the Account of the Book, he published, on the Affairs *de Auxiliis*, without knowing them. "What he suffered

BENNON. BENSERADE.

"fered from Ecclesiastical Judges, made him but
"little wiser. He inveighed, ever after, against Au-
"thors of different Merit, without so much as spar-
"ing *Livy*. So that he became the Terror of the
"Writers of his Time; some of whom durst not pub-
"lish their Compositions, for fear of exposing them
"to his unmerciful Censure (9)."

(9) *Id. Ibid.*

BENNON, Bishop of *Misnia* or *Meissen*, in *Germany*, in the XIth Century, was canonized by *Hadrian* VI. The Bull of the Canonization, dated the Thirty first of *May*, 1523 [*A*], grounds *Bennon*'s Merit, I. On his having been the only Bishop of *Germany*, who was true to the Court of *Rome*, in the Quarrels between *Gregory* VII, and the Emperor *Henry* IV. II. On the Miracles, which he had performed [*B*] in his Life-time, and after his Death. This Canonization had been a long time sollicited at *Rome*, and perhaps had never been obtained, if *Luther* had not shaken off the Pope's Yoke, in the same Country, where the Body of *Bennon* lay: But the Court of *Rome*, thinking, that the Institution of a new Saint, would support the staggering Faith of That Country, yielded, at last, to the Instances of the Bishop of *Meissen*, who went to the Pope with powerful Recommendations from *Charles* V, the Archbishops of *Magdeburg*, and *Saltzburg*, and the Marquisses of *Misnia*. *Luther* was not silent on this Occasion; but published a Treatise in *High-Dutch*, which he entituled, *Against the new Idol, and old Demon*, of Meissen. *Emser* wrote sharply against This Treatise of *Luther*, and boasted insultingly, that, notwithstanding the Invectives of This Enemy of the Church, a wonderful Concourse of People had assisted at the Ceremonies of This new Solemnity; and he presaged, that it would continue for ever. His Prediction was soon convicted of Falshood [*C*]; That of *Bennon* was confuted at the same Time (a) [*D*]. *Emser* thought himself particularly obliged to write, upon this Occasion, against *Luther*; for he had published the Life of *Bennon*, in the Year 1512; wherein, among other things, he alledged divers Reasons, why the Bull of Canonization had not been yet obtained, after so much Expence, and so many Sollicitations (b). There is a strange Mistake in *Moreri*'s Dictionary (c).

(a) *Taken out of Seckendorf's History of Lutheranism, lib. I, pag. 285.*

(b) *Ex eodem Seckendorfio, ib. pag. 232, in Additione.*

(c) *See Permais [A.*

[*A*] *Dated the Thirty first of May* 1523.] We find the same Date in *Moreri*'s Dictionary. And That is not wrong. But we find there also, that Pope *Adrian* IV dispatched This Bull; which is an unpardonable Falsity. *Adrian* IV lived in the XIIth Century.

[*B*] *Grounds his Merit on some Miracles, which he performed.*] The chief of them are; I. That the Keys of his Cathedral, which he had thrown into the River *Elbe*, after he had shut up That Church against the Emperor and his Embassadors, were found in the Belly of a Fish, and carried back to the Prelate. II. That he passed over the *Elbe* dry-shod. III. That he turned Water into Wine. IV. That, with a kick of his Foot, he caused a Fountain to spring up; and this is sufficient ground for the Church of *Rome* to boast, that the Fable of *Pegasus* has had it's Accomplishment among the Christians. V. That he celebrated Mass in two places at one and the same time. VI. That, after his Death, he came, in a Dream, and put out an Eye of *William* Marquis of *Misnia* (1). One may easily guess, that *Luther* did not spare These Miracles.

(1) *Apud Seckendorf, Histor. Luther. lib. i, pag. 285.*

[*C*] *Emser's Prediction was soon convicted of Falshood.*] The Inspectors, or Visitors, who were sent into *Misnia* in the Year 1539, having notified to the Country Priests, that they should conform themselves to the Confession of *Augsburg*, went, soon after, to exhort the Canons of the Cathedral Church of *Meissen* to do the same. Their Dean, *Julius Pflug*, having convened the Chapter, it was resolved, to leave Matters as they stood. Whereupon, they were enjoined not to perform any Act of Religion in the Church, according to the ancient Ritual; and *Bennon*'s Tomb was demolished, as an Object of *Baalistic* Idolatry (2). Behold, then, a Worship, which, instead of being eternal, as *Emser* had prognosticated, was but of fifteen Years continuance. A wise Man ought to be extreamly reserved concerning future Events, even when Appearances are favourable; and I think those are to be pitied, whose Profession requires, that they should keep up the Hopes of the People; for very often they are obliged to make Almanacks against their Knowledge.

(2) *Id. Ibid. lib. iii, pag. 221.*

[*D*] *The Prediction of Bennon was confuted at the same time.*] His Life says, That he declared, when he was dying, that he had obtained, by his Prayers, that the Worship, established in his Cathedral, should never cease. *In eo tamen maxime falsum esse apparet, quod, teste Emsero, moriturus dixerit, precibus suis effectum esse, ut cultus Ecclesiæ Misnensis perpetuus sit futurus* (3). This Worship was singular, and was not to be seen at *Rome* itself. The Intervals of the Psalmody were so contrived, in the Cathedral of *Meissen*, that, every Hour of the Day and Night, they sung the Praises of the Cœlestial Court. *Ut nullum diei aut noctis tempus cantu & Deorum hymnis ac laudibus vacet* (4). *Bennon* died like a false Prophet, if he declared, when he was dying, that this would always continue.

(3) *Ibid. lib. i, pag. 286, litera a.*

(4) *Emserus apud Seckendorf. ibid.*

BENSERADE (a) (ISAAC de), one of the finest Wits of the XVIIth Century, was of *Lions*, near *Roan* (b). He was born a Protestant, as appears by his Christian Name; but was not bred in That Religion; for being yet a Child, when his Father turned Catholic. The Reason why the Bishop, who confirmed him, did not take from him the Name of *Isaac*, is very singular [*A*]. It is said, that his Ancestors were very considerable [*B*]; but every one does not agree to This. When his

(a) *That he spelt his Name in a Letter, which he did me the honour to write to me, the 18th of May, 1685. I found Benserade at the end of the Epistle Dedicatory of the Paraphrase on the nine Lessons of Job. The Abbot Tallemant calls him always Penserade.*

(b) *Discourse concerning the Life of Mr Benserade, before his Poems; Edit of Paris, 1697, and in Holland 1698. Tallemant is the Author of That Discourse.*

[*A*] *The Reason why the Bishop ----- did not take from him the Name of Isaac, is very singular.*] *Benserade* was but seven or eight Years of Age, when the Bishop, who confirmed him, asked him, *If he would have his Jewish Name changed for a more Christian one? With all my Heart*, answered he, *provided you will give me something to boot*. The Prelate, surprized with the Child's Wit, would not change his Name, but said, *We must leave it him; he will make it very illustrious*. This Particular has been communicated to me by a good Hand; and I think it will be found in the Life of *Benserade*, written by the Abbot *Tallemant*, if ever it be printed.

This is what I said in the Year 1694; and my Conjecture has proved true: That Discourse of the Abbot *Tallemant* is to be found at the beginning of *Benserade*'s Works, printed at *Paris* in the Year 1697, and in *Holland* 1698. The Particular, is to be found in it.

[*B*] *It is said, his Ancestors were very considerable.*] It is the Custom for a Person, who is admitted into the *French* Academy, to make the Elogy of Him, to whom he succeeds. Mr *Pavillon*, Successor

his Father died, *he left him very young, with a very small Estate, and very much encumbered; so that he chose rather, as it is said, to give it away, than to go to Law about it* (c). He made himself known to the Court by his Verses, and his Wit, and had the good Fortune to please Cardinal *de Richelieu* [C], and Cardinal *Mazarin* [D]; so that they put him in a Condition, not only to live handsomely, but also to lay up something

(c) Tallemant, ibid.

fessor of Mr *de Benserade*, praised him with great Delicacy: See, here, in what manner he handled what related to his Extraction. "This is not a Place, where the Nobility of This illustrious Man ought to be displayed. Here the Chance of Birth makes no one to be esteemed or despised: Hence it is, that, in the Funeral Pomp of the deceased Members, the Images of their Ancestors are not carried before them; we only take care to expose their Talents, and their Works, to the public View. Let the Elogy of the Deceased be, every where else, adorned with the Name of the ancient Lords of *Maline*; let others reckon, among his Ancestors, Him, who, in the beginning of the last Century, was great Master of the Artillery: my Business, here, is only to speak of That, which made him admired in his Life-time, and will perpetuate his Memory after his Death (1)."

(1) See the Historical Letters of *Feb.* 1692, p. 169, 170.

Here is what is to be found in the Discourse of the Abbot *Tallemant*: "Tho' Mr *de Benserade* spoke but little of his Father, yet he did not forget his Ancestors, one of whom had been Chamberlain to one of our Kings, and Castellan of the Castle of *Milan* - - - - - By the Mother's Side, he was related to the *Vignateurs*, and to the *la Portes*; his Mother bore the last Name, which was That of the Mother of Cardinal *de Richelieu*. —— She would not willingly allow she was related to the Cardinal, saying, often, in her Family, she was not the *la Porte*, they took her for. —— Admiral *de Brizé* looked upon *Benserade* as a Person belonging to him." It is affirmed, in the Epistle dedicatory of his Works (2), that he had the Honour to belong to the great Cardinal *de Richelieu*. I desire you to compare this with the following Passage of the *Menagiana*. By what I have heard, "Mr *de Benserade* was Son of an Attorney of *Gisors*; and I was much surprized, when the Abbot *Regnier* read here, the other Day, Mr *Pavillon*'s Speech, which he made, when he was admitted into the Academy, wherein he gives Mr *de Benserade* a magnificent Genealogy. But I should not esteem him less, if he was of a meaner Birth. The Learned ought to value themselves for being the Sons of their own Works. Mr *de Benserade* had a pretty House at *Gentilli*, and, over the Gate of That House, he had set up a Coat of Arms, with an Earl's Coronet, which he had given himself. One of his Friends, seeing it, said, one Day, *Poets may do these things*) (3)." Observe, that Mr *Pavillon* says nothing of what is mentioned by the Abbot *Tallemant* concerning *Benserade*'s Ancestors; which makes me suspect, that they have followed some general Notions; for they would not have swerved so strangely from Uniformity, if they had followed Genealogical Titles, well proved. Whatever may be said of *Benserade*'s Ancestors, his Father's Obscurity cannot be doubted. Some had heard say, that he was an Attorney of *Gisors*(4), and others, that he had been Justice in *Eyre* (5). His Son made but little mention of him, though he did not forget his Ancestors (6). Would you have a greater Proof of a mean Condition? Take notice of another thing. A great many Persons can prove their Father's Nobility, better than That of their Grand-father, and, if you would oblige them to prove That of their Great-Grand-father, they would find it more difficult still. *Persius* has made this Observation (7). It is quite the contrary here. We must skip over some Degrees, in going back, if we would get clear of Genealogical Darkness. Our *Benserade* finds nothing to please him in his Father, or his Grand-father; he finds his Nobility only in past Ages. It is certain, that the Nobility of Blood is, sometimes, like Those Rivers, which fall down a Precipice, and, having run some Miles under Ground, rise again (8). Genealogical History, which is commonly preceded by fabulous Times, is often interrupted by some Periods of obscure Times. It is a Geographical Map, which has it's Deserts, and unknown Countries. See Mr *Pavillon*, who was

(2) Printed at *Paris*, by *Charles de Sercj*, in the Year 1697.

(3) Continuation of the *Menagiana*, pag. 55, Edit. of Holl.

(4) Menagiana, ibid.

(5) Tallemant's Discourse on the Life of *Benserade*, init.

(6) Id. ibid.

(7) See Remark [*B*], of the Article GENTILIS (*Scipio*).

(8) Such is the *Guadiana* in Spain.

obliged to make a Leap of One hundred and fifty Years back to unite two illustrious Ends in the Family of *Benserade*. I shall make hereafter (9) an *Antithesis* of *Persius*'s Verses, in another Sense.

I know not what to say of one *NICOLAS BENSERADE*, to whom *Erasmus* wrote some Letters (10), and of whom he speaks, as of a very good Man, who had done him much good, and who had some Learning (11). He is called a Civilian (12). Would our Mr *de Benserade* have placed him among his Ancestors?

[C] *He had the good Fortune to please Cardinal* Richelieu.] Mr *Pavillon* informs us, that This Cardinal took care of the Education of *Benserade*. "You have seen, says he (13), in This worthy Member, the Fruit of the Care, which the great Cardinal *de Richelieu* took of his Education; He, who gave Birth to your learned Assembly, educated him in his Youth; and, as Men are only considered by you in relation to their Wit, before you had associated him, he might have boasted, that you were Children of one and the same Father." These Words might induce one to think, that *Benserade* was known to This Cardinal only as a very hopeful young Man, who deserved so much the more That chief Minister's Protection, as he was the Son of a converted Huguenot; but, if we consider the Circumstances of the Time, if we consider, that the *Cleopatra* of *Benserade* was printed in the Year 1630 (14), we cannot doubt, but that he had actually a Share in *Richelieu*'s Esteem, in Quality of an Author, and a fine Wit.

[D] —— *And Cardinal* Mazarin.] Give me leave to insert here a long Passage of a Book, the Title whereof is somewhat surprizing (15). Many Readers will be well pleased to see it here, without being obliged to turn to another Book: Besides, some of them may chance not to have the *Arliquiniana* in their Closets. "Your Story puts me in mind of a Thing, which made *Benserade*'s Fortune: I have it from himself. Were you acquainted with him? Yes, said I, I conversed with him till his Death: He was the quickest Wit, and the most zealous Friend, that ever I saw; he was a good, and gallant, Man, and I will tell you, one Day, some particular things of him. You know then, replied *Arlequin*, that *Benserade* came young, agreeable, and full of merit, to Court. He applied himself to Cardinal *Mazarin*, who loved him, but with such a Friendship, as produced no Advantage to him. *Benserade*, continuing to follow his Genius, made gallant Verses every Day, which gained him a great Reputation. The Cardinal, being one Evening with the King, related to him after what manner he had lived in the Pope's Court, where he had spent his Youth. He said, that he loved the Sciences, but that his chief Application had been to polite Learning, and especially Poetry, wherein he succeeded pretty well; and that he was, at That Pope's Court, what *Benserade* was at That of *France*. Soon after, he retired to his Apartment. *Benserade* happened to come in, an Hour after; and his Friends told him what the Cardinal had said; they had scarce ended, when *Benserade*, being filled with Joy, left them bluntly, without saying any thing. He ran to the Cardinal's Apartment, and knocked as hard as he could, to be heard. The Cardinal was just gone to Bed; *Benserade* was so pressing, and made so much Noise, that they were obliged to let him in. He went, and fell on his Knees by the Bolster of his Eminence's Bed, and, having begged a thousand Pardons for his Rudeness, he told him what he had heard, and thanked him, with an inexpressible Ardour, for the Honour he had done him in comparing himself to Him, as to the Reputation he had for Poetry; adding withal, that he was so proud of it, that he could not contain his Joy, and that he should have died at his Door, if he had been hindred from coming to pay him his Acknowledgment for it. This Zeal pleased the "Cardinal

(9) In Remark [*E*], of the Article GENTILIS (*Scipio*).

(10) See the 21st and 23th Letters of the 5th Book of *Erasmus*. One of them is dated in the Year 1499; and the other in the Year 1498.

(11) In the Table of *Erasmus*'s Letters.

(12) *Erasmus* ibid. See also Epist. 74, lib. 5, pag. 323.

(13) Historical Letters, of *Feb.* 1692, pag. 171.

(14) See Remark [*O*].

(15) *Entretiens des Arlequiniana*. I cannot see why they chose rather to say Arliquiniana, than Arlequiniana, since every one says Arlequin, and not Arliquin.

BENSERADE. 751

something for his latter Years. He had some Pensions assigned him *on a Bishoprick*, and *two Abbeys* (d) [E]; so that he might be looked upon as *a kind of Ecclesiastic* (e). The Queen-Mother gave him a Pension of Three thousand Livres, when, upon the Death of Cardinal *de Richelieu*, he lost his Pension (f). He found means to subsist at Court, by means of the Thousand Crowns of the Queen-Mother, *and by That of some rich and liberal Ladies* (g). I have read somewhere, that the Court had resolved to depute him to the Queen of *Sweden*; but it was not put in Execution [F]. His Sonnet

(d) Menage, An. Baillet, Article 14c. See also towards the end of Remark [D].
(e) See the Anti Baillet, ibid.
(16) Aristiquiniana, pag. 231. Edit. of Holland.
(17) The Abbot Tallemant, ubi supra.
(18) Tallemant, ibid.
(19) I wrote this in Capital Letters, to show the Opposition between the Abbot Tallemant, and the Author of the Aristiquiniana, who says, that Benserade would have been a Bishop, if he had been willing to be a Churchman. See Citat. (16).
(20) Tallemant, ibid.
(21) Ibid.

" Cardinal very much. He assured him of his Pro
" tection, and promised him that he would not be
" useless to him; and indeed, six Days after, he sent
" him a small Pension of Two thousand Livres;
" some time after, he had other considerable Pen
" sions on Abbeys; and he might have been a
" Bishop, if he would have been a Churchman (16)."
The Abbot *Tallemant* will not agree to this latter
Fact. See the following Remark.

[E] *He had some Pensions assigned him on a Bishopric, and two Abbeys.*] He obtained one from Cardinal *de Richelieu*, "from the Time that his first Works
" appeared: it was continued to him till That Cardi
" nal's Death; and he would, perhaps, have found
" the same Protection with the Duchess of *Aiguillon*,
" if the four following Verses, which he made after
" the Cardinal's Death, had not offended her very
" much:

Cy-gist, ouy gist, par la mort-bleu,
Le Cardinal de Richelieu,
Et ce qui cause mon ennuy,
Ma pension aveecque luy.

*Here lies, ay here doth lie, morbleu,
The Cardinal de Richelieu,
And, what is worse, my Pension too.*

" This Pension was pretty considerable, as I have
" been assured; which was a terrible Loss to him,
" and which would have very much incommoded him,
" if it had not been made up by another of Three
" thousand Livres, which the Queen-Mother gave
" him (17)." Let us admire here the Power of the
Habit of Jesting. A Poet, who has a turn this way,
will rather waste his Fortune, than lose the Opportunity of a Jest, even the most unnatural Opportunity,
and the most opposite to Decency: for what can be
conceived more indecent, than to jest on the Death
of the greatest Man that ever was in the Ministry of
France? And if, for this reason alone, Pleasantry be
improper, it is still more so, when the Poet, who
jests on that Subject, had received a considerable Pension from the deceased. I cannot blame the Duchess
of *Aiguillon* for suppressing this Pension; She was less
to be blamed for it, than Mr *Benserade*. But let us
proceed to other Favours, with which this fine Wit
was gratified. Cardinal *Mazarin* procured him a
" Pension of a thousand Crowns on the Abbey of St
" Eloy —— and, when he died, left him a Pension of
" Two thousand Livres on the Bishopric of *Mende*.
" Lastly, *Benserade* had yet another Pension of Two
" thousand Livres on an Abbey of the Abbot *de Fe
" rilles*, called *Haut-Villiers*. — Besides this, he
" had a yearly Rent of Five hundred Crowns on the
" Town-house of *Lyons*, and a great deal of ready
" Money (18)." He would willingly " have had a
" Title; and perhaps they would not grant him this
" Favour, because he had not, at first, dedicated
" himself wholly to the Church. But, if he did not
" obtain That, which he HAD EARNESTLY
" DESIRED (19), he met with something, which
" he did not expect (20)." We are told, afterwards
in what manner he received the Three hundred Pistols, which the King sent him one Morning (21).
That Prince gave Ten thousand Livres for the Figures, wherewith the *Roundo's* of *Benserade* on *Ovid's*
Metamorphoses were adorned.

The Abbot *Tallemant* says, " It may perhaps be
" wondered at, that, being so well to pass as he was,
" he jested so much on his Poverty: But, in answer
" to this, we need only distinguish the times; it was
" at his first coming to Court." If the Dates were
well enquired into, it would perhaps be found, that
This Apology is not right, and that Mr *Benserade*
complained of Poverty, even when he did not feel the
Inconveniencies of it. He would not be the only

Poet, who has been guilty of This Fault; and it is
an Irregularity, which deserves more to be censured,
than That, for which *Seneca* was blamed, who praised
and recommended Poverty in the midst of an excessive
Opulency. It is better to do this, than to complain
of being poor, when one is in very good Circumstances. However it be, our *Benserade* is an example,
which may be alledged against the Author of a pretty
Roundo, which I mention elsewhere (22), and which
begins thus, *Le bel Esprit au siecle de Marot*. His
Verses helped him to attain a pretty good Fortune,
and put him in a Condition to be able to lend the
Ladies a Coach and Footmen. Doubtless, he deserved a Reward; but they should not have assigned
him Pensions on the Revenues of the Church, *non
hos quæsitum munus in usus*. See the Remark [G]
of the Article THOMAS. There is no question,
but several other Wits envied him, as well on account of his Coach, as because he had the Advantage
of frequently dining at the best Houses in *Paris*. One
of them (23) composed a Sonnet with this Conclusion:

Il frequente les bonnes tables,
Et je ne mange que chez moi:
J'en connois de plus miserables (24).

*Abroad to Dinner he can roam;
But I, alas! must eat at home.*

This is the taste of the ancient Parasites.

Si tristi domicœnio laboras,
Turani, potes esurire mecum (25).

*If there no Invitation be,
Turanius, you may fast with me.*

Let us observe, that this Sonnet " was very improper
" at that Time: for sickness and weakness obliged
" Mr *de Benserade*, towards the latter end of his
" Life, to dine seldom abroad, and to make few
" Visits (26)."

[F] *The Court had resolved to depute him to the
Queen of* Sweden; *but it was not put in Execution.*]
I have read this in a Letter of *Costar* to the Marchioness of *Lavardin*. *Costar's* words deserve to be set
down; since they inform us, that *Benserade* was not
in very good Circumstances at that time. It is an ill
Custom among ingenious Gentlemen not to date their
Letters. If *Costar* had dated his, we should know the
Year, wherein *Benserade* was to have had This Employment. " You have been informed, that the
" Queen sends him to *Sweden*, and that he will set out
" in a Week or ten Days. He has waited in vain, a
" long time, at *Paris*. I do not know whether *Stock
" holm*, and the Northern Air, will be more favour
" able to his Fortune, than That of the Court has
" been. I am sure, that all the Ice and Snow of the
" North will not be able to extinguish That noble
" Fire, which animates him, and that the Presence of
" the bravest and most ingenious of Queens will
" inspire him with things, worthy to be conceived
" under a better Heaven, and milder Climate (27)."
See, in the Collection of the fine Pieces of the *French*
Poets, the Jest, which This Embassador made on the
Meanness of his Equipage. *Scarron* could not be
silent on the Miscarriage of this Deputation: See how
he dates an Epistle to the Countess *de Ficsque*;

L'an que le Sieur de Benserade
N'alla point à son Ambassade (28).

*The Year, in which the Sieur Benserade did not go
upon his Embassy.*

This does not inform us, in what Year it was. I
cannot tell why Mr *Tallemant* says, that some One
made

(22) In the New Letters against Maimbourg, pag. 59. & seq.

(23) The Abbot Esprit.

(24) This Sonnet was made on Job. Tallemant, ubi supra.

(25) Mart. Epigr. 80, lib. 5. See also Epigr. 78, 79, lib. 12.

(26) Tallemant's Discourses on Benserade.

(27) Costar, Letter 16, of Vol. I, pag. 430.

(28) Tom. V, pag. 231. Speak of the Collection published by the Author of the Journey into Spain.

VOL. I. 9 D

BENSERADE

Sonnet of *Job*, compared with That of *Urania*, raised his Fame greatly [G]; for how great an Honour was it, to be the Head of a Party against *Voiture* (*b*), and to have, on *Parnassus*, the Faction of the *Jobelins*, disputing the Ground with the Faction of the *Uranists*? It is certain, This Dispute divided the whole Court, and the Wits, and that some very illustrious Persons declared, against *Voiture*, for *Benserade*. The latter succeeded wonderfully in the Verses, which he made for Interludes [H]; but he miscarried in his *Roundo*'s upon *Ovid* (*i*). He was admitted, somewhat late, into the *French Academy*, since it was in the Year 1674; and he was then above sixty Years of Age. He succeeded *Chapelain* in this Place, and made his Elogy, which displeased the Count *de Rabutin* (*k*), and which was rather an Homage paid to Custom, than an Effect of Sincerity. Some Years before his Death, *he applied himself to pious Works, and translated almost all the Psalms* (*l*): Another Homage paid to Custom;

(h) He was the Author of the Sonnet of Urania.
(i) See the Menagiana, pag. 189, of Edit. 2. of Holland.
(k) See that Count's Letters, Part IV, Lett. 91.
(l) Tallemant's Discourse on Benserade.

made these two Verses *in his Gazettes*; for *Scarron*'s Epistles ought not to be called by That Name.

[G] *His Sonnet of* Job - - - - - - *raised his Fame greatly*] This Sonnet, and That of *Urania*, occasioned a World of Verses, which may be seen in the Collection of choice Pieces. I believe, that, during the Course of This Contest, one of the finest and most ingenious Pieces was the *Glose à Mr Esprit* (29). *Sarrazin* composed it: he had declared for the Sonnet of *Urania*. *Balzac* wrote a severe Censure of these two Sonnets, which is to be found at the End of his *Christian Socrates*. When one examines this Censure, one cannot but say, that there are some excellent Pieces, which have Imperfections. There are certain Beauties and Graces, which shine in such a Manner, in the midst of the Faults, which escaped the Author, that These Faults are not taken notice of. But, after all, I do not see, that these two Sonnets pass, at this time, for the best Pieces of their Authors. See what a good Critic (30) said of them: "Many "Persons have concerned themselves in this Contest "(31); and it is carried to such a Height, that con- "siderable Wagers are laid in favour of the one, and "of the other. But it is to be feared, that the same "thing may happen to these two Pieces, that hap- "pened to Those two Sonnets, which divided *Par- "nassus* into two famous Factions, under the Names "of the *Jobelins*, and the *Uranins*. For, being ex- "amined more narrowly, they lost a great deal of "their Worth and Esteem.

The Author of the Epistle which serves as a Preface to the new Translation of *Persius* and *Juvenal* (32), relates a curious Particular, which I cannot omit. "Thus (33) a great Prince, who knew a great "deal, but who had still a better Taste, than Capa- "city, for good things, judged so well, in two "small Verses, of the two famous Sonnets, which formerly amused the whole Court, and divided it into "two Cabals of Wits, whose War was very inno- "cent. *Voiture* had some formidable Partisans; and "so had *Benserade*: but, in truth, the Decision of "the Prince of *Conti*, which Nature alone dictated "to him, gave the Cause to the *Jobelins*, and That "without Appeal. This is the Decree.

L'un est plus grand, plus achevé;
Mais je voudrois avoir fait l'autre.

The One is more Grand, and more Perfect; but I would rather have been the Author of the Other.

"The first Verse relates to *Voiture*, and the second "to *Benserade*; who, I believe, was very well sa- "tisfied with the wish of a Judge, who was so much "the more incorruptible, as, in reading the terms, "which he made use of, every Body perceives he "judged without any partiality." The Abbot *Talle- mant* makes no mention of these two Verses of the Prince of *Conti*; though he says, that the Prince said, he never saw a finer Sonnet than That of *Job*. "The "End of it, *said his Highness*, is the most lucky in "the World; but, though the other Verses are very "gallant, yet they seem rather careless, than polished "and finished." Madam *de Longueville* declared for the Sonnet of *Voiture* (34). Note, that *Benserade* made his Sonnet *upon sending the Paraphrase, he had composed, on* Job, *to a Lady* (35); observe this, I say, as a Proof of the prophane Licence, which amorous Poets give themselves. Ought the Patience of *Job*, That Canonical, Divine, and Sacred, Example, to serve as an Introduction, or Text, to a Declaration of Love? Ought not a Christian Poet to have more respect for the Histories of the Bible? Ought he to have set his Patience, and his pretended Misery, above That of *Job*, under pretence that he was in love, and durst not declare it?

[H] *He succeeded wonderfully in the Verses, which be made for Interludes.*] These Verses were of quite a new Invention; They characterized, at the same time, the Poetical Deities, and the Persons, who represented them. The Author of the *News from the Republic of Letters*, has mentioned This Singularity by the by. "Mr *de Benserade* read (36) a Piece of "his own Composition, which was wonderfully ap- "plauded. It is an abridged Picture of the forty "Academists, as to their Persons, their Talents, Ad- "ventures, and Fortunes. He speaks freely of every "one of them; but with That ingenious and inimi- "table Turn, which he made use of in his Verses "for Interludes, personally proper to the Ladies and "Lords of the Court, who were to appear in the "Entries (37)." Mr *Perrault* explained this much better: Let us see what he says of it; "*I am going to "speak of another* Kind of Poetry, which has been ad- "ded to the Ancients; I mean the admirable Verses, "which Mr *de Benserade* made for the King's Inter- "ludes. Heretofore, when they made *Stanza's*, up- "on *Jupiter*, for Instance, who, making his Entry, "strikes the Cyclops with his Thunder-bolt, those "*Stanza's* spoke only of *Jupiter*, as *Jupiter*, and not "at all of the Person, who represented him. But "Mr *de Benserade* turns his Verses in such a manner, "that they are equally understood of both; and, as "the King generally represented *Jupiter*, sometimes "*Neptune*, and other times *Mars*, or the *Sun*, no- "thing is more admirable, than the delicate and art- "ful Manner, in which he praises him, without ad- "dressing himself to him. The Person, who is re- "presented, and the Actor, are both pointed at; "which creates a double Delight, by giving two "things to be understood at one time, which, being "separately fine, become still finer, when joined to- "gether (38)." I add a third Witness to these two, because he describes the Verses in question more fully in some Respects, and because he supplies me with a Proof of two following Remarks. "We have lost, "*says he* (39), a fine Wit, who excelled in the Art "of fine and agreeable Rallery, both in his Conversa- "tion, and in his Writings; especially in the inge- "nious Verses for Interludes, which he made several "Years for the whole Court. He was an Original "in this Kind; the Ancients have not supplied him "with any Model of This Sort of Rallery, and no "one has hitherto succeeded in imitating it. He "joined, to the Description of the Gods, and God- "desses, and other Persons, who were represented "in these Interludes, some lively and natural Pictures "of the Courtiers, who represented them: He often "discovered their Inclinations, their Amours, and "even their most private Adventures, in so fine, so "pleasing, and so nice, a manner, that those, whom "he pointed at, were the first, who were pleased "with it, and that his Jests did not affect them with "Resentment, or Vexation, which is an essential "Mark of their Perfection." See also the first Letter of the second Part of the Count *de Rabutin*, and the Discourse of the Abbot *Tallemant*. In That Discourse you will find, that *Benserade* had a Quarrel with the President de *Perigni*, and with *Moliere*, who had both made Verses for Interludes. Which shews, that he desired to be the only Person, who should be employed in this Business.

(29) You will find it among Sarrazin's Poems, pag. 26, Edit. of 1658, in 12mo.

(30) Mr Sallo, in the Journal of the Learned, Jan. 26, 1665, pag. 48, Edit. of Holl.

(31) It is That, which was raised on the Jocunde of Mr de Bouillon, Secretary to the late Duke of Orleans, and on the Joconde of Mr de la Fontaine.

(32) Made by the Jesuit Jerom Tarteron, and printed at Paris, in 1689.

(33) That is to say, in judging by what passes in ourselves when we read.

(34) Tallemant's Discourse on Benserade. He relates some Particulars concerning the War composed, &c.

(35) Id. ib.

(36) The Day, when Mr Corneille the younger was admitted into the French Academy.

(37) Month of January, 1685, p. 37.

(38) Parallel of the Ancients and Moderns, Tom. II, pag. 112, Edit. Holl.

(39) Collection of witty Sayings, printed by the Widow Cramoisi, 1693, pag. 204, Edit. Holl. This Book is ascribed to Mr de Calliere, of the French Academy, and Plenipotentiary of France, at the Treaty of Ryswick.

[I] *It*

BENSERADE. 753

(m) See the Hiſtorical Mercury of Nov. 1691, pag. 537.

(n) The Abbot Tallemant, ubi ſupra.

(o) Hiſtorical Mercury, Nov. 1691, pag. 537.

Cuſtom; but which may alſo proceed from a good Principle [*I*]. He died in the Month of *November*, 1691, in his Eighty ſecond Year (*m*); others ſay, that he died before he was eighty Years of Age (*n*). He had a Penſion from the Duke of *Orleans*, and an Apartment in the Royal Palace (*o*). He was a very honeſt Man, and of an admirable Converſation; having a good Talent at Jeſting [*K*], and telling People their Faults, without making them angry [*L*]. He had a bold way with him, which made him behave familiarly towards thoſe of the firſt Quality; ſo that he might ſay what he would, without being contradicted; nay, he ſeemed to have an aſcendant over the moſt conſiderable Perſons. ——— His Familiarity had even ſomething imperious in it; for he was not contented with taking the Liberty of contradicting others, but would not ſuffer his own Compoſitions to be criticized, and defended them ſo conceitedly, that thoſe very Perſons, whom he conſulted, could not ſpeak their Thoughts without expoſing themſelves to his Anger (*p*). He was ſincere, and very officious, eſpecially to the Ladies; for his Coach, and his Servants, were always at their Service (*q*). He was not learned [*M*]; but I would not alledge, as a Proof of his Ignorance, that he could not tell, one Day, what Difference there is between the *Hamadryads* and the *Dryads* [*N*]. He began early to appear in Print; for it is ſaid, that his Tragedy of *Cleopatra* was printed in the Year 1630; which made ſome ſay, that he was *more than a* Jubilate *Author* [*O*]. *Furetiere* abuſed him too

(p) Abbot Tallemant, ibid.

(q) Ibid.

---

(40) Tallemant's Diſcourſe on Benſerade.

(41) Citat. (39).

(42) Collection of witty Sayings, pag. 24, 25.

(43) Pavillon's Speech made to the French Academy. See Hiſtorical Letter, Feb. 1692. pag. 170.

(45) Furetiere.

(4?) Pag. 19. of Factum II.

[*I*] *It was perhaps in compliance with Cuſtom, that he tranſlated the Pſalms in his old Age; which might alſo proceed from a good Principle.*] I am the more inclined to believe This proceeded from a good Principle in Mr *de Benſerade*, becauſe his Submiſſion to God was very great during his laſt Sickneſs. Let us quote the Abbot *Tallemant* for it. "No Man " could begin his Life with more Gallantry, nor " end it with more Piety, or a greater Submiſſion " to the Will of God, than Mr *de Benſerade*. He " ſuffered ſuch violent Pains, that *Job*, whoſe Patience " he had celebrated, did hardly ſuffer ſharper; they " were ſo terrible, that one of a leſs lively Tem" per, and much leſs ſenſible than he was, could not " have been able to bear them (40)."

[*K*] *He had good Succeſs in Jeſting.*] A Paſſage, which I have juſt now quoted (41), ſhews, that he was Maſter of this Talent. Here is another Teſtimony, taken from the ſame Author. It is a Teſtimony, which may be called *practical*; for it conſiſts in an Example. "A Courtier was ſuſpected of being " Impotent, and would not own it; he meet *Benſe*" *rade*, who had often jeered him about it, and ſaid " to him, Sir, notwithſtanding all your poor jeſting, " my Wife is lately brought to Bed, *Alas! Sir*, re" plied *Benſerade, the World never doubted of your* " *Lady* (42)." You may find ſome of his witty Sayings in the Continuation of the *Menagiana*, and in the Diſcourſe of the Abbot *Tallemant*.

[*L*] *He told People their Faults, without making them angry.*] Nothing is more true, than the Saying, *Obſequium amicos, veritas, odium parit*, that is, *Friends are made by Complaiſance, and Enemies by ſpeaking Truth*. They, therefore, who know how to make Truth appear without That odious Look, which commonly attends it, muſt needs have a very ſingular Dexterity. This was the Talent, which *Benſerade* was praiſed for by his Succeſſor. "What a wonder" ful Addreſs, to make the moſt paſſionate Men " bear jeſting, and to praiſe the Modeſt, without " offending their Modeſty; to ſpeak the Truth in " the midſt of a Court, without prejudicing his For" tune, and to divert thoſe very Perſons, whoſe " faults he reproved. Amiable Cenſor, whoſe inge" nious Verſes, being purged from the Gall of Satire, " found the admirable Art of reproving All, and of" fending none (43)." Mr *Pavillon* cannot be accuſed of having carried the Matter too far, though what is ſaid in ſome Factums (44) ſhould be true; for there is no general Rule, but will admit of an Exception: It is the Ignorance of the Factums, who may be ſuſpected of overſtraining things. He ſays (45), that *Benſerade* "had ſet up for a Gallant in the old Court, " by Songs and Ballad-Verſes, which had gained him " a Reputation during the Reign of bad Taſte, Double " Meanings, and Points, which ſtill keep their Credit " with him. They have drawn upon him, *continues* " *he*, ſome Threats, and melancholy Adventures, " which have ſerved by way of Date to certain bur" leſque Gazettes." At Page 28 of the third *Factum*, he ſays, that "the ſcandalous Liſt, *which* Benſerade " *drew up, of the Academy*, and which he had the " Aſſurance to read publickly in one of the ſolemn " Aſſemblies, *contained* ſuch ſhocking and outrageous

" things, that they drew upon him the Threats of a " Perſon of the firſt Quality, who was concerned in " them; inſomuch that, notwithſtanding his Impru" dence, he was obliged to ſuppreſs it out of reſpect " to his own Shoulders (46)."

[*M*] *He was not Learned*] This was ſo well known, that no ſcruple was made of owning it, when Mr *Pavillon* was admitted into the *French* Academy, a Day favourable to Mr *Benſerade*, wherein they were rather diſpoſed to give him more than his Due, than to take from him what belonged to him. See, here, how Mr *Charpentier* expreſſed himſelf in the Anſwer he made to the Diſcourſe of the new Academiſt. " The Society has loſt one of it's Ornaments in Mr " *de Benſerade*: He was an original Wit, and owed " all his Reputation to himſelf alone. He equalled " the Ancients, without borrowing any thing of " them; NEITHER WERE THEY VERY WELL " KNOWN TO HIM; and, if any of their Thoughts " have appeared in his Writings, it was rather an " effect of Chance, than of Imitation. He ſhewed, " that one could ſtill produce ſomething new under " the Sun; and this Character of Novelty was ſo na" tural to him, that, whenever he would forſake it, " he was no more the ſame Man; and the Correſ" pondence, which he held with the Graces, became " interrupted, when he followed other Ideas, than " his own." I do not wonder that this want of Erudition was not ſuppreſs'd; for it afforded matter for a delicate and refined Elogy.

[*N*] *He could not explain the Difference between the* Hamadryads, *and the* Dryads.] The Thing is This: We ſhall ſee, that he came off with a Piece of Wit. "Being one Day at the Opera, in the Box of " the Duke of *Orleans*, the King's Brother, the Du" cheſs of *Orleans* aſked him, What difference there " was between the *Hamadryads*, and the *Dryads*? " He found himſelf much perplexed; but, not think" ing it fit to be ſilent, and perceiving, that an Arch" biſhop, and a Biſhop, waited in the Paſſage for the " Ducheſs's going out, being unwilling to ſhew their " Croſiers in the Box, he replied, *There was as much* " *difference as between Biſhops, and Archbiſhops*. This " immediately raiſed a laugh, and, the Ducheſs re" peating it the next Day at her *Toilet*, ſome one, " looking upon a Clergyman, his Friend, ſaid, point" ing to him, *Here is one your Highneſs may make a* " Dryad, *and* Hamadryad *of, whenever you are* " *pleaſed to go about it ſeriouſly* (47)." Mr *Benſerade*'s Perplexity in this Caſe does not ſeem to me a true Sign of Ignorance; for I am ſure, that the Queſtion of the Ducheſs of *Orleans* would have put ſeveral celebrated Regent Doctors to a ſtand (48). Theſe things are better known when we firſt leave the College, than after we have grown old in more ſublime Studies.

[*O*] *He was more than a* Jubilate *Author*.] This Expreſſion is borrowed from a Cloyſter. A Monk of fifty Years Profeſſion, is a *Jubilate* Religious, who is excuſed from *Matins*, and the Rigors of the Rule, in ſome Houſes (49). The Convents have formed This Expreſſion on the Duration of the Jewiſh *Jubilee*, which was of fifty Years (50). See how Mr *Menage* proves, that Mr *Benſerade was more than a Jubi-*

(46) The Abbot Tallemant, ubi ſupra.

(47) Tallemant, ibid.

(48) See the Article DRYADES.

(49) See Furetiere, at the Word JUBILE.

(50) Ibid.

BENSERADE. BERAULD.

too much in his *Factums* (r). *Sarrasin* had a fling at him, in the *Funeral Pomp of Voiture*: It is He, whom he calls *Rousselin de Grenade*, in the third Chapter of *The great Chronicle of the noble* Vetturius; and he makes use of this Name, because *Benserade* was red-haired [P]; and because he used to say, in jest, and by reason of the Resemblance of Names, that he was descended from the *Abencerrages*. I found this written with a Pen, in the Margin of a Copy of *The Funeral Pomp of* Voiture, in possession of a Person, who knew the Secret History of that Time. It appears by this Chapter of *Sarrasin*, that *Benserade* had supplanted *Voiture*, in the House of Madam de Saintot [Q]. I was in hopes to have found many things relating to the Life of Mr *de Benserade*, in the Collection of the finest Pieces of the French Poets (s); The Title assured me of it; but, when I came to read the Page, referred to in the Table, I did not meet with one Line of History in it.

(r) See pag. 18, of Factum II, and pag. 27, of the IIId Edit. of Holland.

(s) This Collection is in five Volumes. The Author of the Memoirs, and Journey to Straux published it at the Year 1602. It was presently printed at Amsterdam.

a Jubilate Author. He supposes, that the *Cleopatra* of This Author was printed in the Year 1630, and then goes on in this manner; "He died in the "Year 1691, aged eighty Years: So that he wrote "That Piece Sixty one Years ago; and I suppose, "that he was at least twenty Years of Age when "he composed it. Moreover, it is to be observed, "that a Piece for the Stage was seldom printed "until a Year after it had been acted the first "Time (51)."

Mr *Menage* is mistaken, in supposing, that The *Cleopatra* of our Author was printed in the Year 1630; and I am surprized, that, having so many Opportunities of coming at the Truth of this Fact, at *Paris*, he neglected to inform himself, or to employ, in the Enquiry, some of those young Persons, who attended his *Mercurials*. By Accident, I have met with a Copy of the first Edition of the *Cleopatra* of *Benserade* (52); and have found, by this means, that This Piece was printed for *Antony de Sommaville*, in 4to, and finished the Twenty ninth of March, 1636.

Let us add, to this, these Words of the Abbot *Tallemant*. "He had scarce left the College, when "he produced two or three Dramatic Pieces; "I have seen two of them, one of which was en- "tituled, *Ibis* and *Hiante*, and the other *Marc* "*Antony* (53): Both of them had pretty good Success; But, if he loved Comedy, he was no less "fond of the Actresses; and it is said, that, with "the late Marquis d' *Armentieres*, who was then "an Abbot, he left the *Sorbonne*, where their Parents would have had them study, and went al- "most every Day to the *Hotel de Bourgogne*, where "they met their Mistresses, who were *la Valiere*, "and the Fair *Reze* (54)."

[P] *Benserade was red haired*] The Abbot *Tallemant* believes, that *Benserade* loved the fair *Reze*, "because of the likeness of their Hair: Her Hair "was of a lively fair Colour; as for him, he con- "fessed freely, that he was red haired, and called "himself so, and thereupon compared himself with "some of the greatest Lords of the Court, without "troubling himself whether it would please them or "not (55)."

[Q] *He had supplanted* Voiture, *in the House of Madam de Saintot.*] *Sarrazin* expresses himself thus: *How* Vetturius *came to the Court of Queen* Lionelle de Galle: *How he fell in Love with her, and how he was driven from thence by the Intrigues of* Hunault d'Armorique, *and of* Rousselin de Grenade. The Manuscript Notes of my Copy (56) inform me, that Madam *de Saintot* was denoted under the Name of *Lionelle de Galle*, because of *Gaillonet*, her Father's House. Mr *de la Hunaudaye*, who was a *Breton*, was denoted by *Hunault d' Armorique*.

(51) Menagiana, pag. 33 &, Edit. 1, of Holl.

(52) It is the Orthography of his Name, both in the beginning, and at the end of the Epistle Dedicatory, and in the King's Privilege.

(53) It is likely the same, which Mr Menage calls Cleopatra.

(54) Tallemant's Discourse on Benserade.

(55) Ibid.

(56) See the words the end of the Text of this Article.

BERAULD (NICOLAS), in *Latin Beraldus*, ought to be reckoned among the Learned of the XVIth Century. He was Tutor to Admiral *de Coligny* [A]. *Erasmus* praises him in more than one place [B], and confesses, that, passing through *Orleans*, in his Way to *Italy*, he lodged at his House [C], and received many Favours from

[A] *He was Tutor to Admiral* de Coligny.] See here the Proof of it. "Natus est hic Gaspar anno "MDXVII. mensis Feb. die XVI. qui cum puer in- "dolem virtutis atque ingenii mirificam ostenderet, "mater cum patre mortuo bonis literis ab ineunte "ætate imbuendum curavit: eique Nicolaum Beraul- "dum, qui tum eruditionis laude in primis totius "Galliæ florebat præceptorem attribuit (1). — "*This Gaspar was born in the Year* 1517, *the sixteenth of February; who discovering, in his Youth, surprizing Talents of Virtue and Wit, his Mother and deceased Father took care to train him up very early to Learning; and, for this Purpose, put him under the Tuition of* Nicolas Berauld, *the most famous Person for his Learning in all* France." The ancient Life of This Admiral says no more; but That, which was published in the Year 1686, has more Circumstances. It informs us, that "*Berauld* "was first of all made Tutor to the Elder, who, "having abundance of Wit, made a great Pro- "gress under so good a Master (2). Afterwards "he was also *Gaspar*'s Tutor, and did not find him "of a more penetrating Wit (for few such were "found), but of a Spirit more disposed to Obedience, "so that, in a little time, he not only taught him "*Latin*, but also Philosophy. As Mr *de Montmo- "renci*, who was but newly made Constable, loved "his *Sister*, and *her Children*, he found time, not- "withstanding his great Occupations, to take care "of the Education of his Nephews; wherefore he "ordered *Berauld* to come to him regularly once a "Week, and to give him a true Account of all, "that he should observe in them, whether good "or bad. Now *Berauld*, being come to him, ac- "cording to his Command, and having told him, "that he was more satisfied with *Gaspar*, than with "*Odet*; The Constable took the one for the other, "and told him, he knew how to remedy it, for "that he designed *Gaspar* for the Church; and "that *Odet*, as the eldest, should keep up the Honour "of his Family. — *Berauld*, being surprized at this "Answer, asked him, Whether it was requisite, that "an Ecclesiastic should be ignorant, and a Man of the "World learned? This Discourse of *Berauld* made "the Constable perceive, that he had mistaken the "Matter; and he was very well pleased to hear, "that *Gaspar* had so good a Disposition for Learn- "ing, and that there was reason to hope something "good of him. But, *Berauld* having related this "Conversation to his Scholar, he was so afraid of "being made a Churchman, that they could no lon- "ger prevail with him to look into a Book.

[B] *Erasmus praises him, in more than one place.*] What he says of him, in his *Ciceronianus*, is a Mixture of good and bad: for, if on the one hand he allows him the Talent of Speaking well, he says, on the other hand, that he had not the Talent of Writing well, and represents him as very indolent. "Agnosco dictionis illaborato fluxu Pino non diffi- "milem: verum is in hoc genere nunquam nervos "intendit suos, dicendo quam scripto felicior. Quid "possit, satis divino, sed est magni laboris fugitan- "tior (3). — *I acknowledge, he is not unlike* "Pinus, *in the easy flow of his Style: but he never "exerts himself this way, being a happier Speaker, "than Writer. What he is capable of doing, I can "easily divine; but he is of an indolent Disposition, "and hates Trouble."* In the following Remark, the Praises he gives him are more pure, and in greater Number. Observe, that he dedicated his Book, *de Conscribendis Epistolis*, to him, in the Year 1522.

[C] *He lodged at his House*] Let us set down the whole Passage: it will afford us a Point of Criticism on the Modern Historian of Admiral *de Coligny*. "Nicolaus

(1) Vita Gasp. Colinii, pag. 33, 34, Edit. Ultraject. Ann. 1645.

(2) Life of Caspar de Coligny, pag. 8, 9.

(3) Erasm. in Ciceron. pag. 74.

BERAULD.

from him. We learn thereby, that *Berauld* lived at *Orleans*. Some say he was born there [D]; but others affirm, he was of *Languedoc* [E]. He wrote upon *Pliny* [F]; of which Father *Hardouin* has made no mention, in his excellent Catalogue of the Commentators on That ancient Author. He expressed a just Concern, in his Preface, for the Abuses of the Press. Doubtless, the Reader will be well pleased to see his Complaint [G], and the Catalogue of some other Pieces, which he published [H]. One thing has been lately reported, whereby it appears, that he was an honest

"Nicolaus Beraldus lepide nimirum hospitalis tesseræ meminit in subscriptione sua. Nam memini cum olim essem *Aureliæ Italiam* aditurus me hominis hospitio usum, atque apud eum dies aliquot sanè quam benignè comiterque habitum. Etiam nunc audire mihi videor linguam illam explanatam ac volubilem, suaviterque tinnientem & blandè canoram vocem, orationem paratam ac pure fluentem: videre os illud amicum & plurimum humanitatis præ se ferens, supercilii nihil: mores venustos, commodos, faciles minimeque molestos: quin & interulam sericam velut apophoretum obtulit abituro, virque ab homine impetravi ut liceret recusare (4). ——— Nicolas Berauld *makes diverting mention of our former Acquaintance, in his Subscriptions. For I remember, when I was at Orleans, designing to go to Italy, I was entertained in a very friendly manner at his House for some Days. Even now I fancy I hear That voluble, sweet, and harmonious, Voice, That ready and flowing Elocution: I have now before my Eyes That friendly, and humane, Aspect; Than graceful, easy, and genteel, Behaviour: And, upon my Departure, he presented me with a silken Vest, which I could scarce prevail with him to permit me to refuse.*" This Letter is dated the Twenty first of *February*, 1516: from whence it may be inferred, that *Berauld* was not young, when he was made Preceptor to the Sons of the Marshal *de Chattillon*. But how shall we reconcile That Volubility of Tongue, which *Erasmus*, an Ear-Witness, ascribes to him, with the following Words? " The Admiral had two things in " him, which seemed extreamly opposite, *viz.* a great " Vivacity of Wit, and a very slow Speech; so that " one would have said, that he mused upon what " he was going to say. The Politicians would have " it to be a Piece of Cunning to gain time to ob-" serve those with whom he had to do. ----- It " is much more likely, that it was a Fault, which " he had contracted by the constant Attendance up-" on his Master, *Nicolas Berault*, in whom the same " Thing was observed (5)."

[D] *Some say, that he was born at* Orleans] *Nicolai Beraldi* AURELII ---- *dialogus*. ---- *The Dialogue of* Nicolas Beraldus *of* Orleans. Thus speaks *Gesner* (6). See also *Rocolles*, Page 214, of the true History of *Calvinism*. I shall set down his Words in the following Remark.

[E] *Others affirm, that he was of* Languedoc.] " Their Mother, *Louise de Montmorency,* assisted with " the Advice of her Brother, took care of their Edu-" cation, and gave them *Nicolas Berault*, born in " *Languedoc,* for their Tutor, but he had acquired " Literature at *Paris,* whither he came very young." These Words are in the eighth Page of the new Life of the Admiral. *Gesner* might be deceived by the long Abode, which *Berauld* made at *Orleans,* where he was Professor of the Civil-Law, if I am not mistaken. *Rocolles* speaks of it thus, at the Two hundred and fourteenth Page of the true History of *Calvinism:* Nicolas Berauld, *of* Orleans, *A great* CIVILIAN. *Gesner* mentions a Speech of *Berauld*, *de Jurisprudentia vetere ac novitia.*

[F] *He wrote upon* Pliny.] He is the third of the Commentators on That Author, mentioned by *Erasmus. Hermolaus Barbarus* is the first (7), *Budæus* the second, and *John Cæsareus* the fourth. " Post hunc *(Budæum)* Nicolaus Beraldus, homo su-" pra peritiam humanarum literarum, Mathematicæ " etiam pulchrè callens, quodque hic vel præcipuum " erat sani judicii, non minore studio quam religione " vesatus est in hoc labore. Nuper omnium po-" stremus Joannes Cæsareus, in omni genere lite-" rarum exercitatissimus, non infelicem operam præ-" stitit (8). ----- *After* Budæus, Nicolas Berauld, " *a Man skilled beyond the Knowledge of human Li-" terature, well versed likewise in Mathematicks, per-*

" *formed This Task, and, what demonstrated the " Soundness of his Judgment, with no less Religion, " than Care. Last of all,* Joannes Cæsareus, *a " thorough learned Man, bestowed his Pains not un-" successfully.*" *Erasmus* speaks thus, in the Preface to *Pliny*, which was printed at *Basil*, by *Froben,* in the Year 1525. He assures us, that he had corrected many Passages, and that *Pliny* had never appeared in a better Condition. *In cæteris item ita vigilatum est, ut meo periculo non dubitem polliceri nunquam hactenus existisse Plinium f litius tractatum* (9). Nevertheless Father *Hardouin* says nothing of this Edition, and he only reckons *Cæsarius* (so he calls him) among those, who wrote on some Part of *Pliny.* He ascribes to him only some *Scholia* on what relates to Fishes, in the ninth Book. Mr *Chevillier* goes, then, too far, in these Words of the One hundred ninety first Page of his Origin of Printing at *Paris:* " I wondered, when I saw, that nothing was " said, there, of *John Cæsarius*, and that no men-" tion was made of his Work, " neither in the Preface, nor in the List of the chief " Editions of That famous Author, which was in-" serted in the first Volume (10)." This will serve as a Note, or Appendix, to what is said concerning the Omission of *Berauld,* in the Text of the Article.

[G] *His Complaint of the Abuses of the Press.*] *James Fontaine,* Professor of the Civil-Law in the University of *Paris* ---- very much approves the Advice, which *Nicolas Berauld* gave to Sovereigns, to redress this Evil, and to make E-dicts to remove all those from the noble Art of Printing, who, for want of Learning, should be judged uncapable of exercising it. Quare prudentissimè in Præfatione operis sui Plinian admonet longè eruditissimus Nicolaus Beraldus, ut aliquo publico decreto insolentissima ista ignorantum Impressorum audacia reprimatur; quibus hoc debemus studiosi, quòd pro unaquaque literâ inveni-mus plagam, pro Syllabâ crucem, pro libro tormentum. Sed rei indignitas, quæ loqui compulit, etiam tacere cogit. ----- *The very learned* Be-rauld *very prudently advises, in the Preface to his Work on* Pliny, *to repress, by public Decree, the uncommon Impudence of ignorant Printers; to whom the Learned owe That Perplexity and Torment, which every Letter and Syllable of a Book affords them* (11)." These Words of *James Fontaine* are to be found in the Elogy, which he made upon *Bertholdus Rembolt* a famous Printer. *It occurs in the Sexte of the Decretals, printed, by* Chevalon, *in the Year* 1520 (12).

[H] *Some other Pieces, which he published*] Here are Those, which *Gesner* mentioned: Dialogus, quo rationes explicentur, quibus dicendi ex tempore facultas parari potest; æque ipsa dicendi ex tempore facultate; at *Lyons,* 1534: De Jurisprudentia vetere ac novitia oratio, cum eruditâ ad antiquorum lectionem ac studium exhortatione, at *Lyons,* 1533: Notes on the *Rusticus,* and on the *Nutricia,* of *Politian.* It is true, that *Gesner* is not positive, as to this last Work. Fertur etiam in Politiani Nutricia scripsisse, si bene memini (13). *Jodocus* Badius, dedicating the second Part of *Politian*'s Works to *Lewis de Berquin*, in the Year 1512, excuses himself as well as he can, for not having yet printed the *most learned, and most solid Epistle,* which *Berauld* had composed against *Laurentius Valla,* and dedicated to his good Friend, *Lewis de Berquin*. *Rocolles* says, that This Work of *Berauld* was entituled, *Of Recrimination, against* Laurentius Valla, Anthony *of* Palermo, *and* Bartholomew Ficius (14). The Catalogue of the *Bodleian* Library mentions a *Dictionarium Græco-Latinum Nicolai Beraldi,* printed at *Paris,* in the Year 1521, and another Book, entituled *Syderalis abyssus,* printed at the same Place, in 1514. [*I*] He

VOL. I.   9 E

BERAULD. BERAULT.

honest Man [*I*]. He was very much esteemed by *Stephen Poncher*, Bishop of *Paris*, and afterwards Archbishop of *Sens* (*a*), a Prelate of great Authority in the Kingdom, and a Patron of Learning. His Son, FRANCIS BERAULD, was a very learned Man. He understood *Greek* well, and taught it at *Montbeillard*, in the Year 1554 (*b*). He taught at *Lausanne*, when *Beza* went thither in 1549 (*c*). He taught there also, in the Year 1557 (*d*). He was at *Geneva* in the Year 1561 (*e*). He was Principal of the College of *Montargis*, in the Year 1571 (*f*); from whence he went to *Rochel*, to exercise the like Employment (*g*). He was a good *Greek* and *Latin* Poet (*h*). It is unnecessary to observe, that he was a Protestant. He translated some Books of *Appian* [*K*].

[*I*] *He was an honest Man.*] Madam *de Chatillon*, and her Brother, the Constable *de Montmorency*, had a Mind to make a Churchman of *Gaspar de Coligny*, and, knowing from him, that it was against his Inclination, *he ordered Berault to insinuate their Pleasure to him, thinking that, as he had all along governed his youthful Spirit, he knew better how to prevail with him, than any one else.* They represented to him, that his Scholar might forget him in the Profession of Arms; but that, in an Ecclesiastical State, he would always stand in need of him, and load him with Benefices. *They could not have taken a more cunning way to engage him to do what they desired: But Berault, who was more honest, than interested, instead of using all the Endeavours, which they expected,* only represented to his Pupil the Advantages of the Dignity of a Cardinal, and at the same time pointed out to him the Dangers of it, and advised him not to ingage in it against his Inclination (15).

[*K*] *He translated some Books of* Appian.] *Henry Stephens* made choice of him to translate *Annibal's Wars*, and Those of *Spain*. " Sicut hosce duos Libellos " à me ex Italia (uti dixi) allatos primus edidi, ita " etiam primus latinè vertendos curavi, & quidem " delecto ad id munus viro Græcæ linguæ non pa- " rum perito, Francisco Beraldo Aurelianensi (16). " ---- *As I was the First, who published these* " *two Books, which, as I said, I had brought with* " *me from Italy, so was I the First, who got them* " *translated into Latin, having, for that Purpose,* " *made choice of* Francis Berauld *of Orleans, a Man* " *not a little skilled in the Greek Language.*" He shews, in his Notes, why he preferred *Francis Berauld*'s Translation before That of *Cælius Secundus Curio*.

BERAULT (CLAUDE), Author of *The Commentary on* Statius, in usum Delphini, died at *Paris*, in the Month of *March*, 1705. He was *Regius* Professor of *Syriac*, after the Death of Mr *d'Herbelot*.

BERAULT (MICHAEL), Minister, and afterwards Professor of Divinity at *Montauban*, flourished about the end of the XVIth Century, and beginning of the XVIIth. He became very considerable among Those of his Party. He *had been a Monk*, if we may believe *Scaliger*, who gives him the Character of *a learned and able Man* (*a*). He was pitched upon, in 1593, to dispute against *Perron*, in the Conference of *Mante*, as I have said in another Place (*b*); and he published a Work against the same *Perron*, in the Year 1598 [*A*]. During the Civil-Wars, he greatly favoured the Interests of the Duke *de Rohan*, and he published, with That View, several Pieces, which brought him into Trouble [*B*]. In 1605, he *almost publickly made Interest*, to be appointed Deputy to the General Assemblies of the Protestants (*c*). He informs us of an *Æra*, which is very curious: I mean That, which induced many Protestant Divines of *France* to begin to read the Fathers (*d*).

[*A*] *He published a Work against the same* Perron, *in* 1598.] It was printed at *Montauban*, by *Dennis Haultin*, and dedicated to the Magistrates, and People, of the Town. It is an Octavo of Four hundred ninety eight Pages, entituled, *A short and clear Defence of the Vocation of the Ministers of the Gospel against the Reply of Messire* James Davy, *Bishop of* Evreux, *drawn up Article by Article from the same Reply.*

[*B*] ---- *Some Pieces, which brought him into Trouble.*] The King's Commissary at the National Synod of *Charenton*, in 1631, demanded, among other things, " That the Ministers should be prohibited " from meddling with State Affairs (1). This was aimed at *Beraud*, Minister of *Montauban*, a Man of a warm Spirit, and who went fast. During the last Troubles, he had written a Book, in which, not satisfied with justifying the taking up of Arms, he undertook to maintain, that the Ministers themselves had a Call to bear them, and to shed Blood. " The Commissary aggravated the Importance of " This Opinion, which was dangerous in such a Man, " as *Beraud*, who, besides the Quality of Minister, " had That likewise of Professor of Divinity. He " first pronounced the Condemnation of the guilty " Person, and then ordered the Synod to censure " him. Before they could give any Answer in the " Affair of *Beraud*, it was necessary to hear him (2). " He owned the Book; he pretended, he had not " taught in it the Doctrine he was charged with, " and excused whatever was suspicious in it from " the Malice of the Times. He said, there were, " indeed, some ambiguous Expressions in it; and that " he detested the Consequence, which was drawn from " them. The King's Commissary would not admit of this " kind of Excuse; and he convicted *Beraud* of having " expresly written, in a Preface to his Book, the " Things, of which he was accused. So that he " was severely censured by the Synod, who treated " the Expressions of his Book as scandalous Terms, " which he had improperly made use of. This Do- " ctrine was condemned, and the Ministers were " forbid to teach it. In the mean time, *Beraud* " was secluded the Synod; and, before his re-esta- " blishment, he incurred a fresh Censure on the " Part of the Commissary."

After the Deputies of the Synod had harangued the King, *Berauld* was permitted to take his Seat in the Assembly (3).

BERENGARIUS (PETER), of *Poitiers*, Disciple of *Abelard*, espoused his Master's Interest very much, who was condemned by a Council (*a*) in 1140; and because he looked upon St *Bernard* as the chief Cause of his Condemnation, he wrote most vehemently against him. He published *An Apology for Abelard* (*b*), wherein he

BERENGARIUS.

he sets forth, that his Enemies prepared the Judgment of the Trial amidst their Cups [*A*], and that the accused, seeing the ill Disposition of his Judges, desired, that his Cause might be referred to the Pope [*B*]; that, nevertheless, they condemned him, and that St *Bernard* prepossessed the Holy Father, with so much Diligence, that *Abelard* was speedily condemned at *Rome*, without being heard [*C*], and even without giving him time to appear before the Tribunal, to which he had appealed. Upon this the Apologist relates the Reasons, which might be alledged in favour of St *Bernard*, viz. *That the Zeal of* GOD's *House had eaten him up*; *that the Leprosy, which disfigured the Body of the Church, would have spread all over it, if the Evil had not been stifled in it's Birth*; *and that, to save the Readers the trouble of turning over several Volumes, it had been thought fit to give a short List of* Abelard's *pernicious Propositions*. He, who made Those Extracts, cannot be excused; and, whether St *Bernard* alone was at the Trouble of doing it, or whether, besides the Propositions extracted by him, he produced Those, which others supplied him with, it is certain, that This Passage of his Life does little Honour to his Memory [*D*]. The List, which he produced, contained some things, which *Abelard* had never said, nor

[*A*] *He sets forth, in his Apology for* Abelard, *that his Enemies prepared the Judgment of the Trial amidst their Cups.*] A more satirical Description cannot be seen, than That, which *Berengarius* gives of the Preliminaries of That Synodal Judgment. He says that, after the Fathers of the Council had well eat and drank, they caused *Peter Abelard*'s Writings to be read to them. While it was read to them, they stamped with their Feet, they laughed, they jeered, they drank; and when they heard any thing, which was new to their Ears, they gnashed their Teeth against the Author, and demanded of each other, If they would suffer such a Monster to live? They had drank so much, that they fell asleep; so that, when their Reader met with some suspicious Passages, and asked, If they did not condemn it? They started out of their Sleep, and said, half asleep, some *damnamus*, and others only *namus*. *Berengarius*'s Words have greater force, than mine; therefore give me leave to produce them. He applies the Thoughts of the ancient *Latin* Poets very prettily.

" Post aliqua Pontifices insulære, pedem pedi ap-
" plodere, ridere, nugari conspiceres, ut facile qui-
" libet judicaret illos non CHRISTO vota persolvere,
" sed Baccho. Inter hæc salutantur cyphi, pocula
" celebrantur, laudantur vina, Pontificum guttura ir-
" rigantur. —— Lethæi potio succi Pontificum cor-
" da jam sepelierat. Ecce, inquit Satyricus,

- - - - - inter pocula quærunt
Pontifices saturi quid dia poëmata narrent.

" Denique cum aliquid subtile divinumque sonabat
" quod auribus pontificalibus erat insolitum, audien-
" tes omnes dissecabantur cordibus suis, & stridebant
" dentibus in Petrum, & oculos talpæ habentes in
" Philosophum, hoc, inquiunt, sineremus vivere mon-
" strum. — Cujus (*vini*) calor ita incesserat cere-
" bris, ut in somni letargiam oculi omnium solveren-
" tur. Inter hæc sonat lector, stertit auditor. Alius
" cubito innititur ut det oculis suis somnum, alius
" super molle cervical dormitionem palpebris suis
" molitur, alius super genua caput reclinans dormitat.
" Cum itaque lector in Petri satis aliquod reperiret
" spinetum, surdis exclamabat auribus Pontificum,
" *damnatis?* Tunc quidam vix ad extremam syllabam
" expergefacti, somnolenta voce, capite pendulo,
" *damnamus* ajebant. Alii vero damnantium tumul-
" tu excitati, decapitata prima syllaba, *namus* inqui-
" unt." I cannot forbear inserting here this short Story. A Judge was wont to fall asleep sometimes on the Bench: " One Day the President, gathering
" the Votes of the Court, and coming to ask his:
" he answered, starting out of his Sleep, and not
" being quite awake, *That his Opinion was, that the*
" *Man should be beheaded. But the Business in hand*
" *is about a Meadow*, said the President; *Let it be*
" *mowed then*; replied the Judge (1)." *Balzac* had perhaps read this in a burlesque Piece of *Francis Hotman*, disguised under the Name of *Matago de Matagonibus*, against *Matharel*. " Nota omnibus,
" says be, est historia de eo qui cum dormiens à præ-
" side excitatus & sententiam interrogatus esset, semi-
" somnis dixit, suspendatur, suspendatur, credens
" criminalem processum esse. Cui præses, quinimo,
" inquit, agitur de prato; ergo defalcetur, respondit
" ebrius."

[*B*] *Seeing the ill Disposition of his Judges, he appealed to the Pope.*] *Otho Frisingensis* says, that *Abelard* apprehended he should be overwhelmed by popular Tumults, and that, to avoid this Misfortune, he demanded to be referred to the Court of *Rome*. *Dum de fide sua discuteretur, seditionem populi timens, Apostolicæ sedis præsentiam appellavit* (2). He had reason to distrust a Mob, animated by the Declamations of his Accusers, who cried him down as a Destroyer of the most Holy Mysteries of the Gospel.

[*C*] *At the Instigation of St Bernard, he was condemned without being heard.*] The same Injustice was done him, in the Council of *Soissons*, and this was done on a very ill Pretence; which was, That they feared the Subtilty of his Logic, and the Force of his Eloquence. *Libros quos ediderat propria manu ab Episcopis igni dare coactus est, nulla sibi respondendi facultate, eo quod discepandi in eo peritia ab omnibus suspecta haberetur, concessa* (3). The President d'*Argentri*, had reason to find fault, that, upon such an account, they should transgress one of the most Sacred Laws of Justice; that *No Man ought to be condemned unheard*; *audiatur & altera pars*.

Qui statuit aliquid parte inaudita altera,
Æquum licet statuerit, haut æquus fuerit (4).

He, who determines any thing, without hearing the other side, though he determines right, is unjust.

Here is what He, who published *Peter Abelard*'s Works, says of That Author; " Quæritur eum non
" fuisse auditum in Concilio contra eum coacto, quod
" omnes quantumvis docti & subtiles ejus acumen in-
" genii, linguæ versatilis volubilitatem, eloquentiæ
" flumen aureum, vel potius fulmen igneum & tri-
" fulcum, syllogifmorum gryfos & contorta enthyme-
" mata, reformidarint (5). —— *He complains, that*
" *Abelard was not heard, in the Council, which was*
" *called against him*; *because All of them, learned and*
" *subtile as they were, dreaded the Acuteness of his Wit,*
" *the Volubility of his Tongue, the golden Flow, or*
" *rather Lightning, of his Eloquence, with the Sub-*
" *tilty and Pointedness of his Syllogisms and Enthy-*
" *mema*'s

[*D*] —— *this Proceeding of St Bernard does little Honour to his Memory.*] Zeal and Solitude made him very choleric, and very credulous, if we may believe the same Author (6). This Observation was made by a more ancient Author, though it has not retained all the Impressions of it's Original; for see what *Otho Frisingensis* says: " Erat autem Bernardus Clareval-
" lensis Abbas tam ex Christianæ religionis fervore
" zelotypus, quam ex habitudinali mansuetudine quo-
" dammodo credulus, ut & Magistros, qui humanis
" rationibus seculari sapientia confisi nimium inhæ-
" rebant, abhorreret, & si quicquam ei Christianæ
" fidei absonum de talibus diceretur, facile aurem
" præberet (7). —— Bernard, *Abbot of* Clairvaux,
" *was both passionately zealous for the Christian*
" *Religion, and, thro' an habitual Mildness of Dis-*
" *position, a little too credulous*; *insomuch, that he*
" *abhorred those Teachers, who, depending too worldly*
" *Wisdom, stuck too much to human Reason*; *and,*
" *whenever they were reported to him to have ad-*
" *vanced any Doctrine contrary to the Christian Faith,*
" *he*

(1) Balzac, Aristip. pag. 199.

(2) Otho Frising. de gestis Frider. lib. I, c. 48.

(3) Id. ibid. cap. 47.

(4) Seneca Medea, Act. II, sc. II.

(5) Argentré apud Franc. Amboesium, Præf. Apolog. ad opera Abælardi.

(6) Argentré, ibid.

(7) Otho Frising. de Gest. Frid. lib. 1, c. 47.

BERENGARIUS.

nor written; and some things, which *Abelard* never understood according to the Sense, which was imputed to him (c). This is what the Apologist intended to shew, in the second Part of his Work; but he did not write it; and he had his Reasons for it [E]. In the mean time, he gave St *Bernard* to understand, in the first Part, that he should not persecute others on account of their Doctrine, since his own Writings were not free from Errors. He maintained, against him, That he had taught a Thing, which he would not have failed to insert, as a monstrous Doctrine, in his Extracts out of *Abelard*, if *Abelard* had wanted it (d). This Recrimination of *Berengarius* was useless; he had to do with one of those privileged Persons, who acquire the Benefit of Impunity, by the great Services, which they pretend they have done to the Cause [F]. He had no better Success in representing to That Informer the Indulgence, which was shewn to the Errors of some Fathers of the Church. Besides This Piece of *Berengarius*, we have two Letters of his, one to the Bishop of *Mende*, the other against the *Carthusians*. They are printed with *Abelard*'s Works. He supports, in all his Writings, the Character of a fiery, sowre, Spirit, which *Petrarch* gave him [G]; but he says, that his Invective against the *Carthusians* was

" he readily believed it." Thus the Providence of God dispenses good and evil. Most of Those, who have a great Zeal, become credulous and suspicious, and easily conceive an extraordinary Animosity against Those, whom they suspect; They write Letter upon Letter against them (8); They alarm the Consciences of others, and give themselves no rest, 'till they have inspired their Prepossessions into every Body. If a Book is to be examined, God knows how difficult it is for them them to understand the true Sense of the Author, and to put the most equitable Construction upon his Words. See the Remark [*I*].

[*E*] *He did not write the second Part of his Apology for Abelard; and he had his Reasons for it.*] Perhaps he did not give the true Reason of his Silence. This Reason was, probably, the fear of stirring up all the Monks, and the Clergy, against him, and of being exposed thereby to the People's Indignation, and a thousand Mischiefs. He knew how odious he had made himself by the first Part of his Book; but the second would have much more exasperated the People. The first contained only hard Words, and Reproaches, with some Recriminations, which could do but little Prejudice to St *Bernard*; but the second would have convicted him of Knavery, or Ignorance, and consequently of being an unjust Persecutor. The plainer the thing had been, the more angry they would have been with *Berengarius*, the Destroyer of an holy Reputation, so usefully established in the Minds of People. So that he found it more proper to be silent, and to justify his Silence by shameful Nonsense. He declared, that Time had made him wise, and that he had embraced St *Bernard*'s Opinion, and refused to protect Doctrines, which founded ill, though they were not bad in the main: Lastly, That if he had said any thing against the Man of God, he desired it should be looked upon as said in jest, and not in earnest. *Processu temporis meum sapere crevit: & in sententiam Abbatis pedibus, ut dicitur, ivi. Nolui esse patronus capitulorum objectorum Abelardo, quia etsi sanum saperent, non sane sonabant. ----- Si quid in personam hominis Dei joco, legatur non serio* (9). And yet, a little before, he had said, that his Censure of St *Bernard* was well grounded. It is the true Sense of these Words: *Legant eruditi viri Apologeticum quem edidi, & si dominum Abbatem justè non argui, licenter me redarguant.* Is not this the Nonsense of a Man, who dares not say, that he is in the right, and who is ashamed to confess, that he is in the wrong?

[*F*] *He had to do with one of those privileged Persons, who acquire the Benefit of Impunity by the great Services, which they pretend they have done to the Cause.*] St *Bernard* had a very agreeable Stile: The whole World was over-run with the Productions of his Pen; his Books flew every where; and were in great Numbers. *Mirantur homines in te liberalium disciplinarum ignaro tantam ubertatem facundiae, qua emissiones tuae jam cooperuerunt universam superficiem terrae* (10). The Reputation of his Sanctity, Zeal, and Miracles, was no less spread, than That of his Pen. *Jamdudum sanctitatis tuae odorem ales per orbem fama dispersit, praeconsavit merita, miracula declamavit* (11). With all these Advantages, he was able to ruin any Man's Reputation; much less could

so great a Philosopher, as *Abelard*, expect to pass for Orthodox in spite of him. *Berengarius* has very happily represented the Authority of the Man of God in this manner, " Damnatur, proh dolor! absens, " inauditus, & inconvictus. Quid dicam, quidve non " dicam? Bernarde,

Nil opus est bello, veniam pacemque rogamus,
Porrigimus junctas ad tua lora manus.
Jura cadent rerum, vertetur sanctio legum,
Si vis, si mandas, si fic decernis agendum,
Quem penes arbitrium est & vis & norma loquendi (12).

" He is condemned, alas! absent, unheard, and un-
" convicted. What shall I say, or what shall I not
" say? O Bernard,

*Enough of War; henceforth let Discord cease;
Vanquish'd, to Thee we humbly sue for Peace;
Right shall be Wrong, Unlawful Law shall be;
For Right and Law depend alone on Thee.*

Where is the Orthodoxy, that can hold out against such Accusers? The People are so much prepossessed, that they will scarce suffer one to make a Defence; It cannot be done without charging the Promoter of the Process, and the Informer, with Calumny; but there is no enduring This. *What? shall we suffer so great a Servant of God to be defamed, as an egregious Calumniator? God forbid; the Honour of the Church is too much concerned in it.* Thus an inconsiderable private Man may say; " I shall be Ortho-
" dox, or Heterodox, according as such a one pleases;
" for, if he attacks my Doctrine, they neither dare,
" nor can, absolve me: My Justification would disgrace
" him, and would rejoice the Enemy too much.
" In vain might I accuse him, in my turn; no re-
" gard would be had to it: I have not laboured
" for the Good of the Church like him; I do not
" deserve the Immunities, which are due to his Stu-
" dies, and indefatigable Vigilance. A great many
" People would take it ill, that I should dare to pu-
" blish Apologies, and would say to me, if they durst
" speak their Mind, what *Caligula* said to his Bro-
" ther. *What? Do'st Thou take an Antidote against*
" *Cæsar* (13)? I should seem to them worthy of a
" new Accusation, because I did not sink under the
" first." *Quintus Scævola*, who was one of the honestest Men of his Time, was treated in the same manner: " Diem Scævola dixit postea quam compe-
" rit eum posse vivere: cum ab eo quaereretur quid
" tandem accusaturus esset eum, quem pro dignita-
" te ne laudare quidem quisquam satis commode
" posset, ajunt hominem (ut erat furiosus) respon-
" disse, quod non totum telum corpore recepisset
" (14). ----- When he found Scævola was out of
" Danger, be entered an Action, against him; and,
" being asked, what he had to alledge against a Per-
" son, whose Merit deserved the highest Praise, the
" enraged Fellow is said to have replied, Because he
" did not receive the whole Weapon in his Body."

[*G*] *He supported, in all his Writings, the Character of a fiery, and sowre, Spirit, which Petrarch had given him*] These are *Petrarch*'s Words in his Apology: " Damnavit Bernardus Claravallensis Abbas
" Petrum

BERENGARIUS.

was only designed to reclaim them from their detracting Temper (e). They, who have said, that he was of a small Stature, have misunderstood the Author they quote (f). At the bottom, the Reproaches of Heterodoxy, which he made to St *Bernard*, are meer Cavils, and serve only to shew, that, when a Man insists too rigidly on certain Expressions, without putting on That Spirit of Equity, which looks for the Sense of an Author in the Design, and Principles, of his Works, it is easy for him to discover Erroneous Propositions. I do not pretend, that all the Errors, imputed to *Abelard*, have as bad a Foundation as This [H]; but it cannot be denied, as to the greatest part of them [I]; and therefore St *Bernard*'s Friends had now just Reason to complain, that some Errors are found in his Works, by making use of his own Method against him. It is for the Advantage of the Public, that some Men should be obliged to cry out,

— — — — — Eheu
Quàm temerè in nosmet legem sanximus iniquam! (g)

— — — — *unthinking that we are,*
T' establish Precedents against ourselves.

(e) Volui retraere in eis immoderatam licentiam linguae, quia velut quidem Geometrae totum orbem mensurabant. *Ibid.* pag. 323.

(f) See Remark [G].

(g) Horat. Sat. lii, lib. 1, ver. 66.

The
" Petrum Abaelardum literatum quondam virum.
" Huic iratus Berengarius Pictaviensis vir, & ipse
" non infacundus ac discipulus Petri, contra Bernar-
" dum librum unum scripsit, non magni quidem
" corporis, sed INGENTIS ACRIMONIAE. De
" quo postmodum à multis increpatus se excusavit
" quod adolescens scripsisset, & quod sibi viri sancti-
" tas nondum penitus nota esset. - - - - - Bernard,
" Abbot of Clairvaux, condemned Peter Abelard, a
" very learned Man. Enraged at This, Berengarius,
" of Poitiers, himself not ineloquent, and besides a
" Disciple of Peter, wrote one Piece against Bernard,
" not very bulky indeed, but of Great Acrimony.
" Being reprehended by many for it, he pleaded, in
" his Excuse, that he wrote it in his Youth, when
" he was not as yet sufficiently acquainted with the
" Sanctity of Bernard." Francis d'Amboise, not considering this Passage with sufficient Attention, found in it, that *Berengarius* was a little Man; " De Be-
" rengario - - - - - Petrarcha in Apologia ait ipsum
" fuisse facundum, non magni corporis, sed ingentis
" acrimoniae (15). - - - - - Petrarch, *in his Apology,
" says, that he was an eloquent Man, of Small Sta-
" ture, but great Acrimony.*" This ought to teach Authors, and, first of all, myself, to be continually on their Guard against those Distractions of Mind, which are so often the Cause, that we apply, to one thing, what Those, whom we transcribe, have said of another.

(15) Pref. Apologet. ad Opera Abel.

[H] *The Reproaches of Heterodoxy, which he made to St Bernard, are meer cavils.* — *The Errors imputed to Abelard have not All as bad a Foundation as This.*] For example, no wrong was done him, in accusing him of having too far extended the Power of Free-will, and the Necessity of Grace too little. He expressed himself so clearly upon This (16), that whoever should undertake to justify him, would imitate the Insincerity of Those, who, on other questions, maintain, that he was an Heretic. Neither must there be any cavilling about certain Articles, which it is difficult not to adopt, when once the Doctrine of Free-will is embraced. We may, therefore, say, that it is very true, that *Abelard* had a good Indulgence for sins of Ignorance, and that he damned no body for *Philosophical Sin* (17). He seems also to me to have taught plainly, that JESUS CHRIST did not die to redeem us from the Tyranny of the Devil; but that the Love, which GOD shewed to Mankind by the Incarnation of his SON, should incline us to love him reciprocally; and to follow the Instructions, and the example, of an Incarnate GOD. This Doctrine is half Socinian, and, according to St *Bernard*, whoever maintains it deserves better to be confuted, than to be cudgelled. *Annon justius os loquens talia fustibus tunderetur, quam rationibus refelleretur* (18)? Here is another offensive Doctrine; *viz.* that Things, which never were, nor ever shall be, are not possible. This was, without doubt, *Abelard's* Opinion (19); and I do not see, that They, who say, that GOD is determined by his Infinite Wisdom to do what is most worthy of himself, can consistently with themselves deny This Philosopher's Doctrine. See the Remark [M]. I omit some other Opinions, which might reasonably have been imputed to him, and which are either true, or indifferent to Religion.

(16) See his Exposition of the Epistle to the Romans, pag. 652, & seq.

(17) See his Works, pag. 470, 591, 592.

(18) Bernard. Epist. ad Innoc. Papam.

(19) See pag. 1112, 1117, of his Works.

[I] — *but it cannot be denied as to the greatest Part of them.*] This Assertion was falsely imputed to him: " Deus pater plena est potentia, Filius quaedam
" potentia, Spiritus Sanctus nulla potentia. - - - - -
" GOD *the* FATHER *is Full Power, The* SON *Some
" Power, The* HOLY GHOST *No Power.*" They, who are most partial to St *Bernard*, own, that he did not apprehend the Author's Opinion. " Abaelardi
" mentem assecuti non videntur S. Bernardus, Abbas
" S. Theodorici, & Anonymus, qui ipsi tribuunt, &c.
" (20). — St *Bernard, Abbot of S.* Theodoric, *and
" an Anonymous Author, do not seem to have under-
" stood* Abelard's *Meaning, when They impute to him,
" &c.* Non ideo in Sabellianam aut Arianam hae-
" resim impegit, non Trinitatem destruxit, non blas-
" phemiam dixit in Spiritum Sanctum, non Deorum
" novorum annuntiator fuit, ut maximi illi viri fer-
" vore disputationis abrepti ipsi improperarunt (21). —
" *He was not a Sabellian, or an Arian, he did
" not destroy the Trinity, he did not blaspheme against
" the* HOLY GHOST, *he was not a setter forth of
" new Gods, as these Great Men, carried away by
" the Heat of Disputation, have hastily asserted.*" The Thing speaks of itself, when the whole Passage of *Abelard* is examined. He was found a Heretic in these words: " Spiritus quamvis ejusdem substantiae
" sit cum patre & filio, unde etiam Trinitas ὁμοίου-
" ος, id est, unius substantiae, praedicatur, minimè
" tamen ex substantia patris aut filii, si proprie loqui-
" mur, esse dicendus est, quod oportet ipsum ex pa-
" tre vel filio gigni, sed magis ex ipsis habet pro-
" cedere. — *The Spirit, though he be of the same
" Substance with the* FATHER *and the* SON, *whence
" the Trinity is said to be* ὁμοίουσιος, *or Consubstan-
" tial, yet he must not be said to be of the Substance
" of the* FATHER *and* SON, *properly speaking, be-
" cause he must be begotten of the* FATHER *or* SON,
" *or rather proceed from them.*" But, if the Laws of Equity had been ever so little followed, it might have been apprehended, that he acknowledges the Substance of That Doctrine, and that he has nothing Particular, but one of Those Abstractions of Logic, which will always be unavoidable by Those, who will argue about the Difference of the Three Persons. He was charged with teaching that the HOLY GHOST is the Soul of the World (22), and that there is no sin, either in Action, or in the Will, or in Lust, or in the Pleasure, which excites it, and that we should not desire to stifle these things. He maintains, in his Apology, that he had never said, nor wrote, such a Proposition (23). There is mention made of an Apology, which he published, wherein he partly denied the Propositions, that were objected against him, as to the words, and altogether as to the Sense. *Ad Cluniacensem Caenobium se contulit. Apologeticum scribens praedictorum capitulorum, partim verba, ex toto autem sensum negans* (24).

But there is some reason to believe, that This Apology is lost (25). In That, which we have, he maintains, that he never wrote one of the Books, from which some of the Doctrines, which are imputed to him, were taken, and that That Work is ascribed to him with the same Malice, or with the same Ignorance, as all the Propositions of the Catalogue:
" Sed sicut caetera contra me capitula, ita & hoc quo-

(20) Natalis Alexander, Saec. xi, xii, Part. III, pag 19.

(21) Id. Ib, pag. 21.

(22) Nothing is worse grounded than This. See Father Alexander, ibid. pag. 27.

(23) Oper. Abael. pag.

(24) Otho Frising. Hb. i, cap. 49.

(25) See the Notes of Andrew du Chesne, on Abelard's Relation, pag. 1161, 1162.

VOL. I. 9 F " que

BERENGARIUS.

The Mischief is, that the Event does not always prove prejudicial to the Aggressor; for we see, to this Day, the unfortunate *Abelard* covered with Shame and Ignominy [K], whilst his Adversary is invoked as a Saint. He had been condemned at *Soissons*, in a Council, where the Pope's Legate presided; which Legate understood nothing of the State of the Question [L]. *Gerson* believed, that the famous *Berengarius*, who denied the Real Presence, was a Scholar of *Peter Abelard* (*h*); perhaps he took him for Him, who makes the Subject of This Article; however he is mistaken, since *Abelard* was not ten Years of Age, when the Adversary of the Real Presence died.

They, who would know more particularly, whether *Berengarius* had Reason to pretend, that *Abelard* was not an Heretic, who deserved the Persecutions, which were raised against him, will do well to consult Mr *du Pin*, who passes an equitable Judgment on This Man's Doctrine; and particularly on the fourteen Propositions extracted out of his Works, and read in the Council of *Sens*. It cannot be denied, says he (*i*), but that his Opinions concerning the Mystery of the Trinity were Orthodox, and that he believed the three Divine Persons to be of the same Nature. I shall set down all that he has said about this Proposition of *Abelard*; GOD cannot do but what he does [M]. It is a more important and difficult Question, than can be imagined. I shall

(*h*) *Gerson, Oper. Tom. iv. Alphabeto 69, Lit. Q. fol. 212.*

(*i*) *Du Pin, Biblioth. of the Ecclesiastical Authors, Tom. IX, pag. 121. Edit. of Holl.*

" que per malitiam vel ignorantiam prolatum est." *Berengarius*, his Apologist, denied it with more restriction. " Indiculum vidimus, in quo non Petri " dogmata, sed nefandi commenti capitula legimus. " —— Hæc & alia indiculus tuus continet, quorum " quædam, fateor, Petrus & dixit & scripsit, quædam " verò neque protulit neque scripsit. Quæ autem " dixerit, & quæ non dixerit, & quam Catholica " mente ea quæ dixerit senserit, secundus arrepti " Operis tractatus Christiana disputatione ardentur & " inpigrè declarabit (26). —— *I have seen an Index,* " *in which I have read, not the Tenets of* Peter, *but* " *Articles maliciously invented.* —— *Your Index con-* " *tains These and Others, some of which, I confess,* " Peter *both spoke, and wrote, and some he never* " *either produced, or wrote. What he has said, and* " *what he has not said, and with how Catholic a Dis-* " *position he conceived what he has said, The second* " *Treatise of the Work, complained of, will warmly* " *and zealously declare, in a Christian Disputation.*" Some accuse *Abelard* of having taught, *that there are as many Heavens, as Days in the Year*; and they add, that he was answered, *That he supposed so great a number of them, that he might secure one, which would fit him* (27). But this is rather Jesting than Disputing. It was, therefore, a very great Piece of Injustice to give the Cause for the Accuser, without knowing, whether the Accused acknowledged the Work, out of which These Propositions were extracted, for his own; whether he owned, that they were faithfully extracted; whether he understood them in the Accuser's Sense, &c? And the Pope, who, from the Extracts, condemned the Books to be burnt, and *Abelard* to a Cloyster, without informing himself, whether *Abelard* taught those things, was more unjust, than the Synod of *Sens*. The Accuser's Letters, and the Messenger, whom he sent to the Court of *Rome*, and who said all that was necessary to make *Abelard* odious (28), compleated the Oppression. *Francis d' Amboise* has described very lively the Part, which St *Bernard* acted in This whole Process. It was That of a Trumpeter sounding the Charge, and That of an Incendiary setting Fire to the Powder (29): since he sent to the Pope all the filth he could collect, and which ill affected Persons had gathered either out of his Adversary's Writings, or Lectures, or out of the Papers, which were published under his Name. And, therefore, I do not wonder, that *Horstius* inveighed against *Francis d' Amboise* (30): but I cannot tell whether he censured him for a thing, which deserved it; I mean for having said, that *Peter* the Venerable wrote to *Innocent* II, that *Abelard*, oppressed by the Vexations of some Men, who treated him as an Heretic, appealed to the Holy See. *Ait Abælardum* —— *gravatum vexationibus quorundam qui illi nomen hæretici quod calidè abominabatur imponere volebant, Majestatem Apostolicam se appellasse*. Whoever wrote thus to the Pope, plainly laid the Blame upon St *Bernard*: but This Business was not transacted in this Manner. *Peter* the Venerable said only, that *Abelard* gave out, he was persecuted. *Quæstivimus quo tenderet, gravatum se vexationibus, &c. Majestatem Apostolicam se appellasse responsit.*

[K] *We see, to this Day, the unfortunate* Abelard *covered with shame and ignominy.*] Thus he is charged

(26) *Bereng. in Oper. Abel. p. 320.*

(27) *Garasse, in his Summary of Divinity, pag. 304. and in his Curious Doctrine, pag. 266.*

(28) *Quod melius Nicæ laus iste meus, imo & vester, viva referet voce. Bernard. Epist. ad Innoc. II. in Operib. Abal. pag. 275.*

(29) *Hoc classico mulsi a arma spiritualia excitati sunt — Admovet suces Incendia ut comurat d'murus mm ab co (P.nt.ce) e t nu cat. A-ela: Pref. Abel.*

(30) *Notis in Bernard. sol. 37.*

to the end of the World with all the Errors, which were imputed to him in the Council of *Sens.*, and with several others. *Peter of Pergamo* charges him with denying, that GOD is the Author of all Good, that he is a simple Being, that he alone is Eternal, and that every thing, which exists, is either Creator, or Creature (31). *Bernard of Luxenburg* ascribes the same Things to him, upon the Credit of the other. *Prateolus* has followed *Bernard* (32), and has been copied by the Jesuit *Gaultier* (33). *Belæforêt*, and *du Haillan*, have done like *Prateolus*. The Writers of the Catalogues of Heretics, who like Sheep follow one another, *Sanderus*, *Alphonsus de Castro*, &c. have not failed to adopt these Accusations. But, on the other hand, They, who inserted him in the Catalogue of the Witnesses of the Truth (34), knew not what they did: He had indeed some particular Opinions about the Eucharistical Accidents; but it was rather in supposing the Real Presence, than in denying It.

[L] *The Legate, who condemned him, understood nothing of the State of the Question.*] After the Condemnation was pronounced, one of the Accusers muttered, that he had read in *Abelard's* Book, that GOD the Father is the Only Almighty (35). The Legate, having a very good Ear, heard it, and answered, that they ought not so much as to believe, that a Child was capable of falling into so great an Error, since, according to the common and public Faith, there are three Almighties. A Doctor, laughing at the Legate, could not forbear quoting these words of St *Athanasius*; *Et tamen non tres omnipotentes, sed unus omnipotens. —— And yet there are not Three Almighties, but One Almighty*. His Bishop censured him for it; but he was boldly answered with a Passage of *Daniel*, concerning ignorant Judges, who deserve more to be condemned than Those, whom they judge. " Sic fatui filii " *Israel*, non judicantes neque quod verum est cog- " noscentes condemnastis filium Israël. Revertimini " ad judicium, & de ipso judice judicata." He added of his own: " qui talem judicem quasi ad instru- " ctionem fidei & correctionem erroris instituistis, " qui cum judicare deberet, ore se potius condem- " navit. —— *Who have set up such a Judge, as it* " *were for Instruction in the Faith, and Correction* " *of Error, who, when he ought to have judged,* " *condemned himself out of his own Mouth.*"

[M] *Mr Du Pin's Judgment on This Proposition of* Abelard, *GOD cannot do but what he does.*] Neither does he deny, that Power, Wisdom, and Love, are Attributes common to the three Divine Persons; nay he declares the contrary in express words: " but he attributes Power to the FATHER, Wisdom " to the SON, and Love to the HOLY GHOST, by " by way of Appropriation; in which he does not " seem to recede from the Doctrine of the Fathers " and Divines. But he does not think, and speak, " as others do, in the Third Proposition, wherein he " maintains, that GOD cannot do but what he does, " and cannot do all that he does not; not but that he " acknowledges, that the Power of GOD in itself " can extend to other Objects; but he pretends, that, " being considered as joined to the Wisdom and Will " of GOD, he cannot will, or do any thing, but " what he wills, and actually does (36)." You will see this more at large in the Substance, which Mr *du Pin*

(31) *Petr. Pergam. apud Bern. Lutzenberg. Catal. Hæret.*

(32) *Prateol. Elench. Hæret.*

(33) *Gaulk. Chronol.*

(34) *See the Life of Abelard, by Thomasius, printed in the first Part of the Historia Sapientia & Stultitiæ, at Hall, in Germany, in 1693.*

(35) *Oper. Abæl. p. 24.*

(36) *Du Pin, Biblioth. of Ecclesiastical Authors, Tom. IX, pag. 122, Edit. Holl.*

BERENICE.

shall add to this, that the Protestants are more inclined to condemn *Abelard* [N], than many Catholics are, and I shall quote a Passage of Mr *Joli*, a Canon of *Notre Dame* at *Paris*.

Pin has given of one of *Abelard's* Works (37). "In the third Book, he treats particularly of the Power of GOD; and he maintains, that GOD can do but what he does, and cannot do all that he does not, because GOD can do but what he wills: now he cannot have the Will to do any thing but what he does, because he does necessarily will all that is fit to be done; from whence it follows, that, whatever he does not, is not fit to be done; that he cannot have the Will to do it; and consequently that he cannot do it. He himself confesses, that this Opinion is peculiar to him; that scarce any body else approves of it; that it seems contrary to the Doctrine of the Saints, and to Reason, and to derogate from the greatness of GOD. Hereupon he raises a difficult Objection against himself: *A Reprobate*, says he, *may be saved; but he cannot be saved except GOD saves him: therefore GOD can save him, and consequently do something, which he does not*. He answers, that it may be said indeed, that this Man may be saved, as to the Possibility of human Nature, which is capable of Salvation; but that it cannot be said, that GOD can save him, with relation to GOD himself, because it is impossible, that GOD should do what he ought not to do: He explains this by divers Examples: A Man that speaks may hold his Tongue; but a Man that does actually speak cannot be silent: the Voice may be heard, but a deaf Man cannot hear it: a Field may be manured, though a Man cannot manure it, *&c* (38)."

I may perhaps examine this Doctrine in one of the Remarks on the Article WICLIFFE.

[N] *The Protestants are more inclined to condemn* Abelard *than many Catholics.*] "*Hornbeck*, at the beginning of his *Apparatus ad controversias & disputationes Socinianas*, observes *Abelard's* Heresies. ——*Prateolus* in his *Specimen Apologeticum antiGuaitrianum* (39) *accusationibus Jacobi Gualterii Jesuitis oppositum*, in his fifth Defence, *de fide implicita*, gives likewise an article Description of *Abelard*, and of his Opinions, and shews at large, "*Pontificios, & nominatim Jesuitas, in multis cum Abailardo convenire:* —— *that the Roman Catholics, and particularly the Jesuits, agree in many things with Abelard.* He draws a Parallel between them, and shews, in another Place of That fifth Defence, *Quàm pulchrè Socinianis præluxerit, minimè obscurum est:* ——— *that it is well known how he prepared the way to Socinianism.* *Beckmannus,* in his Theological Exercitations, *Exercit. 2* says, that, Socinus hunc errorem, Christum pro peccatis nostris non esse mortuum, è lacunis veterum hausit; quippe, quem Christi 1140, in Galliis Petrus Abailardus (quem Bernardus & Otho Frisingensis Abailardum, Platina Baillardum, vocant) idem docuit (40). ——— Socinus *borrowed This Error (that Christ did not die for our Sins) from the Ancients; since, in the Year 1140,* Peter Abelard *(whom Bernard and Otho of Frisingen call* Abailard*, and* Platina Baillard*) taught the same in* France. *Joly*, a Canon of *Notre Dame* at *Paris* ———— says, in his Treatise of the Restitutions of Great Men, That *Abelard's* Enemies, being jealous of his Reputation, did so much impose upon St *Bernard*, who proceeded honestly in the matter, that we find, that the Book of the Sentences was condemned to be burnt under the Name of *Abelard*, as being the Author of it; though it was of *Peter Lombard*, Bishop of *Paris*: a Work, nevertheless, adds he, which is known to be canonized in the *Sorbonne;* and on which all the Scholastic Divinity is founded. He says again, That the same *Abelard* was very much abused and persecuted by the Monks of *St Den's* in *France*, and by St *Gildas* (41) that observe two things, upon This Passage of Mr *Ancillon*, the one is, that, in effect, *Abelard's* Opinions, about the Doctrine of Grace, are much the same with Those, which the Jesuits maintain. But Mr *du Pin* observes, that, if This Author's Doctrine "be not conformable to St *Augustin's* Doctrine "———— neither is it Pelagian, nor Semipelagian, "since he acknowledges the Necessity of Grace for "the beginning of good Actions, and maintains only, that GOD has given an equal Grace to all "Men, whereof every one may make a good use, "or reject it (43)." The second thing I have to observe, is, that I shall enquire, in another place, whether the Book of the Sentences, condemned to be burnt under the Name of *Abelard*, be That of *Peter Lombard*.

BERENICE, the Name of several Women and Cities. We shall speak of some of These Women; and, as to the Cities, we shall only observe, that *Ortelius* reckons nine of them, and that the two chief were in *Africa*, one in *Pentapolis*, and the other in the Red-Sea. The latter received This Name in honour of *Berenice,* the Mother of *Ptolomy Philadelphus* (a), and the other in honour of *Berenice,* the Wife of *Ptolomy*, the Third of That Name (b). *Berenice* is a *Greek* Name [A].

[A] Berenice *is a Greek Name.*] It was formed from That of φερενίκη, that is to say, *Victory-Bearer,* by the *Macedonians,* who changed *Ph.* into *B.* See *Plutarch* (1), and *Steph. Byzantinus* (2). Hence it is, that some Authors call Her *Pherenice,* whom others call *Berenice.* There are some, who, instead of *Berenice,* say, in *Latin, Beronice.*

BERENICE, Daughter, Sister, and Mother, of some Persons, who carried the Prize at the Olympian Games (a), obtained, by reason of such Singularity, leave to assist at Those Games, which had been forbidden other Women, by a public Decree [A]. Some say she obtained This Privilege, before her Son was Victor [B]. It

[A] *She obtained the Privilege of assisting at the Olympic Games; which had been forbidden Women by a public Decree.*] This Prohibition supposes, that They did not trust to the Suggestions of Decency and natural Modesty. The Champions were stark naked; which alone ought to have banished the fair Sex from These Shews: Nevertheless, They did not rely upon This: Laws were made, and published, to forbid Women the Sight of These Exercises. Thus far there was no harm in it: They were sensible of the great Power of Curiosity: But who would not condemn the extream and cruel Rigour of These new Legislators? They ordered, that, if any Woman was surprized in These Assemblies, or if she passed the River during That Time, she should be thrown headlong from the Top of a Hill (1). It is no wonder, that no Woman suffered this terrible Punishment (2). The Sight of some naked Men could not be a Charm, or Allurement, strong enough to have blinded her to so great Danger; and, if there was found a Woman, who did not observe this Prohibition, it was because she thought she ran no hazard; for she was disguised in Man's Apparel, and did not think, that a single Leap would betray her. She was probably so overjoyed to see her Son become Conqueror, that She threw herself a little too merrily over the Barrier: Nay, how do we know, but that her Cloaths catched in

BERENICE

It was enough, that they knew her Father, and her Brothers, had obtained This Advantage, and that they saw her, accompanied by her victorious Brothers, present her Son, ready to dispute these kind of Crowns. *Pausanias*'s Narrative differs from this, and is, perhaps, better. He says, that the Inhabitants of *Elis* made a Law, which condemned all Women, who, by stealth, should be present at the Olimpic Games, or pass over the *Alpheus* (*b*), on any Occasion whatever, during the Time, which was forbid them, to be cast headlong from a Rock (*c*). There was but One, who disobeyed this Order; her Name was *Callipatira*, according to some, *Pherenice* according to others [C]. After the Death of her Husband, she pretended to be One of Those, who instructed young Men in the Exercise of the Olympic Games, and, under This Disguise, she presented herself in the Field of Battle with her Son, whom she brought thither as an Athlet, whom she had instructed, and who prepared himself for the Combat. Seeing her Son obtain the Victory, she leaped over a Barrier, which served as an Inclosure to the Masters of the Combatants, and discovered her Sex by This Action. She would have been proceeded against according to the Laws, were it not that the Judges thought they ought to acquit her, because they found, that her Father, and her Brothers, and now her Son, had obtained the Prizes of Those Games: So much Glory, in One Family, procured This Lady her Pardon. But They made a Law, that, for the future, the Masters of the Athlets themselves should come naked to Those Shews. It must not be forgotten, that This *Berenice* was the Daughter of That *Diagoras* the *Rhodian*, who was so famous in the Public Games of *Greece* (*d*). I do not know whether any Modern Commentator observes This. It is easy to find out in what Time This *Berenice* lived [D].

(*b*) It is the Name of a River, near which the Olympian Games were celebrated.
(*c*) Pausan. lib. v, pag. 153.
(*d*) See Remark [C].

in something, by an unfortunate Accident? However it was, she afforded, without thinking of it, a new Spectacle, which disturbed the Solemnity, and occasioned a Tryal, from which she came off victoriously. I say, *without thinking of it*; for we must not believe, what a learned Critic says, that she put off her Cloaths, to discover her Sex, when she saw her Son's Victory. " Scribit autem (*Pausanias*) ne- " mini fuisse suspectam, donec viso filio victore ve- " stem, abjiceret mulieremque se ostenderet (3). ---- " But Pausanias *writes, that she passed unsuspected,* " 'till, *seeing her Son come off Victor, she threw* " *aside her Cloaths, and discovered, that she was a* " *Woman.*" He is in the wrong to ascribe This to *Pausanias*, who intended no more, than that The Lady, getting over the Barrier, discovered a Nakedness, which ought to have been concealed. These are his *Greek* Words: Τὸ ἔρυμα ἐν ᾧ τὰς γυμνασὰς ἔχουσιν ἀπειλημμένες τοῦτο ὑπερπηδᾶσα ἡ καλλινίκατειρα ἐγυμνώθη. Septimenium id, quo magistras seclusos habent, transiliens nudata est (4). *Romulus Amasæus* has mis-translated it, *transiliuit veste posita*, as *Sylburgius* has observed.

[*B*] *Some say, that she obtained This Privilege, before her Son was Victor.*] *Valerius Maximus* affirms it; these are his Words: " Pherenices quoque non " vulgaris honos, cui soli omnium fœminarum gym- " nico spectaculo interesse permissum est, cum ad " Olympia filium Euclea certamen ingressurum ad- " duxisset Olympionico patre genita, fratribus eam- " dem palmam assecutis latera ejus cingentibus (5). " ---- *Uncommon was the Honour paid to Pherenice,* " *who alone, of all other Women, had the Privilege* " *of being present at the Athletic Games: This Lady,* " *born of a Father, who had been crowned a Victor,* " *and attended by her Brothers, who had all obtained* " *the same Honours, presented her Son* Eucles *to con-* " *tend for the Prize at the Olympic Games.*" *Ælian* says the same thing, and that the Cause was pleaded, and that *Pherenice* gained it (6). There is no room to doubt, but that *Euclea*, in *Valerius Maximus*, is the Name of the young Champion, who was brought into the Lists by *Berenice*. *Pausanias* does not call him so; but *Pisidorus*, or *Pisirodus* (7). It ought not to be conjectured, that *Euclea*, in the *Greek* Authors, who supplied *Valerius Maximus* with This Event, was the Epithet of the Games, and not the Name of the Champion, and that the *Latin* Writer, for want of Attention, took an Epithet for a Proper Name: I say This Conjecture ought not to be mentioned,

(3) Scheferius in Ælian, lib. x. cap. 1.
(4) Pausan. lib. 5, pag. 153.
(5) Val. Maxim. lib. viii, sub fin.
(6) Ælian. lib. x, cap. 1.
(7) Pausan. ubi supra; he says, Πισίδωρος, *and* lib. 6, pag. 284, Πισείδωρος; *the one ought to be corrected, by the other; for it is plain, that one and the same Person is meant in both the Passages. It is best to read* Pisidorus *in both.*

since we find an Athlet called *Eucles*, who was, at least, *Berenice*'s Nephew (8). It must be said, then, that some *Greek* Authors gave her Son the Name of *Eucles*, and that *Valerius Maximus* followed them. See the following Remark.

[*C*] *Her Name was* Callipatira *according to some,* Pherenice *according to others*] This *Pausanias* observes, in his fifth Book (9): but, in the sixth (10), he seems plainly to prove, that *Callipatira*, and *Pherenice*, were two Sisters, Daughters of the famous Athlet *Diagoras*. He says, that *Diagoras* had the good Fortune to obtain some Victories, and to have three Sons, who obtained some, and four Daughters, whose Sons likewise carried the Prizes. He says DAUGHTERS, in the Plural Number; from whence it must be concluded, that *Diagoras*'s two Grand-children, of whom he speaks, were not Brothers, but only first Cousins, Sons of two Sisters. He calls one of These two Grand-children, *Eucles*, and the other *Pisidorus*. He says, that *Eucles* was the Son of *Callionax*, and of *Callipatira*, Daughter of *Diagoras*. He does not name the Mother of *Pisidorus*; but says only, that his Mother, disguised like a Master of the young *Athlets*, brought him into the Lists of the Combatants. I say again, that, since he speaks of *Diagoras*'s Daughters in the Plural Number, and since he says, that *Diagoras*'s Grand-sons, by the Daughters side, had obtained some Victories, he must have pretended, that the Mother of *Eucles*, and the Mother of *Pisidorus*, were Sisters: Now the Name of *Eucles*'s Mother was *Callipatira*; we may, therefore, reasonably think, that the Name of *Pisidorus*'s Mother was not *Callipatira*, but *Pherenice*; for it is the Name, which many give her, in the fifth Book of *Pausanias*: and, if some called Her *Callipatira*, who, under the Disguise of a Master of the *Athlets*, brought her Son *Pisidorus* to the Combat of the *Olympian* Games, it must be attributed to the same Causes, which make so many careless Writers confound the Actions of one Person with Those of another.

[*D*] *In what Time This* Berenice *lived.*] *Pausanias* informs us, that she was the Daughter of *Diagoras*, and Sister of *Dorieus* (11). Now *Dorieus* fought for the *Lacedæmonians*, against the *Athenians*, at the time that *Conon* was General of the latter (12); and, therefore he flourished about the XCVth Olympiad. Consult the Remark [*D*] of the Article DIAGORAS *the Rhodian*, in which I enquire when he lived.

(8) Apud Pausan. lib. vi, p. 183, 184.
(9) P. 153.
(10) P. 184.
(11) Pausan. lib. 6. pag. 184.
(12) Idem. pag. 183.

BERENICE, a courageous and revengeful Woman, having lost her Son, by the Contrivance of *Laodice*, mounted, well armed, on a Chariot, and pursued the Murtherer so briskly, that she killed him. His Name was *Cæneus*, and had only executed a Royal Order. She missed him, in throwing her Javelin at him, but killed him with a Stone; afterwards she drove her Chariot over him, and retired,

through

BERENICE. 763

through the Enemy's Troops, to the House, where she believed her Son's Body was hid. This we find in *Valerius Maximus* (a). There is some Probability, that This Author has confounded what relates to two different Persons. The Commentators are puzzled about it [*A*]. See the Remark.

(a) *Valer. Maxim.* lib. ix. cap. 10. sub. fin.

[*A*] *Valerius Maximus has confounded what relates to two different Persons. The Commentators are puzzled about it.*] *Oliverius*, who wrote long Notes on *Valerius Maximus*, full of trivial Erudition, pretends, that the *Berenice* in question was also called *Laodice*, and that she was Sister of *Mithridates*, who waged a long War with the *Romans*. Whereupon, he relates, that This Lady was first married to *Ariarathes*, King of *Cappadocia*; that her second Husband was *Nicomedes*, King of *Bithynia*; and that the two Sons, which she had by *Ariarathes*, having been killed by *Mithridates*, the one immediately, and the other mediately, she armed herself, and pursued *Cæneus*, who had executed the Order of *Mithridates*, and punished him, as *Valerius Maximus* relates. I observe, against This, I. That *Valerius Maximus* was so far from intending to speak of a Woman, whose Name was *Berenice*, or *Laodice*, that he remarks, that *Laodice* caused the Son of *Berenice* to be killed. II. The first Part indeed of our Commentator's Narrative is to be found in *Justin* (1); but we do not find there, that the Sister of *Mithridates*, who was the Wife of *Ariarathes*, and of *Nicomedes*, had any other Name, than That of *Laodice*. III. We do not find there, that the second Son of *Ariarathes* and *Laodice* was killed by Order of *Mithridates*; we find, on the contrary, that he died of Sickness. *Nec multo post adolescens ex ægritudine collectâ infirmitate decedit* (2). IV. The latter Part of This Narrative is manifestly contradicted by *Justin*: See in what manner he relates, that *Laodice* endeavoured to revenge herself of her Brother, after having lost her two Sons. *Nicomedes*, her second Husband, suborned a very handsome Youth, to make it believed, that there remained yet a third Son of *Ariarathes*, and sent *Laodice* to *Rome* with Orders to testify, that *Ariarathes* had left three Sons, whereof the last was yet living, and demanded his Father's Kingdom of the *Romans*. It is too bold to advance several Facts, with their Circumstances, without being able to cite Authorities for them. Where did *Oliverius* read, that the Sister of *Mithridates* mounted on a Chariot, and pursued *Cæneus*, the Murtherer of her second Son, &c? I shall observe, by the way, that *Freinshemius*

FAULTS of *Oliverius*, the Commentator on *Valerius Maximus*.

(1) *Justin.* lib. xxviii. cap. i, ii.

(2) Ibid. lib. xxvii, c iii.

had no reason to accuse *Justin* of contradicting himself, or of confounding History prodigiously (3). *Justin* spoke of two *Laodices*, married to two *Ariarathes's*. The first killed five of her Children, after the Death of her Husband, and would have killed the sixth, the only one that remained, if her Relations had not prevented it (4). The People got rid of This furious Woman. The second *Laodice* married That Son of *Ariarathes*, who was the only remaining one. This will plainly appear in another Place (5). I wish *Justin* was guilty of no other Confusions, and Contradictions.

Father *Cantel* observes, that *Oliverius* was in the wrong to ascribe the Action, which *Valerius Maximus* relates, to *Mithridates*'s Sister. He believes, that *Valerius Maximus* meant *Berenice*, and *Laodice*, Wives of *Antiochus Theus*, and both Daughters of *Ptolomy Philadelphus*. It is not universally agreed, that they were Sisters: *Polyænus*, quoted by one of Father *Cantel*'s Fraternity (6), says, that *Laodice*, the Wife of *Antiochus Theus*, was her Husband's Sister, and Daughter of *Antiochus Soter*. As for *Berenice*, the other Wife of *Antiochus Theus*, it is generally agreed, that she was the Daughter of *Ptolomy Philadelphus*. Nevertheless, Father *Cantel* is not to be condemned; he has *Appian*'s Authority for what he says (7). He has some reason to believe, that *Valerius Maximus* meant the Wives of *Antiochus Theus*; but he should have censured him for having made an Addition to the sad Fate of *Berenice*. The Valour, which That Author ascribes to his *Berenice*, and her good Success, mentioned by him, against her Son's Murtherer, do not agree with the Wife of *Antiochus*; for she was so far from being able to revenge her Son's Death, that she was cruelly murdered, with him, in the Place, whither she had fled. But it is true, that it was one *Laodice*, who was the cause of This Misfortune (8). But, since Father *Cantel* believed, that the Author, whom he commented, had the History of the Wives of *Antiochus Theus* in view, he should not have marked the Six hundred sixty fourth Year of *Rome* in the Margin: This Chronology differs too much from That, which belongs to These two Princesses (9).

(3) See *Orphrion's Justin* pag. 548.

(4) *Justin.* lib. xxxvii. cap. i.

(5) *In the Art.* CAPPADOCIA, *Rem. [F]*, n. III.

EXAMINATION of the Opinion of Father *Cantel*, One of the Commentators on *Valerius Maximus*.

(6) *By F.* Hardouin, *in Plin.* lib. 7, cap. 12, pag. 25.

(7) *Appian.* in *Syriac.* circa finem.

(8) *See Justin.* lib. xxvii, cap.i.

(9) *Antiochus Theus* began to reign about the Year of Rome 492. See *Calvisius*, and *Anno Mundi* 3689.

BERENICE, Daughter of *Ptolomy Auletes*, King of *Egypt*, succeeded her Father before his Death. I do not find, that she excited the *Egyptians* to expel him (a); and there is some probability, that they were inclined, of themselves, to get rid of a troublesome Yoke, without being animated to it by Her: But it is certain, that, as soon as the Father was driven out, the Daughter was crowned [*A*]. This banished Prince implored the Assistance of the *Romans*, and obtained, at last, that *Gabinius*, Governor of *Syria*, should endeavour to restore him. *Pompey* performed it; for the People of *Rome*, relying on some Verses of the *Sybil*, would not concern themselves with This Re-establishment. On the other side, *Berenice* did her utmost Endeavours to maintain herself on the Throne; and, though she feared the *Romans*, she made no Proposals of Accommodation to her Father, nor shewed him any Civility (b). And, believing that a Husband would be of great Use to her, she invited a Prince, whose Name was *Seleucus*, descended from the Kings of *Syria*, and shared with him her Bed, and her Scepter. She was soon weary of him, not finding him a Man of any Merit; and caused him to be killed (c). Afterwards she cast her Eyes on *Archelaus*, the Son of him, who had forsaken the Party of *Mithridates*, to join

(a) *See Remark [C].*

(b) *'Επιστεῖλαι μὲν ἐ- δὲν πρὸς αυτὸν και- μένην τῆς Πομπίκης ἐ- τρωτε, τα̣ γα̣νο̣- μένων 'Ρωμαίων μετα- νοε̣σθαι μετα- βαλ ουκ εν τοῖς μετα- μεν μανδα- τι Πτολε- μαίω εχι- θμητη. Dio,* lib. 39, pag. 130.

(c) *See Remark [C].*

[*A*] *As soon as the Father was driven out, the Daughter was crowned*] *Strabo* observes, that That Prince had three Daughters, and that the eldest, who was legitimate, was placed on the Throne (1). This Narrative is not exact, if it be supposed, that *Porphyry* gives a true Account of This Revolution; for he affirms, That *Cleopatra*, or *Tryphæne*, and *Berenice*, Daughters of *Ptolomy*, reigned together, the first Year of their Father's Flight, and that, *Tryphæne* being dead, her Sister *Berenice* reigned two Years alone (2). This shews, that *Berenice* was not the eldest, and confirms my Opinion, that she did not plot to dethrone the King: The Suspicion rather falls on her Sister *Tryphæne*. I do not pretend to deny, that it is possible Ambition might prompt them to favour the Malecon-

(1) *Strabo,* lib. xvii. pag. 547.

(2) *Porphyr. apud Eusebium, in Chron.* pag. 60. *Edit. Scaligeri* 1658.

tents, and open a way to the Throne for themselves, by the Deposition of their Father; I pretend only, that the ancient Books do not contain this Fact. Mr *Baudelot* maintains the contrary (3); but I am certain, that, if what he alledges out of *Dio Cassius*, *Porphyry*, and *Photius*, be examined, his Opinion will not be found to be confirmed thereby. His strongest Allegation is, that *Ptolomy*, stifling all fatherly Affection, caused his Daughter *Berenice* to be put to Death for what she had done. It is plain, that, without making her an Accomplice in the Revolt of the *Egyptians*, one may think she was guilty enough in her Father's Judgment, by considering only, that she accepted the Crown, and used all manner of means to maintain her Usurpation.

(3) *Baudelot de Dairval's History of Priamus Auletes,* pag. 121, 127, &c. seq.

VOL. I. 9 G [*B*] She

BERENICE.

join with *Sylla*. She offered herself to him in Marriage [B], and promised him, that he should share in her Royalty. He was, then, in *Gabinius*'s Army; and he might easily have been hindered from going to *Berenice*, if *Gabinius* had not rather, for his particular Interest, given him the Liberty to marry That Princess [C]. *Archelaus* married her, and put himself at the Head of Her Army to repel the *Romans*, who pretended to restore King *Ptolomy*. He was slain in Battle; *Ptolomy* re-entered *Alexandria*, and caused his rebellious Daughter to be put to death without Mercy (*d*). Such was the Fate of *Berenice*. A modern Author has very well unfolded the Intrigues

(*d*) Ex Dione, lib. xxxix, pag. 130, 131.

[B] *She offered herself to Archelaus in Marriage.*] I have reason to say This; but Father *Noris* had no reason to say it. " Archelaus à Berenice spe nuptiarum Alexandriam evocatus, eadem upsen ducta, copias contra Gabinium ducens, victus prælio occubuit, mense regni sexto, ex Strabone, lib. 12. pag. 385 (4). ----- Archelaus, *being invited to Alexandria by Berenice, upon an Offer of Marriage, after having wedded her, lead an Army against Gabinius, and fell in Battle, in the sixth Month of his Reign, according to Strabo, lib. 12. pag. 385.*" Had I had no other Author to quote but *Strabo*, I would not have said, as Father *Noris* did, that *Berenice* gained him, by a Promise of Marriage. I do not find in *Strabo*, that That Princess had any Thought of *Archelaus*; I find only that the *Egyptians*, having expelled their King *Ptolomy*, sought for a Prince of the Royal Blood, to marry him to *Berenice*, and that *Archelaus*, knowing this, offered himself to them, under the supposed Quality of the Son of *Mithridates Eupator*, and was accepted, and reigned six Months. Ταύτη ζητοῦμένη ἀνδρὸς βασιλικη γένες ἀνεγγυήσειεν ἑαυτῷ τοῖς συμπράκτοις, προποιησάμενος Μιθριδάτη τοῦ Εὐπάτορο υἱὸς εἶναι, καὶ παραδεχθεὶς, ἐβασίλευσεν ἐξ μῆνας (5). *Ei cum quæreretur maritus regio sanguine natus, dedit se Archelaus auxiliaris suis, simulavitque se filium esse Mithridatis Eupatoris, itaque receptus sex menses regno potitus est.* This affords us an Example of the great Care, with which a Writer ought to relate what he finds in Authors. The least Liberty, he takes, is sufficient sometimes to injure a Person's Honour. It is not decent, or becoming the Dignity of a Queen, to offer herself in Marriage, and to entice a young Man by the Hopes of marrying her. It belongs to her Subjects to procure a suitable Match for her; which is the Account *Strabo* gives in relation to *Berenice*. The Case should not therefore have been represented as Father *Noris* has done it, or else he should have quoted other Authors, than *Strabo*. If *Dio* had been quoted, *Berenice* might have been decried as a Princess, who, after having usurped the Throne of Him, to whom she owed her Life, went in quest of an Husband, and offered herself, and her Crown, as a Price of the Protection she stood in need of. See the following Remark.

[C] *Gabinius, who could have hindered him from going to Berenice, chose to let him espouse This Princess.*] *Gabinius* presently discovered *Archelaus*'s Design, and secured him; which might have put an end to The Business: But, fearing he should not find Difficulty enough in the restoring *Ptolomy* to have room to demand all the Sums, which That Prince had promised, he ordered the matter so, that his Re-establishment met with some Obstacles. In this View, he found no better Expedient, than to suffer *Archelaus* to put himself at the Head of the Rebels. *Archelaus* passed for a Man of Courage, and had a great Reputation: To drive him from *Alexandria* seemed a great Exploit to *Gabinius*, for which he might honourably demand great Rewards from *Ptolomy*. Besides, *Gabinius* did not release his Prisoner, 'till he had extorted a great Sum from him (6): So that he took Money on all Hands, that is of both Parties. A notable Instance of the Tricks that are plaid to Sovereigns. Sometimes one Campaign would end a War, if Generals, for their private Advantage, did not dexterously supply the Enemy with an After-game. Take notice, they were obliged to spread a Report, that *Archelaus* had made his Escape (7). *Gabinius*, being well paid for the leave he had given him to escape, pretended, without doubt, to be angry with Those, who kept him. A new Scene of The Comedy! But I observe, that *Strabo* knew nothing of all this Management of *Gabinius*. He says, that *Archelaus* was brought to *Berenice*, without *Gabinius*'s Privacy. Λαθὼν δὲ τοῦτον

(a) Noris's Cenotaph. Pisan, pag. 225.

(5) Strabo, lib. xii, pag. 384. See also lib. xvii, pag. 548.

(6) Ex Dione, lib. xxx x, pag. 131.

(7) Dio, ibid.

κομίζεται διά τινὸς (or τίνων) εἰς τὴν βασίλισσαν, καὶ ἀναδείκνυται βασιλεὺς. Eo (Gabinio) *nesciente, per amicos quosdam ad Reginam deductus, rex declaratus fuit* (8). Thus he frees that *Roman* General from a great Reproach. *Strabo* clears *Berenice* in great Measure, and induces us to believe, that she was not guilty of her Father's Expulsion. He says plainly, that That Prince was expelled by the Inhabitants of *Alexandria*, who afterwards set the Eldest of his three Daughters on the Throne, and caused one *Cybiosactes* to come from *Syria*, who pretended to be descended from the Kings of *Syria*, and gave him the Queen in Marriage. She, being displeased with the Baseness she observed in him, caused him to be strangled a few Days after. It is said, that he caused *Alexander*'s Body to be put into a Glass Coffin, to appropriate to himself That of massy Gold, out of which he took it. I have read this Fact in a Modern Writer, who quotes *Strabo* and *Suetonius*, two Authors, who say not a word of it (9). The latter says in general, that That Prince was sordidly avaricious. " Alexandrini Cybiosacten eum " (*Vespasianum*) vocare perseverarunt, cognomine " unius è regibus suis turpissimarum sordidum (10). " ------ *The Inhabitants of* Alexandria *continued to* " *nick-name* Vespasian Cybiosactes, *from one of their* " *Kings, who was most sordidly covetous.*" Τοῦτον μὲν ἐν ὀλίγων ἡμερῶν ἀπεπραγάλλισεν ἡ Βασίλισσα, ᾗ φέρουσα τὸ ἀύναυσον αὐτῇ καὶ τὸ ἀνελεύθερον: They are *Strabo*'s Words: *Hunc intra paucos dies regina strangulavit, cum ejus sordes illiberalitatemque pati non posset* (11).

You will tell me, that, in the foregoing Page, That Writer mentions one *Ptolomy*, who being come from *Syria*, had carried off The golden Urn, but drew no profit from This Action, being soon overthrown: But how do you know, that This is to be understood of *Berenice*'s Husband? Do you not see, that *Strabo* gives only the Title of *Cybiosactes* to the latter, and that he gives the Name of *Ptolomy*, and the Sirname of *Coccus*, and *Parisactus*, to the other? Ἐσύλησε δ᾿ αὐτὸν ὁ Κόκκης καὶ Παρίσακτος ἐπικληθεὶς Πτολεμαῖος: *aureum Ptolemæus cognomento Coccus & subditicius rapuit* (12). Do you not know, that *Dion* calls Him, that was married to *Berenice*, *Seleucus* (13)? Can it be believed, that, if *Strabo* had pretended to speak of the same Man, in the Five hundred forty sixth, and Five hundred forty seventh Pages, he would have expressed himself as he does? There is no Word, or Phrase, in his Narrative, which insinuates, that the *Syrian*, who carried away the golden Tomb, is the same *Cybiosactes*, whom *Berenice* put to Death. Nevertheless, read the learned Reflexions of Mr *Baudelot*, who believes, as well as the Abbot *de St Real*, that *Cybiosactes*, and *Ptolomy Coccus*, are one and the same Person (14).

[D] *Archelaus was slain in Battle.*] This does not agree with the seventeenth Book of *Strabo*, where we read, that *Ptolomy*, being re-established in his Kingdom, caused his Daughter, and his Son-in-law *Archelaus*, to be put to Death. Καταχθεὶς ὑπὸ Γαβινίου Πτολεμαῖος, τόν τε Ἀρχέλαον ἀναιρεῖ καὶ τὴν Θυγατέρα. *Ptolemæus, à Gabinio reductus, Archelaum ac Filiam interimit* (15). But I had rather depend on the twelfth Book of *Strabo*, than on the seventeenth; because *Plutarch* plainly confirms, what *Strabo* relates in the twelfth Book, that *Archelaus* was slain in Battle. Τοῦτον μὲν ἐν Ταξινίοις ἀνεῖλεν ἐν παραδόξῳ, καταγωνίζων τὸν Πτολεμαῖον. *Eum Gabinius Ptolemæum reducens in pugna occidit* (16). *Plutarch* sets forth, that *Marc Antony* performed several courageous Actions in *Gabinius*'s Army, when *Ptolomy* was re-established, and that he did likewise an Act of Humanity, which was much praised; namely, that he caused the Body of his Friend *Archelaus* to be fought for, and made a splendid Funeral for him. Is not this a Proof, that *Archelaus*

(8) Strabo, lib. xvii, pag. 548.

(9) *The Abbot de St Real*, al, in his *Cesarion*, Entret II, pag. 78.

(10) Suetonius *in* Vespas. cap. xix.

(11) Strabo, lib. xvii, pag. 548.

(12) Ib. pag. 546.

(13) Dio, lib. xxxix, pag. 130.

(14) Baudelot de Dairval's Hist. of *Ptolomy Auletes*, pag. 170.

(15) Strabo, lib. xvii, pag. 548.

(16) Ibid. lib. xii. pag. 384.

BERENICE.

trigues, which were carried on at *Rome*, for the Re-eſtabliſhment of *Ptolomy* ; but he is miſtaken as to the Circumſtances of *Archelaus*'s Detention [*E*].

(17) Plutarch. M. Antonio, pag. 917.

Archelaus was killed in Battle? Τοχρτως γαρ αυτω ευνεθης και ξιν⊕. ἐπολεμει μεν αναγκαιως ζωντι, τω δε σωμα τετοντ⊕. ἐξευρων, και κοσμησας βασιλικως ἐκηδευσε. *Nam quùm familiaritas ei cum illo & jus hoſpitii interceſſiſſet, bellum cum vivente geſſit neceſſario, corpus interfecti requiſitum regio cultu funeravit* (17). *Dio Caſſius* relates the matter in ſuch a manner, as plainly ſhews, that *Archelaus* was killed in the Fight, which decided the Quarrel between the Father and the Daughter, and that, after That Victory of *Gabinius*, the *Egyptians* were obliged to open the Gates of *Alexandria* to *Ptolomy*, who cauſed *Berenice* and divers others to be put to Death. [*E*] *A Modern Author* —— *is miſtaken as to the Circumſtances of* Archelaus'*s Detention*.] The Modern Author, whom I mean, is the Abbot *de Saint Real*. See the *Ceſarion*, which he publiſhed in the Year 1685. The Miſtake, which I deſign to take notice of, conſiſts in his ſuppoſing, that *Archelaus* departed privately *from Gabinius* to marry the Queen of *Egypt* (18); and that, being taken Priſoner in a Battle, after the *Romans* had made themſelves Maſters of *Peluſium*, *Gabinius gave him the Aſſiſtance, which was neceſſary for his Eſcape*, upon paying a great Ranſom (19). *Dio Caſſius*, whom he quotes, ſays, in expreſs Words, that *Gabinius* let *Archelaus* eſcape, before the Army marched towards *Peluſium*, and before there was any Battle (20).

(18) St Real, Ceſarion. pag. 80. Edit. Holl. 1685.

(19) Ibid. pag. 82.

(20) Dio, lib. xxxix, pag. 131.

BERENICE, Daughter of *Coſtobarus*, and *Salome*, Siſter of *Herod the Great* [*A*], was firſt married to *Ariſtobulus*, Son of the ſame *Herod*, and of *Mariamne*, and lived unhappily enough with him ; for, becauſe he had a Brother married to the Daughter of *Archelaus*, King of *Cappadocia*, he often upbraided *Berenice* with having undermatched himſelf in marrying her, and that, in ſo doing, he had made himſelf much inferior to his Brother. *Berenice*, all in Tears, reported theſe, and other Diſcourſes, to her Mother, and incenſed her greatly: Inſomuch, that *Salome*, who had a great Power over *Herod*, made him jealous of *Ariſtobulus*, and was the chief Cauſe that induced That cruel Father to make away with him (*a*). Though *Berenice* had five Children (*b*), ſhe married again with a Brother of *Antipater*'s Mother ; which *Antipater* was *Herod*'s Son. Having loſt This ſecond Huſband, ſhe went to *Rome*, and gained the Eſteem of *Auguſtus* : But, above all, ſhe inſinuated herſelf into the Favour of *Antonia*, the Wife of *Druſus* [*B*], which, afterwards, ſtood her Son *Agrippa* in good ſtead. The firſt time the latter went to *Rome*, his Mother *Berenice* was yet living [*C*] ; but, the ſecond time he went thither, ſhe was dead.

(*a*) Joſeph. de Bell. Jud. lib. l. c. 17.

(*b*) Three Sons and two Daughters : The Sons were Agrippa, the firſt of That Name, King of Judæa ; Herod, King of Chalcis, and Ariſtobulus: The Daughters were Herodias, and Mariamne. Ibid. c. 18.

[*A*] *She was Daughter of* Coſtobarus, *and of* Salome, *Siſter of* Herod the Great] *Joſephus* ſays ſo in expreſs Words: It is, therefore, through want of Memory, that Dr *Mountague* queſtions, whether it was ever determined, that *Berenice* was the Daughter of *Coſtobarus*, or of *Joſeph*. *Quam* (Berenicen ſcilicet Salomes) *vel è Coſtobaro vel Joſepho, nam non minime pro certo traditum, genuerat* (1). *Cornelius à Lapide* believed falſly, that *Herod* was the Father of our *Berenice* (2).

[*B*] *She inſinuated herſelf into the Favour of* Antonia.] There is a Paſſage in *Strabo*, which deſerves to be produced. Καισαρ και τες υἱες ἐτιμησε τω Ἡρωδε και την ἀδελφην Σαλωμην, και την ταυτης θυγατερα Βερενικην: That is; *The Emperor honoured the Sons of* Herod, *and his Siſter* Salome, *and* Berenice, *the Daughter of* Salome (3). It is probable, theſe two Women went together to *Rome*, to diſpute the Kingdom of *Judea* with *Archelaus*, the Son of *Herod* : for it is known, that *Salome* went thither, at That Time, with her Family (4).

[*C*] *The firſt time* Agrippa *went to* Rome, *his Mother* Berenice *was yet living*.] For we read, in *Joſephus*, that *Agrippa* lived familiarly with *Druſus*, the Son of *Tiberius* ; and that he acquired the Friendſhip of *Antonia*, the Wife of *Druſus*, the Brother of *Tiberius*, by reaſon of the Eſteem, which *Antonia* had for *Berenice*, the Mother of *Agrippa* (5). That Hiſtorian adds, that *Agrippa*, out of reſpect to his Mother, reſtrained his Natural Inclination, which prompted him to be laviſh of his Fortune ; but that, after her Death, he was ſo prodigal, that he quite exhauſted it. Having neither Money nor Credit left, he returned to *Judea*, from whence, after divers Adventures, he came back to *Rome*, and went to ſalute *Tiberius* in the Iſland of *Capreæ*. He was, at firſt, very well received by him ; but he had, afterwards, good need of *Antonia*'s Protection. I do not know, where *Noldius* had read, that *Berenice* died at *Antonia*'s Houſe (6).

(1) Montacut. in Apparat. V. n. 74, p. 151. apud Noldium, de vita & peſtis Herodum pag. 297.

(2) Corn. à Lap. in Act. xxv. ver. 13. pag. 363. apud Noldium, ibid. pag. 296.

(3) Strabo, lib. xvi, pag. 526.

(4) Joſeph. Antiq. lib. xvii, cap. 11.

(5) Ibid. lib. xviii, cap. 8.

(6) Noldius de Vita & Geſtis Herodum. p. 297.

BERENICE, Grand-daughter of the foregoing, and Daughter of *Agrippa*, the firſt of That Name, King of *Judæa*, was much talked of on account of her Amours. She was betrothed to one *Marc*, the Son of *Alexander Lyſimachus*, *Alabarche* ; but he died before the Marriage was conſummated. A little after, ſhe was married to her Uncle *Herod*, who, at the Requeſt of *Aprippa*, both his Brother, and Father-in-law, was made King of *Chalcis*, by the Emperor *Claudius* (*a*). She was but ſixteen Years of Age, when her Father died (*b*). She loſt her Huſband in the eighth Year of the Emperor *Claudius* (*c*), and behaved very ill in her Widowhood ; for the general Opinion was, that ſhe committed Inceſt with her Brother *Agrippa*. To put a ſtop to Theſe Reports, ſhe endeavoured to marry again, and offered herſelf to *Polemon*, King of *Cilicia*, provided he would change his Religion (*d*). It will eaſily be believed, that ſhe required this Condition rather out of Vanity, or Policy, than out of Zeal ; but it is no uncommon thing for a zealous, and amorous, Woman to ſet up for a Converter. *Polemon*, having more Regard to the Riches, than the Reputation, of the Lady, who courted him, accepted her Offers, cauſed himſelf to be circumciſed, and married her : And, if he did not continue all his Life-time in the Bonds of This Marriage, it was not his own Fault, but That of *Berenice* ; ſince This lewd Woman left him, and returned whither ſhe pleaſed [*A*]. He forſook Judaiſm

(*a*) Joſeph. Antiq. lib. xix, cap. 4.

(*b*) Ib. c. 7.

(*c*) Ibid. xx, cap. 3.

(*d*) Ib. c. 5.

[*A*] *This lewd Woman left* Polemon, *her Huſband, and returned whither ſhe pleaſed*.] I ſhall here tranſcribe A Paſſage, which is full of Faults. *That* Berenice, *of whom our* Xiphilinus *makes mention, was the Daughter of* Archelaus, *and the Wife of* Herod, *after whoſe Death, ſhe married* Polemon *King of* Lycia, *whom ſhe left*, propter nimietatem coitus, ut quidam dixerunt, ſays Jolephus, lib. 20. cap. 2. This is what

BERENICE.

(e) Ibid.

daism immediately, to return to his first Religion (e). *Berenice*'s ill Life did not hinder her from practising the Jewish Observances. She had made a Vow, and, to accomplish it, she went to *Jerusalem*, and submitted to the Custom, which was, That before any Person offered his Sacrifices, he spent thirty Days in Prayer, and Supplication, without drinking Wine, and had his Head shaved. Whilst she observed these Ceremonies, she received a thousand Affronts from the *Roman* Soldiers, and was in Danger of her Life: In vain did she go bare-foot, to interceed for the People with the Governor *Florus*; she obtained nothing, not so much as the Civilities, (f) Id. de Bell. Jud. lib. ii, c. 26. which her Quality, and Sex, made indispensable (f). She was still in Favour with her Brother *Agrippa*; and she seconded him in his Design of preventing the Desolation of the *Jews*, by exhorting them to submit to the *Romans*. But all these Ex-(g) Ib. cap. xviii, xxix. hortations, accompanied with Tears, proved ineffectual (g); so that *Berenice*, either to avoid being involved in the Ruin of the Nation, or to exercise her Parts, went to *Vespasian* and *Titus*, and gained the one so fortunately by her Liberality, and the other by her Beauty [B], that she was in a fair way of becoming a *Roman* Empress. She ensnared *Titus*, and saw the Hour, that, of a favoured Gallant, he would become her Husband [C]: But the Murmurs of the *Roman* People frustrated her Hope; she

---

(1) They are at the end of the French Translation of Xiphilinus, by Antony de Bandole, and printed at Paris, in 1610, in 4to.

what I find in the Annotations of the Sieur *de Canque* on the History of *Dio Cassius*, abridged by *Xiphilinus* (1). Let us observe, in the first place, that the *Berenice*, spoken of in those Words, is the Mistress of *Titus*; and then let us reckon up the Faults. I. She was not the Daughter of *Archelaus*. II. *Polemon* was not King of *Lycia*. III. The Reason, why she left him, was not because he performed, too often, what is called the Conjugal Duty. It was rather a quite contrary reason. For see how the *Jewish* Historian, quoted by the Author of the Annotations, expresses himself: ὰ μὲν ὑπὸ πολλῦ συνέχοντο γαμῷ, ἀλλὰ Βερνίκη δι᾽ ἀκολασίαν, ὡς ἔφασαν, καταλείπει τὸν Πολέμωνα. Id tamen conjugium diuturnum non fuit, propter intemperantiam, ut

(2) Joseph. Antiq. Jud. lib. xx, cap. 5. (and rot cap. 2.) pag. 693.

fertur, discedente ab eo Berenice (2). If This Author had consulted the Translation of *Gencbrard*, he would not have fallen into the Error, which he has committed; he would have read there; *This Marriage did not continue long; and it is said, that it was by reason of *Berenice's* Intemperance, who left him.* Granting, that the Words of the *Jewish* Author, considered in themselves, may have I know not what ambiguity, which may make one doubt, whether the Matter in question be the Husband's, or the Wife's Irregularity, was there no means to remove the Ambiguity? Was it not sufficient to observe the ill Life of *Berenice*? They, who know how she lived, will readily acknowledge, that she could not be displeased with a Man, for being indefatigable in the Exercises of Love. All Persons, *Berenice* among the rest, generally speaking, admit of This Maxim, *Too*

(3) Id arbitror a primis in vita esse utile, ut ne quid nimia. Terentius, in And in Act. i. Sc. i. See also in Erasmus, Ch. I. i, Cent vi. n. 96. pag. 526. several such like Sentences.

much of Nothing (3); but the Varieties are infinite, when the Question is to fix the bounds between *too much* and *enough*: Opinions are very different. If the Constitution of *Berenice* be no Argument against the general Thesis, it is One against the Application of it; it is not affected by it; it calls That Mediocrity, which others call Excess. It is not indeed such, as literally fulfils the Sentence of the thirtieth Chapter of *Proverbs*: " Tria sunt insaturabilia, & quartum " & terra quæ non satiatur aqua; ignis vero nunquam " dicit, sufficit. ----- *There are three things, that* " *are never satisfied, yea a fourth, which saith not,* " *It is enough; The Grave, and The Womb, The* " *Earth, that is not filled with Water; and the* " *Fire, that saith not, It is enough:*" or such, as falsifies That of *Pindar*;

(4) Pindar, Nemeus Od. vii. p. 180. See a like Sentence of Homer, in Remark [E], of the Article XENOPHANES.

- - - - - 'Αναπαύσις

Ἐν παντὶ γλυκεῖα ἔργῳ. Κόρον δ᾽ ἔχει
Καὶ μέλι καὶ τὰ τερπν᾽ ἄνθε᾽ Ἀφροδίσια (4).

In ev'ry Exercise, 'tis best
Alternately to work and rest:
Honey, and Love's inviting Joy,
Too largely if we taste them, cloy.

But, at last, it gives the Lie to This Maxim; *Nature is satisfied with a little*.

The Author, whom I refute, should rather have placed *Polemon's* Offence in the Defect, than in the Excess, and compared That Monarch with the first Husband of Queen *Joan* of *Naples*. It is true,

Polemon came off cheaper than the other; for he did not lose his Life, as the other did.

Some Caviller will perhaps tell me, that Mr *de Canque's* meaning is, that *Berenice* forsook *Polemon*, because he was not able to supply her amorous Desires; but I maintain, that the Words are not ranged in such a manner as to be so understood. Whatever his Thought was, they plainly signify, what I suppose, and, consequently, they represent *Berenice* as a Woman of a most extraordinary Humour. See what I shall quote out of the Letters of the Count *de Bussi Rabutin*, in the Remark [D] of the Article G L E I- C H E N.

[B] *She gained Vespasian by her Liberality, and Titus by her Beauty*] *Tacitus* informs us, that This Lady intrigued to place the Crown on *Vespasian's* Head. I do not wonder at it; she had more to hope for from him, than from his Competitors, if he came to the Empire. " Mox per occultos suorum nuntios " excitus ab urbe Agrippa, ignaro adhuc Vitellio, " celeri navigatione properaverat. Nec minore animo " regina Berenice partes juvabat, florens ætate forma- " que, & seni quoque Vespasiano magnificentia mu- " nerum grata (5). ——— *Afterwards*, Agrippa, upon (5) Tacit. Histor lib. ii, cap. 81. " *secret Intelligence from Those of his Party, left the* " *City, and set sail with all Expedition.* Queen " *Berenice, with equal Resolution, favoured his De-* " *signs, being then in the Flower of her Youth and* " *Beauty, and agreeable to old Vespasian on account of* " *the Magnificence of her Presents*." The same Historian informs us, that *Titus* loved her, and that it was thought she was the cause, why he did not finish his Journey, but return into *Judæa*, after he heard of *Galba's* Death at *Corinth*. " Fuere qui accensum " desiderio Berenices reginæ vertisse iter crederent. " Neque abhorrebat à Berenice juvenilis animus: sed (6) Ibid. cap. ii. " gerendis rebus nullum ex eo impedimentum (6). — " *Some believed, that the Love of* Berenice *stopped his* " *Journey; nor indeed was he averse to the Lady; but* " *This was no Interruption to his Affairs.*" This Historian refutes Calumny in two words: He owns, This Queen touched the Heart of *Titus*; but he declares, it was but an amorous Amusement, which did not prevent him from attending to his Affairs.

[C] *She saw the Hour ——— that* Titus *would become her Husband*.] *Agrippa*, and his Sister *Berenice*, took a Journey to *Rome*, in the fourth Consulship of *Vespasian*; great Honour was done them; she lodged in the Palace; she lay with *Titus*; and began to dispose of all things like a lawful Wife: But *Titus*, understanding, that the People were scandalized at it, sent her away. This is what *Xiphilinus* relates (7); (7) In Vespasiano. and he observes, that *Berenice* was, then, in her Prime, and in great Lustre. Βερνίκη δὲ ἰσχυρῶς τε ἤκμει. *Berenice maxime florebat* (8). Nevertheless, (8) Xiphil. in Vespas. she was then Forty four Years of Age; for the fourth Consulship of *Vespasian* fell in the Year of J E S U S pag. 222. C H R I S T 72 (9), and she was sixteen Years of (9) See Calvisius. Age, when her Father died (10), that is to say, the third Year of the Emperor *Claudius* (11), which (10) Joseph. Antiq. lib. was the Forty fourth of J E S U S C H R I S T. This 19, cap. 7. may be easily calculated. Besides, she entred young into the Lists, and had contended vigorously, and (11) Ibid. without Intermission; she had a Husband, and perhaps Children, in the sixteenth Year of her Age: She had had a second Husband, and some Gallants, and yet
she

BERENICE. 767

she retained only the Title of the Emperor's Mistress, or Concubine. In the XVIIth Century, the *French* Stage resounded with the Amours of *Titus* and *Berenice* [D]. She had too beautiful a Sister for them to love each other [E]. The Holy Scripture makes mention of *Berenice* [F]. Great Mistakes have been committed in relation to This Princess.

she was in her greatest Lustre at Forty four Years of Age. This was enough to expose her to Envy. *Suetonius* observes, that the Separation was with Regret on both sides. " Nec minus Ibido *(suspecta erat in* " *Tito)* propter exoletorum & spadonum greges, " propterque insignem reginæ Berenices amorem, " cui etiam nuptias pollicitus ferebatur. ---- Bere- " nicem statim ab urbe dimisit invitus invitam (12). " ---- Nor *was Titus less suspected of Lust, on ac-* " *count of the many Catamites and Eunuchs, as also* " *from his remarkable Love for Berenice, to whom* " *he is said to have promised Marriage.* ---- *He* " *immediately dismissed Berenice from the City, to* " *the great Regret of both.*" *Titus* did himself great Violence in sending away *Berenice*, to put a stop to the Complaints of Slanderers. *Berenice* was much vexed at being sent away: no doubt she would rather have suffered the Continuance of Calumny: And, if it be true, that *Titus* had promised her Marriage, as was reported, we may very well believe, that the loudly exclaimed against the Unfaithfulness of Men. It is probable, that, to moderate her Grief, *Titus* represented to her, that it is was a Sacrifice he was obliged to make to the Murmurs of the whole City; but that, after having given way to This Torrent for a while, they should meet again. It is certain, that *Berenice* behaved, as if she had been sent away in this manner: Some time after she returned to *Titus*; but the got nothing by it; for he would not hear of her any more. I believe, *Xiphilinus* is the only Historian, who has observed, that *Berenice* was sent away twice, the first time in the Reign of *Vespasian*, and the second in That of *Titus*. Ὁ δε δὴ Τίτος οὐδέν ὅτε φονικὸν ὅτε ἐρωτικὸν μοναρχήσας ὑπέδειξεν, ἀλλὰ χρηστὸς καίπερ ἐπιβουλευθεὶς, καὶ σώφρων καίτοι καὶ τῆς Βερενίκης ἐς Ῥώμην αὖθις ἐλθούσης, ἐγένετο (13). *Titus*, *from the Time that he became* " *sole Emperor, neither committed Slaughter, nor was* " *a Slave to Love; but was courteous, though plotted a-* " *gainst; and chast, though Berenice was returned to* " *the City.* *Xiphilinus* probably is not mistaken, tho' *Aurelius Victor*, and the other Historians, mention but one Dismission. " Ut subiit pondus regium, " ---- Berenicem nuptiis suas (speranten regredi domum " ---- præcepit (14). ---- *When he had taken* " *upon him the Royal Authority, he commanded Be-* " *renice, who was in Hopes of being married to him,* " *to return home.*" These Words of *Aurelius Victor*, compared with what he had said before, convict him of extream Negligence. He says, here, that *Berenice* was in hopes of marrying *Titus*, and he had said, just before, that she was his Wife. " Cœci- " nam Consularem, adhibitum cœnæ, vix dum tri- " clinio egressum, ob suspicionem stupratæ Berenices " UXORIS SUÆ, jugulari jussit. ---- Cœcina, *of* " *Consular Dignity, whom he had invited to his* " *Table, had scarce left it, when, by the Emperor's* " *Order, he was put to Death, on Suspicion of having* " *violated his Wife Berenice.*" Let us infer from hence, that *Berenice* lent an Ear to other Lovers, besides the Emperor. This is common enough in the Mistresses of great Princes. I cannot pass over an Error of *Noldius*. He says, in Page 408, that *Dio Cassius*, or *Xiphilinus*, are mistaken in placing *Berenice's* Divorce under the Reign of *Vespasian*, since *Aurelius Victor* affirms, that *Titus* did not send her away, 'till after he had taken Possession of the Crown. Ut subiit Pondus Regium (15). This *Noldius* says, Page 408; but, at Page 409, he affirms, that *Berenice* returned to *Rome*, to make a new Attempt on *Titus's* Heart, and that her Design miscarried. He quotes *Xiphilinus* for This. What! After having said, that an Author is mistaken, should we affirm what he advances? Should we prove it by his Testimony?

[D] *In the XVIIth Century, the French Stage resounded with the Amours of* Titus *and* Berenice.] Two Pieces, entitled *Berenice*, were acted at the same time: One was composed by *Corneille*, and the other by *Racine*; each of them had it's Partizans: The Abbot *de Villars* published some Critical Observations on both. I should not have known, that he

is the Author of Those Observations, if I had not read these Words in the *Sentimens de Cleanthe* (16) " Would you have questioned it, if you had recollect.d " the Critic on the two *Berenices* ? ---- For what " reason should we have escaped That Critic on two " excellent Poets, one of whom did not vouchsafe " to answer him, and the other declared, in but two " Words, why he did not answer him (17)?" Here are some Extracts, which seem to me worthy of the Place I give them. " I am very sorry, *says* " *a Lady, writing to the Count* de Rabutin, *that* " I cannot send you the *Berenice* of *Racine*, this " Day; I expect it from *Paris*, and I am sure it " will please you; but, for that Purpose, you must " have a refined Tenderness; for no Woman ever " carried Love and Delicacy so far as she does. " Good God! What a pretty Mistress! And what " pity it is, that a single Character cannot make a " good Piece: *Racine's* Tragedy would be perfect " (18)." The Count answered her: " I have just " now read *Berenice*. I do not find so much Ten- " derness in it, as I expected. I remember, that, " when I pretended to have some, I could have " out-done *Berenice*: *Titus* does not seem to me " to love her so much as he says, since he uses " no Endeavours, in her favour, with the Senate, " and the People of *Rome*. He yields immediately " to the Remonstrances of *Paulinus*, who, finding " him shaken, brings the People, and Senate, of " *Rome*, to engage him; whereas, if he had spoken " resolutely to *Paulinus*, he would have found eve- " ry one ready to submit to his Will. I would " have done so myself; and, by this means, I should " have joined Love and Glory together. As for " *Berenice*, if I had been in her Place, I would " have done as she did, that is, I would have left " *Rome* full of Rage against *Titus*; but *Antiochus* " should not have been the better for it (19)." Here is the Reply, that was made to him. " Your " Heart is not so indifferent as I believed it to be, " since you remember still, that you could have out- " done *Berenice* in Point of Tenderness, and you " must have carried it to a very high Pitch, to " have surpassed her: I commend, and esteem, you " for it. He, who pretends to Love, must not do " it by halves (20)." From these three Passages, we learn, what Judgment was passed on Mr *Racine's Berenice*, and how much the Ladies are naturally inclined to approve of Those Hearts, which have the utmost Tenderness. I do not find, that the Count *de Rabutin's* Criticism is well grounded; for he would have had the Poet falsify an Event, which ought to be preserved on the Stage. *Berenice's* Dismission is so well known in History, that they, who had not found it in the Tragedy, might justly have exclaimed against the Author. Without doubt, Mr *Racine* foresaw this; and it is probable this was the Reason, why he represented *Titus's* Passion inferior to That of the Lady: This might displease the Fair Sex; but the Author found, that this Inconvenience did not equal the other.

[E] *She had too beautiful a Sister, for them to love each other*.] *Josephus* observes, that *Drusilla*, the Sister of *Berenice*, listened to the Proposals of *Felix*, Governor of *Judæa*, to secure herself from her Sister's Jealousy, who could not endure, that she (*Drusilla*) should be so beautiful. *Drusilla* was courted by *Felix*, whilst she was married to *Azizus*, King of *Emesenians*. She yielded, and married *Felix*, and she even seems to have abjured the Jewish Religion (21). The Hatred of Brothers is great; and some Maxims might be quoted upon this Subject; but, it I am not mistaken, the Hatred of Sisters exceeds it. We may touch upon this in some other Place (22).

[F] *The Holy Scripture makes mention of* Berenice] We find, in the Twenty fifth Chapter of the *Acts*, that *Agrippa* and *Berenice* came to *Cæsarea*, to salute *Festus*, and that, having been told of St *Paul*, who was then in Prison, they had a mind to hear him; and that, for this Purpose, they went to the Place of Audience, with great Pomp (23), and heard St *Paul*.

9 H [G] *Great*

BERENICE.

Princess [G]. I could not take notice of all the Queens, who have born this Name. I shall remark some Errors of *Moreri* [H], *Hofman*, *Charles Stephens*, &c. [I].

[G] *Great Mistakes have been committed in relation to This Princess.*] Sabellicus believed, that she was the Wife of *Aristobulus*, and afterwards of *Antipater* (24). This is to confound two *Berenices*, *viz.* the Grand-mother, and the Grand-daughter, together: The former was married, the first time, to *Aristobulus*, and, the second time, to an Uncle of *Antipater*, and not to *Antipater* himself. This is, then, a second Mistake of *Sabellicus*. As for the *Berenice*, whom he speaks of (the Mistress of *Titus*) she had neither of These two Husbands. I shall set down a Passage of *Juvenal*, which is, doubtless, to be understood of the latter *Berenice*, who was beloved by *Titus*, and who was suspected of Incest with her Brother *Agrippa*;

Grandia tolluntur crystallina; maxima rursus
Myrrhina, deinde adamas notissimus, & Berenices
In digito factus pretiosior: hunc dedit olim
Barbarus incestæ, dedit hunc Agrippa sorori,
Observant ubi festa mero pede sabbata Reges,
Et vetus indulget senibus clementia porcis (25).

*Rich Chrystals of the Rock she takes up there,
Huge Agat Vases, and old China Ware:
Then* Berenice's *Ring her Finger proves,
More precious made by her incestuous Loves;
And infamously dear: A Brother's Bribe;
Eo'n* God's *Anointed, and of* Judah's *Tribe;
Where barefoot they approach the sacred Shrine,
And think it only Sin to feed on Swine.*
DRYDEN.

The Scholiast of *Juvenal* understands, here, by *Berenice*, a Sister of *Ptolomy*, King of *Egypt*, and, by *Agrippa*, a Son of *Julia*, Daughter of *Augustus*; That Son of *Juba*, and of *Agrippa*, whom *Tiberius* put to Death, after the Decease of *Augustus* (26). To say no worse, it is prodigious Carelessness in This Scholiast; for it appears plainly, upon a little attention, that *Juvenal* speaks of an *Agrippa*, who lived in *Judæa*, which can no ways agree with the Son of *Julia*. Besides that, according to *Noldius*'s Observation (27), no one ever said, that *Agrippa*, and his unchaste Sister *Julia*, were ever accused of Incest. It is not easy to reprove the Scholiast on the other Point, because the repeating of the Word *dedit* made some learned Men believe, that the Poet supposes here two Persons, who gave each a Diamond of great Value to his Sister; I. A King of *Egypt*. II. An *Agrippa*. This Explication is not good. The whole must relate to *Agrippa*, King of the *Jews*, and to his Sister *Berenice*: And we learn a Particular here, which *Josephus* did not touch upon; namely, that *Berenice* received a Diamond of great Value from her Brother, and that she wore it, which caused their incestuous Love to make the greater Noise. *Baronius* thought, that *Juvenal* alluded to a precious Stone, mentioned by *Pliny*, which *Ptolomy*, King of *Egypt*, gave to his Wife, who was also his Mother, as *Baronius* pretends. *Alluderse videtur pretioso lapidi, quem prius dedit Ptolomæus Ægypti Rex uxori simul & matri. Verum Plinius tradit fuisse topazion* (28). A modern Author, whom I have already quoted several times (29), finds many Faults in This Opinion of the Annalist. I. *Juvenal* speaks of a Diamond, enchased, or set in a Ring; but the precious Stone, mentioned by *Pliny*, was a rough Topaz, which was afterwards made into a Statue. II. It was not *Ptolomy*, who gave This Topaz to his Mother; but it was *Polemon*, Governor of the Island, wherere the Topaz was found, who gave it to *Berenice*, Mother of the King, that succeeded Him, who then reigned. III. *Pliny* does not say, that *Ptolomy Philadelphus* made a Present of This Stone to his Wife *Arsinoë*, who was also his Sister; he says only, that they made a Statue of *Arsinoë*, the Wife of *Ptolomy Philadelphus*, of That Stone, and that This Statue was four Cubits high, and that it was consecrated in a Temple, which was called *The Golden Temple*. We may add a fourth Censure; which is, That we do not find, that any King of *Egypt* married his own Mother, and that This agrees less with the Father of *Ptolomy Philadelphus*, than with any other. It is of his Wife, that *Pliny* speaks, when he says, that the Topaz in question was brought to Queen *Berenice*. I am much less surprized at these Faults of *Baronius*, than to find Father *Harduin* of Opinion, that *Juvenal*'s Words are to be understood of the Diamond of the same *Berenice*, mentioned by *Pliny*, the Wife of *Ptolomy Lagus*, and Mother of *Ptolomy Philadelphus* (30). The *Juvenal Variorum* contains many Mistakes in relation to *Berenice*. There is in it a Note, which says, that the *Berenice*, mentioned by That Poet, was Queen of *Judæa*, and *Herod*'s Wife; that, according to others, he meant *Berenice*, *Herod*'s Wife, and, after her Husband's Death, Mistress to her Brother *Agrippa*, that is, to *Agrippa*, her Husband's Brother. This is all wrong; for, in the first Place, here are two different *Herods*, which they have not taken care to distinguish by any Mark whatever. One of them must be He, who slew the Children of *Bethlehem*; the other must be the King of *Chalcis*, Brother of *Agrippa*, the first of That Name. Now, the first of the two *Herods* had no Wife, whose Name was *Berenice*; and there was no *Berenice*, Queen of *Judæa*. Neither was there any *Berenice* in *Judæa*, whose Incest consisted in the Love of her Brother-in-law. The Incest, mentioned by *Josephus*, and *Juvenal*, consists in the Amours of *Agrippa*, the second of That Name, with his own Sister *Berenice*. That, which deceived the Author of the Annotation, is, that *Berenice* was the Widow of *Herod*, King of *Chalcis*, and Brother of an *Agrippa*, when her Love for *Agrippa* was spoken of: But the *Agrippa*, of whose Brother she was Widow, was not He, with whom she committed Incest. She was Daughter of That other *Agrippa*, and Sister to This. There is another Remark in the *Juvenal Variorum*, the Author of which calls himself *Lubin*. This *Lubin* makes use of a pleasant manner of arguing. After having said, that *Herod Agrippa* was *Berenice*'s Brother, he proves, that the Love of That *Agrippa* for *Berenice* was Incest, because she had been married to her Uncle *Herod*. *Herodes Agrippa dedit incestæ suæ sorori Berenice, cum qua incestum commiserat,* ὑπότε *quæ ante nupta erat patruo suo Herodi. N:ldius*, who observed two Faults in This *Variorum*, and who placed them to the Account of *Schrevelius*, the Compiler of That Commentary (31), took no notice of This.

[H] *I shall remark some Errors of* Moreri.] The first *Berenice*, of whom he speaks, is the Mother of *Ptolomy Philadelphus*, King of *Egypt*. What he says of her is not to be found in the Author, whom he quotes (32). The second is the Daughter of *Ptolomy Philadelphus*, and Wife of *Ptolomy Evergetes*: He quotes *Ælian*, and *Justin*, who do not say what he relates. He should have quoted *Hyginus* (33), who mentions what relates to this Queen's Head of Hair. As for the Temple of *Berenice the Guardian*, I confess, I cannot discover the Source of it, and, therefore, I dare not affirm, that *Moreri* has advanced a Falshood. I have many suspicions about it. He should have remembered, that he had said, in the Article of ARSINOE *the Daughter of Antiochus Soter*, that *Berenice*, the Wife of *Ptolomy Evergetes*, was the Daughter of *Magas* King of *Cyrene* (34), and Brother of *Ptolomy Philadelphus*, and, consequently, Uncle of *Ptolomy Evergetes*. At that time, *Berenice*, the Wife of *Ptolomy Evergetes*, was but his first Cousin; at present, she is his own Sister. Every one sees how much such Variations confound the Readers, and are sufficient to make them weary of the Study of a Dictionary. Such a Chaos should be cleared, by observing, who They are, that relate things one way, and who Those, that relate them another way. The third *Berenice*, according to *Moreri*, is Sister to the second, and Wife of *Antiochus Soter*, King of *Syria*. He should have said *Antiochus Theus*, and not *Antiochus Soter*; the former was the Son of the latter, and was married to a Daughter of *Ptolomy Philadelphus*, whose Name was *Berenice* (35). The fourth is the Daughter of *Ptolomy Auletes*. I have made an Article about her; see the Remarks of it. The fifth is *Berenice* the Sister of *Agrippa* II of That Name. What *Moreri* says, that This Princess was *with her Brother Agrippa in the Year 55, when St Paul pleaded his Cause in their Presence, and in That of the Proconsuls* Felix *and* Pontius (36) Festus, supposes

BERGAMO. 769

supposes that Those two *Proconsuls* commanded in *Judæa* at the same time, which is false (37). He ought not to have quoted *Strabo*; for what He says relates to another *Berenice*, whom *Moreri* forget, viz. the Grandmother of *Titus*'s Mistress.

[*1*] - - - - - *Of* Hofman, Charles Stephens, &c.] I. *Hofman*'s first Mistake consists in affirming, that the *Berenice*, mentioned by *Juvenal*, was the Daughter of *Herod* the *Ascalonite* (38), and Wife of her Brother *Agrippa*. This is, at least, a double, or tripple, Mistake; for That *Herod* had no Daughter, whose Name was *Berenice*, nor a Son, whose Name was *Agrippa*: She, whom *Juvenal* speaks of, was Daughter of the first *Agrippa*, and was never married to her Brother *Agrippa*, the second of That Name; it was only believed, that She had an incestuous Commerce with him. St *Chrysostom* was mistaken, or spoke figuratively, when he called her the Wife of *Agrippa* (39). II. It is a second Mistake to say, that the *Berenice*, whom *Titus* loved, is different from Her, whom *Juvenal* mentions. *Hofman* makes them different, since he treats of Her, who was *Titus*'s Mistress, in an Article apart. III. It is not true, that the *Berenice* of *Juvenal* made a Journey to *Jerusalem*, with her Head shaved and bare-footed. *Hofman* should have said, that, in order to accomplish a Vow, she went to *Jerusalem*, where she observed the Ceremonies required in such Cases; which were, that, before any Sacrifices were offered, they put up Prayers for thirty Days, had their Heads shaved, and abstained from Wine. This is all that *Josephus* tells us concerning This Journey of *Berenice* (40). It is true, he observes, that she went bare-footed to the Governor's Audience; but this cannot be said to be a Journey to *Jerusalem*. IV. What signifies it to quote the Twenty fifth Chapter of the *Acts*, and the sixteenth Book of *Strabo*, immediately after having said, that *Berenice* went to *Jerusalem*, with her Head shaved, and bare-footed? Is This mentioned in the Book of the *Acts*? And does not *Strabo* speak of a *Berenice*, who was the Grand-mother of This: LLOYD has committed the first and third Fault of *Hofman*; and it is from

Him, that the latter transcribed them. CHARLES STEPHENS falsifies *Pliny*'s Testimony; He makes him say, That *Ptolomy Philadelphus* built a fine Town on the Red-Sea, and called it *Berenice*, after his Mother's Name. *Pliny* says only, that That Town bore the Name of *Ptolomy Philadelphus*'s Mother. *Berenice, Oppidum matris Philadelphi nomine* (41). This puts me in mind of a Fault of *Hofman*, which I had omitted: He makes *Pliny* say, that That *Berenice* gave her Name to a City, which She caused to be built. Thus much concerning the first Fault of *Charles Stephens*. The second is his having said, that there was a *Berenice*, the Daughter of *Herod* the *Ascalonite*, who married her Brother *Agrippa*. We have already found This Fault in *Lloyd*, and *Hofman*; *Lloyd* took it from *Charles Stephens*. Some one will tell me perhaps; " you misunderstand these Words;
" *Berenice, Herodis Ascalonitæ filia, quæ nupsit*
" *etiam Agrippæ fratri* (42). You explain them, as
" if the Meaning of them were, that *Berenice* mar-
" ried her own Brother; but they must be under-
" stood in this Sense; that she was married to *Agrip-*
" *pa*'s Brother, which is the Sense of *Lloyd* and *Hof-*
" *man*'s Words. *Berenice Herodis Ascalonitæ filia,*
" *Agrippæ fratris uxor.*" I answer, That I explain the *Latin* Words of these three Authors in the most natural Sense; and that, since the two latter confirm the Words alledged; by the Authority of *Juvenal*, they meant, without doubt, that *Agrippa* was the Husband, and not the Husband's Brother. I can, at least, convict them of a Falsity: They suppose, that *Berenice*, the Wife of *Agrippa*'s Brother, was the Daughter of *Herod* the *Ascalonite*: This is false; she was the Daughter of *Agrippa*, the first of That Name, who married her to his Brother *Herod*, King of *Chalcis*. The third Fault is, his quoting *Strabo* for the pretended Daughter of *Herod* the *Ascalonite*; whereby it appears, that *Charles Stephens* knew not, that *Strabo* speaks only of the Daughter of *Salome*. That Daughter makes a separate Article in his Dictionary: which shews, that he did not take the one for the other, but that he fancied to himself two distinct Persons; which might pass for a fourth Mistake.

BERGAMO (JAMES PHILIP de), an *Augustin* Monk, was born at *Bergamo*, in the Year 1434. He composed, in *Latin*, a *Chronicle* from the Creation of the World, down to the Year 1503 [*A*], and a Treatise of *Illustrious Women*. He was of a very considerable Family [*B*], and became a Monk in the Year 1451 [*C*]. He had a particular Devotion for *Nicolas Tollentin*, by whose Intercession he believed himself to have been cured of the Plague, in 1474 (*a*). He died at *Bergamo*, in the Year 1518, in the Monastery of his Order, of which he had been Prior, and had repaired it at a very great Expence (*b*). Consult *Moreri*'s Dictionary, under the Word FORESTA. What you meet with faulty, there, may be corrected by comparing it with This Article.

[*A*] *He composed, in Latin, A Chronicle from the Creation of the World down to the Year* 1503.] *Vossius* observes, that the first Edition is of *Brescia*, and that it ends at the Year 1485, and not 1436, as *Possevin* affirms (1). *Bellarmin* has committed the same Mistake (2). The second Edition is of *Venice*, and comes down to the Year 1503. *Vossius* says, that the Author remarks, at the end of the Book, that he was then Sixty nine Years of Age. This Work was re-printed at *Paris*, in the Year 1535, with a *Continuation* down to That Time. It was translated into *Italian*, and published, at *Venice*, in the Year 1540, in Folio. This Edition contains *Additions* to the Work of the first Compiler, down to the Year 1539. The Author of these Additions was one *Bernardino Bindoni*, of *Milan*. I am of Opinion, that *Philip* of *Bergamo* continued the Work after the Year 1503, and that Part of what follows was His; but This *Italian* Version does not distinguish the Additions, which came from another Hand. I have not found, at the end of the Year 1503, that the Author gives us the Account of his Age, as related by *Vossius*.
This Chronicle is tolerably good, especially as to the Times, near which the Author lived. He has taken care to distinguish the Famous Men, who lived in each Century, and he gives us some Particulars relating to the Moderns, which are curious enough. *Gesner*, in 1544, knew no Edition of This Book (3).
[*B*] *He was of a very considerable Family*] It was That of the *Foresti*. *Matthew de Bergamo*, who was of this noble Family, and a very learned Civilian, obtained, of the Emperor *Lewis* of *Bavaria*, very great Privileges, both for himself, and his Posterity. He was created a Count *Palatin*, with the Right of instituting Notaries, Doctors, Knights, and Judges, in every part of *Italy*, and of legitimating Bastards, &c. A List of all these Privileges is to be met with in Our Author's Chronicle (4). They have been confirmed by all the Lords, who have been in Possession of *Bergamo*. The Letters Patents of this Grant of *Lewis* of *Bavaria* were dated at *Trent*, the twentieth of *January*, 1330 (5).
[*C*] *He became a Monk, in the Year* 1451.] He affirms, somewhere in his Chronicle, according to *Vossius*, that *John Rochus* admitted him into his Convent, with some other young Persons, in the Year 1451; but I find, in the *Italian* Version of This Chronicle, that it was *John* of *Novara*, Superior of the *Augustins* of *Bergamo*, who associated him to his Order, the first of *May*, 1451. He had been speaking of *John Rochus*, Reformer of the *Augustins*, and their General, who died at *Mantua*, in the Year 1461, aged seventy Years. Immediately after, he speaks of *John* of *Novara*, who had strongly seconded *John Rochus* in the Work of Reforming the Order, and who succeeded him in the Dignity of Prior of the Convent of *Crema*, in consequence of which he was promoted to the same Office in the Convent of *Bergamo*. They, who have the *Latin* Edition, which *Vossius* made use of, may examine whether he is mistaken. The *Italian*, which I consult, was made from the Edition of *Paris*, corrected from many Errors.

[*A*] *I shall*

BERGIER. BERIGARDUS.

BERGIER (NICOLAS), was born at *Reims*, in the Year 1557. He studied there in the new University, which the Cardinal of *Lorrain* had lately established, and was also a Teacher in it for some Years. From the College he went to the Count *de Saint Soupplet*, Great Bailiff of the Province, to be Tutor to his Children, and, afterwards, embraced the Profession of an Advocate, in which he had very good Success. The Inhabitants of the City of *Reims*, who knew his Merit and Capacity, made him their Syndic, and deputed him often to *Paris*, upon the Affairs of the City. This brought him acquainted with several learned Men, and, amongst others, with Mess. *Peiresc*, and *Du Puy*, to whom he communicated the Design of his Book of the *High-Ways of the Roman Empire*, and who encouraged him greatly to put it in Execution. For this End, Mr *Peiresc* communicated to him the Map of *Peutinger* (*a*). But of all the Friends, and Patrons, which his good Qualities procured him, the chief, and most famous, was *Nicolas de Bellievre*, President *a Mortier*, in the Parliament of *Paris* ; who procured him a Brief of the Crown, constituting him Historiographer, with a Pension of Two hundred Crowns, and entertained him at his House, where he spent the Remainder of his Life. He died the fifteenth of *September*, 1623, in the Castle of *Grignon*, belonging to Monf. *de Bellievre*. The Epitaph, which That illustrious President made to the Memory of his Friend, is to be found at the beginning of *The History of Reims*, printed in 1629 (*b*). I shall speak, below, of *Bergier*'s Works [*A*]. See also, at the end of this Dictionary, the Dissertation *on the Day*, Remark [*B*].

(*a*) *See Caffendus, in the Life of Peiresc.*

(*b*) *A Memoir, communicated by Mr Ouinet, Keeper of the Cabinet of Medals of Lewis XIV. I give it as I received it.*

[*A*] *I shall speak of Bergier's Works.*] Besides the *History of the High-ways of the Roman Empire*, he composed also *le bouquet Royal*, which is a Relation of the Coronation of *Lewis* XIII, printed at *Reims*, in the Year 1637 ; A Treatise of *Day-break*, printed at *Reims*, in the Year 1629, and which had been printed at *Paris*, in the Year 1617, under the Title of *Archemeron* (1); *Le dessein de l' Histoire de Reims*, printed in 1637. He wrote the Life of St *Albert*, with the History of the Translation of his Body from *Reims* to *Brussels*, in the Year 1612, at the Request of the Archduke *Albert*. He received a Chain of Gold as a Reward, sent him by that Prince ; but the Work was not printed ; and the Manuscript is in the Hands of the Author's Heirs, with some other Papers, written with his own Hand, concerning *the Excellency of Learning ; and the Antiquity and Excellency of Poetry, and Speculative Music* (2).

(2) *Consult my Dissertation on the Day, at the end of the last Volume, and chiefly in Remark [B].*

(3) *Taken from a Memoir, communicated by Mr Ouinet.*

BERIGARDUS (CLAUDIUS), one of the most subtile Philosophers of the XVIIth Century, was of *Moulins*. He acquired such a Reputation in the University of *Paris*, that the Great Duke of *Florence* drew him to That of *Pisa* (*a*). He taught Philosophy, there, twelve Years (*b*) ; after which, he was invited to *Padua*, for the same Profession. He was discharging it honourably, when, in 1643, he published a Book at *Udina*, which greatly displeased several Divines [*A*], though it was approved by the Holy Office. He had published another at *Florence*, in the Year 1632 (*c*). His Cut, prefixed to the Book, printed in the Year 1643, makes him Fifty one Years of Age ; but the Year of the Century is not marked.

(*a*) *See the Preface to his Circulus Pisanus, in lib. 8. Physicor. Aristot.*

(*b*) *See his first Epistle dedicatory.*

(*c*) *Intituled, Dubitationes, Galileae, Lyncei.*

[*A*] *He published a Book —— which greatly displeased several Divines*] The Title of it is *Circulus Pisanus*. See, here, the Judgment, which an Archdeacon of *Canterbury* passed on it. " Hunc (Cæsalpinum) eâdem impietatis viâ & ratione non modò secutus est, sed superavit, Claudius Berigardus Molinensis, qui unà cum impiâ Aristotelis disciplinâ obsoletam illam quoque veterum Ionicorum (quemadmodum de iis ipse censuit ac alii plerique censuerunt) revocavit ; cùm enim disputationes suas dialogorum consuetudine perscripsit, sermonem in duas personas Charilaum & Aristæum distribuit, quorum alter Aristotelem, qui præter materiam, quendam primum motorem, providentiæ tamen expertem, posuit, alter antiquos istos defendit, quos omnia corporea esse velle, nullumque primum motorem ab universo corporeo distinxisse putavit. Atque adeo uno eodémque opere diversas cùm Epicureæ tum Peripateticæ impietatis rationes adornavit, quanquam Aristotelis disciplinam fusiùs & ardentiùs excoluit, atque eam potissimum quàm libro Physicor im octavo, librisque de Coelo & rerum Generatione, tradidit, quibus universam mundi fabricam sine Providentiâ architectrice extruxisse se putat Philosophus. Neque nefaria sua dogmata dispersè uno aut altero capite (ut Cæsalpinus) insinuavit, sed apertè omnem Peripateticæ impietatis rationem secutus est, neque nimis providentiam ut ille ë rerum naturâ tollere satis habuit, nisi & falsè dictis (qualia vir non admodum facetus potuit) increparet (1). —— Hunc autem sicut & Cæsalpinum, quanquam multò uteriùs rem tractavit, & quidem integrum peripateticæ impietatis systema descripsit, hoc loco redarguere operæ pretium non existimo, quòd in uno Aristotele vincantur qui ab eo steterunt omnes (2). —— *He* (Cæsalpinus) *was not only followed but surpassed, in this Way and Method of Impiety*, by Claudius Berigardus *of Moulins ; who, together with the blasphemous Doctrine of Aristotle, revived That of the ancient Ionians, obsolete both in his own, and the Opinion of Others : for, writing his Disputations in the Way of Dialogue, he divides the Discourse between two Persons, Charilaus and Aristippus ; of whom the One defends Aristotle, who, besides Matter, supposed a certain First Mover, but denied a Providence, the Other vindicates those ancient Philosophers, who, he supposed, would have every thing to be corporeal, and to have made no distinction between the first Mover, and the Corporeal Universe. And thus, in one and the same Work, has he displayed the different Arguments both of the Aristotelean and Peripatetic Impiety, though he more largely and zealously cultivated the Doctrines of Aristotle, That in particular, which he has delivered in the Eighth Book of his Physics, and his Book, de Coelo & Rerum Generatione, in which the Philosopher pretends to have raised the Fabric of the Universe without an Architectal Providence. Nor has he insinuated his wicked Tenets in One or Two Chapters (as Cæsalpinus has done) but has openly espoused the whole Peripatetic Impiety ; nor was he satisfied, like him, with destroying a Providence, but (which requires no very great Degree of Wit) must ridicule and laugh at the Notion. ----- But it is not worth my while, at present, to confute this Author, any more than Cæsalpinus, though he has handled the Subject much more copiously, and indeed delineated a complete System of Peripatetic Impiety, because, in Aristotle alone, All his Followers stand condemned.*" Mr *de Villenandy*, a French Minister (3), passes the same Judgment ; for he looks upon *Berigardus* as a great Favourer of *Pyrrhonism*, and a Propagator of Impiety : " Vestigiis ejus (Pomponatii) institit Berigardus *in Circulis Pisanis* sub sæculi hujus initium. Quanta ab his, nonnullisque alia ejusdem ordinis doctoribus, malorum seges in scientiis,

(1) *Samuel Parker, Disput. de Deo, &c. pag. 6*.

(2) *Ib. ibid. pag. 68.*

(3) *He was Professor of Philosophy at Saumur, at the Revocation of the Edict of Nantes, and has been since Rector of the Walloon College at Leyden.*

BERYTUS. 771

(a) Petrus de Villemandy, in Scepticismo debellato, pag. 11.

"scientiis, societate civili, & religione luxuriarit, nonunt eruditi (4). —— Berigardus in his Circuli Pisani tried in His (Pomponatius's) Steps, about the beginning of this Century. The Learned know what a plentiful Crop of Evils has sprung up, by means of these and the like Teachers, in The Sciences, in Civil Society, and in Religion." He explains himself more fully in another place. "Ipsorum quidem dubitationes, contendendique pruritus, eò usque non evagantur, ut vel Divinam Providentiam, vel etiam Existentiam, aperte summoveant: ita tamen procedunt eorum nonnulli, ut summovere velle videantur: utcunque fit, suspecta est admodum eorum religio ac fides. Cum, ex. g. Claudius Berigardus, in Circulis suis Pisanis, res omnes Physicas, imo & Divinas plerasque, ex principiis Aristotelia ita declarat & astruit, ut easdem illas ex oppositis Anaximandri hypothesibus, purum atheismum redolentibus, continuò impugnet ac subvertat; an quicquam in rebus Physicis stabile & immotum relinquit? Nonne contrà perpetuâ suâ illâ libratione cunctas suspendit? Deinde quò tendit assumpta hæc Anaximandri hypothesis, quam Berigardus Aristotelicæ longè præfert, nisi eò ut in Supremi Numinis ejusque Providentiæ locum infinitam quandam materiam, infinitis corporibus dissimilaribus, ex seipsis mobilibus, conflatam, hoc est, in Veri Dei locum

(5) Id. ibid. pag. 23, 25.

" Cæcam Naturam substituat (5)? —— Their Scepticism, and Itch of Disputation, do not run such lengths, as openly to set aside the Providence, or Existence, of Gods; yet some of them proceed so far, that they seem inclined to deny both: be it as it will, there is great reason to suspect their Religion and their Faith. For instance, when Claudius Berigardus, in his Circuli Pisani, so lays down and establishes all Physical Effects, and even many Divine, upon Aristotle's Principles, as immediately to attack, and overthrow, them by the Opposite Hypotheses of Anaximander, which favour of downright

"Atheism, can he be said to have left any thing certain, and that may be depended upon, in Natural Philosophy? On the contrary, does he not bring every thing into doubt by his continual Wavering? Lastly, whither tends this Hypothesis of Anaximander, which Berigardus has assumed, and prefers to That of Aristotle, but to substitute an infinite Matter, composed of infinite dissimilar, self-moving, Corpuscles, in the Room of a Supream Deity, and his Providence; that is, Blind Nature in the Room of the True God?" He quotes him, page 100, as having said a Thing, which is full of Libertinism; but it is worth remarking, that the Words, which he ascribes to him, and which are printed in Italics, are not to be found in his Work. These are his Words. "Ex iis duci quidem notionem Virtutis cujuidam, quæ omnia dispouerit, ac sapientissime regat, sed hanc nihil aliud esse, quam Universi totius corporei vigorem, ab ipso solâ ratione distinctum. cujus Universi singulæ partes, divinitatis participes, se ipsis misceantur ad omnia componenda, nullo alio Intellectu ordinante, quam sua ipsorum energia, perinde ad finem optimum tendente ac si ab aliqua mente dirigerentur (6). —— Hance we reduce the Notion of a certain Virtue, which disposed, and most wisely governs, all things; but that This Virtue is nothing else but the Energy of the whole corporeal Universe, and is distinct from it only in the Order of our Ideas; that All things are formed by the Intermixture of the several Parts of This Universe, each partaking of Divinity, and ranged in order by no other Intellect, than their own Energy, tending as surely to the best end, as if directed by any Mind whatever." Mr de Villemandy should, therefore, have told his Readers, that he did not quote the Text of Berigardus, but the Paraphrase of his Thought. I have quoted That Author, in the Article RUFINUS, Remark [C].

(6) Villemandy, ubi supra, pag. 100. He quotes Berigard. Circulor. Pisanor. Parte II. Circulo 19.

(a) Stephan. Byzant. in voce Βηρυτός.

(b) See Berkelius, in Steph. Byzantino, voce Βηρυτός.

(1) Nam, & Beroeam appellatam esse auctor est Eusebius in Chron. Harduin. in Plin. lib. v. cap. 20. pag. 524.

(2) Guil. Grotius de viris Jurisconsf. lib. II, cap. 6. pag. 144.

(3) Scalig. Animad. in Euseb. n. 1733. pag. 130.

(4) Menagius, Jur. Civil. Amœnit. cap. xxiv. pag. 132.

(5) It is in the first Title of the fourth Book.

(6) Bertrand de vitis Jurisconf. p. 4.

(7) Mr Menage, and Will. Grotius, as cited above, consute him.

(8) Justinian. Præfat. in Digesta de juris docendi ratione.

(9) That is, Rome, and Constantinople.

BERYTUS, a maritime Town of Phœnicia, near Mount Libanus, was also called Beroë [A]. It was said, that Saturn built it (a). It had a good Harbour, the Description whereof is to be found in the Itinerary of John Phocas (b). Strabo says, that it was ruined by Trypho, and rebuilt by the Romans (c). It was Augustus, who rebuilt it (d), and made a Colony of it, which was called Julia Felix (e), and enjoyed the Jus Italicum (f). Agrippa led two Legions thither (g). It was one of the three Cities, in which the Civil-Law was publickly taught [B]; The other two were Rome, and Constantinople. There is some reason to believe, that there were more Professors in Berytus, than in either of the other two [C]. The Conflagrations, Inundations, and Earthquakes, which ruined it several Times, did not hinder the Law-Schools from

(c) Strabo, lib. xvi. pag. 520.

(d) Euseb. in Chron. n. 2103.

(e) Plinius, lib. v. cap. 20. p. 574.

(f) Ulpianus de Censibus apud Scalig. Animadv. n. 1003, pag. 171.

(g) Strabo, ubi supra.

[A] It was also called Beroë.] Neither the Testimony of Eusebius, alledged by Father Harduin (1), nor That of Stephanus Byzantinus, alledged by William Grotius (2), serve me for a Proof; for I have not found, that Eusebius, or Stephanus Byzantinus, say so. My Proofs are Those, which Scaliger found in the Epigrams of John Barbucallus, on the burning of Berytus, and in the Forty first Book of the Dionysiaca of Nonnus (3), and Those, which Mr Menage discovered in the third Book of the same Dionysiaca (4), and in an Epigram of the Anthologia (5), where Bertrand (6) would, without Reason, have changed the Word Βηρόη into That of Βηρυτός (7).

[B] It was one of the three Cities, in which the Civil-Law was publickly taught.] In all the Roman Empire, there were but these three Cities, which were permitted to have Schools of Law. This is surprizing, when we consider the Extent of That Empire; and more surprizing still, when we think of the many Universities, which are at present in Europe. What a Change of Customs? The seven United-Provinces, which are but a Point in the Map, in comparison of the Roman Monarchy, have twice or thrice as many Schools of Civil-Law, as there were in That vast State. Let us prove what ought to be proved: " Hæc autem tria volumina (they are Justinian's " Words) (8) à nobis composita tradi eis tam in regiis " urbibus (9), quàm in Berytiensium pulcherrima civitate (quam & legum nutricem benè quis appellet) " tantummodo voluimus: quod jam & à retro principibus constitutum est, & non in aliis locis, quæ à " Majoribus tale non meruerint privilegium. —— We " will, that these Three Volumes, composed by us, be

" delivered only to Those of the Royal Cities (Rome " and Constantinople) and the flourishing City of " Berytus, which may deservedly be called The Nursery of The Law: it having been so constituted and " appointed by Our Predecessors, and no other Places " having deserved to enjoy such a Privilege." These Words inform us, that the Predecessors of Justinian fixed the number of the Schools of Civil-Law to Three; but it is not known, at what time This was done. The first, who, in Mr Menage's Opinion (10), has mentioned the School of Berytus, is Gregory Thaumaturgus (11), who lived under Alexander Severus. The Ecclesiastical History of Eusebius makes mention of a young Martyr, who suffered death under the Reign of Maximian, and who had studied at Berytus (12). That School was, then, very flourishing (13). It was no less so, when Zachary of Mitylene wrote against Ammonius: He calls Berytus μητέρα τῶν νόμων, parentem legum. He flourished in the VIth Century. His Treatise is in the eleventh Volume of the Bibliotheca Patrum, in the Edition of Paris, 1644.

(10) Menag. Amœnit. Juridic. p. 133.

(11) In Orationes Paneqyrica, ad Origenem.

(12) Eusebius de Martyrib. Palæstinæ, cap. 4. pag. 323.

(13) See Bertrand in Vitis Juriscap. 5, who quotes lib I, C. qui ætate excus.

[C] There were more Professors in Berytus, than in either of the other two.] The Title Se studiis liberalibus urbis Romæ & Constantinopolitanæ, in the Theodosian Code, and in That of Justinian, informs us, that there were but two Professors of Law at Rome, and two at Constantinople. Now, as Justinian addresses the Constitution, de juris docendi ratione, to eight Professors of Law, we must conclude, that there were four of them in the School of Berytus. See Mr Menage (14).

(14) Menag. ubi supra.

VOL. I. N°. XXV. 9 I [D] The

from being set up there again [D]. The Metropolitan Dignity, which *Theodosius* the Younger granted to the Bishops of *Berytus*, was only titular [E].

[D] *The Conflagrations*, &c. *did not hinder the Law Schools from being set up there again.*] For proof of this, I will give you the following Words of *Francis Balduin*. " Berytum Syriæ " urbem fuisse nutricem legum Ro. alt. nostr. " Just. ut & Jurisprudentiæ Eunapius vocat, & " ante utrumque Nonnus multo magis. Quid igi- " tur? Tempore Constantii terræ motu convulsam " fuisse ait Cedrenus. Sed fuisse restitutam & tempore " Justiniani nostri floruisse constat. Cum vero Justi- " nianus jam illi suos juris civilis libros explicandos " tradidisset, ecce horribiliori terræ motu cum audi- " toribus & doctoribus absorpta est. Testis est Aga- " thias. Sed idem testis est eo casu minime deterri- " tum Justinianum fuisse quominus illam instauraret. " Ergo rursus instauratam esse quo magis semper ex- " taret sedes jurisprudentiæ. Mirum vero, ecce " paulo post inundationem & incendio iterum vastatam " esse lego. Nam id testatur vetus liber Græcorum " Epigrammatum. Necdum tamen cessarunt talibus " tempestatibus quá afflictæ jurisprudentiæ opem ferre " debuerunt (15). ——— Berytus, *a City of Syria, was* " *called, by* Justinian, *the Nursery of the Roman* " *Law*; *by* Eunapius, *the Mother of the Civil-Law*; *and by* Nonnus, *before them both, much more.* " *What then?* Cedrenus *tells us, it was thrown down* " *by an Earthquake in the Time of* Constantius. *But* " *we know, that it was rebuilt, and that it was in a* " *flourishing Condition in the Reign of our* Justinian. " *But no sooner had* Justinian *delivered to it his Books* " *of Civil-Law, to be explained, but it was swal-* " *lowed up, together with it's Auditors and Doctors,* " *by a more dreadful Earthquake.* Agathias *testifies* " *This. But the same Author informs us, that* Justi- " *nian was not in the least deterred by this Accident* " *from rebuilding it. It was therefore restored, that* " *it might for ever be The Seat of Law. Yet, strange* " *to relate! I read, that it was, very soon after,* " *destroyed by an Inundation, and Conflagration. This*

" *is testified by an old Book of* Greek *Epigrams. Yet* " *these great Calamities did not prevent Those, whose* " *Duty it was, from succouring the Distressed Law.* [E] *The Metropolitan Dignity* ——— *if it's Bishop was only titular.*] *Theodosius* the Younger, being imposed upon by *Eustathius*, Bishop of *Berytus*, made this Decree (16). " Propter multas justaique causas " Metropolitano nomine & dignitate civitatem Bery- " tum decernimus exornandam, jam suis virtutibus " coronatam. Igitur hæc quoque Metropolitanam " habeat dignitatem, Tyro nihil de suo jure deroge- " tur. Sit illa mater Provinciæ majorum nostrorum " beneficio; hæc nostro. ——— *Many and just Reasons* " *moving us thereto, we decree, that the City of* " Berytus, *already crowned with it's Virtues, be* " *adorned with the Metropolitan Title and Dignity,* " *saving to* Tyre *it's full Rights and Privileges. Be* " *She the Mother of the Province, by the Favour of* " *our Predecessors; This by Our Own.*" The Emperor declares, that he will not lessen the Rights of the Metropolis of *Tyre* in any manner whatever: He did not pretend, then, that the Bishop of *Berytus* struck at any of Those Rights. Nevertheless, *Eustathius*, spurred by Ambition, usurped Authority over many Churches, which depended on the Metropolis of *Tyre*. Complaints were made of it to the Council of *Chalcedon*, who restrained him within his Bounds; and the Privilege, which *Theodosius* had granted him, was like That, which *Marcian* afterwards granted to the City of *Chalcedon*. " Chalcedonensem civitatem, in qua sanctæ " fidei concilium gestum est, Metropolis privilegia " habere sancimus, nomine tantum, salva videlicet " Nicomediensium civitati propria dignitate. ——— " *We decree, that* Chalcedon, *where was held a Coun-* " *cil of the Holy Faith, shall enjoy the Privileges of* " *a Metropolis, in Name only, that is saving the* " *just Dignity of the City of* Nicomedia." Consult Father *Noris* (17).

(15) Francifcus Balduinus, ad L. fi pact. C. de part. sub fin.

(16) It is in the 11th Book of the Code of Justinian. Tit. xxi.

(17) Noris de anno & epochis Syro Mace-donum Differt. 4. cap. 3. p. 40., 401. Edit. Lipf. 1696.

St BERNARD, Abbot of *Clairvaux*, flourished in the XIIth Century. He acquired so great an Esteem, that the whole Weight of the Church seemed to lie on his Shoulders, and that Kings and Princes made choice of him for the general Arbitrator of their Differences [A]. It is certain, that he had very great Talents, and a great deal of Zeal; but some pretend, that his Zeal made him too jealous of Those, who acquired a great Name by the Study of Human Learning; and they add, that his mild and easy Temper rendered him too credulous, when he heard any ill Report of Those learned Persons. They believe, that, by reason of these Principles, he suffered himself to be too much prejudiced against *Abelard* [B]. It is difficult to imagine, that he was free from human Passions, when he made it his whole Business to procure Anathemas against all Those, who appeared to him to be Heterodox: But it is very easy to conceive, that his great Reputation, and the Ardour, with which he sollicited the Condemnation of his Adversaries, imposed upon the Judges, and made the accused Persons sink under the Weight of Those irregular Proceedings. However it be, he verified the Interpretation

[*A*] *He acquired so great an Esteem, that* ——— *Princes made choice of him for the general Arbitrator of their Differences.*] It will not be improper, upon this Occasion, to hear *Francis d'Amboise*: thus he expresses himself. " Plus favoris in " humilitate adeptus, quam Salomon in omni gloria " sua, ita omnes in sui admirationem ——— ad fa- " mam sui nominis, ad sui amorem & observantiam, " rapuit, ut ad eum totius Orbis Vota concurrerent, " ut ab ejus monitis & exemplis tota res monastica " & ecclesiastica penderet visa sit, ut ab ejus oraculis " Præsules, Principes, Populi, consilium expeterent, " eumque induciarum ac pacis arbitrum agnoscerent, " & se ejus orationibus omnes Ordines cupiverint " esse commendari (1). ——— *Having gained more* " *Favour in his Humility, than* Solomon *in all his* " *Glory, he was so generally admired and beloved,* " *that he had the good Wishes of the whole World,* " *that Monastic and Ecclesiastical Affairs seemed* " *wholly to depend on his Precepts and Example; that* " *he was consulted as an Oracle by high and low,* " *and acknowledged as the Arbiter both of Truces* " *and of Peace, and that all Orders of Men desired* " *to be recommended to his Prayers.*

[*B*] *His Zeal made him jealous* ——— *and his easy Temper made him credulous* ——— *with regard to learned Men, and particularly* Abelard.] I have quoted a long Passage of *Francis d'Amboise*, in the preceding Remark: here is another still longer. " Pace " igitur Sancti Abbatis liceat dicere quod de eo au- " sus est Annalibus mandare ejus discipulus, Clarævallensis quondam Monachus, demum Abbas Morimontanus, Otho, Episcopus, Frisingensis, Leopoldi Pii Marchionis Austriæ filius, Frederici I. Ænobarbi, cujus vitam scripsit, patruus, qui quam- " vis Abbatem suum in magna habuerit veneratione, " tamen scribit eum ex Religionis Christianæ fervore " zelotypum, & ex habitudinali (sic enim loquitur) " mansuetudine quodammodo credulum, ut Magistros " qui humanis rationibus & seculari sapientiæ confi- " denter nimium inhærebant abhorreret, & de ulti- " bus sinistrum quid recitanti facile aurem præberet, " juxta illud Festi, τὰ πολλὰ γράμματα εἰς μα- " νίαν περιξρέπει. ——— fieri potuit ut sibi in ani- " mum induxerit quasdam esse dicta act scripta ab " Abælardo quæ non essent, aut quæ in pejorem " partem accipi non deberent (2)." ——— *Let* " *me, therefore, by the Holy Abbot's Leave, repeat* " *what*

(1) Fr. Ambrosius Præfat Operibus Abelardi præfixa.

(2) Ibid.

BERNARD.

tation of his Mother's Dream. She dreamed, when she was with Child of him, that she should be delivered of a white Dog, whose Barking should be very sonorous [C]. Being frighted at this Dream, she consulted an honest Monk, who said to her, *Be of good Courage; you will have a Son, who shall keep* GOD's *House, and bark much against the Enemies of the Faith* [D]. St Bernard did more, than the Prediction imported; for he barked sometimes against chimerical Enemies, against Errors, which were either meer Trifles, or unjust Interpretations of the Words and Thoughts of others (*a*): And, whether he was in the right, or in the wrong, he could give the Alarm admirably, and make the Thunder of his Triumphs resound [E]. He was more successful in exterminating the Heterodox, than in the Ruin of Infidels; and yet he attacked the latter, not only with the Force of his Eloquence, but with the extraordinary Arms, likewise, of Prophecy. By this means he increased the Troops of the *Crusade* more than can be expressed; but all the fair Promises, with which he fed them, vanished in Smoke; and, when it was complained, that he had sent a vast Number of Christians to the Slaughter, without stirring out of his Country, he came

"what has been recorded, in *Annals*, by a Disciple of
"His, formerly a Monk of Clairvaux, I mean Otho, Bi-
"shop of Frisingen, Son of Leopold the Pious, Marquis
"of Austria, and Uncle of Frederic I. Ænobarbus,
"whose Life he wrote; who, though he held his
"Abbot in great Veneration, yet writes, that he was
"blinded by a mistaken Zeal for the Christian Reli-
"gion, and, through an habitual Mildness of Temper,
"was become very credulous; insomuch, that he had
"in abhorrence Those Teachers, who too confidently
"adhered to Human Reasons, and worldly Wisdom, and
"readily believed every Thing ill, which was reported
"of such Persons; according to That of Festus, Much
"Learning hath made thee mad. *And this, perhaps,
"occasioned him to take it into his Head, that some
"things were said, or written, by Abelard, which
"were not, or which should not have been taken in
"a bad Sense."

[C] *His Mother dreamed ----- she should be delivered of a white Dog, whose Barking should be very sonorous.*] Her Mother was *Aletha*; her Husband, the Father of St *Bernard*, was called *Tesselinus*.
"Cum mater Aletha uxor Tesselini in utero gesta-
"ret, somnio vidit praesagium futuri partus, catel-
"lum scilicet se pariturum totum candidum, in
"dorso subrusum, & claré latrantem (3). ----
"*His Mother Aletha, the Wife of* Tesselinus,
"*being with Child, saw, in a Dream, a Presage
"of the future Birth; to wit, a little white Dog,
"with a reddish Back, and barking with a shrill
"Tone."

[D] *An honest Monk told her ----- she should have a Son ------ who should bark much against the Enemies of the Faith.*] I shall again quote Francis d'*Amboise*. "Cui (*Aletha*) de illo terricula-
"mento anxiae & sciscitanti respondit religiosus qui-
"dam vaticinii spiramine afflatus: optimi catuli mater
"eris, qui Domus Dei custos futurus, validos pro
"ea contra inimicos fidei edituros est latratus (4).
"---- Aletha, *greatly terrified, enquired of a cer-
"tain Monk, who, with a Spirit of Prophecy, said
"to her; you shall be the Mother of a most excel-
"lent little Dog, who shall guard the House of* GOD,
"*and bark strongly against the Enemies of the Faith.*"
He does not descend to the particular Explication of the *White* and *Red*, as others do, who say, That the Whiteness of This Dog signified, that St *Bernard* would be mild and courteous to the Friends of the House; that is, to pious Persons: And, that the Redness of the Dog signified, that he would be wild and fierce to the Impious, and Strangers; and that he would bark continually at them (5): For it is the Property of a good Dog to caress his Master's Friends and Domesticks; and to fly with great Fury at Strangers, with continual barking, and even with biting. *In peregrinos ferus & atrox eos cauda erecta continuis latratibus, imo morsibus, interdum insectetur* (6). *Francis d'Amboise*, omitting this Distinction of the two Colours, observes, that St *Bernard* confirmed the Prophecy, and spared no body. *Firmavit vaticinium nec enim ulli pepercit* (7). He fell upon *Abelard, Arnauld of Bresse, Peter de Bruys, Gilbert Porretanus*, &c. In a Word, they do not do him Justice, who call him only a Hound, or a Mastiff Dog; he may, in some sense, be compared to *Nimrod*, and stiled, *A mighty Hunter before the Lord* (8).

Give me leave to digress a little concerning the Dream of St *Bernard*'s Mother It was a lucky Thought of Him, who explained it; for, in short, can there be a better Symbol of Vigilance, than a Dog? Can there be a more natural Image of the Assaults, given to Error, as well *viva voce*, as in Writing, than the Barking of a Dog? Only we must take care not to carry the Comparison too far; since there are but too many Persons, in all Countries, and in all Ages, who, to avoid being called dumb Dogs, bark in Season, and out of Season, and bite, and tear, all who do not please them. Those Dogs, that were kept at *Rome*, to guard the Capitol, were designed to make a Noise at the approach of Robbers: And, for that Reason, it was not thought strange, that they barked in the Night, if they heard any body; for it is an unseasonable Time, which gives ground for Suspicions; and, therefore, they let them bark, whether Those, whom they heard go by, were honest Men, or Thieves: But, if these Dogs had barked, in the Day-time, at Those who came to the Temple to pay their Devotion, They would have had their Legs broken. I borrow this from an ancient *Roman*; the Application is easy to be made. "Anseribus cibaria publice locantur, & canes alun-
"tur in Capitolio ut significent si fures venerint. At
"fures internoscere non possunt, significant tamen,
"si qui noctu in Capitolium venerint: & quia id
"est suspiciosum, tametsi bestiae sunt, tamen in eam
"partem potius peccant quae est cautior. Quod si
"luce quoque canes latrent quum deos salutatum ali-
"qui venerint, opinor iis crura suffringantur, quod acres
"sint etiam tum quum suspicio nulla sit (9)." The Public maintains you to guard the Truth; make a Noise, then, against all Comers, if you have Ingenuity enough to compare yourself to a Dog, who cannot discern any Person through the Darkness of the Night. If you are in Darkness, either by reason of your Incapacity, or because Passions cloud your Judgment, and if you have the Honesty to acknowledge the Obscurity, which surrounds you, you ought to be excused; but if you pretend to the Quality of a Great Doctor, who acts only for the Glory of GOD, without any Motive of Personal Revenge; and, if, nevertheless, you involve a great Number of good Men in your Informations, your Libels, and Denunciations, you deserve to be punished; you are unworthy of your Station; you are a Dog, that falls indifferently on Friends and Foes; which must needs cause a thousand Disorders. You are one of those *English* Mastiffs, on which the Jesuit *Maimbourg* once employed one of the four Parts of his Sermon (10). Many Pamphlets, stuffed with Lamentations, and Extracts of complaining Letters, have appeared in *Holland* within these few Years, as if a very considerable Part of the Ministers, fled from *France*, had conspired to introduce the most abominable Errors, wherever they are dispersed (11). But, after all, not one guilty Person has been discovered, what Pains soever have been taken to do it. Ought such Dogs, destitute of Discernment, to go unpunished?

[E] *He could give the Alarm, admirably, and make the Thunder of his Triumphs resound.*] I only tread in the Steps of the Sieur d'*Amboise*, a very good Catholic. He observes, that St *Bernard*'s Letters, written to the Prelates of *Rome*, and to the Pope,

BERNARD. BEROALDUS.

came off with saying, that the Sins of Thofe, who had taken up the Crofs, had prevented the Effect of his Prophecies [F]. There is no Impoftor, but may fhelter himfelf behind fuch an Intrenchment. St *Bernard* was canonized: He is one of the greateft Saints in the *Romifh* Communion; and it is pretended, that he wrought a world of Miracles, both in his Life-time, and after his Death. Obferve, that he once went up to his Neck into the Water, to free himfelf from the Temptation, into which the Sight of a Woman had led him (*b*). The beft Edition that we have of his Works, is That of 1690. It is the fecond, which the learned Father *Mabillon* took care to procure. The Journalifts of *Leipfic* have fpoken very exactly of it (*c*): It is accompanied with feveral learned Prefaces. It is acknowledged, in one of them, that St *Bernard* taught, that the Souls of the Bleffed are received into Heaven, and into the Society of the Angels, as foon as they are feparated from their Bodies, but that they enjoy only the Sight of the Humanity of JESUS CHRIST, and not the Sight of GOD.

Pope, were the fitteft in the World to prejudice and exafperate, them againft *Abelard*; they mentioned nothing but Sacrileges, Lyons, and Dragons. "Le-
"gite, fi placet, librum, quem dicit, Theologiæ,
"legite & illum, quem dicunt, fententiarum, nec
"non & illum qui infcribitur, Scito te ipfum, &
"animadvertite quantæ ibi filvefcant fegetes facri-
"legiorum & errorum. ---- Leonem evafimus, fed
"incidimus in Draconem (12). ---- *Read, I befeech
"you, his Book* (as he calls it) *of Divinity*; *Read
"another* (as it is called) *of his Sentences, and
"That entituled,* Know thy felf; *and obferve how
"plentifully Sacrilege and Error fprings up in them.
"----- We have efcaped a Lion, but are fallen in-
"to the Claws of a Dragon."* He was not contented to write in his own Name, but dictated fome Letters for the Archbifhop of *Reims*, and three of his Suffragans, in which they demanded the Thunders of the Court of *Rome*; and, when they had obtained the Condemnation of the Propofitions, they had fent to the Pope, they publifhed it abroad as a compleat Victory; though, at the bottom, the Pope had pronounced nothing againft *Abelard*'s Perfon. Their Flourifhes, and the great Stir they made, prevented every where the Caufe of the Accufed from being heard. They prepoffeffed the Minds of every one. Thefe are the common Artifices of Caballers; I do not fay, that others never make ufe of them. "At
"accufatores potentiffimi, tanquam albis equis trium-
"phantes, lætum pæana cantarunt, victoriamque fuam
"toto orbe diffeminarunt; ita ut mifer Ille inaudi-
"tus apud probos quamplurimos male audiret, &
"ejus exemplaria, quæ Galliam Italiamque fplen-
"dore colluftrarant, tanquam horrendi criminis car-
"mina vel voracibus rogis cremanda traderentur,
"vel in fitu, fqualore, & cinere veterum bibliothe-
"carum latitantia putrefcerent. (13). ----- *But his
"moft powerful Accufers, triumphing as it were on
"white Horfes, fang a joyful Pæan, and fpread their
"Victory over all the World*; *infomuch, that the
"poor Wretch was condemned, unheard, by many
"good Men, and his Works, which were the Orna-
"ment of France and Italy, like blafphemous, or ob-
"fcene, Poems, were either thrown into the Fire,
"or rotted in old dufty Libraries."*

[*F*] When *he was reproached with the ill Succefs
of his Crufade, he came off with faying, that the
Sins of the Croifes has prevented the Effects of his
Prophecies.*] This is, in truth, the whole Center of his Manifefto (14); for, if he alledges the Example of *Mofes*, to fhelter himfelf under the inviolable Authority of fo great a Name, it is becaufe he pretended, that the Members of the *Crufade* were no lefs polluted with Crimes, than the Children of *Ifrael*, and that therefore both had diverted the Effects of the Promifes. See what a modern Philofopher (15) thought upon This.

BEROALDUS (MATTHEW) [*A*], born at *Paris*, taught the *Hebrew* Tongue at *Orleans*, in 1565. Thofe of *Rochel* offered him an Employ in their College, in the Year 1571 (*a*). I believe he did not accept of it. He was in *Sancerre*, when the Marfhal *de la Châtre* befieged it, a little after the Maffacre of *Paris* (*b*); and He did the Inhabitants great Services by his wife and courageous Counfels [*B*]. At his leaving *Sancerre*, he retired to *Sedan*, where he read Hiftorical Lectures. Some were offended at the manner, in which it is pretended, that he fpoke of *Francis I*, in his Lectures [*C*]. I cannot tell at what time he was Minifter of *Geneva* [*D*]; but it

[*A*] *He was called* MATTHEW.] *Theophilus Raynaud*, by Miftake, calls him *Michael* (1). *Thomafius*, I find, doubts, whether This be a Miftake (2): He fhould not have doubted of it.

[*B*] *And did the Inhabitants of Sancerre great Services by his wife and courageous Counfels.*] D'*Aubigné* obferves this in two Places. "The *Sancerrois*,
"fays he (3), compofed alfo a Council, in which
"they found themfelves particularly happy in Be-
"*roaldus*, formerly *Hebrew* Reader at *Orleans*. He
"accompanied his Counfels with Courage. ----
"The Befieged, being very much aftonifhed at this
"News, wanted to be fupported by their Paftors;
"but chiefly ftood in need of the wife and coura-
"geous Counfels of *Beroaldus*; according to which,
"they refolved to endure all the Miferies of a Siege,
"and that they, who would not confent to it,
"fhould be thrown over the Walls (4)."

[*C*] *Some were offended at the manner, in which
it is pretended, that he fpoke of Francis I, in his Le-
ctures.*] A Minifter, who was then at *Sedan*, and who abjured his Religion afterwards, publifhed what follows. "It is to be noted, that *Matthew Beroal-
"dus*, a learned Man among them, and one of their
"Profeffors, being retired from *Sancerre* to *Sedan*,
"was defired, by the Prefident *la Louëtte*, and fome
"others, to read fome Lectures; which he did in
"the fame Place, where they preach, and delivered
"a Syftem of Chronology, which he faid he had
"made. Now, being come to the Reign of King
"*Francis* I, a Prince of Glorious Memory, &
"whom we may juftly call the Father of Learning,
"and Reftorer of Sciences, in This Kingdom of
"*France*; Advantages, which cannot be fufficiently
"valued, and which all *Europe* felt afterwards: Be-
"ing, I fay, come to the Reign of This Great and
"Virtuous Prince, he fpoke fo impudently, and ir-
"reverently, of him, and of his moft Illuftrious,
"and moft Chriftian, Pofterity, that I know not one
"Man, breathing the Air of *France*, but would have
"been fcandalized at it. The Prefident, the Baylif,
"and other Magiftrates, and all the Minifters, re-
"fiding then at *Sedan*, were prefent; who, if they
"had had a Chriftian, and *French*, Heart, and not
"ungrateful for the Benefits arifing from Learning,
"which That Good Prince revived, would certain-
"ly have been offended at it as well as myfelf, and
"would not have tolerated fuch a Perfon. At leaft,
"the Prefident, and others, who had Authority in
"the City, fhould have given Notice of it to the
"Lord of the Place, who, being well affected to
"the Good of The Crown, and the King's Service,
"would, I am fure, have punifhed him according
"to his Deferts. But as was fmothered. I fpoke
"of it myfelf to the Prefident, fhewing him fome
"other Faults, which the faid *Beroaldus* had com-
"mitted in Chronology; and I exhorted him, by the
"Obedience, which we all owe to our Prince; and
"for

it cannot be queſtioned, that he was ſo; and, ſince he taught Philoſophy there, in the Year 1576 (c), there is ſome reaſon to believe, that he exerciſed the Miniſtry, there, at that time. He publiſhed a Book of Chronology, in the Year 1575, in which there is, doubtleſs, much Learning, but little Solidity. In ſtriving to do Honour to the Scripture, he loſes himſelf in a Labyrinth, which he cannot get out of. He pretends, that no other Guide is to be followed, in the Doctrine of Times, but the Writings inſpired by GOD [*E*]. *Scaliger* has plainly ſhewed the Inſufficiency of this Hypotheſis; but he has inveighed too much againſt The Author. *Moreri* goes too far, when he affirms, that, beſides the *Latin* Chronology, *there appeared many other Works* of Beroaldus, and that he *died about the Year* 1575, *or* 76. *La Croix du Maine*, whom he quotes, does not ſay ſo; but only, that *Beroaldus* was no longer living in the Year 1584, and that it was probable, his other Compoſitions would be publiſhed by the Care of his Son, the Sieur *de Verville*.

(c) *See Remark* [*D*].

" for the Honour of our Nation, to perform his
" Duty in it; who anſwered me ſomewhat coldly,
" that he could have wiſhed it had not been ſaid,
" and that it was, in truth, a Piece of Imprudence.
" Yet he made his Report of my Remonſtrance;
" which incenſed them the more againſt me; tho'
" without any outward Appearance of it, except a
" few croſs Looks: but they waited for an Opportunity (5)." I am willing this Diſcourſe ſhould be as much ſuſpected of Falſhood, as any one pleaſes; and, if it be talſe, ſo much the better for this Dictionary; which ought principally to contain the Errors of other Books. Let this be ſaid with reſpect to a great many other Paſſages, which ſhall be quoted.

[*D*] *I cannot tell, at what time be was Miniſter of Geneva.*] *Beza* does not determine it; He only gives *Beroaldus* the Quality of his Colleague in the Church, which imports, as *Colomies* (6) well obſerves, that *Beroaldus* exerciſed the Miniſtry at *Geneva*. He alſo taught Philoſophy there, as the ſame *Colomies* obſerves (7), and as may be proved by the Epiſtle Dedicatory, which *Lambert Danæus* prefixed to the Treatiſe of Hereſies It is ſaid there, that, in 1576, *Matthew Beroaldus* taught Philoſophy at *Geneva*. Here are *Beza*'s own Words: *Aliam igitur rurſus rationem iniit*

vir beatæ memoriæ, & meus ſuperioribus annis in hac Eccleſia collega, Beroaldus (8). I believe *Beroaldus* went to be Profeſſor at *Geneva*, after he had been ſo at *Sedan*. *Scaliger* ſays, that *be read with great Applauſe, and was admired at Sedan, and at Geneva, where there were ſome great Men* (9).

[*E*] *He would have no other Guide — than the Writings inſpired by* GOD.] In conſequence of this Maxim, he ſtruck *Cambyſes*, and *Darius*, the Son of *Hyſtaſpes*, out of the Catalogue of the Kings of *Perſia*: for, ſays he, *Theſe Names appear no where in the Scripture* : — *quæ nomina, quia nunquam extant in Scriptura, è nobis ſunt prætermiſſa* (10). *Vaſſius* pretends, that he is miſtaken as to the Fact; and that, if he was right in that Reſpect, he would, nevertheleſs, be much to blame in denying the Exiſtence of Thoſe Kings, under pretence that the Scripture makes no mention of them. *Scaliger* calls this manner of explaining the Times Fanatical and Prophetical (taking the laſt Word in an odious Senſe) and maintains, that, if the prophane Authors had not ſupplied us with ſome Light, the Chronology of the Scripture could never have been dientangled. *Actum erat de Chronologia ſacra, abſque exoticis monumentis foret* (11). He calls *Parcus Hierophantam Beroaldinum*.

(5) Defence of *Matthew de Launo*, and *Henry Pennetier*, lately Miniſters, &c. pag. 32. *This Book was printed at Paris, in* 1577.

(6) Colomeſii Gallia Orient. p. 46.

(7) Ibid. pag. 45.

(8) Beza in Acta Apoſtol. cap. xiii. ver. 30, where he treats *of the 450 Years, that paſſed from Joſhua to Samuel.*

(9) In Scaligerania.

(10) Beroald, lib. iii. Chron. c. 8. apud Voſſium de Scient. Mathem. pag. 233.

(11) In elenchoChronol. prophetic., pag. 5, apud Voſſium, ibid.

BEROALDUS (FRANCIS), Sieur *de Verville*, Son of the foregoing, was born at *Paris* [*A*], the Twenty eighth of *April*, 1558 (a). He was a Man of Learning and Parts; but he did not make choice of proper Materials to perfect his natural Gifts. He took the pains to tranſlate *Polyphilus*'s Dream (b), and afterwards to compoſe a Piece of the ſame Stamp; it was entituled, *The Travels of Fortunate Princes*; which he called *Steganographical*. He wrote ſeveral Books of Chymiſtry, and ſeveral Tomes of Romances (c) [*B*], which are very tedious, and little better, than the Writings of *Nerveze*, and the Sieur *des Eſcuteaux*. Perhaps he would have done better to have continued exerciſing himſelf on the ſame Subjects, by which he appeared firſt in public. Being but Twenty two Years of Age, he publiſhed ſome Commentaries on the Mechanics of *James Beſſon* (d). He had ſcarce tried his Fortune this way, but he ran after the Philoſopher's Stone. In the Year 1583, were publiſhed *His Spiritual Apprehenſions, Poems, and other Philoſophical Works, with ſome Enquiries after the Philoſopher's Stone* (e). The Year after, he publiſhed a Poem, entituled, *The Idea of a Republic* (f).

(a) La Croix du Maine, pag. 480.

(b) Sorel Biblioth. Franç. pag. 373.

(c) Ib pag. 177, 256.

(d) Printed at *Lyons*, in 1580, and 1581, at La Croix du Maine ſays, pag. 91.

(e) La Croix du Maine, pag. 92.

(f) Idem. pag. 480.

[*A*] *He was born at* Paris] Mr *de Marolles* ought, then, to ſtrike him out of the Liſt, which he has given, of the Illuſtrious *Tourangeaux* (1).

[*B*] *He wrote ſeveral kinds of tedious Romances.*] He was Author of *The Adventures of* Florida*, Minerva's Cloſet, The Maid of Orleans, The Hiſtory of Herodias*, " and ſome other Works, wherein he introduces ſome Lords and Ladies, whoſe Converſa-

" tions are not very ingenious; but, what is to be
" eſteemed therein, is, the Sentiments of Honour
" and Virtue, which are the fineſt in the World,
" with many Secrets of Nature and Art, by means
" whereof many extraordinary things are performed;
" whereas the ancient *Romanus* referred every thing to
" Magic, for want of Invention and Learning (2)."

(1) Memoirs, pag. 255.

(2) Sorel Bibl. Franç. pag. 177.

BERQUIN (LEWIS *de*,) a Gentleman of the Country of *Artois*, was burnt for the Proteſtant Religion, at *Paris*, the Twenty ſecond of *April*, 1529 [*A*]. He was

(*A*) In the Diſcourſe concerning the Church, at the end of the Life of Henry IV.

(5) The Night following, which was the Eve of St Martin, the *Com* was over France, blighted all which cauſed a Famine, and Plague, in diſorers Places. Beza Hiſt. Eccleſ. lib. i. pag. 8.

[*A*] *He was burnt, at* Paris*, the Twenty ſecond of April* 1529.] We have a Proof of this Chronology in a Letter of *Eraſmus*, dated the firſt of *July* 1529 (1). It contains an ample Relation of the Life and Death of *Lewis de Berquin*. It is expreſsly noted there, that he was burnt *decimo Calend. Majas*. The Proof would fix the Day of his Death, were it not for another Letter of *Eraſmus* (2), in which the Execution of *Berquin* is placed on the ſeventeenth of *April*, XV *Calend. Majas* (3). This Letter is dated the ninth of *May* 1529. All, that *Eraſmus* can do,

is to fix us to the Month of *April* 1529; we muſt look on all the other Varieties as Miſtakes. *Mezerai* is miſtaken in the Year, and perhaps alſo in the Day: He affirms, that *Berquin* was burnt on the Twenty firſt of *April*, of the Year 1528 (4). *John Crepin*, in the Acts of the Martyrs, places the Death of This Perſon in the Month of *May*, in general, 1529 *Beza* places it on the Tenth of *November*, in the ſame Year (5), both in his Eccleſiaſtical Hiſtory, and in another Work. *Frugibus nocte poſt interitum illius proxima (qui fuit undecimus dies Novembris anno Domini*

(1) The 4th of the 22th B k, pag. 1272.

(2) To. 4th of the note L ck.

(3) E in. D. ... men. to b... can it pag. 425.

VOL. I. 9 K

BERQUIN.

was Lord of a Village, of which he bore the Name *(a)*, and was very much esteemed in the Court of *France*, and honoured with the Title of the King's Counsellor *(b)*. He lived a good Life, and regularly observed the Precepts of the Church. He was a Layman, and unmarried; yet he was never censured, in relation to his Chastity. *Erasmus*, who had learned these Particulars from some Persons, whom he could depend upon, adds, that they had also informed him, that *Berquin* abhorred *Lutheranism (d)*, and that the great Crime, which was found in him, was, that he openly professed to hate morose and peevish Divines, and Monks, who were no less fierce, than ignorant *(e)*. He spoke very ill of them publickly. This paved the way to a bloody War, that began with a Quarrel, which he had with one of the most violent Inquisitors of That Time *(f)* [B]. It was not long before they accused him as an Heretic: Certain Propositions were extracted from a Book, which he had published; whereupon he was Imprisoned; but the Judges, finding no Crime in him, acquitted him [C]. The Accusers pretended, that he had escaped Punishment by the Royal Authority; as for him, he said he was not beholden to any thing but the Justice of his Cause; and he behaved as formerly. He translated some of *Erasmus*'s Books into *French* [D], and added something of his own to them. Immediately, *Noel Beda*, and his Emissaries, began a new War; They extracted several Things out of Those Books, and, having informed against them, as pernicious Errors, they occasioned the Author's second Imprisonment. The Cause being judged, some Monks went to tell him the definitive Sentence, which was passed upon him: Which was, that his Books should be burnt; that he should retract his Errors, and submit to such Satisfactions, as should be prescribed to him; and that

mini 1329.) *in tota Gallia frigore perustis, & gravis-sima tum fame tum etiam peste consequuta* (6). *Spondanus* plainly shews, that *Beza* is in an Error, by the fourth Letter of the Twenty fourth Book of *Erasmus*, which, being dated the first of *July* 1529, mentions *Berquin*'s Execution; but he is afterwards mistaken, when he gives the Reason, why he thinks, that *Beza* falsified That Date (7). He says, It was done to make what was to be said on the Judgments of GOD more probable. *Beza* says, that Heaven declared for *Berquin*, and reversed the Sentence of the Judges, because, the following Night, the Frost spoiled all the Corn in the Kingdom; from whence a great Famine, and Mortality, ensued. *Judicium Sententia veluti cœlitus rescissa triumpharit, frugibus nocte*, &c (8). Nothing was more easy than to criticize *Beza* with Justice on this Point: For first, it is to dispose of the particular Providence of GOD a little too rashly, to say, that the Plagues, which desolate a whole Kingdom, are a Vengeance for the unjust Death of one Man. In the second place, Frost can do but little damage to Corn, the tenth, or eleventh, of *November*. They sow at that time, almost all the Kingdom over: and it is at least very certain, that the greatest Part of what is sowed is out of danger at that time. So that, if *Beza* had, with a premeditated Design, falsified the Date, he would have taken care not to pitch upon the Eve, or the Day, of *St Martin*. The right Time, noted by *Erasmus*, was much properer for his Reflexion; for Cold may hurt the Fruits of the Earth towards the end of *April*. Thus you see how *Spondanus* might have confuted the moral Reflexion of *Beza*. If he had criticized him from my first Consideration, he would have disarmed himself; for he is as much accustomed, as any one, to say, that such or such Evils happen as Punishments for This or That. One of Those, who wrote against *Maimbourg*'s History of *Calvinism* (9), observes, that *Berquin* was executed, *the Twenty second of* March, *on the Eve of St Martin, the Pope, in the Place Maubert*. What he adds of *Dr Merlin*, and which I shall relate below (10), persuades me, that he copied *Beza*: only he took notice, that, the Month of *November* not being a Time, wherein Corn can receive any damage by the Cold, he sought another for *St Martin*'s Eve.

Let it not be wondered at, that the Day of such a Martyrdom was not well known to the Protestant Writers, and that they have variously reported The Date of it. The Battle of *Cerisoles*, the Death of *Antony de Bourbon*, King of *Navarre*, the Barricades of *Paris*, in the Time of *Henry* III, were not better dated by great Authors. See the Extract, which Mr *Bernard* gave, of a Book of Father *du Londel*, in his *News from the Republic of Letters*, page 224, of the Month of *February*, 1699.

[B] *He had a Quarrel with one of the most violent Inquisitors.*] *Berquin* was no Coward; he must have had a great Courage, since he feared neither an *A Quercu*, nor a *Noel Beda*. He durst, not only defend himself against them, but even attack them: *Beza* praises him for it. " Adsuit autem animi tanta gene-
" rositas, ut maxime omnium tunc metuendos crabro-
" nes in ipsis eorum cavis, Bedam videlicet & a Quer-
" cu (de quibus scripserat, procul illos configens,
" *Erasmus*, Lutetiæ Betam sapere & Quercum con-
" cionari) Matæologorum ejus seculi principes, in ipso
" eorum sterquilinio sit ausus non modo utcunque
" lacessere, sed impetatis etiam accusatos non unius
" anni certamine tum voce tum scriptis strenuè exer-
" cere (11). —— *He was a Man of such Courage, that*
" *he ventured, not only to attack, upon their own*
" *Dunghill, but vigorously to pursue, with an Action*
" *of Impiety, during a Contest of more than one Year,*
" *both in Speech and Writing, Those most formidable*
" *Hornets,* Beda *and a* Quercu, *of whom* Erasmus,
" *lashing them at a Distance, wrote, that, at* Paris,
" *a Birch-Tree pretended to Learning, and an Oak to*
" *Oratory*." See, here, what *Erasmus* says, concerning the Process, wherein *Berquin* was the Aggressor. " Non enim solùm promittebat sibi absolutio-
" nem, verumetiam victoriam esse in manibus, sed
" malle seriùs aliquanto finiri causam, quo magnificen-
" tiùs triumpharet. Jamque mutatis vicibus, ipsam
" facultatem sacratissimam, monachos & Beddaicos
" reos peragebat impietatis. Nam quædam arcana
" deprehenderat in illorum actis (12) —— *For he*
" *not only promised himself an honourable Acquittal,*
" *but even that he had the Victory in his Hands; he*
" *was willing that the Determination of the Cause*
" *should be protracted, that he might triumph the*
" *more splendidly. And now, changing Hands, he*
" *brought an Action of Impiety against the most sa-*
" *cred Order, The Monks, and Bedaists: for he had*
" *discovered some secret Transactions of Theirs.*" See the Remark [A], of the Article BEDA, Citation (7).

[C] *He was accused as an Heretic —— but the Judges —— acquitted him.*] He' was accused of condemning the Custom, which Preachers have, of invoking the Holy Virgin, instead of invoking the HOLY GHOST. It is said, that he did not approve, that the Holy Virgin should be called the *Fountain of Grace*, and that, in the Evening Hymn, she should be called our Hope and our Life. He said, that This was more applicable to JESUS CHRIST, and that the Scripture does not favour the Modern Usage. These are the Trifles, for which he was imprisoned, and in danger of being treated as an Heretic. *Ob hujusmodi nænias ductus est in carcerem, reus hæreseos periclitatus est. At Judices, ubi viderunt causam esse nullius momenti, absolverunt hominem* (13). I do not wonder so much, that *Erasmus* called them Trifles, as that *Berquin* was acquitted upon such Opinions.

[D] *He translated some of* Erasmus's *Books into French.*] Among others, *The Panegyric on Marriage* (14), *The Manual of the Christian Soldier* (15), and *The Complaint of Peace.* See the Remark [K].

[E] *If*

BERQUIN. 777

that, if he refused, He should himself be burnt. Being a Man of an inflexible and intrepid Spirit, he would not submit to any thing; and he would probably have been burnt, if some Judges, perceiving the excessive Animosity of the Accusers, had not contrived the Matter so, that the Business was examined again. Many are of Opinion, that this was done at the Recommendation of the Lady Regent, Mother of *Francis* I, to save *Berquin*. During these Transactions, *Francis* I returned from *Spain*; and, hearing of the Danger his Counsellor was in, from the Faction of *Beda*, he wrote to the Parliament to take great care of what should be done, and that he would hear *Lewis de Berquin*'s Cause himself. Some time after, The Prisoner was set at Liberty: This raised his Courage in such a manner, that he was so bold, as to accuse his Accusers (g): He brought an Action of Irreligion against them, and flattered himself with obtaining a compleat Victory (h). If he had followed the judicious Advice of *Erasmus*, he would have looked upon it as a great Triumph, not to be oppressed by these Men [E], instead of hoping to bring them to Reason. But if, on the one Side, he came off the worse for having had the Boldness to resist, to their Face, Those, with whom *Erasmus*, for very good Reasons, advised him to have nothing to do [F]; it was, on the other side, a great Advantage to him; because, by falling a Victim to their Hatred, he procured to himself the Crown of Martyrdom. He was imprisoned the third time; the Sentence pronounced against him, condemned him to make the *Amende Honorable* for his Errors (i), and to suffer perpetual Imprisonment [G]. He refused to submit to This Sentence: He would have acknowledged, thereby, that his Opinions were erroneous; so that he was condemned, as an obstinate Heretic, to be strangled in the *Greve* (k), and afterwards burnt (l). He suffered Death with an extraordinary Constancy. He was about forty Years of Age. It is said, that the Monk, who attended him on the Scaffold, declared, that he observed in him some Signs of Abjuration [H]. But see what *Erasmus*

[E] *If he had followed the Advice of* Erasmus, *he would have looked upon it as a great Triumph not to be oppressed by Those Men.*] Few Persons of Sense, and who are used to reflect on what they see, or read, will think on *Berquin*'s Conduct, without applying to him the Fable of the Wolf and the Crane. He was not satisfied with having escaped out of the Hands of his Accusers, but he would also have the Prize and Honour of the Victory, as a Reward of his Contest: Is not This to imitate the Crane, who required a Reward, after having got her Neck, whole and safe, from out of a very dangerous Passage?

Ingrata es, inquit, ore quæ nostro caput
Incolume abstuleris, & mercedem postulas (16).

You are ungrateful, after drawing your Neck, safe, out of my Mouth, to demand a Reward.

These Verses of *Horace* may be very well applied to *Berquin*:

Cervi luporum præda rapacium
Sectamur ultro, quos opimus
Fallere, & effugere est triumphus (17).

*We, like the Stag, the brinded Wolf provoke;
And, when Retreat is Victory,
Rush on, though sure to die.*

CREECH.

[F] --- *With whom* Erasmus, *for very good Reasons, advised him to have nothing to do.*] He had received Letters from *Berquin*, but had never seen him; and, fearing to be involved in the Prosecutions against Innovators, he was not very well satisfied to find his own Thoughts, with Those of *Berquin* (18), in one and the same Book; and he exhorted the latter to be quiet, or, at least, not to expose him to Danger. " Your Adversaries, *said he to him*, will " never own the Crime, of which you accuse them; " think that *Beda* is an Hydra with several Heads; " you have to do with an immortal Enemy; a Faculty, " a Society, never dies; do not trust to the Protection " of the Prince. The Favour of Kings is change- " able; an Informer prejudices them; the Fear they " have of Churchmen, and their Desire of being " no more fatigued with their importante Sollici- " tations, force them to grant them what they de- " mand." Here are his *Latin* Words. " Crebris " epistolis hortatus sum, ut vel arte quâpiam semet " extricaret à causa, purâ curarent amici, ut præ- " textu regiæ legationis longius proficisceretur: for-

" tassis Theologos passuros ut causa tempore evane- " sceret, nunquam passuros ut impietatis crimen, quod " illis objiciebat, agnoscerent. Etiam atque etiam " cogitaret qualis excetra esset Bedda, quotque capi- " tibus affiaret venenum: Tum expenderet sibi cum " immortali adversario rem esse; facultas enim non " moritur: simul illud cogitaret, qui cum tribus " monachis belligeraret, eum cum multis phalangi- " bus habere rem, non solum opulentis ac potenti- " bus, verum etiam improbissimis, & in omni ma- " larum artium genere instructis. Illos non con- " quieturos, donec ei procuraffent exitium, etiamsi " causam haberet meliorem quàm habuit CHRISTUS, " neque plus satis fideret Regis præsidio. Principum " enim favores esse temporarios, ac delatorem artibus " facilè in diversum trahi illorum affectus. Postremò, " ut nihil horum accidat, magnos etiam Principes " vel delassari talium improbitate, vel metu non- " nunquam cogi ut cedant (19)."

[G] *The Sentence, pronounced against him, condemned him to make the* Amende Honorable, *and to suffer perpetual Imprisonment.*] I have followed the *Acta Martyrum of John Crepin*; but I shall observe, wherein the Relations differ. *Beza* makes no mention of an *Amende Honorable*; and he says, that *Berquin*'s Books were to be burnt in the Presence of the Author, which *Crepin* does not remark. *Erasmus* mentions four Heads of Punishment; the Books were to be burnt; the Author was to recant; his Tongue was to be bored through, and himself to suffer perpetual Imprisonment (20). *Beza*, and *Crepin*, have not forgot this latter Head. *Erasmus* adds, that the Cause was judged by twelve Commissaries; that *Budæus*, who was one of them, exhorted *Berquin*, before his Condemnation, to retract (21); that *Berquin*, having heard the Sentence, appealed to the King, and to the Pope, and that the Judges, full of Indignation on that Account, condemned him to be burnt the next Day. *Erasmus* relates all this on Hear-say (22). See the Remark [K].

[H] *The Monk, who attended him on the Scaffold, declared, That he had observed in him some Signs of Abjuration.*] A Person (23), whom *Erasmus* thought worthy of Credit, wrote to him, that he asked This Monk, If *Berquin* had not acknowledged his Errors, at his last Breath? And that the Monk answered him, He had; and seemed to have no manner of doubt, but that *Berquin*'s Soul was in the Abode of the Blessed. *Erasmus*'s Friend was near the Place of Execution, and gave him a faithful Account of it. He informed him, that no one could hear the Speech, which *Berquin* made to the People, the Archers making a great Noise on purpose to drown

" it

BERQUIN.

mus said upon This [*I*]. Beza believed (*m*), that *Berquin* would have been, in *France*, what *Luther* was in *Germany*, if *Francis* I had done for him, what the Duke of *Saxony* did for *Luther*. It is certain, that he was a Man of great Parts, and of great Courage. *Nicholas Berauld* was one of his beft Friends, as *Badius Afcenfius* affirms, in dedicating the Works of *Politian* to them.

Since the firft Impreffion of this Article, a Book has been publifhed, wherein the different Proceedings againft *Lewis de Berquin* are well cleared up. I fhall give the Subftance of them in the laft Remark of This Article.

it: No one cried Jesus, when the Sufferer was ftrangled, though it be commonly practifed towards facrilegious Men, and Parricides (24). If what *Beza* relates were true, we fhould certainly find it in *Erafmus*'s Relation: His Friend would not have kept it fecret. *Beza* fays, "that Dr *Merlin*, at that "Time Penitentiary of *Paris*, who went with him "to the Place of Execution, could not forbear fay-"ing aloud to the People, after his Death, to the "great Regret of his Accufers, and Judges, that, "perhaps, for above an hundred Years paft, no one "had died a better Chriftian, than *Berquin* (25)." It is probable, *Beza*, afterwards, difcovered the Falf-hood of This; for, if he had believed the Thing to be true, why fhould he not have placed it in his *Icones?* It is certain, that many pious Frauds are handed about in fuch Cafes, which an Hiftorian ought to diftruft.

[*I*] See *what Erafmus fays upon this*.] He freely declares, that he believed the *Francifcan*, who attended *Berquin* on the Scaffold, told a Lie: He adds, that "it is always their Cuftom in fuch Cafes. Thefe "pious Frauds ferve to maintain them in the Ho- "nour of having vindicated Religion, and to juftify "to the People Thofe, who have accufed and con- "demned Hereticks." *At ego Francifcani dictis nihil habeo fidei, præfertim quum hoc fit ipfis folenne, poft extinctum hominem fpargere rumores, quòd in incendio cecinerit palinodiam, quo fimul & vindicatæ religionis laudem auferant, & multitudinis invidiam calumniaque fufpicionem effugiant* (26). He knew, from the firft Hand, fome of thefe Frauds, which had been practifed at *Bruffels*; and he relates them in few Words. If People were reafonable, they would make fuch Accufers and Judges ftand in awe of them; for, in fhort, can any thing be conceived more fhock-ing, when it is examined without Prejudice, than to reprefent to one's felf a Man condemned to the Flames, becaufe he will not violate the Faith, which he has fworn to the True God? But the Authors of thefe Executions were fo far from fearing any thing on that Account, that they became more infolent for it: for they were in hopes to render themfelves more formidable. This was one of the Inconvenien-cies, which *Erafmus* found in the Execution of poor *Berquin*. *Periculum eft, ne Befidus fua fponte plus fatis infanientibus nimium accedat animorum* (27).

[*K*] There has appeared a Work, *in which the Proceedings againft* Berquin *are well cleared up*.] It is *A Treatife of the Origin of Printing at* Paris, by Mr *Chevillier*. Thus he gives an Account of Thefe Proceedings The thirteenth of *May*, in the Year 1523, the Parliament caufed *Lewis de Berquin*'s Books to be feized, *and ordered, that they fhould be communicated to the Faculty of Theology to have their Opinion concerning them*. *They found upon him the Book* De Abrogandâ Miffâ, *with fome others of* Luther *and* Melancthon; *and feven or eight Treatifes, whereof he was the Author, fome entituled*, Specu-lum Theologaftrorum. De Ufu & Officio Miffæ, &c. Rationes Lutheri, quibus omnes Chriftianos effe Sa-cerdotes molitur fuadere; The Debate of Piety and Superftition. *They found alfo fome Books, which he had tranflated into French, as,* The Reafons why Luther tranflated the Decretals, and all the Books of the Canon Law, to be publickly burnt: La Triade Romaine; *and others*. *The Faculty, having examined thefe Books, judged, that they plainly contained* Lu-ther's *Herefies and Blafphemies*. *Their Opinion is dated Friday the Twenty fixth of* July, 1523, *and addreffed to the Court of Parliament*. *After having cenfured each Book in particular, they concluded, that all of them ought to be burnt; that* Ber-quin, *having made himfelf a Defender of the* Lutheran *Herefies, ought to be obliged to make a publick abjuration, and to be forbidden to compofe any Book, for the future, or make any Tranflation pre-judicial to the fame* (28). "The Parliament order-"ed, that this Opinion fhould be fignified to him.

"He anfwered, in Writing, and verbally, to it, in "the Prefence of the Judges. Upon his Anfwer, "he was made Prifoner, the firft Day of *Auguft*, "and, four Days after, his Sentence was read to "him, which fent him back to the Tribunal of the "Bifhop of *Paris*, to be judged by him, on the "Cafes refulting from the Procefs. The eighth of "*Auguft*, the King caufed him to be taken out of the "Prifons of the Epifcopal Court, by Captain *Fre-*"*deric*, and brought the Caufe before his Council, "where he was judged by the Chancellor, *and* "*condemned to abjure fome heretical Propofitions*; "*which he did*. Thefe are the Terms of the "Regifters of the Parliament. He was no fooner "delivered from this Danger, but he began again "to utter Herefies in his Books, and in his "Difcourfe; and, to be lefs obferved, he retired "into the Diocefe of *Amiens*, where he offended "the People, and the Clergy, in fuch a manner, "that the Bifhop was obliged to come to *Paris*, "and make his Complaint to the Parliament, who "caufed him to be taken up; and he was declared "a Relapfed Heretic, by the Sentence of two Coun- "fellors of the Court, chofen to take Cognizance of "the Fact of Herefy, and invefted with the Autho- "rity of the Holy See, by a Brief of Pope *Clement* "VII, dated the twentieth of *May*, 1525, regiftered "in the Court, which the Queen Regent had ob- "tained from *Rome*, in the King her Son's Abfence. "Thefe Ecclefiaftical Judges gave him up to the "Parliament, as to the Secular Power. His Procefs "had been committed to a Counfellor. The Morn- "ing when it was to be reported, the Parliament re- "ceived a Letter from the King, who was returned "from *Spain*, dated the firft of *April*, 1526, where- "by he ordered the Proceedings to be ftopped: "And, at laft, after many Letters written, he fent "a Lieutenant of his Guards, with the Provoft of "*Paris*, who took him out of Jail, kept him fome "time in the *Louvre*, and gave him his Liberty (29). "The Faculty of Divinity having cenfured *Erafmus*'s Colloquies, the Univerfity prohibited the reading and teaching them in the Colleges. "Then *Berquin* "wrote to *Erafmus*, that the matter ought not to "be delayed any longer; that he ought to join with "him; that now was the time to ruin all the Au- "thority of the Doctors in the Church, and to cry "them quite down, the Occafion being favourable. "*Nunc tempus effe, ut Theologos omnis in pofterum* "*detraheretur auctoritas*. His Caufe remained in "fufpenfe. It confifted in a Sentence, pronounced "againft him by two Counfellors, Judges delegated "by the Pope (which *Erafmus* afcribes to the Prior "of the *Carthufians*, to That of the *Celeftins*; and "to a Third, whom he does not name). It con- "fifted alfo in a Reproach, which he had made to "the Faculty of Theology, for having approved "the impious Doctrine, as he falfly called it, of "Doctor *Beda*. - - - - Puffed up with the Protection, "which he had received from the Court, flattering "himfelf with the vain Hopes of deftroying the "Faculty, and uttering Errors continually, he would "purfue his Abfolution, contrary to *Erafmus*'s Coun- "fels, who advifed him, very wifely, to defift from "this Enterprife, and to leave the Kingdom. ------ "Twelve Commiffaries were deputed to judge him; "who, having found him convicted of Herefy, cau- "fed him to be arrefted. They had agreed toge- "ther, that his Books fhould be burnt, that his "Tongue fhould be bored, and that he fhould be "only condemned to a perpetual Imprifonment, pro- "vided he would abjure his Herefy. The Learned "*William Budæus*, who was one of his Judges, "did his utmoft, for three Days, to perfwade him "to fave his Life, by recanting his Errors: But, "not being able to conquer his Obftinacy, Sentence "was pronounced againft him, and he was burnt at "the Grève, in the Month of *April*, 1529 (30)."

BERSALA

BERSALA. 781

BERSALA [*A*] (ANNE), Daughter, and chief Heiress, of *Wolfard de Borselle* (*a*), and of *Charlotte de Bourbon-Montpenfier* (*b*), who were married the seventeenth of *June*, 1468, was the Wife of *Philip* of *Burgundy*, Son of *Antony* of *Burgundy*, Lord of *Bevres*, one of the Natural Sons of *Philip The Good*, Duke of *Burgundy* (*c*). She brought him, for her Dowry, the Lordship of *Vere* [*B*], and that of *Flushing*, and some others; and had one Son, and two Daughters by him. Her own Father, and her Husband's Father, made a very great Figure [*C*]. This Lady's Merit, and some Passages concerning her Conduct, and her Misfortunes, shall be the Subject of our last Remark [*D*]. We shall, there, see, among other things, that *Erasmus* greatly esteemed her.

(a) Fabert. Hist. of the Dukes of *Burgundy*, Part I, pag. 162.
(b) Anselm. Hist. of the Royal Family, pag. 272.
(c) Pontus Heuterus, Rerum Burgundic. lib. vi. pag. 7.

[*A*] BERSALA.] Thus *Erasmus* latinizes the vulgar Name BORSELLE.
[*B*] *She brought her Husband the Lordship of Vere.*] It is in *Zealand*, in the Island of *Walcheren*, and has been since erected into a Marquisate. It is vulgarly called *Teer-Vere*.
[*C*] *Her own Father, and her Husband's Father, made a very great Figure.*] For it is said (1), that *Wolfard de Borselle's* first Wife was *Mary, the Daughter* of *James* I, *King* of *Scotland*, *who brought him the Country of Boncam* (2); and that he was a Marshal of *France* (3). It is more certain he was made a Knight of the Golden Fleece (4). *Lewis Gollut* places him in the List, and calls him Count *de Grand-Pré*. Mr Fabert does the like; but I can scarce believe, that they are in the right; for I find, that *Antony* of *Burgundy*, Natural Son of *Philip The Good*, was made Earl of *Grand-Pré*, and of *Chateau-thierri*, by *Lewis* XI, in the Year 1478 (5), which is about the time that *Wolfard de Borselle* received the Collar of the Order. If we had no other Proof of the Rank he held, than his Marriage with a Daughter of *Lewis* of *Bourbon*, Earl of *Montpenfier*, and Dauphin of *Auvergne*, third Son of *John* I, Duke of *Bourbon*, we could not doubt, but that he made a great Figure in the World. Thus much concerning the Father of *Anne de Borselle*. Let us say a Word of her Father-in-law, and of her Husband. *Antony* of *Burgundy*, sirnamed the *Great Bastard*, was made Knight of the Golden Fleece in the Year 1456 (6). He obliged the *Moors* to raise the Siege of *Ceuta*; he led the Vanguard at the Battle of *Grandson* (7), and remained Prisoner in That of *Nancy*. He entered, afterwards, into the Service of *Lewis* XI, who gave him very fine Lands, as I have already said (8). *Charles* VIII granted him Letters of Legitimation, in the Year 1485, and made him Knight of the Order of *St Michael*. From the Marriage of This Bastard of *Burgundy* with *Mary de la Vieville*, contracted in the Year 1459, proceeded *Philip* of *Burgundy*, Lord of *Bevres*, *who was made Admiral and Governour* of *Artois, and Knight of the Fleece*, at *Bruges, in the Year* 1478. *He was also provided with the Government of the Earldom of Flanders*; and he married *Anne de Borselle* (9).
[*D*] *This Lady's Merit, and some Passages concerning her Conduct - - - - shall be the Subject of our last Remark.*] If we believe *Erasmus*, She was extreamly obliging and generous. " Vivi pervenimus, fays he, in a Letter dated in the Month of " February, 1497, ad Annam Principem Verianam. " Quid ego tibi de hujus mulieris comitate, benig- " nitate, liberalitate memorem? Scio rhetorum am- " plificationes suspectas haberi solere, præsertim iis " qui ejus artificii rudes non sunt. At hic me nihil " allevare, imo re vinci artem nostram, mihi credas " velim. Nihil unquam produxit rerum natura aut " prudentius, aut candidius, aut benignius (10). - - " *I have lived to see Anne, Princess of Vere. Need* " *I tell you of this Lady's Courtesy, Good-Nature,* " *and Liberality? I know, Rhetoricians are usually* " *suspected of Amplification, especially by Those, who* " *are not unacquainted with the Art. But, here,* " *believe me, I exaggerate nothing; the Subject is* " *even too great for me. Nature never produced so* " *much Modesty, Prudence, Candor, and Humanity.*" He had but lately received a thousand Marks of her Kindness and Liberality. " Tam illa in nos bene- " fica fuit - - - - tantis illa me officiis cumulavit, nul- " lis a me studiis provocata (11). - - - - *She was so* " *beneficent to me, she heaped so many Favours* " *on me, unasked.*" The Year following, he wrote a Letter to his good Friend *James Battus*, who was Tutor to This Lady's only Son: See, here, in what Terms he praised her: " O te beatum, ô " superis charum, si tu litos scopulos enavigâris: si

(1) Fabert. Hist. of the Dukes of *Burgundy*, Tom. I. pag. 162.
(2) I believe it ought to be Buchan.
(3) Anselme, History of Great Officers, pag. 252.
(4) Gollut, Memoirs of *Burgundy*, pag. 744.
(5) Anselm. Geneal. of the Royal Family, pag. 221.
(6) Ibid. pag. 220.
(-) *The Year* 1476.
(8) *Above, Citat.* (5).
(9) *Taken out of Father* Anselm, p. 220, 221.
(10) Erasm. Epist. xiv, lib. iv. pag. 265.
(11) Id. ib.

" felicitate tuâ, quæ mihi quidem summa videtur, " fine invidia frui possis. Quod ut fore confidam, " dominæ virtus facit, cui superos omnes propitios, " benéque volentes esse, non dubito. Evenit mihi, " mi Batte, in ista, quod in te sæpenumero solet, " ut tum ardentius amare, mirarique incipiam, quum " absum. Bone Deus, qui candor, quæ comitas in " amplissima fortuna, quæ animi lenitas in tantis in- " juriis, quæ hilaritas in tantis curis; tum quæ ani- " mi constantia, quæ vitæ innocentia, quod in lite- " ratos studium, quæ in omnes affabilitas (12). - - " *O happy Thou, and Favourite of Heaven, if you* " *can sail clear of these Rocks, and enjoy That Hap-* " *piness, which appears to me the greatest possible,* " *without provoking the Envy of others. That this* " *will be your happy Lot, I cannot doubt, when I* " *reflect on the Goodness of the Lady you serve, on* " *whom Heaven, I am sure, will always smile. It* " *happens to me, dear Battus, in regard to This* " *Lady, as it is wont with respect to yourself; I* " *begin to love, and admire, her with the greatest* " *Ardor, when I am absent from her. Good God!* " *What Candor, what Courtesy, amidst the amplest* " *Fortune! What Lenity of Mind, amidst such great* " *Injuries! What Chearfulness amidst so many Cares!* " *Then, what Constancy of Soul! What Innocence of* " *Life! What Liberality to Men of Learning!* " *What Affability to All!*"
I would not mention the Letter he wrote to this same Friend, in the Year 1500, if it did not testify This Lady's Liberality to the Clergy. He wished she would make choice of him for an Object of her Bounty, since the Productions of the Pen were more lasting, than the Voice of Preachers: He adds (13), that he would go into *Italy* to take his Doctor's Degree, which could not be done without such Expence, as he found himself unable to support, if she did not open her Purse for his Assistance. " Ostendes quanto amplius ego sim " meis literis decus dominæ allaturus, quam alii, quos " alit, Theologi. Nam illi vulgaria concionantur, " ego scribo quæ semper sint victura. Illi indoctè " nugantes, uno aut altero in templo audiuntur: mei " libri à Latinis, à Græcis, ab omni gente toto " orbe legentur. Ejusmodi indoctorum Theologo- " rum permagnam ubique esse copiam, mei similem " vix multis seculis inveniri; nisi forte adeò superfti- " tiosus ea, ut religio tibi sit in amici negotio menda- " ciolis aliquot abuti. Deinde ostendes nihilo illam " pauperiorem futuram, si ut Hieronymus jam depra- " vatus, si ut vera Theologia instauretur, aliquot au- " reis adjuverit, cum tanta ex illius opibus turpissimè " pereant (14). - - - - *You will shew this Lady, how* " *much greater Honour it will be to her to be celebra-* " *ted in my Writings, than in Those of some other Di-* " *vines, whom she supports. They preach vulgar Things;* " *I write what will live for ever. They, illiterate* " *Triflers, are listened to in one or two Churches at* " *most: My Works are read by Latins, by Greeks, by* " *every Nation in the whole World. You will tell* " *her, that there is every where great Plenty of such* " *illiterate Divines, but that many Ages scarce pro-* " *duce a single* Erasmus: *unless, perhaps, you make* " *a Conscience of being a little to favour your Friend.* " *Lastly, you will shew her, that she will not be the* " *poorer, if she contributes a little of That Gold, she* " *is so lavish of on the most unworthy Objects, to-* " *wards restoring St Jerom, now greatly corrupted,* " *and True Divinity.*" She found herself embarrassed in the Year 1498, and even under a kind of Confinement. " Apud dominam Veriensis oppidi res hoc " erant loco, ut nec colloqui fine summo periculo po- " tuerim, nec abire fine gravi suspicione. Nosti cau- " sam Præpositi, qui ut nunc in vinculis est, ita do- " mina in tutela (15). - - - - *The Affairs of the Prin-* " *cess of Vere were in such a State, that I could nei-* " *ther*

(12) Id. Epist. xiv. lib. iv. pag. 293.
(13) *See the 47th Letter of the 8th Book.*
(14) Id. Epist. xlvii, lib. vii. pag. 449.
(15) Id. Epist. xxiii. lib. ix, pag. 482. It is dated from Paris, 1498. See also the 37th Letter of the same Book.

VOL. I.   9 L

BERTELIER.

"ther converse with her without the greatest Danger, nor depart without being greatly suspected. You know the Cause of the Provost, who as he is now in Bonds, so the Lady is in Custody." Matters did not go better the following Year. " Veriana duris Fatis premitur, ut sublevanda potius, quam oneranda, videatur (16). —— The Princess of Vere is greatly distressed, and seems herself to stand in need of Assistance, rather than to be further burthened." But the Steddiness of her Courage against ill Fortune was a fine Subject of Praise. See the Letter, which Erasmus wrote to her in the Year 1500. I shall borrow but one Passage from it: It will inform us, that she was married very young; and that, being a Widow, after an uncomfortable Marriage, she would not marry again, though many Suitors offered themselves, with great Sollicitations. " Nam te quidem non tam in viduis, quàm in virginibus, pono: siquidem quod olim puella admodum nupsisti, id quidem partim parentum autoritati, partim generi propagando darum: & ejusmodi fuit conjugium, ut non tam fit imputanda voluptas, quàm patientia spectata. Quod autem nunc ista adhuc ætate virenti, & penè puellari, nulla procorum instantiâ possis à continentiæ proposito divelli, quod in fortunâ tam affluenti tam nihil indulges tibi, id ego non viduitatem, sed virginitatem existimo: in quo si, ut confido, perseverabis, ego te, mihi crede audacter, non in adolescentularum choro, quarum, ut ait Scriptura, non est numerus, non in octoginta Solomonis concubinis, sed in quinquaginta Reginis, & Hieronymo quidem, ut spero, approbante, annumervero (17). ——— For I reckon you, not among the Widows, but the Virgins; since you married very young, and That, partly in obedience to the Commands of your Parents, and partly for the Sake of Posterity: and since your Marriage was such, as must be considered rather as the Trial of your Patience, than the Gratification of your Desires. Now, since, in the Flower of your Youth, no Sollicitation of Suitors can divert you from a determined State of Continency; since, amidst such an Affluence of Fortune, you so little indulge yourself; I esteem the Matter as a Virgin, than a Widow; which State if you persist in, as I trust you will, believe me, I shall reckon you, not in the Company of young Maids, of which, the Scripture says, there is no number; not among the fourscore Concubines of Solomon; but among the fifty Queens, with the Consent, I hope, of St Jerom himself."

I must say something of her only Son *Adolphus* of *Burgundy*. He was Admiral of *Flanders*, and made Knight of the *Golden-Fleece*, at Brussels, in the Year 1516. *Erasmus praised him for his good Qualities, and dedicated his Book of Virtue to him*. He died at his Castle of Bevres in *Flanders*, the seventh of December, 1540 (18). He left a Son, and two Daughters; the latter left some Posterity (19); but the Son had no Children by his Wife *Louisa de Croy*, who was Daughter of *Philip de Croy*, Duke of *Arschot* (20). He was made Marquis of *Veer-Vere* by *Charles* V (21); and, in the Year 1546, he received the Collar of the Order of the *Golden Fleece* (22). He died in the Year 1558 (23). The sixteenth Letter of the tenth Book of *Erasmus* is written to *Adolphus* of *Burgundy*; *Principi Veriano*. It is dated from *London*, 1512. The same Year he wrote to him, from *Paris*, a very excellent Letter, which is, in some Editions, at the End of the *Enchiridion militis Christiani*.

BERTELIER (PHILIBERT), Register of the inferior Court of Justice at *Geneva*, where he was born, should not have had a place in this Dictionary, had not his Article been proper to be the Supplement of another (a); and to shorten That of *Calvin*, which, probably, will be very long. This *Bertelier* lived in the middle of the XVIth Century. He distinguished himself only by his vile Actions; but, as he committed one, which pleased the Controversists much, since it supplied them with ample Matter to defame *Calvin's* Memory, this gave occasion to his being quoted as a Person of Consequence; and gave him a Figure in some considerable Writings (b). He pretended, that the Republic of *Geneva* had sent him to *Noyon*, with orders to make an exact Enquiry, there, into *Calvin's* Life and Conversation; and that, having performed his Commission, he found, that *John Calvin* had been convicted of Sodomy; and that, at the Bishop's Request, the Punishment of Fire was commuted into That of being branded with the *Flower-de-luce*. He boasted to have an Act, signed by a Notary, which certified the Truth of the Process and Condemnation. *Bolsec* affirms (c), that He, and many Others, had seen That Act; and This is the Ground of That horrid Accusation, so much spoken of, and which has been inserted in many Books. The matter of Fact, whether *Calvin* was branded with a hot Iron, for the Crime of Pederasty, is only grounded on the Authority of *Bolsec*, who affirms, that he saw the Act, which *Bertelier* brought from *Noyon*. We shall see, in the Article BOLSEC, that his Testimony is of no weight in Things, which are laid to *Calvin's* Charge. That *Bertelier* cannot be better; for he was an ill Liver, and against whom Sentence of Death had been pronounced [A]; and who,

[A] *He was a Person of an ill Life, and against whom Sentence of Death had been pronounced.*] Mr *Drelincourt*, Minister of *Paris*, will supply me with a Proof of this Fact, which the boldest Sophister cannot deny. He has inserted the Extract of a Letter, which he received from Mr *Lullin*, Counsellor, and ancient Syndic of *Geneva*, in a Book, printed at *Geneva*, and licensed by the Republic (1): These are the Contents of That Extract.

" In the mean time, I shall not refuse, for your " particular Satisfaction, to acquaint you with what " I have learned, and what I can assure you I have " just now read, in the ancient Records of our " Council: wherein I find, that *Philip Bertelier* " was a Native of This City, and had the Office " of *Secretary* (which is elsewhere called *Register*) " *of the Inferior Court of Justice;* which Post is " much below That of *Secretary of State*, which " he is said to have had; and that, being accused " of Sedition and Conspiracy against This State, and " Church, he ran away, and, not appearing to an- " swer for himself, was condemned, as being attaint- " ed, and convicted, of Those Crimes, to lose his " Head, by a Sentence pronounced against him, the " sixth of *August*, 1555. About two Years after, " he went to Law with a private Person of this " City, in a foreign Court of Justice, whither he " had fled; and, it being requisite, for the Honour " and Interest of our Republic, and of That private " Person, to make This perfidious Man known, an " Attestation was granted of the Judgment, given " against him, in the Terms, which you shall see " in the following Copy, dated the fifth of *February*, " 1557. This is the true Character of *Bertelier*, " whose Testimony is so much extolled in the Book " of the late Cardinal *de Richelieu*. As for what con- " cerns his being sent, or deputed, to *Noyon*, to make " a Report of *Calvin's* Life, it is a Fact not only " falsly supposed, and whereof no kind of Mention " is made in our Records; but it is also contrary to " all probability. For, besides that no Envoy, or " Deputy, was ever sent from our City, upon pub- " lic Business, who was not in a higher Station, than " That of *Bertelier*; and that such Employs are on- " ly given to Counsellors of the little Council; It is " notorious, as you know, that we had some consi- " derable

BERTELIER. 783

who, besides, had no Party against him, in *Geneva*, more inexorable than *Calvin* [B]. It is no ways necessary, in order to confute this Accusation, to make use of the just Exceptions, which invalidate the Testimony of these two Persons (d). There is, in the Act itself, an infallible Mark of Reprobation [C]; and nothing surprizes me more, than to see so great a Person, as *Cardinal de Richelieu*, depend on this piece of *Bertelier* [D], and alledge, as his principal Reason, that the Republic

(d) *See Rivet Catholi. Orthodox. Oper. Tom. III. pag. 8. & seq. and in Jesuita Vapulante, cap. ii. pag. 401, & seq. e used Tomwhere be shews Lesseus, that, by his own Rules, Bertelier and Bolsec can be no Evidence against Calvin.*

"derable Persons of *Noyon* in our City, who retired
" hither, with *Calvin*, soon after him: And, among
" others, a Canon, whose Name was Mr *Collement*,
" and Mr *de Normandie*, Lieutenant-Civil of the
" City of *Noyon*, whose Family is still One of the
" most considerable among us, and from which I am
" descended by the Mother's Side; by whose means,
" it was very easy to receive all the Information, which
" could have been desired, without going farther.
" Add to this, that it is certain, This *Bertelier* was
" always *Calvin*'s Enemy; because he had often reprimanded, and censured him for his vicious and
" scandalous Life; and that he had strenuously opposed his wicked and pernicious Designs. This
" appears by *Calvin*'s Letters to *Viretus*, and to *Bullinger*, in the Months of *September*, and *November*,
" 1553; in which he cries him down as a vicious
" and audacious Man: *Beza* represents, likewise, the
" wicked Qualities of *Bertelier*, in *Calvin*'s Life (2)."
Here follows the Copy of the Attestation of the Republic of *Geneva*, against *Philibert Bertelier* (3).
" We, the Syndics and Council of *Geneva*, to All
" Those, to whom these Presents shall come, do cer-
" tify, that, on the sixth of *August*, of the Year
" 1555, was publickly given, and pronounced, by
" Sound of Trumpet, a criminal Sentence against
" *Philibert Bertelier*, and his Accomplices, named
" in the said Sentence; by which, for the horrid and
" detestable Crimes of Conspiracy against the Holy
" Institution, and Christian Reformation, and against
" this City, and the public Good and Tranquillity
" thereof, the said *Philibert Bertelier*, as one of the
" Authors of the Conspiracy, and an Enemy to this
" City, and to the Peace, Union, and Tranquillity
" thereof, has been condemned to be bound, and
" brought to the Place of *Champel*; there to have
" his Head cut off; his Body to be quartered, and
" his Members to be set up in the four most eminent
" Places round about this City, for an Example to
" others, who shall commit such Crimes: This we
" attest and certify. And, therefore, we have
" ordered, and commanded, these Presents to be
" given under our usual Seal, and signed by our Secretary. Given at *Geneva*, the fifth of *February*, 1577."

[B] *He had no Party against him — — more inexorable than Calvin.*] *Bertelier*, having been excommunicated, in the Year 1552, by the Consistory of *Geneva* (4), made his Complaint to the Senate. The Ministers were sent for, to give their Reasons for it; and both Parties being heard, the Senate confirmed the Excommunication. Eighteen Months after, *Bertelier* had recourse again to the Senate, who, after having heard *Calvin*'s Opposition, pronounced, that *Bertelier* should be admitted to the Holy Sacrament. As soon as *Calvin* heard this News, he desired the *Syndics* to assemble the Senate; and, when they were met, he represented his Reasons, and concluded, with an Oath, that he would rather lose his Life, than give his Consent, that such a Man should receive the Lord's Supper (5). This is what *Calvin* wrote himself. His Historian will tell us more of it (6). The Clamour, which was raised against the Ministers, as if, in some respects, they had invaded the Rights of the Sovereignty, was the Reason, why the Council of Two hundred ordered, that the final Judgment of Causes of Excommunication should belong to the Senate; and that the Senate might abuse the excommunicated, as they should think fit. By virtue of this Decree, the Senate granted Letters of Absolution to *Bertelier*, which were sealed with the Seal of the Republic. The Sacrament was to be administred within two Days, when *Calvin* came to hear of what had past; he soon resolved what to do, and preached against the Contempt of the Sacrament; he raised his Voice, lifted up his Hands, and said, that he would imitate St *Chrysostom*; that he would not oppose Force to Force, but that he would rather suffer himself to be massacred, than that his Hands should present the Holy Mysteries to Those, who had been judged unworthy of them: This was a Thunder-bolt, which confounded *Bertelier*'s Faction; so that it was not thought fit, that he should present himself to the Communion. The next Day after the Sacrament, *Calvin*, accompanied by his Consistory, desired leave of the Senate, and of the Council of Two hundred, to speak to the People about this Matter, for as much as it concerned the Abrogation of a Law, made by the People. This made so great an Impression on the People's Minds, that it was resolved the *Swiss Cantons* should be consulted about it; and that the Decree of the Two hundred should be suspended; but that none should say, that the ancient Regulations had been in the least infringed. *In eam sententiam animis non mediocriter immutatis itum est, ut suspenso illo Diaceseorum decreto statueretur petendum esse à quatuor civitatibus Helveticis judicium, nec interea præjudicium ullum fieri receptis legibus oportere* (7). By this means the Consistory obtained a compleat Victory, and, in a manner, made the Senate, and the Council of Two hundred, buckle to. What would they not have done in a Democratical Country? Is it possible to rule over Men, who tell the People, from the Pulpit, that they had rather suffer themselves to be killed, than consent, that Holy Things should be prophaned? St *Chrysostom*'s Example, properly alledged, is an artful way of threatning the Government on an Insurrection.

[C] *There is, in the Act itself, an infallible Sign of Reprobation.*] No one knows when it was drawn up, or by whom, or the Names of the Witnesses, or, in general, any of the Circumstances, which are never forgotten, except when People fear to supply Those with Arms, whose Interest it is to deny a Thing. What I am going to say, carries a much greater Force with it. If *Bertelier*'s Act had not been suppositious, there would have been, at *Noyon*, authentic and public Testimonies of the Trial, and Punishment, in question; and, therefore, They would have been published, as soon as the Catholic Religion began to suffer by *Calvin*'s Means. Unless we suppose a continual, and more unheard of Miracle, than was ever yet known, the Inhabitants of *Noyon* would not have kept the Secret, and spared the Reputation of a Countryman of theirs, who was so odious to them (8). I carry this Thought farther in another place (9), and observe that it is there as it is. I add, that, if what *Bertelier* said was true, he would have had his Paper, when he fled from *Geneva*: I mean, that his pretended Commission would have preceded the Matter, for which he was condemned to death in the Year 1555; for it is plain, that he had not the Commission, he boasted of, after That time. But can any one believe, that, before the Year 1555, when Those, who were called Hereticks, durst not shew themselves, for fear of being burnt, a Deputy from *Geneva* should go boldly to *Noyon*, to inform himself of *Calvin*'s Life? Who will believe, that, if *Bertelier* had made an authentic Act of *Calvin*'s Infamy in the Year 1554, he would have kept it so close, that the Public should have no knowledge of it before the Year 1577? Was it not a Piece, which the Clergy of *France* would have bought for it's weight in Gold? But why do I lose time in confuting such a ridiculous Romance, as This is?

[D] *It is surprizing to see Cardinal* de Richelieu *depend on This Piece of* Bertelier.] "That, *says* he "(10), which ought to pass for an undeniable Con- " viction of the Crimes, imputed to *Calvin*, is, that " ever since he was charged with This Accusation, " the Church of *Geneva* has neither proved the con- " trary, nor even denied the Report, which *Berte- " lier*, sent by Those of That City, made at *Noyon*. " This Report was signed by the most eminent Per- " sons of the City of *Noyon*, and made with all usual " Forms of Justice: And by the same Report it ap- " pears, that That Arch-Heretic, having been con- " victed of an abominable Sin, punishable only by " Fire, the Punishment, which he had deserved.

(2) *Dreline. Defence of Calvin. pag. 148.*

(3) *It is in Mr Drellincourt's Book, pag. 151.*

(4) *It is of him, that these Words of Calvin's Letter to Bullinger, (which is the 163d,) must be understood. Quodam obstreperes suas libidines & multa flagitia, cærne usu privatus donec respisceret.*

A VICTORY obtained by the Consistory of *Geneva*, against the Magistrates.

(5) *Ex Epistola Calvini ad Viretum. It is the 154th, and is dated Septem. 4. 1553.*

(6) *Beza, in Vita Calvini ad Ann. 1553.*

(7) *Beza, ib.*

(8) *In 1551, Public Prayers and Processions were made at Noyon, on a false Report of Calvin's Death, to thank God for it. Non dubito quin me patriæ esse superstitem. Ita urbem mortuam lugere cogent (Calvin says this on occasion of the Fire, which happened that City in the Year 15(2,) re anno obsit inter mortalium morem solennes habuisse. It supplicationes, ut de Christo triumpharet. Calvin, Epist. 140, dated Decemb. 5, 1553.*

(9) *In Remark* [K], *of the Article* BOLSEC, *and more amply in Remark* [U], *of the Article* BEZA.

(10) *A Method to convert Those, who have separated themselves from the Church, lib. II, cap. 10, pag. 319.*

" was,

public of *Geneva* did not undertake to ſhew the Falſhood of This Piece [E]. This is not a Place to examine, whether they had reaſon to make light of This Lie [F]. There is no Article of a Dictionary more uſeful to a Reader, than This [G].

" was, by the Interceſſion of his Biſhop, commuted " into That of the *Flower-de-luce*. And the Church " of *Geneva*, which does not deny This Report con- " cerning *Calvin*'s Life, would not have failed to " have done it, if they had believed, that it could " have been done without offending againſt Truth." Is it not ſtrange, that a chief Miniſter of State, whoſe Credit was not inferior to That of the King, ſhould depend on a blind Act, which an inconſiderable Phyſician of *Lyons* had pretended to have ſeen in the Hands of a mean Perſon? An inconſiderable private Man muſt, then, have had more credit, than Cardinal *de Richelieu*, to find out the old Records of *Noyon*? The Truth is, This Cardinal made all imaginable Enquiry into the pretended Proceedings againſt *John Calvin*, at *Noyon*, and that he diſcovered nothing (11); and yet he maintained the Affirmative on the Credit of *Jerome Bolſec*. Can ſuch a ſtrange Conduct be excuſed? Mr *Drelincourt* cannot believe, that That great Man was guilty of it, and lays all the Blame on Thoſe, who publiſhed the Book, entituled, *Methode pour convertir*, &c (12).

[E] ---- *And alleage, as his chief Reaſon, That the Republic of* Geneva *did not undertake to ſhew the Falſhood of this Piece*] In the foregoing Remark, we have ſet down Cardinal *Richelieu*'s own Words: They ſhew, that he lays his Streſs on the Silence of the Republic of *Geneva*. Mr *Drelincourt* ſhews him, by ſome plain Inſtances, that there is nothing more falſe, nor more abſurd, than to pretend, that They, who ſuffer an Accuſation to be ſpread abroad againſt themſelves, give occaſion to believe, that They are convinced it is well-grounded. The firſt of theſe Examples is Cardinal *Richelieu* himſelf: "That Thoſe, " who could not bear his Elevation, and his Power, " ſaid ſtrange things of him; and that ſome of Thoſe " Things have been publiſhed, and ſome Books have " been filled with them. Becauſe no Juridical Infor " mation has been made to juſtify the contrary, muſt " we therefore believe, that the Relations of That " Illuſtrious Cardinal, and Thoſe, who honour his " Memory, look upon Thoſe Things as certain " Truths (13)?". *Rivetus*, Profeſſor of Divinity at *Leyden*, made uſe of the like Reaſoning, in anſwer to an Objection of *Leſſius*, taken from the Silence of *Calvin*'s good Friends. "*Itane?* Ergo quotieſ " cunque libuerit infami alicui ægyrtæ crimina con " fingere in viros bonos, neceſſariumne erit libellos " illos famoſos diſcutere, ut homines iſti, ſi tamen " homines, qui famam aucupantur ex adverſariorum " nomine, applaudant ſibi, quod tandem repererint " qui ſe cum illis voluerint componere, & exiſtima " rint talia eſſe reſponſione digna, quæ contemptu " potius erant diluenda (14). —— *What! Shall " it be neceſſary, as often as an infamous Fellow " invents an Accuſation againſt Good Men, to re " fute his libellous Books; and thus give ſuch Men, " if they deſerve the Name of Men, who build their " own Fame on the Reputation of their Adverſaries, " an Opportunity of triumphing, in that they have found " Perſons, who will enter the Liſts with Them, and " think Theſe Things worthy of an Anſwer, which deſerve " to be refuted rather with Contempt?*" Here is a Jeſuit, who agrees perfectly with Theſe Miniſters. "How long is it, ſince it is not allowable to be ſilent, " without being looked upon as convicted of the " Crimes, which are imputed to us? It does not " appear, That This is the Opinion of the Wiſeſt, " and of Thoſe, whoſe Example may ſerve as a Rule " to others. Who is ignorant, how many fooliſh " things the Enemies of *France* are uſed to publiſh " againſt it, in their Gazettes, and Libels? Who " does not know how many infamous and abomi " nable Reports Mr *Jurieu* has ſpread againſt the " Popes, and againſt the Church of *Rome*, in his " *Parallel*, in his *Prejugez*, and in ſo many other " Books, with which he fills the World? So that, " if the King does not keep Perſons on purpoſe to " confute Theſe Foreign Gazettes, in every Parti " cular; if more are to be found among the " Catholics, who will loſe their Time in confuting, " ſeriouſly, theſe idle Fancies of Mr *Jurieu*, that

(11) *See the Defence of Calvin, by Mr Drelincourt, p. 9.*

(12) Ib. pag. 71. See alſo pag. 14 ?, &c.

THAT the Silence of an accuſed Perſon concludes no thing in certain Caſes. Some curious Examples of This.

(13) *Drelincourt, ibid. pag. 84.*

(14) *Rivet. Oper. Tom. Iii, pag. 9, & 490.*

" the Popes have pretended to Univerſal Monarchy: " that, in order to it, they have occaſioned a Schiſm " between the *Greeks* and the *Latins*; that, after " wards, to end the Quarrel, they have ---- *&c.* " I ſay, unleſs the King, or the Pope, take care " to have theſe Fooleries, and Slanders, refuted, " will not the Gazetteer of *Holland*, and Mr *Ju " rieu*, have reaſon to ſay, *They dare not anſwer; " there is therefore reaſon to believe, they cannot do " it?* Would the Author of the *Morale Pratique* have " condemned them upon ſuch an Account? I am " willing to believe, he would be aſhamed to own " it. Why, then, might not the Jeſuits neglect " to anſwer Libels, which are, in their Opinion, " no leſs fabulous, nor leſs deſpicable, than the Ga " zettes of *Amſterdam*, and the Hiſtorical or Pro " phetical Syſtems of Mr *Jurieu?* Ought they to " be more nice in Point of Reputation, than Thoſe, " whom GOD has placed over us? Ought they not, " or at leaſt may they not, after Theſe great Ex " amples, deſpiſe what concerns only their particu " lar Honour (15)?"

[F] *This is not a Place to examine, whether They had reaſon to make Light of This Lie.*] Mr *Drelincourt*, and Father *le Tellier*'s, Maxim is in general very good and true; but there are ſome particular Caſes, wherein it is better not to make uſe of it. I ſhall not decide whether the Republic of *Geneva* had done better to make a public Declaration againſt *Bolſec*, in relation to the pretended Deputation of *Bertelier*. It ſeems at firſt ſight, that the Advantage, which the Catholic Controverſiſts have pretended to draw from the Silence of That Republic, ſhews, that they were in the wrong to be ſilent, I mean, not to make it appear, by a public Act, that Theſe Perſons were impudent Liars: But They, who conſider, that nothing can ſtop the Pens of a Sort of Men, and that, if you ſilence them In one Point, they will turn to ſomething elſe, will eaſily perceive, that an Act of the Republic of *Geneva* would not have ended This Diſpute. I agree to the Maxim, that, ſometimes, the beſt way to be revenged of an impudent Calumniator, is to return him no Anſwer (16). However I believe, that *Beza* did not well apply this Maxim, when he made uſe of it in relation to *Bolſec*. An Anſwer would have puffed him up with Vanity; and he would have concluded from it, that his Slanders had touched the Proteſtants to the quick, which would have filled him with Joy. I grant it: But it had been better to have let him enjoy This Pleaſure, attended with the infamous Character of a public Calumniator, which a good Anſwer would have branded him, than to give him, and others, a Pretence to boaſt, that the Republic could not deny the Matter in queſtion. *Qui tacet conſentire videtur.* Theſe Truths, which are called Maxims, no leſs claſh with each other, than Errors, and Truths.

[G] *There is no Article of a Dictionary more uſeful to a Reader, than This.*] One of the greateſt Uſes, which may be drawn from Reading, is, to learn the Weakneſſes of the Heart of Man, and the ill Effects of Prejudices in Point of Religion. Can there be a more remarkable Inſtance of it, than This? What muſt not a Man naturally be, or what will he not become, by a blind and furious Zeal for Religion, ſince a Monk, who turned a Proteſtant Phyſician, and afterwards a Popiſh Phyſician, and who was expelled two or three times, with a Brand of Infamy, from the Places where he was ſettled, no ſooner produces an Accuſation on the Credit of a Fugitive, condemned to death, upon refuſing to appear before his Judges, an Accuſation, than which none was ever worſe contrived, and worſe proved, but it is adopted, and conveyed from Book to Book; a thouſand Conſequences are drawn from it; and Authors of the firſt Rank, the great Cardinal *Richelieu* himſelf, propoſe it to the Heretics as a powerful Motive of Converſion: And all this *propter majorem Dei gloriam?* O QUANTUM EST IN REBUS INANE (17)!

(15) Father le Tellier's Defence of the New Chriſtians. Part I, pag. 25, 30.

(16) Genus ultionis eſt eripere ei qui fecit contumeliæ voluptatem. Solent cicere, miſerum me, puto non intellexiſſe! Adeo fructus contumeliæ in ſenſu & indignatione patientis eſt, at optime Seneca cap. 17, de Conſt. Sapientis. Hanc fructum gerebat Belſecus, quem ei ademit veritas ſapientia. *Rivet. Oper. Tom. III. pag. 496.*

(17) *Perſius, Sat. I, ver. 1.*

BERTRAM

BERTRAM. BERULLE.

BERTRAM (CORNELIUS BONAVENTURA), born at *Thouars*, in *Poitou*, was a considerable Man, in the XVIth Century, for his Knowledge in the Oriental Languages. He studied *Hebrew* at *Paris*, under *Angelus Caninius*, and, afterwards, at *Cahors*, with the Civilian *Francis Roaldus*. He had much ado to avoid being massacred, at *Cahors*, in the Year 1572; but, at last, he made his escape, and fled to *Geneva*; where, at the end of two Years, he was made *Hebrew* Professor, in the room of *Rodolphus Cevalier*. He wrote several considerable Books, during his abode at *Geneva* [*A*], and continued to apply himself to his Studies, when he went to *Franckenthal*, in the *Palatinate*. He published a Book, there, in the Year 1586, entituled, *Lucubrationes Franckenthalenses*. He left That Post to go to *Lausane*, where the Magistrates of *Bern* offered him a Professorship, which he exercised 'till his Death, which happened in the Year 1594. He was in his climacterical Year, when he died (*a*), by which we may judge, that he was born in the Year 1531. It must be forgot, that he was a Minister, and that he exercised That Office in *Geneva* (*b*); where he married *Genevieve Denoße*, Niece of *Beza*'s first Wife, in whose House she had been educated from her Youth. She was very tenderly beloved by her Aunt (*c*). *Bertram* was a good Critic, as *Beza*, *Caſaubon*, and several other learned Persons, have publickly acknowledged (*d*).

(*a*) *Taken from Thuanus, at the End of Book* 109.

(*b*) *See Beza's Preface to Mercerus in Jobum, printed in* 1573.

(*c*) *Ant. Feyus, de vita & obitu Th. Bezæ*, pag. 43.

(*d*) *See Colomeſii Galli. Oriental.* pag. 73. 74.

[*A*] *He wrote several considerable Books during his abode at Geneva.*] He published the *Thesaurus of Sanctes Pagninus*, with Additions, part whereof he took out of the Writings of *Mercerus* and *Cevalier*, and the rest he supplied out of his own Stock. He published, also, a *Comparatio Grammaticæ Hebraicæ & Aramææ*, and a Treatise *de Politia Judaica*. *Thuanus* knew no more of them: He places this last Treatise above the other Books, composed by This Author. *Qui ex omnibus ejus operibus maxime commendatur* (1). He might have added, that *Bertram* contributed, as much as any one, to the Edition of the Commentary of *Mercerus* on the Book of *Job*. This is acknowledged in the Preface: " Cæterum " ne fua quidem laude fraudandus Cornelius noster " videtur, ejusdem Merceri quondam diſcipulus & " nunc meus in hac Ecclesia Collega. Huic siqui- " dem non parva ex parte debetur istius libri editio, " cum vix alius reperiri potuiße videretur, qui hæc " à Mercero minutiſſimis characteribus ac fugien- " tibus penè literis in adverſariis deſcripta legendo " conſequeneretur (2). — *Nor muſt we deny due* " *Praiſe to our Cornelius Bertram, formerly a Diſ-* " *ciple of Mercerus, and at preſent my Colleague in* " *This Church; to whom we are not a little indebted* " *for the Publication of This Book; there being ſcarce* " *any other Perſon capable of decyphering the exceed-* " *ing ſmall, and almoſt inviſible, Characters of Mer-* " *cerus in his Adverſaria.*" Mr *Simon* mentions another Work of *Bertram*; he ſays, that This Profeſſor, aſſiſted by *Beza*, *la Faye*, *Rotan*, *Jaquemot*, and *Goulart*, reviſed the *French* Tranſlation of the Bible in the Year 1588, and *that, being more learned in the Hebrew Tongue, than all thoſe, who had preceeded him, he took a great deal more Liberty in the Reformation, which he made, both in the Tranſlation, and in the Notes* (3). What Mr *Simon* says farther concerning This Reviſion, is not only to be found in his *Critical Hiſtory*, but alſo in the Supplement to *Moreri*'s Dictionary. I obſerve, that, according to *Thuanus*, the Work, entituled *Lucubrationes Franckenthalenſes* (4), was publiſhed in the Year 1586, and entituled ſo, becauſe the Author lived at *Franckenthal*. How then, may it be ſaid to me, could he *have a hand in the Reviſion, which was made at Geneva, in the Year* 1581. This is no difficulty at all. When Mr *Simon* ſays, that *another Reformation of the Tranſlation of Geneva was made in the Year* 1588, he intends only to mark the Date of the Impreſſion, and does not pretend, that the whole Work was done in the Year 1588. It is well known, that ſuch Reviſions commonly take up ſeveral Years. So that *Bertram* might have been the chief Director of This, though it was not printed 'till a long time after he was gone from *Geneva*. I add, that he was, particularly, the Author of the Figures of This Bible, and of their Explication (5). Theſe Words of the Preface, prefixed to This Bible, muſt therefore be underſtood of Him. " We have alſo added ſome Fi- " gures, but at the end, and out of the Body of this " Work, which may ſerve for the underſtanding of " ſeveral Paſſages, wherein a learned Perſon of our " Society, who is very well verſed in the *Hebrew* " Tongue, and in the reading of the Old Teſtament, " has been particularly concerned." Mr *Colomies* has applied them to our *Bertram* (6).

(1) *Thuan. lib. 109. ſub fin.*

(2) *Beza in Præfat. illius Commentarii.*

(3) *Critical Hiſt. of the Old Teſtament, lib. iii. chap. 24.* pag. 347.

(4) *To give the whole Title, we muſt add here, ſeu Specimen expoſitionum in difficiliores utriuſque Teſtamenti locorum. In Mr Simon's Critical Hiſtory, and in the Supplement to Moreri's Dictionary, it is Franckellenſes, inſtead of Franckenthallenſes.*

(5) *Teſſier, Elog. de Mr de Thou, Tom. II.* pag. 202.

(6) *In Colomeſia Orientali,* pag. 73.

BERULLE (PETER *de*), Cardinal, and Founder of the Fathers of the Oratory in *France*, was born the 4th of *Febr.* 1575, and died the 2d of *October*, 1629 (*a*). You will find many Particulars concerning him in *Moreri*'s Dictionary, and in Mr *Perrault*'s *Illuſtrious Men*; but you wil! not find, in either of them, that he was expoſed to the Laſh of the *Carmelites* [*A*], who induſtriouſly decried him as a very diſhoneſt Man; nor that he oppoſed the Deſign, which Cardinal *Richelieu* had formed, of humbling

(*a*) *Perrault's Illuſtrious Men,* Part I, pag. 30, 34.

[*A*] *He was expoſed to the Laſh of the Carmelites.*] This is what I have read in a Book of the Biſhop of *Belles* (1). " Mr *de Berulle*, being Supe- " rior of the Oratory —— was made Superior, by " Delegation and Commiſſion from the Pope, of " certain Nuns of great Piety and Edification (2), " whom he had brought from *Spain*, and intro- " duced into *France*. The Monks of the ſame Order, " who wanted to have the Direction of Them, " clamoured loudly both at *Rome*, and in *France*. " But, failing of Succeſs (becauſe, at the Court of " *Rome*, The Direction of Nuns by Monks is held " in Abhorrence, for Reaſons, which Experience " ſufficiently evinces) they ſet themſelves to libel " him; they called him Anti-Pope, concealed Hu- " guenot, impious Wretch, Libertine; in ſhort, they " threw the moſt ſcandalous Reflexions upon him. " They accuſed his Morals, cenſured his Doctrine, " and blackened his Reputation every way; at laſt, " Theſe Contradictions, by a wonderful Providence " of GOD, who can bring Good out of Evil, and " Light out of Darkneſs, gave birth to thoſe excel- " lent Works of the State and Glories of JESUS; " and That of his Life; which dazzled the Eyes " of his Adverſaries, and ſtruck them dumb." Some of them arrived to ſuch a Pitch of Raſhneſs and Preſumption as to maintain, that the Pope could not give the Direction of Nuns to any but Monks of the ſame Order (3). There is, among the Works of Cardinal *Berulle*, a Narrative of the Quarrel, which The *Carmelites* had with him. Their Pretence was a certain Memorial, which he had drawn up, by way of Formulary for a new kind of Vow (4). It was a Vow of Servitude to JESUS CHRIST, and the *Virgin Mary*. This Author did not anſwer their Writings; but he compoſed a Diſcourſe *Of the State and Glories of* JESUS, as an Apology for his Memorial. " Inſtead of Anſwer, and Reply, *ſays he* (5), " after ten Years of Patience and Silence, after three " Years of Storms and Tempeſts, raiſed in *France* and " *Italy*, by Spirits fit for this Employ, after many " Calumnies,

(1) *The Antiboulic, in anſwer to the Anti Coton,* p. 141.

(2) *That is, Carmelite Nuns.*

(3) *Ibid.* pag. 202.

(4) *This Memorial is in the Works of Cardinal Berulle,* pag. 278, &c. *Edit. of Paris, in* 1657, *in Folio*.

(5) *Part III of his Works.*

VOL. I   9 M

humbling the House of *Austria* [B]; nor that it was pretended, that he died by Poison [C]. What I shall say of the Edition of his Works will rectify an Oversight of *Moreri* [D]. I shall refute, likewise, an Error of Mr *Perrault* [E]. Cardinal *Berulle* had a Brother, a Counsellor of State, one of whose Grand-sons was Master of the Requests, Intendant at *Lyons*, and afterwards First President of the Parliament of *Grenoble* (b). The Brother of this latter was called The Abbot *de Berulle*, and was Master of the Requests, and Prior of *St Romain du Puy*, near *Lyons*, and died about the End of the Month of *June*, 1704 (c).

(b) Mercure Gallant, of July, 1704. pag. 99.
(c) Ibid. pag. 100.

" Calumnies, and six injurious and diffamatory Li-
" bels, industriously spread, even in foreign Coun-
" tries; I produce This Discourse in Evidence, and
" produce it, not to speak of their Persons, their
" Designs, their Conduct; but, to speak of JESUS."
[B] *He opposed the Design ---- of humbling the House of* Austria] He was seconded by *Marillac*, Keeper of the Seals, and *by some other Members of the Privy-Council of* Mary de Medicis (6). The Reasons, which They alledged, against succouring the Duke of *Mantua*, are to be found in Mr *le Vas-for* (7), who adds; " *Berulle*, a Man, whose Poli-
" tics are of a Religious Turn, displayed them in
" a Council of the Queen-Mother, and supported
" them by the false Arguments, which his mystical Divi-
" nity, and his Imagination, naturally lively and fer-
" tile, suggested to him in Abundance. The Keeper
" of the Seals listened to him, as to a Prophet in-
" spired from Heaven. *Berulle* spoke to him after
" his own Heart. ——— Certain *Carmelite* Nuns of
" the Fauxbourg *St Jaques*, great Visionaries, whom
" *Berulle*, their Director, the Keeper of the Seals,
" and the Queen-Mother, consulted as Oracles,
" greatly applauded the Project (8). GOD had re-
" vealed to them, in their Prayers, and their Exta-
" sies, that such was his Will (9)." We shall see, in the following Remark, how This Historian excuses his Wishing, that the House of *Austria* might not be humbled.

The Political Will of Cardinal *de Richelieu* shews us the Partiality of Cardinal *Berulle* for *Spain*. I shall cite This Passage. " Your Majesty (*it is* Car-
" *dinal* Richelieu, *who addresses himself to* Lewis
" XIII) might, by this means, have for ever freed
" the *Grisons* from the Tyranny of the House of
" *Austria*, if *Fargis*, your Embassador in *Spain*, had
" not, at the Sollicitation of Cardinal *Berulle*, with-
" out your Knowledge, and contrary to the express
" Orders of your Majesty (as he has since confessed),
" made a very disadvantageous Treaty, to which
" you at last adhered, to please the Pope, who pre-
" tended to have some Interest in This Affair (10)."
The Abbot *Richard* cites these Words, in his Histo-ry of Father *Joseph*, after having said, that " The
" Treaty, made by the Lord du *Fargis*, ---- was
" disclaimed, because he had not followed the In-
" structions of Father *Joseph* (11)." He adds, that it was resolved in the King's Council, to take no notice of this Fault of *du Fargis*: but that, " instead
" of ratifying what he had done, another Project
" should be sent him, agreeable to which he might
" rectify the first; which The Embassador accord-
" ingly executed (12)."

[C] *It was pretended, that he died by Poison*]

" He died suddenly, as he was saying Mass -----
" This Accident made it suspected, by several, that
" *Richelieu* had poisoned him. The Duke of *Or-
" leans* insinuates This in a Letter to the King.
" Cardinal *Berulle*, my *Cousin*, says *Gaston*, did me
" very great Service, in my Reconciliation with the
" Queen my Mother. But it proved fatal to him,
" since his Death followed so soon after *. Is not
" This to carry the Malignity too far? *Berulle* was
" in a languishing Condition more than a Year. The
" noble Parts, in him, were found injured, and
" corrupted. Perhaps the Censorious might look
" upon it as the Effect of a slow Poison, sent him
" by *Richelieu*, who was chagrined at his Rise.
" However it be, *Berulle* was universally acknow-
" ledged to be a perfectly good Man. If he was
" out in his Politics, it was owing to the Tender-
" ness of his Conscience, and to a false Zeal for
" Religion, which made him sincerely think, that his
" Opinion was more advantageous to the Good of
" the State, and the Re-establishment of the *Romish
" Worship in* France, *and other Countries* (13)."
Observe, that *le Vassor* neither rejects, nor adopts, the Calumny of the Cardinal's Enemies. It is a Sign he did not think it very probable.

[D] *What I shall say of the Edition of his Works will rectify an Oversight of Mr* Moreri] Part of the Works of Cardinal *Berulle* had been printed at different Times during his Life; the other Part was found among his Manuscripts (14). *Francis Bour-goign*, at the Request of the Fathers of the Oratory, whose General he was, caused them to be collected into one Body (15). Father *Gibieuf*, who knew more of them than any other, ranged them in order, and enriched them with *Arguments and Summaries* (16). They were printed at *Paris*, in the Year 1644, in Folio; and a second Edition was published at the same Place, in 1657, in Folio. Father *Bour-gign* (17) dedicated them to the Queen-Regent, *Anne of Austria*: and added a Preface, which is not, as Mr *Moreri* pretends, an *Abridgment of the Life* of *Berulle*, but rather an Elogy on his Piety, and a general Idea of his Works.

[E] *I shall refute an Error of Mr* Perrault] He affirms, that Cardinal *Berulle*, having conducted the Princess *Henrietta Maria* into *England*, gained there *the Love and Veneration of every one* (18). Yet we read, as follows, in a Letter, which This Cardinal wrote to That Princess, the Twenty sixth of *October*, 1625. " The Duke of *Buckingham* is pleased to
" make great Complaint to the King, by his Con-
" fident Mr *Gerbieres*, who arrived ten or twelve
" Days after me, that I had conspired, and attempted,
" in *England*, against his Life and Fortune (19)."

BEVERNINGK (JEROM), was one of the ablest Men, of the XVIIth Century, for Embassies, and important Negotiations. He was originally descended from a noble Family of *Prussia* [A]; but he was born at *Tergou*, in *Holland*, the Twenty fifth of *April*, 1614. That Town, which boasts, with reason, of having produced so great a Man, saw him in the Number of it's Counsellors, in the Year 1645; and in the Number of it's Burgomasters, in the Year 1668. He was deputed by it, in the Year 1646, to the States of the Province, where he gave such good Proofs of his Capacity, that, not long after, they employed him in Affairs of Consequence.

[A] *He was originally descended from a noble Family of* Prussia.] His Grandfather, *John Van* BEVERNINGK, a Gentleman of *Prussia*, came into *Holland* in the Year 1575, with the Count de *Hohenlo*. The States gave him a Company of Foot. He was made afterwards Lieutenant-General of the Artillery. He married the Daughter of *Dirck Loncq*, Burgo-Master of the City of *Tergou*, and Treasurer General of the Province of *Holland*. From This Marriage proceeded *Melchior Van* BEVERNINGK, Cap-tain of Foot in the Service of the States General, and Commander of the Castles of *Argenteau* and *Dalem*. He married *Sibylla Standert*, Daughter of *Leonard Standert*, Esq; Captain of Foot, and Governor of *Knodseuburch*, over against *Nimegen*, and of *Catherine Hauffart*, Daughter of *Francis Hauffart*, Chamberlain to the Queen of *Hungary*. Our Mr *Van Beverningk* proceeded from the Marriage of *Melchior Van Beverningk*, and *Sibylla Standert*.

BEVERNINGK.

In the Year 1650, the States of *Holland* deputed him, with Mr *Van Brederode*, to the States of *Utrecht*, to defire them to be at the Extraordinary Affembly of the United Provinces, which was to be held at the *Hague*. In 1651, the fame States of *Holland* deputed him to affift at That Great Affembly of the United Provinces. In the Year 1653, the City of *Tergou* deputed him to the Affembly of the States General. The fame Year, he was fent to the Protector, and the Republic, of *England*, in the Quality of Deputy Extraordinary: The Year following, This Character was changed into That of Embaffador Extraordinary. He concluded the Peace between *Holland* and *England*, the Twenty eighth of *April*, 1654. During the Courfe of this Embaffy, he had the Office of Treafurer General of the United Provinces conferred upon him. He poffeffed it 'till the Year 1665; and it was his own Fault that he held it no longer; for the States General defired him to continue in That Office, and did not confent to the laying down his Commiffion, 'till they faw, that neither their Reafons, nor their Intreaties, could prevail upon him. He received a very advantageous Teftimony, that they were perfectly fatisfied with his Conduct; and they gave him, in particular, fome Marks of the Efteem they had for his Perfon *(a)*. In the Year 1659, he had the good Fortune to contribute, with other Deputies, to the compofing the Differences, which were raifed In the Province of *Groningen*. It may be faid, that he was born for this kind of good Fortune; which appears by the many Treaties of Peace, or Alliance, which he concluded [*B*]. He was twice fent to *Cleves*, in the Year 1666. The firft Time, he concluded a very ftrict Alliance with his Electoral Highnefs of *Brandenburg* (*b*); the fecond time, he concluded a Peace with the Bifhop of *Munfter* (*c*). The Year following, being invefted with the Character of Embaffador, he concluded the Treaty of Peace with *England*, at *Breda* (*d*). In 1668, he was fent in the Quality of Embaffador Extraordinary to *Aix la Chapelle*, for the Treaty of Peace between *France* and *Spain*; which Treaty was concluded the fecond of *May*. In the fame Year 1668, he was nominated to go, with Prince *Maurice* of *Naffau*, in the Quality of Embaffador Extraordinary to the Emperor; but the States General changed their Mind as to That Embaffy. The States of *Holland* gave Mr *Van Beverningk* fome Marks of their Regard for his important Services (*e*). In the Year 1671, he went to the Court of *Spain*, in the Quality of Embaffador Extraordinary, to difpofe his Catholic Majefty to a Negotiation about his Differences with *France*, and he fucceeded in it to the Satisfaction of his Mafters. In the Year 1672, he followed the Prince of *Orange* to the Army, as Deputy of the States. After this he had a Mind to live a quiet Life, and thought he ought to be fatisfied with the Glory he had acquired, and that he had performed all that a good Subject owes to his Country; but his Country wanted him too much to let him enjoy a retired Life. The redoubled Inftances of the States, and of the Prince of *Orange*, obliged him, in the Year 1673, to engage himfelf in one of the moft important Negotiations, that had yet occurred. I mean the Conferences at *Cologne*. At firft, the City of *Aix la Chapelle* had been chofen, to negotiate the Peace between the Princes, who were then at War; but it was found more proper to go to *Cologne*. Mr *Van Beverningk* appeared there with the Character of Embaffador Extraordinary. The carrying off of the Prince of *Furftenberg* produced the Effect, which was expected from That bold Attempt, *viz.* the breaking off of the Conferences in relation to *France*. Neverthelefs, the Negotiation was continued with the Allies of that Crown; and it was done with all manner of Succefs; for Mr *Van Beverningk* brought the Elector of *Cologne*, and the Bifhop of *Munfter*, back again into the Alliance of the States General (*f*). He was made Curator of the Univerfity of *Leyden*, in the Year 1673. It is an Office, which is not commonly given but to Thofe, who have ferved their Country in great Employments. When he expected to enjoy the Repofe, which he had fo long wifhed for, he found himfelf engaged in a moft difficult Negotiation: He was fo earneftly follicited to go to *Nimegen*, in the Quality of Embaffador Plenipotentiary from the Republic, for the General Peace, that, after having excufed himfelf feveral times, he could not refufe That important and laborious Commiffion. The Obftacles, which he was to overcome, cannot be expreffed:

[*B*] *The many Treaties of Peace, or Alliance, which he concluded*] Here is a Paffage, which, in a long Parenthefis, will ferve as a Commentary upon thefe Words. "Monfieur *Patius* (1) being "Embaffador in *Spain*, and having, by his great "Capacity, preferved, and increafed, in the Queen "of *Spain*, and her Council, the good Impreffions, "which Monfieur *Van Beverningk* (a Man born to "make Peace in the World, having given it, in "*Cromwel's* Time, and afterwards at *Breda*, to the "*Engl: b*, and *Dutch*, at *Cleves* to the Bifhop of "*Munfter*, at *Aix la Chapelle* to the *French* and *Spa-* "*niards*, and, lately, at *Cologne*, to the Archbifhop "of *Cologne*, and to the Bifhop of *Munfter*, and hav- "ing not a little contributed to the Peace, lately "made with *England*, and who, for that reafon, "might well be called the *Peace-Maker*) had made "upon them, to oppofe early, by juft and effectual "Means, the Ambition of the *French*; *Stoupe* does "not know any other way of revenging himfelf up- "on him, but by Calumny, and falfly accufing him "of being an *Arminian*. He is alfo foolifhly afraid, "that, if Mr *Patius should go through Swifferland*, "*he would not come off very cheap*. I am fure, that, "if he fhould happen to pafs by that Country, the "*Swifs*, as well the Proteftant, as the Catholic, "*Cantons*, would receive him with their ufual Civi- "lity, and with the Refpect due to his Character, "and to his great Merit, and that they would give "him public Thanks for having fo much contributed "to the Prefervation of Religion, and the Liberty of "*Europe*." This is to be found in an Anfwer, which was made to Mr *Stoupe's* Letter about the Religon of the *Dutch* (2).

[*C*] *The*

preffed: A lefs confummate Induftry and Experience, than His, could never have compaffed it; for, except the *French* Embaffadors, almoft all the reft made it much more their their Bufinefs to retard the Treaty of Peace, than to advance it. Neverthelefs, after the taking of *Ghent*, it feemed, that the Peace was become, at laft, a neceffary Evil for *Holland*; and People were fo fenfible of the fatal Confequences, which the taking of That Place might have, that they ardently defired an end of the War. Mr *Van Beverningk* had Orders to go to the King of *France*, at his Camp of *Wetteren* (g); and, after the Reception he met with [C], it was no longer doubted, but that a Peace would be concluded. It was figned, between *France* and *Holland*, the tenth of *Auguft*, 1678; after which, Mr *Van Beverningk* ferved effectually, as a Mediator, to conclude That between *France* and *Spain*, the eleventh of *September*, in the fame Year. He alfo concluded a Treaty of Peace, and of Commerce, between *Sweden*, and the States General, the twelfth of *October*, 1679. After fo many honourable, and happy, Negotiations, he enjoyed, at laft, That quiet Life, which he had fo long wifhed for. He retired to a fine Lordfhip (b), which he had, a fmall League from *Leyden*, where he chiefly employed himfelf in the Culture of all forts of Plants, which he fent for from all Parts of the World. But this pleafant and innocent Occupation, fo like That, which fome great Princes have betaken themfelves to, after their Triumphs, and the Government of the State, did not hinder him from regarding the Common-Wealth of Learning. He exercifed his Function of Curator of the Univerfity, with great Vigilance. He felt the beginning of his laft Sicknefs, a little after having fpent one Morning in perufing the Manufcripts of the famous Library of *Ifaac Voffius*, which had lately been bought for the Univerfity of *Holland* (i). As foon as he was got into his Coach again, he began to fhudder. This was the beginning of a Fever, which encreafed daily, and of which he died, the thirtieth of *October*, 1690, at the Age of Seventy fix Years. His Wife furvived him (k); but he had no Children by her; fo that as he was an only Son, no Perfon remains to bear his Name, in this Country. He was buried at *Tergou*, in a Marble Chapel, which he had built. His Relations caufed his Epitaph to be engraved on a Touchftone. It is a fine Infcription, which may be feen entire in the Remark [D]. It contains an Abridgment of a Life, which might fill

(g) *He arrived there May 30, 1678.*
(b) *The Name of it is, Oud-Teilingen.*
(i) *That of Leyden.*
(k) *She was born at Amfterdam, May 11, 1635; Her Name is Joan le Gillon, She is originally of a noble Family of Picardy.*

[C] *The Reception he met with from the King of France.*] See the Anfwer, which the King of *France* gave to the Letter of the States General, and the Memorial, which he ordered to be delivered to Mr *Van Beverningk*, with the fame Anfwer. There is nothing in it, but what tends to facilitate the Advancement of the Peace; the Stile is mild and civil; and many Advances are made in it. Every Body may be convinced of it (3). There was a particular Circumftance in This Embaffy, which is not known, but deferves to be fo. It fhews, on one fide, the Diftinction, with which the King of *France* regarded the Perfon, who had been fent to him, and, on the other fide, with what Principles of Honour, and Difintereftednefs, Mr *Van Beverningk* behaved himfelf. When he came away from *Wetteren*, the King would make him a Prefent of two of his Pictures, enriched with Jewels, each of which were worth about Eight hundred Livres. It is not ufual to give two Pictures, but one only. He anfwered the Perfon, who offered him This Prefent from the King, that he thanked His Majefty for the Honour; but that he did not think proper to accept of it. Neverthelefs, he made a Prefent to the Bearer of the two Pictures, as if he had accepted of Them. The King's Letter to the States contains, among other things, that the Sieur *Van Beverningk's Perfon and Conduct had been very acceptable to him*.

[D] *His Epitaph may be feen entire in the Remarks.*] Here it is: The Lines are placed here, as they are in the Original:

Perilluftris. ac generofus. vir
HIERONYMUS. VAN. BEVERNINGK,
Theilingæ. Toparcha.
Senator. Judex. Conful. Goudanus.
In. confeffu. præpot: ord. gen: Affeffor
Idem. aliquoties. extra. ordin:
Communi. Belgicæ. Fœd: ærario. Præfectus
Lycei. Batavorum. Curator
In Hifpan: & Fœd: Belg: finibus. regundis Adjutor.
Legatus Wilhelmo. III. in exercitu. datus.
Weftmonafterium. Cliviam. II. Bredam
Aquisgranum. Bruxellas. Madritum
Coloniam. Agripp: Noviomagum:

(3) *All this is inferted in the 2d Part of the 3d Vol. of The Acts and Memoirs of the Negotiations of the Peace of Nimegen, pag. 407, Edit. Amft. 1680.*

Ad. Gall: item. Regem.
Wetteræ. Morinorum. caftra habentem.
Cum poteftate. res. componendi. miffus.
Ad. Cæfarem. vero. defignatus. Orator.
Re. nifi. perfecta. nunquam. reverfus.
De. maximi. præterea. momenti. rebus. domi
De. amicitiis. parandis
Et. fœderibus. pangendis foris,
A. Patriæ. Patribus. paffim
Feliciter. confultus. & adhibitus.
Natus. Goudæ. xxv. April. MDCXIV.
Mortuus. Theilingæ. xxx. Octob: MDCXC
Satur. honorum
Hoc. monumento. conditur
Cum
Optima. vitæ. fortunarum. que. focia
Joanna. Le Gillon
Nata. Amft. xi. Maji. MDCXXXV
Mortua.
ΘΑΝΑΤΩ. ΠΑΝΤΕΣ. ΟΦΕΙΛΟΜΕΘΑ.

The very Illuftrious and Noble
JEROM VAN BEVERNINGK;
Lord of Teilingen;
Senator, Judge, and Counfellor, of Tergou;
Deputy in the General Affembly of the States;
Sometimes Deputy Extraordinary;
Treafurer General of the United Provinces;
Curator of the Univerfity of Leyden;
Affiftant in fettling the Boundaries of Spain, and the United Provinces.
Deputy of the States in the Army of William. III.
Sent Plenipotentiary to
Weftminfter, *To* Cleves *twice*, *To* Breda,
To Aix la Chapelle, *To* Bruffels, *To* Madrid,
To Cologne, *To the French King*,
Encamped at Wetteren.
Appointed Embaffador to the Emperor,
He returned not, 'till he had finifhed his Negotiation.
Confulted, with fuccefs.

BEVERNINGK. BEZANITES.

fill a whole Volume; and, if Mr *Van Beverningk* had taken the pains to compose some Memoirs concerning his Embassies, it would be the most instructive, and most curious Book, that could be seen. He always succeeded in his Negotiations; which is an Honour, whereof we find but few Examples among those, who have had the Management of so many public Affairs. He was laborious and industrious, and never discouraged at any thing (*l*). The *French* and *Dutch* Writers equally praise him. I could alledge many Proofs of it; but shall be satisfied with producing what Mr *de Wicquefort* [E], and Mr *de Saint Didier* [F], have said of him. As for Sir *William Temple*, he seems to be a little vexed at the signing of the Treaty of *Nimegen*; but, notwithstanding, he owns, that Mr *Van Beverningk* put a Stop to the Complaints of his Enemies (*m*). He might have said, that the Magistrates of *Amsterdam* wrote a very obliging Letter to him, in which they thanked him for the Conclusion of the Peace (*n*). They assured him, that they had taken much Pains with the Members of the States of *Holland*, that he might be employed in That Negotiation. They knew very well, that they stood in need of such a Man, as He, to make it succeed. The Town, where he was born, shewed him, upon that Occasion, how much they esteemed him. The City of *Tergou* made him a Present of two Silver Handirons, in the Year 1679, in Consideration of the last Treaty of Peace, and for other important Services, done to the State and the City.

In Domestic Affairs of the greatest Consequence,
And in public Treaties abroad,
By the Fathers of his Country.
He was born at Tergou, April 25. 1614;
Died at Teilingen, Octob. 30, 1690;
Full of Honours;
And lies buried, in This Monument,
With
The best Companion of his Life and Fortunes,
JOANNA LE GILLON;
Born at Amsterdam, May 11, 1635.
Died.
DEATH IS A DEBT WE ALL MUST PAY.

[E] *What Mr Wicquefort ——— said of him.*] "*Jerom Beverningk* is, doubtless, one of the ablest Men of the United Provinces for Negotiations. The City of *Tergou*, which otherwise does not want able Men, deputed him several times to the Assemblies of the States of the Province of *Holland*, and to the Colleges of the Generality, and he always perfectly answered what might be expected from his great Ability. It was He, who, in the Year 1654, made the Treaty with *Oliver Cromwell*, which gave Peace to the United Provinces; but it had like to have involved them in a Civil War, because the Interests of the Prince of *Orange*, according to some, had not been well managed in it. The Province of *Holland* was so well satisfied with the Service he did them at That Juncture, that They procured him the Office of Treasurer General, that is to say, of first Minister of the United Provinces. There is no Affair, though ever so difficult, but what he can clear up, when he will apply himself to it. If any one desires proofs of it, he need only look into the Treaty, which he concluded at *Cleves*, with the Bishop of *Munster*, in the Year 1666. Nor was He less successful in his Negotiations at *Madrid*, concerning the important Interests of the Provinces of the *Netherlands*. If he did not succeed at *Congres*, it must be imputed to the Ill disposition of the Parties concerned, and to the unlucky Juncture of Affairs, rather than to his Way of managing Things. Hence it is, that he was intrusted with the whole Negotiation at *Nimegen*; and the States made choice of him to go, and conclude it with the most Christian King near *Ghent*. He is weary of so many Employments; so that, whereas others strive for them, he avoids them; choosing rather to enjoy himself in his Country Retirement, than to be troubled with the Cares, which Business brings upon him, and which are often no less troublesome to him, than to Those, who negotiate with him. A better Pen, than mine, is requisite to draw up Mr *Van Beverningk*'s Character, because, it all the Parts of it be well examined, it will be found, that, abating his uneven Temper, there is nothing in him, but what is Excellent (4)."

[F] ——— *and Mr de Saint Didier.*] Of all the Places, where this Author speaks of Mr *Van Beverningk*, I shall select but these three. "Mr *Van Beverningk*'s quick Return, occasioned by this News (5), which made him set out from his House, to repair to *Nimegen*, with all speed, confirmed the Conjecture of a private Agreement between *Holland* and *France*. This Embassador appeared to be so zealous for the true Interest of his Country, that, if any private Negotiation was to be expected, it could not be by any other means (6). ——— He is a Man of a quick Wit, who knows what is best, and attains to it the shortest way. He is Vigilant and Laborious. He has been employed by the States in several Embassies, and in all the Treaties, which have been made since 1650; but he loves a retired Life, and it was with some kind of uneasiness, that he left his Country House near *Leyden*, to go to *Nimegen* (7). ——— Mr *Van Beverningk* is a Man of no less Ability, than Dispatch (8)."

BEZANITES, or BEZANIANS, an imaginary Sect, which never existed but in the Heads of some Makers of Catalogues of Heretics. There would be reason to wonder, that such absurd Writings, as Those Catalogues are, have not been suppressed in their Birth, by Persons of Authority; I say, there would be reason to wonder at it, if it were not known, that Those Persons of Authority are very often the least knowing, and the most persuaded of this wrong Maxim, *that one may use indifferently Fraud or Force against one's Enemy*; ——— *dolus an virtus quis in hoste requirat* (*a*)? These Persons did not perceive, that those Catalogues, being full of impertinent and notorious Falsities, were only proper to inspire the Heretics with a very great Contempt for the Writers of the prevailing Party. They only considered the Advantage, which would accrue from the Heretics being thought to be divided into a thousand Sects. However it be, if *Prateolus* may be believed (*b*), there arose a Sect under the Reign of *Charles* V, and under the Pontificate of *Julius* III, about the Year 1550 (*c*), which was called the *Bezanites*, or the *Bezanians*, from *Theodorus Beza*. The only Proof, that he could bring for it, would be, that he had read such a Thing in a Book of *Lindanus*; for it is very true, that *Lindanus* says so (*d*); but without quoting any Body. That which is very certain, is, that one

BEZANITES. BEZA.

one might boldly lay any Wager, though never so great, to be paid to Those, who could prove, that some People, in the XVIth Century, made a separate Sect, in the Quality of *Beza*'s Disciples. The same may be said in relation to a great many other Sects, which fill up the Alphabet of *Prateolus*. Perhaps the chief Reason, which induced him to mention the pretended Sect of the *Bezanites*, was the Desire of adorning his Work with the Calumnies, which were published against *Beza* [*A*]. If, instead of rewarding *Lindanus*, they had punished him for his Lies [*B*], he would not have been transcribed by so many Persons, among whom a *Carthusian* of *Germany* is, doubtless, the most ridiciculous [*C*].

[*A*] *Prateolus would not, perhaps, have mentioned the Bezanians, but for the desire of adorning his Work with the Calumnies which were published against Beza.*] My Conjecture will appear very probable to Those, who shall consider, that, *Prateolus* having but five or six Lines to bestow upon his pretended *Bezanites*, has filled seven or eight Pages with the most disgraceful Things, he could find, against That famous Minister, in the Writings of *Lindanus, Claudius de Sainctes*, and *John le Virl*. Besides, he misrepresents and relates unfaithfully what he takes from them. I am going to give an Example of it. *Lindanus* had quoted *Peter Viretus*, who said, that some Schoolmasters took delight in repeating, a thousand times, to their Scholars, that *a Man is happy, when he can trample upon the Fear of Death, and infernal Torments*. It is a Passage of *Virgil*. *Testatur P. Viretus lib. 2. de Minist. Verba esse quædam ludimagistros ex illo Epicuri grege porcos, qui in scholis soleant suis sæpe scholasticis occinere illum vere beatum qui, uti est apud Virgilium,*

—— *metus omnes, & inexorabile Fatum
Subjecit pedibus, strepitumque Acherontis avari* (1).

Lindanus adds, that *Beza* had rendered himself suspected of the like Epicureism, as his Brethren of *Paris* and *Orleans* witness. What does *Prateolus*? He maintains, that *Lindanus* had said, that, when *Beza* was Schoolmaster, he often repeated This Passage of *Virgil* to his Scholars (2). Is not This to falsify an Author? Afterwards, *Lindanus*, who had quoted, hitherto, no Authority against *Beza*, quotes one *Fabricius* (3), who accuses That Minister of having sold his Benefices, and of loving the Fair Sex to excess. *Beneficia ecclesiastica —— publice venderet, & alienas uxores permoleret tam familiariter, ut publicus matronarum haberetur maritus*. This is soon said; but where are the Proofs?

[*B*] *Instead of rewarding* Lindanus, *they should have punished him for his Lies*.] It is certain, that *Prateolus* has ranged a great many Sects in an Alphabetical Order, which never existed, and that he had no other Authority for it, than *Lindanus*. Father *Gaultier*, a Jesuit, gives us a List of these same Sects, in his Chronographical Table, on *Prateolus*'s Testimony. If he is not his only Author, he is at least his chief Authority. An hundred Authors have spoken, and do still speak, of these Sects on the Credit of That Jesuit. Observe the prodigious and horrible Propagation of the Fault of a single Writer, I mean *Lindanus*. When one considers, that This Author, having been preferred to a small Bishopric, was afterwards promoted to a greater, and received great Honours at *Rome* (4), and that none of all the Superiors, to whom he was to give an account of his Conduct, censured him for the Boldness, with which he had created so many Sects (5); it can be no longer wondered at, that there should be so many Liars, among Those, who engage in Controversies. If *Lindanus*'s Superiors had required him to prove, that certain Disciples of *Beza*, distinct from Those of *Calvin*, and from Those of the other Reformers, had formed a great, or small, Body, separate from the other Sectaries; and if, for want of good Proofs, they had condemned him to the Punishment of public Impostors, and declared him unqualified for meddling with holy Things, they had established a Precedent, which would have reclaimed all credulous, or deceitful, Writers, who report so many Falsities. But, instead of bringing him into trouble for it, they looked upon him as a valiant Champion of the Catholic Cause, and raised him more and more. Who would therefore scruple to calumniate Heretics? One might apply these Words of *Horace* to That Author:

Ulla si Juris tibi pejerati
Pœna, Barine, nocuisset unquam;
Dente si nigro fieres, vel uno
  Turpior ungue:
Crederem. Sed tu simul obligasti
Perfidum votis caput, enitescis
Pulchrior multo, juvenumque prodis
  Publica cura.
Expedit matris cineres opertos
Fallere, & toto taciturna noctis
Signa cum cœlo, gelidaque divos
  Morte carentes (6).

*Barine, did Revenge o'retake,
And blast as oft as you deceive;
Were but one Nail, or Tooth, more black,
Thy Vows I would at last believe:
But still more fair, more bright thy Face,
More Crowds of Lovers flock to view,
At each false Oath procured a Grace,
And tempted Thee to prove untrue.
It profits thee to be forsworn
By all that other Mortals fear,
Th' Eternal Gods, thy Mother's Urn,
By whirling Heav'n, and ev'ry Star.*
CREECH.

There is another Reflexion, which would well deserve to be weighed. If the Question had been to defame the Taylors, or some other Tradesmen of an Imperial City, *Lindanus*, I believe, would not have affirmed any thing publickly, without being certain of the Fact; but, because Religion, and the Glory of God, was concerned in it, he published all that came into his Head, without any Examination, or Remorse. So that, if we consider the matter well, the Zeal of Controversists, instead of increasing their Virtue, stifles the Knowledge, and all the Scruples, which might keep them in the way of Probity, in Things purely Human. QUOD NOTANDUM (7).

[*C*] Lindanus*'s Lies have been most ridiculously transcribed by a* Carthusian *of* Germany.] His Name is *Theodorus Petreius* —— his *Catalogus Hæreticorum* was printed in the Year 1628. See what *Hoornbeeck* said of it in his *Summa Controvers.* pag. 321.

(1) Lindanus, Dubitantis, Dial. ii, pag. 246.

(2) Prateol. in Elencho Hæret. pag. 94.

(3) Michael Fabricius pro Fran. Balduino.

(4) Valer. Andreas Bibl. Belg. pag. 583, 584.

(5) He made them out of nothing, ix præludio ex nihilo sumens, si ita est, & in talibus Creations.

(6) Horat. Od. viii. lib. ii.

(7) See Remark [*O*] of the Article CAYET.

BEZA

BEZA (THEODORUS), one of the chief Pillars of the Reformed Church, was of *Vezelai*, in *Burgundy*. He was nobly born, both by his Father's and Mother's Side [*A*], the Twenty fourth of *June*, 1519. He was hardly weaned, when his Uncle,

[*A*] *He was born Noble, both on his Father's and Mother's Side.*] His Father, who was Bailiff of *Vezelai*, was called *Peter de Beze*, his Mother's Name was *Mary Bourdelot*. "P. à *Beza ejus oppidi præ-
" fecto, & Maria Bourdelotia, utroque Dei gratia
" genere nobili (utinam vero potius veri Dei cogni-
" tione imbuto) & integræ famæ parente natus. ——
" Born of Peter Beza, Bailiff of That Town, and
" Mary Bourdelot, both, by God's Grace, of noble
" Birth, and unblemished Fame; I wish I could rather
" say, instructed in the Knowledge of the True GOD."
Beza, who speaks in this manner, in an Epistle Dedicatory

BEZA.

Uncle, *Nicolas Beza*, Counsellor in the Parliament of *Paris*, would have him at his House, where he was very affectionately educated, 'till the beginning of *December*, 1528 (*a*), when he was sent to *Melchior Wolmar*, at *Orleans*, who had a wonderful Skill in instructing Youth. He lodged seven Years at *Wolmar*'s House, who improved him wonderfully in Classical Learning, and instructed him in Religion, out of the Word of GOD (*b*); that is, he educated him in the Protestant Religion. *Wolmar* had been sent for to *Bourges*, by the Queen of *Navarre*, to teach the *Greek* Tongue there. He left That Employment, and returned into *Germany*, his Country, in the Year 1535. Then *Beza* was sent to study the Law at *Orleans*. This Study pleased him but little: He spent the best of his Time in reading good *Greek* and *Latin* Authors, and composing Verses. He made such good ones, that he distinguished himself by them, in a particular manner; insomuch that he was taken notice of and beloved by the most learned Men in the University of *Orleans*. He took his Licentiate's Degree, there, in the Year 1539 (*c*), and went to *Paris*, where some good Preferments were provided for him [B], which combated for some time the Resolution he had taken to return to *Wolmar*, and make public Profession of the Reformation. The Pleasures of *Paris*, the Honours, which were offered him, and a great many other Snares of Satan, he says, did not choak the good Seed; he never forsook the Resolution of renouncing Popery, though the Temptations of the World made him Irresolute [C]. He had provided against Those of the Flesh by a Marriage of Conscience (*d*); that is to say, by a Promise, which he made to a Woman, to marry her publickly, as soon as the Obstacles, which hindered him at That Time, should be removed, and, in the mean time, not to engage himself in the Ecclesiastical State. He faithfully performed These two Promises; but a dangerous Sickness was necessary to extricate him from the Snares, which entangled him in the Mire. The frightful Image of approaching Death made him renew so earnestly the Vow, he had formerly made, to profess the Reformed Religion, that, as soon as he had recovered sufficient Health to travel, he fled to *Geneva*, with This Woman. He arrived there the Twenty fourth of *October*, 1548; and, before he resolved upon what Course of Life he should take, he went to see *Melchior Wolmar*, at *Tubingen*. The Year following, he accepted the Professorship of the *Greek* Tongue at *Lausanne*;

(*a*) *Antony la Faye, de vita & ob tu Th. B. læ, pag. 9, anticipates six Years, and it must here be says, that Beza was sent, at five Years of Age, to be educated by Wolmar, at Orleans. Mr Teissier, Addit. to the Elogies, Tom. II, pag. 352, says the same thing.*

(*b*) *Vera plaetatis cognitione ex Dei verbo tanquam limpidissimo fonte petita tu me ita imbuit ut, &c. Beza, Ep. ad M. Wolmarum. See Ici i u, Ciarlei i (e).*

(*c*) *Anno Domini 1530. Col. II. Augu t, quum annum ætatis vicesimum etiam incensus Id ibid. He reckons twenty be was already in his 21st Year.*

(*d*) *See Rem. his [C] and [T].*

---

(1) *It is That of his Confession of Faith, which he publashed in Latin, in 1560. See Citat. (e), of this Article.*

(2) *Beza ad Chandum de Maintes, Apolog'a Alteri, sub. fin.*

(3) *Verheiden, p 209, who says he was still living, is mistaken.*

(4) *Beza Epist. ad Melch. Wolmarum.*

(5) *Ibid.*

dicatory to *Wolmar* (1), tells us elsewhere, that his Ancestors had been rich for several Generations, and great Benefactors to the Church. "Sum enim ego "(ne nescias) Dei gratia, non ex Monachis, non ex "adulterio, vel stupro, sed honestis avis & atavis "prognatus; &, ne ad allegorias tuas confugias, scito "Bezarum familiam, si forte quæcunque ante ducen"tos & amplius annos in Monachos superstitiose lar"gita est reciperet, tam fore locupletem quam ægre "hodie sese in sua inopia tuetur (2).——— *You are to* "*know, that I am not the Offspring of Monks, that* "*I was not begotten in Adultery or Whoredom, but* "*am sprung from honest Parents, and reputable An*"*cestors; and, that you may not fly to your Allegories,* "*know, that the Family of the Beza's, if it could re*"*cover what it has superstitiously bestowed on Monks* "*for Two hundred Years, and more, would be as* "*wealthy, as it is now scarce able to support itself in* "*it's Poverty.*"

[B] *He went to Paris, where some good Preferments were provided for him.*] His Uncle, the Counsellor, had been dead seven Years (3); but another Uncle, Abbot of *Froidmont*, had no less kindness for This Nephew. He designed to have resigned to him his Abbey, worth Fifteen thousand Livers yearly Rent; which, with two other good Benefices, which *Beza* was already provided with, and which had been procured him without his Knowledge, would have put him in a very good way. "Huc accedebat quod duobus pin"guibus & opimis Beneficiis me alioqui macrum ado"lescentem, & præterea, quod vere testor, istarum "rerum prorsus ignarum & absentem, onerarunt, quo"rum vectigalia aureos coronatos annuos plus minus "septingentos æquabant (4)." Besides, his elder Brother was very ill, and could not live long; the Succession to his Benefices was an approaching Hope. He died soon after; and This Death increased *Beza*'s Income considerably. *Ex Fratris morte auctiores mihi reditus essent facti* (5). It is easy to judge, that a young Man, so well settled already, and who had such great Talents, many Friends and Relations, and an uncommon Reputation, built on the Success of his *Latin* Verses, which the Public had seen, might promise to himself all sorts of Preferments. "Quum"que mihi præter illa impedimenta, quæ ante "commemoravi, triplicem laqueum Satanas circun"dedisset, nempe voluptatum illecebras quæ sunt in "ea civitate maximæ; gloriolæ dulcedinem, quam

"ego non parvam, ex meorum præsertim Epigram"matum editione, ipsius quoque M. Antonii Flami"nii doctissimi poëtæ, & quidem Itali, judicio eram, "consequutus; spem denique maximorum honorum "mihi propositam, ad quos ex ipsis aulicis proceribus "aliquot me vocabant, incitabant amici, pater & "patruus hortari non definebant; voluit Deus Opt. "Max. ut - - - - - tandem ex his quoque periculis "evaderem (6). - - - - - - *And though, besides the* "*Obstacles, already mentioned,* Satan *laid a triple* "*Snare for me; to wit, the Allurements of Pleasure,* "*which are very great in That City; the Sweets of* "*Fame, which I had acquired no small Degree of,* "*particularly by the Publication of my Epigrams, and* "*in the Opinion even of the very learned Italian Poet* "*M. Antony Flaminius; lastly, the Hopes given me* "*of the greatest Honours, to which some of the Cour*"*tiers themselves invited me, my Friends prompted,* "*and my Father and Uncle perpetually exhorted me,* "*to accept of; yet it pleased* God - - - - - *to extri*"*cate me even out of these Dangers.*"

[C] *The Temptations of the World made him irresolute.*] This ought to be no wonder to us. At such an Age, a witty and handsome Man, who wants nothing to divert himself, has much ado to resist Temptation. In vain did the Woman, to whom *Beza* had promised Marriage, put him in mind of marrying her; the Revenue of the Benefices, which he must have renounced, confuted all her Instances: One may easily believe what *Beza* says upon it. But the Force, with which He, at last, broke these Bonds, is so much the more admirable. "Quum mihi & juveni & à meis otio, pecunia, re"bus denique omnibus potius quam consilio, abun"danti, Satanas omnia illa impedimenta derepente "objecisset, fateor me inani illarum rerum splendore "& vanis blanditiis ita fuisse pellectum, ut me to"tum huc & illuc abripi facile paterer ——— Uxo"rem mihi despondi, sed clam, id tamen fateor & "uno tantum & altero ex piis amicis conscio, par"tim ne cæteros offenderem, partim quod adhuc "non satis possem à sceleratis illis pecuniæ quam ex "sacerdotiis, de quibus ante dixi, percipiebam, ut "impurus canis ab uncto corio, abstlerreri. ——— Ego "tum interea semper in luto hærere, instantibus meis "ut tandem certum aliquod vitæ genus amplecterer, "& patruo mihi omnia deferente, adeo ut quum "una ex parte me premeret conscientia, & conjux "de promisso appellaret; ex altera vero personatus "Satan

(6) *Ibid.*

792 BEZA.

Lausanne; and, after having exercised it about nine or ten Years, he returned to Geneva [D], where he was admitted a Minister (e). During these nine Years, he did not confine himself to Greek Lectures; he read some also, in French, on the New Testament [E], which were for the Instruction, and Consolation, of several Refugees of both Sexes, who lived at Lausanne. He published several Books during his Abode in that City [F]; and, before he quitted the Professorship, which he exercised

"Satan mihi placidissimo vultu blandiretur, & ex "fratris morte auctiores mihi reditus essent facti, "quasi omnis consilii inops inter istas animi curas "jacerem (7). —— *I confess, I suffered myself to "be easily carried away with the empty Show, and "Allurements, of Those Temptations, which Satan "suddenly threw in my way, when I was young, idle, "and fuller of Money, than Discretion. —— I en-"tered into a Contract of Marriage, but secretly; "yet with the Privacy, I must confess, of one or "two of my pious Friends, partly that I might not "offend the rest, and partly because I still hankered "after the wicked Profits of those Benefices, I be-"fore spoke of. —— In the mean time I continued "plunged in the Mire, notwithstanding the Instances "of my Friends, that I would, at length, embrace "some settled way of Life, and the ready Compliance "of my Uncle in every thing; insomuch that, on the "one side, Conscience pressing me, and the Lady cal-"ling me to the Performance of my Promise; and, "on the other side, allured by worldly Temptations, "and an Encrease of my Income by the Death of "my Brother, I remained utterly Irresolute and In-"determined."*

[D] *After having exercised the Greek Professor-ship about nine or ten Years at* Lausanne, *he returned to* Geneva.] This is what he says himself, in his Answer to *Claudius de Saintes. Novem circiter an-nos Græcas literas docussi* (8). *Antony la Faye* has made use of an even Number, *viz.* ten Years compleat; *Inciderunt postea tempora, quæ* Bezam ad *migrandum* Lausaniæ, ubi D E C E M annos integros *hæserat Græca docendi munere defungens, induxe-runt* (9). *Beza was, afterwards, induced to "go to* Lausanne, *where he taught Greek* T E N *"whole Years."* Beza, in another Place of his Books, says, that from *Lausanne* he returned to *Geneva*, after ten Years stay there. *"Inde vero tan-"dem, id est post annum decimum —— in hunc "urbem iterum tanquam in placidissimum por-"tum redii* (10). Neither He, nor *la Faye*, have judged it proper to explain all the Reasons of his leaving *Lausanne*: What they say of it does not hinder us from suspecting, that there was I know not what in it, which would be fit for secret Memoirs. *"Inciderunt Tempora, quæ* Bezam "ad migrandum Lausanna induxerunt. —— Beza "*was induced to go to* Lausanne (11). —— Inde "—— *partim quod* meipsum cuperem Theologiæ totum "consecrare, partim alias ob causas quas nihil hic "attinet commemorare - - - in hanc urbem - - - - "redii (12). —— *I returned from thence to this "City, partly that I might dedicate myself wholly "to Divinity, and partly for Reasons, which it sig-"nifies nothing to repeat here."* His Enemies, who made Mountains of Mole-hills, published, that he had been expelled. That City. See *Lindanus*, at the Hundred fifty second Page of the second Dialogue of his *Dubitantius*; and *Baudouin*, in his third Answer, *fol.* 146. verso, where he says, *Docuit Lau-janna multis annis - - - - illinc turpiter atque igno-miniose pulsus.* —— He taught many Years at Lau-sanne, *from whence he was expelled with Ignominy.* This is false; but there was something, I know not, which gave occasion to this Lie. Mr *Teissier* mistook one thing for another, when he said, that Beza exercised the Professorship of Philosophy, for ten Years, at *Lausanne* (13).

One of my Friends (14), a famous Professor at *Lausanne*, having read what goes before, used all his Endeavours to help me to some Explanations; but his Endeavours proved vain: However, I here give you an Abstract of his Letter, which is of some Moment. "I thought I could have given you some "Light into *Beza's* Life, and particularly as to his "leaving This University to go to *Geneva*. You "intimate, that there is something concealed in this "matter. I know it has been reported, and even "an Author, whose Name I have forgot, says, that "it was because he had got his Maid with Child;

"But, if it had been so, it would have been known "at *Geneva*, as well as here; and he would not "have gone away honourably, *Bona cum venia Am-"plissimi Magistratus Bernensis*, as he says in his "Letter to his Preceptor *Wolmar*: And, to conclude, "he would not have come every Year, as he did, "to *Lausanne*, and have been so well received. "They shewed him so much Respect, that the Coun-"cil used to go out, and meet him, as our Memoirs "testify." I am uncertain whether the Author, meant here, be not *Reboul* (15). That satirical Writer, who was beheaded at *Rome* for his Pasquinades (16).

[E] *He read Lectures, in French, on the New Testament*.] He made choice, at first, of the Epistle to the *Romans*, and afterwards of Those of St *Peter*. They were, as it were, the Seeds of That great Work, which he published some time after; I mean his *Latin* Translation of the New Testament with Notes. He revised it several Times, and made many Corrections in it. None but Those, who are ignorant of the Difficulty of such a Work, will think it strange, that he should make some Alterations in each Edition. *Illas tamen aliquoties emendatas ab ipso mirabitur nemo, qui operis difficultatem cum dignitate conjunctam, ut decet, perpenderit* (17). It is true, This created some Trouble to Those, who had made use of the first Editions: They were always in Fear, that a new one would come out, which would overthrow what they had looked upon as certain; but, to be honest at This, is to be angry with Nature, which will have our Knowlede to be very limited, and to increase by Degrees. Cruel Reproaches were made against *Beza* on this Account. "Nisi quis "septies tuas Novi Testamenti editiones emat, nes-"ciet quid ajas aut quid neges. Memini typogra-"phum eruditum Hieronymum Commelinum hoc "mihi ante decennium dixisse, quod crebra muta-"tione consilii hoc tantum adeptus es ut plurimi "nihili faciant Novum Testamentum litera læsum at-"que sensu flexiloquum. Et olim quidam Doctor "Cantabrigiensis mihi retulit, quod Cantabrigiæ plu-"res aversati sunt religionem ducti per te ad cre-"dendum quod Novum Testamentum depravatum "est, sicut per Edwardum Livilejum quod Vetus "ulceratum (18). - - - - - - *One must purchase your "seven Editions of the New Testament, to know what "you affirm or deny. I remember a learned Printer, "Jerom* Commelinus, *told me, ten Years ago, that, "by frequently altering your Mind, you had gained "This, that many Persons had no Dependance on "Your New Testament. And, not long ago, a certain "*Cambridge *Doctor informed me, that many at* Cam-"bridge *disregarded Religion, being induced, by "you, to believe, that the New Testament is corrupt, "as they had been, by* Edward Livilejus, *that the "old one is very much so."*

Note, that the first Edition of the Work of *Beza* is of the Year 1556. He published a second, ten Years after, and dedicated it to the Queen of *England*. The fifth Edition came out in the Year 1598. He dedicated it again to the same Queen, by a new Epistle, and suppressed the first: He should not have suppressed it; for it explains, at large, the Method, and Design, of the Author.

[F] *He published several Books during his Abode at* Lausanne.] The first was a French Tragi-Comedy, entituled *Abraham's Sacrifice. Jacomot* translated it into *Latin*, in the Year 1598. Almost at the same time *James Brunon* translated it into the same Language, at *Amsterdam*. It has passed through several Impressions. Let us see what *Pasquier* says of it. *About the same time,* Theodorus Beza *lived, a fine* Latin *and* French *Poet. He composed, in* French Vaise, Abraham's Sacrifice *so much to the Life, that, in reading it formerly, it drew Tears from my Eyes* (19). *Beza* went frequently to *Geneva*, during the Vacations, to visit *Calvin*, who exhorted him to dedicate his Talents to the Service of the Church, and who advised him, particularly,
to

exercised there, he made a Journey into *Germany*, with the Character of a Deputy [G]. He had, then, the Pleasure of conferring with *Melanchthon*. Having settled at *Geneva*, in the Year 1559, he attached himself to *Calvin* in a particular manner, and, in a little time, was made his Colleague in the Church, and University. He was sent to *Nerac*, at the Instigation of some Great Persons of the Kingdom, to convert the King of *Navarre*, and to confer with him about Matters of Consequence (*f*). This happened when the *Guises* had invaded the King's Authority, under the Reign of *Francis* II, to the Prejudice of the Princes of the Blood. The King of *Navarre* having signified, both by Letters, and by Deputies, that he desired *Beza* should assist at the Conference of *Poissi*, the Senate of *Geneva* readily consented to it. No better Choice could have been made for the Good of the Cause. *Beza* spoke

(*f*) Cumque eo de rebus gravissimis communicaret, sed potissimum et illius animo, si Deus aspiraret, versa religionis gustum aliquem instillaret. *Ant. Fayus de vita & obitu Th. Bezæ, pag. 21.*

to finish what *Marot* had begun. *Beza* followed this Advice, and translated, into *French* Verse, the Hundred *Psalms*, which remained to be translated. They were printed, with the King's Privilege, in 1561. The *Translation of the Remainder of the Psalms* of *David* shews what he could do, though he has not so happily succeeded as *Clement Marot* in his fifty (20). After he had recovered from the Plague, he made an Ode to return thanks to GOD for it. It is pretended, that *Jodelle* made this Tetrastich at that Time.

(20) Ibid.

Beze fut lors de la peste accueilli
Qu'il retouchoit cette harpe immortelle;
Mais pourquoi fut Beze d'elle assailli?
Beze assailloit la peste à tous mortelle (21).

(21) We shall examine, in the Article JODELLE, whether it is to be, who composed This Tetrastich.

Beza was seized with the Plague, when he was retouching This Immortal Lyre. But why was Beza attacked by It? Beza attacked That General Mortality, The Plague.

A REFLEXION on the Book de Puniendis Hæreticis.

One of the most remarkable Works, published by *Beza*, during his Abode at *Lausanne*, was the Treatise *de Hæreticis à Magistratu puniendis*. He published it in answer to the Book, which *Castalio*, disguised under the Name of *Martinus Bellius*, had composed on That important Subject, a little after the Execution of *Servetus* (22). *Castalio* treated the general Thesis of Toleration: *Beza* maintained, against him, that the Magistrates ought to punish Hereticks, The Author of his Life maintains, that This Work was published very seasonably to settle fluctuating Minds; *Scriptum utriusque Beza tum refutavit, tempore in speciem importuno, sed re ipsa opportunissimo ad cohibendos levium hominum in Religione fluctuantium vagos & incertos æstus* (23). It cannot be denied, that the Fear of Capital Punishment is of great Force, towards silencing Those, who may have any Doubts to propose against the prevailing Religion, and to maintain the Unity of External Communion: But it is with the Doctrine, which authorises This Practice, as it is with the Invention of Bombs and Carcasses, and of all kinds of Machines of War. They, who make use of them first, draw great Advantages from them, and, whilst they are the strongest, Things go very well with them: But, when they are the weakest, They are destroyed by their own Inventions. If *Beza's* Party had been the strongest all the World over, and if it could have maintained it's Superiority, the Doctrine, *de Puniendis Hæreticis*, would have done great Service: It would have repressed the Zeal, or the shuffling Humour, of Innovators; but, because, within a quarter of a League of *Geneva*, They were exposed to the Caprices of the strongest, and did not know whether GOD would permit the Sect of *Socinus* to prevail, It was very imprudent to maintain, that the Magistrates ought to inflict the Punishment of Death on Hereticks: A present Advantage ought not to blind our Eyes so much, as to hinder us from reflecting on the Consequences: On such an Occasion, the Maxim of *Regulus* is to be made use of:

(22) Servetus was burnt at Geneva, in 1553.

(23) Fayus, in vita Bezæ, pag. 17. Note, that by utrusque he means Lælius Socinus & Castalio.

Hoc caverat mens provida Reguli,
Dissentientis Conditionibus
Fœdis, & exemplo trahenti
Perniciem veniens in ævum (24).

(24) Horat. Od. v, l. iii.

Wise Regulus *did This prevent;*
He scorn'd base Terms, which Carthage *sent,*

Nor wou'd he e'er, by his Advice,
Tempt future Times to Cowardice.

CREECH.

I do not mention the other Reasons, which may confute this Doctrine; I dwell only on That of Expediency, alledged by the Writer of *Beza's* Life. This Expediency is but a Trifle in comparison of the Evil, which the Book *de Puniendis Hæreticis* produces daily; for, whenever the Protestants complain of the Persecutions, which they suffer, the Right, which *Calvin* and *Beza* have acknowledged in the Magistrates, is alledged against Them: Hitherto we have seen no one, who has not come off wretchedly, as to This Objection *ad hominem*. But let us proceed to other Books, published by *Beza*, before he left *Lausanne*. He published a short Explanation of Christianity, *ex Doctrina de æterna Dei Prædestinatione*; an Answer to *Joachim Westphalus*, concerning the Lord's Supper; two Dialogues on the same Subject, against *Tillemannus Hesbusius* (25); and an Answer to *Castalio*, concerning the Doctrine of Predestination. *Beza*, at that time, had not as yet tempered his Fire, and his gay Disposition, which made him let fall I know not what Railleries in his Works, which he expunged, when he published new Editions. " In iis quidem (dialogis) " postea quædam liberiore calamo quàm rei qua de " agebatur majestati conveniebat scripta mutavit, ut " & in nonnullis aliis scriptis, è quibus jocos aliquot " (ut erat ingenio lepido & faceto dum ætate adhuc " vigente esset) postquam maturior factus est, & " *Σπέργως φροντίδας* in consilium adhibuisset, e-" rasit (26)."

(25) The one entituled, Κρυπθο-καλβίνος, the other ἀκυθλοπαυμενος.

(26) Antonius Fayus, in vita Bezæ, pag. 17.

I express myself thus, as a Translator of the Words of *Antony la Faye*: for, if I would follow the Judgment of some Lutheran Authors, I should be obliged to make use of Terms, which exceed Raillery. *Conrad Schlusselburgius* pretends, that there are such scurrilous and lewd Revilings in *Beza's* Works, that they become Those only, who have had no other School, than the Stews. What he has said upon This, has been carefully gathered up by the Author of the *Calvino-Turcismus*. I can only cite Him, not having the Book of That famous Lutheran. " Omis- " sis aliis, Theodorum Bezam exempli gratia pro- " ponit, ex cujus scriptis, *non modo contra Papistas*, " *sed etiam Lutheranos, hoc* (inquit) *abundè potest* " *demonstrari. Et hæc adeo sunt vera, ut ipsos Sa-* " *cramentarios pigeat & pudeat futilitatum & blas-* " *phemiarum, quas Beza sine metu divinæ majesta-* " *tis evomuit, sicut ipse Lavatherus fateri cogitur,* " *& aliqui nobiliores Calvinistæ apud ipsum Bezam* " *conquesti sunt. Et quanquam Beza excuset omnia,* " *vocans sanctam urbanitatem: hæc tamen urbanitas* " (inquit iste Patriarcha) *non Theologus in pietatis* " *schola versantes, sed lenones effrontes, & scurras* " *spurciloquos in ludo meretricio a Thaïda vel* " *Candida profuga eruditos decet. Unde haud* " *dubii noster ille Beza flosculos suarum elegantia-* " *rum decerpsit.* Mox fortius urgens æque probans " hoc de Bezæ maledico & elumbi in disputationibus " & scriptionibus charactere. *Si quis* (inquit) *de* " *hac re ambigere velit, ille duos famosissimos dialo-* " *gos Bezæ contra D. Hesbusium legat, qui certè* " *non ab homine, sed ab ipso incarnato Beelzebub,* " *exarati esse videntur. Horret animus blasphemias* " *obscænas, & diabolico atramento tinctas, referre,* " *quas iste impurus convitiator & Athous in dialogis* " *illis, in articulo gravissimo, blasphemè impiè & scur-* " *riliter eructavit.* Certè adeo sunt fœdæ, ut ipse " Beza paulò post, quo speciosiùs priorem editionem " supprimeret, secundam procurarit, in qua septem
" folia

spoke well; he knew the World; he had a ready Wit, and much Learning. His Speech was heard with attention, till he touched upon the Real Presence. An Expression, which he made use of, caused a murmuring [H]. In the remaining part of this Conference, he behaved like a Man of great Capacity, and never suffered himself to be surprized by the Artifices of the Cardinal of *Lorrain*. He did not return to *Geneva*, when the Conference was ended; for, being a *Frenchman*, *Catherine de Medicis* would have him stay in his own Country. He preached often at the Queen of *Navarre*'s, at the Prince of *Condé*'s, and in the Suburbs of *Paris*. After the Massacre at *Vaſſi* (g), he was deputed to the King, to complain of That Action. The

(g) March 1, 1562.

---

(27) Gulielmus Reginaldus, in Calvino-Turciſmo, lib. iii. cap. 19. p. 671, 672. *He quotes* Conrad. Schlusselb. in Theol. Calvinist. lib. i. fol. 92. In Præfat. lib. iii. fol. 34, 35, & lib. ii. fol. 77, 78, 127.

" folia integra omisit, & loca plurima expunxit quæ
" erant in editione priori. Quanquam iste bonus &
" gravis Superintendens, hac qualicunque castigatione
" non contentus, optat *ut non modò isti dialogi in*
" *univerſum, ſed ſimul alia ejus omnia impia &*
" *blaſphema ſcripta, quæ ſunt plurima, abolerentur,*
" *ne à teneris, piis, & caſtis hominibus viderentur*
" *in æternum*. Sic ille (27). ---- *Omitting others*,
" *he propoſes* Theodore Beza *as an Instance; from*
" *whoſe Writings*, not only against the Papists, but
" even the Lutherans, This *(he ſays)* may be
" abundantly demonstrated. And These Things
" are so true, that the Sacramentarians them-
" selves are tired, and aſhamed, of the Follies
" and Blaſphemies, which *Beza*, without Fear of
" the Divine Majesty, has given vent to; as *La-*
" *vatherus* himself is forced to acknowledge, and
" some of the more noble Calvinists have complained
" to *Beza* himself. And, though Beza *excuſes it all*,
" *by calling it* Pious Raillery; yet This Raillery
" *(ſays* the Patriarch*)* is more becoming of the
" Stews, than Divines, brought up in the School
" of Piety. And, indeed, *Beza* seems to have ga-
" thered the Flowers of his Elegances in the former.
" *Afterwards, as a farther and ſtronger Proof of This*
" *ſlanderous Character of Beza in his Diſputations,*
" *and Writings*; If any one *(ſays he)* is not ſatiſ-
" fied of the Truth of This, let him read the two
" infamous Dialogues of *Beza* against *Heſhuſius*,
" which certainly appear to be the Work, not
" of a Man, but of *Beelzebub* himself incarnate. I
" tremble to repeat the obſcene and diabolical Blaſ-
" phemies, which This filthy Slanderer, and Athe-
" istical Writer, has impiouſly and ſcurrilouſly poured
" forth, in theſe Dialogues, on the most important
" Article. *Indeed They are ſo foul, that Beza him-*
" *ſelf, that he might have the better Colour for ſuppreſ-*
" *ſing the firſt Edition, procured a ſecond*, in which
" he omitted ſeven entire Leaves, and expunged
" ſeveral Paſſages, which were in the former Edi-
" tion. *Though This good Superviſor, not ſatisfied*
" *with this Correction, wiſhes*, that Theſe Dialogues,
" as also all his other wicked and blaſphemous Wri-
" tings, which are many in number, were entirely
" aboliſhed, that they might never more be ſeen
" by conſcientious, pious, and chaſt Men. *Thus far*
" *He.*" Remember, that this Conrad is a very paſ-
fionate Writer.

[G] *He made a Journey into* Germany, *with the Character of a Deputy*.] This was the Reason of his Journey. An Aſſembly of Those of the Reformed Religion was detected, at *Paris*, in the Year 1557. It consisted of Four hundred Perſons, whereof ſeven were burnt, and the rest impriſoned (28). The Churches had Recourſe to some Princes of *Germany*, to endeavour to obtain the Lives of Thoſe poor Prisoners from *Henry* II. *Farel*, *Beza*, and *John Budæus*, Son of the great *William Budæus*, were the three Deputies, who went to the Court of the Elector *Palatine*, to That of the Landgrave of *Heſſe*, and to That of the Duke of *Wirtemberg*, in the Year 1558. These three Princes earneſtly recommended the Cauſe of Thoſe Prisoners; but the Court of *France* paid little Regard to Theſe Recommendations. *Beza*, as he paſſed through *Franckfort*, had the Pleaſure of ſpeaking with *Melanchthon* (29). This is what *Antony la Faye* ſays; but, according to *Beza*, the Motive to This Journey was, to deſire the Interceſſion of Thoſe Princes for the Vallies of *Piedmont*, which were, then, in Poſſeſſion of the King of *France*, that is, in the Year 1557 (30). He acknowledges, neverthelesſ, in the Life of *Calvin*, that That Interceſſion was deſired for the Priſoners at *Paris*, and that it was not made in vain. " Par-

(28) *According to* Beza, in vita Calvini, *about* 30 *were taken, and the reſt fled*.

(29) Fayus, in vit. Bez*æ*, pag. 17.

(30) Beza ad Cl. de Xaintes, Apolog. i. Oper. Tom. II. pag. 235.

" tim intervenientium Germanorum Principum le-
" gatione, quam ſumma celeritate Calvinus procura-
" vit, tempeſtas illa nonnihil conquievit (31). - - - -
" *The Storm was ſomething appeaſed, partly by the*
" *Interpoſition of ſome* German *Princes, which* Calvin,
" *with great Expedition, procured*." He finds fault with *Claudius de Xaintes*, who placed This Journey in the Year 1556.

[H] *An Expreſſion, which be made uſe of at the Conference of* Poiſſy, *cauſed a murmuring*.] The Expreſſion was This: " We ſay, that the Body of
" Jesus Christ is as far from the Bread and
" Wine, as the higheſt Heaven is remote from the
" Earth (32)." Let us ſee, now, what the Effect of it was; and let us make uſe of *Beza*'s own Words.
" This ſingle Expreſſion (though many others, as
" contrary and repugnant to the Doctrine of the
" Church of *Rome*, had been ſaid by him) was the
" Cauſe, that the Prelates began to ſtir, and to mur-
" mur, ſome ſaying *blaſphemavit*; others aroſe to
" be gone, not being able to do any thing worſe,
" becauſe of the King's Preſence: Among others,
" Cardinal *de Tournon*, Dean of the Cardinals, who
" was ſeated in the chief Place, required of the
" King, and the Queen, that Silence might be im-
" poſed on *Beza*, or that He, and his whole Com-
" pany, might be permitted to retire. Neither the
" King, nor any of Princes, ſtirred; and audience
" was given to proceed. Silence being made, *Beza*
" ſaid; I deſire you, Sirs, to hear the Concluſion,
" which will ſatisfy you: And then he returned to
" his Diſcourſe, which he continued to the end (33)."
Catharine de Medicis ſaid, in her Letter to Mr *de Rennes*, Embaſſador of *France* at the Emperor's Court,
" That *Beza*, ſpeaking of the Sacrament, forgot
" himſelf, in a Compariſon, ſo abſurd and offen-
" ſive to the Ears of all the Aſſiſtants, that ſhe
" was near ſilencing him, and ſending all the
" Miniſters away, without ſuffering them to pro-
" ceed any farther: but that ſhe abſtained from it,
" least People ſhould go away imbued with his Do-
" ctrine, without having heard what ſhould be
" anſwered him (34)." Obſerve the *Parentheſis*, which the Historian made uſe of (35). Nothing will better diſcover the Weakneſs of Mens Minds. An old Cardinal, and many Biſhops are ſcandalized, are going away, and cry out *Blaſphemy*: for what? Becauſe they heard a Miniſter ſay, that Jesus Christ is not corporeally preſent in the Symbols of the Bread and Wine of the Euchariſt; for it is what That Expreſſion, *ſo offenſive to the Ears of all the Aſſiſtants*, amounts to: Can there be a worſe grounded, or more childish, Cauſe of Offence? When People teach, that the Body of Jesus Christ is preſent but in one Place at one Time, and that it is always ſeated in Paradice at the Right-Hand of God, They plainly maintain, that it is as remote from the Sacrament of the Euchariſt, as Paradiſe is from the Earth. Now the Prelates of the Conference of *Poiſſy* could not be ignorant, that the Miniſters teach, that the Humanity of Jesus Christ is always in Heaven, at the Right-Hand of God; and that it can be preſent but in one Place at one Time; and They could not expect, that *Beza* would not explain the Doctrine of his Party; They ſhould not, therefore, have been offended at this Expreſſion (for once again, it adds nothing to the Doctrine of the Miniſters); or elſe They went to the Aſſembly with This Perſuaſion, that the Miniſters would betray their Opinions, and only endeavour to deceive the King. I ſee but one Thing, which can excuſe the Irritation of the Prelates. It may be ſaid, that ſome Expreſſions offend us, though they import no more, than ſome Expreſſions, at which we are not offended

(31) Beza in vita Calvini.

(32) Beza Hiſt. Ecclesiaſt. lib. iv. pag. 516.

(33) Ibidæ pag. 521.

(34) Apud Maimbourg. Hiſt. of Calviniſm, pag. 223, 224. Le Laboureur, Addit. to Caſtelnau, Tom. I. pag. 763, *pro-duces the Queen's Letter*.

(35) (*The many others, as contrary and repugnant to the Doctrine of the Church of* Rome, *had been ſaid by him*.) Beza Hiſt. Ecclesſ. *A* Reflexion *on the Offence, which the Prelates took, at the Conference of* Poiſſy.

BEZA. 791

The Civil-War followed soon after; during which the Prince of *Condé* kept him with Him. *Beza* was at the Battle of *Dreux*, as a Minister [*I*]. During the Imprisonment of the Prince, he always kept with Admiral *de Coligni*, and did not return to *Geneva*, 'till after the Peace of 1563. He did not see *France* again 'till 1568, and That was in order to go to *Vezelai*, where his Presence was necessary [*K*]. He had written several Books after his Return to *Geneva*; and he published others after his Return from *Vezelai* [*L*]. He returned into *France* again, in the Year 1571, to assist at the National Synod of *Rochel*, of which he was elected Moderator. The following Year he assisted at That of *Nimes*, and opposed the Faction of *John Morel*, who designed to introduce a new Discipline. The Prince of *Condé* sent for him to *Strasburg*, in the Year 1574, in order to send him to Prince *John Casimir*, Administrator of the *Palatinate*; which shews, that it was well known, that he understood other Things, besides Lectures, and Books. The Conference of *Mombelliard*, in

offended. For Example, the Parts, which Modesty does not permit to name, may be denoted by modest Words; and yet These Words signify the same thing, as Those, which are called obscene. If the latter are offensive, it is not because of the Thing itself, which They signify, but because we think, that He, who uses them, against Custom, does not pay us That Respect, which Decency requires (36). Upon This Footing, The Bishops of *Poissi* might be more offended at the Minister's Doctrine, represented by a Comparison, than at the same Doctrine nakedly and plainly represented: But then, their Scandal was not grounded on a Zeal for Religion: For the Comparison, which *Beza* alledged, is not more contrary to GOD, or to the Christian Faith, than the plainest Exposition of the Doctrine of the Protestants. It was not, then, for the Interest of GOD, that they were scandalized; but only because they supposed, that the Minister did not pay sufficient Respect to his Auditors, when he made use of such Expressions. They, who would make such an Apology for These Prelates, would ascribe to them a most criminal Vanity. What shall we say then? Is it better to say, that They acted like Children; that They were not offended at the Things, but at the Words? This would not be for their Honour. I am surprized, that such a grave Historian, as *Mezerai*, durst say, that This Proposition of *Beza* was passionate, and offensive; that *Beza* was ashamed of it himself; and that it strangely offended the Ears of the Catholics; and that the Prelates trembled with Horror at it (37). It is plain, *Mezerai* thinks These great Tremblings reasonable; and he makes himself ridiculous by it; for it is the same thing, to say; *The Body of* Jesus Christ *is not present in the Holy Sacrament*; and to say, *It is at an infinite Distance from it.*

[*I*] *He was at the Battle of* Dreux, *as a Minister*.] I add This Clause, least any of my Readers should suspect, that he assisted there, to fight, and handle the Sword. *Claudius de Xaintes* reproaches him for it. This is *Beza*'s Answer. " Interfui sane prælio, &
" inchoanti & definenti (quidni enim hoc facerem
" eo rite vocatus?) & quidem quod magis mireris
" palliatus, non armatus: nec mihi quisquam vere
" vel cædem cujusquam vel fugam objecerit (38),
" ————— *I was indeed present at the Battle*;
" (*and why should I not, being properly called?*) *and,*
" *which you will more wonder at, in the Habit of my*
" *Order, not armed: nor can any one justly charge me*
" *with the Slaughter of one Man, or with Flight.*

[*K*] *He went to* Vezelai, *where his Presence was necessary.*] *Nicolas de Beze,* Bailiff of *Vezelai,* fled to *Geneva* for Religion, where he died, a little while after, of the Plague, at the House of *Theodorus,* his Brother by the Father's Side. The latter, having a Mind to order the Affairs of the Family of the deceased, and to endeavour at the same time to save Part of his Estate, took a Journey to *Vezelai. Hæc fuit occasio Bezæ Vezelios suos revisendi, partim ut fratris defuncti liberis prospiceret, partim ut nonnullas Patrimonii sui Reliquias dispersas colligeret, quod & fecit quantum locus, tempus, & res permiserunt* (39). He endeavoured to persuade a Sister, which he had in a Nunnery, to forsake the Church of *Rome.* She was an old Nun, very obstinate in her Religion, who would not listen to her Brother's Remonstrances (40).

[*L*] *He had written several Books after his Return to* Geneva; *and he published others after his Return from* Vezelai.] Soon after his Settlement in the Church of *Geneva,* he drew up a *Confession of Faith* in *Latin,* which he had formerly written in *French,* to justify himself to his Father, and to endeavour The good old Man's Conversion. He published This Confession in *Latin,* dedicated to his good Master *Melchior Wolmar,* in the Year 1560. His Pen was quiet, whilst he followed, in the Armies, either the Prince of *Condé,* or Admiral *de Coligni;* but, as soon as he returned to *Geneva,* he wrote two *Answers,* the one to *Castalio* (41), and the other to *Francis Baudouin.* Afterwards, he attacked *Brentius,* and *James Andreas,* upon their Doctrine of Ubiquity; and then wrote his Book *de Divortiis & Repudiis,* against *Bernardin Ochinus,* who had written in Favour of Polygamy. He attacked also the Errors of *Flacius Illyricus.* He answered *Claudius de Xaintes, Selneccerus, James Andreas,* and *Pappus, &c.* and turned *David's Psalms* into all sorts of *Latin* Verses. He published a Treatise of the *Sacrament,* and a Book against *H. sinannus;* some *Sermons* on the Passion of Jesus Christ, and on the Canticle of Canticles; a Translation of That Canticle into *Lyric* Verse; and an Answer to *Genebrard,* to whom That Translation had given new Occasion to repeat his Slanders. In 1590, he published his Treatise *de Excommunicatione & Presbyterio,* against *Thomas Erastus.* Some time after, he examined the Book of *Saravia, de Ministrorum Evangelii gradibus.* I omit the Titles of some other Books; They may be seen in the Lists, which *Antony la Faye* has placed at the end of his Work, *de vita & obitu Theodori Bezæ,* from whence I have borrowed what I have just now said. I have not met with, there, all the Productions of *Beza*'s Pen. The *Icones* of the Illustrious Persons, who set their Hand to the Work of the Reformation (42), is not mentioned there, nor the *Ecclesiastical History of the Reformed Churches.* This last Work is very curious; It extends from the Year 1521, to the Peace of the thirteenth of *March* 1563. I do not wonder, that They have not inserted in This List the ingenious, but too burlesque, Letter of *Benedictus Passavantius* to the President *Lizet* (43). *La Faye* makes no mention of it; but, as for some other satirical or burlesque Pieces, which some attribute to *Beza,* he maintains, that they are mistaken. " Dicteriis plenos libros compoſuit, Harangusam ad
" Cardinalem Lothariugum, de furoribus Gallicis,
" vitam Catharinæ Mediceæ, & similis notæ chartas.
" Atqui tam verum est libros illos fuisse compositos à
" *Beza,* quàm verum est (quod isti ignoranter & te-
" merè deblaterant) ab Amiralii ministro scriptum fu-
" isse librum, cui nomen est Matagonis de Matagoni-
" bus (44). ——— *He wrote Books, full of satirical In-*
" *vectives, The Speech to the Cardinal of* Lorrain,
" *concerning the Madness of the* French *Nation, The*
" *Life of* Catharine *of* Medicis, *and the like. And*
" *it is as true, that these Pieces were written by Beza,*
" *as it is true (which these Persons ignorantly and*
" *rashly blab out) that the Book, entituled* Matagonis
" *de* Matagonibus, *was written by The Admiral's Mi-*
" *nister.*"
Garasse maintains, that *Beza,* " gives himself, jestingly, the Name of FRANTOPIN, in writing
" against Dr *de Xaintes,* in That little *Macaronic* Book,
" which begins with These Words; *Tu facis bene de*
" *sufficiente, Domine Magister noster, post habere bibi-*
" *tum quatuor bonas fides de vestro vino Sorbonnico, in*
" *dejunando Theologaliter, &c* (45)." He attributes also a Book to him, entituled, *A Parallel of* Henry II *with* Pilate (46). Observe, that there is a great Fault in the List of *Antony la Faye*: It does not mention the Date of the first Editions, nor when, and how many times, the Books of *Beza* were reprinted.

[*M*] The

BEZA.

in 1586, engaged him against *James Andreas*, a Divine of *Tubingen*. *Beza* would have had the Dispute managed syllogistically; but he was obliged to yield to the Desires of his Adversary, who would not be confined to the Rules of Syllogisms. The Success of This Dispute was as usual [M]; each Party boasted to have gained the Victory, and published an Account accordingly. *Beza* lost his Wife, in the Year 1588; but this Domestic Affliction, great as it was, did not hinder him from going to the Synod, which Those of *Bern* had assembled. The Doctrine of *Samuel Huberus*, concerning our Justification before GOD, which, he said, consisted in an inherent Quality (b), was there condemned. *Beza* married again, the same Year, to a Widow, who survived him [N]. The Inconveniencies of old Age began to come upon him, in the Year 1597, and obliged him to speak but seldom in public; and, at last, he desisted altogether from it, in the beginning of the Year 1600. His poetical Vein was not so dried up, in the Year 1597, but that he wrote some Verses, full of Fire, against the Jesuits, occasioned by the Report, which was spread of his Death

[M] *The Success of the Dispute of* Mombelliard *was as usual.*] *Antony la Faye* asserts this: "Utrinque placide discessum est sine lite, aut amarulentia; sed nullo fructu, ut fere semper in talibus palæstris publicis contingere solet (47). ——Both *Parties retreated peaceably, without Strife, or Bitterness ; but with no Advantage gained on either side, as is usual in such Kind of Public Disputes.*" Some Gentlemen, who had left *France* for their Religion, and had fled to *Mombelliard*, gave occasion to This Dispute. The Count of *Mombelliard* desired the Canton of *Berne* to name Deputies, to confer with the Divines of *Wirtemberg*; he desired also the Republic of *Geneva* to send *Beza* to the Conference; This he did in compliance with the Desire of the Refugees. *Abraham Musculus*, Minister of *Bern*, and *Peter Huberus*, Professor of the *Greek* Language in the same City, were the *Swiss* Deputies: *Beza*, and *Antony la Faye*, were the Deputies of *Geneva*. *James Andreas*, and *Luke Osiander*, were the chief Deputies of *Wirtemberg*. Most of them heard only *Beza* and *James Andreas*, and saw but little Light in This Dispute of several Days, because it was not managed syllogistically; for, when Two Persons answer each other, by long Discourses, it is almost impossible to perceive, whether they remove the Difficulties. "Jacobus Andreas perpetua & declamatoria oratione utebatur. Quare illius vestigiis insistere Beza coactus est. Unde non tam facilis, expedita, aut perspicua fuit tota illa dierum aliquot disceptatio (48). —— *James Andreas used a long and declamatory Way of Speaking.* Beza *was, therefore, obliged to do the same. Hence it was, that This Dispute, which lasted so many Days, was not at all cleared up.*" A Man is scarce ever worsted upon these occasions, if he knows but how to prattle. The Parties agreed not to publish the Relation of This Conference; but, when it was known, that Letters were dispersed all over *Germany*, which were read in the Courts of Princes, and in private Conversations, and that These Letters proclaimed the Victory of *James Andreas*, and that, at last, the Divines of *Wirtemberg* had published the Conference with Marginal Notes; *Beza* was obliged to publish a Counter-Relation.

I have lately read, in a Work of *Abraham Scultetus*, that The Political Reasons, as well on the Part of the *French* Refugees, as on that of the Count of *Mombelliard*, contributed much more to the appointing this Conference, than the Theological Reasons. The Refugees sent for *Beza*, because they thought, that, if he conferred amicably with Dr *Andreas*, about the Controverted Matters, They should live more easy in the County of *Mombelliard*, and that, perhaps, the Duke of *Wirtemberg* might come over to their Side. As for the Count, he had been an *Ubiquitarian* in his Youth; but, having heard *Beza's* Sermons and Lectures, he declared freely, that he had seen many things at *Geneva*, and in *Swisserland*, of which *James Andreas* had never spoken a word to him, and that he had scarce seen any thing there, of what the same Doctor had often told him. *Geneva, & in Helvetia, vidi multa, de quibus nihil, pauca eorum, de quibus sæpe audivi ex D. Jacobo* (49). This was to declare, that That Person had not drawn the Picture of the *Calvinists* very faithfully. From that time, the Count was more kind to the Reformed, and afforded a Retreat to Those, who fled from *France* for their Religion. But, when it was represented to him, that the Duke of *Wirtemberg* had no Son, and that the House of *Austria* would not suffer a Favourer of the *Huguenots* to inherit That Duke's Succession; I say, when it was represented to him, that he had made himself suspected, both by his Journey to *Geneva*, and by his Kindness to the *French* Refugees, he consented to the Dispute between Dr *Andreas* and *Beza*; but his Aim was not so much to promote the Truth, as to clear himself from the Suspicion of *Calvinism*. *Non tam ut veritati consuleret, quam ut se de Calvinismo purgaret* (50). This is what *Daniel Tossa* replied to *Christopher Pezelius*, who had asked him the Reason of the Conference of *Mombelliard*. *Scultetus*, who relates it (51), was at Dinner, where This was said (52). If we had a Collection of such like Tabletalk, as large as That, which is found in *Plutarch's* Works, we might learn a great many curious Things from it.

[N] *He married again, the same Year, to a Widow, who survived him.*] The Name of his first Wife was *Claudine Denosse:* See below the Remark [Y]. Their Marriage continued forty Years: The Name of his second Wife was *Catherine de la Plane*, who took great Care of him as long as he lived. *Catherina Plania, Astensis, Francisci Taruffi Januensis Vidua, quæ ei usque ad ultimum Spiritum magno subsidio fuit* (53). *Patin* is mistaken, when he says, that *Stephen Pasquier* wrote some Verses on the three Marriages of *Beza*.

Uxores ego tres vario sum tempore nactus,
Cum juvenis, tum vir, factus & inde senex.
Propter opus prima est validis mihi juncta sub annis,
Altera propter opes, tertia propter opem (54).

The Meaning of These Verses is: *I married three Wives, at several times; in my Youth, in my Manhood, and in my Old-Age. I married the first Wife for the Delights of Love ; the second, because she was Rich; the third, that she might nurse me in my Infirmities.* But This could not agree with *Beza*, since he had not had three Wives. Some say, that *Pasquier* made these Verses on himself (55). He, who observes This, is, nevertheless, in the Error of *Guy Patin* concerning *Beza's* three Wives. *He married again, for the third time, at seventy Years of Age, and had sent word of it to his intimate Friend* Junius, *a* Dutchman (56), *in these Words:* If it be a Folly to marry again at seventy Years of Age, I have lately committed it. *He was an old Cock, which could not break off from* Venus's *Chariot, to which he had been burnassed from his Youth* (57). These are the Words of a credulous Monk, who is but seldom well-informed of what he says. If He, and *Patin*, had consulted the nineteenth Book of *Stephen Pasquier's* Letters, They would have spoken with more exactness. *Pasquier* relates, that, having heard it said, that *Theodora Beza* was married again, *he wrote This Tetrastich in Favour of the Person, who should marry three Wives* (58). *Beza's* second Wife was wonderfully careful of him; He left her Heiress of all his Estate in *Geneva*. " Eorum quæ Genevæ habebat hæredem ex asse instituit Catharinam Planiam conjugem suam ; qua senectutem ipsius sustentante, & gloriam ex officiis assiduis erga ipsum, annorum septendecim spatio, quærente, vivebat (59). ———— *He left* Catharine *de la* Plane, *his Wife, who supported his old Age, and placed all her Glory in taking the greatest Care of him, for seventeen Years, sole Heiress of his Estate at* Geneva." *Beza* never had any Children (60).

[O] He

BEZA.

Death, and that, before he expired, he had made Profession of the *Romish* Faith [O]. The last Verses, which he composed, were a *Votiva Gratulatio*, to *Henry* IV, after he had been kindly received by him, near *Geneva*, in the Month of *December*, 1600 (*i*) [P]. He lived 'till the thirteenth of October, 1605, and preserved his Good Sense to the last [Q], and expressed great Sentiments of Piety with his last Breath. He was a Man of an extraordinary Merit, and who did his Party very great Services [R]. He was

(i) La Faye, pag. 61, says, in 1599, but is mistaken.

[O] *He wrote Verses —— on occasion of the Report that was spread of his Death —— and that he had made Profession of the Romish Faith.*] They, who invented, and spread, this Story, were but little acquainted with the True Interest of Their Church. These kind of Frauds may be spread, to some advantage, against a Sect, which has neither Authors, nor Printers; but They must needs be prejudicial, when they are boldly employed against a Church, which has a thousand Presses, and Pens, in her Bosom, which let nothing fall to the Ground, and take the Ball at the first rebound. Was it not great Folly to imagine, that the Protestants would lose such a fair Opportunity of exclaiming against Monkish Impostures and Cheats, and to draw many thundering Conclusions from their Assurance in reporting a Falshood, which was so easy to be confuted? The Ministers of *Geneva* were not silent on This Occasion. They published two Pieces, attended with all the Authenticity necessary to refute This foolish Lie: One of These Pieces was in *Latin*, and the other in *French*. *Editus nomine suo publicis duobus scriptis, altero Latine (cui Beza redivivus nomen fecerunt) altero Gallice* (61). *Beza,* in a Letter to *William Stuckius,* confuted the same Story (62); and the Jesuit *Clement du Puy,* who was looked upon as the Inventor of This Fable, drew a shower of satirical Verses on himself in particular, and on his own Order in general, which *Beza's* Muses, old as they were, made very formidable (63). It was easy to forsee This; so that They were but dimsighted Persons, as to their own Interests, who invented such a Romance. There are rash Persons in all Communions. See the Article BELLARMIN, Remark [E].

I must not omit, that the Jesuits asserted, that this Story was invented by the Protestants, to be imputed to them. See the *Scaligerana*, under the Word *Vellerus*, and the Notes on the Book, entituled, *La Confession de Sanci,* wherein you will find an Abstract of the Letter, which they published, in 1598, *under the Name of a Savoyard Gentleman,* in which *they maintained, that The pretended Latter, which was attributed to Them, about the Death, and Conversion, of Theodorus Beza, was a meer Imposture of Beza himself, and the Bezæans at Geneva.* The Author of the Notes observes, that *Stephen Pasquier* had no regard to This, and that the Jesuit *Richeome* gave out, as certain, the Story of This Minister's Conversion, in a Book, reprinted in the Year 1599 (64).

Observe, that, in 1591, there was a Report, that *Beza* was dead. This false News was written by a Minister to M*r du Plessis Mornai,* which inflamed him in these Terms: *You have made me sorrowful by the Death of Beza, quam nondum certò accepi, quanquam jam olim animo præcepi. We have lost three or four Stars; I see nothing but thick Clouds over us.* This we find in the Ninty fourth, and Ninty fifth Pages of the second Volume of his Memoirs.

[P] *He was kindly received ----- by Henry* IV.] D*r Spon* reports the Speech, which *Beza* made to That Prince, and the King's Answer (65). M*r de Perefixe* thought, falsly, that *Henry* IV entered into *Geneva,* and that he was harangued there by This Minister (66). He received the Deputies of *Geneva* at *Luyset* (67), a Quarter of a League from S*t Catherine's* Fort, which Fort was two Leagues from *Geneva. Thuanus* says, that the King made *Beza* a Present of Five hundred Crowns (68).

[Q] *He was sensible to the last.*] His Historian makes no mention of what *Thuanus* observes concerning This Venerable Old Man's Memory. " Præsen-
" tium memoriam debilitata quippe mente evanidam
" amiserat, præteritorum dum ingenio valebat im-
" pressam servaverat. Itaque & totos Psalmos He-
" braicè, & quodcumque caput ex B. Pauli Epistolis
" proposuisses, integrum Græcè recitabat, nec in iis
" quæ olim didicerat judicio carebat, sed quæ dixerat
" statim obliviscebatur (69)." The Meaning of this is, that, in divers Respects, *Beza's* Memory was very good, and very bad; very good, as to Things which he had learned during the Vigor of his Mind; (for he could repeat all the *Psalms* in *Hebrew*, and all S*t Paul's* Epistles in *Greek*, by heart), and very bad, as to Things present; for, a little after having said any thing, he forgot, that he had said it. He continued in This Condition almost two Years, if we may believe *Thuanus,* who seems to have been furnished with very good Memoirs on this Head. And, indeed, *Casaubon* affirms, that, in Point of Erudition, *Beza* shewed himself, in the latter Years of his Life, such as he had appeared Twenty Years before. He discoursed so clearly upon ancient History, that one would have thought he had just been reading *Plutarch*, and the like Authors. He spoke *Latin*, and sometimes *Greek*, as before: But, after having amply discoursed on the Subject of the new King of *England*, he would, often, ask, in the same Conversation, Whether it was true, that Queen *Elizabeth* was dead? " Venerandus senex Theodorus
" Beza cum per longinquitatem ætatis factus sit ob-
" liviosus, adeo ut post frequentes de novo Rege
" Angliæ sermones subinde me rogaret de Regina,
" an verum esset quod fama jactaret, illam satis con-
" cessisse. Idem tamen in literis visus nobis esse
" quem ante annos viginti noveramus. Loquitur
" Latinè, interdum & Græcè, ut antea: audivimus
" de historia veteri differentem è re nata locule-
" tissimè, ut videretur recens esse à lectione Plutarchi
" & id genus autorum (70)." *Thuanus* was mis-informed of the Circumstances of *Beza's* Death; He says, that This Minister, as he was going out to Church, was seized with a sudden Convulsion, of which he died. The Truth is, that, for some Weeks, his Strength declined visibly, and that there was nothing sudden, or unexpected, in his Death. See *la Faye,* pag. 65, 66.

[R] *He did his Party great Services.*] *Leti* relates, that *Sixtus* V. caused two Conferences to be held, at which he was present, to deliberate about the means of depriving the Protestant Party of the great Support they had in the Person of *Theodorus Beza* (71). What could be said more to the Honour of This Minister, than the representing him as a Man, who made the Pope, and Cardinals, uneasy, as to Affairs of State; for there was no Controversy in the Case? *Leti* pretends, that, in the Year 1587, the Deputy of the King of *Navarre*, to the *Cantons*, made use of *Beza's* good Offices, to obtain some Levies in their Country; That *Beza* went from Town to Town, over all the Protestant *Cantons*, and that he animated the *Swiss* in such a manner, that they furnished Prince *Casimir* with great Sums; that the Catholic *Cantons*, seeing this, informed the Court of *Rome* of the great Prejudice this Person did to the Catholic Cause; that, upon This, *Sixtus* V caused two Conferences to be held, the Result whereof was, that all manner of means should be employed, to oblige this Minister to leave *Geneva*; after which, nothing would be more easy than the Conversion of That City; and that the Conversion of *Geneva* would be the total Ruin of Heresy, both in *Swisserland*, and *France*; that M*r de Sales,* Bishop of *Geneva*, being at That Time at *Rome*, was desired to declare, in the Pope's Presence, by what means he thought they might dislodge This old Minister from his Post; that he declared, the only means was, to supply the Duke of *Savoy* with necessary Forces for the Conquest of *Geneva*; that *Beza*, not doubting, but there was a Design upon his Life, would take such care of himself, that they must not expect any enterprize against his Person would succeed; that, after This Discourse of M*r de Sales*, the Design was laid aside of getting rid of This Minister by Assassination, or by Poison; forasmuch as they were informed, that his Highness of *Savoy* had tried all Expedients for This Purpose in vain.

I have three things to observe upon this Narrative. I. *Antony la Faye* does not say, that *Beza* made a Journey

(61) Fayus, pag. 59.

(62) See also the Preface of his New Testament, Edit. 1598.

(63) Ant. la Faye has these Verses of Beza, pag. 60, 61.

(64) Taken from the Notes on The Confession of Sanci, pag. 427, &c. Edit. 1699.

(65) Spon. Hist. of Geneva, l. iii. pag. 319. Edit. of Utrecht, 1685.

(66) Perefixe, Life of Henry IV.

(67) Matthieu, Hist. of the Peace, lib. iv. pag. 661. La Faye calls this Place Eluctetum; Thuanus, lib. 132, Luisellum.

(68) Thuan. lib. 125. pag. 229.

(69) Id. lib. 134. pag. 2082.

(70) Casaubon. Epist. 297. ad Scaliger.

(71) Leti, vita di Sisto V. Part II. lib. iii. pag. 262, & seq. Edit. 1686.

BEZA, it is said, was the Subject of some Consultations at *Rome*.

ATTEMPTS against his Person.

VOL. I. 9 F

BEZA.

was expofed to a great Number of Slanders and Calumnies: But he made both *Catholics*, and *Lutherans*, fee, that he knew how to defend himfelf, and that he had both Teeth and Claws. He had a great fhare in *Scaliger*'s Efteem [*S*]. I criticize *Moreri* only in five Things [*T*]. *Mezerai* treats This Minifter very ill; he adopts the Story for Truth, which had been fpread, of an Accufation of Sodomy, entered againft *Beza*, before the Parliament of *Paris*; and another Story of his running away with *Candida*, a Taylor's Wife. This appears unworthy of a judicious Hiftorian [*U*].
The

a Journey to *Swifferland*, in the Year 1587; and yet he feldom forgets thefe fort of things. An Expedition like This, the Effects of which were, it is faid, fo great, and of fuch general Influence for the Good of the Caufe, could not have been unknown to, or fuppreffed by, him. II. *Francis de Sales* was not Bifhop of *Geneva*, under *Sixtus* V: *Clement* VIII made him Coadjutor of That Bifhoprie. III. The Difcourfe, which is afcribed here to This Prelate, does not agree with Thefe Words of *Moreri*; *Beza, with whom* Francis de Sales *had fome Conferences at* Geneva, *confeffed to him, that the Catholic Religion was the only true Religion* (72). Upon fuch a Confeffion, the Prelate would have advifed The Pope to offer all manner of Dignities to This Minifter. The Defcription of the Care, which it was faid, at *Rome*, that *Beza* took of his Life, is hyperbolical. " Non faceva paffo, fenza un cumulo grande " di precautioni, è fenza pigliar cento & mille mi- " fure, non coftumando di praticar niffuno, fenza " effer ficuro d'un inveterata conofcenza, ne lafciava " domeftici in fua Cafa, della di cui fede non ne " foffe ficuro ultro che qui fuo perverfi Settarii lo " cuftodivano come fuoi Demoni tutelari, nè ufciva " mai di Cafa fenza haverne cinque ò fei à lato, è " quel che importa, che per maggior ficurezza non " metteva mai li piedi fuori della Citta (73)." The Meaning of This is; " that he never ftirred without " the utmoft Precaution; that he converfed with " none but his moft intimate Acquaintance; that his " very Domefticks were only Thofe of his Sect; that " he never went abroad without five or fix of them " about him; and that, for the greater Security, he " never fet foot out of the City." But it is true, that he made ufe of Precaution. See one of his Pieces againft *Claudius de Xaintes*. You will find, there, that They upbraided him with not daring to go out of *Geneva*, for fear of being killed, like another *Cain*, by the firft, who fhould meet him. *Geneva pedem non audes efferre, ne te quifquis invenerit ut alterum Cain occidat*. He anfwered, that, if God called him to it, he would go any where without Fear; though he was not ignorant of the Ambufhes, which were laid for him, and which he would avoid as prudently as he could. " Etfi mihi appofitos à tuis illis & veneficos & fi- " carios non ignoro (hae funt enim artes Romanae) " quorum etiam unus jam hic deprehenfus poenas " dedit .... Interea me fane libens domi contineo, " & veftras infidias quam prudentiffimè poffum " evito (74)."

[*S*] *He had a great Share in* Scaliger's *Efteem*.] This appears by his *Epicedium* on *Beza*'s Death. He inferted an ill Prefage in it, which proved falfe. *Addito etiam de fato urbis in qua deceffit omine, quod tamen hactenus eventu caruit* (75). It is ninety Years, more or lefs, fince *Thuanus* made This Obfervation, and it has not hitherto (76) appeared, that *Scaliger*'s Prefage has been confirmed in the leaft. It was not one of Thofe Poetical Predictions, which are of no greater Confequence, than Thofe of a Fanatical Commentator on St *John*'s Revelation. Nor do I believe, that the Defire of comparing *Beza* to St *Auguftin*, which might have ingaged an hundred other Poets to hazard This Prediction, made *Scaliger* fpeak in This manner. It is very probable, that, confidering the State of Things, He feared for the City of *Geneva* the Fate of That of *Hippo*, which was taken by the *Vandals*, a little after the Death of it's Bifhop. So that it was rather a Political Conjecture, than a Poetical Rapture. The Event has proved it to be fo; which fhews, that the fureft way is not to judge at all of Things to come. *Scaliger*'s ill Prefage is This;

Utque Dei famulo non Hippo fuperftite capta eft,
  Cum quateret Lybicas Vandalus Hoftia opes,
Indulfit tibi fic praefentia numinis, ifto
  Cernere ne poffes ulteriora malo.

Atque utinam celeres rapiant procul omina venti,
  Et potius mendax finxerit ifta metus.
Sed te felicem, &c.

And, as, fecure 'till holy Auftin died,
Hippo, untaken, ftem'd the Vandal Tide;
So Heav'n withholds, in Kindnefs, from Thy Eyes
Approaching Ills, and greater Miferies.
Far may the Winds the lucklefs Omen bear;
May it be nothing but the Child of Fear;
Yet Happy Thou, &c.

There are certain Things in the *Scaligerana*, to the Difadvantage of *Beza*; but do we ceafe to efteem a Man, when, for Example, we make no Difficulty to confefs, that the many Affairs, he was concerned in, and the Multitude of Books, he compofed, hindered him from acquiring much Learning?

[*T*] *I criticize* Moreri *only in five Things*.] I. *Beza* was not yet paft Childhood, when he was brought to *Paris*: His Mother carried him thither, as foon as he was weaned. *Mater ──── mariti imperio obfecuta Lutetiam ufque me* RECENS ABLACTATUM *perduxit*. *Beza* writes This to *Wolmar*. II. We fhall fee below (77), whether we ought to believe, *That a fcandalous Epigram drew the Refentment of Juftice on Beza ──── and that he was accufed of a more horrible Crime*, than Fornication, and that his Debaucheries brought a Difeafe upon him. III. It is not true, that *Calvin* often procured important Commiffions for *Beza*, that he might *affift at fome Conferences againft the Lutherans*. I do not think there were any Conferences, during *Calvin*'s Life, at which *Beza* was prefent; for the Difpute of the Year 1557 muft not be reckoned; Chance brought it about (78): It was but a trifling Bufinefs; They went into *Germany* upon another Defign. IV. It is not true, that *Beza* is the Author of the Confeffion of Faith of the Reformed Churches. The Confeffion of Faith, which he compofed firft in *French*, and afterwards in *Latin*, is a different Piece from the Confeffion of the Churches. V. *Beza* did not prefide in the Synod of *Nimes*, in the Year 1572. The following Faults are to be imputed to *Moreri*'s Printers: They have placed *Beza*'s Birth in the Year 1619, inftead of 1519. They have quoted *Antony Pale De vita & obitu Theod. Beze*: It fhould be *Antony la Faye, and Beza*.

[*U*] *What* Mezerai *fays, appears unworthy of a judicious Hiftorian*.] If he had been contented to fay, that we read, in many printed Pieces, that *Beza* was accufed of This abominable Crime, it would be no ftrange Thing; for he would have faid nothing but what is very true. Perhaps Two hundred Authors might be quoted, who, tranfcribing one another, have fpoken of This Procefs. *Mezerai* goes much farther; He maintains the Thing? he warrants it; and can produce no Proof for it; This may be called the Conduct of a rafh Hiftorian. Let us fet down his Words. " He may, without prejudice to any Religion, " very well be called a very wicked Man, and a " Soul wholly corrupted; who, like a filthy Harpy, " fpoiled the moft Holy Things with his malicious " Railleries; and whofe Heart brooded nothing but " bloody, and altogether execrable, Defigns. Nei- " ther was there any manner of Villany, wherewith " he did not defile his Youth; the Poems, whereof " he defigned to cover the Lewdnefs with the Title " of *Juvenilia*, make fufficient mention of it: But, " befides, it is certain, that he fled to *Geneva*, to " avoid the Punifhment, he deferved, for the Sodo- " my, whereof he was accufed before the Parlia- " ment of *Paris*; and that he carried his *Candida* " away with him, who was a Taylor's Wife, and " who was yet living in the beginning of This Cen- " tury, after he had fold certain Benefices, which he " had of his Uncle, and, among others, the Priory
" of

BEZA.

The Poems, entituled *Juvenilia*, have raised great Clamours [*X*]. It cannot be denied, that they contained Verses too licentious, and little becoming the Chastity of Christian Muses; but, if the Author's Enemies had been reasonable, they would rather have praised him for the Grief he expressed for them (*k*), than have put an

---

" of *Longjumeau*; beginning, in this manner, the " Reformation of his Life, with Simony and Adultery (79)." Mr *Maimbourg* gives only a Paraphrase of These Words of *Mezerai*, when he drew an horrible Picture of *Beza* (80); but, instead of following the Example of *Mezerai*, who quotes no body, he quotes *Bolsec*, *Spondanus*, *Florimond de Remond*, *Claudius de Xaintes*, &c. Had he had better Witnesses, he would, doubtless, have produced them; so that it is unquestionable, that *Mezerai* had no other Authorities, than Those, which *Maimbourg* quotes. Once again, This is most shameful in so famous and illustrious an Historiographer. Truly, an Historian would write very pretty Stories, should he mention all the abusive Language, which Controvertists give each other, of what Religion soever they be. They are not to be believed in personal Facts, with which they reproach their Adversaries, unless they support them with authentic Acts; so that *Mezerai*, having only followed *Claudius de Xaintes*, and *Florimond de Remond*, who brought no Proofs for Their Slanders, has injured himself greatly with Persons of Judgment.

Suffer me to make an Observation here, which may be of use in the Discussion of personal Facts. Several Authors have maintained, I. That *Beza* left *France*, to avoid the Consequences of a Process of Sodomy, which, they say, was entered against him, in the Parliament of *Paris*. II. That he carried a certain Taylor's Wife away with him. *Beza* has publickly maintained, that they were two enormous Calumnies; that he had lived an unblameable Life at *Paris*; and that he left it, neither out of Fear, nor for Debt, but for his Religion; and that he had never attempted his Neighbour's Wife, any more than the Kingdom of the *Indies*. *Lutetiâ inculpatâ & bonâ integrâque existimatione* — *vixisse*. *Inde non fuga, non clam, non vi, non metu, non ære alieno oppressum (quæ tu mihi falsissime & mendacissime impingis) sed unius religionis studio* — — *ad veram Ecclesiam justis itineribus ultro concessisse.* — — — *Coram Deo juratus testari possum non magis unquam mihi contigisse ut cujusquam uxoris pudicitiam attentarem, quam ut Indorum regnum invaderem* (81). Thus far, no Man of any Religion whatsoever is obliged to believe, that *Beza* was either innocent, or guilty; no one is obliged to believe, either that his Minister would not deny an infamous Crime, if he was not innocent of it; or that his Priest would advance a heinous Accusation, if it were not true. The Reader, therefore, must suspend his Judgment, 'till the Accusation be proved: But, on the other side, he must give it for the accused Person, when he sees, that the Accusation remains without Proof, and chiefly in the Circumstances, which I am going to mention. If the Fact in question be of such a nature, that it may be proved authentically; and, if the Accuser want neither Good-will, nor Industry, it must be concluded, that, if they do not prove it, They are Calumniators. This is sufficient to convict *Beza*'s Accusers of Calumny. A Process, entered against a Prior of *Longjumeau*, before the Parliament of *Paris*, is a Thing, which may be easily verified. The Accusers, Their Attorney, Their Petition, The Commission of Information, The Verbal Process of the Commissioners, are settled Persons, or Pieces, which are preserved by public Authority; and it can never be thought, that a wretched Fellow, who flies away as fast as he can, has Credit enough to abolish the Proceedings, and to silence the Complaints of the Party against him. The Taylor, whose Wife was said to have been debauched, lived as long as the pretended Seducer; so that it was easy for him to bring his legal Deposition. How comes it then, that such a one as *Claudius de Xaintes*, and so many Ecclesiastics, who publickly accused *Beza*, could never produce any Vouchers, nor a formal Deposition of This Taylor? Perhaps *Beza*'s obliging Language disarmed them: On the contrary, he treated Them like Dogs; his Jests, and his ill Language, pierced them through and through; and all their Writings breathe the most violent Hatred. So that They had, on the one side, all imaginable means of coming at Proofs; and, on the other, a most passionate Desire of finding Them; and yet they have not produced Them. From whence any equitable Person ought to conclude, that They are meer Calumniators.

This is the Substance of my whole Argument. The Thing is of such a Nature, that, if it were true, legal, and authentic, Proofs would not be wanting. The Accusers have all the Skill, and all the Address, necessary for finding these Proofs: They have the greatest Interest in the World in finding Them: They have not found them; It must, therefore, be concluded, that it is, because there were none. There were none; it must, then, be again concluded, that the Thing in question was false and chimerical.

I have enlarged on This Thought, because it may serve to clear up the Uncertainties, occasioned by so many rash Writers, who transcribe the most heinous Accusations from one another, without attempting to prove them; whilst, on the other Hand, the Accused, and their Friends, do not cease to cry out against the Calumny.

[*X*] *The Poems, entituled* Juvenilia, *raised great Clamours.*] They were printed at *Paris*, in the Year 1548, in the Printing-House of *Jodocus Badius Ascensius*, by *Conrad Badius*, for himself, and *Robert Stephens*, with a Licence of the Parliament for Three Years. The Author's Effigies is in the second Page; wherein he is said to have been, then, Twenty nine Years of Age. He dedicated This Work to his Professor *Melchior Wolmar*. These Poems consist of *Silvæ*, *Elegies*, *Epitaphs*, *Pictures*, *Icones*, and *Epigrams*. It is in vain to tell the Controvertists, that *Beza* produced these lewd Poems before he was a Protestant; for he himself contradicts Those, who make such an Apology for him. He acknowledges, that, from sixteen Years of Age, he had imbibed the Knowledge of the pure Gospel; and that, when he abjured Popery outwardly, he had long before made a Vow of that Abjuration (82). The first thing he returns GOD thanks for, in his Testament, is, *quod anno ætatis suæ* 16 *verâ Christianæ Religionis cognitione ac luce donatus sit* (83). *Note*, that *Morton*, having confessed, in the first Edition of his *Catholic Apology*, that *Beza*, while he was a Papist, was such as he is represented; *erat, erat, sed dum in volutabro vestro miser hæserat — dum Papista hircus fuit, &c* (84), has corrected This in the second Edition, and maintained that *Beza* always had the Character of an honest Man. *Brerleius* took the Advantage of the first Edition (85). It is in vain, likewise, to have recourse to Recrimination; for neither *Muretus*, nor *John della Casa*, nor an hundred other Poets, who had no Reformation, nor any new Church to set up, were obliged to distinguish themselves by a singular Virtue and Piety. The shortest way is, to place These Poems of *Beza* among the Sins of his Youth, for which he asked Pardon both of God and the Public (86). It is certain, that he endeavoured to suppress them (87), as much as his Enemies endeavoured to revive them; and, if he consented, at the Age of Seventy eight Years, to a new Edition of his *Latin* Verses, he did not design Those should be inserted, which gave offence. I wonder the contrary was believed (88); for not only the Authors, who are quoted, do not say, that *Beza* gave ALL *his Verses, to be printed with the fairest Characters, that were to be found at the* Stephens's; but it is certain also, that the Edition, which then was made, does not contain the licentious Verses of the *Juvenilia*. Consider well These Words of *la Faye*. " Accidit ut de Bezæ poë- " matis ageretur, & generof. D. Zaftrizellus peteret " à Beza sibi donari illa carmina, quæ cum ipse, tum " Paludius, vita digna judicarent. Id quum impetrâs- " sent, Beza concedente, curavit ille in unum colli- " gi Sylvas, Elegias, Epitaphia, Epigrammata, Ico- " nes, Emblemata, Catonem Censorium, & ut ele- " gantissimis typographii Stephaniani formis excude- " rentur effecit anno 1597 (89). — *The Discourse* " *happened to turn upon* Beza's *Poems*; *and* D. Zastri- " sellus *desired* Beza *to give him those Pieces, which* " *both He, and* Paludius (he was *Zastrisellus's* Tutor) " *should think worthy of being preserved*. Beza *con-* " *senting, He took care, that his* Sylvæ, *Elegies,* " *Epitaphs,*

---

(79) Mezerai, Hist. of France, Vol. III. pag. 64.

(80) Maimb. Hist. of Calvinism, pag. 217.

THE WAY to know whether an Accusation be false.

(81) Beza, Apolog. altera ad Claud. de Xaintes, Oper. Tom. II. pag. 359.

(82) Epist. Dedicator. Confessionis Fidei ad Wolmarum.

(83) Fayus, in vita Bezæ, pag. 73.

(84) Morton, Apol. Cathol. Part I. lib. ii. cap. xxi.

(85) Brerleii Apol. Protest. p. 550.

(86) See the Preface to his Poems, addressed to Andrew Dudithius, dated May 14, 1569; his Notes on Matth. i. 19; his Answer to Claudius de Xaintes, &c.

(87) Ant. Fayus, in vita Bezæ, pag. 9, 10.

(88) Jugem. sur les Poëtes, Num. 1336.

(89) Ant. Fayus, p. 59.

BEZA.

an ill Construction upon the Epigram on *Candida* and *Audebert* [*Y*]: They accused him of having a Hand in the Murther of the Duke of *Guise*; This we may examine in the Article POLTROT. They have said, that he wished to return into the Bosom of the Catholic Church [*Z*]. It is not true, that a *Dominican* confounded him in a Dispute [*AA*]. We shall see, in another Place (*l*), whether *Bolsec* may be credited.

(*l*) In the Article BOLSEC. Remark [*L*].

After having committed the Fault of publishing his *Juvenilia*, I think there was no other way left for him to avoid suffering for it, but to live a very obscure Life, or very remote from Theological Disputes; for, under what Figure soever he had appeared, his Enemies would have taken Advantage of This Blot, to lessen his Reputation. He had This chiefly to fear in whatever Party he should signalize himself in point of Controversy. And it is not to be questioned, but that, if the same Arms, he made use of against the Papists, had been employed, by him, against the Protestants, some

---

(90) Enfans celebres, Art. 56.

(91) In Vol. I. pag. 386. & seq.

(92) Taken from the xix Sermon on 2 Tim. iii.

(93) In Pag. 398.

(94) Apolog. Altern ad Claud. de Xaintes, Oper Tom. II. pag. 359, 360. See also his Epistle dedicatory to his Poems.

(95) Epist. Dedicator. Poëmatum. See also the second Address to Claudius de Xaintes, pag. 360.

(96) In Scaligerana, at the Word Beza.

(97) Ant. Fayus, in vita Bezæ, pag. 54.

(98) See the Description Maimbourg gives of him; History of Calvinism, pag. 217. It appears, by the Scaligerana, that Beza had the Presence of a Prince. Fuit valde pulcher senex — fuit valde præstanti Forma, ut judicaretur aliquis principis.

" Epitaphs, Epigrams, Icones, Emblems, and Cato
" Censorius, *should be collected together, and had
" them printed, with the most beatiful Types, which
" the Stephens's Printing-House could furnish, in the
" Year 1597.*" Mr Baillet has shewed his Civility, and his Equity (90).

You will find a good Justification of *Beza* in the Critical Miscellanies of Mr *Ancillon* (91): He relates a fine Passage of Mr *Daillé* (92), whereby we learn, that the Infidels reproached the Primitive Church, that they gave their best Employments to Those, *whom the Scandal of their Ill Lives had rendered odious and infamous among the Pagans*. Mr *Ancillon* refers us to his Apology for *Calvin*, *Luther*, *Zuinglius*, and *Beza* (93).

[*Y*] *An Ill Construction was put upon the Epigram on Candida and Audebert.*] There is nothing so ill grounded, as the enormous Accusation built on This Epigram. See the Article AUDEBERT. They who pretend, that the *Candida* of *Beza* was his Wife, are mistaken: for *Beza*'s Wife was never with Child; and there are some Verses on *Candida*'s Pregnancy in the *Juvenilia* of This Author. *Quænam illa est Candida? uxor mea scilicet, quam in meis versiculis prægnantem superis commendo, quam uxor mea nunquam etiam conceperit* (94). I have not been able to discover any Thing concerning *Beza*'s Wife, except that she was of no high Birth; and that their Correspondence began four Years before they left the Kingdom, and before they married in the Face of the Church. Her Husband gives a good Character of her. " Uxorem mihi ea quam illa tempora ferebant " ratione ―― quatuor circiter annos ante volunta-
" rium meum exilium desponfi, genere quidem im-
" parem, fed ea virtute præditum mulierem cujus me
" pœnitere ab eo tempore minime oportuerit (95). *Scaliger* says, that she was the Daughter of an Advocate, and barren; and afterwards cries out, *What a foolish Woman* (96)*!* The Historian of the Husband speaks otherwise of Her; He praises her for several good Qualities, and chiefly for her conjugal Affection; but it is the common Stile of Those, who write the Life of a Learned Person; His Wife, if ever he had any, is always a Woman of great Merit, and of a peaceable Temper. The Funeral Orations of Professors never omit This Topic, though The Makers of them have but too often a *Socrates* to praise. However it be, let us see the Elogy of *Beza*'s first Wife. " Anno 1588. mense Aprili è vivis excessit Claudia
" Denossa Bezæ conjux, cum qua conjunctissime &
" honestissime vixerat annos quadraginta. Fuit illi
" casus hic gravissimus: erat enim fœmina multum
" laudata, sedula, frugi, & viri sui in primis studio-
" sa (97). ――――― *In the Month of April, 1588, died* Claudia Denossa, *the Wife of* Beza, *with whom he lived forty Years lovingly and honourably. This was a very great Misfortune to him; for she was a Lady of great Merit, Diligent, Thrifty, and particularly careful of her Husband.*" Not a word of her Family: This makes me question, what *Scaliger* says, that she was the Daughter of an Advocate: And besides, would *Beza* have confessed so freely, that he had married beneath himself, if his Wife had been the Daughter of an Advocate of *Paris*? This Under-matching has something in it, which I cannot unravel, and which leaves room for Suspicion. *Beza*, as handsome as an *Adonis* (98), Polite, Learned, Witty, wanting no Money, under-matches himself! One of Those, who have answered *Maimbourg*'s History of *Calvinism*, denies, that the *Candida* of *Beza* is one *Dame* Claudia, *a Taylor's Wife*; and, among other Reasons, He makes use of this; *When* Beza *speaks of the Clasp, he complains, that* coërcet globulos duos rubentes, intra cæca jubet manere claustra; *These Expressions*, says he, *of a Woman's Breast, do not suit a Taylor's Wife* (99). Who told him, that a Taylor's Wife of *Paris* might not wear a Clasp in Those Days, to hide her Breasts? This Apologist makes some minute Observations, which he would have done better to have suppressed.

I cannot give credit to what I have read in one of Mr *Ancillon*'s Works, which is, that *Beza*'s first Wife was Frances de St Marcel d' Avençon, *Sister of a Bishop of* Grenoble, *and the Widow of* Nicolas Odetuoud, *Brother of* John IV, *First Consul of the same City of* Grenoble, *her first Husband, and of* Philip de Poy, *Lord of* Fiancé, *her second Husband* (100). Such an eminent Nobility cannot agree with the Under-matching, which the pretended Third Husband confesses so ingenuously. Besides, Mr *Ancillon* had not well informed himself of what concerns *Beza*'s Marriages; He admits three of Them, and applies to them *Pasquier*'s Epigram (101), which I have set down in the Remark [*N*].

[*Z*] *He is charged with wishing to return into the Bosom of the Catholic Church.*] See, in the Remark [O], the Report, that was spread, of his dying a good Catholic, in the Year 1597. I have an Author to quote here, whose Name and Temper agree very well (102). " Did he not lately most humbly supplicate our most
" Christian King to obtain for him the Absolution
" of our Holy Father? The same Prince told it, two
" several times, to a Prelate; and I am sure he
" would not revoke it for all the Huguenotism in
" the World. Cry out, and murmur at it, as much
" as you will. The Sieur *Corneille*, a late Minister,
" told me, that the same *Beza*, advising him to for-
" sake all their Errors, and return to the Faith of
" the Catholic Church, protested to him, that he
" would do the same, if he could easily get out of
" *Geneva*. If you have a Mind to know more of it,
" he will tell you the Day, the Place, and his Dis-
" course, with so many Particulars, that you cannot
" doubt of it, &c.". Thus the *Franciscus Feuardentius* speaks of *Beza*. One is amazed to see him quote *Henry* IV, with so much Confidence; as for the Ex-Minister, *Corneille*, his Quotation signifies nothing. Compare This with the Remark [*R*], towards the End.

[*AA*] *It is not true, that a Dominican confounded him in a Dispute.*] *Alfonsus Fernandez* relates, in his Annals of the Dominicans, printed at *Salamanca*, in the Year 1617, that Father *Sebastian Michaeb*, a Religious of the Order of St *Dominic*, mortified the Pride of the Huguenots in *Montpellier*, and chiefly That of *Beza*, who travelled often from *Geneva* to *Montpellier*. *Rivetus* says, upon This, that, at the Time of This pretended Triumph, *Beza* was in his Eighty first Year; and that he was not in a Condition to undertake long Journeys; and that it is certain, that, neither in that Year, nor after, did he set Foot out of the Territories of *Geneva*. " Cum tamen certum sit
" *Bezam, tum octuagesimum primum annum agentem, illo anno nec potuisse, si voluisset, Montempessulanum adventare, nec ab illo tempore Geneva excessisse, aut saltem fines Genevensium* (103)." I do not believe, that, in any time of his Life, This Minister made frequent Journeys from *Geneva* to *Montpellier*. We have seen (104), that They reproached him for not daring to go out of *Geneva*. *Rivetus*

(99) See the Book, entituled, The true History of Calvinism, pag. 171.

(100) Ancillon, Melange Critique, Tom. I. pag. 379.

(101) Id. Ibid. pag. 405.

(102) Feuardent. Enervationesque ministeriales, Book iii. chap. 24. pag. 327.

(103) Rivetus in Jesuita vapulante, Oper. Tom. III. p. 479. *In this Treatise of* Rivetus *are divers other Answers to* Bezæ's *Adversaries.*

(104) *At the end of Remark* [*R*].

BEZA. 797

some Reformed Writers would have thrown in his Teeth his *Audebert*, and his *Candida* [*BB*]. Among the *Roman* Catholics, He, who treated him with the greatest Moderation, is more easy to be pointed out, than He, who treated him with the greatest Anger. They, who have shewn some Moderation and Equity towards him, are but a few in Number; They, who have discharged the Fury of their Animosities against him, are numberless: But I do not believe, there are many, whose Passion is so extravagant, as That of the Author of the *Doctrine Curieuse*. I shall mention one of his Calumnies [*CC*]: It is so strange, that one can hardly believe one's own Eyes in a Thing of this Nature. He was publickly censured for it by a Catholic

---

(105) Ant. Fayus, in vita Bezæ, pag. 19.

Rivetus did not know, that, in the Year 1601, *Beza* went to *Lausanne* (105); he took, then, his final leave of That City.

[*BB*] *Some Reformed Writers would have twitted him with his Audebert and his Candida.*] We should presume too much upon the Privileges of Orthodoxy, and belie Experience, if we should believe, that all Those, who write in the Defence of Truth, resist the Impressions of Resentment in such a Manner, as to see only, in the Writings of their Adversaries, what Justice requires they should find in Them. *Beza's* Epigram on *Audebert* is, at the bottom, but a witty Conceit: It is free from the Abominations, which the Missionaries pretend to discover in it; but, to see this Purity in it, one must either be the Author's Friend, or have no Partiality for, or against, him; for, when once a Man is very angry, and would be revenged for the Injuries he has received from an Author, He gives a criminal Turn to his Words. The Protestants of the Confession of *Geneva* do not doubt, but that Those of the Confession of *Augsburg* are Part of That True Church, which leads to Heaven: Nevertheless, some of the *Lutherans* were so offended, because *Beza* had written against their Party, that they adopted the Slanders of the *Roman* Catholics, as to his *Juvenilia*. See here a long Passage of the *Calvino-Turcismus*, in which we see the Sentiments of a famous Lutheran Divine. " Et quanquam Theodorus

* Conrad. Schlusselburg. Calvinist. Theolog. l. ii. fol. 72.

" Beza aliter de vita moribusque Calvini scribat, tamen contra Theodorum Bezam isti arguunt hæc esse
" verissima, nec unquam luculenter & solidè à Cal-
" vinistis refutata. Nam quod ad Bezæ testimonium

† Idem. lib. 2. fol 92.

" attinet, quum *Theodorus Bezam* (inquiunt) * eadem
" hæresi, & eodem ferme peccato nobilitatus sit, ut
" historia de Candida meretricula (& Audeberto) te-
" status; nemo ipsi hac in parte fidem habere potest.
" Nihil certè apud hominem moderatum & æquum
" valere potest ejus quæcunque vehementissima licet
" contestatio, si verum est quod juxta istos †, Certò
" constat Theodorum Bezam à pueritia imbibisse vatum
" impudicitiam, & impudentiam, totamque æta-
" tem explendis suis libidinibus & cupiditatibus,
" ac describendis suis amoribus, & ulisscendis suis
" rivalibus exercuisse, atque in meretricum lenam,
" & cynædum transformatum esse. De quo item con-

‡ Fol. 93.

" stat & hoc ‡, quod obscænissimos versus scripsit
" ad Germanum Audebertium Aurelium, & eundem
" tanquam Adonidem à Theodoro Beza factum esse

(106) Guilielmus Reginaldus, in Calvino-Turcismo, lib. ii. cap. 11. p. 274.

" (106). —— And, though Beza gives a different
" Account of the Life and Character of Calvin, yet
" They contend, against Theodore Beza, that these
" things are most true, and that they were never
" clearly and solidly refuted by the Calvinists. For,
" as to the Testimony of Beza, since Theodore Beza
" (say They) was remarkable for the same Heresy, and
" almost the same Crime, as appears from the Story
" of the Harlot Candida (and Audebert); no one can
" believe him upon this Head. And, indeed, his
" strongest Attestation can have no weight with a Man
" of Moderation and Equity, if what They say be
" true; viz. It is notorious, that Beza, from his In-
" fancy, had imbibed the Immodesty and Impudence
" of the Poets, and had spent his whole Life, in
" gratifying his lustful Inclinations, in describing his
" Amours, and revenging himself on his Rivals, and
" that he was metamorphosed both into a Bawd, and a
" Catamite. Of whom it is likewise true, that he
" wrote the most obscene Verses to Germanus Aude-
" bert, who is described by Theodore Beza as another
" Adonis." The same Blindness, which engaged *Schlusselburgius* to write such things, would have appeared in some Reformed Authors, if *Beza* had fol-

lowed the Footsteps of *Claudius de Xaintes*, or of *Ronsard* (107); if he had been Chaplain to the Duke of *Guise* at the Battle of *Dreux*; if he had harangued against The Protestants at the Conference of P[...]; in a word, if he had persecuted them by his Books, Intrigues, Sermons, Journies, &c. Let us say, then, that the Glory, he acquired, in maintaining the Cause of the Reformed, with great Zeal, caused his Poems to be taken notice of, which, without This, had never been exclaimed against: And, if it were permitted to compare Small Faults with Great Ones (108), One might remember, here, what shall be said in another Place of *John de la Casa*. His *Capitolo del Forno* would have remained unknown, with so many other more infamous Poems, if he had not been raised to the Function of an Inquisitor. To conclude, I add, that, if *Beza* had been a great Persecutor of the *Huguenots*, and exposed to their Libels for his *Juvenilia*, the Writers of the other Party would have maintained, that there was no harm in the Epigram upon *Audebert* and *Candida*, and that a Man must be given over to a Spirit of Slander, a perpetual Ch[ar]acter of Here[s]y, to, &c.

[*CC*] *I shall mention one of Garasse's Calumnies against Beza.*] " The Fourth, who was guilty of a
" great Piece of Folly in relation to the Sacrament,
" was *Beza*; for This Man, who had Wit enough
" to make a lascivious Epigram, though he commit-
" ted childish Faults in the Quantity of his *Latin*
" Verses, never spoke of any Thing relating to Di-
" vinity, without exposing himself to the Derision of
" the Learned. *George Fabricius* tells us, *In respon-*
" *sione ad Apologiam Bezæ*, that the said Arch Here-
" tic, being at the Conference of *Poissi*, made a long
" Discourse, in the Form of a Paraphrase, on the
" Words of the Consecration, in which he equally
" shewed his Malice, and his Folly. For, said he,
" Sirs, I must inform you, that there is an essential
" Error crept into the New Testament, in the Words
" of the Consecration; for, whereas we read, Hoc est
" corpus meum; Hic est calix meus *, it should cer-
" tainly be read in the Negative; Hoc NON EST cor-
" pus meum; Hic NON EST calix meus †, and that
" CHRIST pronounced so in express Terms; but that
" the Evangelists, and St Paul, who were our LORD
" JESUS CHRIST's Secretaries, have, unfortunately,
" or through too much Precipitation, forgotten the Ne-
" gative, as it appears often, continues he, in the Pan-
" dects of Florence, and the Civilians observe, that
" Those, who transcribed them, have often forgot the
" Negative, and, by that means, made some Laws
" quite contrary to the Intention of the Founder: Thus,
" said Beza, the Evangelists, having forgotten the
" NON, are the cause, that we debate, at this Day,
" a most clear Truth: For, what probability is there,
" that the Body of CHRIST should be contained in a
" little roundish Wafer? I say, Sirs, that Non plus
" est in COENA, quàm in COENO; He is as much in
" the Mire, as in the Sacrament. At this Discourse,
" the Doctors, and particularly Espencæus, and Clau-
" dius de Xaintes, were in a manner stupified with
" Astonishment, seeing the Impudence and Folly of
" the Man: And Claudius de Xaintes to confound
" him having produced the Confession of Augsburg,
" which the Calvinists of France had embraced, which
" has these Words in express Terms: CHRIST cor-
" pus in Eucharistia ADESSE: Beza answered, that it
" ought to be corrected; that the same Fault was in
" it, as in the Evangelists; and that, by changing
" one Letter, it might be read ABESSE; viz. that
" the Body of JESUS CHRIST was absent from the
" Eucharist (109)." We shall see how This absurd Discourse

BEZA.

Catholic Writer [*DD*]: But he was not ashamed of it, and chose rather to make use

Discourse of Father *Garasse* was confuted by a Person of his own Communion.

[*DD*] *He was publickly censured for it by a Catholic Writer.*] I mean, by the same Mr *Ogier*, who wrote in favour of *Balzac*, some time after, and who was a very good Preacher. He did not put his Name to the Book, which he entituled, *Jugement & Censure du Livre de la doctrine curieuse de François Garasse*, and which he published at *Paris*, in the Year 1623. However, it is certainly known, that he was the Author of it. Never was Writer so bore down, or crushed by his Adversary, as *Garasse* was by Mr *Ogier*, in relation to This silly Story. The Censurer did two things: First, he shewed, by three Reasons, that nothing is more absurd, than to suppose, that *Beza* spoke in this Manner; and, afterwards, he proved, that the Witness, quoted by *Garasse*, did not say what was imputed to him.

Let us see his three Reasons. "Is it likely, that "*Beza*, one of the chief Ministers of the Conference "of *Poissy*, held such a Discourse, as *Garasse* fathers "upon him, and said that we must read, *Hoc non* "*est corpus meum*; since That cursed Corruption "does not only ruin the Catholic Belief concerning "the Holy Sacrament of the Eucharist; but also "That of the Heretics, and of *Beza*, and his own "Party. Certainly, if our LORD had said, *This is* "*not my Body*, as the Catholics could not conclude the "Reality of the Body from That Expression; so the "*Zuinglians* could not draw Their Signification of "Body from it; and much less the *Calvinists* their "Flowings, Irradiations, Participations, of the Body "of CHRIST, which They add to the Significa- "tion; since he would absolutely have said, *This is* "*not my Body*. Add to this Consideration, that one "must be, not only a Beast, as *Garasse* says, but "worse than a Beast, more insensible than a Log, "more stupid than a Lump of Lead, to entertain "such a Thought, that our Lord JESUS CHRIST "said, *Hoc non est*, &c. For *cui bono*? Wherefore "should he tell his Disciples, that the Bread was "not his Body, rather than any other Meat, that "was on the Table; nay, rather than the Table "itself? Besides, What Coherence, what Conse- "quence, what Reasoning is there in These Words; "*This is not my Body, which is given for you*; *This is* "*not my Blood*, &c. without adding any explanatory "Words, to denote which was That Body, and "That Blood, which was to be given, and shed, "for the Salvation of Mankind? As for myself, I "own, that, though I consider these Words never "so attentively, I cannot conceive any Reason, or "Consequence, in Them; and I firmly believe, that "one must be a Fool, and a Mad-Man, to be able "to find any. Finally, Who will believe, that *Beza* "made, at the Conference of *Poissy*, that fine Speech, "which *Garasse* ascribes to him, who presented This "Form of Confession concerning the Eucharist to "the Bishops with his own Hands? *Confitemur* "CHRISTUM JESUM *in sua sancta Cœna nobis of-* "*ferre, dare, & exhibere veram substantiam corporis* "*& sanguinis per operationem Spiritus Sancti*; ---- "*We confess, that* CHRIST JESUS, *in the Eucharist,* "*offers, gives, and exhibits to us the true Substance* "*of Flesh and Blood, by the Operation of the Holy* "*Spirit*. And what follows; as may be read in "the Answer of *Claude de Xaintes* to *Beza*'s Apo- "logy. And, though These fine Words, so Ortho- "dox in Appearance, vanish into airy Notions, and "Figures; yet in what manner soever they be taken, "they are inconsistent with That pretended Nega- "tive (110)."

(110) *Jugement & Censure de la Doctrine Curieuse,* chap. viii. pag. 89, 90.

He tells us, afterwards, of the Comparison he made between *Garasse*'s Narrative, and That of the Ci- vilian, *Gabriel* (111) *Fabricius*, whom *Garasse* had quoted for the Voucher of his Story. He relates, "That *Francis Bauduin*, alias *Balduin*, having de- "serted the Sect of the *Calvinists*, was, a long time, "exposed to their Calumnies, and Curses. Besides, "----- he composed very learned Treatises against "*Calvin*'s Doctrine, and, among others, a Preface "to an Edition, which he published, of *Optatus*

(111) *And not George, as Garasse had said, for which the Prior Ogier cersures him,*

"*Milevitanus*, with this Superscription *Joanne Lu-* "*camio* (112)." He adds (113); "If the Ministers "hated This Civilian much, They feared him no less, "because of his Ability, and profound Learning; "insomuch that all the Works of the Catholic Do- "ctors, wherein any Point of their Doctrine was "solidly confuted, were ascribed by Them to *Bal-* "*duin*. It happening, then, that Dr *de Xaintes*, af- "terwards Bishop of *Evreux*, having composed a "Book entituled, *Examen doctrinæ Calvinianæ &* "*Bezanæ de Cœna Domini* (114); *Beza* wrote an "Apology by way of Answer to it, wherein he "furiously inveighs against *Balduin*, as the chief "Author of the *Examen*. De *Xaintes* answered by "a Reply, entituled, *Responsio ad Apologiam Theod.* "*Bezæ*, &c. And, on the other side, *Gabriel Fa-* "*bricius* undertook to defend his Master *Balduin*'s "Cause, and composed a Libel, entituled, *Gab. Fa-* "*bricii Responsio ad Bezam Vrxeliam Eceboliam* (115), "which, to speak properly, is a Menyppæan Satire, "wherein he displays *Beza* in all his Colours, never "calling him by any other than a Feminine Name, "treating him, as the most lascivious and profligate "Woman in the World, and using the keenest "Strokes, that Satire can invent against an Enemy. "It is out of This little Book, that *Garasse* ---- "took That Speech of *Beza*, at the Conference of "*Poissy*, which might be tolerated, if *Fabricius* had "made him harangue in the same manner, that "*Rapin* makes Cardinal *de Pelve* discourse, in the "*Catholicon*. But it is so far from being so, that "there is nothing that looks like a Speech in all the "Book. *Fabricius* says only, that *Beza*, without "racking his Brain with so many Forms of Confes- "sion, Commentaries, and Explanations of this Pas- "sage, *Hoc est corpus meum*, should have said, with "the utmost Boldness, that it is an Error of the Tran- "scribers, who, instead of *Hoc non est*, as the Evan- "gelists wrote it, have carelesly left out the Ne- "gative, and wrote *Hoc est*, &c. Here are *Fabri-* "*cius*'s own Words, in the seventeenth Page of "my Copy. *Et fortasse ut tandem te expedias,* "*& tot commentariorum plaustra facessere jubeas, re-* "*curres ad talem emendationem: & quia nostri cor-* "*rectores dicunt in ipsis etiam Pandectis Florentinis,* "*sæpe deesse negationem, tu tali artificio statim te* "*liberes, & adversariis os obstruas, præsertim cum* "*alios multos Evangeliorum locos similiter scilicet e-* "*mendaris, partim ex conjectura, partim ex manu-* "*scriptis, ut ais, exemplaribus*. From which Words "it is as clear as the Sun at Noon-day, that *Fabri-* "*cius* means This; *Eum qui semel verecundiæ fines* "*transierit, naviter oportet esse impudentem*. ---- "*That He, who has once transgressed the Bounds of* "*Modesty, may persevere in Impudence*: That, since "*Beza* had the Assurance to corrupt the Scriptures "in several Passages of less moment, He might car- "ry his Impudence farther, and corrupt This Pas- "sage, *Hoc est corpus meum*, substituting, in the "room of it, *Hoc non est*, &c. The following Im- "posture of *Garasse* is of the same Stamp, when "he says, That *Claudius de Xaintes*, hearing *Beza* "speak in This Manner, produced the Confession "of *Augsburg*, to confound him, which has these "Words, *Christi corpus in Eucharistia adesse*; and "that *Beza* answered, that it ought to be read *abesse*. "*Garasse* wonders at *Beza*'s Folly; and I admire "at *Garasse*'s Stupidity, who hopes to make his "Readers believe, that *Beza*, who would never "subscribe to the Confession of *Augsburg*, notwith- "standing all the Entreaties of the Cardinal *de Lor-* "*rain*, nor give his Opinion about That Confes- "sion, made This foolish and impertinent Reply "to Dr *de Xaintes*. ---- The Truth is, *Fabricius* "derides *Beza* according to his usual Custom: *Ubi* "*id voteris*, says he, *facile deinde efficies, quod præ-* "*terea suscipis, ut persuadeas, tam fuisse bactenus te-* "*mulentos omnes Protestantes*, &c. ---- *When you* "*shall have proved This, you will then induce us to be-* "*lieve, what you farther suspect, that the Protestants* "*have been hitherto, in general, so besotted, &c.* "*And a little after*; *Ingenua profecto & ingeniosa*

(112) *Jugement & Censure de la Doctrine Curieuse*, p. 91.

(113) *Ibid.* pag. 92. & seqq.

(114) *Printed at Paris, in 1567.*

(115) *Printed at Paris, 1567, in 8vo.*

"*fuerit*

use of a pitiful Shift, than to confess the Truth [*EE*]. I have read, somewhere, in his Works, that *Sturmius* affirmed, that *Beza* might truly say, *I believe but one thing, which is, That I believe nothing* (*m*). What Calumny is this! *Prateolus* must be reckoned among the Authors, who have been the most diligent Transcribers of the

(*m*) *Note, that* Beza, Apol. i. ad Claudi m Oper. Tom. II. pag. 224. *said that of* Francis Baudou n. Vir fane nullius fidei, ut tanquam alter Socrates vere po sit Illud usurpare, Ηδε οιδα μηδεν quod nihil credo.

(116) Ibid. pag. 95.

" *fuerit illa tua emendatio, ut ubi in eorum de cœna*
" *confessione scriptum est corpus adesse, scribatur abesse.*
" *Facilem enim lapsum obrui scriptoris fuisse, in tanta*
" *affinitate unius literulæ.* Certainly, it would be
" an ingenious Correction, if instead of *adesse*, as the
" Confession of *Augsburg* has it, you should read
" *abesse*; and, if you should say, that it is an Er-
" ror, easily crept into the Text, through the Care-
" lessness of some drunken *German*, by reason of the
" Affinity and Resemblance between the two Letters,
" *d* and *b* (116)." You may be sure, This Censurer did not forget to insult *Garasse* for his Boldness in mentioning This Circumstance, that *the Doctors, and particularly* Espencæus, *and* Claudius de Xainctes, *were struck with Amazement*. He ends with a very good Reflexion. " This way of proceeding, *says*
" *he* (117), is greatly prejudicial to the Conversion
" of Erring Souls, and particularly of Those, which
" *Garasse* pretends to bring over to the Church by
" means of his Book. For, pray tell me, what He-
" retic, what Atheist, would trust him, after he
" has been surprized in so manifest a Falshood?
" Who will not presume, that a thousand Absur-
" dities, which he relates of several Heretical Au-
" thors, are of the same Stamp, and that he quotes
" the Ancients with as little Sincerity as the Mo-
" derns? - - - - I have it from good Hands, that
" the chief Reason, which retained the great *Casau-*
" *bon* in the Errors, wherein he was brought up,
" was his having perceived the like Tricks in some
" modern Divines, which made him conceive a very
" bad Opinion of Those, who would triumph over
" their Enemies with false Colours."

(117) Ibid. pag. 96, 97.

Errors of Mr *Ogier*.

Let us observe some small Mistakes in This Judicious Censurer. The Reason, why the Protestants calumniated *Baudouin*, was not because he had forsaken Their Religion, and composed learned Works to confute Them. See the Remark [*H*] of his Article; where you will find, that he drew their Indignation upon him for having concerned himself with some Intrigues, wherein they thought there was a Design of destroying them, under Pretence of reconciling both Religions. You will find there, that they took him for the Author of a small Piece, which *Cassander* had written, and which was not a Book of Controversy, but rather an Explication of the Duty of a good Man in the Condition the Church was then in. In short, you will find there, that The Slanders preceded the Preface to *Optatus Milevitanus*. To these Faults of the Prior Ogier may be added these others. The Protestants imputed only the Anonymous Book of *George Cassander* to *Baudouin*. It is false, that *Beza* looked upon him as the chief Author of the *Examen Doctrinæ Calvinianæ*, written by *Claude de Xaintes*; He was contented to say, that *Baudouin* had supplied This Doctor with some Things, which consisted much more of Matters of Fact, than Arguments.

[*EE*] *He chose rather to make use of a pitiful Shift, than to confess the Truth*] First of all, he supposes, that the Question is only, *Whether* Fabricius *spoke those Words seriously, or by way of Irony*

(118) Garasse. Apologe de la Doctrine Curieuse, chap. xxvi. pag. 349.

(118)? He confesses afterwards, that his Adversary builds on the seventeenth Page of *Fabricius*'s Book; and then he expresses himself thus: " Not to mul-
" tiply Words in vain, I answer, that, not having
" *Fabricius*'s Book at present in my Possession, to
" verify the Passage, and not being able to prove
" it, what Diligence soever I could use, I must
" refer myself to the Truth of my Extracts, which
" I made very punctually above twelve Years ago;
" by which I perceive, that Monsieur *Augier* did,
" out of Simplicity or Cunning, what the Mini-
" sters do maliciously in the Books of the ancient
" Fathers; for he took one Part of the Passage,
" which was favourable to him, and dropped the
" other. - - - - - To prove, then, that *Fabricius* did
" not speak ironically, and that he did not falsly
" accuse *Beza* of having substituted a Negative in

" the sacred Words of the Evangelists, he shews evi-
" dently, in the Sequel of his Discourse, that *Beza*'s
" Belief was such, and that he had certainly cor-
" rupted the Passages of the Gospel. These are his
" Words, which deserve to be seriously considered.
" Ipse Illyricus de illa explicatione & INVENTIONE
" Bezana loquens, vocat phantasticam inventionem,
" qualis est amantium in Pictura & Poësi, ut ibi suos
" amores esse somnient, ubi non sunt. Illum absens
" absentem auditque videtque ; & ita, inquiebat Illy-
" ricus, se cum CHRISTO in Eucharistia Beza gessit,
" ut Phædria cum Thaide apud Terentium, cum
" ait; Volo ut cum milite isto præsens absens sies
" & mecum tota sis; Ita Beza sua illa phantastica &
" imaginosa inventione vult ut CHRISTUS in Eucha-
" ristia præsens & absens siet, & ita sit ut non esse di-
" catur. - - - - *The* Illyrian *himself, speaking of This*
" *Explication and* INVENTION *of Beza, calls it a*
" *fantastical Invention, like That of Lovers, in*
" *Painting or Poetry, who fancy the beloved Object*
" *to be, where it is not. Thus, said he,* Beza *dealt*
" *with* CHRIST *in the Eucharist, as* Phædria, *in Te-*
" *rence, does with* Thais, *when she says* ; *Though*
" *in Company with This Soldier, I would have you*
" *be absent, and only present with me. Thus* Beza,
" *in That fantastical and imaginary Discovery, would*
" *have* CHRIST *to be present in Absence, and so to*
" *exist, as to be said not to exist.* Monsieur *Augier*
" may plainly see by these Words, that *Fabricius*,
" whom he represents to us as a Buffoon, purposely
" to lessen his Authority, did not speak jestingly,
" as he supposes, but with all the Seriousness, which
" such Matters deserve (119)." The Insincerity, which reigns in these Words of Father *Garasse*, cannot be sufficiently represented. An indigent Layman, living in a Place remote from great Cities, might make use of This Excuse, *I could not procure such a Book; I could not verify such a Passage*; but, if he lived at *Paris*, and if His Honour engaged him to justify a Quotation, there would be reason to laugh at This Excuse, and to call it a Cheat. But *Garasse* was, then, at *Paris*; so that he might easily have found *Fabricius*'s Book ; and no Author was ever more obliged to purge himself from Calumny. It was therefore prodigious Confidence, and invincible Obstinacy, to say, *I could not find This Book, what Diligence soever I used*. What! Shall a Jesuit, who can be supplied by the Libraries of his Order, in the furthermost Part of a Province, with any Book he stands in need of, tell us, that he could not find, at *Paris*, the Work he quoted? His Adversary could meet with it there, and does not say, that he used any Diligence to find it. Why had he not Recourse to That Copy, if all other Helps failed him? Mr *Ogier* durst not have refused him; His Refusal would have been a Proof of *Garasse*'s Innocence. There is something worse still; This Jesuit took a Passage of *Fabricius* out of his Collections, and gave it as the Sequel of That, which his Adversary had mentioned; I say, as a Sequel artificially suppressed by his Adversary. But it appears plainly, that Mr *Ogier* suppresses nothing, and that *Fabricius*'s Words, which Francis *Garasse* quoted, relate to another Thing. What would have become of him, if the Reply, which Mr *Ogier* was going to make, had not been stopped by the Reconciliation between them? Would he have found new means to have dispensed with himself from fairly acknowledging his Calumny, Rashness, Imposture, and Impudence?

(119) Id. ib. pag. 350.

I shall say it often; I shall not be weary of repeating it; It is very useful to collect Examples of the Insincerity of Authors, and the Pieces, which it has occasioned. It were to be wished, that such Men, as *Langius* and *Gruterus*, had spent Part of the Time they bestowed upon *Polyanthea*'s, in making such Compilations. *Garasse* would have often appeared in them; He was a Satirical, Hot-headed, Scurrilous, and Rash Man, who told a Lie boldly, and denied it afterwards. It was his Interest, that the

Doctrine

BEZA.

the abusive Language against This Minister. He omitted nothing of what *Surius*, and such like Writers, had collected (*n*). Cardinal *Richelieu* made use, in his *Method*, of some of Their Rhapsodies. I shall remark against him [*FF*]. Let us not forget, that *Beza* was buried in *St Peter's Cloyster*, and not in the *Burying-place of* Plein-palaix, *because the Savoyards had boasted, that they would take him up, and send him to* Rome (*o*). La Faye says, that This was done for some Reasons, which it was not necessary to mention. The Feuillant *Peter de St Romuald* brings a ridiculous Charge against him, when he accuses him of Rebellion, in having stiled Queen *Elizabeth* Queen of France [*GG*]. I am

Doctrine of Those, who hold, that a Man, who dies in the Service of People infected with the Plague, is a Martyr, should be true. See *Theophilus Raynaud*, in the Treatise *de Martyrio per Pestem*. He says, that Father *Garasse* was persuaded, by the reading That Book, that the Crown of Martyrdom was to be obtained by that means, and was induced thereby to expose himself to the Danger of the Plague (120). He died in That Manner; and had published so many Calumnies, and discovered so much Knavery, that scarce any Thing but a true Martyrdom could expiate such Crimes. Observe, that some Persons will rather sacrifice their Lives, than a false Point of Honour; *Garasse* would not own his Calumnies upon any Account, and made no Difficulty to shut himself up with Those, who had the Plague (121).

[*FF*] *A Remark against Cardinal* Richelieu.] Let us first set down his Words. " *Beza*, being an Ecclesiastic, and in Possession of some Benefices, forsook the Church of *Rome*, at the time when the Parliament summoned him to appear before them, about an extreamly wanton and scandalous Poem *, he had composed; but, knowing himself to be guilty of such great Excess, he answered that *August* Senate only by his Flight, and retired to *Geneva* †. To learn what he was, we need no other Witness than himself, having discovered, by the Verses, which he made in Imitation of *Catullus* and *Ovid*, that he gives himself up to an enormous and monstrous Lewdness (122), for which reason, his own Fraternity call him The Shame of *France*, a *Simonist*, a Man guilty of all Vices, and even of That, which drew Fire from Heaven ‡." This is what The Cardinal says, in the tenth Chapter of the second Book of his *Method*, pages 321, 322, of the Edition of *Paris*, 1663. Mr *Martel*, Professor of Divinity at *Montauban*, and at *Puylaurens*, before the Revocation of the Edict of *Nantes*, and, since That Revocation, at *Bern*, opposes the Testimony of *Stephen Pasquier* against These Words of the Cardinal, and adds, That *it is not a Frenchman, who called* Beza *a Simonist, and a Sodomite. It is* Costerus, *a Flemish Writer and a Jesuit*. I cannot tell by what *Rhetorical Figure they pretend to rank him among the Fraternity of our Ministers* (123). As for what he says of *Costerus*, he refers us to the Twenty first Chapter of the second Book of the first Part of *Morton's* Catholic Apology; where, it is certain, the *Latin* Words, quoted by the Cardinal, *Galliae probrum, &c.* are to be found, as taken from the first Chapter of the third Book of One of *Costerus's* Works. This Cardinal, or Those, who published his *Method*, cannot be excused for This false Quotation: They found it necessary, that the Name of a *Reformed* Writer should appear next to the *Galliae probrum, &c.* For, though it should be proved, that *Costerus's* Words are to be seen in the Writings of the *Lutheran Schlusselburgius*, it would not justify them; since it is very evident, that That *Lutheran* cannot pass for one of *Beza's* Fraternity. As for what remains, it must be confessed, that a *Flemish* Jesuit was not the First, who charged *Beza* with such Abominations. *Costerus* did but transcribe several *Frenchmen*, and by name, *Claudius de Xaintes*. A Chronological Mistake of the Cardinal might be taken notice of: He says, in a Marginal Note, that *Beza* retired to *Geneva*, in the Year 1554, aged Fifty five Years of Age. He should have said, in the Year 1548, being Twenty nine Years of Age.

[*GG*] *Peter de St Romuald ridiculously accuses him of Rebellion, in stiling* Queen Elizabeth *Queen of* France.] "This same Year, 1581, *says he* (125), "*Theodore Beza*, Minister of *Geneva*, published his "Book, entituled, *Icones Virorum illustrium pietate & doctrina*, which he dedicated to *Elizabeth*, Queen "of *England*, stiling her *Queen of France*. Cer"tainly, a *Frenchman* cannot use such Terms, with"out declaring himself a bad Subject; for it is say"ing, that the King, his Master, is an Usurper, and "that the Crown does not belong to him, but to ano"ther. Can This be done in a printed Book, with"out Felony and Treason? But what better can we "expect from an Heretic?" He has repeated the same Charge, Word for Word, in another Book (126); which proves, that he was thoroughly satisfied with This Remark; which, however, is childish, nonsensical, and superstitious. I excuse him Errors of Fact; such as, that the *Icones of Beza* came out in 1581, and that they were dedicated to the Queen of *England*. It was to *James*, King of *Scotland*, that the Author dedicated Them, the first of *March* 1580; and it is the Year 1580, which I find marked in my Copy: But if our Feuillant is to be pardoned for such Mistakes, as These, he cannot be excused the Error of *Right*, into which he is fallen. I confess, that *Beza*, in dedicating his Remarks on the New Testament to Queen *Elizabeth*, gives her the Title of *Angliae, Franciae, Hiberniae, & circumjacentium Insularum Regina*: but it is absurd to pretend, that This is *felonious* and *treasonable*, and that the King of *France* is thereby determined to be an *Usurper*. For I. *Beza* ought not to be considered, at That Time, as a Subject of the King of *France*: he had renounced his Country for the Sake of his Religion, and had taken Shelter in foreign Lands: he was become a Citizen of *Geneva*, and actually exercised, there, the Office of Professor, and Minister. II. A Private Person, who, in a Letter, gives Princes the Titles, which they usually assume, does not set himself up as a Judge of their Pretensions; he does but follow the Usage, which he finds established; and, when he complies with the Formulary of Subscriptions, he does not engage himself to examine, whether such or such Titles are justly assumed, or no. I go farther, and say, III. that, even when we doubt whether a Prince has a Right to a Kingdom, we observe the Usage of Subscriptions, in an Epistle Dedicatory, or other Letter. *Beza*, for example, fully persuaded, that *Charles* IX, and *Henry* III, lawfully possessed *France*, yet gives *Elizabeth* the Titles, which she assumed in *England*. It is, therefore, the utmost impertinence, to conclude, that he treated the King of *France* as an Usurper. In the IV, and last, place, I say, that Usage, or Custom, authorizes Those, who give the same Titles to Possessors, and Pretenders, and that the Latter, 'till they have renounced their Titles, and Pretensions, are called Kings, or Lords, of such a Country, at the same time that the actual Possessors are acknowledged as Kings, or Lords, of the same Country. We have, among other Examples, the Conduct, which *France* observed towards *Uladislas* King of *Poland*, and *Gustavus Adolphus* King of *Sweden*. We were in strict Alliance with the One, and even as King of *Sweden*; yet we did not scruple to give the other the Title of King of *Sweden*. Mr *le Laboureur* has inserted, in his Account of *Poland* (127), a Letter, which was written by the King of *France* to King *Uladislas*, the Twenty fourth of *November* 1645, at the time when there was such strict Friendship between Queen *Christina*, and *France*. The Subscription of the Letter is: *To the most High, most Excellent, and most Mighty Prince, our dear and well-beloved Cousin, The King of Poland and Sweden*. A *Spanish* Author, who, in dedicating a Book to the most Christian King, stiled him *King of France and Navarre*, would not, I believe, be called to an Account for it, in a Time of Amity. Nor do I think, the Grand Signior would be such a *Turk*, as to punish a *Greek* Bishop, who, in writing to the Duke

BEZA. BIBLIANDER.

I am surprized, that *Balzac* quarrels with certain anonymous Persons on the same Account [*HH*].

Duke of *Savoy*, should call him *King of Cyprus*, or, in writing to the King of *Spain*, should stile him *King of Jerusalem*; and who, in case of an Accusation, should reply, that he had innocently followed the Usage of Inscriptions, without intending to derogate, in the least, from the Fidelity, which he owed his Highness. Is there any Prince in *Christendom*, who does not acknowledge Two Kings of *Navarre*; One in *France*, and the Other in *Spain*; the One only titular, the other in actual Possession? Does This gives occasion for Complaints, or Threats? Would an *Englishman* be prosecuted, who, in an Epistle Dedicatory to *Lewis* XIV, should stile him *King of France*, or *King of the French*, which is the same Thing? Are not the Kings of *France* so stiled, in *England*, not only in common Conversation, but even in Histories, and Public Acts?

[*HH*] *I am surprized, that Balzac quarrels with some anonymous Persons, on the same Account.*] I shall produce his Words, without refuting them; since That is sufficiently done in the preceding Remark. " Let Those, who have lost Countries, " flatter themselves with Those, which They re- " tain. It may serve by way Amusement, or Play- " Thing, formed by the Imagination, after the loss " of essential Things. It would be cruelty to refuse " their Grief this light Consolation. Queen *Eliza- " beth* of *England* may stile herself Queen of *France*, " and the *English* may speak the Language of their " Mistress. Let them, if They please. But I can- " not allow *Frenchmen* to talk thus. It was well " said by a *Frenchman*, speaking of King *James*, " Successor of *Elizabeth*; *He has certainly too much " of a Name, or too little of a Kingdom*; and, *if " the King of France be at London, whom will he " send Embassadors to at Paris*? However, as it is " every where the Custom to speak improperly, and " as every Thing in the World is a Farce, This may " be allowed among the rest. But it must be plaid " in *England*, and not in *France*, or Places un- " der the Protection of *France*. A *Frenchman* can- " not use such Terms, without forgetting, that he " is a *Frenchman*, without declaring himself a bad " Subject, without saying, that the King his Master " is an Usurper. Publickly to degrade his Prince, " to give his Crown to another Prince by a solemn " and printed Acknowledgment, can This be done " without the Crime of Felony? I think not, Sir! " and, for fear of putting myself farther into a Pas- " sion, let us change the Discourse (128)." I fancy (128) Balzac, Entret. xii. pag. 384, 385.
he glances at *Theodore Beza*, and that *Peter de St Romuald* has only transcribed him.

It will not, perhaps, be improper to remark, that *Noel Beda* had before had the same Quarrel with *Erasmus*, on account of the Dedication of One of his Books to the King of *England*. See the Remark [*B*] of the Article BEDA, Citation (11).

BIBLIANDER (THEODORUS), Professor of Divinity at *Zurich*, in the XVIth Century, was born at *Bischoffsel* (*a*), near *St Gal*, in *Swisserland*. He was an universal Scholar (*b*); but he excelled chiefly in the Exposition of the Scripture. He was Professor of Divinity at *Zurich*, from the Year 1532, to 1560, and died of the Plague in the same City, the Twenty fourth of *September* 1564 (*c*). If any one asks, Why his Professorship ended before his Life? I answer, That it was, because he stirred certain Questions, which caused some Disturbances [*A*], in which he departed too much from the common Doctrine of the Protestants, about Predestination. To prevent the Schism, which might have arisen from too long a Contest upon Those Points, it was thought proper to declare *Bibliander Emeritus*; I mean, to treat him as a *Veteran*, and to give him to understand, that his Age, and his long Services, required, that, as a Reward, They should grant him a quiet Life, and an honourable Dismission. I cannot tell whether he apprehended the true meaning of this Compliment, or whether it vexed him; but I know, that he left off teaching. As he understood the *Oriental* Languages, he set about a new Edition of the *Koran*, the Text of which he corrected according to the Rules of Criticism, by comparing the *Arabic* and *Latin* Copies together. He added to it the Life of *Mahomet*, and his Successors, and an Apologetical Preface, which raised a great Outcry [*B*]. He published several other

(*a*) *In Latin Episcopicella, or Episcopocella.*

(*b*) *Vir fœcundissimi ingenii, & Theologiæ exegeticæ commurus* in *Helvetia passim*. Hottinger. in Biblioth. Tigurina, pag. 72.

(*c*) Id. Hottinger, ibid. Thuanus, Bucholcer, Melchior Adam, &c. *place his Death on the 26th of November.*

[*A*] *He stirred certain Questions, which caused some Disturbance.*] Pantaleon has not specified These Questions; he says only, They were little agreeable to the common Opinion, and that *Bibliander* lost Part of his Authority upon That Account. *Pantaleon scribit ante obitum motas ab ipso fuisse quæstiones quasdam novas & insolentes unde auctoritati aliquid decesserit, sed quales illæ fuerint quæstiones, non addit* (1). But Henry Alting has not expressed himself in general Terms; He says, that *Bibliander* had embraced *Erasmus*'s Errors concerning Predestination, and that, for this Reason, Those of *Zurich* discharged him from the Functions of his *Office*, under Pretence, that his Old-age made him unfit for it, and put Peter Martyr *in his Place* (2). This latter Fact is not to be contested, under Pretence, that *Peter Martyr* was called to *Zurich* in the Year 1556, to succeed *Pelican*. He might have been Professor at *Zurich* for some Years, and yet succeed *Bibliander*; for all Professors of Divinity have not the same Functions assigned them. See, below, the Remark [*E*], at the end.

[*B*] *He added, to the Version of the Koran, an Apologetical Preface, which raised a great Outcry.*]

The Title of it is, *Apologia ad reverendissimos patres ac dominos, episcopos & doctores Ecclesiæ Christianæ, in qua rationes redduntur editionis voluminis quod continet Alcoranum & ejus confutationes, & vitas Mahumetis atque successorum ipsius*. This Work was printed by *Oporin*, in the Year 1543, in Folio (3). *Bibliander* corrected the Text of the *Koran*, by comparing the *Latin* and *Arabic* Manuscripts together, and made some Marginal Notes, which shew, or refute, the Absurdities of That Book. This did not hinder the *Spanish* Inquisitors from condemning This Edition of the *Koran*; They condemned not only the Prefaces, but the *Koran* itself (4). This is as clear as the Day; and yet some Authors say, that They only condemned the impious Prefaces, and the pernicious Notes, which are in *Bibliander*'s Edition. Father *Theophilus Reynaud* maintains, that the *Koran* itself deserves to be proscribed, and shews, that *San-Barcillus*, who says, that the Index forbids the reading of it, only because of the Pieces, which *Bibliander* added to it, argued but weakly (5). I set down That Jesuit's Remark somewhat at length, that the Reader may have a more particular Notion of *Bibliander*'s Design. We shall see, that This Minister did

(1) Melchior Adam in vit. Theol. pag. 403.

(2) Altingii Theol. Histor Loc. iv. apud Teissier, Addit. to Thuan. Tom. I. pag. 255.

(3) Note, *that the Preface of Bibliander was printed by itself, in the Year 1638, by the Care of John Fabricius of Dantzic.*

(4) See the Index librorum prohibitorum, pag. 765, Edit. 1667.

(5) Theoph. Raynaudus, Erotem. de malis & bonis libris, n. 141, pag. 200.

VOL. I. 5 R

BIBLIANDER.

other Books [C], and composed a great many, which were never printed, the Manuscripts whereof are kept in the Library of *Zurich* (*d*). He had a hand in a Translation of the Scripture (*e*). I have endeavoured in vain to find out what Age he was of when he died : I give no Credit to *Melchior Adam*; and I wonder he was not sensible of his Error [D]. *Moreri* relates very ill what he takes from *Thuanus*, concerning *Bibliander* [*E*].

I am

(*d*) Hottinger in Biblioth. Tigurina, pag. 72, 73.

(*e*) *See* Remark [*E*].

did not think it proper, that the Books of Adversaries should be destroyed. " Tractans hoc punctum " Antonius Sanctarellus *Tract. de hæresi*, c. 14. dub. " unico, *propositione* 7. ait, Alcoranum per se non " prohiberi, sed ratione scholiorum impiorum, no- " tarumque ac prætationum Lutheri ac Melanchto- " nis, quibus Basiliensis editio Alcorani, per Theo- " dorum Bibliandrum damnatæ memoriæ scriptorum " adornata, contaminatur. Hoc verè & rectè autor " ille. Et addere æquè poterat, ipsius Bibliandri " Apologiam, qua Alcorano patrocinatus est, dig- " nissimam fuisse quæ consigeretur. Omnium quippe " librorum prohibitorum indemnitati studet meribi- " bulus ille, usque adeò, ut non erubuerit contra " Theodosii & Valentiniani Imperatorum legem de " comburendis Nestorii libris grunnire Hæc igitur " concedo Sanctarello. Sed addit quo everti videan- " tur quæ sic sunt constituta ; addit enim rationem, " cur Alcoranus prohibeatur, esse, quia in eo agitur " de Religione nationis, hoc tempore maximè po- " tentis, & ad corporum voluptates patentissimum " ostium aperientis ; quæ sunt valida corruptelæ il- " lectamenta. Hæc, inquam, ratio monstrare vide- " tur, Alcoranum non veteri tantùm ratione impia- " rum Bibliandri annotationum, vel ratione Præfa- " tionum Lutheri ac Melanchtronis, sed per se ac " ratione contextus ipsiusmet Alcorani, quo Aposto- " licæ hami, quos divinus, apponuntur (6). ----- " Antonius Sanctarellus, *handling This Point*, in *his* " *Treatise of Heresy*, chap. 14. Prop. 7. *says, that* " *the Koran is not prohibited on it's own Account,* " *but by reason of the impious Scholia, Notes, and* " *Prefaces, of* Luther *and* Melanchthon, *which de-* " *file the* Basil *Edition of the* Koran, *by* Theodore " Bibliander *of accursed Memory. This is justly and* " *truly observed by This Author. And he might,* " *with equal Justice, have added, that the Apology* " *of* Bibliander *himself, in which he patronizes the* " Koran, *was most worthy of Censure. For* This *Sot* " *pleads for the Indemnity of all prohibited Books,* " *so far as impudently to arraign the Edict of the Em-* " *perors* Theodosius *and* Valentinian *for the burning* " *of* Nestorius's *Books. Thus far, then,* Sanctarellus " *is right. But he adds, what seems to overthrow* " *This Determination. For he adds, that the Reason,* " *why the* Koran *is prohibited, is, because it treats* " *of the Religion of a Country, at This Time very* " *powerful, and which opens a wide Door to corpo-* " *real Pleasures, the Source of all Corruption. This* " *Reason, I say, seems to prove, that the* Koran *is* " *not only forbidden on account of the impious Anno-* " *tations of* Bibliander, *or the Prefaces of* Luther " *and* Melanchthon, *but on it's own Account, on Ac-* " *count of the very Text of the* Koran, *on which* " *The Hooks of Apostacy, which I have spoken of, do* " *hang*."

(6) Id. ibid. n. 342, pag. 203.

[C] *He published several other Books.*] Here are the Titles of some of Them : *Evangelica Historia, quam scripsit B* Marcus, &c. *una cum vita Johannis Marci Evangelistæ collecta ex probatioribus auctoribus,* at *Basil,* 1551. He added to it the *Protevangelium Jacobi,* for which he was censured. *Expositio vaticinii de restitutione Israëlis, de instauranda urbe Jerusalem & Templo, terraque dividenda rursus in tribus, quod ultimis octo capitibus Ezechielis legitur.* This Work was inserted in the Commentaries of Pelican on the Scripture. *Purgatio scriptorum Joannis Oecolampadii, & Ulrici Zuinglii, qua & aliâ eorum obiter defenduntur contra calumniatores.* This Piece was printed before *Zuinglius*'s Works. *De fatis Monarchiæ Romanæ somnium Vaticinium Esræ Prophetæ explicatum non conjectatione privata, sed demonstratione Theologica, Historica & Mathematica. Ad Julium III Papam & cæteros Ecclesiæ Romanæ præsides consideratio de Judæorum & Christianorum defectione à Christo, & Ecclesia & fide Catholica: iterumque de Judæorum & Christianorum conversione*

ad Christum Jesum, & Ecclesiam Dei simsam & fidem Catholicam, at *Basil* 1553. *De summa Trinitate & fide Catholica,* at *Basil* 1555. *De mysteriis salutiferæ passionis, & mortis Jesu Messiæ expositionis historicæ, libri tres,* in the same Place, 1555.

[D] *I wonder* Melchior Adam *was not sensible of his Error.*] He affirms, that *Bibliander* was born in the Year 1514 (7), and that, at last, he died very old, in the Year 1564. *valde senex.* Can this be said of a Man of fifty Years of Age? He adds, that his poring too much on Books had so weakened his Sight, that, coming one Morning into his Stove, in his declining Age, and seeing his Cat playing on a Table, he took her to be his Maid, and bid her good-morrow. " Ex nimiis studiis ætate declivi " ἀμβλυωπίαν contraxit. Accidit ergo ut aliquando, " cum diluculo surrexisset, hypocaustum ingressus " feli in mensa gesticulanti, ancillam suam esse ratus, " faustum fuerit diem precatus, quem felis, ut po- " tuit, resalutavit." A fine Circumstance, and most worthy to be transmitted to future Ages !

(7) If this were so, it would have been observed, as something very extraordinary, that he had been made Professor of Divinity in the Year 1532; but no one observes it.

[E] *Moreri relates very ill what he borrows from* Thuanus ?] It is not true, that *Thuanus* places *Bibliander's* Death on the Twenty ninth of *November* : He makes use of this Expression ; VI *Kalend. Decembris* ; which signifies the Twenty sixth of *November*. II. It is true, that he speaks of *Leo the Jew*. He made use of these Words, *Leo Judæ,* which must be translated *Leo Judæ,* or *Leo of Juda*. But it is very true, that *Bibliander* was One of Those, who put the last Hand to the Bible of *Leo Juda,* to That Bible, which is called the *Zurich* Bible, and which was printed in That City in the Year 1543. *Leo Juda* had advanced very far in the *Latin* Translation of the Scripture when he died ; and he made his Colleagues promise, that they would finish This Work. *Quem Leo Judæ inchoaverat, & moriens ut opus persequeretur Collegis in fidem religionis adactis transcripserat* (8). Bibliander *translated the last eight Chapters of* Ezekiel, Daniel, Job, Ecclesiastes, *the Songs of Songs, and the Forty eight* Psalms, *which remained to be translated.* Peter Cholin *made the Translation of the Greek Books, which the Protestants call* Apocrypha (9). It is of *Cholin* only, that *Thuanus* says, he understood the *Greek* Tongue very well. *Bibliander Chuuredi Pellicani & Petri Cholini Tugiensis Græcæ linguæ peritissimi opera adjutus*. Moreri *does not* translate This well by The'se Words ; Bibliander, *assisted by* Conrad Pelican, *and by* Peter Cholin, *was learned Men in the* Greek *Tongue*. This is his third Fault. The fourth is much more considerable. *A long time after,* says he, *the* Spanish *Divines caused This Bible of* Zurich *to be reprinted at* Lyons, *having been revised by* William Roville (10). Here are *Thuanus's Latin* Words ; *Hispani Theologi diu post recognitam per* Gulielmum Rouillium *denuo Lugduni excudendam curaverunt.* William Roville *is the Printer of Lyons, whom Those Divines employed ; but it was not He, who revised the Translation, but the* Spanish *Divines themselves.* Father *Simon* makes no mention of This Edition of *Lyons*; He says, that *the Divines of* Salamanca *caused This Bible to be reprinted in fair Characters at* Salamanca, *and made very small Alterations in it* (11). It is no wonder, that honest Mr *du Rier,* of the *French* Academy, has ill translated *Cicero, Seneca,* and *Livy,* since he has committed so many Faults in translating *Thuanus*. For *Moreri* does but transcribe *du Rier's* Translation in This Place. As for what *Thuanus* says, that *John* Stuckius *was put in* Bibliander's *Place,* This neither agrees with *Alting*, who says, that *Peter* Martyr succeeded *Bibliander*; nor with *Hottinger,* who says, that *Josias* Simler succeeded him for a time (12) ; and that *Stuckius*, having been some time the Substitute of *James* Ammien, Professor of Rhetoric, and Logic, was ordinary Professor of Divinity, from the Year 1571, to the Year 1607 (13). It is cer-

(8) Thuan. lib. xxxv, pag. 726.

(9) Simon, Hist. Critique du Vieux Test. pag. 324.

(10) In the *Latin* Edition published by Mr Teissier, there is Rauville.

(11) Simon, ubi suprà, pag. 323.

(12) Rudæ donatus, lautiùsalem ad tempus tradidit D. Josiæ Simlero. Hottinger. in Biblioth. Tigur. pag. 72.

(13) Id. ib. pag. 169.

tain,

I am just informed (f), that it is found, in the Prosopography of *Pantaleon*, that he lived sixty Years [F], being born in 1504, and dying in 1564. (f) *By Mr Brestet.*

tain, that, when *Bibliander* resigned his Professorship, *Stuckius*, a young Man of eighteen Years of Age, was, then, in *France* (14). He was at *Paris* the Year following, where he received a Commission to join with *Peter Martyr* in the Conference of *Poissy*. He continued a long time in *France*; afterwards he went into *Italy*; and he did not begin to have any Academical Offices at *Zurich*, before the Year 1568. Nevertheless, it is affirmed, in his Life, that he succeeded *Bibliander* in the Office of Professor of the *Old Testament* (15). This was in the Month of *February*, 1571. *Bibliander* had been dead a long Time. No matter for That; his Office continued vacant many Years: There are many Examples of This. *Thuanus* is not so exact in This Point, as he should have been; for all his Readers will believe, that *Stuckius* was made Professor of Divinity in the Year 1564. He should have told us, what Year *Stuckius* had This Professorship conferred upon him.

[F] *That he lived Sixty Years.*] This we find in the *German* Edition of the *Prosopographia* (16), not in the *Latin* Edition (17) where we see on the contrary, that he died in the Year 1560, being about fifty Years old. *Pantaleon* discovered this Error, and corrected it in the *German* Edition.

(14) Melch. Adam. in vitis Theol. pag. 767.

(15) Ibid. pag. 770.

(16) *Printed at Basil, for Leonard Ossen,* 1578, *in Folio.*

(17) *Printed at Basil, for Nicolas Brylinger.*1566, *in Fol.*

The End of the First VOLUME.

RESERVED BOOK

Usually books are lent out for two weeks, but there are exceptions and the borrower should note carefully the date stamped above. Fines are charged for overdue books at the rate of five cents a day; for reserved books the rate is twenty-five cents a day. (For detailed regulations please see folder on "Loan of Books.") Books must be presented at the desk if renewal is desired

CPSIA information can be obtained
at www.ICGtesting.com
Printed in the USA
LVHW022340310323
743150LV00005B/81